Library Service

79 258 883 5

2010

The International WHO'S WHO

73rd Edition

Routledge
Taylor & Francis Group

LONDON AND NEW YORK

First published 1935

© **Routledge 2009**
Albert House, 4th Floor, 1-4 Singer Street, London, EC2A 4BQ, United Kingdom
(Routledge is an imprint of the Taylor & Francis Group, an **informa** business)

All rights reserved. No part of this
publication may be photocopied, recorded,
or otherwise reproduced, stored in a retrieval system
or transmitted in any form or by any
electronic or mechanical means without the
prior permission of the copyright owner.

ISBN-10: 1-85743-510-9
ISBN-13: 978-1-85743-510-8
ISSN: 0074-9613

MILTON KEYNES LIBRARIES	
79 258 883 5	
HJ	2693003
QR920.02 INT	£395.00

Series Editor: Robert J. Elster
Associate Editor: Amy Tyndall
Assistant Editor: Joanne Corsan
Freelance Editorial Team: Gerard Delaney, Annabella Gabb, Sue Leckey, Justin Lewis

PUBLISHER'S NOTE

The *International Who's Who* has been published annually since 1935 and provides biographical information on the most famous and talented men and women in the world today. We select the entries entirely on merit and our book is recognised by librarians in every country as a standard reference source in its field. It is compiled in our editorial offices at Albert House, 1-4 Singer Street, London, EC2A 4BQ, England. We wish to make it clear that the Europa Biographical Reference Series has no connection with any other business purporting to produce a publication with the same title or a similar title to ours.

The Publishers make no representation, express or implied, with regard to the accuracy of the information contained in this book and cannot accept any legal responsibility for any errors or omissions that may take place.

Typeset by Data Standards Limited, Frome
Printed and bound by Polestar Wheatons, Exeter

2010

The International WHO'S WHO

ABBREVIATIONS

CBiol	Chartered Biologist
CBIM	Companion of the British Institute of Management
CBS	Columbia Broadcasting System
CC	Companion of the Order of Canada
CChem	Chartered Chemist
CCMI	Companion of the Chartered Management Institute (formerly CIMgt)
CCP	Chinese Communist Party
CD	Canadian Forces Decoration; Commander Order of Distinction
Cdre	Commodore
CDU	Christlich-Demokratische Union
CE	Civil Engineer; Chartered Engineer
CEAO	Communauté Economique de l'Afrique de l'Ouest
Cen.	Central
CEng	Chartered Engineer
CENTO	Central Treaty Organization
CEO	Chief Executive Officer
CERN	Conseil (now Organisation) Européen(ne) pour la Recherche Nucléaire
CFR	Commander of the Federal Republic of Nigeria
CGM	Conspicuous Gallantry Medal
CGT	Confédération Général du Travail
CH	Companion of Honour
Chair.	Chairman; Chairwoman; Chairperson
CHB	Companion of Honour of Barbados
ChB	Bachelor of Surgery
Chem.	Chemistry
ChM	Master of Surgery
CI	Channel Islands
CIA	Central Intelligence Agency
Cia	Compagnia (Company)
Cía	Compañia (Company)
CID	Criminal Investigation Department
CIE	Companion of the (Order of the) Indian Empire
Cie	Compagnie (Company)
CIEE	Companion of the Institution of Electrical Engineers
CIMgt	Companion of the Institute of Management (now CCMI)
C-in-C	Commander-in-Chief
CIO	Congress of Industrial Organizations
CIOMS	Council of International Organizations of Medical Science
CIS	Commonwealth of Independent States
CLD	Doctor of Civil Law (USA)
CLit	Companion of Literature
CM	Canada Medal; Master in Surgery
CMEA	Council for Mutual Economic Assistance
CMG	Companion of (the Order of) St Michael and St George
CNAA	Council for National Academic Awards
CNRS	Centre National de la Recherche Scientifique
CO	Colorado; Commanding Officer
Co.	Company; County
COI	Central Office of Information
Col	Colonel
Coll.	College
Colo	Colorado
COMECON	Council for Mutual Economic Assistance
COMESA	Common Market for Eastern and Southern Asia
Comm.	Commission
Commdg	Commanding
Commdr	Commander; Commandeur
Commdt	Commandant
Commr	Commissioner
CON	Commander of Order of Nigeria
Conf.	Conference
Confed.	Confederation
Conn.	Connecticut
Contrib.	Contributor; contribution
COO	Chief Operating Officer
Corp.	Corporate
Corpn	Corporation
Corresp.	Correspondent; Corresponding
CP	Communist Party; Caixa Postal (Post Office Box)
CPA	Certified Public Accountant; Commonwealth Parliamentary Association
CPhys	Chartered Physicist
CPP	Convention People's Party (Ghana)
CPPCC	Chinese People's Political Consultative Conference
CPSU	Communist Party of the Soviet Union
cr.	created
CSc	Candidate of Sciences
CSCE	Conference on Security and Co-operation in Europe
CSI	Companion of the (Order of the) Star of India
CSIRO	Commonwealth Scientific and Industrial Research Organization
CSSR	Czechoslovak Socialist Republic
CStJ	Commander of (the Order of) St John of Jerusalem
CT	Connecticut
Cttee	Committee
CUNY	City University of New York
CV	Commanditaire Vennootschap
CVO	Commander of the Royal Victorian Order
d.	daughter(s)

DArch	Doctor of Architecture
DB	Bachelor of Divinity
DBA	Doctor of Business Administration
DBE	Dame Commander of (the Order of) the British Empire
DC	District of Columbia
DCE	Doctor of Civil Engineering
DCL	Doctor of Civil Law; Doctor of Canon Law
DCM	Distinguished Conduct Medal
DCMG	Dame Commander of (the Order of) St Michael and St George
DCnL	Doctor of Canon Law
DComm	Doctor of Commerce
DCS	Doctor of Commercial Sciences
DCT	Doctor of Christian Theology
DCVO	Dame Commander of the Royal Victorian Order
DD	Doctor of Divinity
DDR	Deutsche Demokratische Republik (German Democratic Republic)
DDS	Doctor of Dental Surgery
DE	Delaware
Dec.	December
DEcon	Doctor of Economics
DEd	Doctor of Education
DEFRA	Department for Environment, Food and Rural Affairs
Del.	Delegate; Delegation; Delaware
Denbighs.	Denbighshire
DenD	Docteur en Droit
DenM	Docteur en Medicine
DEng	Doctor of Engineering
Dep.	Deputy
Dept	Department
DES	Department of Education and Science
Desig.	Designate
DèsL	Docteur ès Lettres
DèsSc	Docteur ès Sciences
Devt	Development
DF	Distrito Federal
DFA	Doctor of Fine Arts; Diploma of Fine Arts
DFC	Distinguished Flying Cross
DFM	Distinguished Flying Medal
DH	Doctor of Humanities
DHist	Doctor of History
DHL	Doctor of Hebrew Literature
DHSS	Department of Health and Social Security
DHumLitt	Doctor of Humane Letters
DIC	Diploma of Imperial College
DipAD	Diploma in Art and Design
DipAgr	Diploma in Agriculture
DipArch	Diploma in Architecture
DipEd	Diploma in Education
DipEng	Diploma in Engineering
DipMus	Diploma in Music
DipScEconSc	Diploma of Social and Economic Science
DipTh	Doctor of Theology
Dir	Director
Dist	District
DIur	Doctor of Law
DIurUtr	Doctor of both Civil and Canon Law
Div.	Division; divisional
DJur	Doctor of Law
DK	Most Esteemed Family (Malaysia)
DL	Deputy Lieutenant
DLit(t)	Doctor of Letters; Doctor of Literature
DLS	Doctor of Library Science
DM	Doctor of Medicine (Oxford)
DMD	Doctor of Dental Medicine
DMedSc	Doctor of Medical Science
DMilSc	Doctor of Military Science
DMunSci	Doctor of Municipal Science
DMS	Director of Medical Services
DMus	Doctor of Music
DMV	Doctor of Veterinary Medicine
DO	Doctor of Ophthalmology
DPH	Diploma in Public Health
DPhil	Doctor of Philosophy
DPM	Diploma in Psychological Medicine
DPS	Doctor of Public Service
Dr	Doctor
DrAgr	Doctor of Agriculture
DrIng	Doctor of Engineering
DrIur	Doctor of Laws
DrMed	Doctor of Medicine
DrOecPol	Doctor of Political Economy
DrOecPubl	Doctor of (Public) Economy
DrPhilNat	Doctor of Natural Philosophy
Dr rer. nat	Doctor of Natural Sciences
Dr rer. pol	Doctor of Political Science
DrSc(i)	Doctor of Sciences
DrScNat	Doctor of Natural Sciences
DS	Doctor of Science
DSC	Distinguished Service Cross
DSc(i)	Doctor of Sciences
DScS	Doctor of Social Science
DSM	Distinguished Service Medal

ABBREVIATIONS

AAA	Agricultural Adjustment Administration
AAAS	American Association for the Advancement of Science
AAF	Army Air Force
AASA	Associate of the Australian Society of Accountants
AB	Bachelor of Arts; Aktiebolag; Alberta
ABA	American Bar Association
AC	Companion of the Order of Australia
ACA	Associate of the Institute of Chartered Accountants
ACCA	Associate of the Association of Certified Accountants
Acad.	Academy; Académie
Accad.	Accademia
accred	accredited
ACIS	Associate of the Chartered Institute of Secretaries
ACP	American College of Physicians
ACS	American Chemical Society
ACT	Australian Capital Territory
ADC	Aide-de-camp
Adm.	Admiral
Admin(.)	Administrative; Administration; Administrator
AE	Air Efficiency Award
AERE	Atomic Energy Research Establishment
AF	Air Force
AFC	Air Force Cross
ADB	African Development Bank
affil.	affiliated
AFL	American Federation of Labor
AFM	Air Force Medal
AG	Aktiengesellschaft (Joint Stock Company)
Agric.	Agriculture
a.i.	ad interim
AIA	Associate of the Institute of Actuaries; American Institute of Architects
AIAA	American Institute of Aeronautics and Astronautics
AIB	Associate of the Institute of Bankers
AICC	All-India Congress Committee
AICE	Associate of the Institute of Civil Engineers
AIChE	American Institute of Chemical Engineers
AIDS	Acquired Immune Deficiency Syndrome
AIEE	American Institute of Electrical Engineers
AIME	American Institute of Mining Engineers; Associate of the Institution of Mining Engineers
AIMechE	Associate of the Institution of Mechanical Engineers
AIR	All-India Radio
AK	Alaska; Knight of the Order of Australia
Akad.	Akademie
AL	Alabama
Ala	Alabama
ALS	Associate of the Linnaean Society
Alt.	Alternate
AM	Alpes Maritimes; Albert Medal; Master of Arts; Member of the Order of Australia
Amb.	Ambassador
AMICE	Associate Member of the Institution of Civil Engineers
AMIEE	Associate Member of the Institution of Electrical Engineers
AMIMechE	Associate Member of the Institution of Mechanical Engineers
ANC	African National Congress
ANU	Australian National University
AO	Officer of the Order of Australia
AP	Andhra Pradesh
Apdo	Apartado
APEC	Asia and Pacific Economic Co-operation
approx.	approximately
appt	appointment
apptd	appointed
apt	apartment
AR	Arkansas
ARA	Associate of the Royal Academy
ARAM	Associate of the Royal Academy of Music
ARAS	Associate of the Royal Astronomical Society
ARC	Agriculture Research Council
ARCA	Associate of the Royal College of Art
ARCM	Associate of the Royal College of Music
ARCO	Associate of the Royal College of Organists
ARCS	Associate of the Royal College of Science
ARIBA	Associate of the Royal Institute of British Architects
Ariz.	Arizona
Ark.	Arkansas
ARSA	Associate of the Royal Scottish Academy; Associate of the Royal Society of Arts
ASEAN	Association of South-East Asian Nations
ASLIB	Association of Special Libraries and Information Bureaux
ASME	American Society of Mechanical Engineers
Asoc.	Asociación
Ass.	Assembly

Asscn	Association
Assoc.	Associate
ASSR	Autonomous Soviet Socialist Republic
Asst	Assistant
ATV	Associated Television
Aug.	August
autobiog.	autobiography
AZ	Arizona
b.	born
BA	Bachelor of Arts; British Airways
BAAS	British Association for the Advancement of Science
BAFTA	British Academy of Film and Television Arts
BAgr	Bachelor of Agriculture
BAgrSc	Bachelor of Agricultural Science
BAO	Bachelor of Obstetrics
BAOR	British Army of the Rhine
BArch	Bachelor of Architecture
Bart	Baronet
BAS	Bachelor in Agricultural Science
BASc	Bachelor of Applied Science
BBA	Bachelor of Business Administration
BBC	British Broadcasting Corporation
BC	British Columbia
BCC	British Council of Churches
BCE	Bachelor of Civil Engineering
BChir	Bachelor of Surgery
BCL	Bachelor of Civil Law; Bachelor of Canon Law
BCom(m)	Bachelor of Commerce
BCS	Bachelor of Commercial Sciences
BD	Bachelor of Divinity
Bd	Board
BDS	Bachelor of Dental Surgery
BE	Bachelor of Education; Bachelor of Engineering
BEA	British European Airways
BEcons	Bachelor of Economics
BEd	Bachelor of Education
Beds.	Bedfordshire
BEE	Bachelor of Electrical Engineering
BEM	British Empire Medal
BEng	Bachelor of Engineering
Berks.	Berkshire
BFA	Bachelor of Fine Arts
BFI	British Film Institute
BIM	British Institute of Management
biog.	biography
BIS	Bank for International Settlements
BL	Bachelor of Laws
BLA	Bachelor of Landscape Architecture
Bldg	Building
BLit(t)	Bachelor of Letters; Bachelor of Literature
BLL	Bachelor of Laws
BLS	Bachelor in Library Science
blvd	boulevard
BM	Bachelor of Medicine
BMA	British Medical Association
BMus	Bachelor of Music
Bn	Battalion
BNOC	British National Oil Corporation
BOAC	British Overseas Airways Corporation
BP	Boîte Postale
BPA	Bachelor of Public Administration
BPharm	Batchelor of Pharmacy
BPhil	Bachelor of Philosophy
Br.	Branch
Brig.	Brigadier
BS	Bachelor of Science; Bachelor of Surgery
BSA	Bachelor of Scientific Agriculture
BSc	Bachelor of Science
Bt	Baronet
Bucks.	Buckinghamshire
c.	child; children; circa
CA	California; Chartered Accountant
Calif.	California
Cambs.	Cambridgeshire
Cand.	Candidate; Candidature
Cantab.	of Cambridge University
Capt.	Captain
Cards.	Cardiganshire
CB	Companion of the (Order of the) Bath
CBC	Canadian Broadcasting Corporation
CBE	Commander of the (Order of the) British Empire
CBI	Confederation of British Industry

ALPHABETIZATION KEY

The list of names is alphabetical, with the entrants listed under surnames. If part of an entrant's first given name is in parentheses, this will not affect his or her alphabetical listing.

All names beginning Mc and Mac are treated as though they began Mac, e.g. McDowell before MacEachen, MacFarlane after McFadyen, Macharski before McHenry.

Names with Arabic prefixes are normally listed after the prefix except when requested by the entrant. In the case of surnames beginning De, Des, Du, van or von the entries are normally found under the prefix. Names beginning St are listed as if they began Saint, e.g. St Aubin de Teran after Sainsbury. As a general rule Chinese names are alphabetized under the last name.

In the case of an entrant whose name is spelt in a variety of ways, who is known by a pseudonym or best known by another name, a cross reference is provided, e.g.:

Kadhafi, Col Mu'ammar Muhammed al- (see Gaddafi, Col Mu'ammar Muhammed al-).

Le Carré, John (see Cornwell, David John Moore).

Lloyd, Chris(tine) Marie Evert (see Evert, Chris(tine) Marie).

FOREWORD TO THE 73rd EDITION

This is the 73rd edition of THE INTERNATIONAL WHO'S WHO, which since its first publication in 1935 has become the standard reference work on the world's most famous and influential men and women. The current edition contains more than 22,000 entries, of which more than 1,000 appear here for the first time.

In compiling THE INTERNATIONAL WHO'S WHO, our aim is to create a reference book that answers the needs of readers seeking information on the lives of our most gifted contemporaries. We choose the entries entirely on merit and for their continuing interest and importance. Some are household names in every continent. Others are noted for their contributions in specialized fields or for their role in the political, economic, social or cultural life of their particular countries. The scope and diversity of the book is reflected in the range of activities represented, which includes architecture, art, business, cinema, diplomacy, engineering, fashion, journalism, law, literature, medicine, music, photography, politics, science, sport, technology and theatre.

Each year new entrants are sent questionnaires with a request to supply biographical details. All existing entrants are also contacted, so that they may have an opportunity to make necessary additions and amendments. Supplementary research is done by the Editor and the Europa editorial department to ensure that the book is as up-to-date as possible upon publication. Valuable assistance is also provided by consultants and experts in particular fields or with specialized knowledge of certain countries.

The introduction contains a list of abbreviations and international telephone codes. The names of entrants whose death has been reported over the past year are included in the Obituary. There is also a section on Reigning Royal Families.

The biographical information contained in this 73rd edition, as well as information on past entrants, deceased entrants and entrants from the wide range of other Europa biographical sources, is provided online in WORLD WHO'S WHO. Using the product's sophisticated search functions, researchers can easily and quickly access the rich biographical data in the comprehensive Europa biographical database. As well, online users can take advantage of the quarterly updating cycle that ensures the data is as current as possible. Details of this resource are available at www.worldwhoswho.com

Not many countries have their own who's who, and not all national who's whos are published annually. THE INTERNATIONAL WHO'S WHO 2010 represents in one volume a library of information from all countries that is not found elsewhere and is unrivalled in its balance and coverage.

May 2009

OBITUARY

Innocenti, Antonio	6 September 2008
Iordache, Stefan	14 September 2008
Ito, Kiyoshi	10 November 2008
Jacobs, Klaus J.	11 September 2008
Jagan, Janet	28 March 2009
Jarre, Maurice Alexis	29 March 2009
Jeyaretnam, J.B.	30 September 2008
Johnson, Russell	7 August 2007
Jones, James Larkin (Jack)	21 April 2009
Jordan, Hamilton	20 May 2008
Joshi, Damayanti	19 September 2004
Kabui, Joseph	7 June 2008
Kagel, Mauricio	18 September 2008
Kahn-Ackermann, Georg	6 September 2008
Kanovitz, Howard	2 February 2009
Kantrowitz, Adrian	14 November 2008
Kantrowitz, Arthur Robert	29 November 2008
Kaplicky, Jan	14 January 2009
Karmel, Peter Henry	30 December 2008
Ke, Ting-Sui	29 April 2000
Keeble, Sir (Herbert Ben) Curtis	6 December 2008
Kennet, Lord Wayland Young	7 May 2009
Kerr, Deborah Jane	16 October 2007
Khalil, Mustafa	7 June 2008
Kiet, Vo Van	11 June 2008
Kim, HE Cardinal Stephen Sou-Hwan	16 February 2009
Kirkup, James Harold	10 May 2009
Kitt, Eartha Mae	25 December 2008
Kolff, Willem Johan	11 February 2009
Knopf, Alfred Jr	14 February 2009
Lagergren, Gunnar Karl Andreas	27 December 2008
Laghi, Pio	10 January 2008
Lamb, Willis Eugene, Jr	15 May 2008
Lang, Andrew Richard	30 June 2008
Lapid, Joseph (Tommy)	1 June 2008
Lapidus, Ted	29 December 2008
Latyshev, Col-Gen. Pytor Mikhailovich	2 December 2008
Leblond, Charles Philippe	10 April 2007
Leonard, Hugh	12 February 2009
Léontieff, Alexandre	2 March 2009
Levey, Sir Michael Vincent	28 December 2008
Liao, Bingxiong	22 September 2006
Liao, Lt. Gen Hansheng	5 October 2006
Liao, Shantao	6 June 1997
Li, Jiulong	19 November 2003
Li, Ximing	8 November 2008
Liberaki, Margarita	2001
Loomis, Henry	2 November 2008
Lu, Wenfu	9 August 2005
Ma, Hong	28 October 2007
MacCormick, Sir (Donald) Neil	5 April 2009
Maddox, Sir John Royden	12 April 2009
Mailer, Norman Kingsley	10 November 2007
Makeba, Miriam	9 November 2008
Manekshaw, Field Gen. Sam Hormuzji Framji Jamshedji	26 June 2008
Manyika, Elliott T.	6 December 2008
Massevitch, Alla G.	6 May 2008
Maximova, Ekaterina Sergeyevna	28 April 2008
Mellers, Wilfrid Howard	17 May 2008
Melles, Carl	25 April 2004
Mellink, Machteld Johanna	24 February 2006
Mitchell, Adrian	20 December 2008
Monette, Richard Jean	9 September 2008
Monory, René Claude Aristide	11 April 2009
Moore, Robin James	4 January 2009
Mordyukova, Nonna (Noyabrina) Viktorovna	6 July 2008
Mortimer, Sir John Clifford	16 January 2009
Motlana, Nthato Harrison	30 November 2008
Mouriño Terraza, Juan Camilo	4 November 2008
Mphahlele, Ezekiel (Es'kia)	27 October 2008
Mu'alla, Sheikh Rashid bin Ahmad al-,	2 January 2009
Mudenda, Elijah	2 November 2008
Muir Wood, Sir Alan (Marshall)	1 February 2009
Mwanawasa, Levy Patrick	19 August 2008
Nasir, Amir Ibrahim	22 November 2008
Negahban, Ezatollah	2 February 2009
Negeri Sembilan, Tuanku Ja'afar ibni al-Marhum Tuanku Adbul Rahman	27 December 2008
Newman, Paul	26 September 2008
Nielsen, Inga	10 February 2008
Nissel, Siegmund Walter	23 May 2008
Nixon, Sir Edwin Ronald	17 August 2008
North, John David	31 October 2008
Nye, Peter Hague	13 February 2009
O'Brien, Conor Cruise	18 December 2008
Okun, Daniel Alexander	10 December 2007
Osipyan, Yuri Andreyevich	10 September 2008
Osman, Osman Ahmed	April 1999

Pak, Song-chol	28 October 2008
Palade, George Emil	7 October 2008
Papadopoulos, Tassos	12 December 2008
Pavlicek, Frantisek	29 September 2004
Pelissier, Jacques Daniel Paul	2 December 2008
Pell, Claiborne de Borda	1 January 2009
Peng, Huanwu	28 February 2007
Perisin, Ivo	30 October 2008
Phounsavanh, Nouhak	9 September 2008
Piccard, Jacques Ernest Jean	1 November 2008
Picht, Robert	24 September 2008
Pinter, Harold	24 December 2008
Piontek, Heinz	26 October 2003
Pippard, Sir (Alfred) Brian	21 September 2008
Ploritis, Marios	29 December 2006
Pollack, Sydney	26 May 2008
Prabhakar, Vishnu	11 April 2009
Pristavkin, Anatoliy Ignatevich	11 July 2008
Pugovkin, Mikhail Ivanovich	25 July 2008
Purdy, James	13 March 2009
Qi, Gong	30 June 2005
Quinlan, Sir Michael Edward	26 February 2009
Rakowski, Mieczys?aw Franciszek	8 November 2008
Religa, Zbigniew Eugeniusz	8 March 2009
Richards, Frederic Middlebrook	11 January 2009
Richardson, Natasha Jane	18 March 2009
Ritchie, J. Murdoch	9 July 2008
Robertson, Sir Lewis	24 November 2008
Robinson, Sir Albert Edward Phineas	17 January 2009
Rogers, Edward Samuel (Ted)	2 December 2008
Rooke, Sir Denis Eric	2 September 2008
Rothschild, Edmund Leopold de	17 January 2009
Rúfus, Milan	11 January 2009
Russell, John	23 August 2008
Russell-Johnston, Lord David Russell Russell-Johnston	27 July 2008
Russert, Tim	13 June 2008
Rytkheu, Yuriy Sergeyevich	15 May 2008
Sabah, Sheikh Saad al-Abdullah as-Salim as-	13 May 2008
Sabiston, David Coston jr	26 January 2009
Saint Laurent, Yves (Henri Donat)	1 June 2008
Salpeter, Edwin E.	25 November 2008
Sargeson, Alan McLeod	29 December 2008
Schevill, James Erwin	29 January 2009
Schulz, Mikhail	9 October 2006
Schwartz, Jacob T.	2 March 2009
Seamans, Robert Channing, Jr	28 June 2008
Setubal, Olavo Egydio	27 August 2008
Shi, Qingyun	2002
Shields, Sir Robert	3 October 2008
Shinohara, Kazuo	15 July 2006
Shivas, Mark	11 October 2008
Sidki, Aziz	January 2008
Sidorov, Veniamin A.	20 December 2006
Simonet, Henri	15 February 1996
Simplot, J.R.	25 May 2008
Simutis, Anicetas	8 March 2006
Singh, Vishwanath Pratap	27 November 2008
Singh Gurjar, Govind	6 April 2009
Sinowatz, Fred	11 August 2008
Slaoui, Driss	7 February 1999
Slynn of Hadley, Lord Gordon Slynn	7 April 2009
Snodgrass, William DeWitt	13 January 2009
Snow, Tony	12 July 2008
Solomon, Yonty	26 September 2008
Solzhenitsyn, Aleksandr Isayevich	3 August 2008
Song, Defu	13 September 2007
Sorsa, Kalevi	16 January 2004
Southall, Ivan Francis	15 November 2008
Southam, Gordon Hamilton	1 July 2008
Spekreijse, Henk	20 October 2006
Stadtman, Earl Reece	7 January 2008
Stanley, Julian	12 August 2005
Stead, Rev. (George) Christopher	28 May 2008
Stent, Gunther	12 June 2008
Stephens, Olin James II	13 September 2008
Stokes, Donald Gresham	21 July 2008
Stumpf, Paul Karl	10 February 2007
Styles, Margretta	20 November 2005
Sugita, Katsuyuki	30 March 2008
Suliotis, Elena	4 December 2004
Sun, Dao Lin	28 December 2007
Surjeet, Harkishan Singh	1 August 2008
Suzman, Dame Helen	1 January 2009
Syquia, Enrique P.	1 February 2005
Szajna, Józef	24 June 2008
Szczepanski, Jan	2004
Tan, Haosheng	28 September 2005
Tan, Jiazhen	1 November 2008

OBITUARY

Tang, Zhisong	21 July 2008	Walters, Sir Alan Arthur	3 January 2009
Templeton, Sir John Marks	8 July 2008	Wang, Yung-ching	15 October 2008
Terkel, Louis (Studs)	31 October 2008	Watkins, Winnifred May	3 October 2003
Thomson of Monifieth, George Morgan	3 October 2008	Watson, Lyall	25 June 2008
Thorpe, James	4 January 2009	Weatherstone, Dennis	13 June 2008
Troshev, Col-Gen. Gennady Nikolayevich	14 September 2008	Weber, John William	23 May 2008
Underwood, Cecil H.	24 November 2008	Weller, Thomas Huckle	23 August 2008
Updike, John Hoyer	27 January 2009	White, Robert M. II	19 November 2008
Urwin, Gregory (Greg)	11 August 2008	Wijetunga, Dingiri Banda	21 September 2008
Utzon, Jørn	29 November 2008	Wild, John Paul	10 May 2008
Van Allan, Richard	4 December 2008	Winkler, Jan	16 February 2009
Van Bruggen, Coosje	10 January 2008	Woytowicz-Rudnicka, Stefania	1 September 2005
Van der Klauuw, Christoph Albert	16 March 2005	Wright, Barbara	3 March 2009
Van Kesteren, John	11 July 2008	Wyeth, Andrew	16 January 2009
Vansittart, Peter	4 October 2008	Wu, Jinghua	19 October 2007
Varennikov, Valentin Ivanovich	6 May 2009	Xie, Jin	18 October 2008
Varley, Lord Eric Graham Varley	29 July 2008	Yao, Zhen	4 November 2005
Venkataraman, Ramaswamy	27 January 2008	Yoshimura, Akira	7 July 2006
Vieira, Brig Gen Joao Bernardo	2 March 2009	Young, Hon. Sir John (McIntosh)	6 October 2008
Viljoen, Gerrit van Niekerk	29 March 2009	Zhang, Haoruo	27 March 2004
Vinogradov, Vladimir Viktorovich	29 June 2008	Zhang, Taiheng	29 January 2005
von Dassanowsky, Elfi (Elfriede)	2 October 2007	Zienkiewicz, Olgierd Cecil	2 January 2009
Waelsch, Salome G.	7 November 2007	Zou, Chenglu	23 November 2006
Walde, Thomas	11 October 2008		

ABBREVIATIONS

DSO	Companion of the Distinguished Service Order
DSocSc	Doctor of Social Science
DST	Doctor of Sacred Theology
DTech	Doctor of Technology
DTechSc(i)	Doctor of Technical Sciences
DTheol	Doctor of Theology
DTM	Diploma in Tropical Medicine
DTM&H	Diploma in Tropical Medicine and Hygiene
DUP	Diploma of the University of Paris
DUniv	Doctor of the University
E	East; Eastern
EBRD	European Bank for Reconstruction and Development
EC	European Commission; European Community
ECA	Economic Co-operation Administration; Economic Commission for Africa
ECAFE	Economic Commission for Asia and the Far East
ECE	Economic Commission for Europe
ECLA	Economic Commission for Latin America
ECLAC	Economic Commission for Latin America and the Caribbean
ECO	Economic Co-operation Organization
Econ.	Economic
Econs	Economics
ECOSOC	Economic and Social Council
ECSC	European Coal and Steel Community
ECWA	Economic Commission for Western Asia
ed	educated; edited
Ed.	Editor
ED	Efficiency Decoration; Doctor of Engineering (USA)
EdD	Doctor of Education
Edin.	Edinburgh
EdM	Master of Education
Edn	Edition
Educ.	Education
EEC	European Economic Community
EFTA	European Free Trade Association
eh	Ehrenhalben (Honorary)
EIB	European Investment Bank
EM	Edward Medal; Master of Engineering (USA)
Emer.	Emerita; Emeritus
Eng	Engineering
EngD	Doctor of Engineering
ENO	English National Opera
EPLF	Eritrean People's Liberation Front
ESA	European Space Agency
ESCAP	Economic and Social Commission for Asia and the Pacific
ESCWA	Economic and Social Commission for Western Asia
est.	established
ETH	Eidgenössische Technische Hochschule (Swiss Federal Institute of Technology)
Ets	Etablissements
EU	European Union
EURATOM	European Atomic Energy Community
Exec.	Executive
Exhbn	Exhibition
Ext.	Extension
f.	founded
FAA	Fellow of Australian Academy of Science
FAAS	Fellow of the American Association for the Advancement of Science
FAATS	Fellow of the Australian Academy of Technological Sciences
FACC	Fellow of the American College of Cardiology
FACCA	Fellow of the Association of Certified and Corporate Accountants
FACE	Fellow of the Australian College of Education
FACP	Fellow of American College of Physicians
FACS	Fellow of the American College of Surgeons
FAHA	Fellow Australian Academy of the Humanities
FAIA	Fellow of the American Institute of Architects
FAIAS	Fellow of the Australian Institute of Agricultural Science
FAIM	Fellow of the Australian Institute of Management
FAO	Food and Agriculture Organization
FAS	Fellow of the Antiquarian Society
FASE	Fellow of Antiquarian Society, Edinburgh
FASSA	Fellow Academy of Social Sciences of Australia
FBA	Fellow of the British Academy
FBI	Federal Bureau of Investigation
FBIM	Fellow of the British Institute of Management
FBIP	Fellow of the British Institute of Physics
FCA	Fellow of the Institute of Chartered Accountants
FCAE	Fellow Canadian Academy of Engineering
FCGI	Fellow of the City and Guilds of London Institute
FCIA	Fellow of the Chartered Institute of Arbitrators
FCIB	Fellow of the Chartered Institute of Bankers
FCIC	Fellow of the Chemical Institute of Canada
FCIM	Fellow of the Chartered Institute of Management
FCIS	Fellow of the Chartered Institute of Secretaries
FCMA	Fellow of the Chartered Institute of Management Accountants
FCO	Foreign and Commonwealth Office
FCSD	Fellow of the Chartered Society of Designers
FCT	Federal Capital Territory
FCWA	Fellow of the Institute of Cost and Works Accountants (now FCMA)
FDGB	Freier Deutscher Gewerkschaftsbund
FDP	Freier Demokratische Partei
Feb.	February
Fed.	Federation; Federal
FEng	Fellow(ship) of Engineering
FFCM	Fellow of the Faculty of Community Medicine
FFPHM	Fellow of the Faculty of Public Health Medicine
FGS	Fellow of the Geological Society
FGSM	Fellow of the Guildhall School of Music
FIA	Fellow of the Institute of Actuaries
FIAL	Fellow of the International Institute of Arts and Letters
FIAM	Fellow of the International Academy of Management
FIAMS	Fellow of the Indian Academy of Medical Sciences
FIAP	Fellow of the Institution of Analysts and Programmers
FIArb	Fellow of the Institute of Arbitrators
FIB	Fellow of the Institute of Bankers
FIBA	Fellow of the Institute of Banking Associations
FIBiol	Fellow of the Institute of Biologists
FICE	Fellow of the Institution of Civil Engineers
FIChemE	Fellow of the Institute of Chemical Engineers
FID	Fellow of the Institute of Directors
FIE	Fellow of the Institute of Engineers
FIEE	Fellow of the Institution of Electrical Engineers
FIEEE	Fellow of the Institute of Electrical and Electronics Engineers
FIFA	Fédération Internationale de Football Association
FIJ	Fellow of the Institute of Journalists
FilLic	Licentiate in Philosophy
FIM	Fellow of the Institute of Metallurgists
FIME	Fellow of the Institute of Mining Engineers
FIMechE	Fellow of the Institute of Mechanical Engineers
FIMI	Fellow of the Institute of the Motor Industry
FInstF	Fellow of the Institute of Fuel
FInstM	Fellow of the Institute of Marketing
FInstP	Fellow of the Institute of Physics
FInstPet	Fellow of the Institute of Petroleum
FIPM	Fellow of the Institute of Personnel Management
FIRE	Fellow of the Institution of Radio Engineers
FITD	Fellow of the Institute of Training and Development
FL	Florida
Fla	Florida
FLA	Fellow of the Library Association
FLN	Front de Libération Nationale
FLS	Fellow of the Linnaean Society
FMedSci	Fellow of the Academy of Medical Sciences
fmr(ly)	former(ly)
FNI	Fellow of the National Institute of Sciences of India
FNZIA	Fellow of the New Zealand Institute of Architects
FRACP	Fellow of the Royal Australasian College of Physicians
FRACS	Fellow of the Royal Australasian College of Surgeons
FRAeS	Fellow of the Royal Aeronautical Society
FRAI	Fellow of the Royal Anthropological Institute
FRAIA	Fellow of the Royal Australian Institute of Architects
FRAIC	Fellow of the Royal Architectural Institute of Canada
FRAM	Fellow of the Royal Academy of Music
FRAS	Fellow of the Royal Astronomical Society; Fellow of the Royal Asiatic Society
FRBS	Fellow of the Royal Society of British Sculptors
FRCA	Fellow of the Royal College of Anaesthetists
FRCM	Fellow of the Royal College of Music
FRCO	Fellow of the Royal College of Organists
FRCOG	Fellow of the Royal College of Obstetricians and Gynaecologists
FRCP	Fellow of the Royal College of Physicians
FRCPE	Fellow of the Royal College of Physicians, Edinburgh
FRCPGlas	Fellow of the Royal College of Physicians (Glasgow)
FRCPI	Fellow of the Royal College of Physicians of Ireland
FRCPath	Fellow Royal College of Pathologists
FRCR	Fellow Royal College of Radiology
FRCS	Fellow of the Royal College of Surgeons
FRCSE	Fellow of the Royal College of Surgeons, Edinburgh
FRCVS	Fellow of the Royal College of Veterinary Surgeons
FREconS	Fellow of the Royal Economic Society
FREng	Fellow of the Royal Academy of Engineering
FRES	Fellow of the Royal Entomological Society
FRFPS	Fellow of the Royal Faculty of Physicians and Surgeons
FRG	Federal Republic of Germany
FRGS	Fellow of the Royal Geographical Society
FRHistS	Fellow of the Royal Historical Society
FRHortS	Fellow of the Royal Horticultural Society
FRIBA	Fellow of the Royal Institute of British Architects
FRIC	Fellow of the Royal Institute of Chemists
FRICS	Fellow of the Royal Institute of Chartered Surveyors
FRMetS	Fellow of the Royal Meteorological Society
FRNCM	Fellow of the Royal Northern College of Music
FRPS	Fellow of the Royal Photographic Society
FRS	Fellow of the Royal Society
FRSA	Fellow of the Royal Society of Arts
FRSAMD	Fellow of the Royal Scottish Academy of Music and Drama
FRSC	Fellow of the Royal Society of Canada; Fellow of the Royal Society of Chemistry
FRSE	Fellow of the Royal Society of Edinburgh

FRSL	Fellow of the Royal Society of Literature
FRSM	Fellow of the Royal Society of Medicine
FRSNZ	Fellow of the Royal Society of New Zealand
FRSS	Fellow of the Royal Statistical Society
FRSSA	Fellow of the Royal Society of South Africa
FRTS	Fellow of the Royal Television Society
FSA	Fellow of the Society of Antiquaries
FSIAD	Fellow of the Society of Industrial Artists and Designers
FTI	Fellow of the Textile Institute
FTS	Fellow of Technological Sciences
FWAAS	Fellow of the World Academy of Arts and Sciences
FZS	Fellow of the Zoological Society
GA	Georgia
Ga	Georgia
GATT	General Agreement on Tariffs and Trade
GB	Great Britain
GBE	Knight (or Dame) Grand Cross of (the Order of) the British Empire
GC	George Cross
GCB	Knight Grand Cross of (the Order of) the Bath
GCIE	Knight Grand Commander of (the Order of) the Indian Empire
GCMG	Knight (or Dame) Grand Cross of (the Order of) St Michael and St George
GCSI	Knight Grand Commander of (the Order of) the Star of India
GCVO	Knight (or Dame) Grand Cross of the Royal Victorian Order
GDR	German Democratic Republic
Gen.	General
GHQ	General Headquarters
GLA	Greater London Authority
Glam.	Glamorganshire
GLC	Greater London Council
Glos.	Gloucestershire
GM	George Medal
GmbH	Gesellschaft mit beschränkter Haftung (Limited Liability Company)
GOC	General Officer Commanding
GOC-in-C	General Officer Commanding-in-Chief
Gov.	Governor
Govt	Government
GPO	General Post Office
Grad.	Graduate
GRSM	Graduate of the Royal School of Music
GSO	General Staff Officer
Hants.	Hampshire
hc	honoris causa
HE	His Eminence; His (or Her) Excellency
Herefords.	Herefordshire
Herts.	Hertfordshire
HH	His (or Her) Highness
HI	Hawaii
HIV	human immunodeficiency virus
HLD	Doctor of Humane Letters
HM	His (or Her) Majesty
HMS	His (or Her) Majesty's Ship
Hon.	Honorary; Honourable
Hons	Honours
Hosp.	Hospital
HQ	Headquarters
HRH	His (or Her) Royal Highness
HSH	His (or Her) Serene Highness
HSP	Hungarian Socialist Party
HSWP	Hungarian Socialist Workers' Party
Hunts.	Huntingdonshire
IA	Iowa
Ia	Iowa
IAAF	International Association of Athletics Federations
IAEA	International Atomic Energy Agency
IATA	International Air Transport Association
IBA	Independent Broadcasting Authority
IBRD	International Bank for Reconstruction and Development (World Bank)
ICAO	International Civil Aviation Organization
ICC	International Chamber of Commerce
ICE	Institution of Civil Engineers
ICEM	Intergovernmental Committee for European Migration
ICFTU	International Confederation of Free Trade Unions
ICI	Imperial Chemical Industries
ICOM	International Council of Museums
ICRC	International Committee for the Red Cross
ICS	Indian Civil Service
ICSID	International Centre for Settlement of Investment Disputes
ICSU	International Council of Scientific Unions
ID	Idaho
Ida	Idaho
IDA	International Development Association
IDB	Inter-American Development Bank
IEA	International Energy Agency
IEE	Institution of Electrical Engineers
IEEE	Institution of Electrical and Electronic Engineers

IFAD	International Fund for Agricultural Development
IFC	International Finance Corporation
IGAD	Intergovernmental Authority on Development
IISS	International Institute for Strategic Studies
IL	Illinois
Ill.	Illinois
ILO	International Labour Organization
IMCO	Inter-Governmental Maritime Consultative Organization
IMechE	Institution of Mechanical Engineers
IMF	International Monetary Fund
IMO	International Maritime Organization
IN	Indiana
Inc.	Incorporated
Ind.	Indiana; Independent
Insp.	Inspector
Inst.	Institute; Institution
Int.	International
INTERPOL	International Criminal Police Organization
INTUC	Indian National Trades Union Congress
IOC	International Olympic Committee
IPU	Inter-Parliamentary Union
ISO	Companion of the Imperial Service Order
ITA	Independent Television Authority
ITU	International Telecommunications Union
ITV	Independent Television
IUPAC	International Union of Pure and Applied Chemistry
IUPAP	International Union of Pure and Applied Physics
Jan.	January
JCB	Bachelor of Canon Law
JCD	Doctor of Canon Law
JD	Doctor of Jurisprudence
JMK	Johan Mangku Negara (Malaysia)
JP	Justice of the Peace
Jr	Junior
JSD	Doctor of Juristic Science
Jt(ly)	Joint(ly)
JUD	Juris utriusque Doctor (Doctor of both Civil and Canon Law)
JuD	Doctor of Law
JUDr	Juris utriusque Doctor (Doctor of both Civil and Canon Law); Doctor of Law
Kan.	Kansas
KBE	Knight Commander of (the Order of) the British Empire
KC	King's Counsel
KCB	Knight Commander of (the Order of) the Bath
KCIE	Knight Commander of (the Order of) the Indian Empire
KCMG	Knight Commander of (the Order of) St Michael and St George
KCSI	Knight Commander of (the Order of) the Star of India
KCVO	Knight Commander of the Royal Victorian Order
KG	Royal Knight of the Most Noble Order of the Garter
KGB	Committee of State Security (USSR)
KK	Kaien Kaisha
KLM	Koninklijke Luchtvaart Maatschappij (Royal Dutch Airlines)
KNZM	Knight of the New Zealand Order of Merit
KP	Knight of (the Order of) St Patrick
KS	Kansas
KStJ	Knight of (the Order of) St John of Jerusalem
KT	Knight of (the Order of) the Thistle
Kt	Knight
KY	Kentucky
Ky	Kentucky
LA	Louisiana; Los Angeles
La	Louisiana
Lab.	Laboratory
Lancs.	Lancashire
LDP	Liberal Democratic Party
LDS	Licentiate in Dental Surgery
Legis.	Legislative
Leics.	Leicestershire
LenD	Licencié en Droit
LèsL	Licencié ès Lettres
LèsSc	Licencié ès Sciences
LG	Lady of (the Order of) the Garter
LHD	Doctor of Humane Letters
LI	Long Island
LicenDer	Licenciado en Derecho
LicenFil	Licenciado en Filosofía
LicMed	Licentiate in Medicine
Lincs.	Lincolnshire
LittD	Doctor of Letters
LLB	Bachelor of Laws
LLC	Limited Liability Company
LLD	Doctor of Laws
LLL	Licentiate of Laws
LLM	Master of Laws
LLP	Limited Liability Partnership
LM	Licentiate of Medicine; Licentiate Midwifery
LN	League of Nations
LPh	Licentiate of Philosophy
LRAM	Licentiate of the Royal Academy of Music
LRCP	Licentiate of the Royal College of Physicians

ABBREVIATIONS

LSE	London School of Economics and Political Science
Lt	Lieutenant
Ltd	Limited
Ltda	Limitada
LTh	Licentiate in Theology
LVO	Lieutenant, Royal Victorian Order
m.	married; marriage; metre(s)
MA	Massachusetts; Master of Arts
MAgr	Master of Agriculture (USA)
Maj.	Major
MALD	Master of Arts in Law and Diplomacy
Man.	Management; Manager; Managing; Manitoba
MArch	Master of Architecture
Mass	Massachusetts
Math.	Mathematics; Mathematical
MB	Bachelor of Medicine; Manitoba
MBA	Master of Business Administration
MBE	Member of (the Order of) the British Empire
MBS	Master of Business Studies
MC	Military Cross
MCC	Marylebone Cricket Club
MCE	Master of Civil Engineering
MCh	Master of Surgery
MChD	Master of Dental Surgery
MCL	Master of Civil Law
MCom(m)	Master of Commerce
MCP	Master of City Planning
MD	Maryland; Doctor of Medicine
Md	Maryland
MDiv	Master of Divinity
MDS	Master of Dental Surgery
ME	Maine; Myalgic Encephalomyelitis
Me	Maine
MEconSc	Master of Economic Sciences
MEd	Master in Education
mem.	member
MEng	Master of Engineering (Dublin)
MEP	Member of European Parliament
MFA	Master of Fine Arts
Mfg	Manufacturing
Mfrs	Manufacturers
Mgr	Monseigneur; Monsignor
MI	Michigan; Marshall Islands
MIA	Master of International Affairs
MICE	Member of the Institution of Civil Engineers
MIChemE	Member of the Institution of Chemical Engineers
Mich.	Michigan
Middx	Middlesex
MIEE	Member of the Institution of Electrical Engineers
Mil.	Military
MIMarE	Member of the Institute of Marine Engineers
MIMechE	Member of the Institution of Mechanical Engineers
MIMinE	Member of the Institution of Mining Engineers
Minn.	Minnesota
MInstT	Member of the Institute of Transport
Miss.	Mississippi
MIStructE	Member of the Institution of Structural Engineers
MIT	Massachusetts Institute of Technology
MJ	Master of Jurisprudence
MLA	Member of the Legislative Assembly; Master of Landscape Architecture
MLC	Member of the Legislative Council
MM	Military Medal
MLitt	Master in Letters
MM	Military Medal
MMus	Master of Music
MN	Minnesota
MNOC	Movement of Non-Aligned Countries
MO	Missouri
Mo.	Missouri
MOH	Medical Officer of Health
Mon.	Monmouthshire
Mont.	Montana
Movt	Movement
MP	Member of Parliament; Madhya Pradesh
MPA	Master of Public Administration (Harvard)
MPh	Master of Philosophy (USA)
MPhil	Master of Philosophy
MPolSci	Master of Political Science
MPP	Member of Provincial Parliament (Canada)
MRAS	Member of the Royal Asiatic Society
MRC	Medical Research Council
MRCP	Member of the Royal College of Physicians
MRCPE	Member of the Royal College of Physicians, Edinburgh
MRCS	Member of the Royal College of Surgeons
MRCSE	Member of the Royal College of Surgeons, Edinburgh
MRCVS	Member of the Royal College of Veterinary Surgeons
MRI	Member of the Royal Institution
MRIA	Member of the Royal Irish Academy
MRIC	Member of the Royal Institute of Chemistry
MRP	Mouvement Républicain Populaire
MS	Mississippi; Master of Science; Master of Surgery
MSc	Master of Science
MScS	Master of Social Science
MSP	Member Scottish Parliament
MT	Montana
MTS	Master of Theological Studies
MUDr	Doctor of Medicine
MusB(ac)	Bachelor of Music
MusD(oc)	Doctor of Music
MusM	Master of Music (Cambridge)
MVD	Master of Veterinary Medicine
MVO	Member of the Royal Victorian Order
MW	Master of Wine
N	North; Northern
NAS	National Academy of Sciences (USA)
NASA	National Aeronautics and Space Administration
Nat.	National
NATO	North Atlantic Treaty Organization
Naz.	Nazionale
NB	New Brunswick
NBC	National Broadcasting Corporation
NC	North Carolina
ND	North Dakota
NE	Nebraska; North East
NEA	National Endowment for the Arts
Neb.	Nebraska
NEDC	National Economic Development Council
NERC	Natural Environment Research Council
Nev.	Nevada
NF	Newfoundland
NGO	Non-Governmental Organization
NH	New Hampshire
NHS	National Health Service
NI	Northern Ireland
NIH	National Institutes of Health
NJ	New Jersey
NL	Newfoundland and Labrador
NM	New Mexico
Northants.	Northamptonshire
Notts.	Nottinghamshire
Nov.	November
NPC	National People's Congress
nr	near
NRC	Nuclear Research Council
NS	Nova Scotia
NSF	National Science Foundation
NSW	New South Wales
NT	Northern Territory
NU	Nunavut Territory
NV	Naamloze Vennootschap; Nevada
NW	North West
NWT	North West Territories
NY	New York (State)
NZ	New Zealand
NZIC	New Zealand Institute of Chemistry
O	Ohio
OAPEC	Organization of Arab Petroleum Exporting Countries
OAS	Organization of American States
OAU	Organization of African Unity
OBE	Officer of (the Order of) the British Empire
OC	Officer of the Order of Canada
Oct.	October
OE	Order of Excellence (Guyana)
OECD	Organisation for Economic Co-operation and Development
OEEC	Organization for European Economic Co-operation
OFS	Orange Free State
OH	Ohio
OHCHR	Office of the United Nations High Commissioner for Human Rights
OIC	Organization of the Islamic Conference
OJ	Order of Jamaica
OK	Oklahoma
Okla	Oklahoma
OM	Member of the Order of Merit
ON	Ontario; Order of Nigeria
Ont.	Ontario
ONZ	Order of New Zealand
OP	Ordo Praedicatorum (Dominicans)
OPCW	Organization for the Prohibition of Chemical Weapons
OPEC	Organization of the Petroleum Exporting Countries
OPM	Office of Production Management
OQ	Officer National Order of Québec
OR	Oregon
Ore.	Oregon
Org.	Organization
OSB	Order of St Benedict
OSCE	Organization for Security and Co-operation in Europe
Oxon.	of Oxford University; Oxfordshire
PA	Pennsylvania
Pa	Pennsylvania
Parl.	Parliament; Parliamentary

PC	Privy Councillor
PCC	Provincial Congress Committee
PdB	Bachelor of Pedagogy
PdD	Doctor of Pedagogy
PdM	Master of Pedagogy
PDS	Partei des Demokratischen Sozialismus
PE	Prince Edward Island
PEI	Prince Edward Island
Pembs.	Pembrokeshire
PEN	Poets, Playwrights, Essayists and Novelists (Club)
Perm.	Permanent
PGCE	Postgraduate Certificate in Education
PhB	Bachelor of Philosophy
PhD(r)	Doctor of Philosophy
PharmD	Docteur en Pharmacie
Phila	Philadelphia
PhL	Licentiate of Philosophy
PLA	People's Liberation Army; Port of London Authority
PLC	Public Limited Company
PLO	Palestine Liberation Organization
PMB	Private Mail Bag
pnr	partner
PO(B)	Post Office (Box)
POW	Prisoner of War
PPR	Polish Workers' Party
PPRA	Past President of the Royal Academy
PQ	Province of Québec
PR	Puerto Rico
PRA	President of the Royal Academy
Pref.	Prefecture
Prep.	Preparatory
Pres.	President
PRI	President of the Royal Institute (of Painters in Water Colours)
PRIBA	President of the Royal Institute of British Architects
Prin.	Principal
Priv Doz	Privat Dozent (recognized teacher not on the regular staff)
PRO	Public Relations Officer
Proc.	Proceedings
prod.	producer
Prof.	Professor
Propr	Proprietor
Prov.	Province; Provincial
PRS	President of the Royal Society
PRSA	President of the Royal Scottish Academy
PSM	Panglima Setia Mahota
Pty	Proprietary
Publ.(s)	Publication(s)
Publr	Publisher
Pvt.	Private
PZPR	Polish United Workers' Party
QC	Québec; Queen's Counsel
QGM	Queen's Gallantry Medal
Qld	Queensland
QPM	Queen's Police Medal
QSO	Queen's Service Order
q.v.	quod vide (to which refer)
RA	Royal Academy; Royal Academician; Royal Artillery
RAAF	Royal Australian Air Force
RAC	Royal Armoured Corps
RACP	Royal Australasian College of Physicians
RADA	Royal Academy of Dramatic Art
RAF	Royal Air Force
RAFVR	Royal Air Force Volunteer Reserve
RAM	Royal Academy of Music
RAMC	Royal Army Medical Corps
RAOC	Royal Army Ordnance Corps
RC	Roman Catholic
RCA	Radio Corporation of America; Royal Canadian Academy; Royal College of Art
RCAF	Royal Canadian Air Force
RCM	Royal College of Music
RCP	Romanian Communist Party
RCP	Royal College of Physicians
RCPI	Royal College of Physicians of Ireland
Regt	Regiment
REME	Royal Electric and Mechanical Engineers
Rep.	Representative; represented
Repub.	Republic
resgnd	resigned
retd	retired
Rev.	Reverend
RI	Rhode Island
RIBA	Royal Institute of British Architects
RMA	Royal Military Academy
RN	Royal Navy
RNR	Royal Naval Reserve
RNVR	Royal Naval Volunteer Reserve
RNZAF	Royal New Zealand Air Force
RP	Member Royal Society of Portrait Painters
RPR	Rassemblement pour la République
RSA	Royal Scottish Academy; Royal Society of Arts
RSC	Royal Shakespeare Company; Royal Society of Canada
RSDr	Doctor of Social Sciences
RSFSR	Russian Soviet Federative Socialist Republic
RSL	Royal Society of Literature
Rt Hon.	Right Honourable
Rt Rev.	Right Reverend
RVO	Royal Victorian Order
RWS	Royal Society of Painters in Water Colours
s.	son(s)
S	South; Southern
SA	Sociedad Anónima; Société Anonyme; South Africa; South Australia
SAARC	South Asian Association for Regional Co-operation
SADC	South African Development Community
SAE	Society of Aeronautical Engineers
Salop.	Shropshire
SALT	Strategic Arms Limitation Treaty
Sask.	Saskatchewan
SB	Bachelor of Science (USA)
SC	Senior Counsel; South Carolina
SCAP	Supreme Command Allied Powers
ScB	Bachelor of Science
ScD	Doctor of Science
SD	South Dakota
SDak	South Dakota
SDLP	Social and Democratic Liberal Party
SDP	Social Democratic Party
SE	South East
SEATO	South East Asia Treaty Organization
Sec.	Secretary
SEC	Securities and Exchange Commission
Secr.	Secretariat
SED	Sozialistische Einheitspartei Deutschlands (Socialist Unity Party of the German Democratic Republic)
Sept.	September
S-et-O	Seine-et-Oise
SHAEF	Supreme Headquarters Allied Expeditionary Force
SHAPE	Supreme Headquarters Allied Powers in Europe
SJ	Society of Jesus (Jesuits)
SJD	Doctor of Juristic Science
SK	Saskatchewan
SLD	Social and Liberal Democrats
SM	Master of Science
SOAS	School of Oriental and African Studies
Soc.	Society; Société
SpA	Societá per Azioni
SPD	Sozialdemokratische Partei Deutschlands
Sr	Senior
SRC	Science Research Council
SRL	Société a responsabilité
SSM	Seria Seta Mahkota (Malaysia)
SSR	Soviet Socialist Republic
St	Saint
Staffs.	Staffordshire
STB	Bachelor of Sacred Theology
STD	Doctor of Sacred Theology
STL	Licentiate of Sacred Theology
STM	Master of Sacred Theology
str.	strasse
Supt	Superintendent
SW	South West
SWAPO	South West Africa People's Organization
TA	Territorial Army
TD	Teachta Dála (member of the Dáil); Territorial Decoration
Tech.	Technical; Technology
Temp.	Temporary
Tenn.	Tennessee
Tex.	Texas
ThB	Bachelor of Theology
ThD	Doctor of Theology
THDr	Doctor of Theology
ThM	Master of Theology
TN	Tennessee
Trans.	Translation; Translator
Treas.	Treasurer
TU(C)	Trades Union (Congress)
TV	television
TX	Texas
UAE	United Arab Emirates
UAR	United Arab Republic
UCLA	University of California at Los Angeles
UDEAC	L'Union Douanière et Economique de l'Afrique Centrale
UDR	Union des Démocrates pour la République
UED	University Education Diploma
UK	United Kingdom (of Great Britain and Northern Ireland)
UKAEA	United Kingdom Atomic Energy Authority
UMIST	University of Manchester Institute of Science and Technology
UMNO	United Malays National Organization
UN(O)	United Nations (Organization)

ABBREVIATIONS

UNA	United Nations Association
UNCED	United Nations Council for Education and Development
UNCHS	United Nations Centre for Human Settlements (Habitat)
UNCTAD	United Nations Conference on Trade and Development
UNDCP	United Nations International Drug Control Programme
UNDP	United Nations Development Programme
UNDRO	United Nations Disaster Relief Office
UNEF	United Nations Emergency Force
UNEP	United Nations Environment Programme
UNESCO	United Nations Educational, Scientific and Cultural Organisation
UNFPA	United Nations Population Fund
UNHCR	United Nations High Commissioner for Refugees
UNICEF	United Nations International Children's Emergency Fund
UNIDO	United Nations Industrial Development Organization
UNIFEM	United Nations Development Fund for Women
UNITAR	United Nations Institute for Training and Research
Univ.	University
UNKRA	United Nations Korean Relief Administration
UNRRA	United Nations Relief and Rehabilitation Administration
UNRWA	United Nations Relief and Works Agency
UNU	United Nations University
UP	United Provinces; Uttar Pradesh
UPU	Universal Postal Union
Urb.	Urbanizacion
US	United States
USA	United States of America
USAAF	United States Army Air Force
USAF	United States Air Force
USAID	United States Agency for International Development
USN	United States Navy
USNR	United States Navy Reserve
USPHS	United States Public Health Service
USS	United States Ship
USSR	Union of Soviet Socialist Republics
UT	Utah
UWI	University of the West Indies
VA	Virginia

Va	Virginia
VC	Victoria Cross
VI	(US) Virgin Islands
Vic.	Victoria
Vol.(s)	Volume(s)
VSO	Voluntary Services Overseas
VT	Vermont
Vt	Vermont
W	West; Western
WA	Washington (State); Western Australia
Warwicks.	Warwickshire
Wash.	Washington (State)
WCC	World Council of Churches
WCT	World Championship Tennis
WEU	Western European Union
WFP	World Food Programme
WFTU	World Federation of Trade Unions
WHO	World Health Organization
WI	Wisconsin
Wilts.	Wiltshire
WIPO	World Intellectual Property Organization
Wis.	Wisconsin
WMO	World Meteorological Organization
WNO	Welsh National Opera
Worcs.	Worcestershire
WRAC	Women's Royal Army Corps
WRNS	Women's Royal Naval Service
WTO	World Trade Organization
WV	West Virginia
WVa	West Virginia
WWF	World Wildlife Fund
WY	Wyoming
Wyo.	Wyoming
YMCA	Young Men's Christian Association
Yorks.	Yorkshire
YT	Yukon Territory
YWCA	Young Women's Christian Association

INTERNATIONAL TELEPHONE CODES

To make international calls to telephone and fax numbers listed in the book, dial the international code of the country from which you are calling, followed by the appropriate code for the country you wish to call (listed below), followed by the area code (if applicable) and telephone or fax number listed in the entry.

	Country code	+ or − GMT*
Afghanistan	93	+4½
Albania	355	+1
Algeria	213	+1
Andorra	376	+1
Angola	244	+1
Antigua and Barbuda	1 268	−4
Argentina	54	−3
Armenia	374	+4
Australia	61	+8 to +10
Australian External Territories:		
Australian Antarctic Territory	672	+3 to +10
Christmas Island	61	+7
Cocos (Keeling) Islands	61	+6½
Norfolk Island	672	+11½
Austria	43	+1
Azerbaijan	994	+5
Bahamas	1 242	−5
Bahrain	973	+3
Bangladesh	880	+6
Barbados	1 246	−4
Belarus	375	+2
Belgium	32	+1
Belize	501	−6
Benin	229	+1
Bhutan	975	+6
Bolivia	591	−4
Bosnia and Herzegovina	387	+1
Botswana	267	+2
Brazil	55	−3 to −4
Brunei	673	+8
Bulgaria	359	+2
Burkina Faso	226	0
Burundi	257	+2
Cambodia	855	+7
Cameroon	237	+1
Canada	1	−3 to −8
Cape Verde	238	−1
Central African Republic	236	+1
Chad	235	+1
Chile	56	−4
China, People's Republic	86	+8
Special Administrative Regions:		
Hong Kong	852	+8
Macao	853	+8
China (Taiwan)	886	+8
Colombia	57	−5
Comoros	269	+3
Congo, Democratic Republic	243	+1
Congo, Republic	242	+1
Costa Rica	506	−6
Côte d'Ivoire	225	0
Croatia	385	+1
Cuba	53	−5
Cyprus	357	+2
'Turkish Republic of Northern Cyprus'	90 392	+2
Czech Republic	420	+1
Denmark	45	+1
Danish External Territories:		
Faroe Islands	298	0
Greenland	299	−1 to −4
Djibouti	253	+3
Dominica	1 767	−4
Dominican Republic	1 809	−4
Ecuador	593	−5
Egypt	20	+2
El Salvador	503	−6

	Country code	+ or − GMT*
Equatorial Guinea	240	+1
Eritrea	291	+3
Estonia	372	+2
Ethiopia	251	+3
Fiji	679	+12
Finland	358	+2
Finnish External Territory:		
Åland Islands	358	+2
France	33	+1
French Overseas Regions and		
Departments:		
French Guiana	594	−3
Guadeloupe	590	−4
Martinique	596	−4
Réunion	262	+4
French Overseas Collectivities:		
French Polynesia	689	−9 to −10
Mayotte	262	+3
Saint-Barthélemy	590	−4
Saint-Martin	590	−4
Saint Pierre and Miquelon	508	−3
Wallis and Futuna Islands	681	+12
Other French Overseas Territory:		
New Caledonia	687	+11
Gabon	241	+1
Gambia	220	0
Georgia	995	+4
Germany	49	+1
Ghana	233	0
Greece	30	+2
Grenada	1 473	−4
Guatemala	502	−6
Guinea	224	0
Guinea-Bissau	245	0
Guyana	592	−4
Haiti	509	−5
Honduras	504	−6
Hungary	36	+1
Iceland	354	0
India	91	+5½
Indonesia	62	+7 to +9
Iran	98	+3½
Iraq	964	+3
Ireland	353	0
Israel	972	+2
Italy	39	+1
Jamaica	1 876	−5
Japan	81	+9
Jordan	962	+2
Kazakhstan	7	+6
Kenya	254	+3
Kiribati	686	+12 to +13
Korea, Democratic People's Republic (North Korea)	850	+9
Korea, Republic (South Korea)	82	+9
Kosovo	381†	+3
Kuwait	965	+3
Kyrgyzstan	996	+5
Laos	856	+7
Latvia	371	+2
Lebanon	961	+2
Lesotho	266	+2
Liberia	231	0
Libya	218	+1
Liechtenstein	423	+1
Lithuania	370	+2

	Country code	+ or − GMT*		Country code	+ or − GMT*
Luxembourg	352	+1	Spain	34	+1
Macedonia, former Yugoslav republic	389	+1	Sri Lanka	94	+5½
Madagascar	261	+3	Sudan	249	+2
Malawi	265	+2	Suriname	597	−3
Malaysia	60	+8	Swaziland	268	+2
Maldives	960	+5	Sweden	46	+1
Mali	223	0	Switzerland	41	+1
Malta	356	+1	Syria	963	+2
Marshall Islands	692	+12	Tajikistan	992	+5
Mauritania	222	0	Tanzania	255	+3
Mauritius	230	+4	Thailand	66	+7
Mexico	52	−6 to −7	Timor-Leste	670	+9
Micronesia, Federated States	691	+10 to +11	Togo	228	0
Moldova	373	+2	Tonga	676	+13
Monaco	377	+1	Trinidad and Tobago	1 868	−4
Mongolia	976	+7 to +9	Tunisia	216	+1
Montenegro	382	+1	Turkey	90	+2
Morocco	212	0	Turkmenistan	993	+5
Mozambique	258	+2	Tuvalu	688	+12
Myanmar	95	+6½	Uganda	256	+3
Namibia	264	+2	Ukraine	380	+2
Nauru	674	+12	United Arab Emirates	971	+4
Nepal	977	+5¾	United Kingdom	44	0
Netherlands	31	+1	United Kingdom Crown Dependencies	44	0
Netherlands Dependencies:			United Kingdom Overseas Territories:		
Aruba	297	−4	Anguilla	1 264	−4
Netherlands Antilles	599	−4	Ascension Island	247	0
New Zealand	64	+12	Bermuda	1 441	−4
New Zealand's Dependent and Associated Territories:			British Virgin Islands	1 284	−4
Tokelau	690	−10	Cayman Islands	1 345	−5
Cook Islands	682	−10	Diego Garcia (British Indian Ocean Territory)	246	+5
Niue	683	−11	Falkland Islands	500	−4
Nicaragua	505	−6	Gibraltar	350	+1
Niger	227	+1	Montserrat	1 664	−4
Nigeria	234	+1	Pitcairn Islands	872	−8
Norway	47	+1	Saint Helena	290	0
Norwegian External Territory:			Tristan da Cunha	290	0
Svalbard	47	+1	Turks and Caicos Islands	1 649	−5
Oman	968	+4	United States of America	1	−5 to −10
Pakistan	92	+5	United States Commonwealth Territories:		
Palau	680	+9	Northern Mariana Islands	1 670	+10
Palestinian Autonomous Areas	970 or 972	+2	Puerto Rico	1 787	−4
Panama	507	−5	United States External Territories:		
Papua New Guinea	675	+10	American Samoa	1 684	−11
Paraguay	595	−4	Guam	1 671	+10
Peru	51	−5	United States Virgin Islands	1 340	−4
Philippines	63	+8	Uruguay	598	−3
Poland	48	+1	Uzbekistan	998	+5
Portugal	351	0	Vanuatu	678	+11
Qatar	974	+3	Vatican City	39	+1
Romania	40	+2	Venezuela	58	−4½
Russian Federation	7	+2 to +12	Viet Nam	84	+7
Rwanda	250	+2	Yemen	967	+3
Saint Christopher and Nevis	1 869	−4	Zambia	260	+2
Saint Lucia	1 758	−4	Zimbabwe	263	+2
Saint Vincent and the Grenadines	1 784	−4			
Samoa	685	−11			
San Marino	378	+1			
São Tomé and Príncipe	239	0			
Saudi Arabia	966	+3			
Senegal	221	0			
Serbia	381	+1			
Seychelles	248	+4			
Sierra Leone	232	0			
Singapore	65	+8			
Slovakia	421	+1			
Slovenia	386	+1			
Solomon Islands	677	+11			
Somalia	252	+3			
South Africa	27	+2			

* The times listed compare the standard (winter) times in the various countries. Some countries adopt Summer (Daylight Saving) Time— i.e. +1 hour—for part of the year.

† Mobile telephone numbers for Kosovo use either the country code for Monaco (377) or the country code for Slovenia (386).

Note: Telephone and fax numbers using the Inmarsat ocean region code 870 are listed in full. No country or area code is required, but it is necessary to precede the number with the international access code of the country from which the call is made.

REIGNING ROYAL FAMILIES OF THE WORLD

Biographical entries of most of the reigning monarchs and of certain other members of the reigning royal families will be found in their appropriate alphabetical order in the biographical section of this book. The name under which they can be found in the text of the book will be listed in this section in bold type.

BAHRAIN

Reigning King

HM SHEIKH HAMAD BIN ISA AL-KHALIFA;b. 28 January 1950; succeeded 6 March 1999 as Ruler of Bahrain on the death of his father, Sheikh Isa bin Sulman al-Khalifa; acceded as Amir 6 March 1999; proclaimed King 14 February 2002; married 1968, Shaikha Sabeeka bint Ibrahim al-Khalifa; six sons, four daughters.

Crown Prince

HH Sheikh Salman bin Hamad al-Khalifa.

BELGIUM

Reigning King

HM KING ALBERT II; b. 6 June 1934; succeeded to the throne 9 August 1993, on the death of his brother, King Baudouin I; married 2 July 1959, Donna Paola Ruffo di Calabria (Queen Paola) (b. 11 September 1937).

Children of the King

Crown Prince Philippe, Duke of Brabant, b. 15 April 1960; married 4 December 1999, Mathilde d'Udekem d'Acoz; daughter, Princess Elisabeth, b. 25 October 2001; son, Prince Gabriel, b. 20 August 2003; son, Emmanuel, b. 4 October 2005.

Princess Astrid, b. 5 June 1962; married 22 September 1984, Archduke Lorenz; son, Prince Amedeo, b. February 1986; daughter, Princess Maria Laura, b. August 1988; son, Prince Joachim, b. December 1991; daughter, Princess Louisa-Maria, b. October 1995; daughter, Princess Laetitia Maria, b. 23 April 2003.

Prince Laurent, b. 19 October 1963; married 12 April 2003, Claire Coombs; daughter, Princess Louise, b. February 2004; son, Prince Aymeric, b. December 2005; son, Prince Nicolas, b. December 2005.

Parents of the King

King Léopold III, b. 3 November 1901, died 25 September 1983; married 1st 4 November 1926, Princess Astrid of Sweden (Queen Astrid) (b. 17 November 1905, died 29 August 1935); married 2nd 11 September 1941, Mary Lilian Baels (died 7 June 2002); three children.

Brother and Sister of the King

Joséphine Charlotte, Princess of Belgium, b. 11 October 1927, died January 2005; married 9 April 1953, Prince (later Grand Duke) Jean of Luxembourg (b. 5 January 1921, died 10 January 2005); three sons, two daughters.

King Baudouin I, b. 7 September 1930, died 31 July 1993; married 15 December 1960, Fabiola Fernanda María de las Victorias Antonia Adelaida de Mora y Aragón.

BHUTAN

The Druk Gyalpo (Dragon King)

HM DASHO JIGME KHESAR NAMGYAL WANGCHUCK; b. 21 February 1980; succeeded to the throne 14 December 2006, on the abdication of his father, the Druk Gyalpo Jigme Singye Wangchuk.

Parents of the King

King Jigme Singye Wangchuck, b. 11 November 1955; succeeded to the throne 24 July 1972; crowned 2 June 1974; abdicated 14 December 2006; married Queen Ashi Tshering Yandon Wangchuck (b. 21 June 1959); ten children.

Brothers and Sisters of the King

HRH Princess Chimi Yangzom Wangchuck, b. 10 January 1980.

HRH Princess Sonam Dechen Wangchuck, b. 5 August 1981.

HRH Princess Dechen Yangzom Wangchuck, b. 2 December 1981.

HRH Princess Kesang Choden Wangchuck, b. 23 January 1982.

HRH Prince Jigyel Ugyen Wangchuck, b. 16 July 1984.

HRH Prince Khamsum Singye Wangchuck, b. 6 October 1985.

HRH Prince Jigme Dorji Wangchuck, b. 14 April 1986.

HRH Princess Euphelma Choden Wangchuck, b. 6 June 1993.

HRH Prince Ugyen Jigme Wangchuck, b. 11 November 1994.

BRUNEI

Reigning Sultan and Yang di-Pertuan

HM Sultan Haji HASSANAL BOLKIAH MU'IZUDDIN WADDAULAH; b. 15 July 1946; succeeded as 29th Sultan 5 October 1967, on the abdication of his father, Sultan Haji Omar Ali Saifuddien II; crowned 1 August 1968; married 29 July 1965, Raja Isteri Pengiran Anak Hajjah Saleha; two sons, four daughters; also married 28 October 1981, Mariam Abd Aziz (divorced 2003); two sons, two daughters; also married 19 August 2005, HRH Pengiran Isteri Azrinaz Mazhar Hakim; one son.

Crown Prince

HRH Prince Haji al-Muhtadee Billah, b. 17 February 1974; proclaimed Crown Prince 10 August 1998; married 9 September 2004, HRH Pengiran Anak Isteri Pengiran Anak Sarah binti Pengiran Salleh Ab Rahaman.

Brothers of the Sultan

HRH Prince Mohamed Bolkiah, b. 27 August 1947.

HRH Prince Haji Sufri Bolkiah, b. 31 July 1951.

HRH Prince Haji Jefri Bolkiah, b. 6 November 1954.

CAMBODIA

Reigning King

KING NORODOM SIHAMONI; b. 14 May 1953; elected King October 2004, following the abdication of his father, King Norodom Sihanouk.

Parents of the King

King Norodom Sihanouk b. 31 October 1922; elected King 1941; abdicated 1955; took oath of fidelity to vacant throne 1960; elected Head of State 1960, on the death of his father; deposed 1970; elected as King 24 September 1993; abdicated October 2004; married Queen Norodom Monineath Sihanouk.

Brothers and Sisters of the King

Princess Buppha Devi, b. 8 January 1943.

Prince Yuvaneath, b. 17 October 1943.

Prince Norodom Ranariddh, b. 2 January 1944.

Prince Ravivong, b. 1944, died 1973.

Prince Chakrapong, b. 21 October 1945.

Prince Naradipo, b. 10 February 1946, died 1976.

Princess Soriya Roeungsey, b. 1947, died 1976.

Princess Kantha Bopha, b. 1948, died 14 December 1952.

Prince Khemanourak, b. 1949, died 1975.

Princess Botum Bopha, b. 1951, died 1976.

Princess Socheata, b. 1953, died 1975.

Prince Narindrapong, b. 18 September 1954, died 8 October 2003.

Princess Arunrasmy, b. 2 October 1955.

DENMARK

Reigning Queen

HM QUEEN MARGRETHE II; b. 16 April 1940; succeeded to the throne 14 January 1972, on the death of her father, King Frederik IX; married 10 June 1967, Count Henri Marie Jean André de Laborde de Monpezat (HRH Prince Consort Henrik) (b. 11 June 1934).

Children of the Queen

HRH Crown Prince Frederik André Henrik Christian, b. 26 May 1968; married 14 May 2004, Mary Elizabeth Donaldson (HRH Crown Princess

Mary Elizabeth) (b. 5 February 1972); son, HRH Prince Christian Valdemar Henri John, b. 15 October 2005; daughter, b. 21 April 2007.

HRH Prince Joachim Holger Waldemar Christian, b. 7 June 1969; married 18 November 1995, Alexandra Christina Manley (Alexandra Christina, Countess of Frederiksborg) (b. 30 June 1964) (divorced 2005); son, HH Prince Nikolai William Alexander Frederik, b. 28 August 1999; son, HH Prince Felix Henrik Valdemar Christian, b. 22 July 2002.

Parents of the Queen

King Frederik IX, b. 11 March 1899 (son of King Christian X and Queen Alexandrine), died 14 January 1972; married 24 May 1935, Princess Ingrid of Sweden (b. 28 March 1910, died 7 November 2000).

Sisters of the Queen

HRH Princess Benedikte Astrid Ingeborg Ingrid, b. 29 April 1944; married 3 February 1968, Prince Richard zu Sayn-Wittgenstein-Berleburg (b. 29 October 1934); son, Prince Gustav, b. 12 January 1969; daughter, Countess von Pfeil und Klein-Ellguth (formerly Princess Alexandra), b. 20 November 1970, (married, two children); daughter, Princess Nathalie, b. 2 May 1975.

HM Queen Anne-Marie Dagmar Ingrid of the Hellenes, b. 30 August 1946; married 18 September 1964, HM King Constantine II of the Hellenes (b. 2 June 1940); daughter, Princess Alexia, b. 10 July 1965, (married, three children); son, Prince Pavlos, b. 20 May 1967, (married, four children); son, Prince Nikolaos, b. 1 October 1969; daughter, Princess Theodora, b. 9 June 1983; son, Prince Philippos, b. 26 April 1986.

JAPAN

Reigning Emperor

His Imperial Majesty EMPEROR AKIHITO; b. 23 December 1933; succeeded to the throne 7 January 1989, on the death of his father, Emperor Hirohito; enthroned 12 November 1990; married 10 April 1959, Shoda Michiko (Empress Michiko) (b. 20 October 1934).

Children of the Emperor

The Crown Prince Naruhito (fmrly Hiro no Miya), b. 23 February 1960; married 9 June 1993, Owada Masako (The Crown Princess Masako) (b. 9 December 1963); daughter, Princess Aiko (Toshi no Miya), b. 1 December 2001.

Prince Akishino (Fumihito, fmrly Aya no Miya), b. 30 November 1965; married 29 June 1990, Kawashima Kiko (Princess Kiko) (b. 11 September 1966); daughter, Princess Mako, b. 23 October 1991; daughter, Princess Kako, b. 29 December 1994; son, Prince Hisahito, b. 6 September 2006.

Kuroda Sayako (fmrly Nori no Miya, then Princess Sayako), b. 18 April 1969; married 15 November 2005 (relinquished Royal claim), Kuroda Yoshiki (b. 17 April 1965).

Parents of the Emperor

Emperor Hirohito, b. 29 April 1901, died 7 January 1989 (known as Emperor Showa); married 26 January 1924, Princess Kuni Nagako (b. 6 March 1903, died 16 June 2000); seven children.

JORDAN

Reigning King

KING ABDULLAH II IBN AL-HUSSEIN; b. 30 January 1962; succeeded to the throne 7 February 1999, on the death of his father, King Hussein Ibn Talal; married 10 June 1993, Rania al-Yassin (Queen Rania al-Abdullah) (b. 31 August 1970).

Children of the King

HRH Prince Hussein, b. 28 June 1994.

HRH Princess Iman, b. 27 September 1996.

HRH Princess Salma, b. 26 September 2000.

HRH Prince Hashem, b. 30 January 2005.

Parents of the King

King Hussein ibn Talal, b. 14 November 1935, died 7 February 1999; married 1st Dina bint Abdelhamid (Queen Dina) (divorced), one child; married 2nd Antoinette Gardner (Princess Muna) (divorced 1972), four children; married 3rd Alia Toukan (Queen Alia) (deceased), two children; married 4th Lisa Najeeb Halaby (Queen Noor) (b. 23 August 1951), four children.

Brothers and Sisters of the King

Princess Alia, b. 13 February 1956; married 1st 11 July 1977, Nasser Wasfi Mirza (divorced 1983); son, Prince Hussein Mirza, b. 12 February 1981; married 2nd 30 July 1988, Mohammad Farid as-Saleh; son, Talal as-Saleh, b. 12 September 1989; son, Abdel Hamid as-Saleh, b. 15 November 1991.

Prince Feisal, b. 11 October 1963; married 10 August 1987, Alia at-Tabaa (Princess Alia); daughter, Princess Ayah, b. 11 February 1990; son, Prince Omar, b. October 1993; daughter, Princess Aisha, b. 1996; daughter, Princess Sarah, b. 1996.

Princess Zein, b. 23 April 1968; married 3 August 1989, Majdi Farid as-Saleh; son, Jaafar as-Saleh, b. 9 November 1990; daughter, Jumana as-Saleh.

Princess Aisha, b. 23 April 1968; married 26 July 1990, Zeid Juma'a; son, Aoun Juma'a, b. 27 May 1992; daughter, Muna Juma'a.

Princess Haya bint al-Hussein, b. 3 May 1974; married 10 April 2004, Sheikh Muhammad bin Rashid al-Maktoum (Ruler of Dubai).

Prince Ali, b. 23 December 1975; married 23 April 2004, Rym Brahimi; daughter, Jalilah, b. 16 September 2005.

Prince Hamzah, b. 29 March 1980; married 2003, Princess Noor bint Asem Ben Nayef.

Prince Hashim, b. 10 June 1981; married 15 April 2006, Fahdah Mohammed Abu Neyan.

Princess Iman, b. 24 April 1983.

Princess Raiyah, b. 9 February 1986.

KUWAIT

Reigning Amir

SHEIKH SABAH AL-AHMAD AL-JABER AS-SABAH; b. 1928; succeeded as Amir 29 January 2006, following the abdication of Sheikh Saad al-Abdullah as-Salim as-Sabah.

Crown Prince

HH Sheikh Nawaf al-Ahmad al-Jaber as-Sabah; b. 1937; proclaimed Crown Prince 20 February 2006.

LESOTHO

Reigning King

KING LETSIE III; b. 17 July 1963; installed as King 12 November 1990, abdicated 25 January 1995, reinstalled 7 February 1996, following the death of his father, King Moshoeshoe II on 15 January, crowned 31 October 1997; married 18 February 2000, Karabo Anna Mots'oeneng (Queen 'Masenate Mohato Bereng Seeiso).

Children of the King

Crown Princess Senate Mary Mohato Seeiso, b. 7 October 2001.

Princess 'MaSeeiso Mohato Seeiso, b. 20 November 2004.

Prince Lerotholi Mohato Seeiso, b. 18 April 2007.

LIECHTENSTEIN

Reigning Prince

HSH PRINCE HANS-ADAM II, Duke of Troppau and Jägerndorf, Count of Rietberg; b. 14 February 1945; succeeded 13 November 1989, on the death of his father, Prince Franz Josef II; married 30 July 1967, Countess Marie Aglaë Kinsky von Wchinitz und Tettau (Princess Marie).

Children of the Prince

Hereditary Prince Alois Philipp Maria, b. 11 June 1968; appointed permanent representative 15 August 2004, performing the duties of Head of State from that time; married 3 July 1993, Duchess Sophie in Bavaria (b. 28 October 1967); son, Prince Joseph Wenzel, b. 24 May 1995; daughter, Princess Marie Caroline, b. 17 October 1996; son, Prince Georg, b. 20 April 1999; son, Prince Nikolaus, b. 6 December 2000.

Prince Maximilian, b. 16 May 1969; married 29 January 2000, Angela Gisela Brown; son, Alfonso, b. 18 May 2001.

Prince Constantin, b. 15 March 1972; married 17 July 1999, Countess Marie Kalnoky; son, Moritz, b. 27 May 2003; daughter, Gina, b. 23 July 2005.

Princess Tatjana, b. 10 April 1973; married 5 June 1999, Philipp von Lattorff; son, Lukas, b. 13 May 2000; daughter, Elisabeth, b. 25 January 2002; daughter, Marie Teresa, b. 18 January 2004; daughter, Camilla, b. 4 November 2005; daughter, Anna, b. 3 August 2007.

Brothers and Sisters of the Prince

Prince Philipp, b. 19 August 1946; married 11 September 1971, Isabelle de l'Arbre de Malander; son, Prince Alexander, b. 19 May 1972; son, Prince Wenzeslaus, b. 12 May 1974; son, Prince Rudolf, b. 7 September 1975.

Prince Nikolaus, b. 24 October 1947; married 20 March 1982, Princess Margaretha of Luxembourg (b. 15 May 1957); daughter, Princess Maria-Annunciata, b. 12 May 1985; daughter, Princess Marie-Astrid, b. 26 June 1987; son, Prince Joseph-Emmanuel, b. 7 May 1989.

Princess Nora, b. 31 October 1950; married 11 June 1988, Vicente Marques de Mariño (died 22 July 2002); daughter, Teresa Maria, b. 21 November 1992.

Prince Wenzel, b. 19 November 1962, died 28 February 1991.

LUXEMBOURG

Reigning Monarch

HRH GRAND DUKE HENRI ALBERT FÉLIX MARIE GUILLAUME; b. 16 April 1955; succeeded 7 October 2000, on the abdication of his father, Grand Duke Jean; married 14 February 1981, Maria Teresa Mestre.

Children of the Grand Duke

HRH Prince Guillaume Jean Joseph Marie, b. 11 November 1981; proclaimed Hereditary Grand Duke 18 December 2000.

Prince Félix Léopold Marie Guillaume, b. 3 June 1984.

Prince Louis Xavier Marie Guillaume, b. 3 August 1986.

Princess Alexandra Josephine Teresa Charlotte Marie Wilhelmina, b. 16 February 1991.

Prince Sébastien Henri Marie Guillaume, b. 16 April 1992.

Parents of the Grand Duke

Former Grand Duke Jean Benoit Guillaume Marie Robert Louis Antoine Adolphe Marc d'Aviano, b. 5 January 1921; married 9 April 1953, Joséphine Charlotte, Princess of Belgium (b. 11 October 1927, died 10 January 2005).

Brothers and Sisters of the Grand Duke

Princess Marie-Astrid, b. 17 February 1954; married 6 February 1982, Charles Christian of Habsburg Lorraine, Archduke of Austria; daughter, Marie-Christine Anne Astrid Zita Charlotte of Habsburg Lorraine, b. 31 July 1983; son, Prince Imre, b. 8 December 1985; son, Prince Christophe, b. 2 February 1988; son, Prince Alexander, b. 26 September 1990; daughter, Princess Gabriella, b. 26 March 1994.

Prince Jean, b. 15 May 1957; married 27 May 1987, Hélène Suzanne Vestur (divorced); daughter, Marie-Gabrielle, b. 8 December 1986; son, Constantin Jean Philippe, b. 22 July 1988; son, Wenceslas, b. 17 November 1990; son, Carl-Johann, b. 15 August 1992.

Princess Margaretha, b. 15 May 1957; married 20 March 1982, Prince Nikolaus of Liechtenstein (b. 24 October 1947); daughter, Princess Maria-Annunciata, b. 12 May 1985; daughter, Princess Marie-Astrid, b. 26 June 1987; son, Prince Joseph-Emmanuel, b. 7 May 1989.

Prince Guillaume, b. 1 May 1963; married 24 September 1994, Sibilla Weiller; son, Paul-Louis, b. 4 March 1998; son, Léopold, b. 2 May 2000; daughter, Charlotte, b. 2 May 2000; son Jean b. 13 July 2004.

MALAYSIA

Yang di-Pertuan Agong (Supreme Head of State)

HM The Sultan of Terengganu, Tuanku Mizan Zainal Abidin; b. 22 January 1962; elected as 13th Yang di-Pertuan Agong 13 December 2006, crowned 26 April 2007.

Timbalan Yang di-Pertuan Agong (Deputy Supreme Head of State)

HRH The Sultan of Kedah, Tuanku Haji Abdul Halim Mu'adzam Shah ibni al-Marhum Sultan Badlishah.

The Hereditary Rulers

There are nine hereditary rulers who qualify for and elect the positions of Yang di-Pertuan Agong and Timbalan Yang di-Pertuan Agong.

HRH The Sultan of Johor, Tuanku Mahmood Iskandar ibni al-Marhum Sultan Ismail.

HRH The Sultan of Kelantan, Tuanku Ismail Petra ibni al-Marhum Sultan Yahaya Petra.

The Yang di-Pertuan Besar of Negeri Sembilan, Tuanku Ja'afar ibni al-Marhum Tuanku Abdul Rahman.

HRH The Sultan of Pahang, Haji Ahmad Shah al-Musta'in Billah ibni al-Marhum Sultan Abu Bakar Ri'ayatuddin al-Mu'adzam Shah.

HRH The Sultan of Perak, Tuanku Azlan Muhibuddin Shah ibni al-Marhum Sultan Yusuf Izuddin Ghafarullah Shah.

HRH Tuanku Syed Sirajuddin al-Marhum Syed Putra Jamalullail, The Raja of Perlis.

HRH The Sultan of Selangor, Tuanku Sharafuddin Idris Shah Salahuddin Abdul Aziz Shah.

MONACO

Reigning Monarch

HSH PRINCE ALBERT II; b. 14 March 1958; succeeded 6 April 2005, on the death of his father, Prince Rainier III.

Parents of the Prince

HSH Prince Rainier III, Louis Henri Maxence Bertrand, b. 31 May 1923, died 6 April 2005; married 18 April 1956, Grace Patricia Kelly (b. 12 November 1929, died 14 September 1982).

Sisters of the Prince

Princess Caroline Louise Marguerite, b. 23 January 1957; married 1st 28 June 1978, Philippe Junot (divorced 1980, marriage annulled 1992); married 2nd 29 December 1983, Stefano Casiraghi (died 3 October 1990); son, Andrea Albert Pierre, b. 8 June 1984; daughter, Charlotte Marie Pomeline, b. 3 August 1986; son, Pierre Rainier Stefano, b. 5 September 1987; married 3rd 23 January 1999, Prince Ernst August of Hanover; daughter, Princess Alexandra of Hanover, b. 20 July 1999.

Princess Stéphanie Marie Elisabeth, b. 1 February 1965; married 1 July 1995, Daniel Ducruet (divorced 4 October 1996); son, Louis Robert Paul, b. 26 November 1992; daughter, Pauline Grace Maguy, b. 4 May 1994; daughter, Camille Marie Kelly, b. 15 July 1998.

MOROCCO

Reigning King

HM KING MOHAMMED VI; b. 21 August 1963; succeeded to the throne 23 July 1999, on the death of his father, King Hassan II; married 21 March 2002, HRH Princess Lalla Salma Bennani.

Children of the King

HRH Crown Prince Moulay Hassan, b. 8 May 2003.

HRH Princess Lalla Khadija, b. 28 February 2007.

Father of the King

HM King Hassan II, b. 9 July 1929, died 23 July 1999.

Brothers and Sisters of the King

HRH Princess Lalla Meryem, b. 26 August 1962; married September 1984, Fouad Filali (divorced 1996).

HRH Princess Lalla Asma, b. 29 September 1965; married 7 June 1987, Khalid Bouchentouf.

HRH Princess Lalla Hasna, b. 19 November 1967; married 13 December 1991, Khalid Benharbit.

HRH Prince Moulay Rachid, b. 20 June 1970.

NEPAL

Reigning King

HM KING GYANENDRA BIR BIKRAM SHAH DEV; b. 7 July 1947; succeeded to the throne 4 June 2001, on the death of his nephew, King Dipendra (who had succeeded 1 June 2001, on the death of his father, King Birendra); married 1 May 1970, Princess (now Queen) Komal Rajya Laxmi Devi Shah (b. 18 February 1951).

Children of the King

HRH Crown Prince Paras Bir Bikram Shah Dev, b. 30 December 1971; proclaimed Crown Prince 26 October 2001; married 25 January 2000, HRH Crown Princess Himani Rajya Laxmi Devi Shah (b. 1 October 1976); daughter, Princess Purnika Rajya Laxmi Devi Shah, b. 11 December 2000; son, Prince Hridayendra Bir Bikram Shah Dev, b. 30 July 2002; daughter, Princess Kritika Rajya Laxmi Devi Shah, b. 16 October 2003.

Princess Prearana Rajya Laxmi Devi Shah; married 22 January 2003, Raj Bahadur Singh.

THE NETHERLANDS

Reigning Queen

HM QUEEN BEATRIX WILHELMINA ARMGARD; b. 31 January 1938; succeeded to the throne 30 April 1980, on the abdication of her mother, Queen Juliana (now Princess Juliana); married 10 March 1966, Prince Claus George Willem Otto Frederik Geert Jonkheer van Amsberg (b. 6 September 1926, died 6 October 2002).

Children of the Queen

Prince Willem-Alexander Claus George Ferdinand, Prince of Orange (heir to the throne), b. 27 April 1967; married 2 February 2002, Máxima Zorreguieta (b. 17 May 1971); daughter, Princess Catharina-Amalia Beatrix Carmen Victoria, b. 7 December 2003; daughter, Princess Alexia

Juliana Marcella Laurentien, b. 26 June 2005; daughter, Ariane Wilhelmina Máxima Ines, b. 10 April 2007.

Prince Johan Friso Bernhard Christiaan David, b. 25 September 1968; married 24 April 2004 (relinquished right to the throne and membership of the Royal House), Mabel Wisse Smit; daughter, Emma Luana Ninette Sophie, b. 26 March 2005.

Prince Constantijn Christof Frederik Aschwin, b. 11 October 1969; married 17 May 2001, Laurentien Brinkhorst (b. 25 May 1966); daughter, Princess Eloise Sophie Beatrix Laurence, b. 8 June 2002; son, Prince Claus-Casimir Bernhard Marius Max, b. 21 March 2004; daughter, Leonor Marie Irene Enrica, b. 3 June 2006.

Parents of the Queen

Princess Juliana of the Netherlands, Princess of Orange-Nassau, Duchess of Mecklenburg, Princess of Lippe-Biesterfeld, b. 30 April 1909, died 30 March 2004; married 7 January 1937, Prince Bernhard Leopold Frederik Everhard Julius Coert Karel Godfried Pieter of the Netherlands, Prince of Lippe-Biesterfeld (b. 29 June 1911, died 1 December 2004).

Sisters of the Queen

Princess Irene Emma Elisabeth, b. 5 August 1939; married 29 April 1964, Prince Carlos Hugo of Bourbon Parma (divorced 1981); son, Prince Carlos Javier Bernardo, b. 27 January 1970; son, Prince Jaime Bernardo, b. 13 October 1972; daughter, Princess Margarita Maria Beatriz, b. 13 October 1972; daughter, Princess Maria Carolina Christina, b. 23 June 1974.

Princess Margriet Francisca, b. 19 January 1943; married 10 January 1967, Pieter van Vollenhoven; son, Prince Maurits Willem Pieter Hendrik, b. 17 April 1968; son, Prince Bernhard Lucas Emmanuel, b. 25 December 1969; son, Prince Pieter-Christiaan Michiel, b. 22 March 1972; son, Prince Floris Frederik Martÿn, b. 10 April 1975.

Princess Maria Christina, b. 18 February 1947; married 28 June 1975, Prince Jorge Guillermo (divorced 1996); son, Prince Bernardo Federico Tomás, b. 17 June 1977; son, Nicolas Daniel Mauricio, b. 6 July 1979; daughter, Princess Juliana Edenia Antonia, b. 8 October 1981.

NORWAY

Reigning King

HM KING HARALD V; b. 21 February 1937; succeeded to the throne 17 January 1991, on the death of his father, King Olav V; sworn in 21 January 1991; married 29 August 1968, Sonja Haraldsen (HM Queen Sonja) (b. 1937).

Children of the King

Princess Märtha Louise, b. 22 September 1971; married 24 May 2002, Ari Mikael Behn (b. 1972); daughter, Maud Angelica Behn, b. 29 April 2003; daughter, Leah Isadora Behn, b. 8 April 2005.

HRH Crown Prince Haakon, b. 20 July 1973; married 25 August 2001, Mette-Marit Tjessem Høiby (HRH Crown Princess Mette-Marit) (b. 19 August 1973); daughter, HRH Princess Ingrid Alexandra, b. 21 January 2004; son, Prince Sverre Magnus, b. 3 December 2005.

Sisters of the King

Princess Ragnhild Alexandra, b. 9 June 1930; married 15 May 1953, Erling Lorentzen; three children.

Princess Astrid Maud Ingeborg, b. 12 February 1932; married 12 January 1961, Johan Martin Ferner; five children.

OMAN

Reigning Sultan

SULTAN QABOOS BIN SAID AS-SAID; b. 18 November 1940; assumed power 23 July 1970, after deposing his father, Sultan Said bin Taimur (b. 13 August 1910, died 19 October 1972); married 1976.

QATAR

Reigning Amir

HH SHEIKH HAMAD BIN KHALIFA ATH-THANI; b. 1950; assumed power 27 June 1995, after deposing his father, Sheikh Khalifa bin Hamad ath-Thani (b. 1932); married Sheikha Mozah bint Nasser al-Missned; five sons, two daughters.

Children of the Amir

HH Sheikh Tamim bin Hamad bin Khalifa ath-Thani, b. 3 June 1980; proclaimed heir apparent 8 August 2003; married 8 January 2005, Sheikha Jawahar bint Hamad bin Sohaim ath-Thani.

Sheikh Jassim bin Hamad ath-Thani

Sheikh Joaan bin Hamad ath-Thani

Sheikh Khalifa bin Hamad ath-Thani

Sheikh Mohammed bin Hamad ath-Thani

Sheikha al-Mayassa bint Hamad ath-Thani

Sheikha Hind bint Hamad ath-Thani

SAMOA

O le Ao o le Malo (Head of State)

HH Tuiatua Tupua Tamasese EFI; b. 1938; elected Head of State 15 June 2007.

SAUDI ARABIA

Reigning King

HM KING ABDULLAH IBN ABD AL-AZIZ AS-SA'UD; b. 1924; succeeded to the throne, 1 August 2005, on the death of his brother, King Fahd.

Brothers of the King include

King Saud ibn Abd al-Aziz as-Sa'ud, b. 1902, acceded 9 November 1953 (following the death of his father, King Abd al-Aziz as-Sa'ud), relinquished the throne 2 November 1964, died 23 February 1969.

King Faisal ibn Abd al-Aziz as-Sa'ud, b. April 1906, acceded 2 November 1964, died 25 March 1975; children include son, Prince Sa'ud al-Faisal as-Sa'ud, b. 1941; son, Prince Turki al-Faisal ibn Abd al-Aziz as-Sa'ud, b. 15 February 1945.

HRH Prince Mohammed ibn Abd al-Aziz as-Sa'ud, b. 1909, died 28 November 1988.

King Khalid ibn Abd al-Aziz as-Sa'ud, b. 1913, acceded 25 March 1975, died 13 June 1982.

King Fahd ibn Abd al-Aziz as-Sa'ud, b. 1923, acceded 13 June 1982, died 1 August 2005.

HRH Crown Prince Sultan ibn Abd al-Aziz as-Sa'ud, b. 5 January 1928; children include son, HRH Prince Bandar ibn Sultan ibn Abd al-Aziz as-Sa'ud, b. 2 March 1949.

HRH Prince Talal ibn Abd al-Aziz as-Sa'ud, b. 1934; children include son, Prince Walid ibn Talal.

HRH Prince Nayef ibn Abd al-Aziz as-Sa'ud, b. 1934.

HRH Prince Salman ibn Abd al-Aziz as-Sa'ud, b. 13 December 1936.

SPAIN

Reigning King

HM KING JUAN CARLOS I; b. 5 January 1938; succeeded to the throne 22 November 1975; married 14 May 1962, Princess Sofia of Greece (HM Queen Sofía) (b. 2 November 1938, daughter of the late King Paul of the Hellenes and Queen Frederica).

Children of the King

HRH Princess (Infanta) Elena, b. 20 December 1963; married 18 March 1995, Don Jaime de Marichalar y Saénz de Téjada (b. 7 April 1963); son, Felipe Juan Froilán de Todos los Santos, b. 17 July 1998; daughter, Victoria Federica, b. 9 September 2000.

HRH Princess (Infanta) Cristina, b. 13 June 1965; married 4 October 1997, Iñaki Urdangarin (b. 15 January 1968); son, Juan Valentín de Todos los Santos, b. 29 September 1999; son, Pablo Nicolás, b. 6 December 2000; son, Miguel de Todos los Santos, b. 30 April 2002; daughter, Irene, b. 5 June 2005.

HRH Prince Felipe de Borbón, The Prince of Asturias, Prince of Girona, Prince of Viana, Duke of Montblanc, Count of Cervera, Lord of Balaguer, b. 30 January 1968; married 22 May 2004, HRH Princess Letizia Ortiz Rocasolano (Princess of Asturias) (b. 15 September 1972); daughter, Princess (Infanta) Leonor, b. 31 October 2005; daughter, Princess (Infanta) Sofía, b. 29 April 2007.

Parents of the King

Don Juan de Borbón y Battenberg, Count of Barcelona, b. 20 June 1913, died 1 April 1993; married 1935, Doña María de las Mercedes de Borbón y Orléans (died 1 January 2000).

SWAZILAND

Reigning Monarch

KING MSWATI III; b. 19 April 1968; proclaimed Crown Prince September 1983, following the death of his father the previous year; installed as head of state 25 April 1986.

Father of the King

King Sobhuza II, b. 22 July 1899, died 21 August 1982.

SWEDEN

Reigning King

HM KING CARL XVI GUSTAF; b. 30 April 1946; succeeded to the throne 15 September 1973, on the death of his grandfather, King Gustaf VI Adolf; married 19 June 1976, Silvia Renate Sommerlath (HM Queen Silvia) (b. 23 December 1943).

Children of the King

HRH Crown Princess Victoria Ingrid Alice Désirée, Duchess of Västergötland, b. 14 July 1977.

HRH Prince Carl Philip Edmund Bertil, b. 13 May 1979.

HRH Princess Madeleine Thérèse Amelie Josephine, b. 10 June 1982.

Parents of the King

Prince Gustaf Adolf, Duke of Västerbotten, b. 22 April 1906, died 26 January 1947; married 20 October 1932, Sibylla, Princess of Saxe-Coburg and Gotha (b. 18 January 1908, died 28 November 1972).

Sisters of the King

Princess Margaretha, b. 31 October 1934; married 30 June 1964, John Ambler (b. 1924); daughter, Sibylla Louise, b. 14 April 1965; son, Charles Edward, b. 14 July 1966; son, James Patrick, b. 10 June 1969.

Princess Birgitta, b. 19 January 1937; married 25 May 1961, Prince Johann Georg of Hohenzollern (b. 1932); son, Carl Christian, b. 5 April 1962; daughter, Desirée, b. 27 November 1963; son, Hubertus, b. 10 June 1966.

Princess Désirée, b. 2 June 1938; married 5 June 1964, Baron Niclas Silfverschiöld (b. 1934); son, Carl Otto Edmund, b. 22 March 1965; daughter, Christina Louise Ewa Madeleine, b. 29 September 1966; daughter, Hélène Ingeborg Sibylla, b. 20 September 1968.

Princess Christina, b. 3 August 1943; married 15 June 1974, Tord Magnuson (b. 1941); son, Carl Gustaf Victor, b. 8 August 1975; son, Tord Oscar Fredrik, b. 20 June 1977; son, Victor Edmund Lennart, b. 10 September 1980.

THAILAND

Reigning King

HM KING BHUMIBOL ADULYADEJ, (King Rama IX); b. 5 December 1927; succeeded to the throne 9 June 1946, on the death of his brother, King Ananda Mahidol; crowned 5 May 1950; married 28 April 1950, Mom Rajawongse Sirikit Kitiyakara (Queen Sirikit) (b. 12 August 1932).

Children of the King

Princess Ubol Ratana, b. 5 April 1951; married August 1972, Peter Ladd Jensen (relinquished royal claim); daughter, Khun Ploypailin, b. 12 February 1981; son, Khun Poomi, b. 16 August 1983; daughter, Khun Sirikittiya, b. 18 March 1985.

HRH Crown Prince Maha Vajiralongkorn, b. 28 July 1952; proclaimed Crown Prince 28 December 1972; married 3 January 1977, Mom Luang Soamsawali Kitiyakara (b. 1957) (divorced); daughter, Princess Bajrakitiyabha, b. 7 December 1978; partner, Yuvadhida Polpraserth; four sons (no royal claim); daughter, HRH Princess Siriwanwari Nariratana, b. 8 January 1987 (elevated status by royal command 15 June 2005); married 10 February 2001, Mom Srirasmi Mahidol na Ayudhya (HRH Princess Srirasmi, The Royal Consort) (b. 9 December 1971); son, HRH Prince Teepangkorn Rasmichoti, b. 29 April 2005.

HRH Princess Maha Chakri Sirindhorn, b. 2 April 1955.

HRH Princess Chulabhorn, b. 4 July 1957; married 7 January 1982, Flight Lieutenant Virayuth Didyasarin; daughter, Princess Siribhachudabhorn, b. 8 October 1982; daughter, Princess Aditayadornkitikhun, b. 5 May 1984.

Parents of the King

Prince Mahidol Adulyadej of Songkla, b. 1 January 1892, died 24 September 1929; married 1920, Sangwal Talabhat (Princess Mahidol of Songkla) (b. 21 October 1900, died 18 July 1995).

Brother and Sister of the King

Princess Galyani Vadhana Krom Luang Naradhiwas Rajanagarindra, b. 1923, died 2 January 2008.

King Ananda Mahidol, b. 20 September 1925, died 9 June 1946; elected to succeed to the throne 2 March 1935.

TONGA

Reigning King

HM KING George Tupou V; b. 4 May 1948; succeeded to the throne 10 September 2006, on the death of his father, King Taufa'ahau Tupou IV.

Parents of the King

King Taufa'ahau Tupou IV, b. 4 July 1918, died 10 September 2006; succeeded to the throne 15 December 1965; married 1947, Princess Halaevalu Mata'aho 'Ahome'e (Queen Halaevalu Mata'aho) (b. 1926).

Brothers and Sisters of the King

HRH Princess Salote Mafile'o Pilolevu Tuku'aho Tuita, Princess Regent, b. 17 November 1951; married 21 July 1976, Captain Ma'ulupekotofa Tuita (known as Honourable Tuita).

HRH Prince Fatafehi Alaivahamama'o Tuku'aho (known as Honourable Matu), b. 17 December 1954, died 17 February 2004; married (relinquished royal claim).

HRH Crown Prince Tupouto'a Lavaka (fmrly known as Prince 'Ulukalala-Lavaka-Ata), b. 12 July 1959; proclaimed Crown Prince 11 September 2006; married 11 December 1982, Nanasipau'u Vaea (Princess Nanasipau'u); three children.

UNITED ARAB EMIRATES

Reigning Rulers

Ruler of Abu Dhabi: HH Sheikh KHALIFA BIN ZAYED AN-NAHYAN; succeeded to the throne 2004.

Ruler of Dubai: HH Sheikh MUHAMMAD BIN RASHID AL-MAKTOUM; succeeded to the throne 4 January 2006; married 10 April 2004, HRH Princess Haya bint al-Hussein of Jordan.

Ruler of Sharjah: HH Sheikh SULTAN BIN MUHAMMAD AL-QASIMI; succeeded to the throne 1972.

Ruler of Ras al-Khaimah: HH Sheikh SAQR BIN MUHAMMAD AL-QASIMI; succeeded to the throne 1948.

Ruler of Umm al-Qaiwain: HH Sheikh RASHID BIN AHMAD AL-MU'ALLA; succeeded to the throne February 1981.

Ruler of Ajman: HH Sheikh HUMAID BIN RASHID AN-NUAIMI; succeeded to the throne 1981.

Ruler of Fujairah: HH Sheikh HAMAD BIN MUHAMMAD ASH-SHARQI; succeeded to the throne 1974.

UNITED KINGDOM

Reigning Queen

HM QUEEN ELIZABETH II; b. 21 April 1926; succeeded to the throne 6 February 1952, on the death of her father, King George VI; crowned 2 June 1953; married 20 November 1947, HRH Prince Philip, Duke of Edinburgh, Earl of Merioneth, Baron Greenwich, KG, KT, OM, GBE, AC, QSO (b. 10 June 1921), son of Prince Andrew of Greece and Princess Alice of Battenberg (Mountbatten).

Children of the Queen

HRH Prince Charles Philip Arthur George, The Prince of Wales, Duke of Cornwall, Duke of Rothesay, Earl of Chester, Earl of Carrick, Baron of Renfrew, Lord of the Isles and Great Steward of Scotland, KG, KT, GCB, OM, AK, QSO, ADC (heir-apparent), b. 14 November 1948; married 1st 29 July 1981, Lady Diana Frances Spencer (The Princess of Wales) (divorced 1996, died 1997); son, Prince William Arthur Philip Louis of Wales, b. 21 June 1982; son, Prince Henry Charles Albert David of Wales, b. 15 September 1984; married 2nd 9 April 2005, Camilla Parker Bowles (HRH The Duchess of Cornwall) (b. 17 July 1947).

HRH Princess Anne Elizabeth Alice Louise, The Princess Royal, KG, KT, GCVO, QSO, b. 15 August 1950; married 1st 14 November 1973, Captain Mark Phillips (divorced 1992); son, Peter Mark Andrew Phillips, b. 15 November 1977; daughter, Zara Anne Elizabeth Phillips, b. 15 May 1981; married 2nd 12 December 1992, Vice Admiral Timothy Laurence, CB, MVO, ADC.

HRH Prince Andrew Albert Christian Edward, The Duke of York, Earl of Inverness, Baron Killyleagh, KS, KCVO, ADC, b. 19 February 1960; married 23 July 1986, Sarah Ferguson (The Duchess of York) (b. 15 October 1959) (divorced 1996); daughter, Princess Beatrice Elizabeth Mary of York, b. 8 August 1988; daughter, Princess Eugenie Victoria Helena of York, b. 23 March 1990.

HRH Prince Edward Antony Richard Louis, The Earl of Wessex, KS, KCVO, ADC, b. 10 March 1964; married 19 June 1999, Sophie Rhys-Jones (HRH The Countess of Wessex) (b. 20 January 1965); daughter, Lady Louise Alice Elizabeth Mary Windsor, b. 8 November 2003; son, James Alexander Philip Theo, Viscount Severn, b. 17 December 2007.

Parents of the Queen

King George VI, b. 14 December 1895 (son of King George V and Queen Mary), died 6 February 1952; married 26 April 1923, Lady Elizabeth Angela Marguerite Bowes-Lyon (Queen Elizabeth The Queen Mother) (b. 4 August 1900, died 30 March 2002).

Sister of the Queen

Princess Margaret Rose, Countess of Snowdon, CI, GCVO, b. 21 August 1930, died 9 February 2002; married 6 May 1960, Antony Armstrong-Jones (Earl of Snowdon, GCVO) (divorced 1978); son, David Albert Charles, Viscount Linley, b. 3 November 1961, (married, two children); daughter, Lady Sarah Frances Elizabeth Chatto (née Armstrong-Jones), b. 1 May 1964, (married, two children).

The full titles of Queen Elizabeth II are as follows:

United Kingdom
"Elizabeth the Second, by the Grace of God, of the United Kingdom of Great Britain and Northern Ireland and of Her other Realms and Territories Queen, Head of the Commonwealth, Defender of the Faith."

Canada
"Elizabeth the Second, by the Grace of God, of the United Kingdom, Canada and Her other Realms and Territories Queen, Head of the Commonwealth, Defender of the Faith."

Australia
"Elizabeth the Second, by the Grace of God, Queen of Australia and Her other Realms and Territories, Head of the Commonwealth."

New Zealand
"Elizabeth the Second, by the Grace of God, Queen of New Zealand and Her Other Realms and Territories, Head of the Commonwealth, Defender of the Faith."

Jamaica
"Elizabeth the Second, by the Grace of God, Queen of Jamaica and of Her other Realms and Territories Queen, Head of the Commonwealth."

Barbados
"Elizabeth the Second, by the Grace of God, Queen of Barbados and of Her other Realms and Territories, Head of the Commonwealth."

The Bahamas
"Elizabeth the Second, by the Grace of God, Queen of the Commonwealth of The Bahamas and of Her other Realms and Territories, Head of the Commonwealth."

Grenada
"Elizabeth the Second, by the Grace of God, Queen of the United Kingdom of Great Britain and Northern Ireland and of Grenada and Her other Realms and Territories, Head of the Commonwealth."

Papua New Guinea
"Elizabeth the Second, Queen of Papua New Guinea and of Her other Realms and Territories, Head of the Commonwealth."

Solomon Islands
"Elizabeth the Second, by the Grace of God, Queen of the Solomon Islands and of Her other Realms and Territories, Head of the Commonwealth."

Tuvalu
"Elizabeth the Second, by the Grace of God, Queen of Tuvalu and of Her other Realms and Territories, Head of the Commonwealth."

Saint Lucia
"Elizabeth the Second, by the Grace of God, Queen of Saint Lucia and of Her other Realms and Territories, Head of the Commonwealth."

Saint Vincent and the Grenadines
"Elizabeth the Second, by the Grace of God, Queen of Saint Vincent and the Grenadines and of Her other Realms and Territories, Head of the Commonwealth."

Belize
"Elizabeth the Second, by the Grace of God, Queen of Belize and of Her Other Realms and Territories, Head of the Commonwealth."

Antigua and Barbuda
"Elizabeth the Second, by the Grace of God, Queen of Antigua and Barbuda and of Her other Realms and Territories, Head of the Commonwealth."

Saint Christopher and Nevis
"Elizabeth the Second, by the Grace of God, Queen of Saint Christopher and Nevis and of Her other Realms and Territories, Head of the Commonwealth."

The Republics of India, Ghana, Cyprus, Tanzania, Uganda, Kenya, Zambia, Malawi, Singapore, Botswana, Guyana, Nauru, The Gambia, Sierra Leone, Bangladesh, Sri Lanka, Malta, Trinidad and Tobago, Seychelles, Dominica, Kiribati, Vanuatu, Maldives, Namibia, Mauritius, South Africa, Fiji, Pakistan, Cameroon and Mozambique, together with the Federation of Malaysia, the Kingdom of Lesotho, the Kingdom of Swaziland, the Kingdom of Tonga, the Independent State of Samoa and the Sultanate of Brunei, recognize the Queen as "Head of the Commonwealth".

OBITUARY

Abascal Carranza, Carlos María	2 December 2008	Cuevas Cancino, Francisco	18 February 2008
Abd Al-Halim Abu Ghazala, Muhammed	6 September 2008	Cuevas Salvador, José Maria	27 October 2008
Aitmatov, Tchinguiz Torekulovich	10 June 2008	Dahlbeck, Eva	8 February 2008
Alatas, Ali	11 December 2008	Darwish, Mahmoud	9 August 2008
Aleksei II	5 December 2008	Dassin, Jules	31 March 2008
Alfonsín Foulkes, Raúl	31 March 2009	Davis, Sir Thomas Robert Alexander Harries	23 July 2007
Annakin, Kenneth	22 April 2009	Dearing, Lord Ronald Ernest Dearing	19 February 2009
Armstrong, Anne	30 July 2008	Debakey, Michael Ellis	11 July 2008
Arnell, Richard Anthony Sayer	10 April 2009	Del Pino y Calvo-Sotelo, Rafael	14 June 2008
Baah-Wiredu, Kwadwo	24 September 2008	DeLuise, Dom	4 May 2009
Ba Swe, U	1987	Desailly, Jean	11 June 2008
Bachrach, Howard L.	26 June 2008	Dia, Mamadou	25 January 2009
Baddiley, Sir James	17 November 2008	Diddley, Bo	2 June 2008
Balanandan, E.	19 January 2009	Douglas, Margaret Elizabeth	20 August 2008
Ballard, James Graham (J.G.)	19 April 2009	Druon, Maurice Samuel Roger Charles	14 April 2009
Barendrecht, Wouter	5 April 2009	Dulles, HE Cardinal Avery	12 December 2008
Barnes, Clive Alexander	19 November 2008	Eliel, Ernest	18 September 2008
Barron, John Penrose	16 August 2008	Elliott, Osborn	28 September 2008
Barry, Brian Michael	10 March 2009	Engel, Karl	2 September 2006
Basnet, R. B.	18 August 2007	Faillard, Hans	5 August 2005
Bata, Thomas John	1 September 2008	Fanthorpe, Ursula Askham	28 Aprill 2009
Battle, Lucius Durham	13 May 2008	Febres Cordero Rivadeneira, León	15 December 2008
Baxandall, Michael David Kighley	12 August 2008	Fedorov, Boris Grigorievich	20 November 2008
Bazan, Dominador Kaiser Baldomero	August 2006	Fehn, Sverre	23 February 2009
Beaudoin, Hon. Gérald-A.	10 September 2008	Feilden, Sir Bernard Melchior	14 November 2008
Beck, Beatrix Marie	30 November 2008	Fellgett, Peter	15 November 2008
Bekhtereva, Natalya Petrovna	22 June 2008	Fergason, James L.	9 December 2008
Benda, Ernst	2 March 2009	Filali, Abdellatif	20 March 2009
Benney, Adrian Gerald Sallis	26 June 2008	Fischer, Ernst Otto	23 July 2007
Berri, Claude	12 January 2009	Flindt, Flemming Ole	3 March 2009
Berrill, Sir Kenneth	30 April 2009	Foote, (Albert) Horton Jr	4 March 2009
Bessmertnova, Natalia	19 February 2008	Fort, Dame Maeve Geraldine	18 September 2008
Betti, HE Cardinal Umberto	1 April 2009	Foss, Lukas	1 February 2009
Beutler, Ernest	5 October 2008	Fox Bassett, Nigel	26 October 2008
Beyer, Frank	20 April 2008	Francois Poncet, Michel	19 February 2005
Bide, Sir Austin (Ernest)	11 May 2008	Frankenhaeuser, Marianne	5 October 2005
Birla, Krishna Kumar	30 August 2008	Frankevich, Yevgeniy Leonidovich	21 April 2006
Bourges, Yvon	18 April 2009	Franklin, John Hope	25 March 2009
Bowie, Stanley Hay Umphray	3 September 2008	French, Marilyn	2 May 2009
Braibant, Guy	25 May 2008	Furgler, Kurt	23 July 2008
Brennan, Séamus	9 July 2008	Fursenko, Aleksander Aleksandrovich	30 June 2008
Brewer, Derek Stanley	23 October 2008	Gajdusek, Daniel Carleton	12 December 2008
Bullock, Peter	2 April 2008	Garn, Stanley Marion	31 August 2007
Burcham, William Ernest	5 November 2008	George, Rt Hon. Sir Edward Alan John	18 April 2009
Butler, (Frederick) Guy	26 April 2001	Geremek, Bronislaw	13 July 2008
Calisher, Hortense	13 January 2009	Ghattas, HE Cardinal Stephanos II (Andreas Ghattas)	20 January 2009
Camilleri, Charles	3 January 2009	Gilmour of Craigmillar, Lord Ian (Hedworth John Little Gilmour)	21 September 2007
Candea, Virgil	16 February 2007		
Capa, Cornell	23 May 2008	Gillespie, Charles Anthony Jr	7 March 2008
Cardiff, Jack	22 April 2009	Glistrup, Mogens	1 July 2008
Carruth, Hayden	29 September 2008	Glossop, Peter	7 September 2008
Cartan, Henri Paul	13 August 2008	Gonzalez Zumarraga, Antonio José	13 October 2008
Carver, John Henry	25 December 2004	Goodwin, Leonard George	25 November 2008
Caso, Carlo	7 July 2007	Goumba, Abel	11 May 2009
Chadwick, Sir Henry	17 June 2008	Gray, Simon James Holliday	6 August 2008
Chahine, Youssef	27 July 2008	Greevy, Bernadette	26 September 2008
Chandra, Avinash	1991	Grindrod, Most Rev. John Basil Rowland	3 January 2009
Chang, Xiangyu	1 June 2008	Guo, Xiexian	1998
Chapin, Schuyler Garrison	7 March 2009	Haavikko, Paavo Juhani	6 October 2008
Chino, Tadao	17 July 2008	Hadzipasic, Ahmet	23 July 2008
Chon, Chol-hwan	June 2004	Haider, Jorg	11 October 2008
Chung, (Raymond) Arthur	23 June 2008	Harris, Rene	5 July 2008
Clark, William, Jr	22 January 2008	Helms, Jesse	4 July 2008
Cleveland, Harlan	30 May 2008	Henderson, Sir (John) Nicholas	16 March 2009
Clyde, James John	6 March 2009	Hermon, John	6 November 2008
Coburn, John	7 November 2006	Hersom, Naomi	27 June 2008
Colomer Viadel, Vicente	13 May 2006	Hibbert, Christopher	21 December 2008
Conombo, Joseph	20 December 2008	Hickox, Richard Sidney	23 November 2008
Conté, Gen. Lansana	22 December 2008	Hightower, Rosella	3 November 2008
Cook, Beryl	28 May 2008	Hoffman, Grace	26 July 2008
Cooke, Jean Esme Oregon	6 August 2008	Holmes, George Arthur	29 January 2009
Cookson, Richard Clive	17 December 2008	Hopper, Wilbert Hill (Bill)	3 July 2006
Corbally, John E.	23 July 2004	Houthakker, Hendrik Samuel	15 April 2008
Corbett, Michael M.	16 September 2007	Hua, Guofeng	20 August 2008
Corsten, Severin	18 October 2008	Huang, Kun	6 August 2005
Cotton, Sir William (Bill) Frederick	11 August 2008	Húlse, Gúnther	30 November 2004
Couzens, Sir Kenneth	4 August 2004	Huntington, Samuel Phillips	24 December 2008
Crichton, (John) Michael	4 November 2008	Huo, Yingdong	7 November 2006
Cuckney, John Graham	30 October 2008	Hurwicz, Leonid (Leo)	24 June 2008

THE INTERNATIONAL WHO'S WHO

2010

A

AARNES, Asbjørn Sigurd, DPhil; Norwegian academic; b. 20 Dec. 1923, Vågbø; s. of Halvor Aarnes and Alida Olsen; m. Berit Alten 1950 (died 2002); one s. one d.; ed Univ. of Oslo and Ecole Normale Supérieure, Paris; Prof. of European Literature, Univ. of Oslo 1964, Dir Inst. d'Études Romanes 1966–70; Pres. Norwegian Acad. of Language and Literature 1966–84; mem. Norwegian Acad. of Science, various editorial bds and cttees; Chevalier, Ordre nat. du Mérite; Légion d'honneur; Officier des Palmes académiques. *Publications:* J. S. Welhaven 1955, Gérard de Nerval 1957, Idé og Tanke (series co-ed.) 1960–1985, Nicolas Boileau 1961, Det poetiske fenomen 1963, Litterært Leksikon 1964, Pierre Le Moyne 1965, Ved Veiskille: natur og rasjonalitet 1974, Maine de Biran 1976, Thorleif Dahls Kulturbibliotek (ed.) 1979–2001, René Descartes 1980, Debatten om Descartes: innvendinger og svar 1982, Fransk tanke og idéliv: Cartesianske perspektiver 1981, Henri Bergson 1989, Perspektiver og profiler i norsk poesi 1989, Cartesianische Perspektiven von Montaigne bis Paul Ricoeur 1991, Emmanuel Levinas (ed.), Den Annens humanisme 1996, Underveis mot den Annen (ed.) 1998, Stadier i fransk idéliv, Barokk, klassisisme, romantikk 1998, Ut av fatning: Samtaler med Hall Bjørnstad 2001, Poesien hos Olav Nygard: Et dikteralbum 2004; as editor: Jules Lequier: Mellom frihet og nødvendighet 2003, Dryadens hind: Om et dikt av Emil Boyson 2004, Råka av Røyndom 2006, Gertroffen vom Wirklichen 2009; as co-editor: Stemmer i tiden 1998, Den annen front 1998, Den etiske vending 2000, Fransk poesi i nordisk gjendiktning 2000, Lyset i Nord 2008. *Address:* Ostadalsveien 9, 0753 Oslo 7, Norway. *Telephone:* 22500789 (home). *Fax:* 22500789 (home).

AARON, David L., MA; American diplomatist; *Senior International Adviser, Dorsey & Whitney LLP;* b. 21 Aug. 1938, Chicago; m. Chloe W. Aaron; one c.; ed Occidental Coll. Calif. and Princeton Univ.; entered Foreign Service 1962; Political and Econ. Officer, Guayaquil, Ecuador; Int. Relations Officer, Dept of State 1964–66; Political Officer, NATO, Paris 1966; Arms Control and Disarmament Agency; Sr Staff mem. Nat. Security Council 1972–74; Legis. Asst to Senator Walter Mondale 1974–75; Task Force Leader, Senate Select Cttee on Intelligence 1975–76; mem. staff, Carter-Mondale presidential campaign; Transition Dir with Nat. Security Council and CIA 1976–77; Deputy Asst to Pres. for Nat. Security Affairs 1977–81; Vice-Pres. Oppenheimer & Co. Inc. 1981–85, Dir Oppenheimer Int. 1984; Sr Adviser, Mondale presidential campaign; writer and lecturer, Lantz-Harris Agency 1985–93; consultant, 20th Century Fund 1990–92, Sr Fellow 1992–93; US Rep. to OECD 1993; US Special Envoy for Cryptography 1996; Under-Sec. of Commerce for Int. Trade 1997–2001; Sr Int. Adviser, Int. Trade Practice Group, Dorsey & Whitney LLP 2000–; Dr hc (Occidental Coll.); Nat. Defense Medal. *Television:* The Gulf War (script), Miracle on 44th Street: The Action Studio (script). *Publications:* State Scarlet 1987, Agent of Influence 1989, Crossing by Night 1993; articles in newspapers and journals. *Address:* Dorsey & Whitney LLP, 1001 Pennsylvania Avenue, NW, Suite 300, Washington, DC 20004, USA (office). *Telephone:* (202) 442-3000 (office); (202) 442-3645. *Fax:* (202) 442-3199 (office). *E-mail:* aaron.david@dorseylaw.com (office). *Website:* www.dorseylaw.com (office).

AAVIKSOO, Jaak, PhD; Estonian politician, academic and government official; *Minister of Defence;* b. 11 Jan. 1954, Tartu; m.; three c.; ed Tartu Univ. and Inst. of Physics, Estonian Acad. of Science; Jr, Sr and Chief Researcher, Inst. of Physics, Estonian Acad. of Science 1976–92; Prof. of Physics, Tartu Univ. 1992, First Pro-rector 1992–95, Head Inst. of Experimental Physics and Tech. 1996–98, Rector 1998–2007; Minister of Culture and Educ. 1995, of Educ. 1996, of Defence 2007–; mem. Estonian Acad. of Science 1994, Academia Europaea 2004, Estonian Physics Soc., American Physical Soc., American Optics Soc., European Physics Soc.; Order of the Nat. Coat of Arms (Estonia) 1999, Large Cross of Merit (Germany) 2000, Ordre nat. du Mérite 2001, Order of White Rose (Finland) 2001, Medal of Merit, City of Tartu 2002, Order of the White Star, Class Two (Estonia) 2006; Dr hc (Turku Univ.) 2003. *Publications include:* over 100 research papers. *Address:* Ministry of Defence, Sakala 1, Tallinn 15094, Estonia (office). *Telephone:* 717-0010 (office). *Fax:* 717-0001 (office). *E-mail:* jaak.aaviksoo@kmin.ee (office). *Website:* www.mod.gov.ee (office).

ABAH ABAH, Polycarpe; Cameroonian politician; b. 1954; ed Univ. of Yaounde 1, Univ. of the Sorbonne, Paris, France; Dir Gen. of Taxes 1994–2004; Minister of the Economy and Finance 2004–07; Gov. for Cameroon, IMF 2006–07; arrested on allegations of fraud, corruption and embezzling public funds March 2008; Africa Finance Minister of the Year, The Banker magazine 2006. *Address:* c/o Ministry of the Economy and Finance, BP 13750, Quartier Administratif, Yaoundé, Cameroon (office).

ABAKANOWICZ, Magdalena; Polish artist, weaver and sculptor; b. 20 June 1930, Falenty, nr Warsaw; d. of Konstanty Abakanowicz and Helena Abakanowicz; m. Jan Kosmowski 1956; ed Acad. of Fine Arts, Warsaw; mem. Soc. of Authors ZAIKS; work includes monumental space forms of woven fibres, cycles of figurative sculptures of burlap, wood and clay, cast metal, stone, drawings, paintings with collage and gouache; Prof., Acad. of Fine Arts, Poznań 1979–90; mem. Presidential Council for Culture 1992; Hon. mem. American Acad. of Arts and Letters 1996; Commdr's Cross with Star, Order of Polonia Restituta 1998, Officier des Arts et Lettres, Paris 1999, Cavaliere nell Ordine Al Merito della Repubblica Italiana 2000,; Dr hc (RCA, London) 1974, (Rhode Island School of Design, Providence) 1992, (Acad. of Fine Arts, Łódź) 1997, (Pratt Inst., New York) 2000, (Massachusetts Coll. of Art, Boston) 2001, (School of the Art Inst. of Chicago) 2002, (Acad. of Fine Arts, Poznań) 2002; Minister of Culture and Art Prize (1st Class) 1965, Gold Medal VIIIth Int. Biennale of Arts, São Paulo 1965, Gottfried von Herder Prize 1979, Alfred Jurzykowski Foundation Award 1982, New York Sculpture Center Award 1993, Leonardo da Vinci World Award of Arts 1997, Visionaries! Award, American Craft Museum 2000, Lifetime Achievement Award, Int. Sculpture Center, New York 2005. *Works include:* Sculpture for Elbląg, relief woven composition for North Brabant Prov. Bldg, Netherlands; three-dimensional woven forms: Abakans Figurative sculptures, seated figures, Backs, Incarnations, War Games, Crowds, Hands-like Trees, Mutants, Birds; large outdoor installations: Katarsis, Italy, Negev, Israel, Space of Dragon, S Korea, Space of Nine Figures, Germany, Becalmed Beings, Hiroshima, Japan and others. *Leisure interests:* swimming, walking in the countryside and forests. *Address:* ul. Bzowa 1, 02-708 Warsaw, Poland. *Telephone:* (22) 8486379 (home). *Fax:* (22) 8486379 (home). *E-mail:* magdalena@abakanowicz.art.pl. *Website:* www.abakanowicz.art.pl.

A-BAKI, Ivonne, BA, BArch, MPA; Ecuadorean diplomatist and artist; *President, Andean Parliament;* b. Guayaquil; m. Sammi A-Baki; two s. one d.; ed Sorbonne Univ., Paris, France and Harvard Univ., USA; fmr Dir Conflict Man. Group, Harvard Univ., del. to confs in Geneva 1984, Lausanne 1985; Adviser to Pres. on Ecuador–Peru peace negotiations –1998; Consul-Gen., then Hon. Consul in Lebanon; Consul-Gen. in Boston, Mass; apptd Amb. to USA 1999; unsuccessful cand. for Pres. of Ecuador 2002; Minister of Foreign Trade, Industrialization, Fishing and Competition 2003–05; Pres. Andean Parl. 2007–; painter, numerous exhbns in museums, galleries and pvt. collections in Europe, N and S America and Middle East; f. Harvard Foundation for the Arts; Artist-in-Residence, Harvard Univ. 1991–98; Pres. Arts and Community Renewal Coalition, Boston, Beyond Boundaries Foundation; Order of Merit; Honorato Vasquez Order; Keys of the City of Coral Gables, Florida; numerous other awards. *Address:* Office of the President, Andean Parliament, Avenida 13 No. 70-61, Santafé de Bogotá, Colombia (office). *Telephone:* (1) 217-3357 (office). *Fax:* (1) 348-2805 (office). *E-mail:* correo@parlamentoandino.org (office). *Website:* www.parlamentoandino.org (office).

ABAL, Sam; Papua New Guinea politician; *Minister for Foreign Affairs, Trade and Immigration;* fmr Minister for Provincial Affairs, fmr Minister for Inter-Govt Relations, Minister for Foreign Affairs, Trade and Immigration 2007–; MP for Wabag; mem. Nat. Alliance Party. *Address:* Department of Foreign Affairs, Central Government Offices, Kumul Ave, Post Office, Wards Strip, Waigani, National Capital District, Papua New Guinea (office). *Telephone:* 3271311 (office). *Fax:* 3254467 (office). *Website:* www.pngonline.gov.pg (office).

ABALAKIN, Victor Kuz'mich, DPhysMathSc; Russian astronomer; *Adviser, Russian Academy of Sciences;* b. 27 Aug. 1930, Odessa, Ukraine; m.; two c.; ed Odessa State Univ.; jr researcher, Inst. of Geophysics, USSR Acad. of Sciences 1953–55, Inst. for Theoretical Astronomy, USSR Acad. of Sciences 1955–57, Head of Div. 1965–83; Sr Researcher, Odessa Astronomical Observatory 1960–63; Docent, Odessa State Univ. 1963–65; Dir Main Astronomical Observatory, Russian Acad. of Sciences 1983–2000, Adviser 2000–; Corresp. mem. USSR (now Russian) Acad. of Sciences 1987–, Adviser 2000–; mem. Int. Acad. of Ecology, Man and Nature Protection Sciences 1997–; main research in theoretical astronomy, stellar dynamics, history of astronomy; Hon. mem. Russian Acad. of Cosmonautics 1998, Russian Acad. of Natural Sciences; Hon. Citizen of Tucson, Arizona, USA; Medal of the Merits for Fatherland, 2nd class 2006; "For Labour Valour" Medal (USSR) 1976, State Prize (USSR) 1982. *Publications:* seven books including Foundations of Ephemeris Astronomy 1979, Laser Ranging to the Moon 1981; numerous papers. *Leisure interests:* reading classical and modern belles lettres. *Address:* Central (Pulkovo) Astronomical Observatory, Russian Academy of Sciences, 196140 St Petersburg, Pulkovskoye Shosse 65, Bldg 1 (office); 191024 St Petersburg, 162 Nevsky Prospect, Apt 9, Russia (home). *Telephone:* (812) 723-4900 (office); (812) 723-4400 (office); (812) 717-2881 (home). *Fax:* (812) 723-1922 (office);

(812) 717-2881 (home). *E-mail:* vicabal@gmail.com (office); vicabal@hotmail .com (office). *Website:* www.gao.spb.ru (office).

ABALKHAIL, Sheikh Mohamed Ali, BA; Saudi Arabian government official and financial executive; b. 1935, Buraida; s. of Ali Abdullah Abalkhail and Fatima Abdulaziz Othaim; m. 1966; two s. two d.; ed Cairo Univ.; began career as Asst Dir of Office of Minister of Communications, later Dir; Dir-Gen. of Inst. of Public Admin; Deputy Minister of Finance and Nat. Econ., then Vice-Minister, Minister of State, Minister for Finance and Nat. Econ. 1975–95; fmr Chair. Riyadh Bank, Riyadh; Chair. Centre for Econ. and Man. Studies; mem. JP Morgan Int. Council; decorations from Belgium, Egypt, France, Niger, Pakistan, Saudi Arabia, Sudan, Germany, Morocco, Spain. *Leisure interests:* reading, sports. *Address:* PO Box 287, Riyadh 11411, Saudi Arabia; J.P. Morgan Chase & Company, 270 Park Avenue, New York, NY 10017, USA (office). *Telephone:* (1) 478-1722; (1) 476-6965. *Fax:* (1) 478-1904. *E-mail:* abakhail@kfshhub.kfshrc.edu.sa (office).

ABALKIN, Leonid Ivanovich, PhD, DEcon; Russian economist; *Director of Science, Institute of Economics, Russian Academy of Sciences;* b. 5 May 1930, Moscow; m. Anna Vartanovna Abalkina (née Satarova) 1953; one s. one d.; ed Moscow Inst. of the Economy, State Econ. Inst. of Moscow; teacher, Deputy Dir agricultural school 1953–58; Sr Teacher and Lecturer in Political Economy, Moscow Inst. of the Economy 1961–66, Chair holder 1966–76; Prof., Acad. of Social Sciences 1976–78, Head, Faculty of Political Econ. 1978–86; Dir Inst. of Econs, USSR (now Russian) Acad. of Sciences 1986–2004, Dir of Science 2004–, Corresp. mem. USSR (now Russian) Acad. of Sciences 1984–87, mem. 1987–, mem. of Presidium 1988–; mem. CPSU 1956–91, mem. Cen. Cttee 1990–91; USSR People's Deputy 1989–91; Deputy Chair. State Comm. on Improving Man., Planning and Economy Mechanism, USSR Council of Ministers 1987–89; Deputy Prime Minister, Chair. State Comm. for Econ. Reforms 1989–91; adviser to Pres. Gorbachev 1991; mem. Bd Int. Foundation of Econ. and Social Reforms 1991–; mem. Govt's Econ. Crisis Group 1998–; Ed.-in-Chief Voprosy Ekonomiki 1992–, Ekonomicheskoe naslediye, Pamitniki ekonomicheskoi mysli; mem. New York Acad. of Sciences 1993–, Int. Acad. of Man. 1994–, Int. Econs Acad. of Eurasia 1997–; Pres. N. Kondratieff Int. Foundation 1992–; Vice-Pres. Int. Union of Economists, Free Econ. Soc. of Russia 1992–; columnist, Trud; mem. bds of EKO and Voprosy ekonomiki; Hon. mem. Moscow Intellectual Business Club 1992–; Order of People's Friendship 1986; Order for Distinguished Service to the Nation 2000. *Publications:* Political Economy and Economic Policy 1970, Final Economic Results 1978, Direction – Acceleration 1986, New Type of Economic Thinking 1987, Perestroika – Ways and Problems 1989, Missed Chance – A Year and a Half in the Soviet Union Government 1991, To the Goal Through Crisis: Destiny of Economic Reform 1992, At the Crossroads – Thoughts About Russia's Fate 1993, The Crisis Grip 1994, To Self-Perception of Russia 1995, Zigzags of Fate – Disappointments and Hopes 1996, Postponed Changes – The Lost Year 1997, Russia – The Choice 1998, Saving Russia 1999, Russian School of Economic Thought – In Search of Identity 2000, The New Century's Challenge 2001, The Logic of Economic Growth 2002, Russia: In Search of Identity (essays) 2002, Strategy: Choice of the Course 2003, Russia's Strategic Answer to the Calls of the New Era; numerous articles in Soviet press on theoretical problems of political economy under socialism. *Leisure interests:* chess, gardening. *Address:* Institute of Economics, Academy of Sciences of Russia, 117218 Moscow, Nakhimovsky Prospekt 32; 117334 Moscow, 38-8-89 Zelinskogo str., Russia (home). *Telephone:* (495) 129-02-54 (office); (495) 135-10-85 (home). *Fax:* (495) 718-0511. *E-mail:* abalkin@inst-econ.org.ru (office). *Website:* www.inst-econ.org.ru (office).

ABAZA, Mohammed Maher, BSc; Egyptian engineer, business executive and fmr politician; *Chairman, Midtap Company;* b. 12 March 1930, Sharkia; s. of Muhamed Osman Abazah; m. Ezdehar Abo El-Ela 1955; one s. one d.; ed Cairo Univ. and studies in W Germany and Sweden; engineer, Dept of Hydroelectric Power, Ministry of Public Works 1951–64; several sr positions in Egyptian Electricity Authority 1964–73; First Under-Sec. of State, Ministry of Electricity and Energy 1975–80, Minister of Electricity and Energy 1980–99; Chair. Midtap Co., Midor Electricity Co., Petrosport Co., Emarat Misr Co.; mem. Bd EMG Co.; Pres. Int. Asscn for Electricity Generation, Transmission and Distribution (Afro-Asian region) 1996–99; mem. numerous nat. and int. scientific cttees; mem. World Energy Ccouncil, IEEE, Thomas Alva Edison Foundation, Int. Council on Large Electrical Systems (CIGRE), Int. Conf. on Electricity Distribution (CIRED); The Greatest Nile Medal, Golden Medal of Distinction, Order of the Repub. (First Class, Egypt, France, Poland, Niger), Royal Order of the Polar Star (Grand Cross, Sweden), Grand Cross of the Order of Merit (FRG, Italy), Order of the Grand Cross (Italy), Cross of the Order of Merit (Italy), Grand Cross of the Order of Merit (First Class) (Finland), Order of the State (First Class, Yugoslavia), Order of Merit (Greece), Order of the State (First Class, Syria, Cen. African Repub.). *Publications:* several articles in trade journals and for int. confs. *Leisure interests:* philately, photography, reading, swimming. *Address:* 22 El Badia Street, Heliopolis, Cairo (office); 8 Taha Hussein Street, Zamalek, Cairo, Egypt (home). *Telephone:* (2) 2918398 (office); (2) 4142028 (office); (2) 7357201 (home). *Fax:* (2) 4147515 (office). *E-mail:* midtap@midtap.com.eg (office).

ABBADO, Claudio; Italian conductor; *Chief Conductor and Music Director, Lucerne Festival Orchestra;* b. 26 June 1933, Milan; one c.; ed Giuseppe Verdi Conservatory, Milan and Acad. of Music, Vienna with Hans Swarowsky; debut at La Scala, Milan in concert celebrating tercentenary of A. Scarlatti 1960; conducted opening of La Scala season 1967; Music Dir Teatro alla Scala, Milan 1968–86, Vienna Philharmonic Orchestra 1972–86, London Symphony Orchestra 1979–88, Vienna State Opera 1986–91; Principal Conductor Chamber Orchestra of Europe 1981; Principal Guest Conductor Chicago Symphony Orchestra 1982–85; Gen. Music Dir City of Vienna 1987–; Music Dir and Principal Conductor Berlin Philharmonic Orchestra 1989–2002; Artistic Dir Salzburg Easter Festival 1994; Chief Conductor and Music Dir Lucerne Festival Orchestra 2003–; f. European Community Youth Orchestra 1978, La Filharmonica della Scala 1982, Gustav Mahler Jugendorchester, Vienna 1986, Wien Modern (Modern Vienna) Contemporary Art Festival 1988, Vienna Int. Competition for Composers 1991, Encounters in Berlin (Chamber Music Festival) 1992; has conducted on tours worldwide, with numerous orchestras; guest conductor Rome 2005, Tokyo 2006, Carnegie Hall 2007; Dr hc (Aberdeen) 1986, (Ferrara) 1990, (Cambridge) 1994; Mozart Medal (Vienna) 1973, Gold Medal, Int. Gustav Mahler Gesellschaft (Vienna) 1985, Amadeus (Ferrara) 1996, award from the Presidency of the Council of Ministers 1997, Athena-Giovani e Cultura Award (Univ. of Milan) 1999, Premio Nonino 1999, Opernwelt Review Conductor of the Year 2000, Oscar della Lirica 2001, Praemium Imperiale 2003, MIDEM Classical Lifetime Achievement Award 2005; Grand Cross, Order of Merit (Italy) 1984, Grand Croix, Légion d'Honneur, Bundesverdienstkreuz (Germany) 1992, Ehrenring, City of Vienna 1994, Das Grosse Verdienstkreuz mit Stern (Germany) 2002. *Recordings include:* Mahler's Symphony No. 6 (Gramophone Award for Recording of the Year 2006) 2005, Mozart's Die Zauberflöte (Gramophone Award for Best Opera Recording) 2006. *Publications:* Musica sopra Berlino (Nonino Award 1999) 1998, Suite Concertante from the Ballet Hawaii 2000, La Casa del Suoni (juvenile). *Address:* Askonas Holt Ltd, Lincoln House, 300 High Holborn, London, WC1V 7JH, England (office). *Telephone:* (20) 7400-1700 (office). *Fax:* (20) 7400-1799 (office). *E-mail:* info@askonasholt.co.uk (office). *Website:* www.askonasholt.co.uk (office).

ABBAS, Mahmud, (Abu Mazen), PhD; Palestinian politician and head of state; *President;* b. 1935, Safad, Galilea; ed Damascus Univ., Syria, Moscow Univ., Russia; civil servant, UAE –1967; co-f. Fatah (largest political party in The Palestine Nat. Liberation Movt), mem. Cen. Cttee 1964–; elected to Palestine Liberation Org. (PLO) Exec. Cttee 1980, Head Pan-Arab and Int. Affairs Dept 1984, Sec.-Gen. PLO Exec. Cttee 1996–2004, Chair. 2004–; Exec. Pres. Palestinian Nat. Authority (PNA) known internationally as Palestinian Authority (PA) 2005–; participated in Middle East Peace Conf., Washington, DC and in Norwegian-mediated peace talks with Israel; Prime Minister, Palestinian Authority (PA) 2003. *Address:* Office of the President, Ramallah, Palestinian Autonomous Areas. *E-mail:* fateh@fateh.org. *Website:* www.p-p-o .com; www.fateh.net.

ABBOTT, Anthony (Tony) John, CMG, OBE; British diplomatist; b. 9 Sept. 1941, Ashton-under-Lyne, England; s. of Walter Abbott and Mary Abbott (née Delaney); m. Margaret Stuart Green 1962; three s. one d.; ed All Souls School, Salford, De La Salle Coll., Pendleton; joined British diplomatic service 1959, Vice Consul, Khorramshahr, Iran 1963–65, Helsinki, Finland 1965–68, Press Officer, FCO, London 1969–72, Passport Officer, Lusaka, Zambia 1972–75, Consul, Santiago, Chile 1976–80; with UK Presidency Secr. to EC 1981; on secondment to British Overseas Trade Bd 1981–82; Consul, Lisbon, Portugal 1983–87; First Sec., later Deputy High Commr, Calcutta, India 1987–91; EC Monitor, Croatia 1991; Chief of EC Monitoring Mission, Bosnia-Herzegovina 1991; Deputy Head, Training Dept, FCO 1992–93; Consul-Gen., Perth, Australia 1993–97; Gov. of Montserrat 1997–2001; Head of Pitcairn Logistics Team, New Zealand 2001–; Officer, Order of Dom Enfante d'Enrique (Portugal) 1985; EC Monitoring Medal for Services in Former Yugoslavia 1994. *Leisure interests:* travel, driving, golf, all spectator sports, beating Australia at anything. *Address:* 5 Rye View Maisonettes, The Gardens, East Dulwich, London, SE22 9QB, England (home).

ABBOUD, A. Robert, LLB, MBA; American banker and business executive; *President, A. Robert Abboud and Company;* b. 29 May 1929, Boston, Mass.; s. of Alfred Abboud and Victoria Abboud; m. Joan Grover Abboud 1955; one s. two d.; ed Harvard Coll., Harvard Law School, Harvard Business School; Asst Cashier, Int. Dept, First Nat. Bank of Chicago 1960, Asst Vice-Pres. Int. 1962, Vice-Pres. 1964, Sr Vice-Pres. 1969, Exec. Vice-Pres. 1972, Vice-Chair. 1973, Deputy Chair. of Bd 1974–75, Chair. of Bd 1975–80; Pres., COO and Dir Occidental Petroleum Corpn 1980–84; Pres. A. Robert Abboud and Co. (pvt investment co.), Fox Grove, Ill. 1984–; Chair. Braeburn Capital Inc. 1984–92; Chair. and CEO First City Bancorp of Tex. Inc., Houston 1988–91, First City Nat. Bank of Houston 1988–91; Co-Chair. and Ind. Lead Dir Ivanhoe Energy Inc., Vancouver 2006–; fmr mem. Bd of Dirs AAR Corpn, Dir Cities Service, ICN Biomedicals, ICN Pharmaceuticals, Inland Steel Co., AMOCO, Hartmarx Corpn, Alberto-Culver Co.; Bronze Star, Purple Heart, US Marine Corps 1952 Baker Scholar, Harvard Business School 1958. *Publications:* Introduction of US Commercial Paper in Foreign Markets: Premature and Perilous? 1970, A Proposed Course for US Trade and Investment Policies 1971, A Proposal to Help Reverse the Narrowing Balance in the US Balance of Trade 1971, The Outlook for a New Monetary System 1971, Opportunities for Foreign Banks in Singapore 1971, The International Competitiveness of US Banks and the US Economy 1972, Money in the Bank: How Safe Is It? 1988. *Address:* A. Robert Abboud & Co., 960 II Route 22, #212, Fox River Grove, IL 60021 (office); 209 Braeburn Road, Barrington Hills, IL 60010, USA (home). *Telephone:* (847) 639-0101 (office); (847) 658-4808 (home). *Fax:* (847) 639-0233 (office). *E-mail:* araco@mc.net (office).

ABDALLAH, Abdelwahab; Tunisian government official; *Minister of Foreign Affairs;* b. 14 Feb. 1940, Monastir; fmr head several press agencies; Presidential Aide 1990–; Minister of Foreign Affairs 2005–. *Address:* Ministry of Foreign Affairs, ave de la Ligue des états arabes, Tunis, Tunisia (office). *Telephone:* (71) 847-500 (office). *E-mail:* mae@ministeres.tn (office). *Website:* www.diplomatie.gov.tn (office).

ABDALLAHI, Sidi Ould Cheikh; Mauritanian politician and head of state; b. 1938, Aleg; m.; three s. one d.; ed William Ponty School, Senegal, Univ. of Dakar, Senegal and Univ. of Grenoble, France; Dir of Planning, Second Plan for the Econ. and Social Devt of Mauritania 1968–71; served in several govt positions including Minister of State for Nat. Economy 1971–78; Econ. Adviser, Kuwait Fund for Arab Econ. Devt, Kuwait 1982–85, Head of Econs and Finance, Niger Div. 1989–2003; Minister of Hydraulics and Energy 1986–87, of Fisheries and Maritime Economy 1987–89; Pres. of Mauritania 2007–08 (ousted in coup). *Address:* c/o Office of the President, National Assembly, BP 184, Nouakchott, Mauritania (office).

ABDEL-MALEK, Anouar I., DLit, PhD; Egyptian academic and writer; *Adviser, National Centre for Middle East Studies;* b. 23 Oct. 1924, Cairo; s. of Iskandar Abdel-Malek and Alice Zaki Ibrahim; m. Karin Konigseider 1961; one d.; ed Coll. de la Sainte Famille, British Inst., Ain Shams Univ., Cairo and Univ. de Paris-Sorbonne; leading mem. Egyptian Nat. and Progressive Movt 1941–; official, Nat. Bank of Egypt, Cairo 1941–42, Crédit Foncier Egyptien, Cairo 1943–46; Jt Ed. Actualité, Cairo 1950–59; journalist, Le Journal d'Egypte, Cairo 1950–59; contrib. to Rose el-Yusef, Al-Magallah, Al-Masa, Cairo 1950–59; teacher of philosophy, Lycée Al-Hurriya, Cairo 1958–59; Research Asst, Ecole Pratique des Hautes Etudes, Paris 1959–60; Research Lecturer, later Research Reader, Research Prof., CNRS, Paris 1960–, Dir of Research 1970–90, Hon. Dir 1990–; Project Co-ordinator, The UN Univ., Tokyo 1976–86; Prof. of Sociology and Politics, Faculty of Int. Relations, Ristumeikan Univ., Kyoto 1989–92; Prof. Emer. of Philosophy, Ain Shams Univ. 1998–; Adviser Nat. Centre for Middle East Studies, Cairo 1990–; mem. Bd and Adviser, Centre for Asian Studies, Cairo Univ. 1994–; writer, Al-Ahram 1995; mem. exec. cttee, EEC Int. Sociological Asscn 1970–74 (vice-pres. 1974–78), Egyptian Council for Foreign Affairs 2002–, IISS, Int. Political Science Asscn, Royal Inst. for Int. Affairs, Chatham House, London 2007–; Visiting Prof., Univ. of Santiago, Chile 1969, Ain Shams 1975, Québec 1986, Cairo 1992; Visiting Fellow, Clare Coll., Cambridge 1985, Life Assoc. 1986–; Ed. Library of the Contemporary Orient 1989, Ideas of the New World 1991; Prix du Jury de l'Amitié Franco-Arabe, Paris 1965, Gold Medal, Nasser Higher Mil. Acad. 1976, State Prize in the Social Sciences 1996, Prize for Best Book, Cairo 2001, Gold Medal, Faculty of Econs and Political Sciences, Cairo Univ. 2003. *Publications include:* Egypte, société militaire 1962, Studies on National Culture 1967, Idéologie et renaissance nationale: l'Egypte moderne 1969, La pensée politique arabe contemporaine 1970, Sociologie de l'impérialisme 1970, La dialectique sociale 1972, The Army and National Movements 1974, Spécificité et Théorie sociale 1977, Intellectual Creativity in Endogenous Culture 1983, East Wind 1983, The Transformation of the World 1985, The Egyptian Street and Thought 1989, Creativity and the Civilizational Project 1991, Endogenous Intellectual Creativity in the Arab World 1994, Towards a Civilizational Strategy 2005, On the Origins of the Civilizational Question 2005, Along the Path Towards a New Egypt 2005, China in the Eyes of Egyptians 2006, Patriotism is the Solution 2006. *Leisure interests:* music, opera, ballet, theatre, cooking, swimming, walking, table-tennis, travelling, meditation. *Address:* 48 Nehru Street, 11351 Heliopolis, Cairo, Egypt (home). *Telephone:* (2) 634-3977 (home). *Fax:* (2) 634-3977 (home). *E-mail:* anouarmalek@hotmail.com (home).

ABDEL-MEGUID, Ahmed Esmat, LLB, PhD; Egyptian diplomatist and lawyer; *President, Arab and African Arbitrators' Society;* b. 22 March 1923, Alexandria; s. of Mohamed Fahmy Abd al-Meguid; m. Eglal Abou-Hamda 1950; three s.; ed Faculty of Law, Alexandria Univ. and Univ. of Paris; Attaché and Sec., Embassy, London 1950–54; Head British Desk, Ministry of Foreign Affairs 1954–56, Asst Dir Legal Dept 1961–63, Head Cultural and Tech. Assistance Dept 1967–68; Counsellor, Perm. Mission to European Office of UN, Geneva 1957–61; Minister Counsellor, Embassy, Paris 1963–67; Official Spokesman of Govt and Head Information Dept 1968–69; Amb. to France 1969–70; Minister of State for Cabinet Affairs 1970–72; Head, Perm. Del. to UN 1972–83; Minister of Foreign Affairs 1984–91; Deputy Prime Minister 1985–91; Sec.-Gen. League of Arab States 1991–2001; pvt. law practice 2001–; Chair. Cairo Preparatory Conf. for Geneva Peace Conf. 1977; fmr Dir Cairo Int. Arbitration Centre, Pres. Arab and African Arbitrators' Soc. 2001–; mem. Politbureau, Nat. Democratic Party, Int. Law Asscn, Advisory Council of the Inst. for Int. Studies, took part in UN confs on the Law of the Sea 1959, on Consular Relations 1963 and on the Law of Treaties 1969; mem. Int. Center for Settlement of Investment Disputes, World Bank, Washington DC, High Level Advisory Panel of OAU; mem. Bd of Trustees, American Univ., Cairo (AUC), French Univ., Cairo; Ordre nat. du Mérite 1967, Grand Croix 1971, 1st Class Decoration, Arab Repub. of Egypt 1970 and numerous foreign decorations; Dr hc (Louvain) 1998, (Khartoum) 1998; Hon. PhD (American Univ., Cairo) 2002. *Publications:* Time of Defeat and Victory 1999, Positions and Challenges in the Arab World 2003; several articles in Revue Egyptienne de Droit International. *Address:* 78 El Nile Street, Apt 23, Giza, Cairo, Egypt (home). *Telephone:* (202) 37489111 (also fax) (office); (202)37489001 (home).

ABDEL-RAHMAN YOUSSEF, Ali, BSc, MSc, PhD; Egyptian construction engineer, academic and fmr university administrator; ed Cairo Univ., McGill Univ. and Univ. of New Brunswick, Canada; instructor, Dept of Construction Eng, Cairo Univ. 1974–76, Asst Prof. 1976–81, Assoc. Prof. 1981–86, Prof. of Concrete Construction Design 1986–, Dir of Construction Eng Lab., Faculty of Eng. 1991–, Vice Dean of Educ. and Student Affairs 1995–2001, Dean Faculty of Eng 2001–04, Pres. of Cairo Univ. 2004–08; Chair. Centre for Support of Architectural and Eng Designs; mem. Scientific Cttee Housing and Building Nat. Research Centre; State Prize for Eng Sciences 1985. *Address:* c/o Office of the President, Cairo University, Giza, Egypt (office).

ABDEL-RAZEQ, Omar, PhD; Palestinian economist, academic and government official; b. 3 July 1958, Salfit, West Bank; studied in USA 1980s; Prof. of Econs, An-Najah Univ., Nablus; mem. Islamic Resistance Movt (Hamas; Harakat al-Muqawama al-Islamiyya); Sr Research Fellow, Palestine Econ. Policy Research Inst.; Minister of Finance 2006. *Address:* c/o Ministry of Finance, POB 795, Sateh Marhaba, Al-Birah/Ramallah; POB 4007, Gaza, Palestinian Autonomous Areas (office).

ABDELKERIM, Mahamat Nour; Chadian government official; trained in French military schools; fmr rebel leader United Front for Democratic Change (FUC), signed peace deal with govt 2006; f. Rally for Democracy and Liberty (RDL) 2005; Minister of Nat. Defence March–Dec. 2007. *Address:* c/o Ministry of National Defence, BP 916, N'Djamena, Chad (office).

ABDELLAH, Faye Glenn, BA, MA, EdD, ScD; American nurse, psychologist and naval officer; ed Teachers' Coll., Columbia Univ., Rutgers Univ.; Chief Nurse Officer and Deputy Surgeon General, US Public Health Service (first woman) 1981–89, retd with rank of Rear Adm.; Founding Dean and Prof., Grad. School of Nursing, Uniformed Services Univ. of Health Sciences 1993–2002; Charter Fellow, American Acad. of Nursing, later Vice-Pres. and Pres.; mem. Nat. League for Nursing, American Public Health Asscn, NAS, Inst. of Medicine, Asscn of Mil. Surgeons of US; several academic awards including 12 hon. degrees; Presidential Award Sigma Theta Tau 1987, 2005, Allied Signal Award 1989, Gustav O. Lienhard Award from Inst. of Medicine 1992, Living Legend Award from American Acad. of Nursing 1994, elected Nat. Women's Hall of Fame, 2000, and numerous other awards and honours. *Publications include:* Better Patient Care through Nursing Research (with E. Levine) 1986; more than 135 publs (books, monographs and articles). *Leisure interests:* piano, swimming. *Address:* 313 Chanel Road, Annandale, VA, 22003, USA (home). *Telephone:* (703) 941-2932 (home).

ABDÉRÉMANE HALIDI, Ibrahim; Comoran politician; b. 1954, Anjouan Island; fmr philosophy teacher in secondary schools; fmr mem. Chuma Party; Minister of Interior 1990; fmr Leader, Union des démocrates pour le développement (UDD); Prime Minister of the Comoros Jan.–May 1993; Minister of Transport, Tourism, Posts and Telecommunications 1996–97; presidential cand., Anjouan Island 2002, 2006, ind. cand. supported by Convention pour le renouveau des Comores (CRC). *Address:* c/o Convention pour le renouveau des Comores (CRC), Moroni, The Comoros.

ABDESSALAM, Belaid, BA; Algerian politician; b. July 1928, Dehemcha; m.; four s. two d.; ed Grenoble Univ.; fmr Hon. Pres. Union Générale des Etudiants Musulmans Algériens (UGEMA); Instructor Front de Libération Nationale (FLN) School, Oujda; Political Adviser in Cabinet of M. Ben Khedda 1961; in charge of Econ. Affairs, FLN Provisional Exec. 1962; Pres., Dir-Gen. Soc. Nat. pour la Recherche, la Production, le Transport, la Transformation et la Commercialisation des Hydrocarbures (SONATRACH) 1964–66; Minister of Industry and Energy 1966–77 (retaining SONATRACH post 1965–66), of Light Industry 1977–84; Prime Minister of Algeria and Minister of Economy 1992–93; Pres. of Special Econ. Comm. of Cen. Cttee of FLN 1979–81; Chair. Council OAPEC 1974. *Address:* c/o Office of the Prime Minister, Palais du Gouvernement, Algiers, Algeria.

ABDIC, Fikret 'Babo' (Papa); Bosnia and Herzegovina/Croatian politician and business executive; b. 29 Sept. 1939, Donji Vidovec; Dir Agrokomerc co. 1980s; charged with fraud in Fmr Yugoslavia 1987, convicted, sentenced to two years' imprisonment, acquitted on appeal 1989; Co-Founder (with Alijah Izetbegovic), Party of Democratic Action (PDA); set up autonomous region of W Bosnia in defiance of cen. Govt in Sarajevo 1993, his forces were crushed by Pres. Izetbegovic 1995; fled to Croatia in 1995, f. pvt. food co.; f. political party Democratic People's Union (DNZ) 1996; accused of war crimes by Bosnia 2001; extradition to Bosnia repeatedly refused by Croatian Govt on account of his Croatian citizenship; sentenced by Croatian court to 20 years' imprisonment for war crimes committed during Bosnian war 1993–95 July 2002; permitted by Bosnian Election Comm. to run for Muslim post in three-man inter-ethnic presidency while still in prison Oct. 2002.

ABDILDIN, Serikbolsyn Abdildayevich, DEcon,; Kazakhstani politician; *Leader, Communist Party of Kazakhstan;* b. 25 Feb. 1937, Kyzylkesek, Semipalatinsk; m.; one d. one s.; ed Kazakh Nat. Agric. Univ., KasGoz Post-Grad. Coll.; mem. CP of Soviet Union 1964–91; Minister of Agric. 1976–90; mem. CP of Kazakhstan (CPK) 1981–91, apptd First Sec. (Leader) 1996–; Deputy in Majlis (Nat. Ass.) 1990–93, 1999–2004, First Speaker 1991–93; joined Socialist Party of Kazakhstan (SPK) 1993; Cand. in Kazakh Presidential Elections 1999; joined Democratic Choice of Kazakhstan (DCK—opposition movt) 2001; Prof. Kazakh Nat. Agric. Univ. 1995–. *Publications:* more than 60 scientific publs 1964–2007. *Address:* Communist Party of Kazakhstan, Karasai batyr 85/312, Almaty, Kazakhstan (office). *Telephone:* (727) 265-11-19 (office); (701) 722-42-49 (home). *E-mail:* kpk_rk@mail.ru (office).

ABDIU, Fehmi, DrIur; Albanian judge; *Member, Constitutional Court;* b. 5 Jan. 1944, Dibra; m.; two c.; ed Faculty of Law, Tirana Univ., Teachers' Training School, Peshkopi; Judge, Fieri Dist Court 1968–73, Deputy Chief 1974–77, Chief 1977–85; Chief Tirana Dist Court 1989–90; Judge, Supreme Court 1985–89, Deputy Chief 1990–92; mem. Parl. 1991–98; mem. Constitutional Court 1998–, Pres. 1998–2004; Golden Order Naim Frashëri 2004. *Publications include:* The Politic According to the Constitution and Laws, Constitution and the Constitutional Court of the Republic of Albania, The Constitution, the Law and the Justice, Civil Action During Criminal Process. *Address:* President of the Constitutional Court, c/o Ministry of Justice, Ministria e Drejtësisë, Bulevard Dëshmorët e Kombit, Tirana (office); Bulevard "Zhan D'Ark" Pallati 4, Ap. 1, Kati 9, Tirana, Albania (home). *Telephone:* (5) 426-9174 (office); (5) 422-8125 (home). *Fax:* (5) 422-8357 (office). *Website:* www.gjk.gov.al (office).

ABDOU MADI, Mohamed; Comoran politician and diplomatist; b. 1956, Mjamaoue; m.; four c.; ed Algeria, Poland; tax insp. Moroni 1988; convicted of fraud, served sentence as a domestic servant; Perm. Sec., CTRAP (org. funded by UNDP to implement reforms in civil service) –1994; Sec.-Gen. Rassemblement pour la Démocratie et le Renouveau (RDR); Prime Minister of the Comoros 1994, also responsible for Public Works; Minister of Justice, Public Affairs, Employment, Professional Training, Admin. Decentralization and Institutional Reform 1998; Adviser, Embassy in Madagascar 2000; joined govt of Anjouan leader Colonel Mohamed Bacar 2007, govt removed from office by combined Comoros and African Union force 2008.

ABDOULAYE, Souley; Niger politician and business executive; fmr banker; Minister of Commerce, Transport and Tourism 1993–94; Prime Minister of Niger 1994–95; Minister of Transport 1996–97, of Interior 1997; mem. Convention démocratique et social—Rahana (CDS). *Address:* c/o Convention démocratique et social—Rahama, BP 11973, Niamey, Niger. *Telephone:* 20-74-19-85.

ABDOULAYE DIALLO, Ahmadou, DESS; Malian economist and politician; *Minister of the Economy, Industry and Commerce;* b. 16 March 1959, Bazi; m.; four c.; ed Inst. polytechnique rural de Katibougou, Centre d'études financières économiques et bancaires, Paris; Head of Dept of Control and Analysis, Malian Office of Livestock and Meat (OMBEVI) and Head of Planning Unit, Ministry of Natural Resources and Livestock 1985–89; Dir of Public Debt, Autonomous Debt Financing Fund (now Directorate–Gen. of Public Debt) 1991–94, tech. adviser to Fund Dir 1994–98; analyst, African Solidarity Fund 1998–2002, Dir of Studies and Projects 2003–05, of Operations 2007–08; econ. adviser to Pres. of Mali 2002; Minister of the Economy, Industry and Commerce 2008–. *Address:* Ministry of the Economy, Industry and Commerce, BP 234, Koulouba, Bamako, Mali (office). *Telephone:* 222-51-56 (office). *Fax:* 222-01-92 (office).

ABDRASHITOV, Vadim Yusupovich; Russian film director; b. 19 Jan. 1945, Kharkov, Ukraine; s. of Yusup Sh. Abdrashitov and Galina Abdrashitov; m. Natella G. Toidze; one s. one d.; ed Moscow State Inst. of Cinematography (VGIK); mem. Russian Film Acad., Russian Union of Cinematographers; Order of the Fatherland, Fourth Class 2006; RSFSR State Prize 1984, State Prize of the USSR 1991, People's Artist of Russia 1996,. *Films include:* Witness for the Defence (USSR Riga Prize) 1977, The Turning 1978, Foxhunting 1980, The Train Has Stopped 1982, The Parade of the Planets 1984, Plumbum, or a Dangerous Game (Gold Medal at Venice Festival 1987) 1986, The Servant (Alfred Bauer Prize 1989) 1988, Armavir 1991, The Play for a Passenger (Silver Bear Award, Berlin Festival 1995) 1995, Time of the Dancer 1997, Magnetic Storms 2003. *Address:* 119270 Moscow, 3d. Frunzenskaya 9, Apt 211, Russia. *Telephone:* (495) 242-35-54.

ABDRISAEV, Baktybek, PhD; Kyrgyzstani diplomatist, scientist and academic; *Distinguished Visiting Professor, Utah Valley University;* b. 17 April 1958, Bishkek; s. of Dyushen Abdrisaev and Kalicha Jakypova; m. Cholpon Akmatalieva; two c.; ed Bishkek Polytechnical Inst. (now Kyrgyz Tech. Univ.), Inst. of Electronics, Acad. of Sciences of Belarus; Jr Scientific Fellow, Bishkek Polytechnical Inst. 1980–84; Sr Scientific Fellow 1987–88; Scientific Fellow, Inst. of Physics, Acad. of Sciences of Kyrgyz Repub. 1988–91, Sr Scientific Fellow 1991–92; staff expert, Pres.'s Dept of Int. Relations 1992–93, Head of Dept 1993–96; mem. Parl. 1995–2000; Amb. to USA and Canada 1996–2005; currently Distinguished Visiting Prof., Utah Valley Univ., USA; mem. European Acad. of Natural Sciences 2004–, Russian Acad. of Natural Sciences 2005–; Hon. Prof., Int. Univ. of Kyrgyzstan 2006; Union of Youth of Kyrgyzstan Scientific Achievement Award 1992. *Publications:* Kyrgyzstan's Voice in Washington 2005; more than 80 scientific articles and presentations on applied optics and diplomacy. *Leisure interests:* hiking, table tennis. *Address:* Utah Valley University, Department of History and Political Science, 800 West University Parkway, Orem, UT 84058, USA (office). *Telephone:* (801) 863-8351 (office). *Fax:* (801) 863-7013 (office). *E-mail:* abdrisba@uvu.edu (office). *Website:* www.uvsc.edu/plsc (office).

ABDUL, Paula; American singer and choreographer; b. 19 June 1962, San Fernando, CA; d. of Harry Abdul and Lorraine Abdul; m. 1st Emilio Estevez 1992 (divorced 1994); m. 2nd Brad Beckerman 1996; ed Van Nuys High School, Northridge Coll. Calif. State Univ.; choreographer, LA Laker basketball cheerleaders; several bands, including Duran Duran, Toto, The Pointer Sisters, ZZ Top; scenes in films Bull Durham, Coming To America, The Waiting Game, The Doors, Touched By Evil, Junior High School; City of Crime video (from film Dragnet); worldwide performances as singer include tours throughout USA, UK, Japan and Far East; f. Co Dance (dance co.); judge, American Idol: The Search for a Superstar (TV series) 2002–; Rolling Stone Award for Best Female Singer 1989, American Music Awards for Favorite Pop/Rock Female Vocalist 1989, 1992, Billboard Magazine Top Female Pop Album 1990, Grammy Award for Best Music Video (for Opposites Attract) 1991, Starlight Foundation Humanitarian of the Year, Los Angeles 1992. *Choreography:* pop videos: The Jacksons and Mick Jagger's Torture, George Michael's Monkey, Janet Jackson's Control, Nasty (MTV Video Award for best choreography 1987), When I Think Of You, What Have You Done For Me Lately; television: Dolly Parton Christmas Special, Tracey Ullman Show (Emmy Award for best choreography) 1989. *Recordings include:* albums: Forever Your Girl 1989, Shut Up And Dance (The Dance Mixes) 1990, Spellbound 1991, Head Over Heels 1995, Greatest Hits 2000. *Address:* Third Rail Entertainment, Tri-Star Bldg, 10202 W Washington Avenue, Suite 26, Culver City, CA 90232, USA (office). *Website:* www.paulaabdul.com (office).

ABDUL-GHANI, Abdulaziz, MA; Yemeni politician and economist; *Speaker, Shoora Council;* b. 4 July 1939, Haifan, Taiz; s. of Abdulghani Saleh and Tohfa Moqbel; m. Aseya Hamza 1966; five s. one d.; ed Teacher's High School, Aden Coll., Colorado Coll. and Univ. of Colorado, USA; teacher, Balquis Coll., Aden 1964–67; Minister of Health, San'a 1967–68, of Economy 1968–69, 1970–71; Prime Minister 1975–80, 1983–90, 1994–97; Chair. Tech. Office, Supreme Council for Devt 1969–70; mem. Command Council 1975–78; Vice-Pres. of

Yemen Arab Repub. 1980–83; mem. Perm. Cttee of Presidential Advisory Council and mem. Gen. Cttee (Politburo) 1982; mem. Gen. People's Congress (GPC) 1982–, Asst Sec.-Gen. to GPC 1991–95; mem. Presidential Council 1990–94; Speaker, Shoora Council 2001–; Dir Yemen Bank for Reconstruction and Devt 1968; Gov. Cen. Bank of Yemen 1971–75; Lecturer, Univ. of San'a 1972–74; Chair. Yemen Oil Co. 1971, Supreme Council for Reconstruction of Earthquake Affected Areas 1982; mem. Yemeni Econ. Soc.; Mareb Sash (First Class) 1987; Decoration of Unity; Sash of Al-Fateh (Libya); Sash of King Abdul Aziz (Saudi Arabia); Decoration of Merit (Lebanon); Hon. PhD. *Leisure interests:* swimming, hiking. *Address:* Shoora Council, San'a (office); Haddah Street, San'a, Yemen (home). *Telephone:* (9671) 227802 (office); (9671) 440450 (home). *Fax:* (9671) 227816 (office). *E-mail:* aghani@y.net.ye (office).

ABDUL HADI, Mahdi, PhD; Palestinian research institute director; *Chairman, Palestinian Academic Society for the Study of International Affairs (PASSIA);* ed Bradford Univ., UK; Co-Founder and Ed. Al-Fajr daily newspaper 1972–74; Co-Founder and Gen. Sec. Council for Higher Educ. in the West Bank 1977–80; Founder and Pres. Arab Thought Forum, Jerusalem 1977–81; special adviser to Ministry of Occupied Land Affairs, Amman, Jordan 1985–86; Founder and Chair., Bd of Trustees, Palestinian Academic Soc. for Study of Int. Affairs (PASSIA) 1987–; mem. Arab Thought Forum, Amman 2002; occasional guest lecturer on Palestinian issues at local colls, univs and insts; mem. Jerusalem Arab Council, Palestinian Council for Justice and Peace, Assoc. of Palestinian Policy Research Insts; Fellow, Center for Int. Affairs, Harvard Univ. 1985, Salzburg Int. Seminar 1986; mem. Black Sea Univ. Foundation, Bucharest 1990, IISS, London, EuroMeSCo network, Arab Social Science Research Network. *Publications:* Awakening Sleeping Horses 2000; numerous articles, monographs and essays in newspapers and journals. *Address:* The Palestinian Academic Society for the Study of International Affairs, POB 19545, Jerusalem (office). *Telephone:* 2-6264426 (office). *Fax:* 2-6282819 (office). *E-mail:* passia@palnet.com (office). *Website:* www.passia.org (office).

ABDUL-JABBAR, Kareem; American basketball coach and fmr professional basketball player; b. (Ferdinand Lewis Alcindor, Jr), 16 April 1947, New York; s. of Lewis Alcindor and Cora Alcindor; ed Power Memorial High School, UCLA; graduated as the leading scorer in UCLA history (2,325 points); played for Nat. Basketball Asscn (NBA) Milwaukee Bucks 1969–75, for NBA Los Angeles Lakers 1975–89; All NBA First Team 1971–74, 1976–77, 1980–81, 1984, 1986; NBA All-Defensive First Team 1974–75, 1979–81; retd from game 1989; Asst Coach Alchesay High School (Whiteriver, AZ) 1999–2000; Asst Coach NBA LA Clippers 2000; Asst Coach NBA Indiana Pacers 2002; Head Coach USBLs Oklahoma Storm 2002; Asst Coach Los Angeles Lakers 2005–; NBA career records include: most minutes (57,446), most points (33,387), most field goals made (15,837), most field goals attempted (28,307), most blocks (3,189); first player in NBA history to play 20 seasons; 1,560 games played; 18 NBA All-Star games played; All-City 1963–65, All-American 1963–65, Consensus All-American 1963–65, First Team All-America 1967, 1968, 1969, Nat. Player of the Year 1967, 1969, Nat. Collegiate Athletic Asscn (NCAA) Tournament Most Outstanding Player 1967, 1968, 1969, Naismith Award Winner 1969, NBA Rookie of the Year 1970, NBA Most Valuable Player—MVP 1971, 1972, 1974, 1976, 1977, 1980, NBA Finals MVP 1971, 1975, Sports Illustrated Sportsman of the Year 1985, elected to Basketball's Hall of Fame 1995. *Address:* The Los Angeles Lakers, Inc., 555 North Nash Street, El Segundo, CA 90245, USA (office). *Telephone:* (310) 426-6000 (office). *Fax:* (310) 426-6115 (office). *Website:* www.nba.com/lakers (office).

ABDUL LATIF, Pehin Dato' Jaya; Brunei diplomatist; b. 1939; m.; six c.; ed Univ. of Manchester, UK; Govt Deputy Agent, London 1981–82; Commr to Malaysia 1982–84, High Commr 1984–86; Amb. to the Philippines 1986–87; Perm Rep. of Brunei Darussalam to the UN 1987–93; Amb. to USA 1993–97; High Commr to UK 1997; Pres. Brunei State Youth Council 1977–80; fmr mem. World Assembly of Youth, World Assembly of Muslim Youth and Asian Youth Council. *Address:* c/o Ministry of Foreign Affairs (Kementerian Hal Ehwal Luar Negeri), Bandar Seri Begawan, BD 2710, Brunei (office).

ABDUL-RAHMAN, Tan Sri Datuk Omar, MVD, MRCVS, FASc; Malaysian professor of veterinary pathology and university administrator; *President and CEO, Malaysia University of Science and Technology (MUST);* b. 9 Nov. 1932, Kota Bharu, Kelantan; three c.; ed Sydney and Queensland Univs, Australia and Univ. of Cambridge, UK; Demonstrator in Veterinary Pathology, Queensland Univ. 1959; Veterinary Research Officer, Veterinary Research Inst., Ipoh 1960–67, Sr Research Officer 1967–70, Deputy Dir 1971–72; Foundation Prof. and Dean, Faculty of Veterinary Medicine and Animal Sciences, Universiti Putra Malaysia 1972–78, Prof. of Veterinary Pathology 1982–2001, Deputy Vice-Chancellor 1982–84; apptd Pres. Malaysian Scientific Asscn 1984, currently Adviser; fmr Pres. Asscn of Veterinary Surgeons Malaysia–Singapore; mem. Nat. Council for Scientific Research and Devt, Malaysia, Nat. Comm. for UNESCO, Nat. Devt Planning Cttee of Malaysia 1984; Adviser to Prime Minister on Science and Tech. 1985–2001; Exec. Chair. Venture Capital for Tech. Acquisition 2001–07; currently Pres. and CEO Malaysia Univ. of Science and Tech. (MUST); Founding Chair. Commonwealth Partnership for Tech. Man. (CPTM); Founding Pres. and Sr Fellow, Malaysian Acad. of Sciences; Pres. Malaysian Asscn of Professional Speakers 2006–; Founding Chair. Malaysian Tech. Devt Corpn, Tech. Park Malaysia Corpn; Founding Jt Chair. Malaysian Industry-Govt Group for High Tech.; Founding Fellow, Islamic Acad. of Sciences; Fellow, Acad. of Sciences for the Third World; mem. Editorial Advisory Bd Tropical Veterinarian (journal) 1983–; Exec. Chair. Kumpulan Modal Perdana Sdn Bhd; mem. Bd of Dirs OSK Ventures Int. Bhd, Green Packet Bhd, Encorp Bhd, Kotra Industries Bhd, Great Wall Plastic Industries Bhd, BCT Technology Bhd; Hon. Fellow, Nat.

Acad. of Sciences of Kyrgyz Repub.; Dr hc (Stirling) 1986, (Melbourne), (Guelph), (Bristol), (Queensland); Asean Achievement Award (Science) 1993, Fook Ying Tung South East Asia Prize 1998, Tun Abdul Razak Award (Int. Category) 2000; Darjah Mulia Seri Melaka (state award), Johan Setia Mahkota, Johan Mangku Negara and Panglima Setia Mahkota (fed. awards). *Publications:* over 100 publs on science and tech. *Address:* MUST Ehsan Foundation, Malaysia University of Science and Technology, Unit GL33 (Ground Floor), Block C, Kelana Square, 17, Jalan SS7/26, 47301 Petaling Jaya, Selangor D.E; Malaysian Association of Professional Speakers, c/o Suite 47-4, 4th Floor, PJ Highway Centre, Jalan 51/205, 46050 Petaling Jaya, Selangor, Malaysia. *Telephone:* (3) 78806863 (office). *Fax:* (3) 78806525 (office). *E-mail:* tsomar@must.edu.my (office); info@maps.org.my (home). *Website:* www.must.edu.my (office).

ABDULAI, Yesufu Seyyid Momoh; Nigerian economist and international organization official; b. 19 June 1940, Auchi; s. of Momoh Abdulai and Haijia Fatimah Abdulai; m. Zene Makonnen Abdulai 1982; three s. one d.; ed Mount Allison Univ. and McGill Univ., Canada; taught econs in Canada; Tech. Asst to Exec. Dir (Africa Group I), World Bank Group, Washington, DC 1971–73, Adviser to Exec. Dir 1973–78, Alternate Exec. Dir for Africa Group 1 1978–80, Exec. Dir 1980–82, Vice-Chair. Jt Audit Cttee Exec. Bd 1980–82; Chair. Jt Secr. African Exec. Dirs of World Bank Group and the IMF 1975–77; Man. Dir and CEO Fed. Mortgage Bank of Nigeria 1982–83; Dir-Gen. OPEC Fund for Int. Devt 1983–2003; mem. Prize Cttee, Arab Gulf Programme for UN Devt Orgs (AGFUND) Int. Prize for Pioneering Devt Projects; Grand Decoration of Honour (Austria) 2004. *Leisure interests:* sport, reading, photography, listening to music. *Address:* c/o Prize Committee, AGFUND, PO Box 18371, Riyadh 11415, Saudi Arabia.

ABDULATIPOV, Ramazan Gadzhimuradovich, DPhilSc; Russian/Dagestan politician and diplomatist; *Ambassador to Tajikistan;* b. 4 Aug. 1946, Guerguta, Dagestan; m.; two s. one d.; ed Dagestan State Univ.; mem. CPSU 1973–91; CP work 1974–76; Sr Teacher, Dagestan Pedagogical Inst. 1975–76; Head of Murmansk Higher School of Marine Eng 1978–87; Head of Sector, Div. of Int. Relations of CPSU Cen. Cttee 1988–90; RSFSR People's Deputy 1990–93, Chair. Council of Nationalities 1990–93; elected to Council of Fed. 1993, Deputy Chair. 1994–96; mem. State Duma 1995–97; Deputy Prime Minister 1997–98, Minister of Nat. Policy 1998–99; Rep. of Saratov Region in Council of Fed. 2000–05; Amb. to Tajikistan 2005–; Pres. Ass. of Nations of Russia 1998–; participant of numerous peace-making missions on N Caucasus; Pres. Fed. of UNESCO Clubs in Russia; mem. Russian Acad. of Natural Sciences. *Publications:* Lenin's Policy of Internationalism in USSR, Internationalism and the Spiritual and Moral Development of the Peoples of Dagestan, What is the Essence of Your Being?, Power and Conscience, Nature and Paradoxes of National Consciousness Authority of Sense, Ethnic Question and State Structure of Russia: From Cran Tower to the Kremlin Gates, Inscriptions. *Leisure interests:* painting, aphoristic poetry. *Address:* Embassy of the Russian Federation, 734000 Dushanbe, Kuchai Abu Ali ibni Sino 29/31, Tajikistan (office). *Telephone:* (372) 235-70-65 (office). *Fax:* (372) 235-88-06 (office). *E-mail:* rambtadjik@rambler.ru (office). *Website:* www.rusembassy.tajnet.com (office); www.abdulatipov.ru.

ABDULLA, Ahmed; Maldivian newspaper publisher and fmr government official; *Chairman, Miadhu News;* b. 26 Sept. 1949, Malé; s. of Abdullah Hassan and Hawwa Fulhu; m.; one s. three d.; fmr Amb. to Sri Lanka and India; fmr Minister of Health, of Information, Arts and Culture; Acting Minister of Foreign Affairs 2005; Minister of Environment, Energy and Water 2005–08 (resgnd); mem. Dhivehi Raiyyithunge Party –2008; Owner and Chair. Miadhu newspaper. *Leisure interests:* calligraphy, reading, sports fishing, badminton, swimming. *Address:* G. Mescot, Lonuziyaarai Magu, Malé (home); Miadhu News, G. Mascot, Koimalaa Hingun, Malé 20-02, Maldives (office). *Telephone:* 3322557 (home); 3320700 (office). *Fax:* 3321504 (home); 3320500 (office). *E-mail:* miadhu@dhivehinet.net.mv (office). *Website:* www.miadhu.com.mv (office).

ABDULLAH, Abdullah, DMed; Afghan ophthalmologist and politician; *Secretary-General, Massoud Foundation;* b. 5 Sept. 1960, Kabul; s. of Gullam Mahyuddin and Siddiqa Mahyuddin; one s. three d.; ed Faculty of Medicine, Kabul Univ.; Mujahidin activist, Jamiat-i-Islami group, Sr Spokesman 1996; Deputy Minister of Foreign Affairs, Northern Alliance 1999, Minister 1999–2001; participated in Future of Afghanistan Govt Talks, Bonn Nov. 2001; Minister of Foreign Affairs, Afghan Interim Authority Dec. 2001–June 2002, Afghan Transitional Authority 2002–04, of Afghanistan 2004–06; Sec.-Gen. Massoud Foundation 2006–. *Leisure interests:* music, swimming, ping-pong. *Address:* 2N Street Kart-e-Parwan, Kabul, Afghanistan (home). *Website:* www.masoudfoundation.com.

ABDULLAH, Tun Ahmad Shah; Malaysian state official and civil servant; *Yang di-Pertua Negeri of Sabah;* b. 9 Dec. 1946, Kampung Inanam; m. Datin Dayang Masuyah Awang Japar; three s. one d.; ed La Salle Secondary School, South Devon Coll., UK, Indiana State Univ., USA; Customs Officer, Royal Customs Dept 1968–69, Asst Dist Officer, Beaufort 1969–78, seconded to Nat. Rice and Padi Bd 1979–83; Sec. State Public Services Comm. 1983–87; Dir Missionary of the Sabah Islamic Council 1988–94; Sec. Home Affairs and Research 1994–95; Dept Dir Sabah Public Services 1995–98, Deputy State Sec. 1998–2002; Yang di-Pertua Negeri (Head of State) of Sabah 2003–; Deputy Pres. Bajau Arts and Cultural Ass. *Address:* Dewan Ungangan Negeri Sabah, Aras 4, Bangunan Dewan Undangan Negeri Sabah, Peti Surat 11247, Kota Kinabalu 88813, Malaysia (office). *Telephone:* (88) 427533 (office). *Fax:* (88) 427333 (office). *E-mail:* webmaster@sabah.gov.my (office). *Website:* www.sabah.gov.my (office).

ABDULLAH, Burhanuddin, MA; Indonesian central banker and economist; b. 10 July 1947, Garut; ed Padjadjaran Univ. Bandung, Mich. State Univ., USA; joined Bank Indonesia 1979; worked in Credit Dept 1981, later with Econ. Research and Statistics Dept, then Personal Asst to Gov.; joined IMF, Washington, DC 1989, Asst Exec. Dir 1990–93; Head Econ. Co-operation and Int. Trade Div., Indonesia 1993–95; Deputy Dir for Int. Affairs 1995–96; Deputy Dir Econ. Research and Monetary Policy Dept 1996–98; Deputy Gov. Bank Indonesia 2000–03, Gov. 2003–08, also Gov of IMF for Indonesia; Co-ordinating Minister of Econ. Affairs 2001. *Address:* c/o Bank Indonesia, Jalan M. H. Thamrin 2, Jakarta Pusat 10110, Indonesia (office).

ABDULLAH, Farooq, MB; Indian physician and politician; b. 21 Oct. 1937, Srinagar, Kashmir; s. of Sheikh Mohammad Abdullah and Begum Abdullah; m. Mollie Abdullah 1968; one s. three d.; Chief Minister, Jammu and Kashmir 1982–84, 1986–90, 1996–2002; Pres. State Cen. Labour Union, Jammu and Kashmir Nat. Conf.; Chair. Jammu and Kashmir Muslim Auquaf Trust, Sher-i-Kashmir Nat. Medical Inst. Trust, Sher-i-Kashmir Inst. of Medical Sciences; mem. Parl. 1980–82; mem. India Int. Centre; Gen. Sec. Indo-Arab Friendship Soc., Nat. Integration Council; Patron Jammu and Kashmir Nat. Conf.; Nat. Solidarity Award 1998, Eminent Personality of the Year, Indian Medical Asscn 1999. *Leisure interests:* golf, photography, gardening, music. *Address:* Jammu and Kashmir National Conference, Mujahid Manzil, Srinagar 190 002 (office); 5 Pritvi Raj Road, New Delhi 110 01, India. *Telephone:* (194) 271500 (office). *E-mail:* farooq.abdullah@hotmail.com (home).

ABDULLAH, Omar Farooq, BCom; Indian politician; *Chief Minister of Jammu and Kashmir;* b. 10 March 1970, Rochford, UK; s. of Farooq Abdullah and Mollie Abdullah; m. Payal Abdullah; two s.; ed Sydenham Coll., Mumbai; Pres. Youth Nat. Conf.; elected to 12th Lok Sabha, mem. Parl. for Srinagar Constituency (Nat. Conf. Party) 1998, re-elected to 13th Lok Sabha 1999; mem. Cttee of Transport and Tourism, Consultative Cttee, Ministry of Tourism 1998–99; Minister of State for Commerce and Industry 1999–2001, for External Affairs 2001–02; Pres. Jammu and Kashmir Nat. Conf. (JKNC) 2002–; Chief Minister of Jammu and Kashmir 2009–. *Address:* Jammu and Kashmir National Conference, Mujahid Manzil, Srinagar 190 002, India (office). *Telephone:* (194) 271500 (office).

ABDULLAH, Yousuf bin al-Alawi bin; Omani government minister and diplomatist; *Minister responsible for Foreign Affairs;* b. 1942, Salalah; s. of Abdullah bin Alawi; ed Egypt, univ. studies in political science, UK; joined Diplomatic Service 1970, Second Sec. Ministry of Foreign Affairs 1972, postings to Cairo and Beirut; Amb. to Lebanon 1973; Under-Sec. Ministry of Foreign Affairs 1974, Minister of State 1982, Minister responsible for Foreign Affairs 1997–; First Grade Sultan Qaboos Decoration, Order of Merit, Egypt, Officier, Légion d'honneur, France, Grand Decoration of Honour, Austria, Cavaliere Grande Croce, Italy and other foreign decorations. *Address:* Ministry of Foreign Affairs, PO Box 252, Muscat 113, Oman (office). *Telephone:* 699500 (office). *Fax:* 699589 (office); 699531 (office). *E-mail:* mfaoman@omantel.net.om (office). *Website:* www.mofa.gov.om (office).

ABDULLAH II IBN AL-HUSSEIN, HM King of Jordan; head of state and army officer; b. 30 Jan. 1962, Amman; s. of the late King Hussein Ibn Talal and of Princess Muna al-Hussein; m. Rania al-Yassin 1993 (Queen Rania); two s. two d.; ed Islamic Educ. Coll., St Edmund's School, Surrey, UK, Deerfield Acad., USA, Sandhurst Mil. Acad. and Univ. of Oxford, UK; succeeded to the throne 7 Feb. 1999; commissioned Second Lt 1981, Reconnaissance Troop Leader 13th/18th Bn Royal Hussars (British Army), FRG and England; rank of First Lt 1984; Platoon Commdr and Co. second-in-command 40th Armoured Brigade, Jordan, Commdr Tank Co. 91st Armoured Brigade 1985–86 (rank of Capt.); Tactics Instructor Helicopter Anti-Tank Wing, 1986–87; undertook advanced studies in int. affairs at School of Foreign Service, Georgetown Univ., Washington, DC 1987–88; Commdr of a co. 17th Tank Bn, 2nd Guards Brigade then Bn second-in-command (rank of Maj.) 1989; attended Command and Staff Coll., Camberley, UK 1990; Armour Rep. Office of the Insp. Gen. 1991, Commdr 2nd Armoured Car Regt, 40th Brigade (rank of Lt Col) 1992; promoted to rank of Col 1993; Deputy Commdr Jordanian Special Forces Jan.–June 1994; promoted to the rank of Brig. 1994 and assumed command of Royal Jordanian Special Forces; Commdr of Special Operations Command 1997–; Pres. Jordan Nat. Football Fed.; Hon. Pres. Int. Tourism Golden Rudder Soc.; Head Nat. Cttee for Tourism and Archaeological Film Production 1997–. *Leisure interests:* car racing, (fmr Jordanian Nat. Rally Racing Champion), water sports, scuba diving, collecting ancient weapons and armaments. *Address:* Royal Hashemite Court, Amman, Jordan. *Website:* www.kingabdullah.jo.

ABDURIXIT, Abdulahat; Chinese politician; *Chairman, Regional People's Congress, Xinjiang Uygur Autonomous Region;* b. March 1942, Yining, Xinjiang; ed Xinjiang Eng Coll.; joined CCP 1960; engineer then Vice-Pres. Xinjiang Uygur Autonomous Region Construction Survey and Design Acad., Vice-Dir Xinjiang Uygur Autonomous Region Planning Comm.; Vice-Chair. Xinjiang Uygur Autonomous Region 1965–93; Chair. Xinjiang Uygur Autonomous Region 1993–2003; apptd Vice-Sec. CCP Xinjiang Uygur Autonomous Region Cttee 1993; mem. CCP 15th Cen. Cttee 1997–2002, 16th Cen. Cttee 2002–07; Chair. Regional People's Congress, Xinjiang 2003–. *Address:* c/o People's Government of Xinjiang Uygur Autonomous Region, Urumqi, Xinjiang, People's Republic of China.

ABDYKARIMOV, Oralbai; Kazakhstani politician; b. 18 Dec. 1944, Kievka, Karaganda region; m. Abdykarimova Jamal; three s. one d.; ed Alma-Ata Higher CPSU School, Karaganda State Univ.; leading posts in Komsomol and CP organs of Kazakhstan; Deputy Head, then Head of Admin. Office of Pres. of Kazakhstan; Chair. Mazhilis (Parl.); Chair. Higher Disciplinary Council, State Comm. for Fight with Corruption; mem. Senate (Parl.) 1999–, Chair. of

Senate 1999–2004; Sec. of State and presidential adviser 2004–07; Chair. Nur Otan party public council on fighting corruption 2007–; fmr mem. Security Council of Kazakhstan; Order Barys. *Address:* Light Of The Fatherland People's Democratic Party (Nur Otan), 050000 Almaty, Abylai khana 79, Kazakhstan (office). *Telephone:* (727) 279-78-00 (office). *Fax:* (727) 279-40-66 (office). *E-mail:* partyotan@nursat.kz (office). *Website:* www.ndp-nurotan.kz (office).

ABE, Nobuyasu; Japanese diplomatist and fmr UN official; *Ambassador to Switzerland;* b. 9 Sept. 1945, Akita; m. Akiko Sugawara; two s.; ed Univ. of Tokyo, Amherst Coll., Mass, USA; entered Foreign Service 1967, has held variety of positions in fields of arms control and disarmament; served in Perm. Missions to Int. Orgs, Geneva 1977–79, UN, New York 1987–90, 1996–97, Int. Orgs, Vienna 1999–2001; Pvt. Sec. to Foreign Minister Kiichi Miyazawa 1974–76; Dir of Policy Planning 1984–86; Sous-Sherpa for G7 Summits 1992–94; Consul-Gen. of Japan, Boston, Mass, USA 1994–96; Dir-Gen. for Arms Control and Science Affairs, Tokyo 1997–99; Amb. to Saudi Arabia 2001–03; UN Under-Sec.-Gen. for Disarmament Affairs, New York 2003–06; Amb. to Switzerland 2006–; Int. Fellow, Weatherhead Center for Int. Affairs, Harvard Univ. 1986–87. *Address:* Embassy of Japan, Engestr. 53, Postfach, 3000 Bern 9, Switzerland. *Telephone:* 313002222. *Fax:* 313002255. *E-mail:* eojs@bluewin.ch. *Website:* www.ch.emb-japan.go.jp.

ABE, Shinzo, LLB; Japanese politician; s. of the late Shintaro Abe (died 1991); grandson of the late Nobusuke Kishi; ed Faculty of Law, Seikei Univ., Univ. of Southern Calif., USA; began career with Kobe Steel Ltd –1982; Exec. Asst to Minister for Foreign Affairs 1982–87; Pvt. Sec. to Chair. of Gen. Council, Liberal Democratic Party (LDP) 1987–87, Pvt. Sec. to Sec.-Gen. 1987–93, Dir of LDP Social Affairs Div. 1999–2000, Sec.-Gen. 2003–04, Acting Sec.-Gen. 2004, Pres. 2006–07; mem. House of Reps (Yamaguchi Pref., 4th Electoral Dist) 1993–, mem. Standing Cttee on Foreign Affairs 1993–99, on Health and Welfare 1999–2000, on Security 1999–2000; Deputy Chief Cabinet Sec. 2000–01, 2001–03, Chief Cabinet Sec. 2005–06, Prime Minister 2006–07 (resgnd). *Publications include:* Utsukushii Kuni E (Toward a Beautiful Country) 2006. *Address:* Liberal-Democratic Party—LDP (Jiyu-Minshuto), 1-11-23, Nagata-cho, Chiyoda-ku, Tokyo 100-8910, Japan (office). *Telephone:* (3) 3581-6211 (office). *Website:* www.jimin.jp (office); newleader.s-abe.or.jp.

ABED DE ZAVALA, Sheila R.; Paraguayan lawyer and environmentalist; *Chairman, Commission on Environmental Law, International Union for Conservation of Nature;* ed Universidad Nacional de Asunción; Environmental Law & Policy Prof. in the Masters Programme on Environmental Eng, Universidad Nacional de Asunción; Founder and Exec. Dir IDEA (Instituto de Derecho y Economía Ambiental), Asuncion, Paraguay 1996–; past Gen. Coordinator Alianza Regional para Políticas de Conservación en América Latina y el Caribe (Regional Alliance for Conservation Policies in Latin America and the Caribbean); mem. Comm. on Environmental Law, Int. Union for Conservation of Nature 2000–, currently Chair.; mem. Grupo Zapallar on Trade and Environment(S American coalition of NGOs and individual mems); has represented the Paraguayan Govt before UN Framework Convention on Climate Change; has represented civil society in Biodiversity and Ramsar Conventions. *Publications:* co-author of eight publs. *Address:* International Union for Conservation of Nature, Rue Mauverney 28, Gland 1196, Switzerland (office); Instituto de Derecho y Economia Ambiental, Asunción, Paraguay (office). *Telephone:* (22) 999-0000 (IUCN) (office). *Fax:* (22) 999-0002 (IUCN) (office). *E-mail:* sheila.abed@iucn.org (office). *Website:* www.iucn.org (office); www.idea.org.py (office).

ABEL, Edward William, CBE, PhD, DSc; British chemist and academic; *Emeritus Professor of Inorganic Chemistry, University of Exeter;* b. 3 Dec. 1931, Mid-Glamorgan; s. of Sydney J. Abel and the late Donna Maria Grabham; m. Margaret R. Edwards 1960; one s. one d.; ed Bridgend Grammar School, Glamorgan, Univ. Coll. Cardiff and Northern Polytechnic, London; Research Fellow, Imperial Coll. London 1957–59; Lecturer and Reader, Univ. of Bristol 1959–71; Prof. of Inorganic Chem. Univ. of Exeter 1972–97, Deputy Vice-Chancellor 1991–94, now Emer. Prof.; Visiting Prof., Univ. of BC 1970, Univ. of Japan 1971, Tech. Univ. of Brunswick 1973, ANU, Canberra 1990; mem. Council, Royal Soc. of Chem. (RSC) 1978–82, 1983–2002, Pres. RSC 1996–98, Ed.-in-Chief Tutorial Chemistry Texts (10 vols) 1999; Chair. Scientific Affairs Bd, Univ. Grants Cttee 1986–89; Hon. Fellow, Univ. of Cardiff 1999; Hon. DUniv (Univ. of N London); Hon. DSc (Exeter) 2000, (Univ. of Glamorgan); Tilden Medal, RSC 1981. *Publications:* Organometallic Chemistry Vols 1–25 (ed.) 1970–1995, Comprehensive Organometallic Chemistry I (ed.) (nine vols) 1984, II (14 vols) 1995. *Leisure interest:* gardening. *Address:* 1A Rosebarn Avenue, Exeter, Devon, EX4 6DY, England (home). *Telephone:* (1392) 270272 (home).

ABELA, George, BA, LLB, LLM, PhD; Maltese lawyer, politician and head of state; *President;* b. 22 April 1948, Qormi; s. of George Abela and Ludgarda Abela (née Debono); m. Margaret Abela 1976; one s. one d.; ed Univ. of Malta; fmr attorney in pvt. practice, specialising in civil, commercial and industrial law; legal consultant to Gen. Workers' Union 1975–2000; fmr legal adviser to Medical Asscn of Malta; Pres. Qormi FC –1982, Pres. Malta Football Asscn 1982–92; Deputy Leader in charge of Party Affairs, Malta Labour Party 1992–96; legal adviser to Prime Minister of Malta 1996–97; fmr Dir Cen. Bank of Malta; fmr Exec. Dir Bank of Valletta PLC; Pres. of Malta 2009–. *Address:* Office of the President, The Palace, Valletta VLT, 1190, Malta (office). *Telephone:* 21221221 (office). *Fax:* 21241241 (office). *E-mail:* president@gov.mt (office). *Website:* www.president.gov.mt (office).

ABELE, John E., BS; American medical device industry executive (retd); *Chairman, FIRST;* m. Mary Abele; three c.; ed Amherst Coll.; several exec. positions with medical device firms in 1960s including with Advanced Instruments Inc.; joined Medi-tech 1969 then f. Cooper Scientific 1970 and acquired Medi-tech, Pres. 1970–83, helped develop, manufacture and market first steerable catheter; f. (with Peter Nicholas) Boston Scientific Corpn 1979, Dir 1979–, Chair. 1979–95, Vice-Chair. and Founder, Office of the Chair. 1995–96 (retd); Founder Chair. Argosy Foundation (pvt.family foundation) 1997–; Chair. FIRST (For Inspiration and Recognition of Science and Technology) Foundation; mem. and Hon. Fellow, Soc. of Interventional Radiology. *Address:* FIRST, 200 Bedford St., Manchester, NH 03101, USA (office). *Telephone:* (603) 666-3906 (office). *Fax:* (603) 666-3907 (office). *Website:* www.usfirst.org (office); www.argosyfnd.org.

ABELEV, Garry Israyelevich; Russian immunologist; *Head of Laboratory, N. N. Blokhin Cancer Research Centre, Russian Academy of Medical Sciences;* b. 10 Jan. 1928, Moscow; s. of Israel Abelev and Eugenia Abelev; m. 1st Elfrida Cilart 1949 (died 1996); two s.; m. 2nd Galina Deichman 1999; ed Moscow State Univ.; joined N. F. Gamaleya Inst. of Epidemiology and Microbiology, held several positions including Sr Lab. Technician, Researcher, Head of Lab., Head of Dept 1950–77; Head of Lab. Inst. of Carcinogenesis, N. N. Blokhin Cancer Research Centre 1977–; Prof., Moscow State Univ.; Corresp. mem. USSR (now Russian) Acad. of Sciences 1987–, mem. 2000–; mem. American Acad. of Immunology; conducts research on immunology of tumours, immunochemistry, cell biochemistry; mem. Bd New York Inst. of Cancer, New York Acad. of Sciences; Hon. mem. American Asscn of Immunologists, European Soc. of Cancer Researchers; Gold Medal Cancer Research Inst. (USA) 1975, USSR State Prize 1978, Abbot Prize 1990, Honourable Scientist of Russia 1999, Triumph Prize 2001, Calling Prize 2004. *Publications:* Virusology and Immunology of Cancer 1962, Alpha-Feto-Protein: 25 Years of Study, Tumour Biology 1989, An autobiographical sketch: 50 years in cancer immunochemistry (in 'Comprehensive Biochemistry', ed. G. Semenza) 2007; articles in scientific journals of Russia, Western Europe and USA. *Leisure interests:* music, history of science. *Address:* N.N. Blokhin Cancer Research Centre, Russian Academy of Medical Sciences, 115478 Moscow, Kashirskoye Shosse 24, Russia (office). *Telephone:* (495) 323-59-10 (office). *Fax:* (495) 324-12-05 (office). *E-mail:* abelev@crc.umos.ru (office). *Website:* www.ronc.ru (office); garriabelev.narod.ru (home).

ABERBACH, David, BA, BSc, MLitt, DPhil; British academic; *Professor of Jewish Studies, McGill University;* b. 17 Oct. 1953, London; s. of the late Prof. Moshe Aberbach and of Rose Aberbach (née Firsht); m. Mimi Skelker 1980; three d.; ed Talmudical Acad. of Baltimore, Univ. Coll., London, Univ. of Oxford, Tavistock Clinic, Open Univ.; Lecturer, Univs of Oxford and Cambridge, Leo Baeck Coll. and Cornell Univ. 1982–86; Visiting Asst Prof., McGill Univ. 1986–87, Assoc. Prof., Dept of Jewish Studies 1987–2006, Prof. 2006–; Visiting Prof., Univ. Coll. London 1992–93, 1998, 2001–02; Academic Visitor, Sociology Dept, LSE 1992–93, 1994–98, 2001–03, Govt Dept, LSE 2004, 2006, 2008–. *Publications:* At the Handles of the Lock: Themes in the Fiction of S. J. Agnon 1984, Bialik 1988, Surviving Trauma: Loss, Literature and Psychoanalysis 1989, Realism, Caricature and Bias: The Fiction of Mendele Mocher Sefarim 1993, Imperialism and Biblical Prophecy 750–500 BCE 1993, Charisma in Politics, Religion and the Media: Private Trauma, Public Ideals 1996, Revolutionary Hebrew, Empire and Crisis 1998, The Roman-Jewish Wars and Hebrew Cultural Nationalism (co-author) 2000, Major Turning Points in Jewish Intellectual History 2003, C.N. Bialik: Selected Poems (ed.) 2004, Jewish Cultural nationalism: origins and influences 2008, Moshe Aberbach, Jewish Education and History: Continuity, Crisis and Change (ed.) 2009. *Leisure interests:* cinema, painting, coastal path hiking. *Address:* Department of Jewish Studies, McGill University, 3438 McTavish, Montreal, PQ H3A 1X9, Canada (office); 32 Ravenshurst Avenue, London, NW4 4EG, England (home). *Telephone:* (514) 398-5009 (office). *Website:* www.arts.mcgill.ca/programs/jewish (office).

ABHISIT, Vejjajiva (Mark), BA, M.Phil., LLB; Thai economist and politician; *Prime Minister;* b. 3 Aug. 1964, Newcastle-upon-Tyne, England; s. of Dr Athasit Vejjajiva and Dr Sodsai Vejjajiva; m. Dr Pimpen Sakuntabhai; two c.; ed Eton Coll., Univ. of Oxford, UK, Ramkhamhaeng Univ.; fmr Lecturer, Chulachomklao Royal Mil. Acad. and Faculty of Econs, Thammasat Univ.; mem. Parl. (Democrat) for Bangkok 1992–2001, Democrat Party List 2001–06, Democrat Party List Zone 6 2007–, Govt Spokesperson 1992–94, Deputy-Sec. to the Prime Minister for Political Affairs 1994, Chair. House Educ. Affairs Cttee 1995, Chair. Cttee to Consider the Nat. Educ. Bill of 1999 1998, Minister to the Prime Minister's Office 2001; Deputy Leader Democrat Party (Prachatipat) 1999, Leader 2005–; Prime Minister 2008–; Kt Grand Cordon of the Most Noble Order of the Crown of Thailand 1998, Kt Grand Cordon (Special Class) of the Most Exalted Order of the White Elephant 1999. *Address:* Office of the Prime Minister, Government House, Thanon Nakhon Pathom, Bangkok 10300 (office); Democrat Party (Prachatipat), 67 Thanon Setsiri, Samsen Nai, Phyathai, Bangkok 10400, Thailand. *Telephone:* (2) 280-3526 (office). *Fax:* (2) 282-8792 (office). *E-mail:* webmaster@opm.go.th (office). *Website:* www.opm.go.th (office); www.democrat.or.th; www.abhisit.org.

ABILDAYEV, Bolot; Kyrgyzstani business executive and fmr government official; *General Director, Gazprom Neft Asia;* Minister of Finance 2002–05; Gen. Dir Gazprom Neft Asia 2006–. *Address:* Gazprom, 117997, Moscow, 16 Nametkina Street, V-420, GSP-7, Russia (office). *Telephone:* (495) 719-30-01 (office). *Fax:* (495) 719-83-33 (office). *E-mail:* gazprom@gazprom.ru (office). *Website:* www.gazprom.com (office).

ABILOV, Geldimyrat; Turkmenistani central banker; First Deputy Chair. Cen. Bank of Turkmenistan 2005-06, Chair. 2006–; Rep. of Turkmenistan at World Bank and Asian Devt Bank. *Address:* Central Bank of Turkmenistan, 744000 Aşgabat, ul. Bitarap, Turkmenistan (office). *Telephone:* (12) 38-10-27 (office). *Fax:* (12) 51-08-12 (office). *E-mail:* merkez3@online.tm (office).

ABIRACHED, Robert, DèsSc; French writer and academic; *Professor Emeritus, University of Paris X;* b. 25 Aug. 1930, Beirut, Lebanon; m. Marie-France de Bailliencourt 1974; one s. one d.; ed Lycée Louis-le-Grand and Ecole Normale Supérieure, Paris; Attaché, CNRS 1960–64; Drama Critic, Nouvel Observateur 1964–66; Literary and Drama Critic, La Nouvelle Revue Française 1956–72; Lecturer, later Prof., Univ. of Caen 1969–81; Prof. and Dir Dept of Drama, Univ. of Paris X 1988–99, Prof. Emer. 1999–; Prof., Conservatoire nat. supérieur d'art dramatique 1993–97; Dir Theatre and Exhbns, Ministry of Culture 1981–88; Pres. Int. Festival of Francophones, Limoges 1990–2000, Observatory of Cultural Politics, Grenoble, 1991–2001; Officier, Légion d'honneur; Commdr du Mérite; Commdr des Arts et Lettres; Commdr des Palmes académiques; Prix Sainte-Beuve. *Plays:* Tu connais la musique? 1972, Giacomo Casanova comédien (in Italian) 1997. *Television:* La Consultation, Agnès, Agnès, Le dernier mot. *Publications:* Casanova ou la dissipation (essay) 1961, l'Emerveillée (novel) 1963, Tu connais la musique? (play) 1971, La crise du personnage dans le théâtre moderne (essay) 1978, Le théâtre et le Prince tome I: L'Embellie 1992, La décentralisation théâtrale (four vols) (ed.) 1992–95, Le Théâtre et le Princetome tome II: Un système fatigué 2003. *Address:* 4 rue Robert-Turquan, 75016 Paris, France (home). *Telephone:* 1-45-27-23-49 (home). *E-mail:* robert.abirached@orange.fr (home).

ABIYEV, Col-Gen. Safar Akhundbala oğlu; Azerbaijani politician and army officer; *Minister of Defence;* b. 27 June 1950, Baku; ed Baku Troops Command Acad., Frunze Acad., Moscow; served in Azerbaijani Army, attaining rank of Col-Gen.; currently Minister of Defence. *Address:* Ministry of Defence, 1139 Baku, Azarbaycan pr, Azerbaijan (office). *Telephone:* (12) 439-41-89 (office). *Fax:* (12) 492-92-50 (office).

ABIZAID, Gen. John; American army officer (retd) and consultant; *Senior Partner, JPA Partners LLC;* m.; three c.; ed US Mil. Acad., West Point, Harvard Univ., Univ. of Jordan, Amman; began career with 82nd Air Airborne Div., Fort Bragg, N Carolina; fmr infantry commdr; led Ranger rifle co. during invasion of Grenada 1983; led 1st infantry div., 504th Parachute Infantry Regt; 66th Commdt US Mil. Acad.; Asst to Chair. of Jt Chiefs of Staff 1993; fmr Dir of Strategic Plans and Policy, Jt Staff, later Dir of the Jt Staff; Deputy Commdr, then Commdr for Combined Forces Command, US Cen. Command 2003–07 (retd); Sr Pnr, JPA Partners LLC (consulting firm), Nev. 2007–; Annenberg Distinguished Visiting Fellow, Hoover Inst., Stanford Univ. 2007–; mem. Bd of Dirs RPM International Inc. 2008–; Montgomery Fellow, Dartmouth Coll. 2008; Legion of Merit; Defense Distinguished Service Medal, Army Distinguished Service Medal, Bronze Star. *Address:* c/o Board of Directors, RPM International, 2628 Pearl Rd., Mediana, OH 44258, USA.

ABLAZA, Gerardo C., Jr, AB; Philippine telecommunications industry executive; *President and CEO, Globe Telecom Inc.;* b. 1953; ed De La Salle Univ.; began career at Unilever; several positions at Citibank NA 1983–97 including Country Business Man. for Philippines and Guam 1996–97 and Vice-Pres. Citibank NA Singapore for Consumer Banking; joined Ayala Corpn, assigned to Globe Telecom Inc. as Exec. Vice–Pres. and COO 1997, Pres. and CEO 1998–, mem. Man. Cttee, Ayala Corpn 1998–, also Sr Man. Dir and Chair. Innove Communications (subsidiary); mem. Bd of Dirs Bank of The Philippine Islands 2001–; Asia Business Leadership Award and CEO Choice of the Year Award, TNT 2004. *Address:* Globe Telecom Inc., Globe Telecom Plaza (Pioneer Highlands), Pioneer Corner, Madison Street 1552, Mandaluyong City, Philippines (office). *Telephone:* (632) 730-2000 (office). *Website:* www1.globe.com.ph (office).

ABOULELA, Leila, MSc; Sudanese writer; b. 1964, Cairo, Egypt; m.; three c.; ed The Sisters' School, Khartoum, Univ. of Khartoum and London School of Econs, UK; lived in Aberdeen, Scotland 1990–2000; fmr lecturer in statistics and part-time research asst in Scotland; began writing 1992; co-writer of plays broadcast on BBC Radio 4; currently lives in Abu Dhabi. *Publications:* The Translator (novel) 1999, The Museum (short story) (Caine Prize for African Writing) 2000, Coloured Lights (novel) 2001, Minaret (novel) 2005; work included in anthologies Scottish Short Stories 1996, Ahead of its Time 1998. *Address:* c/o Stephanie Cabot, The Gernert Company, 136 East 57th Street, New York, NY 10022, USA (office). *Telephone:* (212) 838-7777 (office). *Fax:* (212) 838-6020 (office). *E-mail:* info@thegernertco.com (office). *Website:* www .thegernertco.com (office).

ABOUMRAD, Daniel Hajj; Mexican telecommunications executive; *CEO, América Móvil;* b. 1966, Mexico City; s.-in-law of Carlos Slim Helú; ed Anáhuac Univ.; Dir América Móvil SA de CV, CEO 2000–; CEO Hulera Euzkadi SA de CV; mem. Bd of Dirs Carso Global Telecom, América Telecom, Grupo Carso SA de CV, Radiomóvil Dipsa SA de CV, Telefonos de Mexico (Telmex). *Address:* América Móvil SA de CV, Lago Alberto 366, Colonia Anáhuac, 11320 México, DF, Mexico (office). *Telephone:* (55) 25813947 (office). *Fax:* (55) 25813948 (office). *E-mail:* info@americamovil.com (office). *Website:* www.americamovil.com (office).

ABOVA, Tamara Yevgenyevna, DJur; Russian professor of law; *Head, Centre of Civil Studies and Sector of Civil Law, Civil and Arbitration Procedure, Institute of State and Law, Russian Academy of Sciences;* b. 18 Nov. 1927; m.; one s.; ed Moscow Inst. of Law; Sr Consultant, USSR Ministry of Transport 1959–64; Sr Researcher 1964, Head of Sector 1987, later Head of Centre of Civil Studies and Sector of Civil Law, Civil and Arbitration Procedure, Inst. of State and Law, Russian Acad. of Sciences; Arbitrator, Int. Commercial Arbitration Court, Chamber of Commerce and Industry, Vice-Chair. Arbitrator, Maritime Arbitration Comm. 2006–; mem. Scientific-Consultative Council, Supreme State Arbitration Court of Russian Fed.; Expert Council on Civil Legislation in State Duma (Parl.) of Russian Fed.; participant in USSR and Russian Women's Movt; Honoured Scientist of the Russian Fed. 2006. *Publications:* more than 135 works on civil law, civil procedure, arbitration etc. *Leisure interests:* music, theatre, art exhbns. *Address:* Centre of Civil Studies, IGPRAN, 119841 Moscow, Znamenka str. 10, Russia (office). *Telephone:* (495) 291-17-09 (office). *Fax:* (495) 291-85-74 (office). *E-mail:* islran@rinet.ru (office).

ABRAGAM, Anatole, DPhil; French physicist and academic; *Professor Emeritus, Collège de France;* b. 15 Dec. 1914, Griva-Semgallen, Russia; s. of Simon Abragam and Anna Maimin; m. 1st Suzanne Lequesme 1944 (died 1992); m. 2nd Nina Gordon 1996; ed Lycée Janson, Sorbonne, Univ. of Oxford, UK; Research Assoc., CNRS 1946; joined French Atomic Energy Comm. 1947, Physicist, later Sr Physicist 1947–55, Head of Magnetic Resonance Lab. 1955–58, Head of Solid State Physics and Nuclear Physics Dept 1959–65, Dir of Physics 1965–70, Dir of Research 1971–80; Prof. of Nuclear Magnetism, Collège de France 1960–85, now Prof. Emer.; Pres. French Physical Soc. 1967; mem. Acad. of Sciences 1973–; Foreign mem. Royal Soc. 1983, NAS, Russian Acad. of Sciences 1999; Hon. Fellow, American Acad. of Arts and Sciences; Hon. Fellow, Merton and Jesus Colls, Oxford 1976, Magdalen Coll., Oxford 2002; Grand Croix, Ordre nat. du Mérite; Commdr, Légion d'honneur, des Palmes académiques; Dr hc (Kent) 1968, (Oxford) 1976 and others; Holweck Prize, London Physical Soc. 1958, Grand Prix Cognacq-Jay, Acad. of Sciences 1970, Lorentz Medal 1982, Mateucci Medal 1992, Lomonosov Medal 1995 and others. *Publications:* Discovery of Anomalous Hyperfine Structure in Solids 1950, Dynamic Polarization in Solids 1957, The Principles of Nuclear Magnetism 1961, Nuclear Anti-ferromagnetism 1969, Electron Paramagnetic Resonance of Transition Elements (with B. Bleaney) 1970, Nuclear Pseudomagnetism 1971, Nuclear Ferromagnetism 1973, Nuclear Magnetism: Order and Disorder (with M. Goldman) 1982, Reflexions of a Physicist 1985, La physique avant toute chose 1987, Time Reversal 1989. *Leisure interest:* English and Russian literature. *Address:* Collège de France, 3 rue d'Ulm, 75231 Paris (office); 33 rue Croulebarbe, 75013 Paris, France (home). *Telephone:* 1-47-07-62-57 (home). *Fax:* 1-44-27-17-04 (office). *E-mail:* abragam@physique.ens.fr (office). *Website:* www.college-de-france.fr/site/ins_pro/p1001667426147.htm (office).

ABRAHAM, E. Spencer, JD; American consultant and fmr politician; *Chairman and CEO, The Abraham Group LLC;* b. 12 June 1952, East Lansing, Mich.; s. of Eddie Abraham and Juliette Sear Abraham; m. Jane Abraham; three c.; ed Michigan State Univ. and Harvard Law School; attorney, Lansing, Mich. 1980–; Prof., Thomas M. Cooley Law School, Lansing 1981–; Chair. Mich. Republican Party 1983–90; Chair. Mich. Del. Republican Nat. Convention 1984; Chair. Presidential Inaugural Cttee, Mich. 1985; Deputy Chief of Staff to Vice-Pres. Dan Quayle (q.v.) 1991–93; Co-Chair. Nat. Republican Congressional Cttee 1991–93; Counsel to Canfield, Paddock and Stone 1993–94; Senator from Mich. 1995–2001; US Sec. of Energy 2001–04 (resgnd); Founder, Chair. and CEO The Abraham Group LLC (consulting firm), Washington, DC 2004–; Chair. AREVA, Inc. 2006–; mem. Bd of Dirs Occidental Petroleum; Distinguished Visiting Fellow, Hoover Inst., Stanford Univ. –2008, co-Chair. Cttee for Justice 2005–08; mem. Electricity Advisory Bd (also Sec.) 2001; mem. Mich., American and DC Bar Asscns; Co-founder Federalist Soc. *Address:* The Abraham Group LLC, 600 Fourteenth Street, NW, Suite 500, Washington, DC 20005 (office); Areva Inc., 4800 Hampden Lane, Suite 1100, Bethesda, MD 20814, USA (office). *Telephone:* (202) 393-7700 (Abraham Group) (office). *Fax:* (202) 393-7701 (Abraham Group) (office). *Website:* www.abrahamgroupllc.com (office); www.areva.com (office).

ABRAHAM, F(ahrid) Murray; American actor; b. 24 Oct. 1939, Pittsburgh; m. Kate Hannan 1962; two c.; ed Texas Univ.; Prof., Brooklyn Coll. 1985–; Dir No Smoking Please, Time & Space Ltd Theatre, New York; numerous Broadway plays, musicals, TV appearances and films; Obie Award (for Uncle Vanya) 1984, Golden Globe Award 1985, Los Angeles Film Critics Award 1985. *Films include:* Amadeus (Acad. Award 1985) 1985, The Name of the Rose 1987, Russicum 1987, Slipstream, Hard Rain, Personal Choice, Eye of the Widow 1989, An Innocent Man 1990, Mobsters 1991, Bonfire of the Vanities 1991, By The Sword 1992, Last Action Hero 1993, Surviving the Game 1994, Nostradamus 1994, Mighty Aphrodite 1995, Children of the Revolution 1996, Mimic 1997, Star Trek IX 1998, Falcone 1999, Muppets from Space 1999, Finding Forrester 2000, I cavalieri che fecero l'impresa 2001, 13 Ghosts 2001, Joshua 2002, The Bridge of San Luis Rey 2004, And Quietly Flows the Don 2004, Peperoni ripieni e pesci in faccia 2004, A House Divided 2006, The Stone Merchant 2006, Perestroika 2007, Come le formiche 2007, Carnera: The Walking Mountain 2008; narrator Herman Melville, Damned in Paradise 1985, OBS 1985,. *Stage appearances:* The Wonderful Ice Cream Suit 1965, The Man in the Glass Booth 1968, 6 Rms Rivvu 1972, Bad Habits 1974, The Ritz 1976, Teibele and Her Demon 1979, Landscape of the Body 1977, The Master and Margarita 1978, King Lear 1981, Frankie and Johnny in the Clair de lune 1987, A Month in the Country 1995. *TV includes:* Dream West 1986, The Betrothed 1989, Largo Desolato 1990, A Season of Giants 1991, The First Circle 1992, Il Caso Dozier 1993, Journey to the Center of the Earth 1993, Larry McMurty's Dead Man's Walk 1996, Color of Justice 1997, Esther 1999, Noah's Ark 1999, Excellent Cadavers 1999, The Darkling 2000, Dead Lawyers 2004, The Final Inquiry 2006, Life, Shark Swarm 2008. *Address:* c/o Paradigm, 10100 Santa Monica Boulevard, Suite 2500, Los Angeles, CA 90067, USA.

ABRAHAM, Gen. Hérard; Haitian politician and army officer (retd); b. 28 July 1940; enlisted in Haitian army, rose to rank of Lt-Gen.; supported coup against Duvalier 1986; Minister of Foreign Affairs 1987–88; Acting Pres. of Haiti after street protests forced Pres. Prosper Avril into exile 1990; helped to crush coup attempt by Roger Lafontant Jan. 1991; retd from army, settled in Miami, Fla 1991; made radio address from Fla calling on Pres. Jean-Bertrand Aristide to resign Feb. 2004; Minister of the Interior 2004–05, of Foreign Affairs and Religion 2005–06. *Address:* c/o Ministry of Foreign Affairs and

Religion, Blvd Harry S. Truman, Cité de l'Exposition, Port-au-Prince, Haiti (office).

ABRAHAM, Ronny; French judge and professor of international law; *Judge, International Court of Justice;* b. 5 Sept. 1951, Alexandria, Egypt; ed Univ. of Paris II, Inst. d'Études Politiques, Ecole Nat. d'Admin, Paris; Prof., Inst. d'Études Politiques, Paris –1998; Assoc. Prof., Univ. of Paris X, Nanterre 1997–2003; Assoc. Prof. of Public Int. Law and Human Rights, Univ. of Paris II, Panthéon-Assas 2004–; Admin. Tribunal Judge 1978–85, 1987–88; Asst Dir Office of Legal Affairs, Ministry of Foreign Affairs 1986–87, Dir of Legal Affairs 1998–; Maître des requêtes 1988–2000; Counseiller d'État 2000–; Govt Commr within the judicial system 1989–1998; Judge, Int. Court of Justice 2005–(09); Rep. of France to many cases before Int. Court of Justice, European Court of Human Rights, Court of Justice of the EC and int. arbitral tribunals; mem. Cttee of Experts for the Improvement of Procedures for the Protection of Human Rights 1986–98, Chair. 1987–2004; Chair. Jt Consultative Cttee OECD 1994–98; Del. to UN Gen. Ass. 1998–2004; Chair. French Del. to Ass. of States Parties to Rome Statute of Int. Criminal Court 2002–04; Head of French Del. to Cen. Comm. for Navigation of the Rhine 1998–, Chair. 2002–03; mem. Bd Soc. française pout le droit int.; mem. European Group of Public Law. *Publications:* numerous books, papers and articles in professional journals on int. and European law. *Address:* International Court of Justice, Peace Palace, 2517 KJ The Hague, The Netherlands (office). *Telephone:* (70) 3022323 (office). *Fax:* (70) 3649928 (office). *E-mail:* information@icj-cij.org (office). *Website:* www.icj-cij.org (office).

ABRAHAMIAN, Hovik, CandMedSci; Armenian politician; *Chairman (Speaker), Azgayin Zhoghov (National Assembly);* b. 24 Jan. 1958, Mekhchyan, Ararat region; m.; three c.; ed Yerevan Automobile Road Vocational Coll., Yerevan Inst. of Nat. Economy, trained in burn surgery at Moscow Surgery Inst.; mil. service in Soviet Army 1977–79; Div. Head, Burastan Cognac Factory 1990–91; Dir Artashat Wine and Cognac Factory 1991–95; mem. Republican Party of Armenia, mem. Exec. Bd; mem. Azgayin Zhoghov (Nat. Ass.) first convocation 1995–99, re-elected for Constituency No. 17, Ashtarak 2008–, Chair. (Speaker) 2008–; Chair. Artashat City Council Exec. Cttee 1995–96; Mayor of Artashat 1996–98; Marzpet (Gov.) of Ararat 1998–2000; Minister of Regional Admin and Urban Devt Co-ordination 2000–01, of Regional Admin 2001–02, of Regional Admin and Infrastructure Co-ordination 2002–05, of Territorial Admin endowed with functions of Co-ordinating Minister 2005–07; mem. Security Council 2005–; Deputy Prime Minister and Minister of Territorial Admin 2007–08; Sec.-Gen. Presidential Staff April—Sept. 2008; Man. A-948 scientific discipline of project presented by Int. Scientific-Tech. Centre; Chair. Yerevan State Econs Univ. Bd; mem. Yerevan State Univ. Bd; Anania Shirakatsi Medal, Prime Minister's Commemorative medal, Marshall Baghramyan Medal, Fridtjof Nansen Commemorative Gold Medal. *Address:* Office of the Speaker, Azgayin Zhoghov (National Assembly), 0095 Yerevan, Marshal Baghramian Street 19, Armenia (office). *Telephone:* (10) 58-82-25 (office). *Fax:* (10) 52-98-26 (office). *E-mail:* abrahamyan@parliament.am (office). *Website:* www.parliament.am (office).

ABRAHAMS, Ivor, RA; British sculptor and painter; b. 10 Jan. 1935, Lancs.; s. of Harry Abrahams and Rachel Kalisky; m. 1st Victoria Taylor 1966 (divorced 1974); one s. (deceased); m. 2nd Evelyne Horvais 1974; one s.; ed Wigan Grammar School, Lancs., St Martin's School of Art and Camberwell School of Art, London; Visiting Lecturer in Sculpture and Drawing, Birmingham Coll. of Art 1960–64, Coventry Coll. of Art 1964–68; Visiting Lecturer, RCA, Slade School of Fine Art and Goldsmith's Coll. of Art 1970–80; Winston Churchill Fellow 1990, Fellow Royal Soc. of British Sculptors 1994; Visiting Lecturer, RA Schools; Fellow Royal Soc. of British Sculptors. *Television:* subject of several TV documentaries including Ivor Abrahams/Review BBC 2 1972, Museum of Drawers/Arena produced by Alan Yentob BBC 2 1979. *Publications:* Oxford Garden Sketchbook, Tales & Poems by E. A. Poe (illustrator 20 images), A Philosophical Enquiry into the Sublime and Beautiful Edmund Burke (illustrator 15 images) 1979. *Leisure interests:* books, postcards, golf. *Address:* c/o Royal Academy of Arts, Burlington House, Piccadilly, London, W1V 0DS, England. *Telephone:* (20) 8961-2792 (home). *Fax:* (20) 8961-2792 (home). *E-mail:* ieabrahams@onetel.com (home).

ABRAHAMSEN, Egil, MSc, DTech; Norwegian scientist; b. 7 Feb. 1923, Hvaler; s. of Anker Christian Abrahamsen and Aagot Abrahamsen (née Kjoelberg); m. Randi B. Wiborg 1951; one s. two d.; ed Polytechnical Univ. of Norway, Univ. of Calif., Berkeley, USA, Univs of Durham, Newcastle upon Tyne, UK; Surveyor, Det Norske Veritas 1952–54, Sr Surveyor 1954–57, Prin. Surveyor 1957–75, Deputy Pres. 1966, Vice-Pres. 1967, Pres. 1967–85; Ed. European Shipbuilding 1955–60; Chair. and mem. numerous cttees; Chair. Bd of A/S Veda 1967–70, Bd of Dirs A.S. Computas 1967–83, Norsk Hydro 1985–92, The Abrahamsen Cttee 1984–86; Chair. Norwegian Telecom 1980–95, Royal Caribbean Cruise Line A/S (RCCL) 1985–89, OPAK 1985–, I. M. Skaugen 1990–99, Eikland 1990–99, Kosmos 1988–92, IKO Group 1988–92; Innovation 1990–2004; mem. Bd Den Norske Creditbank 1983–88; Kt Commdr, Order of the Lion (Finland) 1983, Commdr, Order of St Olav (Norway) 1987; Chevalier, Légion d'honneur 1987, Ordre nat. du Mérite 1990, and numerous other decorations. *Leisure interests:* skiing, tennis. *Address:* Maaltrostveien 35, 0786 Oslo, Norway (home). *Telephone:* 91-71-40-05 (home); 22-49-18-78 (office). *Fax:* 22-49-18-78 (office). *E-mail:* egiab@online.no (home).

ABRAHAMSON, Gen. James Alan; American air force officer (retd) and business executive; *Chairman and CEO, StratCom International LLC;* b. 19 May 1933, Williston, ND; s. of Norval S. Abrahamson and Thelma B. Helle; m. Barbara Jean Northcott 1959 (died 1985); one s. one d.; ed Massachusetts Inst. of Tech. and Univ. of Oklahoma; commissioned USAF 1955, Lt-Gen. 1982, Gen. 1987; Flight Instructor, Bryan AF Base, Tex. 1957–59; Spacecraft Project Officer Vela Nuclear Detection Satellite Programme, LAAF Station 1961–64; Fighter Pilot, Tactical Air Command 1964; Astronaut USAF Manned Orbiting Lab. 1967–69; mem. staff, Nat. Aeronautics and Space Council, White House 1969–71; Commdr 4950th Test Wing USAF 1973–74; Insp. Gen. AF Systems Command 1974–76; Dir F-16 Fighter Programme 1976–80; Deputy Chief of Staff for Systems, Andrews AF Base, Md 1980–81; Assoc. Admin. for Space Transportation System, NASA HQ 1981–84; Dir Strategic Defence Initiative Org. 1984–89; Pres. Transportation Sector, Exec. Vice-Pres. for Devt Hughes Aircraft Co. 1989–92; Chair. Bd Oracle Corpn 1992–95; Lecturer in Astronautics, AIAA 1993; moved to International Air Safety LLC, Washington, DC 1995; Founder and currently Chair. and CEO StratCom International LLC; mem. Nat. Advisory Bd Childhelp USA; numerous awards and medals. *Leisure interests:* sports, music, poetry. *Address:* StratCom International LLC, 20112 Marble Quarry Road, Keedysville, MD 21756-1508, USA (office). *Telephone:* (301) 432-8950 (office). *Fax:* (301) 432-2657 (office). *E-mail:* GenAbe@aol.com.

ABRAMOVICH, Roman Arkadyevich; Russian business executive and fmr politician; b. 24 Aug. 1966, Saratov, Russian SFSR, USSR; s. of Arkadii Nakhimovich Abramovich and Irina Vassilyevna Abramovich; m. 1st Olga Abramovich; m. 2nd Irina Malandina (divorced 2007); two s. three d.; ed Industrial Inst., Ukhta, Komi, Moscow Gubkin Inst. of Oil and Gas; f. cos Supertechnologia-Shishmarev, Elita, Petroltrans, GID, NPR 1992–95; Head of Moscow Office Runicom SA, Switzerland 1993–96; f. (with Boris Berezovskii) Jt Stock Co. P.K. Trust 1995; f. cos Mekong, Centurion-M, Agrofert, Multitrust, Oilimpex, Sibreal, Forneft, Servet, Branko, Vektor-A 1995–96; Founder and Dir-Gen. Runicom Ltd Gibraltar 1997–99; Dir Moscow br. Sibneft 1996–97, Dir Sibneft 1996–2005; acquired major interest in Evraz Group S.A. (steel and mining cos) 2006–; mem. State Duma 1998–2000; Gov. of Chukot Autonomous Okrug 2000–08 (resignation rejected by Pres. Putin 2007, accepted 3 July 2008), Head of Govt 2001–08, mem. Chukot Autonomous Okrug Duma 2008–; Owner, Chelsea Football Club (UK) 2003–; Order of Honour 2006; named by Expert (Russian business magazine) as Person of the Year (jtly) 2003. *Address:* Evraz Group S.A., 127006 Moscow, ul. Dolgorukovskaya 15, Bldgs 4 and 5, Russia (office). *Telephone:* (495) 232-1370 (office). *Fax:* (495) 232-1359 (office). *Website:* www.evraz.com (office).

ABRAMS, Hon. Elliott, MA, JD; American government official; *Deputy Assistant to the President and Deputy National Security Adviser for Global Democracy Strategy, National Security Council;* b. 24 Jan. 1948, New York, NY; m. Rachel Abrams; three c.; ed Harvard Coll., Harvard Law School, LSE, UK; Chief of Staff, Special Counsel for Senator Daniel P. Moynihan 1977–79; Asst Sec. of State for Int. Org. Affairs 1981, for Human Rights and Humanitarian Affairs 1981–85, for Inter-American Affairs 1985–89; Sr Fellow, Hudson Inst. 1990–96; Pres. Ethics and Public Policy Center 1996–2001; mem. US Comm. on Int. Religious Freedom 1999–2001, Chair. 2000–01; Special Asst to Pres. and Sr Dir for Democracy, Human Rights and Int. Operations 2001–02, Special Asst to Pres. and Sr Dir for Near East and North African Affairs 2002–05, Deputy Asst to Pres. and Deputy Nat. Security Adviser for Global Democracy Strategy 2005–; mem. Council on Foreign Relations; Sec. of State's Distinguished Service Award 1988. *Publications:* Shield and Sword 1995, Security and Sacrifice: Isolation, Intervention, and American Foreign Policy 1995, Faith or Fear: How Jews Can Survive in a Christian America 1997, Honor Among Nations: Intangible Interests and Foreign Policy 1998, Undue Process: A Story of How Political Differences are Turned into Crimes 1998, Close Calls: Intervention, Terrorism, Missile Defense, and "Just War" Today 1998, Secularism, Spirituality, and the Future of American Jewry 1999, The Influence of Faith 2001, Democracy How Direct?: Views from the Founding Era and the Polling Era 2002. *Address:* National Security Council, The White House, 1600 Pennsylvania Avenue, NW, Washington, DC 20500, USA (office). *Telephone:* (202) 456-9373 (office). *Fax:* (202) 456-7106 (office). *E-mail:* eabrams@nsc.eop.gov (office). *Website:* www.whitehouse.gov/nsc (office).

ABRAMS, Herbert Leroy, MD; American radiologist and academic; *Professor Emeritus of Radiology, School of Medicine, Stanford University;* b. 16 Aug. 1920, New York; s. of Morris Abrams and Freda Abrams (née Sugarman); m. Marilyn Spitz 1943; one s. one d.; ed Cornell Univ., State Univ. of New York; began medical practice at Stanford Univ., faculty mem., School of Medicine 1951–67, Dir Div. Diagnostic Roentgenology 1961–67, Prof. of Radiology 1962–67; Philip H. Cook Prof. of Radiology, Harvard Univ. 1967–85, Prof. Emer. 1985–, Chair. Dept of Radiology 1967–80; Radiologist-in-Chief, Peter Bent Brigham Hosp., Boston 1967–80; Chair. Dept of Radiology, Brigham & Women's Hosp., Boston 1981–85; Radiologist-in-Chief, Sidney Farber Cancer Inst., Boston 1974–85; Prof. of Radiology, Stanford Univ. Medical School 1985–90, Prof. Emer. 1990–, also Mem.-in-Residence and Dir Project on Disabled Leadership, Center for Int. Security and Cooperation (CISAC) 1985–; Clinical Prof. Univ. of California Medical School 1986–; Ed.-in-Chief Postgraduate Radiology 1983–99, Cardiovascular and Interventional Radiology 1976–85; R.H. Nimmo Visiting Prof., Univ. of Adelaide 1976; numerous lectureships; mem. Int. Blue Ribbon Panel on Radiation Effects Research Foundation, Hiroshima and Nagasaki; mem. numerous medical asscns; Fellow, Nat. Cancer Inst.; Hon. Fellow, Royal Coll. of Radiology, Royal Coll. of Surgeons (Ireland); Gold Medal, Asscn of Univ. Radiologists 1984, Gold Medal, Radiological Soc. 1995, 2000, Gold Medal, Soc. of Cardiovascular and Interventional Radiology 2000. *Publications include:* Congenital Heart Disease 1965, Coronary Arteriography: A Practical Approach 1983, Ed. Abrams Angiography 1983, The President has been Shot: Confusion, Disability and the 25th Amendment in the Aftermath of the Assassination Attempt on Ronald Reagan 1992, The History of Cardiac Radiology 1996, Health Risks from Exposure to Low Levels of Ionizing Radiation 2004, numerous reports and articles for professional periodicals. *Leisure interests:* English and American literature, tennis, music. *Address:* CISAC, Stanford University,

Encina Hall, Stanford, CA 94305-6165; Stanford University School of Medicine, 300 Pasteure Drive, Stanford, CA 94305; 714 Alvarado, Stanford, CA 94305, USA (home). *Telephone:* (650) 725-4873; (415) 723-6258 (office); (415) 424-8552 (home). *Fax:* (650) 723-0089; (415) 725-7296. *E-mail:* hlabrams@stanford.edu (office). *Website:* www-radiology.stanford.edu (office); siis.stanford.edu/people/herbertlabrams (office).

ABRAMS, Norman, AB, JD; American university administrator and academic; *Acting Chancellor, University of California, Los Angeles;* b. 1933, Chicago, Ill.; ed Univ. of Chicago; Ed.-in-Chief University of Chicago Law Review while a student; fmr Assoc. in Law, Columbia Univ. Law School; Research Assoc. and Dir Harvard-Brandeis Cooperative Research for Israel's Legal Devt, Harvard Law School –1959; mem. staff, UCLA 1959–, on leave from UCLA serving as Special Asst to US Attorney Gen. in Criminal Div., US Dept of Justice 1966–67, now Prof. Emer., UCLA School of Law, teaches and writes on fed. criminal law, anti-terrorism law and evidence, Assoc. Dean of Law School 1989–91, Vice-Chancellor of Academic Personnel 1991–2001, Interim Dean of Law School 2003–04, Acting Chancellor UCLA 2006–07. *Publications include:* Evidence: Cases and Materials (ninth edn, co-author with Berger, Mansfield and Weinstein), Anti-Terrorism and Criminal Enforcement (second edn) 2005, Federal Criminal Law and Its Enforcement (fourth edn, co-author with Beale) 2006. *Address:* UCLA Law School, Los Angeles, CA 90095-1405, USA (office). *Telephone:* (310) 794-4056 (office). *Fax:* (310) 206-6489 (office). *E-mail:* abrams@law.ucla.edu (office). *Website:* www.law.ucla.edu (office).

ABRAMSKY, Dame Jennifer (Jenny), DBE, BA; British radio producer, editor and broadcasting industry executive; *Chair, Heritage Lottery Fund;* b. 7 Oct. 1946; d. of Chimen Abramsky and the late Miriam Abramsky (née Nirenstein); m. Alasdair D. MacDuff Liddell 1976; one s. one d.; ed Holland Park School and Univ. of East Anglia; joined BBC Radio as Programme Operations Asst 1969, Producer, The World at One 1973, Ed. PM 1978–81, Producer Radio Four Budget Programmes 1979–86, The World at One 1981–86, Ed. Today programme 1986–87, News and Current Affairs Radio 1987–93, est. Radio Four News FM 1991, Controller BBC Radio Five Live 1993–96, Dir Continuous News Services, BBC (including Radio Five Live, BBC News 24, BBC World, BBC News Online, Ceefax) 1996–98, Dir BBC Radio 1998–2000, BBC Radio and Music 2000–06, Head, Audio and Music Group 2006–08, also in charge of BBC Radio Drama and Popular Music TV 2007–08, mem. Exec. Bd; Chair., Heritage Lottery Fund 2008–; mem. Econ. and Social Research Council 1992–96, Editorial Bd British Journalism Review 1993–; Vice-Chair. Digital Radio Devt Bureau 2002–; mem. Bd of Dirs Hampstead Theatre 2003–, Chair. 2005–; mem. Bd of Govs BFI 2000–06; News Int. Visiting Prof. of Broadcast Media, Exeter Coll., Oxford 2002; Radio Acad. Fellowship 1998; Hon. Prof. Thames Valley Univ. 1994; Hon. RAM 2002; Hon. MA (Salford) 1997; Woman of Distinction, Jewish Care 1990, Sony Radio Acad. Award 1995. *Leisure interests:* theatre, music. *Address:* Heritage Lottery Fund, 7 Holbein Place, London, SW1W 8NR, England (office). *Telephone:* (20) 7591-6000 (office). *Fax:* (20) 7591-6001 (office). *E-mail:* enquire@hlf.org.uk (office). *Website:* www.hlf.org.uk (office).

ABRAMSON, Jill, BA; American newspaper editor; *News Managing Editor, New York Times;* b. 1954; m. Henry Griggs; two c.; ed Harvard Univ.; Ed.-in-Chief Legal Times, Washington, DC 1986–88; Deputy Bureau Chief and investigative reporter, Wall Street Journal 1988–97; joined New York Times 1997, Enterprise Ed., Washington Bureau 1997–99, Washington Ed. 1999–2000, Washington Bureau Chief 2000–03, News Man. Ed. 2003–; Nat. Press Club Award 1992. *Publications include:* Where They Are Now 1986, Strange Justice (with Jane Mayer) 1994. *Address:* New York Times, 620 Eighth Avenue, New York, NY 10018, USA (office). *Telephone:* (212) 556-8000 (office). *E-mail:* managing-editor@nytimes.com (office). *Website:* www.nytimes.com (office).

ABRASH, Mahmoud Aref al-; Syrian politician; Speaker, Majlis ash-Sha'ab (People's Ass.) 2003–. *Address:* Majlis ash-Sha'ab (People's Assembly), Damascus, Syria (office). *Telephone:* (11) 3324045 (office). *Fax:* (11) 3712532 (office). *E-mail:* info@parliament.gov.sy (office). *Website:* www.parliament.gov.sy (office).

ABRASZEWSKI, Andrzej, MA, LLD; Polish diplomatist and international organization official; *Member, United Nations Advisory Committee on Administration and Budgetary Questions (ACABQ);* b. 4 Jan. 1938, Paradyz; s. of Antoni Abraszewski and Maria Zaleska; m. Teresa Zagorska; one s.; ed Cen. School for Foreign Service, Warsaw and Copernicus Univ., Toruń; researcher, Polish Inst. for Int. Affairs, Warsaw 1962–71; Sec. Polish Nat. Cttee on the 25th anniversary of the UN 1970; Counsellor to the Minister for Foreign Affairs, Dept of Int. Orgs, Ministry of Foreign Affairs, Warsaw 1971–83; mem. Polish del. to Gen. Ass. of the UN 1971–90, with rank of Amb. 2001–, mem. Ad Hoc Working Group on UN's programme and budget machinery 1975, mem. Advisory Cttee on Admin. and Budgetary Questions (ACABQ) 1977–82, 2001–, Vice-Chair. 2006–07; Vice-Chair. Admin. and Budgetary Cttee of Gen. Ass. 1979, Chair. 1982; mem. Cttee on Contribs 1983–88 (Vice-Chair. 1987–88), mem. Cttee for Programmes and Co-ordination (Vice-Chair. 1989, Chair. 1990); Asst to Deputy Minister for Foreign Affairs 1984–90; mem. UN Jt Inspection Unit 1991–2000, Vice-Chair. 1993, 1998, Chair. 1994; Prize of the Minister for Foreign Affairs, Prize of the Minister of Finance. *Publications:* various publs on UN affairs. *Leisure interests:* boating, skiing, swimming. *Address:* United Nations Advisory Committee on Administrative and Budgetary Questions, Room CB-60, New York, NY 10017 (office); 338 East 44th Street, Apt. 14F, New York, NY 10017, USA. *Telephone:* (212) 963-7456 (office). *Fax:* (212) 963-6943 (office). *E-mail:* abraszewski@un.org (office). *Website:* www.polandun.org (office); www.un.org/ga/acabq (office).

ABREHE, Berhane; Eritrean politician; *Minister of Finance;* Acting Minister of Land, Water and Environment 1998; currently Minister of Finance; mem. Bd of Govs, African Devt Bank Group, Eritrea, Eastern and Southern African Trade and Devt Bank. *Address:* Ministry of Finance, POB 896, Asmara, Eritrea (office). *Telephone:* (1) 118131 (office). *Fax:* (1) 127947 (office).

ABREU, Alcinda António de; Mozambican politician; *Minister of Environmental Affairs;* b. 13 Oct. 1953, Nova-Sofala; ed Universidad Eduardo Mondlane, Univs of Johannesburg and London; Deputy Gen. Sec. Organização da Juventude Moçambicana 1977–91; mem. Parl. 1977–94; Minister of Social Welfare Co-ordination 1994–97, of Foreign Affairs and Co-operation 2005–08, of Environmental Affairs 2008–; apptd by FRELIMO as mem. Nat. Elections Comms responsible for organizing municipal elections in 1998 and general election 1999; elected to Political Cttee, FRELIMO 2002–. *Address:* Ministry of Environmental Co-ordination, Avda Acordos de Lusaka 2115, CP 2020, Maputo, Mozambique (office). *Telephone:* 21466245 (office). *Fax:* 21465849 (office). *E-mail:* jwkacha@virconn.com (office). *Website:* www.micoa.gov.mz (office).

ABRIKOSOV, Alexei Alexeyevich; American (b. Russian) physicist; *Distinguished Scientist, Argonne National Laboratory;* b. 25 June 1928, Moscow; s. of Aleksei Ivanovich Abrikosov and Fanny Davidovna Vulf; m. Svetlana Yuriyevna Bun'kova 1977; two s. one d.; ed Moscow Univ.; Postgraduate Research Assoc., then Scientist and Sr Scientist, Inst. of Physical Problems, USSR (now Russian) Acad. of Sciences 1948–65; Head of Dept, Landau Inst. of Theoretical Physics, USSR (now Russian) Acad. of Sciences 1965–88, Dir Inst. of High Pressure Physics 1988–91; Distinguished Scientist, Argonne Nat. Lab., Ill., USA 1991–; Research Assoc., then Asst Prof. and Prof., Moscow Univ. 1951–68; Prof., Gorky Univ. 1971–72; Prof., Moscow Physical Eng Inst. 1974–75, Chair. Theoretical Physics, Moscow Inst. of Steel and Alloys 1976–91; mem. USSR (now Russian) Acad. of Sciences 1964, American Acad. of Arts and Sciences 1991, NAS 2000; Foreign mem. Royal Soc. 2001; Fellow, American Physics Soc. 1992; Hon. ScD (Moscow) 1955; Hon. DS (Lausanne) 1975, (Bordeaux) 2003, (Loughborough) 2004, (Tsukaba) 2005, (Hong Kong) 2005; Lenin Prize 1966, Fritz London Award 1972, USSR State Prize 1982, Landau Prize 1989, John Bardeen Prize 1991, Nobel Prize in Physics 2003. *Publications:* Quantum Field Theory Methods in Statistical Physics 1962, Introduction to the Theory of Normal Metals 1972, Fundamentals of Metal Theory 1987 and works on plasma physics, quantum electrodynamics, theory of superconductors, magnetism, astrophysics, quantum liquids and semi-metals. *Leisure interest:* skiing. *Address:* Argonne National Laboratory, 9700 South Cass Avenue, Argonne, IL 60439, USA (office). *Telephone:* (630) 252-5482 (office); (630) 252-6525 (office). *Fax:* (630) 252-7777 (office). *E-mail:* abrikosov@anl.gov (office). *Website:* www.anl.gov (office).

ABRIL, Victoria; Spanish actress; b. (Victoria Mérida Rojas), 14 July 1959, Madrid; m.; two s. *Films include:* Obsesión 1975, Robin and Marian 1975, Robin Hood 1975, Caperucita Roja 1975, Cambio de Sexo 1975, La Bien Plantada 1976, Doña Perfecta 1976, Esposa y Amante 1977, La Muchacha de las Bragas de Oro 1979, Asesinato en el Comité Central 1981, La Guerrillera 1981, La Colmena 1982, La batalla del Porro 1982, Le Bastard 1982, La Lune dans le Caniveau 1982, Sem Sombra de pecado 1982, J'ai Epousé un Ombre 1982, Rio Abajo 1982, Bajo el Signo de Piscis 1983, Le Voyage 1983, Las Bicicletas son para el Verano 1983, L'Addition 1983, Rouge George 1983, La noche más Hermosa 1984, Padre Nuestro 1984, After Dark 1984, L'Addition 1984, La Hora Bruja 1985, Tiempo de Silencio 1985, Max mon Amour 1985, Vado e Torno 1985, El Lute 1987, El Placer de Matar 1987, Barrios Altos 1987, El Juego más Divertido 1987, Ada dans la Jungle 1988, Baton Rouge 1988, Sandino 1989, Atame 1989, A solas Contigo 1990, Amantes 1990, Tie Me Up! Tie Me Down! 1991, High Heels 1992, Lovers (Silver Bear for Best Actress, Berlin Film Festival) 1992, Intruso 1993, Kika 1993, Jimmy Hollywood 1994, Casque Bleu 1994, Nadie Hablará de Nosotras Cuandro Hayamas Muerto (Best Actress, Cannes) 1995, Gazon Maudit 1996, Freedomfighters 1996, La femme du cosmonaute 1998, Between Your Legs 1999, Mon Père, Ma Mère, Mes Frères et Mes Soeurs 1999, 101 Reykjavik 2001, Sin Noticias de Dios 2002, Don't Tempt Me 2003, Incautos 2003, Septimo Dia El 2004, Cause Toujours 2004, Incautos 2004, Escuela de Seduccion 2004, Les Gens Honnêtes vivent en France 2005, Carne de Neón 2005, Tirante el Blanco 2006, Les Aristos 2006, 1 Camino de los Ingleses 2006. *Theatre includes:* Obras de Mihura, Company Tirso de Molina 1977, Viernes, día de libertad, Company L. Prendes 1977, Nuit d'Ivresse, Paris 1986. *Address:* c/o Alsira García-Maroto, Gran Via 63–3° izda, 28013 Madrid, Spain.

ABRIL-MARTORELL HERNÁNDEZ, Fernando; Spanish business executive; *Managing Director, Grupo Credit Suisse España;* s. of Fernando Abril Martorell; began career with JP Morgan; Gen. Man. Corp. Finance, Telefónica SA 1997–99, Pres. Telefónica Publicidad e Información (TPI) 1998–2000, COO Telefónica SA 2000, mem. Bd of Dirs 2001, Man. Dir 2001–03; currently Man. Dir Grupo Credit Suisse España; mem. Bd of Dirs Cintra 2004–, Portugal Telecom, Telecomunicaciones de Sao Paulo (Telesp). *Address:* Grupo Credit Suisse España, Paseo de Recoletos, 17, 28004 Madrid, Spain (office). *Telephone:* (91) 5959999 (office). *E-mail:* departamento.marketing@credit-suisse.com (office). *Website:* www.credit-suisse.es (office).

ABSALON, Julien; French mountain biker; b. 16 Aug. 1980, St Amé; m. Emilie; winner World Jr Championships, Mont St Anne 1998, U23 Category, European Championships 2001, 2002; Silver Medal, Elite Category, World Cup 2003; Gold Medal, Cross Country Cycling, Athens Olympics 2004, World Championships, Les Gets 2004, Livigno 2005, Rotorua 2006, Fort William 2007, Beijing Olympics 2008; Silver Medal, European Championships 2005; 17 World Cup wins (as of Aug. 2008); currently rides for Spanish mountain bike trade team Orbea. *Leisure interests:* snowboarding, paragliding, motorcross. *E-mail:* athlet-go@wanadoo.fr. *Website:* www.absalon-julien.com; www.orbea.com (office).

ABSE, Dannie, DLitt, LRCP, MRCS, FRSL; British writer, poet and physician; b. 22 Sept. 1923, Cardiff, Wales; s. of Rudolph Abse and Kate Shepherd; m. Joan Mercer 1951; one s. two d.; ed St Illtyd's Coll. Cardiff, Univ. Coll. Cardiff, King's Coll. London and Westminster Hosp., London; first book of poems published while still a medical student 1948; qualified as doctor 1950; Squadron-Leader RAF 1951–55; doctor in charge of chest clinic at Cen. Medical Establishment, Cleveland Street, London 1954–89; writer-in-residence, Princeton Univ., NJ, USA 1973–74; Pres. Poetry Soc. 1979–92; Fellow Welsh Acad. 1993; council mem. Royal Soc. of Literature; Hon. Fellow, Univ. of Wales Coll. of Medicine 1999; Hon. DLitt (Univ. of Wales) 1989, (Glamorgan) 1997; Welsh Arts Council Literature Prize 1971, 1987, Henry Foyle Award 1964, Jewish Chronicle Award, Cholmondeley Award 1983, 1985. *Publications:* poetry: Funland and Other Poems 1973, Way Out in the Centre 1981, White Coat, Purple Coat: Collected Poems 1948–1988 1989, Remembrance of Crimes Past 1990, On the Evening Road 1994, Arcadia, One Mile 1998, Running Late (Roland Mathias Award 2007) 2006; editor: Voices in the Gallery 1986, The Music Lover's Literary Companion (with Joan Abse) 1989, The Hutchinson Book of Post-War British Poets 1989, Twentieth-Century Anglo-Welsh Poetry 1997, New and Collected Poems 2003; fiction: Pythagoras (a play), Ash on a Young Man's Sleeve 1954, Some Corner of an English Field 1956, O Jones, O Jones 1970, Ask the Bloody Horse 1986, The View from Row G (three plays) 1990, There was a Young Man from Cardiff 2001, The Strange Case of Dr Simmonds and Dr Glas 2002; other: Journals from the Ant Heap 1986, Intermittent Journals 1994, A Welsh Retrospective 1997, Goodbye, Twentieth Century 2001, The Two Roads Taken 2003, The Presence (memoir) (Wales Book of the Year English language prize 2008) 2007; contributions: BBC and various publs in the UK and USA. *Leisure interests:* chess, supporting Cardiff City Football Club. *Address:* United Agents, 12–26 Lexington Street, London, W1F 0LE (office); 85 Hodford Road, London, NW11 8NH, England (home). *Telephone:* (20) 3214-0800 (office). *Fax:* (20) 3214-0801 (office). *E-mail:* info@unitedagents.co.uk (office). *Website:* www.unitedagents.co.uk (office).

ABSHIRE, David Manker, PhD; American diplomatist and administrator; *President and CEO, Center for the Study of the Presidency;* b. 11 April 1926, Chattanooga, Tenn.; s. of James Ernest Abshire and Phyllis Patten Abshire; m. Carolyn Sample Abshire 1957; one s. four d.; ed Baylor School, Chattanooga, US Mil. Acad., West Point, NY, Georgetown Univ., Washington, DC; co-f. Center for Strategic and Int. Studies, Georgetown Univ. 1962, Exec. Dir 1962–70, Chair. 1973–82, Pres. 1982–83, Vice-Chair. 1999–; Asst Sec. of State for Congressional Relations 1970–73; Perm. Rep. to NATO 1983–87; Special Counsellor to Pres. Jan.–April 1987; Chancellor Center for Strategic and Int. Studies (CSIS) April–Dec. 1987, Pres. 1988–, Vice-Chair. 1999–; Co-ed. Washington Quarterly 1977–83; Chair. US Bd for Int. Broadcasting 1974–77; Dir Nat. Security Group, Transition Office of Pres.-elect Reagan 1980–81; Pres. and CEO, Center for the Study of the Presidency 1999–; Pres. Richard Lounsbery Foundation of New York 2002–; mem. Congressional Cttee on the Org. of Govt for the Conduct of Foreign Policy 1973–75; mem. Bd Procter & Gamble 1987–96, Ogden Corpn, BP American Advisory Bd; mem. Advisory Bd Pres.'s Task Force on US Govt Int. Broadcasting 1991; Order of Crown (Belgium), Commdr Ordre de Léopold (Belgium), Order of the Lion of Finland (1st Class) 1994, Order of the Liberator (Argentina) 1999, Order of Sacred Treasure Gold and Silver Star (Japan) 2001; Pres. Civilian Service Award 1989, Medal of the Pres. of the Italian Repub., Senate, Parl. and Govt, Medal of Diplomatic Merit (Rep. of Korea) 1993, US Mil. Acad. Castle Award 1994, Distinguished Graduate Award, John Carroll Award for Outstanding Service by a Georgetown Univ. Alumnus. *Publications include:* International Broadcasting: A New Dimension of Western Diplomacy 1976, Foreign Policy Makers: President vs. Congress 1979, The Growing Power of Congress 1981, Preventing World War III: A Realistic Grand Strategy 1988, The Global Economy 1990, Putting America's House in Order: The Nation as a Family 1996, Report to the President-Elect 2000: Triumphs and Tragedies of the Modern Presidency 2000. *Leisure interest:* historical literature. *Address:* Center for Study of the Presidency, 1020 19th Street, NW, Suite 250, Washington, DC 20036 (office); 311 South St Asaph Street, Alexandria, VA 22314, USA (home). *Telephone:* (202) 872-9800 (office); (703) 836-2892 (home). *Fax:* (202) 872-9811 (office); (703) 836-2992 (home). *E-mail:* center@thepresidency.org (office). *Website:* www.thepresidency.org (office).

ABU GHAZALA, Field Marshal Muhammad Abd al-Halim (see Abd al-Halim Abu Ghazala, Field Marshal Muhammad).

ABU-GHAZALEH, Talal; Palestinian/Jordanian management consultant and intellectual property expert; *Chairman of the Management Board, Talal Abu-Ghazaleh International;* b. 22 April 1938, Jaffa; m. Nuha Salameh; two s. two d.; ed American Univ. of Beirut; Founder and Chair. Man. Bd Talal Abu-Ghazaleh Int. (TAGI) (mem. firm of Grant Thornton Int.), regional holding group of professional firms operating through 34 offices in Arab World and comprising, among others Talal Abu-Ghazaleh & Co. (TAGCO), Abu-Ghazaleh Consultancy & Co. (AGCOC), Al-Dar Consulting Co. (ADCO), Talal Abu-Ghazaleh Assocs. Ltd (TAGA), Arab Int. Projects Co. (AIPC), The First Projects Man. Co. (FPMC), Talal Abu-Ghazaleh Int. Man. Inc. (TAGIMI), TMP Agents, Arab Bureau for Legal Services (ABLE), Al-Dar Gen. Trading Co. (ADTCO); Chair. Arab Knowledge Man. Soc. (fmrly Arab Man. Soc.) 1989–; Chevalier, Légion d'honneur and decorations from Tunisia, Kuwait, Bahrain and Jordan; Hon. DHumLitt (Canisius Coll. Buffalo, NY) 1988. *Publications:* Taxation in the Arab Countries, The Abu-Ghazaleh English–Arabic Dictionary of Accounting, Trade Mark Laws in the Arab Countries. *Address:* Talal Abu-Ghazaleh International, TAGI House, Queen Noor Street, Shmeisani, Amman; PO Box 921100, Amman 11192, Jordan. *Telephone:* (6) 5669603. *Fax:* (6) 5696284. *E-mail:* tagi@tagi.com. *Website:* www.tagi.com.

ABU-HAMMOUR, Muhammed, MA, PhD; Jordanian economist and government official; *Chairman, Executive Privatization Commission;* b. 1961, Salt; m.; two s. two d.; ed Yarmouk Univ., Univ. of Jordan, Univ. of Surrey, UK; Researcher, Public Finance Div., Cen. Bank of Jordan 1987–91, Chief, External Economy and Balance of Payments Div. 1992–94, Chief, Public Finance Div. 1997–98; Advisor to Minister of Finance 1998–2000, Vice-Chair., Evaluation of Monetary, Financial and Econ. Situations Cttee 1999–; Chair., Fiscal Monitoring Unit 1999, Sec. Gen., Ministry of Finance 2000–03; Minister of Industry and Trade July–Oct. 2003; Minister of Finance 2003–05; Chair. Exec. Privatization Comm. 2005–; mem., Gen. Budget Cttee 1990, Evaluation of the Monetary, Financial and Econ. Situations Cttee 1992–93, Cttee Studying Priorities of Public Expenditure of Govt 1998, Cttee Evaluating Public Debt Management System 1998, Tech. Cttees 1998–99, Cttee Crystallizing and Formulating Nat. Strategy for Privatization and Privatization Law 1999, Jordanian delegation for negotations on debt rescheduling 1999, Cttee following-up implementation of Nat. Information System on Jordanian Legislation 1999; mem. Cttee Guiding Plan for Econs Major, Al-Balqa' Applied Univ.; mem. Bd of Dirs Jordan Phosphate Mines Co., Jordan Nat. Bank, The Jordanian Hashemite Fund for Human Devt; fmr mem. Bd of Dirs Jordan Telecom, Royal Jordanian, Arab Bank, Social Security Corpn, Nat. Resources Investment and Devt Corpn, Deposit Insurance Corpn, Jordan Petroleum Refinery Co. Ltd; part-time lecturer to grad. students in Econs, Univ. of Jordan 1998–; Best Minister of Finance of the Year in the Middle East, Euromoney Emerging Markets magazine, Washington, DC 2004. *Publications:* Property Tax in Jordan 1987, Factors Affecting Debt Service Ratio in Jordan 1988, The Impact of Financial Assistance and External Loans on Balance of Payments and Money Supply 1989, The Impact of Budget Deficit on GNP, BOP and Money Supply in Jordan 1990, The Instruments of Islamic Internal Debt 1992, Attracting Foreign Direct Investment in Jordan 1993, Measuring Taxable Capacity and Tax Effort in Jordan 1998. *Address:* Executive Privatization Commission, Jordan Investment Board, PO Box: 893, Amman 11821, Jordan (office). *Telephone:* (6) 5608400 (office). *Fax:* (6) 5608416 (office). *E-mail:* info@jib.com.jo (office). *Website:* www.jordaninvestment.com (office).

ABU JAFAR, Mohammad, ACMA; Bangladeshi business executive; fmr Finance Man. Everbest Shipping Agencies Ltd; fmr Chair. Bangladesh Steel and Engineering Corpn. *Address:* c/o Bangladesh Steel and Engineering Corporation, BSEC Bhaban, 102 Kazi Nazrul Islam Avenue, Dhaka 1215, Bangladesh.

ABU MAZEN (see ABBAS, Mahmud).

ABU-NIMAH, Hasan; Jordanian diplomatist; *Director, Royal Institute for Inter-Faith Studies;* b. 11 Sept. 1935, Battir, Jerusalem; s. of Abdul Rahim Abu-Nimah and Fatima Othman Oweinah; m. Samira Al-Najjar; three c.; ed Al-Ummah Coll., Bethlehem, American Univ. of Beirut, Birkbeck Coll., London; fmr political commentator, Amman Broadcasting Service and Lecturer, Teacher Training Centre, Ramallah, Jordan; Third Sec., Embassy, Kuwait 1965–67, Second Sec., Embassy, Iraq 1967–70, First Sec. in USA 1970–72, with Foreign Ministry, Amman 1972–73, Counsellor, Embassy, UK 1973–77, Amb. to Belgium (also accred to Netherlands and Luxembourg) 1978–90, to Italy 1990–95; Perm. Rep. to UN 1995–2000; Dir Royal Inst. for Inter-Faith Studies; also currently adviser to Prince El-Hassan bin Talal; contribs to Electronic Intifada and Electronic Iraq (online publs), Green Left Weekly 2003, The Daily Star, Al-Rai; weekly articles in The Jordan Times and Al-Ghad; Order of Grand Cross of Crown of Belgium, Order of Independence of Jordan, Grade I, Order of Al-Kawkab of Jordan, Medal of Pope Paul VI, Order of Grand Cross of Merit, Italy. *Leisure interests:* hunting, reading, researching, writing. *Address:* PO Box 132, Jubeihah, Amman 11941, Jordan (home). *Telephone:* (9626) 461-8051 (office); (9626) 534-1360 (home). *Fax:* (9626) 461-8053 (office). *E-mail:* hasan.abunimah@riifs.org (office); abunimah@nol.com.jo (home).

ABU ZAYD, Karen Koning; American UN official; *Commissioner-General, United Nations Relief and Works Agency for Palestine Refugees in the Near East (UNRWA);* b. 21 Aug. 1941, Youngstown, Ohio; m. Abdul Abu Zayd 1969; two c.; fmr Lecturer in Political Science and Islamic Studies, Makerere Univ., Uganda and Jubu Univ., Sudan; joined UNHCR 1981, worked on various emergencies across Africa, served as UNHCR Chief of Mission during Bosnian war, Chef du Cabinet to High Commr Sadako Ogata, and Regional Rep. to USA and Caribbean 1981–2000; Deputy Commr-Gen. UNRWA 2000–05, Commr-Gen. 2005–. *Address:* UNWRA Headquarters Gaza, Gamal Abdul Nasser Street, Gaza City, Palestinian Autonomous Areas (office); PO Box 140157, Amman 11814, Jordan (office); UNWRA Liaison Office New York, Chief Liaison Officer Maher Nasser, One United Nations Plaza, Room DC1-1265, New York, NY 10017, USA (office). *Telephone:* (8) 677-7333 (office); (212) 963-2255 (NY) (office). *Fax:* (8) 677-7555 (office); (212) 935-7899 (NY) (office). *E-mail:* unrwa-pio@unrwa.org (office). *Website:* www.un.org/unrwa (office).

ABUBAKAR, Gen. Abdulsalami; Nigerian international official, fmr head of state and army officer; b. 13 June 1942, Minna; ed Minna, Bida, Kaduna; joined Nigerian Army 1963, with UN peace-keeping force in Lebanon 1978–79, Chief of Defence Staff and Chair. Jt Chiefs of Staff of the Armed Forces 1993–98, fmrly active in Cttee of W African Chiefs of Staff; Commdr in Chief 1998; Head of Govt of Nigeria 1998–99; apptd UN Special Envoy to Democratic Repub. of the Congo 2000; Head of Commonwealth Observer Mission to Oversee Zimbabwe's Parl. Elections 2000, Mission to Monitor Pres. Elections in Zimbabwe March 2002.

ABUBAKAR, Alhaji Atiku; Nigerian politician; b. 25 Nov. 1955, Jada, Adamawa State; ed Adamawa Prov. Secondary School, Yola, Ahmadu Bello Univ., Zaira; with Customs and Excise Dept 1969–89; joined People's Democratic Movt (PDM) 1989; fmr Gov. Adamawa State; mem. People's Democratic Party (PDP) 1998–2006; Chair. Nat. Econ. Council; Head Fed. Exec. Council meeting 1999; Vice-Pres. of Nigeria 1999–2007; mem. Action Congress (AC) Party 2006–, unsuccessful AC cand. for Pres. of Nigeria 2007; mem. Finance Cttee World Constitution and Parl. Asscn, World Citizens; Turaki Adamawa 1988. *Address:* c/o Action Congress, Plot 779 Ona Cres., Maitama, Abuja, Nigeria. *Telephone:* (9) 4139999.

ABULHASAN, Mohammad Abdulla, BA; Kuwaiti diplomatist and government official; b. 12 Jan. 1943, Kuwait; m.; five c.; ed Univ. of Cairo, Egypt; with Ministry of Foreign Affairs 1965–68; mem. Kuwait Mission to UN, Geneva 1968–73; First Sec. in Kuwait and Tehran 1973–75; Amb. to People's Repub. of China 1975–78, to Yugoslavia (also non-resident Amb. to Hungary and GDR) 1978–81; Amb. and Perm. Rep. to UN, New York (also non-resident Amb. to Cuba, Argentina and Mexico) 1981–2003; Minister of Information 2003–06; currently Adviser to Amiri Diwan; Rep. of Kuwait at Movt of Non-Aligned Countries Summits, India 1983, Zimbabwe 1986, Yugoslavia 1989, Indonesia 1992 and Colombia 1995; mem. Del. to UN Summit of the Child, New York 1990, Earth Summit, Rio de Janeiro 1992 and Social Summit, Copenhagen 1995; Chair. Third Cttee (Social, Humanitarian and Cultural), 43rd Session of UN Gen. Ass. 1988; Pres. Pledging Conf. for Devt Activities 1989, High Level Cttee on Review of Tech. Co-operation among Developing Countries 1989; Vice-Pres. UN Gen. Ass. for 39th (1984), 44th (1989), 47th (1992) and 50th (1995) Sessions; Chair. Bd of Trustees, Islamic Cultural Center, New York 1982–; decorated by Govts of Argentina and Yugoslavia. *Address:* Al Diwan Al Amiri, Sief Palace, Building 100, Kuwait. (office).

ABYKAYEV, Nurtai Abykayevich; Kazakhstani politician and diplomatist; *Ambassador to the Russian Federation;* b. 15 May 1947, Jambul (now Taraz), Almaty Oblast; m.; three c.; ed S.M. Kirov Ural Polytech. Inst., Alma–Ata (Almaty) Higher CP School; has rank of Amb.; engineer Almaty factory of heavy machine construction 1972–76; CP functionary 1976–88; First Sec. of Cen. Cttee 1988–89; Asst to First Sec. Cen. Cttee CP of Kazakh SSR 1989–90; Head Adm. of Pres. and Prime Minister Repub. of Kazakhstan, mem. Nat. Security Council 1990–95, also served as Chair.; Amb. to UK (also accred to Denmark, Norway and Sweden) 1995–96; First Asst to Pres. of Kazakhstan 1996–99, fmr Head of Presidential Admin; First Deputy Minister of Foreign Affairs 1999; Amb. to Russian Fed. 2002–03, 2007–; Chair. of Senate 2003–07. *Address:* Embassy of Kazakhstan, 101000 Moscow, Chistoprudnyi bulv. 3a, Russia (office). *Telephone:* (495) 927-17-01 (office). *Fax:* (495) 608-15-49 (office). *E-mail:* kazembassy@kazembassy.ru (office). *Website:* www .kazembassy.ru (office).

ACCARDO, Salvatore; Italian violinist and conductor; b. 26 Sept. 1941, Turin; s. of Vincenzo Accardo and Ines Nea Accardo; m. Resy Corsi 1973; ed Conservatorio S. Pietro a Majella, Naples and Chigiana Acad., Siena; first professional recital 1954; won 1st prize Geneva Competition aged 15 and 1st prize Paganini Competition aged 17; repertoire includes concertos by Bartók, Beethoven, Berg, Brahms, Bruch, Paganini, Penderecki, Prokofiev, Saint-Saëns, Sibelius, Stravinsky and Tchaikovsky; plays with world's leading conductors and orchestras including Amsterdam Concertgebouw, Berlin Philharmonic, Boston Symphony, Chicago Symphony, Cleveland, La Scala, Milan, Santa Cecilia, Rome, BBC Symphony, London Symphony and Philharmonia; also appears as soloist/dir with the English, Scottish and Netherlands Chamber Orchestras; Artistic Dir Naples Festival; Cavaliere di Gran Croce 1982; numerous music prizes include Caecilia Prize (Brussels) and Italian Critics' Prize for recording of the Six Paganini Concertos and Diapuson d'Or for recording of the Sibelius Concerto. *Recordings include:* the Paganini Concertos and Caprices (Deutsche Grammophon), concertos by Beethoven and Brahms, complete works for violin and orchestra by Bruch, concertos by Mendelssohn, Dvořák, Sibelius and Tchaikovsky (Philips/Phonogram). *Publications:* Edn Paganini Sixth Concerto, Paganini: Variations on "Carmagnola". *Leisure interests:* hi-fi, electronics, sport, cooking. *Address:* c/o Agenzia Resia Srl Rappresentanze e Segreterie Internazionali Artistiche, Via Manzoni 31, 20121 Milan, Italy.

ACCONCI, Vito Hannibal, MFA; American writer, artist and architect; *Owner, Acconci Studio Inc.;* b. 24 Jan. 1940, Bronx, New York; s. of Amilcar Acconci and Catherine Colombo; ed Holy Cross Coll., Worcester, Mass, Univ. of Iowa; public comms include: The Palladium, New York 1986, Coca Cola Co., Atlanta 1987, St Aubin Park, Detroit 1990, Autry Park, Houston 1990, Embarcadero Promenade, San Francisco 1992, Arvada Art Center, Arvada, Colo 1992, La Fontaine Avenue School, Bronx, New York 1992, Storefront for Art and Architecture, New York 1993, Mur Island, Graz 2003, Roof Like A Liquid Flung Over the Plaza, Tennessee 2004, Open-Book Store, Armory Art Fair, New York 2007; several awards from New York State Council of the Arts 1976, Guggenheim Foundation Fellowship 1979, Nat. Endowment for the Arts, Skowhegan Award 1980. *Leisure interests:* architecture, movies, music. *Address:* Acconci Studio Inc., 20 Jay Street, #215, Brooklyn, New York, NY 11201 (office). *Telephone:* (718) 852-6591 (office). *Fax:* (718) 624-3178 (office). *E-mail:* studio@acconci.com (office). *Website:* www.acconci.com (office).

ACCOYER, Bernard; French physician and politician; *President, Assemblée Nationale;* b. 12 Aug. 1945, Lyon (Rhône); head of clinic, specialising in Oto-Rhino-Laryngology (Ear, Nose and Throat) 1976; Mayor and mem. Municipal Council, Annecy-le-Vieux (Haute-Savoie) 1989–; mem. Conseil Général, Haute-Savoie 1992–98; mem. Assemblée Nationale (Haute-Savoie (1ère)) 1993– (re-elected 1997, 2002, 2007), First Vice-Chair. Union pour un Mouvement Populaire Parl. Group 2002–04, Chair. 2004–07; Pres. Assemblée Nationale 2007–, mem. Cultural, Family and Social Affairs Cttee. *Address:* Casier de la Poste, Palais Bourbon, 75355 Paris 07 SP (office); 49 Ave. de Genéve, 7400 Annecy-le-Vieux; Mairie, 74940 Annecy-le-Vieux, France. *Telephone:* 4-50-23-86-33 (office). *Fax:* 4-50-27-66-90 (office). *E-mail:* baccoyer@assemblee-nationale.fr (office); bernard.accoyer@wanadoo.fr. *Website:* www.assemblee-nationale.fr/12/tribun/fiches_id/230.asp (office).

ACHARYA, Shailaja, MA; Nepalese politician; b. 8 May 1944, Biratnagar; d. of the late Dr Pinaki Prasad and of Indira Acharya; ed Banaras Hindu Univ., India; imprisoned for political reasons aged 16; Pres. Democratic Socialist Youth League 1967–68; Ed. Tarun (Youth) political magazine of Nepali Congress Party while in exile in India 1972–74; Convener Nat. Social Cttee, Nepali Congress Party 1984–89, sr leader Nepali Congress Party; mem. Cen. Action Cttee 1991, which launched People's Movt, culminating in the restoration of multi-party democracy in Nepal; mem. House of Reps (Parl.) 1991; apptd Minister of Agric. 1992; Deputy Prime Minister and Minister for Water Resources 1998. *Leisure interests:* yoga, meditation. *Address:* Nepali Congress Party, Bhansar Tole, Teku, Kathmandu (office); Ward No. 9, Biratnagar, Nepal. *Telephone:* (1) 4227748 (office); (21) 524960. *Fax:* (1) 4227747 (office). *E-mail:* ncparty@ntc.net.np (office). *Website:* www .nepalicongress.org.np (office).

ACHEBE, (Albert Chinualumogu) Chinua, BA, FRSL; Nigerian writer, poet and academic; *Charles P. Stevenson Jr Professor of Languages and Literature, Bard College;* b. 16 Nov. 1930, Ogidi, Anambra State; s. of the late Isaiah O. Achebe and Janet N. Achebe; m. Christie C. Okoli 1961; two s. two d.; ed Govt Coll., Umuahia and Univ. Coll., Ibadan; Producer, Nigerian Broadcasting Corpn, Lagos 1954–58, Regional Controller, Enugu 1958–61, Dir Voice of Nigeria, Lagos 1961–66; Sr Research Fellow, Univ. of Nigeria, Nsukka 1967–72; Rockefeller Fellowship 1960–61; UNESCO Fellowship 1963; Foundation mem. Asscn of Nigerian Authors 1982–, Pres. 1981–86; mem. Gov. Council, Lagos Univ. 1966, mem. E. Cen. State Library Bd 1971–72; Founding Ed., Okike 1971–; Prof. of English, Univ. of Mass 1972–75, Univ. of Conn. 1975–76, Univ. of Nigeria, Nsukka 1976–81, Prof. Emer. 1985–; Charles P. Stevenson Jr Prof. of Languages and Literature, Bard Coll. 1991–; Pro-Chancellor and Chair. of Council, Anambra State Univ. of Tech., Enugu, Nigeria 1986–88; Regents Lecturer, UCLA 1984; Founding Ed. African Writers' Series (Heinemann) 1962–72; Dir Heinemann Educational Books (Nigeria) Ltd, Nwamife (Publishers), Enugu; mem. Tokyo Colloquium 1981; Visiting Distinguished Prof. of English, City Coll., New York 1989; Montgomery Fellow and Visiting Prof., Dartmouth Coll., Hanover 1990; Visiting Fellow, Ashby Lecturer, Clare Hall, Cambridge 1993; Scottish Arts Council Neil Gunn Int. Fellow 1975; Fellow, Ghana Asscn of Writers 1975; Goodwill Amb. (UN Population Fund) 1998–; Hon. mem. American Acad. of Arts and Letters 1982; Hon. Fellow, Modern Language Asscn of America 1974; Hon. DUniv, Hon. DLitt (16 times), Hon. DHL (eight times), Hon. LLD (three times), Dr hc (Open Univ.) 1989; Margaret Wrong Memorial Prize 1959, Nigerian Nat. Trophy 1960, Jock Campbell New Statesman Award 1965, Commonwealth Poetry Prize 1972, The Lotus Prize (Afro-Asian writers) 1975, Order of the Federal Republic (Nigeria) 1979, Nigerian Nat. Merit Award 1979, Nonino Prize (Italy) 1994, Campion Medal, New York 1996, Nat. Creativity Award 1999, Friedenspreis (Germany) 2002, Man Booker Int. Prize 2007. *Publications:* fiction: Things Fall Apart 1958, No Longer at Ease 1960, The Sacrificial Egg and Other Stories (short stories) 1962, Arrow of God 1964, A Man of the People 1966, Chike and the River (juvenile) 1966, How the Leopard Got his Claws (juvenile, with John Iroaganachi) 1972, Girls at War (short stories) 1973, The Flute (juvenile) 1978, The Drum (juvenile) 1978, African Short Stories (ed., with C. L. Innes) 1984, Anthills of the Savannah 1987, The Heinemann Book of Contemporary African Short Stories (ed., with C. L. Innes) 1992, Telling Tales (contrib. to charity anthology) 2004; poetry: Beware, Soul-Brother and Other Poems 1971, Christmas in Biafra and Other Poems 1973, Don't Let him Die: An Anthology of Memorial Poems for Christopher Okigbo (ed., with Dubem Okafor) 1978, Aka Weta: An Anthology of Igbo Poetry (ed., with Obiora Udechukwu) 1982, Home and Exile 2000, Collected Poems 2004; non-fiction: Morning Yet on Creation Day (essays) 1975, The Trouble with Nigeria (essays) 1983, Hopes and Impediments: Selected Essays 1965–87 1988, Essays and Poems: Another Africa (ed., with Robert Lyons) 1998, Home and Exile (essays) 2000; contrib. to New York Review of Books, Transition, Callaloo. *Leisure interest:* music. *Address:* David Higham Associates, 5–8 Lower John Street, Golden Square, London, W1F 9HA, England (office); Bard College, PO Box 41, Annandale-on-Hudson, NY 12504, USA (office). *Telephone:* (845) 758-7325 (office). *E-mail:* achebe@bard .edu (office). *Website:* www.bard.edu/academics/programs/langlit (office).

ACHENBACH, Christoph, PhD; German business executive and consultant; *Partner, INTES Akademie für Familienunternehmen;* b. 1958, Münster; m.; three c.; ed Univs of Münster and Cologne; with Strategic Planning Dept, Quelle Schickedanz AG & Co., Fürth 1989–91, Man. Planning and Controlling Speciality Mail Order Dept 1993–94; Gen.-Man. Optofot (optics and photography chain) 1991–93; Head, Office of the Man. Bd, Schickedanz Holding Stiftung & Co. KG 1994–97; apptd mem. Man. Bd Quelle AG 1997, Chair. 2001–04; mem. Man. Bd Karstadt Quelle AG 2001–04, Chair. 2004–05; mem. Man. Bd Neckermann Versand AG, Frankfurt am Main 2002–04; mem. Exec. Bd Versandhaus Klingel GmbH; fmr CEO Bell Group; Pnr, INTES Akademie für Familienunternehmen (consultant for family businesses) 2008–. *Address:* INTES, Kronprinzenstraße 46, 53173 Bonn-Bad Godesberg, Germany (office). *Telephone:* (228) 36780 (office). *E-mail:* info@intes-beratung.de (office). *Website:* www.intes-online.de (office).

ACHIDI ACHU, Simon; Cameroonian politician; b. 1934, Santa Mbu; ed Cameroon Protestant Coll., Bali, Yaoundé Univ., Univ. of Besançon, France, Nat. School of Magistracy, Yaoundé; worked as agricultural Asst, Cameroon Devt Corpn before entering univ.; fmr interpreter, Presidency, Yaoundé, Chief

Accountant, Widikum Council, Pres. N W Prov. Co-operative Union Ltd; Minister-del. in charge of State Reforms 1971; Minister of Justice and Keeper of the Seals 1972–75; worked in pvt. business 1975–88; mem. Parl. (Rassemblement démocratique du peuple camerounais) 1988–92; Prime Minister of Cameroon 1992–96. *Leisure interests:* farming, football. *Address:* c/o Rassemblement démocratique du peuple camerounais, Palais des Congrès, BP 867, Yaoundé, Cameroon. *Telephone:* 221-2417. *E-mail:* rdpc@rdpcpdm .cm. *Website:* www.rdpcpdm.cm.

ACHUTHANANDAN, V(elikkakathu) S(ankaran); Indian politician; *Chief Minister of Kerala;* b. 20 Oct. 1923, Punnapra, Alappuzha, Kerala; s. of Sri. Sankaran and Smt. Accamma; m. Smt. K. Vasumathy; one s. one d.; lost parents at early age, forced to give up studies after 7th standard in school; started working by helping elder brother in village cloth shop, later took up job of meshing coir to make ropes at coir factory; began trade union activities and joined State Congress 1938; mem. Communist Party of India (CPI) 1940; imprisoned for five and a half years during Freedom Struggle period and went underground for a further four and half years; mem. State Secr. of CPI 1957; left CPI Nat. Council to form Communist Party of India (Marxist)—CPI(M) 1964, Sr Leader of CPI(M) in Kerala; active in famous Punnapra-Vayalar uprising; State Sec. Kerala CPI(M) 1980–92, mem. Politburo 1985–2007; elected mem. Kerala Legis. Ass. 1967, 1970, 1991, 2001, 2006; Leader of Opposition, Kerala Legis. Ass. 1992–96, 2001–06; mem. Legis. Ass. for Malampuzha constituency, Palghat Dist 2006–; Chief Minister of Kerala 2006–; popularly known as 'Comrade VS'. *Leisure interest:* reading. *Address:* Room No. 141, Third Floor, North Block, Government Secretariat, Thiruvananthapuram 1, Kerala (office); Cliff House, Nanthancode, Thiruvananthapuram 3, Kerala, India (home). *Telephone:* (471) 2333812 (office); (471) 2314853 (home). *Fax:* (471) 2333489 (office). *E-mail:* chiefminister@keralacm .gov.in (office). *Website:* www.keralacm.gov.in (office).

ACKEREN, Robert Van; German filmmaker, screenwriter and producer; b. 22 Dec. 1946, Berlin; s. of Max Van Ackeren and Hildegard Van Ackeren; ed in film studies, Berlin; Prof. of TV and Film, Acad. of Media Arts, Cologne; German Film Prize, Ernst Lubitsch Prize, Federal Film Prize (FRG), Max Ophüls Prize, Prix Celuloide, Premio Incontri Int., Prix Cinedecouverte, El Premio Cid, Prix L'âge d'or. *Films:* Einer weiss mehr 1964, Wham 1965, Sticky Fingers 1966, Nou Nou 1967, Ja und Nein 1968, Für immer und ewig 1969, Blondie's No. 1 1971, Küss mich, Fremder 1972, Harlis 1973, Der letzte Schrei 1975, Belcanto 1977, Das andere Lächeln 1978, Die Reinheit des Herzens 1980, Deutschland Privat 1981, Die flambierte Frau 1983, Die Tigerin 1985, Die Venusfalle 1987, Die Wahre Geschichte von Männern und Frauen 1992. *Address:* Academy of Media Arts, Peter-Welter-Platz 2, 50676 Cologne (office); Kurfürstendamm 132A, 10711 Berlin, Germany (home). *Telephone:* (221) 20189-0. *Fax:* (221) 20189-124. *E-mail:* presse@khm.de. *Website:* www.khm .de.

ACKERMAN, F. Duane, BS, MS, MBA; American telecommunications industry executive (retd); *Chairman Emeritus, BellSouth Corporation;* b. 1942, Plant City, Fla; m.; four c.; ed Rollins Coll., Winter Park, Fla, Massachusetts Inst. of Tech.; various posts with BellSouth Group, including Pres. and CEO, BellSouth Telecommunications 1992–95, Vice Chair. and COO, BellSouth Corpn 1995–97, Pres., CEO 1997–98, Chair. and CEO 1998–2006 (retd) 1996–2005, now Chair. Emer.; fmr Chair. Nat. Council on Competitiveness, Georgia Research Alliance; fmr Vice-Chair. Nat. Security Telecommunications Advisory Cttee; mem. Bd of Dirs Home Depot, United Parcel Service of America, Inc. 2007–, Allstate Corpn; mem. Pres.'s Council of Advisors on Science and Tech.; fmr mem. US Homeland Security Advisory Council; Trustee, Rollins Coll.; fmr Gov. Soc. of Sloan Fellows, MIT. *Address:* 1155 Peachtree St., NE, Suite 2000, Atlanta, GA 30308-7628, USA.

ACKERMAN, Valerie (Val) B.; American lawyer, sports executive and fmr basketball player; *President, Board of Directors, USA Basketball;* m. Charlie Rappaport; two d.; ed Univ. of Virginia, UCLA; fmr professional basketball player in France; Assoc. Simpson Thacher and Bartlett (law firm), New York 1986–88; Attorney and Sr Exec. Nat. Basketball Asscn 1988–96; mem. Bd of Dirs USA Basketball 1990–, Pres. 2005–; Founding Pres. Women's Nat. Basketball Asscn 1996–2005; mem. Exec. Cttee Naismith Memorial Basketball Hall of Fame; mem. Bd of Dirs Girls Inc., NYC Sports Devt Corpn; mem. Nat. Bd of Trustees for March of Dimes; Silver Anniversary Award, Nat. Collegiate Athletic Asscn 2006. *Address:* USA Basketball, 5465 Mark Dabling Boulevard, Colorado Springs, CO 80918-3842, USA (office). *Telephone:* (719) 590-4800 (office). *Fax:* (719) 590-4811 (office). *Website:* www.usabasketball .com (office).

ACKERMANN, Ronny; German professional skier; b. 6 May 1977; winner, Gundersen and Sprint Disciplines, World Cup, Trondheim, Norway 2004; second, Gundersen Discipline, World Cup, Oberhof, Germany 2004; winner Sprint Discipline, World Cup, Ruhpolding, Germany 2005; second, Sprint Discipline, World Cup, Seefeld, Austria 2005; third, Gundersen Discipline 2005; second, Mass Start, World Cup, Sapporo, Japan 2005; winner, Gundersen Discipline, World Ski Championships, Oberstdorf, Germany 2005; third, Sprint Discipline, World Cup, Lahti, Finland 2005; second, Gundersen Discipline, World Cup, Lahti 2005; third, Gundersen Discipline, World Cup, Oslo, Norway 2005; third, Sprint Discipline, World Cup, Oslo 2005; mem. Rhoener WSV Dermbach skiing club. *Address:* c/o Martina Reichel, Deutsche Sport-Marketing GmbH, Schaumainkai 91, 60596 Frankfurt am Main, Germany. *Telephone:* (69) 695801-11. *Fax:* (69) 695801-30. *E-mail:* martina.reichel@dsm-olympia.de. *Website:* www.ronnyackermann.de.

ACKLAND, Joss (Sidney Edmond Jocelyn), CBE; British actor; b. 29 Feb. 1928, London; s. of Norman Ackland and Ruth Izod; m. Rosemary Jean Kirkcaldy 1951 (died 2002); two s. (one deceased) five d.; ed Dame Alice Owens School, Cen. School of Speech Training and Dramatic Art; has worked in theatre since 1945; repertory includes Stratford-upon-Avon, Arts Theatre, Buxton, Croydon, The Embassy, Coventry, Oxford, Pitlochry; tea planter in Cen. Africa 1954–57; disc jockey in Cape Town 1955–57; mem. Old Vic Theatre Co. 1958–61; Artistic Dir Mermaid Theatre 1961–63; Dir The Plough and the Stars; mem. Drug Helpline, Amnesty Int. *Theatre roles include:* Falstaff in Henry IV, Parts I and II, Hook and Darling in Peter Pan, Clarence Darrow in Never the Sinner, Mitch in A Streetcar Named Desire, Brassbound in Captain Brassbound's Conversion, Sir in The Dresser (nat. tour), Petruchio in The Taming of the Shrew (nat. tour), Gaev in The Cherry Orchard, Gus in Hotel in Amsterdam, Sam in Collaborators, Ill in The Visit, Eustace Perrin State in The Madras House, John Tarleton in Misalliance, Weller Martin in The Gin Game, Captain Shotover in Heartbreak House. *West End musical roles include:* Squeezum in Lock Up Your Daughters, Romain Gary in Jean Seburg, Jorrocks in Jorrocks, Frederic in A Little Night Music, Perón in Evita, Captain Hook and Mr Darling in Peter Pan – the Musical. *Films include:* Seven Days to Noon 1949, Crescendo 1969, The House That Dripped Blood, Villain, Great Expectations, The Four Musketeers, Royal Flash, England Made Me, Lady Jane 1984, A Zed and Two Noughts 1985, The Sicilian 1986, To Kill a Priest 1987, White Mischief 1988, Lethal Weapon II, The Hunt for Red October, To Forget Palermo, Tre Colonne in Cronaca 1989, The Object of Beauty, The Sheltering Desert, The Bridge, A Murder of Quality 1990, Voices in the Garden 1992, Georgino, Occhio Pinocchio 1993, Nowhere to Run 1993, The Bible, Miracle on 34th Street, Mad Dogs and Englishmen, A Kid at the Court of King Arthur, Citizen X 1994, Daisies in December, Till the End of Time, Surviving Picasso, Deadly Voyage 1995, Swept from the Sea 1996, Firelight 1997, Game of Mirrors, Son of Sandokan, Milk, Passion of Mind 1998, Mumbo Jumbo 2000, K19: The Widowmaker 2001, No Good Deed 2001, I'll Be There 2002, A Different Loyalty 2004, Asylum 2005, These Foolish Things 2006, How About You 2007, Flawless 2007. *Radio roles includes:* Macbeth in Macbeth, The King in The King and I, Honoré Lachailles in Gigi, God in The Little World of Don Camillo, Victor Hugo in Les Misérables, The Dog in Investigations of a Dog, Socrates in The Trial and Death of Socrates 2008, Big Daddy in Cat on a Hot Tin Roof 2008. *TV appearances include:* Kipling, The Man Who Lived at the Ritz, When We are Married, The Lie, The Barretts of Wimpole Street, Shadowlands, A Woman Named Jackie, First and Last, They Do It with Mirrors, Deadly Voyage, Under the Sun, The Icon, Above and Beyond, Moscow Zero. *Publication:* I Must Be in There Somewhere (autobiog.) 1989. *Leisure interests:* writing, painting, reading, 32 grandchildren, six great-grandchildren. *Address:* The Old Rectory, Clovelly, North Devon, EX39 5TA, England. *Telephone:* (1237) 431848. *E-mail:* ackland@sosi.net.

ACKROYD, Norman, RA, FRCA; British artist; b. 26 March 1938, Leeds; s. of the late Albert Ackroyd and Clara Briggs; m. 1st Sylvia Buckland 1963 (divorced 1975); two d.; m. 2nd Penelope Hughes-Stanton 1978; one s. one d.; ed Cockburn High School, Leeds, Leeds Coll. of Art, Royal Coll. of Art; Tutor in Etching, Cen. School of Art and Design 1965–93; Prof. of Etching, Univ. of Indiana 1970; comms include: Haringey Cultural Centre 1985, Lloyds Bank Tech. Centre, London 1990, British Airways 1991, Freshfields, London 1992, Tetrapak, London 1993; elected Royal Academician 1991; Sr Fellow, RCA 2000; British Int. Print Biennale Prize 1974, 1982, Royal Soc. of Etchers and Engravers 1984, 85, Bronze Medal, Frechen, Germany 1986. *Television includes:* Artists in Print (Etching) 1981, A Prospect of Rivers 1988. *Publications include:* Landscapes and Figures, Etchings (with William McIllvannry) 1973, The Pictish Coast (with Douglas Dunn) 1988, St Kilda: The Furthest Island 1989, Windrush 1990. *Leisure interests:* British history, archaeology, cricket. *Address:* c/o Royal Academy of Arts, Piccadilly, London, W1V 0DS, England (office). *Telephone:* (20) 7378-6001 (office). *E-mail:* membershipoffice@royalacademy.org.uk (office).

ACKROYD, Peter, CBE, MA, FRSL; British writer; b. 5 Oct. 1949, London; s. of Graham Ackroyd and Audrey Whiteside; ed St Benedict's School, Ealing, Clare Coll., Cambridge and Yale Univ., USA; Literary Ed. The Spectator 1973–77; Jt Man. Ed. 1978–82; Chief Book Reviewer The Times 1986–; Mellon Fellow, Yale Univ.; Hon. Fellow, Clare Coll., Univ. of Cambridge 2008; Hon. Fellow, RIBA 2009; Hon. DLitt (Univ. of Exeter), (London Guildhall), (City Univ.), (Univ. Coll., London), (Brunel Univ.) 2006. *Play:* The Mystery of Charles Dickens 2000. *Television:* Charles Dickens (BBC 2), Peter Ackroyd's London (BBC 2) 2004, The Romantics (BBC 2) 2006. *Publications:* fiction: The Great Fire of London 1982, The Last Testament of Oscar Wilde (Somerset Maugham Prize 1984) 1983, Hawksmoor (Whitbread Award for Fiction 1986, Guardian Fiction Award 1986) 1985, Chatterton 1987, First Light 1989, English Music 1992, The House of Doctor Dee 1993, Dan Leno and the Limehouse Golem 1994, Milton in America 1996, The Plato Papers 1999, The Clerkenwell Tales (short stories) 2003, The Lambs of London 2004, The Fall of Troy 2006, The Casebook of Victor Frankenstein 2009; non-fiction: Notes for a New Culture 1976, Dressing Up: Transvestism and Drag: The History of an Obsession 1979, Ezra Pound and his World 1980, T. S. Eliot (RSL W. H. Heinemann Award 1985, Whitbread Award for Biography 1985) 1984, Dickens 1990, Introduction to Dickens 1991, Blake 1995, The Life of Thomas More 1998, London: The Biography 2000, Dickens: Public Life and Private Passion 2002, The Collection 2002, Albion: The Origins of the English Imagination 2002, Illustrated London 2003, The Beginning: Voyages Through Time (juvenile) 2003, Chaucer 2004, Shakespeare: The Biography 2005, Brief Lives – Newton 2006, Thames: Sacred River 2007, Poe: A Life Cut Short 2008; poetry: London Lickpenny 1973, Country Life 1978, The Diversions of Purley 1987. *Address:* Anthony Sheil Associates Ltd, 43 Doughty Street, London, WC1N 2LF, England (office). *Telephone:* (20) 7405-9351 (office).

ACLAND, Sir Antony (Arthur), KG, GCMG, GCVO; British diplomatist; b. 12 March 1930, London; s. of the late Brig. P. B. E. Acland; m. 1st Clare Anne Verdon 1956 (died 1984); two s. one d.; m. 2nd Jennifer McGougan (née Dyke)

1987; ed Eton Coll., Christ Church, Oxford; joined diplomatic service 1953; at Middle East Centre for Arab Studies 1954; served in Dubai 1955, Kuwait 1956; Foreign Office 1958–62; Asst Pvt. Sec. to Sec. of State 1959–62; mem. UK Mission to UN 1962–66; Head of Chancery, UK Mission, Geneva 1966–68; FCO 1968–, Head of Arabian Dept 1970–72; Prin. Pvt. Sec. to Foreign and Commonwealth Sec. 1972–75; Amb. to Luxembourg 1975–77, to Spain 1977–79; Deputy Under-Sec. of State, FCO 1980–82, Perm. Under-Sec. of State and Head of Diplomatic Service 1982–86; Amb. to USA 1986–91; Provost of Eton 1991–2000; Chancellor Order of St Michael and St George 1994–2005; Dir Shell Transport and Trading 1991–2000, Booker PLC 1992–99; Chair. of the Council of the Ditchley Foundation 1991–96, Chair. Tidy Britain Group 1991–96, Pres. 1996–2002; Pres. Exmoor Soc. 2007; Trustee Nat. Portrait Gallery 1991–99, Esmée Fairbairn Foundation 1991–2005; Hon. DCL (Exeter) 1988, (William and Mary Coll., USA) 1990, (Reading) 1991. *Leisure interests:* country pursuits, reading. *Address:* Staddon Farm, nr Winsford, Minehead, Somerset, TA24 7HY, England (home). *Telephone:* (1643) 831489 (home).

ACOGNY, Germaine; Senegalese/French dancer, choreographer and teacher; *Artistic Director, L'ecole des sables;* b. 1944, Porto Novo, Benin; m. Helmut Vogt; moved to France 1962, returned to Dakar to found pvt. professional dance studio; Dir Mudra Africa Int. Dance School, Dakar 1977–1982; worked in Brussels with Maurice Béjart; dancer, choreographer with Peter Gabriel (q.v.) 1984; first solo performance Sahel 1984; collaborated with drummer Arona N'Diaye to stage Ye'ou, the Awakening 1985; performance at World of Music and Dance Festival 1993; co-f. (with Helmut Vogt) Studio-Ecole-Ballet-Theatre of the Third World, Toulouse, France; f. The School of Sands (L'École des sables maison int. de danse), Toubab Dialaw, Senegal 1995; f. Jant Bi Dance Co.; Artistic Dir Dance Section, Afrique en Creations/AFAA (French Asscn for Artistic Action) 1997–2000; also Artistic Dir Contemporary African Dance Competition; Tchourai Solo 2001–, Fagaala (with Kota Yamazaki) 2004–, organiser annual three-month workshop for African dancers and choreographers; London Dance and Performance Award for Ye'ou, the Awakening 1991, Bessie Award 2007; Chevalier de L'Ordre du Merite, Officier des Arts et des Lettres of the French Republic, Chevalier de L'Ordre National du Lion of Senegal. *Dance:* Ye'ou The Awakening 1988, Afrique, ce corps memorable 1990, YEWA, Eau Sublime, for dance Biennale Lyon 1994, Le Coq est Mort (The Rooster is Dead) 2001, Tchourai 2001, Fagaala 2004. *Television:* Regard de Femmes, Double Je (Pivot), Ecole des Sables (documentary), Tchourai (documentary). *Publications:* African Dance 1980, Tchourai 2005. *Address:* Jant-Bi/L'ecole des sables, Toubab Dialaw, BP 22626 Dakar-Ponty (office); Association Jant Bi, BP 22626, 15523 Dakar, Senegal. *Telephone:* (221) 8363619 (office). *Fax:* (221) 8363619 (office). *E-mail:* jant-bi@sentoo.sn (office); jant-bi.acogny@wanadoo.fr (office). *Website:* www .jant-bi-acogny.com (office).

ACOSTA, Carlos; Cuban ballet dancer; b. 1973, Havana; ed Nat. Ballet School of Cuba; guest appearances with numerous int. ballet cos 1989–91; guest dancer, English Nat. Ballet 1991–92; dancer, Nat. Ballet of Cuba 1992–93; Prin. Dancer, Houston Ballet 1993–; Prin. Guest Artist, The Royal Ballet, London 1998–; Prix de Lausanne Gold Medal 1990, Spanish Vegnale Dance Prix 1990, Grand Prix and Gold Medal, Fourth Annual Ballet Competition, Paris 1990, Grand Prix, Third Juvenile Dance Competition 1991, Int. Critics' Prize Chile, Nat. Dance Awards Best Male Dancer 2004, Outstanding Achievement in Dance, Laurence Olivier Awards 2007. *Performances include:* English Nat. Ballet: Polovtsian Dances from Prince Igor 1991, The Nutcracker 1992, Cinderella 1992; Nat. Ballet of Cuba: Giselle 1994, Don Quixote 1994, Swan Lake 1994; Houston Ballet: The Nutcracker 1993, Swan Lake, La Bayadère, Don Quixote; Royal Ballet: In the middle, somewhat elevated 1998, Raymonda, La Fille mal gardée, Swan Lake, My Brother, My Sisters, Giselle, Rhapsody, Le Corsaire, The Nutcracker 2000, Coppelia 2000, Shadowplay 2000, Don Quixote 2001, Apollo 2002, Tocororo 2003, La Fille mal gardée 2005. *Publication:* No Way Home: A Cuban Dancer's Story (biog.) 2007. *Address:* Royal Opera House, Covent Garden, London, WC2E 9DD, England (office). *Telephone:* (20) 7304-4000 (office). *Fax:* (20) 7212-9469 (office). *Website:* www.royaloperahouse.org (office).

ACOSTA URQUIDI, Mariclaire, BA; Mexican diplomatist and international organization official; *Director, Americas, International Center for Transitional Justice;* ed Nat. Autonomous Univ. of Mexico (UNAM), Univ. of Essex, UK; Founding mem. and fmr Pres. Mexican Comm. for the Defence and Promotion of Human Rights; fmr Exec. Dir Mexican Acad. of Human Rights; fmr Under-Sec. for Human Rights and Democracy, Ministry of Foreign Relations; fmr Special Adviser to OAS Sec.-Gen.on civil soc. affairs; currently Americas Dir. Int. Center for Transitional Justice, New York; del. to numerous confs on human rights issues including OHCHR, Geneva 2003; fmr adviser Bd of Social Convergence for Civil Orgs; involved in human rights evaluation projects for int. orgs including Dutch Agency for Int. Co-operation and Ford Foundation. *Address:* International Center for Transitional Justice, 5 Hanover Square, Floor 24, New York, NY 10004, USA (office). *Telephone:* (917) 637-3800 (office). *Fax:* (917) 637-3900 (office). *E-mail:* macosta@ictj.org (office). *Website:* www .ictj.org (office).

ACQUAVELLA, William; American art dealer and gallery owner; *Owner, Acquavella Galleries;* s. of the late Nicholas Acquavella (founder of Acquavella Galleries) and of Edythe Acquavella; m. Donna Acquavella; two s. one d.; ed Westminster School, Simsbury, Conn., Washington and Lee Univ., Lexington, Va; began by working for his father at Acquavella Galleries 1960, has sold major paintings and sculpture to pvt. collectors and museums world-wide, gallery has presented exhbns of Claude Monet, Edgar Degas, Paul Cézanne, Alfred Sisley, Pierre-Auguste Renoir, Camille Pissarro, Amedeo Modigliani, Pierre Bonnard, Yves Tanguy, Fernand Léger, Pablo Picasso, Henri Matisse, Robert Rauschenberg, Lyonel Feininger, Alberto Giacometti, Joan Miró, Lucian Freud and James Rosenquist; fmr Pres. Art Dealers Asscn of America; mem. Bd Westminster School. *Leisure interests:* tennis, golf, skiing. *Address:* Acquavella Galleries, Inc., 18 East 79th Street (between Madison and Fifth Avenues), New York, NY 10075, USA (office). *Telephone:* (212) 734-6300 (office). *Fax:* (212) 794-9394 (office). *E-mail:* info@acquavellagalleries.com (office). *Website:* www.acquavellagalleries.com (office).

ACZÉL, János D., PhD, FRSC; Canadian (b. Hungarian) mathematician and academic; *Distinguished Professor Emeritus and Adjunct Professor, Department of Pure Mathematics, University of Waterloo;* b. 26 Dec. 1924, Budapest; s. of Dezső Aczél and Irén Aczél; m. Susan Kende 1946; two d.; ed D. Berzsenyi High School, Univ. of Budapest; teaching asst, Univ. of Budapest 1946–48; Statistician, Metal Workers' Trade Union, Budapest 1948; Asst Prof., Univ. of Szeged 1948–50; Assoc. Prof. and Dept Head, Tech. Univ., Miskolc 1950–52; Dept Head, Assoc. Prof. then Prof., L. Kossuth Univ., Debrecen 1952–65; Prof., Univ. of Waterloo, Ont., Canada 1965–, Distinguished Prof. 1969–93, Distinguished Prof. Emer. and Adjunct Prof. 1993–; many visiting professorships and fellowships, N America, Europe, Africa, Asia and Australia 1963–; Chair. Int. Symposia on Functional Equations 1962–96, Hon. Chair. 1997–; mem. Canadian Math. Soc., American Math. Soc., New York Acad. of Science; Fellow, Royal Soc. of Canada 1971 (Convener Math. Div. 1974–75, Chair. Acad. of Science Editorial Cttee 1977–78); Foreign Fellow, Hungarian Acad. of Sciences 1990; donor, L. Fejér-J. Aczél Scholarship, Univ. of Waterloo; Dr hc (Karlsruhe) 1990, (Graz) 1995, (Katowice) 1996, (Miskolc) 1999, (Debrecen) 2003; M. Beke Award, J. Bolyai Math. Soc. 1961, Award of Hungarian Acad. of Sciences 1962, Cajal Medal, Nat. Research Council of Spain 1988, Kampé de Feriet Award, Int. Conf. on Information Processing and Man. of Uncertainty in Knowledge-Based Systems 2004. *Publications:* more than 300 articles and ten books, including Lectures on Functional Equations and their Applications 1966 (republished 2006), A Short Course on Functional Equations Based upon Recent Applications to the Social and Behavioral Sciences 1987, Functional Equations in Several Variables (with J. Dhombres) 1989, (enlarged Russian trans.) 2003; Hon. Ed.-in-Chief Aequationes Math; Ed. Theory and Decision Library, Series B and seven int. mathematical journals. *Leisure interests:* reading, swimming, walking. *Address:* Department of Pure Mathematics, University of Waterloo, Waterloo, Ont., N2L 3G1, Canada (office). *Telephone:* (519) 888-4567, ext. 3784 (office). *Fax:* (519) 725-0160 (office). *E-mail:* jdaczel@ math.uwaterloo.ca (office). *Website:* www.math.uwaterloo.ca (office).

ADA, Gordon Leslie, AO, DSc, FAA; Australian microbiologist and academic; *Professor Emeritus, John Curtin School of Medical Research, Australian National University;* b. 6 Dec. 1922, Sydney; s. of W. L. Ada and Erica Flower; m. Jean MacPherson 1946; three s. one d.; ed Fort Street Boy's High School, Sydney and Univ. of Sydney; Research Scientist, Nat. Inst. for Medical Research, London 1946–48, Walter and Eliza Hall Inst., Melbourne 1948–68 (Head of Unit 1962–68); Fellow, Australian Acad. of Science 1964, Council mem. 1972–75, Foreign Sec. 1977–81; Pres. Australian Biochemical Soc. 1966–67; Head, Dept of Microbiology, John Curtin School of Medical Research, ANU 1968–88, now Prof. Emer. and Visiting Fellow, Div. of Immunology and Cell Biology; Pres. Australian Soc. for Immunology 1975–76; mem. and Chair. Scientific Council, Int. Agency for Research on Cancer, Lyon; mem. Scientific and Tech. Advisory Cttee, WHO, UNDP and World Bank Special Programme on Tropical Diseases; mem. Global Advisory Council for Medical Research, WHO 1981–84, Chair. WHO Programme on Vaccine Devt 1984–, consultant, WHO 1988–; Assoc. Dir then Dir Johns Hopkins School of Hygiene and Public Health, Baltimore, Md, USA 1988–91, mem. Johns Hopkins Soc. of Scholars 2001. *Publications:* Antigens, Lymphoid Cells and the Immune Response (with G. J. V. Nossal) 1971; about 180 scientific papers on virology and immunology. *Leisure interests:* sailing, music, walking.

ADABASHYAN, Aleksander Artemovich; Russian scriptwriter, artist and actor; b. 8 March 1945, Moscow; m. Shadrina Yekaterina Igorevna; two d.; ed Moscow (Stroganov) Higher School of Art and Design; began career as art dir working with Nikita Mikhalkov (q.v.). *Films include:* At Home Among Strangers, A Stranger at Home (art dir) 1975, Kinsfolk 1982, Unfinished Piece for Mechanical Piano (scriptwriter/co-scriptwriter) 1997, Five Evenings (actor) 1979, Several Days in the Life of Oblomov 1980, Trans-Siberian Express 1978, The Slave of Love (artistic designer) 1976, Mado, Poste Restante (dir) 1992, The President and His Niece (actor) 2000. *Address:* Novy Arbat str. 31, Apt 36, 121099 Moscow, Russia. *Telephone:* (495) 205-00-89.

ADACHI, Naoki, LLB; Japanese business executive; *President and CEO, Toppan Printing Company Ltd;* ed Chuo Univ.; joined Sales Dept, Toppan Printing Co. Ltd 1962, rising through over 20 different positions, including Man., Domestic Operations –2003, Pres. and CEO 2003–. *Address:* Toppan Printing Company Ltd, 1, Kanda Izumi-cho, Chiyoda-ku, Tokyo, 101-0024, Japan (office). *Telephone:* (3) 3835-5111 (office). *Fax:* (3) 3835-0674 (office). *Website:* www.toppan.co.jp (office).

ADADA, Rodolphe; Republic of the Congo politician; b. 1946; fmr Minister of Economy, Finance and Budget, Repub. of the Congo; Minister of Foreign Affairs, Co-operation and Francophone Affairs 1997–2007; UN and African Union joint Special Rep. to Darfur 2007–. *Address:* c/o Ministry of Foreign Affairs, Co-operation and Francophone Affairs, BP 2070, Brazzaville, Republic of the Congo (office). *Telephone:* 81-10-89 (office). *Fax:* 81-41-61 (office). *Website:* www.unamid.unmissions.org (office).

ADAM, Lt-Gen. Anbaree Abdul Sattar; Maldivian army officer (retd), politician and diplomatist; *High Commissioner to India;* has served as Dir and Dir-Gen. of Nat. Security, Minister of State for Defence and Nat. Security, Chief of Staff of Nat. Security Services (NSS), and Deputy C-in-C of NSS and of Police since 1967; currently High Commr to India (also accred to Nepal and Bhutan). *Address:* High Commission of the Maldives, E-45, Greater Kailash

II, New Delhi 110 048, India (office). *Telephone:* (11) 51435701 (office). *Fax:* (11) 51435709 (office). *E-mail:* admin@maldiveshighcom.co.in (office). *Website:* www.maldiveshighcom.co.in (office).

ADAM, Sir Kenneth (Ken), Kt, OBE; British film designer; b. (Klaus Hugo Adam), 5 Feb. 1921, Berlin, Germany; ed St Paul's School, London Univ.; moved with family to UK 1934; studied architecture; served six years in RAF in World War II; started film career as draughtsman on set of This Was a Woman 1947; production designer of seven James Bond films; production designer of Goldeneye: Rogue Agent video game 2004. *Films include:* Artistic Dir: The Devil's Pass, Soho Incident, Around the World in Eighty Days; Production Designer: Golden Earrings 1947, Curse of the Demon 1957, Dr No 1962, Woman of Straw 1964, Goldfinger 1964, Dr. Strangelove 1964, Thunderball 1965, Funeral in Berlin 1966, Goodbye Mr Chips 1969, Diamonds Are Forever 1971, Sleuth 1972, The Last of Sheila 1973, Barry Lyndon (Acad. Award) 1975, Patriots, Chitty Chitty Bang Bang, The Spy Who Loved Me 1977, Pennies from Heaven 1981, King David 1985, Agnes of God 1985, Crimes of the Heart 1986, The Deceivers 1988, The Freshman 1990, The Doctor 1991, Company Business 1991, Undercover Blues 1993, Addams Family Values 1993, The Madness of King George (Acad. Award 1994) 1994, Boys on the Side 1995, Bogus 1996, In and Out 1997, The Out-of-Towners 1999, Taking Sides 2001; designed sets for La Fanciulla del West, Royal Opera House, London.

ADAM, Robert, RIBA, FRSA; British architect; *Director, Robert Adam Architects;* b. 10 April 1948, Hants.; s. of Robert W. Adam and Jessie M. Adam; m. Sarah J. Chalcraft 1970; one s. one d.; ed Canford School and Regent Street Polytechnic (now Univ. of Westminster); Co-founder Robert Adam Architects (fmrly Winchester Design) 1986, Dir 2000–; Founder and Chair. Popular Housing Group 1995–; Chair. INTBAU; mem. Planning and Urban Design Group, RIBA 1995–, Chair. Pres Special Working Party 1995, mem. Council RIBA 1999–, Hon. Sec. 2001–03, Trustee RIBA Trust 2003–; Chair. Faculty of Fine Art, British School at Rome 1993–97 (mem. 1989), Vice-Chair. Council 1997–99; mem. Architecture Club Cttee 1987–, English Heritage London Advisory Group 1996–2002, Dept of the Environment Good Practice Guidance on Design in the Planning System Project Sounding Bd 1997, Comm. for Architecture and the Built Environment 1999–2003; lectures including tours in USA and Russia; Trustee Maria Nobrega Charitable Trust 2003–; contrib. to numerous TV and radio programmes; Bannister Fletcher Prize 1973, Rome Scholarship 1973–74, Commendation, London Borough of Richmond-upon-Thames Conservation and Design Awards Scheme 1991, Winner, Copper Roofing Competition Copper Devt Assoc. 1995, Elmbridge Borough Council Design/Conservation Award 1998, RIBA Southern Region Nat. Housebuilder Design Award, Best Partnership Devt Commendation for Roman Court, Rocester 2000, Marsh Country Life Awards 2001. *Projects:* primary care centre and housing for the elderly, Pulborough, W Sussex, new country houses in Hants., Cambridge, Yorks., S Oxon., Glos., Wilts., Bucks., Dorset; restaurant and display buildings, Nagano Prefecture Japan, roof garden, Daimaru Dept Store, Osaka Japan, new villages for the Duchy of Cornwall, Shepton Mallet and Midsomer Norton, new town centre, Rocester, Staffs., village extension in Trowse, nr Norwich, master plan for St Andrew's Hosp., Northampton, master plan for new dist, Leith Scotland, new co. HQ, Dogmersfield Park, Humanities Library, Univ. of Oxford, new library for Ashmolean Museum, Oxford, Solar House, W Sussex, Millennium Temple Pvt. Estate, Hants., alterations repairs and additions to Heveningham Hall and Park, Suffolk, new offices, Piccadilly, London. *Works in public collections:* V&A Contemporary Furniture Collection (Pembroke table for Alma Furniture Co.), RIBA Drawings Collection Tower of the Orders. *Publications:* Classical Architecture – A Complete Handbook 1990, Buildings by Design 1994; numerous articles in nat. newspapers, magazines and journals. *Leisure interests:* medieval history, ceramics. *Address:* Robert Adam Architects, 9 Upper High Street, Winchester, Hants., SO23 8UT, England (office). *Telephone:* (1962) 843843 (office). *Fax:* (1962) 843303 (office). *E-mail:* admin@robertadamarchitects.com (office). *Website:* www .robertadamarchitects.com (office).

ADAM, Theo; German singer (bass-baritone); b. 1 Aug. 1926, Dresden; s. of Johannes Adam and Lisbeth Adam (née Dernstorf); m. Eleonore Matthes 1949; one s. one d.; ed Gymnasium and Conservatory; engagements with Dresden State Opera 1949, Bayreuth Festival 1952–80, Salzburg Festival 1969, 1970, 1980–89, 1992, 1995; mem. Deutsche Staatsoper, Berlin 1953–; has appeared with Vienna and Munich State Operas since 1967; Pres. of Curatorium Oper, Dresden 1985–; sang at Semper Opera House, Dresden 1985; staged Graun's Cesare e Cleopatra, Berlin State Opera 1992; performed at Royal Festival Hall, London 1994, Berlin Staatsoper 1997; retd from stage 2006; numerous recordings; Österreichischer Kammersänger, Bayerischer Kammersänger; Nat. Prize (First Class) of GDR. *Publications:* Seht, hier ist Tinte, Feder, Papier 1980, Die 100 Rolle, Wie schön ist doch die Musik 1996. *Leisure interest:* swimming. *Address:* Opéra et Concert, 37 rue de la Chaussée d'Antin, 75009 Paris, France (office); Schillerstrasse 14, 01326 Dresden, Germany (home). *Telephone:* 1-42-96-18-18 (office); (351) 2683997 (home). *Fax:* 1-42-96-18-00 (office). *E-mail:* agence@opera-concert.com (office); adamloschwit@freenet.de (office). *Website:* www.opera-concert.com (office).

ADAMI, Franco; Italian sculptor; b. 19 Nov. 1933, Pisa; s. of Toscano Adami and Giuseppina Bertoncini; m. Jacqueline Sylvius; one s. two d.; ed Leonardo da Vinci Inst., Pisa, Scuola d'Arte, Cascina and School of Fine Arts, Florence; Sculpture Prize of Cascina 1957; Prix Fernand Dupré for sculpture (France) 1981, Prix Charles Oulmont, Fondation de France 1987. *Leisure interests:* antiques. *Address:* Via del Vicinato 13, Pontestrada, 55045 Piatrasanta, Italy; 250 rue du Faubourg Saint-Antoine, 75012 Paris, France. *Telephone:* (058) 471317. *Fax:* (058) 471317.

ADAMIA, Revaz, PhD; Georgian biologist, politician and fmr diplomatist; *Director, G. Eliava Institute of Bacteriophage, Microbiology and Virology;* b. 20 July 1952, Tbilisi; ed Tbilisi Univ., Moscow School of Political Research of the Council of Europe, Harvard Kennedy School of Governance; Jr Research Asst, Giorgi Eliava Inst. of Microbiology and Virology 1974, Sr Research Asst 1982–88, Head, Lab. of Biotechnology and Genetic Eng 1988–92; mem. Parl. 1992-2002, Chair. Cttee on Defense and Security 1995–2000, Chair. Citizens' Union of Georgia Parl. faction 2000–01; Vice-Pres. Council of Europe Parl. Ass. 2000–01; Perm. Rep. to UN, New York 2002–06, Chair. Disarmament Comm. 2004; Dir G. Eliava Inst. of Bacteriophages, Microbiology and Virology, Tbilisi 2006–; George Soros Award. *Publications:* more than 100 articles on Biochemistry, Molecular Biology, Politics and Int. Relations. *Address:* G. Eliava Institute of Bacteriophage, Microbiology and Virology, 3, Gotua Street, 0160 Tbilisi, Georgia (office). *Telephone:* (32) 38-16-04 (office). *E-mail:* radamia@gmail.com; adamia@pha.ge (office). *Website:* www.eliava -institute.org (office).

ADAMISHIN, Anatoly Leonidovich, CandHistSc; Russian diplomatist, fmr politician and business consultant; *President, Association of Euro-Atlantic Co-operation;* b. 11 Oct. 1934, Kiev, USSR (now Ukraine); m. Svetlana Adamishina; one d.; ed Moscow State Univ.; diplomatic service 1957–; Third, then Second Sec., Embassy, Rome 1959–65; Counsellor in First European Countries Dept, Ministry of Foreign Affairs 1965–71, Counsellor in Dept of Gen. Int. Problems 1973–78, Head of First European Dept 1978–86; mem. of Collegium, Ministry of Foreign Affairs 1979; Deputy Minister of Foreign Affairs 1986–90; mem. State Duma (Parl.) 1993–95, First Deputy Minister 1992–94; Pres. USSR Comm. for UNESCO 1987–90; USSR (now Russian) Amb. to Italy 1990–92, to UK 1994–97; Minister for Co-operation with CIS Countries 1997–98; Vice-Pres. Systema Corpn 1998–2004; currently Pres. Asscn of Euro-Atlantic Co-operation; Head of Chair and Prof., Russian Acad. of State Service 1998; mem. Yabloko 2004–; several decorations from USSR including Red Banner; Grand Cross (Italy) 1992. *Television:* Diplomat's Notes (series) 2003. *Publications:* The Decline and Revival of the Great Power (La Plejade Award, Rome 1995, Best Publication of the Year, International Life, Moscow 2000) 1993, The White Sun of Angola 2001. *Leisure interests:* classical music, opera, tennis. *Address:* Association of Euro-Atlantic Co-operation, 119034 Moscow, 3 ul. Prechistenka (office); Apt 170, 2/1 Kutuzovski, Moscow, Russia (home). *Telephone:* (495) 203-62-71 (office); (495) 243-53-81 (home). *Fax:* (495) 230-22-29 (office); (495) 243-53-81 (home). *E-mail:* aeac@mail.ru (office); adamishin@dialup.ptt.ru (home). *Website:* aeac.narod.ru (office).

ADAMKUS, Valdas; Lithuanian politician and head of state; *President;* b. 3 Nov. 1926, Kaunas; m. Alma Adamkienė; ed Munich Univ., Univ. of Ill., Ill. Inst. of Tech.; resistance movt, World War II; left Lithuania; on staff World YMCA, Sec.-Gen. and Chair. Chief Physical Training and Sports Cttee; emigrated to USA 1949; worked in Chicago sports cars factory, draftsman eng co.; f. Academic Sports Club of American Lithuanians 1951; Chair. Bd of Santara Cen. of Lithuanian Students in USA 1957–58; Vice-Chair., Chair. Santara-Sviesa Fed. of Lithuanian Émigrés 1958–67; mem. Bd Lithuanian Community in USA 1961–64; Deputy Chair. Cen. Bd, mem., Chair. American Lithuanian Community; Chair. Org. Cttee World Lithuanian Games 1983; fmr Head Scientific Research Cen. Environment Protection Agency, Admin. for Mid-W Regions Environment Protection Agency, USA, active participation in political life of Lithuania 1993–; Pres. of Lithuania 1998–2002, 2004–; UNESCO Goodwill Amb. for the Construction of Knowledge Socs 2003–; Grand Cross of the Order of Falcon, Iceland 1998, Grand Cross of the Order of St. Olof, Norway 1998, First Class, Order of Yaroslav the Wise, Ukraine 1998, Collar and Grand Cross of the Order of Mary's Land, Estonia 1999, Grand Cross of the Order of the Saviour, Greece 1999, Class Collar and Grand Cross of the Order for Service, Italy 1999, Order of the White Eagle, Poland 1999, Grand Cross of the Order for Service, Malta 1999, Grand Cross of the Order for Service, Hungary 1999, Grand Cross of the Order of Friendship, Kazakhstan 2000, Collar and Grand Cross of the Order of Three Stars, Latvia 2001, Grand Cross Légion d'Honneur, France 2001, Collar of the Order of the Star of Romania 2001, Order of St. Meshrop Mashtots, Armenia 2002, Collar and Grand Cross of the Order of the White Rose, Finland 2002, Order of Special Merit, Uzbekistan 2002, Order of Vytautas the Great with golden collar, Lithuania 2003, Golden Collar and Grand Cross of the Order of the White Star, Estonia 2004, Order of Isabel the Catholic with Collar, Spain 2005, Special Class of the Grand Cross of the Order for Service, Germany 2005, Grand Cross of the Order of Leopold, Belgium 2006; Dr hc (Vilnius) 1989, (Indiana St Joseph Coll.) 1991, (Northwestern Univ.) 1994, (Kaunas, American Catholic Univs) 1998, (Lithuanian Agricultural Univ., Ill. Inst. of Tech.) 1999, (Lev Gumilev Euro-Asian Univ. Kazakhstan) 2000, (De Paul Univ. Chicago, Law Univ. of Lithuania) 2001, (Vytautas Magnus Univ., Lithuania) 2002, (Lithuanian Acad. of Physical Educ.) 2004, (Yerevan State Univ., Armenia, Baku State Univ., Azerbaijan) 2006; Gold Medal, US Environment Protection Agency, US Distinguished Service Award, Int. Environmental Award 1988. *Address:* Office of the President, S. Daukanto 3/8, Vilnius 01021, Lithuania (office). *Telephone:* (5) 266-4154 (office). *Fax:* (5) 266-4145 (office). *E-mail:* bozena.krasovskaja@president.lt (office); info@president.lt (office). *Website:* www.president.lt (office); www.adamkus.lt (office).

ADAMOV, Yevgeny Olegovich, DTechSc; Russian politician, engineer and academic; *Research Supervisor, I. Kurchatovn Institute of Power Engineering;* b. 28 April 1939, Moscow; m.; two d.; ed Moscow Aviation Inst.; engineer, Deputy Dir I. Kurchatov Inst. of Power Eng. (NIKIET) 1962–86, Research Supervisor 1998–; Prof., Moscow Aviation Inst. 1965–; took part in Chernobyl Nuclear Power Station recovery work May–Aug. 1986; Dir Constructor-Gen. Research Inst. of Energy Tech. 1986–98, Scientific Dir 2001; Minister of Nuclear Energy 1998–2001; arrested in Switzerland 2005 on fraud charges at request of USA, won court decision to be extradited to Russia 2006; mem.

Russian Acad. of Eng, New York Acad. of Sciences; Badge of Honour. *Publications:* over 100 books, papers and articles on man., econs of energy resources, nuclear energy, informatics. *Leisure interest:* reading books. *Address:* c/o NIKIET, 107140 Moscow, Krasnoselskaya M. str. 2/8 a/y 788, Russia. *Telephone:* (495) 264-46-10 (office). *Fax:* (495) 632-29-72 (office). *Website:* www.nikiet.ru/rus/index.html (office).

ADAMS, Bryan, OC; Canadian/British rock singer, songwriter, musician (guitar) and photographer; b. 5 Nov. 1959, Kingston, Ont.; numerous world-wide tours; 15 Juno Awards, Recording Artist of the Decade, Canada, Grammy Award, American Music Award. *Recordings:* albums: Bryan Adams 1980, You Want It You Got It 1981, Cuts Like A Knife 1983, Reckless 1984, Into The Fire 1987, Waking Up The Neighbours 1991, So Far So Good 1992, Live! Live! Live! 1995, 18 'Til I Die 1996, MTV Unplugged 1987, On A Day Like Today 1998, The Best Of Me 2000, Spirit: Stallion of Cimarron (film soundtrack) 2002, Room Service 2004, 11 2008. *Publications:* Bryan Adams: The Official Biography 1995, Made in Canada (photographs by Bryan Adams). *Address:* The Leighton-Pope Organisation, 8 Glenthorne Mews, 115a Glenthorne Road, Hammersmith, London, W6 0LJ, England (office). *Telephone:* (20) 8741-4453 (office). *Fax:* (20) 8741-4289 (office). *E-mail:* info@l-po.com (office); info@bryanadams.com. *Website:* www.bryanadams.com.

ADAMS, Gerard (Gerry); Northern Irish politician and author; *President, Sinn Féin;* b. 6 Oct. 1948, Falls Road, Belfast; s. of the late Gerard Adams and of Annie Hannaway; m. Colette McCardle 1971; one s.; ed St Mary's Christian Brothers School, Belfast; worked as a barman; Founder-mem. NI Civil Rights Asscn; mem. Belfast Housing Action Cttee; interned in Long Kesh under suspicion of being a terrorist March 1972; released to take part in secret London talks between Sec. of State for NI and Irish Republican Army (IRA) July 1972; re-arrested 1973, attempted to escape from Maze Prison, sentenced to 18 months' imprisonment, released Feb. 1977; charged with membership of Provisional IRA Feb. 1978, freed after seven months because of insufficient evidence for conviction; Vice-Pres. Sinn Féin 1978–83, Pres. 1983–; MP for Belfast West 1983–92, 1997–; mem. NI Ass. for Belfast West 1998– (Ass. suspended 11 Feb. 2000 and 14 Oct. 2002); involved in peace negotiations with British Govt; Thorr Award, Switzerland 1995. *Publications:* Falls Memory, Politics of Irish Freedom, Pathway to Peace 1988, Cage 11 (autobiog.) 1990, The Street and Other Stories 1992, Selected Writings 1994, Our Day Will Come (autobiog.) 1996, Before the Dawn (autobiog.) 1996, An Irish Voice 1997, An Irish Journal 2001. *Address:* Sinn Féin, 51–55 Falls Road, Belfast, BT12 4PD, Northern Ireland (office). *Telephone:* (28) 9022-3000 (office). *Fax:* (28) 9022-0045 (office). *E-mail:* sfwestbelfast@talk21.com (office). *Website:* www.sinnfein.ie (office).

ADAMS, John Coolidge; American composer and conductor; b. 15 Feb. 1947, Worcester, MA; ed Harvard Univ.; appearances as clarinettist and conductor; Head, Composition Dept, San Francisco Conservatory of Music 1971–81; Adviser on new music, San Francisco Symphony Orchestra 1978–82, Composer-in-Residence 1982–85; conducted Nixon in China at 1988 Edinburgh Festival; Creative Adviser, St Paul Chamber Orchestra, MN 1988–89; The Death of Klinghoffer premiered at Brussels, Lyon and Vienna 1991 (London premiere at Barbican Hall 2002); I Was Looking at the Ceiling performed at Berkeley, New York, Paris, Edinburgh and Hamburg 1995; Artistic Advisor, Los Angeles Philharmonic Orchestra 2009–; Guggenheim Fellowship 1982, Fellow, BAC&S 2005; Grawemeyer Award for Music Composition 1995, Opera News Award 2008, Nat. Endowment for the Arts Opera Award 2009. *Compositions include:* opera: Nixon in China 1987, The Death of Klinghoffer 1991, I Was Looking at the Ceiling and Then I Saw the Sky 1995; orchestral works: Shaker Loops 1978, Common Tones in Simple Time 1979, Harmonium 1980, Grand Pianola Music 1981–82, Harmonielehre 1984–85, The Chairman Dances 1985, Short Ride in a Fast Machine 1986, Tromba Lontana 1986, Fearful Symmetries 1988, The Wound-Dresser 1989, Eros Piano 1989, El Dorado 1991, Violin Concerto 1993, Gnarly Buttons 1996, A Flowering Tree 2008; chamber and ensemble works: Christian Zeal and Activity 1973, China Gates 1977, Phrygian Gates 1977, Chamber Symphony 1992, John's Book of Alleged Dances 1994, Road Movies 1995, Naïve and Sentimental Music 1998, El Niño 2000, Guide to Strange Places 2001, On the Transmigration of Souls (Pulitzer Prize for Music 2003, Grammy Awards for Best Classical Album, Best Orchestral Performance, Best Classical Contemporary Composition 2005, Classical BRIT Award for Contemporary Music 2005) 2002, Doctor Atomic Symphony 2005, The Dharma at Big Sur 2003, My Father Knew Charles Ives (Classical BRIT Award for Contemporary Composer 2007) 2003, Son of Chamber Symphony 2007. *Publication:* Hallelujah Junction (auto-biog.) 2008. *Address:* c/o Jane Brown, Harrison Parrott, 5–6 Albion Court, London, W6 0QT, England (office). *Telephone:* (20) 7229-9166 (office). *Fax:* (20) 7221-5042 (office). *E-mail:* info@harrisonparrott.co.uk (office). *Website:* www.harrisonparrott.co.uk (office); www.earbox.com.

ADAMS, Paul Nicholas, BA; British business executive; *Chief Executive, British American Tobacco PLC;* b. 12 March 1953, Manchester; s. of Peter Charles Adams and Joan Adams; m.; one s. two d.; ed Culford School and Ealing Coll.; began career with Shell UK; Marketing Dir Beecham Int. 1983–86; Vice-Pres. of Marketing for Europe, Pepsi-Cola Int. 1986–91, also Man. Dir Pepsi Cola de France and Area Vice-Pres. for Scandinavia; joined British American Tobacco PLC 1991, Regional Dir for Asia Pacific 1991–99, for Europe 1999–2001, Man. Dir 2002–03, Chief Exec. 2004–; mem. Exec. Cttee Transatlantic Business Dialogue; mem. Trilateral Comm.; Founding mem. Global Business Leaders Alliance Against Counterfeiting. *Leisure interests:* family, theatre, rugby, shooting. *Address:* British American Tobacco PLC, Globe House, 4 Temple Place, London, WC2R 2PG, England (office). *Telephone:* (20) 7845-1936 (office). *Fax:* (20) 7845-2184 (office). *E-mail:* info@bat.com (office). *Website:* www.bat.com (office).

ADAMS, Phillip Andrew, AO, AM, FRSA; Australian writer, broadcaster and film-maker; b. 12 July 1939; m. 1st (divorced); three d.; m. 2nd Patrice Newell; one d.; ed Eltham High School; columnist and critic 1956–; Chair. Film, Radio and TV Bd 1972–75; founder-mem. Australia Council 1972–75; Vic. Govt Rep. Australian Children's TV Foundation 1981–87; Pres. Vic. Council for Arts 1982–86; Chair. Australian Film Inst. 1975–80, Australian Film Comm. 1983–90, Comm. for the Future 1985–90, Nat. Australia Day Council 1992–96; Foundation Chair., Australian Centre for Social Innovation 2009–; mem. Bd Ausflag 1990–; mem. Cttee for the Centenary of Fed. 1994; worked with Families in Distress 1985–, Montsalvat Artists' Soc. 1986–, CARE Australia 1995–97; mem. Bd Nat. Museum of Australia 1996–97, Festival of Ideas 1999; mem. Council, Adelaide Festival 1996; Hon. DUniv (Griffith Univ.) 1998, (Univ. of S Australia) 2004, Hon. DLitt (Edith Cowan Univ.) 2003, (Univ. of Sydney); Sr ANZAC Fellow 1981, Hon. Fellow, Australian Acad. of the Humanities 2008; Raymond Longford Award 1981, Australian Arts Award 1987, Australian Humanist of the Year 1987, CSICOP Award for Responsibility in Media (New York) 1996, Australian Republican of the Year 2006, Human Rights and Equal Opportunity Comm. Human Rights Medal 2006. *Films include:* Jack and Jill: A Postcript 1970, The Naked Bunyip 1971, The Adventures of Barry McKenzie 1972, Don's Party 1975, The Getting of Wisdom 1976, Grendel Grendel Grendel 1980, We of the Never Never 1982, Lonely Hearts 1982, Fighting Back 1983. *Radio includes:* Compere, Late Night Live (ABC). *Television includes:* Death and Destiny, Short and Sweet (ABC), Adam's Australia (BBC), The Big Question, Face the Press (SBS). *Publications:* Adams With Added Enzymes 1970, The Unspeakable Adams 1977, More Unspeakable Adams 1979, The Uncensored Adams 1981, The Inflammable Adams 1983, Adams Versus God 1985, Harold Cazneaux: The Quiet Observer (with H. Ennis) 1994, Classic Columns 1994, The Penguin Book of Australian Jokes (with P. Newell) 1994, The Penguin Book of Jokes from Cyberspace (with P. Newell) 1995, The Big Questions (with P. Davies) 1996, The Penguin Book of More Australian Jokes 1996, Kookaburra 1996, Emperors of the Air 1997, Retreat from Tolerance? 1997, More Big Questions (with P. Davies) 1998, The Penguin Book of Schoolyard Jokes (with P. Newell) 1998, A Billion Voices 1999, The Penguin Book of All New Australian Jokes (with P. Newell) 2000, Adams Ark 2004, Adams vs. God: The Rematch 2007. *Leisure interests:* archaeology, reading. *Address:* c/o Radio National, ABC, GPO Box 9994, Sydney, NSW 2001, Australia (office). *E-mail:* philadams@ozemail.com.au (home).

ADAMS, Richard George, MA, FRSA, FRSL; British novelist; b. 9 May 1920, Newbury, Berks.; s. of Dr E. G. B. Adams, FRCS and Lilian Rosa Adams (née Button); m. Barbara Elizabeth Acland 1949; two d.; ed Bradfield Coll., Berks. and Worcester Coll., Oxford; army service 1940–46; Home Civil Service 1948–74; Pres. Royal Soc. for the Prevention of Cruelty to Animals 1980–82; Writer-in-Residence, Univ. of Florida, 1975, Hollins Coll., Va 1976; Carnegie Medal 1972, Guardian Award for Children's Fiction 1972, Medal of California Young Readers' Asscn 1977. *Publications:* Watership Down 1972 (filmed 1974), Shardik 1974, Nature Through the Seasons, The Tyger Voyage 1976, The Plague Dogs 1977 (filmed 1982), The Ship's Cat 1977, Nature Day and Night 1978, The Girl in a Swing 1980 (filmed 1988), The Unbroken Web (The Iron Wolf) 1980, Voyage Through the Antarctic 1982, Maia 1984, The Bureaucats 1985, A Nature Diary 1985, Occasional Poets: anthology (ed. and contrib.) 1986, The Legend of Te Tuna 1986, Traveller 1988, The Day Gone By (autobiog.) 1990, Tales From Watership Down 1996, The Outlandish Knight 2000, Daniel 2006. *Leisure interests:* chess, ornithology, folk-song, country pursuits, fly-fishing, travel. *Address:* 26 Church Street, Whitchurch, Hants., RG28 7AR, England (home). *E-mail:* water.bow@virgin.net (office).

ADAMS, Robert McCormick, Jr., PhD; American anthropologist and academic; *Adjunct Professor, Department of Anthropology, University of California, San Diego;* b. 23 July 1926, Chicago, Ill.; s. of Robert McCormick Adams and Janet Adams (née Lawrence); m. Ruth Salzman Skinner 1953; one d.; ed Univ. of Chicago; Instructor, Univ. of Chicago 1955–57, Asst Prof. 1957–61, Assoc. Prof. 1961–62, Prof. 1962–84, Dir Oriental Inst. 1962–68, 1981–83, Prof. of Anthropology 1963, Dean of Social Sciences 1970–74, 1979–80, Univ. Provost 1982–84; Sec., Smithsonian Inst. 1984–94; Homewood Prof., Johns Hopkins Univ. 1984; Adjunct Prof., Univ. of Calif., San Diego 1993–; Chair. Ass. of Behavioral and Social Sciences, Nat. Research Council 1973–76; Visiting Prof., Harvard Univ. 1962, 1977, Univ. of Calif., Berkeley 1963; Annual Prof., Baghdad School, American Schools of Oriental Research 1966–67; Fellow, Inst. for Advanced Study, Berlin 1995–96; conducted field research in Iraq, Iran, Mexico, Saudi Arabia and Syria; Lewis Henry Morgan Prof., Univ. of Rochester 1965; Councillor, NAS 1981 (mem.); mem. American Acad. of Arts and Sciences, American Anthropological Asscn, AAAS, Middle East Studies Asscn, American Philosophical Soc., German Archaeological Inst.; Trustee, Nat. Opinion Research Center 1970–94, Nat. Humanities Center 1976–83, Russell Sage Foundation 1978–91, Santa Fe Inst. 1989–; Great Cross of Vasco Nuñez de Balboa (Panama) 1993; numerous hon. degrees; UCLA Medal 1989, Distinguished Service Award. Soc. for American Archaeology 1996. *Publications:* Land Behind Baghdad: A History of Settlement on the Diyala Plains 1965, The Evolution of Urban Society: Early Mesopotamia and Prehispanic Mexico 1966, (with H. J. Nissen) The Uruk Countryside 1972, Heartland of Cities 1981, (with N. J. Smelser and D. J. Treiman) Behavioral and Social Science Research: A National Resource (two vols) 1982, Paths of Fire 1996. *Leisure interests:* skiing, mountaineering. *Address:* University of California, San Diego, Department of Anthropology, 9500 Gilman Drive, La Jolla, CA 92093-0532 (office); PO Box ZZ, Basalt, CO 81621, USA. *Telephone:* (202) 965-0456 (home); (303) 927-3380 (home). *E-mail:* rmadams@ucsd.edu (office). *Website:* www.anthro.ucsd.edu (office).

ADANI, Gautam S.; Indian business executive; *Executive Chairman, Adani Group;* b. 24 June 1962, Ahmedabad; s. of Shantilal Adani and Shantaben

Adani; m. Priti Adani; two s.; ed CN Vidyalay School, Ahmedabad; began career in diamond trade, Mahindra Bros, Mumbai 1978; f. plastics factory, Ahmedabad 1981; f. Adani Group 1988 with interests in commodities trading, power generation, coal mining and agric., currently Exec. Chair. *Leisure interests:* yoga. *Address:* Adani Group, Adani House, Near Mithakhali Six Roads, Navarangpura, Ahmedabad 380 009, India (office). *Telephone:* (79) 25555-555 (office). *Fax:* (79) 26565-500 (office). *Website:* www.adanigroup.com (office).

ADCOCK, Fleur, OBE, MA, FRSL; British writer; b. 10 Feb. 1934, Papakura, New Zealand; d. of Cyril John Adcock and Irene Robinson; m. 1st Alistair Teariki Campbell 1952 (divorced 1958); two s.; m. 2nd Barry Crump 1962 (divorced 1966); ed Victoria Univ. Wellington; Asst Lecturer, Univ. of Otago 1958, Asst Librarian 1959–61; with Alexander Turnbull Library 1962; with FCO 1963–79; freelance writer 1979–; Northern Arts Fellowship in Literature, Univs of Newcastle upon Tyne and Durham 1979–81; Eastern Arts Fellowship, Univ. of E Anglia 1984; writer-in-residence, Univ. of Adelaide 1986; mem. Poetry Soc.; Festival of Wellington Poetry Award 1961, New Zealand State Literary Fund Award 1964, Buckland Award 1967, 1979, Jessie MacKay Award 1968, 1972, Cholmondeley Award 1976, New Zealand Nat. Book Award 1984, Arts Council Writers' Award 1988. *Publications:* The Eye of the Hurricane 1964, Tigers 1967, High Tide in the Garden 1971, The Scenic Route 1974, The Inner Harbour 1979, Below Loughrigg 1979, The Oxford Book of Contemporary New Zealand Poetry (ed.) 1982, Selected Poems 1983, The Virgin and the Nightingale: Medieval Latin Poems 1983, Hotspur: A Ballad for Music 1986, The Incident Book 1986, The Faber Book of 20th Century Women's Poetry 1987, Orient Express: Poems by Grete Tartler (trans.) 1989, Time Zones 1991, Letters from Darkness: Poems by Daniela Crasnaru (trans.) 1991, High Primas and the Archpoet (ed. and trans.) 1994, The Oxford Book of Creatures (ed. with Jacqueline Simms) 1995, Looking Back 1997, Poems 1960–2000 (Queen's Gold Medal for Poetry 2006) 2000. *Address:* 14 Lincoln Road, London, N2 9DL, England. *Telephone:* (20) 8444-7881.

ADDIS, Richard James, MA; British journalist, newspaper industry executive and consultant; *Founder, Shakeup Media;* b. 23 Aug. 1956; s. of Richard Thomas Addis and Jane Addis; m. Eunice Minogue 1983 (divorced 2000); one s. two d.; ed West Downs, Rugby, Downing Coll., Cambridge; with Evening Standard 1985–89; Deputy Ed. Sunday Telegraph 1989–91; Exec. Ed. Daily Mail 1991–95; Ed. Daily Express 1995–98, The Express on Sunday 1996–98; Consultant Ed. Mail on Sunday 1998–99; Ed. The Globe and Mail, Toronto 1999–2002; Asst Ed. and Design Ed., Financial Times 2002–06; f. Shakeup Media, London 2006; mem. Bd of Govs York Univ., Toronto; Hon. Gov. York Univ., Canada 2002. *Leisure interests:* dancing, tennis, elementary music-making, mountains. *Address:* Shakeup Media, 4th Floor, 54-55 Margaret St, London, W1W 8SH, England (office). *Telephone:* (7899) 968427 (office). *E-mail:* richard@shakeupmedia.com (office). *Website:* www.shakeupmedia.com (office).

ADDISON, Mark Eric, CB, MA, MSc, PhD; British fmr civil servant; b. 22 Jan. 1951; s. of Sydney Robert James Addison and Prudence Margaret Addison (née Russell); m. Lucinda Clare Booth 1987; ed Marlborough Coll., St John's Coll., Cambridge, City Univ. and Imperial Coll., London; with Dept of Employment 1978–95, Pvt. Sec. to Parl. Under-Sec. of State 1982, Pvt. Sec. to Prime Minister 1985–88; Regional Dir London Training Agency 1988–91, Dir Finance and Resource Man. 1991–94; Dir Safety Policy Health and Safety Exec. 1994–97; Dir Better Regulation Unit, Office of Public Service 1997–98; Chief Exec. Crown Prosecution Service 1998–2001; Dir-Gen. Operations and Service Delivery, Dept for the Environment, Food and Rural Affairs 2001–05, Acting Perm. Sec. 2005, Chief Exec. Rural Payments Agency 2006; mem. Bd of Dirs Salix Finance Ltd; Dir (non-exec.) The Nat. Archives. *Leisure interests:* British motorbikes, windsurfing, photography. *Address:* c/o Board of Directors, Salix Finance, 25 Southampton Buildings, London, WC2A 1AL, England (office). *Telephone:* (20) 3043-8800 (office). *Fax:* (20) 3043-8799 (office). *E-mail:* info@salixfinance.co.uk (office).

ADDO-KUFUOR, Kwame, MA, BChir, FRCP; Ghanaian politician and physician; b. 14 July 1940, Kumasi, Ashanti Region; ed Achimota School, Univ. Coll. Medical Hosp., London, Univ. of Cambridge and Middlesex Medical School Hosp., UK; worked at several hosps including W Suffolk Gen. Hosp., Edmonds, St Charles Hosp., London, Old Church Hosp., Essex, St Helier Hosp., London 1970s; fmr Medical Dir, Kufuor Clinic, Kumasi; fmr Inspector of Examinations for Final Bachelor of Medicine, Univ. of Ghana Medical School; fmr Chair. of Operations, Prisons Council of Ghana; elected MP (NPP —New Patriotic Party) for Manhyia, served on House Cttee, Health Cttee, Cttee on Selection; Chair. Cabinet Cttee on Governance; fmr Shadow Minister of Health; fmr Acting Minister of Interior; Minister of Defence 2001–07, of Interior 2008–09; Lecturer (part-time), Dept of Medicine, School of Medical Sciences (KNUST); fmr mem. NPP Nat. Council and Chair. Health Cttee; fmr Chair. Jesus Coll. Cambridge UN Students Asscn; fmr Pres. Ghana Medical Asscn; fmr Rep. for W Africa to Confed. of African Medical Asscns; Hon. Sec. Medical Students Asscn, Jesus Coll., Cambridge. *Publications:* Safe Motherhood in the Upper West Region of Ghana (Ed.); several articles in medical journals. *Leisure interests:* music, gardening, football, swimming, watching boxing. *Address:* c/o New Patriotic Party, C912/2 Duade Street, Kokomlemle, POB 3456, Accra (office); 95 Obenesu Crescent, East Contonments, Accra, Ghana (home). *Telephone:* (21) 227951 (office); (21) 777797 (home). *Fax:* (21) 224418 (office); (21) 773951 (home). *E-mail:* npp@africanonline.com.gh.

ADEDEJI, Adebayo, the Asiwaju of Ijebu and Olotu'fore of Ijebu-Ode, MPA, PhD; Nigerian economist; *Executive Director, African Centre for Development and Strategic Studies;* b. 21 Dec. 1930, Ijebu-Ode; s. of L. S. Adedeji; m. Susan Aderinola Ogun 1957; eight s. three d.; ed Ijebu-Ode Grammar School, Univ.

Coll., Ibadan, Univ. Coll., Leicester and Harvard Univs; Asst Sec., Ministry of Econ. Planning, W Nigeria 1958–61, Prin. Asst Sec. (Finance) 1962–63; Deputy Dir Inst. of Admin, Univ. of Ife 1963–66, Dir 1967– (on leave of absence 1971); Prof. of Public Admin, Univ. of Ife 1968– (on leave of absence 1971); Nat. Manpower Bd 1967–71; Fed. Commr for Econ. Devt and Reconstruction 1971–75; Chair. Directorate, Nigerian Youth Services Corps 1973–75; UN Under-Sec.-Gen. and Exec. Sec. UN Econ. Comm. for Africa 1975–91, Founder and Exec. Dir African Centre for Devt and Strategic Studies (ACDESS) 1992–; Chair. Senate of UN Inst. for Namibia 1975; Founder and Ed., Quarterly Journal of Administration 1967–75; Fellow, Nigerian Inst. of Man., Nigerian Econ. Soc., African Acad. of Sciences, African Asscn for Public Admin and Man.; Pres. Nigerian Econ. Soc. 1971–72; Pres. African Asscn for Public Admin and Man. 1974–83; Vice-Chair. Asscn of Schools and Inst. of Admin of Int. Inst. of Admin. Sciences 1970–; Head of Commonwealth Observer Group for Kenya's gen. elections Dec. 2002; mem. Advisory Bd on Human Security, UN Trust Fund for Human Security; Hon. DLitt (Ahmadu Bello Univ.); Hon. LLD (Dalhousie Univ., Univ. of Calabar, Univ. of Zambia); Hon. DSc (Obafemi Awolowo Univ.); numerous foreign decorations and awards. *Publications:* A Survey of Highway Development in Western Nigeria 1960, Nigerian Administration and its Political Setting (ed.) 1969, Nigerian Federal Finance: Its Development, Problems and Prospects 1969, Local Government Finance in Nigeria: Problems and Prospects (co-ed.) 1972, Management Problems and Rapid Urbanisation in Nigeria (co-ed.) 1973, The Tanzania Civil Service, A Decade After Independence 1974, Developing Research on African Administration: Some Methodological Issues (co-ed.) 1974, Africa, The Third World and the Search for a New Economic Order 1977, Africa and the New International Economic Order: A Reassessment 1979, The Indigenization of the African Economy 1981, Economic Crisis in Africa: African Perspectives on Development Problems and Potentials (co-ed.) 1985, Towards the Dawn of the Third Millennium and the Beginning of the Twenty-First Century 1986, Towards a Dynamic African Economy: Selected Speeches and Lectures 1975–1986 1989, African Within the World 1993, South Africa and Africa: Within or Apart? 1996, Nigeria: Renewal from the Roots? 1997, Comprehending and Mastering African Conflicts 1999. *Leisure interests:* photography, lawn tennis, golf, walking. *Address:* African Centre for Development and Strategic Studies (ACDESS), Obafemi Awolowo Way, POB 203, Molipa, Ijebu-Ode, Nigeria (office). *Telephone:* 37-432208 (office); 37-433000 (home). *Fax:* 1-269-1746 (office). *E-mail:* adebayo_adedeji@acdess.org (office).

ADELI, Seyed Muhammad Hossein, PhD; Iranian economist, banker and diplomatist; *Chairman and CEO, Ravand Institute for Economic and International Studies;* b. 1952, Ahwaz; m. Khadijeh Aryan; two s. one d.; temp. Attaché in Canada 1979–80; Dir-Gen. of Econ. Affairs, Ministry of Foreign Affairs 1982–86; Amb. to Japan 1987–89; Gov. Bank Markazi Iran (Cen. Bank of Iran) 1990–95; Amb. to Canada 1995–99; Deputy Minister for Econ. Affairs, Ministry of Foreign Affairs 1999–2004; Amb. to UK 2005; Founder, Chair. and CEO Ravand Inst. for Econ. and Int. Studies (think tank), Tehran. *Leisure interest:* reading. *Address:* Ravand Institute for Economic and International Studies, Unit 6-2, 1479 Jam Building, Vali-e Asr Avenue, Tehran, 19668-43116, Iran (office). *Telephone:* (21) 22019734 (office). *Fax:* (21) 22019735 (office). *E-mail:* contact@ravandinstitute.com (office). *Website:* www.ravandinstitute.com (office).

ADELMAN, Irma Glicman, BS, MA, PhD; American economist, academic and international consultant; *Professor Emerita of Economics and Agricultural and Resource Economics, University of California, Berkeley;* b. 14 March 1930, Romania; d. of the late Jacob Max Glicman and Raya Etingon; m. Frank Louis Adelman 1950 (divorced 1979); one s.; ed Univ. of Calif., Berkeley; Asst Prof., Stanford Univ. 1960–62; Assoc. Prof., Johns Hopkins Univ. 1962–66; Prof. of Econs, Northwestern Univ. 1967–72; Sr Economist, Devt Research Centre, IBRD 1971–72; Prof. of Econs, Univ. of Maryland 1972–79; Consultant, US Dept of State 1963–72, IBRD 1968–, ILO, Geneva 1973–; Fellow, Netherlands Inst. of Advanced Study, Cleveringa Chair, Leiden Univ. 1977–78; Prof. of Econs and Agric. and Resource Econs, Univ. of Calif., Berkeley 1979–94, Prof. Emer. 1994–; Vice-Pres. American Econ. Asscn 1979–80, Distinguished Fellow 2004; Fellow, American Acad. of Arts and Sciences, Econometric Soc., Royal Soc. for the Encouragement of the Arts, American Agricultural Econs Asscn; Order of the Bronze Tower (S Korea) 1971. *Publications:* Theories of Economic Growth and Development 1964, Society, Politics and Economic Development (with C. T. Morris) 1967, Economic Growth and Social Equity in Developing Countries (with C. T. Morris) 1973, Income Distribution Planning (with Sherman Robinson) 1978, Comparative Patterns of Economic Development: 1850–1914 (with C. T. Morris) 1988, Village Economies (with J. Edward Taylor) 1996, The Visible and Invisible Hand: The Case of Korea 2002. *Leisure interests:* art, theatre, music. *Address:* Agriculture and Resource Economics Department, 207 Gianninni Hall, University of California at Berkeley, Berkeley, CA 94720-3310 (office); 10 Rosemont Avenue, Berkeley, CA 94708, USA (home). *Telephone:* (510) 642-6417 (office); (510) 527-5280 (home). *Fax:* (510) 643-8911. *E-mail:* adelman@are.berkeley.edu (office). *Website:* are.berkeley.edu/~adelman (office).

ADELMAN, Kenneth Lee, PhD; American lobbyist and fmr government official; *Senior Counselor, Edelman Public Relations;* b. 9 June 1946, Chicago, Ill.; s. of Harry Adelman and Corinne Unger; m. Carol Craigle 1971; two d.; ed Grinnell Coll., Georgetown Univ.; with US Dept of Commerce 1968–70; Special Asst, VISTA, Washington, DC 1970–72; Liaison Officer, AID 1975–76; Asst to Sec. of Defense 1975–77; Sr Political Scientist, Stanford Research Inst., Arlington, Va 1977–81; Amb. and Deputy Perm. Rep. to UN 1981–83; Dir Arms Control and Disarmament Agency (ACDA) 1983–88; Vice-Pres. Inst. of Contemporary Studies 1988–; mem. Defense Policy Bd. Advisory Cttee; Sr Counselor, Edelman Public Relations, Washington, DC; fmr Exec. Dir USA for Innovation; mem. Exec. Bd Noel Foundation; mem. Advisory Bd Princeton

Review; Sec. Bd Trustees Freedom House; mem. Bd Shakespeare Theatre, Washington, DC; Instructor in Shakespeare, Georgetown Univ. 1977–79; taught at George Washington Univ.; Co-Host Tech Cen. Station. *Publications:* The Great Universal Embrace 1989, The Defense Revolution (with Norman Augustine q.v.) 1990, Shakespeare in Charge: The Bard's Guide to Leading and Succeeding on the Business Stage (with Norman Augustine) 1999, and articles in newspapers, magazines and professional journals. *Address:* Edelman Public Relations, International Square, 1875 Eye Street, NW, Suite 900, Washington, DC 20006, USA (office). *Telephone:* (202) 371-0200 (office). *Fax:* (202) 371-2858 (office). *E-mail:* washington.dc@edelman.com (office). *Website:* www.edelman.com/offices/us/dc (office).

ADELSOHN, Ulf, LLB; Swedish politician and business executive; *Chairman, Swedish Railways;* b. 4 Oct. 1941, Stockholm; s. of Oskar Adelsohn and Margareta Adelsohn; m. Lena Liljeroth 1981; one s. one d.; legal adviser, Real Estate Co., Stockholm City 1968–70; Man.'s Asst, Swedish Confed. of Professional Asscns 1970–73; Commr, Street and Traffic Dept, Stockholm City Admin 1973–76; Mayor and Finance Commr 1976–79; Minister for Transport and Communications 1979–81; mem. Riksdagen (Parl.) 1982–88; Leader Moderata Samlingspartiet (Conservative Party) 1981–86; County Gov. of Stockholm 1992–2001; Chair. Luftfartsverket (Civil Aviation Authority) 1992–2002, Skansen (open air museum) 1998–2004; Chair. Swedish Railways 2002–, Swedish Hotel and Restaurants Asscn 2001–; Sr Adviser Stockholm Chamber of Commerce, Ogilvy; King's Medal of the 12th Dimension with Ribbon of the Order of the Seraphims. *Publications:* Torsten Kreuger, Sanningen på väg (Torsten Kreuger, Truth on its Way) 1972, Kommunalmän: Hur skulle ni göra om det vore era egna pengar? (Local Politicians: What Would You Do If It Was Your Money?) 1978, Ulf Adelsohn Partiledare 1981–86 (Leader of the Party 1981–86) 1987, Priset för ett liv (The Price for a Life) 1991. *Leisure interests:* ice hockey, tennis. *Address:* Strandvägen 35, 114 56 Stockholm, Sweden. *Telephone:* (8) 212502 (office). *E-mail:* ulf.adelsohn@shr.se (office).

ADENIJI, Oluyemi, BA; Nigerian diplomatist, politician and international organization official; b. 22 July 1934, Ijebu-Ode; m.; ed Nigerian Coll. of Arts, Science and Tech., Ibadan, Univ. Coll., Ibadan, Univ. of London, UK; joined Foreign Service 1960; Minister, Perm. Mission to UN, New York 1970–73; served in embassies in Washington, DC, Freetown, Sierra Leone, and Accra, Ghana; apptd Amb. to Austria and Perm. Rep. to IAEA 1976; Amb. to Switzerland and Perm. Rep. to UN, Geneva 1977–81; with Ministry of Foreign Affairs 1981–87; Amb. to France 1987–91; Dir-Gen. Ministry of Foreign Affairs 1991–94; Special Rep. of the UN Sec.-Gen. for the Central African Republic (MINURCA); apptd Special Rep. of the UN Sec.-Gen. for Sierra Leone and Chief of UN Mission in Sierra Leone (UNAMSIL) 1999; Minister of Foreign Affairs 2003–06, of Internal Affairs 2006–07; apptd Chief Mediator Nat. Dialogue and Reconciliation Cttee est. to resolve issues stemming from power-sharing deal in Kenya March-July 2008. *Address:* c/o Ministry of Internal Affairs Area 1, Secretariat Complex, Garki, Abuja, Nigeria.

ÁDER, János, DrIur; Hungarian politician; *Deputy Speaker, Hungarian National Assembly;* b. 9 May 1959, Csorna; m.; four c.; ed Révai Miklós Grammar School, Győr, Eötvös Loránd Univ., Budapest; law clerk, Budapest District VI Council 1983–84; researcher, Inst. of Sociology, Hungarian Acad. of Sciences 1986–90; joined Fed. of Young Democrats (FIDESZ) 1988, mem. Nat. Election Cttee 1989, campaign chief for 1990 parliamentary elections and for both parliamentary and local elections in 1994, Chair. Steering Cttee 1992–93, party Vice-Pres. 1993–2002, Exec. Vice-Pres. 1995–97, 1999–2000, 2001–02, Parl. Group Leader 2002–06; mem. Parl. 1990–98; Deputy Speaker of Nat. Ass. and mem. House Cttee 1997–98, 2006–, Speaker, Nat. Ass. 1998–2002. *Leisure interests:* angling, soccer. *Address:* Hungarian National Assembly, 1357, Budapest, Kossuth tér 1-3, Hungary (office). *Telephone:* (1) 441-4000 (office); (1) 441-4808 (office). *Fax:* (1) 441-4062 (office). *E-mail:* janos .ader@parlament.hu (office). *Website:* www.parlament.hu (office).

ADÈS, Thomas Joseph Edmund, MA, MPhil; British composer, pianist and conductor; *Artistic Director, Aldeburgh Festival;* b. 1 March 1971, London; s. of Timothy Adès and Dawn Adès; ed Univ. Coll. School, Guildhall School of Music, King's Coll., Cambridge, St John's Coll., Cambridge; solo recitalist with the Composers' Ensemble 1992; PLG Young Concert Artists Platform concert at the Purcell Room 1993; Composer in Assoc., Hallé Orchestra 1993–95; Lecturer, Univ. of Manchester 1993–94; Fellow Commoner in Creative Arts, Trinity Coll., Cambridge 1995–97; Benjamin Britten Prof. of Music, RAM 1997–99; Musical Dir Birmingham Contemporary Music Group 1998–2000; Artistic Dir Aldeburgh Festival 1999–; conducted the BBC Symphony Orchestra at the BBC Proms, London 2002; Lutine Prize, GSM 1986, winner Paris Rostrum, for best piece by composer under 30 1994, Royal Philharmonic Prize 1997, Elise L. Stoeger Prize 1996, Royal Philharmonic Soc. Award for Large-scale Composition 1997, 2005, Salzburg Easter Festival Prize 1999, Ernst von Siemens Prize 1999, Grawemeyer Prize 2000, Hindemith Prize 2001, ISCM Young Composers Award 2002. *Compositions:* Five Eliot Landscapes 1990, Chamber Symphony 1990, Catch 1991, Darkness Visible 1992, Under Hamelin Hill 1992, Fool's Rhymes 1992, Still Sorrowing 1993, Life Story 1993, Living Toys 1993, … but all shall be well 1993, Sonata da Caccia 1994, The Origin of the Harp 1994, Arcadiana 1994, Powder Her Face 1995, Traced Overhead 1995–96, These Premises are Alarmed 1996, Asyla 1997, Concerto Conciso 1997–98, America (A Prophecy) 1999, January Writ 1999, Piano Quintet 2000, Brahms 2001, The Tempest (Olivier Award for outstanding achievement in opera 2005, Royal Philharmonic Soc. award for large-scale composition 2005) 2004, Tevot (Royal Philharmonic Soc. Award for large-scale composition) 2007. *Television includes:* Music for the 21st Century: Thomas Adès (Channel 4), Powder her Face (Channel 4). *Address:* c/o Faber Music Ltd, 74–77 Great Russell Street, London, WC1B 3DA, England (office). *Telephone:*

(20) 7908-5310 (office). *Fax:* (20) 7908-5339 (office). *E-mail:* sally.cavender@ fabermusic.com (office). *Website:* www.fabermusic.com (office).

ADESIDA, Ilesanmi, BS, MS, PhD, FIEEE; American (b. Nigerian) electrical engineer, academic and university dean; *Donald Biggar Willett Professor of Engineering and Dean, College of Engineering, University of Illinois at Urbana-Champaign;* ed Univ. of California, Berkeley; worked briefly at Cornell Univ. and then as univ. admin. in Nigeria; joined faculty, Univ. of Illinois at Urbana-Champaign 1987, currently Donald Biggar Willett Prof. of Eng, Dept of Electrical and Computer Eng, Researcher, Beckman Inst. for Advanced Science and Tech. and at Coordinated Science Lab., also Dir Center for Nanoscale Science and Tech., fmr Dir Micro and Nanotechnology Lab., Interim Dean, Coll. of Eng 2005–06, Dean 2006–; mem. Nat. Acad. of Eng, Minerals, Metals and Materials Soc., Materials Research Soc., Soc. for Eng Educ.; Fellow, AAAS, American Vacuum Soc., Optical Soc. of America; US citizen 2002. *Publications:* numerous scientific papers in professional journals on applications of advanced semiconductor processing and in manufacturing of high-speed microelectronic devices and circuits. *Address:* Office of the Dean, College of Engineering, University of Illinois at Urbana-Champaign, 306 Engineering Hall, MC 266, 1308 West Green Street, Urbana, IL 61801, USA (office). *Telephone:* (217) 333-2150 (office). *Fax:* (217) 244-7705 (office). *E-mail:* info@engr.uiuc.edu (office). *Website:* engineering.illinois.edu (office).

ADESINA, Segun, DEd; Nigerian professor of education; *Vice-President, African University Institute;* b. 5 Jan. 1941, Abeokuta, Ogun State; s. of Samuel Adesina and Georgiette Adesina; m. 1968; five c.; ed Loyola Coll., Nigerian Coll. of Arts, Science and Tech., Univ. of Ife and N Illinois and Columbia Univs, USA; history tutor, Loyola Coll. 1965–66; Asst Lecturer in Educ., Univ. of Lagos Coll. of Educ. 1967–69, Lecturer 1969–75; Sr Lecturer, Univ. of Lagos Faculty of Educ. 1975–77, Assoc. Prof. 1977–78, Prof. of Educ. 1988–2000, now Dir Inst. of Educ.; fmr Prof. of Educ., Ilorin Univ.; Visiting Prof. and Provost, Univ. of Ife, Adeyemi Coll. of Educ., Ondo 1984–85; Exec. Sec. Nigerian Educational Research Council 1987; Adviser on Educ. UN Office, Geneva 1975–76; consultant, UNESCO, Senegal 1984; Vice-Pres. African Univ. Inst., Imeko, Ogun State 2005–; Fellow, Nigerian Inst. of Admin. Man.; Assoc., Inst. of Personnel Man.; mem. Nigerian Inst. of Man., Presidential Cttee on Brain Drain; Obamoyegun of Ondo; Bajiki of Afon; Okonomo of Imeko. *Publications:* Primary Education in Nigeria: A Book of Readings, Planning and Educational Development in Nigeria (co-ed.) 1978, The Development of Modern Education in Nigeria 1988, Growth Without Development: Nigeria's Educational Experience 1914–2004 2006, Universal Basic Education in Nigeria: Prospects and Challenges 2007. *Leisure interest:* Gospel music. *Address:* PO Box 41, Abeokuta, Nigeria (home). *Telephone:* (803) 5638515 (mobile) (office); (39) 232226 (home); (803) 4388120 (mobile) (home).

ADESOLA, Akin Oludele, MD, MCh, FRCS (Eng), FACS; Nigerian physician and academic; b. 6 Nov. 1930, Aba, Nigeria; s. of Bamgboye F. Adesola and Felicia A. Adesola; m. Oyebola Sodeinde 1959; two d.; ed Abeokuta Grammar School, Univ. of Ibadan, Queen's Univ., Belfast, Royal Coll. of Surgeons of England, Univ. of Rochester, USA; surgical tutor, Queen's Univ. Belfast 1959–61; Sr Buswell Fellow, Univ. of Rochester, New York, USA 1963–64; Prof. of Surgery, Univ. of Lagos 1967–88; Pres. W Africa Soc. of Gastroenterology 1967–72, Nigerian Surgical Research Soc. 1975–79, W Africa Coll. of Surgeons 1975–77; Chair. Nat. Orthopaedic Hosps Man. Bd 1977–78, Health Educ. Research and Man. Services 1989, Bd of Trustees W African Coll. of Surgeons 1991, Nat. Cttee on Medical Care and Training 1991; Vice-Chancellor Univ. of Ilorin 1978–81, Univ. of Lagos 1981–88; Chair. Asscn of Commonwealth Univs 1984–85, Nat. Bd of Dirs, Leadership for Environment and Development (LEAD) Int. Inc. 1998; mem. Albert Schweitzer Int. Nomination Council 1984–, Commonwealth Expert Group on Distance Educ. 1986–88; Fellow, Nigerian Acad. of Science 1986–; Consultant on Higher Educ. to IBRD 1988, to Canadian Int. Devt Agency 1988; Ed. Nigerian Medical Journal 1970–80; mem. editorial Bd British Journal of Surgery 1968–80; mem. Expert Panel Comm. on Commonwealth Studies, Commonwealth Secr. 1995, Rockefeller Foundation, New York 1996–; Dir Imperial Coll. London, UK 2000–; Prof. Emer. Univ. of Lagos 2001–; Hon. LLD (Queen's Univ. Belfast) 1989; Symons Medal for Distinguished Service to Commonwealth Univs 1987, Distinguished Visitor Award, Carnegie Corpn of New York 1988, Adesuyi Prize for Outstanding Contributions to Health in West Africa (West African Health Community) 1993. *Publications:* Coronary Thrombosis: The Influence of Meterological Changes 1960, Hyperparathyroidism and the Alimentary Tract 1960, Adult Intussusception in Western Nigeria 1964, Influence of Vasoactive Agents on Ascites 1965, Chronic Gastritis and Duodenal Ulcer in Nigerians 1974, Endoscopy in Upper Gastrointestinal Disease in Nigerians 1978, Technology in a Developing Economy 1983, The Nigerian University System: Meeting the Challenges of Growth in a Depressed Economy 1991, Anatomy of Service 1997, Nigerian Universities and a Nation in Crisis 1999, The State of Education in Nigeria – An Overview 2000, A Bridge Endowed (autobiography) 2007. *Leisure interests:* golf, swimming, music. *Address:* 1 Ajani Olujare Street, Surulere, POB 51218, Falomo-Ikoyi, Lagos, Nigeria. *Telephone:* (1) 583-4470. *Fax:* (1) 583-4470. *E-mail:* akinadesola@nigol.net.ng (home).

ADEWOYE, Omoniyi, PhD; Nigerian academic and fmr politician; b. 27 Oct. 1939, Inisa, Osun State; s. of the late Chief James Woye and Victoria Fadunke Woye; m. Margaret Titilayo 1967; five d.; ed Kiriji Memorial Coll., Igbajo, Univ. of Ibadan, Univ. of London, Columbia Univ., New York; Lecturer in History, Univ. of Ibadan 1968–75, Sr Lecturer 1975, Prof. of History 1984–2000, Vice-Chancellor 1996–2000, Prof. Emer. 2000–; Commr for Econ. Devt, Western State 1975–76; Commr for Finance and Econ. Devt, Oyo State 1976–77; Fed. Commr for Econ. Devt 1977–79; First Chair. Council of Ministers, Econ. Community of W African States 1977–78; Chair. Council of Ministers, Nigerian–Niger Jt Comm. 1977–78; Consultant to Econ. Comm. for Africa on Econ. Integration in W Africa 1982–83; Hon. Treas. Historical Soc. of Nigeria 1972–77; Woodrow Wilson Dissertation Scholarship (Columbia Univ.) 1967, Afgrad Fellowship (USA) 1964–68; Chair. Bd of Fellows, Osun Anglican Community 2005–. *Publications:* The Legal Profession in Nigeria 1865–1962 1977, The Judicial System in Southern Nigeria 1854–1954 1977, Law and the Management of Change 2003; numerous articles on law and development in Africa. *Leisure interests:* gardening, reading, writing, music. *Address:* University of Ibadan, PO Box 7321, Ibadan, Nigeria. *Telephone:* 806019706 (office); 8042117560 (home). *E-mail:* omoniyiadewoye@yahoo.com.

ADEY, Christopher, FRAM, FRCM, FRWCMD; British conductor; *Chief Conductor and Artistic Director, Royal Oman Symphony Orchestra;* b. 19 Feb. 1943, London; m. Catherine Cave 1965 (divorced 1985); one s.; ed Royal Acad. of Music, London; violinist with Hallé Orchestra 1963–65, London Philharmonic Orchestra 1967–71; Assoc. Conductor, BBC Scottish Symphony Orchestra 1973–76, Ulster Orchestra 1981–83; Conductor and Prof. Royal Coll. of Music (RCM) 1979–92, Dir of Orchestral Studies, RCM Jr Dept 1973–84; Principal Conductor, Nat. Youth Orchestra of Wales 1996–2002; Chief Conductor and Artistic Dir, Royal Oman Symphony Orchestra 2001–; Conductor in Residence, Wells Cathedral School 2001–; freelance conductor appearing as guest conductor with major orchestras in UK, Europe and South Africa; Cycle of the complete Martinu symphonies for BBC 1975; Commemorative Medal of Czechoslovakian Govt 1986. *Publication:* Orchestral Performance: A Guide for Conductors and Players 1998. *Address:* c/o Richard Haigh, Performing Arts, 6 Windmill Street, London, W1P 1HF, England (office); 137 Anson Road, Willesden Green, London, NW2 4AH, England (home). *Telephone:* (20) 7255-1362 (office). *Fax:* (20) 7631-4631 (office). *E-mail:* info@performing-arts.co.uk (office). *Website:* www.performing-arts.co.uk (office).

ADHIKARI, Bharat Mohan; Nepalese politician; Deputy Prime Minister and Minister of Finance 2004–05; mem. Communist Party of Nepal (Unified Marxist-Leninist) (UML); currently under house arrest. *Address:* c/o Ministry of Finance, Foreign Aid Co-ordination Division, POB 12845, Kathmandu, Nepal (office).

ADIE, Kathryn (Kate), OBE, BA; British journalist, broadcaster and author; b. 19 Sept. 1945; d. of Babe Dunnett (née Issit) and adopted d. of the late John Wilfrid Adie and of Maud Adie (née Fambely); ed Sunderland Church High School, Univ. of Newcastle; technician and producer BBC Radio 1969–76; reporter BBC TV South 1977–78, BBC TV News 1979–81, corresp. 1982–89, Chief News Corresp. 1989–2003, presenter, From Our Own Correspondent, BBC Radio 4; freelance journalist, broadcaster and TV presenter 2003–; Visiting Fellow, Univ. of Bournemouth 1998–; Hon. Prof., Sunderland Univ. 1995; Hon. Fellow, Royal Holloway, Univ. of London 1996; Freeman of Sunderland 1990; Hon. MA (Bath) 1987, (Newcastle) 1990; Hon. DLitt (City Univ.) 1989, (Loughborough) 1991, (Sunderland) 1993, (Robert Gordon) 1996, (Nottingham) 1998, (Nottingham Trent) 1998; Hon. MUniv (Open Univ.) 1996; Royal Television Soc. News Award 1981, 1987, Monte Carlo Int. News Award 1981, 1990, BAFTA Richard Dimbleby Award 1989. *Publications:* The Kindness of Strangers (autobiog.) 2002, Corsets to Camouflage: Women and War 2003, Nobody's Child: The Lives of Abandoned Children 2005, Into Danger 2008. *Address:* POB 317, Brentford, London, TW8 8WX, England (office). *Telephone:* (20) 8838-2871 (office).

ADING, Jack; Marshall Islands accountant and politician; *Minister of Finance;* accountant, Pacific Resources for Educ. and Learning 1994–2007; Senator for Enewetak Atoll 2007–; Minister of Finance 2008–; mem. United People's Party (UPP). *Address:* Ministry of Finance, POB D, Majuro MH 96960, Marshall Islands (office). *Telephone:* (625) 8320 (office). *Fax:* (625) 3607 (office). *E-mail:* secfin@ntamar.net (office).

ADJANI, Isabelle; French actress; b. 27 June 1955; two s.; ed Lycée de Courbevoie; Pres. Comm. d'Avances Sur Recettes 1986–88. *Films:* Faustine et le bel été 1972, la Gifle 1974, l'Histoire d'Adèle H. 1975 (Best Actress, New York Critics 1976), le Locataire 1976, Barocco 1977, Violette et François 1977, Driver 1977, Nosferatu 1978, les Soeurs Brontë 1978, Possession 1980 (Best Actress, Cannes 1981), Clara et les chics types 1980, Quartet 1981 (Best Actress, Cannes 1982), l'Année prochaine si tout va bien 1981, Antonieta 1982, l'Eté meurtrier 1983 (Best Actress César 1984), Mortelle randonnée 1983, Subway 1985, Ishtar 1987, Camille Claudel 1988 (Best Actress César 1989, Best Actress Award, Berlin Film Festival 1989), La Reine Margot 1994 (Best Actress César 1995), Diabolique 1996, Paparazzi 1998, La Repentie 2002, Adolphe 2002, Bon Voyage 2003, Monsieur Ibrahim et les Fleurs du Coran 2003. *Theatre:* la Maison de Bernarda Alba 1970, l'Avare 1972–73, l'Ecole des femmes 1973, Port-Royal 1973, Ondine 1974, Mademoiselle Julie 1983. *TV appearances include:* le Petit bougnat 1969, le Secret des flamands 1972, l'Ecole des femmes 1973, Top à Sacha Distel 1974, Princesse aux petits pois 1986, Figaro 2008, La Journée de la jupe 2008. *Address:* c/o Artcomédia, 20 avenue Rapp, 75017 Paris, France.

ADJAYE, David, OBE, MA; British/Tanzanian architect; b. 1966, Dar-es-Salaam, Tanzania; ed Royal Coll. of Art; reformed studio as Adjaye/Associates 2000, won Idea Store competition to design two new-build libraries in East London, the first, nr Canary Wharf, opened July 2004 and won RIBA Building Award in 2005, the second, five-storey flagship library/community centre with top floor café and dance/yoga studio, opened Oct. 2005; ongoing projects include prototype house in Nanjing, China, visual arts bldg for London-based orgs inIVA/Autograph, Stephen Lawrence Educational Centre and Museum of Contemporary Art, Denver; fmr Lecturer at RCA; currently unit tutor at Architectural Asscn, London; RIBA First Prize Bronze Medal 1993. *Works*

include: Elektra House, Whitechapel, London 1998–2000, Dirty House Shoreditch, London 2001–02, Idea Store, Chrisp Street, Poplar, London (community centre) 2001–04, Idea Store Whitechapel, Whitechapel, London (flagship community centre) 2001–05, Nobel Peace Center, Oslo, Norway (exhbn centre) 2002–05, T–B A21 Olafur Eliasson Pavilion, Venice Biennale, Venice, Italy (art installation) 2005. *Radio:* hosted BBC Radio programme which featured an interview with Oscar Neimeyer, also interviewed Indian architect Charles Correa 2005. *Television:* co-presented two TV series of Dreamspaces for BBC (six-part series on modern architecture); presented BBC documentary Building Africa: The Architecture of a Continent 2005. *Publications:* Houses: Recycling, Reconfiguring, Rebuilding 2005, Making Public Buildings 2006. *Address:* Adjaye/Associates, 23–28 Penn Street, London, N1 5DL, England (office). *Telephone:* (20) 7739-4969 (office). *Fax:* (20) 7739-3484 (office). *E-mail:* info@adjaye.com (office). *Website:* www.adjaye.com (office).

ADJI, Boukary; Niger economist, banker and politician; *Président du Conseil d'Administration, Banque Regionale de Solidarite—Niger;* Minister of Finance 1983–87; Deputy Gov. Banque Centrale des Etats de l'Afrique de l'Ouest—BCEAO (Cen. Bank of West African States) –1996, 1997–2002; Prime Minister of Niger Jan.–Dec. 1996; Prés. du Conseil d'Admin, Banque Regionale de Solidarite—Niger 2005–. *Address:* Banque Regionale de Solidarite—Niger, Avenue de l'Amitié, BP 10584, Immeuble Marina, Niamey, Niger (office). *Telephone:* 20-73-95-48 (office). *Fax:* 20-73-95-49 (home). *E-mail:* brsniger@groupebrs.com (office). *Website:* www.groupebrs.com/accueil_filiale.php?id=24 (office).

ADKERSON, Richard C., BS, MBA; American business executive; *President and CEO, Freeport-McMoRan Copper & Gold Inc.;* ed Mississippi State Univ., Advanced Man. Program of Harvard Business School; Professional Accounting Fellow, SEC, Washington, DC and a Presidential Exchange Exec. 1976–78; Pnr and Man. Dir Arthur Andersen & Co. –1989 (headed Worldwide Oil and Gas Industry Practice); joined Freeport-McMoRan 1989, currently Pres. and CEO Freeport-McMoRan Copper & Gold Inc., also Co-Chair. McMoRan Exploration Co. (MMR); Pres. Mississippi State Univ. Foundation Bd of Dirs, Chair. State of the Future capital campaign, mem. University's Advisory Bds for the Coll. of Business and Industry and the Agribusiness Inst.; Chair. Int. Council on Mining and Metals; mem. Exec. Bd Int. Copper Asscn, M.D. Anderson Cancer Center Bd of Visitors, Business Council of New Orleans and the River Region, Devt Bd of Fellowship of Christian Athletes of New Orleans, Bd of New Orleans Police and Justice Foundation, Louisiana State Univ. Ourso Coll. of Business Exec. Bd of Advisors, Xavier Univ. Pres.'s Council, New Orleans Baptist Theological Seminary Foundation Bd; Trustee, The Nat. World War II Museum; Outstanding Accounting Alumnus of Mississippi State Univ. 1989, Outstanding Alumnus of Mississippi State Univ.'s Coll. of Business and Industry 1991, Richard C. Adkerson School of Accountancy est. by Mississippi State Univ. in his honour. *Address:* Freeport-McMoRan Copper & Gold, One North Central Avenue, Phoenix, AZ 85004-4414, USA (office). *Telephone:* (602) 366-8100 (office). *E-mail:* info@fcx.com (office). *Website:* www.fcx.com (office).

ADKISSON, Perry Lee, PhD; American entomologist and academic; *Distinguished Professor of Entomology Emeritus and Chancellor Emeritus, Texas A&M University;* b. 11 March 1929, Hickman, Arkansas; s. of Robert L. Adkisson and Imogene Adkisson (née Perry); m. 1st Frances Rozelle 1956 (died 1995); one d.; m. 2nd Goria Ray 1998; ed Univ. of Arkansas, Kansas State Univ. and Harvard Univ.; Asst Prof. of Entomology Univ. of Missouri 1956–58; Assoc. Prof. of Entomology Texas A&M Univ. 1958–63, Prof. of Entomology 1963–67, Head Dept of Entomology 1967–78, apptd Distinguished Prof. of Entomology 1967, currently Distinguished Prof. Emer., Vice-Pres. for Agric. and Renewable Resources 1978–80, Deputy Chancellor for Agric. 1980–83, Deputy Chancellor 1983–86, Chancellor 1986–91, Chancellor Emer. 1991–, Regent's Prof. 1991–95; Consultant Int. AEC, Vienna 1969–74; Chair. Texas Pesticide Advisory Comm. 1972; mem. Panel on Integrated Pest Control FAO, Rome 1971–78; mem. NAS, Governing Bd Int. Crop Research Inst. for Semi-Arid Tropics 1982–88, Standing Cttee for Int. Plant Protection Congresses 1984–, Texas Science and Tech. Council 1986–88, Advisory Cttee, Export-Import Bank of the US 1987; Alexander Von Humboldt Award 1980, Distinguished Service Award, American Inst. of Biological Sciences 1987, Distinguished Alumni Award (Ark. Univ.) 1990, Wolfe Prize in Agric. 1994–95, World Food Prize 1997, Medallion Alumni Award, Kansas State Univ. 1999 and numerous other awards. *Publications:* Controlling Cotton's Insect Pests: A New System 1982; several papers on insect diapause and other entomological topics. *Leisure interests:* gardening, fishing. *Address:* Texas A&M University, Entomology Department, TAMU 2475, College Station, TX 77843-2475 (office); The Reed House, 1 Reed Drive, College Station, TX 77843, USA (home). *Telephone:* (979) 680-9128 (office); (409) 845-2516 (home). *Website:* insects.tamu.edu (office).

ADLER, Julius, AB, MS, PhD, FAAS; American biologist, biochemist and academic; *Professor Emeritus, Department of Biochemistry, University of Wisconsin;* b. 30 April 1930, Edelfingen, Germany; s. of Adolf Adler and Irma Stern; m. Hildegard Wohl 1963; one s. one d.; ed Harvard Univ. and Univ. of Wisconsin; emigrated to USA 1938, naturalized US citizen 1943; Postdoctoral Fellow, Washington Univ., St Louis 1957–59, Stanford Univ. 1959–60; Asst Prof., Depts of Biochemistry and Genetics, Univ. of Wisconsin 1960–63, Assoc. Prof. 1963–66, Prof. 1966–96, Prof. Emer. 1997–, Edwin Bret Hart Prof. 1972; Steenbock Prof. of Microbiological Sciences 1982–92; mem. American Acad. of Arts and Sciences, American Philosophical Soc., NAS, Wis. Acad. of Sciences, Arts and Letters; Fellow, American Acad. of Microbiology, Wisc. Acad. of Sciences, Arts, and Letters 1996; Behring Lecturer, Philips Univ. of Marburg 1989, Hartman-Müller Memorial Lecturer, Univ. of Zürich 1984; Dr hc

(Tübingen) 1987, (Regensburg) 1995; Selman A. Waksman Microbiology Award, NAS 1980, Otto-Warburg Medal, German Soc. of Biological Chem. 1986, Hilldale Award, Univ. of Wisconsin 1988, R. H. Wright Award, Simon Fraser Univ. 1988, Abbott-American Soc. for Microbiology Lifetime Achievement Award 1995, William C. Rose Award, American Soc. for Bio chem. and Molecular Biology 1996. *Publications:* research papers on the behaviour of simple organisms, especially bacteria, research on the behaviour of fruit flies. *Address:* 457C Biochemistry Addition, Department of Biochemistry, 433 Babcock Drive, University of Wisconsin, Madison, WI 53706-1544 (office); 1234 Wellesley Rd., Madison, WI 53705, USA. *Telephone:* (608) 262-3693 (office). *E-mail:* adler@biochem.wisc.edu (office). *Website:* www.biochem.wisc.edu (office).

ADLERCREUTZ, (Carl) Herman (Thomas), MD, PhD; Finnish clinical chemist and academic; *Professor Emeritus and Head, Institute for Preventative Medicine, Nutrition and Cancer, Folkhälsan Research Centre, Biomedicum, University of Helsinki;* b. 10 April 1932, Helsinki; s. of Erik Adlercreutz and Elisabeth Adlercreutz; m. 1st Marie-Louise Gräsbeck 1956 (divorced 1974); m. 2nd Sirkka T. Neva 1976; one s. two d.; ed Univ. of Helsinki, Folkhälsan Research Centre; specialist training in internal medicine 1961–64; Research Fellow, Hormone Lab. Dept of Obstetrics and Gynaecology, Karolinska Hosp., Stockholm 1958–61; Resident in Internal Medicine, Univ. of Helsinki 1961–64, Acting Asst Prof. of Internal Medicine 1964, Assoc. Prof. of Clinical Chem. 1965–69, Acting Prof. of Clinical Chem. 1967–69, Prof. of Clinical Chem. 1969–97; Chief Physician, Central Lab. Helsinki Univ. Central Hosp. 1965–97; Research Prof., Acad. of Finland 1983–88; Head, Inst. for Preventive Medicine, Nutrition and Cancer, Folkhälsan Research Centre 1997–; mem. 13 foreign socs, numerous editorial bds of journals, Comm. on Health and Science Asscn of European Olympic Cttees 1985–93; Hon. mem. Polish Soc. for Laboratory Diagnostics, Finnish Soc. for Clinical Chem., Finnish Soc. for Nutrition Research; Kt (First Class), Order of the White Rose 1983, Kt of Johanniternorden of the St Johannis vom Spital zu Jerusalem (Germany) 1992; Medal of Japan Foundation for Cancer Research, Tokyo 1984, The Tenth D. R. Edwards Medal 1987, J.W. Runeberg Award 1991, Medal of the Faculty of Medicine, Tartu Univ. (Estonia) 1992, Silver Medal of Univ. of Helsinki 1992, Bronze Paavo Nurmi Memorial Medal (Finland) 1992, Egon Diczfalusy Lecture Medal, Karolinska Inst., Stockholm 2001, and other awards and distinctions. *Publications:* more than 620 original publs mainly in the fields of steroid hormones, endocrinology, sports medicine, nutrition, phytoestrogens and cancer. *Leisure interests:* gardening, fishing, sport. *Address:* Institute of Clinical Medicine and Folkhälsan Research Centre, Biomedicum, University of Helsinki, PO Box 63, 00014 Helsinki (office); Riskutie 13, 00950 Helsinki, Finland (home). *Telephone:* (9) 19125380 (office); (9) 3250258 (home); 50-5114430 (mobile); (9) 3250327 (home). *Fax:* (9) 19125382 (office); (9) 3250327 (home). *E-mail:* herman.adlercreutz@helsinki.fi (office). *Website:* www.folkhalsan.fi (office).

ADLEŠIĆ, Đurđa; Croatian politician; *Deputy Prime Minister;* b. 18 April 1960, Bjelovar; m.; one c.; ed Univ. of Zagreb; mem. Croatian Social Liberal Party (HSLS) 1990–, Vice-Pres. 2000–06, Pres. 2006–; mem. Sabor (Parl.) 1995–, mem. Cttee for Family, Youth and Sports, Cttee for War Veterans, Pres. HSLS Group of Deputies 1998–, Vice-Pres. Sabor 2004–08; Mayor of Bjelovar 2001–08; Deputy Prime Minister 2008–; cand. in 2005 presidential election; fmr Vice-Pres. Comm. for Determining the Victims of War. *Address:* c/o Office of the Prime Minister, 10000 Zagreb, trg sv. Marka 2, Croatia (office). *Telephone:* (1) 4569222 (office). *Fax:* (1) 6303023 (office). *E-mail:* premijer@vlada.hr (office). *Website:* www.vlada.hr (office).

ADNI, Daniel; Israeli/British pianist; b. 6 Dec. 1951, Haifa; ed High Schools in Haifa and Tel-Aviv, Conservatoire of Music in Paris; first recital in Haifa 1963; professional debut, London 1970; New York debut 1976; has played at most musical centres in the world including UK, Germany, Israel, USA, Japan, South Africa, Switzerland, Norway, Netherlands, Romania, Australia, New Zealand, Finland, Austria; has taught masterclasses including at Dartington Summer School (UK); made over 20 records for EMI-His Master's Voice; First Prize, Paris Conservatoire, First Prize, Young Concert Artists' Auditions, New York. *Leisure interests:* cinema, theatre, bridge, walks, sightseeing. *Address:* c/o 64A Menelik Road, London, NW2 3RH, England. *Telephone:* (20) 7794-4076. *Fax:* (20) 7794-4076. *E-mail:* danieladni@waitrose.com (home).

ADOLFO; American fashion designer; b. (Adolfo F. Sardiña), 15 Feb. 1933, Cardenas, Matanzas, Cuba; ed St Ignacio de Loyola Jesuit School, Havana; served in Cuban Army; apprentice, Cristóbal Balenciaga millinery salon, Paris 1950–52; apprentice millinery designer, Bergdorf Goodman, New York 1953–54; designer Emme (milliners), New York 1954–62; worked as unpaid apprentice, Chanel, New York summers of 1957, 1966; Owner and Head Designer, Adolfo Inc., New York 1962–93; f. Adolfo Enterprises (licensing firm) 1993; Designer, Adolfo Menswear Inc. and Adolfo Scarves Inc., New York 1978; created perfume line for Frances Denny, New York 1979; f. Adolfo F. Sardiña Trust; mem. Council, Fashion Designers of America 1982. *Address:* 60 East 42nd Street, Suite 1134, New York, NY 10165, USA. *Telephone:* (212) 682-1977.

ADOUKI, Martin, DJur; Republic of the Congo diplomatist; *Ambassador and Diplomatic Adviser to the President;* b. 8 April 1942, Makoua; ed Bordeaux and Paris Univs and Int. Inst. of Public Admin., Paris; Information Officer for the Group of African, Caribbean and Pacific Countries (ACP) in Brussels and attended negotiations between the ACP and the EEC; fmrly Lecturer in Law at the Marien Ngouabi Univ., Brazzaville and later Special Adviser to the Prime Minister; Perm. Rep. to the UN 1985–94, to UN Security Council 1986–87, Pres. UN Security Council 1986–87, Chair. UN African Group Sept. 1986, Rep. of Chair. of OAU to UN 1986–87, Head Congo Del. to 43rd Session of Gen. Ass. 1988; mem. of the Zone of Peace and Co-operation in the South Atlantic 1988–90, mem. Del. of UN Special Cttee on the Verification of Elections in Namibia 1989, Vice-Pres. UN Gen. Ass. (44th Session) 1989; Observer on the Gen. Elections in Nicaragua Feb. 1990, Head Del. to World Summit for Children Sept. 1990; Chair. 4th Cttee of 45th Session of Gen. Ass. 1990–91; Amb. and Diplomatic Adviser to Pres. 1998–. *Address:* c/o Ministry of Foreign Affairs and Co-operation, BP 2070, Brazzaville, Republic of the Congo.

ADRIANO, Dino B., FCCA; British business executive; *Chairman, Oxfam Activities Ltd;* b. 24 April 1943; s. of Dante Adriano and Yole Adriano; m. Susan Rivett 1996; two d.; ed Strand Grammar School and Highgate Coll.; articled clerk, George W. Spencer & Co. 1959–64; Accounting Dept trainee J. Sainsbury PLC 1964–65, Financial Accounts Dept 1965–73, Br. Financial Control Man. 1973–80, Area Dir Sainsbury's Cen. and Western Area 1986–89, Asst Man. Dir 1995–96, Deputy Chief Exec. 1996–97, Jt Group Chief Exec. 1997–98, Group Chief Exec. 1998–2000, Chair., Chief Exec. Sainsbury's Supermarkets Ltd 1997–2000; Gen. Man. Homebase 1981–86, Man. Dir 1989–95, Deputy Chief Exec. 1996–97; Dir Laura Ashley PLC 1996–98; Trustee Oxfam 1990–96, 1998–, Adviser on Retail Matters 1996–98, Vice-Chair. 2001–, currently Chair. Oxfam Activities Ltd; Trustee Women's Royal Voluntary Service 2001–; Chair. Bd of Govs Thames Valley Univ. 2004–. *Leisure interests:* opera, music, soccer, cookery. *Address:* Oxfam Activities Ltd, Oxfam House, 274 Banbury Road, Oxford Oxon., OX2 7DZ, England. *Website:* www.oxfam.org.uk.

ADVANI, Lal Krishna; Indian politician, fmr journalist and social worker; *Leader of the Opposition;* b. 8 Nov. 1927, Karachi (now in Pakistan); s. of Kishinchand Advani and Gyani Advani; m. Kamala Jagtiani 1965; one s. one d.; ed St Patrick's High School, Karachi, D.G. Nat. Coll., Hyderabad, Sind, Govt Law Coll., Bombay (now Mumbai); joined Rashtriya Swayam Sevak Sangh (RSS, social work org.) 1942, Sec. of Karachi br. 1947; joined Bharatiya Jana Sangh (BJS) 1951; party work in Rajasthan –1958, Sec. of Delhi State Jana Sangh 1958–63, Vice-Pres. 1965–67; mem. Cen. Exec. of BJS 1966; Jt Ed. BJS paper Organizer 1960–67; mem. interim Metropolitan Council, Delhi 1966, Leader of Jana Sangh Group 1966; Chair. Metropolitan Council 1967; mem. Rajya Sabha 1970, Head of Jana Sangh Parl. Group 1970; Pres. BJS 1973–77 (inc. in Janata); detained during emergency 1975–77; Gen. Sec. Janata Party Jan.–May 1977; Minister of Information and Broadcasting 1977–79, of Home Affairs and of Kashmir Affairs 1998–99, of Home Affairs 1999–2004; Deputy Prime Minister of India 2002–04; Gen. Sec. Bharatiya Janata Party 1980–86, Pres. 1986–90, 1993–2005; Leader of Opposition, Lok Sabha 1990–91, 1991–96, 2004–. *Publications:* A Prisoner's Scrap-Book, The People Betrayed. *Leisure interests:* theatre, cinema, books. *Address:* 1835/16, Kasturbhai Block, Din Dayal Bhawan, J.P. Chowk, Khanpur, Ahmedabad (home); 30 Prithviraj Raj Road, New Delhi 110 003, India (home). *Telephone:* (11) 23794124 (New Delhi) (home). *Fax:* (11) 23017419 (New Delhi) (home). *E-mail:* advanilk@sansad.nic.in (office). *Website:* www.bjp.org (office).

ADYRKHAYEVA, Svetlana Dzantemirovna; Russian/Ossetian ballerina and ballet teacher; *Director, Svetlana Adyrkhayeva Ballet Studio;* b. 12 May 1938, Khumalag, North Ossetia; d. of Taissya Gougkayeva and Dzantemir Adyrkhayev; m. Alexey Zakalinsky 1966; one d.; ed Leningrad Choreographic School, Theatre Acad. of Russia; danced with Glinka Theatre of Opera and Ballet, Chelyabinsk 1955–58; with Odessa Opera and Ballet 1958–60; dancer at Bolshoi Theatre 1960–88; USSR People's Artist 1984; Dir Svetlana Adyrkhayeva Ballet Studio, Moscow. *Principal parts include:* Odette-Odile, Princess Florine, Woman of the Bronze Mountain (Prokofiev's Stone Flower), Zarema (Asafiev's Fountain of Bakhchisaray), Mehmene Banu (Melikov's Legend of Love), Aegina (Khatchaturyan's Spartacus), Kitri (Minkus's Don Quixote). *Leisure interests:* reading, travelling. *Address:* 121099 Moscow, 1st Smolensky per. 9, Apt. 74, Russia. *Telephone:* (495) 241-13-62.

ADZÉ, Jean-Marie; Gabonese politician and fmr diplomatist; Amb. to France 2002–08; Mayor of Akiéni, Haut-Ogooue Prov. 2008–. *Address:* Office of the Mayor, Akiéni, Haut-Ogooue Province, Gabon.

AFANASIYEV, Yuri Nikolaevich, DHistSc; Russian historian, academic and politician; *Honorary President, Russian State University for the Humanities;* b. 5 Sept. 1934, Maina, Ulyanovsk region; m.; two c.; ed Moscow State Univ., Acad. of Social Sciences; mem. CPSU 1956–90; instructor, then sec. Comsomol org. in Krasnoyarsk Region 1957–64, mem. of Comsomol Cen. Cttee 1964–71; Deputy Head of Div. 1971, Lecturer, Higher Comsomol School 1971, Pro-Rector 1972–83; Sr Researcher, Inst. of World History USSR Acad. of Sciences 1983–87; Rector Moscow Inst. of History and Archives (now Russian Humanitarian Univ.) 1987–; Founder and Rector Russian State Univ. for the Humanities 1991–2002, Hon. Pres. 2003–; USSR People's Deputy 1989–91, mem. of Interregional Deputies' Group, People's Deputy of Russia 1991–92; Co-Chair. Democratic Russia Movt 1991–92. *Publications:* numerous articles and over 10 books on problems of Russian history and contemporary politics including Russia on the Crossroads (three vols) 2000, Dangerous Russia 2001. *Address:* Russian State University for the Humanities, 125993 Moscow, Miusskaya sq. 6, Russia (office). *Telephone:* (495) 250-63-36 (office); (495) 921-41-69 (home). *Website:* rggu.com (office).

AFANASSIEVSKY, Nikolay Nikolayevich; Russian diplomatist; b. 1 Oct. 1940, Moscow; m.; one s.; ed Moscow Inst. of Int. Relations; mem. CPSU 1968–91; Attaché, Embassy, Cameroon, 1964–66; with Ministry of Foreign Affairs 1966–76; del. to UN Gen. Ass. 1969; del. to CSCE, Geneva, Helsinki; 1973–75; Counsellor, Ministry Counsellor, Embassy, Paris 1976–83; Deputy Chief of First European Dept, Ministry of Foreign Affairs 1983–86, Chief 1986–90; Amb. to Belgium and liaison to NATO 1990–94; Deputy Minister of Foreign Affairs 1994–98; Amb. to France 1999–2002, to Poland 2002–06.

Address: c/o Ministry of Foreign Affairs, 119200 Moscow, Smolenskaya-Sennaya pl. 32/34, Russian Federation.

AFEWERKI, Issaias; Eritrean head of state; *President;* b. 2 Feb. 1946, Asmara; trained as engineer; joined Eritrean Liberation Front (ELF) 1966, mil. training in China 1966, Leader fourth regional area ELF 1968, Gen. Commdr ELF 1969; Founding mem. Eritrean People's Liberation Front (now People's Front for Democracy and Justice—PFDJ 1977), fmr Asst Sec. Gen., Sec. Gen. 1987; Chair. State Council, Nat. Ass.; Sec. Gen. Provisional Govt of Eritrea 1991; assumed power May 1991; elected Pres. of Eritrea by Nat. Ass. 1993–. *Address:* Office of the President, PO Box 257, Asmara, Eritrea. *Telephone:* (1) 122132. *Fax:* (1) 125123.

AFFLECK, Ben; American actor; b. 15 Aug. 1972, Berkeley, Calif.; m. Jennifer Garner 2005; two d. *Films include:* School Ties 1992, Buffy the Vampire Slayer, Dazed and Confused, Mallrats 1995, Glory Daze, Office Killer, Chasing Amy 1997, Going All the Way 1997, Good Will Hunting (also screenplay with Matt Damon q.v., Acad. Award and Golden Globe for Best Original Screenplay 1997), Phantoms 1998, Armageddon 1998, Shakespeare in Love 1998, Reindeer Games 1999, Forces of Nature 1999, Dogma 1999, Daddy and Them 1999, The Boiler Room 1999, 200 Cigarettes 1999, Bounce 2000, The Third Wheel (also producer) 2000, Pearl Harbor 2001, The Sum of All Fear 2002, Changing Lanes 2002, Daredevil 2003, Gigli 2003, Paycheck 2003, Jersey Girl 2004, Surviving Christmas 2004, Man About Town 2006, Hollywoodland 2006, Smokin' Aces 2006, Gone Baby Gone (dir and producer) 2007. *Television includes:* Voyage of the Mimi, Against the Grain, Lifestories: Families in Crisis, Hands of a Stranger, Daddy. *Address:* 2401 Main Street, Santa Monica, CA 90405; c/o Patrick Whitesell, Endeavor Agency, 9701 Wilshire Boulevard, 10th Floor, Beverly Hills, CA 90212, USA.

AFRAH, Mohammed Qanyare; Somali politician and business executive; fmr militia leader, Mogadishu; fmr Chair. United Somali Congress; unsuccessful cand. for Pres. 2004; Minister of Nat. Security 2004–06; mem. Transitional Parl. 2004–; handed over militia weapons to govt 2007. *Address:* Transitional Parliament, Mogadishu, Somalia (office).

AFXENTIOU, Afxentis C., MA (Econ); Cypriot banker and government official; b. 11 Dec. 1932, Larnaca; s. of Costas Afxentiou and Terpsichore Panayi; m. 1st Stella Vanezis 1957 (deceased); one s. one d.; m. 2nd Egli Pattichis 1981; ed Pancyprian Commercial Lyceum, Larnaca, Athens School of Econs and Business and Univ. of Georgia; with Hellenic Mining Co. Group 1955–62; with Ministry of Finance 1962–82, Perm. Sec. 1973–79, Minister of Finance 1979–82; Gov. Cen. Bank of Cyprus 1982–2002 (retd); fmr Gov. for Cyprus, IMF 1982, fmr Gov. for Cyprus, IBRD; fmr Vice-Chair. Bd of Dirs Cyprus Devt Bank Ltd. *Leisure interests:* reading, walking, swimming. *Address:* 3 Idis Street, Parisinos, Strovolos, Nicosia, Cyprus (home).

AG HAMANI, Ahmed Mohamed; Malian politician; b. 1942; Rep. of Mali to EC and Head of Mission to ECSE and Euratom 2000, Amb. in Brussels 2001; Prime Minister of Mali and Minister of African Integration 2002–04. *Address:* c/o Office of the Prime Minister, quartièr du Fleuve, BP 790, Bamako, Mali (office).

AGA KHAN IV, HH Prince Karim, Spiritual Leader and Imam of Ismaili Muslims, KBE, BA; British; b. 13 Dec. 1936, Creux-de-Genthod, Geneva; s. of the late Prince Aly Salomon Khan and of Princess Joan Aly Khan (late Viscountess Camrose, née Joan Barbara Yarde-Buller); m. 1st Sarah Frances Croker-Poole 1969 (divorced 1995); two s. one d.; m. 2nd Princess Gabriele zu Leiningen (Begum Inaara Aga Khan) 1998; one s.; ed Le Rosey, Switzerland, Harvard Univ., USA; became Aga Khan on the death of his grandfather Sir Sultan Mahomed Shah, Aga Khan III, GCSI, GCIE, GCVO 1957; granted title of His Highness by Queen Elizabeth II 1957, of His Royal Highness by the Shah of Iran 1959; Founder and Chair. Aga Khan Foundation 1967, Aga Khan Award for Architecture 1977–, Inst. of Ismaili Studies 1977–, Aga Khan Fund for Econ. Devt, Geneva 1984, Aga Khan Trust for Culture 1988, Aga Khan Agency for Microfinance 2005–; Founder and Chancellor Aga Khan Univ., Pakistan 1983–, Univ. of Cen. Asia 2001–; Founder Pres. Yacht Club Costa Smeralda, Sardinia; mem. Royal Yacht Squadron 1982–; Hon. Prof., Univ. of Osh, Kyrgyzstan 2002; Hon. FRIBA 1991; Hon. mem. AIA 1992; Foreign Hon. mem. American Acad. of Arts and Sciences; Commdr Ordre du Mérite Mauritanien 1960, Grand Croix, Ordre du Prince Henry du Gouvernement Portugais 1960, Ordre Nat. de la Côte d'Ivoire 1965, de la Haute-Volta 1965, Ordre Nat. Malgache 1966, Ordre du Croissant Vert des Comores 1966, Grand Cordon Ordre du Tadj de l'Empire d'Iran 1967, Nishan-i-Imtiaz, Pakistan 1970, Cavaliere di Gran Croce dell'Ordine al Merito della Repubblica (Italy) 1977, Grand Officier de l'Ordre Nat. du Lion (Senegal) 1982, Nishan-e-Pakistan, Pakistan 1983, Grand Cordon of Ouissam-al Arch (Morocco) 1986, Cavaliere del Lavaro (Italy) 1988, Commdr, Légion d'honneur (France) 1990, Gran Cruz de la Orden del Mérito Civil, Spain 1991, Grand Croix, Order of Merit (Portugal) 1998, Order of Friendship (Tajikistan) 1998, Order of Bahrain (First Class) 2003, Hon. CC 2004, Grã-Cruz da Ordem Militar de Cristo (Portugal) 2005; Hon. LLD (Peshawar Univ.) 1967, (Univ. of Sind) 1970, (McGill Univ.) 1983, (McMaster Univ.) 1987, (Univ. of Wales) 1993, (Brown Univ.) 1996; Hon. DLitt (London) 1989 (Toronto) 2004; Hon. DHumLitt (American Univ. of Beirut) 2005; Dr hc (Evora, Portugal) 2006; Thomas Jefferson Memorial Foundation Medal in Architecture, Univ. of Virginia 1984, AIA Honor Award 1984, La Medalla de Oro del Consejo Superior de Colegios de Arquitectos, Spain 1987, Médaille d'Argent Acad. d'Architecture, Paris 1991, Huésped de Honor de Granada, Spain 1991; Hadrian Award, World Monuments Fund (USA) 1996, Gold Medal, City of Granada (Spain) 1998; Insignia of Honour, Union Int. des Architectes 2001, State Award of Peace and Progress, Kazakhstan 2002, Vincent Scully Prize (USA) 2005, Die Quadriga (Germany) 2005, Carnegie Medal of Philanthropy 2005. *Leisure interests:* breeding race-horses, yachting, skiing. *Address:* Aiglemont, 60270 Gouvieux, France.

AGAFANGEL, His Eminence (Savvin Alexey Mikhailovich), Metropolitan of Odessa and Izmail, Kand.Theol; Ukrainian Orthodox ecclesiastic; b. 2 Sept. 1938, Burdino, Lipetsk Region; s. of Savvin Mikhail Petrovick and Savvina Marpha Federovna; ed Odessa Seminary, Moscow Theological Acad.; took monastic vows 1965; ordained as archimandrite 1967; Rector Odessa Seminary 1967–75; Bishop of Vinnitsa and Bratslav 1975–81; ordained as Archbishop 1981, Archbishop of Vinnitsa and Bratslav 1981–89; ordained as Metropolitan 1989, Metropolitan of Vinnitsa and Bratslav 1989–92; Metropolitan of Odessa and Izmail 1992–; People's Deputy of Ukraine 1990–94; Rector Odessa Seminary 1993–98; rep. of Russian Orthodox Church in Ukraine; Dr. hc (Kiev) 1995; Order of the Holy Cross (Jerusalem Patriarchate) 1981, Order of Friendship of Peoples 2003; UN Peace Medal 1988, Ukrainian President's Award, 2nd Rank 1999, 1st Rank 2003, Imperial Culture Award, Union of Writers of Russia 2005. *Address:* Pushkinskaya St 79, Odessa 65012 (office); Monastery of the Dormition, Mayatchny pereulok 6, Odessa 65038, Ukraine (home). *Telephone:* (48) 746-3037 (home). *Fax:* (48) 746-3038 (office). *E-mail:* lebed@farlep.net (office). *Website:* www.provoslav.odessa.net.

AGAKHANOV, Khalnazar Amannazarovich; Turkmenistani diplomatist and politician; *Ambassador to Russia;* b. 25 Feb. 1952, Ashgabat; m.; three c.; ed Samarkand State Inst. of Co-operation; trader, Ashgabat 1969–87; First Deputy Chair. Turkmenpotrebsoyuz 1987–91; Minister of Trade 1991–94, of Trade and Resources 1994–98, of Trade and Foreign Econ. Relations 1998–99; Amb. to Kazakhstan 1999–2000, to Russia 2000–; Order of Galkynysh, For Love for Homeland and Gairat Medals. *Leisure interests:* chess, reading books, pop and folk music. *Address:* Embassy of Turkmenistan, Filippovskii per. 22, 121019 Moscow, Russia (office). *Telephone:* (095) 291-66-36 (office). *Fax:* (095) 291-09-35 (office).

AGAM, Tan Sri Hasmy, BA, MA; Malaysian diplomatist; *Executive Chairman, Institute of Diplomacy and Foreign Relations, Ministry of Foreign Affairs;* b. 3 Feb. 1944, Malacca; m.; two d.; ed Univ. of Malaya, Kuala Lumpur, Fletcher School of Law and Diplomacy, Tufts Univ., USA; joined Foreign Ministry as Asst Sec. 1968, various positions in Ministry and in missions in Saigon, Washington, DC, Hanoi and London; seconded to Nat. Inst. of Public Admin as Head, Centre for Int. Relations and Diplomacy 1981; Amb. to Libya (also accred to Malta) 1986–88, to France (also accred to Portugal) 1990–92; Alt. Perm. Rep. to UN, Alt. Del. to Security Council 1988–90; Dir-Gen. Relations with ASEAN, Foreign Ministry 1993, Deputy Sec.-Gen. for Int. Orgs and Multilateral Econs 1994–96; Alt. Perm. Rep. to UN 1996–98, apptd Perm. Rep. 1998; mem. Sec.-Gen.'s Advisory Bd on Disarmament Matters; currently Exec. Chair. Institute of Diplomacy and Foreign Relations (IDFR), Ministry of Foreign Affairs; adjunct Prof., Northern Univ. of Malaysia, Int. Islamic Univ. Malaysia, Nat. Univ. of Malaysia; Panglima Setia Mahkota, Panglima Jasa Negara, Darjah Mulia Seri Melaka, Johan Setia Mahkota, Kesatria Mangku Negara. *Address:* Institute of Diplomacy and Foreign Relations, Ministry of Foreign Affairs, Jalan Wisma Putra, 50602 Kuala Lumpur, Malaysia (office). *Telephone:* (3) 21491001 (office). *Fax:* (3) 21445640 (office). *E-mail:* hasmy@idfr.gov.my (office). *Website:* www.idfr.gov.my (office).

AGAM, Yaacov; Israeli artist; b. (Jacob Gipstein), 1928, Rishon Le-zion; m. Clila Agam 1954; two s. one d.; ed Bezalel School of Art, Jerusalem, Atelier d'art abstrait, Paris; travelling retrospective exhbn Paris (Nat. Museum of Modern Art), Amsterdam, Düsseldorf, Tel-Aviv 1972–73. *Works include:* Transformes Musicales 1961, Double Metamorphosis, Shalom Liner 1964, Sculptures in the City, Reims 1970, sculpture and mural, President's mansion, Israel 1971, Water-Fire fountain, St Louis 1971, Pompidou Room, Elysée Palace 1972, environment, Elysée Palace, Paris 1972, mobile wall, School of Science, Montpellier 1972, design and realization of a square in La Défense, Paris, including water fountain and monumental sculpture 1973, Villa Regina, Miami (biggest painting in the world, at 300,000 square feet) 1984, Homage to Mondrian (a whole building), LA 1984, Fire-Water Fountain, Tel-Aviv 1986, Visual Educ. System 1986, MS Celebration cruise ship 1987, Grand Prix Artec 1989, Nagoya, MS Fantasy cruise ship 1990; films produced include Recherches et inventions 1956, Le désert chante, 1957. *Publications:* 36 books covering his non-verbal visual learning method (visual alphabet). *Address:* 26 rue Boulard, Paris 75014, France. *Telephone:* 1-43-22-00-88.

AGANBEGYAN, Abel Gezevich; Russian/Armenian economist; b. 8 Oct. 1932, Tbilisi, Georgia; s. of Galina A. Aganbegyan; m. Zoya V. Kupriyanova 1953; one s. one d.; ed Moscow State Econ. Inst.; mem. CPSU 1956–91; Economist, Gen. Econ. Dept, State Cttee for Labour and Wages 1955–61; Head of Lab., Inst. of Econs and Industrial Eng, Siberian Branch of USSR Acad. of Sciences 1961–67, Dir Inst. of Econs and Industrial Eng 1967–85; Prof. of Econs, Novosibirsk State Univ.; Prof. Acad. of Nat. Econ.; Chair. Cttee for Study of Productive Forces and Natural Resources 1965–; Rector Acad. of Nat. Economy 1989–2002; mem. Presidium; Chair. All-Union Club of Managers; Corresp. mem. USSR (now Russian) Acad. of Sciences 1964, mem. 1974, Acad.-Sec. Dept of Econ. 1986–89; Foreign mem. Bulgarian and Hungarian Acads. of Sciences; Corresp. FBA; two Orders of Lenin; Dr. hc (Alicante and Łódź). *Publications:* Wages and Salaries in the USSR 1959, On the Application of Mathematics and Electronic Machinery in Planning 1961, Some Questions of Monopoly Price Theory with Reference to the USA 1961, Economical-Mathematical Analysis of Input-Output Tables in USSR 1968, System of Models of National Economy Planning 1972, Management of the Socialist Enterprises 1979, Management and Efficiency: USSR Economy in 1981–85 1981, Siberia—not by Hearsay (with Z. Ibragimova) 1981, Economic Methods in Planned Management (with D. Kazakevich) 1985, Enterprise: Managing Scientific and Technological Progress (with V. Rechin) 1986; The Challenge:

Economics of Perestroika 1987, Moving the Mountain: Inside Perestroika 1989, Measures and Stages of Improving USSR Economy 1991. *Address:* c/o Academy of National Economy, 119571 Moscow, Prospect Vernadskogo 82, Russia. *Telephone:* (495) 434-83-89 (office). *Website:* www.ane.ru (office).

AĞAOĞLU, Adalet; Turkish writer; b. 1929, Ankara; d. of Mustafa Sümer and İsmet Sümer; m. Halim Ağaoğlu 1954; ed Univ. of Ankara; worked for Türkiye Radyo Televizyon Kurumu (TRT) 1953–73; freelance writer 1973–; Dr hc (Ohio State Univ.) 1998; Sedat Simavi Prize, Orhan Kemal Prize, Madarali Prize, Pres. of the Turkish Repub. Grand Prize for Culture and the Arts 1995. *Publications include:* (in Turkish) novels: Lying Down to Die 1973, The Mince Rose of My Mind 1977, A Wedding Party 1978, Summer's End 1980, Four or Five People 1984, No... 1987, Shiver of Soul 1990, Curfew (in trans.) 1997; short stories: High Tension (Sait Faik Prize) 1974, The First Sound of Silence 1978, Come On, Let's Go 1982; plays: Three Play (Prize of Turkish Language Inst.) 1956, Plays 1982, Too Far, Much Closer (Is Bankasi Grand Award for the Theatre) 1991. *Leisure interests:* reading, writing. *Address:* Piyasa Cad, Bülbül Sok, 10/5 Ceviz Apt, Büyükdere, Istanbul, Turkey. *Telephone:* (1) 1422636.

AGAPOV, Lt-Gen. Boris Nikolayevich; Russian politician; b. 6 Feb. 1946, Bakhazden, Turkmenistan; m.; one s. two d.; ed Alma-Ata Higher Commanding School, Far E Univ., Frunze Mil. Acad.; served in border forces in Middle Asia and Afghanistan; Deputy C-in-C border forces of Russia, Head of Chief Operation Dept 1991–93; Vice-Pres. Repub. of Ingushetia 1993–97; Deputy Sec. Security Council responsible for Inter-ethnic Problems and Emergency Situations June 1997, Deputy Exec. Sec., CIS Exec. Cttee 1998; Co-Chair. Movt for Equality and Justice 1999; Rep. of Altai Repub. to Fed. Council 2002–05, Rep. of Sakhalin Oblast 2005–07. *Address:* c/o Federation Council, 103426 Moscow, ul. B. Dmitrovka 26, Russia.

AGARWAL, Anil; Indian business executive; *Executive Chairman, Vedanta Resources plc;* b. 1953; m.; two c.; f. Sterlite Gold Ltd (now Sterlite Industries) 1976, currently Chair. and Man. Dir, cr. Vedanta Resources plc (diversified metals and mining group) after Sterlite acquired Shamsher Sterling, CEO 1979–2005, Exec. Chair. 2005–. *Address:* Vedanta Resources plc, 16 Berkeley Street, London, W1J 8DZ, England (office). *Telephone:* (20) 7629-6070 (office). *Fax:* (20) 7629-7426 (office). *Website:* www.vedantaresources.com (office).

AGARWAL, Bina, PhD; Indian economist and academic; *Professor of Economics, Institute of Economic Growth, University of Delhi;* b. Jabalpur, India; ed Univ. of Delhi, Univ. of Cambridge, UK, Delhi School of Econs; Research Assoc., Council for Social Devt 1972–74; Visiting Fellow, Inst. of Devt Studies, Univ. of Sussex, UK 1978–79, Research Fellow, Science Policy Research Unit 1979–80; Assoc. Prof. of Econs, Inst. of Econ. Growth, Univ. of Delhi 1981–88, Prof. 1988–, Head, Population Research Centre 1996–98; Fellow, Bunting Inst., Radcliffe Coll. 1989–91; mem. Harvard Center for Population and Devt Studies 1990–91; Visiting Prof., Harvard Univ. Cttee on Degrees in Women's Studies 1991–92, First Daniel H.H. Ingalls Visiting Prof. March–Sept. 1999; Visiting Scholar, Inst. for Advanced Study, Princeton 1995; Visiting Prof., Univ. of Michigan 2003; Visiting Prof. and Winton Chair Holder, Univ. of Minnesota 2004, Visiting Research Fellow, Ash Inst., Kennedy School of Govt, Harvard Univ. 2006; mem. numerous nat. and int. editorial bds, advisory cttees and consultancies; Padma Shri 2008; Dr hc (Inst. of Social Studies, The Hague) 2007; K.H. Batheja Award 1995–96, Edgar Graham Book Prize 1996, Ananda Kentish Coomaraswamy Book Prize 1996, Malcolm Adisheshiah Award for Distinguished Contributions to Development Studies 2002, Ramesh Chandra Award for Outstanding Contributions to Agricultural Economics 2005. *Publications:* Mechanization in Indian Agriculture 1983, Cold Hearths and Barren Slopes: The Woodfuel Crisis in the Third World 1986, A Field of One's Own: Gender and Land Rights in South Asia 1994, Structures of Patriarchy: State, Community and Household in Modernizing Asia (ed.) 1988, Women, Poverty and Ideology in Asia (co-ed.) 1989, Women and Work in the World Economy 1991; Psychology, Rationality and Economic Behaviour: Challenging Assumptions (co-ed.) 2005, Capabilities, Freedom and Equality: Amartyr Sen's Work from a Gender Perspective (co-ed.) 2006; numerous articles in learned journals on property rights, environment, agricultural technology, poverty, political economy of gender, and related topics. *Leisure interests:* writing poetry, painting, reading literature and biography, nature walks, movies. *Address:* Institute of Economic Growth, University Enclave, University of Delhi, Delhi 110007, India (office). *Telephone:* (11) 27667101 (office). *Fax:* (11) 27667410 (office); (11) 24353393 (home). *E-mail:* bina@iegindia.org (office). *Website:* www.iegindia.org (office); www.binaagarwal.com (home).

AGARWAL, Sudarshan, LLB; Indian fmr lawyer and fmr politician; b. 19 June 1931, Ludhiana; m. Usha Agarwal; one s. one d.; Sec.-Gen. Rajya Sabha 1981–93, participated in several parl. confs and int. goodwill dels world-wide; mem. Nat. Human Rights Comm. Judge of the Supreme Court 2000–03; Gov. of Uttaranchal (now Uttarakhand) 2003–07, of Sikkim 2007–08; currently involved in community work; Pres. Delhi Gymkhana Club 1986–88; Trustee Amity Business School, Sanskriti Pratishthan cultural centre; fmr Chair. Uttaranchal State Red Cross Soc., State Child Welfare Council; Chief Returning Officer, Indian presidential election 1982, 1992; mem. and Past Pres. Rotary Club of Delhi, Dist Gov. Rotary Int., Dir, Rotary Int., mem. and Chair. several Rotary Int. Cttees, Chair. Rotary Foundation (India) 1992–2002, Trustee, Rotary Service to Humanity Awards Trust; helped establish voluntary Blood Banks in Delhi and Dehradun-Uttarakhand; est. free boarding school for girls from disadvantaged families in Dehradun-Uttarakhand; Hon. DSc (Gurukul Univ., Uttaranchal); Rotary Foundation's citation for Meritorious Service and Rotary Foundation Distinguished Service Award. *Leisure interest:* gardening. *Address:* c/o Raj Bhavan, 57 Tughlakabad Institutional Area, New Delhi, 110024, India (office); C-312, Defence Colony, New Delhi, 110024, India (home). *Telephone:* (11) 29054065 (office); (11) 24332676 (home). *Fax:* (11) 26056333 (office). *E-mail:* sud.agarwal@gmail.com.

AGASSI, Andre; American professional tennis player (retd); b. 29 April 1970, Las Vegas, Nev.; s. of Mike Agassi and Elizabeth Agassi; m. 1st Brooke Shields (q.v.) 1997 (divorced 1999); m. 2nd Steffi Graf (q.v.); one s.; coached from age 13 by Nick Bollettieri, strength coach Gil Reyes; turned professional 1986; semi-finalist, French Open 1988, US Open 1988, 1989; mem. US team that defeated Australia in Davis Cup Final 1990; defeated Stefan Edberg to win inaugural ATP World Championship, Frankfurt 1991; finalist French Open 1990, 1991, US Open 1990, 1995, 2002, Wimbledon 1999; won Wimbledon 1992, US Open 1994, 1999, Canadian Open 1995, Australian Open 1995, 2000, 2001, 2003, French Open 1999; winner Olympic Games tennis tournaments 1996; Asscn of Tennis Professionals World Champion 1990; one of only five players to have won all four Grand Slam titles; winner of 59 singles titles and one doubles title; retd 2006; f. Andre Agassi Charitable Foundation to help at-risk youth in Las Vegas 1994; f. Agassi Enterprises, Inc. *Address:* International Management Group, 1 Erieview Plaza, Suite 1300, Cleveland, OH 44114; Andre Agassi Charitable Foundation, 3960 Howard Hughes Parkway, Suite 750, Las Vegas, NV 89109. USA. *Website:* www.agassifoundation.org.

AGASSI, Shai, BSc; Israeli business executive; *CEO, Better Place;* b. April 1968, Tel-Aviv; s. of Reuven Agassi; m.; two s.; ed Technion (Israeli Inst. of Tech.); computer programmer, Army Intelligence, Israeli Army; f. QuickSoft (software distribution co.) 1990, Menahel Inc. 1991, TopManage 1992, QuickSoft Media 1994; f. TopTier Software 1992, Chair. 1996–99, Chief Exec. 1999–2001; Chief Exec. SAP Portals (later SAP Markets) 2001–02, mem. Exec. Bd SAP AG, Walldorf 2002–07, Top Tech. Developer 2003, Pres. Product and Tech. Group 2003–07, consultant 2007–; (resgnd) his position to pursue interests in alternative energy and climate change; Founder and CEO Better Place (fmrly Project Better Place) 2007–. *Leisure interests:* reading technology books. *Address:* Better Place, 1070 Arastradero Road, Suite 220, Palo Alto, CA 94304, USA (office). *Telephone:* (650) 845-2800 (office). *Fax:* (650) 845-2850 (office). *Website:* www.betterplace.com (office); www.sap.com.

AGBOYIBO, (Appolinaire) Yawovi; Togolese politician and lawyer; b. 1943; ed in Togo, Senegal, France and Côte d'Ivoire; fmr Head of Nat. Human Rights Comm.; Leader, Action Cttee for Renewal (CAR) party, jailed for six months for defaming Togolese Prime Minister Aug. 2001, freed as gesture of appeasement March 2002; cand. in presidential elections 2003; led inter-Togolese dialogue in Burkina Faso helping to broker agreement to form a power-sharing cabinet Aug. 2006; Prime Minister of Togo Sept. 2006–07. *Address:* Comité d'action pour le Renouveau (CAR), 58 ave du 24 janvier, BP06, Lomé, Togo (office). *Telephone:* 222-05-66 (office). *Fax:* 221-62-54 (office). *E-mail:* yagboyibo@bibway.com (office).

AGEE, William J., MBA; American business executive; b. 5 Jan. 1938, Boise, Ida; s. of Harold J. Agee and Suzanne Agee; m. 1st Diane Weaver 1957; one s. two d.; m. 2nd Mary Cunningham 1982; one d.; ed Stanford Univ., Boise Junior Coll., Univ. of Idaho, Harvard Univ.; with Boise Cascade Corpn 1963–72; Sr Vice-Pres. and Chief Financial Officer, Bendix Corpn 1972–76, Pres. and COO 1976–77, Chair. and CEO 1977–83, Pres. 1977–79; CEO Semper Enterprises, Inc. (now Semper Pnrs) 1983–; Chair., Pres. and CEO Morrison Knudsen Corpn 1988–95; Dir ASARCO, Equitable Life Assurance Soc. of US, Dow Jones & Co. Inc., Econ. Club of Detroit, Detroit Renaissance Inc., Nat. Council for US–China Trade, Gen. Foods Corpn, Detroit Econ. Growth Corpn 1978–, United Foundation, Nat. Council for US–China Trade; mem. Conf. Bd, Council on Foreign Relations, Business Roundtable, American and other insts of CPAs, Bd of Dirs, Assocs of Harvard Business School 1977, United Negroes Coll. Fund 1977; Chair. Gov.'s Higher Educ. Capital Investment Advisory Cttee, Pres.'s Industrial Advisory Sub-Cttee on Econ. and Trade Policy 1978–79, Advisory Council Cranbrook Educational Community 1978, Trustee 1978; Trustee Urban Inst., Cttee for Econ. Devt 1977, Citizen Research Council, Mich. 1977; numerous hon. degrees. *Leisure interests:* tennis, golf, swimming. *Address:* 1733 Fir Hill, Saint Helena, CA 94574-2356, USA.

AGHILI, Shadmehr; Iranian singer, musician and actor; b. 27 Jan. 1973, Tehran; singer and writer of popular songs. *Film:* Par e Parvaz (also composed soundtrack). *Recordings include:* Bahare Man 1998, Mosaafer 1999, Dehati 2000, Naghmehaye Mashreghi 2001, Pare Parvaz 2002, Khiali Nist 2004, Adam Foroush 2004, Popcorn 2006. *Website:* www.shadmehr.us.

AGIUS, Marcus Ambrose Paul, MA, MBA; British business executive and investment banker; *Chairman, Barclays plc;* b. 22 July 1946, Walton-on-Thames; s. of the late Alfred Victor Louis Benedict Agius and Ena Eleanora Hueffer; m. Kate Juliette de Rothschild 1971; two d.; ed Univ. of Cambridge and Harvard Business School; grad. trainee with Vickers PLC 1968–70; Man. Dir Lazard 1984–89, Vice Chair. and Man. Dir Lazard Frères & Co. LLC 1989–2002, Deputy Chair. Lazard LLC 2002–06, Chair. Lazard Bank Ltd 2002–06; mem. Bd of Dirs BAA (British Airports Authority) PLC 1995–2006, Deputy Chair. 1998–2002, Chair. 2002–06; mem. Bd of Dirs Barclays PLC 2006–, Chair. 2007–; Sr Ind. Dir (non-exec.) BBC 2006–; Chair. Foundation and Friends of Royal Botanic Gardens, Kew 2004–. *Leisure interests:* gardening, shooting, skiing. *Address:* Barclays plc, 1 Churchill Place, Canary Wharf, London, E14 5HP (office); 25 Chelsea Square, London, SW3 6LF, England (home). *Telephone:* (20) 7116-1000 (office). *Fax:* (20) 7116-7780 (office). *E-mail:* info@barclays.com (office). *Website:* www.barclays.com (office).

AGLUKKAQ, Leona; Canadian politician; *Minister of Health;* fmr Asst Deputy Minister of Human Resources, Regional Govt of Nunavut; fmr Minister of Health and Social Services and Minister Responsible for Status of Women, Exec. Council of Nunavut; Deputy Clerk, Nunavut Legis. Ass. 2000–02, mem. Legis. Ass. 2004–08; MP for Nunavut 2008–; Minister for Health 2008–; mem. Conservative Party of Canada. *Address:* Health Canada, Brooke Claxton Building, Tunney's Pasture, Ottawa, ON K1A 0K9, Canada (office). *Telephone:* (613) 957-2991 (office). *Fax:* (613) 952-1154 (office). *E-mail:* info@hc-sc.gc.ca (office). *Website:* www.hc-sc.gc.ca (office).

AGNELLI, Roger, BEcons; Brazilian mining executive; *President and CEO, Vale;* b. 3 March 1959; ed Fundação Armando Álvares Penteado, São Paulo; began career with Bradesco Group 1981, Exec. Dir Bradesco Bank 1998–2000, Pres. and CEO Bradespar SA 2000–01; Chair. Companhia Vale do Rio Doce (CVRD) 2000–01 (now called Vale), Pres. and CEO 2001–; Dir Spectra Energy (USA), Duke Energy (USA) 2004–, Suzano Petroquimica SA, Petrobras-Petroleo Brasileiro SA, INCO Ltd 2006–; Dir (non-exec.) Asea Brown Boveri, (ABB) 2002–; fmr Counselor, São Paulo Power and Light Co., Companhia Siderurgica Nacional; mem. Conselho de Desenvolvimento Economico e Social (Econ. and Social Devt Council, CDES); mem. Int. Investments Council for S Africa; mem. Int. Advisory Cttee, NYSENext; O Globo Faz Diferença Award 2007, Latin Trade Bravo Business Leader of the Year 2007. *Address:* Vale, Av. Graça Aranha, 26, 20030-900 Rio de Janeiro RJ, Brazil (office). *Telephone:* (21) 3814-4477 (office). *Fax:* (21) 3814-4040 (office). *E-mail:* info@vale.com (office). *Website:* www.vale.com (office).

AGNELLI, Susanna; Italian politician and international organization official; *President, Italian Telethon Foundation;* b. 24 April 1922, Turin; sister of the late Giovanni Agnelli and of Umberto Agnelli; m. Urbano Rattazz 1945 (divorced); six c.; Mayor of Monte Argentario 1974–84; mem. Parl. 1976–83; mem. European Parl. 1979–81; Senator 1983; mem. Nat. Council, Republican Party until 1992; Jr Minister, Ministry of Foreign Affairs 1986–91; Minister of Foreign Affairs 1992–96; Adviser, John F. Kennedy School of Govt Council of Women World Leaders, Harvard Univ. 1998–; mem. Int. Comm. on Missing Persons 1998–, Bd of Dirs of Int. Center for Missing and Exploited Children 1999–; Pres. Italian Telethon Foundation 1992–, 'Il Faro' Foundation 1997–; Hon. Pres. AMREF Italy; Hon. LLD (Mt Holyoke Coll., MA) 1981. *Publications include:* We Always Wore Sailor Suits 1975, Ricordati Gualeguaychù 1982, Addio, addio mio ultimo amore 1985, Questo libro è tuo 1993; numerous articles in magazines and newspapers. *Leisure interest:* writing. *Address:* Comitato Telethon Fondazione ONLUS, Via G. Saliceto 5A, 00161 Rome (office); Piazza Navona 49, 00186 Rome, Italy (home). *Telephone:* (06) 440151 (office). *Fax:* (06) 44202032 (office). *E-mail:* info@telethon.it (office). *Website:* www.telethon.it (office).

AGNELO, HE Cardinal Geraldo Majella; Brazilian ecclesiastic; *Archbishop of São Salvador da Bahía;* b. 19 Oct. 1933, Juiz de Fora; s. of Antônio Agnelo and Silvia Spagnolo Agnelo; ordained priest 1957; elected Bishop of Toledo 1978; Bishop of Londrina 1982; resgnd 1991; Archbishop of São Salvador da Bahía 1999–; cr. Cardinal (Cardinal-Priest of San Gregorio Magno alla Magliana Nuova) 2001. *Address:* Archdiocese of São Salvador da Bahía, Rua Martin Afonso de Souza 270, 40100–050 Salvador, Bahía (office); Avenida Cardeal da Silva 26, Casa 33, 40220–140 Salvador, Bahía, Brazil (home). *Telephone:* (71) 328-6699 (office); (71) 331-2738 (home). *Fax:* (71) 328-0068 (office); (71) 261-5243 (home). *E-mail:* contato@arquidiocesedesalvador.org.br (office).

AGNEW, Harold Melvin, PhD; American physicist and academic; *Adjunct Professor, University of California, San Diego;* b. 28 March 1921, Denver, Colo; s. of Sam E. Agnew and Agusta Agnew (née Jacobs); m. Beverly Jackson 1942; one s. one d.; ed Univs of Denver and Chicago; Los Alamos Scientific Lab. 1943–46, Alt. Div. Leader 1949–61, Leader Weapons Div. 1964–70, Dir Los Alamos Scientific Lab. 1970–79; Pres. GA Technologies Inc. 1979–85, Dir 1985–; New Mexico State Senator 1955–61; Scientific Adviser, Supreme Allied Commdr in Europe, Paris 1961–64; Chair. Army Scientific Advisory Panel 1965–70, mem. 1970–74; Chair. Gen. Advisory Cttee, US Arms Control and Disarmament Agency 1972–76, mem. 1976–80; mem. Aircraft Panel, Pres.'s Scientific Advisory Cttee 1965–73, USAF Scientific Advisory Bd 1957–69, Defense Scientific Bd 1965–70, Govt of NM Radiation Advisory Council 1959–61; Sec. NM Health and Social Services 1971–73; mem. Aerospace Safety Advisory Panel, NASA 1968–74, 1986, White House Science Council 1982–89; Adjunct Prof., Univ. of Calif., San Diego 1988–; mem. Woodrow Wilson Nat. Fellowship Foundation 1973–80; Dir Charles Lee Powell Foundation 1993–; Fellow, American Physical Soc.; mem. NAS, Nat. Acad. of Eng; Ernest Orlando Lawrence Award 1966, Enrico Fermi Award, Dept of Energy 1978, Los Alamos Nat. Lab. Medal 2001. *Leisure interests:* crafts, gardening, skiing, golf, tennis, fishing. *Address:* 322 Punta Baja Drive, Solana Beach, CA 92075, USA. *Telephone:* (858) 481-8908. *Fax:* (858) 481-8908. *E-mail:* hmabja@sdsc.edu (office).

AGNEW, Jonathan Geoffrey William, MA; British investment banker; *Chairman, LMS Capital plc;* b. 30 July 1941, Windsor; s. of the late Sir Geoffrey William Gerald Agnew and Hon. Doreen Maud Jessel; m. 1st Hon. Agneta Joanna Middleton Campbell 1966 (divorced 1985; died 2002); one s. two d.; m. 2nd Marie-Claire Dreesmann 1990; one s. one d.; ed Eton Coll. and Trinity Coll., Cambridge; with The Economist 1964–65, IBRD 1965–67; with Hill Samuel & Co. 1967–73, Dir 1971; Morgan Stanley & Co. 1973–82, Man. Dir 1977; with J.G.W. Agnew & Co. 1983–86; Chief Exec. ISRO 1986; with Kleinwort Benson Group PLC 1987–93, Chief Exec. 1989–93; Chair. Limit PLC 1993–2000, Henderson Geared Income & Growth Trust PLC 1995–2003 (Dir 1995–2003), Gerrard Group PLC 1999–2000, LMS Capital plc 2006–; Chair. (non-exec.) Leo Capital plc; Dir and Chair. The Cayenne Trust PLC 2006–, Ashmore Global Opportunities Fund; Dir (non-exec.) Thos. Agnew & Sons Ltd 1969–; Dir (non-exec.) Nationwide Building Soc. 1997–2007, Deputy Chair. (non-exec.) 1999–2002, Chair. 2002–07; Dir (non-exec.) Beazley Group PLC 2002–, Chair. 2003–; Dir (non-exec.) Jarvis PLC 2003–04; Dir Soditic Ltd 2001–04, LMS Capital plc (fmrly Leo Capital plc) 2006–; Sr Ind. Dir Rightmove plc 2006–; mem. Council Lloyd's 1995–98. *Address:* LMS Capital plc, Carlton House, 33 Robert Adam Street, London, W1U 3HR (office); Flat E, 51 Eaton Square, London, SW1W 9BE, England (home). *Telephone:* (20) 7935-3555 (office); (20) 7235-7589 (home). *Fax:* (20) 7935-3737 (office). *E-mail:* enquiries@lmscapital.com (office). *Website:* www.lmscapital.com (office).

AGNEW, (Morland Herbert) Julian, MA, FRSA; British art dealer; *Chairman, Thomas Agnew & Sons Ltd;* b. 20 Sept. 1943, London; s. of the late Sir Geoffrey William Gerald Agnew and Hon. Doreen Maud Jessel; m. 1st Elizabeth Margaret Moncrieff Mitchell 1973 (divorced 1992); one s. two d.; m. 2nd Victoria Burn Callander 1993; one s.; ed Eton Coll. and Trinity Coll., Cambridge; joined Thomas Agnew & Sons Ltd 1965, Dir 1968, Man. Dir 1987–92, Chair. 1992–; Pres. British Antique Dealers Asscn 1979–81; Chair. Soc. of London Art Dealers 1986–90. *Leisure interests:* opera, music, books, tennis, golf. *Address:* Thomas Agnew & Sons Ltd, 8 Grafton St, London, W1S 4EL (office); 76 Alderney Street, London, SW1 4EX (home); Egmere Farm House, Egmere, nr Walsingham, Norfolk, England (home). *Telephone:* (20) 7290-9250 (office). *Fax:* (20) 7629-4359 (office). *E-mail:* julianagnew@agnewsgallery.co.uk (office). *Website:* www.agnewsgallery.com (office).

AGNEW, Sir Rudolph (Ion Joseph), Kt, FRSA; British business executive; b. 12 March 1934; s. of Rudolph John Agnew and Pamela Geraldine Agnew (née Campbell); m. Whitney Warren 1980; ed Downside School; Commissioned Officer, 8th King's Royal Irish Hussars 1953–57; joined Consolidated Gold Fields PLC 1957, apptd Exec. Dir 1973, Deputy Chair. 1978–82, Group Chief Exec. 1978–89, Chair. 1983–89, mem. Cttee of Man. Dirs 1986–89; Chief Exec. Amey Roadstone Corpn 1974–78, Chair. 1974–77; Chair. and CEO TVS Entertainment 1990–93; apptd Chair. Stena Int. BV (fmrly Sealink Stena Line) 1990, Federated Aggregates PLC 1991–95, Bona Shipholding Ltd, Bermuda 1993–98, LASMO PLC 1994–2000, Redland PLC 1995–97, Star Mining Corpn 1995–98; Jt Chair. Global Stone Corpn (Canada) 1993–94; Dir (non-exec.) New London PLC 1985–96, Standard Chartered PLC 1988–97, Newmount Mining Corpn, USA 1989–98, Hanson PLC 1989–91; Vice-Pres. Nat. Asscn of Boys Clubs; mem. Council WWF (UK) 1989– (Trustee 1983–89); Fellow, Game Conservancy. *Leisure interest:* shooting. *Address:* 7 Eccleston Street, London, SW1X 9LX, England.

AGON, Jean-Paul; French business executive; *CEO, L'Oréal Group;* b. Paris; three c.; ed Hautes Etudes Commerciales; joined L'Oréal Paris Group and worked in sales and marketing 1978–81, Gen. Man. Consumer Products Div., Greece 1981–86, Gen. Man. L'Oréal Paris 1986–89, Int. Man. Dir Luxury Products Div., Biotherm 1989–94, Gen. Man. L'Oréal Germany 1994–97, Man. Dir L'Oréal Group's Asia zone 1997–2001, Pres. and CEO L'Oréal USA 2001–06, CEO L'Oréal 2006–. *Address:* L'Oréal SA, 41 rue Martre, 92117 Clichy Cedex, France (office). *Telephone:* 1-47-56-70-00 (office). *Fax:* 1-47-56-80-02 (office). *E-mail:* info@loreal.com (office). *Website:* www.loreal.com (office).

AGOSTINI, Giacomo (Ago); Italian motorcylist; b. 16 June 1942, Brescia; rode for Morini 1961–64; understudy to Mike Hailwood at MV Augusta 1965, number one rider 1966–73, 1976–77; rode for Yamaha 1974–76; 311 wins; a record 122 Grand Prix wins (54 at 350 cc, 68 at 500 cc); 12 Isle of Man TT wins (350 cc: 1966, 1967, 1968, 1969, 1970, 1972; 500 cc: 1967, 1968, 1969, 1970, 1971, 1972); 18 Italian championship wins; a record 15 World Championship wins (350 cc: 1968, 1969, 1970, 1971, 1972, 1973, 1974; 500 cc: 1966, 1967, 1968, 1969, 1970, 1971, 1972, 1975); shares (with Mike Hailwood) record for most races won in a season (19 in 1970); AMA Motorcycle Hall of Fame 1999, named Grand Prix Legend, Fédération Internationale de Motocyclisme (FIM) 2000. *Address:* c/o Media Affairs Office, Laureus World Sports Awards, 15 Hill Street, London, W1J 5QT, England (office). *Website:* www.giacomo-agostini.com.

AGRAWAL, Prabhu Lal, PhD; Indian business executive and engineer; b. 22 Oct. 1926, Udaipur, Rajasthan; s. of Tilok Chand Agrawal and Narayan Devi Agrawal; m. Pushpa Devi 1948; one s. one d.; ed Banaras Hindu Univ. and Univ. of Sheffield, UK; Asst Prof., College of Mining and Metallurgy, Banaras Hindu Univ. 1947–54, Reader 1954–56; Tech. Officer Rourkela Steel Plant, then Sr Fuel Engineer, then Asst Chief Fuel Engineer, then Supt Energy and Economy Dept 1957–65, then Chief Supt 1965–66, Asst Gen. Supt 1966–69, Gen. Man. 1971–78; Gen. Supt Alloy Steels Plant 1969–70; Gen. Supt Bokaro Steel Ltd 1970–71; Chair. Steel Authority of India 1978–80; Tech. Adviser PT Krakatan Steel, Jakarta 1980–86; Dir Secure Meters Ltd; mem. judging panel for Prime Minister's Trophy for Best Operating Integrated Steel Plant 1992–97, 2000–01; Pres. Indian Inst. of Metals 1978, Hon. mem. 1980; Trustee Sevamandir 1987–; Holkar Fellow, Banaras Hindu Univ.; Bundesverdienstkreuz (1st Class) 1981; Uttar Pradesh Govt Book Prize for Audyogik Indhan, Nat. Metallurgists Day Award 1966, FIE Foundation Award, India 1981, Tata Gold Medal, Indian Inst. of Metals 1981, Platinum Medal, Indian Inst. of Metals 1993, Lifetime Achievement Award, Govt of India 2005. *Publications:* Audyogik Indhan (Hindi); several tech. papers and reports. *Leisure interests:* reading, social work, walking. *Address:* Narayan Villa, 56-A New Fatehpura, Sukhadia Circle, Udaipur 313004, India (home). *Telephone:* (294) 2560380 (office). *Fax:* (294) 2560380 (office). *E-mail:* prabhuagrawal@yahoo.com (office).

AGRAWALA, Surendra Kumar, MA, LLD; Indian university administrator and professor of law; *Professor Emeritus, University of Pune;* b. 18 Jan. 1929, Bilgram; s. of the late Radha Krishna and Tara Devi; m. Prof. Dr Raj Kumari Agrawala 1959; one s.; ed Allahabad and Lucknow Univs and Harvard Law School; Lecturer in Law, Lucknow Univ. 1953–62; Reader in Law, Aligarh Muslim Univ. 1962–65; Prof. and Head of Dept, Univ. of Pune 1965–85, now Prof. Emer.; Vice-Chancellor, Agra Univ. 1985–88; Sec.-Gen. Asscn of Indian

Univs 1988–93; fmr mem. Governing Council, Indian Inst. of Science, Bangalore, Acad. Council, J. Nehru Univ., Court, Aligarh Muslim Univ.; Convener, UGC Advisory Panel on Law; numerous professional appointments, cttee memberships etc.; UGC Nat. Lecturer in Law 1974, K.M. Munshi Memorial Lecturer, Indian Law Inst. 1983, Banerjee Research Prize 1962, Best Univ. Teacher Award, Maharashtra Govt 1979. *Publications:* International Law: Indian Courts and Legislature 1965, Essays on the Law of Treaties (ed.) 1972, Legal Education in India: Problems and Perspectives (ed.) 1973, Proposed Indian Ombudsman 1971, Aircraft Hijacking and International Law 1975, New Horizons of International Law (ed.) 1983, Public Interest Litigation in India 1985; about 50 articles in anthologies and legal journals. *Leisure interests:* reading, writing, travel and sightseeing. *Address:* 3/454 Vishwas Khand, Gomtinagar, Lucknow, UP, India. *Telephone:* (522) 2309515.

AGRÉ, HE Cardinal Bernard; Côte d'Ivoirian ecclesiastic; *Archbishop of Abidjan;* b. 2 March 1926, Monga, Abidjan; ordained priest 1953; consecrated Bishop 1968; Bishop of Yamoussoukro 1992–95; Archbishop of Abidjan 1995–; cr. Cardinal 2001; Commdr de l'Ordre Nat. 1992. *Address:* Archevêché, av. Jean Paul II, 01 BP 1287, Abidjan 01, Côte d'Ivoire (office). *Telephone:* 20211246 (office); 20212308 (office); 20212299 (home). *Fax:* 20214022 (office).

AGRE, Peter C., BA, MD; American physician, molecular biologist and academic; *President-Elect, American Association for the Advancement of Science;* b. 1949, Northfield, Minn.; ed Theodore Roosevelt High School, Minneapolis, Augsburg Coll., Minneapolis, Johns Hopkins Univ., Baltimore; Fellow, Univ. of North Carolina 1974–81; Fellow, Depts of Medicine and Cell Biology, Johns Hopkins Univ., Baltimore, Md 1981–2005, Prof. of Biological Chem. 1993–2005; Vice-Chancellor, Science and Tech. of Chem. and Public Policy Studies and Prof. of Cell Biology and Public Policy Studies, Duke Univ. Medical Center 2005–, mem. Chancellor's Science Advisory Council 2006–07; mem. NAS 2000–, American Acad. of Arts and Sciences 2003–, AAAS (mem. Bd Dirs, Pres.-Elect 2011); Founding mem. Scientists and Engineers for America (mem. Bd of Advisors); Nobel Prize in Chem. (jt recipient) for his discovery of aquaporins 2003, Distinguished Eagle Scout Award. *Publications include:* numerous specialist papers, including cross-country skiing (has participated in the Vasaloppet ski race). *Address:* Office of the the Vice-Chancellor for Science and Technology, Duke University Medical Center, 108 Davison Building, Durham, NC 27708, USA (office); American Association for the Advancement of Science, 1200 New York Avenue, NW, Washington, DC 20005, USA (office). *Telephone:* (919) 684-2255 (Durham) (office); (202) 326-6400 (Washington, DC) (office). *E-mail:* peter.agre@duke.edu (office); webmaster@aaas.org. *Website:* www.dukehealth.org (office); www.aaas.org.

AGREST, Diana, DipArch; American architect and urban designer; *Co-founder and Partner, Agrest and Gandelsonas Architects;* b. 1945, Buenos Aires; m. Mario Gandelsonas; ed Univ. of Buenos Aires, École Pratique des Hautes Études and Centre du Recherche d'Urbanisme, Paris, France; Prof., Columbia, Princeton and Yale Univs, USA 1973–96; currently Prof. of Architecture, Cooper Union, New York; Pnr (with husband), Agrest and Gandelsonas Architects, New York; f. Diana Agrest Architectural Firm, New York; fmr Fellow, Inst. for Architecture and Urban Studies, New York 1972–84; Design Excellence Award, AIA NY State 2002, Design Excellence Award, AIA New York City 2002, Design Merit Award, Soc. of Registered Architects 2002, Masterwork Award, Municipal Art Soc. 2002, NY State Council on the Arts Grant 2003, AIA Brunner Award Grant 2004. *Architectural and urban design works include:* Melrose Community Center, New York, urban design for Shanghai, People's Repub. of China, plan for West Midtown Manhattan, New York, farm in Sagaponack, NY, house in Sagaponack, farm in Uruguay, Des Moines Vision Plaza, Ia, duplex on Central Park West, Manhattan, house in Majorca, Spain. *Publications include:* A Romance with the City: The Work of Irwin S. Chanin, Architecture from Without: Theoretical Framings for a Critical Perspective, Agrest and Gandelsonas Works (co-author), The Sex of Architecture; articles on architecture in numerous int. publs. *Leisure interest:* film-making. *Address:* Agrest and Gandelsonas Architects, 176 Grand Street, 2nd Floor, New York, NY 10013, USA (office). *Telephone:* (212) 625-3800 (office). *Fax:* (212) 625-3816 (office). *E-mail:* agrest@ag-architects.com (office). *Website:* www.ag-architects.com (office).

AGUADO, Victor M., MSc, MEng; Spanish international official, aviation executive and engineer; b. 9 June 1953; m. Paloma Sierra de Aguado; one s. two d.; ed Polytechnic Univ., Madrid, MIT, USA; student trainee, Lufthansa 1975; Man. of Tech. Standards, Maintenance Airforce Base, Albacete 1977–78; Systems Engineer in civil and mil. air traffic Man., Mitre Corpn, Boston, USA 1978–83; Programme Dir Civil Aviation Authority, Madrid 1983–84; Exec. Adviser to Sec. of State for Aerospace and Telecommunications Affairs 1984–85; Chair. Inter-Govt Task Force on major aerospace programmes 1984–85; Deputy Dir-Gen. in Spanish Admin 1985–88, Dir-Gen. 1988–90; apptd CEO ISDEFE SA Systems Engineering and Consulting Co., Madrid 1990; Air Navigation Commr ICAO, Montréal, Canada, later Pres. of Air Navigation 1996–2000; Dir-Gen. Eurocontrol (European Org. for the Safety of Air Navigation), Brussels 2001–08; Grand Cross of the Aeronautical Order of Merit, Spain; Global NavCom '97 Laurel Award. *Address:* c/o Eurocontrol, 96 rue de la Fusée, 1130 Brussels, Belgium (office).

AGUILAR MARMOLEJO, María de los Dolores, MA, PhD; Mexican international organization executive; *Director General, Inter-American Children's Institute (IIN-OAS);* b. 1966; ed Universidad La Salle, México, Univ. of Santiago de Compostela, Spain; extensive experience as a teacher; has worked with Univ. of Anahuac and Technological Univ. of Mexico; currently Prof. of Basic Educ., with grad. studies in philosophy, Universidad La Salle, México; recognized instructor in workshops and adviser on schoolwork consultancy; lectures on issues of family, children, health, educ., policy and organizational devt, among others; mem. Partido Acción Nacional (Nat. Action Party—PAN) 1984–, cand. for various elective offices at local level; Deputy to Fed. Dist Legis. Ass. 1997–2000; worked for Nat. System for Integral Devt of the Family 2001–08, served as adviser to Directorate-Gen., Deputy Dir Care Unit to the Vulnerable Population and CEO for Child Welfare; participated in design of 'Diagnóstico de la Familia Mexicana' basic tool for the analysis, design and implementation of public policies on the family 2003–05; Dir-Gen. Inter-American Children's Inst. (IIN-OAS) 2008–. *Address:* Inter-American Children's Institute, Avenida 8 de Octubre 2904, Montevideo 11600, Uruguay (office). *Telephone:* (2) 487-2150 (office). *Fax:* (2) 487-3242 (office). *E-mail:* direcciongral@iinoea.org (office). *Website:* www.iin.oea.org (office).

AGUILERA, Christina Maria; American singer; b. 18 Dec. 1980, Staten Island, NY; m. Jordan Bratman 2005; one s.; appeared on US Star Search TV talent show aged eight; joined cast of Orlando-based TV show, The New Mickey Mouse Club aged 12; intensive worldwide promotional touring 1997–; solo artist 1998–; numerous TV and live appearances; Grammy Award for Best New Artist 2000, ALMA Award for Best New Entertainer 2000, Billboard Award for Female Vocalist of the Year 2000, Q Award (for Dirrty) 2003, Grammy Award for Best Female Pop Vocal Performance (for Beautiful) 2004, (for Ain't No Other Man) 2007, MTV Europe Music Award for Best Female Artist 2006. *Film appearance:* Magic Isle 2003. *Recordings include:* albums: Christina Aguilera 1999, Mi Reflejo (Billboard Latin Music Award for Best Pop Album of the Year 2001) 2000, My Kind Of Christmas 2000, Just Be Free 2001, Stripped 2002, Back to Basics 2006. *Address:* Irving Azoff, 3500 W Olive Avenue, Suite 600, Burbank, CA 91505, USA (office); c/o RCA Records, 1540 Broadway, New York, NY 10036, USA. *E-mail:* info@rcarecords.com. *Website:* www.christinaaguilera.com.

AGUILERA, Isabel, MBA; Spanish business executive; *President, General Electric Spain and Portugal;* b. 1961, Seville; two c.; ed Univ. of Seville, Instituto de Empressa, Madrid; studied architecture and urban planning; Dir of Distribution and Marketing Communications Compaq Spain 1985–88; Marketing Man. Hewlett-Packard Spain 1989–95; with Airtel 1995–97; Man. Dir for Spain, Portugal and Italy, Dell Computer SA 1997–2002; COO and mem. Man. Cttee NH Hoteles 2002–06; Man. Dir Google Spain and Portugal 2006–08; Pres. General Electric Spain and Portugal 2008–; mem. Bd of Dirs Indra Sitemas 2006–, Pulsar Technologies, APD; Int. Dir Instituto de Empresa; ranked by Fortune magazine amongst 50 Most Powerful Women in Business outside the US (45th) 2002, ranked 20th by The Financial Times amongst 25 Most Important Women in Business in Europe 2004. *Address:* c/o General Electric Company, 3135 Easton Tpke, Fairfield, CT 06828-0001, USA (office). *Website:* www.ge.com/es (office).

AGUIRRE URIOSTE, Luis Fernando, MSc, PhD; Bolivian biologist, conservationist and academic; *Researcher and Professor, Centre for Biodiversity and Genetics, Universidad Mayor de San Simon;* ed Universidad Mayor de San Andres, La Paz, Antwerp Univ., Belgium; f. Bolivian Bat Conservation Programme of BIOTA (one of four major programmes at Centro de Estudios en Biologia Teorica y Aplicada) to protect bats through educ. and practical habitat conservation throughout Bolivia; currently Researcher and Prof., Centre for Biodiversity and Genetics, Universidad Mayor de San Simon; mem. Scientific Advisory Bd of Bat Conservation International, Network of Educators of Conservation Biology (AMNH), Int. Union for Conservation of Nature Chiropteran Specialist Group; Assoc. Ed. Acta Chiropterologica, Mastozoologia Neotropical, Revista Boliviana de Ecologia, Ecologia en Bolivia; reviewer for several int. scientific journals, including Conservation Biology, Biotropica, Acta Chiropterologica, Ecography, Journal of Tropical Ecology, Journal of Mammalogy; Pres. Asociacion Boliviana de Investigadores de Mamiferos 2005–; Adjunct Researcher, Center for Environmental Research and Conservation, Columbia Univ., New York, USA 2006–; Devt Cooperation Prize, Belgian Cooperation Program 2005, Oliver P. Person Award, American Soc. of Mammalogists 2006, Whitley Award in memory of Daniel Kelly, Rufford Maurice Laing Foundation 2007. *Publications:* more than 30 scientific papers in professional journals. *Address:* Centro de Biodiversidad y Genética, Universidad Mayor de San Simón, Calle Sucre y parque la Torre, Cochabamba, Bolivia (office). *Telephone:* (4) 4231765 (office). *E-mail:* laguirre@fcyt.umss.edu.bo (office). *Website:* www.fcyt.umss.edu.bo/investigacion/biodiversidad (office).

ÁGÚSTSSON, Helgi; Icelandic diplomatist; b. 16 Oct. 1941, Reykjavik; s. of Ágúst H. Pétursson and Helga Jóhannesdóttir; m. Hervör Jónasdóttir 1963; three s. one d.; ed Commercial Coll. of Iceland and Univ. of Iceland; joined Ministry for Foreign Affairs 1970; First Sec. and Counsellor, London 1973–77; Dir Defence Div. Ministry for Foreign Affairs and Icelandic Chair. US-Icelandic Defence Council 1979; Minister-Counsellor, Washington, DC 1983–87; Deputy Perm. Sec., Ministry for Foreign Affairs 1987; Amb. to UK (also accred to Ireland, Netherlands and Nigeria) 1989–94; Perm. Sec., Ministry for Foreign Affairs 1995–99; Amb. to Denmark (also accred to Lithuania, Turkey, Israel and Romania) 1998–99, to USA (also accred to Argentina, Brazil, Chile, El Salvador, Guatemala, Mexico and Uruguay) 2002–06; Chief of Protocol, Ministry of Foreign Affairs –2009; fmr Pres. Icelandic Basketball Fed.; Hon. GCVO; Grand Cross of Dannebrog, Kt Commdr of White Rose, Grand Cross of Mérito Civil, Kt Commdr of Pole Star, Grand Cross of the Order of the Falcon, Grand Cross Oranje-Nassau Order, Grand Cross Norwegian Service Order, Grand Cross IMR. *Leisure interest:* salmon fishing, music, chess, theatre. *Address:* Ministry for Foreign Affairs, Rauðarárstíg 25, 150 Reykjavík, Iceland (office). *Telephone:* 5459900 (office). *Fax:* 5622373 (office). *E-mail:* helgiandheba@simnet.is (office). *Website:* www.utanrikisraduneyti.is (office).

AGUT BONSFILLS, Joaquim, BSc, MBA; Spanish media executive; *Director General, CIRSA Gaming Corporation;* ed Univ. Polytécnica de Catalunya, Barcelona, Univ. de Navarra; joined Synthese SA as Dir of Business Devt, Barcelona, Gen. Man. 1980; worked for family-owned co. Agut SA (later acquired by Gen. Electric) 1982; various sr positions with Gen. Electric (GE), including Vice-Pres. and Gen. Man. of Marketing and Sales, Pres. and CEO GE Power Controls, Pres. and CEO GE Nat. Exec. for Spain and Portugal, Chair. Pan European GE Quality Council, Leader of European Corp. Exec. Council (CEC); Chair. Terra Networks –2000; Exec. Chair. Terra Lycos (following merger of Terra and Lycos 2000) 2000–04; Chair. and CEO Endemol Group 2004–06; Dir Gen., CIRSA Gaming Corpn 2006–; Young Businessman of the Year Award 1984. *Address:* CIRSA, Edificio CIRSA, Carretera de Castellar, 298, 08226 Barcelona, Spain (office). *Telephone:* (93) 7396700 (office). *E-mail:* cirsa@cirsa.com (office). *Website:* www.cirsa.com (office).

AGUTTER, Jennifer (Jenny) Ann; British actress and dancer; b. 20 Dec. 1952, Taunton; d. of Derek Brodie Agutter and Catherine Agutter (née Lynam); m. Johan Tham 1990; one s.; ed Elmhurst Ballet School; film debut in East of Sudan 1964; has appeared in numerous TV films, dramas and series and on stage with RSC and Nat. Theatre. *Plays include:* The Tempest, Spring Awakening, Hedda Gabler, Betrayal, The Unified Field, Breaking the Code, Love's Labour's Lost, Peter Pan. *Films include:* Ballerina 1964, Gates of Paradise 1967, Star 1968, I Start Counting, The Railway Children 1969, Walkabout, Logan's Run 1975, The Eagle Has Landed, Equus, The Man in the Iron Mask, Riddle of the Sands, Sweet William, The Survivor 1980, An American Werewolf in London 1981, Secret Places 1983, Dark Tower 1987, King of the Wind 1989, Child's Play 2 1991, Freddie as Fro 7 1993, Blue Juice 1995, English Places, English Faces 1996, The Parole Officer 2001, At Dawning 2001, Number 1, Longing. Number 2, Regret 2004, Heroes and Villains 2006, Irina Palm 2007. *TV includes:* Amy 1980, Not a Penny More, Not a Penny Less 1990, The Good Guys, Puss in Boots 1991, Love Hurts 1994, Heartbeat 1994, September 1995, 1996, The Buccaneers 1995, And The Beat Goes On 1996, A Respectable Trade 1997, Bramwell 1998, The Railway Children 2000, Spooks 2002, The Alan Clark Diaries 2004. *Publication:* Snap 1983. *Leisure interest:* photography. *Address:* c/o Marmont Management, Langham House, 308 Regent Street, London, W1B 3AT, England.

AHADI, Anwar al-Haq, MBA, PhD; Afghan banker, politician and professor of political science; *Minister of Finance;* b. 12 Aug. 1951, Jigdalai, Sarobi Dist; s. of Abdul Haq; m. Fatima Gailani; ed Hibibiya High School, American Univ. of Beirut, Lebanon, Northwestern Univ., Chicago, USA; fmr mem. of staff Continental Bank of Chicago; joined Afghan Mellat Party (Afghan Social Democratic Party) 1969, elected to Supreme Council 1987, 1990, Pres. 1995–; Asst Prof. of Political Sciences, Carlton Univ. 1984; Banking Dir, Continental Elona Bank, Chicago 1985–87; Prof. of Political Sciences, Providence Univ. 1987–2002; Gov. Da Afghanistan Bank (Cen. Bank of Afghanistan) 2002–04; Minister of Finance 2004–. *Address:* Ministry of Finance, Pashtunistan Wat, Kabul, Afghanistan (office). *Telephone:* (75) 2004199 (office). *Fax:* (20) 2103439 (office). *E-mail:* info@mof.gov.af (office). *Website:* www.mof.gov.af (office).

AHARONOV, Yakir, BSc, PhD; Israeli physicist and academic; *Professor of Physics, Tel-Aviv University; Distinguished Professor, University of South Carolina;* b. 1932; ed Technion (Israel Inst. of Tech.), Haifa, Univ. of Bristol, England; Research Assoc., Brandeis Univ., Waltham, Mass, USA 1960–61; Asst Prof., Yeshiva Univ. 1961–64, Assoc. Prof. 1964–67, Prof. 1967–73; Prof. of Physics, Tel-Aviv Univ. 1967–; Distinguished Prof., Univ. of SC, USA 1973–; mem. Israeli Nat. Acad. of Science 1990–, NAS 1993–; Fellow, American Physical Soc. 1981–; Hon. DSc (Technion – Israel Inst. of Tech.) 1992, (Univ. of SC) 1992, (Univ. of Bristol) 1997; Hon. DUniv (Buenos Aires) 1999 Weizmann Prize in Physics 1984, Rothschild Prize in Physics 1984, Israeli Nat. Prize in Physics 1989, Elliot Cresson Medal 1991, Hewlett-Packard Europhysics Prize 1995, Wolf Prize in Physics (jt recipient) 1998. *Publications:* over 140 papers in learned journals. *Address:* School of Physics, Tel-Aviv University, POB 39040, Tel-Aviv 69978, Israel (office). *Telephone:* (3) 640-8159 (office). *E-mail:* beatriz@post.tau.ac.il (office). *Website:* www.minerva.tau.ac.il (office).

AHERN, Bertie; Irish accountant and politician; b. 12 Sept. 1951, Dublin; s. of Cornelius Ahern and Julia Ahern (née Hourihane); m. Miriam Patricia Kelly 1975 (separated); two d.; ed Rathmines Coll. of Commerce (now Dublin Inst. of Tech.), Univ. Coll., Dublin; TD (Fianna Fáil Party) for Dublin-Finglas 1977–81, Dublin Cen. 1981–, Pres. Fianna Fáil 1994–; mem. Dublin City Council 1978–88, Lord Mayor 1986–87; Asst Chief Whip 1980–81; Fianna Fáil Spokesman on Youth Affairs 1981–82; Govt Chief Whip and Minister of State, Depts of the Taoiseach and of Defence March–Dec. 1982; Opposition Chief Whip 1982–84; Fianna Fáil Front Bench spokesman on Labour 1984–87; Minister for Labour 1987–91, for Finance 1991–94, for Industry and Commerce Jan. 1993; Deputy Prime Minister (Tánaiste) and Minister for Arts, Culture and the Gaeltacht Nov.–Dec. 1994; Leader of the Opposition 1994–97; Prime Minister (Taoiseach) of Ireland 1997–2008 (resgnd); Pres. European Council Jan.–June 2004; mem. Bd of Govs IMF 1991–94, World Bank 1991–94; Chair. European Investment Bank 1991–92; Chair. Dublin Millennium Cttee 1988; fmr mem. Bd of Govs Univ. Coll. Dublin, Dublin Port and Docks Bd, Eastern Health Bd, Dublin Chamber of Commerce; Grand Cross, Order of Merit with Star and Sash (Germany) 1991. *Leisure interests:* sports, reading. *Address:* Constituency Office, St. Luke's, 161 Lower Drumcondra Road, Dublin 9, Republic of Ireland (office).

AHERN, Dermot, BCL; Irish politician; *Minister for Justice, Equality and Law Reform;* b. Feb. 1955, Drogheda, Co. Louth; s. of Jeremiah Ahern and Gertrude Alice Ahern (née McGarrity); m. Maeve Coleman; two d.; ed Marist Coll., Dundalk, Univ. Coll., Dublin, Inc. Law Soc. of Ireland; solicitor 1976–; mem. Louth Co. Council 1979–91; mem. Fianna Fáil 1987–; mem. various parl. cttees; Asst Govt Whip 1988–91; Minister of State at Depts of the Taoiseach and Defence, Govt Chief Whip 1991–92; Minister for Social, Community and Family Affairs 1997–2002, for Communications, Marine and Natural Resources 2002–04, Minister for Foreign Affairs 2004–08, Minister for Justice, Equality and Law Reform 2008–; mem. British-Irish Parl. Body 1991–97 (Co-Chair. 1993–95). *Address:* Department of Justice, Equality and Law Reform, 94 St Stephen's Green, Dublin 2, Ireland (office). *Telephone:* (1) 6028202 (office). *Fax:* (1) 6615461 (office). *E-mail:* info@justice.ie (office). *Website:* www.justice.ie (office).

AHLENIUS, Inga-Britt, BBA; Swedish diplomatist, auditor and UN official; *Under-Secretary-General for Internal Oversight Services, United Nations;* b. 19 April 1939, Karlstad; d. of Stig-Olof Grigholm and Inga Montan; three c.; ed Stockholm School of Econs; worked in Econ. Secr. Handelsbanken 1962–63, 1964–68; worked in Dept for Medium-Term Credits, Soc. Tunisienne de Banque, Tunisia 1963–64; Head Section Int. Dept and Budget Dept Ministry of Finance 1975–80, Head Ministerial Dept 1980–87, Head Budget Dept 1987–93; Auditor Gen. Nat. Audit Office 1993–2003; Auditor Gen. of Kosovo 2003–05; UN Under-Sec.-Gen. for Internal Oversight Services 2005–; Chair. Governing Bd European Org. for Supreme Audit Insts. (EUROSAI) 1993–96, Auditing Standards Cttee, Int. Org. Supreme Audit Insts. (INTOSAI) 1995–2003; Public mem. Int. Auditing and Assurance Standards Bd 2005–; mem. Cttee of Ind. Experts in the EU 1999; Dr hc (Royal Inst. of Tech. Stockholm), (Univ. of Lund). *Address:* United Nations Office of Internal Oversight Services, United Nations Plaza, New York, NY 10017, USA (office). *Telephone:* (212) 963-6196 (office). *E-mail:* ahlenius@un.org (office). *Website:* www.un.org/Depts/oios (office).

AHLMARK, Per, BA; Swedish politician, journalist, novelist and poet; *Adviser, Elie Wiesel Foundation for Humanity;* b. 15 Jan. 1939, Stockholm; s. of Prof. Axel Ahlmark; m. 1st (divorced); one s. one d.; m. 2nd Bibi Andersson (q.v.) 1978 (divorced); m. 3rd Lilian Edström; one s.; Leader of Young Liberals 1960–62; columnist for Expressen 1961–95, for Dagens Nyheter 1997–; mem. Parl. 1967–78; Deputy Chair. Swedish-Israeli Friendship Org. 1970–97; mem. Council of Europe 1971–76; mem. Royal Comms. on Literature, Human Rights, etc. in the 1970s; Leader, Folkpartiet (Liberal Party) 1975–78; Deputy Prime Minister and Minister of Labour 1976–78; Deputy Chair. Martin Luther King Fund 1968–73; Chair. Swedish Film Inst. 1978–81; Founder and Deputy Chair. Swedish Comm. Against Antisemitism 1983–95; Adviser to Elie Wiesel Foundation for Humanity, New York 1987–; mem. UN Watch, Geneva 1993–; mem. Acad. Universelle des Cultures, Paris; Fellow Wissenschaftskolleg zu Berlin 1998–99; Hon. Fellow, Hebrew Univ., Jerusalem 1992; Defender of Jerusalem Award, New York 1986. *Publications:* An Open Sore, Tyranny and the Left, many political books, essays and numerous articles, three books of poetry, one novel. *Leisure interest:* books. *Address:* Folkungag 61, 11622 Stockholm, Sweden.

AHLSEN, Leopold; German writer; b. 12 Jan. 1927, Munich; m. Ruth Gehwald 1964; one s. one d.; Gerhart Hauptmann Prize, Schiller-Förderungspreis, Goldener Bildschirm, Hörspielpreis der Kriegsblinden, Silver Nymph of Monte Carlo, Bundesverdienstkreuz and other awards. *Publications:* 13 plays, 23 radio plays, 68 television plays, seven novels. *Leisure interest:* joinery. *Address:* Waldschulstrasse 58, 81827 Munich, Germany (home). *Telephone:* (89) 4301466 (home). *Fax:* (89) 4301466 (home).

AHLSTRÖM, Krister Harry, MSc; Finnish business executive; *Vice-Chairman, StoraEnso;* b. 29 Aug. 1940, Helsinki; s. of Harry F. Ahlström and Asta A. Ahlström (née Seege); m. Anja I. Artto 1974; one s. four d.; ed Helsinki Univ. of Technology; Product Engineer, Gen. Man. and mem. Bd of Man. Oy Wärtsilä Ab 1966–81; Dir and mem. Exec. Bd A. Ahlström Corpn 1981–82, Pres. and CEO 1982–98, Chair. 1998–99; currently Vice-Chair. StoraEnso, Nordea Securities; Chair. Confed. Finnish Employers 1986–92, Fed. of Finnish Metal, Eng and Electrotechnical Industries 1992–96, Orgalime (Organisme de Liaison des Industries Métalliques Européennes) Brussels 1994–96; Chair. Bd of the Research Inst. of the Finnish Economy. *Leisure interests:* sailing (World winner 8mR 1975), skiing. *Address:* c/o A. Ahlström Corporation, PO Box 329, Eteläesplanadi 14, 00101 Helsinki (office); Kvarnvägen 2A2 00140 Helsinki, Finland (home). *Telephone:* (10) 8884761 (office); 500 500788 (home). *Fax:* (10) 8884729 (office); (9) 625560 (home). *E-mail:* krister.ahlstrom@ahlstrom.com (office). *Website:* www.StoraEnso.com (office); www.ahlstrom.com (office).

AHMAD, Maniruddin; Bangladeshi business executive; fmr Chair. Bangladesh Jute Mills Corpn. *Address:* c/o Bangladesh Jute Mills Corporation, Adamjee Court (Annexe), 115–120 Motijheel C/A, Dhaka 1000, Bangladesh (office).

AHMAD, Salman; American composer, songwriter, musician (guitar) and medical doctor; b. 12 Dec. 1963, Lahore, Pakistan; s. of Ejaz Ahmad and Shahine Khan; m. Samina Haq; ed Tappan Zee High School, King Edward Medical Coll., MBBS; early childhood spent travelling the world; returned to Pakistan to study medicine 1982; began musical career in band Vital Signs 1991; founder mem., Junoon (with Ali Azmat and Brian O'Connell) 1990–, banned by Pakistani authorities for criticism of govt corruption early 1990s; upon invitation of UN Sec.-Gen., Kofi Annan, performed at UN Gen. Ass. (first band to play at Gen. Ass.); tours throughout Asia, N America, Middle E and Europe; UN Goodwill Amb. on the issue of HIV/AIDS 2001; appearances in Pakistani TV dramas; currently lives in New York; Jazbe-e-Junoon selected as official song of cricket world cup, hosted by Pakistan 1996; Channel V Music Award for Int. Group 1998, UNESCO Award for Outstanding Achievement in Music and Peace 1999, BBC Asia Award 1999. *Television:* The Rockstar and the Mullah (producer, VH1 documentary) 2002. *Recordings include:* albums:

with Junoon: Junoon 1990, Talaash 1993, Inquilaab 1995, Khashmakash 1996, Azaadi 1997, Parvaaz 1999, Andaz 2001, The Millennium Edition (compilation) 2000, Daur-e-Junoon 2002, Dewaar 2003; solo: Infiniti 2005. *Leisure interests:* cricket, reading, films, theatre. *Address:* Junoon Inc., 210 Old Tappan Road, Tappan, NY 10983, USA (office). *E-mail:* saminadr@gmail .com (office); info@junoon.com. *Website:* www.junoon.com.

AHMAD, Shamshad, MA; Pakistani diplomatist; m.; two s.; ed Univ. of Punjab; diplomatic postings to Tehran 1968–69, Dakar 1969–72, Paris 1972–74, Washington, DC 1977–80; with Mission to UN (Chair. Political Cttee UN Council for Namibia and mem. UN Cttee on Palestine) 1980–81, Consul Gen. 1981–85; Dir-Gen. Ministry of Foreign Affairs 1985–87; Amb. to Repub. of Korea 1987–90, to Iran 1990–92; Sec.-Gen. Econ. Cooperation Org., Tehran 1992–96; Special Sec., Ministry of Foreign Affairs 1996–97, Foreign Sec. 1997–2000; Perm. Rep. to UN, New York 2000–02; mem. ESCAP Panel of Eminent Persons on Human Resources Devt 1994. *Address:* c/o Ministry of Foreign Affairs, Constitution Avenue, Islamabad, Pakistan (office).

AHMAD, Sufyan; Ethiopian politician; currently Minister of Finance and Econ. Devt and Cooperation. *Address:* Ministry of Finance and Economic Development and Cooperation, POB 1037, Addis Ababa, Ethiopia (office). *Telephone:* (11) 1552800 (office). *Fax:* (11) 1550118 (office). *E-mail:* media2@ telecom.net.et.

AHMADINEJAD, Mahmoud, PhD; Iranian politician and head of state; *President;* b. 1956, Garmsar; ed Iran Univ. of Science and Tech. (IUST); joined Islamic Revolutionary Guards Corps 1986; Prof. of Civil Eng, IUST 1989–; Advisor for Cultural Affairs to Minister of Culture and Higher Educ. 1993; fmr Vice-Gov., then Gov. Maku and Khoy; Gov. –Gen. Ardabil prov. 1993–97; Mayor of Tehran 2003–05; Pres. of Iran 2005–; mem. Cen. Council, Islamic Soc. of Engineers; mem. Iran Tunnel Soc., Iran Civil Eng Soc. *Publications include:* numerous articles on political, social, cultural and economic topics. *Address:* Office of the President, Palestine Avenue, Azerbaijan Intersection, Tehran, Iran (office). *E-mail:* webmaster@president.ir (office). *Website:* www .president.ir (office); www.mardomyar.com; www.ahmadinejad.ir.

AHMADJONOV, Muhammadjon A.; Uzbekistani politician; *Chairman, O'zbekiston Liberal Demokratik Partiyasi (Liberal Democratic Party of Uzbekistan);* b. 1955, Kuva, Farg'ona Viloyat; m.; three c.; mem. and Chair. O'zbekiston Liberal Demokratik Partiyasi (Liberal Democratic Party of Uzbekistan) 2004–. *Address:* O'zbekiston Liberal Demokratik Partiyasi, 100015 Tashkent, Mirobod tumani, Nukus ko'ch. 73A, Uzbekistan (office). *Telephone:* (71) 133-28-46 (office). *E-mail:* uzlidep@intal.uz (office).

AHMED, Aneesa; Maldivian politician; *Deputy Speaker, People's Majlis;* b. 29 Sept. 1949, Malé; divorced; one s. one d.; ed studied nursing in India and Australia; staff nurse, Govt Hosp., Male' 1973–77, Sister-in-Charge 1978–80; mem. People's Special Majlis (Presidential nominee) 1979–85, 1993–97, apptd by Pres. 1997–99, mem. People's Majlis for Mulaku Atoll 1999–, Leader Parl. Group Dhivehi Rayyithunge Party 2006–, Deputy Speaker of People's Majlis 2008–; Under-Sec., Ministry of Foreign Affairs 1980–81; Asst to Exec. Sec., Pres. Office 1981–82, Presidential Aide 1982–89, Sr Presidential Aide 1989–92, Dir-Gen. Foreign Relations, Pres.'s Office 1992–98; Deputy Minister of Women's Affairs and Social Security 1998–2002, Minister of Women's Affairs, Family Devt and Social Security 2002–04, of Health 2004–05, of the Pres.'s Office 2005–08. *Leisure interests:* reading, walking. *Address:* M Lonuveli, Raiveri Hingun, Malé 20-02, Maldives (home); People's Majlis, Malé (office). *Telephone:* 3326566 (home). *Website:* www.majlis.gov.mv/pm/ english/index.php (office).

AHMED, Azzam al-, BA; Palestinian politician; b. 1947, Jenin; m.; three c.; ed Baghdad Univ., Iraq; Head, Gen. Union of Palestinian Students (GUPS) in Iraq 1971–74, Deputy Head GUPS Exec. Cttee 1974–80; PLO Rep. to Iraq 1979–94; joined Fatah 1989, served in several sr positions, mem. Revolutionary Council 1989; mem. Parl. 1996–, Minister of Public Works 1996–2003, Minister of Telecommunications and IT 2003, Head, Fatah bloc in Palestinian Legis. Council –2007; Deputy Prime Minister March–June 2007. *Address:* c/o Fatah (Harakat at-Tahrir al-Watani al-Filastin—Palestine National Liberation Movement), Gaza, Palestinian Autonomous Areas. *E-mail:* fateh@fateh .net. *Website:* www.fateh.net.

AHMED, Fakhruddin, BA, MA, PhD; Bangladeshi economist, civil servant and fmr central banker; *Honourable Chief Adviser, in charge of Cabinet Division, of the Ministry of Establishment and the Ministry of Information;* b. 1 May 1940, Munshiganj, British India; s. of Dr Mohiuddin Ahmed and Firoza Akhter Khatun; m. Neena Ahmed; one s.; ed Dhaka Univ., Williams Coll., USA, Princeton Univ., USA; began career as Lecturer in Econs, Dhaka Univ.; served in Civil Service of Pakistan and in Govt of Bangladesh –1978, lastly as Jt Sec., Econ. Relations Div., Ministry of Finance; several sr positions at World Bank, Washington, DC, USA 1978–2001; Gov. Bangladesh Bank 2001–05; Chair. Palli Karma-Sahayak Foundation (apex fund) 2005–07; Hon. Chief Adviser of Caretaker Govt of Bangladesh, in charge of Cabinet Div., of Ministry of Establishment, of Ministry of Home Affairs and of Election Comm. Secr. 2007–08, Honourable Chief Adviser, in charge of Cabinet Div. of the Ministry of Establishment and the Ministry of Information 2008–. *Address:* Honourable Chief Adviser's Office, Old Sangshad Bhaban, Tejgaon, Dhaka, Bangladesh (office). *Telephone:* (2) 8151157 (office). *Fax:* (2) 8113244 (office). *E-mail:* info@pmo.gov.bd (office). *Website:* www.pmo.gov.bd (office).

AHMED, Maj. Hafizuddin; Bangladeshi army officer (retd) and politician; fmr Minister of Water Resources, of Commerce; mem. Standing Cttee and Vice-Pres. Bangladesh Jatiyatabadi Dal (Bangladesh Nationalist Party), apptd Sec.-Gen. of faction Oct. 2007–. *Address:* Bangladesh Jatiyatabadi Dal, Banani Office, House 23, Road 13, Dhaka, Bangladesh (office). *Telephone:* (2) 8819525 (office). *Fax:* (2) 8813063 (office). *E-mail:* bnpbd@e-fsbd.net (office). *Website:* www.bnpbd.com (office).

AHMED, Iajuddin, BSc, MS, PhD; Bangladeshi soil scientist, academic, politician and head of state; *President;* b. 1 Feb. 1931, Nayagoan, Munshiganj Dist; s. of the late Maulvi Mohammad Ibrahim; m. Anwara Begum; three c.; ed Munshiganj Haraganga Coll., Dhaka Univ., Univ. of Wisconsin, USA; Asst Prof., Dept of Soil Sciences, Dhaka Univ. 1963, Assoc. Prof. 1964–1973, Prof. 1973, Chair. of Dept 1968–69, 1976–79, Provost, Salimullah Muslim Hall 1975–1983, Dean, Faculty of Biological Sciences 1989–1990, 1990–91; Visiting Prof., Cornell Univ. 1983, German Tech. Univ., Berlin 1984, Gatinzens Univ., Germany 1984; adviser to caretaker govt 1991; Chair. Public Service Comm. 1991–93; Chair. Univ. Grants Comm. 1995–99; fmr Chancellor, State Univ. of Bangladesh; Pres. of Bangladesh 2002–, Chief Adviser (Head of Caretaker Govt), Minister of Foreign Affairs, of Defence, of Home Affairs 2006–07; mem. Bangladesh Jatiyabadi Dal (Bangladesh Nationalist Party); mem. Int. Soil Science Asscn, Indian Soil Science Asscn, Bangladesh Soil Science Asscn, Asiatic Soc.; Ibrahim Memorial Gold Medal 1987–88, Sri Gjyan Atish Dipanker Gold Medal 1990, Ekushey Award for Educ. 1995. *Address:* President's Secretariat, Old Sansad Bhaban, Dhaka, Bangladesh (office).

AHMED, Jameel Yusuf; Pakistani civil servant; *Co-Chief, Citizen Police Liaison Committee;* b. 10 May 1946, Hyderabad Deccan, India; s. of Yusuf Ahmed and of Amina Yusuf; m.; one s. two d.; ed Karachi Polytechnic Inst.; industrialist in paper cone mfg co. 1969; convenor Citizen Police Liaison Cttee (CPLC) Reporting Cell (est. to restore confidence in police service) 1989, Co-Chief CPLC 1990–, mem. numerous police reform cttees; mem. Bd of Govs Karachi Public Transport and Social Educ. Soc. (KPTC) 1999–; mem. Advisory Bd Interior Div., Fed. Ministry of the Interior 2000–; Hon. Sec. Bd of Govs Al-Murtaza School Network Charitable Trust 1989–, Chair. Steering Cttee Professional Devt Centre, Al-Murtaza 2001–; mem. Man. Cttee Zainabia Housing Trust 1990–, Steering Cttee NGO Resource Centre, Aga Khan Foundation 2001–; Founder and Trustee Panah Women's Shelter 2001–; Sitara-e-Shujaat 1992, Mulla Asghar Memorial Int. Award for Excellence in Educ. 2002. *Address:* CPCL-Central Reporting Cell, Sindh Governor's Secretariat, Gate No. 4, Abdullah Haroon Road, Karachi - 75580 (office); 37-L/1, Block-6, PECHS, Karachi, Pakistan (home). *Telephone:* (21) 568222 (office); (21) 4546428 (home). *Fax:* (21) 5683336 (office). *E-mail:* clcp@gerrys.net (office); juchief@hotmail.com (home).

AHMED, Kamal U.; Bangladeshi television executive; *Director General, Bangladesh Television;* fmr Ed. BBC Bangla Service, London, UK; currently Jt Sec. of Information and Dir Gen. Bangladesh Television. *Address:* National Broadcasting Authority Bhaban, 121 Kazi Nazrul Islam Avenue, Shahbagh, Dhaka - 1000, Bangladesh (office). *Telephone:* (2) 861-6606 (office). *Fax:* (2) 862-4839 (office). *E-mail:* dg@btv.gov.bd (office). *Website:* www.btv.gov.bd (office).

AHMED, Khurshid, BA, LLB; Pakistani trade union official; *General-Secretary, Pakistan Workers Federation;* b. 13 July 1936, Lahore; s. of Bashid Ahmad Dar and Naseem Ahmed (née Begum); m. Sahaira Nasreen; two s. four d.; active in trade union movt in Pakistan 1956–; Chair. Bukhtiar Memorial Computer Training Centre, Lahore, Faisalabad, Gujranwala and Hyderabad; Vice-Pres. ILO Conf., Geneva 1986; Gen.-Sec. Pakistan Workers Fed. and Pakistan Wapda Hydroelectric Cen. Labour Union; mem. Pakistan Tripartite Cttee, Pakistan Workers Labour Comm., Nat. Industrial Relations Comm.; Sec. and Trustee Bukhtiar Labour Welfare Trust; Ed. Pak Workers. Pakistan Workers journal; elected mem. ILO Governing Body, Geneva since early 1970s; Rep., Int. Workers Group; Sitara Imtaz of Pakistan. *Publications include:* (in Urdu) Trade Union Struggle in Pakistan, Trade Union Struggle of WAPDA Workers, International Labour Organisation, The Challenge of the 21st Century and the Role of the Working Class of Pakistan, Socio-Economic Problems Facing the Working Class of the Country, Responsibility of the Labour Movement of Pakistan; (in English) Dignity of Labour, Journalism on Labour Issues, History of Labour Movement in Pakistan; regular contrib. to nat. press on current labour issues. *Address:* Bakhtiar Labour Hall, 28-Nisbat Road, Lahore, Pakistan (office); Sadiq Colony, Mumtaz Street, Ghari Shau, Lahore, Pakistan (home). *Telephone:* (42) 7222192 (office); (42) 7229419 (office); (42) 6363097 (home). *Fax:* (42) 7239524 (office). *E-mail:* gs@pwf.org.pk (office). *Website:* www.pwf.org.pk (office).

AHMED, Mahmud Yayale, MA, BA; Nigerian civil servant and government official; *Secretary to the Government of the Federation;* b. 15 April 1952, Shira, Bauchi State; s. of Mallam Ahmadu; m.; seven c.; ed Ahmadu Bello Univ., Zaria; began his civil service career, Bauchi State 1977; served as Vice Prin., Makurdi community secondary school; Deputy Sec., Ministry of Animal Health and Forestry Resources 1982–83; Acting Perm. Sec., Ministry of Rural Devt and Cooperatives 1983–84; based at Ministry of Finance and Econ. Planning 1984–86; joined Fed. Civil Service 1986, served in various posts including Admin. Officer I, Sec. CIPBS, Dir Finance and Accounts, Dir-Gen., Perm. Sec. and Head of Service of the Fed.; fmr mem. Council, Bauchi Coll. of Arts and Science, Coll. of Educ., Azare, Coll. of Legal and Islamic Studies, Misau; Minister of Defence 2007–08; Sec. to the Govt of the Fed. 2008–; Ajiyan Katagum, Akowonio of Idanre Kingdom; Hon. LLD (Abuja), Hon. DLit (Bayero Univ., Kano). *Address:* Office of the Head of State, New Federal Secretariat Complex, Shehu Shagari Way, Central Area District, Abuja, Nigeria (office). *Telephone:* (9) 5233536 (office).

AHMED, Lt-Gen. Moeen U.; Bangladeshi army officer; *Chief of Army Staff;* m. Begum Naznin Moeen; one s. one d.; ed Defence Services Command and Staff Coll., Mirpur, US Army Command and Staff Coll., Harvard Univ., Centre for Security Studies of Hawaii, USA; began mil. service 1975, fmr positions include Weapons Training Officer, Platoon Commdr Bangladesh

Mil. Acad., Brigade Maj., Infantry Brigade, Grade One Staff Officer, Mil. Operations Directorate, Army HQ, Col Infantry Div., Directing Staff Defence Services Command and Staff Coll., Sr Instructor Army Wing, later Chief Instructor, Commdt School of Infantry and Tactics, Mil. Sec. and Master Gen. of Ordnance, Army HQ, promoted to rank of Lt-Gen. 2005, Chief of Army Staff 2005–; fmr Defence Adviser, High Comm. in Pakistan; served with UN Assistance Mission for Rwanda (UNAMIR); Force Commdr's Commendation, US Forces Commendation. *Address:* Office of the Chief of Army Staff, Army Headquarters, GS Branch, Dhaka, Bangladesh (office). *Telephone:* (2) 8752348 (office). *Fax:* (2) 8754455 (office). *E-mail:* itdte@army.mil.bd (office). *Website:* www.bangladesharmy.org (office).

AHMED, Moudud, MA; Bangladeshi politician and barrister; b. 1940, Noakhali; s. of the late Bara Moulana; m. Hasna Jasimuddin; two s.; ed Dhaka Univ.; fmr Gen. Sec. E Pakistan House, UK; took an active part in struggle for independence, organizing External Publicity Div. of Bangladesh Govt in exile; Ed. Bangladesh (weekly); lawyer, Bangladesh Supreme Court 1972–74; Gen. Sec. Cttee for Civil Liberties Legal Aid 1974; imprisoned during State of Emergency 1974; Head, Bangladesh del. to 32nd Session UN Gen. Ass. 1977; Adviser to Pres. 1977; Minister of Communications 1985–86, Deputy Prime Minister in charge of Ministry of Industries 1986–88, Prime Minister and Minister of Industry 1988–89, Vice-Pres. 1989–90; under house arrest 1990–91, imprisoned Dec. 1991, later released; Minister of Law, Justice and Parl. Affairs 2001–06; facing charges of possession of contraband liquor June 2007; Visiting Fellow South Asian Inst. of Heidelberg Univ., Harvard Univ. Centre for Int. Affairs, Univ. of Oxford, UK. *Publications:* Bangladesh Contemporary Events and Documents, Bangladesh Constitutional Quest for Autonomy 1974, Democracy and the Challenge of Development: A Study of Politics and Military Interventions in Bangladesh. *Address:* Islam Chamber, 9th floor, 125/A, Motijheel C/A, Dhaka 1000, Bangladesh (office). *Telephone:* (2) 9888694 (home).

AHMED, Ougoureh Kifleh; Djibouti politician; *Minister of Defence;* Leader Front pour la Restauration de l'Unité et de la Démocratie (FRUD–a splinter group in Afar guerilla movt) 1994, currently Sec.-Gen.; fmr Minister for the Public Office and Admin. Reforms; fmr Minister of Agric.; currently Minister of Defence. *Address:* Ministry of Defence, BP 42, Djibouti (office). *Telephone:* 352034 (office).

AHMED, Qazi Hussain, MSc; Pakistani politician; *Chairman, Jamaat-e-Islami Pakistan;* b. 1938, Dist of Nowshera, North-West Frontier Prov. (NWFP); s. of Qazi Muhammad Abdul Rab; m.; four c.; ed Islamic Coll., Peshawar; teacher; mem. Jamaat-e-Islami Pakistan (JIP) 1970–, fmr Pres. Peshawar Br., Party Sec., Pres. for NWFP, Sec.-Gen. of JIP 1978–87, Chair. 1987–; mem. Senate of Pakistan 1986–96, resigned in protest against corrupt political system, re-elected 2002–; mem. Muttahida Majlis-e-Amal alliance 2002–, Pres. 2004–. *Leisure interest:* poetry. *Address:* Jamaat-e-Islami Pakistan, Mansoorah, Multan Road, Lahore 54570 (office); Ziarat Kaka Sahib, Nowshera District, NWFP, Pakistan (home). *Telephone:* (42) 5419504 (office). *Fax:* (42) 5419505 (office). *E-mail:* uroobah@pol.com.pk (office). *Website:* www.jamaat.org.

AHMED, Salahuddin, BSc, MA, LLM; Bangladeshi lawyer and government official; *Attorney-General;* b. 8 Feb. 1948, Dhaka; ed London School of Econs, UK, Dhaka Univ., Colombia Univ., USA; Asst Prof., Dept of Econs, Dhaka Univ. 1971–77, Asst Prof., Inst. of Business Admin, Dhaka Univ. 1980–83; began practising law 1980, lawyer at High Court 1982–2008; Assoc. Counsel, Dr Kamal Hossain & Assocs (law firm), Dhaka –2008; Additional Attorney-Gen. 2007–08, Attorney-Gen. 2008–; mem. Supreme Court Bar Asscn, Human Rights Bangladesh, South Asian Asscn for Regional Co-operation in Law, Bangladesh Chapter. *Address:* Office of the Attorney General, Bangladesh Supreme Court, Dhaka 2 (office); c/o Dr Kamal Hossain & Associates, Chamber Building, 2nd Floor, 122-124 Motijheel CA, Dhaka 1000, Bangladesh. *Telephone:* (2) 433585 (office). *E-mail:* info@minlaw.gov.bd (office).

AHMED, Salehuddin, MA, PhD; Bangladeshi central banker; *Governor and Chairman, Bangladesh Bank;* m.; two c.; ed Dhaka Univ., McMaster Univ., Canada; Lecturer in Econs, Dhaka Univ. 1970; joined civil service and served in various admin. capacities, including in Centre on Integrated Rural Devt for Asia and the Pacific, Dhaka; fmr Dir-Gen. Bangladesh Acad. for Rural Devt, Comilla, NGO Affairs Bureau of Office of the Prime Minister; Man. Dir Palli Karma Sahayak Foundation (apex funding agency of macro-credit operations in Bangladesh) 1996–2005; Gov. and Chair. Bangladesh Bank (cen. bank) 2005–; mem. advisory bodies of several govt and non-govt agencies in Bangladesh; Distinguished Alumni Award, McMaster Univ. 2006. *Publications:* more than 60 books, reports and journal articles. *Address:* Bangladesh Bank, Motijheel C/A, PO Box 325, Dhaka 1000, Bangladesh (office). *Telephone:* (2) 7120106 (office). *Fax:* (2) 9566212 (office). *E-mail:* governor@bangla.net (office). *Website:* www.bangladeshbank.org (office).

AHMED, Shahabuddin, MA; Bangladeshi fmr head of state and judge; b. 1930, Pemai of Kendua, Greater Mymensingh Dist; s. of Talukder Risat A. Bhuiyan (deceased); two s. three d.; ed Dhaka Univ., Lahore Civil Service Acad., Univ. of Oxford, UK; joined Civil Service of Pakistan 1954 as Sub-Div. Officer, later Additional Deputy Commr; transferred to Judicial Br. 1960; fmr Additional Dist and Sessions Judge, Dhaka and Barisal; fmr Dist and Sessions Judge, Comilla and Chittagong; fmr Registrar High Court of E Pakistan; elevated to High Court Bench 1972; apptd Judge of Appellate Div., Supreme Court of Bangladesh 1980; Chief Justice 1990, 1991–95; Chair. Labour Appellate Tribunal 1973–74, Bangladesh Red Cross Soc. 1978–82, Comm. of Inquiry into police shootings of students 1983, Nat. Pay Comm. 1984; Vice-Pres. League of Red Cross and Red Crescent Soc., Geneva, Switzerland; Acting Pres. of Bangladesh 1990–91, Pres. 1996–2001; Hon. Master Hon. Soc.

of Gray's Inn, London. *Address:* House Dal Motia, nr Mohammadpur, Dhaka, Bangladesh.

AHMED, Hon. Sheikh Riaz, BA, LLB; Pakistani judge; b. 9 March 1938, s. of the late Sheikh Mansoor Ahmed; Asst Advocate Gen. Punjab 1974–1980, Advocate Gen. 1980–84; Judge Lahore High Court 1984, Chief Justice June–Nov. 1997; Judge Supreme Court 1995–2002, Chief Justice 2002–04. *Address:* c/o Supreme Court of Pakistan, Constitution Avenue, Islamabad, Pakistan.

AHMED, Air Chief Marshal Tanvir Mehmood, MSc; Pakistani air force officer; *Chief of Air Staff;* b. 1952; m.; four c.; ed Pakistan Air Force (PAF) Public School, Sargodha, PAF Acad., Risalpur, Turkish Air War Coll. and Nat. Defence Coll., Islamabad; joined PAF and took fighter and operational conversion courses, qualified flying instructor and combat commdr on fighter aircraft, commanded Fighter Squadron, F-16s Flg Wing, PAF Base, Sargodha and PAF Acad., Risalpur, Deputy Dir in Operations Br., Personal Staff Officer to two Air Chiefs, Dir F-16 project, Sr Air Staff Officer at Northern Air Command, Peshawar and Dir-Gen. Air Weapons Complex, Wah, served as Deputy Chief Air Staff Admin and Operations; served in UAE Air Force as fighter instructor pilot; Vice-Chief of Air Staff 2003–06, Chief of Air Staff 2006–; Sitara-i-Basalat, Sitara-i-Imtiaz (Mil.), Hilal-i-Imtiaz (Mil.). *Address:* Office of the Chief of Air Staff, Ministry of Defence, Pakistan Secretariat, No. II, Rawalpindi 46000, Pakistan (office). *Telephone:* (51) 9271107 (office). *Fax:* (51) 9271113 (office).

AHMETI, Ali; Macedonian politician; *President, Democratic Union for Integration;* b. 4 Jan. 1959, Zajas, Kičevo municipality; m.; one s. one d.; ed Prishtina Univ.; political activist as student; imprisoned for taking part in demonstrations by Kosovo Albanians 1981; granted asylum in Switzerland 1986; active in dissident People's Movt of Kosovo throughout 1980s; Founding mem. Kosovo Liberation Army 1996; Co-founder Democratic Union for Integration 1999, Pres. 2002–; elected mem. Parl. 2002; elected Supreme Commdr and Political Rep. of Nat. Liberation Army in Macedonia 2001; formed multi-ethnic coalition Govt with Prime Minister Branko Crvenkovski's Together for Macedonia coalition Oct. 2002. *Address:* 1200 Tetova, Reçicë e vogël, Rruga 170 nr. 2 (office); Parliamentary Assembly Buildings, 1000 Skopje, Stojan Andov, 11 Oktomvri bb, Former Yugoslav Republic of Macedonia (office). *Telephone:* (4) 4334398 (office). *Fax:* (4) 4334397 (office). *E-mail:* bdi@bdi.org.mk (office). *Website:* www.bdi.org.mk (office).

AHMETI, Vilson; Albanian politician; b. 5 Sept. 1951; ed Univ. of Tirana; engineer, Vehicles Workshop, Tirana 1973–78; mem. Foreign Trade Dept Makina-Import 1978–87; Deputy Minister of Food 1987; Minister of Industry March–June 1991, of Food June–Dec. 1991; Prime Minister of Albania 1991–92; convicted of abusing power Sept. 1993, sentenced to two years' imprisonment, case abandoned due to lack of evidence 1995.

AHN, Hyun-soo; South Korean short-track speed skater; b. 23 Nov. 1985, Seoul; ed Korea Nat. Sport Univ.; began speed skating at Myungji Elementary School aged eight; debut for S Korea, Olympic Games, Salt Lake City, USA 2002; bronze medal, 500m, World Championships, Beijing 2005; silver medal, 1000m and Overall, World Championships, Montreal 2002, 1000m, Warsaw 2003, 1000m and 5000m Relay, Beijing 2005; gold medal, 5000m Relay, World Championships, Montreal 2002, 1500m, 5000m Relay and Overall 2003, 1000m, 1500m, 5000m Relay and Overall, World Championships, Gothenburg 2004, 1500m and Overall, World Championships, Beijing 2005; World Cup ranking: third, 500m and 1000m 2002/03, second, 1500m 2002/03, 500m 2003/05, 1000m and 1500m 2004/05, 1000m 2005/06, first, 1000m and 1500m 2003/04, 500m and 1500m 2005/06, third, Overall 2004/05, second, Overall 2002/03, first, Overall 2003/04, 2005/06; bronze medal, 500m, Olympic Games, Turin 2006; gold medal, 1000m, 1500m and 5000m Relay, Olympic Games, Turin 2006. *Leisure interest:* watching movies. *Address:* c/o Korea Skating Union, Room 412, Olympic Center, 88 Bangyee-Dong, Songpa-Ku, Seoul 138-749, Republic of Korea. *Telephone:* (2) 422-6165. *Fax:* (2) 423-8097. *E-mail:* skating@sports.or.kr. *Website:* www.skating.or.kr.

AHO, Esko Tapani, MA; Finnish politician and organization executive; *President, Finnish National Fund for Research and Development (Sitra);* b. 20 May 1954, Veteli; s. of Kauko Kaleva Aho and Laura Kyllikki (née Harjupatana) Aho; m. Kirsti Hannele Söderkultalahti 1980; two s. one d.; Chair. Youth Org. of the Centre Party 1974–80, Chair. Finnish Centre Party (KESK) 1990–2002; Political Sec. to Minister of Foreign Affairs 1979–80; Trade Agent, Kannus 1980–; mem. Parl. 1983–; Prime Minister of Finland 1991–95; presidential cand. 2000; Lecturer, Harvard Univ., USA; currently Pres. Finnish Nat. Fund for Research and Development (Sitra). *Leisure interests:* literature, tennis, theatre. *Address:* Sitra, Itämerentori 2, PL 160, 00181 Helsinki, Finland (office). *Telephone:* (9) 618991 (office). *Fax:* (9) 645072 (office). *E-mail:* aho.esko@sitra.fi (office). *Website:* www.sitra.fi (office).

AHRENDS, Peter, AADipl, RIBA; British architect; *Director, Ahrends, Burton and Koralek;* b. 30 April 1933, Berlin, Germany; s. of Steffen Bruno Ahrends and Margarete Marie Sophie Ahrends (née Visino); m. Elizabeth Robertson 1954; two d.; ed King Edward VII School, Johannesburg, Architectural Asscn, London; research into decoration in Islamic Architecture 1956; Visiting Critic and/or External Examiner Kumasi Univ., Architectural Asscn School of Architecture, Nova Scotia Tech. Univ., Univ. of Strathclyde; with Steffen Ahrends & Partners, Johannesburg 1957–58; with Denys Lasdun & Partners 1959–60; with Julian Keable & Partners; teacher, Architectural Asscn School of Architecture 1960–61; f. architectural practice Ahrends, Burton and Koralek 1961, Partner, Dir 1961–; Visiting Prof., Kingston Polytechnic 1983–84; teacher and conducted workshops Architectural Asscn School of Architecture, Canterbury Art School, Univ. of Edinburgh, Winter School, Edinburgh, Plymouth Polytechnic, Plymouth Art School; Prof., Bartlett

School of Architecture and Planning, Univ. Coll. London 1986–89; comms include Trinity Coll. Library, Dublin 1961 and Arts Faculty Bldg 1979, Chichester Theological Coll. residential bldg (Grade II listed) 1965, Templeton Coll. (Grade II listed), Oxford 1969, Nebenzahl House, Jerusalem 1972, Habitat Warehouse & Showroom, Wallingford 1974, Residential Bldg, Keble Coll. (Grade II* listed), Oxford 1976, Nat. Gallery Extension 1982–85, Cummins Engines Factory, Shotts 1983, J. Sainsbury Supermarket, Canterbury 1984, W. H. Smith Retail HQ, Swindon, Phase I 1985, Phase 2 1995, Office Devt for Stanhope Trafalgar 1990, St Mary's Hosp., Newport, Isle of Wight 1990, John Lewis Dept Store, Kingston 1990, White Cliffs Heritage Centre, Dover 1991, Poplar Footbridge, London Docklands 1992, Docklands Light Railway, Beckton Extension Stations 1993, Techniquest Science Centre, Cardiff 1995, Whitworth Art Gallery Sculpture Court 1995, Insts of Tech. at Waterford 1998, Tralee 2001, and Blanchardstown, Ireland 2002, Loughborough Univ. Business School 1998, Dublin Dental Hosp. extension 1998, Waterford Visitor Centre 1999, New British Embassy, Moscow 2000, Carrickmines Croquet and Lawn Tennis Club 2000, Dublin Inner City Devt Study 2000, Co. Offices at N Tullamore, Offaly 2002, Riding Tipperary 2004, Cork 2007, Dublin Corpn NEIC Civic Centre 2000–01, housing at Newcastle West and Limerick, Ireland 2004, Arts Faculty Ext., Trinity Coll., Dublin 2002, Galway Co. Council Civic Offices Ext., New Library and HQ 2002, Bexhill Town Centre Devt Plan 2004, Riverside building, Trinity Buoy Wharf, London, John Wheatley College, Glasgow; mem. Design Council; Chair. UK Architects Against Apartheid 1988–93; Design Adviser, London Devt Agency; RIBA Good Design in Housing Award 1977, RIBA Architecture Award 1978, 1993, 1996, 1999, Structural Steel Design Award 1980, Structural Steel Design Commendation 1993; RIAI Architecture Award 1999, Gulbenkian Museum of the Year Award 1999, Designs on Democracy Competition Winner. *Publications:* Ahrends, Burton & Koralek, Architects (monograph) 1991; collaborations: The Architecture of ABK 2002; numerous articles in professional journals. *Leisure interests:* architecture and architecture-related interests. *Address:* Ahrends Burton & Koralek, 7 Chalcot Road, London, NW1 8LH, England (office). *Telephone:* (20) 7586-3311 (office). *Fax:* (20) 7722-5445 (office). *E-mail:* abk@abklondon.com (office). *Website:* www.abk.co.uk (office).

AHRENDTS, Angela, BA; American retail executive; *CEO, Burberry Ltd;* b. New Palestine, Ind.; m. Gregg Ahrendts; one s. two d.; ed Ball State Univ.; Pres. Donna Karan International 1989–96; Exec. Vice-Pres. Henri Bendel 1996–98; Vice-Pres. Merchandising and Design, Liz Claiborne Inc. 1998–99, Sr Vice-Pres. Corp. Merchandising and Group Pres. for Modern Brands 1999–2002, Exec. Vice-Pres. 2002–05; Exec. Dir Burberry Ltd Jan. 2006–, CEO July 2006–; ranked by Forbes Magazine amongst 100 Most Powerful Women (66th) 2007, ranked by Fortune magazine amongst 50 Most Powerful Women in Business outside the US (18th) 2007, ranked by the Financial Times amongst Top 25 Businesswomen in Europe (11th) 2007. *Address:* Burberry Ltd, 18–22 Haymarket, London, SW1 4DQ, England (office). *Telephone:* (20) 7968-0412 (office). *Fax:* (20) 7318-2666 (office). *Website:* www.burberry.com (office); www.burberryplc.com (office).

AHRWEILER, Hélène, DenHist, DèsL; French university professor and administrator; *Rector, University of Europe, Paris;* b. 28 Aug. 1926, Athens, Greece; d. of Nicolas Glykatzi and Calliroe Psaltides; m. Jacques Ahrweiler 1958; one d.; ed Univ. of Athens; Sorbonne Paris; Research Worker CNRS 1955–67, Head of Research 1964–67; apptd Prof. Sorbonne 1967, now Prof. Emer.; Pres. Univ. de Paris I 1976–81; Rector Acad., Chancellor Univs of Paris 1982–89; Chair. and Pres. Terra Foundation for the Arts (Chicago); Sec.-Gen. Int. Cttee of Historical Sciences 1980–90; Vice-Pres. Conseil d'Orientation du Centre Georges Pompidou 1975–89, Conseil Supérieur de l'Education Nationale 1983–89; Pres. Centre Georges Pompidou 1989–91; currently Rector, Univ. of Europe, Paris; Pres. Comité d'Ethique des Sciences (CNRS) 1994; Pres. Admin Council, European Cultural Centre of Delphi, Nat. Theatre, Athens; mem. Greek, British, Belgian, German and Bulgarian Acads; Commdr de la Légion d'honneur; Commdr Ordre nat. du Mérite; Commdr des Arts et Lettres; Officier des Palmes académiques; numerous foreign decorations; Dr hc (London, New York, Belgrade, Harvard (USA), Lima, New Brunswick (Canada), Athens Social Science Univ., American Univ. of Paris, Haifa, Fribourg). *Publications:* Byzance et la Mer 1966, Etudes sur les structures administratives et sociales de Byzance 1971, l'Idéologie politique de l'empire byzantin 1975, Byzance: les pays et les territoires 1976, Geographica 1981, The Making of Europe 2000, Les Européens 2001; three volumes of poetry in Greek; contribs to numerous books. *Leisure interests:* tennis, swimming. *Address:* 28 rue Guynemer, 75006 Paris, France (home). *Telephone:* 1-42-22-08-47 (home). *Fax:* 1-45-44-46-49 (home).

AHSAN, Chaudhry Aitzaz; Pakistani barrister, writer, human rights activist and politician; b. 27 Sept. 1945, Murree, Punjab; ed Aitchison Coll. and Government Coll., Lahore, Univ. of Cambridge, UK; called to the Bar, Gray's Inn, London 1967; came first in Cen. Superior Services examination but refused to join govt service during mil. rule of Gen. Ayub Khan; currently Sr Advocate, Supreme Court; Pres. Supreme Court Bar Asscn; fought cases in defence of Benazir Bhutto 2001 and fmr Prime Minister Nawaz Sharif, successfully represented Chief Justice Iftikhar Mohammad Chaudhry in Supreme Court of Pakistan 2007; began political career 1970s; mem. Pakistan People's Party (PPP); elected to Punjab Ass. and inducted into prov. cabinet, given portfolio of Information, Planning and Devt 1977 (resgnd); expelled from PPP; became an active leader of Movt for the Restoration of Democracy (MRD) following coup by Gen. Mohammad Zia-ul-Haq, rejoined PPP during martial law period, jailed several times as a political prisoner without trial for active participation in MRD movt; elected to Nat. Ass. from Lahore as PPP cand. 1988, re-elected 1990, lost seat 1993, elected to Senate 1994, Leader of House and Leader of Opposition 1996–99, re-elected to Nat. Ass. as PPP cand. for his traditional seat in Lahore, as well as from Bahawalnagar in Southern Punjab 2002, mem. Standing Cttee on Interior and Standing Cttee on Public Accounts; Fed. Minister for Law and Justice, Interior, Narcotics Control 1988–90; has been under arrest periodically for his involvement in effort to restore Iftikhar Mohammad Chaudhry as Chief Justice of Pakistan following suspension of constitution and removal of Chief Justice Chaudhry from the bench by Pres. Pervez Musharraf 2007; Founder and Vice-Pres. Human Rights Comm. of Pakistan; Asian Human Rights Defender Award, Asian Human Rights Comm., Hong Kong 2008, Award for Distinction in Int. Law and Affairs, New York State Bar Asscn 2008. *Publications:* The Indus Saga and the Making of Pakistan (also Urdu trans., Sindh Sagar Aur Qyam-e-Pakistan), Divided by Democracy (with Lord Meghnad Desai). *Address:* Supreme Court Bar Association of Pakistan, Supreme Court of Pakistan Building, Constitution Avenue, Islamabad, Pakistan (office). *Telephone:* (51) 9215185 (office). *Fax:* (51) 9214862 (office). *E-mail:* info@scbap.org (office). *Website:* www.scbap.org (office).

AHTISAARI, Martti; Finnish diplomatist and fmr head of state; *Chairman, Crisis Management Initiative;* b. 23 June 1937, Viipuri; s. of Oiva Ahtisaari and Tyyne Ahtisaari; m. Eeva Irmeli Hyvärinen 1968; one s.; ed Univ. of Oulu; joined Finnish Ministry for Foreign Affairs 1965, worked in various positions in Ministry's Bureau for Tech. Cooperation 1965–72, Asst Dir 1971–72; Deputy Dir Ministry for Foreign Affairs, Dept for Int. Devt Co-operation 1972–73; mem. Govt Advisory Cttee on Trade and Industrialisation Affairs of Developing Countries 1971–73; Amb. to Tanzania 1973–76 (also accred to Zambia, Somalia and Mozambique 1975–76); mem. Senate of UN Inst. for Namibia 1975–76; UN Commr for Namibia 1977–81, Special Rep. of Sec.-Gen. for Namibia 1978; Under-Sec. of State in charge of Int. Devt Co-operation, Ministry for Foreign Affairs 1984–86; UN Envoy, Head of operation monitoring Namibia's transition to independence 1989–90, Sr Envoy, participated in peace-making efforts in fmr Yugoslavia 1992–93; Pres. of Finland 1994–2000; EU's Special Envoy on Crisis in Kosovo 1999, Special Envoy of the Sec.-Gen. of the UN for the Future Status Process for Kosovo 2005–08; mem. observer group on Austrian Govt's human rights record 2000; Co-Insp. of IRA arms dumps 2000–01; Head UN fact-finding mission into Israeli operation in Jenin refugee camp 2002; Chair. Int. Crisis Group –2004; mem. Bd War-torn Societies Project Int., Balkan Children and Youth Foundation; mem. Open Soc. Inst. Int. Adviser's Group, Exec. Bd of Int. Inst. for Democracy and Electoral Assistance –2003, Jt Advisers' Group Soros Foundations; Chair. Global Action Council of Int. Youth Foundation, Int. Bd WSP Int., founder and Chair. Crisis Man. Initiative, Helsinki 2000–; Chair. Int. Crisis Group –2004; Co-Chair. EastWest Inst. –2005; Chair. Supervisory Bd Finnish Nat. Opera; mem. Bd of Trustees Averett Univ., Inter Press Service Int. Asscn; Hon. Chair. Pro Baltica Forum, Advisory Cttee of Eurasia Foundation, Int. Cttee of Vyborg Library; Hon. Trustee American-Scandinavian Foundation; mem. Steering Cttee Northern Research Forum; Patron Koeppler Appeal; mem. Bd of Dirs Elcoteq SE, UPM-Kymmene, Naantali Music Festival, EUSTORY; Hon. AO 2002, Order of the Companion of Oliver Tambo 2004; Dr hc (Univ. of Oulu) 1959, 1989, (Bentley Coll., Waltham, Mass) 1990, (Kasetsart Univ., Bangkok) 1995, (Univ. of Turku) 1995, (Helsinki School of Econs and Business Admin) 1996, (Univ. of Palermo, Argentina) 1997, (Univ. of Helsinki) 1997, 2006, (Univ. of Moscow (MGIMO) 1997, (Kyiv) 1998, (Univ. of Tech., Espoo) 1998, (Univ. of Namibia) 2000, (Columbia Univ.) 2000, (Univ. of Jyväskylä) 2000, (Averett Coll.) 2001, (American Univ., Bulgaria) 2005; Franklin D. Roosevelt Four Freedoms Award 2000, Hessen Peace Prize 2000, J. William Fulbright Award for Int. Understanding 2000, European Centre for Common Ground European Peacebuilder Award 2003, European Foundation for Culture Euro-Atlantic Bridge Prize 2003, American-Scandinavian Foundation Golden Medal 2006, Friends of the UN Common Humanity Award 2006, Manfred Wörner Medal, German Ministry of Defence 2007, Geuzenmedal, Geuzen Resistance 1940–1945 Foundation 2008, Delta Prize for Global Understanding, Univ. of Georgia and Delta Air Lines 2008, Chair.'s Award of Int. Crisis Group for outstanding contributions to conflict prevention and resolution in Europe, Asia and Africa 2008, Félix Houphouët-Boigny Peace Prize, UNESCO 2008, Nobel Peace Prize 2008. *Leisure interests:* golf, music, reading. *Address:* Crisis Management Initiative, Pieni Roobertinkatu 13B, 00130 Helsinki, Finland (office). *Telephone:* (9) 4242810 (office). *Fax:* (9) 4242810 (office). *E-mail:* cmi.helsinki@cmi.fi (office). *Website:* www.cmi.fi (office).

AHUJA, Sanjiv, BE, MS; Indian telecommunications industry executive; *Chairman, Orange UK;* ed Delhi Univ., Columbia Univ., NY, USA; various exec. positions at IBM, including head of telecommunications software div. 1990s; fmr Pres. Telcordia Technologies; CEO Comstellar Technologies –2003; COO Orange 2003–04, CEO 2004–07, Chair. Orange UK 2007–. *Address:* Orange, UK Corporate Headquarters, 50 George Street, London, W1U 7DZ, England (office). *Telephone:* (20) 7984-1600 (office). *Fax:* (20) 7984-1601 (office). *Website:* www.orange.com (office).

AI, Weiwei; Chinese artist; *Artistic Director, China Art Archive and Warehouse;* b. 1957, Beijing; s. of Ai Qing; m. Lu Qing; ed Beijing Film Acad.; freelance curator, cultural advisor and architect; Co-founder art group The Stars 1979; est. loft-gallery China Art Archive and Warehouse (CAAW), Beijing 1998, currently Artistic Dir; collaborated with Swiss firm Herzog de Meuron as architectural consultant for Olympic Stadium ('Bird's Nest') for 2008 Olympic Games in Beijing; Lifetime Achievement Award, Chinese Contemporary Art Awards 2008. *Address:* China Art Archive and Warehouse, POB 100102-43, Beijing 100102, People's Republic of China (office). *Telephone:* (10) 84565152 (office). *Fax:* (10) 84565154 (office). *E-mail:* caaw@public.gb.com.cn (office). *Website:* www.archivesandwarehouse.com (office); www.aiweiwei.com (office).

AI, Zhongxin; Chinese painter; b. 13 Oct. 1915, Shanghai; m. Qian Lily 1977; ed Nanjing Central Univ. and in USSR; Prof., Cen. Inst. of Fine Arts 1954–, Deputy Dir 1980, fmr Pres.; mem. Chinese Artists Asscn, currently Deputy Councillor; Consultant, China Oil Painting Soc. Society. *Works include:* Yellow River, Road to Ulumci, Seashore, Over the Snowy Mountain. *Publications:* Study of Xu Beihong, On Style of Painting, etc. *Address:* c/o Chinese Artists Assocation, Beijing, People's Republic of China.

AIBEL, Howard James, BA, DJur; American lawyer, arbitrator and business executive; b. 24 March 1929, New York; s. of David Aibel and Anne Aibel; m. Katherine W. Webster 1952; three s.; ed Harvard Coll., Harvard Law School; admitted New York Bar 1952, served as Vice-Pres. of Asscn of the Bar of New York City, Chair. Cttee on Fed. Legislation, Assoc. White & Case, New York 1952–57; with Gen. Electric Co. 1957–64, Anti-Trust Litigation Counsel GE 1960–64; Trade Regulation Counsel ITT Corpn, New York 1964–66, Vice-Pres., Assoc. Gen. Counsel 1966–68, Gen. Counsel 1968–92, Sr Vice-Pres. 1969–87, Exec. Vice-Pres. 1987–94, Chief Legal Officer 1992–94; Pres. Harvard Law School Asscn of New York City 1992–93; Partner, Le Boeuf Lamb Greene & McRae LLP 1994–99, mem. counsel 1999–2001; fmr Trustee, Chair. Advisory Bd School of Law, Bridgeport Univ. 1989–91, Chair. Exec. Cttee Bd of Dirs American Arbitration Asscn 1992–95, Chair. Bd of Dirs 1995–98; Bd of Dirs Alliance of Resident Theaters, New York 1986–, Chair. 1989–2002, Chair. Emer. 2002–; Vice-Chair., Trustee The Fund for Modern Courts 1985–95, Vice-Pres. Harvard Law School Asscn 1994–2002; mem. American Law Inst., New York State, American Bar Asscn; mem. Bd of Dirs Sheraton Corpn 1982–94, Farrel Corp. 1994–2005; Life Fellow American Bar Foundation; Trustee Int. Bar Asscn Foundation, Lawyers' Cttee for Civil Rights under Law 1991–95; consulting Trustee Nature Centre for Environmental Activities of Westport; Trustee, Sacred Heart Univ., Fairfield, Conn. 2004–; Commr, Town of Weston Conservation Comm.; Harold S. Geneen Man. Award 1994. *Leisure interests:* theatre, bird study, photography. *Address:* 183 Steep Hill Road, Weston, CT 06883-1924, USA (home). *Telephone:* (203) 227-0738 (home). *Fax:* (203) 454-2072 (home). *E-mail:* hjaibel@post.harvard.edu (home).

AICHINGER, Ilse; Austrian writer; b. 1 Nov. 1921, Vienna; m. Günter Eich (died 1972); ed Universität Wien; fmrly worked with Inge Scholl at Hochschule für Gestaltung, Ulm; later worked as a reader for S. Fischer (publrs), Frankfurt and Vienna; Förderungspreis des Österreichischen Staatspreises 1952, Preis der Gruppe 47 1952, Literaturpreis der Freien und Hansestadt Bremen 1954, Immermannpreis der Stadt Düsseldorf 1955, Literaturpreis der Bayerischen Akad. 1961, Nyell Sachs-Preis, Dortmund 1971, City of Vienna Literature Prize 1974, Georg Tracke Prize 1979, Petrarca Prize 1982, Belgian Europe Festival Prize 1987, Town of Solothurn Prize 1991, Joseph-Breitbach-Preis 2000. *Publications include:* Die Grössere Hoffnung (novel) 1948, Knöpfe (radio play) 1952, Der Gefesselte (short stories) 1953, Zu keiner Stunde (dialogues) 1957, Besuch im Pfarrhaus (radio play) 1961, Wo ich wohne (stories, dialogues, poems) 1963, Eliza, Eliza (stories) 1965, Nachricht von Tag (stories) 1970, Schlechte Worter 1976, Meine Sprache und Ich Erzählungen 1978, Radio Plays, Selected Poetry and Prose by Ilse Aichinger 1983, Kleist, Moos, Fasane 1987, Collected Works (eight vols) 1991, Film und Verhängnis 2001. *Address:* c/o Fischer Verlag, POB 700480, 60008 Frankfurt, Germany.

AIDA, Takefumi, PhD; Japanese architect and academic; b. 5 June 1937, Tokyo; s. of Takeshi Aida and Chiyo Aida; m. Kazuko Aida 1966; one s. one d.; ed School of Architecture, Waseda Univ., Tokyo; qualified architect 1967; Prof., Shibaura Inst. of Tech., Tokyo 1976–2000, Prof. and Dean Dept of Architecture and Eng 1991–94; major works include: Memorial at Iwo-Jima Island, Tokyo 1983, Toy Block House X, Shibuya, Tokyo 1984, Tokyo War Dead Memorial Park, Bunkyo, Tokyo 1988, Saito Memorial Hall, Shibaura Inst. of Tech., Tokyo 1990, Community Centre, Kawasato 1993, Funeral Hall, Mizuho 1998, Nenseiji Temple 2001; Japan Architects' Asscn Annual Prize for Newcomers 1982, 2nd Prize Int. Doll's Houses Competition, England 1983. *Publications:* Architecture Note, Toy Block Houses 1984, Toy Block House X 1986, Takefumi Aida Buildings and Projects 1990, The Works of Takefumi Aida 1998, The Collected Edition of Takefumi Aida 1998. *Leisure interest:* Shogi. *Address:* 1-3-2 Okubo, Shinjuku-ku, Tokyo 169-0072, Japan (home). *Telephone:* (3) 3205-1585 (home). *Fax:* (3) 3209-7960 (home). *E-mail:* t-aida@kt.rim.or.jp (office).

AIDEED, Hussein; Somali politician; *Deputy Prime Minister and Minister of Public Works and Housing;* b. 1963; s. of Gen. Mohamed Farah Aideed (died 1996); mem. Habr Gedir clan; m. 1st; m. 2nd 1995; one d.; m. 3rd (divorced); one d.; immigrated to USA 1978, obtained American citizenship; joined US Marine Corps Reserve 1987, attained position of Corporal; translator, US-led peacekeeping force in Somalia 1992; public works clerk, Water Supply and Roads Maintenance Dept, W Covina City Hall, Southern Calif. –1995; returned to Somalia 1995; led reorganisation of clan militia and armed conquest of Baidoa 1995; Leader Somali Nat. Alliance (SNA) 1996–; Co-Chair. Somali Reconciliation and Restoration Council (SRRC); participated in peace talks on future of Somalia, Nairobi, Kenya 2002; imprisoned in Nairobi on charges of failing to pay debts 2002; Deputy Prime Minister 2004–; Minister of Internal Affairs 2004–07, of Public Works and Housing 2007–. *Address:* Ministry of Public Works and Housing, Mogadishu, Somalia (office). *Telephone:* 252-1-534889 (office). *Fax:* 252-5-974242 (office). *E-mail:* publicworks_housing@somali-gov.info (office). *Website:* www.somali-gov.info/newspages/ministerpublicworks (office).

AIDOO, Ama Ata; Ghanaian writer and academic; *Visiting Professor of Africana Studies and Creative Writing, Brown University;* b. Abeadzi Kyiakor, Gold Coast (now Ghana); one d.; Lecturer, Cape Coast Univ. 1970–73; Consultant Prof., Phelps-Stokes Fund Ethnic Studies Program, Washington 1974–75; consultant at univs, acads and research insts in Africa, Europe and USA; Prof. of English, Univ. of Ghana; Minister of Educ. 1982–83; fmr Fellow of Advanced Creative Writing Program, Stanford Univ.; currently Visiting Prof. of Africana Studies and Creative Writing, Brown Univ., also Writer-in-Residence; Chair. African Regional Panel of the Commonwealth Writers' Prize 1990, 1991; fmr mem. Bd of Dirs Ghana Broadcasting Corpn, Artis Council of Ghana, Ghana Medical and Dental Council; Fellow, Inst. for African Studies; Millenium Award for Literary Excellence, Ghana's Excellence Awards Foundation 2005, Woman of Substance Award, African Women's Devt Fund 2005. *Publications include:* novels: Our Sister Killjoy or Reflections from a Black-Eyed Squint 1977, Changes: A Love Story (Commonwealth Writers Prize for the Africa region 1993) 1991; poetry: Someone Talking to Sometime 1985, Birds and Other Poems; plays: The Dilemma of a Ghost 1965, Anowa 1970, Changes: A Love Story 1991; short stories: No Sweetness Here 1970, The Eagle and The Chicken and Other Stories 1987, The Girl Who Can and Other Stories 1999; numerous contribs to magazines and journals. *Address:* Department of Africana Studies, Brown University, Box 1904, 155 Angell Street, Providence, RI 02912, USA (office). *Telephone:* (401) 863-3137 (office). *Fax:* (401) 863-3559 (office). *E-mail:* Ama_Ata_Aidoo@brown.edu (office). *Website:* www.brown.edu/Departments/Africana_Studies (office).

AIELLO, Danny; American actor; b. 20 May 1933, New York; s. of Daniel Louis Aiello and Frances Pietrocova; m. Sandy Cohen 1955; three s. one d. *Theatre includes:* Lamppost Reunion 1975 (Theatre World Award), Gemini 1977 (Obie Award 1977), Hurlyburly 1985. *Films include:* Bang the Drum Slowly 1973, The Godfather II 1976, Once Upon a Time in America 1984, The Purple Rose of Cairo 1985, Moonstruck 1987, Do the Right Thing 1989 (Boston Critics Award, Chicago Critics Award, L.A. Critics Award, all for Best Supporting Actor), Harlem Nights 1989, Jacob's Ladder 1990, Once Around 1991, Hudson Hawk 1991, The Closer 1991, 29th Street 1991, Mistress 1992, Ruby 1992, The Pickle 1992, The Cemetery Club 1992, The Professional 1994, Prêt-a-Porter 1994, Léon 1994, City Hall 1995, Power of Attorney 1995, Two Days in the Valley 1996, Mojave Moon 1996, Two Much 1996, A Brooklyn State of Mind 1997, Bring Me the Head of Mavis Davis 1998, Wilbur Falls 1998, Mambo Cafe 1999, 18 Shades of Dust 1999, Prince of Central Park 2000, Dinner Rush 2000, Off Key 2001, The Russian Job 2002, Marcus Timberwolf 2002, The Last Request 2002, Mail Order Bride 2003, Zeyda and the Hitman 2004, Brooklyn Lobster 2005, Lucky Number Slevin 2006, The Last Request 2006. *TV films include:* The Preppie Murder 1989, A Family of Strangers 1993 (Emmy Award), The Last Don (mini-series) 1997, Dellaventura (series) 1997, The Last Don II (mini-series) 1998. *Address:* William Morris Agency, 1 William Morris Place, Beverly Hills, CA 90212, USA.

AIGRAIN, Jacques, PhD; Swiss/French business executive; b. 1954; m., two c.; ed Dauphine Univ., Sorbonne; joined JP Morgan 1981, served as co-head of investment banking client coverage, fmr mem. Man. Cttee; joined Swiss Reinsurance Co. (Swiss Re) as Head, Financial Services Business Group and mem. Exec. Bd Cttee 2001, CEO 2004–09; mem. Bd of Dirs Swiss Int. Air Lines 2001–, Chair. Audit Cttee. *Address:* c/o Swiss Reinsurance Co., Mythenquai 50/60, 8022 Zurich, Switzerland (office).

AIKEN, Linda H., PhD, FAAN, FRCN, RN; American nurse, sociologist and academic; *Claire M. Fagin Leadership Professor in Nursing, Professor of Sociology, and Director, Center for Health Outcomes and Policy Research, University of Pennsylvania;* b. 29 July 1943, Roanoke; d. of William Jordan and Betty Philips Harman (née Warner); one s. one d.; ed Univ. of Florida, Univ. of Texas, Univ. of Wisconsin; nurse, Univ. of Florida Medical Center 1964–65, Instructor, Coll. of Nursing 1966–67; Instructor, School of Nursing, Univ. of Missouri 1967–70, Clinical Nurse Specialist 1967–70; Lecturer, School of Nursing, Univ. of Wisconsin 1973–74; Program Officer, Robert Wood Johnson Foundation 1974–76, Dir of Research 1976–79, Asst Vice-Pres. 1979–81, Vice-Pres. 1981–87; Claire M. Fagin Leadership Prof. in Nursing and Prof. of Sociology and Dir Center for Health Outcomes and Policy Research, Univ. of Pennsylvania 1988–; mem. Pres. Clinton's Nat. Health Care Reform Task Force 1993; Commr Physician Payment Review Comm. Nat. Advisory Council, US Agency for Health Care Policy and Research; Assoc. Ed. Journal of Health and Social Behaviour 1979–81; Jessie M. Scott Award, American Nurses Asscn 1984, Nurse Scientist of the Year Award 1991, Best of Image Award 1991, Distinguished Pathfinder Research Award 2001, Barbara Thoman Curtis Award, American Nurses Asscn 2002, Individual Codman Award, Jt Comm. on Accreditation of Healthcare Orgs 2003. *Publications:* Nursing in the 1980s: Crises, Challenges, Opportunities (ed.) 1982, Evaluation Studies Review Annual 1985 (co-ed. with B. Kehrer) 1985, Applications of Social Science to Clinical Medicine and Health Policy (co-ed. with D. Mechanic) 1986, Charting Nursing's Future (co-ed. with C. Fagin) 1991, Hospital Restructuring in North America and Europe 1997, Advances in Hospital Outcomes Research 1998, Accounting for Variation in Hospital Outcomes: Cross-National Study 1999; contribs to professional journals. *Address:* University of Pennsylvania, Center for Health Outcomes and Policy Research, NEB 332R, 420 Guardian Drive, Philadelphia, PA 19104-6096 (office); 2209 Lombard Street, Philadelphia, PA 19146-1107, USA (home). *Telephone:* (215) 898-9759 (office); (215) 898-5673 (home). *Fax:* (215) 573-2062 (office). *E-mail:* laiken@nursing.upenn.edu (office). *Website:* www.nursing.upenn.edu/chopr (office).

AILES, Roger Eugene, BFA; American television producer and communications executive; *Chairman, Fox Television Stations;* b. 15 May 1940, Warren, OH; s. of Robert Eugene Ailes and Donna Marie Ailes (née Cunningham); m. Elizabeth Tilson 1998; one c.; ed Ohio Univ.; Assoc. Dir KYW-TV, Cleveland 1962–63, Producer and Dir 1963–65; Producer Mike Douglas Show, Westinghouse Broadcasting Corpn, Phila 1965–67, Exec. Producer 1967–68; political and media consultant to presidential campaigns of

Richard M. Nixon 1968, Ronald Reagan 1984, and George Bush 1988; resgnd from political consulting 1992; Chair. Ailes Communications Inc., NY 1969–92; Exec. Vice-Pres. TV News Inc. 1975–76; Pres. CNBC, NBC 1993–96; Pres. and Program Host, America's Talking, NBC, NY 1993–96; Chair. and CEO Fox News 1996–, Exec. Ed. FOXNews.com 2000–, Chair. Fox TV Stations 2005–, also Head Twentieth TV; fmr consultant WCBS-TV; Vice-Pres. Conf. Personal Mans; mem. American Fed. of TV and Radio Artists, Dirs Guild of America, Radio and TV News Dirs Asscn; Hon. PhD (Ohio Univ.); Award for Shakespeare Production, Fine Arts Magazine 1964, Emmy Award (twice) for The Mike Douglas Show 1967, 1968, Liberty Bell Award, Advertising Alliance Phila 1971, Commendation Award for Contrib. to Communications, Ohio Univ. 1972, Silver Circle Award, Nat. Acad. TV Arts and Sciences 1999, First Amendment Leadership Award, Radio and TV News Dirs Foundation 2006. *Productions include:* Mother Earth, Broadway Museum (play) 1972, Hot-L Baltimore (play, four Obie Awards 1973) 1973–76, The Last Frontier 1974, Television and the Presidency (Emmy Award) 1984, Fellini: Wizards, Clowns and Honest Liars 1977, Tomorrow: Coast to Coast 1981, The Rush Limbaugh Show 1992–96, A Current Affair, The Maury Povich Show, The Leeza Show, An All-Star Salute to Our Troops 1991. *Publications:* You Are the Message: Secrets of the Master Communicators (co-author with Jon Kraushar) 1987; articles in popular magazines and professional journals. *Address:* Fox News, 1211 Avenue of the Americas, New York, NY 10036, USA (office). *Website:* www.foxnews.com (office).

AILLAGON, Jean Jacques; French politician and cultural official; *Director, Palazzo Grassi;* b. 2 Oct. 1946, Metz; s. of Charles Aillagon and Anne-Marie Louis; two c.; ed Univs of Toulouse and Nanterre; Prof. of History and Geography, Lycée de Tulle 1973–76; Deputy Dir Ecole Nat. Supérieure des Beaux-Arts 1978–82; Admin. Musée Nat. d'Art Moderne (Centre Pompidou) 1982–85; Asst to Dir of Cultural Affairs of City of Paris 1985–88; Del.-Gen. for Cultural Programmes of City of Paris 1988–93; Dir-Gen. Vidéothèque de Paris 1992–93; Dir of Cultural Affairs of City of Paris 1993–96; Pres. Centre Georges Pompidou 1996–2002; Minister of Culture and Communication 2002–04; Pres. and Dir-Gen. TV5 Monde 2005–06; Dir Palazzo Grassi, Venice 2006–; Pres. comm. organizing year 2000 celebrations 1999–2001; Artistic Dir Commissariat for France–Egypt Year 1996–98; Chevalier, Ordre Nat. du Mérite, des Palmes académiques, Légion d'honneur. *Address:* Palazzo Grassi, Campo San Samuele, 3231, CP 708, 30124, Venice, Italy. *Telephone:* (041) 5231689. *Fax:* (041) 5286218. *Website:* www.palazzograssi.it.

AILLERET, François; French government official; *President, Association Française de Normalisation (AFNOR);* b. 7 June 1937; s. of Pierre Ailleret and Denise Nodé-Langlois; m. Chantal Flinois 1963; four c.; ed Ecole Polytechnique, Ecole Nationale des Ponts et Chausseés; served in Algeria and Côte d'Ivoire in early 1960s; various appointments at Paris Airport 1967–80; joined Electricité de France (EdF) 1980, Deputy Dir-Gen. 1987, Dir-Gen. 1994–96, Vice-Pres. 1996, Pres. EdF Int. 1996–2003, Hon. CEO 2003–; Pres. Int. Union of Electricity Producers and Distributors (UNIPEDE) 1997–2000; Admin. Pechiney 1996–2003; currently Pres. Asscn Française de Normalisation (AFNOR); Chair. French Energy Council 1998–2004; mem. Conseil Economique et Social (Nat.) 1999; Pres., Conseil d'Administration, Institut Pasteur 2005–; Officier de la Légion d'honneur; Commdr Ordre nat. du Mérite; Croix de la Valeur militaire. *Address:* EdF, 151 boulevard Haussmann, 75008 Paris (office); 33 rue Desnouettes, 75015 Paris, France (home). *Telephone:* 1-40-42-26-70 (office). *Fax:* 1-40-42-77-78 (office). *E-mail:* francois.ailleret@edf.fr (office). *Website:* www.pasteur.fr/english.html (office).

AIMÉ, Jean-Claude C., MBA; Haitian international civil servant; b. 10 Sept. 1935, Port-au-Prince; s. of Christian F. Aimé and Carmen Amelia Gautier; m. 1st Elizabeth B. Bettison 1963 (divorced 1991); m. 2nd Lisa M. Buttenheim 1992; ed Harvard Coll., Univ. of Pennsylvania, USA; joined UN 1962, Programme Officer Tunis 1963–64, Asst Resident Rep. UNDP Algiers 1964–67, ILO Geneva 1967–69, Deputy Perm. Rep. UNDP Amman 1969–71, UN Relief Operation Dacca 1971–72, Rep. East African Community Arusha UNDP 1972–73, Resident Rep. UNDP Amman 1973–77, Sr Adviser UNIFIL Naqoura 1978, UN Sr Adviser in the Middle East 1979–82, Dir Office of Under-Secs-Gen. for Special Political Affairs 1982–88, Exec. Asst to Sec.-Gen. 1989–92, Asst Sec.-Gen., Chief of Staff 1992–96, Exec. Sec. UN Compensation Comm., Geneva 1997–2000. *Leisure interests:* music, reading, squash, hunting. *Address:* c/o Ministry of Foreign Affairs and Religion, blvd Harry S. Truman, Cité de l'Exposition, Port-au-Prince, Haiti. *Telephone:* 222-8482. *Fax:* 223-1668.

AIMÉE, Anouk; French actress; b. (Françoise Dreyfus), 27 April 1932, Paris; d. of Henry Dreyfus and Geneviève Durand; m. 2nd Nico Papatakis 1951; one d.; m. 3rd Pierre Barouh 1966; m. 4th Albert Finney (q.v.) 1970 (divorced 1978); ed Ecole de la rue Milton, Paris, Ecole de Barbezieux, Pensionnat de Bandd, Inst. de Megève and Cours Bauer-Therond; film and TV actress 1955–; Commdr des Arts et des Lettres, Golden Globe Award 1968, Prix Féminin, Cannes. *Theatre includes:* Sud 1954, Love Letters 1990, 1994. *Films include:* Les mauvaises rencontres 1955, Tous peuvent me tuer, Pot bouille and Montparnasse 19 1957, La tête contre les murs 1958, Les drageurs 1959, La dolce vita, Le farceur, Lola, Les amours de Paris, L'imprévu 1960, Quai Notre Dame 1960, Le jugement dernier 1961, Sodome et Gomorrhe 1961, Les grands chemins 1962, Education sentimentale 1962, Huit et demi 1962, Un homme et une femme 1966, Un soir un train 1967, The Appointment 1968, Model Shop 1968, Justine 1968, Si c'était à refaire 1976, Mon premier amour 1978, Salto nel vuoto 1979, La tragédie d'un homme ridicule 1981, Qu'est-ce qui fait courir David? 1982, Le Général de l'armée morte 1983, Vive la vie 1984, Le succès à tout prix 1984, Un homme et une femme: vingt ans déjà 1986, Docteur Norman Bethune 1992, Les Marmottes 1993, Les Cent et une nuits 1995, Prêt-à-porter 1995, Une pour toutes 2000, La Petite prairie aux bouleaux 2003, Ils se mariérent et eurent beaucoup d'enfants 2004, De particulier à particulier 2006. *Television:* Une page d'amour 1979, L'Île bleue 2001, Des voix dans le jardin, Napoléon 2002, Claude Lelouch, on s'aimera (narrator) 2007. *Leisure interests:* reading, life, human rights. *Address:* c/o Artmédia, 20 avenue Rapp, 75007 Paris, France (home).

AINI, Martin; Papua New Guinea politician; mem. Parl. for Kavieng, New Ireland province; fmr Vice-Minister Assisting the Prime Minister; Minister of Defence 2006–07 (resgnd); mem. Pangu (Papua New Guinea Unity) Pati. *Address:* c/o Department of Defence, Murray Barracks, Free Mail Bag, Boroko 111, NCD, Papua New Guinea (office).

AINSLEY, John Mark; British singer (tenor); b. 9 July 1953, Crewe; s. of John Alwyn Ainsley and Dorothy Sylvia Ainsley (née Anderson); pnr William Whitehead; ed Royal Grammar School, Worcester, Madgalen Coll., Oxford; debut in Stravinsky's Mass, Royal Festival Hall 1984; many concert performances from 1985 with Taverner Consort, New London Consort and London Baroque; appearances in Mozart Masses at The Vienna Konzerthaus with Heinz Holliger, Handel's Saul at Götingen with John Eliot Gardiner, the Mozart Requiem under Yehudi Menuhin at Gstaad and Pulcinella at the Barbican under Jeffrey Tate; other concerts with the Ulster Orchestra and the Bournemouth Sinfonietta; debut in USA at Lincoln Center in Bach's B Minor Mass with Christopher Hogwood 1990; opera debut at the Innsbruck Festival in Scarlatti's Gli Equivoci nel Sembiante, at the ENO in the Return of Ulysses 1989; title role in Méhul's Joseph for Dutch Radio, Handel's Acis in Stuttgart and Solomon for Radio France under Leopold Hager; has sung Mozart's Tamino for Opera Northern Ireland and Ferrando for Glyndebourne Touring Opera; sang Ferrando at Glyndebourne 1992, Don Ottavio 1994, Haydn's The Seasons with the London Classical Players; BBC Proms Concerts, London 1993, Stravinsky concert under Andrew Davis at Royal Festival Hall 1997, Monteverdi's Orfeo for the Munich Opera Festival 1999, Jupiter in Semele for ENO 1999, Bach's St Matthew Passion at the BBC Proms 2002, Skuratov in From the House of the Dead for Amsterdam, Vienna and Aix en Provence Festivals, 2007, Captain Vere in Billy Budd for Frankfurt Opera 2007, Emilio in Partenope for ENO 2008, title role in Idomeneo and Bazajet in Tamerlano for Munich Opera Festival 2008; Grammy Award for Best Opera Recording 1995, Munich Festival Prize 1999, Royal Philharmonic Soc. Singer Award 2007. *Recordings include:* Handel's Nisi Dominus under Simon Preston, Purcell's Odes with Trevor Pinnock, Mozart's C Minor Mass with Christopher Hogwood, Great Baroque Arias with the King's Consort, Acis and Galatea, Saul. *Address:* Askonas Holt, Lincoln House, 300 High Holborn, London, WC1V 7JH, England (office). *Telephone:* (20) 7400-1700 (office). *Fax:* (20) 7400-1799 (office). *E-mail:* info@askonasholt.co.uk (office). *Website:* www .askonasholt.co.uk (office).

AINSLIE, Charles Benedict (Ben), CBE; British sailor; b. 5 Feb. 1977, Macclesfield; s. of Roddy Ainslie (skipper of 'Second Life' in first Whitbread Round the World Race 1973–74) and Susan Ainslie; ed Peter Symonds Coll., Winchester, Hants., Truro School, Truro, Cornwall; started sailing in Restronguet Creek, Cornwall aged eight; three gold medals in successive Olympic Games (Laser Class, Sydney 2000, Finn Class, Athens 2004, Finn Class, Beijing 2008), also won silver medal in Laser Class at Atlanta Olympic Games 1996; other competitive results include Laser Radial European Champion 1993, Laser Radial World Champion 1993, Youth World Champion 1995, Laser European Champion 1996, 1998, 1999, 2000, Laser World Champion 1998, 1999, Finn European Champion 2002, 2003, Finn World Champion 2002, 2003, 2004 (first Briton to win three consecutive Finn titles), 2005; joined Team New Zealand in late 2004 to compete in America's Cup 2007; announced by British America's Cup Campaign 'Origin' as skipper for 33rd America's Cup challenge in 2009 Sept. 2007; secured fifth world title at Finn Gold Cup in Melbourne 2008 (most successful Finn sailor ever); Hon. mem. Royal Cornwall Yacht Club, Stokes Bay Sailing Club, Restronguet Sailing Club, Hayling Island Sailing Club; Hon. degree in Sports Science (Univ. Coll. of Chichester); British Young Sailor of the Year 1995, British Yachtsman of the Year 1995, 1999, 2000, 2002, Sports Writers' Asscn Best Int. newcomer 1996, Int. Sailing Fed. (ISAF) World Sailor of the Year 1998, 2002. *Leisure interests:* cycling, flying, football, cricket, golf. *E-mail:* jo.grindley@intotheblue.biz (office). *Website:* www.benainslie.com (office).

AIPIN, Jeremy Danilovich; Russian author and politician; *Deputy Chairman, Khanty-Mansisky State Duma;* b. 27 June 1948, Varyegan, Khanty-Mansisky Dist; s. of Danil Romanovich Aipin and Vera Savljevna Aipina; m.; two d.; ed Gorky Inst. of Literature; People's Deputy 1990–91; Pres. Asscn of Aboriginal Peoples of the North, Siberia and Far East of Russia (now Asscn of Aboriginal People of the North, Siberia and Far East of Russia) 1993; Co-founder Democratic Choice of Russia Party in Khanty-Mansysk Autonomous Region 1994; mem. State Duma, Deputy Chair. Cttee on Nat. Affairs 1993–96, Deputy Chair. of Duma 2002–, Chair. Ass. of Native People's Reps 2002–; Honoured Cultural Figure of Khanty-Mansisky, Order of the Fatherland, 1st class 2006; Honoured Achiever in Culture 1998, Khanty-Mansisky Governor's Prize 1999, Star of the Morning Dawn. *Publications include:* In the Shadow of the Old Cedar 1981, In Wait for the First Snow 1990, Doomed for Destruction 1994, By the Dying Fire 1998, I am Listening to the Earth 2002, and other works about peoples of N Russia. *Leisure interests:* hunting, fishing, reindeer breeding. *Address:* Mira str. 628011 Khanty-Mansisk, (office); Lenina str. 39, apt. 27 628011 Khanty-Mansisk, Russia (home). *Telephone:* (34671) 2-45-78 (office); (34671) 2-25-57 (home). *Fax:* (34671) 2-14-35 (office). *E-mail:* aipin@dumahmao.ru (office).

AIREY, Dawn Elizabeth, MA, FRSA, FRTS; British television executive; *Chairman and CEO, Channel 5 Broadcasting Ltd;* b. 15 Nov. 1960, Preston, Lancs.; one d.; ed Kelly Coll., Girton Coll. Cambridge; with Cen. TV 1985–93; ITV Network Centre 1993–94; Channel 4 1994–96; Channel 5 1996–2002,

Chief Exec. 2000–02; Man. Dir Sky Networks 2002–06; CEO Iostar (TV production and distribution co.) April 2007 (resgnd); Dir of Global Content, ITV 2007–08, mem. Bd of Dirs 2008; Chair. and CEO Channel 5 Broadcasting Ltd 2008–; Vice-Pres. Royal TV Soc. 2002–; mem. Bd of Dirs (non-exec.) Taylor Nelson Sofres 2007–; Exec. Chair. Media Guardian Edinburgh Int. TV Festival 2001–06; mem. Bd Int. Emmy Awards; Olswang Business Woman of the Year 2000. *Leisure interests:* cinema, tennis. *Address:* Channel 5 Broadcasting Ltd, 22 Long Acre, London, WC2E 9LY, England (office). *Telephone:* (20) 7421-7270 (office). *Website:* www.five.tv (office).

AIRLIE, 13th Earl of; **David George Patrick Coke Ogilvy,** KT, GCVO, PC, RVO; British business executive; b. 17 May 1926, London; s. of 12th Earl of Airlie, KT, GCVO, MC and Lady Alexandra Marie Bridget Coke; m. Virginia Fortune Ryan 1952; three s. three d.; ed Eton Coll.; Chair. Schroders PLC 1977–84, Ashdown Investment Trust Ltd 1968–84, J. Henry Schroder Bank AG (Switzerland) 1977–84, Baring Stratton Investment Trust PLC 1986–2000; Chair. Gen. Accident Fire and Life Assurance Corpn PLC 1987–97; Dir J. Henry Schroder Wagg & Co. Ltd 1961–84, Schroder, Darling and Co. Holdings Ltd (Australia) 1977–84, Schroders Inc. (USA) 1977–84, Schroder Int. Ltd 1973–84, Scottish & Newcastle Breweries PLC 1969–83; Dir Royal Bank of Scotland Group PLC 1983–93; Lord Chamberlain of the Queen's Household 1984–97; Lord Lt of Angus 1989–2001; Capt.-Gen. of the Royal Co. of Archers 2004–; Chancellor Univ. of Abertay, Dundee 1994–; Chair. Historic Royal Palaces 1998–2002; Pres. Nat. Trust for Scotland 1998–2002; Gov. Nuffield Hosps; Hon. Pres. Scout Asscn in Scotland 1988–2002, JP Angus 1990; Hon. LLD (Dundee) 1990. *Address:* Cortachy Castle, Kirriemuir, Angus, DD8 4LY, Scotland (home); 36 Sloane Court West, London, SW3 4TB, England (home). *Telephone:* (1575) 540231. *Fax:* (1575) 540223 (office); (1575) 540570109. *E-mail:* office@airlieestates.com (office). *Website:* www.airlieestates.com (office).

AITCHISON, Craigie Ronald John, CBE; British artist; b. 13 Jan. 1926, Scotland; s. of the late Rt Hon. the Lord Aitchison and of Lady Aitchison; ed Slade School of Fine Art, London; British Council/Italian Govt Scholarship for Painting 1955; Edwin Austin Abbey Premier Scholarship 1970; Lorne Scholarship 1974–75; Arts Council Bursary 1976; works in public collections including Tate Gallery, Arts Council of GB, Contemporary Art Soc., London, Scottish Nat. Gallery of Modern Art, Scottish Arts Council, Walker Art Gallery, Liverpool and Newcastle Region Art Gallery, NSW, Australia, British Council Exhbn, Israel Museum, Jerusalem 1992; fmr RA, resgnd 1997, rejoined 1998; Prizewinner John Moores Liverpool Exhbn 1974–75, Johnson's Wax Award for Best Painting at Royal Academy Summer Exhbn 1982, Korn Ferry Int. Award, Royal Academy Summer Exhbn 1989, 1991, Jerwood Foundation Prize 1994, Nordstern Art Prize 2000. *Address:* c/o Royal Academy of Arts, Burlington House, Piccadilly, London, W1V 0DS, England.

AITMATOV, Askar Chingizovich, Kyrgyzstani politician; b. 5 Jan. 1959, Frunze (now Bishkek); s. of the late Chingiz Aitmatov; ed Moscow State Univ.; mem. staff Div. of Middle Asia, Ministry of Foreign Affairs, USSR 1982–83, Information Dept 1987–90; seconded to USSR Embassy in Istanbul 1983–87; mem. Political Information Dept, Ministry of Foreign Affairs, Kyrgyzstan 1990–92, Deputy Minister of Foreign Affairs 1992–94, Minister 2002–05; Acting Perm. Rep. to UN, New York 1994–96; Adviser, Office of the Pres. 1996–98, Head of Dept of Foreign Policy 1998–2002, Minister of Foreign Affairs 2002–05. *Address:* c/o Ministry of Foreign Affairs, Erkindik Boulevard, 54, 720021 Bishkek, Kyrgyzstan (office).

AITMATOV, Ilghiz Torokulovich, PhD, DTechSc; Kyrgyzstani geologist; *Director, Institute of Physics and Mechanics of Rocks, Kyrgyz National Academy of Sciences;* b. 8 Feb. 1931, Frunze (now Bishkek); s. of Torokul Aitmatov and Naghima Aitmatova (née Abdulvaliyeva); m. Rosalia Jamankulovna Jenchuraeva 1961; one s. two d.; ed Moscow Inst. of Geological Survey, USSR Acad. of Sciences, Inst. of Mining; foreman, engineer, head anti-avalanche surveillance service, Kyrgyz Geological Dept 1954–57; doctoral studies USSR Acad. of Sciences, Inst. of Mining (Moscow) 1957–60; jr researcher, Head of Lab., Deputy Dir Inst. of Physics and Mechanics of Rocks, Kyrgyz Nat. Acad. of Sciences, Head of Lab. 1960–68, Deputy Dir 1968–79, Dir 1970–88, Pres. 1990–94, Dir 1994–, Academician-Sec., Dept of Physical, Math. and Earth Sciences 1988–90; Corresp. mem. Kyrgyz Nat. Acad. of Sciences 1986, mem. 1988–, mem. Political Council, People's Republican Party of Kyrgyzstan 1992–95; mem. Parliament (Supreme Council) of Kyrgyz Repub. 1990–91; mem. Pres. Council 1990–94; Pres. Kyrgyz Acad. of Sciences 1990–93; mem., Russian Acad. of Mining Sciences (Moscow), Int. Engineering Acad. (Moscow) and other int. acads. 1995–2003; Kyrgyzstan SSR State Prize 1984, USSR State Prize 1989, Merited Worker of Science of Kyrgyzstan; other medals and awards. *Achievement:* Scientific Discovery Phenomena of Saltatory Release of Residual Stresses in Rocks (co-author) 1998. *Publications:* more than 250 papers on rock and mass geomechanics, including seven monographs, 15 inventions and one scientific discovery. *Address:* Institute of Physics and Mechanics of Rocks, National Academy of Sciences, ul. O. Mederova 98, 720035 Bishek (office); 98 ul. Toktoghula, Apartment 9, 720000 Bishkek, Kyrgyzstan (home). *Telephone:* (312) 54-11-15 (office); (312) 66-21-89 (home). *Fax:* (312) 54-11-17 (office); (312) 68-00-47 (home). *E-mail:* ifmgp@yandex.ru (office); djam@freenet.kg (home). *Website:* www.ifmgp.narod.ru (office).

AIZAWA, Hideyuki, LLB; Japanese politician; *Chairman of Financial Reconstruction Commission, Ministry of State;* b. 4 July 1919; m. Yoko Aizawa; three s.; ed Univ. of Tokyo; mem. House of Reps, Tottori Pref. 1976–2003; Vice-Minister of Finance; Vice-Chair. Policy Affairs Research Council Liberal Democratic Party (LDP); Dir-Gen. Research Bureau, Treasury Bureau, (LDP); Chair. Cttee on Judicial Affairs, Cttee on Foreign Affairs; Dir-Gen. Econ. Planning Agency, Minister of State 1990; Chair. Extraordin-

ary Cttee on Revitalizing Securities and Bond Markets (LDP) 2000–, Financial Reconstruction Comm., Ministry of State 2001–. *Publications include:* A Day in My Life (autobiog.), From the Forest of Ta Taru (novel), Flower and After (photo album). *Leisure interests:* golf, photography. *Address:* 2-2-1-721, Nagata-cho, Chiyoda-ku, Tokyo 100-8981 (office); 7-10-3, Seijo, Setaya-ku, Tokyo 167-0066 (home); c/o Liberal Democratic Party, 1-11-23 Nagata-cho, Chiyoda-ku, Tokyo 100-8910, Japan. *Telephone:* (3) 3508-7207 (office); (3) 3484-1234 (home); (3) 3581-6211. *Fax:* (3) 3502-3399 (office); (3) 3483-0017 (home). *E-mail:* aizawahideyuki@mbg.sphere.ne.jp (office). *Website:* www.mars.sphere.ne.jp/aizawa/ (office).

AIZAWA, Masuo, MSc, PhD; Japanese research institute director and academic; *President, Tokyo Institute of Technology;* b. 1942, Yokohama; ed Yokohama Nat. Univ., Grad. School of Science and Eng, Tokyo Inst. of Tech.; Research Assoc., Chemical Resources Lab., Tokyo Inst. of Tech. 1971–80; Assoc. Prof., Inst. of Material Science, Tsukuba Univ. 1980–86; Assoc. Prof., Faculty of Eng, Tokyo Inst. of Tech. 1986, Prof. 1986–94, Dean of Faculty of Bioscience and Biotechnology 1994–96, 1998–2000, Vice-Pres. Tokyo Inst. of Tech. 2000, Pres. 2001–; Advising Prof., Shanghai Jiaotong Univ. 2003–; fmr Pres. Electrochemical Soc. of Japan, Int. Soc. of Molecular Electronics and Biocomputing, Intelligent Materials Forum; fmr Vice-Pres. Chemical Soc. of Japan; Chemical Soc. of Japan Award, Outstanding Achievement of the Electrochemical Soc. 2002. *Address:* Tokyo Institute of Technology, 2-12-1 Ookayama, Meguro-ku, Tokyo 152-8550, Japan (office). *Telephone:* (3) 5734-2001 (office). *Fax:* (3) 5734-3446 (office). *E-mail:* titech.pres@jim.titech.ac.jp (office). *Website:* www.titech.ac.jp (office).

AJAYI, Jacob Festus Ade, PhD; Nigerian professor of history; *Chairman of the National Committee, Slave Routes Project, United Nations Educational, Scientific and Cultural Organization (UNESCO);* b. 26 May 1929, Ikole-Ekiti; s. of the late Chief E. Ade Ajayi and Comfort F. Bolajoko Ajayi; m. Christie Akinleye-Martins 1956; one s. four d.; ed Igbobi Coll. Lagos, Higher Coll. Yaba, Univ. Coll. Ibadan, Univ. Coll. Leicester and King's Coll. London; tutor, Ibadan Boys' High School 1948–49, 1951–52; Fellow, Inst. of Historical Research 1957–58; Lecturer, Sr Lecturer, Univ. of Ibadan 1958–63, Prof. of History 1963–89; Fellow, Center for Advanced Study in the Behavioural Sciences, Stanford 1970–71; Vice-Chancellor, Univ. of Lagos 1972–78; Pro-Chancellor, Ondo State Univ., Ado-Ekiti 1984–88; mem. UN Univ. Council 1974–80, Chair. 1976–77; Chair. Int. African Inst. 1975–87; mem. Bureau, Asscn of African Univs 1973–80, Vice-Pres. 1976–80; mem. Bureau, Int. Asscn of Univs 1980–90; Pres. Historical Soc. of Nigeria 1972–81; mem. UNESCO scientific cttee for drafting The General History of Africa (Ed. Vol. VI) 1970–93, Council, Nat. Univ. of Lesotho 1976–82, OAU Group of Eminent Persons for Reparation 1992–, editorial Bd Encyclopaedia of Sub-Saharan Africa 1995–; Chair. Nat. Cttee on the UNESCO Slave Routes Project 2003–; mem. Bd of Dirs of SOWSCO 1994–; Corresp. Fellow Royal Historical Soc., UK; Hon. Fellow, SOAS (Univ. of London) 1994; Hon. LLD (Leicester) 1975; Hon. DLitt (Birmingham) 1984, (Ondo State Univ.) 1992; Bd of Trustees Nigerian Merit Award 1996–; Bobapitan of Ikole-Ekiti and Onikoyi of Ife 1983; Nigerian Nat. Order of Merit (NNOM) 1986; Officer of the Fed. Repub. (OFR) 2002; Univ. of Lagos Anniversary Gold Medal 1987, Distinguished Africanist Award (African Studies Asscn of USA) 1993. *Publications include:* Milestones in Nigerian History 1962, Yoruba Warfare 1964, Christian Missions in Nigeria, 1841–91: The Making of a New Elite 1965, Cementing Partnership: The Story of WAPCO 1960–90 1990, History and the Nation and other Addresses 1990, History of the Nigerian Society of Engineers 1995, The African Experience with Higher Education 1996, Tradition and Change: Essays of J F Ade Ajayi (ed. Toyin Falola) 2000, A Patriot to the Core: Bishop Ajayi Crowther (with Akinseye-George) 2001, Kayode Eso: The Making of a Judge 2002; ed. or co-ed. of various vols on African history. *Leisure interests:* table tennis, dancing. *Address:* PO Box 14617, University of Ibadan, Ibadan (office); 1, Ojobadan Avenue, Bodija, Ibadan, Nigeria (home). *Telephone:* (2) 8100064 (office); (2) 8101588 (home). *Fax:* (2) 8100064 (office). *E-mail:* jadeas@skannet.com.

AJIBOLA, Hon. Prince Bola; Nigerian lawyer and judge; *President, African Concern;* b. 22 March 1934, Lagos; s. of Oba A. S. Ajibola and Adikatu Ashakun Ajibola; m. Olu Ajibola 1961; three s. two d.; ed Holborn Coll. of Law, London Univ.; called to the English Bar (Lincoln's Inn) 1962; Prin. Partner, Bola Ajibola & Co., Lagos, Ikeja, Abeokuta and Kaduna, specializing in commercial law and int. arbitration; fmr Attorney-Gen. and Fed. Minister of Justice; mem. Int. Court of Justice, The Hague 1991–94; mem. Nigerian del. to UN Gen. Ass. 1986; Temporary Pres. UN Gen. Ass., 17th Special Session on Narcotic Drugs 1990; Chair. Task Force for Revision of the Laws of the Fed. 1990; initiated first African Law Ministers Conf., Abuja 1989; Chair. Gen. Council of the Bar, Disciplinary Cttee of the Bar, Advisory Cttee on the Prerogative of Mercy; Founder and Pres. African Concern 1996–; Founder Islamic Movt for Africa 1996; mem. Nigeria Police Council, Int. Law Comm., Perm. Court of Arbitration, The Hague, ICC Court of Arbitration, Int. Maritime Arbitration Comm., Paris, Panel of Int. Arbitrators, London Inst. of Arbitrators, Int. Advisory Cttee of World Arbitration Inst., USA; Judge and Vice-Pres. IBRD Tribunal, Washington, DC 1995; Vice-Pres. Inst. of Int. Business Law and Practice, Paris; Nat. Chair. World Peace Through Law Centre; Ed. Nigeria's Treaties in Force 1970–1990, All Nigeria Law Reports 1961–1990; Ed.-in-Chief, Justice; Gen. Ed. Fed. Ministry of Justice Law Review Series (7 vols); Fellow, Chartered Inst. of Arbitrators, Nigerian Inst. of Advanced Legal Studies; mem. Nigerian Bar Asscn (Pres. 1984–85), African Bar Asscn, Int. Bar Asscn, Asscn of World Lawyers, ICC, Commonwealth Law Asscn, World Arbitration Inst., Soc. for the Reform of Criminal Law; Hon. LLD (Buckingham) 1996. *Publications:* Principles of Arbitration 1980, The Law and Settlement of Commercial Disputes 1984, Law Development and Administration in Nigeria 1987, Integration of the African Continent Through

Law 1988, Banking Frauds and Other Financial Malpractices in Nigeria 1989, Women and Children under Nigerian Law 1990, Scheme Relating to Mutual Assistance in Criminal Matters and the Control of Criminal Activities within Africa and numerous other books on other legal topics. *Address:* 141 Igbosere Road, Lagos, Nigeria.

AJODHIA, Jules Rattankoemar; Suriname politician; Vice-Pres. and Prime Minister of Suriname 1991–96, 2000–05; mem. Verenigde Hervormings Partij (VHP). *Address:* c/o Verenigde Hervormings Partij, Paramaribo, Suriname.

AJZENBERG-SELOVE, Fay, BS, PhD; American (b. Russian) nuclear physicist and academic; *Professor of Physics Emeritus, University of Pennsylvania;* b. 1926; ed Univ. of Michigan, Univ. of Wisconsin, Columbia Univ., New York; came to USA aged 15 after escaping Nazi takeover of France; carried out post-doctoral research at California Inst. of Tech. (CalTech); Faculty mem. Haverford Coll. 1957–70; fmr Prof. of Physics, Univ. of Pennsylvania, now Prof. of Physics Emer.; Chair. IUPAP Comm. on Nuclear Physics 1978–81; mem. Nuclear Science Advisory Cttee, Dept of Energy/NSF 1977–80; mem. American Physical Soc. (Chair. Div. of Nuclear Physics 1973–74), AAAS (mem. Governing Council 1974–80); Dr hc (Smith Coll.) 1995, (Michigan State Univ.) 1997, (Haverford Coll.) 1999; Guggenheim Fellow 1965–66, Christian and Mary Lindback Foundation Award for Distinguished Teaching 1991, Faye Ajzenberg-Selove Scholarship named in her honour 1998, Nicholson Medal for Humanitarian Service, American Physical Soc. 1999, Distinguished Alumni Fellow Award, Dept of Physics, Univ. of Wisconsin 2001, Nat. Medal of Science 2007. *Achievements include:* organized first session of American Physical Soc. meeting to deal with women in physics, helped found American Physical Soc.'s Cttee on Women in Physics. *Publications:* Nuclear Spectroscopy, Energy Levels of Light Nuclei (five vols) 1986, 1987, 1988, 1990, 1991, A Matter of Choices: Memoirs of a Female Physicist (autobiography) 1994. *Address:* 2N34, David Rittenhouse Laboratory, Department of Physics and Astronomy, University of Pennsylvania, 209 South 33rd Street, Philadelphia, PA 19104-6396, USA (office). *Telephone:* (215) 898-8159 (office); (215) 898-5645 (office). *Fax:* (215) 898-2010 (office). *E-mail:* fay@pobox.upenn.edu (office); fay@physics.upenn.edu (office). *Website:* www.upenn.edu (office).

AKAGAWA, Jiro; Japanese writer; b. 29 Feb. 1948, Fukuoka; m. Fumiko Serita 1973; one d.; ed Toho-gakuen High School; fmr proof-reader for Japan Soc. of Mechanical Engineers; mem. Japanese Mystery Writers' Asscn 1977–; All Yomimono Debut Writers' Award 1976; Kadokawa Publishing Book Award 1980. *Publications:* more than 500 works including novels: The School Festival for the Dead 1977, Ghost Train 1978, The Deduction of Tortoiseshell Holmes 1978, High School Girl with a Machine Gun 1978, The Requiem Dedicated to the Bad Wife 1980, Virgin Road 1983, Chizuko's Younger Sister 1989, The Ghost Story of the Hitokoizaka-Slope 1995. *Leisure interests:* classical music, watching movies. *Address:* 40-16-201 Ohyama-cho, Sibuya-ku, Tokyo 151-0065, Japan (home).

AKAIKE, Hirotugu, DSc; Japanese mathematician and academic; *Professor Emeritus, The Institute of Statistical Mathematics;* b. Nov. 1927; ed Tokyo Univ.; joined Inst. of Statistical Math., Tokyo 1952, Head of Second Section, First Div. 1962–73, Dir Fifth Div. 1973–85, Prof. and Dir Dept of Prediction and Control 1985–86, Dir-Gen. Inst. of Statistical Math. 1986–94, Prof. Emer. 1994–; Head of Dept of Statistical Science, Univ. for Advanced Studies 1988–94, Prof. Emer. 1994–; mem. Science Council of Japan 1988–91; Medal with Purple Ribbon 1989, Order of the Sacred Treasure (Gold and Silver Star) 1996; Ishikawa Prize, Union of Japanese Scientists and Engineers 1972, Okochi Prize, Okochi Memorial Foundation 1980, Asahi Prize 1989, Japan Statistical Soc. Prize 1996, Kyoto Prize in Basic Sciences, The Inamori Foundation 2006. *Publications:* Modern Society and Mass Communication, Lectures on Mass Communication, Vol. 5 (with R. Hidaka) 1955, Views on Public Opinion (co-author) 1955, Statistical Analysis and Control of Dynamic Systems (with T. Nakagawa) 1972, Probability and Statistics (co-author) 1985, Special Topics of Statistics (co-author) 1986, Theory of Time Series (co-author) 1988, Statistical Analysis and Control of Dynamic Systems (with T. Nakagawa) 1988, Practice of Time Series Analysis II (co-author) 1995; numerous papers in professional journals. *Address:* The Institute of Statistical Mathematics, 4-6-7 Minami-Azabu, Minato-ku, Tokyo 106-8569, Japan (office). *Telephone:* (3) 3446-1501 (office). *E-mail:* info@ism.ac.jp (office). *Website:* www.ism.ac.jp (office); tswww.ism.ac.jp/kitagawa/HomePage/akaike.html (office).

AKAKA, Daniel Kahikina; American politician; *Senator from Hawaii;* b. 11 Sept. 1924, Honolulu; s. of Kahikina Akaka and Annie Kahoa; m. Mary M. Chong 1948; four s. one d.; ed Univ. of Hawaii; schoolteacher, Hawaii 1953–60; Vice-Prin., Prin. Ewa Beach Elementary School, Honolulu 1960–64; Prin. Pohakea Elementary School 1964–65, Kaneohe Elementary School 1965–68; Dir Hawaii Office of Econ. Opportunity 1971–74; Special Asst Human Resources Office of Gov. of Hawaii 1975–76; program specialist, Hawaii Compensatory Educ. 1978–79, 1985–91; mem. 95th–101st Congresses from 2nd Dist of Hawaii 1977–90; Senator from Hawaii 1990–; Democrat. *Address:* 141 Hart Senate Bldg, Washington, DC 20510-0001, USA. *Telephone:* (202) 224-6361 (office). *Fax:* (202) 224-2126 (office). *Website:* akaka.senate.gov (office).

AKALAITIS, JoAnne, BA; American theatre director and academic; *Wallace Benjamin Flint and L. May Hawver Flint Professor of Theater, Bard College;* b. 29 June 1932, Chicago; d. of Clement Akalaitis and Estelle Mattis; m. Philip Glass 1965 (divorced 1974); one s. one d.; ed Univ. of Chicago and Stanford Univ. Grad. School; Artistic Dir New York Shakespeare Festival 1991–92; Wallace Benjamin Flint and L. May Hawver Flint Prof. of Theater, Bard Coll.

2003–; Rockefeller Playwright Fellow; Rosamund Gilder Fellow; Guggenheim Fellow 1978; Co-founder Mabou Mines (avant-garde theatre co.), New York 1970; recipient of five Obies for distinguished direction, Edwin Booth Award, Rosamund Gilder Award for Outstanding Achievement in Theatre. *Works directed include:* Beckett's Cascando 1976, Dressed Like an Egg 1977, Dead End Kids 1980, A History of Nuclear Power (writer and dir of play and film), Request Concert (Drama Desk Award) 1981, The Photographer 1983, Beckett's Endgame 1984, Genet's The Balcony 1985, Green Card (writer and dir) 1986, Greg Büchner's Leon & Lena (and Lenz) 1987, Genet's The Screens 1987, Cymbeline 1989, 'Tis Pity She's a Whore 1992, Henry IV (Pts I & II) 1991, Woyzeck 1992, In the Summer House 1993. *Publication:* Green Card. *Leisure interest:* cooking. *Address:* Theater Program, Division of the Arts, Bard College 30 Campus Road, Annandale-on-Hudson, NY 12504-5000, USA. *Telephone:* (845) 758-7936. *E-mail:* akalaiti@bard.edu. *Website:* www.bard.edu/academics/programs/arts.

AKAMATSU, Ryoko; Japanese academic, diplomatist and civil servant; *President, Japanese Association of International Women's Rights;* b. 24 Aug. 1929, Osaka; d. of Rinsaku Akamatsu and Asaka Akamatsu; ed Tsuda Coll. and Univ. of Tokyo; joined Ministry of Labour 1955, Dir Women Workers' Div. 1970–72; Dir-Gen. Yamanashi Labour Standard Bureau 1975–78; Counsellor in charge of Women's Affairs, Prime Minister's Office 1978–79; Minister, Perm. Mission to UN, New York 1979–82; Dir-Gen. Women's Bureau, Ministry of Labour 1982–85; Amb. to Uruguay 1986–89; Pres. Japan Inst. of Workers' Evolution 1989–93; Prof., Bunkyo Gakuin Univ. 1992–2003; Minister of Educ., Science, Culture and Sports 1993–94; Pres. Japanese Asscn of Int. Women's Rights; Councillor, Asian Women's Fund; Grand Cordon of the Order of the Rising Sun 2003. *Publications:* Girls Be Ambitious (autobiog.) 1990, Beautiful Uruguay 1990, Enacting Laws of Equal Employment Opportunity for Men and Women 2003. *Leisure interests:* reading, swimming, listening to classical music. *Address:* Japanese Association of International Women's Rights, c/o Office of Prof. Yasuko Yamashita, Bunkyo Gakuin University, 1-19-1Mukougaoka Bunkyou-ku, Tokyo 113-8668, Japan. *E-mail:* info@JAIWR.org. *Website:* www.JAIWR.org.

AKASAKA, Kiyotaka, MA; Japanese diplomatist and UN official; *Under-Secretary-General, Department of Communications and Public Information, United Nations;* b. 1948, Osaka; ed Kyoto Univ. and Trinity Coll., Cambridge, UK; joined Foreign Ministry 1971; held several posts at Secr. of GATT 1988–91, WHO 1993–97; Deputy Dir-Gen. Multilateral Co-operation Dept, Ministry of Foreign Affairs 1997–2000; Perm. Rep., UN, New York 2000–01; Consul-Gen. Embassy in Sao Paulo 2001–03; Deputy Sec.-Gen. OECD 2003–07; Under-Sec.-Gen., Dept of Communications and Public Information, UN 2007–; Rep. to Kyoto Conf. on Climate Change 1997; Vice-Chair. Prep. Cttee World Summit on Sustainable Devt, Johannesburg 2002. *Publications:* The GATT and the Uruguay Round Negotiations; The Cartagena Protocol on Biosafety and numerous journal articles on trade, the environment and sustainable devt. *Address:* Department of Communications and Public Information, United Nations, New York, NY, 10017, USA (office). *Telephone:* (212) 963-1234 (office). *Fax:* (212) 963-4879 (office). *Website:* www.un.org (office).

AKASHI, Yasushi; Japanese diplomatist; *Chairman, Japan Center for Conflict Prevention;* b. 19 Jan. 1931, Akita; m.; two c.; ed Univ. of Tokyo, Univ. of Virginia, Fletcher School of Law and Diplomacy and Columbia Univ.; Political Affairs Officer UN Secr. 1957–74; Chair. Univ. Seminar on Modern East Asia 1963–64; Amb. at Perm. Mission to UN, New York 1974–79; UN Under-Sec.-Gen. for Public Information 1979–87, for Disarmament Affairs 1987; UN Rep. in Cambodia 1992; Special Envoy to Fmr Yugoslavia 1994–95; UN Under-Sec. for Humanitarian Affairs 1996–97, UN Emergency Relief Co-ordinator 1997–98; Chair. Japan Center for Conflict Prevention 1999–, Int. Peace Co-operation Council 2002–; has represented Japan in Gen. Ass. and numerous UN confs and orgs; Chair. Budget and Finance Cttee Governing Council UNDP 1978; mem. Advisory Cttee on Admin. and Budgetary Questions 1974, 1977; Assoc. Columbia Univ. Seminars; Chair. Conf. of Mid-Career Asian Leaders on Devt 1967; Pres. Council on Population, Japan Asscn for the Study of the UN; Dir Int. Peace Acad., Better World Soc.; Sec. Founding Cttee UN Univ.; fmr Visiting Lecturer, Univ. of Tokyo, Int. Christian Univ., Tokyo and Sophia Univ.; currently Visiting Prof., Ritsumeikan Univ. *Publications:* The United Nations 1965, From the Windows of the United Nations 1984, The Lights and Shadows of the United Nations 1985 and numerous articles. *Address:* Japan Center for Conflict Prevention, 2-14-11 Yushima, Bunkyo-ku, Tokyo 113-0034, Japan (office). *Telephone:* (3) 3834-2651 (office). *Fax:* (3) 3834-2652 (office). *E-mail:* contact@jccp.gr.jp (office). *Website:* www.jccp.gr.jp (office).

AKAYEV, Askar Akayevich, DTech; Kyrgyzstani politician; *Professor of Mathematics, Moscow State University 'M. V. Lomonsov';* b. 10 Nov. 1944, Kyzyl-Bairak Kemin Dist; s. of Akai Tokoyev and Ossel Tokoyeva; m. Mairam Akayeva 1970; two s. two d.; ed Leningrad Inst. of Precise Mechanics and Optics; lecturer; Prof. Frunze (now Bishkek) Politech. Inst. 1972–73, Chair. 1976–86; Prof. Inst. of Precise Mechanics and Optics 1973–76; Head of Science Dept Cen. Cttee Kyrgyz CP 1986–87; mem. CPSU 1981–91 (resgnd); fmr mem. Cen. Cttee Kyrgyz CP, Vice-Pres., Pres. Kirghiz SSR Pres. Kyrgyz SSR Acad. of Sciences 1987–90; fmr mem. CPSU Constitutional Compliance Cttee; fmr mem. USSR Supreme Soviet Cttee on Econ. Reform 1991; Exec. Pres. Kyrgyz SSR 1990, Pres. of Kyrgyzstan 1990–2005; Prof. of Mathematics, Moscow State University 'M. V. Lomonsov' 2005–; Academician, Int. Acad. of Informatisation, Canada 1997; Hon. Academician Int. Eng Acad. and of Int. Acad. of Creation 1996; Albert Einstein Award 1999, Devotion to Peace and Good Award, Russia 2000, WIPO Gold Medal 2001, Elizabeth Haub Award for Environmental Diplomacy 2003. *Publications:* Methods of Data Optical

Processing 1992, Diplomacy of the Silk Road 1999, The Memorable Decade 2001, Kyrgyz Statehood and National Epos 'Manas' 2002, The Difficult Road to Democracy 2002, more than 80 articles on radiophysics and politics. *Leisure interests:* travelling with the family, mountain skiing, mountaineering. *Address:* Moscow State University 'M. V. Lomonsov', 119992 Moscow, Leninskie Gory, Russia (office). *Telephone:* (095) 939-10-00 (office). *Fax:* (095) 939-01-26 (office). *E-mail:* office@akaev.kg (office); mmf@mech.math .msu.su (office). *Website:* www.askarakaev.kg (office); www.msu.ru (office).

AKBAROV, Otabek Khamidullayevich; Uzbekistan diplomatist; *Ambassador to UK;* b. 19 Dec. 1967, Tashkent; m. Nisso Akbarova; two s.; ed Tashkent State Univ., Netherlands Inst. of Int. Relations, Geneva Centre for Security Policy; Sr Insp., Consular Dept, Ministry of Foreign Affairs 1993–94, Third Sec., Dept of European Countries 1994–95; Second Sec., Embassy in Brussels 1995–98; First Sec. and Acting Head of Unit, Dept of European Countries, Ministry of Foreign Affairs 1998–2000; First Sec., Embassy in Paris 2000–04; Dir Dept of Cooperation with Countries of Europe, Ministry of Foreign Affairs 2004–07; Amb. to UK 2007–. *Leisure interests:* literature, films, nature, tennis, cycling. *Address:* Embassy of Uzbekistan, 41 Holland Park, London, W11 3RP, England (office). *Telephone:* (20) 7229-7679 (office). *Fax:* (20) 7229-7029 (office). *E-mail:* info@uzbekembassy.org (office). *Website:* www.uzbekembassy.org (office).

AKCHURIN, Renat Suleimanovich, DrMed; Russian cardiovascular surgeon; *Professor and Head, Department of Cardiovascular Surgery, Russian Cardiological Centre;* b. 2 April 1946, Andijan, Uzbekistan; m. Natalya Pavlovna Akchurina; two s.; ed Inst. of Medicine (now Seehenov Acad. of Medicine); gen. practitioner, polyclinics 1970–73; Ordinator, Jr, Sr Researcher, Inst. of Clinical and Experimental Medicine 1973–84; in Baylor Univ., Texas, USA 1984; Surgeon, Prof. and Head, Dept of Cardiovascular Surgery, Russian Cardiological Centre 1984–; Corresp. mem. Russian Acad. of Medical Sciences 1997; performed first heart and lung transplantation operations in USSR; performs about 100 bypass operations a year, performed a bypass operation on Pres. Yeltsin 1996; patented several inventions of medical instruments; USSR State Prize 1982, Russian Fed. State Prize 2001, Russian Govt Prize 2004, Paul Harris Fellow, Rotary International. *Publications include:* more than 300 scientific papers and articles. *Leisure interests:* music, hunting, cooking. *Address:* Cardiology Scientific Centre, Cherepkovskaya str. 15A, 121552 Moscow, Russia (office). *Telephone:* (495) 149-00-69 (office). *E-mail:* rsakchurin@list.ru (office); 3ko@list.ru (office).

AKEIL, Ahmad Abdallah al-; Saudi Arabian banker; Chair. Arab Bank for Econ. Devt in Africa (Banque arabe pour le développement économique en Afrique—BADEA); mem. Bd of Dirs Arab Nat. Bank. *Address:* Arab Bank for Economic Development in Africa, Sayed Abd ar-Rahman el-Mahdi Street, PO Box 2640, Khartoum 11111, Sudan (office). *Telephone:* (1) 83773646 (office). *Fax:* (1) 83770600 (office). *E-mail:* badea@badea.org (office). *Website:* www .badea.org (office).

AKENSON, Donald Harman, BA, MEd, PhD, DLitt, DHum, FRSA, FRSC, FRHistS; Canadian historian and academic; *Douglas Professor of Canadian and Colonial History, Queen's University;* b. 22 May 1941, Minneapolis, Minn.; s. of Donald Nels Akenson and Fern L. Harman Akenson; ed Yale and Harvard Univs; Allston Burr Sr Tutor, Dunster House, Harvard Coll. 1966–67; Assoc. Prof. of History, Queen's Univ., Kingston, Ont. 1970–74, Prof. 1974–, currently Douglas Prof. of Canadian and Colonial History; Beamish Research Prof., Inst. of Irish Studies, Univ. of Liverpool 1998–2002; Guggenheim Fellow 1984–85; Hon. DLitt (McMaster) 1995, (Guelph) 2000; Hon. DHumLitt (Lethbridge) 1996; Hon. LLD (Regina) 2002; Hon. DLH (Queen's Univ. Belfast) 2008; Chalmers Prize 1985, Landon Prize 1987, Grawemeyer World Peace Prize 1993, Molson Laureate 1996 and many other awards and distinctions. *Publications:* The Irish Education Experiment 1970, The Church of Ireland: Ecclesiastical Reform and Revolution 1800–1885 1971, Education and Enmity: The Control of Schooling in Northern Ireland 1920–50 1973, The United States and Ireland 1973, A Mirror to Kathleen's Face: Education in Independent Ireland 1922–60 1975, Local Poets and Social History: James Orr, Bard of Ballycarry 1977, Between Two Revolutions: Islandmagee, Co. Antrim 1798–1920 1979, A Protestant in Purgatory: Richard Whately: Archbishop of Dublin 1981, The Irish in Ontario: A Study of Rural History 1984, Being Had: Historians, Evidence and the Irish in North America 1985, The Life and Times of Ogle Gowan 1986, Small Differences: Irish Catholics and Irish Protestants, 1815–1921 1988, Half the World from Home: Perspectives on the Irish in New Zealand 1990, Occasional Papers on the Irish in South Africa 1991, God's Peoples: Covenant and Land in South Africa, Israel and Ulster 1992, The Irish Diaspora, A Primer 1993, Conor: A Biography of Conor Cruise O'Brien 1994, If the Irish Ran the World: Montserrat 1630–1730, Surpassing Wonder: The Invention of the Bible and the Talmuds 1998, Saint Saul: A Skeleton Key to the Historical Jesus 2000, Intolerance: The E. Coli of the Human Mind 2004, An Irish History of Civilization (two vols) 2006, Some Family – The Mormons and How Humanity Keeps Track of Itself 2007; novels: The Lazar House Notebooks 1981, Brotherhood Week in Belfast 1984, The Orangeman: The Edgerston Audit 1987, At Face Value: The Life and Times of Eliza McCormack 1990. *Address:* Department of History, Queen's University, Kingston, ON, K7L 3N6, Canada (office). *Telephone:* (613) 533-2155 (office). *Fax:* (613) 533-6822 (office). *Website:* www.queensu.ca/ history (office).

AKERLOF, George Arthur, BA, PhD; American economist and academic; *Koshland Professor of Economics, University of California, Berkeley;* b. 17 June 1940, New Haven, Conn.; m. Janet L. Yellen; one s.; ed Massachusetts Inst. Tech., Yale Univ.; Asst Prof., Univ. of Calif., Berkeley 1966–70, Assoc. Prof. 1970–77, Prof. 1977–78, Koshland Prof. 1980–; Visiting Prof., Indian Statistical Inst. 1967–68; Research Assoc., Harvard Univ. 1969; Sr Staff Economist, Pres.'s Council of Econ. Advisers 1973–74; Visiting Research Economist, Special Studies Section, Bd of Govs of the Fed. Reserve System 1977–78; Cassel Prof. with respect to Money and Banking, LSE 1978–80; Sr Fellow, The Brookings Inst. 1994–; Vice-Pres. American Econ. Asscn; mem. Bd of Dirs Nat. Bureau for Economic Research 1997–; Assoc. Ed. several journals on econs; Guggenheim Fellow; Fellow Inst. for Policy Reform; numerous hon. lectureships; Nobel Prize in Econs 2001 (jt recipient); numerous other awards and prizes. *Publications:* An Economic Theorist's Book of Tales 1984, Animal Spirits: How Human Psychology Drives the Economy, and Why It Matters for Global Capitalism (with Robert Shiller) 2009. *Address:* Department of Economics, 549 Evans Hall, #3880, University of California, Berkeley, CA 94720-3880, USA (office). *Telephone:* (510) 642-5837 (office). *Fax:* (510) 642-6615 (office). *E-mail:* akerlof@econ.berkeley.edu (office). *Website:* emlab.berkeley.edu/users/akerlof/index.shtml (office).

AKERMANN, Markus; Swiss business executive; *CEO, Holcim Ltd;* b. 25 Jan. 1947; ed Univ. of St Gallen, Univ. of Sheffield, UK; with Swiss Banking Corpn 1975–78; joined Holcim Ltd 1978, served in posts including Latin America Area Man. 1987, mem. Exec. Cttee 1993–2002, mem. Bd of Dirs and CEO 2002–, Chair. Man. Bd Holcim Foundation; mem. Bd of Dirs ACC Ltd, India. *Address:* Holcim Ltd, Hagenholzstrasse 83, 8050 Zurich, Switzerland (office). *Telephone:* (58) 850-68-68 (office). *Fax:* (58) 850-68-69 (office). *E-mail:* info@holcim.com (office). *Website:* www.holcim.com (office).

AKERS-JONES, Sir David, KBE, CMG, JP, MA; British civil servant; b. 14 April 1927; s. of Walter George Jones and Dorothy Jones; m. Jane Spickernell 1951 (died 2002); one s. (deceased) one d.; ed Worthing High School and Brasenose Coll., Oxford; with British India Steam Navigation Co. 1945–49; Malayan Civil Service 1954–57; Hong Kong Civil Service 1957–86, Sec. for New Territories and for Dist Admin, Hong Kong Govt 1973–85, Chief Sec. 1985–86; Acting Gov. Hong Kong 1986–87; Hong Kong Affairs Adviser to China 1993–97; Chair. Nat. Mutual Asia Hong Kong (later AXA China Region) 1988–2001, Hong Kong Housing Authority 1988–93, Global Asset Man. Hong Kong 1988–; Dir Hysan Devt Co. Ltd, The Mingly Corpn Ltd; Vice-Pres. WWF Hong Kong 1995–, Hong Kong Girl Guides; Hon. Pres. Outward Bound Trust (Hong Kong) 1986–; Hon. mem. RICS; Hon. DCL (Kent Univ.) 1987; Hon. LLD (Chinese Univ. of Hong Kong) 1988; Hon. DScS (City Univ., Hong Kong) 1993; Grand Bauhinia Medal (Hong Kong) 2003. *Leisure interests:* painting, gardening, walking and music. *Address:* Flat 1, Floor 25, Bamboo Grove, 80 Kennedy Road, Hong Kong Special Administrative Region, People's Republic of China (home). *Telephone:* (852) 2491-9319 (office); (852) 2491-9319 (home). *Fax:* (852) 2491-1300 (home). *E-mail:* akersjon@pacific.net.hk (home).

AKHEDJAKOVA, Liya Medjidovna; Russian actress; b. 9 June 1938, Dniepropetrovsk; d. of Medjid Salekhovich Akhedjakov and Yulia Aleksandrovna Akhedjakova; m. Vladimir Nikolayevich Persyanov; ed State Inst. of Theatre Art; actress, Moscow Theatre of Young Spectator 1953–71, Sovremennik Theatre 1971–; leading roles in classical and contemporary plays including Shakespeare, Tennessee Williams; People's Artist of Russia, State Prize, Nike Prize. *Films include:* Garage, Office Romance, Blessed Heavens, Twenty Days Without War, Lost Bus, Pretty Face 1990, Promised Heaven 1991, Seven-Forty 1992, Moscow Vacation 1995, Dandelion Wine 1997, Old Hags 2000. *Leisure interest:* travel. *Address:* 117415 Moscow, Udaltsova str. 12, Apt. 153, Russia (home). *Telephone:* (495) 921-63-48 (office); (495) 131-60-41 (home).

AKHMADULINA, Isabella (Bella) Akhatovna; Russian poet; b. 10 April 1937, Moscow; d. of Ahat Akhmadulin and Nadya Akhmadulina (née Lazareva); m. 1st Yevgeniy Yevtushenko (q.v.) 1960; m. 2nd Yuriy Nagibin; m. 3rd Boris Messerer 1974; m. 4th Gennadi Mamlin; ed Gorky Inst. of Literature, Moscow; Sec. USSR (now Russian) Writers' Union 1986–91, mem. Bd Russian PEN-Centre 1989–92; Hon. mem. American Acad. of Arts and Letters 1977; Order of Friendship of Peoples 1984; State Prize of USSR 1989, Pushkin Prize 1994, Russian President's Prize 1998, Alfred Tepfer Prize, State Prize of the Russian Fed. 2004. *Publications:* Fire Tree 1958, The String 1962, The Rain 1963, My Ancestry 1964, Summer Leaves 1968, The Lessons of Music 1969, Fever and Other New Poems 1970, Tenerezza 1971, Poems 1975, The Dreams About Georgia 1977, The Candle 1978, The Snowstorm 1978, The Mystery 1983, The Garden 1987, The Seaboard 1991, Selected Works (vols 1–3) 1996, The Ancient Style Attracts Me 1997, Beautiful Features of My Friends 1999, and trans from Georgian. *Address:* 125319 Moscow, Chernyachovskogo str. 4, Apt 37, Russia. *Telephone:* (495) 151-22-00.

AKHMETOV, Danial Kenzhetayevich, BEng, BEcons; Kazakhstani politician; *Minister of Defence;* b. 15 June 1954, Pavlodar; m.; two c.; ed Pavlodar Industry Inst.; fmr racing cyclist; fmr Deputy Prime Minister and Minister of Industry, Energy, Transport and Communications; Akim (Gov.) Pavlodar Oblast 1995–97, 2001–03; Akim (Gov.) Northern Kazakhstan Oblast 1997–99; Deputy, then First Deputy Prime Minister 1999–2001; Prime Minister of Kazakhstan 2003–07 (resgnd); Minister of Defence 2007–. *Address:* Ministry of Defence, 010000 Astana, Beibitshilik 51A, Kazakhstan (office). *Telephone:* (7172) 33-78-89 (office). *Fax:* (7172) 33-78-89 (office). *Website:* www.mod.kz (office).

AKHMETOV, Rinat Leonidovych, BA; Ukrainian business executive; b. 21 Sept. 1966, Donetsk; m.; two c.; ed Donetsk State Univ.; f. Donetsk City Bank; Head, Donetsk Industrial Group (conglomerate of steel and mining cos); prin. shareholder, System Capital Man. (SCM) (holding co. with controlling shares in more than 90 cos); Pres. Shaktar Donetsk football club 1996–; Deputy, Verkhovna Rada (Supreme Council) 2006–; mem. Partiya Regioniv (Party of Regions); Founder, Foundation for Effective Governance, Kyiv. *Address:* System Capital Management, 83001 Donetsk, vul. Postysheva 117 (office); Verkhovna Rada (Supreme Council), 01008 Kyiv, vul. M. Hrushevskoho 5,

Ukraine (office). *Telephone:* (44) 255-35-69 (Verkhovna Rada) (office). *Fax:* (62) 334-99-08 (office). *E-mail:* Akhmetov.Rinat@rada.gov.ua (office). *Website:* www.scm.com.ua (office); www.shakhtar.com.

AKHTAR, Muhammad, MSc, PhD, FRS; British/Pakistani biochemist and academic; *Professor Emeritus of Biochemistry, University of Southampton;* b. 23 Feb. 1933, Punjab, India; s. of Muhammad Azeem Chaudhry; m. Monika E. Schürmann 1963; two s.; ed Govt Coll. Sargodha, Govt Coll. Lahore, Univ. of Punjab and Imperial Coll., London; Research Scientist, Research Inst. for Medicine and Chem., Cambridge, Mass, USA 1959–63; Lecturer in Biochemistry, Univ. of Southampton 1963–66, Sr Lecturer 1966–68, Reader 1968–73, Prof. 1973–98, Head, Dept of Biochemistry 1978–93, Chair. School of Biochemical and Physiological Sciences 1983–87, Prof. Emer. of Biochemistry 1998–; Founding Fellow Third World Acad. of Sciences, Treasurer, mem. Council 1993–98, Vice-Pres. 1998–2004; mem. Council Royal Soc. 1983–85; mem. Biochemical Soc. Cttee 1983–86; Hon. DSc (Karachi) 2000; Sitara-I-Imtiaz (Pakistan), Flintoff Medal, Royal Soc. of Chem. 1993, TWAS Medal 1996. *Publications:* numerous articles in biochemical and chemical journals. *Address:* Department of Biochemistry, University of Southampton, Southampton, SO16 7PX, England (office). *Telephone:* (23) 8059-4338 (office); (23) 8059-4323 (office).

AKHTAR, Shamshad, BA, MSc, MA, PhD; Pakistani economist and central banker; *Governor, State Bank of Pakistan;* b. Hyderabad, Sindh Prov.; ed Univ. of Punjab, Quaid-e-Azam Univ., Univ. of Sussex and Paisley Coll. of Tech. (now Univ. of Paisley), UK, Harvard Univ., USA; briefly worked at planning offices in Pakistan at Fed. and Sindh Govt levels; economist, World Bank mission in Pakistan 1980–90; Sr then Prin. Financial Sector Specialist, Asian Devt Bank (ADB) 1990–98; Man. and Coordinator for APEC Finance Ministers' Group 1998–2001, Dir Govt Finance and Trade Div. for E and Cen. Asia Dept, then Deputy Dir Gen. SE Asia Dept 2001–04, Dir Gen. 2004–05; Gov. (first woman) State Bank of Pakistan 2006–; Visiting Fellow, Harvard Univ. Dept of Econs 1987; Best Cen. Bank Gov. in Asia, Emerging Markets newspaper 2007, Cen. Bank Gov. of the Year in Asia, Banker Magazine 2008, named one of Ten Outstanding Asian Women Leaders by Asian Wall Street Journal 2008. *Publications:* numerous papers on econs and finance. *Address:* State Bank of Pakistan, Central Directorate, I. I. Chundrigar Road, PO Box 4456, Karachi 2, Pakistan (office). *Telephone:* (21) 9212400 (office). *Fax:* (21) 9217234 (office). *E-mail:* shamshad.akhtar@sbp.org.pk (office); governor .office@sbp.org.pk (office). *Website:* www.sbp.org.pk (office).

AKHTAR, Tasleem, MBBS, DCh, MRCP FRCP; Pakistani paediatrician, medical research officer and academic; *Chief of Research and Academic Advancement, Fatima Memorial College of Medicine and Surgery;* b. 1 Sept. 1944, Village Jhanda, Tehsil Dist; m.; one s. one d.; ed Khyber Medical Coll., Univ. of Peshawar, Royal Coll. of Physicians, London, UK, Royal Coll. of Physicians and Surgeons, Edinburgh, UK; est. Neonatal Unit, Khyber Medical Coll. 1976, Sr Medical Research Officer Pakistan Medical Research Council (PMRC) Research Centre 1979–1980, Research Dir 1980, Exec. Dir PMRC 1994–2004, Chair. 1996–99; currently Chief of Research and Academic Advancement, Fatima Memorial Coll. of Medicine and Surgery, Lahore; Dir Prov. Health Services Acad., Dept of Health, Govt of North-West Frontier Prov. (NWFP) 1999–2000; Gen. Sec. Pakistan Paediatric Asscn, NWFP Br. (PPA–NWFP) 1980–82, 1984–86, Pres. 1982–84, Vice-Pres. PPA Centre 1990; Chief Ed. Pakistan Journal of Medical Research, PMRC; Asst Ed. Pakistan Paediatric Journal, Lahore; mem. Hosp. Monitoring Cttee, Ministry of Health; mem. Governing Bd Nat. Inst. of Health, Islamabad; mem. Bd of Dirs NWFP Health Foundation, The Network for Consumer Protection; mem. Forum on Telemedicine in Pakistan, Tech. Resource Mobilization Unit 2001–02; American Public Health Asscn Award for Most Successful Int. Collaboration 1997. *Address:* Fatima Memorial Hospital, Shadman, Lahore, Pakistan (office). *Telephone:* 111-555-600 (office). *Fax:* 7570586 (office). *E-mail:* tasleem.akhtar@fmsystem.org (office); akhtar_tasleem@hotmail.com. *Website:* www.fmsystem.org (office).

AKIHITO, Emperor of Japan; b. 23 Dec. 1933, Tokyo; s. of the late Emperor Hirohito and of Empress Nagako; m. Michiko Shoda 1959; two s. (including Crown Prince Naruhito) one d.; ed Gakushuin schools and Faculty of Politics and Econs Gakushuin Univ.; official investiture as Crown Prince 1952; succeeded 7 Jan. 1989; crowned 12 Nov. 1990; has undertaken visits to some 37 countries and travelled widely throughout Japan; Hon. Pres. or Patron, Asian Games 1958, Int. Sports Games for the Disabled 1964, Eleventh Pacific Science Congress 1966, Japan World Exposition 1970, Int. Skill Contest for the Disabled 1981; mem. Ichthyological Soc. of Japan; Hon. Sec. Int. Conf. on Indo-Pacific Fish 1985; Hon. mem. Linnean Soc. (London). *Publications:* 25 papers in journal of Ichthyological Soc. of Japan. *Leisure interests:* taxonomic study of gobiid fish, natural history and conservation, history, tennis. *Address:* The Imperial Palace, 1-1 Chiyoda, Chiyoda-ku, Tokyo 100, Japan. *Telephone:* (3) 32131111.

AKIKUSA, Naoyuki, BA; Japanese business executive; *Chairman and Representative Director, Fujitsu Ltd;* b. 12 Dec. 1938, Tochigi; m.; two c.; ed Waseda Univ.; joined Fujitsu Ltd as Systems Engineer 1961, Gen. Man., Public Service Systems Eng Div. 1977–86, Group Sr Vice-Pres., System Eng Group 1986–91, mem. Bd of Dirs 1988–, Sr Vice-Pres. 1991–92, Exec. Vice-Pres. 1992–98, Pres. 1998–2000, Pres. and CEO 2000–03, Chair. and Rep. Dir 2003–; Vice-Chair. Japan Electronics and Information Tech. Industries Asscn (JEITA) 1998–99, Chair. 1999–2000; Vice-Chair. Communications and Information Network Asscn of Japan (CIAJ) 1998, Bd of Councillors, Japan Fed. of Econ. Orgs (Keidanren) 2000; Co-Chair. Cttee on Trade & Investment, Japan Business Fed. (JBF) 2004–; mem. World Econ. Forum, Industrial Re-birth Council. *Leisure interest:* tennis. *Address:* Fujitsu Ltd, Shiodome City Centre, 1-5-2, Higashi-Shimbashi, Minato-ku, Tokyo 105-7123, Japan (office). *Telephone:* (3) 6252-2175 (office). *Fax:* (3) 6252-2783 (office). *Website:* www.fujitsu .com (office).

AKILOV, Akil Gaibullayevich; Tajikistani politician and engineer; *Chairman, Council of Ministers (Prime Minister) and Minister of Construction;* b. 2 Feb. 1944, Leninabad (now Khujand); m.; three c.; ed Moscow Inst. of Construction and Eng; various posts in construction orgs, Leninabad (now Sogdh) Viloyat 1960–76; worked for CP 1976–93; Minister of Construction of Tajikistan 1993–94; Deputy Prime Minister 1994–96; First Deputy Chair. Leninabad Viloyat 1996–99; Chair. Council of Ministers (Prime Minister) and Minister of Construction 1999–; mem. People's Democratic Party of Tajikistan. *Address:* Secretariat of the Prime Minister, 734023 Dushanbe, Xiyoboni Rudaki 80, Tajikistan (office). *Telephone:* (372) 21-18-71 (office). *Fax:* (372) 21-51-10 (office).

AKINKUGBE, Oladipo Olujimi, Atobase of Ife, Babalofin of Ijebu-Igbo, Adingbuwa of Ondo, Ikolaba Balogun Basegun of Ibadan, MD, DPhil, DTM&H, FRCP; Nigerian professor of medicine; *Professor Emeritus, University of Ibadan;* b. 17 July 1933, Ondo; s. of Chief Odofin David Akinkugbe and Chief (Mrs) Grace Akinkugbe; m. Dr Folasade Dina 1965; two s.; ed Govt Coll., Ibadan, Univ. Coll., Ibadan, Univs of London, Liverpool and Oxford; Lecturer in Medicine, Univ. of Ibadan 1964–66, Sr Lecturer 1966–68, Prof. 1968–95, Prof. Emer. 1996–, Dean of Medicine 1970–74, Chair. of Cttee of Deans 1972–74, mem. Council 1971–74; Visiting Prof. of Medicine, Harvard Univ. 1974–75; Principal, Univ. Coll., Ilorin 1975–77; Vice-Chancellor Univ. of Ilorin 1977–78, Ahmadu Bello Univ. 1978–79; Pro-Chancellor and Chair. Council, Port Harcourt Univ. 1986–90; Pres. Nigerian Asscn of Nephrology 1987–89, Nigerian Hypertension Soc. 1992–95; mem. Scientific Advisory Panel CIBA Foundation, Council of Int. Soc. of Hypertension, WHO Expert Cttees on Cardiovascular Diseases, Smoking Control, Professional and Tech. Educ. of Medical and Auxiliary Personnel, Sr Consultant 1983–84, WHO Advisory Cttee on Health Research 1990; Visiting Fellow, Balliol Coll., Oxford 1981–82; Visiting Prof. of Medicine, Univ. of Oxford 1981–82; mem. Bd of Trustees, Obafemi Awolowo Foundation, Nigerian Heartcare Foundation 1994–, Chair. 2000– (also mem. Governing Council), Nigerian Educare Trust 1995, The Social Sciences and Reproductive Health Research Network 1996, Ajumogobia Science Foundation; Chair. Bd of Man., Univ. Coll. Hosp. Ibadan 2000–04; Pres. African Heart Network 2001; Founding Pres. Nigerian Soc. for Information, Arts and Culture 2001–; Patron Sickle Cell Asscn of Nigeria; mem. several editorial bds; Fellow Nigerian Acad. of Science; Hon. Fellow Univ. of Ibadan 1998; Nigerian Nat. Order of Merit 1997, Commdr Order of the Niger 1979, Commdr Order of the Fed. Repub. of Nigeria 2004, Officier, Ordre Nat. de la République de Côte d'Ivoire; Hon. DSc (Ilorin) 1982, (Fed. Univ. Tech. Akure) 1994, (Port-Harcourt) 1997, (Ogun State Univ.) 1998; Searle Distinguished Research Award 1989, Life Achievement Award, Nigerian Acad. of Science 2004, Boehringer Ingelheim Award, Int. Soc. of Hypertension 2004. *Publications include:* High Blood Pressure in the African 1972, Priorities in National Health Planning 1974 (ed.), Hypertension in Africa (ed.) 1975, Cardiovascular Diseases in Africa (ed.) 1976, Clinical Medicine in the Tropics – Cardiovascular Disease 1986, Nigeria's Health in the 90s (co-ed.) 1996, A Compendium of Clinical Medicine (ed.) 1999; many papers on hypertension and renal disease. *Leisure interests:* bird-watching, music, gardening. *Address:* Department of Medicine, University of Ibadan, Ibadan, Oyo State (office); The Little Summit, Olubadan Aleshinloye Way, Iyaganku, Ibadan, Nigeria (home). *Telephone:* (2) 2315463 (office); (2) 2317717. *E-mail:* akin.ooihc@skannet.com (office).

AKIYA, Einosuke; Japanese religious leader; b. 15 July 1930, Tokyo; s. of Jubei Akiya and of Yuki Akiya; m. Akiko Ishida 1957; two s.; ed Waseda Univ.; with Soka Gakkai 1951–, Young Men's Div. Chief 1956–59, Youth Div. Chief 1959–66, Dir 1961–62, Vice-Gen. Dir 1962–67, Gen. Admin. 1967–70, Vice-Pres. 1970–81, Pres. 1981–2006, Chair. Exec. Guidance Conf. 2006–; Ed.-in-Chief Seikyo Shimbun 1968, Rep. Dir 1975–81, Pres. 1987–90, Exec. Adviser 1990–2006; Gen. Dir Soka Gakkai Int. 1981–92, Exec. Counsellor 1992–95, Deputy Pres. 1995–2007, Counsellor 2007–. *Leisure interests:* reading, music, theatre. *Address:* Soka Gakkai Headquarters, 32 Shinano-machi, Shinjuku-ku, Tokyo 160-8583, Japan (office). *Telephone:* (3) 3353-7111 (office). *Website:* www.sgi.org (office).

AKIYAMA, Kotaro; Japanese newspaper executive; *President and CEO, The Asahi Shimbun Company;* Man. Ed. Asahi Shimbun –2005, Pres. and CEO The Asahi Shimbun Co. 2005–, Chair. Compliance Cttee 2006–; mem. Bd Dirs TV Asahi Corpn, NSK (Japanese Newspaper Publrs and Eds Asscn). *Address:* The Asahi Shimbun Company, 5-3-2 Tsukiji, Chuo-ku, Tokyo 104-8011, Japan (office). *Telephone:* (3) 3545-0131 (office). *Fax:* (3) 3545-8450 (office); (3) 3545-0358 (office). *Website:* www.asahi.com (office).

AKIYAMA, Yoshihisa; Japanese business executive; *Chairman, Kansai Electric Power Company;* Chair. Kansai Electric Power Co., Chair. Kansai Econ. Fed. (Kankeiren); Chair. Kansai Asscn of Corp. Execs 1994–95; Chair. IIS Japan (non-profit making org.); Dir Japan Productivity Center for Socio-Econ. Devt. *Address:* Kansai Electric Power Co, 3–22 Nakanoshima 3-chome, Kita-ku, Osaka 530-8270, Japan (office). *Telephone:* (6) 6441-8821 (office). *Fax:* (6) 6441-0569 (office). *E-mail:* postmaster@kepco.co.jp (office). *Website:* www.kepco.co.jp (office).

AKOL, Lam; Sudanese politician; *Minister of Cabinet Affairs;* fmr Sr mem. Sudan People's Liberation Army (SPLA) (Southern Sudanese opposition movt); participated in armed rebellion with Dr Riek Machar that split the rebel movt; signed Fashoda Agreement with Sudanese Govt 1997; Minister of Transport 1997; involved in peace process negotiations with ASAP 2003; Minister of Foreign Affairs 2005–07, of Cabinet Affairs 2007–; mem. Justice

Party. *Publications:* SPLM/SPLA: Inside an African Revolution. *Address:* Ministry of Cabinet Affairs, Khartoum, Sudan (office).

AKRAM, Wasim (see WASIM Akram).

AKSU, Abdülkadir; Turkish politician; b. 12 Oct. 1944, Diyarbakır; m.; two c.; ed Ankara Univ.; fmrly Security Dir, Malatya, Acting Gov. of Kahramanmaraş, Deputy Security Dir, Gov. and Mayor of Rize, Gov. of Gaziantep; Deputy for Motherland Party 1987; Minister of Internal Affairs 1989–91, 2002–07 (resgnd); State Minister for GAP; Union of Journalists Bureaucrat of the Year 1986, Siyaset Magazine Policy Maker of the Year 2002, Siyaset Magazine Minister of the Year 2002–03. *Address:* c/o Ministry of Internal Affairs, İçişleri Bakanlığı, Bakanlıklar, Ankara, Turkey.

AKSYONOV, Vasiliy Pavlovich; Russian physician, writer and academic; *Professor Emeritus, George Mason University;* b. 20 Aug. 1932, Kazan; s. of Pavel V. Aksyonov and Yevgeniya Ginzburg; m. 1st Kira L. Mendeleva 1957; m. 2nd Maya A. Karmen; one s.; ed Leningrad Medical Inst.; practised as a physician 1956–60, Moscow Tubercular Dispensary 1960–61; professional writer 1960–; was stripped of Soviet citizenship while Guest Lecturer, UCLA 1980; taught at Johns Hopkins Univ. and Goucher Univ.; Robinson Prof. of Russian Literature and Writing, George Mason Univ., USA 1987–2004, Prof. Emer. 2004–; mem. Union of Russian Writers; mem. Editorial bd Yunost; Russian citizenship restored 1990; Ordre des Arts et des Lettres. *Publications:* novels: Colleagues 1960, Starry Ticket 1961, 1970, Oranges from Morocco 1963, Time, My Friend, Time 1964, The Empty Barrels 1968, Love of Electricity 1971, My Grandpa is a Monument 1972, The Box Inside Which Something Knocks (children's book) 1976, Our Golden Ironware 1980, The Burn 1980, The Island of Crimea 1981, An Aristopheana 1981, Paper Landscape 1983, The Right to the Island 1983, Say 'Cheese' 1985, In Search of a Genre 1986, In Search of Melancholy Baby 1987, Our Garden Fronburg 1989, The Moscow Saga 1993, The Negative of a Positive Hero 1996, New Sweet Style 1998, Volteryantsy i Volteryanki (Russian Booker Prize) 2004, Moskva Kva-Kva 2006, Redkie zemli 2007; collected stories: Catapult 1964, Half-Way to the Moon 1966, Wish You Were Here 1969; screenplay for films: Colleagues, My Young Friend, When They Raise the Bridges, Travelling 1967, The Murmar House 1972; play: On Sale 1965; travel: An Unusual Journey 1963, Twenty-Four Hours Non-Stop 1976, The Steel Bird and Other Stories 1978; reminiscences; Pupil of the Eye 2005; jt ed. Metropol 1979, Four Temperaments (comedy) 1979. *Leisure interests:* music, travelling, running.

AKSYUCHITS, Viktor Vladimirovich; Russian politician and Orthodox philosopher; *Chairman, Orthodox Social Service Foundation;* b. 27 Aug. 1949, Vardantsy, Minsk region, USSR (now Belarus); m. 2nd; five c.; ed Riga Navigation School, Moscow State Univ.; served in navy 1969–72; mem. CPSU 1971–78; seasonal worker in Siberia and Far East 1978–88; Founder Orthodox Unity Church; ed Vybor (journal); Chair. Duma (Bd) of Political Council, Russian Christian Democratic Movt 1990–98; Chair. Orthodox Brotherhood Resurrection 1990–96; People's Deputy of Russia 1990–93; mem. Duma of Russian People's Congress 1992–96; Lecturer, State Acad. of Slavic Culture 1996–2003; adviser to Deputy Prime Minister Boris Nemtsov 1997–98; Chair. Bd of Dirs Orthodox Social Service Foundation 2000–. *Publications:* six books on Christian philosophy and philosophy of history; numerous articles on political science and culturology. *Address:* Matveevskaya, 10-2-234, 119517 Moscow, Russia (home). *Telephone:* (985) 991-5669 (home). *E-mail:* aksyu@mail.ru (office).

AKUFO-ADDO, Nano Addo Dankwa, BSc (Econs); Ghanaian politician and lawyer; s. of Edward Akufo-Addo (fmr Chief Justice and Pres. Second Repub.) and Adeline Akufo-Addo; m. Rebecca Akufo-Addo (née Griffiths-Randolph); five c.; ed Lancing Coll., Sussex, UK, Univ. of Ghana, Legon; called to English Bar (Middle Temple) 1971, Ghanaian Bar 1975; Assoc. Counsel, Coudert Freres (US law firm), Paris office, France 1971–75; Jr mem. U.V. Campbell 1975–79; Sr Partner and Co-Founder Prempeh & Co.; Gen. Sec. People's Movt for Freedom and Justice 1977–78;; mem. Gen. Legal Council 1991–96, Gen. Council, Ghana Bar Asscn 1991–96 (Vice-Pres. Greater Accra Regional Br. 1991–96); Founder and first Chair. Ghana Cttee on Human and People's Rights; mem. Nat. Council and Nat. Exec. Cttee, New Patriotic Party (NPP) 1992–2000; mem. Parl. (NPP) for Abuakwa constituency 1996–2000, Chair. NPP Internal Affairs Cttee, NPP Legal and Constitutional Affairs Cttee, Sec. NPP Political Cttee, Sec. NPP Policy Advisory Cttee 1996, Standing Cttee on Subsidiary Legislation 1997–2001; Ranking Minority mem. Parl.'s Select Cttee on Constitutional, Legal and Parl. Affairs 1997–2001; Minister of Foreign Affairs 2000–07; NPP cand. for Pres. of Ghana 2008; Chair. DHL, Ghana Ltd, Kinesec Communications Co. Ltd; Hon. Fellow Legon Hall, Univ. of Ghana. *Leisure interests:* listening to music, sports. *Address:* c/o New Patriotic Party, C912/2 Duade St, Kokomlemle, POB 3456, Accra-North, Ghana. *Telephone:* (21) 227951. *Fax:* (21) 224418. *E-mail:* npp@africanonline.com.gh.

AKUNIN, Boris; Russian (b. Georgian) writer; b. (Grigory Shalvovich Chkhartishvili), 1956, Georgia; ed Moscow State Univ.; Deputy Ed.-in-Chief Inostrannaya Literatura (magazine) –2000; Ed.-in-Chief Anthology of Japanese Literature (20 vols); Chair. Exec. Bd Pushkin Library (Soros Foundation). *Publications:* (names in trans.) fiction: Azazel, Special Errands, Counsellor of State, Coronation or the Last of the Novels, Lover of Death Vol One, Lover of Death Vol Two, Pelagia and the White Bulldog, Pelagia and the Black Monkey, Pelagia and the Red Rooster, The Winter Queen, Leviathan, Turkish Gambit, The Death of Achilles, Jack of Spades, The Decorator, The Diamond Chariot, F.M. 2006, Special Assignments 2007, Pelagia and the Black Monk 2007, The State Counsellor 2008; non-fiction: Tales for Idiots (essays), The Writer and Suicide; contrib. to numerous reviews and criticisms, numerous trans of Japanese, American and English literature. *Address:* Poema Press Publications, Zvezdny blvd 23, 129075 Moscow, Russia (office). *Telephone:* (495) 925-42-05 (home). *E-mail:* erikavoronova@mtu-net.ru (office). *Website:* www.akunin.ru (office).

ALABBAR, Mohamed Ali, BA; United Arab Emirates government official and real estate development executive; *Chairman, Emaar Properties PJSC; Director General, Dubai Department of Economic Development;* b. Dubai; ed Albers School of Business and Econs, Univ. of Seattle, USA; joined Dubai Central Bank 1981; Gen. Man. Al Khaleej Investments, Singapore –1992; Vice Chair. Dubai Aluminium Co. Ltd 1992–2003; Founder and Chair. Emaar Properties PJSC 1997–; Dir Gen. Dubai Dept of Econ. Devt and mem. Dubai Exec. Council; mem. Bd of Dirs UAE Stocks and Commodities Authority; Vice Chair. Dubai World Trade Centre 1992–2002; Chair. UAE Golf Asscn. *Address:* Emaar Properties PJSC, POB 9440, Dubai, United Arab Emirates (office). *Telephone:* (4) 3673333 (office). *Fax:* (4) 3673000 (office). *E-mail:* enquiry@emaar.ae (office). *Website:* www.emaar.com (home).

ALAGIAH, George, OBE; British journalist, broadcaster and writer; *Presenter, Six O'Clock News and World News Today, British Broadcasting Corporation (BBC);* b. 22 Nov. 1955, Sri Lanka; m.; two s.; ed St John's Coll., Portsmouth and Univ. of Durham; family moved to Ghana 1960; worked in print journalism for South Magazine 1982–89; joined the BBC 1989, Leading Foreign Corresp. specializing in Africa and the developing world, BBC's Africa Corresp., Johannesburg 1994–98, Presenter The World News on BBC 4 2002, Presenter BBC Six O'Clock News 2003–, World News Today, BBC World; has interviewed many internationally prominent figures; has contributed to The Guardian, Daily Telegraph, The Independent and Daily Express newspapers; Patron NAZ Project, Parenting, Educ. and Support Forum, Fairtrade Foundation; Critics' Award and Golden Nymph Award, Monte Carlo TV Festival 1992, Best Int. Report, Royal TV Soc. 1993, Best TV Journalist Award, Amnesty Int. 1994, One World Broadcasting Trust Award 1994, James Cameron Memorial Trust Award 1995, Bayeux Award for War Reporting 1996, Media Personality of the Year, Ethnic Minority Media Awards 1998, BAFTA Award (part of BBC Team) for coverage of Kosovo conflict 2000. *Publications:* A Passage to Africa 2001, The Day That Shook the World, A Home from Home (autobiog.) 2006. *Address:* BBC, Room 1640, Television Centre, Wood Lane, London, W12 7RJ, England (office). *Telephone:* (20) 8743-8000 (office). *Fax:* (20) 8743-7882 (office). *Website:* www.bbc.co.uk (office).

ALAGNA, Roberto; French singer (tenor); b. 7 June 1963, Clichy-sous-Bois; m. 1st (deceased); m. 2nd Angela Gheorghiu (q.v.) 1996; ed studied in Paris, France and Italy; debut as Alfredo in La Traviata, Glyndebourne Touring Opera at Plymouth 1988; Met, New York debut as Rodolfo 1996; appearances worldwide at Covent Garden, London, Monte Carlo, Vienna Staatsoper, Théâtre du Châtelet, Paris, La Scala, Milan, Chicago and at the New York Met; repertoire includes Rodolfo (La Bohème), Edgard (Lucia di Lammermoor), Rigoletto, L'Elisir d'amore, Roméo, Don Carlos, Roberto Devereux, Duke of Mantua, Don Carlos, Alfredo, L'Amico Fritz, La Rondine, Faust; winner Pavarotti Competition 1988, Personalité Musicale de l'Année 1994, Laurence Olivier Award for Outstanding Achievement in Opera 1995, Victor Award for Best Singer 1997; Chevalier, Ordre des Arts et des Lettres. *Recordings include:* Duets and Arias (with Angela Gheorghiu), La Bohème 1996, Don Carlos 1996, La Rondine 1997. *Address:* Theateragentur Dr Germinal Hilbert, Maximilianstrasse 22, 80539 Munich, Germany (office). *Telephone:* (89) 290 7470 (office). *Fax:* (89) 290 74790 (office). *E-mail:* agentur@hilbert.de (office). *Website:* www.hilbert.de (office); www.alagna.com.

ALAÏA, Azzeddine; French fashion designer; b. Tunis; ed Ecole des Beaux Arts, Tunis; studied sculpture; worked with dressmakers specializing in copies of Parisian haute couture in Tunis and then began making his own designs for pvt. clients in Tunis; moved to Paris 1957; worked briefly at Christian Dior before moving to Guy Laroche workrooms for two seasons; also worked in Paris as cook and housekeeper; began made-to-order dressmaking business in 1960s; set up first atelier in Faubourg Saint Germain 1965–84; first ready-to-wear show, Bergdorf Goodman store, New York 1982; first Azzedine Alaïa boutique opened in Beverly Hills 1983; moved to Marais district of Paris 1984; retrospective exhbn Museum of Modern Art, Bordeaux 1985; named Best Designer of Year by French Ministry of Culture 1985. *Address:* 18 rue de la Verrérie, Paris, France.

ALAIN, Marie-Claire; French organist; b. 10 Aug. 1926, Saint-Germain-en-Laye; d. of Albert Alain and Magdeleine Alain (née Alberty); m. Jacques Gommier 1950; one s. one d.; ed Institut Notre Dame, Saint-Germain-en-Laye, Conservatoire Nat. Supérieur de Musique, Paris; organ teacher, Conservatoire de Musique de Paris; Lecturer, Summer Acad. for organists, Haarlem, Netherlands 1956–72; organ teacher, Conservatoire de Musique de Rueil-Malmaison 1978–94; numerous concerts world-wide 1955–; lecturer at numerous univs throughout world; expert on organology to Minister of Culture, Commission des Orgues des Monuments Historiques 1965–2002; Commdr, Légion d'honneur, Commdr, Ordre du Mérite, Commdr, Ordre des Arts et des Lettres; Hon. DHumLitt (Colorado State Univ.); Hon. DMus (Southern Methodist Univ., Dallas, Boston Conservatory); Dr hc (Acad. Sibelius, Helsinki); numerous prizes for recordings and performances, including Buxtehudepreis (Lübeck, Germany), Prix Léonie Sonning (Copenhagen, Denmark), Prix Franz Liszt (Budapest) 1987. *Recordings:* over 250 records, including complete works of J. Alain, C.P.E. Bach, J.S. Bach, C. Balbastre, G. Böhm, N. Bruhns, D. Buxtehude, L.N. Clérambault, F. Couperin, L.C. Daquin, C. Franck, N. de Grigny, J.A. Guilain, G.F. Handel, J. Haydn, F. Mendelssohn, A. Vivaldi. *Publication:* Notes critiques sur l'œuvre d'orgue de Jehan Alain 2001. *Address:* 4 rue Victor Hugo, 78230 Le Pecq, France. *Telephone:* 1-30-87-08-65. *Fax:* 1-30-61-43-61.

ALAINI, Mohsin Ahmed; Yemeni politician and diplomatist; *Deputy Chairman, Consultative Council;* b. 20 Oct. 1932, Bani Bahloul, N Yemen; m. Aziza Abulahom 1962; two s. two d.; ed Faculty of Law, Cairo Univ. and the Sorbonne, Paris; schoolteacher, Aden 1958–60; Int. Confed. of Arab Trade Unions 1960–62; Minister of Foreign Affairs, Yemeni Repub. Sept.–Dec. 1962, 1974–80; Perm. Rep. to UN 1962–65, 1965–66, 1967–69; Minister of Foreign Affairs May–July 1965; Prime Minister Nov.–Dec. 1967, 1974–80; Amb. to USSR 1968–70; Prime Minister, Minister of Foreign Affairs Feb. 1971, 1971–72, 1974–75; Amb. to France Aug.–Sept. 1974, 1975–76, to UK 1973–74, to FRG 1982–84, to USA 1984–97; Perm. Rep. to UN 1980–82; Deputy Chair. Consultative Council 1997–. *Publications include:* Battles and Conspiracies against Yemen 1957, Fifty Years of Mounting Sands (autobiog.) 2000. *Leisure interests:* reading, exercising. *Address:* 8 Wissa Wassif Street, Giza, Cairo, Egypt (home); PO Box 72922, San'a, Yemen. *Telephone:* (1) 441185 (Yemen) (office); (2) 5702423 (Cairo). *Fax:* (2) 5762423 (Cairo) (home).

ALAM, A. I. M. Nazmul; Bangladeshi business executive; fmr Chair. Bangladesh Steel and Engineering Corporation (BSEC). *Address:* c/o Bangladesh Steel and Engineering Corporation, BSEC Bhaban, 102 Kazi Nazrul Islam Avenue, Dhaka 1215, Bangladesh.

ALAMI, Raz Mohammad; Afghan engineer and airline executive; fmr Acting Pres. Ariana Afghan Airlines; fmr Sec., Ministry of Transport and Civil Aviation, currently Tech. Deputy Minister of Transport. *Address:* Ministry of Transport and Aviation, Ansari Wat, Kabul, Afghanistan (office). *Telephone:* (20) 2101031 (office); (799) 360360.

ALAPAYEV, Marat O.; Kyrgyzstani central banker; *Chairman, National Bank of the Kyrgyz Republic;* m.; two c.; fmr Lecturer, Dept of Political Economy, Osh Pedagogical Teacher Training Coll.; worked as a broker in the securities market; Chair. Bakai Bank 1998–2006; Head, Cttee of Dirs Manas Int. Airport 2005–06; Acting Chair. Nat. Bank of the Kyrgyz Repub. (Kyrgyz Respublikasynyn Uluttuk Banky) April 2006, Chair. April 2006–. *Address:* Kyrgyz Respublikasynyn Uluttuk Banky, 101 T. Umetaliev str., 720040 Bishkek, Kyrgyzstan (office). *Telephone:* (312) 66-90-11 (office). *Fax:* (312) 61-07-30 (office). *E-mail:* mail@nbkr.kg (office). *Website:* www.nbkr.kg (office).

ALARCÓN DE QUESADA, Ricardo; Cuban diplomatist and politician; *President of National Assembly;* b. 21 May 1937; s. of Roberto Alarcón de Quesada; m. Margarita Maza; one d.; ed Univ. de Habana; Head of Student Section, Prov. Office of 26 July Revolutionary Movt 1957–59; Pres. Univ. Students' Fed., Sec. Union of Young Communists; Dir for Regional Policies (Latin America), Ministry of Foreign Affairs 1962–66; mem. Governing Council of Inst. for Int. Politics, Ministry of Foreign Affairs, Deputy Minister of Foreign Affairs 1978, mem. Tech. Advisory Council 1980; Perm. Rep. of Cuba to the UN 1966–78; Pres. UNDP 1976–77; Alt. mem. Cen. Cttee of CP of Cuba 1980–; mem. Politburo of CP 1992–; Perm Rep. to UN 1990; Minister of Foreign Affairs 1992–94; Pres. Nat. Ass. of People's Power 1993–. *Address:* Asamblea Nacional del Poder Popular, Havana, Cuba; 42 Street No. 2308 e/23 and 25 Streets, Municipio Playa, Cuba.

ALARCÓN MANTILLA, Luis Fernando, MSc; Colombian politician and engineer; *President, Flota Mercante Grancolombiana SA;* b. Aug. 1951, Bucaramanga; m.; ed Univ. of the Andes and MIT; engineer with Mejía Millan y Perry Ltd and Prof. of Civil Eng Univ. of the Andes 1980–83; Head of Public Investment Unit, Nat. Dept of Planning 1983–84; Dir-Gen. of Budget, Ministry of Finance and Public Credit 1984–86; economist at Banco Internacional de Desarrollo, Washington DC 1986; Vice-Minister at Ministry of Finance and Public Credit 1986–87, Minister 1987–91; currently Pres. Flota Mercante Grancolombiana SA; mem. of Governing Council for Foreign Trade, Bd of Banco de la República, Nat. Council for Econ. and Social Policy 1987–. *Address:* Flota Mercante Grancolombiana, SA Edif. Grancolombiana, Carrera 13, No 27-75, Apdo Aéreo 4482, Santa Fe de Bogotá, Colombia (office). *Telephone:* (1) 286-0200 (office). *Fax:* (1) 286-9028 (office).

ALARCON RIVERA, Fabián Ernesto, PhD; Ecuadorean politician; b. 1947, Quito; m. Lucía Peña; two s. one d.; ed Pontifical Catholic Univ.; councillor Quito 1969; fmr Prefect of Pinchincha Prov.; fmr Deputy to Congress (three times), fmr Speaker of Congress (three times); Acting Pres. of Ecuador 6–10 Feb. 1997, Pres. of Ecuador 1997–98; arrested on charges of illegally hiring personnel March 1999; mem. Frente Radical Alfarista, Leader 2002. *Address:* c/o Frente Radical Alfarista (FRA), Quito, Ecuador.

ALBACETE CARREIRA, Alfonso; Spanish painter; b. 14 March 1950, Málaga; s. of Alfonso Albacete and María Carreira; m. Luisa Gómez 1986; one s. one d.; studied painting, with Juan Bonafé and architecture; studied painting Valencia 1969, then in Paris; first one-man exhbn, Madrid 1972; first exhbn USA, Center for Contemporary Art, Chicago 1989; works included in numerous collections of contemporary art including Chase Manhattan Bank, New York, White House Collection, Washington, Collection Dobe, Zurich, Museo Reina Sofia, Madrid. *Leisure interests:* botany, architecture. *Address:* Vegap, Centro de Madrid, Gran Vía 16, 5 planta, 28013 Madrid, Spain (office); Joaquín Maruía López, 23–7° C, 28015 Madrid, Spain (office). *Telephone:* (91) 5326632 (office); (91) 5491140 (office). *Fax:* (91) 5315398 (office). *E-mail:* infomad@vegap.es (office). *Website:* www.vegap.es (office).

ALBANESE, Thomas (Tom), BS, MS; American mining industry executive; *Chief Executive, Rio Tinto Group;* b. 1957; m. Mary Albanese (neé Ross); two d.; ed Univ. of Alaska Fairbanks; COO Nerco Minerals –1993, Gen. Man. Rio Tinto plc Greens Creek mine (after acquisition of Nerco by Rio Tinto), Admiralty Island, Alaska 1993–95, Group Exploration Exec., London 1995–98, Vice-Pres. Eng and Tech. Services, Kennecott Utah Copper 1998–2000, CEO Industrial Minerals Group, Rio Tinto 2000–04, CEO Copper Group and Head, Exploration, London 2004, Dir Group Resources, Rio Tinto Group, Melbourne –2006, mem. Bd of Dirs Rio Tinto plc and Rio Tinto Ltd 2006–, Chief Exec. Rio Tinto Group 2007–; mem. Bd of Dirs Palabora Mining Co. 2004–06, Ivanhoe Mines 2006–07; mem. Exec. Cttee Int. Copper Asscn 2004–06. *Address:* Rio Tinto plc, 5 Aldermanbury Square, London, EC2V 7HR England (office); Rio Tinto Ltd, 120 Collins Street, Melbourne, Vic. 3000, Australia (office). *Telephone:* (20) 7781-2000 (London) (office); (3) 9283-3333 (Melbourne) (office). *Fax:* (20) 7781-1800 (London) (office); (3) 9283-3707 (Melbourne) (office). *E-mail:* info@riotinto.com (office). *Website:* www.riotinto.com (office).

ALBAR, Datuk Seri Syed Hamid bin Syed Jaafar; Malaysian politician; *Minister of Home Affairs and Internal Security;* mem. BN-UMNO Party; mem. Parl. for Kota Tinggi; Minister in the Prime Minister's Dept and Minister of Law *c.* 1993; Minister of Defence *c.* 1997; Minister of Foreign Affairs *c.* 1999–2008; Minister of Home Affairs and Internal Security 2008–. *Address:* Ministry of Home Affairs (Kementerian Hal Ehwal Dalam Negeri), Blok D2, Parcel D, Pusat Pentadbiran Kerajaan Persekutuan, 62546 Putrajaya, Malaysia (office). *Telephone:* (3) 88863000 (office). *Fax:* (3) 88891613 (office). *E-mail:* azmi@mofa.gov.my (office). *Website:* www.moha.gov.my (office).

ALBARN, Damon; British singer, musician (keyboards) and songwriter; b. 23 March 1968, Whitechapel, London; s. of Hazel Albarn and Keith Albarn; ed Stanway Comprehensive, Colchester, East 15 Drama School, Debden; mem. and lead singer, Blur (fmrly named Seymour) 1989–; live appearances and tours worldwide; founder mem. and Musical Dir of 'virtual band', Gorillaz 1998–, collaborating with numerous guest artists; founder mem., The Good The Bad and The Queen 2006–; with Blur: BRIT Awards for Best Single, Best Video, Best Album, Best Band 1995, Q Awards for Best Album 1994, 1995; with Gorillaz: Q Awards for Best Video, for Best Producer 2005, Digital Music Award for Top Online Band, for Best Use of Digital Platforms 2005, MTV Europe Music Award for Best Group 2005, Grammy Award for Best Pop Collaboration with Vocals (for Feel Good Inc.) 2006, NME John Peel Music Innovation Award 2006, Ivor Novello Award for Songwriter of the Year 2006, Q Inspiration Award 2007. *Film:* Face 1997. *DVD:* with Gorillaz: Phase One: Celebrity Take Down 2002, Phase Two: Slow Boat to Hades 2006. *Compositions:* wrote film scores for Ravenous (with Michael Nyman) 1998, Ordinary Decent Criminal 1999, 101 Reykjavík (with Einar Örn Benediktsson) 2000; wrote theatre score for Monkey: Journey to the West 2007. *Recordings include:* albums: with Blur: Leisure 1991, Modern Life Is Rubbish 1993, Parklife 1994, The Great Escape 1995, Blur 1997, 13 1999, The Best Of Blur 2000, Think Tank 2003; with Gorillaz: Gorillaz 2001, G-Sides 2002, Laika Come Home 2002, Demon Days 2005, D-Sides 2007; solo: Mali Music (various contributors) 2002, Democrazy 2003; with The Good The Bad and The Queen: The Good The Bad and The Queen 2007. *Leisure interests:* football, Tae Kwon Do. *Address:* CMO Management International Ltd, Studio 2.6, Shepherds East, Richmond Way, London, W14 0DQ, England (office). *Telephone:* (20) 7316-6969 (office). *Fax:* (20) 7316-6970 (office). *E-mail:* reception@cmomanagement.co.uk (office). *Website:* www.cmomanagement.co.uk (office); www.blur.co.uk; www.gorillaz.com; www.thegoodthebadandthequeen.com.

ALBEE, Edward Franklin, III; American playwright; b. 12 March 1928, Va; adopted s. of Reed Albee and Frances Cotter; ed Lawrenceville and Choate Schools, Washington, Valley Forge Mil. Acad., Pa and Trinity Coll., Hartford; Comm. Chair. Brandeis Univ. Creative Arts Awards 1983, 1984; Pres. The Edward F. Albee Foundation Inc.; Distinguished Prof., Univ. of Houston 1988–2003; mem. Dramatists Guild Council, PEN America, The American Acad., Nat. Inst. of Arts and Letters; Tony Awards 1963, 1996, 2002, Gold Medal, American Acad. and Inst. of Arts and Letters 1980; inducted, Theater Hall of Fame 1985, Kennedy Center Award 1996, Nat. Medal of Arts 1996, Special Tony Award for Lifetime Achievement 2005. *Plays include:* The Zoo Story (Vernon Rice Award 1960) 1958, The Death of Bessie Smith 1959, The Sandbox 1959, Fam and Yam 1959, The American Dream (Foreign Press Asscn Award 1961) 1960, Who's Afraid of Virginia Woolf? (Drama Critics' Circle Award for Best Play) 1961–62, stage adaptation of The Ballad of the Sad Café (Carson McCuller) 1963, Tiny Alice 1964, Malcolm (from novel by James Purdy) 1965, A Delicate Balance (Pulitzer Prize 1966) 1966, Everything in the Garden (after a play by Giles Cooper) 1967, Box 1968, Quotations from Chairman Mao Tse-tung 1968, All Over 1971, Seascape (Pulitzer Prize 1975) 1974, Listening 1975, Counting the Ways 1976, The Lady from Dubuque 1977–79, Lolita (adapted from Vladimir Nabokov) 1979, The Man Who Had Three Arms 1981, Finding the Sun 1982, Marriage Play 1986–87, Three Tall Women (Pulitzer Prize 1994) 1990–91, Fragments 1993, The Play About the Baby 1996, The Goat, or, Who is Sylvia? 2000, Occupant 2001, Peter and Jerry (Act 1: Home Life, Act 2: The Zoo Story) 2004, Me, Myself and I 2007. *Leisure interest:* collecting art. *Address:* 14 Harrison Street, New York, NY 10013 (office); PO Box 697, Montauk, NY 11954, USA (home). *Telephone:* (212) 226-2020 (office). *E-mail:* albee@albeefoundation.org (office). *Website:* www.albeefoundation.org (office).

ALBERDI, Inés, Doctorado en Ciencias Políticas y Sociología; Spanish sociologist, international organization official and academic; *Executive Director, United Nations Development Fund for Women (UNIFEM);* b. 11 Feb. 1948, Seville; m.; one s. one d.; ed Universidad Complutense de Madrid; Asst Prof., Dept of Sociology, Universidad Complutense de Madrid 1971–75, Prof. Encargada 1975–78, Adjunct Prof. 1978, Adjunct Prof. of Sociology 1980–84, Titular Prof. of Sociology 1984–88, 1990–91, Prof. of Sociology 1993–2008; Visiting Scholar, Dept of Sociology, Georgetown Univ., Washington, DC 1978–79, Assoc. Researcher 1988–89; Univ. Prof. of Sociology, Univ. of Saragossa 1991–93; Dir for Research, Centre for Sociological Research 1992–93; Dir Masters programme 'Women's Studies and Equality Opportunity Policies' organized by School of Doctors and Lawyers in Political Sciences and Sociology and sponsored by Main Directorate of Woman of CAM 1994–96; Deputy in Madrid

Ass. 2003–07; Exec. Dir UNIFEM 2008–; Adviser for Women in Devt, IDB 1989–90; served as expert for Equal Opportunities Unit of EC on networks Family and Work and Diversification of Occupational Choices for Women 1998–2000; mem. Bd UN Int. Research and Training Inst. for Advancement of Women (INSTRAW) 1986–89; Eisenhower Fellowship 1998. *Publications include:* Guía didáctica para una orientación no sexista Ministerio de Educación y Ciencia 1988, Estudio Sociológico sobre las viudas en España (second edn; co-author) 1989, La situación social de las viudas en España. Aspectos Cuantitativos (co-author) 1990, Matrimonios y Parejas (co-author) 1994, Informe sobre la situación de la familia en España 1994, Lo personal es político. El movimiento feminista en la transición ((co-author) 1996, La nueva familia española 1999, Las mujeres jóvenes en España 2000, Les dones joves a Espanya Fundació 2001, Violencia: Tolerancia Cero (with Luis Rojas Marcos) 2005, Los hombres jóvenes y la paternidad 2007. *Address:* UNIFEM Headquarters, 304 East 45th Street, 15th Floor, New York, NY 10017, USA (office). *Telephone:* (212) 906-6400 (office). *Fax:* (212) 906-6705 (office). *E-mail:* ines .alberdi@unifem.org (office). *Website:* www.unifem.org (office).

ALBERT II, HSH Prince of Monaco (Albert Alexandre Louis Pierre), BA; b. 14 March 1958; s. of the late Prince Rainier III of Monaco, and the late Princess Grace (née Kelly); ed Albert I High School, Amherst Coll., Mass, USA; ranked as 1st Class Ensign (Sub-Capt.); Pres. Monegasque Del. to Gen. Ass., UN 1993–; Chair. of several sports feds and cttees; Chair. Organizing Cttee, Monte Carlo Int. Television Festival 1988–; Deputy Chair. Princess Grace Foundation of Monaco; named Prince Regent of Monaco 31 March 2005, became Sovereign Prince of Monaco upon death of father Prince Rainier III 6 April 2005, enthroned 12 July 2005; Hon. Pres. Int. Athletic Foundation, Int. Modern Pentathlon Union, World Beach Volleyball, hon. citizen of Forth Worth 2000, Hon. Chair. Jeune Chambre Economique, Monaco Aide et Présence, hon. mem. St Petersburg Naval Ass., Int. Inst. for Human Rights, Hon. Prof. of Int. Studies, Tarrant County Coll., Fort Worth 2000; Grand Cross, Order of Grimaldi 1958, Grand Officier, Nat. Order of the Lion of Senegal 1977, Grand Cross, Order of Saint-Charles 1979, Kt Grand Cross, Equestrian Order of the Holy Sepulchre of Jerusalem 1983, Grand Officer, Legion of Honour 1984, Col of the Carabineers 1986, Chevalier, Order of Malta 1989, Grand Officer, Merite Int. du Sang 1994, Grand Cross, National Order of Merit 1997, Grand Cross, Nat. Order of Niger 1998, Grand Cross of the Jordanian Renaissance (Nahdah medal) 2000, Grand Cross, Order of the Sun of Peru 2003, Grand Cross, Order Juan Mora Fernandez, Costa Rica 2003, Order of Stara Planina, Bulgaria 2004; Dr hc (Pontifical Univ., Maynooth) 1996. *Address:* Palais Princier, BP 518, MC 98015, Monaco. *Website:* www .palais.mc.

ALBERT II, HM, King of the Belgians; b. 6 June 1934, Brussels; s. of King Léopold III and Queen Astrid (fmrly Princess of Sweden); m. Donna Paola Ruffo di Calabria 1959; two s. Crown Prince Philippe, Prince Laurent, one d. Princess Astrid; fmrly Prince of Liège; succeeded to the throne 9 Aug. 1993, on the death of his brother King Baudouin I; Pres. Caisse Générale d'Epargne et de Retraite 1954–92; Pres. Belgian Office of Foreign Trade 1962–93; Pres. Belgian Red Cross 1958–93. *Address:* Office of HM the King, The Royal Palace, Rue Brederode 16, 1000 Brussels, Belgium (office). *Telephone:* (2) 551-20-20 (office). *Website:* www.monarchie.be.

ALBERT, Calvin; American sculptor; b. 19 Nov. 1918, Grand Rapids, Mich.; s. of Philip Albert and Ethel Albert; m. Martha Neff 1941; one d.; ed Inst. of Design, Chicago, Art Inst. of Chicago and Archipenko School of Sculpture; Teacher, New York Univ. 1949–52, Brooklyn Coll. 1947–49, Inst. of Design 1942–46; Prof. of Art, Pratt Inst. 1949–85, Prof. Emer. 1985–; sculpture and drawings in collections of Whitney Museum, Metropolitan Museum, Jewish Museum, Art Inst. of Chicago, Detroit Inst. of Arts, Univ. of Nebraska, Chrysler Museum of Art and Nelson-Atkins Museum of Art; Fulbright Advanced Research Grant to Italy 1961; Tiffany Grants 1963, 1965; Guggenheim Fellowship 1966; Nat. Inst. of Arts and Letters Award 1975. *Publication:* Figure Drawing Comes to Life (with Dorothy Seckler) 1987. *Leisure interest:* boating.

ALBERT, Delia Domingo; Philippine diplomatist; *Ambassador to Germany;* b. 11 Aug. 1942, Baguio City; d. of Jesus Domingo and Nemesia Domingo; m. Hans Albert; one d.; ed Univ. of the Philippines, Inst. for Int. Studies, Geneva, Switzerland, Diplomatic Inst., Salzburg, Austria, Boston Univ. Overseas, Bonn, Germany, Inst. for Political Science and Strategic Studies, Kiel, Germany, Kennedy School of Govt, Harvard Univ., USA; Asst, Office of Sec. of Foreign Affairs, Dept of Foreign Affairs 1967; assigned to Philippines Mission to UN, Geneva and attended confs of UN Specialized Agencies in Geneva and Vienna; rep. The Philippines in various diplomatic capacities in Romania, Hungary, FRG, GDR, Australia (also accred to Nauru, Tuvalu and Vanuatu); Dean of Diplomatic Corps, Australia 2001; Under-Sec. for Int. Econ. Relations and Philippine Sr Official for APEC 2001–03; Sec. of Foreign Affairs 2003–04; Presidential Adviser for Multilateral Cooperation and Devt 2004–05, concurrently Presidential Envoy for Mining 2005; Amb. to Germany 2005–; fmr Dir-Gen. ASEAN Nat. Secr. of the Philippines (served as Sec.-Gen. of Conf. Secr. of Fourth APEC Econ. Leaders' Meeting, The Philippines 1996); Kt Commdr's Cross of the Order of Merit with Star (FRG) 1992, Order of Sikatuna (rank of Datu); Dr hc (Philippine Women's Univ.) 2003; Outstanding Woman in Public Service, Nat. Council for Women of the Philippines 2005. *Leisure interest:* golf. *Address:* Embassy of the Philippines, Uhlandstr. 97, 10715 Berlin, Germany (office). *Telephone:* (30) 8649500 (office). *Fax:* (30) 8732551 (office). *E-mail:* info@philippine-embassy.de (office). *Website:* www.philippine-embassy.com (office).

ALBERTI, Sir Kurt George Matthew Mayer, MA, DPhil, FRCP; British physician; *National Director for Emergency Access, Department of Health;* b. 27 Sept. 1937, Koblenz, Germany; s. of the late William Peter Matthew Alberti and Edith Elizabeth Alberti; m. 1st 1964; m. 2nd Stephanie Anne Amiel 1998; three s.; ed Univ. of Oxford; Research Fellow, Harvard Univ. 1966–69; Research Officer, Univ. of Oxford 1969–73; Prof. of Chemical Pathology, Univ. of Southampton 1973–78; Prof. of Clinical Biochemistry and Metabolic Medicine, Univ. of Newcastle 1978–85, Prof. of Medicine 1985–2002, Dean 1995–97; Prof. of Metabolic Medicine, Imperial Coll. London 1999–2002, Sr Research Fellow 2002–; Nat. Dir for Emergency Access, Dept of Health 2002–; Dir Research and Devt, Northern and Yorkshire Regional Health Authority 1992–95; Pres. Royal Coll. of Physicians 1997–2002; Fellow Acad. of Medicine, Singapore, Hong Kong, Coll. of Physicians, Sri Lanka, Thailand, SA; Hon. DMed (Århus), (Southampton) 2000, (Athens) 2002; Hon. DSc (Cranfield) 2005, (Warwick) 2005. *Publications:* Ed. International Textbook of Diabetes Mellitus 1997 and more than 1,000 papers, reviews and edited books. *Leisure interests:* jogging, hillwalking, crime fiction, opera. *Address:* 57 Lancaster Avenue, West Norwood, London, SE27 9EL, England (home). *Telephone:* (191) 222-6602 (office). *Fax:* (191) 222-0723 (office); (20) 8766-7132 (home). *E-mail:* george.alberti@ncl.ac.uk (office).

ALBERTSSON, Per-Åke, PhD; Swedish biochemist and academic; *Professor Emeritus of Biochemistry, Lund University;* b. 19 March 1930, Skurup; s. of Albert Olsson and Frideborg Olsson; m. 1st Elisabet Godberg 1955 (divorced 1978); five s. one d.; m. 2nd Charlotte Erlanson 1978; three d.; ed Swedish High School, Ystad and Univs of Lund and Uppsala; Lecturer in Biochemistry, Univ. of Uppsala 1960–65; Prof. of Biochemistry, Univ. of Umeä 1965–75, Univ. of Lund 1975–, now Prof. Emer.; Research Zoologist, UCLA 1961–62; Visiting Prof., Stanford Univ. 1971–72, Univ. of Calif., Berkeley 1984–85; mem. Swedish Acad. of Sciences, Swedish Acad. of Eng Sciences, Royal Physiographic Soc. of Lund, Röda Kapellet (symphonic band), City Council of Lund 1991–94; mem. Bd Lunds Energi AB, Bioenter HB; Gold Medal, Swedish Acad. of Eng Sciences, Gold Medal, Swedish Chemical Soc., Bror Holmberg Medal. *Publications:* Partition of Cell Particles and Macromolecules; over 140 scientific publs in journals. *Leisure interests:* playing music with flute, recorder, trombone and euphonium. *Address:* Department of Biochemistry, Box 124, 22100 Lund, Sweden (office). *Telephone:* (46) 222-8190 (office). *Fax:* (46) 222-4534 (office). *E-mail:* Per-Ake.Albertsson@biokem.lu.se (office). *Website:* www.biokem.lu.se (office).

ALBERTY, Robert Arnold, BA, MS, PhD, FAAS; American chemist and academic; *Professor Emeritus of Chemistry, Massachusetts Institute of Technology;* b. 21 June 1921, Winfield, Kan.; s. of Luman H. Alberty and Mattie (née Arnold) Alberty; m. Lillian Jane Wind 1944; one s. two d.; ed Lincoln High School, Lincoln, Neb., Univ. of Nebraska and Univ. of Wisconsin; Instructor, Chem. Dept, Univ. of Wis. 1947–48, Asst Prof. 1948–50, Assoc. Prof. 1950–56, Prof. 1956–57, Assoc. Dean of Letters and Science 1962–63, Dean of Grad. School 1963–67; Prof. of Chem., MIT 1967–91, Prof. Emer. 1991–; Dean, School of Science 1967–82; mem. NAS 1965–, American Acad. of Arts and Sciences 1968–, Inst. of Medicine 1973–; Chair. Comm. on Human Resources, Nat. Research Council 1971–77; Dir Colt Industries 1978–88; Dir Inst. for Defense Analysis 1980–86; Chair. Cttee on Chem. and Public Affairs, ACS 1980; Pres. Physical Chem. Div. IUPAC 1991–93; Dr hc (Nebraska) 1967, (Lawrence) 1967; Eli Lilly Award for research in enzyme kinetics 1956. *Publications:* Experimental Physical Chemistry (co-author) 1962, Physical Chemistry (co-author) 2001. *Leisure interest:* designing and building a summer cabin. *Address:* Massachusetts Institute of Technology, Room 6-215, 77 Massachusetts Avenue, Cambridge, MA 02139-4307 (office); 931 Massachusetts Avenue, Cambridge, MA 02139-3171, USA (home). *Telephone:* (617) 253-2456 (office). *Fax:* (617) 253-7030 (office). *E-mail:* alberty@mit.edu (office). *Website:* web.mit.edu/chemistry/www/index.html (office).

ALBERY, Tim; British theatre and opera director; b. 20 May 1952, *Plays directed include:* War Crimes 1981, Secret Gardens 1983, Venice Preserv'd 1983, Hedda Gabler 1984, The Princess of Cleves 1985, Mary Stuart 1988, As You Like It 1989, Berenice 1990, Wallenstein 1993, Macbeth 1996, Attempts on Her Life 1997, Nathan the Wise 2004. *Operas directed include:* (for ENO) Billy Budd 1988, Beatrice and Benedict 1990, Peter Grimes 1991, Lohengrin 1993, From the House of the Dead 1997, La Bohème 2000, War and Peace 2001, Lohengrin 2006; (for Opera North) The Midsummer Marriage 1985, The Trojans 1986, La Finta Giardiniera 1989, Don Giovanni 1991, Don Carlos 1992, Luisa Miller 1995 Così fan Tutte 1997, Katya Kabanova 1999, Cosi Fan Tutte 2004, One Touch of Venus 2004, 2005; (for Welsh Nat. Opera) The Trojans 1987, Nabucco 1995; (for Scottish Opera) The Midsummer Marriage 1988, The Trojans 1990, Fidelio 1994, The Ring Cycle 2003, Don Giovanni 2006; (for Australian Opera) The Marriage of Figaro 1992; (for Netherlands Opera) Benvenuto Cellini 1991, La Wally 1993, Beatrice and Benedict 2001; (for Bayerische Staatsoper) Peter Grimes 1993, Simon Boccanegra 1995, Ariadne Auf Naxos 1996; (for Batignano Festival, Italy) The Turn of the Screw 1983; (for Bregenz Festival, Austria) La Wally 1990; (for Royal Opera House) Cherubin 1994; (for Metropolitan Opera, New York) Midsummer Night's Dream 1996, The Merry Widow 2000; (for Minnesota Opera) Passion 2004, (for Canadian Opera Company, Toronto) Rodelinda 2005, Gotterdammerung 2006. *Address:* c/o Harriet Cruickshank, Cruickshank Cazenove, 97 Old South Lambeth Road, London, SW8 1XU, England (office). *Telephone:* (20) 7735-2933 (office). *Fax:* (20) 7582-6405 (office). *E-mail:* office@ cruickshankcazenove.com (office).

ALBERY, Wyndham John, MA, DPhil, FRS, FRSC; British professor of physical chemistry; b. 5 April 1936, London; s. of the late Michael James Albery and Mary Lawton Albery; ed Winchester Coll., Balliol Coll., Oxford; Nat. Service 1955–56; Weir Jr Research Fellow 1962, Fellow in Physical Chem., University Coll., Oxford 1964–78; Lecturer, Physical Chem., Univ. of Oxford 1964–78; Prof. of Physical Chem., Imperial Coll., London 1978–89, Visiting Prof. 1989; Master of University Coll., Oxford 1989–97; Visiting Prof.,

Harvard Univ. 1989; Chair. Burton-Taylor Theatre Man. Cttee 1990–93; Gov. Rugby School 1987–99; Fellow, Winchester Coll. 1989–99; Tilden Lecturer, Royal Soc. of Chemistry (RSC) 1978; Hon. DSc (Kent) 1990; Electrochemistry Medal, RSC 1989. *Publications:* Ring-Disc Electrodes 1971, Electrode Kinetics 1975; (two musicals with John Gould) Who Was That Lady? 1970, On the Boil 1972. *Leisure interest:* theatre. *Address:* 35 Falmouth House, Hyde Park Place, London W2 2NT, England. *Telephone:* (20) 7262-3909.

ALBRECHT, Ernst Carl Julius, Dr rer. pol; German politician and economist (retd); b. 29 June 1930, Heidelberg; s. of Carl Albrecht, MD and Dr Adda Albrecht (née Berg); m. Dr Heidi Adele Stromeyer 1953; five s. two d.; ed Univs of Tübingen, Cornell, Basle, Bonn; Attaché to Council of Ministers, ECSC 1954; Sec. of Common Market section of Brussels conf. for preparation of Treaties of Rome 1956; CEO to EEC Commr Hans von der Groeben 1958; Deputy Head of Comm. del. at negotiations with Denmark, Ireland, Norway and UK for accession to EEC 1961–63; Dir-Gen. for Competition, EEC Comm. 1967–70; Financial Dir Bahlsens Keksfabrik, biscuit mfrs 1971–76; mem. Landtag (Parl.) for Lower Saxony 1970–90, Minister-Pres. of Lower Saxony 1976–90; personal consultant to Pres. and Prime Minister of Kyrgyzstan 1995–2005; mem. CDU; Grosskreuz der Bundesrepublik Deutschland. *Publication:* Der Staat – Idee und Wirklichkeit (The State – Idea and Reality) 1976–90, Erinnerungen (Memoirs) 1999. *Address:* Am Brink 2B, 31303 Burgdorf, Germany. *Telephone:* (5136) 977900 (office); (5136) 977900 (home). *Fax:* (5136) 977901 (office).

ALBRECHT, Karl; German business executive; b. 1920, Essen; co-f. Albrecht Discount (now ALDI) with brother Theo Albrecht (q.v.) 1948, fmr CEO ALDI Süd, Co-CEO ALDI Group –1994, Chair. 1994–2002. *Address:* c/o ALDI Group, Eckenbergstrasse 16, Postfach 13 01 110, 45307 Essen, Germany (office).

ALBRECHT, Theo; German business executive; *Co-Chairman, ALDI Group;* co-f. Albrecht Discount (now ALDI) with brother Karl Albrecht (q.v.) 1948, fmr head of ALDI Nord, currently Co-Chair. ALDI Group; Chair. Markus Stiftung. *Address:* ALDI Group, Eckenbergstrasse 16, Postfach 13 01 110, 45307 Essen, Germany (office). *Telephone:* (20) 185930 (office). *Fax:* (20) 18593319 (office). *Website:* www.aldi.com (office).

ALBRIGHT, Madeleine Korbel, BA, MA, PhD; American diplomatist, international affairs adviser and fmr government official; *Principal, Albright Group LLC;* b. 15 May 1937, Prague, Czechoslovakia; d. of Joseph Korbel and Anna Speeglova; m. Joseph Albright 1959 (divorced 1983); three d.; ed Wellesley Coll. and Columbia Univ.; Prof. of Int. Affairs, Georgetown Univ. 1982–83; Head, Center for Nat. Policy 1985–93; chief legis. asst to Democratic Senator Edmund Muskie 1976–78; mem. Nat. Security Council staff in Carter Admin 1978–81; adviser to Democrat cands Geraldine Ferraro 1984 and Michael Dukakis 1988; Perm. Rep. to UN 1993–97 (first foreign-born holder of this post); Sec. of State 1997–2001 (highest-ranking woman in history of US govt); Co-founder and Prin. The Albright Group LLC 2001–; Chair. Nat. Democratic Inst. for Int. Affairs, Washington, DC 2001–; Chair The PEW Global Attitudes Project; Pres. Truman Scholarship Foundation; mem. Bd NY Stock Exchange; mem. Council on Foreign Relations, American Political Science Asscn, American Asscn for Advancement of Slavic Studies. *Publications:* Poland: The Role of the Press in Political Change 1983, Madam Secretary: A Memoir 2003, The Mighty and the Almighty: Reflections on Faith, God and World Affairs 2006; numerous articles. *Address:* The Albright Group LLC, 901 15th Street, NW, Suite 1000, Washington, DC 20005, USA (office). *Telephone:* (202) 842-7222 (office). *Fax:* (202) 354-3888 (office). *Website:* www.thealbrightgroupllc.com (office).

ALBURQUERQUE DE CASTRO, Rafael, DJur; Dominican Republic politician; *Vice-President;* b. 14 June 1940, Santo Domingo; ed Univ. of Santo Domingo, Sorbonne, Université de Paris, France; fmr Minister of Labour; Vice-Pres. of Dominican Repub. 2004–. *Address:* Administrative Secretariat of the Presidency, Palacio Nacional, Avenida México, esq. Dr Delgado, Santo Domingo, DN, Dominican Republic (office). *Telephone:* 686-4771 (office). *Fax:* 688-2100 (office). *E-mail:* prensa@presidencia.gov.do (office). *Website:* www .presidencia.gov.do (office).

ALCHOURON, Guillermo E.; Argentine farmer, lawyer and politician; b. 4 Nov. 1933; m. María Elina Albin Etchart; two s. three d.; ed Univ. of Buenos Aires; farmer specializing in breeding of Dutch, Argentine and Jersey dairy cattle and milk production at Coronel Brandsen Estate; mem. Bd of Dirs Argentine Rural Soc. 1969–96, Pres. 1984–90; Pres. Argentine Soc. of Jersey Dairy Cattle; Counsellor, Foundation for Latin American Econ. Research 1969–; Adviser, Argentine Council for Int. Relations 1987–; Deputy for Acción de la República 1999–; mem. Exec. Council, Int. Fed. of Agric. Producers; Gov. World Econ. Forum for Food and Farming Production; Pres. Agric. Soc.; mem. Acción por la República (AR); decorations from Spain, France, USA, Germany and Italy. *Leisure interests:* golf, tennis, cattle-raising. *Address:* Acción por la República (AR), Buenos Aires; La Juanita, Coronel Brandsen, Argentina.

ALCKMIN, Geraldo José Rodrigues; Brazilian politician; b. 7 Nov. 1952, Pindamonhangaba, São Paulo; m. Maria Lúcia Ribeiro Alckmin; three c.; ed Universidade de Taubaté Medical School; worked in São Paulo Public Service Hosp.; elected to Pindamonhangaba City Council 1973–77, Mayor 1977–82 (youngest Brazilian mayor); elected as Fed. Deputy 1983–87, 1987–94, Co-founder Brazilian Social Democracy Party (Partido da Social Democracia Brasileira—PSDB) 1988; Vice-Gov. of São Paulo 1994–2001, Gov. 2001–06; cand. in presidential elections Oct. 2006; cand. in São Paulo mayoral elections 2008. *Address:* c/o Partido da Social Democracia Brasileria, SGAS, Quadra 607, Edif. Metrópolis, Asa Sul, 70200-670 Brasília DF, Brazil (office).

ALDA, Alan, BS; American actor; b. 28 Jan. 1936, New York; s. of the late Robert Alda and Joan Browne; m. Arlene Weiss; three d.; ed Fordham Univ.; performed with Second City 1963; Trustee Museum of TV and Radio, Rockefeller Foundation; Pres. Appointee Nat. Comm. for Observance of Int. Women's Year 1976; Co-Chair. Nat. ERA Countdown Campaign 1982; five Emmy Awards (Best Actor, Best Dir and Best Writer), two Dirs' Guild Awards, Writers' Guild Award, seven People's Choice Awards, Humanitas Award for Writing, five Golden Globe Awards for M*A*S*H, elected to TV Acad. Hall of Fame 1994. *Films include:* Gone Are the Days 1963, Paper Lion 1968, The Extraordinary Seaman 1968, The Moonshine War 1970, Jenny 1970, The Mephisto Waltz 1971, To Kill a Clown 1972, California Suite 1978, Same Time Next Year 1978, The Seduction of Joe Tynan (also wrote screenplay) 1979, Crimes and Misdemeanours (D.W. Griffith Award, NY Film Critics' Award) 1989, Whispers in the Dark 1992, And the Band Played On 1993, Manhattan Murder Mystery 1993, White Mile 1994, Canadian Bacon 1995, Everybody Says I Love You 1996, Murder at 1600 1997, Mad City 1997, The Object of My Affection 1998, What Women Want 2000, The Aviator 2004, Resurrecting the Champ 2007; actor, dir, writer of films: The Four Seasons 1981, Sweet Liberty 1986, A New Life 1987, Betsy's Wedding 1990. *Broadway appearances include:* The Owl and the Pussycat, Purlie Victorious, Fair Game for Lovers, The Apple Tree, Our Town (London) 1991, Jake's Women 1992, etc. *TV includes:* The Glass House 1972, M*A*S*H 1972–83, Tune in America 1975, Kill Me If You Can (film) 1977, Club Land 2001, The Killing Yard 2001, The West Wing (series) 2004–06; devised series We'll Get By 1975; Fair Game for Lovers (Theatre World Award); And The Band Played On 1993, White Mile 1994. *Publication:* Never Have Your Dog Stuffed (memoir) 2006, Things I Overheard While Talking to Myself 2007. *Address:* c/o Martin Bregman Productions, 641 Lexington Avenue, New York, NY 10022, USA.

ALDANA VILLANUEVA, Brig.-Gen. Carlos Humberto; Guatemalan army officer and government official; fmr Vice-Minister of Nat. Defence, Minister of Nat. Defence 2004–05. *Address:* c/o Ministry of National Defence, Antigua Escuela Politécnica, Avda La Reforma 1-45, Zona 10, Guatemala City, Guatemala (office).

ALDER, Berni Julian, PhD; American theoretical physicist; *Professor Emeritus of Applied Science, University of California, Davis;* b. 9 Sept. 1925, Duisburg, Germany; s. of Ludwig Alder and Ottilie Gottschalk; m. Esther Romella Berger 1956; two s. one d.; ed Univ. of California, Berkeley and California Inst. of Tech.; Instructor, Univ. of Calif., Berkeley 1951–54; Theoretical Physicist, Univ. of Calif. Lawrence Livermore Nat. Lab. 1955–93; Prof. of Applied Science, Univ. of Calif., Davis 1987–93, Prof. Emer. 1993–; NSF Sr Post Doctoral Fellow, Weizman Inst. (Israel) and Univ. of Rome 1963–64; Van der Waals Prof., Univ. of Amsterdam 1971; Guggenheim Fellow, Univ. of Cambridge, UK and Leiden, Netherlands 1954–55; Assoc. Prof., Univ. of Paris 1972; Hinshelwood Prof., Univ. of Oxford 1986; Lorentz Prof., Univ. of Leiden 1990; G.N. Lewis Lecturer 1984, Kistiakowsky Lecturer 1990, Royal Soc. Lecturer 1991, Grad. Lecturer 2000; Ed. Journal of Computational Physics; mem. NAS; Fellow Japanese Promotion of Science 1989, American Physics Soc.; ACS Hildebrand Award 1985, Berni J. Alder Prize est. by European Physical Soc. 1999, IUPAP Boltzmann Prize 2002. *Publications:* Methods of Computational Physics 1963, many chapters in books and articles in journals. *Leisure interests:* hiking, skiing, gardening. *Address:* Lawrence Livermore National Laboratory, PO Box 808, Livermore, CA 94551-0808 (office); 1245 Contra Costa Drive, El Cerrito, CA 94530, USA (home). *Telephone:* (925) 422-4384 (office); (510) 231-0137 (home). *Fax:* (925) 423-4371 (office). *E-mail:* alder1@llnl.gov (office).

ALDER, Jens, BSc, MBA; Swiss business executive; *President and CEO, TDC A/S;* b. 1957; ed Swiss Fed. Inst. of Tech. (ETH), Zürich, INSEAD, Fontainebleau, France; trained as electrical engineer; began career with Standard Telephon & Radio AG; various exec. positions Alcatel STR AG, Motor Columbus AG, Alcatel Schweiz AG; Head of Network Services Business Unit and mem. Man. Bd Swisscom AG 1998–99, CEO 1999–2006; Pres. and CEO TDC A/S 2006–; Pres. Schweizerische Gesellschaft für Konjunkturforschung; mem. Man. Bd Swiss Information and Telecommunications Tech. Asscn (SICTA), Swiss Employers' Fed. *Leisure interest:* skiing. *Address:* TDC A/S, Nørregade 21, 0900 Copenhagen C, Denmark (office).

ALDERDICE OF KNOCK, Baron (Life Peer), cr. 1996, of Knock, in the City of Belfast; **John Thomas Alderdice,** MB, BCh, BAO, FRCPsych, KCFO; British politician and psychiatrist; *Commissioner, Independent Monitoring Commission;* b. 28 March 1955, Lurgan, Co. Antrim; s. of Rev. David Alderdice and Helena Alderdice (née Sheilds); m. Joan Margaret (née Hill) 1977; two s. one d.; ed Ballymena Acad., Queen's Univ., Belfast; Royal Coll. of Psychiatrists; apptd Consultant Psychotherapist, Eastern Health and Social Services Bd (EHSSB) 1988; Dir NI Inst. of Human Relations 1991–94; Exec. Medical Dir, S and E Belfast Health and Social Services Trust 1993–97; mem. Alliance Party of NI 1978–, mem. Exec. Cttee 1984–98, Chair. Policy Cttee 1985–87, Vice-Chair. 1987, Leader 1987–98; contested Belfast E 1987, 1992, NI European Parl. elections 1989; Councillor, Belfast City Council 1989–97; Leader of Del. to Inter-Party and Inter-Govt Talks on the Future of NI 1991–92; Leader of Del. at Forum for Peace and Reconciliation (Dublin Castle) 1994–96; mem. NI Forum for Political Dialogue 1996–98; Vice-Pres. European Liberal Democrat and Reform Party 1999–2003, Exec. Cttee mem. 1987–2003, Treas. 1995–99; Vice-Pres. Liberal Int. 1992–99, Deputy Pres. 1999–2005, Pres. 2005–, Chair. Human Rights Cttee 1999–2005; mem. House of Lords 1998–; mem. NI Ass. (Belfast E) 1998–2002, Speaker 1998–2004 (NI Ass. suspended Oct. 2002); Commr, Ind. Monitoring Comm. 2003–; mem. BMA, Asscn Psychoanalytic Psychotherapy; Trustee Ulster Museum 1993–97; Hon. Lecturer, Faculty of Medicine, Queen's Univ. Belfast 1991–99; Hon. Prof., Faculty of Medicine, Univ. of San Marcos, Lima (Peru) 1999; Hon. Fellow, Royal Coll. of Physicians of Ireland 1997, Royal Coll. of Psychiatrists 2001; W. Averell Harriman Award for Democracy 1998, John F. Kennedy Profiles in Courage Award 1998, Silver Medal of Congress of Peru 1999, Medal of Honour of Peru Coll. of Medicine 1999, Extraordinary Meritorious Service to Psychoanalysis, Int. Psychoanalytical Asscn 2005. *Publications include:* articles on psychology of violent conflict and terrorism. *Leisure interests:* music, singing, gastronomy. *Address:* House of Lords, London, SW1A 0PW, England (office). *Telephone:* (20) 7219-5050 (office). *E-mail:* alderdicej@parliament.uk (office). *Website:* homepage .ntlworld.com/john.alderdice.

ALDERS, Hans; Dutch politician; b. 17 Dec. 1942; ed vocational school; fmr junior man. in an employment agency; mem. Gelderland Prov. Ass. 1978, Leader Partij van de Arbeid (PvdA) Group 1979; mem. Parl. 1982, Sec. PvdA Parl. Group 1987–89; Minister of Housing, Physical Planning and the Environment 1989–94; Commr of the Queen, Prov. of Groningen 1995–. *Address:* c/o Province of Groningen, Martinikerkhof 12, Postbus 610, 9700 AP, Groningen, Netherlands.

ALDINGER III, William F.; American business executive; b. 1947; ed Baruch Coll.; Dir, Chair. and Chief Exec. Household Finance Inc. 1996–2002, then Chair. and Chief Exec. Household Int. (after acquisition of Household Finance by HSBC) –2005 (retd); Dir IL Tools Inc. 1998–, Mastercard Int., AT&T Inc., KKR Financial Corpn, Charles Schwab Corpn; Dr hc (Baruch Coll.) 2005; Distinguished Alumnus Award, Baruch Coll. 2004, Adam Smith Business Citizen Medal 2004. *Address:* c/o Board of Directors, AT&T Inc., 175 East Houston, San Antonio, TX 78205-2233, USA (office).

ALDISS, Brian Wilson, OBE, FRSL; British writer, critic and actor; b. 18 Aug. 1925, Norfolk; m. 2nd Margaret Manson 1965 (died 1997); two s. two d.; ed Framlingham Coll. and West Buckland School; fmr soldier, draughtsman, bookseller and film critic; Literary Ed. Oxford Mail 1957–69; Pres. British Science Fiction Asscn 1960–65; Jt-Pres. European Science Fiction Cttees 1976–80; Chair. John W. Campbell Memorial Award 1976–77; Chair. Cttee of Man. Soc. of Authors 1977–78; mem. Literature Advisory Panel, Arts Council 1978–80; Chair. Cultural Exchanges Cttee of Authors 1978; Judge, Booker McConnell Prize 1981; Pres. World SF 1982–84; Ed. S.F. Horizons 1964–; Vice-Pres. H.G. Wells Soc., W. Buckland School 1997–; Hon. DLitt 2000; Ditmar Award for World's Best Contemporary Science Fiction Writer 1969, first James Blish Award for Excellence in Criticism 1977, Pilgrim Award 1978, John W. Campbell Award 1983, Kurt Lasswitz Award 1984, IAFA Distinguished Scholarship Award 1986, J. Lloyd Eaton Award 1988, Prix Utopie (France) 1999, Grand Master of Science Fiction 2000. *Opera:* Oedipus on Mars. *Plays (author):* SF Blues, Kindred Blood in Kensington Gore, Monsters of Every Day (Oxford Literary Festival) 2000, Drinks with The Spider King (Florida) 2000; acted in own productions 1985–2002. *Publications:* The Brightfount Diaries 1955, Space, Time & Nathaniel 1957, Non-Stop (Jules Verne Award 1977) 1958, The Male Response 1959, Hothouse (Hugo Award 1962) 1962, The Airs of Earth 1963, The Dark Light Years 1964, Greybeard 1964, Earthworks 1965, Best Science Fiction Stories of Brian W. Aldiss 1965, The Saliva Tree (Nebula Award) 1965, Cities and Stones: A Traveller's Jugoslavia 1966, Report on Probability A 1968, Barefoot in the Head 1969, Intangibles Inc., 1969, A Brian Aldiss Omnibus 1969, The Hand-Reared Boy 1970, The Shape of Further Things 1970, A Soldier Erect 1971, The Moment of Eclipse (British Science Fiction Asscn Award 1972) 1971, Brian Aldiss Omnibus 2 1971, Penguin Science Fiction Omnibus (ed.) 1973, Comic Inferno 1973, Billion Year Spree (III Merit Award 1976) 1973, Frankenstein Unbound (made into film directed by Roger Corman) 1973, The Eighty-Minute Hour 1974, Hell's Cartographers (ed.) 1975, Space Odysseys, Evil Earths, Science Fiction Art 1975, The Malacia Tapestry, Galactic Empires (two vols) 1976, Last Orders, Brothers of the Head 1977, Perilous Planets 1977, A Rude Awakening 1978, Enemies of the System 1978, This World and Nearer Ones 1979, Pile 1979, New Arrivals, Old Encounters 1979, Moreau's Other Island 1980, Life in the West 1980, An Island Called Moreau 1981, Foreign Bodies 1981, Helliconia Spring 1982, Science Fiction Quiz 1983, Helliconia Summer 1983, Seasons in Flight 1984, Helliconia Winter 1985, The Pale Shadow of Science 1985, ... And the Lurid Glare of the Comet 1986, Trillion Year Spree (Hugo Award 1987) 1986, Ruins 1987, Forgotten Life 1988, Science Fiction Blues 1988, Best SF Stories of Brian W. Aldiss 1988, Cracken at Critical 1989, A Romance of the Equator 1990, Bury My Heart at W. H. Smith's 1990, Dracula Unbound 1991, Remembrance Day 1993, A Tupolev Too Far 1993, Somewhere East of Life 1994, The Detached Retina 1995, At the Caligula Hotel (poems) 1995, The Secret of this Book 1995, Songs from the Steppes of Central Asia 1996, The Twinkling of an Eye 1998, The Squire Quartet (four vols) 1998, When the Feast is Finished 1999, White Mars 1999, Supertoys Last All Summer Long (made into Kubrick–Spielberg film A.I. 2001) 2001, The Cretan Teat 2001, Super-State 2002, Researches and Churches in Serbia 2002, The Dark Sun Rises (poems) 2002, Affairs in Hampden Ferrers 2004, Jocasta 2005, Sanity and the Lady 2005, Harm 2007, A Science Fiction Omnibus (ed) 2007; contributions: TLS, Nature. *Leisure interests:* the past, the future, obscurity. *Address:* Hambleden, 39 St Andrew's Road, Old Headington, Oxford, OX3 9DL, England. *Telephone:* (1865) 762464. *Fax:* (1865) 744435. *E-mail:* aldiss@dial.pipex.com (office). *Website:* www .brianwaldiss.com.

ALDOSHIN, Sergey Mikhailovich, DChem; Russian chemist; *Director, Institute of Problems of Chemical Physics;* b. 1953, Krasny Pochinski, Kadom Dist; ed Rostov State Univ.; Dir Inst. of Problems of Chemical Physics, Chernogolovka 1997–; Vice-Dir MSU Branch Chernogolovka; mem. Presidium, Russian Acad. of Sciences; Gold Medal for Contrib. to World Science and Int. Collaboration 2003. *Publications:* numerous scientific papers. *Address:* Institute of Problems of Chemical Physics, 1 Semenov av., 142432 Chernogolovka, Moscow Region, Russia (office). *Telephone:* (495) 785-70-48 (office).

Fax: (096) 52-49-676 (office). *E-mail:* sma@icp.ac.ru (office). *Website:* www.icp .ac.ru (office).

ALDOURI, Mohammed A., BL, PhD; Iraqi diplomatist and professor of law; b. 1942, Baghdad; ed Baghdad Univ. and Dijon Univ., France; Lecturer Coll. of Law and Political Science, Baghdad Univ. 1973–82, Head Dept of Law 1982–83, Prof. of Int. Law and Dean of Law Coll. 1983–98; Dir-Gen. Iraqi Cultural Relations Office, Ministry of Higher Educ. 1975–78; mem. UN Cttee for Civil and Political Rights 1980–84, also Rep. of Iraq to Comm. for Human Rights; Head of Human Rights and Legal Depts, Ministry of Foreign Affairs 1994–96, 1998; Perm. Rep. to UN, Geneva 1999–2001, New York 2001–03. *Address:* c/o Permanent Mission of Iraq to the United Nations, 14 East 79th Street, New York, NY 10021, USA (office).

ALDRIDGE, (Harold Edward) James; British author and journalist; b. 10 July 1918, White Hills, Vic., Australia; s. of William Thomas Aldridge and Edith Quayle Aldridge; m. Dina Mitchnik 1942; two s.; with Herald and Sun, Melbourne, Australia 1937–38, Daily Sketch and Sunday Dispatch, London 1939; with Australian Newspaper Service and North American Newspaper Alliance (as war corresp.), Finland, Norway, Middle East, Greece, USSR 1939–45; corresp. for Time and Life, Tehran 1944; Rhys Memorial Award 1945, New South Wales Premier's Literary Award 1986; Lenin Peace Prize 1972. *Plays:* 49th State 1947, One Last Glimpse 1981. *Publications:* Signed with Their Honour 1942, The Sea Eagle 1944, Of Many Men 1946, The Diplomat 1950, The Hunter 1951, Heroes of the Empty View 1954, Underwater Hunting for Inexperienced Englishmen 1955, I Wish He Would Not Die 1958, Gold and Sand (short stories) 1960, The Last Exile 1961, A Captive in the Land 1962, The Statesman's Game 1966, My Brother Tom 1966, The Flying 19 1966, Living Egypt (with Paul Strand) 1969, Cairo: Biography of a City 1970, A Sporting Proposition 1973, The Marvellous Mongolian 1974, Mockery in Arms 1974, The Untouchable Juli 1975, One Last Glimpse 1977, Goodbye Un-America 1979, The Broken Saddle 1982, The True Story of Lilli Stubek (Australian Children's Book of the Year 1985) 1984, The True Story of Spit Mac Phee (Guardian Children's Fiction Prize) 1985, The True Story of Lola MacKellar 1993, The Girl From the Sea 2003, The Wings of Kitty St Clair 2006. *Leisure interests:* trout and salmon fishing. *Address:* Curtis Brown Ltd, Haymarket House, 28–29 Haymarket, London, SW1Y 4SP, England (office). *Telephone:* (20) 7393-4400 (office). *Fax:* (20) 7393-4401 (office). *E-mail:* info@ curtisbrown.co.uk (office). *Website:* www.curtisbrown.co.uk (office).

ALDRIN, Buzz, DSc; American astronaut, author and scientist; *Chairman, Starcraft Enterprises;* b. 20 Jan. 1930, Montclair, NJ; s. of the late Col Edwin E. Aldrin and Marion Moon; m. 1st (divorced 1978); two s. one d.; m. 2nd Lois Driggs Cannon 1988; ed US Mil. Acad. and Massachusetts Inst. of Tech.; fmr mem. USAF; completed pilot training 1952; flew combat missions during Korean War; later became aerial gunnery instructor, Nellis Air Force Base, Nev.; attended Squadron Officers' School at Air Univ., Maxwell Air Force Base, Ala; later Flight Commdr 36th Tactical Fighter Wing, Bitburg, Germany; completed astronautics studies at MIT 1963; selected by NASA as astronaut 1963; Gemini Target Office, Air Force Space Systems Div., LA, Calif. 1963; later assigned to Manned Spacecraft Center, Houston, Tex.; pilot of backup crew for Gemini IX mission 1966; pilot for Gemini XII 1966; backup command module pilot for Apollo VIII; lunar module pilot for Apollo XI, landed on the moon 20 July 1969; Commdt Aerospace Research Pilot School 1971–72; Scientific Consultant, Beverly Hills Oil Co., LA; Chair. Starcraft Enterprises 1988–, Starcraft Boosters Inc. 1996–, ShareSpace Foundation 1998–, Nat. Space Soc.; Fellow, American Inst. of Aeronautics and Astronautics; Hon. mem. Royal Aeronautical Soc.; retd from USAF 1972; Pres. Research & Eng Consultants Inc. 1972–; consultant to JRW, Jet Propulsion Lab.; several hon. degrees; Medal of Freedom, USA and numerous other awards. *Publications:* First on the Moon: A Voyage with Neil Armstrong (with Michael Collins) 1970, Return to Earth (with Wayne Warga) 1974, Men From Earth (with Malcolm McConnell) 1989, Encounter with Tiber (with John Barnes) 1996, The Return (with John Barnes) 2000, Reaching for the Moon 2005. *Leisure interests:* scuba diving, snow skiing, star gazing. *Address:* 10380 Wilshire Boulevard, Suite 703, Los Angeles, CA 90024, USA (office). *Telephone:* (310) 278-0384 (office); (310) 278-0384 (home). *Fax:* (310) 278-0388 (office); (310) 278-0388 (home). *E-mail:* starbuzz2@aol.com (office). *Website:* www.buzzaldrin.com (office).

ALEBUA, Rt Hon. Ezekiel, PC; Solomon Islands politician; fmr Deputy Prime Minister; Prime Minister of the Solomon Islands 1986–89; Premier Guadalcanal prov.; mem. Solomon Islands United Party (SIUPA). *Address:* c/o Office of the Prime Minister, Honiara, Solomon Islands.

ALEGRE, Norberto José d'Alva Costa; São Tomé and Príncipe politician; fmr Minister of Econ. and Finance; Prime Minister of São Tomé e Príncipe 1992–94; mem. Partido de Convergência Democrática Grupo de Reflexão. *Address:* c/o Partido de Convergência Democrático Grupo de Reflexão, São Tomé, São Tomé e Príncipe.

ALEKPEROV, Avaz Akber oğlu, BEcons; Azerbaijani politician; b. 23 July 1952; m.; ed Azerbaijan State Economy Inst.; accountant, Baku Head Construction Dept 1973; mil. service, Brest region 1973–74; economist, Chief Economist, Chief of Planning Dept then Deputy Chief of Econ. Affairs in Azergurashdirmakandtikinti Trust, Ministry of Rural Construction 1975–81; Chief of Planning and Finance Dept, Cabinet of Ministers 1981–84; Deputy Chief of Econ. Dept 1984–91; Chief of Azerbaijan Br., USSR Pension Fund 1991; Chair. Exec. Bd, Pension Fund of Azerbaijan Repub. 1991–92; Chair. State Social Protection Fund 1992–99; Minister of Finance 1999–2006. *Address:* c/o Ministry of Finance, Samed Vurghun küç. 83, 1022 Baku, Azerbaijan (office).

ALEKPEROV, Vagit Yusufovich, DEcon; Russian-Azerbaijani business executive; *President and Director, Lukoil;* b. 1 Sept. 1950, Baku, Azerbaijan;

m.; one s.; ed Azizbekov Inst. of Oil and Chem., Azerbaijan; worked in oil industry in Azerbaijan and Western Siberia 1968–75; worked as engineer for Kasporneft, Surgntneftegaz.Bashneft cos 1975–84; Dir Kogalymneftegas (oil-extraction co.) 1984–90; Deputy, then First Deputy Minister of Oil and Gas Industry of USSR 1990–91; Chair. Bd Imperial Bank, Petrocommercial Bank; Founder, mem. Bd of Dirs and Pres. Lukoil 1993–, Chair. 1993–2000, currently Chair. Man. Cttee; Deputy Chair. Oil Exporters Union of Russia; Vice-Pres. Int. Oil Consortium; mem. Russian Acad. of Natural Sciences; awarded four orders and eight medals; winner of two Russian Govt prizes. *Publication:* Vertical Integrated Oil Companies in Russia. *Leisure interests:* travel, spending time with family and friends. *Address:* Lukoil, Sretenskii bulv. 11, 101000 Moscow, Russia (office). *Telephone:* (495) 627-44-44 (office). *Fax:* (495) 625-70-16 (office). *E-mail:* pr@lukoil.com (office). *Website:* www .lukoil.com (office).

ALEKSANDROV, Aleksandr Pavlovich, PhD; Russian cosmonaut and pilot; b. 20 Feb. 1943, Moscow; m. Natalia Valentinovna Aleksandrova; one s. one d.; ed Baumann Tech. Inst., Moscow; mem. CPSU 1970; after service in Soviet Army started work with Space Programme 1964–; took part in elaboration of control system of spacecraft, Cosmonaut since 1978, participated in Soyuz-T and Salyut programmes; successfully completed 149-day flight to Salyut-7 orbital station with V.A. Lyakhov 1983 and effected spacewalk, July 1987, with A. Victorenko and M. Fares; joined Yurii Romanenko in space, returned to Earth Dec. 1987; completed 160-day flight on Mir Space Station; Chief, Dept of Crew Training and Extra Vehicular Activity at Energya design and production firm; mem. Extra Vehicular Activity Cttee, IAF 1994–; Academician Int. Informatization Acad. 1997; Hero of Soviet Union 1983, 1987, Hero of Syria. *Address:* Khovanskaya str. 3, 27, 129515 Moscow, Russia. *Telephone:* (495) 513-67-88 (office); (495) 215-56-19 (home). *Fax:* (495) 513-61-38.

ALEKSANDROV, Kiryll Sergeyevich, DPhysMathSc; Russian physicist; *Director, Kirensky Institute of Physics and Counsellor, Russian Academy of Sciences;* b. 9 Jan. 1931, St Petersburg; s. of Sergey Aleksandrov and Ljubov' Aleksandrov; m. Inga Chernjavskaja 1959; one d.; ed Leningrad Electrotech. Inst.; worked as researcher, Inst. of Crystallography; researcher, Vice-Dir Kirensky Inst. of Physics, Siberian br. of USSR (now Russian) Acad. of Sciences, Krasnoyarsk 1958–83, Dir 1983–; Corresp. mem. USSR Acad. of Sciences 1971, mem. 1984, Counsellor 2004–; Chair. Scientific Council on Physics of Segnetoelectrics and Dielectrics, Dept of Gen. Physics and Astronomy, Russian Acad. of Sciences; Vice-Chair. Krasnoyarsk Scientific Centre of Russian Acad. of Sciences; USSR State Prize in Science 1989. *Publications:* Perovskite-like Crystals (co-author) 1997, Perovskites, Modern and Future (co-author) 2004; works in the field of crystal physics, structural phase transitions, physics of materials. *Leisure interests:* numismatics, mushroom hunting. *Address:* L. Kirensky Institute of Physics, 600036 Akademgorodok, Krasnoyarsk, Russia. *Telephone:* (3912) 43-26-35 (office); (3912) 44-41-75 (home). *Fax:* (3912) 43-89-23. *E-mail:* kaleks@iph.krasn.ru (office). *Website:* www.kirensky.ru (office).

ALEKSANDROV, Vassily Yegorovich; Russian pilot and aviation executive; *Director-General, Tupolev Aviation Scientific-Technical Complex;* b. 6 May 1947, Istra, Moscow region; m.; one d.; ed Tambov Higher Aviation School of Pilots, Yuri Gagarin Mil. Aviation Acad., Mil. Acad. of Gen. Staff; pilot in mil. air forces of Russian Fed., Squadron Commdr, Regt Commdr; Dir Tambov Higher Aviation School; Deputy Commdr Air Forces Siberian Mil. Command; Dir Research Inst., Ministry of Defence; Chair. Bd of Dirs Tupolev Aviation Scientific-Tech. Complex (mfrs of strategic bombers and passenger liners) 1997–98, Dir-Gen. 1998–; Corresp. mem. Russian Acad. of Aviation. *Address:* Tupolev Aviation Scientific-Technical Complex, akademik Tupolev emb. 15, 111250 Moscow, Russia (office). *Telephone:* (495) 785-53-38 (office). *Fax:* (495) 261-08-68 (office). *Website:* www.tupolev.ru/English (office).

ALEKSASHENKO, Sergey Vladimirovich; Russian investment banker and fmr government official; *President, Antanta Capital Investment Group;* b. 23 Dec. 1959, Likino-Dulevo, Moscow Region; m.; two c.; ed Moscow State Univ.; mem. of staff Moscow Inst. of Econs and Math., USSR Acad. of Sciences 1986–90; leading expert USSR State Comm. on Econ. Reform; Exec. Dir Inst. of Russian Union of Industrialists and Entrepreneurs 1991–93, Dir.-Gen. 1995; Deputy Minister of Finance 1993–95; First Deputy Chair. Cen. Bank of the Russian Fed. 1995–98; Chair. Audit Comm.; Chair. Asscn of Current Stock Exchanges of Russia 1995–; First Deputy Chair. Observation Council Savings Bank 1996–99; Head Centre of Devt Analytical Group 1999–; Deputy Dir-Gen. Interros (holding co.) 2000, Man. Dir —2004; Pres. Antanta Capital Investment Group 2004–. *Publications:* Battle for the Rouble, Alma Mater; over 100 publs on fiscal and econ. matters. *Leisure interests:* photography, diving. *Address:* Antanta Capital Investment Group, 19, building 1, Lyalin Per., Moscow 105062, Russia. *Telephone:* (495) 775-5100. *Fax:* (495) 783-9627. *E-mail:* mail@antcm.ru. *Website:* www.antcm.ru.

ALEKSEEV, Aleksander Yuryevich; Russian diplomatist and politician; *Permanent Representative to the Council of Europe;* b. 20 Aug. 1946, Moscow; m.; one d.; ed Moscow Inst. of Int. Relations; diplomatic posts abroad, including in India and in Ministry of Foreign Affairs of USSR and Russia; Amb. to Pakistan 1993; Dir 3 Asian Dept, Ministry of Foreign Affairs; Perm. Rep. to OSCE 2001–04; Deputy Minister of Foreign Affairs 2004–07; Perm. Rep.to Council of Europe 2007—. *Address:* Office of the Permanent Representative to the Council of Europe, 75 allee de la Robertsau, 67000 Strasbourg, France (office). *Telephone:* (388) 24-20-15 (office). *Fax:* (388) 24-19-74 (office). *E-mail:* representationpermderussie@wanadoo.fr (office).

ALEKSEEVA, Tatyana Ivanovna, DrSc, PhD; Russian anthropologist, biologist and academic; *Principal Researcher, Research Institute and Museum of Anthropology, Moscow State University;* b. 7 Dec. 1928, Kazan; d. of Ivan Sharabrin and Varvara Majorova; m. Valery Alekseev (deceased); ed Moscow State Univ.; Jr, Sr, Leading, Prin. Researcher, Research Inst. and Museum of Anthropology 1955–; Prin. Researcher, Inst. of Archaeology 1992–; Corresp. mem. USSR (now Russian) Acad. of Sciences 1991, mem. 2000–; research in study of influence of geographical and social medium on aboriginal population; mem. Asscn of Human Biologists; Pres. Russian br. of European Anthropological Asscn; Foreign mem., Montenegro Acad. of Science and Art; Hon. mem. World Org. of Mongolian Studies 1997; Hon. Res., Moscow State Univ. 1997; Order of Friendship 1999; Medal of Moscow 1997. *Publications include:* Origin and Ethnic History of Russian People 1965, Ethnogenesis of East Slavs 1973, Geographical Medium and Biology of Man 1977, Adaptive Processes in Populations of Man 1986, Neolithic Population of the Eastern Europe Forest Zone 1997, Eastern Slavs: Anthropology and Ethnic History 1999, Homo Sungirensis Upper Palaeolithic Man: Ecological and Evolutionary Aspects of the Investigation 2000, Anthropology of Medieval Vlakhs in Comparative Study: on data on Mistikhaly Burial Site 2003. *Leisure interests:* riding, pets. *Address:* Research Institute and Museum of Anthropology, Moscow State University, 125009 Moscow, Mokhovaya str. 11 (office); 119420 Moscow, ul. Profsoyuzhaya 43-1, Apt 125, Russia (home). *Telephone:* (495) 203-35-98 (office); (495) 331-32-73 (home). *Fax:* (495) 203-3554 (office). *E-mail:* homo@ antropos.msu.ru (office).

ALEKSEYEV, Sergey Sergeyevich, DJur; Russian lawyer; *Chairman, Council of Research Centre of Private Law;* b. 28 July 1924; m.; two d.; ed Sverdlovsk Inst. of Law; teacher, Prof., Head of Chair Sverdlovsk (now Yekaterinburg) Inst. of Law 1949–; Dir Inst. of Philosophy and Law Ural Div. of USSR Acad. of Sciences; Corresp. mem. USSR Acad. of Sciences 1987; USSR People's Deputy 1990–91; Chair. USSR Cttee of Constitutional Inspection 1990–91; Chair. Council of Research Centre of Pvt. Law 1992–; author (with A. Sobchak) of one of projects of Constitution of Russia 1991–92; mem. Presidential Council of Russia 1993–95; USSR State Prize, Merited Worker of Science of Russia. *Publications include:* General Theory of Law (Vols 1–2), 1981–82, Theory of Law: Constitutional Concept 1991, Legal Civil Soc. 1991. *Leisure interests:* tourism, mountain skiing, reading. *Address:* Research Centre of Private Law, Yekaterinburg Branch, 620146 Yekaterinburg, Russia (office). *Telephone:* (3432) 28-89-81 (office).

ALEKSIEVICH, Svetlana; Belarusian journalist and writer; b. 31 May 1948, Minsk, Ukraine; ed Minsk Univ.; worked as journalist on local newspaper in early 1970s; Kurt Tucholsky Prize, Swedish PEN Club, Stockholm 1996, Andrej Sinjavskij Prize, Moscow 1997, Triumph Prize 1998, European Understanding Prize for contrib. to a better understanding among European nations 1998, 'Témoin du Monde', Paris 1999, Erich Maria Remarque Peace Prize (Germany) 2001, Nat. Book Critics' Circle Award, New York 2006, Oxfam Novib PEN Award 2007. *Publications include:* non-fiction: Aposhniya svedki. kniga nedzitsyachyh raskaza? 1985, U voyny ne zhenskoe litso (The War's Unwomanly Face) 1985, Tsinkovye mal'chiki (Zinky Boys: Soviet Voices from a Forgotten War) 1991, Zacharavanyya smertsu (Enchanted with Death) 1993, Poslednie svideteli (The Last Witnesses), Charnobyl'skaya malitva (trans. as Chernobyl Prayer: A Chronicle of the Future) 1997. *Address:* c/o Galina Dursthoff, Marsiliusstr. 70, 50937 Cologne, Germany. *E-mail:* svett_al@hotmail.com; galina@dursthoff.de. *Website:* alexievich.info.

ALEKSISHVILI, Aleksi, MPA; Georgian politician; b. 21 Feb. 1974; m.; one s. one d.; ed Tbilisi State Univ. and Duke Univ., Durham, NC, USA; spent five years at Faculty of Econ. Relations, Tbilisi State Univ. 1991–96; fmr Deputy Minister of Finance and First-Deputy Minister of Finance; Pres. Young Economists Soc. of Georgia 1994–2001; Minister of Econ. Devt 2004–2005; Minister of Finance 2005–07; Gov. for Georgia, IMF and World Bank 2005–; mem. Bd of Dirs Nat. Bank of Georgia 2007–; Chair. UN Comm. on Sustainable Devt 2005–06; Program in Int. Devt Policy (PIDP) Summer Internship, Duke Center for Int. Devt and Exec. Educ. 2003, PIDP Fellow 2002–04. *Address:* National Bank of Georgia, 3/5 Leonidze Street, 0105 Tbilisi, Georgia (office). *Telephone:* (32) 44-25-44 (office). *Fax:* (32) 44-25-77 (office). *E-mail:* info@nbg.gov.ge (office). *Website:* nbg.gov.ge (office).

ALEMÁN, Héctor; Panamanian politician; Minister of the Interior and Justice 2004–07. *Address:* c/o Ministry of the Interior and Justice, Avenida Central, entre calle 2da y 3era, San Felipe, Apdo 1628, Panamá 1, Panama (office). *Telephone:* 212-2000 (office). *Fax:* 212-2126 (office).

ALEMÁN HEALY, José Miguel, BA, JD; Panamanian lawyer and fmr government official; *Partner, Arias, Alemán & Mora;* b. 8 May 1956; ed Ripon Coll., Wis., Tulane Univ., USA; admitted to Bar 1981; Vice-Pres. Panamanian Bar Asscn 1990–91; Chair. Fourth Annual Lawyers Congress 1990; Vice-Minister of Govt and Justice 1991, Minister of Foreign Affairs 1999–2002; unsuccessful cand. for Pres. (Vision of the Country) 2004; currently Pnr, Arias, Alemán & Mora (law firm); mem. Bd of Dirs Multi Credit Bank Inc., Compañia Nacional de Seguros, SA, Banex Int. SA, Costa Rica. *Address:* Arias, Alemán & Mora, St Georges Bank & Company Building, 16th Floor, POB 0830-1580, Panamá 9, Panama (office). *Telephone:* 270-1011 (office). *Fax:* 270-0174 (office). *E-mail:* jaleman@aramolaw.com (office). *Website:* www.aramolaw.com (office).

ALEMÁN LACAYO, Arnoldo; Nicaraguan fmr head of state; b. 23 Jan. 1946, Managua; ed Nat. Autonomous Univ.; fmr Leader pro-Somoza Liberal Student Youth Org. in 1960s; imprisoned for alleged counter-revolutionary activity 1980; placed under house arrest 1989; Mayor of Managua 1990; Pres. Fed. of Cen. American Municipalities 1993–95; Leader, Liberal Party Alliance 1996; Pres. of Nicaragua 1997–2001; sentenced to 20 years' imprisonment for corruption Dec. 2003.

ALEMANNO, Gianni, BEng; Italian politician; *Mayor of Rome;* b. 3 March 1958, Bari; m. Isabella Rauti; one s.; ed Univ. of Rome; Prov. Sec., Fronte della Gioventù di Roma 1982; Sec., Movimento Sociale Italiano Youth Div. 1988; fmr mem. Exec. Bd Alleanza Nazionale, becoming Nat. Co-ordinator for Econ. and Social Policy and Vice-Pres., Pres. Rome Div. 2007–; mem. Lazio Regional Council 1990, becoming Vice-Pres. Industrial, Commercial and Trades Comm.; mem. Chamber of Deputies (Parl.) 1994–; Minister of Agric. and Forestry 2001–06; unsuccessful cand. for Mayor of Rome 2006, Mayor of Rome 2008–; Pres. Euro-Mediterranean Conf. on Fisheries and Agric. 2003; Pres. Fondazione Nuova Italia 2006–; f. Area (monthly journal); Dir Aspen Institut Italia; mem. Club alpino italiano; Hon. mem. Kadima World Italia. *Publication:* Intervista sulla destra sociale 2002. *Leisure interest:* mountaineering. *Address:* via Antonio Salandra 18, 00186 Rome (office); Comune di Roma, Via di Campodoglio 1, 00100 Rome; Camera dei Deputati, Palazzo di Montecitorio, 00186 Rome, Italy (office). *Telephone:* (06) 42275000 (office); (06) 0606. *Fax:* (06) 67103590. *E-mail:* posta@giannialemanno.info (office). *Website:* www .giannialemanno.info (home); www.alemannosindaco.net (office); www .comune.roma.it.

ALEMANY, Ellen, BA, MBA; American banking executive; *CEO, Royal Bank of Scotland America;* ed Fordham Univ.; began banking career at Chase Manhattan Bank, Sr Lender in Operations, Structured Trade, and the Media and Electronics Dept 1977–87; with Citigroup 1987–2007, held several sr positions including Exec. Vice-Pres. for Commercial Lending Group (including CitiCapital, Commercial Markets Group, Commercial Real Estate Group), mem. Bd of Dirs Citigroup N.A. and CEO Global Transaction Services –2007, mem. Citigroup's Operating Cttee; CEO Royal Bank of Scotland America, Citizens Financial Group 2007–, also responsible for ABN Amro integration; mem. Fed. Advisory Council 2008–; ranked in the top five of Most Powerful Women in American Banking US Banker survey 2006, 2007, ranked by Forbes magazine amongst 100 Most Powerful Women (26th) 2008. *Address:* Citizens Financial Group, Inc., 1 Citizens Plaza, Providence, RI 02903, USA (office). *Telephone:* (401) 456-7000 (office). *Fax:* (401) 456-7819 (office). *E-mail:* info@ citizensbank.com (office). *Website:* www.citizensbank.com (office); www.rbs .com (office).

ALENCAR GOMES DA SILVA, José; Brazilian politician and business executive; *Vice-President;* b. 17 Oct. 1931, Muriaé; s. of Antonio Gomes da Silva and Dolores Peres Gomes da Silva; m. Mariza Campos Gomes da Silva; three c.; clerk, A Sedutora (textiles store), Muriaé 1946–48; salesperson, Casa Bonfim, Caratinga 1948–50; est. A Queimadeira (textiles store), Caratinga 1950–53; travelling salesman, Tecidos Fernandes SA 1953; co-f. Industria de Macarrão Santa Cruz (pasta factory) 1950s; inherited co. Uniãos dos Cometas from brother Geraldo Gomes da Silva 1959, renamed Geraldo Gomes da Silva Tecidos SA; f. Cia Industrial de Roupas União dos Cometas 1963, renamed Wembley Roupas SA; co-f. Companhia de Tecidos Norte de Minas— Coteminas, Montes Claros 1967; Senator for Tancredo Neves (Liberal Party) 1998–; Vice-Pres. of Brazil 2003–, Minister of Defence 2004–06; Hon. Prof., Fed. Univ. of Juiz de Fora 2003, Admin. Council of Senai/Cetiqt, Rio de Janeiro 2003; Legis. Order of Merit 1985, Cairu Badge of Merit 1985, Officer, Rio Branco Order 1989, Commdr Work Judiciary Merit Order 1991, Grand Cross, Mil. Merit Order 2003, Mil. Judiciary Merit Order 2003, Rio Branco Order 2003, Naval Merit Order 2003, Aviation Merit Order 2003, Defence Merit Order 2003; Dr hc (Fed. Univ. of Viçosa) 2002, (State Univ. of Minas Gerais Unimontes de Montes Claros) 2004; Prominent Businessman, Medal of the Trade Asscn of Minas Gerais 1970, 1975, Industrial Merit Badge 1976, Great Medal of the Inconfidência 1983, Santos Dumont Merit Medal 1985, Alferes Tiradentes Medal, Bicentennarian of the Inconfidência Mineira 1989, Commemorative Medal of the Day of the State of Minas Gerais 1989, Great Trade Merit Medal 1987, Municipal Merit Badge 2003, Public Prosecutor Ozanam Coelho Medal 2003, Great Necklace of Order of the Public Ministry of the Fed. Dist and Territories 2003, Legis. Municipal Great Merit Necklace, Municipal Chamber of Belo Horizonte 2003, Peacemaker's Medal 2003. *Address:* Gabinete do Senador, Anexo II, 1 Andar, Gab. 57, Ala Senador Tancredo Neves, Senado Federal, 70165-900 Brasília (office); Companhia de Tecidos Norte de Minas—Coteminas, Matrix Unit, Av. Magalhaes Pinto, No. 4000, Bairro Planalto, 39404-166 Montes Claros, MG, Brazil (office). *Telephone:* (38) 3215-7777 (office). *Fax:* (38) 3217-1633 (office). *E-mail:* jose .alencar@senado.gov.br (office).

ALENTOVA, Vera Valentinovna; Russian actress; b. 21 Feb. 1942; m. Vladimir Menshov; one d.; ed Studio School of Moscow Art Theatre; actress at Moscow Pushkin Drama Theatre 1965; Order of Friendship 2001; State Prize of USSR 1981, Grand Prix Saint Michel, People's Artist of Russia 1992. *Theatre roles include:* Last Days, The Warsaw Melody, The Slaves, The Unattainable, Children of the Sun, Scum, Lighting But Not Heating, Chocolate Soldier. *Films include:* Moscow Does Not Trust Tears 1980, Time of Desires 1982, Shirli-Myrli 1995, Son for Father 1997, The Envy of the Gods 2000, The Silver Wedding 2002. *Television:* Bal'zakovsky vozrast, ili Vse muzikhi svo (series) 2004, Samara Gorodok (miniseries) 2004, Balzakovskiy vozrast, ili Vse muzhiki svo (series) 2004–05. *Address:* 125047 Moscow, 3d Tverskaya-Yamskaya str. 52, Apt. 29, Russia (home). *Telephone:* (495) 250-85-43 (home).

ALESHIN, Boris S.; Russian business executive and fmr politician; *President and Deputy Chairman, Directors Advisory Council, Avto VAZ OAO;* fmr Chair. State Cttee for Standardization and Metrology; Deputy Prime Minister responsible for Industrial Policy 2003–04, Chair. Comm. on Export Control of the Russian Fed. 2003–04; Head Fed. Agency for Industry 2004–07; Pres. and Deputy Chair. Dirs Advisory Council, AvtoVAZ (Volga Automobile Plant) OAO 2007–. *Address:* Avto VAZ OAO, Yuzhnoye shosse 36/ 49, Tolyatti, 445633, Samara obl., Russia (office). *Telephone:* (8482) 73-82-43

(office). *Fax:* (8482) 73-71-71 (office). *E-mail:* press@vaz.ru (office). *Website:* www.lada-auto.ru (office).

ALEXANDER, (Andrew) Lamar, JD; American politician; *Senator from Tennessee;* b. 3 July 1940, Knoxville, Tenn.; s. of Andrew Lamar Alexander and Genevra F. Rankin; m. Leslee K. (Honey) Buhler 1969; two s. two d.; ed Vanderbilt and New York Univs; mem. Bar of La. and Tenn.; law clerk to presiding justice, US Court of Appeals (5th circuit), New Orleans; Assoc. Fowler, Rountree, Fowler & Robertson, Knoxville 1965; Legislative Asst to Senator Howard Baker 1967–68; Exec. Asst to Bryce Harlow, White House Congressional Liaison Office 1969–70; Pnr, Dearborn & Ewing, Nashville 1971–78; Gov. of Tenn. 1979–87; Chair. Leadership Inst. Belmont Coll. Nashville 1987–88; Pres. Univ. of Tenn. 1988–90; mem. Pres.'s Task Force on Federalism; Chair. Nat. Govs Asscn 1985–86, Pres.'s Comm. on Americans Outdoors 1985–87; mem. Bd of Dirs Corporate Child Care Inc., Nashville, Martin Marietta Corpn Bethesda, Md; Sec. of Educ. 1991–93; Counsel, Baker, Donelson, Bearman and Caldwell 1993–98; pvt. practice 1999–; Chair. Republican Neighborhood Meeting 1993–; Senator from Tenn. 2003–, Chair. Cttee on Foreign Relations Sub-Cttee on African Affairs; Republican; recipient of various awards and distinctions. *Publications:* Steps Along the Way 1986, Six Months Off 1988, We Know What We Do 1995. *Leisure interest:* piano. *Address:* United States Senate, SD B-40, Suite 2, Washington, DC 20510, USA. *Telephone:* (202) 224-4944 (office). *Fax:* (202) 228-3398 (office). *Website:* alexander.senate.gov (office).

ALEXANDER, Anthony J., LLB; American business executive; *CEO, President and Director, FirstEnergy Corporation;* b. Akron; ed Univ. of Akron Law School; fmr Dir, COO and Head of UK Operations, Hanson PLC; fmr Exec. Ohio Edison (merged with other utility cos into FirstEnergy Corpn 1997); Pres. and COO FirstEnergy Corpn –2003, Pres. and Acting CEO 2003–04, CEO, Pres. and Dir 2004–; mem. Bd Dirs Imperial Tobacco, Misys PLC, Cookson Group PLC, Platinum Investment Trust PLC; mem. Republican Nat. Cttee's Team 100 2000; apptd to Energy Dept Transition Team by US Pres. George W. Bush 2000; Bush Pioneer 2000. *Address:* FirstEnergy Corporation, 76 South Main Street, Akron, OH 44308, USA (office). *Telephone:* (800) 646-0400 (office). *Fax:* (330) 384-3866 (office). *E-mail:* thowson@ firstenergycorp.com (office). *Website:* www.firstenergycorp.com (office).

ALEXANDER, Bill, BA; British theatre director; b. 23 Feb. 1948, Hunstanton, Norfolk; s. of Bill Paterson and Rosemary Paterson; m. Juliet Harmer 1978; two d.; ed St Lawrence Coll. Ramsgate and Keele Univ.; began career at Bristol Old Vic directing Shakespeare and the classics and contemporary drama; joined RSC 1977, Assoc. Dir 1978–91, Hon. Assoc. Artistic Dir 1991–; productions for RSC include: Tartuffe, Richard III 1984, Volpone, The Accrington Pals, Clay, Captain Swing, School of Night, A Midsummer Night's Dream, The Merry Wives of Windsor; other theatre work at Nottingham Playhouse, Royal Court Theatre, Victory Theatre, New York and Shakespeare Theatre, Washington, DC; Artistic Dir Birmingham Repertory Co. 1993–2000, productions include: Othello, The Snowman, Macbeth, Dr. Jekyll and Mr. Hyde, The Alchemist, Awake and Sing, The Way of the World, Divine Right, The Merchant of Venice, Old Times, Frozen, Hamlet, The Tempest, The Four Alice Bakers, Jumpers, Nativity (co-author) 1999, Quarantine 2000, Twelfth Night 2000, An Enemy of the People (Theatre Clwyd) 2002, Frozen, Mappa Mundi (RNT) 2002, The Importance of Being Ernest (Northampton) 2002, Titus Andronicus (RSC) 2003, King Lear (RSC) 2004, The School of Night (Mark Taper Forum, Los Angels) 2008; Olivier Award for Dir of the Year 1986. *Film:* The Snowman 1998. *Leisure interest:* tennis. *Address:* Rose Cottage, Tunley, Glos., GL7 6LP, England (home). *Telephone:* (1285) 760555 (office). *Fax:* (1285) 760494 (office). *E-mail:* bill2juliet@btinternet.com (office).

ALEXANDER, Brooke, BA; American art dealer and publisher; b. 26 April 1937, Los Angeles; s. of Richard H. Alexander and Marion C. Alexander; m. Carolyn Rankin 1967; two d.; ed Yale Univ.; f. Brooke Alexander Inc. to publish and distribute graphic art 1968, expanded co. 1975; f. Brooke Alexander Editions, opened separate gallery for graphics 1989; partner in Madrid gallery, Galería Weber, Alexander y Cobo 1991–; mem. Governing Bd Yale Univ. Art Gallery 1988–. *Address:* Brooke Alexander Editions, 59 Wooster Street, New York, NY 10012-4349, USA (office). *Telephone:* (212) 925-4338 (office). *Fax:* (212) 941-9565 (office). *E-mail:* info@baeditions.com (office). *Website:* www.baeditions.com (office).

ALEXANDER, Christopher, BS, MS, PhD; British architect, academic, consultant and writer; *Professor in the Graduate School and Emeritus Professor of Architecture, University of California, Berkeley;* b. 4 Oct. 1936, Vienna, Austria; m. Margaret Moore 2008; two d.; ed Oundle, Trinity Coll., Cambridge, Harvard Univ.; fmrly with Center for Cognitive Studies, Harvard, with Jt Center for Urban Studies, Harvard Univ. and MIT 1959–63; Prof. of Architecture, Univ. of Calif., Berkeley 1963–, now Prof. Emer., Research Prof. in the Humanities 1965, Prof. in Grad. School, Univ. of Calif., Berkeley 1998–; Visiting Fellow, Rockefeller Foundation Villa Serbelloni 1965; founder, Pres., Dir Center for Environmental Structure 1967–; Trustee Prince of Wales's Inst. for Architecture 1991–97; Chair. Bd of Dirs PatternLanguage.com, Berkeley, Calif. 1999–; Center for Environmental Structure has undertaken around 200 projects, including town and community planning world-wide; Fellow, Harvard Univ. 1961–64, American Acad. of Arts and Sciences 1996; mem. Swedish Royal Acad. 1980–; Best Bldg in Japan Award 1985, Seaside Prize 1994, numerous other awards and prizes. *Major works include:* 35 bldgs of New Eishin Univ., Tokyo, Linz Café, Linz, village school, Gujarat, low-cost housing in Mexico and Peru, Shelter for the Homeless, San José, numerous pvt. houses and public bldgs on four continents. *Publications include:* Notes on the Synthesis of Form 1964, The Oregon Experiment 1975, A Pattern Language 1977, The Timeless Way of Building 1979, The Linz Café 1981, A New Theory of Urban Design 1984, The Nature of Order (four vols): The

Phenomenon of Life 1998, The Process of Creating Life 1998, The Luminous Ground 1998, A Vision of the Living World 1998; over 200 articles in design journals. *Address:* The Center for Environmental Structure, 2701 Shasta Road, Berkeley, CA 94708, USA (office); Meadow Lodge, Binsted, near Arundel, W Sussex, BN18 0LQ, England (home). *Telephone:* (510) 841-6166 (office). *Website:* www.patternlanguage.com (office); www.livingneighborhoods.org (office).

ALEXANDER, Clifford L., LLD; American fmr government official and lawyer; *President, Alexander & Associates, Inc.;* b. 21 Sept. 1933, Harlem, New York; s. of Clifford Alexander and Edith Alexander (née McAllister); m. Adele Logan 1959; one s. one d.; ed Harvard Univ., Yale Univ.; practised as lawyer in New York, partner in Verner, Liipfert, Bernhard, McPherson and Alexander, law firm; Foreign Affairs Officer, Nat. Security Council Staff 1963–64; Deputy Special Asst, later Deputy Special Counsel to Pres. Lyndon Johnson 1964–67; Chair. Equal Employment Opportunity Comm. 1967–69, resgnd; mem. Comm. for the Observance of Human Rights 1968; Special Amb. to Swaziland 1968; Partner in Arnold & Porter, law firm; news commentator and host, Cliff Alexander–Black on White TV programme 1971–74; Prof. of Law, Howard Univ. 1973–74; US Sec. of the Army 1977–80; Pres. Alexander & Assocs Inc. 1981–; mem. Bd of Dirs Pennsylvania Power & Light Co.; Adjunct Prof., Georgetown Univ.; Prof. Howard Univ., Washington, DC; mem. Bd of Dirs. Mexican-American Legal Defense and Educ. Fund, Dreyfus Third Century Fund Inc., MCI Corpn, Dreyfus Common Stock Fund, Dreyfus Tax Exempt Fund; mem. American and DC Bar Asscns; fmr mem. Bd Overseers Harvard Univ.; Trustee, Atlanta Univ.; mem. Community and Friends Bd, Kennedy Center; Hon. LLD (Univ. of Maryland, Atlanta Univ.); Frederick Douglass Award and other decorations. *Address:* Alexander & Associates, Inc., 400 C Street, NE, Washington, DC 20002-5818 (office); 512 A Street, SE, Washington, DC 20003-1139, USA (home). *Telephone:* (202) 546-0111 (office).

ALEXANDER, Rt Hon Douglas Garven, LLB, MA, PC; British politician and solicitor; *Secretary of State for International Development;* b. 26 Oct. 1967, Glasgow; m. Jacqueline Christian; one s. one d.; ed Park Mains High School, Erskine, Vancouver, Univ. of Edinburgh, Univ. of Pennsylvania; press steward, Michael Dukakis US presidential campaign and staff mem. of Democratic Senator, USA 1988; Parl. Researcher and speech writer for MP Gordon Brown 1990; qualified as solicitor 1993; unsuccessful cand. in Perth and Kinross by-election 1995, Perth gen. election 1997; MP for Paisley South (following by-election) 1997–2005, for Paisley and Renfrewshire 2005–; Minister for E-Commerce and Competitiveness, Dept of Trade and Industry 2001–02; Minister of State, Cabinet Office 2002–04; Minister for the Cabinet Office and Chancellor of the Duchy of Lancaster 2003–04; Minister of State, Trade, Investment and Foreign Affairs, FCO and Dept of Trade and Industry 2004–05; Minister of State for Europe, FCO 2005–06; Secretary of State for Transport and for Scotland 2006–07, for Int. Devt 2007–; mem. Nat. Exec. Cttee, Labour Party; Gen. Election Campaign Coordinator 1999–2001. *Address:* Department for International Development, 1 Palace Street, London, SW1E 5HE (office); 2014 Mile End Mill, Abbey Mill Business Centre, Seedhill Road, Paisley, SW1A 0AA, England (office). *Telephone:* (20) 7023-0000 (office); (141) 561-0333 (constituency) (office). *Fax:* (1355) 843632 (office); (141) 561-0334 (constituency) (office). *E-mail:* enquiry@dfid.gov.uk (office). *Website:* www.dfid.gov.uk (office); www.douglasalexander.labour.co.uk (home).

ALEXANDER, Héctor, MA, PhD; Panamanian economist and politician; *Minister of the Economy and Finance;* ed Univ. of Panama, Univ. of Chicago and Univ. of St Thomas, Fla, USA, Catholic Univ. of Chile; Prof. of Microeconomics, Analysis and Project Evaluation, Faculty of Econs, Univ. of Panama; Prof. of Accounting and Microeconomics, Panama Canal Coll.; mem. Tech. Comm. for Incentives to Exports, Ministry of Commerce and Industries; Expositor, Seminar on Economy for Journalists, organized by Repub. Nat. Bank 1976; fmr Minister of Planning and Political Economy; fmr Minister for External Relations; fmr Minister of Property and Treasury; fmr Minister in charge of Commerce and Industry; Sub-Gerente, Zona Libre de Colón; Minister of the Economy and Finance 2007–; Econ. Adviser, Superior Direction, Interoceanica Regional Authority (ARI), Dir of Tech. Planning; mem. of team that negotiated Torrijos-Carter Treaty concerning econ. position of Panama. *Address:* Ministry of the Economy and Finance, Edif. Ogawa, Vía España, Apdo 5245, Panamá 5, Panama (office). *Telephone:* 507-7008 (office). *E-mail:* prensa@mef.gob.pa (office). *Website:* www.mef.gob.pa (office).

ALEXANDER, Helen Anne, CBE, MA, MBA; British business executive; *Adviser, Bain Capital Ltd;* b. 10 Feb. 1957; d. of the late Bernard Alexander and Tania Alexander (née Benckendorff); m. Tim Suter 1985; two s. one d.; ed Hertford Coll. Oxford, Institut Européen d'Admin des Affaires (INSEAD), France; with Gerald Duckworth 1978–79, Faber & Faber 1979–83; joined The Economist Group 1984, Man. Dir Economist Intelligence Unit 1993–96, Group CEO 1997–2008; Adviser, Bain Capital 2008–; Vice-Pres. CBI; Dir (non-exec.) Northern Foods PLC 1994–2003, British Telecom PLC 1998–2002, Centrica PLC, Rolls-Royce PLC; Trustee Tate Gallery; Gov. St Paul's Girls' School; Hon. Fellow, Hertford Coll., Oxford. *Address:* Bain Capital Ltd, Devonshire House, 6th Floor, Mayfair Place, London, W1J 8AJ, England (office). *Telephone:* (20) 7514-5252 (office). *Fax:* (20) 7514-5250 (office). *Website:* www.baincapital.co.uk (office).

ALEXANDER, Jane; American actress and organization official; b. 28 Oct. 1939, Boston; d. of Thomas Bartlett and Ruth Quigley; m. 1st Robert Alexander 1962 (divorced 1969); one s.; m. 2nd Edwin Sherin 1975; ed Sarah Lawrence Coll., Edinburgh Univ.; Guest Artist-in-Residence, Oklahoma Arts Inst. 1982; Chair. Nat. Endowment for Arts 1993–97; Francis Eppes Prof., Florida State Univ. 2002–04; mem. Bd of Dirs Women's Action for Nuclear Disarmament 1981–88, Film Forum 1985–90, Nat. Stroke Asscn 1984–91, American Birding Asscn 2007–; mem. Bd of Trustees Wildlife Conservation Soc. 1997–2007, The MacDowell Colony 1997–2008, Arts Int. 2000–05; Hon. DFA (The Juilliard School) 1994, (North Carolina School of Arts) 1994, (The New School of Social Research) 1996, (Smith Coll.) 1999, (Pa State Univ.) 2000; Hon. PhD (Univ. of Pa) 1995, (Duke Univ.) 1996 and numerous other hon. degrees; Lifetime Achievement Award, Americans for Arts 1999, Harry S. Truman Award for Public Service 1999, Directors' Guild of America Award 2002. *Broadway appearances include:* The Great White Hope (Tony Award 1969) 1968–69, Find Your Way Home 1974, Hamlet 1975, The Heiress 1976, Goodbye Fidel 1980, Night of the Iguana 1988, Shadowlands 1990–91, The Visit 1992, The Sisters Rosensweig 1993, Honour 1998. *Other stage appearances include:* Antony and Cleopatra 1981, Hedda Gabler 1981, Approaching Zanzibar 1989, The Cherry Orchard 2000, Mourning Becomes Electra 2002, Rose and Walsh 2003. *Film appearances include:* The Great White Hope 1970, All the President's Men 1976, Kramer vs. Kramer 1979, Brubaker 1980, Sweet Country 1986, Glory 1989, The Cider House Rules 1999, Sunshine State 2002, The Ring 2002, Fur: An Imaginary Portrait of Diane Arbus 2006, Feast of Love 2007. *TV appearances include:* Eleanor and Franklin 1976, Playing for Time (Emmy Award 1980) 1980, Kennedy's Children 1981, A Marriage: Georgia O'Keeffe and Alfred Stieglitz 1991, Stay the Night 1992, The Jenifer Estess Story 2001, Carry Me Home 2004, Warm Springs (Emmy Award 2005) 2005, Tell Me You Love Me 2007. *Publications:* The Bluefish Cookbook (with Greta Jacobs) 1979, (co-trans.) The Master Builder (Henrik Ibsen), Command Performance: An Actress in the Theater of Politics 2000. *Leisure interest:* bird watching. *Address:* c/o Samuel Liff, William Morris Agency, 1325 Avenue of the Americas, New York, NY 10019, USA.

ALEXANDER, Jonathan James Graham, DPhil, FBA, FSA; British/American art historian and academic; *Professor of Fine Arts, New York University;* b. 20 Aug. 1935, London; s. of Arthur Ronald Brown and Frederica Emma Graham (who m. 2nd Boyd Alexander); m. 1st Mary Davey 1974 (divorced 1994); one s.; m. 2nd Serita Winthrop 1996 (divorced 2001); ed Magdalen Coll., Oxford; Asst, Dept of Western Manuscripts, Bodleian Library, Oxford 1963–71; Lecturer, History of Art Dept, Univ. of Manchester 1971–73, Reader 1973–87; Prof. of Fine Arts, Inst. of Fine Arts, New York Univ. 1988–; Lyell Reader in Bibliography, Univ. of Oxford 1982–83; Sandars Lecturer, Univ. of Cambridge 1984–85; Visiting Prof., Univ. Coll. London 1991–92; Fellow, Medieval Acad. of America 1999; John Simon Guggenheim Memorial Foundation Fellowship 1995–96, Distinguished Visiting Fellowship, La Trobe Univ. 1997; Visiting Fellow, All Souls Coll., Oxford 1998; J. Clawson Mills Fellow, Metropolitan Museum of Art, New York 2002; Samuel H Kress Prof., Center for Advanced Study in the Visual Arts (CASVA), Nat. Gallery of Art, Washington DC 2004–05; Panizzi Lectures, British Library, London 2007–08; Hon. Fellow, Pierpont Morgan Library 1995; Prix Minda de Gunzburg 1987. *Publications:* Illuminated Manuscripts in the Bodleian Library, Oxford (with Otto Pächt) (three vols) 1966, 1970, 1973, Italian Illuminated Manuscripts in the library of Major J. R. Abbey (with A. C. de la Mare) 1969, Norman Illumination at Mont St Michel *c.* 966–1100 1970, The Master of Mary of Burgundy, A Book of Hours 1970, Italian Renaissance Illuminations 1977, Insular Manuscripts 6th–9th Century 1978, The Decorated Letter 1978, Illuminated Manuscripts in Oxford College Libraries, The University Archives and the Taylor Institution (with E. Temple) 1986, Age of Chivalry (co-ed.), Art in Plantagenet England 1200–1400 1987, Medieval Illuminators and their Methods of Work 1993, The Painted Page: Italian Renaissance Book Illumination 1450–1550 (ed.) 1994, The Towneley Lectionary (introduction) 1997; articles in Burlington Magazine, Arte Veneta, Pantheon, Art Bulletin etc. *Leisure interests:* music, gardening. *Address:* Institute of Fine Arts, 1 East 78th Street, New York, NY 10021, USA (office). *Telephone:* (212) 992-5876 (office). *Fax:* (212) 992-5807 (office). *Website:* www.ifa.nyu.edu (office).

ALEXANDER, Meena, BA, PhD; American (b. Indian) poet, writer and academic; *Distinguished Professor of English and Women's Studies, Hunter College and the Graduate School and University Center, City University of New York;* b. 17 Feb. 1951, Allahabad, India; d. of George Alexander and Mary Kuruvilla Alexander; m. David Lelyveld 1979; one s. one d.; ed Univ. of Khartoum, Sudan, Univ. of Nottingham, UK; Lecturer, Univ. of Hyderabad 1977–79, Reader 1979; Asst Prof., Fordham Univ. 1980–87; Asst Prof., Hunter Coll. and the Grad. School and Univ. Center, CUNY 1987–89, Assoc. Prof. 1989–92, Prof. of English 1992–99, Distinguished Prof. of English and Women's Studies 1999–; Comm. for Poetry Int., Royal Festival Hall, London 2002; mem. Jury, Fifteenth Neustadt Int. Award in Literature 1997–98; mem. Selection Cttee Lila Wallace Reader's Digest Awards in Literature 1998; mem. Modern Language Asscn, PEN American Center; Altrusa Int. Award 1973, MacDowell Fellow 1993, 1998, Poet-in-Residence, American Coll., Madurai 1994, Artist/Humanist-in-Residence, Intercultural Resource Centre, Columbia Univ. 1995, Int. Writer in Residence, Arts Council of England 1995, Lila Wallace Writer in Residence, Asian American Renaissance, Minnesota 1995, Poetry Award, New York State Foundation for the Arts 1999, Poet-in-Residence, Nat. Univ. of Singapore 1999, Residency at Château Lavigny, Fondation Ledig-Rowohlt 2001, Imbongi Yesizwe Poetry Int. Award (S Africa) 2002, Fellowship, Centre for Place, Culture and Politics, CUNY Grad. Center 2001–02, Hunter Coll. Faculty Fellowship 2002, Fulbright Sr Scholar Award, Mahatma Gandhi Univ., India 2002–03, Bellagio Award, Rockefeller Foundation 2003, Martha Walsh Pulver Residency for a Poet, Yaddo 2005, Fulbright Sr Specialist Award, Univ. of Venice Ca' Foscori 2006, Elector, American Poet's Corner, Cathedral of St John the Divine, New York 2006–, John Simon Guggenheim Fellowship 2008, Camargo Foundation Fellowship, 2008. *Publications:* The Poetic Self: Towards a Phenomenology of Romanticism 1979, Stone Roots (poems) 1980, House of a Thousand Doors (poems and prose) 1988, Women in Romanticism: Mary Wollstonecraft, Dorothy Wordsworth and Mary Shelley 1989, The Storm: A Poem in Five Parts 1989,

Nampally Road (novel) 1991, Night-Scene: The Garden (poem) 1992, Fault Lines (memoir) 1993 (new expanded edn 2003), River and Bridge (poems) 1995, The Shock of Arrival: Reflections on Postcolonial Experience (poems and prose) 1996, Manhattan Music (novel) 1997, Illiterate Heart (poems) (PEN Open Book Award 2002) 2002, Raw Silk (poems) 2004, Indian Love Poems (ed.) 2005, Quickly Changing River 2008; contribs to books, anthologies and periodicals. *Leisure interests:* walking, watching old movies, cooking. *Address:* PhD Program in English, CUNY Graduate Center, 365 Fifth Avenue, New York, NY 10016 (office); English Department, Hunter College, CUNY, 695 Park Avenue, New York, NY 10065, USA (office). *Telephone:* (212) 817-8344 (Grad. Center) (office); (212) 772-5167 (Hunter Coll.) (office). *E-mail:* malexander@gc.cuny.edu (office). *Website:* www.meenaalexander.com; www1.cuny.edu/academics/oaa/distinguished/view.html?prof=2.

ALEXANDER, Padinjarethalakal Cherian, DLitt; Indian government official; b. 20 March 1921, Kerala; s. of Jacob Cherian and Mariama Cherian; m. Ackama Alexander 1942; two s. two d.; ed India and UK; Indian Admin. Service, Kerala Cadre 1948; Devt Commr Small Scale Industries 1960–63; Sr Adviser, Centre for Industrial Devt, UN, New York 1963–66; Chief UN Project on Small Industries and Chief Adviser to Govt of Iran 1970–73; Devt Commr Small Scale Industries 1973–75; Sec. Foreign Trade, later Commerce Sec. 1975–78; Sr Adviser, later Exec. Dir and Asst Sec.-Gen. Int. Trade Centre, UNCTAD-GATT, Geneva 1978–81; Prin. Sec. to Prime Minister of India 1981–85; High Commr in UK 1985–88; Gov. Tamil Nadu 1988–89, Maharashtra 1993–2002 (resgnd); mem. Raja Sabha (Parl.) 2002–; Hon. LLD (Pondicherry) 1994; Kanchi Parmacharya Prize for Nat. Eminence in Admin. 2000. *Publications:* The Dutch in Malabar, Buddhism in Kerala, Industrial Estates in India, My Years with Indira Gandhi, The Perils of Democracy, India in the New Millennium, Through the Corridors of Power. *Leisure interest:* reading. *Address:* 12, Mother Teresa Crescent, New Delhi 110001, India.

ALEXANDER, Robert McNeill, CBE, MA, PhD, DSc, FRS; British zoologist and academic; *Professor Emeritus of Zoology, University of Leeds;* b. 7 July 1934, Lisburn, Northern Ireland; s. of Robert Priestley Alexander and Janet Alexander (née McNeill); m. Ann Elizabeth Coulton 1961; one s. one d.; ed Tonbridge School and Univ. of Cambridge; Lecturer, Univ. Coll. of North Wales, Bangor 1958–69; Prof. of Zoology, Univ. of Leeds 1969–99, Prof. Emer. 1999–; Sec. Zoological Soc. of London 1992–99; Vice-Pres. Soc. for Experimental Biology 1993–95, Pres. 1995–97; Pres. Int. Soc. for Vertebrate Morphology 1997–2001; Ed. Proceedings of the Royal Society B 1998–2004; mem. Academia Europaea 1996, European Acad. of Sciences 2004; Hon. mem. American Soc. of Zoologists (now Soc. for Integrative and Comparative Biology) 1986; Foreign Hon. mem. American Acad. of Arts and Sciences 2001; Hon. Fellow, Zoological Soc. of London 2003; Hon. DSc (Aberdeen) 2002; Dr hc (Wageningen) 2003; Scientific Medal, Zoological Soc. of London 1969, Linnean Medal for Zoology, Linnean Soc. of London 1979, Muybridge Medal, Int. Soc. for Biomechanics 1991, Borelli Award, American Soc. for Biomechanics 2003. *Publications:* Functional Design in Fishes 1967, Animal Mechanics 1968, Size and Shape 1971, The Chordates 1975, The Invertebrates 1979, Locomotion of Animals 1982, Optima for Animals 1982, Elastic Mechanisms in Animal Movement 1988, Dynamics of Dinosaurs and Other Extinct Giants 1989, Animals 1990, Exploring Biomechanics 1992, The Human Machine 1992, Bones 1994, Energy for Animal Life 1999, Principles of Animal Locomotion 2003, Human Bones 2004; numerous scientific papers. *Leisure interests:* history of biology and history of tableware. *Address:* School of Biology, University of Leeds, Leeds, LS2 9JT (office); 14 Moor Park Mount, Leeds, LS6 4BU, England (home). *Telephone:* (113) 3432911 (office); (113) 2759218 (home). *Fax:* (113) 3432911 (office). *E-mail:* r.m.alexander@leeds.ac.uk (office).

ALEXANDER, Wendy, MA, MBA; British politician; b. Glasgow, Scotland; m. Brian Ashcroft; two c.; ed Park Mains High School, Erskine, Pearson Coll., Canada, Univ. of Glasgow, Univ. of Warwick and Institut Européen d'Admin des Affaires (INSEAD), France; fmr int. man. consultant with Booz Allen & Hamilton; apptd Special Adviser to Sec. of State for Scotland 1997; MSP (Labour) for Paisley N 1999–, Minister for Communities 1999–2000, for Enterprise and Lifelong Learning 2000–01, for Enterprise, Transport and Lifelong Learning 2001–02, mem. Finance Cttee, Education Cttee, co-convenor Cross-Party Group in Scottish Parl. for Scottish Economy, Leader, Scottish Labour Party 2007–08 (resgnd); Visiting Prof., Univ. of Strathclyde Business School 2002–; wrote weekly column in Daily Record newspaper 2007; mem. Transport and Gen. Workers' Union, Royal Soc. for the Protection of Birds, Amnesty Int; Scottish Politician of the Year (Channel 4) 2000, Johnnie Walker Award (Scottish Politician of the Year) 2005. *Publications include:* First Ladies of Medicine 1986; contribs to The World is Ill Divided: Women's Work in Scotland 1992, The State and the Nations 1996, The Ethnicity Reader 1997, New Gender Agenda 2000, Chasing the Tartan Tiger 2003, New Wealth for Old Nations (co-ed.) 2003, Donald Dewar, Scotland's First First Minister (ed.) 2005. *Leisure interests:* ornithology, Scottish Islands. *Address:* The Scottish Parliament, Edinburgh, EH99 1SP (office); Abbey Mill Business Centre, Mile End, 12 Seedhill Road, Paisley, PA1 1JS, Scotland (office). *Telephone:* (131) 348-5852 (office). *Fax:* (131)348-6949 (office). *E-mail:* Wendy.Alexander.msp@scottish.parliament.uk (office). *Website:* www.scottish.parliament.uk/msps/biographies/n-pais.htm (office); www.wendyalexandermsp.org.uk.

ALEXANDER KARADJORDJEVIC, HRH Crown Prince of Serbia; b. 17 July 1945, London, England; s. of HM King Peter II of Yugoslavia and HRH Princess Alexandra of the Hellenes and Denmark; m. 1st HRH Princess Maria da Gloria of Orléans and Bragança 1972 (divorced 1983); m. 2nd Katherine Batis 1985; three s.; ed Le Rosey, Switzerland, Gordonstoun, Scotland, Culver Mil. Acad., USA, Royal Mil. Acad., UK; commissioned in British Army, 16th/5th The Queen's Royal Lancers, rank of Acting Capt. 1971; business exec. working in Rio de Janeiro, New York, Chicago and London; in exile from birth, visited Belgrade for the first time Oct. 1991, established residence in The Royal Palace, Belgrade 2001; British Army Ski Champion 1972. *Leisure interests:* skiing, scuba diving, underwater photography, family. *Address:* The Royal Palace, Belgrade, Serbia (home). *Telephone:* (11) 3064000 (office). *Fax:* (11) 3064040 (office). *E-mail:* office@royalfamily.org (office). *Website:* www.royalfamily.org (office).

ALEXANDRA, HRH Princess (see Ogilvy, the Hon. Mrs Angus).

ALEXANDRE, Boniface; Haitian judge; three c.; fmr lawyer with Cabinet Lamarre; Judge, Supreme Court 1990s, Chief Justice 2002–04; Acting Pres. March 2004–06; currently Lecturer, Univ. of Port-au-Prince. *Address:* c/o Office of the President, Palais National, rue de la République, Port-au-Prince, Haiti (office).

ALEXEEV, Dmitri Konstantinovich; Russian pianist; b. 10 Aug. 1947, Moscow; s. of Konstantin Alekseyev and Gertrude Bolotina; m. Tatiana Sarkisova 1970; one d.; ed Moscow Conservatoire; studied under Dmitri Bashkirov; performs regularly in Russia, in UK and throughout Europe and USA and has toured Japan, Australia etc.; has performed with London Philharmonic Orchestra, London Symphony Orchestra, City of Birmingham Symphony Orchestra, the Royal Philharmonic Orchestra, St Petersburg Philharmonic Orchestra, Berlin Philharmonic, Chicago Symphony Orchestra, Philadelphia Orchestra, Royal Concertgebouw Orchestra of Amsterdam, Israel Philharmonic and the Munich Bavarian Radio Orchestra; worked with Ashkenazy, Boulez, Semyon Bychkov, Dorati, Giulini, Jansons, Muti, Kent Nagano, Rozhdestvensky, Salonen, Klaus Tennstedt, Michael Tilson Thomas, Sian Edwards, Valery Gergiev, Andrew Litton, Yuri Temirkanov, Mstislav Rostropovich, Lynn Harrell, Truls Mørk, Yuri Bashmet, Joshua Bell and Barbara Hendricks; prizewinner Int. Tchaikovsky Competition, Moscow 1974, 5th Leeds Int. Piano Competition 1975 and other int. competitions; received Edison Award, Netherlands for his recording of the complete Rachmaninov Preludes. *Recordings:* works by Bach, Brahms, Chopin, Grieg, Liszt, Medtner, Prokofiev, Rachmaninov, Schumann, Shostakovich and Scriabin. *Address:* c/o IMG Artists, The Light Box, 111 Power Road, London, W4 5PY, England (office). *Telephone:* (20) 7957-5800 (office). *Fax:* (20) 7957-5801 (office). *E-mail:* artistseuropa@imgartists.com (office). *Website:* www.imgartists.com (office).

ALEXEEVA, Ludmilla; Russian human rights activist; *Chairwoman and President, Moscow Helsinki Group;* forced to immigrate to USA in 1977, returned to Russia 1993; co-f. Moscow Helsinki Group, currently Chair. and Pres.; Pres. Int. Helsinki Fed. 1996–2004; mem. Presidential Council on Assistance of Insts of Civil Society and Human Rights; Co-Chair All-Russia Civil Congress; Olof Palme Prize (Jtly) 2004, Human Rights Award, Human Rights First 2005. *Publications include:* Soviet Dissent 1985. *Address:* Moscow Helsinki Group, 107045 Moscow, Grand Golovin per, Bldg 22, p 1, Russia (office). *Telephone:* (495) 207-60-69 (office). *E-mail:* mhg-main@online.ptt.ru (office). *Website:* www.mhg.ru (office).

ALEXEYEV, Nikolay Gennadyevich; Russian conductor; *Artistic Director and Principal Conductor, Estonian National Symphony Orchestra;* b. 1 May 1956, Leningrad; s. of Gennady Nikolayevich Alexeyev and Tamara Andreyevna Alexeyeva; m. Nina Yefimovna Alexeyeva; two s.; ed Glinka Choir School, St Petersburg State Conservatory; Chief Conductor Ulyanovsk Philharmonic Orchestra 1983–2001; Prin. Guest Conductor Zagreb Philharmonic and Estonian Nat. Symphony 1994–97; Artistic Dir and Prin. Conductor Estonian Nat. Symphony Orchestra 2000–; performs with leading orchestras, Symphony Orchestra, Moscow, Russian Nat. Orchestra, Moscow Philharmonic, tours in Europe, USA, Japan; Assoc. Prin. Conductor St Petersburg Philharmonic 2000–; Prize Int. H. von Karajan Music Competition 1982, Int. V. Talikh Competition 1985. *Address:* Estonian National Symphony Orchestra, Estonia pst. 4, 10148 Tallinn, Estonia (office); St Petersburg Philharmonia, Mikhailovskaya str. 2, St Petersburg, Russia (office). *Telephone:* 614-7787 (Estonia) (office); (812) 931-75-88 (office); (812) 271-04-90 (home). *Fax:* 631-3133 (Estonia) (office). *E-mail:* erso@erso.ee (office). *Website:* www.erso.ee (office).

ALEXIS, Francis, LLM, PhD; Grenadian politician, author and lawyer; *Leader, People's Labour Movement;* b. 3 Oct. 1947, Grenada; s. of John Everest Alexis and Anastasia Omega Alexis; m. Margaret de Bique 1973; three d.; ed Grenada Boys' Secondary School, Univ. of West Indies, Hugh Wooding Law School and Univ. of Cambridge; fmr clerk, Jonas Brown & Hubbards Ltd, Grenada; later civil servant, Grenada; Sr Lecturer in Law and Deputy Dean, Faculty of Law, Univ. of West Indies; barrister-at-law, Grenada; MP 1984–; Minister of Labour, Co-operatives, Social Security and Local Govt 1984–87; Attorney-Gen. and Minister of Legal Affairs and Labour 1987; Opposition MP 1987–90; Founder-mem. and Deputy Leader New Nat. Party 1986, Nat. Democratic Congress 1987–95; Attorney-Gen. and Minister of Legal Affairs and Local Govt 1990–95; Acting Prime Minister on various occasions 1990–95; Leader Govt Business, House of Reps in Parl. 1990–95, Grenada Nat. Del. to Commonwealth Parl. Asscn UK 1986, to Windward Islands Political Union Talks 1991–92, to UN Gen. Ass. 1993, Canada 1994; Father of House of Reps in Parl. 1995–; Founder-mem., Leader Democratic Labour Party, now People's Labour Movement 1995–; Vice-Pres. Grenada Bar Asscn 1997–98. *Publications:* Commonwealth Caribbean Legal Essays 1981, Changing Caribbean Constitutions 1983, H. Aubrey Fraser: Eminent Caribbean Jurist 1985, The Constitution and You 1991; articles in law journals. *Leisure interests:* reading, writing, music. *Address:* Church Street, St George's (office); St Paul's, St

George's, Grenada (home). *Telephone:* 440-6743 (office); 440-2378 (home). *Fax:* 440-6591.

ALEXIS, Jacques Edouard, MSc; Haitian politician and university rector; *Rector, Université Quisqueya;* b. 21 Sept. 1947, Gonaïves; m.; five c.; ed Faculty of Agronomics and Veterinary Medicine, State Univ. of Haïti, Laval Univ.; Prof., Univ. of Quisqueya 1990–, Rector, 1990–96, 2005–, Co-ordinator, Office of Institutional Devt 2003–05; Minister of Nat. Educ., Youth and Sport 1996–99, of Culture 1997–99, of the Interior and Local Govt 1999–2001; Prime Minister 1998–2001, 2006–08; Pres. Educ. et Société Foundation 2001–. *Address:* Office of the Rector, Université Quisqueya, Angle Rue Charéron et Boulevard Harry Truman, Port-au-Prince, Haiti (office).

ALFANO, Angelino; Italian lawyer and politician; *Minister of Justice;* b. 31 Oct. 1970, Agrigento; ed Catholic Univ. of Sacro Cuore, Milan; mem. Sicilian Regional Ass. 1996–2001; mem. Camera dei Deputati (Parl.) representing Sicily 1 constituency 2001–; Regional Sec., Forza Italia 2005–08, with Popolo della Libertà party 2008–; Minister of Justice 2008–. *Address:* Ministry of Justice, Via Arenula 71, 00186 Rome, Italy (office). *Telephone:* (06) 68851 (office). *Fax:* (06) 68897342 (office). *E-mail:* ufficio.stampa@giustizia.it (office). *Website:* www.giustizia.it (office); www.angelinoalfano.it.

ALFARO, Andreu; Spanish sculptor; b. 5 Aug. 1929, Valencia; s. of Andrés Alfaro and Teresa Hernández; m. Dorothy Hofmann 1954; three c.; began work as sculptor in Valencia 1958; joined Grupo Parpalló and participated in various collective exhbns 1959–62; monumental open-air sculptures in Valencia, Barcelona, Madrid, Nuremberg, Cologne, Frankfurt, Munich; Gold Medal Salón Internacional de Marzo 1964, Premi Jaume I, Barcelona 1980, Premio Nacional de Artes Plásticas 1981, Premi Creu de Sant Jordi, Barcelona 1982, Premi Alfons Roig, Valencia 1991, Premio Urbanismo, Arquitectura y Obras Públicas, Ayuntamiento de Madrid 1991, Premio Tomás Francisco de Prieto, Fundación Casa de la Moneda de Madrid 1995. *Publications:* El Arte visto por los artistas 1987, Doce artistas de vanguardia en el Museo del Prado 1991; articles in reviews. *Address:* Urbanización Sta. Bárbara 138R, 46111 Rocafort, Valencia, Spain. *Telephone:* (96) 1310956.

ALFARO ESTRIPEAUT, Roberto; Panamanian business executive and fmr diplomatist; *President, Association of Panamanian Business Executives (APEDE);* m.; five c.; ed George Washington Univ., USA, Inst. of Higher Studies in Admin., Venezuela, Canal Zone Coll., Center for Studies of Insurance Admin.; Gen. Man. Financeria de Seguros SA 1994–97; Pres. Bd of Dirs Aseguradora La Unión 1997–99; Gen. Man. Proexport Int. Devt. Inc. 1998–99; Treasurer Bd of Dirs, Corporación Panameña de Energia SA 1998–99; Vice-Minister of Commerce and Industry, Govt of Panama 1990–91, Minister 1991–94; Amb. to Italy (with concurrent accreditation to Malta) 2000–02, to USA 2003–04; Pres. Asscn of Panamanian Business Execs 2008–. *Address:* Association of Panamanian Business Executives (APEDE), Avenida Balboa, Calle 42 Bella Vista, Apdo 0816-06785, Panamá, Panama (office). *Telephone:* 227-3511 (office). *Fax:* 227-1872 (office). *Website:* apede.org (home).

ALFEROV, Zhores Ivanovich, DPhysMathSc; Russian physicist; *Chairman, St Petersburg Scientific Centre;* b. 15 March 1930, Vitebsk; m.; two c.; ed Leningrad Electrotech. Inst.; Researcher, Head of Lab., Ioffe Inst. of Physics and Tech., USSR Acad. of Sciences 1972–87; Dir 1987–; Corresp. mem. USSR (now Russian) Acad. of Sciences 1972, mem. 1979; Vice-Pres. 1991–; Chair. Leningrad (now St Petersburg) Scientific Centre 1990–; mem. State Duma 1995–; Ed.-in-Chief Physics and Tech. of Semiconductors; mem. Acad. of Sciences of Germany, Poland, USA, European Physical Soc., and many others; Hon. Citizen of St Petersburg; USSR, Lenin and State Prizes, Karpinsky Prize, Nobel Prize for Physics 2000, Stuart Ballantine Gold Medal, Hewlett-Packard Europhysics Prize. *Publications:* scientific works on physics and tech. of semiconductors, quantum electronics. *Leisure interest:* history of Second World War. *Address:* St Petersburg Scientific Centre, Universitetskaya nab. 5, St Petersburg 199034 (office); Ioffe Physico-Technical Institute, Polytechnicheskya str. 26, St Petersburg 194021 (office); Jacques Duclos str. 8/3-82, St Petersburg 194223, Russia (home). *Telephone:* (812) 328-23-11 (office); (812) 552-58-55 (home). *Fax:* (812) 328-37-87 (office). *E-mail:* zhores.alferov@pop.ioffe.rssi.ru (office).

ALFIE, Isaac; Uruguayan politician and economist; b. 1962; ed in USA; Dir of Macroeconomic Programming, Ministry of Economy 2000, Macroeconomic Policy Adviser –2003; Minister of Economy and Finance 2003–04; Gov. and Exec. Dir for Uruguay, Inter-American Devt Bank (IDB). *Address:* c/o Ministry of Economy and Finance, Colonia 1089, 3°, 111000 Montevideo, Uruguay (office).

ALGABID, Hamid; Niger politician; *Chairman, Rassemblement pour la démocratie et le progrès—Djamaa (RDP);* b. 1941, Tamont; m.; five c.; ed Abidjan Univ.; fmr Minister of State for Planning, Commerce and Transportation; fmr Minister Del. for Finance; Prime Minister of Niger 1983–88; Sec.-Gen. Org. of the Islamic Conf. 1989–96; currently Chair. Rassemblement pour la démocratie et le progrès—Djamaa (RDP); presidential cand. 1999, 2004. *Address:* c/o Organisation of the Islamic Conference, Kilo 6, PO Box 178, Jeddah 2411, Saudi Arabia.

ALHEGELAN, Sheikh Faisal Abdul Aziz; Saudi Arabian diplomatist; b. 7 Oct. 1929, Jeddah; s. of Sheikh Abdul Aziz Al-Hegelan and Fatima Al-Eissa; m. Nouha Tarazi 1961; three s.; ed Faculty of Law, Fouad Univ., Cairo; Ministry of Foreign Affairs 1952–54; served in Embassy in Washington, DC 1954–58; Chief of Protocol in Ministry 1958–60; Political Adviser to HM King Sa'ud 1960–61; Amb. to Spain 1961–68, to Venezuela and Argentina 1968–75, to Denmark 1975–76, to UK 1976–79, to USA 1979–83, to France 1996–2003; Minister of State and mem. Council of Ministers (Saudi Arabia) April–Sept. 1984, of Health 1984–96, Chair. Bd of Dirs, Saudi Red Crescent Soc. 1984–, Saudi Anti-Smoking Soc. 1985–; Chair. Bd of Trustees, Saudi Council for Health Specialties 1992–; Order of King Abdulaziz, Gran Cruz Cordon of King Abdul Aziz, Order of Isabela la Católica (Spain), Gran Cordón, Orden del Libertador (Venezuela), Grande Oficial, Orden Riobranco (Brazil), May Grand Decoration (Argentina); Hon. KBE. *Leisure interests:* bridge, golf. *Address:* PO Box 25557, Riyadh 11576, Saudi Arabia.

ALI, Ahmad Mohamed, LLB, DPA; Saudi Arabian development banker; *Chairman of the Board of Executive Directors and President, Islamic Development Bank;* b. 13 April 1934, Medina; s. of Mohamed Ali and Amina Ali; m. Ghada Mahmood Masri 1968; one s. three d.; ed Cairo Univ., Univ. of Michigan, New York State Univ.; Dir Scientific and Islamic Inst., Aden 1958–59; Deputy Rector King Abdul Aziz Univ., Jeddah 1967–72; Deputy Minister of Educ. for Tech. Affairs 1972–75; Pres. Islamic Devt Bank 1975–93, 1995–, currently also Chair. Bd of Exec. Dirs; Sec.-Gen. Muslim World League 1993–95; mem. King Abdul Aziz Univ. Council, King Saud Univ., Oil and Minerals Univ., Islamic Univ., Imam Mohammed Ben Saud Univ.; mem. Admin. Bd Saudi Credit Bank, Saudi Fund for Devt. *Publications:* numerous articles and working papers on Islamic econs, banking and educ. *Leisure interests:* cycling, walking. *Address:* Islamic Development Bank, PO Box 5925, Jeddah 21432, Saudi Arabia (office). *Telephone:* (2) 6361400 (office). *Fax:* (2) 6366871 (office). *E-mail:* idbarchives@isdb.org.sa (office). *Website:* www.isdb.org (office).

ALI, Ahmed Thasmeen; Maldivian politician; *Minister of Atolls Development;* mem. People's Majlis (Parl.), Deputy Speaker; fmr Deputy Dir Ministry of Trade and Industry; Minister of Home Affairs 2005–07, of Atolls Devt 2007–; Chair. Bd Dirs Dhiraagu 2005–; Regional Rep. CPA. *Address:* Ministry of Atolls Development, Faashana Building, Boduthakurufaanu Magu, Malé 20-05, Maldives (office). *Telephone:* 3323070 (office). *Fax:* 3327750 (office). *E-mail:* minister@atolls.gov.mv (office). *Website:* www.atolls.gov.mv (office).

ALI, Amadou; Cameroonian politician; *Deputy Prime Minister;* Sr Minister in charge of Justice 2000–04; Deputy Prime Minister 2004–; mem. Rassemblement démocratique du peuple camerounais (RDPC). *Address:* c/o Office of the Prime Minister, Yaoundé, Cameroon (office). *Telephone:* 223-8005 (office). *Fax:* 223-5735 (office). *Website:* www.spm.gov.cm (office).

ALI, Anwar, MSc; Pakistani nuclear physicist and administrator; *Chairman, Pakistan Atomic Energy Commission;* ed Univ. of Punjab, Govt Coll., Lahore, Univ. of Birmingham, UK; worked as Dir at Dr A. Q. Khan Research Laboratories (KRL, fmr Eng Research Lab.); joined Pakistan Atomic Energy Comm. (PAEC) as Asst Scientific Officer 1967, one of pioneers of PAEC's Uranium Enrichment Project-706, Kahuta Research Labs, played key role in PAEC's Directorate of Tech. Devt, Mem. (Tech.) PAEC 2001–, Chair. PAEC 2006–; played key role in formative years of Nat. Defence Complex in developing guidance and control system for Shaheen-I rocket; mem. team of scientists and engineers who carried out nuclear tests at Ras Koh Hills, Chagai region 1998; Hilal-e-Imtiaz; Special Commendation from Chief of Army Staff and Chair. Jt Chiefs of Staff Cttee, Pres.'s Medal for Pride of Performance. *Address:* Pakistan Atomic Energy Commission, PO Box 1114, Islamabad, Pakistan (office). *Telephone:* (51) 9209032 (office). *Fax:* (51) 9204908 (office). *E-mail:* feedback@paec.gov.pk (office). *Website:* www.paec.gov.pk (office).

ALI, Mahfoudh Ould Mohamed; Mauritanian politician and lawyer; b. 1954, Nouadhibou; ed Secondary School, Atar, Ecole Nat. d'Admin, Nouakchott; with Customs Directorate-Gen. 1976–78; pvt. law practise 1978–82; State Auditor 1982–92; Dir Treasury 1992–97; Gov. Banque Centrale de Mauritanie (cen. bank) 1997–2003; Mayor of Nouadhibou 2001–; Minister of Finance 2003–05. *Address:* c/o Ministry of Finance, BP 181, Nouakchott, Mauritania (office).

ALI, Lt-Gen. Moses, BSc; Ugandan army officer and politician; b. 5 April 1939, Meliaderi, Atabo Parish, Pakele Div., Adjumani Dist.; ed Old Kampala Sr Secondary School, Staff Coll. Camberley and Holborn Coll. London, UK; mil. training as Cadet Officer and Paratrooper Instructor; Officer-in-Charge, Uganda Paratrooper School 1969–71, apptd Commdt 1971; elected mem. of Parl. (Adjumani Dist.); Minister of Provincial Educ. 1973; served as Minister of Finance, Minister of Internal Affairs, Minister of Youth, Culture and Sports, Second Deputy Prime Minister and Minister of Tourism, Trade and Antiquities; First Deputy Prime Minister and Minister of Disaster Preparedness and Refugees –2006; Chair. W Nile Parl. Group; fmr Gov. African Devt Bank; fmr Chair. Cabinet Econ. Cttee, Cen. Tender Bd; mem. Nat. Resistance Council, Moyo Dist.; fmr Del. to Constitutent Ass. for E Moyo Dist. *Address:* c/o Office of the Prime Minister, POB 341, Kampala, Uganda (office).

ALI, Muhammad; American fmr boxer; b. (Cassius Marcellus Clay), 17 Jan. 1942, Louisville, Ky; s. of Cassius Marcellus Clay Sr and Odessa L. Grady; m. 1st Sonji Roi (divorced 1966); m. 2nd Belinda Boyd (Khalilah Toloria) 1967 (divorced 1977); m. 3rd Veronica Porche 1977 (divorced 1986); m. 4th Yolanda Williams 1986; two s. seven d.; ed Louisville; amateur boxer 1954–60, Olympic Games Light-Heavyweight Champion 1960; turned professional 1960, won World Heavyweight title Feb. 1964, defeating Sonny Liston; adopted name Muhammad Ali 1964; stripped of title after refusing to be drafted into US Army 1967, won case in US Supreme Court and returned to professional boxing 1970; regained World Heavyweight title Oct. 1974, defeating George Foreman in Zaïre; lost title to Leon Spinks 1978, regained title from Spinks 1978; 56 victories in 61 fights up to Dec. 1981; lost to Larry Holmes Oct. 1980; mem. of US Black Muslim movt; Special Envoy of Pres. Carter to Africa 1980 (to urge boycott of Olympic Games), of Pres. Bush to Iraq 1990 (prior to Operation Desert Storm); lit Olympic flame, Atlanta 1996; fmr mem. Peace Corps Advisory Council; Hon. Consul-Gen. for Bangladesh in Chicago Feb. 1978; Athlete of the Century, GQ Magazine, Lifetime Achievement Award,

Amnesty Int., named Messenger of Peace, UN 1999, Presidential Medal of Freedom 2005. *Film appearances include:* The Greatest 1976, Freedom Road (TV) 1978, Freedom Road 1980. *Publications:* The Greatest: My Own Story (autobiog.) 1975, Healing (with Thomas Hauser) 1996, More Than a Hero (with Hana Ali) 2000. *Address:* PO Box 160, Berrien Springs, MI 49103, USA.

ALI, Brig.-Gen. Muhammad Nasser Ahmad; Yemeni army officer and government official; Minister of Defence 2006–. *Address:* Ministry of Defence, POB 4131, San'a, Yemen (office). *Telephone:* (1) 252640 (office). *Fax:* (1) 252375 (office).

ALI, Muhammad Shamsher, PhD; Bangladeshi professor of physics; *Vice-Chancellor, Southeast University;* b. 9 Nov. 1940, Bheramara, Kushtia; ed Dhaka Univ. and Univ. of Manchester, UK; scientific officer, Atomic Energy Comm. 1961–65, Sr Scientific Officer 1965–69, Prin. Scientific Officer 1975–82; Dir Atomic Energy Centre, Dhaka 1970–78; Prof. of Physics, Univ. of Dhaka 1982; currently Vice-Chancellor, Southeast Univ. Dhaka; mem. Advisory Cttee, Bangladesh Atomic Energy Comm. 1977–87; Sr Assoc. Int. Centre for Theoretical Physics, Trieste; Gen. Sec. Bangladesh Asscn of Scientists and Scientific Professions 1978–81; Fellow, Bangladesh Physical Soc., Bangladesh Acad. of Sciences 1978, Islamic Acad. of Sciences, mem. Council 1989–94; mem. New York Acad. of Sciences; Hon. Prof. of Physics, Dhaka Univ. 1973, Hon. Mem. World Innovation Foundation 2006; Khan Bahadur Ahsanullah Gold Medal 2004. *Publications:* over 70 research papers on nuclear physics. *Address:* Office of the Vice-Chancellor, Southeast University, House 64/B, Road 18, Banani, Dhaka 1213 (office); c/o Bangladesh Academy of Sciences, National Science and Technology Museum Bhaban, Agargaon, Dhaka 1207, Bangladesh. *Telephone:* (2) 88604567 (office). *Fax:* (2) 9892914 (office). *E-mail:* info@seu.ac.bd (office); seqeba@bol-online.com. *Website:* www.seu.ac.bd (office).

ALI, Sheikh Razzak, LLB, MA; Bangladeshi politician and diplomatist; b. 1928, Khulna; ed Univ. of Dhaka; fmr reporter and journalist with Daily Pakistan; Asst Ed. 'Enterprise' 1952; Chief Reporter and Commercial Ed. Daily Pakistan Observer 1954–58; practised law in Khulna, lawyer of High Court –1990, 1997–2001; participated in Language Movt 1952, War of Liberation 1971; joined Bangladesh Nat. Party (BNP) 1978, fmr Pres. Khulna Dist BNP, fmr Vice-Chair. BNP Cen. Cttee, fmr mem. BNP Standing Cttee, now mem. LDP; rep. Bangladesh in UN Gen. Ass. 1980; elected mem. Parl. 1970, 1991, 1996; State Minister for Law and Justice 1991; Deputy Speaker of Parl. April–Oct. 1991, Speaker 1991–96; High Commr to UK 2001–02; Pres. and Gen. Sec. Khulna Bar Asscn 1964, 1972; Pres. Jessore Bar Asscn 1984–86; Founder-Prin. Khulna City Coll.; Founder Khulna Suburban Coll.; Founder-Pres. Khulna Shiromony Eye Hosp. *Address:* c/o Liberal Democratic Party, Dhaka, Bangladesh (office).

ALI, Tariq; Pakistani political activist and writer; b. 21 Oct. 1943, Lahore; pnr Susan Watkins; two d. one s.; ed Punjab Univ., Univ. of Oxford; Editorial Dir Verso 1999–; mem. editorial bd New Left Review 1982–; mem. Fourth International. *Publications:* fiction: Redemption 1990, Shadows of the Pomegranate Tree 1992, Fear of Mirrors 1998, The Book of Saladin 1999, The Stone Woman 2000, The Illustrious Corpse 2003, A Sultan in Palermo 2005; non-fiction: The Thoughts of Chairman Harold (compiler) 1967, The New Revolutionaries: A Handbook of the International Radical Left (ed.) 1969, Pakistan: Military Rule or People's Power? 1970, The Coming British Revolution 1972, Chile: Lessons of the Coup: Which Way to Workers' Power? (with Gerry Hedley) 1974, 1968 and After: Inside the Revolution 1978, Trotsky for Beginners 1980, Can Pakistan Survive? 1983, What is Stalinism? (ed.) 1984, The Stalinist Legacy: Its Impact on Twentieth-Century World Politics (ed.) 1984, An Indian Dynasty: The Story of the Nehru-Gandhi Family 1985, Street Fighting Years: An Autobiography of the Sixties 1987, Revolution from Above: Where is the Soviet Union Going? 1988, Moscow Gold (with Howard Brenton) 1990, 1968: Marching in the Streets (with Susan Watkins) 1998, Ugly Rumours (with Howard Brenton) 1998, Masters of the Universe?: NATO's Balkan Crusade (ed.) 2000, The Clash of Fundamentalisms: Crusades, Jihads and Modernity 2002, The Clash of Fundamentalisms: Bush in Babylon: Recolonising Iraq 2003, Rough Music 2005, Pirates of the Caribbean: Axis of Hope 2006, The Duel: Pakistan on the Flight Path of American Power 2009; contribs to periodicals, including London Review of Books. *Address:* c/o Verso, 6 Meard Street, London, W1F 0EG, England. *Website:* www.tariqali.org.

ALI, Zine al Abidine Ben; Tunisian politician and head of state; *President;* b. 3 Sept. 1936, Hammam Sousse; m. Leila Ben Ali; three c.; ed as grad. in electronics, Saint-Cyr Military Acad. (France), Chalons-sur-Marne School of Artillery (France), Special School of Intelligence and Security (USA); Head of Mil. Security 1958–74; Mil. and Naval Attaché, Rabat, Morocco 1974–77; mem. of Cabinet for Minister of Nat. Defence, Dir-Gen. Nat. Security 1977–80; Amb. to Poland 1980–84; Sec. of State for Nat. Security 1984–85, Minister of the Interior 1986–87, Minister of State for the Interior May–Nov. 1987, Pres. of Tunisia Nov. 1987–; mem. politbureau of Parti Socialiste Destourien (PSD) 1986, Sec.-Gen. PSD 1986, Chair. Rassemblement Constitutionnel Démocratique (RCD); Order of Merit of Bourguiba, Order of Independence, Order of the Repub., several foreign orders. *Leisure interests:* computers, music, sports. *Address:* Présidence de la République, Palais de Carthage, Tunis, Tunisia. *Website:* www.carthage.tn (office).

ALIA, Ramiz; Albanian fmr head of state; b. 18 Oct. 1925, Shkodër; m. Semiram Alia; ed Party School, Moscow, USSR; active in World War II 1939–45; mem. of political shock 7th brigade; political leader 2nd Div.; fought in Yugoslavia at Kosova, Metohia, Sandjak, Political Commissar of the 5th Div.; First Sec. Cen. Cttee Communist Youth 1949–55; Minister of Educ. and Culture 1955–58; mem. of the Cen. Cttee CP since the 1st Congress 1961–85;

since 4th Congress mem. of the Politburo, Sec. Cen. Cttee CP, First Sec. 1985–90; Vice-Chair. Gen. Council of Democratic Front of Albania; Deputy to People's Ass. from 2nd Legislature; Chair. Presidium of People's Ass. (Head of State) 1982–90; Chair. Presidential Council 1991; Pres. of Albania 1991–92; under house arrest, imprisoned Aug. 1993; sentenced to nine years' imprisonment for abuse of power and violation of citizens' rights July 1994, released July 1995; acquitted of charges of genocide and crimes against humanity Oct. 1997.

ALIBEK, Ken, MD, PhD, ScD; American (b. Kazakhstani) industrial biotechnologist; *President and Chief Scientific Officer, AFG Biosolutions Inc.;* b. Kauchuk, Kazakh Soviet Socialist Repub.; s. of Bayzak Alibekov and Rosa Alibekov; m. Lena Yemesheva 1976; four c.; ed Tomsk Medical Inst.; fmr mem. Communist Party; cadet intern in mil. section of Tomsk Medical Inst. 1973; Jr Lt, later Sr Lt in Soviet Army, rank of Col 1987; mem. staff E European Scientific Br., Inst. of Applied Biochemistry, Omutninsk, Sr Scientist Siberian Br., Berdsk 1976; Deputy Dir (later Dir) Stepnogorsk Biological Research Centre, Deputy Chief Biopreparat Biosafety Div. 1987, First Deputy Chief 1988, working for Soviet Union's offensive biological weapons programme; Dir Biomash 1990–91; visited American mil. and research sites 1991; defected to USA 1992, debriefed by US mil. on Soviet and Russian biological weapons programme, consultant to NIH and numerous US Govt agencies in fields of industrial tech., medical microbiology, biological weapons defence and biological weapons non-proliferation; currently Pres. and Chief Scientific Officer AFG Biosolutions Inc.; Distinguished Prof., George Mason Univ.; Hon. DSc 1988. *Publications:* Biohazard (autobiog. with Stephen Handelman) 1999; more than eighty articles. *Address:* AFG Biosolutions Inc., 20358 Seneca Meadows Parkway, Germantown, MD 20876, USA (office). *Telephone:* (240) 361-1715 (office). *Fax:* (240) 361-1705 (office). *Website:* www.afgbio.com (office).

ALIĆ, Muhidin, LLB; Bosnia and Herzegovina politician; *Minister of Internal Affairs, Federation of Bosnia and Herzegovina;* b. 14 Sept. 1960, Šije, Tešanj Prov.; m.; two c.; ed Sarajevo Univ.; served in Bosnia and Herzegovina Army, then several positions in police force; fmr Sec. Tešanj Municipal Council; fmr Asst Minister of Justice, Minister of Labour, Social Policy and Refugees, Minister of Interior, Zenica-Doboj Canton Govt; Minister of Internal Affairs, Fed. of Bosnia and Herzegovina 2006–. *Address:* Minister of Internal Affairs, 71000 Sarajevo, Mehmeda Spahe 7, Bosnia and Herzegovina (office). *Telephone:* (33) 667246 (office). *Fax:* (33) 207606 (office).

ALIER, Abel, LLM; Sudanese politician and judge; b. 1933, Bor Dist, Upper Nile Prov.; s. of Kwai Alier and Anaai Alier; m. Siama Fatma Bilal 1970; one d.; ed Univs of Khartoum and Yale; fmr advocate; District Judge in El Obeid, Wad Medani and Khartoum –1965; participant in Round Table Conf. and mem. Twelve Man Cttee to Study the Southern Problem 1965; mem. Constitution Comms 1966–67, 1968; fmr mem. Law Reform Comm. and Southern Front; Minister of Supply and Internal Trade 1969–70; Minister of Works 1970–71; Minister of Southern Affairs 1971–72; Vice-Pres. of Sudan 1971–82; Minister of Construction and Public Works 1983–85; mem. Panel of Arbritrators, Perm. Court of Int. Arbitration, The Hague 1988–; apptd head nat. cttee to investigate death of John Garang 2005; Pres. Supreme Exec. Council for the South 1972–78, 1980–81; mem. Political Bureau, Sudanese Socialist Union, Bd of Dirs, Industrial Planning Corpn; mem. Nat. Scholarship Bd; Hon. LLD (Khartoum) 1978. *Leisure interests:* tennis, athletics, reading, history and literature. *Address:* c/o Ministry of Foreign Affairs, POB 873, Khartoum, Sudan.

ALIERTA IZUEL, César; Spanish telecommunications executive; *Executive Chairman and CEO, Telefónica SA;* b. 5 May 1945; fmr stockbroker; Chair. Tabacalera SA 1996–99, Co-Chair. Altadis Group (following merger) 1999–2000; Exec. Chair. and CEO Telefónica SA 2000–; charged with insider trading July 2005 related to sales of Tabacalera shares in 1997; Gov. European Foundation for Quality Man. *Address:* Telefónica SA, Gran Vía 28, 28013 Madrid, Spain (office). *Telephone:* (91) 584-0306 (office). *Fax:* (91) 531-9347 (office). *E-mail:* info@telefonica.com (office). *Website:* www.telefonica.com (office).

ALIMARDONOV, Murodali Mukhamadievich; Tajikistani fmr central banker; Chair. Nat. Bank of Tajikistan 1995–2008; fmr Rep. Gov. EBRD. *Address:* c/o National Bank of the Republic of Tajikistan, 734025 Dushanbe, pr. Rudaki 23/2, Tajikistan (office).

ALIMI, Rashid Muhammad al-; Yemeni politician; *Deputy Prime Minister;* fmr law prof.; Minister of the Interior –2006, 2006–08, Deputy Prime Minister 2006–. *Address:* Ministry of the Interior, San'a, Yemen (office). *Telephone:* (1) 274147 (office). *Fax:* (1) 332511 (office). *E-mail:* info@moi.gov.ye (office). *Website:* www.moi.gov.ye (office).

ALIMOV, Rashid; Tajikistani politician and diplomatist; b. 1953; m.; two c.; ed Tajik Univ.; Chair. Trade Union Cttee Tajik Univ. 1975–77; head of group of lecturers, Cen. Comsomol Cttee of Tajik SSR, instructor, regional and city CP cttees, Dushanbe; mem. Div. of Propaganda, First Sec. Frunze Regional Cttee of Tajikistan CP 1988–89, Second Sec. Dushanbe City CP Cttee 1989; Chair. Comm. on Problems of Youth, Supreme Soviet of Tajikistan 1989–91; State Counsellor to fmr Pres. Nabiyev 1990–92; Minister of Foreign Affairs of Tajikistan 1992–94; Perm Rep. to UN, New York 1994, Deputy Pres. of the Ass. 1999–2000. *Address:* c/o Ministry of Foreign Affairs, Dushanbe, Tajikistan (office).

ALIMOV, Timur; Uzbekistan politician; b. 1936; ed Tashkent Inst. of Irrigation Eng and Agric. Mechanization; engineer on construction of channel in Afghanistan 1960–62; sr engineer, Uzgiprovodkhoz 1962–65; sr engineer, Dir of Tashkent reservoir div. 1965–67; mem. CPSU 1967–91; head of section of water supply and irrigation with Uzbek SSR Council of Ministers 1967–75; Man. Uzbek SSR Council of Ministers 1975–78; Pres. Tashkent Exec. Cttee of Uzbek CP 1978–85; First Sec. of Tashkent Exec. Cttee of Uzbek CP 1985–91; cand. mem. of CPSU Cen. Cttee 1986–90; Adviser to Pres. of Uzbekistan 1991–2005; Chief of Control Inspection Comm. *Address:* c/o Office of the President, Uzbekistansky Prosp. 43, 100163, Tashkent, Uzbekistan.

ALINGTON, William Hildebrand, MArch; New Zealand architect; b. 18 Nov. 1929, Wellington; s. of Edward Hugh Alington and Beatrice McCrie Alington; m. Margaret Hilda Broadhead 1955; one s. two d.; ed Hutt Valley High School, School of Architecture, Auckland Univ. Coll., School of Architecture Univ. of Illinois; architectural cadet and architect, Head Office Ministry of Works, Wellington 1950–65; architect, London Office of Robert Matthew & Johnson-Marshall 1956–57; Pnr, Gabites & Beard 1965–71, Gabites Toomath Beard Wilson & Pnrs 1971–72, Gabites Alington & Edmondson 1972–79, Gabites Porter & Pnrs 1978–83; Sr Pnr, Alington Group Architects 1984–; Asst Ed. NZIA Journal 1964–69; Pres. Architectural Centre 1970–72; Hon. Lecturer, Victoria Univ. of Wellington School of Architecture 1975–85, Tutor 1986–2003; Vice-Pres. and Br. Chair. New Zealand Inst. of Architects 1977–79, mem. Council 1965–79; mem. Wellington Anglican Diocesan Synod 1972–90. *Major works include:* Meteorological Office, Gisborne Courthouse, Upper Hutt Civic Centre, Massey Univ. Halls of Residence, VUW School of Music, Karori Baptist Church, St Mary's Church Extension, New Plymouth. *Publications:* numerous articles in specialist journals. *Leisure interests:* gardening, painting, church government. *Address:* 60 Homewood Crescent, Wellington, New Zealand. *Telephone:* (4) 476-8495. *Fax:* (4) 476-8495 (home). *E-mail:* alington@xtra.co.nz (home).

ALIREZA, Abdullah ibn Ahmed Zainal; Saudi Arabian business executive and politician; *Minister of Commerce and Industry;* fmr adviser to Supreme Econ. Council; fmr Chair. Jeddah Chamber of Commerce and Industry; fmr Cabinet Minister without Portfolio; Minister of Commerce and Industry 2008–; headed team that negotiated Saudi Arabia's to WTO. *Address:* Ministry of Commerce and Industry, POB 1774, Airport Road, Riyadh, Saudi Arabia (office). *Telephone:* (1) 401-2222 (office). *Fax:* (1) 403-8421 (office). *E-mail:* info@commerce.gov.sa (office). *Website:* www.commerce.gov.sa (office).

ALITO, Samuel A., Jr, JD; American judge; *Associate Justice, Supreme Court;* b. 1 April 1950, Trenton, NJ; m. Martha-Ann Bomgardner; one s. one d.; ed Princeton Univ. and Yale Law School; law clerk, Third Circuit US Court of Appeals 1976–77; Asst US Attorney 1977–81; Asst to US Solicitor Gen. 1981–85; Deputy Asst US Attorney Gen. 1985–87; US Attorney 1987–90; Judge, Third Circuit US Court of Appeals 1990–2005; nominated by Pres. George W. Bush for US Supreme Court Oct. 2005. *Address:* Supreme Court of the United States, Washington, DC 20543, USA (office). *Telephone:* (202) 479-3211 (office). *Fax:* (202) 479-3021 (office). *Website:* www.supremecourtus.gov (office).

ALIYEV, İlham Heydar oğlu; Azerbaijani business executive, politician and head of state; *President;* b. 24 Dec. 1961, Baku; s. of the late Heydar Aliyev, fmr Pres. of Azerbaijan; m. Mehriban Aliyeva; three c.; ed Moscow State Univ. of Int. Relations; teacher, Moscow State Univ. of Int. Relations 1985–90; engaged in commercial activity in Moscow and İstanbul 1991–94; First Vice-Pres. State Oil Co. of the Azerbaijani Repub. (SOCAR) 1994–2003; mem. Parl. 1995–2003; Deputy Chair. Yeni Azerbaijan (New Azerbaijan Party) 1999–2001, First Deputy Chair. 2001–; Prime Minister of Azerbaijan Aug. 2003; Pres. of Azerbaijan Oct. 2003–; Pres. Nat. Olympic Cttee 1997–; Leader Del. to Council of Europe; Hon. Prof. L.N. Gumilev Eurasian Nat. Univ., Kazakhstan, Univ. of Nat. and World Economy, Bulgaria, Moscow State Univ.; Order of Heydar Aliyev, of Sheikhulislam (Azerbaijan), Order of The Star of Romania, Order of King Abdul Aziz (Saudi Arabia), Order of Honour (Georgia), Grand Cross, Legion d'honneur, Grand Cross of Order of Merit (Poland); Dr hc (Lincoln Univ., USA, Moscow State Univ., Bilkent Univ., Turkey, Nat. Acad. of Taxes, Ukraine, Petroleum and Gas Univ. of Ploesti, Romania, Kyung Hee Univ., South Korea, Jordan Univ., Corvinus Univ., Hungary); PACE Medal 2004, Ihsan Dogramacı Prize for Int. Relations for Peace (Turkey). *Address:* Office of the President, 1066 Baku, İstiqlaliyet küç. 19, Azerbaijan (office). *Telephone:* (12) 492-17-26 (office). *Fax:* (12) 492-35-43 (office). *E-mail:* office@apparat.gov.az (office). *Website:* www.ilham-aliyev.com (office); www.president.az (office).

ALIYEV, Mukhu Gimbatovich, PhD; Russian/Dagestan politician; *President, Republic of Dagestan;* b. 6 Aug. 1940, Tanusi, Dagestan; m.; two c.; ed Dagestan State Univ.; began career as teacher, then Head Nizhne-Gakvarinskaya Secondary School; Sec. Comsomol Cttee, Dagestan State Univ. 1964–66; First Sec. Makhachkala City Comsomol Cttee 1969–72, Makhachkala Dist CPSU Cttee 1972–85; Bureau Head Dagestan Div. CPSU Cttee 1985–90; First Sec. Dagestan Repub. CPSU Cttee 1990–91; mem. Supreme Soviet of Dagestan (parl.), Vice-Chair. 1991–95; Chair. Econs Cttee, Repub. of Dagestan 1992–94; Chair. Peoples' Ass., Repub. of Dagestan 1999–2006, Pres. of Dagestan 2006–; mem. Council of Feds of Russia 1995–, Deputy Chair. Cttee on Foreign Affairs 1995–2001; fmr mem. Parl. Ass., CIS and Council of Europe; Labour Red Banner 1976, Badge of Honour 1981, For Services to Motherland, class IV 2000, class III 2005. *Publications:* Dagestan Republic: Priorities of National Policy 1996, Unity and Integrity of Dagestan Republic as a Constitutional Principle 1998, Searching for Consent 2002; numerous articles in magazines and journals. *Address:* House of Government, 1 Lenin Square, 367005 Makhachkala, Dagestan (office); 33/1a Korkmasov Street, 367005 Makhachkala, Dagestan, Russia (home). *Telephone:* (8722) 67-30-60 (office); (8722) 67-30-59 (office); (8722) 67-04-96 (home). *Fax:* (8722) 67-30-61 (office). *E-mail:* president@e-dag.ru (office). *Website:* www.president.e-dag.ru (office).

ALIYEV, Natiq Ağa ami oğlu; Azerbaijani oil industry executive and government official; *Minister of Industry and Energy;* Pres. State Oil Co. of the Azerbaijani Repub. (SOCAR) 1993–2005; Minister of Industry and Energy 2005–. *Address:* Ministry of Energy and Industry, 1012 Baku, Hasanbek Zardabi küç. 88, Azerbaijan (office). *Telephone:* (12) 498-78-56 (office). *Fax:* (12) 598-16-78 (office). *E-mail:* pressa@mie.gov.az (office). *Website:* www.mie.gov.az (office).

ALKALAJ, Sven, MS; Bosnia and Herzegovina diplomatist and politician; *Minister of Foreign Affairs;* b. 11 Nov. 1948, Sarajevo; m.; two c.; ed Univ. of Sarajevo and Harvard Univ.; Commercial Man., Petrolinvest, Sarajevo 1975–85; Regional Man. for Middle and Far East Energoinvest, Sarajevo 1985–88, Man. Dir Energoinvest–Thailand 1988–94; Amb. to USA 1994–2000, to OAS 2000–04, to Belgium 2004–07, to NATO 2004–07; Minister of Foreign Affairs 2007–; mem. Party for Bosnia-Herzegovina (SBiH); Silver Badge of Petrolinvest 1994, Sloboda Award. *Address:* Ministry of Foreign Affairs, 71000 Sarajevo, Musala 2, Bosnia and Herzegovina (office). *Telephone:* (33) 281100 (office). *Fax:* (33) 472188 (office). *E-mail:* info@mvp.gov.ba (office). *Website:* www.mvp.gov.ba (office).

ALKATIRI, Mari bin Amude; Timor-Leste politician; *Secretary-General, Frente Revolucionária do Timor Leste Independente (Fretilin);* b. 26 Nov. 1949, Dili; m. Marina Ribeiro; three c.; fmr chartered surveyor; est. Movt for the Liberation of East Timor (Timor-Leste) 1970; Co-Founder and Sec.-Gen. Frente Revolucionário do Timor Leste Independente—Fretilin (Revolutionary Front for an Ind. Timor-Leste) 1974–; lived in political exile, teaching in Mozambique –1999; Minister for Econs in Transitional Admin; Prime Minister of Timor-Leste 2002–06, concurrently Minister for Economy and Devt, then Minister for Devt and the Environment. *Address:* c/o Fretilin, Rua dos Martires da Patria, Dili, Timor-Leste (office). *Telephone:* 3321409 (office). *Website:* fretilin-rdtl.blogspot.com (office).

ALKHANOV, Alu; Russian (Chechen) politician and government official; *Deputy Minister of Justice;* b. 1947; m.; three c.; ed USSR Interior Ministry Acad.; various positions in Ministry of the Interior, Chechen—Nokchi Repub.; Chief of Transport Police Dept 1995–96, of Shakhty Transport Police, Rostov Region 1997–2000, of Groznyi Transport Police 2000–03; Minister of the Interior, Chechen—Nokchi Repub. 2003–04; Pres. of Chechen—Nokchi Repub. 2004–07; Deputy Minister of Justice 2007–. *Address:* Ministry of Justice, 119991 Moscow, Zhitnaya 14, Russian Federation (office). *Telephone:* (495) 955-59-99 (office). *Fax:* (495) 916-29-03 (office). *Website:* www.minjust.ru (office).

ALLAIS, Maurice; French economist and engineer; b. 31 May 1911, Paris; s. of Maurice Allais and Louise Allais (née Caubet); m. Jacqueline Bouteloup 1960; one d.; ed Ecole Polytechnique and Ecole Nat. Supérieure des Mines de Paris; Dept of Mines and Quarries 1937–43; Dir Bureau de Documentation Minière 1943–48; econ. research 1948–70; Prof. of Econ. Analysis, Ecole Nat. Supérieure des Mines de Paris 1944–88; Prof. of Econ. Theory, Inst. of Statistics, Univ. of Paris 1947–68; Dir of Research, CNRS 1954–80; Dir Centre for Econ. Analysis 1946–; Prof., Grad. Inst. of Int. Studies, Geneva 1967–70; Dir Séminaire Clément Juglar d'Analyse Monétaire, Univ. of Paris-X (Nanterre) 1970–85; Foreign Assoc. mem. NAS, Accad. dei Lincei, Russian Acad. of Sciences; mem. Acad. des Sciences Morales et Politiques; Hon. Ingénieur Général au Corps des Mines; Officier Palmes académiques, Chevalier Ordre de l'Economie Nationale, Grand Croix, Ordre Nat. du Mérite, Grand Officier Légion d'honneur; Dr hc (Groningen, Mons, American Univ. of Paris, Lisbon, Hautes Etudes Commerciales, Paris); numerous hon. doctorates from European and American Univs; Lanchester Prize, American Soc. for Operations Research, Gold Medal, Soc. d'Encouragement pour l'Industrie Nationale, CNRS Gold Medal 1978, Prix Laplace, Prix Rivot, Prix Robert Blanché, Grand Prix Zerilli Marimó, Acad. des Sciences Morales et Politiques, Nobel Prize for Econ. Sciences 1988 and other awards. *Publications include:* A la Recherche d'un Discipline Economique 1943, Abondance ou misère 1946, Economie et intérêt 1947, Traité d'économie pure 1952, La gestion des houillères nationalisées et la théorie économique 1953, Les fondements comptables de la macroéconomique 1954, Le pendule paraconique 1957–59, Manifeste pour une société libre 1958, L'Europe unie, route de la prospérité 1960, Le Tiers-Monde au carrefour—Centralisation autoritaire ou planification concurrentielle 1962, L'Algérie d'Evian 1962, The Role of Capital in Economic Development 1963, Reformulation de la théorie quantitative de la monnaie 1965, L'Impôt sur le capital 1966, The Conditions of the Efficiency in the Economy 1967, Growth Without Inflation 1968, Growth and Inflation 1969, La libéralisation des relations économiques internationales 1970, Les théories de l'équilibre économique général et de l'efficacité maximale 1971, Forgetfulness and Interest 1972, The General Theory of Surplus and Pareto's Fundamental Contribution 1973, Inequality and Civilization 1973, La création de monnaie et de pouvoir d'achat par le mécanisme du crédit 1974, The Psychological Rate of Interest 1974, L'inflation française et la croissance 1974, Classes sociales et civilisations 1974, Taux d'expansion de la dépense globale et vitesse de circulation de la monnaie 1975, Inflation répartition des revenus et indexation 1976, L'impôt sur le capital et la réforme monétaire 1977, Expected Utility Hypotheses and the Allais Paradox 1979, La théorie générale des surplus 1980, Frequency, Probability and Chance 1982, The Foundations of the Theory of Utility and Risk 1984, Determination of Cardinal Utility 1985, The Concepts of Surplus and Loss and the Reformulation of the Theories of Stable General Economic Equilibrium and Maximum Efficiency 1985, The Empirical Approaches of the Hereditary and Relativistic Theory of the Demand for Money 1985, Les conditions monétaires d'une économie de marchés 1987, Pour l'indexation; Pour la réforme de la fiscalité 1990, L'Europe face à son avenir 1991, Erreurs et impasse de la construction européenne 1992, Cardinalism 1994, Combats pour l'Europe 1994, L'Anisotropie de l'espace 1997, La crise mondiale d'aujourd'hui 1999, L'Union européene, la mondialisation et le chômage 1999, La mondialisation: La destruction des emplois et de la croissance, L'évidence empirique 2000, Fondements de la dynamique monétaire 2001, La Passion de la Recherche 2001, Un Savant Méconnu 2002, Nouveaux Combats pour l'Europe 2002. *Leisure interests:* history, physics, swimming, skiing. *Address:* 60 boulevard Saint Michel, 75006 Paris (office); 15 rue des Gâtes-Ceps, 92210 St-Cloud, France (home). *Telephone:* 1-40-51-91-88 (office). *E-mail:* mgendrot@club.internet.fr (home). *Website:* allais.maurice.free.fr (office).

ALLAM, Magdi; Egyptian/Italian journalist, editor and author; *Deputy Editor, Corriere della Sera;* b. 22 April 1952, Cairo; ed La Sapienza Univ., Rome; raised in Italy; worked as journalist for several Italian publs, including nat. daily newspaper La Repubblica; currently op-ed. columnist, ad personam Asst Publr and Deputy Ed. Corriere della Sera, Arab and Islamic affairs commentator; appears frequently on nat. TV news shows; co-recipient Dan David Prize, Tel-Aviv Univ. (Israel) 2006. *Publications:* Vincere la paura (Winning Fear), books and articles on relations between Western culture and values and Islamic world. *Address:* Corriere della Sera, Via Solferino 28, 20121 Milano, Italy (office). *Telephone:* (02) 6339 (office). *Fax:* (02) 29009668 (office). *Website:* www.corriere.it/corrforum/corriere/Intro?forumid=291 (office).

ALLAM-MI, Ahmat; Chadian diplomatist; fmr Amb. to France; spokesman for Chadian mediating team during Sudanese peace talks to resolve Darfur crisis 2004; Minister of Foreign Affairs and African Integration 2005–08. *Address:* c/o Ministry of Foreign Affairs and African Integration, BP 746, N'Djamena, Chad (office).

ALLAN, Alexander Claud Stuart (Alex), MA, MSc; British civil servant; *Chairman, Joint Intelligence Committee, Cabinet Office;* b. 9 Feb. 1951; s. of the late Lord Allan of Kilmahew and of Maureen Catherine Flower Stuart-Clark; m. Katie Christine Clemson 1978; ed Harrow School, Clare Coll., Cambridge, Univ. Coll., London; with HM Customs and Excise 1973–76, HM Treasury 1976–92, Prin. Pvt. Sec. to Chancellor of the Exchequer 1986–89; secondments in Australia 1983–84; UnderSec. for Int. Finance 1989–90, for Public Expenditure Policy, 1990–92; Prin. Pvt. Sec. to the Prime Minister 1992–97; High Commr in Australia 1997–2000; e-Envoy Cabinet Office 1999–2000; Permanent Sec., Dept for Constitutional Affairs, later Ministry of Justice 2004–07; Chair. Joint Intelligence Cttee, Cabinet Office 2007–. *Leisure interests:* sailing, Grateful Dead music, cycling, computers, bridge. *Address:* Cabinet Office, 70 Whitehall, London, SW1A 2AS, England (office). *Telephone:* (20) 7276-1234 (office). *E-mail:* alex@whitegum.com (home). *Website:* www.cabinetoffice.gov.uk (office); www.whitegum.com (home).

ALLAN, Andrew Norman, BA, FRTS; British arts and media executive; *Chairman, Codeworks;* b. 26 Sept. 1943, Newcastle-upon-Tyne; s. of Andrew Allan and Elizabeth Allan (née Davidson); m. Joanna Forrest 1978; two s. one d. and two d. from previous m.; ed Univ. of Birmingham; Presenter, ABC Television 1965–66; Producer, Thames TV 1966–69, 1971–75; Head of News 1976–78; Producer, ITN 1970; Dir of Programmes, Tyne Tees TV 1978–83, Deputy Man. Dir 1982–83, Man. Dir 1983–84; Dir of Programes, Cen. Ind. TV 1984–90, Man. Dir 1993–94; Man. Dir Cen. Broadcasting 1990–93; Chief Exec. Carlton TV 1994–95, Dir of Programmes 1996–98 (retd); Dir TV 12 1999–; media consultant 1998–; Gov. Nat. Film and TV School 1993–98; Chair. Birmingham Repertory 2000–, Route 4 PLC 2001–, Codeworks 2004–; Fellow, Royal TV Soc. 1987. *Leisure interests:* reading, dining. *Address:* Codeworks, St Peter's Gate, Charles Street, Sunderland, Tyne and Wear, SR6 0AN, England (office). *Telephone:* (191) 556-1122 (office). *Fax:* (191) 556-1110 (home). *E-mail:* enquiries@codeworks.net (office). *Website:* www.codeworks.net (office).

ALLAN, M. Elyse, BA, MBA; Canadian (b. American) business executive; *President and CEO, General Electric Canada;* m. Don Allan; one s.; ed Dartmouth Coll., Amos Tuck School of Business; began career at General Electric (GE) as consultant in Corp. Marketing Consulting Services group, Bridgeport, Conn. 1984; moved to Canada as Man. Customer Service Program, GE Canada 1988, later Marketing Man. GE Commercial and Industrial Lighting; Dir of Marketing Ont. Hydro; Pres. and CEO Toronto Bd of Trade (first woman) 1995–2004; Pres. and CEO GE Canada 2004–; Chair. Bd of Dirs Providence Healthcare; mem. Nat. Round Table on the Environment and the Economy 2005–; mem. Bd of Dirs Public Policy Forum, Canadian Council of Chief Execs; mem. Bd of Govs Canadian Council on Unity; fmr mem. Bd of Visitors, Rockefeller Centre for Public Policy; Dr hc (Ryerson Univ.) 2005. *Address:* GE Canada, 2300 Meadowvale Blvd, Mississauga, ON L5N 5P9, Canada (office). *Telephone:* (905) 858-6655 (office). *Website:* www.ge.com/can (office).

ALLARD, A. Wayne, DMV; American veterinarian and politician; b. 12 Dec. 1943; m. Joan Malcolm 1967; two d.; ed Colorado State Univ.; early career as veterinarian, Allard Animal Hosp.; mem. Colo State Senate (Republican) 1982–91, Chair. Health, Environment and Insts Cttee, Chair. Senate Majority Caucus; mem. US House of Reps from 4th Dist, Colo 1991–96, mem. House Agric. Cttee 1991–96, House Small Business Cttee 1991–92, House Interior and Insular Affairs Cttee 1991–92, House Cttee on Cttees 1991–94, House Budget Cttee 1993–96, House Natural Resources Cttee 1993–96, Jt Cttee on Reorganization of Congress 1993–96, Chair. House Sub-Cttee of Agric. Conservation, Forest and Water 1995–96; Senator from Colo 1997–2009 (retd), mem. Banking, Urban Affairs Cttee 1997–2009, Environment and Public Works Cttee 1997–2009, Intelligence Select Cttee 1997–2009, Armed Services Cttee and numerous other cttees; fmr health officer, Loveland, Colo; fmr mem. Regional Advisory Council on Veterinarian Medicine, W Interstate Comm. on Higher Educ., Colo Low-Level Radioactive Waste Advisory Cttee; Chair. United Way; Founding mem. AVMA, Colo Veterinarian Medicine Asscn, Larimer Co. Veterinarian Medicine Asscn; mem. Bd Veterinarian Practitioners (charter mem.), American Animal Hosp. Asscn, Nat. Conf. State Legislatures (Vice-Chair. Human Resources Cttee 1987); mem. Loveland Chamber of Commerce. *Address:* POB 2405, Loveland, CO 80539, USA (home).

ALLARDT, Erik Anders, MA, PhD; Finnish university chancellor and sociologist; *Professor of Sociology, University of Helsinki;* b. 9 Aug. 1925, Helsinki; s. of Arvid Allardt and Marita Allardt (née Heikel); m. Sagi Nylander 1947; one s. two d.; ed Univ. of Helsinki, Columbia Univ., New York, USA; Prof. of Sociology, Univ. of Helsinki 1958–, Dean of the Faculty of Social Sciences 1969–70; Pres. Acad. of Finland 1986–91; Chancellor of the Åbo Acad. Univ. 1992–94; mem. European Science Foundation Exec. Council 1987–92, Vice-Pres. 1990–92; mem. Bd Scandinavia-Japan Sasakawa Foundation 1987–96; Founder-mem. Academia Europaea 1988–; Fellow, Woodrow Wilson Int. Center for Scholars 1978–79; Visiting Prof. numerous countries and univs; Commdr of the Swedish Order of the Northern Star; Grand Cross Knight, Icelandic Order of the Falcon 1997; Dr hc (Stockholm) 1978, (Åbo Akademi) 1978, (Uppsala) 1984, (Bergen) 1996, (Copenhagen) 2000. *Publications:* (with Rokkan) Mass Politics: Studies in Political Sociology 1970, Att Ha, Att Älska, Att Vara. Om Välfärd i Norden 1975, Implications of the Ethnic Revival in Modern, Industrialized Society 1979, (with Lysgaard and Sørensen) Sociologin i Sverige, vetenskap, miljö och organisation 1988, The History of the Social Sciences in Finland 1997. *Leisure interest:* playing with grandchildren. *Address:* Department of Sociology, PB 18, 00014 University of Helsinki, Helsinki (office); Unionsgatan 45B 40, 00170 Helsinki, Finland (home). *Telephone:* (9) 19123963 (office); (9) 1354550 (home). *Fax:* (9) 19123967 (office). *E-mail:* erik.allardt@helsinki.fi (office).

ALLAWI, Ali Abdel-Amir, SB, MBA; Iraqi government official and business executive; b. 1947; ed MIT, Harvard Business School, USA; fmr consultant to World Bank and Head, Pan-Arab investment co.; Prof., Univ. of Oxford, UK –2003; Minister of Trade and Minister of Defence, Interim Iraq Governing Council 2003–04, Minister of Finance, Iraqi Transitional Govt 2005–06, then Sr Adviser to Prime Minister of Iraq; mem. United Iraqi Alliance. *Publication:* The Occupation of Iraq: Winning the War, Losing the Peace 2007. *Address:* c/o Ministry of Finance, Khulafa Street, nr ar-Russafi Square, Baghdad, Iraq (office).

ALLAWI, Ayad, MSc, DrMed; Iraqi neurologist and politician; b. 1945; ed Baghdad Univ., London Univ., UK; from prominent Shia family in Baghdad; fmr mem. Ba'ath Party; left Iraq 1971 going first to Beirut then London; survived assassination attempt 1978; formed Iraqi Nat. Accord dissident group 1990, involved in attempted coup against Saddam Hussein 1996; fmr consultant to UNDP, WHO, UNICEF; apptd mem. Iraqi Governing Council 2003, Chair Security Cttee 2003–04; Interim Prime Minister of Iraq 2004–05; Leader, Iraqi Nat. List party. *Address:* Iraqi National List, Baghdad, Iraq. *E-mail:* info@ayadallawi.com. *Website:* www.ayadallawi.net.

ALLCHIN, Frank Raymond, PhD, FBA, FSA; British academic; *Reader Emeritus in Indian Studies, University of Cambridge;* b. 9 July 1923, Harrow; s. of the late Frank MacDonald Allchin and Louise Maude Wright; m. Bridget Gordon 1951; one s. one d.; ed Westminster School, Regent Street Polytechnic School of Architecture, SOAS; Lecturer in Indian Archaeology, SOAS 1954–59; Lecturer in Indian Studies, Univ. of Cambridge 1959–72, Reader 1972–90, Reader Emer. 1990–; Fellow of Churchill Coll., Cambridge 1963–; Jt Dir British Archaeological Mission to Pakistan 1975–92; Dir British Anuradhapura Project, Sri Lanka 1989–93; Jt Founding Trustee, Ancient India and Iran Trust 1978–, Chair. 1995–2004, Chair. Emer. 2004–. *Publications:* co-author: The Birth of Indian Civilization 1968, The Rise of Civilization in India and Pakistan 1982, The Archaeology of Early Historic South Asia 1995, Origins of a Civilization 1997. *Leisure interests:* walking, gardening. *Address:* 2 Shepreth Road, Barrington, Cambridge, CB2 5SB; The Ancient India and Iran Trust, Brooklands House, 23 Brooklands Avenue, Cambridge, CB2 2BG, England. *Telephone:* (1223) 870494; (1223) 356841 (Trust). *Fax:* (1223) 361125 (Trust); 1223 361125. *E-mail:* Indiran@aol.com. *Website:* www.indiran.co.uk.

ALLÈGRE, Claude Jean; French professor of earth sciences and politician; b. 31 March 1937, Paris; s. of Prof. Roger Allègre and Lucette (née Hugoueneq) Allègre; m. Claude Blanche Simon 1967; three s. one d.; ed Lycées Saint-Maur and Saint-Louis, Faculté des Sciences, Paris; Asst, Univ. de Paris 1962–68; Dir of Lab. of Geochemistry and Cosmochemistry, Univ. de Paris VI and VII 1967–; Asst Physician, Inst. de Physique du Globe 1968–70, Dir 1976–86; Prof. of Earth Sciences Univ. de Paris VII 1970–, currently working at Institut de Physique du Globe de Paris; Prof. of Earth Sciences, MIT 1975–76; Special Adviser to Lionel Jospin 1988–92; mem. European Parl. 1989; Minister of Nat. Educ., Research and Tech. 1997–2000; Pres. Admin. Council of Bureau de Recherches Géologiques et Minières 1992–97; Hon. mem. Union Européenne de Géosciences, European Biophysical Soc., Acad. of Arts and Sciences, Boston Philosophical Soc.; Foreign mem. NAS; Crafoord Prize (Sweden) 1986; Officier, Légion d'honneur, Chevalier des Palmes académiques; numerous medals. *Publications include:* L'Ecume de la Terre 1983, De la Pierre à l'Etoile 1985, Les Fureurs de la Terre 1987, Economiser la Planète 1990, Introduction à une Histoire Naturelle 1992, L'Age des Savoires 1993, Ecologie des Villes, Ecologie des Champs 1993, L'Etat de la Planète 1994, La Défaite de Platon 1995, Questions de France 1996, Dieu Face à la Science 1997, Toute Vérité est Bonne à Dire 2000, Vive L'École Libre 2000. *Address:* Institut de physique du globe, Tour 24, BP 89, 4, place Jussieu, 75252 Paris Cedex 05, France. *Fax:* 1-44-27-37-52.

ALLÈGRE, Maurice Marie, LenD; French research co-ordinator and business executive; b. 16 Feb. 1933, Antibes; s. of Guy Allègre and Renée-

Lise Bermond; m. Catherine Pierre 1962; one s. one d.; ed Ecole Polytechnique, Ecole Nat. Supérieure des Mines and Ecole Nat. Supérieure du Pétrole et des Moteurs, Faculté de Droit; Engineer, Direction des Carburants, Ministry of Industry 1957–62; Dir Mines de l'Organisme Saharien 1962–64; Tech. Adviser to Ministry of Finance and Econ. Affairs 1965–67; Délégué à l'Informatique and Pres. Inst. de Recherche d'Informatique et d'Automatique 1968–74; Chief of Nickel Mission to New Caledonia 1975; Asst Dir-Gen. Inst. Français du Pétrole 1976–81; Pres. and Dir-Gen. ISIS 1976–81; Pres. FRANLAB, COFLEXIP 1976–81; Pres. Agence Nat. de Valorisation et de la Recherche (ANVAR) 1982–84; Dir Scientific and Tech. Devt, Ministry of Research and Tech. 1982–84; Dir-Gen. Bureau de Recherches Géologiques et Minières 1984–88, Pres. 1988–92; Pres. Agence Nationale pour la Gestion des Déchets Radioactifs (ANDRA— Nat. Agency for Man. of Radioactive Waste) 1993–98; Pres. Sicav Vauban 1998–2000; Pres. AGRER Asscn 1998–; int. consultant on energy policy and radioactive waste 1998–; Chevalier, Légion d'honneur; Officier, Ordre nat. du Mérite. *Leisure interests:* photography, skiing, sailing. *Address:* 85 rue de Sèvres, 75006 Paris; 50 boulevard d'Aguillon, 06600 Antibes, France. *Telephone:* 1-45-44-94-51 (office).

ALLEN, Charles Lamb, CBE, FRSA, FCMA; British business executive; *Chairman, Global Radio;* b. 4 Jan. 1957; accountant, British Steel 1974–79; Deputy Audit Man. Gallaghers PLC 1979–82; Dir Man. Services Grandmet Int. Services Ltd 1982–85, Group Man. Dir Compass Vending, Grandmet Innovations Ltd 1986–87, Man. Dir Grandmet Int. Services Ltd 1987–88, Man. Dir Compass Group Ltd 1988–91, Chief Exec. Leisure Div., Granada Group 1991–92; Chair. Granada Leisure and Services 1993–2000, CEO LWT (following takeover by Granada) 1994–96 (Chair. 1996), CEO Granada Group PLC 1996–2000, Chair. GMTV 1996–2000, Jt Deputy Chair. Granada Compass PLC 2000, Exec. Chair. Granada PLC 2000–03, CEO ITV PLC (after merger of Granada and Carlton) 2003–06; Chair. Global Radio 2007–; Sr Adviser Goldman Sachs Capital Pnrs 2008–; Chair. Yorkshire Tyne Tees TV 1997–; Chair. M2002 Ltd (Manchester Commonwealth Games); Chair. (non-exec.) EMI Music 2009–; Vice-Chair. London 2012 Ltd (effort to bring 2012 Olympics to London); mem. Bd of Dirs (non-exec.) Tesco PLC 1999–, Endemol 2008–, Virgin Media 2008–; Hon. DBA (Manchester Metropolitan) 1999, (Salford) 2002. *Leisure interests:* visual and performing arts, int. travel and cultures. *Address:* c/o Grandmet Management LLP, 78 Addison Road, London, W14 8EB, England (office). *Telephone:* (20) 7603-8821 (office). *Website:* www .globalradiosales.com/global (office).

ALLEN, Sir Douglas Albert Vivian, GCB see CROHAM, Baron).

ALLEN, Gary James, CBE, DL, DSc, BCom, FCMA, CBIM, FRSA; British business executive; *Senior Director, London Stock Exchange;* b. 30 Sept. 1944, Birmingham; s. of Alfred Allen; m. Judith A. Nattrass 1966; three s.; ed King Edward VI Grammar School, Aston, Birmingham and Univ. of Liverpool; Man. Dir IMI Range Ltd 1973–77; Dir IMI PLC 1978–, Man. Dir and CEO 1986–2001, Chair. 2001–04; Dir (non-exec.) NV Bekaert SA, Belgium 1987–, Nat. Exhbn Centre Ltd 1989–, Marley PLC 1989–97 (Deputy Chair. 1993–97), Birmingham European Airways Ltd 1989–91, The London Stock Exchange PLC (Sr Dir) 1994–, Temple Bar Investment Trust PLC 2001; Chair. Optilon Ltd 1979–84, Eley Ltd 1981–85; mem. Nat. Council CBI 1986–99; mem. Council, Birmingham Chamber of Industry and Commerce 1983–98, Pres. 1991–92, mem. Bd 1994–96; mem. Council Univ. of Birmingham 1985–90 and Hon. Life mem. Court 1984–; mem. Bd Birmingham Royal Ballet 1993–2004; Pres. Midlands Club Cricket Conf. 1995–96; mem. Council Lord's Taverners 1992–2001; Pres. West Midlands Regional Cttee, Lord's Taverners 1994–; Trustee The Lord's Taverners 1995–2001; Trustee Industry in Educ. 1998–2004; Chair. Birmingham Children's Hosp. Appeal 1995–2000; High Sheriff W Midlands 2002; Order of Leopold II (Belgium) 2002; Hon. DSc (Birmingham) 2003. *Leisure interests:* sport, reading, gardening. *Address:* London Stock Exchange, 10 Paternoster Square, London, EC4 M7LS, England (office).

ALLEN, Sir Geoffrey, Kt, PhD, FRS, FRSC, FREng, FInstP, FPRI, FIM; British polymer scientist and university administrator; b. 29 Oct. 1928, Clay Cross, Derbyshire; s. of John James Allen and Marjorie Allen; m. Valerie Frances Duckworth 1972; one d.; ed Clay Cross Tupton Hall Grammar School, Univ. of Leeds; Postdoctoral Fellow, Nat. Research Council, Canada 1952–54; Lecturer, Univ. of Manchester 1955–65, Prof. of Chemical Physics 1965–75; Prof. of Polymer Science, Imperial Coll. of Science and Tech., Univ. of London 1975–76, Prof. of Chemical Tech. 1976–81; Fellow Imperial Coll. 1986, UMIST 1994; Adviser Kobe Steel Ltd 1990–2005; Chair. Science Research Council 1977–81; Head of Research, Unilever PLC 1981–90, Dir of Unilever responsible for Research and Eng 1982–90; Dir (non-exec.) Courtaulds 1987–93; Pres. PRI, SCI 1990–92; mem. Nat. Consumer Council 1993–96; Vice-Pres. Royal Soc. 1991–93; Chancellor Univ. of E Anglia 1994–2003; mem. Royal Comm. on Environmental Protection 1994–2000; Pres. Inst. of Materials 1994–95; Visiting Fellow, Robinson Coll., Cambridge 1980–; Hon. FCGI; Hon. FIM; Hon. FIChemE; Hon. MSc (Manchester); Hon. DSc (Durham, E Anglia) 1984, (Bath, Bradford, Keele, Loughborough) 1985, (Essex, Leeds) 1986, (Cranfield) 1988, (Surrey) 1989, (N London) 1999; Dr hc (Open Univ.). *Leisure interests:* opera, walking, talking. *Address:* 18 Oxford House, 52 Parkside, London, SW19 5NE, England (home). *Telephone:* (20) 8947-7459 (home). *Fax:* (20) 8879-1959 (home). *E-mail:* sirgeoffrey@virgin.net.

ALLEN, George; American business executive and fmr politician; *Reagan Ranch Presidential Scholar, Young America's Foundation;* m. Susan Allen (née Brown); three c.; mem. Va House of Dels 1982–90; mem. US House of Reps, Washington, DC 1991–94; Gov. of Va 1994–98; Senator from Va 2000–07, fmr mem. Commerce, Science and Transportation Cttee, Foreign Relations Cttee, Chair. Sub-Cttee on European Affairs; Reagan Ranch Presidential Scholar, Young America's Foundation 2007–; mem. 'Small b'

Business Cttee; Head, McguireWoods' Business Expansion and Relocation Team, Va; Republican; Jefferson Scholar, American Legis. Exchange Council 1998. *Address:* c/o Young America's Foundation National Headquarters, F.M. Kirby Freedom Center, 110 Elden Street, Herndon, VA 20170, USA.

ALLEN, Dame Ingrid Victoria, DBE, DL, MD, DSc, FRCPath, FMedSci, MRIA; British professor of neuropathology; *Professor Emerita, Queen's University Belfast;* b. 30 July 1932, Belfast; d. of Robert Allen and Doris V. Allen (née Shaw); m. 1st Alan Watson Barnes 1972 (died 1987); m. 2nd John Thompson 1996; ed Ashleigh House School, Belfast, Cheltenham Ladies Coll., Queen's Univ. Belfast; House Officer Royal Victoria Hosp. (RVH), Belfast 1957–58, Sr Registrar 1964–65; Musgrave Research Fellow, Tutor in Pathology, Calvert Research Fellow, Queen's Univ. Belfast (QUB) 1958–64; Sr Lecturer and Consultant in Neuropathology, QUB/RVH 1966–78, Reader and Consultant 1978–79, Prof. Emer. 1997–; Head NI Regional Neuropathology Service 1979–97; mem. MRC 1988–94; Dir for Research and Devt Health and Personal Social Services, NI 1997–2001; Visiting Prof. Univ. of Ulster 1997–; Vice-Pres. Int. Soc. of Neuropathology 1988–92; Fellow Royal Coll. of Pathologists, Vice-Pres. 1993–96; mem. Cttee on Women in Science and Tech., Office of Public Service and Science; mem. numerous editorial bds; Hon. Fellow Int. Soc. of Neuropathology 1997. *Publications:* Greenfield's Neuropathology 1984, McAlpine's Multiple Sclerosis (contrib.) 1990; numerous articles in learned journals on neuropathology, demyelinating diseases, neurovirology, neuro-oncology and biomedical research and devt. *Leisure interests:* reading, sailing, escaping to an island off the NW coast of Ireland. *Address:* Room 113, School of Biology and Biochemistry, Medical Biology Centre, Queen's University Belfast, 97 Lisburn Road, Belfast, BT9 7BL, Northern Ireland (office); 95 Malone Road, Belfast, BT9 6SP, Northern Ireland (home). *Telephone:* (28) 9027-2116 (office); (28) 9066-6662 (home). *Fax:* (28) 9023-6505; (28) 9033-5877 (office). *E-mail:* i.allen@qub.ac.uk (office); ingrid.allen@btinternet.com (home). *Website:* www.qub.ac.uk (office).

ALLEN, John Robert Lawrence, DSc, FRS, FGS, FSA; British geologist, sedimentologist and academic; *Professor Emeritus, University of Reading;* b. 25 Oct. 1932; s. of George Eustace Allen and Alice Josephine (née Formby); m. Jean Mary Wood 1960; four s. one d.; ed St Philip's Grammar School, Birmingham, Univ. of Sheffield; mem. staff, Univ. of Reading 1959–, Prof. of Geology 1972–89, of Sedimentology 1989–93, apptd. Research Prof. Postgrad. Research Inst. for Sedimentology 1993, now Prof. Emer., Visiting Prof. in Archaeology; Assoc. mem. Royal Belgian Acad. of Sciences; Hon. LLD; Lyell Medal, Geological Soc. 1980, David Linton Award, British Geomorphological Research Group 1983, Twenhofel Medal, Soc. of Econ. Paleontologists and Minerologists 1987, G.K. Warren Prize, NAS, USA 1990, Sorby Medal, Int. Asscn of Sedimentologists 1994, Penrose Medal, Geological Soc. of America 1996. *Publications:* Current Ripples 1968, Physical Processes of Sedimentation 1970, Sedimentary Structures 1982, Principles of Physical Sedimentology 1985; numerous contribs. to professional journals. *Leisure interests:* cooking, music, opera, pottery, walking. *Address:* 17C Whiteknights Road, Reading, Berks., RG6 7BY, England. *Telephone:* (118) 926-4621.

ALLEN, John Walter, MA, FRSE; British physicist and academic; *Professor Emeritus of Solid State Physics, University of St. Andrews;* b. 7 March 1928, Birmingham; s. of Walter Allen and Beryl Parsons; m. 1st Mavis Williamson 1956 (died 1972); m. 2nd Hania Szawelska 1981; one s.; ed King Edward's School, Birmingham and Sidney Sussex Coll., Cambridge; RAF Educ. Br. 1949–51; staff scientist, Ericsson Telephones, Nottingham 1951–56; Royal Naval Scientific Service, Services Electronics Research Lab. 1956–68; Visiting Prof. Stanford Univ. 1964–66; Tullis Russell Fellow, Univ. of St Andrew's 1968–72, Reader in Physics, Dir of Wolfson Inst. of Luminescence 1972–81, Prof. of Solid State Physics 1980–93, Prof. Emer. 1993–. *Publications:* some 120 papers in scientific journals including the first account of a practical light-emitting diode 1962. *Leisure interests:* archaeology, traditional dance. *Address:* School of Physics and Astronomy, University of St Andrews, North Haugh, St Andrews, Fife, KY16 9SS (office); 2 Dempster Terrace, St Andrews, Fife, KY16 9QQ, Scotland (home). *Telephone:* (1334) 463331 (office); (1334) 474163 (home). *Fax:* (1334) 463104 (office). *E-mail:* jwa@st-and.ac.uk (office). *Website:* www.st-andrews.ac.uk/~www_pa (office).

ALLEN, Gen. Lew, Jr, MS, PhD; American air force officer (retd); b. 30 Sept. 1925, Miami; s. of the late Lew Allen and Zella Holman; m. Barbara McKelden Frink 1949; two s. three d.; ed Gainesville Junior Coll., US Mil. Acad. West Point, Air Tactical School, Tyndall, Univ. of Illinois; Pilot, Carswell Air Force Base, Tex. 1946–50; Physicist, Los Alamos Scientific Laboratory, NM 1954–57; various posts Kirkland Air Force Base, NM 1957–61; Space Tech. Office and OSD, Washington, DC 1961–65; OSAF, Los Angeles, Calif. 1965–68, 1970–71, OSAF Washington, DC 1968–70; SAMSO, Los Angeles, Calif. 1971–73; c/s, HQ AFSC, Andrews Air Force Base, Md 1973; Deputy to Dir of Cen. Intelligence for the Intelligence Community 1973; Dir NSA and Chief of Cen. Security Service, Fort Meade, Md 1973–77; Commdr, AFSC, Andrews Air Force Base 1977–78; Vice-Chief of Staff USAF April–June 1978, Chief of Staff USAF 1978–82 (retd); Dir Jet Propulsion Lab., Pasadena, Calif. 1982–90; Chair. Draper Lab., Boston 1991–95; mem. Nat. Acad. of Eng 1977–; Defense Distinguished Service Medal, Distinguished Service Medal of the Air Force, Legion of Merit with Two Oak Leaf Clusters, Jt Service Commendation and various other US awards and medals, Order of Nat. Security (Repub. of Korea). *Leisure interests:* racquet ball, scuba diving, jogging. *Address:* c/o Draper Charles Stark Laboratory Inc., 555 Technology Square, Cambridge, MA 02139, USA.

ALLEN, Patrick Linton, CD, PhD; Jamaican school administrator, ecclesiastic and government official; *Governor-General;* b. 7 Feb. 1951, Portland; s. of Ferdinand Allen and Christina Allen; m.; three c.; ed Andrews Univ., USA; Prin. Robins Bay Primary School 1976–78, Hillside Primary School 1978–80;

ordained Seventh Day Adventist pastor 1989; Asst Registrar, Andrews Univ. 1996–98; Pres. Cen. Jamaica Conf. of Seventh Day Adventists 1998–2000, West Indies Union of Seventh Day Adventists 2000–; Gov.-Gen. of Jamaica 2009–; Chair. Bd of Govs Andrews Memorial Hosp., Adventist Devt and Relief Agency, Book and Nutrition Centre Ltd, West Indies Union Investment Man. Ltd. *Address:* Office of the Governor-General, King's House, Hope Road, Kingston 10, Jamaica (office). *Telephone:* 927-6424 (office). *Fax:* 978-6025 (office). *E-mail:* kingshouse@kingshouse.gov.jm (office). *Website:* www.kingshousejamaica.gov.jm (office).

ALLEN, Paul Gardner; American business executive; *Chairman, Vulcan Inc.;* b. 21 Jan. 1953, Seattle, Wash.; ed Lakeside School, Seattle, Wash. State Univ.; co-f. (with Bill Gates) Microsoft Corpn 1975, Gen. Pnr 1975—1977, Vice-Pres. 1977—1981, Exec. Vice-Pres. Research and New Product Devt 1981—1983, (developed Hodgkins Disease and left co.), Sr Strategy Advisor, 2000–; f. Asymetrix Corpn 1985, Starwave Corpn 1992; acquired Marcus Cable 1998, Hollywood Entertainment 1998; founder, Chair. Intervas Research; owner and Chair. Bd Portland (Ore.) Trail Blazers professional basketball team 1988–, Seattle Seahawks professional football team; f. Allen Inst. of Brain Science 2003; sponsor SpaceShipOne private rocket plane venture 2003; f. Experience Music Project, Seattle; Dir Egghead Discount Software 1983–2000, Darwin Molecular Inc.; fmrly owner, Chair., Dir Ticketmaster Holdings Group; founder and Chair. Vulcan Northwest (now Vulcan Inc.) (holding co.) 1987–; f. Paul G. Allen Family Foundation; Life-Time Achievement Award from PC Magazine; inducted into Computer Museum Hall of Fame. *Address:* Vulcan, Inc., 505 5th Avenue, South, Suite 900, Seattle, WA 98104, USA (office). *Telephone:* (206) 342-2000 (office). *Fax:* (206) 342-3000 (office). *Website:* www.vulcan.com (office).

ALLEN, Percival, PhD, FRS; British geologist; b. 15 March 1917, Brede, Sussex; s. of the late Norman Williams Allen and Mildred Kathleen Allen (née Hoad); m. Frances Margaret Hepworth 1941; three s. one d.; ed Rye Grammar School, Univ. of Reading; served in RAF 1941–42; Asst Lecturer, Univ. of Reading 1945–46, Prof. of Geology 1952–82, Prof. Emer. of Geology 1982–; Univ. Demonstrator, Univ. of Cambridge 1946–47, Lecturer 1947–52; Sec. Philpots Quarry Ltd; Dean of Science Faculty, Univ. of Reading 1963–66; Visiting Prof., Univ. of Kuwait 1970; a Vice-Pres. Royal Soc. 1977–79; Pres. Geological Soc. 1978–80; Adviser UNDP Nile Delta Project 1972–75; Geology Consultant, India, for UNESCO/UNDP 1976–77; Algerian Sahara Glacials Expedition 1970; Tibet Geotraverse Follow-up 1986; Chair. Int. Confs Organizing Cttees of Seventh Int. Sedimentology Congress 1967, First European Earth and Planetary Physics Colloquium 1971, First Meeting European Geological Socs 1975; Sec.-Gen. Int. Assoc. of Sedimentologists 1967–71; Chair. Royal Soc. Expeditions Cttee 1974–; Royal Soc. Assessor to NERC 1977–80; Chair. Royal Soc., British Nat. Cttee for Geology 1982–90, British Inst. for Geological Conservation 1987–90; UK Corresp. IGCP Project 245, 1986–91; UK Del. to Int. Union of Geological Sciences, Moscow 1984; Hon. mem. Bulgarian Geological Soc., Geological Asscn, Soc. Econ. Palaeontologists and Mineralogists, Int. Asscn of Sedimentologists; Council mem. Natural Environment Research Council 1971–74; Foreign Fellow, Indian Natural Sciences Acad.; Lyell Medal, Geological Soc. of London 1971. *Publications:* Papers on Purbeck-Wealden (Lower Cretaceous) and Torridonian (Proterozoic) sedimentology in various scientific journals from 1938 onwards. *Leisure interests:* chess, natural history, gardening, bicycling. *Address:* Orchard End, Hazeley Bottom, Hartley Wintney, Hook, Hants., RG27 8LU, England. *Telephone:* (1252) 842229 (home). *Fax:* (1734) 310279.

ALLEN, Richard V.; American academic, international business consultant and fmr government official; *Senior Counselor, APCO Worldwide Inc.;* b. 1 Jan. 1936, Collingswood, NJ; s. of C. Carroll Allen, Sr and Magdalen Buchman; m. Patricia Ann Mason 1957; three s. four d.; ed Notre Dame Univ. and Univ. of Munich; helped found Cen. for Strategic and Int. Studies, Georgetown Univ. 1962; Consultant and fmr Prof., Hoover Inst., Stanford Univ.; with Nat. Security Council 1968–69; mem. Ronald Reagan's staff, campaigns 1976, Bd Govs Ronald Reagan Presidential Foundation 1985; Pres. Richard V. Allen Co., Washington 1982–90, Chair. 1991–; Head Nat. Security Council and Nat. Security Adviser 1981–82; Chair. Fed. Capital Bank 1987; Sr Council for Foreign Policy and Nat. Security Affairs, Repub. Nat. Cttee 1982–88; mem. Bd of Dirs Xsirius Inc. 1991–92; Distinguished Fellow and Chair. Asian Studies Center, The Heritage Foundation 1982; Chair. German-American Tricentenial Foundation 1983; Founding mem. US Nat. Cttee for Pacific Basin 1984; Sr Fellow, Hoover Inst. 1983–; mem. Advisory Bd Catholic Campaign for America 1993–, Nixon Center, Center for Strategic and Int. Studies; mem. Republican Congressional Policy Advisory Bd 1998–, Nat. Security Advisory Group, Defense Policy Bd, Council for Foreign Relations; currently Sr Counselor, APCO Worldwide Inc. (consulting firm), Washington, DC; Order of Diplomatic Merit Ganghwa (Repub. of Korea) 1982; Kt Commdr's Cross (FRG) 1983; Order of Brilliant Star (Repub. of China) 1986; Sovereign Mil. Order of Kts of Malta 1987; hon. degrees (Hanover Coll.) 1981, (Korea Univ.) 1982, Pepperdine Univ. *Publications:* numerous books on political and economic affairs including Peace or Peaceful Coexistence 1966, Communism and Democracy: Theory and Action 1967. *Address:* APCO Worldwide, 1615 L Street, Suite 900, NW, Washington, DC 20036-5623, USA (office). *Telephone:* (202) 778-1000 (office). *Fax:* (202) 466-6002 (office). *E-mail:* information@apcoworldwide.com (office). *Website:* www.apcoworldwide.com (office).

ALLEN, Sharon; American business executive; *Chairman, Deloitte & Touche USA LLP;* fmrly in charge of Portland office, Deloitte & Touche USA LLP, later mem. Bd of Dirs Deloitte & Touche USA LLP and Man. Partner, Deloitte US Firms' Pacific Southwest practice, Los Angeles, currently Chair. (first woman) Deloitte & Touche USA LLP, has served on Client Service Standards Task Force, Partner Admissions Cttee and in many other cttee capacities; mem. Bd of Dirs Los Angeles Area Chamber of Commerce, United Way of Greater Los Angeles, Ind. Colls of Southern Calif., YMCA of Metropolitan Los Angeles; numerous awards for business and community leadership, ranked by Forbes Magazine amongst the 100 Most Powerful Women (96th) 2006, (64th) 2007, (94th) 2008. *Address:* Deloitte & Touche USA LLP, 1633 Broadway, New York, NY 10019-6754, USA (office). *Telephone:* (212) 489-1600 (office). *Fax:* (212) 489-1687 (office). *Website:* www.us.deloitte.com (office); www.deloitte.com (office).

ALLÉN, Sture, DPhil; Swedish professor of linguistics; b. 1928, Göteborg; s. of Bror G. Allén and Hanna Johanson; m. Solveig Janson 1954; three c.; ed Univ. of Göteborg; Asst Prof. of Scandinavian Philology, Göteborg Univ. 1965–70, Prof. of Computational Linguistics 1979–93, Pro-Rector 1980–86, Rector 1982; Assoc. Prof. of Computational Linguistics, Swedish Humanistic Research Council 1970–72, Prof. 1972–79; Perm. Sec. Swedish Acad. 1986–99; mem. Swedish Acad., Royal Soc. of Arts and Sciences of Göteborg, Royal Swedish Acad. of Letters, History and Antiquities, Academia Europaea, Royal Swedish Acad. of Eng. Sciences, Norwegian Acad. of Sciences and Letters, Finnish Soc. of Science and Letters; Corresp. mem. Icelandic Soc. of Sciences; mem. Bd of Dirs Nobel Foundation 1987–99; Hon. mem. Soc. of Swedish Literature in Finland; Medal of King of Sweden in the Ribbon of the Order of Seraphim for Eminent Scientific and Cultural Achievements 1987, Kt Commdr, Order of the White Rose (Finland) 1994, Kt, Order of the Falcon (Iceland) 2007; Dr hc (Swedish Univ. of Åbo) 1988; several awards including Gothenburg City Medal (Gold) 1994, Chester Carlson Research Prize 1988, Margit Påhlson Prize 2000, Chalmers Tech. Univ. Medal 2002. *Radio:* From a Linguistic Point of View (series). *Television:* In Plain Swedish (series). *Publications:* author and co-author of numerous textbooks, dictionaries, glossaries, etc. *Leisure interests:* music, sports. *Address:* Swedish Academy, PO Box 2118, 10313 Stockholm; c/o Språkdata Group, Department of Swedish, Göteborg University, PO Box 200, 40530 Göteborg, Sweden. *Telephone:* (31) 556102 (home). *Fax:* (31) 551890 (home). *E-mail:* sture.allen@svenskaakademien.se (home).

ALLEN, Sir Thomas Boaz, Kt, FRCM; British singer (baritone); b. 10 Sept. 1944, Seaham Harbour, Co. Durham; s. of Thomas Boaz Allen and Florence Allen; m. 1st Margaret Holley 1968 (divorced 1986); one s.; m. 2nd Jeannie Gordon Lascelles 1988; one step-s. one step-d.; ed Robert Richardson Grammar School, Ryhope, Royal Coll. of Music, London; Prin. Baritone, Welsh Nat. Opera 1969–72, Royal Opera House, Covent Garden 1972–78; freelance opera singer 1978–, singing at Glyndebourne Opera 1973, ENO, London Coliseum 1986, La Scala 1987, Chicago Lyric Opera 1990, Royal Albert Hall 2000, London Proms 2002, Royal Opera House, Covent Garden 2003, Metropolitan Opera, New York 2005; Dir Così fan tutte, Samling Opera, The Sage, Gateshead 2005; Prince Consort Prof., Royal Coll. of Music 1994; Hambro Visiting Prof. of Opera, Univ. of Oxford 2000–01, currently Fellow, Jesus Coll.; Pres. British Youth Opera 2000–; Hon. FRAM; Hon. Fellow, Univ. of Sunderland; Hon. MA (Newcastle) 1984; Hon. DMus (Durham) 1988, (Birmingham) 2004; Queen's Prize 1967, Gulbenkian Fellow 1968, Royal Philharmonic Soc. BBC Radio 3 Listeners' Award 2004. *Performances include:* Die Zauberflöte 1973, Le Nozze di Figaro 1974, Così fan Tutte 1975, Don Giovanni 1977, The Cunning Little Vixen 1977 and Simon Boccanegra, Billy Budd, La Bohème, L'Elisir d'Amore, Faust, Albert Herring, Die Fledermaus, La Traviata, A Midsummer Night's Dream, Die Meistersinger von Nürnberg; as producer Albert Herring 2002. *Film:* Mrs Henderson Presents 2005. *Publication:* Foreign Parts: A Singer's Journal 1993. *Leisure interests:* painting, drawing, ornithology, golf, fishing. *Address:* Askonas Holt Ltd, Lincoln House, 300 High Holborn, London, WC1V 7JH, England (office). *Telephone:* (20) 7400-1700 (office). *Fax:* (20) 7400-1799 (office). *E-mail:* info@askonasholt.co.uk (office). *Website:* www.askonasholt.co.uk (office).

ALLEN, Tim; American actor and comedian; b. (Timothy Allen Dick), 13 June 1953, Denver; m. 1st Laura Diebel (divorced); one d.; m. 2nd Jane Hadjuk 2006; ed Western Mich. Univ., Univ. of Detroit; fmr creative dir for advertising agency, Detroit; debut as comedian on Showtime Comedy Club All Stars 1988; Favorite Comedy Actor, People's Choice Award 1995, 1997–99. *TV includes:* Home Improvement (series) 1991–99, Tim Allen: Men Are Pigs 1990, Tim Allen Rewrites America (specials), Showtime Comedy Club All-Stars II 1988, Jimmy Neutron: Win, Lose and Kaboom (voice) 2004. *Films include:* Comedy's Dirtiest Dozen, The Santa Clause 1994, Toy Story (voice) 1995, Meet Wally Sparks 1997, Jungle 2 Jungle 1997, For Richer or Poorer 1997, Galaxy Quest 1999, Toy Story 2 (voice) 2000, Buzz Lightyear of Star Command: The Adventure Begins 2000, Who is Cletis Tout? 2001, Joe Somebody 2001, Big Trouble 2002, The Santa Clause 2 2002, Christmas with the Kranks 2004, The Shaggy Dog 2006, Zoom 2006, The Santa Clause 3: The Escape Clause 2006, Wild Hogs 2007, Redbelt 2007. *Publications:* Don't Stand Too Close to a Naked Man 1994, I'm Not Really Here 1996. *Address:* c/o Messina Baker Entertainment, 955 Carrillo Drive, Suite 100, Los Angeles, CA 90048, USA. *Telephone:* (323) 954-8600.

ALLEN, Woody; American actor, writer, producer and director; b. (Allen Stewart Konigsberg), 1 Dec. 1935, Brooklyn, NY; s. of the late Martin Konigsberg and of Nettie Konigsberg (née Cherry); m. 1st Harlene Rosen (divorced); m. 2nd Louise Lasser 1966 (divorced 1969); m. 3rd Soon-Yi Previn 1997; two adopted d.; one s. with Mia Farrow (q.v.); ed City Coll. of New York and New York Univ.; made his debut as a performer in 1961 at the Duplex in Greenwich Village; has performed in a variety of nightclubs across the USA; produced the play Don't Drink the Water, Morosco Theater 1966, Broadhurst Theatre 1969; made his Broadway debut as Allan Felix in Play it Again, Sam, which he also wrote; during the 1950s wrote for TV performers Herb Shriner 1953, Sid Caesar 1957, Art Carney 1958–59, Jack Paar and Carol Channing, also wrote for the Tonight Show and the Gary Moore Show; Dr hc (Universitat Pompeu Fabra, Spain) 2007; D.W. Griffith Award 1996, San Sebastian Film

Festival Donostia Prize 2004. *Films include:* What's New Pussycat? 1965, Casino Royale 1967, What's Up, Tiger Lily? 1967, Take the Money and Run 1969, Bananas 1971, Everything You Always Wanted to Know About Sex 1972, Play it Again, Sam 1972, Sleeper 1973, Love and Death 1976, The Front 1976, Annie Hall (Academy Awards for Best Dir and Best Writer) 1977, Interiors 1978, Manhattan 1979, Stardust Memories 1980, A Midsummer Night's Sex Comedy 1982, Zelig 1983, Broadway Danny Rose 1984, The Purple Rose of Cairo 1985, Hannah and Her Sisters 1985, Radio Days 1987, September 1987, Another Woman 1988, Oedipus Wrecks 1989, Crimes and Misdemeanors 1989, Alice 1990, Scenes from a Mall, Shadows and Fog 1991, Husbands and Wives 1992, Manhattan Murder Mystery 1993, Bullets Over Broadway 1995, Mighty Aphrodite 1995, Everybody Says I Love You 1996, Deconstructing Harry 1997, Celebrity 1998, Antz (voice only) 1998, Wild Man Blues 1998, Stuck on You 1998, Company Men 1999, Sweet and Lowdown 1999, Small Town Crooks 2000, The Curse of the Jade Scorpion 2001, Hail Sid Caesar! 2001, Hollywood Ending 2002, Anything Else 2003, Melinda and Melinda 2004, Match Point 2005, Scoop 2006, Cassandra's Dream 2007, Vicky Cristina Barcelona 2008. *Television:* Sounds from a Town I Love 2001. *Plays written include:* Don't Drink the Water 1966, The Floating Lightbulb 1981, Death Defying Acts (one act) 1995. *Opera:* as producer: Gianni Schicchi, Los Angeles Opera 2008. *Publications:* Getting Even 1971, Without Feathers 1975, Side Effects 1980, The Complete Prose 1994, Telling Tales (contrib. to charity anthology) 2004, Mere Anarchy 2007, The Insanity Defense 2007; contribs to Playboy and New Yorker. *Leisure interests:* chocolate milk shakes, poker, chess, baseball; also a noted clarinettist. *Address:* 930 Fifth Avenue, New York, NY 10021, USA.

ALLENDE, Isabel; Chilean (b. Peruvian) writer; b. 2 Aug. 1942, Lima, Peru; d. of Tomás Allende and Francisca Llona Barros; m. 1st Miguel Frias 1962; one s. one d.; m. 2nd William Gordon 1988; journalist, Paula women's magazine 1967–74, Mampato children's magazine 1969–74, TV shows and film documentaries 1970–74, El Nacional newspaper, Caracas, Venezuela 1975–84; taught literature at Montclair State Coll., NJ 1985, Univ. of Virginia, Charlottesville 1988, Univ. of California, Berkeley 1989; Goodwill Amb. for Hans Christian Andersen Bicentenary 2004; lecture tours in USA and Europe, speech tours in univs and cols, numerous literature workshops; mem. Academia de Artes y Ciencias, Puerto Rico 1995, Academia de la Lengua, Chile 1989, American Acad. of Arts and Letters 2004; Hon. Citizen of Austin, Tex. USA 1995; Hon. Prof. of Literature, Univ. of Chile 1991; Hon. mem. Acad. of Devt and Peace, Austria 2000; Chevalier, Ordre des Arts et Lettres 1994, Condecoracion Gabriela Mistral (Chile) 1994; Hon. DLitt (New York State Univ.) 1991, (Bates Coll., USA) 1994, (Dominican Coll., USA) 1994, (Columbia Coll., USA) 1996; Hon. DHumLitt (Florida Atlantic Univ.) 1996; Dr hc (Lawrence Univ., USA) 2000, (Mills Coll., USA) 2000, (Illinois Wesleyan Univ.) 2002; Best Novel of the Year (Chile) 1983, Panorama Literario Award (Chile) 1983, Author of the Year (Germany) 1984, Book of the Year (Germany) 1984, Grand Prix d'Evasion Award (France) 1984, Point de Mire Award, Belgian Radio and TV 1985, Quality Paperback Book Club New Voice (USA) 1986, Premio Literario Colima Award (Mexico) 1986, XV Premio Internazionale I Migliori Dell'Anno (Italy) 1987, Mulheres Best Foreign Novel Award (Portugal) 1987, Quimera Libros (Chile) 1987, Book of the Year (Switzerland) 1987, Library Journal's Best Book (USA) 1988, Before Columbus Foundation Award (USA) 1988, Best Novel (Mexico) 1985, Author of the Year (Germany) 1986, Freedom to Write Pen Club (USA) 1991, XLI Bancarella Literary Award (Italy) 1993, Ind. Foreign Fiction Award (UK) 1993, Brandeis Univ. Major Book Collection Award (USA) 1993, Marin Women's Hall of Fame (USA) 1994, Feminist of the Year Award, The Feminist Majority Foundation (USA) 1994, Read About Me Literary Award (USA) 1996, Critics' Choice Award (USA) 1996, Books to Remember Award, American Library Asscn 1996, Gift of HOPE Award, HOPE Educ. and Leadership Fund (USA) 1996, Harold Washington Literary Award, City of Chicago 1996, Malaparte Award, Amici di Capri (Italy) 1998, Donna Città Di Roma Literary Award, Italy 1998, Dorothy and Lillian Gish Prize (USA) 1998, Sara Lee Frontrunner Award (USA) 1998, GEMS Women of the Year Award (USA) 1999, Donna Dell'Anno 1999 Award (Italy) 1999, Books to Remember, The New York Public Library WILLA Literary Award 2000, Excellence in Int. Literature and Arts Award (USA) 2002, The Celebration of Books Amb. Award (USA) 2002, Int. Women's Forum Award (Mexico) 2002, Nopal Award, Cal Poly Pomona (USA) 2003, Cyril Magnin Lifetime Achievement Award (USA) 2003, Premios Iberoamericano de Letrasjose Donoso (Chile) 2003, Premio Personalidad Distinguida, Universdidad del Pacifico (Chile) 2004, Commonwealth Award of Distinguished Service for Literature (USA) 2004. *Plays:* El Embajador 1971, La balada del medio pelo 1973, Los siete espejos 1974. *Publications:* La casa de los espíritus (novel, trans. as The House of the Spirits) 1982, La gorda de porcelana (juvenile short stories) 1983, De amor y de sombra (novel, trans. as Of Love and Shadows) 1984, Cuentos de Eva Luna (short stories, trans. as Stories of Eva Luna) 1989, El plan infinito (novel, trans. as The Infinite Plan) 1991, Paula (memoir) 1994, Afrodita (trans. as Aphrodite) 1998, Hija de la fortuna (novel, trans. as Daughter of Fortune) 1999, Retrato en sepia (novel, trans. as Portrait in Sepia) 2000, La ciudad de las bestias (juvenile novel, trans. as City of the Beasts) 2002, Mi país inventado (memoir, trans. as My Invented Country) (Latino Literacy Now Award for Best Biography 2004) 2003, El reino del dragón de oro (juvenile novel, trans. as Kingdom of the Golden Dragon) (Latino Literacy Now Award for Best Young Adult Fiction 2004) 2003, El Zorro (novel) 2005, El Bosque de los Pigmeos (juvenile novel, trans. as Forest of the Pygmies) 2005, Inés del alma mía (novel, trans. as Inés of My Soul) 2006, La Suma de los Días (memoirs, trans. as The Sum of Our Days) 2007. *Address:* Carmen Balcells, Diagonal 580, Barcelona 21, Spain (office); 116 Caledonia Street, Sausalito, CA 94965, USA. *Fax:* (415) 332-4149. *Website:* www.isabelallende.com.

ALLENDE, Jorge Eduardo, PhD; Chilean biochemist, molecular biologist and academic; *Professor of Biochemistry and Molecular Biology, University of Chile;* b. 11 Nov. 1934, Cartago, Costa Rica; s. of Octavio Allende and Amparo Rivera; m. Catherine C. Connelly 1961; three s. one d.; ed Louisiana State and Yale Univs, USA; Research Assoc., Lab. of Prof. Fritz Lipmann at Rockefeller Univ. 1961–62; Asst Prof., Dept of Biochemistry, Univ. of Chile 1963–68, Assoc. Prof. 1968–71, Prof. of Biochemistry and Molecular Biology 1972–; Pres. Pan American Asscn of Biochemical Socs 1976; mem. Exec. Cttee Int. Union of Biochemistry 1982–91, Int. Cell Research Org. 1976–; mem. Exec. Bd Int. Council of Scientific Unions 1986–90; Regional Co-ordinator Latin American Network of Biological Sciences 1975–97; mem. UNESCO Int. Scientific Advisory Bd 1996–; Chair. Advisory Comm. on Health Research, Pan-American Health Org. 1999–2003; Co-ordinator Science Educ. Program, Inter-Academy Panel; Foreign Assoc. Inst. of Medicine, NAS 1992, NAS 2001–; Fogarty Scholar-in-Residence NIH, USA; Founder-mem. Latin American Acad. of Sciences; mem. Chilean Acad. of Sciences, Pres. 1991–94; Fellow, Third World Acad. of Sciences, Vice-Pres. 2004–06; Hon. mem. Chilean Acad. of Medicine; Grand Cross of Scientific Merit (Pres. of Brazil) 2002; Dr hc (Buenos Aires) 1993; Chilean Nat. Prize in Natural Sciences 1992. *Publications:* more than 140 research articles in learned journals, 25 articles on science policy and science educ. *Leisure interests:* music, reading, swimming. *Address:* Program de Biol. Cel. y Mol., Inst. Cs. Biomed., Facultad de Medicina, Universidad de Chile, Casilla 70086, Santiago 7, Chile (office). *Telephone:* (2) 678-6255 (office). *Fax:* (2) 737-6320 (office). *E-mail:* jallende@ abello.dic.uchile.cl (office).

ALLERT, Richard (Rick) H., AM; Australian financial executive; *Chairman, Coles Group Ltd;* ed Kings Coll., Adelaide; with Carroll Winter & Co. Chartered Accountants 1959–60; joined Peat Marwick Mitchell & Co. 1960, Pnr 1973–79; Sr Pnr, Allert Heard & Co. Chartered Accountants 1979–89; apptd Dir Coles Myer Ltd (renamed Coles Group Ltd 2006) 1995, Chair. 2002–; Chair. AXA Asia Pacific Holdings Ltd, AustralAsia Railway Corpn, Voyages Hotels & Resorts Pty Ltd; Chair. Tourism Australia 2007–; Dir Australian Business Arts Foundation; fmr mem. Review of Business Taxation (Ralph Cttee); Fellow, Inst. of Chartered Accountants (Australia); Hon. DUniv (Univ. of S Australia) 2000. *Address:* Coles Group Ltd, 800 Toorak Road, Tooronga, Vic. 3146, Australia (office). *Telephone:* (3) 9829-3111 (office). *Fax:* (3) 9829-6787 (office). *Website:* www.colesgroup.com.au (office).

ALLEY, Kirstie; American actress; b. 12 Jan. 1951, Wichita, Kan.; m. Parker Stevenson; one s. one d.; ed Univ. of Kan.; People's Choice Award 1998. *Films:* Star Trek II, The Wrath of Khan 1982, One More Chance, Blind Date, Champions 1983, Runaway 1984, Summer School 1987, Look Who's Talking Too 1990, Madhouse 1990, Look Who's Talking Now 1993, David's Mother (TV film) 1994, Village of the Damned 1995, It Takes Two 1995, Sticks and Stones 1996, Nevada 1996, For Richer or Poorer 1997, Deconstructing Harry 1997, Toothless 1997, Drop Dead Gorgeous 1999, The Mao Game 1999, Back By Midnight 2002. *Stage appearances include:* Cat on a Hot Tin Roof, Answers. *Television includes:* Cheers 1987–93, Veronica's Closet 1997, Blonde 2001, Salem Witch Trials (mini-series) 2002, Profoundly Normal 2003, Family Sins 2003, While I Was Gone 2004, Fat Actress (series) 2005, The Minister of Divine 2007, Write & Wrong 2007 and numerous other TV films and series. *Address:* William Morris Agency, 1 William Morris Place, Beverly Hills, CA 90212; Jason Weinberg and Associates, 122 East 25th Street, 2nd Floor, New York, NY 10010, USA.

ALLEYNE, Sir George, Kt, MD, FRCP; Barbadian physician; *Special Envoy of the Secretary-General for HIV/AIDS in the Caribbean, United Nations;* b. 7 Oct. 1932, Barbados; s. of Clinton Alleyne and Eileen Alleyne (née Gaskin); m. Sylvan I. Chen 1958; two s. one d.; ed Harrison Coll., Univ. of the West Indies; Sr Resident, Univ. Hosp. of the W Indies 1963; Research Fellow, Tropical Metabolism Research Unit, Jamaica 1964–72. Prof. of Medicine, Univ. of the W Indies 1972–81, Chair. Dept of Medicine 1976–81; Head Research Unit, Pan American Health Org. 1981–83, Dir Health Programmes 1982–90, Asst Dir 1990–95, Dir 1995–2003, Dir Emer. 2003–; Special Envoy of the UN Sec.-Gen. for HIV/AIDS in the Caribbean 2003–; Chancellor Univ. of the West Indies 2003–; Order of the Caribbean Community 2001; Hon. DSc (Univ. of the W Indies) 1988. *Publications include:* The Importance of Health: A Caribbean Perspective 1989, Public Health for All 1991, Health and Tourism 1992; over 100 articles in major scientific research journals. *Leisure interests:* gardening, reading. *Address:* Pan American Health Organization, 525 23rd Street, NW, Washington, DC 20037, USA (office); Special Envoy of the UN Secretary-General for HIV/AIDS in the Caribbean, UNAIDS, 20 avenue Appia, 1211 Geneva 27, Switzerland (office). *Telephone:* (202) 974-3057 (Washington) (office). *Fax:* (202) 974-3677 (Washington) (office).

ALLFORD, Simon, BA, DipArch, RIBA; British architect; *Partner, Allford Hall Monaghan Morris;* b. 27 July 1961, London; s. of the late David Allford and of Margaret Beryl Allford (née Roebuck); ed Hampstead Comprehensive School, Sheffield Univ., The Bartlett School of Architecture, Univ. Coll. London; with Nicholas Grimshaw 1983–85, BDP 1986–89; Pnr, Allford Hall Monaghan Morris 1989–; Lecturer, Univ. Coll. London 1987–; mem. Architectural Asscn Council 1996–, Hon. Sec. 1991–2001, Hon. Treas. 2001–; Vice-Pres. RIBA 2005–, Chair. RIBA Pres.'s Medals for Architecture; external examiner, visiting lecturer several UK and int. schools; judge various int. competitions; adviser to professional bodies; contrib. to TV and radio programmes; 13 RIBA Awards, BD Office of the Year Award, two Nat. Homebuilder Awards, Royal Fine Arts Comm. Award, five Housing Design Awards, five Civic Trust Awards, MIPIM Award, AIA Award. *Publications:* manual: The Architecture and Office of Allford Hall Monaghan Morris. *Leisure interests:* architecture, Sheffield Wednesday Football Club. *Address:* Allford Hall Monaghan Morris, 2nd Floor, Block C, Morelands, 5–23 Old Street, London EC1V 9HL (office);

232 Bickenhall Mansions, Bickenhall Street, London, W1U 6BW, England (home). *Telephone:* (20) 7251-5261 (office); (20) 7487-5391 (home). *Fax:* (20) 7251-5123 (office). *E-mail:* sallford@ahmm.co.uk (office). *Website:* www.ahmm.co.uk (office).

ALLI, Baron (Life Peer), cr. 1998, of Norbury in the London Borough of Croydon; **Waheed Alli;** British media executive; b. 16 Nov. 1964; ed Norbury Manor School; created Planet 24 Productions Ltd (fmrly 24 Hour Productions) with partner Charlie Parsons, Jt Man. Dir 1992–99; Man. Dir Carlton Productions 1998–2000; Dir Carlton TV 1998–2000; apptd Dir (non-exec.) Chorion 2002, Chair. (non-exec.) 2003–06; Dir Shine Ltd (now Exec. Dir), Castaway TV, Digital Radio Group Ltd, iPublic 2004–; Dir (non-exec.) SMG 2007–; Vice-Pres. UNICEF UK 2003–; Gov. LSE; mem. Teacher Training Agency 1997–98, Panel 2000, Creative Industry Taskforce; mem. Bd English Nat. Ballet 2001–; Chancellor, De Montfort Univ. 2006–; Pres. Croydon Youth Devt Trust. *Address:* House of Lords, London, SW1A 0PW; Shine Ltd, 140 Kensington Church Street, Notting Hill, London, W8 4BN, England (office). *Telephone:* (20) 7985-7000 (office). *Fax:* (20) 7985-7001 (office). *E-mail:* info@shinelimited.com (office). *Website:* www.shinelimited.com (office).

ALLIANCE, Baron (Life Peer), cr. 2004, of Manchester in the County of Greater Manchester; **David Alliance,** CBE, CBIM, FRSA; British business executive; *Chairman, N. Brown Group;* b. June 1932, Kashan, Iran; m. (divorced); three c.; first acquisition, Thomas Hoghton (Oswaldtwistle) 1956; acquired Spirella 1968, then Vantona Ltd, 1975 to form Vantona Group 1975; acquired Carrington Viyella to form Vantona Viyella 1983, Nottingham Mfg 1985, Coats Patons to form Coats Viyella 1986; Group Chief Exec. Coats Viyella 1975–90, Chair. 1989–99; Chair. N. Brown Group (mail order firm) 1968–, Tootal Group PLC 1991–99; Gov. Tel-Aviv Univ. 1989–; Fellow, Royal Soc. for the Encouragement of Arts, Mfrs and Commerce; Fellow, City and Guilds of London Inst.; mem. Prince's Youth Business Trust, Council for Industry and Higher Educ., Univ. of Manchester Foundation, Wiseman Inst.; mem. Liberal-Democrat Party; Hon. Fellow, UMIST, Shenkar Coll. of Textile Tech. and Fashion; Hon. FCGI 1991; Hon. LLD (Manchester) 1989, (Liverpool) 1996; Hon. DSc (Heriot-Watt) 1991;. *Address:* N. Brown Group, Griffin House, 40 Lever Street, Manchester, M60 6ES (office); House of Lords, Westminster, London, SW1A 0PW, England. *Telephone:* (161) 236-8256 (office). *Fax:* (161) 238-2662 (office). *E-mail:* enquiries@nbrown.co.uk (office). *Website:* www.nbrown.co.uk (office).

ALLIES, Bob, MA, DipArch, RIBA, FRSA; British architect and lecturer; *Partner, Allies and Morrison Architects;* b. 5 Sept. 1953, Singapore; s. of Edgar Martyn and Lily Maud; m. Jill Franklin; one s. one d.; ed Reading School, Univ. of Edin.; est. Allies and Morrison Architects with Graham Morrison 1983, Partner 1983–; Lecturer, Univ. of Cambridge 1984–88, George Simpson Visiting Prof., Univ. of Edin. 1995; Visiting Prof., Univ. of Bath 1996–99; mem. Faculty of Fine Arts, British School of Rome, Italy 1997–2002; Kea Distinguished Visiting Prof., Univ. of Maryland, USA 1999; mem. Council Architectural Assen 2005–, Design Panel Comm. for Architecture and the Built Environment 2005–; mem. and Trustee Soc. for the Promotion of New Music 2006–; Rome Scholar in Architecture 1981–82; Medal for Architecture, Edin. Architectural Assen 1977, Building Awards Architectural Practice of the Year 2004. *Architectural works include:* The Clove Bldg (RIBA Award 1991), Pierhead, Liverpool (RIBA Award 1995), Sarum Hall School (RIBA Award 1996), Nunnery Square, Sheffield (RIBA Award 1996), Rosalind Franklin Bldg, Newnham Coll., Cambridge (RIBA Award 1996), British Embassy, Dublin (RIBA Award 1997), Abbey Mills Pumping Station, Stratford (RIBA Award 1997), Rutherford Information Services Bldg, Goldsmiths Coll. London (RIBA Award 1998), Blackburn House (RIBA Award 2000), Blackwell (RIBA Award 2003), One Piccadilly Gardens, Manchester (RIBA Award 2004), The Horniman Museum (RIBA Award 2004), 85 Southwark Street, London (RIBA Building of the Year Award 2004), Fitzwilliam Coll. Gatehouse and Auditorium, Cambridge (RIBA Award 2005), BBC Media Village, White City (RIBA Award 2005), British Council, Lagos, Nigeria (RIBA Int. Award 2006), Girton Coll. Library and Archive (RIBA Award 2006). *Publications include:* Model Futures 1983, Allies and Morrison 1996. *Leisure interest:* contemporary music. *Address:* Allies and Morrison, 85 Southwark Street, London, SE1 0HX (office); 12 Well Road, London, NW3 1LH, England (home). *Telephone:* (20) 7921-0100 (office). *Fax:* (20) 7921-0101 (office). *E-mail:* boballies@alliesandmorrison.co.uk (office). *Website:* www.alliesandmorrison.co.uk (office).

ALLIK, Jüri, PhD; Estonian psychologist and academic; *Professor of Experimental Psychology and Head, Department of Psychology, University of Tartu;* b. 3 March 1949, Tallinn; s. of Karl Allik and Niina Raudsepp; m. Anu Realo Annamari Realo; one s. two d.; ed Moscow Univ., Russia and Tampere Univ., Finland; Prof. of Psychophysics, Univ. of Tartu 1992–2002, Dean, Faculty of Social Sciences 1996–2001, Prof. of Experimental Psychology and Head, Dept of Psychology 2002–; Chair. Estonian Science Foundation; Pres. Estonian Psychological Assen 1988–94, Vice-Pres. 1994–2001; Ed. Trames; Assoc. Ed. European Journal of Personality; Foreign mem. Finnish Acad. of Science and Letters 1997; Order of the White Star, 4th Class (Estonia); Nat. Science Award 1998, 2005. *Publications:* The Five-Factor Model of Personality Across Cultures (co-ed.) 2002; numerous articles in scientific journals on visual perception, comparative study of collectivism vs individualism, the works of Sigmund Freud, and history of psychology. *Address:* Department of Psychology, University of Tartu, Tiigi 78, Tartu 50410, Estonia (office). *Telephone:* (7) 375905 (office). *Fax:* (7) 375900 (office); (7) 376152 (office). *E-mail:* juri.allik@ut.ee (office); jyri@psych.ut.ee (office). *Website:* www.psych.ut.ee/~jyri (office).

ALLIOT-MARIE, Michèle Yvette Marie-Thérèse, MA, DenD, DenScPol; French lawyer and politician; *Minister of the Interior, Overseas Possessions and Territorial Collectivities;* b. 10 Sept. 1946, Villeneuve-le-Roi, Val-de-Marne; d. of Bernard Marie and Renée Leyko; partner, Patrick Ollier; ed Faculté de Droit et des Sciences Econ. de Paris, Faculté des Lettres de Paris-Sorbonne, Univ. de Paris I; Asst Lecturer, Faculté de Droit et des Sciences Econ. de Paris then at Univ. de Paris I 1970–84, Sr Lecturer in Econs and Man. 1984–; Tech. Adviser to Minister of Social Affairs 1972–73, Adviser to Minister of Overseas Territories 1973–74, to Jr Minister for Tourism March–Sept. 1974, Tech. Adviser to Jr Minister for Univs 1974–76, Chef de Cabinet to Jr Minister for Univs then to Minister for Univs 1976–78; Dir, later Pres.-Dir Gen. UTA-Indemnité 1979–84; adviser on Admin. and Public Service Issues, RPR 1981–84, Asst Sec.-Gen. Legal Advisory Cttee 1984–, mem. Cen. Cttee 1984–, Exec. Cttee 1985–, Nat. Sec. for Educ. and Research 1985–; Deputy for Pyrénées-Atlantiques (RPR) 1986; Sec. of State in charge of schools, Ministry of Educ. 1986–88; Nat. Sec. RPR (Research and Planning) 1988–90, Asst Sec.-Gen. (Foreign Relations) 1990–92; Municipal Councillor for Ciboure 1983–89, for Biarritz 1989–91; Deputy for Pyrénées-Atlantiques 1988–; mem. European Parl. (UDF-RPR) 1989; Minister for Youth and Sports 1993–95; mem. and First Vice-Pres. Regional Council of Pyrénées-Atlantiques 1995–2001; Mayor of Saint-Jean-de-Luz 1995–2002; Nat. Sec. RPR for Social Affairs 1997–, mem. Political Cttee 1998–, Nat. Sec. in charge of elections 1999–, Pres. RPR 1999–2002; Minister of Defence and Veterans Affairs 2002–07, of the Interior, Overseas Possessions and Territorial Collectivities 2007–; mem. Political Cttee Alliance pour la France 1998; Pres. Comm. for Defence of Rights and Freedoms 1980–, Foundation for Voluntary Orgs –2000 and many current and fmr offices in women's and children's charitable orgs; Commdr de l'Etoile équatoriale (Gabon), de l'Etoile d'Anjouan (Comoros), du Mérite de l'Educ. Nat. (Côte d'Ivoire), Ordre de la République (Egypt), Palmes Magistrales (First Class) (Peru); ranked by Forbes magazine amongst 100 Most Powerful Women (51st) 2005, (57th) 2006, (11th) 2007. *Publications:* L'actionnariat des salariés 1975, La Décision politique: attention une république peut en cacher une autre 1983, La Grande peur des classes moyennes 1996, La République des irresponsables 1999. *Address:* Ministry of the Interior, place Beauvau, 75008 Paris, France (office). *Telephone:* 1-40-07-60-60 (office). *Fax:* 1-43-59-89-50 (office). *E-mail:* sirp@interieur.gouv.fr (office). *Website:* www.interieur.gouv.fr (office).

ALLISON, Graham Tillett, Jr, AB, MA, PhD; American academic and government official; *Douglas Dillon Professor of Government and Director, Belfer Center for Science and International Affairs, Harvard University;* b. 23 March 1940, Charlotte, NC; s. of Graham T. Allison, Sr and Virginia Wright; m. Elisabeth K. Smith 1968; ed Davidson Coll. and Harvard and Oxford Univs.; Instructor of Govt, Harvard Univ. 1967–68, Asst Prof. of Govt 1968–70, Assoc. Prof. of Politics 1970–72, Prof. of Politics 1972–93, Assoc. Dean and Chair. Public Policy Program, John F. Kennedy School of Govt 1975–77, Dean and Don K. Price Prof. of Politics, John F. Kennedy School of Govt 1977–89, Douglas Dillon Prof. of Govt, John F. Kennedy School of Govt 1989–; Asst Sec. of Defense for Policy and Plans, Dept of Defense, Washington, DC 1993–94; Dir Belfer Center for Science and Int. Affairs, John F. Kennedy School of Govt 1994–; numerous professional appointments; Hon. DPhil (Uppsala Univ.) 1979, Hon. DLaws (Davidson Coll.) 1985, (Univ. of NC at Wilmington) 1992. *Publications include:* Essence of Decision: Explaining the Cuban Missile Crisis 1971, Sharing International Responsibilities: A Report to the Trilateral Commission 1983; co-author: Hawks, Doves and Owls: An Agenda for Avoiding Nuclear War 1985, Fateful Visions: Avoiding Nuclear Catastrophe 1988, Windows of Opportunity: From Cold War to Peaceful Competition 1989, Window of Opportunity: The Grand Bargain for Democracy in the Soviet Union 1991, Beyond Cold War to Trilateral Cooperation in the Asia-Pacific Region 1992, Avoiding Nuclear Anarchy 1996, America's Achilles Heel: Nuclear, Biological, and Chemical Terrorism and Covert Attack 1998, Catastrophic Terrorism 1998, Realizing Human Rights: Moving from Inspiration to Impact 2000, Nuclear Terrorism: The Ultimate Preventable Catastrophe 2004. *Leisure interests:* fishing, tennis. *Address:* Belfer Center for Science and International Affairs, 79 JFK Street, Cambridge, MA 02138 (office); 69 Pinehurst Road, Belmont, MA 02478-1502, USA (home). *Telephone:* (617) 496-6099 (office). *Fax:* (617) 495-1905 (office). *E-mail:* graham_allison@harvard.edu (office). *Website:* bcsia.ksg.harvard.edu (office).

ALLISON, Herbert M., Jr, BA, MBA; American financial industry executive; *President and CEO, Fannie Mae (Federal National Mortgage Association);* b. 24 Aug. 1943, Pittsburgh, Pa; s. of Herbert Allison Sr and Mary Allison (née Boardman); m. Simmin N. Nazemi 1974; two c.; ed Yale and Stanford Univs; four years in USN, including active service in Viet Nam; joined Merrill Lynch & Co. as Banking Assoc. 1974, various man. roles including Head of Human Resources, Chief Financial Officer, becoming mem. Bd, Pres. and COO 1997–99; Nat. Finance Chair. for Senator John McCain's Presidential Election Campaign 1999; Pres. and CEO Alliance for Lifelong Learning 2000–02; Chair., Pres. and CEO TIAA-CREF (Teachers Insurance and Annuity Assen–College Retirement Equities Fund) 2002–08; Pres. and CEO Fannie Mae (Fed. Nat. Mortgage Assen) 2008–; Chair. Business-Higher Educ. Forum; mem. Bd of Dirs New York Stock Exchange 2003–05, Time Warner Inc. 2008–, New York Infirmary–Beekman Downtown Hosp., The Conference Bd Inc.; mem. Fed. Reserve Bank New York Int. Advisory Cttee; mem. Advisory Bd Yale School Man., Advisory Council Stanford Grad. School of Business, Harvard Grad. School Educ. Visiting Cttee; mem. Bd of Trustees Econ. Club New York. *Address:* Fannie Mae, 3900 Wisconsin Avenue Northwest, Washington, DC 20016-2892, USA (office). *Telephone:* (202) 752-7000 (office). *E-mail:* headquarters@fanniemae.com (office). *Website:* www.fanniemae.com (office).

ALLISON, Richard Clark, BA, LLB; American judge; b. 10 July 1924, New York; s. of Albert F. Allison and Anice Allison (née Clark); m. Anne Elizabeth Johnston 1950; two s. one d.; ed Univ. of Virginia; called to New York Bar 1948; practised in New York City 1948–52, 1954–55, 1955–; Partner, Reid &

Priest law firm 1961–87; mem. Iran-US Claims Tribunal, The Hague 1988–; mem. ABA (Chair. Cttee Latin American Law 1964–68, Int. Law Section 1976–77, Nat. Inst. on Doing Business in Far East 1972, Int. Legal Exchange Program 1981–85), Int. Bar Asscn (Chair. Conf. 1986, Ethics Cttee 1986–88); mem. Soc. Int. des Avocats, Inter-American Bar Asscn, American Foreign Law Asscn, American Arbitration Asscn (Int. Panel), Southwestern Legal Foundation, American Soc. of Int. Law, Council on Foreign Relations, American Bar Foundation, Asscn of Bar of City of New York, Inst. for Transnat. Arbitration (Advisory Bd), Raven Soc., SAR, St Andrew's Soc., New York. *Publications:* Protecting Against the Expropriation Risk in Investing Abroad 1988, revised 1998; legal articles. *Address:* Parkweg 13, 2585 JH The Hague, The Netherlands (office); 224 Circle Drive, Manhasset, New York, NY 11030, USA (home). *E-mail:* ra.allison@att.net (office).

ALLISON, Robert J., Jr, BSc; American petroleum industry executive; *Chairman Emeritus, Anadarko Petroleum Corporation;* b. 1939; m. Carolyn Allison; three c.; ed Kansas Univ.; various sr positions with Amoco Production Co. 1959–73; Vice-Pres. of Operations, Anadarko Production Co. (now Anadarko Petroleum Corpn) 1973–76, mem. Bd of Dirs 1976–, Pres. 1976–79, CEO 1979–2002, Chair. 1986–2005 (resgnd), Chair. Emer. 2005–; mem. Bd of Dirs American Petroleum Inst., US Oil & Gas Asscn; mem. Nat. Petroleum Council, Soc. of Petroleum Engineers, Natural Gas Supply Asscn; Dir Freeport-McMoran Copper & Gold; mem. All-American Wildcatters 1991–, Chair. 1999–2000; Assoc. mem. Univ. Cancer Foundation, Univ. of Texas M.D. Anderson Cancer Center; Trustee United Way of Texas Gulf Coast; Dir Spindletop (fmr Pres. and Chair.); mem. Bd of Dirs N. Harris Montgomery Community Coll. Dist Foundation, Sam Houston Area Council, Boy Scouts of America; Offshore Energy Center Pinnacle Award 2002. *Address:* c/o Board of Directors, Anadarko Petroleum Corporation, 1201 Lake Robbins Drive, The Woodlands, TX 77380, USA (office). *Website:* www.anadarko.com (office).

ALLMAND, Warren, OC, PC, QC; Canadian academic and fmr politician; *Visiting Scholar, McGill Institute for the Study of Canada, McGill University;* b. 19 Sept. 1932, Montréal; s. of Harold W. Allmand and Rose Irene McMorrow; one s. two d.; ed Loyola High School, Montreal, St Francis Xavier Univ., NS, McGill Univ., Montréal, Univ. of Paris; called to Quebec Bar 1958, Ont. Bar 1976, Yukon and NWT Bars 1976; MP for Montréal-NDG 1965–93, Minister for Indian and Northern Affairs 1976–77, for Consumer and Corp. Affairs 1977–79; Solicitor-Gen. 1972–76; mem. Exec. World Federalists of Canada 1960–65; Int. Pres. Parliamentarians for Global Action 1984–91; Pres. Int. Centre for Human Rights and Democratic Devt 1997–2002; currently Visiting Scholar, McGill Inst. for the Study of Canada; fmr mem. Parliamentarians for East Timor, Parl. Friends of Tibet, Canadian Civil Liberties Asscn; mem. Quebec Bar Asscn, Liberal Party; Hon. LLD (St Francis Xavier Univ., NS), (St Thomas Univ., NB) 1998; World Peace Award, World Federalists of Canada 1990. *Leisure interests:* ice hockey, long-distance running, skiing, tennis. *Address:* McGill Institute for the Study of Canada, McGill University, 845 Sherbrooke Street West, Montréal, PQ H3A 2T5, Canada (office). *Telephone:* (514) 398-4455 (office). *Fax:* (514) 398-3594 (office). *Website:* www.misc-iecm.mcgill.ca (office).

ALLOTEY, Francis Kofi Ampenyin, MA, PhD, FInstP, FRAS, CIIP; Ghanaian physicist, mathematician and computer scientist; *Director, Institute of Mathematical Sciences;* b. Aug. 1932; ed Imperial Coll. of Science, Tech. and Medicine, London Univ., UK, Univ. of South Bank, London, Princeton Univ., USA; began academic career at Kwame Nkrumah Univ. of Science and Tech. 1960, Head of Dept of Computer Science 1972, full Prof. of Math. 1973 (first Ghanaian), later Pro-Vice-Chancellor Kwame Nkrumah Univ. of Science and Tech.; currently Dir Inst. of Math. Sciences, Ghana; Visiting Scientist, Int. Centre for Theoretical Physics (ICTP), Trieste, Italy 1967–, Chalmers Univ. of Tech., Gothenberg, Sweden 1970–88; Visiting Prof., Clark Atlanta Univ., Ga, USA 1991, Univ. of Michigan, Ann Arbor, USA 1992–97; mem. Scientific Council Int. Inst. of Theoretical and Applied Physics, Ames, Ia, USA 1992–2000, High Level Scientific Expert Review Panel for Int. Centre for Science and High Tech., Trieste 1993, UNESCO Physics Action Council 1992–2000, Scientific Council ICTP 1996–, Int. Planning Cttee for World Year of Physics 2005 2002–, Sub-Cttee on Tech. Transfer of UN Conf. on New and Renewable Energy Sources; Vice-Pres. Preparatory Cttee UN Conf. for Promotion of Int. Peaceful Uses of Nuclear Energy; Vice-Pres. (Western Africa) African Acad. of Sciences; Fellow, Ghana Acad. of Arts and Sciences 1959, Third World Acad. of Sciences 1988, British Computer Soc. 1993, Int. Inst. for Information Tech.; Founding Fellow, African Acad. of Science 1985, Ghana Inst. of Physics 1993; Chartered Physicist (UK) 1993; Chartered Information Tech. Professional (UK) 2004; Patron African Inst. for Math. Sciences; Hon. DSc from four univs; Hon. Fellow, Ghana Inst. of Engineers 1993; Order of Volta (Ghana); Prince Philip Gold Medal Award 1973, Nat. Art and Culture Award for Science 1991, Deserving Scientist Award, Ghana Science Asscn 1995, Martin Luther King Jr/Cesar Chevaz/Rosa Parks Visiting Prof. awarded by US Govt and Univ. of Michigan for contribs to physical and math. sciences and int. co-operation in sciences 1997, Ivory Coast Math. Soc. Medal 1998, World Bank/IMF African Club Distinguished Scientist Award 1998, African Math. Union Medal for quality contrib. to math. sciences and for pioneering and promoting math. in Africa 2000, Millennium Excellence Award (Ghana) 2005, honoured by Ghana by having his image placed on postage stamp 2006. *Address:* Institute of Mathematical Sciences, PO Box LG197, Legon-Accra, East Legon, Greater Accra Region, 00233 Ghana (office). *Telephone:* (21) 501360 (office). *Fax:* (21) 501965 (office). *E-mail:* fka@ghana.com (office). *Website:* imsghana.org (office).

ALLOUACHE, Merzak; Algerian film director and writer; b. 6 Oct. 1944, Algiers; s. of Omar Allouache and Fatma Allouache; m. Lazib Anissa 1962; one d.; worked in Nat. Inst. of Cinema, Algiers, later in Inst. of Film, Paris; after return to Algeria worked as Adviser, Ministry of Culture; Silver Prize, Moscow Festival; Tanit D'Or Prize, Carthage 1979. *Films include:* Our Agrarian Revolution (documentary) 1973, Omar Gatlato, Les aventures d'un héros, L'homme qui regardait les fenêtres 1982, Bab El-Oued City 1994, Lumière et Compagnie 1995, Salut Cousin! 1996, Dans la décapotable 1996, Alger–Beyrouth: Pour Mémoire 1998, Pepe Carvalho: La Solitude du Manager (TV) 1999, À bicyclette (TV) 2001, L'Autre Monde 2001, Chouchou 2003, Bab el seb 2005. *Publications:* Bab El-Oued (novel) 1994.

ALM, John R.; American business executive; *President, CEO and Director, Coca-Cola Enterprises Inc.;* b. 1947; Sr Vice-Pres. and Chief Financial Officer, Coca-Cola Enterprises Inc. 1991–97, Exec. Vice-Pres. and Chief Financial Officer 1997–99, Exec. Vice-Pres. and Prin. Operating Officer April–Oct. 1999, COO 1999–2000, COO and Pres. 2000–04, apptd mem. Bd Dirs 2001, Pres. and CEO 2004–. *Address:* Coca-Cola Enterprises Inc., 2500 Windy Ridge Parkway, Atlanta, GA 30339, USA (office). *Telephone:* (770) 989-3000 (office). *Fax:* (770) 989-3788 (office). *Website:* www.cokecce.com (office).

ALMODÓVAR, Pedro; Spanish film director and screenwriter; b. 25 Sept. 1951, Calzada de Calatrava, Ciudad Real, Castilla La Mancha; fronted a rock band; worked at Telefónica for ten years; started career with full-length super-8 films; made 16mm short films 1974–83; Asturias Prize 2006. *Films as writer and director:* Film político 1974, Dos putas, o historia de amor que termina en boda 1974, El Sueño, o la estrella 1975, Homenaje 1975, La caída de Sódoma 1975, Blancor 1975, Sea caritativo 1976, Muerte en la carretera 1976, Sexo va, sexo viene 1977, Salomé 1978, ¡Folle... folle... fólleme Tim! 1978, Pepe, Luci, Bom y otras chicas del montón 1980, Laberinto de pasiones 1982, Entre tinieblas 1983, ¿Qué he hecho yo para merecer esto? 1985, Matador 1986, La ley del deseo 1987, Mujeres al borde de un ataque de nervios (Felix Award) 1988, ¡Atame! 1990, Tacones lejanos 1991, Kika 1993, La flor de mi secreto 1995, Carne trémula 1997, Todo sobre mi madre (Acad. Award for Best Foreign Language Film) 1999, Hable con ella (BAFTA Award for Best Film not in the English language 2003, Acad. Award for Best Original Screenplay 2003) 2002, La mala educación 2004, Volver (Best Foreign Film Nat. Bd of Review 2006, Goya Award for Best Film, Best Director 2007, Best Foreign Film, London Film Critics' Circle Awards 2007) 2006, Los abrazos rotos 2009. *Films as producer:* Laberinto de pasiones 1982, Mujeres al borde de un ataque de nervios 1988, Acción mutante 1993, Mi nombre es sombra (assoc. producer) 1996, Cuernos de espuma 1996, El Espinazo del diablo 2001, Mi vida sin mí (exec. producer) 2003, La Mala educación 2004. *Publications:* Fuego en las entrañas 1982, The Patty Diphusa Stories and Other Writings 1992. *Address:* c/o El Deseo SA, Ruiz Perelló 15, Madrid 28028, Spain (office); Miramax Films, 18 E 48th Street, New York, NY 10017, USA (office).

ALMOND, Lincoln Carter, LLB; American lawyer and politician; b. 1936, Central Falls, RI; ed Boston Univ.; called to RI Bar 1962; Admin. Town of Lincoln, RI 1963–67; US Attorney, RI Dept of Justice, Providence 1967–78, 1981–93; pvt. law practice 1967–69, 1978–81; Pres. Blackstone Valley Devt Foundation 1993–95; Gov. of Rhode Island 1995–2003; unsuccessful cand. for US Congress (as Ind.) 2004. *Address:* c/o Office of the Governor, 222 State House, Providence, RI 02903-1196, USA.

ALMUNIA AMANN, Joaquín; Spanish politician; *Commissioner for Economic and Monetary Affairs, European Commission;* b. 1948, Bilbao; m.; two c.; ed Univ. of Deusto; economist, various Spanish chambers of commerce in mem. countries of EEC; econ. adviser to Exec. Cttee, Unión General de Trabajo; Sec. for trade union relations, then Head of Dept of Research and Planning, then Head of Perm. Cttee for Political Man., Partido Socialista Obrero Español 1981, Sec.-Gen. 1997–2000; Minister of Labour and Social Security 1982–86; Minister of Public Admin 1987–91; Pres. Socialist Parl. Group 1994–2000, Budget Cttee Congreso de los Diputados 2000; EU Commr for Econ. and Monetary Affairs 2004–. *Publication:* Memorias Políticas 2001. *Address:* Rue de la Loi 200, 1049 Brussels, Belgium (office); Carrera de San Jerónimo, s/n 28014 Madrid, Spain (office). *E-mail:* joaquin.almunia@diputado.congreso.esp (office). *Website:* europa.eu (office); www.almunia.com (office).

ALOGOSKOUFIS, Georgios, MSc, PhD; Greek economist and politician; b. 17 Oct. 1955, Athens; m. Dika Agapitidou; one s. two d.; ed Univ. of Athens, London School of Econs, UK; Researcher Centre of Labour Finance, LSE and Centre for Econ. Policy Research, London 1981–82; Reader and Lecturer, Univ. of London 1984–92; Counsellor, EC 1989–90, World Bank 1991–92; Pres. Council of Financial Experts (SOE), Ministry of Nat. Economy 1992–93; Pres. Inst. of Econ. Studies 1994–96; elected mem. Parl. 1996, mem. Parl. Cttee for Econ. Relations 1996–2004, Parl. Speaker for Political Economy 1997–2004; Minister of the Economy and Finance 2004–09; mem. Exec. Bd European Econ. Asscn 1994–98; Sayers Prize, Univ. of London 1981. *Publications:* La Drachme: du Phoenix à l'euro (Acad. of Athens Prize) 2002. *Leisure interests:* music, tennis. *Address:* c/o Ministry of the Economy and Finance, Odos Nikis 5–7, 101 80 Athens, Greece. *Website:* www.alogoskoufis.gr.

ALOIS PHILIPP MARIA, Hereditary Prince, LLM; Liechtenstein royal; *Permanent Representative of the Head of State;* b. 11 June 1968, Zürich, Switzerland; s. of Prince Hans-Adam II and Princess Marie of Liechtenstein; m. Duchess Sophie in Bavaria 1993; three s. one d.; ed Liechtenstein Grammar School, RMA, Sandhurst, England and Salzburg Univ., Austria; heir to the throne of Liechtenstein; commissioned Second Lt, Coldstream Guards, Hong Kong and London 1988; swore Oath of Allegiance to Constitution alongside his father 1990; worked for auditing firm, London 1993–96; returned to live in Vaduz and given responsibility for various sections of the royal assets; apptd perm. rep. for exercising his father's sovereign powers 15

Aug. 2004. *Address:* Fürstenhaus von Liechtenstein, Schloss Vaduz, Vaduz 9490, Liechtenstein (office). *Telephone:* 2381200 (office). *Fax:* 2381201 (office). *E-mail:* office@sfl.li (office). *Website:* www.fuerstenhaus.li (office).

ALOMAR, Raphaël; French banker and business executive; *Governor, Council of Europe Development Bank;* b. 28 July 1941, Tourcoing; s. of Raphaël Alomar and Jeanne Alomar (née Broutin); m. Nicole Labrunie 1964; three s.; ed Sorbonne, Paris, Ecole des Hautes Etudes Commerciales and Ecole Nationale d'Admin (ENA); Sec.-Gen. Etablissements Broutin 1966–69; Adviser to Gen. Man. Société Générale 1969–86; Prof. of Corp. Financial Man., ENA 1974–82, Pres. Alumni Asscn 1984–96, mem. Bd Dirs 1987–; Assoc. Gen. Man. Cie de Navigation Mixte and of Via Banque 1986–93; Gov. Council of Europe Devt Bank 1993–; Officier, Légion d'honneur; Commdr Order of Isabella the Catholic; Commdr, Order of the Lion of Finland. *Publication:* Financing Business Development 1981. *Address:* Council of Europe Development Bank, 55 avenue Kléber, 75116 Paris, France (office). *Website:* www.coebank.org (office).

ALONEFTIS, Andreas P., MBA, ADipC, FAIA; Cypriot business executive and fmr government official; *Business Manager, IKOS CIF;* b. 24 Aug. 1945, Nicosia; s. of Polycarpos Aloneftis and Charitini Aloneftis; m. Nedi Georghiades 1967; one s. one d.; ed New York Inst. of Finance Coll. of New York Stock Exchange, Southern Methodist Univ., Dallas, Tex., Harvard Univ., Boston, Mass., USA, Henley Management Coll. and Univ. of Middlesex, UK; served in Nat. Guard 1964–66; served 16 years in Cyprus Devt Bank; Gen. Man. and Chief Exec. Officer, Cyprus Investment and Securities Corpn Ltd (CISCO) 1982–88; Minister of Defence 1988–93; Gen. Man. ALICO (Cyprus) 1993–95; Man. Dir CYPRIALIFE Ltd 1995–99; Gen. Man. Insurance, Cyprus Popular Bank Group 1999–2003; Chair. Bd of Govs Cyprus Broadcasting Corpn 2003–06; Exec. Vice-Chair. Alliance Reinsurance Co. Ltd 2003–; Pres. Asscn of Int. Accountants; Open Fellowship, Southern Methodist Univ. 1978, Salzburg Seminar Fellow 1984, Paul Harris Fellow; Fulbright Grantee. *Publications:* numerous articles, working papers and monographs. *Leisure interests:* jogging, reading, cinema, travelling. *Address:* 201 Vashiotis Business Center, 1 Iacovou Tombazi Street, Limassol 3107 (office); 10 Kastellorizo Street, Aglantzia, Nicosia 2108, Cyprus (home). *Telephone:* (25) 814714 (office); (25) 844100 (office); (22) 817970 (home). *Fax:* (25) 814744 (office); (25) 844333 (office); (22) 817971 (home). *E-mail:* andreasa@ikos.com.cy (office); alonefan@cytanet.com.cy (home).

ALONI, Shulamit; Israeli politician and lawyer; b. 1929, Tel-Aviv; three s.; participated in the defence of Jerusalem during the War of Independence; worked as a teacher; columnist for several newspapers; producer of radio programmes dealing with legislation and legal procedures; f. Israel Consumers' Council, Chair. for four years; joined Mapai 1959; mem. Knesset (Labour) 1965–69; f. Ratz Party 1973, CRM Minister without Portfolio June–Oct. 1974, CRM leader and MK 1974–, served on numerous cttees; Minister of Educ. (representing the Meretz coalition) 1992–93, of Communications, Science and Tech. 1993–96; mem. Meretz (coalition party), fmr Chair.; mem. Bd of Dirs Yesh Din (organized to support Palestinian human rights in Occupied Palestinian Territory) 2005–; Israel Prize and Emil Grunzweig Human Rights Award, Asscn for Civil Rights in Israel. *Publications include:* The Citizen and His/Her Country, The Rights of the Child in Israel, The Arrangement – A State of Law and Not a State of Religion, Women as People. *Leisure interests:* reading, theatre, tennis. *Address:* c/o Yesh Din, 11 Rothschild Blvd., 66881 Tel-Aviv, Israel. *Telephone:* (3) 5168563. *Website:* www.yesh-din.org.

ALONSO, Alicia; Cuban ballet dancer, choreographer and ballet director; b. 21 Dec. 1920, Havana; d. of Antonio Martínez and Ernestina del Hoyo; m. 1st Fernando Alonso 1937; m. 2nd Pedro Simón 1975; one s. one d.; ed Ballet School of Sociedad Pro-Arte Musical, Havana, School of American Ballet, USA; mem. American Ballet Caravan 1938–39, American Ballet Theater 1940–41, 1943–48, 1950–55, 1958–60, Ballet Russe, Monte Carlo 1955–59; danced with Greek Theatre, LA, Calif. 1957–59, Washington Ballet 1958; Guest Artist, Teatro Colón, Buenos Aires 1958, Kirov and Bolshoi Ballets 1958, Royal Danish Ballet 1969, Paris Opera 1972, Rome Opera 1987; Founder, Prima Ballerina Assoluta, Choreographer and Gen. Dir Nat. Ballet of Cuba 1948–99; has staged her versions of the major romantic and classical ballets in Paris, Rome, Milan, Naples, Vienna, Mexico, Sofia and Prague; mem. jury several int. ballet competitions, Advisory Council, Ministry of Culture and Nat. Cttee of Writers, Artists' Union of Cuba, Kennedy Center Artistic Cttee, Washington, DC; decorations include Hero of Work, Cuba; Order Félix Varela, Cuba; Order Aguila Azteca, Mexico; Order Isabel la Católica, Spain; Commdr des Arts et Lettres; many awards including Dance Magazine Annual Award 1958, Grand Prix of Paris 1966, 1970, Anna Pavlova Award, Univ. of Dance, Paris 1966, Gold Medal of Barcelona Liceo 1971, Annual Award of Gran Teatro de La Habana 1985. *Publication:* Dialogues with the Dance 1988. *Leisure interests:* films, music, scientific discoveries. *Address:* c/o National Ballet of Cuba, Calzada No. 510 entre D y E, CP 10400, El Vedado, Havana, Cuba. *Telephone:* (7) 55-2948. *Fax:* (7) 33-3317.

ALONSO DÍAZ, Fernando; Spanish racing driver; b. 29 July 1981, Oviedo; s. of José Luis; ed Santo Ángel de la Guarda; began competing on karting circuit at early age, winner of several karting championships at local, regional, nat. and int. levels; World Jr Karting Champion 1996; moved to open-wheel cars 1999, Spanish Nissan Open Series Champion 1999; Formula One debut at Australian Grand Prix 2001; joined Renault team 2002–06, 2007–, with McLaren team 2007; winner Australian Grand Prix 2006, Bahrain Grand Prix 2005, 2006, British Grand Prix 2006, Canadian Grand Prix 2006, Chinese Grand Prix 2005, European Grand Prix 2005, French Grand Prix 2005, German Grand Prix 2005, Hungarian Grand Prix 2003, Japanese Grand Prix 2006, Malaysian Grand Prix 2005, 2007, Monaco Grand Prix 2006, 2007, San Marino Grand Prix 2005, Spanish Grand Prix 2006; winner Driver's Championship (youngest ever Formula One Champion) 2005, 2006; Premio Príncipe de Asturias 2005. *Address:* c/o Renault Formula Ltd, Whiteways Technical Centre, Enstone, Chipping Norton, OX7 4EE, England (office). *Telephone:* (1608) 678000 (office). *Fax:* (1608) 678800 (office). *Website:* www.renaultf1.com (office); www.fernandoalonso.com.

ALONSO SUÁREZ, José Antonio, LicenDer; Spanish politician and lawyer; b. 28 March 1960, Léon; m.; one s.; ed Univ. of Léon; defence lawyer, Torrelavega, Santoña and Pamplona 1985–89; Magistrate, Las Palmas de Gran Canaria 1998–89; Judge, Criminal Court then Prov. Higher Court, Madrid 1989; mem. Congreso de los Diputados (Parl.) for Léon; Minister of Interior 2004–06, of Defence 2006–08; mem. Partido Socialista Obrero Español (Socialist Workers' Party), Spokesman in Congress 2008–; Spokesman, Judges for Democracy Asscn 1994–98, Consejo General del Poder Judicial 2001–04. *Address:* Congreso de los Diputados, Calle Floridablanca 1, 28071 Madrid, Spain (office). *Telephone:* (91) 3906264 (office). *Fax:* (91) 3906711 (office). *E-mail:* secretaria.general@sgral.congreso.es (office). *Website:* www.congreso.es (office).

ALOR KOL, Deng; Sudanese politician; *Minister of Foreign Affairs;* fmr Commdr, Sudan People's Liberation Army (SPLA); attended peace talks in Nairobi 1994; fmr Minister of Cabinet Affairs, Minister of Foreign Affairs 2007–; mem. Sudan People's Liberation Movt (SPLM). *Address:* Ministry of Foreign Affairs, POB 873, Khartoum, Sudan (office). *Telephone:* (183) 773101 (office). *Fax:* (183) 772941 (office). *E-mail:* ministry@mfa.gov.sd (office). *Website:* www.mfa.gov.sd (office).

ALOS, Albert, BSc, DrEng; Spanish electronic engineer, university administrator and academic; *Vice-Chancellor, Pan-African University;* b. 17 Sept. 1939, Barcelona; ed School of Eng, Univ. of Bilbao; Lecturer in Electrical Eng, Univ. of Ife, Lagos and Ibadan, Nigeria 1967; Co-Founder, Lagos Business School (now part of Pan-African Univ.) 1991, Dean 1993–, Vice-Chancellor Pan-African Univ. 2002–; Chair. Ikota Educational Foundation; Vice-Chair. Nigerian Econ. Summit Group; mem. Vision 2010 Cttee, Editorial Advisory Cttee BusinessDay newspaper; Fellow Inst. of Dirs; Distinguished Lecturer Nigerian Soc. of Engineers; Nat. Univs Comm. Award for Dedication and Exemplary Leadership. *Publication:* The Pains & Gains of Growth: Case studies on entrepreneurship. *Address:* Pan-African University, 2 Ahmed Onibudo Street, Victoria Island, Lagos (office); 35 Adeola Hopewell Street, Victoria Island, Lagos, Nigeria (home). *Telephone:* (1) 4616170 (office); (1) 4616173 (home). *E-mail:* aalos@lbs.edu.ng (office). *Website:* www.pau.edu.ng (office).

ALPER, Howard, OC, PhD, FRSC; Canadian chemist and academic; *Professor of Chemistry, University of Ottawa;* b. 17 Oct. 1941, Montreal; s. of Max Alper and Frema Alper; m. Anne Fairhurst 1966; two d.; ed Sir George Williams Univ. and McGill Univ.; NATO Postdoctoral Fellow, Princeton Univ. 1967–68; Asst Prof., State Univ. of New York at Binghamton 1968–71, Assoc. Prof. 1971–74; Assoc. Prof., Univ. of Ottawa 1975–77, Prof. 1977–, Chair. Dept of Chem. 1982–85, 1988–91, 1991–94, Asst Vice-Pres. (Research) 1995–96, Vice-Pres. (Research) 1997–2006; titular mem. European Acad. of Arts, Sciences and Humanities; Guggenheim Fellowship 1985–86; Killam Research Fellow 1986–88; Pres. RSC 2001–03; Assoc. Fellow, Third World Acad. of Sciences 2003; Officier de l'Ordre nat. du mérite 2002; Chemical Inst. of Canada Inorganic Chem. Award 1980, Catalysis Award 1984, Alfred Bader Award in Organic Chem. 1990, Commemorative Medal (125th Anniversary of Canada) 1992, E. W. R. Steacie Award 1993, Urgel-Archambault Prize in Physical Sciences, Math. and Eng (ACFAS) 1996, Chemical Inst. of Canada Medal 1997, Bell Canada Forum Award 1998, Gerhard Herzberg Gold Medal in Science and Eng 2000, Le Sever Memorial Award 2002, Chemical Inst. of Canada Montreal Medal 2003. *Publications:* more than 460 papers and more than 32 patents in the area of organometallic chem. and catalysis. *Address:* Department of Chemistry, University of Ottawa, 10 Marie Curie, D'Iorio 402, Ottawa, Ont. K1N 6N5, Canada (office). *Telephone:* (613) 562-5189 (office). *Fax:* (613) 562-5871 (office). *E-mail:* halper@science.uottawa.ca (office). *Website:* www.chem.uottawa.ca (office).

ALPERN, Robert J., BS, MD; American nephrologist, academic and university administrator; *Dean, School of Medicine, Yale University;* b. 3 Nov. 1950; m. Patricia Preisig; two c.; ed Northwestern Univ., Univ. of Chicago, Columbia Presbyterian, Univ. of California, San Francisco; intern in internal medicine, Columbia Univ. 1976–77, resident in internal medicine 1977–79; Fellow in Nephrology and Renal Physiology, Univ. of California Cardiovascular Research Inst., San Francisco 1979–82, Asst Prof. of Internal Medicine, Univ. of California, San Francisco 1982; Assoc Prof., Texas SW Medical Center, Dallas 1987–90, Chief of Nephrology 1987–98, Prof. of Medicine 1990–2004, Ruth W. and Milton P. Levy Sr Prof. of Molecular Nephrology 1994–2004, also Dean, Texas SW Medical Center 1998–2004; Ensign Prof. of Medicine and Dean, School of Medicine, Yale Univ. 2004–; mem. American Soc. of Clinical Investigation, Asscn of American Physicians, Inst. of Medicine 2007–, American Soc. of Nephrology, Int. Soc. of Nephrology, Soc. of Gen. Physiology, American Physiological Soc., American Heart Asscn; mem. Advisory Council Nat. Inst. of Diabetes and Digestive and Kidney Diseases; mem. Bd of Dirs Abbott Laboratories 2008–; SW Medical Center Outstanding Teaching Award 1999, American Soc. of Nephrology John P. Peters Award 2008. *Publications:* numerous scientific articles and book chapters. *Address:* Office of the Dean, Yale School of Medicine, 333 Cedar Street, New Haven, CT 06510, USA (office). *Telephone:* (203) 785-4672 (office). *E-mail:* Robert.alpern@yale.edu (office). *Website:* www.med.yale.edu/intmed/faculty/alpern.html (office).

ALPERT, Herb; American musician (trumpet), songwriter and record industry executive; b. 31 March 1935, Los Angeles; s. of Louis Alpert and Tillie Goldberg; m. 1st Sharon Mae Lubin 1956 (divorced); two c.; m. 2nd Lani Hall; one d.; ed Univ. of Southern Calif.; co-owner and fmr Pres. Carnival record co., later renamed A&M Record Co., Co-Chair. 1962–94; founder and Co-Chair. Almo Sounds 1994–2002; leader, arranger, own music group, Tijuana Brass 1962–; tours world-wide and numerous concert appearances; f. Herb Alpert Foundation; Lifetime Achievement Award (non-performer), Rock and Roll Hall of Fame Foundation 2005. *Recordings include:* albums: The Lonely Bull 1962, Tijuana Brass 1963, Tijuana Brass Vol. 2 1963, South Of The Border 1964, Whipped Cream & Other Delights 1965, Going Places 1965, What Now My Love 1965, S.R.O. 1966, Sounds Like Us 1967, Herb Alpert's Ninth 1967, Beat Of The Brass 1968, Christmas Album 1968, Warm 1969, The Brass Are Comin' 1969, Summertime 1971, Solid Brass 1972, Four Sider 1973, You Smile, The Song Begins 1974, Coney Island 1975, Just You And Me 1976, Herb Alpert/Hugh Masekela 1978, Rise 1979, Keep Your Eyes On Me 1979, Beyond 1980, Magic Man 1981, Fandango 1982, Blow Your Own Horn 1983, Noche De Amor 1983, Bullish 1984, Wild Romance 1985, Keep Your Eye On Me 1987, Under A Spanish Moon 1988, My Abstract Heart 1989, North On South Street 1991, Midnight Sun 1992, Second Wind 1996, Passion Dance 1997, Colors 1999, Definitive Hits 2001. *Address:* c/o Herb Alpert Foundation, 1414 Sixth Street, Santa Monica, CA 90401, USA. *Website:* www.herbalpert.com.

ALPERT, Joseph Stephen, MD; American physician and university administrator; *Professor of Medicine, University of Arizona;* b. 1 Feb. 1942, New Haven, Conn.; s. of Zelly C. Alpert and Beatrice A. Kopsofsky; m. Helle Mathiasen 1965; one s. one d.; ed Yale and Harvard Univs; Instructor in Medicine, Peter Bent Brigham Hosp., Harvard Univ. 1973–74; Lt-Commdr, USN, Dir Coronary Care Unit, San Diego Naval Hosp. and Asst Prof. of Medicine, Univ. of Calif., San Diego 1974–76; Dir Levine Cardiac Unit and Asst Prof. of Medicine, Peter Bent Brigham Hosp. and Harvard Univ. 1976–78; Dir Div. of Cardiovascular Medicine and Prof. of Medicine, Univ. of Massachusetts Medical School 1978–92, Vice-Chair. Medicine Dept 1990–; Budnitz Prof. of Cardiovascular Medicine 1988–92; Prof., Chair. of Medicine Dept Univ. of Ariz. 1992–; Fulbright Fellow, Copenhagen 1963–64; US Public Health Service Fellow, Harvard and Copenhagen 1966–67; NIH Special Fellow, Harvard 1972–74; Fellow, American Coll. of Physicians, American Coll. of Cardiology (Trustee 1996–2001), American Heart Assen Clinical Council (Vice-Chair. 1991–92, Chair. 1993–95), American Coll. of Chest Physicians; mem. American Bd of Internal Medicine, Bd of Trustees 2001–03; Ed.-in-Chief, American Journal of Medicine 2005–; Gold Medal of Univ. of Copenhagen and other awards, including Gifted Teacher Award, American College of Cardiology 2004. *Publications include:* The Heart Attack Handbook 1978, Physiopathology of the Cardiovascular System 1984, Modern Coronary Care 1990, Diagnostic Atlas of the Heart 1994, Cardiology for the Primary Care Physician 1998, Valvular Heart Disease 2000; co-author of other books including: Manual of Coronary Care 1978, Manual of Cardiovascular Diagnosis and Therapy; author of more than 400 articles in scientific journals. *Leisure interests:* poetry, music, swimming, cycling, cooking, travel. *Address:* Department of Medicine, 6th Floor, Room 6334, Arizona Health Sciences Center, 1501 North Campbell Avenue, Tucson, AZ 85724-5035 (office); 3440 E Cathedral Rock Circle, Tucson, AZ 85718, USA (home). *Telephone:* (520) 626-6138 (office). *Fax:* (520) 626-6604 (office). *E-mail:* jalpert@u.arizona.edu (office). *Website:* www.deptmedicine.arizona.edu (office).

ALPHANDÉRY, Edmond, DèsSc; French economist, politician and business executive; *Chairman, CNP Assurances;* b. 2 Sept. 1943, Avignon; ed Inst. d'études politiques de Paris, Univ. of Chicago, USA; Lecturer, Faculty of Law, Univ d'Aix en Provence and Univ Paris IX Dauphine 1969–71; Sr Lecturer and Dean of Faculty of Econ. Science, Univ de Nantes 1972–74; Assoc. Prof., Univ of Pittsburgh, USA 1975; Prof., Univ of Paris II 1975–93; elected Deputy (mem. Parl.) for Maine and Loire 1978–93, also Vice-Pres. then Pres. Gen. Council of Maine and Loire; mem. Finance Comm., Nat. Ass. 1979–93; Head of Investigatory Mission into European Econ. and Monetary Union 1991; Minister of the Economy 1993–95; Chair. Council of Ministers of the Economy and Finance, EU, Brussels 1995; Chair. Electricité de France (EdF) 1995–98; Founding Pres. Euro 50 Group 1999–; Chair. CNP (Caisse Nat. de Prévoyance) Assurances SA 1998–; mem. Advisory Bd Banque de France 1996–, RWE 1997–2002, Supervisory Bd Bayernwerk AG 1997–98; Dir Crédit Agricole Indosuez, then Calyon 2002–; Dir GDF SUEZ 2008–; Co-Pres. Club of Japanese Investors in France 1998–; Fulbright Award 1967–68. *Publications:* Les politiques de stabilisation (co-author) 1974, Cours d'analyse macroéconomique 1976, Analyse monétaire approfondie 1978, 1986: Le piège 1985, La réforme obligée, sous le soleil de l'Euro 2000. *Address:* CNP Assurances SA, 4 place Raoul Dautry, 75716 Paris Cedex 15, France (office). *Telephone:* 1-42-18-88-88 (office). *Fax:* 1-42-18-93-66 (office). *E-mail:* edmond.alphandery@cnp.fr (office). *Website:* www.cnp.fr (office).

ALSOP, Marin, MusM; American violinist and conductor; *Music Director, Baltimore Symphony Orchestra;* b. 16 Oct. 1956, New York City; d. of LaMar Alsop and Ruth Alsop; ed began piano studies aged two, violin studies aged five; Juilliard Pre-Coll., Yale Univ. and Juilliard School of Music; freelance violinist with New York Symphony Orchestra, Mostly Mozart, New York Chamber Symphony, American Composers Orchestra, several Broadway shows 1976–79; began conducting studies with Carl Bamberger 1979, Harold Farberman 1985; f. String Fever (14-piece swing band) 1981; founder and Dir Concordia Orchestra 1984–; debut with London Symphony Orchestra 1988; Assoc. Conductor Richmond Symphony 1988; studied with Leonard Bernstein, Seiji Ozawa and Gustav Meier, Tanglewood Music Center 1989; Music Dir Eugene Symphony, OR 1989–96, Conductor Laureate 1996–; Music Dir Long Island Philharmonic 1990–96; debut with Philadelphia Orchestra and Los Angeles Philharmonic 1990; Music Dir Cabrillo Music Festival 1992–; Music Dir Colorado Symphony, Denver 1993–; debut Schleswig Holstein Music Festival 1993; Creative Conductor Chair. St Louis Symphony Orchestra 1996–98; Prin. Guest Conductor, Royal Scottish Nat. Symphony 1999–; Prin. Guest Conductor, City of London Sinfonia 1999–; Prin. Conductor Bournemouth Symphony Orchestra (first woman to lead UK symphony orchestra) 2001–07; debut with ENO 2003; teacher, Nat. Orchestral Inst. 1991–, Oberlin Coll. 1998, Interlochen Center for the Arts 1998, Curtis Inst. 1998; Music Dir Baltimore Symphony Orchestra (first woman to head a major US orchestra) 2007–(10); Fellow, American Acad. of Arts and Sciences; Leonard Bernstein Conducting Fellow, Tanglewood Music Festival 1988, 1989, MacArthur Fellow 2005; Hon. DLitt (Gonzaga Univ.) 1995; Stokowski Conducting Competition 1988, Koussevitzky Conducting Prize 1989, ASCAP Award for Adventuresome Programming of Contemporary Music 1991, Univ. of Colorado Distinguished Service Award 1997, State of Colorado Gov.'s Award for Excellence in the Arts 1998, Royal Philharmonic Soc. Conducting Award 2003, Gramophone Artist of the Year 2003, Classical BRIT Award for Female Artist of the Year 2005, Royal Philharmonic Soc. BBC Radio 3 Listeners' Award 2006, Musical America Award for Conductor of the Year 2009. *Recordings include:* Fever Pitch, Fanfares for the Uncommon Woman, Saint-Saens, Blue Monday, Victory Stride, Fiddle Concerto for Violin and Orchestra, Gorgon, Music of Edward Collins, Too Hot to Handel, Barber Vols I–IV, Passion Wheels, Tchaikovsky Symphony No. 4, Bernstein Chichester Psalms. *Address:* c/o Intermusica Artists Management Ltd, 16 Duncan Terrace, London, N1 8BZ, England (office); 21C Media Group Inc., 30 West 63rd Street, Suite 15S, New York, NY 10023, USA (office). *Telephone:* (20) 7278-5455 (Intermusica) (office); (212) 842-0080 (21C) (office). *Fax:* (20) 7278-8434 (Intermusica) (office); (212) 842-0034 (21C) (office). *E-mail:* mail@intermusica.co.uk (office); info@21cmediagroup.com (office); MarinAlsop@aol.com (office). *Website:* www.intermusica.co.uk (office); www.marinalsop.com.

ALSOP, William Allen, OBE, RA, FRSA; British architect; *Director and Chairman, Alsop Architects;* b. 12 Dec. 1947, Northampton; s. of Francis Alsop and Brenda Hight; m. Sheila Bean 1972; two s. one d.; ed Architectural Assen; teacher of sculpture, St Martin's Coll.; worked with Cedric Price; fmrly in practice with John Lyall; designed a ferry terminal in Hamburg; undertook design work on the Cardiff barrage; conducted feasibility studies to recycle the fmr De Lorean car factory in Belfast; designed a govt bldg for Marseilles; est. own practice, collaborates with Bruce Maclean in producing architectural drawings; projects include N Greenwich Station (with John Lyall) 2000, Peckham Library and Media Centre (Stirling Prize) 2000; commissioned to design Fourth Grace, Liverpool 2002–; Prin., Alsop & Störmer Architects 1979–2000; Prin. Dir and Chair. Alsop Architects 2001–; Prof., Technical Univ. of Vienna 1995–; Chair. Architecture Foundation 2001–; Hon. LLD (Leicester) 1996; Dr hc (Nottingham Trent), (Sheffield). *Publications:* City of Objects 1992, William Alsop Buildings and Projects 1992, William Alsop Architect: Four Projects 1993, Will Alsop and Jan Störmer, Architects 1993, Le Grand Bleu-Marseille 1994, Alsop and Störmer: Selected and Current Works 1999, Will Alsop Book 1 1968–1990. *Leisure interest:* fishing. *Address:* Parkgate Studio, 41 Parkgate Road, London, SW11 4NP, England (office). *Telephone:* (20) 7978-7878 (office). *Fax:* (20) 7978-7879 (office). *E-mail:* walsop@alsoparchitects.com (office). *Website:* www.alsoparchitects.com (office).

ALSTON, Philip, BComm, LLM, JSD; Australian academic; *Professor of Law, New York University;* b. 23 Jan. 1950, Melbourne; ed Univ. of Melbourne, Univ. of California, Berkeley, USA; Lecturer and Visiting Prof., Harvard Law School 1984–89, 1993; Assoc. Prof. of Int. Law, Fletcher School of Law and Diplomacy, Tufts Univ., Boston 1985–89; Prof. of Law and Foundation Dir, Centre for Int. and Public Law, ANU 1989–95; Helen L. Deroy Visiting Prof. of Law, Univ. of Mich. 1993; Prof. of Int. Law, European Univ. Inst. 1996–2001, Co-Dir Acad. of European Law 1996–2001, Head of Law Dept 1997–98; Visiting Prof., Woodruff Chair of Int. Law, Univ. of Georgia 2000–01; Prof. of Law, New York Univ. 2001–; Chief of Staff to Cabinet Minister, Australia, 1974–75; Human Rights Officer, UN Centre for Human Rights 1978–1984; Sr Legal Adviser to UNICEF 1984–92; Discrimination Commr for ACT 1992–94; rapporteur, UN Cttee on Econ., Social and Cultural Rights, 1987–90, Chair. 1991–98; UN Special Rapporteur on Extrajudicial, Summary or Arbitrary Executions 2004–; rapporteur, Meeting of Chairs of UN Human Rights Treaty Bodies, 1988, 1990, 1992, 1997–98, Chair. 1990, 1993, 1997–98; mem. Tech. Advisory Group, UN study on Impact of Armed Conflict on Children 1995–97; ind. expert reporting on effectiveness of UN Human Rights Bodies, reports submitted 1989, 1993, 1997; Co-Ed. Australian Yearbook of Int. Law 1991–96, Ed.-in-Chief European Journal of International Law 1996–; Series Co-Ed. Collected Courses of the Academy of European Law 1998–; mem. editorial and advisory bds of numerous int. journals on law and human rights; Chair. Coordinating Cttee for UN Human Rights Special Procedures 2005–06. *Publications include:* The Future of UN Human Rights Treaty Monitoring (co-ed.) 2000, International Human Rights in Context: Law, Politics, Morals (with H. Steiner) 2000, Peoples' Rights (ed. and contrib.) 2001, Economic and Social Rights: A Bibliography 2005, The United Nations and Human Rights: A Critical Appraisal (ed. and contrib.) 2005, Human Rights and Development (ed.) 2005, Neglected Rights 2006; over 100 articles in journals on law and human rights. *Address:* New York University School of Law, Vanderbilt Hall, 40 Washington Square South, Room 305, New York, NY 10012-1099, USA (office). *Telephone:* (212) 998-6173 (office). *E-mail:* philip.alston@nyu.edu (office). *Website:* www.law.nyu.edu (office).

ALSTON, Hon. Richard Kenneth Robert, BA, BCom, MBA, LLM; Australian diplomatist, politician and business executive; b. 19 Dec. 1941, brother of Philip Alston; m. Margaret Mary Alston; two c.; ed Xavier Coll., Melbourne, Melbourne and Monash Univs; Senator for Vic. 1986–2004; Shadow Minister for Communications 1989–90, for Social Security, Child Care and Retirement Incomes 1990–92, for Social Security, Child Care and Superannuation 1992, for Superannuation and Child Care and Shadow Minister Assisting Leader on Social Policy 1992–93, for Communications and the Arts 1994–96; Minister for Communications and the Arts 1996–2003, for Information Tech. 1998–2003; High Commr to UK 2005–08; Deputy Leader of Opposition in Senate 1993–96, of Govt in Senate 1996–2005; Deputy Chair. Senate Standing Cttee on Legal and Constitutional Affairs 1986, Jt Parl. Cttee on Nat. Crime Authority 1987; mem. Senate Standing Cttee on Finance and Public Admin 1987; State Pres. Liberal Party Vic. Div. 1979–82; mem. Amnesty Int. Parl. Group; Nat. Chair. Australian Council for Overseas Aid 1978–83; Chair. Afghan-Australia Council 1987–90; Fed. Pres. UNA of Australia 1977–79; Gov. Nat. Gallery of Australia Foundation; Adjunct Prof., Faculty of Information Tech., Bond Univ., Queensland; mem. Bell Shakespeare Foundation, Melba Foundation; Fellow, Inst. of Dirs 1983–88. *Leisure interests:* Aboriginal art, modern literature, Oriental rugs, jogging, reading, pumping iron. *Address:* c/o Department of Foreign Affairs and Trade, R. G. Casey Building, John McEwen Crescent, Barton, ACT 0221, Australia. *Telephone:* (2) 6261-1111.

ALSTON, Robin Carfrae, OBE, MA, PhD, FSA; Trinidadian bibliographer; *Professor Emeritus of Library Studies, University of London;* b. 29 Jan. 1933, Port-of-Spain; s. of Wilfred Louis Alston and Margaret Louise (née Mackenzie); ed Queen's Royal Coll., Trinidad, Lodge School, Barbados, Rugby School, UK, Univs of British Columbia and Toronto, Canada, Univs of Oxford and London, UK; Teaching Fellow, Univ. Coll. Toronto 1956–58; Lecturer, Univ. of New Brunswick 1958–60; Lecturer in English Literature, Univ. of Leeds 1964–73; Prof. of Library Studies, Univ. of London 1990–98, Prof. Emer. 1998–; Course Dir The History of the Book, School of Advanced Studies, Univ. of London 1993–98; Dir School of Library, Archive and Information Studies, Univ. Coll. London 1990–98; Research Asst to R. E. Watters 1953–54, to Prof. Kathleen Cobum 1962–2004; Research Fellow, Newbery Library, Chicago 1963; has lectured at univs in UK, USA, Canada, Japan, Australia and NZ; fmr Editorial Dir The Nineteenth Century (microform library of texts); Founding mem. British Book Trade Index, Univ. of Newcastle 1985–; Founder, Chair. and Man. Dir Scholar Press 1965–73; Founder and Man. Dir Janus Press 1973–80; Founder Sir Frederick Madden Soc. 1990–, Ed. Occasional Publications of the Madden Society 1990–; Ed. Studies in Early Modern English 1965–70, English Linguistics 1500–1800 (series of 365 vols of facsimile texts published by Scolar Press) 1967–73, European Linguistics (series of 25 vols of facsimile texts) 1967–73, The Lantern 1988; Jt Ed. Leeds Studies in English 1965–70, Leeds Texts and Monographs 1965–70, The Direction Line 1972–79; mem. Editorial Bd The Cambridge History of the Book in Britain 1989–; Founder The Cambridge History of Libraries in Britain and Ireland 1994–; mem. Council, The Bibliographical Soc. 1968–, Publs Cttee 1970–, Vice-Pres. The Bibliographical Soc. 1975–, Pres. 1988–90; Founding mem. and Trustee Ilkley Literature Festival 1973–; mem. Advisory Cttee, British Library Reference Div. 1974–77, Consultant, British Library 1976, 1984; Adviser, Guggenheim Foundation 1978, Early Imprints Project, Australia and New Zealand 1980, Canada Council 1981, Australian Research Grants Cttee 1982, Forschungsgemeinschaft 1983, Nat. Endowment for the Humanities 1984; mem. Advisory Panel Australian Research Grants Cttee 1982, Modern Language Asscn of America for the Wing Project 1978–; External Examiner, Inst. of Bibliography, Univ. of Leeds 1983–89; mem. Governing Bd Common Knowledge (public domain information database in USA) 1989–93; Elector, Munby Fellowship, Univ. of Cambridge 1985–2000, Organizer Munby Fellowship Seminar, Cambridge 1994; adviser on nat. retrospective bibliographical projects being undertaken by the Nat. Libraries of Canada, France, Germany, Sweden, Netherlands, S Africa and Pakistan; Chair. Friends of the Univ. of London Library 1997; Sr Research Fellow, School of Advanced Study, Univ. of London; Hon. FLA; Hon. Research Fellow, Dept of English, Univ. Coll., London 1987–, Inst. of English Studies 1998–; Hon. mem. Grolier Club of Tokyo 1986; Hon. DLitt; Int. Prize for Lithography for developing a new technique for producing continuous tone with litho-graphic plates 1975, Annual Lecturer, Bibliographical Soc. of America 1981, David Murray Lecturer, Univ. of Glasgow 1983, Samuel Pepys Gold Medal, Ephemera Soc. 1984, Smithsonian Inst. Award 1985, Cecil Oldman Lecture and Gold Medal, Univ. of Leeds 1989, Gold Medal, Bibliographical Soc. 1996. *Achievements include:* pioneered gammatype facsimile (Trinity manuscript of Milton's poems) and the introduction of computerised photography in the production of lithographic facsimiles; developed the Prismascope, now used in several research libraries in Europe and N America; developed various new techniques for lithography using modern materials, for recording watermarks in paper, and for reproducing documents without the use of a camera. *Publications include:* Anglo-Saxon Composition for Beginners 1959, Materials for a History of the English Language (two vols) 1960, An Introduction to Old English 1961, A Bibliography of the English Language 1500–1800 (18 of 22 vols published so far) 1965, Dictionary of Early Modern English Pronunciation (assoc. ed.) 1967–73, Bibliography, Machine Readable Cataloguing and the ESTC (with M. J. Jannetta) 1978, Alexander Gil's Logonomia Anglica (1619) (co-ed. with B. Danielsson) 1979, Eighteenth-Century Subscription Lists (with F. J. G. Robinson and C. Wadham) 1983, Eighteenth Century Short Title Catalogue: The British Library Collections (ed.) 1976–83, A Topical Index to the Pressmarks in Use in the British Museum Library, 1843–1973 1986, Index to the Classification Schedules of the Map Collections in the British Library (five vols) 1987, The British Library: Past Present Future 1989, Catalogues of Libraries and Lists of Books in the Department of Manuscripts: A Checklist 1990, A Checklist of Women Writers 1801–1900: Fiction - Verse - Drama: 1801–1900 1990, The Classification of Books in the British Museum Library, 1843–1973 1990, A Handlist to Unpublished Finding-Aids for the London Collections of the British Library 1990, A Handlist of Library Catalogues and Lists of Books and Manuscripts in the British Library Department of

Manuscripts 1991, Books with Manuscript in the British Library 1993, A Catalogue of Books Printed on Vellum in the British Library 1996, Order and Connexion: Studies in Bibliography and the History of the Book (ed.) 1997; numerous specialist articles in periodicals, reviews and printed lectures on lexicography, phonology, historical linguistics, bibliography and the use of computers in the humanities; extensive research on the history of libraries in the British Isles; contribs to the revised Cambridge Bibliography of English Literature, History of English Literature, Times Literary Supplement, The Library, Studio Neophilologica, Publications of the Bibliographical Society of America, Modern Language Review, Philological Quarterly, The Book Collector, Publishing History, The British Library Journal etc.; published more than 2,000 facsimiles of texts in literature, linguistics, history, philoso-phy, religion, art and science. *Address:* 67 Ocean City, St Philip, Barbados (home); 15 Medburn Street, London, NW1 1RJ, England (home). *Telephone:* 416-9097 (St Philip) (home); (20) 7380-1474 (London) (home). *E-mail:* r_alston@sunbeach.net (home). *Website:* www.r-alston.co.uk (office).

ALTANKHUYAG, Norovyn; Mongolian politician; *Chief Deputy Prime Minister;* b. 1958, Ulaangom, Uvs Prov.; ed Mongolian State Univ., Inst. of Man. Devt, Humboldt Univ., Berlin, Germany; Lecturer, Mongolian State Univ. 1981–91; apptd Sec. MSDP 1990, Vice-Chair. 1994–96, Sec.-Gen. 1999; mem. Mongolian Great Khural 1996–2000, 2001–, currently Chief Deputy Prime Minister; Minister of Agric. and Industry April–July 1998, Acting Minister July 1998–Jan. 1999; Chair. Songinohayrhan Democratic Party (DP) 2000–01, Sec.-Gen. DP 2001; Deputy Head, Directorate of Govt Affairs Sept. 2004; Minister of Finance and Economy 2004–06. *Address:* Office of the Chief Deputy Prime Minister, c/o Prime Minister's Office, Government Palace, Sükhbaataryn Talbai 1, Ulan Bator, Mongolia (office). *Telephone:* (11) 322356 (office). *Fax:* (11) 328329 (office).

ALTBACH, Philip G., AB, AM, PhD; American academic; *J. Donald Monan Professor of Higher Education, Boston College;* b. 3 May 1941; s. of Milton Altbach and Josephine Huebsch; m. Edith Hoshino 1962; two s.; ed Univ. of Chicago; Lecturer on Educ., Harvard Univ. 1965–67; Asst Prof., Assoc. Prof., Dept of Educational Policy Studies, Univ. of Wisconsin-Madison 1967–75; Prof., Dept of Educational Org., Admin and Policy, State Univ. of New York, Buffalo 1975, Chair. 1985–88, Dir Comparative Educ. Center 1978–94, Chair. Dept of Social Foundations 1978–82, Adjunct Prof., School of Information and Library Studies 1982, Adjunct Prof., Dept of Sociology 1991; Project Dir NSF study of higher educ. in newly industrializing countries 1988–90; Prof., School of Educ., Boston Coll. 1994–, J. Donald Monan SJ Prof. of Higher Educ. 1996–; Dir Centre for Int. Higher Educ. 1995–; Fulbright Research Prof., Univ. of Bombay 1968; Visiting Prof., Moscow State Univ. 1982, Univ. of Malaya 1983, School of Educ., Stanford Univ. 1988–89; Visiting Fellow, Hoover Inst., Stanford Univ. 1988–89; mem. numerous professional socs; Consultant, Rockefeller Foundation; Sr Assoc. Carnegie Foundation for the Advancement of Teaching 1992–96; lecturer at many int. confs and seminars; N American Ed. Higher Education 1996–2004, Educational Policy 1989–2005; Ed. Review of Higher Education 1998–2004. *Publications:* author or co-author of numer-ous books, book chapters, articles in professional journals etc. *Address:* Boston College, 207 Campion Hall, Chestnut Hill, MA 02467, USA (office). *Telephone:* (617) 552-4236 (office). *E-mail:* altbach@bc.edu (office). *Website:* www.bc.edu/bc/cihe (office).

ALTER, Harvey J., BA, MD; American physician, infectious disease specialist and academic; *Chief, Infectious Disease Section and Associate Director of Research Department, Department of Transfusion Medicine, Warren Magnu-son Clinical Center, National Institutes of Health;* ed Univ. of Rochester, NY, Strong Memorial Hosp., Rochester, Nat. Insts of Health, Bethesda, MD, Univ. of Washington Hosp. System, Seattle, Washington, Georgetown Univ. Hosp., Washington, DC; Instructor in Medicine, Georgetown Univ. School of Medicine 1966–68, Asst Prof. of Medicine 1968–69, Clinical Asst Prof. of Medicine 1969–71, Clinical Assoc. Prof. of Medicine 1971–88, Clinical Prof. of Medicine 1988–; Adjunct Prof., Southwest Foundation for Biomedical Research, San Antonio, TX 1986–; on Faculty, Clinical Research Training Program, NIH 1988–, currently Chief, Infectious Disease Section and Assoc. Dir Research Dept, Transfusion Medicine Warren Magnuson Clinical Center; mem. Scientific Advisory Bd Acrometrix Corpn 1999–; ISBT Liason to Int. Consortium for Blood Safety 2000–; mem. Interagency HCV Working Group 2000–, Scientific Advisory Bd Blood Centers of the Pacific 2000–, Scientific Advisory Bd Hepatitis B Foundation 2002–; Ad Hoc Consultant to Food and Drug Admin (FDA) and Blood Products Advisory Comm. 1997–, Review Panel USAID 1998, FDA Cttee on Emerging Infectious Agents 1999–; Assoc. Ed. Transfusion Medicine Reviews 1986–, Journal of Viral Hepatitis 1994–; Section Ed. 'Hepatology Highlights', Hepatology 2001–; mem. NAS 2002–, Inst. of Medicine 2002–, American Fed. for Clinical Research, American Soc. of Hematology, Int. Soc. of Hematology, Int. Soc. of Blood Transfusion, American Asscn of Blood Banks, Mid-Altantic Asscn of Blood Banks, American Asscn for the Study of Liver Diseases, Asscn of American Physicians; Fellow, American Coll. of Physicians, American Soc. of Internal Medicine; Distinguished Service Medal, USPHS 1977, NIH Directors Award 1986, Emily Cooley Award and Lectureship, American Asscn of Blood Banks 1987, Stanley Davidson Lecturer, Royal Coll. of Physicians, Scotland 1990, Karl Lansteiner Award, American Asscn of Blood Banks 1992, Leon Schiff State of Art Lectureship, American Asscn for the Study of Liver Diseases 1996, Emil von Behring Award Lectureship, Int. Soc. of Blood Transfusion 1996, James Blundell Prize, British Blood Transfusion Service 1999, Laboratory Public Service Nat. Leadership Award 1999, Year 2000 World Health Day Award, American Asscn for World Health 2000, Distinguished Scientist Award, Hepatitis B Foundation 2000, Albert Lasker Award for Clinical Medical Research 2000, Scientific Achievement Award, Hepatitis Foundation International 2001, George Hoyt Whipple Award/Lectureship, U. Roch. 2001, Seymour Kalter

Lectureship, Southwest Foundation for Biomedical Research 2001, Presidential Award, Int. Soc. for Blood Transfusion 2002, Distinguished Scientist Award, American Liver Foundation 2002. *Publications:* numerous articles in scientific journals. *Address:* National Institutes of Health, Warren G. Magunson Clinical Center, Department of Transfusion Medicine, 10 Center Drive, MSC-1184 Building 10, Room 1C711, Bethesda, MD 20892, USA (office). *Telephone:* (301) 496-8393 (office). *Fax:* (301) 402-2965 (office). *E-mail:* halter@dtm.cc.nih.gov (office). *Website:* www.cc.nih.gov (office).

ALTHER, Lisa, BA; American writer, academic and journalist; b. (Elisabeth Greene Reed), 23 July 1944, Kingsport, Tenn.; d. of John Shelton Reed and Alice Greene Reed; m. Richard Alther 1966 (divorced); one d.; ed Wellesley Coll., Radcliffe Coll.; editorial asst, Atheneum Publrs, New York 1967–68; freelance writer 1968–; Lecturer, St Michael's Coll., Winooski, Vt 1980–81; Prof., East Tennessee State Univ. 1999–2000; Basler Chair, East Tennessee State Univ. *Publications:* Kinflicks 1975, Original Sins 1980, Other Women 1984, Bedrock 1990, Birdman and the Dancer 1993, Five Minutes in Heaven 1995, Kinfolks 2007; contrib. to periodicals. *Address:* c/o Martha Kaplan Agency, 115 West 29th Street, New York, NY 10001, USA (office). *Telephone:* (212) 279-7134 (office). *Fax:* (212) 279-6251 (office). *E-mail:* kaplanagency@sprynet.com (office), lisaalther@lisaalther.com (office). *Website:* www.lisaalther.com (office).

ALTMAN, Stuart Harold, BBA, MA, PhD; American health policy researcher, economist and academic; *Sol C. Chaikin Professor of National Health Policy, Heller School for Social Policy and Management, Brandeis University;* b. 8 Aug. 1937, Bronx, New York; s. of Sidney Altman and Florence Altman; m. Diane Kleinberg 1959; three d.; ed City Coll. of New York and UCLA; Labor Market Economist, Fed. Reserve Bd 1962–64; Econ. Consultant and Manpower Economist, Office of Asst Sec. of Defense, Washington, DC 1964–66; Asst Prof. of Econs, Brown Univ. 1966–68, Assoc. Prof. 1968–70; Univ. Fellow and Dir of Health Studies, Urban Inst. 1970–71; Deputy Admin., Office of Health, Cost of Living Council, Dept of Health, Educ. and Welfare 1973–74, Deputy Asst Sec. for Planning and Evaluation (Health) 1971–76; Visiting Lecturer, Grad. School of Public Policy, Univ. of Calif., Berkeley 1976–77; Sol C. Chaikin Prof. of Nat. Health Policy, Heller School, Brandeis Univ. 1977–, Dean 1977–1992; Chair. Prospective Payment Assessment Comm., US Congress 1984–96; currently Chair. Health Industry Forum; Co-Chair. Health Care Task Force for Commonwealth of Mass 2000–04; mem. NAS Inst. of Medicine (mem. Governing Council 1982–83), Bd Robert Wood Johnson Clinical Scholars, Bd Beth Israel Hosp., Brookline, Mass 1979–1991, Bd Tufts New England Medical Center 2002–; Hon. Fellow, American Coll. of Health Care Execs 1996–97. *Publications include:* The Growing Physician Surplus: Will it Benefit or Bankrupt the U.S. Health System? 1982, Ambulatory Care: Problems of Cost and Access (with others) 1983, Will the Medicare Prospective Payment System Succeed? Technical Adjustments Can Make the Difference 1986, Competition and Compassion: Conflicting Roles for Public Hospitals 1989, Strategic Choices for a Changing Health Care System 1996, The Future US Healthcare System: Who Will Care for the Poor and Uninsured? 1997, Regulating Managed Care: Theory, Practice and Future Options 1999, America's Health Care SAFETY NET: Intact but Endangered 2000, Policies for an Aging Society 2002. *Leisure interests:* sailing, cross-country skiing, boating, tennis, golf. *Address:* Heller School for Social Policy and Management, Office 105, POB 549110, Brandeis University, Waltham, MA 02454-9110; 11 Bakers Hill Road, Weston, MA 02493, USA (home). *Telephone:* (781) 736-3803 (office); (781) 891-9144 (home). *E-mail:* altman@brandeis.edu (office). *Website:* heller.brandeis.edu (office).

ALTMANN, Rev. Walter, PhD; Brazilian ecclesiastic and international organization executive; *Moderator, Central Committee, World Council of Churches (WCC);* b. 4 Feb. 1944, Porto Alegre; s. of Friedhold Altmann and Ricarda Altmann, née Sättler; m. Madalena Zwetsch Altmann; four d.; ed studied theology in São Leopoldo, Buenos Aires, Argentina and Hamburg, Germany; parish pastor, Ijui, southern Brazil 1972–74; teacher of systematic theology at Theological Coll., São Leopoldo 1974–, Head of Theological Coll. 1981–87; Dir Ecumenical Inst. for Postgraduate Studies 1989–94; Pres. Latin American Council of Churches 1995–2001; Vice-Pres. Evangelical Church of the Lutheran Confession in Brazil (IECLB) 1998–2002, Pres. 2002–; mem. Council of Lutheran World Fed. 2003–; Moderator Cen. Cttee, World Council of Churches (WCC) 2006–; Award of Merit (category: Theological Reflection), Associated Church Press (ACP) 1990. *Publications:* more than 10 books including Der Begriff der Tradition bei Karl Rahner 1974, Luther and liberation; a Latin American perspective 1992, Nossa fé e suas razões : O Credo Apostólico – história, mensagem, atualidade 2004; 170 articles on Martin Luther, Latin American liberation theology and ecumenism. *Address:* World Council of Churches, PO Box 2100, 150 route de Ferney, 1211 Geneva 2, Switzerland (office). *Telephone:* (22) 791-6111 (office). *Fax:* (22) 791-0361 (office). *E-mail:* moderator-wcc@ieclb.org.br (office). *Website:* www.oikumene.org (office).

ALTON, Roger Martin; British journalist; *Editor, The Independent;* b. 20 Dec. 1947, Oxford; s. of the late Reggie Alton and Jeanine Alton; m. (divorced); one d.; ed Clifton Coll., Exeter Coll., Oxford; grad. trainee, Liverpool Post, then Gen. Reporter and Deputy Features Ed. 1969–74; Sub-Ed. News The Guardian 1974–76, Chief Sub-Ed. News 1976–81, Deputy Sports Ed. 1981–85, Arts Ed. 1985–90, Weekend Magazine Ed. 1990–93, Features Ed. 1993–96, Asst Ed. 1996–98; Ed. The Observer 1998–2007, The Independent 2008–; Editor of the Year, What the Papers Say Awards 2000, GQ Editor of the Year 2005. *Leisure interests:* mountaineering, skiing, films, sports. *Address:* The Independent, Independent House, 191 Marsh Wall, London E14 9RS, England (office). *Telephone:* (20) 7005-2000 (office). *Fax:* (20) 7005-2999 (office). *Website:* www.independent.co.uk (office).

ALTSCHUL, Stephen F., PhD; American mathematician; *Senior Investigator, Computational Biology Branch, National Center for Biotechnology Information;* b. 28 Feb. 1957; ed Harvard Coll., Cambridge, MA and Massachusetts Inst. of Tech.; Guest, Rockefeller Univ., New York 1977–78, Guest Investigator 1984–86; NSF Grad. Fellow, MIT 1981–84; Research Asst, Univ. of N Carolina 1986–87; Postdoctoral Fellow, Nat. Inst. of Diabetes, and Digestive and Kidney Diseases/Math. Research Br., Bethesda, MD 1987–89; Staff Fellow, Nat. Library of Medicine/Nat. Center for Biotechnology Information, Bethesda 1989–91, Sr Staff Fellow 1991–94, Sr Investigator, Computational Biology Br. 1994–, Chair. 1996–98; Adjunct Prof., Univ. of Maryland 2002–; Fellow, American Coll. of Medical Informatics 2001; mem. Advisory Bd Genome Biology 1999–; Pehr Edman Award, Int. Asscn for Protein Structure Analysis and Proteomics 2004. *Publications:* numerous articles in scientific journals. *Address:* Computational Biology Branch, National Center for Biotechnology Information, National Library of Medicine, National Institutes of Health, Bethesda, MD 20894, USA (office). *Telephone:* (301) 435-7803 (office). *Fax:* (301) 480-2288 (office). *E-mail:* altschul@ncbi.nlm.nih.gov (office). *Website:* www.ncbi.nlm.nih.gov (office).

ALTYNBAYEV, General Mukhtar; Kazakhstani air force officer; b. 10 Dec. 1945, Karaganda; m. Gulbanu Rahimbaevna Altynbayeva; one s.; ed Karaganda Aviation Centre, Armavir Air Defence Mil. School, G.K. Jukov Air Defence Mil. Acad.; started career as miner, Karaganda 1962–66; graduated pilot school 1964; became pilot-cadet Kinnel-Cherkassy Aviation Training Centre 1965; held various military command positions including Flight Commdr, Squadron Commdr, Deputy Commdr of training regiment 1972–75, apptd Commdr of a fighter's regiment Ural District 1979; Deputy Div. Commdr then Commdr of Air Defence Div., Turkestan Mil. Dist. 1985–88, Commdr of Air Defence Corps 1992; apptd Air Defence Commdr and Deputy Defence Minister 1992, Air Forces Commdr 1993, Minister of Defence 1996, 2001–06. *Address:* c/o Ministry of Defence, Beibitshilik 51a, Astana 473000, Kazakhstan (office).

ALUVIHARE, Alick; Sri Lankan politician; mem. of Parl. 1961–; fmr Mayor of Matale; Minister in Charge of Rehabilitation 1988; Minister of Post and Telecommunication 1990, Minister of Ports and Shipping 1991; Minister of Home Affairs, Prov. Councils and Local Govt 2001–04. *Address:* c/o Ministry of Home Affairs, Provincial Councils and Local Government, 330 Union Place, Colombo 2, Sri Lanka.

ALVA, Dinkar Shanker, BSc, BSc (Tech.); Indian industrialist; *Chairman, Cotton Textile Export Promotion Council;* b. 2 July 1933, Mangalore, Karnataka; s. of the late Shanker Alva and Kamala Alva; m. Shashikala Alva 1960; one s. one d.; ed Madras Univ.; Asst Weaving Master, Delhi Cloth and Gen. Mills Ltd 1954–58; Industrial Consultant IBCON Pvt. Ltd 1958–60; Sales Exec. Bombay Dyeing and Mfg Co. Ltd 1960–66, Gen. Man. (Sales) 1969–74, Sales Dir 1974–75, Dir 1976–79, Pres. 1979–88, Man. Dir 1988–98; Gen. Man. Anglo-French Textiles Ltd 1966–69; Dir V.T.C. Industries Ltd, Hindustan SPG and WUG Mills Ltd, Banswara Syntex Ltd, Sanghi Polyesters Ltd, Indian Cotton Mills Fed.; Chair. Cotton Textile Export Promotion Council; mem., Man. Cttee All India Exporters' Chamber. *Leisure interests:* music, reading, tennis. *Address:* 18-B L.D. Ruparel Marg, Mumbai 400006, India (home). *Telephone:* (22) 3695419 (home). *Fax:* (22) 3695420 (home). *E-mail:* dinkaralva@hotmail.com (home).

ALVA CASTRO, Luis; Peruvian politician and economist; b. 17 Feb. 1942, Trujillo; ed Univ. Nacional de Trujillo and Univ. Inca Garcilaso de la Vega; fmr Dir Corporación de Desarrollo Económico y Social de la Libertad; Deputy for Libertad; has held various posts in Partido Aprista Peruano including Sec.-Gen. of Northern Regional Org., mem. Political Comm. and Nat. Sec. for Electoral Matters; Chair. Nat. Planning Comm. of Partido Aprista Peruano; Second Vice-Pres. of Repub. 1985–90, Pres. Council of Ministers (Prime Minister) 1985–90, Minister of Economy and Finance 1985–87, of the Interior 2007–08 (resgnd); re-elected to Congress 2001; Pres. Comm. for Integration and Inter-parl. Relations 2001–02; Pres. Econ. Comm. 2001–06; Pres. Andean Parl. Aug.–Dec. 2001, Vice-Pres. 2002–07. *Publications:* La Necesidad del Cambio, Manejo Presupuestal del Perú, En Defensa del Pueblo, Endeudamiento Externo del Perú, Deuda Externa: Un reto para los Latinoamericanos and other books and essays. *Address:* Partido Aprista Peruano, Avda Alfonso Ugarte 1012, Lima, Peru (office). *Telephone:* (1) 4281736 (office). *Website:* www.apra.org.pe (office).

ALVARADO, José Arturo; Honduran banker and government official; b. 28 July 1944, San Pedro Sula; m. Maria Antonieta Arriaga Price de Alvarado; ed Centro Universitario Regional de Norte; Vice-Pres. Citibank NA; Pres., Gen. Man., Bank of Honduras; Exec. Vice-Pres. and Gen. Man., Ficensa Group; Supervisor for Cen. America and Panama, Pacific Financial Group –1990; Prof. of Banking Accountancy, Instituto José Trinidad Reyes; Pres., Honduran Asscn of Banking Insts; Minister of Finance –2004. *Address:* c/o Ministry of Finance, 5a Avda, 3a Calle, Tegucigalpa, Honduras (office).

ALVAREZ, Aida, BA; American journalist and fmr government official; b. Aguadilla, Puerto Rico; ed Harvard Univ.; fmr news reporter and presenter, Metromedia TV, New York; fmr reporter, New York Post; fmr mem. New York City Charter Revision Comm.; fmr Vice-Pres. New York City Health and Hosps Corpn; investment banker, First Boston Corpn New York, San Francisco 1986–93; Dir Office Fed. Housing Enterprise Oversight 1993–97; Dir US Small Business Admin, Washington, DC 1997–2001; Chair. Latino Community Foundation of San Francisco; mem. Bd of Overseers, Harvard Univ. 2000–; mem. Bd of Dirs UnionBanCal Corpn 2004–, Wal-Mart Stores Inc. 2006–; mem. Diversity Advisory Bd Deloitte & Touche LLP; Trustee Latino Community Foundation; fmr mem. Bd of Dirs Nat. Hispanic Leadership Agenda, New York Community Trust, Nat. Civic League; fmr Chair. Bd

Municipal Assistance Corpn/Victim Services Agency, New York; NY State Chair. Gore Presidential Campaign 1988; Nat. Co-Chair. Women's Cttee Clinton Presidential Campaign 1992; mem. Pres. Econ. Transition Team 1992; official spokeswoman for Senator John Kerry during 2004 US presidential elections; Hon. LLD (Iona Coll.) 1985; Front Page Award 1982, Assoc. Press Award for Excellence 1982. *Address:* c/o Board of Directors, UnionBanCal Corporation, 400 California Street, San Francisco, CA 94104, USA (home).

ALVAREZ, Carlos Alberto (Chacho); Argentine politician; *President, Committee of Permanent Representatives, Mercosur;* b. 26 Dec. 1948, Balvanera; m. Liliana Chiernajowsky; one s. three d.; ed Mariano Acosta Coll., Univ. of Buenos Aires; Assessor, Regional Econ. Cttee of Nat. Senate 1983–89; elected Deputy to Nat. Ass. for Fed. Capital 1989–93, 1997–99; left Partido Justicialista and f. Partido Movimento por la Democracia y la Justicia Social (MODEJUSO) 1990; f. Frente Grande; Pres. Frente Grande Bloc in Nat. Constitutional Convention 1994; Founder, Leader Frente del País Solidario—FREPASO 1994–; Vice-Pres. of Argentina 1999–2000 (resgnd); Pres. Cttee of Perm. Reps, Mercosur 2006–. *Address:* Southern Common Market (MERCOSUR/MERCOSUL) (Mercado Común del Sur/Mercado Comum do Sul) Edif. Mercosur, Luis Piera 1992, 1°, 11200 Montevideo, Uruguay. *Telephone:* (2) 412-9024. *Fax:* (2) 418-0557. *E-mail:* sam@mercosur.org.uy. *Website:* www.mercosur.org.uy.

ALVAREZ, Mario Roberto; Argentine architect; b. 14 Nov. 1913, Buenos Aires; m. Jorgelina Ortiz de Rosas 1953; one s. one d.; ed Colegio Nacional, Buenos Aires and Univ. of Buenos Aires; in pvt. practice, Buenos Aires 1937–, as Mario Roberto Alvarez and Assocs 1947–; architect, Ministry of Public Works 1937–42; municipal architect, Avellaneda 1942–47; adviser, Secr. of Public Works, City of Buenos Aires 1958–62; Sec. to World Football Cup Stadium Comm., Buenos Aires 1972–78; Vice-Pres. Cen. Soc. of Architects 1953–55; exhibited, São Paulo Bienal 1957 and several other exhbns of Argentine architecture in Buenos Aires and abroad; Hon. FAIA; Hon. mem. Inst. of City Planning, Peru 1979; Dr hc (La Plata) 1982; Great Prize of the Nat. Fund of Arts 1976; prizewinner in numerous int. architectural competitions. *Address:* Mario Roberto Alvarez y Asociados, Solis 370, Buenos Aires, Argentina. *Website:* www.mariorobertoalvarez.com.ar (office).

ALVAREZ, Ralph, BBA; American business executive; *President and COO, McDonald's Corporation;* ed Univ. of Miami; joined McDonald's 1994, has held several exec. positions including Pres. McDonald's Mexico, Chief Operations Officer and Pres. Cen. Div., McDonald's USA, Pres. McDonald's N America, currently mem. Bd of Dirs, Pres. and COO McDonald's Corpn; mem. Bd of Dirs KeyCorp (nat. bank-based financial services co.); serves on Pres.'s Council and Int. Advisory Bd, Univ. of Miami, Fla; fmr Pres. Ronald McDonald House Charities, Mexico; mem. Bd of Trustees, Field Museum, Chicago. *Address:* McDonald's Corpn, McDonald's Plaza, Oak Brook, IL 60523, USA (office). *Telephone:* (630) 623-3000 (office). *Fax:* (630) 623-5004 (office). *E-mail:* info@mcdonalds.com (office). *Website:* www.mcdonalds.com (office).

ÁLVAREZ MARTÍNEZ, HE Cardinal Francisco; Spanish ecclesiastic; b. 14 July 1925, Santa Eulalia de Ferroñes; ordained priest 1950; consecrated Bishop of Tarazona 1973; Bishop of Calahorra and La Calzada 1976–89, of Orihuela 1989–95; Archbishop of Toledo 1995–; cr. Cardinal 2001. *Address:* Arco de Palacio 3, 45002 Toledo, Spain (office). *Telephone:* (25) 224100 (office); (25) 223439 (home). *Fax:* (25) 222639 (office); (25) 222771 (home).

ÁLVAREZ RENDUELES, José Ramón, LLM, PhD; Spanish central banker, business executive and university professor; *President, ArcelorMittal España SA;* b. 17 June 1940, Gijón; s. of Ramón Alvarez Medina; m. Eugenia Villar 1964; four s. one d.; State Economist 1964; rank of Full Prof. in Public Finance 1973; Head of Econ. Studies in Planning Comm. 1969; Dir Inst. of Econ. Devt 1973; Tech. Sec.-Gen., Ministry of Finance 1973–75, Under-Sec. for Econ. Affairs 1975–76; Sec. of State for Econ. Affairs 1977–78; Gov. Bank of Spain 1978–84; Chair. COFIR 1988–93, Productos Pirelli 1986–, Peugeot España 1996, Aceralia/ArcelorMittal España SA 1997–; Pres. Prince of Asturias Foundation 1996–2008; Gran Cruz Mérito Civil, Gran Cruz Isabel la Católica, Legión d'Honneur (France). *Publications:* Valoración actual de la imposición sobre consumo 1971, La Hacienda pública y el medio ambiente 1973. *Leisure interests:* golf, music, literature, lawn tennis. *Address:* ArcelorMittal España SA, Calle Albacete 3, 28027 Madrid (office); Peguerinos 12-F, 28035 Madrid, Spain (home). *Telephone:* (91) 5969527 (office). *Fax:* (91) 5969366 (office). *E-mail:* jose-r.rendueles@arcelomittal.com (office). *Website:* www.arcelormittal.com (office).

ALVEAR VALENZUELA, María Soledad; Chilean lawyer and politician; b. 17 Sept. 1950, Santiago; d. of Ernesto Alvear and María Teresa Valenzuela; m. Gutenberg Martinez Ocamica 1973; two s. one d.; ed Univ. of Chile; Prof., Faculty of Law and Social Sciences, Univ. of Chile 1973–75; in pvt. legal practice 1973–90; consultant to UN 1987–90; Dir Comisión Preparatoria, Servicio Nacional de la Mujer (women's org.) 1990; Minister, Dir Servicio Nacional de la Mujer 1991; Minister of Justice 1994–99; Leader of Pres. Ricardo Lagos Escobar election campaign 1999; Minister of Foreign Affairs 2000–04; mem. Exec. Council Comisión Interamericana de Mujeres (women's org.) –1990; Orden al Mérito Institucional, Consejo Mundial de Educ. 1991; Pres. Partido Demócrata Cristiano 2004–08, won party nomination to run for presidency of Chile (election Dec. 2005) but withdrew from race; Senator from Santiago East 2006–. *Publications:* Algunas Sugerencias de Modificaciones al Derecho de Familia 1984, Situación de la Mujer Campesina frente a la Legislación 1987, La Mujer Campesina y la Legislación en Colombia 1990. *Leisure interests:* reading, tennis. *Address:* Senado, Santiago Chile (office). *Telephone:* (2) 250-4561 (office). *Fax:* (2) 236-152 (office). *E-mail:* salvear@senado.cl (office). *Website:* www.senado.cl (office); www.soledadalvear.cl.

ALWARD, Peter Andrew Ulrich; British record company executive and classical music consultant; b. 20 Nov. 1950, London; s. of the late Herbert Andrew Alward and Marion Evelyne Schreiber; ed Bryanston School and Guildhall School of Music and Drama; worked for Simrock Music Publrs 1968–70; EMI Records UK 1970–74, European Co-ordinator EMI Classical Div. (Munich) 1975–83, Exec. Producer for all EMI recordings with Herbert von Karajan 1976–89, Man. (UK) Artists and Repertoire 1983, Int. Dir A&R 1985, Vice-Pres. 1989, Sr Vice-Pres. 1997, Pres. EMI Classics 2002–04; mem. Royal Opera House Covent Garden Opera Advisory Bd 1998–99; mem. Bd Trustees Young Concert Artists Trust 1999–2004; mem. Artistic Cttee, Herbert von Karajan Stiftung 2003–; Consultant and mem. European Advisory Bd, The Cleveland Orchestra 2006–; Trustee, Masterclass Media Foundation 2006–; mem. Editorial Advisory Bd, BBC Music 2006–; Dir (Non-Exec.) Royal Opera House/Opus Arte 2007–; mem. Kuratorium Salzburg Int. Stiftung Mozarteum 2008–; Consultant, Bavarian Radio Symphony Orchestra 2008–; Gramophone Special Achievement Award 2004. *Leisure interests:* classical music, painting and sculpture, theatre, books, collecting stage and costume designs, cooking, travelling. *Address:* 24 Midway, Walton-on-Thames, Surrey, KT12 3HZ, England (home). *Telephone:* (1932) 248985 (home). *E-mail:* peter@wotan844.fsnet.co.uk (home).

AMADI, Elechi, BSc; Nigerian writer, fmr teacher, army officer and administrative officer; *Founder and Director, Elechi Amadi School of Creative Writing;* b. 12 May 1934, Aluu, Rivers State; s. of Chief Wonuchukwu Amadi and Enwere Amadi; m. 1st Dorah Nwonne Ohale 1957; m. 2nd Priye Iyalla 1991; four s. eight d.; ed Govt Coll. Umuaphia, Univ. Coll. Ibadan, Brookings Inst., USA; worked as land surveyor 1959–60, teacher 1960–63; army officer (capt.) 1963–66, with 3rd Marine Commandos during civil war 1968–69; Prin. Asa Grammar School 1967; Perm. Sec. Rivers State Govt 1973–83, Commr of Educ. 1987–89, of Lands and Housing 1989–90; Writer-in-Residence and Lecturer, Rivers State Coll. of Educ. 1984–85, Dean of Arts 1985–86, Head Dept of Literature 1991–93; Founder and Dir Elechi Amadi School of Creative Writing 1997–; Chair. Asscn of Nigerian Authors (Rivers State Br.); Fellow, Nigerian Acad. of Educ. 2003–; mem. Order of Fed. Repub.; Hon. DSc (Rivers State Univ. of Science and Tech. 2003; Rivers State Silver Jubilee Merit Award 1992, Ikwerre Ethnic Nationality Merit Award for Literature 1995, Rivers State Silver Jubilee Award 1992, Rivers State Productivity Award 2005. *Publications:* novels: The Concubine 1966, The Great Ponds 1969, The Slave 1978, Estrangement 1986; plays: Isiburu 1973, The Road to Ibadan 1977, Dancer of Johannesburg 1978, The Woman of Calabar 2002; Sunset in Biafra (war diary) 1973; Ethics in Nigerian Culture (philosophy) 1982, Speaking and Singing (papers and poems) 2003. *Leisure interests:* reading, music, playing the piano, billiards. *Address:* PO Box 331, Port Harcourt, Rivers State, Nigeria (home). *Telephone:* (803) 339-8036 (home). *E-mail:* info@elechiamadi.org (office); amadielechi@yahoo.com (home). *Website:* www.elechiamadi.org.

AMADOU, Hama; Niger politician; fmr Man. Dir Niger Broadcasting Bd; fmr Pvt. Sec. to Pres. Seyni Kountche and Pres. Ali Saibou (q.v.); Prime Minister of Niger 1995, 2000–07; now Sec.-Gen. Mouvement national pour une société de développement—Nassara (MNSD). *Address:* c/o Office of the Prime Minister, BP 893, Niamey, Niger (office).

AMADUZZI, Luigi, KCVO; Italian diplomatist; b. 22 March 1937, Naples; s. of Aurelio Amaduzzi; m. Giovanna Amaduzzi; one s. one d.; ed Univ. of Rome; joined diplomatic service 1963; Second Sec., London 1967; First Sec., Moscow 1969; First Sec., later Counsellor, Sec.-Gen.'s Office 1972, Head of Office 1983, 1991; Counsellor, Washington, DC 1975; Amb. to Jordan 1985–88, to Romania 1988; apptd Diplomatic Counsellor to the Pres. 1992; Amb. to UK 1999–2004. *Leisure interests:* tennis, painting. *Address:* c/o Ministry of Foreign Affairs, Piazzale della Farnesina 1, 00194 Rome, Italy. *Telephone:* (06) 36911. *Fax:* (06) 36918899. *E-mail:* relazioni.pubblico@esteri.it. *Website:* www.esteri.it.

AMAMOU, Mohamed; Tunisian diplomatist; b. 7 Oct. 1933, Kairouan; s. of Mohamed Amamou and Zohra Saadi; m. Beya Boujdaria; one s. one d.; ed Collège Sadiki and Inst. des Hautes Etudes; Chargé d'affaires, Jordan 1969–71; Amb. to Zaïre 1972–73; Gen. Consul in Paris 1973–74; Amb. to Lebanon and Jordan 1974–78; Dir of Political Affairs for the Arab World, Ministry of Foreign Affairs 1978–81; Chargé de mission, Ministry of Foreign Affairs 1981–85; Amb. to Morocco and Portugal (resident in Rabat) 1985–87, to Syria 1987–89; Sec. of State for Maghreb Affairs 1989–90; Prin. Adviser to Pres. of Tunisia 1990–91, Minister Adviser 1991; Sec.-Gen. of Arab Maghreb Union 1991–2000; Grand Officier, Ordre de la République Tunisienne; Chevalier, Ordre Indépendance and several foreign decorations. *Address:* c/o Ministry of Foreign Affairs, place du Gouvernement, la Kasbah, 1006 Tunis, Tunisia. *Telephone:* (71) 660-088 (office).

AMAN, Datuk Anifah, BA; Malaysian politician; *Minister of Foreign Affairs;* b. 16 Nov. 1953, Keningau, Sabah; m.; three s.; ed Univ. of Buckingham, UK; Cttee mem., Beaufort Div., Malay Nat. Org. (UMNO) 1991–94, Treasurer 1994–99, Head of Kimanis Div. 2004–; mem. Parl. for Beaufort 1999–; Deputy Minister of Primary Industries 1999–2004, of Plantation Industries and Commodities 2004–08; Minister of Foreign Affairs 2009–; fmr Man. Sabah Football M-League Team; fmr Vice-Pres., Exec. Cttee mem. and Council mem., Football Asscn of Malaysia; fmr Pres. Sabah Football Asscn; Ahli Setia Darjah Kinabalu 1994, Panglima Gemilang Darjah Kinabalu 1998, Darjah Mahkota Pahang 2004; Special Award of Leadership for Sports, Ministry of Culture 1996. *Leisure interests:* football, golf. *Address:* Ministry of Foreign Affairs, Wisma Putra, 1 Jalan Wisma Putra, Presint 2, 62602 Putrajaya, Malaysia (office). *Telephone:* (3) 88874000 (office). *Fax:* (3) 88891717 (office). *E-mail:* webmaster@kln.gov.my (office). *Website:* www.kln.gov.my (office).

AMANI, Michel N'Guessan; Côte d'Ivoirian politician; *Minister of Defence;* b. 1957, Messoukro; fmr teacher of history and geography in various secondary schools in Bouaké, Botro and Bodokro; Sec.-Gen. Front Populaire Ivoirien (FPI) for Bouaké 1990–92, Fed.-Sec. for Centre region 1992; Minister of Nat. Educ. 2000–07, of Defence 2007–. *Address:* Ministry of Defence, Camp Galliéni, côté Bibliothèque nationale, PO Box V241, Abidjan, Côte d'Ivoire (office). *Telephone:* 20-21-02-88 (office). *Fax:* 20-22-41-75 (office).

AMANMYRADOV, Orazgeldy; Turkmenistani politician; *Minister of Internal Affairs;* b. 1970, Dostluk, Akhal Velayat; ed Makhtumkuli Turkmen State Univ.; joined Ministry of Nat. Security 1995, held various positions; Vice-Chancellor Mil. Acad. 2007; Minister of Internal Affairs 2007–. *Address:* Ministry of Internal Affairs, 744000 Aşgabat, pr. Magtymguly 85, Turkmenistan (office). *Telephone:* (12) 35-59-23 (office).

AMANN, Ronald, MSocSc, PhD, FRSA, ACSS; British academic and civil servant (retd); *Emeritus Professor of Comparative Politics, University of Birmingham;* b. 21 Aug. 1943, North Shields; s. of George Amann and Elizabeth Towell; m. Susan Peters 1965; two s. one d.; ed Heaton Grammar School, Newcastle-upon-Tyne and Univ. of Birmingham; Consultant, OECD and Research Assoc. 1965–69; Lecturer, Sr Lecturer in Soviet Science Policy, Univ. of Birmingham 1969–83, Dir Centre for Russian and East European Studies (CREES) 1983–89, Prof. of Comparative Politics 1986–, now Prof. Emer., Dean Faculty of Commerce and Social Science 1989–91, Pro-Vice-Chancellor 1991–94; Chief Exec. and Deputy Chair. Econ. and Social Science Research Council (ESRC) 1994–99; Dir Gen. Centre for Man. and Policy Studies, Cabinet Office 1999–2002; Chair. Centre for Research on Innovation and Competition, Univ. of Manchester; Visiting Fellow, Osteuropa Inst. Munich 1975; Specialist Adviser, House of Commons Select Cttee on Science and Tech. 1976, mem. Steering Cttee, Centre for the Analysis of Risk and Regulation, LSE; Founding Academician, Acad. of Learned Socs. for the Social Services 1999; ind. mem. West Midlands Police Authority 2007–. *Publications:* co-author: Science Policy in the USSR 1969, The Technological Level of Soviet Industry 1977, Industrial Innovation in the Soviet Union 1982, Technical Progress and Soviet Economic Development 1986. *Leisure interests:* walking, modern jazz, cricket. *Address:* c/o Centre for Russian and East European Studies, University of Birmingham, Edgbaston, Birmingham, B15 2TT (office); 26 Spring Road, Edgbaston, Birmingham, B15 2HA, England. *Telephone:* (121) 440-6186.

AMANO, Mari; Japanese diplomatist and international organization executive; *Deputy Secretary-General, Organisation for Economic Co-operation and Development;* m.; three d.; ed Univ. of Tokyo, Hertford Coll., Oxford, UK; career diplomat for over 30 years in Ministry of Foreign Affairs, posts have included service in Econ. Affairs Bureau, Ministry of Foreign Affairs 1980–84, Embassy in Kuwait 1984–87, Perm. Mission to OECD, Paris 1987–92, Minister at Embassies in Thailand 1994–96, USA 1996–98, Deputy Dir-Gen. in Multilateral Co-operation Dept, Ministry of Foreign Affairs 2000–01, Chief Negotiator for Trade Related Investment Measures in Uruguay Round 2000–03, Consul Gen., Houston, Tex. 2001–04; Deputy Exec. Dir Korean Peninsula Energy Devt Org. (KEDO) Secr. 2004–07; Deputy Sec.-Gen. OECD, in charge of Devt Cluster and Policy Coherence dossier 2007–. *Address:* OECD, 2 rue André Pascal, 75775 Paris Cedex 16, France (office). *Telephone:* 1-45-24-82-00 (office). *Fax:* 1-45-24-85-00 (office). *E-mail:* webmaster@oecd .org (office). *Website:* www.oecd.org (office).

AMANPOUR, Christiane, CBE, AB; British broadcasting correspondent; *Chief International Correspondent, Cable News Network (CNN);* b. 12 Jan. 1958, London; d. of Mohammad Amanpour and Patricia Amanpour; m. James Rubin (q.v.) 1998; one s.; ed primary school in Tehran, Iran, Holy Cross Convent, UK, New Hall School, UK and Univ. of Rhode Island, USA; radio producer/research asst, BBC Radio, London 1980–82; radio reporter, WBRU Brown Univ., USA 1981–83; electronic graphics designer, WJAR, Providence, RI 1983; Asst CNN int. assignment desk, Atlanta, GA 1983; news writer, CNN, Atlanta 1984–86; reporter/producer, CNN, New York 1987–90; Int. Corresp. CNN 1990, Sr Int. Corresp. 1994, Chief Int. Corresp. 1996–; assignments have included coverage of Gulf War 1990–91, break-up of USSR and subsequent war in Tbilisi 1991, extensive reports on conflict in Fmr Yugoslavia, Israel and Afghanistan and coverage of civil unrest and political crises in Haiti, Algeria, Somalia, Rwanda, Iran and Pakistan; Fellow, Soc. of Professional Journalists; several hon. degrees including Dr hc (Rhode Island); three Dupont-Columbia Awards 1986–96, nine Emmy Awards, Women, Men and Media Breakthrough Award 1991, named Woman of the Year by New York Chapter of Women in Cable and Telecommunications 1994, George Polk Award 1997, Nymphe d'Honneur, Monte Carlo Television Festival 1997, two News and Documentary Emmy Awards 1999, two George Foster Peabody Awards 1999, Univ. of Missouri Honor Award for Distinguished Service to Journalism 1999, Courage in Journalism Award, Worldfest-Houston Int. Film Festival Gold Award, Livingston Award for Young Journalists, Edward R. Murrow Award for Distinguished Achievement in Broadcast Journalism 2002, Sigma Chi Award, ranked by Forbes magazine amongst 100 Most Powerful Women (72nd) 2005, (79th) 2006, (74th) 2007, (91st) 2008. *Leisure interests:* reading, riding, tennis, swimming, sky-diving. *Address:* CNN International, CNN House, 19–22 Rathbone Place, London, W1P 1DF, England (office). *Telephone:* (20) 7637-6800 (office).

AMARAL, Diogo Freitas do, PhD; Portuguese politician and academic; b. 21 July 1941, Póvoa de Varzim; s. of Duarte P. C. Freitas do Amaral and Maria Filomena Campos Trocado; m. Maria José Salgado Sarmento de Matos 1965; two s. two d.; Prof. of Admin. Law, Lisbon Univ. 1968, Head Dept of Public Law, Prof., Portuguese Catholic Univ. 1978; mem. Council of State 1974–75, Parl. 1975–82, 1992–93; Pres. Centre Democrat Party (CDS) 1974–82, 1988–91; Pres. European Union of Christian Democrats 1981–82; Deputy Prime Minister and Minister for Foreign Affairs 1980–81, Deputy Prime Minister and Minister of Defence 1981–83; Presidential cand. 1986; Pres. 50th Gen. Ass. of UN 1995–96; Minister of Foreign Affairs and Portuguese Communities Abroad 2005–06 (resgnd); Founder, Chair. School of Law, New Univ. of Lisbon 1996–2001; Pres. Fundação Portugal Século XXI 1986–90, PETROCONTROL 1992–2000; Order of Christ, Order of Santiago, Order of Henry the Navigator; Calouste Gulbenkian Prize (twice), Henry the Navigator Prize. *Plays:* O Magnífico Reitor 2001, Viriato 2002. *Publications:* A Utilização do Domínio Público Pelos Particulares 1965, A Execução das Sentenças dos Tribunais Administrativos 1967, Conceito e natureza do recurso hierárquico 1981, Uma Solução para Portugal 1985, Curso de Direito Administrativo I, 1986, II 2001, O Antigo Regime e a Revolução (Memórias Políticas: 1941–76) 1995, História das Ideias Políticas, Vol. I 1998, D. Afonso Henriques. Biografia 2000, Estudios de Direito Público (two vols) 2004, Manual de Introdução ao direito (Vol. I) 2004. *Leisure interests:* music, horses, reading, theatre, writing, political philosophy. *Address:* Av. Fontes Pereira de Melo 35, 12 B, 1050-118, Lisbon, Portugal.

AMARASINGHE, Somawansa; Sri Lankan politician; *Leader, Janatha Vimukhti Peramuna;* mem. and Leader of Peope's Liberation Front (Janatha Vimukhti Peramuna—JVP), f. 1964, party banned following coup attempt 1971, regained legal status 1977, banned again 1983, regained legal status 1994, Amarasinghe is only surviving mem. of JVP Political Bureau, fled to London, UK and continued to provide party leadership from abroad, returned 2004. *Address:* Janatha Vimukthi Peramuna, 198/19 Panchikawattha Road, Colombo 10, Sri Lanka (office). *Telephone:* (11) 4400511 (office). *Fax:* (11) 2786050 (office). *E-mail:* jvplanka@sltnet.lk (office). *Website:* www.jvpsrilanka .com (office).

AMARATUNGA, John E. A.; Sri Lankan politician; mem. Parl. 1978–; Minister of State 1989–90; Minister of Prov. Councils 1990; Minister of Home Affairs and Prov. Councils 1993; Minister of Interior and Christian Affairs 2001–04. *Address:* c/o Ministry of Interior, Colombo, Sri Lanka.

AMARI, Akira; Japanese politician; b. 27 Aug. 1948, Atsugi, Kanagawa; ed Pref. Sr High School, Atsugi, Keio Univ. Law School; worked for Sony Corpn 1972–74; mem. House of Reps of New Liberal Club for Ninami-Kanto, for Kanagawa Pref. 13th Dist 1983–; subsequently joined LDP, Sr Dir LDP Commerce and Industry Panel 1990–95, Chair. 1995; Parl. Vice-Minister of Int. Trade and Industry 1989; Deputy Sec.-Gen. LDP 1999–2001, Chief Deputy Sec.-Gen. 2001; Minister of Labour 1998–99; Chair. House Budget Cttee 2004–05; Minister of Economy, Trade and Industry 2006–08; mem. Japan-Korea Parliamentarians' Union, Japan-China Friendship Parliamentarians' Union. *Leisure interest:* collecting antiques. *Address:* Liberal-Democratic Party (LDP), 1-11-23, Nagata-cho, Chiyoda-ku, Tokyo 100-8910, Japan (office). *Telephone:* (3) 3581-6211 (office). *E-mail:* koho@ldp.jimin.or.jp (office). *Website:* www.jimin.jp (office); www.amari-akira.com.

AMARJARGAL, Rinchinnyamyn, MEcons; Mongolian politician; m.; one s.; ed Moscow Inst. of Econs, Univ. of Bradford, UK; officer, Cen. Council of Mongolian Trade Unions 1982–83; Lecturer, Mil. Acad. and Tech. Univ. 1983–90; Dir Econs Coll., Ulan Bator 1991–96; MP 1996–99, Minister and Acting Minister of External Relations April–Dec. 1998, Prime Minister of Mongolia 1999–2000; mem. Mongolian Nat. Democratic Party (MNPP) Gen. Council; Dr hc (Bradford) 2000. *Address:* c/o Office of the Prime Minister, Ulan Bator, Mongolia (office).

AMATO, Giuliano, LLB, LLM; Italian politician and academic; b. 13 May 1938, Turin; ed Univ. of Pisa, Columbia Univ., USA; Prof. of Italian and Comparative Constitutional Law, Univ. of Rome 1975–97; joined Italian Socialist Party (PSI) 1958, mem. Cen. Cttee 1978–94, Nat. Deputy Sec. 1988–92, Leader –2000, Asst Sec.; mem. Camera dei Deputati for Turin-Novara-Vercelli 1983, 1987–93; Under-Sec. of State, Presidency of Council of Ministers 1983–87, Vice-Pres. Council of Ministers and Minister of the Treasury 1987–89; Deputy Prime Minister of Italy 1987–88, Prime Minister 1992–93, 2000–01; Pres. Italian Antitrust Authority 1994–97; foreign debt negotiator for Albanian Govt 1991–92; Minister for Constitutional Reforms 1998–99; Minister for Treasury 1999–2000; Vice-Pres. EU Special Convention on Pan-European Constitution 2001–06; Senator for Grosseto 2001–06; Minister of Internal Affairs 2006–08; mem. Partito Democratico 2007–; Foreign Hon. mem. American Acad. of Arts and Sciences 2001. *Publications:* Antitrust and the Bounds of Power 1997, Tornare al Futuro 2001, Dialoghi post-secolari 2006, Un altro mondo è possibile? Parole per capire e per cambiare 2006. *Address:* Partito Democratico, Piazza Saint'Anastasia 7, 00186 Rome, Italy (office). *Telephone:* (06) 675471 (office). *Fax:* (06) 67547319 (office). *E-mail:* info@partitodemocratico.it (office). *Website:* www .partitodemocratico.it (office).

AMATONG, Juanita D., BSc, MA; Philippine economist and public finance expert; *Member, Monetary Board, Bangko Sentral ng Pilipinas;* b. 23 March 1935, Bindoy, Negros Oriental; ed Silliman Univ., Dumaguete City, Syracuse Univ. NY, USA; Assoc. Prof., Silliman Univ. 1959–60; tax economist, IMF, Washington, DC 1963–68; Lecturer, Andres Bonifacio Coll., Zamboanga del Norte, Philippines 1968–71; Sr Financial Analyst, Ministry of Finance 1971–83; Special Asst to Prime Minister 1984–86; Asst Sec. (Minister) of Finance 1986–92, Under-Sec. (Deputy Minister) of Finance 1992–95, 2001–03, Sec. (Minister) of Finance 2003–05; Exec. Asst Cen. Bank of Philippines 1984–86; Resident Consultant, Govt Myanmar Consultancy 1992; Exec. Dir, Alt. Exec. Dir, Advisor to Exec. Dir World Bank, IFC and Multilateral Investment Guarantee Agency, Washington, DC 1995–98; consultant, Chemonics International 1998–2000; Man. Pnr, Resource and Measures Assoc. Co. 1999–2000; mem. Monetary Bd Bangko Sentral ng Pilipinas (BSP), Devt Budget Coordinating Cttee, Policy Governing Bd Targeted Interventions for Econ. Reforms and Governance (TIERG) 2004–, Policy Advisory Bd Cities Alliance, World Bank (IBRD) 2005–; mem. Bd Trustees Bantay Katarungan (NGO on sentinel of justice) 2000–, Silliman Univ.; Officer, Philippine Legion of Honors 1998; Outstanding Silliman Univ. Alumnus 1977, First Woman Exec. Dir World Bank Group, Philippine Centennial 1998. *Publications:* Decontrol and its Effects, Taxation of Capital Gains in Developing Countries, The Revenue Importance of Lotteries, The Reconciliation of Government Transaction Statistics: National Accounts, Commission on Audit and Office of Budget and Management Reports 1987, Local Government Fiscal and Financial Management Best Practices 2005. *Leisure interests:* reading, cooking. *Address:* Bangko Sentral ng Pilipinas, Apolinario Mabini, corner Pablo Ocampo Sr Street, Malate, 1004 Manila (office); 21 Masambahin Street, Teacher's Village, Dilliman Quezon City 1100, Philippines (home). *Telephone:* (2) 5212733 (office); (2) 9224647 (home). *Fax:* (2) 5246689 (office). *E-mail:* jamatong@bsp.gov.ph (office). *Website:* www.bsp.gov.ph (office).

AMBANI, Anil D., MBA; Indian business executive; *Chairman and CEO, Anil Dhirubhai Ambani Group;* b. 4 June 1959, Mumbai; s. of the late Dhirubhai Hirachand Ambani and of Kokilaben Dhirubhai Ambani, brother of Mukesh Ambani (q.v.); m. Tina Ambani; two s.; ed Univ. of Bombay (now Mumbai), Univ. of Pennsylvania, USA; apptd Co-CEO Reliance Industries Ltd 1983, currently Vice-Chair., Man. Dir; Dir Reliance Europe Ltd; Dir and Vice-Chair. Indian Petrochemicals Corpn Ltd –2005 (resgnd); Chair. and CEO Anil Dhirubhai Ambani Group (cr. after division of Reliance Industries Ltd and comprising Reliance Energy, Reliance Capital, and Reliance Infocomm) 2005–; mem. Rajya Sabha (upper house of Parl.) 2004–06; Chair. Bd Govs Nat. Safety Council; mem. Bd Govs Indian Inst. of Man., Ahmedabad, Indian Inst. of Tech., Kanpur; Business India Businessman of the Year 1997, Indian Alumni Award, Wharton India Econ. Forum 2001, Bombay Man. Asscn Entrepreneur of the Decade Award 2002. *Address:* Reliance Communications Ltd, I Block, 2nd Floor, Dhirubhai Ambani Knowledge City, Mumbai 400 710, India (office). *Telephone:* (22) 3037-5522 (office). *Fax:* (22) 3037-5577 (office). *E-mail:* anil.ambani@relianceada.com (office). *Website:* www.relianceadagroup.com (office).

AMBANI, Mukesh D., BChemEng, MBA; Indian business executive; *Chairman and Managing Director, Reliance Industries Limited;* b. 19 April 1957, Colony of Aden, Yemen; s. of the late Dhirubhai Hirachand Ambani and of Kokilaben Dhirubhai Ambani, brother of Anil D. Ambani (q.v.); m. Nita Ambani; three c.; ed Univ. Inst. of Chemical Tech., Mumbai, Stanford Univ., USA; joined family-owned Reliance Industries Ltd (India's largest pvt. co.) 1981, Man. Dir 1986–, Chair. 2002–, also Dir Reliance Europe Ltd (Reliance Energy, Reliance Capital, and Reliance Infocomm spun off to brother's co. Anil Dhirubhai Ambani Enterprises 2005); Chair. Bd Indian Petrochemicals Corpn Ltd, FLAG Telecom; Owner Indian Premier League team Mumbai Indians; mem. Prime Minister's Advisory Council on Trade and Industry, Council of Scientific and Industrial Research, Bd Govs Nat. Council of Applied Econ. Research, Advisory Council of the Indian Banks Asscn; Chair. Bd Trustees, Indian Inst. of Software Eng; 'Global Leader for Tomorrow', World Econ. Forum, Switzerland 1994, Business India Businessman of the Year Award 1997, 'Distinguished Alumnus of the Decade', Univ. of Mumbai 1999, Ernst & Young Entrepreneur of the Year Award 2000, rated one of 'India's Most Admired CEOs' in Business Barons-Taylor Nelson Sofres-Mode Survey 2002, Mumbai Man. Asscn Entrepreneur of the Decade Award 2002, ranked first by India Today in The Power List 2003, 2004, Asia Soc. Leadership Award Medal 2004, ranked 42nd amongst the World's Most Respected Business Leaders 2004, ranked second among the four Indian CEOs featured in a survey conducted by Pricewaterhouse Coopers and published in Financial Times, London 2004, World Communication Award for the Most Influential Person in Telecommunications, Total Telecom 2004, chosen by Voice and Data magazine as Telecom Man of the Year 2004, ranked 13th by Fortune magazine in Asia's Power 25 list of The Most Powerful People in Business 2004, chosen as Businessman of the Year by a public poll in India conducted by NDTV 2007, US-India Business Council Leadership Award for 'Global Vision' 2007, Chitralekha Person of the Year Award, Chief Minister of Gujarat 2008. *Address:* Reliance Industries Ltd, Maker Chambers IV, 222, Nariman Point, Mumbai 400 021, India (office). *Telephone:* (22) 22785000 (office). *Fax:* (22) 22870303 (office). *E-mail:* M_Ambani@ril.com (office). *Website:* www.ril.com (office).

AMBARTSUMOV, Yevgeniy Arshakovich, CandHistSc; Russian politician, social scientist, political analyst and journalist; *Professor, Universidad La Salle;* b. 19 Aug. 1929, Moscow; s. of Arshak Ambartsumov and Alexandra Vassilevskaia; m. Nina Ignatovskaia 1978; one s.; ed Moscow Inst. of Int. Relations; with Novoye Vremya 1954–59, Problems of Peace and Socialism 1959–63; Sr Scientific Researcher, Inst. of World Econs and Int. Relations 1956–59, Head of Dept Inst. of World Int. Labour Movt 1966–69; Head of Dept, Inst. of Sociology 1969–73; Head of Dept of Politics, Inst. of Economics of World Socialist System (now Inst. of Int. Economic and Political Studies) 1973–90; Russian People's Deputy 1990–93; Chair. Foreign Affairs Cttee of Russian Supreme Soviet 1992–93; mem. State Duma (Parl.) 1993–94; mem. Presidential Council 1993–95; Amb. to Mexico, also accred to Belize 1994–99; Prof. Universidad La Salle, Mexico 1999–; Order of Aguila Azteca con banda Mexico 1999. *Publications include:* How Socialism Began: Russia under Lenin 1978, NEP: A Modern View 1988, Socialism: Past and Present (ed.) 1990. *Leisure interest:* books. *Address:* Universidad La Salle, Benjamin Franklin 47, Col Condesa, Del. Cuauhtémoc, 06140 México, DF, Mexico. *Telephone:* (55) 26-14-40-79 (Mexico) (home); (495) 332-64-25 (Russia) (home). *Website:* www.ulsa.edu.mx.

AMBARTSUMYAN, Sergey Aleksandrovich, DTech; Armenian state official and scientist; *Honorary Director, Institute of Mechanics;* b. 17 March 1922, Alexandrapol (now Gumry); s. of Alexander G. Ambartsumyan and Anna V. Ambartsumyan; m. Seda A. Ambartsumyan 1949; one s. one d.; Rector Yerevan State Univ. 1977–92; Hon. Dir Inst. of Mechanics 1993–; Academician Armenian Acad. of Sciences 1964– (Vice-Pres. 1975–77), Armenian Eng Acad. 1992–, Armenian Philosophy Acad. 1993–; USSR People's Deputy 1989–91, mem. Supreme Soviet 1979–91; Academician Int. Acad. of Astronautics; mem. Int. Acad. of Sciences, Educ., Industry and Arts 1997–; Foreign mem. Russian Acad. of Sciences 2003; Hon. Pres. Armenian Acad. of Eng 1997–; Hon. mem. Slovak. Acad. of Sciences, Int. Eng Acad. 1991; Hon. Prof., Peninsula Inst. of Information, Tech. and Business 1998; Dr hc (Bratislava) 1984; many awards and prizes. *Publications:* Theory of Anisotropic Shells 1961, Theory of Anisotropic Plates 1967, General Theory of Anisotropic Shells 1974, Magnetoelasticity of Thin Shells and Plates 1977, Different Modulus Theory of Elasticity 1982, Fragments of the Theory of Anisotropic Shells 1990, Some Problems of Electro-magneto-elasticity of Plates 1991, Vibrations and Stability of Current-carrying Elastic Plates 1991, Conductive Plates and Shells in Magnetic Field 1998, Micropolar Theory of Shells and Plates 1999; over 200 articles on mechanics of solids. *Leisure interests:* painting, literature, history. *Address:* Institute of Mechanics, 24 Marshal Bagramian Avenue, 375019 Yerevan, Armenia (office). *Telephone:* (10) 520644 (office); (10) 521503 (office); (10) 532050 (home). *Fax:* (10) 569281. *E-mail:* samb@sci.am (office); samb@sd.am.

AMBRASEYS, Nicholas, PhD, FICE, FREng; British professor of engineering seismology; *Professor Emeritus, Imperial College London;* b. 19 Jan. 1929, Athens, Greece; s. of Neocles Ambraseys and Cleopatra Ambraseys; m. Xeni Stavrou 1955; ed Nat. Tech. Univ. of Athens and Imperial Coll. of Science and Tech., Univ. of London; Prof. of Hydrodynamics, Nat. Tech. Univ. of Athens 1963–64; Lecturer in Soil Mechanics, Imperial Coll., London 1965–68, Reader in Eng Seismology 1968–73, Prof. 1973–94, Head of Eng Seismology Section 1969–94, Sr Research Fellow 1995–, Sr Research Investigator 1996–, currently Prof. Emer.; led UN/UNESCO earthquake reconnaissance missions to Yugoslavia, Iran, Turkey, Pakistan, Romania, Algeria, Italy, E Africa, Nicaragua and Cen. Africa 1963–81; mem. UN Advisory Bd for reconstruction of Skopje 1964–69; Chair. British Nat. Cttee for Earthquake Eng, ICE 1966–76; Vice-Pres. European Asscn of Earthquake Eng 1967–75; mem. and Chair. UNESCO Advisory Cttee on Earthquake Risk 1971–81; mem. Academia Europaea 1996; ; Hon. Fellow, Int. Asscn for Earthquake Eng 1992; Dr hc (Nat. Tech. Univ. Athens) 1993; Busk Medal for Scientific Discovery, Royal Geographical Soc. 1975. *Publications:* A History of Persian Earthquakes (with G. Melville) 1982, The Seismicity of Egypt, Arabia and the Red Sea 1994, Seismicity of Turkey 1995, Seismicity of Central America 2000, Seismicity of Iceland 2000 and over 200 papers in scientific and eng journals. *Leisure interests:* historical geography, archaeology, travel. *Address:* Department of Civil Engineering, Imperial College, London, SW7 2BU; 19 Bede House, Manor Fields, London, SW15 3LT, England (home). *Telephone:* (20) 7589-5111 (office); (20) 8788-4219 (home). *Fax:* (20) 7225-2716 (office). *E-mail:* n.ambraseys@ic.ac.uk (office); ambra@otenet.gr (home).

AMBROSE, Rona, BA, MA; Canadian politician; *Minister of Labour;* b. 15 March 1969, Valley View, Alberta; m. Bruce; ed Univs of Victoria and Alberta; fmr political columnist; fmr owner Ambrose Consulting Ltd; fmr Sr Intergovernmental Officer, Int. and Intergovernmental Relations Dept, Govt of Alberta; MP (Edmonton-Spruce Grove) 2004–; Sr Intergovernmental Affairs Critic, Conservative Official Opposition 2004, later Int. Trade Critic; Minister of the Environment 2006–07; Pres. of the Queen's Privy Council for Canada, Minister of Intergovernmental Affairs and Minister of Western Econ. Diversification 2007–08, Minister of Labour and Vice-Chair. Treasury Bd Cttee 2008–. *Address:* Treasury Board, Corporate Communications, l'Esplanade Laurier, 10th Floor, West Tower, 300 Laurier Avenue West, Ottawa, ON K1A 0R5, Canada (office). *Telephone:* (613) 957-2400 (office). *Fax:* (613) 998-9071 (office). *E-mail:* info@tbs-sct.gc.ca (office). *Website:* www.tbs-sct.gc.ca (office); www.wd.gc.ca (office); www.ronaambrose.com (office).

AMBROZIC, HE Cardinal Aloysius Matthew; Canadian ecclesiastic; *Archbishop Emeritus of Toronto;* b. 27 Jan. 1930, Gabrje, Yugoslavia (now Slovenia); s. of Aloysius Ambrozic and Helen Ambrozic; ed St Augustine's Seminary, Toronto, Univ. of San Tommaso, Rome 1958, Biblicum, Rome, Univ. of Wurzburg; family emigrated to Canada 1948; ordained priest 1955; curate, St Teresa's Parish, Port Colborne, Ont. 1955–56; Prof., St Augustine's Seminary, Toronto 1956–57, 1960–67, 1970–76; Prof. of New Testament Exegesis, Toronto School of Theology 1970–76; Dean of Studies, St Augustine's Seminary, Toronto 1971–76; ordained Auxiliary Bishop, Archdiocese of Toronto 1976–86, Coadjutor Archbishop 1986–90, Archbishop of Toronto 1990–2006, Archbishop Emer. 2006–; mem. Pontifical Council for Pastoral Care of Migrants 1990, Vatican Congregation for Clergy 1991–, Pontifical Council for Culture 1993; cr. Cardinal 1998; mem. Congregation for Divine Worship and Discipline of Sacraments, Congregation for Oriental Churches 1999; apptd to Council of Cardinals for Study of Organizational and Econ. Problems of Holy See 2004; Hon. DD (Univ. of St Michael's Coll.) 1991. *Publications:* The Hidden Kingdom: A Redaction-Critical Study of the References to the Kingdom of God in Mark's Gospel 1972, Remarks on the Canadian Catechism 1974. *Address:* c/o Catholic Pastoral Centre, 1155 Yonge Street, Toronto, ON M4T 1W2, Canada (office).

AMELING, Elisabeth (Elly) Sara; Dutch singer; b. 1938, Rotterdam; m. Arnold W. Beider 1964; ed studied singing with Jo Bollekamp, with Jacoba and Sam Dresden and with Bodi Rapp; studied French art song with Pierre Bernac; recitals in Europe, SA, Japan; debut in USA 1968, annual tours of USA and Canada 1968–, farewell tour 1995; ssng with Concertgebouw Orchestra, New Philharmonic Orchestra, BBC Symphony Orchestra, Berlin Philharmonic, Cincinnati Symphony, San Francisco Symphony, Toronto

Symphony, Chicago Symphony; has appeared in Mozart Festival, Washington, DC 1974, Caramoor Festival 1974, Art Song Festival, Princeton, NJ 1974; teaching selected masterclasses; Knight Order of Orange-Nassau; Dr hc (Univ. of BC) 1981, (Westminster Choir Coll., Princeton, NJ) 1985, (Cleveland Inst. of Music) 1986, (Shenandoa Univ.) 1988; First Prize, Concours Int. de Musique, Geneva, Grand Prix du Disque, Edison Prize, Preis der Deutschen Schallplattenkritik, Stereo Review Record of the Year Award. *Recordings include:* Mozart Concert, Handel Concert, Cantatas (Bach), Mörike Lieder (Wolf), Aimez-vous Handel?, Aimez-vous Mozart?, Christmas Oratorio (Bach), Symphony No. 2 (Mahler), Te Deum (Bruckner), Italienisches Liederbuch (Wolf).

AMELIO, William J., BChemEng, MA; American computer industry executive; b. 25 Nov. 1957; m. Jamie Amelio; ed Lehigh Univ., Sloan Master's Program at Stanford Univ.; with IBM 1979–97, held several Sr Man. positions, including Gen. Man. of Operations for IBM's Personal Computing Div.; Pres. and CEO Honeywell's transportation and power-systems divs, and Head of turbocharging-systems business at Allied Signal Inc. (predecessor of Honeywell International Inc.) 1997–2000; Exec. Vice-Pres. and COO NCR Corpn's Retail and Financial Group 2000–01; Sr Vice-Pres., Asia-Pacific and Japan, Dell Inc. 2001–05; Pres. and CEO Lenovo Group Ltd 2005–09 (resgnd), special adviser to Bd 2009; Co-f. (with his wife) Caring for Cambodia (through Amelio Foundation). *Address:* c/o Lenovo Group Ltd, 1009 Think Place, Morrisville, NC 27560, USA (office).

AMENÁBAR, Alejandro; Spanish/Chilean film director; b. 1973, Santiago, Chile; ed Complutense Univ., Madrid. *Films:* Tésis (Thesis) 1996, Abre los Ojos (Open Your Eyes) 1997, The Others 2001, Mar adentro (The Sea Inside) (Best Foreign Language Film, Nat. Bd of Review, Best Dir, Best Film, Goya Awards 2005, Best Foreign Film, Ind. Spirit Awards 2005, Best Foreign Language Film, Acad. Awards 2005) 2004. *Address:* c/o Dimension Films, 375 Greenwich Street, New York, NY 10012, USA (office).

AMERASINGHE, Chittharanjan Felix, PhD, LLD; Sri Lankan judge and international lawyer; b. 2 March 1933, Colombo; s. of Samson Felix Amerasinghe, OBE and Mary Victorine Abeyesundere; m. Wimala Nalini Pieris 1964; one s. two d.; ed Royal Coll., Colombo, Trinity Hall, Univ. of Cambridge, UK, Harvard Univ. Law School, USA; Supervisor in Law, Trinity Hall, Cambridge Univ. 1955–57; Jr Exec., Caltex Oil Co., Colombo 1959–61; Lecturer in Law, Univ. of Ceylon 1962–65, Sr Lecturer 1965–68, Reader 1968–69, Prof. of Law 1969–71; Counsel, World Bank 1970–75, Sr Counsel 1975–81, Exec. Sec., World Bank Admin. Tribunal 1981–96; Judge UN Tribunal, New York 1997–2000; Judge, Commonwealth Int. Arbitral Tribunal 1999–2002; Consultant in Int. Law, Govt of Ceylon 1963–70; mem. Ceylon Govt Comm. on Local Govt 1969; Adjunct Prof. of Int. Law, School of Law, American Univ. 1991–93; mem. Panel of Arbitrators and Conciliators, Law of the Sea Convention, Int. Centre for Settlement of Investment Disputes, Panel of UN Compensation Comm. for Kuwait; Exec. Council mem. American Soc. of Int. Law 1980–83; Assoc. mem. Inst. de Droit Int. 1981–87, mem. 1987–; mem. Int. Law Asscn 1986–; mem. Sr Editorial Bd, Project on Governing Rules of Int. Law, American Soc. of Int. Law; mem. Hon. Cttee Int. Inst. of Human Rights 1968–; mem. Advisory Bd Int. Inst. of Environmental Law 1987–98, Sri Lanka Journal of Int. Law 1989–, Int. Orgs Law Review 2004–; Sr Fellow (Visiting), Trinity Hall, Univ. of Cambridge 1996–97; Trinity Hall Law Studentship 1956–59, Research Fellowship, Harvard Univ. Law School 1957–58; Hon. Prof. of Int. Law, Univ. of Colombo 1991–94; Henry Arthur Thomas Classical Award, Univ. of Cambridge 1953, Angus Classical Prize 1953, Clement Davies Prize for Law 1955, Major Scholar and Prizeman, Trinity Hall, Cambridge 1953–56, Yorke Prize 1964, Certificate of Merit, American Soc. of Int. Law 1988–89. *Publications:* Some Aspects of the Actio Iniuriarum in Roman-Dutch Law 1966, Defamation and Other Injuries in Roman-Dutch Law 1968, State Responsibility for Injuries to Aliens 1967, Studies in International Law 1969, The Doctrines of Sovereignty and Separation of Powers in the Law of Ceylon 1970, The Law of the International Civil Service (two vols) 1988, Documents on International Administrative Tribunals 1989, Case Law of the World Bank Administrative Tribunal (three vols) 1989, 1991, 1994, Local Remedies in International Law 1990, 2003, Principles of the Institutional Law of International Organizations 1996, 2005, Jurisdiction of International Tribunals 2003, Evidence in International Litigation 2005, Diplomatic Protection 2008; articles in leading law and int. law journals. *Leisure interests:* classical and classical jazz music, art, artifacts, philately, photography, walking. *Address:* 6100 Robinwood Road, Bethesda, MD 20817, USA (home). *Telephone:* (301) 229-2766 (home). *Fax:* (301) 229-4151 (home).

AMES, Bruce Nathan, PhD, FAAS; American biochemist and academic; *Professor, Graduate School, Department of Biochemistry and Molecular Biology, University of California, Berkeley;* b. 16 Dec. 1928, New York; s. of Dr M. U. Ames and Dorothy Andres Ames; m. Dr Giovanna Ferro-Luzzi 1960; one s. one d.; ed Cornell Univ. and California Inst. of Tech., Nat. Inst. of Health, Maryland; Postdoctoral Fellow, NIH 1953–54, Biochemist 1954–60; NSF Fellow, Labs of F. C. Crick, Cambridge and F. Jacob, Paris 1961; Chief Section of Microbial Genetics, Lab. of Molecular Biology, NIH 1962–67; Prof. of Biochemistry, Univ. of California, Berkeley 1968–, Chair. Dept of Biochemistry 1983–89; Sr Research Scientist, Children's Hosp. Oakland Research Inst. 1968–; mem. Nat. Cancer Advisory Bd 1976–82, NAS, American Acad. of Arts and Sciences; Foreign mem. Royal Swedish Acad. of Sciences 1989; ACS Eli Lilly Award 1964, Arthur Flemming Award 1966, Rosenstiel Award 1976, Fed. of American Socs. for Experimental Biology Award 1976, Wankel Award 1978, John Scott Medal 1979, Bolton L. Corson Medal 1980, New Brunswick Lectureship Award, American Soc. for Microbiology 1980, Gen. Motors Cancer Research Fund Charles S. Mott Prize 1983, Gairdner Foundation Award 1983, Tyler Prize for Environmental Achievement 1985, ACS Spencer Award 1986, Roger G. Williams Award in Preventive Nutrition 1989, Gold Medal American Inst. of Chemists 1991, Glenn Foundation Prize 1992, shared Japan Prize 1997, Nat. Medal of Science 1998, Linus Pauling Prize for Health Research 2001, Lifetime Achievement Award of American Soc. for Microbiology 2001, Thomas Hunt Morgan Medal, Genetics Society of America 2004, among the few hundred most-cited scientists in all fields of science. *Publications:* more than 500 scientific papers in areas of operons, biochemical genetics, histidine biosynthesis, mutagenesis, detection of environmental carcinogens and mutagens, oxygen radicals as a cause of aging and degenerative diseases, anti-carcinogens, micronutrient deficiency. *Address:* Children's Hospital Oakland Research Institute, 5700 Martin Luther King Jr. Way, Oakland, CA 94609-1673 (office); University of California, Berkeley, Department of Biochemistry and Molecular Biology, 142 LSA, Room 3200, Berkeley, CA 94720-3200; 1324 Spruce Street, Berkeley, CA 94709, USA (home). *Telephone:* (510) 450-7625 (office). *Fax:* (510) 597-7128 (office). *E-mail:* bnames@uclink4.berkeley.edu (office). *Website:* mcb.berkeley.edu/site (office).

AMES, Michael McClean, OC, PhD, FRSC; Canadian anthropologist and academic; *Professor Emeritus of Anthropology, University of British Columbia;* b. 19 June 1933, Vancouver; s. of Ernest O. F. Ames; m. (separated); one s. one d.; ed Univ. of British Columbia and Harvard Univ.; Asst Prof. of Sociology, McMaster Univ. 1962–64; Asst Prof. Univ. of BC 1964, now Prof. Emer. of Anthropology; Dir Museum of Anthropology, Univ. of BC 1974–97, 2002–04; Co-Ed. of Manlike Monsters; consultant to various museums and projects since 1976; Guggenheim Fellowship 1970–71; Fellow, Canadian Museums Asscn 1996; Soc. of Applied Anthropology in Canada Weaver Tremblay Award 1994, US Western Museums Asscn Dir's Chair Award 2000, Int. Council of Museums Prix d'Excellence 2002. *Publications:* Manlike Monsters on Trial 1980, Museums, The Public and Anthropology 1986, Cannibal Tours and Glass Boxes 1992; articles in academic and museum journals. *Leisure interests:* hiking, photography, running. *Address:* Department of Anthropology-Sociology, The University of British Columbia, 6303 NW Marine Drive, Vancouver, BC V6T 1Z1, Canada (office). *Telephone:* (604) 822-1913 (office). *Fax:* (604) 822-6161 (office). *E-mail:* mames@interchange.ubc.ca (office). *Website:* www.anso.ubc.ca (office).

AMES, Roger; Trinidadian music company executive; b. 1949; with EMI UK 1975–79; staff A & R Dept, Phonogram, PolyGram UK 1979–83, Chair. and CEO PolyGram UK 1991–94, Group Exec. and Vice-Pres. PolyGram Int. Ltd 1996–99, Pres. PolyGram Music Group 1996–99; Gen. Man. London Records 1983, later Man. Dir, purchased back-catalogue of Factory Records; Pres. Warner Music Int. 1999, Chair. and CEO Warner Music Group 1999–2004; Sr Advisor, Time Warner, EMI Music 2005–07; Pres. EMI Music, North America 2007–08, Pres. EMI Music, UK Jan.–May 2008. *Address:* c/o EMI Group Ltd, 27 Wrights Lane, London, W8 5SW, England (office).

AMEY, Julian Nigel Robert, MA; British charitable trust administrator and fmr civil servant; *Chief Executive Officer, Chartered Institution of Building Services Engineers;* b. 19 June 1949; s. of Robert Amey and Diana Amey (née Coles); m. Ann Victoria Brenchley 1972; three d.; ed Wellingborough School, Magdalene Coll., Cambridge; Dir Int. Sales and Marketing Longman Group Ltd 1985–89; Exec. Dir BBC English World Service 1989–94; seconded to Dept of Trade and Industry 1994–96; Dir-Gen. Canning House 1996–2001; Partner The English Place 2001–; CEO Chartered Inst. of Building Services Engineers 2001–; Chair. Anglo-Chilean Soc.; Gov. Bath Spa Univ. Coll., Trinity Coll. London. *Publications:* Spanish Business Directory 1979, Portuguese Business Dictionary 1981. *Leisure interests:* cricket, tennis, travel. *Address:* Chartered Institution of Building Services Engineers, 222 Balham High Road, London, SW12 9BS, England. *Telephone:* (20) 8772-3609. *Fax:* (20) 8673-0822.

AMIGO VALLEJO, HE Cardinal Carlos, OFM; Spanish ecclesiastic; *Archbishop of Seville;* b. 23 Aug. 1934, Medina de Rioseca, Valladolid; ed Faculty of Medicine, Univ. of Valladolid, Cen. Univ. of Madrid; joined Order of Friars Minor (Franciscans); ordained priest in Rome 1960; provincial of Franciscan Prov. of Santiago 1970; Archbishop of Tangier, Morocco 1973–82; consecrated, Church of San Francisco el Grande, Madrid, 1974; acted as mediator to resolve conflicts in Algeria, Libya, Morocco, Mauritania and Tunisia 1976–82; Metropolitan Archbishop of Seville 1982–, Cardinal-Priest of St Mary of Monserrat of the Spanish 2003–; Pres. Episcopal Comm., 5th Centennial of the Evangelization of America 1984, High Bishops of Spain 1996–, Episcopal Comm. of Missions and Cooperation with Churches 1999; del. to Ordinary Ass. of World Synod of Bishops, Vatican City 1977, 1983, 1994, Gen. Conf. of Latin American Episcopate, Dominican Repub. 1992; mem. Exec. Cttee Spanish Episcopal Conf. 1984, Pontifical Comm. for Latin America 1990, 1995, 2000; mem. Pontifical Council for Health 2002; mem. Acads of Buenas Letras, Medicina and Belles Artes of Seville; Orden al Mérito de los Padres de la Patria Dominicana (Dominican Repub.) 1995; Hon. PhD (Tech. Univ. of Cibao, Dominican Repub.) 1995; Silver Medal of Repub. of Panama 2000. *Address:* Arzobispado de Sevilla, Pza. Virgen de los Reyes s/n, 41004, Seville, Spain (office). *Website:* www.diocesisdesevilla.org (office).

AMIN, Mudhaffar, PhD; Iraqi diplomatist; m. Zahr Amin; three c.; ed Univ. of Durham, UK; entered Ministry of Foreign Affairs 1980s; fmr Head of Iraqi Interests Section, Jordanian Embassy, London (Baghdad's only accred diplomat in London at the time). *Address:* c/o Ministry of Foreign Affairs, PO Box 35217, Amman, 11180, Jordan. *Telephone:* (6) 5735150. *E-mail:* inquiry@mfa.gov.jo.

AMIN, Samir, DEcon; Egyptian economist; *Director (Africa Office), Third World Forum;* b. 4 Sept. 1931, Cairo; s. of Farid Amin and Odette Amin; m. Isabelle Eynard 1957; ed Univ. of Paris; Sr Economist, Econ. Devt Org., Cairo

1957–60; Tech. Adviser for Planning to Govt of Mali 1960–63; Prof. of Econs, Univs of Poiters, Paris and Dakar; Dir UN African Inst. for Econ. Devt and Planning 1970–80; Dir Third World Forum (Africa Office), Senegal 1980–. *Publications include:* Trois expériences africaines de développement, Mali, Guinée, Ghana 1965, L'économie du Maghreb (2 vols) 1967, Le développement du capitalisme en Côte d'Ivoire 1968, Le monde des affaires sénégalais 1969, The Maghreb in the Modern World 1970, Neo-colonialism in West Africa 1973, Accumulation on a World Scale 1974, Unequal Development 1976, The Arab Nation 1978, Class and Nation 1980, The Arab Economy Today 1982, Eurocentrism 1989, Delinking: Towards a Polycentric World 1990, Maldevelopment: Anatomy of a Global Failure 1990, The Empire of Chaos 1992, Rereading The Post War Period 1994, Capitalism in the Age of Globalisation 1996, Les défis de la mondialisation 1996, Spectres of Capitalism 1998, L'hégémonisme des Etats-Unis et l'effacement du projet européen 2000. *Leisure interest:* history. *Address:* Third World Forum, B.P. 3501, Dakar, Senegal (office). *Telephone:* 821-11-44 (office). *Fax:* 821-11-44 (office). *E-mail:* ftm@refer.sn (office). *Website:* www.refer.sn/ftm.

AMIN, Sohail; Pakistani diplomatist; *Ambassador to Nepal;* fmr Dir-Gen. for Europe, Ministry of Foreign Affairs; Amb. to Nepal 2005–. *Address:* Embassy of Pakistan, Pushpanjali, Maharajgunj, Chakrapath, POB 202, Kathmandu, Nepal (office). *Telephone:* (1) 4374024 (office). *Fax:* (1) 4374012. *E-mail:* parepktm@wlink.com.np (office).

AMINE SOUEF, Mohamed al-; Comoran politician and diplomatist; apptd Amb. to Egypt (concurrently accred Amb. to the Arab League) 1995; Minister of Foreign Affairs 1999–2002, Minister of State, Minister of Foreign Affairs, Co-operation, Francophone Affairs, with responsibility for Comorans Abroad 2002–06. *Address:* c/o Représentation du Gouvernement, BP 20, Dzaoudzi 97610, Comoros (office).

AMINU, Jibril Muhammed, PhD, FRCP; Nigerian diplomatist and physician; b. 25 Aug. 1939, Song, Adamawa State; m.; eight c.; ed Ahmadu Bello Univ., Zaria, Univ. of Ibadan and London hosps; Prof. of Medicine, specializing in Cardiology and Hypertension, Univ. of Maiduguri 1979–95, Univ. Vice-Chancellor (Pres.) 1980–85; Minister of Educ. 1985–89; Minister of Petroleum and Mineral Resources 1989–92; mem. World Bank Preparatory Cttee on Educ. for All, Jornitien 1990; Chair. First Meeting of the Ministers of Educ. in Sub-Saharan Africa; Vice-Pres. for Africa of the Third World Acad. of Sciences Network of Scientific Orgs; fmr Pres. African Petroleum Producers' Asscn; Pres. OPEC Conf. 1991–92; Del. to Nigerian Nat. Constitutional Conf. 1994–95; Amb. to USA 2000–04; Senator 2003–; Foundation mem. Bd of Trustees, People's Democratic Party of Nigeria 1998; Fellow, Nigerian Acad. of Science 1972, W African Coll. of Physicians 1980; Ordre National de la Légion d'Honneur 2001. *Publications:* Quality and Stress in Nigerian Education 1986, Observations 1987. *Address:* c/o Ministry of Foreign Affairs, Maputo St, Zone 3, Wuse District, Abuja, Nigeria (office).

AMIREDJIBI, Chabua; Georgian writer, editor and politician; b. (Mzechabuk I. Amiredjibi), 18 Nov. 1921, Tbilisi; s. of Irakli Amiredjibi and Maria Nakashidze; m. Tamar Djavakhishvili 1966; four s. (one deceased) two d.; ed Tbilisi State Univ., A. Pushkin Tbilisi Pedagogical Inst.; as student of Tbilisi State Univ. arrested for anti-Soviet activities 1944, sentenced to 25 years' imprisonment in Gulag, released 1959; Dir Advertising-Information Bureau Goskinoprokat 1965–70; Chief Ed. Kino anthology 1970–83; Dir Mematiane documentary film studio 1983–89; mem. Parl. 1992–96; Chair. Defence Fund of Georgia 1992–96; f. PEN Centre of Georgia, Pres. 1994–97, Hon. Chair. 1998–; Publr and Ed.-in-Chief Ganakhlebuli Iveria newspaper 1999–2003; mem. Writers' Union of Georgia 1964–; mem. editorial bds of several journals and newspapers; Honoured Art Worker of Georgia 1987, Order of Honour 1994, Order of King Vakhtang Gorgasili (First Class) 2001; USSR State Prize 1979, Sh. Rustaveli Prize 1994. *Screenplay:* Data Tutashkhia 1979. *Publications:* Road (short stories) 1964, Tales for Children 1966, Data Tutashkhia (novel) 1973, Gora Mborgali (novel) 1994, King George the Excellent (novel) 2003, From the Thoughts 2007. *Leisure interests:* sports, football, basketball. *Address:* 8/45 Tamarashvili Street, 0162 Tbilisi, Georgia (home). *E-mail:* kutsna@posta.ge (office).

AMIS, Martin Louis, BA; British writer; b. 25 Aug. 1949, Oxford; s. of the late Kingsley Amis and of Hilary Bardwell; m. 1st Antonia Phillips 1984 (divorced 1996); two s.; m. 2nd Isabel Fonseca 1998; two d.; ed Exeter Coll., Oxford; Asst Ed., TLS 1971, Fiction and Poetry Ed. TLS 1974–75; Asst Literary Ed., New Statesman 1975–77, Literary Ed. 1977–79; special writer for The Observer newspaper 1980–; Prof., Centre for New Writing, Univ. of Manchester 2007–. *Publications:* fiction: The Rachel Papers (Somerset Maugham Award 1974) 1973, Dead Babies 1975, new edn as Dark Secrets 1977, Success 1978, Other People: A Mystery Story 1981, Money: A Suicide Note 1984, Einstein's Monsters (short stories) 1987, London Fields 1989, Time's Arrow, or, the Nature of the Offence 1991, God's Dice 1995, The Information 1995, Night Train 1997, Heavy Water and Other Stories 1999, Yellow Dog 2003, The Last Days of Muhammad Atta (short stories, novella, essay) 2006, House of Meetings (novella) 2006; non-fiction: My Oxford (with others) 1977, Invasion of the Space Invaders 1982, The Moronic Inferno and Other Visits to America 1986, Visiting Mrs Nabokov and Other Excursions 1993, Experience: A Memoir (James Tait Black Memorial Prize for Biography 2001) 2000, The War Against Cliché (essays and reviews 1971–2000) 2001, Koba the Dread: Laughter and Twenty Million 2002, The Second Plane 2008; contrib. to many publs. *Leisure interests:* tennis, chess, snooker. *Address:* Wylie Agency (UK) Ltd, 17 Bedford Square, London, WC1B 3JA, England (office). *Telephone:* (20) 7908-5900 (office). *Fax:* (20) 7908-5901 (office). *E-mail:* mail@wylieagency.co .uk (office).

AMIT, Maj.-Gen. Meir, MBA; Israeli business executive; b. (Meir Slutsky), 17 March 1921, Tiberias; s. of Shimon Slutsky and Haya Slutsky; m. Yona Kelman 1942; three d.; ed Columbia Univ., New York; mem. Kibbutz Alonim 1939; served in Israeli Defence Forces 1948–68, fmr Head of Mil. Intelligence and Head of Israeli Security Service; Pres. Koor Industries 1968–77; Minister of Transport and Communication 1977; mem. of Knesset 1977–81; man. consultant 1982; Chair. MA'OF 1982–85; Dir Zim Lines, Israel Corpn 1985, Yachin, DSI Teva Pharmaceutical, Lapidot Oil Drilling; Chair. Gen. Satellite Corpn, Spacecom 1982, Satellite Communications, Center for Special Studies; numerous awards include Israel Prize for Personal Achievement and Contribution 2003. *Publications:* Head On, Yes Sir. *Leisure interests:* photography, collecting dolls and educational games. *Address:* 55 Arlazorof Street, Ramat-Gan 52493, Israel (office). *Telephone:* (3) 5477337 (office); (3) 6729777 (home). *Fax:* (3) 5427711; (3) 6725935 (home). *E-mail:* amit173@netvision.net.il (home).

AMITAL, Yehuda; Israeli politician and rabbi; b. 1925, Transylvania; m.; five c.; in Nazi labour camp 1943–44; migrated to Israel 1944; yeshiva studies in Jerusalem; ordained in Jerusalem; joined Haganah during war of independence; Head, Yeshivat Har Etzion 1968–2004; f. Meimad, the Movt for Religious Zionist Renewal 1993; Minister without Portfolio 1995–96; rank of capt. in army reserve. *Address:* c/o Yeshivat Har Etzion, Alon Shevut, Gush Etzion 90433, Israel.

AMMANN, Karl; Swiss wildlife photographer, journalist, author and conservationist; b. 1948, St Gallen; ed St Gallen Grad. School of Econs, Cornell Univ., USA; moved to Kenya to start work with Intercontinental Hotels 1974, spent six months helping Zaïre Govt organize 'The Rumble in the Jungle' boxing match between George Foreman and Muhammad Ali 1974; moved to Cairo to manage hotel 1978; spent two years in Masai Mara Game Reserve to do research for first photographic title, Cheetah 1980; set up eco-tourism camp in Masai Mara 1983, camp in Virunga Mountains, Rwanda 1986, sold camps to concentrate on photography; Media Asia Advertising Award 1991, BBC Wildlife Photographer of the Year, World in Our Hands Award 1996–2000, Dolly Green Award for Artistic Achievement, Genesis Awards 1997, Chimfunshi Pal award in recognition of his work to raise awareness of plight of chimpanzees 1999, Special Genesis Award for media work in exposing bushmeat crisis 2000, Winner, Landscape and Nature category, American Photo, Special Contest Issue No. 5, a Time Magazine Hero of the Environment 2007, Brigitte Bardot International Genesis Award 2008. *Achievements include:* undertook first investigative expedition in Africa looking into apes orphaned by bushmeat trade 1992; initiated campaign with European Zoo Assoc. leading to a two-million signature petition being presented to European Parl. 1995; has also produced images of a hitherto unknown ape Bili Ape. *Television:* documentary: The Cairo Connection (broadcast on SABC2's 50/50) (Environmental Journalist of the Year, South African Broadcasting Corpn 2008). *Publications:* Cheetah 1984, The Hunters and the Hunted 1989, Die Grossen Menschenaffen (photography) 1992, Masai Mara 1993, Gorillas 1998, Little Bull: Growing Up in Africa's Elephant Kingdom 1998, Orangutan Odyssey (photography) 1999, The Great Apes and Humans (co-author) 2001, Great Ape Odyssey (photography) 2002, Eating Apes (with Dale Peterson) (Science Book of the Year, The Economist and Discovery Magazine) 2003, Consuming Nature (photographic title) 2005. *Address:* 25 Joubert Mansions, Jubilee Place, Chelsea, London, SW3 3TH, England. *Telephone:* (176) 22448 (Nairobi) (office); (301) 854-0388 (USA) (office). *Fax:* (176) 32407 (Nairobi) (office); (2) 750035 (Nairobi) (office). *E-mail:* kamman@form-net.com (office). *Website:* www.karlammann.com (office).

AMOAKO, Kingsley Y., BA, MA, PhD; Ghanaian economist; *President, African Center for Economic Transformation;* b. 1947; ed Univ. of Ghana, Univ. of California, Berkeley, USA; with IBRD from the 1970s, Dir Dept of Educ. and Social Policy 1993–95; UN Under-Sec.-Gen. and Exec. Sec. Econ. Comm. for Africa (ECA) 1995–2005; Distinguished African Scholar, Woodrow Wilson Int. Center 2006; Pres. African Center for Econ. Transformation, Accra 2006–; mem. Policy Advisory Bd DATA (debt, AIDS, trade, Africa); Dr hc (Addis Ababa Univ.) 2003, (Kwame Nkrumah Univ. of Science and Tech., Kumasi) 2005. *Address:* c/o DATA, 1400 Eye Street., NW, Suite 600, Washington, DC 20005, USA (office).

AMORIM, Celso Luiz Nunes; Brazilian diplomatist and politician; *Minister of Foreign Affairs;* b. 3 June 1942, Santos, São Paulo; s. of Vicente Matheus Amorim and Beatriz Nunes Amorim; m. Ana Maria Amorim; three s. one d.; ed Rio Branco Inst., Diplomatic Acad. Vienna and London School of Econs; Lecturer in Portuguese, Rio Branco Inst. 1976; Lecturer, Dept of Political Science and Int. Relations, Univ. of Brasília 1977–; Dir-Gen. EMBRAFILME (Brazilian Film Corpn) 1979-1982; Deputy Head of Mission, The Hague 1982–85; Perm. Rep. to UN, GATT and Conf. on Disarmament, Geneva 1991–93 (Pres. 2000), to UN and WTO 1999–2001; Sec. for Int. Affairs, Ministry of Science and Tech. 1987–88; Dir –Gen. for Cultural Affairs, Ministry of Foreign Affairs 1989–90, for Econ. Affairs 1990–91, Sec.-Gen. 1993, Minister of Foreign Affairs 1993–94, 2003–; Perm. Rep. to UN, New York 1995–99; Amb. to UK 2001–02; Chair. UN Security Council Resolution Sanctions Cttee on Kosovo 1998–99, UN Security Council Panels on Iraq 1999, Governing Body ILO 2000, Council for Trade in Services, WTO 2001; Perm. mem. Dept of Int. Affairs, Inst. of Advanced Studies, Univ. of São Paulo; mem. Canberra Comm. on Elimination of Nuclear Weapons 1966, Int. Task Force on Security Council Peace Enforcement 1997; Foreign Policy Asscn Medal (USA) 1999. *Publications:* several works on political theory, int. relations, cultural policies and subjects connected with science and tech. *Leisure interests:* reading, travel, art, cinema. *Address:* Ministry of Foreign Affairs, Palácio do Itamaraty, Esplanada dos Ministérios, Bloco H, 70170-900, Brasília DF,

Brazil (office). *Telephone:* (61) 3411-6161 (office). *Fax:* (61) 3225-1272 (office). *Website:* www.mre.gov.br (office).

AMOS, Daniel P., BS; American insurance industry executive; *Chairman and CEO, AFLAC Inc.;* b. Pensacola, FL; ed Univ. of Georgia; joined AFLAC Inc. 1973, Sales Dept 1973–83, Pres. 1983–87, COO 1987–90, CEO AFLAC Inc. and mem. Bd 1990–, Chair. 2001–; mem. Bd of Dirs Synovus Financial Corpn, Southern Co.; mem. Bd of Trustees, Children's Healthcare of Atlanta, House of Mercy of Columbus; fmr mem. Consumer Affairs Advisory Cttee, Securities and Exchange Comm.; fmr Chair. Japan America Soc. of Georgia, Univ. of Georgia Foundation; Dr Martin Luther King Jr. Unity Award, Anti-Defamation League's Torch of Liberty Award. *Address:* AFLAC Worldwide Headquarters, 1932 Wynnton Road, Columbus, GA 31999, USA (office). *Telephone:* (706) 323-3431 (office); (800) 992-3522 (office). *Fax:* (706) 324-6330 (office). *Website:* www.aflac.com (office).

AMOS, Baroness (Life Peer), cr. 1997, of Brondesbury in the London Borough of Brent; **Valerie Ann Amos,** MA; British politician; b. 13 March 1954, Guyana; d. of E. Michael Amos and Eunice V. Amos; ed Univs of Warwick, Birmingham and East Anglia; Race Relations Adviser, London Borough of Lambeth 1981–83; Women's Adviser, London Borough of Camden 1983–85; Head of Training and Devt, London Borough of Hackney 1985–87, Head of Man. Services 1988–89; Chief Exec. Equal Opportunities Comm. 1989–94; Dir Fraser Bernard 1994–98; Govt Whip 1998–2001; Parl. Under-Sec. of State, FCO 2001–03; Sec. of State for Int. Devt 2003; Leader of the House of Lords 2003–07; Commr Fulbright Comm. 2009–; Dir Hampstead Theatre 1992–98; Deputy Chair. Runnymede Trust 1990–98; mem. Advisory Cttee Centre for Educ. Devt Appraisal and Research, Univ. of Warwick 1991–98, Gen. Advisory Council BBC, King's Fund Coll. Cttee 1992–98, Council Inst. of Employment Studies 1993–98, Advisory Bd Global Health Group, Univ. of California; Trustee Women's Therapy Centre 1989–; Hon. LLD (Warwick) 2000, (Staffordshire) 2000, (Manchester) 2001, (Bradford) 2007, (Birmingham) 2008. *Address:* House of Lords, London, SW1A 0PW, England (office). *Telephone:* (20) 7219-3000 (office). *E-mail:* amosv@parliament.uk (office).

AMOUR, Salmin; Tanzanian politician; *Vice-Chairman, Revolutionary Party of Tanzania;* Pres. and Chair. Supreme Revolutionary Council of Zanzibar 1990–2000; Vice-Chair. Chama Cha Mapinduzi (Revolutionary Party of Tanzania). *Address:* Chama Cha Mapinduzi, Kuu Street, POB 50, Dodoma, Tanzania (office). *Telephone:* (61) 2282 (office).

AMOYAL, Pierre Alain Wilfred; French violinist; b. 22 June 1949, Paris; s. of Dr Wilfred Amoyal and Vera Amoyal (née Popravka); m. 2nd Leslie Chabot 1988; ed Cours d'Etat, Vanves, Conservatoire Nat. Supérieur de Musique, Paris, Univ. of Southern Calif., USA; studied with Jascha Heifetz; invited by Sir Georg Solti to perform Berg's violin concerto with Orchestre de Paris 1971; invited by Pierre Boulez to perform Schoenberg's Concerto with Orchestre de Paris 1977; recital debut at Carnegie Hall 1985; numerous performances throughout the world with orchestras including Berlin Philharmonic, Vienna Symphony Orchestra, Filarmonica della Scala, Milan, Royal Philharmonic, New Philarmonia, l'Orchestre Nat. de France, Residentie-Orkest, The Hague; Prof. of Violin, Conservatoire Nat. Supérieur de Musique, Paris 1977–88; Lausanne Conservatory 1987–, Co-founder (with Alexis Weissenberg) and Artistic Dir Lausanne Summer Music Acad. 1991; f. Camerata of Lausanne 2002, ensemble orchestra of young musicians; Chevalier, Ordre des Arts et des Lettres; First Prize, Conservatoire de Versailles 1960, Conservatoire Nat. Supérieur de Musique, Paris 1962, for chamber music, Conservatoire Nat. Supérieur de Musique, Prix Ginette Neveu, Prix Paganini, Prix Enesco 1970, Grand Prix du Disque 1974, 1977, Prix du Rayonnement de la Fondation Vaudoise pour la Promotion et la Creation artistique 2002, Prix de Lausanne 2006. *Recordings include:* Symphonie espagnole (Lalo), Violin Concerto (Mendelssohn), Concertos Nos 1 and 2 and Two Sonatas (Prokofiev), Tartini's concertos, Third Concerto, Havanaise and Rondo Capriccioso (Saint-Saëns), Concerto No. 1 (Bruch), Concerto (Glazunov), Sonatas (Fauré), Horn Trio (Brahms), Concertos (Mozart), Concerto (Sibelius), Concerto (Tchaikovsky), Sonatas (Brahms), Concerto (Schoenberg). *Leisure interests:* photography, literature, sport. *Address:* Conservatoire de Lausanne, Haut Ecole de la Musique, Rue de la Grotte 2, 1002 Lausanne, Switzerland (office). *E-mail:* pierre.amoyal@cdlhem.ch (office). *Website:* www.amoyal.com.

AMUDUN, Niyaz; Chinese party and government official; *Chairman, Standing Committee of 8th Xinjiang Uygur Autonomous Regional People's Congress;* b. 1932, Xinjiang Uygur Autonomous Region, Luntai; joined CCP 1953; Sec. CCP Autonomous Prefectural Cttee, Xinjiang Uygur Autonomous Region, Korla 1955–60; mem. CCP Autonomous County Cttee, Secr. Xinjiang Uygur Autonomous Region, Luntai 1960–62; Deputy Dir Commerce Dept, Xinjiang Uygur Autonomous Region 1962–1966, Supply and Marketing Cooperatives 1962–66; Mayor Urumqi City, Xinjiang Uygur Autonomous Region 1966–67; Deputy Sec. CCP Autonomous City Cttee, Urumqi City 1973–78, Sec. 1973–78; Deputy to 4th NPC 1975, Vice-Chair. Ethnic Affairs Cttee 1978–83; Vice-Chair. Govt of Xinjiang Uygur Autonomous Region 1979–83; Chair. Standing Cttee of Xinjiang Uygur Autonomous Region People's Congress 1983–; Deputy Sec. CCP Xinjiang Uygur Autonomous Region Cttee 1985–, Sec. Political Science and Law Cttee 1985–; Chair. Xinjiang Uygur Autonomous Regional 8th People's Congress 1985, Standing Cttee of 7th Xinjiang People's Congress 1989–93, of 8th Xinjiang Uygur Autonomous Regional People's Congress 1993–; Del., 13th CCP Nat. Congress 1987, 15th Nat. Congress 1997–2002; Deputy, 8th NPC 1993–98; mem. Cen. Comm. for Discipline Inspection, CCP Cen. Cttee. *Address:* Standing Committee of Xinjiang Uygur Autonomous Region People's Congress, Urumqi, People's Republic of China.

AMUM OKECH, Pagan; Sudanese politician; *Secretary-General, Sudan People's Liberation Movement (SPLM);* b. Malakal; joined Sudan People's Liberation Army (SPLA) 1983, served as mil. and civilian admin., Malakal, Bahr al-Ghazal, Melut, apptd civilian admin., Kapoeta 1991, fmr commdr SPLM/A operations in eastern Sudan, fmr mem. SPLM negotiating team for the CPA (Comprehensive Peace Agreement), Sec.-Gen. SPLM 2005–; currently also Diplomatic Affairs Advisor to Pres. of Sudan; fmr Sec.-Gen. Nat. Democratic Alliance. *Address:* SPLM General Headquarters, Khartoum, Sudan (office). *E-mail:* info@splmtoday.com (office). *Website:* www.splmtoday.com (office).

AMUNUGAMA, Sarath, PhD; Sri Lankan politician; *Minister of Enterprise Development and Investment Promotion;* b. 10 July 1939; m.; fmr Spokesman for People's Alliance (PA); elected mem. Parl. for Kandy Dist; Minister of Northern Rehabilitation 2000; Minister of Culture 2000; Minister of Finance –2005, of Public Admin and Home Affairs 2005–07, of Enterprise Devt and Investment Promotion 2007–. *Address:* Ministry of Enterprise Development and Investment Promotion, 25th Level, West Tower, World Trade Centre, Echelon Square, Colombo 1, Sri Lanka (office). *Telephone:* (11) 2394951 (office). *Fax:* (11) 2424960 (office). *E-mail:* secedip@sltnet.lk (office). *Website:* www.atned.lk (office).

AMURO, Namie; Japanese singer; b. 20 Sept. 1977, Okinawa; m. Sam Maruyama; ed Okinawa Actor's School; mem. of group Super Monkeys 1992, left group for short period, returned in 1994; solo artist 1995–; Japan Records Award 1996. *Singles include:* (with Super Monkeys) Paradise Train, Try Me, Tiayo No Season, (solo) Stop the Music, Body Feels Exit, Chase the Chance, Don't Wanna Cry, You Are My Sunshine, Sweet 19 Blues, Can You Celebrate. *Albums include:* (solo) Sweet 19 Blues 1996, Concentration 20 1997, 181920 1998, Genius 2000 2000, Break the Rules 2000, Style 2003, Queen of Hip-Pop 2005, Play 2007. *Address:* c/o Avex Trax, Room 3608-10, Windsor House, 311 Gloucester Road, Causeway Bay, Hong Kong Special Administrative Region, People's Republic of China. *Website:* www.avexnet.or.jp/amuro; www.amuro.com.

AMUSÁTEGUI DE LA CIERVA, José María; Spanish banker; *Chairman, Banco Vitalicio DE Espana SA DE Seguros;* b. 12 March 1932, San Roque; s. of Antonio Amusátegui de la Cierva and Dolores Amusátegui de la Cierva; m. Amalia de León 1988 (divorced); six c.; ed Colegio de Huérfanos de la Armada and Univ. of Madrid; state lawyer, Minister of Finance, Gerona 1959–70; Deputy Chair. Instituto Nacional de Industria 1970; Deputy Chair. Prodinsa 1974; Chair. Intelsa 1975, Astilleros Españoles 1980; Deputy Chair. Instituto Nacional de Hidrocarburos 1981; Chair. Campsa 1982; Man. Dir, Deputy Chair. Banco Hispano Americano 1985, Chair. 1991–99, also Pres.; Chair. Banco Cen. Hispano 1992–99; Co.-Chair. Banco Santander Cen. Hispanoamericano (BSCH, now Banco Santander Cen. Hispano SA) 1999–2002, Hon. Chair. 2002–; currently Chair. Banco Vitalicio DE Espana SA DE Seguros; Grand Cross of Civil Merit. *Leisure interests:* motorcycling, astronomy, botany. *Address:* Banco Vitalicio DE Espana SA DE Seguros, Paseo de Gracia, 11, 08007 Barcelona (office); Banco Santander Central Hispano SA, Alcalá 49, 28014 Madrid, Spain. *Telephone:* (93) 4840100 (office). *Website:* www.vitalicio.es (office).

AN, Zhendong; Chinese government official and engineer; *Vice-Chairman, Central Committee of the Jiusan Society;* b. 5 Sept. 1930, Tangshan, Hebei Prov.; ed Hebei Engineering Coll. 1951; engineer, Railway Admin, Electric Power Div., Heilongjiang Prov., Qiqihar City 1952–58; engineer, Heilongjiang Silicon Rectifier Factory, Harbin City 1963–67; Engineer, Deputy Factory Dir Harbin Rectifier Equipment Factory 1967–81; Chief Engineer, 2nd Light Industry Bureau 1981–82; joined Jiusan Soc. 1981, Vice-Chair. 6th, 7th, 8th, 9th and 10th Cen. Cttee Jiusan Soc. 1997–; Vice-Gov. Heilongjiang 1983–90; Vice-Chair. Standing Cttee Heilongjiang Prov. People's Congress 1990–93; mem. 6th NPC 1983–88, 7th NPC 1988–93, 8th NPC 1993–98; mem. 9th CPPCC Nat. Cttee, Standing Cttee 1998–2003; Vice-Pres. Chinese Package Soc.; Dir Chinese Industry Econ. Soc.; main inventions include: Signal and Radio Telephone in Railroad Cars 1958, Fire-fighting Automatic System in Cities 1963, Explosion-proof Rectifier Equipment in Coal Mines 1973, Power Factor Electricity Regulator 1976; named Model Worker of Special Grade of Harbin, Model Worker of Heilongjiang Prov. *Address:* c/o People's Congress Standing Committee of Heilongjiang, Nangang District, Harbin 150001, People's Republic of China.

AN MIN; Chinese university professor; b. (Wang, An Min), 15 March 1922, Shandong; s. of Wang Jingxuan and Zhou Ailian; m. Wu Pei (Wu Guangrui) 1951; one s. one d.; ed Ming Hsien High School and Nat. Cen. Univ.; mem. Friends Ambulance Unit 1941–49; mem. Faculty China Agric. Univ. 1949–, Head Dept Animal Science 1979–82, Pres. Univ. 1982–87; Vice-Chair. Scientific and Tech. Cttee Ministry of Agric. 1983–87, Consultant 1987–; Head Animal Science Section Nat. Academic Degree Cttee 1984–92; Section Head Nat. Foundation for Natural Science 1986–; Pres. Domestic Animal and Poultry Information Centre 1984–87; Dir Int. Goat Asscn 1982, China Int. Conf. Centre for Science and Tech. 1984–; Vice-Chair. Chinese Asscn of Agricultural Sciences 1983–87; Chief Ed. Chinese Journal of Animal Science 1980–84; mem. Standing Cttee China Asscn of Animal Science and Veterinary Medicine 1986–, China Asscn for Science and Tech. 1987–91, Nat. Awarding Cttee of Natural Science 1987–91; Deputy Chief Ed. China Agricultural Encyclopedia, Vol. Animal Science 1988–; Chief Ed. Biography of Chinese Scientists, Vol. Agricultural Animal Science 1989–; Dir Dept of Taiwan, Hong Kong and Macao Affairs, Ministry of Foreign Trade and Econ. Co-operation 1991; Assoc. Chief Ed. China Animal Science 1993–; mem. Steering Cttee Small Ruminant Production System Network of Asia 1990–; mem. Agricultural Consultant Group, Beijing Municipality 1990–; Nat. Award for Tech. Support in Agric. Sciences 1981, 1984, Educ. Award for Outstanding Profs

1985, 1988 and other awards. *Publications:* Animal Reproduction and Reproductive Physiology 1984, Reproductive Hormones, Farm Animal Reproduction and its Genetical Improvement 1990, English-Chinese Dictionary of Animal Science and Technology 1991. *Leisure interests:* music, theatre and travel. *Address:* 303 Building 15, 3 Yuan Ming Yuan West Road, Beijing 100094, People's Republic of China (home). *Telephone:* (10) 6273-2955 (home). *Fax:* (10) 6273-1274 (home). *E-mail:* wh15@vip.sina.com (home).

AN QIYUAN, BEng; Chinese government official and fmr geologist; *Chairman, CPPCC Shaanxi Provincial Committee;* b. 1933, Lingtong Co., Shaanxi Prov.; ed Dept of Geology, Northwest China Univ.; joined CCP 1953; leader geological team of Songliao Petroleum Prospecting Bureau 1958–59; Dir of Oil Mine and Chief, Underground Operation Section of 1st HQ Oil Extracting in Daqing 1964–65; Dir Petroleum Geophysics Prospecting Bureau, Ministry of Petroleum 1973–77; Deputy Dir State Seismological Bureau 1977–80, Dir 1982–88; mem. Standing Cttee CCP Shaanxi Prov. Cttee, Sec. CCP Xian Municipal Cttee 1988; mem. Standing Cttee CPPCC Comm. for Inspecting Discipline 1992–94; Sec. CCP Shaanxi Prov. Cttee 1994–97; Chair. CPPCC Shaanxi Prov. Cttee 1998–; mem. 9th CPPCC Nat. Cttee 1998–2003. *Publications:* Developing Shaanxi Province and Enriching the People by Grasping the Keystone and Fulfilment. *Leisure interest:* reading. *Address:* Shaanxi Provincial Committee, Xian, Shaanxi Province, People's Republic of China. *Telephone:* (29) 85581418 (office); (29) 85581417 (office); (29) 85581410 (home); (29) 85581398 (home).

ANAND, A. S., LLD; Indian judge; *Chairman, National Human Rights Commission;* b. 1 Nov. 1936; ed Jammu and Lucknow Univs, Univ. of London, UK; enrolled as Advocate Bar Council 1964; practised in criminal, constitutional and election law, Punjab & Haryana High Court –1975; apptd Additional Judge, Jammu & Kashmir High Court 1975, Chief Justice 1985–89; Chief Justice Madras High Court 1989–91; Judge, Supreme Court of India 1991–98, Chief Justice 1998–2001; Chair. Nat. Human Rights Comm. 2003–. *Address:* National Human Rights Commission, Faridkot House, Copernicus Marg, New Delhi, PIN 110001, India (office). *Telephone:* 23382514 (office); 23384863 (office). *E-mail:* chairnhrc@nic.in (office). *Website:* nhrc.nic.in (office).

ANAND, Bal Krishan, MB, BS, MD; Indian physiologist; b. 19 Sept. 1917, Lahore; s. of V. D. Anand and Saraswati Anand; m. Kamla Puri 1942; one s. two d.; ed Government Coll. and K.E. Medical Coll., Lahore; Prof. of Physiology, Lady Hardinge Medical Coll., New Delhi 1949–57, All India Inst. of Medical Sciences, New Delhi 1957–74 (Dean 1964–74), Prof. Emer. 1977–; Pres. XXVI Int. Congress of Physiological Sciences, New Delhi 1974; Asst Dir WHO (SE Asia) 1974–77; Dir Inst. of Medical Sciences, Srinagar 1982–85; Vice-Chancellor, Banaras Hindu Univ., Varanasi 1978; Pres. Indian Nat. Acad. of Medical Sciences; Pres. Nat. Bd of Examinations 1979–82; Pres. Asscn for Advancement of Medical Educ. 1984–86; Chair. Post-grad. Cttee of Medical Council of India 1985–91; Chair. Physiology Cttee of Indian Nat. Science Acad. 1988–91, Governing Council Vallahbhai Patel Chest Inst., Univ. of Delhi 1997–; Visiting Prof., Pennsylvania Univ. School of Medicine 1968; Commonwealth Visiting Prof., Univ. of London 1966; Rockefeller Foundation Fellow at Yale Univ. School of Medicine 1950–51; Fellow Nat. Acad. of Medical Sciences, Nat. Science Acad., Indian Acad. of Sciences; Hon. mem. Fed. of Asia Oceanic Physiological Soc. 1994; Hon. DSc (Banaras) 1983; Indian Council of Medical Research Sr Research Award 1962, Watumull Foundation Award in Medicine 1961, Sir Shanti Swaroof Bhatnagar Memorial Award for Scientific Research in Medicine 1963, Padma Shri 1966, Medical Council of India Silver Jubilee Research Award 1969, Dr B. C. Roy Award for Eminent Medical Man 1984. *Publications:* several specialized articles. *Leisure interests:* academic literature, photography, tennis, hiking. *Address:* B9/21, Vasant Vihar, New Delhi, India (home). *Telephone:* 6142627.

ANAND, Dev, BA; Indian actor and filmmaker; *Head, Navketan International Films;* b. (Dharamdev Pishorimal), 26 Sept. 1923, Gurdaspur; m. Kalpana Kartik; one s. one d.; ed Govt Coll., Lahore, Pakistan; est. Navketan Studios; Padma Bhushan 2001, Dada Saheb Phalke Award 2002. *Films include:* Hum Ek Hain 1946, Kaala Pani (Filmfare Award for Best Actor 1955) 1954, The Guide (Filmfare Award for Best Actor 1966) 1965, Des Pardes 1978, Hare Rama Hare Krishna, Bullet, Manzil, Barsaat, Jaal, Paying Guest, Censor 2001, Ishk Ishk Ishk, Taxi Driver, Tere Ghar Ke Samne, Aman ke Farishtey 2002, Love at Times Square 2003, Mr. Prime Minister 2005. *Address:* Anand, 42 Pali Hill, Zig-Zag Road, Bandra (West), Mumbai 400 050 (office); 2 Irish Park, Juhu, Mumbai 400 049, India (home). *Telephone:* (22) 26487417 (office); (22) 26202609 (home). *Fax:* (22) 26487421 (office). *E-mail:* navketan1@hotmail .com (office). *Website:* www.navketanfilms.com (office).

ANAND, Viswanathan; Indian chess player; b. 11 Dec. 1969; s. of K. Viswanathan and Susila Viswanathan; m. Aruna Anand; Int. Master (aged 15) 1984; first Indian Int. Grandmaster 1987; World Jr Champion 1987; beat fmr world champions Mikhail Tal and Boris Spassky at 4th Int. Games Festival 1989; captained Indian team at Chess Olympiad, Manila 1992; has participated in numerous int. chess tournaments 1987–; placed No. 2 in PCA ranking 1995; World Chess Champion 2000; FIDE World Cup Champion 2002, 2007, 2008; Padma Shri 1987, Padma Bhushan 2000; Dr hc (Jawaharlal Nehru Technological Univ., Hyderabad) 1988; Arjuna Award 1985, Nat. Citizens' Award 1987, Shri Rajiv Gandhi Award 1988, Rajiv Gandhi Khel Ratna Award 1991–92, K Birla Award 1995, Sportstar Millenium Award 1998, Oscar Best Chess Player 1997, 1998, 2003, 2004. *Address:* 7 (old No. 4) II Cross Street, Customs Colony, Besant Nagar, Chennai 600 090, India (home); c/o FIDE, 9 Avenue de Beaumont, Lausanne 1012, Switzerland (office).

ANANDASANGAREE, Veerasingham; Sri Lankan politician; *President, Tamil United Liberation Front;* b. 15 June 1933, Point Pedro; s. of the late S.

Veerasingham and Ratnam; m.; four c.; ed Sri Somaskanda Coll., Christian Coll. Atchuvely, Hartley Coll., Zahira Coll.; fmr teacher, Hindu Coll., Jaffna, Poonakri MMV, Kotelawela GTM School, Ratmalana, Christ King Coll., Ja-Ela; lawyer 1967–83; joined All Ceylon Tamil Congress 1966, Youth Front Pres. 1970; Chair. Karaichi Village Council 1965–68, Karaichi Town Council 1968–69; joined Tamil United Front (later Tamil United Liberation Front), Propaganda Sec. Tamil United Liberation Front 1976–1983, mem. Politburo 1983–93, Sr Vice-Pres. 1993–2002, Acting Pres. 1998–2001, Pres. 2002–; UNESCO Madanjeet Singh Prize for the promotion of tolerance and non-violence 2006. *Address:* Tamil United Liberation Front, 30/1B Alwis Place, Colombo 3, Sri Lanka (office). *Telephone:* (11) 2347721 (office). *Fax:* (11) 2347721 (office).

ANANIASHVILI, Nina Gedevanovna; Georgian/Russian ballet dancer; *Artistic Director, State Ballet of Georgia;* b. 28 March 1963, Tbilisi, Georgia; d. of Gedevan Ananiashvili and Lia Gogolashvili; m. Gregory Vashadze 1988; ed State Choreographic Schools of Georgia and Bolshoi Theatre, Moscow; Prima Ballerina, Bolshoi Ballet 1981–, Prin., American Ballet Theater (ABT) 1993–; has performed on tour world-wide with New York City Ballet, Royal Ballet, Royal Danish Ballet, Kirov Ballet, Royal Swedish Ballet, Ballet de Monte Carlo, The Munich Ballet and others; Artistic Dir State Ballet of Georgia 2004–; numerous awards include Grand Prix Int. Ballet Competition, Jackson 1986, People's Artist Repub. of Georgia and of Russia, State Prize of Russia 1992, State Prize of Georgia 1993, Order for Outstanding Service to Fatherland (Russia) 2000, Dance Magazine Award for Outstanding Achievements, USA 2002. *Dance:* over 100 roles including Giselle, Odette/Odile (Swan Lake), Aurora (Sleeping Beauty), Raimonda, Juliet (Romeo and Juliet), Nikya (La Bayadère), Kitri (Don Quixote). *Leisure interests:* antique books, modern painting. *Address:* Tbilisi Opera and Ballet Theatre, 0108 Tbilisi, Rustaveli Ave. 25, Georgia (office); Frunzenskaya nab. 46, Apt. 79, 119270 Moscow, Russia. *E-mail:* ballet@comtv.ru (home). *Website:* www.opera.ge (office).

ANANICH, Boris Vasilyevich; Russian historian; b. 4 March 1931, Leningrad; m.; one d.; ed Leningrad State Univ.; Chief Researcher St Petersburg Br. Inst. of History, USSR Acad. of Sciences; Corresp. mem. USSR (now Russian) Acad. of Sciences 1990, mem. 1994; research in history of Russia 19th–20th centuries, econ. history, internal policy. *Publications include:* Russia and International Capital 1897–1914, Essays on History of Financial Relations 1976, Banking Houses in Russia 1860–1914, Essays on History of Private Businesses 1991, numerous articles. *Address:* Institute of History, Russian Academy of Sciences, Petrozavodskaya str. 7, 197110 St Petersburg, Russia. *Telephone:* (812) 235-41-98 (office).

ANASTASE, Roberta Alma; Romanian politician; *Chairwoman, Chamber of Deputies;* b. 27 March 1976, Ploieşti; mem. European Parl. 2007–; elected Deputy for Prahova constituency 2008–; Chair. Camera Deputaţilor (Chamber of Deputies) 2009–. *Address:* Camera Deputaţilor, 050563 Bucharest, Palatul Parlamentului, Str. Izvor 2–4, Sector 5, Romania (office). *Telephone:* (21) 4021444 (office). *Fax:* (21) 4022149 (office). *E-mail:* secretar.general@cdep .ro (office). *Website:* www.roberta.anastase.eu (office); www.cdep.ro (office).

ANASTASIADES, Nikos; Cypriot politician and lawyer; *President, Dimokratikos Synagermos (Democratic Rally);* b. 1946, Limassol; m. Andri Moustakoudes; two d.; ed Univ. of Athens, Univ. of London, UK; practising lawyer, Limassol 1972–; Dist Sec. Youth Org. of Dimokratikos Synagermos (DISY – Democratic Rally Party) 1976–85 (Pres. 1987–90), Vice-Pres. DISY 1985–86, 1990–93, Parl. Leader DISY 1993–97, Deputy Pres. 1995–97, Pres. 1997–; mem. Parl. 1981–, Speaker House of Reps 1996–2001. *Address:* Dimokratikos Synagermos, PO Box 25303, 25 Pindarou Street, 1061 Nicosia, Cyprus (office). *Telephone:* (2) 883164 (office). *Fax:* (2) 753821 (office). *E-mail:* disy@disy.org.cy (office). *Website:* www.disy.org.cy (office).

ANAYA, Rudolfo, MA; American academic and author; *Professor Emeritus, University of New Mexico;* b. 30 Oct. 1937, Pastura, NM; s. of Martin Anaya and Rafaelita Mares; m. Patricia Lawless 1966; ed Albuquerque High School, Browning Business School, Univ. of New Mexico; teacher, Albuquerque public schools 1963–70; Dir Counseling Center, Univ. of Albuquerque 1971–73; Lecturer, Univ. Anahuac, Mexico City 1974; Prof., Dept of Language and Literature, Univ. of New Mexico 1974–93, Prof. Emer. 1993–; Founder, Ed. Blue Mesa Review 1989–93; Martin Luther King, Jr/César Chávez, Rosa Parks Visiting Prof., Univ. of Michigan, Ann Arbor 1996; currently Assoc. Ed. The American Book Review; Bd Contributing Ed. The Americas Review; Advisory Ed. Great Plains Quarterly; f. PEN-NM, Teachers of English and Chicano Language Arts 1991; Founder, Pres. NM Rio Grande Writers Asscn; mem. Bd Before Columbus Foundation; mem. Nat. Asscn of Chicano Studies; Hon. DHumLitt (Albuquerque) 1981, (Marycrest Coll.) 1984, (New England) 1992, (Calif. Lutheran Univ.) 1994, (New Hampshire) 1997; Hon. PhD (Santa Fe) 1991; Hon. DLitt (New Hampshire) 1996; recipient of numerous awards including National Endowment for the Arts Fellowship 1980, New Mexico Governor's Award for Excellence and Achievement in Literature 1980, W. K. Kellogg Foundation Fellowship 1983–86, New Mexico Eminent Scholar Award 1989, Rockefeller Foundation Residency Bellagio, Italy 1991, Excellence in the Humanities Award, New Mexico Endowment for the Humanities 1995, Tomás Rivera Mexican American Children's Book Awards 1995, 2000, Distinguished Achievement Award, Western Literature Asscn 1997, Arizona Adult Authors Award, Arizona Library Asscn 2000, Wallace Stegner Award Center of the American West 2001, National Medal of Arts 2001, National Asscn of Chicano/Chicana Studies Scholar 2002. *Plays:* Billy the Kid, Who Killed Don José?, Matachines, Angie, Ay, Compadre, The Farolitos of Christmas, Bless Me, Ultima 2009. *Publications include:* Bless Me, Ultima 1972 (Premio Quinto Sol Award 1971), Heart of Aztlan 1976, Tortuga 1979 (American Book Award, Before Columbus Foundation 1979), Cuentos: Tales from the Hispanic Southwest (trans.) 1980, The Silence of the Llano (short stories) 1982, The Legend of La Llorona 1984, The Adventures of Juan Chicaspatas (poem) 1985, A Chicano in China 1986, Lord of the Dawn, The Legend of Quetzalcoatl 1987, Alburquerque 1992 (PEN-WEST Fiction Award 1993), The Anaya Reader (anthology) 1994, Zia Summer 1995, The Farolitos of Christmas (children's fiction) 1995, Jalamanta, A Message from the Desert 1996, Rio Grande Fall 1996, Maya's Children (children's fiction) 1997, Descansos: An Interrupted Journey (with Estevan Arellano and Denise Chávez) 1997, Isis in the Heart 1998, Shaman Winter 1999, Farolitos for Abuelo (children's fiction) 1999, My Land Sings 1999, Roadrunner's Dance 2000, Elegy for Cesar Chavez 2000, The Santero's Miracle (children's fiction) 2004, Serafina's Stories 2004, Jemez Spring 2005, The Man who Could Fly and other stories 2006; short stories in literary magazines in USA and internationally; has also ed. various collections of short stories. *Leisure interests:* reading, travel, apple orchards. *Address:* 5324 Cañada Vista NW, Albuquerque, NM 87120-2412, USA (home). *Fax:* (505) 899-0014 (home).

ANCRAM, 13th Marquis of Lothian; **Michael Andrew Foster Jude Kerr,** PC, QC, DL, LLB, MA; British politician; b. 7 July 1945; s. of 12th Marquess of Lothian and Antonella, Marchioness of Lothian; m. Lady Jane Fitzalan-Howard 1975; two d.; ed Ampleforth, Christ Church Coll., Oxford, Univ. of Edinburgh; fmr columnist, Daily Telegraph (Manchester edn); fmr partner in tenanted arable farm; called to Scottish Bar 1970, practised law 1970–79; MP for Berwickshire and East Lothian Feb.–Oct. 1974, Edinburgh S 1979–87, for Devizes 1992–; mem. House of Commons Energy Select Cttee 1979–83; Parl. Under-Sec. of State, Scottish Office 1983–87; Parl. Under-Sec., NI Office 1993–94, Minister of State 1994–96; Shadow Cabinet Spokesman for Constitutional Affairs 1997–98; Chair. Conservative Party 1998–2001, Deputy Leader 2001–; Shadow Sec. of State for Foreign and Commonwealth Affairs 2001–05, for Int. Affairs 2003–04, for Int. Devt 2004–05; Vice-Chair. Conservative Party in Scotland 1975–80, Chair. 1980–83; Chair. Northern Corp. Communications 1989–91; Dir CSM Parl. Consultants 1988–92; mem. Bd Scottish Homes 1988–90. *Leisure interests:* skiing, fishing, photography, folk-singing. *Address:* House of Commons, Westminster, London, SW1A 0AA, England (office). *Telephone:* (20) 7219-5072 (office). *Fax:* (20) 7219-2528 (office). *Website:* www.ancram.com (office); www.michaelancram.com (office).

ANDAYA, Rolando G., BSc, DIur; Philippine politician; *Secretary of the Budget and Management;* ed De La Salle Univ., Ateneo de Manila Univ.; Head Exec. Asst to Chair., Securities and Exchange Comm. 1996, Hearing Officer 1996–98; mem. House of Reps 1998–, Chair. Cttee on Appropriations 2001–; Sec. of the Budget and Man. 2006–; Dr hc (Bulacan State Univ.) 2002. *Address:* Department of the Budget and Management, DBM Bldg, Gen. Solano Street, San Miguel, Manila, The Philippines (office). *Telephone:* (2) 7354807 (office). *Fax:* (2) 7357814 (office). *E-mail:* dbmtis@dbm.gov.ph (office). *Website:* www.dbm.gov.ph (office).

ANDELY, Rigobert Roger; Republic of the Congo banking executive and fmr government official; *Vice-Governor, Banque des Etats de l'Afrique Centrale;* Vice-Gov. Banque des Etats de l'Afrique Centrale (BEAC) 1998–2002, 2005–; Minister of the Economy, Finance and the Budget 2002–04; Deputy Chair. Comm. Bancaire de L'Afrique Centrale (COBAC). *Address:* Banque des Etats de l'Afrique Centrale, 736, Avenue Monseigneur Vogt, 1917 Yaoundé, Cameroon (office). *E-mail:* beac@beac.int (office). *Website:* www.beac.int (office).

ANDERS, Edward, MA, PhD; American professor of chemistry; *Horace B. Horton Professor Emeritus, University of Chicago;* b. 21 June 1926, Liepaja, Latvia; s. of Adolph Alperovitch and Erica Leventals; m. Joan Elizabeth Fleming 1955; one s. one d.; ed Univ. of Munich, Germany, Columbia Univ., USA; Instructor in Chem., Univ. of Ill. at Urbana 1954–55; Asst Prof. of Chem. Univ. of Chicago 1955–60, Assoc. Prof. 1960–62, Prof. 1960–73, Horace B. Horton Prof. of Physical Sciences 1973–91, Prof. Emer. 1991–; Visiting Prof. Calif. Inst. of Tech. 1960, Univ. of Berne 1963–64, 1970, 1978, 1980–81, 1983, 1987–88, 1989–90; Research Assoc. Field Museum of Natural History 1968–91; Fellow American Acad. of Arts and Sciences 1973–; mem. NAS 1974–; Assoc. Royal Astronomical Soc., UK 1974–; Fairchild Distinguished Scholar, Calif. Inst. of Tech. 1992–93; Hon. DChem (Latvian Acad. of Sciences) 2000; Cleveland Prize, AAAS 1959, Smith Medal, NAS 1971, Leonard Medal, Meteoritical Soc. 1974, Goldschmidt Medal, Geochemical Soc. 1990, Kuiper Prize, American Astronomical Soc. 1991, Hess Medal (American Geophysical Union) 1995. *Publications:* over 260 articles in scientific journals. *Leisure interests:* classical music, hiking, photography. *Address:* Department of Chemistry, University of Chicago, 5735 S Ellis Ave, Chicago IL 60637, USA.

ANDERSEN, Ib; Danish ballet dancer; *Artistic Director, Ballet Arizona;* b. 14 Dec. 1954, Copenhagen; s. of Ingolf Andersen and Anna Andersen; ed with Royal Danish Ballet; ballet dancer, Royal Danish Ballet 1973–80, Prin. Dancer 1975–80; Prin. Dancer, New York City Ballet 1980–94; Ballet Master Pittsburgh Ballet Theater 1997–97; Artistic Dir Ballet Ariz. 2000–; Nijinsky Prize. *Address:* Ballet Arizona, 3645 East Indian School Road, Phoenix, AZ 85018, USA (office). *Telephone:* (602) 381-0184 (home). *E-mail:* info@balletaz .org (office). *Website:* www.balletaz.org (office).

ANDERSEN, Mogens; Danish painter; b. 8 Aug. 1916, Copenhagen; s. of the late Einar F. T. Andersen and Erna Ingeborg (née Andersen); m. Inger Therkildsen 1947; one s. one d.; ed in Copenhagen under art master P. Rostrup Boyesen; art teacher, Copenhagen 1952–59, Acad. de la Grande Chaumière, Paris 1963; mem. Cttee Danish Art Exhbn Arrangement 1956–58; Pres. Danish State Art Foundation 1977–80; mem. Royal Acad. of Fine Arts 1956, Prof. 1970–72; mem. PEN Club; paintings hung in Modern Museum, Skopje 1965, Bridgestone Museum, Tokyo, Kunstmuseum, Malmø, Kongelige Bibliotek, Copenhagen and many other museums in Denmark, Sweden, Norway, Poland and USA; Chevalier, Légion d'honneur, Ordre des Arts et

Lettres; Kt of Dannebrog; Eckersberg Medal 1949, Thorvaldsen Medal 1984 and other awards. *Major works:* Composition in Niels Bohr Inst., Copenhagen 1955, Mural, Cen. Library, Copenhagen 1958–59, Composition in Cen. Library, Århus 1964, October, State Art Museum 1964, Mural, Gentofte Town Hall 1971, Restaurante Copenhagen, Paris 1973, Handelsbanken, Copenhagen 1975, Northern Feather Inst., Danmarks Tekniske Højskole 1979, Panum-institutet, Copenhagen 1981, Kunstmuseum, Bochum 1981, Musikhuset, Århus 1982, Metalskolen, Holstebro, Skäfogaard, Mörke Konstmuseum, Lund, Mural in Sejs Church, Denmark 1989. *Publications:* Moderne fransk malerkunst 1948, Omkring Kilderne 1967, Nødigt, Men Dog Gerne 1976, Ungdomsrejsen 1979, Om Kunst og Samfund 1980, Huset 1986, Punktum, Punktum, Komma, Streg 1994, Efterayn 2002. *Address:* Strandagervej 28, 2900 Hellerup, Copenhagen, Denmark. *Telephone:* (39) 62-02-66.

ANDERSEN, Ronald Max, MS, PhD; American sociologist and academic; *Wasserman Professor Emeritus, School of Public Health, UCLA;* b. 15 Feb. 1939, Omaha, Neb.; s. of Max Adolph Andersen and Evangeline Dorothy Andersen (née Wobbe); m. Diane Borella 1965; one d.; ed Univ. of Santa Clara and Purdue Univ.; Research Assoc. Purdue Farm Cardiac Project, Dept of Sociology, Purdue Univ. 1962–63; Assoc. Study Dir Nat. Opinion Research Center, Univ. of Chicago 1963–66, Research Assoc. Center for Health Admin. Studies 1963–77; Instructor Grad. School of Business, Univ of Chicago 1966–68, Asst Prof. 1968–72, Asst Prof. Dept of Sociology 1970–72, Assoc. Prof. Grad. School of Business, then Prof. 1974–90; Assoc. Dir Center for Health Admin. Studies 1977–80, Dir and Dir Grad. Program in Health Admin. 1980–90; Chair. Ed. Bd Health Admin. Press, Chicago, Ill. 1980–83, 1988–; Wasserman Prof. of Health Services and Prof. of Sociology, UCLA School of Public Health 1991–2006, Chair. Dept of Health Services 1993–96, 2000–03, Wasserman Prof. Emer. 2006–; mem. numerous cttees., advisory panels etc.; mem. American Sociological Asscn, American Statistical Asscn, American Public Health Asscn; Fellow Inst. of Medicine, mem. Royal Soc. of Science, Uppsala; Hon. doctorate (Purdue Univ.); Baxter Allegiance Prize 1999, Distinguished Investigator Award Asscn for Health Services Research, Leo G. Reeder Award for Distinguished Service to Medical Sociology. *Publications:* author and co-author of numerous books, monographs, book chapters and articles in professional journals. *Address:* UCLA School of Public Health, 650 Charles E. Young Drive South, Los Angeles, CA 90095-1772 (office); 10724 Wilshire Boulevard, Apartment 312, Los Angeles, CA 90024-4453, USA (home). *Telephone:* (310) 206-1810 (office). *Fax:* (310) 825-3317 (office). *E-mail:* randerse@ucla.edu (office). *Website:* www.ph.ucla.edu/hs/andersen.html (office).

ANDERSEN, Torkild, MSc, DPhil; Danish physicist and academic; *Professor Emeritus of Physics, University of Århus;* b. 19 June 1934, Randers; m. Inger Bloch-Petersen 1957; one s. one d.; ed Tech. Univ. Copenhagen; industrial chemist 1958–59; Asst and Assoc. Prof. of Chem., Univ. of Århus 1958–71, Prof. of Physics (Atomic Physics) 1971–2001, Prof. Emer. 2001–; Postdoctoral Fellow, Univ. of Cambridge 1961–63; Visiting Prof., Univ. of Colo 1984–85, Flinders Univ., S Australia 1988, 1994; mem. Bd Carlsberg Foundation 1996–2004; mem. Royal Danish Acad. of Science 1979–; N. Bjerrum Prize 1972. *Publications:* over 200 scientific contribs to chemistry and physics journals. *Address:* Institute of Physics and Astronomy, University of Århus, Nordre. Ringgade, 8000 Århus C (office); 37 Klokkerbakken, 8210 Århus V, Denmark (home). *Telephone:* 89-42-37-45 (office). *Fax:* 86-12-07-40 (office). *E-mail:* fystor@phys.au.dk (office).

ANDERSON, (Angus) Gerry, MBE; British filmmaker; b. 14 April 1929, Hampstead, London; s. of Joseph Anderson and Deborah Anderson; m. 1st Betty Wrightman 1952; two d.; m. 2nd Sylvia Thamm 1961 (divorced); one s.; m. 3rd Mary Robins 1981; one s.; ed Willesden Co. Secondary School; trainee, Colonial Film Unit 1943; Asst Ed. Gainsborough Pictures 1945–47; Dubbing Ed. 1949–53; Film Dir Polytechnic Films 1954–55; co-founder Pentagon Films 1955, AP Films 1956, AP Merchandising 1961; Dir of TV commercials 1961, 1988–92; Chair. Century 21 Org. 1966–75; Pres. Thames Valley and Chiltern Air Ambulance 2002; Hon. Fellow, British Kinematograph Sound and TV Soc.; Silver Arrow Award. *Television series include:* Adventures of Twizzle (52 shows) 1956, Torchy the Battery Boy (26 shows) 1957, Four Feather Falls (52 shows) 1958, Supercar (39 shows) 1959, Fireball XL5 (39 shows) 1961, Stingray (39 shows) 1962–63, Thunderbirds (32 shows screened in 20 countries) 1964–66 (Royal Television Soc. Silver Medal), Captain Scarlet (32 shows) 1967, Joe 90 (30 shows) 1968, The Secret Service (13 shows) 1968, UFO (26 shows) 1969–70, The Protectors (52 shows) 1971–72, Space 1999 (48 shows) 1973–76, Terrahawks (39 shows) 1982–83, Dick Spanner (26 shows) 1987, Space Precinct 1993–95, Lavender Castle 1997, Firestorm 2002; numerous TV commercials. *Films:* Thunderbirds are Go 1966, Thunderbird 6 1968, Doppelganger 1969. *Leisure interests:* walking, gardening.

ANDERSON, Bradbury H., BA; American retail executive; *Vice-Chairman and CEO, Best Buy Company Inc.;* b. 1950, Sheridan, WY; m. Janet Anderson; two s.; ed Waldorf Coll., Forest City, Ia, Univ. of Denver; began career as salesman, Sound of Music Inc. (predecessor to Best Buy), various man. positions Best Buy Co. Inc. 1973, including Vice-Pres. 1981, Dir 1986–, Pres. and COO 1991–2002, Vice-Chair. 2001–, CEO 2002–; Dir Best Buy Children's Foundation; Dir Junior Achievement Inc. 2000–, Int. Mass Retail Asscn, American Film Inst.; Trustee, Minn. Public Radio Bd; mem. Waldorf Coll. Bd of Regents 1998–; Waldorf Coll. Alumni Distinguished Service Award 1997, Retail Merchandiser Retail Exec. of the Year 2002. *Leisure interests:* cycling, reading biographies, theatre, music. *Address:* Best Buy Co., Inc., Corporate Headquarters, 7601 Penn Avenue South, Richfield, MN 55423, USA (office). *Telephone:* (612) 291-1000 (office). *Fax:* (612) 292-4001 (office). *E-mail:* info@ bestbuy.com (office). *Website:* www.bestbuy.com (office).

ANDERSON, Campbell McCheyne, BEcons; Australian business executive; b. 17 Sept. 1941, Sydney; s. of Allen Taylor Anderson and Ethel Catherine Rundle; m. Sandra Maclean Harper 1965; two s. one d.; ed Armidale School, NSW, Univ. of Sydney; audit clerk, Priestley and Morris 1958–59; with Boral Ltd 1962–69; Gen. Man. then Man. Dir Reef Oil and Basin Oil 1969–72; with Burmah Oil Australia Ltd 1972–73, New York 1973–74, Div. Dir, then Chief Financial Officer, Burmah Oil Trading Ltd, UK 1974–75, Dir 1975–76, Exec. Dir Burmah Oil Co. Ltd 1976–82, Man. Dir Burmah Oil PLC 1982–85; Man. Dir Renison Goldfields Consolidated Ltd 1985, Man. Dir and CEO 1986–93, Dir Consolidated Gold Fields PLC 1985–89; Chair. Ampolex Ltd 1991–96, Dir 1996–97; Man. Dir North Ltd 1994–98; Chair. Energy Resources Australia Ltd 1994–98; Pres. Business Council of Australia 1999–2000; Chair. Southern Pacific Petroleum 2001–07; Man. Dir and Dir of numerous cos in UK and overseas; Pres. Australia/Japan Soc. of Vic. 1995–98; mem. Bd of Dirs Aviva Australia Holdings Ltd 1999–, IBJ Bank Australia 1999–2003, Reconciliation Australia 2001–07; Assoc. Australian Soc. of Certified Practising Accountants; mem. Sentient Council 2001–. *Leisure interests:* golf, shooting, horse-racing, swimming. *Address:* 77 Drumalbyn Road, Bellevue Hill, NSW 2023, Australia. *Telephone:* (4) 1751-2187. *Fax:* (2) 9327-5035.

ANDERSON, Christopher (Chris), BEcons; Australian journalist; b. 9 Dec. 1944; s. of C. F. Anderson and L. A. Anderson; m. Gabriella Douglas 1969; one s. one d.; ed Picton High School, NSW, Univ. of Sydney, Columbia Univ., New York; journalist and political commentator 1962–76; Deputy Ed., later Ed., The Sun-Herald 1976–79; Deputy Ed., later Ed., The Sydney Morning Herald 1980–83, Ed.-in-Chief 1983–88; Man. Dir and Group Ed. Dir John Fairfax Ltd 1987–90, Chief Exec. 1990–91; Man. Ed. Australian Broadcasting Corpn 1993–95; Chief Exec. TV New Zealand Ltd 1995–97; CEO Optus Communications 1997–2004; mem. Bd, Austrade 2004–07. *Leisure interests:* cricket, reading.

ANDERSON, Don L., PhD, FAAS; American geophysicist; *Eleanor and John R. McMillan Chair in Geophysics, Caltech;* b. 5 March 1933, Frederick, Md; s. of Richard Andrew and Minola Andrew (née Phares); m. Nancy Lois Ruth 1956; one s. one d.; ed Rensselaer Polytechnic Inst. and California Inst. of Tech.; Geophysicist, Chevron Oil Co. 1955–56; Geophysicist, Geophysics Research Directorate, Air Force Cambridge Research Center 1956–58; Research Fellow, Calif. Inst. of Tech. 1962–63, Asst Prof. 1963–64, Assoc. Prof. 1964–68, Prof. 1968–, Dir Seismological Lab. 1967–89; Eleanor and John R. McMillan Chair. in Geophysics, Caltech 1990–; Ed. Physics of the Earth and Planetary Interiors 1977; Assoc. Ed. Tectonophysics, Physics and Chemistry of the Earth, Journal of Geodynamics etc.; Pres. American Geophysical Union 1988–90, Past Pres. 1990–92; mem. Space Science Bd, Geophysics Research Forum (Chair. 1984–86), Bd on Earth Sciences of NAS, Arthur L. Day Award Cttee NAS (Chair. 1989–90) and several other cttees and bds; Fellow American Geophysical Union (Pres. 1986–88), Geological Soc. of America, NAS, Royal Astronomical Soc., American Philosophical Soc.; Guggenheim Fellow 1998; mem. Seismological Soc. of America; Sloan Foundation Fellow 1964–67; H. Burr Steinbach Visiting Scholar, Woods Hole Oceanographic Inst. 1995; Distinguished Scientists Lecture Series, Trinity Univ. 1995; Cloos Memorial Scholar, Johns Hopkins Univ. 1989; Hon. Foreign Fellow, European Union of Geosciences; Hon. DSc (Rensselaer Polytechnic Inst.) 2000; J. B. Macelwane Award, American Geophysical Union 1966, Sr Fulbright-Hays Award (Australia) 1975, AAAS Newcomb Cleveland Prize 1976–77, NASA Distinguished Scientific Achievement Award 1977, Emil Wiechert Medal, German Geophysical Soc. 1986, Arthur L. Day Medal, Geological Soc. of America 1987, Gold Medal, Royal Astronomical Soc. 1988, Bowie Medal, American Geophysical Union 1991, Crafoord Prize 1998, Nat. Medal of Science 1998, Guggenheim Fellowship 1998. *Address:* Seismological Laboratory 252-21, California Institute of Technology, Pasadena, CA 91125 (office); 669 Alameda Street, Altadena, CA 91001, USA (home). *Telephone:* (626) 395-6901 (office); (626) 797-7426 (home). *Fax:* (626) 564-0715.

ANDERSON, Donald Thomas, AO, BSc, PhD, DSc, FRS; Australian biologist and academic; *Professor Emeritus of Biology, University of Sydney;* b. 29 Dec. 1931, Eton, UK; s. of Thomas Anderson and Flora Anderson; m. Joanne T. Claridge 1960; one s.; ed Univs of London, UK, and Sydney; Lecturer in Zoology, Univ. of Sydney, Australia 1958, Sr Lecturer 1963, Reader 1968, Prof. 1972, Challis Prof. of Biology 1984–91, Prof. Emer. 1992–; Visiting Prof., King's Coll., London 1970; Kowalevsky Medal 2001. *Publications:* Embryology and Phylogeny in Annelids and Arthropods 1973, Barnacles 1994, Atlas of Invertebrate Anatomy 1996, Invertebrate Zoology 1998. *Leisure interests:* photography, gardening. *Address:* 5 Angophora Close, Wamberal, NSW 2260, Australia. *Telephone:* (2) 4384-7218 (home).

ANDERSON, Gillian, BFA; American actress; b. 9 Aug. 1968, Chicago; d. of Edward Anderson and Rosemary Anderson; m. 1st Errol Clyde Klotz (divorced); one d.; m. 2nd Julian Ozanne 2004 (divorced 2006); two s.; ed DePaul Univ., Chicago, Goodman Theater School, Chicago; worked at Nat. Theatre, London; appeared in two off-Broadway productions; Golden Globe Awards 1995, 1997, Screen Actors' Guild Awards 1996, 1997, Emmy Award 1997. *Films:* Three at Once 1986, A Matter of Choice 1988, The Turning 1992, Princess Mononoke (voice, English-language version) 1997, Chicago Cab 1998, The X-Files 1998, The Mighty 1998, Playing By Heart 1998, The House of Mirth 2000, The Mighty Celt 2005, Tristram Shandy: A Cock and Bull Story 2005, The Last King of Scotland 2006, Straightheads 2007, The X Files: I Want to Believe 2008, How to Lose Friends & Alienate People 2008. *Plays include:* Absent Friends (Manhattan Theater Club) (Theater World Award 1991) 1991, The Philanthropist (Along Wharf Theater) 1992, What the Night is For (Comedy Theatre, London, Whatsonstage.com Theatregoers' Choice Best Actress Award 2003) 2002, The Sweetest Swing in Baseball (Royal Court Theatre, London) 2004. *Television:* Home Fire Burning (film) 1992, The X-Files 1993–2002, When Planes Go Down (film) 1996, Future Fantastic (series presenter, BBC), Bleak House (series, BBC) 2005. *Address:* 10100 Santa Monica Blvd, Suite 1300, Los Angeles, CA 90067-4003, USA (office). *Website:* www.gilliananderson.ws.

ANDERSON, Sir John Anthony, Kt, KBE, FCA; New Zealand banker; *Chief Executive and Director, National Bank of New Zealand;* b. 2 Aug. 1945, Wellington; m. Carol M. Anderson 1970; two s. one d.; ed Christ's Coll. and Victoria Univ. of Wellington; Deloitte Haskins & Sells (chartered accountants), Wellington 1962–69; Guest & Bell (sharebrokers), Melbourne 1969–72; joined South Pacific Merchant Finance Ltd, Wellington 1972, Chief Exec. and Dir 1979; Deputy Chief Exec. Nat. Bank of NZ (following merger of Southpac and Nat. Bank) 1988, Chief Exec. and Dir 1990–; Chair. NZ Merchant Banks Asscn 1982–89, Petroleum Corpn of NZ Ltd 1986–88, NZ Bankers Asscn 1992, 1999, 2000; Dir NZ Steel Ltd 1986–87, Lloyds Merchant Bank (London) 1986–92, Lloyds Bank NZA (Australia) 1989–97; Chair NZ Cricket Bd 1995–, NZ Sports Foundation Inc. 1999–2002; Pres. NZ Bankers Inst. 1990–2001; Dir Exec. Bd Int. Cricket Council 1998–; other professional and public appointments, affiliations etc.; Commemoration Medal 1990. *Leisure interests:* rugby, cricket, golf, bridge. *Address:* The National Bank of New Zealand Ltd, 170–186 Featherston Street, PO Box 1791, Wellington 6000 (office); 5 Fancourt Street, Karori, Wellington 5, New Zealand (home). *Telephone:* (4) 802-2220 (office). *Fax:* (4) 802-2517 (office).

ANDERSON, John Bayard, LLM, JD; American politician; *Chairman, Center for Voting and Democracy;* b. 15 Feb. 1922, Rockford, Ill.; s. of E. Albin Anderson and the late Mabel Ring; m. Keke Machakos 1953; one s. four d.; ed Univ. of Illinois, Harvard Law School; admitted to Ill. Bar 1946; practised law, Rockford, Ill. 1946–48, 1950–52, 1955–56; Instructor, Northeastern Univ. Law School 1948–49; State Dept Career Diplomatic Service 1952–55; Winnebago County, Ill., State's Attorney 1956–60; Congressman, 16th Dist, Ill. 1960–80; mem. US House of Reps 1960–79; Chair. House Republican Conf. 1969–79; ind. cand. for US Pres. 1980; Chair. Nat. Unity Party; Political Commentator WLS-TV, Chicago 1981; Visiting Prof. of Political Science, Brandeis Univ. 1985, Univ. of Mass 1985–, Ore. State Univ. 1986, Nova Univ. Center for Study of Law 1987–2002; Pres. and CEO World Federalist Asscn 1992–; Lecturer, US State Dept 1994–; Pres. and Chair. of Bd, Center for Voting and Democracy 1993–; Lecturer in Political Science, Bryn Mawr Coll. 1985; Visiting Prof. of Law, Washington Coll. of Law of American Univ., Washington, DC 1997–; fmr Trustee, Trinity Coll., Deerfield, Ill.; Hon. LLD (Ill., Wheaton Coll., Shimer Coll., Biola Coll., Geneva Coll., North Park Coll., Houghton Coll., Trinity Coll., Rockford Coll.). *Publications:* Between Two Worlds: A Congressman's Choice 1970, Vision and Betrayal in America 1975, Congress and Conscience (ed.) 1970, The American Economy We Need But Won't Get 1984, A Proper Institution: Guaranteeing Televised Presidential Debates 1988. *Leisure interest:* writing occasional commentary or opinion piece on political affairs, lecturing. *Address:* Center for Voting and Democracy, 6930 Carroll Avenue, Suite 610, Takoma Park, MD 20912; 418 7th Street, SE, Washington DC 20002-5257 (office); 3300 36th Street, NE, Fort Lauderdale, FL 33308-6754, USA; 4120 48th Street, NW, Washington DC 20016 (home). *Telephone:* (202) 546-3950 (office); (954) 262-6183 (office); (954) 566-8491 (home); (202) 546-3950 (home). *Fax:* (202) 546-3749 (office); (202) 362-1831 (home). *E-mail:* j.anderson@wfa.org (office); jbafed@aol.com (home). *Website:* www.fairvote.org; wfa.org (office).

ANDERSON, John Duncan, MA; Australian fmr politician; b. 14 Nov. 1956; s. of D. A. Anderson; m. Julia Gillian Robertson 1987; one s. three d.; ed Kings School, Parramatta, St Paul's Coll., Univ. of Sydney; fmr farmer and grazier; MP for Gwydir, NSW 1989–2007; Deputy Leader Nat. Party of Australia (NPA) 1993–99, Leader 1999–2005; Shadow Minister for Primary Industry 1993–96; Minister for Primary Industries and Energy 1996–98, for Transport and Regional Devt 1997–2005, Deputy Prime Minister 1999–2005 (resgnd). *Leisure interests:* farming, shooting, reading, photography, motoring. *Address:* 206 Conadilly Street, Gunnedah, NSW 2380, Australia (home).

ANDERSON, June, BA; American singer (soprano); b. 30 Dec. 1952, Boston; ed Yale Univ.; concert and oratorio singer; performances at Metropolitan, New York, New York City Opera, Milwaukee Florentine Opera, San Diego Opera, Seattle Opera, Royal Opera, London, La Scala, Milan. *Roles include:* Queen of the Night in The Magic Flute, New York City Opera 1978, title role in Lucia di Lammermoor, Milwaukee Florentine Opera 1982 and Chicago 1990, Gulnara in Il Corsaro, San Diego Opera Verdi Festival 1982, I Puritani, Edmonton Opera 1982–83, title role in Semiramide, Rome Opera 1982–83 and Metropolitan Opera 1990, Rosina in The Barber of Seville, Seattle Opera and Teatro Massimo 1982–83, Cunigonde in Candide 1989, Metropolitan Opera debut as Gilda in Rigoletto 1989, title role in Luisa Miller, La Fenice, Venice 2006; concert and oratorio vocalist: Chicago Pops Orchestra, Handel Festival Kennedy Center, Denver Symphony, St Louis Symphony, Cincinnati Symphony, Maracaibo (Venezuela) Symphony. *Address:* Askonas Holt, Lincoln House, 300 High Holborn, London, WC1V 7JH, England (office). *Telephone:* (20) 7400-1700 (office). *Fax:* (20) 7400-1799 (office). *E-mail:* info@askonasholt.co.uk (office). *Website:* www.askonasholt.co.uk (office); www.june-anderson.com.

ANDERSON, Laurie P., MFA; American performance artist, musician (keyboards, violin) and writer; b. 5 June 1947, Wayne, Ill.; d. of Arthur T. Anderson and Mary Louise Anderson (née Rowland); m. Lou Reed 2008; ed Columbia Univ., Barnard Coll.; instructor in Art History, City Coll., CUNY 1973–75; freelance critic, Art News, Art Forum; composer and performer in multi-media exhbns; Artist-in-Residence, ZBS Media 1974, NASA 2005–; Guggenheim Fellow 1983; Dr hc (Art Inst. of Chicago), (Philadelphia Coll. of the Arts); Gish Prize 2007. *Film performances:* Carmen, Personal Service Announcements, Beautiful Red Dress, Talk Normal, Alive From Off Center,

What You Mean We?, Language Is A Virus, This Is The Picture, Sharkey's Day, Dear Reader, Home of the Brave (writer, dir, performer) 1986, Puppet Motel (CD-ROM) 1995. *Recordings include:* O Superman 1981, Big Science 1982, United States 1983, Mister Heartbreak 1984, Strange Angels 1989, Bright Red 1994, The Ugly One With The Jewels And Other Stories 1995, Live At Town Hall, New York City 2002; film scores: Home Of The Brave 1986, Swimming To Cambodia, Monster In A Box. *Publications:* The Package 1971, October 1972, Transportation, Transportation 1973, The Rose and the Stone 1974, Notebook 1976, Artifacts at the End of a Decade 1981, Typisch Frac 1981, United States 1984, Empty Places: A Performance 1989, Laurie Anderson's Postcard Book 1990, Stories from the Nerve Bible 1993. *E-mail:* press@difficultmusic.com (office). *Website:* www.laurieanderson.com (office).

ANDERSON, Michael; British film director; b. 30 Jan. 1920, London; one s.; ed in France. *Films include:* (Co-Dir) Private Angelo (with Peter Ustinov) 1949; (Dir) Waterfront 1950, Hell is Sold Out 1952, Night Was Our Friend, Dial 17, Will Any Gentleman?, The House of The Arrow 1952, The Dam Busters 1954, Around the World in Eighty Days 1956, Yangtse Incident 1957, Chase a Crooked Shadow 1957, Shake Hands with the Devil 1958, Wreck of the Mary Deare 1959–60, All the Fine Young Cannibals 1960, The Naked Edge 1961, Flight from Ashiya (in Japan) 1962, Operation Crossbow 1964, The Quiller Memorandum 1966, The Shoes of The Fisherman 1969, Pope Joan 1970–71, Doc Savage (in Hollywood) 1973, Conduct Unbecoming 1974, Logan's Run (MGM Hollywood) 1975, Orca—Killer Whale 1976, Dominique 1977, The Martian Chronicles 1978, Bells 1979–80, Murder by Phone, Second Time Lucky, Separate Vacations, Sword of Gideon, Jeweller's Shop, Young Catherine, Millennium, Summer of the Monkeys, The New Adventures of Pinocchio 1999. *Address:* c/o Film Rights Ltd, 113–117 Wardour Street, London, W1C 3TD, England.

ANDERSON, Olive Ruth, BLitt, MA, FRHistS; British historian and academic; *Emerita Professor of History, Queen Mary, University of London;* b. 27 March 1926, Edinburgh; d. of Donald H. F. Gee and Ruth Gee (née Clackson); m. Matthew Smith Anderson 1954 (died 2006); two d.; ed King Edward VI Grammar School, Louth, Lincs., St Hugh's Coll., Oxford; Asst Lecturer in History, Westfield Coll., Univ. of London 1949–56, Lecturer 1958–69, Reader 1969–86, Prof. and Head of Dept 1986–89, Prof. and Deputy Head of Dept, Queen Mary & Westfield Coll. (now Queen Mary) 1989–91, Prof. Emer. and Hon. Research Fellow 1991–, Fellow 1995–; James Ford Special Lecturer, Oxford Univ. 1992; mem. Acad. Council Univ. of London 1989–91 (Exec. Cttee 1990–91); Councillor Royal Historical Soc. 1986–90, Vice-Pres. 1991–95, Hon. Vice-Pres. 2001–; Trustee Theodora Bosanquet Trust 1995–98; mem. Finance Cttee British Fed. of Women Grads Charitable Foundation 1996–99, Grants Cttee 1998–2002. *Publications:* A Liberal State at War 1967, Suicide in Victorian and Edwardian England 1987. *Address:* 45 Cholmeley Crescent, Highgate, London, N6 5EX, England (home).

ANDERSON, Paul M., BS, MBA; Australian business executive; b. 1 April 1945, USA; m. Kathy Anderson; two d.; ed Univ. of Washington, Stanford Univ.; joined Ford Motor Co. 1969, Planning Man. 1972–74; Dir Corp. Planning Texas Eastern Corpn 1977–80, Pres. Texas Eastern Synfuels Inc. and Project Dir Tri-State Synfuels Co. 1980–82, Vice-Pres. Planning and Eng, Texas Eastern Corpn 1982–85, Sr Vice-Pres. Financial and Diversified Operations 1985–90; Vice-Pres. Finance and Chief Finance Officer Inland Steel Industries Inc. 1990–91; Exec. Vice-Pres., then Pres. Panhandle Eastern Pipe Line Co. 1991–93; Pres., CEO PanEnergy Corpn 1995–97, Chair. 1997, Dir, Pres., COO Duke Energy Corpn (merger between Duke Power and PanEnergy Corpn 1997) 1997–98, Chair., CEO 2003–07; Man. Dir, CEO Broken Hill Pty Co. Ltd (later BHP Ltd, now BHP-Billiton) 1998–2001; Dir Kerr-McGee Corpn, Baker Hughes Inc., Temple-Inland, Inc. *Leisure interest:* motorcycling. *Address:* c/o Duke Energy, 526 South Church Street, Charlotte, NC 28202-1904, USA (office).

ANDERSON, Paul S., BS, PhD; American chemist; ed Univs of Vermont and New Hampshire; Postdoctoral appointment with Prof. Meinwaid at Cornell Univ., NY; joined Merck Sharp & Dohme Research Labs 1964, later Sr Research Chemist, then Research Fellow, then Dir Medicinal Chem. Dept, later Vice-Pres. for Chem. at West Point research facility –1994 (retd), Sr Vice-Pres. Chemical and Physical Sciences, DuPont-Merck Pharmaceuticals Co., Wilmington, Del. 1994–98, (became Dupont Pharmaceuticals Co. 1998) 1998–2001, co. acquired by Bristol-Myers Squibb 2001, Vice-Pres. Drug Discovery, Bristol-Myers Squibb 2001–02; mem. Bd Dirs MDS, Inc., Albany Molecular Research, Inc. 2002–, and other cos; mem. Scientific Advisory Bd Vertex Pharmaceuticals, Inc. 2004–; Chair. Medicinal Chem. Div., ACS 1987, Gordon Research Conf. on Medicinal Chem. 1991; Pres. ACS 1997; mem. NIH Study Section on Bioorganic Chem. and Natural Products 1985–88, Chair. 1988–89; fmr mem. NIH Nat. Advisory Gen. Medicinal Sciences Council, Nat. Research Council, Bd on Chemical Sciences and Tech.; mem. Bd Dirs Chemical Heritage Foundation; Founding mem. Exec. Advisory Council Univ. of Kansas School of Pharmacy; Trustee Gordon Research Confs; Hon. DSc (Univ. of Vermont) 1998; Hon. DChem (Univ. of New Hampshire) 2001; ACS E. B. Hershberg Award 1995, ACS Award in Industrial Chem. 2001, Soc. for Chemical Industry Perkin Medal 2002, Nat. Acad. of Sciences Award for Chem. in Service to Society 2003, ACS Priestley Medal 2006. *Address:* Albany Molecular Research, Inc., 21 Corporate Circle, PO Box 15098, Albany, NY 12212-5098, USA (office). *Telephone:* (518) 464-0279 (office). *Fax:* (518) 464-0289 (office). *Website:* www.albmolecular.com (office).

ANDERSON, Paul Thomas; American film director; b. 1 Jan. 1970, Studio City, Calif.; s. of the late Ernie Anderson; ed Montclair Coll. Prep. High School; began career as production Asst on TV films. *Films include:* The Dirk Diggler Story 1988, Cigarettes and Coffee 1993, Hard Eight 1996, Boogie Nights (Boston Soc. of Film Critics Award), Magnolia (Golden Bear Award) 1999, Punch-Drunk Love 2002, Couch (TV) 2003, Blossoms and Blood 2003, There Will Be Blood 2007. *Address:* c/o The Endeavor Agency, 9601 Wilshire Blvd., 10th Floor, Beverly Hills, CA 90212, USA.

ANDERSON, Porter Warren, Jr, PhD; American microbiologist and academic; *Professor Emeritus of Pediatrics, University of Rochester;* worked at Children's Hosp. Medical Center, Boston and continued at Univ. of Rochester Medical Center, NY 1968–, now Prof. Emer. of Pediatrics; Albert Lasker Clinical Research Award for groundbreaking work in devt and commercialization of Hemophilus influenza type b vaccine 1996. *Address:* University of Rochester Medical Center, Department of Pediatrics 601 Elmwood Avenue, Rochester, NY 14642, USA (office). *Telephone:* (585) 275-2121 (office). *Website:* www.urmc.rochester.edu (office).

ANDERSON, Reid Bryce; Canadian ballet director; *Artistic Director, The Stuttgart Ballet;* b. 1 April 1949, New Westminster, BC; Prin. Dancer, Stuttgart Ballet 1969–83, Ballet Master 1983–85; Artistic Dir Ballet of British Columbia 1987–89, Nat. Ballet of Canada 1989–96, Stuttgart Ballet 1996–; has staged works for Royal Ballet, Royal Danish Ballet, Ballet of the Teatro alla Scala in Milan, Australian Ballet, Deutsche Staatsoper in Berlin, Hamburg Ballett, Teatro de Colon in Buenos Aires, Boston Ballet, Rome Opera Ballet, Norwegian National Ballet; Bundesverdienstkreuz; John Cranko Prize 1989, 1996. *Address:* Stuttgarter Ballett, Oberer Schlossgarten 6, 70173 Stuttgart, Germany (office). *Telephone:* (711) 2032235 (office). *Fax:* (711) 2032491 (office). *Website:* www.stuttgart-ballet.de (office).

ANDERSON, Richard H., JD; American airline industry executive; *CEO, Delta Air Lines, Inc.;* b. Galveston, Tex.; m. Susan Anderson; ed Univ. of Houston, South Tex. Coll. of Law; joined Continental Airlines 1987, served as Staff Vice-Pres. and Deputy Gen. Counsel; joined Northwest Airlines 1990, served as Sr Vice-Pres., Tech. Operations and Airport Affairs, Exec. Vice-Pres., COO and CEO 2001–04; Exec. Vice-Pres. UnitedHealth Group 2004–07, also served as Pres. Commercial Markets Group; mem. Bd of Dirs and CEO Delta Air Lines, Inc. 2007–; mem. Bd of Dirs Cargill Inc. and Medtronic Inc. *Address:* Delta Air Lines Inc., PO Box 20706, 1030 Delta Blvd, Atlanta, GA 30320-6001, USA (office). *Telephone:* (404) 715-2600 (office). *Fax:* (404) 715-5042 (office). *E-mail:* info@delta.com (office). *Website:* www.delta.com (office).

ANDERSON, Robert Geoffrey William, MA, DPhil, FRSE, FSA, FRSC; British museum director; *Director, British Museum;* b. 2 May 1944, London; s. of Herbert Patrick Anderson and Kathleen Diana Burns; m. Margaret Elizabeth Callis Lea 1973; two s.; ed Woodhouse School, Finchley, St John's Coll., Oxford; Keeper Science Museum, London 1980–84; Dir Royal Scottish Museum 1984–85, Nat. Museums of Scotland 1985–92, British Museum 1992–; Curator School of Advanced Study, Univ. of London 1994–; Pres. British Soc. for the History of Science 1988–90, Scientific Instrument Comm. of the Int. Union of the History and Philosophy of Science 1982–97; mem. Bd Boerhaave Museum, Leiden 1995–99, Trustee 1994–; Hon. FSA (Scotland) 1991; Hon. Fellow St John's Coll. Oxford; Hon. DSc (Edinburgh) 1995, (Durham) 1998; Dexter Award (ACS) 1986. *Publications:* The Playfair Collection 1978, Science in India 1982, Science, Medicine and Dissent (ed.) 1987, A New Museum for Scotland (ed.) 1990, Joseph Black: A Bibliography (with G. Fyffe) 1992, Making Instruments Count (co-author) 1993, The Great Court at the British Museum 2000. *Address:* The British Museum, Great Russell Street, London, WC1B 3DG, England. *Telephone:* (20) 7636-1555 (office). *Fax:* (20) 7323-8480 (office). *E-mail:* randerson@thebritishmuseum.ac.uk (office).

ANDERSON, Sir Roy Malcolm, Kt, PhD, DIC, FRS, FIBiol, ARCS; British scientist, academic and university administrator; *Rector, Imperial College London;* b. 12 April 1947, Herts.; s. of James Anderson and Betty Watson-Weatherburn; m. 1st Dr Mary Joan Mitchell 1975 (divorced 1989); m. 2nd Claire Baron 1990; ed Duncombe School, Bengeo, Richard Hale School, Hertford, Imperial Coll., Univ. of London; IBM Research Fellow, Univ. of Oxford 1971–73; Lecturer, King's Coll., Univ. of London 1973–77; Lecturer, Imperial Coll. 1977–80, Reader 1980–82, Prof. of Parasite Ecology 1982–93, Head of Dept of Biology 1984–93; Linacre Prof., Univ. of Oxford 1993–2000, Head of Dept of Zoology 1993–98, Dir The Wellcome Trust Centre for the Epidemiology of Infectious Disease 1993–2000; Head of Dept of Infectious Disease Epidemiology, Imperial Coll. Faculty of Medicine, Univ. of London 2000–08, Prof. of Infectious Disease Epidemiology 2007–, Rector Imperial Coll. London 2008–; seconded to Ministry of Defence as Chief Scientific Adviser 2003–07; Genentech Visiting Prof., Univ. of Washington 1998; James McLaughlin Visiting Prof., Univ. of Texas 1999; Chair. Infection and Immunity Panel for Wellcome Trust 1990–92, Terrestrial Life Sciences Cttee, Nat. Environment Research Council (NERC), Science Advisory Council, DEFRA 2004–; Council mem. NERC 1988–91, Advisory Council on Science and Tech. (ACOST) 1989–91, Royal Soc. 1989–92, Zoological Soc. 1988–90; mem. Bd of Dirs AIDS Policy Unit 1988–89, Spongiform Encephalopathy Advisory Cttee (SEAC) 1997–2003; mem. Science Advisory Bd, Bill and Melinda Gates Foundation 'Grand Challenges in Global Health 1998–2002'; mem. Acad. of Medical Sciences 1998, Academia Europaea 1998; Trustee The Wellcome Trust 1991–92, Gov. 1992–2000; Patron Virgin Health Care Foundation; Fellow, Royal Soc. of Tropical Medicine and Hygiene; Fellow, Merton Coll., Oxford 1993–2000; Foreign mem. Inst. of Medicine, NAS 2000–; Hon. FRCPath 1999–; Hon. FRSS 2002–; Hon. MRCP; Hon. Fellow Linacre Coll., Oxford 1997–; Hon. ScD (East Anglia) 1997, (Stirling) 1998; Zoological Soc. Scientific Medal 1982, Huxley Memorial Medal 1983, C. A. Wright Memorial Medal 1986, David Starr Jordan Prize 1986, Chalmers Medal 1988, Weldon Medal 1989, John Grundy Lecture Medal 1990, Frink Medal 1993, Joseph Smadel Lecture and Medal, Infectious Diseases Soc. of America 1994, Distinguished Statistical Ecologist Award 1998. *Publications:* Population Dynamics of Infectious Disease Agents: Theory and Applications (ed.) 1982,

Population Biology of Infectious Diseases (co-ed. with R.M. May) 1982, Infectious Diseases of Humans: Dynamics and Control (with R.M. May) 1991. *Leisure interests:* hill walking, croquet, natural history, photography. *Address:* Rector's Office, Level 4 Faculty Building, Imperial College London, Exhibition Road London, London, SW7 2AZ, England (office). *Telephone:* (20) 7594-5001 (office). *E-mail:* rector@imperial.ac.uk (office); roy.anderson@imperial.ac.uk (office). *Website:* www3.imperial.ac.uk/rector (office).

ANDERSON, Ruth, BA; British professional business services executive; *Vice-Chairman, KPMG LLP;* b. Northern Ireland; ed Univ. of Bradford; joined KPMG LLP (UK unit of KPMG) 1976, apptd Partner 1989, mem. Bd Dirs (first woman on bd of large professional services firm in UK) 1998–2004, Vice-Chair. 2005–. *Leisure interests:* theatre, cinema, gardening. *Address:* KPMG LLP, 8 Salisbury Square, London, EC4Y 8BB, England (office). *Telephone:* (20) 7311-1000 (office). *E-mail:* ruth.anderson@kpmg.co.uk (office). *Website:* www.kpmg.co.uk (office).

ANDERSON, Theodore Wilbur, PhD; American statistician and academic; *Professor Emeritus of Statistics and Economics, Stanford University;* b. 5 June 1918, Minneapolis, Minn.; s. of Theodore Wilbur Anderson and Evelynn Johnson Anderson; m. Dorothy Fisher 1950; one s. two d.; ed North Park Coll., Northwestern Univ., Princeton Univ.; Research Assoc. Cowles Comm. for Research in Econs, Univ. of Chicago 1945–46; Instructor in Math. Statistics, Columbia Univ. 1946–47, Asst Prof. to Prof. 1947–67, Chair. of Dept 1956–60, 1964–65, Dir Office of Naval Research, Dept of Math. Statistics 1950–68; Prof. of Statistics and Econs, Stanford Univ. 1967–88, Prin. Investigator NSF Project, Dept of Econs 1969–83, Dept of Statistics 1983–92; Prin. Investigator Army Research Office Project, Dept of Statistics 1982–92; Academic Visitor, Imperial Coll. of Science and Tech., UK; Visiting Prof. of Math., Univ. of Moscow; Visiting Prof. of Statistics, Univ. of Paris 1967–68; Academic Visitor, LSE 1974–75, Univ. of Southern Calif. 1989; Research Consultant, Cowles Foundation for Research in Econs 1946–60; Consultant, Rand Corpn 1949–66; Fellow, Center for Advanced Study in the Behavioral Sciences 1957–58, Visiting Scholar 1972–73, 1980; Distinguished Scholar, Calif. Inst. of Tech. 1980; Visiting Prof. of Econs, Columbia Univ. 1983–84, New York Univ. 1983–84; Sabbaticant, IBM Systems Research Inst. 1984; Research Assoc. Naval Postgraduate School 1986–87; Visiting Distinguished Prof. of Norwegian Council for Scientific and Industrial Research, Univ. of Oslo 1989; Pres. Inst. of Math. Statistics 1963, mem. Council; Vice-Pres. American Statistical Soc. 1971–73; Chair. Section U, Statistics, AAAS 1990–91; mem. NAS 1976–, Econometric Soc., Inst. of Math. Statistics (mem. Council), Royal Statistical Soc., UK, American Math. Soc., Bernoulli Soc. for Math. Statistics and Probability, Indian Statistical Inst., Int. Statistical Inst., Statistical Soc. of Canada; Foreign mem. Norwegian Acad. of Science and Letters 1994; Fellow Acad. of Arts and Sciences 1974–; Hon. DLit (North Park Coll.) 1988; Hon. DSc (Northwestern Univ.) 1989; Hon. PhD (Oslo) 1997, Dr hc (Athens); Guggenheim Fellow, Univs of Stockholm and Cambridge 1947–48, R.A. Fisher Award, Cttee of Pres. of Statistical Socs 1985, Distinguished Alumnus Award, North Park Coll. 1987, Samuel S. Wilks Memorial Medal, American Statistical Asscn 1988, Award of Merit, Northwestern Univ. Alumni Asscn 1989. *Publications:* An Introduction to Multivariate Statistical Analysis 1958, 1984, 2003, The Statistical Analysis of Time Series 1971, A Bibliography of Multivariate Statistical Analysis (with S.D. Gupta and G. Styan) 1972, Introductory Statistical Analysis (with S. Sclove) 1974, An Introduction to the Statistical Analysis of Data (with S. Sclove) 1978, 1986, A Guide to MINITAB for the Statistical Analysis of Data (with B. Eynon) 1986, Collected Papers of T. W. Anderson 1943–85 1990, The New Statistical Analysis of Data (with J. D. Finn) 1996 and some 165 articles in statistical journals; ed. and fmr ed. of numerous specialist journals. *Leisure interests:* tennis, swimming, travelling. *Address:* Department of Statistics, Sequoia Hall, Stanford University, Stanford, CA 94305-4065 (office); 746 Santa Ynez Street, Stanford, CA 94305-8441, USA (home). *Telephone:* (650) 723-4732 (office); (650) 327-5204 (home). *Fax:* (650) 725-8977 (office). *E-mail:* Twa@stat.stanford.edu (office). *Website:* www-econ.stanford.edu (office).

ANDERSON, Wesley (Wes) Wales; American film director; b. 1 May 1969, Houston, Tex.; ed St John's School, Univ. of Tex.; Best New Filmmaker Award, MTV Movie Awards 1996. *Films:* dir, writer, producer: Bottle Rocket (short) 1994, Bottle Rocket 1996, Rushmore (Best Dir, Ind. Spirit Awards, New Generation Award, LA Film Critics Asscn) 1998, The Royal Tenenbaums 2001, The Life Aquatic with Steve Zissou 2004, The Darjeeling Limited 2007; producer: The Squid and the Whale 2005. *Address:* c/o United Talent Agency Inc., 9560 Wilshire Boulevard, Suite. 500, Beverly Hills, CA 90212, USA (office). *Telephone:* (310) 273-6700 (office). *Website:* www.wesanderson.org.

ANDERSON, Sir (William) Eric (Kinloch), Kt, KT, MA, DLitt, FRSE; British educationist; b. 27 May 1936, Edinburgh; s. of W. J. Kinloch Anderson and Margaret Harper; m. Anne Elizabeth Mason 1960; one s. one d.; ed George Watson's Coll., Univ. of St Andrews and Balliol Coll., Oxford; Asst Master, Fettes Coll., Edinburgh 1960–64, 1966–70, Gordonstoun School 1964–66; Headmaster, Abingdon School 1970–75, Shrewsbury School 1975–80, Eton Coll. 1980–94, Provost 2000–09; Rector, Lincoln Coll. Oxford 1994–2000; mem. Visiting Cttee of Memorial Church, Harvard 2001–07; Trustee Nat. Heritage Memorial Fund 1996–98, Chair. 1998–2001, Royal Collection Fund 2000–06, Shakespeare Birthplace Trust 2001–; Chair. Cumberland Lodge 1997–2009. *Publications:* The Journal of Walter Scott (ed.) 1972, The Percy Letters (Vol. IX) 1988, The Sayings of Sir Walter Scott 1995; articles and reviews. *Leisure interests:* theatre, golf, fishing. *Address:* c/o Provost's Lodge, Eton College, Windsor, Berks., SL4 6DH, England (office). *Website:* www.etoncollege.com (office).

ANDERSSON, Göran Bror (Benny); Swedish composer and musician (keyboards); b. 16 Dec. 1946, Stockholm; m. 1st Frida Lyngstad 1978 (divorced 1981); m. 2nd Mona Nörklit 1981; two s. one d.; songwriter with Björn Ulvæus 1966–; duo with Ulvæus as The Hootennanny Singers; partner in production with Ulvæus at Polar Music 1971; mem. pop group, ABBA 1973–82; winner, Eurovision Song Contest 1974; worldwide tours; concerts include Royal Performance, Stockholm 1976, Royal Albert Hall, London 1977, UNICEF concert, New York 1979, Wembley Arena 1979; reunion with ABBA, Swedish TV This Is Your Life 1986; continued writing and producing with Ulvæus 1982–; produced musical Mamma Mia! with Ulvæus, West End, London 1999–; World Music Award for Best Selling Swedish Artist 1993, Ivor Novello Special International Award (with Björn Ulvaeus) 2002. *Film:* ABBA: The Movie 1977, Mamma Mia! 2008. *Compositions include:* ABBA songs (with Ulvaeus); musicals: Chess (with lyrics by Tim Rice) 1983, Mamma Mia! (with Ulvaeus) 1999, Kristina Från Duvemåla (based on Vilhelm Moberg's epic novels, Utvandrarna). *Recordings:* albums: with Ulvaeus: Happiness 1971; with ABBA: Waterloo 1974, ABBA 1976, Greatest Hits 1976, Arrival 1977, The Album 1978, Voulez-Vous 1979, Greatest Hits Vol. 2 1979, Super Trouper 1980, The Visitors 1981, The Singles: The First Ten Years 1982, Thank You For The Music 1983, Absolute ABBA 1988, ABBA Gold 1992, More ABBA Gold 1993, Forever Gold 1998, The Definitive Collection 2001; singles include: with ABBA: Ring Ring 1973, Waterloo 1974, Mamma Mia 1975, Dancing Queen 1976, Fernando 1976, Money Money Money 1976, Knowing Me Knowing You 1977, The Name Of The Game 1977, Take A Chance On Me 1978, Summer Night City 1978, Chiquitita 1979, Does Your Mother Know? 1979, Angel Eyes/Voulez-Vous 1979, Gimme Gimme Gimme (A Man After Midnight) 1979, I Have A Dream 1979, The Winner Takes It All 1980, Super Trouper 1980, On And On And On 1981, Lay All Your Love On Me 1981, One Of Us 1981, When All Is Said And Done 1982, Head Over Heels 1982, The Day Before You Came 1982, Under Attack 1982, Thank You For The Music 1983. *Publication:* Mamma Mia! How Can I Resist You? (with Björn Ulvaeus and Judy Craymer) 2006. *Address:* Södra Brobänken 41A, 111 49 Stockholm, Sweden. *Website:* www.abbasite.com.

ANDERSSON, Bibi; Swedish actress; b. 11 Nov. 1935; d. of Josef Andersson and Karin Andersson; m. 1st Kjell Grede 1960; one d.; m. 2nd Per Ahlmark (q.v.) 1978 (divorced); ed Terserus Drama School and Royal Dramatic Theatre School, Stockholm; Malmö Theatre 1956–59, Royal Dramatic Theatre, Stockholm 1959–62, 1968–; appearances at Uppsala Theatre 1962–. *Plays include:* Erik XIV 1956, Tre systrar 1961, King John 1961, Le balcon 1961, La grotte 1962, Uncle Vanya 1962, Who's Afraid of Virginia Woolf? 1963, As You Like It 1964, After the Fall 1964–65, The Full Circle 1973, Twelfth Night 1975, The Night of the Tribades 1977, Twelfth Night 1980, Antigone 1981, A Streetcar Named Desire 1981, 1983, L'oiseau bleu 1981, Prisoners of Altona 1982, The Creditors 1984–85, Ett gästabud i Pestens tid 1986, Loner 1994. *Films include:* Sjunde inseglet (The Seventh Seal) 1956, Smultronstället (Wild Strawberries) 1957, Nära livet (The Brink of Life) 1958, Sommarnöje Sökes (Summer House Wanted) 1958, Djävulens öga (Eye of the Devil) 1961, Älskarinnen (The Mistress) 1962, För att inte tala om alla dessa kvinnor (All Those Women) 1964, Juninatt (June Night) 1965, Ön (The Island) 1965, Syskonbädd (My Sister, My Love) 1966, Persona 1966, Duel at Diablo 1966, Story of a Woman 1968, The Girls 1969, The Kremlin Letter 1970, A Passion, The Touch 1971, Scenes from a Marriage 1974, I Never Promised You a Rose Garden, La rivale 1976, An Enemy of the People 1976, Quintet 1979, Svarte Fugler 1982, Berget på månens baksida 1982, The Hill on the Other Side of the Moon 1983, Sista leken 1984, Huomenna 1986, Pobre mariposa 1986, Svart gryning 1987, Babette's Feast 1987, Fordringsägare 1988, Litt et Art 1989, A Passing Season 1992, The Butterfly's Dream 1994, Drømspel 1994, Det blir aldrig som man tänkt sig 2000, Elina: Som om jag inte fanns 2002, När mörkret faller 2006. *Television:* Wallenberg: A Hero's Story 1985, Måsen 1988, The Secret of Nandy 1990, Till Julia 1991, Blank päls och starka tassar 1993, Längtans blåa blomma (miniseries) 1998, The Lost Prince 2003, Return of the Dancing Master 2004. *Address:* Tykövägen 27, Lidingö 18161, Sweden (home).

ANDERSSON, Claes, DMed; Finnish politician, psychiatrist, writer and poet; b. 30 May 1937, Helsinki; s. of Oscar Andersson and Ethel Hjelt; m. Katriina Kuusi 1970; six c.; novelist and poet 1974; mem. Parl. 1987–; Minister, Ministry of Educ. 1995–98; fmrly mem. Finnish People's Democratic League 1970–90, mem. Left-Wing Alliance 1990–, Chair. 1990; Chair. Finland's Swedish Union of Writers; Vice-Pres. Information Centre of Finnish Literature 1985–; Eino-Leino Prize 1985, five times recipient of State Prize of Literature, Bellmanpriset 2007. *Publications:* novels: Bakom bilderna 1972, Den fagraste vår 1976, En mänske börjar likna sin själ 1983, Mina tolv politiska år 2000, Har de sett öknen blomma? 2006; poetry: Ventil 1962, Som om ingenting hänt 1964, Staden heter Helsingfors 1965, Samhället vi dör i 1967, Det är inte lätt att vara villaägare i dessa tider 1969, Bli, tillsammans 1970, Rumskamrater 1974, Jag har mött dem 1976, Genom sprickorna i vårt ansikte 1977, Trädens sånger 1979, Tillkortakommanden 1981, Under 1984, Det som blev ord i mig 1987, Mina bästa dagar 1987, Som lyser mellan gallren 1989, Huden där den är som tunnasi 1991, Dikter från havets botten 1993, En lycklig mänska 1996, Dessa underbara stränder, förber glidande 2002, Mörkret regnar stjärnor 2002, Det är kallt, det brinner 2004, Tidens framfart 2005; 20 stage plays and several radio plays and an opera libretto. *Leisure interest:* amateur jazz piano. *Address:* Eduskunta, Parliament of Finland, 00102 Helsinki, Finland (office). *Telephone:* (9) 4323172 (office). *E-mail:* claes.andersson@parliament.fi (office). *Website:* www.eduskunta.fi (office).

ANDERSSON, Harriet; Swedish actress; b. 14 Feb. 1932, Stockholm; began career in chorus at Oscars Theatre; subsequently appeared in reviews and then started serious dramatic career at Malmö City Theatre 1953; now appears regularly at Kunigliga Dramatiska Teatern, Stockholm; Swedish Film Asscn plaque. *Films include:* Summer with Monica 1953, Sawdust and Tinsel 1953, Women's Dreams 1955, Dreams of a Summer Night 1955, Through a Glass Darkly (German Film Critics' Grand Prize) 1961, All Those

Women 1964, Cries and Whispers 1973, One Sunday in September 1963, To Love (Best Actress Award, Venice Film Festival) 1964, Adventure Starts Here 1965, Stimulantia 1965–66, Rooftree 1966, Anna 1970, Siska 1962, Dream of Happiness 1963, Loving Couples 1964, For the Sake of Friendship 1965, Vine Bridge 1965, The Serpent 1966, The Deadly Affair 1967, The Girls 1968, The Stake, Happy End 1999, Dogville 2003, Bip Bop Bip Bop Bap 2006. *Television includes:* Belinder auktioner 2003, Swedenhielms 2003. *Theatre includes:* Anne Frank in The Diary of Anne Frank, Ophelia in Hamlet, The Beggar's Opera and plays by Chekhov. *Address:* c/o Sandrew Film & Theater AB, Box 5612, 114 86 Stockholm, Sweden.

ANDERSSON, Leif Christer Leander, MD, PhD; Finnish pathologist and academic; *Professor of Pathology, University of Helsinki;* b. 24 March 1944, Esse; s. of Herman Alfons Andersson and Elvi Alina Häll; m. Nea Margareta Gustavson 1971 (died 2003); one s. two d.; ed Univ. of Helsinki; Visiting Investigator, Univ. of Uppsala, Sweden 1975–76, Scripps Clinic and Research Inst., La Jolla, Calif., USA 1989–90; Prof. of Pathology, Univ. of Helsinki 1981–; Research Prof., Finnish Acad. of Science 1987–92; Prof. of Pathology, Karolinska Inst., Stockholm, Sweden 1996–2000, Head of Pathology, Karolinska Hosp. 1997, Foreign Adjunct Prof. 2004–; Head of Diagnostics, Div. of Pathology and Medical Genetics, Helsinki Univ. Hosp. 2002–03; Chair. Finnish Cancer Inst. 2003–; Pres. Finnish Soc. of Sciences and Letters, Helsinki 2007–; Anders Jahres Medical Prize, Univ. of Oslo 1981, Finska Läkaresällskapets Prize 1985, E.J. Nyström Prize, Finnish Soc. of Sciences and Letters 2003, Runeberg Prize 2007. *Publications:* about 320 original publs on cell biology, immunology, haematology, oncology and pathology. *Leisure interest:* happy jazz. *Address:* University of Helsinki, Haartman Institute, Department of Pathology, PO Box 21 (Haartmaninkatu 3), 00014 Helsinki, Finland (office). *Telephone:* (9) 1911 (office). *Fax:* (9) 1912-6675 (office). *E-mail:* leif.andersson@helsinki.fi (office).

ANDERTON, James Patrick (Jim); New Zealand politician; *Minister of Agriculture, for Biosecurity, of Fisheries and of Forestry;* b. 21 Jan. 1938, Auckland; m.; three s. one d.; ed Seddon Memorial Tech. Coll., Auckland Teachers' Training Coll; teacher for two years; Child Welfare Officer Educ. Dept, Wanganui; Catholic Youth Movt Organiser 1960–65; Sec. Catholic Diocesan Office, Auckland 1967–69; Export Man. UEB Textiles 1969–70; Man. Dir Anderton Holdings 1971–; City Councillor Manukau 1965–68, Auckland 1974–77, Councillor Auckland Regional Authority 1977–80; joined Labour Party 1963, held posts at Electorate, Regional and Exec. levels, Pres. NZ Labour Party (NZLP) 1979–84, mem. Policy Council 1979–89; MP for Sydenham 1984–; resigned from Labour Party 1989 and formed New Labour Party; re-elected MP for Sydenham (now Wigram) 1990 as NZLP cand.; elected first leader of Alliance Party (formed 1991); Deputy Prime Minister 1999–2002; Minister for Econ. Devt, for Industry and Regional Devt 1999–2005, for Public Trust Office and Audit Dept 1999–2002, currently Minister of Agric., for Biosecurity, of Fisheries and of Forestry; Leader Progressive Party 2004–. *Leisure interests:* chess, cricket and classical guitar. *Address:* Ministry of Agriculture and Forestry, 25 The Terrace, POB 2526, Wellington, New Zealand (office). *Telephone:* (4) 819-0100 (office). *Fax:* (4) 474-4111 (office). *E-mail:* info@maf.govt.nz (office). *Website:* www.maf.govt.nz (office).

ANDÒ, Salvatore; Italian politician and academic; *Lecturer in Public Law, University of Catania;* b. 13 Feb. 1945, Jonia, Catania; m.; two c.; Chair. Consiglio Nazionale delle Opere Universitarie; Prov. Exec. Fed. of Young Socialists 1963–69; mem. Prov. Exec. Cttee Catania Fed. of Italian Socialist Party (PSI) 1974–, mem. Exec. of Fed. 1975–, Deputy Sec. 1978–, mem. Regional Cttee PSI; Parl. Deputy 1979–; Minister of Defence 1992–93; currently Lecturer in Public Law, Univ. of Catania. *Address:* Università degli Studi di Catania, Facoltà di Scienze Politiche, Palazzo Calì, via Vittorio Emanuele II 49, 95131 Catania, Italy (office). *Telephone:* (095) 533651 (office). *Fax:* (095) 531058 (office). *Website:* www.fscpo.unict.it (office).

ANDO, Tadao; Japanese architect; b. 13 Sept. 1941, Osaka; m. Yumiko Kato 1970; one c.; began as professional boxer; taught himself architecture by observing bldgs in Africa, America, Europe; Founder, Dir Tadao Ando Architect and Assocs 1969–; Visiting Prof., Columbia, Harvard, Yale Univs; exhbn at RIBA 1993; Gold Medal of Architecture (French Acad.), Carlsberg Architecture Prize, Pritzker Prize 1995, Imperial Praemium Prize 1996, RIBA Royal Gold Medal 1997. *Works include:* school for Benetton, Northern Italy, the Church of Light, Osaka, Japan, Children's Museum, Hyogo, Japan, Water Temple, Osaka, Rokko Housing nr Osaka. *Publications include:* Tadao Ando 1981, Tadao Ando: Buildings, Project, Writings 1984. *Address:* Tadao Ando Architect and Associates, 5-23 Toyosaki, 2-chome, Kita-ku, Osaka 531, Japan.

ANDON, Nick Leon, BA, MSc; Micronesian politician and financial administrator; m. Marpellina Dereas; two c.; ed Truk High School, Univ. of Guam, Grossmont Coll. El Cajon CA, San Diego State Univ., United States Int. Univ. (USIU) San Diego; Coordinator Territorial Econ. Opportunity Office 1977–78; Program Developer Office of Aging 1980–81, Trust Territory of Pacific Islands (TTPI) Saipan, Program Coordinator 1981–83; Man. Analysis Budget Office 1983–84; Admin. Div. Grants Man. 1990–97, FSM Nat. Govt; Dir Budget 1984–90, 1997–98, Dir Treasury 1998–2000, Chuuk State Govt; State Man. FSM Telecommunications Chuuk Station 2000–03; Sec. Dept of Finance and Admin, FSM Nat. Govt 2003–; Chair. Bd Chuuk Public Utility Corpn (CPUC) 1997–2001; Chair. Chuuk State Financial Control Comm. 2002–03; Sec. Bd Bank of FSM 1999–2007; Chair. Bd of Trustees Chuuk State Health Care Plan (CSHCP) 2001–. *Address:* c/o Department of Finance and Administration, POB PS-158, Palikir, Pohnpei FM 96941, Federated States of Micronesia (office).

ANDOV, Stojan; Macedonian politician and economist; b. 1935; ed Skopje Univ., Belgrade Univ.; worked as economist; political activities since late 1980s; one of founders and mem. Exec. Bd Liberal Party of Macedonia 1990; Deputy Chair. Repub. Exec. Cttee; mem. Union Veche (Parl.) of Yugoslavia; took part in negotiations between Yugoslavia and EC; Amb. of Yugoslavia to Iraq; Del. to Nat. Ass. Repub. of Macedonia 1990–, Chair. 1990–96, Pres. Nat. Ass. 2001; Acting Pres. of Macedonia Oct. 1995–Jan. 1996; Head, faction Reform Forces of Macedonia-Liberal Party, Co-Chair. 1996. *Address:* Sobranje, 1000 Skopje, 11 Oktombri bb, Macedonia (office). *Telephone:* (2) 112255 (office). *Fax:* (2) 237947 (office). *E-mail:* sgjorgi@assembly.gov.uk (office). *Website:* www.assembly.gov.mk/sobranje.

ANDRÁSFALVY, Bertalan, PhD, DSc; Hungarian politician, ethnographer and academic; *Professor Emeritus, University of Pécs;* b. 17 Nov. 1931, Sopron; s. of Károly Andrásfalvy and Judit Mezey; m. Mária Gere; three s.; ed Budapest Univ.; with Museum of Szekszárd 1955, Transdanubian Research Inst. of the Hungarian Acad. of Sciences 1960–76, Archives of Baranya Co. and Museum of Pécs –1985; Exec., later Dept Head Ethnographic Research Group, Hungarian Acad. of Sciences; Assoc. Prof., Univ. of Pécs 1989–93, Prof. 1993–2001, Prof. Emer. 2001–; mem. Cttee Hungarian Democratic Forum; mem. of Parl. 1990–94; Minister of Culture and Public Educ. 1990–93; Hon. mem. Finnish Literature Soc.; Grand Silver Medal with Ribbon (Austria), Order of Merit Medium Cross with Star (Hungary), Grosse Verdienstkreutz (Germany), Grand Cross of Lion's Order of Knighthood (Finland); Eriksson Prize of the Swedish Royal Acad., István Győrffy Memorial Medal of Hungarian Ethnographic Soc. *Publications:* Contrasting Value Orientation of Peasant Communities, Die traditionelle Bewirtschaftung der Überschwemmungsgebiete in Ungarn, European Culture of the Hungarian People, Vom 'Nutzen' der Volkskunst und der Volkskunde, Duna-Drava Nemzeti Park (co-author) 2001, Folyamatok es Fordulopontok (co-author) 2003, Hagyomany es Jovendo: Nepismereti Tanulmanyok 2004. *Leisure interest:* gardening. *Address:* Főútca 26, 7694 Hosszúhetény, Hungary (home). *Telephone:* (72) 490-473 (home). *Fax:* (72) 490-473 (home). *E-mail:* mariberci@t-online.hu (home).

ANDRE 3000, (Dré); American rap artist; b. (Andre Benjamin), 27 May 1975, Georgia; ed Tri-City High School, Atlanta; mem., Outkast (with Big Boi) 1992–, signed to LaFace Records; designed Outkast Clothing line; Source Award for Best New Rap Group of the Year 1995, American Music Awards for Best Hip Hop/R&B Group 2003, 2004, Grammy Award for best urban/ alternative performance 2004, World Music Awards for Best Group, Best Pop Group, Best Rap/Hip-Hop Artist 2004, MTV Europe Best Group Award 2004, Best Song Award, Best Video Award (both for Hey Ya) 2004. *Recordings include:* albums: Southernplayalisticadillacmuzik 1994, ATLiens 1996, Aquemini 1998, Stankonia 2000, Big Boi And Dre Present... 2002, Speakerboxxx/The Love Below (Grammy Awards for Album of the Year, Best Rap Album 2004, American Music Award for Best Rap/Hip-Hop Album 2004) 2003, My Life In Idlewild 2005, Idlewild 2006. *Address:* William Morris Agency, 1325 Avenue of the Americas, New York, NY 10019, USA (office); c/o LaFace Records, A&R Department, 1 Capital City Plaza, 3350 Peachtree Road, Suite 1500, Atlanta, GA 30326, USA. *Telephone:* (212) 586-5100 (office). *Fax:* (212) 246-3583 (office). *Website:* www.outkast.com.

ANDRE, Carl; American sculptor; b. 16 Sept. 1935, Quincy, Mass; s. of George H. Andre and Margaret M. Andre (née Johnson); ed Phillips Acad., Andover, Mass, served in US Army 1955–56; went to New York 1957; worked as freight brakeman and conductor of Pennsylvania Railroad 1960–64; first public exhbn 1964, numerous public collections in USA and Europe. *Address:* c/o Paula Cooper, 534 West 21st Street, New York, NY 10011-2812; Konrad Fischer, Platanestrasse 7, 40233 Düsseldorf, Germany; Cooper Station, PO Box 1001, New York, NY 10276, USA (home). *Telephone:* (212) 255-1105 (New York); (211) 68-59-08 (Düsseldorf).

ANDRÉ, Maurice; French musician (trumpet); b. 21 May 1933, Alès, Gard; s. of Marcel André and Fabienne Volpélière; m. Lilianne Arnoult 1956; four c.; ed Conservatoire nat. supérieur de musique, Paris; apprenticed as coal miner before undertaking formal music studies; trumpet soloist Orchestre des Concerts Lamoureux 1953–60, Orchestre Philharmonique de l'ORTF 1953–62, Orchestre de l'Opéra-Comique 1962–67; played in jazz groups and chamber orchestras; now soloist with world's leading orchestras; specialises in baroque and contemporary music; Prof. of Trumpet, Paris Conservatoire 1967–1978; has made about 300 recordings, including 30 trumpet concertos; Chevalier, Légion d'honneur, Commdr, Ordre des Arts et des Lettres; won Prix d'honneur for cornet 1952, premier prix for trumpet 1953, first prize Geneva Int. Competition 1955, Munich Int. Competition 1963, Schallplattenpreis, Berlin 1970, Victoire de la musique 1987. *Leisure interests:* pen and ink drawing, gardening, swimming, sculpture in wood and stone. *Address:* c/o Harry Lapp Organisation, 9 avenue de la Liberté, 67000 Strasbourg, France (office).

ANDREA, Pat; Dutch artist; b. 25 June 1942, The Hague; s. of Kees Andrea and Metty Naezer; m. 1st Cecile Hessels 1966 (divorced 1983); m. 2nd Cristina Ruiz Guiñazu 1993; three s. one d.; ed Royal Acad. of Fine Arts, The Hague; paints in figurative style, focusing on personal deformities, people in dramatic situations, sex and violence in suspense; represented in MOMA, New York, Centre Pompidou, Paris and Frissiras Museum, Athens; Prof. Ecole Nat. Supérieur des Beaux Arts, Paris 1998–, Corresp. Académie des Beaux Arts Institut de France; Royal Subsidy for painting 1963, 1972; Jacob Maris Prize 1968. *Films:* (with Fred Compain) Du crime consideré comme un des Beaux Arts 1981, Journal de Patagonie 1985, (with Marie Binet) L'aventure Pat Andrea 2002, (with Jorge Amat) La puñalada Pat Andrea 2004. *Publications:* (with H. P. de Boer) Nederlands gebarenboekje 1979, 2004, (with J. Cortazar) La Puñalada 1982, Pat Andrea: conversations avec Pierre Sterckx 1993.

Address: 52 avenue F.V.Raspail, 94110 Arcueil, France (office). *Telephone:* (1) 45-47-89-08 (office). *Fax:* (1) 45-47-89-08 (office).

ANDREANI, Jacques; French fmr diplomatist; b. 22 Nov. 1929, Paris; m. 1st Huguette de Fonclare; one s. one d.; m. 2nd Donatella Monterisi 1981; one s. one d.; ed Inst. d'Etudes Politiques, Univ. of Paris and Ecole Nat. d'Admin; Sec. French Embassy, Washington, DC 1955–60, Moscow 1961–64; Ministry of Foreign Affairs 1964–70; Deputy Rep. of France, NATO, Brussels 1970–72; Head, French Del. to CSCE, Helsinki and Geneva 1972–75; Asst Sec. for European Affairs, Ministry of Foreign Affairs 1975–79; Amb. to Egypt 1979–81; Dir of Political Affairs, Ministry of Foreign Affairs 1981–84; Amb. to Italy 1984–88; Chief of Staff, Ministry of Foreign Affairs 1988–89; Amb. to USA 1989–95; Special Asst to Minister of Foreign Affairs 1995–97; Commdr Légion d'honneur; Commdr Ordre Nat. du Mérite. *Publication:* L'Amérique et nous 2000. *Leisure interests:* arts, music, golf. *Address:* 40 rue Bonaparte, 75006 Paris, France (home). *Telephone:* 1-43-26-14-92 (home). *Fax:* 1-43-26-60-82 (home). *E-mail:* jandrean@noos.fr (home).

ANDREAS, Glenn Allen, BA, JUDr; American business executive; *Chairman and Chief Executive Officer, Archer Daniels Midland Co.;* b. 22 June 1943, Cedar Rapids, Ia; s. of Glenn Allen Andreas and Vera Yates; m. Toni Kay Hibma 1964; one s. two d.; ed Valparaiso Univ., Ind., Valparaiso Univ. School of Law; attorney, US Treasury Dept 1969–73; with Legal Dept, Archer Daniels Midland Co. 1973–86, Treasurer 1986–, Chief Financial Officer of European Operations 1989–94, Vice-Pres. and Counsel to Exec. Cttee 1994–96, mem. Office of CEO 1996–97, Pres., CEO 1997–99, Chair., CEO 1999–. *Leisure interest:* golf. *Address:* Archer Daniels Midland Company, 4666 Faries Parkway, PO Box 1470, Decatur, IL 62526-5666, USA (office). *Telephone:* (217) 424-5426 (office). *Fax:* (217) 424-4266 (office). *Website:* www.admworld.com (office).

ANDREEV, Aleksandr Fyodorovich, DrPhysSc; Russian physicist; *Vice-President, Russian Academy of Sciences;* b. 10 Dec. 1939, Leningrad; s. of Fyodor Andreev and Nina Andreeva; m. Tamara Turok 1960; one d.; ed Moscow Physico-Tech. Inst.; Jr then Sr Researcher 1964–79, Prof. 1979–; Deputy Dir USSR Acad. of Sciences, Kapitza Inst. for Physical Problems 1984–91, Dir 1991–; Lorentz Prof., Univ. of Leiden 1992; Ed.-in-Chief Priroda 1993–, JETP 1997–; Corresp. mem. USSR (now Russian) Acad. of Sciences 1981–87, mem. 1987, Vice-Pres. 1991–; Chair. Comm. for State Scientific Stipends; Foreign mem. Finnish Acad. of Science and Letters 2002, Georgian Acad. of Sciences 2002; Lomonosov Prize, USSR Acad. of Sciences 1984, Lenin Prize 1986, Carus-Medaille de Deutschen Akad. der Naturforscher Leopoldina, Carus-Preis der Stadt Schweinfurt 1987, Simon Memorial Prize (UK) 1995, Kapitza Gold Medal, Russian Acad. of Sciences 1999. *Address:* Academy of Sciences, Kapitza Institute for Physical Problems, Kosygin Street 2, 119334 Moscow, Russia (office). *Telephone:* (495) 137-32-48 (office). *Fax:* (495) 651-21-25 (office). *E-mail:* andreev@kapitza.ras.ru (home). *Website:* www.kapitza.ras.ru (office).

ANDREI, Ştefan; Romanian politician; b. 29 March 1931, Podari-Livezi, Dolj County; ed Inst. of Civil Eng, Bucharest; Asst Prof. Inst. of Civil Eng and Inst. of Oil, Gas and Geology, Bucharest 1956–63; mem. Union of Communist Youth (UCY) 1949–54; joined student movt 1951; mem. Exec. Cttee Union of Student Asscns 1958–62; mem. Bureau Cen. Cttee UCY 1962–65; mem. Romanian Communist Party (RCP) 1954–89; Alt. mem. Cen. Cttee RCP 1969–72, mem. 1972–89; First Deputy Head of Int. Section Cen. Cttee 1966–72; Sec. Cen. Cttee 1972–78; alt. mem. Exec. Political Cttee 1974–89; mem. Perm. Bureau, Exec. Political Cttee 1974–84; Minister for Foreign Affairs 1978–85; Secr. Cen. Cttee 1985–87; Deputy Prime Minister 1987–89; mem. Grand Nat. Ass. 1975–89; mem. Nat. Council Front of Socialist Democracy and Unity 1980–89; several Romanian orders and medals.

ANDREJEVS, Georgs, DMed; Latvian politician, diplomatist, physician and scientist; b. 30 Oct. 1932, Tukums; m. Anita Andrejeva; one s. one d.; ed Latvian Medical Inst.; paramedic, Riga first aid station 1953–59; Head of Dept, P. Stradiņs Clinic, Riga 1959–62, Asst 1962–64, teacher 1964–74; Asst Prof., Head Dept of Surgery, Chief Anaesthesiologist and Reanimatologist of Ministry of Health 1962–92; Head of Dept and Prof., Riga Inst. of Medicine 1974–90; Head of Dept, Latvian Acad. of Medicine 1994–95; Founder Latvijas ceļš (Latvian Way) party 1993; mem. Latvian People's Front; Deputy to Latvian Repub. Supreme Council; Sec. Comm. for Foreign Affairs of Supreme Council; Minister of Foreign Affairs 1992–94; mem. Saima (Parl.) 1993–95; Amb. to Canada 1995–98, to Council of Europe 1998–2004; Chair. Council of Europe Ministers' Deputies 2000–01, Council of Europe Cttee of Ministers' Working Party on Co-operation between the Council of Europe and the EU 2001–03; mem. European Parl. (Group of the Alliance of Liberals and Democrats for Europe) 2004–, Vice-Chair. Cttee on the Environment, Public Health and Food Safety, mem. Del. to EU-Armenia, EU-Azerbaijan and EU-Georgia Parl. Cooperation Cttees, Substitute mem. Del. to EU-Croatia Jt Parl. Cttee; mem. Latvian Acad. of Sciences 1995–, European Asscn of Anaesthesiologists 1997–; Fellow, Royal Coll. of Anaesthetists, UK 1995; doyen d'âge, Council of Europe diplomatic corps; Commdr, Order of the Three Stars. *Address:* European Parliament, Bâtiment Altiero Spinelli, ASP 08G318, 60 rue Wiertz, 1047 Brussels, Belgium (office); Akmenu iela 15, 1048 Riga, Latvia. *Fax:* (2) 284-9548 (office). *E-mail:* gandrejevs@europarl.eu.int (office). *Website:* www.europarl.eu.int (office).

ANDREN, Anders, LèsL, MBA; Swedish business executive; b. 30 July 1939, Gothenburg; s. of Erik Andren and Birgit Flodin; m. Monika Grohmann 1967; one s.; ed Univ. of Stockholm and Institut européen de l'admin des affaires (INSEAD); Dir-Gen. Electrolux Canarias SA 1968–70, Electrolux Belgique 1971–74; Pres.-Dir-Gen. Electrolux SA France 1974–93, fmr Chair., Man. Dir; fmr Pres. Supervisory Bd, Arthur Martin (now Hon. Pres.); Pres.-Dir Gen.

Groupe Esab SA France 1992–95, Direct Ménager France 1993–98; f. Domus France SA 1998; Hon. Pres. Swedish Chamber of Commerce in France; Chevalier, Légion d'honneur. *Address:* 13 Boucle d'en bas, 60270 Gouvieux, France (home).

ANDREOLI, Kathleen Gainor; American professor of nursing and university dean; *Dean Emerita, College of Nursing, Rush University;* b. 22 Sept. 1935, Albany, NY; d. of John Edward Gainor and Edmunda Ringelmann Gainor; m. Thomas Eugene Andreoli 1960 (divorced); one s. two d.; ed Georgetown Univ. and Vanderbilt Schools of Nursing and Univ. of Alabama School of Nursing, Birmingham; Staff Nurse, Albany Hosp. Medical Center, New York 1957; instructor, various schools of nursing 1957–70; Educational Dir, Physician Asst Program, Dept of Medicine, School of Medicine, Univ. of Alabama 1970–75, subsequently Asst Prof. then Assoc. Prof. of Nursing 1970–79, Prof. of Nursing 1979; Prof. of Nursing, Special Asst to Pres. for Educational Affairs, Univ. of Texas Health Science Center, Houston 1979–82, Vice-Pres. for Educational Services, Interprofessional Educ. and Int. Programs 1983–87; Vice-Pres. Nursing Affairs and John L. and Helen Kellogg Dean of Coll. of Nursing Rush Univ., Chicago 1987–2005, Dean Emer. 2005–; Ed. Heart and Lung, Journal of Total Care 1971; mem. Bd of Dirs American Asscn of Colleges of Nursing 1998–2000; mem. Nat. Advisory Nursing Council V.H.A. 1992, Advisory Bd Robert Wood Johnson Clinic Nursing School Program, Visiting Cttee Vanderbilt Univ. School of Nursing, Editorial/Advisory Bd The Nursing Spectrum 1996–, Advisory Bd Major Diseases: Diabetes Mellitus and Hypertension 1999, numerous other bodies; mem. Inst. of Medicine of NAS, Inst. of Medicine of Chicago; Fellow American Acad. of Nursing; Founders Award, NC Heart Asscn 1970, Distinguished Alumni Awards, Vanderbilt Univ. and Univ. of Alabama, Birmingham; Sigma Theta Tau Dean's Award 2003; numerous other awards. *Publications:* Comprehensive Cardiac Care (jtly) 1983; numerous articles in professional journals. *Leisure interests:* music, art, reading, bicycling, travelling. *Address:* Rush University Medical Center, 600 South Paulina Street, Suite 1080, Chicago, IL 60612-3806 (office); 1212 South Lake Shore Drive, Chicago, IL 60605-2402, USA (home). *Telephone:* (312) 942-7117 (office); (312) 266-8338 (home). *Fax:* (312) 942-3043 (office). *E-mail:* Kathleen_G_Andreoli@rush.edu (office). *Website:* www.rushu.rush.edu/nursing (office).

ANDREOTTI, Giulio; Italian politician and journalist; *Co-Founder, European Democracy;* b. 14 Jan. 1919, Rome; s. of Philip Andreotti; m. Livia Danese 1945; two s. two d.; ed Univ. of Rome; Pres., Fed. of Catholic Univs in Italy 1942–45; Deputy to the Constituent Ass. 1945 and to Parl. 1946– (Life Senator 1992–); Under-Sec. in the Govt of De Gasperi and Pella 1947–53; Minister for the Interior in Fanfani Govt 1954; Minister of Finance 1955–58, of Treasury 1958–59, of Defence 1959–60, 1960–66, March–Oct. 1974, of Industry and Commerce 1966–68, for the Budget and Econ. Planning and in charge of Southern Devt Fund 1974–76, Chair. Christian Democratic Parl. Party in Chamber of Deputies 1948–72; Prime Minister 1972–73, 1976–79, 1989–92; Chair. Foreign Affairs Cttee, Chamber of Deputies; Minister of Foreign Affairs 1983–89; Co-Founder European Democracy 2001–; immunity lifted May 1993, charged with consorting with the Mafia March 1995, acquitted 1999; charged with complicity in murder Nov. 1995, acquitted 1999, prosecution urged appeals court to reconsider, sentenced to 24 years' imprisonment Nov. 2002; Hon. LLD (Beijing Univ.) 1991. *Publications:* Ed. of Concretezza 1954–76, A Ogni morte di Papa 1980, Gli USA Visti da Vicino 1983, Diari 1976–79, Lives: Encounters with History Makers 1989, The USA Up Close 1992, Cosa Loro 1995, De Prima Republica 1996.

ANDRESEN, Brit, MArch; Norwegian architect and academic; *Professor of Architecture, University of Queensland;* ed Univ. of Trondheim; awarded scholarship to study housing in The Netherlands; won competition to co-design Burrell Museum (with John Meunier and Barry Gasson), Glasgow, UK; fmr part-time teacher of architecture, Univ. of Cambridge and Architectural Asscn, UK; currently Prof. of Architecture, Univ. of Queensland, Australia; fmr Visiting Prof., UCLA, USA; Co-founder Andresen O'Gorman Architects (with Peter O'Gorman); Fellow, Royal Australian Inst. of Architects (RAIA); RAIA Gold Medal (first woman to receive medal) 2002. *Architectural works include:* Burrell Museum (Glasgow), Rosebury House (Brisbane), Ocean View House (Mt Mee), Mooloomba House (Point Lookout), Moreton Bay Houses (Wynnum). *Publications include:* articles on architecture in professional journals. *Address:* School of Architecture, University of Queensland, Brisbane, Queensland 4072, Australia (office). *Telephone:* (7) 3365-3780 (office). *E-mail:* b.andresen@uq.edu.au (office).

ANDRETTI, Mario; American business executive and fmr racing driver; b. 28 Feb. 1940, Montona, Italy; s. of Alvise Andretti and Rina Andretti; m. Dee Ann Hoch 1961; two s. one d.; began racing career in Nazareth, Pa aged 19; Champ Car Nat. Champion 1965, 1966, 1969, 1984; winner of Daytona 500 1967; winner of 12 Hours of Sebring 1967, 1970, 1972; winner of Indianapolis 500 1969; USAC Nat. Dirt Track Champion 1974; Formula One World Champion 1978; winner of Int. Race of Champions 1979; all-time Champ Car lap leader (7,587); all-time leader in Champ Car pole positions won (67); oldest race winner in recorded Champ Car history; retd from active driving 1994; Commdr, Order of Merit; Driver of the Year 1967, 1978, 1984, Driver of the Quarter Century 1992, Driver of the Century 1999–2000, FIA Gold Medal for Motor Sport 2007, Library of Congress Living Legend 2008. *Achievements:* 111 career wins, 52 Champ Car victories (USAC & CART), 12 Formula One victories (FIA), 9 Sprint Car victories (USAC), 9 Midget victories (ARDC, NASCAR & USAC), 7 Formula 5000 victories (SCCA/USAC), 7 World Sports Car victories (FIA), 5 Dirt Track victories (USAC), 4 Three-Quarter Midget victories (ATQMRA), 3 IROC victories, 2 stock car victories (NASCAR & USAC), 1 non-championship race. *Publication:* Mario Andretti: A Driving Passion (autobiog.). *Leisure interests:* golf, snowmobiling, tennis, opera.

Telephone: (248) 335-3535 (office). *Fax:* (248) 335-3352 (office). *E-mail:* info@ sportsmanagementnetwork.com (office). *Website:* www .sportsmanagementnetwork.com (office); www.marioandretti.com (home).

ANDREW, Christopher Robert (Rob), MBE; British professional rugby union coach and fmr professional rugby union player; *Elite Rugby Director, Rugby Football Union;* b. 18 Feb. 1963, Richmond, Yorks.; m. Sara Andrew 1989; two d.; ed Univ. of Cambridge; chartered surveyor; fly-half; fmr mem. Middlesbrough, Cambridge Univ., Nottingham, Gordon (Sydney, Australia) clubs; mem. Wasps Club 1987–91, 1992–96, Capt. until 1989–90; with Toulouse 1991–92, Barbarians, Newcastle 1996–; int. debut England versus Romania 1985; Five Nations debut England versus France 1985; Capt. England team, England versus Romania, Bucharest 1989; mem. Grand Slam winning team 1991, 1992; record-holder for drop goals in ints; retd from int. rugby 1995, returned 1997–99; Devt Dir Newcastle Rugby Football Club 1996–2006; Elite Rugby Dir, Rugby Football Union (RFU) 2006–. *Publication:* A Game and a Half 1995. *Leisure interests:* gardening, pushing a pram, golf. *Address:* Rugby Football Union, Rugby House, Rugby Road, Twickenham, Middlesex TW1 1DS, England (office). *Telephone:* (870) 405-2000 (office). *E-mail:* media@therfu.com (office). *Website:* www.rfu.com (office).

ANDREWS, Anthony; British actor; b. 1 Dec. 1948, Hampstead, London; m. Georgina Simpson; one s. two d.; ed Royal Masonic School, Herts.; started acting 1967. *TV appearances include:* Doomwatch, Woodstock 1972, A Day Out, Follyfoot, Fortunes of Nigel 1973, The Pallisers, David Copperfield 1974, Upstairs, Downstairs 1975, French Without Tears, The Country Wife, Much Ado About Nothing 1977, Danger UXB 1978, Romeo and Juliet 1979, Brideshead Revisited 1980, Ivanhoe 1982, The Scarlet Pimpernel 1983, Columbo 1988, The Strange Case of Dr. Jekyll and Mr. Hyde 1989, Hands of a Murderer 1990, Lost in Siberia 1990, The Law Lord 1991, Jewels 1992, Ruth Rendell's Heartstones, Mothertime, David Copperfield 2000, Love in a Cold Climate (miniseries) 2001, Cambridge Spies (miniseries) 2003. *Films Include:* The Scarlet Pimpernel, Under the Volcano, A War of the Children, Take Me High 1973, Operation Daybreak 1975, Les Adolescents 1976, The Holcroft Covenant 1986, Second Victory 1987, Woman He Loved 1988, The Light-horsemen 1988, Hannah's War 1988, Lost in Siberia (also producer) 1990, Haunted (also co-producer) 1995, Last Night 2007. *Plays:* 40 Years On, A Midsummer Night's Dream, Romeo and Juliet, One of Us 1986, Coming into Land 1986, Dragon Variation, Tima and the Conways, My Fair Lady 2003–04, The Woman in White 2005, The Letter 2007.

ANDREWS, David, SC, BCL; Irish fmr politician, international organization official and barrister; *Chair, Irish Red Cross;* b. 15 March 1935, Dublin; s. of Christopher Andrews and Mary Coyle; m. Annette Cusack; two s. three d.; ed Mount St Joseph's Cistercian Coll., Co. Tipperary, Univ. Coll. Dublin and King's Inns, Dublin; mem. Dáil 1965–2002; Parl. Sec. to Taoiseach 1970–73; Govt Chief Whip 1970–73; Minister of State, Dept of Foreign Affairs 1977–79, Dept of Justice 1978–79; Minister for Foreign Affairs 1992–93, for Defence and the Marine 1993–94, for Defence July–Oct. 1997, for Foreign Affairs 1997–2000; Opposition Spokesman on Tourism and Trade 1995–97; mem. New Ireland Forum, Consultative Ass. of Council of Europe, British-Irish Inter parl. Body 1990–92; Chair. Irish Red Cross 2000–; mem. Fianna Fáil; Chevalier, Légion d'Honneur 2006. *Leisure interests:* cinema, sport, walking. *Address:* Irish Red Cross, 16 Merrion Square, Dublin 2 (office); 102 Avoca Park, Blackrock, Dublin, Ireland (home). *Telephone:* (1) 6424600 (office); (1) 6623851 (home). *Fax:* (1) 6614461 (office). *Website:* www.redcross.ie (office).

ANDREWS, John Hamilton, AO, MArch, FTS, RIBA; Australian architect; b. 29 Oct. 1933, Sydney; s. of the late K. Andrews; m. Rosemary Randall 1958; four s.; ed N Sydney Boys' High School, Univ. of Sydney, Harvard Univ.; pvt. practice, Toronto, Canada 1962, Sydney 1970–; mem. Staff, Univ. of Toronto School of Architecture 1962–67, Chair. and Prof. of Architecture 1967–69; mem. Visual Arts Bd, Australia Council 1977–80, Bd mem. 1988–90; Chair. Architecture and Design Comm., Australia Council 1980–83, Founding Chair. Design Arts Bd, 1983–88; Architectural Juror, Australian Archives Nat. Headquarters Building 1979, Parl. House Competition 1979–80, The Peak, Hong Kong 1983, Hawaii Loa Coll. 1986, Gov. Gen.'s Medals, Canada 1986; mem. Bd Australia Council 1988–; Assoc. NZ Inst. of Architects; Foundation mem. Australian Acad. of Design 1990; Fellow, Royal Architectural Inst. of Canada, Australian Acad. of Technological Science; Life Fellow, Royal Australian Inst. of Architects; ; Hon. FAIA; Hon. DArch (Sydney) 1980; Centennial Medal (Canada) 1967, Massey Medal (Canada) 1967, Arnold Brunner Award, US Acad. of Arts and Letters 1971, American Inst. of Architects Honour Award 1973, Gold Medal, Royal Australian Inst. of Architects 1980, Advance Australia Award 1982, Sulman Medal (Australia) 1983, Design Excellence 25 Year Award, Ontario Asscn of Architecture, Scarborough Coll. 1989. *Principal works:* Scarborough Coll., Toronto, Harvard Grad. School of Design, Harvard Univ., Cameron Offices, Canberra, American Express Tower, Sydney, Intelsat HQ Bldg, Washington, DC, Hyatt Hotel, Perth, Convention Centre, Darling Harbour, Sydney, Convention Centre and Hyatt Hotel, Adelaide, World Congress Centre and Eden on the Yarra Hotel, Melbourne, The Octagon (office bldg), Parramatta, Sydney, NSW, Veterinary Conf. Centre, Univ. of Sydney, NSW. *Publication:* Architecture: A Performing Art 1982. *Leisure interests:* fly fishing, surfing. *Address:* John Andrews International, 'Colleton', Cargo Road, Orange, NSW 2800 (office); 'Colleton', Cargo Road, Orange, NSW 2800, Australia (home). *Telephone:* (2) 6365-6223 (office). *Fax:* (2) 6365-6211 (office).

ANDREWS, Dame Julie Elizabeth, DBE; British actress and singer; b. (Julia Wells), 1 Oct. 1935, Walton-on-Thames, Surrey; m. 1st Tony Walton 1959 (divorced 1968); one d.; m. 2nd Blake Edwards 1969; one step-s. one step-d. and two adopted d.; ed voice lessons with Lillian Stiles-Allen; first stage appearance aged 12 as singer, London Hippodrome; played in revues and concert tours; debut in Starlight Roof, London Hippodrome 1947; work for UN Devt Fund for Women; Academy Award for Best Actress 1964, three Golden Globe Awards 1964, 1965, Emmy Award 1987, BAFTA Award 1989, Kennedy Center Honor 2001, Screen Actors' Guild Lifetime Achievement Award 2006. *Theatre:* Starlight Roof (London Hippodrome) 1947, Cinderella (London Palladium), The Boy Friend (Broadway) 1954, My Fair Lady 1956–60, Camelot (Broadway) 1960–62, Putting it Together 1993, Victor, Victoria 1995–96. *Films:* Mary Poppins 1963, The Americanization of Emily 1964, The Sound of Music 1964, Hawaii 1965, Torn Curtain 1966, Thoroughly Modern Millie 1966, Star! 1967, Darling Lili 1970, The Tamarind Seed 1973, 10 1979, Little Miss Marker 1980, S.O.B. 1980, Victor/Victoria 1981, The Man Who Loved Women 1983, That's Life 1986, Duet For One 1986, The Sound of Christmas (TV) 1987, Our Sons (TV) 1991, Relative Values 1999, The Princess Diaries 2001, Shrek 2 (voice) 2004, The Princess Diaries 2: Royal Engagement 2004, The Cat That Looked at a King 2004, Shrek the Third (voice) 2007, Enchanted (voice) 2007. *TV appearances include:* High Tor 1956, The Julie Andrews Hour 1972–73, Great Performances Live in Concert 1990, The Julie Show (ABC) 1992, Eloise at the Plaza 2003, Eloise at Christmastime 2003. *Recordings:* albums: My Fair Lady (Broadway cast recording) 1956, The Lass With The Delicate Air 1957, Julie Andrews Sings 1958, Rose Marie 1958, Camelot (Broadway cast recording) 1960, Don't Go In The Lion's Cage Tonight 1962, Heartrending Ballads and Raucous Ditties 1962, Julie & Carol at Carnegie Hall (with Carol Burnett) 1962, Mary Poppins (film soundtrack) 1964, The Sound Of Music (film soundtrack) 1965, A Christmas Treasure 1968, Star! 1968, Darling Lili 1969, TV's Fair Julie 1972, The Secret of Christmas 1977, Christmas With Julie Andrews 1982, Love Me Tender 1983, Broadway's Fair Julie 1984, Love Julie 1989, At The Lincoln Center (with Carol Burnett) 1989, The King And I (studio cast) 1992, Broadway: The Music of Richard Rodgers 1994, Here I'll Stay: The Words of Alan Jay Lerner 1996, Nobody Sings It Better 1996. *Publications:* Mandy (as Julie Andrews Edwards) 1972, Last of the Really Great Whangdoodles 1973, The Great American Mousical (as Julie Andrews Edwards, with Emma Walton Hamilton) 2006, Home (auto-biog.) 2008. *Leisure interests:* skiing, riding. *Address:* c/o William Morris Agency, 1 William Morris Place, Beverly Hills, CA 90212, USA (office). *Telephone:* (310) 850 4550 (office). *Fax:* (310) 248 5650 (office). *E-mail:* nd@wma.com (office).

ANDREWS, Nancy C., BS, MS, MD, PhD; American physician, biologist and academic; *Dean, School of Medicine, Duke University;* b. 29 Nov. 1958, Syracuse, NY; m. Bernard Mathey-Prevot; one s. one d.; ed Yale Univ., Massachusetts Inst. of Tech., Harvard Univ. Medical School; joined faculty of Harvard Univ. Medical School 1991, becoming George Richards Minot Prof. of Pediatrics 2003, then Leland Fikes Prof. of Pediatrics, Dean for Basic Sciences and Grad. Studies 2003–07; Investigator, Howard Hughes Medical Inst. 1993–2006; Attending Physician in Hematology and Oncology, Children's Hosp., Boston –2003; fmr Distinguished Physician, Dana-Farber Cancer Inst., Boston; Chancellor for Academic Affairs and Dean of Medicine, Duke Univ. 2007–; Pres. American Soc. of Clinical Investigation; mem. American Acad. of Arts and Sciences 2007–, NAS Inst. of Medicine; Samuel Rosenthal Prize for Excellence in Academic Pediatrics 1998, American Fed. for Medical Research Foundation Outstanding Investigator Award in Basic Science 2000, Soc. for Pediatric Research E. Mead Johnson Award 2002, Harvard Medical School Dean's Leadership Award for Advancement of Women 2004. *Publications include:* over 100 peer-reviewed articles and 16 book chapters. *Address:* Dean's Suite, Duke University School of Medicine, Davison Building, 200 Trent Drive, Durham, NC 27710, USA (office). *Telephone:* (919) 684-8111 (office). *E-mail:* nancy.andrews@duke.edu (office). *Website:* medschool.duke .edu (office).

ANDREYEV, Vladimir Alekseyevich; Russian actor and stage director; *Director, Yermolova Theatre; Chairman, Drama Faculty of the Russian Theatre Academy;* b. 27 Aug. 1930; m. Natalia Selezneva; one s. one d.; ed State Inst. of Theatre Arts Cinema (GITIS); actor with Yermolova Theatre Moscow 1952–70, Chief Dir 1970–85, 1990–; teaches concurrently at GITIS, Prof. 1978–; Chief Dir of Maly Theatre, Moscow 1985–88; mem. CPSU 1962–92; mem. Int. Acad. of Theatre; currently Dir of Yermolova Theatre and Chair., Drama Faculty of Russian Theatre Acad.; USSR People's Artist 1985; Stanislavsky State Prize 1980, 1993, State Prize of Russia 1990, Govt Prize for Theatre Arts 1994, 2001. *Roles include:* Aleksey in V. Rozov's It's High Time!, Vasilkov in Ostrovsky's Crazy Money, Golubkov in Bulgakov's Flight, Sattarov in Valeyev's I Give You Life, Dorogin in Zorin's Lost Story, Writer in Bunin's Grammar of Love. *Productions include:* Vampilov's plays: Last Summer in Chulimsk and The Duck Hunt; Money for Mary (based on a work by V. Rasputin), The Shore (based on Yuriy Bondarev's novel), Uncle Vanya, Three Sisters (Chekhov). *Publication:* I Remember with an Open Heart. *Leisure interests* fine art, architecture, football, politics. *Address:* Yermolova Theatre, Tverskaya 5, 103009 Moscow; Tverskaya 9-60, 202009 Moscow, Russia (home). *Telephone:* (495) 203-87-03; (495) 629-48-57 (home). *E-mail:* yermolova@theatre.ru.

ANDRIANARIVO, Tantely René Gabrio; Malagasy politician; Prime Minister of Madagascar, Chief of Govt, Minister of Finances and Economy 1998–2002; sentenced to 12 years' hard labour for abuse of office Dec. 2003.

ANDRIANOV, Nikolai Yefimovich; Russian fmr gymnast; b. 14 Oct. 1953, Vladimir; m. Lyubov Burda; two s.; ed Moscow Inst. of Physical Culture; holds record for most Olympic medals won by a man: 15 Olympic medals (1972, 1976, 1980) including gold medals in free-style exercises 1972, in all-round competitions, on the rings, in jumps 1976, team championships and in jumps 1980; world champion 1974, 1978, 1979; numerous champion titles of Europe and USSR; Chief Coach USSR (now Russian) team, currently coaches in Japan; Merited Master of Sports 1972, Int. Gymnastics Hall of Fame 2001.

Address: Russian Federation of Gymnastics, 119871 Moscow, Luzhnetskaya nab. 8, Russia (office). *Telephone:* (495) 201-13-42 (office); (9222) 23924 (home).

ANDRIEŞ, Andrei, DPhys-MathSc; Moldovan physicist; *Director, Centre of Optoelectronics of the Institute of Applied Physics, Academy of Sciences of Moldova;* b. 24 Oct. 1933, Chişinău (Kishinev); s. of Mihail Andrieş and Maria Andrieş; m. Lidia Vasilievna Klimanova 1959; one s.; ed Kishinev Univ., Ioffe Inst. of Physics and Tech., Leningrad; researcher Inst. of Applied Physics, Acad. of Sciences Moldavian SSR 1962–64, Learning Sec. 1964–71, Head of Lab. Inst. of Applied Physics 1971–, Gen. Learning Sec. 1984–89, Dir Centre of Optoelectronics 1993–; Corresp. mem. Acad. of Sciences Moldavian SSR (now Acad. of Sciences of Moldova) 1978, mem. 1984, Pres. 1989–2004, Hon. Pres. 2004–; Gen. Dir Research and Educational Networking Asscn of Moldova (RENAM) 2004–; State Prize of Moldova 1983, 2001; Merited Scientific Researcher 1984; mem. Eng. Acad. of Russian Fed. 1992, New York Acad. of Sciences 1995, Int. Scientific Acad. of Life, the Universe and Nature, Toulouse 1997, Cosmanautics Acad.; more than forty patents; Hon. Mem. Romanian Acad., American-Romanian Acad. of Arts, Science and Humanities; Order of the Repub. of Moldova 1996; State Prize 1983, Int. Acad. of Rating Tech. and Sociology, Golden Fortune Award 2002, Stanford R. Ovahinsky Award for Excellence in Non-Crystalline Chalcogenides 2005; numerous other decorations and awards. *Publications:* over 450 works, including five monographs on physics of non-crystalline chalcogenides and new materials for photographic processes. *Leisure interests:* reading, travel. *Address:* Centre of Optoelectronics, Institute of Applied Physics, Academy of Sciences of Moldova, Str. Academiei 1, 2028 Chişinău (office); Str. Alexandrescu 13/62, 2008 Chişinău, Moldova (home). *Telephone:* (22) 73-98-05 (office); (22) 75-16-70 (home). *Fax:* (22) 73-98-05; (2) 27-60-14. *E-mail:* presidium@asm.md (office). *Website:* www.asm.md (office).

ANDRIESSEN, Franciscus H.J.J.; Dutch politician and economist; b. 2 April 1929, Utrecht; ed Univ. of Utrecht; Dir Catholic Inst. for Housing 1954–72; mem. of Second Chamber, States-Gen. (Parl.) 1967–77, First Chamber 1980–; Minister of Finance 1977–80; Commr for Competition Policy and Relations, European Parl., Comm. of European Communities 1981–84; for Agric. and Fisheries 1984–85, for Agric. and Forestry 1986–89, for External Relations and Trade Policy 1989–93; special adviser to KPMG 1993–1999; Pres. Inst. of the Euro 1993–2001; Prof. of European Integration, Univ. of Utrecht 1990–99; mem. Catholic People's Party, Christian Democratic Appeal; Kt, Order of the Lion; Grand Cross of Order of Orange-Nassau, of Order of Leopold II; Commdr du Mérite agricole. *Address:* clôs Henri Vaes l, 1950 Kraainem, Netherlands (home). *Telephone:* (32) 27315857 (home).

ANDRIKIENĖ, Laima Liucija, DEcon; Lithuanian politician and academic; b. 1 Jan. 1958, Druskininkai; m. (husband deceased); one s.; ed Druskininkai Secondary School, Druskininkai Seven-Year Music School, Vilnius State Univ., Univ. of Manchester, UK; engineer, Computing Centre, Lithuanian Research Inst. of Agricultural Econs 1980–82, Researcher, Sr Researcher 1982–88; British Council Post-Doctoral Fellow, Univ. of Manchester 1988–89; Asst to Deputy Chair. Council of Ministers, Lithuanian SSR 1989–90; Deputy, Supreme Soviet 1990; signatory to Act on Re-establishment of Ind. State of Lithuania 1990; mem. Independence Party 1990–92; mem. Seimas (Parl.) (mem. Foreign Affairs Cttee, Vice-Chair. June–Oct. 2000, European Affairs Cttee 1998–2000) 1992–2000; Co-founder Homeland Union Party (Lithuanian Conservatives) 1993, mem. Bd 1993–98; Minister of Trade and Industry 1996, of European Affairs 1996–98; Head, Lithuanian Parl. Del. to Baltic Ass. 1998–2000 (Chair. Presidium 1998–99, 2000); Founder and Chair. Homeland People's Party 1999–2001; mem. Union of the Right 2001–03, Homeland Union 2003–; Chair. Bd Laitenis UAB, Vilnius 2001–03; consultant, Asscn of Lithuanian Chambers of Commerce, Industry and Crafts 2002–; Assoc. Prof., Dept of Political Science, Law Univ. of Lithuania 2002–04, Dir Inst. of EU Policy and Man. 2002–03, Dean Faculty of Public Man. 2003–04; mem. European Parl. (Group of the European People's Party (Christian Democrats) and European Democrats) 2004–, mem. Cttee on Budgets, Sub-cttee on Human Rights, Del. to EU-Moldova Parl. Co-operation Cttee; Pew Fellowship Scholar, School of Foreign Service, Georgetown Univ., Washington, DC 1996; Dr hc (Kingston Univ.) 2007; Grand Officier, l'Ordre nat. du Mérite 1997, Cross of Commdr of the Order of the Lithuanian Grand Duke Gediminas 2004; Independence Medal of Repub. of Lithuania 2000, Medal of the Baltic Ass. 2003. *Publications include:* more than 60 articles and academic monographs on foreign policy, EU policies and man., interest groups and lobbying, econ. reform, agricultural econs and human rights. *Address:* European Parliament, Bâtiment Altiero Spinelli, ASP 11E153, 60 rue Wiertz, 1047 Brussels, Belgium (office); 8/26 Liejyklos Street, 01120 Vilnius, Lithuania. *Telephone:* (5) 212-2360; 699-05062 (Mobile). *Fax:* (2) 284-9858 (office). *E-mail:* llandrikiene@europarl.eu.int (office); info@laimaandrikiene.lt. *Website:* www.europarl.eu.int (office); www.laimaandrikiene.lt; www.culture.lt/LLA.

ANDRIYAN, (Alexander Gennadyevich) Chetvergov; Russian ecclesiastic; *Metropolitan of Moscow and All-Russia;* Bishop of Kazan and Vyatsk 2001–04; Metropolitan of Moscow and All-Rus 2004–; mem. Belokrinitskii Concord of Old Believers (Old Ritualists—Staroobryatsy). *Address:* 109052 Moscow, ul. Rogozhskii pos. 29, Russian Federation (office). *Telephone:* (495) 361-51-92 (office).

ANDRIYASHEV, Anatoliy Petrovich; Russian zoologist and academic; *Professor, Zoological Institute, Russian Academy of Sciences;* b. 19 Aug. 1910, Montpellier, France; s. of P. E. Waitashevsky and N. Y. Andriasheva; m. Nina N. Savelyeva 1934; two d.; ed Leningrad Univ.; postgraduate, Research Assoc., Asst Prof., Leningrad Univ. 1933–39; Sevastopol Biological Scientific Station 1939–44; Chief, Antarctic Research Div., Zoological Inst., USSR (now Russian) Acad. of Sciences 1944–, Prof. 1970–; Vice-Pres. European Ichthyological Union 1979–82, Hon. mem. 1982–; Arctic and Bering Sea expeditions 1932, 1936, 1937, 1946, 1951; Antarctic expeditions 1955–58, 1971–72, 1975–76; Mediterranean and N Atlantic expedition 1979; Corresp. mem. USSR (now Russian) Acad. of Sciences 1966, Chief Scientist Zoological Inst. 1986–; Fellow, Russian Acad. of Natural Sciences 1994; Ed.-in-Chief Journal of Ichthyology 1977–88; Hon. Arctic explorer of the USSR (now Russia) 1947–; Hon. Foreign mem. American Soc. of Ichthyologists and Herpetologists; Soros Hon. Prof. 1996; State prizewinner 1971, Leo S. Berg Academic Prize 1992. *Publications:* works on ichthyology, marine zoogeography and Antarctic biology, feeding habits of fishes, Liparidae taxonomy; Liparid Fishes of the Southern Ocean (monograph) 2003. *Leisure interest:* skiing. *Address:* Zoological Institute, Universitetskaya Nab. 1, Russian Academy of Sciences, 199034 St Petersburg (office); Savushkina str. 15, Apt 120, 197193 St Petersburg, Russia (home). *Telephone:* (812) 328-06-12 (office); (812) 430-59-69 (home). *Fax:* (812) 328-29-41 (office). *E-mail:* antarct@zin.ru (office). *Website:* www.zin.ru (office).

ANDROSCH, Hannes, PhD; Austrian business executive and fmr politician; b. 18 April 1938, Vienna; m. Brigitte Schärf; two d.; ed Hochschule für Welthandel, Vienna; Asst Auditor Fed. Ministry of Finance 1956–66; Sec. Econ. Affairs Section, Socialist Parl. Party 1963–66, Vice-Chair. 1974–85; mem. Nationalrat (Nat. Council) 1967–85; Minister of Finance 1970–81; Vice-Chancellor 1976–81; Chair. and Gen. Man. Creditanstalt-Bankverein 1981–87; Chair. Österreichische Kontrolbank AG 1985–86; Pres. Supervisory Bd Austria Technologie & Systemtechnik AG (A.T. & S.); f. AIC Androsch International Management Consulting GmbH 1989; Chief Shareholder Salinen and Lenzing cos; Grand Gold Medal of Honour. *Address:* AIC Androsch International Management Consulting GmbH, Opernring 1/R/3, 1010 Vienna, Austria (office). *Telephone:* (1) 586-10-54 (office). *Fax:* (1) 586-10-54-30 (office). *E-mail:* office@aic.co.at (office). *Website:* www.androsch.com (office).

ANDRUS, Cecil D.; American business executive, consultant and politician; *Chairman, Andrus Center for Public Policy, Boise State University;* b. 25 Aug. 1931, Hood River, Ore.; s. of Hal S. Andrus and Dorothy (Johnson) Andrus; m. Carol M. May 1949; three d.; ed Oregon State Univ.; served USN 1951–55; mem. Idaho Senate 1961–66; State Gen. Man. Paul Revere Life Insurance Co. 1967–70; Gov. of Idaho 1971–77, 1987–95; Chair. Nat. Govs Conf. 1976; Sec. of Interior 1977–81; Dir Albertson's Inc. 1985–87, 1995–, Coeur d'Alene Mines 1995–, Key Corp. 1996–, Rentrak Corpn; Chair. Andrus Center for Public Policy 1995–; of Counsel to Gallatin Group 1995–; Democrat; Hon. LLD (Gonzaga Univ., Spokane, Wash. 1975, Whitman Coll., Albertson Coll. of Idaho, Oregon State Univ., Univ. of Idaho, Idaho State Univ., Univ. of New Mexico); Conservationist of the Year, Nat. Wildlife Fed. 1980, Ansel Adams Award, Wilderness Soc. 1985, Audubon Medal 1985, Torch of Liberty Award, B'nai B'rith 1991, William Penn Mott Jr Park Leadership Award, Nat. Parks Conservation Asscn 2000. *Publication:* Cecil Andrus: Politics Western Style 1998. *Leisure interests:* hunting, fishing, golf. *Address:* The Gallatin Group, 350 North Ninth Street, Suite 202, Boise, ID 83702-5468 (office); Andrus Center for Public Policy, Boise State University, POB 852, Boise, ID 83701, USA. *Telephone:* (208) 336-1986 (Gallatin) (office); (208) 426-4218 (Andrus Center). *Fax:* (208) 426-4208 (Andrus Center). *Website:* www.gallatingroup.com (office); www.andruscenter.org.

ANDSNES, Leif Ove; Norwegian pianist; b. 7 April 1970, Stavanger; ed Bergen Music Conservatory; debut, Oslo 1987; British debut with Oslo Philharmonic, Edinburgh Festival 1989; US debut with Cleveland Orchestra under Neeme Järvi 1990; recitals in London, Berlin, Vienna, Amsterdam, New York (Carnegie Hall); performed with Orchestre Nat. de France, Berlin Philharmonic, Chicago Symphony, BBC Symphony, London Symphony, LA Philharmonic, Japan Philharmonic, New York Philharmonic; soloist, Last Night of the Proms 2002; Co-Artistic Dir Risør Music Festival; Commdr Royal Norwegian Order of St Olav 2002; first prize Hindemith Competition, Frankfurt am Main, prizewinner at other int. competitions, Levin Prize (Bergen) 1988, Norwegian Music Critics' Prize 1988, Grieg Prize (Bergen) 1990, Dorothy B. Chandler Performing Arts Award, Los Angeles 1992, Gilmore Prize 1997, Royal Philharmonic Soc. Instrumentalist Award 2000, Gramophone Award for Best Concerto Recording 2000, for Best Instrumental Recording 2002. *Recordings include:* Rachmaninov Piano Concerto 1 and 2 (Classical BRIT Award for Instrumentalist of the Year 2006, Gramophone Award for Best Concerto Recording 2006) 2005, Horizons (Classical BRIT Award for Instrumentalist of the Year 2007) 2006, also works of Brahms, Chopin, Grieg, Janacek, Liszt, Schumann. *Address:* c/o Kathryn Enticott, IMG Artists, The Light Box, 111 Power Road, London, W4 5PY, England (office). *Telephone:* (20) 7957-5800 (office). *Fax:* (20) 7957-5801 (office). *E-mail:* cclarkson@imgartists.com (office). *Website:* www.imgartists.com (office); www.andsnes.com.

ANEFAL, Sebastian L., BS; Micronesian politician; *Governor of Yap;* b. 21 Jan. 1952, Guror, Gilman, State of Yap; m. Marita Phillip; two s. three d.; ed Yap High School, Sherwood High School, Ore., USA, Univ. of Guam, Agana, Guam, Eastern Ore. State Univ., La Grande, Ore., Micronesian Occupational Coll., Repub. of Palau, Ore. Coll. of Education, Univ. of Hawaii, Ore. State Univ., USA; radio announcer/reporter, WSZA Radio Station, Yap 1970; Asst Dorm Man. Eastern Ore. State Univ. 1972–74; Sec. Educ. for Self-Governmental Task Force 1974; Classroom Instructor in Social Studies, Dept of Educ. 1975–80, Chief of Fed. Programs 1980–82, Chief of Community Outreach Aug.–Dec. 1982, ECIA (US Govt's Educ. Consolidation and Improvement Act of 1981) Chapter I Coordinator July–Sept. 1982, Man. and Support Admin. 1982–87; Public Information Program Coordinator, Office of the Plebiscite Commr, Yap Jan.–June 1982; Convention Sec., Yap Constitutional Convention March–Aug. 1982; Dir Dept of Public Affairs, Yap 1987–88, Dept of Resources and Devt 1988–91, Office of Planning and Budget 1991–95;

Special Consultant to Gov. of State of Yap 1991–95, 2007–; Chief of Gilman (Municipality), Yap 1992–2007; Sec. of Dept of Resources and Devt, FSM Nat. Govt 1995–98, Dept of Econ. Affairs 1998–2003, Dept of Foreign Affairs 2003–07; Vice-Chair. Tourist Comm. 1975; mem. Nat. Disaster Control Bd 1976; Yap SPEA Coordinator, Festival of Arts, Papua New Guinea 1980; Chair. Elementary and Secondary Educ. Act (ESEA) Title IV State Advisory Council, Trust Territory of the Pacific Islands (TTPI) 1980; Chair. UN Day Cttee; Ed. 1981; mem. Old Age Program Advisory Bd 1983, COM Bd of Regents 1984–93, EPA Bd (TTPI/FSM) 1985–87; mem. Bd of Dirs Micronesia Maritime Authority 1989–95; Chair. Bd of Govs Pacific Island Devt Bank 1989–95; Chair. Bd of Nat. Fisheries Corpn 1990–; Vice-Chair. Bd of Dirs Yap Econ. Devt Authority 1990–95; Pres. Yap Fishing Corpn 1990–95; Vice-Pres. Yap Purse Seiners Corpn 1990–95; mem. Bd of Dirs Yap Cooperative Asscn 1990–95, Micronesia Longline Fishing Co. 1990–, FSM Devt Bank 1990–2004; Gov. of Yap 2007–; American Field Service Scholarship 1969–72, Trust Territory Social Sciences Scholarship 1972, UNESCO Fellowship in Ethnic Heritage to the Gilbert Islands 1978. *Publications include:* Social Studies Curriculum Guide (ed.) 1980, Tabinaw Rodad (social studies text book) (co-ed.) 1980. *Leisure interests:* spear fishing, hunting, sailing, guitar playing, photography. *Address:* Office of the Governor, POB 39, Colonia, Yap, FM 96943, The Federated States of Micronesia (office).

ANELL, Lars Evert Roland, MA, MBA; Swedish consultant; *Chairman, Stockholm Environment Institute;* b. 23 Oct. 1941, Katrineholm, Sweden; s. of Evert Andersson and Margit Andersson; m. Kerstin Friis 1966; one s. three d.; ed Stockholm School of Econs, Univ. of Stockholm; served in Ministry of Finance 1966–70, Dir for Planning and Research, Ministry for Foreign Affairs 1970–80, Dir Gen. Swedish Agency for Research Co-operation with Developing Countries 1980–83, Sr Advisor Prime Minister's Office 1983–86; Perm. Rep. of Sweden to UN orgs in Geneva 1986 and EU; Chair. GATT Council 1990–91; Sr Vice-Pres. AB Volvo 1992–2001, currently Sr Adviser to CEO; currently Chair. of Bd Stockholm Environment Inst. *Publications:* The Other Society 1969, Should Sweden be Asphalted? 1971, Recession, The Western Economies and the Changing World Order 1981, Economic Crises in Theory and Practice 1986. *Address:* Hantverkargalan 34, 112 21 Stockholm, Sweden (home). *Telephone:* (8) 650-64-43 (home). *E-mail:* lars.anell@chello.se (home).

ANFIMOV, Nikolai Appolonovich; Russian scientist; *General Director, Central Institute of Machine Construction;* b. 29 March 1935, Russia; m.; one s.; ed Moscow Inst. of Physics and Tech.; Head of Group, Head of Sector, Research Inst. of Heat Processes 1958–73, Head of Div., Deputy Dir Central Research Inst. of Machine Construction 1973–2000, Dir 2000–02, Gen. Dir 2002–; Corresp. mem. Russian Acad. of Sciences 1984, mem. 1997; State Prize of Russia. *Publications include:* Problems of Mechanics and Heat Exchange in Space Tech. 1982, Numerical Modelling in Aerohydrodynamics 1986 and numerous scientific works on heat exchange and heat protection in high-speed, high-temperature regimes, heat regimes of spaceships, radiation gas dynamics. *Leisure interest:* tennis. *Address:* Central Institute of Machine Construction, Pionerskya str. 4, 141070 Korolyev, Moscow Region, Russia (office). *Telephone:* (495) 513-50-01 (office); (495) 238-40-67 (home). *Fax:* (495) 274-00-25 (office). *Website:* www.tsniimash.ru (office).

ANGELINI, HE Cardinal Fiorenzo; Italian ecclesiastic; *President Emeritus, Pontifical Council for Pastoral Assistance to Health Care Workers;* b. 1 Aug. 1916, Rome; ordained priest 1940; elected Titular Bishop of Messene 1956, consecrated 1956; Archbishop 1985; Cardinal Deacon of Santo Spirito in Sassia 1991, Cardinal Priest 2002–; Pres. Pastoral Assistance to Health Care Workers, Roman Curia, 1989–96, Pres. Emer. 1996–; mem. Congregation for Evangelization of the Peoples, Papal Council on the Family, Papal Comm. on Latin America. *Address:* c/o Pontifical Council for Pastoral Assistance to Health Care Workers, Via della Conciliazione, 3, 00193 Rome; Via Anneo Lucano 47, 00136 Rome, Italy.

ANGELL, Wayne D., PhD; American economist; b. 28 June 1930, Liberal, Kansas; s. of Charlie Francis Angell and Adele Thelma Angell (née Edwards); m.; four c.; ed Univ. of Kansas; Prof., Univ. of Ottawa 1956, Dean 1969–72; mem. Kansas House of Reps 1961–67; Dir Fed. Reserve Bank, Kansas City 1979–86; mem. of Fed. Reserve Bd 1986–94; Chief Economist, Sr Man. Dir Bear Sterns & Co. Inc. 1994–2001; with Angell Econs, Arlington Va, 2001–. *Leisure interest:* tennis. *Address:* Angell Economics, 1600 North Oak Street, Suite 1915, Arlington, VA 22209, USA (office). *E-mail:* wangell@comcast.net (office).

ANGELOPOULOS, Theo; Greek film director; b. 27 April 1935, Athens; s. of Spyridon Angelopoulos and Katerina Krassaki; m. Phoebe Economopoulou 1979; three d.; ed Univ. of Athens, Univ. Paris-Sorbonne, Inst. des Hautes Etudes Cinématographiques, Paris; film critic for Athens daily Dimokratiki Allaghi 1964–67; co-founder Contemporary Cinema (film journal) 1969; Chair. jury Eurasia Int. Film Festival 2005; Lecturer, Univ. of Brussels; Dr hc (Univ. Libre de Bruxelles) 1995, (Paris X Nanterre) 1999, (Univ. of Essex) 2001, (Univ. Stendhal Grenoble 3) 2004, (Univ. of Sheffield) 2007, (Univ. of Rome) 2008, (Univ. of West Macedonia) 2008; Chevalier des Arts et Lettres 1985, Officier des Arts et Lettres 1997, Officier, Légion d'honneur 1992, Grand Officer, Order of Merit (Italy) 2005. *Films include:* Formix Story 1965, Broadcast 1968 (Critics' Prize, Thessaloniki Film Festival), Reconstruction (George Sadoul Award, Thessaloniki Film Festival Awards for Best Director, Best Cinematography, Best Film, Critics' Prize, Best Foreign Film, special mention at Berlin Forum) 1970, Days of '36 (FIPRESCI Award, Berlin, Thessaloniki Film Festival Awards for Best Director and Best Cinematography 1973, Dir's Fortnight, Cannes Film Festival 1973) 1972, The Travelling Players (FIPRESCI Grand Prix, Cannes Film Festival 1975, Interfilm Award, Berlin 1975, Best Film of the year, Golden Age Award, Brussels 1976, Best Film of the Year, British Film Inst. 1976, Best Film, Thessaloniki Film Festival, Grand Prix of the Arts, Japan, Best Film of the Year, Japan, Best Film in the World 1970–1980, Italian Critics' Asscn, FIPRESCI 40th Best Film in the History of Cinema) 1974–75, The Hunters (Official Selection, Cannes Film Festival 1977, Golden Hugo Award, Chicago Film Festival 1978) 1976–77, Megalexandros (Venice Film Festival Awards: Gold Lion, FIPRESCI Award, New Cinema Award) 1980, One Village One Inhabitant (documentary) 1981, Athens: Return to Acropolis (documentary) 1983, Voyage to Cythera (Best Screenplay and FIPRESCI Awards, Cannes Film Festival, Critics Award, Rio Film Festival) 1984, The Bee Keeper (Official Selection, Venice Film Festival) 1986, Landscape in the Mist (FIPRESCI Award and Silver Lion for Best Dir, Venice Film Festival, CICAE Art House Prize 1988, Pasinetti Award 1988, Golden Hugo Award and Silver Plaque for Best Cinematography, Chicago Film Festival 1988, Félix Award for Best European Film of the Year 1989) 1988, The Suspended Step of the Stork (Official Selection, Cannes Film Festival 1991) 1991, Ulysses Gaze (Grand Prix du Jury and FIPRESCI Award, Cannes Film Festival, Félix Prize for Best European Film of the Year) 1995, Eternity and a Day (Palme d'Or, Cannes Film Festival, Catholic Church Ecumenical Prize) 1998, The Weeping Meadow (Official Selection, Berlinale 2004) 2004, The Dust of Time 2008. *Publications:* numerous screenplays. *Leisure interest:* cultivating tomatoes. *Address:* Solomou 18, 106 82 Athens, Greece (office). *Telephone:* 383-9120 (office). *Fax:* 382-0582 (office). *E-mail:* info@theoangelopoulos.com (office). *Website:* www.theoangelopoulos.gr (office).

ANGELOPOULOS-DASKALAKI, Gianna, LLB; Greek business executive, politician and sports administrator; b. 1955, Heraklion, Crete; m. Theodore Angelopoulos; two s. one d.; ed Aristotelian Univ., Thessaloniki; mem. Athens municipal council; mem. Parl. (New Democracy Party) 1989–90; Vice-Chair. John F. Kennedy School of Govt, Harvard Univ. 1994–; Pres. Athens 2004 Olympic Games Bid Cttee 1998–2000, Athens 2004 Olympic Cttee 2000–04; apptd Ambassador at Large by Greek Govt 1998; mem. Athens Bar Asscn; man. family-owned shipping business; Hellenic Public Radio Phidippides Award 1997, ranked 49th by Fortune magazine amongst 50 Most Powerful Women in Business outside the US 2002, Archbishop Iakovos Leadership 100 Award for Excellence 2008. *Address:* c/o Ministry of Foreign Affairs, 1st Vas. Sofias Avenue, 106 71 Athens, Greece (office).

ANGELOU, Maya; American writer, poet and academic; b. (Marguerite Johnson), 4 April 1928, St Louis; d. of Bailey Johnson and Vivian Baxter; one s.; Assoc. Ed. Arab Observer 1961–62; Asst Admin., teacher, School of Music and Drama, Univ. of Ghana 1963–66; Feature Ed. African Review, Accra 1964–66; Reynold's Prof. of American Studies, Wake Forest Univ. 1981–; teacher of modern dance, Rome Opera House, Hambina Theatre, Tel-Aviv; has written several film scores; contrib. to numerous periodicals; Woman of Year in Communication 1976; numerous TV acting appearances; mem. Bd of Govs Maya Angelou Inst. for the Improvement of Child and Family Educ., Winston-Salem State Univ., NC 1998–; distinguished visiting prof. at several univs; mem. various arts orgs; Hon. Amb. to UNICEF 1996–; more than 50 hon. degrees; Horatio Alger Award 1992, Grammy Award Best Spoken Word or Non-Traditional Album 1994, Lifetime Achievement Award for Literature 1999, Nat. Medal of Arts, numerous other awards. *Plays:* Cabaret for Freedom 1960, The Least of These 1966, Gettin' Up Stayed On My Mind 1967, Ajax 1974, And Still I Rise 1976, Moon On a Rainbow Shawl (producer) 1988. *Theatre appearances include:* Porgy and Bess 1954–55, Calypso 19576, The Blacks 1960, Mother Courage 1964, Look Away 1973, Roots 1977, How To Make an American Quilt 1995 (feature film 1996). *Films directed include:* Down in the Delta 1998. *Publications include:* I Know Why the Caged Bird Sings 1970, Just Give Me A Cool Drink of Water 'Fore I Die 1971, Georgia, Georgia (screenplay) 1972, Gather Together In My Name 1974, All Day Long (screenplay) 1974, Oh Pray My Wings Are Gonna Fit Me Well 1975, Singin' and Swingin' and Gettin' Merry Like Christmas 1976, And Still I Rise 1976, The Heart of a Woman 1981, Shaker, Why Don't You Sing 1983, All God's Children Need Travelling Shoes 1986, Now Sheba Sings the Song 1987, I Shall Not Be Moved 1990, Gathered Together in My Name 1991, Wouldn't Take Nothing for my Journey Now 1993, Life Doesn't Frighten Me 1993, Collected Poems 1994, My Painted House, My Friendly Chicken and Me 1994, Phenomenal Woman 1995, Kofi and His Magic 1996, Even the Stars Look Lonesome 1997, Making Magic in the World 1998, A Song Flung up to Heaven 2002, Hallelujah! The Welcome Table 2005, Amazing Peace (long poem) (Quill Award for Poetry 2006) 2005. *Address:* Lordly and Dame Inc., 51 Church Street, Boston, MA 02116, USA. *Telephone:* (617) 482-3593. *Fax:* (617) 426-8019. *E-mail:* mayaangelou@lordly.com. *Website:* www.mayaangelou.com.

ANGENOT, Marc, DPhil, FRSC; Canadian academic; *James McGill Professor of Social Discourse Theory, McGill University;* b. 21 Dec. 1941, Brussels; s. of Marcel Angenot and Zoé-Martha DeClercq; m. 1st Joséphine Brock 1966 (divorced 1976); one s. one d.; m. 2nd Nadia Khouri 1981; one d.; ed Univ. Libre de Bruxelles; James McGill Prof. of Social Discourse Theory, McGill Univ. 1967–; Assoc. Dir Ecole des Hautes Etudes en Sciences Sociales, France 1985; Northrop Frye Prof. of Literary Theory, Univ. of Toronto 1994; Vice-Pres. Acad. des Lettres et Sciences Humaines, Royal Soc. of Canada 2001; Killam Fellowship 1987; Chevalier des Palmes académiques (France); Prix Biguet, Acad. Française 1983, Prix des Sciences Humaines ACFAS (Canada) 1996, Award for High Distinction in Research, McGill Univ. 2001, Prix du Québec 'Léon Gérin' 2005. *Publications:* Le Roman populaire 1975, Les Champions des femmes 1977, Glossaire pratique de la critique contemporaine 1979, La Parole pamphlétaire 1982, Critique de la raison sémiotique 1985, Le Cru et le faisandé 1986, Le Centenaire de la Révolution 1989, Ce que l'on dit des Juifs en 1889 1989, Mille huit cent quatre-vingt neuf 1989, L'Utopie collectiviste 1993, La Propagande socialiste 1996, Idéologies du ressentiment 1996, Colins et le socialisme rationnel 1999, La critique au service de la Révolution 2000, Religions de l'humanité et sciences de l'histoire 2000, D'où venons-nous, où allons-nous? 2001, L'Antimilitarisme 2003, La démocratie, c'est le mal 2004, Rhétorique de l'anti-socialisme 2004, Le marxisme dans les Grands récits 2005, Dialogues de sourds 2008, En quoi sommes-nous encore pieux? 2008. *Address:* Arts Building, 853 Sherbrooke St. West, Montreal, PQ H3A 2T6 (office); 4572 Harvard Avenue, Montreal, PQ H4A 2X2, Canada (home). *Fax:* (514) 398-8557 (office).

ANGERER, Paul; Austrian conductor, composer and instrumentalist; b. 16 May 1927, Vienna; s. of Otto Angerer and Elisabeth Angerer; m. Anita Rosser 1952; two s. two d.; ed Hochschule für Musik und darstellende Kunst, Vienna; viola player, Vienna Symphony 1947, leading solo viola player 1953–57; viola player, Tonhalle Zürich 1948, Suisse Romande Orchestra, Geneva 1949; Dir and Chief Conductor, Chamber Orch. of Wiener Konzerthausgesellschaft 1956–63; composer and conductor, Burgtheater, Vienna and Salzburg and Bregenz festivals 1960–; Perm. Guest Conductor, Orchestra Sinfonica di Bolzano e Trento "Haydn" 1964–90; First Conductor, Bonn City Theatre 1964–66; Music Dir Ulm Theatre 1966–68; Chief of Opera, Salzburger Landestheater 1967–72; Dir SW German Chamber Orch., Pforzheim 1971–82; Prof. Hochschule, Vienna 1983–92; Moderator ORF 1984–2001, Radio Stephansdorn 2001; Leader of Concilium Musicum; several prizes including Austrian State Prize 1956, Theodor Körner Prize 1958, Vienna Cultural Prize 1983, Cultural Prize of Lower Austria 1987; Nestroy-Ring, City of Vienna 1998; Austrian Order of Honour for Sciences and Arts Class 2001. *Works include:* orchestral pieces, chamber works, viola and piano concertos, a dramatic cantata, television opera, works for organ, harp, viola, harpsichord, etc.; numerous recordings both as soloist and conductor. *Publications:* Und s'ist elles noch wehr! Briefe eines Eipeldaners, Mozart auf Reisen: Reisebriefe Leopold Mozarts aus Wren 1762–63, 1767–69, 1773, aus Paris und London 1763, aus Italien 1771–73. *Address:* Esteplatz 3/26, 1030 Vienna, Austria. *Telephone:* (1) 7141271. *Fax:* (1) 7141271. *E-mail:* PaulAngerer@concilium.at (home).

ANGREMY, Jean-Pierre, (Pierre-Jean Rémy); French diplomatist and writer; b. 21 March 1937, Angoulême; s. of Pierre Angremy and Alice Collebrans; m. 1st Odile Cail (divorced); one s. one d.; m. 2nd Sophie Schmit 1986 (divorced); one s.; ed Institut d'études politiques, Paris, Brandeis Univ., USA, Ecole nationale d'admin; served in Hong Kong 1963–64, Beijing 1964–66, London 1966–71, 1975–79; Cultural, Scientific and Tech. Relations, Paris 1971–72; seconded to ORTF 1972–75; seconded to Ministry of Culture and Communication (Dir Theatre Dept) 1979–84; Consul, Florence 1984–87; Dir-Gen. Cultural, Scientific and Tech. Relations 1987–90; Amb. to UNESCO 1990–94; Dir Acad. de France, Rome 1994–97; Pres. Bibliothèque Nationale de France 1997–2002, Années France–Chine 2003–05, mem. Acad. française 1988; Commdr, Légion d'honneur, des Arts et Lettres; Officier, Ordre nat. du. Mérite. *Publications include:* Désir d'Europe 1995, Le Rose et la Blanc 1997, Callas, une Vie 1997, Retour d'Hélène 1997, Aria Di Roma 1998, La Nuit de Ferrare 1999, Demi-Siècle 2000, Etat de Grâce et Dire Perdu 2001, Berlioz 2002, Chambre noire de Pekin 2004, Dictionnaire amoureux de l'Opéra 2004, and numerous other publs. *Leisure interests:* collecting books and photographs. *Address:* 63 Boulevard Saint-Michel, 75005 Paris, France (home). *Telephone:* 1-47-05-29-10 (home). *Fax:* 1-47-05-29-10 (home). *E-mail:* angremy@wanadoo.fr (home).

ANGULA, Nahas Gideon, BEd, MA, MEd; Namibian politician; *Prime Minister;* b. 22 Aug. 1943, Onyaanya; m. Katrina Tangeni Namalenga; four c.; ed Oniipa Boy's School, Engela Boy's School, Ongwediva Training Coll., Oshigambo Jr Secondary School, Nkumbi Int. Coll., Univ. of Zambia, Columbia Univ., New York, Univ. of Manchester, UK; became active in SWAPO 1967, went into exile to Zambia 1967; Sec. for Educ., SWAPO Politburo; returned from exile 1989; Head of Dept, Voter Registration, SWAPO Election Directorate, Windhoek 1989; mem. Constituent Ass. 1989, Nat. Ass. 1990–; Minister of Educ., Sport and Culture 1990–95, of Higher Educ., Training and Employment Creation 1995–2005; nominated as one of three SWAPO presidential cands 2004; Prime Minister of Namibia 2005–. *Publication:* The African Origin of Civilisation and the Destiny of Africa (co-ed.) 2000. *Address:* Office of the Prime Minister, Robert Mugabe Avenue, PMB 13338, Windhoek, Namibia (office). *Telephone:* (61) 2879111 (office). *Fax:* (61) 230648 (office). *Website:* www.opm.gov.na (office).

ANGUS, Sir Michael Richardson, Kt, BSc, DL, CIMgt; British company director; b. 5 May 1930, Ashford, Kent; s. of William Richardson Angus and Doris Margaret Breach; m. Eileen Isabel May Elliott 1952; two s. one d.; ed Marling School, Stroud, Univ. of Bristol; served in RAF 1951–54; joined Unilever PLC 1954, Marketing Dir Thibaud Gibbs, Paris 1962–65, Man. Dir Research Bureau 1965–67, Sales Dir Lever Brothers, UK 1967–70, Dir Unilever PLC and Unilever NV 1970–92, Toilet Preparations Co-ordinator 1970–76, Chemicals Co-ordinator 1976–80, Regional Dir N America 1979–84, Chair. and CEO Unilever United States Inc., New York 1980–84, Chair. and CEO Lever Brothers Co., New York 1980–84, Vice-Chair. Unilever PLC 1984–86, Chair. 1986–92, also Vice-Chair. Unilever NV; Vice-Pres. Netherlands-British Chamber of Commerce 1990–94; Deputy Pres. CBI 1991–92, 1994–95, Pres. 1992–94; Chair. RAC Holdings Ltd 1999; Gov. Ashridge Man. Coll. 1974–, Chair. of Govs 1991–2002; Jt Chair. Netherlands-British Chamber of Commerce 1984–89; Chair. of Govs Royal Agricultural Coll., Cirencester 1992–2005, Vice-Pres. 2005–; Dir (non-exec.) Whitbread PLC 1986–2000 (Deputy Chair. Jan.–Aug. 1992, Chair. 1992–99), Thorn EMI PLC 1988–93, British Airways PLC 1988–2000 (Deputy Chair. 1989–2000), Halcrow Group 1999–; Dir Nat. Westminster Bank PLC 1991–2000 (Deputy Chair. 1991–94), The Boots Co. PLC 1994–2000 (Chair. 1994–98, Deputy Chair. 1998–2000); Chair. Leverhulme Trust 1984–2008; mem. Council, British Exec. Service Overseas 1986–2000 (Pres. 1998); mem. Council of Man., Ditchley Foundation 1994–; Commdr of Order of Oranje Nassau 1992; Hon.

DSc (Bristol) 1990, (Buckingham) 1994; Hon. LLD (Nottingham) 1996; Holland Trade Award 1990. *Leisure interests:* countryside, wine and mathematical puzzles. *Address:* Cerney House, North Cerney, Cirencester, Glos., GL7 7BX, England (home). *Telephone:* (1285) 831300 (home). *Fax:* (1285) 831676 (home).

ANGYAL, Stephen John, OBE, PhD, DSc, FAA; Australian (b. Hungarian) chemist and academic; *Professor Emeritus of Organic Chemistry, University of New South Wales;* b. 21 Nov. 1914, Budapest; s. of Charles Engel and Maria Szanto; m. Helga Ellen Steininger 1941; one s. one d.; ed Pazmany Peter Univ., Budapest; Research Chemist, Chinoin Pharmaceutical Works, Budapest 1937–40; Research Chemist, Nicholas Pty Ltd, Melbourne, Australia 1941–46; Lecturer, Univ. of Sydney 1946–52; Nuffield Dominion Travelling Fellow 1952; Assoc. Prof. of Organic Chem., Univ. of NSW 1953–60, Prof. 1960–80, Prof. Emer. 1980–, Dean of Science 1970–79; Foreign mem. Hungarian Acad. of Science 1990; H.G. Smith Memorial Medal, Royal Australian Chem. Inst. 1958, Haworth Medal and Lectureship, Royal Soc. of Chem. 1980, ACS Hudson Award 1987. *Publications:* Conformational Analysis (with others) 1965; about 200 research publs in chemical journals. *Leisure interests:* swimming, skiing, bushwalking, music. *Address:* 304 Sailors Bay Road, Northbridge, NSW 2063, Australia (home). *Telephone:* (2) 9958-7209 (home). *Fax:* (2) 9385-6141 (office). *E-mail:* s.angyal@unsw.edu.au (home).

ANH, Gen. Le Duc; Vietnamese army officer and fmr head of state; b. 1 Dec. 1920, Thua Thien-Hue; mem. Dang Cong Sang Viet Nam (CP); led Viet Cong combat units during Viet Nam War; Deputy Minister of Defence 1980–87, Minister of Nat. Defence 1987–92; mem. CP Politburo 1981, Secr.; Pres. of Viet Nam 1992–97. *Address:* c/o Office of the President, Hanoi, Viet Nam.

ANISTON, Jennifer; American actress; b. 11 Feb. 1969, Sherman Oaks, Calif.; d. of John Aniston; m. Brad Pitt (q.v.) 2000 (divorced 2005); ed New York High School of the Performing Arts. *Theatre includes:* For Dear Life, Dancing on Checker's Grave. *Films include:* Leprechaun 1993, She's the One 1996, Dream for an Insomniac 1996, 'Til There Was You 1996, Picture Perfect 1997, The Object of My Affection 1998, Office Space 1999, The Iron Giant 1999, Rock Star 2001, The Good Girl 2002, Bruce Almighty 2003, Along Came Polly 2004, Derailed 2005, Rumor Has It... 2005, Friends with Money 2006, The Break-Up 2006, Management 2008, Marley & Me 2008, He's Just Not That Into You 2009. *TV includes:* Molloy (series) 1989, The Edge, Ferris Bueller, Herman's Head, Friends (Emmy Award for Best Actress 2002, Golden Globe for Best TV Actress in a Comedy 2003) 1994–2004. *Address:* 5750 Wilshire Blvd, Los Angeles, CA 90036; Creative Artists Agency, 9830 Wilshire Boulevard, Beverly Hills, CA 90212-1825, USA (office). *Telephone:* (310) 288-4545 (office). *Fax:* (310) 288-4800 (office). *Website:* www.caa.com (office); www.jenniferaniston.com.

ANJARIA, Shailendra J.; Indian international finance official; b. 17 July 1946, Bombay; s. of Jashwantrai J. Anjaria and Harvidya Anjaria; m. Nishigandha Pandit 1972; two d.; ed Univ. of Pennsylvania, Yale Univ. and London School of Econs; economist, Exchange and Trade Relations Dept, IMF 1968; IMF office, Geneva 1973; Div. Chief 1980; Asst Dir and Adviser, Exchange and Trade Relations Dept 1986; Asst Dir N African Div. of African Dept 1988; Dir External Relations Dept IMF 1991–99, Sec. IMF 1999–2008. *Address:* c/o International Monetary Fund, 700 19th Street, NW, Washington, DC 20431, USA (office).

ANKA, Paul, OC; Canadian/American singer, songwriter and actor; b. 30 July 1941, Ottawa, Ont.; m. Marie Ann Alison de Zogheb 1963 (divorced); five d.; numerous TV appearances worldwide, live performances; mem. BMI; Chevalier, Ordre des Arts et Lettres. *Films:* Girls Town 1959, The Private Lives of Adam and Eve 1960, Look in Any Window 1961, The Longest Day 1962, Captain Ron 1992, Ordinary Magic 1993, Mad Dog Time 1996, 3000 Miles to Graceland 2001. *Television:* The Paul Anka Show (series host) 1982, Perry Mason: The Case of the Maligned Mobster 1991. *Compositions:* theme for The Tonight Show 1962, theme music for films, The Longest Day, No Way Out, Atlantic City, and contrib. songs to numerous other films; some 900 songs, including It Doesn't Matter Any More (for Buddy Holly) 1959, My Way (for Frank Sinatra) 1969, She's A Lady (for Tom Jones) 1971, Puppy Love (for Donny Osmond); other songs performed by artists, including Elvis Presley, Barbra Streisand, Linda Ronstadt, The Sex Pistols, Nina Simone, Gipsy Kings and Robbie Williams. *Recordings include:* albums: The Fabulous Paul Anka And Others 1956, Paul Anka 1958, My Heart Sings 1959, Paul Anka Sings His Big 15 1959, Vol. II 1962, Vol. III 1962, Paul Anka Swings For Young Lovers 1959, Anka At The Copa 1960, It's Christmas Everywhere 1960, Diana 1962, Young Alive & In Love! 1962, Let's Sit This One Out 1962, Our Man Around the World 1963, Three Great Guys (with Sedaka and Cooke) 1963, Songs I Wish I'd Written 1963, Paul Anka 1964, Paul Anka Italiano 1964, A Casa Nostra 1964, Strictly Nashville 1966, Goodnight My Love 1969, Sincerely 1969, Life Goes On 1969, Paul Anka 70s 1970, Jubilation 1972, My Way 1974, Anka 1974, Feelings 1975, Remember Diana 1975, She's A Lady 1975, Times Of Your Life 1976, The Painter 1977, The Music Man 1977, Listen To Your Heart 1978, Headlines 1979, Both Sides Of Love 1981, Walk A Fine Line 1983, Freedom for the World 1987, Somebody Loves You 1989, Face in the Mirror 1993, After All 1995, Amigos (with others) 1996, A Body Of Work 1998, Rock Swings 2005. *Address:* Paul Anka Productions, 9200 West Sunset Blvd, PH 32, Los Angeles, CA 90069, USA. *E-mail:* paoffice@paulanka.com. *Website:* www.paulanka.com.

ANKUM, Hans (Johan Albert), DJur; Dutch professor of Roman law; *Professor emeritus of Roman law, University of Amsterdam;* b. 23 July 1930, Amsterdam; s. of Leendert Ankum and Johanna Ankum (née Van Kuykhof); m. 1st Joke Houwink 1957 (divorced 1970); m. 2nd Pelline van Es 1971; one s. three d.; ed Zaanlands Lyceum, Zaandam, Univ. of Amsterdam, Univ. of Paris;

Asst, Roman Law and Juridical Papyrology, Univ. of Amsterdam 1956–60; Lecturer in Roman Law and Legal History, Univ. of Leyden 1960–63, Prof. 1963–69; Prof. of Roman Law, Legal History and Juridical Papyrology, Univ. of Amsterdam 1965–95, Prof. Emer. 1995–; mem. Royal Netherlands Acad. of Arts and Sciences 1986–; Knight, Order of the Dutch Lion 1992; Dr hc (Aix-Marseille) 1985, (Vrije Univ., Brussels) 1986, (Ruhr Universität Bochum) 1995, (Univ. of Belgrade) 2005, (Charles Univ. Prague) 2008; Winkler Prins Award 1970. *Publications:* De geschiedenis der 'Actio Pauliana' 1962; about 300 books and articles on Roman law and legal history. *Leisure interests:* classical music, history of art, travel. *Address:* Faculty of Law, University of Amsterdam, PO Box 1030, 1000 BA, Amsterdam Oudermanhuispoort 4–6 (office); Zonnebloemlaan 8, 2111 ZG, Aerdenhout, Netherlands (home). *Telephone:* (20) 5253751 (office); (23) 5243036 (home). *Fax:* (20) 5253495 (office).

ANLYAN, William George, BS, MD; American professor of surgery, medical consultant and university administrator; *Chancellor Emeritus, Duke University;* b. 14 Oct. 1925, Alexandria, Egypt; s. of Armand Anlyan and Emmy Anlyan; two s. one d.; ed Yale Univ. and Duke Univ. Hosp.; Instructor in Surgery, Duke Univ. School of Medicine 1950–51, Assoc. 1951–53, Asst Prof. of Surgery 1953–58, Assoc. Prof. 1958–61, Prof. 1961–89, Assoc. Dean 1963–64, Dean 1964–69; Assoc. Provost Duke Univ. 1969, Vice-Pres. for Health Affairs 1969–83, Chancellor for Health Affairs 1983–88, Exec. Vice-Pres. 1987–88, Chancellor 1988–90, Chancellor Emer. 1990–; numerous exec. posts, Asscn of American Medical Colls 1965–, Distinguished Service Mem. 1974–, American Medical Asscn 1971–74, American Surgical Asscn 1964–; mem. Bd of Dirs Asscn for Acad. Health Centers 1971–, Pres. 1974–75; mem. Research Strengthening Group for Special Programme for Research and Training in Tropical Diseases, WHO 1981–85, Chair. Univ. Council's Cttee on Medical Affairs (WHO), Yale Univ. 1987–93; mem. Council Govt-Univ.-Industry Research Roundtable 1984–86; mem. several advisory and research cttees, NC 1965–; Consultant Gen. Surgery, Durham Veterans' Hosp. 1955–73; mem. US dels consulting on health and medical educ., China, Poland, Israel, Egypt, Saudi Arabia, Japan etc.; mem. Bd of Regents Nat. Library of Medicine 1968–71, Chair. 1971–72, Consultant 1972–; mem. Bd of Dirs Wachovia Bank 1970–90, G.D. Searle and Co. 1974–90, Pearle Health Services Inc. 1983–85, NC Inst. of Medicine 1983–, Durham Chamber of Commerce 1988–; mem. Bds of Visitors and Trustees numerous univs; mem. numerous professional socs; mem. Editorial Bd The Pharos 1968–93; Trustee The Duke Endowment 1990–; Hon. DS (Rush Medical Coll.) 1973; Modern Medicine Award for Distinguished Achievement 1974, Gov.'s Award for Distinguished Meritorious Service 1978, Distinguished Surgeon Alumnus, Yale Univ. School of Medicine 1979, The Abraham Flexner Award, Asscn of American Medical Colls 1980, Civic Honor Award, Durham Chamber of Commerce 1981, Award of Merit, Duke Univ. Hosp. and Health Admin Alumni Asscn 1987, Lifetime Achievement Award, Duke Univ. Medical Alumni 1995, Lifetime Achievement Award (for advocacy for medical research), Research America 1997, Distinguished Alumni Service Award, Yale Univ. School of Medicine 1999, Duke Univ. Medal for Distinguished Meritorious Service 2002, N Carolina Award for Science 2002. *Publications:* contrib. and several books; over 100 articles in professional journals on health and surgical topics. *Leisure interests:* piano, tennis. *Address:* Duke University Medical Center, PO Box 3626, 109 Seeley G. Mudd Building, Durham, NC 27710, USA (office). *Telephone:* (919) 684-3438 (office). *Fax:* (919) 684-3518 (office). *E-mail:* anlya001@mc.duke.edu (office). *Website:* www.mc.duke.edu (office).

ANN-MARGRET; American actress, singer and dancer; b. (Ann-Margret Olsson), 28 April 1941, Stockholm, Sweden; m. Roger Smith 1967; film debut in Pocketful of Miracles 1961; five Golden Globe Awards, three Female Star of the Year Awards. *Films include:* State Fair, Bye Bye Birdie, Once a Thief, The Cincinnati Kid, Stagecoach, Murderer's Row, CC & Co., Carnal Knowledge, RPM, The Train Robbers, Tommy, The Twist, Joseph Andrews, Last Remake of Beau Geste, Magic, Middle Age Crazy, Return of the Soldier, I Ought to Be in Pictures, Looking to Get Out, Twice in a Lifetime, 52 Pick-Up 1987, New Life 1988, Something More, Newsies 1992, Grumpy Old Men 1993, Grumpier Old Men 1995, Any Given Sunday 1999, The Last Producer 2000, A Woman's a Helluva Thing 2000, Interstate 60 2002, Taxi 2004, The Break-Up 2006, The Santa Clause 3: The Escape Clause 2006, The Loss of a Teardrop Diamond 2008. *Television includes:* Who Will Love My Children? 1983, A Streetcar Named Desire 1984, The Two Mrs Grenvilles 1987, Our Sons 1991, Nobody's Children, 1994, Following her Heart, Seduced by Madness: The Diane Borchardt Story 1996, Blue Rodeo 1996, Pamela Hanniman 1999, Happy Face Murders 1999, Perfect Murder, Perfect Town 2000, The Tenth Kingdom 2000, A Place Called Home 2004. *Publication:* (with Todd Gold) Ann-Margret: My Story 1994. *Address:* William Morris Agency, One William Morris Place, Beverly Hills, CA 90212, USA.

ANNADIF, Mahamet Saleh; Chadian politician; b. 25 Dec. 1956, Arada; m. twice; eight c.; with Telecommunications Dept, Office Nat. de Postes et Télécommunications (ONPT) 1981–82 (as Head of Research), 1988–89, Dir.-Gen. ONPT 1995–97; Man. Soc. des Télécommunications internationales du Tchad 1990–97; in charge of information and propaganda, Front de libération nationale du Tchad (FROLINAT)/Conseil démocratique révolutionnaire (CDR) 1982–85, Second Vice-Pres. FROLINAT/CDR 1985–88; Sec. of State for Agric. 1989–90; Minister of Foreign Affairs and Co-operation 1997–2003; Commdr Order nat. du Tchad. *Leisure interests:* nature, the countryside. *Address:* Quartier Goudji, Rue de 40m., N'Djamena, Chad (home). *Telephone:* 51-07-51 (home).

ANNAN, Kofi A., GCMG, BA (Econs), MSc; Ghanaian international diplomatist; *President, Kofi Annan Foundation;* b. 8 April 1938; m. Nane Lagergren; one s. two d.; ed Univ. of Science and Tech., Kumasi, Macalester Coll., St Paul, Minn., USA, Institut des Hautes Etudes Internationales, Geneva, Switzerland, Massachusetts Inst. of Tech., USA; held posts in UN ECA, Addis Ababa, UN, New York, WHO, Geneva 1962–71, Admin. Man. Officer, UN, Geneva 1972–74; Alfred P. Sloan Fellow, MIT 1971–72; Chief Civilian Personnel Officer, UNEF, Cairo 1974; Man. Dir Ghana Tourist Devt Co. 1974–76; Deputy Chief of Staff Services, Office of Personnel Services, Office of UNHCR, Geneva 1976–80, Deputy Dir Div. of Admin. and Head Personnel Service 1980–83; Dir of Admin. Man. Service, then Dir of Budget, Office of Financial Services, UN, New York 1984–87, Asst Sec.-Gen., Office of Human Resources Man. 1987–90; Controller Office of Programme Planning, Budget and Finance 1990–92; Asst Sec.-Gen. Dept of Peace-Keeping Operations 1992–93; Under-Sec.-Gen. 1993–96; UN Special Envoy (a.i.) to Fmr Yugoslavia 1995–96; Sec.-Gen. of UN 1997–2006; Pres. Kofi Annan Foundation 2007–; Pres. Global Humanitarian Forum 2007–; Chair. Alliance for a Green Revolution in Africa (AGRA) 2007–, Africa Progress Panel 2007–; Chair., Prize Cttee, Mo Ibrahim Award for Excellence in African Leadership; mem. The Elders; hon. degrees include Hon. DCL (Oxford) 2001; Philadelphia Liberty Medal 2001, Nobel Peace Prize (jtly with UN) 2001, Zayed Prize 2005. *Address:* Rue de Varembe 9-11, 1202 Geneva, Switzerland (office). *Telephone:* 229197520 (office). *Fax:* 229197529 (office). *E-mail:* info@kofiaannan.org (office). *Website:* www.ghf-geneva.org.

ANNAUD, Jean-Jacques, LèsL; French film director and screenwriter; b. 1 Oct. 1943, Juvisy/Orge; s. of Pierre Annaud and Madeleine Tripoz; m. 1st Monique Rossignol 1970 (divorced 1980); one d.; m. 2nd Laurence Duval 1982; one d.; ed Inst. des Hautes Etudes Cinématographiques, Paris and Univ. of Paris, Sorbonne; freelance commercial film dir (500 films) 1966–75; feature film dir 1975–; mem. Institut de France; Officier des Palmes académiques et du Mérite social, Commdr des Arts et Lettres; Grand Prix Nat. du Cinéma, Grand Prix de l'Acad. Française. *Films include:* Black and White in Colour 1976 (Acad. Award for Best Foreign Film), Hot Head 1979, Quest for Fire (César Award) 1981, The Name of the Rose (César Award), The Bear 1988 (César Award), The Lover 1992, Wings of Courage 1994, Seven Years in Tibet 1997, Enemy at the Gates 2001, Two Brothers 2004, Sa majesté Minor 2007. *Leisure interests:* books, old cameras, world travel. *Address:* c/o ICM, 1025 Constellation Boulevard, Los Angeles, CA 90067, USA (office); c/o Repérage, 10 rue Lincoln, 75008 Paris; 9 rue Guénégaud, 75006 Paris, France (home).

ANNE, HRH The Princess (see Royal, HRH The Princess).

ANNESLEY, Sir Hugh (Norman), Kt, QPM; British police officer; b. 22 June 1939, Dublin; m. Elizabeth Ann MacPherson 1970; one s. one d.; ed St Andrew's Prep. School, Dublin and Avoca School for Boys, Blackrock; joined Metropolitan Police 1958; Asst Chief Constable of Sussex with special responsibility for personnel and training 1976; Deputy Asst Commr, Metropolitan Police 1981, Asst Commr 1985; Head Operations Dept, Scotland Yard 1987–89; Chief Constable of the Royal Ulster Constabulary 1989–96; mem. Nat. Exec. Inst., FBI 1986; Exec. Cttee Interpol (British Rep.) 1987–90, 1993–94; mem. Bd Govs Burgess Hill School for Girls 1997, Chair. 2000–. *Leisure interests:* sailing, hockey. *Address:* c/o Brooklyn, Knock Road, Belfast, BT5 6LE, Northern Ireland.

ANNINSKY, Lev Alexandrovich Ivanov, PhD; Russian writer; b. 7 April 1934, Rostov-on-Don; s. of Alexandre Ivanov Anninsky and Anna Alexandrova; m. Alexandra Nikolayevna Ivanova Anninskaya; three d.; ed Moscow State Univ.; freelance literary critic 1956–, cinema critic 1960–, theatre critic 1962–; TV and radio broadcaster 1992–96; fmr Ed. Druzhba Narodov (monthly), Rodina (monthly). *Publications include:* The Core of the Nut: Critical Reviews 1965, Married to the Idea 1971, Literary and Critical Reviews 1977; Hunting for Lev (Lev Tolstoy and Cinematography) 1980, Contacts 1982, Three Heretics: Pisemsky, Melnikov-Pechersky, Leskov 1988, Culture's Tapestry 1991, Elbows and Wings: Literature of the 1980s: Hopes, Reality, Paradoxes 1989, A Ticket to Elysium: Reflections on Theatre Porches 1989, The Sixties Generation 1991, Flying Curtain: Literary-Critical Articles on Georgia 1991, Silver and Black 1997, Bards 1999, Russians plus 2001, numerous titles in Russian, articles on literature, theatre and cinema. *Address:* Udaltsova str. 16, Apt 19, 119415 Moscow, Russia (home). *Telephone:* (495) 131-62-45 (home). *E-mail:* l_anninsky@mtu-net.ru.

ANOSOV, Dmitry Victorovich; Russian mathematician and academic; b. 30 Nov. 1936, Moscow; m.; one d.; ed Moscow State Univ.; mem. of staff Steklov Inst. of Math., Russian Acad. of Sciences (MIAN) 1961–, Head of Dept 1997–; main research in differential equations and affiliated problems of geometry and topology; Corresp. mem. Russian Acad. of Sciences 1990, mem. 1992–; Hon. Prof. Moscow State Univ. 1999; USSR State Prize 1976, Humboldt Prize 1999, Russian Acad. of Sciences Lyapunov Prize (jtly) 2001. *Address:* MIAN, Vavilova str. 42, 119991 Moscow, Russia (office). *Telephone:* (495) 938-37-75 (office). *E-mail:* anosov@mi.ras.ru (office). *Website:* www.mi.ras.ru (office).

ANSARI, Gholamreza, BSc; Iranian diplomatist; *Ambassador to Russia;* b. 22 Nov. 1955, Shahrood; m. Shahih Shirazi; four d.; ed Allameh Tabatabaee Univ., Tehran; Gov.-Gen. Piranshahr City, Deputy Gov.-Gen. Azarbayejan Prov., Supt of Gov.-Gen. of Azarbayejan Prov., Deputy Gen. Dir of Foreign Nationals and Refugees Dept 1980–88; Chargé d'Affaires, Embassy, London 1992–99, Amb. 1999–2000, to Russia (also accred to Turkmenistan) 2005–. *Leisure interests:* reading, jogging, swimming. *Address:* Embassy of Iran, 117292 Moscow, Pokrovskii bulv. 7, Russia (office). *Telephone:* (495) 917-72-82 (office). *Fax:* (495) 230-28-97 (office).

ANSARI, Mohammad Hamid, MA; Indian diplomatist and government official; *Vice-President;* b. 1 April 1937, Kolkata; m. Salma Ansari; ed St Edward's High School, Shimla, St Xavier's Coll., Kolkata, Aligarh Muslim

Univ.; joined Foreign Service 1961, past positions include High Commr to Australia, Amb. to Saudi Arabia, UAE, Afghanistan, Iran, Perm. Rep. to UN, New York; Vice-Chancellor, Aligarh Muslim Univ. 2000–02; Chair. Nat. Comm. for Minorities 2006–07; currently Visiting Prof., Centre for West Asian and African Studies, Jawaharlal Nehru Univ. and Acad. of Third World Studies, Jamia Millia Islamia; Vice-Pres. of India 2007–; Distinguished Fellow, Observer Research Foundation; Padma Shree 1984. *Publications:* numerous articles on West Asian affairs. *Address:* Vice-President's Office, 6 Maulana Azad Road, New Delhi 110 011, India (office). *Telephone:* (11) 23016344 (office). *Fax:* (11) 23018124 (office).

ANSCHUTZ, Philip F., BSc; American business executive; *Chairman, Anschutz Corporation;* b. 1939, Russell, Kan.; ed Univ. of Kan.; f. Anschutz Corpn 1965, Chair. and CEO 1991–; f. Qwest Communication Int., Colorado, Chair. 1993–2002, now mem. Bd of Dirs; Chair. Southern Pacific Rail Corpn, San Francisco 1988–96, Vice-Chair. Union Pacific, San Francisco 1996–; Dir Forest Oil Corpn 1995–; f. Anschutz Entertainment with stakes in LA Kings (professional ice hockey team) 1995–, LA Galaxy and San Jose Earthquakes (professional soccer teams), Los Angeles Lakers (professional basketball team); majority owner Staples Center, LA. *Address:* Anschutz Corpn, 555 17th Street, Suite 2400, Denver, CO 80202-3941 (office); Qwest Communications International, 1801 California Street, Inglewood, CA 80202, USA. *Telephone:* (303) 298-1000 (Anschutz Corpn); (303) 992-1400 (Qwest). *Fax:* (303) 298-8881 (Anschutz Corpn); (303) 992-1724 (Qwest). *Website:* www.qwest.com.

ANSI, Saud bin Salim al-, BA; Omani diplomatist; *Chief of Information Department, Ministry of Foreign Affairs;* b. 23 Dec. 1949, Salalah; s. of Salim Ansi and Sultana Ansi; m. 1976; two s. two d.; ed Beirut Univ.; with Ministry of Information and Culture and of Diwan Affairs 1974–75; Dir Dept of Research and Studies 1976–78; First Sec. Embassy, Tunis 1975–76, Consul-Gen., Karachi 1978–80, Amb. to Djibouti 1980–82, to Kuwait 1982–84; Perm. Rep. to the UN 1984–88; Under-Sec. and Dir-Gen. Council of Environment and Water Resources 1988–89; Sec.-Gen. Council of Educ. and Vocational Training 1990–92; Adviser to Ministry of Nat. Heritage and Culture 1993–94; Chief Information Dept, Ministry of Foreign Affairs 1995–; mem. Bd of Dirs Oman & Emirates Investment Holding Co. *Leisure interests:* reading, writing, sports, travelling. *Address:* PO Box 1128, Ruwi 112, Oman. *Telephone:* 701 207. *Fax:* 704 785.

ANSIMOV, Georgiy Pavlovich; Russian music theatre director; b. 3 June 1922, Ladozhskaya; s. of Pavel Ansimov and Marija Sollertinskaja; m. 1st Irina Miklukho-Maklaj 1944 (died 1991); m. 2nd Lindmila Ansimova; ed Lunarcharsky State Inst. of Theatre (under B.A. Pokrovsky); Stage Dir, Bolshoi Theatre 1955–64, 1980–89; Artistic Dir and main producer, Moscow Operetta Theatre 1964–76; teaches at Lunarcharsky Inst., Prof. 1977–; Czechoslovakia State Prize 1960, USSR People's Artist 1986. *Main productions:* Story of a Real Man (Prokofiev), Carmen, The Tale of Tsar Sultan (Rimsky Korsakov), West Side Story, Orpheus in the Underworld, War and Peace (Prokofiev), Betrothal in the Monastery (Prokofiev), The Golden Cock (Rimsky-Korsakov), Eugene Onegin, The Fiery Angel, Maddalena, The Taming of the Shrew, The Magic Flute, Sunset, Love for Three Oranges, The Tsar-Carpenter. *Publications:* The Director in the Music Theatre 1980, Everything Begins Over Again Always 1983. *Leisure interest:* photography. *Address:* Karetny Ryad 5/10, Apt. 340, 103006 Moscow, Russia (home). *Telephone:* (495) 299-39-53. *Fax:* (495) 290-05-97.

ANSIP, Andrus; Estonian politician; *Prime Minister;* b. 1 Oct. 1956, Tartu; m.; three c.; ed Tartu Univ., Univ. of York; Head of Regional Office, Joint Venture Estkompexim 1988–93; Chair. Radio Tartu Ltd 1994–99; Bankruptcy Trustee, Tartu Commercial Bank 1994–98; mem. Bd Dirs Rahvapank (People's Bank) 1993–95, Fondijuhtide AS 1995–96, Fundmanager Ltd; Chair. Livonia Privatization IF 1995–96; CEO Fondinvesteeringu Maakler AS 1995–96, Investment Fund Broker Ltd; Mayor City of Tartu 1998–2004; Minister of Econ. Affairs and Communications 2004–05; Prime Minister of Estonia 2005–; Officer, Nat. Order of Merit (Malta) 2001, Order of the White Star (Third Class) 2005. *Address:* Office of the Prime Minister, Stenbocki maja, Rahukohtu 3, Tallinn 15161, Estonia (office). *Telephone:* 693-5701 (office). *Fax:* 693-5704 (office). *E-mail:* peaminister@riik.ee (office). *Website:* www.peaminister.ee (office).

ANSTEE, Dame Margaret Joan, DCMG, BSc (Econ), MA; British/Bolivian international organization official, consultant, writer and lecturer; b. 25 June 1926, Writtle, Essex; d. of Edward C. Anstee and Anne A. Mills; ed Chelmsford Co. High School for Girls, Newnham Coll. Cambridge and Univ. of London; Lecturer in Spanish, Queen's Univ. Belfast 1947–48; Third Sec., Foreign Office 1948–52; UN Tech. Assistance Bd Manila 1952–54; Spanish Supervisor, Univ. of Cambridge 1955–56; UN Tech. Assistance Bd Colombia 1956–57, Uruguay 1957–59, Bolivia 1960–65; Resident Rep. UNDP, Ethiopia and UNDP Liaison Officer with ECA 1965–67; Sr Econ. Adviser, Office of Prime Minister, London 1967–68; Sr Asst to Commr in charge of study of Capacity of UN Devt System 1968–69; Resident Rep. UNDP Morocco 1969–72, Chile (also UNDP Liaison Officer with ECLAC) 1972–74; Deputy to UN Under-Sec.-Gen. in charge of UN Relief Operation to Bangladesh and Deputy Co-ordinator of UN Emergency Assistance to Zambia 1973; with UNDP, New York 1974–78; Asst Sec.-Gen. of UN (Dept of Tech. Co-operation for Devt) 1978–87; Special Rep. of Sec.-Gen. to Bolivia 1982–92, for co-ordination of earthquake relief assistance to Mexico 1985–87; Under-Sec.-Gen. UN 1987–93, Dir-Gen. of UN office at Vienna, Head of Centre for Social Devt and Humanitarian Affairs 1987–92, Special Rep. of Sec.-Gen. for Angola and Head of Angolan Verification Mission 1992–93; Adviser to UN Sec.-Gen. on peacekeeping, post-conflict peacebuilding and training troops for UN peacekeeping missions 1994; Chair. Advisory Group of Lessons Learned Unit, Dept of Peacekeeping Operations, UN, New York 1996–2002; Co-ordinator of UN Drug Control Related Activities 1987–91, of Int. Co-operation for Chernobyl 1991–92 and for countering impact of burning oil wells in Gulf War 1991–92; Sec.-Gen. 8th UN Congress on Prevention of Crime and Treatment of Offenders Aug. 1990; writer, lecturer, consultant and adviser (ad honorem) to Bolivian Govt 1993–97, 2002–06 and to UN 1993–2001; consultant to UN Dept of Political Affairs on post-conflict peacebuilding 1996–2001; mem. Advisory Bd UN Studies at Yale Univ. 1994–, Advisory Council Oxford Research Group 1997–, Advisory Bd UN Intellectual History Project 1999–; Trustee Helpage Int. 1994–97; Patron and Bd mem. British Angola Forum 1998–; mem. Pres. Carter's Int. Council for Conflict Resolution 2002–; Vice-Pres. UK/UN Asscn 2002–; mem. Editorial Bd Global Governance 2004–; Hon. Fellow, Newnham Coll. Cambridge 1991; Commdr Ouissam Alaouite, Morocco 1972; Dama Gran Cruz Condor of the Andes, Bolivia 1986; Grosse Goldene Ehrenzeichen am Bande, Austria 1993, Grand Officer, Order of Bernardo O'Higgins, Chile 2006; Dr hc (Essex) 1994; Hon. LLD (Westminster) 1996; Hon. DSc (Econ) (London) 1998; Hon. DIur (Cambridge) 2004; Reves Peace Prize, William and Mary Coll., USA 1993. *Publications:* The Administration of International Development Aid 1969, Gate of the Sun: A Prospect of Bolivia 1970, Africa and the World (co-ed. with R.K.A. Gardiner and C. Patterson) 1970, Desarrollo Diferente para un Pais de Cambios: Salir del Circulo Vicioso de la Riqueza Empobrecedura 1995, Orphan of the Cold War: The Inside Story of the Collapse of the Angolan Peace Process 1992–93 1996, Never Learn to Type: A Woman at the United Nations 2003; numerous articles on UN reforms and peacekeeping, Angola, econ. and social devt. *Leisure interests:* writing, gardening, hill-walking (preferably in the Andes), bird-watching, swimming. *Address:* The Walled Garden, Knill, nr Presteigne, Powys, LD8 2PR, Wales (home); c/o PNUD, Casilla 9072, La Paz, Bolivia. *Telephone:* (1544) 267411 (Wales) (home); (1544) 260331 (Wales) (home).

ANTES, Horst; German painter and sculptor; b. 28 Oct. 1936, Heppenheim; s. of Valentin Antes and Erika Antes; m. Dorothea Grossmann 1961; one s. one d.; ed Heppenheim Coll.; worked in Florence, then Rome; Prof. at State Acad. of Fine Arts, Karlsruhe 1957–59, Berlin 1984–; mem. Acad. der Künste, Berlin, now living in Berlin, Karlsruhe and Tuscany, Italy; Villa Romana Prize, Florence 1962, Villa Massimo Prize, Rome 1963, UNESCO Prize, Venice Biennale 1966, Kulturpreis (Hesse) 1991, Bienal de Sao Paulo 1991. *One-man shows include:* Troisième Biennale de Paris, Museum Ulm, Städtische Galerie Munich, Galerie Stangl Munich, Galerie Defet, Nuremberg, Galerie Krohn, Badenweiler, Gimpel and Hanover Gallery, Zürich and London, Lefèbre Gallery, New York, 10th Biennale São Paulo, Staatliche Kunsthalle Baden-Baden, Kunsthalle Bern, Kunsthalle Bremen, Frankfurter Kunstverein, Badischer Kunstverein Karlsruhe, Galerie Gunzenhauser, Munich, Galerie Brusberg, Hanover and Berlin, Brühl, Schloss Augustenburg, Galerie Valentien, Stuttgart, Nishimura Gallery, Tokyo, Galerie Der Spiegel, Cologne, Kunsthalle, Bremen, Sprengel Museum, Hanover, Wilhelm-Hack Museum, Ludwigshafen, Guggenheim Museum, New York, Galerie Neumann, Düsseldorf, Städt. Galerie, Villingen-Schwerringen u. Kunstverein Hochrhein, Bad Säckingen, Galerie Levy, Hamburg, Freie Akad. der Künste, Hamburg, Galerie Bernd Lutze, Friedrichshafen, Palais Preysing, Munich, Haus der Kunst, Munich, Schloss Mosigkau, Dessau, Berlinische Galerie Pels-Lensden, Berlin, Galerie Organerie-Reinz, Cologne, Prinz Max Palais, Karlsruhe, Galerie Holbein, Lindau, Galerie Meyer-Ellinger, Frankfurt Maine, Galleria d'Arte Narcisco, Turin, Keramik Museum, Stanfen, Galerie Werkstatt, Reinach, Galerie Uwe Sacksofsky, Heidelberg; numerous group exhbns Europe, USA, Japan etc. *Catalogues:* Catalog of Etchings 1962–66 (G. Gerken) 1968, Catolog of Books (W. Euler) 1968, Catalog of Steel Sculptures (H. G. Sperlich) 1976, Catalog of Lithographs (B. Lutze) 1976, 25 Votive (1983/84). *Address:* Hohenbergstrasse 11, 76228 Karlsruhe (Wolfartsweier), Germany. *Telephone:* (721) 491621.

ANTHONY, Rt Hon. (John) Douglas, AC, PC, CH; Australian politician, farmer and business executive; b. 31 Dec. 1929, Murwillumbah; s. of Hubert Lawrence Anthony and Jessie Anthony (née Stirling); m. Margot Macdonald Budd 1957; two s. one d.; ed Murwillumbah High School, The King's School, Paramatta and Queensland Agricultural Coll.; mem. House of Reps 1957–84, Exec. Council 1963–72, 1975–83, Minister for the Interior 1964–67, of Primary Industry 1967–71, for Trade and Industry 1971–72, for Overseas Trade 1975–77, for Minerals and Energy Nov.–Dec. 1975, for Nat. Resources 1975–77, for Trade and Resources 1977–83; Deputy Prime Minister 1971–72, 1975–83; Deputy Leader Nat. Country Party of Australia (now Nat. Party of Australia) 1966–71, Leader 1971–84; Chair. Resource Finance Corp. Pty. Ltd 1987–; fmr Dir Poseidon Gold Ltd; Dir John Swire and Sons Pty Ltd 1988–, Clyde Agric. Ltd 1988–, Normandy Mining Ltd 1996–; Chair. JD Crawford Fund 1986–; Chair. JD Steward Foundation (Univ. of Sydney) 1986–, Commonwealth Regional Telecommunications Infrastructure Fund 1997, Governing Council of Old Parl. House, Canberra 2000; Hon. Fellow Australian Acad. of Technological Sciences and Eng 1990; Hon. LLD (Victoria Univ. of Wellington) 1983; Hon. DUniv (Sydney) 1997; Gold Medal Queensland Agric. Coll. 1985, Canberra Medal 1989, NZ Commemorative Medal 1990. *Leisure interests:* golf, tennis, swimming, fishing. *Address:* PO Box 71, Murwillumbah, NSW 2484, Australia (office). *Fax:* (2) 66723346 (office).

ANTHONY, Kenny Davis, LLB, BSc, PhD; Saint Lucia politician; b. 8 Jan. 1951; ed Univ. of Birmingham, Univ. of the West Indies; Leader, Saint Lucia Labour Party; Prime Minister of Saint Lucia, Minister of Finance, Planning, Devt, Information and the Civil Service 1997–2001, Prime Minister, Minister of Finance, Int. Financial Services, Econ. Affairs and Information 2001–06. *Address:* Tom Walcott Building, 2nd Floor, Jeremie Street, POB 427, Castries, Saint Lucia. *Telephone:* 451-8446. *Fax:* 451-9389. *Website:* www.geocities.com/~slp.

ANTHONY, Lawrence; South African conservationist, environmental activist, explorer and author; *Head of Conservation, Thula Thula Game Reserve;* b. 1950, Johannesburg; m. Françoise Anthony; two s.; was raised in rural Rhodesia (now Zimbabwe), Zambia and Malawi; Head of Conservation, Thula Thula Game Reserve, Zululand, SA; Founder The Earth Org. (pvt., ind., int. conservation and environmental group); rescued animals in Baghdad Zoo at height of US-led Coalition invasion of Iraq 2003; led negotiations with Lord's Resistance Army rebel army in Southern Sudan to raise awareness of the environment and protect endangered species, including last of Northern White Rhinoceros; has served on Nat. Transitional Exec. Cttee during S African Govt's transition from Apartheid, Panel for the Electronic Media that apptd Bd of Dirs of South African Broadcasting Corpn, Cttee that apptd Film Bd of S Africa; Int. mem. The Explorers' Club of New York 2004; mem. S African Asscn for the Advancement of Science; Living Lakes Best Conservation Practice Award, The Global Nature Fund, The Earth Day Medal, Earth Soc. (for his rescue of Baghdad Zoo) 2004, The Earth Trustee Award, Regimental Medal for bravery in Iraq during the Coalition invasion of Baghdad, US Army 3rd Infantry, IAS Freedom Medal, The Umhlatuzi Mayoral Award for Outstanding Community Service, named by journalist Tom Clynes amongst his six most impressive and influential people in a lifetime of reporting 2009. *Publications:* Babylon's Ark: The Incredible Wartime Rescue of the Baghdad Zoo (with Graham Spence) 2007, The Elephant Whisperer (with Graham Spence) 2009. *Address:* Thula Thula Game Reserve, PO Box 87, Heatonville 3881, Zululand, South Africa (office). *Telephone:* (35) 792-8322 (office). *Fax:* (86) 603-7731 (office). *E-mail:* francoise@thulathula.com (office). *Website:* www.thulathula.com (office).

ANTICH VALERO, José; Spanish journalist and newspaper executive; *Director, La Vanguardia;* b. 23 June 1955, La Seu d'Urgell (Lérida); m.; four c.; ed ; writer for Agencia Efe, Barcelona 1977; took part in founding articles of newspaper El Periódico de Catalunya where he started career as political feature writer 1978–82; part of founding team of Catalan edn of El País and worked as political corresp. 1982–94; Chief Political Writer for La Vanguardia 1994–98, coordinator of all political affairs at newpaper 1998–2000, Dir 2000–; VIII Fundación Independiente de Periodismo Camilo José Cela Prize 2004. *Publication:* El Virrey (political study into Jordi Pujol) 1994. *Address:* La Vanguardia, Pelayo 28, 08001 Barcelona, Spain (office). *Telephone:* (93) 4812200 (office). *Fax:* (93) 3185587 (office). *E-mail:* lavanguardia@lavanguardia.es (office). *Website:* www.lavanguardia.es (office).

ANTINORI, Severino, PhD; Italian gynaecologist; b. 1945, Civitella del Tronto; m. Caterina Antinori; two d.; ed Univ. La Sapienza, Rome; Perm. Asst in Obstetrics and Gynaecology, Istituto Materno Regina Elena 1973–80, Prin. Asst 1980–82, Dir Reproductive Physiopathology Service 1985–87; at Ospedale Materno Regina Elena 1978–92; specialist in obstetrics and gynaecology, Univ. Cattolica di Roma 1978; Prof. Univ. degli Studi di Pisa 1993–94, Univ. degli Studi G. D'Annunzio, Chieti 1996–97, 1998–99, Univ. degli Studi di Roma 1998–99; Dir Centro RAPRUI (Ricercatori Associati per la Riproduzione Umana); Vice-Pres. APART (Int. Asscn of Pvt. Assisted Reproductive Tech. Clinics and Laboratories). *Publications:* numerous articles in medical journals. *Address:* Centro RAPRUI, Via Tacito, Quartiere Umbertino di Prati, Rome, Italy (office). *E-mail:* antinori@raprui.org (office). *Website:* www.raprui .org (office).

ANTOINE, Frédéric; Belgian journalist and academic; *Professor, Catholic University of Louvain;* b. 27 Sept. 1955, Uccle; s. of Paul Antoine and Suzanne Degavre; m. Chantal Berque 1982; two s. one d.; ed Catholic Univ. of Louvain; journalist, L'Appel 1977, La Libre Belgique 1978; Research Asst, Communication Dept, Catholic Univ. of Louvain 1979; News Ed. Radio 1180, Brussels 1979; Prof., Media School IAD, Louvain-la-Neuve 1981; Prof., Communication Dept, Catholic Univ. of Louvain 1989–, Dir Research Unit on Mediatic Narrative (RECI) 1991–2000, Head Undergraduate Programme Information and Communication 2006–; Ed. L'Appel 1992–. *Publications:* On Nous a Changé la Télé 1987, La Télévision à Travers ses Programmes 1988, Télévision In: Le Guide des Médias 1989–97; ed. La Médiamorphose d'Alain Vanderbiest 1994; ed. Coupures de Presse 1996, Les Radios et les Télévisions de Belgique 2000, Les Multinationales des Médias 2002, Le Grand Malentendu 2003. *Address:* Ruelle de la Lanterne, Magique 14, 1348 Louvain-la-Neuve (office); L'Appel, Rue du Beau mur 45, 4030 Liège (office); Rue Klipveld 69, 1180 Brussels, Belgium (home). *Telephone:* (1) 47-28-14 (office); (4) 341-10-04 (office); (2) 374-10-81 (home). *Fax:* (1) 47-30-44 (office); (4) 341-10-04 (office); (2) 374-10-81 (home). *E-mail:* antoine@reci.ucl.ac.be (office).

ANTON, Ioan, DEng; Romanian mechanical engineer and academic; *Consulting Professor of Fluid Flow Machinery, University Politechnica Timişoara;* b. 18 July 1924, Vintere; s. of Mihai Anton; m. Viorica Flueraş 1949; one s. one d.; ed Polytech. Inst. of Timişoara; Assoc. Prof., Polytechnic Inst. of Timişoara 1951, Prof. 1962; Dean, Faculty of Mechanical Eng, Polytech. Inst. of Timişoara 1961–63, Head Fluid Flow Machine Dept 1962–73, 1982–90, Rector 1971–81; Corresp. mem. Romanian Acad. 1963–74, mem. 1974–; Dir Tech. Research Centre, Timişoara, Romanian Acad. 1969–70; Dir Research Lab. for Hydraulic Machines, Timişoara 1970–74; Vice-Pres. Nat. Council for Science and Tech. 1973–79; Vice-Pres. Romanian Acad. 1974–90; Dir of Research Centre for Hydrodynamics, Cavitation and Magnetic Fluids, Tech. Univ., Timişoara 1990–; Dir Centre for Fundamental and Advanced Tech. Research, Romanian Acad. 1997–; mem. European Acad. of Sciences and Arts, New York Acad. of Sciences 1997–; Ed.-in-Chief Revue Roumaine des Sciences Techniques; Dr hc (Tech. Univ. of Civil Eng, Bucharest) 1998, (Univ. 'Politechnica' Timişoara) 1999; State Prize 1953, Aurel Vlaicu Prize, Romanian Acad. 1958. *Publications:* Experimental Testing of Fluid Flow Machines (with A. Bărglăzan) 1952, Hydraulic Turbines 1979, Cavitation, Vol.

1 1984, Vol. 2 1985, Hydrodynamics of Bulb Type Turbines and Bulb Type Pump-Turbines (with V. Cîmpeanu and I. Carte) 1988, Energetic and Cavitational Scale-up Effects in Hydraulic Turbines 2002 and over 260 papers on hydraulic machines, cavitation and boiling and magnetic fluids. *Address:* University Politechnica Timişoara, Faculty of Mechanical Engineering, Department of Hydraulic Machines, 300222 Timişoara, Boulevard Mihai Viteazul No. 1, Romania (office). *Telephone:* (256) 403700 (office). *Fax:* (256) 403700 (office). *E-mail:* anton@acad-tim.utt.ro (office).

ANTONACOPOULOS, Lefteris, BSc; Greek business executive; *Chairman and Chief Executive Officer, Hellenic Telecommunications Organization;* b. 1940, Patras; joined Shell 1971, with Shell Chemicals International, London 1979, Dir Human Resources and Public Relations, Shell Hellas, Athens 1981, Man. Dir 1984–89, Pres. and Man. Dir 1992, transferred to Shell International, The Hague, responsible for marketing in Cen. and S Europe 1989, Pres. and Man. Dir, Shell Iberia, Madrid and Lisbon 1996, Transformation Man., Shell London 1998; Pres. Fed. of Oil Marketing Cos 1993–94; mem. Bd Fed. of Greek Industries 1996–, mem. Exec. Cttee 1999–, Pres. 2002–; Chair. and CEO Hellenic Telecommunications Org. (OTE) 2002–; mem. bds several Greek cos 1999–. *Address:* Hellenic Telecommunications Organization (OTE), Administration House, 99 Kifissias Avenue, Maroussi, Athens 15124, Greece (office). *Telephone:* (21) 0 6111000 (office). *Website:* www.ote.gr (office).

ANTONAKAKIS, Dimitris; Greek architect; b. 22 Dec. 1933, Chania, Crete; m. Maria-Suzana Antonakakis (q.v.) (née Kolokytha) 1961; one s. one d.; ed School of Architecture, Nat. Tech. Univ. of Athens; partnership with Suzana Antonakakis (q.v.), Athens 1959–; Asst Instructor in Architecture, Nat. Tech. Univ. of Athens 1959–64, Instructor 1964–78, mem. teaching staff 1978–92; Founder and Co-Prin. (with S. Antonakakis) Atelier 66 1965; mem. and Treas. Admin. Cttee, Greek Architectural Asscn 1962–63; Pres. Asscn of Assts and Instructors, Nat. Tech. Univ. 1975–77; Vice-Pres. Cen. Admin. Cttee, Asscn of Assts and Instructors of Greek Univs 1976–77; mem. Int. Design Seminar, Tech. Univ. Delft 1987, Split 1988; Visiting Prof., MIT, USA 1994–99, Nat. Tech. Univ. of Athens 1997–98; Art Dir Centre for Mediterranean Architecture, Crete 1997–; Corresp. mem. Acad. d'Architecture, Paris; Dr hc (Aristotle Univ. of Thessaloniki) 2007; numerous awards and prizes. *Works include:* Archaeological Museum, Chios 1965–66, Hydra Beach Hotel, Hermionis 1965, vertical addition, house in Port Phaliron 1967–72, miners' housing complex, Distomo 1969, apartment bldg, Emm. Benaki 118, Athens 1973–74, Hotel Lyttos, Heraklion, Crete 1973–82, Zannas House, Philopappos Hill, Athens 1980–82, Gen. Hosp., Sitia, Crete 1982, Ionian Bank br., Rhodes 1983, Heraklion, Crete 1987, Faculty of Humanities, Rethymnon, Crete 1982, Tech. Univ. of Crete, Chania 1982, Summer Theatre, Komotini 1989, Traditional Crafts Centre, Ioannina 1990, Museum of Acropolis, Athens 1990, Art Studio, Aegina 1990, office bldg, 342 Syngrou Ave., Athens 1990, Open-air Theatre, Thessaloniki 1995–96, Pissas House, Iraklio, Crete 1997, Rehabilitation of ancient Agora area, Athens 1997, Museum of Science and Technology, Patras 1999, Kallithea and Ano Patisia railway stations, Athens 2001–02, Kolonaki Square, Athens 2004; several pvt. houses. *Publications:* Le Corbusier Une Petite Maison (trans.) 1998; numerous architectural articles. *Address:* Atelier 66, Emm. Benaki 118, Athens 114-73, Greece (office). *Telephone:* (210) 3300323 (office); (210) 3300328 (home). *Fax:* (210) 3801160 (office). *E-mail:* a66@otenet.gr (office). *Website:* www.a66architects.com (office).

ANTONAKAKIS-KOLOKYTHA, Maria-Suzana; Greek architect; b. 25 June 1935, Athens; m. Dimitris Antonakakis (q.v.) 1961; one s. one d.; ed School of Architecture, Nat. Tech. Univ., Athens; partnership with Dimitris Antonakakis (q.v.), Athens 1959–; Founder and Co-Prin. (with Dimitris Antonakakis) Atelier 66 1965; mem. Admin. Cttee Greek Architects Asscn 1971–72; Pres. Dept of Architecture, Tech. Chamber of Greece 1982–83; mem. Int. Design Seminar, Tech. Univ. Delft 1987, Split 1988; mem. Greek Secr. of UIA 1985–2002; newspaper columnist 1998–; Dr hc (Aristotle Univ. of Thessaloniki) 2007; numerous awards and prizes. *Works include:* Archaeological Museum, Chios 1965–66, Hydra Beach Hotel, Hermionis 1965, vertical additions, House in Port Phaliron 1967–72, miners' housing complex, Distomo 1969, apartment bldg, Emm. Benaki 118, Athens 1973–74, Hotel Lyttos, Heraklion, Crete 1973–82, Zannas House, Philopappos Hill, Athens 1980–82, Gen. Hosp. Sitia, Crete 1982, Ionian Bank branch, Rhodes 1983, Heraklion, Crete 1987, Summer Theatre, Komotini 1989, Art Studio, Aegina 1990, office bldg, 342 Syngrou Ave, Athens 1990, Traditional Crafts Centre, Ioannina 1990, Museum of Acropolis, Athens 1990, Open-air Theatre, Thessaloniki 1995-96, Pissas House, Iraklio, Crete 1997, rehabilitation of ancient Agora area, Athens 1997, Museum of Science and Technology, Patras 1999, Kallithea and Ano Patisia railway stations, Athens 2001–02, New Acropolis Museum, Athens 2001, Kolonaki Square, Athens 2004; several pvt. and holiday houses. *Publications:* numerous architectural articles; trans. Entretien (Le Corbusier) 1971. *Address:* Atelier 66, Emm. Benaki 118, Athens 114-73, Greece (office). *Telephone:* (210) 3300323 (office); (210) 3300328 (home). *Fax:* (210) 3801160 (office). *E-mail:* a66@otenet.gr (office). *Website:* www .a66architects.com (office).

ANTONAKOPOULOS, Gen. Georgios, LLB; Greek army officer; b. 5 Jan. 1943, Patra, Peloponnisos; s. of Antonios Antonakopoulos; m.; two c.; ed Aristotle Univ. of Thessaloniki, Hellenic Nat. Defence Coll., Hellenic Higher Army War Coll.; began career in Hellenic Armed Forces 1967, held positions successively as Artillery Battery Commdr, Instructor Artillery Schools, Staff Officer Infantry Div., Staff Officer Intelligence Div., Commdr Artillery Battalion, Commdr Field Artillery Command, Chief of Staff Mechanized Div., Dir 1st Staff Office Hellenic Army Gen. Staff, Brigade Commdg Gen., Dir. Operation Br. Hellenic Army Gen. Staff, Commdg Gen. XII Mechanized Infantry Div., Commdg Gen. D'Army Corps, Chief of Hellenic Army Gen. Staff, Chief of Hellenic Nat. Defence Gen. Staff 2002–05; Medal for Mil. Valour

Class A and B, Chief of Hellenic Army Gen. Staff Commendation Medal, Star of Merit and Honour, Army Meritorious Command Commendation Medal Class A, Staff Officer Service Commendation Medal Class A, Golden Cross of the Order of Honour, Knight Commdr's Cross of Order of the Phoenix, Knight Commdr's Cross of Order of Honour. *Address:* Ministry of Defence, Mesogeion 151, 15 500 Xolargos, Greece (office). *Telephone:* (210) 6598604 (office). *Fax:* (210) 6443832 (office). *E-mail:* minister@mod.gr (office). *Website:* www.mod.gr (office).

ANTONELLI, HE Cardinal Ennio, DPhil; Italian ecclesiastic; *Archbishop of Florence;* b. 18 Nov. 1936, Todi; ed Seminary of Todi, Pontifical Regional Seminary of Assisi, Pontifical Higher Seminary of Rome, Pontifical Lateran Univ., Rome, State Univ. of Perugia; ordained priest, Nicea 1960; Prof. of Theology, Vice-Rector, then Rector, Seminary of Perugia; Prof. of Theology, Regional Seminary of Assisi; Prof. of Art History, Superior Insts of Assisi and Deruta; apptd Bishop of Gubbio 1982; consecrated by Bishop Grandoni of Orvieto and Todi 1982; Metropolitan Archbishop of Perugia 1988–95; elected Sec.-Gen. of Italian Episcopal Conf. 1995; Archbishop of Florence 2001–; Cardinal Priest of St Andrea delle Fratte 2003–; del. to Special Ass. for Europe, World Synod of Bishops, Vatican City 1999; Pres. Pontifical Council for the Family 2008–. *Address:* Archdiocese di Firenze, Piazza S. Giovanni 3, 50129 Firenze, Italy (office). *Telephone:* 055-271071 (office). *Fax:* 055-2710741 (office). *Website:* www.diocesifirenze.it (office).

ANTONETTI, HE Cardinal Lorenzo; Italian ecclesiastic; b. 31 July 1922, Romagnano Sesia; ordained priest 1945; Archbishop, See of Roselle 1968; Official of State, Roman Curia 1977; Apostolic Nuncio to France 1988; Pro-Pres. of the Admin. of the Patrimony of the Apostolic See 1995–98, Pres. 1998, now Pres. Emer.; Cardinal-Deacon of S. Agnese in Agone 1998–; mem. Pontifical Comm. for Vatican City State. *Address:* Administration of the Patrimony of the Holy See, Palazzo Apostolico, 00120 Città del Vaticano, Italy. *Telephone:* (06) 69884306. *Fax:* (06) 69883141.

ANTONICHEVA, Anna; Russian ballet dancer; *Principal Dancer, Bolshoi Theatre Ballet Company;* b. Baku, Azerbaijan; ed Moscow Academic School of Choreography; joined Bolshoi Theatre Ballet Co. 1991, now Prin. Dancer; Honoured Artist of Russia, Gold Medal, Int. Ballet Competition, Jackson, Miss. 1998. *Ballet:* leading and solo parts include Shirin (Legend of Love), Swan-Princess (Swan Lake), Nikiya (Bayadera), Mirta (Giselle), Juliet (Romeo and Juliet), Frigia (Spartacus), Princess Aurora (Sleeping Beauty), Kitry, Dulcinea (Don Quixote). *Address:* Bolshoi Theatre, Teatralnaya Pl.1. Moscow, Russia. *Website:* www.bolshoi.ru/en.

ANTONIO, Joseph Philippe, LLB; Haitian politician and diplomatist; b. 22 July 1939, Saint-Marc; six c.; ed Port-au-Prince Univ., Ecole Normale Supérieure, Univ. of Geneva, Switzerland; Prof. Nouveau Collège Bird, Haiti 1966–71; Dir-Co-ordinator Haitian Centre of Research and Documentation 1978–91; Chargé d'affaires, UN, New York 1991–94, Perm. Rep. 1995, 1998; Chargé d'affaires, Embassy in Germany 1992–94; Minister of Foreign Affairs and Religion 2001–04. *Address:* c/o Ministry of Foreign Affairs and Religion, boulevard Harry S. Truman, Cité de l'Exposition, Port-au-Prince, Haiti (office).

ANTONOVA, Irina Aleksandrovna; Russian museum researcher; *Director, Pushkin Museum of Fine Arts;* b. 20 March 1922, Moscow; ed Moscow State Univ.; worked in Pushkin Museum of Fine Arts 1945–, Sr Researcher 1945–61, Dir 1961–; organizer of numerous exhbns and regular exchange with museums of Europe and America; f. together with Sviatoslav Richter Festival of Arts December Nights accompanied by art shows 1981–; Vice-Pres. Int. Council of Museums 1980–92, Hon. mem. 1992–; mem. Russian Acad. of Educ. 1989; Corresp. mem. San-Fernando Acad., Madrid; Commdr des Arts et Lettres; State Prize 1995. *Publications:* more than 60 articles on problems of museum man., art of Italian Renaissance, contemporary painting. *Leisure interests:* swimming, cars, music, ballet. *Address:* A.S. Pushkin Museum of Fine Arts, 121019 Moscow, Volkhonka str. 12, Russia. *Telephone:* (495) 203-46-76 (office). *E-mail:* Finearts@gmii.museum.ru (office). *Website:* www.museum.ru/gmii (office).

ANTONOVICH, Ivan Ivanovich, DPhil; Belarusian diplomatist; b. 1937, Brest Region; m.; two d.; ed Minsk State Inst. of Foreign Languages, Inst. of Philosophy and Law; on staff UN Secr. New York 1969–74; Perm. Rep. of Belarus at UNESCO, rep. of Belarus in UN Comm. on Human Rights 1976–77; CP service 1977–87; Pro-Rector, Prof. Acad. of Social Sciences at Cen. Cttee CPSU 1987–90; mem. Politbureau, Sec. Cen. Cttee of Russian CP; advisor to Pres. of Russian-American Univ., Dir programmes of social-political analysis 1991–92; Dir Centre of System Social-Econ. Studies, Pro-Rector (acting) Acad. of Man., Council of Ministers 1992–93; Dir Belarus Inst. of Scientific Information and Prognosis 1993–95; Deputy Minister of Foreign Affairs 1995–97, Minister 1997–98; Dir Inst. of Socio-political Studies, Pres. Admin 1999; mem. Russian Acad. of Social-Political Sciences, Acad. of Geopolitics, Belarus Repub.; Merited Worker of Science, Belarus Repub. *Publications:* 15 books, numerous articles on problems of philosophy and int. relations. *Address:* c/o Ministry of Foreign Affairs, Lenina str. 19, 220050 Minsk, Belarus (office). *Telephone:* (17) 227-29-41 (office).

ANTONY, Arackaparambil Kurian, BA, BL; Indian politician; *Minister of Defence;* b. 28 Dec. 1940, Cherthala, Alappuzha Dist, Kerala; s. of Arackaparambil Kurian Pillai and Aleyamma; m. Elizabeth Antony; two s.; ed Maharajas Coll., Government Law Coll., Ernakulam; mem. Rajya Sabha (Parl.) from Kerala 1985–95, 2005–; fmr Minister of Civil Supplies, Consumer Affairs and Public Distribution; Chief Minister of Kerala 1977–78, 1995–96, 2001–04; Minister of Defence 2006–; Chair. Disciplinary Cttee of All India Congress Cttee. *Address:* Ministry of Defence, South Block, New Delhi 110 011 (office); Anjanam, Easwara Vilasam Road, Thiruvananthapuram 695014, India (home). *Telephone:* (11) 23019030 (office). *Fax:* (11) 23015403 (office). *E-mail:* ak.antony@sansad.nic.in. *Website:* www.mod.nic.in (office).

ANTUNOVIĆ, Željka, MD; Croatian physician and politician; *Deputy President, Social Democratic Party of Croatia (Socijaldemokratska partija hrvatske);* b. 1955, Virovitica; m.; two c.; ed Univ. of Zagreb, Harvard Univ., USA; Head of Finance Section, Sljeme Meat Industry 1980–84; head of finance, housing utilities co., Zagreb 1984–93; Councillor, City of Zagreb Ass. 1993–95, 1997–98; mem. Main Cttee of Social Democratic Party (Socijaldemokratska partija hrvatske— SDP) 1994–95, 1995–, City Cttee of SDP, Zagreb 1997–98, currently Deputy Pres.; mem. Parl. (Croatian Nat. Sabor) 1995–99, 2003–, Pres. Parl. Cttee for Families, Youth and Sport 2005–, mem. Cttee on Equal Opportunities for Women and Men; Pres. Social Democratic Forum of Women in SDP 1995–99; Deputy Prime Minister in charge of Social Affairs 2000–03; Minister of Defence 2002–03; Ed. Accounting and Finance magazine, Croatian Asscn of Accountants and Finance Employees 1993–95. *Address:* Social Democratic Party of Croatia (Socijaldemokratska partija hrvatske), 10000 Zagreb, Iblerov trg 9; Croatian National Parliament, Hrvatski Sabor Trg Svetog Marka 6–7, 1000 Zagreb, Croatia (office). *Telephone:* (1) 4552658 (SDP). *Fax:* (1) 4552842 (SDP). *E-mail:* sdp@sdp.hr. *Website:* www.sdp.hr; www.sabor.hr.

ANUSZKIEWICZ, Richard Joseph, BS, MFA; American artist; b. 23 May 1930, Erie, Pa; s. of Adam Jacob Anuszkiewicz and Victoria Jankowski; m. Sarah Feeney 1960; one s. two d.; ed Cleveland Inst. of Art, Yale Univ., Kent State Univ.; moved to New York City 1957; early positions as conservator Metropolitan Museum of Art and silver designer for Tiffany and Co.; represented in numerous group exhbns including Museum of Modern Art 1960–61, 1963, 1965, Washington Gallery of Modern Art 1963, Tate Gallery, London 1964, Art Fair, Cologne 1967, etc.; represented in perm. collections at Museum of Modern Art, Whitney Museum of American Art, Albright-Knox Art Gallery, Butler Art Inst., Yale Art Gallery, Chicago Art Inst., Fogg Art Museum, Harvard Univ., etc.; Artist-in-Residence Dartmouth 1967, Univ. of Wis. 1968, Cornell Univ. 1968, Kent State Univ. 1968, Charles Foley Gallery, Columbus 1988, Newark Museum 1990, Center for Arts, Vero Beach, Florida 1993. *One-man exhibitions:* at Butler Art Inst., Youngstown, Ohio 1955, The Contemporaries, New York 1960, 1961, 1963, Sidney Janis Gallery, New York 1965–67, Dartmouth Coll. 1967, Cleveland Museum of Art 1967, Kent State Univ. 1968, Andrew Crispo Gallery, New York 1975, 1977, La Jolla Museum of Contemporary Art, Calif. 1976, Univ. Art Museum, Berkeley, Calif. 1977, Columbus Gallery of Fine Arts, Ohio 1977, Galleria Sagittaria, Pordenone, Italy 1988, Galleria Cinche D'Arte Moderna, Ferraro, Italy 1989, Mornzen Co. Ltd, Tokyo 1990, 1991, Vero Beach, Florida 1993. *Publications:* articles in learned journals. *Address:* 76 Chestnut St, Englewood, NJ 07631-3045, USA.

ANWAR, Khurshid, MA; Pakistani diplomatist; *Secretary-General, Economic Cooperation Organization;* ed Fletcher School of Law and Diplomacy, Boston, USA, Univ. of Peshawar; career diplomat, joined Foreign Service 1978, served in missions in Amman, Cairo, Dhaka, London and Ottawa, Additional Foreign Sec. and Head ECO Div., Ministry of Foreign Affairs –2006; Sec.-Gen. ECO 2006–. *Address:* Economic Cooperation Organization Secretariat, No. 1, Golobu Alley, Kamranieh, PO Box 14155- 6176, Tehran, Iran (office). *Telephone:* (21) 22831733 (office); (21) 22292066 (office). *Fax:* (21) 22831732 (office). *E-mail:* registry@ecosecretariat.org (office). *Website:* www.ecosecretariat.org (office).

ANWAR, Sheikh Muhammad, MA; Pakistani television executive; b. 25 March 1943, Amritsar, India; m.; four d.; ed Fairfield Univ., Conn. and Pakistan Admin. Staff Coll.; contract producer/dir and scriptwriter, Pakistan Television (PTV), Lahore 1964–66, programme producer 1966–72, Exec. Producer, News and Current Affairs 1972–79, Deputy Controller, Overseas Div. PTV HQ, Islamabad 1979–80, Programme Man. PTV, Rawalpindi/Islamabad 1980–81; Communications Consultant to the Ministry of Information and Broadcasting, Islamabad 1981–83; Deputy Controller of Programmes PTV HQ, Islamabad 1983–85, Producer Group-8, PTV, Lahore 1985–86, Gen. Man. PTV, Peshawar 1986–87, Controller Programme Planning PTV HQ, Islamabad 1988, Educational TV 1988, Programmes Training Acad. 1989–90, Programmes Admin. 1990–92, Int. Relations 1990–93, Controller Programmes Admin, Sport, Archives 1994–96; Gen. Man. PTV Centre, Lahore 1992–94; Controller PTV Acad., PTV HQ, Islamabad, Exec. Producer, Local Area Transmission, PTV, Lahore 1996–97; Visiting Prof. of Communications, Quaid-e-Azam Univ. of Pakistan Information Services Acad. 1983–90; Examiner Fed. Public Service Comm. (Information Group); Visiting Prof., Fine Arts Dept, Punjab Univ. 1993; mem. Int. Inst. of Communication, London 1981, Royal TV Soc., London 1983–. *Address:* 154-A, Model Town, Lahore, Pakistan (home). *Telephone:* 851169 (home).

ANWAR, Yusuf, SE, MA, LLM, PhD; Indonesian economist, government official and diplomatist; *Ambassador to Japan;* b. Tasikmalaya, West Java; ed Padjajaran Univ., Vanderbilt Univ., US; Pres. and CEO Danareksa Securities and Investment 1992–93; fmr Chair. Jakarta Initiative; Sec.-Gen. Ministry of Finance 1993–95, Chair. Education and Training Agency 1995–98, Chair. Capital Market Supervisory Agency 1998–2000, Minister of Finance and State Enterprises Devt 2004–05; Exec. Dir Asian Devt Bank 2000–04; Amb. to Japan 2006–. *Address:* Embassy of Indonesia, 5-2-9, Higashi Gotanda, Shinagawa-ku, Tokyo 141-0022, Japan (office). *Telephone:* (3) 3441-4201 (office). *Fax:* (3) 3447-1697 (office). *E-mail:* info@indonesian-embassy.or.jp (office). *Website:* www.indonesian-embassy.or.jp (office).

ANYAOKU, Eleazar Chukwuemeka (Emeka), Ndichie Chief Adazie of Obosi, Ugwumba of Idemili, CON, BA, FRSA; Nigerian diplomatist; *International President, World Wide Fund for Nature;* b. 18 Jan. 1933, Obosi; s. of the late Emmanuel Chukwuemeka Anyaoku, Ononukpo of Okpuno Ire and

Cecilia Adiba (née Ogbogu); m. Ebunola Olubunmi Solanke 1962; three s. one d.; ed Merchants of Light School, Oba, Univ. of Ibadan, Univ. of London, UK; Commonwealth Devt Corpn, London and Lagos 1959–62; joined Nigerian Diplomatic Service 1962, mem. Nigerian Perm. Mission to UN, New York 1963–66; seconded to Commonwealth Secr., Asst Dir Int. Affairs Div. 1966–71, Dir 1971–75, Asst Sec.-Gen. of the Commonwealth 1975–77, elected Deputy Sec.-Gen. (Political) Dec. 1977, re-elected, 1984, Sec.-Gen. 1990–2000; Minister of External Affairs, Nigeria Nov.–Dec. 1983; Sec. Review Cttee on Commonwealth Intergovernmental Orgs June–Aug. 1966; Commonwealth Observer Team for Gibraltar Referendum Aug.–Sept. 1967; mem. Anguilla Comm., West Indies Jan.–Sept. 1970; Deputy Conf. Sec., meeting of Commonwealth Heads of Govt, London 1969, Singapore 1971, Conf. Sec., Ottawa 1973, Kingston, Jamaica 1975; Leader, Commonwealth Mission to Mozambique 1975; Commonwealth Observer, Zimbabwe Talks, Geneva Oct.–Dec. 1976; accompanied Commonwealth Eminent Persons Group (EPG) SA 1986; Vice-Pres. Royal Commonwealth Soc. 1975–2000, Pres. 2000–; mem. Council of Overseas Devt Inst. 1979–90, Council of the Selly Oak Colleges, Birmingham 1980–86, Council, Save the Children Fund 1984–90, Council of IISS, London 1987–93, Int. Bd of United World Colleges 1994–2000, World Comm. on Forests and Sustainable Devt 1995–98; Pres. Royal Africa Soc. 2000–; Chair. Presidential Advisory Council on Int. Relations (Nigeria) 2000–; Int. Pres. WWF (World Wide Fund for Nature) 2002–; Freedom of City of London 1998; Hon. Fellow, Inst. of Educ., London 1994, Coll. of Preceptors 1998; Hon. mem. Club of Rome 1992; Commdr of the Order of the Niger (Nigeria) 1982; Order of the Trinity Cross (Trinidad and Tobago) 1999; Hon. GCVO 2000; Hon. DLitt (Ibadan) 1990, (Buckingham) 1994, (Zimbabwe) 1999, (UDFD Sokoto) 2001, (Rhodes, SA) 2001, (UNILORIN) 2002; Hon. DPhil (Ahmadu Bello) 1991; Hon. LLD (Nigeria) 1991, (Aberdeen) 1992, (Reading) 1992, (Bristol) 1993, (Oxford Brookes) 1993, (Birmingham) 1993, (Leeds) 1994, (South Bank, London) 1994, (New Brunswick, Canada) 1995, (North London) 1995, (Liverpool) 1997, (London) 1997, (Nottingham) 1998, (Trinity Coll. Dublin) 1999, (UNIZIK) 2001; Dr hc (Bradford) 1995; Livingston Medal, Royal Scottish Geographical Soc. 1996. *Publications:* The Missing Headlines (vol. of speeches) 1997, essays in various publs. *Leisure interests:* tennis, athletics, swimming, reading. *Address:* Orimili, Okpuno Ire, Obosi, Anambra State, Nigeria.

ANYIM, Anyim Pius, LLM; Nigerian lawyer and senator; *Speaker of the Senate;* b. 10 Feb. 1961, Ishiagu, Ebonyi State; s. of Chief Anyim Ivo Osita and Agnes Anyim; m. Chioma Blessing; two s. one d.; ed Imo State (now Abia State) Univ., Okigwe, Univ. of Jos, Jos; called to Nigerian Bar 1989; Legal Adviser, Directorate of Social Mobilisation (MAMSER) HQ, Abuja 1989–92; Head Protection Dept Nat. Comm. for Refugees HQ, Abuja 1992–97; fmr Registrar, Refugee Appeal Bd; Senator 1999–, Speaker of Senate 2000–; mem. Nigerian Bar Asscn; Fellow Nigerian Environmental Soc., Inst. of Purchasing and Supply Man.; Grand Patron Abuja Chapter, Soc. for Int. Devt (SID); Grand Commdr Order of Niger (GCON); Hon. DPA (Fed. Univ. of Agric., Umudike, Abia State); Hon. DD (Baptist Seminary and Theological Inst., Ogbomoso, Oyo State); Nigeria Nat. Productivity Order of Merit Award, Distinguished Service Award, Nigerian Foundation Inc., Houston, Tex., USA, and other awards. *Leisure interests:* farming, swimming, reading. *Address:* Office of the Speaker of the Senate, National Assembly Complex, PMB 141, Garki, Abuja (office); Legislators Quarters, Apo Mansion, Abuja, Nigeria (home). *Telephone:* (9) 2340505 (office); (9) 2310009 (home). *Fax:* (9) 2341214 (office); (9) 3143660 (home). *E-mail:* panyim@mail.com (office).

ANZAI, Yuichiro, BEng, MEng, PhD; Japanese university administrator and academic; *President, Keio University;* ed Keio Univ.; Instructor, Dept of Admin Eng, Faculty of Eng, Keio Univ. 1971–79, Asst Prof. 1979–85, Prof., Dept of Electrical Eng, Faculty of Science and Tech. 1988–96, Prof., Center for Computer Science, Grad. School of Science and Tech. 1989–2000, Chair. Grad. School of Science and Tech. and Dean of Faculty of Science and Tech. 1993–2001, Prof., Dept of Information and Computer Science 1996–, Prof., School of Open and Environmental Systems, Grad. School of Science and Tech. 2000–, Pres. Keio Univ. 2001–; Postdoctoral Research Fellow, Dept of Psychology and Computer Science, Carnegie-Mellon Univ., Pittsburgh, USA, 1976–78, Visiting Asst Prof., Dept of Psychology 1981–82; Assoc. Prof., Dept of Behavioral Science, Faculty of Letters, Hokkaido Univ. 1985–88; Visiting Prof., McGill Univ., Canada 1990; Pres. Japan Asscn of Pvt. Colls and Univs 2003, Fed. of Japanese Pvt. Colls and Univs Asscns 2003; Chair. Fed. of All Japan Pvt. Schools Asscns 2003; Gen. Man. 'Biosimulation' Leading Project, Ministry of Educ., Culture, Sports, Science and Tech.; Chair. Sub-div. on Cen. Council for Educ.; mem. Science Council of Japan, Admin. Council Univ. of Tsukuba, Council of Univ. Man., Tohoku Univ., Strategic Council on Intellectual Property, Cabinet Office; mem. Council for Univ. Establishment and School Corpn, Ministry of Educ., Culture, Sports, Science and Tech.; Exec. Dir Research Org. of Information and Systems, Governing Bd Japan Asscn for Philosophy of Science; Vice-Chair. Asscn of Pacific Rim Univs (Vice-Chair. Steering Cttee); Pres. Information Processing Soc. of Japan; fmr Pres. Japanese Cognitive Science Soc.; fmr mem. Council Bd Japan Soc. for Philosophy of Science, Council Bd Japan Soc. for Neuroscience; fmr Dir The Soc. of Instrument and Control Engineers, Japan Soc. for Eng Educ.; fmr mem. Life Science Cttee Council for Science and Tech., Informatics Cttee Council for Science and Tech.; Commdr, Ordre des Palmes académiques 2005; Dr hc (Ecole Centrale de Nantes, France) 2007; Best Tech. Paper Award, Soc. for Instrumental and Control Engineers 1972, Best Paper Award, Information Processing Soc. of Japan 1988, Achievement Award, Japanese Soc. for Artificial Intelligence 2001. *Address:* Office of the President, Keio University, 2-15-45 Mita, Minato-ku, Tokyo 108-8345, Japan (office). *Telephone:* (3) 5427-1627 (office). *Fax:* (3) 5427-1626 (office). *E-mail:* president@info.keio.ac.jp (office). *Website:* www.pre.keio.ac.jp (office).

AOKI, Mikio; Japanese politician; *Chairman, LDP Diet Affairs Committee, House of Councillors;* b. 8 June 1934, Taisha; m. Reiko Aoki; two s. one d.; ed Waseda Univ., Tokyo; Sec. to Noboru Takeshita 1958–66; Pres. Taisha Fishery Co-operative 1966; mem. Shimane Prefectural Ass. 1967–86; mem. House of Councillors 1986–; mem. Special Cttee on Disasters, Budget Cttee, Special Cttee on Land and Environment; Vice-Chair. LDP Diet Affairs Cttee 1986; Parl. Vice-Minister of Finance 1991; Chair. House of Councillors Cttee on Agric., Forestry and Fisheries 1994; Deputy Sec.-Gen. LDP, Upper House Sec.-Gen. 1998; Chief Cabinet Sec. and Dir.-Gen. Okinawa Devt Agency 1999–2000; elected to House of Councillors 2001–, Dir-Gen. Personnel Bureau, Chair. Fed. of Kyoto Prefecture Liberal Democratic Party Brs, Chair. LDP Diet Affairs Committee, House of Councillors 2002–; Chair. LDP Fed. of Shimane Pref. 1989, Shimane Fed. of Land Improvement Asscns 1995. *Leisure interests:* golf, reading. *Address:* c/o Liberal-Democratic Party—LDP (Jiyu-Minshuto), 1-11-23, Nagata-cho, Chiyoda-ku, Tokyo 100-8910, Japan (office). *Telephone:* (3) 3581-6211 (office). *Website:* www.jimin.jp (office).

AOUN, Gen. Michel; Lebanese politician and fmr army officer; *President, Free Patriotic Movement Party;* b. 18 Feb. 1935, Haret Hreik; m. Nadia El Chami; three d.; attended Christian school, Beirut; enrolled in mil. school 1955; trained as artilleryman; training courses Châlons-sur-Marne, France 1958–59, Fort Seale, USA 1966, Ecole Supérieure de Guerre, France 1978–80; became Brigade Gen. 1984; C-in-C of Army 1984; following abandoned presidential elections of Sept. 1988, outgoing Pres. Gemayel named him prime minister of interim mil. admin; following assassination of Pres. Mouawad in Nov. 1989, he refused to accept authority of successor, Pres. Elias Hrawi; evicted from Baabda Presidential Palace by Syrian forces, refuge in French Embassy 1990–91, in exile in France 1991; returned to Lebanon May 2005, elected mem. Majlis Alnwab (Nat. Ass.) June 2005; Head of Change and Reform Parliamentary Bloc 2005–; Pres. Free Patriotic Movement Party. *Publications:* Une Certaine Vision du Liban 2007. *Address:* Street 17th, Rabieht, Lebanon (office). *E-mail:* claudineaoun@gmail.com (office). *Website:* www.tayyar.org (office).

APANG, Gegong; Indian politician; b. 8 July 1949, Rumgong; Minister of Agric. 1977–78; Chief Minister of Arunachal Pradesh 1980–99, 2003–07; mem. Lok Sabha (Parl.) 1998–99; Leader United Democratic Front (later merged with Bharatiya Janata Party) 2003–04; joined Indian National Congress 2004. *Address:* c/o Chief Minister's Secretariat, Itanagar, Arunachal Pradesh, India.

APEL, Karl-Otto, DPhil; German academic; *Professor Emeritus of Philosophy, University of Frankfurt am Main;* b. 15 March 1922, Düsseldorf; s. of Otto Apel and Elisabeth Gerritzen; m. Judith Jahn 1953; three d.; ed Univs of Bonn and Mainz; Prof. of Philosophy, Univ. of Kiel 1962–69, Univ. of Saarbrücken 1969–72, Univ. of Frankfurt am Main 1972–90, Prof. Emer. 1990–; many hon. degrees; Galileo Galilei Int. Prize 1988, F. Nietzsche Int. Prize 1989. *Publications include:* Idee der Sprache in der Tradition des Humanismus 1963, Transformation der Philosophie (translated as Towards a Transformation of Philosophy 1980) 1973, Der Denkweg von C. Peirce (translated as Charles Peirce: From Pragmatism to Pragmaticism 1981) 1975, Die Erklären: Verstehen-Kontroverse in transzendentalpragmatischer Sicht (translated as Understanding and Expectation: A Transcendental Peripatetic Perspective 1984) 1979, Diskurs und Verantwortung (Vol. 1) 1988, (Vol. 2) 1999, Towards a Transcendental Semiotics (selected essays) 1994, Ethics and the Theory of Rationality (selected essays) 1996, Auseinandersetzungen 1998, From a Transcendental-Semiotic Point of View 1998, The Response of Discourse Ethics 2001. *Leisure interest:* history of art. *Address:* Am Schillertempel 6, 65527 Niedernhausen, Germany (home). *Telephone:* 06127-2170 (home). *Fax:* 06127-2058 (home). *E-mail:* karl-otto.apel@main-rheiner.de (home).

APELOIG, Yitzhak, BSc, MSc, PhD; Israeli research institute administrator and chemist; *President, Technion—Israel Institute of Technology;* b. 1 Sept. 1944, Buchara, Uzbekistan; m. Zipora Zaltzberg; two s.; ed Hebrew Univ. of Jerusalem; family emigrated to Israel 1947; Postdoctoral Research Fellow, Princeton Univ., NJ, USA 1974–76; joined Faculty of Chem., Technion—Israel Inst. of Tech., Haifa 1976, Full Prof. 1988–, Chair incumbent 1993–, Dean, Faculty of Chem. 1995–99, Pres. Technion—Israel Inst. of Tech. 2001–, mem. numerous Technion cttees, including Promotion and Tenure Cttees; Visiting DAAD (Deutscher Akademischer Austausch Dienst—German Academic Exchange Service) Fellow and Prof., Universität Erlangen-Nornberg 1979, 1985, 1992; Visiting Prof., Tel-Aviv Univ. 1983, 1986, Cornell Univ., Ithaca, NY, USA 1983–84; Louis Klein Visiting Professorship in Australian Univs 1986; Visiting DAAD Prof., Technische Universität Berlin 1985, 1991; Visiting JSPS (Japan Soc. for the Promotion of Science) Prof., Kyushu Univ. 1991, Sendai Univ. 1999; Visiting Alexander von Humboldt Prof. 1994, Technische Universität Berlin and Universität Ulm 1997; Visiting Prof., Univ. of Utah, Salt Lake City, USA 2000; Co-founder and Co-Dir Lise Meitner Center for Computational Chem. 1996–; Chair. Asscn of Univ. Pres in Israel 2004; Chair. IUPAC Conf. on Physical Organic Chem., Haifa 1990, Fourth World Congress of Theoretically Oriented Chemists, Jerusalem 1996, Symposium on Frontiers in Electronic Structure Calculations, Haifa 1998; mem. numerous nat. scientific cttees and scientific advisory cttees of int. confs; mem. Acting Bd Israel Chemical Soc.; mem. Editorial Bds Journal of the Chemical Society, Perkin Transactions II, Progress in Physical Organic Chemistry, Journal of Computational Chemistry, Theoretical Chemical Accounts, Silicon Chemistry, Molecules; Dr hc (Tech. Univ. of Berlin) 2006; Pres.'s Prize for Distinction in Chem. Studies, Hebrew Univ., Jerusalem, Yashinski Prize for Distinguished PhD Thesis, Hebrew Univ. 1974, Bat-Sheba de Rothschild Fellow 1977–78, Technion Award for Academic Excellence 1988, Henri Gutwirth Prize for Excellence in Research, Technion 1991, 1993, Sr Scientist Exchange Fellow (Italy) 1993, granted a Minerva Center in Computational Quantum Chem. 1996, Distinguished Teacher Award, Technion Student Asscn 1986,

1993, 1997, JSPS Sr Visiting Prof. Award 1991, 1999, Alexander von Humboldt–Lise Meitner Sr Research Award 1994–99, Coulson Lecturer, Univ. of Georgia, USA 2002, Israel Chemical Soc. Prize 2002. *Publications:* more than 170 publs in int. scientific journals on organosilicon chem., computational chem., mechanistic organic chem., reactive intermediates; co-ed four books (with Z. Rappoport) on Chemistry of Organic Silicon Compounds, one book (with Z. Rappoport) on Chemistry of Organic Germanium, Tin and Lead Compounds and two special journal issues dedicated to computational chem. *Address:* Office of the President, Technion—Israel Institute of Technology, Technion City, Haifa 32000, Israel (office). *Telephone:* (4) 8292595 (office); (4) 8292597 (office). *Fax:* (4) 8292000 (office). *E-mail:* president@tx.technion.ac.il (office). *Website:* www.technion.ac.il/technion/chemistry/staff/apeloig (office).

APICELLA, Lorenzo Franco, BA, DipArch, RIBA, FCSD, FRSA; Italian architect and designer; *Partner, Pentagram Design Ltd;* b. 4 Feb. 1957, Ravello; s. of Belfiore Carmine Apicella and Carmina Apicella (née Nolli); ed Univ. of Nottingham, Canterbury Coll. of Art, Royal Coll. of Art, UK; Asst Architect, Skidmore Owings & Merill, Houston, Tex., USA 1981; Project Architect, CZWG Architects, London 1982; Consultant Architect, Visiting Lecturer, Canterbury Coll. of Art 1983–86; Head of Architecture Interiors and Exhbn Design, Imagination, London 1986–89, f. Apicella Assocs Architecture & Design, London 1989; Pnr, Pentagram Design Ltd, London 1998–2006, 2008–, Pnr Pentagram Design San Francisco 2006–08; contrib. to TV and radio programmes; Design Week Annual Awards Winner 1990, 1991, Designers Minerva Award 1993, RIBA Award 1999, Aluminium Imagination Awards 1993, 1997, IDSA Award 2001, Art Directors Club 80th Annual Awards 2001. *Address:* Pentagram, 11 Needham Road, London, W11 2RP (office); 29 Saville Road, London, W4 5HG, England (home). *Telephone:* (20) 7229-3477 (office); (20) 8995-1552 (home). *Fax:* (20) 7727-9932 (office). *E-mail:* apicella@pentagram.co.uk (office). *Website:* www.pentagram.com (office).

APONTE MARTÍNEZ, HE Cardinal Luis; American (Puerto Rican) ecclesiastic; b. 4 Aug. 1922, Lajas; s. of Santiago Evangelista Aponte and Rosa Martinez; ed St Ildefonso Seminary, San Juan and St John's Seminary, Boston, Mass, USA; ordained priest 1950; Curate, Patillas, then Pastor of Santa Isabel; Sec. to Bishop McManus, Vice-Chancellor of Diocese of Ponce 1955–57; Pastor of Aibonito 1957–60; Chaplain to Nat. Guard 1957–60; Auxiliary Bishop of Ponce and Titular Bishop of Lares 1960–63; Bishop of Ponce 1963–64; apptd. Archbishop of San Juan 1964; created Cardinal by Pope Paul VI 1973; Dir of Devt for Catholic Univ. of Puerto Rico 1960–63, fmr Chancellor; Pres. Puerto Rican Episcopal Conf. 1966; Hon. LLD (Fordham) 1966; Hon. STD (Inter-American Univ. of Puerto Rico) 1969. *Address:* Urb. San Ignacio, 1763 San Alejandro, San Juan, Puerto Rico 00927-6814. *Telephone:* (787) 274-8956 (home). *Fax:* (787) 751-5112 (home).

APPEL, Frank, MSc, PhD; German scientist and business executive; *Chairman and CEO, Deutsche Post World Net;* b. 1961; ed Univ. of Munich, Eidgenössische Technische Hochschule (ETH), Zurich, Switzerland; Consultant and Project Man. Dir, McKinsey & Co., Frankfurt/Main 1993–99, Partner-mem. German Business Man., McKinsey & Co. 1999–2000; Man. Dir, Corp. Devt, Deutsche Post AG 2000–02, mem. Man. Bd Deutsche Post World Net in charge of int. mail and logistics div. 2002–08, Chair. and CEO 2008–, Chair. Supervisory Bd Deutsche Postbank AG; mem. Bd of Dirs Williams Lea Holdings PLC, Williams Lea Group Ltd, Exel Investment Ltd, Exel Ltd, Tibbett & Britten Group Ltd. *Address:* Deutsche Post World Net, Charles-de-Gaulle-Strasse 20, 53113 Bonn, Germany (office). *Telephone:* (228) 182-630-01 (office). *Fax:* (228) 182-630-99 (office). *E-mail:* info@dpwn.de (office). *Website:* www.dpwn.de (office).

APPIAH, Kwame Anthony Akroma-Ampim Kusi, PhD; American (b. British) academic and writer; *Laurance S. Rockefeller University Professor of Philosophy and the University Center for Human Values, Princeton University;* b. 8 May 1954, London; s. of Joe Appiah and Peggy Appiah; partner, Henry David Finder; ed Ullenwod Manor School for Boys, Port Regis and Bryanston School, UK, Kwame Nkrumah Univ. of Science and Tech., Ghana, Univ. of Cambridge, UK; raised in Ghana; taught at Univ. of Ghana; has held position of Prof. of Philosophy and/or Prof. of African Studies and African-American Studies at Univ. of Cambridge, Yale Univ., Cornell Univ., Duke Univ., Harvard Univ. 1991–2002; Laurance S. Rockefeller Univ. Prof. of Philosophy and Univ. Center for Human Values, Princeton Univ. 2002–; Juror, Neustadt Prize, Univ. of Oklahoma 2001; mem. American Philosophical Soc. 2001, American Acad. of Arts and Letters 2008; Hon. DLitt (Richmond) 2000, (Colgate) 2003, (Bard Coll.) 2004, (Fairleigh Dickinson) 2006, (Swarthmore Coll.) 2006, (Dickinson Coll.) 2008; Phi Beta Kappa Speaker, Harvard Commencement 2000, Tanner Lecturer, Cambridge Univ. 2001; Annisfield-Wolf Book Award 1993, Herskovits Award, African Studies Asscn 1993, Annual Book Award, N American Soc. for Social Philosophy 1996, Ralph J. Bunche Award, American Political Science Asscn 1997, Gustavus Myers Center Award 1997, Morehouse Coll. Candle in the Dark Award in Educ. 2003, Arthur Ross Book Award, Council on Foreign Relations 2007, Joseph B. and Toby Gittler Prize 2008. *Publications include:* Assertion and Conditionals 1985, For Truth in Semantics 1986, Necessary Questions: An Introduction to Philosophy 1989, Avenging Angel (novel) 1991, In My Father's House: Africa in the Philosophy of Culture (essays) (Annisfield-Wolf Book Award 1993, African Studies Asscn Herskovits Award 1993) 1992, Nobody Likes Letitia (novel) 1994, Another Death in Venice (novel) 1995, Color Consciousness: The Political Morality of Race (with Amy Gutman) (North American Soc. for Social Philosophy Annual Book Award) 1996, The Ethics of Identity 2005, Cosmopolitanism: Ethics in a World of Strangers (Council on Foreign Relations Arthur Ross Award) 2006, Experiments in Ethics 2007; Ed.: Early African-American Classics 1990; Co-Ed. with Henry Louis Gates, Jr: Critical Perspectives Past and Present (series) 1993, Identities (essays) 1995, The Dictionary of Global Culture 1996, Africana: The Encyclopedia of African and African American Experience 1999; with Peggy Appiah: Bu Me Bé: The Proverbs of the Akan; with Martin Bunzl: Buying Freedom 2007. *Address:* Department of Philosophy, 208 Marx Hall, Princeton University, Princeton, NJ 08544-1006, USA (office). *Telephone:* (609) 258-4302 (office). *Fax:* (609) 258-1502 (office). *E-mail:* kappiah@princeton.edu (office); anthony_appiah@msn.com (home). *Website:* web.princeton.edu/sites/philosph (office); www.appiah.net (home).

APPLEBY, Malcolm Arthur; British artist; b. 6 Jan. 1946, Beckenham, Kent; s. of James William Appleby and Marjory Stokes; m. Philippa Swann; one d.; ed Hansdown Co. Secondary Modern School, Beckenham School of Art, Ravensbourne Coll. of Art, Cen. School of Arts and Crafts, Sir John Cass School of Art, RCA; career artist, designer and engraver; Littledale Scholar 1969, Liveryman Worshipful Co. of Goldsmiths 1991; Hon. DLitt (Heriot-Watt) 2000. *Leisure interests:* garden, work, family. *Address:* Aultbeag, Grandtully, Perthshire, PH15 2QU, Scotland. *Telephone:* (1887) 840484. *Fax:* (1887) 840785 (home).

APPLEWHAITE, Lolita; Barbadian government official, international organization executive and academic; *Deputy Secretary-General, Caribbean Community and Common Market (CARICOM);* fmr Perm. Sec., Ministry of Educ., Youth and Culture; fmr Dir Centre for Int. Services, Univ. of the West Indies, Mona, Jamaica; fmr Deputy Regional Authorising Officer, Caribbean Community (CARICOM) Secr., Georgetown, Guyana, currently Deputy Sec.-Gen. *Address:* Caribbean Community Secretariat, PO Box 10827, Turkeyen Greater, Georgetown, Guyana (office). *Telephone:* (2) 222-0001 (office). *Fax:* (2) 222-0171 (office). *E-mail:* info@caricom.org (office). *Website:* www.caricom.org (office).

APPY, Bernard; Brazilian economist and banker; *Chairman, Banco do Brasil SA;* ed Faculty of Econs, Univ. of Sao Paolo; fmr Prof. of Econs, Pontificia Universidade Catolica do Sao Paolo (PUC-SP), Unicamp; Pnr Luciano Coutinho & Assocs (LCA—consultancy) 1995–2002; joined Ministry of Finance 1994, served as Sec. for Econ. Policies 2005–06, Deputy Minister of Finance 2003–05, 2006–08; Econ. Advisor to Pres. of Brazil 2008–; currently Chair. Banco do Brasil SA; fmr mem. Bd of Dirs The Brazilian Devt Bank (BNDES). *Address:* Banco do Brasil SA, SBS Qd. 01 Bloco C - Edifício Sede III, 24th Floor, 70073-901 Brasília, DF, Brazil (office). *Telephone:* (61) 310-3409 (office). *Fax:* (61) 310-2561 (office). *Website:* www.bb.com.br/appbb/portal/index.jsp (office).

APTED, Michael David; British film director; b. 10 Feb. 1941, Aylesbury; m. 1st (divorced); two s.; m. 2nd Dana Stevens; one s.; ed Downing Coll., Cambridge; started career as researcher, Granada TV 1963, then worked as investigative reporter for World in Action; feature film dir 1970s–. *Films include:* The Triple Echo 1972, Stardust 1975, The Squeeze 1977, Agatha 1979, The Coal Miner's Daughter 1980, Continental Divide 1981, P'TangYang Kipperbang, Gorky Park 1983, Firstborn 1984, Critical Condition, Gorillas in the Mist 1988, Class Action 1990, Incident at Oglala, Thunderheart 1992, Blink 1993, Moving the Mountain 1993, Nell 1994, Extreme Measures 1996, Inspirations 1997, Me and Isaac Newton 1999, The World Is Not Enough 1999, Enigma 2001, Enough 2002, Lipstick 2002, Amazing Grace 2006. *Television includes:* (dir) episodes of Coronation Street, comedy series The Lovers, children's series Folly Foot, Another Sunday and Sweet F.A., Kisses at Fifty, Poor Girl, Jack Point, Up documentary series including 28 Up and 35 Up, 42: Forty-two Up 1998, Always Outnumbered 1998, Nathan Dixon 1999, Married in America 2002, Rome (series, Dirs Guild of America Best Director of Dramatic Series 2006) 2005, 49 Up 2005. *Publications:* 7 Up 1999. *Address:* United Agents, 12–26 Lexington Street, London, W1F 0LE, England (office). *Telephone:* (20) 3214-0800 (office). *Fax:* (20) 3214-0801 (office). *E-mail:* info@unitedagents.co.uk (office). *Website:* unitedagents.co.uk (office).

AQUINO, (Maria) Corazon (Cory), BA; Philippine fmr politician and fmr head of state; b. 25 Jan. 1933, Tarlac Prov.; d. of José Cojuangco, Sr; m. Benigno S. Aquino, Jr 1954 (assassinated 1983); one s. four d.; ed Raven Hill Acad., Philadelphia, Notre Dame School, New York, Mount St Vincent Coll., New York; in exile in USA with her husband 1980–83; mem. United Nationalist Democratic Org. (UNIDO) 1985–; Pres. of the Philippines (after overthrow of régime of Ferdinand Marcos) 1986–92; Founder and Chair. Benigno S. Aquino Foundation; Chair. Emer. PinoyME Foundation; f. People Power Movt 2003; mem. Bd of Dirs Sanyo Electric Co. Ltd (first woman and first non-Japanese); mem. Bd of Govs Asian Inst. of Man.; Trustee Children's Hour; numerous hon. doctorates; William Fulbright Prize for Int. Peace 1996, Ramon Magsaysay Award for Int. Understanding 1998, David Rockefeller Award for Bridging Leadership 2005. *Address:* c/o People Power People Movement, Unit 2C Classica I Building, H.V. dela Costa Street, Salcedo Village, Makati City, Metro Manila, Philippines. *Website:* www.coryaquino.ph.

ARAD, Ron; British designer and architect; *Professor of Design Product, Royal College of Art;* b. 24 April 1951, Tel-Aviv, Israel; ed Jerusalem Acad. of Art and Architectural Asscn; Founder One Off Ltd 1981–94, Ron Arad Assocs 1989–; Prof. of Product Design, Hochschule, Vienna 1994–97; Prof. of Design Product, RCA 1997–; Oribe Art and Design Award, Japan 2001, Giò Ponti Int. Design Award, Denver, CO 2001, Barcelona Primavera Int. Award for Design 2001, Architektur & Wohnen Designer of the Year 2004. *Exhibitions:* Nouvelles Tendences, Centre Georges Pompidou 1989, Ron Arad Recent Works, Tel-Aviv Museum of Art 1990, One Off and Short Runs, Centre for Contemporary Arts (Warsaw, Kraków, Prague) 1993, L'Esprit du Nomade, Cartier Foundation, Paris 1994, Sticks and Stones, Vitra Design Museum, Touring Exhbn 1990–95, Ron Arad at the Powerhouse Museum, Sydney 1997,

Before and After Now, Victoria and Albert Museum 2000, Delight in Dedark, Galeria Marconi 2001, Paperwork, Galeria Marconi 2002, Centre d'Art Santa Monica, Barcelona 2003, Von Mensch zu Mensch, Sparda Bank, Münster 2003, Ron Arad Studio Works 1981–2003, Louisa Guinness Gallery, London 2003, Ron Arad in der Galerie Stefan Vodgt, Galerie der Moderne, Munich 2003, *Lo-rez-dolores-tabula-rasa*, Galeria Marconi 2004. *Leisure interests:* tennis, ping-pong. *Address:* Arad Associates, 62 Chalk Farm Road, London, NW1 8AN, England (office). *Telephone:* (20) 7284-4963 (office). *Fax:* (20) 7379-0499 (office). *E-mail:* info@ronarad.com (office). *Website:* www.ronarad.co.uk (office).

ARAGALL GARRIGA, Giacomo Jaime; Spanish singer (tenor); b. 6 June 1939, Barcelona; s. of Ramon Aragall and Paola Garriga; m. Luisa Aragall 1964; three s.; ed with Jaume Francisco Puig, Barcelona and Vladimiro Badiali, Milan; winner int. competition, Busseto; debut at Teatro La Fenice de Venezia, Palermo, Metropolitan, New York 1968; has sung in more than 100 opera productions at Gran Teatre del Liceu; numerous prizes include Peseta de Oro and Medalla de Plata for appearing at 1992 Olympics, Barcelona, Medalla de Oro de Bellas Artes 1992, etc. *Performances include:* El Amico Fritz, La Bohème (La Scala, Milan), Madame Butterfly, La Favorita, La Traviata, Faust, Tosca, etc. *Address:* 2wise Artist Management, Ronda Sant Pere 29 2°- 3ª, 08010 Barcelona, Spain (office). *Telephone:* (93) 3041168 (office); 630 021 281 (mobile) (office). *E-mail:* miguelpons@2wiseartist.com (office). *Website:* www.2wiseartist.com (office).

ARAGHCHI, (Seyed) Abbas, BA, MA, PhD; Iranian diplomatist; *Ambassador to Japan;* b. 1962, Tehran; m. Bahareh Araghchi; three c.; ed School of Int. Relations, Tehran, Azad Univ., Univ. of Kent, UK; expert, Int. Affairs Div., Ministry of Foreign Affairs 1988–91, Deputy Dir for Islamic Forums, Regional and Non-Aligned Movt 1991–92, Chargé d' Affairs, Perm. Mission to Org. of Islamic Conf., Jeddah, Saudi Arabia 1992; Sr Researcher, Inst. for Political and Int. Studies (research inst. affiliated to Ministry of Foreign Affairs) 1995–97, Head, Center for Persian Gulf and Middle East Studies 1997–98, Dir Gen. 1998–2000, Editor in Chief Journal of Foreign Policy 1998–99; Lecturer, Faculty of International Relations 1995–99, Rector 2003–05; Amb. to Finland (also accred to Estonia) 1999–2003; Dir Western Europe Affairs, Foreign Ministry 2003–05; Deputy Foreign Minister for Legal and Int. Affairs 2005–08; Amb. to Japan 2008–. *Address:* Embassy of Iran, 3-13-9, Minami Azabu, Minato-ku, Tokyo 106-0047, Japan (office). *Telephone:* (3) 3446-8011 (office). *Fax:* (3) 3446-9002 (office). *E-mail:* sjei@gol.com (office). *Website:* www.iranembassyjp.com (office).

ARAGONA, Giancarlo, LLB; Italian diplomatist; *Ambassador to UK;* b. 14 Nov. 1942, Messina; ed Univ. of Messina; joined Ministry of Foreign Affairs, Rome 1969, First Sec., Vienna 1972–74, Consul, Italian Consulate, Freiburg 1974–77, Counsellor, Lagos 1977–80, Directorate-Gen. for Political Affairs, Ministry of Foreign Affairs 1980, later Dept for Co-operation and Devt, First Counsellor, London 1984–87, First Counsellor, Perm. Mission of Italy to NATO, Brussels 1987–92, Diplomatic Adviser, Ministry of Defence 1992–94, Deputy Head of Staff to Foreign Minister 1994–95, Head of Staff 1995–96, Sec.-Gen. OSCE, Vienna 1996–99, Amb. to Russia 1999–2001, Dir-Gen. for Multilateral Political Affairs and Human Rights 2001–04, Amb. to UK 2004–; Hon. KCVO. *Address:* Embassy of Italy, 14 Three Kings Yard, London, W1K 4EH, England (office). *Telephone:* (20) 7312-2200 (office). *Fax:* (20) 7313-2230 (office). *E-mail:* ambasciata.londra@esteri.it (office). *Website:* www.amblondra.esteri.it (office).

ARAIZA ANDRADE, Francisco José; Mexican singer (tenor) and teacher; *Professor, Stuttgart Musikhochschule, Opernstudio Zurich; Head, International Hugo Wolf Akademie;* b. 4 Oct. 1950, Mexico City; s. of José Araiza and Guadalupe Andrade; m. 1st Vivian Jaffray (divorced); one s. one d.; m. 2nd Ethery Inasaridse; one s. one d.; ed Univ. of Mexico City and Nat. School of Music, Mexico City and Munich Acads of Music; first engagement as lyric tenor in Karlsruhe, Germany 1974; debut as Ferrando in Così fan Tutte 1975; debut at Zurich Opera House with Almaviva 1976, perm. mem. 1978–; has become one of the leading tenors world-wide, performing at all the major opera houses in London, Paris, Munich, Berlin, Madrid, Barcelona, Milan, Parma, New York, Chicago, San Francisco, as well as recitals accompanied by piano or orchestra; named Kammersänger by Vienna State Opera 1988; has participated in festivals of Salzburg (debut under von Karajan 1980), Hohenems, Bayreuth, Edinburgh, Pesaro, Verona, Macerata, Aix-en-Provence, Orange, Garmisch; Prof., Stuttgart Musikhochschule 2003–, Int. Opernstudio, Zurich 2005–; Head of Int. Hugo Wolf Akad. 2007–; Deutscher Schallplattenpreis, Orphée d'Or, Mozart Medal, Univ. of Mexico City, Otello d'Oro, Goldener Merkur, Best Performer Award, Munich 1996, Dr A. Ortiz Tirado Medal (Sonora, Mexico) 2008. *Films include:* videos: Manon, Faust, La Cenerentola (two), Falstaff, Die Entführung aus dem Serail, Don Giovanni, Die Schöpfung, Recital Tokio, Die Zauberflöte (two), Così fan tutte, Mozart Gala Verona 1 & 2, Bach Magnificat, Francisco Araiza – I am a Romantic, Fast ein Gentleman. *Television includes:* Melodien zum Muttertag 2000, Gala der Europahilfe 2000, Kein Schöner Land 2000, Zauber der Musik mit André Rieu 2002, Sternstunden der Musik 2003. *Recordings include:* The Magic Flute, Faust, Das Lied von der Erde, Die schöne Müllerin, Don Giovanni, Idomeneo, Rossini's Messa di Gloria, 200 Jahre La Fenice, Die Winterreise, La Bohème, Berlioz' Requiem. *Address:* c/o Opern-Agentur und Artists' Mgt Lewin, Tal 28, 80331 Munich, Germany (office). *Telephone:* (89) 29161662 (office). *Fax:* (89) 29161667 (office). *E-mail:* tschaidse@opern-agentur.com (office); faraiza@aol.com (home). *Website:* www.opern-agentur.de (office); www.francisco-araiza.ch (home).

ARAKAWA, Shoshi, BA; Japanese business executive; *Chairman, President, CEO and Representative Director, Bridgestone Corporation;* b. 8 April 1944; ed Tokyo Univ.; joined Bridgestone Tire Co. 1968, Man. Exec. Secretarial Office 1988–91, Gen. Man. F21 Planning and Promotion Project Group 1991–92, Man. Dir Bridgestone Tire Co. Thailand 1992–97, mem. Bd of Dirs 1997–, Gen. Man. China Dept 1997–2001, Dir Asia and Oceania Div. 1998–2001, CEO and Chair. Bridgestone/Firestone Europe SA 2001–06, Chair., Pres., CEO and Rep. Dir Bridgestone Corpn 2006–, also serves as Chief Risk-Management Officer. *Address:* Bridgestone Corpn, 10-1, Kyobashi 1-chome, Chuo-ku, Tokyo 104-8340, Japan (office). *Telephone:* (3) 3567-0111 (office). *Fax:* (3) 3535-2553 (office). *E-mail:* info@bridgestone.co.jp (office). *Website:* www.bridgestone.co.jp (office).

ARAKI, Minoru S. (Sam), BS, MS; American aeronautics engineer (retd); b. 12 July 1931, Saratoga, Calif.; ed Stanford Univ.; joined Lockheed Missiles & Space Co. in 1958 as Sr Scientist, held numerous positions including Asst Chief Engineer, Devt 1975–76, Dir Systems Eng 1976–78, Dir Advanced Systems, Space Systems Division (SSD) 1978–83, Vice-Pres. Space Systems Div., Vice-Pres. and Program Man. Milstar programs 1983, Vice-Pres. and Asst Gen. Man. SSD 1985–87, Pres. and Gen. Man. SSD 1987–88, also a Vice-Pres. of Lockheed Corpn, Exec. Vice-Pres. Lockheed's Missiles and Space Systems Group 1988–95, Pres. Lockheed Martin Missiles & Space Co. 1995–2007 (retd); mem. Nat. Acad. of Eng; Fellow, American Astronautical Soc.; AIAA Von Braun Award for Excellence in Space Program Man. 2004, Charles Stark Draper Prize, Nat. Acad. of Eng (co-recipient) 2005, named a Pioneer of Nat. Reconnaissance by Nat. Reconnaissance Office. *Address:* c/o National Academy of Engineering, 500 Fifth Street, NW, Washington, DC 20001, USA.

ARAM I (KESHISHIAN), His Holiness, Catholicos of Cilicia, PhD; Lebanese ecclesiastic; b. 1947; ed Seminary of the Armenian Apostolic Church, Antelias, Near East School of Theology, Beirut, American Univ. of Beirut, Fordham Univ., New York, USA, WCC Graduate School of Ecumenical Studies, Bossey, Switzerland, Univ. of Oxford, UK; ordained priest 1968; named to WCC Faith and Order Comm. 1975; locum tenens of diocese of Lebanon 1978; Primate 1979; ordained Bishop 1980; elected to Cen. Cttee of WCC 1983, youngest person and first Orthodox to be elected Moderator of Cen. Cttee of WCC 1991–2005; Catholicos of the See of Cilicia of the Armenian Apostolic Church 1995–; mem. Oriental–Eastern Orthodox and Oriental Orthodox–Roman Catholic bilateral dialogues; Hon. mem. Pro-Oriente Catholic Ecumenical Foundation, Vienna, Austria. *Publications:* 12 publs including Conciliar Fellowship: A Common Goal 1990, The Challenge to be a Church in a Changing World 1997. *Address:* c/o World Council of Churches, 150 route de Ferney, POB 2100, 1211 Geneva 2, Switzerland (office).

ARAMBURUZABALA LARREGUI, María Asunción; Mexican business executive; *Vice-Chairman, Grupo Modelo;* d. of Pablo Aramburuzabala Ocaranza; m. 1st; two c.; m. 2nd Antonio O. Garza, Jr 2005; worked as accountant at Mexican securities firm; Pnr, Vice-Chair. and mem. Exec. Cttee Grupo Modelo SA de CV (brewing co.) 1996–; Vice-Chair. and mem. Exec. Cttee Grupo Televisa SA 2002; CEO Tresalia Capital SA de CV; mem. Bd of Dirs Grupo Financiero Banamex-Accival, SA de CV, Banco Nacional de Mexico, SA, America Movil, SA de CV; ranked by Fortune magazine amongst 50 Most Powerful Women in Business outside the US (14th) 2002, (13th) 2003, (11th) 2004, (14th) 2005, (14th) 2006, (26th) 2007, ranked by Forbes magazine amongst 100 Most Powerful Women (78th) 2004, (53rd) 2005. *Address:* Grupo Modelo SA de CV, Campos Elíseos #400, 8th Floor, Colonia Lomas de Chapultepec, 11000 Mexico City, DF (office); Grupo Televisa SA, 2000 Avenida Vasco De Quiroga Santa Fe, 01210 Mexico City, DF, Mexico (office). *Telephone:* (55) 5283-3600 (Grupo Modelo) (office); (55) 5261-2000 (Grupo Televisa) (office). *Fax:* (55) 5280-6718 (Grupo Modelo) (office); (55) 5261-2494 (Grupo Televisa) (office). *Website:* www.gmodelo.com.mx (office); www.televisa.com (office).

ARANA SEVILLA, Mario; Nicaraguan politician and banker; *President, Central Bank of Nicaragua;* Minister of Devt, Industry and Commerce –2005, of Finance and Public Credit 2005–06; currently Pres., Central Bank of Nicaragua; fmr Gov. for Nicaragua IMF, World Bank and IDB, Int. Finance Corpn. *Address:* Banco Central de Nicaragua, Carretera Sur, Km 7, Apdos 2252/3, Zona 5, Managua, Nicaragua (office). *Telephone:* (2) 65-0500 (office). *Fax:* (2) 65-0561 (office). *E-mail:* bcn@bcn.gob.ni (office). *Website:* www.bcn.gob.ni (office).

ARANGIO-RUIZ, Gaetano; Italian professor of law; b. 10 July 1919, Milan; s. of Vincenzo Arangio-Ruiz and Ester Mauri Arangio-Ruiz; ed Univ. of Naples; Prof. of Int. Law, Univ. of Camerino 1952–54, Univ. of Padua 1955–67, Univ. of Bologna 1968–74; Prof. of Int. Law, Univ. of Rome 1974–, now Prof. Emer.; mem. Iran-United States Claims Tribunal, The Hague 1989–; Visiting Prof., Virginia Univ. Law School 1965, European Cen., Johns Hopkins School of Advanced Int. Studies 1967–75; Lecturer, Hague Acad. of Int. Law 1962, 1972, 1977, 1984; mem. UN Int. Law Comm. 1985–96; Special Rapporteur on State Responsibility 1987–96; mem. Int. Law Inst.; Dr hc (Univ. Panthéon-Assas, Paris II, France) 1997; Giuseppe Capograssi Prize 1990, Scanno Law Prize 2001. *Publications include:* Rapporti contrattuali fra Stati e organizzazione internazionale 1950, Gli enti soggetti 1951, Sula dinamica della base sociale 1954, The Normative Role of the UN General Assembly (Hague Rec.) Vol. III 1972, Human Rights and Non-Intervention in the Helsinki Final Act (Hague Rec.) Vol. IV 1977, The UN Declaration on Friendly Relations and the System of the Sources of International Law 1979, le Domaine réservé, General Course in International Law (Hague Rec.) Vol. V 1990, Non-Appearance Before the International Court of Justice (report to the Int. Law Inst.) International Law Institute Yearbook 1991, On the Security Council's 'Law-Making', Rivista di Diritto Internazionale 2000, Dualism Revisited: International Law and Interindividual Law, Rivista di Diritto Internazionale 2003, Article 39 of the ILC First-Reading Articles on State Responsibility, *ibidem*, The ICJ Statute, The Charter and Forms of Legality Review of Security

Council Decisions, Liber Amicorum Cassese 2003, Customary Law, on the theory of 'spontaneous' international custom, Droit du Pouvoir, Pouvoir du Droit 2007, International Law and Interindividual Law: New Perspectives on the Divide Between National and International Law (co-eds J. Nijman and A. Nollkaemper) 2007, La Persona Internazionale dello Stato 2008. *Address:* c/o Iran-United States Claims Tribunal, Parkweg 13, 2585 JH The Hague, Netherlands (office); Corso Trieste 51, interno 4, 00198 Rome, Italy (home). *Telephone:* (70) 3520064 (office); (06) 8559720 (home); (70) 3551371 (Netherlands) (home); (0564) 819200 (Italy) (home). *Fax:* (70) 3502456 (office).

ARANGO, Jeronimo; Mexican (b. Spanish) retail industry executive; b. 1926, Spain; f. CIFRA retail chain (entered jt venture with Wal-Mart Stores in early 1990s and renamed Wal-Mart de México), fmr Chair. and CEO; mem. Bd of Dirs Wal-Mart 1997; owner of luxury resort in Acapulco, Mexico. *Address:* c/o Wal-Mart de México, SA de CV, Boulevard Manuel Avila Camacho 647, Delegación Miguel Hidalgo, 11220 México, DF, Mexico (office).

ARÁOZ ESPARZA, Ántero Flores; Peruvian lawyer, politician and academic; b. 28 Feb. 1942, Lima; ed Pontifical Catholic Univ. of Peru, Univ. of the Pacific, Nat. Univ. of San Marcos, Lima; Prof., Faculty of Law, Univ. of Lima, Faculty of Law, Univ. of St Martín de Porres, Inst. of Govt, Univ. of St Martín de Porres; visiting prof. at numerous univs; Expository Pres. Peruvian Inst. of Humanistic Studies; Dir Estudio Flores-Aráoz & Asociados S.C. de R.L.; Vice-Pres. Sociedad de Beneficencia Pública de Lima 1980–85; Vice-Pres. and Pres. Caja de Ahorros de Lima (Savings Bank of Lima) 1980–85; Pres. Lotteries of Lima and Callao 1980–85; Metropolitan Regidor of Lima 1987–89, Dir Caja Municipal de Crédito Popular; Nat. Deputy 1990–92, mem. Constituent Congress 1993–95, Congressman of the Repub. 1995–, re-elected 2000, 2001, 2006, fmr mem. Consultative Comm., Ministry of Integration, Consultative Comm., Sec. of State of Integration, Consultative Comm. of Integration, Ministry of Industries, Tourism and Integration; mem. Consultative Cttee, Constitutional Comm. of Congress 2006–07, Consultative Comm., Ministry of Justice, Pres. Congress of the Repub. 2004–05, Pres. Constitutional Comm. Regulation of the Congress of the Repub. 2005–06; Minister of Defence 2007–08 (resgnd); Rep. of Peru before the OAS 2007; Vice-Pres. Cttee against the Territory of the OAS 2007; mem. Peruvian Del. to Socio-Econ. Advisory Cttee (CAES) of Cartagena Agreement for several years; mem. and Pres. Partido Popular Cristiano –2007; mem. Unidad Nacional (Nat. Unity); columnist in various media; Hon. Prof. at several univs; Gran Cruz de la Orden José Gregorio Paz Soldán, Decoration 'Hipólito Unanue', Gran Cruz del Congreso de la República, Gran Cruz de la Orden del Sol; decorations from Colombia, Chile, Russian Fed. and Morocco; decorations of Peruvian Navy, Air Force, Nat. Police; Dr hc from several univs. *Publication:* Autoritarismo o Democracia 2006. *Address:* Unidad Nacional, Calle Ricardo Palma 1111, Miraflores, Lima, Peru (office). *Telephone:* (1) 2242773 (office).

ARARKTSYAN, Babken Gurgenovich, PhD; Armenian politician; *Chairman, Armat Movement;* b. 1944, Yerevan; m.; three c.; ed Yerevan State Univ., Moscow State Univ., Steklov Inst. of Math. USSR (now Russian) Acad. of Sciences; researcher, Computation Cen. and Inst. of Math. Armenian Acad. of Sciences 1968–75; researcher, Inst. of Scientific and Tech. Information 1975–77; concurrently Prof., Head of Dept Yerevan State Univ. 1977–; Chair. Armat Centre for Devt of Democracy and Civil Soc. 1999–; mem. Cttee Karabakh, mem. Exec. Bd of Armenian Nat. Movt 1988; mem., First Deputy Chair. Supreme Council of Armenia 1990–91, Chair. 1991–95; Chair. Armenian Parl. 1991–95; elected mem. Nat. Ass. Repub. of Armenia 1995–99, Chair. 1995–98; Chair. Armat Movt 1999–. *Publications:* over 30 scientific articles and textbooks. *Leisure interests:* music, literature, tennis. *Address:* Armat Centre, 26 Buzand Street, 375010 Yerevan (office); 3 Tamanian Street, #35, 375009 Yerevan, Armenia (home). *Telephone:* (10) 540512 (office); (10) 548440 (home). *Fax:* (10) 540511 (office); (10) 522099 (home). *E-mail:* armat@acc.am (office). *Website:* www.ac.am/~armat (office).

ARASKOG, Rand Vincent; American business executive; *Director, ITT Industries, Inc.;* b. 30 Oct. 1931, Fergus Falls, Minn.; s. of Randolph Victor Araskog and Hilfred Mathilda Araskog; m. Jessie Marie Gustafson 1956; one s. two d.; ed US Mil. Acad. and Harvard Univ.; special Asst to Dir, Dept of Defense, Washington, DC 1954–59; Dir Marketing, Aeronautical Div., Honeywell Inc., Minneapolis 1960–66; Vice-Pres. ITT, Group Exec. ITT Aerospace Electronics, Components and Energy Group, Nutley, NJ 1971–76; Pres. 1979–85, CEO ITT Corpn, New York 1979–80, Chair. Bd and Exec. and Policy Comms. 1980–98, also Dir, Chair., Pres., CEO ITT Holdings Inc., New York, 1995–98, mem. Bd Dirs ITT Industries 1980–, Chair. Nat. Security Telecommunications Advisory Cttee 1983–; mem. Bd of Dirs Rayonier, Inc., Int. Steel Group, Inc., Cablevision Systems Corpn; mem. Bd of Govs, Aerospace Industries Asscn, Exec. Council, Air Force Asscn; Officier, Légion d'honneur, Grand Officer Order of Merit (Italy). *Publications:* ITT Wars 1989, numerous articles. *Address:* ITT Industries Inc., 4 West Red Oak Lane, White Plains, NY 10604, USA (office). *Telephone:* (914) 641-2000 (office). *Fax:* (914) 696-2950 (office). *Website:* www.ittind.com (office).

ARASTOU, Seyed Mojtaba; Iranian diplomatist and international official; fmr Amb. and Perm. Rep. to UN, Vienna; fmr Amb. to Switzerland; fmr Dir-Gen. Protocol Dept, Ministry of Foreign Affairs; various positions with ECO, Sec.-Gen. 2002–03. *Address:* c/o Economic Co-operation Organization, 1 Golbon Alley, Kamranieh Street, POB 14155-6176, Tehran, Iran (office).

ARAÚJO, María Consuelo; Colombian politician; b. 1971, Cesar Prov.; m.; one c.; ed Externado Univ. of Colombia, Columbia Univ., New York, Univ. of Milan, Sorbonne, Paris; teaching asst, Externado Univ. of Colombia; Vice-Minister's Asst, Ministry of Law and Justice; Foreign Trade Adviser, Agricultural and Rural Devt Ministry; President's Asst, Communications Dept Chief, Housing Programme Dir, Rural and Industrial Bank; Commercial Dir Bermudez y Valenzuela Finance Co.; Botanic Garden Dir, Bogota; Recreation and Sports Inst. Dir, Bogota; Minister of Culture 2002–06, of Foreign Affairs 2006–07 (resgnd); mem. Bd of Dirs Bogota Aqueduct and Sewer Enterprise, Nat. Network of Botanical Gardens, Recreational and Sportive Local Inst., Capital Channel, Inst. for Childhood Protection; Ciudad de Bogota Civil Meritory Order. *Leisure interests:* music, film. *Address:* c/o Ministry of Foreign Affairs, Palacio de San Carlos, Calle 10a, No 5-51, Bogotá, DC, Colombia (office).

ARAÚJO PERDOMO, Fernando, DEng; Colombian politician and engineer; b. 1955, Cartagena; s. of Alberto Araújo Merlano and Judith Perdomo; m.; four s.; ed Javeriana Pontifical Univ.; Gen. Man. Empresas Públicas de Cartagena 1983–84; Dir Gen. Inmuebles Nacional 'MOPT' 1985–86; fmr Prof. of Engineering, Jorge Tadeo Lozano Univ., Univ. of Cartagena; Minister of Devt 1998–2000; captured and held hostage by Revolutionary Armed Forces of Colombia (FARC) 2000–06; Minister of Foreign Affairs 2007–08; unsuccessful cand. in Cartagena mayoral elections 1998; fmr Pres. Colombian Chamber of Construction (CAMACOL); fmr mem. Bd of Dirs El Universal (magazine), Hotel Las Américas Beach Resort. *Leisure interests:* sport, reading. *Address:* c/o Ministry of Foreign Affairs, Palacio de San Carlos, Calle 10a, No 5-51, Bogotá, DC, Colombia (office).

ARAZOV, Rejepbay; Turkmenistani geologist, politician and trade union official; b. 1947, Shakhman, Krasnovodsk region; ed Turkmen State Polytech. Inst.; joined Kumdagneft co. 1963; Minister of Petroleum, Natural Gas and Mineral Resources 1998–2000; Head of Admin. Balkan region 2000–01; Chair. Majlis (Parl.) 2001–02; Minister of Defence 2002–03, First Deputy Prime Minister –2003; Chair. Nat. Centre of Trade Unions of Turkmenistan 2003–. *Address:* c/o Ministry of Defence, ul. Nurberdy Pomma 15, Ashgabat, Turkmenistan.

ARBASINO, Alberto; Italian author, essayist and critic; b. 22 Jan. 1930, Voghera; ed Univ. of Milan; Ed. Italo Calvino 1957; began literary career writing reports for the weekly Il Mondo from Paris and London; also worked for newspapers Il Giorno and later Il Corriere della sera; has collaborated with la Repubblica since 1975; mem Group 63; hosted programme Match on RAI2 1977, Che tempo che fa by Fabio Fazio 2006; Deputy Italian Parl. (elected as ind. for Italian Republican Party) 1983–87; Cavaliere di Gran Croce Ordine al Merito della Repubblica Italiana 1995. *Publications:* Le piccole vacanze 1957, L'Anonimo lombardo 1959, Fratelli d'Italia 1963, Parigi o cara 1960, La narcisata – La controra 1964, Certi romanzi 1964, Grazie per le magnifiche rose 1966, La maleducazione teatrale 1966, Off-Off 1968, Due orfanelle 1968, Super Eliogabalo 1969, Sessanta posizioni 1971, I Turchi 1971, Certi romanzi – La Belle Epoque per le scuole 1977, Il principe costante 1972, La bella di Lodi 1972, Amate Sponde (con Mario Missiroli) 1974, Specchio delle mie brame 1974, La narcisata 1975, In questo Stato 1978, Un paese senza 1980, Matine 1983, Il meraviglioso, anzi 1985, La caduta dei tiranni 1990, Mekong 1994, Lettere da Londra 1997, Passeggiando tra i draghi addormentati 1997, Paesaggi italiani con zombi 1998, Le muse a Los Angeles 2000, Rap! 2001, Marescialle e libertini 2004, Dall'Ellade a Bisanzio 2006; most works later published in revised edns; contrib. to L'illustrazione italiana, Officina, Il Mondo, Tempo presente, Il Verri, Espresso, il Giorno, la Repubblica. *Address:* c/o La Repubblica Gruppo Editoriale L'Espresso Div. La, Piazza dell'Indipendenza 11B, 00185 Rome, Italy. *Telephone:* (06) 49821. *Fax:* (06) 49822923. *E-mail:* larepubblica@repubblica.it. *Website:* www.repubblica.it.

ARBATOV, Aleksander Arkadyevich, DrEcons; Russian geologist; b. 4 Sept. 1938, Moscow; ed Moscow Inst. of Oil; researcher, participated in geological expeditions Ministry of Geology, USSR 1960–62; researcher All-Union Research Inst. of Geological Studies 1962–76; Head of lab. All-Union Inst. of System Studies USSR (now Russian) Acad. of Sciences 1976–89; mem. staff Comm. on Natural Resources, Russian Acad. of Sciences 1989–, Chair. 1996–, currently Deputy Chair. Russian Acad. of Sciences; Deputy Chair. Council for the Study of Productive Forces of the Econ. Devt of Russia; mem. Russian Acad. of Natural Sciences 1993; Vice-Pres. Russian Asscn of Power Econs; mem. Int. Asscn of Power Econs; mem. editorial bd journals Natural Resources Forum, The Energy Journal. *Publications:* numerous scientific articles, Oil and Gas in the 15 Republics of the Former USSR (5 vol. treatise). *Address:* KEPS, Vavilova str. 7, 117822 Moscow (office); SOPS, ul. Vavilova 7, GSP-7, 117997 Moscow, Russia (office). *Telephone:* (495) 135-45-29 (KEPS) (office). *E-mail:* director@sops.ru (office). *Website:* sopssecretary.narod.ru (office).

ARBATOV, Aleksei Georgiyevich, DrHistSc; Russian politician; *Deputy Chairman, State Defence Committee;* b. 17 Jan. 1951, Moscow; s. of Georgiy Arkadyevich Arbatov (q.v.) and Svetlana Pavlovna Goriacheva; m.; one d.; ed Moscow Inst. of Int. Relations; researcher, then Head of Div., Inst. of World Econ. and Int. Relations (IMEMO), USSR (now Russian) Acad. of Sciences 1976–, Head Centre of Geopolitical and Mil. Prognoses 1992; Dir Centre on Disarmament and Strategic Stability of Asscn of Foreign Policy; adviser in different UN bodies; mem. State Duma (Parl.) 1993–99; Deputy Chair. State Defence Cttee 1994–; mem. faction Yabloko, mem. Cen. Council Yabloko Movt (now Yabloko Party). *Publications:* numerous papers and articles on problems with Russian foreign policy, int. relations and US political system. *Address:* State Duma of the Russian Federation, 1 Okhotny Ryad Street, 103265 Moscow, Russia (office). *Telephone:* (495) 292-80-23 (office). *Fax:* (495) 292-80-23 (office).

ARBATOV, Georgiy Arkadyevich, DHistSc; Russian administrator and academician; *Honorary Director, Institute for US and Canadian Studies, Russian Academy of Sciences;* b. 19 May 1923, Kherson; s. of Arkady Michailovich Arbatov and Anna Vasilievna Arbatova; m. Svetlana Pavlovna Goriacheva 1948; one s.; ed Moscow Inst. for Int. Relations; Soviet Army

1941–44; mem. CPSU 1943–91; ed. in publishing house for foreign literature and periodicals (Voprosy filosofii, Novoe vremya, Kommunist) 1949–60; Columnist Problems of Peace and Socialism 1960–62; Section Chief at Inst. of World Econ. and Int. Relations of USSR Acad. of Sciences 1962–64; worked for CPSU Cen. Cttee 1964–67; Dir Inst. for US and Canadian Studies (ISKRAN), USSR (now Russian) Acad. of Sciences 1967–95, Hon. Dir 1995–; Deputy USSR Supreme Soviet 1974–89; People's Deputy of the USSR 1989–91; personal adviser to Mikhail Gorbachev (q.v.) and other Soviet leaders including Brezhnev and Andropov and to Boris Yeltsin –1993; mem. Cen. Auditing Comm. of CPSU 1971–76; Cand. mem. and mem. CPSU Cen. Cttee 1976–89; mem. Palme Comm. 1980–91; mem. USSR (now Russian) Acad. of Sciences 1974; Order of the Red Star 1943; Badge of Honour 1962; Order of the October Revolution 1971; Order of Lenin 1975; Order of the Great Patriotic War, 1st Rank 1985. *Publications:* The System (published in USA) 1993 and other books and articles on history of Russian–American relations, disarmanent, world econs, including A Delayed Recovery 1991. *Address:* Institute for US and Canadian Studies, 2/3 Khlebny per., Moscow G-69, 121814, Russia (office). *Telephone:* (495) 290-58-75 (office). *Fax:* (495) 200-12-07 (office). *E-mail:* iskran@rambler.ru (office). *Website:* www.iskran.ru (office).

ARBER, Werner; Swiss microbiologist and academic; b. 1929, Gränichen, Aargau; m.; two c.; ed Aargau Gymnasium, Eidgenössische Technische Hochschule, Zürich and Univ. of Geneva; Asst at Lab. of Biophysics, Univ. of Geneva 1953–58 1960–62, Dozent, then Extraordinary Prof. of Molecular Genetics 1962–70; Research Assoc., Dept of Microbiology, Univ. of Southern California, USA 1958–59; Visiting Investigator, Dept of Molecular Biology Univ. of California, Berkeley 1970–71; Prof. of Microbiology, Univ. of Basel 1971–96, Rector 1986–88; Pres. Int. Council of Scientific Unions (ICSU) 1996–99; Nobel Prize for Physiology or Medicine (jtly) 1978. *Address:* c/o Department of Microbiology, Biozentrum der Universität Basel, 70 Klingelbergstrasse, 4056 Basel, Switzerland (office). *Telephone:* (61) 2672130. *Fax:* (61) 2672118.

ARBHABHIRAMA, Anat, PhD; Thai scientist; *Adviser to the Board of Directors, Bangkok Mass Transit System Public Company, Ltd.;* b. 13 Jan. 1938, Bangkok; s. of Arun Arbhabhirama and Pathumporn Arbhabhirama; m. Mrs Benjarata 1966; three s.; ed Chulalongkorn Univ., Bangkok, Asian Inst. of Tech., Bangkok, Colorado State Univ.; Vice-Pres. for Acad. Affairs and Provost, Asian Inst. of Tech. 1979–80; Deputy Minister of Agric. and Co-operatives 1980, Minister 1980–81; Head, Regional Research and Devt Center, Asian Inst. of Tech. 1981–84; Pres. Thailand Devt Research Inst. 1984–87; Chair. Intergovernmental Council of the Int. Hydrological Programme, UNESCO 1984–88; Gov. Petroleum Authority of Thailand 1987; Chair. PTT Exploration and Production Co. Ltd 1988, The Aromatics Co. Ltd (Thailand) 1990; currently Adviser to Bd of Dirs Bangkok Mass Transit System Public Co. Ltd; mem. Council of Trustees and Bd of Dirs Thailand Devt Research Inst. (TDRI), Petroleum Inst. of Thailand; Outstanding Researcher of the Year 1987, Companion (Fourth Class) of Most Admirable Order of Direkgunabhorn 2003. *Publications:* numerous articles and papers on water resources and hydraulics. *Leisure interests:* golf, jogging, chess. *Address:* c/o TDRI, 565 Ramkhamaeng 39 (Thepleela 1), Wangthonglang, Bangkok 10310, Thailand.

ARBIA, Silvana, LLD; Italian judge; *Registrar, International Criminal Court;* b. 1953; ed Univ. of Padua; prosecutor and judge in Venice, Rome and Milan Courts of Appeal 1979–; mem. Italian Del., Diplomatic Conf. on drafting statute of Int. Criminal Court Rome 1998; Judge, Supreme Court and Court of Cassation of Italy 1999; Sr Trial Attorney, Int. Criminal Tribunal for Rwanda 1999, becoming Acting Chief of Prosecutions and Chief of Prosecutions; Registrar, Int. Criminal Court, The Hague 2008–. *Publications:* several essays and books on human rights and children's rights. *Address:* International Criminal Court, Maanweg 174, 2516 AB The Hague, Netherlands (office). *Telephone:* (70) 515-85-15 (office). *Website:* www.icc-cpi.int (office).

ARBOUR, Louise, CC, BA, LLL; Canadian judge (retd) and UN official; b. 10 Feb. 1947, Montréal; one s. two d.; ed Collège Regina Assumpta, Montréal, Université de Montréal; articling, Legal Dept, City of Montréal 1970; called to Québec Bar 1971, Ont. Bar 1977; law clerk, Supreme Court of Canada 1971–72; Research Officer, Law Reform Comm. and mem. Criminal Procedure Project 1972; Lecturer in Criminal Procedure, Osgoode Hall Law School, York Univ., Toronto 1974, Asst Prof. 1975, Assoc. Prof. 1977–87, Assoc. Dean July–Dec. 1987; called to Bar, Ont. 1977; Judge, Supreme Court of Ont. (High Court of Justice) 1987–90; Judge, Court of Appeal for Ont. 1990–96; apptd by Order-in-Council as Commr to conduct inquiry into certain events at Prisons for Women, Kingston April 1995; Chief Prosecutor, Int. Criminal Tribunals for Fmr Yugoslavia and Rwanda, The Hague 1996–99; Puisne Judge, Supreme Court of Canada 1999–2004; UN High Commr for Human Rights 2004–08; Vice-Pres. Canadian Civil Liberties Asscn –1987; Lifetime mem. l'Asscn des jurists d'expression française de l'Ontario 1992–, Int. Council, Inst. for Global Legal Studies, Washington Univ. School of Law, Saint Louis, Mo. 2001; mem. Advisory Bd International Journal of Constitutional Law 2001–; mem. Bd of Eds Journal of International Criminal Justice 2003–; mem. Bd of Trustees, Int. Crisis Group 2000–; Hon. Prof., Univ. of Warwick, UK 1999–2004; Hon. mem. American Soc. of Int. Law 2000, Golden Key Nat. Honour Soc. 2000; Hon. Bencher Gray's Inn, London, England 2001; Hon. Fellow, American Coll. of Trial Lawyers 2003; Hon. LLD (York) 1995, (Law Soc. of Upper Canada, New Brunswick, Laurentian Univ., Université du Québec à Montréal) 1999, (Université Libre de Bruxelles, Univ. of Victoria, Kingston Royal Mil. Coll., Chicago-Kent Coll. of Law, Université de Montréal, McMaster Univ., Univ. of Western Ontario, Univ. of Toronto, Univ. of Glasgow, Queen's Univ., Carleton Univ.), (Mount Saint Vincent Univ., Univ. of King's Coll., Université de Moncton, Memorial Univ., St John's, Newfoundland, Windsor Univ., Con-

cordia Univ., Univ. of British Columbia) 2001, (Lakehead Univ.) 2002, (Université de Picardie Jules Verne, St Francis Xavier Univ., Antigonish, NS) 2003; Hon. DUniv (Ottawa) 1997; Médaille de l'Université de Montréal 1995, Achievement Award, Women's Law Asscn, Toronto 1996, G. Arthur Martin Award, Criminal Lawyers' Asscn 1998, First Recipient Toronto 1999 Medal of Honour, Int. Asscn of Prosecutors 1998, Medal of Honour, Int. Asscn of Prosecutors 1999, Médaille du Mérite, Institut de recherches cliniques de Montréal 1999, Fondation Louise Weiss Prize, Paris 1999, Second Annual Service to Humanity Award, Pennsylvania Bar Foundation 2000, Franklin and Eleanor Roosevelt Four Freedoms Medal (Freedom from Fear), Roosevelt Study Centre, Middleburg, Netherlands 2000, Women of Distinction Award, Toronto Hadassah-Wizo 2000, Peace Award, World Federalists of Canada 2000, Lord Reading Law Soc.'s Human Rights Award 2000, Wolfgang Freidman Memorial Award, Columbia Law School 2000, Eid-ul-Adha Award, Asscn of Progressive Muslims of Ontario 2000, Médaille du Barreau du Québec 2001, Nat. Achievement Award, Jewish Women Int. of Canada 2001, Stefan A. Riesenfeld Symposium Award, Berkeley Journal of International Law 2002, McGill Centre for Research and Teaching on Women Person of the Year 2002 Award 2002, 2002 Year Award, Prix de la Fondation Justice dans le Monde de l'Union internationale des Magistrats 2002, Médaille de la Faculté de droit de l'Université de Montréal 2003, inducted into Int. Hall of Fame – International Women's Forum 2003, Médaille 125e anniversaire, Faculté de droit, Asscn des diplômés en droit, Université de Montréal 2003. *Publications:* numerous articles on criminal procedure, human rights, civil liberties and gender issues. *Address:* c/o OHCHR-UNOG, 8–14 Avenue de la Paix, 1211 Geneva 10, Switzerland.

ARBULÚ GALLIANI, Gen. Guillermo; Peruvian government official and army officer; b. 1922, Trujillo; m. Bertha Tanaka de Azcárate; one s. two d.; ed Chorillos Mil. Acad.; Sub-Lt, Eng Corps 1943, Lt 1946, Capt. 1949, Maj. 1955, Lt-Col 1959, Col 1964, Brig.-Gen. 1971, Div. Gen. 1975–; fmr Chief of Staff, 1st Light Div.; fmr Dir of Logistics; fmr Chief of Operations, Armed Forces Gen. Staff; fmr Dir of Mil. Eng Coll.; fmr Instructor, Higher War Coll.; fmr Adviser to Ministries of Mining and Fisheries; fmr Pres. Empresa Pública de Servicios Pesqueros (State Fishing Corpn); Pres. Jt Armed Forces Command; Prime Minister and Minister of Defence 1976–78, Amb. to Chile 1978–79, to Spain 1979–80; del. to Latin American Conf. of Ministers of Labour; rep. of Ministry of Foreign Affairs to negotiations for Andean Pact; rep. to 11th American Mil. Congress; Commdr Mil. Order of Ayacucho; Grand Officer of Peruvian Crosses of Aeronautical Merit, Naval Merit; Grand Cross, Peruvian Order of Mil. Merit; Grand Officer, Mayo Cross of Mil. Merit (Argentina); Jorge Chávez Award. *Address:* c/o Ministry of Foreign Affairs, Lima, Peru.

ARCAND, Denys; Canadian film director; b. 25 June 1941, Deschambault, Québec; ed Univ. of Montreal; worked at Office Nat. du Film, Canada 1962–65; Vice-Pres. Asscn des Réalisateurs et Réalisatrices de films du Québec. *Films directed:* Seul ou avec d'autres (co-dir) 1962, Champlain (short) 1963, Les Montrealistes (short) 1964, La Route de l'Ouest (short) 1965, Montreal, un jour d'été and Parcs atlantiques (shorts) 1966, Volleyball 1967, On est au coton 1969, Québec: Dupléssis et après 1970, La maudite galette 1971, Réjeanne Padovani 1972, Gina 1974, La lutte des travailleurs d'hôpitaux (short) 1975, Le confort et l'indifférence 1980, Empire Inc. (TV) 1982, Le crime d'Ovide Plouffe 1984, Le déclin de l'empire américain 1986, Jésus de Montréal 1989 (Cannes Jury Prize 1989), Love and Human Remains 1993, Poverty and Other Delights, Stardom 2001, The Barbarian Invasions (Cannes Best Screenplay, Critics' Choice Award, Best Foreign Language Film 2004, Acad. Award, Best Foreign Language Film 2004) 2003.

ARCAYA, Ignacio; Venezuelan diplomatist; b. 3 June 1939, Caracas; m.; two c.; ed Cen. Univ. of Venezuela; Third Sec. Perm. Mission to UN in Geneva 1966–68, Second Sec., Ministry for Foreign Affairs 1968–69, First Sec., Mission to OAS, Washington, DC 1969–72, Counsellor Inst. of Foreign Trade, Ministry of Foreign Affairs 1972–75, Minister Counsellor of Econ. Affairs, Embassy in Paris 1975–78, Amb. to Australia (also accred to NZ, Fiji and the Philippines) 1978–84; Sec.-Gen. Asscn of Iron Ore Exporting Countries 1984–88; Amb.-at-Large, Ministry of Foreign Affairs 1988, Amb. to Chile 1989–92, to UK (also accred to Ireland) 1992–95, to Argentina 1995–98, to USA 2001–02; Minister of the Interior and Justice, then Acting Pres. 1999; Perm. Rep. to UN, New York 2000. *Address:* c/o Ministry of Foreign Affairs, Torre MRE, esq. Carmelitas, Avda Urdaneta, Caracas, 1010, Venezuela. *Telephone:* (212) 862-1085 (office). *Fax:* (212) 864-3633 (office). *E-mail:* criptogr@mre.gov.ve (office).

ARCE CATACORA, Luis Alberto, MSc; Bolivian government official; *Minister of Finance;* b. 28 Sept. 1963, La Paz; m.; three c.; ed Universidad Mayor de San Andrés, Univ. of Warwick, UK; with Cen. Bank of Bolivia 1988–2006; fmr consultant Natsuky Co., Nacida Co., Centro de Estudios para el Desarrollo Laboral y Agrario, Sistema Contable Computarizado; Minister of Finance 2006–. *Publications include:* numerous journal articles. *Address:* Ministry of Finance, Edif. Palacio de Comunicaciones, Avda Mariscal Santa Cruz, La Paz, Bolivia (office). *Telephone:* (2) 237-7234 (office). *Fax:* (2) 235-9955 (office).

ARCHER, David, BS, PhD; American oceanographer and academic; *Professor, Department of the Geophysical Sciences, University of Chicago;* b. 15 Sept. 1960; ed Indiana Univ., Univ. of Washington; Asst Prof. of Geophysical Sciences, Univ. of Chicago 1993–97, Adjunct Prof. of Environmental Sciences 1996–, Assoc. Prof. of Geophysical Sciences 1997–2001, Full Prof. of Geophysical Sciences 2001–; Lamont Fellow Postdoctoral Fellowship, Lamont Doherty Earth Observatory, Columbia Univ., New York 1990–92, Postdoctoral Research Scientist 1992–93, Adjunct Prof. 1994–; Contributing Ed. realclimate.org (climate science blog site). *Publications:* Global Warming: Understanding the Forecast 1992, The Long Thaw: How Humans are

Changing the Next 100,000 Years of Earth's Climate 2008; more than 70 scientific papers in professional journals on the global carbon cycle and its relation to global climate, with special focus on ocean sedimentary processes. *Address:* HGS 419, Department of the Geophysical Sciences, 5734 South Ellis Avenue, University of Chicago, Chicago, IL 60637, USA (office). *Telephone:* (773) 702-0823 (office). *Fax:* (773) 702-9505 (office). *E-mail:* d-archer@uchicago.edu (office). *Website:* geosci.uchicago.edu (office).

ARCHER, Lady Mary Doreen, MA, PhD, FRSC; British chemist and hospital administrator; *Chairman, Cambridge University Hospitals NHS Foundation Trust;* b. 22 Dec. 1944; d. of the late Harold Norman Weeden and the late Doreen Weeden (née Cox); m. Jeffrey Howard Archer (now Baron Archer of Weston-super-Mare q.v.) 1966; two s.; ed Cheltenham Ladies' Coll., St Anne's Coll. Oxford, Imperial Coll. London; Jr Research Fellow, St Hilda's Coll. Oxford 1968–71; temporary Lecturer in Chem., Somerville Coll. Oxford 1971–72; Research Fellow, Royal Inst. of GB 1972–76; Lector in Chem., Trinity Coll. Cambridge 1976–86; Fellow and Coll. Lecturer in Chem., Newnham Coll. Cambridge 1976–86; Sr Academic Fellow, De Montfort Univ. 1990–; Visiting Prof., Dept of Biochemistry, Imperial Coll. London 1991–2000, Visiting Prof., Centre for Energy Policy and Tech. 2001–03; Visitor, Univ. of Herts. 1993–2004; Trustee Science Museum 1990–2000, Cambridge Foundation 1997–2004; mem. Council, Royal Inst. 1984–85, 1999–2001, Cheltenham Ladies Coll. 1991–2000; Chair Nat. Energy Foundation 1990–2000, Pres. 2000–; mem. Bd of Dirs Anglia TV Group 1987–95, Mid Anglia Radio 1988–94, Cambridge & Newmarket FM Radio (now Heart) 1988–97; Dir, Cambridge Univ. Hosps NHS Foundation Trust 1992–, Vice-Chair. 1999–2002, Chair. 2002–; Chair. East of England Stem Cell Network 2004–08; Chair. UK Univ. Hosps Choirs Group 2008–; mem. Council of Lloyd's 1989–92; Pres. Guild of Church Musicians 1989–, Solar Energy Soc. 2001–; Hon. DSc (Herts.) 1994; Energy Inst. Melchett Medal 2002, Inst. of Chem. of Ireland Eva Philbin Award 2007. *Publications:* Rupert Brooke and The Old Vicarage, Grantchester 1989, Clean Energy from Photovoltaics (co-ed.) 2001, Molecular to Global Photosynthesis (co-ed.) 2004, Transformation and Change: the 1702 Chair of Chemistry at Cambridge (co-ed.) 2004, Solar Photon Conversion in Nanostructured and Photoelectrochemical Systems (co-ed.) 2008; contribs to chemical journals. *Leisure interests:* reading, writing, singing. *Address:* Management Offices, Cambridge University Hospitals NHS Foundation Trust, Hills Road, Cambridge, CB2 2QQ (office); The Old Vicarage, Grantchester, Cambridge, CB3 9ND, England (home). *Telephone:* (1223) 217510 (office); (1223) 840213 (home). *Website:* www.cuh.org.uk.

ARCHER, Robyn, AO, BA, DipEd; Australian singer, performer and writer; b. 18 June 1948, Adelaide; d. of the late Clifford Charles Smith and Mary Louisa Wohling; ed Enfield High School, Adelaide Univ.; singer 1952–; recorded ten albums including Brecht, Weill and Eisler repertoire; has toured world-wide in recital, concert and cabaret performances; has sung with Australian and Adelaide Chamber Orchestras, Adelaide, Melbourne and Tasmanian Symphony Orchestras; numerous TV appearances in Australia and UK; has written over 100 songs; writing for theatre includes Songs from Sideshow Alley, The Pack of Women (also Dir), Cut & Thrust Cabaret (also Dir), Café Fledermaus, See Ya Next Century, Ningali, A Star is Torn, Comes a Cropper; writing for TV includes The One That Got Away; also writes for radio; Artistic Counsel Belvoir Street Theatre 1986; Artistic Dir Nat. Festival of Australian Theatre 1993–95, Adelaide Festival 1998, 2000, Melbourne Int. Festival of Arts 2002–04; Artistic Advisor Australia Day, Hannover Festival EXPO 2000; Creative Consultant Melbourne Museum 1995–98; Creator and Inaugural Artistic Dir, Ten Days on the Island, Tasmania 2001–05; Artistic Dir Liverpool Capital of Culture Festival 2004; Chair. Community Cultural Devt Bd, Australia Council 1993–95; Commonwealth Appointee to Centenary of Fed. Advisory Cttee 1994; mem. Bd Dirs Int. Soc. of Performing Arts, Council Victorian Coll. of the Arts, Adelaide Festival Centre Trust; Trustee Don Dunstan Foundation; Artistic Dir The Light in Winter (Federation Square, Melbourne) 2009; currently artistic adviser to Govts of S Australia and Western Australia; Patron Australian Art Orchestra, Arts Law Centre, Australian Script Centre, Brink Productions, Globalism Inst.; fmr mem. Bd Helpmann Acad.; fmr Patron Nat. Affiliation of Arts Educators; Inaugural Amb. Adelaide Festival Centre Trust; Amb. Adelaide Football Club; Chevalier des Arts et Lettres 2000, Federation Medal 2001, Officer of the Crown (Belgium) 2008; Hon. DUniv (Flinders); Sydney Critics' Circle Award 1980, Henry Lawson Award 1980, Australian Creative Fellowship 1991–93, Australian Record Industry Award for Best Soundtrack for Pack of Women 1986, for Best Children's Album for Mrs Bottle 1989, Exec. Woman of the Year, Australian Women's Network 1998, S Australia Arts and Culture Award 1998, 2000, Int. Citation of Merit, Int. Soc. of Performing Arts, New York 2006. *Performance roles include:* Annie I in The Seven Deadly Sins 1974, 1993, Jenny in The Threepenny Opera 1976, Brect Compilations, Never the Twain, To Those Born Later, Sung and Unsung, Brecht & Co, Pierrot Lunaire, Out of the East, Mrs Peachum in The Threepenny Opera 1999. *One-woman shows include:* Tonight Lola Blau (Australian tour), A Star is Born (two Australian tours, Theatre Royal, Stratford East and Wyndham's Theatre, London West End). *Theatre directed:* The Pack of Women (Australian tour), Cut and Thrust Cabaret (London), Scandals (Australian tour), On Parliament Hill (Sydney), ABC (Sydney), Akwanso Fly South (Adelaide Festival and Australian tour), Mayday (Darwin and Hobart), Labour of Love (Darwin and Hobart), Le Chat Noir (Brisbane and Canberra), The Bridge (Perth), Accidental Death of an Anarchist (Adelaide and Sydney), Boy Hamlet (Brisbane), January (Tim Finn/Dorothy Porter), Toughnut Cabaret (Pittsburgh) 2009. *Publications include:* The Robyn Archer Songbook 1980, Mrs Bottle Burps 1983, The Pack of Women 1986, A Star is Torn 1986; for theatre: Kold Komfort Kaffee 1977, The Pack of Women 1981, Cut & Thrust Cabaret 1984, Songs from Sideshow Alley 1986, Il Magnifico 1987, Akwanso Fly South 1988, Poor Johanna 1983, The Hanging of Minine Thwaites 1983, A Star is Torn 1979, Scandals 1985, Ningali 1992, Architektin 2008; contrib. to The All Australian HaHa Book 1983, Australia Fair 1984, Mrs Bottle's Absolutely Blurtingly Beautiful World-Beating Burp 1990, Cafe Fledermaus 1990, Penguin Anthology of Contemporary Australian Women's Writing 1991, Loaves and Fishes 1991, Hope and Fear 1995, The Myth of the Mainstream 2004, Australian Greats 2008, Essentially Creative (Griffith Review) 2009. *Address:* c/o Rick Raftos Management, Box 445, Paddington, NSW 2021, Australia (office). *Telephone:* (2) 9281-9622 (office). *Fax:* (2) 9212-7100 (office). *Website:* www.robynarcher.com.au (home).

ARCHER OF WESTON-SUPER-MARE, Baron (Life Peer), cr. 1992, of Mark in the County of Somerset; **Jeffrey Howard Archer;** British writer and fmr politician; b. 15 April 1940, London; s. of William Archer and Lola Archer (née Cook); m. Mary Doreen Archer (q.v.) (née Weeden) 1966; two s.; ed Wellington School and Brasenose Coll., Oxford; mem. GLC for Havering 1966–70; MP for Louth (Conservative) 1969–74; Deputy Chair. Conservative Party 1985–86; mem. House of Lords 1992–; sentenced to four years' imprisonment for perjury and perverting the course of justice July 2001, released July 2003. *Plays:* Beyond Reasonable Doubt 1987, Exclusive 1989, The Accused (writer and actor) 2000. *Film:* Bridget Jones's Diary (as himself) 2001. *Television:* three advertisements. *Publications:* Not a Penny More, Not a Penny Less 1975, Shall We Tell the President? 1977, Kane and Abel 1979, A Quiver Full of Arrows 1980, The First Miracle (with Craigie Aitchison) 1980, The Prodigal Daughter 1982, First Among Equals 1984, A Matter of Honour 1985, A Twist in the Tale (short stories) 1988, As the Crow Flies 1991, Honour Among Thieves 1993, Twelve Red Herrings (short stories) 1994, The Fourth Estate 1996, The Collected Short Stories 1997, The Eleventh Commandment 1998, To Cut a Long Story Short (short stories) 2000, A Prison Diary Vols I and II 2002, Sons of Fortune 2003, A Prison Diary Vol. III 2004, False Impression 2006, Cat O' Nine Tales (short stories) 2006, The Gospel According to Judas 2007, A Prisoner of Birth 2008, Paths of Glory 2009. *Leisure interests:* theatre, cricket, auctioneering. *Address:* 93 Albert Embankment, London, SE1 7TY, England. *E-mail:* questions@jeffreyarcher.co.uk. *Website:* www.jeffreyarcher.co.uk.

ARCULUS, Sir Ronald, KCMG, KCVO, MA, FBIM; British fmr diplomatist; b. 11 Feb. 1923, Birmingham; s. of the late Cecil Arculus, MC and Ethel Lilian Arculus; m. Sheila Mary Faux 1953; one s. one d.; ed Solihull School, Exeter Coll., Oxford and Imperial Defence Coll.; served in Fourth Queen's Own Hussars 1942–45 (attained rank of Capt.); Foreign Office 1947; San Francisco 1948–50; La Paz 1950; Ankara 1953–56; Foreign Office 1957–60; First Sec. (Commercial), Washington 1961–65; Dir of Trade Devt, New York 1965–68; Imperial Defence Coll. 1969; Head of Science and Tech. Dept, FCO 1970–73; Minister (Econ.), Paris 1973–77; Amb. to Law of Sea Conf. 1977–79; Amb. to Italy 1979–83; Special Adviser to Govt on Channel Tunnel trains 1987–88; Dir Glaxo PLC 1983–91, Consultant 1992–95; Chair. Kensington Soc. 1999–2001, Pres. 2001–; Dir of Appeals, King's Medical Research Trust 1984–88; Trustee Glaxo Trustees Ltd 1988–93; Gov. British Inst., Florence 1984–93; Consultant London and Continental Bankers Ltd 1985–90, Trusthouse Forte 1983–86; Freeman of the City of London; Hon. Fellow, Exeter Coll., Oxford 1989. *Leisure interests:* travel, fine arts, music, antiques. *Address:* 20 Kensington Court Gardens, London, W8 5QF, England (home).

ARDALAN, Nader, MArch; American architect and planner; *Senior Vice-President and Director of Design, KEO International Consultants;* b. 9 March 1939, Tehran, Iran; s. of Abbas Gholi Ardalan and Faranguis Davar Ardalan; m. 1st Laleh Bakhtiar 1962 (divorced 1976); one s. two d.; m. 2nd Shahla Ganji 1977; one s.; ed New Rochelle High School, Carnegie-Mellon Univ. and Harvard Univ. Grad. School of Design; designer, S.O.M. 1962–64; Chief Architect, Nat. Iranian Oil Co. 1964–66; Design Partner, Aziz Farmanfarmaian & Assocs 1966–72; Man. Dir Mandala Collaborative Tehran/Boston 1972–79; Prof. of Design, Tehran Univ. Faculty of Fine Arts 1972–77; Pres. Nader Ardalan Assocs 1979–92; Prin. Jung/Brannen Assocs Inc., Boston 1983–94; Man. Prin. Jung/Brannen Assocs Inc., Abu Dhabi 1992; Sr Vice-Pres. and Dir of Design KEO Int. Consultants 1994–; Visiting Prof. Harvard Univ. Grad. School of Design 1977–78, 1981–83, Yale Univ. 1977, MIT 1980; various other professional appointments; Aga Khan Award Steering Cttee 1976–80; King Fahd Award 1987; design awards. *Publications:* Sense of Unity 1972, Habitat Bill of Rights 1976, Pardisan, Environmental Park 1976, Blessed Jerusalem 1985; articles in leading professional journals. *Leisure interests:* the study of sacred architecture, photography, swimming, hunting. *Address:* 20 Williams Street, Suite 245, Wellesley, MA 02481, USA (home); KEO International Consultants, PO Box 3679, Safat 13037, Kuwait. *Telephone:* (965) 243-8011. *Fax:* (965) 244-3969. *E-mail:* nadera@keoic.com (office).

ARDANT, Fanny; French actress; b. 22 March 1949, Monte Carlo; d. of Lt-Col Jean Ardant and Jacqueline Lecoq; three c.; Grand Prix Nat., Ministry of Culture. *Films include:* Les Chiens 1979, Les uns et les autres, The Woman Next Door, The Ins and Outs, Life is a Novel, Confidentially Yours, Benevenuta, Desire, Swann in Love, Love Unto Death, Les Enragés, L'Eté prochain, Family Business, Affabulazione, Melo, The Family, La Paltoquet, Three Sisters, Australia, Pleure pas my love, Adventure of Catherine C., Afraid of the Dark, Rien que des mensonges, La Femme du déserteur, Amok, Colonel Chabert, Beyond the Clouds, Ridicule, Elizabeth, La Débondade, Le Fils du Français, Le Dîner et le Libertin 2000, Callas Forever 2002, 8 Femmes 2002, Nathalie 2003, L'odore del Sangue 2004, El Año del diluvio 2004, Paris, je t'aime 2006, Roman de gare 2007, The Secrets 2007, Hello Goodbye 2008. *Theatre includes:* Polyeucte, Esther, The Mayor of Santiago, Electra, Tête d'Or. *Leisure interest:* music (piano). *Address:* Artmédia, 10 avenue George V, 75008 Paris, France (office).

ARDEBERG, Arne Lennart, PhD; Swedish professor of astronomy and astrophysics; *Director, Lund Observatory;* b. 10 Nov. 1940, Malmö; s. of Kurt

Ardeberg and Elly Ardeberg; m. Margareta Vinberg 1969; one s. two d.; ed Lund Univ.; staff astronomer, Lund Observatory 1965–69; staff astronomer, European Southern Observatory, La Silla, Chile 1969–73; Assoc. Prof. Lund Observatory 1973–79; Astronomical Dir European Southern Observatory, La Silla 1979–81, Dir 1981–83; Dir Lund Observatory 1983–1998, 2004–, Nordic Optical Telescope Scientific Asscn 1984–95; apptd. Dean, Faculty of Science, Lund Univ. 1987–98, Vice-Pres., Lund Univ. 1998–2002; Chair. European Telescope Consortium Euro50 2001–; Deputy Project Man. European Extremely Large Telescope 2004–; mem. Swedish Nat. Research Policy Working Group; mem. Royal Physiographical Soc. (Sweden) 1980–, Royal Swedish Acad. of Sciences 1983– (Chair. Astronomy and Space Research Bd), Royal Soc. of Sciences (Sweden) 1986–; Wallmark Prize (Royal Swedish Acad. of Sciences) 1977. *Publications:* 250 publs in int. journals and books on astronomy, physics and related technology. *Leisure interests:* mountaineering, forestry, literature. *Address:* Lund Observatory, Room B 256, Box 43, 22100 Lund (office); Blåmesvägen 2, 24735 Södra Sandby, Sweden (home). *Telephone:* (46) 222-72-90 (office); (46) 46-570-16 (home). *Fax:* (46) 222-46-14 (office). *E-mail:* arne@astro.lu.se (office). *Website:* www.astro.lu.se (office).

ARDEN, John; British playwright and novelist; b. 26 Oct. 1930, Barnsley; s. of Charles Alwyn Arden and Annie Elizabeth Layland; m. Margaretta Ruth D'Arcy (q.v.) 1957; five s. (one deceased); ed Sedbergh School, King's Coll., Cambridge and Edinburgh Coll. of Art; British Army Intelligence Corps 1949–50; architectural asst 1955–57; Fellow in Playwriting, Univ. of Bristol 1959–60; Visiting Lecturer (Politics and Drama), New York Univ. 1967; Regent's Lecturer, Univ. of California, Davis 1973; Writer in Residence, Univ. of New England, Australia 1975; mem. Corrandulla Arts and Entertainment Club 1973, Galway Theatre Workshop 1975; PEN Short Story Prize 1992, V. S. Pritchett Short Story Prize 1999, Evening Standard Drama Award 1960, Arts Council Playwriting Award (with Margaretta D'Arcy) 1972. *Plays:* All Fall Down 1955, The Waters of Babylon 1957, Live Like Pigs 1958, Serjeant Musgrave's Dance 1959, The Happy Haven (with Margaretta D'Arcy) 1960, The Business of Good Government (with Margaretta D'Arcy) 1960, Wet Fish 1962, The Workhouse Donkey 1963, Ironhand 1963, Ars Longa Vita Brevis (with Margaretta D'Arcy) 1964, Armstrong's Last Goodnight 1964, Left Handed Liberty 1965, Friday's Hiding (with Margaretta D'Arcy) 1966, The Royal Pardon (with Margaretta D'Arcy) 1966, Muggins is a Martyr (with Margaretta D'Arcy and C.A.S.T.) 1968, The Hero Rises Up (musical with Margaretta D'Arcy) 1968, Two Autobiographical Plays 1972, The Ballygombeen Bequest (with Margaretta D'Arcy) 1972, The Island of the Mighty (with Margaretta D'Arcy) 1972, The Non-Stop Connolly Show (with Margaretta D'Arcy) 1975, Vandaleur's Folly (with Margaretta D'Arcy) 1978, The Little Gray Home in the West (with Margaretta D'Arcy) 1978, The Making of Muswell Hill (with Margaretta D'Arcy) 1979. *Radio:* The Life of Man 1956, The Bagman 1969, Keep Those People Moving (with Margaretta D'Arcy) 1972, Pearl 1977, Don Quixote (adaptation) 1980, Garland for a Hoar Head 1982, The Old Man Sleeps Alone 1982, The Manchester Enthusiasts (with Margaretta D'Arcy) 1984, Whose is the Kingdom? (with Magaretta D'Arcy) 1988, A Suburban Suicide (with Margaretta D'Arcy) 1994, Six Little Novels of Wilkie Collins (adaptation) 1997, Woe Alas, the Fatal Cashbox! 1999, Wild Ride to Dublin 2003, Poor Tom Thy Horn is Dry 2003. *Television:* Soldier Soldier 1960, Wet Fish 1962, Profile of Sean O'Casey (documentary, with Margaretta D'Arcy) 1973. *Publications:* essays: To Present the Pretence 1977, Awkward Corners (with Margaretta D'Arcy) 1988; novels: Silence Among the Weapons 1982, Books of Bale 1988, Jack Juggler and the Emperor's Whore 1995; short stories: Cogs Tyrannic 1991, The Stealing Steps 2003. *Leisure interests:* antiquarianism, mythology. *Address:* c/o Casarotto Ramsay Ltd, Waverley House, 7–12 Noel Street, London, W1F 8GQ, England (office). *Telephone:* (20) 7287-4450 (office). *Fax:* (20) 7287-9128 (office). *E-mail:* info@casarotto.co.uk (office).

ARDEN, Rt Hon. Dame Mary (Howarth), DBE, PC, MA, LLM; British judge; *Lady Justice of Appeal;* b. 23 Jan. 1947; d. of the late Lt-Col E. C. Arden and of M. M. Arden (née Smith); m. Sir Jonathan Hugh Mance 1973; one s. two d.; ed Huyton Coll., Girton Coll., Cambridge, Harvard Law School, USA; called to the Bar, Gray's Inn 1971; admitted to Lincoln's Inn 1973, Bencher 1994; QC 1986; Dept of Trade and Industry Inspector Rotaprint PLC 1988–91; Attorney Gen. Duchy of Lancaster 1991–93; Judge of High Court of Justice, Chancery Div. 1993–2000; Chair. Law Comm. 1996–99; Lady Justice of Appeal 2000–; Bar mem. Law Soc.'s Standing Cttee on Company Law 1976–; mem. Financial Law Panel 1993–2000, Steering Group, Company Law Review 1998–2001; Fellow, Girton Coll. Cambridge; Hon. Fellow, Liverpool John Moores Univ. 2006; Hon. DUniv (Essex) 1997; Hon. LLD (Liverpool) 1998, (Warwick) 1999, (Royal Holloway and Bedford New Coll., London) 1999, (Nottingham) 2002; The Times Woman of Achievement Lifetime Award in 1997. *Publications:* Buckley on The Companies Acts (Jt Gen. Ed.) 2000; contrib. to numerous books, articles in legal journals. *Leisure interests:* reading, swimming. *Address:* Royal Courts of Justice, Strand, London, WC2A 2LL, England. *Telephone:* (20) 7947-6402 (office). *Fax:* (20) 7947-7201 (office).

ARDITO BARLETTA, Nicolás, PhD, MS; Panamanian politician and economist; b. 21 Aug. 1938, Aguadulce, Coclé; s. of Nicolás Ardito Barletta and Leticia de Ardito Barletta; m. María Consuelo de Ardito Barletta; two s. one d.; ed Univ. of Chicago and N Carolina State Univ.; Cabinet mem. and Dir Planning 1968–70; Dir Econ. Affairs Org. of American States 1970–73; Minister of Planning 1973–78; Negotiator of econ. aspects of Panama Canal Treaties 1976–77; Vice-Pres. World Bank for Latin America and Caribbean 1978–84; Founder and first Pres. Latin American Export Bank (BLADEX) 1978; Pres. Latin American Econ. System (SELA) Constituent Ass.; Pres. of Panama 1984–85; Gen. Dir of Int. Centre for Econ. Growth 1986–95; Dir Autoridad de la Región Interoceanía (ARI) 1995–2000; Chair. Asesores Estrategicos; mem. Bd of Dirs of several corpns, banks and policy insts including Superintendencia de Bancos 2006–(14). *Publications:* numerous publications on econ. and social devt issues. *Leisure interests:* tennis and music. *Address:* PO Box 0830, 00378 Panamá 9, Panama. *Telephone:* 264-6675. *Fax:* 223-6488. *E-mail:* asesores@cwpanama.net.

ARDZINBA, Vladislav Grigoriyvich, DHisSc; Georgian (b. Abkhaz) politician and historian; b. 14 May 1945, Eshera; m. Svetlana Ardzinba; one d.; ed Sukhumi Pedagogical Inst.; mem. CPSU 1967–91; researcher, Inst. of Oriental Sciences, Moscow 1969–87; Dir D. Gulia Abkhaz Inst. of Language, Literature and History, Georgian Acad. of Sciences 1987–90; USSR People's Deputy 1989–91; Chair. Supreme Soviet of Abkhazia 1990–94; leader of independence movt, self-proclaimed Repub. of Abkhazia, Pres. 1994–2004. *Publications:* Rituals and Myths of Ancient Anatolia 1985; numerous papers.

AREF, Mohammad Reza, BEng, MS, PhD; Iranian electronics engineer, politician and academic; *Professor, Department of Electrical Engineering, Sharif University of Technology;* b. 1941, Yazd; ed Tehran Univ., Stanford Univ., USA; politically active as student, supporter of Ayatollah Khomeini, arrested by secret police 1963; mem. of Muslim students org. during stay in US, subsequently head of that org.; has held a number of govt posts including Minister of Posts, Telegraphs and Telecommunications, Deputy Minister of Culture and Higher Educ. in charge of Students' Affairs 1981–82 and Advisor to Minister of Culture and Higher Educ.; Head of Tehran Univ. 1984–88; First Vice-Pres. of Iran 2001–05; currently Prof., Electrical Engineering Dept, Sharif Univ. of Tech.; First Prize, Nat. Math. Competition 1959, Isfahan Tech. Univ. Scholarship. *Address:* Department of Electrical Engineering, Sharif University of Technology, POB 11365-8639, Tehran, Iran (office). *Telephone:* (21) 6005419 (office). *Fax:* (21) 6012983 (office). *E-mail:* aref@sharif.edu (office). *Website:* www.sharif.edu (office).

ARENDARSKI, Andrzej, PhD; Polish politician, business executive and university lecturer; *President, Polish Chamber of Commerce;* b. 15 Nov. 1949, Warsaw; m. Agnieszka Łypacewicz; three s. one d.; ed Warsaw Univ.; teacher, East Dembowski Secondary School, Warsaw 1972–73, Inst. of Philosophy and Sociology of Polish Acad. of Sciences, Warsaw 1973–75; mem. Solidarity Trade Union 1980–; Ed.-in-Chief, underground journal Zeszyty Edukacji Narodowej 1981–82; co-f. Agric.-Industrial Soc., Konin 1988; mem. Soc. for Econ. and Econ. Action, Warsaw 1988–; co-f. Social Movt for Econ. Initiatives SPRING 1988; Deputy to Sejm (Parl.) 1989–93; mem. Liberal Democratic Congress (KLD) 1989–94, Deputy Chair. KLD 1989–94, mem. KLD Political Council 1991–94, now Chair.; Pres. Polish Chamber of Commerce 1990–; Minister of Foreign Econ. Co-operation 1992–93; Chair. Polish-Ukrainian Chamber of Commerce 1996–; Sec.-Gen. Polish Asscn Industry, Commerce and Finance 1997–; Chair. Polish-American Small Business Consultation Fund; CEO Tel-Emergo, Telephony Service Providers. *Publications:* contribs to underground journals 1981–89; co-author: Polska lat 80-tych: Analiza stanu obecnego i perspektywy rozwoju sytuacji politycznej w Polsce 1984, Stan środowiska przyrodniczego 1984. *Leisure interests:* travel, sailing, art of cooking. *Address:* Krajowa Izba Gospodarcza, ul. Trębacka 4, 00-074 Warsaw, Poland. *Telephone:* (22) 630-96-00 (office). *Fax:* (22) 827-46-73 (office). *E-mail:* aarendarski@kig.pl (office). *Website:* www.kig.pl/english/index.htm (office).

ARENS, Moshe; Israeli politician, academic and diplomatist; b. 7 Dec. 1925, Lithuania; ed Massachusetts and California Insts of Tech., USA; Assoc. Prof. of Aeronautical Eng, Technion (Israel Inst. of Tech.), Haifa; Deputy Dir Israel Aircraft Industries, Lod; Amb. to USA 1982–83; Minister of Defence 1983–84, 1999, without Portfolio –1987, of Foreign Affairs 1988–90, of Defence 1990–92; Adviser to Prime Minister 2001; elected to Knesset (Likud), mem. Knesset Finance Cttee 1973; Israel Defence Prize 1971; Assoc. Fellow, AIAA. *Publications:* Broken Covenant 1994, several books on propulsion and flight mechanics. *Address:* c/o Likud, 38 Rehov King George, Tel-Aviv 61231, Israel.

ARENY CASAL, Francesc; Andorran politician; b. 28 June 1959, Canillo; Mayor of Canillo 1988–95; Pres. Unio Pro-Turisme, Canillo 1987; mem. Partit Liberal d'Andorra; Síndic-Gen. (Speaker of the Gen. Council) 1997–2005. *Address:* c/o Consell General, Andorra la Vella, Andorra (office).

ARGERICH, Martha; Argentine pianist; b. 5 June 1941, Buenos Aires; ed studied with V. Scaramuzzo, Friedrich Gulda, Nikita Magaloff, Madeleine Lipatti and Arturo Benedetto Michaelangeli; debut Buenos Aires 1949; London debut 1964; soloist with world's leading orchestras; with Chamber Orchestra of Europe, Barbican Hall, London 1991; Schumann Concerto, BBC London Proms 2000; Officier, Ordre des Arts et Lettres 1996, Accademica di Santa Cecilia di Roma 1997; First Prize Busoni Contest and Geneva Int. Music Competition 1957, Int. Chopin Competition, Warsaw 1965, Praemium Imperiale Award (Japan) 2005, three Grammy Awards. *Address:* Jacques Thelen Agence Artistique, 15 Avenue Montaigne, 75008 Paris, France (office). *Telephone:* 1-56-89-32-00 (office). *Fax:* 1-56-89-32-01 (office). *E-mail:* jthelen@wanadoo.fr (office). *Website:* jacquesthelen.com (office).

ARGUETA, Manlio; Salvadorean writer and librarian; b. 24 Nov. 1935, San Miguel; lived in exile in Costa Rica for many years since 1973; Dir Biblioteca Nacional de El Salvador 1996. *Publications:* En el costado de la luz (poetry) 1968, Un hombre por la patria 1968, El valle de las Hamacas 1977, Caperucita en la zona roja 1977, Un día en la vida (Univ. of Cen. America Prize) 1980, Cuscatlán (novel) 1987, Milagro de la Paz (novel) 1996, Siglo de O(g)ro 1997. *Address:* Biblioteca Nacional, 4ta Calle Oriente y Avda Mons. Oscar A. Romero # 124, San Salvador, El Salvador (office). *Telephone:* 2221-2099 (office). *Fax:* 2221-8847 (office). *Website:* www.binaes.gob.sv (office).

ARGUETA ANTILLÓN, José Luis; Salvadorean economist, academic and university administrator; *Professor, Faculty of Economic Sciences, University of El Salvador;* b. 16 July 1932, El Salvador; s. of Tomás Antillón and Andrea Argueta; m. María Luz Márquez 1969; four s. two d.; ed Univs of El Salvador and Chile; Prof., Univ. of El Salvador 1964–67, Sec. Faculty of Econ. Sciences 1967–69, Prof., Faculty of Investigative Econs 1974–78, Asst Dir to the Dir 1973–74, Dir 1985–86, Asst to Acting Rector 1979–80, Rector 1986, now Prof.; Prof. and Researcher, Cen. American Univ. 1980–85; Dr hc (Univ. of Simón Bolívar, Colombia); Economist of the Year 1985. *Publications include:* Manual de Contabilidad Nacional 1967, La Economía Salvadoreana—Algunos Elementos de Análisis 1984, La Reedición de Reforma Universitaria de Córdoba—Una Necesidad Histórica 1989. *Leisure interest:* sport. *Address:* Final 25 Avenida Norte, Universidad de El Salvador, Facultad de Ciencias Económicas, San Salvador, El Salvador. *Telephone:* 2243-0472. *Fax:* 225-7922. *E-mail:* antillon@navegante.com.sv.

ARGUETA DE BARILLAS, Marisol; Salvadorean lawyer and diplomatist; *Minister of Foreign Affairs;* b. 1968; m. Carlos R. Barillas; three d.; ed Univ. of Oxford, UK, New York Univ., USA; fmr Asst Prof. of Constitutional Law and Political Law, El Salvador; Alt. Rep. to UN, New York 1990–97; Minister Counselor Embassy in Washington DC 1997–99; Gen. Dir of Foreign Policy, Ministry for Foreign Affairs –2004; Adviser to Minister of Foreign Affairs 2004–08, Minister of Foreign Affairs 2008–; fmr Vice-Pres. OAS Nat. Authorities Meeting for the Devt of Women; mem. Bd of Dirs Hogares CREA-El Salvador, Salvadorean Foundation for the Elderly, Int. Inst. for Women; mem. Oxford Union Soc. *Address:* Ministry of Foreign Affairs, Calle El Pedregal, Blvd Cancillería, Ciudad Merliot, Antiguo Cuscatlan, El Salvador (office). *Telephone:* 2231-1000 (office). *Fax:* 2243-9656 (office). *E-mail:* webmaster@rree.gob.sv (office). *Website:* www.rree.gob.sv (office).

ARGUS, Donald (Don) Robert, AO; Australian banker and business executive; *Chairman, BHP Billiton;* b. 1 Aug. 1938, Bundaberg; s. of Dudley Francis Argus and Evelyn Argus; m. Patricia Anne Argus 1961; three d.; ed Royal Melbourne Inst. of Tech., Harvard Univ.; Chief Man. Corp. Lending, Nat. Australia Bank Ltd 1983, then Gen. Man. Credit Bureau, then Gen. Man. Group Strategic Devt, then Exec. Dir and COO, Man. Dir, CEO 1990–99; Chair. Australian Bankers' Asscn 1992–94; Dir Broken Hill Pty Co. Ltd (BHP Ltd) 1996–, Chair. 1999–, Chair. BHP Billiton Ltd, BHP Billiton Plc 2001–, Chair. Nomination Cttee; Chair. Brambles Industries Ltd 1999–2008; Dir Southcorp Ltd 1999–, Australian Foundation Investment Co. Ltd 1999–; mem. Int. Advisory Council Allianz AG 2000–, Int. Advisory Cttee to New York Stock Exchange Bd of Dirs 2005–. *Leisure interests:* hockey, golf, reading. *Address:* BHP Billiton Ltd, BHP Billiton Centre, 180 Lonsdale Street, Melbourne, Vic. 3000, Australia (office). *Telephone:* (3) 9609-3891 (office). *Fax:* (3) 9609-3588 (office). *E-mail:* kerry.a.eastlake@bhpbilliton.com (office). *Website:* www.bhpbilliton.com (office).

ARGYROS, George L.; American business executive and diplomatist; b. 1937, Detroit; m. Julia; three c.; ed Chapman Univ.; co-owner AirCal 1981–87; owner Seattle Mariners professional baseball team 1981–89; mem. Advisory Cttee for Trade Policy and Negotiations US Trade Amb. –1990; mem. Bd Fed. Home Loan Mortgage Corpn (FreddieMac) 1990–93; Amb. to Spain and Andorra 2001–04; Chair. and CEO Arnel and Affiliates CA –2001; Gen. Pnr Westar Capital, Chair. 1976–2001, mem. Bd Trustees, Chapman Univ. 2001–; mem. Bd Trustees, California Inst. of Technology (CalTech); fmr Chair. Bd Orange Co. Council Boy Scouts of America; founding Chair. Nixon Center, Washington DC, fmr Chair. Richard Nixon Library and Birthplace Foundation; fmr Chair., Treas., Horatio Alger Asscn; Chair. Bd of Dirs Beckman Foundation; fmr mem. Bd of Dirs Rockwell Int. Corpn, First American Corpn, DST Systems Inc., Newhall Land and Farming Co., Tecstar, Doskocil Manufacturing Co., Harper Leather Goods Inc., Verteq Inc. *Address:* c/o Arnel and Affiliates, 949 South Coast Drive, Suite 600, Costa Mesa, CA 92626, USA (office). *Telephone:* (714) 481-5000 (office). *Fax:* (714) 481-5055 (office).

ARHABI, Abd al-Karim Ismail al-, MA; Yemeni politician; *Deputy Prime Minister for Economic Affairs and Minister of Planning and International Cooperation;* b. 1947, Alssadah, Ibb Prov.; ed Martin Luther Univ., Germany, academic and field training in USA, Germany and UK; worked in pvt. sector 1977–79; Gen. Dir Industrial Estate Authority 1979–81; Man. Dir Yemeni Industrial Bank 1981–94; Head of Small Enterprise Devt Unit 1994; est. and was Man. Dir Social Fund for Devt 1996; Minister of Social Affairs and Labour 2001–06; Deputy Prime Minister for Econ. Affairs and Minister of Planning and Int. Cooperation 2006–. *Address:* Ministry of Planning and International Cooperation, PO Box 175, San'a, Yemen (office). *Telephone:* (1) 250101 (office). *Fax:* (1) 251665 (office). *E-mail:* info@mpic-yemen.org (office). *Website:* www.mpic-yemen.org (office).

ARHAR, France, BA, MA, PhD; Slovenian business executive and fmr central banker; b. 24 April 1948, Ljubljana; ed Univ. of Ljubljana; joined Nat. Bank of Slovenia 1971, Head of Section 1974–76, Asst Gen. Man. Int. Div. 1976–78, Gen. Man. Int. Div. and Asst Gov. 1978–88; Gen. Man. Corp. Finance LHB Int. Handelsbank, Frankfurt 1988–91; Gov. Bank of Slovenia 1991–2001; Chair. Man. Bd Vzajemna (pvt. health insurer) 2001–03, Bank Austria Creditanstalt d.d. Ljubljana (currently UniCredit Banka Slovenija d.d.) 2003–; Asst Prof. of Int. Econ. Law, Faculty of Law, Univ. of Ljubljana 1988, Asst Prof. of Int. Finance and Int. Financial Law 2005; trainee, Linklaters & Paines Pnrs, London, UK 1979, Hessische Landensbank Frankfurt 1982; Pres. Ethics Cttee of the Int. Forum for Scientific Research in Pharmaceutical Cos, Slovenian Cttee for Negotiations on Succession by the Vienna Agreement, Council of Slovene Nat. Theatre, Ljubljana; Deputy Pres. Supervisory Bd, Bank Asscn of Slovenia; mem. Man. Cttee, Univ. of Ljubljana, mem. Council of the Faculty of Econs; mem. Govt Strategic Council on the Economy; mem. ILO, Geneva. *Publications include:* three books on foreign trade, int. finance and int. econ. law and over 80 articles. *Address:* Slovenian People's Party, Beethovnova ulica 43, 1000 Ljubljana, Slovenia (office). *Telephone:* (1) 2418820 (office). *Fax:* (1) 2511741 (office). *Website:* www.sls.si (office).

ARIARAJAH, Wesley, ThM, MPhil, PhD; Sri Lankan ecclesiastic; *Professor of Ecumenical Theology, Drew University;* b. 2 Dec. 1941, Jaffna; s. of Ponniah David Seevaratnam and Grace Annalukshmi (née Sinnapu); m. Christine Shyamala Chinniah 1974; three d.; ed Madras Christian Coll., India, United Theological Coll., Bangalore, India, Princeton Seminary, NJ, USA, Univ. of London, UK; ordained in Methodist Church; Minister, Methodist Church of Sri Lanka, Jaffna 1966–68; Lecturer, Theological Coll. Lanka, Pilimatalawa 1969–71; Chair. North and East Dist, Methodist Church, Jaffna 1974–81; mem. staff WCC programme on Dialogue with People of Living Faiths, Geneva 1981–83, Dir 1983–93, Deputy Sec.-Gen. WCC 1993–97; currently Prof. of Ecumenical Theology, Drew Univ., NJ; delivered Sixth Lambeth Interfaith Lecture 1987. *Publications:* Dialogue 1980, The Bible and People of Other Faiths 1986, Hindus and Christians: A Century of Protestant Ecumenical Thought, Did I Betray the Gospel?: The Letters of Paul and the Place of Women 1996, Not Without My Neighbour: Issues in Interfaith Dialogue 1998, Axis of Peace: Christian Faith in Times of Violence and War 2004; contrib. articles to specialist journals. *Leisure interest:* reading. *Address:* Seminary Hall, School of Theology, Drew University, Madison, NJ 07940 (office); 34B Loantaka Way, Madison, NJ 07940, USA (home). *Telephone:* (973) 408-3979 (office); (973) 360-9296 (home). *Fax:* (973) 408-3808 (office). *E-mail:* wariaraj@drew.edu (office); ariarajah@hotmail.com (home).

ARIAS, Inocencio F.; Spanish civil servant and diplomatist; *Consul General in Los Angeles;* b. 20 April 1940; m.; three c.; joined diplomatic service 1967; Dir of Diplomatic Information Office, Ministry of Foreign Affairs 1980–82, 1985–88, 1996–97; Under-Sec. Ministry of Foreign Affairs 1988–91; State Sec. for Int. Co-operation for Iberoamerican Affairs 1991–93; Gen. Dir Real Madrid 1993–95; Perm. Rep. to UN, New York 1998–2004; currently Consul Gen. Los Angeles, Calif.; fmr Prof. of Int. Relations, Univ. Complutense, Univ. Carlos III, Madrid; 30 Spanish and foreign decorations. *Publications include:* numerous papers and contribs; Confesiones de un diplomático, Tres Mitos del Real Madrid. *Address:* Consulate of Spain, 5055 Wilshire Blvd., Suite 860, Los Angeles, CA 90036, USA (office). *Telephone:* (323) 938-0158 (office). *Fax:* (323) 938-0112 (office). *E-mail:* inocencio.arias@maec.es (office). *Website:* www.maec.es/consulados/losangeles (office).

ARIAS-SALGADO Y MONTALVO, Fernando; Spanish diplomatist; b. 3 May 1938, Valladolid; s. of Gabriel Arias-Salgado y Cubas and Maria Montalvo; m. María Isabel Garrigues López-Chicheri 1969; one s. one d.; ed Univ. of Madrid, Coll. of Lawyers, Madrid; entered Diplomatic School 1963; Sec. Perm. Del. of Spain to UN 1966–68; Adviser, UN Security Council 1968–69; Asst Dir-Gen. Promotion of Research, Ministry of Educ. and Science 1971, Asst Dir-Gen. of Int. Co-operation, Ministry of Educ. and Science 1972; Legal Adviser, Legal Dept (Int. Affairs), Ministry of Foreign Affairs 1973–75, Dir 1983–85; Counsellor, Spanish Del. to Int. Court of Justice 1975; Tech. Sec.-Gen. Ministry of Foreign Affairs 1976; Dir-Gen. Radiotelevisión Española 1977–81; Amb. to UK 1981–83, to Tunisia 1993–96, to Morocco 2001–04; Consul-Gen. for Spain, Zürich 1985–90; Perm. Rep. to Int. Orgs in Vienna 1990–93. *Address:* c/o Ministry of Foreign Affairs and Co-operation, Plaza de la Provincia 1, 28012, Madrid, Spain.

ARIAS SÁNCHEZ, Oscar, PhD; Costa Rican politician, academic and head of state; *President;* b. 13 Sept. 1940, Heredia; s. of Juan Rafael Arias Trejos and Líllyan Sánchez Cortes; m. Margarita Penõn; one s. one d.; m.; ed Univ. of Costa Rica, Univ. of Essex, UK; Prof., School of Political Sciences, Univ. of Costa Rica 1969–72; Financial Adviser to Pres. of Repub. 1970–72; Minister of Nat. Planning and Econs Policy 1972–77; Int. Sec. Liberación Nacional Party 1975, Gen. Sec. 1979–83, 1983; Congressman in Legis. Ass. 1978–82; Pres. of Costa Rica 1986–90, 2006–; f. Arias Foundation for Peace and Human Progress 1988; mem. Bd Cen. Bank 1972–77, Vice-Pres. 1970–72; ad hoc Comm. mem. Heredia's Nat. Univ. 1972–75; mem. Bd Tech. Inst. 1974–77; mem. Rector's Nat. Council 1974–77; mem. Bd Int. Univ. Exchange Fund, Geneva 1976; mem. North–South Roundtable 1977; has participated in numerous int. meetings and socialist conventions; instrumental in formulating the Cen. American Peace Agreement 1986–87; campaigned for constitutional admendment to allow presidential re-election 2000, constitutional court ruled in favor of re-election 2004, announced intention to run for president 2004; approx. 50 hon. degrees; Nobel Peace Prize 1987, Martin Luther King Award 1987, Príncipe de Asturias Award 1988, shared Philadelphia Liberty Medal 1991, and other awards. *Publications:* Pressure Groups in Costa Rica 1970 (Essay's Nat. Award 1971), Who Governs in Costa Rica? 1976, Latin American Democracy, Independence and Society 1977, Roads for Costa Rica's Development 1977, New Ways for Costa Rican Development 1980 and many articles in newspapers and in nat. and foreign magazines. *Address:* Ministry of the Presidency, 2010 Zapote, Apdo 520, 1000, San José; Arias Foundation for Peace and Human Progress, Apdo 8-6410-1000, San José, Costa Rica. *Website:* www.arias.or.cr.

ARIAS SÁNCHEZ, Rodrigo, LLM; Costa Rican politician; *Minister of the Presidency;* b. 1946, brother of Oscar Arias Sánchez; ed Univ. of Costa Rica, Univ. of Pennsylvania, USA; Prof. of Commercial Law, Univ. of Costa Rica 1971–73; attorney, then legal adviser, Dir and Vice-Pres. Bolsa Nacional de Valores 1971–85, Man. 1997–2003; Chair. Ingenio Taboga SA 1974–; Pres. Municipality of Heredia 1974–86; Minister of the Presidency 1986–99, 2006–. *Address:* Office of the Presidency, 520-2010 Zapote, San José, Costa Rica (office). *Website:* www.casapres.go.cr (office).

ARIBAUD, Jean Roch; French diplomatist and civil servant; *Prefect of Seine-Saint-Denis;* b. 30 Nov. 1943, Carcassonne (Aude); s. of Jean-Baptiste Aribaud and Suzanne Boyer; m. Claire Thépot 1970; three s.; ed Balwyn High School, Australia, Lycée Condorcet, Faculté des lettres, Paris, Ecole nat. d'admin; Dir Office of Prefect, Eure-et-Loir 1971–74; Deputy Prefect Briançon 1974–77; Chef de Cabinet Sec. of State for Youth and Sport 1977, then Tech.

Adviser to Sec. of State for Overseas Depts and Territories 1978–80; Deputy Dir Social and Cultural Affairs, Sec. of State for Overseas Depts and Territories 1980–85; Asst Dir, Local Communities Dept, Ministry of Interior 1985–89; Prefect Lozère 1989–92, Yonne 1992–93, seconded Prefect and Adviser on Interior Affairs, Principality of Monaco 1993–97, Prefect Seine-Saint-Denis 2001–; High Commr in French Polynesia 1997–2001; Chevalier, Légion d'honneur, des Palmes académiques; Officier, Ordre nat. du Mérite, du Mérite agricole, de Saint-Charles (Monaco); Commdr du Mérite, Ordre Souverain de Malte; Médaille d'or Jeunesse et des Sports. *Leisure interest:* running. *Address:* c/o Ministry of the Interior, Internal Security and Local Freedoms, Place Beauvau, 75008 Paris, France.

ARIDJIS, Homero; Mexican author, poet and diplomatist; *President Emeritus, International PEN;* b. 6 April 1940, Contepec, Michoacán; m. Betty Ferber 1965, two d.; ed Autonomous Univ. of Mexico 1961; lecturer in Mexican literature at univs in USA; Cultural Attaché, Embassy in Netherlands 1972, later Amb. to Switzerland and the Netherlands; Man. Cultural Inst., Michoacán, Dir Festival Int. de Poesia 1981, 1982, 1987; f. Review Correspondencias; Chief Ed. Dialogos; Visiting Prof., Univ. of Indiana and New York Univ.; Poet-in-Residence, Columbia Univ. Translation Center, New York; co-f. Pres. Grupo de los Cien 1985 (100 internationally renowned artists and intellectuals active in environmental affairs); Nichols Chair in the Humanities and the Public Sphere, Univ. of Calif. at Irvine; Pres. International PEN 1997–2003, Pres. Emer. 2003–; Guggenheim Fellow 1966–67, 1979–80; Hon. DHumLitt (Indiana) 1993; Global 500 Award 1987, Novedades Novela Prize 1988, Grinzane Cavour Prize for Best Foreign Fiction 1992, Prix Roger Caillois, France 1997, Presea Generalisimo José María Morelos, City of Morelia 1998, Environmentalist of the Year Award, Latin Trade Magazine 1999, John Hay Award, Orion Soc. 2000, Forces for Nature Award, National Resources Defense Council 2001, Green Cross Millennium Award for Int. Environmental Leadership, Global Green, USA 2002. *Publications include:* poetry: Los ojos desdoblados 1960, Antes del reino 1963, Ajedrez-Navegaciones 1969, Los espacios azules 1969 (Blue Spaces 1974), Quemar las naves 1975, Vivir para ver 1977, Construir la muerte 1982, Obra poética 1960–86 1987, Imágenes para el fin del milenio 1990, Nueva expulsión del paraíso 1990, El poeta en peligro de extinción 1992, Tiempo de ángeles 1994, Ojos de otro mirar 1998 (Eyes to See Otherwise: Selected Poems of Homero Aridjis 2002), El ojo de la ballena 2001; prose: La tumba de Filidor 1961, Mirándola dormir 1964, Perséfone 1967 (Persephone 1986), El poeta niño 1971, Noche de independencia 1978, Espectáculo del año dos mil 1981, Playa nudista y otros relatos 1982, 1492 vida y tiempos de Juan Cabezón de Castilla 1985, El último Adán 1986, Memorias del nuevo mundo 1988, Gran teatro del fin del mundo 1989, La leyenda de los soles 1993, El Señor de los últimos días: Visiones del año dos mil 1994, ¿En quién piensas cuando haces el amor? 1996, Apocalipsis con figuras 1997, La montaña de las mariposas 2000, El silencio de Orlando 2000, La zona del silencio 2002. *Address:* International PEN, 9–10 Charterhouse Buildings, Goswell Road, London, EC1M 7AT, England. *Telephone:* (20) 7253-4308. *Fax:* (20) 7253-5711. *E-mail:* intpen@dircon.co.uk. *Website:* www.internatpen.org.

ARIDOR, Yoram, BA, MJur; Israeli politician and lawyer; b. 24 Oct. 1933, Tel-Aviv; m.; three c.; ed Hebrew Univ. of Jerusalem; mem. Knesset 1969–88, Chair. Cttee for Interior and Environmental Affairs 1975–77, Chair. Sub-Cttee for Constitutional Law 1975–77, mem. Cttee for Legislation and Justice 1969–81, Deputy Minister in Prime Minister's office 1977–81; Minister of Finance 1981–83, also of Communications Jan.–July 1981; Chair. Herut (Freedom) Movt in Histradrut (Gen. Fed. of Labour) 1972–77, mem. Cen. Cttee Herut Movt 1961–90, Chair. Secr. 1979–87; Amb. to UN 1990–92; fmr Gov. IMF. *Address:* 38 Haoranim Street, Ramat-Efal, Israel (home).

ARIE, Thomas Harry David, CBE, MA, BM, DPM, FRCP, FRCPsych, FFPHM; British psychiatrist and academic; *Professor Emeritus of Health Care of the Elderly, University of Nottingham;* b. 9 Aug. 1933, Prague, Czechoslovakia; s. of the late Dr O. M. Arie and H. Arie; m. Eleanor Aitken 1963; one s. two d.; ed Balliol Coll., Oxford; Sr Lecturer in Social Medicine, London Hosp. Medical Coll. 1962–74; Consultant Psychiatrist for Old People, Goodmayes Hosp. 1969–77; Foundation Prof. and Head, Dept of Health Care of the Elderly, Univ. of Nottingham 1977–95, Prof. Emer. 1995–; Visiting Prof., NZ Geriatrics Soc. 1980, Univ. of the Negev 1988, UCLA 1991, Univ. of Keele 1997; Consultant Psychiatrist to the Nottingham Hosps 1977–95; Vice-Pres. Royal Coll. of Psychiatrists 1984–86, Chair. Specialist Section on Old Age 1981–86; Sec. Geriatric Psychiatry Section, World Psychiatric Asscn 1983–89, Chair. 1989–93; mem. Standing Medical Advisory Cttee for the Nat. Health Service 1980–84, Cttee on the Review of Medicines 1981–91, Registrar Gen.'s Medical Advisory Cttee 1990–94; Gov. Centre for Policy on Ageing 1992–98; Council mem., Vice-Chair. Royal Surgical Aid Soc. (AgeCare) 1995–2007, Vice-Pres. 2008; Hon. Fellow, Royal Coll. of Psychiatrists 2001; Dhole-Eddlestone Memorial Prize, British Geriatrics Soc. 1996; Int. Psychogeriatric Asscn Life Award 1999, Founders' Medal, British Geriatrics Soc. 2005. *Publications:* Ed. Health Care of the Elderly 1981, Recent Advances in Psychogeriatrics (Vol. 1) 1985, (Vol. 2) 1992; papers on the care of the aged, old age psychiatry, epidemiology and educ. *Address:* Cromwell House, West Church Street, Kenninghall, Norfolk, NR16 2EN, England (home). *Telephone:* (1953) 887375 (home).

ARIGONI, Duilio, DScTech; Swiss chemist and academic; *Professor Emeritus of Organic Chemistry, Swiss Federal Institute of Technology (ETH);* b. 6 Dec. 1928, Lugano; s. of Bernardino Arigoni and Emma Arigoni (née Bernasconi); m. Carla Diener 1958 (died 1998); two s. one d.; ed Swiss Fed. Inst. of Tech. (ETH), Zürich; Lecturer in Organic Chem., ETH Zürich 1961–62, Assoc. Prof. 1962–67, Prof. 1967–96, Prof. Emer. 1996–; Visiting Prof., Harvard Univ., USA 1969, 1983, Technion, Haifa, Israel 1970, Univ. of Cambridge 1981; Prof.-

at-Large, Cornell Univ. 1980–87, Univ. of Innsbruck, Austria 2003; mem. Deutsche Akad. der Naturforscher Leopoldina 1976, Academia Europaea, London 1989, Accad. Nazionale delle Scienze, Rome 1991, European Acad. of Sciences, Brussels 2004; Foreign mem. Royal Soc., London 1991; Foreign Assoc. NAS, Washington, DC 1998; Hon. FRSC 1978; Hon. mem. French Chem. Soc. 1976, Italian Chem. Soc. 1981, American Acad. of Arts and Sciences, Boston 1988, Associé étranger, Acad. des Sciences, Paris 2005; Dr hc (Université de Paris-Sud) 1982; Davy Medal, Royal Soc., London 1983, R.A. Welch Award, Welch Foundation, USA 1985, ACS Arthur C. Cope Award 1986, Wolf Prize, Israel 1989, Marcel Benoist Prize, Switzerland 1992 and other prizes and awards. *Publications:* over 200 publs in scientific journals. *Leisure interest:* music, especially Bach, Mozart. *Address:* Laboratorium für Organische Chemie, ETH Hönggerberg, HCI H307, Wolfgang-Pauli-Strasse 10, 8093 Zürich (office); Im Glockenacker 42, 8053 Zürich, Switzerland (home). *Telephone:* (44) 632-2891 (office); (44) 381-1383 (home). *Fax:* (44) 632-1154 (office). *E-mail:* arigoni@org.chem.ethz.ch (office); duilio.arigoni@org.chem.ethz.ch (office). *Website:* www.chab.ethz.ch/forschung/loc/index_EN (office).

ARIKHA, Avigdor; French/Israeli painter and author; b. 28 April 1929, Bukovina; s. of Karl Haim and Pepi (née Korn) Dlugacz; m. Anne Atik 1961; two d.; ed Fine-Art, Bezalel, Jerusalem, Ecole des Beaux Arts, Paris and Sorbonne, Paris; after a short period of abstraction, has painted exclusively from life; painted portrait of HM Queen Elizabeth, The Queen Mother for Scottish Nat. Portrait Gallery 1983, Lord Home 1988; curator Poussin Exhbn, Louvre, Paris 1979, Ingres Exhbn, Frick Collection, New York 1986, Israel Museum, Jerusalem, Musée des Beaux-Arts, Dijon, Museum of Fine Arts, Houston, USA; fmr lecturer at univs in USA and UK; has made several films for TV; Hon. Prof., Nat. Acad. of Fine Arts, China; Chevalier, Ordre des Arts et Lettres, Chevalier, Légion d'honneur 2005; Hon. DPhil (Hebrew Univ., Jerusalem) 1997; Grand Prix des Arts (City of Paris) 1987, Prix des Arts, des Lettres et des Sciences, Fondation du Judaïsme Français, Gold Medal, Tenth Triennial (Milan, Italy) 1954. *Radio:* various programmes for Radio France Culture. *Television:* Avigdor Arikha on Diego Velazquez, BBC 1992, Avigdor Arikha, BBC Omnibus 1992. *Publications:* Ingres: Fifty Life Drawings 1986, Peinture et Regard 1991, On Depiction–Writings on Art 1995; scholarly catalogues for exhbns. etc.; numerous essays and articles. *Address:* c/o Marlborough Fine Art, 6 Albemarle Street, London, W1X 4BY, England (office).

ARIMA, Akito, DSc; Japanese scientist and academic; *Member, House of Councillors;* b. 13 Sept. 1930; s. of Johji Arima and Kazuko Arima; m. Hiroko Aota 1957; one s. one d.; ed Musashi Koto Gakko Coll., Univ. of Tokyo; Visiting Prof., Rutgers and Princeton Univs 1967–68, State Univ. of New York, Stony Brook 1968, USA 1971–73; Prof. of Physics, Faculty of Science, Univ. of Tokyo 1975, Dir Computer Centre 1981–87, Dean of the Faculty of Science 1985–87, Vice-Pres. Univ. of Tokyo 1987–89, Pres. 1989–93; Pres. Inst. of Physical and Chemical Research (RIKEN) 1993–98; Minister of Educ. and Dir Gen. of Science and Tech. Agency 1998–99; currently mem. House of Councillors; mem. Science Council of Japan 1985–94; Das Grosse Verdienstkreuz (Germany) 1990, Order of Orange Nassau (Netherlands) 1991; Hon. DSc (Univ. of Glasgow); Nishina Memorial Prize 1978, Humboldt Prize 1987, John Price Wetherill Medal 1990, Bonner Prize 1993, Japan Acad. Prize 1993. *Publication:* Interacting Boson Model 1987. *Leisure interests:* Haiku, calligraphy, reading. *Address:* RM223, Sangiin-Kaikan 2-1-1, Nagata-cho, Chiyoda-ku, Tokyo 100-8962, Japan. *Telephone:* (3) 3508-8223. *Fax:* (3) 5512-2223. *E-mail:* akito_arima@sangiin.go.jp.

ARINZE, HE Cardinal Francis A., DD, STL; Nigerian ecclesiastic; *Prefect of Congregation Emeritus for Divine Worship and the Discipline of the Sacraments;* b. 1 Nov. 1932, Eziowelle, Onitsha; s. of Joseph Arinze Nwankwu and Bernadette M. Arinze; ed Bigard Memorial Seminary, Nigeria, Urban Univ., Rome and Univ. of London; ordained 1958; consecrated Bishop (Titular Church of Fissiana) 1965; Archbishop of Onitsha 1967; cr. Cardinal 1985; Pres. Pontifical Council for Inter-Religious Dialogue 1984–2002; Prefect of Congregation for Divine Worship and the Discipline of the Sacraments 2002–08, Emer. 2009–; Hon. PhD (Univ. of Nigeria) 1986; Hon. LLD (Catholic Univ. of America) 1998; Hon. DD (Wake Forest Univ., USA) 1999, (Univ. of Our Lady of the Lake, USA) 2003; Hon. DH (Univ. of Santo Tomas, Philippines) 2001, DD hc (Christendom Coll., VA) 2004. *Publications:* Partnership in Education 1965, Sacrifice in Ibo Religion 1970, Answering God's Call 1983, Alone With God 1986, Church in Dialogue 1990, Meeting Other Believers 1997, Brücken Bauen 2000, The Holy Eucharist 2001, Religions for Peace 2002, Trust in Divine Providence 2003, God's Invisible Hand 2003. *Leisure interests:* tennis, reading. *Address:* Congregation for Divine Worship and the Discipline of the Sacraments, Palazzo delle Congregazioni, Piazza Pio XII 10, 00193 Rome, Italy (home). *Telephone:* (06) 69884316 (home). *Fax:* (06) 69883499 (home). *E-mail:* cultdiv@ccdds.va (home). *Website:* www.vatican.va/roman_curia/congregations/ccdds (home).

ARISMUNANDAR, Wiranto, MSc; Indonesian mechanical engineer, academic and politician; *Professor of Mechanical Engineering, Institut Teknologi Bandung;* b. 19 Nov. 1933, Semarang; s. of Raden Arismunandar and Raden Roro Sri Wuryan; m. Nyi Raden Sekarningrum Wirakusumah; three s., three d.; ed Univ. of Indonesia, Purdue and Stanford Univs, USA; Research Assoc., Dept of Mechanical Eng, Stanford Univ. 1961–62; training in rocket propulsion, Japan 1965; Vice-Chair. Indonesian Nat. Inst. of Aeronautics and Space 1978–89; Prof. of Mechanical Eng, Inst. of Tech., Bandung 1973–, Pres. 1988–97; Minister of Educ. and Culture 1998; Sr Scientist, Indonesian Agency for the Assessment and Application of Tech.; technological adviser, Indonesian Aircraft Industry 1979–; Consultant, Indonesian Nat. Atomic Energy Agency; mem. People's Consultative Council 1992–97, Consultative Bd

Indonesian Islamic Council; Chair. Patent Appeal Cttee, Ministry of Justice; mem. Nat. Energy Cttee, World Energy Conf., Nat. Telecommunication Council, Indonesian Nat. Cttee; mem. Indonesian Nat. Research Council, AIAA, Indonesian Aeronautics and Astronautics Inst., Soc. of Automotive Engineers of Indonesia (Founding mem.) and many other nat. and int. eng bodies; Chief Ed. Teknology magazine; Fellow, Islamic Acad. of Sciences; Satyalancana Dwidya Sistha Medal of Merit 1968, 1983, 1989, 1992, Satyalancana Karya Satya (First Class) 1990, Satyalancana Karya Satya for 30 years' service, Bintang Jasa Utama 1998. *Publications:* 13 books and more than 100 papers. *Leisure interests:* sport, photography. *Address:* Institut Teknologi Bandung, Department of Mechanical Engineering, Ganesa 10, Bandung 40132 (office); Bukit Dago Utara I/6, Bandung 40135, Indonesia (home). *Telephone:* (22) 2534118 (office); (22) 2503558 (home). *Fax:* (22) 2534212 (office); (22) 2503558 (home). *E-mail:* wiranto@lmbsp.ms.itb.ac.id (office). *Website:* lmbsp.ms.itb.ac.id (office).

ARISMUNANDAR, Lt-Gen. Wismoyo; Indonesian army officer; brother-in-law of fmr Pres. Suharto; fmrly special forces Commdr; fmr Army Deputy Chief, Army Chief 1993–. *Address:* c/o Ministry of Defence and Security, Jalan Merdeka Barat 13, Jakarta 10110, Indonesia (office).

ARISTIDE, Jean Bertrand, PhD; Haitian fmr head of state and fmr ecclesiastic; b. Salut; m. Mildred Trouillot 1996; one d.; Roman Catholic priest; expelled from Salesian Order 1988; resgnd from priesthood Nov. 1994; Pres. of Haiti Feb.–Oct. 1991, 1993–96, Feb. 2001–04; in exile in Caracas, Venezuela Oct. 1991; returned Oct. 1993 after resignation of junta; fled to Africa following civil unrest Feb. 2004; Research Fellow in African Languages, Univ. of SA 2004–07. *Publications:* Haiti and the New World Order 1995, Dignity 1996, Eyes of the Heart 2000. *Address:* c/o Centre for African Renaissance Studies, PO Box 392, UNISA, 0003 Pretoria, South Africa.

ARKHIPOVA, Irina Konstantinovna; Russian singer (mezzo-soprano); b. 2 Jan. 1925, Moscow; d. of Vetoschkin Konstantin and Galda Evdokija; m. Piavkò Vladislav; one s.; ed Inst. of Architecture, Moscow with Nadezda Malysheva, Moscow Conservatoire with L. Savransky; stage debut as soloist (Lubasha) of Tsar's Bridge with Sverdlovsk Opera and Carmen with Bolshoi Theatre 1956, leading soloist –1958; mem. CPSU 1963–91; mem. USSR Supreme Soviet 1962–66; People's Deputy 1989–91; Prof., Moscow Conservatoire 1982–; Pres. Int. Union of Musicians, Irina Arkhipova Foundation; opera performances and song recitals since 1956 at Milan, Vienna, Paris, London and in USA; performs Russian, French and Italian repertoire, roles include Carmen, Amneris in Aida, Hélène in War and Peace, Eboli in Don Carlos; mem. Acad. of Creative Endeavours 1991, Int. Acad. of Sciences 1994; co-f. Irina Arkhipova Foundation 1993; People's Artist of USSR 1966, Lenin Prize 1978, Hero of Socialist Labour 1984, People's Artist of Kyrgyzstan 1993, State Prize 1997. *Publications:* My Muses 1992, Music of Life 1997. *Address:* 103009 Moscow, Bryusov per. 2/14, Apt. 27, Russia (home). *Telephone:* (495) 290-64-03 (office); (495) 229-43-07 (home). *E-mail:* info@arhipova.org (office). *Website:* www.arhipova.org/en (office).

ARKIN, Alan Wolf; American actor, director and author; b. 26 March 1934; s. of David Arkin and Beatrice Arkin; m. 2nd Barbara Dana; one s.; m. 3rd Suzanne Newlander; two s. from first marriage; ed Los Angeles City Coll., Los Angeles State Coll., Bennington Coll.; made professional theatre debut with the Compass Players, St Louis 1959; later joined Second City group, Chicago 1960; made New York debut at Royal, in revue From the Second City 1961; played David Kolvitz in Enter Laughing 1963–64 (Tony Award 1963), appeared in revue A View Under The Bridge 1964, Harry Berline in Luv. *Films include:* Enter Laughing (New York Film Critics Theatre World Award 1964) 1964, The Russians Are Coming, The Russians Are Coming (Golden Globe Award) 1966, Women Times Seven 1967, Wait Until Dark 1967, Inspector Clouseau 1968, The Heart is a Lonely Hunter 1968, Popi 1969, Catch-22 1970, Little Murders (also Dir) 1971, Last of the Red Hot Lovers 1972, Freebie and the Bean 1974, Rafferty and the Gold Dust Twins 1975, Hearts of the West (Best Supporting Actor Award) 1975, The In-Laws 1979, The Magician of Lublin 1979, Simon 1980, Chu Chu and the Philly Flash 1981, Improper Channels (Canadian Acad. Award) 1981, The Last Unicorn 1982, Joshua Then and Now (Canadian Acad. Award) 1985, Coupe de Ville 1989, Havana 1990, Edward Scissorhands 1990, The Rocketeer 1990, Glengarry Glen Ross 1992, Indian Summer 1993, So I Married an Axe Murderer 1993, Steal Big, Steal Little 1995, Mother Night 1995, Grosse Point Blank 1997, Gattaca 1998, The Slums of Beverly Hills 1998, Jakob the Liar 1999, Arigo 2000, America's Sweethearts 2001, Thirteen Conversations About One Thing 2001, Counting Sheep 2002, Noel 2004, Eros 2004, The Novice 2004, Firewall 2006, Little Miss Sunshine (Screen Actors' Guild Award for Outstanding Performance by a Cast 2007, BAFTA Award for Best Supporting Actor 2007, Acad. Award for Best Supporting Actor 2007) 2006, The Santa Clause 3: The Escape Clause 2006, Raising Flagg 2006, Rendition 2007, Get Smart 2008. *TV appearances include:* The Love Song of Barney Kempinski 1966, The Other Side of Hell 1978, The Defection of Simas Kudirka 1978, Captain Kangaroo, A Deadly Business 1986, Escape from Sobibor, Necessary Parties, Cooperstown, Taking the Heat, Doomsday Gun, Varian's War 2001, The Pentagon Papers 2003, And Starring Pancho Villa as Himself 2003, Noel 2004. *Theatre includes:* dir: Eh? at the Circle in the Square, 1966, Hail Scrawdyke 1966, Little Murders, 1969, White House Murder Case 1970, The Sunshine Boys, Eh? 1972, Molly 1973, Joan Lorraine 1974, Power Plays (also wrote and directed), Promenade Theatre 1998, The Sorrows of Stephen, Room Service. *Publications:* Tony's Hard Work Day, The Lemming Condition, Halfway Through the Door, The Clearing 1986, Some Fine Grampa! 1995, One Present from Flekmans 1998, Cassie Loves Beethoven 1999. *Address:* c/o The Endeavor Agency, 9601 Wilshire Blvd, 10th Floor, Beverly Hills, CA 90212, USA (office). *Telephone:* (310) 248-2000 (office). *Fax:* (310) 248-2020 (office).

ARLACCHI, Pino; Italian politician and international organization official; b. 21 Feb. 1951, Gioia Tauro, Reggio Calabria; m.; two c.; Assoc. Prof. of Applied Sociology, Univ. of Calabria 1982–85, Univ. of Florence 1988–94; apptd Prof. of Sociology, Univ. of Sassari 1994; elected to Chamber of Deputies 1994–95, to Senate 1995–97; Vice-Pres. Parl. Comm. on the Mafia; UN Under-Sec.-Gen. and Dir-Gen. UN Vienna Office 1997–2002; Exec. Dir UN Office for Drug Control and Crime Prevention 1997–2002; fmr Pres. Int. Asscn for the Study of Organized Crime; Hon. Pres. Giovanni Falcone Foundation 1992–; Fellow, Ford Foundation. *Publications:* numerous publs on int. organized crime. *Address:* c/o Vienna International Centre, PO Box 500, 1400 Vienna, Austria (office).

ARLMAN, Paul, MA; Dutch international civil servant and trade association administrator; *Secretary-General, Federal European Securities Exchanges;* b. 11 July 1946, Bussum; s. of Evert Arlman and Corrie Jacobs; m. Kieke Wijs 1971; one s. one d.; ed Hilversum Grammar School, Rotterdam Econ. Univ., Peace Research Inst., Groningen and Nice European Inst., France; served in the Treasury, The Hague 1970–74, as Treasury Rep. to the Netherlands Embassy, Washington DC 1974–78; Div. Chief Treasury, The Hague 1978–81, Dir and Deputy Asst Sec. Int. Affairs 1981–86; Exec. Dir IBRD, IDA, IFC, MIGA 1986–90; mem. Bd of Dirs, EIB 1981–86, Chair. Bd Policy Cttee 1983–84; Sec.-Gen. Amsterdam Stock Exchange 1991–96; Dir Int. Affairs Amsterdam Exchanges 1997–98; Sec.-Gen. Fed. European Securities Exchanges 1998–; mem. Bd European Capital Market Inst.; mem. Peters Cttee on Corp. Governance, mem. Bd Int. Corp. Govt Inst.; scholarships from Royal Dutch Shell, Ministry of Educ. and European Comm. *Leisure interests:* literature, tennis, skiing, outdoor sports. *Address:* Federation European Securities Exchange, Rue du Lombard 41, 1000 Brussels, Belgium (office); Jan van Nassaustraat 33, 2596 BM The Hague, Netherlands (home). *Telephone:* (2) 551-01-80 (office); (70) 3244938 (home). *Fax:* (2) 512-49-05 (office); (70) 3240458 (home). *E-mail:* arlman@fese.be (office); paul@arlman.com (home). *Website:* www.fese.org (office).

ARMACOST, Michael Hayden, MA, PhD; American diplomatist, politician and administrator; *Shorenstein Distinguished Fellow, Asia Pacific Research Center, Institute for International Studies, Stanford University;* b. 15 April 1937, Cleveland, Ohio; s. of George H. Armacost and Verda Gay Armacost (née Hayden); brother of Samuel Henry Armacost (q.v.); m. Roberta June Bray 1959; three s.; ed Carleton Coll., Friedrich Wilhelms Univ., Columbia Univ.; Assoc. Prof. of Govt, Pomona Coll., Claremont, Calif. 1962–70; Wig Distinguished Prof. 1966; Special Asst to Amb., American Embassy, Tokyo 1972–74, Amb. to Philippines 1982–84, to Japan 1989–93; mem. Policy Planning, Staff Dept, Washington, DC 1974–77; Sr Staff mem., Nat. Security Council, Washington, DC 1977–78; Dep. Asst Sec. Defence, Int. Security Affairs Defence Dept, Washington, DC 1978–79; Principal Deputy Asst Sec. E Asian and Pacific Affairs 1980–81; Undersec. Political Affairs 1984–89; mem. Council on Foreign Relations; Visiting Prof. of Int. Relations, Int. Christian Univ., Tokyo 1968–69; Pres. Brookings Inst., Washington, DC 1995–2002, Trustee 2002–, White House Fellow 1969–70; currently Shorenstein Distinguished Fellow, Asia Pacific Research Center, Stanford Institute for Int. Studies; Superior Honour Award, State Dept 1976; Distinguished Civilian Service Award, Defence Dept 1980; Presidential Distinguished Service Award; Sec. of State Distinguished Service Award. *Publications:* The Politics of Weapons Innovation 1969, The Foreign Relations of United States 1969, Friends or Rivals 1996. *Leisure interests:* reading, music, golf. *Address:* Asia Pacific Research Center, Stanford University, Encina Hall, Room E301, Stanford, CA 94305-6055, USA (office). *Telephone:* (650) 724-4002 (office). *Fax:* (650) 723-6530 (office). *E-mail:* armacost@stanford.edu (office). *Website:* fsi.stanford.edu/people/michaelharmacost (office).

ARMACOST, Samuel Henry, BA, MBA; American business executive; *Chairman, SRI International;* b. 1939, Newport News, Va; brother of Michael Hayden Armacost (q.v.); m. Mary Jane Armacost 1962; two d.; ed Denison Univ., Granville, Ohio, Stanford Univ.; joined Bank of America as credit trainee 1961; London branch 1969–71; State Dept Office of Monetary Affairs (executive exchange programme) 1971–72; Head Europe, Middle East and Africa Div., London 1977–79; Cashier Bank of America and Treasurer of its Holding Co. Bank-America Corpn 1979–80; Pres. and CEO Bank of America and Bank-America Corpn 1981–86, Chair. and CEO 1986 (resgnd); Investment Banker Merrill Lynch and Co. 1987; Man. Dir Merrill Lynch Capital Markets 1987–1990; Man. Dir Weiss, Peck & Greer LLC 1990–98; Chair. SRI Int. (fmrly Stanford Research Inst.) 1998–; mem. Bd of Dirs ChevronTexaco Corpn 2001–, Callaway Golf Co., The James Irvine Foundation, Del Monte Foods Co., Scios Inc., Exponent Inc., Sarnoff Corpn, Bay Area Council; mem. Exec. Bd Bay Area Science Infrastructure Consortium (BASIC). *Address:* SRI International, 333 Ravenswood Avenue, Menlo Park, CA 94025-3493, USA (office). *Telephone:* (650) 859-2000 (office). *Fax:* (650) 326-5512 (office). *Website:* www.sri.com (office).

ARMANI, Giorgio; Italian fashion designer and business executive; *Chairman, President and Chief Executive Officer, Giorgio Armani SpA;* b. 11 July 1934, Piacenza; s. of the late Ugo Armani and of Maria Raimondi; ed Univ. of Milan; window dresser, then Asst Buyer, La Rinascente, Milan 1957–64; Designer and Product Developer Hitman (menswear co. of Cerruti Group) 1964–70; freelance designer for several firms 1970; f. Giorgio Armani SpA with Sergio Galeotti 1975, achieved particular success with unconstructed jackets of mannish cut for women, trademarks also in babywear, underwear, accessories, perfume; appeared on cover of Time 1982; patron Sydney Theatre Co.; Grand'Ufficiale dell'ordine al merito 1986, Gran Cavaliere 1987; Dr hc (RCA, London) 1991, (Univ. of the Arts, London) 2006, (Polytechnic Univ., Milan) 2007; numerous awards including Cutty Sark 1980, 1981, 1984, 1986, 1987, (First Designer Laureate 1985), Ambrogino d'Oro, Milan 1982, Int.

Designer Award, Council of Fashion Designers of America 1983, L'Occhio d'Oro 1984, 1986, 1987, 1988, L'Occhiolino d'Oro 1984, 1986, 1987, 1988, Time-Life Achievement Award 1987, Cristobal Balenciaga Award 1988, Woolmark Award, New York 1989, 1992, Senken Award, Japan 1989, Award from People for the Ethical Treatment of Animals, USA 1990, Fiorino d'Oro, Florence, for promoting Made in Italy image 1992, Hon. Nomination from Brera Acad., Milan 1993, Aguja de Oro Award, Spain, for Best Int. Designer 1993, Telva Triunfador Award, Madrid, for Best Designer of the Year 1993. *Leisure interests:* cinema, music, books. *Address:* Giorgio Armani SpA, 650 Fifth Avenue, New York, NY 10019 (office); Via Borgonuovo 21, 20121 Milan, Italy (office); Giorgio Armani SpA, 114 Fifth Avenue, New York, NY 10011, USA (office). *Telephone:* (02) 723181 (Milan) (office). *Fax:* (02) 72318549 (Milan) (office). *Website:* www.giorgioarmani.com (office).

ARMATRADING, Joan, MBE, BA; British singer and songwriter; b. 9 Dec. 1950, St Kitts, West Indies; d. of Amos Ezekiel Armatrading and Beryl Madge Benjamin; moved to Birmingham, UK 1958; began professional career in collaboration with lyric-writer Pam Nestor 1972; tours worldwide; Hon. Fellow, John Moores Univ., Liverpool, Univ. of Northampton; Hon. DLitt (John Moores Univ., Liverpool), (Aston Univ., Birmingham); Hon. DMus (Birmingham). *Recordings include:* albums: Whatever's For Us 1973, Back To The Night 1975, Joan Armatrading 1976, Show Some Emotion 1977, Me Myself I 1980, Walk Under Ladders 1981, The Key 1983, Secret Secrets 1985, The Shouting Stage 1988, Hearts and Flowers 1990, The Very Best of 1991, Square the Circle 1992, What's Inside 1995, Lovers Speak 2003, Into the Blues 2007. *Leisure interests:* British comics, vintage cars. *Address:* c/o JABA CDs, 72 New Bond Street, London, W1Y 9DD, England (office). *Website:* www.joanarmatrading.com (office).

ARMEY, Richard (Dick) Keith, BA, MA, PhD; American economist and fmr politician; *Chairman, Freedom Works Inc.;* b. 7 July 1940, Cando, ND; s. of Glen Armey and Marion Gutschlog; m. Susan Byrd; four s. one d.; ed Jamestown Coll., ND and Univs of N Dakota and Oklahoma; mem. Faculty of Econs, Univ. of Montana 1964–65; Asst Prof., West Texas State Univ. 1967–68, Austin Coll. 1968–72; Assoc. Prof., North Texas State Univ. 1972–77, Chair. Dept of Econs 1977–83; mem. US House of Reps from 26th Tex. Dist 1985–2002; Majority Leader, House of Reps 1995–2002; retd from Congress 2002; mem. Republican Party; Sr Policy Adviser and Co-Chair. Homeland Security Task Force, DLA Piper Rudnick Gray Cary 2003–; also currently Chair. Freedom Works Inc., Washington, DC; Hon. Patron, Univ. of Dublin Philosophical Soc. 2008. *Publications:* Price Theory 1977, The Freedom Revolution 1995, The Flat Tax 1996, Armey's Axioms 2003. *Address:* Freedom Works, 600 Pennsylvania Avenue NW, North Building, Suite 700, Washington, DC 20004 (office); DLA Piper Rudnick Gray Cary, 500 Eighth Street, NW, Washington, DC 20004, USA (office). *Telephone:* (202) 783-3870 (Freedom Works) (office); (202) 799-4316 (DLA Piper) (office). *Fax:* (202) 942-7649 (Freedom Works) (office); (972) 813-6249 (DLA Piper) (office). *Website:* www.freedomworks.org (office).

ARMFIELD, Diana Maxwell, RA, RWS, CSIA; British painter; b. 11 June 1920, Ringwood, Hants.; d. of Joseph Harold Armfield and Gertrude Mary Uttley; m. Bernard Dunstan 1949; three s.; ed Bedales School, Bournemouth Art School, Slade School of Art, Cen. School of Arts and Crafts, London; teacher, Byam Shaw School of Art 1959–80; Artist in Residence, Perth, Australia 1985, Jackson, Wyoming, USA 1989; Assoc. Royal Acad. 1989–1991, full mem. 1991–; mem. Royal Soc. of Painters in Watercolours (ARWS) 1977–, Royal Water Colour Soc. 1983–; Hon. mem. New English Art Club, Pastel Soc., Royal Acad. 1989–; Hon. retd mem. Royal Cambrian Acad., Royal W of England Acad.; Hunting Finalist Prize 1980, 1981. *Publications:* Painting in Oils, Drawing; subject of book The Art of Diana Armfield by Julian Halsby. *Leisure interests:* music, gardening. *Address:* 10 High Park Road, Kew, Richmond, Surrey, TW9 4BH, England; Llwynhir, Parc, Bala, Gwynedd, LL23 7YU, Wales. *Telephone:* (20) 8876-6633 (Richmond). *Fax:* (20) 8876-6633 (Richmond).

ARMITAGE, Richard Lee; American fmr diplomatist; *President, Armitage International LC;* b. 1945; ed US Naval Acad.; US naval officer served Viet Nam –1973; US Defense Attache Office Saigon 1973–75; consultant, Pentagon 1975, posted Tehran, Iran –1976; private sector 1976–78; Admin. Asst to Kan. Senator Robert Dole, 1978–80; Sr Advisor, Interim Foreign Policy Advisory Bd 1980; Deputy Asst Sec. of Defense, E Asia and Pacific Affairs 1981–83, Asst Sec. of Defense, Int. Security Affairs 1983–89; Presidential Special Negotiator, Philippines Mil. Bases Agreement and Special Mediator for Water, Middle East 1989–92; Special Emissary to King Hussein, Jordan 1991; Coordinator, Emergency Humanitarian Assistance 1992; Dir, assistance to new independent states (NIS), fmr Soviet Union 1992–93; Pres. Armitage Associates LLC 1993–2001; Deputy Sec. of State 2001–05; Pres. Armitage Int. LC 2005–; mem. Bd of Dirs ManTech Int. Corpn 2005–, ConocoPhillips Co. 2006–, Transcutaneous Technologies Inc. (TTI) 2006–; mem. Bd of Trustees Center for Strategic and Int. Studies (CSIS); Distinguished Public Service (four times), Outstanding Public Service, State Dept Distinguished Honor Award, numerous US mil. decorations, decorations from govts of Thailand, Repub. of Korea, Bahrain, Pakistan; Dept of Defense Medal, Sec. of Defense Medal, Presidential Citizens Medal. *Address:* Armitage International LC, 2300 Clarendon Blvd, Suite 601, Arlington, VA 22201-3392, USA (office). *Telephone:* (703) 248-0344 (office). *Fax:* (703) 248-0166 (office). *Website:* www.armitageinternational.net (office).

ARMITT, John, CBE; British transport industry executive, construction manager and engineer; *Chairman, Engineering and Physical Sciences Research Council (EPSRC);* civil engineer, John Laing Construction Co., Jt Man. Dir 1963–93; Project Man. Channel Tunnel Rail Link 1992–97; CEO Union Railways 1993–97, selected route and oversaw parl. legislation for Channel Tunnel–London St Pancras Station Rail Link; CEO Costain (eng and construction group) 1997–2001, negotiated co-operation agreement with Skanska; CEO Railtrack PLC 2001–02, Network Rail 2002–07; Chair. UK Engineering and Physical Sciences Research Council (EPSRC) 2007–, Olympic Delivery Authority 2007–; Dir Major Projects Asscn; fmr Chair. Anglo-French venture to build Second Severn Crossing. *Address:* Engineering and Physical Sciences Research Council, Polaris House, North Star Avenue, Swindon, SN2 1ET, England (office). *Telephone:* (1793) 444000 (office). *Website:* www.epsrc.ac.uk (office).

ARMSTRONG, Billie Joe; American singer and musician (guitar); b. 17 Feb. 1972, San Pablo, CA; m. Adrienne Nesser 1994; two s.; founding mem., Sweet Children, renamed Green Day 1989–; numerous tours and television appearances; side projects include Pinhead Gunpowder, Screeching Weasel, The Network and Foxboro Hot Tubs; Australian MTV Awards for Best Group 2005, for Best Rock Video (for American Idiot) 2005, MTV Award for Best Rock Video, Best Group Video (both for Boulevard of Broken Dreams), Best Group, MTV Viewer's Choice Award 2005, Kerrang! Awards for Best Band on the Planet, Best Live Act 2005, NME Award for Best Video (for American Idiot) 2005, MTV Europe Music Award for Best Rock 2005, Billboard 200 Album Group of the Year 2005, Billboard Music Awards for Pop Group of the Year, for Hot 100 Group of the Year, for Rock Artist of the Year, for Rock Song of the Year (for Boulevard of Broken Dreams), for Modern Rock Artist of the Year 2005, Grammy Award for Record of the Year (for Boulevard of Broken Dreams) 2006, BRIT Award for Best Int. Group 2006, ASCAP Awards for Creative Voice, and for Song of the Year (for Boulevard of Broken Dreams) 2006. *Recordings include:* albums: with Green Day: 39/Smooth 1990, Kerplunk 1991, Dookie 1994, Insomniac 1994, Nimrod 1997, Warning 2000, International Superhits (compilation) 2001, Shenanigans 2002, American Idiot (Grammy Award for Best Rock Album 2005, MTV Europe Music Award for Best Album 2005, American Music Award for Favorite Pop/Rock Album 2005, BRIT Award for Best Int. Album 2006) 2004, 21st Century Breakdown 2009; with The Network: Money Money 2020 2003; with Foxboro Hot Tubs: Stop Drop and Roll!!! 2008. *E-mail:* info@greenday.com (office). *Website:* www.greenday.com.

ARMSTRONG, C. Michael, BS; American business executive; *Chairman, Johns Hopkins Medicine;* b. 18 Oct. 1938, Detroit, Mich.; s. of Charles H. Armstrong and Zora Jean Armstrong (née Brooks); m. Anne Gossett 1961; three d.; ed Miami Univ., Dartmouth Inst.; joined IBM Corpn 1961, Dir Systems Man. Marketing Div. 1975–76, Vice-Pres. Market Operations East 1976–78, Pres. Data Processing Div. 1978–80, Vice-Pres. Plans and Controls, Data Processing Product Group 1980–84, Asst Group Exec. 1980–83, Group Exec. 1983–92, Sr Vice-Pres. 1984–92, fmrly Pres. IBM Corpn Europe, Pres. and Dir Gen. World Trade (Europe, Middle East, Africa) 1987–89; Chair. World Trade Corpn 1989–92; Chair., CEO Hughes Aircraft Co. 1992–93, Hughes Electronics Corpn 1993; Chair., CEO AT&T 1997–2002; Chair. Comcast Corpn 2002–04; Chair. Johns Hopkins Medicine 2005–; Chair. Pres.'s Export Council 1994; Visiting Prof. of Practice of Man., MIT Sloan School of Man.; Chair. FCC Network Reliability and Inter-Operability Council 1999; Dir HCA Inc. 2004–; mem. Bd of Dirs. Citigroup, Nat. Cable TV Asscn.; mem. Supervisory Bd Thyssen-Bornemisza Group, Council on Foreign Relations, Nat. Security Telecommunications Advisory Cttee, Defence Policy Advisory Cttee on Trade (DPACT), numerous univ. advisory bds; mem. Bd of Trustees of Carnegie Hall, The Johns Hopkins Univ.; Hon. LLD (Pepperdine Univ.) 1997, (Loyola Marymount Univ.) 1998. *Address:* Johns Hopkins Medicine, 733 North Broadway, Baltimore, MD 21205, USA (office). *Website:* www.hopkinsmedicine.org (office).

ARMSTRONG, Clay M., BA, MD; American physiologist and academic; *Professor of Physiology, School of Medicine, University of Pennsylvania;* ed Rice Univ., Houston, Tex., Washington Univ. School of Medicine, St Louis, Mo.; intern, Univ. of Chicago Clinics 1960–61; Multiple Sclerosis Soc. Research Fellowship, Neurology Dept, Washington Univ. School of Medicine 1961; Research Assoc., NIH 1961–64; Asst Prof. of Physiology, Duke Univ. 1966–69; Assoc. Prof., Univ. of Rochester, NY 1969–75, Prof. of Physiology, Univ. of Rochester School of Medicine 1974–75; Prof. of Physiology, Univ. of Pennsylvania School of Medicine 1976–, mem. Neurosciences Grad. Group; mem. NAS, Biophysical Soc., Soc. of Gen. Physiologists (Pres. 1985–86), Physiological Study Section, American Physiological Soc. 1975–79 (Chair. 1979), Inst. of Medicine 1996; mem. Editorial Bd Journal of General Physiology 1976–, Journal of Neurophysiology 1980–84; Trustee Marine Biological Lab., Woods Hole, MA 1980–93; Hon. Research Assoc., Univ. Coll., London, UK 1964–66; Scholarship, Washington Univ. School of Medicine 1956–60, Teacher of the Year, Freshman Medical Class, Univ. of Rochester 1973, K.S. Cole Award, Biophysical Soc. 1975, Bowditch Lecturer, American Physiological Soc. 1975, Distinguished Lecturer, Soc. of Gen. Physiologists, IUPAB Meeting 1986, Distinguished Alumnus, Rice Univ. 1995, Louisa Gross Horwitz Prize 1996 (co-recipient), Albert Lasker Award for Basic Medical Research 1999, Jacob Javits Neuroscience Research Award, NIH. *Publications:* numerous articles in scientific journals. *Address:* B701 Richards Building, Department of Physiology, 3700 Hamilton Walk, University of Pennsylvania, Philadelphia, PA 19104-6085, USA (office). *Telephone:* (215) 898-7816 (office). *Fax:* (215) 573-5851 (office). *E-mail:* carmstro@mail.med.upenn.edu (office). *Website:* www.med.upenn.edu (office).

ARMSTRONG, David John, BA; Australian journalist and media executive; *Director, Post Publishing, Bangkok;* b. 25 Nov. 1947, Sydney; s. of Allan E. Armstrong and Mary P. Armstrong; m. Deborah Bailey 1980 (deceased); two d.; ed Marist Brothers High School, Parramatta, Univ. of NSW; Ed. The Bulletin 1985–86; Deputy Ed. The Daily Telegraph 1988–89; Ed. The Australian 1989–92, Ed.-in-Chief 1996–2002; Ed. The Canberra Times

1992–93; Ed. South China Morning Post, Hong Kong 1993–94, Ed.-in-Chief 1994–96; Ed.-in-Chief, South China Morning Post 2003–05; mem. Bd Dirs Post Publishing 2004–, Pres. and COO 2005–08, mem. Exec. Cttee 2006–08; mem. Bd Dirs HFP-Post 2006–; mem. Asian Bd Int. Newspaper Marketing Asscn 2006–; Australian Centenary Medal 2003. *Leisure interests:* reading, golf. *Address:* Bangkok Post Building, 136 Na Ranong Road, off Sunthorn Kosa Road, Klong Toey, Bangkok 10110, Thailand (office). *Telephone:* (2) 240-3700 (office). *Fax:* (2) 240-3679 (office). *E-mail:* david@bangkokpost.co.th (office); wansao365@gmail.com (office). *Website:* www.bangkokpost.com (office).

ARMSTRONG, David Malet, AO, BA, BPhil, PhD, FAHA, FBA; Australian academic and writer; *Professor Emeritus of Philosophy, University of Sydney;* b. 8 July 1926, Melbourne; s. of Cdre J. M. Armstrong and Philippa Suzanne Marett; m. Jennifer Mary de Bohun Clark 1982; ed Dragon School, Oxford, UK, Geelong Grammar School, Sydney Univ., Exeter Coll., Oxford, Univ. of Melbourne; Asst Lecturer in Philosophy, Birkbeck Coll., London, UK 1954–55; Lecturer, Sr Lecturer in Philosophy, Univ. of Melbourne 1956–63; Challis Prof. of Philosophy, Univ. of Sydney 1964–91, Prof. Emer. 1992–; mem. Bd Quadrant magazine; mem. US Acad. of Arts and Science; Hon. DLitt (Nottingham). *Publications:* Berkeley's Theory of Vision 1961, Perception and the Physical World 1961, Bodily Sensations 1962, A Materialist Theory of the Mind 1968, Belief, Truth and Knowledge 1973, Universals and Scientific Realism 1978, The Nature of the Mind and Other Essays 1983, What is a Law of Nature? 1983, Consciousness and Causality (with Norman Malcolm) 1984, A Combinatorial Theory of Possibility 1989, Universals: An Opinionated Instruction 1989, Dispositions: A Debate (with C. B. Martin and U. T. Place) 1996, A World of States of Affairs 1997, The Mind-Body Problem: An Opinionated Introduction 1999, Truth and Truthmakers 2004; contribs to scholarly books and journals. *Leisure interest:* genealogy. *Address:* 206 Glebe Point Road, Glebe, NSW 2037, Australia (home). *Telephone:* (2) 9660-1435 (home). *Fax:* (2) 9660-8846 (home). *E-mail:* david.armstrong@arts.usyd.edu.au (office).

ARMSTRONG, Dido Florian Cloud de Bounevialle (see Dido).

ARMSTRONG, Gillian May, AM; Australian film director; b. 18 Dec. 1950, Melbourne; d. of Raleigh Edward Armstrong and Patricia May Armstrong; m.; two d.; ed Swinburne Art Coll., Fine Arts Degree of Nat. Australian Film & TV School, Sydney; mem. Dirs' Guild of America, Acad. of Motion Picture Arts and Sciences; Patron Sydney Film Festival, Flickerfest Short Film Festival, Nat. Gallery of Victoria; Companion of the Australian Rotary Health Research Fund; Hon. Doctorate in Film (Swinburne Univ.) 1998; Hon. DLitt (Univ. of NSW) 2000; numerous awards including Women in Hollywood Icon Award 1988, Dorothy Arzner Directing Award, USA 1993. *Feature films include:* The Singer and The Dancer 1976, My Brilliant Career (Best Film and Best Dir, Australian Film Inst. Awards, Best First Feature British Film Critics Award) 1979, Starstruck 1982, Mrs Soffel 1984, High Tide (Best Film, Houston Film Festival, Grand Prix Festival Int. de Creteil, France) 1987, Fires Within 1990, The Last Days of Chez Nous 1991, Little Women 1995, Oscar and Lucinda 1997, Charlotte Gray 2001, Unfolding Florence 2005, Death Defying Acts 2006. *Address:* c/o HLA Management, 87 Pitt Street, Redfern, NSW 2016, Australia (office). *Telephone:* (2) 9310-4948 (office). *Fax:* (2) 9310-4113 (office). *E-mail:* hla@hlamgt.com.au (office). *Website:* www.hlamgt.com.au (office).

ARMSTRONG, Greg L., BS, CPA; American oil executive; *Chairman and CEO, Plains All American Pipeline LP;* ed Southeastern Okla State Univ.; joined Plains Resources 1981, Corp. Sec. 1981–88, Vice-Pres. and Chief Financial Officer (CFO) 1984–91, Treas. 1984–97, Sr Vice-Pres. and CFO 1991–92, Exec. Vice-Pres. and CFO June–Oct. 1992, Pres. and COO Oct.–Dec. 1992, Pres., CEO and Dir 1992–2001, Chair. and CEO Plains All American Pipeline LP 2001–; mem. Bd Dirs Petroleum Club of Houston, Varco Int. Inc. 2004–; mem. Texas SE Regional Bd Trustees, IPAA. *Address:* Plains All American Pipeline LP, 333 Clay Street, Suite 1600, Houston, TX 77002, USA (office). *Telephone:* (713) 646-4100 (office). *Fax:* (713) 646-4572 (office). *E-mail:* info@paalp.com (office). *Website:* www.paalp.com (office).

ARMSTRONG, Rt Hon. Hilary Jane, PC, BSc; British politician; b. 30 Nov. 1945, Sunderland; d. of the late Rt Hon Ernest Armstrong and Hannah P. Armstrong (née Lamb); m. Paul D. Corrigan 1992; ed Monkwearmouth Comprehensive School, Sunderland, West Ham Coll. of Tech., Univ. of Birmingham; mem. Labour Party 1960–; teacher with VSO, Murray Girls' High School, PO Mwatate, Kenya 1967–69; social worker, Newcastle City Social Services Dept 1970–73; community worker, Southwick Neighbourhood Action Project, Sunderland 1973–75; Lecturer in Community and Youth Work, Sunderland Polytechnic (now Univ. of Sunderland) 1975–86; Councillor, Durham City Council 1985–87; MP (Labour) for Durham NW 1987–; Frontbench Spokesperson on Educ. (under-fives, primary and special educ.) 1988–92, on Treasury Affairs 1994–95; Parl. Pvt. Sec. to Leader of the Opposition 1992–94; mem. Nat. Exec. Labour Party 1992–97; Minister of State Dept of Environment, Transport and the Regions 1997–2001; Parl. Sec. to HM Treasury and Govt Chief Whip 2001–06; Cabinet Office Minister, Minister for Social Exclusion and Chancellor of the Duchy of Lancaster 2006–07; fmr Vice-Pres. Nat. Children's Homes; fmr mem. British Council; fmr mem. Bd VSO; fmr mem. Manufacturing Science Finance (MSF) Union. *Leisure interests:* reading, theatre, watching football. *Address:* House of Commons, Westminster, London, SW1A 0AA (office); North House, 17 North Terrace, Crook, Co. Durham, DL15 9AZ, England (home). *Telephone:* (20) 7276-2020 (office); (1388) 767065 (home). *Fax:* (1388) 767923 (home). *E-mail:* hilary@hilaryarmstrong.com. *Website:* www.hilaryarmstrong.com.

ARMSTRONG, Lance; American professional cyclist; b. 18 Sept. 1971, Plano, Texas; s. of Linda Armstrong; m. Kristin Richard 1998 (divorced 2003); three c.; US Nat. Amateur Champion 1991; mem. US Olympic team 1992, 1996, 2000 (bronze medal); mem. US Postal Service Pro Cycling Team 1998–2004, Discovery 2004–; winner numerous races including US Pro Championship, World Championships 1993, Clasica San Sebastian, Tour Du Pont 1995, Tour Du Pont 1996, Tour de Luxembourg 1998, Tour de Suisse 2001, Criterium du Dauphine Libere 2002, Criterium du Dauphine Libere 2003, Tour de France 1999–2005 (first to win seven Tours); survived testicular cancer 1996; f. Lance Armstrong Foundation for Cancer 1996; retd after completion of 2005 Tour de France; came out of retirement and joined Astana team 2008; Sports Illustrated Sportsman of the Year 2002. *Publications:* It's Not About the Bike, The Lance Armstrong Performance Programme, Every Second Counts (with Sally Jenkins) 2003. *Address:* c/o Capital Sports Ventures, 803 Presslar, Austin, TX 78703 (office); Lance Armstrong Foundation, PO Box 13026, Austin, TX 78711, USA (office). *Website:* www.lancearmstrong.com (office).

ARMSTRONG, Neil A., FRAeS; American astronaut, professor of engineering and business executive; *Chairman Emeritus, EDO Corporation;* b. 5 Aug. 1930, Wapakoneta, Ohio; s. of Stephen Armstrong; m. Janet Shearon; two s.; ed Purdue Univ. and Univ. of Southern California; naval aviator 1949–52, flew combat missions during Korean War; joined NASA Lewis Flight Propulsion Laboratory 1955, later transferred to NASA High Speed Flight Station, Edwards, Calif., as aeronautical research pilot, was X-15 project pilot flying to over 200,000 ft. and at approx. 4,000 mph; other flight test work included X-1 rocket research plane, F-100, F-101, F-104, F5D, B-47 and the paraglider; selected as astronaut by NASA Sept. 1962; command pilot for Gemini VIII 1966; backup pilot for Gemini V 1965, Gemini XI 1966; flew to the moon in Apollo XI July 1969, first man to set foot on the moon 20 July 1969; Chair. Peace Corps Nat. Advisory Council 1969; Deputy Assoc. Admin. for Aeronautics, NASA, Washington 1970–71; Prof. of Eng, Univ. of Cincinnati 1971–79; Chair. Cardwell Int. Ltd 1979–81; Chair. CTA Inc. 1982–92, AIL Systems Inc. 1989–2000, EDO Corpn 2000–2002; Dir numerous cos; mem. Pres.'s Comm. on Space Shuttle 1986, Nat. Comm. on Space 1985–86; mem. Nat. Acad. of Eng; Fellow, Soc. of Experimental Test Pilots, AIAA; Hon. Fellow Int. Astron. Fed.; Hon. mem. Int. Acad. of Astronautics; numerous decorations and awards from 17 countries including Presidential Medal of Freedom, NASA Exceptional Service Award, Royal Geographical Soc. Gold Medal and Harmon Int. Aviation Trophy 1970, Rotary National Award for Space Achievement 2004. *Address:* EDO Corporation, 60 East 42nd Street, Suite 5010, New York, NY 10165, USA (office). *Telephone:* (212) 716-2000 (office). *Fax:* (212) 716-2049 (office). *Website:* www.edocorp.com (office).

ARMSTRONG, Robin Louis, BA, PhD, FRSC; Canadian physicist and academic; *Professor Emeritus of Physics, University of Toronto;* b. 14 May 1935, Galt, Ont.; s. of Robert Dockstader Armstrong and Beatrice Jenny Armstrong (née Grill); m. Karen Elisabeth Hansen 1960; two s.; ed Univ. of Toronto and Univ. of Oxford, UK; RSC Rutherford Memorial Fellowship 1961; Asst Prof. of Physics, Univ. of Toronto 1962–68, Assoc. Prof. 1968–71, Prof. 1971–90, Adjunct Prof. 1990–99, Prof. Emer. 1999–; Assoc. Chair. Physics, Univ. of Toronto 1969–74, Chair. 1974–82, Dean Faculty of Arts and Science 1982–90, Adjunct Prof. 1990–99; Visitante Distinguido, Univ. of Córdoba, Argentina 1989; Pres. and Prof. of Physics, Univ. of New Brunswick 1990–96; Adviser to Pres., Wilfrid Laurier Univ. 1997–2000; Pres. Canadian Inst. for Neutron Scattering 1986–89, Canadian Asscn of Physicists 1990–91; Dir Canadian Inst. for Advanced Research 1981–82, Huntsman Marine Lab. 1983–87; mem. Research Council of Canadian Inst. for Advanced Research 1982–2000, Natural Science and Eng Research Council of Canada (NSERC) 1991–97 (mem. Exec. 1992–97, Vice-Pres. 1994–97), Bd of Dirs Canadian Arthritis Network (Chair. 2003–), Research and Devt Advisory Panel, Atomic Energy of Canada Ltd 1999– (Vice-Chair. 2004–05, Chair. 2006–07); Exec. Dir College Univ. Consortium Council 2006–; Hon. DSc (Univ. of New Brunswick) 2001; Herzberg Medal 1973, Medal of Achievement (Canadian Asscn of Physicists) 1990, Commemorative Medal for 125th Anniversary of Canadian Confed. 1992, Preston High School Hall of Fame 2007. *Publications:* over 180 research articles on condensed matter physics in numerous journals. *Leisure interests:* golf, gardening. *Address:* Suite 803, 383 Ellis Park Road, Toronto, ON M6S 5B2 (home); University of Toronto, Department of Physics, 60 St George Street, Toronto, Ont., M5S 1A7, Canada. *Telephone:* (416) 979-2165 ext. 254 (office); (416) 760-9146 (home); (519) 475-6737. *E-mail:* rarmstrong@cucc-ontario.ca (office); robinl.armstrong@sympatico.ca (home). *Website:* www.physics.utoronto.ca (office).

ARMSTRONG, Sheila Ann, FRAM; British singer (soprano); b. 13 Aug. 1942, Ashington, England; d. of William R. Armstrong and Janet Armstrong; m. David E. Cooper 1980 (divorced 1999); ed Hirst Park Girls' School, Ashington, Northumberland and Royal Acad. of Music; sang Despina in Così fan tutte at Sadler's Wells 1965, Belinda in Dido and Aeneas, Glyndebourne 1966, Mozart's Pamina and Zerlina and Fiorila in Rossini's Il Turco in Italia, Glyndebourne; sang in the premiere of John McCabe's Notturni ed Alba at Three Choirs Festival 1970; New York debut with New York Philharmonic 1971; sang with Los Angeles Philharmonic under Mehta; Covent Garden debut as Marzelline in Fidelio 1973; sang Donizetti's Norina and Mozart's Donna Elvira for Scottish Nat. Opera; concert engagements included Messiah at the Concertgebouw, tour of the Far East with the Bach Choir, Britten's Spring Symphony, Strauss' Four Last Songs with Royal Philharmonic, Elgar's Oratorios and the Sea Symphony by Vaughan Williams; Pres. Kathleen Ferrier Soc., trustee Kathleen Ferrier Award; Fellow Hatfield Coll., Univ. of Durham 1992; mem. Royal Philharmonic Soc.; Hon. MA (Newcastle); Hon. DMus (Durham) 1991; Mozart Prize 1965, Kathleen Ferrier Memorial Award 1965. *Recordings include:* Samson, Dido and Aeneas, Mozart's Requiem, Carmina Burana, Elgar's Apostles, The Pilgrim's Progress, Cantatas by Bach, Haydn's Stabat Mater, Beethoven's Ninth Symphony, Mahler's 2nd and 4th,

'Spring Symphony', Child of Our Time, Semele, Fauré Requiem, Rachmaninov's The Bells, Grieg's Pier Gynt Suite, Fauré's Requiem, Schubert's Lazarus. *Leisure interests:* collecting keys, interior decoration and design, flower-arranging, sewing, gardening and garden design.

ARMSTRONG-JONES, Baron (see Snowdon, Earl of).

ARMSTRONG OF ILMINSTER, Baron (Life Peer), cr. 1988, of Ashill in the County of Somerset; **Robert Temple Armstrong,** GCB, CVO, MA; British fmr civil servant; b. 30 March 1927, Oxford; s. of Sir Thomas Armstrong and of Lady Armstrong (née Draper); m. 1st Serena Mary Benedicta Chance 1953 (divorced 1985); two d.; m. 2nd (Mary) Patricia Carlow 1985; ed Eton Coll. and Christ Church, Oxford; Asst Prin. Treasury 1950–55, Pvt. Sec. to Econ. Sec. 1953–54; Pvt. Sec. to Chancellor of the Exchequer (Rt Hon. R. A. Butler) 1954–55; Prin. Treasury 1955–64; Asst Sec. Cabinet Office 1964–66; Asst Sec. Treasury 1966–68; Prin. Pvt. Sec. to Chancellor of the Exchequer (Rt Hon. Roy Jenkins) 1968; Under-Sec. Treasury 1968–70; Prin. Pvt. Sec. to the Prime Minister 1970–75; Deputy Under-Sec. of State, Home Office 1975–77, Perm. Under-Sec. of State 1977–79; Sec. of the Cabinet 1979–87; Perm. Sec. Man. and Personnel Office 1981–87; Head, Home Civil Service 1981–87; Chair. Biotechnology Investments Ltd 1989–2000; Chair. Forensic Investigative Assocs PLC 1997–2003; Chair. Hestercombe Gardens Trust 1995–2005, Bd of Govs Royal Northern Coll. of Music 2000–05; Sec. Radcliffe Cttee on Monetary System 1957–59; Sec. to the Dirs, Royal Opera House, Covent Garden 1968–87, Dir 1988–93; Dir Bristol and West Bldg Soc. 1988–97 (Chair. 1993–97), Bank of Ireland and other cos; Chair. Bd of Trustees, Victoria and Albert Museum 1988–98; mem. Rhodes Trust 1975–97; Fellow, Eton Coll. 1979–94; Chancellor, Univ. of Hull 1994–2006; Pres. The Literary Soc. 2004–; Trustee Leeds Castle Foundation 1987– (Chair. 2001–); Hon. Student, Christ Church 1985; Hon. Bencher, Inner Temple 1986; Hon. LLD. *Leisure interest:* music. *Address:* House of Lords, Westminster, London, SW1A 0PW, England. *Telephone:* (20) 7219-4983. *Fax:* (20) 7219-1259.

ARNAOUD ALI, Idriss; Djibouti politician; *President, National Assembly;* b. 1945, Ali-Sabieh; m.; four c.; Deputy, Nat. Ass. 1997–, Pres. 2003–; Sec.-Gen. Rassemblement pour le Progrés; fmr Dir Air Djibouti. *Address:* National Assembly, Djibouti, Djibouti.

ÁRNASON, Kristinn F., LLM; Icelandic diplomatist; *Director, Defence Department, Ministry of Foreign Affairs;* b. 5 Jan. 1954, Reykjavík; m.; three c.; ed Univ. of Iceland, Univ. of Exeter, UK, Univ. of Oslo, Norway; solicitor in pvt. attorney's office 1979–80, 1982, for Fed. of Employees 1983–85; First Sec. Ministry of Foreign Affairs 1985–87; Deputy Perm. Rep. to Int. Orgs, Geneva 1987–92; Chief Negotiator and Spokesman on Fisheries, Ministry of Foreign Affairs 1992–94, Dir for External Trade 1994–98; apptd Amb. 1997; Amb. to Slovakia and Poland 1999–2002, to Norway and Czech Repub. 1999–2003, to Egypt 2000–03; Dir Defence Dept, Ministry for Foreign Affairs 2003–. *Address:* Department of Defence, Ministry of Foreign Affairs, Raudarárstíg 25, 150 Reykjavík, Iceland (office). *Telephone:* 5459900 (home). *Fax:* 5622373 (office). *E-mail:* external@utn.stjr.is (office). *Website:* www.mfa.is (office).

ARNAUD, Jean-Loup, LenD; French government official; b. 25 Sept. 1942, Paris; s. of Raoul Arnaud and Emilienne Lapeyre; m. Lucienne Lavallée 1966; one d.; ed Faculté de Droit, Paris and Ecole Nat. d'Admin; Auditor, Cour des Comptes 1969, Advisory Counsellor 1976; assigned to Datar 1971–72; Tech. Counsellor, Cabinet of Sec. of State, André Rossi; assigned to financial aspects of reform of ORTF 1974–75; Advisory Counsellor, Cour des Comptes 1976; Tech. Counsellor, Cabinet of Minister of Culture and Environment 1977; Chief of Centre, Centre Nat. de la Cinématographie 1978; official in charge of relations with cinema, Soc. Nat. de Programme de France-Régions 3 (FR3) 1979–82; Admin. Soc. Française de Production Cinématographique 1983–; Head, Dept of Cinema, Ministry of Culture and Communication 1986; Dir-Gen. Soc. d'Edition de Programmes de Télévision 1987–; Admin. Fondation Européenne des métiers de l'image et du son (Femis) 1987; Dir-Gen. Télé-Hachette 1989–; Vice-Pres. Union syndicale de la production audiovisuelle 1990–; Magistrate Cour des comptes; mem. Admin. Council of France 3 1993–; Pres. Asscn pour le crédit de l'épargne des fonctionnaires de Paris et sa région 1997–; Deputy Mem. Comité fiscal, douanier et des changes 2000–; Pres. 4th Section of Second Chamber of Cour des Comptes 2001–. *Address:* Cour des comptes, 13 rue Cambon, 75001 Paris (office); 57 avenue du Maine, 75014 Paris, France (home).

ARNAULT, Bernard; French business executive; *Chairman and CEO, LVMH;* b. 5 March 1949, Roubaix; s. of Jean Arnault and Marie-Jo Arnault (née Savinel) m. 1st Anne Dewavrin 1973 (divorced); two c.; m. 2nd Hélène Mercier 1991; three s.; ed Ecole Polytechnique; joined Ferret-Savinel (family construction co.) 1971, Pres. 1978–84; lived in USA 1981–84; took over Boussac Saint-Frères (parent co. of Dior) 1985; CEO LVMH (luxury goods group which includes Louis Vuitton bags, Moët et Chandon champagne, Parfums Christian Dior, Hennessy and Hine cognac) 1989–, Chair. 1992–, Chair. Christian Dior SA; Pres. Bd of Dirs Montaigne 1997–; Owner Phillips auction house 1999– (merged with Bonhams & Brooks 2001); fmr Dir Diageo; through holding co. Financière Agache owns fashion houses Dior, Lacroix and Céline and dept store Bon Marché; Commdr, Légion d'honneur 2007, Officier, Ordre nat. du Mérite. *Publication:* La Passion créative 2000. *Leisure interests:* music, tennis. *Address:* 11 rue François 1er, 75008 Paris; LVMH, 22 avenue Montaigne, 75008 Paris, France (office). *Telephone:* 1-44-13-22-22 (office). *Fax:* 1-44-13-22-23 (office). *E-mail:* info@lvmh.com (office). *Website:* www.lvmh.com (office).

ARNETT, Emerson James, QC, BA, LLM; Canadian lawyer and business executive; b. 29 Sept. 1938, Winnipeg, Man.; s. of Emerson Lloyd Arnett and Elsie Audrey Rhind; m. Edith Alexandra Palk 1964; four c.; ed Univ. of Man., Harvard Univ.; civil litigation section, Dept of Justice, Ottawa 1964–65; Assoc.

Pitblado and Hoskin (law firm), Winnipeg 1965–66; Asst to Exec. Vice-Pres. Vickers and Benson Advertising, Toronto 1966–67; Assoc./Pnr, Davies, Ward and Beck (law firm), Toronto 1968–73; Pnr, Stikeman, Elliott (law firm), Toronto 1973–97, Resident Pnr, Washington, DC, 1993–96; Pres. and CEO Molson Inc. 1997–2000; Dir Mirabaud Asset Management (Canada) Inc. 2002–. *Publications:* Doing Business (co-ed.); numerous law review and newspaper articles and conf. papers. *Leisure interests:* shooting, skiing, hiking, reading. *Address:* c/o Board of Directors, Mirabaud Asset Management (Canada) Inc., 161 Bay Street, Suite 2706, Toronto, Ont. M5J 2S1, Canada (office). *Telephone:* (416) 572-2039 (office). *Fax:* (416) 572-4170 (office).

ARNETT, Peter; American journalist and television reporter; b. 1934, New Zealand; m. (divorced); two c.; ed Waitaki Coll., Oamaru, New Zealand; with Associated Press (AP) 1960–; war corresp. in Viet Nam, Middle East, Nicaragua, El Salvador and Afghanistan; special writer for AP, New York; joined Cable News Network (CNN) 1981–99; served as corresp. in Moscow for two years; later nat. security reporter, Washington, DC; CNN corresp. Baghdad 1991; Chief Foreign Corresp. ForeignTV.com, New York 1998, then reporter MSNBC, fired for making unauthorized remarks to state-run Iraqi TV 2003, then briefly reporter in Iraq for Daily Mirror (UK newspaper); Pulitzer prizewinner. *Publication:* Live from the Battlefield 1994. *Leisure interests:* collector of books and oriental statuary.

ARNOLD, Armin, PhD, FRSC; Swiss/Canadian academic, writer and critic; b. 1 Sept. 1931, Zug, Switzerland; s. of Franz Arnold and Ida Baumgartner; ed Univs of Fribourg, London and Zürich; Asst Prof. of German, Univ. of Alberta 1959–61, McGill Univ. 1961–64, Assoc. Prof. 1964–68, Prof. 1968–84, Auxiliary Prof. 1984–89; Dozent, Höhere Wirtschafts- und Verwaltungsschule, Olten 1984–93, Baden 1994–. *Publications include:* D.H. Lawrence and America 1958, James Joyce 1963, Die Literatur des Expressionismus 1966, Friedrich Dürrenmatt 1969, Prosa des Expressionismus 1972, Kriminalromanführer 1978, Alfred Doeblin 1996, etc. *Address:* 9E Rang Ste-Anne de la Rochelle, Québec J0E 2B0, Canada; Rauchlenweg 332, 4712 Laupersdorf, Switzerland.

ARNOLD, Eve; American photographer; b. Philadelphia; m. Arnold Arnold (divorced); one s.; ed New School for Social Research; joined Magnum Photographic Agency 1951, became full mem. 1955; moved to UK 1962; has worked for Sunday Times, Time, Life, others; worked in UK, USA, China, fmr USSR; subjects include Marilyn Monroe, Joan Crawford, John and Anjelica Huston, Francis Bacon, Yves Montand, Margot Fonteyn, Rudolph Nureyev, Malcolm X, photographs examining the status of women and numerous other topics; Fellow, Royal Photographic Soc. 1995; Hon. OBE 2003; Dr hc (Univ. of St. Andrews, Scotland) 1997, (Staffordshire Univ.) 1997, (Richmond, the American Int. Univ. in London) 1997; Lifetime Achievement Award, American Soc. of Magazine Photographers 1980, Master Photographer, Int. Center of Photography 1995. *Publications include:* The Unretouched Woman 1976, In China (Nat. Book Award) 1980, In America 1983, Marilyn for Ever 1987, Marilyn Monroe: An Appreciation 1987, Private View: Inside Baryshnikov's American Ballet Theatre 1988, The Great British 1991, Eve Arnold: In Retrospect (Kraszna-Krausz Book Award) 1996, Eve Arnold: The Hand Book 2004. *Address:* c/o Magnum Photos London, 63 Gee Street, London, EC1V 3RS (office); 26 Mount Street, London, W1Y 5RB, England (home). *Telephone:* (20) 7490-1771 (office).

ARNOLD, Hans Redlef, PhD; German diplomatist (retd), writer and academic; *Lecturer, Academy of Political Science, Munich;* b. 14 Aug. 1923, Munich; s. of Karl Arnold and Anne-Dora Volquardsen; m. Karin Baroness von Egloffstein 1954; three d.; ed Univ. of Munich; joined Foreign Service, FRG; served Embassy, Paris 1952–55, Foreign Office, Bonn 1955–57, Embassy, Washington, DC 1957–61, Foreign Office 1961–68, sometime head of Foreign Minister Willy Brandt's office; Amb. to the Netherlands 1968–72; Head, Cultural Dept, Foreign Office 1972–77; Amb. to Italy 1977–81; Insp.-Gen. German Foreign Service 1981–82; Amb. and Perm. Rep. to UN and Int. Orgs, Geneva 1982–86; Lecturer, Acad. of Political Science, Munich; several nat. and foreign decorations. *Publications:* Cultural Export as Policy? 1976, Foreign Cultural Policy 1980, The March (co-author) 1990, Europe on the Decline? 1993, Germany's Power 1995, Europe To Be Thought Anew: Why and How Further Unification? 1999, Security for Europe (co-ed.) 2002, How Much Unification Does Europe Need? 2004; regular contribs to periodicals and newspapers. *Address:* 83083 Riedering-Heft, Germany. *Telephone:* (8032) 5255. *E-mail:* hans.arnold@gmx.net (home).

ARNOLD, James R., MA, PhD; American chemist, space scientist and academic; *Harold C. Urey Emeritus Professor of Chemistry, University of California, San Diego;* b. 5 May 1923, Metuchen, NJ; s. of Abraham S. Arnold and Julia J. Arnold; m. Louise C. Arnold 1952; three s.; ed Princeton Univ.; Asst Princeton 1943, Manhattan Project 1943–46; Fellow, Inst. of Nuclear Studies, Univ. of Chicago 1946; Nat. Research Fellow, Harvard 1947; Asst Prof., Univ. of Chicago 1949–55; Assoc. Prof., Princeton Univ. 1956–58; Assoc. Prof., Dept of Chem., Univ. of Calif., San Diego 1958–60, Prof. 1960–92, Harold C. Urey Prof. 1983–92; Assoc. Ed. Moon 1972–; Dir Calif. Space Inst. (SIO), Univ. of Calif., San Diego 1980–89, interim Dir 1996–97; Prin. Investigator Calif. Space Grant Consortium 1989–2003; recipient of lunar samples from Apollo and Soviet missions; mem. of NAS, AAAS, ACS, American Acad. of Arts and Sciences; Nat. Council of World Federalists 1970–72; Guggenheim Fellow, India 1972–73; specialized in field of cosmic-ray produced nuclides, meteorites, lunar samples and cosmochemistry; asteroid 2143 is named for him 'Jimarnold'. *Publications:* over 100 articles in scientific reviews and journals. *Address:* University of California at San Diego, Department of Chemistry, Code 0524, La Jolla, CA 92093, USA. *Telephone:* (858) 534-2908. *Fax:* (619) 534-7840. *E-mail:* jarnold@ucsd.edu. *Website:* www-chem.ucsd.edu (office).

ARNOLD, Luqman; British business executive and banker; *Partner, Corsair Capital LLC;* b. April 1950, Calcutta; m.; one s.; ed Oundle School, Univ. of London; with Mfrs Hanover Corpn, London, Hong Kong and Singapore 1976–82; with First Nat. Bank (Dallas), Singapore and London 1972–76; with Credit Suisse First Boston, London and Tokyo 1982–92, responsible for Asia Pacific origination, Private Placements, Cen. and Eastern Europe, later Head of Investment Banking, New Business, mem. Operating Cttee; sabbatical year (research into drivers and outlook for cross-border institutional investment flows) 1992–93; Global Head of Investment Banking, Paribas Capital Markets, Banque Paribas, London 1993–95, Group Head of Business Devt, Paris 1995–96; CEO Asia Pacific UBS AG, Singapore and Tokyo 1996–98, COO, London 1998–99, Chief Financial Officer and Head of Corp. Centre, Zurich 1999–2001, Pres. and Chair., Exec. Bd, Zurich 2001; CEO Abbey National 2002–04; Pnr Corsair Capital LLC 2005–; mem. Devt Council, Univ. of the Arts London; Chair. Design Museum; Trustee Architecture Foundation.

ARNOLD, Roseanne (see Roseanne).

ARNOLD, Susan E., BA, MBA; American business executive; b. 8 March 1954, Pittsburgh, Pa; ed Univs of Pennsylvania and Pittsburgh; joined Procter & Gamble in 1980, held series of marketing and man. positions including Man. Noxell Products, Int. Div. (Canada) 1990–92, Gen. Man. deodorant business in US 1993, Vice-Pres. and Gen. Man. Deodorants/Old Spice and Skin Care Products in US 1996–97, Vice-Pres. and Gen. Man. North American Laundry and Fabric Conditioner Products 1997–99, Pres. Global Personal Beauty Care 1999–2000, Pres. Global Cosmetics and Skin Care 2000–02, Pres. Global Personal Beauty Care and Feminine Care 2002–04, Vice-Chair. and Pres. Global Beauty Care, Oral Care, Personal Health and Pharmaceuticals 2004–09 (resgnd); mem. Bd Dirs Walt Disney Co., McDonald's, Catalyst, Save the Children; mem. Clinton Global Initiative; Advertising Age Top Marketer and One of the 21 to Watch in the 21st Century, Year 2000 YWCA Career Woman of Achievement 2000, ranked by Fortune magazine amongst 50 Most Powerful Women in Business in the US (32nd) 2002, (31st) 2003, (20th) 2004, (17th) 2005, (10th) 2006, (seventh) 2007, ranked by Forbes magazine amongst 100 Most Powerful Women (16th) 2004, (56th) 2005, (24th) 2006, (29th) 2007, (49th) 2008. *Leisure interests:* triathlon, surfing. *Address:* c/o The Procter & Gamble Co., 1 Procter & Gamble Plaza, PO Box 599, Cincinnati, OH 45201-0599, USA (office).

ARNOLD, Vladimir Igorevich, DSc; Russian mathematician and academic; *Professor and Chief Scientific Researcher, Steklov Mathematical Institute, Russian Academy of Sciences;* b. 12 June 1937, Odessa; s. of Igor Vladimorovich Arnold and Nina Alexandrovna Isakovich; m. Voronina Elionora Aleksandrovna 1976; one s.; ed Moscow State Univ.; Asst Prof., then Prof., Moscow State Univ. 1961–86; Prof. and Chief Scientific Researcher, Steklov Math. Inst., Russian Acad. of Sciences, Moscow 1986–; Prof., Université Paris-Dauphine 1993–2005, Hon. Prof. 2005–; Corresp. mem. USSR (now Russian) Acad. of Sciences 1984–90, mem. 1990–; Foreign mem. Académie des Sciences, Paris, NAS, USA, Academia Lincei, Rome, Royal Soc., London, Acad. of Arts and Sciences, Boston, USA, London Math. Soc., American Philosophical Soc., European Acad.; Dr hc (Univ. P. et M. Curie, Paris) 1979, (Warwick, UK) 1988, (Utrecht) 1991, (Bologna) 1991, (Universidad Complutense de Madrid) 1994, (Toronto) 1997, (Université Paris-Dauphine) 2005; Moscow Math. Soc. Prize 1958, Lenin Prize 1965, Crafoord Prize 1982, Lobachevsky Prize 1992, Harvey Prize 1994, ADION Medal 1995, Wolf Prize 2001, American Physics Soc. Prize 2001. *Publications:* Ergodic Problems in Classical Mechanics (with A. Avez) 1967, Mathematical Methods of Classical Mechanics 1974, Catastrophe Theory 1981, Singularity Theory and its Applications (Vols 1, 2) 1982, 1984, Huygens and Barrow, Newton and Hooke 1990, Partial Differential Equations 1995, Topological Methods in Hydrodynamics 1997, Arnold Problems 2000, and other publs. *Leisure interests:* skiing, canoeing, hiking. *Address:* Steklov Mathematical Institute, 8 Gubkina Street, GSP-1 Moscow 119991, Russia (office). *Website:* www.mi.ras.ru (office).

ARNON, Ruth, PhD; Israeli immunologist and academic; *Paul Ehrlich Professor of Immunology, Weizmann Institute of Science;* b. 1 June 1933, Tel-Aviv; one s. one d.; ed Hebrew Univ., Jerusalem, Weizmann Inst. of Science, Rehovot; Visiting Scientist, Rockefeller Inst., New York, USA 1960–62, Univ. of Washington, Seattle, USA 1968–69; Assoc. Prof., Weizmann Inst. of Science 1971, Head, Dept of Chemical Immunology 1973–74, 1975–78, Prof. 1975, now Paul Ehrlich Prof. of Immunology, Dir MacArthur Center for Parasitology 1984–89, Dean, Faculty of Biology 1985–93, Vice-Pres. 1988–93, Vice-Pres. for Int. Scientific Relations 1995–97; Visiting Scientist, UCLA 1977–78, Institut Pasteur, Paris, France 1983, 1998, Walter and Eliza Hall Inst., Melbourne, Australia 1994, Imperial Cancer Research Fund, London, UK 1995, Rockefeller Foundation's Bellagio Conf. and Study Center, Lake Como, Italy 1995; Sec.-Gen. Int. Union of Immunological Socs 1989–93; Pres. European Fed. of Immunological Socs 1983–86; mem. Steering Cttee WHO Task Force on Immunological Methods for Fertility Control 1972–77, European Molecular Biology Orgs (EMBO); mem. Israel Acad. of Sciences and Humanities 1990– (Chair. Science Div. 1995–2001), Vice-Pres. 2004–; Advisor for Science to Pres. of Israel 2001–; Chevalier de la Légion d'honneur 1994; Robert Koch Prize in Medical Sciences (Germany) 1979, Jimenez Diaz Award (Spain) 1986, Fogarty Scholarship, NIH, USA 1996, 1997–98, Wolf Prize 1998, Rothschild Prize 1998, Israel Prize in Medical Research 2001. *Publications:* more than 350 articles, chapters and books on immunology and biochemistry. *Address:* Department of Immunology, Wolfson Building, 431A, Weizmann Institute of Science, 76100 Rehovot, Israel (office). *Telephone:* (8) 934-4017 (office). *Fax:* (8) 946-9712 (office). *E-mail:* ruth.arnon@weizmann.ac.il (office). *Website:* www.weizmann.ac.il (office).

ARNOTT, Struther, CBE, FRSE, FRS; British university vice-chancellor, scientist and academic; *Visiting Professor and Senior Research Fellow, Biological Structure and Function Division, Faculty of Medicine, Imperial College London and University of London School of Pharmacy;* b. 25 Sept. 1934; s. of Charles McCann and Christina Struthers Arnott; m. Greta Edwards 1970; two s.; ed Hamilton Acad., Lanarkshire and Glasgow Univ.; Scientist, MRC Biophysics Research Unit, King's Coll. London 1960–70, Demonstrator in Physics 1960–67, Dir of Postgraduate Studies in Biophysics 1967–70; Prof. of Molecular Biology, Purdue Univ., West Lafayette, Ind. 1970–86, Head, Dept of Biological Sciences 1975–80, Vice-Pres. for Research and Dean, Graduate School 1980–86; Sr Visiting Research Fellow, Jesus Coll. Oxford 1980–81; Nuffield Research Fellow, Green Coll. 1985–86; Principal and Vice-Chancellor, St Andrews Univ. 1986–2000, Leverhulme Fellow 2000–02; Haddow Prof. Inst. for Cancer Research 2000–03; Visiting Prof. and Sr Research Fellow, Imperial Coll. of Science, Tech. and Medicine, London 2003–; Visiting Prof., Univ. of London School of Pharmacy 2004–; Guggenheim Memorial Foundation Fellow 1985; Gov. Sedbergh School 1986–2000; Hon. ScD (St Andrews, USA) 1994; Hon. DSc (Purdue) 1998; Hon. LLD (St Andrews) 1999. *Publications:* papers in learned journals on structures of fibrous biopolymers, especially nucleic acids and polysaccharides and techniques for visualizing them. *Leisure interests:* birdwatching, botanizing. *Address:* Cancer Research UK, Biomolecular Structure Group, School of Pharmacy, University of London, 29–39 Brunswick Square, London, WC1N 1AX (office); 1 Yorkshire, South Parade, Bawtry, DN10 6JH, England (home). *Telephone:* (07929) 629769 (mobile) (office). *E-mail:* s.arnott@pharmacy.ac.uk (office); No1Yorkshire@onetel.com (home). *Website:* www.bmsg.pharmacy.ac.uk (office).

ARNOUL, Françoise; French actress; b. (Françoise Gautsch), 9 June 1931, Constantine, Algeria; d. of Gen. Arnoul Gautsch and Jeanne Gradwohl; m. Georges Cravenne (divorced); ed Lycée de Rabat, Lycée Molière, Paris and Paris Conservatoire; Chevalier de la Légion d'honneur; Officier des Arts et Lettres. *Films include:* L' Épave 1949, Nous irons à Paris 1950, La maison Bonnadieu 1951, La plus belle fille du monde 1951, Le désir et l'amour 1952, Les compagnons de la nuit 1953, Les amants du Tage 1955, French-Cancan 1955, Des gens sans importance 1955, Thérèse Etienne 1958, La chatte 1958, Asphalte 1958, La bête à l'affût 1959, Le bal des espions 1960, La chatte sort ses griffes 1960, La morte-saison des amours 1960, Les Parisiennes 1962, Le Congrès s'amuse 1966, Le Dimanche de la vie 1967, spañolas en Paris 1970, Van der Valk 1972, Dialogue d'exiles 1975, Dernière sortie avant Roissy 1977, Ronde de Nuit 1984, Nuit Docile 1987, Voir L'Éléphant 1989, Années campagne, Les 1992, Les Cent et une nuits de Simon Cinéma 1995, Temps de chien 1996, Post coïtum animal triste 1997, Photo de famille 2000, Merci pour le geste 2000,; theatre debut in Les Justes (Camus), Versailles 1966. *Television includes:* La Guêpe 1965, Le Petit théâtre de Jean Renoir 1970, Van der Valk und das Mädchen 1972, La Mort d'un enfant 1974, Lockruf des Goldes (mini-series) 1975, L' Automate 1981, Les Brus 1981, Mon enfant, ma mère 1981, Vivre ma vie 1982, L' Amour s'invente 1982, Un garçon de France 1985, L' Herbe rouge 1985, La Garçonne 1988, L' Étrange histoire d'Emilie Albert 1989, Héloïse 1991, Billard à l'étage 1996, Une patronne de charme 1997, L' Alambic 1998, Duval: Un mort de trop 2001. *Leisure interest:* dancing. *Address:* 53 rue Censier, 75005 Paris, France (home).

ARNOULT, Erik, (Erik Orsenna), DèsScEcon, PhD; French civil servant and writer; b. 22 March 1947, Paris; s. of Claude Arnoult and Janine Arnoult (née Bodé); m. 2nd Catherine Clavier; one s. one d.; ed Ecole Saint-Jean de Béthune, Versailles, Institut d'Etudes Politiques, Paris, Univ. of Paris I, London School of Economics; Lecturer, Inst. d'Etudes Politiques, Paris 1975–80, Ecole Normale Supérieure 1977–81; Literary Ed. Editions Ramsay 1977–81; Sr Lecturer, Université de Paris I 1978–81; Tech. Adviser to Ministry of Co-operation and Devt 1981–83, to Minister of Foreign Affairs 1990–92; Cultural Adviser to Pres. of Repub. 1983–90; Maître des Requêtes, Conseil d'Etat 1985–, Sr mem. 2000–; Pres. Centre Int. de la Mer 1991–, Ecole Nat. Supérieure du Paysage 1995–; Vice-Pres. Cytale Soc. 2000–; mem. Foundation for World Agric. and Rural Life 2006–, Acad. Française. *Film screenplay:* Indochine (co-writer) (Acad. Award for Best Foreign Film). *Publications:* Loyola's blues 1974, Espace national et déséquilibre monétaire 1977, La Vie comme à Lausanne 1977 (Prix Roger Nimmier), Une comédie française 1980, L'Exposition coloniale (novel) (Prix Goncourt) 1988, Grand Amour 1993, Histoire du monde en neuf guitares 1996, Deux Etés (novel) 1996, Longtemps (novel) 1998, Portrait d'un homme heureux, André Le Nôtre 1613–1700 2000, La Grammaire est une chanson donce 2001, Madame Bâ 2003, Les Chevaliers du Subjonctif 2004, Portrait du Gulf Stream 2005, Voyage aux pays du coton 2006 (Prix du livre d'économie), La révolte des accents 2007. *Leisure interest:* yachting. *Address:* Conseil d'Etat, 1 place du Palais Royal, 75001 Paris (office); 8 passage Sigaud, 75013 Paris, France (home).

ARNS, HE Cardinal Paulo Evaristo; Brazilian ecclesiastic; *Archbishop Emeritus of São Paulo;* b. 14 Sept. 1921, Forquilhinha, Criciúma, Santa Catarina; s. of Gabriel and Helena Steiner Arns; ed Univ. de Paris and Ecole des Hautes Etudes, Paris; ordained priest 1945; taught theology and French, Univ. Católica de Petrópolis; pastoral work in Petrópolis; apptd. Auxiliary Bishop of São Paulo 1966, apptd. Archbishop of São Paulo 1970–98, Archbishop Emer. 1998–; Cardinal-Priest of St Anthony of Padua in via Tuscolana 1973; Grand Chancellor of Pontificia Univ. Católica de São Paulo; mem. Sacred Congregation for the Sacraments (Vatican); mem. UN Int. Independent Comm. on Humanitarian Issues; Hon. LLD (Notre Dame, Ind., USA); Nansen Prize (UN) 1985. *Publications:* numerous works and trans on religious and racial topics, including A Quem iremos, Senhor? 1968, Comunidade: União e Ação 1972, Sê Fiel 1977, Em Defesa dos Direitos Humanos 1978, Convite para Rezar 1978, Presença e Força do Cristão 1978,

Discutindo o Papel da Igreja 1980, Os Ministérios na Igreja 1980, O que é Igreja 1981, Meditações para o Dia-a-Dia (Vols 1–4) 1981–83, Pensamentos 1982, Olhando o Mundo com São Francisco 1982, A Violência em nossos Dias 1983, Para Ser Jovem Hoje 1983, Santos e Heróis do Povo 1984. *Address:* Avenida Higienopolis, 890, C.P. 6778, 01064 São Paulo, S.P., Brazil. *Telephone:* (11) 826-0133. *Fax:* (11) 825-6806.

ARORA, Sunil; Indian business executive; fmr Jt Sec. (Policy and Planning); Chair. and Man. Dir Indian Airlines 2002–; Man. Dir Air India 2003–. *Address:* Air India Building, Nariman Point, Mumbai 400 021, India. *Telephone:* (22) 22024142.

ARP, Fredrik, BA; Swedish automobile industry executive; *President and CEO, Volvo Car Corporation;* b. 1953, Köping; m. Suzanne Arp; four c.; ed Lund Univ.; salesman Tarkett France, Swedish Match Group, later Div. Man. for Flooring; with Tyre Div., Trelleborg Group 1985, Vice-Pres. 1996; Pres. and CEO PLM (now Rexam) 1996–99; Pres. and CEO Trelleborg AB 1999–2005; Pres. and CEO Volvo Car Corpn 2005–; Chair. Thule AB; mem. Bd of Dirs Hilding Anders SACC–NY; DEcon hc (Lund). *Leisure interests:* golf, skiing. *Address:* Volvo Car Corporation, Gunnar Engellaus Väg, 405 31 Gothenburg, Sweden (office). *Telephone:* (31) 590000 (office). *Website:* www .volvocars.com (office).

ARPEY, Gerard J., BBA, MBA; American airline industry executive; *Chairman, President and CEO, AMR Corporation and American Airlines;* b. 26 July 1958; m. Lisa Arpey; two s. one d.; ed Univ. of Texas, Austin; joined American Airlines 1982, Financial Analyst 1982–83, Sr Financial Analyst 1983–85, Man. Financial Analysis 1985–87, Dir Airline Profitability Analysis 1987–88, Man. Dir Financial Analysis 1988, Man. Dir Financial Planning 1988–89, Vice-Pres. Financial Planning and Analysis 1989–92, Sr Vice-Pres. Planning 1992–95, Sr Vice-Pres. Finance and Planning and Chief Financial Officer 1995–99, Exec. Vice-Pres., Operations 2000–02, Pres. and COO 2002–03, mem. Bd Dirs, Pres. and CEO AMR Corpn and American Airlines Inc. 2003–, Chair. 2004–; Dir Dallas Museum of Art; mem. The Business Council, Advisory Council McCombs School of Business at Univ. of Texas. *Leisure interest:* private pilot (holds a FAA Multi-Engine Instrument Pilot Rating). *Address:* AMR Corporation, 4333 Amon Carter Boulevard, Fort Worth, TX 76155, USA (office). *Telephone:* (817) 963-1234 (office). *Fax:* (817) 967-9641 (office). *E-mail:* info@amrcorp.com (office). *Website:* www.amrcorp.com (office); www.aa.com (office).

ARQUETTE, Patricia; American actress; b. 8 April 1968; d. of Lewis Arquette and Mardi Arquette; m. 1st Nicolas Cage (q.v.) 1995 (divorced); m. 2nd Thomas Jane 2006; one s. one d. *Films:* Pretty Smart 1986, A Nightmare on Elm Street 3: Dream Warriors 1987, Time Out 1988, Far North 1988, The Indian Runner 1991, Prayer of the Rollerboys 1991, Ethan Frome 1993, Trouble Bound 1993, Inside Monkey Zetterland 1993, True Romance 1993, Holy Matrimony 1994, Ed Wood 1994, Beyond Rangoon 1995, Infinity 1995, Flirting with Disaster 1996, The Secret Agent 1996, Lost Highway 1997, Nightwatch 1998, In the Boom Boom Room 1999, Goodbye Lover 1999, Stigmata 1999, Bringing out the Dead 1999, Little Nicky 2000, Human Nature 2001, Holes 2003, Tiptoes 2003, Deeper than Deep 2003, Fast Food Nation 2006,. *TV includes:* Daddy 1987, Dillinger 1991, Wildflower 1991, Betrayed by Love 1994, Toby's Story 1998, The Hi-Lo Country 1998, The Badge 2002, Medium (series) (Emmy Award for Best Actress in a Drama 2005) 2005–09. *Address:* c/o U.T.A., 9560 Wilshire Boulevard, 5th Floor, Beverly Hills, CA 90212, USA.

ARQUETTE, Rosanna; American actress; b. 10 Aug. 1959, New York; d. of Lewis Arquette and Mardi Arquette; m. 1st (divorced); m. 2nd James N. Howard (divorced); m. 3rd. John Sidel 1993; f. Flower Child Productions. *Films include:* Gorp 1980, S.O.B. 1981, Off the Wall 1983, The Aviator 1985, Desperately Seeking Susan 1985, 8 Million Ways to Die 1986, After Hours 1986, Nobody's Fool 1986, The Big Blue 1988, Life Lessons, Black Rainbow 1989; Wendy Cracked a Walnut 1989, Sweet Revenge 1990, Baby, It's You 1990, Flight of the Intruder 1990, The Linguini Incident 1992, Fathers and Sons 1992, Nowhere to Run 1993, Pulp Fiction 1994, Search and Destroy 1995, Crash 1996, Liar 1997, Gone Fishin' 1997, Buffalo '66 1997, Palmer's Pick Up 1998, I'm Losing You 1998, Homeslice 1998, Floating Away 1998, Hope Floats 1998, Fait Accompli 1998, Sugar Town 1999, Palmer's Pick Up 1999, Pigeonholed 1999, Interview with a Dead Man 1999, The Whole Nine Yards 2000, Too Much Flesh 2000, Things Behind the Sun 2001, Big Bad Love 2001, Good Advice 2001, Diary of a Sex Addict 2001, Gilded Stones 2004, Dead Cool 2004, Max and Grace 2005, Iowa 2005, Kids in America 2005, Welcome to California 2005, I-See-You.Com 2006, Ball Don't Lie 2008, Growing Op 2008. *TV films include:* Harvest Home, The Wall, The Long Way Home, The Executioner's Song, One Cooks, the Other Doesn't, The Parade, Survival Guide, A Family Tree, Promised a Miracle, Sweet Revenge, Separation, The Wrong Man, Nowhere to Hide, I Know What You Did, The Law and Mr. Lee 2003, Rush of Fear 2003, The L Word (series) 2004–07, What About Brian (series) 2006–07. *Address:* c/o Abrams Artists Agency, 9200 Sunset Blvd, 11th Floor, Los Angeles, CA 90069, USA (office).

ARRABAL, Fernando; Spanish writer; b. 11 Aug. 1932, Melilla; s. of Fernando Arrabal and Carmen Terán González; m. Luce Moreau 1958; one s. one d; ed Univ. of Madrid; political prisoner in Spain 1967; Founder "Panique" Movt with Topor, Jodorowsky, etc.; Officier, Ordre des Arts et des Lettres 1984, Chevalier, Légion d'honneur 2005; "Superdotado" Award 1942, Ford Foundation Award 1959, Grand Prix du Théâtre 1967, Grand Prix Humour Noir 1968, Obie Award 1976, Premio Nadal (Spain) 1983, World's Theater Prize 1984, Medalla de Oro de Bellas Artes (Spain) 1989, Prix du Théâtre (Acad. Française) 1993, Prix Int. Vladimir Nabokov 1994, Premio de Ensayo Espasa 1994, Grand Prix Soc. des Gens de Lettres 1996, Grand Prix de la

Méditerranée 1996, Medal of Centre for French Civilization and Culture, New York 1997, Prix de la Francophonie 1998, Premio Mariano de Cavia 1998, Prix Alessandro Manzoni di Poesia 1999, Premio Nacional de las Letras, Premio Eninci Cine y Literatura 2000, Premio Nacional de Teatro 2001, Premio Ercilla Teatro 2001. *Publications:* plays: numerous plays including Le cimetière des voitures, Guernica, Le grand cérémonial, L'architecte et l'Empereur d'Assyrie, Le jardin des délices, Et ils passèrent des menottes aux fleurs, Le ciel et la merde, Bella ciao, La Tour de Babel, L'extravagante réussite de Jésus-Christ, Karl Marx et William Shakespeare, Les délices de la chair, La traversée de l'empire, Luly, Cielito, Fando et Lis, Lettre d'amour; novels: Baal Babylone 1959, L'enterrement de la sardine 1962, Fêtes et rites de la confusion 1965, La tour prends garde, La reverdie, La vierge rouge, Bréviaire d'amour d'un haltérophile, L'extravagante croisade d'un castrat amoureux 1991, La tueuse du jardin d'hiver 1994, El Mono 1994, Le Funambule de Dieu 1998, Ceremonia por un teniente abandonado 1998, Porté disparu 2000, Levitación 2000; poetry includes: La pierre de la folie 1963, 100 sonnets 1966, Humbles paradis 1983, Liberté couleur de femme 1993, Arrabalesques 1994, Passion, Passions 1997, Le Frénétique du Spasme 1997; essays: numerous, including Le Panique, Le New York d'Arrabal, Lettre au Général Franco, Greco 1970, Lettre à Fidel Castro 1983, Goya-Dali 1992, La Dudosa Luz del Día 1994. *Films:* directed and written: Viva la Muerte, J'irai comme un cheval fou, L'arbre de Guernica, L'odyssée de la Pacific, Le cimetière des voitures, Adieu Babylone!, J.-L. Borges (Una Vida de Poesía) 1998. *Leisure interest:* chess. *Address:* 22 rue Jouffroy d'Abbans, Paris 75017, France (home). *Fax:* 1-42-67-01-26 (home). *E-mail:* fernando.arrabal@orange .fr (home); arrabalf@gmail.com (home). *Website:* www.arrabal.org.

ARRAYED, Jawad bin Salem al-; Bahraini politician; *Deputy Prime Minister;* b. 23 Sept. 1940; ed Cairo Univ., Leeds Univ., UK; Public Prosecution Dir 1969–71; Minister of Labour and Social Affairs 1971–73; Minister of State for Cabinet Affairs 1973–82; Minister of Health and Chair. Environmental Protection Cttee 1982–95, Minister of State 1995–99; Minister of State for Municipalities and Environmental Affairs 1999–2002; Minister of Justice 2002–05; Advisor to Prime Minister on Legal Affairs 2005–06; Deputy Prime Minister 2006–; mem. Hon. Soc. of Gray's Inn; mem. al-Wifaq party. *Address:* c/o Office of the Prime Minister, POB 1000, Government House, Government Rd, Manama, Bahrain.

ARREDONDO MILLÁN, Gonzalo; Bolivian politician; Minister of Nat. Defence 2003–05. *Address:* c/o Ministry of National Defence, Plaza Avaroa, esq. Pedro Salazar y 20 de Octubre, La Paz, Bolivia (office).

ARRILLAGA, Josu, PhD, FRS (NZ), FIEE, FIEEE; Spanish/New Zealend electrical engineer and academic; *Professor Emeritus of Electrical Engineering, University of Canterbury, New Zealand;* b. 21 Jan. 1934; s. of José María and María Mercedes Arrillaga; m. Greta Robinson 1968; two s. two d.; ed in Spain and Univ. of Manchester Inst. of Science and Tech.; Industrial Engineer, ISOLUX, Spain 1955–59; A.E.I. Engineer, Manchester 1959–61; Research student UMIST 1961–66; Lecturer, Univ. of Salford 1966–67; Lecturer and Sr Lecturer, UMIST 1967–75, Head Power Systems and High Voltage 1970–75; Prof. of Electrical Eng, Univ. of Canterbury, NZ 1975–, Head Dept of Electrical and Electronic Eng 1986–91, James Cook Sr Research Fellow 2002–04; EPCA Fellow 2004–; Johns Hopkins Prize, IEE 1975, Uno Lamm Medal, IEEE 1997, Int. Power Quality Award 1997, IPENZ Pres. Gold Medal 1999, Royal Soc. (NZ) Silver Medal for Tech. Innovation 1999, Royal Soc. (NZ) John Scott Medal 2003, IEE Award 2004; NZ Order of Merit (MNZM)2006. *Publications:* twelve books including AC-DC Power System Analysis 1998, Power System Quality Assessment 2000, Power System Electromagnetic Transients Simulation 2002, Power System Harmonics 2003; 300 technical articles. *Leisure interest:* gardening. *Address:* 2/77 Hinau Street, Christchurch, New Zealand (home). *Telephone:* (3) 348-8492 (home). *Fax:* (3) 364-2761 (office). *E-mail:* arrillj@elec.canterbury.ac.uk (office).

ARRINDELL, Sir Clement Athelston, GCMG, GCVO, QC; Saint Christopher and Nevis civil servant and lawyer; b. 16 April 1932, St Kitts, West Indies; s. of George E. Arrindell and Hilda I. Arrindell; m. Evelyn Eugenia O'Loughlin 1967; ed St Kitts-Nevis Grammar School (Island Scholar 1948) and Lincoln's Inn, London; practising barrister-at-law 1959–66; Dist Magistrate 1966–74; Chief Magistrate 1975–77; Puisne Judge 1978–81; Gov. of St Kitts-Nevis 1981–83; Gov.-Gen. of St Christopher and Nevis 1983–95. *Leisure interests:* gardening, piano playing, classical music. *Address:* The Lark, Bird Rock, Saint Christopher and Nevis, West Indies.

ARROW, Kenneth Joseph, PhD; American economist and academic; *Professor Emeritus of Economics and Operations Research, Stanford University;* b. 23 Aug. 1921, New York; s. of Harry I. Arrow and Lillian Arrow; m. Selma Schweitzer 1947; two s.; ed The City College, Columbia Univ.; Capt. USAF 1942–46; Research Assoc. Cowles Comm. for Research in Econ., Univ. of Chicago 1947–49; Asst Assoc. and Prof. of Econs, Statistics and Operations Research, Stanford Univ., 1949–68; Prof. of Econs, Harvard Univ., 1968–79; Prof. of Econs and Operations Research, Stanford Univ., 1979–91, Prof. Emer. 1991–; mem. NAS, American Acad. of Arts and Sciences, American Philosophical Soc., Finnish Acad. of Sciences, British Acad., Inst. of Medicine, Pontifical Acad. of Social Sciences; Pres. Int. Soc. for Inventory Research 1983–90, Int. Econ. Asscn, Econometric Soc., American Econ. Asscn, Soc. for Social Choice and Welfare; Dir various cos; Order of the Rising Sun (Japan); Hon. LLD (City Univ., Univ. of Chicago, Washington Univ., Univ. of Pennsylvania, Ben-Gurion Univ., Harvard Univ., Univ. of Cyprus, Univ. of Buenos Aires); Hon. Dr of Social and Econ. Sciences (Vienna); Hon. ScD (Columbia Univ.) 1973; Hon. DSocSci (Yale) 1974; Hon. LLD (Hebrew Univ. Jerusalem) 1975, Hon. DPolSci (Helsinki) 1976; Hon. DLitt (Cambridge) 1985, (Harvard) 1999; Hon. DUniv (Uppsala) 1995; Hon. PhD (Univ. of Tel-Aviv) 2001; Dr hc (Univ. René Descartes) 1974, (Univ. Aix-Marseille III) 1985,

(Univ. of Cyprus) 2000; Nobel Memorial Prize in Econ. Science 1972, John Bates Clark Medal, Von Neumann Prize, Medal of Univ. of Paris 1998, Nat. Medal of Science 2006. *Publications:* Social Choice and Individual Values 1951, 1963, Studies in the Mathematical Theory of Inventory and Production (with S. Karlin and H. Scarf) 1958, Studies in Linear and Nonlinear Programming (with L. Hurwicz and H. Uzawa) 1958, A Time Series Analysis of Inter-industry Demands (with M. Hoffenberg) 1959, Public Investment, The Rate of Return and Optimal Fiscal Policy (with M. Kurz) 1970, Essays in the Theory of Risk-Bearing 1971, General Competitive Analysis (with F. H. Hahn) 1971, The Limits of Organization 1973, Studies in Resource Allocation Processes (with L. Hurwicz) 1977, Collected Papers 1983–85, Social Choice and Multicriterion Decision Making (with H. Raynaud) 1985; more than 240 articles in learned journals. *Leisure interests:* walking, music. *Address:* Department of Economics, Stanford University, Stanford, CA 94305-6072 (office); 580 Constanzo Street, Stanford, CA 94305, USA (home). *Telephone:* (650) 723-9165 (office). *Fax:* (650) 725-5702 (office). *E-mail:* arrow@stanford .edu (office). *Website:* www-econ.stanford.edu/faculty/arrow.html (office).

ARROYO, Mary Kalin, BSc, PhD, FLS, FRSNZ; Chilean biologist and academic; *Director, Institute of Ecology and Biodiversity;* ed Univ. of Canterbury, Christchurch, New Zealand, Univ. of California, Berkeley, USA; Postdoctoral Research Fellow, Stanford Univ./New York Botanical Garden 1971–72; Titular Prof. of Biology, Universidad de Chile, Dir Inst. of Ecology and Biodiversity; Head of Ind. Scientific Comm. of the Rio Condor Project (jt collaboration between Chilean scientific community and Chilean forestry industry); her studies have led to the design of an improved system of protected areas in Chile, 68,000 hectares of the Condor River drainage basin have been protected; Corresp. mem. Botanical Soc. of America 1995, NAS 1999, Chilean Acad. of Sciences 2003; mem. Third World Acad. of Sciences 2004; Condecoración al Mérito 'Amanda Labarca' 1996; Percival Memorial Prize in Botany, Univ. of Canterbury 1966, Premio Cultural 'Angel Faivovich' 1982, Guggenheim Fellow 1984, Cátedra Presidencial en Ciencias, 1997–99, Medalla Rectoral, Universidad de Chile 1998, Premio Fundación BBVA a la Investigación a la Biología de la Conservación 2004, Volvo Environment Prize (Sweden) 2005. *Publications:* numerous papers on reproductive systems of plants, studies of complete communities and conservation. *Address:* Millenium Centre for Advanced Studies in Ecology and Biodiversity Research, University of Chile, Castilla 653, Santiago, Chile (office). *Telephone:* (2) 2760351 (office). *Fax:* (2) 2715464 (office). *E-mail:* southern@abello.dic.uchile .cl (office). *Website:* www.ieb-chile.cl/focus/people_focus1/MaryKalin.php (office).

ARSALA, Hedayat Amin, PhD; Afghan politician and economist; nephew of Pir Gailani; ed high school in Kabul, George Washington Univ., Washington, DC, USA; ethnic Pashtun descended from Jabar Khel tribe; foreign language trainer for three consecutive Peace Corps training programmes in USA; started his professional career at World Bank Youth Professional Program 1969, held various econ. and sr operational posts 1969–87; returned to Afghanistan to join Afghan resistance to Soviet occupation 1987–89, served as Sr Adviser and mem. Afghan Mujahideen Unity Council; Minister of Finance, Transitional Govt of Afghanistan 1989–92; Minister of Foreign Affairs 1993–96; Sr mem. Exec. Council of Loya Jirga (traditional council of Afghan tribal leaders) 1998–; played key role in Intra-Afghan Bonn Conf. following fall of the Taliban regime 2001; apptd Vice-Chair. and Minister of Finance of the interim admin 2001; named one of four Vice-Pres, Transitional Islamic State of Afghanistan 2001–04, Chair. Ind. Civil Services Admin Reform Comm., adviser to Cen. Statistics Office and Afghan Econ. Cooperation Cttee; mem. Afghan Nat. Security Council; Minister of Commerce and Sr Presidential Adviser 2004–06, Sr Minister in the Cabinet 2006–. *Address:* c/o Office of the President, Gul Khana Palace, Presidential Palace, Kabul, Afghanistan (office). *E-mail:* webmaster@afghanistangov.org (office). *Website:* www .president.gov.af (office).

ARSENIS, Gerasimos; Greek politician and economist; b. 1931, Cephalonia; m. Louka Katseli; three s. one d.; ed Univ. of Athens and Massachusetts Inst. of Tech.; worked for UN 1960; Dir Dept of Econ. Studies, OECD Research Centre 1964–66, Sr Official, Prebisch Group, UN 1966–73; Dir UNCTAD 1973; Gov. Bank of Greece 1981–84; Minister of Nat. Economy 1982–84, of Finance and Nat. Economy 1984–85, of Merchant Marine June–July 1985, of Defence 1993–96, of Educ. and Religious Affairs 1996–99; expelled from PASOK 1986; f. Democratic Initiative Group 1987, Leader 1987–89; returned to PASOK 1989, mem. Exec. Bureau 1990–; mem. Parl. for Athens Dist 1990–. *Address:* 23 Sina Street, 106 801 Athens, Greece (office). *Telephone:* (21) 03644558 (office). *Fax:* (21) 03603558 (office). *E-mail:* garsenis@otenet.gr (office). *Website:* www.garsenis.gr (office).

ARSENISHVILI, Georgy, DrTechSc; Georgian politician, mathematician and academic; b. 1942, Khirsa, Signakhi Region; m.; two c.; ed Tbilisi State Univ.; Jr Researcher, Inst. of Applied Math., Sr Researcher, Docent and Deputy Dean Tbilisi State Univ. 1970–73; at Heidelberg Univ. 1973–74; Dean, Chair of Applied Math., Methods Prof., Tbilisi Univ. 1978–; State Rep. of Pres. of Georgia to Kakhetia Dist 1995–2000; Minister of State 2000–02; mem. Int. Acad. of Communications. *Publications:* over 50 scientific works on probability theory and statistical math., application of math. methods to humanitarian and nat. science fields, econ. geography.

ARTAMONOV, Sergey Pavlovich, DEcon; Russian educationist; b. 10 Feb. 1947, Moscow; ed Higher Mil. School, Diplomatic Acad.; main area of research interest: devt of the econ. potential of European govts in accordance with int. law; First Vice-Pres. Acad. of Russian Encyclopedias; Vice-Pres. Acad. of the Comprehensive Russian Encyclopedia; Exec. Sec. Acad. of Mil. Sciences; Rector Inst. of Professionalization; Dir Centre of Econ.-Legal Educ.; Dir.-Gen. Int. Inst. of Marketing, Vice-Pres. Int. Commercial Univ.; Councillor Expert Council, State Duma 1996–; mem., Sec.-Gen. Russian Acad. of Natural Sciences; Vice-Pres. Int. Acad. of Sciences; Vice-Pres. Int. Asscn of Writers; mem. Russian Pres.'s Political Consultancy Council; Dr hc (Dresden Acad. of Sciences); numerous awards and prizes. *Publications:* more than 100 scientific works. *Leisure interest:* sport. *Address:* State Duma, Okhotny Ryad 1, 103265 Moscow, Russia (office). *Telephone:* (495) 292-80-00 (office); (495) 453-98-03 (home).

ARTÉS-GÓMEZ, Mariano; Spanish professor of mechanics; *University Professor and Head of Mechanics Department, Universidad Nacional de Educación a Distancia;* b. 5 March 1947, Murcia; s. of Mariano Artés and Elisa Gómez; m. María José Caselles 1973; three s.; ed Universidad Politécnica de Madrid, Int. Centre for Theoretical Physics, Trieste; Asst Prof. of Mechanics, Universidad Politécnica de Madrid 1971–78, Assoc. Prof. 1979–80; Prof. Universidad de Oviedo 1980–81; Prof. and Head of Dept of Mechanics, Universidad Nacional de Educación a Distancia 1981–, Vice-Rector for Research 1986, Dean of Faculty of Industrial Eng 1987, Rector 1987–96; mem. Asocs Española de Informática y Automática, Asocs Española de Ingeniería Mecánica, Soc. for Research into Higher Educ. (UK); Premio Citema 1975, Premio Extraordinario de Doctorado 1977, Laurel de Murcia 1987. *Publications:* El Papel Instrumental de la Informática en el Proceso Educativo 1975, Dinámica de Sistemas 1979, Mecánica 1982, numerous articles on informatics in educ. and applied mechanics. *Leisure interests:* music, reading. *Address:* Universidad Nacional de Educación a Distancia, Ciudad Universitaria, 28040 Madrid, Spain (office). *Telephone:* (1) 3986016 (office). *Fax:* (1) 3986037 (office). *E-mail:* infouned@adm.uned.es (office). *Website:* www.uned.es/ (office).

ARTHUIS, Jean Raymond Francis Marcel; French politician; b. 7 Oct. 1944, Saint-Martin du Bois, Maine-et-Loire; s. of Raymond Arthuis and Marthe Cotin; m. Brigitte Lafont 1971; one s. one d.; ed Coll. Saint-Michel, Château-Gontier, Ecole Supérieure de Commerce, Nantes and Inst. d'Etudes Politiques, Paris; chartered accountant, Paris 1971–86; Mayor of Château-Gontier 1971–2001; mem. Conseil, Gen., Mayenne, Château-Gontier canton 1976–, Pres. 1992–; Senator from Mayenne (Centrist Group) 1983–86, 1988–95; Sec. of State, Ministry of Social Affairs and Employment 1986–87, Ministry of Econ., Finance and Privatization 1987–88; Spokesman on Budget in Senate 1992–95; Minister of Econ. Devt and Planning May–Aug. 1995, of Econ. and Finance 1995–97; Vice-Pres. Force Démocrate (fmrly Centre des démocrates sociaux) 1995–; Vice-Pres. Nouvelle Union pour la Démocratie Française (UDF) 1998; Pres. Union centriste du Sénat 1998–2002, Financial Comm. in Senate 2002–; Chevalier du Mérite Agricole, Commandeur de l'Ordre du Mérite, Germany. *Publications:* Justice sinistrée, Démocratie en danger (co-author) 1991, Les Délocalisations et l'emploi 1993, Dans les coulisses de Bercy, Le Cinquième pouvoir 1998, Mondialisation, la France à Contre Emploi 2007. *Address:* SENAT, Palais du Luxembourg, 75291 Paris Cedex 06 (office); Conseil général de la Mayenne, 39 rue Mazagran, BP 1429, 53014 Laval Cedex (office); 8 rue René Homo, 53200 Château-Gontier, France (home).

ARTHUR, James Greig, PhD, FRS, FRSC; Canadian mathematician and academic; *University Professor, Department of Mathematics, University of Toronto;* b. 18 May 1944, Hamilton; s. of John G. Arthur and Katherine (née Scott) Arthur; m. Dorothy P. Helm 1972; two s.; ed Univ. of Toronto, Yale Univ.; Instructor, Princeton Univ. 1970–72; Asst Prof., Yale Univ. 1972–76; Prof., Duke Univ. 1976–79; Prof. of Math., Univ. of Toronto 1979–87, Univ. Prof. 1987–; Sloan Fellow 1975–77, Stracie Memorial Fellowship 1982–84; Vice-Pres. American Math. Soc. 1999–2001, Pres. 2005–07; Fellow, Royal Soc. of Canada 1980, Royal Soc. (UK) 1992; Guggenheim Fellowship 2000; Dr hc (Univ. of Ottawa) 2002; Synge Award in Math. 1987, Henry Marshall Tory Medal 1997, Canadian Gold Medal for Science and Eng 1999, Wilbur Lucius Cross Medal, Grad. School of Yale Univ. 2000, Killam Prize 2004. *Publications:* numerous scientific papers and articles. *Leisure interests:* tennis, squash, golf. *Address:* Department of Mathematics, University of Toronto, Toronto, Ont. M5S 3G3 (office); 23 Woodlawn Avenue West, Toronto, Ont. M4V 1G6, Canada (home). *Telephone:* (416) 978-4524 (office). *E-mail:* arthur@ math.toronto.edu (office). *Website:* www.math.toronto.edu (office).

ARTHUR, Rt Hon. Owen, PC; Barbadian politician and economist; b. 17 Oct. 1949; m. Beverley Jeanne Batchelor 1978; ed Harrison Coll., Univ. of W Indies, Cave Hill, Univ. of W Indies, Mona; Research Asst, Univ. of W Indies, Jamaica 1973; Asst Econ. Planner, Chief Econ. Planner Nat. Planning Agency, Jamaica 1974–79; Dir of Econs, Jamaica Bauxite Inst. 1979–81; Chief Project Analyst, Ministry of Finance, Barbados 1981–83; lecturer Dept of Man., Univ. of W Indies, Cave Hill 1986, Resident Fellow 1993; Senator 1983–84; Parl. Sec. Ministry of Finance 1985–86; mem. Barbados Labour Party (BLP), Chair. 1993–96; Prime Minister of Barbados, Minister of Defence and Security, Finance and Econ. Affairs and for the Civil Service Sept. 1994–2008. *Publications:* The Commercialisation of Technology in Jamaica 1979, Energy and Mineral Resource Development in the Jamaican Bauxite Industry 1981, The IMF and Economic Stabilisation Policies in Barbados 1984. *Leisure interests:* gardening, cooking. *Address:* Barbados Labour Party, Grantley Adams House, 111 Roebuck Street, Bridgetown, Barbados (office). *Telephone:* 429-1990 (office). *Fax:* 427-8792. *E-mail:* will99@caribsurf.com (office). *Website:* labourparty.wordpress.com (office).

ARTHURS, Harry William, OC, BA, LLM, FRSC, FBA; Canadian professor of law and political science; *University Professor Emeritus and President Emeritus, York University;* b. 9 May 1935, Toronto; s. of Leon Arthurs and Ellen H. Arthurs (née Dworkin); m. Penelope Geraldine Ann Milnes 1974; two s.; ed Univ. of Toronto, Harvard Univ., USA; Asst, Assoc. then full Prof. of Law, Osgoode Hall Law School, York Univ., Ont. 1961–, Dean of Law School 1972–77, Pres. York Univ. 1985–92, Pres. Emer. 1992–, Univ. Prof.

1995–2005, Univ. Prof. Emer. 2005–; Assoc. Canada Inst. of Advanced Research 1995–98; mediator and arbitrator in labour disputes 1962–85; author, lecturer 1961–; Bencher, Law Soc. of Upper Canada 1979–83; mem. Econ. Council of Canada 1978–81; Chair. Consultative Group, Research and Educ. in Law 1980–84; Chair. Council of Ont. Univs 1987–89; Commr to Review Federal Labour Standards 2004–06; mem. Ontario Expert Comm. on Pensions 2006–08; Order of Ontario; Hon. LLD (Sherbrooke, McGill, Brock, Montreal, Toronto, York Univs, Law Soc. of Upper Canada); Hon. DLitt (Lethbridge); Hon. DCL (Windsor); Killam Prize for Social Sciences, Canada Council 2002, Laskin Prize for Contrib. to Labour Law 2002, ILO Decent Work Research Prize (co-winner) 2008. *Publications:* Industrial Relations and Labour Law in Canada (co-author) 1984, Law and Learning (Report on Legal Research and Education in Canada) 1984, Without the Law: Administrative Justice and Legal Pluralism in Nineteenth Century England 1985, Fairness at Work (Report on Federal Labour Standards) 2006, A Fine Balance (Report on Pensions) 2008. *Address:* Osgoode Law School, York University, 4700 Keele Street, North York, Ont., M3J 1P3 (office); 11 Hillcrest Park, Toronto, Ont., M4X 1E8, Canada (home). *Telephone:* (416) 736-5407 (office). *Fax:* (416) 736-5736 (office). *E-mail:* harthurs@osgoode.yorku.ca (office).

ARTHUS-BERTRAND, Yann Marie; French photographer; b. 13 March 1946, Paris; s. of Claude Arthus-Bertrand and Jeanne Arthus-Bertrand (née Schildge); m. 2nd Anne Thual 1984; three s.; early career as asst dir and actor 1963–66; worked on wildlife reserve, Allier River 1966–76; balloon pilot, Masai Mara Reserve, Kenya 1976–78; f. Altitude agency (aerial photographs) 1991, cr. Earth from Above project 1995, Six Billion Others project 2003, Good Planet 2005; elected Académie des Beaux-Arts 2006. *Publications:* more than 60 books of photographs including Lions 1981, Three Days in France 1989, La terre vue du ciel (The Earth from Above) 1999 (updated annually), 365 jours pour réfléchir sur la terre 2000 (updated annually), Etre Photographe 2003, Agenda Chevaux 2005, Bestiaux 2006. *Address:* Altitude, Domaine de Longchamp, Carrefour de Longchamp, 75116 Paris, France (office). *E-mail:* yannab@club-internet.fr (office). *Website:* www.yannarthusbertrand.com.

ARTSCHWAGER, Richard Ernst, BA; American artist; b. 26 Dec. 1923, Washington, DC; m. 1st Elfriede Wejmelka 1947 (divorced 1970); one d.; m. 2nd Catherine Kord 1972 (divorced 1989); m. 3rd. Molly O'Gorman (divorced 1993); one s. one d.; m. 4th Ann Sebring 1995; ed Cornell Univ.; studied with Amedee Ozenfant, New York 1949–50; baby photographer 1950–53; cabinet-maker 1953–65; has exhibited with Richard Bellamy and Leo Castelli also many group and one-man shows in USA and Europe 1963–. *Publication:* The Hydraulic Door Check 1967. *Address:* P.O. Box 12, Hudson, NY 12534-0012, USA.

ARTUCIO RODRIGUEZ, Alejandro, DJur, DScS; Uruguayan diplomatist; *Permanent Representative, United Nations, Geneva;* b. 22 Aug. 1934; m.; two c.; ed Univ. of Repub.; Chief Counsel and Commr, Int. Comm. of Jurists, Geneva 1985–2005; Perm. Rep. of Uruguay to UN, New York 2004–06, to UN, Geneva 2007–; Special Rapporteur on Equatorial Guinea, UN High Comm. on Human Rights 1993–99; Chief Counsel for Human Rights, UN Verification Mission in Guatemala (MINUGUA) 1997; fmr mem. Governing Council, Inst. of Legal and Social Studies, Uruguay, Governing Council Assocn for Prevention of Torture, Geneva, Advice Council, Int. Service for Human Rights, Geneva, International Consulting Council, Legal and Social Studies Center, Argentina. *Address:* Office of the Permanent Representative of Uruguay to the United Nations, Rue de Lausanne 65 (4th Floor), 1202 Geneva, Switzerland (office). *Telephone:* 227318366 (office). *Fax:* 227315650 (office). *E-mail:* mission.uruguay@urugi.ch (office).

ARTZT, Alice Josephine, BA; American classical guitarist, writer and teacher; b. 16 March 1943, Philadelphia, PA; d. of Maurice Gustav Artzt and Harriett Green Artzt; m. Bruce B. Lawton, Jr; ed Columbia Univ. and studied composition with Darius Milhaud and guitar with Julian Bream, Ida Presti and Alexandre Lagoya; taught guitar at Mannes Coll. of Music, New York 1966–69, Trenton State Univ. 1977–80; world-wide tours as soloist 1969–94; f. Alice Artzt Guitar Trio (with M. Rutscho and R. Burley) 1989; toured in duo with R. Burley; fmr mem. Bd of Dirs Guitar Foundation of America (Chair. 1986–89); several Critics' Choice Awards. *Recordings include:* Bach and His Friends, Guitar Music by Fernando Sor, Guitar Music by Francisco Tarrega, 20th Century Guitar Music, English Guitar Music, The Music of Manuel Ponce, The Glory of the Guitar, Virtuoso Romantic Guitar, Musical Tributes, Variations, Passacaglias and Chaconnes, American Music of the Stage and Screen, Alice Artzt Classic Guitar, Alice Artzt Plays Original Works. *Publications:* The Art of Practicing, The International GFA Guitarists' Cookbook (ed.), Rhythmic Mastery 1997; numerous articles in guitar and music periodicals. *Leisure interests:* hi-fi, travel, Chaplin movies. *Address:* 51 Hawthorne Avenue, Princeton, NJ 08540, USA (home). *Telephone:* (609) 921-6629 (home). *E-mail:* guitartzt@aol.com (home).

ARTZT, Edwin Lewis, BJ; American business executive; *Executive Director, Barilla G.E.R. SpA;* b. 15 April 1930, New York; s. of William Artzt and Ida Artzt; m. Ruth N. Martin 1950; one s. four d.; ed Univ. of Oregon; Account Exec. Glasser Gailey Advertising Agency, Los Angeles 1952–53; joined Proctor & Gamble Co., Cincinnati 1953, Brand Man. Advertising Dept 1956–58, Assoc. Brand Promotion Man. 1958–60, Brand Promotion Man. 1960, 1962–65, Copy Man. 1960–62, Advertisement Man. Paper Products Div. 1965–68, Man. Products Food Div. 1968–69, Vice-Pres. 1969, Vice-Pres., Acting Man. Coffee Div. 1970, Vice-Pres., Group Exec. 1970–75, Dir 1972–75, 1980–95; Group Vice-Pres. Procter & Gamble Co., Europe, Belgium 1975–80; Pres. Procter & Gamble Int. 1980–89, Chair., CEO 1995–99; Vice-Chair. Procter & Gamble Co. 1980–89, Chair. 1989–95, CEO 1995–99; Exec. Dir Barilla G.E.R. SpA 1995–; Martin Luther King, Jr Salute to Greatness Award 1995, Leadership Conf. on Civil Rights Pvt. Sector Leadership Award 1995. *Address:* 9495 Whitegate Lane, Cincinnati, OH 45243, USA (home).

ARUNGA, June, LLB; Kenyan journalist and film company executive; *Founder and President, Open Quest Media LLC;* b. 1981; ed Univ. of Buckingham, UK, Univ. of Nairobi; Founder and Pres. Open Quest Media LLC (film and TV production co.), New York, USA 2006–; Vice-Pres. New Liberty Films LLC; Assoc. Ed. AfricanLiberty.org; mem. Bd of Advisors Global Envision (USA), The Inter-Region Econ. Network (Kenya), Grassroot Free Markets (Hawaii), The Bastiat Soc., Charleston, SC; mem. Creative Council, Moving Pictures Inst., New York; H.B. Earhart Grad. Fellow of Law; Sr Fellow, Istituto Bruno Leoni, Milan, Italy; Fellow, IMANI Center for Policy and Educ., Int. Policy Network, London, UK; honoured by Clutch magazine as one of 21 International Women of Power 2008. *Television:* writer/host of The Devil's Footpath (BBC TV) 2004, co-presenter/subject of Africa: Who is to Blame? (BBC World TV) 2005, writer/producer of Africa's Ultimate Resource (Victory Studios) 2005, The Cell-Phone Revolution in Kenya (BBC Newsnight mini-documentary) 2007. *Publication:* The Cell-Phone Revolution in Kenya (co-author) 2007. *Address:* Open Quest Media LLC, 119 W 72nd Street (No. 158), New York, NY 10023, USA (office). *Telephone:* (206) 719-6485 (office). *E-mail:* junearunga@openquestmedia.com (office). *Website:* www.openquestmedia.com (office); junearunga.typepad.com/openquest/2007/10/index.html (office).

ARUTIUNIAN, Alexander Grigor; Armenian composer; b. 23 Sept. 1920, Yerevan; s. of Gregori Arutiunian and Eleanor Arutiunian; m. Irina Odenova Tamara 1950; one s. one d.; ed Komitas Conservatory, Yerevan and Workshop at House of Armenian Culture, Moscow; mem. CPSU 1952–91; Artistic Dir Armenian Philharmonic 1954–; Prof. of Composition, Komitas Conservatory 1962–; USSR State Prize 1949, People's Artist of the USSR 1970, Armenian State Prizes 1970, 1986, Kentucky Coll. Orpheus Award 1983, Khachaturian Prize 1986. *Compositions include:* Cantata on the Motherland 1949, Trumpet concerto 1950, Concertino for piano and orchestra 1951, Symphony 1957, Legend of the Armenian People for soloists, choir and orchestra 1961, French Horn concerto 1962, Concertino for cello 1964, Sinfonietta 1966, Sayat-Nova (opera) 1969, vocal series Memorial to Mother 1970, Piano concertos 1971, 1983, Reverend Beggars (musical comedy) 1972, Theme and Variations for trumpet and orchestra, Rhapsody for piano, percussion and string orchestra 1974, Oboe concerto 1977, Symphony for choir and percussion 1982, Armenian Scenes (brass quintet) 1984, concertos for flute and string orchestra 1985, for violin and string orchestra 1988, for trombone and orchestra 1990, for tuba and orchestra 1991, Suite for clarinet, violin and piano 1992, Rhapsody for trumpet and wind orchestra 1992, Suite for oboe, clarinet and piano 1994; chamber and vocal music, music for theatre and cinema. *Address:* Demirchian str. 25, Apt. 19, 375002 Yerevan, Armenia. *Telephone:* (10) 524785. *Fax:* (10) 151938.

ARUTYUNYAN, Khosrov Melikovich; Armenian politician; b. 30 May 1948, Yerevan; m.; two c.; ed Yerevan Polytech. Inst.; Head of Lab., Head of Dept, Dir Ashtarak br., Byurokan Observatory 1977–82; lecturer, Yerevan Polytechnic Inst. 1978–82; Dir knitted goods factory 1983–87, Chair. Municipal Cttee Charentsavan Dist 1991; mem. Armenian Supreme Soviet 1990–92; Chair. Comm. on problems of local self-governing 1990–92; mem. Parl. 1993–; Prime Minister of Armenia 1992–93; Deputy Chair. State Legal Comm., Adviser to Prime Minster 1995–; Pres. Nat. Ass. 1998; Minister for Territorial Govt 1999–2000. *Address:* National Assembly, 19 Marshal Bughramyan Avenue, 375095 Yerevan, Armenia. *Telephone:* (10) 524614. *Fax:* (10) 529826.

ARYAL, Krishna Raj, MEd, MA; Nepalese politician, educationist and diplomatist; b. Dec. 1928, Kathmandu; m. Shanta Laxmi 1956; one s.; ed Durbar High School, Tri-Chandra Coll., Allahabad Univ., India, Univ. of Oregon, USA Lecturer, Nat. Teachers' Training Centre 1954–56; Prof. Coll. of Educ., Dir Publs Govt Educ. Devt Project 1956–59; Ed. Education Quarterly 1956–59, Nabin Shikshya 1956–59; Founder, Admin. and Prin. Shri Ratna Rajya Laxmi Girls' Coll. 1961–71; Asst Minister for Educ. 1971–72, Minister of State 1972–73, Minister 1973–75, Minister of Foreign Affairs 1975–79; Amb. to France also accred to Spain, Italy, Portugal and Israel and Perm. Del. to UNESCO 1980–84; Chair. Asian Group and mem. Bureau Group 77, UNESCO 1982–83; Hon. mem. Raj Sabha 1985–90, Rastriya Panchayat (unicameral legis.) 1986–90; fmr Sec. Cricket Asscn of Nepal; Chair. Brahmacharya Ashram; Exec. mem. World Hindu Fed.; Gorakha Dakhinbahu (1st Class); Grand Cordon of Yugoslav Star; Order of the Rising Sun, 1st Class (Japan); Grand Officier, Order Nat. du Mérite (France), Order of Civil Merit, 1st Class (Spain) and other decorations. *Publications include:* Monarchy in the Making of Nepal (in English), Education for the Development of Nepal (in English), The Science of Education (in Nepalese). *Address:* 17/93 Gaihiri Dhara, Kathmandu, Nepal (home).

ARYSTANBEKOVA, Akmaral Khaidarovna, PhD, DSc; Kazakhstani politician and diplomatist; *Ambassador-at-Large, Ministry of Foreign Affairs;* b. 12 May 1948, Alma-Ata (now Almaty); d. of Khaidar Arystanbvekov and Sharbanu Bekmanovna Nurmuhamedova; ed Kazak State Univ.; mem. Staff Dept of Chem., Kazak State Univ. 1975–78; Chief of Dept and Sec. Cen. State Cttee, Kazak Komsomol 1978–83; mem. Supreme Council Kazakstan 1985–90, Presidium 1987–90; Minister of Foreign Affairs 1989–91; Rep. of Kazakhstan at Perm. Mission of the fmr USSR 1991–92; Perm. Rep. and Amb., Perm. Mission of Kazakstan to UN 1992–99; Amb. to France 1999–2003; currently Amb.-at-Large, Ministry of Foreign Affairs; Deputy Chair. Kazak Friendship Soc. 1983–84; Chair. Presidium Kazakh Soc. for Friendship and Cultural Relations with Foreign Countries 1984–89; Medal of Supreme Soviet of USSR 1970, 1981, Kurmat Order 1996. *Publications:* United Nations and Kazakhstan 2002, Kazakhstan in the UN: History and

Perspectives 2004, Globalization 2007; numerous contribs to periodicals. *Leisure interests:* classical music, piano. *Address:* Ministry of Foreign Affairs, 010000 Astana, Beibitshilik 11 (office); 050000, Almaty, Aiteke-Bi, 65, Kazakhstan (home). *Telephone:* (7172) 32-76-69 (office); (7272) 72-07-40 (home). *Fax:* (7172) 32-76-67 (home); (7272) 72-01-03 (home). *E-mail:* mta_almaty@mail.ru (home). *Website:* www.mfa.kz (office).

ARZALLUZ ANTÍA, Xabier; Spanish politician and lawyer; *President, Basque Nationalist Party;* b. 1932; fmr Jesuit priest; mem. Euzko Alderdi Jeltzalea/Partido Nacionalista Vasco (EAJ/PNV) (Basque Nationalist Party) 1968–, now Pres. *Address:* Ibáñez de Bilbao 16 (Sabin Etxea), 48001 Bilbao, Spain (office). *Telephone:* (94) 40359400 (office). *Fax:* (94) 40359412 (office). *E-mail:* prensa@eaj-pnv.com (office). *Website:* www.eaj-pnv.com (office).

ARZÚ IRIGOYEN, Alvaro Enrique; Guatemalan politician; b. 14 March 1946, Guatemala City; ed Univ. of Rafael, Landívar; Dir Guatemalan Tourist Inst. 1978–81; Mayor of Guatemala City 1986–91, 2004–07; unsuccessful presidential cand. 1990; Leader, Partido de Avanzada Nacional (PAN) 1991; Minister of Foreign Relations 1991; Pres. of Guatemala 1996–2000; del. to Cen. American Parl. 2000–04; Dr hc (Univ. of St Paul, Chicago); Prince of Asturias and Int. Cooperation Award 1997, Feliz Houphout Boigny Prize (UNESCO), Galardón Monseñor Leonidas Proaño Award, Latin American Asscn for Human Rights. *Achievements include:* fmr squash nat. champion. *Leisure interests:* soccer, swimming, cycling, golf, horse riding. *Address:* Partido de Avanzada Nacional (PAN), 7A Avda 10-38, Zona 9, Guatemala City, Guatemala (office). *Telephone:* 2334-1702 (office). *Fax:* 2331-9906 (office).

ARZUMANYAN, Aleksander Robertovich; Armenian politician and diplomatist; b. 24 Dec. 1959, Yerevan; m.; two c.; ed Yerevan State Univ.; Eng Yerevan Research Inst. of Automatic Systems of City Man. 1985–88; Dir Information Cen. Armenian Nat. Movt 1989–90; Asst Chair. of Supreme Council of Armenia 1990–91; Rep. of Armenia to N America 1991–92; Chargé d'affaires to USA 1992–93; Perm. Rep. to UN 1992; rank of Amb. 1992; took part and headed dels of Armenia to int. meetings; elected Deputy Chair. 49th Gen. UN Ass., concurrently mem. Gen. Cttee of UN and mem. Appellation Cttee on resolutions of Admin. Court of UN 1994; Chair. Regional Group for Eastern Europe 1992–96; Minister of Foreign Affairs 1996–98. *Address:* c/o Mashal Bagramyan str. 10, 375019 Yerevan, Armenia.

ASADA, Teruo; Japanese business executive; *President and CEO, Marubeni Corporation;* joined Marubeni Corpn in 1972, has held several exec. positions, including Man. Exec. Officer, Chief Information Officer, Sr Man. Exec. Dir and Dir, mem. Bd of Dirs 2005–, Pres. and Rep. Dir Marubeni Corpn 2008–. *Address:* Marubeni Corpn, 42 Ohtemachi 1-chome, Chiyoda-ku, Tokyo 100-8088, Japan (office). *Telephone:* (3) 3282-2111 (office). *Fax:* (3) 3282-4241 (office). *E-mail:* info@marubeni.com (office). *Website:* www.marubeni.com (office).

ASADOV, Oktai S.; Azerbaijani engineer and politician; *Chairman, Milli Majlis (National Assembly);* b. 3 Jan. 1955, Shaharjik village, Gafan Dist; m.; two c.; ed Azerbaijan Chem. Inst.; early position at Baku Air Conditioning Factory; Sr Engineer, Azerbaijan Special Installation and Construction Co. 1979–81; Sr Engineer, Azerbaycantexqurashdirma 1981–83, Head of Dept No. 1 1983–89; CEO Santexqurashdirma Industrial Union 1989–96; Pres. Absheron Regional Jt Stock Water Co. 1996–2004; Pres. Azersu Jt Stock Co. 2004–; mem. New Azerbaijan Party 1999–; Deputy, Milli Majlis (Nat. Ass.) 2000–, Chair. 2005–. *Address:* Milli Majlis (National Assembly), 1152 Baku, Parlament pr. 1, Azerbaijan (office). *Telephone:* (12) 439-97-50 (office). *Fax:* (12) 493-49-43 (office). *E-mail:* azmm@meclis.gov.az (office). *Website:* www .meclis.gov.az (office).

ASALI, Saif Mahyoub al-; Yemeni politician; Minister of Finance 2006–07, of Industry and Commerce 2007–. *Address:* Ministry of Industry and Commerce, PO Box 22210, San'a, Yemen (office). *Telephone:* (1) 252345 (office). *Fax:* (1) 251557 (office). *E-mail:* most@y.net.ye (office). *Website:* www .most.org.ye (office).

ASAMOAH, Obed Y., JSD; Ghanaian politician and lawyer; b. 6 Feb. 1936, Likpe Bala, Volta Region; s. of William Asamoah and Monica Asamoah; m. Yvonne Wood 1964; two s. one d.; ed Achimota Secondary School, Woolwich Polytechnic, London, King's Coll. London and Columbia Univ., New York; called to the Bar, Middle Temple, London 1960; upon return to Ghana practised as solicitor and advocate of Supreme Court of Ghana; Lecturer, Faculty of Law, Univ. of Ghana, Legon 1965–69; fmr Chair. Bd of Dirs of Ghana Film Industry Corpn, Ghana Bauxite Co.; mem. Constituent Ass. which drafted Constitution for Second Repub. of Ghana 1969; elected to Parl. (Nat. Alliance of Liberals) 1969; mem. Constituent Ass. which drafted third Republican Constitution 1979; Gen. Sec. United Nat. Convention 1979, All People's Party 1981; Minister of Foreign Affairs 1982–97; Attorney-Gen. and Minister of Justice 1993–2001; Chair. Nat. Democratic Congress 2002–05; mem. Ghana Bar Asscn; has served on several int. and public orgs; Patron Democratic Freedom Party; Order of the Star of Ghana 2001. *Publications:* The Legal Significance of the Declaration of the General Assembly of the United Nations 1967; articles in legal journals. *Leisure interests:* reading, farming. *Address:* PO Box 14581, Accra, Ghana. *Telephone:* (21) 668414 (home); (20) 811-99-11 (mobile). *E-mail:* obed@obedasamoah.com (home).

ASANO, Tadanobu; Japanese actor; b. 27 Nov. 1973, Yokohama; m. Chara (q.v.) 1994; one d. one s.; TV debut in school drama series Kinpachi Sensei 1989; film debut in Bataashi Jingyo (Swimming Upstream) 1990; model for designers Takeo Kikuchi and Jun Takahashi; singer in (local rock band) Mach 1.67; appearances on TV programmes and commercials. *Films include:* Bataashi Jingyo (Swimming Upstream) 1990, Aitsu 1991, Fried Dragon Fish 1993, 119 (Quiet Days of Firemen) 1994, Maboroshi no Hikari (Maborosi) 1995, Picnic 1996, Helpless 1996, Swallowtail 1996, Yume no ginga (Labyrinth of Dreams) 1997, Neji-shiki 1998, Samehada Otoko to Momojiri Onna (Shark Skin Man and Peach Hip Girl) 1998, Love & Pop 1998, Away with Words 1999, Sôseiji (Man with Sword) 1999, Hakuchi 1999, Gohatto (Taboo) 1999, One Step on a Mine – It's All Over 1999, Gojoe Senkei 2000, Kaza-Hana 2000, Party7 2000, Distance 2001, Koroshiya 1 (Ichi the Killer) 2001, Mizu no onna (Woman of Water) 2002, Akarui mirai (Bright Future) 2003, Watashi no guranpa (My Grandpa) 2003, Last Life in the Universe 2003 (Upstream Prize for Best Actor Venice Film Festival), Zatôichi 2003, Kôhî jikô 2003, Dead End Run 2003, The Taste of Tea 2004, Vital 2004, Survive Style 5+ 2004, Chichi to kuraseba 2004, Ranpo jigoku 2005. *Website:* www.asanotadanobu.com.

ASANTE, Samuel Kwadwo Boaten, LLM, JSD; Ghanaian lawyer and international legal consultant; *Chairman, Ghana Arbitration Centre;* b. 11 May 1933, Asokore; s. of Daniel Y. Asante and Mary Baafi; m. Philomena Margaret Aidoo 1961; two s. three d.; ed Achimota School, Univs of Nottingham and London, UK and Yale Univ. Law School, USA; State Attorney in the Ministry of Justice of Ghana 1960–61; Lecturer in Law and Acting Head of Law Dept, Univ. of Ghana 1961–65; Lecturer, Univ. of Leeds, UK 1965–66; Attorney World Bank, Washington, DC 1966–69; Adjunct Prof. of Law, Howard Univ. Law School, Washington, DC 1967–69; Solicitor-Gen. of Ghana 1969–74; mem. Arbitration Panel, Int. Cen. for Settlement of Investment Disputes, Washington, DC 1971–; Chair. Public Agreements Review Cttee of Ghana 1972–77; Deputy Attorney-Gen. of Ghana 1974–77; Chief Legal Adviser, UN Comm. on Transnational Corpns, New York 1977–83, Dir 1983–92; Chair. Cttee of Experts on Ghana Constitution 1991; Dir UN Legal Advisory Services for Devt 1992–93; Dir Int. Third World Legal Studies Asscn, New York; installed as Paramount Chief of Asante-Asokore, Ashanti, Ghana 1995–; Chair. Ghana Public Utilities Regulatory Comm. 1997–2002, Ghana Arbitration Centre 1997–; mem. Bd of Dirs Int. Devt Law Inst., Rome; Taylor Lecturer, Lagos Univ. 1978; Consultant, Commonwealth Secr., African Devt Bank and UNITAR; guest lecturer, numerous univs and insts world-wide; Guest Fellow, Berkeley Coll., Yale Univ. 1964–65; fmr Sterling, Fulbright and Aggrey Fellow; Fellow of World Acad. of Arts and Sciences 1975, Ghana Acad. of Arts and Sciences 1976 (Pres. 2002–); Visiting Fellow, Clare Hall, Cambridge, UK 1978–79, Life mem.; Visiting Prof., Temple Univ. Law School, Philadelphia 1976; Patron Int. Centre for Public Law, Inst. of Advanced Legal Studies, Univ. of London; mem. Int. Bar Asscn, Exec. Council, American Soc. of Int. Law 1979, Gen. Legal Council, Ghana, Advisory Bd, Foreign Investment Law Journal-ICSID Review, Int. Court of Arbitration of ICC 1993–2002 and of several other int. arbitral panels; Ghana Book Award. *Publications:* Property Law and Social Goals in Ghana 1976, Transnational Investment Law and National Development 1979 and various articles in law journals. *Leisure interests:* tennis, golf, reading biographies. *Address:* S.K.B. Asante & Associates, PO Box GP 18615, Accra, Ghana (office). *Telephone:* (21) 678973 (office); (21) 678776 (office). *Fax:* (21) 678776 (office). *E-mail:* drskba@ghana.com (office).

ASASHORYU AKINORI; Mongolian sumo wrestler; b. (Dolgorsuren Dagvadorj), 27 Sept. 1980, Ulan Bator; m.; travelled to Japan aged 16; national championship (Makuuchi) debut in 1999; first victory in Nov. 2002 in only 24th tournament (joint quickest victory in Sumo history); eight titles in total, also one Makushita title, one Sandamne title, one Jonidian title; promoted to Ozeki rank in Nov. 2002, became 68th wrestler to reach Yokozuna level (highest rank) March 2003 (first non-Japanese or non-American to reach Yokozuna level), only active Yokozuna Jan. 2004–; career record 330-109-5; three Outstanding Performance awards, three Fighting Spirit prizes.

ÅSBRINK, Erik, BSc, BA; Swedish fmr politician and business executive; *Chairman, Commission on Business Confidence;* b. 1 Feb. 1947, Stockholm; m. Anne-Marie Lindgren; three c.; ed Univ. of Stockholm, Stockholm School of Econs; worked at Inst. for Soviet and E European Econ. Affairs 1972; Nat. Inst. of Econ. Research 1972–74; Ministry of Finance 1974–76; Ministry of the Budget 1976–78; Research Sec., parl. group of Social Democratic Party (SDP) 1978–82; Under-Sec. of State, Ministry of Finance 1982–90; Minister for Fiscal and Financial Affairs, Ministry of Finance 1990–91, Minister of Finance 1996–99; currently Chair. Comm. on Business Confidence (govt comm.); Man. Dir Vasakronan AB 1993–, Pres. –1996; mem. Bd First Nat. Pension Insurance Fund 1982–85; Chair. Lantbrukskredit AB 1983–85; Chair. State Housing Finance Corpn 1984–85; Chair. Governing Bd Sveriges Riksbank 1985–90; mem. Bd Fourth Nat. Pension Insurance Fund 1985–90; Vice-Chair. Systembolaget AB 1986–90; mem. Bd AB Vin & Sprit AB (Swedish Wine and Spirits Corpn) 1986–90, 1993–, AB Trav & Galopp 1989–90, Sparbanken Sverige AB 1991–93; Chair. Sparbanken Första 1992, Confortia AB 1993–, Swedish Bond Promotion 1993–; mem. Bd ABB Investment Man. 1993–, SkandiaBanken 1994–, Swedish Concert Hall Foundation 1995–, SNS, Centre for Business and Policy Studies 1995–. *Address:* c/o Ministry of Finance, Drottninggt. 21, 103 33 Stockholm, Sweden.

ASEFI, Tariq, BS; Afghan aerospace engineer and organisation executive; *CEO and President, Afghan Chamber of Commerce;* ed Univ. of California, USA; more than 16 years' experience in man., construction, finance, design and planning in semiconductor and pharmaceutical industries; currently CEO and Pres. Afghan Chamber of Commerce. *Address:* Afghan Chamber of Commerce, 39270 Paseo Padre Parkway #343, Fremont, CA 94538, USA (office). *Fax:* (267) 790-8203 (office). *E-mail:* Info@Afghanchamber.com (office). *Website:* www.afghanchamber.com (office).

ASGHAR, Muhammad, LLB, DPhil (Oxon.); French (b. Pakistani) physicist and academic; *Professor, Laboratoire de Physique Subatomique et de Cosmologie;* b. 7 June 1936, Pakistan; s. of Muhammad Fazal and Bibi Fazal; m.; one c.; ed Univ. of Punjab, Univ. of Oxford, UK; with Pakistan Inst. of Tech., Nilore, also worked at atomic energy research stations at Harwell, UK and Saclay, France; Assoc. Prof., Univ. of Bordeaux 1968–71; physicist, Inst. Laue-Langevin (ILL), Grenoble 1971–78, CCR Euratom, Ispra 1978–80, Centre d'Etudes Nucléaires, Grenoble 1980–81; Prof. of Physics, Houari Boumedienne Univ., Algiers 1981–94, Laboratoire de Physique Subatomique et de Cosmologie, Grenoble 1994–; field of research: low-energy nuclear physics and fundamental physics, specialist in nuclear fission and nuclear energy, has coordinated int. teams in major experiments at high flux nuclear reactor, ILL, Grenoble; Fellow, Islamic Acad. of Sciences 1998. *Publications:* more than 200 research papers. *Leisure interest:* writing poetry in English, French and Persian. *Address:* Laboratoire de Physique Subatomique et de Cosmologie, 53 avenue des Martyrs, 38026 Grenoble (office); 12 rue des Aberlles, 38240 Meylan, France (home). *Telephone:* (4) 76-28-40-00 (office); (4) 76-18-00-22 (home). *Fax:* (4) 76-28-40-04 (office). *E-mail:* masgharfr@yahoo.fr (office).

ÁSGRÍMSSON, Halldór; Icelandic politician; *Secretary General, Nordic Council of Ministers;* b. 8 Sept. 1947, Vopnafjörður; s. of Ásgrímur Halldórsson and Guðrún Ingólfsdóttir; m. Sigurjóna Sigurðardóttir; three d.; ed Co-operative's Commercial Coll. and commerce univs in Bergen and Copenhagen; Certified Public Accountant 1970; Lecturer in Auditing and Accounting, Univ. of Iceland 1973–75; mem. Parl. 1974–78, 1979–; mem. Bd Cen. Bank of Iceland 1976–83, Chair. 1981–83; mem. Nordic Council 1977–78, 1979–83, 1991–95, Chair. 1982–83, Chair. Icelandic Del. 1982–83, mem. Presidium 1991–94, Chair. Liberal Group 1992–94; Minister of Fisheries 1983–91, of Nordic Co-operation 1985–87, 1995, of Justice and Ecclesiastical Affairs 1988–89, of Foreign Affairs and External Trade 1995–2004; Prime Minister and Minister of the Statistical Bureau of Iceland 2004–06 (resgnd); Vice-Chair. Framsóknarflokkurinn (Progressive Party) 1980–94, Chair. 1994–2006; Vice-Pres. Liberal Int. 1994–99; Sec.-Gen. Nordic Council of Ministers 2007–; Kt of Order of Falcon of Iceland. *Address:* Nordic Council of Ministers, Store Strandstraede 18, 1255 Copenhagen K, Denmark (office). *Telephone:* 33-96-03-22 (office). *E-mail:* ha@norden.org (office). *Website:* www.norden.org (office).

ASH, Sir Eric Albert, Kt, CBE, PhD, FRS, FCGI, FIEE, FIEEE, FInstP, FREng; British professor of physical electronics; b. 31 Jan. 1928, Berlin, Germany; s. of Walter Ash and Dorothea Ash (née Schwarz); m. Clare Babb 1954; five d.; ed Univ. Coll. School and Imperial Coll., London; Research Fellow, Stanford Univ. 1952–54; Research Asst, Queen Mary Coll., London 1954–55; Research Engineer, Standard Telecommunications Labs Ltd 1955–63; Sr Lecturer, Univ. Coll. London 1963–65, Reader 1965–67, Prof. of Electrical Eng 1967–80, Pender Prof. and Head, Dept of Electronic and Electrical Eng 1980–85, Prof. of Electrical Eng 1993–97, Prof. Emer. 1997–; Rector, Imperial Coll. London 1985–93; Dir (non-exec.) British Telecom 1987–93, Student Loans Co. PLC 1994–; Chair. BBC Science Advisory Cttee 1987–; Chair. of Council, Vice-Pres. Royal Inst. 1995– (fmr Sec., Man.); Treasurer, Royal Soc. 1997–2002; Trustee, Science Museum 1987–93, Wolfson Foundation 1988–; Foreign mem. Nat. Acad. of Eng, Russian Acad. of Sciences; Chevalier, Ordre nat. du Mérite 1990; hon. degrees from Aston, Leicester, Edinburgh, New York Polytechnic, INPG Grenoble, Westminster, Sussex, Glasgow, Surrey Univs and Chinese Univ. of Hong Kong; Faraday Medal of the IEE 1980, Royal Medal of the Royal Soc. 1986. *Publications:* papers on topics of physical electronics in various eng and physics journals. *Leisure interests:* music, skiing, writing. *Address:* 11 Ripplevale Grove, London, N1 1HS, England (home). *Telephone:* (20) 7607-4989 (home). *Fax:* (20) 7700-7446 (home). *E-mail:* eric_ash99@yahoo.co.uk (home).

ASH, Roy Lawrence, MBA; American business executive; b. 20 Oct. 1918, Los Angeles, Calif.; s. of Charles K. Ash and Fay Ash (née Dickinson); m. Lila M. Hornbek 1943; three s. two d.; ed Harvard Univ.; Pvt. to Capt., USAF 1942–46; Chief Financial Officer, Hughes Aircraft Co. 1949–53; co-founder and Dir, Litton Industries Inc. 1953–72; Pres. 1961–72; mem. Bd of Dirs Bankamerica Corpn 1968–72, 1976–91, Bank of America NT and SA 1964–72, 1978–91, Global Marine Inc. 1965–72, 1975–81, Pacific Mutual Life Insurance Co. 1965–72, Sara Lee Corpn 1979–90; Dir Los Angeles World Affairs Council 1968–72, (Pres. 1970–72), 1978–91; Chair. President's Advisory Council on Exec. Org. 1969–71; Asst to the Pres. of the USA for Exec. Man. 1972–75; Dir US Office of Man. and Budget 1973–75; Chair. and CEO AM Int. 1976–81; Co-Chair. Japan–California Asscn 1965–72, 1980–81; Vice-Chair. Los Angeles Olympic Organizing Cttee 1979–84; mem. Bd and Chair. LA Music Center Opera 1988–93; mem. The Business Roundtable 1977–81, Bd of US Chamber of Commerce 1979–85; mem. Bd of Trustees, Calif. Inst. of Tech. 1967–72; Trustee Cttee for Econ. Devt 1970–72, 1975–; Kt of Malta; Hon. LLD (Pepperdine) 1976; Horatio Alger Award 1966. *Address:* 1900 Avenue of the Stars, #1600, Los Angeles, CA 90067-4407 (office); 655 Funchal Road, Los Angeles, CA 90077, USA (home). *Telephone:* (310) 553-6244 (office); (310) 472-6661 (home). *Fax:* (310) 203-9530 (office).

ASHANTI; American hip-hop and R&B singer, songwriter and actress; b. (Ashanti Douglas), 13 Oct. 1980, Glen Cove, NY; signed record deal when 14 years old; guest vocalist with artists, including Big Punisher, Ja Rule, J. Lo, Big Pun, Fat Joe, Notorious B.I.G.; solo artist 2002–; MOBO Award for Best R&B Act 2002, American Music Awards for Best New Pop/Rock Artist, Best New Hip Hop/R&B Artist 2003. *Television appearances:* Polly (musical film), American Dreams (one episode) 2002, Buffy the Vampire Slayer (one episode) 2003, The Muppets' Wizard of Oz (TV film) 2005. *Film appearances:* Bride & Prejudice 2004, Coach Carter 2005, John Tucker Must Die 2006, Resident Evil: Extinction 2007. *Recordings include:* albums: Ashanti 2002, Foolish/Unfoolish: Reflections on Love 2002, Chapter II 2003, Ashanti's Christmas 2003, Concrete Rose 2004, The Declaration 2008. *Address:* c/o Universal Records, 2220 Colorado Avenue, Santa Monica, CA 90404, USA (office). *Website:* www.ashantimusic.net.

ASHBERY, John Lawrence, MA; American poet, author, critic and academic; *Charles P. Stevenson, Jr Professor of Languages and Literature, Bard College;* b. 28 July 1927, Rochester, NY; s. of Chester F. Ashbery and Helen L. Ashbery; ed Deerfield Acad., Mass, Harvard, Columbia and New York Univs; asst, Literature Dept, Brooklyn (NY) Public Library 1949; copywriter, Oxford Univ. Press, New York 1951–54, McGraw-Hill Book Co. 1954–55; went to France as a Fulbright Scholar 1955–56, 1956–57, lived there 1958–65; Art Critic, Int. edn New York Herald-Tribune, Paris 1960–65; Co-Ed. Locus Solus, Lans-en-Vercors, France 1960–62, Art and Literature, Paris 1964–67; Art Critic, Art International, Lugano 1961–63, New York Magazine 1978–80, Newsweek 1980–85; Paris corresp. Art News, New York 1964–65, Exec. Ed. 1965–72; Prof. of English and Co-Dir MFA Program in Creative Writing, Brooklyn Coll., NY (CUNY) 1974–90, Distinguished Prof. 1980–90, Distinguished Prof. Emer. 1990–; Poetry Ed. Partisan Review, New York 1976–80; Charles Eliot Norton Prof. of Poetry, Harvard Univ. 1989–90; Charles P. Stevenson, Jr Prof. of Languages and Literature, Bard Coll., Annandale-on-Hudson, NY 1990–; Chancellor Acad. of American Poets 1988–99; Leader, Fondation d'Art de La Napoule 1989; Poet Laureate, New York State 2001–03, MtvU (to promote poetry in US universities) 2007–; mem. American Acad. of Arts and Letters 1980–, American Acad. of Arts and Sciences 1983–; works translated into more than 20 languages; Chevalier des Arts et Lettres 1993; Officier, Légion d'honneur 2002; Hon. DLitt (Southampton Coll. of Long Island Univ.) 1979, (Univ. of Rochester, NY) 1994, (Harvard Univ.) 2001; recipient of numerous awards, grants and honours, including two Guggenheim Fellowships 1967, 1973, MacArthur Fellow 1985–90, Horst Bienek Prize for Poetry (Bavarian Acad. of Fine Arts) 1991, Ruth Lilly Prize for Poetry 1992, Antonio Fraternelli Int. Prize for Poetry (Accad. Nazionale dei Lincei, Rome) 1992, Robert Frost Medal (Poetry Soc. of America) 1995, Grand Prix de Biennales Internationales de Poésie (Brussels) 1996, Gold Medal for Poetry (American Acad. of Arts and Letters) 1997, Bingham Poetry Prize 1998, Walt Whitman Citation of Merit (State of New York and New York State Writers' Inst.) 2000, Signet Soc. Medal for Achievement in the Arts 2001, Wallace Stevens Award (Acad. of American Poets) 2001. *Plays:* The Heroes 1952, The Compromise 1956, The Philosopher 1963, Three Plays 1978. *Publications include:* poetry: Turandot and Other Poems 1953, Some Trees 1956, The Tennis Court Oath 1962, Rivers and Mountains 1966, The Double Dream of Spring 1970, Three Poems 1972, The Vermont Notebook 1975, Self-Portrait in a Convex Mirror (Pulitzer Prize 1975, Nat. Book Award 1975, Nat. Book Critics' Circle Award 1975) 1975, Houseboat Days 1979, As We Know 1979, Shadow Train 1981, A Wave 1984, Selected Poems 1985, April Galleons 1987, Flow Chart 1991, Hotel Lautréamont 1992, And the Stars Were Shining 1994, Can You Hear, Bird 1995, Wakefulness 1998, Girls on the Run 1999, Your Name Here 2000, As Umbrellas Follow Rain 2001, Chinese Whispers 2002, Where Shall I Wander 2005, Notes from the Air: Selected Later Poems 2007; novel: A Nest of Ninnies (with J. Schuyler) 1969; essays and criticism: Fairfield Porter 1983, R. B. Kitaj (with others) 1983, Reported Sightings: Art Chronicles 1957–1987 1989, Other Traditions (The Charles Eliot Norton Lectures at Harvard) 2000; numerous translations from French including works by Raymond Roussel, Max Jacob, Alfred Jarry, Antonin Artaud and Pierre Martory, including Every Question but One 1990, The Landscape is behind the Door 1994. *Address:* c/o George Borchardt Inc., 136 East 57th Street, New York, NY 10022-2707; Bard College, Department of Languages and Literature, PO Box 5000, Annandale-on-Hudson, NY 12504-5000, USA (office). *Telephone:* (845) 758-7290 (office). *Website:* www.bard.edu/academics/programs/langlit (office).

ASHBURTON, 7th Baron, cr. 1835; **John Francis Harcourt Baring,** Kt, KG, KCVO, MA, DL, FIB; British merchant banker; b. 2 Nov. 1928, London; s. of 6th Baron Ashburton and Hon. Doris Mary Therese Harcourt; m. 1st Susan Mary Renwick 1955 (divorced 1984); two s. two d.; m. 2nd Sarah Crewe 1987; ed Eton Coll. and Trinity Coll., Oxford; Chair. Barings PLC 1985–89 (Dir (non-exec.) 1989–94), Baring Bros & Co. Ltd 1974–89 (a Man. Dir 1955–74); Dir Trafford Park Estates Ltd 1964–77; Royal Insurance Co. Ltd 1964–82, (Deputy Chair. 1975–82); Dir Outwich Investment Trust Ltd 1965–86 (Chair. 1968–86), British Petroleum Co. 1982–95 (Chair. 1992–95), Dunlop Holdings 1981–84, Bank of England 1983–91, Baring Stratton Investment Trust PLC 1986–98 (Chair. 1986–98), Jaguar PLC 1989–91; mem. British Transport Docks Bd 1966–71; Vice-Pres. British Bankers Asscn 1977–81; mem. Pres.'s Cttee CBI 1976–79, Gen. Council CBI 1976–80; Chair. Accepting Houses Cttee 1977–81, NEDC Cttee on Finance for Industry 1980–87; Pres. Overseas Bankers Club 1977–78; Rhodes Trustee 1970–79, Chair. 1987–98; Trustee Nat. Gallery 1981–87; Trustee and Hon. Treas. Police Foundation 1989–2001; mem. Exec. Cttee Nat. Art Collections Fund 1989–99; mem. Council Baring Foundation 1971–98, Chair. 1987–98; mem. Southampton Univ. Devt Trust 1986–96 (Chair. 1989–96); mem. Winchester Cathedral Trust 1989– (Chair. 1993–2006); Lord Warden of the Stannaries, Duchy of Cornwall 1990–94, Receiver-Gen. 1974–90; High Steward Winchester Cathedral 1991–; DL Hants. 1994–; Fellow, Eton Coll. 1982–97; Hon. Fellow, Hertford Coll., Oxford 1976, Trinity Coll., Oxford 1989. *Address:* Lake House, Northington, Alresford, Hants., SO24 9TG, England (office). *Telephone:* (1962) 738728 (office).

ASHBY, Michael Farries, CBE, PhD, FRS, FREng; British professor of engineering materials; *Royal Society Research Professor and Principal Investigator, Engineering Design Centre, University of Cambridge;* b. 20 Nov. 1935; s. of Lord Ashby and Elizabeth Helen Farries; m. Maureen Stewart 1962; two s. one d.; ed Campbell Coll., Belfast, Queens' Coll., Cambridge; Asst, Univ. of Göttingen, FRG 1962–65; Asst Prof., Harvard Univ., USA 1965–69, Prof. of Metallurgy 1969–73; Prof. of Eng Materials, Univ. of Cambridge 1973–89, Royal Soc. Research Prof., Dept of Eng 1989–; currently Royal Acad. Visiting Prof., RCA, London; Ed. Acta Metallurgica 1974–96, Progress in

Materials Science 1995–; mem. Akad. der Wissenschaften zu Göttingen 1985–, American Acad. of Arts and Sciences 1993–; Foreign mem. US Nat. Acad. of Eng 1990; Fellow Royal Swedish Acad. of Eng Sciences 1985–, Inst. of Metals, UK 1991; Hon. Life mem. Soc. Francaise de Materiaux 1990, Materials Research Soc. of India 1990, Materials Research Soc. of the USA 1990; Hon. MA (Harvard) 1969; Dr hc (Leuven) 1990, (Royal Inst. of Tech., Stockholm) 1995, (Tech. Univ. of Lisbon) 1996; L.B. Pfeil Medal, Metals Soc. 1975, Rosenheim Medal, Metals Soc. 1979, Mehl Medal, American Soc. for Metals 1983, Amourers and Brasiers Medal, Royal Soc. 1985, A.A. Griffiths Medal, Metals Soc. 1985, Acta Metallurgica Gold Medal 1986, Hume-Rothery Award, American Soc. for Metals 1988, Paul Bergsoe Medal, Danish Metallurgical Soc. 1989, Materials Medal, Soc. Francaise de Materiaux 1990, Hatfield Memorial Lecturer, Royal Soc. of Great Britain 1992, Von Hippel Award, Materials Research Soc. of the USA 1992, Gold Medal, Fed. of European Materials Socs 1993, Luigi Losana Medal, Associazione Italiana di Metallurgia 1993, Campbell Lecturer, American Soc. for Metals 1994, The Körber Prize 1996, Platinum Medal, Inst. of Materials, London 1998, Hirsch Lecturer, Univ. of Oxford 1998, A. Cemal Eringen Medal, SES, USA 1999. *Publications:* Deformation Mechanism Maps 1982, Engineering Materials (Vol. 1) 1989, (Vol. 2) 1996, Cellular Solids 1997, Materials Selection in Design (2nd edn) 1999, Materials and Design – The Art and Science of Product Design 2002, Materials and the Environment 2009. *Leisure interests:* music, design, watercolour painting. *Address:* 51 Maids Causeway, Cambridge, CB5 8DE (home); University of Cambridge, Department of Engineering, Trumpington Street, Cambridge, CB2 1PZ, England (office). *Telephone:* (1223) 303015 (home); (1223) 332635 (office). *Fax:* (1223) 332662 (home). *E-mail:* mfa2@eng.cam.ac.uk (office). *Website:* www-edc.eng.cam.ac.uk/people/mfa2.html (office).

ASHCROFT, Frances Mary, BA, PhD, ScD, FRS, FMedSci; British physiologist and academic; *Royal Society GlaxoSmithKline Research Professor of Physiology, University of Oxford;* b. 15 Feb. 1952; d. of John Ashcroft and Kathleen Ashcroft; ed Talbot Heath School, Bournemouth; Girton Coll., Cambridge; MRC Training Fellow in Physiology, Univ. of Leicester 1978–82; Demonstrator in Physiology, Oxford Univ. 1982–85, EPA Cephalosporin Jr Research Fellow, Linacre Coll. 1983–85, Royal Soc. Univ. Research Fellow in Physiology 1985–90, Lecturer in Physiology, Christ Church 1986–87, Trinity Coll. 1988–89 (Sr Research Fellow 1992–; Tutorial Fellow in Medicine, St Hilda's Coll. 1990–91; Univ. Lecturer in Physiology 1990–96, Prof. of Physiology 1996–2001, Royal Soc. GlaxoSmithKline Research Prof. 2001–; G. L. Brown Prize Lecturer 1997, Peter Curran Lecturer, Yale Univ. 1999; mem. European Molecular Biology Org.; Dr hc (Open Univ.) 2003, (Univ. of Leicester) 2007; Frank Smart Prize, Univ. of Cambridge 1974, Andrew Culworth Memorial Prize 1990, G. B. Morgagni Young Investigator Award 1991, Charter Award, Inst. of Biology 2004. *Publications:* Insulin-Molecular Biology to Pathology (jtly) 1992, Ion Channels and Disease 2000, Life at the Extremes 2000, and numerous articles in scientific journals. *Leisure interests:* reading, walking, writing, sailing. *Address:* Department of Physiology, Anatomy and Genetics, Sherrington Bldg, Parks Road, Oxford, OX1 3PT, England (office). *Telephone:* (1865) 285810 (office). *Fax:* (1865) 285812 (office). *E-mail:* frances.ashcroft@dpag.ox.ac.uk (office). *Website:* www.dpag.ox.ac.uk (office); oxion.physiol.ox.ac.uk/oxion.php (office); www.dpag.ox.ac.uk/research/ion_channels/ashcroft/ashcroft_research (office).

ASHCROFT, John David, JD; American lobbyist and fmr politician; *Chairman, Ashcroft Group LLC;* b. 9 May 1942, Chicago; m. Janet Elise; two s. one d.; ed Yale Univ. and Univ. of Chicago; admitted, Missouri State Bar, US Supreme Court Bar; Assoc. Prof. SW Missouri State Univ. Springfield; legal practice, Springfield, Mo. until 1973; State Auditor, Missouri 1973–75, Asst Attorney-Gen. 1975–77, Attorney-Gen. 1977–84; Gov. of Missouri 1985–93; Senator from Missouri 1995–2001; US Attorney Gen. 2001–04 (resgnd); f. Ashcroft Group, LLC (lobbying firm) 2006; apptd mem. of Faculty, Regent Univ. 2006; recordings as gospel singer. *Publications:* College Law for Business (with Janet Elise), It's the Law 1979, Never Again 2006. *Address:* The Ashcroft Group, LLC, 1399 New York Avenue, NW, Suite 950, Washington, DC 20005, USA (office). *Telephone:* (202) 942-0202 (office). *Fax:* (202) 942-0216 (office). *E-mail:* info@ashcroftgroupllc.com (office). *Website:* www.ashcroftgroupllc.com (office).

ASHCROFT, Baron (Life Peer), cr. 2000, of Chichester in the County of West Sussex; **Michael Ashcroft;** Belizean/British business executive and diplomatist; *Chairman and CEO, Carlisle Holdings Ltd;* b. 4 March 1946; m.; three c.; ed St Catherine's Acad., Belize City, Norwich School, Mid-Essex Coll.; fmr Chair. and CEO BHI Corpn, Belize; Chair. and Chief Exec. ADT Ltd (fmrly Hawley Group Ltd and now Tyco Int. Ltd), Bermuda 1977–97, Dir (non-exec.) 1997–2002; currently Chair. and CEO Carlisle Holdings Ltd; Trade and Investment Adviser to Belize High Comm. in London 1984–89; Belize's Itinerant Amb. to EEC 1989; Econ. Adviser, Embassy of Belize, USA 1998–99; Perm. Rep. of Belize to UN 1998–2000; Treas. Conservative Party, UK 1998–2001; Head of Aspen Int. Devt Co.; fmr Chair. Bd of Trustees, Crimestoppers, UK, Industry in Educ., UK, Prospect Educational Trust, UK; fmr Chair. Michael A. Ashcroft Foundation, Belize and UK; Chancellor Anglia Polytechnic Univ. 2001–. *Publication:* Dirty Politics, Dirty Times 2006, Victoria Cross Heroes 2007. *Address:* House of Lords, Westminster, London, SW1A 0PW, England (office); Carlisle Holdings Ltd, 60 Market Square, Belize City, Belize (office). *Telephone:* (501) 227-2660 (Belize) (office). *Fax:* (501) 227-5474 (Belize) (office). *Website:* www.carlisleholdings.com (office).

ASHDOWN OF NORTON SUB-HAMDON, Baron (Life Peer), cr. 2001, of Norton Sub-Hamdon in the County of Somerset; **Sir Jeremy John Durham (Paddy) Ashdown,** GCMG, KBE, PC; British politician; b. 27 Feb. 1941, Delhi, India; s. of John W. R. D. Ashdown and Lois A. Ashdown; m. Jane Courtenay 1961; one s. one d.; ed Bedford School; served in Royal Marines 1959–71, rank of Capt.; joined Diplomatic Service, First Sec. Mission to UN, Geneva 1971–76; Commercial Man.'s Dept, Westland Group 1976–78; Sr Man., Morlands Ltd 1978–81; employee, Dorset Co. Council 1982–83; Parl. Spokesman for Trade and Industry 1983–86; Liberal/SDP Alliance Spokesman on Education and Science 1987; Liberal MP for Yeovil 1983–88, Liberal Democrat MP for Yeovil 1988–2001; Leader Liberal Democrats 1988–99; UN Int. High Rep. to Bosnia and Herzegovina 2002–06. *Publications:* Citizen's Britain: A Radical Agenda for the 1990s 1989, Beyond Westminster 1994, The Ashdown Diaries 1988–1997 2000, The Ashdown Diaries Vol. II 1997–1999 2001, Swords and Ploughshares 2007, A Fortunate Life 2009. *Leisure interests:* walking, gardening, wine making. *Address:* House of Lords, Westminster, London, SW1A 0PW, England (office). *Telephone:* (20) 7219-3000 (office). *Fax:* (20) 7219-5979 (office).

ASHER, Jane; British actress, food industry executive and writer; b. 5 April 1946, London; d. of the late Richard A. J. Asher and of Margaret Eliot; m. Gerald Scarfe (q.v.); two s. one d.; ed North Bridge House, Miss Lambert's Parents' Nat. Educational Union; has appeared in numerous films, on TV and the London stage and has written several best-selling books; Proprietor Jane Asher Party Cakes Shop and Sugarcraft 1990–; designer, consultant for Sainsbury's cakes 1992–99; Pres. Nat. Autistic Soc.; spokesperson and consultant to Heinz Frozen Desserts 1999–2001; Cookware and Gift Food Designer for Debenhams 1998–2005; creator of Home Baking Mixes for Victoria Foods 1999–; Hon. LLD. *Films include:* Greengage Summer, Masque of the Red Death, Alfie 1966, Deep End, Henry the Eighth and his Six Wives 1970, Success is the Best Revenge, Dreamchild, Paris By Night 1988, Tirante el Blanco 2006, Death at a Funeral 2007. *Plays include:* Henceforward..., School for Scandal 1990, Making It Better 1992, The Shallow End 1997, Things We Do for Love 1998, House and Garden 2000, What the Butler Saw 2001, Festen 2004. *Television includes:* Closing Numbers 1994, The Choir 1995, Good Living 1997, Crossroads 2003, Miss Marple 2004, New Tricks 2005, Holby City 2007. *Publications include:* The Moppy Stories 1987, Keep Your Baby Safe 1988, Calendar of Cakes 1989, Eats for Treats 1990, Time to Play 1993, Jane Asher's Book of Cake Decorating Ideas 1993; novels: The Longing 1996, The Question 1998, Losing It 2002, Cakes for Fun 2005. *Leisure interests:* reading, Times crossword. *Address:* 24 Cale Street, London, SW3 3QU, England; United Agents, 12–26 Lexington Street, London, W1F 0LE, England (office). *Telephone:* (20) 3214-0800 (office). *Fax:* (20) 3214-0801 (office). *E-mail:* info@unitedagents.co.uk (office). *Website:* www.unitedagents.co.uk (office).

ASHIDA, Akimitsu; Japanese business executive; *Representative Director and President, Mitsui Osk Lines Ltd;* joined Mitsui OSK Lines Ltd 1967, positions held include Dir 1st Regular Line, Dir of Planning, Man. Dir, Sr Man. Dir, Sr Man. Exec. Officer, Vice-Pres., Exec. Vice-Pres., Pres. and Dir, Rep. Dir and Exec. Pres. 2005–. *Address:* Mitsui OSK Lines Ltd, 1-1 Toranomon, 2-chome, Tokyo 105-8688, Japan (office). *Telephone:* (3) 3587-6224 (office). *Fax:* (3) 3587-7734 (office). *E-mail:* info@mol.co.jp (office). *Website:* www.mol.co.jp (office).

ASHIDA, Jun; Japanese fashion designer; *President, Jun Ashida Co. Ltd;* b. 21 Aug. 1930, Kyoto; s. of Sadao Ashida and Ritsuko Ashida; m. Tomoko Tomita 1960; two d.; ed Tokyo High School; studied under Jun-ichi Nakahara 1948–52; consultant designer to Takashimaya Dept Store 1960; est. Jun Ashida Co. Ltd and Jun Ashida label 1963, Pres. 1963–; exclusive designer to HIH Crown Princess (now Empress) Michiko 1966–76, designs for several mems of Imperial family; presented first collection in Paris 1977; launched Miss Ashida and Jun Ashida for Men labels 1985–86; opened shop Jun Ashida Paris 1989; designed uniforms for Japanese Pavilion, Expo World Fair, Seville 1992, All Nippon Airways, Fuji Xerox, Imperial Hotel, Nomura Securities, Idemitsu Kosan, Tokyo Kaijo, Japanese team at Olympic Games, Atlanta 1996; mem. Postal Service Council of Ministry of Posts and Telecommunications; Japanese Hans Christian Andersen Goodwill Amb. 2005; Cavaliere, Ordine al Merito (Italy) 1989, Ufficiale 2003, Officier, Ordre nat. du Mérite (France) 2000, Officier, Ordre nat. du Mérite (Luxembourg) 2006, Order of the Rising Sun, Gold Rays with Neck Ribbon (Japan) 2006; FEC Award (Japan) 1971, Purple Ribbon Medal (Japan) 1991. *Publications:* Young Man (essays) 1986, Jun Ashida, 30 Years of Design 1993, Patches of Unshaven Beard 1998; articles on fashion and lifestyle in daily newspapers. *Leisure interests:* tennis, golf. *Address:* 1-3-3 Aobadai, Meguro-ku, Tokyo 153-8521, Japan (office). *Telephone:* (3) 3463-8631 (office). *Fax:* (3) 3463-9638 (office). *E-mail:* secretary@jun-ashida.co.jp (office). *Website:* www.jun-ashida.co.jp (office).

ASHKENASI, Shmuel; American violinist; b. 11 Jan. 1940, Tel-Aviv, Israel; m. Mihaela Ionescu Ashkenasi; two s.; ed Musical Acad. of Tel Aviv, Curtis Inst. of Music, Philadelphia; concert violinist since 1962; First Violinist, Vermeer String Quartet; Prof. of Music and Artist-in-Residence, Univ. of Northern Illinois 1969–2007; also taught at Roosevelt Univ., Chicago and Musikhochshcule Lübeck, Germany; mem. teaching faculty, Curtis Inst. of Music 2007–; First Prize, Merryweather Post Contest, Washington, DC 1958, Finalist, Queen Elizabeth Competition, Brussels 1959, Second Prize, Tchaikovsky Competition, Moscow 1962. *Leisure interests:* tennis, chess. *Address:* The Curtis Institute of Music, 1726 Locust Street, Philadelphia, PA 19103, USA (office). *Telephone:* (215) 893-5252 (office). *Fax:* (215) 893-9065 (office). *Website:* www.curtis.edu (office).

ASHKENAZY, Vladimir; Icelandic (b. Russian) pianist and conductor; *Principal Conductor and Artistic Adviser, Sydney Symphony Orchestra;* b. 6 July 1937, Gorky, USSR; s. of David Ashkenazy and Evstolia Ashkenazy (née Plotnova); m. Thorunn Sofia Johannsdóttir 1961; two s. three d.; ed Cen. Music School, Moscow and Moscow Conservatoire; Prin. Guest Conductor, Philharmonia 1982–83; Music Dir Royal Philharmonic Orchestra 1987–94,

Deutsches Symphonie-Orchester Berlin (fmrly Berlin Radio Symphony) 1989–99; Chief Conductor Czech Philharmonic Orchestra 1998–2003; Music Dir EUYO (European Union Youth Orchestra) 2002–; Music Dir NHK Symphony, Tokyo 2004–07; apptd Artist Laureate, Royal Liverpool Philharmonic Orchestra during Liverpool's tenure as European City of Culture 2008; Principal Conductor and Artistic Adviser, Sydney Symphony Orchestra 2009–; Hon. RAM; Icelandic Order of the Falcon; Hon. DMus (Nottingham) 1995; Second Prize, Int. Chopin Competition, Warsaw 1955, Gold Medal, Queen Elizabeth Int. Piano Competition, Brussels 1956, Jt Winner (with John Ogdon) Int. Tchaikovsky Piano Competition, Moscow 1962. *Publication:* Beyond Frontiers (with Jasper Parrott) 1985. *Address:* Harrison Parrott, 5–6 Albion Court, London, W6 0QT, England (office). *Telephone:* (20) 7229-9166 (office). *Fax:* (20) 7221-5042 (office). *E-mail:* info@harrisonparrott.co.uk (office). *Website:* www.harrisonparrott.com (office).

ASHKIN, Arthur, AB, PhD; American physicist (retd); b. 2 Sept. 1922; ed Columbia Coll., Cornell Univ.; technician, Columbia Coll. Radiation Lab. 1942–45; researcher AT&T Bell Laboratories 1952, Head of Laser Science Research Dept 1963–92, (retd); mem. Nat. Acad. of Eng, NAS 1996–; Fellow American Physical Soc., AAAS, IEEE, Optical Soc. of America; IEEE Quantum Electronics Award, Optical Soc. of America Townes Award, Rank Prize in Opto-Electronics, Optical Soc. of America Ives Medal/Quinn Award, American Physical Soc. Joseph F. Keithley Award 2003. *Achievements:* inventor of 'optical tweezers'; holder of 47 patents. *Publications:* many research papers. *Address:* c/o Lucent Technologies, 600 Mountain Avenue, Murray Hill, NJ 07974-0636, USA (office).

ASHMAWY, Muhammad Saïd al-, BA; Egyptian lawyer and writer; b. 1 Dec. 1932; Asst of Dist Attorney, Alexandria 1954; Dist Attorney 1956; Judge 1961; Chief Prosecutor, Cairo 1973; Counsellor of State for Legislation 1977; Chief Justice High Criminal Court, Cairo 1985. *Publications:* Roots of Islamic Law 1979, Political Islam 1987, Islamic Caliphate 1990, Religion for the Future 1992, Veil and Tradition in Islam 1995, The Conflict between Arabs and Israel 1997, Reason in Islam 1998, Book of Ethics 1999, Egyptian Roots of Judaism 2001, Clash of Nations 2002. *Leisure interests:* music, driving, tennis. *Address:* 9 Gezira al-Wosta Street, Zamalek, Cairo 11211, Egypt (home). *Telephone:* (2) 735-2060 (home). *Fax:* (2) 735-2060 (home). *E-mail:* ashmawy2@hotmail.com (home).

ASHMORE, Adm. of the Fleet Sir Edward (Beckwith), GCB, DSC; British naval officer; b. 11 Dec. 1919, Queenstown (now Cobh), Ireland; s. of Vice-Adm. L. H. Ashmore, C.B., DSO and T. V. Schutt; m. Elizabeth Mary Doveton Sturdee 1942; one s. one d.; ed Royal Naval Coll., Dartmouth; served HMS Birmingham, Jupiter, Middleton 1938–42; qualified Communications 1943; Staff, C-in-C Home Fleet 1944; Cruiser Squadron British Pacific Fleet 1945–46; mentioned in despatches 1946; Russian interpreter and Asst Naval Attaché, British Embassy, Moscow 1946–47; Squadron Communications Officer 3rd Aircraft Carrier Squadron 50; Commdr 1950; HMS Alert 1952–53; Capt. 1955; Capt. (F) 6th Frigate Squadron, Commdg Officer HMS Blackpool 1958; Dir of Plans, Admiralty and Ministry of Defence 1960–62; Commdr British Forces Caribbean Area 1963–64; Rear-Adm. 1965; Asst Chief of Defence Staff, Signals 1965–67; Flag Officer, Second-in-Command, Far East Fleet 1967–68; Vice-Adm. 1968; Vice-Chief Naval Staff 1969–71; Adm. 1970; C-in-C Western Fleet Sept.–Oct. 1971; C-in-C Fleet 1971–73; Chief of Naval Staff and First Sea Lord 1974–77; Chief of Defence Staff Feb.–Aug. 1977; First and Principal Naval ADC to Her Majesty the Queen 1974–77; Adm. of the Fleet 1977–; Dir Racal Electronics Ltd 1978–97; Gov. Sutton's Hosp. in Charterhouse 1975–2000; Distinguished Service Cross 1942; Order of the Bath 1974. *Publication:* The Battle and the Breeze 1997. *Leisure interest:* travel. *Address:* c/o Naval Secretary, Victory Building, HM Naval Base, Portsmouth, Hants., England.

ASHRAWI, Hanan Daoud Khalil, BA, MA, PhD; Palestinian politician, organization executive and academic; *Media Director and Spokesperson, League of Arab States;* b. 8 Oct. 1946, Ramallah (then part of British Mandate of Palestine); d. of Daoud Mikhail (a founder of Palestinian Liberation Org. — PLO) and Wadi'a Ass'ad; m. Emile Ashrawi; two d.; ed American Univ. of Beirut, Univ. of Virginia, USA; joined mainstream PLO Fatah faction; Prof. of English Literature, Birzeit Univ., West Bank 1973–90, mem. Faculty 1973–95, Chair. English Dept 1973–78, 1981–84, Dean of Faculty of Arts 1986–90; activist, Palestinian Women's Movt 1974–; f. Birzeit Univ. Legal Aid Cttee/Human Rights Action Project 1974; joined Intifada Political Cttee 1988, served on its Diplomatic Cttee 1988–93; official spokeswoman for Palestinian Del. to Middle East peace process 1991–93, mem. Leadership/Guidance Cttee and Exec. Cttee of del.; mem. Advisory Cttee Palestinian Del. at Madrid Peace Conf. on Middle East; mem. Palestinian Ind. Comm. for Palestinian Repub., Head 1993–95; Founder and Commr Gen. Palestinian Ind. Comm. for Citizens' Rights 1993–95; mem. Palestinian Legis. Council 1996– (re-elected on a nat. list, The Third Way 2006); Palestinian Authority Minister of Higher Educ. and Research 1996–98 (resgnd in protest against political corruption); f. MIFTAH (Palestinian Initiative for the Promotion of Global Dialogue and Democracy) 1998; currently Human Rights Commr (semi-official ombudsman) and mem. Palestinian Council; Media Dir and Spokesperson Arab League 2001–; Olof Palme Prize 2002, Sydney Peace Prize 2003, ranked 96th by Forbes magazine amongst 100 Most Powerful Women 2004. *Publications:* numerous poems, short stories and papers and articles on Palestinian culture, literature and politics, including Anthology of Palestinian Literature (ed., The Modern Palestinian Short Story: An Introduction to Practical Criticism, Contemporary Palestinian Literature under Occupation, Contemporary Palestinian Poetry and Fiction, Literary Translation: Theory and Practice; A Passion for Peace 1994, This Side of Peace: A Personal Account (memoirs) 1995. *Address:* Arab League, PO Box 11642, Arab League Building, Tahrir

Square, Cairo, Egypt (office). *Telephone:* (2) 5750511 (office). *Fax:* (2) 5775726 (office). *Website:* www.arableagueonline.org (office); www.miftah.org (office).

ASHTAL, Abdalla Saleh al-, MA; Yemeni diplomatist; b. 5 Oct. 1940, Addis Ababa, Ethiopia; m. Vivian Eshoo al-Ashtal; one s. one d.; ed Menelik II Secondary School, American Univ. of Beirut and New York Univ.; Asst Dir Yemeni Bank for Reconstruction and Devt, San'a 1966–67; mem. Supreme People's Council, Hadramout Prov. 1967–68, Gen. Command Yemeni Nat. Liberation Front 1968–70; Political Adviser, Perm. Mission to UN 1970–72, Sr Counsellor 1972–73, Perm. Rep. 1973–2002; Non-Resident Amb. to Canada 1974, to Mexico 1975–79, to Brazil 1985–91 (Pres. Security Council 1991). *Address:* c/o Ministry of Immigrants' and Foreign Affairs, PO Box 1994, San'a, Yemen.

ASHTON OF UPHOLLAND, Baroness (Life Peer), cr. 1999, of St Albans in the County of Hertfordshire; **Catherine Margaret Ashton,** BSc, PC; British economist and politician; *Commissioner for Trade, European Commission;* b. 20 March 1956; d. of Harold Ashton and Clare Ashton; m. Peter Kellner; one s. one d.; ed London Univ.; Admin. Sec., Campaign for Nuclear Disarmament 1977–79; Man. Coverdale Org. 1979–81; Dir of Public Affairs, Business in the Community 1983–89; policy adviser 1989–98; Parl. Under-Sec. of State and Govt Spokesperson, Dept for Educ. and Skills 2001–04, Early Years and School Standards 2001–02, Early Years and Childcare 2002, Sure Start (also Dept for Work and Pensions) 2002–04; Govt Spokesperson for Children 2003–; Parl. Under-Sec. of State and Govt Spokesperson, Dept for Constitutional Affairs/Ministry of Justice 2004–07, Leader House of Lords and Lord Pres. of the Council 2007–08; Commr for Trade, EU Comm. 2008–; Chair. Hertfordshire Health Authority 1998–2001; House Magazine Minister of the Year 2005, Channel 4 Peer of the Year 2005, Stonewall Politician of the Year 2006. *Address:* European Commission, 200 rue de la Loi-Wetstraat, 1049 Brussels, Belgium (office). *Telephone:* (2) 299-11-11 (office). *Fax:* (2) 298-86-57 (office). *Website:* ec.europa.eu/commission_barroso/ashton (office).

ASHWORTH, Sir John Michael, Kt, PhD, DSc; British biologist; *Chairman, Barts and the London NHS Trust;* b. 27 Nov. 1938, Luton; s. of Jack Ashworth and Mary Ousman; m. 1st Ann Knight 1963 (died 1985); one s. three d.; m. 2nd Auriol Stevens 1988; ed Exeter Coll., Oxford, Univ. of Leicester, Brandeis Univ., USA, Univ. of California, San Diego; Harkness Fellow, Commonwealth Fund, New York, NY 1965–67; Lecturer, Biochemistry Dept, Univ. of Leicester 1967–71, Reader 1971–73; Prof., Biology Dept, Univ. of Essex 1973–79; Chief Scientist, Cen. Policy Review Staff, Cabinet Office 1976–81; Under-Sec. Cabinet Office 1979–81; Vice-Chancellor, Univ. of Salford 1981–89; Dir LSE and Political Science 1990–96; Chair. Bd Nat. Computer Centre 1983–91, Nat. Accreditation Council for Certification Bodies 1984–88, British Library 1996–2001; mem. Bd of Granada TV 1987–89, Dir Granada Group 1990–2002; Dir J. Sainsbury 1993–96, Strategic Health Authority, NE London 2002–03; mem. Council Inst. of Cancer Research 1998–; Chair. Bd Barts and the London National Health Service (NHS) Trust 2003–; Hon. Fellow LSE 1997; Hon. DSc (Salford) 1991, Hon. LLD (Leicester) 2005; Colworth Medal of Biochemical Soc. 1972. *Publications:* Ed.: Outline Studies in Biology; author: Cell Differentiation 1973, The Slime Moulds (with J. Dee) 1976, over 100 papers on biological, biochemical and educational topics in scientific journals. *Leisure interest:* sailing. *Address:* Garden House, Wivenhoe, Essex, CO7 9DB, England. *Telephone:* (1206) 822256 (home). *E-mail:* john .ashworth@britishlibrary.net (home).

ASIM, Mohamed, BA, MA, PhD; Maldivian diplomatist; *High Commissioner to UK;* b. 1960; m. Mariyam Ali Manik; one s. one d.; ed American Univ. of Beirut, Lebanon, California State Univ., Sacramento, USA, Australian Nat. Univ., Canberra, Australia; early govt career as Admin. Officer, Ministry of Educ. 1982; Personnel Services Officer, Pres.'s Office 1983, then Sr Research Officer, Int. Div.; Presidential Aide 1990–92; Dir Employment Affairs 1992–96, Dir-Gen. 1996–99; Dir-Gen. Public Service Div. of Pres.'s Office 1999–2004; High Commr to Sri Lanka 2004–07, to UK 2007–; Pres. Colombo Plan Council 2004–; Grad. Asst, School of Business and Public Admin, Calif. State Univ. 1983–85; taught professional short courses in human resources man. at ANU, Canberra 1996–98; represented Maldives at numerous confs including Commonwealth Meeting of Small States, Windhoek, Namibia 1985, Third Asia Pacific Conf. on Public Admin, Katmandu, Nepal 1991; mem. Maldives del. to Commonwealth Heads of States and Govts Meeting, Kuala Lumpur, Malaysia 1989. *Address:* High Commission of the Maldives, 22 Nottingham Place, London, W1U 5NJ, England (office). *Telephone:* (20) 7224-2135 (office). *Fax:* (20) 7224-2157 (office). *E-mail:* info@maldiveshighcommission.org (office). *Website:* www.maldiveshighcommission.org (office).

ASKEW, Reubin O'Donovan, JD; American politician, lawyer and academic; b. 11 Sept. 1928, Muskogee, Okla; s. of Leo G. Askew and Alberta N. O'Donovan; m. Donna L. Harper 1956; one s. one d.; ed Escambia Co. Public School System, Fla State Univ., Univ. of Fla Coll. of Law and Denver Univ.; pnr in law firm, Pensacola, Fla 1958–70; Asst Co. Solicitor, Escambia Co., Fla 1956–58; mem. State of Fla House of Reps 1958–62; State Senate 1962–70; Gov. of Fla 1971–79; US Trade Rep. 1979–81; dir in law firm, Miami 1981–88; Dir Akerman, Senterfitt and Eidson 1988–96; Chair. Educ. Comm. of USA 1973; Chair. Southern Govs Conf. 1974–78, Chair. Nat. Democratic Govs Conf. 1976, Nat. Govs Conf. 1976–77; Chair. Presidential Advisory Bd on Ambassadorial Appointments 1977–79, Select Comm. on Immigration and Refugee Policy 1979; Visiting Fellow, Inst. of Politics, Harvard Univ. 1979; Chubb Fellow, Yale Univ.; Distinguished Service Prof., Fla Atlantic Univ., Fort Lauderdale 1991; Eminent Scholar, Reubin O'D Askew School of Public Admin and Policy, Fla State Univ. 2000–; Sr Fellow, Fla Inst. of Govt 2001–; Democrat; Dr hc (Univ. of Notre Dame, Stetson Univ., Rollins Coll., Eckerd Coll., Fla Southern Coll., Saint Leo Coll., Miami Univ., Bethune-Cookman Coll., Univ. of West Fla, Barry Univ., Univ. of Fla, Univ. of Tampa, Belmont

Abbey Coll.); John F. Kennedy Award, Nat. Council of Jewish Women 1973, Hubert Harley Award (American Judicature Soc.) 1973, Nat. Wildlife Fed. Award 1972, Outstanding Conservationist of Year Award, Fla Audubon Soc. 1972, Herbert H. Lehman Ethics Award 1973, Salvation Army Gen. William Booth Award 1973, Distinguished Community Service Award, Brandeis Univ., Ethics and Govt Award, Common Cause; Order of COIF (Hon.) Coll. of Law, Univ. of Fla, Albert Einstein Distinguished Achievement Award, Yeshiva Univ. *Publications:* Trade Services and the World Economy 1983, Opinion: Public Welfare 1984. *Address:* Reubin O'D Askew School of Public Administration and Public Policy, Florida State University, PO Box 12487, Tallahassee, FL 32317, USA (office). *Telephone:* (840) 487-1870 (office). *Fax:* (840) 487-0041 (office). *E-mail:* raskew@fsu.edu (office). *Website:* askew.fsu .edu (office).

ASKEY, Thelma J., BA; American diplomatist and international organization executive; *Deputy Secretary-General, Organisation for Economic Co-operation and Development;* ed Tennessee Technological Univ., Univ. of Tennessee, George Washington Univ.; worked for several years sr staffer and counsel on US House of Reps Committee on Ways and Means, Staff Dir Trade Sub-cttee, helped develop strategy for enactment and implementation of N America Free Trade Agreement (NAFTA), Uruguay Round of WTO, Africa Growth and Opportunity Act, and other trade agreements 1994–98; Commr US Int. Trade Comm. –2000; Dir US Trade and Devt Agency, Washington, DC 2001–07; Deputy Sec.-Gen. OECD in charge of Global Relations 2007–. *Address:* OECD, 2 rue André Pascal, 75775 Paris Cedex 16, France (office). *Telephone:* 1-45-24-82-00 (office). *Fax:* 1-45-24-85-00 (office). *E-mail:* news .contact@oecd.org (office). *Website:* www.oecd.org (office).

ASKONAS, Brigitte Alice, PhD, FRS, FMedSci; British/Canadian immunologist; *Fellow, Imperial College London;* b. 1 April 1923; d. of the late Charles F. Askonas and Rose Askonas; ed McGill Univ., Montreal, Canada and Univ. of Cambridge, UK; Research Student, School of Biochemistry, Univ. of Cambridge 1949–52; Immunology Div., Nat. Inst. for Medical Research, London 1953–88, Head 1977–88; Dept of Bacteriology and Immunology, Harvard Medical School, Boston, Mass, USA 1961–62; Basel Inst. for Immunology, Switzerland 1971–72; Visiting Prof., Dept of Medicine, St Mary's Hosp. Medical School, London 1988–95; attached to Dept of Immunology 1992–96; attached to Molecular Immunology Group, Weathersall Inst. of Molecular Medicine, John Radcliffe Hosp., Oxford 1989–; Visiting Prof., Dept of Cellular Molecular Biology, Imperial Coll. London 1995–, Fellow 2000–; Hon. mem. American Soc. of Immunology, Soc. Française d'Immunologie, British Soc. of Immunology, German Soc. of Immunology; Hon. DSc (McGill Univ.) 1987. *Publications:* more than 200 scientific papers in biochemical and immunological journals and books. *Leisure interests:* art, travel, music. *Address:* Department of Cellular Molecular Biology, Imperial College London, Sir Alexander Fleming Building, London, SW7 2AZ (office); 23 Hillside Gardens, London, N6 5SU, England (home). *Telephone:* (20) 8348-6792 (home). *Fax:* (20) 7584-2056 (office). *E-mail:* b.askonas@imperial.ac.uk (office). *Website:* www3 .imperial.ac.uk/lifesciences/divisions/cellandmolecularbiology (office).

ASLAKHANOV, Col-Gen. Aslanbek Akhmedovich, CandJur; Chechen politician; *Representative of Chechen Republic in State Duma (Parliament);* b. 11 March 1947, Novye Atagi; m.; two c.; ed Kharkov State Pedagogical Inst., Acad. of USSR; teacher Moscow Mining Inst. 1965–67; numerous positions in USSR Ministry of Internal Affairs 1967–, investigator, then Head of Dept, then Sr Inspector, then Deputy Head, then Head of Div., Chief Inspector Organizational Dept 1981–89; head of successful operation to end hijacking of an aircraft in N Caucasus 1989; Pres. All-Russian Asscn of Security Veterans and Courts; mem. Soviet of Nationalities, USSR Supreme Soviet 1989–91; elected to State Duma (Parl.) 2000, representing Chechen Repub.; Adviser to Pres. Putin 2003–; numerous awards. *Leisure interests:* free-style wrestling, sport. *Address:* State Duma, Okhotny Ryad 1, 103265 Moscow, Russia . *Telephone:* (495) 292-02-04.

ASMAL, Kader, LLM, MA; South African politician and lawyer; b. 1934, Stanger; m. Louise Parkinson; two s.; ed Stanger High School, Univ. of SA, London School of Econs, Trinity Coll. Dublin and Springfield Teachers' Training Coll.; law teacher, Trinity Coll., Dublin for 27 years (during 30-year exile), Dean, Faculty of Arts, Trinity Coll., Dublin 1980–86; barrister, Lincoln's Inn, London and King's Inn, Dublin; returned from exile 1990; Prof. of Human Rights Univ. of Western Cape 1990–94; Minister for Water Affairs and Forestry, Govt of Nat. Unity 1994–99, of Educ. 1999–2004; Chair. World Comm. of Dams 1997–; Pres. Irish Council for Civil Liberties 1976–90; f. Irish Anti-Apartheid Movt 1963, Chair. –1991; mem. Constitutional Comm. of ANC 1986–93, ANC Nat. Exec. Comm. 1991–, Nat. Comm. for Emancipation of Women 1992–, Nat. Ass. on ANC's Nat. List 1994–; Chair. Portfolio Cttee on Defence 2004–05; mem. ANC negotiating team at Multi-Party Negotiating Forum 1993; Légion d'Honneur, 2005; Hon. Fellow LSE; Hon. LLD (Queen's Univ. Belfast) 1997, (Trinity Coll. Dublin) 1998, (Univ. of Cape Town) 1999; Hon. PhD (Rhodes Univ.) 1997; UNESCO Prize for Teaching and Devt of Human Rights 1985, Gold Medal, WWF, SA 1996, Int. Stockholm Water Prize 2000. *Publications:* Reconciliation Through Truth (co-author) 1997, Legacy v Freedom- The ANC's Human Rights Tradition 2005; over 150 articles on legal and political aspects of apartheid, labour law, Ireland and decolonization. *Leisure interests* watching cricket, gardening, Ian Rankin books. *Address:* Parliament, PO Box 15, Cape Town 8000 (office); 37 Alma Road, Rosebank, Cape Town 7700, South Africa (home). *Telephone:* (21) 6852479 (home). *Fax:* (21) 6898298 (home). *E-mail:* kasmal@parliament.gov.za (office); kasmal@ iafrica.com. *Website:* www.parliament.gov.za (office).

ASNER, Edward (Ed); American actor and film producer; b. 15 Nov. 1929, Kansas City; m. 1st Nancy Sykes 1957; three c.; m. 2nd Cindy Gilmore 1998; one s. with Carol Jean Vogelman; ed Univ. of Chicago; film and TV actor 1961–; Pres. Screen Actors Guild 1981–85; f. Quince Productions, Inc. (production co.); seven Emmy Awards, five Golden Globe Awards, Ralph Morgan Award, Screen Actors Guild 2000, Lifetime Achievement Award 2002. *Film appearances include:* Fort Apache the Bronx 1981, JFK 1991, The Golem 1995, Hard Rain 1998, The Batchelor 1999, Above Suspicion 2000, Mars and Beyond 2000, The Animal 2001, The Confidence Game (also co-producer) 2001, Academy Boyz 2001, Fair Play 2002, The Commission 2003, Missing Brendan 2003, Elf 2003, Crab Orchard 2006, All In 2005, Sleeping Dogs Lie 2005, Ways of the Flesh 2006; numerous TV film appearances. *Films produced:* Payback (TV) 1997, A Vision of Murder: The Story of Donielle (TV) (exec. producer) 2000. *TV series include:* The Mary Tyler Moore Show (as Lou Grant) (five Emmy Awards) 1970–77, Lou Grant (as Lou Grant) 1977–82. *Address:* Quince Production, Inc, 12400 Ventura Blvd., #371, Studio City, CA 91604. *Telephone:* (323) 436-0677. *Fax:* (323) 436-0246.

ASO, Taro; Japanese politician; *Prime Minister;* b. 20 Sept. 1940; m.; two c.; ed Gakushuin Univ., Stanford Univ., USA and London School of Econs, UK; joined Aso Cement Co. Ltd 1966, Pres. 1973–79; mem. House of Reps for Fukuoka Prefecture 8th Dist 1979–; Parl. Vice-Minister, Ministry of Educ., Science and Sports 1988; Chair. Standing Cttee on Foreign Affairs 1991; Minister of State for Econ. Planning 1996; mem. Judge Indictment Cttee 1998; apptd Minister of State for Econ. and Fiscal Policy 2001–03; Minister for Public Man., Home Affairs, Posts and Telecommunications 2003–05, of Foreign Affairs 2005–07; Prime Minister 2008–; Dir Educ. Div., LDP Policy Research Council 1990, Dir Foreign Affairs Div. 1992, Deputy Sec.-Gen. LDP 1993, Deputy Chair. Policy Research Council 1999, Dir-Gen. LDP Treasury Bureau 2000, Chair. Policy Research Council 2001–, Sec.-Gen. 2007, 2008, Pres. 2008–; mem. Japan Olympic Shooting Team, Montréal 1976; Pres. Japan Jr Chamber of Commerce 1978. *Address:* Office of the Prime Minister, 1-6-1, Nagata-cho, Chiyoda-ku, Tokyo 100-8968 (office); Liberal-Democratic Party (Jiyu-Minshuto), 1-11-23, Nagata-cho, Chiyoda-ku, Tokyo, 100-8910, Japan (office). *Telephone:* (3) 3581-2361 (office); (3) 3581-6211 (office). *Fax:* (3) 3581-1910 (office). *E-mail:* koho@ldp.jimin.or.jp (office). *Website:* www.kantei .go.jp (office); www.jimin.jp (office).

ASSAD, Asma al-, BSc; Syrian state official and investment banker; *First Lady;* b. 11 Aug. 1975, Acton, London, UK; d. of Dr Fawaz Akhras and Sahar Akhras; m. Bashar al-Assad 2000; two s. one d.; ed Queen's Coll. secondary school, London and King's Coll., Univ. of London; economist, Hedge Fund Man., Deutsche Bank, London 1996–97; Investment Banker, Mergers and Acquisitions for Biotechnology Cos, JP Morgan, London, New York, Paris 1998–2000; First Lady of Syria 2001–, state visits to Tunisia, Spain, Morocco, France, Italy, Qatar, UK, The Vatican; represented Syria in talks with Bank of England concerning Syrian econ. reform, London 2002, with UNESCO concerning educ. and literacy, with Arab Women's Org. on the improvement of women's status in the Arab world; Founder and Chair. The Syria Trust for Devt 2001; introduced and championed rights for the disabled in Syria, including comprehensive legislation; hosted numerous int. confs, including the Women in Business Conf. (largest ever gathering of business women in Middle East) 2002; Chair. the Syrian Org. for the Disabled; mem. World Links Arab Region Advisory Council, Higher Council in Arab Women's Org.; Patron Syrian Comm. for Family Affairs, Damascus Arab Capital of Culture (UNESCO) 2008; Hon. Chair. Special Olympics, Syria; Hon. PhD (La Sapienza Univ., Rome) 2004; Arab First Lady of the Year 2008, Italian Presidency Gold Medal of the Year 2008. *Leisure interest:* horse-riding, skiing, cycling. *Address:* Office of HE Mrs al-Assad, Rawda Square, Damascus, Syria (office). *Telephone:* (11) 334-2342 (office); (11) 223-1112 (office). *Fax:* (11) 334-3022 (office). *E-mail:* fares.kallas@mopa.gov.sy (office). *Website:* www.assad.org (office).

ASSAD, Lt-Gen. Bashar al-; Syrian ophthalmologist, army officer and head of state; *President;* b. 11 Sept. 1965, Damascus; s. of the late Hafiz al-Assad (Pres. of Syria 1971–2000) and Anissa Makhlouf; m. Asmaa al-Akhras 2001; one s.; ed Al-Huria High School, Damascus; trained as an ophthalmologist; Capt., Medical Corps 1994, fmr commdr armoured div., Syrian Armed Forces, apptd. Col 1999; C-in-C Armed Forces 2000–; Pres. of Syria 2000–. *Leisure interest:* surfing the net. *Address:* Office of the President, Damascus, Syria (office). *Website:* www.assad.org (office).

ASSAF, Ibrahim ibn Abd al-Aziz al-, PhD; Saudi Arabian politician and economist; *Minister of Finance;* b. 28 Jan. 1949, Ayoun Al-Jawa, Qassim; m.; four c.; ed King Saud Univ. Riyadh, Univ. of Denver, Colo State Univ., USA; Teaching Asst King Abdulaziz Mil. Acad. (KAMA) Riyadh 1971–82, Asst Prof. 1982–86, Head Dept of Admin. Sciences 1982–86; Visiting Lecturer Staff's Acad. 1982–83; Econ. Adviser Saudi Fund for Devt 1982–86; Alt. Exec. Dir IMF Saudi Arabia, Washington, DC 1986–89; Exec. Dir World Bank Saudi Arabia, Washington, DC 1989–95; Minister of Finance and Nat. Economy 1996–; Chair. Bd, Public Investment Fund, Pension and Retirement Fund, Saudi Fund Devt, Real Estate Devt Fund; Gov. for Saudi Arabia, Islamic Devt Bank, World Bank Group, IMF, Arab Funds and Financial Insts.; mem. Bd Supreme Econ. Council, Higher Advisory Council for Petroleum and Minerals, Saudi Arabian Oil Company (SAUDI ARAMCO), Gen. Investment Authority, Supreme Tourism Authority, Higher Council Islamic Affairs, Higher Council for Univs, Civil Service Council, Manpower Council, Mil. Service Council, Higher Council for Civil Defense, Saudi Econ. Asscn. *Address:* Ministry of Finance, Airport Road, Riyadh, 11177, Saudi Arabia (office). *Telephone:* (1) 405-0000 (office). *Fax:* (1) 401-0583 (office). *E-mail:* Minister@mof.gov.sa. *Website:* www.mof.gov.sa.

ASSELBORN, Jean; Luxembourg politician; *Deputy Prime Minister and Minister of Foreign Affairs and Immigration;* b. 27 April 1949; m. Sylvie Hubert 1980; two d.; ed Athénée de Luxembourg and Univ. of Nancy; left school to work for Uniroyal Labs 1967; became involved in trade-union movt, elected to post of Youth Rep. of Fed. of Luxembourg Workers (Lëtzebuerger Aarbechterverband, precursor to current OGB-L or Ind. Fed. of Trade Unions of Luxembourg); joined civil admin of Luxembourg City 1968–69; returned to Steinfort to serve in local admin 1969; Admin. Inter-municipal Hosp., Steinfort 1976; Mayor of Steinfort 1982–2004; elected to Luxembourg Parl. 1984–, Head, Parl. Group of Luxembourg Socialist Workers' Party (LSAP) 1989, Chair. LSAP 1997, Vice-Pres. Luxembourg Parl. 1999–2004, mem. Cttee of the Regions of the EU; Vice-Pres. European Socialist Party 2000–04; Deputy Prime Minister and Minister for Foreign Affairs and Immigration 2004–. *Address:* Ministry of Foreign Affairs and Immigration, Hôtel St Maximin, 5 rue Notre-Dame, 2240 Luxembourg Ville, Luxembourg (office). *Telephone:* 478-1 (office). *Fax:* 22-31-44 (office). *E-mail:* officielle.boite@mae.etat.lu (office). *Website:* www.mae.lu (office).

ASSENMACHER, Ivan, MD, DSc; French professor of physiology; *Professor Emeritus of Physiology, University of Montpellier;* b. 17 May 1927, Erstein; s. of Ivan Assenmacher and Mary Assenmacher (née Wetzel); m. Violette Rochedieu 1952; two s. (one s. deceased); ed Univs of Strasbourg and Paris; Asst, Faculty of Medicine, Univ. of Strasbourg 1950–53; Asst Prof., Histophysiology Lab., Coll. de France, Paris 1953–57, Sub-Dir 1957–59; Assoc. Prof., Univ. of Montpellier 1959–62, Prof. Physiology 1962–95, Prof. Emer. 1995–; Head of Neuroendocrinology Lab., CNRS, Montpellier 1967–92; Exchange Prof. of Physiology, Univ. of Calif., Berkeley 1976, 1982; mem. Acad. des Sciences 1982, Academia Europaea 1990; mem. Consultative Cttee for Univs, Paris 1967–80, 1986–91, Nat. Cttee for Scientific Research, Paris 1967–75, 1980–86, Gutachtergruppe für Neuroendokrinologie 1975–85 and Neuropeptide 1985–92, Deutsche Forschungsgemeinschaft, Bonn, Nat. Consultative Cttee for a Code of Ethics for Life and Health Sciences 1986–91, French Nat. Comm. for UNESCO 1997–2001, Higher Council for Scientific and Technological Research, Paris 1992–95; Officier, Légion d'honneur, Ordre nat. du Mérite, des Palmes académiques; Insigne des Réfractaires 1944–45. *Publications:* Photorégulation de la Reproduction (with J. Benoît) 1970, Environmental Endocrinology (with D.S. Farner) 1978, Endocrine Regulations as Adaptive Mechanisms to the Environment (with J. Boissin) 1987. *Leisure interest:* music. *Address:* Laboratory of Neuroendocrinology, Department of Health Sciences, University of Montpellier II, 34095 Montpellier (office), 419 avenue d'Occitanie, 34090 Montpellier, France (home). *Telephone:* (4) 67-52-28-25 (office); (4) 67-63-22-20 (home). *Fax:* (4) 67-52-28-25 (office).

ASSOWEH, Ali Farah; Djibouti politician; *Minister of Economy, Finance and Planning, in charge of Privatization;* Minister of Economy, Finance and Planning, in charge of Privatization 2005–; Gov. for Djibouti IMF, World Bank, Int. Finance Corpn, Islamic Devt Bank 2005–. *Address:* Ministry of the Economy, Finance and Planning, BP 13, Djibouti, Djibouti (office). *Telephone:* 353331 (office). *Fax:* 356501 (office). *E-mail:* cabmefpp@intnet.dj (office); dfe@intnet.dj (office). *Website:* www.ministere-finances.dj (office).

ASTAKHOV, Pavel Alekseyevich, LLM; Russian barrister; b. 8 Sept. 1966, Moscow; m. Astakhova Svetlana; two s.; ed Higher KGB School, Univ. of Pittsburgh, USA; legal adviser, pvt. practice 1989–; has worked in Spain, France, USA, Greece, Czech Repub. –1990; Founder, Head Advocates' Group, P. Astakhov 1990–; Rep., Int. Business Centre, Moscow 1990–; Chair. Moscow City Bar Asscn; mem. Moscow City Collegiate of Advocates. *Leisure interests:* collecting lenses, hunting, shooting, boxing. *Address:* Advocates Bureau, Barshchevsky & Co., Strioteley str. 8, korp. 2, 119311 Moscow, Russia (office). *Telephone:* (495) 930-23-00 (office). *Fax:* (495) 930-23-00 (office). *E-mail:* astakhov@bbp.ru (office); pavel@astakhov.ru (office). *Website:* advocate.org (office); astakhov.ru (office).

ASTAKHOV, Yevgeny Mikhailovich, CandHist; Russian diplomatist; b. 9 March 1937, Moscow; m.; one d.; ed Tashkent Pedagogical Inst., Moscow State Inst. of Int. Relations, Diplomatic Acad., USSR Ministry of Foreign Affairs; on staff USSR Embassy, Brazil 1963–65, Attaché 1965–68, Third Sec. 1968–69, Second Sec. 1971–73, First Sec. 1973–75; Third Sec., Div. of Latin America, USSR Ministry of Foreign Affairs 1969–71; First Sec., European Dept, USSR Ministry of Foreign Affairs 1977–78; First Sec. USSR Embassy, Spain 1979–80; Counsellor 1980–85; Head of Sector IEO 1985–87, Deputy Head 1987–90; Deputy Head, First European Dept, USSR Ministry of Foreign Affairs 1990; Amb. to Nicaragua 1990, to Honduras 1991, to El Salvador 1992; Russian Amb. to Uruguay 1999–2000, to Argentina 2000–04; observer at Latin America Asscn of Integration.

ASTAPHAN, Gerald Anthony Dwyer; Saint Christopher and Nevis politician; *Minister of National Security, Immigration and Labour;* Minister of Tourism, Commerce and Consumer Affairs 2003–05, of Nat. Security, Immigration and Labour 2005–. *Address:* Ministry of National Security, Immigration and Labour, Pelican Mall, Basseterre, Saint Christopher and Nevis (office). *Telephone:* 465-2521 (office). *Fax:* 466-1896 (office). *E-mail:* natsec@caribsurf.com (office).

ASTLEY, Philip Sinton, CVO, BA; British diplomatist; b. 18 Aug. 1943; s. of Bernard Astley and Barbara Astley (née Sinton); m. Susanne Poulsen 1966; two d.; ed St Albans School, Magdalene Coll., Cambridge; Asst Rep., British Council, Madras 1966–70, London 1970–73; First Sec. FCO 1973–76, 1982–86, Copenhagen 1976–79; First Sec. and Head of Chancery, East Berlin 1980–82; Econ. Counsellor and Consul-Gen., Islamabad 1986–90; Deputy Head of Mission, Copenhagen 1990–94, Head of Human Rights Policy Dept, FCO 1994–96; Asst Under-Sec. of State, FCO and HM Vice-Marshal of the Diplomatic Corps 1996–99; Amb. to Denmark 1999–2003. *Address:* c/o Foreign and Commonwealth Office, London, SW1A 2AH, England (office).

ASTORI, Danilo; Uruguayan economist and politician; *Minister of Economy and Finance;* b. 1940, Montevideo; m.; four c.; ed Univ. of the Repub., Montevideo; econs researcher in govt agric. agencies and econ. consultant to

UN agencies 1961–89; consultant to Head of Frente Amplio party 1984–; f. Asamblea Uruguay party 1994; elected as Senator 1995–2000, re-elected 2000–05; Minister of Economy and Finance 2005–. *Address:* Ministry of Finance and Economy, Colonia 1089, 3°, 11100 Montevideo, Uruguay (office). *Telephone:* (2) 9021017 (office). *Fax:* (2) 9021277 (office). *Website:* www.mef.gub.uy (office).

ÅSTRÖM, Jan, MSc; Swedish business executive; *President and CEO, Svenska Cellulosa Aktiebolaget;* b. 21 March 1956; m.; two c.; ed Royal Swedish Inst. of Tech. Stockholm; Paper Mill Man. Modo Paper, Husum Mill 1989–93; Man. Dir Svenska Cellulosa Aktiebolaget (SCA) Packaging 1993–96, Business Group Pres. SCA Fine Paper, Germany 1996–99; Pres. and CEO Modo Paper AB, Stockholm 1999–2000; Exec. Vice-Pres. and Deputy CEO SCA 2000–02, Pres. and CEO 2002–. *Address:* Svenska Cellulosa Aktiebolaget, Box 7827, 103 97 Stockholm, Sweden (office). *Telephone:* (8) 7885100 (office). *Fax:* (8) 6607430 (office). *Website:* www.sca.com (office).

ASTRUC, Alexandre, LèsL; French film director, writer and journalist; b. 13 July 1923, Paris; s. of Marcel Astruc and Huguette Haendel; m. Elyette Helies 1983; ed Lycée de Saint-Germain-en-Laye, Lycée Henri IV and Faculté des Lettres, Paris; journalist and film critic since 1945; TV reporter for Radio Luxembourg 1969–72; Film Critic, Paris Match 1970–72; contributor to Figaro-Dimanche 1977–; Chevalier, Légion d'honneur; Officier, l'Ordre nat. du Mérite; Commdr des Arts et Lettres; various film prizes and other awards. *Films directed include:* Le rideau cramoisi 1952, Les mauvaises rencontres 1955, Une vie 1958, La proie pour l'ombre 1960, Education sentimentale 1961, Evariste galois 1965, La longue marche 1966, Flammes sur l'Adriatique 1968, Sartre par lui-même 1976; also TV films and series. *Publications:* Les vacances 1945, La tête la première, Ciel de cendres 1975, Le serpent jaune 1976, Quand la chouette s'envole 1978, Le permissionnaire 1982, Le roman de Descartes 1989, De la caméra au stylo 1992, L'autre versant de la colline 1993, Evadiste galois 1994, Le montreur d'ombres 1996, La France au coeur 2000, Un rose en hiver 2006. *Leisure interests:* mathematics, literature. *Address:* 168 rue de Grenelle, 75007 Paris, France (home). *Telephone:* 1-47-05-20-86 (home).

ASTURIAS, HRH The Prince of; Felipe de Borbón, (Prince of Girona, Prince of Viana, Duke of Montblanc, Count of Cervera, Lord of Balaguer), LLB, MA; Spanish; b. 30 Jan. 1968, Madrid; s. of King Juan Carlos I and Queen Sofia of Spain; m. Letizia Ortiz Rocasolano 2004; two d.; ed Santa Maria de los Rosales, Madrid, Lakefield Coll., Canada, Gen. Mil. Acad., Zaragoza, Naval Coll., Marin, Air Force Gen. Acad., San Javier, Madrid Autonomous Univ., Georgetown Univ., USA; heir to the throne; received dispatches as Infantry Lt, Sub-Lt and Lt of the Air Arm 1989, holds mil. ranks of Commdr of the General Land Army Corps (Infantry), Lt Commdr in the General Navy and Commdr of the General Air Force; qualified helicopter pilot; numerous official visits to countries in Europe, Latin America, Middle East, Asia and Australasia 1995–; named Eminent Person for UN Int. Year of Volunteers 2001; mem. Olympic sailing team, Barcelona 1992; established Prince of Asturias Foundation; Hon. Pres. Codespa Foundation, Asscn of European Journalists, Spain. *Address:* c/o The Royal Household of HM the King, La Zarzuela Palace, Madrid, Spain (office). *Website:* www.casareal.es.

ASYLMURATOVA, Altynai; Kazakhstani ballerina and artistic director; *Artistic Director, Vaganova Ballet Academy;* b. 1962, Alma-Ata (now Almaty); m. Konstantin Zaklinsky; one d.; ed Vaganova Ballet School, Leningrad (now St Petersburg); dancer with Kirov (now Mariinsky) Ballet 1980, then Prin. Dancer; numerous foreign tours including Paris 1982, USA, Canada 1987; Artistic Dir Vaganova Ballet Acad, St. Petersburg 2000–; Honoured Artist of Russia 1983, Baltika Prize 1998, Golden Sophit 1999, People's Artist of Russia 2001,. *Roles include:* Odette/Odile in Swan Lake, Shirin in Legend of Love, Kitzi in Don Quixote, Aurora in Sleeping Beauty, Nike in Boyaderka, Giselle. *Address:* Vaganova Ballet Academy, 2 Rossi Street, St Petersburg 191023, Russia (office). *Fax:* (812) 315-53-90 (office). *E-mail:* umo@vaganova.ru (office). *Website:* www.vaganova.ru (office).

ATAEVA, Aksoltan Toreevna; Turkmenistani diplomatist, politician and medical practitioner; *Permanent Representative, United Nations;* b. 6 Nov. 1944, Ashgabat; m. Tchary Pirmoukhamedov 1969; one s. one d.; ed Turkmenistan State Medical Inst., Ashgabat; doctor, Hosp. No. 1, Ashgabat 1968–79, Asst to Chief Doctor 1979–80; Vice-Dir Regional Health Dept, Ashgabat 1980–85; Vice-Minister of Health 1985–90, Minister 1990–94; Minister of Social Security 1994–95; Amb. and Perm. Rep. to UN 1995–; mem. Democratic Party 1992–, Khalk Maslakhaty (Supreme People's Council of Turkmenistan) 1993–; Pres. Trade Unions of Turkmenistan 1994–95; Hon. Assoc. of Int. Acad. of Computer Sciences and Systems, Kiev, Ukraine 1993; Hon. Cand.Sci, Hon. DrMed (Russian Scientific Research Inst. for Social Hygiene and Health Care Man.) Neutrality Order, Gairat Medal 1992, Medal for Love of Motherland 1996, Order of Gurbansoltan Eje 1997, Order of Bitaraplyk 1999, Order for the Great of Independent Turkmenistan. *Publications:* 108 publs and two monographs on health and maternity care. *Leisure interests:* books, arts, sports. *Address:* Permanent Mission of Turkmenistan to UN, 866 UN Plaza, Suite 424, New York, NY 10021, USA. *Telephone:* (212) 486-8908 (office). *Fax:* (212) 486-2521 (office). *E-mail:* turkmenistan@un.int (office).

ATAMBAYEV, Almazbek Sharshenovich; Kyrgyzstani engineer and politician; *Chairman, Social Democratic Party of Kyrgyzstan (PSD);* b. 17 Sept. 1956, Alamudun, Chui Oblast; ed Moscow Inst. of Man.; engineer with Kyrgyz SSR Ministry of Communications 1980–81; Sr Engineer with DU-4, Frunze (now Bishkek) 1981–83; held position in Presidium of Supreme Soviet, Kyrgyz SSR 1983–87; Deputy Chair. Exec. Cttee Pervomaisky Dist Council of People's Deputies, Frunze 1987–89; Founder and Head, Forum (business firm)

1989; Deputy in Jogorku Kenesh (Parl.) 1995–2000; Gen.-Dir Kyrgyzavtomash 1997–99; Chair. Social Democratic Party of Kyrgyzstan (PSD) 1999–; Minister of Industry, Trade and Tourism 2005-06 (resgnd); Co-Chair. Opposition For Reforms movt 2006; Prime Minister March–Nov. 2007; unsuccessful presidential cand. 2000; Dank Medal 1999. *Address:* Social Democratic Party of Kyrgyzstan, 720000 Bishkek, Alma-Atinskaya 4B /203, Kyrgyzstan (office). *Telephone:* (312) 43-15-07 (office).

ATANASIU, Teodor; Romanian politician; b. 23 Sept. 1962, Cugir, Alba Co.; m.; one c.; ed Faculty of Mechanics, Cluj-Napoca Polytechnic, Open Univ. Business School; engineer, U.M. Cugir 1987–95, Chief of Workshop 1995–96, Dir 1997–2001; joined Nat. Liberal Party (PNL) 1990, mem. Perm. Cen. Bureau 2001–02, mem. Exec. Cttee 2005–; Councillor, Cugir Local Council 1992–96, Alba Co. Council 1996–2004 (Pres. of Council 2004); Parl. Expert, Chamber of Deputies 2001–04; Minister of Nat. Defence 2004–06 (resgnd); Dir APA-CTTA SA, Alba Iulia 1996–97, FPS (State Devt Fund), Bucharest 1997–2000; Deputy Dir-Gen., SC Cugir SA 1997–2001; Man. Palplast Sibiu SA 2001–04, B&M Direct Consulting Cugir 2003–04. *Address:* National Liberal Party (NLP) (Partidul Naţional Liberal) (PNL), 70112 Bucharest, Bd. Aviatorilor 86, Romania (office). *Telephone:* (21) 2310795 (office). *Fax:* (21) 2317511 (office). *E-mail:* dre@pnl.ro (office). *Website:* www.pnl.ro (office).

ATANASOF, Alfredo; Argentine politician; b. 1949; mem. Gremios Solidarios Group; official, Gen. Confed. of Labour; fmr Minister of Labour, Employment and Social Affairs; apptd Cabinet Chief 2002. *Address:* c/o General Secretariat to the Presidency, Balcarce 50, 1064 Buenos Aires, Argentina (office).

ATANASOV, Georgi Ivanov; Bulgarian politician; b. 23 June 1933, Pravoslaven, Plovdiv; ed Faculty of History, Univ. of Sofia; mem. Bulgarian CP (BCP) 1956–; First Sec. Sofia Komsomol City Cttee 1953–62; mem. Komsomol Political Bureau and Sec. of Cen. Cttee 1962–65, First Sec. 1965–68; Cand. mem. BCP Cen. Cttee 1962–66, Head of Dept of Science and Educ., 1968–76, mem. BCP Cen. Cttee 1966; mem. Dept of Admin., 1976–78, Sec. 1977–86; mem. Political Bureau 1986; Deputy Chair. State Planning Cttee 1980–81; Chair. Cttee on State Control 1981–84; Pres. Council of Ministers 1986–90; charged with embezzlement Oct. 1992, convicted Nov. 1992; granted presidential pardon Aug. 1994.

ATANGANA MEBARA, Jean-Marie; Cameroonian politician; Minister of Higher Educ. 1997–2002; Pres. Int. Inst. of Admin. Sciences 2001–04; Minister of State and Sec.-Gen. Presidency of Cameroon 2002–06; Minister of State and Minister of External Relations 2006–07. *Address:* c/o Ministry of External Relations, Yaoundé, Cameroon (office).

ATAYEV, Gurbanmurat; Turkmenistani government official; First Deputy Minister of Petroleum, Natural Gas and Mineral Resources –2005, Minister of Petroleum, Natural Gas and Mineral Resources 2005–07; Acting Head, Turkmengaz (state natural gas co.) 2005. *Address:* c/o Ministry of Petroleum, Natural Gas and Mineral Resources, 744000 Aşgabat, ul. 2002 28, Turkmenistan (office).

ATHEL, Saleh Abdul Rahman al-, PhD; Saudi Arabian professor of mechanical engineering and university president; b. Al-Rus; m.; several c.; ed Stanford and Texas Univs; joined teaching staff of King Saud Univ., becoming Vice-Dean, Coll. of Eng 1974–75, Dean 1975–76, Vice-Pres. for Grad. Studies and Research 1976–84; Pres. King Abdulaziz City for Science and Tech., Riyadh; mem. UN World Comm. on Environment and Devt, UN Advisory Cttee on Science and Tech. for Devt, Saudi Working Cttee for Educ. Policy and Scientific Cttee Pio Manza Int. Research Centre; fmr mem. Exec. Cttee Org. for Islamic Co-operation Ministerial Cttee of Scientific and Tech. Co-operation; mem. ASME; Fellow Islamic Acad. of Sciences, Vice-Pres. 1986–90. *Publications:* a book on eng structures, trans of three books, more than 50 articles. *Address:* Islamic Academy of Sciences, PO Box 830036, Amman, Jordan (office). *Telephone:* (55) 23385 (office). *Fax:* (55) 11803 (office).

ATHERTON, David, OBE, MA, LRAM, LTCL, LGSM; British conductor; *Conductor Laureate, Hong Kong Philharmonic Orchestra;* b. 3 Jan. 1944, Blackpool; s. of Robert Atherton and Lavinia Atherton; m. Ann Gianetta Drake 1970; one s. two d.; ed Univ. of Cambridge; Répétiteur, ROH 1967–68, Resident Conductor 1968–79; Co-Founder and Artistic Dir London Sinfonietta 1968–73, 1989–91; youngest-ever conductor at ROH and Henry Wood Promenade Concerts, London 1968; debut Royal Festival Hall, London 1969, La Scala, Milan 1976, San Francisco Opera 1978, Metropolitan Opera, New York 1984; has conducted performances in Europe, Middle East, Far East, Australasia, N America 1970–; Artistic Dir and Conductor, London Stravinsky Festival 1979–82, Ravel/Varèse Festival 1983–84; Prin. Conductor and Artistic Adviser, RLPO 1980–83, Prin. Guest Conductor 1983–86; Music Dir and Prin. Conductor, San Diego Symphony Orchestra 1980–87; Prin. Guest Conductor BBC Symphony Orchestra 1985–89; Music Dir and Prin. Conductor, Hong Kong Philharmonic Orchestra 1989–2000, Conductor Laureate 2000–; Founder and Artistic Dir Mainly Mozart Festival, Southern Calif. and Northern Mexico 1989–; Prin. Guest Conductor BBC Nat. Orchestra of Wales 1994–97; Co-Founder, Pres. and Artistic Dir Global Music Network 1998–2002; Conductor of the Year Award, Composers' Guild of GB 1971, Edison Award 1973, Grand Prix du Disque Award 1977, Koussevitzky Award 1981, Int. Record Critics' Award 1982, Prix Caecilia 1982. *Publications:* The Complete Instrumental and Chamber Music of Arnold Schoenberg and Roberto Gerhard (ed.) 1973, Pandora and Don Quixote Suites by Roberto Gerhard (ed.) 1973; contrib. to The Musical Companion 1978, The New Grove Dictionary 1981. *Leisure interests:* travel, films, theatre, computers. *Address:* Askonas Holt Ltd, Lincoln House, 300 High Holborn, London, WC1V 7JH, England (office). *Telephone:* (20) 7400-1700 (office). *Fax:* (20) 7400-1799

(office). *E-mail:* info@askonasholt.co.uk (office). *Website:* www.askonasholt.co.uk (office).

ATHERTON, Michael Andrew, OBE; British fmr professional cricketer; b. 23 March 1968, Manchester; s. of Alan Atherton and Wendy Atherton; ed Manchester Grammar School and Downing Coll. Cambridge; right-hand opening batsman; leg-spin bowler; played for Cambridge Univ. 1987–89 (Capt. 1988–89), Lancs. 1987–2001; England debut 1989, 115 tests to 1 May 2000, 54 as Capt. (England record), scoring 7,728 runs (average 37.69) including 16 centuries (to 1 Jan. 2002); scored 18,349 first-class runs (47 centuries) to end of 2000–01 season, including 1,193 in debut season; toured Australia 1990–91, 1994–95 (Capt.); 54 limited-overs ints (43 as Capt.) to 20 Aug. 1998; toured SA 1995–96, Zimbabwe and NZ 1996–97, West Indies 1998; mem. team touring Australia 1998–99, SA 1999–2000, Pakistan and Sri Lanka 2000–01; retd 2001; cricket commentator for Channel 4; Wisden Cricketer of the Year 1991, Cornhill Player of the Year 1994. *Publications:* A Test of Cricket 1995, Opening Up (autobiog.) 2002, Gambling 2007. *Leisure interests:* decent novels, good movies, food, wine, travel, most sports, music. *Address:* c/o Channel 4 Television, 124 Horseferry Road, London, SW1P 2TX, England (office). *Telephone:* (20) 7396-4444 (office). *E-mail:* email@cricket4.com (office). *Website:* www.channel4.com (office).

ATHFIELD, Ian Charles, DipArch, CNZM; New Zealand architect; *Director, Athfield Architects Limited;* b. 15 July 1940, Christchurch; s. of Charles Leonard Athfield and Ella Agnes Taylor; m. Nancy Clare Cookson 1962; two s.; ed Christchurch Boys High School, Auckland Univ. School of Architecture; a Prin. of Structon Group Architects, Wellington 1965–68; Dir Athfield Architects Ltd (own practice) 1968–; Professional Teaching Fellowship, Victoria Univ. of Wellington 1987–88; Pres. NZ Inst. of Architects 2006–08, NZ APEC Architect 2006–; Dir Auckland Property Enterprise Bd; Hon. DLitt (Victoria Univ. of Wellington) 2000; winner Int. Design Competition for Housing, Manila, Philippines 1976; winner of over 80 design awards including AAA Award 1968, 1972, NZIA Silver Medal 1970, Bronze Medal 1975, Gold Medal 1982, Jt Supreme Award 2003, 2007, NZ Tourist and Publicity Design Award 1975, jt winner Design Competition for Low Cost Housing, Fiji 1978, AAA Monier Design Award 1983, NZIA Nat. Design Award 1984, 1985, 1986, 1987, 1988, 1989, 1993, 1997, 1998, 1999, 2003, 2006, 2007, 2008, Environmental Design Award 1986, NZ Wool Bd Award 1987, 1991, NZ Commemoration Medal 1990, NZIA Gold Medal 2004, Wellington Architectural Centre Award for Most Significant Architect 1946–2006. *Television:* Today Tonight, TVNZ 1980, Ian Athfield, TVNZ 1989, Deconstructing Athfield, TVNZ 2004. *Films:* Architect Athfield, NZ Film Unit 1977, Architect of Dreams: Ian Athfield, Messenger Films, 2008. *Publications:* Architecture: an Involvement 1963, The Architecture of Self-Help Communities 1978, Joyful Architecture 1980. *Leisure interests:* building, gardening. *Address:* 105 Amritsar Street, Khandallah, POB 3364, Wellington 6140, New Zealand (office). *Telephone:* (4) 499-1727 (office). *Fax:* (4) 499-1960 (office). *E-mail:* ath@athfieldarchitects.co.nz (office). *Website:* www.athfieldarchitects.co.nz.

ATIQUR RAHMAN, A. K. M., PhD; Bangladeshi economist, diplomatist and academic; *Ambassador to Bhutan;* fought during war of independence in 1971; fmr Assoc. Prof., later Prof. and Chair. Dept of Econs, North South Univ., Dhaka, Head of Inst. of Devt, Environmental and Strategic Studies; fmrly with Centre for Studies in Int. Relations and Devt, Kolkata; joined Ministry of Foreign Affairs 1986; fmr Second Sec., later First Sec., Embassy in Rome; Consul-Gen. Embassy in Hong Kong 2003–04; Dir-Gen. Ministry of Foreign Affairs –2007; Amb. to Bhutan 2007–; Vice-Pres. Mercantile Bank Ltd. *Address:* Embassy of Bangladesh, PO Box 178, Upper Choubachu, Thimphu, Bhutan (office). *Telephone:* (2) 322539 (office). *Fax:* (2) 322629 (office). *E-mail:* bdoot@druknet.bt (office); akmatiq@northsouth.edu (office).

ATIYAH, Sir Michael Francis, Kt, OM, MA, PhD, ScD, FRS, PRSE; British mathematician and academic; *President, Royal Society of Edinburgh;* b. 22 April 1929, London; s. of Edward Selim Atiyah and Jean Atiyah (née Levens); m. Lily Brown 1955; three s.; ed Victoria Coll., Egypt, Manchester Grammar School and Trinity Coll. Cambridge; Research Fellow, Trinity Coll., Cambridge 1954–58, Hon. Fellow 1976, Master 1990–97, Fellow 1997–; Fellow, Pembroke Coll., Cambridge 1958–61 (Hon. Fellow 1983), Univ. Lecturer 1957–61; Reader, Oxford Univ. and Fellow St Catherine's Coll., Oxford 1961–63, Hon. Fellow 1991; Savilian Prof. of Geometry, Univ. of Oxford and Fellow, New Coll., Oxford 1963–69, Hon. Fellow 1999; Prof. of Mathematics, Inst. for Advanced Study, Princeton, NJ 1969–72; Royal Soc. Research Prof., Oxford Univ. 1973–90, Fellow, St Catherine's Coll., Oxford 1973–90; Dir Isaac Newton Inst. of Math. Sciences, Cambridge 1990–96; Chancellor Univ. of Leicester 1995–2005; Pres. Royal Soc. of Edinburgh 2005–; Pres. London Math. Soc. 1974–76, Pres. Math. Asscn 1981; mem. Science and Eng Research Council 1984–89; Pres. Pugwash Confs 1997–2002; mem. Council Royal Soc. 1984–85, Pres. 1990–95; Foreign mem. American Acad. of Arts and Sciences, Swedish Acad. of Sciences, Leopoldina Acad. (Germany), NAS, Acad. des Sciences (France), Royal Irish Acad., Third World Acad. of Science, Indian Nat. Science Acad., Australian Acad. of Sciences, Chinese Acad. of Sciences, American Philosophical Soc., Ukrainian Acad. of Sciences, Russian Acad. of Sciences, Georgian Acad. of Sciences, Venezuelan Acad. of Sciences, Accad. Nazionale dei Lincei, Royal Spanish Acad. of Sciences, Norwegian Acad. of Science and Letters; Hon. Prof., Univ. of Edinburgh 1997–; Hon. Fellow, Darwin Coll., Cambridge 1992, Hon. FREng 1993, Hon. Faculty of Actuaries 1999, Univ. of Wales Swansea 1999; Commdr Order of the Cedars, Gold Order of Merit, Lebanon, Order of Andreas Bello (Venezuela); Hon. DSc (Bonn, Warwick, Durham, St Andrew's, Dublin, Chicago, Edinburgh, Cambridge, Essex, London, Sussex, Ghent, Reading, Helsinki, Leicester, Rutgers, Salamanca, Montreal, Waterloo, Wales, Queen's-Kingston, Keele, Birmingham, Lebanon, Open, Brown, Oxford, Prague, Chinese, Hong Kong, Heriot-

Watt, York Univs, American Univ. of Beirut), Dr hc (UMIST) 1996; Fields Medal, Int. Congress of Mathematicians, Moscow 1966, Royal Medal of Royal Soc. 1968, De Morgan Medal, London Math. Soc. 1980, Copley Medal of Royal Soc. 1988, Feltrinelli Prize, Accad. Nazionale dei Lincei 1981, King Faisal Int. Prize for Science 1987, Benjamin Franklin Medal, American Philosophical Soc., Nehru Medal, Indian Nat. Science Acad., Abel Prize, Norwegian Acad. of Sciences (jtly with Isadore Singer) 2004. *Publications:* K-Theory 1966, Commutative Algebra 1969, Geometry and Dynamics of Magnetic Monopoles 1988, Collected Works (five vols) 1988, vol. 6 2005, The Geometry and Physics of Knots 1990. *Leisure interests:* gardening, music. *Address:* University of Edinburgh, Room 5619, School of Mathematics, Mayfield Road, Edinburgh, EH9 3JZ (office); Royal Society of Edinburgh, 22–26 George Street, Edinburgh, EH2 2PQ (office); 3/8 West Grange Gardens, Edinburgh, EH9 2RA, Scotland (home). *Telephone:* (131) 650-4886 (office); (131) 240-5022; (131) 667-0898 (home). *E-mail:* M.atiyah@ed.ac.uk (home). *Website:* www.maths.ed .ac.uk (office); www.royalsoced.org.uk.

ATIYAT, Talal Moh'd Ismail, BBA, MA; Jordanian civil servant; b. 28 Dec. 1951, Amman; Chief of Div., Revenue Dept; Dir of Admin., UNESCO office; Dir of Finance, Co-operative Bank; Asst Gen. Dir, Dir of Devt Admin., Jordan Co-operative Corpn 1995–. *Leisure interest:* reading. *Address:* Jordan Co-operative Corporation, Amman (office); PO Box 930008, Housing Bank Complex, Amman, Jordan. *Telephone:* 665171 (office); 711530 (home).

ATKINS, Dame Eileen June, DBE; British actress; b. 16 June 1934; d. of Arthur Thomas Atkins and of the late Annie Ellen Elkins; m. Bill Shepherd; ed Latymer Grammar School, Edmonton and Guildhall School of Music and Drama; Laurence Olivier Award 2003. *Stage appearances include:* Twelfth Night, Richard III, The Tempest 1962, The Killing of Sister George (Best Actress, Evening Standard Awards) 1965, The Cocktail Party 1968, Vivat! Vivat Regina! (Variety Award) 1970, Suzanne Andler, As You Like It 1973, St Joan 1977, Passion Play 1981, Medea 1986, The Winter's Tale, Cymbeline (Olivier Award) 1988, Mountain Language 1988, A Room of One's Own 1989, Exclusive 1989, The Night of the Iguana 1992, Vita and Virginia 1993, Indiscretions 1995, John Gabriel Borkman 1996, A Delicate Balance 1997 (Evening Standard Award), The Unexpected Man (Olivier Award) 1998, 2000–01, Honor (Laurence Olivier Award) 2003, The Retreat from Moscow 2003–2004, There Came a Gypsy Riding 2007, The Sea 2008, The Female of the Species 2008. *Films include:* Equus 1974, The Dresser 1984, Let Him Have It 1990, Wolf 1994, Cold Comfort Farm 1995, Jack and Sarah 1995, The Avengers 1998, Women Talking Dirty 1999, Gosford Park 2002, The Hours 2003, Cold Mountain 2003, Vanity Fair 2004, Ask the Dust 2006, Scenes of a Sexual Nature 2006, Evening 2007, Wild Target 2008. *Radio work includes:* adaptation of To the Lighthouse 2000, Restless 2009. *TV appearances include:* The Duchess of Malfi, Sons and Lovers, Smiley's People, Nelly's Version, The Burston Rebellion, Breaking Up, The Vision, Mrs Pankhurst in In My Defence (series) 1990, A Room of One's Own 1990, The Lost Language of Cranes 1993, The Maitlands 1993, Talking Heads 2 1998, Madame Bovary 2000, The Sleeper 2000, Wit 2001, Bertie and Elizabeth 2001, The Lives of Animals 2002, Cranford 2007 (BAFTA for Best Actress, Emmy Award for Best Supporting Actress), Waking the Dead 2007. *Co-creator:* Upstairs Downstairs, The House of Eliott television series. *Adaptation:* Mrs Dalloway (Evening Standard Film Award) 1999. *Leisure interests:* books, cats. *Address:* c/o Paul Lyon Maris, ICM, Oxford House, 76 Oxford Street, London, W1D 1BS (office); 2 The Moorings, Strand on the Green, Chiswick, London, W4 3PG, England (home). *Telephone:* (20) 7636-6565 (office); (20) 8994-6577. *Fax:* (20) 7323-0101 (office).

ATKINSON, Sir Anthony Barnes (Tony), Kt, MA, FBA; British economist and academic; *Warden, Nuffield College, University of Oxford;* b. 4 Sept. 1944, Caerleon; m. Judith Mary Mandeville 1965; two s. one d.; ed Cranbrook School, Kent and Churchill Coll., Cambridge; Prof. of Econs, Univ. of Essex 1970–76; Head, Dept of Political Economy, Univ. Coll. London 1976–79; Prof. of Econs, LSE 1980–92; Prof. of Political Economy, Univ. of Cambridge, Fellow, Churchill Coll. 1992–94; Warden, Nuffield Coll. Oxford 1994–; Ed. Journal of Public Economics 1972–97; mem. Royal Comm. on Distribution of Income and Wealth 1978–79, Retail Prices Index Advisory Cttee 1984–90, Pension Law Review Cttee 1992–93, Conseil d'Analyse Economique 1997–2001; Fellow, St John's Coll., Cambridge 1967–70; Fellow, Econometric Soc. 1984, Pres. 1988; Vice-Pres. British Acad. 1988–90; Pres. of the European Econ. Asscn 1989; Pres. Int. Econ. Asscn 1989–92, Royal Econ. Soc. 1995–98; Hon. mem. American Econ. Asscn 1985; Chevalier Légion d'honneur; Hon. Dr rer. pol (Univ. of Frankfurt); hon. degrees from Univ. of Liège 1989, Athens Univ. of Econs 1991, Univ. of Stirling 1992, Univ. of Edin. 1994 and numerous others; UAP Prix Scientifique 1986, Frank E. Seidman Distinguished Award in Political Economy 1995. *Publications:* Poverty in Britain and the Reform of Social Security 1969, Unequal Shares 1972, The Economics of Inequality 1975, Distribution of Personal Wealth in Britain (with A. Harrison) 1978, Lectures on Public Economics (with J.E. Stiglitz) 1980, Social Justice and Public Policy 1983, Parents and Children (with A. Maynard and C. Trinder), Poverty and Social Security 1989, Economic Transformation in Eastern Europe and the Distribution of Income (with J. M. Micklewright) 1992, Public Economics in Action 1995, Incomes and the Welfare State 1996, Poverty in Europe 1998, The Economic Consequences of Rolling Back the Welfare State 1999, Social Indicators (jtly) 2002. *Leisure interest:* sailing. *Address:* Nuffield College, Oxford, OX1 1NF (office); 39 Park Town, Oxford, OX2 6SL, England (home). *Telephone:* (1865) 278520 (office); (1865) 556064 (home). *E-mail:* tony .atkinson@nuf.ox.ac.uk (office).

ATKINSON, Conrad; British artist; b. 15 June 1940, Cleator Moor, Cumbria; m. Margaret Harrison 1967; two d.; ed Whitehaven Grammar School, Carlisle and Liverpool Colls of Art and Royal Acad. Schools, London; Granada Fellow in Fine Art 1967–68; Churchill Fellow in Fine Art 1972; Fellow in Fine Art, Northern Arts 1974–76; Lecturer, Slade School of Fine Art 1976–79; Visual Art Adviser to GLC 1982–86; Power Lecturer, Univ. of Sydney 1983; Artist-in-Residence, London Borough of Lewisham 1984–86, Edin. Univ. 1986–87; Adviser, Visual Arts Policy, Labour Party 1985–86. *Leisure interest:* rock and roll music. *Address:* c/o Ronald Feldman Gallery, 31 Mercer Street, New York, NY 10013, USA; 172 Erlanger Road, London, SE14 5TJ, England (home). *Telephone:* (20) 7639-0308 (home).

ATKINSON, Sir Frederick John, Kt, KCB, MA; British economist; b. 7 Dec. 1919, London; s. of George E. Atkinson and Elizabeth S. Cooper; m. Margaret Grace Gibson 1947; two d.; ed Jesus Coll., Oxford Univ.; Lecturer, Jesus and Trinity Colls, Oxford 1947–49; Econ. Adviser, Cabinet Office 1949–51, at Embassy, Washington 1951–54 and at Treasury 1955–69; Chief Econ. Adviser, Dept of Trade and Industry 1970–73; Asst Sec.-Gen. OECD 1973–75; Deputy Sec. Chief Econ. Adviser, Dept of Energy 1975–77; Chief Econ. Adviser, Treasury 1977–79; Hon. Fellow, Jesus Coll., Oxford 1979–. *Publication:* (jt author) Oil and the British Economy 1983. *Leisure interest:* reading. *Address:* 26 Lee Terrace, Blackheath, London, SE3 9TZ; Tickner Cottage, Church Lane, Aldington, Kent, TN25 7EG, England. *Telephone:* (20) 8852-1040; (1233) 720514.

ATKINSON, Harry Hindmarsh, PhD (Cantab); British physicist; b. 5 Aug. 1929, Wellington, New Zealand; s. of the late Harry Temple Atkinson and Constance Hindmarsh Atkinson (née Shields); m. Anne Judith Barrett 1958; two s. one d.; ed Canterbury Univ. Coll., NZ, Corpus Christi Coll. and Cavendish Lab., Univ. of Cambridge; Asst Lecturer in Physics, Canterbury Univ. Coll., NZ 1952–53; Research Asst, Cornell Univ., USA 1954–55; Sr Research Fellow, AERE, Harwell 1958–61; Head, General Physics Group, Rutherford Lab. 1961–69; Staff Chief Scientific Adviser to UK Govt, Cabinet Office 1969–72; Head, Astronomy, Space and Radio Div., Science Research Council 1972–78, UnderSec. and Dir, Astronomy, Space and Nuclear Physics 1983–86; UnderSec. and Dir of Science, Science and Eng Research Council 1983–88, UnderSec. and Dir (Special Responsibilities) 1988–92, Consultant 1992–; Chief Scientist (part-time) UK Loss Prevention Council 1990–98; Consultant North Comm. on Future of Oxford Univ. 1995–97; Chair. Anglo-Dutch Astronomy Cttee 1981–88, Steering Cttee, Inst. Laue Langevin (ILL), Grenoble 1984–88; UK Del. Council, European Space Agency 1973–87, Vice-Chair. 1981–84, Chair. 1984–87; UK Del. Intergovernmental Panel on High Energy Physics 1983–91, Council of European Synchrotron Radiation Facility 1986–88; Assessor Univ. Grants Cttee 1987–89, Consultant 1995–97; UK mem. S African Astronomical Observatory Cttee 1979–83, Anglo-Australian Telescope Bd 1979–88; mem. Working Group on Int. Collaboration, Cabinet Office 1989, NI Cttee of Univ. Funding Council 1989–93; Co-ordinator Australia, NZ, UK Science Collaboration 1989–94; Chair. Govt Task Force on Potentially Hazardous Near Earth Objects 2000; mem. Advisory Council on Science and Tech. (ACOST)'s Working Group on Int. Collaboration, Cabinet Office 1989, European Science Foundation Working Group on Near Earth Objects 2001; Consultant to Hong Kong Govt's Univ. Grants Cttee 1993–95, Univ. of Oxford's Comm. on the Future of the University 1995–96. *Address:* Atkinson Associates, Bampton, Oxon., OX18 2JN, England.

ATKINSON, Kate, BA; British writer and playwright; b. 1951, York; m. (divorced); two d.; ed Univ. of Dundee; fmrly home help, teacher and short story writer for women's magazines; writer 1988–; Woman's Own Short Story Competition 1986, Ian St James Award 1993, E. M. Forster Award, American Acad. of Arts and Letters 1997. *Plays include:* Nice 1996, Abandonment 2000. *Publications:* Behind the Scences at the Museum (novel) (Whitbread First Novel award and Book of the Year 1996, Boeker Prize, SA, Livre Book of the Year, France) 1995, Human Croquet (novel) 1997, Emotionally Weird (novel) 2001, Not the End of the World (short stories) 2002, Case Histories (novel) 2004, One Good Turn (novel) 2006, When Will There be Good News? (British Book Award for Best Read of the Year 2009) 2008; contrib. short stories to Daily Telegraph, BBC2, BBC Radio 4, Daily Express, Daily Mail, Scotsman. *Address:* c/o Transworld Publishers Ltd, 61–63 Uxbridge Road, London, W5 5SA, England (office). *Website:* www.booksattransworld.co.uk (office); www .kateatkinson.co.uk.

ATKINSON, Sir Robert, Kt, DSC, RD, BSc (Eng), FREng, FIMech; British business executive (retd); b. 7 March 1916, Tynemouth, Northumberland; s. of Nicholas Atkinson and Margaret Atkinson; m. 1st Joyce Forster 1941 (died 1973); one s. one d.; m. 2nd Margaret Hazel Walker 1977; ed Christ Church School, Tynemouth Grammar School, Univ. of London, McGill Univ., Canada; served during World War II (DSC and two bars; mentioned in despatches); Man. Dir William Doxford 1957–61; Tube Investments 1961–67; Unicorn Industries 1967–72; Chair. Aurora Holdings 1972–84; Chair. and Chief Exec. British Shipbuilders 1980–84; James Clayton Gold Medal 1961, MOD Arctic Medal 2006. *Publications:* The Design and Operating Experience of an Ore Carrier Built Abroad 1957, Some Crankshaft Failures: Investigations into Causes and Remedies 1960, The Manufacture of Crankshafts (North East Coast of Engineers and Shipbuilders Gold Medal) 1961, British Shipbuilders' Offshore Division 1962, Productivity Improvement in Ship Design and Construction 1983, The Development and Decline of British Shipbuilding 1999, Some Experiences of an Ancient Mariner 2006. *Leisure interests:* salmon and trout fishing, walking, gardening. *Address:* South Downs, 1 Little Hayes Lane, Itchen Abbas, Winchester, SO21 1XA, England (home). *Telephone:* (1962) 779610 (home).

ATKINSON, Roger, BA, PhD; British environmental scientist and academic; *Professor of Environmental Science and Chemistry, University of California, Riverside;* ed Univ. of Cambridge; Post-doctoral Researcher, Nat. Research Council of Canada, Ottawa 1969–71, York Univ. Centre for Research in Experimental Space Science, Downsview, Ont. 1971–72; Asst Research Chemist, Statewide Air Pollution Research Center, Univ. of California,

Riverside 1972–76, Assoc. Research Chemist 1976–78, 1980–81, Research Chemist 1981–, Prof. of Environmental Science and Chem. 1990–, Assoc. Dir Dept of Environmental Sciences 1990–92, Interim Dir 1993–96, Dir 1996–2005; Sr Scientist, Shell Research Ltd, Thornton Research Centre, Chester 1978–79; Sr Scientific Adviser, Environmental Research and Technology Inc., Westlake Village, Calif. 1979–80; mem. ACS, American Geophysical Union, AAAS. *Publications:* numerous specialist publs on atmospheric chem. *Address:* Air Pollution Research Center, University of California, Riverside, Fawcett Laboratory 123, Riverside, CA 92521-0312, USA (office). *Telephone:* (951) 827-4191 (office). *E-mail:* roger.atkinson@ucr.edu (office). *Website:* www.chem.ucr.edu/faculty/atkinson/atkinson.html (office).

ATKINSON, Rowan Sebastian, MSc; British actor and writer; b. 6 Jan. 1955; s. of the late Eric Atkinson and of Ella Atkinson; m. Sunetra Sastry 1990; ed Durham Cathedral Choristers' School, St Bees School and Univs of Newcastle and Oxford; stage appearances include: Beyond a Joke, Hampstead 1978, Oxford Univ. revues at Edinburgh Fringe, one-man show, London 1981, The Nerd 1985, The New Revue 1986, The Sneeze 1988, Oliver! 2008–. *TV appearances:* Not the Nine O'Clock News 1979–82, Blackadder 1983, Blackadder II 1985, Blackadder the Third 1987, Blackadder Goes Forth 1989, Mr Bean (13 episodes) 1990–96, Rowan Atkinson on Location in Boston 1993, Full Throttle 1994, The Thin Blue Line 1995–96, Unseen Bean 1995. *Films:* Never Say Never Again 1983, The Tall Guy 1989, The Appointments of Dennis Jennings 1989, The Witches 1990, Four Weddings and a Funeral 1994, Hot Shots – Part Deux 1994, Bean: The Ultimate Disaster Movie 1997, Blackadder – Back and Forth 2000, Maybe Baby 2000, Rat Race 2002, Scooby Doo 2002, Johnny English 2003, Love Actually 2003, Mickey's PhilharMagic (voice) 2003, Keeping Mum 2005, Mr. Bean's Holiday 2007. *Leisure interests:* motor cars, motor sport. *Address:* c/o PBJ Management Ltd, 7 Soho Street, London, W1D 3DQ, England (office). *Telephone:* (20) 7287-1112 (office). *Fax:* (20) 7287-1191 (office). *E-mail:* general@pbjmgt.co.uk (office).

ATLANTOV, Vladimir Andreevich; Russian singer (tenor); b. 19 Feb. 1933, Leningrad; ed Leningrad Conservatory (pupil of Natalya Bolotina); mem. CPSU 1966–88; joined Leningrad Kirov 1963; further study, La Scala, Milan 1963–65; won Tchaikovsky Competition 1966 and Int. Contest for Young Singers, Sofia 1967; soloist with Moscow Bolshoi Theatre 1968–88, with Vienna State Opera 1987–, Kammersänger 1987; major roles include German in The Queen of Spades, José in Carmen, Otello, Cavaradossi in Tosca; many tours and recordings; RSFSR People's Artist 1972, USSR People's Artist 1976. *Address:* c/o Wiener Staatsoper, Opernring 2, 1015 Vienna, Austria. *Fax:* (1) 51444-2330.

ATOPARE, Sir Sailas, GCMG; Papua New Guinea civil servant; b. 1951, Kabiufa, Eastern Highlands Prov.; m.; ed Jones Missionary Coll., Rabaul, E New Britain Prov.; fmrly Agric. Officer, Dept of Agric., Stocks and Fisheries, Asst Transport Man., Dept of Works and Supply, Man. and Sec. Assro-Watabung Rural Devt Corpn; mem. Nat. Parl. for Goroka Open, Eastern Highlands Prov. 1977; Gov.-Gen. 1997–2003; Sec.-Gen. Papua New Guinea Coffee Growers' Asscn; KStJ. *Leisure interests:* playing golf, going to church. *Address:* c/o Government House, PO Box 79, Port Moresby 121, Papua New Guinea (office).

ATRASH, Muhammad al-, PhD; Syrian banker, politician and international organization official; b. 13 Nov. 1934, Tartous; s. of Hassan Sayed al-Atrash and Aziza Sayed al-Atrash; m. Felicia al-Atrash 1958; two s. one d.; ed American Univ., Beirut, Lebanon, American Univ., Washington, DC, USA, London School of Econs; joined Cen. Bank of Syria 1963, Research Dept 1963, Head of Credit Dept 1966–70; Alt. Exec. Dir IMF 1970–73; Deputy Gov. Cen. Bank of Syria 1974; Exec. Dir IBRD 1974–76, IMF 1976–78; Del. to Second Cttee of UN Gen. Ass., to UNCTAD and other int. econ. confs 1963–70; part-time Lecturer, Univ. of Damascus 1963–70; mem. Deputies of IMF Interim Cttee of the Bd of Govs on Reform of Int. Monetary System 1972–74; Assoc. mem. IMF Interim Cttee 1974–76, ex officio mem. 1976–78; Minister of Economy and Foreign Trade 1980–82; Minister of Finance 2001–03. *Publications:* articles in Al-Abhath (Quarterly of the American Univ. of Beirut) 1963, 1964, 1966; several articles on int. political economy, regional econs, Arab–Israeli conflict etc. *Leisure interests:* swimming, walking, reading books on history and literature. *Address:* c/o Ministry of Finance, BP 13136, rue Jule Jammal, Damascus, Syria.

ATTALI, Bernard; French business executive; *Senior Advisor, TPG Capital;* b. 1 Nov. 1943, Algiers; s. of the late Simon Attali and Fernande Abecassis; twin brother of Jacques Attali (q.v.); m. Hélène Scebat 1974; one d.; ed Lycée Gauthier, Algiers, Lycée Janson-de-Sailly, Paris, Faculté de Droit, Paris, Inst. d'Etudes Politiques, Paris and Ecole Nat. d'Admin; auditeur, Cour des Comptes 1968, adviser 1974; on secondment to Commissariat Général du Plan d'Equipement et de la Productivité 1972–74; Délégation à l'Aménagement du Térritoire et à l'Action Regionale (Datar) 1974–80, 1981–84; Finance Dir Soc. Club Mediterranée 1980–81; Pres. Regional Cttee of EEC 1981–84; Pres. Groupe des Assurances Nationales 1984–86; Pres. Banque pour l'Industrie Française 1984–86; Adviser on European Affairs, Commercial Union Assurance 1986–88, Chair. Air France 1988–93; Pres. Supervisory Council, Sociétés Epargne de France 1986–88, Commercial Union Lard 1986–88; Pres. Euroberlin 1988, Union de Transports Aériens 1990, Asscn des Transporteurs Aériens Européens 1991; Vice-Pres. Supervisory Bd BIGT 1995; Admin. Aérospatiale 1989, Air Inter 1990; Chief Adviser Revenue Court 1991–93; Chair. Supervisory Bd Banque Arjil (part of Lagadère) 1993–96; Chair. Bankers Trust Co. France 1996–99; Vice-Pres. Investment Banking in Europe Div., Deutsche Bank 1999–2000; currently mem. European Bd Orrick Rambaud Martel, Bd Air Canada, Bd Baccarat; Commdr, Légion d'honneur; Commdr, Ordre nat. du Mérite. *Publication:* Les Guerres du Ciel 1994. *Address:* 6 rue Christophe Colomb, 75008 Paris (office). *Telephone:* 1-53-57-00-61 (office). *Fax:* 1-53-57-00-66 (office). *E-mail:* battali@tpg.com (office). *Website:* www.tpg.com (office).

ATTALI, Jacques; French international bank official and writer; *President, Attali et Associés;* b. 1 Nov. 1943, Algiers; s. of the late Simon Attali and of Fernande Abecassis; twin brother of Bernard Attali (q.v.); m. Elisabeth Allain 1981; one s. one d.; ed Ecole Polytechnique, Inst. d'Etudes Politiques de Paris, Ecoles des Mines de Paris, Ecole Nat. d'Admin; started career as mining engineer, then Lecturer in Econs, Ecole Polytechnique; Auditeur, Council of State; Adviser to the Pres. 1981–91; State Councillor 1989–91; Pres. EBRD, London 1991–93; Pres. Attali et Associés (ACA) 1994–; mem. Council of State 1981–90, 1993–; Admin. KeeBoo 2000–; Pres. Attali Comm. (est. to evaluate means of liberalising econ. growth in France) 2007–; columnist for L'Express magazine; Dr hc (Univ. of Kent, Univ. of Haifa). *Publications:* Analyse économique de la vie politique 1972, Modèles politiques 1973, Anti-économique (with Marc Guillaume) 1974, La parole et l'outil 1975, Bruits, Essai sur l'économie politique de la musique 1976, La nouvelle économie française 1977, L'ordre cannibale 1979, Les trois mondes 1981, Histoires du temps 1982, La figure de Fraser 1984, Un homme d'influence 1985, Au propre et au Figuré 1988, La vie éternelle (novel) 1989, Millennium: Winners and Losers in the Coming World Order 1991, 1492 1991, Verbatim (Tome I) 1993, Europe(s) 1994, Verbatim (Tome II) 1995, Economie de l'Apocalypse 1995, Tome III 1996, Chemins de Sagesse 1996, Au delà de nulle part 1997, Dictionnaire du XXIe siècle 1998, Les portes du ciel 1999, La femme du menteur 1999 (novel), Fraternités 1999, Blaise Pascal ou le génie français 2000, Bruits 2001, Nouv'Elles 2002 (novel), L'homme nomade 2003, La Confrérie des Eveillés 2004 (novel), Karl Marx ou l'esprit du Monde 2004, Une brève histoire de l'avenir 2007. *Address:* Attali et Associés 27, rue Vernet, 75008 Paris, France. *Telephone:* 1-53-57-38-38 (office). *Fax:* 1-47-23-09-91 (office). *Website:* www.aeta.net/fr (office).

ATTALIDES, Michalis A., PhD; Cypriot diplomatist, sociologist and academic; *Dean, School of Humanities, Social Sciences and Law, Intercollege, Nicosia;* b. 1941; m.; two c.; ed London School of Econs, UK and Princeton Univ., USA; Lecturer in Sociology, Univ. of Leicester 1966–68; sociologist, Cyprus Town and Country Planning Project 1968–70; counterpart of UNESCO expert, Social Research Centre, Cyprus 1971, 1973–74; mil. service 1972; Guest Lecturer Otto Suhr Inst., Free Univ. of Berlin 1974–75; journalist 1975–76; worked in Int. Relations Service, House of Reps of Cyprus 1977–89, Dir 1979–89; Amb., Dir of Political Affairs Division B (Cyprus question), Ministry of Foreign Affairs 1989–91; Amb. of Cyprus to France (also accred to Morocco, Portugal and Spain) 1991–95, Amb. to Belgium (also accred to Luxembourg) and Perm. Del. of Cyprus to EU 1995–98, High Commr in UK 1998–2000; Perm. Sec., Ministry of Foreign Affairs 2000–01; Rep. of Govt of Cyprus Del. to Convention on the Future of Europe 2002–03; Dean, School of Humanities, Social Sciences and Law, Intercollege, Nicosia 2003–; Grand Officier, Ordre Nat. du Mérite. *Publications:* Cyprus: Nationalism and International Politics 1980, Social Change and Urbanization in Cyprus: A Study of Nicosia 1971. *Address:* 8 Sachtouris Street, Nicosia 1080, Cyprus (home). *E-mail:* mattali@spidernet.com.cy (home).

ATTALLAH, Naim Ibrahim, FRSA; British publisher and financial adviser; *Chairman, Namara Group;* b. 1 May 1931, Haifa, Palestine; s. of Ibrahim Attallah and Genevieve Attallah; m. Maria Nykolyn 1957; one s.; ed Coll. des Frères, Haifa and Battersea Polytechnic, London; Propr Quartet Books 1976–, Women's Press 1977–, Robin Clark 1980–, Pipeline Books 1978–2000, The Literary Review 1981–2001, The Wire 1984–2000, Acad. Club 1989–96, The Oldie 1991–2001; Group Chief Exec. Asprey PLC 1992–96, Deputy Chair. Asprey (Bond Street) 1992–98; Man. Dir Mappin and Webb 1990–95; Exec. Dir Garrard 1990–95; Chair. Namara Group of cos 1973–, launched Parfums Namara 1985, Avant L'Amour and Après L'Amour 1985, Naïdor 1987, L'Amour de Namara 1990; Hon. MA (Surrey) 1993; Retail Personality of the Year, UK Jewellery Awards 1993. *Films produced:* The Slipper and the Rose (with David Frost q.v.) 1975, Brimstone and Treacle (Exec. Producer) 1982 and several TV documentaries. *Theatre:* Happy End (Co-Presenter) 1975, The Beastly Beatitudes of Balthazar B. (Presenter and Producer) 1981, Trafford Tanzi (Co-Producer) 1982. *Publications:* Women 1987, Singular Encounters 1990, Of a Certain Age 1992, More of a Certain Age 1993, Speaking for the Oldie 1994, A Timeless Passion 1995, Tara and Claire (novel) 1996, Asking Questions 1996, A Woman a Week 1998, In Conversation with Naim Attallah 1998, Insights 1999, Dialogues 2001, The Old Ladies of Nazareth 2004, The Boy in England (memoir) 2005, In Touch with His Roots: a Second Memoir 2006, Fulfilment & Betrayal 2007. *Leisure interests:* classical music, opera, theatre, cinema, photography and fine arts. *Address:* 25 Shepherd Market, London, W1J 7PP, England (home). *Telephone:* (20) 7499-2901 (home). *Fax:* (20) 7499-2914 (home). *E-mail:* nattallah@aol.com (office).

ATTANASIO, Paul; American screenwriter; m. Katie Jacobs; one d.; ed Harvard Univ., Harvard Law School; began career as a journalist; film critic for Washington Post 1984–87. *Films include:* Quiz Show 1994, Disclosure 1994, Donnie Brasco 1997, Sphere 1998, The Sum of All Fears 2002, The Good German 2006, The Bourne Ultimatum 2007. *TV series include:* Doctor, Doctor 1989, Homicide: Life on the Street 1993, Gideon's Crossing (also producer) 2000, R.U.S./H. (also producer) 2002, House (exec. producer) 2004–. *Address:* c/o CAA, 9830 Wilshire Blvd., Beverly Hills, CA 90212-1825, USA.

ATTAR, Mohamed Saeed al-, PhD; Yemeni politician and diplomatist; b. 26 Nov. 1927; m.; one s. five d.; ed Sorbonne, Paris; Research Assoc. Sorbonne and Inst. de Développement, Paris 1959–62; Gen. Man. Yemen Bank for Reconstruction and Devt 1962–65, Chair. 1965–68; mem. High Econ. Comm. 1962–68; Ministry of Econ. 1965–68; Perm. Rep. of Yemen Arab Repub. to UN 1968–71, 1973–74; Roving Amb. 1971–73; Under-Sec.-Gen. of UN and Exec. Sec. Econ. Comm. for Western Asia (ECWA) 1974–85; Deputy Prime Minister,

Minister of Devt and Chair. Cen. Planning Org. 1985; Deputy Prime Minister and Minister of Industry 1990–95; Pres. Gen. Investment Authority 1993; Deputy Prime Minister and Minister of Oil and Mineral Resources 1995; fmr Perm. Rep., UN Geneva; mem. Supreme Council for Oil; many other public appointments; MARIB Legion decoration (Yemen); Légion d'honneur. *Publications include:* La Révolution Yemenite 1964; articles in magazines and newspapers. *Address:* c/o Ministry of Planning and International Co-operation, POB 175, San'a, Yemen (office).

ATTAR, Najah al-, PhD; Syrian academic and politician; *Second Vice-President, responsible for Cultural Policy;* b. 1933, Damascus; sister of Issam al-Attar, currently in exile in Europe; m. Dr Majed Al-Azmeh; one s., one d.; ed Damascus Univ., Univ. of Edinburgh, UK; schoolteacher in Damascus 1960–62; Dir of Composition and Literature Translation, Ministry of Culture 1962, Minister of Culture and Nat. Guidance (first woman minister) 1976–2000, served as spokeswoman for Syrian Govt early 1980s, co-f. Nat. Symphonic Orchestra 1995, initiated construction of Syrian Opera House; Dir Centre for the Dialogue of Civilisations 2002–06; mem. Bd Kalamoun Univ., Dayr Atiya 2003–; Pres. Bd of Trustees, Syrian Virtual Univ. 2003–; Second Vice-Pres. of Syria (first woman and first non-Baath Party mem.), responsible for Cultural Policy 2006–; Friendship Among People's Order, fmr USSR, Polish Culture Order, Order of Merit of Supreme Officer, France 1983, Order of League of Honour, rank of Commdr, France 1992, Order of Great Lady, Malta Knights, Order of Holy Cross, Poland 1999, Order of Holy Treasure of Grand Sash, Japan 2002, Medallion of Honour, Chile 2004, Order of Katrina the Great, Acad. of Security, Defense and Law, Russian Fed. 2007. *Publications:* For Us to Be or Not to Be (2 vols), The Literature of War, Who Remembers Those Days?, A Diary, Life's Questions, Coloured Words, The Revolutionary Fabric Between March and November, Spain, Hemingway and the Bulls; weekly newspaper and magazine columns; numerous articles; literary criticism titles (forthcoming). *Address:* c/o Office of the President, Damascus, Syria (office). *Telephone:* (11) 3323023 (office). *Fax:* (11) 3341404 (office). *E-mail:* center-cs@mail.sy (office).

ATTAS, Haydar Abu Bakr al-; Yemeni politician; fmr Minister of Construction; Prime Minister of People's Democratic Repub. of Yemen 1985–86; Pres. (following overthrow of Govt of Ali Nasser Mohammed,) 1986–90; Prime Minister of Repub. of Yemen 1990–94. *Address:* c/o Office of the Prime Minister, San'a, Yemen.

ATTENBOROUGH, Sir David Frederick, Kt, OM, CH, CVO, CBE, MA, FRS; British broadcaster, naturalist and writer; b. 8 May 1926, London; s. of the late Frederick Attenborough and of Mary Attenborough; brother of Lord Attenborough (q.v.); m. Jane Elizabeth Ebsworth Oriel 1950 (died 1997); one s. one d.; ed Wyggeston Grammar School, Leicester and Clare Coll., Cambridge; served with RN 1947–49; editorial asst in publishing house 1949–52; with BBC Television 1952–73, Producer of zoological, archaeological, travel, political and other programmes 1952–64, Controller BBC 2 1964–68, Dir of Programmes, TV 1969–73; writer, presenter BBC series: Tribal Eye 1976, Wildlife on One, annually 1977–2004, Life on Earth 1979, The Living Planet 1984, The First Eden 1987, Lost World, Vanished Lives 1989, The Trials of Life 1990, Life in the Freezer 1993, The Private Life of Plants 1995, The Life of Birds 1998, State of the Planet 2000, The Blue Planet (narrator) 2001, The Life of Mammals 2002, Life in Cold Blood 2008; Huw Wheldon Memorial Lecturer, RTS 1987; Pres. BAAS 1990–91, Royal Soc. for Nature Conservation 1991–96; mem. Nature Conservancy Council 1975–82; Fellow, Soc. of Film and Television Arts 1980; Int. Trustee, World Wild Life Fund 1979–86; Trustee, British Museum 1980–2000, Science Museum 1984–87, Royal Botanical Gardens, Kew 1986–92; Hon. Fellow, Clare Coll., Cambridge 1980, UMIST 1980, Inst. of Biology; Order of Merit; Hon. DLitt (Leicester, London, Birmingham, City); Hon. DSc (Liverpool, Ulster, Sussex, Bath, Durham, Keele, Heriot-Watt, Bradford, Nottingham); Hon. LLD (Bristol, Glasgow) 1977; Hon. DUniv (Open Univ.) 1980, (Essex) 1987, Antwerp 1993; Dr hc (Edin.) 1994; Special Award, Guild of TV Producers 1961, Silver Medal, Royal TV Soc. 1966, Silver Medal, Zoological Soc. of London 1966, Desmond Davis Award, Soc. of Film and TV Arts 1970, UNESCO Kalinga Prize 1982, Medallist, Acad. of Natural Sciences, Philadelphia 1982, Founders Gold Medal, Royal Geographical Soc. 1985, Int. Emmy Award 1985, Encyclopedia Britannica Award 1987, Kew Award 1996, Edin. Medal, Edin. Science Festival 1998, BP Natural World Book Prize 1998, Faraday Prize, Royal Soc. 2003, Int. Documentary Asscn Career Achievement Award 2003, Raffles Medal, Zoological Soc. of London 2004, Caird Medal, Nat. Maritime Museum 2004, British Book Awards Lifetime Achievement Award 2004. *Publications:* Zoo Quest to Guiana 1956, Zoo Quest for a Dragon 1957, Zoo Quest in Paraguay 1959, Quest in Paradise 1960, Zoo Quest to Madagascar 1961, Quest under Capricorn 1963, The Tribal Eye 1976, Life on Earth 1979, The Zoo Quest Expeditions 1982; The Living Planet 1984, The First Eden, The Mediterranean World and Man 1987, The Trials of Life 1990, The Private Life of Plants 1994, The Life of Birds (BP Natural World Book Prize) 1998, The Life of Mammals 2002, Life on Air (memoirs) 2002, Life in the Undergrowth 2005, Life in Cold Blood 2008. *Leisure interests:* music, tribal art, natural history. *Address:* 5 Park Road, Richmond, Surrey, TW10 6NS, England.

ATTENBOROUGH, Michael; British theatre director; *Artistic Director, Almeida Theatre Company;* b. 1950; s. of Richard Attenborough (Baron Attenborough of Richmond) (q.v.) and Sheila Sim; m. Jane Seymour 1971 (divorced); ed Univ. of Sussex; Assoc. Dir Mercury Theatre, Colchester 1972–74; Assoc. Dir Leeds Playhouse 1974–79, Young Vic Theatre 1979; Dir Palace Theatre, Watford 1980–84, Hampstead Theatre 1984–89; Prin. Assoc. Dir RSC 1990–2002; Artistic Dir Almeida Theatre Co. 2002–; Vice-Chair. Royal Acad. of Dramatic Art. *Productions include:* RSC: The Herbal Bed, Romeo and Juliet, Othello, Pentecost, Henry IV Parts 1 and 2; Almeida

Theatre: The Mercy Seat, Five Gold Rings. *Address:* Almeida Theatre, Almeida Street, Islington, London, N1 1TA, England (office). *Telephone:* (20) 7288-4900 (office). *Fax:* (20) 7288-4901 (office). *Website:* www.almeida.co.uk (office).

ATTENBOROUGH, Baron (Life Peer), cr. 1993, of Richmond-upon-Thames in the London Borough of Richmond-upon-Thames; **Richard (Samuel) Attenborough,** Kt, CBE; British actor, producer and director; b. 29 Aug. 1923; s. of the late Frederick Attenborough and of Mary Attenborough; brother of Sir David Attenborough (q.v.); m. Sheila Beryl Grant Sim 1945; one s. (Michael Attenborough (q.v.)), two d.; ed Wyggeston Grammar School, Leicester, Royal Acad. of Dramatic Art, London; first stage appearance as Richard Miller in Ah! Wilderness, Palmers Green 1941; West End debut in Awake and Sing 1942; first film appearance In Which We Serve 1942; joined RAF 1943; seconded to RAF Film Unit for Journey Together 1944, demobilised 1946; returned to stage 1949; formed Beaver Films with Bryan Forbes (q.v.) 1959, Allied Film Makers 1960; Goodwill Amb. for UNICEF 1987–; mem. British Actors' Equity Asscn Council 1949–73, Cinematograph Films Council 1967–73, Arts Council of GB 1970–73; Chair. Actors' Charitable Trust 1956–88 (Pres. 1988–), Combined Theatrical Charities Appeals Council 1964–88 (Pres. 1988–), BAFTA 1969–70 (Vice-Pres. 1971–94), Royal Acad. of Dramatic Arts 1970 (mem. Council 1963–), Capital Radio 1972–92 (Life Pres. 1992–), Help a London Child 1975–, UK Trustees Waterford-Kamhlaba School, Swaziland 1976– (Gov. 1987–), Duke of York's Theatre 1979–92, BFI 1981–92, Goldcrest Films and TV 1982–87, Cttee of Inquiry into the Arts and Disabled People 1983–85, Channel Four TV 1987–92 (Deputy Chair. 1980–86), British Screen Advisory Council 1987–96, European Script Fund 1988–96 (Hon. Pres. 1996); Gov. Nat. Film School 1970–81, Motability 1977–; Pres. Muscular Dystrophy Group of GB 1971– (Vice-Pres. 1962–71), The Gandhi Foundation 1983–, Brighton Festival 1984–95, British Film Year 1984–86, Arts for Health 1989–, Gardner Centre for the Arts, Sussex Univ. 1990– (Patron 1969–82); Dir Young Vic 1974–84, Chelsea Football Club 1969–82; Trustee Tate Gallery 1976–82, 1994–96, Tate Foundation 1986–, Foundation for Sport and the Arts 1991–; Patron Kingsley Hall Community Centre 1982–, RA Centre for Disability and the Arts, Leicester 1990–; Pro-Chancellor Sussex Univ. 1970–98, Chancellor 1998–; Fellow King's Coll. London 1993, Fellow BAFTA; Freeman of Leicester 1990; Hon. Fellow BFI 1992, Nat. Film and TV School 2001; Commdr des Arts et Lettres; Chevalier, Légion d'honneur; Hon. DLitt (Leicester) 1970, (Kent) 1981, (Sussex) 1987; Hon. DCL (Newcastle) 1974; Hon. LLD (Dickinson, Penn.) 1983; Evening Standard Film Award for 40 Years' Service to British Cinema 1983, Martin Luther King, Jr Peace Prize 1983, Padma Bhushan, India 1983, European Film Awards Award of Merit 1988, Shakespeare Prize for Outstanding Contrib. to European Culture 1992, Dilys Powell Award 1995, Patricia Rothermere Award, Evening Standard Theatre Awards 2004. *Stage appearances include:* The Little Foxes 1942, Brighton Rock 1943, The Way Back Home (Home of the Brave) 1949, To Dorothy a Son 1965, Sweet Madness 1952, The Mousetrap 1952–54, Double Image 1956–57, The Rape of the Belt 1957–58. *Film appearances include:* School for Secrets, The Man Within, Dancing with Crime, Brighton Rock, London Belongs to Me, The Guinea Pig, The Lost People, Boys in Brown, Morning Departure, Hell is Sold Out, The Magic Box, Gift Horse, Father's Doing Fine, Eight O'Clock Walk, The Ship that Died of Shame, Private's Progress, The Baby and the Battleship, Brothers in Law, The Scamp, Dunkirk, The Man Upstairs, Sea of Sand, Danger Within, I'm All Right Jack, Jet Storm, S.O.S. Pacific, The Angry Silence (also co-prod.) 1959, The League of Gentlemen 1960, Only Two Can Play, All Night Long 1961, The Dock Brief, The Great Escape 1962, Seance on a Wet Afternoon (also prod., Best Actor, San Sebastian Film Festival and British Film Acad.), The Third Secret 1963, Guns at Batasi (Best Actor, British Film Acad.) 1964, The Flight of the Phoenix 1965, The Sand Pebbles (Hollywood Golden Globe) 1966, Dr. Doolittle (Hollywood Golden Globe), The Bliss of Mrs. Blossom 1967, Only When I Larf 1968, The Last Grenade, A Severed Head, David Copperfield, Loot 1969, 10 Rillington Place 1970, And Then There Were None, Rosebud, Brannigan, Conduct Unbecoming 1974, The Chess Players 1977, The Human Factor 1979, Jurassic Park 1992, Miracle on 34th Street 1994, The Lost World: Jurassic Park 1997, Elizabeth 1998, Puckoon 2002. *Produced:* Whistle Down the Wind 1961, The L-Shaped Room 1962. *Directed:* Young Winston (Hollywood Golden Globe) 1972, A Bridge Too Far (Evening News Best Drama Award) 1976, Magic 1978, A Chorus Line 1985, Grey Owl 2000, Closing the Ring 2004. *Produced and directed:* Oh! What a Lovely War (16 int. Awards), Gandhi (eight Oscars, five BAFTA Awards, five Hollywood Golden Globes, Dirs' Guild of America Award for Outstanding Directorial Achievement) 1980–81, Cry Freedom (Berlinale Kamera, BFI Award for Tech. Achievement) 1987, Chaplin 1992, Shadowlands 1993 (Alexander Korda Award for Outstanding British Film of the Year, BAFTA), In Love and War 1997, Grey Owl 2000. *Publications:* In Search of Gandhi 1982, Richard Attenborough's Chorus Line (with Diana Carter) 1986, Cry Freedom, A Pictorial Record 1987, Entirely Up To You (autobiog., co-author) 2007. *Leisure interests:* music, collecting art, watching football. *Address:* Old Friars, Richmond Green, Richmond, Surrey, TW9 1NQ, England.

ATTERSEE, Christian Ludwig; Austrian artist; b. 28 Aug. 1940, Pressburg; s. of Christian Ludwig and Susanne Ludwig; ed Akad. für Angewandte Kunst, Vienna; has worked as an artist since 1963; more than 400 one-man exhbns in USA, Germany, France, Netherlands, Italy, Austria, Switzerland, including Venice Biennale 1984; Prof., Universität für angewandte Kunst, Vienna 1990–; Austrian Cross of Honour for Science and Art 1st Class 2005; Grand Austrian State Prize 1997, Lovis Corinth Prize of the Künstlergilde Esslingen, Germany 2004. *Publications:* Attersee Werksquer 1962–82, Attersee, Biennale Venedig 1984. *Leisure interest:* sailing. *Address:* Atelier/ Archiv Attersee, Tuchlauben 17/4/7, 1010 Vienna, Austria. *E-mail:* attersee@ utanet.at. *Website:* www.attersee-christian-ludwig.com.

ATTIYAH, Abdullah bin Hamad al-, BA; Qatar politician; *Second Deputy Premier and Minister of Energy, Industry, Electricity and Water;* b. 1952, Qatar; m.; six c.; ed Univ. of Alexandria, Egypt; joined Ministry of Finance and Petroleum 1972, Head Dept of Int. and Public Affairs 1973–86, Dir Office of Minister 1986–89; Dir Office of Minister of Interior and Acting Minister of Finance and Petroleum 1989–92; Minister of Energy and Industry 1992–99, 2001–, of Energy, Industry, Electricity and Water 1999–2000, Second Deputy Premier 2003–; Chair. State Planning Council 1998–; Deputy Chair. Q-Tel 1987–95; Chair. Gulf Helicopters 1975–; mem. Bd of Dirs Gulf Airways Corpn 1986–2002; Man. Dir and Chair. of Bd Qatar Petrol Co. 1992–; fmr Head Al-Sadd Sports Club; Chair. Qatar Amateur Radio Asscn 1992–, Qatar Gen. Electricity and Water Corpn 1999–. *Leisure interests:* reading, fishing, amateur radio, football, travelling. *Address:* Second Deputy Premier, Ministry of Energy and Industry POB 3212, Doha, Qatar (office). *Telephone:* 4835666 (office). *Fax:* 4836999 (office). *E-mail:* chairman@qp.com.qa. *Website:* www.qp.com.qa (office).

ATTRIDGE, Harold W., PhD; American academic; *Dean and Lillian Claus Professor of New Testament, Yale Divinity School;* b. Nov. 1946; ed Boston Coll., Cambridge Univ., UK, Hebrew Univ. of Jerusalem, Israel, Harvard Univ.; Asst Prof. of New Testament, Perkins School of Theology, Southern Methodist Univ. 1977–82, Assoc. Prof. of New Testament 1982–85; Assoc. Prof., Dept of Theology, Univ. of Notre Dame 1985–87, Prof., Dept of Theology 1988–97, Dean, Coll. of Arts and Letters 1991–97; Prof. of New Testament, Yale Univ. Divinity School 1997–, Dean 2002–; mem. Soc. of Biblical Literature 1969–, Chair. SW Region Progam 1980–81, mem. Annual Meeting Program Cttee 1985–88, Cttee on Research and Publs 1990–93, Devt Cttee 1995– (Vice-Pres. 2000), Finance Cttee 2001– (Pres. 2001); mem. Catholic Biblical Asscn 1974–, Int. Asscn for Coptic Studies 1975–, American Philosophical Asscn 1976–, Soc. for New Testament Studies 1981–; mem. Editorial Bd Catholic Biblical Quarterly 1983–90, Journal of Biblical Literature 1982–87, 1996–2001, Hermeneia Commentary Series 1984–; Editorial Consultant, Harvard Theological Review 1978–90; Ed., Soc. of Biblical Literature, Texts and Trans: Pseudepgrapha Series 1979–85, Early Christian Literature Series 1990–95;; Nat. Endowment for the Humanities Summer Research Stipend 1982; John Simon Guggenheim Fellowship 1983–84. *Publications:* The Testament of Job 1974, The Syrian Goddess 1976, The Interpretation of Biblical History in the Antiquitates Judaicae of Flavius Josephus 1976, First-Century Cynicism in the Epistles of Heraclitus 1976, Philo of Byblos, The Phoenician History 1981, Nag Hammdi Codex I (The Jung Codex) 1985, Hebrews: A Commentary on the Epistle to the Hebrews 1989; numerous articles; ed. of eleven books. *Address:* Yale Divinity School, 409 Prospect Street, New Haven, CT 06511, USA (office). *Telephone:* (203) 432-5304 (office). *E-mail:* harold.attridge@yale.edu (office). *Website:* www.yale.edu/divinity (office).

ATWOOD, Margaret Eleanor, CC, AM, FRSC; Canadian writer and poet; b. 18 Nov. 1939, Ottawa, Ont.; m. Graeme Gibson; one d.; ed Victoria Coll., Univ. of Toronto, Radcliffe Coll. and Harvard Univ., Cambridge, Mass; Lecturer in English, Univ. of British Columbia, Vancouver 1964–65; Instructor in English, Sir George Williams Univ., Montreal 1967–68, Univ. of Alberta 1969–70; Asst Prof. of English, York Univ., Toronto 1971; Writer-in-Residence, Univ. of Toronto 1972–73, Maquarie Univ., Australia 1987, Trinity Univ., San Antonio, Tex. 1989; Berg Chair, New York Univ. 1986; Pres. Writers' Union of Canada 1981–82, International PEN (Canadian Centre—English Speaking) 1984–86; MFA Hon. Chair, Univ. of Alabama, Tuscaloosa 1985; Foreign Hon. mem. American Acad. of Arts and Sciences 1988; Order of Ont. 1990, 125th Anniversary of Canadian Confederation Commemorative Medal 1992, Chevalier, Ordre des Arts et Lettres 1994, Order of Literary Merit (Norway) 1996, Markets Initiative Order of the Forest 2006; Hon. DLitt (Trent) 1973, (Concordia) 1980, (Smith Coll., Mass) 1982, (Toronto) 1983, (Mount Holyoke) 1985, (Waterloo) 1985, (Guelph) 1985, (Oxford) 1998; Hon. LLD (Queen's Univ.) 1974; Dr hc (Victoria Coll.) 1987, (Université de Montréal) 1991, (Leeds) 1994, (McMaster) 1996, (Lakehead) 1998, (Oxford) 1998, (Cambridge) 2001, (Algoma) 2001, (Harvard) 2004, (Sorbonne Nouvelle) 2005, (Literary and Historical Soc., Univ. Coll. Dublin) 2005; E.J. Pratt Medal 1961, Pres.'s Medal, Univ. of Western Ontario 1965, First Prize, Centennial Comm. Poetry Competition 1967, Union Poetry Prize, Chicago 1969, Bess Hoskins Prize for Poetry, Chicago 1974, City of Toronto Book Award 1977, Canadian Bookseller's Asscn Award 1977, Periodical Distributors of Canada Short Fiction Award 1977, St Lawrence Award for Fiction 1978, Radcliffe Grad. Medal 1980, Molson Award 1981, Guggenheim Fellowship 1981, Welsh Arts Council Int. Writer's Prize 1982, Periodical Distributors of Canada and the Foundation for The Advancement of Canadian Letters Book of the Year Award 1983, Ida Nudel Humanitarian Award 1986, Toronto Arts Award 1986, Los Angeles Times Fiction Award 1986, Ms. Magazine Woman of the Year 1986, Arthur C. Clarke Award for Best Science Fiction 1987, Commonwealth Literary Prize (regional winner) 1987, 1994, Silver Medal for Best Article of the Year, Council for Advancement and Support of Educ. 1987, Humanist of the Year Award 1987, YWCA Women of Distinction Award 1988, First Prize, Nat. Magazine Award for Environmental Journalism 1988, Canadian Booksellers Asscn Author of the Year 1989, 1996, Harvard Univ. Centennial Medal 1990, John Hughes Prize, Welsh Devt Bd 1992, Commemorative Medal for the 125th Anniversary of Canadian Confed. 1992, Best Local Author, NOW Magazine Readers' Poll 1995, 1997, 1998, 1999, 2000, 2003, 2004, Nat. Arts Club Medal of Honor for Literature 1997, London Literature Award 1999, Int. Crime Writers' Asscn Dashiell Hammett Award 2001, Canadian Booksellers Asscn People's Choice Award 2001, Radcliffe Medal 2003, Harold Washington Literary Award 2003, Banff Centre Nat. Arts Award 2005, Edinburgh Int. Book Festival Englightenment Award 2005, Chicago Tribune Literary Prize 2005, Premio Príncipe de Asturias, Spain 2008. *Radio script:* The Trumpets of Summer (CBC Radio) 1964. *Television screenplays:* The Servant Girl (CBC) 1974, Snowbird 1981, Heaven on Earth (with Peter Pearson) 1986. *Recordings:* The Poetry and Voice of Margaret Atwood 1977, Margaret Atwood Reads From A Handmaid's Tale, Margaret Atwood Reads Unearthing Suite 1985, audio edns of her novels. *Publications:* poetry: Double Persephone 1961, The Circle Game (Gov.-Gen.'s Award 1966) 1964, Kaleidoscopes Baroque 1965, Talismans for Children 1965, Speeches for Doctor Frankenstein 1966, The Animals in That Country 1968, The Journals of Susanna Moodie 1970, Procedures for Underground 1970, Power Politics 1971, You Are Happy 1974, Selected Poems 1976, Marsh, Hawk 1977, Two-Headed Poems 1978, True Stories 1981, Notes Towards a Poem That Can Never Be Written 1981, Snake Poems 1983, Interlunar 1984, Selected Poems II: Poems Selected and New 1976–1986 1986, Selected Poems 1966–1984 1990, Margaret Atwood Poems 1965–1975 1991, Morning in the Burned House (Trillium Award for Excellence in Ontario Writing 1995) 1995; fiction: The Edible Woman 1969, Surfacing 1972, Lady Oracle 1976, Dancing Girls (short stories) 1977, Life Before Man 1979, Bodily Harm 1981, Encounters with the Element Man 1982, Murder in the Dark (short stories) 1983, Bluebeard's Egg (short stories) 1983, Unearthing Suite 1983, The Handmaid's Tale (Gov.-Gen.'s Award 1986) (adapted for the screen by Harold Pinter and directed by Volker Schlöndorf 1990) 1985, Cat's Eye (Torgi Talking Book—CNIB 1989, City of Toronto Book Award 1989, Coles Book of the Year 1989, Foundation for the Advancement of Canadian Letters/Periodical Marketers of Canada Book of the Year 1989) 1988, Wilderness Tips (short stories) (Govt of Ont. Trillium Award (with Jane Urquhart) for Excellence in Ontario Writing 1992, Periodical Marketers of Canada Book of the Year Award 1992) 1991, Good Bones (short stories) 1992, The Robber Bride (Canadian Authors' Asscn Novel of the Year 1993, Trillium Award for Excellence in Ontario Writing 1994, Commonwealth Writers' Prize for the Canadian and Caribbean Region 1994, Sunday Times Award for Literary Excellence 1994, Swedish Humour Asscn's Int. Humourous Writer Award 1995) 1993, Bones and Murder 1995, The Labrador Fiasco 1996, Alias Grace (Giller Prize 1996, Premio Mondello 1997, Salon Magazine Best Fiction of the Year 1997) 1996, The Blind Assassin (Booker Prize 2000) 2000, Oryx and Crake 2003, Telling Tales (contrib. to charity anthology) 2004, Bottle 2004, The Penelopaid 2005, The Tent (short stories) 2006, Moral Disorder (short stories) 2006, The Door 2007; juvenile: Up in the Tree 1978, 2006, Anna's Pet 1980, For the Birds 1990, Princess Prunella and the Purple Peanut 1995, Rude Ramsay and the Roaring Radishes 2003, Bashful Bob and Doleful Dorinda 2004; non-fiction: Survival: A Thematic Guide to Canadian Literature 1972, Days of the Rebels 1815–1840 1977, Second Words: Selected Critical Prose 1982, Strange Things: The Malevolent North in Canadian Literature 1995, Negotiating with the Dead: A Writer on Writing 2002, Moving Targets: Writing With Intent 1982–2004 2004, Curious Pursuits: Occasional Writing 2005, Writing with Intent: Essays, Reviews, Personal Prose 1983–2005 2005, The Penelopiad: The Myth of Penelope and Odysseus 2005, Payback: Debt and the Shadow Side of Wealth 2008; editor: The New Oxford Book of Canadian Verse in English (ed.) 1982, The Oxford Book of Canadian Short Stories in English (with Robert Weaver) 1986, The Canlit Foodbook 1987, The Best American Short Stories (with Shannon Ravenel) 1989, The New Oxford Book of Canadian Short Stories in English (with Robert Weaver) 1995; reviews and critical articles have appeared in Canadian Literature, Maclean's, Saturday Night, This Magazine, New York Times Book Review, Globe and Mail, National Post, The Nation, Books In Canada, Washington Post, Harvard Educational Review, and many others; works have been translated into many languages, including French, German, Italian, Urdu, Estonian, Roumanian, Serbo-Croatian, Catalan, Turkish, Russian, Finnish, Dutch, Danish, Norwegian, Swedish, Portuguese, Greek, Polish, Japanese, Icelandic, Spanish, Hebrew. *Address:* c/o McClelland & Stewart, 75 Sherbourne Street, 5th Floor, Toronto, ON M5A 2P9, Canada (office). *Telephone:* (416) 598-1114 (office). *Fax:* (416) 598-7764 (office). *E-mail:* mail@mcclelland.com (office). *Website:* www.mcclelland.com (office); www.owtoad.com.

ATZMON, Moshe; Israeli conductor; b. (Miklos Groszberger), 30 July 1931, Budapest, Hungary; m. 1954; two d.; ed Tel-Aviv Acad. of Music, Jerusalem Acad. of Music, Guildhall School of Music, London; left Hungary for Israel 1944; played the horn professionally in various orchestras for several years; has conducted in Israel, England, Australia, Germany, Sweden, Norway, Switzerland, Spain, Finland, Italy, Austria, Turkey and USA; Chief Conductor, Sydney Symphony Orchestra 1969–71; Chief Conductor, North German Radio Symphony Orchestra 1972–74; Musical Dir Basel Symphony Orchestra 1972–86; Chief Conductor Tokyo Metropolitan Orchestra 1979–83, Nagoya Philharmonic Orchestra 1987–92, Conductor Laureate 1992–; Musical Dir Dortmund Opera House and Philharmonic Orchestra 1991–93; second prize Dimitri Mitropoulos Competition for Conductors, New York 1963, Leonard Bernstein Prize 1963, First Prize, Int. Conductors Competition, Liverpool, England 1964. *Leisure interests:* reading, travelling. *Address:* Patrick Garvey Management, 40 North Parade, York YO30 7AB, England (office). *Telephone:* (1904) 621222 (office). *Fax:* (1723) 330050 (office). *E-mail:* patrick@patrickgarvey.com (office). *Website:* www.patrickgarvey.com (office).

AUBERGER, Bernard, Ing Civil, LenD; French banker; *Judge, Tribunal de Commerce de Paris;* b. 5 Dec. 1937, Gennevilliers; s. of Paul Auberger and Jeanne Auberger (née Geny); m. Christine Baraduc 1963; three s. one d.; ed Ecole des Mines, Paris, Inst. d'Etudes Politiques, Paris, Ecole Nat. d'Admin, Paris; Investigating Officer, French Ministry of Finance 1966–70; Adviser to Gen. Man. Crédit Nat., Paris 1970–72; Financial Attaché, French Embassy, New York 1972–74; Dir of Cabinet for UnderSec. for Finance 1974; attached to Industrial Relations Cttee 1974–75; Dir Production and Trade, French Ministry of Agric. 1975–80; Cen. Man. Société Générale 1983–86; Gen. Man. Caisse Nat. de Crédit Agricole 1986–88; Insp. Gen. of Finances 1988; Advisor to Pres. of Paluel-Marmont 1990; Pres. Cortal Bank 1991–98, Banque Directe 1994–2001; Vice-Pres., Dir-Gen. Crédit du Nord 1993–94, Chair., CEO 1994–95; Pres. Asscn Opéra Comique-Salle Favart 1994–2001; Dir Compagnie Bancaire 1991–98, Banque Paribas 1994–97; Judge, Tribunal de Commerce de Paris 1998–; mem. Econ. and Social Council 1982–; Officier Ordre nat. du Mérite, Chevalier du Mérite agricole, Officier Légion d'honneur. *Leisure interest:* opera. *Address:* 193 Boulevard St Germain, 75007 Paris, France (home). *Telephone:* 1-45-48-94-11 (home).

AUBERT, Guy, PhD; French scientist and academic; *Scientific Adviser, Commissariat a l'Energie Atomique;* b. 9 May 1938, Les Costes, Hautes-Alpes; s. of Gontran Aubert and Marguerite Vincent; m. 1st 1962; two d.; m. 2nd 1998; ed Ecole normale supérieure de Saint-Cloud; Research Assoc. Lab. d'Electrostatique et de Physique du Metal, CNRS, Grenoble; Titular Prof. Univ., Scientifique et Médicale de Grenoble 1970, Vice-Pres. in Charge of Research 1981–84; Scientific Del. of CNRS for Rhône-Alpes region 1981–83; Dir Ecole Normale Supérieure de Lyon 1985–94; Dir-Gen. CNRS 1994–97; Extraordinary mem. Conseil d'Etat 1997–2000; Dir-Gen. CNED 2000–03; Scientific Adviser to Commissariat a l'Energie Atomique 2003–; mem. French Physics Soc.; Officier, Légion d'honneur, Ordre nat. du Mérite; Commdr des Palmes académiques; Chevalier du Mérite agricole. *Publications:* papers in scientific journals. *Leisure interests:* skiing, tennis. *Address:* Université de Poitiers, Présidence, 15 rue de l'Hôtel Dieu, 86034 Poitiers Cedex (office); 34T, rue des Feuillants, 86000 Poitiers, France (home). *Telephone:* (5) 49-45-43-39 (office). *Fax:* (5) 49-36-62-34 (office). *E-mail:* guy.aubert@ext.univ-poitiers.fr (office).

AUBERT, Pierre; Swiss politician and lawyer; b. 3 March 1927, La Chaux-de-Fonds; s. of the late Alfred Aubert and Henriette Erni Aubert; m. Anne-Lise Borel 1953; one s. one d.; ed Univ. of Neuchatel; mem. of local Ass., La Chaux-de-Fonds 1960–68, Pres. 1967–68; mem. Legis. Ass. of Canton of Neuchâtel 1961–75, Pres. 1969–70; Labour mem. Council of States 1971–77; mem. Fed. Council (Govt) 1978–87, Vice-Pres. Jan.–Dec. 1982; Pres. of Switzerland Jan.–Dec. 1983, Jan.–Dec. 1987; Head of Fed. Foreign Affairs Dept 1978–87. *Leisure interests:* camping, boxing, skiing, cycling, theatre, watches.

AUBOUIN, Jean Armand, DèsSc; French academic; b. 5 May 1928, Evreux; s. of Jean Aubouin and Yvonne Joubin; m. Françoise Delpouget 1953; two d.; ed Lycées Buffon and St-Louis, Ecole Normale Supérieure (St-Cloud) and Univ. of Paris; Lecturer, Univ. of Paris 1952–61, Prof. 1961–90 (Univ. Pierre et Marie Curie from 1969), Emer. Prof.; mem. Acad. of Sciences, Inst. of France 1981–, Vice-Pres. 1986–88, Pres. 1989–90; mem. Univ. Consultative Cttee 1967–73, Nat. Cttee CNRS 1976–84; Pres. Soc. Géologique de France 1976, Cttee de Télédétection du CNES (Centre National d'Etudes spatiales) 1974–78, 23rd Int. Geological Congress 1980, Cttee Geological Map of the World 1984–92, Scientific Advisory Bds of GPF (Géologie profonde de la France) program 1982–86, Bureau de Recherches Géologiques et Minières 1982–91, Inst. Français de Recherche pour l'Exploitation de la Mer 1985–90; mem. Scientific Advisory Bds Planning Cttee Int. Programme of Ocean Drilling 1980–84, Fondation de France 1984–87 Inst. Français du Pétrole 1985–91;,; mem. Bd of Dirs Office de Recherche Scientifique d'Outre-mer 1984–88, Bureau de Recherche Géologique et Minières 1989–92, Inst. Océanographique, Paris and Monaco 1994– (Pres. Comité Perfectionnement 1992–); mem. Conseil Supérieur Recherche et Technologie 1983–87; Pres. French Cttee of Int. Decade for the Reduction of Natural Disasters 1990–93; mem. Advisory Bd Parc Naturel du Verdun 1996–2000; f. and mem. Acad. des Technologies 2000–; Admin. Chancellery Acad. de Nice 1996–, Acad. de Paris 2000–04; Foreign mem. Accad. dei Lincei, Italy 1974–, USSR (now Russia) Acad. of Sciences 1976–, Acad. of Athens, Greece 1980–, Academia Europaea 1988–, Acad. of Zagreb, Croatia 1990–, Acad. Royale Sciences, Arts et Lettres de Belgique 1994–, Deutsche Akad. der Naturforscher Leopoldina 1995–, Acad. de la Latinité 2000–; Hon. mem. Geological Soc. of London 1976–, Soc. Physique Histoire Naturelle (Geneva) 1990–, Geological Soc. of Greece 2001–; Hon. Fellow, Geological Soc. of America 1980–; Chevalier, Ordre des Palmes académiques 1965, Ordre Nat. du Mérite 1981, Légion d'honneur 1989; Dr hc (Athens) 1992; CNRS Medal 1959, Prix Viquesnel de la Soc. Géologique de France 1962, Prix Charles Jacob Acad. des Sciences 1976, Museo de la Plata Medal 1977, Argentina, Dumont Medal, Soc. Géologique de Belgique 1977, Ville de Paris Medal 1980, Gaudry Prize, Soc. Géologique de France 1990, Gold Medal, Acad. Royale des Sciences de Belgique 1990. *Publications:* Géologie de la Grèce septentrionale 1959, Geosynclines 1965, Manuel de Cartographie (co-ed.) 1970, Précis de Géologie (co-ed., four vols) 1968–79, approx. 400 scientific articles. *Leisure interests:* reading, mountain walking and swimming at sea. *Address:* Académie des technologies, Grand Palais des Champs Elysées, Porte C, Avenue Franklin D. Roosevelt, 75008 Paris, France (office). *Telephone:* 1-53-85-44-44 (office); (4) 93-86-03-76 (home). *Fax:* 1-53-85-44-45; (4) 93-86-03-76 (home). *E-mail:* jean.aubouin@academie-technologies.fr (office).

AUBRY, Martine Louise Marie; French politician; *First Secretary, Socialist Party;* b. 8 Aug. 1950, Paris; d. of Jacques Delors (q.v.) and Marie Lephaille; m. 1st Xavier Aubry; one d.; m. 2nd Jean Louis Brochon 2004; ed Inst. Saint-Pierre-Fourier, Lycée Paul-Valéry, Faculté de Droit, Paris, Inst. des Sciences Sociales du Travail, Inst. d'Etudes Politiques, Paris and Ecole Nat. d'Admin; Ministry of Labour 1975–79; Instructor, Ecole Nat. d'Admin 1978; Dir of preparations for econ. competition for admin. of Univ. Paris-Dauphine 1978; civil admin., Conseil d'Etat 1980–81; Deputy Dir Pvt. Office of Minister of Labour 1981; special assignment for Minister of Social Affairs and Nat. Solidarity 1983–84; Dir of Labour Relations, Ministry of Labour 1984–87; Maître des Requêtes, Conseil d'Etat 1987; Deputy Dir-Gen. Pechiney 1989–91; Minister of Labour, Employment and Professional Training 1991–93; Pres. FACE 1993–97; First Asst Mayor of Lille 1995–2001, Mayor 2001–; Vice-Pres. Lille Urban Council 1995–; mem. Nat. Ass. for Nord region (Socialist Party) 1997–2002; Minister of Employment and Social Affairs 1997–2000; Nat. Sec. Socialist Party 2000–05, First Sec. 2008–; joined Reformer (think tank) 2000; mem. club Le Siècle; Int. Press Prize, Le Trombinoscope 1999. *Publications include:* Le Choix d'Agir 1994, Petit dictionnaire pour lutter contre l'extrême droite (jtly) 1995, Il est grand temps... 1997, C'est quoi la solidarité? 2002, Muscler sa conscience du bonheur en trente jours 2004, Quel projet pour la gauche? 2004, Une vision pour espérer, une volonté pour transformer 2004, Agir contre les discriminations 2006. *Leisure interests:* tennis, skiing. *Address:* Reformer, 22 bis rue Gabriel Péri, 91300 Massy; Parti Socialiste, 10 rue de Solférino, 75333 Paris Cédex 07 (office); Mairie, B.P. 667, 59033 Lille Cédex France. *Telephone:* 1-40-63-68-59 (Reformer); 1-45-56-77-00 (office). *Fax:* 1-47-05-15-78 (office). *E-mail:* reformer@reformer.fr; infosp@parti-socialiste.fr (office). *Website:* www.parti-socialiste.fr (office); www.reformer.fr.

AUCHINCLOSS, Louis Stanton, LLB, DLitt; American author and lawyer; b. 27 Sept. 1917; s. of Joseph Howland Auchincloss and Priscilla Auchincloss (née Stanton); m. Adele Lawrence 1957; three s.; ed Groton School, Yale Univ. and Univ. of Virginia; admitted to New York Bar 1941, Assoc. Sullivan and Cromwell 1941–51, Hawkins, Delafield and Wood, New York 1954–58, Pnr 1958–86; Lt, USN 1941–45; Pres. American Acad. of Arts and Letters 1997–2000; Pres. Museum of the City of New York; mem. Nat. Inst. of Arts and Letters; Living Landmark, New York Landmarks Conservancy 2000, Nat. Medal of Arts Award 2005. *Publications:* The Indifferent Children 1947, The Injustice Collectors 1950, Sybil 1952, A Law for the Lion 1953, The Romantic Egoists 1954, The Great World and Timothy Colt 1956, Venus in Sparta 1958, Pursuit of the Prodigal 1959, House of Five Talents 1960, Reflections of a Jacobite 1961, Portrait in Brownstone 1962, Powers of Attorney 1963, The Rector of Justin 1964, Pioneers and Caretakers 1965, The Embezzler 1966, Tales of Manhattan 1967, A World of Profit 1969, Motiveless Malignity 1969, Edith Wharton: A Woman in Her Time 1971, I Come as a Thief 1972, Richelieu 1972, The Partners 1974, A Winter's Capital 1974, Reading Henry James 1975, The Winthrop Covenant 1976, The Dark Lady 1977, The Country Cousin 1978, Persons of Consequence 1979, Life, Law and Letters 1979, The House of the Prophet 1980, The Cat and the King 1981, Watchfires 1982, Exit Lady Masham 1983, The Book Class 1984, Honorable Men 1985, Diary of a Yuppie 1986, Skinny Island 1987, The Golden Calves 1988, Fellow Passengers 1989, The Vanderbilt Era 1989, J. P. Morgan 1990, The Lady of Situations 1991, False Gods 1992, Three Lives 1993, Tales of Yesteryear 1994, Collected Stories 1994, The Style's the Man 1994, The Education of Oscar Fairfax 1995, The Man Behind the Book 1996, La Gloire 1996, The Atonement 1997, Woodrow Wilson 2000, The Scarlet Letters 2003, East Side Story 2004; contributions to New York Review of Books, New Criterion. *Address:* 1111 Park Avenue, New York, NY 10028, USA (home).

AUCOTT, George William, BS; American business executive; b. 24 Aug. 1934, Philadelphia; s. of George William Aucott and Clara Anna Aucott (née Nagel); m. Ruth Tonetta Heller 1956; one s. two d.; ed Ursinus Coll., Collegeville, Pa and Harvard Univ.; served in US army 1957–60; joined Firestone Tire & Rubber Co. 1956, Pres. Firestone Industrial Products Co. 1978, Firestone Canada Inc. 1978–80, Vice-Pres. Mfg parent co., Akron, Ohio 1980; Pres. and COO Firestone Int. 1982–91, Pres., COO World Tire Group 1988, then Chair. Firestone (now retd), mem. Bd of Dirs and Exec. Vice-Pres. of Corpn 1986; fmr Chair. and CEO Motor Coach Industries; mem. Bd Dirs Akron United Way 1968–73; Pres. and Dir Akron YMCA 1969–73; mem. Bd of Dirs Rubber Mfrs Asscn, Rubber Asscn.

AUDIBET, Marc; French fashion designer; b. 1955, Boulogne-sur-Seine; celebrated in fashion world for his research into stretch fabrics and their use in garments without hooks, eyes, buttons or zippers, expertise acquired while working as an assistant to Emanuel Ungaro in 1972, and then as designer for Pierre Balmain, Madame Gres and Nino Cerruti; presented first collection in 1975; took over design at house of Christian Aujard 1977–81; designed for Basile and Laure Biagiotti 1981–84; continued with own label until 1988 when he designed for Parallel; collaborated with Azzedine Alaia to work closely with Du Pont on project to mix Lycra with fabrics such as satin and silk 1984, became textile adviser to Du Pont and helped create and launch single and two-way stretch fabrics made from Du Pont's Lycra; has continued to design and create seamless garments made from Lycra mixed with a wide range of other fabrics such as cotton, silk, linen and wool; also designed for Hermes 1990s; designed nine collections for Prada 1990–96; worked as consultant for Italian house of Trussardi; designer for Salvatore Ferragamo 2000–02; Artistic Adviser to Vionnet 2007–08. *Address:* Vionnet, 21 place Vendôme, 75001 Paris, France (office). *Telephone:* 1-44-77-93-60 (Press enquiries) (office). *Fax:* 1-44-77-93-70 (Press enquiries) (office).

AUDRAIN, Paul André Marie; French business executive; b. 17 May 1945, Chambéry, Savoie; s. of Jean Audrain and Margueritte Gubian; m. Danièle Pons 1967; two s.; ed Lycée d'Etat de Chambéry, Lycée du Parc Lyon, Ecole Supérieure des Sciences Economiques et Commerciales, Paris; Engineer, IBM France 1969–70; Financial and Admin. Dir Aiglon, Angers 1970–74; Financial Dir Christian Dior 1974–79, then Sec. Gen., Financial and Admin. Dir 1979–84, Chair. and CEO 1984–85, Pres. 1985–86; Int. Dir Financière Agache 1986–87; Chair. and CEO Christian Lacroix 1987–88, Pierre Balmain 1988–89; CEO Société Crillon 1990–93, Int. Consulting & Licensing; Chevalier Ordre nat. du Mérite 1985. *Address:* 27 rue du Phare, Port Navalo, 56 640 Arzon (home); 20 Boulevard du Montparnasse, 75015 Paris, France. *Telephone:* 1-44-49-98-70 (office); (2) 97-53-85-45 (home). *E-mail:* polaudrain@wanadoo.fr (home).

AUDRAN, Stéphane (see Dacheville, Colette).

AUERBACH, Frank Helmuth; British (b. German) artist; b. 29 April 1931, Berlin; s. of Max Auerbach and Charlotte Auerbach; m. Julia Wolstenholme 1958; one s.; ed St Martin's School of Art, London, Royal Coll. of Art; works in public collections in UK, Australia, Brazil, USA, Mexico, Israel, SA, Canada; Silver Medal for Painting, Royal Coll. of Art. *Address:* c/o Marlborough Fine Art, 6 Albemarle Street, London, W1S 4BY, England. *Telephone:* (20) 7629-5161.

AUGUST, Bille; Danish film director; b. 9 Nov. 1948; ed Christer Stroholm School of Photography, Stockholm, Danish Film School; worked as camera-man on Homewards at Night, Manrape, The Grass is Singing, Love, before making first feature film 1978; Hans Christian Andersen Prize 2003. *Television includes:* The World is So Big, So Big, May, Three Days with Magnus, Buster's World (series), episode of The Young Indiana Jones, Detaljer. *Feature films:* In My Life 1978, Zappa 1983, Twist and Shout 1986, Pelle the Conqueror 1989 (Oscar for Best Foreign Film, Palme d'Or, Cannes Film Festival, Golden Ram, Stockholm, Golden Globe, LA), The Best Intentions 1991, The House of the Spirits, Smilla's Feeling for Snow, A Song for Martin 2001, Return to Sender 2004, Goodbye Bafana 2007.

AUGUSTINE, Norman Ralph, BSc, MSc, FIEEE; American aerospace indus-try executive; b. 27 July 1935, Denver, Colo; s. of Ralph Harvey Augustine and Freda Irene Augustine (née Immenga); m. Margareta Engman 1962; two c.; ed Princeton Univ.; Research Asst, Princeton Univ. 1957–58; Program Man., Chief Engineer Douglas Aircraft Co. Inc., Santa Monica, Calif. 1958–65; Asst Dir of Defense Research and Eng, Office of US Sec. for Defense, Washington, DC 1965–70; Vice-Pres. Advanced Systems, Missiles and Space Co., LTV Aerospace Corpn, Dallas 1970–73; Asst Sec. of the Army, The Pentagon, Washington 1965–70, Under-Sec. 1973–75; Vice-Pres. Operations, Martin Marietta Aerospace Corpn, Bethesda, Md 1977–82, Pres. Martin Marietta Denver Aerospace Co. 1982–85, Sr Vice-Pres. Information Systems 1985, Pres. COO 1986–87, Vice-Chair. and CEO 1987–88, Chair. and CEO 1988–95; Pres. Lockheed Martin 1995–96, Pres. CEO 1996–97, Chair. –1997, Chair. Exec. Cttee, Bd of Dirs 1997–98; mem. Bd of Dirs Phillips Petroleum Co. (now ConocoPhillips), Procter & Gamble Co., Black and Decker Corpn; fmr mem. Bd of Dirs Riggs Nat. Bank Corpn; mem. NATO Group of Experts on Air Defence 1966–70, NASA Research and Tech. Advisory Council 1973–75; Chair. NASA Space Systems and Tech. Advisory Bd 1985–89; fmr Chair. Nat. Acad. of Eng (NAE) Council, now Chair. Nat. Acads Philanthropy Council; Chair. American Red Cross 1992–2001; Prof. Princeton Univ. 1997–; Fellow AIAA, IEEE, American Acad. of Arts and Sciences, Royal Aeronautical Soc., American Astronautical Soc.; mem. Int. Acad. of Astronautics, New York Acad. of Sciences, Nat. Acad. of Eng; fmr Pres. Boy Scouts of America; 18 hon. degrees including Hon. DEng (Princeton) 2007; Distinguished Service Medal, Dept of Defense five times, Goddard Medal, AIAA 1988, Nat. Eng Award, American Asscn of Eng Socs 1991, Nat. Medal of Tech. 1997, AAAS Philip Hauge Abelson Prize 2005, Public Welfare Medal, Nat. Acad. of Sciences 2006, Harold W. McGraw, Jr. Prize in Educ. 2006, Bower Award for Business Leadership 2007. *Publications:* Augustine's Laws, The Defense Revolution (co-author) 1990, Augustine's Travels 1997, Shakespeare in Charge: The Bard's Guide to Leading and Succeeding on the Business Stage (with K. Adelman) 2001. *Address:* c/o Princeton University, C232 Engineering Quadrangle, Princeton, NJ, 08544-5263, USA.

AUGUSZTINOVICS, Maria, PhD, DEconSci; Hungarian economist and academic; *Consultant, Institute of Economics, Hungarian Academy of Sci-ences;* b. 12 Feb. 1930, Budapest; m. Gabor Fekecs; one s.; ed Budapest Univ. of Econs; at Ministry of Finance 1955–61; at Nat. Planning Bureau 1961–84; Sr Research Adviser, Inst. of Econs, Hungarian Acad. of Sciences 1984–2000 (retd), Consultant 2000–; Prof. of Econs, Budapest Univ. of Econs (now Corvinus Univ.) 1986, now Hon. Prof.; Visiting Prof., Univ. of Michigan, USA 1969; lecturing tour at several univs in India and Bangladesh 1975; Visiting Research Fellow, Int. Inst. for Applied Systems Analysis, Laxenburg, Austria 1982; Visiting Prof., Wesleyan Univ., Conn., USA 1988, La Trobe Univ., Melbourne, Australia 1993; Sec. Cttee of Econs, Hungarian Acad. of Sciences 1958–78, Vice-Chair. 1993–; mem. UN Cttee for Devt Policy (Vice-Chair.) 1978–84, Council of Habilitations, Budapest Univ. of Econs 1994–, Council of European Soc. for Population Econs 1996–; Vice-Chair. Hungarian Asscn of Economists 1995–; mem. Editorial Bd Journal of Policy Modeling, Acta Oeconomica, Közgazdasági Szemle; Fellow, Econometric Soc. 1976–. *Publica-tions:* numerous articles on macroeconomic aspects and models of the human life-cycle (over-lapping generations, life-cycle theory, human capital), eco-nomic demography, pension econs. *Address:* Institute of Economics, Hungar-ian Academy of Sciences, Budaörsi út 45 1112 Budapest, Hungary (office). *Telephone:* (1) 816-4253 (office); (23) 344-226 (home). *Fax:* (1) 816-3136 (office); (23) 344-226 (home). *E-mail:* auguszti@econ.core.hu (office). *Website:* econ .core.hu/english/inst/auguszti.html (office).

AUKIN, David, BA, FRSA; British theatre, film and television producer; b. 12 Feb. 1942, Harrow; s. of Charles Aukin and Regina Aukin; m. Nancy Meckler 1969; two s.; ed St Paul's School, London and St Edmund Hall, Oxford; co-founder Foco Novo and Jt Stock Theatre cos and admin. producer for various fringe theatre groups 1970–75; Admin. Dir Hampstead Theatre 1975–79, Dir 1979–84; Dir Leicester Haymarket Theatre 1984–86; Exec. Dir Royal Nat. Theatre of Great Britain 1986–90; Pres. Soc. of West End Theatres 1988–90; Head of Drama, Channel 4 TV 1990–97, Head of Film 1997–98; Jt Chief Exec. HAL Films 1998–2000; Producer and Man. Dir David Aukin Productions Ltd 2001–. *Films produced include:* Mansfield Park 1998, Elephant Juice 1999, About Adam 2000, The Hamburg Cell 2004, Mrs. Henderson Presents 2005. *Address:* c/o Act Productions Ltd, 20–22 Stukeley Street, London WC2B 5LR, England (office). *Website:* actproductions.co.uk (office).

AULENTI, Gae; Italian architect and designer; b. 4 Dec. 1927, Palazzolo dello Stella, Udine; d. of Aldo Aulenti and Virginia Gioia; m. (divorced); one d.; ed Milan Polytechnic; mem. editorial staff, Casabella-Continuità review 1955–65; Asst, Venice Faculty of Architecture 1960–62, Milan Faculty of Architecture 1964–67; own architecture, exhbn design, interior design, industrial design, stage design practice, Milan 1956–; solo exhbn, Padiglione d'Arte Contemporanea (PAC), Milan 1979; group exhbn Museum of Modern Art, New York 1972; mem. Jury The Grand Egyptian Museum int. architec-tural competition Giza-Cairo 2002; Hon. mem. American Soc. of Interior Designers 1967; Hon. Fellow, American Inst. of Architects 1990; Chevalier de la Légion d'honneur 1987; Cavaliere di Gran Croce, Rome 1995; Kt, Grand Cross, Order of Merit of Italian Repub. 1995; Hon. DFA (RI School of Design, USA) 2001; Int. Prize for Italian Pavilion, Milan Triennale 1964, Praemium Imperiale for Architecture, Japan Art Asscn, Tokyo 1991. *Major recent works:* conversion of Gare d'Orsay into museum, Paris 1980–86; new interior design of Musée Nat. d'Art Moderne, Centre Georges Pompidou, Paris 1982–85; restoration of Palazzo Grassi, Venice 1986; conversion of Palau Nacional into Museu Nacional d'Art de Catalunya, Barcelona 1987–2004; new access ramp to S. Maria Novella railway station, Florence 1990; Italian Pavilion at EXPO '92, Seville 1992; Città degli Studi, Biella 1987–; conversion of San Francisco Old Main Library into Asian Art Museum 1996–2003; new HQ for Nat. Film Hall, Milan 1999; renovation of fmr Papal Stables at Quirinale as temp. exhbn gallery, Rome 1999; redevelopment of Piazza Cadorna, Milan 2000; Museo and Dante underground stations and redesign of Piazza Cavour and Piazza Dante, Naples 1999–; new lakeside in Meina-Novara 2001–; redevelopment of Palavela Turin to host figure skating and short track competitions at 2006 Olympic Winter Games. *Exhibition installations:* Futurism 1986, Balthus 2001–02 and other exhbns at Palazzo Grassi, Venice, The Italian Metamor-phosis 1943–1968, Guggenheim Museum, New York 1994; 1950–2000: Theater of Italian Creativity New York 2003; new installation at Estensi Castle Ferrara 2004–; Arti & Architettura 1900–2000, Palazzo Ducale, Genova 2004–2005. *Industrial design:* furniture, lamps, objects for Kartell, Knoll, Fontana Arte, Louis Vuitton, Tecno, Venini, Zanotta etc. *Publications:* Gae Aulenti (by Margherita Petranzan) 2002 (Italy), 2003 (USA). *Leisure interests:* collecting paintings and sculptures. *Address:* 4 piazza San Marco, 20121 Milan, Italy (office). *Telephone:* (2) 8692613 (office). *Fax:* (2) 874125 (office). *E-mail:* aulenti@tin.it (office).

AULETTA, Mino, LLD; Italian lawyer; *President, Court of Arbitration for Sport;* b. Milan; currently attorney, Milan High Court and Court of Appeal; Legal Counsel, also Int. Athletic Foundation, Monaco, Yacht Club of Monaco; fmr mem. Legal Comm., Int. Univ. Sports Fed., Monaco; Acting Pres. Court of Arbitration for Sport 2007–08, Pres. 2008–. *Address:* Court of Arbitration for Sport, Château de Béthusy, Avenue de Beaumont 2, 1012 Lausanne, Switzerland (office). *Telephone:* (21) 613-50-00 (office). *Fax:* (21) 613-50-01 (office). *E-mail:* info@tas-cas.org (office). *Website:* www.tas-cas.org (office).

AULETTA ARMENISE, Giampiero, BEcons; Italian banking executive; *CEO, Unione di Banche Italiane SpA;* b. 1957, Rome; m.; three c.; ed Univ. of Rome, La Sapienza; with Bonifiche Siele Finanziaria Group 1978–98; Head of Analyses, Planning and Investments Dept, then Head of Financial Control and Risk Monitoring Dept, Banco Ambrosiano Veneto 1995–98, Man. Planning, Investments and Financial Control Sector, Banca Intesa 1998–2002; CEO Banca Popolare Commercio e Industria 2002–03, Banche Popolari Unite Group 2003–07, Unione di Banche Italiane SpA 2007–, mem. Bd of Dirs Banca Popolare di Bergamo SpA, Banca Popolare Commercio e Industria SpA, Banca Popolare di Ancona SpA, Banca Carime SpA, Centrobanca SpA, Banco di Brescia SpA. *Address:* Unione di Banche Italiane SpA, Piazza Vittorio Veneto 8, 24122 Bergamo, Italy (office). *Telephone:* (035) 392111 (office). *Website:* www.ubibanca.it (office).

AUMANN, Robert J., BS, SM, PhD; Israeli mathematician, economist and academic; *Professor Emeritus, The Hebrew University;* b. 8 June 1930, Frankfurt am Main, Germany; s. of Siegmund and Miriam Aumann (née Landau); m.; five c.; ed City Coll. of NY and MIT, USA; Instructor, Dept of Math., Hebrew Univ. of Jerusalem 1956–58, Lecturer 1958–61, Sr Lecturer 1961–64, Assoc. Prof. 1964–68, Prof. 1968–2001, Prof. Emer. 2001–, Fellow, Inst. for Advanced Studies 1979–80, mem. Center for the Study of Rationality 1991–; Research Assoc., Princeton Univ. 1960–61; Visiting Prof., Yale Univ. 1964–65, Univ. of Calif., Berkeley 1971, 1985–86, Univ. Catholique de Louvain 1972, 1978, 1984, Stanford Univ. 1975–76, 1980–81, NY Univ. 1997; External Prof. (part-time), Tel Aviv Univ. 1969–93; Prof. (part-time), Center for Game Theory, Econs Dept, State Univ. of NY (SUNY), Stony Brook 1986–89, 1991–2007; Visiting Scholar, Cowles Foundation for Research in Econs, Yale Univ. 1989; Nemmers Prof. of Econs, Northwestern Univ. 1999–2000; Assoc. Ed. Journal of Econ. Theory 1974–79, Econometrica 1975–78, Journal of the European Math. Soc. 2000–; mem. Editorial Bd Int. Journal of Game Theory 1971–, Journal of Math. Econs 1974–, SIAM Journal on Applied Math. 1976–80, Games and Econ. Behavior 1989–; Pres. Israel Math. Union 1990–92, Game Theory Soc. 1998–2003; mem. Inst. for Math., Univ. of Minn. 1984, Math. Sciences Research Inst., Berkeley 1985–86, Fellow Econometric Soc. 1966–, mem. Council 1977–82, Exec. Cttee 1982–85; mem. NAS 1985, Israel Acad. of Sciences and Humanities 1989; Corresp. Fellow, British Acad. 1995; Foreign Hon. mem., American Acad. of Arts and Sciences 1974, Hon. mem. American Econ. Asscn 1993–; Dr hc (Univ. of Bonn) 1988, (Univ. Catholique de Louvain) 1989, (Univ. of Chicago) 1992, (City Univ. of New York) 2005, Bar Ilan Univ.) 2005; Israel Prize in Econs 1994, Lanchester Prize in Operations Research 1995, Erwin Plein Nemmers Prize in Econs, Northwestern Univ. 1998, EMET Prize in Econs, Prime Minister of Israel 2002, Von Neumann Prize in Operations Research 2005, Sveriges Riksbank Prize in Econ. Sciences in Memory of Alfred Nobel 2005. *Publications:* Values of Non-atomic Games (with L. S. Shapley) 1974, Repeated Games with

Incomplete Information (with M. Maschler) 1995; numerous articles in professional journals and conf. papers on game theory, econ. theory and theory of choice. *Leisure interests:* skiing, hiking, cooking, Talmud study. *Address:* Center for Rationality, The Hebrew University, 91904 Jerusalem, Israel (office). *Telephone:* (2) 6586254 (office). *Fax:* (2) 6513681 (office). *E-mail:* raumann@math.huji.ac.il (office). *Website:* www.ma.huji.ac.il/raumann (office); www.ratio.huji.ac.il (office).

AUMONT, Jacques; French author and professor of film aesthetics; *Director of Studies, École des hautes études en sciences sociales;* b. 1942, Avignon; m. Lyang Kim; two c.; ed École polytechnique, École nationale supérieure des télécommunications; began career as engineer, ORTF (nat. broadcasting co.) 1965–70; film reviewer, Les Cahiers du cinéma 1967–74; Dir Editions de l'Etoile 1970–74; Lecturer in Cinema, Univ. of Paris III 1970–, later Prof. of Film Aesthetics; Dir of Studies, École des hautes études en sciences socials (EHESS) 1995–; mem. of various film festival juries and selection cttees; visiting lecturer at numerous foreign establishments, including Berkeley, Madison, Iowa City, Nijmegen, Lisbon; Chevalier des Palmes académiques. *Publications include:* Montage Eisenstein 1979, Esthétique du film (co-author) 1983, L'analyse des films (co-author) 1988, L'oeil interminable 1989, L'image 1990, Du visage au cinéma 1992, À quoi pensent les films 1997, De l'ésthetique au présent 1998, Dictionnaire critique et théorique du cinéma (co-author) 2001, Ingmar Bergman 2003, Matière d'images 2005; over 200 reviews in periodicals. *Leisure interests:* piano/chamber music. *Address:* Université Paris-3, 13 rue Santeuil, 75005 Paris, France (office). *Telephone:* 1-45-87-42-38 (office). *Fax:* 1-45-87-48-94 (office). *E-mail:* aumont@ehess.fr (office). *Website:* www.ehess.fr (office).

AUNG SAN SUU KYI, BA; Myanma politician; b. 19 June 1945, Rangoon; d. of the late Gen. Aung San and of Khin Kyi; m. Michael Aris 1972 (died 1999); two s.; ed St Francis Convent, Methodist English High School, Lady Shri Ram Coll., Delhi Univ., St Hugh's Coll., Oxford; Asst Sec. Advisory Cttee on Admin. and Budgetary Questions UN Secr., New York 1969–71; Resident Officer, Ministry of Foreign Affairs, Bhutan 1972; Visiting Scholar Centre for SE Asian Studies, Kyoto Univ., Japan 1985–86; Fellow, Indian Inst. of Advanced Studies 1987; Co-Founder, Gen. Sec. Nat. League for Democracy 1988 (expelled from party), reinstated as Gen. Sec. Oct. 1995; returned from UK 1988, under house arrest 1989–95, house arrest lifted July 1995, placed under de facto house arrest Sept. 2000, released unconditionally May 2002, arrested following Depayin massacre 30 May 2003, held in secret detention for over three months before being returned to house arrest, house arrest extended by one year 25 May 2007, mil. junta extended her house arrest another year 27 May 2008; Hon. mem. Bd Council Int. Inst. for Democracy and Electoral Assistance (IDEA) 2003; numerous hon. degrees; Rafto Prize 1990, Sakharov Prize 1990, European Parl. Human Rights Prize 1991, Nobel Peace Prize 1991, Simón Bolívar Prize 1992, Liberal Int. Prize for Freedom 1995, Jawaharlal Nehru Award for Int. Understanding 1995, Freedom Award of Int. Rescue Cttee 1995, Free Spirit Prize, Freedom Forum USA 2003, US Congressional Gold Medal 2008, ranked by Forbes magazine amongst 100 Most Powerful Women (45th) 2004, (15th) 2005, (47th) 2006, (71st) 2007, (38th) 2008. *Publications:* Aung San 1984, Burma and India: Some Aspects of Colonial Life Under Colonialism 1990, Freedom from Fear 1991, Towards a True Refuge 1993, Freedom from Fear and Other Writings 1995. *Address:* c/o National League for Democracy, 97B West Shwegondine Road, Bahan Township, Yangon, Myanmar.

AURA, Matti Ilmari, LLM; Finnish politician and business executive; b. 18 June 1943, Helsinki; s. of Teuvo Ensio Aura and Kielo Kaino Kivekäs; m. Marja H. Hiippala 1967; two s.; ed Munkkiniemi High School and Univ. of Helsinki; lawyer, Finnish Export Credit Ltd 1968–69, Confed. of Finnish Industries 1970–71; Man. Dir Cen. Bd of Finnish Wholesale and Retail Assen 1972–85; Gen. Man. Cen. Chamber of Commerce of Finland 1986; apptd Minister of Transport and Communications 1997–99. *Address:* Louhentie 1 H 25, 02130 Espoo, Finland (home). *Telephone:* (358) 465610 (home).

AURAKZAI, Lt-Gen. Ali Mohammad Jan; Pakistani army officer (retd) and government administrator; b. 1 Dec. 1947; s. of Haji Khial Din and Naze Gul Aurakzai; m. Mujahida Khanum; three s. one d.; ed Peshawar Univ., Balochistan Univ.; fmr Commdr 11th Corps, Peshawar; fmr Adjutant-Gen. of Gen. HQ; Gov. of North-West Frontier Prov. 2006–08 (resgnd); Sitara-e-Basalat 1999, Hilal-e-Imtiaz (Mil.) 2000, Hilal-e-Imtiaz (Civil) 2004. *Leisure interests:* music, hunting. *Address:* House #2, Street 2, Sector 2, DHA Phase 1, Morgah, Islamabad, Pakistan (home). *Telephone:* (51) 5788298 (home). *E-mail:* ali.aurakzai@hotmail.com (office).

AURBACH, Gerhard, Dr rer. pol; German administrative official; b. 19 July 1936, Neuburg/Donau; m. Jennifer Thompson; two d.; ed Univ. of Munich; Asst, Univ. of Munich; fmr consultant, IFO Inst. (Econ. Research Inst.) Munich, Fed. Ministry of Transport 1960–63; Admin. European Conf. of Ministers of Transport (ECMT) 1963, Prin. Admin. 1970, Head, Transport Policy Div. 1975, Deputy Sec.-Gen. 1986, apptd Sec.-Gen. ECMT 1992. *Publications:* articles on transport econs and policy. *Leisure interests:* history, classical music, skiing, tennis. *Address:* c/o European Conference of Ministers of Transport, 2 rue André Pascal, 75116 Paris Cedex 16, France.

AUROUX, Jean; French politician; b. 19 Sept. 1942, Thizy, Rhône; s. of Louis Auroux and Jeanne Auroux (née Masson); m. Lucienne Sabadie 1967; one s. one d.; ed Lycée Jean Puy, Roanne, Université Claude Bernard de Lyon; City Councillor, Roanne 1976–88, Mayor 1977–2001; mem., then Vice-Pres. Regional Ass. of Rhône-Alpes 1977–81; Pres. Dist de l'Agglomération Roannaise (now Communauté d'Agglomération du Grand Roanne) 1991–2001; Parti Socialiste Nat. Del. for Housing 1978; mem. Nat. Ass. 1978–81, 1986–88, mem. Finance Cttee; mem. Production and Exchange Cttee; Minister of Labour 1981–82, Minister Del. attached to Social Affairs Ministry, in charge of Labour Affairs 1982–83, Sec. of State at Ministry of Industry and Research in Charge of Energy 1983–84, at Ministry of Urban Planning, Housing and Transport 1984–85, Minister 1985–86; Pres. Socialist Group in Nat. Ass. 1990–93; Pres. Fédération des Maires des Villes Moyennes 1988–2001; mem. Conseil Nat. des Villes, Comité de Décentralisation; Chevalier Légion d'honneur; Officier Ordre nat. du Mérite. *Publication:* Géographie économique à usage scolaire, Rapport sur les nouveaux droits des travailleurs. *Address:* Parti Socialiste, 10 rue de Solférino, 75007 Paris (office); c/o Fédération des Villes Moyennes, 42 boulevard Raspail, 75007 Paris, France. *Telephone:* (4) 77-23-20-13 (office).

AUSHEV, Lt-Gen. Ruslan Sultanovich; Russian/Ingush politician; b. 29 Oct. 1954, Volodarskoye, Kokchetav Region, USSR (now Kazakhstan); s. of Sultan Aushev and Tamara Aushev; m. Aza Ausheva 1983; two s. two d.; ed Ordzhonikidze Gen. Troops School, M. Frunze Mil. Acad.; Commdr motorized infantry co., then platoon 1975–80; Chief of HQ, then Commdr motorized Bn in Afghanistan 1980–82; Chief of Regt HQ in Afghanistan 1985–87; Commdr motorized infantry regt, then Deputy Commdr motorized infantry div. Far East Command 1987–91; at Council of Heads of Govts of CIS countries 1991–92; USSR People's Deputy 1989–91; Head of Admin in newly formed Ingush Repub. Nov.–Dec. 1992; Pres. Repub. of Ingushetiya 1993–2001 (resgnd); mem. Fed. Council of Russia 1993–2000, Rep. of Ingushetiya to Fed. Council 2002–03; fmr Chair. Political Council, Rossiiskaya Partiya Mira (Russian Party of Peace); Hero of Soviet Union (Gold Star). *Leisure interest:* football.

AUST, Stefan; German journalist and writer; *Editor, Der Spiegel;* b. 1 July 1946, Stade; m. Ulrike Meinhof; Ed. Concrete magazine 1966–69; staff mem. NDR TV 1970–72; journalist Panorama (political magazine) 1972–86; Chief Ed. Der Spiegel TV 1988–94, Ed.-in-Chief Der Spiegel 1994–; Man. Dir. Der Spiegel TV GmbH 1995–; fmr. TV host with talkshow Talk in the Tower, currently Host Spiegel-TV; Goldenen Kamera 2005. *Publications include:* The Baader Meinhof Complex 1985, Stammheim (film script) 1986, Mauss: A German Agent 1988, The Pirate 1990. *Address:* Der Spiegel, Brandstwiete 19/ Ost-West-Strasse 23, 20457 Hamburg, Germany (office). *Telephone:* (40) 30070. *Fax:* (40) 30072247. *E-mail:* spiegel@spiegel.de (office). *Website:* www .spiegel.de (office).

AUSTEN, K(arl) Frank, MD; American professor of medicine; *Astra Zeneca Professor of Respiratory and Inflammatory Diseases, Department of Medicine, Brigham and Women's Hospital;* b. 14 March 1928, Akron, Ohio; s. of Karl Arnstein and Bertle J. Arnstein; m. Jocelyn Chapman 1959; two s. two d.; ed Amherst Coll. and Harvard Medical School; Intern in Medicine, Mass. Gen. Hosp. 1954–55, Asst Resident 1955–56, Sr Resident 1958–59, Chief Resident 1961–62, Asst in Medicine 1962–63, Asst Physician 1963–66; Capt., US Army Medical Corps, Walter Reed Army Inst. of Research 1956–58; U.S.P.H.S. Postdoctoral Research Fellow, Nat. Inst. for Medical Research, Mill Hill, London, UK 1959–61; Physician-in-Chief, Robert B. Brigham Hosp. Boston 1966–80; Physician, Peter Bent Brigham Hosp. Boston 1966–80; Chair. Dept Rheumatology and Immunology, Brigham and Women's Hosp., Boston 1980–95, Dir Inflammation and Allergic Diseases Research Section, Div. of Rheumatology and Immunology 1995, now Astra Zeneca Professor of Respiratory and Inflammatory Diseases; Asst in Medicine, Harvard Medical School 1961, Instr. 1962, Assoc. 1962–64, Asst Prof. 1965–66, Assoc. Prof. 1966–68, Prof. 1969–72, Theodore Bevier Bayles Prof. of Medicine 1972–; Pres. Int. Soc. of Immunopharmacology 1994; numerous cttee assignments, guest lectureships, etc.; mem. numerous professional orgs; recipient of numerous prizes and awards. *Publications:* numerous publications on immunology, etc. *Leisure interests:* skiing, jogging, gardening. *Address:* Department of Medicine, Brigham and Women's Hospital, Smith Building, Room 638, One Jimmy Fund Way, Boston, MA 02115, USA (office). *Telephone:* (617) 525-1300 (office). *Fax:* (617) 525-1310 (office). *E-mail:* jmiccile@rics.bwh .harvard.edu (office). *Website:* www.hms.harvard.edu/dms/immunology (office).

AUSTER, Paul, BA, MA; American writer and poet; b. 3 Feb. 1947, Newark, NJ; s. of the late Sam Auster and Queenie Auster; m. 1st Lydia Davis 1974 (divorced 1982); one s.; m. 2nd Siri Hustvedt 1982; one d.; ed Columbia High School, NJ, Columbia Coll., New York, Columbia Univ., New York; worked as census taker; oil tanker utility man. on the Esso Florence; moved to Paris, France 1971, returned to USA 1974; worked as translator; Tutor in Storywriting and Trans., Princeton Univ. 1986–90; juror, Cannes Film Festival 1997; mem. PEN; Nat. Endowment for the Arts fellowships 1979, 1985; Prix Médicis Étranger 1993; Commandeur, Ordre des Arts et des Lettres. *Screenplays:* Smoke 1995, Blue in the Face 1995, Lulu on the Bridge 1998. *Publications:* fiction: City of Glass 1985, Ghosts 1986, The Locked Room 1986, In the Country of Last Things 1987, Moon Palace 1989, The Music of Chance 1990, Leviathan 1992, Mr Vertigo 1994, Timbuktu 1999, True Tales of American Life 2001 (aka I Thought My Father Was God) 2001, The Book of Illusions 2002, Oracle Night 2003, The Brooklyn Follies 2005, Travels in the Scriptorium 2006, Man in the Dark 2008; non-fiction: White Spaces 1980, The Invention of Solitude 1982, The Art of Hunger 1982, Hand to Mouth (memoir) 1989, The Red Notebook 1995, Why Write? 1996, Translations 1996, Collected Prose 2003; poetry: Unearth 1974, Wall Writing 1976, Fragments From Cold 1977, Facing the Music 1980, The Random House Book of Twentieth-Century French Poetry (ed.) 1982, Disappearances: Selected Poems 1988, Collected Poems 2003, Collected Poems 2007. *Address:* Carol Mann Agency, 55 Fifth Avenue, New York, NY 10003, USA (office). *Website:* www.paulauster.co.uk.

AUSTIN, Colin François Lloyd, DPhil, FBA; British classical scholar; *Emeritus Fellow, Trinity Hall, University of Cambridge;* b. 26 July 1941, Melbourne, Australia; s. of the late Lloyd James Austin; m. Mishtu Mazumdar

1967; one s. one d.; ed Lycée Lakanal, Paris, Manchester Grammar School, Jesus Coll. Cambridge (Scholar), Christ Church Oxford (Sr Scholar) and Freie Universität, West Berlin; Research Fellow, Trinity Hall, Univ. of Cambridge 1965–69, Dir of Studies in Classics 1965–2005, Emer. Fellow 2008–; Asst Lecturer in Classics, Univ. of Cambridge 1969–73, Lecturer 1973–88, Reader in Greek Language and Literature 1988–98, Prof. of Greek 1998–2008, Prof. Emer. 2008–; Hallam Prize 1961, Browne Medal 1961, Porson Prize 1962. *Publications:* Nova Fragmenta Euripidea 1968, Menandri Aspis et Samia 1969–70, Comicorum Graecorum Fragmenta in papyris reperta 1973, Poetae Comici Graeci (with R. Kassel): Vol. I Comoedia Dorica, Mimi, Phlyaces 2001, Vol. II Agathenor—Aristonymus 1991, Vol. III 2 Aristophanes, Testimonia et Fragmenta 1984, Vol. IV Aristophon—Crobylus 1983, Vol. V Damoxenus—Magnes 1986, Vol. VI 2 Menander, Testimonia et Fragmenta apud Scriptores Servata 1998, Vol. VII Menecrates-Xenophon 1989, Vol. VIII Adespota 1995, Posidippi Pellaei Quae Supersunt Omnia (jtly) 2002, Aristophanes Thesmophoriazusae (jtly) 2004. *Leisure interests:* cycling, philately, wine tasting. *Address:* Trinity Hall, Cambridge, CB2 1TJ (office); 7 Park Terrace, Cambridge, CB1 1JH, England (home). *Telephone:* (1223) 332500 (office); (1223) 362732 (home). *Fax:* (1223) 332537 (office).

AUSTRIAN, Neil R.; American business executive; b. 1940; fmr CEO Doyle, Dane, Bernbach (advertising co.); Chair. and CEO Showtime/The Movie Channel –1987; Man. Dir Dillon, Read & Co. 1987–91; Pres. and COO Nat. Football League (NFL) 1991–99; mem. Bd of Dirs Office Depot Inc. 1998–, CEO and Interim Chair. 2004–05; mem. Bd of Dirs DirecTV Group, Viking Office Products 1988–98; mem. Advisory Bd Mid-Ocean Pnrs. *Address:* c/o Board of Directors, Office Depot Inc., 2200 Old Germantown Road, Delray Beach, FL 33445, USA (office).

AUTEUIL, Daniel; French actor; b. 24 Oct. 1950, Algeria; s. of Henri Auteil and Yvonne Auteil; two d. (one with Emmanuelle Béart q.v.); worked in musical comedies in Paris; screen debut in L'Agression 1974; stage appearances include Le Garçon d'Appartement 1980; Chevalier des Arts et des Lettres. *Films:* Attention les Yeux 1975, La Nuit Saint-Germain des Près 1976, L'Amour Violé 1976, Monsieur Papa 1977, Les Héros n'ont pas Froid aux Oreilles 1978, A Nous Deux 1979, Bête Mais Discipliné 1979, Les Sous-Doués 1980, La Banquière 1980, Clara et les Chics Types 1980, Les Hommes Préfèrent les Grosses 1981, Les Sous-Doués en Vacances 1981, T'empêches Tout le Monde de Dormir 1981, Pour Cent Briques t'as Plus Rien 1981, L'Indic 1982, Que les Gros Salaires Lèvent le Doigt 1982, P'tit Con 1983, Les Fauves 1983, Palace 1983, L'Arbalete 1984, L'Amour en Douce 1984, Jean de Florette (César for Best Actor 1986) 1985, Manon des Sources (César for Best Actor 1986, Best Actor Award, Cannes Film Festival) 1985, Le Paltoquet 1986, Quelques Jours Avec Moi 1988, Romuald and Juliette 1989, Lacenaire 1989, Ma Vie Est Un Enfer 1991, Un Coeur en Hiver 1992, Ma Saison Préférée 1992, Quelques Jours Avec Moi, L'Elegant Criminel, Tout Ça Pour Ça 1993, La Séparation 1994, La Reine Margot 1994, Ma Saison Préférée 1994, The Eighth Day 1996, Les Voleurs 1998, La Fille sur le Pont, The Lost Son 1999, La Veuve de Saint Pierre 2000, Sade 2000, The Escort 2000, Le Placard 2001, L'Adversaire 2002, Aprés vous 2003, Pourquoi (pas) le Brésil 2004, 36 Quai des Orfèvres 2004, L'Un reste, l'autre part 2005, Caché 2005, Peindre ou faire l'amour 2005, La Doublure 2006, L'Entente cordiale 2006, Mon meilleur ami 2006, N (Io e Napoleone) 2006, Dialogue avec mon jardinier 2007. *Address:* c/o Artmédia, 20 avenue Rapp, 75007 Paris, France (office).

AVDEEV, Aleksander Alekseyevich; Russian politician and diplomatist; *Ambassador to France;* b. 8 Sept. 1946, Kremenchug, USSR (now Ukraine); m.; one s.; ed Moscow State Inst. of Int. Relations; diplomatic service with USSR Ministry of Foreign Affairs 1968–; Second, First Sec., USSR Embassy, France 1977–85; Counsellor; Head of Sector, First European Dept, USSR Ministry of Foreign Affairs 1985–87; USSR Amb. to Luxembourg 1987–90; First Deputy Head, First European Dept, Ministry of Foreign Affairs 1990–91; USSR Deputy Minister of Foreign Affairs 1991–92; Amb. at Large, Russian Ministry of Foreign Affairs 1992–; Amb. to Bulgaria 1992–96; Deputy Minister of Foreign Affairs 1996–98, First Deputy Minister 1998–2002, Amb. to France 2002–. *Address:* Embassy of Russia, 40–50 Boulevard Lannes, 75116 Paris, France (office). *Telephone:* 1-45-04-05-50 (office); 1-42-22-18-42 (home). *Fax:* 1-45-04-17-65 (office); 1-45-49-39-20 (home). *E-mail:* ambrus@wanadoo.fr (office). *Website:* www.france.mid.ru (office).

AVDEYEV, Alexander Alexeyevich; Russian politician; *Minister of Culture;* b. 8 Sept. 1946, Kremenchuk, Poltava Region, Ukrainian Soviet Repub.; m.; one s.; ed Moscow State Inst. of Int. Relations, Ministry of Foreign Affairs; joined Soviet Union diplomatic corps 1968, first posting as Advisory Sec. of Gen. Consul Div. of Soviet Union in Annaba, Algeria 1968–71, worked in Soviet Embassy in Algiers with rank of Attaché 1971–73, worked in central body of Ministry of Foreign Affairs (MFA), Moscow 1973–77, Second, later First Sec., Embassy in Paris 1977–85, Chief of First European Div. with rank of Counsellor, MFA 1985–87; Amb. to Luxembourg 1987–90; First Deputy Chief of First European Directorate, MFA 1990–91, Deputy Minister of External Relations 1991–92, Special Envoy 1992, Head of Dept of CIS Affairs 1992; Amb. to Bulgaria 1992–96; Deputy Minister of Foreign Affairs 1996–98, First Deputy Minister of Foreign Affairs 1998–2002; Amb. to France 2002–08 (also accred to Monaco 2007–08); Minister of Culture 2008–; Honour 'For Services to the Fatherland', 4th Degree 1999, Order of Honour, Order of Friendship; Laureate of 'Best Feathers of Russia' Award, Russian Trade Union of Television Employees, House of Russian Press, Professional Writers' Union and Union of Journalists and Int. Asscn of Journalists ASMO-Press 1999, Laureate of journal Mezhdunarodnaya Zhizn (International Life) for publication of several articles 2000. *Address:* Ministry of Culture, Moscow 109074, 7 Kitaygorodskiy proezd, Russia (office). *Telephone:* (495) 928-38-72

(office); (495) 625-11-95 (office). *Fax:* (495) 628-17-91 (office). *E-mail:* apd@mkmk.ru (office). *Website:* www.mkmk.ru (office).

AVEN, Peter Olegovich, PhD; Russian economist; *President, Alfa Bank;* b. 16 March 1955, Moscow; s. of Oleg I. Aven; m.; two c.; ed Moscow State Univ.; researcher, All-Union Inst. for Systems Studies, USSR (now Russian) Acad. of Sciences 1981–88; Int. Inst. of Applied System Analysis, Laxenburg, Austria 1989–91, First Deputy Minister of Foreign Affairs, Chair. Cttee of Foreign Econ. Relations 1991–92; Russian Minister of Foreign Econ. Relations Feb.–Dec. 1992; mem. State Duma 1993–94; Pres., Deputy Chair. of Bd Alfa Bank 1994–, Chair. Bd of Dirs, Alfastrakhovaniye (Alfa Insurance) 2007–; Chair. Bd of Dirs STS Television 1998, Golden Telecom Inc. 2001–; Co-Chair. Bd of Dirs CTC Media; mem. Bd Competitiveness and Entrepreneurship Council, Bolshoi Theatre; Trustee Russian Econ. School, Nat. Asscn for Nat. Financial Reporting Standards; lectures internationally on econ. devts in Russia; several int. awards, named Russia's Most Admired Exec. in the Financial Services by Institutional Investor magazine 2004. *Publications:* The International Economy 2003; numerous books, scientific papers and articles on econ. and trade issues and reform of the rural economy. *Leisure interests:* the arts, theatre, collecting early 20th century Russian art. *Address:* Alfa Bank, 27 Kalanchevskaya st, 107078 Moscow, Russia (office). *Telephone:* (495) 620-91-91 (office). *Fax:* (495) 974-24-56 (office). *E-mail:* mail@alfabank.ru (office). *Website:* www.alfabank.ru (office).

AVERCHENKO, Vladimir Alexandrovich, CandEcon; Russian politician and engineer; b. 23 July 1950, Belaya Kalitva, Rostov Region; m.; three c.; ed Novocherkassk Polytech. Inst., New York Univ.; army service 1969–71; on staff Belokalitvinsky City CPSU Cttee 1975–80; constructor major industrial sites Rostov Region; Head of Itominstroi, then Promstroi Rostov Region 1980–89; Deputy Chair. Novocherkassk City Exec. Cttee 1989–91; First Vice-Maj. Novocherkassk 1991–98; Deputy Gov., Minister of Econ., Int. and Foreign Relations, Rostov Region 1998–99; concurrently Head Econ. Council Asscn of Social-Econ. Devt N Caucasus; Deputy State Duma, People's Deputies Group 1999; Head Del. of Fed. Ass. in Parl. Ass. of Black Sea Econ. Co-operation (PACHES); Deputy Chair. State Duma 2000–03; Dir Fed. Agency for Construction and Housing Economy 2004–05; state awards and int. Award for contrib. to devt of free market relations between Russia and CIS countries 1994. *Publications:* numerous publs, eight books on man., investment policy, ecology. *Leisure interests:* chess, basketball, collecting figurines of lions, collecting coins. *Address:* c/o State Duma, Okhotny Ryad 1, 103265 Moscow, Russia (office). *Telephone:* (495) 292-84-40 (office). *Fax:* (495) 292-52-23 (office).

AVERINTSEV, Sergey Sergeyevich, DPhil; Russian philologist; *Head, Department of Christian Culture, Moscow University;* b. 10 Dec. 1937; m.; one s. one d.; ed Moscow Univ.; Researcher, Sr Researcher, Head of Div., Leading Researcher Inst. of World Literature, USSR Acad. of Sciences 1965–88, Head of Section 1982–92; Prof., Moscow Univ. 1991, Head Dept of Christian Culture 1992–; Prof., Inst. für Slavistik, Vienna Univ. 1994–; Corresp. mem. USSR (now Russian) Acad. of Sciences 1987; mem. Russian Acad. of Natural Sciences; mem. Acad. Universelle de Culture 1991, Academia Europaea 1992, Acad. dell Science Social, Rome 1994; Pres. Asscn of Culturologists of Russia; Chair. Bible Soc. of Russia; USSR People's Deputy 1989–91; USSR State Prize 1991, Leopold Lucas Prize, Tübingen Univ. 1995, Russia State Prize 1996. *Publications:* works on history and theory of literature, studies of Ancient Byzantine, Latin and Syrian Literature, on history of Russian and West European Poetry including Plato and Greek Literature 1973, Poetry of Early Byzantine Literature 1977, From the Banks of Bosphorus to the Banks of Efrat 1987, contribs to the Encyclopedia of Myths and Tales of Peoples of the World. *Address:* Moscow University, Vorob'yevy Gory, Philological Faculty, 119899 Moscow, Russia. *Telephone:* (495) 939-20-08; (495) 939-54-38.

AVERY, Bryan Robert, MA, DipArch, RIBA; British architect and designer; b. 2 Jan. 1944, Aston Tirrold, Berks.; one d.; ed Brockenhurst Co. High School, Leicester Coll. of Art and Univ. of Essex; specialised in component devt and industrialized bldg techniques 1967–69; studied history and theory of architecture, Univ. of Essex 1969–70; worked in various architect practices 1970–78; f. Avery Assocs 1978–; Minerva Award for Nat. Film Theatre, UNESCO Award for Advanced Tech. Housing; awards for Museum of the Moving Image: PA Award for Innovation 1988, Civic Trust Award 1989; City Heritage Award for Plantation House 1992; awards for No. 1 Neathouse Place: Aluminium Imagination Architectural Awards 1997, British Construction Industry Award 1997, Glassex Award 1997, Westminster Soc.'s Award 1997, Nat. Lighting Design Awards 1997, British Council for Offices Award 1998, Civic Trust Commendation 1998, British Inst. of Architectural Technologists 1999, Millennium Products Award 1999; awards for BFI London IMAX Cinema: Millennium Products Award 1999, FX International Interior Design Awards 1999, British Construction Industry Awards 1999, Comedia Creative City Award for Urban Innovation 2000, Civic Trust Award 2000, National Drywall Awards 2001; awards for Royal Acad. of Dramatic Art: Camden Design Award Commendation 2001, ADAPT Trust Access Award 2001, RIBA Award 2001, Civic Trust Commendation 2002, British Inst. of Architectural Technologists Commended Award 2002, Open Award for Tech. Excellence in Architectural Tech. 2002, United States Inst. of Theater Technicians Merit Award 2003, Building Quality Awards Excellence in Inclusive Design Award 2003. *Artistic achievements:* major bldgs completed include Museum of the Moving Image 1987–88, Nat. Film Theatre foyers and bookshop 1989, No. 1 Neathouse Place 1997, IMAX Cinema for the British Film Inst. 1999, Royal Acad. of Dramatic Art (RADA) 2000; work in progress includes regeneration of the London Transport Museum, the Innovation Centre at Oakham School and a major West End commercial redevelopment; major design and research projects include Advanced Tech. Housing Project, Wilderness City Project and

Ecological Beacons Project. *Publications:* numerous articles in the UK and abroad. *Leisure interests:* film, theatre, country walking. *Address:* Avery Associates Architects, 270 Vauxhall Bridge Road, London, SW1V 1BB, England (office). *Telephone:* (20) 7233-6262 (office). *Fax:* (20) 7233-5182 (office). *E-mail:* enquiries@avery-architects.co.uk (office). *Website:* www.avery-architects.co.uk (office).

AVICE, Edwige, LèsL; French consultant and fmr politician; b. 13 April 1945, Nevers; d. of Edmond Bertrant and Hélène Guyot; m. Etienne Avice 1970; ed Cours Fénelon, Nevers, Lycée Pothier, Orléans, Univ. of Paris; worked for Nat. Cttee for Housing Improvement 1970; Int. Dept, Crédit Lyonnais 1970–73; on staff of Dir-Gen. of Paris Hosps 1973–78; Pres. Asscn Démocratique des Français de l'Etranger 1991–93; mem. Parti Socialiste (PS) 1972, mem. Exec. Bureau 1977, Nat. Secr. 1987–94, PS Nat. Del. for Nat. Service; mem. Nat. Ass. 1978–81, 1986–88; Minister-Del. for Free Time, Youth and Sports 1981–84; Sec. of State attached to the Minister of Defence 1984–86; Minister-Del. attached to the Minister for Foreign Affairs 1988–91; Minister of Co-operation and Devt 1991–93; Conseillère de Paris 1983–88; Pres. and Dir-Gen. Financière de Brienne 1993–2005, Chair Brienne Council and Finance 1993–2005; currently Assoc. Dir BIPE (econ. consultancy); Pres. Int. Defence Council 1999–2003. *Publication:* Terre d'élection 1993. *Leisure interests:* travelling, music, swimming, walking, fencing. *Address:* BIPE, Le Vivaldi, 11/13 rue René Jacques, 92138 Issy-les-Moulineaux Cedex, France (office). *Telephone:* 1-70-37-23-23 (office). *Fax:* 1-70-37-23-00 (office). *E-mail:* contact@bipe.fr (office). *Website:* www.bipe.com (office).

ÁVILA, Rodrigo, BEng, BA; Salvadorean police officer and politician; b. 25 June 1965, San Salvador; three d.; ed N Carolina State Univ. and Gainesville Coll., Ga, USA, courses in police specialization at FBI Acad. and police admin at Texas A&M Univ., USA; rose through ranks of police force to serve as Deputy Chief of Police Operations Feb.–June 1994, Chief of Police 1994–99, 2006–08; Deputy Head of Alianza Republicana Nacionalista (ARENA) Bench in Congress 2000–03; cand. in mayoral elections for Santa Tecla 2003; Deputy Minister for Security 2003–06; ARENA party cand. for Pres. of El Salvador 2008. *Address:* Alianza Republicana Nacionalista (ARENA), Prolongación Calle Arce 2423, entre 45 y 47 Avda Norte, San Salvador, El Salvador (office). *Telephone:* 2260-4400 (office). *Fax:* 2260-5918 (office). *E-mail:* info@arena.com.sv (office). *Website:* www.arena.com.sv (office).

AVILDSEN, John Guilbert; American film director, cinematographer and editor; b. 21 Dec. 1935, Ill.; s. of Clarence John Avildsen and Ivy Avildsen (née Guilbert); m. Tracy Brooks Swope 1987; two s. one d.; ed New York Univ.; Advertising Man. Vespa Motor Scooters 1959; served in US Army 1959–61; Asst Dir Greenwich Village Story 1961; worked as asst cameraman and production man.; with Muller, Jordan & Herrick Industrial Films 1965–67; mem. Dirs' Guild of America, Motion Picture Photographers' Union, Motion Picture Eds Union, Writers' Guild of America. *Films include:* Turn On to Love 1967, Sweet Dreams 1968, Guess What We Learned in School Today 1969, Joe 1970, Cry Uncle 1971, Save the Tiger 1972, Inaugural Ball 1973, W.W. and the Dixie Dancekings 1974, Rocky (Acad. Award for Best Dir) 1976, Slow Dancing in the Big City 1978, The Formula 1980, Neighbors 1981, Traveling Hopefully 1982, A Night in Heaven 1983, The Karate Kid 1984, Happy New Year 1985, The Karate Kid II 1986, For Keeps 1987, The Karate Kid III 1989, Lean on Me (Image Award, Nat. Asscn for the Advancement of Colored People) 1989, Rocky V 1990, The Power of One 1992, 8 Seconds 1994, Save the Everglades (documentary), A Fine and Private Place, Coyote Moon 1998. *Television:* From No House to Options House (Emmy Award). *Address:* c/o United Talent Agency Dan Aloni, 9560 Wilshire Blvd., Fl. 5, Beverly Hills, CA 90212-2401, USA.

AVINERI, Shlomo; Israeli academic; *Professor of Political Science, Hebrew University of Jerusalem;* b. 20 Aug. 1933, Bielsko, Poland; s. of Michael Avineri and Erna Groner; m. Dvora Nadler 1957; one d.; ed Shalva Secondary School, Tel-Aviv, Hebrew Univ., Jerusalem and London School of Econs; has lived in Israel since 1939; Prof. of Political Science, Hebrew Univ. Jerusalem 1971–, Dir Eshkol Research Inst. 1971–74, Dean of Faculty of Social Sciences 1974–76; Dir-Gen. Ministry of Foreign Affairs 1976–77; Dir Inst. for European Studies, Hebrew Univ. 1997–; visiting appointments at Yale Univ. 1966–67, Wesleyan Univ., Middletown, Conn. 1971–72, Research School of Social Sciences, ANU 1972, Cornell Univ. 1973, Univ. of California 1979, Queen's Coll., New York 1989, Univ. of Oxford 1989; mem. Int. Inst. of Philosophy 1980–; Fellow, Woodrow Wilson Center, Washington, DC 1983–84; Visiting Prof., Cardozo School of Law, New York 1996–97, 2000–01, Brookings Inst., Washington, DC 1991, Cen. European Univ., Budapest 1994, Northwestern Univ., Evanston 1997, Carnegie Endowment for Int. Peace, Washington, DC 2000–01; Fellow, Collegium Budapest 2002; British Council Scholarship 1961, Rubin Prize in the Social Sciences 1968, Naphtali Prize for study of Hegel 1977, Present Tense Award for Study of Zionism 1982, Carlyle Lecturer, Univ. of Oxford 1989, Israel Prize 1996, Life Award, Israel Political Science Asscn 2005. *Publications:* The Social and Political Thought of Karl Marx 1968, Karl Marx on Colonialism and Modernization 1968, Israel and the Palestinians 1971, Marx's Socialism 1972, Hegel's Theory of the Modern State 1973, Varieties of Marxism 1977, The Making of Modern Zionism 1981, Moses Hess – Prophet of Communism and Zionism 1985, Arlosoroff – A Political Biography 1989, Communitarianism and Individualism (co-author) 1992, Herzl's Diaries 1998, Identity and Integration 1999, The Law of Religious Identity (co-author) 1999, Identities in Transformation 2002, Herzl – An Intellectual Biography (in Hebrew) 2007. *Address:* Faculty of Social Sciences, Hebrew University of Jerusalem, Mount Scopus, Jerusalem (office); 10 Hagedud Ha-ivri Street, Jerusalem, Israel (home). *Telephone:* (2) 588-3286 (office); (2) 563-0862 (home). *Fax:* (2) 588-1333 (office). *E-mail:* shlomo.avineri@huji.ac.il (office).

AVNET, Jonathan Michael, BA; American film company executive and film director; b. 17 Nov. 1949, Brooklyn, New York; m. Barbara Brody; one s. two d.; ed Sarah Lawrence Coll., Univ. of Pennsylvania, Conservatory for Advanced Film Studies; Reader United Artists, LA 1974; Dir Creative Affairs, Sequoia Pictures, LA 1975–77; Pres. Tisch/Avnet Productions, LA 1977–85; Chair. Avnet/Kerner Co., LA 1985–; Pres. Allied Communications Inc.; Trustee LA Co. Opera; Fellow American Film Inst.; mem. Dirs' Guild of America, Writers' Guild of America, Acad. of Motion Pictures Arts and Sciences. *Films:* Dir and Producer: Fried Green Tomatoes at the Whistle Stop Cafe (three Golden Globes), The War, Up Close and Personal, George of the Jungle, 88 Minutes 2007, Righteous Kill 2008; Producer, Exec. Producer: Risky Business, Men Don't Leave, Less than Zero, When a Man Loves a Woman, Mighty Ducks, Deal of the Century, Miami Rhapsody, Three Musketeers; Exec. Producer: The Burning Bed, Silence of the Heart, Heatwave (four Cable Ace Awards, including Best Picture), Do You Know the Muffin Man, No Other Love, Steal This Movie. *Television:* Producer, Writer, Dir (series): Call to Glory 1984–85 (Golden Reel Award), Between Two Women (Emmy Award). *Leisure interests:* basketball, skiing, biking.

AVOKA, Cletus, LLB; Ghanaian politician and lawyer; *Minister of the Interior;* ed Univ. of Ghana; Chair. Public Tribunal for Northern Ghana 1983–84; mem. Parl. (Nat. Democratic Congress) for Bawku W 1992–2005; Minister of State 1995–97, Minister of Lands and Forestry 1997, of Environment, Science and Tech. 1998, of the Interior 2009–; worked in pvt. legal practice, Accra 2005–09. *Address:* Ministry of the Interior, POB M42, Accra, Ghana (office). *Telephone:* (21) 684400 (office). *Fax:* (21) 684408 (office).

AVRIL, Pierre; French academic; *Professor Emeritus, University of Paris;* b. 18 Nov. 1930, Pau; s. of Stanislas Avril and Geneviève Camion; m. Marie-Louise Hillion 1959; one s.; Asst, Pierre Mendès France 1955–62, Ed.-in-Chief Cahiers de la République 1960–62; Sub-Ed., Soc. Gen. de Presse 1962–69; Prof., Faculté de Droit de Poitiers 1972–79, Univ. de Paris X 1979–88, Inst. d'études politiques 1982–97, Univ. de Paris II 1988–99; mem. Conseil supérieur de la magistrature 1998–2002; Pres. Comm. de réflexion sur le statut pénal du Président de la République 2002; mem. Comité scientifique de la Comm. Nat. des archives constitutionnelles 2002–; Hon. Pres., Association Française de Droit Constitutionnel 2005. *Publications:* Le Régime politique de la Ve République 1964, Droit parlementaire (with others) 1988; Un président pour quoi faire? 1965, Essais sur les partis politiques 1990, La Ve République – histoire politique et constitutionnelle 1994, Les conventions de la Constitution 1997. *Address:* 48 rue Gay-Lussac, 75005 Paris, France (home). *Telephone:* 1-43-26-36-43 (home).

AVRIL, Brig.-Gen. Prosper; Haitian politician and army officer; ed Mil. Acad. Haiti and Univ. of Haiti Law School; fmr adviser to deposed Pres. Jean-Claude Duvalier; adviser to mil.-civilian junta headed by Gen. Namphy (q.v.) and mem. Nat. Governing Council 1986; Commdr Presidential Guard 1988; major participant in June 1988 coup which overthrew civilian Govt of Leslie Manigat; leader of coup which deposed regime of Gen. Namphy Sept. 1988; Pres. of Haiti 1988–90.

AWAD, Muhammad Hadi; Yemeni diplomatist; b. 5 May 1934; m. Adelah Moh'd Hadi Awad 1956; one s. three d.; ed Murray House Coll. of Educ.; teacher 1953–59; Educ. Officer 1960–62; Chief Insp. of Schools 1963–65; Vice-Prin. As-Shaab Coll. 1965–67; Perm. Rep. to Arab League 1968–70, concurrently Amb. to UAR, also accred to Sudan, Lebanon, Libya and Iraq; Perm. Sec. Ministry of Foreign Affairs 1970–73; Amb. to UK 1973–80, concurrently to Spain and Sweden 1974–80, to Denmark, Portugal, the Netherlands 1975–80; Amb. to Tunisia and Perm. Rep. to the Arab League 1980–91; Dir Western Europe Dept, Ministry of Foreign Affairs 1990–95; Amb. to People's Repub. of China (also accred to Viet Nam and Thailand) 1995–2000; mem. Supanen 2001. *Leisure interest:* photography. *Address:* c/o Ministry of Foreign Affairs, PO Box 19262, San'a, Yemen.

AWADALLAH, Bassem, PhD; Jordanian government official; b. 1964; ed Georgetown Univ., USA, London School of Econs, UK; worked in investment banking, UK 1986–91; Econ. Sec. to the Prime Minister of Jordan 1992–96, Econ. Adviser 1996–99; Dir Econ. Dept, Royal Hashemite Court 1999–2001; Minister of Planning and Int. Co-operation 2001–Feb. 2005; Minister of Finance April 2005–June 2005; Al Kawkab and Al Istiqlal Decorations of the First Order of the Hashemite Kingdom of Jordan; Al Hussein Medal for Distinguished Service, Royal Hashemite Award for Distinguished Service 1995. *Address:* c/o Ministry of Finance, POB 85, Amman 11118, Jordan (office).

AWOONOR, Kofi Nyidevu, PhD; Ghanaian writer, teacher, diplomatist and politician; b. 13 March 1935, Wheta; s. of Kosiwo Awoonor and Atsu Awoonor; m.; five s. one d.; ed Univ. of Ghana, Univ. Coll., London and State Univ. of NY, Stony Brook; Research Fellow, Inst. of African Studies; Man. Dir Film Corpn, Accra; Longmans Fellow, Univ. of London; Asst Prof. and later Chair. Comparative Literature Program, State Univ. of NY; Visiting Prof., Univ. of Texas, Austin and New School of Social Research, New York; detained in Ghana for allegedly harbouring leader of coup 1975; on trial 1976, sentenced to one year's imprisonment Oct. 1976, pardoned Oct. 1976; fmr Chair. Dept of English and Dean of Faculty of Arts, Univ. of Cape Coast; Sec.-Gen. Action Congress Party; Amb. to Brazil 1984–90 (also accred to Cuba 1988–90); Perm. Rep. to UN 1990–94; currently Minister of State; Contributing Ed., Transition and Alcheringa; Longmans and Fairfield Fellowships; Gurrey Prize for Poetry, Nat. Book Council Award for Poetry 1979, Dillons Commonwealth Prize for Poetry (Africa Div.) 1989, Order of the Volta 1977, Agbonugla of ANLO 1997, Agbaledzigla of the Wheta Traditional Area 1998. *Publications:* poetry: Rediscovery 1964, Messages 1970, Night of My Blood 1971, House by the Sea 1978, Until the Morning After (collected poems); prose: This Earth My

Brother 1971, Guardians of the Sacred Word 1973, Ride Me Memory 1973, Breast of the Earth 1974 (history of African literature), Traditional African Literature (series, ed.), Alien Corn (novel) 1974, Where is the Mississippi Panorama 1974, Fire in the Valley: Folktales of the Ewes 1980, The Ghana Revolution, Ghana: A Political History 1990, Comes the Voyage at Last 1991, The Caribbean and Latin American Notebook 1992, Africa the Marginalized Continent. *Leisure interests:* jazz, walking, tennis, hunting. *Address:* c/o Secretariat for Foreign Affairs, POB M212, Accra, Ghana. *Telephone:* (21) 665415 ext. 119 (office); (21) 503580 (home). *Fax:* (21) 660246 (office).

AWORI, Arthur Moody; Kenyan politician and business executive; b. 5 Dec. 1927, Butere; s. of Jeremiah and Maria Awori; m.; ed Chartered Inst. of Secretaries; MP for Funyula constituency 1983–; numerous posts as Asst Minister under Pres. Daniel arap Moi, including Asst Minister for Educ.; left Kanu Party late 2002 to join new Narc alliance; Minister of Home Affairs 2002–05, Vice-Pres. 2003–05; fmr Chair. Western Province Kanu MPs Parl. Group; Chair. Francis Da Gama Rose Group 1981–; Dir East Africa Building Soc., Akiba Bank Ltd, Mercantile Life and General Insurance Co. Ltd, Macmillan Publrs Kenya Ltd, Securicor Security Services Ltd; Chair. Asscn for the Physically Disabled of Kenya; proprietor of Gulumwoyo Ltd, Western Sunrise Properties Ltd, Mocian Ltd, Rose Mareba Ltd, Mareba Enterprises Ltd; Sec. to the Bd of East African Industries (EAI); Elder of the Burning Spear. *Leisure interests:* tennis, swimming. *Address:* c/o Office of the Vice President, Jogoo House 'A', Taifa Road, POB 30520, Nairobi, Kenya (office).

AXEL, Richard, MD; American biochemist and academic; *Professor of Biochemistry and Molecular Biophysics, Columbia University;* b. 1946; ed Columbia Coll., Johns Hopkins Univ. School of Medicine; began academic career as Fellow, Columbia Univ. Inst. of Cancer and Nat. Inst. of Health; currently Prof. of Biochemistry and Molecular Biophysics, Columbia Univ. and Prof. of Pathology, Columbia Univ. Coll. of Physicians and Surgeons; Investigator, Howard Hughes Medical Inst. (HHMI); mem. NAS, American Philosophical Soc., American Acad. of Arts and Sciences; Eli Lilly Award in biological chemistry, Richard Lounsberry Award, NAS, Bristol-Myers Squibb Award for distinguished achievement in neuroscience research, Gairdner Foundation Int. Award, Nobel Prize in Physiology or Medicine (jtly with Linda B. Buck, q.v.) 2004. *Address:* Columbia University Medical Center, Room 1014, 701 West 168 Street, New York, NY 10032 (office); Howard Hughes Medical Institute, 4000 Jones Bridge Road, Chevy Chase, MD 20815-6789, USA (office). *Telephone:* (212) 305-6915 (office); (301) 215-8500 (office). *Fax:* (212) 923-7249 (office). *E-mail:* ra27@columbia.edu (office). *Website:* cpmcnet.columbia.edu/dept/gsas/biochem/faculty/axel.html (office); cpmcnet.columbia.edu/dept/neurobeh/axel (office); www.hhmi.org (office).

AXELROD, David M., BA; American political consultant and government official; *Senior Advisor to the President;* b. 22 Feb. 1953, New York City; m. Susan Landau 1979; ed Univ. of Chicago; reporter and columnist, Chicago Tribune newspaper 1977–84; Communications Man. then Co-Dir Paul Simon's US Senate campaign in Illinois 1984; Founding Pnr, Axelrod & Assocs (political consultancy firm, now AKP&D Message and Media) 1985–; worked on mayoral campaigns of Harold Washington, Dennis Archer, Michael R. White, Anthony A. Williams, Lee P. Brown and John F. Street; worked with John Edwards' Presidential campaign team and Barack Obama's Senate campaign 2004; consultant for gubernatorial campaigns of Eliot Spitzer in New York and Deval Patrick in Massachusetts 2006; chief political advisor to Rahm Emanuel in US House of Reps election 2006; chief strategist and media advisor for Barack Obama's presidential campaign 2007–08; Sr Advisor to Pres. of USA, The White House 2009–. *Address:* The White House Office, 1600 Pennsylvania Ave, NW, Washington, DC 20500, USA (office). *Telephone:* (202) 456-1414 (office). *Fax:* (202) 456-2461 (office). *Website:* www.whitehouse.gov (office); www.akpmedia.com (office).

AXER, Erwin; Polish theatre producer and director; b. 1 Jan. 1917, Vienna, Austria; s. of Dr Maurycy Axer and Fryderyka Schuster; m. Bronisława Kreczmar 1945 (died 1973); two s.; ed Nat. Acad. of Theatrical Art, Warsaw; Asst Producer, Nat. Theatre, Warsaw 1938–39; Actor Polish Drama Theatre, Lvov, USSR 1939–41; Artistic Dir, Teatr Kameralny, Łódź 1946–49; Dir and Producer, Teatr Współczesny (Contemporary Theatre), Warsaw 1949–81; Dir and Chief Producer, Nat. Theatre, Warsaw 1954–57; Asst Prof. Producers' Dept, State Higher Theatrical School, Łódź 1946–49, Warsaw 1949–55, Extraordinary Prof. 1955–66, Prof. Ordinary 1966–81, Prof. Emer. 1981–; mem. Presidential Council for Culture 1992–95; Commdr 's Cross, Order of Polonia Restituta, Great Cross, Order of Polonia Restituta 1996; Order of Banner of Labour (1st Class); State Prizes for Artistic Achievement 1951, 1953, 1955, 1962, Nagroda Krytyki im. Boya-Żeleńskiego (Critics Award) 1960, and other awards and prizes. *Productions include:* Major Barbara (Shaw) 1947, Niemcy (Kruczkowski) 1955, Kordian (Słowacki) 1956, Pierwszy dzień wolności 1959, Iphigenia in Tauris 1961, Kariera Arturo Ui (Brecht), Warsaw 1962, Leningrad 1963, Three Sisters (Chekhov) 1963, Düsseldorf 1967, Androcles and the Lion (Shaw), Warsaw 1964, Tango (Mrożek), Warsaw 1965, Düsseldorf 1966, Die Ermittlung (Weiss), Warsaw 1966, Le Piéton de l'Air (Ionesco), Warsaw 1967, Maria Stuart (Schiller), Warsaw 1969, Dwa Teatry (Szaniawski), Leningrad 1969, Matka (Witkiewicz), Warsaw 1970, Porträt eines Planeten, Düsseldorf 1970, Old Times and Macbeth, Warsaw 1972, Uncle Vanya, Munich 1972, Ein Fest für Boris, Vienna (Kainz Award) 1973, Maria Stuart (Schiller), Vienna 1974, King Lear (Bond), Warsaw, 1974, Endgame (Beckett), Vienna 1976, Kordian, Warsaw 1977, Seagull (Chekhov), Vienna 1977, Biedermann und die Brandstifter (Max Frisch), Zürich 1978, Krawiec (Tailor by Mrożek), Warsaw 1979, Wesele (Wyspiański), New York 1962, Our Town, Leningrad 1979, John Gabriel Borkman, Zürich 1979, Triptychon (Frisch), Warsaw 1980, Die Schwärmer (Musil), Vienna 1980, Triptychon (Frisch), Vienna 1981, Amphitryon (Kleist), Vienna 1982, Till Damascus (Strindberg), Munich 1983, Reigen (Schnizler), Vienna 1983, Vinzenz (Musil), Vienna 1985, Am Ziel (Bernhard), Berlin 1987, Nachtasyl (Gorky), Berlin 1987, Theatermacher (Bernhard), Warsaw 1990, When We Dead Awaken (Ibsen), Hamburg 1990, Emigranci (Mrożek), Bregenz 1990, Mein Kampf (Tabori), Hamburg 1992, The Widows, Warsaw 1992, Love in Crimea (Mrożek), Warsaw 1994, Ambassador 1995, Warsaw Semiramida (Wojtyszko) 1996, Am Ziel (Bernhard), Warsaw 1997, Androcles and the Lion (Shaw), Poznań 1999, Easter (Strindberg), Warsaw 2001. *Television:* plays by Frisch, Mrożek, Dürrenmatt and others, Warsaw 1962–, Tango (Mrożek,), Düsseldorf 1966, Die Schwärmer (Musil), Vienna 1980. *Publications include:* Listy ze sceny I (Letters from the Stage) 1955, Listy ze sceny II 1957, Sprawy teatralne (Theatrical Things) 1966, Cwiczenia pamięci (Exercises of the Memory Series I) 1984, Exercises of the Memory Series II 1991, Exercises of the Memory Series III 1998, Exercises of the Memory Series IV 2003, Kłopoty młodości, kłopoty starości 2006, From the Memory 2006; essays, serial, articles on theatre. *Address:* ul. Odyńca 27 m.11, 02-606 Warsaw, Poland (home). *Telephone:* (22) 844-01-16 (home); (8) 25-03-54 (home). *Fax:* (22) 825-52-17 (office).

AXFORD, David Norman, MA, MSc, PhD, CEng, FIEE, FRMetS; British meteorologist; b. 14 June 1934, London; s. of Norman Axford and Joy A. Axford (née Williams); m. 1st Elizabeth A. Stiles 1962 (divorced 1980); one s. two d.; m. 2nd Diana R. J. Bufton 1980; three step-s. one step-d.; ed Merchant Taylors School, Plymouth Coll., St John's Coll. Cambridge and Southampton Univ.; Scientific Officer, Kew Observatory 1960–62; Sr Scientific Officer, various RAF stations 1962–68; Prin. Scientific Officer, Meteorological Research Flight, Royal Aircraft Establishment, Farnborough 1968–76; Asst Dir (SPSO) Operation Instrumentation Branch 1976–80; Asst Dir (SPSO), Telecommunications 1980–82; Deputy Dir Observational Services 1982–84; Dir of Services and Deputy to Dir-Gen. Meteorological Office 1984–89; Pres. N Atlantic Ocean Station Bd 1982–85; Chair. Cttee of Operational World Weather Watch System Evaluations -N Atlantic (CONA) 1985–89; Deputy Sec.-Gen. World Meteorological Org., Geneva 1989–1995, Special Exec. Adviser to Sec.-Gen. Jan.–May 1995; Consultant Meteorologist 1995–; Consultant to Earthwatch Europe, Oxford 1996–2000; Chair. of Trustees Stanford in the Vale Public Purposes Charity 2000–02, Clerk/Corresp. 2002–; Hon. Sec. Royal Meteorological Soc. 1983–88, Vice-Pres. 1989–91, Chair. Accreditation Bd 1999–2004, Sec. Special Group on Observations and Instruments 1999–2001; Trustee Thames Valley Hospice, Windsor 1996–98; mem. Exec. Cttee British Asscn of Former UN Civil Servants (BAFUNCS) 1996–2004, Vice-Chair. 1998, Chair. 1999–2004, Vice-Pres. 2004–; Chartered Meteorologist of Royal Meteorological Soc. 1994–; Vice-Pres. and Treas. European Meteorological Soc. 2002–05; Chair., Stanford-in-the-Vale Local History Soc. 2004–; Trustee, Friends of the Ridgeway 2008–; Groves Award 1972. *Publications:* articles in professional journals. *Leisure interests:* home and garden, food and wine, Tibetan terrier, 12 grandchildren, local and family history. *Address:* Honey End, 14 Ock Meadow, Stanford-in-the-Vale, Oxon., SN7 8LN, England. *Telephone:* (1367) 718480.

AXFORD, Sir William Ian, Kt, MSc, ME, PhD, FRS; British/New Zealand scientist and academic; *Director Emeritus, Max Planck Institut für Aeronomie;* b. 2 Jan. 1933, Dannevirke, NZ; s. of John Edgar Axford and May Victoria Axford (née Thoresen); m. Catherine Joy Lowry 1955; two s. two d.; ed Canterbury Univ. Coll., NZ, Univs of Manchester and Cambridge, UK; mem. staff Defence Research Bd, Canada 1960–62; Assoc. Prof., then Prof. of Astronomy, Cornell Univ., USA 1963–67; Prof. of Physics and Applied Physics, Univ. of California, San Diego, USA 1967–74; Ed. Journal of Geophysical Research 1969–73; Scientific mem. and Dir Max Planck Inst. für Aeronomie 1974–82, 1985–2002, Dir Emer. 2002–; Vice-Chancellor, Victoria Univ. of Wellington 1982–85; Pei Ling Chan Chair, Univ. of Alabama 2002–04; Regents' Prof., Univ. of California, Riverside 2003; Adjunct Prof., Auckland Univ. of Tech. 2004–; Pres. Cttee on Space Research 1986–94; Vice-Pres. Scientific Cttee on Solar Terrestrial Physics 1986–90; Chair. Foundation for Research, Science and Tech., NZ 1992–95; Pres. European Geophysical Soc. 1990–92; Chair. Marsden Fund, NZ 1994–98; Vice-Pres. Asia Oceania Geosciences Soc.; Assoc., Royal Astronomical Soc.; Fellow, American Geophysical Union; Foreign Assoc. NAS; mem. Academia Europaea; Hon. FRSNZ; Hon. mem. European Geophysical Soc.; Hon. Prof., Univ. of Gottingen; Hon. DSc (Canterbury, NZ) 1996, (Victoria, NZ) 1999; Appleton Award, Union Radio-Scientifique Int., J. A. Fleming Award, American Geophysical Union, AIAA Space Award, Tsiolkovski Medal, Chapman Medal, Royal Astronomical Soc. 1994, NZ Science and Tech. Medal, Royal Soc. of NZ 1994, Scientist of the Year and New Zealander of the Year 1995. *Publications:* more than 300 articles on various aspects of astrophysics, cosmic ray physics, space physics and general historical subjects, In Soso's Web (with T.K. Breus). *Leisure interests:* family history, writing on historical topics. *Address:* 2 Gladstone Road, Napier, New Zealand (home); Max Planck Institut für Aeronomie, Max-Planck-Str. 2, 37191 Katlenburg-Lindau, Germany (office). *Telephone:* (6) 8352188 (home). *Fax:* (6) 8352176 (home). *E-mail:* ian@axford.org (home). *Website:* www.axford.org (home).

AXWORTHY, Lloyd, BA, MA, PhD, OM, OC; Canadian academic administrator and fmr politician; *President and Vice-Chancellor, University of Winnipeg;* b. 21 Dec. 1939; s. of Norman Joseph Axworthy and Gwen Jane Axworthy; m. Denise Ommaney 1984; two s. one d.; ed United Coll. (now Univ. of Winnipeg), Princeton Univ.; Asst Prof. of Political Science, Univ. of Winnipeg 1964–79, Dir Inst. of Urban Studies 1970–79, Pres. and Vice-Chancellor 2004–; mem. Man. Legis. 1973–79; mem. House of Commons 1979–; MP for Winnipeg Fort-Garry 1979–88, for Winnipeg South-Centre 1988–2000; Minister of Employment and Immigration 1980–83, Minister responsible for Status of Women 1980–81; Minister of Transport 1983–84; Minister of Human Resources Devt and Minister of Western Econ. Diversification 1993–96, of Foreign Affairs

1996–2000; UN Special Envoy to Ethiopia and Eritrea 2004–; Dir and CEO Liu Centre for the Study of Global Issues, Univ. of British Columbia 2001–04; Chair. Human Security Centre for UN Univ. for Peace, State of the World Forum, Comm. on Globalization; mem. Cttee High Level Comm. for the Empowerment of the Poor, UNDP 2005–; Head, OAS Electoral Observation Mission to Peru 2006; mem. Bd Univ. of Winnipeg Foundatioo, MacArthur Foundation, Human Rights Watch (Chair. Advisory Board For Americas Watch), Lester B. Pearson Coll., Univ. of the Arctic, Pacific Council on Int. Policy, Churchill Gateway Devt Corpn; mem. Advisory Bd Port of Churchill, Ethical Globalization Initiative; mem. Liberal Party; Hon. Fellow, American Acad. of Arts and Sciences, Hon. Chair. Canadian Landmine Foundation; mem. Order of Canada, Order of Manitoba; Dr hc (Queen's, Lakehead, Victoria, Denver, Niagara, Winnipeg, Dalhousie, Guelph); Peace Award, North-South Inst., Senator Patrick J. Leahy Award, Vietnam Veterans of America Foundation, Madison Medal, Princeton Univ., CARE Int. Humanitarian Award. *Publication:* Navigating a New World: Canada's Global Future 2003. *Leisure interest:* golf. *Address:* President's Office, University of Winnipeg, 3W02, 515 Portage Avenue, Winnipeg, Manitoba, R3B 2E9 (office); c/o Liberal Party of Canada, 81 Metcalfe Street, Suite 400, Ottawa, Ont., K1P 6M8, Canada. *Telephone:* (204) 786-9214 (office). *Fax:* (204) 786-1693 (office). *E-mail:* president@uwinnipeg.ca (office). *Website:* www.uwinnipeg.ca/index/admin-president (office).

AYALA, Francisco Jose, PhD; American (naturalized) biologist, geneticist and academic; *Donald Bren Professor of Biological Sciences and University Professor, University of California, Irvine;* b. 12 March 1934, Madrid, Spain; s. of Francisco Ayala and Soledad Ayala (née Pereda); m. Hana Lostakova 1985; two s. (by previous m.); ed Univ. of Madrid and Columbia Univ.; Research Assoc. Rockefeller Univ., New York 1964–65, Asst Prof. 1967–71; Asst Prof., Providence Coll., RI 1965–67; Assoc. Prof., later Prof. of Genetics, Univ. of Calif., Davis 1971–87, Dir Inst. of Ecology 1977–81, Assoc. Dean of Environmental Studies 1977–81; Distinguished Prof. of Biology, Univ. of Calif., Irvine 1987–89, Donald Bren Prof. of Biological Sciences 1989–, Univ. Prof. 2003–; Pres. AAAS 1994–95; Pres.-Elect Sigma Xi, The Scientific Research Soc. 2003–04, Pres. 2004–05; mem. NAS, American Acad. of Arts and Sciences, American Philosophical Soc. (Pres. Cttee of Advisers on Science and Tech. 1994–2001); Dr hc (León) 1982, (Madrid) 1986, (Barcelona) 1986, (Athens) 1991, (Vigo) 1996, (Islas Baleares) 1998, (Valencia) 1999, (Bologna) 2001, (Vladivostok) 2002, (Masaryk) 2003; US Nat. Medal of Science 2001. *Publications:* Studies in the Philosophy of Biology 1974, Molecular Evolution 1976, Evolution 1977, Evolving: The Theory and Processes of Organic Evolution 1979, Population and Evolutionary Genetics 1982, Modern Genetics 1984 and more than 880 scientific articles. *Leisure interests:* travel, reading, collecting fine art. *Address:* Department of Ecology and Evolutionary Biology, University of California, Irvine, CA 92697 (office); 2 Locke Court, Irvine, CA 92617, USA (home). *Telephone:* (949) 824-8293 (office). *Fax:* (949) 824-2474 (office). *E-mail:* fjayala@uci.edu (office). *Website:* ecoevo.bio.uci.edu/faculty/ayala/ayala.html (office).

AYALA-CASTAÑERES, Agustín, MS, DBiol; Mexican professor of micropaleontology; b. 28 Aug. 1925, Mazatlán; s. of Agustín Ayala and María Luisa Castañares; m. Alma Irma López 1957; one s. two d.; ed Universidad Nacional Autónoma de México (UNAM) and Stanford Univ.; micropaleontologist, Pemex 1950–54; Prof. of Paleontology, Inst. Politécnico Nacional (IPN) 1955–60; Head Dept of Micropaleontology and Marine Science Dept Inst. of Geology, UNAM 1956–67; Prof. of Micropaleontology, Faculty of Sciences, UNAM 1961–, Head Dept of Biology 1965–67, Dir Inst. Biología 1967–73; full-time researcher, Centro de Ciencias del Mar y Limnología, UNAM 1970–81; Coordinator of Scientific Investigation, UNAM 1973–80; Assoc. Researcher, Scripps Inst. of Oceanography, Univ. of Calif., San Diego 1968–; Chair. Nat. Cttee Scientific Cttee on Oceanic Research (SCOR) 1971–; Dir Plan para Crear una Infraestructura en Ciencias y Tecnologías del Mar, México-UNESCO 1974–80; Pres. Acad. de la Investigación Científica 1975–76; Chair. Intergovernmental Oceanographic Comm., UNESCO 1977–82; Exec. Dir Programa Nacional de Ciencia y Tecnología para el Aprovechamiento de los Recursos Marinos (PROMAR-CONACyT) 1974–80; Chair. Org. Cttee Jt Oceanographic Ass., Mexico 1988; mem. Bd Trustees, Int. Center for Living Aquatic Resources Man. 1989–94; Gen. Coordinator, Interinstitutional Comms for Evaluation of Higher Educ. 1991–; Fellow, Geological Soc. of America; mem. Int. Asscn of Plant Taxonomy and Nomenclature, American Soc. of Ecology, American Soc. of Petroleum Geologists, Soc. of Econ. Paleontologists and Mineralogists, etc.; Dr hc (Bordeaux) 1988. *Publications:* 52 articles on fossil foraminifera, marine geology, coastal lagoons and science policy. *Address:* Apartado Postal 70-157, México 04510 DF (office); 43 Cerro del Jabalí, México 04320 DF, Mexico (home).

AYALA-LASSO, José; Ecuadorean diplomatist and international civil servant; b. 29 Jan. 1932, Quito; m.; four c.; ed Pontificia Universidad Católica del Ecuador, Universidad Cen. del Ecuador, Université Catholique de Louvain, Belgium; several foreign affairs postings including at embassies in Tokyo, Seoul, Beijing, Rome; Minister of Foreign Affairs 1977, 1997–99; fmr Amb. to Belgium, Luxembourg, Peru, EEC; Lecturer, Int. Law Inst., Universidad Cen. del Ecuador; Deputy Legal Sec. Perm Comm. for the South Pacific; Perm. Rep. to UN, New York 1989–94, Chair. Security Council Cttee concerning Fmr Yugoslavia 1991; Chair. working group to establish post of High Commr for Human Rights 1993; UN High Commr for Human Rights 1994–97; Amb. to Holy See 1999–2002; Grand Cross, Nat. Order of Merit (Ecuador), numerous decorations from Japan, Belgium, Brazil, etc. *Address:* c/o Ministry of Foreign Affairs, Avda 10 de Agosto y Carrión, Quito, Ecuador.

AYALON, Admiral Ami, MA; Israeli politician and naval officer (retd); *Founding Director, The People's Voice;* b. 1945, Kibbutz Ma'agan; ed Bar-Ilan Univ., Naval War Coll., Newport, RI and Harvard Univ., USA; drafted into Flotilla 13 elite commando unit, Israeli Navy, commissioned officer, participated in hundreds of secret missions, served with distinction in Six Day and Yom Kippur wars, Commdr Israeli Navy 1992–96 (retd); Dir Shin-Beit (Israeli internal security service) 1996–2000; Co-Founding Dir The People's Voice (with Sari Nusseibeh—civil org. advocating two states for Israel and Palestine secured through non-violent means) 2000–; mem. Labour Party 2004–; Ribbon of Valour (Israel), Medal of Supreme Bravery (Israel), Quality Govt Kt Award. *Address:* The People's Voice, Ramat Gan, Israel. *Telephone:* 3-7538888. *Fax:* 3-7538887. *E-mail:* mifkad@mifkad.org.il. *Website:* www.mikkad.org.il.

AYALON, Daniel, BA, MBA; Israeli fmr diplomatist; *Co-Chairman, Nefesh B'Nefesh;* b. 1955, Tel-Aviv; m. Anne Ayalon; two d.; ed Tel-Aviv Univ., Bowling Green State Univ., USA; fmr Capt. Armored Corps, Israel Defense Forces; sr finance exec. before joining Foreign Service; Deputy Chief of Mission, Panama 1991–92; Dir Bureau of Israel's Amb. to UN, New York 1993–97, Deputy Foreign Policy Adviser to fmr Prime Ministers Ehud Barak and Benjamin Netanyahu 1997–2001, Chief Foreign Policy Adviser to Prime Minister Ariel Sharon 2002, Amb. to USA 2002–06; Co-Chair. Nefesh B'Nefesh, Jerusalem 2006–. *Address:* Nefesh B'Nefesh, Beit Ofer, 5 Nachum Hefzadi, Jerusalem, 95484, Israel (office). *Fax:* (2) 6595701 (office). *E-mail:* dayalon@nbn.org.il (office). *Website:* www.nbn.org.il (office).

AYARI, Chedli, LenD, DèsSc(Econ); Tunisian economist, diplomatist and politician; *Vice–President, National Consultative Counsel on Scientific Research and Technology;* b. 24 Aug. 1933, Tunis; s. of Sadok and Fatouma Chedly; m. Elaine Vatteau 1959; three c.; ed Collège Sadiki and Inst. de Hautes Etudes; with Société Tunisienne de Banque 1958; Asst Faculté de Droit et des Sciences Economiques et Politiques, Tunis 1959; Econ. Counsellor, Perm. Mission of Tunis at UN 1960–64; Exec. Dir IBRD 1964–65; Dean, Faculté de Droit, Tunis 1965–67; Dir CERES 1967–69; Sec. of State in charge of Plan 1969–70; Minister of Nat. Educ., Youth and Sport 1970–71; Amb. to Belgium Feb.–March 1972; Minister of Nat. Economy 1972–74, of Planning 1974–75; Chair. of Bd and Gen. Man. Arab Bank for Econ. Devt in Africa 1975; Prof. of Economics, Agrégé de Sciences Economiques, Tunis; Assoc. Prof. Univ. of Aix-Marseilles 1989–; mem. UN Cttee of Planning for Devt; currently Vice Pres., Nat. Consultative Counsel on Scientific Research and Tech.; Dr hc (Aix-Marseilles) 1972; Grand Officier Légion d'honneur, Grand Cordon, Ordre de la République. *Publications:* Les Enjeux méditerranéens 1992, La Méditerranée economique 1992; books and articles on econ. and monetary problems. *Leisure interest:* music. *Address:* Rue Tanit, Gammarth, La Marsa, Tunis, Tunisia (home). *Telephone:* 270-038.

AYASSOR, Adji Othèth, LLD; Togolese lawyer and politician; *Minister of Finance, Budget and Privatization;* b. 1952; m.; four c.; ed Univ. of Bordeaux, France, Univ. of Wisconsin, USA; fmr Prof. of Law, Lomé Univ.; fmr Prof., École nationale d'administration (ENA), Lomé; int. consultant and expert on educ.; mem. Nat. Assembly (Parl.) for Doufelgou Pref.; Dir-Gen. Ministry of Educ. 1990–2006; Sec.-Gen. Cabinet Office 2006–07; Minister of Finance, Budget and Privatization 2007–. *Address:* Ministry of Finance, Budget and Privatization, Lomé, Togo (office).

AYATSKOV, Dmitry Fedorovich, DHistSc; Russian politician; *Assistant to the Presidential Representative, Volga Federal District;* b. 9 Nov. 1950, Stolypino, Saratov Region; s. of Fedor Kuzmich Ayatskov and Anna Petrovna Ayatskov; m.; one s. one d.; ed Saratov Inst. of Agric., Moscow Cooperation Inst.; machine-operator, electrician in kolkhoz; army service 1969–71; chief agronomist in kolkhozes, leading posts on major enterprises of region (Tantal, Saratovskoye) 1977–92; Vice-Mayor of Saratov 1992–96; Head of Admin, Saratov Region 1996–2005, Gov. 1996–2005; Asst to the Presidential Rep., Volga Fed. Dist 2005–; mem. Council of Fed. of Russia 1993–2000; mem. Our Home is Russia 1995–99; mem. United Russia Political Party 2001; numerous decorations including Order of Honour 1996, Orders for Merits to the Homeland, First and Second Rank 1997, 2000, Golden Order in the Name of Russia 2004, Order of the Rev. Sergiy Radonezhsky, Second Rank 2005. *Publications:* more than 50 articles on local govt and econ. devt of the Russian Federation. *Leisure interest:* history, collecting watches, sport, hunting, fishing. *Address:* Kreml, kor. 1, 603082 Nizhnii Novgorod, Russia (office). *Telephone:* (8312) 31-46-07 (office). *Fax:* (8312) 31-47-51 (office). *Website:* www .pfo.ru (office).

AYCKBOURN, Sir Alan, Kt, CBE, FRSA; British playwright and theatre director; b. 12 April 1939, London; s. of Horace Ayckbourn and Irene Maud Ayckbourn (née Worley); m. 1st Christine Helen Roland 1959 (divorced 1997); two s.; m. 2nd Heather Elizabeth Stoney 1997; ed Haileybury; on leaving school went straight into the theatre as stage manager and actor with various repertory cos in England; Founder mem. Victoria Theatre Co., Stoke on Trent 1962–64; Drama Producer, BBC Radio 1964–70; Artistic Dir Stephen Joseph Theatre, Scarborough 1971–2008; Prof. of Contemporary Theatre, Oxford 1992; Hon. Fellow, Bretton Hall Coll. 1982, Cardiff Univ. 1995; Hon. Prof., Univ. of Hull 2007; Hon. DLitt (Hull) 1981, (Keele, Leeds) 1987, (Bradford) 1994; Dr hc (York) 1992, (Wales Cardiff) 1995, (Open Univ.) 1998, (Manchester) 2003; Variety Club of Great Britain Playwright of the Year 1974, Lifetime Achievement Award (Writers' Guild) 1993, John Ederyn Hughes Rural Wales Award for Literature 1993, Yorkshire Man of the Year 1994, Montblanc de la Culture Award for Europe 1994, Sunday Times Literary Award for Excellence 2001, Yorkshire Arts and Entertainment Personality, Yorkshire Awards 2005; inducted into American Theater Hall of Fame 2009. *Plays:* Mr Whatnot 1963, Relatively Speaking 1965, How the

Other Half Loves 1969, Ernie's Incredible Illucinations 1969, Family Circles 1970, Time and Time Again 1971, Absurd Person Singular (Evening Standard Award for Best New Comedy 1973) 1972, The Norman Conquests (Evening Standard Award for Best New Play 1974, Plays and Players Award for Best New Play 1974) 1973, Jeeves (book and lyrics for Andrew Lloyd Webber musical) 1975 (rewritten as By Jeeves – British Regional Theatre Awards for Best Musical 1996), Absent Friends 1974, Confusions 1974, Bedroom Farce 1975, Just Between Ourselves (Evening Standard Award for Best New Play 1977) 1976, Ten Times Table 1977, Joking Apart (Co-winner Plays and Players Award for Best New Comedy 1979) 1978, Family Circles 1978, Sisterly Feelings 1979, Taking Steps 1979, Suburban Strains (musical play with music by Paul Todd) 1980, Season's Greetings 1980, Me, Myself & I (with Paul Todd) 1981, Way Upstream 1981, Intimate Exchanges 1982, It Could Be Any One Of Us 1983, A Chorus of Disapproval (London Evening Standard Award, Olivier Award and DRAMA Award for Best Comedy 1985) 1984 (film 1988), Woman in Mind 1985, A Small Family Business (London Evening Standard Award for Best New Play 1987) 1987, Henceforward... (London Evening Standard Award for Best Comedy 1989) 1987, A View from the Bridge (Plays and Players Director of the Year Award) 1987, Man of the Moment (London Evening Standard Award 1990) 1988, Mr A's Amazing Maze Plays (TMA/Martini Regional Theatre Award for Best Show for Children and Young People 1993) 1988, The Revengers' Comedies 1989, Invisible Friends 1989, Body Language 1990, This Is Where We Came In 1990, Callisto 5 1990 (rewritten as Callisto 7 1999), Wildest Dreams 1991, My Very Own Story 1991, Time of My Life 1992, Dreams From a Summer House (with music by John Pattison) 1992, Communicating Doors (Writers' Guild of GB Award for Best West End Play 1996) 1994, Haunting Julia 1994, A Word from our Sponsor (with music by John Pattison) 1995, The Champion of Paribanou 1996, Things We Do For Love (Lloyds Pvt. Banking Playwright of the Year Award 1997) 1997, Comic Potential 1998, The Boy Who Fell Into A Book 1998, House & Garden 1999, Whenever (with music by Denis King) 2000, Damsels in Distress (trilogy: GamePlan, FlatSpin, RolePlay) 2001, Snake in the Grass 2002, The Jollies 2002, Sugar Daddies 2003, Orvin – Champion of Champions (with music by Denis King) 2003, My Sister Sadie 2003, Drowning On Dry Land 2004, Private Fears in Public Places 2004, Miss Yesterday 2004, Improbable Fiction 2005, The Girl Who Lost Her Voice 2005, If I Were You 2006, Life and Beth 2008. *Publications:* fiction: majority of plays have been published; non-fiction: Conversations with Ayckbourn (with I. Watson) 1981, The Crafty Art of Playmaking 2002. *Leisure interests:* music, cricket. *Address:* c/o Casarotto Ramsay & Associates Ltd, Waverley House, 7–12 Noel Street, London, W1F 8GQ, England (office). *Telephone:* (20) 7287-4450 (office). *Fax:* (20) 7287-9128 (office). *E-mail:* info@casarotto.uk.com (office). *Website:* www.casarotto.uk.com (office); www.alanayckbourn.net (home).

AYER, Ramani, BS, DEng, PhD; American insurance industry executive; *Chairman and CEO, The Hartford Financial Services Group Inc.;* ed Indian Inst. of Tech., Mumbai, Drexel Univ., Philadelphia; joined The Hartford Financial Services Group Inc. 1973, Asst Sec. and Staff Asst to Chair. 1979, Vice-Pres. HartRe (subsidiary co.) 1983, Pres. Hartford Specialty Co. 1986, Sr Vice-Pres. The Hartford 1989, Exec. Vice-Pres. 1990, mem. Bd Dirs 1991–, COO 1991–97, Chair., Pres. and CEO 1997–2007, Chair. and CEO 2007–, also Chair. Hartford Life; Chair. BusinessLINC, Metro Hartford Alliance; Dir American Insurance Asscn, Insurance Information Inst., Financial Services Roundtable, Hartford Hosp.; Trustee, Drexel Univ.; mem. Business Roundtable. *Address:* The Hartford Financial Services Group, Inc., Hartford Plaza, 690 Asylum Avenue, Hartford, CT 06115-1900, USA (office). *Telephone:* (860) 547-5000 (office). *Fax:* (860) 547-2680 (office). *E-mail:* info@thehartford.com (office). *Website:* www.thehartford.com (office).

AYÉVA, Zarifou; Togolese politician; *President, Parti pour la démocratie et le renouveau (PDR);* b. 22 April 1942, Sokode; m.; ed Collège Moderne de Sokodé, Lycée Classique de COCODI, Abidjan, Univ. of Mons, Belgium; Financial Dir SGGG, Lomé 1969–73, Head Sales Dept 1973–85; Lecturer Univ. of Lomé 1975–77; Asst Gen. Dir Société Nlle de Sidérurgie 1977–79, Gen. Dir 1979–82; Minister of Commerce and Transport 1978, of Information 1979; Dir CODIS 1983–, STOP-FEU-TOGO 1986–; Minister of State, Minister of Foreign Affairs and African Integration 2005–07; Pres. Parti pour la démocratie et le renouveau (PDR) 1991–. *Address:* Parti pour la démocratie et le renouveau (PDR), Lomé, Togo (office).

AYISSI, Henri Eyebe, PhD; Cameroonian politician; *State Minister for External Relations;* ed Nat. Advanced School of Admin. and Magistracy; Minister of Urban Affairs 1990–92; Inspector of Gen. Affairs, Ministry of Higher Educ. 1998; fmr mem. Nat. Census Comm. and Inspector-Gen. of elections; State Minister for External Relations 2007–. *Address:* Ministry of External Relations, Yaoundé, Cameroon (office). *Telephone:* 2220-3850 (office). *Fax:* 2220-1133 (office). *Website:* www.diplocam.gov.cm (office).

AYKROYD, Daniel (Dan) Edward; American (b. Canadian) actor; b. 1 July 1952, Ottawa, Canada; s. of Peter Hugh Aykroyd and Lorraine Gougeon Aykroyd; m. 1st Maureen Lewis 1974 (divorced); three s.; m. 2nd Donna Dixon 1984; two d.; ed Carleton Univ., Ottawa; started as a stand-up comedian; worked on Saturday Night Live ensemble TV show (NBC) 1975–79; cr. and performed as The Blues Brothers (with the late John Belushi); Emmy Award 1976–77. *Films include:* 1941 1979, Mr. Mike's Mondo Video 1979, The Blues Brothers (also screenwriter) 1980, Neighbors 1981, Doctor Detroit 1983, Trading Places 1983, Twilight Zone 1983, Ghostbusters 1984, Nothing Lasts Forever 1984, Into the Night 1985, Spies Like Us (also screenwriter) 1985, Dragnet (co-screenwriter) 1987, Caddyshack II 1988, The Great Outdoors 1988, My Stepmother is an Alien 1988, Ghostbusters II 1989, Driving Miss

Daisy 1990, My Girl, Loose Canons, Valkemania, Nothing But Trouble 1991, Coneheads 1993, My Girl II 1994, North, Casper (also co-screenwriter) 1995, Sergeant Bilko (also co-screenwriter) 1996, Grosse Pointe Blank (also co-screenwriter) 1997, Blues Brothers 2000 1997, The Arrow 1997, Susan's Plan 1998 (also dir and screenwriter), Antz (voice) 1999, Diamonds (also dir and screenwriter) 1999, The House of Mirth 2000, Stardom 2000, The Loser 2000, The Devil and Daniel Webster 2001, Pearl Harbor 2001, Evolution 2001, Crossroads 2002, The Curse of the Jade Scorpion 2002, Unconditional Love 2002, Bright Young Things 2003, 50 First Dates 2004, Intern Academy 2004, Christmas with the Kranks 2004, I Now Pronounce You Chuck and Larry 2007. *Albums include:* Briefcase Full of Blues, Made in America, The Blues Brothers, Best of the Blues Brothers. *Address:* c/o Fred Specktor, CAA, 9830 Wilshire Boulevard, Beverly Hills, CA 90212; 9200 Sunset Boulevard, #428, Los Angeles, CA 90069, USA (office).

AYKUT, Imren; Turkish organization official and fmr politician; *President, ÇESAV—Çevre Eğitim Sağlık ve Sosyal Yardımlaşma Vakfı;* b. 1941, Adana; s. of Şevket Şadi and Rahime Aykut; ed Istanbul Univ. and Univ. of Oxford, UK; fmr man. of trades unions; industrial relations expert in Turkish glass industries; fmr Sec.-Gen. Paper Industry Employers' Union; mem. Constitutional Ass. 1981; Deputy, Nat. Ass. 1983–; Minister of Labour and Social Security 1987–91; Govt Spokesperson 1991; Vice-Chair. Inter-Parl. Union Turkish Group 1994–95; State Minister by Premier Minister (Women and Family Affairs) 1996; Minister of Environment 1997–99; Pres. Turkish Inter-Parl. Group 1991; currently Pres. ÇESAV—Çevre Eğitim Sağlık ve Sosyal Yardımlaşma Vakfı (Environment, Educ., Health and Social Solidarity Foundation); mem. Anavatan Partisi (Motherland Party); Order of Isabella Catolica of Spain 1993, Order Grand Cruz Medallion (Chile) 1996; Economist of the Year 1988, chosen one of 100 Most Successful Women of the Century, World Assocn of Women's Clubs 1994. *Publications:* over 40 articles and research papers. *Leisure interests:* hand-made carpets, antiquities. *Address:* ÇESAV, Meşrutiyet Caddesi, Bayındır 2, Sokak No 59/6, 06620 Kızılay, Ankara, Turkey (office). *Telephone:* (312) 4174925 (office). *Fax:* (312) 4252432 (office). *E-mail:* cesav@cesav.org.tr (office). *Website:* www.cesav.org.tr (office).

AYLING, Robert (Bob) John; British business executive; *Chairman, The Sanctuary Group;* b. 3 Aug. 1946; m. Julia Crallan 1972; two s. one d.; ed King's Coll. School, Wimbledon; joined Elborne, Mitchell & Co. 1968; legal adviser on British accession to the EEC 1973–75, Head of Dept of Trade Aviation Law br. 1978 (responsible for parl. bill that led to privatization of British Airways), Under-Sec. for EC, int. trade, competition issues 1981; with British Shipbuilders 1975; joined British Airways (legal and govt affairs) 1985, Co. Sec. 1987, organized legal arrangements concerning BA's privatization 1987 and BA's acquisition of British Caledonian 1988, Dir Human Resources 1988, Dir Marketing and Operations 1991, Group Man. Dir 1993–95, CEO 1996–2000; Dir (non-exec.) Holidaybreak 2003, Chair. 2003–; Dir (non-exec.) Royal & SunAlliance Insurance Group PLC 1993–2004; Chair. New Millennium Experience Co. Ltd. 1997–2000; Chair. The Sanctuary Group 2006–; Gov. King's Coll. School 1996; Hon. LLD (Brunel) 1996. *Address:* The Sanctuary Group PLC, Sanctuary House, 45–53 Sinclair Road, London, W14 0NS, England (office). *Telephone:* (20) 7602-6351 (office). *Fax:* (20) 7603-5941 (office). *E-mail:* info@sanctuarygroup.com (office). *Website:* www.sanctuarygroup.com (office).

AYLWIN AZÓCAR, Patricio; Chilean fmr head of state, lawyer, university professor and consultant; b. 26 Nov. 1918, Viña del Mar; s. of Miguel Aylwin G. and Laura Azócar; m. Leonor Oyarzun Ivanovic 1948; five c.; ed Universidad de Chile; Senator 1965–73, Pres. of Senate 1971–72; Pres. Christian Democrat party (PDC) 1973, 1987–91, Vice-Pres. 1982–89; leader opposition coalition rejecting Gen. Augusto Pinochet in nat. plebiscite Oct. 1988; opposition coalition cand. 1989; PDC cand. for Pres. 1989; Pres. of Chile 1990–94; Pres. Corporación Justicia y Democracia; Hon. Pres. World Democratic Conf. 1997; awarded hon. doctorate degrees from univs in Australia, Canada, Colombia, France, Italy, Japan, Portugal, Spain, and USA and from seven Chilean univs; North-South Prize, Council of Europe 1997, J. William Fulbright Prize for Int. Understanding 1998. *Publications:* El Juicio Arbitral 1943, La Transición Chilena: Discursos escogidos Marzo 1990–92, Crecimiento con Equidad: Discursos escogidos 1992–94, Justicia, Democracia y Desarrollo: Conferencias y discursos 1994–95. *Address:* Teresa Salas No. 786, Providencia, Santiago, Chile. *Telephone:* (562) 3411574. *Fax:* (562) 2042135.

AYNSLEY-GREEN, Sir Albert, Kt, MA, MBBS, DPhil, MRCS, FRCP, FRCPE, FRCPCH, FMedSci; British paediatrician; *National Clinical Director for Children, Department of Health;* b. 30 May 1943; m. Rosemary Boucher 1967; two d.; ed Glyn Grammar School, Epsom and Univs of London and Oxford; House Officer, Guy's Hosp. London, St Luke's Hosp. Guildford, Radcliffe Infirmary, Oxford and Royal Postgraduate Medical School, Hammersmith 1967–70; Wellcome Research Fellow, Radcliffe Infirmary 1970–72, Clinical Lecturer in Internal Medicine 1972–73, Sr House Officer and Registrar in Paediatrics (also John Radcliffe Hosp.) 1973–74; European Science Exchange Fellowship, Univ. Children's Hosp. Zürich 1974–75; Clinical Lecturer in Paediatrics, Univ. of Oxford 1975–78, Univ. Lecturer 1978–83; Prof. of Child Health and Head of Dept, Univ. of Newcastle-upon-Tyne 1984–93; Nuffield Prof. of Child Health, Univ. of London 1993–; Dir of Clinical Research and Devt, Great Ormond St Hosp. and Inst. of Child Health, London 1993–2003; Chair. Nat. Children's Taskforce and Nat. Clinical Dir for Children, Dept of Health 2001–; Fellow, Green Coll. Oxford 1980–83, Royal Coll. of Paediatrics and Child Health; several hon. doctorates. *Publications:* papers on child health. *Leisure interests:* family, walking, music, photography. *Address:* Institute of Child Health, 30 Guilford Street,

London, WC1N 1EH, England (office). *Telephone:* (20) 7813-8391 (office). *Fax:* (20) 7905-2331 (office). *E-mail:* a.aynsley-green@ich.ucl.ac.uk (office). *Website:* www.ich.ucl.ac.uk (office).

AYONG, Most Rev. James Simon, BTheol; Papua New Guinea ecclesiastic; *Archbishop of Papua New Guinea and Bishop of Diocese of Aipo Rongo;* b. 3 Sept. 1944, Kumbun, West New Britain Prov.; s. of Julius Ayong and Margaret Ayong; m. Gawali Ayong 1967; two d. (one deceased); Local Govt Officer 1964–70, 1974–76; Prin. Newton Theological Coll. 1989–93; Archbishop of Papua New Guinea and Bishop of Diocese of Aipo Rongo 1995–; Primate of Anglican Prov. of Papua New Guinea 1996. *Leisure interest:* watching football. *Address:* Anglican Diocese of Aipo Rongo, PO Box 893, Mt Hagen, Western Highlands Province, Papua New Guinea (office). *Telephone:* 542-1131 (office); 542-3727 (home). *Fax:* 542-1181 (office); 542-1181 (home). *E-mail:* achgn@global.net.pg (office); archbishopjayong@hotmail.com (home).

AYRE, Richard James, BA, JP; British journalist; b. 1 Aug. 1949, Newcastle-upon-Tyne; s. of Thomas Henry Ayre and Beth Carson; partner Guy Douglas Burch; ed Univ. Coll., Durham; Pres., Univ. of Durham Students' Union 1969–70; producer and reporter, BBC Northern Ireland 1973–76, Home News Ed., TV News 1979–84, Head of BBC Westminster 1989–92, Controller of Editorial Policy 1993–96, Deputy Chief Exec., BBC News 1996–2000; Chair., Asian & Afro-Carribean Reporters' Trust 1997–2000; mem. Bd Food Standards Agency 2000–; Freedom of Information Adjudicator, Law Soc. 2001–; Chair., Article 19 2002–05; Civil Service Commr 2005–06; Bd mem. for England, Ofcom Content Bd 2006–; Chair., Dairy Partnership 2008–; Benton Fellow, Univ. of Chicago 1984–85. *Address:* The Old Dairy, Burgh Hall, Burgh Parva, Melton Constable, Norfolk, NR24 2PU; 26 Springalls Wharf, Bermondsey Wall West, London, SE16 4TL, England. *Telephone:* (1263) 860939. *E-mail:* richardayre@whats2hide.com (office).

AYUB, Alfredo Elías, BS, MBA; Mexican civil servant and energy industry executive; *General Director, Comisión Federal de Electricidad (CFE);* b. 13 Jan. 1950, Mexico City; ed Anáhuac Univ., Harvard Univ., USA; has held numerous public sector posts including Exec. Co-ordinator of Urban Devt, Secr. of Public Works and Dir, Nat. Fund for Social Activities; worked for nine years at Secr. of Energy, Mines and Govt-Controlled Industry holding positions on Coordinating Comm. of Advisors to Sec., Under-Secr. of Mines and Basic Industry, Under-Secr. of Energy; fmr CEO and Pres. Airports and Auxiliary Services; Gen. Dir Comisión Federal de Electricidad (CFE) 1999–; active in family's real-estate business; fmr Dir School of Eng, Anáhuac Univ.; fmr Chair. Devt Bd, Anáhuac Univ., Mexico Foundation, Harvard Univ. *Address:* Comisión Federal de Electricidad, Rio Rodano 14, Col. Cuauhtemoc, México DF 06598, Mexico (office). *Telephone:* (55) 5229-4400 (office). *Fax:* (55) 5310-4614 (office). *E-mail:* info@cfe.gob.mx (office). *Website:* www.cfe.gob.mx (office).

AYUSHEYEV, Damba Badmayevich; Russian Buddhist leader; b. 1963, Russia; abbot Buddhist monastery Baldan Braybun 1995; elected Head of Buddhists of Russia (Khambo Lama) at conf. of Buddhist clergy, Ulan-Ude 1995–; Shiretuy Buddhist datsan Baldan-Braybun; mem. Presidium of the Interreligious Council of Russia 1998–, Presidium of the Interreligious Council of the CIS 2004–, Council for Co-operation with Religious Union Under the Pres. of the Russian Fed.; Vice-Pres. Asian Buddhist Conf. for Peace. *Address:* c/o Buddist Centre, Petrovsky blvd., 17/1, Suite 35, 103051 Moscow, Russia (office). *Telephone:* (495) 925-16-81 (office).

AYUSO GARCÍA, Joaquín, BEng; Spanish business executive; *CEO, Grupo Ferrovial;* b. 1955, Madrid; ed Univ. Politécnica de Madrid; joined Ferrovial as Site Engineer 1982, becoming Project Supervisor, Group Man., Area Man. and Regional Man., CEO Ferrovial Agromán 1999–2002, currently CEO Grupo Ferrovial and Ferrovial Infraestructuras; First Vice-Chair. Cintra Concesiones de Infraestructuras de Transporte SA; Dir BAA PLC 2006–07; fmr Dir Budimex SA, Poland; Madrid Inst. of Civil Engineers Medal of Honour 2006. *Website:* www.joaquinayuso.com.

AYYUBOV, Yagub Abdulla oğlu; Azerbaijani politician; currently First Deputy Prime Minister; Head of Azeri-Saudi Inter-governmental Econ. Comm. *Address:* c/o Office of the Prime Minister, Lermontov küç. 63, 1066 Baku, Azerbaijan (office). *Telephone:* (12) 492-66-23 (office). *Fax:* (12) 492-91-79 (office).

AZA, Alberto; Spanish diplomatist; *Head of the Royal Household;* b. 22 May 1937, Tetuán, Morocco; s. of Alberto Aza and Marcela Arias; m. María Eulalia Custodio Martí 1963; two s. four d.; ed Univ. of Oviedo and Madrid; joined Diplomatic Service 1965; served in Libreville, Algiers, Rome, Madrid; Dir Cabt. of Prime Minister of Spain 1977–83; Chief Dir OAS, Latin America Dept, Ministry of Foreign Affairs 1983; Minister Counsellor, Lisbon 1983–85; Amb. to OAS, Washington, DC 1985–89 (also accred to Belize); Amb. to Mexico 1990–92, to UK 1992–99; Gen. Dir O.I.D. 2000–02; currently Head of the Spanish Royal Household; Gran Cruz del Mérito Civil 1979; Gran Cruz de la Order del Mérito Naval 1996; Hon. DLitt (Portsmouth) 1997. *Leisure interests:* golf, fishing, walking. *Address:* Palacio de la Zarzuela, Madrid, Spain (office). *Website:* www.sispain.org.

AZAD, Ghulam Nabi, MSc; Indian politician; b. 7 March 1949, Soti village, Doda Dist, Jammu and Kashmir; m. Shrimati Shameem Dev Azad 1980; one s. one d.; ed Kashmir Univ.; mem. Indian Nat. Congress; began his political career in 1973, Block Sec., Congress Cttee, Blessa 1973–75, nominated Pres. Jammu and Kashmir Pradesh Youth Congress 1975–77, Pres. Congress Cttee, Doda Dist 1977, nominated Gen. Sec. All India Youth Congress 1977; Pres. All India Muslim Youth Conf. 1978–81; nominated mem. Congress Working Cttee 1986; Gen. Sec. All India Congress Cttee 1987, re-elected as Gen. Sec. nine

times; Union Deputy Minister for Company Affairs and Law 1982, later Minister of State; re-elected as mem. Parl. for Washim Constituency 1985; apptd Minister of State for Home Affairs 1985, later Minister of State for Food and Civil Supplies; mem. Rajya Sabha 1990–91; Cabinet Minister for Parl. Affairs 1991, later Cabinet Minister for Tourism and Civil Aviation; Pres. Jammu and Kashmir Pradesh Congress Cttee; Union Minister for Urban Devt and Law and Parl. Affairs 2002–05; Chief Minister of Jammu and Kashmir 2005–08 (resgnd). *Address:* c/o Directorate of Information, Jammu and Kashmir Government, Old Secretariat, Mubarak Mandi Complex, Jammu, 180 001, India (office).

AZALI, Col. Assoumani; Comoran politician and fmr head of state; Chief of Staff, Comoran Armed Forces –1999; seized power in coup d'état April 1999; Head of State of the Comoros and C-in-C of the Armed Forces 1999–2002, Fed. Pres. of the Union of the Comoros 2002–06. *Address:* c/o Office of the Head of State, BP 521, Moroni, The Comoros (office).

AZAM, Air Vice-Marshal Fakhrul; Bangladeshi air force officer; joined Air Force, promoted to Air Commodore, to Air Vice-Marshal 2002, Chief of Air Staff 2002–07; Pres. Bangladesh Hockey Fed. *Address:* c/o Air Force Headquarters, Dhaka Cantonment, Bangladesh (office).

AZAM, Ghulam; Bangladeshi politician and professor; b. 7 Nov. 1922, Dhaka; s. of Mawlana Ghulam Kabir and Sayeda Ashrafunnisa; m. Sayeda Afifa Khatun; six s.; joined Tablig Jamaat 1950, Ameer (Leader) Rangpur Dist 1952–54; joined Tamaddin Majlis 1952, Chair. Rangpur Dist 1952–54; joined Jamaat-e-Islami 1954, Sec.-Gen. 1957–1967, Ameer 1967–1971, Ameer Jamaat-e-Islami Bangladesh 1971–2000. *Address:* c/o Jamaat-e-Islami Bangladesh, 505 Elephant Road, Bara Maghbazar, Dhaka, 1215, Bangladesh (office).

AZARNOFF, Daniel Lester, MS, MD; American physician, academic and business executive; *President, D.L. Azarnoff Associates;* b. 4 Aug. 1926, Brooklyn, New York; s. of Samuel J. Azarnoff and Kate Azarnoff; m. Joanne Stokes 1951; two s. one d.; ed Rutgers Univ. and Univ. of Kansas School of Medicine; Instructor in Anatomy, Univ. of Kansas 1949–50, Research Fellow 1950–52, Intern 1955–56, Nat. Heart Inst. Resident Research Fellow 1956–58, Asst Prof. of Medicine 1962–64, Assoc. Prof. 1964–68, Dir Clinical Pharmacology Study Unit 1964–68, Assoc. Prof. of Pharmacology 1965–68, Prof. of Medicine and Pharmacology 1968, Dir Clinical Pharmacology-Toxicology Center 1967–68, Distinguished Prof. 1973–78, Clinical Prof. of Medicine 1982–; Asst Prof. of Medicine, St Louis Univ. 1960–62; Visiting Scientist, Fulbright Scholar, Karolinska Inst., Stockholm, Sweden 1968; Clinical Prof. of Pathology and Prof. of Pharmacology, Northwestern Univ. 1978–85; Prof. of Medicine, Univ. of Kansas Coll. of Health Sciences 1984, Stanford Univ. School of Medicine 1998–2002; Sr Vice-Pres. Clinical Regulatory Affairs, Cellegy Pharmaceuticals 1999–2006; Sr Vice-Pres. Worldwide Research and Devt, G. D. Searle & Co., Chicago 1978, Pres. Searle Research and Devt, Skokie, Ill. 1979–85; Pres. D.L. Azarnoff Assocs, Inc. 1987–; mem. Bd of Dirs De Novo Inc. 1994–95, Oread Inc. 1994–98 (Chair. 1998–), Entropin Inc. 1997–2000; mem. Editorial Bd Drug Investigation 1989–2002; Chair. Cttee on Problems of Drug Safety, NAS 1972–76; consultant to numerous govt agencies; mem. Nat. Comm. on Orphan Diseases, Dept of Health and Human Services; mem. Bd of Dirs Oread Laboratories Inc. 1993; Ed. Review of Drug Interactions 1974–77, Yearbook of Drug Therapy 1977–79; Series Ed. Monographs in Clinical Pharmacology 1977–84; Fellow, American Coll. of Physicians, New York Acad. of Scientists; mem. American Soc. of Clinical Nutrition, American Nutrition Inst., American Fed. of Clinical Research, British Pharmacological Soc., Royal Soc. for the Promotion of Health, Inst. of Medicine (NAS) and others; Burroughs Wellcome Scholar 1964, Markle Scholar 1963–68, Ciba Award for gerontological research 1958, Rector's Medal, Univ. of Helsinki 1968, Oscar B. Hunter Award, American Soc. for Clinical Pharmacology and Therapeutics, Distinguished Alumni Award, Univ. of Kansas School Medicine, Nathanial T. Kwit Memorial Service Award, American Coll. of Clinical Pharmacology. *Publications:* more than 175 publs in scientific and medical journals. *Address:* 610 Edgewood Drive, Rio Vista, CA 94571, USA (office). *Telephone:* (707) 374-2715 (office). *Fax:* (765) 374-2716 (office). *E-mail:* dan@azarnoffassociates.com (office). *Website:* www .azarnoffassociates.com (office).

AZAROV, Mykola Yanovych, PhD; Ukrainian geologist, economist and politician; b. 17 Dec. 1947, Kaluga, Russia; m.; one s.; ed M. Lomonosov Moscow State Univ.; Lab. Man. and Head of Dept, Moscow Research Design Coal Inst. 1976–84; Deputy Dir Ukrainian State Research and Design Inst. of Mining Geology, Geomechanics and Mine Survey, Coal Ministry 1984–95; Chief of State Tax Admin 1996–2002; First Deputy Prime Minister and Minister of Finance 2002–05, 2006–07; apptd Chair. Political Council, Partiya Rehioniv (Party of Regions) 2003; Acting Prime Minister 7–28 Dec. 2004, 5–24 Jan. 2005; mem. Nat. Acad. of Sciences of Ukraine 1997–; Honored Economist of Ukraine 1997. *Publications:* author of numerous books and articles on geology and taxation. *Leisure interests:* reading and painting. *Address:* Partiya Rehioniv (Party of Regions), 01021 Kyiv, vul. Lypska 10, Ukraine (office). *Telephone:* (44) 254-29-20 (office). *Fax:* (44) 254-33-70 (office). *E-mail:* partreg@ln.ua (office). *Website:* www.partyofregions.org.ua (office).

AZCUNA, Adolfo, AB, LLB; Philippine lawyer; b. 16 Feb. 1939; s. of Felipe Azcuna and Carmen Sevilla; m. Maria Asuncion Aunario 1968; one s. three d.; ed Ateneo de Manila and Univ. of Salzburg; elected Del. 1971 Constitutional Convention 1971–73; mem. Constitutional Comm. 1986–87; Press Sec. 1989; Presidential Legal Counsel 1987–90, Presidential Spokesman 1989–90; Pres. Manila Hotel 1997–98; Partner, Azcuna, Yorac, Sarmiento, Arroyo & Chua Law Offices 1992–; Corazon Aquino Fellowship, Harvard Univ. 1990 (deferred). *Publications:* Doing Business in the Philippines, Foreign Judgment Enforcement in the Philippines, Asian Conflict of Law, The Philippine Writ of Amparo, The Aquino Presidency: Destiny with Valor and Grace. *Leisure interests:* reading, biking, photography. *Address:* Azcuna, Yorac, Sarmiento, Arroyo and Chua Law Offices, G/F, Cedar Mansions II, Amber Avenue, Ortigas Center, Pasig City (office); 140 CRM Avenue, Las Pinas, Metro Manila, Philippines (home). *Telephone:* (2) 633-5981 (office); 801-1685 (home). *Fax:* (2) 633-2820 (office).

AZÉMA, Jean, BEng; French agricultural engineer and insurance executive; *CEO, Groupama SA;* b. 1953; ed Ecole Supérieure d'Agriculture de Purpan, Centre Nat. d'Etudes Supérieures de Sécurité; various positions within Groupe Groupama, including Man. Caisse Régionale des Pyrénées Orientales 1975–78, Caisse Régionale de l'Allier 1979–86, Finance Dir Groupama Cie 1987–95, later Dir of Investment, Consolidation and Insurance, Groupama, Man. Dir Groupama Sud-Ouest 1996–98, Groupama Sud 1998–2000, CEO Caisse Centrale Groupama 2000–04, CEO Groupama SA, Féd. Nat. Groupama, Groupama Holding 2004–; Chair. Féd. Française des Soc. d'Assurance Mutuelles 2001–; Dir Mediobanca, Véolia Environnement, Société Générale. *Address:* Groupama SA, 8–10 rue d'Astorg, 75383 Paris Cedex 08, France (office). *Telephone:* 1-44-56-77-77 (office). *E-mail:* relations.exterieures@groupama.com (office). *Website:* www.groupama.fr (office).

AZESKI, Branko; Macedonian business executive; *President, Managing Board, Economic Chamber of Macedonia;* fmr Gen. Man. Alexandar Palace Hotel; Founder and owner Hit Plus DOOEL, Skopje; Pres. Man. Bd Econ. Chamber of Macedonia 2005–; Pres. Asscn of Balkan Chambers 2005–. *Address:* Economic Chamber of Macedonia, Str. Dimitrie Cupovski 13, 1000 Skopje, Macedonia (office). *Telephone:* (2) 3244000 (office). *Fax:* (2) 3244088 (office). *E-mail:* ic@ic.mchamber.org.mk (office). *Website:* www.mchamber.org.mk (office).

AZHAR, Mohammad; Pakistani politician; mem. Nat. Ass.; fmr Gov. of Punjab; fmr Sr Vice-Pres. Pakistan Muslim League (PML); fmr Pres. PML Quaid-e-Azam Group. *Address:* c/o Pakistan Muslim League (PML), House No. 20-H, Street 10, Sector F-8/3, Islamabad, Pakistan.

AZIM, Athar Vigar Aziz, MA; Pakistani television producer and director; b. 15 June 1948, Karachi; s. of Syed Vigar Azim; ed Punjab Univ., Lahore; with Pakistan Television Corpn (PTV); Best Sports TV Producer (five times), Best Current Affairs TV Producer (twice), Men's Forum Golden Jubilee Award. *Television includes:* numerous reports on current affairs; sports series including Indo-Pakistan cricket series 1978–79, Football World Cup 1986, Hockey Champions Trophy and live coverage of hockey, athletics, squash and other games. *Address:* Pakistan Television Corporation, Karachi TV Centre, Karachi (office); Flat No. GF-3, Block B-1, Sea View Apartment, Defence, Karachi, Pakistan. *Telephone:* (21) 9230161 (PTV) (office); (21) 5843046. *Fax:* (21) 9231068 (PTV) (office).

AZIM, Syed Aftab, MA; Pakistani television producer; b. 19 Dec. 1944, Lucknow, India; s. of Syed Saeem Aziz; m. Ghazala Yasmeen; ed Islamia Coll., Karachi, Univ. of Karachi; Programmes Producer Pakistan TV (PTV) 1967–83, Special Producer of Religious Programmes 1999–; Audio Visual Man., PIA 1984–99; eight PTV Awards in 1972, 1974, 2002, Gold Medal, Silver Jubilee 1989. *Television includes:* documentaries on Japan, Thailand, The Philippines, France, Germany, UK and Saudi Arabia; religious programmes: Quran-e-Hakeem 2001, Haiya Alal Falaah 2002. *Publications include:* Sou-e-Haram (official Govt Hajj book). *Leisure interest:* travel. *Address:* Karachi Television Centre, Stadium Road, Karachi (office); 2/3 Block-E, Myanmar View, Gulshan-e-Igbal, Karachi, Pakistan (home). *Telephone:* (21) 9231178 (office); (21) 4792450 (home). *Fax:* (21) 9231043 (office); (21) 9231068 (home).

AZIMI, Abdul Salam, PhD; Afghan judge, politician and academic; *Chief Justice of the Supreme Court (Stera Mahkama);* ed Kabul Univ. and Univ. of Arizona, USA; fmr univ. prof.; experience in law and educ. also in Pakistan, Middle East and USA; Minister of Educ. 2001–03; mem. Constitutional Comm. to draft a new Afghan Constitution (primary drafter) 2002–03, Vice-Chair. Constitutional Review Comm. 2003; Head of Scientific and Research Centre of the Univ. of Neb. in Afghanistan –2006; legal adviser to Pres. Hamid Karzai 2004–06; Chief Justice of the Supreme Court (Stera Mahkama) 2006–. *Address:* Supreme Court of Afghanistan (Stera Mahkama), Kabul, Afghanistan (office).

AZIMI, Capt. Jahed; Afghan airline executive; fmr pilot, Ariana Afghan Airlines, Pres. 2002–05; fmr Deputy Minister in charge of Admin, Ministry of Transport. *Address:* c/o Ariana Afghan Airlines, PO Box 76, Kabul, Afghanistan (office).

AZIMOV, Rustam S., PhD; Uzbekistani economist and politician; *Deputy Prime Minister, responsible for the Economic Sector and Foreign Economic Relations and Minister of Finance;* b. 1958; ed Tashkent Inst. of Agricultural Engineers; Economist, Yulius Fuchik collective farm; Chief Economist of agricultural amalgamation in Djizak area; Chair. Nat. Bank for Foreign Econ. Activity 1991–98; mem. Oly Majlis (Supreme Ass.) 1994–; Minister of Finance 1998–2000, 2005–; Deputy Prime Minister and Minister of Macroeconomics and Statistics 2000–02; Deputy Prime Minister and Economy Minister 2002–05; Minister of Foreign Econ. Relations July–Nov. 2005; Deputy Prime Minister, responsible for the Econ. sector and Foreign Econ. Relations 2005–; Uzbekistan Del. to Asian Devt Bank; fmr Lecturer in Econs, Tashkent State Univ.; f. Ipak Yuli Bank. *Publications:* numerous articles on econs. *Address:* Ministry of Finance, 100008 Tashkent, Mustaqillik maydoni 5, Uzbekistan (office). *Telephone:* (71) 233-70-73 (office). *Fax:* (71) 244-56-43 (office). *E-mail:* info@mf.uz (office). *Website:* www.mf.uz (office).

AZIMOV, Yakhyo Nuriddinovich; Tajikistani politician; b. 4 Dec. 1947, Khodjend (fmrly Leninabad); m.; one s. two d.; ed Tashkent Inst. of Textile Industry; worked Ura-Tubin Tricot factory 1971–75; engineer, head of rug production, Dir Kairak-Kum rug factory 1975–82; Deputy Chief Engineer, Chief Engineer, Dir-General of rug productions 1982–96; Pres. Jt Stock Co. Kolinkho, Kairakum 1996–; Chair. Council of Ministers (Prime Minister) of Tajikistan 1996–99; Minister of Econs 2000–01. *Address:* c/o Council of Ministers, Rudaki prosp. 42, 743051 Dushanbe, Tajikistan (office).

AZINGER, Paul William; American golfer; b. 6 Jan. 1960, Holyoke, Mass.; m. Toni Azinger; two d.; ed Brevard Jr Coll. and Fla State Univ.; started playing golf aged five; turned professional 1981; won Phoenix Open 1987, Herz Bay Hill Classic 1988, Canon Greater Hartford Open 1989, MONY Tournament of Champions 1990, AT&T Pebble Beach Nat. Pro-Am 1991, TOUR Championship 1992, BMW Int. Open 1990, 1992, Memorial Tournament, New England Classic, PGA Championship, Inverness 1993; GWAA Ben Hogan Trophy 1995; mem. US Ryder Cup Team 1989, 1991, 1993, 2002; mem. Pres. 's Cup 1994, 2000; broadcasting debut as reporter for NBC, 1995 Ryder Cup; analyst American Broadcasting Corpn (ABC) Sports 2005–; PGA Tour Player of the Year 1987, Ben Hogan Award 1995. *Publication:* Zinger (about his fight against cancer). *Leisure interest:* fishing. *Address:* c/o PGA Tour, 112 Tpc Boulevard, Ponte Vedra Beach, FL 33082, USA.

AZIZ, M. Abdul, BA, MA; Bangladeshi judge and government official; b. 30 Sept. 1939, Amboula village, Agailjhara, Barisal; ed Dhaka Univ.; called to Bar, Inner Temple, London, UK 1969; practised as a lawyer in High Court, judge of High Court 1996–2004, judge of Appellate Div. of Supreme Court 2004–05, Chief Election Commr 2005–07. *Address:* c/o Block-5/6, Election Commission Secretariat, Sher-e-Bangla Nagar, Dhaka 1207, Bangladesh (office).

AZIZ, Tan Sri Paduka Rafidah, MEcons; Malaysian politician; b. 4 Nov. 1943, Selama Perak; m. Mohammed Basir bin Ahmad; three c.; ed Univ. of Malaya; tutor, Asst Lecturer, Lecturer and Chair. Rural Devt Div. Faculty of Econs Univ. of Malaya 1966–76; mem. Parl. 1986–; Deputy Minister of Finance 1977–80; Minister of Public Enterprise 1980–88, of Int. Trade and Industry 1988–2008; mem. UMNO Supreme Council 1975–, Chair. Women's Wing 1999–; Ahli Mangku Negara, Datuk Paduka Mahkota Selangor. *Leisure interests:* reading, decoration, music, squash. *Address:* United Malays National Organization (Pertubuhan Kebangsaan Melayu Bersatu), Menara Dato' Onn, 38th Floor, Jalan Tun Ismail, 50480 Kuala Lumpur, Malaysia. *Telephone:* (3) 40429511. *Fax:* (3) 40412358. *E-mail:* email@umno.net.my. *Website:* www.umno-online.com.

AZIZ, Shaukat, BSc, MBA; Pakistani politician and banker; b. 6 March 1949, Karachi; m.; three c.; ed St Patrick's High School, Karachi, Abbottabad Public School, Abbottabad, Govt Islamia Coll., Kasur, Pakistani Business School Inst. of Business Admin, Karachi, Univ. of Karachi; various posts with Citibank including Head of Corp. and Investment Banking, Asia Pacific Region, Head of Corp. and Investment Banking for Cen. and Eastern Europe, Middle East and Africa, Corp. Planning Officer, Citicorp, Man. Dir, Saudi American Bank, Global Head, Pvt. Banking, Vice-Pres. 1969–99; Minister of Finance and Revenue, Econ. Affairs and Statistics and of Planning and Econ. Devt 1999–2004; mem. Senate 2002–04; Prime Minister of Pakistan and Minister of Finance and Revenue, Econ. Affairs and Statistics 2004–07. *Address:* c/o Office of the Prime Minister's Secretariat, Constitution Avenue, F-6/5, Cabinet Division, Cabinet Block, Islamabad, Pakistan. *Telephone:* (51) 9206111.

AZIZ, Ungku Abdul, DEcons; Malaysian academic and university administrator; b. 28 Jan. 1922, London, UK; m. Sharifah Azah Aziz; one d.; ed Raffles Coll. and Univ. of Malaya in Singapore, Waseda Univ., Tokyo, Johore State Civil Service; Lecturer in Econs, Univ. of Malaya in Singapore till 1952; Head, Dept of Econs, Univ. of Malaya, Kuala Lumpur 1952–61, Dean of Faculty 1961–65, Vice-Chancellor 1968–88, Royal Prof. of Econs 1978; Pres. Nat. Co-operative Movement (ANGKASA) 1971, Asscn of SE Asian Institutions of Higher Learning (ASAIHL) 1973–75; Chair. Asscn of Commonwealth Univs 1974–75, Malaysian Nat. Council for ASAIHL, Malaysian Examinations Council 1980–; mem. UN Univ. Council; Corresp. mem. of Advisory Bd, Modern Asian Studies 1973–75; mem. Econ. Asscn of Malaysia, Int. Asscn of Agricultural Economists, Jt Advisory Cttee of FAO, UNESCO and ILO; mem. Nat. Consultative Council and Nat. Unity Advisory Council, Govt of Malaysia; mem. numerous cttees and orgs; Fellow, World Acad. of Arts and Sciences 1965–; Ordre des Arts et Lettres (France) 1965; Hon. DHumLitt (Univ. of Pittsburgh); Hon. EdD (Chulalongkorn Univ., Thailand) 1977; Hon. DJur (Waseda Univ., Japan) 1982; Hon. DLitt (Univ. of Warwick) 1982; Hon. DIur (Univ. of Strathclyde) 1986, (Utara Univ., Malaysia) 1988; Hon. DEcon (Kebangsaan Univ., Malaysia) 1986; Hon. LLD (Buckingham) 1987; Tun Abdul Razak Foundation Award 1978, Japan Foundation Award 1981; Special Award, Muslim Pilgrim Savings Fund Bd 1988; Grand Cordon of the Order of the Sacred Treasure, Emperor of Japan 1989; ASEAN Achievement Award (Educ.) 1992, Int. Academic Prize (City of Fukoka) 1993. *Leisure interests:* jogging, reading and photography.

AZIZ KHAN, Gen. Mohammad; Pakistani army officer; ed Royal Staff Coll.; fmr Chief of Gen. Staff; fmr IV Corps Commdr Lahore; Chair. Jt Chiefs of Staff Cttee 2001–04; mem. Nat. Security Council.

AZIZ M. IBRAHIM, Farouk Abdel, MD, FRCOG; Sudanese professor of obstetrics and gynaecology; b. 12 April 1941, Elgolid; s. of Abdel Aziz Mohamed and Zeinab Ahmed Hassan; m. Amal Abu Bakr Arbab 1975; two s. two d.; ed Univ. of Khartoum; Consultant and Lecturer in Obstetrics and Gynaecology, Univ. of Khartoum 1972, Head of Dept 1974, Assoc. Prof. 1980, Dir EDC 1985, Man. Health Learning Materials Project 1986, Dir Staff Devt

Centre 1990; Dean Ahfad School of Medicine for Girls 1993; Chief Tech. Adviser WHO 1995–. *Publications:* five books on obstetrics and educ., three books on educ., obstetrics and reproductive health and family planning, 16 scientific papers on reproductive health. *Leisure interests:* photography, reading. *Address:* PO Box 543, San'a, Republic of Yemen. *Telephone:* (1) 216 337. *Fax:* (1) 251 216.

AZKOUL, Karim, PhD; Lebanese diplomatist and writer; b. 15 July 1915, Raschaya; s. of Najib Azkoul and Latifah Assaly; m. Eva Corey 1947; one s. one d.; ed Jesuit Univ. of St Joseph, Beirut and Univs of Paris, Berlin, Bonn and Munich; Prof. of History, Arab and French Literature and Philosophy in various colls in Lebanon 1939–46; Dir of an Arabic publishing house and monthly Arabic review The Arab World, Beirut 1943–45; mem. Lebanese Del. to UN, New York 1947–50, Acting Perm. Del. to UN 1950–53; Head of UN Affairs Dept, Ministry of Foreign Affairs 1953–57; Head, Perm. Del. to UN 1957–59, Rapporteur Cttee on Genocide 1948, Humanitarian, Cultural and Social Cttee of Gen. Ass. 1951, Cttee on Freedom of Information 1951; First Vice-Chair. Human Rights Comm. 1958; Chair. Negotiating Cttee for Extra Budgetary Funds 1952–54; Consul-Gen. in Australia and New Zealand 1959–61; Amb. to Ghana, Guinea and Mali 1961–64, to Iran and Afghanistan 1964–66; journalist 1966–68; Prof. of Philosophy, Beirut Coll. for Women 1968–72, Lebanese Univ. 1970–72; Chief Ed. The Joy of Knowledge, Arabic Encyclopedia (10 vols) 1978–; mem. PEN, Emergency World Council, Hague 1971–; Vice-Chair. Cttee for Defence of Human Rights in Lebanon; mem. Bd of Trustees, Bd of Man. of Theological School of Balamand, Lebanon; Order of Cedar (Lebanon), Order of Holy Sepulchre (Jerusalem), Order of St Marc (Alexandria), Order of the Brilliant Star (Repub. of China), Order of Southern Star (Brazil), Order of St Peter and Paul (Damascus). *Publications:* Reason and Faith in Islam (in German) 1938, Reason in Islam (in Arabic) 1946, Freedom (co-author) 1956, Freedom of Association (UN) 1968; trans. into Arabic: Consciencism (Nkrumah) 1964, Arab Thought in the Liberal Age (Albert Hourani) 1969. *Leisure interests:* reading and writing.

AZMAT, Ali; Pakistani musician; b. 1970, Lahore; ed Ashfield Business School, Sydney, Australia; began musical career in band Jupiters, Lahore 1991; founder mem., Junoon (with Salman Ahmad and Brian O'Connell) 1991–, banned by Pakistani authorities for criticism of govt corruption early 1990s; upon invitation of UN Sec.-Gen., Kofi Annan, performed at UN Gen. Ass. (first band to play at Gen. Ass.); tours throughout Asia, N America, Middle East and Europe; Jazbe-e-Junoon selected as official song of cricket world cup, hosted by Pakistan 1996; simultaneous solo career 2002–; Channel V Music Award for Int. Group 1998, UNESCO Award for Outstanding Achievement in Music and Peace 1999, BBC Asia Award 1999. *Film music:* for film Paap (directed by Pooja Bhatt). *Recordings:* albums: with Junoon: Junoon 1990, Talaash 1993, Inquilaab 1995, Khashmakash 1996, Azaadi 1997, Parvaaz 1999, Andaz 2001, The Millennium Edition (compilation) 2000, Daur-e-Junoon 2002, Dewaar 2003; solo: album 2003, Klashinfolk 2008; singles: with Junoon: Jazbe-e-Junoon 1996, Saeein, Ehtesaab 1996, Sayonee 1997, Taara jala. *Address:* Junoon Inc., 210 Old Tappan Road, Tappan, NY 10983, Pakistan (office). *E-mail:* alishan@aliazmat.com (office); info@junoon.com (office). *Website:* www.junoon.com; www.aliazmat.com.

AZMI, Shabana, BA; Indian actress and politician; b. 18 Sept. 1950, Hyderabad; d. of Shaukat Kaifi and Kaifi Azmi; m. Javed Akhtar 1984; ed St Xavier's Coll., Film Inst., Pune; mem. Rajya Sabha (upper house of Parl.) 1997–2003; speaker on women's rights and communication in USA; campaigner on social justice issues; Chair. Nivara Hakk Suraksha Samiti (campaigning org. for upgrading of slum dwellings); Goodwill Amb. United Nations Populations Fund (UNFPA) 1998–; Chair. of Jury Montréal and Cairo Int. Film Festivals; mem. Nat. Integration Council, Advisory Council Endowment Campaign for Chair. in Indian Studies, Columbia Univ.; Visiting Prof., Univ. of Michigan, USA; Soviet Land Nehru Award 1985, Padma Shri Award 1988, Rajiv Gandhi Award for Excellence in Secularism 1994, Yash Bhartiya Award for promoting women's issues, Govt of Uttar Pradesh, King Chevaz Award, Ann Arbor Univ., MI, USA, Gandhi Foundation Int. Peace Award 2006, Crystal Award, World Econ. Forum 2006. *Films include:* nearly 150 films over 30 years, including: Ankur (Nat. Award for Best Actress) 1974, Arth (Nat. Award) 1983, Khandhar (Nat. Award) 1984, Paar (Nat. Award) 1985, Libaas (Int. Best Actress Award, N Korea 1993), Patang (Best Actress Award, Taormina Art Festival 1994), Swami, Bhavna (Filmfare Award), Junoon, Shatranj Ke Khiladi, Parinay, Amardeep, Sparsh, Massom, Doosri Dulhan, Madame Sousatzka, Bengali Night, In Custody, The Journey, Son of the Pink Panther, City of Joy, Fire (Best Actress Award, Chicago Int. Film Festival) 1996, Godmother (Nat. Award 1998), Hari-Bhari: Fertility 2000, Makdee 2002, Tehzeeb 2003, Lakshya 2004, Morning Raga 2004, Waterborne 2005. *Plays:* Nora (Singapore Repertory Theatre), The Waiting Room (Nat. Theatre, London), Sufaid Kundali, Tumhari Amrita. *Television:* Anupama (Hindi serial). *Leisure interests:* reading, singing. *Address:* 702 Sagar Samrat, Green Fields, Juhu, Mumbai 400049, India (home). *Telephone:* (22) 6200066 (home). *Fax:* (22) 26202602 (office). *E-mail:* shabana@vsnl.com (office).

AZNAN, Syed Jaafar, MBA, PhD; Malaysian civil servant and banker; *Vice-President, Trade and Policy and Acting Vice-President, Corporate Resources and Services, Islamic Development Bank;* b. 1947; m.; three c.; ed Univ. of Malaya, Wharton School, USA, Henley Man. Coll./Brunel Univ., UK; civil servant in Malaysia holding several sr positions in various ministries 1970–97; Vice-Pres. Trade and Policy, Islamic Devt Bank, Jeddah, Saudia Arabia 1997–, also currently Acting Vice-Pres. Corp. Resources and Services. *Address:* Islamic Development Bank, PO Box 5925, Jeddah 21432, Saudi Arabia (office). *Telephone:* (2) 6361400 (office). *Fax:* (2) 6366871 (office). *E-mail:* idbarchives@isdb.org (office). *Website:* www.isdb.org (office).

AZNAR LÓPEZ, José María; Spanish politician and academic; *President, FAES Fundación para el Análisis y los Estudios Sociales;* b. 1953, Madrid; m. Ana Botella; two s. one d.; ed Universidad Complutense, Madrid; fmr tax inspector; fmr Chief Exec. Castile-Leon region; joined Rioja br. Alianza Popular 1978, Deputy Sec.-Gen. and mem. Cortes (Parl.) 1982; Premier Castilla y León Autonomous Region 1987; Pres. Partido Popular (PP, fmrly Alianza Popular) 1990–2004; Prime Minister of Spain and Pres. of the Council 1996–2004; currently Pres. FAES Fundación para el Análisis y los Estudios Sociales, Madrid; Distinguished Scholar in the Practice of Global Leadership Georgetown Univ., Washington DC 2004–; Vice-Pres. European Democratic Union (EDC); Pres. Int. Democratic Centre (IDC) 2001; mem. Bd of Dirs News Corp. 2006–; Pres.'s Medal Georgetown Univ. 2004. *Publication:* Ocho años de gobierno: una visión personal de España 2004. *Address:* FAES Fundación para el Análisis y los Estudios Sociales, C/Juan Bravo, 3C, 7°, 28006 Madrid, Spain (office); Mortara Center for International Studies, Edmund A. Walsh School of Foreign Service, Georgetown University, ICC, Suite 304, 37th and O Streets, NW, Washington, DC 20057, USA (office). *Telephone:* (91) 5766857 (office). *Fax:* (91) 5754695 (office). *E-mail:* fundacionfaes@fundacionfaes.org (office); atencion@pp.es (office). *Website:* www.fundacionfaes.org (office); www.georgetown.edu/sfs/mortara (office); www.pp.es (office).

AZNAVOUR, Charles; French/Armenian film actor and singer; b. 22 May 1924; m. 1st Micheline Rugel 1946; m. 2nd Evelyne Plessis 1955; m. 3rd Ulla Thorsel 1967; five c.; ed Ecole Centrale de T.S.F., Centre de Spectacle, Paris; with Jean Dasté Company 1941; Man. Dir French-Music 1965–; Roving UNESCO Amb. to Armenia 1995–; Hon. Pres. Belgrade Film Festival 2003; numerous song recitals in Europe and USA; film music includes: Soupe au lait, L'île du bout du monde, Ces dames préfèrent le mambo, Le cercle vicieux, De quoi tu te mêles Daniela, Douce violence, Les Parisiennes; also author and singer of numerous songs; composer of operetta Monsieur Carnaval 1965, Douchka 1973; Armenian Amb. to Switzerland 2009–; Commdr Légion d'honneur 2004, Commdr des Arts et des Lettres; several prizes; Grand Prix nat. de la chanson 1986, César d'honneur 1997, Molière amical 1999, Time Magazine Entertainer of the Century. *Films include:* La tête contre les murs 1959, Tirez sur le pianiste 1960, Un taxi pour Tobrouk, Le testament d'Orphée, Le diable et les dix commandements, Haute-infidélité 1964, La métamorphose des cloportes 1965, Paris au mois d'août 1966, Le facteur s'en va-t-en guerre 1966, Candy 1969, Les intrus 1973, Sky Riders, Intervention Delta, Folies bourgeoises, Dix petits nègres 1976, The Twist 1976, The Tin Drum 1979, Qu'est-ce qui a fait courir David? 1982, Les fantômes du chapelier 1982, La montagne magique 1983, Vive la vie 1984, Mangeclous 1988, Il Maestro 1992, Les Années Campagne 1992, Pondichéry Dernier Comptoir des Indes 1996, Les Mômes 1999, Judaicaë I 2000, Laguna 2001, Angelina (TV) 2002, Passage du bac (TV) 2002, Ararat 2002, Le Père Goriot 2004, Emmenez-moi 2005. *Recordings include:* albums: Jazznavour 1998, Aznavour 2000, Colore ma vie 2007. *Leisure interests:* photography, do-it-yourself. *Address:* c/o Levon Sayan, 76–78 avenue des Champs-Elysées, bureau 322, 75008 Paris, France. *Website:* www.c-aznavour.com.

AZOUR, Jihad, MS, PhD; Lebanese economist and government official; b. 4 May 1964, Sir Denniye; m. Roula Rizk; ed Assad Univ., Univ. of Paris, IEP Paris, France, Harvard Univ., USA; with McKinsey, Lebanon 1989–93; Program Man. and Advisor to Dir Gen. Asscn d'Economie Financière 1993–94; Man. Pnr, AM&F Consulting 1996–98; consultant IMF and Booz Allen 2005; Prof., American Univ. Beirut; Dir UNDP/World Bank project 1999–2005; Adviser to Ministry of Finance 1999–2004; Minister of Finance 2005–08. *Address:* c/o Ministry of Finance, 4e étage, Immeuble MOF, place Riad es-Solh, Beirut, Lebanon (office).

AZRIELI, David Joshua, OC, CQ, BA, MArch; Canadian designer, architect and philanthropist; *Director, Canpro Investments Ltd;* b. 10 May 1922, Makow, Poland; m. Stephanie Azrieli; four c.; ed Technion Univ., Haifa, Israel, Carleton Univ.; escaped Poland 1939, journeyed secretly through Russia and Cen. Asia 1940–41, sought exile in Palestine 1942; studied architecture in Haifa; served in Israeli Defense and Air Forces 1948; emmigrated to Montreal, Canada 1954; Founding Dir Canpro Investments Ltd, Montreal 1958–, working in commercial real estate markets in Canada, USA and Middle East, designing, developing and building skyscrapers, shopping malls and office towers; est. David Arzieli Fellowship, Concordia Univ.; donated funds to est. David Arzieli School of Architecture, Tel Aviv Univ. 1994 and David J. Arzieli Pavilion, Theatre and Inst. of Grad. Studies in Architecture, Carleton Univ. 2002; Chevalier Ordre Nat. du Québec 1998; Hon. PhD (Concordia, Yeshiva, Technion, Tel Aviv and Carleton Univs); Prime Minister's Jubilee Award (Israel) 1998, Jerusalem Prize, Commemorative Medal on Canada's 125th Anniversary, Golden Jubilee Medal. *Architectural Designs include:* Tel Aviv Enclosed Shopping Mall (first in Israel) 1986, Les Promenades de l'Outaouais, Gatineau, Quebec, Azrieli Centre, Tel Aviv 1998. *Address:* Canpro Investments Ltd, 1155 Sherbrooke Street West, PH-1, Montreal, PQ H3A 2N3, Canada (office). *Telephone:* (514) 282-1155 (office). *Fax:* (514) 849-2036 (office).

AZUELA, Arturo, PhD; Mexican journalist, novelist and academic; b. 30 June 1938, Mexico City; ed Universidad Nacional Autonoma de Mexico; fmr mathematician and violinist in various symphony orchestras; published first novel 1973; fmr Visiting Prof., Univ. of California, Berkeley, Univ. of Nanterre, France, Univ. of Edinburgh, Scotland, Sorbonne and Montpellier, France; Chair. Seminario de Cultura Mexicana; mem. Academia Mexicana de la Lengua 1986–. *Publications:* El tamaño del infierno, La casa de las 1,000 vírgenes, Manifestación de silencios. *Address:* Seminario de Cultura Mexicana, Presidente Masaryk 526, Polanco, México, DF 11560, Mexico. *Telephone:* (55) 5230-7610. *Fax:* (55) 5230-7612. *Website:* www.culturamexicana.org.mx.

AZUMA, Takamitsu, JIA, DArch; Japanese architect; b. 20 Sept. 1933, Osaka; s. of Yoshimatsu Azuma and Yoshiko (née Ikeda); m. Setsuko Nakaoka 1957; one d.; ed Osaka Univ.; designer, Ministry of Postal Service, Osaka 1957–60; Chief Designer, Junzo Sakakura Architect & Assocs, Osaka 1960–63, Tokyo 1963–67; Prin. Takamitsu Azuma Architect & Assocs, Tokyo 1968–85; Instructor, Univ. of Art and Design 1976–78, Tokyo Denki Univ. 1980–82, Tokyo Univ. 1983–85; Instructor, Osaka Univ. 1981–85, Prof. 1985–97, Prof. Emer. 1997–; Instructor, Osaka Art Univ. 1985–87; Architect, Azuma Architects and Assocs 1985–97; Prof., Chiba Inst. of Tech. 1997–; mem. Architectural Inst. of Japan; Visiting Prof., School of Architecture, Washington Univ., St Louis, USA 1985; 1st Prize Kinki Br., Inst. of Architects Competition 1957; Architectural Inst. of Japan Architectural Design Prize 1995. *Publications:* Revaluation of the Residence 1971, On the Japanese Architectural Space 1981, Philosophy of Living in the City 1983, Device from Architecture 1986, Space Analysis of the Urban Residence 1986, White Book about Tower House 1987, On Urban Housing 1997. *Leisure interests:* travelling, reading, computing. *Address:* Azuma Architects & Assocs., 3-6-1 Minami-Aoyama Minato-ku, Tokyo 107-0016 (office); 3-39-4 Jingumae, Shibuya-ku, Tokyo 150-0001, Japan (home). *Telephone:* (3) 3403-5593 (office); (3) 3404-0805 (home).

B

BAALI, Abdallah; Algerian diplomatist; *Special Envoy of the President of Algeria;* b. 19 Oct. 1954, Guelma; m. Rafika Baali; one s. one d.; ed Ecole Nat. d'Admin., New York Univ.; Sec. of Foreign Affairs 1977–82, Head Dept of Communication and Documentation, Foreign Affairs Ministry 1990–92; mem. Perm. Mission to UN, New York 1982–89, Algeria's Alt. Rep. to Security Council 1988–89, Perm. Rep. to UN, New York 1996–2005, Rep. to Security Council 2004–05; Amb. to Indonesia (also accred to Australia, New Zealand and Brunei Darussalam) 1992–96; currently Special Envoy of the Pres. of Algeria; Pres. NPT Review Conf. 2000. *Address:* c/o Office of the President, Présidence de la République, el-Mouradia, Algiers, Algeria (office). *Telephone:* (21) 69-15-15. *Fax:* (21) 69-15-95. *Website:* www.el-mouradia.dz.

BABACAN, Ali, MBA, BSc; Turkish politician; *Deputy Prime Minister and State Minister in charge of coordination of the Economy;* b. 1967, Ankara; m.; two c.; ed Middle East Tech. Univ., Ankara, Northwestern Univ., USA; worked at QRM, Inc., Chicago, Ill. 1992–94; chief adviser to Mayor of Ankara 1994; ran family-owned textile co. 1994–2002; mem. of Grand Nat. Ass., representing Ankara 2002–; Minister of State for Economy 2002–05; Chief Negotiator in accession talks with EU 2005–; Minister of Foreign Affairs 2007–09; Deputy Prime Minister and Minister of State in charge of coordination of the Economy 2009–; Co-founder and Bd Mem., AKP (Adalet ve Kalkinma Partisi/Justice and Devt Party). *Address:* Deputy Prime Ministers' Office, Başbakan yard. ve Devlet Bakanı, Bakanlıklar, Ankara, Turkey (office). *Telephone:* (312) 4191621 (office). *Fax:* (312) 4191547 (office).

BABADJHAN, Ramz; Uzbekistan poet and playwright; b. 2 Aug. 1921; s. of Nasriddin Babadjhan and Salomat Babadjhan; m. 1947; one s. two d.; ed Pedagogical Inst., Tashkent; Deputy Chair. Uzbek Writers' Union; mem. CPSU 1951–91; Chair. Uzbek Republican Cttee on Relations with African and Asian Writers; Pres. Soc. on Cultural Relations with Compatriots Living Abroad 'Vatan' 1990–94; first works published 1935; USSR State Prize 1972. *Publications include:* Dear Friends, Thank You, My Dear, The Heart Never Sleeps, Selected Poetry, A Poet Lives Twice, Living Water, Yusuf and Zuleyha, 1001 Crane, Sides, Uncle and Nephew, You Cannot Deceive a Gipsy. *Leisure interests:* photography, travelling. *Address:* Beshchinar str. 34, 100070 Tashkent, Uzbekistan. *Telephone:* (371) 55-61-06.

BABAEV, Agadzhan Geldyevich, DrGeogSc; Turkmenistani geographer and academic; *Director, Desert Research Institute, Turkmenistan Academy of Sciences;* b. 10 May 1929, Mary; s. of Geldy Babaev and Ogulbek Babaevai; m. Dunyagozel Palvanova 1951; two s. six d.; ed State Pedagogical Inst., Ashkhabad (now Ashgabat), Turkmenistan State Univ.; Head, Geography Dept, Turkmenistan State Univ. 1952–59; Deputy Dir Desert Research Inst., Turkmenistan Acad. of Sciences 1959–60, Dir 1960–99; Chair. Scientific Council for Desert Problems 1967–; Ed.-in-Chief Problems of Desert Devt 1967–; Dir Turkmenistan Research and Training Centre on Desertification Control for ESCAP; Deputy to USSR Supreme Soviet 1979–89; Chair. Turkmenistan Soc. for Chinese-Soviet Friendship; mem. Turkmenistan Acad. of Sciences, Pres. 1975–86, 1989–93; Corresp. mem. USSR (now Russian) Acad. of Sciences 1976; Academician, Islamic Acad. of Sciences 1996–; Vice-Pres. Turkmens of the World Humanitarian Asscn; Deputy, Turkmenistan Parl.; USSR State Prize 1981, Academician Karpinskii Medal 1990, Jerald Piel Medal 1992. *Publications:* 12 monographs, 329 articles for professional journals. *Address:* National Institute of Deserts, Flora and Fauna, 15 Bitarap Turkmenistan Street, Ashgabat 744000 (office); 113 Kosaev Street, Ashgabat 744020, Turkmenistan (home). *Telephone:* (12) 35-73-52 (office); (12) 34-26-24 (home). *Fax:* (12) 39-05-86 (office). *E-mail:* sicm@online .tm (office).

BABANGIDA, Maj.-Gen. Ibrahim Badamasi; Nigerian army officer (retd) and fmr Head of State; b. 17 Aug. 1941, Minna; m. Maryam King 1969; two s. two d.; ed Niger provincial secondary school, Bida, Kaduna Mil. Training Coll. and Indian Mil. Acad.; commissioned 1963, Lt 1966; training with RAC, UK 1966; CO during Biafran Civil War; Co Commdr and Instructor, Nigerian Defence Acad. 1970–72; rank of Maj. then Lt-Col Armoured Corps 1974; trained at US Army Armoury School 1974; promoted to Maj.-Gen.; of Army Duties and Plans 1983; took part in overthrow of Pres. Shehu Shagari 1983; mem. Supreme Mil. Council and Chief Army Staff 1983–85; Pres. of Nigeria following coup overthrowing Maj.-Gen. Muhammadu Buhari (q.v.) 1985–93; Pres. Police Council 1989; Minister of Defence Dec. 1989–90; Hon. GCB 1989. *Publications:* Civil and Military Relationship, The Nigerian Experience 1979, Defence Policy within the Framework of National Planning 1985. *Address:* Minna, Niger State, Nigeria. *Website:* www.ibrahim-babangida.com.

BABANOV, Omurbek T.; Kyrgyzstani business executive and politician; *First Deputy Prime Minister;* opposition activist 2006; fmr mem. of Parl., barred from race in 2007 due to citizenship issues; retd from politics; mem. Social Democratic Party, resgnd 2009; First Deputy Prime Minister 2009–. *Address:* Office of the Prime Minister, 720003 Bishkek, Dom Pravitelstva, Kyrgyzstan (office). *Telephone:* (312) 66-12-20 (office). *Fax:* (312) 66-66-58 (office). *E-mail:* pmoffice@mail.gov.kg (office). *Website:* www.government.gov .kg (office).

BABBAR, Raj; Indian politician, actor and filmmaker; b. 26 June 1952, Agra Dist, Uttar Pradesh; s. of Kaushal Kumar and Shobha Rani; m. Nadira Babbar 1975; two s. one d.; ed NSD, New Delhi; mem. Rajya Sabha 1994–99, Home Affairs Cttee, Rules Cttee, Consultative Cttee, Ministry of Civil Aviation; mem. 13th, 14th Lok Sabha 1999–, mem. Defence Cttee 1999–2000, Energy Cttee; Pres. Jan Morcha party 2006–; acted in more than 150 films and 30

plays; Uttar Pradesh Govt 'Yash Bharti' Award, Punjabi Male Actor of the Millennium, Punjabi American Festival 2000. *Films include:* Shaheed Uddham Singh, LoC, Kyaa Dil Ne Kahaa, The Legend of Bhagat Singh 2002, Talaash 2003, Sheen 2004, Police Force: An Inside Story 2004, Shikaar 2004, Yaaran Naal Baharaan 2005, Bunty Aur Babli 2005, Ek Dhun Banaras Kee 2006, Corporate 2006, UNNS: Love Forever 2006, Ek Jind Ek Jaan 2006, Sirf Romance: Love by Chance 2007, Aap Kaa Surroor: The Moviee 2007. *Leisure interest:* charity work. *Address:* 20 Mahadev Road, New Delhi 110 001; Nepathay 20, Gulmohar Road, J.V.P.D. Scheme, Mumbai 400 049, Maharashtra, India. *Telephone:* (11) 23352728; (11) 3557728; (11) 3352728. *E-mail:* babbar@sansad.nic.in. *Website:* loksabha.nic.in.

BABBITT, Bruce Edward, LLB; American lawyer, business executive and fmr politician; b. 27 July 1938; m. Hattie Coons; two c.; ed Univ. of Notre Dame, Univ. of Newcastle, UK, Harvard Univ. Law School; Attorney-Gen. Ariz. 1975–78; Gov. of Ariz. 1978–87; Pnr, Steptoe & Johnson, Phoenix; US Sec. of Interior 1993–2001; Sec. of Counsel, Environmental Dept, Latham & Watkins LLP (law firm) 2001–; Pres. Raintree Ventures (investment firm), Washington, DC; Chair. World Wildlife Fund 2006–; Chair. Nat. Groundwater Policy Forum 1984; Pres. League of Conservation Voters; Marshall Scholar 1960–62; Democrat; Thomas Jefferson Award, Nat. Wildlife Fed. 1981, Special Conservation Award 1983. *Publications:* Color and Light: The Southwest Canvases of Louis Akin 1973, Grand Canyon: An Anthology 1978, Cities in the Wilderness: A New Look at Land Use in America 2005. *Address:* c/o World Wildlife Fund, 1250 24th Street, NW, PO Box 97180, Washington, DC 20090-7180. *Telephone:* (202) 293-4800. *Website:* www.worldwildlife.org/wildplaces/ unitedstates.cfm.

BABBITT, Milton Byron, DMus, MFA; American composer; b. 10 May 1916, Philadelphia; s. of Albert E. Babbitt and Sarah Potamkin; m. Sylvia Miller 1939; one d.; ed New York and Princeton Univs.; Music Faculty, Princeton Univ. 1938–, Math. Faculty 1943–45, Bicentennial Preceptor 1953–56, Prof. of Music 1966–84, Prof. Emer. 1984–; Dir Columbia-Princeton Electronic Music Center; mem. Faculty, Juilliard School 1971–; Fromm Prof., Harvard Univ. 1988; Guggenheim Fellow 1960–61; MacArthur Fellow 1986–91; mem. American Acad. of Arts and Sciences, American Acad. of Arts and Letters; Hon. DMus (Glasgow); Hon. DFA (Northwestern Univ.); American Acad. of Arts and Letters Award 1959; Gold Medal, Brandeis Univ. 1970; Pulitzer Prize 1982, Schoenberg Inst. Award 1988, William Schuman Award 1992. *Works include:* Music for the Mass 1941, Composition for Four Instruments 1948, Woodwind Quartet 1953, All Set 1957, Vision and Prayer 1961, Philomel 1964, Tableaux 1972, Reflections 1975, Solo Requiem 1977, Paraphrases 1979, Ars Combinatoria 1981, Melismata 1982, The Head of the Bed 1982, Canonic Form 1983, Piano Concerto 1985, Transfigured Notes 1986, The Joy of More Sextets 1986, Whirled Series 1987, Consortini 1989, Emblems 1989, Soli e Duettini 1989–90, Play It Again Sam 1989, Envoi 1990, Preludes, Interludes and Postlude 1991. *Publication:* The Function of Set Structure in the Twelve Tone System 1946. *Leisure interest:* philosophy. *Address:* 222 Western Way, Princeton, NJ 08540-5306, USA.

BABENKO, Hector; Argentine film-maker; b. 7 Feb. 1946, Buenos Aires; eight years in Europe as writer, house painter, door-to-door salesman, film extra etc.; moved to Brazil 1969; Best Foreign Film Award for Pixote (New York Film Critics). *Films:* as writer, dir, producer: Fabuloso Fittipaldi, O 1973, O Rei Da Noite 1976, Pixote 1980, Corazón iluminado 1996, Carandiru 2003; as writer, dir: Lucio Flavio–Passageiro da Agonia 1978, At Play in the Fields of the Lord 1991; as dir, producer: Kiss of the Spider Woman 1985; as producer: Besame Mucho 1987; as dir: Ironweed 1987.

BABESHKO, Vladimir A.; Russian physicist and university official; *Rector, Kuban State University;* b. 30 May 1941; m.; two d.; ed Rostov State Univ.; with Rostov Univ. 1966–82, fmr Asst, Prof., Deputy Dir; Rector Kuban State Univ. 1982–; Chair. Russian S Branch, Int. Acad. of Higher Educ. Sciences; mem. Council for Sciences, Tech. and Educ. under Pres. of Russian Fed. 2004–; mem. Russian Acad. of Sciences 1997–; Order of People's Friendship 1986; Lenin Komsomol Prize 1977, Vavilov Medal 1990, State Award of Russian Fed. in the Field of Science and Eng 2001, Hero of Labour of Kuban Medal 2003, Rector of the Year Hon. Breastplate 2004, 2005, Distinguished Citizen of Krasnodar. *Publications:* author or co-author of more than 300 scientific publs, including five monographs. *Address:* Kuban State University, 149 Libknekhta str., 350040 Krasnodar, Russia (office). *Telephone:* (861) 2199502 (office). *Fax:* (861) 2199517 (office). *E-mail:* babeshko@kubsu.ru (office). *Website:* www.kubsu.ru (office).

BABICH, Mikhail Viktorovich; Russian politician; b. 28 May 1969; m.; two c.; ed Ryazan Higher Mil. School of Communications, Moscow Inst. of Econ. Man. and Law, State Acad. of Man.; sr officer in airborne troops 1990–94; worked in pvt. sector 1995–99; Deputy Dir-Gen. Fed. Agency for Food Market Regulation, Ministry of Agric.; fmr Deputy Gov. Moscow Region, forced to resign following accusations of misappropriating US humanitarian aid; First Deputy Gov. Ivanovskaya Region 2001–02; Chair. of Republican Govt (Prime Minister) of Chechnya Nov. 2002–Jan. 2003 (resgnd); mem. State Duma Dec. 2003–, Deputy Chair. Defence Cttee; Asst to Minister of Econ. Devt 2003–; Dir of election staff, Vladimir Oblast regional branch, United Russia (Yedinaya Rossiya) party; Order of Friendship 2006. *Address:* State Duma, Okhotnyi ryad 1, 103265 Moscow, Russia (office). *Telephone:* (495) 292-83-10 (office). *Fax:* (495) 292-94-64 (office). *E-mail:* www@duma.ru (office). *Website:* www .duma.ru (office).

BABIUC, Victor, PhD; Romanian politician and lawyer; b. 3 April 1938, Răchiţi Commune, Botoşani Co.; s. of Victor Babiuc and Olga Babiuc; m. Lucia Babiuc 1978; one d.; ed Law School of Bucharest, Romanian Acad. for Econ. Studies, Univ. of Bucharest; juridical counsellor, judge in Braşov; Chief Juridical Counsel Ministry of Foreign Trade, Sr Researcher at the World Economy Inst. 1977–90; mem. House of Deputies 1992–; Minister of Justice 1990–91, Minister of the Interior 1991–92; Minister of Nat. Defence 1996–98, Minister of State, Minister of Nat. Defence 1998–2000; mem. Chamber of Deputies for Brasov Ward 2000–04; mem. Democratic Party (PD) 1992–2000, Vice Pres. 1995–2000; mem. Nat. Liberal Party 2000–; Chair. Commercial Arbitration Court, Chamber of Commerce and Industry of Romania (CCIR) 1993–, Pres. CCIR 2005–07; Prof. of Int. Trade Law, Acad. of Econ. Studies of Bucharest 1992–; Chair. Cttee for Investigation into Corruption and Cases of Abuse and for Petitions of the Chamber of Deputies 1992–96; mem. Panel of Arbitrators of American Arbitration Asscn, Moscow, Sofia, Abu Dhabi, Warsaw, New Delhi, Cairo 1991–; mem. Cen. European Acad. of Science and Art 2004–; mem. Nat. Liberal Party; under investigation for bribery 2008–. *Publications:* over 150 publications mainly in the field of econ. legislation and int. trade law. *Leisure interests:* theatre, walking, reading books on politics, history, memoirs. *Address:* Bd Libertatii No. 20, Sector 5, Bucharest, Romania (home).

BABUR, Alamgir; Pakistani diplomatist; *High Commissioner to Bangladesh;* fmr Deputy Perm. Rep., later Acting Perm. Rep. to UN, New York; Dir-Gen. (Americas), Ministry of Foreign Affairs –2005; High Commr to Bangladesh 2005–. *Address:* High Commission of Pakistan, House NE (C)-2, Road No. 71, Gulshan Avenue, Dhaka 1212, Bangladesh (office). *Telephone:* (2) 8825388 (office). *Fax:* (2) 8850673 (office). *E-mail:* parepdka@citech-bd.com (office).

BABURIN, Sergei Nikolaevich, LLD, JSD; Russian politician and academic; *Deputy Chairman, State Duma;* b. 31 Jan. 1959, Semipalatinsk; s. of Nikolay Baburin and Valentina Baburina; m. Tatiana Nikolaevna Baburina; four s.; ed Omsk State Univ., Leningrad State Univ.; mem. CPSU 1981–91; mil. service in Afghanistan 1982–83; worked as lawyer; lecturer, Dean of Law Faculty, Omsk Univ. 1988–90, Professor of Law 1999–; People's Deputy of RSFSR (now Russia); mem. Supreme Soviet 1990–93; mem. Constitutional Comm. 1991–; Co-Chair. Exec. Bd of All Russian Peoples' Union 1991; Co-Chair. Nat. Salvation Front 1992–; mem. State Duma (Parl.) 1995–99, Deputy Chair. 1996–99, 2003–; Chair. All Russian People's Union 1994–2001; Deputy Chair. Parl. Ass. Union of Russia and Belarus 1996–2000; Pres. Inst. of Nat. Reform Strategy 2000–; Deputy Dir for Research, Russian Acad. of Sciences (Inst. of Social and Political Research) 2001–; Chair. Bd Inter-regional Collegium of Advocates of Businessmen and Citizens' Interactions 2001–02; Leader People's Will—Party of National Rebirth (Narodnaya volya—Partiya natsionalnogo vozrozhdeniya) 2001–; Co-Chair. Exec. Council, Motherland–National-Patriotic Union electoral block (Rodina–Narodno-patrioticheskii soyuz). *Publications:* Russian Way: Selected Speeches and Essays 1990–95 1995, Russian Way: Losses and Acquisitions 1997, Territory of State: Law and Geopolitical Problems 1997. *Address:* c/o People's Will—Party of National Rebirth, Verkhnyaya 34/2, 125040 Moscow (office); Inter-regional Collegium of Lawyers, Novogireyevskaya str. 65, Moscow, Russia. *Telephone:* (495) 748-29-49 (office); (495) 176-01-01. *E-mail:* partia-nv@partia-nv.ru (office). *Website:* www.partia-nv.ru (office).

BACA, Susana; Peruvian singer; b. Chortillos, Lima; m. Ricardo Pereira; formed experimental group combining poetry and song; took part in int. Agua Dulce Festival in Lima; with husband f. Instituto Negrocontinuo 1992; first US performance in Brooklyn 1995; one US and six European tours. *Albums include:* Susana Baca 1997, Del Fuego y del Agua 1999, Eco de Sombras 2000, Lamento Negro (early Cuban recordings, Latin Grammy Award for Best Folk Album) 2001, Espiritu Vivo 2002, Travesias 2006. *Publication:* The Cultural Importance of Black Peruvians (co-author with Richard Pereira) 1992. *Address:* c/o Luaka Bop, 195 Chrystie, 901F, New York, NY 10002, USA; c/o Iris Musique, 5 Passage St-Sebastien, 75011 Paris, France. *Website:* www .luakabop.com/susana_baca.

BACALL, Lauren; American actress; b. 16 Sept. 1924, New York; m. 1st Humphrey Bogart 1945 (died 1957); 2nd Jason Robards 1961 (divorced); two s. one d.; fmr model; Commdr des Arts et des Lettres 1995. *Films include:* Two Guys from Milwaukee 1946, To Have and Have Not, The Big Sleep, Confidential Agent, Dark Passage, Key Largo, Young Man with a Horn, Bright Leaf, How to Marry a Millionaire, Woman's World, The Cobweb, Blood Alley, Written on the Wind, Designing Woman, The Gift of Love, Flame over India, Sex and the Single Girl, Harper, Shock Treatment 1964, Murder on the Orient Express 1974, The Shootist 1976, Health 1980, The Fan 1981, Appointment with Death 1988, Mr North 1988, Tree of Hands 1989, A Star For Two 1990, Misery 1990, All I Want for Christmas 1991, A Foreign Field 1993, The Portrait 1993, Prêt à Porter 1995, Le Jour et la Nuit 1996, The Mirror Has Two Faces (Golden Globe 1996, Screen Actors' Guild Award), My Fellow Americans, Day and Night, Diamonds, The Venice Project, Presence of Mind, Dogville 2003, The Limit 2003, Birth 2004, Manderlay 2005, These Foolish Things 2006, The Walker 2007. *Plays:* Goodbye Charlie 1960, Cactus Flower 1966, Applause 1970 (Tony Award, Best Actress in a Musical 1970) (London 1972), Wonderful Town 1977, Woman of the Year 1981 (Tony Award 1981), Sweet Bird of Youth (London) 1985, The Visit (Chichester, UK), Waiting in the Wings. *Publications:* Lauren Bacall By Myself 1978, Lauren Bacall Now 1994, By Myself and Then Some 2005. *Address:* c/o Johnnie Planco, William Morris Agency, 1325 Avenue of the Americas, New York, NY 10019, USA.

BACCOUCHE, Hedi; Tunisian politician; b. 1930; active mem. Tunisian Independence Movt; Pres. Fed. des Étudiants Destouriens; detained by French authorities 1952; Dir PSD Political Bureau –1987; Minister of Social Affairs April–Nov. 1987; Prime Minister 1987–89. *Address:* c/o Office of the Prime Minister, Tunis, Tunisia.

BACH NUÑEZ, Jaume, DArch; Spanish architect; *Titular Professor, Technical Superior University of Architecture, Barcelona;* b. 4 April 1943, Sabadell; s. of Miquel Bach and Josefa Nuñez; m. Carmen Triadó Tur 1978; two s.; ed Tech. Superior Univ. of Architecture, Barcelona (ETSAB); architect, ETSAB 1969, tutor 1972–; in partnership with Gabriel Mora Gramunt (q.v.), Bach/Mora Architects 1976–98; Bach Arquitectes 1998–; Tutor, Int. Lab. of Architecture and Urban Design, Urbino, Italy 1978; Visiting Prof., Univ. of Dublin 1993, Univ. of Hanover 1994; has lectured and shown work in Spain, Germany, Austria, France, Netherlands, Italy, Slovenia, UK, Ireland, Finland, Portugal, Romania, USA, Argentina, Mexico, Venezuela, Chile and Japan; Hon. Mem. Caracas Contemporary Art Museum Foundation; Hon. DArch (Polytechnic Univ. of Barcelona) 1991; various professional awards including eight FAD Prizes and four Brunnel Commendations; ASCER Ceramics Prize 2004. *Works include:* UAB Bellaterra Station 1984, Urban Design Superblock, Olympic Village 1986, Auditorium Reina Sofia 1987, Cellar Raventós i Blanc 1988, grass hockey Olympic stadium, Terrassa 1989, Health Clinic Corachán 1990, Palau Macaya (la Caixa) 1991, Telephone Exchange, Olympic Village, Barcelona 1992, Operating Center FGC 1995, Multicomplex Fleming, Barcelona 1999, social housing, Gavà 2000, Tarragona sea front 2000, Motorcycling World Champion's house 2001, BS-Landscape Office bldg 2001, own house 2003, Tibet House 2004, liturgical adaptation for Parma Cathedral, Italy (First Prize, Int. Invited Competition 2005) 2005, BS-Landscape Office bldg, Barcelona, Can Sant Joan Business Park, Sant Cugat del Valles, Barcelona 2005, Banc Sabadell Center, Sant Cugat del Valles, Barcelona 2007. *Publications include:* Junge Architekten in Europa (co-author) 1983, Young Spanish Architecture (co-author) 1985, Bach/Mora, Contemporary Architectural Catalogues (ed. G. Gili) 1987, Bach – Mora, Architects (ed. G. Gili) 1996, Architecture Guide Spain 1920–2000 1998, Twentieth-Century Architecture Spain 2000, Banc Sabadell Landscape 2003; numerous magazine articles. *Address:* c/o Hercegovina 27 1er 2A, 08006 Barcelona, Spain (office). *Telephone:* (93) 200-29-11 (office). *Fax:* (93) 200-29-98 (office). *E-mail:* j.bach@coac.es (office). *Website:* www.bacharquitectes.com (office).

BACHA, Edmar Lisboa, PhD; Brazilian economist; *Director, Institute of Political and Economic Studies, Casa das Garças;* b. 14 Feb. 1942, Lambari, Minas Gerais; m. Maria Laura Cavalcanti; ed Fed. Univ. of Minas Gerais, Yale Univ., USA; Research Assoc., MIT, Cambridge, Mass, USA 1968–69; Prof. of Econs, Vargas Foundation, Rio de Janeiro 1970–71, Univ. of Brasília 1972–78, Catholic Univ. of Rio de Janeiro 1979–93, Fed. Univ. of Rio de Janeiro 1993–97; Pres. Statistical Office of Brazil, Rio de Janeiro 1985–86; Econ. Adviser to Brazilian Govt 1993; Pres. Nat. Devt Bank, Rio de Janeiro 1995; Senior Consultant, Banco Itaú BBA 1996–; Visiting Prof., Harvard Univ. 1975, Columbia Univ. 1983, Yale Univ. 1984, Univ. of Calif., Berkeley 1988, Univ. of Stanford 1989; Founder and Dir Inst. of Political and Econ. Studies, Casa das Garças 2003–; Pres. Nat. Asscn of Investment Banks (ANDIB) 2000–03; mem. Exec. Cttee, Int. Econ. Asscn, Paris 1987–92, Cttee for Devt Planning, UN, New York 1987–94, Int. Consultative Cttee Yale Univ. 1999–, Consultative Cttee, BrazilFoundation, Rio de Janeiro 2001–, Consultative Cttee Faculdade Pitágoras, Belo Horizonte 2001–, Admin. Cttee Companhia Siderúrgica Nacional (CSN) 2001–03, Admin. Cttee, Banco Itaú BBA 2003–; Hon. mem. Latin American and Caribbean Econ. Asscn (LACEA) 1998–; Grand Officer, Ordem do Cruzeiro do Sul 1995. *Publications:* numerous books and articles inscluding Mitos de uma Decada 1976, Models of Growth and Distribution for Brazil 1980, El Milagro y la Crisis 1986, Social Change in Brazil 1986, Recessão ou Crescimento 1987, Requirements for Growth Resumption in Latin America 1993. *Address:* Institute of Political and Economic Studies, Casa das Garças, Avenida Padre Leonel Franca, Rio de Janeiro, 22451-000, Brazil (office). *Telephone:* (21) 2512-6166 (office). *E-mail:* iepecdg@iepecdg.com (office). *Website:* www.iepecdg.com (office).

BACHCHAN, Amitabh; Indian actor and singer; b. 11 Oct. 1942, Allahabad; s. of Harivansh Rai and Teji Bachchan; m. Jaya Bachchan; one s. one d.; ed Sherwood Coll., Delhi Univ.; host of quiz show Kaun Banega Crorepati (Indian version of Who Wants To Be A Millionaire?); re-launched film co. AB Corpn 2003; apptd '46664' Amb. by Nelson Mandela to raise HIV/AIDS awareness 2004; Ordre national de la Légion d'honneur 2006; Dr hc (De Montfort Univ., Leicester, UK) 2006, (Leeds Metropolitan Univ.) 2007; Shyam Sunder Dyay Kishan Munshi Lifetime Achievement Award 2004. *Films:* over seventy films including Saat Hindustani 1969, Zanjeer 1973, Deewar 1975, Imaan Dharam 1977, Kasme Vaade 1978, Jurmana 1979, Barsaat Ki Ek Raat 1980, Manzil 1981, Shakti 1982, Pet Pyar Aur Paap 1984, Kaun A Kaun Hara 1987, Soorma Bhopali 1988, Jadugar 1989, Agneepath 1990, Ajooba 1991, Insaniyat 1994, Bade Miyan Chote Miyan 1998, Tumhare Liye 1999, Sooryavansham 1999, Kabhi Khushi Kabhi Gham 2001, Baghban 2003, Khakee 2004, Veer-Zaara 2004, Ab Tumhare Hawale Watan Saathiyo 2004, Waqt 2005, Black 2005, Kabhi Alvida Naa Kehna (Never Say Goodbye) 2006, Eklavya – The Royal Guard 2007, Nishabd 2007, Zamaanat 2007, Cheeni Kum 2007. *Television:* presenter Kaun Banega Crorepati? (Who Wants To Be A Millionaire?). *Address:* Pratiksha, 10th Road, JVPD Scheme, Mumbai, 400 049, India (office).

BACHELET JERIA, Verónica Michelle; Chilean politician and head of state; *President;* b. 29 Sept. 1951, Santiago; d. of Gen. Aire Alberto Bachelet (died 1974) and Ángela Jeria; m.; three c.; ed Universidad de Chile, Inter-American Coll. of Defense, Washington, DC, USA; placed in Villa Grimaldi and Cuatro Alamos detention centres for father's resistance to Pinochet regime 1975; lived in Australia, then Germany 1975–80; trained as medical surgeon, podiatrist and epidemiologist, Universidad de Chile; Head of Medical Dept, PIDEE (NGO assisting the children of victims of the military regime); Consultant to Panamerican Health Org. and WHO 1990; mem. Cen. Cttee Socialist Party 1995–, Political Cttee 1998–; Adviser to Under-Sec. of Health 1994–97, to Ministry of Defence 1998–99; Minister of Health 2000–02, of Nat. Defence (first woman in position) 2002–04; Pres. of Chile (first woman) 2006–; ranked by Forbes magazine amongst 100 Most Powerful Women (17th) 2006, (27th) 2007, (25th) 2008. *Address:* Office of the President, Moneda No. 1002, 1298, Santiago, Chile (office). *Telephone:* (2) 690-4000 (office). *E-mail:* contact@msgg.gov.cl (office). *Website:* www.presidencyofchile.cl (office).

BACHELIER, Bernard; French agronomist; *Director, Fondation Pour l'Agriculture et la Ruralité dans le Monde;* b. 27 July 1950, Levallois-Perret; s. of Pierre Bachelier and Claire Pardon; ed Inst. Nat. Agronomique, Paris-Grignon; worked in Africa for several years; Del. for Africa and Indian Ocean, Centre de Coopération Internationale en Recherche Agronomique pour de Développement (Cirad), Paris 1988–90; Pres. Cirad Centre, Montpellier 1993; Head of Devt Research, Ministry of Educ. and Research 1993–96; Dir-Gen. Cirad 1996–2002; Chair., Council of Admin., Centre Nat. d'Etudes Agronomiques des Régions Chaudes (CNEARC) 1998–2003; advisor to minister in charge of Research and New Tech. 2002–04, to Minister for Research and Higher Educ. 2005–; Dir Fondation pour l'agriculture et la ruralité dans le monde (FARM) 2006–; mem. Council for European and Int. Prospective Analysis of Agric. and Food (COPEIAA); Chevalier, Ordre nat. du Mérite, Ordre du Mérite agricole. *Address:* Fondation Pour l'Agriculture et la Ruralité dans le Monde, c/o Crédit Agricole S.A., 91 - 93 boulevard Pasteur, 75015 Paris (office); 9 rue Thérèse, 75001 Paris, France (home). *Telephone:* 1-43-23-61-98 (office). *E-mail:* bernard.bachelier@fondation-farm.org (office). *Website:* www .fondation-farm.org (office).

BACHELOT-NARQUIN, Roselyne, PharmD; French pharmacist and politician; *Minister of Health, Youth and Sports;* b. 24 Dec. 1946, Nevers (Nièvre); d. of Jean Narquin and Yvette Narquin (née Le Dû); m. Jacques Bachelot; one c.; pharmacist, Conseillère général de Maine-et-Loire 1982–88; mem. and Vice-Pres. Regional Council, Pays de la Loire, Pres. Comm. aménagement 1998–; elected Deputy for Maine-et-Loire 1988–; mem. RPR, Sec.-Gen. 1989–92, 2001–, Del.-Gen. for the Status of Women 1992–93, for Labour and Social Exclusion 1995–97, Sec.-Gen. for Labour 1998–2001, mem. Political Bureau RPR; Reporter-Gen. Observatoire de la parité 1995–98; Pres. Nat. Consultative Council for Handicapped Persons 1996–; Minister of Ecology and Sustainable Devt 2002–04, of Health, Youth and Sports 2007–. *Publications include:* Les Maires: fête ou défaite? 2001. *Address:* Ministry of Health, Youth and Sports, 14 avenue Duquesne, 75007 Paris, France (office). *Telephone:* 1-40-56-60-00 (office). *Website:* www.sante.gouv.fr (office).

BACHER, Aron ('Ali'), MB, BCh; South African cricketer, sports administrator and fundraiser; *Executive Director, University of the Witwatersrand (Wits) Foundation;* b. 24 May 1942, Johannesburg; s. of Kopel Bacher and Rose Bacher; m. Shira Ruth Teeger 1965; one s. two d.; ed King Edward VII High School and Univ. of Witwatersrand; right-hand batsman; played for Transvaal 1959–74 (Capt. 1963–74); 12 tests for S Africa 1965–70, four (all won) as Capt.; scored 7,894 first-class runs (18 centuries); toured England 1965; intern, Baragwanath and Natalspruit Hosps; pvt. practice, Rosebank, Johannesburg 1970–79; Man. Dir Delta Distributors (Pty) Ltd 1979–81; Man. Dir The Transvaal Cricket Council 1981–86; Man. Dir The South African Cricket Union 1986–91, United Cricket Bd of South Africa 1991–2000; Exec. Dir 2003 Cricket World Cup 2001–03; South African Sports Award Admin. 1991; Pres. Sports Award Admin. (Cricket) 1997; Exec. Dir Wits Foundation 2003–; Hon. LLD (Witwatersrand, Johannesburg) 2001; South African Sports Merit Award 1972; Paul Harris Fellow Award 1989; Jack Cheetham Memorial Award 1990; Int. Jewish Sports Hall of Fame 1991. *Leisure interest:* jogging. *Address:* 17 Romajador Avenue, Sandhurst Ext. 4, Sandton (home); PO Box 55041, Northlands 2116, South Africa (office). *Telephone:* (11) 717-9702 (office); (11) 783-1263 (home). *Fax:* (11) 717-9720 (office); (11) 883-2597 (home). *E-mail:* greenn@foundationwits.ac.za (office). *Website:* www.wits.ac.za/foundation (office).

BACHIRI, Mohamed, MBA; Moroccan administrator, engineer and business executive; *Chairman, Drapor Port Dredging Company;* b. 14 July 1948, Berkane; s. of Mimoun Bachiri and Aïcha Ouadi; m. Badia Khelfaoui 1972; three c.; ed Ecole Mohammedie d'Ingénieurs, Rabat, Ecole Nationale des Ponts et Chaussées, Paris, France; qualified civil engineer; responsible for public works, Berkane and Nador Provs. 1969; Asst Dir Moroccan Ports 1978; Regional Dir of Public Works, Marrakesh 1983; Dir Nat. Vocational Training 1984; Insp. Gen. Council of Public Works 1991; Founder and Dir Al Handassa Lwatania Eng journal 1981; currently Chair. Drapor Port Dredging Co.; Founding Pres. Public Works Foundation; mem. Bd of Dirs Cen. Dredging Asscn (CEDA), Chair. CEDA–African Section; Royal Decoration of Chevalier for Merit and Knighthood 1998; trophée d'Ingénieur Créateur. *Publications:* Drainage and Environment (ed.), Reference Dredging and Environment; articles and editorials in Al Handassa Lwatania, contrib. to other professional journals. *Leisure interest:* golf. *Address:* Drapor, 5 Rue Chajarat Addor, Q. Palmier, Casablanca (office); 3 Avenue Ma Al Aynine, Agdal, Rabat, Morocco. *Telephone:* (22) 95-91-00 (office); (37) 77-46-24 (home). *Fax:* (22) 23-26-00 (office); (37) 68-14-94 (home). *E-mail:* bachiri@drapor.com (office); bachiri@ iam.net.ma (home). *Website:* www.drapor.com (office); www.ceda-africa.com.

BACHMANN, John William, AB, MBA; American business executive; *Senior Partner, Edward Jones;* b. 16 Nov. 1938, Centralia, Ill.; s. of George Adam Bachmann and Helen Bachmann (née Johnston); m. Katharine I. Butler; one s. one d.; ed Wabash Coll., Crawfordsville, Ind., Northwestern Univ.; broker, Edward Jones, St Louis 1962–63, investment rep. 1963–70, Gen. Pnr 1970–80, Man. Pnr 1980–2003, Sr Pnr 2004–; mem. Bd of Dirs Trans World Airlines 1996–2001, American Airlines Inc., Monsanto Co.; Trustee Wabash Coll. 1980–, Washington Univ.; fmr mem. Bd of Dirs US Chamber of Commerce, Washington, DC 1995–, Chair. 2004–05, Chair. Exec. Cttee 2005–06; fmr Chair. St Louis Regional Chamber and Growth Asscn; Chair. Bd of Visitors Drucker Center, Claremont (Calif.) Grad. School 1987–; fmr Chair. Arts and Educ. Council of Greater St Louis, St Louis Symphony Orchestra; Commr St Louis Art Museum; mem. Nat. Asscn of Securities Dealers (fmr district Chair.), Securities Industry Asscn (Chair. 1976–79), Securities Industry Foundation for Econ. Educ. (Chair. of Trustees 1988–92); Hon. LLD (Wabash Coll.) 1990, (Univ. of Missouri, St Louis) 2003, (Westminster Coll.) 2005. *Address:* Edward Jones, 12555 Manchester Road, St Louis, MO 63131, USA (office). *Telephone:* (314) 515-2626 (office). *Fax:* (314) 515-2622 (office). *E-mail:* john.bachmann@edwardjones.com (office). *Website:* www.edwardjones.com (office).

BACHYNSKI, Morrel Paul, PhD, FRSC, FIEEE; Canadian physicist; *President and CEO, MPB Technologies Inc.;* b. 19 July 1930, Bienfait, Sask.; s. of Nick Bachynski and Karolina Bachynski; m. Slava Krkovic 1959; two d.; ed Univ. of Saskatchewan and McGill Univ.; mem. Scientific Staff, RCA Ltd 1955–58, Dir Microwave Physics Lab. 1958–65; Dir Research 1965–75, Vice-Pres. Research and Devt 1975–76; Pres. and CEO MPB Techs Inc. 1977–; mem. Canadian Asscn of Physicists (Pres. 1968), Asscn of Scientific, Eng and Tech. Community of Canada (Pres. 1974–75), Nat. Research Council of Canada (Chair. on Fusion 1977–87), Science Council of Canada; Fellow, Canadian Aeronautics and Space Inst., American Physical Soc., Canadian Acad. of Eng (Pres. 2003–04); Hon. mem. Eng Inst. of Canada; Hon. LLD (Waterloo) 1993, (Concordia) 1997; Hon. DSc (McGill) 1994; Prix Scientifique du Québec 1974, Canada Enterprise Award 1977, Queen's Silver Jubilee Medal 1977, Canadian Asscn of Physicists Medal 1984, Canadian Research Man. Asscn Award 1988, Prix PME (Quebec) 1988, Canada Award for Business Excellence-Entrepreneurship 1989, 1990, Prix ADRIQ 1991, Canadian Asscn of Physicists Medal for Industrial and Applied Physics 1995, Prix du Québec – Lionel Boulet 2001, Royal Soc. of Canada Thomas W. Eadie Medal 2004. *Publications:* The Particle Kinetics of Plasmas (co-author) 1968; more than 90 publs in scientific and eng journals. *Leisure interest:* tennis. *Address:* 78 Thurlow Road, Montreal, PQ H3X 3G9, Canada (home). *Telephone:* (514) 694-8751 (office); (514) 481-2359 (home). *Fax:* (514) 695-7492 (office). *E-mail:* m.p .bachynski@mpbc.ca (office). *Website:* www.mpbc.ca (office).

BACKE, John David, MBA; American communications industry executive; b. 5 July 1932, Akron, Ohio; s. of John and Ella A. Backe (née Enyedy); m. Katherine Elliott 1955; one s. one d.; ed Miami Univ., Xavier Univ.; various eng, financial and marketing positions at General Electric Co. 1957–66; Vice-Pres. and Dir of Marketing, Silver Burdett Co. 1966–68, Pres. 1968–69; Exec. Vice-Pres. General Learning Corpn 1969, Pres. and CEO 1969–73; Pres. of Publishing Group, CBS Inc. 1973–76, of CBS Inc. (also CEO) 1976–80, Dir of Business Marketing, Corpn of New York 1978; Pres. and CEO Tomorrow Entertainment 1981–84, Chair. 1984; Chair. Cinema Products, Los Angeles 1992–; Founder, Chair. and CEO Backe Group Inc. 1984–; Chair. Station WRGB Schenectady, NY 1983–; Chair. Station WLNS Lansing, Mich. 1984; Chair. Station WKBT Lacrosse, Wis.; Chair. Dorchester Publ Co. Inc., NY 1984; Chair. Kingswood Advertising 1988; Station WDKY-TV, Lexington 1985–93; Gulfshore Publ Co., Naples 1986–; Gulfstream Newspapers, Pompano 1987–; Andrews Communications, Westtown, Pa 1987–; Atlantic Publs, Accomac, Va 1989–; Special Del. to UNESCO Conf. on publishing for Arabic-speaking countries 1972; mem. Nat. Advisory Cttee for Illinois Univ. Inst. for Aviation; Hon. LLD (Miami and Xavier); Cable Ace Award 1988, Oxford Cup, Beta Theta Pi 2005. *Leisure interest:* multi-engine piloting. *Address:* The Backe Group, Inc., 150 Strafford Avenue, Wayne, PA 19087; 399 Park Avenue, 19th Floor, New York, NY 10022, USA (office).

BAČKIS, HE Cardinal Audrys Juozas, BPhil, LTh, DCL; Lithuanian ecclesiastic; *Archbishop of Vilnius;* b. 1 Feb. 1937, Kaunas; ed Inst. Catholique, Paris, Pontifical Gregorian Univ., Rome, Pontifical Lateran Univ., Rome; ordained priest 1961; served in Holy See diplomatic corps in The Philippines 1964–65, Costa Rica 1966–68, Turkey 1969–70, Nigeria 1971–73; with Vatican Secr. of State 1974–88; Titular Archbishop of Meta and Apostolic Pro-Nuncio to Netherlands 1988–91; Archbishop of Vilnius 1991–; cr. Cardinal (Cardinal-Priest of Natività di Nostro Signore Gesù Cristo a Via Gallia) 2001; Grande Oficial da Ordem Militar de Cristo (Portugal) 1981, Grosse Verdienstkreuz mit Stern (Germany) 1982, Grand Officier, Order of the Phoenix (Greece) 1982, Grand Officier, 'Ordre Nat. Honneur et Mérite (Haiti) 1984, Officier, Légion d'Honneur (France) 1984, Gran Oficial, Orden al Merito por Servicios Distinguidos (Peru) 1985, Grande Ufficiale, Ordine al Merito Rep. Italiana 1985, Gran Oficial, Orden de Manuel Amado Guerrero (Panama) 1985, Commdr, Ordre Gran-Ducal de la Couronne de Chene (Luxembourg) 1988, Commendator cum nomismate (Ordo equester S.Sepulcri Hierosolymitani) 1990, Groot Kruis in de Orde van Oranje-Nassau (Netherlands) 1992, Commdr, Royal Norwegian Order of Merit 1998, Order Grand Duke Gediminas (2nd degree) (Lithuania) 2000, Order of Vytautas the Great Grand Cross (Lithuania) 2003; Dr hc (Vilnius Pedagogical Univ.) 1997, (Krakow Pontifical Theological Acad.) 2003. *Address:* Vilnius Archdiocesan Curia, Šventaragio 4, 01122 Vilnius, Lithuania (office). *Telephone:* (2) 223653 (office); (2) 223413 (home). *Fax:* (2) 222807 (office). *E-mail:* curia@vilnensis.lt (office). *Website:* www.vilnius.lcn.lt (office).

BACKLEY, Steve, OBE; British fmr professional athlete; b. 12 Feb. 1969, Sidcup, Kent; s. of John Backley and Pauline Hogg; javelin thrower; coached by John Trower; Commonwealth record-holder 1992 (91.46m); Gold Medal European Jr Championships 1987; Silver Medal World Jr Championships 1988; Gold Medal European Cup 1989, 1997, Bronze Medal 1995; Gold Medal World Student Games 1989, 1991; Gold Medal World Cup 1989, 1994, 1998;

Gold Medal Commonwealth Games 1990, 1994, 2002, Silver Medal 1998; Gold Medal European Championships 1990, 1994, 1998, 2002; Bronze Medal Olympic Games 1992, Silver Medal 1996, 2000; Silver Medal World Championships 1995, 1997; retd 2004; Prin. Javelin Business Strategies 2006–; Athlete of the Year, UK Athletics 2000. *Publication:* The Winning Mind. *Website:* www.javelinstrategies.co.uk; www.stevebackley.com.

BÄCKSTRÖM, Urban, PhD; Swedish banker; *Chief Executive, Confederation of Swedish Enterprise;* b. 25 May 1954, Sollefteå; s. of Sven-Ake Bäckström and Maj-Britt Filipsson; m. Ewa Hintze 1978; one s. one d.; ed Stockholm Univ. and Stockholm School of Econs; Research Asst Inst. for Int. Econ. Studies, Stockholm 1978–80; First Sec. Int. Dept Ministry of Foreign Affairs 1980–82; Chief Economist, Moderate Party 1982–83, 1986–89; Under-Sec. of State, Ministry of Finance 1991–93; Gov. Sveriges Riksbank (Swedish Cen. Bank) 1994–2002; Bd mem. Bank for Int. Settlements 1994–2002, Chair. and Pres. 1999–2002; CEO Skandia Liv 2002–05; CEO Confed. of Swedish Enterprise 2005–. *Address:* Confederation of Swedish Enterprise, Storgatan 19 11482 Stockholm, Sweden (office). *Telephone:* (8) 553 430 00 (office). *Fax:* (8) 553 430 99 (office). *Website:* www.svensktnaringsliv.se (office).

BACKUS, George Edward, SM, PhD, FRSA; American theoretical geophysicist and academic; *Research Professor Emeritus of Geophysics, University of California, San Diego;* b. 24 May 1930, Chicago, Ill.; s. of the late Milo Morlan Backus and of Dora Backus (née Mendenhall); m. 1st Elizabeth E Allen 1961; two s. one d.; m. 2nd Marianne McDonald 1971; m. 3rd Varda Peller 1977; ed Thornton Township High School, Harvey, Ill. and Univ. of Chicago; Asst Examiner, Univ. of Chicago 1949–50; Junior Mathematician, Inst. for Air Weapons Research, Univ. of Chicago 1950–54; Physicist, Project Matterhorn, Princeton Univ. 1957–58; Asst Prof. of Mathematics, MIT 1958–60; Assoc. Prof. of Geophysics, Univ. of Calif. (La Jolla) 1960–62, Prof. 1962–94, Research Prof. 1994–99, Prof. Emer. 1999–; mem. Scientific Advisory Cttee to NASA on Jt NASA/CNES Magnetic Satellites; Co.-Chair. Int. Working Group on Magnetic Field Satellites 1983–92; mem. Visiting Cttee Inst. de Physique du Globe de Paris 1987; Guggenheim Fellowship 1963, 1971; Fellow American Geophysical Union, RSA, Royal Astronomical Soc.; mem. NAS; Foreign mem. Acad. des Sciences de l'Institut de France; Dr hc (Inst. de Physique de Globe, Paris) 1995; Gold Medal, Royal Astronomical Soc. 1986, John Adam Fleming Medal, American Geophysical Union 1986. *Publications:* numerous scientific works 1958–. *Leisure interests:* hiking, swimming, history, reading, skiing. *Address:* Munk Lab 331, Institute of Geophysics and Planetary Physics, Scripps Institution of Oceanography, University of California San Diego, La Jolla, CA 92093-0225 (office); 9362 La Jolla Farms Road, La Jolla, CA 92037, USA (home). *Telephone:* (858) 534-2468 (office); (858) 455-8972 (home). *Fax:* (858) 534-8090 (office). *Website:* www.igpp.ucsd.edu (office); www-mpl.ucsd .edu/cg/people/gbackus.html (office).

BACON, Kevin; American actor; b. 8 July 1958, Philadelphia, Pa; m. Kyra Sedgwick; one s. one d.; ed Manning Street Actor's Theatre; mem. Bacon Brothers band. *Stage appearances include:* Getting On 1978, Glad Tidyings 1979–80, Mary Barnes 1980, Album 1980, Forty-Deuce 1981, Flux 1982, Poor Little Lambs 1982, Slab Boys 1983, Men Without Dates 1985, Loot 1986, Road, Spike Heels. *Film appearances include:* National Lampoon's Animal House 1978, Starting Over 1979, Hero at Large 1980, Friday the 13th 1980, Only When I Laugh 1981, Diner 1982, Footloose 1984, Quicksilver 1985, White Water Summer 1987, Planes, Trains and Automobiles 1987, End of the Line 1988, She's Having a Baby 1988, Criminal Law 1989, The Big Picture 1989, Tremors 1990, Flatliners 1990, Queens Logic 1991, He Said/She Said 1991, Pyrates 1991, JFK 1992, A Few Good Men 1992, The Air Up There 1994, The River Wild 1994, Murder in the First 1995, Apollo 13 1995, Sleepers 1996, Telling Lies in America 1997, Picture Perfect 1997, Digging to China 1997, Wild Things 1998, My Dog Skip 1999, The Hollow Man 1999, Stir of Echoes 1999, Novocaine 2000, We Married Margo 2000, 24 Hours 2001, Trapped 2002, In the Cut 2003, Mystic River 2003, The Woodsman 2004, Cavedweller 2004, Loverboy 2005, Beauty Shop 2005, Where the Truth Lies 2005, The Air I Breathe 2007, Death Sentence 2007, Rails and Ties 2007, Saving Angelo 2007, New York, I Love You 2008, Frost/Nixon 2008. *Television appearances include:* The Gift 1979, Enormous Changes at the Last Minute 1982, The Demon Murder Case 1983, The Tender Age, Lemon Sky, Frasier (voice), Happy Birthday Elizabeth: A Celebration of Life 1997. *Address:* c/o Frank Frattaroli, William Morris Agency, 1 William Morris Place, Beverly Hills, CA 90212, USA. *Website:* www.baconbros.com/site.php.

BACQUIER, Gabriel; French singer (baritone); b. 17 May 1924, Béziers; s. of Augustin Bacquier and Fernande Severac; m. 1st Simone Teisseire 1943; one s.; m. 2nd Mauricette Bénard 1958; one s.; ed Paris Conservatoire; debut at Théâtre Royal de la Monnaie, Brussels 1953; joined Opéra de Paris 1956; debut at Carnegie Hall 1960, Metropolitan Opera, New York 1961; has appeared at the Vienna State Opera, Covent Garden, La Scala, Opéra de Paris and most leading opera houses; repertoire includes Otello, Don Giovanni, Pelléas et Mélisande, Damnation de Faust, Tosca, Falstaff; several recordings; Prix nat. du disque français 1964; Chevalier, Légion d'honneur; Officier, Ordre nat. du Mérite; Commdr des Arts et des Lettres; Médaille de Vermeil, Paris, Victoires de la Musique 1985. *Films include:* La Grande Récré, Falstaff. *Leisure interests:* painting, drawing. *Address:* c/o OIA, 16 avenue Franklin D. Roosevelt, 75008 Paris, France (home).

BÁCS, Ludovic; Romanian composer and conductor; *Professor, Bucharest Conservatory;* b. 19 Jan. 1930, Petrila; s. of Ludovic Bács and Iuliana Bács (née Venczel); m. Ercse Gyöngyver, 1952; two s.; ed Dima Gh. Conservatory, Cluj-Napoca Tchaikovski Conservatory, Moscow, Cluj-Napoca Coll. of Philosophy 1948–49; began career as conductor Symphonic Orchestra of Romanian Radio, also Artistic Dir 1964–; Prof., Bucharest Conservatory 1960–66, 1990–; Assoc. Prof., Transilvania Univ. of Braşov; Conductor Romanian Radio Chamber Orchestra 1990–; f. Musica Rediviva 1966, first group of performers to render ancient Romanian music; has conducted concerts in USSR, Poland, Czechoslovakia, Hungary, Bulgaria, Germany, Holland, Argentina, Switzerland, Spain, France; mem. Romanian Composers' Union; Cultural Merit Award, Medal of Labour, Prize of the Theatre and Music Asscn. *Works include:* orchestration of Bach's Art of the Fugue (on record), numerous adaptations from 15th–18th century music: Bach, Monteverdi, Backfarg, from Codex Caioni a.o.; Suitá de Musicá Veche 17th–18th century, Variations Sinfoniques e Double Fugue sur une Thème Populaire Hongroise, Trois Madrigales pour Choeur, Variations et Fugue sur une Colinde Roumaine, Potpourri sur des Colindes. *Address:* Berthelot 63–64, Bucharest (office); 31 D. Golescu, Sc III, Et V ap. 87, Bucharest 1, Romania (home).

BADAL, Parkash Singh, BA; Indian agriculturist and politician; *Chief Minister of Punjab;* b. 8 Dec. 1927, Abulkhurana, Punjab; s. of the late Raghuraj Singh; m. Surinder Kaur; one s. one d.; entered politics 1947, first elected to Vidhan Sabha 1957; mem. and fmr Pres. Shiromani Akali Dal party; fmr mem. Shiromani Gurdwara Prabandhak Cttee; elected to Ass. 1957, re-elected 1969; Minister for Community Devt Panchayati Raj, Animal Husbandry, Dairying and Fisheries 1969–70; Chief Minister of Punjab 1970–71, 1977–80, 1997–2002, 2007–; imprisoned during State of Emergency 1975–77; elected to Lok Sabha 1977; Minister for Agric. 1977; Leader of Opposition 1980; imprisoned on corruption charges Dec. 2003; Chair. Punjab Arts Council; mem. Nankana Sahib Educational Trust, Ludhiana. *Address:* VPO Badal, Muktsar District (home); Office of the Chief Minister, Government of Punjab, 45, Sector 2, Chandigarh, India (office). *Telephone:* (172) 740737 (home); (172) 740325 (office). *E-mail:* pws@punjabmail.gov.in (office). *Website:* punjabgovt.nic.in (office).

BADAWI, Dato' Seri Abdullah Bin Haji Ahmad, BA; Malaysian politician; b. 26 Nov. 1939, Pulau Pinang; m. Datin Endon bint Datuk Mahmud (died 2005); ed Univ. of Malaya; Asst Sec. Public Service Dept 1964; Asst Sec. MAGERAN 1969; Asst Sec. Nat. Security Council 1971; Dir (Youth), Ministry of Sport, Youth and Culture 1971–74, Deputy Sec.-Gen. 1974–78; Minister without Portfolio, Prime Minister's Dept 1982; Minister of Educ. 1984–86, of Defence 1986–87; mem. UMNO Supreme Council 1982–, Vice-Pres. 1984; Minister of Foreign Affairs 1991; Deputy Prime Minister and Minister of Home Affairs 1998–2003, Prime Minister and Minister of Finance 2003–09 (resgnd). *Address:* c/o Prime Minister's Office (Jabatan Perdana Menteri), Federal Government Administration Center, Bangunan Perdana Putra, 62502 Putrajaya, Malaysia (office). *Website:* www.pmo.gov.my (office).

BADAWI, Zeinab Mohammed-Khair, MA; British (b. Sudanese) journalist and broadcaster; b. 3 Oct. 1959; d. of Mohammed-Khair El Badawi and Asia Malik; m. David Antony Crook 1991; two s. two d.; ed Hornsey School for Girls, St Hilda's Coll. Oxford and Univ. of London; presenter and journalist, current affairs and documentaries on Yorkshire TV 1982–86; current affairs reporter, BBC TV 1987–88; newscaster and journalist, ITN Channel Four News 1988, co-presenter Channel Four News with Jon Snow 1989–98; joined BBC 1998, worked in radio presenting The World Tonight (Radio 4) and BBC World's Newshour, currently presenter The World on BBC Four 2005–; Chair. Africa Medical Partnership Fund; mem. Bd British Council; Trustee, BBC World Service Trust, Nat. Portrait Gallery, British Council, Centre for Contemporary British History; mem. jury for Diageo Africa Business Reporting Award. *Publications:* numerous articles. *Leisure interests:* languages, opera, family, reading. *Address:* c/o Knight Ayton Management, 114 St Martin's Lane, London, WC2N 4BE; BBC Television Centre, Wood Lane, London, W12 7RJ, England (office). *Telephone:* (20) 8576-4440 (office). *Fax:* (20) 8624-8959 (office). *E-mail:* bbc4news@bbc.co.uk (office).

BADER, Kathleen M., BA, MBA; American business executive; ed Loyola Univ., Rome, Italy, Univ. of Calif.; joined Dow Chemical Co. 1972, later Corp. Vice-Pres. of Quality and Business Excellence, Business Group Pres. 2000–04, Chair., Pres. and CEO Cargill Dow LLC (now NatureWorks LLC, jt venture between Dow Chemical and Cargill Inc.) 2004–06 (retd); mem. Bd of Dirs Textron Inc.; mem. Homeland Security Advisory Council; mem. Int. Bd of Dirs Habitat for Humanity, Dean's Council, John F. Kennedy School of Govt; ranked by Fortune magazine amongst 50 Most Powerful Women in Business outside the US (24th) 2001, (17th) 2002, (25th) 2003. *Address:* c/o Board of Directors, Textron Inc., 40 Westminster Street, Providence, RI 02903-2596, USA.

BADHAM, John Macdonald, BA, MFA; American (b. British) film director; b. 25 Aug. 1939, Luton, England; s. of Henry Lee Badham and Mary Iola Hewitt; m. Julia Laughlin 1992; one d.; ed Yale Univ., Yale Drama School; joined Universal Studio as mailroom employee, then tour guide, subsequently Casting Dir and Assoc. Producer; Pres. Great American Picture Show; Chair. Bd JMB Films Inc.; Founder and Pres. Badham Co., Calif. 1975–; currently Prof. and head of Directing Program, Graduate Conservatory of Motion Pictures, Chapman Univ., Orange, Calif.; George Pal Award. *Films include:* The Bingo Long Travelling All-Stars and Motor Kings, Saturday Night Fever 1977, Dracula (Best Horror Film Award, Acad. of Science Fiction, Fantasy and Horror Films) 1979, Whose Life Is It Anyway? (San Rafael Grand Prize) 1981, War Games (Best Dir, Science Fiction/Fantasy Acad.) 1983, Stakeout (also exec. producer) 1987, Disorganized Crime (exec. producer only), Bird on a Wire 1989, The Hard Way 1990, Point of No Return 1993, Another Stakeout (also exec. producer) 1993, Drop Zone (also exec. producer) 1994, Nick of Time (also producer) 1995, Incognito 1997. *Television includes:* The Impatient Heart (Christopher Award 1971), Isn't It Shocking? 1973, The Law, The Gun (Southern Calif. Motion Picture Council Award 1974), Reflections of Murder 1973, The Godchild 1974, The Keegans, Sorrow Floats 1998, Floating Away 1998, The Jack Bull 1999, Footsteps 2003; several series episodes. *Publication:* I'll Be In My Trailer: The Creative Wars Between Directors and Actors

2006. *Address:* MKS 352, Dodge College of Film and Media Arts, Chapman University, One University Drive, Orange, CA 92866, USA. *Telephone:* (714) 628-2798. *Website:* www.badhamcompany.com (office).

BADIAN, Ernst, MA, DPhil, LittD, FBA; American (b. Austrian) historian and academic; *John Moors Cabot Professor Emeritus of History, Harvard University;* b. 8 Aug. 1925, Vienna, Austria; m. Nathlie A. Wimsett 1950; one s. one d.; ed Christchurch Boys' High School, Canterbury Univ. Coll., Christchurch, NZ and Univ. Coll., Oxford; Asst Lecturer in Classics, Victoria Univ. Coll., Wellington 1947–48; Rome Scholar in Classics, British School at Rome 1950–52; Asst Lecturer in Classics and Ancient History, Univ. of Sheffield 1952–54; Lecturer in Classics, Univ. of Durham 1954–65; Prof. of Ancient History, Univ. of Leeds 1965–69; Prof. of Classics and History, State Univ. of NY at Buffalo 1969–71; Prof. of History, Harvard Univ. 1971–82, John Moors Cabot Prof. of History 1982–98, John Moors Cabot Prof. Emer. 1998–; Visiting Prof. and Lecturer at many univs in USA, Canada, Australia, S. Africa, Europe etc.; Fellow, American Acad. of Arts and Sciences, American Numismatic Soc.; Corresp. mem. Austrian Acad. of Sciences, German Archaeological Inst.; Foreign mem. Finnish Acad. of Sciences; Hon. Fellow, Univ. Coll., Oxford; Hon. mem. Soc. for Roman Studies; Cross of Honour for Science and Art (Austria) 1999; Hon. LittD (Macquarie) 1993, (Canterbury) 1999; Conington Prize, Univ. of Oxford 1958. *Publications:* Foreign Clientelae (264–70 BC) 1958, Studies in Greek and Roman History 1964, Polybius 1966, Roman Imperialism in the Late Republic 1967, Publicans and Sinners 1972, From Plataea to Potidaea 1993, Zöllner und Sünder 1997; articles in classical and historical journals. *Leisure interest:* parrots. *Address:* Department of History, Harvard University, Cambridge, MA 02138, USA (office). *Telephone:* (617) 496-5881 (office). *Fax:* (617) 471-0986 (home).

BADINTER, Robert, AM, LLD; French lawyer and professor of law; *President, Court of Conciliation and Arbitration, Organization for Security and Co-operation in Europe;* b. 30 March 1928, Paris; s. of Simon Badinter and Charlotte Rosenberg; m. 1st Anne Vernon 1957; m. 2nd Elisabeth Bleustein-Blanchet 1966; two s. one d.; ed Univ. of Paris, Columbia Univ., New York; Lawyer, Paris Court of Appeal 1951; Prof. of Law, Paris I (Sorbonne) 1974–81; Minister of Justice and Keeper of the Seals 1981–86; Pres. Constitutional Council 1986–95; currently Pres. Court of Conciliation and Arbitration, OSCE; Senator (Hauts de Seine) 1995–. *Play:* C.3.3., Paris 1995. *Publications:* L'exécution 1973, Liberté, libertés 1976, Condorcet (with Elisabeth Badinter) 1988, Libres et égaux: L'émancipation des juifs sous la révolution française 1989, La prison républicaine 1992, C.3.3. 1995, Un antisémitisme ordinaire: Vichy et les avocats juifs 1940–44 1997, L'abolition 2000, Une Constitution européenne 2002, Le plus grand bien 2004, Contre la peine de mort 2006. *Address:* Court of Conciliation and Arbitration within the OSCE, 266 route de Lausanne, PO Box 20, 1292 Chambesy, Geneva, Switzerland (office); 38 rue Guynemer, 75006 Paris, France (home). *Telephone:* 1-45-49-04-59 (home). *Fax:* 1-45-44-87-47 (home). *E-mail:* cca.osce@bluewin.ch (office); r.badinter@senat.fr (office). *Website:* www.osce.org (office); www.senat.fr (office).

BADRAN, Adnan, PhD; Jordanian politician, university president and international organization official; *Chairman, National Centre for Human Rights;* m.; several c.; ed Oklahoma State Univ., Michigan State Univ.; Prof. of Science and Dean Faculty of Science, Univ. of Jordan 1971–76; Pres. Yarmouk Univ. 1976–86; Asst Dir Gen. for Science, UNESCO 1990–93, Deputy Dir Gen. 1993–98; fmr Pres. Philadelphia Univ., Jordan; fmr Minister of Agric. and Minister of Educ.; Prime Minister and Minister of Defence April–Nov. 2005 (resgnd); fmr Sec.-Gen. Higher Council for Science and Tech.; Sec.-Gen. and Fellow, Third World Acad. of Sciences; mem. Arab Thought Forum 1978–, World Affairs Council 1980–, Inst. of Biological Sciences, AAAS 1993–; Fellow, Islamic Acad. of Sciences, mem. Council and Treas. 1999–; Chair. Nat. Center for Human Rights, Jordan 2008–; Dr hc (Sung Kyuakwan Univ., Seoul); Al-Nahda Medal (Jordan), Al-Yarmouk Medal (Jordan), Istilal Medal (Jordan) 1995, Alfonso X Medal (Spain). *Publications:* author and ed. of over 18 books and 90 research papers in the fields of botany, economic devt, educ. and int. co-operation. *Address:* National Centre for Human Rights, PO Box 5503, Amman 11183 (office); PO Box 477, Amman 11941, Jordan (home). *Telephone:* (6) 5931256 (office); (6) 5161880 (home). *Fax:* (6) 5930072 (office); (6) 5165285 (home). *E-mail:* mail@nchr.org.jo (home); abadran@wanadoo.com (home). *Website:* www.nchr.org.jo (office).

BADRAN, Ibrahim, BSc, PhD; Jordanian government official, foundation director and academic; *Assistant President for International Relations and Dean, Faculty of Engineering, Philadelphia University;* b. 19 July 1939, Nablus, Palestine; m.; four c.; ed Univs. of Cairo and London; Lecturer in Electrical Eng, Univ. of Libya, Tripoli 1970–74; Chief Engineer and Head, Electricity Section, Consultancy and Architecture, Ministry of Planning, Baghdad 1974–76; Dir of Planning and Dir of Standards and Specifications, Jordan Electricity Authority 1978–80; Dir of Energy, Ministry of Trade and Industry 1980–84; Sec.-Gen. (Under-Sec.) Ministry of Industry and Trade 1984–85; Sec.-Gen. Ministry of Energy and Natural Resources 1985–90; Adviser to Prime Minister 1991–94; Co-ordinator-Gen. of Peace Process, Ministry of Foreign Affairs 1994–95; Exec. Dir Noor Al-Hussein Foundation 1995–97; Supervisor, Human Rights Unit, Prime Minister's Office; Asst Pres. Philadelphia Univ. 1999–, Dean of Faculty of Eng 2000–; Chair. Bd of Dirs Jordan Glass Co. 1985–87, Commercial Centers Cooperation-Jordan 1984–85, 1990–91; mem. Bd of Dirs Jordan Atomic Energy; mem. Bd Consultance Albayan Magazine; fmr Dir Jordanian Petroleum Refinery, Jordanian Phosphate Co., Jordan Valley Authority, Jordan Water Authority, Jordan Electricity Authority, Jordan Natural Resources Authority, Industrial Bank of Jordan etc.; Gov. for Jordan, IAEA 1982–90; numerous other professional and academic appointments and affiliations; writes weekly column in Aldustou (daily newspaper); Wisam Al Istiqlal of the 1st Order 1990; Hussein Gold Medal for Scientific Distinctions, State Appreciation Award for Human Sciences and Arab Thoughts 2000. *Publications:* Study on the Arab Mind, On Progress and History in the Arab World, Science and Technology in the Arab World, Culture Decline, and other books on aspects of science, tech., nuclear energy, natural resources and devt in the Arab world; two theoretical plays. *Leisure interests:* farming, reading, writing, travelling. *Address:* Philadelphia University, PO Box 1, Amman 19392 (office); 29 Ali Thyabat Street, Tla'a Al Ali, Amman, Jordan (home). *Telephone:* (2) 6374444 (office); (2) 5347777 (home). *Fax:* (2) 6374370 (office); (2) 5344448 (home). *E-mail:* l.badran@philadelphia.edu.jo (office). *Website:* www.philadelphia.edu.jo (office); www.geocities.com/ibbadran (home).

BADRI, Muhammad bin, BSc, PhD; Malaysian chemist and academic; *Dean and Professor, Faculty of Science and Environmental Studies, Universiti Putra Malaysia;* b. May 1943; ed St Francis Xavier Univ., USA, Dalhousie Univ., Canada; teacher 1965–72; Lecturer, Universiti Putra Malaysia 1972–75, Assoc. Prof. 1976–84, Dean and Prof., Faculty of Science and Environmental Studies 1984–; mem. Council of Malaysia Inst. of Chem. 1980–84, Nat. Asscn of Science and Math. Educ., Malaysian Rubber Producers Council, ACS 1984, Bd Rubber Research Inst. of Malaysia, Environmental Quality Council, Ministry of Science, Malaysia; mem. Malaysian del. to IUPAC Comm. on High Temperature and Solid State Chem.; mem. ACS 1984; Founding Fellow, Islamic Acad. of Sciences 1986, Acad. of Sciences, Malaysia 1996. *Address:* Universiti Putra Malaysia, 43400 Serdang, Selangor Darul Ehsan, Malaysia (office). *Telephone:* (3) 89486101 (office). *Fax:* (3) 89483244 (office).

BADUEL, Gen. (retd) Raúl; Venezuelan fmr military officer and fmr politician; b. Guárico State; ed Mil. Acad. of Venezuela; fmr Commdr 42nd Parachute Brigade; fmr Chief of Mil. Staff; Minister of Defence 2006–07; Co-founder Revolutionary Bolivarian Movt 200 (MBR-200); charged with mismanaging govt funds 2008, arrested 2009.

BADURA-SKODA, Paul; Austrian pianist; b. 6 Oct. 1927; s. of Ludwig Badura and Margarete Badura (née Winter); m. Eva Badura-Skoda (née Halfar); two s. two d.; ed Realgymnasium courses in conducting and piano, Konservatorium der Stadt Wien and Edwin Fischer's Master Class in Lucerne; regular concerts since 1948; tours all over the world as soloist and with leading orchestras; conductor of chamber orchestra 1960–; yearly master classes fmrly in Edin., Salzburg and Vienna Festival 1958–63; Artist in Residence, Univ. of Wisconsin, master classes in Madison, Wis. 1966–71; recorded over 200 LP records and CDs including complete Beethoven, Mozart and Schubert sonatas; Austrian Cross of Honour for Science and Arts (First Order) 1976, Bösendorfer-Ring 1978, Chevalier, Legion d'honneur 1992, Commdr des Arts et des Lettres 1997, Grosses Silbernes Ehrenzeichen mit dem Stern der Republik Österreich 2007, Goldenes Ehrenzeichen für die Verdienste um das Land Wien 2007; Dr hc (Mannheim) 2006; First Prize, Austrian Music Competition 1947. *Compositions:* Mass in D, Cadenzas to Piano and Violin Concertos by Mozart and Haydn, completion of 5 unfinished Piano Sonatas by Schubert 1976 and of unfinished Larghetto and Allegro for 2 Pianos by Mozart, Elégie pour Piano 1980, Sonatine Romantique for Violin and Piano 1994, Sonate romantique for Flute (or Violin) and Piano. *Publications:* Interpreting Mozart on the Keyboard (with Eva Badura-Skoda), Die Klaviersonaten von Beethoven (with Jörg Demus) 1970, Interpreting Bach at the Keyboard 1993; Editions of Schubert, Mozart, Chopin; numerous articles. *Leisure interest:* chess. *Address:* c/o DeeAnne Hunstein, 65 West 90th Street, Suite 13F, New York, NY 10024, USA (office); c/o 3116 Live Oak Street, Dallas, TX 75204, USA (home). *Telephone:* (212) 724-2693 (office). *Fax:* (212) 724-9393 (office). *E-mail:* dah@hunsteinartists.com (office); www.hunsteinartists.com (office). *Website:* www.badura-skoda.com.

BAE, Jung Choong; South Korean insurance industry executive; *President and CEO, Samsung Life Insurance Co. Ltd;* currently Pres. and CEO, Samsung Life Insurance Co. Ltd. *Address:* Samsung Life Insurance Building, 150 Taepyong-ro 2-ga, Chung-gu, Seoul 100–716 Republic of Korea (office). *Telephone:* (1) 588-3114 (office). *Fax:* (2) 751-8021 (office). *Website:* www.samsunglife.com (office).

BAEZ, Joan Chandos; American folk singer; b. 9 Jan. 1941, Staten Island, NY; d. of Albert V. Baez and Joan Baez (née Bridge); m. David Harris 1968 (divorced 1973); one s.; ed School of Fine and Applied Arts, Boston Univ.; began career as singer in coffee houses, appeared at Ballad Room, Club 47 1958–68, Gate of Horn, Chicago 1958, Newport, RI, Folk Festival 1959–69, Town Hall and Carnegie Hall, New York 1962, 1967, 1968; gave concerts in black colls in southern USA 1963; toured Europe and USA 1960s–90s, Democratic Repub. of Viet Nam 1972, Australia 1985; recordings with Vanguard Records 1960–72, A & M Record Co. 1972–76, Portrait Records 1977–80, Gold Castle Records 1987–89, Virgin Records 1990–93, Guardian Records 1995–, Grapevine Label Records 1995–; awarded eight gold albums, one gold single; many TV appearances; began refusing payment of war taxes 1964; detained for civil disobedience opposing conscription 1967; speaking tour of USA and Canada for draft resistance 1967–68; Founder and Vice-Pres. Inst. for Study of Non-Violence (now called Resource Center for Non-Violence) 1965–; Founder Humanitas Int. Human Rights Comm. 1979–92; Chevalier, Légion d'honneur; Gandhi Memorial Int. Foundation Award 1988. *Recordings include:* albums: Joan Baez 1960, Joan Baez, Vol. 2 1961, In Concert, part 2 1963, 5 1964, Farewell Angelina 1965, Noel 1966, Joan 1967, Baptism 1968, Any Day Now 1968, David's Album 1969, One Day At A Time 1969, First Ten Years 1970, Carry It On (soundtrack) 1971, Ballad Book 1972, Come From The Shadows 1972, Where Are You Now My Son? 1973, Hits, Greatest and Others 1973, Gracias A La Vida 1974, Contemporary Ballad Book 1974, Diamonds and Rust 1975, From Every Stage 1976, Gulf Winds 1976, Blowin' Away 1977, Best Of 1977, Honest Lullaby 1979, Very Early Joan 1982, Recently 1987,

Diamonds and Rust In The Bullring 1989, Speaking Of Dreams 1989, Play Me Backwards 1992, Rare Live and Classic 1993, Ring Them Bells 1995, Gone from Danger 1997, Dreams 1997, Best Of… 1997, 20th Century Masters: The Millennium 1999, Dark Chords on a Big Guitar 2003, Bowery Songs 2005, Day After Tomorrow 2008. *Publications:* Joan Baez Songbook 1964, Daybreak 1968, Coming Out (with David Harris) 1971, And Then I Wrote… (songbook) 1979, And a Voice to Sing With 1987. *Address:* Diamonds and Rust Productions, PO Box 1026, Menlo Park, CA 94026-1026, USA. *Telephone:* (650) 328-0266. *Fax:* (650) 328-0845. *E-mail:* jbwebpages@aol.com. *Website:* www.joanbaez.com.

BAGABANDI, Natsagiin, PhD, ScD; Mongolian politician; b. 22 April 1950, Zavkhan Prov.; s. of Mendiin Natsag and Rashjamtsiin Dogoo; m. Azadsurengiin Oyunbileg 1971; one s. one d.; ed Refrigeration Jr Coll., Leningrad (now St Petersburg), USSR, Food Tech. Inst. of USSR, Odessa, Acad. of Social Science, Moscow, USSR; machine operator, mechanic and engineer, Ulan Bator City Brewery and Distillery 1972–75; Chief of Dept Mongolian People's Revolutionary Party's (MPRP) Cttee of Tuv Aimag 1980–84; Chief of Div., Div. Adviser Cen. Cttee of MPRP 1987–90; Sec., Deputy Chair. Cen. Cttee of MPRP 1990–92, Chair. Feb.–June 1997; mem. of State Great Hural, Chair. 1992–96; Pres. of Mongolia and C-in-C of the Armed Forces 1997–2005; Hon. Prof., Mongolian Socio-Econ. Inst. 'Explorer XXI'; 70th Anniversary Order of the People's Revolution 1991, 'Golden Star' Olympic Order 1997, Academician Title 'Bilguun Nomch', Mongolian Nomadic Civilization Acad. and 'Ikh-Zasag' Univ. 2000, 'Peace' Order of Russian Fed. 2000, Order of Chinggis Khaan 2000; Dr hc (Nat. Food Tech. Acad. of Odessa, Ukraine) 1995, (Seng-Shui Univ., Japan) 1998, (Ankara Univ., Turkey) 1998, (Alma-Ata Univ., Kazakhstan) 1998, (Mongolian Admin Acad.) 1999, (Mongolian 'Otgontenger' Univ.) 2001, (Mongolian Defense Univ.) 2001, (Sougan Univ., S Korea) 2001, (Mongolian Science and Tech. Univ.) 2002, (Soka Univ., Japan), (Tokyo Univ. of Agric.), (Indiana Univ., USA) 2005, (Hokuriku Univ., Japan) 2007; Sukhbaatar Fund Prize 1996, Peter the Great Int. Prize 2001. *Publications include:* Mongolian Behaviour 1992, The President: Thought and Recommendation Before the New Century 1998, The President: Policy and Objectives Before the New Century 1998, Policy and Mind of the President 2000, Significance of Restoration and Tradition to the Development 2000, Mongolian Intelligence 2001, Policy and Diligence of the President 2001, Thought and Ideas of the President 2001, XXI Century Will Test You 2001, New Era and New Objectives of Mongolian Buddhist Religion 2001, Let Us Respect and Admire Elders 2001, Children, Youths and the President 2001, Multi-Sided National Security 2001, New Century: Adore Consent and Friendship, Develop the Country 2003, New Century: Meaning of Self-reliance upon Globalization, and Globalization upon Self-reliance 2004, New Century: Meaning of Cherishing the Democracy 2005, Policy and Activity of President of Mongolia N. Bagabandi 2005. *Leisure interests:* reading, fishing. *Address:* c/o Mr Ayursaikhan Tumurbaatar, Secretary to Former President N. Bagabandi, State Palace, Ulan Bator 12, Mongolia (office). *E-mail:* ayursaikhan@yahoo.com (office).

BAGÃO FÉLIX, António; Portuguese politician and economist; b. 9 April 1948; fmr Sec. of State for Social Security; Sec. of State for Work and Professional Training 1987; fmr Vice-Pres. Portuguese Cen. Bank; Minister of Social Security and Employment 2002–04; Minister of Finance 2004–05. *Address:* c/o Ministry of Finance, Rua da Alfândega 5, 1100-006 Lisbon, Portugal (office).

BAGAPSH, Sergei Vasilyevich; Georgian (Abkhaz) politician; *'President', 'Republic of Abkhazia';* b. 1949, Sukhumi; ed Georgian Inst. of Agronomy; First Sec. of Abkhaz Komsomol 1980–82, Ochamchire Komsomol 1982–85; Perm. 'Rep. of Abkhaz' leadership in Moscow, Russian Fed. –1997; 'Prime Minister' of self-proclaimed 'Repub. of Abkhazia' 1997–2001; Gen.-Dir ChernoMorEnergo (BlackSeaEnergy) 2001–; 'Minister of Energy' 2001–04; jt cand. in Abkhaz presidential elections (for Amtsakhara and United Abkhazia opposition movts) 2004; 'Pres.' 'Repub. of Abkhazia' 2004–. *Address:* 'Office of the President', 6600 Abkhazia, Sukhumi, Georgia (office). *Telephone:* (122) 2-46-35 (office). *Fax:* (122) 2-71-17 (office). *Website:* www.abkhaziagov.org (office).

BAGAYEV, Sergei Nikolayevich; Russian physicist; *Director, Institute of Laser Physics, Russian Academy of Sciences (Siberia);* b. 9 Sept. 1941; m.; one s.; ed Novosibirsk State Univ.; Jr, Sr Researcher, Head of Lab., Inst. of Physics of Semiconductors, Siberian Br. USSR Acad. of Sciences 1965–78, Head of Lab., Head of Div., Deputy Dir Inst. of Thermal Physics, Siberian Br., USSR Acad. of Sciences 1978–91, Deputy Dir Inst. of Laser Physics, Siberian Br., Russian Acad. of Sciences 1991–92, Dir 1992–; Corresp. mem. USSR (now Russian) Acad. of Sciences 1990, Academician 1993–; research in nonlinear laser spectroscopy of superhigh resolution, laser frequency standards, physics and their applications in precision physical experiments; Order of Friendship 1999, Chevalier Légion d'honneur 2004, Medal of the Order 'For Services to the Motherland' 2006; State Prize of Russian Fed. 1998, V. A. Koptyug Prize, SBRAS/Belarus Nat. Acad. of Sciences 1999. *Publications include:* Laser Frequency Standards 1986, Single-frequency Intracavity Doubled Yb:YAG Ring Laser 2005, Investigation of Transcapillary Exchange by the Laser Method 2005, and numerous articles. *Address:* Institute of Laser Physics, Siberian Branch of Russian Academy of Sciences, Prosp. Lavrentyev 13/3, 630090 Novosibirsk, Russia (office). *Telephone:* (383) 333-24-89 (office). *Fax:* (383) 333-20-67 (office). *E-mail:* bagayev@laser.nsc.ru (office).

BAGAZA, Col Jean-Baptiste; Burundian army officer and politician; *Leader, Parti pour le redressement national (PARENA);* b. 29 Aug. 1946, Rutovu, Bururi Prov.; m. Fausta Bagaza; four c.; ed Ecole des Cadets, Brussels and the Belgian Mil. School, Arlon; fmr Asst to Gen. Ndabemeye; Chief of Staff of the Armed Forces, rank of Lt-Col; led coup to overthrow Pres. Micombero Nov. 1976; Pres. of the Repub. of Burundi 1976–87, also Minister of Defence; Pres. Union pour le progrès national (UPRONA) 1976–87; promoted to Col 1977; currently Leader Parti pour le redressement national (PARENA). *Address:* Parti pour le redressement national (PARENA), Bujumbura, Burundi.

BÅGE, Lennart, MBA; Swedish diplomatist and international organization executive; m.; two c.; ed Stockholm School of Econs; Asst Under-Sec. Ministry of Foreign Affairs; Amb. to Zimbabwe; Head Dept for Int. Co-operation, Ministry of Foreign Affairs, Deputy Dir-Gen. Ministry of Foreign Affairs –2001; Pres. IFAD 2001–09; Chair. UN High-Level Cttee on Programmes, mem. Sec.-Gen.'s High-Level Panel on UN Coherence 2007. *Address:* c/o International Fund for Agricultural Development, Via Paolo di Dono 44, 00142 Rome, Italy (office).

BAGGE, Sverre Hakon, PhD; Norwegian historian and academic; *Professor and Head, Centre for Medieval Studies, University of Bergen;* b. 7 Aug. 1942, Bergen; s. of Sverre Olsen and Gunvor Bagge; m. Guro Mette Skrove; two s. one d.; Lecturer, Univ. of Bergen 1973, Sr Lecturer 1974, Prof. 1991–, Prof., Head Centre for Medieval Studies 2002–; Brage Prize, Clara Lachmann's Prize, Jarl Gallén Prize for Medieval Studies, Univ. of Helsinki 2004. *Publications:* The Political Thought of the King's Mirror 1987, Society and Politics in Snorri Sturluson's Heimskringla 1991, From Gang Leader to the Lord's Anointed 1996, Kings, Politics, and the Right Order of the World in German Historiography *c.* 950–1150. *Address:* Center for Medieval Studies, University of Bergen, PO Box 7800, Villaveien 1A, 5020 Bergen (office); Moldbakken 13, 5035 Bergen, Norway (home). *Telephone:* 55-58-23-25 (office). *Fax:* 55-58-80-90 (office). *E-mail:* sverre.bagge@cms.uib.no (office). *Website:* www.uib.no/cms (office).

BAGGIO, Roberto; Italian fmr professional football player; b. 18 Feb. 1967, Caldogno; s. of Fiorindo Baggio and Matilde Baggio; m. Andreina Fabbri; two d.; with Vicenza 1985, Fiorentina 1985–90, Juventus 1990–95, Milan 1995–97, Bologna 1997–98, Inter Milan 1998–2000, Brescia 2000–04, 318 career goals; played for Italian Nat. Team in 1990, 1994 and 1998 World Cups; FIFA World Player of the Year 1993, European Footballer of the Year 1993. *Leisure interests:* hunting, music. *Address:* Via Bazoli 10, 25127 Brescia, Italy (office). *Telephone:* (30) 241075 (office). *Fax:* (30) 2410787 (office). *E-mail:* info@bresciacalcio.it (office). *Website:* www.bresciacalcio.it (office); www.robertobaggio.com (home).

BAGHDASARIAN, Artur, DJur; Armenian politician; b. 8 Nov. 1968, Yerevan; m.; two c.; ed Yerevan State Univ.; army service 1988–89; Corresp., Head of Dept Avangard newspaper 1989–93; mem. Nat. Ass. 1995–, Chair. 2003–06; Chair. Council on State and Legal Affairs 1998–; Leader Orinats Yerkir party 1998–; Chair. French Univ. of Armenia 2000–; Chair. European Regional Acad. in the Caucasus 2002–. *Publications:* several scientific monographs and articles. *Address:* c/o National Assembly of the Republic of Armenia, Marshal Bagramian St 19, 375095 Yerevan, Armenia (office).

BAGIS, Egemen, MPA, BBA; Turkish politician; *Foreign Policy Advisor to the Prime Minister;* b. 1970, Bingol; m. Beyhan N. Bagis; two c.; ed Baruch Coll., City Univ. of New York, USA; elected to Nat. Ass. for Istanbul 2002–, Foreign Policy Advisor to Prime Minister 2002–; mem. AK Party (Justice and Devt Party), serves as Deputy Chair. for Foreign Affairs; Chair. NATO Parl. Ass. on Transatlantic Relations; Chair. Turkey–USA Inter-Parl. Friendship Caucus; Chair. Advisory Cttee, Istanbul 2010 European Capital of Culture Initiative; Founding Patron, Istanbul Modern Museum, Santral Museum of Art and Industry; fmr Pres. Fed. of Turkish-American Asscns; Hon. mem. Bd of Dirs Siirt Solidarity Foundation. *Address:* Turkish Grand National Assembly, A Blok, Alt Zemin, 3. Banko, No. 3, Bakanliklar, 06543 Ankara, Turkey (office). *Telephone:* (312) 4205908 (office). *Fax:* (312) 4206947 (office). *E-mail:* egemen@egemenbagis.com (office). *Website:* www.egemenbagis.com (office).

BAGLAY, Marat Viktorovich, DJur, DHist; Russian lawyer; b. 13 March 1931, Baku, Azerbaijan; m.; three d.; ed Rostov State Univ., Inst. of State and Law; researcher, Inst. of State and Law 1957–62; Prof., Moscow Inst. of Int. Relations 1962–95; Head of Dept, Inst. of Int. Workers' Movt Acad. of Sciences 1967–77; Pro-Rector and Prof., Acad. of Labour and Social Relations 1977–95; judge, Constitutional Court of Russian Fed. 1996–, Chair. 1997–2003; Corresp. mem. Russian Acad. of Sciences 1997–; mem. Bureau, European Comm. for Democracy Through Law 2005–; Hon. LLD (Baku Univ., Rostov-on-Don Univ., Odessa Nat. Acad. of Law); Merited Scientist of Russia. *Publications include:* Way to Freedom, Constitutional Law of Russian Federation, numerous books and articles. *Address:* Constitutional Court of Russian Federation, Ilyinka str. 21, 103132 Moscow, Russia (office); Venice Commission, Council of Europe, 67075 Strasbourg Cedex, France. *Telephone:* (495) 606-92-25 (office). *Fax:* (495) 606-19-78 (office).

BAGNASCO, HE Cardinal Angelo; Italian ecclesiastic; *Archbishop of Genoa;* b. 14 Jan. 1943, Pontevico; ed Univ. of Genoa; ordained priest, Genoa 1966; served as Prof. of Metaphysics and Atheism, Theological Faculty of Northern Italy, also led archdiocesan liturgical and catechesis offices; fmr diocesan rep. to FUCI (Italian Catholic Fed. of Univ. Students); Bishop of Pesaro 1998–2000, Archbishop of Pesaro 2000–03; Archbishop of the Mil. Ordinariate of Italy 2003–06; Archbishop of Genoa 2006–; has held several posts within Italian Episcopal Conf. (CEI) 2001–, including Pres. Admin. Bd of newspaper Avvenire and Sec. for Schools and Univs 2001–, Pres. CEI 2007–; cr. Cardinal 2007. *Address:* Arcivescovado, Piazza Matteotti 4, 16123 Genoa, Italy (office). *Telephone:* (010) 27-001 (office). *Fax:* (010) 27-00-220 (office). *E-mail:* info@diocesi.genova.it (office). *Website:* www.diocesi.genova.it (office).

BAGRATIAN, Hrant Araratovich; Armenian economist and politician; b. 18 Oct. 1958, Yerevan; m.; one s.; ed Yerevan Inst. of Nat. Econ.; Jr researcher,

Sr researcher Inst. of Econs, Armenian Acad. of Sciences 1982–90; First Deputy Chair. Council of Ministers of Armenian SSR, Chair. State Cttee on Econs 1990; Vice-Prime Minister, Minister of Econs Repub. of Armenia 1991–93; Prime Minister of Armenia 1993–96; Founder and Leader, Azatutiun (Liberty) Party; in pvt. business 1996–.

BAGRI, Baron (Life Peer), cr. 1997, of Regents Park in the City of Westminster; **Raj Kumar Bagri,** CBE; British commodities executive; *Chairman, Minmetco;* b. 24 Aug. 1930; m. 1954; one s. one d.; joined a metals business in Calcutta 1946; moved into int. metals trading 1949; set up UK br. office of an Indian co. 1959; f. own company in UK, Metdist Ltd, which became London Metal Exchange (LME) ring dealing mem. 1970, currently Chair. Minmetco (UK holding co. of Metdist Group of Cos); joined LME's Man. Cttee 1973, apptd. Dir of LME 1983, Vice-Chair. 1990, Chair. 1993–2002, Hon. Pres. 2003–; mem. Advisory Council Prince's Youth Business Trust, Governing Body SOAS; Hon. DSc (City Univ.) 1999, (Nottingham) 2000 Hon. Fellow (London Business School) 2004. *Leisure interest:* cricket. *Address:* Metdist Group, 80 Cannon Street, London, EC4N 6EJ, England. *Telephone:* (20) 7280-0000. *Fax:* (20) 7606-6650.

BAGSHAWE, Kenneth Dawson, CBE, MD, FRCP, FRCR, FRCOG, FRS; British physician and medical oncologist; b. 17 Aug. 1925, Marple, Cheshire; s. of Harry Bagshawe and Gladys Bagshawe; m. 1st Ann A. Kelly 1946 (divorced 1976, died 2000); m. 2nd Sylvia D. Lawler (née Corben) 1977 (died 1996); one s. one d.; m. 3rd Surinder Kanta Sharma 1998; ed Harrow Co. School, London School of Econs and St Mary's Hosp. Medical School, Univ. of London; served RN 1943–46; Research Fellow, Johns Hopkins Hosp. 1955–56; Sr Registrar, St Mary's Hosp. 1956–60; Sr Lecturer in Medicine, Charing Cross Hosp. Medical School 1961–63; Consultant Physician and Dir Dept of Medical Oncology 1961–90, Prof. Emer.; Prof. of Medical Oncology, Charing Cross Hosp. Medical School 1974–90; Chair., Zenyx Scientific Co. Ltd 1996–, Enzacta 1998–; Vice-Chair. Council Cancer Research Campaign 1988–; Pres. Asscn of Cancer Physicians 1986–93, British Asscn for Cancer Research 1990–94; mem. various cancer research cttees etc.; Fellow Royal Coll. of Radiologists; Hamilton Fairley Lectureship 1989; Hon. DSc (Bradford) 1990; Krug Award for Excellence in Medicine 1980; Edgar Gentilli Prize (Royal Coll. of Obstetricians and Gynaeocologists) 1980, Galen Medal (London Soc. of Apothecaries) 1993. *Publications:* Choriocarcinoma 1969, Medical Oncology 1976, Germ Cell Tumours 1983, Antibody Directed Prodrug Therapy 1987 and articles in professional journals. *Leisure interests:* travel, walking, photography, music, art. *Address:* Department of Surgery, 4N, Charing Cross Hospital, London, W6 8RF (office); 115 George Street, London, W1H T5A, England (home). *Telephone:* (20) 8846-7517 (office); (20) 7262-6033 (home). *Fax:* (20) 8846-7516 (office); (20) 7258-1365 (home). *E-mail:* k.bagshawe@ic.ac.uk (home).

BAH, Amadou Lamarana; Guinean diplomatist and government official; b. 1950, Pita; ed Univ. of Havana, Cuba; Lecturer in Hispanic Culture and Civilisation, Gamal Abdel Nasser Univ., Conakry 1976–77; Press Attaché, Office of Pres. 1977–80; First Sec., Embassy in Havana 1980–83, Embassy in Monrovia 1986–87, Embassy in Abidjan 1987–91; First Counsellor, Embassy in Paris 1991–96; Counsellor, Embassy in Lagos 1996–98; Dir Immunities and Privileges Div., Ministry of Foreign Affairs, Co-operation, African Integration and Guineans Abroad 1998–2008, Minister of Foreign Affairs, Co-operation, African Integration and Guineans Abroad 2008. *Leisure interests:* reading, jogging. *Address:* c/o Ministry of Foreign Affairs, Co-operation, African Integration and Guineans Abroad, face au Port, ex-Primature, BP 2519, Conakry, Guinea (office).

BAHARNA, Husain Mohammad al-, PhD; Bahraini politician and lawyer; b. 5 Dec. 1932, Manama; s. of Mohammad Makki Al-Baharna and Zahra Sayed Mahmood; m.; three s. two d.; ed Baghdad Law Coll., Iraq, London Univ. and Cambridge Univ., UK; mem. English Bar (Lincoln's Inn) and Bahraini Bar; Legal Adviser, Ministry of Foreign Affairs, Kuwait 1962–64; Legal Adviser and Analyst Arab Gulf Affairs, Arabian-American Oil Co., Saudi Arabia 1965–68; Legal Adviser, Dept of Foreign Affairs, Bahrain 1969–70; Legal Adviser to the State and mem. Council of State, Pres. Legal Cttee 1970–71; Minister of State for Legal Affairs 1971; mem. Del. of Bahrain to Sixth (Legal) Cttee UN Gen. Ass. 1986, UN Int. Law Comm., Geneva 1987, Del. of Bahrain to Summit of Heads of State of Gulf Co-operation Council 1991; fmr legal adviser and del. to numerous int. confs and summit meetings; Chair. Del. of Bahrain to UN Preparatory Comm. for Int. Sea Bed Authority and Int. Tribunal for Law of the Sea 1983; mem. Cttee of Experts on Control of Transnational and Int. Criminality and for the establishment of the Int. Criminal Court, Siracusa, Italy 1990; Council mem. Centre for Islamic and Middle East Law, SOAS, London Univ., Editorial Bd Arab Law Quarterly; Hon. mem. Euro-Arab Forum for Arbitration and Business Law, Paris; mem. British Inst. of Int. and Comparative Law, American Soc. of Int. Law, Int. Law Asscn, Egyptian Soc. of Int. Law; Assoc. mem. Int. Comm. of Jurists, Int. Law Comm., UN; Arab Historian Medal (Union of Arab Historians) 1986. *Publications:* The Legal Status of the Arab Gulf States 1968, Legal and Constitutional Systems of the Arabian Gulf States (in Arabic) 1975, The Arabian Gulf States – Their Legal and Political Status and their International Problems 1975; articles in learned journals. *Leisure interest:* reading. *Address:* PO Box 790, Manama, Bahrain. *Telephone:* 255633. *Fax:* 270303.

BAHÇELI, Devlet, DEcon; Turkish politician and academic; *Leader, Nationalist Action Party (MHP);* b. 1948, Osmaniye; ed Ankara Econ. and Commercial Sciences Acad., Gazi Univ. Social Sciences Inst.; Sec.-Gen. Turkish Nat. Students Fed. 1970–71; instructor, Ankara Econ. and Commercial Sciences Acad., mem. Faculty of Econ. and Admin. Sciences, Gazi Univ. 1972–87; Sec.-Gen. Nationalist Action Party (MHP) 1987, Leader 1997–; Deputy Prime Minister and State Minister 1999–2002; Founder mem., Pres. of the Financiers and Economists Asscn. *Address:* Milliyetçi Hareket Partisi (Nationalist Action Party), Ceyhun Atif Kansu Cad. 128, Balgat, Ankara, Turkey (office). *Telephone:* (312) 4725555 (office). *Fax:* (312) 4731544 (office). *E-mail:* bilgi@mhp.org.tr (office). *Website:* www.mhp.org.tr (office).

BAHNASSI, Afif, MA, PhD; Syrian academic; *Professor of History of Art and Architecture, Damascus University;* b. 17 April 1928, Damascus; m. 1st Hiba Wadi 1962 (died 1966); m. 2nd Maysoun Jazairi 1971; four s. one d.; ed Univ. of Syria and Sorbonne, Paris; Dir Fine Arts Dept 1959–71; Dir Gen. of Antiquities and Museums of Syria 1972–88; mem. Arab Writers' Union 1967–; Chair. Fine Arts Asscn of Syria 1968–; Prof. of History of Art and Architecture, Damascus Univ. 1988–; co-designer of Martyr Monument 1991, October Monument 1998; Commdr des Arts and des Lettres; First Prize in Islamic Architecture 1991, ICO Award, Jeddah; numerous other awards and medals. *Publications:* General History of Arts and Architecture 1962, L'Esthétique de l'art arabe 1979, Arabic Modern Art 1979, Damascus 1981, L'Art et l'Orientalisme 1983, En Syrie 1986, The Ancient Syria 1987, The Great Mosque of Damascus 1988, Arab Architecture 1994, Dictionnaire d'architecture 1994, Dictionnaire des termes de calligraphie, The Great Mosque of San'a 1996, Aesthetics of al Tawhidi 1997, Criticism of Art 1997, Modernism and Postmodernism 1997, Islamic Tiles 1997, Arab Calligraphy 1997, Interlocution in Islamic Art 2000, Encyclopédie de l'architecture islamique 2002, Formation of Damascus 2002, Damascus – Capital of Umayyad Dynasty 2002. *Leisure interests:* painting, sculpture. *Address:* 4 Gazzi Street, Damascus, Syria. *Telephone:* 3334554 (office); 3311827 (home). *Fax:* 3319368 (home).

BAHR, Egon; German government official and journalist; b. 18 March 1922, Treffurt; m. Dorothea Grob 1945; one s. one d.; journalist 1945–, contrib., Die Neue Zeitung 1948–59, Das Tagesspiegel 1950; Chief Commentator RIAS (Rundfunk im amerikanischen Sektor Berlins) 1950–60; Dir Press and Information Office of Berlin 1960–66; promoted to rank of Amb. in diplomatic service 1967; Dir of Planning Staff, Diplomatic Service 1967–68; Ministerial Dir 1968–69; State Sec., Bundeskanzleramt and Plenipotentiary of the Fed. Govt in Berlin 1969–72; mem. of Parl. (Bundestag) 1972–90; Fed. Minister without Portfolio attached to the Fed. Chancellor's Office 1972–74, for Overseas Devt Aid (Econ. Co-operation) 1974–76; Dir Institut für Friedensforschung und Sicherheitspolitik 1984–94; mem. PEN 1974–, Ind. Comm. on Disarmament and Security 1980–; Grosses Bundesverdienstkreuz; Theodor-Heuss-Preis 1976, Gustav-Heinemann-Bürgerpreis 1982. *Publications:* Was wird aus den Deutschen? 1982, Zum Europäischen Frieden 1988, Zu meiner Zeit 1996, Deutsche Interessen 1998, Nationalstaat: Überholt und unentbehrlich 1999. *Address:* Ollenhauerstrasse 1, 53113 Bonn, Germany.

BAI, Chunli, PhD; Chinese chemist and academic; *Executive Vice-President, Chinese Academy of Sciences;* b. 26 Sept. 1953, Liaoning; s. of Bai Fuxin and Li Fengyun; m. Li Chunfang 1981; one s.; ed Peking Univ., Inst. of Chem., Chinese Acad. of Sciences; Research Asst, Changchun Inst. of Applied Chem., Chinese Acad. of Sciences (CAS) 1978, Research Assoc., Inst. of Chem. 1981–85; Visiting Research Assoc., Calif. Inst. of Tech., USA 1985–87; Assoc. Prof. and Dir Study Group on Scanning Tunnelling Microscopy (STM), Inst. of Chem., CAS 1987–89, Prof. 1989–, Deputy Dir 1992–96, Vice-Pres. CAS 1996–2004, Exec. Vice-Pres. 2004–, Academician 1997–; Dir Nat. Centre of Nanoscience 2004–; Visiting Prof., Inst. for Materials Research, Tohoku Univ., Japan 1991–92; Vice-Pres. China Material Research Soc. 2000–, China Asscn for Science and Tech. 2001–; Sec.-Gen. and mem. Exec. Council Chinese Chemical Soc. 1994–98, Pres. 1999–; Vice-Pres. All-China Youth Fed. 1995–2000; Pres. China Young Scientists' Asscn 1996–; mem. Editorial Advisory Bd Journal of the American Chemical Society, Angewandte Chemie, Advances in Materials; mem. CPPCC 1993–98, Alt. mem. 15th Cen. Cttee 1997–2002, 16th Cen. Cttee 2002–07, 17th Cen. Cttee 2007–; Fellow, Third World Acad. of Sciences 1997–; Foreign mem. Mongolian Acad. of Sciences 2005–, NAS (USA) 2006–; Outstanding Young Scholar, Hong Kong Qiu Shi Science and Tech. Foundation 1995, Ho Leung Ho Lee Prize; numerous prizes and awards. *Publications:* 10 books and more than 250 papers in scientific journals. *Address:* Chinese Academy of Sciences, 52 San Li He Road, Beijing 100864, People's Republic of China (office). *Telephone:* (10) 68597606 (office). *Fax:* (10) 68512458 (office). *E-mail:* clbai@cashq.ac.cn (office).

BAI, Donglu, PhD; Chinese professor of medicinal chemistry; *Professor, Shanghai Institute of Materia Medica, Chinese Academy of Sciences;* b. Feb. 1936, Dinghai Co., Zhejiang Prov.; s. of Bai Daxi and Zhang Yunxiao; m. Ni Zhifang 1969; one d.; ed Shanghai First Medical Coll., Czechoslovak Acad. of Sciences, Prague; Prof., Shanghai Inst. of Materia Medica, Chinese Acad. of Sciences; Science and Tech. Progress Award, Nat. Natural Science Prize 2000. *Publications:* more than 150 papers in scientific journals. *Leisure interest:* stamp collecting. *Address:* Shanghai Institute of Materia Medica, 555 Zuchongzhi Road, Zhangjiang 201203, People's Republic of China (office). *Telephone:* (21) 50805896 (office). *Fax:* (21) 50805896 (office). *E-mail:* dlbai@mail.shcnc.ac.cn (office). *Website:* www.simm.ac.cn (office).

BAI, Enpei; Chinese politician; *Secretary, Chinese Communist Party Yunnan Provincial Committee;* b. Sept. 1946, Qingjian Co., Shaanxi Prov.; ed Northwest Tech. Univ. 1965; sent to do manual labour (Ind. Div. Farm, Shaanxi Prov. Mil. Command) 1970–73; joined CCP 1973; Deputy Dir and Dir Yan'an Diesel Engine Plant, Shaanxi Prov. 1974–83, Deputy Sec. CCP Party Cttee 1974–83; Vice-Sec. CCP Yan'an Prefectural Cttee 1983–90; Sec. CCP Yan'an Prefectural Cttee 1985; Alt. mem. 13th CCP Cen. Cttee 1987–92, 14th CCP Cen. Cttee 1992–97, mem. 15th CCP Cen. Cttee 1997–2002, mem. 16th CCP Cen. Cttee 2002–07, mem. 17th CCP Cen. Cttee 2007–; Head CCP Inner Mongolia Autonomous Regional Cttee, Org. Dept 1990–93, mem. CCP Inner Mongolia Autonomous Regional Cttee Standing Committee 1990–93, Deputy Sec. Inner Mongolia Autonomous Regional Cttee 1993–97; Vice-Sec. CCP

Qinghai Prov. Cttee 1997–99, Sec. 1999–2001; Acting Gov. Qinghai Prov. 1997–1998, Gov. 1998–99; Chair. Qinghai Prov. People's Congress 2000–01; Sec. CCP Yunnan Prov. Cttee 2001–, mem. Standing Cttee 2001–. *Address:* Chinese Communist Party Yunnan Provincial Committee, Kunming, Yunnan Province, People's Republic of China.

BAI, Keming; Chinese journalist and party official; *Vice-Chairman, Committee for Education, Science, Culture and Public Health, National People's Congress;* b. Oct. 1943, Jingbian, Shaanxi Prov.; s. of Bai Jian; ed Harbin Mil. Eng Inst.; joined CCP 1975; worker, Metallurgy and Geology Bureau, Harbin City, Heilongjiang Prov. 1968–70; Teacher Harbin Shipbuilding Inst. 1970–73, National Defence Industry Cttee, Shaanxi Prov. 1973–78; Deputy Div. Chief, Gen. Office, Ministry of Educ. 1978–86, Vice Div. Chief then Deputy Dir 1986–89; Head Educ. Science, Culture and Public Health Group, Research Office of the State Council 1989–93; Sec.-Gen. Propaganda Dept of CCP Cen. Cttee 1993, Deputy Head 1993–2000; Del. 15th CCP Nat. Congress 1997–2002; Deputy Dir CCP Cen. Cttee Gen. Office 2000–01; Pres. CCP Cen. Cttee People's Daily (newspaper) 2000–01; Sec. CCP Hainan Prov. Cttee and Chair. Hainan People's Congress 2001–02; Sec. CCP Prov. Cttee, Hebei Prov. 2002–07; mem. 16th CCP Cen. Cttee 2002–07; Vice-Chair. Cttee for Educ., Science, Culture and Public Health, Nat. People's Congress 2007–. *Address:* National People's Congress, Beijing, People's Republic of China (office). *Website:* npc.people.com.cn (office).

BAI, Lichen; Chinese politician; *Vice-Chairman, 11th National Committee of the Chinese People's Political Consultative Conference;* b. 1941, Lingyuan, Liaoning Prov.; ed Shenyang Agricultural Coll.; technician, Yingkou Agricultural Coll., Agricultural Machinery Inst., Yingkou, Liaoning Prov. 1964–68; joined CCP 1971; clerk, CCP City Cttee Org. Dept, Yingkou 1972–80, Deputy Section Chief Personnel Supervision Bureau 1972–80, Deputy Sec. then Sec. CCP City Cttee, Yingkou 1980–83, Mayor of Yingkou 1983–84; Sec. CCP City Cttee, Panjin City, Liaoning Prov. 1984–85; mem. Standing Cttee CCP Liaoning Prov. Cttee 1985–87; Asst to Gov. Liaoning Prov. 1984–85, Vice-Gov. 1985–86; mem. 13th Cen. Cttee CCP 1987–92, 14th Cen. Cttee CCP 1992–97, 15th Cen. Cttee 1997–2002, 16th Cen. Cttee 2002–07, 17th Cen. Cttee 2007–; Vice-Chair., Acting Chair. and Chair. Ningxia Hui Autonomous Regional People's Govt 1987–97; Deputy Sec. CCP Regional Cttee 1988–97; Sec. CCP Leading Party Group, All-China Fed. of Supply and Marketing Co-operatives 1997–99, Pres. Second Council 1999–2002; Vice-Chair. 9th Nat. Cttee of CPPCC 1998–2003, 10th Nat. Cttee of CPPCC 2003–08, 11th Nat. Cttee of CPPCC 2008–. *Address:* National Committee of the Chinese People's Political Consultative Conference, 23 Taiping Qiao Street, Beijing, People's Republic of China.

BAI, Qingcai; Chinese party and government official; b. 1932, Wutai Co., Shaanxi Prov.; joined CCP 1955; fmr Section Chief, People's Bank of China, Prov. Br., Shanxi Prov.; fmr Dir Prov. Planning Cttee, Gen. Office, Shanxi Prov.; Vice-Gov. Shanxi Prov. 1983–85, 1990–93, Exec. Vice-Gov. 1985–90, Gov. 1993–94; mem. Shanxi Prov. Standing Comm. CCP 1985–90; Del. 13th CCP Nat. Congress 1987–92, 15th CCP Nat. Congress 1997–2002; mem. 7th NPC 1988–93, 8th NPC 1993–98, 9th NPC 1993–2003 (Vice-Chair. Environment and Resource Protection Cttee 1998); Deputy Sec. CCP Shaanxi Prov. Cttee 1990–95; mem. 14th CCP Cen. Cttee 1992–97; Vice-Chair. Second Council, All-China Fed. of Supply and Marketing Co-operatives 1995. *Address:* c/o Standing Committee of the National People's Congress, Beijing, People's Republic of China.

BAI, Shuxian; Chinese ballerina; *Deputy Chairperson, China Dramatists' Association;* b. 1939; ed Beijing Coll. of Dancing; Prin. Dancer, Cen. Ballet Co. 1958, Dir 1984–90; mem. 5th Nat. Cttee CPPCC 1978–82, 6th Nat. Cttee 1983–87, 7th Nat. Cttee 1988–92, 8th Nat. Cttee 1993–97; Vice-Dir Beijing Ballet 1980–; Performing Artist, Longjiang Opera; Perm. mem. Chinese Dancers' Asscn, Chair. 1992–; Vice-Chair. China Fed. of Literary and Art Circles 1996–; Deputy Chair. China Dramatists' Asscn; First Grade Dancer of the Nation, Chinese Opera Plum Blossom Award, Shanghai Theatrical Festival White Magnolia Prize. *Films:* Absurd Baoyu, The Legend of Hua Mulan 1994 (Huabiao prize). *Performances include:* Swan Lake, Giselle, The Fountain of Bakhchisarai, The Emerald, Sylvia, Red Women Army, Song of Yimeng, Song of Jiaoyang. *Address:* Longjiang Opera, No 114, Ashihe Street, Nangong, 150001 Harbin, Heilongjiang Province, People's Republic of China.

BAI, Xueshi; Chinese artist; b. 12 June 1915, Beijing; s. of Dong and Bai Huanzhang; m. Xie Lin; two s. three d.; studied under Liang Shunian; specializes in landscape paintings; fmr teacher Beijing Teachers' Inst. of Arts, Beijing Inst. of Arts; Prof., Cen. Acad. of Arts and Design; Pres. Beijing Research Soc. of Landscape Paintings; mem. Cttee of 7th CPPCC 1988–; exhbns in USA, Japan, Hong Kong. *Works include:* Myriad Peaks Contending, Riverside Village, Riverboats in Springtime, Aspects of Lushan, Lijiang, Cool Waters of Lijiang, Cormorant Fishing, Banks of the Gorge, Li River in the Morning. *Leisure interests:* Beijing opera and weiqi. *Address:* Central Academy of Arts and Design, Beijing, People's Republic of China. *Telephone:* 341308.

BAIGELDI, Omirbek, DrEconSc; Kazakhstani politician; *Deputy Chairman of the Senate;* b. 15 April 1939, Yernazar, Zhambyl Region; m.; three c.; ed Almaty Inst. of Veterinary Sciences, Acad. of Social Sciences Cen. CPSU Cttee; various posts in Dist Dept of Agric. Man. 1962–74; First Deputy Chair. Regional Dept on Agric. Man. 1974–75; First Sec. Kurdai Regional Cttee, Chair. Zhambyl Regional Exec. Cttee, First Sec. Zhambyl Regional Cttee CP of Kazakhstan, Chair. Zhambyl Soviet of People's Deputies 1975–92; Head Zhambyl Regional Admin. 1992–95; Counsellor to Pres. of Kazakhstan 1995–96; Chair. Senate (Parl.) 1996–99, Deputy Chair. 1999–, mem. 1999–; mem. Acad. of Agric. Sciences; Orders Union (Sodruzjestvo) 1991, Kurmet 1995, Otan 1999. *Address:* House of Parliament, Astana, Kazakhstan. *Telephone:* (7172) 32-78-92 (office).

BAILEY, David, CBE, FRPS, FSIAD, FCSD; British photographer and film director; b. 2 Jan. 1938, London; s. of Herbert William Bailey and Gladys Agnes Bailey; m. 1st Rosemary Bramble 1960; m. 2nd Catherine Deneuve 1965; m. 3rd Marie Helvin (divorced 1985); m. 4th Catherine Dyer 1986; two s. one d.; self-taught; photographer for Vogue, UK, USA, France, Italy and advertising photography 1959–; Dir Commercials 1966–, TV documentaries 1968–; photographer for Harpers and Queen 1999; directed and produced TV film Who Dealt? 1993; documentary: Models Close Up 1998; Dir feature film The Intruder 1999; Dr hc (Bradford Univ.) 2001; V&A Award for Outstanding Achievement in Fashion, British Fashion Awards 2004. *Publications:* Box of Pinups 1964, Goodbye Baby and Amen 1969, Warhol 1974, Beady Minces 1974, Mixed Moments 1976, Trouble and Strife 1980, NW1 1982, Black and White Memories 1983, Nudes 1981–84 1984, Imagine 1985, The Naked Eye: Great Photographs of the Nude (with Martin Harrison) 1988, If We Shadows 1992, The Lady is a Tramp 1995, Rock & Roll Heroes 1997, Archive One 1999, Chasing Rainbows 2001, Bailey's Democracy 2005, Pictures that Mark can do 2007. *Leisure interests:* photography, aviculture, travel, painting. *Address:* c/o Robert Montgomery and Partners, 3 Junction Mews, Sale Place, London, W2, England. *Telephone:* (20) 7439-1877. *E-mail:* studio@camera-eye.co.uk (office).

BAILEY, Donovan; Canadian marketing consultant and fmr athlete; *President and CEO, DBX Sport Management;* b. 16 Dec. 1967, Manchester, Jamaica; s. of George Donovan and Icilda Donovan; one d. by Michelle Mullin; ed Sheridan Coll., Oakville; grew up in Jamaica and emigrated to Canada 1981; mem. Canada's winning 4×100m team, Commonwealth Games 1994, Olympic Games 1996; world indoor record-holder for 50m 1996; Canadian 100m record-holder 1995, 1996; world, Commonwealth and Olympic 100m record-holder 1996; retd from athletics 2001; partner in stockbroking, man. and construction co.; Pres. and CEO DBX Sport Management; f. Donovan Bailey Fund to assist Canadian amateur athletes; Sprinter of the Decade, Track and Field News 1999. *Address:* c/o The Donovan Bailey Fund, 468 Wellington Street West, Suite 401, Toronto, Ont. MV5 1E3, Canada (office). *Telephone:* (416) 204-9962. *Website:* www.donovanbailey.com.

BAILEY, Jerry; American professional jockey (retd) and television analyst; b. 29 Aug. 1957, Dallas; s. of James Bailey; m. Suzee; one s.; thoroughbred racing jockey 1974–2006, began career with win at Sunland Park, New Mexico 1974 (Fetch); moved to New York 1982; winner Gulfstream Park Handicap 1990, 1995 (Cigar), 1996, 1997, 1998; 14 Breeders' Cup titles, including Breeders' Cup Classic 1991 (Black Tie Affair), 1993 (Arcangues), 1994 (Concern), (Cigar) 1995, (Saint Liam) 2005, Breeders' Cup Mile (Six Perfections) 2003; winner Belmont 1991 (Hansel); winner Preakness Stakes 1991 (Hansel), 2000 (Red Bullet); winner Hollywood Gold Cup Handicap 1992, 1995 (Cigar), 1998, 1999; winner Woodward Stakes 1992, 1995 (Cigar), 1996 (Cigar), 1998; winner Kentucky Derby 1993 (Sea Hero), 1996 (Grindstone); winner Travers Stakes 1993 (Sea Hero); winner Oaklawn Park Handicap, Pimlico Special, Jockey Club Gold Cup, Don Handicap 1995 (Cigar); winner Massachussets Handicap 1995 (Cigar), 1996 (Cigar), 1998 (Skip Away); winner Dubai World Cup 1996 (Cigar), 1997 (Singspiel), 2001 (Captain Steve); Saratoga riding title 1994, 1995, 1996, 1997, 2000; 16 straight victories on Cigar 1995–96; seven winners on one card, Florida Derby Day 1995; North America's leading money-winning rider 1995–1997 and 2001, 2002; first rider to win more than $20 million in one season (2001); retd 2006 with 5,892 career wins; currently TV analyst for ABC and ESPN; fmr Nat. Pres. Jockeys' Guild; George Woolf Memorial Jockey Award 1992; Mike Venezia Award (New York Racing Asscn) 1993; Eclipse Award for Outstanding Jockey 1995, 1996, 1997, 2000, 2001, 2002, 2003; elected to racing's Hall of Fame 1995, Broward Co. Sports Hall of Fame 2006. *Publication:* Against the Odds: Riding for My Life 2005. *E-mail:* info@jerrybailey.com. *Website:* www.jerrybailey.com.

BAILEY, Michael (Mike) J.; British business executive; ed Westminster Coll., London; Food Service Man., Gardner Merchant 1961, later becoming Man. Dir, Pres., US subsidiary 1985–91; Exec. Vice-Pres. Nutrition Man. Services 1991–93; joined Compass Group PLC 1993, Group Devt Dir 1993–94, CEO N American Div. 1994–99, Group CEO 1999–2005; Fellow, Hotel and Catering Int. Man. Asscn. *Address:* c/o Compass Group PLC, Compass House, Guildford Street, Chertsey, KT16 9BQ, England (office).

BAILEY, Norman A., PhD; American economist, academic and government official; *Mission Manager for Cuba and Venezuela, Office of the Director of National Intelligence;* ed Oberlin Coll. and Columbia Univ.; fmr economist, Mobil Oil Co.; f. Overseas Equity Inc. .(later Bailey, Tondu, Warwick & Co., Inc.), Pres. 1980–84; fmr Prof. of Econs, CUNY; Prof., Center for Strategic and Int. Studies 1980–81; Dir Cttee for Monetary Research and Educ. 1980–81; Sr Dir of Econ. Affairs, Nat. Security Council 1981–83; Special Asst to Pres. Ronald Reagan 1983–89; Pres. Norman A. Bailey Inc. 1984–; Consultant Economist and Sr Fellow, Potomac Foundation, Inc. 2003–06; Adjunct Prof., Inst. of World Politics, Washington DC 2003–06; Mission Man. for Cuba and Venezuela, Office of the Dir of Nat. Intelligence 2006–; Kt Royal Order of Our Lady of the Conception of Vila Vicosa (Portugal); Nat. Security Award, Cold War Commemorative Medal, Medal of the Pan American Soc. *Publications:* The Strategic Plan that Won the Cold War 1999; numerous articles in professional journals. *Address:* Mission for Cuba and Venezuela, Office of the Director of National Intelligence, Washington, DC, 20511 USA (office). *Telephone:* (202) 201-1111 (office). *Website:* www.dni.gov (office).

BAILEY, Norman Stanley, CBE, BMus; British singer (bass-baritone); b. 23 March 1933, Birmingham; s. of the late Stanley Ernest and Agnes Train Bailey (née Gale); m. 1st Doreen Evelyn Simpson 1957 (divorced 1983); two s. one d.; m. 2nd Kristine Ciesinski 1985; ed East Barnet Grammar School,

England, Boksburg High School, South Africa, Prince Edward School, Rhodesia, Rhodes Univ., South Africa, Akad. für Musik und Darstellende Kunst, Vienna; engaged full time at Linz Landestheater, Austria 1960–63, Wuppertaler Bühnen 1963–64, Deutsche Oper am Rhein, Düsseldorf and Duisburg 1964–67; Prin. Baritone English Nat. Opera, Sadler's Wells 1967–71; freelance 1971–; debut at La Scala, Milan 1967, Royal Opera House, Covent Garden 1969, Bayreuth Festival 1969, Paris Opera 1973, Vienna State Opera 1976, Metropolitan Opera, New York 1976; appearances Paris Opera, Edin. Festival, Hamburg State Opera, Munich State Opera; Prof. of Voice, Royal Coll. of Music, London 1990–; Hon. RAM 1981; Hon. DMus (Rhodes) 1986; Sir Charles Santley Memorial Prize 1977. *Major recordings and TV films include:* Der fliegende Holländer, Die Meistersinger von Nürnberg, King Priam, Der Ring des Nibelungen, Macbeth, La Traviata, Falstaff. *Leisure interests:* golf, chess, microcomputing, Concept2 indoor rowing, 13 Million Metre Club (winner, N. American Rowing Challenge 2004); mem. Baha'i World Faith. *Address:* PO Box 655, Victor, ID 83455, USA. *Telephone:* (208) 787-2580 (office). *Fax:* (208) 787-2588 (office). *E-mail:* nbnsbailey@aol.com (office).

BAILEY, Paul, FRSL; British writer; b. (Peter Harry Bailey), 16 Feb. 1937; s. of Arthur Oswald Bailey and Helen Maud Burgess; ed Sir Walter St John's School, London; actor 1956–64, appearing in The Sport of My Mad Mother 1958 and Epitaph for George Dillon 1958; Literary Fellow at Univs. of Newcastle and Durham 1972–74; Bicentennial Fellowship 1976; Visiting Lecturer in English Literature, North Dakota State Univ. 1977–79; Somerset Maugham Award 1968; E. M. Forster Award 1978; George Orwell Memorial Prize 1978. *Publications:* At the Jerusalem 1967, Trespasses 1970, A Distant Likeness 1973, Peter Smart's Confessions 1977, Old Soldiers 1980, An English Madam 1982, Gabriel's Lament 1986, An Immaculate Mistake (autobiog.) 1990, Hearth and Home 1990, Sugar Cane 1993, The Oxford Book of London (ed.) 1995, First Love (ed.) 1997, Kitty and Virgil 1998, The Stately Homo: A Celebration of the Life of Quentin Crisp (ed.) 2000, Three Queer Lives: Fred Barnes, Naomi Jacob and Arthur Marshall 2001, Uncle Rudolf (novel) 2002, A Dog's Life 2003; numerous newspaper articles. *Leisure interests:* visiting churches, opera, watching tennis. *Address:* Rogers, Coleridge and White Ltd., 20 Powis Mews, London W11 1JN, England (office); 2/79 Davisville Road, London, W12 9SH, England (home). *Telephone:* (20) 7221-3717 (office); (20) 8248-2127 (home). *Fax:* (20) 7229-9084 (office). *E-mail:* info@rcwlitagency.com (office). *Website:* www.rcwlitagency.com (office).

BAILEY, Sly; British publishing and media executive; *CEO, Trinity Mirror PLC;* b. (Sylvia Grice), 24 Jan. 1962, London; d. of Thomas Lewis and Sylvia Grice (née Bantick); m. Peter Bailey 1998; ed St Saviours and St Olaves Grammar School for Girls; telephone sales exec. at The Guardian 1984–87; Advertisement Sales Man., The Independent 1987–89; moved to IPC Magazines 1989, Advertising Sales Exec. 1994, mem. Bd of Dirs 1994–2003, Man. Dir TX 1997, CEO 1999–2003; mem. Bd of Dirs and CEO Trinity Mirror PLC 2003–; Dir (non-exec.) Littlewoods PLC April–Sept. 2002, EMI 2004– (Sr Ind. Dir 2007–); mem. Ind. Panel on BBC Charter Review 2004; Dir The Press Asscn; Pres. NewstrAid Benevolent Soc.; Periodical Publrs Asscn Marcus Morris Award for Outstanding Contrib. to Publishing Industry 2002, named as one of 50 Most Powerful Woman in Britain by Management Today 2002, named as one of Britain's Most Influential Woman by Daily Mail 2003, ranked amongst top 20 of MediaGuardian's 100 Most Influential Figures in Media 2003, ranked by Fortune magazine amongst 50 Most Powerful Women in Business outside the US (23rd) 2003, (23rd) 2004, (33rd) 2005, (45th) 2006, ranked by the Financial Times amongst Top 25 Businesswomen in Europe (12th) 2005, (18th) 2006, (25th) 2007. *Leisure interest:* family. *Address:* Trinity Mirror PLC, 1 Canada Square, Canary Wharf, London, E14 5AP, England (office). *Telephone:* (20) 7293-2203 (office). *Fax:* (20) 7293-3225 (office). *E-mail:* sly.bailey@trinitymirror.com. *Website:* www.trinitymirror.com (office).

BAILIE, Robert Ernest (Roy), OBE; British business executive; *Chairman, The Baird Group;* b. 2 June 1943; s. of Robert Bailie and Rosetta Bailie; ed Harvard Business School; joined W&G Baird (later The Baird Group) 1965, Man. Dir 1972, Dir 1977–, Chair. 1982–; Chair. CBI, Northern Ireland 1992–94, Northern Ireland Tourist Bd 1996–2002, 105.8 FM 2005–; Vice-Pres. British Printing Industries Fed. 1997–99, Pres. 1999–2001; Dir Graphic Plates Ltd 1977–, MSO Ltd 1984–, Biddles Ltd 1989–, Thanet Press Ltd 1995–; Dir (non-exec.) Blackstaff Press Ltd 1995–, UTV 1997–, Court, Bank of England 1998–2003, Court, Bank of Ireland 1999–, Corporate Document Services Ltd 2000–. *Leisure interests:* golf, sailing, walking. *Address:* 60 Ballymena Road, Doagh, Ballyclare, Co. Antrim, BT39 0QR, Northern Ireland (home). *Telephone:* (28) 9446-6107 (office); (28) 9334-0383 (home). *Fax:* (28) 9446-6266 (office). *E-mail:* roy.bailie@thebairdgroup.co.uk (office). *Website:* www.thebairdgroup.co.uk (office).

BAILLIE, A. Charles, Jr, BA, MBA; Canadian fmr banker; b. 20 Dec. 1939, Orillia, Ont.; s. of Charles Baillie and Jean G. Baillie; m. Marilyn J. Michener 1965; three s. one d.; ed Trinity Coll., Univ. of Toronto, Harvard Business School, USA; joined The Toronto Dominion Bank 1964, Vice-Pres. and Gen. Man., USA Div. 1979, Sr Vice-Pres. 1981, Exec. Vice-Pres., Corp. and Investment Banking Group 1984, Vice-Chair. 1992, Pres. The Toronto Dominion Bank 1995, CEO 1997–2002, Chair. 1998–2003 (retd); mem. Bd of Dirs The Toronto Dominion Bank, Dana Corpn, Ballard Power Systems Inc., CN 2003–; Chair. and Dir TD Waterhouse Group, Inc.; Chair. Campaign 2000, United Way of Greater Toronto; Chair. Capital Campaign, Shaw Festival; Campaign Co-Chair. Nature Conservancy; Campaign Hon. Chair. Sir Sam Steele Art Gallery; Vice-Chair. Exec. Cttee Business Council on Nat. Issues; mem. Corpn and Hon. Cabinet, Trinity Coll.; Fellow Inst. of Canadian Bankers 1967; Hon. LLD (Queen's Univ.) 2000.

BAILLY, Jean-Paul, MSc; French engineer and business executive; *Chairman and President, La Poste;* b. 29 Nov. 1946, Hénin-Beaumont (Pas-de-Calais); s. of Jean Bailly and Hélène Bailly (née Viénot); m. Michèle Moulard 1972; two s.; ed Lycées d'Oujda, Morocco, Louis-le-Grand and Ecole polytechnique, Paris, Massachusetts Inst. of Tech., USA; engineer, Regie Autonome des Transports Parisiens (RATP) 1970, Chief Consultant SOFRETU for Mexico City Metro 1978–81, Sr Engineer 1981–88, Personnel Dir 1989, Jt Dir-Gen. 1990–94, Pres. and Dir-Gen. 1994–97; Pres. Int. Union of Public Transport (UITP) 1997–2001; Pres. La Poste 2002–, currently also Chair., Chair. Supervisory Bd Postal Bank 2006–; Pres. French Section, Centre européen des entreprises à participation publique (CEEP) 1998–2001; mem. Econ. and Social Council 1994–; Chevalier, Légion dof honneur; Officier, Ordre nat. du Mérite; Pitney Bowes Industry Leadership Award, World Mail Awards, London 2007. *Leisure interest:* tennis. *Address:* La Poste, 44 boulevard de Vaugirard, 75757 Paris Cedex 15, France (office). *Telephone:* 1-55-44-01-01 (office). *Fax:* 1-55-44-01-25 (office). *E-mail:* jean-paul.bailly@laposte.fr (office). *Website:* www.laposte.fr (office).

BAILY, Martin Neil, PhD; American economist and fmr government official; *Senior Fellow, Institute for International Economics;* b. 13 Jan. 1945, Exeter, England; s. of the late Theodore Baily and Joyce Baily; m. Vickie Lyn Baily (née Hyde) 1986; two s. two d.; ed King Edward's School, Birmingham, Christ's Coll., Cambridge, MIT; teaching positions at MIT and Yale Univ. 1972–79; Sr Fellow Brookings Inst. 1979–94, 1996–99; Prof. of Econs, Univ. of Maryland 1989–94; mem. Council of Econ. Advisers 1994–96 in Clinton administration, Chair. and mem. of the Cabinet 1999–2001; Prin. McKinsey and Co. 1996–99, Sr Advisor 2002–; Sr Fellow, Inst. for Int. Econs Washington, DC 2001–; Prizewinner in Econs, Christ's Coll., Cambridge 1967. *Publications:* Macroeconomics, Financial Markets and the International Sector 1994, Efficiency in Manufacturing (Brookings Papers) 1995, Economic Report of the President: 2000, Transforming the European Economy (co-author) 2004. *Leisure interests:* squash, music, travel. *Address:* Institute for International Economics, 1750 Massachusetts Avenue, NW, Washington, DC 20036-1903, USA (office). *Telephone:* (202) 328-9000 (office). *Fax:* (202) 328-5432 (office). *E-mail:* mbaily@iie.com (office). *Website:* www.iie.com (office).

BAILYN, Bernard, PhD; American historian and academic; *Professor Emeritus of History, Harvard University;* b. 10 Sept. 1922, Hartford, Conn.; s. of Charles Manuel Bailyn and Esther Schloss; m. Lotte Lazarsfeld 1952; two s.; ed Williams Coll. and Harvard Univ.; mem. Faculty, Harvard Univ. 1953–, Prof. of History 1961–66, Winthrop Prof. of History 1966–81, Adams Univ. Prof. 1981–93, Prof. Emer. 1993–, James Duncan Phillips Prof. in Early American History 1991–93, Prof. Emer. 1993–; Dir Charles Warren Center for Studies in American History 1983–94; Pitt Prof. of American Hist., Cambridge Univ. 1986–87; Dir Int. Seminar on History of Atlantic World 1995–; Ed.-in-Chief John Harvard Library 1962–70; Co-Ed. Perspectives in American History (journal) 1967–77, 1984–86; mem. American Historical Asscn (Pres. 1981), American Acad. of Arts and Sciences, Nat. Acad. of Educ., American Philosophical Soc.; Foreign mem. Russian Acad. of Sciences, Academia Europaea, Mexican Acad. of History and Geography; Sr Fellow, Soc. of Fellows; Hon. Fellow Christ's Coll., Cambridge Univ.; Corresp. Fellow, British Acad. 1989, Royal Historial Soc.; Trustee Inst. of Advanced Study, Princeton 1989–94; Trevelyan Lecturer, Cambridge Univ. 1971; Jefferson Lecturer, Nat. Endowment for the Humanities 1998; 15 hon. degrees; Robert H. Lord Award, Emmanuel Coll. 1967, Thomas Jefferson Medal 1993, Henry Allen Moe Prize, American Philosophical Soc. 1994, Foreign Policy Asscn Medal 1998; Catton Prize, Soc. American Historians 2000. *Publications:* The New England Merchants in the 17th Century 1955, Massachusetts Shipping 1697–1714: A Statistical Study (jtly) 1959, Education in the Forming of American Society 1960, Pamphlets of the American Revolution 1750–1776, Vol. I (ed.) (Faculty Prize, Harvard Univ. Press) 1965, The Apologia of Robert Keayne (ed.) 1965, The Ideological Origins of the American Revolution (Pulitzer and Bancroft Prizes 1968) 1967, The Origins of American Politics 1968, The Intellectual Migration 1930–1960 (co-ed.) 1969, Law in American History (co-ed.) 1972, The Ordeal of Thomas Hutchinson (Nat. Book Award 1975) 1974, The Great Republic (co-author) 1977, The Press and the American Revolution (co-ed.) 1980, The Peopling of British North America 1986, Voyagers to the West (Pulitzer Prize 1986) 1986, Faces of Revolution 1990, Strangers Within the Realm (co-ed.) 1991, The Debate on the Constitution (two vols, ed.) 1993, On the Teaching and Writing of History 1994, Atlantic History 2005. *Address:* 170 Clifton Street, Belmont, MA 02478-2604 (home); History Department, Harvard University, Cambridge, MA 02138, USA (office). *Website:* fas-www.harvard.edu/~atlantic/bailyn.html (home).

BAIN, Neville Clifford, MCom, LLD, FCA, CMA, FCIS, FIOD; British company director and consultant; *Chairman, Hogg Robinson PLC;* b. 14 July 1940, Dunedin, NZ; s. of Charles Alexander Bain and Gertrude Mae Bain (née Howe); m. Anne Patricia Bain (née Kemp); one s. one d. one step-d.; ed King's High School, Dunedin, Otago Univ., Dunedin, NZ; trainee insp. Inland Revenue, NZ 1957–59; Cost Accountant then Finance Dir Cadbury Schweppes, NZ 1960–75, Commercial Dir and Group Finance Dir Cadbury Schweppes, SA 1975–80, Group Strategy Dir, apptd to Main Bd Cadbury Schweppes PLC 1980–83, Man. Dir Cadbury UK 1983–86, Worldwide Man. Dir Group Confectionery 1986–89, Deputy CEO and Finance Dir Cadbury Schweppes PLC 1989–90, Chief Exec. Coats Viyella PLC 1990–97; Chair. Hogg Robinson PLC 1997–, SHL 1998– (Dir 1997–), The Post Office 1998–2001; Chair. Gartmore Split Capital Opportunities Trust 1999–2001; Deputy Chair. McDowell Alcobevs Ltd (India) 2003–; Dir and Chair. Audit Cttee Biocon Ltd (India) 2000–; Dir United Breweries Ltd (India) 2003–; Dir (non-exec.) Safeway PLC 1993–2000, Scottish & Newcastle PLC 1997–, Gartmore Scotland Investment Trust PLC 1991–2001; mem. Inst. of Dirs (also Fellow and Chair. Audit Cttee), Council for Excellence in Man. and Leadership, Trustee Nat. Centre for Social Research 2002–. *Publications:* Successful Management 1995, Winning Ways through Corporate Governance (with D. Band) 1996, The People Advantage (with Bill Mabey) 1999. *Leisure interests:* sport, walking, music. *Address:* Hogg Robinson PLC, Global House, Victoria Street, Basingstoke, Hants., RG21 3BT, England (office). *Telephone:* (1256) 312609 (office); (1932) 856451 (home). *Fax:* (1256) 346999 (office); (1932) 830899 (home). *E-mail:* neville.bain@hrplc.co.uk (office); bainneville@yahoo.co.uk (home). *Website:* www.hoggrobinson.com (office).

BAINBRIDGE, Dame Beryl, DBE, FRSL; British writer; b. 21 Nov. 1934, Liverpool; d. of Richard Bainbridge and Winifred Bainbridge (née Baines); m. Austin Davies 1954 (divorced); one s. two d.; ed Merchant Taylors' School, Liverpool, Arts Educational Schools, Tring; columnist Evening Standard 1987–93; Hon. DLitt (Liverpool Univ.) 1988; James Tait Black Fiction Prize 1996, Author of the Year 1999, James Tait Black Memorial Prize, British Book Awards 1999, David Cohen Prize, Arts Council of England 2003, Heywood Hill Literary Prize 2004. *Plays:* Tiptoe Through the Tulips 1976, The Warriors Return 1977, It's a Lovely Day Tomorrow 1977, Journal of Bridget Hitler 1981, Somewhere More Central (TV) 1981, Evensong (TV) 1986. *Publications:* A Weekend with Claude 1967, Another Part of the Wood 1968, Harriet Said... 1972, The Dressmaker 1973 (film 1989), The Bottle Factory Outing (Guardian Fiction Award) 1974, Sweet William 1975 (film 1980), A Quiet Life 1976, Injury Time (Whitbread Award) 1977, Young Adolf 1978, Winter Garden 1980, English Journey (TV series) 1984, Watson's Apology 1984, Mum and Mr. Armitage 1985, Forever England 1986 (TV series 1986), Filthy Lucre 1986, An Awfully Big Adventure (staged 1992, film 1995) 1989, The Birthday Boys 1991, Something Happened Yesterday 1993, Collected Stories 1994, Northern Stories (Vol. 5.) (with David Pownall), Every Man For Himself (Whitbread Novel Prize 1996) 1996, Master Georgie 1998, According to Queeney 2001, Front Row (memoirs) 2005. *Leisure interests:* reading, smoking. *Address:* 42 Albert Street, London, NW1 7NU, England. *Telephone:* (20) 7387-3113 (home).

BAINDURASHVILI, Kakha, MA; Georgian politician; *Minister of Finance;* b. 26 Sept. 1978, Tbilisi; ed Tbilisi State Univ., Williams Coll., Williamstown, USA; ed., Prime-News news agency, Tbilisi 1999–2000; consultant, UNDP 2002–04; adviser to the Prime Minister 2004–05; Head of Investment Monitoring Unit, Ministry of Finance 2000–02, Chair. Tax Dept 2006–07, First Deputy Minister of Finance 2007–09, Minister of Finance 2009–; Gov. for Georgia and Vice-Chair. Bd of Govs Asian Devt Bank. *Address:* Ministry of Finance, 0162 Tbilisi, I. Abashidze 70, Georgia (office). *Telephone:* (32) 22-68-05 (office). *Fax:* (32) 93-19-22 (office). *E-mail:* minister@mof.ge (office). *Website:* www.mof.ge (office).

BAINIMARAMA, Cdre Josaia Voreqe, (Frank Bainimarama), OStJ; Fijian military officer; *Prime Minister, Minister of Home Affairs, Immigration and Information and Minister of Finance;* b. 27 April 1954, Kiuva, Tailevu Province; m. Maria Makitalena; six c.; ed Maris Brothers High School, numerous mil. courses and insts; enlisted in Fiji Navy as Ordinary Seaman 1975, commissioned as Ensign 1977, Navigation Officer Aug. 1978, Sub-Lt Nov. 1978, Exec. Officer HMFS Kiro 1979, Commdr HMFS Kikau 1982–84, HMFS Kula 1984–86, Lt Commdr 1986, served with Multinational Force and Observers in Sinai 1986–87, CO and Commdr Fiji Navy 1988, promoted to Capt. 1994, Chief of Staff 1997–99, Cdre and Commdr of Armed Forces 1999–; Head, Interim Mil. Govt of Fiji May–July 2000; Acting Pres. of Fiji (after mil. overthrow of govt of Prime Minister Laisenia Qarase) Dec. 2006–07, Interim Prime Minister Jan. 2007–, also Minister of Home Affairs, Immigration and Information 2007–, Minister of Finance 2008–; fmr Chair. Fiji Rugby Union; Meritorious Service Decoration, Peacekeeping Medal, General Service Medal, Fiji Republic Medal, 25 Anniversary Medal. *Address:* Office of the Prime Minister, PO Box 2353, New Government Buildings, Suva, Fiji (office). *Telephone:* 3211201 (office). *Fax:* 3306034 (office). *E-mail:* pmsoffice@connect.com.fi (office). *Website:* www.fiji.gov.fj (office).

BAINWOL, Mitch, MBA; American music industry executive; *Chairman and CEO, Recording Industry Association of America;* m. Susan; three c.; ed Georgetown Univ., Rice Univ.; fmr Budget Analyst, US Pres. Ronald Reagan's Office of Management and Budget; Chief of Staff US Senator Connie Mack (R-FL); Leadership Staff Dir US Senate 1993–97; Chief of Staff Republican Nat. Cttee 1998; lobbyist Clark & Weinstock 1999; Leader The Bainwol Group 2002–; Chair. and CEO, Recording Industry Asscn of America (RIAA) 2003–. *Address:* c/o Recording Industry Association of America, 1330 Connecticut Avenue NW, Suite 300, Washington, DC 20036, USA (office). *Website:* www.riaa.com (office).

BAIR, Sheila Colleen, BA, JD; American banking official, academic and author; *Chairman, Federal Deposit Insurance Corporation;* b. 3 April 1954, Wilchita, Kan.; d. of Albert Bair and Clara Bair (née Brenneman); m. Scott P. Cooper; one s. one d.; ed Univ. of Kansas, Univ. of Kansas School of Law; called to the Bar, Kan. 1979; Teaching Fellow, Univ. of Arkansas School of Law 1978–79; Advisor, Kan. State Dept of Health 1979–81; Research Dir, Deputy Counsel and Counsel to Senate Majority Leader Robert Dole 1981–88; Of Counsel, Kutak, Rock & Campbell (law firm) 1986–87; Legis. Counsel, New York Stock Exchange, Washington, DC 1988–91, Sr Vice-Pres. for Govt Relations 1995–2000; Commr US Commodity Futures Trading Comm. 1991–95, Acting Chair. 1993; Asst Sec. for Financial Insts, US Dept of the Treasury 2001–02; Dean's Prof. of Financial Regulatory Policy, Isenberg School of Man., Univ. of Massachusetts-Amherst 2002–06; Chair. Fed. Deposit Insurance Corpn 2006–; mem. Insurance Marketplace Standards Asscn, Women in Housing and Finance, Center for Responsible Lending, NASD Ahead-of-the-Curve Advisory Cttee, Mass Savings Makes Cents, ABA, Exchequer Club, Soc. of Children's Book Writers and Illustrators; The Treasury Medal 2002, Distinguished Achievement Award, Asscn of Educ. Publrs 2005, Personal Service Feature of the Year, Author of the Month Award, Highlights Magazine for Children 2002, 2003, 2004, ranked by Forbes magazine amongst 100 Most Powerful Women (second) 2008. *Publications:* Rock, Brock, and the Savings Shock 2006, Isabel's Car Wash 2008. *Address:* Federal Deposit Insurance Corporation, 550 17th Street, NW, Washington, DC 20429, USA (office). *Telephone:* (202) 736-0000 (office). *E-mail:* publicinfo@fdic.gov (home). *Website:* www.fdic.gov (office).

BAIRD, Dugald Euan, MA, LLD, DSc; British business executive; b. 16 Sept. 1937, Aberdeen, Scotland; s. of Dugald Baird and Matilda Deans Tennant; m. Angelica Hartz 1961; two d.; ed Univ. of Aberdeen and Trinity Coll. Cambridge; joined Schlumberger Ltd as field engineer 1960, various field assignments in Europe, Asia, Middle East, Africa until 1974, Personnel Man., Vice-Pres. (Operations) Schlumberger Technical Services, Paris 1974–79; Exec. Vice-Pres. (worldwide wireline operations) Schlumberger Ltd, New York 1979–86, Chair. Bd, Pres. and CEO 1986–2003; Chair. Rolls–Royce PLC 2003–04 (resgnd); mem. Comité Nat. de la Science, France 1998–, Council of Science and Tech., UK 2000–; mem. Bd ScottishPower 2000–; mem. Bd Société Générale Group 2001–; mem. Bd Areva 2001–; Trustee Haven Man. Trust 1994–, Carnegie Inst. of Wash. 1998–; Hon. LLD (Aberdeen) 1995, (Dundee) 1998; Hon. DSc (Heriot-Watt) 1999. *Address:* c/o Rolls-Royce PLC, 65 Buckingham Gate, London, SW1E 6AT, England.

BAIRD, Hon. John Russell (Rusty), PC, BA; Canadian politician; *Minister of Transport, Infrastructure and Communities;* b. 26 May 1969, Ottawa, Ont.; ed Queen's Univ., Kingston, Ont.; Pres. youth wing of Ont. Progressive Conservative Party late 1980s; worked on political staff of Perrin Beatty, Fed. Minister of Nat. Defence, and through subsequent cabinet shifts early 1990s; worked as a lobbyist in Ottawa 1993–95; MPP (Conservative Party of Canada) for Nepean, Legis. Ass. of Ont. 1995–99, for Nepean—Carleton 1999–2005, Parl. Asst to Minister of Labour 1995–97, Parl. Asst to Chair. Man. Bd of Cabinet April–Nov. 1997, Parl. Asst to Minister of Finance Nov. 1997–99, Minister of Community and Social Services and Minister responsible for Francophone Affairs 1999–2002, Minister responsible for Children 2001–02, Chief Govt Whip and Assoc. Minister for Francophone Affairs April–Aug. 2002, Minister for Energy Aug. 2002–03, Leader of Govt in Ont. Legislature 2003, Official Opposition Critic for Finance, Culture, Francophone Affairs, Intergovernmental Affairs and Health 2003–05; Co-Chair. Ont. Conservative Party for fed. elections 2004; left prov. politics to campaign for Fed. House of Commons 2005; MP for Ottawa West-Nepean 2006–; Pres. Treasury Bd 2006–07, also helds ministerial responsibilities for Harbourfront Centre and Toronto Waterfront Revitalization Corpn; Minister of the Environment 2007–08, of Transport, Infrastructure and Communities 2008–; mem. Royal Canadian Legion (Bell's Corners Br.); Life mem. Asscn for Community Living; Hon. mem. Nepean Kiwanis. *Address:* Transport, Infrastructure and Communities Canada, Tower C, 29th Floor, pl. de Ville, 330 Sparks Street, Ottawa, ON K1A 0N5, Canada (office). *Telephone:* (613) 990-2309 (office). *Fax:* (613) 954-4731 (office). *E-mail:* webfeedback@tc.gc.ca (office); bairdj@parl.gc.ca (office). *Website:* www.tc.gc.ca (office); www.johnbaird.com.

BAIRD, Vera, QC, LLB, BA; British barrister, politician and government official; *Solicitor General;* b. 1951, Oldham; m. (died 1979); two step-s.; ed Chadderton Grammar School, Northumbria Univ., Univ. of Teesside; called to the Bar, Gray's Inn 1975; joined Chambers of Michael Mansfield, Tooks Court 1986; Trainer, Criminal Bar Asscn 1999–2002; Visiting Law Fellow, St Hilda's Coll., Oxford 1999; contested Berwick seat in Gen. Election 1983; MP (Labour) for Redcar 2001–, mem. Parl. Jt Select Cttee on Human Rights 2001–03, Work and Pensions 2003–05, Corruption Bill 2003, Armed Forces Bill 2005–06, mem. various Standing Cttees, including Proceeds of Crime Bill 2001–02, Criminal Justice Bill 2003, Domestic Violence Bill 2003–04, Serious Organised Crime and Police Bill 2005; Parl. Pvt. Sec. to Home Sec. 2005–06; Parl. Under-Sec. of State, Dept of Constitutional Affairs 2006–07; Solicitor Gen. 2007–; Visiting Prof., South Bank Univ.; Hon. Fellow, St Hilda's Coll. Oxford, Univ. of Teesside. *Address:* Solicitor General, Attorney General's Office, 20 Victoria Street, London, SW1H 0NF, England (office). *Telephone:* (20) 7271-2406 (office). *Fax:* (20) 7271-2432 (office). *E-mail:* john.peck@attorneygeneral.gsi.gov.uk (office). *Website:* www.attorneygeneral.gov.uk (home).

BAIS, Ramesh; Indian agriculturalist and politician; b. 2 Aug. 1948, Raipur, Madhya Pradesh; s. of the late Khom Pal Bais; m.; one s. two d.; elected Councillor, Raipur Mun. Corpn 1978, mem. Madhya Pradesh Legis. Ass. 1980–84; mem. Lok Sabha 1989, 1996–; Vice-Pres. Madhya Pradesh Bharatiya Janata Party (BJP) 1989–90, 1994–96, mem. BJP Nat. Exec. 1993–; Minister of State for Steel and Mines 1998–2000, for Information and Broadcasting 2000–04, for Environment and Forests Jan.–May 2004; Chair. Seed and Agricultural Devt Corpn of Madhya Pradesh 1992–93. *Leisure interests:* woodcrafting, painting, interior decoration, gardening. *Address:* C-1/8, Tilak Lane, New Delhi 110 001; Ravi Nagar, Raipur 492 001(Chhattisgarh), India. *Telephone:* (11) 2423000 (home); (11) 24323000 (office). *Fax:* (11) 2423000 (home).

BAJA, Lauro Liboon, Jr; Philippine diplomatist; b. 2 May 1937, Alangilan, Batangas; m. Norma Castro; one s. one d.; ed Univ. of the Philippines, Manila, Univ. of Oxford, UK; began career in Dept of Foreign Affairs as Legal Officer, Office Legal Affairs 1962–67, then Chief Treaties Div., Legal Officer, Office Under-Sec. for Admin; Third Sec. then Second Sec., Philippine Embassy in London, UK 1967–72; First Sec., Career Minister, Philippine Mission to UN, New York 1973–76; returned to Philippines; Exec. Dir, Office UN and Other Int. Orgs (UNIO) 1977–79; Chief Coordinator, Special Asst, Office of the Sec. Foreign Affairs (OSEC) 1980–85; Amb. to Brazil 1986–93; Asst Sec., Asian and Pacific Affairs (ASPAC), Manila 1993–97; Amb. to Italy 1997–98; Sr Under-Sec., Dept of Foreign Affairs 1998; Chair. Sixth Legal Cttee, UN Gen. Ass. 2003–; Perm. Rep. to UN, New York 2003–06; Order Grand Cross of Rio Branco 1993, Official Order of Merit 1997, Order of Sikatuna (Datu), Gawad

Mabini Award (rank of Dakilang Kamanong) 1999. *Address:* Department of Foreign Affairs, DFA Bldg, 2330 Roxas Blvd, Pasay City, 1330 Metro Manila, Philippines. *Telephone:* (2) 8344000. *Fax:* (2) 8321597. *E-mail:* webmaster@dfa.gov.ph. *Website:* www.dfa.gov.ph.

BAJAJ, Rahul, LLB, MBA; Indian motor industry executive; *Chairman, Bajaj Auto Ltd;* b. 10 June 1938, Kolkata; m. Rupa Bajaj 1961; two s. one d.; ed St Stephen's Coll., Delhi, Govt Law Coll., Bombay (now Mumbai), Harvard Univ., USA; Dir Bajaj Auto Ltd 1956–60, Chair. and Man. Dir 1972–2008, Chair. 2008–; Chair. Maharashtra Scooters Ltd 1975–; Pres. Asscn of Indian Automobile Mfrs 1976–78, Mahratta Chamber of Commerce and Industries 1983–85; Vice-Chair., then Chair. Mukand Group 1994–; Chair. Devt Council for Automobiles and Allied Industries 1975–77, Indian Inst. of Tech., Mumbai 2003–; mem. Exec. Cttee Confed. of Eng Industry 1978– (Pres. 1979–80), Governing Council, Automotive Research Asscn of India 1972–, Devt Council for Automobiles and Allied Industries 1987–, World Econ. Forum's Advisory Council 1984–; Man of the Year Award, Nat. Inst. of Quality Assurance 1975, Business Man of the Year Award, Business India Magazine 1985, Padma Bhushan 2001. *Address:* Mumbai-Pune Road, Akurdi, Pune 411 035, India (office). *Telephone:* (20) 772851 (office); (20) 82857 (home). *Fax:* (20) 773398 (office). *E-mail:* rahulbajaj@bajajauto.co.in (office).

BAJAMMAL, Abd al-Qadir, BA; Yemeni politician and economist; *Secretary-General, General People's Congress;* b. 18 Feb. 1946, Seiyun-Hadhramout; m. 1976; two s. two d.; ed Cairo Univ.; First Deputy Minister of Planning and Devt, People's Democratic Repub. of Yemen 1978; Lecturer in Econs, Aden Univ. 1978–80; Minister of Industry, Chair. Bd Oil, Mineral and Electricity Authority 1980–85; Minister of Energy and Minerals 1985; mem. Parl. Repub. of Yemen (following union of fmr People's Democratic Repub. of Yemen and fmr Yemen Arab Repub.) 1990–91; Chair. Bd Public Free Zone Authority 1991–94; Deputy Prime Minister 1994–97, 2000–01; Minister of Planning and Devt 1994–97, 1998, of Foreign Affairs 2000–01; Prime Minister of Yemen 2001–07 (resgnd); est. Ministry of Water and Environment and Environment Protection Authority; mem. Gen. People's Congress, Sec.-Gen. 2005–; Advisor to Pres. of Repub. of Yemen; awarded Medal of Yemeni Unity, Medal of Yemeni Revolution, Medal of Yemeni Independence. *Publications:* New Administration Accountancy 1978, The Patterns of Development in the Arab Countries (co-author) 1981, Policies and Guidelines for Privatization in the Republic of Yemen 1994. *Leisure interests:* sports, table tennis. *Address:* General People's Congress, San'a, Yemen (office).

BAJNAI, Gordon; Hungarian economist, business executive and politician; *Prime Minister;* ed Budapest Univ. of Econ. Sciences; with Creditum (financial consulting co.) 1991–93; consultant, EUROCORP Int. Finance plc 1993–94; Dir Corp Finance and Equity Capital Market Div., CA IB Securities plc 1995–2000; CEO Wallis PLC 2000–05, mem. Bd of Dirs 2000–06, Vice-Pres. 2006; Govt Commr for Devt Policy 2006–07; Minister of Local Govt and Regional Devt 2007–08, of Nat. Devt and Economy 2008–09; Prime Minister of Hungary 2009–; Chair. Bd of Dirs Budapest Airport PLC 2006; mem. Bd of Dirs Danubius Radio 1998–99, Graboplast PLC 2001–04, Rába PLC 2003–05; mem. Investment Cttee Equinox Pvt. Equity Fund 1999; mem. Supervisory Bd ZWACK PLC 2003–06; mem. Econ. Council, Budapest Univ. of Econ. Sciences 2006; Officer's Cross, Order of Merit 2006; voted one of the 30 most promising business Cen.-Eastern European execs by Central European Business Review 1999, Young Manager of the Year 2003. *Address:* Office of the Prime Minister, 1055 Budapest, Kossuth Lajos tér 1–3, Hungary (office). *Telephone:* (1) 441-4000 (office). *Fax:* (1) 268-3050 (office). *E-mail:* webmaster@meh.hu (office). *Website:* www.meh.hu (office).

BAJO, Lamin Kaba; Gambian politician; m. Mariama Bajo; serveral c.; joined gendarmerie 1984, rose to position of commdr in mil. police, subsequently Deputy Commdr Mobile Gendarmerie; served as Presidential Guard at State House before July 22nd coup; Commr Western Div.; mem. Armed Forces Provisional Ruling Council 1995; Minister for Interior and Religious Affairs 1995–97, served in Ministry of Youth and Sports and Local Govt and Lands 1997; Amb. to Saudi Arabia 2002–05, Perm. Rep. to OIC; Sec. of State for Foreign Affairs 2005–06. *Address:* c/o Department of State for Foreign Affairs, 4 Col. Muammar Ghadaffi Avenue, Banjul, The Gambia (office).

BAJUK, Andrej, PhD; Slovenian politician and economist; *President, New Slovenia–Christian People's Party;* b. 18 Oct. 1943, Ljubljana; ed Universidad Nacional de Cuyo, Mendoza, Univs of Chicago and Calif., USA; fmr Prof. Universidad Nacional de Cuyo, Mendoza; fmr mem. of staff, World Bank, Washington, DC; various positions at IDB including Exec. Vice-Pres., mem. Bd Dirs, apptd Rep. for Europe, Paris 1994; Prime Minister of Slovenia May–Nov. 2000; f. New Slovenia–Christian People's Party (NSi) (Nova Slovenija—Krščanska ljudska stranka) Aug. 2000, currently Pres.; Minister of Finance 2004–08; Finance Minister of the Year, Financial Times and The Banker. *Address:* New Slovenia–Christian People's Party, 1000 Ljubljana, Cankarjeva 11, Slovenia (office). *Telephone:* (1) 2416650 (office). *Fax:* (1) 2416670 (office). *E-mail:* andrej.bajuk@nsi.si (office). *Website:* www.nsi.si (office).

BAKA, András B., JSD, PhD; Hungarian judge and professor of law; b. 11 Dec. 1952, Budapest; ed St Stephen's High School, Budapest and Eötvös Loránd Univ., Budapest; Research Fellow, Comparative Law Dept Inst. for Legal and Admin. Sciences of Hungarian Acad. of Sciences 1978–82, Sr Research Fellow, Constitutional and Admin. Dept 1982–90; Prof. of Constitutional Law, Budapest School of Public Admin. 1990–; Dir-Gen. and Pres. Bd Budapest School of Public Admin. 1990–; mem. Parl. and Sec. Human Rights Comm. of Hungarian Parl. 1990–91; Judge, European Court of Human Rights 1991–2008, Section Vice-Pres. 2000–08; Visiting Prof., Brown Univ., Providence, RI 1986, Univ. of Virginia 1987, Univ. of Calif. at Berkeley 1987,

Columbia Univ. New York 1987; Prof., Santa Clara Univ. School of Law, Inst. of Int. and Comparative Law, Santa Clara, Calif. 1991; Scientist Award, Hungarian Acad. of Sciences 1988. *Publications:* several publs on minority rights. *Address:* School of Public Administration, 5 Ménesi Street, 1118 Budapest, Hungary (office). *Telephone:* (1) 186-9054 (office). *Fax:* (1) 186-9429 (office).

BAKATIN, Vadim Viktorovich; Russian politician (retd); b. 6 Nov. 1937, Kiselevsk, Kemerovo Dist; s. of Victor Aleksandrovich Bakatin and Nina Afanasievna Bakatina; m. Ludmila Antonovna Bakatina; two s.; ed Novosibirsk Construction Eng Inst., Acad. of Social Sciences; supervisor, chief engineer, Dir of construction works 1960–71; mem. CPSU 1964–91; chief engineer of housing construction combine, Kemerovo 1971–73; Second Sec., Kemerovo City Cttee 1973–75; Sec., Kemerovo Dist Cttee 1977–83; inspector, CPSU Cen. Cttee 1985; First Sec. Kirov Dist Cttee 1985–87; mem. CPSU Cen. Cttee 1986–90; First Sec. Kemerovo Dist Cttee 1987–88; USSR Minister of Internal Affairs 1988–90; mem. Presidential Council Jan.–Nov. 1990; Head KGB Aug.–Dec. 1991, Interrepublican Security Service 1991–92; Vice-Pres. and Dir Dept of Political and Int. Relations, Reforma Fund 1992–98; mem. Bd of Dirs Vostok Capital, mem. Advisory Cttee, Baring Vostok Capital Partners. *Publication:* The Deliverance from the KGB 1992. *Leisure interests:* painting, reading, tennis. *Address:* Baring Vostok Capital Partners, Gasheka str. 7, bldg 1, Ducat Place II, Suite 750, 123056, Moscow, Russia (office). *Telephone:* (495) 967-13-07 (home). *Fax:* (495) 967-13-08 (office). *E-mail:* info@bvcp.ru (office). *Website:* www.bvcp.ru (office).

BAKAYOKO, Youssouf; Côte d'Ivoirian politician and diplomatist; *Minister of Foreign Affairs;* b. 9 April 1943, Bouaké; began diplomatic career 1973; Counsellor, Perm. Mission of Côte d'Ivoire to EU and Int. Orgs in Geneva 1973–83; Minister of Foreign Affairs 2006–. *Address:* Ministry of Foreign Affairs, blvd Angoulvand, BP V109, Abidjan, Côte d'Ivoire (office). *Telephone:* 20-22-71-50 (office). *Fax:* 20-33-23-08 (office). *E-mail:* infos@mae.ci (office). *Website:* www.mae.ci (office).

BAKER, Alan, PhD, FRS; British mathematician and academic; *Professor Emeritus of Pure Mathematics, University of Cambridge;* b. 19 Aug. 1939, London; s. of Barnet Baker and Bessie Baker; ed Stratford Grammar School, University Coll., London and Trinity Coll., Cambridge; Fellow, Trinity Coll., Cambridge 1964–, Research Fellow 1964–68, Dir of Studies in Math. 1968–74; Prof. of Pure Math., Univ. of Cambridge 1974–2006, Prof. Emer. 2006–; Visiting Prof., Stanford Univ. 1974 and other univs in USA, Univ. of Hong Kong 1988, 1999; Guest Prof., ETH, Zürich 1989; mem. Academia Europaea 1998; Hon. Fellow, Indian Nat. Science Acad. 1980; Hon. mem. Hungarian Acad. of Sciences 2001; Dr hc (Univ. Louis Pasteur, Strasbourg) 1998; Fields Medal 1970, Adams Prize 1972. *Publications:* Transcendental Number Theory 1975, A Concise Introduction to the Theory of Numbers 1984, New Advances in Transcendence Theory (ed.) 1988, Logarithmic Forms and Diophantine Geometry (with G. Wüstholz) 2007; papers in scientific journals. *Leisure interests:* travel, photography, theatre. *Address:* Centre for Mathematical Sciences, Wilberforce Road, Cambridge, CB3 0WB (office); Trinity College, Cambridge, CB2 1TQ, England. *Telephone:* (1223) 337999 (office); (1223) 337974 (office); (1223) 338400 (office). *Fax:* (1223) 337920 (office). *E-mail:* a.baker@dpmms.cam.ac.uk (office). *Website:* www.dpmms.cam.ac.uk/site2002/People/baker_a.html (office).

BAKER, Anita; American singer; b. 26 Jan. 1958, Detroit; m. Walter Bridgeforth Jr 1988 (divorced); two s.; mem. funk band, Chapter 8 1976–80; worked as receptionist, Detroit 1980–82; solo singer and songwriter 1982–; Soul Train Awards for Best Single by a Female Artist 1987, for Best R&B Single, Best R&B Song 1989, American Music Award for Favorite Female Soul/R&B Artist 1988, 1990, NAACP Image Award for Best Female Vocalist 1990. *Recordings include:* albums: with Chapter 8: I Just Wanna Be Your Girl 1980; solo: The Songstress 1983, Rapture (Grammy Award for Best Rhythm and Blues Vocal Performance 1987) 1986, Giving You the Best That I Got (Grammy Awards for Best Rhythm and Blues Song, Best Rhythm and Blues Performance by a Female Artist 1988, Best Album 1989, Soul Train Award for Best R&B Album 1989, American Music Award for Favorite Female Soul/R&B Album 1988) 1988, Compositions (Grammy Award for Best Rhythm and Blues Performance, NAACP Image Award for Best Album of the Year) 1990, Rhythm of Love 1994, My Everything 2004, Christmas Fantasy 2005. *Address:* All Baker's Music, 345 North Maple Drive, Beverly Hills, CA 90210, USA.

BAKER, Howard Henry, Jr, LLB; American diplomatist, attorney and fmr politician; b. 15 Nov. 1925, Huntsville, Tenn.; s. of Howard H. Baker and Dora Ladd; m. 1st Joy Dirksen 1951 (died 1993); one s. one d.; m. 2nd Nancy Kassebaum 1996; ed The McCallie School, Chattanooga, Univ. of the South, Sewanee, Tennessee, Tulane Univ. of New Orleans and Univ. of Tennessee Coll. of Law; USNR 1943–46; Pnr, Baker, Worthington, Barnett & Crossley 1949–66; Senator from Tennessee 1967–85; Minority Leader in the Senate 1977–81, Majority Leader 1981–85; Pnr, Baker, Worthington, Crossley, Stansberry & Woolf 1985–87, 1988–95, Baker, Donelson, Bearman & Caldwell, Washington 1995–; mem. law firm Vinson and Elkins 1985–87; White House Chief of Staff 1987–88; Amb. to Japan 2001–05; del. to UN 1976; mem. Council on Foreign Relations 1973–; Int. Councillor, Center for Strategic and Int. Studies 1991–; mem. Inst. of Foreign Affairs 1992–; mem. Bd The Forum for Int. Policy 1993–, Pres.'s Foreign Intelligence Advisory Bd 1985–87, 1988–90; Int. Advisory Bd Barrick Gold Corp., Bd of Regents Smithsonian Inst.; Chair. Cherokee Aviation, Newstar Inc.; mem. Bd of Dirs United Technologies Corpn, Pennzoil Co.; Republican; co-Chair. US Senate Watergate Cttee 1973–74; several hon. degrees; American Soc. of Photographers Award 1993, Presidential Medal of Freedom 1984. *Publications:* No Margin for Error 1980, Howard Baker's Washington 1982, Big South Fork Country 1993, Scott's Gulf 2000. *Leisure interests:* photography, tennis.

Address: c/o Baker, Donelson, Bearman & Caldwell & Berkowitz, 801 Pennsylvania Avenue, NW, Washington, DC 20004, USA.

BAKER, James Addison, III, LLB; American lawyer and fmr government official; *Senior Partner, Baker Botts LLP;* b. 28 April 1930, Texas; s. of James A. Baker, Jr and Bonner Means; m. Susan Garrett 1973; eight c.; ed Princeton Univ. and Univ. of Texas Law School; served in US Marine Corps 1952–54; with law firm Andrews, Kurth, Campbell and Jones, Houston, Tex. 1957–75; Under-Sec. of Commerce under Pres. Ford 1975; Nat. Chair. Ford's presidential campaign 1976; Campaign Dir for George Bush in primary campaign 1980, later joined Reagan campaign; White House Chief of Staff and on Nat. Security Council 1981–85; Trustee, Woodrow Wilson Int. Center for Scholars, Smithsonian Inst. 1977–; Sec. of the Treasury 1985–88, Sec. of State 1989–92; White House Chief of Staff and Sr Counsellor 1992–93; Gov. Rice Univ. 1993; Sr Pnr, Baker Botts LLP 1993–; also currently Sr Counselor, The Carlyle Group; Personal Envoy of UN Sec.-Gen., UN Mission for the Referendum in Western Sahara (MINURSO) 1997–2004 (resgnd); apptd special envoy on Middle East debt by US Pres. George W. Bush 2003; mem. Bd of Dirs Howard Hughes Medical Inst.; Hon. Chair. James A. Baker III Inst. for Public Policy, Rice Univ.; Co-Chair. Iraq Study Group, US Institute of Peace 2006–07. *Publication:* The Politics of Diplomacy 1995. *Leisure interests:* jogging, tennis, hunting. *Address:* Baker Botts LLP, The Warner, 1299 Pennsylvania Avenue, NW, Washington, DC 20004-2400, USA (office). *Telephone:* (202) 639-7778 (office). *E-mail:* james.baker@bakerbotts.com (office). *Website:* www.bakerbotts.com (office).

BAKER, Dame Janet Abbott, CH, DBE, FRSA; British singer (mezzo-soprano); b. 21 Aug. 1933, Hatfield, Yorks.; d. of Robert Abbott Baker and May Baker (née Pollard); m. James Keith Shelley 1957; ed York Coll. for Girls and Wintringham School, Grimsby; Pres. London Sinfonia 1986–; Chancellor Univ. of York 1991–2004; Trustee Foundation for Sport and the Arts 1991–; Hon. Fellow, St Anne's Coll., Oxford 1975, Downing Coll., Cambridge 1985; Hon. DMus (Birmingham) 1968, (Leicester) 1974, (London) 1974, (Hull) 1975, (Oxford) 1975, (Leeds) 1980, (Lancaster) 1983, (York) 1984, (Cambridge) 1984; Hon. LLD (Aberdeen) 1980; Hon. DLitt (Bradford) 1983; Commdr des Arts et des Lettres; Daily Mail Kathleen Ferrier Memorial Prize 1956, Queen's Prize, Royal Coll. of Music 1959, Shakespeare Prize, Hamburg 1971, Grand Prix, French Nat. Acad. of Lyric Recordings 1975, Leonie Sonning Prize (Denmark) 1979; Gold Medal of Royal Philharmonic Soc. 1990, Inc. Soc. of Musicians' Distinguished Music Award 2008. *Publication:* Full Circle (autobiog.) 1982. *Leisure interest:* walking, reading.

BAKER, Rt Rev. John Austin, MA, MLitt, DD; British ecclesiastic; *Emeritus Fellow, Corpus Christi College, Oxford;* b. 11 Jan. 1928, Birmingham; s. of George Austin Baker and Grace Edna Baker; m. Gillian Mary Leach 1974; ed Marlborough Coll., Oriel Coll., Oxford and Cuddesdon Theological Coll.; ordained 1954; Official Fellow, Chaplain and Lecturer in Divinity Corpus Christi Coll., Oxford 1959–73; Lecturer in Theology Brasenose and Lincoln Colls., Oxford; Dorrance Visiting Prof. Trinity Coll., Hartford, Conn. 1967; Canon of Westminster 1973–82; Visiting Prof., King's Coll., London 1974–76; Sub-Dean of Westminster and Lector Theologiae 1978–82; Rector of St Margaret's, Westminster 1978–82; Chaplain to Speaker of House of Commons 1978–82; Bishop of Salisbury 1982–93; mem. Church of England Doctrine Comm. 1967–81, 1984–87, Chair. 1985–87; mem. Standing Comm., WCC Faith and Order Comm. 1983–87; Fellow Emer., Corpus Christi Coll., Oxford 1977–. *Publications include:* The Foolishness of God 1970, Travels in Oudamovia 1976, The Whole Family of God 1981, The Faith of a Christian 1996, Faith: the Country Between Doubt and Hope 2010; numerous theological articles and trans. *Leisure interests:* music. *Address:* 4 Mede Villas, Kingsgate Road, Winchester, Hants., SO23 9QQ, England. *Telephone:* (1962) 861388. *Fax:* (1962) 843089. *E-mail:* johnjillb@talktalk.net (office).

BAKER, Sir John Hamilton, Kt, QC, PhD, LLD, FBA, FRHistS; British legal historian; *Downing Professor of the Laws of England, University of Cambridge;* b. 10 April 1944, Sheffield; s. of Kenneth Lee Vincent Baker and Marjorie Bagshaw; m. 1st Veronica Margaret Lloyd 1968 (divorced 1997); two d.; m. 2nd Fiona Rosalind Holdsworth (née Cantlay) 2002 (died 2005); ed King Edward VI Grammar School, Chelmsford and Univ. Coll. London; Asst Lecturer in Law, Univ. Coll. London 1965–67, Lecturer 1967–70; Barrister Inner Temple, London 1966; Librarian, Squire Law Library, Cambridge 1971–73; Lecturer in Law, Cambridge Univ. 1973–83, Reader in English Legal History 1983–88, Prof. 1988–98, Downing Prof. of the Laws of England 1998–, Fellow of St Catharine's Coll. 1971– (Pres. 2004–07); Visiting Prof., New York Univ. School of Law 1988–; Corresp. Fellow, American Soc. for Legal History 1992; Visiting Fellow, All Souls Coll. Oxford 1995; Jt Literary Dir Selden Soc. 1981–90, Literary Dir 1991–; Fellow of Univ. Coll. London 1991; Hon. Bencher, Inner Temple, London 1988; Hon. Fellow, Soc. for Advanced Legal Studies 1998; Hon. Foreign mem. American Acad. of Arts and Sciences 2001; Hon. LLD (Chicago) 1991; Yorke Prize (Cambridge) 1975; Ames Prize (Harvard Law School) 1985. *Publications:* An Introduction to English Legal History 1971, The Reports of Sir John Spelman 1977, Manual of Law French 1979, The Order of Serjeants at Law 1984, English Legal MSS in the USA (Part I) 1985, The Legal Profession and the Common Law 1986, Sources of English Legal History (with S. F. C. Milsom) 1986, The Notebook of Sir John Port 1987, Readings and Moots at the Inns of Court 1990, English Legal MSS in the USA (Part II) 1990, Cases from the Lost Notebooks of Sir James Dyer 1994, Catalogue of English Legal MSS in Cambridge University Library 1996, Spelman's Reading on Quo Warranto 1997, Monuments of Endless Labours 1998, Caryll's Reports 1999, The Common Law Tradition 2000, The Law's Two Bodies 2001, Readers and Readings 2001, Oxford History of the Laws of England (Vol. VI) 2003, Reports from the Time of Henry VIII, 2003–04, An

Inner Temple Miscellany 2004. *Address:* St Catharine's College, Cambridge, CB2 1RL, England. *Telephone:* (1223) 338317.

BAKER, Sir John William, Kt; British business executive; b. 5 Dec. 1937; s. of Reginald Baker and Wilhelmina Baker; m. 1st Pauline Moore 1962; one s.; m. 2nd Gillian Bullen; ed Harrow Weald Co. Grammar School and Oriel Coll., Oxford; served army 1959–61, Ministry of Transport 1961–70, Dept of Environment 1970–74; Deputy CEO Housing Corpn 1974–78; Sec. Cen. Electricity Generating Bd 1979–80, Bd mem. 1980–89, Jt Man. Dir 1986–89; CEO Nat. Power PLC 1990–95, Chair. 1995–97; Dir (non-exec.) Royal Insurance (now Royal and Sun Alliance Insurance Group) 1995–, currently Deputy Chair.; Dir (non-exec.) The Maersk Co. 1996–, Medeva PLC 1996–2000, EIC 1999–; Deputy Chair. Celltech Group 2000–03; Int. Business Council mem. AP Möller; Chair. Groundwork Foundation 1995–99, World Energy Council Exec. Ass. 1995–98, ENO 1996–2001; mem. Associated Bd, Royal Schools of Music 2000–; mem. Sr Salaries Review Bd 2000–, Chair. 2002–. *Leisure interests:* tennis, bridge, music, theatre. *Address:* Royal & Sun Alliance Insurance Group plc, 30 Berkeley Square, London, W1J 6EW, England (office). *Telephone:* (20) 7636-3450 (office). *Fax:* (20) 7636-3451 (office). *Website:* www.royalsunalliance.com (office).

BAKER, Baron (Life Peer), cr. 1997, of Dorking in the County of Surrey; **Kenneth Wilfred Baker,** PC, CH; British politician and writer; b. 3 Nov. 1934, Newport, Wales; s. of the late W. M. Baker; m. Mary Elizabeth Gray-Muir 1963; one s. two d.; ed St Paul's School and Magdalen Coll., Oxford; nat. service 1953–55; served Twickenham Borough Council 1960–62; as Conservative cand. contested Poplar 1964, Acton 1966; Conservative MP for Acton 1968–70, St Marylebone 1970–83, Mole Valley 1983–97; Parl. Sec. Civil Service Dept 1972–74, Parl. Pvt. Sec. to Leader of Opposition 1974–75; Minister of State and Minister for Information Tech., Dept of Trade and Industry 1981–84; Sec. of State for the Environment 1985–86, for Educ. and Science 1986–89; Chancellor of the Duchy of Lancaster and Chair. Conservative Party 1989–90; Sec. of State for the Home Dept 1990–92; mem. Public Accounts Cttee 1969–70; mem. Exec. 1922 Cttee 1978–81; Chair. Hansard Soc. 1978–81, MTT PLC 1996–97, Business Serve PLC, Northern Edge Ltd, Museum of British History, Belmont Press (London) Ltd, Monstermob, Teather & Greenwood 2003–; Pres. Royal London Soc. for the Blind; Sec. Gen. UN Conf. of Parliamentarians on World Population and Devt 1978; Chair. (non-exec.) Teather & Greenwood PLC, Monstermob, Business Serve; Dir (non-exec.) Hanson 1992–, Stanley Leisure PLC; Chair. Information Cttee, House of Lords 2002–; Companion of Honour 1997. *Publications:* I Have No Gun But I Can Spit 1980, London Lines (ed.) 1982, The Faber Book of English History in Verse (ed.) 1988, The Faber Book of English Parodies (ed.) 1990, Unauthorized Versions (ed.) 1990, The Faber Book of Conservatism (ed.) 1993, The Turbulent Years: My Life in Politics 1993, The Prime Ministers: An Irreverent Political History in Cartoons 1995, The Kings and Queens: An Irreverent Cartoon History of the British Monarchy 1995, The Faber Book of War Poetry (ed.) 1996, Children's English History in Verse (ed.) 2000, The Faber Book of Landscape Poetry (ed.) 2000, George III: A Life in Caricature 2007. *Leisure interests:* collecting books, political cartoons. *Address:* House of Lords, Westminster, London, SW1A 0PW, England (office). *Telephone:* (20) 7219-3000 (office).

BAKER, (Winifred) Mitchell, AB, JD; American software development executive; *Chairperson, Mozilla Foundation;* b. 7 June 1957, Berkeley, Calif.; d. of Theodore and Anne Baker; m.; one s.; ed Univ. of California, Berkeley, Boalt Hall School of Law; Corp. and Intellectual Property Assoc., Fenwick & West LLP 1990–93; Assoc. Gen. Counsel Sun Microsystems 1993–94; Assoc. Gen. Counsel, Netscape Communications Corpn 1994–99; joined Mozilla.org 1998, Gen. Man. (officially known as Chief Lizard Wrangler) Mozilla project 1999–, involved in open-source software devt, creators of Mozilla Firefox and Mozilla Thunderbird, Pres. Mozilla Foundation 2003–05, Chair. 2008–, CEO Mozilla Corpn 2005–08; mem. Bd of Dirs Open Source Applications Foundation 2002–; Time 100, Anita Borg Women of Vision. *Address:* Mozilla Foundation, 1981 Landings Drive, Building K, Mountain View, CA 94043-0801, USA (office). *Telephone:* (650) 903-0800 (office). *Fax:* (650) 903-0875 (office). *E-mail:* mitchell@mozilla.org (office). *Website:* www.mozilla.com (office); blog.lizardwrangler.com (office).

BAKER, Paul Thornell, PhD; American professor of anthropology; *Evan Pugh Professor Emeritus of Biological Anthropology, Pennsylvania State University;* b. 28 Feb. 1927, Burlington, Ia; s. of Palmer Ward Baker and Viola (née Thornell) Laughlin; m. Thelma M. Shoher 1949; one s. three d.; ed Univ. of New Mexico and Harvard Univ.; Research Scientist, US Army Climatic Research Lab. 1952–57; Asst Prof. of Anthropology, Penn. State Univ. 1957–61, Assoc. Prof. 1961–64, Prof. 1965–81, Head Dept of Anthropology 1980–85, Evan Pugh Prof. of Anthropology 1981–87, Evan Pugh Prof. Emer. 1987–; Vice-Pres. Int. Union of Anthropological and Ethnological Sciences 1988–93, Sr Vice-Pres. 1993–98; Pres. Int. Asscn of Human Biologists 1980–89, American Asscn of Physical Anthropologists 1969–71, Human Biology Council 1974–77; Chair. US Man and Biosphere Program 1983–85; mem. NAS; Huxley Medal (Royal Anthropological Soc., London) 1982, Gorjanovic-Krambergeri Medal (Croatian Anthropological Soc.) 1985, Order of the Golden Star with Necklace (Yugoslavia) 1988. *Publications:* The Biology of Human Adaptability (co-ed.) 1966, Man in the Andes: A Multidisciplinary Study of High Altitude Quechua 1976, The Biology of High Altitude Peoples (ed.) 1978, The Changing Samoans: Behavior and Health in Transition 1986, Human Biology (co-author) 1988. *Leisure interest:* sailing. *Address:* 337 Upton Pyne Drive, Brentwood, CA 94513-6458, USA. *E-mail:* nunoa1@aol.com.

BAKER, Raymond, CBE, PhD, FRS; British research scientist and academic; b. 1 Nov. 1936; s. of Alfred Baker and May Golds; m. Marian Slater 1960; one s. two d.; ed Ilkeston Grammar School and Univ. of Leicester; Postdoctoral

Fellow, UCLA, USA 1962–64; Lecturer in Organic Chem., Univ. of Southampton 1964–72, Sr Lecturer 1972–74, Reader 1974–77, Prof. 1977–84; Dir Wolfson Unit of Chemical Entomology 1976–84; Dir of Medicinal Chem. Merck Sharp Dohme Research Labs 1984–89, Exec. Dir 1989–96; Chief Exec. Biotechnology and Biological Sciences Research Council 1996–2001; Visiting Prof., Univ. of Edinburgh 1988–96, Univ. of Leicester 1990–93; Hon. DSc (Nottingham Trent) 1990, (Aston) 1997, (Leicester) 1998, (St Andrews) 1998, (Southampton) 1999. *Publications:* Mechanism in Organic Chemistry 1971; over 300 articles in professional journals. *Leisure interests:* golf, gardening, travel. *Address:* Angeston Court, Uley, Dursley, Glos., GL11 5AL, England (home).

BAKER, Richard; British retail executive; b. 1963; ed Univ. of Cambridge; began career at MG Rover Group; various positions with Mars Inc. in UK, including roles in Nat. Account Man., Marketing and Head of Sales for UK Multiples 1986–1995; COO and Marketing Officer Asda Group Ltd 1995–2003; CEO Boots Group PLC 2003–06, CEO Alliance Boots PLC (after merger with Alliance Unichem) 2006–07. *Address:* c/o Alliance Boots PLC, 4th Floor, 361 Oxford Street, Sedley Place, London, W1C 2JL, England (office).

BAKER, Richard Douglas James, OBE, MA; British broadcaster and author; b. 15 June 1925; s. of Albert Baker and Jane I. Baker; m. Margaret C. Martin 1961; two s.; ed Kilburn Grammar School and Peterhouse, Cambridge; Royal Navy 1943–46; actor 1948; teacher 1949; BBC Third Programme announcer 1950–53; BBC TV newsreader 1954–82; commentator for State Occasion Outside Broadcasts 1967–70; TV introductions to Promenade concerts 1960–95; panellist, Face the Music (BBC 2) 1966–79; presenter, Omnibus (BBC TV) 1983; presenter of various shows on BBC Radio including Start the Week 1970–87, These You Have Loved 1972–77, Baker's Dozen 1978–87, Mainly for Pleasure 1986–92, Comparing Notes 1987–95; presenter, Classic Countdown for Classic FM radio 1995–97, Sound Stories Radio 3 1998–2000, Melodies for You 1999–2003, Your Hundred Best Tunes 2003–; mem. Broadcasting Standards Council 1988–93; Hon. Fellow, London Coll. of Music; Hon. FRCM; Hon. mem. Royal Liverpool Philharmonic Soc.; Hon. LLD (Strathclyde) 1979, (Aberdeen) 1983; TV Newscaster of the Year (Radio Industries Club), 1972, 1974, 1979, BBC Radio Personality of the Year (Variety Club of GB) 1984, Sony Gold Award for Radio 1996. *Publications:* Here is the News (broadcasts) 1966, The Terror of Tobermory 1972, The Magic of Music 1975, Dry Ginger 1977, Richard Baker's Music Guide 1979, Mozart 1982, London, A Theme with Variations 1989, Richard Baker's Companion to Music 1993, Franz Schubert 1997, The Classical Music Quiz Book (compilation) 2006. *Leisure interests:* gardening, music. *Address:* c/o Stephannie Williams Artists, 9 Central Chambers, Wood Street, Stratford upon Avon, CV37 6JQ, England. *Telephone:* (1789) 266272.

BAKER, Russell Wayne, DLitt; American journalist and author; b. 14 Aug. 1925, London Co., Va; s. of Benjamin R. Baker and Lucy E. Robinson; m. Miriam E. Nash 1950; two s. one d.; ed Johns Hopkins Univ.; served USNR 1943–45; with Baltimore Sun 1947–64; mem. Washington Bureau, New York Times 1954–62, author-columnist, editorial page 1962–98; mem. American Acad., Inst. of Arts and Letters; several hon. degrees; Pulitzer Prize for distinguished commentary 1979; Pulitzer Prize for Biography 1983 and other awards. *Publications:* American in Washington 1961, No Cause for Panic 1964, All Things Considered 1965, Our Next President 1968, Poor Russell's Almanac 1972, The Upside Down Man 1977, Home Again, Home Again 1979, So This is Depravity 1980, Growing Up 1982, The Rescue of Miss Yaskell and Other Pipe Dreams 1983, The Good Times (memories) 1989, There's a Country in My Cellar 1990, Russell Baker's Book of American Humor 1993.

BAKEWELL, Dame Joan Dawson, DBE, BA; British broadcaster and writer; b. 16 April 1933, Stockport; d. of John Rowlands and Rose Bland; m. 1st Michael Bakewell 1955 (divorced 1972); one s. one d.; m. 2nd Jack Emery 1975 (divorced 2001); ed Stockport High School for Girls and Newnham Coll., Cambridge; TV critic The Times 1978–81, columnist Sunday Times 1988–90; Assoc. Newnham Coll., Cambridge 1980–91, Assoc. Fellow 1984–87; Gov. BFI 1994–99, Chair. 1999–2003; Dimbleby Award, BAFTA 1995. *TV includes:* Sunday Break 1962, Home at 4.30 (writer and producer) 1964, Meeting Point, The Second Sex 1964, Late Night Line Up 1965–72, The Youthful Eye 1968, Moviemakers at the National Film Theatre 1971, Film 72, Film 73, Holiday 74, 75, 76, 77, 78 (series), Reports Action (series) 1976–78, Arts UK: OK? 1980, Heart of the Matter 1988–2000, My Generation 2000, One Foot in the Past 2000, Taboo (series) 2001. *Radio includes:* Artist of the Week 1998–99, The Brains Trust 1999–, Belief 2000–. *Publications:* The New Priesthood: British Television Today (jtly) 1970, A Fine and Private Place (jtly) 1977, The Complete Traveller 1977, The Heart of the Heart of the Matter 1996, The Centre of the Bed: An Autobiography 2003, The View from Here: Life at Seventy 2007, All the Nice Girls 2009; contribs to journals. *Leisure interests:* theatre, travel, cinema. *Address:* Knight Ayton Management, 10 Argyll Street, London, W1V 1AB, England (office).

BAKHIT, Adnan; Jordanian government official; Head, Nat. Security and Chief of Staff, King's Private Office 2005–. *Address:* c/o The Royal Heshemite Court, Amman, Jordan. *Telephone:* (6) 4637341.

BAKHIT, Maj.-Gen. Marouf al-, PhD; Jordanian government official and military officer (retd); b. 1947; ed Univ. of Jordan, Univ. of Southern Calif., USA, Univ. of London, UK, Royal Jordanian Mil. Coll.; with Jordan Armed Forces 1964–1999, positions including Dir of Studies, Devt, and Procurement and Personnel Affairs; fmr Prof. of Political Science, Vice-Pres. for Mil. Affairs, Muta Univ.; fmr Amb. to Turkey, Israel; fmr Nat. Security Chief; Prime Minister of Jordan and Minister of Defence 2005–07; 14 Jordanian medals. *Address:* c/o Office of the Prime Minister, POB 80, Amman 11180, Jordan (office).

BAKHMIN, Vyacheslav Ivanovich; Russian engineer; b. 25 Sept. 1947, Kalinin (now Tver); m.; one s.; ed Moscow Inst. of Econ. Statistics; researcher Inst. of Molecular Biology 1971–, Inst. of Electronic Man. Machines 1971–73; engineer Computation Cen. Inst. of Information and Electronics 1973–79; Sr engineer Inst. of Public Hygiene and Org. of Public Health 1979–80; mem. human rights movt, arrested and imprisoned 1980–84; engineer, head of group Research Centre at Inst. of Applied Math. 1990; Head Div. of Global Problems and Humanitarian Co-operation Russian Ministry of Foreign Affairs 1991–92; Dir Dept of Int. Humanitarian and Cultural Co-operation 1992–95; Dir Inst. Open Soc. (Soros Foundation) 1995–98; Exec. Dir of Program Block, Social Contract 1998–. *Address:* Ozerkovskaya nab. 18, Moscow, Russia (office). *Telephone:* (495) 787-88-11 (office).

BAKIYEV, Kurmanbek Saliyevich; Kyrgyzstani politician, engineer and head of state; *President;* b. 1 Aug. 1949, Masadan (now Teyyit), Suzdak Dist, Jalal-Abad; s. of Sali Bakiyev; m. Tatyana Vasilyevna Bakiyeva; two s.; ed Kuibyshev (now Samara) Polytechnic Inst., Russia; trained as electrical engineer 1972; served in Soviet Armed Forces 1974–86; electrical engineer, Maslennikov Plant, Kuibyshev 1976–79; Sr Engineer, Head of VTs, then Deputy Chief Engineer, Jalal-Abad Electrical Factory 1979–85; Dir Profil Plant, Kok-Yangak 1985–90; First Sec. CP Kok-Yangak City Council 1990; Deputy Chair. W Jalal-Abad Council of People's Deputies 1991–92; Head of Toguz-Torou Regional Admin 1992–94; Deputy Chair. State Property Fund 1994–95; First Deputy Head, then Head W Jalal-Abad State Admin and Gov. of Jalal-Abad Duban 1995–97; Gov. of Chui Duban 1997–2000; Prime Minister of Kyrgyzstan 2000–02, Acting Prime Minister March–June 2005; mem. Zhogorku Kenesh (Parl.) 2003–05; Acting Pres. of Kyrgyzstan March–Aug. 2005, Pres. Aug. 2005–; Leader, People's Power Movt. *Address:* Office of the President, 720003 Bishkek, Dom Pravitelstva, Kyrgyzstan (office). *Telephone:* (312) 21-24-66 (home). *Fax:* (312) 21-86-27 (office). *E-mail:* office@mail.gov.kg (office). *Website:* www.president.kg (office).

BAKKE, Dennis W., MBA; American business executive; *CEO Emeritus, AES Corporation;* m. Eileen Bakke; ed Univ. of Puget Sound, Harvard Univ.; began career with Fed. Energy Administration; later with Energy Productivity Center, Carnegie Mellon Univ.; Co-founder, AES Corpn Arlington, VA, Pres. and CEO 1994–2002, CEO Emer. 2002–; Pres. The Mustard Seed Asscn. *Publication:* Creating Abundance – America's Least Cost Energy Strategy (Jt author). *Address:* AES Corporation, 1001 North 19th Street, Arlington, VA 22209-1722, USA (office). *Telephone:* (703) 522-1315 (office). *Fax:* (703) 528-4510 (office). *Website:* www.aesc.com (office).

BAKKER, M. Peter; Dutch business executive; *Chairman of the Management Board and CEO, TPG NV;* b. 1961; began career with TS Seeds Holding BV 1984–91; joined PTT Post (later TPG Post) 1991, Finance Dir Parcels Business Unit 1993–95, Dir of Marketing and Sales, PTT Post Logistics 1995–96, Financial Control Dir, TPG Post 1996, mem. Bd of Man. 1997–98, Chief Financial Officer and mem. Bd of Man., TPG NV (following demerger of PTT Post from Royal PTT Nederland NV) 1998–2001, Chair. Man. . Bd and CEO 2001–. *Address:* Neptunusstraat 41–63, 2132 JA Hoofddorp, Netherlands (office). *Telephone:* (20) 500-6000 (office). *Fax:* (20) 500-7000 (office). *Website:* www.tpg.nl (office).

BAKLANOV, Grigoriy Yakovlevich; Russian writer; b. 11 Sept. 1923, Voronezh; s. of Jakov Friedman and Ida Kantor; m. Elga Sergeeva 1953; one s. one d.; ed Gorky Inst. of Literature, Moscow; served as soldier and officer during World War II 1941–45; mem. CPSU 1942–91; Ed.-in-Chief Znamya 1986–93; USSR State Prize 1982, Russian State Prize 1997. *Publications include:* In Snegiri 1954, Nine Days 1958, The Foothold 1959, The Dead Are Not Ashamed 1961, July 41 1964, Karpukhin 1965, Friends 1975, Forever Nineteen 1980, The Youngest of the Brothers 1981, Our Man 1990, Time to Gather Stones 1989, Once it was the Month of May (scenario) 1990, The Moment Between the Past and the Future 1990, Come Through the Narrow Gates 1993, Short Stories 1994, Kondratiy 1995, Short Stories 1996, And Then the Marauders Come (novel) 1996, Life Granted Twice (memoirs) 1999, My General (novel) 2000. *Leisure interest:* gardening. *Address:* Lomonosovsky Prospekt 19, Apt 82, 117311 Moscow, Russia. *Telephone:* (495) 930-12-90. *Fax:* (495) 549-57-67.

BAKLANOV, Oleg Dmitrievich, BEng; Russian politician; *Chairman, Society for Friendship and Co-operation of Russia and Ukraine;* b. 17 March 1932, Kharkov, USSR (now Ukraine); ed All-Union Inst. of Energetics; engineer, Sr engineer, then Dir Kharkov technical appliances plant 1950–55; mem. CPSU 1953–91; gen. Dir of production unit 1975–76; Deputy Minister of Gen. Machine Construction (with special responsibility for the defence industry) in USSR 1981–83, First Deputy Minister 1981–83, Minister 1983–88; mem. CPSU Cen. Cttee 1986–91; Sec. Political Bureau 1988–91; Deputy to Supreme Soviet 1987–89; USSR People's Deputy 1989–91; arrested 22 Aug. 1991 for involvement in failed coup d'état, on trial 1993–94, released on amnesty 1994; active in Communist Movt; mem. Political Council, Russian Public Union 1996–; Chair. Soc. for Friendship and Co-operation of Russia and Ukraine 2000–; Hero of Socialist Labour 1976, Lenin Prize 1982. *Address:* ROS, Szedny Tishinski Pereulok 10, Apt. 9, 123557 Moscow, Russia (office). *Telephone:* (495) 253-18-98.

BAKOYANNIS, Dora; Greek politician; *Minister of Foreign Affairs;* b. 6 May 1954, Athens; d. of Constantine Mitsotakis (fmr Prime Minister) and Marika Yannoukou; m. 1st Pavlos Bakoyannis 1974 (assassinated 1989); one s. one d.; m. 2nd Isidoros Kouvelos 1998; ed German School of Athens and Paris, France, Univ. of Munich, Germany, Univ. of Athens; family fled to Paris to escape mil. dictatorship that ruled Greece 1967–74; worked at Ministry of Econ. Co-ordination and later Ministry of Foreign Affairs 1974–84; Chief of Staff, New Democratic Party 1984–1990; elected Deputy for Evrytania 1990, re-elected three times and later moved candidacy to central Athens; served as Under-Sec. of State 1990, later as Minister of Culture 1992–96; apptd shadow Foreign and Defence Minister 2000; Mayor of Athens (first woman) 2002–06; Minister of Foreign Affairs (first woman) 2006–; Int. Leadership Award, Women's Int. Center 1992, Fontana di Roma Award, 14th Int. Symposium 1993, World Mayor Award 2005, ranked by Forbes Magazine amongst 100 Most Powerful Women (66th) 2006, (67th) 2007, (78th) 2008. *Address:* Ministry of Foreign Affairs, Odos Akadimias 3, 106 71 Athens, Greece (office). *Telephone:* (210) 3681800 (office). *Fax:* (210) 3681433 (office). *E-mail:* dorabakoyiannis@mfa.gr (office). *Website:* www.mfa.gr (office); www.dorabakoyannis.gr (home).

BAKRADZE, Davit, MPA, CandPhys-MathSci; Georgian physicist and politician; *Chairman, Sakartvelos Parlamenti (Georgian Parliament);* b. 1 July 1972, Tbilisi; m.; two c.; ed Georgian Tech. Univ., Georgian-American Inst. of Public Admin, Tbilisi State Univ., Diplomats' Training Course, Swiss Int. Relations Univ. Seminars (SIRUS), Geneva, Defence and Security Studies Course 'Leaders for the 21st Century', G. Marshall European Centre for Security Studies, Garmisch-Partenkirchen, Germany, Sr Course for Officers and Diplomats, NATO Defence Coll., Rome, Italy; First Class State Counsellor; holds diplomatic rank of Chief Minister Counsellor; Deputy Head of Disarmament and Arms Control Div., Politico-Mil. Dept, Ministry of Foreign Affairs 1996–98, Head of Disarmament and Arms Control Div. 1998–2000, Deputy Dir Politico-Mil. Dept 2000–02, Head, Service for Security Issues, Nat. Security Council of Georgia 2002–03, Dir Dept for Int. Security and Conflict Man. 2003–04, Dir Dept for Political Security 2004; mem. Parl. 2004–, Chair. Cttee on European Integration 2004–07, Standing Del. to European Parl., Co-Chair. EU-Georgia Parl. Co-operation Cttee, mem. numerous dels; State Minister on Conflict Resolution Issues 2007–08; Minister of Foreign Affairs Feb.–May 2008; Chair. Sakartvelos Parlamenti (Georgian Parl.) June 2008–; mem. United Nat. Movt (UNP) Party; Special Prize of Pres. of Georgia: Prize for Academic Excellence to the Best Student of Inst. of Public Admin 1996, NATO/EAPC Research Fellowship 1998, Special Gratification from Minister of Foreign Affairs No. 53/2: For Active Participation in Drawing up Adapted Agreements on the Conventional Forces in Europe at OSCE İstanbul Summit 2000, Special Gratification for Significant Professional Achievements in Drawing up Significant Agreements between the States, Pres. of Georgia 2000, Swiss Leadership Award in Int. Relations, Special Award of Grad. Inst. of Int. Studies, Geneva 2005. *Address:* Sakartvelos Parlamenti, 0118 Tbilisi, Rustaveli 8, Georgia (office). *Telephone:* (32) 93-61-70 (office). *Fax:* (32) 99-93-86 (office). *E-mail:* hdstaff@parliament.ge (office). *Website:* www.parliament.ge (office).

BAKRIE, Aburizal, BEng; Indonesian politician and business executive; *Co-ordinating Minister for the People's Welfare;* b. 15 Nov. 1946, Lampung; ed Bandung Inst. of Tech.; Chair. Grup Bakrie & Bros; Pres. ASEAN Business Forum 1991–95; Chair. Indonesian Chamber of Commerce and Industry (Kadin) 1994–2004, now adviser; major shareholder in Bank Nusa, May Bank Nusa International, PT Daya Sarana Pratama and other cos; f. Indonesian Young Entrepreneurs Org. 1972; adviser, Indonesia-Australia Business Council, Jakarta; Co-ordinating Minister for the Economy, Finance and Industry 2005, currently Co-ordinating Minister for the People's Welfare. *Address:* Office of the Co-ordinating Minister for People's Welfare, Jalan Merdeka Barat 3, Jakarta Pusat, Indonesia (office). *Telephone:* (21) 34832544 (office). *Fax:* (21) 3453289 (office). *Website:* www.menkokesra.go.id (office).

BALA-GAYE, Mousa G., BA; Gambian politician; *Secretary of State for Finance and Economic Affairs;* b. 13 Aug. 1946; ed Legon Univ., Univ. of Manchester, UK, IMF Inst.; Asst Sec., Ministry of Works and Communications 1971–73; Sec., Public Service Comm. 1973; Asst Sec., Ministry of Local Govt and Lands 1973; Sr Asst, Ministry of Finance and Trade 1976–79, Under-Sec. 1979–80, Deputy Perm. Sec. 1980–82, Perm. Sec. 1982–86; Exec. Dir African Devt Bank, Abidjan, Côte D'Ivoire 1986–89; Perm. Sec., Office of the Pres. 1989–90; Man. Dir Heron Ltd 1990; Chair. and Man. Dir Afri-Swiss Travel Ltd 1993; Vice-Chair. First Int. Bank Ltd 1999, Acting Chair. 2002; Alt. Dir Senegambia Beach Hotel 2000; Vice-Chair. Int. Trust Insurance Co. Ltd 2000; Sec. of State for Finance and Econ. Affairs 2003–05, for Foreign Affairs March–Oct. 2005, for Trade, Industry and Employment Oct.–Nov. 2005, for Finance and Econ. Affairs Nov. 2005–; fmr mem. Bd Dirs Cen. Bank of The Gambia, Gambia Produce Marketing Bd, Social Security and Housing Finance Corpn, Gambia Nat. Insurance Corpn; del. to numerous int. and multilateral confs and meetings of IMF, World Bank, OPEC Fund, the Commonwealth; Alt. Gov. African Devt Bank, Islamic Devt Bank, World Bank. *Address:* Ministry of Finance and Economic Affairs, The Quadrangle, PO Box 9686, Banjul, The Gambia (office). *Telephone:* 4228291 (office); 4393275 (home). *Fax:* 4227954 (office).

BALABANOV, Alexei O.; Russian film director, producer and scriptwriter; b. 25 Feb. 1959, Sverdlovsk; ed Gorky State Pedagogical Inst.; asst dir Sverdlovsk Film Studio 1983–87; freelance 1987–; co-founder film co. STV; Youth Film Festival Prize, Kiev 1991, Moscow Film Festival Debut Jury Prize 1992, Kinotaur Film Festival, Sochi, Jury Prize 1994 and Best Movie Prize 1997. *Films:* dir: Yegor and Nastya 1989, From the History of Aerostatics in Russia 1990; dir and scriptwriter: Happy Days 1991, The Castle 1994, The Arrival of a Train 1995, Brother 1997, Of Freaks and Men 1998, Brother 2 2000, War (Voyna) (main prize Golden Rose 2002, film festival Kinotavr, Sochi) 2002, River (Reka) 2002, The American (Amerikanets) 2004, Blindman's-Buff (Zhmurki) 2005 (with S. Mokhnachev), It Doesn't Hurt Me (Mne ne bolno) (with S. Mokhnachev) 2006, Burden 200 (Gruz 200) 2007 (prize of the Russian Guild of Film Critics 2007, film festival Kinotavr, Sochi); other: Secrets Shared with a Stranger (producer) 1994, Sergey Eisenstein (producer) 1995. *Address:* STV, Kamennoostrovskii prospect 10, St Petersburg 197101, Russia (office). *E-mail:* kino@ctb.ru (office). *Website:* www.ctb.ru (office).

BĂLĂIŢĂ, George; Romanian writer; b. 17 April 1935, Bacău; s. of Gheorghe Bălăiţă and Constantina Popa Bălăiţă; m. Lucia Gavril 1959; one s.; ed Coll. of Philology; Ed. of cultural review Ateneu (Bacău) 1964–78; Dir Cartea Românească publishing house, Bucharest 1982–90, Ed.-in-Chief Arc 1991–97; Dir Copyro (soc. for defending authors' rights) 1997–; Fulbright stipendiate 1980; Prize of the Romanian Writers' Union 1975, Prize of the Romanian Acad. 1978, Award of Bucharest Writers' Asscn 1994, Opera Omnia Award, Writers' Asscn 2004. *Publications:* novels: Lumea în două zile (The World in Two Days) 1975, Ucenicul neascultător (The Disobedient Apprentice) 1978; essays: A Provincial's Nights 1984, Gulliver in No Man's Land (essays) 1994, Câinele în lesă (Dog on a Leash) (interviews and essays) 2004. *Leisure interests:* music, the arts, his pet dog. *Address:* 115 Victoriei Road, Bucharest (office); 62 Căderea Bastiliei (Copyro), Bucharest; 24–26 Blvd, Lascăr Catargiu, Bucharest, Romania (home). *Telephone:* (1) 3142251 (office); (1) 3171154 (home). *Fax:* (1) 3142251 (office).

BALAKRISHNAN, Arun; Indian chemical engineer and oil industry executive; *Chairman and Managing Director, Hindustan Petroleum Corporation Ltd;* ed Govt Coll. of Eng, Trichur, Kerala Indian Inst. of Man., Bangalore; spent five years as Dir of Planning with Oil Coordination Cttee; several positions in Marketing, Corp. and Human Resources, Hindustan Petroleum Corpn Ltd, Dir Human Resources –2007, Chair. and Man. Dir 2007–; Fellow, All India Man. Asscn; Scroll of Honour, Inst. of Engineers (India). *Address:* Hindustan Petroleum Corpn Ltd, Petroleum House, 17 Jamshedji Tata Road, Mumbai 400 020, India (office). *Telephone:* (22) 2202-6151 (office). *Fax:* (22) 2287-2992 (office). *E-mail:* corphq@hpcl.co.in (office). *Website:* www.hindpetro.com (office).

BALAKRISHNAN, K(onakuppakatil) G(opinathan), BSc, LLM; Indian judge; *Chief Justice;* b. 12 May 1945; enrolled as advocate of Kerala Bar Council 1968; practised civil and criminal law in Erinakulam; apptd a Munsif in Kerala Judicial Service 1973, later resgnd and resumed practice as advocate in Kerala High Court; judge, Kerala High Court 1985–97, Gujarat High Court 1997–98; Chief Justice of High Court of Gujarat 1998–99, of High Court of Judicature, Madras 1999; Judge, Supreme Court 2000–, Chief Justice of India 2007–. *Address:* Supreme Court of India, Tilak Marg, New Delhi 110 001, India (office). *Telephone:* (11) 23388942 (office). *Fax:* (11) 23383792 (office). *E-mail:* supremecourt@nic.in (office). *Website:* www.supremecourtofindia.nic.in (office).

BALANKIN, Alexander Sergeevich, MSc, PhD, DSc; Mexican/Russian scientist and academic; *Professor, National Polytechnic Institute of Mexico;* b. 3 March 1958, Moscow, Russia; ed Moscow Eng Physics Inst.; served as mem. Council of the Union (fmr USSR) for the Physics of Materials Resistance and Fracture (Russia) 1991–92; Full Prof., Monterrey Inst. of Tech. and Higher Educ., Mexico City 1992–97; joined Dept of Electromechanical Eng, Nat. Polytechnic Inst. (IPN) 1997, cr. Lab. of Fracture Mechanics; fmr mem. Advisory Council in Science and Tech. to the Presidency of Mexico; fmr Counsellor of Membership Cttee of Nat. Researcher System; Adviser, Mexican Petroleum Inst., Mexican Transport Inst.; consultant, Mexican Nat. Petroleum Co. (PEMEX); f. Nat. Interdisciplinary Research Group Fractal Mechanics (jt venture between industry and academia) 1998; cr. Inter-university Lab. Fractal Analysis of Complex Systems; mem. Mexican Acad. of Sciences 1998; Fellow, Nat. Researcher System 1998; State Prize of Russian Ministry of Defence 1990, Prize of Acad. of Sciences of USSR 1991, Pleiades Publishing Inc. Prize 1996, First Place Romulo Garza Prize for Research and Technological Devt in Mexico 1996, Nat. Prize of Arts and Sciences in Tech. and Design 2002, Nat. Prize in Financial Research 2004, Lazaro Cardenas' Gold Medal (highest award for Science and Tech. achievements), Pres. of Mexican Repub. 2005, UNESCO Science Prize 2005. *Publications:* five books and more than 120 scientific papers in professional journals on fractal solid mechanics, probabilistic fracture mechanics, fluid flow through porous media mechanics and their eng applications. *Address:* Instituto Politécnico Nacional, CP 07738, Mexico City, DF, Mexico (office). *Telephone:* (55) 5729-6000 (office). *E-mail:* info@ipn.mx (office). *Website:* www.ipn.mx (office).

BALARAM, Padmanabhan, BSc, MSc, PhD; Indian research institute director and molecular biophysicist; *Director, Indian Institute of Science;* ed Fergusson Coll., Pune Univ., Indian Inst. of Tech., Kanpur, Carnegie-Mellon Univ., Pittsburgh, USA; postdoctoral researcher, Dept of Chem., Harvard Univ., USA; Lecturer, Indian Inst. of Science 1973–77, Asst Prof. 1977–82, Assoc. Prof. 1982–85, Prof. 1986–, Astra Prof. of Biological Sciences 1997–2000, Chair. Molecular Biophysics Unit 1995–2000, Chair. Div. of Biological Sciences 2000–05, Dir Indian Inst. of Science 2005–; Assoc. Ed. Indian Journal of Chemical Education 1977–82; mem. Editorial Bd Proceedings of the Indian Academy of Sciences, Chemical Sciences 1980–83, Proceedings of the Indian National Science Academy, Section B 1985–90, Indian Journal of Biochemistry and Biophysics 1989–91, Indian Journal of Chemistry Section B 1985–91, International Journal of Peptide and Protein Research 1984–97, Journal of Peptide Research 1997, Protein Engineering, Design and Selection 2004, Biopolymers (Peptide Science) 2004; mem. Editorial Cttee Current Science 1991–94, Ed. Current Science 1995–; mem. Editorial Advisory Bd Chem Biochem: A European Journal of Chemical Biology 2000–; Fellow, Indian Acad. of Sciences, Indian Nat. Science Acad., Third World Acad. of Sciences; Padma Shri, Govt of India 2002; several awards. *Publications:* one edited book and more than 380 publs on structural biology, protein eng and design. *Address:* Indian Institute of Science, Bangalore 560 012, Karnataka, India (office). *Telephone:* (80) 2360-0690 (office); (80) 2293-2222 (office); (80) 22932337 (Molecular Biology Unit); (80) 23602741 (Molecular Biology Unit). *Fax:* (80) 23260-0936 (office); (80) 23600683 (Molecular Biology Unit); (80)

23600535 (Molecular Biology Unit). *E-mail:* diroff@admin.iisc.ernet.in (office); pb@mbu.iisc.ernet.in. *Website:* www.iisc.ernet.in (office); mbu.iisc.ernet.in/~pbgrp.

BALASSA, Sándor, DLA; Hungarian composer; b. 20 Jan. 1935, Budapest; s. of János Balassa and Eszter Bora; m. Marianna Orosz; one s. one d.; ed Budapest Conservatory and Music Acad. of Budapest; began career as a mechanic; entered Budapest Conservatory at age 17; studied composition under Endre Szervánszky at Budapest Music Acad., obtained diploma 1965; Music Dir Hungarian Radio 1964–80; Teacher of Instrumentation, Music. Acad. Budapest 1981; Erkel Prize 1972, Critics' Prize, Hungarian Radio 1972, 1974, Listeners' Prize, Hungarian Radio 1976, Distinction for Best Work of the Year, Paris Int. Tribune of Composers 1972, Merited Artist of the Hungarian People's Repub. 1978, Kossuth Prize 1983, Bartók-Pásztory Prize 1988, 1999. *Compositions include:* vocal: Eight Songs from Street Rottenbiller 1957, Two Songs to Poems by Dezső Kosztolányi 1957, Two Songs to Poems by Attila József 1958, Five Choruses (for children's choir) 1967, Legenda 1967, Antinomia 1968, Summer Night (for female choir) 1968, Requiem for Lajos Kassák 1969, Cantata Y 1970, Motetta 1973, Tresses 1979, Kyrie (for female choir) 1981, Madaras énekek (for children's choir) 1984, The Third Planet, opera-cantata 1986, Bánatomtól szabadulnék (for female choir) 1988, Oldott kéve (for mixed choir) 1992, Kelet népe (for children's choir) 1992, Damjanich's prayer (for mixed choir) 1993, Chant of Orphans (for mixed choir) 1995, Capriccio (for female choir) 1996, Spring Song, Autumn Song (for female choir) 1997, Woodcutter (for male choir) 1998, Moon-gesang and Sun-anthem (for male choir) 1998, Winter cantata (for children's chorus and string orchestra) 1999, Christmas (for female choir) 1999, Secrets of Heart (for solo tenor and string orchestra) 2002, Songs from Sümegvár Street 2003, A Gólyához (for mixed choir) 2003, Three songs to poems by Albert Wass 2003, Cry in December 2005; opera: Az ajtón kivül (The Man Outside) 1976, The Third Planet 1986, Karl and Anna 1992, Földindulás 2001; instrumental: Dimensioni 1966, Quartetto per percussioni 1969, Xenia 1970, Tabulae 1972, The Last Shepherd 1978, Quintet for Brass 1979, The Flowers of Hajta 1984, Divertimento for two cimbaloms 1992, Sonatina for harp 1993, Little Garland (trio for flute, viola and harp) 1994, Five Brothers (piano) 1994, Jánosnapi muzsika (solo violin) 1994, Vonósnégyes (string quartet) 1995, Bells of Nyirbátor (for twelve brass instruments) 1996, Sonatina for Piano 1996, Preludes and Fantasia for Organ 1996, Duets (for flute and harp) 1998, Pastoral and Rondo (for violin and horn) 1998, Eight Movements for two clarinets 2001, Sonatina II (for piano) 2003, Párosító Hegedüduók (Duet for violins) 2003, Xenia II (nonetto) 2004, Letters from a Reservation (for Cimbalom) 2004, Greeting to Viola (for solo viola) 2004, Three Movements for Cello 2005, Ha szól a Tárogató 2006, Eszterlánc Duets (for flute and violin 2006, Fantasia for Piano 2006, Four Pieces for Cimbalom 2006, Trio I for Strings 2006, Művész utca II/a 2007, Obne Doom-Doom 2007, Trio II for Strings 2008; orchestral: Violin Concerto 1965, Lupercalia 1971, Iris 1972, Chant of Glarus 1978, The Island of Everlasting Youth 1979, Calls and Cries 1980, A Daydreamer's Diary 1983, Three Phantasias 1984, Little Grape and Little Fish 1987, Tündér Ilona 1992, Prince Csaba (for string orchestra) 1993, Bölcske Concerto (for string orchestra) 1993, Dances of Mucsa 1994, Sons of the Sun 1995, Four Portraits 1996, Number 301 Parcel 1997, Pécs Concerto 1998, Hungarian Coronation Music 1998, Hun's Valley (Val d'Anniviers) 1999, Double Concerto (for oboe, horn and string orchestra) 2000, Fantasy (for harp and string orchestra) 2002, Flowers of October 2003, Gödöllö Concerto (for guitar orchestra) 2003, Excursion to the Sun Mountain (for string orchestra) 2003, Concerto (for trumpet) 2004, Szeged concerto (for string orchestra) 2005, Summer Music (for flute and string orchestra) 2005, Civisek Városa 2005, Journeys in Bihar 2005, Lovagi erények dícsérete 2007, Overture and Scenes (for string orchestra) 2007. *Leisure interest:* nature. *Address:* str. 18 Sümegvár, 1118 Budapest, Hungary (home). *Telephone:* (1) 319-7049 (home). *E-mail:* sandor@balassa.hu (home).

BALASURIYA, Stanislaus Tissa, BA, STL; Sri Lankan ecclesiastic; b. 29 Aug. 1924, Kahatagasdigiliya; s. of William Balasuriya and Victoria Balasuriya; ed Univ. of Ceylon, Gregorian Univ., Rome, Oxford Univ., Maris Stella Coll., Negombo, St Patrick's Coll., Jaffna and St Joseph's Coll., Colombo; helped found Aquinas Univ. with Father Peter Pillai 1954, Rector 1964–71; f. Centre for Soc. and Religion, Colombo 1971, Dir 1971–, Citizens Cttee for Nat. Harmony in Sri Lanka 1977–91; Visiting Prof. of Faith and Social Justice, Faculty of Theology, Univ. of Ottawa 1993–94; excommunicated from Catholic Church for refusing to sign 'Profession of Faith' 1997; Ed. Logos, Quest, Voices of the Third World, Social Justice, Sadharanaya; Khan Memorial Gold Medal for Econs. *Publications:* Jesus Christ and Human Liberation, Eucharist and Human Liberation, Catastrophe July '83, Planetary Theology, Mary and Human Liberation, Liberation of the Affluent, Humanization Europe, Indicators of Social Justice, Third World Theology of Religious Life, Right Relationships: Re-rooting of Christian Theology 1991, Doing Marian Theology in Sri Lanka. *Leisure interests:* writing, organic farming. *Address:* Centre for Society and Religion, 281 Deans Road, Colombo 10, Sri Lanka. *Telephone:* 695425.

BALAYAN, Roman Gurgenovich; Armenian film director; b. 15 April 1941, Nagorno-Karabak Autonomous Region; m. Natalia Balayan; two s.; ed Kiev Theatre Inst., USSR; State Prize 1987. *Films include:* The Romashkin Effect, 1973, Kashtanka 1976, Biryuk (Morose) 1978, The Kiss 1983, Dream and Waking Flights 1983, Keep Me Safe, My Talisman 1985, Police Spy 1988, Lady Macbeth of Mtcensk 1989, Two Moons, Three Suns 1998 (dir and writer). *TV:* Who's Afraid of Virginia Woolf 1992, The Tale of the First Love 1995. *Address:* Leningradsky Prosp. 33, Apt. 70, 125212 Moscow, Russia. *Telephone:* (095) 159-99-74.

BALAZS, Artur Krzysztof, MEng; Polish politician, trade union official and farmer; b. 3 Jan. 1952, Ełk; s. of Adam Balazs and Irena Balazs; m. Jolanta Balazs 1973; three d.; ed Agricultural Acad., Szczecin; worked in agric. service of Communal Office, Kołczewo 1974–76; own farm in Łuskowo 1976–; mem. Polish United Workers' Party (PZPR) 1975–81; active in Agric. Solidarity Independent Self-governing Trade Union 1980–81, participant 1st Nat. Congress of Solidarity of Pvt. Farmers Trade Union, Warsaw 1980; participant agric. strikes and co-signatory agreements in Ustrzyki, Rzeszów and Bydgoszcz 1981; mem. All-Poland Founding Cttee of Solidarity of Private Farmers Trade Union, mem. Comm. for Realization of Rzeszów-Ustrzyki Agreements; interned Dec. 1981–Dec. 1982; mem. Presidium of Solidarity Provisional Nat. Council of Farmers 1987; mem. Inter-factory Strike Cttee Szczecin 1988; mem. Civic Cttee attached to Lech Wałęsa, Chair. of Solidarity Trade Union 1988–91; participant Round Table debates, mem. group for union pluralism and team for agric. matters Feb.–April 1989; mem. Episcopate Comm. for the Pastoral Care of Farmers 1989–; Deputy to Sejm (Parl.) 1989–93, 1997–; mem. Solidarity Election Action Parl. Club 1997–; Chair. Sejm Cttee for Admin. and Internal Affairs 1992–93; Vice-Chair. Christian Peasant Party 1990–94, 1995–97, Chair. 1994–95; mem. Nat. Bd Conservative Peasant Party (SKL) 1997–, Vice-Chair. 1998–99, Chair. 2000–02, Chair. Conservative Party–New Poland Movt (SKL–RNP) 2002–; Chair. European Fund for the Devt of Polish Villages 1990–; Minister, mem. Council of Ministers 1989–90, Minister without Portfolio 1991–92; mem. Senate 1995–97; mem. Cttee for Agric.; Minister of Agric. and Rural Devt 1999–2002. *Leisure interests:* press, politics. *Address:* Biuro Poselskie, Artura Balazsa, ul. Garncarska 5/3, 70–377 Szczecin, Poland (office). *Telephone:* (91) 4845643 (office).

BALBINOT, Sergio, MBA; Italian business executive; *Joint Managing Director, Assicurazioni Generali SpA;* b. 8 Sept. 1958, Tarvisio; m.; one s. one d.; began career with business scholarship, EC, Brussels; joined Assicurazioni Generali as graduate trainee, Munich 1983, positions in Trieste, later Zurich 1989, Paris 1992, returned to HQ, Trieste 1995, Gen. Man., Generali Group 2000, Jt Man. Dir 2002–, Deputy Chair. Generali España, Holding de Entidades de Seguros, SA, Madrid, Generali Holding Vienna AG, Vienna, Generali France SA, Paris, Generali China Life Insurance Co. Ltd, Canton; mem. Bd Dirs Generali (Schweiz) Holding, Adliswil Europ Assistance Holding, Paris, Generali Finance BV, Diemen Graafschap Holland Participatie Maatschappij NV, Diemen, Generali Asia NV Diemen, AMB Generali Holding AG, Aachen, Aachener und Münchener Lebensversicherung AG, Aachen, Aachener und Münchener Versicherung AG, Aachen, Commerzbank AG, Frankfurt, Banco Vitalicio de Espana, Barcelona, La Estrella SA, Madrid, Migdal Insurance Holding Ltd, Tel-Aviv, Migdal Insurance & Financial Holdings, Tel-Aviv, Transocean Holding Corpn, New York. *Address:* Assicurazioni Generali SpA, Piazza Duca degli Abruzzi 2, 34132 Trieste, Italy (office). *Telephone:* (40) 6711 (office). *Fax:* (40) 671600 (office). *E-mail:* info@generali.com (office). *Website:* www.generali.com (office).

BALCEROWICZ, Leszek, MBA, DEconSc; Polish politician, economist, academic and fmr central banker; *Professor of Comparative International Studies, Warsaw School of Economics;* b. 19 Jan. 1947, Lipno; s. of Wacław Balcerowicz and Barbara Balcerowicz; m. 1977; two s. one d.; ed Cen. School of Planning and Statistics, Warsaw, St John's Univ., New York; staff Central School of Planning and Statistics (now Warsaw School of Econs), Warsaw 1970–, Inst. of Int. Econ. Relations 1970–80; Head, Research Team attached to Econ. Devt Inst. 1978–81, Scientific Sec. Econ. Devt Inst. 1980–; Prof. of Comparative Int. Studies, Warsaw School of Econs 1992–; mem. Polish United Workers' Party (PZPR) 1969–81; consultant, Network of Solidarity Independent Self-governing Trade Union 1981–84; Deputy Prime Minister and Minister of Finance 1989–91, 1997–2000; Leader Freedom Union (UW) 1995–2000; Pres. Nat. Bank of Poland 2001–07; Deputy to Sejm (Parl.) 1997–2000; fmr mem. Council of Econ. Advisers to Pres. Wałesa; Head Inst. for Comparative Int. Studies, Warsaw School of Econs 1993–; Chair. Council of Centre for Social and Econ. Research, Warsaw 1992–2000; mem. Polish Econ. Soc. 1970–, Vice-Chair. Gen. Bd 1981–82; mem. Polish Sociological Soc. 1983–; mem. Warsaw Civic Cttee Solidarity 1989; 12 hon degrees; Awards of Minister of Science, Higher Educ. and Tech. 1978, 1980, 1981, Ludwig Erhard Prize 1992, Finance Minister of the Year (Euromoney) 1998, Transatlantic Leadership Award (European Inst. of Washington) 1999, Central European Award for Finance Minister of the Year 1999, Friedrich von Hayek Prize (Germany) 2001, Carl Bertelsman Prize 2001, Fasel Foundation Prize for Merits for the Social Market Economy 2002, European Central Banker of the Year (The Banker magazine) 2004, Emerging Markets Award for Emerging Europe's Central Bank Governor of the Year 2004. *Publications:* numerous scientific works on int. econ. relations and problems of econ. systems. *Leisure interests:* basketball, detective stories. *Address:* Warsaw School of Economics, Aleja Niepodległości 162, 02-554 Warsaw, Poland (office). *Telephone:* (22) 5649345 (office). *Fax:* (22) 5649833 (office). *E-mail:* kmsp@sgh.uow.pl (office). *Website:* www.sgh.waw.pl (office).

BALČYTIS, Zigmantas; Lithuanian economist and politician; b. 16 Nov. 1953, Juodziai, Zemaiciu Naumiestis Co., Silute Dist; m. Severina Balčytienė; one s. one d.; ed Faculty of Finance and Accounting, Vilnius State Univ.; project planning office, Ministry of Food Industry 1976–78; Young Communist League 1978–84; Deputy Dir Lithuanian Nat. Philharmonic 1984–89; Man. of Trade Union Affairs and Dir of Training Centre 1989–91; Dir, Vilnius Asphalt and Concrete Factory; Deputy Gov. Vilnius Co. 1994–96; First Deputy Dir of Lithuanian–Hungarian Jt Venture 'Lithun' (now jt stock co.) 1996–2000; mem. Parl. 2000–, Minister of Transport and Communications 2001–05; Minister of Finance and Gov. of EIB for Lithuania 2005–07 (resgnd); Acting Prime Minister June 2006; mem. Social Democratic Party (LSDP); Order of the Cross of the Gunner (Lithuania), Order of the Great Cross (Spain);

Lithuanian Memorial Plaque, Medal of Afanasij Nikitin, Commemorative Medal of 750th Anniversary of King Mindaugas' Coronation, named most meritorious personality in maritime and transport industry, Anatolijus 2004. *Leisure interests:* basketball, hunting, water skiing, fishing, tennis. *Address:* Lithuanian Social Democratic Party (LSDP), Barboros Radvilaites g. 1, Vilnius, 01124, Lithuania (office). *Telephone:* (5) 261-3907 (office). *Fax:* (5) 261-5420 (office). *E-mail:* info@lsdp.lt (office). *Website:* www.lsdp.lt (office).

BALDACCI, John Elias, BA; American state official; *Governor of Maine;* b. 30 Jan. 1955, Bangor, Me; m. Karen Weston; one s.; ed Bangor High School, Univ. of Maine; worked in family restaurant Momma Baldacci's, Bangor; mem. Bangor City Council 1978–81; mem. State Senate, Me 1982–94; mem. US House of Reps 1994–2002; Gov. of Me 2003–; Democrat; Nat. Energy Assistance Dirs Asscn Award 1997, Small Business Assistance Award, NASA, Big M Award, Me State Soc., Washington DC 2000. *Address:* Office of the Governor, 1 State House Station, Augusta, ME 04333, USA (office). *Telephone:* (207) 287-3531 (office). *Fax:* (207) 287-1034 (office). *Website:* www.maine.gov/governor (home).

BALDAUF, Sari Maritta, MSc, DSc; Finnish business executive; b. 10 Aug. 1955, Kotka; ed Helsinki School of Econs and Business Admin; Researcher, Finland Int. Business Operations project, Helsinki School of Econs and Business Admin 1977–78; Training Officer, Finnish Inst. of Exports 1979–80; Market Man. Falcon Communications, Abu Dhabi 1981–82; Planning Man. Nokia Corpn 1983–85, Vice-Pres. Corp. Planning, Nokia Electronics 1985–86, Asst Vice-Pres. Business Devt and Venture Capital, Nokia, New York 1986–87, Vice-Pres. Business Devt, Telenokia 1987–88, Pres. Cellular Systems, Nokia Telecommunications 1988–96, mem. Group Exec. Bd Nokia Corpn 1994, Exec. Vice-Pres. Nokia APAC 1997–98, Pres. Nokia Networks 1998–2003, Exec. Vice-Pres. and Gen. Man. of Networks 2004–05; mem. Bd of Dirs F-Secure Corpn 2006–, YIT Corpn 2006–, Int. Youth Foundation 2000–, Foundation for Econ. Educ. 2002–, SanomaWSOY 2003–, Hewlett-Packard Co. 2006–, CapMan 2007–, Finland-China Trade Asscn 1997–99, Tech. Research Centre of Finland 1998–2001; Chair. Savonlinna Opera Festival; mem. Nat. Cttee for the Information Soc. Issues 1996–2003, Finnish Acad. of Tech., Consultative Cttee of Sibelius Acad. Support Foundation 2003–; mem. Int. Advisory Bd Instituto de Empresa (business school) 2007–; Knight, 1st Class of the Order of the White Rose of Finland 1996; Hon. DTech (Helsinki Univ. of Tech.); ranked by Fortune magazine amongst 50 Most Powerful Women in Business outside the US (14th) 2003, (12th) 2004. *Leisure interest:* classical music, hiking, skiing, spending time with family and friends at her country house. *Address:* c/o Board of Directors, Savonlinna Opera Festival Office, Olavinkatu 27, 57130 Savonlinna, Finland (office).

BALDESCHWIELER, John Dickson, PhD; American chemist and academic; *J. Stanley Johnson Professor and Professor of Chemistry, Emeritus, California Institute of Technology;* b. 14 Nov. 1933, Elizabeth, NJ; s. of Emile L. Baldeschwieler and Isobel M. Dickson; m. Marlene Konnar 1991; two s. one d. from previous m.; ed Cornell Univ. and Univ. of Calif., Berkeley; Asst Prof., Harvard Univ. 1962–65; Assoc. Prof., Stanford Univ. 1965–67, Prof. of Chem. 1967–73; Deputy Dir, Office of Science and Tech. Exec. Office of Pres. of USA 1971–73; Prof. of Chem., Calif. Inst. of Tech. 1973 (now J. Stanley Johnson Prof. and Prof. Emer.), Chair., Div. of Chem. and Chem. Eng 1973–78; Chair., Bd of Dirs Vestar Research Inc. 1981–; mem. numerous advisory cttees and comms; Alfred P. Sloan Foundation Fellow 1962–65; ACS Award in Pure Chem. 1967, William H. Nichols Award 1990, Nat. Medal of Science 2000, ACS Award for Creative Invention 2001. *Publications:* numerous articles in professional journals. *Leisure interests:* hiking, skiing, photography, music, travel. *Address:* Division of Chemistry and Chemical Engineering, 232 Noyes, Mail Code 127-72, California Institute of Technology, Pasadena, CA 91125 (office); PO Box 50065, Pasadena, CA 91115-0065, USA (home). *Telephone:* (626) 395-6088 (office). *Fax:* (626) 568-0402 (office). *E-mail:* jb@caltech.edu (office). *Website:* www.cce.caltech.edu/faculty/baldeschwieler/index.html (office).

BALDESSARI, John, MA; American artist and academic; *Professor of Art, UCLA;* b. 17 June 1931, National City, Calif.; ed San Diego State Univ., Calif., Univ. of Calif., Berkeley, UCLA, Otis Art Inst., Los Angeles, Chouinard Art Inst., Los Angeles; teacher, Calif. Inst. of the Arts, Valencia; Prof. of Art, UCLA 1996–; current projects include solo shows in New York and Europe, books, films, a project at the Deutsche Guggenheim Berlin, and retrospectives at Museum Moderner Kunst Stiftung Ludwig Wien, Vienna and Kunsthaus, Graz, Austria, and Musée d'art contemporain de Nîmes, France; Los Angeles Inst. for the Humanities Fellow, Univ. of Southern Calif. 2002; Hon. DFA (Otis Art Inst. of Parsons School of Design of the New School of Social Research) 2000, (San Diego State Univ.) 2003, (Calif. State Univ.) 2003; Guggenheim Fellowship 1988, Oscar Kokoschka Prize (Austria) 1996, Gov. of Calif.'s Award for Lifetime Achievement in the Visual Arts 1997, Spectrum-International Award for Photography, Foundation of Lower Saxony, Germany 1999, Coll. Art Asscns' Lifetime Achievement Award 1999, Artist Space, New York 2000, Best Web-Based Original Art, AICA USA Best Show Awards 2002, 2nd Place, Best Show Commercial Gallery National for exhibit at Margo Leavin Gallery, US Art Critics Asscn 2003, Americans for the Arts Lifetime Achievement Award, New York 2005, honoured by Rolex Mentor and Protégé Arts Initiative, New York 2005. *Publications:* Throwing a Ball to Get Three Melodies and Fifteen Chords 1975, Close-Cropped Tales 1981, The Life and Opinions of Tristam Shandy (39 photo-collage illustrations for the novel by Laurence Sterne) 1988, The Telephone Book (With Pearls) 1988, Lamb (co-author) 1989, Zorro (Two Gestures and One Mark) 1998, The Metaphor Problem Again (co-author) 1999, Brown and Green and Other Parables 2001; numerous articles and reviews. *Address:* UCLA Department of Art, 11000 Kinross Avenue, Suite 245, Los Angeles, CA 90095, USA (office). *Telephone:* (310) 825-3281 (office). *Website:* www.art.ucla.edu (office); www.baldessari.org.

BALDINI, Stefano; Italian long distance runner; b. 25 May 1971, Castelnovo di Sotto; m. Virna De Angeli; one d.; competes in 5000m., 10000m. and marathon events; holds nat. record for marathon; winner World Half Marathon 1996; Gold Medal Marathon, European Championships 1998, Athens Olympics 2004; Bronze Medal Marathon, World Athletics Championships Edmonton 2001, Paris 2003. *Address:* c/o Italian Olympic Committee, Foro Italico, 00194 Rome, Italy (office). *Telephone:* (06) 36857241 (office). *Fax:* (06) 36857697 (office). *E-mail:* segreteria@coni.it (office). *Website:* www.maratoneti.com/baldini/home.asp.

BALDOCK, Brian Ford, CBE, FRSA, CIMgt, FInstM; British business executive; b. 10 June 1934; s. of Ernest A. Baldock and Florence F. Baldock; m. 1st Mary Lillian Bartolo 1956 (divorced 1966); two s.; m. 2nd Carole Anthea Mason 1968; one s.; ed Clapham Coll. London; army officer 1952–55; Procter & Gamble 1956–61; Ted Bates Inc. 1961–63; Rank Org. 1963–66; Smith & Nephew 1966–75; Revlon Inc. 1975–78; Imperial Group 1978–86; Dir Guinness PLC 1986–96, Group Man. Dir 1989–96, Deputy Chair. 1992–96; Chair. Portman Group 1989–96; Chair. Sygen Int. (fmrly Dalgety) 1992– (Dir 1992–); Dir Marks & Spencer 1996– (Chair. 1999–2000), WMC Communications 1996–99, Cornhill Insurance 1996–2000; Chair. Wellington Group 1998–, Mencap 1998–, First Artist Corpn PLC 2001–; Freeman, City of London 1989. *Leisure interests:* theatre, opera, sport. *Address:* Marks and Spencer PLC, Michael House, Baker Street, London, W1U 8EP, England. *Telephone:* (20) 7935-4422. *Fax:* (20) 7487-2679. *E-mail:* brian.baldock@marks-and-spencer.com. *Website:* www.marksandspencer.com.

BALDWIN, Alexander (Alec) Rae, III; American actor; b. 3 April 1958, Masapequa, NY; s. of Alexander Rae Baldwin, Jr and Carol Baldwin (née Martineau); m. Kim Basinger (q.v.) 1993 (divorced 2002); one d.; ed George Washington and New York Univs, Lee Strasberg Theater Inst.; also studied with Mira Rostova and Elaine Aiken; mem. Screen Actors' Guild, American Fed. of TV and Radio Artists, Actors Equity Asscn; mem. Bd of Dirs People for the American Way. *Stage appearances include:* Loot (Theatre World Award 1986) 1986, Serious Money 1988, Prelude to a Kiss 1990, A Streetcar Named Desire 1992. *Film appearances include:* Forever Lulu 1987, She's Having a Baby 1987, Beetlejuice 1988, Married to the Mob 1988, Talk Radio 1988, Working Girl 1988, Great Balls of Fire 1989, The Hunt for Red October 1990, Miami Blues 1990, Alice 1990, The Marrying Man 1991, Prelude to a Kiss 1992, Glengarry Glen Ross 1992, Malice 1993, The Getaway 1994, The Shadow 1994, Heaven's Prisoners 1995, Looking for Richard 1996, The Juror 1996, Ghosts of Mississippi 1996, Bookworm 1997, The Edge 1997, Thick as Thieves 1998, Outside Providence 1998, Mercury Rising 1998 (also producer), The Confession 1999, Notting Hill 1999, Thomas and the Magic Railroad 2000, State and Main 2000, Pearl Harbor 2001, Cats and Dogs (voice) 2001, Final Fantasy: The Spirit's Within 2001, The Royal Tenenbaums 2001, The Devil and Daniel Webster 2001, Path to War 2002, Dr Seuss' The Cat in the Hat 2003, The Cooler 2003, Along Came Polly 2004, The Last Shot 2004, The Aviator 2004, Elizabethtown 2005, Fun with Dick and Jane 2005, Mini's First Time 2006, The Departed 2006, Running with Scissors 2006, The Good Shepherd 2006, Suburban Girl 2007, Brooklyn Rules 2007, Lymelife 2008, My Best Friend's Girl 2008, Madagascar: Escape 2 Africa (voice) 2008, My Sister's Keeper 2009. *TV appearances include:* The Doctors 1980–82, Cutter to Houston 1982, Knot's Landing 1984–85, Love on the Run 1985, A Dress Gray 1986, The Alamo: 13 Days to Glory 1986, Sweet Revenge 1990, Nuremberg 2000, Path to War 2002, Second Nature 2002, Dreams and Giants 2003, Thomas and Friends: The Best of Gordon 2004, 30 Rock (series) (Golden Globe Award for Best Actor in a Musical or Comedy TV Series 2007, 2009, Screen Actors' Guild Award for Outstanding Performance by a Male Actor in a Comedy Series 2007, 2008) 2006–, Late Show with David Letterman 2008. *Publication:* A Promise to Ourselves: A Journey through Fatherhood and Divorce (with Mark Tabb) 2008. *Website:* www.alecbaldwin.com.

BALDWIN, Sir Jack Edward, Kt, PhD, FRS; British chemist and academic; *Waynflete Professor of Chemistry, University of Oxford;* b. 8 Aug. 1938, London; s. of Frederick C. Baldwin and Olive F. Headland; m. Christine L. Franchi 1977; ed Lewes County Grammar School and Imperial Coll., London; Asst Lecturer in Chem., Imperial Coll. London 1963, Lecturer 1966; Asst Prof., Penn State Univ. 1967, Assoc. Prof. 1969; Assoc. Prof. of Chem., MIT 1970, Prof. 1972–78; Daniell Prof. of Chem., King's Coll., London 1972; Waynflete Prof. of Chem., Univ. of Oxford 1978–, Fellow Magdalen Coll. 1978–; Dir Oxford Centre for Molecular Sciences; Hon. DSc (Warwick) 1988, (Strathclyde); Corday Morgan Medal, Chem. Soc. 1975, Karrer Medal, Univ. of Zürich 1984, Dr P. Janssen Prize (Belgium) 1988, Davy Medal, Royal Soc. 1993, Leverhulm Medal, Royal Soc. 1999, Kitasako Medal 2000. *Publications:* papers in organic and bio-organic chem. in Journal of American Chem. Soc., Journal of Chem. Soc. and Nature. *Address:* Chemistry Research Laboratory, University of Oxford, Mansfield Road, Oxford, OX1 3TA, England (office). *Telephone:* (1865) 275670 (office). *E-mail:* jack.baldwin@chemistry.oxford.ac.uk (office). *Website:* www.chem.ox.ac.uk/researchguide/jbaldwin.html (office).

BALDWIN, Peter, BEE, BA; Australian politician; b. 12 April 1951, Aldershot, UK; ed Univ. of Sydney, Macquarie Univ.; fmr engineer and computer programmer; mem. NSW State Parl. (Upper House) 1976–82; Australian Labor Party mem. for Sydney, House of Reps 1983–98; Minister for Higher Educ. and Employment Services and Minister Assisting Treasurer 1990–93; Minister for Social Security 1993–96; apptd Shadow Minister for Finance 1997; mem. Parl. Cttee on Foreign Affairs, Defence and Trade 1987–90, House of Reps Standing Cttee on Industry, Science and Tech. 1987–90. *Address:* Level 3, 10 Mallet Street, Camperdown, NSW 2050, Australia.

BALE, Christian; British actor; b. 30 Jan. 1974, Haverfordwest, Pembrokeshire, Wales. *Films include:* The Land of Faraway 1987, Empire of the Sun 1987, Henry V 1989, Treasure Island (TV) 1990, Newsies 1992, Swing Kids 1993, Prince of Jutland 1994, Little Women 1994, Pocahontas 1995, The Portrait of a Lady 1996, The Secret Agent 1996, Metroland 1997, Velvet Goldmine 1998, All the Little Animals 1998, A Midsummer Night's Dream 1999, Mary, Mother of Jesus (TV) 1999, American Psycho 2000, Shaft 2000, Captain Corelli's Mandolin 2001, Laurel Canyon 2002, Reign of Fire 2002, Equilibrium 2002, The Machinist 2004, Batman Begins 2005, The New World 2005, Rescue Dawn 2006, Harsh Times 2006, The Prestige 2006, I'm Not There 2007, 3:10 to Yuma 2007, The Dark Knight 2008. *Address:* c/o Endeavor Talent Agency LLC, 9701 Wilshire Boulevard, 10th Floor, Beverly Hills, CA 90210, USA (office). *Telephone:* (310) 248-2000 (office).

BALESTRINI, Nanni; Italian poet, author and artist; b. 2 July 1935, Milan; mem. group of poets called Novissimi and co-founder of Gruppo 63 in Palermo 1963; one of prin. eds of literary magazine Il Verri; co-editor (with Alfredo Giuliani) Quindici magazine 1966–68; has organized numerous confs and exhbns; also a figurative artist, exhibiting in many galleries in Italy and abroad, and at Venice Biennale in 1993. *Publications include:* poetry: Come si agisce 1963, Ma noi facciamone un'altra 1966, Poesie pratiche (anthology) 1954–1969, 1976, Le ballate della signorina Richmond 1977, Blackout 1980, Ipocalisse 1986, Il ritorno della signorina 1987, Osservazioni sul volo degli uccelli, poesie 1954–56 1988, Il pubblico del labirinto 1992, Estremi rimedi 1995, Le avventure complete della signorina 1999, Elettra, operapoesia 2001, Tutto in una volta (antologia) 1954–2003 2003, Sfinimondo 2003; novels: Tristano 1964, Vogliamo tutto 1971, La violenza illustrata 1976, Gli invisibili 1987, L'editore 1989, I furiosi 1994, Una mattina ci siam svegliati 1995, La Grande Rivolta (comprising Vogliamo tutto, Gli invisibili, L'editore) 1999, Sandokan, storia di camorra 2004; other works: Gruppo 63 (anthology, with Alfredo Giuliani) 1964, Gruppo 63. Il romanzo sperimentale 1965, L'Opera di Pechino (with Letizia Paolozzi) 1966, L'orda d'oro (with Primo Moroni) 1988, Paladino 2002, Gruppo 63, L'Antologia (with Alfredo Giuliani) 2002, Parma 1922 (radio drama) 2002; contrib. to many periodicals and journals. *E-mail:* info@nannibalestrini.it (office). *Website:* www.nannibalestrini.it (office).

BALGIMBAYEV, Nurlan Utebovich; Kazakhstani politician; *President, Kazakhoil Co.;* b. 20 Nov. 1947; ed Kazakh Polytech. Inst., Massachusetts Univ. USA; worked in petroleum industry; Minister of Petroleum and Gas Industry 1994–97; Pres. Kazakhoil Co. 1997, 2000–; Prime Minister of Kazakhstan 1997–99. *Address:* Kazakhoil Co., Astana, Kazakhstan.

BALIBAR, Jeanne; French actress; b. 13 April 1968, Paris; d. of Etienne Balibar and Françoise Balibar; pnr, Mathieu Amalric; two s.; ed Univ. de Paris I. *Plays:* Dom Juan (Avignon) 1993, Le Square, Les Bonnes, La Glycine, Clitandre (Comédie Française), Macbeth 1997, Penthesilea 1997, Uncle Vanya (Paris) 2003, Le cadavre vivant (Paris) 2003, Le Soulier de Satin (Paris) 2003. *Films:* La Sentinelle 1992, Un dimanche à Paris 1994, Comment je me suis disputé ... (ma vie sexuelle) 1996, J'ai horreur d'amour 1997, Trois ponts sur la rivière 1999, Sade 2000, Comédie d'innocence 2000, Va savoir 2001, Avec tout mon amour 2001, Intimisto 2001, Une affaire privée 2002, Saltimbank 2003, Code 46 2003, Toutes ces belles promesses 2003, Clean 2004, Mademoiselle Y 2006, Call Me Agostino 2006, J'aurais voulu être un danseur 2007, Ne touchez pas la hache 2007. *Recordings include:* Paramour 2003. *Address:* Zelig, 57 rue de Turbigo, 75003 Paris, France (office).

BALKENENDE, Jan Pieter, DIur; Dutch politician; *Prime Minister;* b. 7 May 1956, Kapelle; ed Free Univ. of Amsterdam; Legal Affairs Policy Officer, Netherlands Univs Council 1982–84; mem. Amstelveen Municipal Council 1982–98, Leader, Council Christen-Democratisch Appèl (CDA) Group 1994–98; Prof. of Econs, Free Univ. of Amsterdam 1993–2002; mem. staff, Policy Inst. of the CDA 1984–98; elected mem. Parl. 1998, Parl. Leader CDA 2001–; Prime Minister of the Netherlands 2002–, also Minister of Gen. Affairs 2002–. *Publications include:* numerous articles on liberal individualism and communitarianism in Dutch society. *Address:* Office of the Prime Minister, Ministry of General Affairs, Binnenhof 20, POB 20001, 2500 EA The Hague (office); c/o Christen-Democratisch Appèl (CDA) (Christian Democratic Appeal), Dr Kuyperstraat 5, POB 30453, 2500 GL The Hague, Netherlands. *Telephone:* (70) 3564100 (office). *Fax:* (70) 3564683 (office). *Website:* www.minaz.nl (office).

BALKHEYOUR, Khalid Ahmed; Saudi Arabian engineer and international organization executive; *President and CEO, Arab Satellite Communications Organization (ARABSAT);* fmr Vice-Pres. Lucent Technologies (Saudi Arabia); fmr Dir of Int. Relations, Saudi Telecommunications Co.; currently Pres. and CEO Arab Satellite Communications Org. (ARABSAT). *Address:* Arab Satellite Communications Organization (ARABSAT), PO Box 1038, Diplomatic Quarter, Riyadh 11431, Saudi Arabia (office). *Telephone:* (1) 4820000 (office). *Fax:* (1) 4887999 (office). *E-mail:* arabsat@arabsat.com (office). *Website:* www.arabsat.com (office).

BALL, Anthony (Tony), MBA; British media executive; *Chairman, Ingenious Media Active Capital;* b. 18 Dec. 1955; ed Kingston Univ.; with Thames TV 1976–88; fmr sports broadcaster for Trans World Int.; with BSB Sport 1988–91; with Int. Man. Group 1991–93; with BSkyB 1993–95; with Fox/Liberty Network 1995–99; Exec. Dir British Sky Broadcasting (BSkyB) 1999–2003, Consultant, News Corporation 2003–; Dir (non-exec.) Marks & Spencer PLC 2000–; mem. Supervisory Bd ProSiebenSat.1 Media 2004–; Chair. Ingenious Media Active Capital 2006–. *Address:* Ingenious Media Active Capital, 100 Pall Mall, London, SW1Y 5NQ, England (office).

BALL, Sir Christopher John Elinger, Kt, MA, FRSA; British academic (retd); b. 22 April 1935, London; s. of the late Laurence Elinger Ball and Christine Florence Mary (née Howe) Ball; m. Wendy Ruth Colyer 1958; three s. three d.; ed St George's School, Harpenden, Merton Coll., Oxford; Second Lt Parachute Regt 1955–56; Lecturer in English Language, Merton Coll., Oxford 1960–61; Lecturer in Comparative Linguistics, SOAS (Univ. of London) 1961–64; Fellow and Tutor in English Language, Lincoln Coll., Oxford 1964–69, Bursar 1972–79, Warden, Keble Coll., Oxford 1980–88; Jt Founding Ed. Toronto Dictionary of Old English 1970; mem. General Bd of the Faculties 1979–82, Hebdomadal Council 1985–89, Council and Exec., Templeton Coll., Oxford 1981–92, Editorial Bd, Oxford Review of Educ. 1984–96, CNAA 1982–88; Chair. Bd of Nat. Advisory Body for Public Sector Higher Educ. in England 1982–88, Oxford Univ. English Bd 1977–79, Jt Standing Cttee for Linguistics 1979–83, Conf. of Colls. Fees Cttee 1979–85, Higher Educ. Information Services Trust 1987–90; Sec. Linguistics Asscn GB 1964–67; Publications Sec. Philological Soc. 1969–75; Gov. St George's School, Harpenden 1985–89, Centre for Medieval Studies, Oxford 1987, Brathay Hall Trust 1988–91, Manchester Polytechnic 1989–91; Founding Fellow in Kellogg Forum for Continuing Education, Oxford Univ. 1988–89, RSA Fellow in Continuing Educ. 1990–92, Dir of Learning 1992–97; Founding Chair. Nat. Advisory Council for Careers and Educational Guidance (NACCEG); Pres. Nat. Campaign for Learning 1995–97, Patron 1998–; Chancellor Univ. of Derby 1995–2003; Founding Chair. The Talent Foundation 1999–2004; Chair. Global Univ. Alliance 2000–; Millennium Fellow, Auckland Univ. of Tech., NZ 2000; Hon. Fellow, Lincoln Coll., Oxford 1981, Merton Coll., Oxford 1987, Keble Coll., Oxford 1989, Manchester Polytechnic 1988, Polytechnic of Cen. London 1991, Auckland Univ. of Tech., NZ 1992, North East Wales Inst. 1996, Oxford Brookes Univ. 2007; Hon. DLitt (CNAA) 1989; Hon. DUniv (Univ. of N London) 1993, (Open Univ.) 2002, (Univ. of Derby) 2003; Hon. DEd (Greenwich Univ.) 1994. *Publications:* Fitness For Purpose 1985, Aim Higher 1989, Higher Education into the 1990s (Jt ed.) 1989, Sharks and Splashes!: The Future of Education and Employment 1991, Profitable Learning 1992, Start Right 1994; poetry (as John Elinger) and various contribs to philological, linguistic and educ. journals. *Address:* 45 Richmond Road, Oxford, OX1 2JJ, England. *Telephone:* (1865) 310800. *Fax:* (1865) 310800 (home).

BALL, James (see Ball, Sir (Robert) James).

BALL, Michael Ashley; British singer; b. 27 June 1962, Bromsgrove; s. of Anthony George Ball and Ruth Parry Ball (née Davies); pnr Cathy McGowan; ed Plymouth Coll., Farnham Sixth Form Coll., Guildford School of Acting; numerous nat. and int. concert tours; co-founder and patron Research into Ovarian Cancer; Variety Club of Great Britain Most Promising Artiste Award 1989, The Variety Club Best Recording Artiste 1998, Theatregoers Club of Great Britain Most Popular Musical Actor 1999. *Theatre appearances include:* Judas/John the Baptist in Godspell (debut), Aberystwyth 1984, Frederick in The Pirates of Penzance, Manchester Opera House 1984, Marius in Les Misérables, London 1985–86, Raoul in The Phantom of the Opera, London 1987–88, Alex in Aspects of Love, London 1989–90, New York (debut) 1990, Giorgio in Passion, London 1996, Alone Together (part of Divas Season), London 2001, Caractacus Potts in Chitty Chitty Bang Bang, London 2002–04, The Woman in White 2005, Hairspray (Olivier Award for Best Actor in a Musical 2008) 2007. *Film:* England My England 1995. *Television:* own TV series 'Michael Ball' 1993, 1994, Royal Variety performances, Michael Ball in Concert (video) 1997, Michael Ball at Christmas 1999; represented UK in Eurovision Song Contest 1992, An Evening with Michael Ball 1998, Lord Lloyd Webber's 50th Birthday 1998. *Recordings include:* albums: Rage of the Heart 1987, Michael Ball 1992, Always 1993, One Careful Owner 1994, The Best of Michael Ball 1994, First Love 1996, Michael Ball – The Musicals 1996, Michael Ball – The Movies 1998, Christmas 1999, Live at the Royal Albert Hall 1999, This Time It's Personal 2000, Centre Stage 2001, Music 2005; stage show cast recordings include Les Miserables 1986, Aspects of Love 1989, West Side Story 1993, Passion 1996, Chitty Chitty Bang Bang 2002. *Leisure interests:* collecting graphic novels and single malt whiskies, country walking, music, theatre. *Address:* c/o Phil Bowdery, Live Nation (Music) UK Ltd, Regent Arcade House, 19-25 Argyll Street, London, W1F 7TS, England. *Telephone:* (20) 7009-3333 (office). *Fax:* (20) 7009-3211 (office). *E-mail:* katie.weston@livenation.co.uk; mbe@michaelball.co.uk (office). *Website:* www.michaelball.co.uk.

BALL, Sir (Robert) James, Kt, MA, PhD, CBIM, FIAM; British economist and academic; *Professor Emeritus of Economics, London Business School;* b. 15 July 1933, Saffron Walden; s. of Arnold James Hector Ball; m. 1st Patricia Mary Hart Davies 1954 (divorced 1970); one s. (deceased) three d. (one d. deceased); m. 2nd Lindsay Jackson (née Wonnacott) 1970; one step-s.; ed St Marylebone Grammar School, Queen's Coll., Oxford, Univ. of Pennsylvania; RAF 1952–54; Research Officer, Univ. of Oxford Inst. of Statistics 1957–58; IBM Fellow, Univ. of Pennsylvania 1958–60; Lecturer, Univ. of Manchester 1960–63, Sr Lecturer 1963–65; Prof. of Econs, London Business School 1984–98, Prof. Emer. 1998–, Deputy Prin. 1971–72, Prin. 1972–84; Dir Barclays Bank Trust Co. Ltd 1973–86, Tube Investments 1974–84, IBM UK Holdings Ltd 1979–95, IBM UK Pensions Trust 1994–; Chair. Legal and General Group PLC. 1980–94, Royal Bank of Canada Holdings (UK) Ltd 1995–98; Dir LASMO 1988–94, Royal Bank of Canada 1990–98; Vice-Pres. Chartered Inst. of Marketing 1991–94; mem. Council British-N American Cttee 1985–98, Research Asscn 1985–, Marshall Aid Commemoration Comm. 1987–94; Econ. Adviser, Touche Ross & Co. 1984–95; Trustee Foulkes Foundation 1984–, Civic Trust 1986–91, The Economist 1987–99, ReAction Trust 1991–93; mem. Advisory Bd IBM UK Ltd 1995–98; Freeman of City of London 1987; Hon. DSc (Aston) 1987; Hon. DSocSc (Manchester) 1988. *Publications:* An Economic Model of the United Kingdom 1961, Inflation and the Theory of Money 1964, Inflation (ed.) 1969, The International Linkage of National Economic Models (ed.) 1972, Money and Employment 1982, The Economics of Wealth Creation (ed.) 1992, The British Economy at the Crossroads 1998, articles in professional journals. *Leisure interests:* chess, fishing, gardening. *Address:* London Business School, Sussex Place, Regent's Park, London, NW1 4SA, England (office). *Telephone:* (20) 7000-8419 (office). *Fax:* (20) 7000-7001 (office). *E-mail:* jball@london.edu (office). *Website:* www .london.edu/economics (office).

BALLADUR, Edouard, LenD; French politician; *Chairman, National Assembly Commission on Foreign Affairs;* b. 2 May 1929, Smyrna, Turkey; s. of Pierre Balladur and Emilie Latour; m. Marie-Josèphe Delacour 1957; four s.; ed Lycée Thiers, Marseilles, Faculté de Droit, Aix-en-Provence, Inst. d'Etudes Politiques, Paris and Ecole Nationale d'Admin; auditor, Conseil d'Etat 1957, Maître des Requêtes 1963; adviser to Dir-Gen. of ORTF 1962–63; mem. Admin. Council of ORTF 1967–68; Tech. Adviser, Office of Prime Minister Georges Pompidou 1966–68; Pres. French soc. for Bldg and Devt of road tunnel under Mont Blanc 1968–81; mem. Admin. Council, Nat. Forestry Office 1968–73; Asst Sec.-Gen. Presidency of Repub. 1969, Sec.-Gen. 1974; Pres. Dir-Gen. Générale de Service Informatique 1977–86; Pres. Compagnie Européenne d'Accumulateurs 1980–86; mem. Conseil d'Etat 1984–88, 1988–; Minister of the Econ., of Finance and Privatization 1986–88; Prime Minister of France 1993–95; Presidential Cand. 1995; Comm. on Foreign Affairs, Nat. Ass. 2002–; mem. Nat. Ass.; Chevalier, Légion d'honneur; Grand-Croix Ordre Nat. du Mérite. *Publications:* l'Arbre de mai 1979, Je crois en l'homme plus qu'en l'Etat 1987, Passion et longueur de temps (with others) 1989, Douze Lettres aux français trop tranquilles 1990, Des Modes et des convictions 1992, Dictionnaire de la réforme 1992, L'Action pour la réforme 1995, Deux ans à Matignon 1995, Caractère de la France 1997, L'Avenir de la différence 1999, Renaissance de la droite, pour une alternance décomplexée 2000. *Address:* Conseil d'Etat, 75100 Paris; Assemblée Nationale, 126 rue de l'Université, 75355 Paris, France.

BALLALI, Daudi T. S.; Tanzanian banking official; m. Anna Muganda; worked for 25 years at IMF, Washington, DC; fmr econ. adviser to Pres. of Tanzania; Gov. and Chair. Benki Kuu Ya Tanzania (Bank of Tanzania) 1998–2008; fmr Chair. Asscn of African Cen. Bank Govs. *Address:* c/o Benki Kuu Ya Tanzania, 10 Mirambo St, POB 2939, Dar es Salaam, Tanzania (office).

BALLANTYNE, Sir Frederick Nathaniel, Kt, GCMG, MD; Saint Vincent and the Grenadines cardiologist and government official; *Governor-General;* b. 5 July 1936; m. Sally Ann Ballantyne; ed Howard Univ. and Syracuse Univ., USA. *Address:* Office of the Governor-General, Government Buildings, Kingstown, Saint Vincent and the Grenadines (office). *Telephone:* 456-1401 (office).

BALLARD, Mark, MA; British consultant, university administrator and fmr politician; *Rector, Edinburgh University;* b. 27 June 1971, Leeds; m. Heather Stacey; one s.; ed Univ. of Edinburgh; with European Youth Forest Action 1994–98; Ed. Reforesting Scotland (journal) 1998–2001; MSP (Green Party) for Lothians 2003–07, mem. Parl. Finance Cttee; fmr consultant for several charities and social enterprises on business devt, promotion and lobbying; Rector Univ. of Edinburgh 2006–; Communications Man. Scottish Council for Voluntary Orgs 2007–; mem. Editorial Bd Scottish Left Review; mem. Friends of the Earth, Sustrans, Campaign for Nuclear Disarmament, Democratic Left Scotland, Reforesting Scotland, Water of Leith Conservation Trust. *Address:* Office of the Rector, Old College, South Bridge, Edinburgh EH8 9YL, Scotland (office). *Telephone:* (131) 650-2160 (office). *E-mail:* rector@ed.ac.uk (office). *Website:* www.rector.ed.ac.uk (office).

BALLARD, Robert D., PhD; American oceanographer; *President, Institute for Exploration;* b. 30 June 1942, Wichita, Kan.; Barbara Earle Ballard; two s. one d.; ed Univs of California, Southern California, Hawaii and Rhode Island; 2nd Lt, US Army Intelligence 1965–67, later transferred to USN 1967–70; served with USN during Vietnam War, Consultant, Deputy Chief of Naval Operations for Submarine Warfare 1984–90, Consultant, Nat. Research Council, Marine Bd Comm. 1984–87, Commdr USNR 1987–2001; Research Assoc. Woods Hole Oceanographic Inst., Cape Cod, Mass. 1969–74, Asst Scientist 1974–76, Assoc. Scientist 1976–83, Sr Scientist 1983–, Founder Deep Submergence Laboratory 1983–, Dir Center for Marine Exploration 1989–95, Emer. 1997–; Visiting Scholar, Stanford Univ. 1979–80, Consulting Prof. 1980–81; Founder and Chair. Jason Foundation for Educ. 1989–; Founder Inst. for Exploration, Mystic, Conn. 1995–, Pres. 1997–; Founder and Pres. Immersion Inst. 2001–; Prof. of Oceanography, URI 2002–; has led or participated in over 100 deep-sea expeditions including discoveries of German battleship Bismarck, RMS Titanic 1985, warships from lost fleet of Guadalcanal, the Lusitania, Roman ships off coast of Tunisia 1997, USS Yorktown 1998; expeditions included first manned exploration of Mid-ocean Ridge, discovery of warm water springs and their fauna in Galapagos Rift, first discovery of polymetallic sulphides; has participated in numerous educ. programmes with major TV networks in Europe, Japan and USA, hosted Nat. Geographic Explorer show 1989–91; Founder Inst. for Archaeological Oceanography, Graduate School of Oceanography, Univ. of Rhode Island 2003; Hon. Dir Explorers Club 1988–; Hon. Dir Sigma Pi Sigma, Physics Soc. 1996–; Dr hc (Clark Univ.) 1986, (Univ. of Rhode Island) 1986, (Southeastern Massachusetts Univ.) 1986, (Long Island Univ.) 1987, (Univ. of Bath, UK) 1988, (Tufts Univ.) 1990, (Lenoir-Rhyne Coll.) 1991, (Skidmore Coll.) 1992, (Worcester Polytechnic Inst.) 1992, (Bridgewater State Coll.) 1993, (Lehigh Univ.) 1993, (Maine Maritime Acad.) 1994, (Massachusetts Maritime Acad.) 1994, (Univ. of Wisconsin) 2000, (Univ. of Hartford) 2001, (Univ. of Delaware) 2001; Distinguished Mil. Grad., US Army 1967, Newcomb-Cleveland Award (American Asscn for the Advancement of Science) 1981, Nat. Geographic Soc. Centennial Award 1988, American Geological Inst. Award 1990, USN Robert Dexter Conrad Award 1992, The Kilby Award 1994, Explorers Medal (Explorers Club) 1995, Nat. Geographic Soc. Hubbard Medal 1996, USN Memorial Foundation Lone Sailor Award 1996, NII Award for Best Internet

Site for Education 1996, American Geophysical Union 'Excellence in Geophysical Education' Award 1997, Commonwealth Award 2000, Lindbergh Award 2001, The Navy League Award Robert M. Thompson Award for Outstanding Leadership 2001, Nat. Humanities Medal 2003; numerous other awards and prizes. *Films:* Secrets of the Titanic (Int. Film Festival Award) 1987, Search for Battleship Bismarck (Emmy Award for Best Documentary) 1990, Last Voyage of the Lusitania (Emmy Award for Best Documentary) 1994. *Publications:* Photographic Atlas of the Mid-Atlantic Ridge 1977, The Discovery of the Titanic (with Rick Archbold) (New York Times and The Times No. 1 Best Seller 1987) 1987, The Discovery of the Bismarck (New York Times and The Times No. 1 Best Seller 1990) 1990, Bright Shark (novel) 1992, The Lost Ships of Guadalcanal (with Rick Archbold) 1993, Explorations (autobiography) 1995, Exploring the Lusitania (with Spencer Dunmore) 1995, Lost Liners (with Rick Archbold) 1997, Return to Midway 1999, The Water's Edge 1999, Eternal Darkness: A Personal History of Deep-Sea Exploration (with Will Hively) 2000, Graveyards of the Pacific 2001, Adventures in Ocean Exploration 2001; non-fiction for children: Exploring the Titanic (Virginia State Reading Asscn Young Readers Award 1993) 1988, The Lost Wreck of the Isis 1990, Exploring the Bismarck 1991, Explorer 1992, Ghost Liners 1998; Deep Sea Explorer (CD-ROM) 1999; has also published more than 57 articles in scientific journals and numerous popular articles. *Leisure interests:* family. *Address:* Institute for Exploration, 55 Coogan Boulevard, Mystic, CT 06355, USA (office). *Telephone:* (860) 572-5955 ext. 602 (office). *E-mail:* lbradt@ife.org (office). *Website:* www.ife.org (office).

BALLE, Francis, DèsSc, PhD; French academic; *Professor, Université de Paris II–Panthéon–Assas;* b. 15 June 1939, Fourmies; s. of Marcel Balle and Madeleine (née Leprohon) Balle; m. Marie Derieux 1972; three d.; ed Inst. d'Etudes Politiques, Univ. de Paris-Sorbonne; philosophy teacher, Ecole Normale d'Oran 1963–65; Asst Lecturer, Faculté des Lettres, Ecole de Journalisme, Algiers 1965–67, Univ. de Paris-Sorbonne 1967–70, Univ. René Descartes, Univ. Paris VI 1970–72; Lecturer, Univ. de Paris II–Panthéon–Assass 1972, Prof. 1978–; Vice-Chancellor Universités de Paris 1986–89; Visiting Prof., Stanford Univ. 1981–83; Pres. statistical Cttee for TV action outside France 1997–; Dir Inst. Français de Presse 1976–86, Inst. de Recherche et d'Etudes sur la Communication 1986–; mem. Conseil Supérieur de l'Audiovisuel 1989–93; Dir Information and New Technologies at Ministry of Nat. Educ. 1993–95, of Scientific Information, Tech. and of Libraries 1995–; Dir French Media Inst. 1997; mem. Conseil d'administration de Radio France 2004–, mem. Fulbright Comm.; Founding Ed. Le Revue Européenne des Médias; Officier, Ordre nat. de la Légion d'honneur 1998, Commandeur 2007, Officier, Palmes académiques; Prize of Acad. des Sciences Morales et Politiques for Médias et Sociétés 1995;. *Publications:* Médias et Sociétés 1980, 2004, The Media Revolution in America and Western Europe 1984, Les nouveaux médias (with Gerard Eymery) 1987, Et si la Presse n'existait pas 1987, La Télévision 1987, Le Mandarin et le marchand 1995, Dictionnaire des médias 1998, Les Médias 2000, Dictionnaire du Web 2002, Les médias, PUF, Que sais-je? 2004, Lexique d'information communication 2006. *Leisure interests:* music, painting. *Address:* Université Panthéon-Assas (Paris II), I.R.E.C., 92 rue d'Assas, 75006 Paris (office); 18 rue Greuze, 75116 Paris, France (home). *Telephone:* 1-55-42-50-31 (office); 1-47-27-78-31 (also fax) (home). *Fax:* 1-43-26-15-78 (office). *E-mail:* balle@u-paris2.fr (office). *Website:* www.u-paris2.fr (office).

BALLESTEROS SOTA, Severiano; Spanish professional golfer; b. 9 April 1957, Pedreña, Santander; s. of Baldomero Ballesteros Presmanes and Carmen Sota Ocejo; m. Carmen Botin Sanz 1988; two s. one d.; professional 1974–2007; won Spanish Young Professional title 1974; 72 int. titles; won Dutch Open and two major European tournaments and, with Manuel Pinero, World Cup 1976; won Opens of France, Switzerland and Japan, four other major tournaments in Europe, Japan and New Zealand and World Cup, with Antonio Garrido 1977; won Opens of Japan, Germany, Kenya, Scandinavia and Switzerland and tournament in USA 1978; British Open Champion (youngest this century) 1979, 1984, 1988; second European and youngest ever winner US Masters 1980; World Matchplay Title 1981, 1982, 1984, 1985; tied Gary Player's record of five victories in World Matchplay with his fifth win 1991; winner US Masters 1980, 1983, Henry Vardon Trophy 1976, 1977, 1978, 1986, Ryder Cup 1979, 1983, 1985, 1987, 1995, 1997 (team captain), British/ Volvo PGA Championship 1983, 1991, Mallorca Open 1988, 1990, 1991, British Masters 1991, Dubai Open 1992, Int. Open 1994, German Masters 1994, Seve Ballesteros Trophy 2000, Royal Trophy 2006, 2007; acted in film Escape to Paradise 1987; mem. Laureus World Sports Acad.; resident of Monaco; Dr hc (St Andrews) 2000; Vardon Trophy 1976, 1977, 1978, 1986, 1988, 1991, Golf Writers Trophy 1979, 1984, 1991, Johnny Walker Golfer Of The Year 1986, 1988, 1991, Príncipe de Asturias Award 1989, BBC Int. Sports Personality of the Year 1984, European Player of the Century 2000, Int. Player Century Award 2001, PGA Recognition Award 2006. *Publications:* Trouble Shooting 1996, Seve: The Official Autobiography 2007. *Leisure interests:* ping-pong, chess, fitness, shooting, reading, music. *Address:* Fairway, SA, Pasaje de Peña 2-4°, 39008 Santander, Spain (office); Houston Palace, 7 Avenue Princess Grace, 39009 Monte Carlo, Monaco (home). *Telephone:* (42) 31-45-12 (Spain) (office). *Fax:* (42) 31-45-59 (Spain) (office). *Website:* www.seveballesteros.com (office).

BALLIN, Ernst Hirsch (see Hirsch Ballin, Ernst).

BALLMER, Steven (Steve) A., BA; American software industry executive; *CEO, Microsoft Corporation;* b. March 1956, Detroit, Ill.; m. Connie Ballmer; three c.; ed Harvard Univ., Stanford Univ. Grad. School of Business; while a student, managed football team, worked on Harvard Crimson newspaper and univ. literary magazine; fmr accountant; Asst Product Man. Procter & Gamble, Vice-Pres. Marketing; Sr Vice-Pres. Systems Software, Microsoft

Corpn, Redmond, WA 1980–, Exec. Vice-Pres. Sales and Support, Pres. 1998, CEO 2000–; Dir Accenture 2001–. *Leisure interests:* exercise, basketball. *Address:* Microsoft Corporation, 1 Microsoft Way, Redmond, WA 98052-8300, USA (office). *Telephone:* (425) 882-8080 (office). *Fax:* (425) 936-7329 (office). *E-mail:* info@microsoft.com (office). *Website:* www.microsoft.com (office).

BALLS, Edward (Ed); British economist and politician; *Secretary of State for Children, Schools and Family;* b. 25 Feb. 1967; s. of Prof. Michael Balls and Carolyn J. Balls; m. Yvette Cooper 1998; one s. two d.; ed Nottingham High School, Keble Coll., Oxford, John F. Kennedy School of Govt, Harvard Univ., USA; Teaching Fellow, Dept of Econs, Harvard Univ. 1989–90; fmr Research Asst Nat. Bureau of Econ. Research, USA; econs leader writer, Financial Times 1990–94; econs columnist, The Guardian 1994–97; Econ. Adviser to Gordon Brown 1994–97; Chief Econ. Adviser to HM Treasury 1999–2004; Research Fellow, Smith Inst. 2004–05; Labour MP for Normanton 2005–, Econ. Sec. to the Treasury 2006–07; Sec. of State for Children, Schools and Family 2007–; Ed. European Econ. Policy 1994–97; mem. Transport and Gen. Workers' Union, Unison, Co-operative Party; Hon. LLD (Nottingham) 2003; Young Financial Journalist of the Year, Wincott Foundation 1992. *Publication:* Reforming Britain's Economic and Financial Policy (co-ed.) 2001, Microeconomic Reform in Britain: Delivering Opportunities for All (co-ed.) 2004. *Address:* House of Commons, Westminster, London, SW1A 0AA, England (office). *Telephone:* (20) 7219-4115 (office). *Fax:* (20) 7219-3398 (office). *E-mail:* sec-of-state.PS@dcsf.gsi.gov.uk (office); ballse@parliament.uk (office). *Website:* www.edballs.com (office).

BALOHA, Viktor; Ukrainian politician; *Chief of the Presidential Secretariat;* b. 15 June 1963, Zavydovo, Mukachev dist, Zakarpatska region; ed Lviv Trade and Econ. Inst.; fmr commodities researcher; Chair. Admin Transcarpathian Oblast 1999–2001, Feb.–Sept. 2005; mem. Verkhovna Rada (Parl.) 2002–05, mem. Our Ukraine party; Mayor of Mukachevo 2004–06; Minister of Emergency Situations 2005–06; Chief of the Presidential Secr. Sept. 2006–. *Address:* Office of the President, 01021 Kyiv, vul. Shovkovichna 12, Ukraine (office). *Telephone:* (44) 226-20-77 (office). *Fax:* (44) 293-61-61 (office). *E-mail:* president@adm.gov.ua (office). *Website:* www.president.gov.ua (office).

BALOI, Oldemiro; Mozambican economist, business executive and politician; *Minister of Foreign Affairs and Co-operation;* Deputy Minister of Co-operation early 1990s; Minister of Industry and Trade and Tourism 1995–2000; active in pvt. business since leaving politics, notably as mem. Bd of Dirs and of Exec. Bd Millennium-BIM (Int. Bank of Mozambique); Minister of Foreign Affairs and Co-operation 2008–. *Address:* Ministry of Foreign Affairs and Co-operation, Av. Julius Nyerere 4, CP 2787, Maputo, Mozambique (office). *Telephone:* 21490222 (office). *Fax:* 21494070 (office). *E-mail:* minec@zebra.uem.mz (office).

BALSAI, István, DIur; Hungarian politician; b. 5 April 1947, Miskolc; s. of József Balsai and Mária Szalontai; m. Ilona Schmidt; two s.; chemical lab. asst 1966; on staff, Faculty of Political and Legal Sciences, Eötvös Loránd Univ., Budapest 1967–72; worked as adviser to Lawyers Asscn, Budapest; mem. Hungarian Democratic Forum 1988; mem. Parl. (Parl. Group of the Magyar Demokrata Fórum (Hungarian Democratic Forum)—MDF) 1990–, Pres. Cttee for Employment and Labour, mem. Cttee on Constitution and Justice, Second Vice-Pres. Hungarian Nat. Group of IPU; Minister of Justice 1990–94; Leader of Legal Cabinet of MDF Parl. Group, 1994–98, Group Leader of MDF 1998–2002; mem. European Parl. (Group of the European People's Party (Christian Democrats) and European Democrats) May–July 2004, mem. Cttee on Constitutional Affairs, Cttee on Petitions; Founding mem. Asscn of Christian Intellectuals 1989–. *Leisure interest:* folk architecture. *Address:* Széchenyi rkp. 19, 1054 Budapest, Hungary. *Telephone:* (1) 441-5139. *Fax:* (1) 441-5978 (office). *E-mail:* istvan.balsai@mdf.parlament.hu (office). *Website:* www.mdf.hu (office).

BALSEMÃO, Francisco Pinto (see Pinto Balsemão).

BALSILLIE, Jim, CA, BCom, MBA; Canadian electronics industry executive; *Co-CEO, Research in Motion Ltd;* b. 1961; ed Univ. of Toronto, Harvard Grad. Business School, USA; trained as accountant and held various positions at Ernst & Young, Toronto, including Sr Assoc., Strategy Consulting Group and Sr Accountant, Entrepreneurial Services Group; Exec. Vice-Pres. and mem. Bd of Dirs Sutherland-Schultz Ltd, Kitchener, Ont. –1992; Chair. Research in Motion Ltd (designer and mfr of wireless products including Blackberry email device), Waterloo, Ont. 1992–2007, Co-CEO 1992–; f. Centre for Int. Governance Innovation (research inst.) 2002; Fellow, Ont. Inst. of Chartered Accountants. *Leisure interest:* triathlete. *Address:* Research in Motion, 295 Phillip Street, Waterloo, ON N2L 3W8, Canada (office). *Telephone:* (519) 888-7465 (office). *Fax:* (519) 888-7884 (office). *Website:* www.rim.net (office).

BALTIMORE, David, PhD; American biologist and university administrator; *President, California Institute of Technology;* b. 7 March 1938, New York, NY; s. of Richard Baltimore and Gertrude Lipschitz; m. Alice Huang 1968; one d.; ed Swarthmore Coll. and Rockefeller Univ.; Postdoctoral Fellow, MIT 1963–64, Albert Einstein Coll. of Medicine, New York 1964–65; Research Assoc., Salk Inst., La Jolla, Calif. 1965–68; Assoc. Prof., MIT 1968–72, Prof. of Microbiology 1972–95, Ivan R. Cottrell Prof. of Molecular Biology and Immunology 1994–97, Inst. Prof. 1995–97; American Cancer Soc. Prof. of Microbiology 1973–83, 1994–97; Dir Whitehead Inst. for Biomedical Research 1982–90; Pres. Rockefeller Univ. 1990–91, Prof. 1990–94; Pres. Calif. Inst. of Tech. 1997–; Pres. Elect AAAS 2006; mem. NIH Advisory Council on AIDS research, Chair. Vaccine Cttee 1997–2002; Eli Lilly Award in Microbiology and Immunology 1971, US Steel Foundation Award in Molecular Biology 1974, Nobel Prize 1975, Nat. Medal of Science 1999, Warren Alpert Foundation Prize 2000, American Medical Asscn Scientific Achievement Award 2002. *Address:* California Institute of Technology, MC 204-31, 1200 East California Boulevard, Pasadena, CA 91125-3100, USA (office). *Telephone:* (626) 395-6301 (office). *Fax:* (626) 449-9374 (office). *E-mail:* baltimo@caltech.edu (office). *Website:* president.caltech.edu (office).

BALTSA, Agnes; Greek singer (mezzo-soprano); b. Lefkas; ed Acad. of Music, Athens and in Munich (Maria Callas Scholarship); opera debut as Cherubino, Frankfurt 1968; debut at Vienna State Opera as Octavian 1970, Salzburg Festival 1970, La Scala, Milan (Dorabella) 1976, Paris Opera and Covent Garden, London (Cherubino) 1976, Metropolitan Opera, New York (Octavian) 1980; mem. Deutsche Oper Berlin 1973–; performs at all maj. opera houses in world and has given concerts in Europe, USA and Japan with Karajan, Böhm, Bernstein, Muti and others; Österreichische Kammersängerin 1980; Deutscher Schallplattenpreis 1983, Prix Prestige Lyrique (French Ministry of Culture) 1984. *Leisure interests:* swimming, fashion. *Address:* c/o Management Rita Schültz, Rütistr 52, 8044 Zurich-Gockhausen, Switzerland.

BALUYEVSKII, Col-Gen. Yurii Nikolayevich; Russian army officer and government official; *Deputy Secretary, Security Council of Russian Federation;* b. 9 Jan. 1947, Trubavets, Drohobych Raion, Lviv Oblast, Ukrainian SSR; ed Leningrad (now St Petersburg) Higher Mil. Command School of Gen. Army, M. Frunze Mil. Acad., Mil. Acad. of Gen. Staff; infantry officer 1970–82; Sr Officer, Operator, and Head of Group Chief Operation Dept of Gen. Staff; First Deputy Commdr of Group, Russian Forces in Caucasus; Deputy Head, Chief Operation Dept of Gen. Staff 1982–2001, First Deputy Chief of Gen. Staff 2001–04, Chief and First Deputy Minister of Defence 2004–08; apptd to Security Council of Russian Fed. 2004, Deputy Sec. 2008–; Order for Service to Motherland in Armed Forces, Order of Audacity; nine medals. *Address:* Security Council of Russian Federation, Moscow, Ipatyevsky per. 4/10, entr. 6, Russia (office). *Telephone:* (495) 206-35-96 (office). *Website:* www.scrf.gov.ru (office).

BALZANI, Vincenzo, Laurea in Chimica cum laude; Italian chemist and academic; *Professor of Chemistry, University of Bologna;* b. 15 Nov. 1936, Forlimpopoli; ed Univ. of Bologna; Asst Prof., Univ. of Bologna 1963–68, Assoc. Prof. 1969–73, Prof. of Chemistry 1973–, Chair. Doctorate in Chemistry Science 2002–, also Dir, Center for the Photochemcail Conversion of Solar Energy 1981–; Asst Prof., Univ. of Ferrara 1968–89; Dir Italian Nat. Research Council /Photochemistry and Radiiation Chemisty Inst. (FRAE) 1977–88; Visiting Prof., Hebrew Univ. of Jerusalem Energy Research Center, Israel 1979; Visiting Prof., Univ. of Strasbourg, France 1990; Dir NATO Science Forum, Taormina 1991; Visiting Prof., Univ. of Leuven, Belgium 1991; Dir ICS School of Photochemistry, Trieste 1993; Visiting Prof., Univ. of Bordeaux, France 1994; mem. Editorial Bd several journals including Nanotechnology 1994–2000, Chemistry European Journal 1995–, Chemical Society Review 1997–98, ChemPhysChem 2000–, Tetrahedron 2003–; mem. Academia Europaea, European Photochemical Asscn, Societa Chimica Italiana; Fellow AAAS, Royal Soc. of Chemistry, Accademia Nazionale delle Scienze del XL, Accademia Nazionale dei Lincei; Dr hc (Univ. of Fribourg) 1989 Univ. of Bologna Miriam Borsari Medal 1960, Italian Chemical Soc. Cannizzaro Gold Medal 1988, Accademia Nazionale dei Lincei Chemistry Award 1992, Porter Medal 2000, French Chemistry Soc. Prix Franco-Italien 2002. *Address:* Dipartimento di Chimica, Università di Bologna, Via Selmi 2, 40126 Bologna, Italy (office). *Telephone:* (51) 209-9560 (office). *Fax:* (51) 209-9456 (office). *E-mail:* vbalzani@ciam.unibo.it (office). *Website:* www.ciam.unibo.it/photochem/balzani.html (office).

BAMBA, Mamadou; Côte d'Ivoirian politician; mem. Parti démocratique de la Côte d'Ivoire—Rassemblement démocratique africain (PDCI—RDA); Minister of State, Minister of Foreign Affairs 2003–06. *Address:* c/o Ministry of Foreign Affairs, Bloc Ministériel, Boulevard, Angoulvand, BP V109, Abidjan, Côte d'Ivoire (office).

BAMBANG YUDHOYONO, Lt-Gen. Susilo, MA; Indonesian politician and head of state; *President;* b. 1949, East Java; m. Ani Herrawati; two s.; ed Indonesian Mil. Acad. and Webster Univ., USA; participated in Operation Seroja (invasion of Timor Leste) and commanded Dili-based Battalion 744 1970s; spent much of mil. career with Kostrad airborne units; mil. training in USA and Europe 1980s–90s; lectured at Army Staff Command Coll . (Seskoad) 1980s; worked in territorial commands in Jakarta and S. Sumatra (Pangdam II/Sriwijaya) mid 1990s; Chief Mil. Observer in Bosnia 1995–96; Chief of the Armed Forces Social and Political Affairs Staff (Kassospol Abri) (renamed Chief of Territorial Affairs (Kaster) Nov. 1998) 1997–2000; retd from active mil. service 2000; Minister of Mines 1999–2000; Co-ordinating Minister for Political Affairs, Security and Social Welfare 2000–04 (resgnd); Pres. of Indonesia Oct. 2004–; UNPKF Medal; Mil. Service medals include Bintang Dharma, Bintang Mahaputera Adipurna, Bintang Republik Indonesia Adipurna. *Address:* Office of the President, Instant Merdeka, Jakarta 10110, Indonesia (office). *Telephone:* (21) 3840946 (office). *Website:* www .presidensby.info (office).

BAMERT, Matthias; Swiss conductor and composer; b. 5 July 1942, Ersigen; m. Susan Exline 1969; one s. one d.; ed studied in Bern and Paris, studied composition with Jean Rivier and Pierre Boulez; asst conductor to Leopold Stokowski 1970–71; Resident Conductor Cleveland Orchestra 1971–78; Music Dir Swiss Radio Orchestra, Basel 1977–83; Prin. Guest Conductor Scottish Nat. Orchestra 1985–90; Dir Musica Nova Festival, Glasgow 1985–90, Lucerne Festival 1992–98; Music Dir London Mozart Players 1993–2000; has appeared with Orchestre de Paris, Rotterdam Philharmonic, Cleveland Orchestra, Pittsburgh Symphony, Montreal Symphony, Royal Philharmonic Orchestra, London, London Philharmonic Orchestra, BBC Philharmonic, City of Birmingham Symphony Orchestra and at BBC Promenade Concerts, London; has toured worldwide; Prin. Conductor and Artistic Adviser Malaysian Philharmonic Orchestra 2005–08; George Szell Memorial Award

1971. *Compositions:* Concertino for English horn, string orchestra and piano 1966, Septuria Lunaris for orchestra 1970, Rheology for string orchestra 1970, Mantrajana for orchestra 1971, Once Upon an Orchestra for narrator, 12 dancers and orchestra 1975, Ol-Okun for string orchestra 1976, Keepsake for orchestra 1979, Circus Parade for narrator and orchestra 1979. *Address:* c/o IMG Artists, The Light Box, 111 Power Road, London, W4 5PY, England (office). *Telephone:* (20) 7957-5800 (office). *Fax:* (20) 7957-5801 (office). *E-mail:* shunt@imgartists.com (office). *Website:* www.imgartists.com (office).

BAMFORD, Sir Anthony (Paul), Kt; British construction executive; b. 23 Oct. 1945; s. of the late Joseph Cyril Bamford and of Marjorie Griffin; m. Carole Gray Whitt 1974; two s. one d.; ed Ampleforth Coll., Grenoble Univ.; joined JCB 1962, Chair. and Man. Dir 1975–; Dir Tarmac 1987–94; Pres. Staffs. Agricultural Soc. 1987–88, Burton-upon-Trent Conservative Asscn 1987–90; Pres.'s Cttee CBI 1986–88; mem. Design Council 1987–89; DL Staffs., High Sheriff Staffs. 1985–86; Chevalier Ordre nat. du Mérite 1989, Commendatore della Repubblica Italiana 1995; Hon. MEng (Birmingham) 1987; DUniv (Keele) 1988; Hon. DSc (Cranfield) 1994; Hon. DBA (Rober Gordon Univ., Aberdeen) 1996; Hon. DTech (Staffordshire) 1998, (Loughborough) 2002; Young Exporter of the Year (UK) 1972, Young Businessman of the Year (UK) 1979, Top Exporter of the Year (UK) 1995. *Leisure interests:* farming, gardening. *Address:* c/o J.C. Bamford Excavators Ltd, Rocester, Uttoxeter, Staffs., ST14 5JP, England.

BAMFORD-ADDO, Joyce; Ghanaian lawyer, judge and politician; *Speaker of Parliament;* b. 26 March 1937, Accra; five c.; called to English Bar 1961, Ghana Bar 1963; practised law 1961–63; Asst State Attorney 1963–65, State Attorney 1965–70, Sr State Attorney 1970–73, Prin. Attorney 1973–76, Chief State Attorney 1976–86, Dir of Public Prosecutions 1986–91; Justice, Supreme Court 1991–2004 (retd); Speaker of Parl. (first woman) 2009–; Ghana Rep. to UN Comm. on the Status of Women 1990, 1991; fmr mem. Ghana Law Reform Comm., Legal Aid Bd, Gen. Legal Council;; Woman of the Year (American Biographical Inst.) 2000. *Address:* Office of the Speaker, Parliament House, Accra, Ghana (office). *Telephone:* (21) 664042 (office). *Fax:* (21) 665957 (office). *E-mail:* clerk@parliament.gh (office). *Website:* www.parliament.gh (office).

BAN, Ki-moon, BA, MPA; South Korean politician, diplomatist and UN official; *Secretary-General, United Nations;* b. 13 June 1944, Eumseong, North Chungcheong; m. Yoo Soon-taek; one s. two d.; ed Seoul Nat. Univ., Kennedy School of Govt, Harvard Univ., USA; early postings include at Embassy in New Delhi, two terms at Embassy in Washington, DC, First Sec., Perm. Observer Mission to UN, New York; fmr Dir UN Div.; Amb. to Austria, also Chair. Preparatory Comm. for the Comprehensive Nuclear Test Ban Treaty Org. (CTBTO) 1999; Dir-Gen. of American Affairs 1990–92; Vice-Chair. South-North Jt Nuclear Control Comm. 1992; Deputy Minister for Policy Planning 1995–96; Nat. Security Adviser to the Pres. 1996–2000; Chef-de-Cabinet to Pres. of UN Gen. Ass. 2001; Vice-Minister 2000, then Foreign Policy Adviser to the Pres.; Minister of Foreign Affairs and Trade 2004–06; Sec.-Gen.-designate UN Oct.–Dec. 2006, Sec.-Gen. 2007–; Order of Service Merit 1975, 1986, Grand Decoration of Honour (Austria) 2001, Grand Cross of Rio Blanco (Brazil) 2002, Gran Cruz del Sol (Peru) 2006; Van Fleet Award, Korea Soc., New York 2005. *Address:* Office of the Secretary-General, United Nations, New York, NY 10017, USA (office). *Telephone:* (212) 963-1234 (office). *Fax:* (212) 963-4879 (office). *Website:* www.un.org/sg (office).

BAN, Shigeru, BArch; Japanese architect and lecturer; *Director, Shigeru Ban Architects;* b. 5 Aug. 1957, Tokyo; ed Southern Calif. Inst. of Architecture and Cooper Union, New York, USA; worked for Arata Isozaki, Tokyo 1982–83; est. Shigeru Ban Architects, Tokyo 1985; Consultant, UNHCR 1995; est. Voluntary Architects Network 1995; Adjunct Prof. of Architecture, Tokohama Nat. Univ. 1995–99, Nihon Univ. 1996–2000; Visiting Prof., Columbia Univ., New York 2000; Prof. of Architecture, Keio Univ. 2001–; Third Kansai Architect Grand Prize, Japan Inst. of Architecture 1996, Japan Inst. of Architecture Best Young Architect of the Year 1997, 18th Tohoku Architecture Prize, Architectural Inst. of Japan 1998, Interior Magazine Best Designer of the Year 2000, World Architecture Awards Best Architecture of the Year in Europe 2001, Matsui Gengo Award 2001, World Architectural Awards Best House of the Year 2002. *Architectural works include:* House of Double Roof 1993, MDS Gallery 1994, Curtain Wall House 1995, Furniture House 1995, Paper Church 1995, Paper Loghouse 1995, Tazawako Station 1997, Wall-less House 1997, 9 Square Grid House 1997, Hanegi Forest 1997, Paper Dome 1998, Ivy Structure House 1998, Japan Pavilion for Expo 2000 Hanover 2000, A Paper Arch, Museum of Modern Art Courtyard, New York 2000, GC Osaka Bldg 2000, Naked House 2000, Day-Care Center 2001, Gymnasium 2001, Paper Art Museum 2002. *Publications include:* Shigeru Ban 1997, Ban Shigeru 1998, Paper Tube Architecture from Kobe to Rwanda 1998, Shigeru Ban—Projects in Progress 1999, Shigeru Ban 2001. *Address:* Shigeru Ban Architects, 5-2-4 Matsubara Ban Building, First Floor, Setagaya, Tokyo 156-0043, Japan (office). *Telephone:* (3) 3324-6760 (office). *Fax:* (3) 3324-6789 (office). *E-mail:* SBA@tokyo.email.ne.jp (office). *Website:* www.dnp.co.jp/millennium/SB/VAN.html (office).

BANDA, Aleke Kadonaphani; Malawi politician and journalist; *President, People's Progressive Movement (PPM);* b. 19 Sept. 1939, Livingstone, Zambia; s. of Eliazar G. Banda and Lilian Phiri; m. Mbumba M. Kahumbe 1961; two s. one d.; ed United Missionary School, Que Que and Inyati School, Bulawayo; Sec. Nyasaland African Congress (NAC), Que Que Branch 1954; Gen. Sec. S. Rhodesia African Students Asscn 1957–59; arrested and detained in Rhodesia 1959, deported to Nyasaland; Founder-mem. Malawi Congress Party (MCP), Sec.-Gen. 1959–73, mem. 1974–; Ed. Nyasaland TUC newspaper Ntendere Pa Nchito and mem. TUC Council 1959–60; Personal Political Sec. to Dr. Hastings Banda 1960–73; Sec. MCP Del. to Lancaster House Conf. resulting in self-govt for Malawi 1960; Sec. to subsequent confs. 1960, 1962; Man. Ed. Malawi News 1959–66; Dir Malawi Press Ltd 1960; Dir-Gen. Malawi Broadcasting Corpn 1964–66; Nat. Chair. League of Malawi Youth and Commdr Malawi Young Pioneers 1963–73; Dir Reserve Bank of Malawi 1965–66; Minister of Devt and Planning 1966–67, of Econ. Affairs (incorporating Natural Resources, Trade and Industry and Devt and Planning) and Minister of Works and Supplies 1967–68, of Trade and Industry (incorporating Tourism, Information and Broadcasting) 1968–69, of Finance and of Information and Tourism 1969–72, of Trade, Industry and Tourism 1972–73; dismissed from Cabinet posts and party 1973, reinstated as mem. party 1974; detained without trial 1980–92; First Vice-Pres. and Campaign Chair. United Democratic Front (UDF) Party 1993–2004; Minister of Finance, Econ. Planning and Devt 1994–97, of Agric. and Irrigation 1997–2000, 2001–03, of Health and Population 2000–01; Pres. People's Progressive Movement (PPM) Jan. 2004–; fmr Chair. Nat. Bank of Malawi. *Leisure interest:* tennis. *Address:* c/o Ministry of Agriculture and Irrigation, PO Box 30134, Capital City, Lilongwe 3, Malawi (office).

BANDA, Joyce, BA; Malawi business executive and politician; *Minister of Foreign Affairs and International Co-operation;* b. 1952, Malemia, Zomba; early career working as sec.; mem. Parl. for Zomba-Malosa constituency; Minister of Foreign Affairs and Int. Co-operation 2006–; mem. United Democratic Front; Chair., Malawi Housing Corpn; mem. Bd Malawi Entrepreneurs Devt Inst., Malawi Polytechnic; Founder and Chair. Nat. Asscn of Business Women 1989, now Exec. Dir; f. Hunger Project, Young Emerging Leader's Network, Joyce Banda Foundation; numerous awards including Africa Prize for Leadership 1997, 100 Heroines Award 1998. *Address:* Ministry of Foreign Affairs and International Cooperation, POB 30315, Capital City, Lilongwe, Malawi (office). *Telephone:* 1789323 (office). *Fax:* 1788482 (office). *E-mail:* foreign@malawi.net (office). *Website:* www.malawi.gov.mw/foreign/foreign.htm (office).

BANDA, Rupia Bwezani; Zambian diplomatist, politician, business executive and head of state; *President;* b. 13 Feb. 1937, Gwenda, Southern Rhodesia (now Zimbabwe); m. Hope Mwansa Makulu 1966; five s.; ed Munali Secondary School, Univ. of Ethiopia, Univ. of Lund, Sweden, Wolfson Coll., Cambridge, UK; UNIP rep. in Europe 1960 to 1964; Amb. to UAR 1965–67, to USA 1967–70; Exec. Chair. Rural Devt Corpn and Gen. Man. Nat. Marketing Bd of Zambia 1970–74; Perm. Rep. to UN, New York 1974–75, Chair. UN Council on Namibia; Minister of Foreign Affairs 1975–76; fmr MP for Munali for many years; Vice-Pres. of Zambia 2006–08, Pres. 2008–; fmr Chair. Chipoza Holdings, Robert Hudson Ltd, Allenwest and Chiparamba Enterprise. *Address:* Office of the President, State House, Independence Avenue, Woodlands, PO Box 30135, Lusaka 10101, Zambia (office). *Telephone:* (1) 266147 (office); (1) 262094 (office). *Fax:* (1) 266092 (office). *Website:* www.statehouse.gov.zm (office).

BANDEEN, Robert Angus, OC, PhD, LLD, DCL, KStJ; Canadian company executive; *President and CEO, Cluny Corporation;* b. 29 Oct. 1930, Rodney, Ont.; s. of John Robert and Jessie Marie (Thomson) Bandeen; m. Mona Helen Blair 1958; four s.; ed Univ. of Western Ontario and Duke Univ., USA; joined Canadian Nat. Railways 1955, Research and Devt Dept 1955–66, Dir of Corporate Planning 1966–68, Vice-Pres. Corporate Planning and Finance 1968–71, Vice-Pres. Great Lakes Region, Toronto 1971–72, Exec. Vice-Pres. Finance and Admin. 1972–74, Pres. 1974–82, CEO 1974–82; Pres. and Chair., Crown Life Insurance Co. 1982–84, Chair. and CEO 1984–85; Pres. Crownx Inc. 1984–85, Vice-Chair. 1985–86; Pres. and CEO Cluny Corpn 1986–; Chair. Bd of Dirs Nat. Challenge Systems Inc.; fmr Chair. Counsel Life Insurance Co., Cytex Inc.; fmr Chancellor Bishop's Univ., Lennoxville, Québec; Gov. Olympic Trust of Canada; Senator Stratford Shakespearean Festival Foundation; Hon. LLD (W Ont.) 1975, (Dalhousie) 1978, (Queens) 1982; Hon. DCL (Bishops) 1978; Salzberg Medal (Syracuse Univ.) 1982. *Address:* Cluny Corporation, 1166 Bay Street, #305, Toronto, Ont., M5S 2X8, Canada. *Telephone:* (416) 922-8238. *Fax:* (416) 928-2729.

BANDERAS, Antonio; Spanish film actor; b. 10 Aug. 1960, Málaga; m. 1st Anna Banderas; m. 2nd Melanie Griffith 1996; began acting aged 14; performed with Nat. Theatre, Madrid for six years. *Films include:* Labyrinth of Passion, El Señor Galíndez, El Caso Almería, The Stilts, 27 Hours, Law of Desire, Matador, Tie Me Up! Tie Me Down!, Women on the Verge of a Nervous Breakdown, The House of Spirits, Interview with the Vampire, Philadelphia, The Mambo Kings, Love and Shadow, Miami Rhapsody, Young Mussolini, Return of Mariaolu, Assassins, Desperado, Evita, The Mask of Zorro 1997, Never Talk to Strangers; Crazy in Alabama (dir), The 13th Warrior, White River Kid (producer), Dancing in the Dark 2000, Malaga Burning (dir) 2000, The Body 2000, Forever Lulu (producer) 2000, Spy Kids 2001, Femme Fatale 2002, Frida 2003, Once Upon a Time in Mexico 2003, Imagining Argentina 2003, Shrek II 2004, The Legend of Zorro 2005, Take the Lead 2006, El Camino de los Ingleses (Summer Rain, Dir) 2006, Bordertown 2007, Shrek the Third (voice) 2007. *Television:* And Starring Pancho Villa as Himself 2003. *Address:* c/o CAA, 9830 Wilshire Boulevard, Beverly Hills, CA 90212, USA; Agents Associés, 201 rue du Faubourg Saint-Honoré, 75008 Paris, France.

BANDIER, Martin, BA, LLD; American lawyer and entertainment business executive; *Chairman and CEO, Sony/ATV Music Publishing;* b. 21 July 1941, New York, NY; m.; three c.; ed Syracuse Univ., Brooklyn Law School; began career with law firm in Manhattan; joined legal dept at LeFrank Organisation, becoming Sr Vice-Pres.; Co-f. Entertainment Co. 1975, Entertainment Music Co. 1985, SBK Entertainment World 1987; Vice-Chair. Thorn EMI 1989–91, CEO EMI Music Publishing 1991–2007, Chair. 1992–2007, mem. Bd of Dirs EMI Group plc 1998–2006; Chair. and CEO, Sony/ATV Music Publishing LLC 2007–; mem. Bd of Dirs United Jewish Appeal, City of Hope, Songwriter's Hall of Fame, Nat. Music Publrs' Asscn, Rock and Roll Hall of Fame; Trustee T.J. Martell Foundation, Syracuse Univ.; mem.

Metropolitan New York Advisory Bd, Nat. Acad. of Recording Arts and Sciences; Abe Olman Publisher Award 1990, Arents Award 1994, Patron of the Arts Award, Songwriters Hall of Fame 2003. *Leisure interests:* playing the piano, golf. *Address:* Sony/ATV Music Publishing LLC, 550 Madison Avenue, Fifth Floor, New York, NY 10022, USA (office). *Telephone:* (212) 833-8000 (office). *Fax:* (212) 833-5552 (office). *E-mail:* info@sonyatv.com (office). *Website:* www.sonyatv.com (office).

BANDLER, Donald K., MA, JD; American diplomatist; *Senior Director, Kissinger McLarty Associates;* m. Jane Bandler; one s. two d.; ed Kenyon Coll., St John's Coll., George Washington Univ.; Dir 'Face to Face', Carnegie Endowment 1978–79; assignments in African Affairs and Congressional relations; Co-ordinator CSCE 1983–85; Head, Political-Mil. Affairs, Paris Embassy 1985–89; Counsellor for Political and Legal Affairs, Bonn 1989–93; Dir Israeli and Arab-Israeli Affairs, Dept of State 1994–95; Deputy Chief of Mission, then Chargé d'affaires, Paris 1995–97; Special Asst to the Pres. and Sr Dir for European Affairs, Nat. Security Council 1997–99; Amb. to Cyprus 1999–2002; Sr Vice Pres., Govt Affairs, Monsanto Co. 2002–04; Sr Dir Kissinger McLarty Assocs 2004–; Légion d'honneur 1998; Superior Honor Award (four times). *Address:* Kissinger McLarty Associates, c/o Kissinger Associates, Inc, 350 Park Avenue, New York, NY 10022, USA (office). *Telephone:* (202) 822-8182 (office). *Website:* www.kmaglobal.com (office).

BANDLER, John William, PhD, DSc (Eng), FIEE, FIEEE, FEIC, FCAE, FRSC; Canadian professor of electrical and computer engineering; *Professor Emeritus, McMaster University;* b. 9 Nov. 1941, Jerusalem; m. 3rd Beth Budd 1990; two d.; ed Imperial Coll. London; Mullard Research Labs, Redhill, Surrey 1966; Univ. of Manitoba 1967–69; McMaster Univ. 1969, Prof. 1974, Prof. Emer. 2000–; Chair. Dept of Electrical Eng, McMaster Univ. 1978–79, Dean of Faculty 1979–81, Dir of Research, Simulation Optimization Systems Research Lab. 1983–; Pres. Optimization Systems Assocs Inc. 1983–97, Bandler Corpn 1997–; ARFTG Automated Measurements Career Award for Automated Microwave Techniques 1994, IEEE Microwave Theory and Techniques Soc. Microwave Application Award 2004. *Publications:* more than 410 papers in journals and books and book chapters. *Address:* Department of Electrical and Computer Engineering, McMaster University, Hamilton, Ont., L8S 4K1, Canada (office). *Telephone:* (905) 525-9140 (office). *Fax:* (905) 523-4407 (office). *Website:* www.sos.mcmaster.ca (office).

BANDURA, Albert, PhD; Canadian psychologist and academic; *David Starr Jordan Professor of Social Science in Psychology, Stanford University;* b. 4 Dec. 1925; ed University of British Columbia and Iowa Univ., USA; Instructor to Prof. of Psychology, Stanford Univ., Calif., USA, 1953–, Chair. Dept of Psychology 1976–77, currently David Starr Jordan Prof. of Social Science in Psychology; Fellow, Center for Advanced Study in the Behavioral Sciences 1969–70; Sir Walter Scott Distinguished Visiting Prof., Univ. of New South Wales, Australia 1988; mem. Bd of Scientific Affairs, American Psychological Asscn 1968–70, mem. Credentials Cttee (Div. 7) 1970, mem. Bd of Convention Affairs 1973, Pres. and Chair. Bd of Dirs 1974, Chair. Council of Reps 1974, Chair. Cttee on Constitutional Issues 1975, Chair. Election Cttee 1975, mem. Comm. on Org. 1978–82; mem. Inst. of Medicine, NAS 1989; Trustee American Psychological Foundation 1975–82; mem. Western Psychological Asscn 1979–82, Chair. Bd of Dirs 1980, Pres. 1980; mem. US Nat. Cttee for the Int. Union of Psychological Sciences 1985–93, Cttee on Int. Affairs of Soc. for Research in Child Devt, 1991–95; Series Ed. on Social Learning Theory 1970–; mem. Editorial Bd Journal of Personality and Social Psychology 1963–77, Journal of Experimental Social Psychology 1967–77, Journal of Experimental Child Psychology 1967–82, Behaviour Research and Therapy 1963–, Journal of Applied Behavior Analysis 1968–72, 1975–78, 1980–81, Behavior Therapy 1970–73, 1989–91, 1992–, Personality: An International Journal 1970–72, Journal of Behavior Therapy and Experimental Psychiatry 1970–, Child Development 1971–77, Journal of Abnormal Psychology 1973, Aggression: An International Interdisciplinary Journal 1974–82, Cognitive Therapy and Research 1977–79, 1982–, Journal of Mental Imagery 1978–, Clinical Behavior Therapy Review 1979–81, Gestalt Therapy: An International Multidisciplinary Journal 1979–, Review of Personality and Social Psychology 1979–85, 1999–, Humboldt Journal of Social Relations 1979–, Psychological Review 1980–82, 1999–, Journal of Cognitive Psychotherapy 1986–, Behaviour Change 1985–, Journal of Anxiety Disorders 1986–91, British Journal of Clinical Psychology 1987–, Annual Review of Psychology 1987–91, Anxiety Stress and Coping 1988–, Psychological Inquiry 1989–, Applied and Preventive Psychology: Current Scientific Perspectives 1991–, Medienpsychologie 1990–2000, Applied Psychology: An International Review 1993–, Social Behavior and Personality: An International Journal 1992–, Media Psychology 1998–; Special Research Fellowship, Nat. Inst. of Mental Health 1969; Guggenheim Fellow 1972; Fellow, American Acad. of Arts and Sciences 1980, Japan Soc. for the Promotion of Science 1982; Hon. Pres. Canadian Psychological Asscn 1999; hon. degrees (Univ. of British Columbia) 1979, (Univ. of Lethbridge) 1983, (Univ. of New Brunswick) 1985, (State Univ. of New York) 1987, (Univ. of Waterloo) 1990, (Freie Universität Berlin) 1990, (Univ. of Salamanca) 1992, (Indiana Univ.) 1993, (Univ. of Rome) 1994, (Leiden Univ.) 1995, (Alfred Univ.) 1995, (Pennsylvania State Univ.) 1999, (Grad. School and Univ. Center, City Univ. of New York) 2002, (Universitat Jaume I) 2002; Distinguished Scientist Award (Div. 12), American Psychological Asscn 1972, Distinguished Scientific Achievement Award, Calif. Psychological Asscn, 1973, Distinguished Contrib. Award, Int. Soc. for Research on Aggression 1980, Distinguished Scientific Contribs Award, American Psychological Asscn 1980, Distinguished Scientist Award, Soc. of Behavioral Medicine, William James Award, American Psychological Soc. 1989, Distinguished Lifetime Contribs Award, Calif. Psychological Asscn 1998, Thorndike Award for Distinguished Contribs of Psychology to Educ., American Psychological Asscn 1999, Lifetime Achievement Award, Asscn for the Advancement of Behavior Therapy 2001, Gold Medal Award for Distinguished Lifetime Contribs to the Advancement of Psychology, American Psychological Foundation 2006. *Publications:* Adolescent Aggression (co-author) 1959, Social Learning and Personality Development (co-author) 1963, Principles of Behavior Modification 1969, Psychological Modeling: Conflicting Theories (ed.) 1971, Aggression: Social Learning Analysis 1973, Social Learning Theory 1977, Social Foundations of Thought and Action: A Social Cognitive Theory 1986, Self-efficacy in Changing Societies (ed.) 1995, Self-efficacy: The Exercise of Control 1997; numerous articles in scientific journals. *Address:* Department of Psychology, Jordan Hall, Bldg 420, 450 Serra Mall, Stanford University, Stanford, CA 94305-2130, USA (office). *Telephone:* (650) 725-2409 (office). *Fax:* (650) 725-5699 (office). *E-mail:* bandura@psych.stanford.edu (office). *Website:* www-psych.stanford.edu (office).

BANERJEE, Milon K.; Indian lawyer; *Attorney-General;* began legal practice in Kolkata in 1955, designated Sr Advocate 1972; Additional Solicitor-Gen. of India 1979–86, Solicitor-Gen. 1986–89, Attorney-Gen. 1992–96, 2004–; Hon. Bencher, Lincoln's Inn, London 2006. *Address:* Office of the Attorney General, Supreme Court of India, Tilak Marg, New Delhi 110 001, India (office). *Telephone:* (11) 3383254 (office). *Fax:* (11) 3782101 (office). *Website:* www.supremecourtofindia.nic.in (office).

BANFIELD, Jillian (Jill) Fiona, BSc, MSc, PhD; Australian scientist and academic; *Professor of Earth and Planetary Science, University of California, Berkeley;* b. 18 Aug. 1959, Armidale, NSW; d. of James E. Banfield and Eve Banfield; m. Perry Smith; two s. one d.; ed Australian Nat. Univ., Johns Hopkins Univ., USA; exploration geologist, Western Mining Corpn 1982–83; Asst Prof., Dept of Geology and Geophysics, Univ. of Wisconsin 1990–95, Assoc. Prof. 1995–99, Prof. 1999–2001, Dept of Chem. 1998–2001; Prof. Dept of Earth and Planetary Science, Univ. of California, Berkeley 2001–, Prof. Dept of Environmental Science, Policy and Man. 2001–, Researcher and mem. geochemistry group, Lawrence Berkeley Nat. Lab.; Assoc. Prof., Mineralogical Inst., Univ. of Tokyo 1996–97, Prof. 1998; John D. and Catherine T. MacArthur Foundation Fellow 1999–2004; John Simon Guggenheim Foundation Fellowship 2000; Distinguished Lecturer, Mineralogical Soc. of America 1994–95, Fellow 1997–; Gast Lecturer, Geochemical Soc. 2000, NSF Earth Science Week Lecturer (Inaugural) 2000, Rosenqvist Lecturer, Norway 2005, Pioneer Lecturer, Clay Minerals Soc. 2005; mem. NAS Bd on Earth Sciences and Resources 2002–05; mem. Mineralogical Soc. of America, Councilor 1997–99, Chair. Roebling Award Cttee 1998, Chair. Mid Career Award Cttee 1998–99, Assoc. Ed. American Mineralogist, Journal of the Mineralogical Society of America 1997–2000; mem. US Dept of Energy, Basic Energy Sciences Geoscience Advisory Cttee; mem. American Soc. for Microbiology; mem. Clay Minerals Soc., Councilor, Student Awards Cttee, Bailey Award Cttee 2000; Geological Soc. of Australia Prize 1978, Award for Outstanding Research, US Dept of Energy 1995, Mineralogical Soc. of America Award 1997, D.A. Brown Medal, ANU 1999, and several other prizes and awards. *Publications:* numerous scientific papers. *Address:* Department of Earth and Planetary Sciences and Department of Environmental Science, Policy and Managment, 128 Hilgard Hall, University of California, Berkeley, CA 94720-4767, USA (office). *Telephone:* (510) 642-3804 (office); (510) 642-5438 (home). *Fax:* (510) 643-9980 (office). *E-mail:* jill@nature.berkeley.edu (office). *Website:* eps.berkeley.edu/~jill (office).

BANGA, M. S.; Indian business executive; *President, Food Division, Unilever PLC;* ed Indian Inst. of Tech., Indian Inst. of Man.; joined Hindustan Lever Ltd (HLL) 1977, various sales and marketing roles, Head of Personal Products Div. 1993–95, Exec. Dir Soaps and Detergents Div. 1995–98, Sr Vice-Pres. Unilever London Hair and Oral Care Divs 1998–2000, Chair. HLL 2000–05, Pres. Food Div., Unilever PLC 2005–. *Address:* Unilever PLC, Unilever House, Blackfriars, London, EC4P 4BQ, England (office). *Telephone:* (20) 7822-5252 (office). *Fax:* (20) 7822-5511 (office). *Website:* www.unilever.com (office).

BANGEMANN, Martin, DJur; German telecommunications executive, lawyer and fmr politician; b. 15 Nov. 1934, Wanzleben; s. of Martin Bangemann and Lotte Telge; m. Renate Bauer 1962; three s. two d.; ed secondary school, Emden and Univs of Tübingen and Munich; mem. Freie Demokratische Partei (FDP) 1963–, Deputy 1969, mem. Regional Exec. Baden-Württemberg FDP 1973–78 (resgnd), mem. Nat. Exec. 1969– (resgnd as Gen. Sec. 1975), Chair. FDP 1985–88; mem. Bundestag 1972–80, 1987–88, European Parl. 1979–84; Minister of Finance 1984–88; EEC (now EU) Commr for Internal Market, Industry, Relations with European Parl. 1989–92, for Industrial Affairs and Tech. 1993–95, for Industrial Affairs, Information and Telecommunications Technologies 1995–99, a Vice-Pres. 1993–95; Dir Telefonica, Madrid 1999, Sr Adviser to Chair. and CEO; Fed. Cross of Merit with Star. *Leisure interests:* philosophy, horticulture. *Address:* c/o Telefonica, Gran Via 28, 28013 Madrid, Spain (office).

BANGURA, Zainab Hawa, BA; Sierra Leone human rights activist and politician; *Minister of Foreign Affairs;* b. (Zainab Sesay), 18 Dec. 1959, Yonibana Chiefdom, Tonkolili Dist, Northern Prov.; ed schools in Magburaka and Freetown; diplomas in the UK on insurance studies and insurance management; apptd Asst Reinsurance Man. Nat. Insurance Co. 1983; f. Women Organized for a Morally Enlightened Nation (WOMEN—first nonpartisan women's political rights org.) 1995; co-f. Campaign for Good Governance 1996; f. Nat. Accountability Group 2001; co-f. Movt for Progress (political party promoting good governance and empowerment of women, youth and the disabled) 2002, nominated Chair., ran as only female cand. in presidential elections May 2002; mem. Steering Cttee World Movt for Democracy; served as Chief Civil Affairs Officer to UN Mission in Liberia; Minister of Foreign Affairs 2007–; fmr Reagan-Fascell Democracy Fellow, The Nat. Endowment for Democracy; Assoc. and Fellow, Chartered Insurance

Inst. (UK) 1991–. *Address:* Ministry of Foreign Affairs, Gloucester Street, Freetown, Sierra Leone (office). *Telephone:* (22) 223260 (office). *Fax:* (22) 225615 (office). *E-mail:* mfaicsl@yahoo.com (office).

BANHAM, Sir John Michael Middlecott, Kt, MA, LLD, DL; British business executive; *Chairman, Johnson Matthey PLC;* b. 22 Aug. 1940, Torquay, Devon; s. of the late Terence Middlecott Banham and of Belinda Joan Banham CBE; m. Frances Favell 1965; one s. two d.; ed Charterhouse, Queens' Coll., Cambridge; with HM Foreign Service 1962–64; Dir of Marketing, Wallcoverings Div., Reed Int. 1965–69; with McKinsey & Co. Inc. 1969, Assoc. 1969–75, Prin. 1975–80, Dir 1980–83; Controller Audit Comm. for Local Authorities in England and Wales 1983–87; Dir-Gen. CBI March 1987–92; Dir Amvescap PLC 1999–; Chair. WestCountry TV Ltd 1992–95, John Labatt Ltd (now Interbrew Ltd) 1992–95, ECI Ventures LLP 1992–, Local Govt Comm. for England 1992–95, Tarmac PLC 1992–2000, Kingfisher 1996–2000, Whitbread PLC 2000–06, Geest PLC 2002–06, Cyclacel Ltd 2002–, Johnson Matthey PLC 2006–; Dir Nat. Westminster Bank 1992–98, Nat. Power PLC 1992–98; Man. Trustee Nuffield Foundation 1988–97; Hon. Treas. Cancer Research Campaign 1991–2002; DL Cornwall 1999; Hon. LLD (Bath) 1987; Hon. DSc (Loughborough) 1989, (Exeter) 1993, (Strathclyde) 1995. *Publications:* Future of the British Car Industry 1975, Realising the Promise of a National Health Service 1977, The Anatomy of Change 1994 and numerous reports for Audit Comm. on educ., social services, housing, etc. 1984–87 and on the economy, skill training, infrastructure and urban regeneration for the CBI 1987–. *Leisure interests:* gardening, walking, music. *Address:* Johnson Matthey PLC, 40–42 Hatton Garden, London, EC1N 8EE (office); Penberth, St Buryan, nr Penzance, Cornwall, England. *Telephone:* (20) 7269-8411 (office). *Fax:* (20) 7269-8478 (office); (1736) 810-722 (home). *E-mail:* sirjohn.banham@westcountrymanagement.co.uk (office); frances@peaver.plus.com (home).

BANI, Father John; Ni-Vanuatu politician; b. 4 July 1941; Pres. of Vanuatu March 1999–2004. *Address:* c/o Office of the President, Port-Vila, Vanuatu.

BANI-SADR, Abolhasan; Iranian economist and politician; b. 1933, Hamadan, W Iran; s. of the Ayatollah Sayed Nasrollah Bani-Sadr; ed Sorbonne and Tehran Univs; supporter of Mossadeq (Prime Minister of Iran 1951–53); joined underground anti-Shah movt 1953; imprisoned after riots over Shah's land reforms 1963; in exile in Paris 1963–79; taught at the Sorbonne; close assoc. of the Ayatollah Ruhollah Khomeini and returned to Iran after overthrow of Shah; Minister of Econ. and Financial Affairs 1979–80; Acting Foreign Minister 1979 (dismissed); Pres. of Iran 1980–81; mem. Supervisory Bd of Cen. Bank of Iran 1979; mem. Revolutionary Council 1979–81 (Pres. 1980–81); fled to France 1981, subsequently formed Nat. Council of Resistance to oppose the Govt (in alliance with Massoud Rajavi, Leader of Mujaheddin Kalq and Abdel-Rahman Ghassemlov, Leader of Democratic Party of Kurdistan, Nat. Democratic Front and other resistance groups), Chair. 1981–84. *Publications:* The Economics of Divine Unity, Oil and Violence, L'espérance trahie 1982 and numerous articles and pamphlets on economics and politics. *Website:* www.banisadr.com.fr.

BANJADE, Yagyamurti; Nepalese lawyer and government official; *Attorney-General;* more than 25 years of legal experience; Attorney-Gen. of Nepal 2006–; mem. Nepal Bar Asscn. *Address:* Office of the Attorney-General, Singh Darbar, Kathmandu, Nepal (office). *Telephone:* (1) 4246860 (office); (1) 4227197 (office). *Fax:* (1) 4227282 (office). *E-mail:* info@attorneygeneral.gov.np (office). *Website:* attorneygeneral.gov.np (office).

BANJO, Ladipo Ayodeji, PhD; Nigerian university administrator and linguist; *Professor Emeritus, University of Ibadan;* b. 2 May 1934, Ijebu-Igbo, Ogun State; s. of the late Ven. and S. A. Banjo; m. Alice Mbamali; two s. two d.; ed Nigerian Coll. of Arts, Science and Tech., Univs of Glasgow and Leeds, UK, Univ. of Calif., Los Angeles, USA, Univ. of Ibadan; Educ. Officer W Nigeria 1960–64 (Sr Educ. Officer Jan.–Oct. 1966); Lecturer, Dept of English, Univ. of Ibadan 1966–71, Sr Lecturer 1971–73, Reader and Acting Head 1973–75, Prof. 1975–97, Head 1981, Dean Faculty of Arts 1977–79, Chair. Cttee of Deans 1978–79, Deputy Vice-Chancellor 1981–84, Vice-Chancellor 1984–91, Prof. Emer. 1997–; Dir Reading Centre 1970–72 (Co-Dir 1966–70); Chair. Int. Panel on English Language, West African Examination Council 1979–85, Advisory Cttee Nat. Language Centre 1980–85; Pres. West African Modern Languages Asscn 1981–; Vice-Pres. Int. Fed. of Languages and Literatures 1985–89, Yoruba Studies Asscn 1985–; J. P. Oyo State 1986–; Pres. and Fellow, Nigerian Acad. of Letters 2000–. *Publications:* Oral English 1971, Letter Writing 1973, Effective Use of English 1976, Developmental English 1985, New Englishes: A West African Perspective (ed. with A. Bamgbose and A. Thomas) 1995, Making a Virtue of Necessity: An Overview of the English Language in Nigeria 1996, In the Saddle: A Vice-Chancellor's Story 1997. *Leisure interests:* music, photography, reading. *Address:* University of Ibadan, PO Box 14341, Ibadan, Oyo State, Nigeria. *Telephone:* (2) 8104863. *Fax:* (2) 8104863. *E-mail:* banjo@ibadan.skannet.com.ng (home).

BANKS, Charles A.; American business executive; b. Greensboro, NC; m.; three c.; ed San Bernardino High School, CA, Hempstead High School, NY, Brown Univ., Providence, RI; active duty, USN 1962–64, rank of Lt, US Naval Reserve 1964–69; joined Peebles Supply Div., Ferguson Enterprises 1967, becoming Gen. Man., Ferguson Herndon and later Regional Man., Southeast Region, Sr Exec. Vice-Pres., Ferguson Enterprises 1987–89, Pres. 1992–2001; mem. Bd, Wolseley PLC 1992, Group CEO 2001–06; mem. Bd of Dirs Bunzl plc, TowneBank/Peninsula; Hon. DrSc (Christopher Newport Univ.). *Leisure interests:* travelling with family, golf, wines. *Address:* c/o Wolseley plc, Parkview 1220, Arlington Business Park, Theale, Reading, RG7 4GA, England (office).

BANKS, Iain Menzies, BA; British writer; b. 16 Feb. 1954, Fife, Scotland; ed Univ. of Stirling; worked as technician, British Steel 1976, IBM, Greenock 1978; writes fiction as Iain Banks and science fiction as Iain M. Banks; Hon. DUniv (Stirling) 1997 (St Andrews) 1997; Hon. DLitt (Napier) 2003; British Science Fiction Asscn Best Novel 1997. *Publications:* as Iain Banks: The Wasp Factory 1984, Walking on Glass 1985, The Bridge 1986, Espedair Street 1987, Canal Dreams 1989, The Crow Road 1992, Complicity 1993, Whit 1995, A Song of Stone 1997, The Business 1999, Look to Windward 2000, Dead Air 2002, Raw Spirit: In Search of the Perfect Dram (non-fiction) 2003, The Steep Approach to Garbadale 2007; as Iain M. Banks: Consider Phlebas 1987, The Player of Games 1988, The State of the Art 1989, Use of Weapons 1990, Against a Dark Background 1993, Feersum Endjinn 1994, Excession 1996, Inversions 1998, The Algebraist 2004, Matter 2008. *Address:* c/o Publicity Department, Time Warner Books UK, Brettenham House, Lancaster Place, London, WC2E 7EN, England. *Telephone:* (20) 7911-8000. *Fax:* (20) 7911-8100. *E-mail:* mail@iainbanks.net. *Website:* www.iainbanks.net.

BANKS, Russell, BA; American writer; b. 28 March 1940, Barnstead, NH; s. of Earl Banks and Florence Banks; m. 1st Darlene Bennett (divorced 1962); one d.; m. 2nd Mary Gunst (divorced 1977); three d.; m. 3rd Kathy Walton (divorced 1988); m. 4th Chase Twichell; ed Colgate Univ. and Univ. of NC at Chapel Hill; fmr teacher of creative writing at Emerson Coll. Boston, Univ. of NH at Durham, Univ. of Ala, New England Coll.; teacher of creative writing, Princeton Univ. 1982–97; Pres. Parl. Int. des Écrivains 2001–; Guggenheim Fellowship 1976; Nat. Endowment for the Arts Fellowships 1977, 1983; Best American Short Stories Awards 1971, 1985, Fels Award for Fiction 1974, O. Henry Awards 1975, St Lawrence Award for fiction 1976, John Dos Passos Award 1985, American Acad. of Arts and Letters Award 1985. *Publications include:* poetry: Waiting to Freeze 1967, 30/6 1969, Snow: Meditations of a Cautious Man in Winter 1974; novels: Family Life 1975, Hamilton Stark 1978, The Book of Jamaica 1980, The Relation of My Imprisonment 1984, Continental Drift 1985, Affliction 1989, The Sweet Hereafter 1991, Rule of the Bone 1995, Cloudsplitter 1998, The Angel on the Roof 2000, The Darling 2004, The Reserve 2008; collected short stories: Searching for Survivors 1975, The New World 1978, Trailerpark 1981, Success Stories 1986; contrib. short stories to magazines and periodicals, including New York Times Book Review, Washington Post, American Review, Vanity Fair, Antaeus, Partisan Review, New England Review, Fiction International, Boston Globe Magazine. *Address:* Steven Barclay Agency, 12 Western Avenue, Petaluma, CA 94952, USA (office); 1000 Park Avenue, New York, NY 10028, USA. *Telephone:* (707) 773-0654 (office). *Fax:* (707) 778-1868 (office). *Website:* www.barclayagency.com (office).

BANKS, Tyra; American model; b. 4 Dec. 1973; d. of Carolyn London; ed Immaculate Heart High School; has modelled since 1991 for Karl Lagerfeld (q.v.), Yves St Laurent, Oscar De La Renta (q.v.), Chanel etc.; featured on covers of Elle, GQ, Sports Illustrated, German Cosmopolitan, Spanish Vogue, Scene, Arena; retd from modeling 2005; f. TYInc. *Video appearances include:* Too Funky by George Michael (q.v.), Black or White by Michael Jackson (q.v.), Love Thing by Tina Turner (q.v.). *Film appearances include:* Black or White 1991, Higher Learning 1995, A Woman Like That (1997, Love Stinks (1999), Love & Basketball (2000), Coyote Ugly (2000, Halloween: Resurrection (2002, Eight Crazy Nights (2002) (voice), Larceny (2004. *Television appearances include:* Inferno (1992, The Apartment Complex (1999, Life-Size (2000); exec. producer America's Next Top Model 2003–; exec. producer and host 'The Tyra Banks Show' (talk show) 2005–. *Publication:* Tyra's Beauty Inside and Out 1998. *Address:* c/o IMG Models, 304 Park Ave South, 12 Floor, New York, NY 10010, USA. *Telephone:* (212) 253-8884. *Fax:* (212) 253-8883. *Website:* tyrashow.warnerbros.com.

BANKS, Victor Franklin, MA; Anguillan politician; *Minister of Finance, Economic Development, Investment and Commerce;* b. 8 Nov. 1947, The Valley; m. Cerise Banks; three c.; ed The Valley Secondary School, Coll. of the Virgin Islands, St Thomas and New School, New York, USA; teacher, The Valley Secondary School 1964–68; Man. Shipping Dept, SARAND, Inc., New York 1974–80; Gov. Liaison Officer, Anguilla 1980–81; elected Deputy to House of Ass. (Anguilla People's Party) for Valley North 1981–84; Minister of Social Services 1981–84; Leader Anguilla Democratic Party 1985–; elected Deputy (Anguilla Democratic Party) for Valley South 1985–; Minister of Finance, Econ. Devt, Investment and Commerce (following formation of coalition govt between Anguilla Democratic Party and Anguilla United Party) 2002–; Pres. Banx Professional Services Ltd 1981–. *Leisure interests:* community work, counselling, political educ., volleyball, squash, handball, duck shooting. *Address:* Ministry of Finance, Economic Development, Investment and Commerce, The Secretariat, The Valley, Anguilla (office). *Telephone:* (264) 497-2545 (office). *E-mail:* ministeroffinance@gov.ai (office). *Website:* www.gov.ai (office).

BANNISTER, (Richard) Matthew, LLB; British broadcasting executive; *Presenter, BBC Radio 5 Live;* b. 16 March 1957; s. of the late Richard Neville Bannister and of Olga Margaret Bannister; m. 1st Amanda Gerrard Walker 1984 (died 1988); one d.; m. 2nd Shelagh Margaret Macleod 1989; one s.; ed King Edward VII School, Sheffield, Nottingham Univ.; Presenter, BBC Radio Nottingham 1978–81; Reporter/Presenter Capital Radio, London 1981–83, Deputy Head News and Talks 1985–87, Head 1987–88; with Newsbeat, BBC Radio 1 1983–85; Man. Ed. BBC Greater London Radio 1988–91, Project Co-ordinator, BBC Charter Renewal 1991–93, Controller BBC Radio 1 1993–96, Dir BBC Radio 1996–98, Head of Production BBC TV 1999–2000; Dir Marketing and Communications Asscn Dec. 2000; Chair. Trust the DJ 2001–; Presenter BBC Radio 5 Live 2002–; mem. Bd Chichester Festival Theatre 1999–. *Leisure interests:* rock music, collecting P. G. Wodehouse first edns. *Address:* Trust the DJ, Units 13–14, Barley Shotts Bus Park, Acklam

Road, London, W10 5YG, England. *Telephone:* (20) 8962-5420. *Fax:* (20) 8962-5455. *E-mail:* contact@trustthedj.com. *Website:* www.trustthedj.com.

BANNISTER, Sir Roger G., Kt, CBE, DM, FRCP; British consultant physician, neurologist, university administrator and fmr athlete; b. 23 March 1929, London; s. of the late Ralph Bannister and of Alice Bannister; m. Moyra Elver Jacobsson 1955; two s. two d.; ed City of Bath Boys' School, Univ. Coll. School, Exeter and Merton Colls, Oxford, St Mary's Hosp. Medical School, London; winner, Oxford and Cambridge Mile 1947–50; Pres. Oxford Univ. Athletic Club 1948; British Mile Champion 1951, 1953, 1954; world record one mile 1954, first sub-four minute mile 1954; Master, Pembroke College, Oxford 1985–93; Hon. Consultant Neurologist, St Mary's Hosp. Medical School, Nat. Hosp. for Neurology and Neurosurgery, London (non-exec. Dir 1992–96), London and Oxford Dist and Region; Chair. St Mary's Hosp. Devt Trust; Chair. Govt Working Group on Sport in the Univs 1995–97; Chair. Clinical Autonomic Research Soc. 1982–84; mem. Physiological Soc., Medical Research Soc. Asscn of British Neurologists; Fellow, Imperial College; Trustee Leeds Castle Foundation 1988–2005, St Mary's Hosp. Medical School Devt Trust 1994–2006; Hon. Fellow, UMIST 1974, Exeter Coll., Oxford 1980, Merton Coll., Oxford 1986, Harris Manchester Coll., Oxford 2007, Brunel Univ. 2008; Hon. LLD (Liverpool) 1972; Hon. DSc (Sheffield) 1978, (Grinnell) 1984, (Bath) 1984, (Rochester) 1986, (Williams) 1987; Hon. MD (Pavia) 1986; Hon. DL (Univ. of Victoria, Canada) 1994, (Univ. of Wales, Cardiff) 1995, (Loughborough) 1996, (Univ. of East Anglia) 1997; Dr hc (Jyvaskylä, Finland); Hans-Heinrich Siegbert Prize 1977. *Publications:* The First Four Minutes (aka Four Minute Mile) 1955, Brain and Bannister's Clinical Neurology (ed.) 1992, Autonomic Failure (co-ed.) 1993; various medical articles on physiology and neurology. *Address:* 21 Bardwell Road, Oxford, OX2 6SV, England. *Telephone:* (1865) 511413.

BANNON, John Charles, BA, LLB; Australian politician; b. 7 May 1943; s. of C. Bannon and Joyce Marion Bannon; m. 1st Robyn Layton 1968 (divorced); one d.; m. 2nd Angela Bannon 1982; ed St Peter's Coll., Univ. of Adelaide; Industrial Advocate, AWU 1969–73; Adviser to Commonwealth Minister of Labour and Immigration 1973–75; Asst Dir S Australian Dept of Labour and Industry 1975–77; mem. House Ass. 1977–93; Minister for Community Devt, Minister for Local Govt, Minister for Recreation and Sport 1978–79; Leader of the Opposition 1979–82; Premier and Treasurer of S Australia, Minister of State Devt and Minister for the Arts 1982–85; Premier and Treasurer of S Australia and Minister for the Arts 1985–89; Premier and Treasurer of S Australia 1982–92; Nat. Pres. Australian Labour Party 1988–91; Dir Australian Broadcasting Corpn 1994–2000, Adelaide Symphony Orchestra Bd 1997–; mem. Council Constitutional Centenary Foundation 1995– (Chair. 1996–); Master St Mark's Coll., Adelaide 2000–; Ed. The New Federalist (Nat. Journal of Australian Fed. History) 1998. *Publications:* The Crucial Colony 1994; articles, monographs on Fed./State relations. *Leisure interests:* running, gardening. *Address:* PO Box 323, Rundle Mall, Adelaide, South Australia 5000, Australia.

BANNY, Charles Konan; Côte d'Ivoirian central banker and economist; *Governor, Central Bank of West African States;* b. 11 Nov. 1942, Divo; m.; four c.; ed Ecole Supérieure des Sciences Economiques et Commerciales, Paris; served as Chargé de Mission, Stabilisation and Support Fund of Agric. Product Prices; Deputy Sec.-Gen. Inter-African Coffee Org., Paris 1970, Sec.-Gen. 1971; Dir of Admin. and Social Affairs, Cen. Bank of West African States (BCEAO) 1976, later Cen. Dir of Securities, Investment, Borrowing and Lending, then Cen. Dir of Research, apptd Nat. Dir of BCEAO for Côte d'Ivoire 1983, Gov. BCEAO 1994–; interim Prime Minister 2005–07. *Address:* Banque centrale des Etats de l'Afrique de l'Ouest, Avenue Abdoulaye Fadiga, B.P. 3108, Dakar, Senegal (office). *Website:* www.bceao.int.

BANVILLE, John; Irish writer; b. 8 Dec. 1945, Wexford; m. Janet Dunham; two s.; ed St Peter's Coll., Wexford; fmrly night copy ed., The Irish Times, Literary Ed. 1988–99, Chief Literary Critic and Assoc. Literary Ed. 1999–2002; Lannan Foundation Award 1998. *Film script:* The Last September 1998. *Plays:* The Broken Jug (after Kleist) 1994, God's Gift (after Kleist's 'Amphitryon') 2000. *Publications include:* novels: Nightspawn 1971, Birchwood 1973, Dr Copernicus 1976, Kepler 1983, The Newton Letter 1985, Mefisto 1987, The Book of Evidence (Guinness Peat Aviation Prize 1989) 1989, Ghosts 1993, Athena 1995, The Untouchable 1996, Eclipse 2000, Shroud 2003, The Sea (Man Booker Prize, Irish Novel of the Year) 2005; as Benjamin Black: Christine Falls 2006, The Silver Swan 2007, The Lemur 2008; non-fiction: Prague Pictures: Portraits of a City 2003; contrib. to New York Review of Books, Irish Times, Guardian, New Republic. *Address:* c/o Ed Victor Ltd, 6 Bayley Street, Bedford Square, London, WC1B 3HE, England (office). *Telephone:* (20) 7304-4100 (office). *Fax:* (20) 7304-4111 (office).

BAO, Wenkui; Chinese agronomist; *Director, Institute of Crop Breeding and Cultivation;* b. 8 May 1916; ed Xiaoshi High School; Calif. Inst. of Tech., USA; began career as Graduate Asst, Nat. Rice and Wheat Improvement Inst., Sichuan Prov.; Prof. Chengdu Univ. 1950; Prof., Chinese Acad. of Agricultural Sciences; Deputy, 5th NPC 1978–83; Dir Inst. of Crop Breeding and Cultivation, Beijing 1981–; Deputy, 6th NPC 1983–88; mem. Dept of Biology, Academia Sinica 1982–. *Address:* Chinese Academy of Agricultural Sciences, Baishiqiao Road, Haidian, Beijing 100081, People's Republic of China.

BAO, Xuding; Chinese government official and business executive; *President, China International Engineering Consulting Corporation;* b. Feb. 1939, Wuxi City, Jiangsu Prov.; ed Shenyang School of Machine Industry, CCP Cen. Party School; joined CCP 1961; Deputy Dir then Dir City Machine Building Industry Bureau, Sichuan Prov. 1986; Dir Sichuan Prov. Econ. Planning Comm. 1986; Vice-Minister of Machine Building and Electronics Industries 1990–93; Vice-Minister of Machine Building Industry 1993–96, Minister 1996–98; Vice-Minister State Devt and Reform Comm. 1998–99; Deputy Sec. CCP Municipal Cttee, Chongqing 1999; Deputy Mayor of Chongqing 1999–2000, Mayor 2000–02; mem. 15th CCP Cen. Cttee 1997–2002; mem. 10th CPPCC Nat. Cttee 2003–; Pres. China Int. Engineering Consulting Corpn 2002–. *Address:* China International Engineering Consulting Corporation, 32 Che Gong Zhuang Xilu, 100044 Beijing, People's Republic of China. *E-mail:* ciecc@ciecc.com.cn. *Website:* www.ciecc.com.cn.

BAPTISTA NETO, Clovis José; Brazilian engineer and international organization executive; *Executive Secretary, Inter-American Telecommunication Commission (Comisión Interamericana de Telecomunicaciones—CITEL);* ed Pontifical Catholic University of Rio de Janeiro; held several sr positions with EMBRATEL (telecommunications operator) 1974–95; held several key positions with Ministry of Communications; fmr Head of Int. Affairs, Brazilian Telecommunications Regulatory Agency, ANATEL; currently Exec. Sec. Inter-American Telecommunication Comm. (Comisión Interamericana de Telecomunicaciones—CITEL), Washington, DC 2000–; participant in confs and int. meetings of ITU, CITEL and WTO, among others; represents OAS at Hemispheric Advisory Bd Inst. for Connectivity in the Americas (Govt-supported Canadian org.). *Address:* Inter-American Telecommunication Commission (CITEL), 1889 F Street, NW, Washington, DC 20006, USA (office). *Telephone:* (202) 458-3004 (office). *Fax:* (202) 458-6854 (office). *E-mail:* citel@oas.org (office). *Website:* www.citel.oas.org (office).

BAQUET, Dean Paul; American journalist and editor; *Assistant Managing Editor and Washington Bureau Chief, New York Times;* b. 21 Sept. 1956, New Orleans; s. of Edward Joseph Baquet and Myrtle (née Romano) Baquet; m. Dylan Landis 1986; one s.; ed Columbia Univ., New York; investigative reporter, New Orleans 1978–84; investigative reporter, Chicago Tribune 1984–87, Chief Investigative Reporter 1987–90; investigative reporter, New York Times 1990–92, Projects Ed. 1992–95, Deputy Metropolitan Ed. 1995, Nat. Ed. 1995–2000, Asst Man. Ed. and Washington Bureau Chief 2007–; Man. Ed. Los Angeles Times 2000–05, Ed. 2005–06; mem. Bd of Dirs Cttee to Protect Journalists; Pulitzer Prize for Investigative Reporting 1988. *Address:* New York Times, 1627 Eye Street, NW, 7th Floor, Washington, DC 20006, USA (office). *Telephone:* (202) 862-0300 (office). *Fax:* (202) 862-0340 (office). *Website:* www.nytimes.com (office).

BAR-ON, Ronnie; Israeli politician and lawyer; b. 1948, Tel-Aviv; m.; three c.; ed Hebrew Univ., Jerusalem; completed mil. service with of Lt-Col, served as judge, Mil. Court of Appeals in Judea, Samaria, Gaza; mem. Cen. Cttee of Israel Bar 1995–2003, also served as mem. Jerusalem Regional Cttee of Israel Bar, Council for the Admin. Courts, Advisory Comm. to the Govt Cos Authority, Public Defenders Comm.; elected to 16th Knesset (parl.) 2003, re-elected 2006; Minister of Nat. Infrastructures and Minister of Science and Tech., January–May 2006, of the Interior 2006–07, of Finance 2007–09; mem. Kadima Party. *Address:* c/o Kadima, Petach Tikva, Tel-Aviv, Israel (office).

BARADEI, Mohammad Mostafa el-, BL, DEA, PhD; Egyptian international organization official and diplomatist; *Director-General, International Atomic Energy Agency;* b. 1942, Cairo; m. Aida el-Kachef; one s. one d.; ed Univ. of Cairo, Grad. Inst. of Int. Studies, Geneva, Switzerland, New York Univ., USA; with Egyptian Ministry of Foreign Affairs, Dept of Int. Orgs 1964–67; mem. Perm. Mission to UN, New York 1967–71; Sr Fellow, Center for Int. Studies, New York Univ. 1973–74; Special Asst to Foreign Minister, Ministry of Foreign Affairs 1974–78; mem. Perm. Mission to UN, Geneva and Alt. Rep. Cttee on Disarmament 1978–80; Sr Fellow and Dir Int. Law and Orgs Programme, UN Inst. for Training and Research, New York 1980–84; Adjunct Prof. of Int. Law, New York Univ. 1981–87; Rep. of Dir-Gen. of IAEA to UN, New York 1984–87, Legal Adviser, then Dir Legal Div., IAEA, Vienna 1987–91, Dir of External Relations 1991–93, Asst Dir-Gen. for External Relations 1993–97, Dir-Gen. IAEA 1997– (re-appointed for third term 2005); mem. Int. Law Asscn, American Soc., of Int. Law, Nuclear Law Asscn; Hon. Patron Trinity's Univ. Philosophical Soc. 2006; Greatest Nile Collar (highest Egyptian civilian decoration); Dr hc (New York Univ., Univ. of Maryland, American Univ., Cairo, Free Mediterranean Univ. (LUM), Bari, Italy, Soka Univ. of Japan, Tsinghua Univ., Beijing, Polytechnic Univ., Bucharest, Universidad Politecnica de Madrid, Konkuk Univ., Seoul, Univ. of Florence, Univ. of Buenos Aires, Nat. Univ. of Cuyo, Argentina, Amherst Coll., Cairo Univ.); Nobel Peace Prize (jt winner with the IAEA) 2005, Franklin D. Roosevelt Four Freedoms Award 2006, James Park Morton Interfaith Award, Golden Plate Award, American Acad. of Achievement, Jit Trainor Award, Georgetown Univ., Human Security Award, Muslim Public Affairs Council, Prix de la Fondation, Crans Montana Forum, El Athir Award (Algeria's highest nat. distinction), Golden Dove of Peace Prize, Pres. of Italy, Award for Distinguished Contrib. to the Peaceful Worldwide Use of Nuclear Tech., World Nuclear Asscn 2007, Mostar Int. Peace Award, Mostar Center for Peace and Multiethnic Cooperation 2007, Peacebuilding Award, EastWest Inst. 2008, Int. Seville NODO Prize for Peace, Security and Inter-Cultural Dialogue 2008, Indira Gandhi Prize for Peace, Disarmament and Devt 2009. *Publications:* The International Law Commission: The Need for a New Direction 1981, Model Rules for Disaster Relief Operations 1982, The Role of International Atomic Energy Agency Safeguards in the Evolution of the Non-Proliferation Regime 1991, The International Law of Nuclear Energy 1993, On Compliance with Nuclear Non-Proliferation Obligations (Security Dialogue) 1996, and articles in int. law journals. *Address:* International Atomic Energy Agency, PO Box 100, Wagramerstrasse 5, 1400 Vienna, Austria (office). *Telephone:* (1) 26000 (office). *Fax:* (1) 26007 (office). *E-mail:* official.mail@iaea.org (office). *Website:* www.iaea.org (office).

BARAK, Lt-Gen. Ehud; Israeli politician, fmr army officer and business executive; *Deputy Prime Minister and Minister of Defence;* b. 12 Feb. 1942, Israel; s. of Israel Brog and Esther Brog; m. Nava Cohen; three d.; ed Hebrew

Univ. Jerusalem and Stanford Univ. Calif.; enlisted in Israeli Defence Force (IDF) 1959; grad. Infantry Officers' course 1962; commando course, France 1963; Armoured Corps Co. Commdrs. course 1968; various command roles; also served in operations br. of Gen. Staff; active service in Six Day War 1967 and Yom Kippur War 1973; Commdr Tank Commdrs' course 1974; Head, Gen. Staff Planning Dept 1982–83; Dir IDF Mil. Intelligence 1983–86; Commdr Cen. Command 1986–87; Deputy Chief of Gen. Staff Israeli Defence Force 1987–91, Chief of Gen. Staff 1991–94; Minister of Interior July–Nov. 1995, of Foreign Affairs 1995–1996; Chair. Israel Labour Party 1997–2001, 2007–; Prime Minister of Israel 1999–2001; Deputy Prime Minister and Minister of Defence 2007–; mem. Knesset (Parl.) and of Parl. Security and Foreign Affairs Cttee 1996; Chair. Barak & Assocs LLC; most decorated soldier in history of IDF. *Leisure interest:* playing the piano. *Address:* Ministry of Defence, Kaplan St, Hakirya, Tel-Aviv 67659 (office); Israel Labour Party, PO Box 62033, Tel-Aviv 61620 (office). *Telephone:* 3-5692010 (Ministry) (office); 3-6899444 (Labour Party) (office). *Fax:* 3-6916940 (Ministry) (office); 3-6899420 (Labour Party) (office). *E-mail:* public@mod.gov.il (office); inter@havoda.org.il (office). *Website:* www.mod.gov.il (office); www.havoda.org.il (office).

BARAKAT, Nayel, PhD, FInstP; Egyptian physicist and academic; *Professor Emeritus of Experimental Physics, Ain Shams University;* b. 22 Sept. 1922, Cairo; s. of M. H. Barakat Bey and N el Safty; m. Afaf Ali Nada 1956; one s. two d.; ed Univs. of Cairo and London; lecturer, Alexandria Univ. 1951–54; lecturer, Ain Shams Univ. 1954–58, Asst Prof. 1958–64, Prof. of Experimental Physics 1964–88, Prof. Emer. 1988–, Dean, Faculty of Science 1971–76; Cultural Counsellor and Dir of Educ. Mission in FRG, Netherlands and Denmark 1976–81; Hon. DSc (London) 1992; Egyptian Nat. Award in Physics 1958, 1963; Nat. Award in Basic Science 1990. *Publications:* 85 papers in specialized journals. *Leisure interests:* Arabic and classical music, photography. *Address:* 4 Ibn Marawan Street, Appt 504, Dokki, Cairo, Egypt. *Telephone:* 3484568.

BARAM, Uzi; Israeli politician; b. 1937, Jerusalem; co-f. Labour Party's Young Guard, Sec. 1966–70; Chair. Young Leadership Dept, World Zionist Org. 1972–75; Chair. Labour Party (Jerusalem br.) 1975–81, Sec.-Gen. 1984–88; Chair. Immigration and Absorption Cttee 1984–92; Minister of Tourism 1992–96, fmrly of Religious Affairs; mem. Knesset 1977–, Foreign Affairs and Defence Cttee. *Address:* c/o Ministry of Foreign Affairs, Hakirya, Romema, Jerusalem 91950, Israel.

BARAMIDZE, Giorgi; Georgian politician; *Vice Prime Minister and State Minister, responsible for European and Euro-Atlantic Integration;* b. 1968, Tbilisi; m. Eka Jafaridze; one d.; ed Polytechnic Inst. of Georgia, George C. Marshall Center for European Security Studies, Germany; Founding mem. Green Party of Georgia 1990; commanded state centre responsible for the search for the missing and for freeing prisoners during war in Abkhazia 1992–93; Chair. Comm. for the Protection of Human Rights and Nat. Minorities 1992–94; mem. Parl. 1992–, Chair. Anti-Corruption Comm. 1996–98, Chair. Defence and Security Cttee 2000–03; Founding mem. Citizen's Union of Georgia 1995, Chair. Parl. Group 1996–98; Research Assoc., Georgetown Univ., Washington, DC, USA 1998–99; Minister of Internal Affairs 2003–04, of Defence June–Dec. 2004; State Minister, responsible for European and Euro-Atlantic Integration 2004–, Deputy Prime Minister 2006–; Cross of Commdr, Order for Merits to Lithuania 2006. *Address:* Office of the Deputy Prime Minister, 0134 Tbilisi, P. Ingorovka 7, Georgia (office). *Telephone:* (32) 93-28-67 (office). *Fax:* (32) 93-27-22 (office). *E-mail:* irinaemikideo@yahoo.com (office). *Website:* www.eu-nato.gov.ge (office).

BARAŃCZAK, Stanisław, PhD; Polish poet, translator, literary critic and academic; *Alfred Jurzykowski Professor of Polish Language and Literature, Harvard University;* b. 13 Nov. 1946, Poznań; m.; one s. one d.; ed Adam Mickiewicz Univ., Poznań; on staff, Nurt magazine, Poznań 1967–71; Asst Lecturer, later Prof., Adam Mickiewicz Univ. 1969–80; Co-Founder Committee for the Defence of the Workers (and of clandestine quarterly Zapis) 1976; in the USA 1981–; Prof. of Slavic Languages and Literatures, Harvard Univ. 1981–84, Alfred Jurzykowski Prof. of Polish Language and Literature 1984–; Co-Founder and Co-Ed. Zeszyty Literackie, Paris 1983–; Assoc. Ed. The Polish Review 1986–87, Ed.-in-Chief 1987–90; mem. American Asscn for Polish-Jewish Studies, American Asscn for Advancement of Slavic Studies, PEN Polish Center, Polish Inst. of Arts and Sciences in America, Polish Writers' Asscn, Union of Polish Authors, Union of Polish Writers Abroad; Chivalric Cross of the Order of Polonia Restituta 1991; Alfred Jurzykowski Foundation Literary Award 1980, Guggenheim Fellowship 1989, Terrence Des Pres Poetry Prize 1989, Special Diploma for Lifetime Achievement in Promoting Polish Culture Abroad, Polish Minister of Foreign Affairs 1993, Co-Winner PEN Best Trans. Award 1996. *Publications:* poetry collections: Korekta twarzy (Face Correction) 1968, Jednym tchem (In One breath) 1970, Dziennik poranny (Morning Diary) 1972, Sztuczne oddychanie (Breathing Underwater) 1974, Ja wiem, że to niesłuszne (I know That It's Wrong) 1977, Atlantyda (Atlantis) 1986, Widokówka z tego świata (A Postcard from This World) 1988, The Weight of the Body 1989, Podróż zimowa (Winter Journey) 1994, Zimy i podroze (Winter and Journeys) 1997, Chirurgiczna precyzja (Surgical Precision) (Nike Prize 1999) 1998; criticism includes: Ironia i Harmonia (Irony and Harmony) 1973, Etyka i poetyka (Ethics and Poetry) 1979, Przed i po (Before and After) 1988, Tablica z Macondo (Board from Macondo) 1990, Ocalone w tłumaczeniu (Saved in Translation) 1992, Fioletowa krowa (Violet Cow) 1993, Poezja i duch h uogólnienia. Wybor esejow 1970–1995 (Poetry and the Spirit of Generalization: Selected Essays) 1996; essays: Breathing Under Water and Other East European Essays 1990; numerous trans of English, American and Russian poetry and of William Shakespeare, including A Fugitive From Utopia: The Poetry of Zbigniew Herbert 1987, The Weight of the Body:

Selected Poems 1989, Panorama der polnischen Literatur des 20. Jahrhunderts (in German) 1997, Polnische Lyrik aus 100 Jahren (in German) 1997; regular contrib. to Teksty Drugie. *Address:* Department of Slavic Languages and Literatures, Barker Center 374, 12 Quincy Street, Cambridge, MA 02138 (office); 8 Broad Dale, Newton Wille, MA 02160, USA. *Telephone:* (617) 495-4065 (office). *Fax:* (617) 496-4466 (office). *E-mail:* barancz@fas.harvard.edu (office). *Website:* www.fas.harvard.edu/~slavic/newsite/main/main.htm (office).

BARBA, Eugenio, MA; Danish theatre director; b. 29 Oct. 1936, Brindisi, Italy; s. of Emanuele Barba and Vera Gaeta; m. Judith Patricia Howard Jones 1965; two s.; ed Univ. of Oslo, Theatre School, Warsaw and Jerzy Grotowski's Theatre Lab. Opole; Founder and Dir Odin Teatret (Interscandinavian Theatre Lab.) 1964–; more than 35 productions 1965–; Founder and Dir Int. School of Theatre Anthropology 1979–; mem. Bd of Advisers, Int. Cttee Théâtre des Nations 1975–80; mem. Bd of Advisers, Int. Asscn of Performing Arts Semiotics 1981–85; adviser, Danish Ministry of Culture 1981–82; UNESCO adviser, Centro de Estudios Teatrales, Museo de Arte Moderno, Bogotá 1983; adviser, Centre of Theatre Exchanges, Rio de Janeiro 1987–; mem. Bd of Advisers, Int. Comparative Literature Asscn 1998; lectures regularly at univs, theatre schools, etc.; Dr hc (Århus) 1988, (Ayacucho) 1998, (Bologna) 1998, (Havana) 2002, (Warsaw) 2003, (Plymouth) 2005, (Hong Kong) 2006; Danish Acad. Award 1980, Mexican Theatre Critics' Prize 1984, Diego Fabbri Prize 1986, Pirandello Int. Prize 1996, Reconnaissance de Mérite Scientifique (Montreal) 1999, Sonning Prize 2000. *Publications include:* In Search of a Lost Theatre 1965, The Floating Islands 1978, Il Brecht dell' Odin 1981, La Corsa dei Contrari 1981, Beyond the Floating Islands 1985, The Dilated Body 1985, Anatomie de l'Acteur (with N. Savarese) 1988, Brechts Aske, Oxyrhincus Evangeliet (two plays) 1986, The Secret Art of the Performer 1990, The Paper Canoe 1992, Theatre – Solitude, Craft, Revolt 1996, Land of Ashes and Diamonds 1999, Arar el cielo 2002; numerous articles, essays etc. *Address:* Nordisk Teaterlaboratorium, Odin Teatret, Box 1283, 7500 Holstebro, Denmark (office). *Telephone:* (45) 97-42-47-77 (office). *Fax:* (45) 97-41-04-82 (office). *E-mail:* odin@odinteatret.dk (office). *Website:* www.odinteatret.dk (office).

BARBARIN, HE Cardinal Philippe Xavier Ignace, MA, PhD; French ecclesiastic; *Archbishop of Lyon;* b. 17 Oct. 1950, Rabat, Morocco; ed Sorbonne, Paris and Institut Catholique, Paris; ordained priest of Créteil 1977; priest in parishes of Notre-Dame d'Alfortville and Notre-Dame de Vincennes 1977–85, St Hilaire de la Varenne 1985–90; asst, Parish of St François de Sales, d'Adamville, St-Maur; Chaplain of St-Maur secondary school 1985–90; Pastor of St Léger Parish, Boissy St Léger 1991–94; Fidei donum priest and Prof. of Theology, Sr Seminary of Vohitsoa, Fianarantsoa, Madagascar 1994–98; Pastor, Bry-sur-Marne, Créteil; Bishop of Moulins 1998; Archbishop of Metropolitan See of Lyon and Primate of Gaul 2002–; cr. Cardinal-Priest of SS. Trinità al Monte Pincio 2003–; Chevalier Légion d'honneur 2002. *Address:* Archdiocese of Lyon, 1 Place de Fourviere, 69321 Lyon, Cedex 05, France (office). *Telephone:* (4) 72-38-80-90 (office). *Fax:* (4) 78-36-06-00 (office). *E-mail:* archeveche.de.lyon@wanadoo.fr (office). *Website:* catholique-lyon.cef.fr (office).

BARBENEL, Joseph Cyril, PhD, FRSE; British bioengineer and academic; *Emeritus Professor, University of Strathclyde;* b. 2 Jan. 1937, London; s. of Tobias Barbenel and Sarah Barbenel; m. Lesley Mary Hyde Jowett 1964; two s. one d.; ed Hackney Downs Grammar School, London, London Hosp. Dental School, Univ. of London, Queen's Coll., Univ. of St Andrews, Univ. of Strathclyde, Glasgow; Dental House Surgeon, London Hosp. 1960; Royal Army Dental Corps 1960–62; gen. dental practice, London 1963; Lecturer, Dental Prosthetics, Univ. of Dundee 1967–69; Lecturer, Univ. of Strathclyde 1970, Sr Lecturer, Bioengineering Unit 1970–82, Reader 1982–85, Prof. 1985–2001, Head Dept 1992–98, Vice-Dean (Research) Faculty of Eng 1997–2001, Prof. Emer. 2001–; Vice-Pres. (Int. Affairs) IPEM; Consulting Prof., Chongqing Univ., China 1986–; Chair. Constitution and Bylaws Cttee, Int. Fed. of Medical and Biological Eng; mem. Admin. Cttee, Int. Union for Physics and Eng Science in Medicine; mem. Council, Chair. (Div. of Socs); Founding Fellow European Alliance for Medical, Biological Eng and Science; Nuffield Foundation Award 1963–66, Pres.'s Medal, Soc. of Cosmetic Scientists 1994, European Pressure Ulcer Advisory Panel Lifetime Achievement Award 2002. *Publications:* Clinical Aspects of Blood Rheology (with Lowe and Forbes) 1981, Pressure Sores (with Lowe and Forbes) 1983, Blood Flow in Artificial Organs and Cardiovascular Prostheses (with co-eds) 1988, Blood Flow in the Brain (with co-eds) 1988, numerous scientific papers. *Leisure interests:* music, theatre, reading. *Address:* Royal College Building, University of Strathclyde, Glasgow, G1 1XW (office); 151 Maxwell Drive, Glasgow, G41, Scotland (home). *Telephone:* (141) 427-0765 (home). *E-mail:* jcbarbenel@btinternet.com (home); j.c.barbenel@strath.ac.uk (office).

BARBER, Brendan; British trade union official; *General Secretary, Trades Union Congress;* b. 3 April 1951, Merseyside; m; two d.; taught in Ghana with VSO; Pres. Students' Union, City Univ., London; worked for Ceramics, Glass and Mineral Products Industrial Training Bd; joined Org. and Industrial Relations Dept, TUC 1975, Head Dept 1987–93, Head Press and Information Dept 1979–87, Deputy Gen. Sec. TUC 1993–2003, Gen. Sec. 2003–; mem. Council of Advisory, Conciliation and Arbitration Service (ACAS) 1995–2004; mem. Court of Bank of England 2004–. *Address:* TUC, Congress House, Great Russell Street, London, WC1B 3LS, England (office). *Telephone:* (20) 7467-1232 (office). *Fax:* (20) 7467-1277 (office). *E-mail:* info@tuc.org.uk (office). *Website:* www.tuc.org.uk (office).

BARBER, Eunice; French athlete; b. 17 Nov. 1974, Freetown, Sierra Leone; d. of Margaret Barber; heptathlete/long jumper; personal best: heptathlon 6889 points (Arles, June 2005), long jump 7.05m (Monaco, June 2003); African record holder heptathlon 6,416 points 1996; Sierra Leone record holder at 100m, high jump, long jump, shot put, javelin, heptathlon; became French citizen 1999; winner, African Championships long jump 1995, European Cup heptathlon 1999, Meeting International d'Arles 1999, 2003, Decastar Talence heptathlon 1999, IAAF World Combined Events Challenge 1999, 2005 (runner up), World Championships heptathlon 1999, 1995 (fouth place), 2003 (runner-up), 2005 (runner up), Hypo-Meeting Götzis heptathlon 2000, 2001, European Cup long jump 2003, World Championships long jump 2003, 2005 (third place); fifth place Olympic Games heptathlon 2000; sixth place World Indoor Championships pentathlon 1997; coach Bob Kersee. *Leisure interests:* fashion, cinema, music, singing, travelling. *Address:* c/o Fédération Française d'Athlétisme, 33 avenue Pierre de Coubertin, 75013 Paris, France. *Telephone:* 1-53-80-74-91. *Fax:* 1-53-80-74-97. *E-mail:* contact_barber@athleteline.com (office). *Website:* www.barber-eunice.com.

BARBER, Lionel, BA; British journalist; *Editor, Financial Times;* b. 1955, London; m.; two c.; ed Univ. of Oxford; journalist, The Scotsman 1978–81; Business Corresp. The Times (London) 1981–85; Washington Corresp. and US Ed. Financial Times 1986–92, Brussels bureau chief 1992–98, News Ed. 1998–2000, Ed. Continental European Edn 2000–02, US Man. Ed. 2002–05, Ed. Financial Times 2005–; Visiting Fellow, European Univ. Inst., Florence, Italy 1996; Woodrow Wilson Foundation Fellow 1991, Eliot-Winant Fellow, British-American-Canadian Foundation 1994; Laurence Stern Fellowship, Washington Post 1985. *Publications include:* Price of Truth: Story of the Reuters Millions (with John Lawrenson) 1984, Not With Honour: Inside the Westland Scandal (co-author) 1986, Britain and the New European Agenda 1998. *Leisure interests:* watching rugby, cycling, reading American Presidential biographies, listening to opera. *Address:* Financial Times, One Southwark Bridge, London, SE1 9HL, England (office). *Telephone:* (20) 7873-3000 (office). *Fax:* (20) 7873-3924 (office). *Website:* www.ft.com (office).

BARBERÁ GUILLEM, Emilio, DrMed; Spanish academic; *Professor of Histology and General Embryology, University del Pais Vasco;* b. 14 Feb. 1946, Valencia; s. of Edelmiro Barberá and Emilia Guillem; two s.; ed Univ. of Valencia; Dir Lab. of Quantitative Biology, Instituto Investigaciones Citológicas, CAMP, Valencia 1969–74; Section Head, Centro Investigaciones Ciudad Sanit. 'La Fe' 1974–76; Investigator, Dept of Pathology, Faculty of Medicine, Valencia 1976–79; Asst Prof., Univ. of Valencia 1976–78, Assoc. Prof. 1978–79; Prof., Univ. of Valladolid 1979–80; Prof. of Histology and Gen. Embryology, Univ. del País Vasco 1980–; Dir Dept of Histology and Cellular Biology 1980, Rector 1986–92; other professional appointments; mem. Real Acad. de Medicina de Valencia, Real Acad. de Medicina de Vizcaya and nine int. biological socs. *Publications:* numerous scientific articles in int. reviews; book chapters. *Leisure interests:* photography, travel. *Address:* Universidad del País Vasco/Euskal Herriko Unibertsitatea, Edificio Rectorado, Apartado de Correos 1397, 48080 Bilbao, Spain. *Telephone:* (34) (4) 463-76-53.

BARBERIS, Alessandro; Italian business executive; *Vice-Chairman, Fiat SpA;* b. 1937, Turin; m.; three c.; trained as engineer; joined Fiat SpA 1964, Dir 1972, Dir Fmb (Fiat Group in Latin America), Brazil 1976–78, Head of Metalworks 1978–1982, Dir-Gen. Magneti Marelli 1982–93, Dir of Industrial Co-ordination Fiat Auto 1993–96, COO 2002, CEO Dec. 2002, then Vice-Chair.; Dir-Gen. Isituto Bancario San Paulo di Torino 1996–97; Pres. Piaggio & C. SpA 1997–2002, Confindustria Toscana 1999, Unione Industriale di Pisa 1999; Chair. CDC Point SpA 2001; Pres. ANCMA (construction asscn). *Address:* Fiat Auto SpA, Corso Agnelli 200, 10135 Turin, Italy (office). *Telephone:* (011) 68311111 (office). *Website:* www.fiat.com (office).

BARBIZET, Patricia Marie Marguerite; French business executive; *Director-General and CEO, Artémis Group;* b. 17 April 1955, Paris; m. Jean Barbizet 1979; one d.; ed Ecole Supérieure de Commerce de Paris; Man. Asst Renault Véhicules Industriels 1977–79, Int. Treas. 1979–82, Group Treas. 1977–84; Financial Dir Renault Crédit Int. 1984–89; Financial Dir Groupe Pinault 1988–90, Deputy Dir-Gen. in charge of Finance and Communication 1990–92, Dir-Gen. Financière Pinault 1992–, Chair. Pinault-Printemps-Redoute (owner of Gucci) and Pres. PPR Group Supervisory Bd 2002–; Admin., Dir-Gen. and CEO Artémis Group 1992–; Chair. and CEO Piasa; Chair. Société Nouvelle du Théâtre Marigny; Dir Christie's Int. PLC, TF1 (also Chair. Audit Cttee), Fnac SA; Pres. French Asscn for Co. Treasurers 1989–92; mem. Supervisory Bd Gucci Group NV (Netherlands), Yves Saint Laurent Parfums, Yves Saint Laurent Couture, Yves Saint Laurent Haute Couture; Perm. Rep. of Artémis on Bd Dirs of Agefi, Bouygues, Sebdo le Point; mem. Man. Bd Château Latour; mem. Conseil des Marchés Financiers; mem. Ed. Cttee Marchés et Techniques Financières; mem. Bd of Dirs Total SA 2008–; Officier de l'Ordre nat. du Mérite; Chevalier de la Légion d'honneur; ranked by Fortune magazine amongst 50 Most Powerful Women in Business outside the US (sixth) 2001, 2002, (15th) 2003, (16th) 2004, (18th) 2005, (19th) 2006, (22nd) 2007. *Leisure interests:* literature, music. *Address:* Artémis, 12 rue François 1er, 75008 Paris (office); 10 rue du Dragon, 75006 Paris, France (home). *Telephone:* 1-44-11-20-52 (office). *Fax:* 1-44-11-20-18 (office). *Website:* international.pprgroup.com (office).

BARBOSA, Rubens Antonio, MA; Brazilian diplomatist and business consultant; b. 13 June 1938, São Paulo; m. Maria Ignez Correa da Costa 1969; one s. one d.; ed Univ. of Brazil, São Paulo and London School of Econs; Exec. Sec. Brazilian Trade Comm. with Socialist Countries of E Europe 1976–84; Chief of Staff of Minister of Foreign Affairs 1985–86; Under-Sec.-Gen. for Multilateral and Special Political Affairs 1986–87; Sec. for Int. Affairs, Ministry of Economy 1987–88; Amb. and Perm. Rep. to Latin American Integration Asscn (ALADI) 1988–91; Pres. Cttee of Reps ALADI 1991–92; Under-Sec.-Gen. for Regional Integration, Econ. Affairs and Foreign Trade, Ministry of Foreign Affairs 1991–93; coordinator Brazilian section of Mercosul (Southern Cone Common Market) 1991–93; Amb. to UK 1994–99, to USA 1999–2004; currently Pres. Conselho Superior de Comércio Exterior de la Federação das Indústrias do Estado de São Paulo; fmr Pres. Asscn of Coffee Producing Countries; business consultant and Pres. Rubens Barbosa & Associados business consultancy firm; Grand Cross, Order of Rio Branco; Commdr Légion d'honneur; Hon. LVO; Hon. GCVO; decorations from Argentina, Mexico and Italy. *Publications:* América Latina em Perspectiva: Integração Regional da Retórica à Realidade 1991; Panorama: Visto de Londres 1998, The Mercosur Codes 2000, O Brasil dos Brasilianistas, um Guia dos Estudos sobre o Brasil nos Estados Unidos (1945–2000) 2002; essays and articles in newspapers and magazines. *Leisure interests:* classical music, tennis. *Address:* Avenida Brigadeiro Faria Lima 2055 9º andar, CEP 01452-001 São Paulo, Brazil (office). *Telephone:* (11) 3039-6330 (office). *Fax:* (11) 3039-6334 (office). *E-mail:* rubarbosa@tevia.com.br.

BARBOSA BORGES, Victor Manuel; Cape Verde politician; fmr Minister of Educ. with portfolio of Human Resources Devt; fmr Minister of Foreign Affairs, Co-operation and Communities. *Address:* c/o Ministry of Foreign Affairs, Co-operation and Communities, Palácio das Comunidades, Achada de Santo António, Praia, Santiago, Cape Verde (office).

BARBOSA GOMES, Joaquim Benedito, LLB; Brazilian judge; *Judge, Supreme Federal Tribunal;* began career as janitor, electoral tribunal, Brasilia; fmr worker, congressional printing press; fmr state prosecutor, Rio de Janeiro; Judge, Supreme Fed. Tribunal May 2003–. *Address:* Supreme Federal Tribunal, Praça dos Tres Poderes, 70175 Brasilia, Brazil (office). *Telephone:* (61) 224-7179 (office). *Fax:* (61) 226-4797 (office). *E-mail:* bndpj@stf.gov.br (office).

BARBOSA PEQUENO, Ovidio Manuel; São Tomé and Príncipe journalist, politician and diplomatist; b. 5 Nov. 1954; m.; ed Pacific Western Univ., Inst. of Tech. of New York, USA; joined diplomatic service, overseas assignments included First Sec., Perm. Mission to UN, New York 1983–90; Sr Ed. Voice of America, Washington, DC 1990–99, headed Angola Bureau 1998–99; returned to diplomatic service and served as Amb. to Taiwan 1999–2004, Minister of Foreign Affairs and Co-operation 2004–06 (resgnd), 2007–08, Perm. Rep. to UN, New York and Amb. to USA (also accred to Canada and Brazil) 2006–07. *Address:* c/o Ministry of Foreign Affairs, Co-operation and Communities, Avda 12 de Julho, CP 111, São Tomé, São Tomé e Príncipe. *Telephone:* 221017.

BARBOT, Ivan, LèsL; French police commissioner and government official; b. 5 Jan. 1937, Ploeuc; s. of Pierre Barbot and Anne Barbot (née Le Calvez); m. Roselyne de Lestrange 1971; three c.; ed Lycée de Saint-Brieuc, Univ. of Paris; Prin. Pvt. Sec. to Chief Commr, Tarn-et-Garonne 1961; Prin. Pvt. Sec., later Dir of Staff to Chief Commr, Haute-Savoie 1962; Dir of Staff, Paris Region Pref. 1967; Deputy Chief Commr, Etampes 1969; Deputy Chief Commr without portfolio, Official Rep. to the Cabinet 1974; Tech. Adviser to Minister of the Interior 1974–77; Sec.-Gen. Seine-Saint-Denis 1977–82; Chief Commr and Supt, Dept de la Charente 1982–85, du Var 1985–87; Dir-Gen. Police Nat. 1987–89; Pres. Interpol 1988–92; Prefect Poitou-Charentes 1989, Vienne 1989–91; with Prime Minister's office, responsible for security 1991–92; Pres. Admin. Council of French concessionary co. for the construction and exploitation of the road tunnel under Mont-Blanc 1992–94; Chair., CEO OFEMA (French Office of Aeronautics Equipment) 1993–97, Chair., CEO SOFEMA (formed after merger with SOFMA) 1997–2004; Officier, Légion d'honneur, du Mérite agricole, Commdr, Ordre nat. du Mérite, Chavalier des Palmes académiques, des Arts et Lettres. *Address:* c/o SOFEMA, 58 ave Marceau, 75008 Paris (office); 4 rue Marguerite, 75017 Paris, France (home).

BARBOUR, Haley Reeves, JD; American state official; *Governor of Mississippi;* b. 22 Oct. 1947, Yazoo City, Miss.; s. of the late Jeptha F. Barbour Jr and LeFlore Johnson; m. Marsha Dickson 1971; two s.; ed Univ. of Mississippi Law School; field rep. Miss. Republican Party 1968, Deputy Exec. Dir 1972–73, Exec. Dir 1973–76; Regional Technician, Bureau of Census 1969–70; Exec. Dir Southern Asscn of Republican State Chairmen 1973–76; Southeastern US Campaign Dir Pres. Ford Cttee 1976; Chair. 3rd Congressional Dist Cttee Miss. 1976–84; Republican nominee, US Senate 1982; Municipal Judge, Yazoo City 1980–81, City Attorney 1981–85; Chair. Republican Nat. Cttee 1993–97; Co-founder, Chair., CEO Barbour Griffith & Rogers LLC (lobbying firm), Washington, DC; Gov. of Miss. 2003–; Dir Deposit Guarranty Corpn; mem. Bd Deposit Guarranty Nat. Bank; mem. Bd Dirs Amtrak, Mobil Telecommunications Technologies Inc.; deacon First Presbyterian Church of Yazoo City. *Publication:* Agenda for America 1996. *Address:* Office of the Governor, POB 139, Jackson, MS 39205, USA (office). *Telephone:* (601) 359-3100 (office). *Fax:* (601) 359-6741 (office). *Website:* www.governor.state.ms.us (office); www.bgrdc.com (office).

BARBOUR, Ian Graeme, BD, PhD; American physicist, theologian and academic; *Carleton Professor Emeritus, Department of Religion, Carleton College;* b. 5 Oct. 1923, Peking (now Beijing), (People's Republic of) China; ed Swarthmore Coll., Duke Univ., Univ. of Chicago, Yale Univ.; Asst Prof., Assoc. Prof. of Physics, Kalamazoo Coll. 1949–53; Asst Prof. of Physics, Assoc. Prof. of Religion, Carleton Coll., Northfield, Minn. 1955–73, Prof. of Religion 1974–86, Winifred and Atherton Bean Prof. of Science, Tech. and Soc. 1981–86, Carleton Prof. Emer., Dept of Religion 1986–; Lilly Visiting Prof. of Science, Theology and Human Values Purdue Univ. 1973–74; Gifford Lecturer Univ. of Aberdeen, Scotland 1989–91; mem. American Acad. of Religion, Soc. for Values in Higher Educ.; Ford Faculty Fellowship 1953–54, Harbison Award for Distinguished Teaching, Danforth Foundation 1963–64, Guggenheim Fellowship 1967–68, Fulbright Fellowship 1967–68, ACLS Fellowship 1976–77, Nat. Endowment for the Humanities Fellowship 1976–77, Nat. Humanities Center Fellow 1980–81, American Acad. of Religion Book Award 1993, Templeton Prize for Progress in Religion 1999. *Publications:* Christianity and the Scientist 1960, Issues in Science and Religion 1966, Science and

Religion: New Perspectives on the Dialogue (ed) 1968, Science and Secularity: The Ethics of Technology 1970, Earth Might Be Fair (ed) 1971, Western Man and Environmental Ethics (ed) 1972, Myths, Models and Paradigms 1974, Finite Resources and the Human Future (ed) 1976, Technology, Environment and Human Values 1980, Energy and American Values (co-author) 1982, Religion in an Age of Science (Gifford Lectures) 1990, Ethics in an Age of Technology 1993, Religion and Science: Historical and Contemporary Issues 1997, When Science Meets Religion 2000, Nature, Human Nature and God 2002; contributions: scientific and religious journals. *Address:* Carleton College, Northfield, MN 55057, USA (home). *E-mail:* ibarbour@carleton.edu (home).

BARBUT, Monique, MPhil(Econs), MA (Econs); French international organization official; *Chairperson and CEO, Global Environment Facility;* b. 22 Aug. 1956; m.; three c.; ed Univ. of Paris I, Grad. Inst. of Int. Studies, IHE, Paris II; several internships in banking, including three months at Volksbank, Zürich, Switzerland 1979; Program Man. Saint-Denis La Réunion, Caisse Centrale de Cooperation Economique 1981–84, Head of Dept of sector-based policies and retrospective evaluation 1984–89, in charge of all public credit and housing cos in French Overseas Depts 1990, at Ministry of Cooperation and Devt 1990–93, in charge of Secr. of French Global Environment Fund (inter-ministerial field) 1994–96; Deputy Dir French Overseas Depts and Territories and Dir Div. in charge of Devt inside same Dept, Agence Française de Développement (AFD) 1996–2000, Exec. Dir at AFD, especially in charge of all activities in French Overseas Depts and Territories, and responsible for all programmes for Pacific, Indian, Caribbean Ocean Islands 2000–02; Dir Div. of Tech., Industry and Econs, UNEP 2003–06; Chair. and CEO Global Environment Facility 2006–; mem. French Govt Del., Earth Summit, Rio de Janeiro, Brazil 1992. *Address:* Global Environment Facility Secretariat, 1818 H Street, NW, Washington, DC 20433, USA (office); 1 rue Frédéric Bastiat, 75008 Paris, France. *Telephone:* (202) 473-3202 (US) (office); 1-42-89-42-33 (France). *Fax:* (202) 522-3240 (office); (202) 522-3245 (office). *E-mail:* mbarbut@thegef.org (office). *Website:* www.thegef.org (office).

BÁRCENA IBARRA, Alicia, BSc, MSc, MPA; Mexican biologist and international organization official; *Executive Secretary, Economic Commission for Latin America and the Caribbean (ECLAC);* b. 5 March 1952; ed Universidad Nacional Autónoma de Mexico (UNAM), Harvard Univ., USA, Instituto Miguel Angel, Mexico; Research Asst, UNAM 1975-76, Assoc. Prof. of Botany, UNAM (Universidad Autónoma Metropolitana) 1976–78; Researcher on Ethnobotany, Instituto Nacional sobre Recursos Bióticos 1978–80; Regional Exec. Dir/Research Coordinator Instituto Nacional de Investigaciones sobre Recursos 1980–82; Under-Sec. of Ecology (Vice-Minister), Secretaría de Desarrollo Urbano y Ecología—SEDUE), Ministry of Urban Devt and Ecology 1982–86; consultant, IDB Aug.–Nov. 1987; Pres. Cultura Ecológica, Civil Soc. Org. in Mexico 1987–88; Dir Gen. Nat. Inst. of Fisheries, SEPESCA (Secretaría de Pesca) 1988-90; Prin. Officer, Programme Unit II, UN Conf. on Environment and Devt, Geneva, Switzerland 1990–92; Exec. Dir Earth Council Foundation, San Jose, Costa Rica 1992–95; Programme Coordinator Global Environmental Citizenship Programme, UNEP 1996–97; Chief Tech. Adviser on Environment and Devt, seconded by UNEP, Regional Bureau for Latin America and the Caribbean, UNDP 1998–99; Chief, Div. of Sustainable Devt and Human Settlements, ECLAC 1999–2003, Deputy Exec. Sec. 2003–06; Deputy Chef de Cabinet, UN, New York Feb.–March 2006, Acting Chef de Cabinet March 2006–07, Under-Sec.-Gen. for Man. 2007–08; Exec. Sec. ECLAC 2008–. *Publications:* The Millenium Development Goals: A Latin American and Caribbean Perspective 2005; numerous articles in professional journals. *Address:* Economic Commission for Latin America and the Caribbean, Casilla de Correo 179-D, Av. Dag Hammarskjöld, 3477 Vitacura, Santiago, Chile (office). *Telephone:* (2) 471-2000 (office). *Fax:* (2) 208-0252 (office). *E-mail:* secretaria.se@cepal.org (office). *Website:* www.eclac.org (office).

BARCHUK, Vasily Vasilievich, CEconSc; Russian politician and economist; *Chairman, Big Pension Fund;* b. 11 March 1941, Komsomolsk-on-Amur; m.; one d.; ed All-Union Inst. of Finance and Econ. USSR Acad. of Nat. Econ.; worked in tax inspection bodies in Khabarovsk Region 1958–72; staff mem. RSFSR Ministry of Finance 1972–84, USSR Ministry of Finance 1986–91, Deputy Minister of Finance April–Nov. 1991; First Deputy Minister of Finance of Russia 1991–92, Minister 1992–93; Chair. of Bd Pensions Fund of Russian Fed. 1993–99; Deputy Chair. Dept of Social Devt, Ministry of Labour and Social Devt 2001–04; Chair. inter-regional non-governmental Big Pension Fund 2004–. *Address:* Big Pension Fund, 28B Balaklavskii prospect, 117452 Moscow, Russia. *Telephone:* (495) 937 65 31 (office). *Fax:* (495) 937 65 32 (office). *E-mail:* info@bigpension.ru (office). *Website:* www.bigpension.ru (office).

BARCO ISAKSON, Carolina, BSc, MBA; Colombian politician and city planner; *Ambassador to USA ;* b. Boston, Mass, USA; d. of fmr Pres. of Colombia, Virgilio Barco; ed Wellesley Coll., Harvard Univ. and Mass Inst. of Tech., USA, Université Libre de Bruxelles, Belgium, Instituto de Empresa, Madrid, Spain; Tech. Consultant and Researcher, OMPU, Caracas, Venezuela 1976, Head of Special Studies, Metropolitan Planning Office 1977–78; Co-Dir Study of Revitalization of Bogota, Nat. Planning Dept, City Planning Dept and Fonade 1985; Head of Program to Recover City Centre, Office of the Mayor, Bogota 1986–88; Coordinator Project to Strengthen Regional Culture, UNDP 1989–90; Int. Cooperation Adviser to Ministry of Devt 1992; Coordinator Project to Support City Housing, Ministry of Devt 1993–95; Adviser to La Candelaria Corpn 1995; Coordinator Study of City Planning for Ciudadela Usme Project 1996; Researcher Coordinator, Universidad de los Andes 1996; Head, Tech. Assistance Project, Fondo Nacional del Ahorro 1996; Dir Study on Environmental Man., Ministry of Environment 1997; Adviser to Strategic

Plan for Bogota 2000, Office of the Mayor 1997; Coordinator Study on Treatment of Bogota Land, City Planning Dept 1988; Coordinator Study of Occupation Trends, Office of Gov. of Cundinamarca 1988; Dir of City Planning, Bogota 1999–2002; Minister of Foreign Affairs 2002–06; Amb. to USA 2006–; mem. Bd of Dirs Lincoln Inst.; Hon. mem. Sociedad Colombiana de Arquitectos 2002; Carlos Martínez Prize for Architecture, Bogotá 1996. *Publications include:* Diagnosis of Central Caracas 1977, The Recovery of City Centers: Operating Plan for Central Bogota (co-author, 27 vols) 1986, Zoning Plan for Central Bogota (co-author) 1988, Land Use Guidelines for Bogota and the Sabana (co-author) 2000; numerous articles and working papers on land use, city zoning regulations, cultural policy and governance. *Address:* Embassy of Colombia, 2118 Leroy Place, NW, Washington, DC 20008, USA (office). *Telephone:* (202) 387-8338 (office). *Fax:* (202) 232-8643 (office). *E-mail:* enwas@colombiaemb.org (office). *Website:* www.colombiaemb.org (office).

BARD, Allen J., PhD; American chemist and academic; *Hackerman-Welch Regents Chair in Chemistry, University of Texas;* b. 18 Dec. 1933, New York; m. Frances Segal 1957; one s. one d.; ed City Coll. of New York and Harvard Univ.; Thayer Scholarship 1955–56; Nat. Science Foundation Postdoctoral Fellowship 1956–58; joined chem. staff of Univ. of Tex., Austin 1958, Prof. of Chem. 1967–, Jack S. Josey Prof. 1980–82, Norman Hackerman Prof. 1982–85, Hackerman-Welch Regents Chair. in Chem. 1985–; consultant to several labs including E.I. duPont, Texas Instruments and several govt agencies; research interests in application of electrochemical methods to study of chemical problems; Vice-Chair. Nat. Research Council; Ed.-in-Chief Journal of American Chemical Soc. 1982–2001; Chair. Nat. Acad. of Sciences Chemical Section 1996–; mem. editorial Bd of numerous journals; Gov. Weizmann Inst. 1995–; mem. ACS, Electrochemical Soc.; Dr hc (Paris) 1986; Ward Medal in Chem. 1955, Harrison Howe Award, ACS 1980, Carl Wagner Memorial Award, Electrochemical Soc. 1981, Bruno Breyer Memorial Medal, Royal Australian Chem. Inst. 1984, Fisher Award in Analytical Chem., ACS 1984, Charles N Reilley Award, Soc. of Electroanalytical Chem. 1984, New York Acad. of Sciences Award in Math. and Physical Sciences 1986, Willard Gibbs Award, ACS 1987, Olin-Palladium Award, Electrochem. Soc. 1987, Oesper Award, Univ. of Cincinnati 1989, NAS Award 1998, Linus Pauling Award 1998, Pittsburgh Analytical Chem. Award 2001, ACS Priestley Medal 2002. *Publications:* Chemical Equilibrium 1966, Electrochemical Methods (with L. R. Faulkner) 1980, Integrated Chemical Systems: A Chemical Approach to Nanotechnology 1994; approx. 700 papers and book chapters; Ed. Electroanalytical Chemistry (15 Vols) 1966–, The Encyclopedia of the Electrochemistry of the Elements, 16 Vols 1973–82. *Address:* Chemistry and Biochemistry Department, University of Texas at Austin, 1 University Station A5300, Austin, TX 78712-0165, USA (office). *Telephone:* (512) 471-3761 (office). *Fax:* (512) 471-0088 (office). *E-mail:* ajbard@mail.utexas.edu (office). *Website:* www.cm.utexas.edu/bard (office).

BARDEM, Javier; Spanish actor; b. 1 March 1969, Las Palmas, Gran Canaria; *Films include:* Jamón, Jamón 1992, Huidos 1992, El Amante bilingüe 1993, Huevos de oro 1993, Días contados 1994, El Detective y la muerte 1994, La Teta y la luna 1995, Boca a boca 1995, La Madre 1995, Más que amor, frenesí 1996, El Amor perjudica seriamente la salud 1997, Airbag 1997, Carne trémula 1997, Perdita Durango 1997, Los Lobos de Washington 1999, Segunda piel 2000, Before Night Falls 2000 (Best Actor Prize, Venice Film Festival 2000), The Dancer Upstairs 2002, Los Lunes al Sol 2002, Collateral 2004, The Three Ages of the Crime 2004, Mar Adentro (The Sea Inside) (Best Actor, Goya Awards 2005) 2004, Goya's Ghosts 2006, No Country for Old Men (Golden Globe for Best Supporting Actor 2008, Outstanding Performance by a Male Actor in a Supporting Role, Screen Actors Guild 2008, Acad. Award for Best Supporting Actor 2008) 2007, Love in the Time of Cholera 2007. *Address:* c/o The Endeavor Agency, 9601 Wilshire Blvd., 10th Floor, Beverly Hills, CA 90210, USA.

BARDER, Sir Brian Leon, KCMG, BA; British diplomatist (retd); b. 20 June 1934, Bristol; s. of Harry Barder and Vivien Young; m. Jane M. Cornwell 1958; two d. one s.; ed Sherborne School and St Catharine's Coll., Cambridge; Colonial Office 1957–64; First Sec. UK Mission to UN, New York 1964–68; FCO 1968–70; First Sec. Moscow 1971–73; Counsellor, Canberra 1973–77; Canadian Nat. Defence Coll. 1977–78; Head of Southern Africa Dept, FCO 1978–82; Amb. to Ethiopia 1982–86; to Poland 1986–88; High Commr in Nigeria and Amb. (non-resident) to Benin 1988–91; High Commr in Australia 1991–94; Know How Fund Diplomatic Training Consultant 1996; mem. Bd of Man. Royal Hosp. for Neurodisability 1996–2003; mem. English-Speaking Union Cttee for Speech and Debate 1996–, Special Immigration Appeals Comm. 1998–2004. *Leisure interests:* politics, classical music, cycling, the internet, polemical blogging, writing to newspapers. *Address:* 20 Victoria Mews, London, SW18 3PY, England (home). *Telephone:* (20) 8355-8394 (home). *E-mail:* brianbarder@compuserve.com (home). *Website:* www.barder.com/ephems (home).

BARDHAN, Ardhendu Bhushan, (Kanu Da), MA, LLB; Indian politician and trade union official; *General-Secretary, Communist Party of India;* b. 25 Sept. 1925, Sylhet (now in Bangladesh); s. of Hemendra Kumar and Sarala Bala; one s. one d.; mem. Maharashtra State Legis. Ass. 1957–1962; Gen.-Sec. Communist Party of India 1996–. *Address:* Communist Party of India, Ajoy Bhavan, Kotla Marg, New Delhi 110 002 (office); Ajoy Bhavan, 15 Com. Indrajit Gupta Marg, New Delhi 110 002, India (home). *Telephone:* (11) 23235546 (office). *Fax:* (11) 23235543 (office). *E-mail:* cpi@cpofindia.org (office). *Website:* www.cpindia.org (office).

BARDIN, Garry Yakovlevich; Russian film director; b. 11 Sept. 1941, Orenburg; m.; one s.; ed Studio-School of Moscow Art Theatre; actor Moscow Gogol Drama Theatre; Stage Dir Moscow Puppet Theatre; animation film dir in studio Soyuzmultfilm 1975–90; also scriptwriter; Founder, Pres. and

Artistic Dir Animated Film Studio Stayer 1991–; Diplomas, Moscow Int. Film Festival, Bilbao Int. Film Festival, Spain, Tampere Int. Film Festival, Finland, Hon. Diploma Krakow Int. Film Festival, Poland, TV Prize, Rennes Int. Film Festival, France, Jury Prizes, Los Angeles Film Festival, USA, Hiroshima Int. Film Festival, Japan, Grand Prix Ruan Int. Film Festival, Annecy Int. Film Festival, France, Golden Dove Prize, Leipzig Int. Film Festival, Germany, Golden Palm Branch Prize, Cannes Film Festival, France, Nika Prize of Russian Acad. of Cinematic Arts (three times), State Prize of Russian Fed. 1999, Golden Prize, New York Int. Film Festival, USA. *Films include:* Dostat do neba (Reach the Sky) 1975, Veselaya karusel (Happy Carousel) (TV) 1976, Letuchiy korabl (Flying Ship) 1979, Pif-paf, oy-oy-oy! 1980, Prezhde my byli ptitsami (We Were Birds Before) 1982, Konflikt (Conflict) 1983, Break! 1985, Banket 1986, Vykrutasy 1988, Seryi volk & Krasnaya Shapochka (aka Grey Wolf and Little Red Riding Hood) 1990, The Coiling Prankster 1990, Chucha (Choo Choo) 1997, Adagio 2000, Chucha 2 (Choo Choo 2) 2002, Chucha 3 (Choo Choo 3) 2005. *Address:* Animated Film Studio Stayer, Otkrytoye shosse 28, korp.6A, 107143 Moscow (office); Lev Tolstoy str. 3, apt. 11, 119021 Moscow, Russia (home). *Telephone:* (495) 167-01-54 (office); (495) 246-45-86 (home). *Fax:* (495) 292-85-11 (office); (495) 167-01-54 (office). *E-mail:* garry@bardin.ru (office). *Website:* www.bardin.ru (office).

BARDINI, Adolfo, DrIng; Italian industrial executive (retd); b. 9 April 1915, Genoa; s. of the late Emilio Bardini and Eugenia Baltuzzi; m. 1st Ernestina Zampaglione 1939; two d.; m. 2nd Mirella Noli Parmeggiani 1972 (deceased); ed Naples Univ.; Gen. Man. Fabbrica Macchine Industriali, Naples 1952–55; Dir and Gen. Man. Nuova San Giorgio, Genoa 1955–62; Dir and Gen. Man. Alfa Romeo SpA 1962–74; Chair. Autodelta SpA 1962–74, ANFIA (Italian Asscn of Motor Vehicle Mfrs) 1975–78, Turin Int. Motor Show 1975–78; Dir CMI SpA, Genoa 1975–82; Pres. CLCA (Comité de Liaison de la Construction Automobile pour les Pays de la Communauté Economique Européenne) 1978–80, Elettronica San Giorgio SpA ELSAG, Genoa 1979–84, Hon. Chair. 1984–94. *Address:* Corso Monforte 36, 20122 Milan, Italy (home). *Telephone:* (02) 784320 (home).

BARDOT, Brigitte; French actress; b. 28 Sept. 1934, Paris; d. of Louis and Anne-Marie (Mücel) Bardot; m. 1st Roger Vadim (died 2000); m. 2nd Jacques Charrier; one s.; m. 3rd Gunther Sachs 1966 (divorced 1969); ed Paris Conservatoire; stage and film career 1952–; Founder, Pres. Fondation Brigitte Bardot; Étoile de Cristal from Acad. of Cinema 1966; Chevalier Légion d'honneur 1985. *Films include:* Les dents longues (uncredited) 1952, Manina: la fille sans voile 1952, Le trou normand 1952, Le portrait de son père 1953, Un acte d'amour 1953, Tradita 1954, Si Versailles m'était conté (uncredited) 1954, Le fils de Caroline chérie 1955, Futures vedettes 1955, Doctor at Sea 1955, Les grandes manoeuvres 1955, La lumière d'en face 1955, Mi figlio Nerone 1956, Cette sacrée gamine 1956, La mariée est trop belle 1956, Helen of Troy 1956, Et Dieu… créa la femme 1956, En effeuillant la marguerite 1956, Une parisienne 1957, Les bijoutiers du clair de lune 1958, En cas de malheur 1958, La femme et le pantin 1959, Babette s'en va-t-en guerre 1959, Voulez-vous danser avec moi? 1959, Le testament d'Orphée, ou ne me demandez pas pourquoi! (uncredited) 1960, L'affaire d'une nuit (uncredited) 1960, La vérité 1960, La bride sur le cou 1961, Amours célèbres 1961, Vie privée 1962, Le repos du guerrier 1962, Le mépris 1963, Une ravissante idiote 1964, Marie Soleil (uncredited) 1965, Viva Maria! 1965, Masculin, féminin: 15 faits précis (uncredited) 1966, A coeur joie 1967, Histoires extraordinaires 1968, Shalako 1968, L'ours et la poupée 1969, Les femmes 1969, Les novices 1970, Boulevard du rhum 1971, Les pétroleuses 1971, Don Juan ou Si Don Juan était une femme… 1973, L'Histoire très bonne et très joyeuse de Colinot trousse-chemise 1973. *Television:* Étoiles et toiles – L'érotisme au cinéma (episode) 1983. *Publications:* Initiales BB 1996 (received Prix Paul Léautaud 1996), Le Carré de Pluton 1999, Un Cri Dans Le Silence 2003. *Address:* Fondation Brigitte Bardot, 28 rue Vineuse, 75116 Paris, France. *Telephone:* 1-45-05-14-60. *Fax:* 1-45-05-14-80. *E-mail:* fbb@fondationbrigittebardot.fr (office). *Website:* www.fondationbrigittebardot.fr (office).

BAREIRO SPAINI, Gen. (retd) Luis Nicanor; Paraguayan military officer and politician; *Minister of Defence;* fmr Commdr Cadets Corps, Mil. Acad., Commdr Army Artillery Corps, Commdr Army Mil. Inst.; fmr Dir Inst. of High Strategic Studies, Ministry of Defence; fmr Dir Inspectorate Gen., Armed Forces; Minister of Defence 2008–. *Address:* Ministry of National Defence, Avda Mariscal López y Vice-Presidente Sánchez, Asunción, Paraguay (office). *Telephone:* (21) 20-4771 (office). *Fax:* (21) 21-1583 (office). *E-mail:* ministro@mdn.gov.py (office). *Website:* www.mdn.gov.py (office).

BAREKZAI, Shukria, (Dawi); Afghan journalist, editor and politician; *Editor-in-Chief, Ayina-e Zan;* b. 1972, Kabul; m.; three d.; ed Univ. of Kabul; organized and funded secret women's schools during Taliban regime; mem. Afghanistan's Constitutional Reviewing Comm. 2001; Founder and Ed.-in-Chief Ayina-e Zan (Women's Mirror) weekly newspaper 2002–; f. Asia Women Org. 2002; mem. Parl. 2005–; Int. Ed. of the Year Award, Worldpress.org 2005. *Address:* Ayina-e Zan (Women Mirror), House 186, St 12, Wazir Akbar Khan, Kabul, Afghanistan (office). *Telephone:* (70) 281864. *E-mail:* womensmirror@hotmail.com; women.mirror@gmail.com; shukriabarakzai@yahoo.com.

BARENBLATT, Grigory Isaakovich, MA, PhD, ScD; Russian mathematician and academic; *Professor-in-Residence, Department of Mathematics, University of California, Berkeley;* b. 10 July 1927, Moscow; s. of Isaak Grigorievich Barenblatt and Nadezhda Veniaminovna Kagan; m. Iraida Nikolaevna Kochina 1952; two d.; ed Moscow Univ., Univ. of Cambridge, UK; Research Scientist, Inst. of Petroleum, USSR Acad. of Sciences, Moscow 1953–61; Prof. and Head, Dept of Mechanics of Solids, Inst. of Mechanics, Moscow Univ. 1961–75; Head, Theoretical Dept, Inst. of Oceanology, USSR Acad. of Sciences 1975–92; G.I. Taylor Prof. of Fluid Mechanics, Univ. of Cambridge 1992–94, Prof. Emer. 1994–; Prof. of Math., Univ. of Calif. at Berkeley 1997–; Foreign mem. American Acad. of Arts and Sciences 1975, Royal Soc. 2000; Fellow, Gonville and Caius Coll., Cambridge 1994–99, Hon. Fellow 1999–; Foreign Assoc. Nat. Acad. of Eng 1992, NAS 1997; mem. Academia Europaea 1993; Hon. DTech (Royal Inst. of Tech., Stockholm) 1989, Hon. D Civil Eng (Turin Polytechnic Inst.) 2005; Laureate, Panetti Gold Medal and Prize 1995, G.I. Taylor Medal, American Soc. of Eng Sciences 1999, J.C. Maxwell Prize, Int. Congress on Industrial and Applied Math. 1999, Accad. Dei Lincei Lagrange Medal 1995, S. P. Timoshenko Medal, American Soc. of Civil Engineers 2005. *Publications:* Similarity, Self-Similarity and Intermediate Asymptotics 1979, Dimensional Analysis 1987, Theory of Fluid Flows in Porous Media (jtly) 1990, Scaling, Self-Similarity and Intermediate Asymptotics 1996, Scaling 2003; articles in scientific journals. *Leisure interest:* historical reading. *Address:* Department of Mathematics, 735 Evans Hall, University of California, Berkeley, CA 94720-3840 (office); 1800 Spruce Street, Apt 102, Berkeley, CA 94709-1836, USA (home). *Telephone:* (510) 642-4162 (office); (510) 849-0155 (home). *Fax:* (510) 642-8204 (office). *E-mail:* gibar@math.berkeley.edu (office). *Website:* math.lbl.gov/barenblatt/barenblatt.html (office); math.berkeley.edu/~gibar (office).

BARENBOIM, Daniel, FRCM; Israeli/Palestinian pianist and conductor; *General Music Director, Deutsche Staatsoper, Berlin;* b. 16 Nov. 1942, Buenos Aires, Argentina; s. of Prof. Enrique and Aida Barenboim (née Schuster); m. 1st Jacqueline du Pré 1967 (died 1987); m. 2nd Elena Bashkirova 1988; two s.; studied piano with his father and other musical subjects with Nadia Boulanger, Edwin Fischer and Igor Markevitch; debut in Buenos Aires aged seven; played Bach D Minor Concerto with orchestra at Salzburg Mozarteum aged nine; has played in Europe regularly 1954–; yearly tours of USA 1957–; has toured Japan, Australia and S America; has played with or conducted London Philharmonic, Philharmonia Orchestra, London Symphony Orchestra, Royal Philharmonic, Chicago Symphony Orchestra, New York Philharmonic, Philadelphia Orchestra, Israel Philharmonic, Vienna Philharmonic, Berlin Philharmonic; frequently tours with English Chamber Orchestra and with them records for EMI (projects include complete Mozart Piano Concertos and late Symphonies); other recording projects include complete Beethoven Sonatas and Beethoven Concertos (with New Philharmonia Orchestra conducted by Klemperer); has appeared in series of masterclasses on BBC TV; presented Festival of Summer Music on South Bank, London 1968, 1969; leading role in Brighton Festival 1967–69; appears regularly at Edinburgh Festival; conductor, Edinburgh Festival Opera 1973; Music Dir Orchestre de Paris 1975–89, Chicago Symphony Orchestra 1991–2006, Hon. Conductor 2006–; Gen. Music Dir Deutsche Staatsoper, Berlin 1992– (Chief Conductor for Life Staatskapelle Berlin 2000–); projects with the late Edward Said, the West-Eastern Divan Workshop 1999–, and the Barenboim-Said Foundation (which promotes music and co-operation through projects targeted at young Arabs and Israelis); Charles Eliot Norton Prof., Harvard Univ. 2006; Maestro Scaligero, La Scala, Milan 2006–; made debut with Metropolitan Opera 2008; Commdr, Légion d'Honneur 2007; Hon. DMus (Manchester) 1997, (Oxford) 2007; Beethoven Medal 1958, Paderewski Medal 1963, Beethoven Soc. Medal 1982, Prix de la Tolérance, Protestant Acad. of Tutzing 2002, Premio Príncipe de Asturias 2002, Grammy Award (for recording of Wagner's Tannhäuser) 2003, Wilhelm Furtwängler Prize (with Staatskapelle Berlin) 2003, Wolf Foundation Prize in Arts 2004, chosen to deliver Reith Lectures 2006, Zwickau Robert Schumann Prize 2006, Conductor of the Year, Echo Klassik Awards 2006, Ernst von Siemens Prize 2006, Hessischer Peace Prize 2006, Goethe Medal 2007, Praemium Imperiale 2007. *Publication:* A Life in Music (jtly) 1991, Parallels and Paradoxes (with Edward W. Said) 2003, La Musica Sveglia il Tempo 2007. *Address:* Opus 3 Artists, 470 Park Avenue South, 9th Floor North, New York, NY 10016, USA (office); c/o Daniel Barenboim Secretariat, 29 rue de la Coulouvrenière, 1204 Geneva, Switzerland. *Telephone:* (212) 584-7500 (office). *Fax:* (646) 300-8200 (office). *E-mail:* info@opus3artists.com (office); danielbarenboim@hotmail.com. *Website:* www.opus3artists.com (office); www.danielbarenboim.com.

BARFIELD, Julia, MBE, RIBA, FRSA; British architect; *Director, Marks Barfield Architects;* b. 15 Nov. 1952; d. of Arnold Robert Barfield and Iolanthe Mary Barfield; m. David Joseph Marks (q.v.) 1981; one s. two d.; ed Godophin and Latymer School, London, Architectural Asscn School of Architecture, London; spent year out from studies with Barriadas, Lima, Peru 1975; Co-founder Tetra Ltd 1978–79, Richard Rogers Partnership 1979–81, Foster Assocs 1981–88; co-f. Marks Barfield Architects with David Marks (q.v.) 1989, London Eye Co. to realize London Eye project 1994; lectures include RA 2000, 2001, RIBA 2000, The Prince's Foundation Urban Villages Forum 2000, Royal Inst. 2001, Cooper-Hewitt Nat. Design Museum, New York 2001, Univ. of Virginia 2006; Civic Trust Awards Assessor; mem. Lambeth Democracy Comm. 2000–01, Design Review Cttee, Comm. for Architecture and the Built Environment (CABE), Architectural Asscn Council 2000–06, Council of Guys and St Thomas'; Gov. Godolphin & Latymer School; RIBA Awards for Architecture 2000, 2004, 2006, London First Millennium Award 2000, Royal Inst. of Chartered Surveyors Award 2000, AIA Design Award 2000, Design Week Special Award 2001, D&AD Awards, Silver and Gold 2001, 2004, Blueprint Award 2001, Architectural Practice of the Year 2001, Civic Trust Award 2002, Queen's Award for Enterprise (for Innovation) 2003, Coolbrands 2003–05, BDI Excellence in Architecture Award 2005. *Leisure interests:* family, travel, art, film. *Address:* Marks Barfield Architects, 50 Bromells Road, London, SW4 0BG, England (office). *Telephone:* (20) 7501-0180 (office). *Fax:* (20) 7498-7103 (office). *E-mail:* jbarfield@marksbarfield.com (office). *Website:* www.marksbarfield.com (office).

BARFOOT, Joan, BA; Canadian novelist and journalist; b. 17 May 1946, Owen Sound, Ont.; ed Univ. of Western Ont.; reporter, Religion Ed. Windsor Star 1967–69; feature and news writer, Mirror Publications, Toronto 1969–73,

Toronto Sunday Sun 1973–75; with London Free Press 1976–79, 1980–94; has taught journalism and creative writing at Univ. of Western Ont.; juror, Books in Canada First Novel Award 1987, Gov.-Gen.'s Award for English Language Canadian Fiction 1995, Trillium Literary Award 1996, 1999; mem. Writers' Union of Canada, PEN Canada; Books in Canada First Novel Award 1978, Marian Engel Award 1992. *Publications:* Abra 1978, Dancing in the Dark 1982, Duet for Three 1985, Family News 1989, Plain Jane 1992, Charlotte and Claudia Keeping in Touch 1994, Some Things About Flying 1997, Getting Over Edgar 1999, Critical Injuries 2001, Luck 2005, Exit Lines 2008. *E-mail:* jbarfoot@sympatico.ca (home). *Website:* www3.sympatico.ca/jbarfoot (home).

BARGHOUTI, Marwan Haseeb, MA; Palestinian resistance leader; b. 6 June 1959, Kobar, Ramallah; m. Fadwa Bargouthi; three s. one d.; ed Bir Zeit Univ.; joined Fatah Movt aged 15; imprisoned for involvement in an intifada (uprising) 1976; placed under admin. detention without charges for six months 1985; deported to Jordan by Israeli authorities for allegedly inciting struggle against occupation 1987; returned to W Bank, Pres. student body, Bir Zeit Univ.; served in PLO in Tunis, cen. liaison officer between PLO and Fatah; helped organize political aspects of the first Intifada 1987; mem. Revolutionary Council of Fatah 1989, Sec.-Gen. in W Bank; returned to Ramallah under Oslo Accords 1994; mem. Palestinian Legis. Council (PLC) 1996, mem. Legal Cttee, Political Cttee, Chair. Parl. Cttee with French Parl.; participated in outbreak of second Intifada in W Bank and Gaza 2000; sponsor of Tanzim (Fatah's operation dept); arrested by Israeli armed forces during incursion into Ramallah April 2002, accused of being the leader of the al-Aqsa Martyrs Brigade, indicted on terrorism charges Aug. 2002; detained by Israel in Maskoubieh Prison, W Jerusalem, trial at Israeli court commenced Sept. 2002, found guilty of organizing suicide attacks which led to five deaths May 2004, given five consecutive life sentences June 2004. *E-mail:* fateh@fateh.org (office). *Website:* www.fateh.net.

BARGHOUTI, Mustafa, MD, MSc; Palestinian politician, human rights activist and physician; *Member, Palestinian Legislative Council;* b. 15 Jan. 1954, Jerusalem; ed trained as medical doctor in fmr Soviet Union, postgraduate training in Jerusalem and Stanford Univ., Calif., USA; lectured at Harvard, John Hopkins and Stanford Univs, also at IISS and Chatham House, London, UK, Brookings Inst., USA, Sydney Inst., Australia; est. Union of Palestinian Medical Relief Cttees 1979, currently Pres.; Co-founder Health, Devt, Information and Policy Inst., Ramallah, Grassroots Int. Protection for the Palestinian People; del. to Madrid Peace negotiations 1991; fmr mem. steering cttee of tech. cttee that prepared establishment of various Palestinian ministries; Co-founder and Sec. Palestinian Nat. Initiative (Mubadara); twice arrested for speaking out against Israeli blockade of Occupied Territories Jan. 2002; presidential cand. (ind.) in Palestinian Authority elections Jan. 2005; mem. Palestinian Legis. Council 2006–. *Publications:* author or co-author of books and research on health devt; numerous articles on civil soc., democracy issues and the political situation in Palestine. *Address:* Union of Palestinian Medical Relief Committees, PO Box 51483, Jerusalem, Israel (office). *Telephone:* (2) 296-9992 (office). *Fax:* (2) 296-9993 (office). *E-mail:* mustafa@hdip.org (home).

BARIANI, Didier, DèsSc; French politician; *Vice-President, Union Pour la Démocratie Française;* b. 16 Oct. 1943, Bellerive sur Allier; m. Chantal Maufroy (divorced); two c.; ed Inst. d'Etudes Politiques de Paris; Chargé de Mission, then Dept Head, Conseil Nat. du Patronat Français 1969–74; Dir, later Chair. Bd of Dirs, Centre de Perfectionnement et de Recherche des Relations Publiques 1974–79; Prin. Pvt. Sec. to Sec. of State for Environment, Ministry of Quality of Life June–Oct. 1974, to Sec. of State in charge of Public Admin, Prime Minister's Office 1974–76; Lecturer, Inst. d'Etudes Politiques de Paris 1975–79; Pres. Paris Fed. of Parti Radical Socialiste (PRS) 1973–78; Sec.-Gen. of Party 1977–79, UDF Deputy for Paris 20th Arrondissement 1978–81, Vice-Pres. UDF Group in Nat. Ass. 1978–81, Exec. Vice-Pres. 1994–97, Nat. Vice-Pres. UDF 1979–83, 1995–97, Pres. UDF, Paris 1999–; Pres. PRS 1979–83; mem. Steering Cttee, Exec. Cttee PRS 1971; mem. UDF Nat. Council 1978–; Paris Councillor 1983, mem. Perm. Comm., Conseil de Paris; Pres. and Dir-Gen. Saemar Saint-Blaise 1983–2001; Mayor 20th Arrondissement, Paris 1983–95, Deputy Mayor of Paris 1983–2001; Sec. of State, Ministry of Foreign Affairs 1986–88; Pres. Parti Radical 1979–83; Nat. Del. of UDF (relations with int. orgs) 1988–92; Man. Soc. INFORG (Information, Communication et Organisation) 1977–; Pres. Parti Radical Fédération Régionale de l'Ile de France 1988–; Exec. Vice-Pres. (in Nat. Ass.) UDF 1994–97, 1999–, Pres. UDF, Paris Council 1999–; Jt Sec.-Gen. responsible for UDF's relations with int. insts 1992–96; mem. Nat. Ass. 1993–97, Vice-Pres. 1995–97; mem. Comm. for Foreign Affairs 1993–97; Titular Judge High Court of Justice 1995–97; Pres. France-Israel Friendship Group 1993–97; Adviser to Mayor of Paris 1995–2001; Co-Producer UDF/RPR Project 'Gouverner ensemble' 1986, 'Projet UDF/RPR pour la France' 1993; Hon. Pres. Parti Radical, Paris Football Club; Chevalier Légion d'honneur, Officier Ordre nat. du Mérite. *Publication:* Les immigrés: pour ou contre la France? 1985, Manifeste des Radicaux (jtly) 1995, Manifestement Radical (jtly) 1996. *Leisure interests:* football, skiing, tennis. *Address:* Groupe UDF-9, Hôtel de Ville de Paris, 75196 Paris RP, France. *Telephone:* 1-42-76-51-27 (office). *Fax:* 1-42-76-64-57 (office). *E-mail:* didier.bariani@paris.fr (office). *Website:* www.paris.fr (office); www.udf.org (office).

BARICCO, Alessandro; Italian writer and playwright; b. 25 Jan. 1958, Turin; music critic, La Repubblica; cultural correspondent, La Stampa; co-founder La Scuola Holden (narrative skills workshop) 1994; collaboration with French band, Air, to produce backing music for City 2003; Assoc. Fandango Libri Publishing House 2005–; several literary prizes. *Television:* L'amore è un dardo 1993, Pickwick, del leggere e dello scrivere 1994, Totem. Letture, suoni, lezioni 1998–2001. *Plays:* Novecento 1994, Davila Roa 1996, Partita Spagnola 2003. *Film:* Lezione 21 2008. *Publications:* novels: Castelli di rabbia (trans. as Lands of Glass) (Premio Selezione Campiello, Prix Médicis étranger) 1991, Oceano Mare (trans. as Ocean Sea) (Premio Viareggio) 1993, Novecento. Un Monologo 1994, Seta (trans. as Silk) 1996, City 1999, Senza sangue (trans. as Without Blood) 2002, Omero, Iliade 2004, Questa Storia 2005; non-fiction: Il Genio in fuga 1988, L'anima di Hegel e le mucche del Wisconsin 1992, Barnum (collection of articles) 1995, Barnum 2 (collection of articles) 1998, Next 2002, I Barbari 2006. *Address:* Fandango Libri, viale Gorizia 19, 00198, Rome, Italy (office); c/o Canongate Books, 14 High Street, Edinburgh, EH1 1TE, Scotland.

BARING, Arnulf Martin, LLD; German academic; b. 8 May 1932, Dresden; s. of Martin Baring and Gertrud Stolze; m.; three d. one s.; ed Univs of Hamburg, Berlin, Freiburg, Columbia Univ., NY, USA, Freie Univ. Berlin, Inst. of Admin. Science, Speyer and Fondation Nat. des Sciences Politiques, Paris; Lecturer, Inst. for Public and Admin. Law, Freie Univ. Berlin 1956–58, in Political Science and Int. Relations 1966–68, Univ. Lecturer, Faculty of Econ. and Social Sciences 1968, Prof. of Political Science, Otto-Suhr-Inst. and John F. Kennedy Inst. 1969–, of Contemporary History and Int. Relations, Dept of History 1976–98 (retd); Research Assoc., Center for Int. Affairs, Harvard Univ. 1968–69; Political Ed. Westdeutscher Rundfunk 1962–64; Guest Prof. Stiftung für Wissenschaft und Politik, Ebenhausen, Sr Research Assoc., Inst. for East-West Security Studies, New York, Fellow, Wilson Int. Center for Scholars, Washington, DC 1986–88; mem. Inst. for Advanced Study, Princeton, NJ 1992–93; Fellow, St Antony's Coll., Oxford 1993–94. *Publications include:* Charles de Gaulle: Grosse und Grenzen (with Christian Tautil) 1963, Aussenpolitik in Adenauers Kanzlerdemokratie 1969, Sehr verehrter Herr Bundeskanzler, Heinrich von Brentano im Briefwechsel mit Konrad Adenauer 1949–64, 1974, Zwei zaghafte Riesen? Deutschland und Japan nach 1945 (co-ed.) 1977, Machtwechsel, Die Ära Brandt-Scheel 1982, Unser neuer Grössenwahn, Deutschland zwischen Ost und West 1988, Deutschland, was nun? 1991, Scheitert Deutschland? 1997, Es lebe die Republik, es lebe Deutschland! 1999; contrib. to Frankfurter Allgemeine Zeitung, Westdeutscher und Norddeutscher Rundfunk, Sender Freies Berlin. *Leisure interests:* travel, rambling. *Address:* Ahrenshooper Zeile 64, 14129 Berlin, Germany. *E-mail:* anfragen@arnulf-baring.de. *Website:* www.arnulf-baring.de.

BARING, Hon. Sir John Francis Harcourt (see Ashburton, Baron).

BARKAT, Nir, BSc; Israeli business executive and politician; *Mayor of Jerusalem;* b. 1959, Jerusalem; m. Beverly Barkat; three d.; ed Hebrew Univ.; served as paratrooper in Israel Defence Forces 1977–83; Co-founder BRM Group (antivirus software co.) 1988, BRM Capital 2000; Co-founder Snunit (nonprofit org. for promotion of use of computer software in elementary educ.); Co-founder Israel Venture Network 2001; Founder Jerusalem Will Succeed party 2003; unsuccessful candidate for Mayor of Jerusalem 2003; mem. Jerusalem City Council 2003–08; Mayor of Jerusalem 2008–; fmr Chair. BackWeb and Checkpoint. *Address:* Jerusalem Municipality, Information Unit, 1 Safra Square, Jerusalem 91007, Israel (office). *Telephone:* 2-6296910 (office). *Website:* www.jerusalem.muni.il/model (office).

BARKAUSKAS, Antanas Stase; Lithuanian government official (retd); b. 20 Jan. 1917, Paparchiai, Lithuania; s. of Stasys Barkauskas and Aleksandra Barkauskas; m. Zoya Yarashunaitė 1961; one s. one d.; ed Higher Communist Party School, Moscow and Acad. of Social Sciences; mem. of Lithuanian Young Komsomol League 1940; Soviet official in Kaunas 1940–41; served in 16th Lithuanian Div. 1942–44; mem. CPSU 1942–90, party official in Kaunas during post-war period; Sec. Vilnius (later Kaunas) Regional Cttee of Lithuanian CP 1950–53; Teacher, Head of Dept, Kaunas Polytechnic Inst. 1953–55; Head of Dept, Cen. Cttee of Lithuanian CP 1959–60, mem. Cen. Cttee 1960–90, Sec. of Cen. Cttee 1961–75, mem. Secr. 1961–91, mem. Politburo 1962–66; Deputy to Supreme Soviet of Lithuania 1959–90, Chair. Supreme Soviet of Lithuanian SSR 1959–75, Pres. of Presidium 1975–85; Deputy to Supreme Soviet of USSR 1974–89, Vice-Chair. of Presidium 1976–85; mem. Cen. Auditing Cttee of CPSU 1976–81; Cand. mem. Cen. Cttee, CPSU 1981–86 (retd); Honoured Cultural Worker of Lithuanian SSR 1967. *Publications:* Country, Culture, Rural Life 1967, Culture and Society 1975, Lithuanian Countryside: Past, Present and Future (in English, French, German, Hungarian and Arabic) 1976, Lithuania: Years and Deeds (in English) 1982. *Leisure interests:* fiction, travelling, sport. *Address:* M.K. Churlionio str. 6, Flat 5, Vilnius, Lithuania. *Telephone:* (2) 62-44-45.

BARKER, David James Purslove, CBE, MD, PhD, FRS, FRCP; British epidemiologist and academic; *Professor of Clinical Epidemiology, University of Southampton;* b. 29 June 1938, London; s. of the late Hugh Barker and Joye Barker; m. 1st Angela Coddington 1960 (deceased); m. 2nd Janet Franklin 1983; three s. two d. and one step-s. two step-d.; ed Oundle School and Guy's Hosp. Univ. of London; Research Fellow, Dept of Medicine, Univ. of Birmingham 1963, Lecturer in Medicine 1966; Lecturer in Preventive Medicine, Makerere Univ. Uganda 1969–72; Sr Lecturer in Clinical Epidemiology and Consultant Physician, Univ. of Southampton 1972–79, Prof. of Clinical Epidemiology 1979–, Dir MRC Environmental Epidemiology Unit 1984–2003; Hon. Consultant Physician, Royal South Hants. Hosp.; Founder FMedSci 1998; Hon. FRCOG 1993; Hon. Fellow, Royal Coll. of Paediatrics; Royal Soc. Wellcome Gold Medal 1994, Feldberg Foundation Award, Prince Mahidol Prize for Medicine. *Publications:* Practical Epidemiology 1973, Epidemiology in Medical Practice (with G. Rose) 1976, Epidemiology for the Uninitiated (with G. Rose) 1979, Fetal and Infant Origins of Adult Disease 1992, Mothers, Babies and Disease in Later Life 1998, The Best Start in Life 2003. *Leisure interests:* writing, drawing, golf, fishing, craic. *Address:* MRC Epidemiology Resource Centre, Southampton General Hospital, Southampton, SO16 6YD (office); Manor Farm, East Dean, nr Salisbury, Wilts., SP5 1HB, England (home). *Telephone:* (23) 8077-7624 (office); (1794) 340016 (home). *Fax:* (23) 8070-4021 (office). *E-mail:* djpb@mrc.soton.ac.uk (office). *Website:* www.mrc.soton.ac.uk (office).

BARKER, Graeme W. W., PhD, FBA; British archaeologist and academic; *Disney Professor of Archaeology and Director, McDonald Institute for Archaeological Research, University of Cambridge;* b. 23 Oct. 1946; ed St John's Coll., Cambridge; Lecturer in Prehistoric Archaeology, Univ. of Sheffield 1972–84; Dir British School at Rome 1984–88; Prof. of Archaeology and Head, School of Archaeology and Ancient History, Univ. of Leicester 1988–2004, Founding Grad. Dean 2000–03, apptd one of three Pro-Vice-Chancellors 2003; Disney Prof. of Archaeology and Dir McDonald Inst. for Archaeological Research, Univ. of Cambridge 2004–; has conducted fieldwork in UK, Italy, Libya, Jordan, Mozambique and Borneo; mem. British Acad.'s Review Cttee of the British Schools and Insts Abroad, British Acad.'s Bd for Acad.-Sponsored Insts and Socs; mem. several editorial panels, including Cambridge University Press 'Manuals in Archaeology', Leicester Univ. Press, Journal of Mediterranean Archaeology; Pres. Prehistoric Soc.; Dan David Prize (jtly) 2005. *Publications:* more than 20 books, including A Mediterranean Valley: Landscape Archaeology as Annales History in the Biferno Valley 1995 (Italian trans. 2001), The Biferno Valley Survey: The Archaeological and Geomorphological Record 1995, Farming the Desert: The UNESCO Libyan Valleys Archaeological Survey (two vols) 1996, Archaeology and Desertification: The Wadi Faynan Landscape Survey 2006; more than 200 papers on subsistence archaeology, forager-farmer transitions, Mediterranean landscape history, desertification, and rainforest foraging and farming. *Address:* Department of Archaeology, University of Cambridge, Downing Street, Cambridge, CB2 3DZ, England (office). *Telephone:* (1223) 339284 (office). *Fax:* (1223) 333536 (office). *E-mail:* director.pa@mcdonald.cam.ac.uk (office). *Website:* www.arch.cam.ac.uk (office); www.mcdonald.cam.ac.uk (office).

BARKER, Patricia (Pat) Margaret, CBE, BSc (Econ), FRSL; British author; b. 8 May 1943, Thornaby-on-Tees; m. David Barker 1978; one s., one d.; ed London School of Econs; taught in colls of further educ. 1965–70; Patron New Writing North; mem. Soc. of Authors, PEN; Hon. Fellow, LSE 1998; Hon. MLitt (Teesside) 1993; Hon. DLitt (Napier) 1996, (Durham) 1998, (Hertfordshire) 1998, (London) 2002; Dr hc (Open Univ.) 1997; Fawcett Prize 1983, Guardian Prize for Fiction 1993, Northern Electric Special Arts Award 1994. *Publications:* novels: Union Street 1982, Blow Your House Down 1984, The Century's Daughter 1986 (retitled Liza's England 1996), The Man Who Wasn't There 1989; trilogy of First World War novels: Regeneration 1991, The Eye in the Door 1993, The Ghost Road (Booker Prize 1995) 1995; Another World 1998, Border Crossing 2001, Double Vision 2003, Life Class 2007. *Address:* Aitken Alexander Associates Ltd, 18–21 Cavaye Place, London, SW10 9PT, England (office). *Telephone:* (20) 7373-8672 (office). *Fax:* (20) 7373-6002 (office). *E-mail:* reception@aitkenalexander.co.uk (office). *Website:* www.aitkenalexander.co.uk (office).

BARKER, Richard (Rick); New Zealand politician; b. 27 Oct. 1951, Greymouth; m.; three c.; ed Greymouth High School, Otago Univ.; various jobs including shop assistant, bartender, storeworker, farmhand, driver, factory worker, quarrier; Nat. Sec. Service Workers' Union; Exec. em. Council of Trade Unions; elected Labour Party MP for Hastings 1993, Minister of Customs 2002–05, for the Community and Voluntary Sector 2004–05, for Courts 2003–08, of Internal Affairs, of Civil Defence, of Veterans' Affairs 2005–08; Trustee Nga Tukimata O Kahungunu; Chair. Hawke's Bay Work Trust; Patron SPELD (Specific Learning Disabilities Federation), Deerstalkers Asscn, Schizophrenics Soc. *Address:* New Zealand Labour Party, Parliament Buildings, Wellington, New Zealand (office). *Telephone:* (4) 471-9998 (office). *Fax:* (4) 473-3579 (office). *E-mail:* contact@labour.org.nz (office). *Website:* www.labour.org.nz (office).

BARKIN, Ellen; American actress; b. 16 April 1955, New York; m. 1st Gabriel Byrne 1988 (divorced); one s.; m. 2nd Ronald Perelman 2000 (divorced 2006); ed City Univ. of New York and Hunter Coll. Ind. *Films:* Diner 1982, Daniel 1983, Tender Mercies 1983, Eddie and the Cruisers 1983, The Adventures of Buckaroo Banzai 1984, Harry and Son 1984, Enormous Changes at the Last Minute 1985, Down by Law 1986, The Big Easy 1987, Siesta 1987, Sea of Love 1989, Johnny Handsome, Switch, Man Trouble 1992, Mac 1993, This Boy's Life 1993, Into the West 1993, Bad Company 1995, Wild Bill 1995, Mad Dog Time 1996, The Fan 1996, Fear and Loathing in Las Vegas, Popcorn, Drop Dead Gorgeous, The White River Kid 1999, Crime and Punishment in Suburbia 2000, Mercy 2000, Someone Like You 2001, Palindromes 2005, Trust the Man 2005, Ocean's Thirteen 2007, Brooklyn's Finest 2009, Happy Tears 2009. *Stage appearances include:* Shout Across the River 1980, Killings on the Last Line 1980, Extremities 1982, Eden Court. *TV appearances include:* Search for Tomorrow, Kent State 1981, We're Fighting Back 1981, Terrible Joe Moran 1984, Before Women Had Wings 1998 (Emmy Award). *Address:* c/o CAA, 9830 Wilshire Boulevard, Beverly Hills, CA 90212, USA (office).

BARLOW, Sir Frank, Kt, CBE; British business executive; *Chairman, Logica PLC;* b. 25 March 1930; s. of John Barlow and Isabella Barlow; m. Constance Patricia Ginns 1950 (died 2000); one s. two d.; ed Barrow Grammar School, Cumbria; with Nigerian Electricity Supply Corpn 1952–59; worked for Daily Times, Nigeria 1960–62; Man. Dir Ghana Graphic 1962–63, Barbados Advocate 1963, Trinidad Mirror Newspapers 1963–64, Daily Mirror 1964–67, King & Hutchings 1967–75; Dir and Gen. Man. Westminster Press 1975–83, CEO Westminster Press Group 1985–90; Dir Economist 1983–99; CEO Financial Times Group 1983–99 (Chair. 1993–96); Man. Dir Pearson PLC 1990–96; Chair. BSkyB 1991–95, Logica PLC 1995–; Pres. Les Echos, Paris 1988–90; Dir Elsevier UK 1991–94; Dir Soc. Européene des Satellites SA 2000–; Chair. Lottery Products Ltd 1997–; Dir Press Asscn 1985–93; Chair. Printers' Charitable Corpn 1995–; Dir Royal Philharmonic Orchestra 1988–93. *Leisure interests:* golf, fell walking, angling. *Address:* Logica PLC, Stephenson House, 75 Hampstead Road, London, NW1 2PL (office); Tremarne, Marsham Way, Gerrards Cross, Buckinghamshire, SL9 8AW, England (home). *Telephone:* (20) 7446-1786 (office). *Website:* www.logica.com (office).

BARLOW, Sir William, Kt, DSc, FREng, FIEE, FIMechE; British engineer; b. 8 June 1924, Oldham; s. of Albert Edward Barlow and Annice Barlow; m. Elaine Mary Atherton Adamson 1948; one s. one d.; ed Manchester Grammar School and Manchester Univ.; English Electric Co. Ltd 1947–68; Man. Dir English Electric Computers 1967–68; Chief Exec. Ransome Hoffmann Pollard Ltd 1969–77, Chair. 1971–77; Chair. Post Office Corpn 1977–80; Dir Thorn EMI PLC 1980–89, Chair. of Eng Group 1980–84; Dir BICC PLC 1980–91, Chair. 1984–91; Chair. Ericsson Ltd 1981–94, Metal Industries Ltd 1980–84, SKF (UK) Ltd 1990–92, Barking Power 1992–93, Parsons Brinckerhoff Ltd 1997–2002; Chair. Design Council 1980–86, Eng Council 1988–90; Dir Vodafone Group (fmrly Racal Telecom) 1988–98, Chemring Group PLC 1994–97 (Chair. 1997–98); Pres. Royal Acad. of Eng 1991–96; Vice-Pres. City and Guilds of London Inst. 1982–93; Gov. London Business School 1979–92; Pres. British Electrotechnical and Allied Mfrs Asscn (BEAMA) 1986–87; Hon. DSc (Cranfield Inst. of Tech.) 1979, (Bath) 1986, (Aston) 1988; Hon. DTech (Liverpool Polytechnic) 1988, (City Univ.) 1989, (Loughborough) 1993; Hon. DEng (UMIST) 1996. *Leisure interests:* golf, racing. *Address:* 4 Parkside, Henley-on-Thames, Oxon., RG9 1TX, England. *Telephone:* (1491) 411101. *Fax:* (1491) 410013.

BÄRLUND, Kaj-Ole Johannes, MSc(Econ); Finnish politician and international organization official; *Director, Environment, Housing and Land Management Division, Economic Commission for Europe, United Nations;* b. 9 Nov. 1945, Porvoo; s. of Elis Bärlund and Meri Bärlund; m. Eeva-Kaisa Oksama 1972; one s. one d.; journalist, Finnish Broadcasting Co. 1967–71; Public Relations Officer, Cen. Org. of Finnish Trade Unions 1971–72; Legis. Sec. Ministry of Justice 1972–79; mem. Parl. 1979–91; Chair. Porvoo City Bd 1979–87, Nat. Cttee on Natural Resources 1979–83; Chair. Swedish Labour Union of Finland 1983–90; mem. Nordic Council, Vice-Chair. Nordic Council Social and Environment Cttee 1983–87; mem. Exec. Bd Finnish Broadcasting Co. 1982–83, Neste Oy 1983–90; Chair. Bureau of the Montreal Protocol 1989–90; Chair. UN/ECE Cttee on Environmental Policy 1991–95; Minister of the Environment 1987–91; Dir-Gen. Nat. Bd of Waters and the Environment 1990–95; Dir-Gen. Finnish Environment Inst. 1995–2001; Dir Environment and Human Settlements Div. (later Environment, Housing and Land Man. Div.) UN ECE 1995–; Chair. Consumers' Union of Finland 1983–90, Peoples of Finland and Russia Friendship Soc. 1991–95, Union of the Pulmonary Disabled in Finland 1993–95; mem. Party Exec., Finnish Social Democratic Party 1984–91, Chair. Environmental Working Group 1981–87; State Publicity Prize (Finland) 1972. *Publications:* Miksi Ei EEC 1971, Palkat Paketissa 1972. *Leisure interests:* tennis, cross-country skiing, literature, roller skating. *Address:* UN ECE Environment, Housing and Land Management Division, Palais des Nations, Office 336, 1211 Geneva 10, Switzerland (home); 229 rue de la Cité, 01220 Divonne-les-Bains, France (home). *Telephone:* (22) 917-23-70 (office); (4) 50-20-44-93 (home). *Fax:* (22) 907-01-07 (office). *E-mail:* kaj.barlund@unece.org (office). *Website:* www.unece.org (office).

BARMANBEK, İmre, BSc; Turkish business executive; *Deputy Chairperson, Doğan Holding;* b. 1942; ed Ankara Univ.; began career as asst tax auditor, Bd of Accountancy Specialists, Ministry of Finance, later Chief Accountant Specialist –1977; fmr State Planning Specialist, State Planning Org.; mem. Tax Appeals Comm. –1977; Chief Financial Officer, jt venture co. formed between Koç and Doğus Akü Industry Inc., later Gen. Man.; Chief Financial Officer, Doğan Group of Companies Holding Inc., mem. Exec. Bd 1999–, CEO 1999–2003, Deputy Chair. 2003–; mem. Turkish Industrialists and Businessmen's Asscn (TÜSİAD); Best Woman Manager of the Year (Turkey) 1999, ranked by Fortune magazine amongst 50 Most Powerful Women in Business outside the US (33rd) 2001, (22nd) 2002, (21st) 2003, (22nd) 2004, (23rd) 2005, (39th) 2006, (43rd) 2007, ranked by Forbes magazine amongst 100 Most Powerful Women (100th) 2006, (88th) 2007. *Address:* Office of the Deputy Chairperson, Doğan Şirketler Grubu Holding A.Ş., Oymacı Sok., 51 Altunizade, Üsküdar, 34662 Istanbul, Turkey (office). *Telephone:* (216) 556-9000 (office). *Fax:* (216) 556-9398 (office). *Website:* www.doganholding.com.tr (office).

BARNABY, Charles Frank, BSc, MSc, PhD; British physicist; *Consultant, Oxford Research Group;* b. 27 Sept. 1927, Andover, Hants.; s. of Charles H. Barnaby and Lilian Sainsbury; m. Wendy Elizabeth Field 1972; one s. one d.; ed Andover Grammar School and Univ. of London; Physicist, UK Atomic Energy Authority 1950–57; mem. Sr Scientific Staff, MRC, Univ. Coll. Medical School 1957–68; Exec. Sec. Pugwash Confs on Science and World Affairs 1968–70; Dir Stockholm Int. Peace Research Inst. (SIPRI) 1971–81; Prof. of Peace Studies, Free Univ., Amsterdam 1981–85; Dir and Scientific Adviser, World Disarmament Campaign (UK) 1982–; Consultant, Oxford Research Group 1998–; Ed. Int. Journal of Human Rights; Hon. DSc (Frei Univ., Amsterdam) 1982, (Southampton) 1996, (Bradford) 2007. *Publications:* Man and the Atom 1971, Preventing the Spread of Nuclear Weapons (ed.) 1971, Anti-ballistic Missile Systems (co-ed.) 1971, Disarmament and Arms Control 1973, Nuclear Energy 1975, The Nuclear Age 1976, Prospects for Peace 1980, Future Warfare (co-author and ed.) 1983, Space Weapons 1984, Star Wars Brought Down to Earth 1986, The Automated Battlefield 1986, The Invisible Bomb 1989, The Gaia Peace Atlas 1989, The Role and Control of Weapons in the 1990s 1992, How Nuclear Weapons Spread 1993, Instruments of Terror 1997, How to Build a Nuclear Bomb and Other Weapons of Mass Destruction 2003; articles in scientific journals. *Leisure interest:* natural history. *Address:* Brandreth, Chilbolton, Stockbridge, Hants., SO20 6HW, England (home).

Telephone: (1264) 860423 (home). *Fax:* (1264) 860868 (home). *E-mail:* frank.barnaby@btinternet.com (home).

BARNALA, Surjit Singh, LLB; Indian politician and lawyer; *Governor of Tamil Nadu;* b. 21 Oct. 1925, Ateli, Gurgaon Dist (now in Haryana); s. of the late Nar Singh and Jasmer Kaur; m. Surjit Kaur 1954; three s. one d.; ed Lucknow Univ.; Shiromani Akali Dal MP for Barnala 1967–77; Educ. Minister of Punjab 1969–71; MP from Sangrur 1977; Union Agric., Irrigation and Food Minister in Janata Govt 1977–80; elected Pres. Shiromani Akali Dal 1985; Chief Minister of Punjab 1985–87; Gov. of Tamil Nadu 1990, 2004–, of Uttaranchal 2000–03, of Andhra Pradesh Jan. 2003–Nov. 04; Admin. of Puducherry 2009–; Minister of Chemicals and Fertilizers 1998–99, of Food 1998–2001; represented India at FAO. *Publication:* Story of an Escape. *Leisure interests:* painting, reading, ecology. *Address:* Secretary to the Governor of Tamil Nadu, Chennai 600 009, India (office). *Telephone:* (44) 25671555 (office). *Fax:* (44) 25672304 (office). *E-mail:* governor@tn.nic.in (office). *Website:* www.tn.gov.in (office).

BARNARD, Eric Albert, PhD, FRS; British biochemist and academic; *Visiting Professor of Pharmacology, University of Cambridge;* b. 2 July 1929, London; m. Penelope J. Hennessy 1956; two s. two d.; ed Davenant Foundation School, King's Coll., Univ. of London; Nuffield Foundation Fellow, King's Coll. 1956–59, Asst Lecturer 1959–60, Lecturer 1960–64; Assoc. Prof. of Biochemical Pharmacology, State Univ. of New York 1964–65, Prof. of Biochemistry 1965–76, Head Biochemistry Dept 1969–76; Rank Prof. of Physiological Biochemistry, Imperial Coll. of Science and Tech., London 1976–85, Chair. Div. of Life Sciences 1977–85, Head Dept of Biochemistry 1979–85; Dir MRC Molecular Neurobiology Unit, Cambridge 1985–92; Dir Molecular Neurobiology Unit, Prof. of Neurobiology, Royal Free Hosp. School of Medicine, London Univ. 1992–; Rockefeller Fellow, Univ. of Calif., Berkeley 1960–61; Guggenheim Fellow, MRC Lab. of Molecular Biology, Cambridge 1971; Visiting Prof., Univ. of Marburg, FRG 1965, Tokyo Univ. 1993; Visiting Scientist, Inst. Pasteur, France 1973; Ed.-in-Chief Receptors and Channels 1993–; Visiting Prof. Dept of Pharmacology, Cambridge Univ. 1999–; mem. American Soc. of Biological Chemists, Int. Soc. of Neurochemistry; cttee mem. MRC; foreign mem. Polish Acad. of Sciences 2000; mem. editorial bd four scientific journals; Josiah Macy Faculty Scholar Award, USA 1975, Medal of Polish Acad. of Sciences 1980, Ciba Medal and Prize 1985, Eastman Kodak Award (USA) 1988, Erspamer Int. Award for Neuroscience 1991, Eli Lilly Prize for European Neuroscience 1998, Thudichum Prize for Molecular Neuroscience 2007. *Publications:* ed. eight scientific books; numerous papers in learned journals. *Leisure interest:* the pursuit of good claret. *Address:* Department of Pharmacology, University of Cambridge, Tennis Court Road, Cambridge, CB2 1PD, England (office). *Telephone:* (1223) 847876 (office). *E-mail:* eb247@cam.ac.uk (office). *Website:* www.phar.cam.ac.uk/research (office).

BARNARD, Lukas Daniël, MA, DPhil; South African intelligence officer and university professor; b. 14 June 1949, Otjiwarongo; s. of Nicolaas Evehardus Barnard and Magdalena Catharina Beukes; m. Engela Brand 1971; three s.; ed Otjiwarongo High School, Univ. of Orange Free State; Sr Lecturer, Univ. of OFS 1976, Prof. and Head, Dept of Political Science 1978; Dir-Gen. Nat. Intelligence Service (fmrly Dept of Nat. Security) 1980–91, Head Constitutional Devt Service 1992; mem. several cttees and bds; S African Police Star for Outstanding Service 1985, Order of the Star of S Africa (Class 1), Gold 1987, Nat. Intelligence Service Decoration for Outstanding Leadership, Gold Nat. Intelligence Service Medal for Distinguished Service, Senior Service Award, Gold (CDS) 1992. *Publications:* one book, 26 articles in popular and technical scientific journals. *Leisure interest:* tennis. *Address:* c/o Constitutional Development, Private Bag X804, Pretoria 0001, South Africa. *Telephone:* 3412400.

BARNDORFF-NIELSEN, Ole Eiler, ScD, RI; Danish mathematician and academic; *Professor, Department of Mathematical Sciences, University of Århus;* b. 18 March 1935, Copenhagen; m. Bente Jensen-Storch 1956; two s. one d.; ed Univ. of Copenhagen, Univ. of Århus; Prof. of Math. Statistics, Inst. of Math., Univ. of Århus 1973–, Scientific Dir Math. Centre 1995–97, MaPhySto (Centre for Math. Physics and Stochastics) 1998–2003; Ed.-in-Chief Bernoulli 1994–2000; mem. Royal Danish Acad. of Sciences and Letters 1980–, Academia Europaea 1990–; Pres. Bernoulli Soc. for Math. Statistics and Probability 1993–95; Hon. Fellow, Int. Statistical Inst., Royal Statistical Soc., Hon. Mem. Danish Soc. for Theoretical Statistics; Dr hc (Univ. Paul Sabatier, Toulouse) 1993, (Katholieke Univ. Leuven) 1999; Humboldt Research Award 2002. *Publications:* Information and Exponential Families in Statistical Theory 1978, Parametric Statistical Models and Likelihood 1988, Asymptotic Techniques for Use in Statistics (with D. R. Cox) 1989, Decomposition and Invariance of Measures with a View to Statistical Transformation Models (with P. Blæsild and P. S. Eriksen) 1989, Inference and Asymptotics (with D. R. Cox) 1994; numerous scientific papers. *Leisure interests:* biography, opera, tennis. *Address:* Department of Mathematical Sciences, University of Århus, 8000 Århus (office); Dalvangen 48, 8270 Højbjerg, Denmark (home). *Telephone:* 89-42-35-21 (office); 86-27-14-42 (home). *E-mail:* oebn@imf.au.dk (home).

BARNES, Brenda C., BA, MBA; American business executive; *Chairman and CEO, Sara Lee Corporation;* ed Augustana Coll. and Loyola Univ., Chicago; held several sr exec. positions in operations, gen. man., sales and marketing, PepsiCo 1976–98 including Vice-Pres. Marketing, Frito-Lay, Business Man. Wilson Sporting Goods, COO PepsiCola North America 1994–96, Pres. and CEO 1996–98; interim Pres. and COO Starwood Hotels & Resorts 1999–2000; Adjunct Prof., Northwestern Univ.'s Kellogg Grad. School of Man. 2002; Guest Lecturer, North Cen. Coll. 2002; mem. Bd of Dirs, Pres. and COO Sara Lee Corpn 2004–05, mem. Bd of Dirs, Pres. and CEO Feb.–Oct. 2005, Chair. and CEO Oct. 2005–; mem. Bd of Dirs The New York Times Co., Staples Inc., Lucas Film Ltd; fmr Dir Avon Products Inc., PepsiAmericas Inc., Sears, Roebuck & Co.; Chair. Bd Trustees Augustana Coll.; mem. Steering Cttee Kellogg Center for Exec. Women at Northwestern Univ.; Hon. DHumLitt (Augustana Coll.) 1997; ranked by Fortune magazine amongst 50 Most Powerful Women in Business in the US (39th) 2004, (third) 2005, (sixth) 2006, (10th) 2007, ranked by Forbes magazine amongst 100 Most Powerful Women (37th) 2004, (eighth) 2005, (ninth) 2006, (19th) 2007, (45th) 2008. *Address:* Sara Lee Corpn, 3 First National Plaza, Chicago, IL 60602-4260, USA (office). *Telephone:* (312) 726-2600 (office). *Fax:* (312) 726-3712 (office). *Website:* www.saralee.com (office).

BARNES, Christopher Richard, CM, PhD, FRSC, PGeol; Canadian geologist and academic; *Project Director, Neptune Canada, University of Victoria;* b. 20 April 1940, Nottingham, England; m. Susan M. Miller 1961; three d.; ed Univs. of Birmingham and Ottawa; NATO Research Fellow, Univ. of Wales, Swansea 1964–65; Asst Prof., Earth Sciences Dept, Univ. of Waterloo 1965–70, Assoc. Prof. 1970–76, Prof. and Chair. 1976–81, Biology Dept 1973–81, Sr Research Fellow, Univ. of Southampton, UK 1971–72; Univ. of Cambridge 1980–81; Prof. and Head, Memorial Univ. of Newfoundland 1981–87; Acting Dir Centre for Earth Resources Research 1984–87; Dir-Gen. Sedimentary and Marine Geosciences, Geological Survey of Canada 1987–89; Dir Centre for Earth and Ocean Research, Univ. of Vic. 1989–2000, Dir School of Earth and Ocean Sciences 1991–2002, Project Dir Neptune Canada 2001–; Pres. Canadian Geoscience Council 1979, Geological Asscn of Canada 1983–84, Acad. of Sciences, RSC 1990–93; mem. Science Council of BC 1991–95, Atomic Energy Control Bd 1996–2000, Canadian Nuclear Safety Comm. 2000–; Geological Asscn of Canada Nat. Lecturer 1978; mem. Acad. of Sciences, Cordoba, Argentina 2003; mem. Order of Canada 1996; Bancroft Award 1982, Past-Pres.'s Medal 1977, Willis Ambrose Medal 1991, Queen's Golden Jubilee Medal 2002, Elkhana Billings Medal 2005. *Publications:* over 160 scientific works in geological journals. *Address:* Neptune Canada, Univ. of Victoria, PO Box 1700, Victoria, BC V8W 2Y2, Canada. *Telephone:* (250) 472-5350 (office). *Fax:* (250) 472-5370 (office). *E-mail:* crbarnes@uvic.ca (office). *Website:* www.neptunecanada.ca (office).

BARNES, John Arundel, DSC, MA, DPhil, FBA; British/Australian sociologist and academic; *Fellow, Churchill College, University of Cambridge;* b. 9 Sept. 1918, Reading, Berks.; s. of Thomas D. Barnes and M. Grace Barnes; m. Helen F. Bastable 1942; three s. one d.; ed Christ's Hosp., St John's Coll. Cambridge, Univ. of Cape Town and Balliol Coll. Oxford; served RN 1940–46; Research Officer, Rhodes-Livingstone Inst. Northern Rhodesia 1946–49; Lecturer, Dept of Anthropology, Univ. Coll. London 1949–51; Fellow, St John's Coll. Cambridge 1950–53; Simon Research Fellow, Univ. of Manchester 1951–53; Reader in Anthropology, London School of Econs 1954–56; Prof. of Anthropology, Univ. of Sydney 1956–58, ANU 1958–69; Fellow, Churchill Coll. Cambridge 1965–66, 1969–; Prof. of Sociology, Univ. of Cambridge 1969–82; Visiting Fellow, ANU 1978–79, 1984–92, Program Visitor 1993–98; Fellow, Acad. of Social Sciences, Australia; Distinguished Service Cross 1944; Wellcome Medal 1950, Rivers Medal 1959, Royal Anthropological Inst. *Publications:* Marriage in a Changing Society 1951, Politics in a Changing Society 1954, Three Styles in the Study of Kinship 1971, The Ethics of Inquiry in Social Science 1977, Who Should Know What? 1979, Models and Interpretations 1990, A Pack of Lies 1994. *Address:* Churchill College, Cambridge, CB3 0DS, England. *Telephone:* (1223) 276297.

BARNES, Jonathan, FBA; British academic; b. 26 Dec. 1942, Much Wenlock; s. of the late A. L. Barnes and K. M. Barnes; m. Jennifer Mary Postgate 1964; two d.; ed City of London School and Balliol Coll., Oxford; Lecturer in Philosophy, Exeter Coll., Oxford 1967–68, Fellow, Oriel Coll., Oxford 1968–78, Balliol Coll., Oxford 1978–94; Prof. of Ancient Philosophy, Univ. of Oxford 1989–94, Univ. of Geneva 1994–2002, Univ. of Paris IV–Sorbonne 2003–06; visiting posts at Univ. of Chicago 1966–67, Inst. for Advanced Study, Princeton 1972, Univ. of Mass 1973, Univ. of Tex. 1981, Wissenschaftskolleg zu Berlin 1985, Univ. of Alberta 1986, Univ. of Zurich 1987, Istituto Italiano per la Storia della Filosofia 1989, 1994, 1999, Ecole Normale Supérieure, Paris 1996, Scuola Normale di Pisa 2002; mem. L'Acad. scientifique, Geneva, Aristotelian Soc., Mind Asscn; Hon. Fellow American Acad. of Arts and Sciences 1999, Oriel Coll., Oxford 2007–; Condorcet Medal 1996, John Locke Lecturer, Univ. of Oxford 2004. *Publications:* The Ontological Argument 1972, Aristotle's Posterior Analytics 1975, The Presocratic Philosophers 1979, Doubt and Dogmatism (with M. F. Burnyeat and M. Schofield) 1980, Aristotle 1982, Science and Speculation (with J. Brunschwig and M. F. Burnyeat) 1982, The Complete Works of Aristotle 1984, The Modes of Scepticism (with J. Annas) 1985, Early Greek Philosophy 1987, Matter and Metaphysics (with M. Mignucci 1988, Philosophia Togata (with M. Griffin) Vol. I 1989, Vol. II 1997, The Toils of Scepticism 1991, Sextus Empiricus: Outlines of Scepticism (with J. Annas) 1994, The Cambridge Companion to Aristotle 1995, Logic and the Imperial Stoa 1997, The Cambridge History of Hellenistic Philosophy (with K. Algra, J. Mansfield and M. Schofield) 1999, Porphyry: Introduction 2003. *Address:* Les Charmilles, 36200 Ceaulmont (home); 12 blvd Arago, 75013 Paris, France (home). *E-mail:* jonathanbarnes@wanadoo.fr (home).

BARNES, Julian Patrick, (Dan Kavanagh, Basil Seal), BA; British writer; b. 19 Jan. 1946, Leicester, England; m. Pat Kavanagh (died 2008); ed City of London School, Magdalen Coll. Oxford; lexicographer, Oxford English Dictionary Supplement 1969–72; Asst Literary Ed. New Statesman 1977–79, reviewer 1977–81, TV critic 1979–82; Contributing Ed. New Review, London 1977–78; Deputy Literary Ed. Sunday Times, London 1979–81; TV Critic The Observer 1982–86; Hon. Fellow Magdalen Coll., Oxford 1996–; Somerset Maugham Award 1981, Geoffrey Faber Memorial Prize 1985, E. M. Forster Award, US Acad. of Arts and Letters 1986, Gutenberg Prize 1987, Grinzane Cavour Prize, Italy 1988, Shakespeare Prize, Germany 1993;

Officier, Ordre des Arts et des Lettres 1995. *Publications:* Metroland 1980, Before She Met Me 1982, Flaubert's Parrot (Geoffrey Faber Memorial Prize, Prix Médicis 1986) 1984, Staring at the Sun 1986, A History of the World in 10½ Chapters 1989, Talking it Over (Prix Femina Etranger 1992) 1991, The Porcupine 1992, Letters From London 1990–95 (articles) 1995, Cross Channel (short stories) 1996, England, England 1998, Love, etc. 2000, Something to Declare (essays) 2002, In the Land of Pain, by Alphonse Daudet (ed. and trans.) 2002, The Lemon Table (short stories) 2004, The Pedant in the Kitchen 2004, Arthur & George 2005, Nothing to be Frightened Of 2008; as Dan Kavanagh: Duffy 1980, Fiddle City 1981, Putting the Boot In 1985, Going to the Dogs 1987. *Address:* United Agents, 12–26 Lexington Street, London, W1F 0LE, England (office). *Telephone:* (20) 3214-0800 (office). *Fax:* (20) 3214-0801 (office). *E-mail:* info@unitedagents.co.uk (office). *Website:* unitedagents.co.uk (office); www.julianbarnes.com.

BARNES, Peter John, MA, DM, DSc, FRCP, FMedSci, FRS; British medical scientist and academic; *Professor and Head of Thoracic Medicine, National Heart and Lung Institute, Imperial College London;* b. 29 Oct. 1946, Birmingham; s. of the late John Barnes and Eileen Barnes; m. Olivia Harvard-Watts 1976; three s.; ed Leamington Coll., Cambridge Univ., Oxford Univ. Clinical School; medical positions Oxford, Brompton Hosp., Nat. Hosp., Univ. Coll. Hosp. 1972–78; Sr Registrar Hammersmith Hosp. 1979–82; Sr Lecturer, Consultant Physician Royal Postgrad. Medical School 1982–85 (MRC Research Fellow 1978–79); Prof. of Clinical Pharmacology, Cardiothoracic Inst. 1985–87, of Thoracic Medicine, Nat. Heart and Lung Inst. 1987–; Hon. Consultant, Physician Royal Brompton Hosp. 1987–; MRC Travelling Fellow, Cardiovascular Research Inst., San Francisco 1981–82; numerous awards. *Publications:* Asthma: Basic Mechanics and Clinical Management, The Lung: Scientific Foundations 1991, Pharmacology of the Respiratory Tract 1993, Conquering Asthma 1994, Molecular Biology of Lung Disease 1994, Asthma (two vols) 1997, Airway Disease 2003, An Atlas of COPD 2004. *Leisure interests:* ethnic art, foreign travel, gardening. *Address:* Department of Thoracic Medicine, National Heart and Lung Institute (Imperial College), Dovehouse Street, London, SW3 6LY (office); 44 Woodsome Road, London, NW5 1RZ, England (home). *Telephone:* (20) 7351-8174 (office); (20) 7485-6582 (home). *Fax:* (20) 7351-5675 (office). *E-mail:* p.j.barnes@imperial.ac.uk (office). *Website:* www1.imperial.ac.uk/medicine (office).

BARNETT, Correlli Douglas, CBE, MA; British historian; *Fellow, Churchill College, Cambridge;* b. 28 June 1927, Norbury, Surrey; s. of Douglas A. Barnett and Kathleen M. Barnett; m. Ruth Murby 1950; two d.; ed Trinity School, Croydon and Exeter Coll. Oxford; Intelligence Corps 1945–48; North Thames Gas Bd 1952–57; public relations 1957–63; Keeper of Archives, Churchill Coll. Cambridge 1977–95; Defence Lecturer, Univ. of Cambridge 1980–83; Fellow, Churchill Coll., Cambridge 1977–; mem. Council, Royal United Services Inst. for Defence Studies 1973–85; mem. Cttee London Library 1977–79, 1982–84; Winston Churchill Memorial Lecturer, Switzerland 1982; Hon. DSc (Cranfield Univ.) 1993; Hon. Fellow, City and Guilds of London Inst. 2003; Screenwriters' Guild Award for Best British TV Documentary (The Great War) 1964; FRSL Award for Britain and Her Army 1971; Chesney Gold Medal Royal United Services Inst. for Defence Studies 1991. *Television includes:* The Great War (BBC TV) 1964, The Lost Peace (BBC TV) 1966, The Commanders (BBC TV) 1972. *Publications:* The Hump Organisation 1957, The Channel Tunnel (with Humphrey Slater) 1958, The Desert Generals 1960, The Swordbearers 1963, Britain and Her Army 1970, The Collapse of British Power 1972, Marlborough 1974, Bonaparte 1978, The Great War 1979, The Audit of War 1986, Hitler's Generals 1989, Engage the Enemy More Closely 1991 (Yorkshire Post Book of the Year Award 1991), The Lost Victory: British Dreams, British Realities 1945–1950 1995, The Verdict of Peace: Britain Between Her Yesterday and the Future 2001. *Leisure interests:* gardening, interior decorating, eating, idling, mole-hunting. *Address:* Catbridge House, East Carleton, Norwich, Norfolk, NR14 8JX, England (home). *Telephone:* (1508) 570410 (home). *Fax:* (1508) 570410 (home).

BARNETT, Baron (Life Peer), cr. 1983, of Heywood and Royton in Greater Manchester; **Joel Barnett,** PC, JP; British politician and accountant; b. 14 Oct. 1923; s. of Louis and Ettie Barnett; m. Lilian Goldstone 1949; one d.; ed Derby Street Jewish School, Manchester Central High School; Certified Accountant 1974; Sr Partner accountancy practice, Manchester 1953–74, 1979–80; served Royal Army Service Corps and British Mil. Govt in Germany; mem. Borough Council, Prestwich, Lancs. 1956–59; Labour cand. for Runcorn Div. of Cheshire 1959; MP for Heywood and Royton Div. of Lancashire 1964–83, mem. House of Commons Public Accounts Cttee 1965–71, Chair. 1979–83; mem. Public Expenditure Cttee 1971–74, Select. Cttee on Tax Credits 1973–74; Vice-Chair. Parl. Labour Party Econ. and Finance Group 1966–67, Chair. 1967–70, 1972–74; Opposition Spokesman on Treas. Matters 1970–74; Chief Sec. to the Treas. 1974–79, mem. Cabinet 1977–79; mem. Hallé Cttee 1982–93; Vice-Chair. Bd of Govs, BBC 1986–93; Chair., Dir, consultant to a number of cos; Chair. British Screen Finance Ltd 1985–95, Hansard Soc. for Parl. Govt 1984–95; Pres. Royal Inst. of Public Admin. 1989–92, Children's Medical Charity Trust PLC; Hon. Fellow Birkbeck Coll., London Univ. 1992; Trustee Victoria and Albert Museum 1984–96, Open Univ. Foundation 1995–; Gov. Birkbeck Coll., Hon. Fellow 2002; Hon. Treas. Manchester Fabian Soc. 1953–65; Hon. Visiting Fellow, Univ. of Strathclyde 1980–83; Hon. LLD (Strathclyde) 1983. *Publication:* Inside the Treasury 1982. *Leisure interests:* walking, conversation, reading, good food. *Address:* 92 Millbank Court, 24 John Islip Street, London, SW1P 4LG (home); 7 Hillingdon Road, Whitefield, Manchester, M45 7QQ, Lancs., England (home). *Telephone:* (20) 7828-4620 (London) (home); (161) 766-3634 (Manchester).

BARNETT, Peter Leonard, AM; Australian journalist, broadcaster and administrator; *Company Chairman, Light Technologies Pty Ltd;* b. 21 July 1930, Albany, Western Australia; s. of Leonard Stewart and Ruby Barnett; m. Siti Nuraini Jatim 1970; one s.; ed Guildford Grammar School, Western Australia, Univ. of Western Australia; Canberra Rep. and Columnist, The Western Australian 1953–57; SE Asia Corresp., Australian Broadcasting Comm. 1961, 1963, 1964, Jakarta Rep. 1962, New York and UN Corresp. 1964–67, Washington Corresp. 1967–70; News Ed. Radio Australia, Melbourne 1971–72, Washington Corresp. 1972–80, Controller, Melbourne 1980–84, Dir 1984–89; Exec. Dir Australian Broadcasting Corpn 1984–89; fmrly Exec. Dir Media Centre, Islamic Council of Victoria; currently Co. Chair., Light Technologies Pty Ltd; convenor, Melbourne City Circle; mem. editorial Bd Dialogue/Asia Pacific; Australia Award 1988. *Publication:* Foreign Correspondence 2001. *Leisure interests:* swimming, literature, musical composition. *Address:* Light Technologies Pty Ltd, 50 Market Street, Melbourne 3000 (office); 66/46 Lansell Road, Toorak, Vic. 3142, Australia (home). *Telephone:* (3) 9649-7770 (office); (3) 9827-5979 (home). *E-mail:* peter@lighttechnologies.com.au (office); plsnb@netspace.net.au (home).

BARNEVIK, Percy Nils, MBA; Swedish business executive; *Chairman, Hand in Hand International;* b. 13 Feb. 1941, Simrishamn; s. of Einar Barnevik and Anna Barnevik; m. Aina Orvarsson 1963; two s. one d.; ed Gothenburg School of Econs, Stanford Univ., USA; Man. Corp. Devt, Group Controller, Sandvik AB 1969–74, Pres. US subsidiary 1975–79, Exec. Vice-Pres. parent co. 1979–80, Chair. Sandvik AB 1983; Pres. and Chief Exec. ASEA AB, Västerås 1980–87; Pres. and CEO ABB Ltd 1988–96, Chair. 1996–2001; Dir Skanska 1986–92, Chair. 1992–97; Chair. Investor AB 1997–2002, AstraZeneca PLC 1999–2005; mem. Bd of Dirs General Motors Corpn 1996–2009, Du Pont Co. 1991–98; Adviser, Hand in Hand India (charity) 2000–, also Chair. Hand in Hand International; Fellow, Royal Acad. of Eng 1998; mem. of numerous professional orgs; recipient of several hon. degrees and numerous awards. *Address:* 10 Hill Street, London W1J 5NQ, UK, Nacka, Sweden (office). *Telephone:* (207) 514-5091 (office). *Fax:* (207) 514-5099 (office). *E-mail:* info@handinhandinternational.org.uk (office). *Website:* www.hihseed.org (office).

BARNEY, Matthew, BA; American film director, actor, artist and sculptor; b. 25 March 1967, San Francisco, Calif.; s. of Marsha Gibney; pnr Björk; one d.; ed Capital High School, Yale Univ.; Europa 2000 Prize, 45th Venice Biennale 1996, Guggenheim Museum Hugo Boss Award 1996, James D. Phelan Art Award in Video, Bay Area Video Coalition, San Francisco Foundation 1999, Glen Dimplex Award, Irish Museum of Modern Art, Dublin 2001. *Films include:* Cremaster 4 1995, Cremaster 1 1996, Cremaster 5 1997, March of the Anal Sadistic Warrior 1998, Cremaster 2 1999, Cremaster 3 2002, De Lama Lamina 2005, Drawing Restraint 9 2005, Destricted 2006, Matthew Barney: No Restraint (documentary) 2007. *Address:* c/o Gladstone Gallery, 515 West 24th Street, New York, NY 10011, USA. *Telephone:* (212) 206-9300. *Fax:* (212) 206-9301. *E-mail:* info@gladstonegallery.com. *Website:* www.gladstonegallery.com/barney.asp?id=605; www.cremaster.net; www.drawingrestraint.net.

BARNIER, Michel; French politician; *Minister for Agriculture and Fisheries;* b. 9 Jan. 1951, l'Isère; m.; three c.; ed Ecole Supérieure de Commerce, Paris; Pvt. Office of the Ministers for the Environment, Youth and Sport and for Trade and Craft Industries 1973–78; Departmental Councillor for Savoie 1973; mem. Nat. Ass. for Savoie 1978–93; Chair. Departmental Council of Savoie 1982; Co-Pres. Organizing Cttee for XVIth Olympic Games, Albertville and Savoie 1987–92; Minister of the Environment 1993–95; Minister of State for European Affairs 1995–97; Senator for Savoie 1997; Chair. French Assn of Council of European Municipalities and Regions 1997; Pres. Senate Del. for the EU 1998; EU Commr for Regional Policy and Institutional Reform 1999–2004, Special Adviser to EU Pres. Barroso 2006–07; Minister of Foreign Affairs 2004–05, for Agriculture and Fisheries June 2007–; Chevalier, Légion d'honneur. *Publications:* Vive la politique 1985, Le défi écologique, chacun pour tous 1990, L'Atlas des risques majeurs 1992, Vers une mer inconnue 1994. *Address:* Ministry of Agriculture and Fisheries, 78, rue de Varenne, 75349 Paris 07, France (office). *Telephone:* 1-49-55-49-55 (office). *Fax:* 1-49-55-40-39 (office). *E-mail:* ressource@agriculture.gouv.fr (office). *Website:* www.agriculture.gouv.fr (office).

BARNSLEY, Victoria, OBE; British publisher; *CEO, HarperCollins UK;* b. 4 March 1954; d. of the late Thomas E. Barnsley and Margaret Gwyneth Barnsley (née Llewellin); m. Nicholas Howard 1992; one d. one step-s.; ed Loughborough High School, Beech Lawn Tutorial Coll., Edinburgh Univ., Univ. Coll. London, York Univ.; with Junction Books 1980–83; founder, Chair. and CEO Fourth Estate 1984–2000; CEO HarperCollins UK 2000–, also for Australia, New Zealand, India and South Africa 2008–; Trustee Tate Gallery 1998–; Dir Tate Enterprises Ltd 1998–; council mem. Publishers Asscn 2001–, Vice-Pres. 2009–(10). *Address:* HarperCollins, 77–85 Fulham Palace Road, London, W6 8JB, England (office). *Telephone:* (20) 8307-4000 (office). *Fax:* (20) 8307-4440 (office). *E-mail:* contact@harpercollins.co.uk (office). *Website:* www.harpercollins.co.uk (office).

BAROIN, François, MA; French politician and lawyer; b. 21 June 1965, Paris; m. Valérie Broquisse 1991 (divorced 2006); three c.; ed Inst. of Higher Man. Studies (ISG), Paris; town councillor for Nogent-sur-Seine, Aube 1989; Deputy for Aube (Union for a Popular Movement—UMP), Assemblee Nationale 1993–95, 1997–2005, 2007–; Mayor of Troyes 1995–2001; Sec. of State and Govt Spokesperson 1995–97; Pres. Town Community Council, Troyes 2001–; barrister in pvt. law firm, Paris 2001–; Vice-Pres. Nat. Ass. 2002–05; Spokesperson UMP 2003–; Minister of Overseas France 2005–07, Minister of the Interior, Internal Security and Local Freedoms March–May 2007. *Leisure interests:* hunting, fishing, reading, chess, sports. *Address:* Hôtel de Ville, Place Alexandre Israël, 10000 Troyes, France (office). *E-mail:* fbaroin@assemblee-nationale.fr (office); francoisbaroin3@aol.com. *Website:* www.francoisbaroinblog.org.

BARON, Franklin Andrew Merrifield; Dominican business executive, politician and diplomatist; b. 19 Jan. 1923, Dominica; s. of Alexander Baron and O. M. Baron; m. Sybil Eva McIntyre 1973; ed Dominica Grammar School, St Mary's Acad.; Man. A.A. Baron & Co. 1939–45, partner 1945–78, sole owner 1987–; mem. Dominica Legis. and Exec. Councils 1954–60; rep. of Dominica to Fed. Talks 1956–60; Founder and Political Leader, Dominica United People's Party 1957–66; Minister of Trade and Production 1956–60; Chief Minister and Minister of Finance 1960–61; Man. Dir Franklyn Hotels Ltd 1970–75; Man. Sisserou Hotel 1975–76; Chair. Dominica Tourist Bd 1970–72, Dominica Electricity Services 1983–91, Nat. Commercial Bank of Dominica 1986–90, Fort Young Hotel Co. Ltd 1986–, New Chronicle Newspaper 1990–96, Paramount Printing Ltd 1992–; Propr The Chronicle 1996–; Adviser, Barclays Bank Int. 1976–84; non-resident Amb. to USA 1982–95; Perm. non-resident Rep. to UN and to OAS 1982–95, Chair. OAS 1985, 1993; non-resident High Commr in UK 1986–92; mem. Industrial Devt Corpn 1984–88; Dominica Award of Honour. *Leisure interests:* gardening, reading. *Address:* 14 Cork Street, PO Box 57, Roseau (office); Syb Bar Aerie, Champs Fleurs, Eggleston, Dominica (home). *Telephone:* 4480415 (office); 4488151 (home). *Fax:* 4480047 (office). *E-mail:* thechronicle@cwdom.dm (office); frankb@cwdom.dm (home). *Website:* www.dachronicle.com (office).

BARON, Martin, BA, MBA; American journalist; *Editor, The Boston Globe;* b. Tampa, FL; ed Lehigh Univ.; state reporter, business writer The Miami Herald 1976–79; joined Los Angeles Times 1979, apptd Business Ed. 1983, Asst . Man. Ed. for 'Column One' 1991, Ed. Orange Co. Edn 1993; joined The New York Times 1996, Assoc. Man. Ed. responsible for night-time news operations 1997–99; Exec. Ed. The Miami Herald 1999–2002; Ed. The Boston Globe 2002–; Pulitzer Prize 2001, Ed. of the Year, Editor & Publisher Magazine 2002. *Address:* The Boston Globe, 135 Morrissey Boulevard, POB 2378, Boston, MA 02107-2378, USA (office). *Telephone:* (617) 929-2000 (office). *Fax:* (617) 929-3192 (office). *E-mail:* news@globe.com (office). *Website:* www .boston.com (office).

BARÓN CRESPO, Enrique; Spanish politician; b. 1944, Madrid; m.; one s.; ed Calasancio de las Escuelas Pías Coll., Instituto Católico de Dirección de Empresas, Ecole Supérieure des Sciences Economiques et Commerciales, Paris; mem. Federación Universitaria Democrática Española; mem. Unión Sindical Obrero 1964; ran legal and econ. consultancy with Agapito Ramos; mem. Convergencia Socialista and Federación de Partidos Socialistas (FPS); negotiated electoral coalition of FPS with the Partido Socialista Obrero Español (PSOE); mem. Congress of Deputies 1977–, PSOE Spokesman for Econ. Affairs, Public Finance and the Budget 1977–82; Minister of Transport and Tourism 1982–85; mem. European Parl. 1986–, Pres. 1989–92; Chair. Parl. Group, Party of European Socialists 2000–. *Publications:* Population and Hunger in the World, Europa 92, Europe at the Dawn of the Millennium. *Leisure interests:* jazz, painting, walking, skiing. *Address:* Parlement Européen, ASP 6H 263, rue Wiertz 60, 1047 Brussels, Belgium. *Telephone:* (2) 284-5490 (office). *Fax:* (2) 284-9490 (office).

BARR, Roseanne (see Roseanne).

BARR, William Pelham, MA, JD; American lawyer and business executive; *Executive Vice-President and General Counsel, Verizon Communications Inc.;* b. 23 May 1950, New York; s. of Donald Barr and Mary Ahern; m. Christine Moynihan 1973; three d.; ed Columbia Univ., George Washington Univ.; staff officer CIA Washington 1973–77; barrister 1977–78; law clerk to US Circuit Judge 1977–78, Assoc. Shaw, Pittman, Potts & Trowbridge 1978–82, 1983–84, Partner 1985–89, 1993–; Deputy Asst Dir Domestic Staff Policy The White House, Washington 1982–83; Asst Attorney Gen. Office of Legal Counsel US Dept of Justice, Washington 1989–91; Attorney Gen. of USA 1991–93; Exec. Vice.-Pres., Gen. Counsel GTE Corpn (now Verizon Communications Inc.), Washington 1994–; mem. Virginia State Bar Asscn, DC Bar Asscn. *Address:* Verizon Communications Inc, 140 West Street, New York, NY 10007, USA (office). *Telephone:* (212) 395-2121 (office). *Fax:* (212) 869-3265 (office). *Website:* www.verizon.com (office).

BARRAK, Saad H. al-, BSc, MSc, PhD; Kuwaiti engineer and business executive; *Deputy Chairman and Managing Director (CEO), Zain;* ed Ohio and Harvard Univs, USA, Univ. of London, UK; fmr Chair. IT Soft, Cairo, Arab Telecom; Dir (non-exec.) Arab Man. Asscn, Cairo; Man. Dir International Turnkey Systems –2002; Deputy Chair. and Man. Dir (CEO) MTC (renamed Zain 2007), mem. Exec. Bd Celtel International; fmr Vice-Chair. Social Devt Office, Amiri Diwan, Kuwait; E-businessman of the Year Award 2003, Middle East CEO of the Year Award in the Information Communication Tech. sector 2005. *Address:* Zain Head office, Shuwaikh, Airport Road, Kuwait POB 22244, Safat, 13083 Kuwait (office). *E-mail:* info@zain.com (office). *Website:* www .zain.com (office).

BARRAULT, Marie-Christine; French actress; b. 21 March 1944, Paris; d. of Max-Henri Barrault and Marthe Valmier; m. 1st Daniel Toscan de Plantier (divorced); one s. one d.; m. 2nd Roger Vadim 1990 (died 2000); ed Conservatoire national d'art dramatique; Officer des Arts et des Lettres, Chevalier de la Legion d'honneur. *Theatre includes:* Andorra, Othon, Un couple pour l'hiver, Travail à domicile, Conversation chez les Stein sur Monsieur de Goethe absent, Dylan, cet animal étrange, Partage du midi, L'Etrange intermède, Même heure l'année prochaine, Enfin seuls!, La Cerisaie, Le bonheur des autres qui a peur de Virginia Woolf, La mènagerie de verre, Barrage contre le pacifique. *Films include:* Ma nuit chez Maude 1966, Le distrait 1970, Cousin, cousine 1975 (Prix Louis Delluc), Du côté des tennis 1976, L'état sauvage 1978, Femme entre chien et loup 1978, Ma chérie 1979, Stardust Memories 1980, L'amour trop fort 1981, Un amour en Allemagne 1983, Les mots pour le dire 1983, Un amour de Swann 1984, Pianoforte 1985, Le jupon rouge 1987, Adieu je t'aime 1988, Sanguines 1988,

Prisonnières 1988, Un été d'orage 1989, Dames galantes 1990, L'amour nécessaire 1991, Bonsoir 1994, C'est la tangente que je préfère 1997, La dilettante 1999, Azzurro 2000, Berlin Niagara 2000, Les amants de Mogador 2002, L'empreinte de l'ange 2004. *Musical:* L'homme rêvé 2000. *Television includes:* Marie Curie (series; Nymphe d'argent, Monte Carlo TV Festival 1991, 7 d'Or for best comedienne 1991), Le vieil ours et l'enfant 2001, Garonne (mini-series) 2002, Le don fait à Catchaires 2003, La deuxième vérité 2003, Rêves en France 2003, Droit d'asile 2003, Saint-Germain ou La négociation 2003, L'empreinte de l'ange 2004, Parlez-moi d'amour 2005, Ange de feu (mini-series) 2006. *Publication:* Le Cheval dans la pierre 1999. *Address:* c/o Cinéart – Marie Laure Munich, 36 rue de Ponthieu, 75008 Paris, France.

BARRÉ-SINOUSSI, Françoise Claire, DèsSc; French scientist; *Head of Retroviruses Unit, Institut Pasteur;* b. 30 July 1947, Paris; d. of Roger Sinoussi and Jeanine Fau; m. Jean-Claude Barré 1978; ed Lycée Bergson, Faculty of Science Paris VII and Paris VI; Research Asst, Inst. nat. de la Santé et de la recherche médicale (Inserm) 1975–80, Researcher 1980–86, Dir of Research 1986–; Head of Lab., Biology of Retroviruses Unit, Inst. Pasteur 1988–92, Head of Unit 1993–; mem. Governing Council Int. AIDS Soc. (IAS) 2006–; Chevalier, Ordre nat. du Mérite, Légion d'honneur; Prize of Fondation Körber pour la promotion de la Science européenne 1986, Prize of Acad. de médecine 1988, Faisal Prize for Medicine 1993, Prix du Rayonnement Français 2003, Nobel Prize in Medicine (jtly) 2008; inducted into Women in Tech. Int. Hall of Fame 2006. *Publications:* over 200 scientific publs including co-author of publ. in Science that first reported discovery of a retrovirus later named HIV 1983. *Leisure interests:* theatre, reading. *Address:* Institut Pasteur, Unité de Biologie des Rétrovirus, 25 rue du Docteur Roux, 75724 Paris cedex 15, France (office). *Telephone:* 1-45-68-80-00 (office). *E-mail:* fbarre@pasteur.fr (office). *Website:* www.pasteur.fr (office).

BARREIRO, Magdalena; Ecuadorean academic and government official; b. 1954; ed Escuela Politécnica del Ejército, MIT Sloan School of Man., Ill. Inst. of Tech.; worked in financial recovery unit Cen. Bank of Ecuador 1992–96; Dir financial analysis and valuation for privatisation Conam (admin. body of Office of the Pres.) 1997–98; Prof. of Finance Universidad San Francisco de Quito 2000–05; apptd Deputy Minister for Economy and Finance April 2005, Minister of Economy and Finance August–Dec. 2005. *Address:* c/o Ministry of the Economy and Finance, Avda 10 de Agosto 1661 y Jorge Washington, Quito, Ecuador (office).

BARREIRO FAJARDO, Georgina; Cuban politician, lawyer and banker; b. 1964; lawyer in finance and credit; Vice-Pres. Cen. Bank of Cuba –2003; Minister of Finance and Prices 2003–09; Head of Systems of Payment and Man., Risles; Dir Cen. Bank of Cuba. *Address:* c/o Ministry of Finance and Prices, Calle Obispo 211, Havana, Cuba (office).

BARRERA, Marco Antonio; Mexican boxer; b. 17 Jan. 1974, Iztacalco; m.; one s.; professional flyweight boxing debut age 15; known as 'Baby-Faced Assassin'; winner Super Flyweight Title, Mexico 1992, NABF Super Flyweight Title 1993, WBO Super Bantamweight Title 1995, 1998, Ring Featherweight Title, WBC Super Featherweight Title 2004; 65 fights, 61 wins, four losses, 42 knockouts. *Address:* MarcoBarrera.com, 3331 Palm Avenue, #A11, San Diego, CA 92154, USA (office). *Website:* www .marcobarrera.com.

BARRERA DE IRIMO, Antonio; Spanish business executive and politician; *Chairman, Bull International;* Pres. Telefónica 1964–73; fmr Vice-Pres. of Spain and Minister of Finance; fmr Chair. Sema Group PLC; Chair. Bull Int. 2002–, Bull (Spain) SA; fmr Chair. Pechiney and Générale des Eaux; fmr mem. Bd Banco Hispano Americano. *Address:* Bull (España) SA, Paseo de las Doce Estrellas 2, Campo de las Naciones, 28042 Madrid, Spain (office). *Telephone:* (91) 3939393 (office). *Fax:* (91) 3939395 (office). *Website:* www.bull .com (office).

BARRETO OTAZÚ, César Amado, MA; Paraguayan economist and politician; *Minister of Finance;* ed Universidad Nacional de Asunción, Pontificia Universidad Católica de Chile; with Entidad Binacional Itaipú 1988–94; Econ. Adviser, Nat. Econ. Equipment, Ministry of Finance 1997–98; Product Man., Cash Man. and Trade, Citibank NA, Paraguay Br. 1998–2000; Founding Pnr, Macroanálisis Consultora 1999; Project Man., Hutchison Telecom Paraguay SA Jan.–Oct. 2001, Gen. Man. 2001–02, Exec. Dir 2002–05; Exec. Dir Devt in Democracy 2004–05; Pres. Directory and Gen. Man. Agencia Financiera de Desarrollo 2005–07; Minister of Finance 2007–; fmr Prof. of Int. Economy and Master's Programme in Economy and Finances, Universidad Católica de Asunción. *Address:* Ministry of Finance, Sede Central: Chile 252, 1220 Asunción, Paraguay (office). *Telephone:* (21) 440010 (office). *Fax:* (21) 448283 (office). *E-mail:* info@hacienda.gov.py (office). *Website:* www.hacienda.gov.py (office).

BARRETT, Colleen C.; American airline industry executive; *President and Corporate Secretary, Southwest Airlines Co.;* b. 14 Sept. 1944, Bellows Falls, VT; m. (divorced); one s.; ed Becker Jr Coll., Worcester, Mass; Exec. Asst to Herb Kelleher (Southwest Airlines founder) at his law firm –1978; joined Southwest Airlines Co. 1978, Corp. Sec. 1978–, Vice-Pres. Admin 1986–90, Exec. Vice-Pres. Customer Services 1990–2001, Pres. 2001–; mem. Bd of Dirs, Better Business Bureau of Metropolitan Dallas Inc. 2002–, JCPenney Co. Inc. 2004–; mem. Int. Women's Forum 1985–; mem. numerous political, civic, charitable and business bds and cttees; mem. Hon. Bd of Advisors, Nat. Soc. of High School Scholars 2003–; numerous awards and honours including The Most Powerful Woman in Travel, Travel Agent Magazine, Top Women Execs, Women's Enterprise 1999, Tex. Business Woman of the Year, Tex. Women's Chamber of Commerce 2001, America's Most Powerful Business Women, Fortune Magazine 2001, Kupfer Distinguished Exec. Award 2002, Women's Leadership Exchange Compass Award 2002, Best Managers, BusinessWeek

2002, 50 Most Powerful Women in Business, Fortune Magazine 2002, 2003, Distinguished Women's Award, Northwood Univ. 2003, ranked by Forbes magazine amongst 100 Most Powerful Women 2004–07, Horatio Alger Award 2005. *Address:* Southwest Airlines, PO Box 36647-ICR, Dallas, TX 75235-1647, USA (office). *Telephone:* (214) 792-4306 (office). *Fax:* (214) 792-7676 (office). *E-mail:* vickie.shuler@wnco.com (office). *Website:* www.southwest.com (office).

BARRETT, Craig R., BS, MS, PhD; American computer industry executive; *Chairman, Intel Corporation;* b. 29 Aug. 1939, San Francisco, Calif.; m. Barbara Barrett; one s. one d.; ed Stanford Univ.; Assoc. Prof., Dept of Materials Science and Eng, Stanford Univ. 1964–74; NATO Postdoctoral Fellowship, Nat. Physical Lab., England 1964–65; Fulbright Fellowship, Tech. Univ. of Denmark 1972; joined Intel Corpn as a Tech. devt man. 1974, Vice-Pres. 1984–87, Sr Vice-Pres. 1987–90, Exec. Vice-Pres. 1990–92, mem. Bd Dirs 1992–, COO 1993–97, Pres. 1997–2005, CEO 1998–2005, Chair. 2005–(09); Chair. UN Global Alliance for Information and Communication Technologies and Devt; Co-Chair. Business Coalition for Student Achievement, Nat. Innovation Initiative Leadership Council, Achieve, Inc.; apptd to Pres.'s Advisory Cttee for Trade Policy and Negotiations and to American Health Information Community; mem. Nat. Govs' Asscn Task Force on Innovation America, Nat. Infrastructure Advisory Council, Cttee on Scientific Communication and Nat. Security, US-Brazil CEO Forum; mem. Bd Dirs US Semiconductor Industry Asscn, Nat. Action Council for Minorities in Eng, Dossia, Nat. Forest Foundation, TechNet and Science Foundation Arizona; mem. Bd of Trustees US Council for Int. Business, Advisory Bd Clinton Global Initiative Educ.; mem. and fmr Chair. Nat. Acad. of Eng; Hardy Gold Medal, American Inst. of Mining and Metallurgical Engineers. *Publications:* Principles of Engineering Materials; more than 40 tech. papers on the influence of the microstructure of materials. *Leisure interests:* hiking, skiing, horse riding, cycling, fly-fishing. *Address:* Intel Corporation, 2200 Mission College Boulevard, Santa Clara, CA 95052-1537, USA (office). *Telephone:* (408) 765-8080 (office). *Fax:* (408) 765-9904 (office). *E-mail:* info@intel.com (office). *Website:* www.intel.com (office).

BARRETT, Matthew W., OC; Canadian banker; b. 20 Sept. 1944, Co. Kerry, Ireland; ed Harvard Business School; joined Bank of Montreal, London, England 1962; moved to Canada 1967; Vice-Pres. Man. Services, Bank of Montreal 1978, Vice-Pres. BC Div. 1979, Sr Vice-Pres. Eastern and Northern Ont. 1980, Sr Vice-Pres. and Deputy Gen. Man. Int. Banking Group 1981, Sr Vice-Pres. and Deputy Group Exec. Treasury Group 1984, Exec. Vice-Pres. and Group Exec. Personal Banking 1985, Pres. and COO 1987, CEO 1989–99, Chair. Bd of Dirs 1990–99; Group CEO Barclays plc 1999–2004, Chair. 2004–06; Trustee, First Canadian Mortgage Fund; Dir Harris Bankcorp. Inc. and subsidiaries, Nesbitt Burns Inc., Molson Cos Ltd, Seagrams Co. Ltd; Hon. LLD (St Mary's Univ., Halifax, NS, York Univ., Ont., Concordia Univ., Univ. of Waterloo, Acadia Univ.); Hon. DCL (Bishop's Univ.) 1993; Harvard Business School Alumni Achievement Award 1997. *Leisure interests:* fly-fishing, tennis, reading. *Address:* c/o Barclays Group, 1 Churchill Place, London, E14 5HP, England (office).

BARRIE, George Napier, BA, LLD; South African professor and advocate; *Special Professor, Faculty of Law and Researcher, Centre for the Study of International Law in Africa, University of Johannesburg;* b. 10 Sept. 1940, Pietersburg; m. Marie Howell 1970; two s. one d.; ed Pretoria Univ., Univ. of S Africa and Univ. Coll., London, UK; State Advocate, Supreme Court 1964–69; Sr Law Adviser, Dept of Foreign Affairs 1970–80; Prof. of Int. and Constitutional Law, Rand Afrikaans Univ. 1981–, Dean Faculty of Law 2001–04; Visiting Prof., Free Univ. of Brussels 1992; Leader of S African del. to numerous int. confs; mem. S African del. to Int. Bar Asscn Conf. 1984, Nat. Council on Correctional Services 1996–; Special Prof., Faculty of Law and Researcher, Centre for Study of Int. Law in Africa, Univ. of Johannesburg 2005–. *Publications include:* Topical International Law 1979, Self-Determination in Modern International Law 1995 and numerous works and articles on int. and constitutional law; co-author: Nuclear Non-Proliferation: The Why and the Wherefore 1985, Constitutions of Southern Africa 1985, Law of South Africa 1986, Law of the Sea 1987, Bill of Rights Compendium 1996, Managing African Conflicts 2000. *Leisure interests:* long distance running, long distance cycling. *Address:* Faculty of Law, University of Johannesburg, PO Box 524, Auckland Park, Johannesburg 2006, South Africa (office). *Telephone:* (11) 7044376 (home). *Fax:* (11) 4892049 (office); (11) 7044376 (home). *E-mail:* barriegm@telkomsa.net (home). *Website:* www.general.rau.ac.za/law (office).

BARRINGTON, Edward John, BA, MA; Irish civil servant and diplomatist; b. 26 July 1949, Dublin; m. Clare O'Brien 1972; one s.; ed Univ. Coll. Dublin; Third Sec. Dept of Foreign Affairs, EC Div. 1971–73, First Sec. 1973–75, First Sec. EC Perm. Rep. Office, Brussels 1975–80, First Sec. Press Section, HQ Aug.–Dec. 1980, Counsellor Political Div., HQ 1980–85, Asst Sec.-Gen. Admin. Div., HQ 1985–89, Asst Sec.-Gen. EC Div., HQ 1989–91, Asst Sec.-Gen. Political Div. and Political Dir, HQ 1991–95, Deputy Sec. 1995; Amb. to UK 1995–2001; currently Hon. Prof., Research Inst. for Irish and Scottish Studies, Univ. of Aberdeen, UK; Visiting Research Fellow, Inst. for British-Irish Studies, Univ. Coll. Dublin; Hon. DUniv (Univ. of North London) 2001. *Leisure interests:* cinema, hiking, jazz, theatre. *Address:* Sun Villa, Mauritius Town, Rosslare Strand, Co. Wexford, Ireland (home). *Telephone:* (53) 32880 (home).

BARRINGTON, Sir Nicholas John, KCMG, CVO, MA, FRSA; British diplomatist; b. 23 July 1934; s. of the late Eric A. Barrington and Mildred Bill; ed Repton School and Clare Coll., Cambridge; joined HM Diplomatic Service 1957; served Kabul 1959, UK Del. to European Communities, Brussels 1963, Rawalpindi 1965, Tokyo 1972–75, Cairo 1978–81; Minister and Head, British

Interests Section, Tehran 1981–83; Minister and Head, UN New York 1981–83; Coordinator for G7 London Summit 1984; Asst Under-Sec. of State, FCO 1984–87; Amb. to Pakistan 1987–89, High Commr 1989–94, also Amb. (non-resident) to Afghanistan 1994; Trustee, Ancient India and Iran Trust, Cambridge 1992–; Trustee Museum of British Empire and Commonwealth, 1996–; served on various bodies linking Britain with Asia and Christianity with Islam; Hon. Fellow, Clare Coll. Cambridge 1992; Order of the Sacred Treasure, Japan 1975. *Publication:* A Passage to Nuristan 2005. *Leisure interests:* theatre, drawing, prosopography, Persian poetry. *Address:* 2 Banhams Close, Cambridge, CB4 1HX, England (home). *Telephone:* (1223) 360802 (home).

BARRINGTON-WARD, Rt Rev. Simon, KCMG, MA, DD, DLitt; British ecclesiastic; *Assistant Bishop of Ely;* b. 27 May 1930, London; s. of Robert McGowan Barrington-Ward and Margaret A. Radice; m. Dr Jean Caverill Taylor 1963; two d.; ed Eton Coll., Magdalene Coll. Cambridge and Westcott House, Cambridge; ordained, diocese of Ely 1956; Chaplain, Magdalene Coll. Cambridge 1956–60; Lecturer, Ibadan Univ. Nigeria 1960–63; Fellow and Dean of Chapel, Magdalene Coll. Cambridge 1963–69, Hon. Fellow 1991–, Hon. Asst Chaplain 1999–; Prin., Church Missionary Soc. Coll., Selly Oak, Birmingham 1969–74; Gen. Sec. Church Missionary Soc. 1974–85; Canon, Derby Cathedral 1975–85; Chaplain to HM The Queen 1983–85; Bishop of Coventry 1985–97; Chair. Int. and Devt Affairs Cttee, Gen. Synod of Church of England 1986–96; Prelate to the Most Distinguished Order of St Michael and St George 1989–2005; Asst Bishop of Ely 1997–; Hon. Fellow, Magdalene Coll., Cambridge 1977–, Hon. Asst Chaplain 1999–; Hon. DD (Wycliffe Coll. Toronto) 1983; Hon. DLitt (Warwick Univ.) 1988; Dr hc (Anglia-Ruskin Univ., Cambridge) 2008. *Publications:* Love Will Out 1988, Christianity Today 1988, The Weight of Glory 1991, Why God? 1993, The Jesus Prayer 1996, Praying the Jesus Prayer Together 2001, revised edn 2008); articles and book chapters. *Leisure interests:* hill walking, music, cycling, calligraphy. *Address:* 4 Searle Street, Cambridge, CB4 3DB, England (home). *Telephone:* (1223) 740460 (home). *E-mail:* sb292@cam.ac.uk (home).

BARRIOS DE CHAMORRO, Violeta; Nicaraguan politician, publisher and fmr head of state; *President, Fundación Violeta Chamorro;* b. 18 Oct. 1929, Rivas; m. Pedro Joaquín Chamorro (died 1978) 1950; two s. two d.; ed Our Lady of the Lake Catholic School, San Antonio and Blackstone Coll., USA; mem. and Dir Sociedad Interamericana de Prensa 1978–89, Prensa Freedom Comm. 1978–89; Pres. and Dir-Gen. La Prensa (daily newspaper) 1978–89; Nat. Opposition Union cand. for Pres. 1989–90; Pres. of Nicaragua 1990–97, also Minister of Nat. Defence 1990; Founder and Pres. Fundación Violeta Chamorro; Grand Cross of the Order of Isabel la Católica (Spain) 1991, Grand Collar of the Order of the Aztec Eagle (Mexico) 1993, Grand Cross of the Order of Merit (Germany) 1996; six hon. degrees including Hon. LLD (American Univ., Washington, DC) 1997; Hon. DH (Catholic Univ. of Nicaragua Redemptores Mater) 1995; Dr hc (American Univ., Managua) 1998, (Univ. for Peace, Costa Rica) 1999; numerous nat. and int. awards including Louis Lyon Prize, Harvard Univ. 1986, American Soc. Gold Ensign Award 1990, Int. Rescue Cttee Freedom Award 1990, Int. Peace Asscn Woman for Peace Award 1990, Pan-American Devt Foundation Inter-american Leadership Award 1991, Lutheran Univ. of Calif. Thomas Wade Landry Award 1991, The Path to Peace Foundation Award 1997. *Publication:* Dreams of the Heart (autobiog.) 1996. *Address:* Fundación Violeta Chamorro, Plaza España, Edificio Málaga, Módulo B-9, Managua, Nicaragua (office). *Telephone:* (2) 68-6500 (office). *Fax:* (2) 68-6502 (office). *E-mail:* violetabch@ibw.com.ni (office). *Website:* www.violetachamorro.org.ni (office).

BARRO, Robert Joseph, PhD; American economist and academic; *Professor of Economics, Harvard University;* b. 28 Sept. 1944, New York; four c.; ed Harvard Univ., California Inst. of Tech.; Prof. of Econs, Harvard Univ. 1987–; Sr Fellow Hoover Inst., Stanford Univ. 1995–; Viewpoint Columnist, Business Week 1998–; Frank Paish Lecturer, Meeting of Royal Econ. Soc., Oxford, 1985; Henry Thornton Lecturer, City Univ. Business School, London 1987; Horowitz Lecturer, Israel 1988; Lionel Robbins Lecturer, LSE 1996; Hoover Inst. Nat. Fellowship 1977–78; John Simon Guggenheim Memorial Fellowship 1982–83; Fellow Econometric Soc. 1980–; American Acad. of Arts and Sciences 1988–. *Publications:* Determinants of Economic Growth: A Cross-Country Empirical Study, Getting it Right: Markets and Choice in a Free Society, Economic Growth. *Address:* Department of Economics, Harvard University, Cambridge, MA 02138, USA (office). *Telephone:* (617) 495-3203 (office); (781) 894-8184 (home). *Fax:* (617) 496-8629 (office). *E-mail:* rbarro@harvard.edu (office). *Website:* www.economics.harvard.edu (office).

BARRON, Sir Donald James, Kt, DL, BCom, CA; British business executive; b. 17 March 1921, Edinburgh; s. of Albert Gibson Barron and Elizabeth Macdonald; m. Gillian Mary Saville 1956; three s. two d.; ed George Heriot's School, Edinburgh, Univ. of Edinburgh; served with King's Own Scottish Borderers 1941–45; joined Rowntree & Co. Ltd 1952, Dir 1961, Vice-Chair. 1965; Chair. Rowntree Mackintosh Ltd 1966–81; Vice-Chair. Midland Bank PLC 1981–82 (Dir 1972–87), Chair. 1982–87; mem. Bd of Banking Supervision 1987–89; Dir Canada Life Assurance Co., Toronto 1980–96; Vice-Chair. Canada Life Assurance Co. of Great Britain 1983–91, Chair. 1991–94 (Dir 1980–96); Dir Canada Life Unit Trust Mans 1980–96 (Chair. 1982), 3i Group PLC 1980–91; mem. Council of CBI 1966–81, Soc. Science Research Council 1971–72, Univ. Grants Cttee 1972–81, Council Inst. of Chartered Accountants of Scotland 1980–81, Council of British Inst. of Man. 1979–80; Trustee, Joseph Rowntree Foundation 1966–73, 1975–96, Chair. 1981–96; mem. NEDC 1983–85; Dir Clydesdale Bank 1986–87; Gov. London Business School 1982–89; Treas. Univ. of York 1966–72, Pro-Chancellor 1982–94; Chair. York Millennium Bridge Trust 1998–2002; Dr hc (Loughborough) 1982, (Heriot-Watt) 1983, (CNAA) 1983, (Edinburgh) 1984, (Nottingham) 1985,

(York) 1986. *Leisure interests:* golf, tennis, travelling, gardening. *Address:* Greenfield, Sim Balk Lane, Bishopthorpe, York, YO23 2QH, England (home). *Telephone:* (1904) 705675 (home). *Fax:* (1904) 700183 (home).

BARRON, Eric J., BS, MS, PhD; American geologist, oceanographer and academic; *Director, National Centre for Atmospheric Research;* b. 26 Oct. 1951, Lafayette, Ind.; ed Florida State Univ., Univ. of Miami; Cray Supercomputing Fellowship, Nat. Center for Atmospheric Research, Boulder, Colo 1976, Postdoctoral Research Fellow 1980, Scientist, Climate Section 1981–85, Dir 2008–; Assoc. Prof., Univ. of Miami 1985–86; Dir Earth System Science Center and Assoc. Prof. of Geosciences, Pennsylvania State Univ. 1986–, Prof. of Geosciences 1989–, Dir Earth and Mineral Sciences Environment Inst. 1998–2003, Distinguished Prof. of Geosciences 1999–, Dean, Coll. of Earth and Mineral Sciences 2002–06, Trustee, Univ. Corpn for Atmospheric Research 2002–, mem. Bd of Govs Jt Oceanographic Insts, Inc. 2003–; Jackson Chair in Earth System Science and Dean, Jackson School of Geosciences, Univ. of Texas at Austin 2006–; Ed.-in-Chief Palaeogeography, Palaeoclimatology, Palaeoecology 1985–91, Earth Interactions (electronic journal) 1995-99; Ed. Global and Planetary Change 1988–96; Assoc. Ed. Journal of Climate 1989–95; mem. Editorial Bd Geology 1982–89, Palaeogeography, Palaeoclimatology, Palaeoecology 1984–85, 1992–, Geotimes 1994–96, Consequences 1994–2000, Global Change Encyclopedia (Oxford Univ. Press) 1998; Chair. Nat. Research Council (NRC) Climate Research Cttee 1990–96, Co-Chair. Bd on Atmospheric Sciences 1997–99, Chair. 1999–; mem. NRC Cttee on Global Change Research, Assessment of NASA Post-2000 Plans, Climate Change Science, Human Dimensions of Global Change, Panel on Grand Environmental Challenges, Cttee on Tools for Tracking Chemical, Biological, and Nuclear Releases in the Atmosphere: Implications for Homeland Security; fmr Chair. Science Exec. Cttee for NASA's Earth Observing System and NASA's Earth Science and Applications Advisory Cttee, US Global Change Research Program Forum on Climate Modeling, Allocation Panel for the Interagency Climate Simulation Lab., US Nat. Cttee for PAGES, NSF Earth System History Panel; mem. Geological Soc. of America, American Geophysical Union (Chair. Selection Cttee, Ed. Paleoceanography, Biogeochemical Cycles 1995, 1997) 1991; Fellow, American Geophysical Union, American Meteorological Soc. 1995, AAAS 2004; Fellow, Nat. Inst. for Environmental Science, Univ. of Cambridge, UK 2002; Honors Student, Florida State Univ. 1969–73, Texaco Fellow 1975–77, Outstanding Student Award, Miami Geological Soc. 1977–78, Koczy Fellowship (most outstanding student in last year of study) 1979–80, Smith Prize (most creative dissertation) 1980, Excellence of Presentation Award, Soc. of Econ. Paleontologists and Mineralogists 1988, Hon. Mention for Excellence of Presentation Award, Soc. of Econ. Paleontologists and Mineralogists 1989, Wilson Research Award, Coll. of Earth and Mineral Sciences, Pennsylvania State Univ. 1992, Provost Award for Collaborative Instruction and Curricular Innovations 1992, 1993, Excellence of Presentation Award, Soc. of Sedimentary Geology (SEPM) 1993, American Geophysical Union Fellow 1993, Hon. Mention for Excellence of Presentation (Poster), American Asscn of Petroleum Geologists 1993, Distinguished Lecturer, American Asscn of Petroleum Geologist 1997, Wilson Teaching Award, Coll. of Earth and Mineral Sciences 1999, NASA Outstanding Earth Science Educ. Product (Discover Earth: Earth-as-a-System) 1999, NASA Group Achievement Award for Research Strategy for the Earth Science Enterprise 2001, Frontiers in Geophysics Lecturer, American Geophysical Union 2002, NASA Distinguished Public Service Medal 2003. *Publications:* numerous scientific papers in professional journals on climatology, numerical modelling and Earth history. *Address:* National Centre for Atmospheric Research, PO Box 3000, Boulder, CO 80307-3000, USA (office). *Telephone:* (303) 497-1111 (office). *E-mail:* barron@ucar.edu (office). *Website:* www.ucar.edu (office).

BARROSSO, John Anthony; American surgeon and politician; *Senator from Wyoming;* b. 21 July 1952; m. Linda Nix (divorced); two c.; orthopedic surgeon in pvt. practice, Casper, Wyo.; ran unsuccessfully for Republican nomination for Senator 1996, elected to Wyo. State Senate 2002, re-elected 2006, served as Chair. Transportation, Highways and Mil. Affairs Cttee, mem. Labor, Health and Social Services Cttee, Select Cttee on Legis. Tech., Dept of Health Advisory Council; apptd Senator from Wyo. (upon death of Senator Craig Thomas) 2007–; Chief of Staff Wyo. Medical Center; State Pres. Wyo. Medical Soc.; Pres. Nat. Asscn of Physician Broadcasters; mem. American Medical Asscn Council of Ethics and Judicial Affairs; physician for Professional Rodeo Cowboy's Asscn; mem. Bd of Dirs Presidential Classroom; mem. Casper Chamber of Commerce, Casper Rotary Club; Wyo. Physician of the Year, Wyo. Nat. Guard Medal of Excellence, Veterans of Foreign Wars Legislative Service Award. *Publications:* Keeping Wyoming Healthy, Caring for Wyoming's Seniors newspaper columns. *Address:* Office of Senator John Barrosso, The Senate, Washington DC 20510; 4140 Centennial Hills Blvd., Casper, WY 82609, USA (office). *Telephone:* (307) 265-7205 (office). *E-mail:* barrasso@senate.wyoming.com (office).

BARROT, Jacques, LenD; French politician; *Vice-President and Commissioner for Justice, Freedom and Security, European Commission;* b. 3 Feb. 1937, Yssingeaux, Haute-Loire; s. of Noël Barrot and Marthe Pivot; one s. two d.; ed Coll. d'Yssingeaux and Faculté de Droit, Paris and Inst. d'Etudes Politiques, Paris; Deputy to Nat. Ass. (Union Centriste) 1967–74, 1978, (Union pour la Démocratie Française) 1981–95, 1997–2002, (UMP) 2002–03, Pres. UMP Group 2002–04; Councillor, Haute-Loire Regional Council 1966–2004, Pres. 1976–2004; Sec. of State, Ministry of Equipment 1974–78; Minister of Commerce and Working Classes 1978–79, of Health and Social Security 1979–81; Pres. Conseil-Gen. Haute-Loire 1976–2004; Mayor of Yssingeaux 1989–2001; Minister of Labour, Social Dialogue and Participation 1995–97, EU Commissioner for Regional Policy and Institutional Reform 2004, for Transport 2004–08, for Justice, Freedom and Security 2008–; Pres. Nat. Union for Environmental Improvement 1991–93; mem. Fondatems du "Dialogue et Initiations". *Publications:* Les Pierres de l'avenir 1978, Notre contrat pour l'alternance 2002, L'Europe n'est pas ce que vous croyez 2007. *Leisure interest:* mountain sports. *Address:* Rue de la Loi 200, 1049 Brussels, Belgium (office); Rue Beuve-Méry, 43200 Yssingeaux, France (home). *Telephone:* (2) 299-11-11 (office). *Fax:* (2) 295-01-38 (office). *Website:* europa.eu (office).

BARROW, Dean Oliver, MA, LLM; Belizean politician; *Prime Minister and Minister of Finance;* b. 2 March 1951, Belize City; ed Univ. of West Indies and Center for Advanced Int. Studies, Univ. of Miami, USA; elected (United Democratic Party—UDP)) to Belize City Council 1983; elected to Nat. Ass. (UDP) for Queen Square Div. 1984–89; Deputy Leader UDP 1990, currently Leader; Minister of Foreign Affairs and Econ. Devt 1984–86; Attorney-Gen. 1986–89; apptd Deputy Prime Minister, Minister of Foreign Affairs and Econ. Devt and Attorney-Gen. 1993, also Minister of Nat. Security, Immigration and Nationality Matters 1995; Prime Minister 2008–, Minister of Finance 2008–; Pnr, Barrow and Williams (law firm). *Address:* Office of the Prime Minister, Sir Edney Cain Bridge, Belmopan (office); United Democratic Party, South End Bel-China Bridge, POB 1898, Belize City, Belize (office). *Telephone:* 822-2345 (office); 227-2576 (office). *Fax:* 822-3323 (office); 227-6441 (office). *E-mail:* primeministerbelize@btl.net (office); info@udp.org.bz (office). *Website:* www.udp.org.bz (office).

BARROW, John David, BSc, DPhil, FRS, FRAS, CPhys, FInstP, FRSA; British academic and astrophysicist; *Professor of Mathematical Sciences, University of Cambridge;* b. 29 Nov. 1952, London; s. of the late Walter Henry Barrow and Lois Miriam Barrow (née Tucker); m. Elizabeth Mary East 1975; two s. one d.; ed Van Mildert Coll., Durham Univ., Magdalen Coll., Oxford; Lindemann Fellow, Astronomy Dept, Univ. of Calif., Berkeley 1977–78, Miller Fellow, Physics Dept 1980–81; Research Lecturer, Astrophysics Dept, Univ. of Oxford 1978–80; Lecturer, Astronomy Centre, Univ. of Sussex 1981, later Sr Lecturer, Prof. 1989–99, Dir Astronomy Centre 1995–99; Prof. of Math. Sciences, Univ. of Cambridge 1999–, Fellow, Clare Hall 1999– (Vice-Pres. 2004–07), Gresham Prof. of Astronomy 2003–07, Emer. Gresham Prof. of Astronomy, Gresham Coll. 2007–, Gresham Prof. of Geometry 2008–; Gordon Godfrey Visiting Prof., Univ. of NSW 2000, 2003; First Eastern Visiting Cambridge Prof. (China and Hong Kong) 2005; Li Ka Shing Foundation Visiting Scholar (China and Hong Kong) 2006; Dir Millennium Math. Project 1999–; mem. Int. Soc. for Science and Religion (ISSR) 2002; Nuffield Fellow 1986–87, Leverhulme Royal Soc. Fellow 1992–93, PPARC Sr Fellow 1994–; Hon. Prof., Nanjing Univ. 2005–; Hon. DSc (Hertfordshire) 1999, (Szczecin) 2007, (Durham) 2008; Gifford Lecturer (Univ. of Glasgow) 1988, Samuel Locker Prize 1989, Scott Memorial Lecture (Leuven) 1989, Collingwood Lecture (Durham) 1990, Spinoza Lecture (Amsterdam) 1993, George Darwin Lecture (Royal Astronomical Soc.) 1993, Elizabeth Spreadbury Lecture (Univ. Coll. London) 1993, Templeton Award 1995, BBV Lectures (Spain), Robert Boyle Memorial Lecture (Oxford) 1996, RSA Lecture 1999, Kelvin Medal 1999, LMS Lectures 2000, Flamsteed Lecture (Derby) 2000, Tyndall Lecture (Bristol) 2001, Darwin Lecture (Cambridge) 2001, Whitrow Lecture (Royal Astronomical Soc.) 2002, Premi Ubu (Italy) 2002, Brasher Lecture (Kingston) 2002, Italgas Prize 2003, Gresham Lectures (London) 2003, Newton Lecture (Grantham) 2004, Hubert James Lecture (Purdue) 2004, Von Weizsäcker Lectures (Hamburg) 2004, McCrea Centenary Lecture (Sussex) 2004, Wood Memorial Lecture (Newcastle) 2005, Lacchini Prize 2005, Hamilton Lecture (Dublin) 2005, Queen's Anniversary Prize 2005, Templeton Prize 2006, Knight Lecture (Bath) 2006, Borderlands Lecture (Durham) 2007, Boyle Lecture (St Mary-le-Bow) 2007, Roscoe Lecture (Liverpool) 2007, Kallen Lecture (Lund) 2007, Phillips Lecture (Cardiff) 2008, Faraday Medal (Royal Soc., London) 2008, Faraday Prize Lecture (Royal Soc., London), 2009. *Plays:* Infinities (dir Luca Ronconi) 2002, 2003, Ciutat de les Arts Escèniques (dir Vicente Genovés) (Italian Theatre Prize, Premi Ubu 2002) 2002. *Publications:* The Left Hand of Creation 1983, L'Homme et le Cosmos 1984, The Anthropic Cosmological Principle 1986, The World Within the World 1988, Theories of Everything 1991, Perche il Mondo è Matematico? 1992, Pi in the Sky 1992, The Origin of the Universe 1994, The Artful Universe 1995, Impossibility 1998, Between Inner Space and Outer Space 1999, The Universe that Discovered Itself 2000, The Book of Nothing 2000, The Constants of Nature 2002, Science and Ultimate Reality (ed.) 2003, The Infinite Book 2005, The Artful Universe Expanded 2005, New Theories of Everything 2007, Cosmic Imagery 2008, 100 Essential Things You Didn't Know You Didn't Know 2008. *Leisure interests:* athletics, books, theatre, writing. *Address:* Centre for Mathematical Sciences, University of Cambridge, Wilberforce Road, Cambridge, CB3 0WA, England (office). *Telephone:* (1223) 766696 (office). *Fax:* (1223) 765900 (office); (1223) 309509 (home). *E-mail:* j.d.barrow@damtp.cam.ac.uk (office). *Website:* www.cms.cam.ac.uk (office).

BARROW, Viscountess Lady Waverley Ursula Helen, MA; Belizean economist and diplomatist; b. 31 Oct. 1955; d. of Raymond Hugh Barrow and Rita Helen Barrow; m. Viscount Waverley; one s.; ed Newnham Coll., Cambridge, UK; Econ. Devt Planner, Planning Unit, Govt of Belize 1978; consultant for small business affairs, urban planning and marketing, Frazier & Assocs 1979–85; Counsellor and Deputy High Commr in London 1988–89, High Commr 1993–98; Perm. Rep. to UN, New York 1989–91; Asst Dir Commonwealth Secr. 1991–93; Amb. to the EU, Belgium, France, Germany and the Holy See 1993–98; mem. Bd of Dirs Belize Telecommunications Ltd 2004; awarded Belize Open Scholarship 1974, Cambridge Commonwealth Trust Scholarship 1985. *Address:* c/o Board of Directors, Belize Telecommunications Ltd, St Thomas Street, Belize City, Belize.

BARRY, Edward William, BA; American publishing executive; b. 24 Nov. 1937, Stamford, Conn.; s. of Edward Barry and Elizabeth Cosgrove; m. Barbara H. Walker 1963; one s. one d.; ed Univ. of Conn.; Pres. The Free Press,

New York 1972–82, Oxford Univ. Press Inc., New York 1982–2000; Sr Vice-Pres. Macmillan Publishing Co., New York 1973–82; mem. Exec. Council, Professional and Scholarly Publications 1993; mem. Advisory Bd Pace Univ. Grad. Program in Publishing 1990–; mem. Bd of Dirs Asscn of American Publrs 1995; Trustee Columbia Univ. Press 2000–; Hon. LittD (Univ. of Oxford) 2000. *Address:* 266 Old Poverty Road, Southbury, CT 06488-1769, USA (home). *Telephone:* (212) 251-0416 (office). *E-mail:* edwardbarry@cs.com (office).

BARRY, John, OBE; British composer; b. (Jonathan Barry Prendergast), 3 Nov. 1933, York; formed group The John Barry Seven 1957–62; stage musical, Billy 1974; composer of film scores 1959–; Fellow BAFTA 2005–. *Compositions for film:* Beat Girl 1959, Drumbeat 1959, Never Let Go 1960, Girl on a Roof 1961, The Amorous Prawn 1962, Stringbeat 1961, Man in The Middle 1962, Dr No 1962, The L-Shaped Room 1962, It's All Happening 1963, Zulu 1963, From Russia with Love 1963, A Jolly Bad Fellow 1964, Séance on a Wet Afternoon 1964, Goldfinger 1964, Boy on a Bicycle 1965, The Party's Over 1965, Mister Moses 1965, Four in the Morning 1965, The Knack 1965, The Ipcress File 1965, King Rat 1965, Passion Flower Hotel 1965, Thunderball 1965, Dutchman 1966, The Chase 1966, Born Free (Acad. Awards for Best Original Song, Best Original Score 1967) 1966, The Wrong Box 1966, The Quiller Memorandum 1966, You Only Live Twice 1967, The Whisperers 1967, Boom 1968, Petulia 1968, Deadfall 1968, The Lion in Winter 1968, Midnight Cowboy (Acad. Award for Best Original Score) 1969, On Her Majesty's Secret Service 1969, Monte Walsh 1970, Mary Queen of Scots 1971, The Last Valley 1971, They Might Be Giants 1971, Walkabout 1971, Lolita My Love 1971, Alice's Adventures in Wonderland 1971, Diamonds Are Forever 1971, Follow Me! 1972, Bang Bang 1973, A Doll's House 1973, The Tamarind Seed 1974, The Dove 1974, The Man with the Golden Gun 1974, The Day of the Locust 1975, Robin and Marian 1976, King Kong 1976, The White Buffalo 1977, The Deep 1977, First Love 1977, The Betsy 1978, Game of Death 1978, Starcrash 1979, Hanover Street 1979, Moonraker 1979, The Black Hole 1979, Somewhere in Time 1980, Night Games 1980, Inside Moves 1980, Raise the Titanic 1980, Touched by Love 1980, The Legend of the Lone Ranger 1981, Body Heat 1983, Hammett 1982, Frances 1982, Murder by Phone 1982, The Golden Seal 1983, High Road to China 1983, Octopussy 1983, Mike's Murder 1984, Until September 1984, The Cotton Club 1984, A View To A Kill 1985, Jagged Edge 1985, Out of Africa (Acad. Award for Best Original Score, Golden Globe for Best Original Score) 1985, A Killing Affair 1986, Howard the Duck 1986, Peggy Sue Got Married 1986, Hearts of Fire 1987, The Living Daylights 1987, Masquerade 1988, Dances with Wolves (Acad. Award for Best Original Score) 1990, Chaplin 1992, Indecent Proposal 1993, Ruby Cairo 1993, My Life 1993, The Specialist 1994, Cry, the Beloved Country 1995, The Scarlet Letter 1995, Across the Sea of Time 1995, Swept from the Sea 1997, Mercury Rising 1998, Playing by Heart 1998, Beyondness of Things 1999, A Song of Africa 2000, The Last Valley 2001, Enigma 2001. *Composition for television:* Drumbeat (series) 1959, Juke Box Jury (series theme) 1959, Discs a Go-Go (series theme) 1961, Impromptu (series) 1964, The Newcomers (series theme) 1965, Vendetta (series theme) 1966, The Persuaders (series theme) 1971, The Adventurer (series theme) 1972, Great Mysteries (series theme) 1973, The Glass Menagerie (film) 1973, Love Among the Ruins (film) 1975, Eleanor and Franklin (film) 1976, The War Between the Tates (film) 1977, Young Joe, the Forgotten Kennedy (film) 1977, The Gathering (film) 1977, The Corn is Green (film) 1979, Willa (film) 1979, The Witness (film) 1992. *Recordings include:* albums: Elizabeth Taylor in London 1963, Sophia Loren in Rome 1965, Eternal Echoes 2001. *Address:* c/o J. H. Cohn LLP, 1212 Avenue of the Americas, 24th Floor, New York, NY 10036, USA (office). *Telephone:* (212) 826-6000 (office). *Fax:* (212) 421-2583 (office).

BARRY, Marion Shepilov, Jr; American politician; b. 6 March 1936, Itta Bena, Miss.; s. of Marion S. Barry and Mattie Barry; m. 1st Effi Barry 1978; one s.; m. 2nd Cara Masters Barry 1994; ed LeMoyne Coll., Fisk Univ., Univ. of Tennessee; Dir of Operations, Pride Inc., Washington, DC 1967; co-founder, Chair. and Dir Pride Econ. Enterprises, Inc., Washington, DC 1968; mem. Washington DC School Bd 1971–74; mem. Washington DC City Council 1974–78, 2004–; Mayor of Washington, DC 1979–91; arrested and charged with possessing cocaine Jan. 1990; convicted, imprisoned for 6 months for possessing cocaine; re-elected Mayor 1995–98. *Address:* Office of Councilmember Marion Barry Council of the District of Columbia, 1350 Pennsylvania Avenue, NW, Suite 102, Washington, DC 20004, USA (office). *Telephone:* (202) 724-8045 (office); (202) 698-2185 (office). *Fax:* (202) 698-2388 (office). *Website:* www.dccouncil.washington.dc.us/BARRY (office).

BARRY, Nancy Marie, BA, MBA; American banking executive; *President, NBA Enterprise Solutions to Poverty;* b. 1949; ed Stanford Univ., Harvard Business School; joined World Bank 1975, various sr positions including Head of Global Industry Devt Div., Chair. Donor's Cttee on Small and Medium Enterprises, Founding mem. CGAP Policy Advisory Group; Pres. Women's World Banking 1990–2006, mem. Bd of Trustees 1981–; Social Entrepreneur in Residence, Harvard Business School 2006, advisor to Social Cos and Poverty initiative; f. Nancy Barry Assocs (NBA) 2006–, Founder and Pres. NBA Enterprise Solutions to Poverty 2006–; Chair. Donald A. Strauss Foundation; mem. Council on Foreign Relations; Founding mem. Advisory Bd Harvard Business School Social Enterprise Initiative; mem. Asia Soc. Asian Social Issues Cttee; Outstanding Women in Finance and Consulting, HBS Women's Student Asscn 2001, Forbes Exec. Women's Summit Trailblazer Award 2002, Kellogg-McKinsey Award for Distinguished Leadership 2004, ranked by Forbes magazine amongst 100 Most Powerful Women (98th) 2004, (98th) 2005. *Address:* c/o Advisory Board, Social Enterprise Initiative, Loeb House, 3rd Floor, Soldiers Field, Boston, MA 02163, USA (office). *Telephone:* (617) 495-6421 (office). *Fax:* (617) 496-7416 (office). *Website:* www.hbs.edu/socialenterprise (office).

BARRYMORE, Drew; American film actress and producer; b. 22 Feb. 1975, Los Angeles; d. of the late John Barrymore, Jr and of Jaid Barrymore; m. 1st Jeremy Thomas 1994 (divorced); m. 2nd Tom Green 2001 (divorced 2001); appeared in dog food commercial 1976; film debut in TV movie Suddenly Love 1978; f. Flower Films (production co.); apptd Amb. for Hunger, WFP 2007. *Films include:* Altered States 1980, E.T.: The Extra-Terrestrial 1982, Irreconcilable Differences 1984, Firestarter 1984, Cat's Eye 1985, See You In The Morning 1988, Far From Home 1989, Motorama 1991, Guncrazy 1992, Poison Ivy 1992, Beyond Control: The Amy Fisher Story 1992, No Place to Hide 1993, Doppelganger 1993, Wayne's World 2 1993, Bad Girls 1994, Inside the Goldmine 1994, Boys On The Side 1995, Batman Forever 1995, Mad Love 1995, Scream 1996, Everyone Says I Love You 1996, All She Wanted 1997, Best Men 1997, Never Been Kissed (also producer) 1998, Home Fries 1998, The Wedding Singer 1998, Ever After 1998, Titan A.E. (voice) 2000, Charlie's Angels (also producer) 2000, Donnie Darko (also producer) 2001, Riding in Cars With Boys 2001, Confessions of a Dangerous Mind 2002, Duplex (also producer), So Love Returns (also producer), Charlie's Angels: Full Throttle (also producer) 2003, Fifty First Dates 2004, Fever Pitch 2005, The Perfect Catch 2005, Music and Lyrics 2006, Lucky You 2007, He's Just Not That Into You 2007, South of the Border (voice) 2008, Grey Gardens 2008. *Address:* c/o Creative Artists Agency LCC (CAA-LA), 2000 Avenue of the Stars, Los Angeles, CA 900671, USA (office).

BARSALOU, Yves; French banking executive; *Chairman, Crédit Foncier de Monaco;* b. 18 Sept. 1932, Bizanet; s. of Marcell Barsalou and Marie-Louise Salvan; m. Claire-Marie Vié 1955; two s.; ed Ecoles de Carcassonne et Narbonne; mem. Dept Centre of Young Farmers 1957–67; Pres. Caisse Locale de Crédit Agricole de Narbonne 1974–; mem. Cen. Cttee, then Vice-Pres. Caisse nat. du Crédit agricole (CNCA) 1981–88, Pres. 1988–2000, Chair. CNCA 1989; Vice-Pres. Fed. Nationale du Crédit Agricole (FNCA) 1992–2000; mem. Plenary Comm., Fed. nat. du Crédit agricole 1975–77, Dir 1977–81, Pres. 1982–92; Vice-Pres., Pres. Fed. Int. du Crédit Agricole (CiCa) 1993–2001; Vice-Pres. Bd Crédit Agricole Indosuez 1996–2001; Chair. Crédit Foncier Monaco 1999–; mem. Bd of Dirs TotalFinaElf 2000–03; mem. Conseil econ. et social, numerous cttees; Hon. Chair. Credit Agricole; Commdr, Légion d'honneur, Mérite agricole. *Address:* Crédit Foncier de Monaco, 11 Boulevard Albert 1er 98012 Monaco (office); rue Jean-Jacques Rousseau, 11200 Bizanet, France (home). *Telephone:* 93-10-20-00 (office). *Fax:* 93-10-23-50 (office). *E-mail:* contact@cfm.mc (office). *Website:* www.cfm.mc (office).

BARSHAI, Rudolf Borisovich; Russian/British conductor; b. 28 Sept. 1924, Labinskaya, Krasnodar Territory; s. of Boris and Maria Barshai; ed Moscow Conservatoire; performed in chamber ensembles with Shostakovich, Richter, Oistrakh, Rostropovich; Founder and Artistic Dir Moscow Chamber Orchestra 1956–77; Prin. Conductor and Artistic Adviser, Bournemouth Symphony Orchestra 1982–96; Guest Conductor Orchestre Nat. de France; numerous tours abroad; author of orchestrations and arrangements for chamber orchestra of old and contemporary music; Hon. DMus (Southampton). *Address:* Askonas Holt Ltd, Lincoln House, 300 High Holborn, London, WC1V 7JH, England (office); Homberg Str. 6, 4433 Ramlinsburg, Switzerland (home). *Telephone:* (20) 7400-1700 (office). *Fax:* (20) 7400-1799 (office); (61) 931-35-64 (home). *E-mail:* info@askonasholt.co.uk (office). *Website:* www.askonasholt.co.uk (office); www.rudolfbarshai.com.

BARSHCHEVSKY, Mikhail Yuryevich; Russian lawyer; *Representative of the Government of the Russian Federation to the Constitutional Court, the Supreme Court and the Supreme Arbitration Court;* b. 27 Dec. 1955, Moscow; m. Olga Barkalova; one d.; ed All-Union Inst. of Law; legal consultant in Moscow butter factory 1973–79; Sr Legal Consultant, Dept of Trade, Reutov Town 1979–80; Founder, Head Moscow Lawyers 1991–, (Barschevsky and Partners Co. 1993–), defended Obshchaya Gazeta newspaper 1993, Oblik TV Co. 1997; TV arbiter, What? Where? When? 1997–; Prof., State Acad. of Law, Moscow State Jurists' Acad.; Govt Rep., Constitutional Court, Supreme Court, Higher Arbitration Court 2001–; Chair. Moscow Inst. of Econs, Politics and Law; mem. Bd All Russian Co-ordination Council for Public-Political Union, Moscow Region 1999–; mem. Russian Acad. of Natural Sciences, Russian Acad. of Lawyers, Moscow Collegiate of Advocates 1980–2001; Advocate of Honour, Plevako Gold Medal 2000. *Publications:* seven books and over 100 legal publs. *Leisure interests:* theatre, chess, travelling. *Address:* Krasnopresnenskaya emb. 2, 103274 Moscow, Russia (office). *Telephone:* (495) 205-40-51 (office). *Fax:* (495) 205-65-25 (office).

BARSHEFSKY, Charlene, BA, JD; American lawyer and fmr government official; *Senior International Partner, Wilmer Cutler Pickering LLP;* ed Univ. of Wisconsin; Pnr, Steptoe & Johnson (law firm), Washington, DC 1975–93; Deputy US Trade Rep. 1993–96, Acting US Trade Rep. April–Nov. 1996, US Trade Rep. 1997–2001; Sr Int. Pnr, Wilmer Cutler Pickering LLP (law firm) 2001–; mem. Bd American Express 2001–, Estée Lauder Cos 2001–, Idenix Parmaceuticals Inc. 2002–, Starwood Hotels & Resorts Worldwide Inc. 2001–, Intel Corpn 2004–. *Address:* Wilmer Cutler Pickering LLP, 2445 M Street, NW, Washington, DC 20037, USA. *Telephone:* (202) 663-6000 (office). *Fax:* (202) 663-6363 (office). *Website:* www.wilmer.com (office).

BARSTOW, Dame Josephine Clare, DBE, BA; British singer; b. 27 Sept. 1940, Sheffield; d. of Harold Barstow and Clara Barstow; m. 1st Terry Hands 1964 (divorced 1968); m. 2nd Ande Anderson 1969 (died 1996); ed Birmingham Univ.; taught English in London area for two years; debut in operatic profession with Opera for All 1964; for short time co. mem. Welsh Nat. Opera, then ENO; now freelance singer in all nat. opera houses in UK and in Paris, Vienna, Salzburg, Zürich, Geneva, Turin, Florence, Cologne, Munich, Berlin, USSR, Chicago, San Francisco, New York, Houston and many other American opera houses; Hon. DMus (Birmingham, Kingston, Sheffield Hallam), (Leeds) 2007; Fidelio Medal. *Chief roles:* Violetta in La Traviata, Leonora in Forza del

Destino, Elisabeth in Don Carlos, Lady Macbeth, Leonore in Fidelio, Sieglinde, Arabella, Salome, Chrysothemis, Amelia, The Marschallin, Tosca, Mimi, Minnie, Manon Lescaut, Emilia Marty, Jenůfa, Katya Kabanova, Medea, Renata in The Fiery Angel, Katerina Ismailova, Kostelnicka in Jenůfa, Marie in Wozzeck, Gloriana, Lady Billows in Albert Herring; world premières of Tippett, Henze and Penderecki. *Film:* Gloriana 2000, Owen Wingrave 2001. *Recordings include:* Verdi Recital Record with ENO Orchestra and Mark Elder, Amelia with Herbert von Karajan, Anna Maurant in Street Scene, Kate in Kiss Me Kate, Four Finales, Gloriana, Albert Herring. *Leisure interests:* farming (cattle) and breeding Arabian horses. *Address:* Musichall International, Vicarage Way, Ringmer, BN8 5LA, England (office). *Telephone:* (1273) 814240 (office). *Fax:* (1273) 813637 (office). *E-mail:* info@musichall.uk.com (office). *Website:* www.musichall.uk.com (office).

BART, Hon. Delano Frank, LLB; Saint Christopher and Nevis lawyer, politician and international official; *Permanent Representative, United Nations;* b. 28 Oct. 1952; ed Basseterre Senior School, Matthew Bolton Tech. Coll., Birmingham, Queen Mary Coll. and Inns of Court School, London, UK; teacher, Molineux All Age School 1970–72; part-time Lecturer in Law, Coll. of Distributive Justice, London 1977–79; admitted to Bar of England and Wales 1977, of Anguilla 1984, of Saint Christopher and Nevis 1984, of Antigua and Barbuda 1989; in pvt. practice from Chambers, The Temple, London 1977–95, appeared in variety of criminal and civil rights cases; Asst Counsel to Comm. of Inquiry, Bahamas 1993–94; Legal Rep. of Govt 1995–2001; mem. Legal Affairs Cttee Org. of Eastern Caribbean States 1995–; various positions with CARICOM 1995–, including mem. Legal Affairs Cttee, Attorney-Gen. to Caribbean Asscn of Regulators of Int. Business (CARIB), mem. Del. to Heads of Govt Meetings, Barbados, Bahamas, Canada; Head Del. to Defence Ministerial of the Americas Meetings 1995, 1996, 1998, 2000; head numerous other govt dels including Commonwealth Law Ministers Conf., Malaysia; Attorney-Gen. and Minister of Justice and Legal Affairs 2001–04, Minister of Justice 2006–06; Perm. Rep. to UN 2006–; mem. Lincoln's Inn, London 1976; Del. to Talks on Drafting Saint Christopher and Nevis Constitution 1982; fmr Exec. mem. Soc. of Black Lawyers in England and Wales. *Leisure interests:* music, art, reading, swimming. *Address:* Permanent Mission of Saint Christopher and Nevis to the United Nations, 414 East 75th Street, 5th Floor, New York, NY 10021, USA (office); #45 Horizon Villa, Frigate Bay, Basseterre, Saint Christopher and Nevis (home). *Telephone:* (212) 535-1234 (office); (869) 465-3581 (home). *Fax:* (212) 535-6854 (office). *E-mail:* sknmission@aol.com (office). *Website:* www.stkittsnevis.org.

BARTELSKI, Lesław, LLM; Polish writer; b. 8 Sept. 1920, Warsaw; s. of Zygmunt and Zofia Ulanowska; m. Maria Zembrzuska 1947; one s. one d.; ed Univ. of Warsaw; mem. of resistance movement 1939–44; mem. Sztuka i Naród (Art and Nation) 1942–44; Co-Ed. Nowiny Literackie 1947–48, Nowa Kultura 1953–63, Kultura 1963–72; mem. Presidium of Gen. Council, Union of Fighters for Freedom and Democracy 1969–79, Deputy Pres. 1979–90; mem. PEN; Chair. Warsaw Branch, Polish Writers' Asscn 1972–78, mem. Polish Writers' Asscn 1984–, Deputy Pres. 1989–2000, Hon. Pres. 2000–; mem. Bd, Janusz Korczak Int. Asscn; Visiting Prof., Univ. of Warsaw 1970–71, 1977–78; Vice-Pres. Warsaw City Council 1973–80; Lecturer on Cultural Research, Pvt. Higher School of Commerce 1993–96; Commdr's Cross, Order of Polonia Restituta, Order of Banner of Labour (2nd Class), Order of Cyril and Methodius (1st Class) Bulgaria, Cross of Valour, Warsaw Insurgent Cross, Partisan's Cross; State Prize (3rd Class) 1951, Prize of Minister of Defence (2nd Class) 1969, Pietrzak Prize 1969, 1985, Warsaw Prize 1969, Prize of Minister of Culture and Art 1977 (1st Class), Award of Pres. of Warsaw 1990, Reymont Prize 1998. *Publications:* poems: Przeciw zagładzie 1948; novels include Ludzie zza rzeki 1951, Pejzaż dwukrotny 1958, Wodorosty 1964, Mickiewicz na wschodzie 1966, Dialog z cieniem 1968, Niedziela bez dzwonów 1973, Krwawe skrzydła 1975, Rajski ogród 1978; essays: Genealogia ocalonych 1963, Jeździec z Madary 1963, Cień wojny 1963, Walcząca Warszawa 1968, Z głową na karabinie 1974, Pamięć żywa 1977, Polscy pisarze współcześni 1944–74 (biographical dictionary) 1977, Kusociński 1979, Pieśń niepodległa 1988, Czas bitew 1993, Polscy pisarze współcześni 1939–91 (biographical dictionary) 1995; monograph: Powstanie Warszawskie 1965, Mokotów 1944, 1971, Pułk AK Baszta 1990, Krzyż AK 1993, Getto 1999; fiction: Zlota Mahmudia (The Golden Mahmudia, made into film 1987); non-fiction: Warsaw Ghetto Thermopolye 2005. *Leisure interests:* history of the Second World War, sport. *Address:* ul. F. Joliot Curie 17 m. 1, 02-646 Warsaw, Poland. *Telephone:* (22) 844-31-10.

BARTENSTEIN, Martin, PhD; Austrian politician and business executive; *Minister for Economic Affairs and Labour;* b. 3 June 1953, Graz; m.; five c.; ed Akademisches Gymnasium, Miami Univ., OH, USA, Karl Franzens Univ., Graz; joined Lannacher Heilmittel GmbH (family-owned pharmaceutical co.) 1978, Man. Dir 1980–86; Chief Exec. Genericon Pharma GesmbH 1986–90; mem. Bd of Dirs Pharmavit AG, Budapest 1990; Chair. Asscn of Young Austrian Industrialists 1988; mem. Austrian People's Party (Österreichische Volkspartei—ÖVP), Party Spokesman on Industry 1991; Deputy Regional Chair. Styrian People's Party 1991; mem. (ÖVP) Nat. Ass. 1991–; State Sec., Fed. Ministry for Public Economy and Transport 1994; Minister for the Environment 1995, for Environment, Youth and Family Affairs 1996, for Econ. Affairs and Labour 2000–; Chair. Cancer Relief Fund for the Children of Styria 1988–92, Austrian Cancer Relief Fund for Children 1993–. *Address:* Ministry of Economic Affairs and Labour, Stubenring 1, 1011 Vienna, Austria (office). *Telephone:* (1) 711-00-0 (office). *Fax:* (1) 713-79-95 (office). *E-mail:* service@bmwa.gv.at (office). *Website:* www.bmwa.gv.at (office).

BARTH, Else M.; Norwegian/Dutch professor of logic and analytical philosophy; b. 3 Aug. 1928, Strinda, Norway; m. Hendrik A.J.F. Misset 1953; ed Univs of Oslo, Trondheim, Amsterdam and Leyden; Reader in Logic, Utrecht Univ. 1971–77; Prof. of Analytical Philosophy, Groningen Univ. 1977–87, of Logic and Analytical Philosophy 1987–; Pres. Evert Willem Beth Foundation 1976; mem. Royal Netherlands Acad. of Arts and Sciences, Norwegian Soc. of Sciences. *Publications:* The Logic of the Articles in Traditional Philosophy. A Contribution to the Study of Conceptual Structures 1974, Perspectives on Analytic Philosophy, in Mededelingen der Koninklijke Nederlandse Akad. van Wetenschappen, afd. Letterkunde, Nieuwe Reeks 1979, From Axiom to Dialogue – A Philosophical Study of Logics and Argumentation (with E. C. W. Krabbe) 1982, Argumentation: Approaches to Theory Formation. Containing the Contributions to the Groningen Conference on the Theory of Argumentation, October 1978 (ed., with J. L. Martens) 1982, Problems, Functions and Semantic Roles – A Pragmatist's Analysis of Montague's Theory of Sentence Meaning (co-ed. with R. T. P. Wiche) 1986; numerous contribs to learned journals and published lectures. *Leisure interests:* music, cultural and political philosophy, literature, skiing. *Address:* Nachtegaallaan 26, 2224 JH Katwijk aan Zee (home); Filosofisch Instituut, University of Groningen, Westersingel 19, 9718 CA Groningen (office); Kamperfoelieweg 16, 9765 HK Paterswolde, Netherlands. *Telephone:* (50) 636146 (office); (5907) 4315 (Paterswolde); (1718) 13353 (Katwijk aan Zee).

BARTH, John M.; American business executive; *Chairman, Johnson Controls Inc.;* b. 1946; ed Carnegie-Mellon Univ., Gannon Univ., Northwestern Univ. Inst. for Man.; joined Johnson Controls Inc. 1969, various man. positions including Dir Johnson Controls Automotive Systems Group 1990, mem. Bd of Dirs 1997–, Pres. and COO 1998, CEO 2002, Chair. 2004–. *Address:* Johnson Controls Inc., 5757 North Green Bay Avenue, POB 591, Milwaukee, WI 53201, USA (office). *Telephone:* (414) 524-1200 (office). *Fax:* (414) 524-2077 (office). *Website:* www.johnsoncontrols.com (office).

BARTH, John Simmons, MA; American novelist and academic; *Professor Emeritus in the Writing Seminars, Johns Hopkins University;* b. 27 May 1930, Cambridge, Md; s. of John J. Barth and Georgia Simmons; m. 1st Harriette Anne Strickland 1950 (divorced 1969); two s. one d.; m. 2nd Shelly Rosenberg 1970; ed Johns Hopkins Univ.; Instructor Pennsylvania State Univ. 1953, Assoc. Prof. until 1965; Prof. of English, State Univ. of New York at Buffalo 1965–73, Johns Hopkins Univ. 1973–91, Prof. Emer. 1991–; Rockefeller Foundation Grant; Brandeis Univ. Citation in Literature; Hon. LittD (Univ. of Maryland); Hon. DHL (Pennsylvania State Univ.) 1996; Nat. Acad. of Arts and Letters Award, Nat. Book Award 1973, F. Scott Fitzgerald Award 1997, President's Medal, Johns Hopkins Univ. 1997, PEN/Malamud Award 1998, Lifetime Achievement Award, Lannan Foundation 1998, Lifetime Achievement in Letters Award, Enoch Pratt Soc. 1999. *Publications:* The Floating Opera 1956, The End of the Road 1958, The Sot-Weed Factor 1960, Giles Goat-Boy 1966; Lost in the Funhouse (stories) 1968, Chimera 1972, Letters 1979, Sabbatical 1982, The Friday Book (essays) 1984, The Tidewater Tales: A Novel 1987, The Last Voyage of Somebody the Sailor 1991, Once Upon a Time 1994, On With the Story (stories) 1996, Coming Soon!!! (novel) 2001, The Book of Ten Nights and a Night (stories) 2004, Three Roads Meet (novella) 2005, The Development (stories) 2008. *Address:* The Writing Seminars, 135 Gilman Hall, Johns Hopkins University, 3400 North Charles Street, Baltimore, MD 21218, USA. *Telephone:* (410) 167-563. *Website:* www.jhu.edu/writsem.

BARTH, (Thomas) Fredrik (Weybye), MA, PhD; Norwegian social anthropologist; b. 22 Dec. 1928, Leipzig; s. of Prof. Tom Barth and Randi Barth; m. Unni Wikan 1972; one s.; ed Berg School, Oslo and Univs. of Chicago, USA and Cambridge, England; Research Fellow in Social Anthropology, Univ. of Oslo 1953–61; Prof. of Social Anthropology, Univ. of Bergen 1961–72, Univ. of Oslo 1973–86; Research Fellow, Ministry of Educ. and Science 1987–; Prof. of Anthropology, Boston Univ., USA; Visiting Prof. Columbia Univ. 1960, Univ. of Khartoum 1963–64, Yale Univ. 1972, Johns Hopkins Univ. 1977, Univ. of Calif. Berkeley 1980, City Univ. NY 1987, Emory Univ. 1989–96, Harvard Univ. 1996–97; Sir James Frazer Memorial Lecturer, Cambridge 1983; Sir Thomas Huxley Memorial Lecturer, London 1989; Hon. Life Fellow Royal Anthropological Inst. 1968; Hon. Life mem. Int. Union of Anthropological and Ethnological Sciences 1993; Dr. hc (Memorial Univ., Canada) 1988, (Univ. of Edin.) 1996; Retzius Gold Medal, Royal Swedish Soc. 1988, Lifetime Achievement Award, IUAES Comm. on Nomadic Peoples 1998. *Publications:* Political Leadership Among Swat Pathans 1959, Nomads of South Persia 1961, Models of Social Organization 1964, Ethnic Groups and Boundaries 1969, Ritual and Knowledge among the Baktaman of New Guinea 1975, Selected Essays 1981, Sohar 1983, The Last Wali of Swat 1985, Cosmologies in the Making 1987, Balinese Worlds 1993. *Leisure interests:* travel, art. *Address:* Rödkleivfaret 16, 0788 Oslo, Norway. *Telephone:* (47) 22-147483. *Fax:* (47) 22-145748.

BARTHOLOMEOS I, Patriarch, DCnL; Turkish ecclesiastic; *Archbishop of Constantinople (New Rome) and Ecumenical Patriarch;* b. 29 Feb. 1940, Hagioi Theodoroi, Island of Imvros; s. of Christos Archondonis and Merope Archondonis; ed Theological School of Halki, Pontifical Oriental Inst., Rome, Ecumenical Inst. Bossey, Switzerland and Univ. of Munich; mil. service 1961–63; ordained deacon 1961, priest 1969; Asst Dean, Theological School of Halki 1968; elevated to rank of Archimandrite 1970; Admin. Pvt. Patriarchal Office of Ecumenical Patriarch Dimitrios 1972–90; Metropolitan, See of Philadelphia, Asia Minor 1973; mem. Holy and Sacred Synod 1974; Metropolitan of Chalcedon 1990–91; Archbishop of Constantinople (New Rome) and Ecumenical Patriarch 1991–; mem. Exec. and Cen. Cttees, WCC 1991–; Dr hc (Athens), (Holy Cross Orthodox School of Theology, Brookline, Mass). *Address:* Chief Secretariat of the Holy and Sacred Synod of the Ecumenical Patriarchate, Greek Orthodox Church, Rum Ortodoks Patrikhanesi, 34220 Fener-Haliç, Istanbul, Turkey (office). *Telephone:* (212) 5319671 (office). *Fax:* (212) 5349037 (office). *Website:* www.patriarchate.org (office).

BARTHOLOMEW, Reginald; American diplomatist and business executive; *Chairman, Merrill Lynch Italy;* b. 17 Feb. 1936, Portland, Maine; m.

Rose-Anne Dognin; three s. one d.; ed Dartmouth Coll., Chicago Univ.; instructor, Chicago Univ. 1961–64; Wesleyan Univ., Conn. 1964–68; Deputy Dir Policy Planning Staff, Dept of State 1974; Deputy Dir Politico-Mil. Affairs Bureau 1977, Dir 1979–81; with Nat. Security Council 1977–79; Special Cyprus Co-ordinator 1981–82; Special Negotiator for US–Greek defence and econ. co-operation negotiations 1982–83; Amb. to Lebanon 1983–86, to Spain 1987–89, to NATO 1992–93; Special Envoy of Pres. Clinton to Bosnia 1993; Amb. to Italy 1993–97; Vice-Chair., Man. Dir Merrill Lynch Europe Holdings Ltd 1997, Chair. Merrill Lynch, Italy; mem. Council on Foreign Relations. *Address:* Merrill Lynch, Largo Fontanella Borghese, 00186 Rome, Italy (office).

BARTKUS, Gintautas; Lithuanian politician and lawyer; *Assistant Professor, Vilnius University;* b. 30 June 1966, m.; two c.; ed Vilnius State Univ., Helsinki Univ., Jean Moulin Univ., Lyon, France; Adviser to Dir Dept of Nat. Lithuanian Govt 1990–92; Visiting Prof., John Marshall Law School, Chicago, USA 1993–96; Founder and Pnr, Law Co. Lideika, Petrauskas, Valiunas and Pnrs 1990–2000; mem. Working Group for Drafting the Civil Code of Lithuania 1992–2000; Asst Prof., Vilnius Univ. 1989–; Minister of Justice of Lithuania 2000–01. *Address:* Vilnius University, Universiteto 3, 2734 Vilnius (office); Jurevicius, Balciunas & Partners, Subaciaus 7, 01008 Vilnius, Lithuania. *Telephone:* (2) 62-37-79 (office); (5) 274-24-00. *Fax:* (2) 22-35-63 (office). *E-mail:* Gintautas.Bartkus@lt.eylaw.com (office).

BARTLETT, Jennifer, BA, BFA, MFA; American artist; b. 14 March 1941, Long Beach, Calif.; ed Mills Coll., Oakland, Calif., Yale Univ. School of Art and Architecture; taught art at Univ. of Connecticut 1964–72, School of Visual Arts, New York 1972–77; first New York exhbn, Alan Saret's SoHo gallery 1970; works in numerous collections, including Museum of Modern Art, Metropolitan Museum of Art, Whitney Museum of American Art, New York; Art Gallery of S Australia, Adelaide, Rhode Island School of Design, Yale Univ. Art Gallery and Walker Art Center, Minneapolis; numerous public commissions; large-scale murals and other works include: Rhapsody 1976, Swimmers Atlanta (Richard B. Russel Fed. Bldg, Atlanta, GA) 1979; 270 steel plates for Inst. for Scientific Information, Phila; murals for AT&T Bldg, New York; sculpture and other objects for Volvo Corpn's HQ, Göteborg, Sweden; Harris Prize, Art Inst. of Chicago 1976, Award of American Acad. and Inst. of Arts and Letters 1983, American Inst. of Architects Award 1987. *Solo exhibitions include:* The Brooklyn Art Museum 1985, Cleveland Museum of Art 1986, Paula Cooper Gallery, NY 1987, Milwaukee Art Museum 1988, Galerie Mukai, Tokyo 1989, Knoedler Gallery, London 1990, Richard Gray Gallery, Chicago 1991, Randolf-Macon Woman's Coll., Lynchberg, Va 1992, Santa Fe Inst. of Fine Arts 1993, Baldwin Gallery, Aspen, Colo 1994, Hiram Butler Gallery, Houston 1995, Richard Gray Gallery, Chicago 1996, Gagosian Gallery, Beverly Hills, Calif. 1997, Numark Gallery, Washington, DC 1998, Richard Gray Gallery, Chicago 1999, Greenberg Van Doren Fine Art, NY 2000, Richard Gray Gallery, Chicago 2001, Greenberg Van Doren Gallery, NY 2003, Locks Gallery, Phila 2004, Rosenbaum Contemporary, Boca Raton, Fla 2005. *Address:* 134 Charles Street, New York, NY 10014, USA (office). *Website:* www.richardgraygallery.com.

BARTLETT, John Vernon, CBE, MA, FREng, FICE; British consulting engineer (retd); b. 18 June 1927, London; s. of the late Vernon F. Bartlett and of Olga (née Testrup) Bartlett; m. Gillian Hoffman 1951; four s.; ed Stowe School and Trinity Coll., Cambridge; engineer, John Mowlem & Co., Ltd 1951–57; joined Mott Hay & Anderson (now Mott MacDonald Group) 1957, Partner 1966, Chair. 1973–88, Consultant 1988–95; Chair. British Tunnelling Soc., 1977–79; Pres. Inst. of Civil Engineers 1982–83; mem. Governing Body Imperial Coll. London 1991–95; Master Worshipful Co. of Engineers 1992–93; Founder Bartlett Library, Nat. Maritime Museum Cornwall (NMMC) 2002; Telford Gold Medals 1971, 1973; S.G. Brown Medal, Royal Soc. 1973. *Publications:* Tunnels: Planning, Design and Construction (with T.M. Megaw) 1981, Ships of North Cornwall 1996; various professional papers. *Leisure interests:* sailing, maritime history. *Address:* 6 Cottenham Park Road, Wimbledon, London, SW20 0RZ, England (home). *Telephone:* (20) 8946-9576 (home).

BARTLETT, Neil, BSc, PhD, FRS; British/American chemist and academic; *Professor Emeritus of Chemistry, University of California, Berkeley;* b. 15 Sept. 1932, Newcastle-upon-Tyne; s. of Norman Bartlett and Ann Willins Bartlett (née Vock); m. Christina Isabel Cross 1957; three s. one d.; ed Heaton Grammar School, Newcastle-upon-Tyne, King's Coll., Durham Univ.; Sr Chem. Master, The Duke's School, Alnwick, Northumberland 1957–58; Faculty mem. Dept of Chem., Univ. of British Columbia, Canada 1958–66; Prof. of Chem., Princeton Univ., NJ, USA 1966–69; Scientist, Bell Telephone Labs, Murray Hill, NJ 1966–69; Prof. of Chem., Univ. of California, Berkeley 1969–94, Prof. Emer. 1994–, Prin. Investigator, Lawrence Berkeley Nat. Lab. (LBNL) 1969–99, Guest Sr Scientest 1998–; Brotherton Visiting Prof., Chem. Dept, Univ. of Leeds 1981; Erskine Visiting Fellow, Univ. of Canterbury, NZ 1983; Visiting Fellow, All Souls Coll. Oxford 1984; Assoc., Inst. Jozef Stefan, Slovenia; mem. Leopoldina Acad., Halle 1969, European Acad. of Science 2004; Corresp. mem. Göttingen Acad. 1977, American Acad. of Arts and Sciences 1977, NAS 1979; Associé Etranger Acad. des Sciences, France 1989, Academia Europaea 1998; Foreign Fellow, Royal Soc. of Canada 2001; Hon. FRSC 2002; Hon. DSc (Waterloo) 1968, (Colby Coll.) 1971, (Newcastle-upon-Tyne) 1981, (McMaster) 1992, (British Columbia) 2006; Dr hc (Bordeaux) 1976, (Ljubljana) 1989, (Nantes) 1990; Hon. LLD (Simon Fraser) 1993, Hon. Dr rer. nat (Freie Univ. Berlin) 1998; Research Corpn Award 1965, Dannie Heineman Prize 1971, Robert A. Welch Award 1976, W. H. Nichols Medal, USA 1983, Moissan Fluorine Centennial Medal, Paris 1986, Prix Moissan 1988, ACS Award for Distinguished Service to Inorganic Chem. 1989, ACS Pauling Medal 1989, ACS Award for Creative Work in Fluorine Chem. 1992, Bonner Chemiepreis 1992, Pierre Duhem Lecturer, Bordeaux Univ. 1998, Davy Medal, Royal Soc. (London) 2002, Grand Prix de la Fondation Internationale de la Maison de la Chimie (Paris) 2004. *Achievements (miscellaneous):* preparation of the first compound of a noble gas ($XePtF_6$), characterization of the first salt of oxidized oxygen (O_2^+), synthesis and structural characterization of the metastable fluorides ÅgF3and NiF3and synthesis of new semi-conducting pseudo-graphite materials such as C3B, C5N and BC2N. *Publications:* The Chemistry of the Monatomic Gases (with F. O. Sladky, A. H. Cockett and K. C. Smith) 1973, Noble-Gas Compounds (with D. T. Hawkins and W. E. Falconer) 1978, The Oxidation of Oxygen and Related Chemistry 2001; more than 160 scientific papers including reports on the first preparation of the oxidized oxygen cation O2+and the first true compound of a noble gas. *Leisure interests:* watercolour painting, antique silver. *Address:* Lawrence Berkeley National Laboratory, Room 3307, Building 70A, Berkeley, CA 94720 (office); 6 Oak Drive, Orinda, CA 94563, USA (home). *Fax:* (510) 486-6033 (office). *E-mail:* N-Bart@cchem.berkeley.edu (office). *Website:* chem.berkeley.edu (office).

BARTOLI, Cecilia; Italian singer (coloratura mezzo-soprano) and recitalist; b. 4 June 1966, Rome; d. of Pietro Angelo Bartoli and Silvana Bazzoni; ed Accademia di Santa Cecilia, Rome; professional career began with TV appearance aged 19; US debut in recital at Mostly Mozart Festival, New York 1990; Paris debut as Cherubino in The Marriage of Figaro, Opéra de Paris Bastille 1990–91 season; debut, La Scala, Milan in Rossini's Le Comte Ory 1990–91 season; appeared as Dorabella in Così fan tutte, Maggio Musicale, Florence 1991; debut with Montreal Symphony Orchestra and Philadelphia Orchestra 1990–91 season; recitals in collaboration with pianist András Schiff since 1990; appeared in Marriage of Figaro and Così fan tutte conducted by Daniel Barenboim in Chicago Feb. 1992; debut at Salzburg Festival 1992; appeared in recital at Rossini bicentenary celebration at Lincoln Center, New York 1992; has appeared with many leading conductors including the late Herbert von Karajan, Claudio Abbado, Riccardo Chailly, Myung-Whun Chung, William Christie, Charles Dutoit, Adam Fischer, Nikolaus Harnoncourt, Christhopher Hogwood, James Levine, Sir Neville Marriner, Zubin Mehta, Riccardo Muti, Giuseppe Sinopoli and the late Sir George Solti; particularly associated with the operas of Mozart and Rossini; highlights of the 2000–01 season included Cenerentola in Munich, Così fan tutte and Don Giovanni in Zurich, concert performances of Haydn's Orfeo with Hogwood in Birmingham, Amsterdam, Bremen and Paris, orchestral appearances with Harnoncourt and the Berlin Philharmonic in Berlin, Barenboim and the Chicago Symphony in Chicago and New York, Boulez and the London Symphony Orchestra in London and Amsterdam, Chailly and the Concertgebouw Orchestra in Amsterdam, all-Vivaldi concerts with the Giardino Armonico in Merano, Zurich, Paris, Lindau, Liechtenstein, New York, Vancouver, Los Angeles and San Francisco, baroque music concerts with the Akademie für Alte Musik in Oslo, Goteborg, Stockholm, Helsinki and Vienna; Hon. mem. Royal Acad. of Music 2005; Chevalier, Ordre des Arts et des Lettres; two Grammy Awards for Best Classical Vocal Album 1994, Deutsche Schallplatten Preis, La Stella d'Oro, Italy, Caecilia Award, Belgium, Diapason d'Or, France, Best Opera Recording of the Year for La Cenerentola, Japan, Classical BRIT Award for Female Artist of the Year 2004, Echo Klassik Award for Female Singer of the Year 2008. *Recordings include:* albums: Rossini Arias, Rossini Songs, Mozart Arias, Rossini Heroines, Chants d'amour, If You Love Me 1992, Mozart Portraits 1995, An Italian Songbook 1997, Cecilia Bartoli – Live Vivaldi Album 1999, Cecilia & Bryn, Il Turco in Italia, Mitridate, Rinaldo, Armida in Italy, The Salieri Album, The Vivaldi Album, Gluck Italian Arias, Opera proibito 2005, Maria (Gramophone Award for Best Recital 2008) 2007. *Address:* MusicArt Management AG, PO Box 123, 8702 Zollikon-Zurich, Switzerland (office). *Website:* www.ceciliabartolionline.com.

BARTON, Anne, PhD, FBA; American professor of English; *Fellow, Trinity College, University of Cambridge;* b. 9 May 1933; d. of Oscar Charles Roesen and Blanche Godfrey Williams; m. 1st William Harvey Righter 1957; m. 2nd John Bernard Adie Barton 1969; ed Bryn Mawr Coll. and Univ. of Cambridge, UK; Lecturer History of Art, Ithaca Coll., New York 1958–59; Rosalind Carlisle Research Fellow, Girton Coll. Cambridge 1960–62, Official Fellow in English 1962–72; Asst Lecturer, Univ. of Cambridge 1962–64, Lecturer 1964–72; Hildred Carlile Prof. of English and Head Dept of English, Bedford Coll., London 1972–74; Fellow and Tutor in English, New Coll., Oxford and Common Univ. Fund Lecturer 1974–84; Prof. of English, Univ. of Cambridge 1984–2000; Fellow, Trinity Coll., Cambridge 1986–; mem. Editorial Bds, Studies in English Literature 1976–, Romanticism 1995–; mem. Academia Europaea; Hon. Fellow, Shakespeare Inst., Univ. of Birmingham, New Coll., Oxford; Rose Mary Crawshay Prize, British Acad. 1990. *Publications:* Shakespeare and the Idea of the Play 1962; Ben Jonson, Dramatist 1984, The Names of Comedy 1990, Byron: Don Juan 1992, Essays, Mainly Shakespearean 1994; numerous essays in journals. *Leisure interests:* opera, fine arts. *Address:* Trinity College, Cambridge, CB2 1TQ, England (office). *Telephone:* (1223) 338466 (office); (1223) 338466 (home). *E-mail:* ab10004@hermes.cam.ac.uk (office).

BARTON, Jacqueline K., AB, PhD; American chemist and academic; *Arthur and Marian Hanisch Memorial Professor of Chemistry, California Institute of Technology;* b. 7 May 1952, New York City; d. of William Kapelman and Claudine Kapelman (née Gutchen); m. Prof. Peter Brendan Dervan 1990; ed Barnard Coll. and Columbia Univ., New York; Visiting Research Assoc., Dept of Biophysics, Bell Labs 1979; Postdoctoral Fellow, Bell Labs and Yale Univ. 1980; Asst Prof. of Chem. and Biochemistry, Hunter Coll., CUNY 1980–82; returned to Columbia Univ. 1983, Assoc. Prof. of Chem. and Biological Sciences 1985–86, Prof. 1986–89; Prof., California Inst. of Tech. 1989–, currently Arthur and Marian Hanisch Memorial Prof. of Chem.; mem. NSF

Chem. Advisory Cttee 1985–88, NIH Metallobiochemistry Study Section 1986–90 (Chair. 1988–90); mem. Bd of Dirs Dow Chemical Co. 1993–, currently Chair. Environment, Health and Safety Cttee and mem. Governance and Compensation Cttees; Fellow, American Acad. of Arts and Sciences 1991, American Philosophical Soc. 2000, NAS 2002; fmr Fellow, Sloan Foundation; fmr NSF Presidential Young Investigator; Hon. DSc (Knox Coll.) 1991, (Williams Coll.) 1992, New Jersey Inst. of Tech. 1993, (Kenyon Coll.) 1994, (Lawrence Univ.) 1994, (Skidmore Coll.) 1997, (Yale Univ.) 2005; NSF Predoctoral Fellow 1975–78, NIH Postdoctoral Fellow 1979–80, Harold Lamport Award, New York Acad. of Sciences 1984, NSF Alan T. Waterman Award 1985, Camille and Henry Dreyfus Teacher-Scholar 1986–91, ACS Award in Pure Chem. 1988, ACS Eli Lilly Award in Biological Chem. 1987, ACS Baekeland Medal 1991, Fresenius Award 1986, University Medal, Barnard Coll. 1990 and Columbia Univ. 1992, MacArthur Foundation Fellowship 1991, ACS Garvan Medal 1992, ACS Tolman Medal 1994, Mayor of New York's Award in Science and Tech. 1988, Havinga Medal 1995, Paul Karrer Medal 1996, ACS Nichols Medal 1997, Weizmann Women and Science Award 1998, ACS Ronald Breslow Award in Biomimetic Chem. 2003, Willard Gibbs Award, Chicago Section of ACS 2006. *Publications:* more than 250 publs in scientific journals on the application of transition metal complexes as tools to probe recognition and reactions of double helical DNA. *Address:* Department of Chemistry, M/C 127-72, California Institute of Technology, 1200 East California Blvd, Pasadena, CA 91125-7200, USA (office). *Telephone:* (626) 395-6075 (office). *Fax:* (626) 577-4976 (office). *E-mail:* jkbarton@caltech.edu (office). *Website:* www.its.caltech.edu/~jkbgrp (office).

BARTON, Rev. John, MA, DPhil, DLitt, FBA; British academic; *Oriel and Laing Professor of the Interpretation of Holy Scripture, Oriel College, University of Oxford;* b. 17 June 1948, London; s. of Bernard A. Barton and Gwendolyn H. Barton; m. Mary Burn 1973; one d.; ed Latymer Upper School, London and Keble Coll. Oxford; Jr Research Fellow, Merton Coll. Oxford 1973–74; Univ. Lecturer in Theology, Univ. of Oxford 1974–89, Reader in Biblical Studies 1989–91; Fellow, St Cross Coll. Oxford 1974–91; Oriel and Laing Prof. of the Interpretation of Holy Scripture and Fellow, Oriel Coll. Oxford 1991–; Canon Theologian of Winchester Cathedral 1991–2003; mem. Norwegian Acad. of Arts & Sciences 2008; Hon. DrTheol (Bonn) 1998. *Publications:* Amos's Oracles Against the Nations 1980, Reading the Old Testament 1984, Oracles of God 1986, People of the Book? 1988, Love Unknown 1990, What is the Bible? 1991, Isaiah 1–39 1995, The Spirit and the Letter 1997, Making the Christian Bible 1997, Ethics and the Old Testament 1998, The Cambridge Companion to Biblical Interpretation 1998, Oxford Bible Commentary 2001, Joel and Obadiah 2001, The Biblical World 2003, Understanding Old Testament Ethics 2003, The Original Story (with J. Bowden) 2004, Living Belief 2005, The Nature of Biblical Criticism 2007, The Old Testament: Canon, Literature, Theology 2007. *Address:* Oriel College, Oxford, OX1 4EW, England (office). *Telephone:* (1865) 276537 (office). *E-mail:* john.barton@oriel.ox.ac.uk (office). *Website:* www.oriel.ox.ac.uk (office).

BARTON, John Bernard Adie, CBE, MA; British drama director and adaptor; *Advisory Director, Royal Shakespeare Company;* b. 26 Nov. 1928, London; s. of Sir Harold Montagu Barton and Lady Joyce Barton (née Wale); m. Anne Righter 1968; ed Eton Coll. and King's Coll., Cambridge; Drama Lecturer, Univ. of Berkeley, Calif. 1953–54; Fellow, King's Coll. Cambridge 1954–59; Asst Dir (to Peter Hall) RSC 1959, Assoc. Dir 1964–91, Advisory Dir 1991–. *Productions for RSC include:* The Wars of the Roses (adapted, edited, co-directed) 1963, Love's Labour's Lost 1965, 1978, All's Well That Ends Well, Julius Caesar, Troilus and Cressida 1968–69, Twelfth Night, When Thou Art King 1969–70, Othello, Richard II, Henry V 1971, Richard II 1973, Dr. Faustus, King John (co-dir), Cymbeline (co-dir) 1974–75, Much Ado About Nothing, Troilus and Cressida, The Winter's Tale, King Lear, A Midsummer Night's Dream, Pillars of the Community 1976, The Way of the World 1978, The Merchant of Venice, Love's Labour's Lost 1978, The Greeks 1980, Hamlet 1980, Merchant of Venice, Two Gentlemen of Verona 1981, Titus Andronicus 1981, La Ronde 1982, Life's a Dream 1984, The Devils 1984, Waste 1985, Dream Play 1985, The Rover 1986, The Three Sisters 1988, Coriolanus 1989, Peer Gynt 1994, 1995, Cain 1995; also School for Scandal, London 1983, For Triumph Apollo 1983, The Vikings 1983; for Nat. Theatre, Oslo: Peer Gynt 1990, Measure for Measure, As You Like It 1991–92; The War That Still Goes On 1991, Tantalus, Denver Center Theater Co. 2000. *Television productions:* Playing Shakespeare 1982, Mallory's Morte d'Arthur 1983, The War That Never Ends (scriptwriter) 1990. *Publications:* The Hollow Crown 1962, The Wars of the Roses 1970, The Greeks 1981, Playing Shakespeare 1982, Tantalus 2000. *Leisure interests:* travel, chess, work. *Address:* 14 De Walden Court, 85 New Cavendish Street, London, W1W 6XD, England. *Telephone:* (20) 7580-6196. *Fax:* (20) 7580-6196 (office).

BARTON, Nicholas Hamilton (Nick), PhD, FRS, FRSE; British biologist and academic; *Professor of Evolutionary Biology, University of Edinburgh;* ed Univ. of East Anglia; Demonstrator, Dept of Genetics, Univ. of Cambridge 1980–82; Lecturer, Dept of Genetics and Biometry, Univ. Coll. London 1982–90; staff mem., Univ. of Edinburgh 1990–, Prof. of Evolutionary Biology 1994–; Handling Ed. Evolution 2008–; mem. Editorial Bd Public Library of Science 2003; David Starr Jordan Prize 1994, Pres.'s Award, American Soc. of Naturalists 1998, Wolfson Merit Award 2005, Darwin Medal, Royal Soc. 2006, Darwin-Wallace Medal and Award (co-recipient), Linnean Soc. 2008. *Publications:* numerous scientific papers in professional journals on hybrid zones, speciation and multi-locus evolution, and on understanding the evolution of traits which depend on interactions between large numbers of genes. *Address:* Room 126, Ashworth Labs, School of Biological Sciences, University of Edinburgh, Michael Swann Building, King's Buildings, Mayfield Road, Edinburgh, EH9 3JR, Scotland (office). *Telephone:* (131) 650-5509 (office).

E-mail: n.barton@ed.ac.uk (office). *Website:* bartongroup.icapb.ed.ac.uk (office).

BARTOŠEK, Karel, DPhil; Czech historian and writer; *Editor, Nouvelle Alternative;* b. 30 June 1930, Skutec; s. of Karel Bartošek and Frantiska Stepanková; m. Suzanne Bartošek (née Chastaing) 1959; one s. two d.; ed Charles Univ., Prague; Research Asst, Inst. of History, Czechoslovak Acad. of Sciences 1960–68; resgnd 1969; stoker 1972–82; researcher, Inst. d'Histoire du Temps Présent, CNRS 1983–99; Ed. Nouvelle Alternative 1986–. *Publications:* Les Aveux des archives 1996, Le Livre noir du communisme, crimes, terreurs, répressions (co-author) 1997, Czech Prisoner 2001. *Leisure interests:* swimming, skiing. *Address:* 6 rue du Moulin de la Pointe, 75013 Paris, France. *Telephone:* 1-45-81-44-69.

BARTOV, Omer, DPhil; Israeli/American historian and academic; *John P. Birkelund Distinguished Professor of European History, Brown University;* ed Univ. of Oxford, UK; fmrly at Rutgers Univ.; currently John P. Birkelund Distinguished Prof. of European History and Prof. of History, Brown Univ.; Visiting Fellow, Davis Center, Princeton Univ.; Jr Fellow, Soc. of Fellows, Harvard Univ.; mem. American Acad. of Arts and Sciences; Fellow, Nat. Endowment for the Humanities, Alexander von Humboldt Foundation, Radcliffe Inst. for Advanced Study, Harvard Univ. 2002–03; Guggenheim Fellow 2003–04, American Acad., Berlin 2007, NEH Fellowship 2008–09. *Publications include:* The Eastern Front 1941–45: German Troops and the Barbarisation of Warfare 1985, Hitler's Army 1991, Murder in Our Midst (Fraenkel Prize in Contemporary History) 1996, Mirrors of Destruction 2000; Ed.: The Holocaust: Origins, Implementation, Aftermath 2000; Co-Ed.: In God's Name: Genocide and Religion in the Twentieth Century 2001, Germany's War and the Holocaust 2003, The Crimes of War: Guilt and Denial in the Twentieth Century 2002, The "Jew" in Cinema 2005, Erased: Vanishing Traces of Jewish Galicia in Present-Day Ukraine 2007; numerous book chapters, articles and reviews in several languages. *Address:* Brown University, Department of History, Peter Green House, 79 Brown Street, Box N, Providence, RI 02912, USA (office). *Telephone:* (401) 863-1375 (office). *Fax:* (401) 863-1040 (office). *E-mail:* Omer_Bartov@brown.edu (office). *Website:* www.brown.edu (office).

BARTZ, Carol; American business executive; *CEO, Yahoo! Inc.;* b. 1949; one d.; ed Univ. of Wisconsin; fmr Man. Product Line and Sales, Digital Equipment Corpn and 3M Corpn; various roles with Sun Microsystems rising to Exec. Officer 1983–92; Chair., Pres. and CEO Autodesk, Inc. 1992–2009; CEO Yahoo! Inc. 2009–; mem. Bd of Dirs BEA Systems, Cisco Systems, Network Appliance, TechNet, Foundation for the Nat. Medals of Science and Tech., New York Stock Exchange; mem. Pres. Bush's Council of Advisors on Science and Tech.; Hon. DHumLitt (New Jersey Inst. of Tech.); Hon. DSc (Worcester Polytechnic Inst.); Hon. DLitt (Williams Woods Univ.); Soc. of Manufacturing Engineers Donald C. Burnham Manufacturing Man. Award 1994, Women in Tech. Int. Hall of Fame 1997, Horatio Alger Award 2000, Ernst & Young's Northern Calif. Master Entrepreneur of the Year Award 2001, Ada Lovelace Award, Asscn for Women in Computing 2003, Avatar Award for Women of Excellence, Nat. Asscn of Female Execs 2003, Spirit of Life Award, City of Hope 2004, named by San Francisco Business Times amongst the 100 Most Influential Women in Business 2004, named by Business Week in Women in Technology List 2004, Exemplary Community Leadership Award, Nat. Conf. for Community and Justice 2004, Women in Tech. Int. Hall of Fame, ranked by Forbes magazine amongst 100 Most Powerful Women (90th) 2004, (86th) 2005, ranked by Fortune magazine amongst 50 Most Powerful Women in Business in the US (31st) 2005, named by The Wall Street Journal as one of 50 Women to Watch 2005, named by Barron's amongst The World's 30 Most Respected CEOs 2005. *Address:* Yahoo! Incorporated, 701 1st Avenue, Sunnyvale, CA 94089, USA (office). *Telephone:* (408) 349-3300 (office). *Fax:* (408) 349-3301 (office). *E-mail:* CorporateSecretary@yahoo-inc.com (office). *Website:* www.yahoo.com (office).

BARUCH, Jordan J., ScD; American engineer and academic; *President, Jordan Baruch Associates;* ed James Madison High School, Brooklyn, NY, Brooklyn Coll., Massachusetts Inst. of Tech.; three years' service in US Army during WWII; Asst Prof., MIT 1948–71; Faculty mem. Grad. School of Business Admin, Harvard Univ. 1970–74; Prof. of Business Admin, Tuck School of Business, and Prof. of Eng, Thayer School of Eng, Dartmouth Coll. 1974–77; Founding Pnr and Vice-Pres. Bolt Beranek & Newman (BBN), left co. 1966–68, Dir –1977; Dept Gen. Man. MEDINET Dept, General Electric 1966–68; Founding mem. and Dir Boston Broadcasters, Inc. (Channel 5, Boston) –1977; Asst US Sec. of Commerce for Science and Tech., Washington, DC 1977–81; led establishment of first Chinese man. school on industrial use of science and tech.; Pres. Jordan Baruch Assocs, Chevy Chase, Md 1981–; has worked in Africa, India, Indonesia and Jordan; Founder Trans-Atlantic Inst. of American Jewish Cttee and US/Israel Binational Industrial Research and Devt Foundation; mem. American Bd Ben Gurion Univ., Israel Oceanic and Limnological Research Foundation; fmr mem. Bd of Regents, Nat. Library of Medicine; mem. Nat. Acad. of Eng (NAE) 1974, NAE Fellow and Augustine Sr Scholar 2001; Fellow, Acoustical Soc. of America, IEEE, American Acad. of Arts and Sciences, AAAS, New York Acad. of Science; has been honoured by China and Israel for his work in and with those countries, Arthur M. Bueche Award 2007. *Achievements:* invented affordable multi-loudspeaker system, a colorimeter for pathology labs, instruments for cardiac and neurosurgery operating suites, and first US multi-station computer system for hosps. *Publications:* Innovation Explosion – Using Intellect and Software to Revolutionize Growth Strategies (co-author) 1997; 12 patents and numerous articles in professional journals. *Address:* 5630 Wisconsin Ave, Chevy Chase, MD 20815, USA (office).

BARYSHNIKOV, Mikhail (Misha); Russian/American ballet dancer; *Artistic Director, Baryshnikov Arts Center;* b. 28 Jan. 1948, Riga, Latvia; s. of Nikolay Baryshnikov and Aleksandra (née Kisselov) Baryshnikova; one d.; ed Riga Ballet School and Kirov Ballet School, Leningrad; mem. Kirov Ballet Co. 1969–74; guest artist with many leading ballet cos including American Ballet Theater, Nat. Ballet of Canada, Royal Ballet, Hamburg Ballet, FRG, Ballet Victoria, Australia, Stuttgart Ballet, FRG, Alvin Ailey Co., USA 1974–; joined New York City Ballet Co. 1978, resgnd 1979; Artistic Dir, American Ballet Theater 1980–89; Co-Founder (with Mark Morris) and Dir White Oak Dance Project 1990–2002; founder and Artistic Dir, Baryshnikov Arts Center, New York 2005–; launched perfume Misha 1989; Gold Medal, Varna Competition, Bulgaria 1966, First Int. Ballet Competition, Moscow, USSR 1968, Nijinsky Prize, First Int. Ballet Competition, Paris Acad. de Danse 1968, Kennedy Center Honors, Nat. Medal of Honor, Commonwealth Award. *Ballets (world premières):* Vestris 1969, Medea 1975, Push Comes to Shove 1976, Hamlet Connotations 1976, Other Dances 1976, Pas de Duke 1976, La Dame De Pique 1978, L'Après-midi d'un Faune 1978, Santa Fe Saga 1978, Opus 19 1979, Rhapsody 1980. *Films:* The Turning Point 1977, White Nights 1985, Giselle 1987, Dancers 1987, Dinosaurs 1991. *Television:* appeared in episodes of Sex and the City 2003–04. *Choreography:* Nutcracker 1976, Don Quixote 1978, Cinderella 1984. *Publications:* Baryshnikov at Work 1977, Moments in Time 2005. *Address:* Baryshnikov Arts Center, 450 West 37th Street, Suite 501, New York, NY 10018, USA (office). *Telephone:* (646) 731-3200 (office). *Fax:* (646) 731-3207 (office). *E-mail:* info@bacnyc.org (office). *Website:* www.bacnyc .org (office).

BARZANI, Masoud; Iraqi (Kurdish) politician; *President, Kurdistan Region and Leader, Kurdistan Democratic Party;* b. 16 Aug. 1946, Mahabad, Iran; s. of Mustafa Barzani, founder of Kurdistan Democratic Party (KDP); m.; five s. three d.; ed Tehran Univ.; father forced to flee to USSR 1946, returned to Iraq following overthrow of Iraqi monarchy in 1958; reunited with his father, family returned to their home village of Barzan; KDP launched armed struggle to defend Kurdish people 1961, joined Peshmerga forces 1962; participated in del. that signed autonomy agreement with Govt in Baghdad March 1970; engaged in renewed Kurdish armed struggle 1970s; succeeded his father as Pres. of KDP 1979–; requested help from Iraqi Govt to capture city of Erbil from rival Patriotic Union of Kurdistan (PUK) 1995; led KDP in establishing a govt in Iraqi Kurdistan with PUK; mem. Iraqi Governing Council following invasion of Iraq 2003, Pres. Council April 2004; elected first Pres. Kurdistan Region in Iraq by Kurdistan Nat. Ass. June 2005–. *Publication:* Mustafa Barzani and the Kurdish Liberation Movement (with Ahmed Ferhani) (three vols in Arabic; first vol. also in English and Turkish). *Leisure interests:* reading and football. *Address:* Office of the President, Kurdistan Regional Government, Erbil, Iraq (office). *E-mail:* info@krg.org (office); party@kdp.se (office). *Website:* www.krg.org (office); www.kdp.se (office).

BARZANI, Nechirvan Idris; Iraqi (Kurdish) politician; *Prime Minister, Kurdistan Regional Government;* b. 21 Sept. 1966, Barzan, southern Kurdistan; grandson of Mustafa Barzani, founder of Kurdistan Democratic Party (KDP), nephew of Masoud Barzani, Pres. of Kurdistan Region; m. Nabila Barzani; two c.; ed Tehran Univ.; family forced to flee to Iran 1975; often accompanied his father and sr KDP mem. Idris Barzani on his missions abroad; political science studies in Tehran cut short due to sudden death of his father 1987; took up active role in Kurdish politics, working in KDP youth orgs, rose rapidly through ranks of KDP; first elected to leadership of KDP in 1989, re-elected 1999; participated in negotiations with Iraqi Govt following Gulf War 1991; Deputy Prime Minister of KDP's controlled region in Iraqi Kurdistan 1996–99, Prime Minister 1999–2006, first Prime Minister of unified Govt of Kurdistan Region 2006–. *Leisure interest:* Kurdish and Persian poetry. *Address:* Office of the Prime Minister, Council of Ministers Building, Kurdistan Regional Government, Erbil, Iraq (office). *E-mail:* info@krg.org (office). *Website:* www.krg.org (office).

BARZEL, Amnon, MSc; Israeli art writer, critic, consultant and museum director; b. 5 July 1935, Tel Aviv; m. Shafrira Glikson 1956; one s. one d.; ed Hebrew Univ., Jerusalem, Sorbonne, Paris; Art Consultant for City of Tel Aviv 1975–76; Curator Biennale of Venice, Italy 1976–78, 1980, 'Two Environments', Forte Belvedere, Florence and Castle of Prato, Italy 1978, São Paulo Biennale, Brazil 1985; Founding Curator 'Contemporary Art Meetings', Tel Hai, Israel 1980–83, Villa Celle Art Spaces Collection, Giuliano Gori, Prato, Italy 1981–82; Founding Dir Centre of Contemporary Art Luigi Pecci, Prato, Italy 1986–, Dir School for Curators 1991–; Consultant for creation of Museum of Contemporary Art, Florence, Italy 1989; mem. Curatorial Cttee for Int. Sculpture Center (ISC), Washington, DC, USA 1990. *Publications:* Isaac Frenel 1973, Dani Karavan 1978, Art in Israel 1986, Europe Now 1988, Julian Schnabel 1989, Enzo Cucchi 1989, Contemporary Russian Artists (jt ed.) 1990. *Leisure interests:* poetry, holy contemporary philosophy. *Address:* Centro per l'Arte Contemporanea Luigi Pecci, Viale della Repubblica 277, 50047 Prato (office); Via Giovanni Prati, 26, 50124 Florence, Italy (home). *Telephone:* (0574) 570620 (office); (055) 220098 (home).

BARZUN, Jacques Martin, AB, PhD, FRSA, FRSL; American writer and academic; *Professor Emeritus, Columbia University;* b. 30 Nov. 1907, Créteil, France; s. of Henri Martin and Anna-Rose Barzun; m. 1st Mariana Lowell 1936 (died 1979); two s. one d.; m. 2nd Marguerite Lee Davenport 1980; ed Lycée Janson de Sailly and Columbia Univ.; Instructor in History, Columbia Univ. 1929, Asst Prof. 1938, Assoc. Prof. 1942, Prof. 1945, Dean of Graduate Faculties 1955–58, Dean of Faculties and Provost 1958–67, Seth Low Prof. 1960–67, Univ. Prof. 1967–75; Prof. Emer. 1975–; Literary Adviser, Scribner's 1975–93; fmr Dir Council for Basic Educ., New York Soc. Library, Open Court Publications Inc., Peabody Inst.; mem. Advisory Council, Univ. Coll. at Buckingham, Editorial Bd Encyclopedia Britannica 1979–; mem. Acad. Delphinale (Grenoble), American Acad. of Arts and Letters (Pres. 1972–75, 1977–78), American Historical Asscn, Royal Soc. of Arts, American Arbitration Asscn, American Philosophical Soc., Royal Soc. of Literature, American Acad. of Arts and Sciences; Extraordinary Fellow, Churchill Coll., Cambridge 1961; Chevalier de la Légion d'honneur, Presidential Medal of Freedom 2004; Gold Medal for Criticism, American Acad. of Arts and Letters. *Publications:* The French Race: Theories of its Origins and their Social and Political Implications Prior to the Revolution 1932, Race: A Study in Modern Superstition 1937, Of Human Freedom 1939, Darwin, Marx, Wagner: Critique of a Heritage 1941, Romanticism and the Modern Ego (revised edn as Classic, Romantic, and Modern) 1943, Introduction to Naval History (with Paul H. Beik, George Crothers and E. O. Golob) 1944, Teacher in America 1945, Berlioz and the Romantic Century 1950, God's Country and Mine: A Declaration of Love Spiced with a Few Harsh Words 1954, Music in American Life 1956, The Energies of Art: Studies of Authors, Classic and Modern 1956, The Modern Researcher (with Henry F. Graff) 1957, Lincoln the Literary Genius 1959, The House of Intellect 1959, Science, the Glorious Entertainment 1964, The American University: How it Runs, Where it is Going 1968, On Writing, Editing and Publishing: Essays Explicative and Horatory 1971, A Catalogue of Crime (with Wendell Hertig Taylor) 1971, The Use and Abuse of Art 1974, Clio and the Doctors: Psycho-History, Quanto-History and History 1974, Simple and Direct: A Rhetoric for Writers 1975, Critical Questions 1982, A Stroll with William James 1983, A Word or Two Before You Go 1986, The Culture We Deserve 1989, Begin Here: On Teaching and Learning 1990, An Essay on French Verse for Readers of English Poetry 1991, From Dawn to Decadence: 500 Years of Western Cultural Life 2000, A Jacques Barzun Reader 2001; editor: Pleasures of Music 1950, The Selected Letters of Lord Byron 1953, New Letters of Berlioz (also trans.) 1954, The Selected Writings of John Jay Chapman 1957, Modern American Usage; translator: Diderot: Rameau's Nephew 1952, Flaubert's Dictionary of Accepted Ideas 1954, Evenings with the Orchestra 1956, Courteline: A Rule is a Rule 1960, Beaumarchais: The Marriage of Figaro 1961; contrib. of articles to various scholarly and non-scholarly periodicals and journals. *Address:* 18 Wolfeton Way, San Antonio, TX 78218, USA.

BAS, Philippe; French politician; b. 20 July 1958, Paris; ed Inst. of Political Studies, Nat. School of Man., Paris; mem. Council of State 1987–92; Advisor to Minister of Social Affairs, Health and Towns and to Minister of State for Health 1993–94; Asst Dir, Cabinet of Minister of Social Affairs, Health and Towns 1994–95; Dir, Cabinet of Minister of Employment and Social Affairs 1995–97; Social Affairs Advisor to Pres. of France 1997–2000; Asst Sec.-Gen., Cabinet of Pres. 2000–02, Sec.-Gen. 2002–07; Minister of Health and Social Protection 2007. *Publications:* L'Afrique Australe dans la Tourmente (with Denis Tersen) 1988. *Address:* c/o Ministry of Health and Social Protection, 8 ave de Ségur, 75007 Paris, France (office).

BASANG; Chinese party official; b. (Galsang), 1937, Lang, Tibet; ed Tibetan Minorities Inst. 1956; served as a slave to the Landlord of Chika 1947–56; joined the CCP 1959; Vice-Chair. Tibet Autonomous Region Revolutionary Cttee 1968–79; Sec. Secr. CCP Cttee Tibet 1971–77; Chair. Women's Fed. of Tibet 1973; mem. 10th CCP Cen. Cttee 1973; Chair. Langxian Co. Revolutionary Cttee 1974; mem. Standing Cttee 4th NPC 1975; 5th NPC 1978; Deputy Head Leading Group for Party Consolidation CCP Cttee Tibet 1977; Sec. CCP 4th Tibet Autonomous Regional Cttee 1977; Deputy Sec. 5th Autonomous Regional Cttee 1977; mem. CCP 11th Cen. Cttee 1977; Deputy for Tibet to 5th NPC 1978; Vice-Chair. People's Govt of Tibet 1979–83; mem. 12th CCP Cen. Cttee 1982–86; mem. Cen. Discipline Inspection Comm., CPPCC; Vice-Chair. CPPCC 6th Tibet Regional Cttee 1993. *Address:* Chinese Communist Party, Tibet Autonomous Region, Lhasa, People's Republic of China.

BASANT ROI, Rameswurlall, GCSK, MA (Econs); Mauritian banker; *Governor, Bank of Mauritius;* b. 17 Aug. 1946; ed Dehli School of Econs, Univ. of Delhi, India; joined Bank of Mauritius 1976, Research Officer 1976–84, Asst Dir Dept of Research 1984–87, Dir 1987–98, Gov. 1998–. *Publications include:* several papers on econs including Monetary Policy Making in Mauritius (co-author with Maxwell Fry) 1995. *Address:* Bank of Mauritius, Sir William Newton Street, PO Box 29, Port Louis (office); 15 Couvent de Lorette, Vacoas, Mauritius (home). *Telephone:* (230) 212-6127 (office). *Fax:* (230) 208-9204 (office). *E-mail:* bomrd@bow.intnet.mu (office). *Website:* bom.intnet.mu (office).

BASELITZ, Georg; German artist; b. 23 Jan. 1938, Deutschbaselitz, Saxony; m. Elke Kretzschmar 1962; two s.; ed Gymnasium, Kamenz, Kunstakad. E. Berlin and Akad. der Künste, W. Berlin; Instructor Staatliche Akad. der Bildenden Kunste, Karlsruhe 1977–78, Prof. 1978–83; Prof. Hochschule der Kunste, Berlin 1983–2003; works in public collections including Berlinische Galerie and Staatliche Museen zu Berlin, Berlin, Kunsthalle, Hamburg, Sammlung Ludwig, Cologne, Staatsgalerie Stuttgart, Pinakothek der Moderne, Munich, Statens Museum for Kunst, Copenhagen, Museum Moderner Kunst Stiftung Ludwig, Vienna, Stedelijk Museum, Amsterdam, Centre Pompidou, Paris, Musée d'art moderne et contemporain, Strasbourg, Ludwig Museum, Budapest, Museo Nacional Centro de Arte Reina Sofia, Madrid, Kunstmuseum, Basel, Russian State Museum, St Petersburg, Tate Gallery, London, Scottish Nat. Gallery of Modern Art, Edinburgh, Museum of Fine Arts, Boston, The Art Inst., Chicago, Metropolitan Museum of Art and Museum of Modern Art, New York, Nat. Gallery of Art, Washington, DC, Toronto Art Gallery, Ludwig Museum for Int. Art, Beijing, Nat. Museum of Modern Art Tokyo, Museum of Contemporary Art, Sydney; Commdr de l'Ordre des Arts et Lettres 2002; Kaiserring Prize, Goslar 1986, Rhenus Art Prize, Mönchen-Gladbach 1999, Julio González Prize, Valencia 2001,

Niedersächsischer Staaspreis 2003. *Publications:* books, pamphlets, manifestos and articles. *Address:* Schloss Derneburg, 31188 Holle, Germany.

BĂSESCU, Traian; Romanian politician, head of state and fmr naval officer; *President;* b. 4 Nov. 1951, Basarabi, Constanţa Co.; m.; two d.; ed Inst. of Civil Marine Mircea cel Bătrân and Norwegian Acad.; Officer Grades III, II and I, Romanian Navy 1976–81, Capt., Merchant Navy 1981–87; Head Navrom Agency, Antwerp 1987–89; Gen. Dir State Inspectorate of Civil Navigation, Ministry of Transportation 1989–90, Under-Sec. of State and Head of Naval Transportation Dept 1990–91, Minister of Transport 1991–92, 1996–2000; mem. Democratic Party (PD), Pres. 2001–04; mem. Chamber of Deputies 1992–96, 1996–2000; Vice-Pres. Chamber of Deputies Comm. for Industry and Services 1992–96; investigated for corruption and fraud 1996; Dir electoral campaign for Petre Roman (pres. cand.) 1996; Co-Pres. Justice and Truth Alliance (DA) 2003–; Mayor of Bucharest 2000–04; Pres. of Romania 2004– (suspended from post April–May 2007). *Address:* Office of the President, 060116 Bucharest, Palatul Cotroceni, Str. Geniului 1–3, Sector 5, Romania (office). *Telephone:* (21) 4100581 (office). *Fax:* (21) 4103858 (office). *E-mail:* presedinte@basescu.ro (home); presedinte@presidency.ro (office). *Website:* www.basescu.ro (home); www.presidency.ro (office).

BASHA, Lulzim, LLM; Albanian politician; *Minister of Foreign Affairs;* b. 12 June 1974, Tirana; m. Aurela Basha; one d.; ed Utrecht Univ., Netherlands; mem. war crimes investigation team of Serbian forces in Kosovo 1998–99; Legal Adviser, Justice Dept, UN Mission in Kosovo (UNMIK) 2000–01, Deputy Chief of Cabinet of Dir of Justice Dept 2001–02, Special Adviser for Transition, Justice Dept 2002–05; mem. Democratic Party of Albania (Partia Demokratike e Shqipërisë, PDSh) 2005–, Co-ordinator Cttee for Policy Orientation 2005–, Nat. Council 2005–, mem. Presidency 2005–, Spokesman of Gen. Election Campaign May–July 2005; mem. Parl. 2005–, Minister of Public Works, Transport and Telecommunications 2005–07, of Foreign Affairs 2007–. *Address:* Ministry of Foreign Affairs, Bulevardi Gjergj Fishta 6, Tirana, Albania (office). *Telephone:* (4) 362170 (office). *Fax:* (4) 235899 (office). *E-mail:* ministri@mfa.gov.al (office). *Website:* www.mfa.gov.al (office).

BASHIR, Attalla Hamad, BSc, MA, PhD; Sudanese diplomatist and international organization official; b. 23 Aug. 1946, Dongola; m.; one s. one d.; ed Khartoum Univ., Syracuse Univ., New York, USA, Acad. of Commerce, Bucharest, Romania; joined diplomatic service 1971; served in Kuwait, Bahrain, Czechoslovakia, Hungary, Malta, Italy, Romania, Ethiopia; Amb. to GDR 1989–90, to Rep. of Korea 1990–93; Amb. to Saudi Arabia and Perm. Rep. to Islamic Devt Bank and Org. of the Islamic Conf. 1995–97; Amb. to Netherlands and Resident Rep. to Int. Court of Justice 1997–2000; Dir-Gen. Bilateral and Regional Relations, Ministry of External Relations –2000; Exec. Sec. Intergovernmental Authority on Devt (IGAD) 2000–08; Guwang Hwa Medal for Merit for outstanding diplomatic service (Govt of S Korea) 1993. *Leisure interests:* drawing, painting. *Address:* c/o Intergovernmental Authority on Development, BP 2653, Djibouti (office).

BASHIR, Marie Roslyn, AC, CVO, MBS; Australian state governor and professor of psychiatry; *Governor of New South Wales;* b. Narrandera; d. of M. Bashir; m. Sir Nicholas Shehadie 1957; three c.; ed Sydney Girls High School, Univ. of Sydney; fmr teacher Univs of Sydney and NSW; Foundation Dir, Rivendell Child Adolescent and Family Service 1972–87; Dir Community Health Services, Cen. Sydney 1987–93; Clinical Prof. of Psychiatry, Univ. of Sydney 1993–2001; Consultant to NSW Juvenile Justice Facilities 1993–2000; Area Dir of Mental Health Services, Cen. Sydney 1994–2001; Sr Consultant to Aboriginal Medical Service, Redfern and Kempsey 1996–2001; Gov. of NSW 2001–; currently Chancellor Univ. of Sydney; Co-Chair. NSW Mental Health Strategy for Aboriginal People; mem. Amnesty Int., Nat. Trust, NSW Camellia Research Soc., Tandanya Nat. Aboriginal Cultural Centre; Patron Sydney Symphony and Opera Australia; mem. numerous univ. cttees, medical research bodies, mental health bds; involved in establishment of post grad. medical training in psychiatry in Viet Nam and other medical educ. visits to Laos and Cambodia; Fellow Royal Australian and NZ Coll. of Psychiatrists (FRANZ) 1971–; named Mother of the Year NSW 1971. *Publications include:* research papers and publs on child, adolescent, refugee and Aboriginal mental health issues. *Leisure interests:* int. affairs, Australian history, early Australian antique furniture, classical music, opera, Aboriginal art, growing camellias. *Address:* Office of the Governor, Macquarie Street, Sydney, NSW 2000, Australia (office). *Website:* www.parliament.nsw.gov.au (office).

BASHIR, Munir Abdul al-Aziz; Iraqi composer and performer; b. 28 Sept. 1930, Mosul; s. of Bashir Abdul Aziz; m. Gecsy Iren 1961; two s.; ed high school and Fine Arts Inst. Baghdad; Instructor, Fine Arts Acad. 1946–60; Dir Community Arts Acad. 1950–56; Head, Music Dept Baghdad Radio and TV 1949–60; Art Adviser and Gen. Dir Music Dept Iraqi Ministry of Culture and Information 1973–93; Gen. Dir Babylon Int. Festival 1986–91; Vice-Pres. Int. Music Council (UNESCO) 1986–91; Sec.-Gen. Arab Acad. of Music 1974–; has performed solo Ud in more than 50 countries since 1954 and made many recordings; recipient of numerous honours and awards including Tchaikovsky Medal (USSR), Chopin Medal (Poland), UNESCO Int. Prize and decorations from France, Spain, Poland, Italy, Jordan, Cuba etc. *Leisure interest:* reading. *Address:* Arab Academy of Music, Al-Mansour, PO Box 1650, Baghdad; The National Music Conservatory, PO Box 926687, Baghdad, Iraq. *Telephone:* 962-2-687620. *Fax:* 962-2-687621.

BASHIR, Lt-Gen. Omar Hassan Ahmad al-; Sudanese head of state and army officer; *President and Prime Minister;* b. 1 Jan. 1944, Hoshe Bannaga, Anglo-Egyptian Sudan; ed Sudan Mil. Acad., Egyptian Mil. Acad., Cairo; fought in Egyptian army during 1973 war with Israel; career army officer rising to rank of Brig., then Lt-Gen.; overthrew Govt of Sadiq al-Mahdi in coup 30 June 1989; Chair. Revolutionary Command Council for Nat. Salvation 1989–; Minister of Defence 1989–93; Pres. and Prime Minister of Sudan 1993–; Chair. Ass. Intergovernmental Authority on Devt 2000–01; charged with genocide by Int. Criminal Court (ICC) 14 July 2008, warrant issued for his arrest on two counts of war crimes and five counts of crimes against humanity in Darfur (first ICC warrant for a serving head of state) 4 March 2009. *Address:* Revolutionary Command Council, Khartoum, Sudan (office).

BASHIR, Salah ed-Din al-, MA, PhD; Jordanian lawyer, academic and politician; b. 1966; ed Univ. of Jordan, Harvard Law School, USA, McGill Univ., Canada; Adjunct Prof. of Law, Univ. of Jordan 1996–, also Dir Centre for Strategic Studies 1999; fmr Minister of Industry and Trade, fmr Minister of State for Cabinet Affairs, fmr Minister of Justice; Minister of Foreign Affairs 2007–09; Man. Pnr Abu Ghazaleh Legal Services; mem. Econ. Consultative Council 1999; Founder and Sr Man. Pnr Int. Business Legal Assocs (IBLAW); Co-Chair. Jordanian–American Comm. for Educational Exchange. *Address:* c/o Ministry of Foreign Affairs, POB 35217, Amman 11180, Jordan (office).

BASHKIROV, Dmitri Aleksandrovich; Russian pianist and academic; *Professor Titular, Escuela Superior de Música Reina Sofia;* b. 1 Nov. 1931, Tbilisi; s. of Alexandr Bashkirov and Ester Ramendik; m. Natalya Bashkirova 1987; one s.; one s. from second marriage; one d. from a previous marriage; ed Moscow P. I. Tchaikovsky State Conservatory; studied in Tbilisi under A. Virsaladze, Moscow State Conservatory under A. Goldenweiser; concerts since 1955 in more than 30 countries; participated in Wiener Festwochen, Verbier, Switzerland, Helsinki, Granada, Ruhr Piano Fest, Germany and other festivals; repertoire includes works by Mozart, Schumann, Brahms, Debussy, Prokofiev; Moscow State Conservatory 1957, Prof. 1976–90; mem. jury numerous int. competitions; Prof. classes Acad. Mozarteum Salzburg, Sibelius Acad. Helsinki, Acad. of Music Jerusalem, Paris National Conservatory and others in London, Vienna, New York, Los Angeles, Lisbon, Stockholm; Prof. Internat. Acad. di Musica, Como, Italy 1992–; fmr Prof. Moscow Conservatory; Chair. Piano Dept Queen Sofia Higher School of Music, Madrid 1991–, now Titular Prof.; currently Prof. Titular, Escuela Superior de Música Reina Sofia; Hon. Prof., Schanchaj ConservatoriumGrand Prix M. Long Int. Competition (Paris) 1955; People's Artist of Russia, Hon. R. Schumann Medal (Zwickau, Germany), Hon. Medal, Univ. Autónoma de Madrid, Hon. Prix Ruhr pianisten festivals. *Music:* more than 30 recordings on various labels, including Melodia, RCD, EMI, Erato and Harmonia Mundi. *Address:* Studencheskaja 31, app. 74, Moscow, Russia (home); San Antonio 17, Pozaelo, Madrid, Spain (home). *Telephone:* (91) 351-1060 (office); (495) 249-37-41 (home). *Fax:* (91) 357-0788 (office); (495) 249-37-41 (home).

BASHMACHNIKOV, Vladimir Fedorovich, DEcon; Russian politician; *President, Association of Farmers' and Agricultural Co-operatives of Russia;* b. 27 March 1937; m.; three d.; ed Urals State Univ.; worker, deputy chair. kolkhoz, Sverdlovsk Region 1959–62; teacher, docent, Prof., Urals State Univ. 1962–65; Founder All-Russian Inst. of Labour (now All-Russian Inst. of Econ. and Man. in Agric.) 1964–72, Deputy Dir 1972–84; consultant Econ. Dept Cen. Cttee CPSU 1984–89; mem. Cttee on Land Reform Cen. Cttee CPSU 1989–91; active participant movt for privatization of land; mem. State Duma; mem. faction Our Home Russia; mem. Cttee on Agrarian Problems 1995–; Pres. Asscn of Farmers' and Agric. Co-operatives of Russia 1991–; Chair. Union of Land-Owners of Russia 1994; mem. Co-ordination Council, Round Table Business of Russia. *Publications:* over 150 books and articles on org. of labour in agric. *Address:* Association of Farmers' and Agricultural Co-operatives of Russia, Orlikov per 3, Suite 405, 107139 Moscow, Russia (office). *Telephone:* (495) 204-40-27 (office).

BASHMET, Yuri Abramovich; Russian violist and conductor; *Founder and Artistic Director, Moscow Soloists;* b. 24 Jan. 1953, Rostov-on-Don; m. Natalia Bashmet; one d.; ed Moscow State Conservatory; concerts since 1975; gave recitals and played with maj. orchestras of Europe, America and Asia; played in chamber ensembles with Sviatoslav Richter, Vladimir Spivakov, Victor Tretyakov and others; restored chamber repertoire for viola, commissioned and was first performer of music by contemporary composers, including concertos by Alfred Schnittke, Giya Kancheli, Aleksander Tchaikovsky; first viola player to give solo recitals at leading concert halls including Tchaikovsky Hall, Moscow, Concertgebouw, Amsterdam, La Scala, Milan, Suntory Hall, Tokyo; Founder and Artistic Dir Chamber Orchestra Soloists of Moscow 1989–; founder, Artistic Dir and conductor, Moscow Soloists 1992–; Artistic Dir and Chief Conductor Young Russian Symphony Orchestra 2002–; f. Yuri Bashmet Int. Competition for Young Viola Players 1994–; Artistic Dir Dec. Nights Festival, Moscow 1998–; Founder and Artistic Dir Elba Music Festival 1998–; f. Yu. Bashmet Viola Competition, Moscow 1999–; f. Int. Foundation to award Shostakovich Prize annually; prize winner of int. competitions in Budapest 1975, Munich 1976; People's Artist of Russia 1986, State Prize of Russia 1993, Sonning Prize (Denmark) 1995, Russian Biographic Soc. Man of the Year 2000, Olympus Nat. Award 2003. *Address:* Van Walsum Management, 4 Addison Bridge Place, London W14 8XP, England (office); Briyusov per. 7, Apt. 16, 103009 Moscow, Russia (home). *Telephone:* (20) 7371-4343 (office); (095) 561-66-96 (office); (495) 229-73-25 (home). *Fax:* (20) 7371-4344 (office). *E-mail:* vwm@vanwalsum.com (office). *Website:* www.vanwalsum.com (office); www.yuribashmet.com.

BASILASHVILI, Oleg Valeriyanovich; Russian actor; b. 26 Sept. 1934, Moscow; m. Galina Mshanskaya; two d.; ed Moscow Art Theatre; debut Leningrad Theatre of Lenin's Komsomol 1956–59; leading actor Leningrad (now St Petersburg) Bolshoi Drama Theatre of Tovstonogov 1959–; several leading roles, including Gayev (The Cherry Orchard), Voynitsky (Uncle Vanya), Khlestakov (The Government Inspector); active participant of democratic movt since end of 1980s, People's Deputy of Russia 1990–93; Order of Friendship 1994, Order Merit to Fatherland Fourth Degree 2004;

People's Actor of Russia 1977, State Prize of Russia 1978, USSR People's Actor 1984, Laureat Golden Soffit 1997. *Films include:* Alive Corpse 1969, Business Love Affair 1977, Autumn Marathon 1979, Railway Station for Two 1983, The Promised Heaven 1991, The Prophecy 1992, The Ticket in the Red Theatre 1994, Heads and Tails 1995, The Romanovs: An Imperial Family 2000, Poisons or the World History of Poisoning 2001, Idiot (TV) 2003; Dorogaya Masha Berezina 2004, The Master and Margarita (TV) 2005, Sonka – Zolotaya Ruchka (Sonka – Golden Pen) 2006; numerous TV productions. *Address:* Borodinskaya str. 13, Apt 58, 196180 St Petersburg, Russia (home). *Telephone:* 113-55-56 (home).

BASIN, Yefim Vladimirovich, DEcon; Russian fmr politician and engineer; *First Vice-President, Inzhtranstroy Corporation;* b. 3 Jan. 1940, Khislovichi, Tambov Region; m.; one s. one d.; ed Belarus Inst. of Transport Eng, Acad. of Nat. Econs; Master, Chief Engineer, Head, Yaroslavl Construction Dept 1962–69; Deputy Man., Chief Engineer, Gortransstroi, Gorky (now Nizhny Novgorod) 1969–72; Head Construction Dept, Pechorstroi 1972–78; First Deputy Head Glavbamstroi 1980–86; USSR Deputy Minister of Transport Construction; Head, Glavbamstroi and Bamtransstroi production cos 1986–90; Deputy, State Duma of RSFSR; mem. Supreme Soviet; Chair. Cttee on Construction, Architecture and Housing 1990–92; Chair. State Cttee on Problems of Architecture and Construction 1992–94; Minister of Construction 1994–97; Chair. State Cttee on Construction Policy 1997–98; First Deputy Head, Complex of Perspective Construction, then Head, Dept of Construction Devt, Moscow Govt May–Oct. 1998; Chair. State Cttee on Construction, Architecture and Housing Policy 1998–99; First Vice-Pres. Transstroy Corpn 1999–; Hero of Socialist Labour 1990, Merited Constructor of Russian Fed. 1998, State Prize of Russian Fed. 1998. *Leisure interests:* hunting, tennis, tourism. *Address:* Inzhtranstroy, Sadovaya-Spasskaya str. 21/1, 107217 Moscow, Russia. *Telephone:* (495) 777-79-04 (office). *Fax:* (495) 777-73-78 (office). *E-mail:* nzm@transstroy.ru (office). *Website:* www.ingtransstroy.ru (office).

BASINGER, Kim; American actress; b. 8 Dec. 1953, Athens, Ga; d. of Don Basinger; m. 1st Ron Britton 1980 (divorced 1990); m. 2nd Alec Baldwin (q.v.) 1993 (divorced 2002); one d.; model 1971–76; first TV role 1976; f. Skyfish Productions (film production co.). *Films include:* Hard Country 1981, Mother Lode 1982, Never Say Never Again 1982, The Man Who Loved Women 1983, The Natural 1984, 9½ weeks 1985, Fool for Love 1985, No Mercy 1986, Batman 1989, The Marrying Man 1990, Too Hot to Handle 1991, Final Analysis 1992, Cool World 1992, The Real McCoy 1993, Getaway 1994, Wayne's World II 1994, Pret-a-Porter 1994, LA Confidential 1997 (Acad. Award and Golden Globe for Best Supporting Actress), Bless the Child 2000, I Dreamed of Africa 2000, People I Know 2002, 8 Mile 2003, Elvis Has Left the Building 2004, Cellular 2004, The Door in the Floor 2004, The Sentinel 2006, Even Money 2006, The Burning Plain 2008. *Address:* CAA, 9830 Wilshire Boulevard, Beverly Hills, CA 90212; c/o Judy Hofflund, Hofflund Polone, 9465 Wilshire Boulevard, Suite 820, Beverly Hills, CA 90212; Skyfish Productions, 725 Arizona Avenue, Suite 100, Santa Monica, CA 90401, USA.

BASIR, Tan Sri Ismail; Malaysian banker; b. 1927, Taiping, Perak State; ed Serdang Agricultural Coll. and Durham Univ.; Lecturer, Universiti Pertanian Malaysia; Asst Agricultural Officer Serdang Agricultural Coll.; Dir Agric. Dept, Dir-Gen. Agric., later Exec. Dir Johore State Devt Corpn; Chair. Nat. Padi and Rice Authority 1981, Food Industries Malaysia 1981; Exec. Chair. Bank Bumiputra Malaysia Bhd. 1985; Head BMF, Kewangan Bumiputra, Bumiputra Merchant Bankers 1985; Dir Bank Negara 1981 and of several other cos; Chair. Malaysian Airport Holdings Berhad –2003.

BAŠKA, Jaroslav; Slovak politician; *Minister of Defence;* b. 5 April 1975, Považská Bystrica; m.; three c.; ed Electro-Technical Faculty, Žilina Univ.; Matador Púchov 1998–2000; Project Man. for information systems 1999–2000; Asst Dir for Econ 2001–02; mem. Parl. (Smer-Sociálna demokracia) 2002–06, mem. Perm Del. to Parl. Ass. of Council of Europe 2002–06; Mayor of Dohňany 2003–06; State Sec., Ministry of Defence 2006–08, Minister of Defence 2008–. *Address:* Ministry of Defence, Kutuzovova 7, 832 47 Bratislava, Slovakia (office). *Telephone:* (2) 4425-0320 (office). *Fax:* (2) 4425-3242 (office). *E-mail:* kovacovaz@mod.gov.sk (office). *Website:* www.mosr.sk (office).

BASOLO, Fred, PhD, FAAS; American chemist and academic; *Morrison Professor Emeritus of Chemistry, Northwestern University;* b. 11 Feb. 1920, Coello, Ill.; s. of John Basolo and Catherine Basolo; m. Mary P. Basolo 1947; one s. three d.; ed Southern Illinois Normal Univ. and Univ. of Illinois; Research Chemist, Rohm & Haas Chemical Co. 1943–46; Instructor, subsequently Asst Prof., Assoc. Prof. and Prof. of Chem., Northwestern Univ. 1946–, Chair. of Chem. Dept 1969–72, Morrison Prof. of Chem. 1980–90, Charles E and Emma H. Morrison Prof. Emer. 1990–; NATO Distinguished Prof., Tech. Univ. of Munich 1969; NATO Sr Scientist Fellow, Italy 1981; numerous visiting lectureships USA, Australia, Europe and Asia; Ed.-in-Chief Chemtracts 1988–; Assoc. Ed. Inorganic Chemica Acta Letters 1977–; mem. Editorial Bd Inorganica Chemica Acta 1967– and other publs; Hon. Prof. Lanzhou Univ., China 1985; Chair. Chem. Section, AAAS 1979; mem. ACS (mem. Bd of Dirs 1982–84, Pres. 1983), NAS, Chemical Soc. (London); Hon. mem. Italian Chemical Soc.; Foreign mem. Accademia Naz. dei Lincei, Italy; Corresp. mem., Chemical Soc. of Peru 1983; Fellow, American Acad. of Arts and Sciences 1983, Japanese Soc. for the Promotion of Science 1979; Guggenheim Fellow, Copenhagen 1954–55; Sr Nat. Research Foundation Fellow, Rome 1962–63; Hon. DSc (Southern Ill.) 1984; ACS Award for Research in Inorganic Chem. 1964, Award for Distinguished Service in Inorganic Chem. 1975, Dwyer Medal Award 1976, Oesper Memorial Award 1983, IX Century Medal of Bologna Univ. 1988, Harry and Carol Mosher Award 1990, Padua Univ. Medal 1991, Chinese Chemical Soc. Medal 1991, Chemical Pioneer Award (American Inst. of Chemists) 1992, Humboldt Sr US Scientist Award 1992, Gold Medal Award (American Inst. of Chemists) 1993, Joseph Chatt Medal (RSC) 1996, Josiah Willard Gibbs Medal (ACS) 1996, numerous other awards and honours. *Publications:* Mechanisms of Inorganic Reactions (with R. G. Pearson), Co-ordination Chemistry (with R. C. Johnson—several edns in trans.); more than 350 scientific publs. *Address:* Department of Chemistry, Northwestern University, 2145 Sheridan Road, Evanston, IL 60208, USA (office). *Telephone:* (847) 491-3793 (office). *E-mail:* basolo@chem.northwestern.edu (office). *Website:* www.chem.northwestern.edu (office).

BASS, Ronald (Ron); American songwriter and screenwriter; b. 1942, Los Angeles, Calif.; ed Yale Univ., Harvard Law School; began career as entertainment lawyer. *Films include:* screenplays: Code Name: Emerald, Black Widow, Gardens of Stone, Rain Man (Acad. Award 1988), Sleeping with the Enemy, The Joy Luck Club, When a Man Loves a Woman 1994, Dangerous Minds 1995, Waiting to Exhale, My Best Friend's Wedding 1997, What Dreams May Come 1998, Stepmom 1998, Entrapment 1999, Snow Falling on Cedars 1999, Passion of Mind 1999, The Lazarus Child (exec. prod.) 2004, Mozart and the Whale 2005, Just Like Heaven 2005. *Television includes:* Dangerous Minds (series), Moloney. *Publications:* novels: The Perfect Thief 1978, Lime's Crisis 1982, The Emerald Illusion 1984. *Address:* c/o Creative Artists Agency, 9830 Wilshire Boulevard, Beverly Hills, CA 90212, USA.

BASSANI, Giuseppe Franco, DrSc; Italian professor of physics; *President, Italian Physical Society;* b. 29 Oct. 1929, Milan; s. of Luigi Bassani and Claretta Riccadonna; m. Serenella Figini 1959; one s. one d.; ed Univ. of Pavia and Univ. of Illinois, USA; research physicist, Argonne Nat. Lab. 1960–65; Prof. of Physics, Univ. of Pisa 1965–70, Univ. of Rome 1970–80, Scuola Normale Superiore, Pisa 1980–; Pres. Italian Physical Society 1999–; Nat. mem. Accad. dei Lincei; Dr hc (Toulouse) 1979, (Lausanne) 1986, (Purdue Univ., West Lafayette, USA) 1994; Italgas Prize for Materials Science 1996. *Publications:* Electronic States and Optical Transitions in Solids (co-author) 1975, Fisica dello Stato Solido (co-author) 2000 and articles in professional journals. *Leisure interest:* history. *Address:* Lungarno Pacinotti 18, 56126 Pisa, Italy (home); Italian Physical Society, via Saragozza 12, 40123 Bologna, Italy. *Telephone:* 051-331554 (office). *Fax:* 051-581340 (office). *Website:* www.sif.it (office).

BASSET, Lytta, DTheol; Swiss theologian, writer and academic; *Professor and Vice-Dean, Faculty of Theology, University of Neuchâtel;* m.; three c.; ed Univs of Strasburg and Geneva; missionary work in India, Iran, Djibouti, French Polynesia and USA 1970–; fmr Lecturer in Philosophy and Theology, Faculty of Theology, Univ. of Lausanne; currently Prof. and Vice-Dean, Faculty of Theology, University of Neuchâtel. *Publications include:* Le pardon original 1995, La joie imprenable 1998, Moi, je ne juge personne 1998, Guérir du malheur 1999, Le pouvoir de pardonner 1999, Culpabilité 2000, La fermeture à l'amour 2000, Histoire et Herméneutique 2002, Sainte colère 2002; numerous articles and essays on Protestant theology. *Address:* University of Neuchâtel, Faculty of Theology, Faubourg de l'Hôpital 41, 2000 Neuchâte, Switzerland (office). *Telephone:* 327181907 (office). *E-mail:* Lytta.Basset@unine.ch (office). *Website:* www2.unine.ch/theol (office).

BASSETT, Angela; American actress; b. 16 Aug. 1958, New York; ed Yale School of Drama. *Theatre includes:* Colored People's Time 1982, Antigone, Black Girl, The Mystery Plays 1984–85, The Painful Adventures of Pericles, Prince of Tyre 1986–87, Joe Turner's Come and Gone 1986–87, Ma Rainey's Black Bottom, King Henry IV (Part I) 1987. *Films include:* F/X 1986, Kindergarten Cop 1990, Boyz 'N the Hood 1991, City of Hope 1991, Critters 4, Innocent Blood 1992, Malcolm X 1992, Passion Fish 1992, What's Love Got to Do with It 1993 (Golden Globe Award Best Actress 1994), Strange Days 1995, Panther 1995, Waiting to Exhale 1995, A Vampire in Brooklyn 1995, Contact 1997, How Stella Got Her Groove Back 1998, Music of the Heart 1999, Supernova 2000, Boesman and Lena 2000, The Score 2001, Sunshine State 2002, Masked and Anonymous 2003, The Lazarus Child 2004, Mr 3000 2004, Akeelah and the Bee 2005, Time Bomb 2006, Meet the Robinsons (voice) 2007. *TV films include:* Line of Fire: The Morris Dees Story 1991, The Jacksons: An American Dream 1992, A Century of Women 1994. *Address:* c/o Doug Chapin Management, Suite 430, 9465 Wilshire Boulevard, Beverly Hills, CA 90212, USA (office).

BASSEY, Dame Shirley Veronica, DBE; British popular singer; b. 8 Jan. 1937, Tiger Bay, Cardiff, Wales; d. of the late Henry Bassey and Eliza Bassey (née Mendi); one d.; m. 1st Kenneth Hume 1961 (divorced 1965; deceased); m. 2nd Sergio Novak 1971 (divorced 1981); one d. (deceased) one adopted s.; sang at Astor Club, London; signed up for Such is Life by impresario Jack Hylton 1955; started making records 1956; appeared in cabaret New York 1961; Artist for Peace, UNESCO 2000; Int. Amb., Variety Club 2001; many awards including 20 Gold Discs and 14 Silver Discs for sales in UK, Netherlands, France, Sweden and other countries; Best Female Singer (TV Times) 1972, 1973, (Music Week) 1974, Best Female Entertainer (American Guild of Variety Artists) 1976, Britannia Award for Best Female Singer 1977. *Film:* La Passione 1996. *Singles include:* Banana Boat Song, As I Love You, Kiss Me Honey Honey Kiss Me, As Long As He Needs Me, theme song for film Goldfinger 1964, Diamonds Are Forever 1971. *Albums include:* Born to Sing the Blues 1958, And I Love You So 1972, Magic is You 1978, Sassy Bassey 1985, I Am What I Am 1984, New York, New York 1991, Great Shirley Bassey 1999, Thank You For the Years 2003, Get the Party Started 2007. *Address:* Mr Mills, c/o Mrs Victoria Settepassi, 31 Avenue Princesse Grace, 98000 MC, Monaco (office). *E-mail:* basseyoffice@libello.com. *Website:* www.dameshirleybassey.com.

BASSIOUNI, Muhammad Abd al-Aziz; Egyptian diplomatist; b. 31 July 1937, Cairo; s. of Abdel Aziz Bassiouny; m. Nagwa Elsabouny; one s. one d.; ed

Egyptian Mil. Acad.; served in Egyptian Army 1956–80; mem. teaching staff, Mil. Acad. 1959–66; Mil. Attaché to Syria 1968–76, Liaison Officer between Egyptian and Syrian Commands, War of Oct. 1973; Brig.-Gen. in Egyptian Army 1978; Mil. Attaché to Iran 1978–80; joined Foreign Service 1980; Counsellor, then Minister Plenipotentiary, Embassy, Tel-Aviv 1980, Amb. to Israel 1986–2000; participated in all Egyptian-Israeli talks on normalization of relations and on Taba dispute; twelve mil. decorations from Egyptian Army; High Medal of Honour for Bravery with rank of Kt, Syria; Dr hc (Ben Gurion Univ., Israel) 1995. *Publications:* several articles on Egyptian-Israeli relations, the peace process and the Taba talks. *Leisure interests:* sport, reading. *Address:* c/o Ministry of Foreign Affairs, Corniche en-Nil, Cairo, Egypt (office).

BASSOLE, Bazomboué Léandre, MA; Burkinabè diplomatist; b. 21 Sept. 1946, Koudougou; s. of the late Bassole Baourla and of Kanki Eyombie; m. Louise Ouedraogo 1975; four s. one d.; ed Higher Educ. Centre, Ouagadougou, Univ. of Bordeaux and Int. Inst. for Public Admin., Paris; Counsellor State Protocol Dept, Legal Affairs and Claims Dept and Int. Co-operation Dept of Ministry of Foreign Affairs 1975–76, Dir for Admin. and Consular Affairs 1976–77; Second Counsellor, later First Counsellor, Upper Volta Embassy, Paris 1977–81; First Counsellor, Perm. Mission of Upper Volta to the UN 1981–82, Chargé d'affaires 1982–83, Perm. Rep. of Upper Volta (now Burkina Faso) to the UN 1983–86; Amb. to USA March–Aug. 1986; Minister of External Affairs and Co-operation 1986–87; Amb. to Canada 1988–91, to Côte d'Ivoire 1991–2001. *Leisure interests:* classical music, soccer, cycling, swimming, movies. *Address:* c/o Ministry of Foreign Affairs, 03 BP 7038, Ouagadougou 03, Burkina Faso (office).

BASSOLET, Djibril Ypéné; Burkinabé government official; *Joint United Nations-African Union Chief Mediator for Darfur;* b. 30 Nov. 1957, Nouna; ed Collège Charles Luanga de Nouna, Prytanée Militaire de Kadiogo, Université de Ouagadougou, Académie Royale Militaire de Meknès, Ecole Nationale de la Gendarmerie, Abidjan, Côte d'Ivoire, Ecole Supérieure de la Gendarmerie, Maisons Alfort, France; served as Commdt, Gendarmerie Nationale (nat. police force) 1983–95, served in various sr positions including Chef d'Etat-Major (head of police force) 1997–99; Minister-Del. for Security 1999–2000, Minister for Security 2000–07, Minister of Foreign Affairs and Regional Co-operation 2007–08; Jt UN —African Union Chief Mediator for Darfur 2008–; Officier et Commandeur de l'Ordre Nat. de Burkina Faso, Médaille d'honneur Militaire, Médaille d'honneur de la Police, Officier de l'Ordre Nat. du Lion (Senegal), Commandeur de l'Ordre du Mérite du Niger, Commandeur de l'Ordre du Mérite du Gabon, Officier de l'Ordre National du Mérite. *Address:* Department of Peace-keeping Operations, Room S-3727-B, United Nations, New York, NY 10017, USA (office); UNAMID, El Fasher, Sudan (office). *Telephone:* (212) 963-8077 (office). *Fax:* (212) 963-9222 (office). *Website:* www .un.org/Depts/dpko (office); unamid.unmissions.org (office).

BASTARRECHE SAGUES, Carlos, LLB; Spanish diplomatist and academic; *Permanent Representative, European Union;* b. 1950, Madrid; m. Rosalía Gómez-Pineda Goizueta; four c.; entered diplomatic corps 1976; Spanish Embassy, Bucharest 1976–79, Sec., Conf. for Spanish Accession to EU, Perm. Mission of Spain to EU, Brussels 1979–84, Adviser to Sec. of State for EU Affairs, Madrid 1984–85, Asst Dir-Gen. for EU Co-ordination, Secr. of State for EU Affairs 1986–90, Dir-Gen. of Legal and Institutional Co-ordination 1990–91, Asst Perm. Rep. to EU 1991–96, Sec.-Gen. of Foreign Political and EU Affairs 1996–2000, Sec.-Gen. of European Affairs 2000–02, Perm. Rep. to EU 2002–; Prof. of Community Affairs, Escuela Diplomatica. *Address:* Permanent Mission of Spain to the European Community, 52 blvd du Régent, 1000 Brussels, Belgium (office). *Telephone:* (2) 509-86-11 (office). *Fax:* (2) 511-19-40 (office). *E-mail:* carlos.bastarreche@reper.mae.es (office). *Website:* www.es-ue.org (office).

BÁSTI, Juli; Hungarian actress; b. 10 Aug. 1957, Budapest; d. of Lajos Básti and Zsuzsa Zolnay; one s.; ed Acad. of Dramatic Arts, Budapest; mem. Csiky Gergely Theatre Co., Kaposvár 1980–85, Katona József Theatre Co. 1985–; Best Actress Award, San Remo 1982, Moscow 1985, Award for Best Acting in Theatre in Budapest 1985, Jászay Marit Prize 1985, Kossuth Prize 1993. *Stage roles include:* Beatrice (The Changeling), Ophelia (Hamlet), Helena (Midsummer Night's Dream), Lady Anne (Richard III), Mother Ubu (King Ubu), Masha (Three Sisters), Anna Andrejevna (The Government Inspector), Anna Petrovna (Platonov); musicals: Velma Kelly in Chicago, Sally in Cabaret 1993. *Films:* Wasted Lives 1980, The Red Countess 1983, The Followers 1983, Laura 1986, The Horoscope of Jesus Christ 1988, A Hecc 1989, The Holidaymaker 1990, A Távollét hercege 1991, The Bride of Stalin 1991, A Nyaraló (The Summer Guest) 1992, Az Álommenedzser 1992, Pá Drágám 1994, Irány Kalifornia! (Let's Go to California!) 1997, Egy tél az Isten háta mögött (One Winter Behind God's Back) 1999, Kínai védelem (Chinese Defence) 1999, Egyszer élünk 2000, Fehér alsó 2000, Film 2000, Üvegtigris 2001, Csocsó, avagy éljen május elseje! (May Day Mayhem!) 2001, Valami Amerika (A Kind of America) 2002, Kísértések (Temptations) 2002, A Hídember 2002, Tea (TV series) 2002, Szent Iván Napja 2003, Magyar vándor 2004. *Leisure interest:* forests. *Address:* Krecsányi utca 6, 1025 Budapest, Hungary. *Telephone:* 2742219 (home).

BASTIAN, Edward H., BBA, CPA; American business executive; *President and Chief Financial Officer, Delta Air Lines, Inc.;* b. 1957; m. Anna Bastian; four c.; ed St Bonaventure Univ.; fmr Partner Price Waterhouse, NY, becoming Strategic Planning Partner; fmr Vice-Pres. Finance and Controller Frito-Lay International, becoming Vice-Pres. of Business Processes Re-engineering, later Vice-Pres. of Finance, PepsiCo International (parent co.); Vice-Pres. of Finance and Controller, Delta Air Lines, Inc. 1998–2000, Sr Vice-Pres. 2000–05, Chief Financial Officer 2005–, Pres. 2007–; Sr Vice-Pres. and Chief Financial Officer Acuity Brands June–July 2005; mem. Int. Bd of Dirs Habitat for Humanity, Woodruff Arts Center, Atlanta. *Address:* Delta Air

Lines Inc., PO Box 20706, 1030 Delta Blvd, Atlanta, GA 30320-6001, USA (office). *Telephone:* (404) 715-2600 (office). *Fax:* (404) 715-5042 (office). *E-mail:* info@delta.com (office). *Website:* www.delta.com (office).

BASTIDAS CASTILLO, Adina Mercedes; Venezuelan economist and politician; *Executive Director, Inter-American Development Bank;* ed Central Univ. of Venezuela; Rep. of Venezuela to Inter-American Devt Bank, Washington, DC 1999–2000, currently Exec. Dir for Venezuela; Vice-Pres. of Venezuela 2000–02; Minister of Production and Commerce 2002. *Address:* Inter-American Development Bank (IDB), 1300 New York Avenue, NW, Washington, DC 20577, USA (office). *Telephone:* (202) 623-1000 (office). *Fax:* (202) 623-3096 (office). *E-mail:* pic@iadb.org (office). *Website:* www.iadb.org (office).

BASTOS, Márcio Thomaz de; Brazilian politician and lawyer; b. 30 July 1935, Cruzeiro, São Paulo; m. Maria Leonor de Castro Bastos; one s. one d.; ed Univ. of São Paulo; criminal lawyer 1957–, involved in over 700 cases including acting for the prosecution of Chico Mendes, Lindomar Castilho and Pimenta Neves; Minister of Justice 2003–07; co-founder Action for the Citizenship Movt; fmr Pres. Ordem dos Advogados do Brasil (Brazil bar asscn). *Address:* c/o Ministry of Justice, Esplanada dos Ministérios, Bloco T, 4° Andar, 70064-900 Brasília, DF, Brazil (office).

BASU, Jyoti, BA; Indian politician and lawyer; *Leader, Communist Party of India—Marxist (CPI—M);* b. 1914; ed Loreto Day School, St Xavier's School, St Xavier's Coll.; went to England to study law, called to Middle Temple Bar 1939; during stay in England actively associated with India League and Fed. of Indian Students in England, Sec. of London Majlis and came in contact with CP of Great Britain; returned to Calcutta 1940; joined undivided CP of India; a leader of fmr Eastern Bengal Railroad Workers' Union; elected to Bengal Legis. Council 1946; after Partition remained a mem. of W Bengal Legis. Ass.; arrested for membership of CP after party was banned 1948, but released on orders of High Court; became Chair. Editorial Bd Swadhinata; mem. W. Bengal Legis. Ass. 1952–72; fmr Sec. Prov. Cttee of CP, mem. Nat. Council, Cen. Exec. Cttee and Nat. Secr. until CP split 1963; subsequently mem. Politbureau, CPI—M, currently Leader; imprisoned 1948, 1949, 1953, 1955, 1963, 1965; Deputy Chief Minister and Minister in charge of Finance in first United Front Govt 1967, Deputy Chief Minister in second United Front Govt; narrowly escaped assassination attempt while campaigning in Bihar 1972; mem. Legis. Ass., W Bengal for Satgachia 1977; subsequently Leader of Left Front Legislature Party; Chief Minister of W Bengal 1977–2000. *Address:* Communist Party of India—Marxist, A. K. Gopalan Bhavan, 27–29 Bhai Vir Singh Marg, New Delhi 110 001, India (office). *Telephone:* (11) 23344918 (office). *Fax:* (11) 23747483 (office). *E-mail:* cpim@vsnl.com (office); cpimwb@vsnl.com (office). *Website:* www.cpim.org (office).

BAT-ÜÜL, Erdeniin; Mongolian politician; b. 1 July 1957, Ulan Bator; m. B. Delgertuja 1977; two s. one d.; teacher, First Constructing Tech. Training School, Ulan Bator 1981–82, secondary school, Höbsögöl Prov. 1982–85; scientist, Observatory of Acad. of Sciences 1985–89; Founder-mem. Mongolian Democratic Union, mem. Gen. Co-ordinating Council 1989–, Gen. Co-ordinator Political Consultative Centre 1990–; Deputy to Great People's Hural 1990–92, 1996–; mem. Political Consultative Centre of Mongolian Democratic Party 1992–; mem. Gen. Council and Dir Political Policy Inst. of Mongolian Nat. Democratic Party 1992–, Regional Sec. 1993–, Gen. Sec. and Presidium of Co-ordinating Council of Mongolian Democratic Union 1993–. *Address:* Mongolian National Democratic Party, Ulan Bator (office); Suchbaatar District 1-40,000, 62-1-4 Ulan Bator, Mongolia (home). *Telephone:* 372810 (office); 321105 (home). *Fax:* 372810.

BATALOV, Aleksey Vladimirovich; Russian film actor and director; b. 20 Nov. 1928, Moscow; m. Gitana Azkad'yevna Leonchenko; two d.; ed Moscow Arts Theatre Studio; actor with Cen. Theatre of Soviet Army 1950–53; with Moscow Art Academic Theatre 1953–60; film debut 1954; teacher VGIK 1976–, Prof. 1979–; Order of Lenin, People's Artist of USSR 1976, Hero of Socialist Labour and other decorations. *Roles include:* Aleksei Zhurbin in A Large Family 1954, Sasha in The Rumyantsev Case 1956, Boris in The Cranes Are Flying 1957, Gusev in Nine Days in One Year 1962, Pavel Vlasov in Mother 1964, Gurov in The Lady with the Lap-dog 1965, Golubkin in The Flight 1971, Georgi Ivanovich in Moscow Does Not Believe in Tears 1980, Rokovyye Yaytsa 1996. *Films directed:* The Overcoat 1960, The Three Fat Men 1966, The Living Corpse 1969, The Flight 1971, The Gambler 1973. *Publication:* Fate and Craftsmanship 1984. *Address:* VGIK, Wilhelm Pieck str. 3, 129226 Moscow (office); Serafimovicha 2, Apt. 91, 109072 Moscow, Russia (home). *Telephone:* (495) 181-13-14 (office); (495) 238-16-29 (home).

BATALOV, Andrei Yevgenyevich; Russian ballet dancer; b. 22 April 1974, Izhevsk, Udmurt Repub., Russia; ed Vaganova Acad. of Russian Ballet, St Petersburg; Prin. Dancer Maly Theatre of Opera and Ballet 1992–94; with Mariinsky Theatre 1994–, Prin. Dancer 1996–; also currently Prin. Dancer Danish Royal Theatre of Opera and Ballet (Danish Royal Ballet); Int. Ballet Competition, Nagoya, Japan, First Prize and Gold Medal 1996, Int. Ballet Competition, Budapest, Second Prize and Silver Medal 1996, Int. Ballet Competition, Perm, First Prize and Gold Medal, The Mikhail Baryshnikov Prize 1996, Int. Ballet Competition, Paris, First Prize and Gold Medal 1996, VIII Int. Ballet Competition, Moscow, Grand Prix 1997. *Roles in ballets include:* James (La Sylphide), Blue Bird (Sleeping Beauty), Prince (Nutcracker), Peasants' Pas de Deux (Giselle), Clown (Legend of Love), Bozhok and Solor (La Bayadère), Basil (Don Quixote), Ali (Le Corsaire), Golden Slave (Sheherazada), Lescaut (Manon Lescaut), Ondine (Matteo), The Prodigal Son (Prodigal Son), Pas de Deux (Diana and Acteon). *Address:* c/o Concert Agency Intrada Co., Ltd, POB 94, 190008 St.Petersburg; c/o Mariinsky Theatre, 1

Teatralnaya Square, St. Petersburg, Russia (office). *Website:* www.mariinsky.ru.

BATBAYAR, Bat-Erdeniin, BSc; Mongolian politician and scientist; b. 1955, Arkhangai Prov.; ed Mongolian State Univ., Imperial Coll., Univ. of London, UK; teacher at secondary school, Hentii Prov. 1982–84; scientist, Inst. of Microbiology 1984–; Founding mem. Democratic Socialist Movt; Founding mem. Mongolian Social Democratic Party, Chair. 1990–94; mem. State Great Hural 1996–2000; Minister of Finance 1998–99 (resgnd). *Address:* Mongolian Social Democratic Party, PO Box 578, Ulan Bator 11, Mongolia. *Telephone:* 322055; 328425. *Fax:* 322055.

BATBOLD, Sükhbaataryn; Mongolian business executive and politician; *Minister of External Affairs;* b. 1963; mem. Parl.; Vice-Minister of Foreign Affairs 2003–05; Minister of Trade and Industry 2005, of External Affairs 2008–; mem. Mongolian People's Revolutionary Party; fmr Chair. Mongolian Devt Strategy Inst.; majority shareholder in Altai Holding LLC. *Address:* Ministry of External Affairs, Enkh Taivny Örgön Chölöö 7a, Sükhbaatar District, Ulan Bator, Mongolia (office). *Telephone:* (11) 262788 (office). *Fax:* (11) 322127 (office). *E-mail:* mongmer@magicnet.mn (office).

BATCHELOR, Paul John; Australian financial services executive; b. 22 Sept. 1950, Sydney; s. of John Eastley Batchelor and Patricia Fay Batchelor (née Smith); m. Therese Batchelor 1974; three s.; partner Touche Ross & Co. 1981–85; Financial Dir Nat. Mutual Royal Bank 1985–87; Exec. Dir of Operations Westmax 1987–89; Dir Retail Asia Man. 1993–96; Group Chief Financial Officer and Group Exec. Australasia Fiji Colonial Mutual Assurance Soc. Ltd 1995–97; Chief Financial Officer AMP Ltd 1997–99, Man. Dir and CEO 1999–2002; Dir Jardine CMG Life Holdings Ltd 1994–, Colonial Mutual Funds 1993–, Colonial Mutual Funds Man. Ltd 1993–, Colonial Investment Man. Ltd 1993–, Colonial State Bank 1995–, Jacques Martin Pty Ltd 1993–; mem. Business Council of Australia, Financial Sector Advisory Council, Investment Advisory Cttee, Australian Olympic Foundation; Fellow, Inst. of Charted Accountants. *Address:* c/o AMP, AMP Sydney Core Building, 33 Alfred Street, Sydney, NSW 2000, Australia (office).

BATE, Jennifer Lucy, OBE, BA, FRCO, FRSA, LRAM, ARCM; British organist; b. 11 Nov. 1944, London; d. of Horace Alfred Bate and Dorothy Marjorie Bate; ed Univ. of Bristol; Shaw Librarian, LSE 1966–69; full-time concert career 1969–; has performed world-wide; has organized several teaching programmes; collaboration with Olivier Messiaen 1975–92; designed portable pipe organ with N. P. Mander Ltd 1984 and a prototype computer organ 1987; gives masterclasses world-wide and lectures on a wide range of musical subjects; mem. Inc. Soc. of Music; British Music Soc., vice-pres., Royal Philharmonic Soc., Royal Soc.; hon. Italian citizenship for services to music 1996; Hon. DMus (Bristol) 2007; F.J. Read Prize, Royal Coll. of Organists, Young Musician 1972, voted Personnalité de l'Année, France 1989, one of the Women of the Year, UK 1990–97, Grand Prix du Disque (Messiaen), Diapason d'Or, Prix de Répertoire, France, Preis der deutschen Schallplattenkritik, Germany and MRA Award for 18th century series From Stanley to Wesley. *Compositions:* Toccata on a Theme of Martin Shaw, Introduction and Variations on an Old French Carol, Four Reflections, Homage to 1685: Four Studies, The Spinning Wheel, Lament, An English Canon, Variations on a Gregorian Theme. *Recordings:* Complete Works of Messiaen, Complete Works of Franck, An English Choice, Virtuoso French Organ Music, Panufnik: Metasinfonia, Vivaldi Double and Triple Concertos, Jennifer Bate and Friends, Jennifer Plays Vierne, From Stanley to Wesley on period instruments, Reflections: The Organ Music of Jennifer Bate, Samuel Wesley Organ Music, The Wesleys and their Contemporaries, Complete Works of Felix Mendelssohn, Complete Organ Works of Peter Dickinson. *Television:* South Bank Show on Messiaen, La Nativité du Seigneur (Channel 4). *Publications:* Grove's Dictionary of Music and Musicians, Organist's Review. *Leisure interests:* cooking, theatre, philately, gardening. *Address:* c/o Andrew Roberts, 28 Oakenbrow, Sway, Lymington, Hampshire SO41 6DY, England (office); 35 Collingwood Avenue, Muswell Hill, London, N10 3EH, England (office). *Telephone:* (1590) 582060 (office); (20) 8883-3811 (office). *Fax:* (1590) 682060 (office); (20) 8444-3695 (office). *E-mail:* andrew.roberts15@virgin.net (office); jenniferbate@classical-artists.com (office). *Website:* www.classical-artists.com/jbate.

BATE, (Andrew) Jonathan, CBE, PhD, FBA, FRSL; British academic; *Professor of Shakespeare and Renaissance Literature, University of Warwick;* b. 26 June 1958, Sevenoaks, Kent; s. of Ronald Montagu Bate and Sylvia Helen Bate; m. 1st Hilary Gaskin 1984 (divorced 1995); m. 2nd Paula Jayne Byrne 1996; two s. one d.; ed St Catharine's Coll., Cambridge; Harkness Fellow, Harvard Univ. 1980–81; Research Fellow, St Catharine's Coll., Cambridge 1983–85, Hon. Fellow 2000–; Fellow, Trinity Hall, Cambridge, Lecturer 1985–90; King Alfred Prof. of English Literature, Univ. of Liverpool 1991–2003; Prof. of Shakespeare and Renaissance Literature, Univ. of Warwick 2003–; Research Reader, British Acad. 1994–96; Leverhulme Personal Research Prof. 1999–2004; Gov. Bd RSC, Ed. Shakespeare Edition; Hon. Fellow, St Catharine's Coll., Cambridge; Calvin & Rose Hoffman Prize 1996, NAMI NY Book Award 2003. *Radio:* features and reviews for BBC Radio 3 and Radio 4. *Television:* South Bank Show and other arts programmes. *Publications:* Shakespeare and the English Romantic Imagination 1986, Charles Lamb: Essays of Elia (ed.) 1987, Shakespearean Constitutions: Politics, Theatre, Criticism 1730–1830 1989, Romantic Ecology: Wordsworth and the Environmental Tradition 1991, The Romantics on Shakespeare (ed.) 1992, Shakespeare and Ovid 1993, The Arden Shakespeare: Titus Andronicus (ed.) 1995, Shakespeare: An Illustrated Stage History (ed.) 1996, The Genius of Shakespeare 1997, The Cure for Love (novel) 1998, The Song of the Earth 2000, John Clare: A Biography (Hawthornden Prize 2003, James Tait Black Memorial Prize 2004) 2003, I Am: The Selected Poetry of John Clare (ed.)

2003, Andrew Marvell: Complete Poems (ed.) 2005, William Shakespeare: Complete Works (ed.) 2007, Soul of the Age: The Life, Mind and World of William Shakespeare 2008. *Leisure interests:* gardening, tennis, walking, opera, home. *Address:* Wylie Agency Ltd, 17 Bedford Square, London, WC1B 3JA (office); Department of English, Room H513, University of Warwick, Coventry, CV4 7AL, England (office). *E-mail:* j.bate@warwick.ac.uk (office). *Website:* www2.warwick.ac.uk/fac/arts/english (office).

BATEMAN, Barry Richard James, BA; British investment executive; *Vice-Chairman, Fidelity International Ltd.;* b. 21 June 1945; m. Christine Bateman; one s.; ed Univ. of Exeter; investment analyst, Hoare Govett 1967–72, Research Dir 1972–75; Marketing Dir Datastream 1975–81; Sr Marketing Dir Fidelity Int. Man. Ltd 1981–86, Man. Dir Fidelity Investment Ltd 1986–97, Pres. Fidelity Int. Ltd 1991–2001, Vice-Chair. 2001–; Chair. Unit Trust Asscn 1991–93; mem. Bd Dirs Colt Group 1996–, Chair. (non-exec.) 2003–. *Address:* Fidelity International Ltd, Oakhill House, 130 Tonbridge Road, Hildenborough, Tonbridge, Kent, TN11 9DZ, England (home). *Telephone:* (1732) 361144 (home). *Fax:* (1732) 777441 (office). *Website:* www.fidelity-international.com (office).

BATEMAN, Robert McLellan, OC, BA, RCA; Canadian artist; b. 24 May 1930, Toronto; s. of Joseph W. Bateman and Anne Bateman (née McLellan); m. 1st Suzanne Bowerman 1960; two s. one d.; m. 2nd Birgit Freybe 1975; two s.; ed Forest Hill Collegiate Inst., Toronto, Univ. of Toronto, Ontario Coll. of Educ.; high school art teacher for 20 years; began full-time painting 1976, numerous museum exhbns since 1959, including the Smithsonian Inst. 1987, Nat. Museum of Wildlife Art, Jackson, WY 1997, Everard Read Gallery, Johannesburg 2000, Gerald Peters Gallery, Santa Fe 2004; Master Artist, Leigh Yawkey Woodson Museum 1982; mem. Advisory Council, Ecotrust; mem. Bd Jane Goodall Inst., Canada; mem. Advisory Bd Pollution Probe, Advisory Bd Pollution Probe, Advisory Council Ecotrust; mem. Royal Canadian Acad. of Arts; Hon. Dir Kenya Wildlife Fund, Sierra Legal Defense Fund, EcoJustice Canada; Hon. Chair. Harmony Foundation, Victoria; Hon. Life mem. Audubon Soc., Canadian Wildlife Fed., Sierra Club, Fed. of Canadian Artists 1983–, RCA; Order of British Columbia 2001; Hon. DFA; Hon. DLitt; Hon. DSc; Hon. LLD; Queen Elizabeth II Jubilee Medal 1977, Soc. of Animal Artists Award of Excellence 1979, 1980, 1981, 1986, 1990, Master Artist, Leigh Yawkey Woodson Art Museum 1982, Member of Honour Award, World Wildlife Fund 1985, Lescarbot Award, Canadian Govt 1992, Rachel Carson Award 1996, Golden Plate Award, American Acad. of Achievement 1998, One of 20th Century's 100 Champions of Conservation, US Nat. Audubon Soc. 1998, Rungius Medal 2001, Pres.'s Medal, Sir Edmund Hillary Foundation of Canada 2005, Human Rights Defender Award, Amnesty International 2007 and numerous other awards. *Publications:* with Ramsay Derry: The Art of Robert Bateman 1981, The World of Robert Bateman 1984; with Rick Archbold: Robert Bateman: An Artist in Nature 1990, Robert Bateman: Natural Worlds 1996, Safari 1998, Thinking Like a Mountain 2000; with Kathryn Dean: Birds 2002; with Ian Coutts: Backyard Birds 2005; with Nancy Kovacs: Birds of Prey 2007. *Address:* PO Box 115, Fulford Harbour, Salt Spring Island, BC V8K 2P2, Canada (office). *E-mail:* rb@gulfislands.com (office). *Website:* www.robertbateman.ca (office); www.batemanideas.com (office).

BATENIN, Vyacheslav Mikhailovich, DrPhys-MathSc; Russian physicist and academic; *Director, Institute of High Temperatures (IVTAN), Russian Academy of Sciences;* b. 12 March 1939; m.; one s.; ed Moscow Energy Inst.; Engineer, Sr Engineer, Deputy Dir Inst. of High Temperatures USSR (now Russian) Acad. of Sciences 1962–, Dir 1987–; corresp. mem. USSR Acad. of Sciences 1987. *Publications include:* works on physics of gas explosion and low-temperature plasma, problems of applied superconductivity and magnetic hydrodynamics, unconventional energy sources. *Leisure interests:* tennis, travelling. *Address:* Institute of High Temperatures (IVTAN), Izhorskaya str. 13/19, 127412 Moscow, Russia (office). *Telephone:* (495) 484-23-11 (office); (495) 331-32-52 (home). *Fax:* (095) 484-82-00 (office). *Website:* oivt.nm.ru (office).

BATES, Kathy; American actress; b. 28 June 1948, Memphis, Tenn.; d. of Langdon Doyle Bates and Bertye Kathleen (née Talbot); m. Tony Campisi 1991; ed White Station High School, Southern Methodist Univ.; singing waitress Catskill mountains, cashier Museum of Modern Art, Manhattan; Mary Pickford Award, Int. Press Acad. 2007. *Theatre work includes:* Varieties 1976, Crimes of the Heart 1979 (won Pulitzer Prize 1981), The Art of Dining 1979, Goodbye Fidel 1980, Chocolate Cake 1980, Extremities 1980, The Fifth of July 1981, Come Back to the 5 & Dime Jimmy Dean, Jimmy Dean 1982, 'night, Mother 1983 (Outer Critics Circle Award), Days and Nights Within 1985, Rain of Terror 1985, Deadfall 1985, Curse of the Starving Class 1985, Frankie and Johnny in the Clair de Lune 1987 (Obie Award), The Road to Mecca 1988. *Films include:* Taking Off 1971, Straight Time 1978, Summer Heat 1987, Arthur 2 on the Rocks 1988, High Stakes 1989, Dick Tracy 1990, White Palace 1990, Men Don't Leave 1990, Misery 1990 (Acad. Award for Best Actress 1991, Golden Globe Award from Hollywood Foreign Press Asscn), Prelude to a Kiss 1991, At Play in the Fields of the Lord 1991, The Road to Mecca 1991, Fried Green Tomatoes at the Whistle Stop Café 1991, Used People 1992, A Home of Our Own 1993, North 1994, Curse of the Starving Class 1994, Diabolique 1996, The War at Home 1996, Primary Colors 1998, Swept from the Sea 1998, Titanic 1998, A Civil Action 1999, Dash and Lilly 1999, My Life as a Dog 1999, Bruno 2000, Rat Race 2001, American Outlaws 2001, About Schmidt 2002, Love Liza 2002, Evelyn 2003, The Tulse Luper Suitcases: The Moab Story 2003, The Ingrate 2004, Little Black Book 2004, Around the World in 80 Days 2004, The Bridge of San Luis Rey 2004, Rumor Has It 2005, Charlotte's Web (voice) 2006, Bee Movie (voice) 2007, Fred Claus 2007, Christmas Is Here Again (voice) 2007, P.S., I Love You 2007, The Golden

Compass 2007. *TV work includes guest roles in:* The Love Boat, St Elsewhere, Cagney & Lacey, LA Law, China Beach, All My Children, Six Feet Under. *TV films include:* Johnny Bull, Uncommon Knowledge, No Place like Home, One for Sorrow—Two for Joy, Signs of Life, Murder Ordained, Straight Time, Hostages, The West Side Waltz 1995, The Late Shift (Golden Globe 1997) 1996, Annie 1999, My Sister's Keeper 2002. *Address:* c/o Susan Smith and Associates, 121 N San Vicente Blvd, Beverly Hills, CA 90211-2303, USA.

BATESON, (Paul) Patrick (Gordon), PhD, FRS; British ethologist and academic; *Professor Emeritus of Ethology, University of Cambridge;* b. 31 March 1938, Chinnor Hill, Oxon.; s. of Richard Gordon Bateson and Solvi Helene Berg; m. Dusha Matthews 1963; two d.; ed Westminster School, Univ. of Cambridge; Stanford Medical Centre, Univ. of Calif.; Jr Research Fellow, King's Coll. Cambridge 1964–68, Sr Research Fellow 1968–69, Official Fellow 1969–84, Professorial Fellow 1984–88, Provost 1988–2003, Life Fellow 2003–; Sr Asst in Research Sub-Dept of Animal Behaviour, Univ. of Cambridge 1965–69, Dir 1976–80, Lecturer in Zoology 1969–78, Reader in Sub-Dept of Animal Behaviour 1978–84, Prof. of Ethology 1984–2005, Prof. Emer. 2005–; Pres. Zoological Soc. of London 2004–; mem. Council Museums and Galleries Comm. 1995–2000; Trustee, Inst. for Public Policy Research 1988–95; Biological Sec., Royal Soc. 1998–2003; Foreign mem. American Philosophical Soc. 2006–; Scientific Medal, Zoological Soc. of London 1976, Asscn for Study of Animal Behaviour Medal 2001. *Publications:* Defended to Death (co-author) 1983, Perspectives in Ethology (ten vols; co-ed.) 1973–93, Growing Points in Ethology (co-ed.) 1976, Mate Choice (co-ed.) 1983, Measuring Behaviour (co-author) 1986, The Domestic Cat: The Biology of its Behaviour (co-ed.) 1988, The Development and Integration of Behaviour (co-ed.) 1991, Design for a Life: How Behaviour Develops (co-author) 1999. *Address:* Sub-Department of Animal Behaviour, Department of Zoology, University of Cambridge, Madingley, Cambridge, CB3 8AA (office); The Old Rectory, Rectory Street, Halesworth, Suffolk, IP19 8BL, England (home). *Telephone:* (1223) 331338 (office); (1954) 210301 (office); (1986) 873182 (home). *Fax:* (1223) 336676 (office). *E-mail:* ppgb@cam.ac.uk (office). *Website:* www.zoo.cam.ac.uk/zoostaff/bateson (office).

BATIZ CAMPBELL, Enrique; Mexican conductor; *Principal Conductor, Orquesta Sinfónica del Estado de México;* b. 4 May 1942, Mexico City, DF; s. of José Luis Bátiz and María Elena Campbell; m. 1st Eva María Zuk 1965 (divorced 1983); one s. one d.; m. 2nd Elena Campbell Lombardo; ed Centro Universitario México, Southern Methodist Univ., Dallas, Tex., USA, Juilliard School, New York, Warsaw Conservatoire, Poland; founder and prin. conductor Orquesta Sinfónica del Estado de México 1971–83, 1990–; Artistic Dir Orquesta Filarmónica de la Ciudad de México 1983–90; Prin. Guest Conductor Royal Philharmonic Orchestra, London 1984–; Guest Conductor with 130 orchestras; decorated Officer, Order of Rio Branco (Brazil) 1986. *Leisure interest:* swimming. *Address:* Cerrada Rancho de los Colorines No. 11, Col Huipulco Tabla del Llano, Código Postal 14380, Zona Postal 22, México, DF, 7, 34, Mexico. *Telephone:* (525) 671-4216 (Agent); (72) 14 46 84 (office). *Fax:* (72) 15 62 16.

BATKHUYAG, Jamyandorjiin, MA, PhD; Mongolian economist and politician; *Minister of Defence;* b. 1964; ed , Univ. of Colorado at Denver, USA; fmr Lecturer, Mongolian Nat. Univ. and Higher Polytechnic; fmr Sr Adviser on Econ. Policy to Prime Minister; fmr Learned Sec. and Dir Inst. of Finance and Econs; mem. Great Khural (Parl.) 2004–; Minister of Defence 2007–; mem. Nat. New Party. *Address:* Ministry of Defence, Government Bldg 7, Dandaryn Gudamj, Bayanzürkh District, Ulan Bator, Mongolia (office). *Telephone:* (11) 458495 (office). *Fax:* (11) 451727 (office). *E-mail:* mdef@mongol.net (office). *Website:* www.pmis.gov.mn/mdef (office).

BATLINER, Gerard, DrIur; Liechtenstein lawyer; *Arbitrator, Court of Conciliation and Arbitration, Organization for Security and Co-operation in Europe;* b. 9 Dec. 1928, Eschen; s. of Andreas Batliner and Karolina Batliner; m. Christina Negele 1965; two s.; ed Grammar School, Schwyz, Switzerland and Univs of Zürich, Fribourg, Paris and Freiburg im Breisgau; practice at Co. Court of Principality of Liechtenstein 1954–55; lawyer, Vaduz 1956–62, 1970–; Vice-Pres. Fortschrittliche Bürgerpartei (Progressive Burgher Party) 1958–62; Deputy Mayor of commune of Eschen 1960–62; Head of Govt of Principality of Liechtenstein and Minister of Justice 1962–70; attorney-at-law 1970–; Pres. Liechtenstein Parl. 1974–77, Vice-Pres. 1978–81; Head of Liechtenstein Parl. Del. to the Council of Europe 1978–81; a Vice-Pres. Parl. Ass., Council of Europe 1981–82; mem. European Comm. on Human Rights 1983–90, European Comm. for Democracy Through Law (Venice Comm.) 1991–2003 (Vice-Pres. 1999–2001, Pres. Sub-comm. on Constitutional Reform); Arbitrator at Court of OSCE 1995–; merger and partnership, Batliner Wanger Batliner, Attorneys at Law 2002–; Chair. Scientific Council of Liechtenstein-Inst. 1987–97, mem. 1998–; Dir at Ed.'s Office, Liechtenstein Politische Schriften (Liechtenstein Political Publications) 1972–98; mem. Liecthensteinische Akademische Gesellschaft, Liechtensteinische Gesellschaft für Umweltschultz Historischer Verein, Liechtensteinische Kunstgesellschaft; Grand Cross of the Liechtenstein Order of Merit, Grand Silver Cross of Honour (Austria); Hon. DrIur (Basel) 1988, (Innsbruck) 2001; Fürstlicher Justizrat 1970. *Publications include:* Grundlagen einer liechtensteinischen Politik: Kleinstaatliche Variationen zum Thema der Integration 1972, Denkmodelle: Die volkerrechtlichen und politischen Beziehungen zwischen dem Furstentum Liechtenstein und der Schweizerischen Eidgenossenschaft 1973, Zu heutigen Problemen unseres Staates – Gegebenheiten, Ziele und Strategien 1976, Zur heutigen Lage des liechtensteinischen Parlaments 1981, Liechtenstein und die europäische Integration 1989, Die Siechtensteinische Rechtsordnung und die Europaische Menschenrechtskonvention 1990, Schichten der liechtensteinischen Verfassung 1993, Einfuhrung in das liechtensteinische Verfassungsrecht 1994, Aktuelle Fragen des liechtensteinischen Verfassungsrechts 1998, Der konditionierte Verfassungsstaat 2001, and other publs, essays and speeches in the field of political science. *Address:* Am Schrägen Weg 2, PO Box 185, 9490 Vaduz, Liechtenstein (office). *Telephone:* 239-78-78 (office). *Fax:* 239-78-79 (office). *E-mail:* office@bwb-law.li (office). *Website:* www.bwb-law.li (office).

BATLLE IBÁÑEZ, Jorge Luis, LLD; Uruguayan fmr head of state; b. 25 Oct. 1927; m. Mercedes Menafra; one s. one d.; ed Universidad de la República; journalist 1946–76; mem. Parl. (Partido Colorado) 1959–63, 1963–67; blacklisted by mil. Govt, frequently arrested 1973–84; Senator Partido Colorado 1985–90, 1995–99; co-author constitutional reform project 1996; Pres. of Uruguay 2000–05. *Address:* c/o Office of the President, Casa de Gobierno, Edif. Libertad, Avda Luis Alberto de Herrera 3350, esq. Avda José Pedro Varela, Montevideo, Uruguay (office).

BATT, Neil Leonard Charles, AO, BA; Australian politician; *Victorian Manager, Australian Health Insurance Association;* b. 14 June 1937, Hobart; s. of Clyde Wilfred Luke Batt and Miriam (née Wilkie) Batt; m. 1st Anne Cameron Teniswood 1962 (divorced 1986); three d.; m. 2nd Dr Karen Green 1986; one s., two d.; ed Hobart High School, Univ. of Tasmania; secondary school teacher 1960–61 and 1964–66; mem., House of Ass., Tasmanian Parl. 1969–80, 1986–89; Minister of Transport and Chief Sec. 1972–74, Minister for Educ. 1974–77, Deputy Premier and Treasurer 1977–80, Minister for Forests 1978–80, Minister for Finance 1979–82; Nat. Pres. Australian Labor Party 1978–80; Dir TNT Group of Cos. for Vic. and Tasmania 1982–86, Resident Dir TNT Man. Pty Ltd 1982–86; Leader of Opposition 1987–89; fmr Exec. Dir Health Benefits Council of Vic.; Chair. Heine Man. Ltd 1995–2000; Victorian Man. Australian Health Insurance Asscn 2001–; Vice-Pres. Int. Diabetes Inst.; mem. Bd Netwealth Ltd; Ombudsman for Tasmania 1989–91; mem. Jackson Cttee; Trustee, Nat. Gallery of Vic. 1983–86, Treas. 1984–86; Commr of Commonwealth Serum Labs 1983–86, Chair. 1984–86; mem. Bd of Australian Opera 1983–96. *Publications:* The Great Depression in Australia 1970, The Role of the University Today 1977, Information Power 1977. *Leisure interests:* swimming, yachting. *Address:* 16 Kooyong Road, North Caulfield, Vic. 3161, Australia.

BATT, Philip (Phil) Eugene; American fmr politician and farmer; b. 4 March 1927, Wilder, Idaho; m. Jacque Fallis 1948; one s. two d.; Chair. Idaho State Republican party; fmr mem. Idaho State Senate; fmr Lt-Gov. of Idaho; Gov. of Idaho 1995–99; first Pres. Idaho Food Producers; Dir Wilder Farm Labor Cttee; Chair. Otter for Idaho political campaign 2005. *Publications:* The Compleat Phil Batt: A Kaleidoscope 1999, Life as a Geezer 2002. *Address:* c/o Vista Book Gallery, 1116 South Vista Avenue, Boise, ID 83705, USA.

BATTEN, Alan Henry, PhD, DSc, FRSC; Canadian (b. British) astronomer; b. 21 Jan. 1933, Whitstable, England; s. of George Cuthbert Batten and Gladys Batten (née Greenwood); m. Lois Eleanor Dewis 1960; one s. one d.; ed Wolverhampton Grammar School, Univs of St Andrews and Manchester; Research Asst, Univ. of Manchester and Jr Tutor, St Anselm Hall of Residence 1958–59; Post-doctoral Fellow, Dominion Astrophysical Observatory, Victoria, BC, Canada 1959–61, staff mem. 1961–91, Sr Research Officer 1976–91, Guest Worker 1991–; Visiting Erskine Fellow, Univ. of Canterbury, NZ 1995; Vice-Pres. Astronomical Soc. of Pacific 1966–68; Pres. Canadian Astronomical Soc. 1974–76, Royal Astronomical Soc. of Canada 1976–78 (Hon. Pres. 1994–98), Comm. 30 of Int. Astronomical Union 1976–79, Comm. 42 1982–85; Vice-Pres. Int. Astronomical Union 1985–91; mem. Advisory Council, Centre for Studies in Religion and Society, Univ. of Vic. 1993–2002 (Chair. 1997–2000), 2006–; mem. Editorial Bd, Journal of Astronomical History and Heritage 1998–; Sessional Lecturer in History, Univ. of Victoria 2003–04; mem. Craigdarroch Research Awards Cttee, Univ. of Victoria 2004–06; Queen's Silver Jubilee Medal 1977. *Publications:* The Determination of Radial Velocities and their Applications (co-ed.) 1967, Extended Atmospheres and Circumstellar Matter in Close Binary Systems (ed.) 1973, Binary and Multiple Systems of Stars 1973, Resolute and Undertaking Characters: The Lives of Wilhelm and Otto Struve 1988, Algols (ed.) 1989, Astronomy for Developing Countries (ed.) 2001; nearly 200 scientific papers. *Leisure interest:* campanology. *Address:* Dominion Astrophysical Observatory, 5071 West Saanich Road, Victoria, BC V9E 2E7 (office); 2987 Westdowne Road, Victoria, BC V8R 5G1, Canada (home). *Telephone:* (250) 363-0009 (office); (250) 592-1720 (home). *Fax:* (250) 363-0045 (office). *E-mail:* alan.batten@nrc.gc.ca (office).

BATTEN, Sir John Charles, KCVO, MD, FRCP; British physician; b. 11 March 1924; s. of the late Raymond Wallis Batten and of Gladys Charles; m. Anne Margaret Oriel 1950; one s. two d. (and one d. deceased); ed Mill Hill School, St Bartholomew's Medical School; Jr appointments, St George's Hospital and Brompton Hospital 1946–58; Surgeon Capt., Royal Horse Guards 1947–49; Physician, St George's Hosp. 1958–79, Brompton Hosp. 1959–86, King Edward VII Hosp. for Officers 1968–89, King Edward VII Hosp., Midhurst 1969–89; Physician to HM Royal Household 1970–74, Physician to HM the Queen 1974–89, Head HM Medical Household 1982–89; Dorothy Temple Cross Research Fellow, Cornell Univ. Medical Coll., New York 1954–55; Deputy Chief Medical Referee, Confederation Life Insurance Co. 1958–74, Chief Medical Officer 1974–95; Examiner in Medicine, London Univ. 1968; Marc Daniels Lecturer, Royal Coll. of Physicians 1969; Croonian Lecturer, Royal Coll. of Physicians 1983; mem. Bd of Govs, Brompton Hosp. 1966–69, Medical School Council, St George's Hosp. 1969, Man. Cttee, King Edward VII Hospital Fund, Council, Royal Soc. of Medicine 1970, Chair. Medical and Survival Cttee RNLI 1992–94, Life Vice-Pres. 2000–; Censor, Royal Coll. of Physicians 1977–78, Sr Censor 1980–81, Vice-Pres. 1980–81; Hon. Physician to St George's Hospital 1980–, Royal Brompton Hosp. 1986–; Consultant to King Edward VII Convalescent Home, Isle of Wight 1975–85; Pres. Cystic Fibrosis Trust 1986–2003, Medical Protection Soc. 1987–95. *Publications:*

articles in medical books and journals. *Address:* 7 Lion Gate Gardens, Richmond, Surrey, TW9 2DF, England. *Telephone:* (20) 8940-3282.

BATTENBERG, J. T., III, BEng, MBA; American business executive; ed Kettering Univ., Columbia Univ., Harvard Univ.; various positions with General Motors (GM), including Ass. Plant Superintendent, Production Man. and Plant Man., Man. Dir GM Continental, Belgium, and Gen. Man., GM Overseas Truck Operations, England, Vice-Pres., Buick-Oldsmobile-Cadillac (B-O-C) Luxury Car Div. 1986, later B-O-C Vice-Pres. and Group Exec., Vice-Pres. and Group Exec., GM Automotive Components Group (ACG) 1992–94, Sr Vice-Pres. 1994, Exec., Vice-Pres., GM July 1995–99, Pres. Delphi Corpn (fmrly ACG Worldwide) 1995–2005 (retd), later also Chair. and CEO; Dir Sara Lee Corpn –2006 (resgnd), Covisint, Columbia Univ. Business School, Kettering Univ., Nat. Advisory Bd, J.P. Morgan Chase, Detroit Renaissance, Econ. Club of Detroit; mem. Business Roundtable, Business Council, Group of 100, Soc. of Automotive Engineers; charged of accounting fraud by SEC 2006; Int. Business Council World Trader of the Year 1998, US-Mexico Chamber of Commerce Double Eagle Leadership Award, Shingo Prize 1999, Harvard Business Club Stateman of the Year 2002. *Address:* c/o Delphi Corporation World Headquarters, 5725 Delphi Drive, Troy, MI 48098-2815, USA (office).

BATTERSBY, Sir Alan Rushton, Kt, PhD, DSc, ScD, FRS; British chemist and academic; *Professor Emeritus, University of Cambridge;* b. 4 March 1925, Leigh; s. of William Battersby and Hilda Battersby; m. Margaret Ruth Hart 1949 (died 1997); two s.; ed Leigh Grammar School, Univ. of Manchester, St Andrews Univ.; Lecturer in Chem., St Andrews Univ. 1948–53, Univ. of Bristol 1954–62; Prof. of Organic Chem., Univ. of Liverpool 1962–69, Univ. of Cambridge 1969–92, Prof. Emer. 1992–; Baker Lectureship, Cornell Univ. 1984, Robert Robinson Lectureship 1985, Marvel Lectureship, Illinois, USA 1989, Gilman Lectureship, Iowa, USA 1989, Kurt Alder Lectureship, Univ. of Cologne, Germany 1991, Romanes Lectureship, Univ. of Edin. 1993, Univ. Lectureship, Ottawa 1993, William Dauben Lectureship, Univ. of Calif., Berkeley, USA 1994, Alexander Cruickshank Lectureship, Gordon Confs, USA 1994, Linus Pauling Distinguished Lectureship, Ore. State, USA 1996, IAP Lectureship, Columbia, USA 1999; Hon. LLD (St Andrew's) 1977; Hon. DSc (Rockefeller) 1977, (Sheffield) 1986, (Bristol) 1994, (Liverpool) 1996; Corday-Morgan Medal and Prize 1961, Tilden Lectureship and Medal 1963, Hugo Müller Lectureship and Medal 1972, Flintoff Medal 1975, Paul Karrer Medal 1977, Davy Medal 1977, Max Tishler Award and Lectureship (Harvard) 1978, W von Hofmann Award and Lectureship 1979, Medal for Chemistry of Natural Products 1979, Pedlar Lectureship and Medal 1980, Roger Adams Award and Medal, ACS 1983, Davy Medal, Royal Soc. 1984, Havinga Medal 1984, Longstaff Medal 1984, Royal Medal 1984, Antonio Feltrinelli Int. Prize for Chem., Accad. Nazionale dei Lincei, Italy 1986, Varro Tyler Award, Purdue, USA 1987, Medal of Soc. Royale de Chimie, Belgium 1987, Adolf Windaus Medal and Lectureship German Chemical Soc. 1987, Wolf Foundation Chemistry Prize 1989, Arun Guthikonda Award and Lectureship, Columbia Univ., USA 1991, W. von Hofmann Memorial Medal 1992, Tetrahedron Prize 1995, Hans-Herloff Inhoffen Medal and Prize, Germany 1997, Robert A. Welch Award, USA 2000, Copley Medal, Royal Soc. 2000, Robert B. Woodward Career Award, USA 2004. *Publications:* numerous papers in the major chemical journals. *Leisure interests:* trout fishing, camping, hiking, gardening, classical music. *Address:* c/o University Chemical Laboratory, Lensfield Road, Cambridge, CB2 1EW (office); 20 Barrow Road, Cambridge, CB2 2AS, England (home). *Telephone:* (1223) 336400 (office); (1223) 363799 (home). *Fax:* (1223) 336362.

BATTISTON, Giuseppe, (Beppe Battiston); Italian actor; b. 22 July 1968, Udine; acting debut in Italia–Germania 4–3 1990. *Films include:* Italia–Germania 4–3 (Italy–Germany 4–3) 1990, Un'Anima divisa in due (A Soul Split in Two) 1993, Le acrobate (The Acrobat) 1997, Il più lungo giorno 1998, Pane e tulipani (Bread and Tulips) (David di Donatello Award for Best Supporting Actor 2000, Ciak d'Oro for Best Supporting Actor 2000) 2000, Guarda il cielo: Stella, Sonia, Silvia (Watch the Sky: Stella, Sonia, Silvia) 2000, Chiedimi se sono felice (Ask Me If I'm Happy) 2000, La forza del passato (The Power of the Past) 2002, Nemmeno in un sogno 2002, Un aldo qualunque 2002, Agata e la tempesta (Agata and the Storm) 2004, L'Uomo perfetto 2005, La bestia nel cuore (The Beast in the Heart; aka Don't Tell (UK)) 2005, La tigre e la neve (The Tiger and the Snow) 2005, Apnea 2005, Non prendere impegni stasera 2006, Uno su due (One Out of Two) 2006, A casa nostra (Our Country) 2006, La fine del mare 2007, Non pensarci (Don't Think About It) 2007, Giorni e nuvole (Days and Clouds) 2007, La giusta distanza (The Right Distance) 2007, Le pere di Adamo (voice) 2007, Amore, bugie e calcetto 2008. *Television includes:* L'Avvocato (episode La prova del fuoco) 2003, Al di là delle frontiere (mini-series) 2004, Una famiglia in giallo (mini-series) 2005, La notte breve 2006.

BATTLE, Kathleen Deanna, MMus; American singer (soprano); b. Portsmouth, OH; d. of Ollie Layne Battle and Grady Battle; ed Coll.-Conservatory of Music, Univ. of Cincinnati; professional debut in Brahms Requiem, Cincinnati May Festival, then Spoleto Festival, Italy 1972; debut Metropolitan Opera, New York as shepherd in Wagner's Tannhäuser 1977; regular guest with orchestras of New York, Chicago, Boston, Philadelphia, Cleveland, LA, San Francisco, Vienna, Paris and Berlin, at Salzburg, Tanglewood and other festivals and at the maj. opera houses including Metropolitan, New York, Covent Garden, London, Paris and Vienna; season 1985–86 appearances included Sophie in Der Rosenkavalier and Susanna in Figaro, Metropolitan New York, US premiere parts of Messiaen's St Francis of Assisi with Boston Symphony Orchestra and recitals USA and in Toronto, Paris, Vienna and Florence; season 1986–87 appearances included Zerbinetta in Ariadne auf Naxos and Adina in L'Elisir d'amore, Metropolitan New York and recitals in Japan, London, Salzburg and Vienna; planned recordings include Fauré Requiem; Dr hc (Cincinnati and Westminster Choir Coll., Princeton), Grammy Award 1987, 1988. *Recordings include:* Brahms Requiem and Songs, Mozart Requiem, Don Giovanni, Seraglio and concert arias, Verdi's Un Ballo in Maschera and Berg's Lulu Suite; New Year's Eve Gala, Vienna. *Leisure interests:* gardening, cooking, sewing, piano, dance. *Address:* Columbia Artist Management Inc., 1790 Broadway, New York, NY 10019-1412, USA (office). *Telephone:* (212) 841-9500 (office). *Fax:* (212) 841-9744 (office). *E-mail:* info@cami.com (office). *Website:* www.cami.com (office).

BATTS, Warren Leighton; American business executive and academic; *Adjunct Professor of Strategic Management, Graduate School of Business, University of Chicago;* b. 4 Sept. 1932, Norfolk, Va; s. of John Leighton Batts and Allie Belle (née Johnson) Batts; m. Eloise Pitts 1957; one d.; ed Georgia Inst. of Tech., Harvard Business School; with Kendall Co. 1963–64; Exec. Vice-Pres. Fashion Devt Co. 1964–66; Vice-Pres., Douglas Williams Assocs 1966–67; Founder, Triangle Corpn 1967, Pres. and Chief Exec. Officer 1967–71; Vice-Pres., Mead Corpn 1971–73, Pres. 1973–80, CEO 1978–80; Pres. Dart Industries 1980–81, Pres. Dart & Kraft 1981–86; Chair. Premark Int. Inc. 1986–97, CEO 1986–96; Chair., CEO Tupperware Corpn 1996–97; now Adjunct Prof. of Strategic Man. Graduate School of Business, Univ. of Chicago; mem. Bd Dirs, Nat. Assen of Corpn Dirs. 2000–, Chicago Climate Exchange, Methode Electronics; Trustee Northwestern Univ. 1989, Children's Memorial Hospital, Chicago 1984–. *Address:* Graduate School of Business, University of Chicago, 1101 East 58th Street, Chicago, IL 60637, USA (office). *Telephone:* (312) 867-0417 (office). *Fax:* (312) 867-0800 (office). *E-mail:* fwbatts@gsb.uchicago.edu (office). *Website:* www.gsb.uchicago.edu (office).

BATU, Bagen; Chinese party and government official; b. 1924, Zhenlai Co., Jilin Prov.; s. of Chen and Ne Garibu; m. 1950; three d.; joined CCP 1946; Deputy 1st, 2nd, 4th, 5th, 6th and 7th Inner Mongolia Autonomous Regional People's Congress, Chair. 1983–93; mem. Presidium 4th, 5th, 6th and 7th Autonomous Regional People's Congress; Deputy for Inner Mongolia 4th, 5th, 6th and 7th NPC; mem. Presidium 6th, 7th NPC; Vice-Chair. Autonomous Regional Govt Inner Mongolia 1979–83; Alt. mem. Cen. Cttee CCP 1982–92; mem. Standing Cttee 8th CPPCC and Vice-Chair. Ethnic Affairs Cttee CPPCC 1993–97; Leader 8th Prov. Spoken and Written Mongolian Language Co-ordination Group 1983–; Vice-Chair. China Sports Assen for the Elderly 1992; Vice-Pres. China Yellow River Culture, Econs and Devt Research Inst. 1993; Pres. Inner Mongolia Yellow River Culture, Econs and Devt Research Inst. 1995. *Leisure interests:* tennis, calligraphy. *Address:* Building 4, Inner Yard, 1 Qingcheng Lane, Huhhot 010015, People's Republic of China.

BATUMUBWIRA, Antoinette, MA; Burundian government official; m. Jean-Marie Ngendahayo; two d.; ed Univ. of Bordeaux III, France; emigrated to Finland as refugee 2003; fmr Planning Officer, Uudenmaa Employment and Econ. Devt Centre; returned to Burundi; Minister of External Relations and Int. Co-operation 2005–09. *Publications:* The Route Towards Integration: The Share of Everyone 2004. *Address:* c/o Ministry of External Relations and International Co-operation, Bujumbura, Burundi (office).

BATURIN, Yuri Mikhailovich, DJur; Russian politician, cosmonaut, lawyer and journalist; *Deputy Commander of the Cosmonaut Corps;* b. 12 June 1949, Moscow; m.; one d.; ed Moscow Inst. of Physics and Tech., All-Union Inst. of Law, Moscow State Univ. School of Journalism, Mil. Acad. of Gen. Staff; worked in research production union Energia 1973–80; Inst. of State and Law USSR (now Russian) Acad. of Sciences 1980–91; Research Scholar, Kennan Inst. for Advanced Russian Studies, The Woodrow Wilson Center, Washington, DC, USA 1991; on staff of Pres. Mikhail Gorbachev Admin 1991; mem. Pres.'s Council 1993–; Asst to Pres. on legal problems 1993–94, on Nat. Security Problems 1994–96; mem. Council on Personnel Policy of Pres. 1994–97; Sec. Defence Council of Russian Fed. 1996–97; Asst to Pres., Chair. Cttee for Mil. Ranks and Posts 1995–97; columnist, Novaya Gazeta newspaper 1997–; cosmonaut and test pilot of the Cosmonaut Corps 1998–, Deputy Commr 2000–, participated in space flight to Mir Station Aug. 1998, second space flight to Int. Space Station 2001; Prof. of Computer Law, Moscow Inst. of Eng and Physics; Prof., Moscow Inst. of Physics and Tech.; Prof., School of Journalism, Moscow Univ., Pres. of the School, Media Law and Policy Center; Chair. Center for Anti-Corruption Research and Initiative Transparency Int. 2000–; Union of Journalists Prize 1990, Award for Outstanding Contribution to Mass-Media Law 1997, Themis Award 1998. *Films:* documentaries: Tuch-and-go in Space 1997, Ladder to Heaven 2000. *Publications:* drafts of the laws on the freedom of the press of the USSR 1989 and of Russia 1991, Problems of Computer Law 1991. *Address:* Y. Gagarin Centre for Cosmonaut Training, Zvezdny Gorodok, 141160 Shchelkovsky Raion, Moskovskaya oblast, Russia (office). *Telephone:* (495) 526-38-83 (office). *E-mail:* baturin@medialaw.ru (office); TIRussia@libfl.ru (office).

BAUCHARD, Denis M(ichel) B(ertrand), BA; French diplomatist; *Senior Fellow, Institut français des relations internationales;* b. 20 Sept. 1936, Paris; s. of Charles Bauchard and Marguerite Duhamel; m. Geneviève Lanoë 1961; two s. two d.; ed Inst. of Political Studies, Ecole nat. d'administration; Civil Admin., Ministry of Finance 1964–66, 1968–74; Financial Attaché Nr and Middle East, French Embassy, Beirut 1966–68; Asst to Minister 1974–76; Financial Counsellor, French Mission to UN 1977–81; Deputy Asst Sec., Ministry of Foreign Affairs 1981–85; Asst Sec. 1986–89; Amb. to Jordan 1989–93; Asst Sec. Ministry of Foreign Affairs (N Africa and Middle East) 1993–96; Chief of Staff to Minister of Foreign Affairs 1996–97; Amb. to Canada 1998–2001; Pres. Institut du Monde Arabe 2002–04; Sr Fellow, Institut Français de Relations Internationales 2004–; Adviser, Gen. Dir Agence française de Developpement 2005–; Officier, Légion d'honneur, Ordre nat. du Mérite. *Publications:* Le jeu mondial des pétroliers 1970, Economie financière des collectivités locales 1972. *Address:* IFRI, 27 rue de la Procession, 75015 Paris (office); 91 rue de Rennes, 75006 Paris, France (home).

Telephone: 1-40-61-60-82 (office); 1-45-44-18-05 (home). *Fax:* 1-40-61-60-82 (office). *E-mail:* bauchard@ifri.org (office); denis.bauchard@wanadoo.fr (home). *Website:* www.ifri.org (office).

BAUCHEREL, Jean-Luc; French insurance industry executive; *Chairman, Groupama SA;* joined Groupama SA 1975, Dir Morbihan Mutual 1975–78, mem. Exec. Bd 1978–, mem. Bd of Dirs Groupama Bretagne 1992–, Vice-Chair. 1996–2000, Chair. 2000–05, Chair. Groupama Loire-Bretagne 2002–, Chair. Fédération Nationale Groupama and Groupama SA 2004–, also Dir Groupama Holding. *Address:* Groupama SA, 8-10, rue d'Astorg, Paris Cedex 08 75383, France (office). *Telephone:* 1-44-56-77-77 (office). *Website:* www.groupama.com (office).

BAUCUS, Max S., LLB; American politician; *Senator from Montana;* b. 11 Dec. 1941, Helena, Mont.; m. Wanda Minge 1983; one s.; ed Helena High School, Stanford Univ. and Stanford Law School; staff attorney, Civil Aeronautics Bd, Washington, DC 1967–69; legal staff, Securities and Exchange Comm. 1969–71; legal Asst to Chair. SEC 1970–71; private law practice, Missoula, Mont. 1971; Acting Exec. Dir and Cttee Coordinator, Mont. Constitutional Convention; elected to Montana State Legislature 1972; two terms in US House of Reps for Mont. Western Dist, mem. House Appropriations Cttee and Deputy Whip; Senator from Montana 1979–; Chair. Senate Int. Trade Sub-Cttee of Finance, Senate Environment and Public Works Cttee, Senate Agric. and Intelligence Cttee, Finance Cttee 2001; mem. several other sub-cttees; Democrat. *Address:* 511 Hart Senate Building, Washington, DC 20510–0001, USA (office). *Telephone:* (202) 224-2651 (office). *Fax:* (202) 224-0515 (office). *Website:* baucus.senate.gov (office).

BAUDO, Serge; French conductor; *Honorary Musical Director, Orchestre Symphonique de Prague (FOK);* b. 16 July 1927, Marseille; s. of Etienne Baudo and Geneviève Tortelier; m. Madeleine Reties 1947; one s. one d.; ed Conservatoire nat. supérieur de musique, Paris; Music Dir Radio Nice 1957–59; Conductor Paris Opera Orchestra 1962–66; titular Conductor and Orchestral Dir a.i. Orchestre de Paris 1968–70; Music Dir Opéra de Lyon 1969–71, Orchestre Nat. de Lyon 1971–87; Hon. Musical Dir Orchestre Symphonique de Prague (FOK) 2001–; has conducted many of world's leading orchestras; Founder Berlioz Festival, Lyon 1979–89; Officier Légion d'honneur, Ordre des Arts et Lettres; Chevalier Ordre nat. du Mérite; numerous prix du disque and other awards. *Films:* music for Le Monde sans Soleil 1964. *Address:* Les Hauts du Ferra, 2901 Chemin Charré, 13600 Ceyreste, France (home); Matthias Vogt, 1714 Stockton Street, Suite 300, San Francisco, CA 94133-2930, USA. *Telephone:* (415) 788-8073. *Fax:* 4-42-83-07-57 (home); (530) 684-5535. *E-mail:* matthias.vogt@usa.net (office).

BAUDOUIN, Jean-Louis, BA, BCL, PhD; Canadian professor of law and judge; *Judge, Court of Appeal of Québec;* b. 8 Aug. 1938, Boulogne, France; s. of Louis Baudouin and Marguerite Guerin; m.; four d.; ed Univ. of Paris, McGill Univ., Montreal, Canada; admitted to Bar of Québec 1959; Prof. of Law, Univ. of Montreal 1963–; Commr, Law Reform Comm. of Canada 1976–78, Vice-Chair. 1978–80; Judge, Court of Appeal, Québec 1989–; mem. RSC; Dr hc (Sherbrooke) 1990, (Paris) 1994, (Namur) 1998, (Ottawa) 2001; Médaille du Burreau de Québec 1988. *Publications:* Les Obligations 1970–2004, La Responsabilité Civile 1973–2006, Le Secret Professionnel 1964, Produire l'Homme: de quel Droit? 1987, Ethique de la Mort, Droit à la Mort 1992. *Leisure interests:* skiing, fishing, wine-tasting. *Address:* Court House, #17.95, 1 Notre Dame East, Montreal, Québec, H2Y 1B6 (office); 875 Antonine Maillet, Montreal, Québec, H2V 2Y6, Canada (home). *Telephone:* (514) 393-4863 (office); (514) 270-1884 (home). *Fax:* (514) 873-0376 (office). *E-mail:* jlbaudouin@justice.gouv.qc.ca (office).

BAUDRIER, Jacqueline; French journalist; b. 16 March 1922, Beaufai; m. 1st Maurice Baudrier (divorced); m. 2nd Roger Perriard 1957; ed Univ. of Paris; political reporter, Actualités de Paris news programme and foreign news reporter and presenter on various news programmes, Radiodiffusion-Télévision Française 1950–60; Sec.-Gen. Soutien fraternel des journalistes 1955; Ed.-in-Chief of news programmes, Office de Radiodiffusion-Télévision Française (ORTF) 1963–66, in charge of main news programme 1966–68; Asst Dir of radio broadcasting, in charge of information 1968–69; Dir of Information, 2nd TV channel (A2) 1969–72; Dir 1st TV channel network (TF1) 1972–74; Chair. Radio-France (nat. radio broadcasting co.) 1975–81; mem. Bd of Dirs Télédiffusion de France (nat. TV broadcasting co.) 1975–81; Pres. Communauté radiophonique des programmes de langue française 1977–79; Vice-Chair. Programming Comm. Union européenne de radiodiffusion 1978, re-elected 1980; Perm. Rep. of France to UNESCO 1981–85; mem. Exec. Cttee, UNESCO 1984–85, Comm. nat. de la Communication et des Libertés 1986–89; columnist Quotidien de Paris 1989; Pres. Cosmo Communications 1989–95; columnist, mem. Bd L'Observatoire de la Télévision 1993–; Pres. Channel 5 TV Programming Comm. 1995; Vice-Pres. Nat. Comm. for UNESCO 1996; Chevalier, Légion d'honneur, Officier, Ordre nat. du Mérit; Prix Maurice Bourdet 1960, Prix Ondes 1969, numerous other awards; . *Address:* La Cinquième, 8 rue Marceau, 92136 Issy-les-Moulineaux Cedex (office); 60 quai Louis Blériot, 75016 Paris, France (home).

BAUGH, Kenneth, MD; Jamaican politician and physician; *Deputy Prime Minister and Minister of Foreign Affairs and Foreign Trade;* b. Montego Bay, St James; m. Vilma Baugh; two s. one d.; ed Univ. of W Indies, Royal Coll. of Surgeons; MP for N W St James 1980–89, currently for St Catherine West Central; fmr Deputy Leader of the Opposition; fmr Minister of Health; Shadow Minister for Health and Environment –2007; Deputy Prime Minister and Minister of Foreign Affairs and Foreign Trade Sept. 2007–; mem. Jamaica Labour Party (currently Chair.). *Leisure interests:* art, drawing, swimming. *Address:* Office of the Deputy Prime Minister, 1 Devon Road, Kingston 10, Jamaica (office). *Telephone:* 929-8880 (office). *Fax:* 929-8459 (office). *E-mail:* info@cabinet.gov.jm (office); mfaftjam@cwjamaica.com (office). *Website:* www.cabinet.gov.jm (office); www.mfaft.gov.jm (office).

BAULCOMBE, David Charles, BSc, PhD, FRS; British botanist and academic; *Professor of Botany and Royal Society Research Professor, University of Cambridge;* m.; four c.; ed Univs of Leeds and Edinburgh; Post-doctoral Fellow, McGill Univ., Montréal, Canada 1977–78, Univ. of Georgia, Athens, Ga, USA 1978–80; Higher Scientific Officer, Plant Breeding Inst., Cambridge 1980–86, Prin. Scientific Officer 1986–88; joined The Sainsbury Lab., Norwich 1988, Sr Research Scientist and Head of Lab. 1990–93, 1999–2003; Prof., Univ. of East Anglia 2002–07; Prof. of Botany and Royal Soc. Research Prof., Univ. of Cambridge 2007–; mem. Editorial Bd The Plant Journal 1991–, Virology 1996–, Physiological and Molecular Plant Pathology 1999–, EMBO Reports 1999–, EMBO Journal (also Sr Advisor) 2005–, Genome Biology 2005–; mem. Scientific Advisory Bd, Nat. Inst. for Biological Sciences, Beijing, People's Repub. of China 2006–09, Nat. Inst. of Chemical Physics and Biophysics, Tallinn, Estonia, Science Foundation Ireland 2004–07; Panel mem. Health and Safety Exec. Scientific Advisory Cttee on Genetic Modification (Contained Use) 2004–07; Pres. Int. Soc. of Plant Molecular Biology 2003–04; mem. European Molecular Biology Org. 1997, Academia Europaea 2002; Foreign Assoc. mem. NAS 2005; Hon. Prof., Univ. of East Anglia 1998–2002; Prix des Cerealiers de France for work on hormonally regulated genes of cereals 1990, Kumho Science Int. Award in Plant Molecular Biology and Biotechnology 2002, Kumho Cultural Foundation (S Korea) 2002, Ruth Allen Award, American Phytopathology Soc. 2002, Wiley Prize in Biomedical Science, Wiley Foundation, Rockefeller Univ. (co-recipient) 2003, M.W. Beijerinck Virology Prize, Royal Netherlands Acad. of Arts and Sciences 2004, Massry Prize, Massry Foundation, Univ. of Southern California (co-recipient) 2005, Royal Medal, Royal Soc. 2006. *Publications:* numerous scientific papers in professional journals. *Leisure interests:* music, sailing, hill walking. *Address:* Department of Plant Sciences, University of Cambridge, Downing Street, Cambridge, CB2 3EA, England (office). *Telephone:* (1223) 339386 (office). *Fax:* (1223) 333953 (office). *E-mail:* david.baulcombe@plantsci.cam.ac.uk (office). *Website:* www.plantsci.cam.ac.uk/Baulcombe (office).

BAULIEU, Etienne-Emile, DenM, DèsSc; French physician, biochemist and academic; *Honourary Professor, Collège de France;* b. 12 Dec. 1926, Strasbourg; s. of Léon Blum and Thérèse Lion; m. Yolande Compagnon 1947; one s. two d.; ed Lycée Pasteur, Neuilly-sur-Seine, Faculté de Médecine and Faculté des Sciences, Paris; Intern, Paris Hosps. 1951–55; Chef de Clinique, Faculté de Médecine, Paris 1955–57, Assoc. Prof. of Biochemistry 1958; Visiting Scientist, Dept of Obstetrics, Gynaecology and Biochemistry, Columbia Univ. New York 1961–62; Dir Research Inst. 33, Hormones Lab., Inst. Nat. de la Santé et de la Recherche Médicale (INSERM) 1963–97; Prof. of Biochemistry, Faculté de Médecine de Bicêtre, Univ. Paris-Sud 1970; Prof. at Collège de France 1993, a chair. 1994, now Hon. Prof.; Consultant, Roussel Uclaf; mem. Editorial Bds several French and int. journals; mem. and Past Pres. INSERM, Fondation pour la Recherche Médicale Française; Pres. Société Française d'Endocrinologie 1975; Vice-Pres. Acad. of Sciences 2000–02, Pres. 2003–; mem. Organizing Cttee Karolinska Symposia on Reproductive Endocrinology, NCI-INSERM Cancer and Hormones Programme (Past French Scientific Chair.), fmr mem. Scientific Advisory Bd WHO Special Programme in Human Reproduction; mem. Endocrine Soc., USA 1966–, Royal Soc. of Medicine, London 1972–, Inst. de France (Acad. des Sciences) 1982– (Vice-Pres. 2000–02, Pres. 2003–04), New York Acad. of Sciences 1985–; Foreign Assoc. mem. NAS 1990–; mem. Expert Advisory Panel, Int. Fed. of Gynaecology and Obstetrics (FIGO) 1997–; Mem. Emer. Academia Europaea 1997–; developed RU486 abortion pill and anti-aging pill from human hormone, DeHydroEpiAndrosterone (more commonly known as DHEA); Hon. mem. American Physiological Soc. 1993, Acad. Nationale de Médecine 2002; Chevalier Ordre nat. du Mérite 1967; Officier Ordre du Mérite du Gabon 1979; Commdr Légion d'honneur 1990, Grand Officier de la Légion d'honneur 2003; Dr hc (Ghent) 1991, (Tufts) 1991, (Karolinska Inst.) 1994, (Worcs. Foundation, Shrewsbury) 1994; Reichstein Award, Int. Soc. of Endocrinology 1972, Grand Prix Scientifique 1989 de la Ville de Paris 1974, First European Medallist of Soc. of Endocrinology (GB) 1985, Albert & Mary Lasker Clinical Research Award 1989, American Acad. of Achievement Golden Plate Award 1990, Premio Minerva, Rome 1990, Christopher Columbus Discovery Award in Biomedical Research (Genoa and NIH) 1992, Nat. Award, American Assn for Clinical Chem. 1992, Grand Prix Scientifique, Fondation pour la Recherche Médicale, Paris 1994, Ken Myer Medal (Australia) 2000, Int. Acad. of Humanism Laureat 2002, Charles H. Sawyer Distinguished Lecture 2003 and numerous other prizes and awards. *Publications:* Génération pilule 1989, Hormones 1990, Contraception: Constraint or Freedom?; numerous specialist papers. *Address:* c/o Institut de France, 23 quai de Conti, 75006 Paris, France (office). *Telephone:* 1-49-59-18-82 (office). *Fax:* 1-49-59-92-03 (office).

BAUM, Bernard René, MSc, PhD, FRSC; Canadian scientist; *Principal Research Scientist, Eastern Cereal and Oilseed Research Centre, Agriculture Canada;* b. 14 Feb. 1937, Paris, France; s. of Kurt Baum and Marta Berl; m. Danielle Habib 1961; one d.; ed Hebrew Univ., Jerusalem; Research Scientist, Plant Research Inst., Dept of Agric., Ottawa, Canada 1966–74; Sr Research Scientist, Biosystematics Research Inst., Agric. Canada, Ottawa 1974–80, Prin. Research Scientist, Biosystematics Research Centre 1980–90, Prin. Research Scientist, Centre for Land and Biological Resources Research 1990–95, Eastern Cereal and Oilseed Research Centre 1996–; Section Chief, Cultivated Crops Section 1973–77, Section Head, Vascular Plants Section 1982–87, Acting Dir, Geostrategy Div., Devt Policy Directorate 1981–82; mem. Acad. of Sciences (RSC) 1981, Botanical Soc. of America, Soc. Botanique de France, Int. Assn for Plant Taxonomy and other socs; Founder-mem. Hennig

Soc.; Fellow, Linnean Soc., London; George Lawson Medal, Canadian Botanical Asscn 1979. *Publications:* Material of an International Oat Register 1973, Oats: Wild and Cultivated. A Monograph of the Genus Avena 1977, The Genus Tamarix 1978, Barley Register 1985, Triticale Register; more than 290 scientific publs. *Leisure interests:* swimming long distance, running 10k, pilates, classical music. *Address:* Eastern Cereal and Oilseed Research Centre, Agriculture Canada, Central Experimental Farm, 960 Carling Avenue, Ottawa, ON K1A 0C6, Canada (office). *Telephone:* (613) 759-1821 (office). *Fax:* (613) 759-1701 (office). *E-mail:* bernard.baum@agr.gc.ca (office); baumbd@sympatico.ca (home). *Website:* www.agr.gc.ca/index_e.php (office).

BAUM, Warren C., PhD; American international finance official; b. 2 Sept. 1922, New York; s. of William Baum and Elsie Baum; m. Jessie Scullen 1946; two d.; ed Columbia and Harvard Univs; with Office of Strategic Services 1942–46; Economic Co-operation Admin. 1949–51; Mutual Security Agency 1952–53; Economist, RAND Corpn 1953–56; Chief, Office of Network Study, Fed. Communications Comm. 1956–59; Economist, European Dept World Bank 1959–62; Div. Chief, European Dept 1962–64; Asst Dir in charge of Transportation, Projects Dept 1964–68; Deputy Dir Projects Dept 1968; Assoc. Dir, Projects 1968–72; Vice-Pres. Projects Staff 1972–83, Vice-Pres. 1983–86; Chair. Consultative Group on Int. Agricultural Research 1974–83, Chair. Emer. 1984–. *Publications:* The Marshall Plan and French Foreign Trade 1951, The French Economy and the State 1956, Investing in Development 1985.

BAUM, HE Cardinal William Wakefield, STD, STL; American ecclesiastic; b. 21 Nov. 1926, Dallas, Tex.; s. of Harold E. White and Mary Leona White (née Hayes), step-father Jerome C. Baum; ed Kenrick Seminary, St Louis and Univ. of St Thomas Aquinas, Rome; ordained to priesthood 1951; Assoc. Pastor, St Aloysius, St Therese's and St Peter's parishes, Kan. City, Mo. 1951–56; Instructor and Prof., Avila Coll., Kan. City 1954–56; 1958–63; Admin. St Cyril's Parish, Sugar Creek, Mo. 1960–61; Hon. Chaplain of His Holiness the Pope 1961; Peritus (Expert Adviser), Second Vatican Council 1962–65; First Exec. Dir Bishops' Comm. for Ecumenical and Interreligious Affairs, Washington, DC 1964–67, Chair. 1972; mem. Jt Working Group of Reps of Catholic Church and World Council of Churches 1965–69; mem. Mixed Comm. of Reps of Catholic Church and Lutheran World Fed. 1965–66; Chancellor, Diocese of Kan. City, St Joseph 1967–70; Hon. Prelate of His Holiness the Pope 1968; Pastor, St James Parish, Kan. City 1968–70; Bishop, Diocese of Springfield-Cape Girardeau 1970; mem. Synod of Bishops 1971; Archbishop of Washington 1973–80; Chancellor of the Catholic Univ. 1973–80; cr. Cardinal 1976; Prefect, Sacred Congregation for Catholic Educ. 1980–91; Major Penitentiary of Apostolic Penitentiary, Roman Curia 1990–2001, Major Penitentiary Emer. of Apostolic Penitentiary 2001–; Permanent Observer-Consultant for Vatican Secr. for Promoting Christian Unity; Chair. USCC-NCCB Doctrine Cttee, Cttee for Pastoral Research and Practices; mem. Secr. for Non-Christians; Hon. DD (Muhlenberg Coll., Allentown, Pa 1967, Georgetown Univ., Wash., St John's Univ., Brooklyn, NY). *Publications:* The Teaching of HE Cardinal Cajetan on the Sacrifice of the Mass 1958, Considerations Toward the Theology on the Presbyterate 1961. *Leisure interests:* reading, music. *Address:* c/o Apostolic Penitentiary, Palazzo della Cancelleria 1, 00186 Rome, Italy. *Telephone:* (06) 69887526. *Fax:* (06) 69887557.

BAUMAN, Robert Patten, BA, MBA; American business executive; b. 27 March 1931, Cleveland; s. of John Nevan Bauman, Jr and Lucille Miller Patten; m. Patricia Hughes Jones 1961; one s. one d.; ed Ohio Wesleyan Univ., Harvard Business School; joined Gen. Foods Corpn 1958, Corp. Vice-Pres. 1968, Group Vice-Pres. 1970, Exec. Vice-Pres. and Corp. Dir 1972–81; Dir Avco Corpn 1980, Chair. and CEO 1981–85; Vice-Chair. and Dir Textron Inc. 1985–86; Chair. and Chief Exec. Beecham Group 1986–89, CEO SmithKline Beecham 1989–94; Chair. British Aerospace PLC 1994–98, BTR PLC, London 1998–99; fmr mem. Bd of Dirs BTR plc, CIGNA Corpn, Hathaway Holdings, Inc., Morgan Stanley Dean Witter and Russell Reynolds Assocs, Inc., Union Pacific Corpn, Cap Cities/ABC Inc., Bolero.net, Reuters; Trustee, Ohio Wesleyan Univ. *Publication:* Plants as Pets 1982, From Promise to Performance 1997. *Leisure interests:* growing orchids, paddle tennis, jogging, tennis, photography, golf, sailing. *E-mail:* RPBauman@aol.com (office).

BAUMAN, Zygmunt, MA, PhD; British academic and writer; *Professor Emeritus of Sociology, University of Leeds;* b. 19 Nov. 1925, Poznań, Poland; s. of Maurycy Bauman and Zofia Bauman (née Cohn); m. Janina Bauman (née Lewinson) 1948; three d.; ed Univ. of Warsaw; held Chair of Gen. Sociology, Univ. of Warsaw 1964–68, Prof. Emer. 1968–; Prof. of Sociology, Tel-Aviv Univ. 1968–71; Prof. of Sociology, Univ. of Leeds 1971–91, Prof. Emer. 1991–; mem. British Sociological Asscn, Polish Sociological Asscn; Krzyz Walecznych (Poland) 1945; Dr hc (Oslo) 1997, (Lapland) 1999, (Uppsala) 2000, (Prague) 2001, (Copenhagen) 2001, (Sofia) 2001, (West of England) 2002, (London) 2003, (Leeds) 2004, (Gotenburg) 2005, (Leeds, Metropolitan) 2007, (Kaunas) 2008, (New School, NY) 2008, (Aberdeen) 2009, (Copenhagen Business School) 2009; Amalfi Prize for Sociology and Social Sciences 1989, Theodor W. Adorno Prize 1998. *Publications:* Culture as Praxis 1972, Hermeneutics and Social Science 1977, Memories of Class 1982, Legislators and Interpreters 1987, Modernity and the Holocaust 1989, Modernity and Ambivalence 1990, Intimations of Postmodernity 1991, Thinking Sociologically 1991, Mortality, Immortality and Other Life Strategies 1992, Postmodern Ethics 1993, Life in Fragments 1995, Postmodernity and Its Discontents 1996, Globalization: The Human Consequences 1998, Work, Consumerism and the New Poor 1998, In Search of Politics 1999, Liquid Modernity 2000, Individualized Society 2000, Community: Seeking Safety in an Uncertain World 2001, Society Under Siege 2002, Liquid Love: On the Frailty of Human Bonds 2003, Wasted Lives: Modernity and its Outcasts 2003, Europe: An Unfinished Adventure 2004, Liquid Life 2005, Liquid – Modern Fears 2006, Has Ethics a Chance in a Society of Consumers? 2008, The Art of Life 2008; contrib. to scholarly journals and general periodicals. *Leisure interest:* photography. *Address:* 1 Lawnswood Gardens, Leeds, LS16 6HF, England (home). *E-mail:* janzygbau@aol.com (home).

BAUMANIS, Aivars; Latvian lawyer, journalist and diplomatist; b. 23 Dec. 1937, Riga; s. of Arturs Baumanis and Elza Finks; m. Anita Baumanis 1979; three s. one d.; ed Latvian Univ.; investigator, City Police Dept of Riga 1961–64; corresp. foreign news desk of Latvian Radio 1964–71; ed. Liesma (magazine) 1971–74; corresp., Padomfu Faunatne (newspaper) 1974–80; Exec. Sec. Furmala (newspaper) 1980–88, Ed.-in-Chief 1986–88; Dir Latvian br. Novosti News Agency 1988–90; Dir Latvian News Agency Leta 1990–91; Amb. and Perm. Rep. of Latvia to UN 1991–98; Amb. to Denmark 1998–2005; Amb. and Head, Press Review Div., Ministry of Foreign Affairs 2005–09. *Publications:* articles in various Latvian newspapers and magazines 1966–91. *Leisure interests:* jazz, movies, literature. *Address:* Ministry of Foreign Affairs, Brīvības blvd 36, Riga 1395, Latvia (office). *Telephone:* 732-1311 (office). *Fax:* 732-1309 (office). *E-mail:* mfa.cha@mfa.gov.lv (office). *Website:* www.am.gov.lv (office).

BAUMANN, Herbert Karl Wilhelm; German composer and conductor; b. 31 July 1925, Berlin; s. of Wilhelm and Elfriede (née Bade) Baumann; m. Marianne Brose 1951; two s.; ed Berlin Classical High School, Schillergymnasium and Int. Music Inst.; conductor, Tchaikovsky Symphony Orchestra 1947; composer and conductor, Deutsches Theater, Berlin 1947–53, Staatliche Berliner Bühnen: Schillertheater and Schlossparktheater 1953–70, Bayerisches Staatsschauspiel: Residenztheater, Munich 1971–79; freelance composer 1979–; numerous published compositions and recordings, including the ballets Alice in Wonderland and Rumpelstilzgen, Three Concertos, Music for Strings, Chamber Music for Wind, Ballade, Concerti da Camera, Metamorphosen (chamber music); Mem. of Honour, BDZ 1990; Bundesverdienstkreuz 1998; Diploma of Honour Salsomaggiore, Italy 1981, GEMA 1998; Silbernes Ehrenzeichen GDBA 1979. *Works include:* stage music for more than 500 plays, 40 TV plays and the ballets Alice in Wonderland and Rumpelstilzgen, music for radio, cinema and television, orchestral, chamber and choral works, several suites for plucked instruments, music for strings, music for wind instruments, three concertos and works for organ. *Films:* Das Jahrhundert des Kindes, Die Stadt von morgen, Menschen in der Stadt, König Fußball, Timpi Tox und Ali Bum, Berlin Sketchbook. *Leisure interests:* travelling and wandering, reading, especially books on fine arts. *Address:* Franziskanerstrasse 16, Apt 1419, 81669 Munich, Germany (home). *Telephone:* (89) 480 77 45 (home). *Fax:* (89) 480 77 45 (home). *E-mail:* hkwbau@t-online.de. *Website:* www.komponisten.net/baumann.

BAUMANN, Karl-Hermann, Dipl.-Kfm, Dr.rer.oec; German business executive; b. 22 July 1935, Dortmund; Asst, Dept of Business Admin, Univ. of Saarland, Saarbrücken 1964–70; joined Siemens AG 1970, various positions in Corp. Finance Div. 1970–78, Sr Vice-Pres. Siemens Capital Corpn, NY and Siemens Corpn, Iselin, NJ, USA 1978–83, Head of Corp. Financial Accounting Div., Munich 1983–84, Vice-Pres. Siemens AG 1984–88, apptd to Bd of Man. 1987, apptd mem. Exec. Cttee 1988, Head of Corp. Finance 1988–98, Chair. Supervisory Bd Siemens AG 1998–2005; mem. Supervisory Bds Allianz AG 1998–2001, Bayer Schering Pharma AG (fmrly Schering AG) 1994–2009, Deutsche Bank AG 1989–2005, E.ON AG 1998–2008, Linde AG 1998–2008, MG Technologies AG 1998–2003, Thyssen Krupp AG 1998–2005. *Address:* Siemens AG, Wittelsbacherplatz 2, 80333 Munich, Germany (office). *Telephone:* (89) 636-32005 (office). *Fax:* (89) 636-32025 (office). *Website:* www.siemens.com (office).

BAUMEISTER, Wolfgang, Dr rer. nat (Habil.); German biochemist and academic; *Professor and Head of Department of Structural Biology, Max Planck Institute of Biochemistry;* b. 1946, Wesseling; ed Univs of Münster, Bonn and Düsseldorf; worked at Cavendish Lab., Cambridge, UK 1970s, Lecturer in Biophysics 1978–83; Prof., Univs of Düsseldorf and Munich; Group Leader, Max Planck Inst. of Biochemistry, Martinsried 1983–88, Dir and Head of Dept of Structural Biology 1988–; mem. several acads, including American Acad. of Arts and Sciences; Hon. Prof. of Physics, Tech. Univ. of Munich; Otto Warburg Medal, Schleiden Medal, Louis Jeantet Prize for Medicine, Stein and Moore Award, Harvey Prize in Science and Tech., Technion – Israel Inst. of Tech. 2005. *Publications:* numerous scientific papers in professional journals on cellular protein quality control. *Address:* Department of Molecular Structural Biology, Max Planck Institute of Biochemistry, Am Klopferspitz 18, 82152 Martinsried, Germany (office). *Telephone:* (89) 8578-2642 (office); (89) 8578-2387 (office). *Fax:* (89) 8578-2641 (office); (89) 8578-3557 (office). *E-mail:* baumeist@biochem.mpg.de (office). *Website:* www.biochem.mpg.de/baumeister (office).

BAUMOL, William Jack, PhD; American economist and academic; *Professor of Economics, New York University;* b. 26 Feb. 1922, New York; s. of Solomon Baumol and Lillian Baumol; m. Hilda Missel 1941; one s. one d.; ed Coll. of City of New York and Univ. of London; jr economist, US Dept of Agriculture 1942–43, 1946; Asst Lecturer, London School of Econs 1947–49; Asst Prof., Dept of Econs, Princeton Univ. 1949–52, Prof. of Econs 1952–92, Prof. Emer. and Sr Research Economist 1992–; Prof. of Econs, New York Univ. 1971–, Dir C.V. Starr Center for Applied Econs 1983–2000; Pres. Eastern Econ. Asscn 1978–79, Asscn of Environmental and Resource Economists 1979, American Econ. Asscn 1981, Atlantic Econ. Soc. 1985; mem. NAS, Accademia Nazionale de Lincei, Rome 2001; Hon. Fellow, LSE; Hon. Prof. Univ. of Belgrano 1996; Dr hc (Princeton Univ. Joseph D. Green) 1968, (Stockholm School of Econs) 1971, (Univ. of Basel) 1973, (Univ. of Lille) 1997; Frank E. Seidman Award, Political Econ. 1987, Henry H. Villand Research Award 1997, Int. Award for Entrepreneurship and Small Business Research, Swedish Foundation for

Small Business Research and Swedish Business Devt Agency 2003. *Publications:* more than 30 books including: Economic Dynamics 1951, Business Behavior, Value and Growth 1959, Economic Theory and Operations Analysis 1961, Performing Arts: The Economic Dilemma (with W. G. Bowen) 1966, Theory of Environmental Policy (with W. E. Oates) 1975, Economics, Environmental Policy and the Quality of Life (with W. E. Oates and S. A. Batey Blackman) 1979, Economics: Principles and Policy (with A. S. Blinder) 1979, Contestable Markets and the Theory of Industry Structure (with J. C. Panzar and R. D. Willig) 1982, Productivity Growth and US Competitiveness (co-ed. with K. McLennan) 1985, Superfairness: Applications and Theory 1986 (Best Book in Business, Man. and Econs, Asscn of American Publishers), Microtheory: Applications and Origins 1986, Productivity and American Leadership: The Long View (with S. A. Batey Blackman and E. N. Wolff) (Hon. Mention, American Publrs Asscn Annual Awards for Excellence in Publishing 1989) 1989, The Information Economy and the Implications of Unbalanced Growth (with L. Osberg and E. N. Wolff) 1989, The Economics of Mutual Fund Markets: Competition versus Regulation (co-author) 1990, Perfect Markets and Easy Virtue: Business Ethics and the Invisible Hand (co-author) 1991, Entrepreneurship, Management and the Structure of Payoffs 1993, Toward Competition in Local Telephony (with G. Sidak) 1994, Convergence of Productivity: Cross-National Studies and Historical Evidence (with R. R. Nelson and E. N. Wolff) 1994, Transmission Pricing and Stranded Costs in the Electric Power Industry (with J. G. Sidak) 1995, Assessing Educational Practices: The Contribution of Economics (with W. E. Becker) 1995, Baumol's Cost Disease: The Arts and Other victims (co-ed. R. Towse) 1997, Global Trade and Conflicting National Interests 2000, Welfare Economics (with C. A. Wilson) 2001, The Free-Market Innovation Machine: Analyzing the Growth Miracle of Capitalism 2002, Downsizing in America: Reality, Causes, and Consequences (with A. S. Blinder and E. N. Wolff) 2003, Growth, Industrial Organization and Economic Generalities 2003, and 500 articles in professional journals. *Leisure interests:* woodcarving, painting. *Address:* Department of Economics, New York University, 269 Mercer Street, New York, NY 10003 (office); 100 Bleecker Street, Apt 29A, New York, NY 10012, USA (home). *Telephone:* (212) 998-8943 (office). *Fax:* (212) 995-3932 (office). *E-mail:* william.baumol@nyu.edu (office). *Website:* www.econ.nyu.edu (office).

BAUSCH, Pina; German dancer and choreographer; *Artistic Director, Tanztheater Wuppertal Pina Bausch GmbH;* b. 27 July 1940, Solingen; one s.; ed Folkwang School, Essen, Juilliard School, New York; scholarship from German Academical Exchange Service to USA as Special Student of Juilliard School of Music, New York; mem. Dance Company Paul Sanasardo and Donya Feuer, danced at Metropolitan Opera New York, New American Ballet 1960–62; became soloist, Folkwang-Ballett 1962, Artistic Dir, Choreographer and Dancer 1969–73; Dir and Choreographer Tanztheater Wuppertal (renamed Tanztheater Wuppertal Pina Bausch) 1973, directed first 'Ein Fest in Wuppertal', marking 25th anniversary of Tanztheater Wuppertal 1998, further festivals 2001, 2004; guest performances include Schwetzinger Festival, Festival of The Two Worlds, Spoleto, Festival Jacob's Pillow/USA, Salzburg Festival, Stuttgart, Rotterdam, The Hague, London, Manchester 1973; has worked with choreographers Kurt Jooss, Antony Tudor, Lucas Hoving, Hans Züllig, Peter Pabst and especially with dancer and choreographer Jean Cebron; Head Dance Dept, Folkwang Hochschule Essen 1983–89; Artistic Dir Folkwang-Tanzstudio 1983–; choreographed Le Sacre du Printemps (The Rite of Spring) for the Ballet de L'Opéra National de Paris 1997; directed the opera Herzog Blaubarts Burg (Duke Bluebeard's Castle) by Béla Bartok for the Festival Int. d'Art Lyrique d'Aix-en-Provence under the musical direction of Pierre Boulez 1998; staged choreography of Orpheus und Eurydike with the Ballet de L'Opéra Nat. de Paris 2005; Freeman City of Wuppertal 1997; Hon. Public Relations Amb. of the Repub. of Korea 2005; Chevalier Légion d'honneur 2003, Commdr Ordre des Arts et des Lettres 1991, Cruz da Ordem Militar de Santiago de Espada (Portugal) 1994, Orden Pour le Mérite 1997, Bundesverdienstkreuz (First Class) 1986, Großes Verdienstkreuz mit Stem und Schulterband 1997, Commdr's Cross, Order of Grand Duke Gediminas 2003, Komturkreuz des Verdienstordens (Italy) 2004, Orden al Mérito Artístico y Cultural Pablo Neruda' des Consejo Nacional de la Cultura y las Artes de Chile 2007; Dr hc (Bologna) 1999; Laureate hc der Juilliard School, New York 2006; Direzione Onoraria, Accad. Nazionale di Danza, Rome 2006; Folkwang Leistungspreis 1958, Förderpreis für junge Kunstler des Landes Nordrhein-Westfalen 1973, Eduard von der Heydt Prize, Wuppertal 1978, Critics' Prize (Dance), El Circulo de Criticos de Arte (Italy) 1980, Simba Theatre Prize (Italy) 1982, UBU Prize, Miglior Spettacoto Straniero (Italy) 1983, 1997, German Critics' Prize, Akad. der Kunste, Berlin 1984, New York Dance and Performance Bessie Award 1984, Dance Critics' Soc. Prize (Japan) 1987, 'Toleranzorden', Wuppertaler Karnevalvereins 1988, Prize, Int. Academia Medicea 'Lorenzo il Magnifico', Florence 1990, Premio Aurel Milloss in context of Premio Gino Tani, Rome 1990, Prize, Zentrums BRD des Internationalen Theaterinstituts e.V. (ITI) zum Welttheatertag 1990, UBU Prize (Italy) 1990, NRW State Prize 1990, Prize for Dance, Soc. des Auteurs et Compositeurs dramatique, Paris 1991, Rheinischer Kulturpreis, Sparkassenstiftung zur Förderpreis rheinischen Kulturgutes, Dusseldorf 1991, Int. Prize 'Fontana di Roma', Centro Internazionale Arte e Cultura la Sponda 1991, Prize, Danza+Danza magazine, Treviso 1991, Una Vita per la Danza Prize, Positano 1991, UNESCO Picasso Medal, Munich 1993, Eduard von der Heydt Prize, Wuppertal Dance Theatre Ensemble 1993, German Dance Prize, Deutschen Berufsverbandes für Tanzpädagogik e.V. 1995, Joana Maria Gorvin Prize, Deutschen Akad. der Schonen Kunste, Berlin 1995, Berlin Theatre Prize 1997, Prize of Stiftung Preußische Seehandlung 1997, Harry Edmonds Award, International House, New York 1998, Bambi 98 (Kultur) 1998, European Theatre Prize 1998, Samuel H. Scripps American Dance Festival Award 1999, Praemium Imperiale for Theatre and Film, Japan Art Asscn 1999, Life Time Achievement Award, Istanbul Festival 2000, Int. Asscn of Performing Arts Award 2000, Hansischer Goethe Prize 2001, Harbourfront Centre World Leaders Prize, Toronto 2001, Bessies Award, New York 2002, Spanish World Art Prize, Valldigna 2003, Nijinsky Award, Monte Carlo 2004, Golden Mask for Best Foreign Production, Golden Mask Festival of Performing Arts, Moscow 2005, Wuppertal Econ. Prize for City Marketing 2005, Golden Schwebebahn vom Stadtverband der Burger- und Bezirksvereine Wuppertal 2005, Commissioner of the Year Award, European Voice magazine 2005, Leader of a Partnership Award, International Chamber of Commerce of Lithuania 2005, Laurence Olivier Award, London, for Nelken 2006, Special Award from TV3 news service during the traditional awards ceremony, Lietuvos Garbė (Lithuania's Honour) 2006, Wladislav Grabski Award for contrib. to business, Polish Confed. of Pvt. Employers (LEWIATAN). *Films:* performed in Federico Fellini's film E la nave va 1982, directed Die Klage der Kaiserin (The Complaint of the Empress) 1990, performed in Pedro Almodovar's film Hable con ella with excerpts from Café Müller and Masurca Fogo by Pina Bausch 2001. *Choreographed works include:* Fragment (for Folkwang Ballett, music by Béla Bartók) 1968, Im Wind der Zeit (music by Mirko Dorner, staging of Kurt Jooss' version of Henry Purcell's The Fairy Queen for Schwetzinger Festival) (Prize, Second Int. Choreographic Competition, Cologne 1969) 1969, Nachnull 1970, Ballet Aktionen für Tänzer 1971, Tannhäuser-Bacchanal 1972, Wiegenlied 1972, Fritz, 1974, Iphigenie auf Tauris 1974, Ich bring dich um die Ecke 1974, Adagio – Fünf Lieder von Gustaf Mahler 1974, Orpheus und Eurydike 1975, Frühlingsopfer 1975, Die Sieben Todsünden 1976, Blaubart – Beim anhören einer Tonbandaugnahme von Béla Bartóks 'Duke Bluebeard's Castle' 1977, Komm Tanz mit Mir 1977, Renate Wandert aus 1977, Er nimmt sie an der Hand und führt sie in das Schloss, die anderen Folgen… 1978, Café Müller (Critics' Award, Edinburgh 1992) 1978, Kontakthof 1978, Arien 1979, Keuschheitslegende 1979, Ein Stück von Pina Bausch 1980, Bandoneon 1980, Walzer 1982, Nelken 1982, Auf dem Gebirge hat Man ein Geschrei gehört 1984, Two Cigarettes in the Dark 1985, Viktor 1986, Ahnen 1987, Palermo Palermo 1989, Tanzabend II 1991, Das Stück mit dem Schiff 1993, Ein Trauerspiel 1994, Danzón 1995, Nur Du 1996, Der Fensterputzer 1997, Masurca Fogo 1998, Lissabon-Projekt 1998, O Dido 1999, Kontahof 200, Wiesenland 2000, Agua 2001, Für die Kinder von Gestern, Heute und Morgen 2002, Nefés 2003, Ten Chi 2004, Rough Cut 2005. *Film directed:* Die Klage der Kaiserin (The Plaint of the Empress) 1989. *Address:* Tanztheater Wuppertal, Postfach 20-18-13, 42218 Wuppertal, Germany (office). *Telephone:* (202) 5634253 (office). *Fax:* (202) 5638171 (office). *E-mail:* info@pina-bausch.de (office). *Website:* www.pina-bausch.de (office).

BAUTIER, Robert-Henri; French archivist and museum curator; b. 19 April 1922, Paris; s. of the late Edgar Bautier and Suzanne Voyer; m. Anne-Marie Regnier 1948; one d.; ed Ecole des Chartes, Sorbonne and Ecole des Hautes Etudes; archivist, Nat. Archives 1943; Head Archivist, Archives départementales de la Creuse 1944–45; assigned to Ecole Française de Rome 1944–45, head of research for CNRS in Italy 1948–58; Keeper, Archives de France 1948; Prof. Ecole Nat. des Chartes 1961–90; Head, Musée du château de Langeais 1990–92; Curator Musée Jacquemart-André, Chaalis Abbey 1992–2000; Pres. Comm. Int. de Diplomatique 1980 (then Hon. Pres.); Cttee Historic and Scientific Works, Ministry of Nat. Educ. 1989–, Soc. Française d'Héraldique et Sigillographie, Soc. de l'histoire de France, Soc. Nat. des Antiquaires de France, Monumenta Germaniae Historica (Munich), comité français des sciences historiques mem. Inst. de France (Acad. des Inscriptions et Belles Lettres) 1974–; Assoc. Fellow, British Acad.; Fellow, Medieval Acad. of America; Assoc. mem. Acad. royale des Sciences, des Lettres et des Beaux-Arts de Belqique (Brussels), Académie internationale d'Héraldique, Accad. Santa Chiara (Genova) etc.; Fellow of numerous French provincial acads and learned socs; Officier, Légion d'honneur, Ordre nat. du Mérite, Commdr des Palmes académiques, des Arts et des Lettres and other decorations; Dr hc (Univ. of Rome). *Publications:* numerous books and more than 300 articles in learned journals. *Address:* 13 rue de Sévigné, 75004 Paris; Les Rabuteloires, 45360 Chatillon-sur-Loire, France. *Telephone:* 1-48-87-23-38.

BAVČAR, Igor, BSc; Slovenian business executive and fmr politician; *Chairman, Istrabenz Group;* ed Univ. of Ljubljana; journalist, including Chief Ed., Tribuna, Science Critic Journal and KRT Publications, early 1980s; Man. Ada Graf Computer Co. 1986–88; f. Human Rights Council 1988, Dir 1988–90; Minister of the Interior 1990–93; mem. Nat. Ass. 1993–2000, Minister without Portfolio for European Affairs 1997–2000, Minister for European Affairs 2000–02; Chair. Istrabenz Group 2002–. *Leisure interests:* nature, sports. *Address:* Istrabenz Group, C. Zore Perelllo Godina 2, 6000 Koper, Slovenia (office). *Telephone:* (5) 6621500 (office). *Fax:* (5) 6621515 (office). *E-mail:* info@istrabenz.si (office). *Website:* www.istrabenz.si (office).

BAVIN, Rt Rev. Dom Timothy John, MA; British monk; b. 17 Sept. 1935, Northwood, England; s. of Edward Bavin and Marjorie Bavin; ed St George School, Windsor, Brighton Coll., Worcester Coll., Oxford Univ., Cuddesdon Coll.; Asst Priest, St Alban's Cathedral, Pretoria 1961–64; Chaplain, St Alban's Coll., Pretoria 1964–69; Asst Priest, Uckfield, Sussex, England 1969–71; Vicar, Church of the Good Shepherd, Brighton 1971–73; Dean of Johannesburg 1973–74, Bishop 1974–84; Bishop of Portsmouth, England 1985–95; Monk, Order of St Benedict, Alton Abbey 1996–; mem. Oratory of the Good Shepherd 1987–95; Hon. Fellow, Royal School of Church Music 1991. *Publications:* Deacons in the Ministry of the Church 1986, In Tune with Heaven (ed.) 1992. *Leisure interests:* music, walking, gardening. *Address:* Alton Abbey, Alton, Hants., GU34 4AP, England.

BAWDEN, Nina Mary, CBE, MA, JP, FRSL; English novelist; b. 19 Jan. 1925, Ilford, Essex; d. of Charles Mabey and Ellaline Ursula May Mabey; m. 1st H. W. Bawden 1947; two s. (one deceased); m. 2nd Austen S. Kark 1954 (died 2002); one d. two step-d.; ed Ilford Co. High School, Somerville Coll., Oxford;

Asst, Town and Country Planning Asscn 1946–47; JP, Surrey 1968; Pres. Soc. of Women Writers and Journalists 1981–; Hon. Fellow, Somerville Coll., Oxford; mem. PEN; council mem. Soc. of Authors; Yorkshire Post Novel of the Year Award 1976, Edgar Allan Poe Award, Phoenix Award 1993, S. T. Dupont Golden Pen Award for Services to Literature 2004. *Publications:* Who Calls the Tune 1953, The Odd Flamingo 1954, The Solitary Child 1956, Devil by the Sea 1958, Just Like a Lady 1960, In Honour Bound 1961, Tortoise by Candlelight 1963, A Little Love, A Little Learning 1965, A Woman of My Age 1967, The Grain of Truth 1969, The Birds on the Trees 1970, Anna Apparent 1972, George Beneath a Paper Moon 1974, Afternoon of a Good Woman 1976, Familiar Passions 1979, Walking Naked 1981, The Ice House 1983, Circles of Deceit (also adapted for TV) 1987, Family Money (also adapted for TV) 1991, In My Own Time (autobiog.) 1994, A Nice Change 1997, Dear Austen 2005; for children: The Secret Passage 1963, The Runaway Summer 1969, Carrie's War 1973 (Phoenix Award 1993) (also adapted for BBC TV 2003), The Peppermint Pig 1975 (Guardian Prize for Children's Literature 1975), The Finding 1985, Princess Alice 1985, Keeping Henry 1988, The Outside Child 1989, Humbug 1992, The Real Plato Jones 1993, Granny the Pig 1995, Off the Road 1998, Ruffian on the Stair 2001. *Leisure interests:* theatre, cinema, travel, croquet, friends. *Address:* Curtis Brown Ltd, Haymarket House, 28–29 Harmarket, London, SW1Y 4SP (office); 22 Noel Road, London, N1 8HA, England; 19 Kapodistriou, Nauplion 21100, Greece. *Telephone:* (20) 7393-4400 (office); (20) 7226-2839 (office). *Fax:* (20) 7393-4401 (office); (20) 7359-7103. *E-mail:* info@curtisbrown.co.uk (office). *Website:* www.curtisbrown.co.uk (office).

BAWOYEU, Jean Alingue; Chadian politician; b. 18 Aug. 1937, N'Djamena; s. of Marc Alingue Bawoyeu and Tabita Poureng; m. Esther Azina 1960; three s. four d.; fmr Pres. of Nat. Ass.; Prime Minister of Chad 1991–92; Chair. Union pour la Démocratie et la République; Presidential Cand. for elections 2001. *Address:* BP 1122, N'Djamena, Chad.

BAXENDELL, Sir Peter (Brian), Kt, CBE, BSc, ARSM, FREng; British petroleum engineer; b. 28 Feb. 1925, Runcorn; s. of Lesley Wilfred Edward Baxendell and Evelyn Mary Baxendell (née Gaskin); m. Rosemary Lacey 1949; two s. two d.; ed St Francis Xavier's Coll., Liverpool, Royal School of Mines, Imperial Coll., London; with Royal Dutch/Shell Group 1946–95; Anglo-Egyptian Oilfields 1947–50; Compañía Shell de Venezuela 1950–63; Tech. Dir Shell-BP Nigeria 1963–66, Man. Dir 1969–72; Shell Int. London, Eastern Region 1966–69; Chair. Shell UK 1973–79; Man. Dir Royal Dutch/Shell Group 1973–85; Vice-Chair. Cttee of Man. Dirs 1979–82, Chair. 1982–85; Dir Shell Transport and Trading Co. 1973–95 (Chair. 1979–85); Dir Hawker Siddeley Group 1984–91, Chair. 1986–91; Dir Inchcape PLC 1986–93; Dir Sun Life Assurance Co. of Canada 1986–97; mem. Univ. Grants Cttee 1983–89; Fellow, Imperial Coll. Science and Tech., London 1983, mem. Governing Body 1983–99 (Deputy Chair. 1992–99); Commdr Order of Orange-Nassau; Hon. DSc (Heriot-Watt) 1982, (Queen's, Belfast) 1986, (London) 1986, (Loughborough) 1987. *Leisure interests:* fishing, tennis. *Address:* c/o Royal Dutch/Shell Group, Shell Centre, London, SE1 7NA, England.

BAXTER, Glen; British artist; b. 4 March 1944, Leeds; s. of the late Charles Baxter and of Florence Baxter; m. Carole Agis; one s. one d.; ed Cockburn Grammar School, Leeds and Leeds Coll. of Art; has exhibited his drawings in New York, San Francisco, Venice, Amsterdam, Lille, Munich, Tokyo and Paris and represented UK at the Sydney Biennale 1986, Adelaide Festival 1992, Hôtel Furkablick (Switzerland) 1993; major retrospectives at Musée de l'Abbaye Sainte-Croix, Les Sables d'Olonne, France 1987, 'Une Ame en Tourment', Centre nat. de l'art imprimé Chatou, Paris; illustrated Charlie Malarkey and the Belly Button Machine 1986; tapestry commissioned by French Govt to commemorate 8th centenary of death of Richard the Lion-Heart. *Television:* The South Bank Show: Profile of Glen Baxter 1983. *Publications:* The Impending Gleam 1981, Atlas 1982 and Glen Baxter: His Life: The Years of Struggle 1983, Jodhpurs in the Quantocks 1986, Welcome to the Weird World of Glen Baxter 1989, The Billiard Table Murders, A Gladys Babbington Morton Mystery 1990, Glen Baxter Returns to Normal 1992, The Collected Blurtings of Baxter 1993, The Further Blurtings of Baxter 1994, The Wonder Book of Sex 1995, Glen Baxter's Gourmet Guide 1997, Blizzards of Tweed 1999, Podium 2000, The Unhinged World of Glen Baxter 2001, Trundling Grunts 2002. *Leisure interests:* marquetry, snood retrieval. *Address:* c/o Chris Beetles Gallery, 10 Ryder Street, St James's, London, SW1Y 6QB, England (office). *E-mail:* Glen.Baxter@tesco.net. *Website:* www.glenbaxter.com (home).

BAXTER, Rodney James, ScD, GradDip(Theol), FRS, FAA; Australian (b. British) mathematical physicist and academic; *Visiting Fellow, Mathematical Sciences Institute, Australian National University;* b. 8 Feb. 1940, London, England; s. of Thomas J. Baxter and Florence Baxter; m. Elizabeth A. Phillips 1968; one s. one d.; ed Bancroft's School, Essex, Trinity Coll., Cambridge and Australian Nat. Univ.; Reservoir Engineer, Iraq Petroleum Co. 1964–65; Research Fellow, ANU 1965–68, Fellow 1971–81, Prof., Dept of Theoretical Physics, Research School of Physical Sciences 1981–, jtly with School of Math. Sciences 1989–, now Visiting Fellow; Asst Prof., MIT, USA 1968–70; Royal Soc. Research Prof., Univ. of Cambridge 1992; Pawsey Medal, Australian Acad. of Science 1975, IUPAP Boltzmann Medal 1980, Dannie Heineman Prize, American Inst. of Physics 1987, Massey Medal, Inst. of Physics 1994, Onsager Prize, American Physical Soc. 2006. *Publication:* Exactly Solved Models in Statistical Mechanics 1982, contrib. to professional journals. *Leisure interest:* theatre. *Address:* Centre for Mathematics and Its Applications, Mathematical Sciences Institute, Building 27, Australian National University, Canberra, ACT 0200, Australia (office).

BAYAR, Sanjaagiin (Sanjiin); Mongolian politician and diplomatist; *Prime Minister;* b. 1956, Ulan Bator; ed Moscow State Univ.; fmr officer, Ulan Bator City Ass. and Nairamdal Dist Office 1978–79; officer Gen. HQ Nat. Defence Army 1979–83; journalist and ed., Novosti Mongolii newspaper, Chief Ed. and Gen. Ed. Montsame news agency 1983–88; Deputy Head of Admin Agency, Mongolian Radio TV 1988–90; mem. Nat. Congress 1990–92; Head, Strategy and Research Center, Ministry of Defence 1992–97; Chief of Staff, Office of the Pres. 1997–2001; Amb. to Russian Fed. 2001–05; Chair. Mongolian People's Revolutionary Party 2005–07, Chair. 2007–; Prime Minister of Mongolia 2007–. *Address:* State Palace, Sükhbaatayrn Talbai 1, Ulan Bator (office); Mongolian People's Revolutionary Party, Sukhbaatar District, UB-14191, Ulan Bator, Mongolia (office). *Telephone:* 50067805 (office). *Fax:* 50067805 (office). *E-mail:* contact@mprp.mn (office). *Website:* www.mprp.mn (office).

BAYARDI, José, MD; Uruguayan physician and politician; *Minister of National Defence;* b. 30 June 1955, Montevideo; Deputy (Vertiente Artiguista) Cámara de Representantes (Parl.) 1990–; Deputy Minister of Nat. Defence 2005–08, Minister of Nat. Defence 2008–; Chair. Vertiente Artiguista 1994–2001. *Address:* Ministry of National Defence, Edif. General Artigas, Avda 8 de Octubre 2628 Montevideo, Uruguay (office). *Telephone:* (2) 4872828 (office). *Fax:* (2) 4809397 (office). *E-mail:* rrpp.secretaria@mdn.gub.uy (home). *Website:* www.mdn.gub.uy (office).

BAYARTSAIKHAN, Nadmidyn; Mongolian academic and politician; b. 27 Jan. 1971, Ulan Bator; m.; two c.; fmr Lecturer and Prof.; mem. Parl., fmr Chair. Standing Cttee on Budget; Minister of Finance 2006–07; mem. Mongolian People's Revolutionary Party (MPRP); fmr Pres. Nat. Asscn of Mongolian Agricultural Cooperatives (NAMAC). *Address:* Mongolian People's Revolutionary Party, Baga Toiruu 37/1, Ulan Bator, Mongolia (office). *Telephone:* (11) 320432 (office). *Fax:* (11) 323503 (office). *E-mail:* contact@mprp.mn (office). *Website:* www.mprp.mn (office).

BAYE, Nathalie; French actress; b. 6 July 1948, Mainneville; d. of Claude Baye and Denise Coustet; one d. by Johnny Hallyday; ed Conservatoire nat. d'art dramatique de Paris; Femme en or—Trophée Whirlpool 2000. *Stage appearances include:* Galapages 1972, Liola 1973, les trois soeurs 1978, Adriana Monti 1986, Les fausses confidences 1993, La parisienne 1995. *Films include:* Two People 1972, La nuit américaine 1973, La gueule ouverte 1974, La Gifle 1974, Un jour la fête 1974, Le voyage de noces 1975, Le plein de super 1976, Mado 1976, L'homme qui aimait les femmes 1977, Monsieur Papa 1977, La communion solennelle 1977, La chambre verte 1978, Mon premier amour 1978, La mémoire courte 1978, Sauve qui peut 1979, Je vais craquer 1979, Une semaine de vacances 1980, Provinciale 1980, Beau-père, Une étrange affaire, L'ombre rouge 1981, Le retour de Martin Guerre 1981, La balance (César for Best Actress 1983) 1982, J'ai épousé une ombre 1982, Notre histoire 1983, Rive droite, rive gauche 1984, Détective 1984, Le neveu de Beethoven 1985, Lune de Miel 1985, De guerre lasse 1987, En toute innocence 1988, La Baule-les-Pins 1990, Un week-end sur deux 1990, The Man Inside 1990, L'Affaire Wallraff 1991, La Voix 1992, Mensonges 1993, La machine 1994, Les soldats de l'espérance 1994, Enfants da salud 1996, Si je t'aime... prends garde à toi 1998, Food of Love 1998, Paparazzi 1998, Vénus beauté 1999, Une liaison pornographique 1999, Ça ira mieux demain 2000, Selon Matthieu, Barnie et ses petites contrariétés 2001, Absolument fabuleux 2001, Catch Me If You Can 2002, La Fleur du mal 2003, Les Sentiments 2003, France Boutique 2003, Une vie à t'attendre 2004, L'un reste, l'autre part 2005, Le Petit Lieutenant (César Award for Best Actress 2006) 2005, Ne le dis à personne 2006, Mon fils à moi 2006. *Address:* c/o Artmédia, 20 avenue Rapp, 75007 Paris, France (office).

BAYER, Oswald; German ecclesiastic and professor of theology; b. 30 Sept. 1939, Nagold; s. of Emil Bayer and Hermine Bayer; m. Eva Bayer 1966 (deceased 1993); ed Tübingen, Bonn and Rome, Italy; Vicar, Evangelische Landeskirche, Württemberg 1964; Asst Univ. of Tübingen 1965–68; Evangelical Stift, Tübingen 1968–71; Pastor, Tübingen 1972–74; Prof. of Systematic Theology, Univ. of Bochum 1974–79, Univ. of Tübingen 1979–, Dir Inst. of Christian Ethics 1979–95; Ed. Zeitschrift für Systematische Theologie und Religionsphilosophie 1986–2006. *Publications:* numerous books and essays on theological and philosophical topics. *Address:* Kurhausstr. 138, 53773 Tübingen (office); Am Unteren Herrlesberg 36, 72074 Hennef, Germany (home). *Telephone:* (2242) 918951 (office). *E-mail:* oswaldbayer@unitybox.de (office).

BAYERO, Alhaji Ado; Nigerian administrator; *Emir of Kano;* b. 25 July 1930, Kano; s. of Alhaji Abdullahi Bayer, Emir of Kano; m. Halimatu Sadiya; ed Kano Middle School; clerk, Bank of West Africa; MP, Northern House of Ass. 1955–57; Chief of Kano Native Authority Police 1957–62; Amb. to Senegal 1962–63; 13th Emir of Kano 1963–; Chancellor, Univ. of Nigeria, Nsukka, E Nigeria 1966–75, Chancellor Univ. of Ibadan 1975–85. *Leisure interests:* photography, riding, reading. *Address:* c/o University of Ibadan, Ibadan, Nigeria.

BAYH, Evan, BS, JD; American politician; *Senator from Indiana;* b. 26 Dec. 1955, Terre Haute, Ind.; s. of Birch Evans Bayh Jr and Marvella Hern; m.; ed Indiana Univ. and Univ. of Virginia; Sec. of State of Indiana 1987–89; Gov. of Indiana 1989–97; partner Baker & Daniel Assocs. Indianapolis 1997; Senator from Indiana 1999–; Democrat. *Address:* 463 Russell Senate Office Building, Washington, DC 20510-0001; 10 West Market Street, Suite 1650, Indianapolis, IN 46204-2934, USA. *Telephone:* (202) 224-5623 (office). *Website:* bayh.senate.gov (office).

BAYI, Filbert, BSc (Educ.); Tanzanian sports administrator and fmr athlete; *Secretary-General, National Olympic Committee;* b. (Habiye), 22 June 1953, Karatu, Arusha Region; s. of the late Sanka Bayi and of Magdalena Qwaray; m. Anna Lyimo 1977; two s. two d.; ed Univ. of Texas at El Paso, USA; joined Air Transport Battalion (TPDF), Dar es Salaam; beat Tanzanian Nat. Champion over 1,500m, Dar es Salaam 1972; 1,500m Gold Medal Nat. Championships, Dar es Salaam 1972, All African Games, Lagos, Nigeria (record time) 1973; first competed Europe June 1973; 1,500m Gold Medal (and world record), Commonwealth Games, Christchurch, New Zealand 1974; 1,500m Gold Medal, All African Games, Algiers, Algeria 1978; 1,500m Silver Medal Commonwealth Games, Edmonton, Canada 1978; 3,000m Steeplechase Silver Medal, Olympic Games, Moscow, USSR 1980; Athletic Nat. Coach; Army Chief Coach ATHL; Sec. TAAA Tech. Cttee, Tanzania Olympic Cttee; mem. TAAA Exec. Cttee, IAAF Tech. Cttee; IAAF Athletic Coaching Lecturer; Nat. Chief Instructor and Athletic Coach; IOC Nat. Course Dir; Exec. mem. Nat. Olympic Cttee, Sec.-Gen. Nat. Olympic Cttee 2002–; Gen. Chair. Bd of Dirs Filbert Bayi Nursery, Primary and Secondary School; United Repub. of Tanzania Medal 1995. *Leisure interests:* reading, sports, watching TV, talking to children. *Address:* Filbert Bayi Nursery and Primary School—Kimara, Morogoro Road, PO Box 60240, Dar es Salaam, Tanzania. *Telephone:* (22) 2420635 (office); (22) 2420634 (home). *Fax:* (22) 2420178 (office); (22) 2420178 (home). *E-mail:* fbayi@ud.co.tz (office); fsbayi@yahoo.com (home). *Website:* www.filbertbayischools.org (home).

BAYKAM, Bedri; Turkish painter, writer and politician; b. 26 April 1957, Ankara; s. of Suphi Baykam and Mutahhar Baykam; m. Sibel Yağci; one s.; ed French Lycée, Istanbul, Univ. of Paris I (Panthéon-Sorbonne), France, Calif. Coll. of Arts and Crafts, Oakland, Calif., USA; 86 solo exhbns Paris, Brussels, Rome, New York, Istanbul, Munich, Stockholm, Helsinki, London 1963–99; mem. Cen. Bd CHP (Republican Party of the People) 1995–98; f. Piramid Publishing 1998; Founder The Patriotic Movement 2005; Painter of the Year, Nokta magazine 1987, 1989, 1990, 1996–97, Best Artist and Best Performance, Art Jonction, Cannes 1994. *Major art works include:* The Prostitute's Room 1981, The Painting 1985, This Has Been Done Before 1987, Livart 1994, The Years of 68 1997, Curatorial Schizophrenia 2005. *Publications include:* The Brain of Paint (Boyanin Beyni) 1990, Monkey's Right to Paint 1994, Mustafa Kemal's on Duty Now 1994, Secular Turkey Without Concession 1995, Fleeting Moments, Enduring Delights 1996, His Eyes Always Rest on Us 1997, The Color of the Era 1997, The Years of 68 (Vols 1 and 2) 1998–99, I'm Nothing but I'm Everything 1999, The Last Condottiere of the Millennium, Che 2000, The Bone 2000 (English trans. 2005), The Millennium Crack 2002, End of the Empire of Fear 2004. *Leisure interests:* tennis, football, music, pool. *Address:* Piramid Publishing, Palanga Cad. 33/23, Ortaköy, Istanbul (office); Palanga Cad 33/23, Ortaköy, Istanbul 80840, Turkey (home). *Telephone:* (212) 2584464 (office); (212) 2580809 (home). *Fax:* (212) 2273465 (office). *E-mail:* bedbay@tnn.net (office); bedbay@turk.net (home). *Website:* www.bedribaykam.com (office).

BAYLEY, John Oliver, MA, FBA, CBE; British academic; b. 27 March 1925; s. of F. J. Bayley; m. 1st (Jean) Iris Murdoch 1956 (died 1999); m. 2nd Audhild Villers 2000; ed Eton Coll. and New Coll., Oxford; served in army 1943–47; mem. St Antony's and Magdalen Colls, Oxford 1951–55; Fellow and Tutor in English, New Coll., Oxford 1955–74; Warton Prof. of English Literature and Fellow, St Catherine's Coll., Oxford 1974–92; Heinemann Literary Award. *Publications:* In Another Country (novel) 1954, The Romantic Survival: A Study in Poetic Evolution 1956, The Characters of Love 1961, Tolstoy and the Novel 1966, Pushkin: A Comparative Commentary 1971, The Uses of Division: Unity and Disharmony in Literature 1976, An Essay on Hardy 1978, Shakespeare and Tragedy 1981, The Order of Battle at Trafalgar 1987, The Short Story: Henry James to Elizabeth Bowen 1988, Housman's Poems 1992, Alice (novel) 1994, The Queer Captain (novel) 1995, George's Lair (novel) 1996, The Red Hat 1997, Iris and the Friends: A Year of Memories 1999, Widower's House 2001, Hand Luggage – An Anthology 2001, The Power of Delight – A Lifetime in Literature: Essays 1962–2002 2005. *Address:* c/o St Catherine's College, Manor Road, Oxford, OX1 3UJ, England.

BAYLEY, Stephen Paul, MA; British design consultant, writer, exhibition organiser and museum administrator; *Principal, Eye-Q Ltd.;* b. 13 Oct. 1951, Cardiff; s. of Donald Bayley and Anne Bayley; m. Flo Fothergill 1981; one s. one d.; ed Quarry Bank School, Liverpool, Univ. of Manchester, Univ. of Liverpool School of Architecture; Lecturer in History of Art, Open Univ. 1974–76, Univ. of Kent 1976–80; Dir Conran Foundation 1981–89; Dir Boilerhouse Project, Victoria and Albert Museum London 1982–86; Founding Dir then Chief Exec. Design Museum 1986–89; Prin. Eye-Q Ltd (design consultancy) 1991–; Creative Dir New Millennium Experience Co. 1997–98 (resgnd); design and architecture Corresp., The Observer; lectured throughout the UK and abroad; Fellow Liverpool Inst. of Performing Arts 2000; Hon. Fellow, Univ. of Wales Inst., Cardiff 2007; Chevalier des Arts et Lettres (France) 1990; Periodical Publrs Asscn Magazine Columnist of the Year 1995. *Publications include:* In Good Shape 1979, The Albert Memorial 1981, Harley Earl and the Dream Machine 1983, Conran Directory of Design 1985, Sex, Drink and Fast Cars 1986, Commerce and Culture 1989, Taste 1991, General Knowledge 1996, Labour Camp 1998, Moving Objects (ed.) 1999, General Knowledge 2000, Sex: An Intimate History (ed.) 2001, Dictionary of Idiocy 2003, Life's a Pitch 2007, Design: Intelligence made Visible 2007, Cars 2008. *Leisure interests:* travel-related services, solitary sports, books. *Address:* 176 Kennington Park Road, London, SE11 4BT, England (office). *Telephone:* (20) 7820-8899. *Fax:* (20) 7820-9966 (office). *E-mail:* guru@stephenbayley.com (office).

BAYM, Gordon Alan, AM, PhD, FAAS; American physicist and academic; *Professor of Physics, University of Illinois;* b. 1 July 1935, New York; s. of Louis Baym and Lillian Baym; two s. two d.; ed Cornell Univ., Harvard Univ.; Fellow, Universitetets Institut for Teoretisk Fysik, Copenhagen 1960–62; Lecturer, Univ. of Calif., Berkeley 1962–63; Prof. of Physics, Univ. of Ill., Urbana 1963–; Visiting Prof., Univs. of Tokyo and Kyoto 1968, Nordita, Copenhagen 1970, 1976, Niels Bohr Inst. 1976, Univ. of Nagoya 1979; Visiting Scientist, Academia Sinica, Beijing 1979; mem. Advisory Bd Inst. of Theoretical Physics, Santa Barbara, Calif. 1978–83; mem. Sub-Cttee on Theoretical Physics NSF 1980–81, Physics Advisory Cttee 1982–85; mem. Nuclear Science Advisory Cttee, Dept of Energy/NSF 1982–86; mem. Editorial Bd Procs. NAS 1986–92; Trustee Assoc. Univ. Inc. 1986–90; Fellow American Acad. of Arts and Sciences, American Physical Soc.; Research Fellow, Alfred P. Sloan Foundation 1965–68; NSF Postdoctoral Fellow 1960–62; Trustee, Assoc. Univs Inc. 1986–90; Assoc. Ed. Nuclear Physics; mem. American Astronomical Soc., Int. Astronomical Union, NAS; Sr US Scientist Award, Alexander von Humboldt Foundation 1983. *Publications:* Quantum Statistical Mechanics (jt author) 1962, Lectures on Quantum Mechanics 1969, Neutron Stars 1970, Neutron Stars and the Properties of Matter at High Density 1977, Landau Fermi-Liquid Theory (jt author) 1991. *Leisure interests:* photography and mountains. *Address:* Loomis Laboratory of Physics, University of Illinois, 1110 West Green Street, Urbana, IL 61801, USA. *Telephone:* (217) 333-4363. *Fax:* (217) 333-9819.

BAYMENOV, Alikhan Mukhamediyevich; Kazakhstani politician; *Chairman, Bright Road—Democratic Party of Kazakhstan;* b. 25 March 1959, Karaganda; held numerous govt posts including Head of Presidential Admin 1998–99; Minister of Labour and Social Security 2000–01; Co-founder Democratic Choice of Kazakhstan party 2001; Co-founder and Chair. Bright Road—Democratic Party of Kazakhstan (Ak Zhol) 2002–; unsuccessful presidential cand. 2005. *Address:* Bright Road—Democratic Party of Kazakhstan (Ak Zhol), 010000 Astana, Imanov 18/7, Kazakhstan (office). *Telephone:* (7172) 22-10-66 (office). *Fax:* (7172) 22-14-50 (office). *E-mail:* oral@kepter.kz (office). *Website:* www.akzhol.kz (office).

BAYNE, Sir Nicholas Peter, KCMG, MA, DPhil; British diplomatist (retd); *Fellow, International Trade Policy Unit, London School of Economics;* b. 15 Feb. 1937, London; s. of the late Capt. Ronald Bayne, RN and of Elizabeth Bayne (née Ashcroft); m. Diana Wilde 1961; three s. (one deceased); ed Eton Coll. and Christ Church, Oxford; joined HM Diplomatic Service 1961; served in Manila 1963–66, Bonn 1969–72; seconded to HM Treasury 1974–75; Financial Counsellor, Paris 1975–79; Head of Econ. Relations Dept, FCO 1979–82; Royal Inst. of Int. Affairs 1982–83; Amb. to Zaïre (also accred to Congo, Rwanda, Burundi) 1983–84; Amb. and Perm. Rep. to OECD, Paris 1985–88; Deputy Under-Sec. of State, FCO 1988–92; High Commr in Canada 1992–96; Fellow, Int. Trade Policy Unit, LSE 1997–. *Publications:* Hanging Together: The Seven-Power Summits (with R. Putnam) 1984, Hanging In There: The G7 and G8 Summit in Maturity and Renewal 2000, The Grey Wares of North-West Anatolia and their Relations to the Early Greek Settlements 2000, The New Economic Diplomacy (with S. Woolcock) 2003, Staying Together: The G8 Summit Confronts the 21st Century 2005. *Leisure interests:* reading, sightseeing. *Address:* 2 Chetwynd House, Hampton Court, Surrey, KT8 9BS, England.

BAYROU, François; French politician; *President, Mouvement démocrate;* b. 25 May 1951, Bordères, Basses-Pyrénées; s. of Calixte Bayrou and Emma Sarthou; m. Elisabeth Perlant; three s. three d.; ed Lycée de Nay-Bourdettes, Lycée Montaigne, Bordeaux and Univ. of Bordeaux III; fmr school teacher; Prof., Pau 1974–79; special attachment to Office of Minister of Agric. 1979; Ed.-in-Chief, Démocratie Moderne (weekly) 1980–; Nat. Sec. Centre des Démocrates Sociaux (now Force démocrate) 1980–86, Deputy Sec.-Gen. 1986–94, Pres. 1994–97 (then merged into Nouvelle UDF then into Union pour la Démocratie Française (UDF)), Gen. Del. (UDF) 1989–91, Sec. Gen. 1991–94, Pres. 1998–2007; Pres. Mouvement démocrate 2007–; Conseiller Gen. Pau 1982–93, 2008–; Pres. Conseil Gen. des Pyrénées-Atlantiques 1992–; Conseiller Régional, Aquitaine 1982–86; Town Councillor, Pau 1988–92; Adviser to Pierre Pflimlin (Pres. of Ass. of EC) 1984–86; Deputy to Nat. Ass. 1986–93, 1997–99, 2002–; Minister of Nat. Educ. 1993–95, also of Higher Educ., Research and Professional Training 1995–97; mem. European Parl. 1999–2002; presidential cand. 2002, 2007. *Publications include:* La Décennie des mal-appris 1990, Le roi libre 1994, Henri IV, le roi libre 1994, le Droit au sens 1996, Saint-louis 1997, Henri IV 1998, L'Edit de Nantes 1998, Hors des sentiers battus 1999, Relève 2001, Oui : Plaidoyer pour la Constitution européenne 2005, Au nom du Tier-Etat 2006. *Leisure interests:* raising horses, literature. *Address:* 34 Rue Henri Faisans, 64000 Pau (office); Mouvement Démocrate, 133 Bis Rue de l'Université, 75007 Paris (office); 27 rue Duboué, 64000 Pau, France (home). *Telephone:* 5-59-30-61-91 (office); 1-53-59-20-00 (office). *E-mail:* f.bayrou@udf.org (office); fbayrou@assemblee-nationale.fr (office). *Website:* www.bayrou.fr.

BAYÜLKEN, Ümit Halûk; Turkish diplomatist; b. 7 July 1921, Istanbul; s. of Staff Officer H. Hüsnü Bayülken and Melek Bayülken; m. Valihe Salci 1952; one s. one d.; ed Lycée of Haydarpasa, Istanbul and Univ. of Ankara (Political Sciences); with Ministry of Foreign Affairs 1944–; Reserve Officer in Army 1945–47; Vice-Consul, Frankfurt (Main) 1947–49; First Sec., Bonn 1950–51; Ministry of Foreign Affairs 1951–53; First Sec. Turkish Perm. Mission to UN 1953–57, Counsellor 1957–59; Turkish Rep. to London Jt Cttee on Cyprus 1959–60; Dir-Gen., Policy Planning Group, Ankara 1960–63, Deputy Sec.-Gen. for Political Affairs 1963–64, Sec.-Gen. 1964–66; Amb. to UK 1966–69, concurrently accred to Malta 1968–1969; Perm. Rep. of Turkey to UN 1969–71; Minister of Foreign Affairs 1971–74; Sec.-Gen. CENTO 1975–77; Sec.-Gen. of the Presidency 1977–80; Minister of Defence 1980–83; mem. of Parl. from Antalya 1983–87; Pres. Atlantic Treaty Asscn (Turkey) 1987–90; Pres. of Turkish Parl. Union 1992–; Hon. mem. Mexican Acad. Int. Law, etc.; Hon. GCVO (UK), Order of Isabel la Católica (Spain), Grosses Bundesverdienstkreuz (FRG), numerous other int. awards. *Publications:* lectures, articles, studies and essays on minorities, Cyprus, principles of foreign policy, int. relations and disputes, including the Cyprus Question in the UN 1975, Collective Security and Defence Organizations in Changing World Conditions 1976, Turkey and the Regional Security Interests 1991. *Leisure interests:* music, painting, reading. *Address:* Nergiz Sokak No. 15/20, Cankaya, Ankara, Turkey. *Telephone:* (212) 1270858.

BAZER, Fuller W., MSc, PhD; American biologist and academic; *Regents Fellow, O.D. Butler Chair in Animal Science, Vice-President for Research and Associate Dean for Agricultural and Life Sciences, Texas A&M University;* ed Centenary Coll. of La, La State Univ., N Carolina State Univ.; Grad. Research Prof. in Animal Science, NC State Univ., then Research Prof. in Paediatrics, Univ. of Fla –1992; joined Faculty of Biosciences, Tex. A&M Univ. 1992, currently holds several positions including Regents Fellow, Prof. and O.D. Butler Chair in Animal Science, Vice-Pres. for Research and Exec. Assoc. Dean for Agricultural and Life Sciences and Dir Centre for Animal Biotechnology, Inst. of Biosciences and Tech. (Dir IBT 1994–2001); fmr Pres. and Ed.-in-Chief, Biology of Reproduction Journal, Soc. for the Study of Reproduction (SSR); fmr Assoc. Dir Tex. Agricultural Experimental Station; co-f. Gordon Research Conf. on Reproductive Tract Biology; Fellow AAAS; Tex. A&M Vice Chancellor for Agric. Award in Excellence for Research, L.E. Casida Award for Grad. Educ., American Soc. of Animal Science Physiology and Endocrinology, distinguished service awards from Soc. for the Study of Reproduction Research, Biotechnology 94, Distinguished Achievement in Agric. Award, Gamma Sigma Delta 1996, Alexander von Humboldt Research Award in Agric. 2000, Wolf Prize for Agric. 2003, SSR Research Award, SSR Distinguished Award, SSR Carl G. Hartman Award 2004. *Publications:* Endocrinology of Pregnancy (Ed.) 1998; numerous articles in professional journals. *Address:* Department of Animal Science, 442 D Kleberg, Mail Stop 2471, Texas A&M University, College Station, TX 77843-2471, USA (office). *Telephone:* (979) 862-2659 (office). *Fax:* (979) 862-2662 (office). *E-mail:* fbazer@cvm.tamu.edu (office). *Website:* cerh.tamu.edu, www.ibt.tamhsc.edu (office).

BAZHANOV, Yevgeny Petrovich, CSc, DHist; Russian diplomatist, scientist and journalist; *Vice-Rector for Research, Diplomatic Academy of the Ministry of Foreign Affairs;* b. 5 Nov. 1946, Lvov, Ukraine; m.; ed Nanyan Univ., Singapore, Moscow Inst. of Int. Relations, Inst. of the Far East, Diplomatic Acad., Inst. of Oriental Studies; mem. staff, USSR Ministry of Foreign Affairs 1970–73; Vice-Consul, USSR Gen. Consulate, San Francisco 1973–79; Counsellor, USSR Embassy in Beijing 1981–85; consultant, Int. Dept, Cen. CPSU Cttee; mem. Exec. Cttee Asscn for Dialogue and Co-operation in Asian-Pacific Region 1991; mem. Nat. Cttee on Security, 1996; Vice-Rector for Research, Diplomatic Acad. of the Ministry of Foreign Affairs 1991–; Hon. Prof., People's Univ., Beijing, China 1999; mem. Int. Ecological Acad., Acad. of Humanitarian Research, Acad. of Political Sciences, USA, Asscn of Russian Sinologists 1986–, Nat. Cttee on Trade and Econ. Co-operation with the Pacific-Asian Countries, Asscn of Russian Diplomats 1999–, Political Science Asscn, Asscn of Asian Studies, Russia's Council on Foreign Policy; Distinguished Scholar of the Russian Fed. 1997; numerous prizes for journalistic and scholarly articles. *Publications:* China and the World 1990, Studies in Contemporary International Development. Vols I–III 2002 and 14 other books and over 1,000 articles and book chapters on world affairs, foreign policies and Russia's internal and foreign policy. *Address:* Diplomatic Academy of the Ministry of Foreign Affairs, Moscow 119992, 53/2, Ostozhenka (office); 12165 Moscow, 30 Kutuzovsky Av. #462, Russia (home). *Telephone:* (495) 208-94-61 (office); (495) 249-15-60 (home). *Fax:* (495) 208-94-66 (office). *E-mail:* icipu@online.ru (office). *Website:* www.dipacademy.ru/english (office).

BAZIN, Henry; Haitian politician; ed in France; trained as economist; fmr consultant to UN on Third World Affairs; fmr Minister of Finance, Minister of Economy and Finance –2006. *Address:* Ministry of Economy and Finance, Palais des Ministrères, rue Monseigneur Guilloux, Port-au-Prince, Haiti (office).

BAZIN, Marc Louis, LenD; Haitian politician; *President, Mouvement pour l'Instauration de la Démocratie en Haïti (MIDH);* b. 6 March 1932, Saint-Marc; s. of Louis Bazin and Simone St Vil; m. Marie Yolène Sam 1981; ed Lycée Petion, Port-au-Prince, Univ. of Paris, Solvay Inst. Brussels and American Univ. Washington, DC; Admin. Asst Ministry of Foreign Affairs 1950; Prof. of Civic Educ. Lycée Petion, Haiti 1951; Legal Adviser, Cabinet Rivière (real estate agency), Paris 1958; Lecturer in Commercial Law, Paris 1960; Tech. Adviser, Treasury Dept, Rabat, Morocco 1962, Deputy Gen. Counsel 1964; Technical Adviser, Ministry of Finance, Rabat 1965; Sr Loan Officer, IBRD, Washington, DC 1968; Deputy Chief IBRD Mission in West Africa, Ivory Coast 1970; Div. Chief, IBRD, Washington, DC 1972; Dir Riverblindness Program, WHO, Upper Volta 1976; Man. Dir Industrial Devt Fund, Port-au-Prince 1980; Minister of Finance and Econ. Affairs 1982; Special rep. of IBRD at UN 1982; Div. Chief for int. orgs IBRD 1986; Pres. Mouvement pour l'Instauration de la Démocratie en Haiti (MIDH) allied with ANDP 1986–; Prime Minister of Haiti 1992–93; Officer, Order of the Ouissam Alaouite (Morocco), Kt of Nat. Order of Merit (Burkina Faso). *Address:* Mouvement pour l'Instauration de la Démocratie en Haïti (MIDH), 114 ave Jean Paul II, Port-au-Prince, Haiti. *Telephone:* 245-8377.

BAZOLI, Giovanni; Italian lawyer, academic and banking executive; *Chairman, Sanpaolo IMI SpA;* b. 18 Dec. 1932, Brescia; Prof. of Law, Faculty of Econs, Univ. Cattolica di Milano; Chair. Banca Intesa SpA 1982–2006, Chair. Supervisory Bd Sanpaolo IMI (following merger between Banca Intesa and Sanpaolo) 2007–, also Chair. Intesa Sanpaolo; apptd Dir Fondazione Giorgio Cini 1987, Chair. 1999–; Chair. Mittel SpA, Istituto Studi Direzionale SpA; Deputy Chair. Banca Lombarda, Editrice La Scuola SpA; Dir Banco di Brescia, Italian Banking Asscn, Alleanza Assicurazione SpA; Nat. Dir FAI (Fondo per l'Ambiente Italiano); mem. Gen. Advisory Bd Assonime, Exec. Cttee Istituto Paolo VI, Council of Conservationists of Ambrosiana Library; Cavaliere del Lavoro 2000, Cavaliere di Gran Croce 2002, Officier Légion d'Honneur (France) 2002; Hon. DUniv (Univ. of Macerata) 1997, (Univ. of Udine) 2001. *Address:* Banca Intesa SpA, Piazza San Carlo 156, 10121 Turin, Italy (office). *Telephone:* (011) 5551 (office). *E-mail:* info@sanpaoloimi.comt (office). *Website:* www.intestasanpaolo.com (office).

BAZZAZ, Saad al-, MA; Iraqi journalist and broadcaster; *Editor-in-Chief, Azzaman Daily;* b. 18 April 1952, Mosul; ed Univ. of Baghdad, Arab League Inst. for Researches and Studies, Univ. of Exeter, England; Dir Iraqi TV Second Channel 1974–79; Dir Iraqi Cultural Centre, London 1979–84; Gen. Man. Nat. House for Printing and Distribution, Baghdad 1984–86; Gen. Man. Iraq News Agency 1986–88; Gen. Dir Iraqi TV and Radio 1988–90; Ed.-in-Chief, Al-Jammhoria 1990–92; left Iraq Oct. 1992; founder and Ed.-in-Chief, Azzaman Press and Publication Co., London 1997–2003, Baghdad 2003–. *Publications include:* Alhijrat (Migrations) 1972, Searching for the Sea Birds 1976, Future of the Boy and the Girl 1980, Future of Radio Broadcasts 1980, The Secret War 1987, The Scorpion 1987, At 6:30 Hours: Secrets of FAO Battle 1988, A War Gives Birth to Another 1992, Ashes of War 1995, The Generals are the Last to Know 1996, Kurds in Iraqi Question 1996. *Address:* Azzaman Daily, Baghdad, Iraq (office). *Website:* www.saadbazzaz.com (office).

BBUMBA, Syda, BComm, MBA; Ugandan politician; *Minister of Finance;* b. 7 Jan. 1952; m.; Commr, Interim Electoral Comm. 1996; mem. Parl. 1996–; Minister of State for Dept of Econ. Monitoring, Office of the Pres. 1996–99; Minister of Energy and Mineral Devt 1999–2006, of Gender, Labour and Social Services 2006–09, of Finance 2009–; mem. Nat. Resistance Movt. *Address:* Ministry of Finance, Appollo Kaggwa Road, Plot 2/4, POB 8147, Kampala, Uganda (office). *Telephone:* (41) 4707000 (office). *Fax:* (41) 4230163 (office). *E-mail:* webmaster@finance.go.ug (office).

BEACH, David Hugh, PhD, FRS; British molecular biologist; b. 18 May 1954, London; s. of Gen. Sir Hugh Beach and Estelle Beach; ed Winchester Coll., Peterhouse, Cambridge, Univ. of Miami, USA; Postdoctoral Fellow, Univ. of Sussex 1978–82; Postdoctoral Fellow, Cold Spring Harbor Lab., NY 1982–83, Jr then Sr Staff Investigator 1984–89, Tenured Scientist 1992– (Sr Staff Scientist 1989–97, Adjunct Investigator 1997–2000); Investigator, Howard Hughes Medical Inst. 1990–97; Adjunct Assoc. Prof., State Univ. of NY at Stony Brook 1990–97; f. Mitotix Inc. 1992; Founder and Pres. Genetica Inc. 1996–; Hugh and Catherine Stevenson Prof. of Cancer Biology, Univ. Coll. London 1997–; Eli Lilly Research Award 1994; Bristol-Myers Squibb Award 2000; Raymond Bourgine Award 2001. *Publications:* numerous papers in scientific journals. *Address:* Wolfson Institute for Biomedical Research, Cruciform Building, University College London, Gower Street, London, WC1E 6BT (office); 15 Springalls Wharf, 25 Bermondsey Wall West, London, SE16 4TL, England (home). *Telephone:* (20) 7679-6762 (office). *Fax:* (20) 7679-6793 (office). *E-mail:* d.beach@ucl.ac.uk (office); dhbeach@btinternet.com (home). *Website:* www.ucl.ac.uk/wibr.

BEALE, Graham; British chartered accountant and business executive; *Chief Executive, Nationwide Building Society;* one s. one d.; ed Coll., Univ.; joined Nationwide Building Society 1985, held several sr and gen. man. positions, including Man. Dir of a wholly owned property co. and Divisional Dir of Commercial Lending, mem. Bd of Dirs and Group Finance Dir 2003–07, Chief Exec. 2007–; Dir (non-exec.) Visa Europe Ltd, Visa Europe Services. *Address:* Nationwide Building Society, Pipers Way, Swindon, Wilts., SN38 1NW, England (office). *Telephone:* (1793) 656789 (office). *Fax:* (1793) 455341 (office). *E-mail:* info@nationwide.co.uk (office). *Website:* www.nationwide.co.uk (office).

BEALES, Derek Edward Dawson, LittD, FBA; British historian and academic; *Professor Emeritus of Modern History, Sidney Sussex College, University of Cambridge;* b. 12 June 1931, Felixstowe; s. of the late Edward Beales and Dorothy K. Dawson; m. Sara J. Ledbury 1964; one s. one d.; ed Bishop's Stortford Coll. and Sidney Sussex Coll., Cambridge; Research Fellow, Sidney Sussex Coll. Cambridge 1955–58, Fellow 1958–; Asst Lecturer in History, Univ. of Cambridge 1962–65, Lecturer 1965–80, Prof. of Modern History 1980–97, Prof. Emer. 1997–; Stenton Lecturer, Univ. of Reading 1992, Birkbeck Lecturer, Trinity Coll., Cambridge 1993; Recurring Visiting Prof., Cen. European Univ., Budapest 1995–; Ed. Historical Journal 1971–75; mem. Standing Cttee for Humanities, European Science Foundation 1994–99; Leverhulme 2000, Emer., Fellowship 2001–03; Prince Consort Prize, Univ. of Cambridge 1960, Henry Paolucci/Walter Bagehot Prize, Intercollegiate Studies Inst., Wilmington, Del. 2004. *Publications:* England and Italy 1859–60 1961, From Castlereagh to Gladstone 1969, History and Biography 1981, History, Society and the Churches (with G. Best) 1985, Joseph II, Vol. I: In the Shadow of Maria Theresa 1987, Mozart and the Habsburgs 1993, Sidney Sussex Quatercentenary Essays (with H. B. Nisbet) 1996, The Risorgimento and the Unification of Italy (2nd edn with E. Biagini) 2002, Prosperity and Plunder: European Catholic Monasteries in the Age of Revolution 2003, Enlightenment and Reform in the 18th Century 2005, Joseph II, Vol. II: Against the World 2009. *Leisure interests:* music, walking, bridge. *Address:* Sidney Sussex College, Cambridge, CB2 3HU, England (office). *Telephone:* (1223) 338833 (office). *E-mail:* derek@beales.ws.

BEALL, Donald Ray, BS, MBA; American business executive; *Partner, Dartbrook Partners LLC;* b. 29 Nov. 1938, Beaumont, Calif.; s. of Ray C. Beall and Margaret Beall (née Murray); m. Joan Frances Lange 1961; two s.; ed San Jose State Coll. and Univ. of Pittsburgh; various financial and management positions, Ford Motor Co., Newport Beach, Calif., Philadelphia and Palo Alto, Calif. 1961–68; Exec. Dir Corporate Financial Planning, Rockwell Int., El Segundo, Calif. 1968–69, Exec. Vice-Pres. Electronics Group 1969–71; Exec. Vice-Pres. Collins Radio Co., Dallas 1971–74; Pres. Collins Radio Group, Dallas, Rockwell Int. 1974–76, Pres. Electronics Operations 1976–77, Exec. Vice-Pres. 1977–79; Pres. Rockwell Int. (now Rockwell Collins) 1979–88, COO 1979–88, Chair., CEO 1988–98, CEO 1988–97, Chair. Exec. Cttee 1998, mem. Bd Dirs 2001–, Chair. 2001–02; mem. Pres.'s Export Council 1981–85; mem.

Foundation Bd of Trustees Univ. of Calif., Irvine 1988–; mem. Bd of Dirs Conexant Systems, Proctor & Gamble; Overseer, Hoover Inst.; Trustee Calif. Inst. of Tech.; mem. Business Council; founding mem. New Majority, Orange Co.; currently Pnr Dartbrook Pnrs LLC. *Leisure interests:* tennis and boating. *Address:* Dartbrook Partners, 5 Civic Plaza, #320, Newport Beach, CA 92660; c/o Board of Directors, Rockwell Collins, Inc., 400 Collins Road, NE, Cedar Rapids, IA 52498, USA. *Telephone:* (319) 295-1000 (office). *Fax:* (319) 295-5429 (office). *E-mail:* collins@rockwellcollins.com (office). *Website:* www .rockwellcollins.com (office).

BEAN, Charles Richard, PhD; British economist; *Deputy Governor, Bank of England;* b. 16 Sept. 1953; ed Brentwood School, Emmanuel Coll., Cambridge, Massachusetts Inst. of Tech., USA; Econ. Asst, Short-Term Forecasting Div., HM Treasury 1975–79, Econ. Adviser, Monetary Policy Div. 1981–82; Lecturer in Econs, LSE 1982–86, Reader 1986–90, Prof. 1990–2000, Deputy Dir Centre for Econ. Performance 1990–94, Head of Econs Dept 1999–2000; Visiting Prof., Stanford Univ. 1990, Reserve Bank of Australia 1999; mem. Monetary Policy Cttee, Bank of England 2000–, Exec. Dir and Chief Economist 2000–08, Deputy Gov., Monetary Policy 2008–. *Address:* Bank of England, Threadneedle Street, London, EC2R 8AH, England (office). *Telephone:* (20) 7601-4999 (office). *Fax:* (20) 7601-3047 (office). *Website:* www .bankofengland.co.uk (office).

BEAN, Sean; British actor; b. 17 April 1958, Sheffield, Yorks.; ed Royal Acad. of Dramatic Art; professional debut as Tybalt in Romeo and Juliet, Watermill Theatre, Newbury. *Stage appearances include:* The Last Days of Mankind and Der Rosenkavalier at Citizens' Theatre, Glasgow, Lederer in Deathwatch, Young Vic Studio, Who Knew Mackenzie? and Gone, Theatre Upstairs, Royal Court, Starvling in Midsummer Night's Dream and Romeo in Romeo and Juliet, RSC, Stratford-upon-Avon 1986, Captain Spencer in The Fair Maid of the West, RSC, London, Macbeth in Macbeth, Albery Theatre, London 2002. *Films:* Winter Flight 1984, Samson and Delilah 1985, Caravaggio 1986, Stormy Monday 1988, War Requiem 1989, How to Get Ahead in Advertising 1989, Windprints 1990, The Field 1990, In the Border Country 1991, Prince 1991, Patriot Games 1992, Shopping 1994, Black Beauty 1994, Goldeneye 1995, When Saturday Comes 1996, Anna Karenina 1997, Airborne 1998, Ronin 1998, Bravo Two Zero 1999, Essex Boys 2000, Don't Say a Word 2001, The Lord of the Rings: The Fellowship of the Ring 2001, Tom and Thomas 2002, The Lord of the Rings: The Two Towers 2002, Equilibrium 2002, The Big Empty 2003, The Lord of the Rings: The Return of the King 2003, Troy 2004, National Treasure 2004, Flightplan 2005, North Country 2005, The Dark 2005, The Island 2005, Silent Hill 2006, The Hitcher 2007, True North 2007, Outlaw 2007, Far North 2008. *Radio work:* A Kind of Loving, The True Story of Martin Guerre, Saturday Night and Sunday Morning. *TV appearances include:* Lorna Doone 1990, Small Zones 1990, Wedded 1990, My Kingdom for a Horse (series) 1991, Clarissa 1991, Tell Me That You Love Me 1991, Fool's Gold: The Story of the Brink's-Mat Robbery 1992, Sharpe's Rifles 1993 (also several Sharpe episodes in subsequent years), Lady Chatterley 1993, A Woman's Guide to Adultery 1993, Scarlett (miniseries) 1994, Jacob 1994, Extremely Dangerous 1999, Henry VIII 2003, Pride (voice) 2004, Faceless 2006. *Address:* c/o ICM Ltd, Oxford House, 76 Oxford Street, London, W1D 1BS, England. *Telephone:* (20) 7636-6565. *Fax:* (20) 7323-0101.

BEARN, Alexander Gordon, MD, FACP; American (b. British) pharmaceut-ical industry executive and professor of medicine; *Executive Officer Emeritus, American Philosophical Society;* b. 29 March 1923, Cheam, England; s. of Edward Gordon Bearn; m. Margaret Slocum 1952; one s. one d.; ed Epsom Coll. and Guy's Hospital, Univ. of London; Postgraduate Medical School, London 1949–51; Asst to Prof., Rockefeller Univ., New York, USA 1951–64, Prof. 1964–66, Adjunct Prof., Visiting Physician 1966–; Prof. and Chair. Dept of Medicine, Cornell Univ. Medical Coll. 1966–77; Physician-in-Chief, New York Hosp. 1966–77; Stanton Griffis Distinguished Medical Prof. 1976–80; Prof. of Medicine, Cornell Univ. Medical Coll. 1966–89, Prof. Emer. 1989–; Sr Vice-Pres., Medical and Scientific Affairs, Merck Sharp & Dohme Int. 1979–88; mem. Council Fogarty Centre, NIH 1990–; Exec. Officer American Philosophical Soc. 1997–; mem. NAS; Pres. American Soc. of Human Genetics 1971; Lowell Lecture, Harvard Univ. 1958; Hon. MD (Catholic Univ., Korea); Dr hc (René Descartes, Paris); Alfred Benzon Prize (Denmark); American Coll. of Nutrition Award 1972, American Philosophical Society's Benjamin Franklin Medal for Distinguished Achievement in the Sciences 2001. *Publi-cations:* Progress in Medical Genetics (ed.) 1962–87, Cecil Loeb Textbook of Medicine (assoc. ed.) 1963, 1967, 1971, 1975, Archibald Garrodi and the Individuality of Man 1993, 1999; numerous articles in medical and scientific journals. *Leisure interest:* aristology. *Address:* American Philosophical Soci-ety, 104 S Fifth Street, Philadelphia, PA 19106 (office); 241 South 6th Street, #2111, Philadelphia, PA 19106, USA (home). *Telephone:* (215) 440-3435 (office). *Fax:* (215) 440-3436 (office). *Website:* www.amphilsoc.org (office).

BEARPARK, Andrew, BSc; British security industry executive and fmr international organization official; *Vice-President, Special Projects, Olive Group LLC;* ed Univ. of London; with UK Overseas Devt Admin. (ODA) responsible for Devt programmes in Asia and Africa 1973–86, Head of Information and Emergency Aid Dept, responsible for programmes in Bosnia, Rwanda, N Iraq and Somalia 1991–97, Press Sec. to ODA Minister Baroness Chalker 1991–95; Deputy High Rep. for Reconstruction and Return Task Force, Sarajevo 1998–2000; Deputy Special Rep. for Reconstruction and Econ. Devt, UN Interim Admin. Mission in Kosovo 2000; fmr Dir of Reconstruction, Coalition Provisional Authority, Baghdad; currently Vice-Pres. Special Pro-jects, Olive Group LLC (pvt. security co.); Pvt. Sec. to Prime Minister Margaret Thatcher 1986–89, responsible for Home Affairs, then Parl. Affairs, Chief of Staff to Lady Thatcher 1990–91; f. Punchline (Public Relations consultancy) 1989. *Address:* Olive Group FZ-LLC, POB 502356, Dubai, United Arab Emirates (office). *Telephone:* (4) 3912935 (office). *Fax:* (4) 3912907 (office). *E-mail:* info@olivegroup.com (office). *Website:* www.olivegroup.com (office).

BÉART, Emmanuelle; French actress; b. 14 Aug. 1965, Gassin; d. of Guy Béart (q.v.) and Geneviève Galéa; one d. with Daniel Auteuil (q.v.); ed drama school; began acting career with appearance as a child in Demain les Momes 1978. *Films:* Un Amour Interdit, L'Enfant Trouvé 1983, L'Amour en Douce 1984, Manon des Sources 1985, Date with an Angel 1987, A Gauche en Sortant de l'Ascenseur 1988, Les Enfants du Désordre 1989, Capitaine Fracasse 1990, La Belle Noiseuse 1991, J'Embrasse Pas 1991, Un Coeur en Hiver 1991, Ruptures 1992, L'Enfer 1993, Mission Impossible 1995, Nelly and M. Arnaud 1995, Time Regained 1999, Les Destinées Sentimentales 2000, La Repetition 2001, 8 Femmes 2002, Strayed 2003, Histoire de Marie et Julien 2003, Nathalie 2003, À boire 2004, D'Artagnan et les trois mousquetaires 2005, Un fil à la patte 2005, L'Enfer 2005, A Crime 2006, Le Héros de la famille 2006, Les Témoins 2007.

BÉART, Guy; French singer, composer, engineer and author; b. 16 July 1930, Cairo, Egypt; s. of David Behart-Hasson and Amélia Taral; one s. one d. (Emmanuelle Béart (q.v.)); ed Lycée Henri IV, Paris and Ecole Nat. des Ponts et des Chaussées; music transcriber, Prof. of Math., then Eng 1952–57; subsequently made debut in cabaret in Paris; composed songs for Zizi Jeanmaire, Juliette Greco, Patachou, Maurice Chevalier, etc.; recitalist in various Paris theatres and music-halls; composer of more than 200 songs, also film music (including L'Eau vive, Pierrot la tendresse and La Gamberge); author and producer of TV series Bienvenue 1966–72; Chevalier, Légion d'honneur, Officier, Ordre Nat. du Mérite, Commdr des Arts et des Lettres, Grand Prix, Acad. du Disque 1957, Grand Prix du Disque, Acad. Charles Cros 1965, Grand Prix de la chanson Sacem 1987, Prix Balzac 1987, Grand Médaille de la Chanson Française (Académie Française) 1994. *Publications:* Couleurs et colères du temps 1976, L'Espérance polle 1987, Il est temps 1995. *Leisure interest:* chess. *Address:* Editions Temporel, 2 rue du Marquis de Morès, 92380 Garches, France (office).

BEASLEY, David Muldrow, JD; American politician; *Chairman, National Advisory Committee on Rural Health and Human Services, US Department of Health and Human Services;* b. 26 Feb. 1957, Lamar, SC; s. of Richard L. Beasley and Jacqueline A. Blackwell; m. Mary Wood Payne; two d., two s.; ed Clemson Univ. and Univ. of Southern Carolina; practising attorney Beasley, Ervin & Warr; Rep. for SC State, Dist 56 1979–92; Majority Leader, SC House of Reps 1987; Gov. of S. Carolina 1995–98; Prin. Bingham Consulting Group 1999–2001; Fellow Inst. of Politics, Kennedy School of Govt, Harvard Univ. 1999; Prin., Bingham Consulting Group 1999–2001; mem. Bd of Trustees, Francis Marion Coll. 1988-91, Univ. of South Carolina 1990–91; unsuccessful campaign for US Senate 2004; Chair. Nat. Advisory Cttee on Rural Health and Human Services, US Dept of Health and Human Services 2004–; Republican; Dr hc (Univ. of South Carolina), (The Citadel), (Charleston Southern Univ.), (Regent Univ.), Medical Univ. of South Carolina,) Coll. of Charleston), (Bob Jones Univ.), (Newberry Coll.); American Swiss Foundation Friendship Award 1996, John F. Kennedy Profile in Courage Award 2003. *Address:* c/o National Advisory Committee on Rural Health and Human Services, c/o Office of Rural Health Policy, Health Resources and Services Administration, 5600 Fishers Lane, 9A-55, Rockville, MD 20857, USA. *Telephone:* (301) 443-0835. *Fax:* (301) 443-2803. *Website:* ruralcommittee.hrsa.gov.

BEATH, John Arnott, MA, MPhil, FRSE, FRSA; British economist and academic; *Professor of Economics, School of Economics and Finance, Univer-sity of St Andrews;* b. 15 June 1944, Thurso, Caithness, Scotland; s. of James Beath and Marion McKendrick Beath (née Spence); m. Monika Schröder 1980; ed Hillhead High School, Glasgow, Univs of St Andrews, London, Pennsylva-nia and Cambridge; Thouron Scholar, Univ. of Pennsylvania 1968–71, Fels Fellow 1971–72; Research Officer, Univ. of Cambridge 1972–79, Fellow, Downing Coll. 1978–79; Lecturer, then Sr Lecturer, Univ. of Bristol 1979–91; Prof. of Econs, Univ. of St Andrews 1991–, Head, School of Social Sciences 1997–2003; Chair. Econ. Research Inst. of Northern Ireland 2003–; mem. Doctors' and Dentists' Review Body 2003–; Sec.-Gen. Royal Economic Soc. 2008–. *Publications include:* Economic Theory of Product Differentiation. *Leisure interests:* gardening, golf, walking. *Address:* School of Economics and Finance, Room G5W, University of St Andrews, St Andrews, Fife, KY16 9AL, Scotland (office). *Telephone:* (1334) 462421 (office). *Fax:* (1334) 462444 (office). *E-mail:* jab@st-and.ac.uk (office). *Website:* www.st-andrews.ac.uk/economics (office).

BEATRIX WILHELMINA ARMGARD, HM Queen of The Netherlands; b. 31 Jan. 1938, Baarn; d. of Queen Juliana (died 2004) and Bernhard, Prince of the Netherlands; m. Claus George Willem Otto Frederik Geert Jonkheer von Amsberg 10 March 1966 (died 2002); children: Prince Willem-Alexander Claus George Ferdinand, Prince of Orange, b. 27 April 1967; Prince Johan Friso Bernhard Christiaan David, b. 25 Sept. 1968; Prince Constantijn Christof Frederik Aschwin, b. 11 Oct. 1969; ed Baarn Grammar School, Leiden State Univ.; succeeded to the throne on abdication of her mother 30 April 1980; Hon. KG; ranked 35th by Forbes magazine amongst 100 Most Powerful Women 2004. *Address:* c/o Government Information Service, Press and Publicity Department, Binnenhof 19, 2513 AA The Hague, Netherlands. *Telephone:* (70) 3564136. *Website:* www.koninklijkhuis.nl/english/.

BEATSON, Sir Jack, Kt, QC, DCL, LLD, FBA; British judge; *Justice of the High Court, Queen's Bench Division;* b. 3 Nov. 1948, Haifa, Israel; s. of the late John James Beatson and Miriam White; m. Charlotte H. Christie-Miller 1973; one s. (deceased) one d.; ed Whittingehame Coll. Brighton and Brasenose Coll. Oxford; Lecturer in Law, Univ. of Bristol 1972–73; Fellow and Tutor in Law, Merton Coll. Oxford 1973–93, Hon. Fellow 1994–; Rouse Ball Prof. of Law,

Univ. of Cambridge 1993–2003, Chair. Faculty of Law 2001–03; Fellow, St John's Coll. Cambridge 1994–2003, Hon. Fellow 2005–; Dir Centre for Public Law, Cambridge 1997–2001; QC 1998; Deputy High Court Judge 2000–03, Justice of the High Court, Queen's Bench Div. 2003–; Visiting Prof., Osgoode Hall Law School, Toronto 1979, Univ. of Va Law School 1980, 1983; Distinguished Visiting Prof., Univ. of Toronto 2000; Sr Visiting Fellow, Nat. Univ. of Singapore 1987; Visiting Fellow, Univ. of W Australia 1988; Law Commr for England and Wales 1989–94; Recorder of Crown Court 1994–2003; Pres. British Acad. of Forensic Science 2007–09; mem. Competition Comm. 1995–2001; Bencher, Inner Temple. *Publications:* Administrative Law: Cases and Materials (2nd edn) (with M. Matthews), The Use and Abuse of Restitution 1991; Jt Ed. Chitty on Contracts (28th edn 1999), Good Faith and Fault in Contract Law 1995, Jt Ed. European Public Law 1998, Anson's Law of Contract (28th edn 2001), Human Rights: The 1998 Act and the European Convention (with S. Grosz and P. Duffy), Jt Ed. Unjustified Enrichment: Cases, materials and Texts 2003, Jt Ed. Jurists Uprooted: German Speaking Émigré Lawyers in Twentieth Century Britain 2004, Human Rights: Judicial Protection in the UK (co-author) 2009. *Leisure interest:* attempting to relax. *Address:* Royal Courts of Justice, Strand, London, WC2A 2LL, England.

BEATTIE, Ann, MA; American writer; *Edgar Allan Poe Professor of Literature and Creative Writing, University of Virginia;* b. 8 Sept. 1947, Washington; d. of James Beattie and Charlotte Crosby; m. Lincoln Perry; ed American Univ. and Univ. of Connecticut; Visiting Asst Prof. Univ. of Virginia, Charlottesville 1976–77, Visiting Writer 1980; Briggs Copeland Lecturer in English, Harvard Univ. 1977; Guggenheim Fellow 1977; currently Edgar Allan Poe Prof. of Literature and Creative Writing, Univ. of Virginia; mem. American Acad. and Inst. of Arts and Letters (Award in Literature 1980), PEN, Authors' Guild; Hon. LHD (American Univ.); PEN/Bernard Malamud Award 2000. *Publications:* Chilly Scenes of Winter 1976, Distortions 1976, Secrets and Surprises 1979, Falling in Place 1990, Jacklighting 1981, The Burning House 1982, Love Always 1985, Where You'll Find Me 1986, Alex Katz (art criticism) 1987, Picturing Will 1990, What Was Mine (story collection) 1991, My Life Starring Dara Falcon 1997, Park City: New and Selected Stories 1998, Perfect Recall 2001, The Doctor's House 2002, Follies 2005. *Address:* c/o Scribner, Simon & Schuster, 1230 Avenue of the Americas, New York, NY 10020, USA.

BEATTY, (Henry) Warren; American actor; b. 30 March 1937, Richmond, Virginia; s. of Ira Beatty and Kathlyn Maclean; brother of Shirley Maclaine (q.v.); m. Annette Bening (q.v.) 1992; one s. three d.; ed Stella Adler Theatre School; Fellow, BAFTA 2002; Hon. Chair. Stella Adler School of Acting 2004; Commdr Ordre des Arts et Lettres; Irving Thalberg Special Acad. Award 2000, recipient of Kennedy Center Honors 2004, Golden Globe Cecil B DeMille Award 2007, American Film Inst. Life Achievement Award 2008. *Film appearances include:* Splendor in the Grass 1961, Roman Spring of Mrs. Stone 1961, All Fall Down 1962, Lilith, 1965, Mickey One 1965, Promise Her Anything 1966, Kaleidoscope 1966, Bonnie and Clyde 1967, The Only Game in Town 1969, McCabe and Mrs. Miller 1971, Dollars 1972, The Parallax View 1974, Shampoo (producer and co-screenwriter) 1975, The Fortune 1976, Heaven Can Wait (producer, co-dir and co-screenwriter) 1978, Reds (producer, dir, Acad. Award for Best Dir 1981) 1981, Ishtar 1987, Dick Tracy 1989, Bugsy 1991, Love Affair, Bulworth (also dir) 1998, Town and Country 2001, Dean Tavoularis: The Magician of Hollywood (documentary) 2003, One Bright Shining Moment (documentary) 2005. *Theatre roles include:* A Loss of Roses 1960. *TV appearances include:* Studio One and Playhouse 90, A Salute to Dustin Hoffman 1999. *Address:* c/o Risa Gertner, CAA, 9830 Wilshire Boulevard, Beverly Hills, CA 90212-1825, USA (office). *Telephone:* (310) 288-4545 (office). *Fax:* (310) 288-4800 (office). *Website:* www.caa.com (office).

BEATTY, Hon. Perrin, BA; Canadian business executive and fmr politician; *President and CEO, Canadian Manufacturers & Exporters;* b. 1 June 1950, Toronto; s. of George Ernest Beatty and Martha (Perrin) Beatty; m. Julia Kenny 1974; two s.; ed Upper Canada Coll., Univ. of Western Ont.; Special Asst to Minister of Health, Ont.; mem. House of Commons 1972–93; Minister of State for Treasury Bd 1979; Minister of Nat. Revenue 1984–85; Solicitor-Gen. for Canada 1985–86, Acting Solicitor-Gen. 1989; Minister of Defence 1986–89, of Nat. Health and Welfare 1989–91, of Communications 1991–93, of External Affairs 1993; Pres. and CEO CBC 1995–2000, Canadian Mfrs & Exporters 1999–; mem. Special Jt Cttee on Constitution 1978, Chair. Progressive Conservative Caucus Cttee on Supply and Services, Spokesperson on Communications; Co-Chair. of Standing Jt Cttee on Regulations and Other Statutory Instruments; Caucus spokesperson on Revenue Canada; Chair. of Caucus Cttee on Fed. Prov. Relations and of Progressive Conservative Task Force on Revenue Canada 1983. *Leisure interests:* music, travel, technology and reading. *Address:* Canadian Manufacturers & Exporters, 1 Nicholas Street, Suite 1500, Ottawa, Ont. K1N 7B7, Canada (office). *Website:* www.cme-mec.ca (office).

BEAUCE, Thierry M. de, LenD; French government official; b. 14 Feb. 1943, Lyon; s. of Bertrand Martin de Beauce and Simone de Beauce (née de la Verpillere); two d.; ed Univ. of Paris and Ecole Nat. d'Admin; Civil Admin., Ministry of Cultural Affairs 1968–69; seconded to Office of Prime Minister 1969–73; Tech. Adviser, Pvt. Office of Pres. of Nat. Ass. 1974; seconded to Econ. Affairs Directorate, Ministry of Foreign Affairs 1974–76; Cultural Counsellor, Japan 1976–78; Second Counsellor, Morocco 1978–80; Vice-Pres. for Int. Affairs Société Elf Aquitaine 1981–86; Dir-Gen. of Cultural, Scientific and Tech. Relations, Ministry of Foreign Affairs 1986–87; State Sec. attached to Minister of Foreign Affairs 1988–91; Adviser to the Pres. for African Affairs 1991–94; Vice-Pres. of Conf. for Yugoslavia 1992; Amb. to Indonesia 1995–97; Special Adviser to Chair. and CEO for Int. Affairs Vivendi Universal (became

Vivendi 2006) 1997–, fmr Sr Exec. Vice-Pres. for Int. Affairs, Vivendi Environnement; Pres. MEDEF Int. for Middle East 1998–; Deputy Pres. Asscn of Democrats 1989–; Chevalier, Légion d'honneur. *Publications:* Les raisons dangereuses (essay) 1975, Un homme ordinaire (novel) 1978, L'Ile absolue (essay) 1979, Le désir de guerre 1980, La chute de Tanger (novel) 1984, Nouveau discours sur l'universalité de la langue française 1988, Le livre d'Esther 1989, La République de France 1991, La nonchalence de Dieu 1995, L'archipel des épices 1998, L'absent de Marrakech 2006. *Address:* Vivendi, 42 Avenue de Friedland, 75380 Paris (office); 45 rue de Richelieu, 75001 Paris, France (home). *Telephone:* 1-71-71-10-00 (office). *Fax:* 1-71-71-10-01 (office). *Website:* www.vivendi.com.

BEAUDET, Alain, MD, PhD; Canadian physician and neuroscientist; *President, Canadian Institutes of Health Research;* b. Montréal; ed Univ. of Montréal; Postdoctoral Research, Centre d'études nucléaires, Saclay, France 1977–79, Univ. of Zürich Brain Research Inst., Switzerland 1979–80; Researcher, Montréal Neurological Inst. 1980, becoming Assoc. Dir of Research 1985–92; Head of Neurobiology Group, McGill Univ., Montréal 1988–96, becoming Prof. of Neurosciences; Pres. and CEO Fonds de la recherche en santé du Québec 2004–08; Pres. Canadian Insts of Health Research 2008–; Pres. Canadian Asscn for Neuroscience 1995–97; Officier, Ordre des Palmes académiques 2007; Dr hc (Univ. Pierre et Marie Curie, France) 2007; Asscn francophone pour le savoir Prix Adrien-Pouliot 2004. *Publications:* around 500 publications. *Address:* Office of the President, Canadian Institutes of Health Research, 160 Elgin Street, 9th Floor, Ottawa, ON K1A 0W9, Canada (office). *Telephone:* (613) 941-2672 (office). *Fax:* (613) 954-1800 (office). *Website:* www.cihr-irsc.gc.ca (office).

BEAUDOIN, Laurent, CC, BA, MComm, CA, FCA; Canadian financial executive; *Chairman, Bombardier Inc.;* b. 1938, Laurier Station, PQ; m.; one s.; ed St-Anne Coll., NS, Univ. of Sherbrooke, PQ; began career with Beaudoin, Morin, Dufresne & Asocs Chartered Accountants 1961–63; Comptroller, Bombardier Ltd 1963–64, Gen. Man. 1964–66, Pres. 1966–79, Chair. and CEO 1979–99, Chair. Bd and Exec. Cttee Bombardier Inc. 1999–, CEO 2004–08; Co-Chair. Regroupement Économie et Constitution 1991; mem. Advisory Bd LAZARD Canada 2000–, Carlyle Group (Canada) 2001–; mem. Bd of Dirs Championnat des Amériques 2003; Officer Ordre Nat. du Québec, Golden Emblem of Merit, Prov. Govt of Upper Austria 1999; Hon. PhD (Univ. of Montreal, York Univ.), Hon. DBA (Univ. of Sherbrooke), Hon. DEcon (Univ. of St-Anne), Hon. DCL (Bishop's Univ.), DJur (Univ. of Toronto, McGill Univ.), DEng (Carleton Univ.); Canadian Business Leader Award, Univ. of Alberta 1991, CEO of the Year, The Financial Post 1991, Canada's Int. Exec. of the Year, Int. Chamber of Commerce 1992, Laureate Award in Aeronautics/Propulsion, Aviation Week & Space Tech. Magazine 1993, CD Home Award, Canadian Aeronautics and Space Inst. 1995, Canadian Business Leadership Award, Harvard Business Club of Toronto 1996, Prix de Carrière, Conseil du Patronat du Québec 1997, Int. Distinguished Entrepreneur Award, Univ. of Man. 1998, Entreprise du siècle au Québec Award, Revue Commerce 1998, Lifetime Achievement Award, Ernst and Young Entrepreneur of the Year Program in Québec 2000, Golden Hon. Medal for Duties to the City of Vienna 2001, Canadian Youth Business Foundation Lifetime Achievement Award 2006. *Address:* Bombardier Inc., 800 René-Lévesque Boulevard West, Montreal, PQ H3B 1YB, Canada (office). *Telephone:* (514) 861-9481 (office). *Fax:* (514) 861-7053 (office). *E-mail:* piero.scaramuzzi@defence.bombardier.com (office). *Website:* www.bombardier.com (office).

BEAUDOIN, Pierre; Canadian business executive; *President and CEO, Bombardier Inc.;* ed Brébeuf Coll., McGill Univ., Montréal; worked as Canadian Customer Service Man. for BIC Sport Inc.; helped to organize the Marine Products Div. of Bombardier 1985, Vice-Pres. Product Devt for Sea-Doo/Ski-Doo (following fusion of marine products and snowmobile divs Oct. 1990) 1990–92, Exec. Vice-Pres. Sea-Doo/Ski-Doo Div., Bombardier Inc. 1992–94, Pres. 1994–96, Pres. and COO Bombardier Recreational Products 1996–2001, also responsible for Bombardier-Rotax, Pres. Bombardier Aero-space, Business Aircraft Feb.–Oct. 2001, mem. Bd of Dirs, Pres. and COO Oct. 2001–04, Exec. Vice-Pres. Bombardier Inc. 2004–08, Pres. and CEO 2008–. *Address:* Bombardier Inc., 800 René-Lévesque Boulevard West, Montréal, PQ H3B 1YB, Canada (office). *Telephone:* (514) 861-9481 (office). *Fax:* (514) 861-7053 (office). *E-mail:* piero.scaramuzzi@defence.bombardier.com (office). *Website:* www.bombardier.com (office).

BEAUMONT, (John) Michael, OBE, CEng; British engineer (retd); *Seigneur of Sark;* b. 20 Dec. 1927, Egypt; s. of the late Lionel Beaumont and Enid Beaumont (née Ripley); m. Diana La Trobe-Bateman 1956; two s.; ed Loughborough Coll.; Chief Stress Engineer, Beagle Aircraft 1965–69, Chief Tech. Engineer 1969–70; Sr Engineer, Guided Weapons, Filton 1970–74; inherited Fief of Sark 1974. *Leisure interests:* theatre, music, gardening. *Address:* La Seigneurie de Sark, Channel Islands, GY9 0SF (office). *Telephone:* (1481) 832017 (office). *Fax:* (1481) 832628 (office). *E-mail:* seigneur@sark.gg (office). *Website:* www.sark.gov.gg (office).

BEAUMONT, Lady Mary Rose, BA (Hons); British art historian and academic; b. (Mary Wauchope), 6 June 1932, Petersfield; d. of Charles Edward Wauchope and Elaine Margaret Armstrong-Jones; m. Lord Beaumont of Whitley, The Rev. Timothy Wentworth Beaumont 1955; one s. (one s. deceased) two d.; ed Prior's Field School, Godalming, Surrey, Courtauld Inst. of Fine Art, Univ. of London; f. Centre for the Study of Modern Art, Inst. of Contemporary Arts (ICA) 1972; art critic for Art Review 1978–96; Lecturer in Modern Art for Christies' Educ. 1978–2001; Exhbn curator for British Council in E Europe and Far East 1983–87; Exhbn Curator The Human Touch, Fischer Fine Art Gallery 1986, The Dark Side of the Moon, Rhodes Gallery 1990, Three Scottish Artists, Pamela Auchincloss Gallery, New York 1990; Picker Fellow Kingston Polytechnic 1986–87; Lecturer in Humanities,

Dept City & Guilds School of Art 1996–2008; mem. Exec. Cttee of Contemporary Art Soc. 1979–89, Advisory Cttee Govt Art Collection 1994–2001; Hon. Fellow, Royal Soc. of British Sculptors. *Publications include:* An American Passion: The Susan Kasen Summer and Robert D. Summer Collection of Contemporary British Painting (contrib. artists' profiles) 1995, Open Studio: Derek Healey 1997, Jean MacAlpine: Intervals in Light 1998, Carole Hodgson 1999, George Kyriacou 1999, Jock McFadyen: A Book About a Painter (contrib.) 2000, New European Artists Vol. I (contrib.) 2000. *Leisure interests:* reading novels, listening to opera. *Address:* 40 Elms Road, London, SW4 9EX, England (home). *Telephone:* (20) 7498-8664 (home). *Website:* www.cityandguildsartschool.ac.uk/index.html.

BEAZLEY, Hon. Kim Christian, MA, MPhil; Australian politician; b. 14 Dec. 1948, Perth; s. of Kim Edward Beazley; m. 1st Mary Beazley 1974 (divorced 1989); two d.; m. 2nd Susie Annus 1990; one d.; ed Hollywood Sr High School, Perth, Univ. of Western Australia, Univ. of Oxford, UK; fmr Lecturer in Social and Political Theory, Murdoch Univ. Perth; MP for Swan 1980–96, for Brand 1996–2007; Minister for Aviation 1983–84, for Defence 1984–90, for Transport and Communications 1990–91, of Finance 1991, of Employment, Education and Training 1991–93, of Finance 1993–96; Deputy Prime Minister 1995–96; Special Minister of State 1983–84; Leader of the House 1988–96; Leader of Australian Labor Party 1996–2001, 2005–06. *Leisure interests:* reading, swimming, watching cricket. *Address:* c/o Australian Labor Party, Centenary House, 19 National Circuit, Barton, ACT 2600, Australia (office).

BÉBÉAR, Claude; French business executive; *Chairman of the Supervisory Board, AXA Group;* b. 29 July 1935, Issac; s. of André Bébéar and Simone Bébéar (née Veyssière); m. Catherine Dessagne 1957; one s. two d.; ed Lycées of Périgueux and St Louis, Paris, Ecole Polytechnique, Paris; joined Ancienne Mutuelle (renamed Mutuelles Unies 1978) 1958, CEO 1975–82; Chair. and CEO AXA Group 1982–2000, Chair. Man. Bd 1996–2000, Chair. Supervisory Bd 2000–, Chair FINAXA (holding co.); mem. Bd of Dirs Schneider Electric SA 1986–2003, BNP Paribas 2000–, Vivendi 2002–, mem. supervisory Bd 2005–; Founder AXA Atout Cœur (humanitarian asscn) 1991; Hon. Pres. Inst. des Actuaires Français 1989–; Chair. Institut du Mécénat de la Solidarité; Founder and Chair. L'Institut Montaigne 2001–; Commdr, Légion d'honneur, Officier, Ordre Nat. du Mérite. *Publications:* Le courage de réformer 2002, Ils vont tuer le capitalisme 2003. *Address:* AXA Group, 25 avenue Matignon, 75008 Paris, France (office). *Telephone:* 1-40-75-71-81 (office). *Fax:* 1-40-75-57-95 (office). *Website:* www.axa.com (office).

BEBIĆ, Luka; Croatian agricultural engineer and politician; *Speaker, Hrvatski Sabor (Croatian Parliament);* b. 21 Aug. 1937, Desne-Kula Norinska; m.; two c.; ed Faculty of Agric., Sarajevo; mem. Croatian Democratic Union (HDZ) 1989–, mem. Hrvatski Sabor (Parl.) since Croatia's independence, Deputy Speaker, Parl., mem. and Vice-Chair. Cttee for Consideration and Political System, Chair. Club of Reps of HDZ 2003–08, Pres. (Speaker) of Sabor (Ass.) 2008–; Minister of Defence July–Sept. 1991. *Address:* Office of the Speaker, Sabor, 10000 Zagreb, Trg sv. Marka 6–7, Croatia (office). *Telephone:* (1) 4569222 (office). *Fax:* (1) 16303010 (office). *E-mail:* sabor@sabor.hr (office); predsjednik@sabor.hr (office). *Website:* www.sabor.hr/Default.aspx?sec=715 (office).

BECHERER, Hans Walter, MBA; American business executive; b. 19 April 1935, Detroit, Mich.; s. of Max Becherer and Mariele Specht; m. Michele Beigbeder 1959; one s. (deceased) one d.; ed Trinity Coll., Hartford, Conn. and Munich and Harvard Univs; Exec. Asst Office of Chair. Deere & Co., Moline, Ill. 1966–69; Gen. Man. John Deere Export, Mannheim, Germany 1969–73; Dir Export Marketing, Deere & Co., Moline, Ill. 1973–77, Vice-Pres. 1977–83, Sr Vice-Pres. 1983–86, Exec. Vice-Pres. 1986–87, Pres. 1987–90, COO 1987–89, CEO 1989–2000, Chair. 1990–2000; mem. Bd of Dirs Schering-Plough Corpn 1989–, Honeywell International Inc., Chase Manhattan Corpn and Chase Manhattan Bank (now JPMorgan Chase & Co.) 1998–; fmr mem. Bd of Dirs Allied Signal Inc.; mem. The Business Roundtable 1989–, Chase Manhattan Bank Int. Advisory Cttee 1990–98, The Business Council 1992–; Trustee Cttee for Econ. Devt 1990. *Address:* c/o Board of Directors, JPMorgan Chase & Company, 270 Park Avenue, New York, NY 10017, USA (office).

BECHERT, Heinz, DPhil; German academic; *Professor of Indology, University of Göttingen;* b. 26 June 1932, Munich; s. of the late Rudolf Bechert and of Herta Bechert; m. Marianne Würzburger 1963; ed Univs of Munich and Hamburg; Research Asst, Univ. of Saarbrücken 1956–61; Univ. of Mainz 1961–64; Prof. of Indology, Univ. of Göttingen 1965–; Visiting Prof., Yale Univ., USA 1969–70, 1974–75; Research Fellow, Japan Soc. for the Promotion of Science 1990; mem. Akad. der Wissenschaften, Göttingen 1968, Acad. Royale de Belgique 1973, Royal Swedish Acad. of Literature, History and Antiquities 1988, Academia Europaea 1989. *Publications:* author and ed. of 30 books and 212 contribs in academic journals. *Address:* Hermann-Föge-Weg 1A, 37073 Göttingen, Germany. *Telephone:* (551) 485765.

BECHTEL, Marie-Françoise; French jurist; *Conseiller d'Etat;* b. 19 March 1946, Coarraze, Basses Pyrénées; d. of Gaston Cassiau and Marie Cassiau (née Sahores); one s. one d.; ed Univ. de Paris-Sorbonne, Ecole Nat. d'Admin.; secondary school teacher 1972–75; civil servant at Ecole Nat. d'Admin. 1978–80; Officer, Council of State 1980–84, Counsel 1984–85, Sr mem. 1996–; Adviser to Minister of Justice 1992–93, to Minister of the Interior 1999–2000; Dir Ecole Nat. Admin. 2000–02; Tech. Adviser to Minister of Nat. Educ. 1984–86; Sr Lecturer, Inst. d'Etudes Politiques 1983–87; Vice-Pres. UN Cttee of Experts on Admin. Reforms 2002–06, mem. 2006–. *Publications:* contribs to Revue Française d'administration publique on institutions, organization, justice, civil rights etc. 1983–99, to "Ofer dire non", Fayard, Pais 2005; Rapport général du Comité pour la révision de la Constitution 1993. *Leisure interest:* modern art. *Address:* Conseil d'Etat, place du Palais Royal, 75001

Paris RP (office); 29 boulevard Edgard Quinet, 75014 Paris, France (home). *Telephone:* 1-40-20-87-80 (office). *Fax:* 1-43-20-59-53 (home). *E-mail:* marie-francoise.bechtel@conseil-etat.fr (office). *Website:* www.conseil-etat.fr (office).

BECK, Aaron T., MD; American psychotherapist and academic; *Professor Emeritus of Psychiatry, University of Pennsylvania;* b. 18 July 1921, Providence, RI; m.; four c.; ed Brown Univ., Yale Univ. Medical School; fmr Assoc. Ed. Brown Daily Herald; Resident in Pathology, RI Hosp. 1946; Resident in Neurology, Cushing Veterans Admin Hosp., Framingham, MA; Fellow Austin Riggs Center, Stockbridge; Asst Chief of Neuropsychiatry, Valley Forge Army Hosp.; joined Dept of Psychiatry, Univ. of Pa 1954, currently Prof. Emer. of Psychiatry; developed field of cognitive behaviour therapy research; funded research investigations of psychopathology of depression, suicide, anxiety disorders, alcoholism, drug addiction and personality disorders 1959–; f. Beck Inst. for Cognitive Therapy and Research; fmr Visiting Scientist, Medical Research Council, Oxford, Visiting Fellow, Wolfson Coll., Visiting Prof. Harvard, Yale and Columbia Univs; mem. Inst. of Medicine, NAS; consultant or mem. several review panels, Nat. Inst. of Mental Health; served on editorial bds several professional journals; Hon. DMedSc (Brown Univ.), Hon. DHumLitt (Assumption Coll.); Brown Univ.: Phi Beta Kappa, Francis Wayland Scholarship, Bennet Essay Award, Gaston prize for Oratory; MERIT Award, Nat. Inst. of Mental Health, American Psychiatric Asscn Research Award, Sarnat Award, Inst. of Medicine, Albert Lasker Clinical Medical Research Award 2006. *Publications:* over 450 articles and author or co-author of 23 books. *Address:* Psychopathology Research Unit, 3535 Market Street, Room 2032, Philadelphia, PA 19104-3309, USA (office). *Fax:* (215) 573-3717 (office). *E-mail:* abeck@mail.med.upenn.edu (office). *Website:* www.med.upenn.edu/suicide/beck/index.html (office). www.beckinstitute.org (office).

BECK, Rev. Brian Edgar, MA, DD; British ecclesiastic; b. 27 Sept. 1933, London; s. of the late A. G. Beck and C. A. Beck; m. Margaret Ludlow 1958; three d.; ed City of London School, Corpus Christi Coll., Cambridge and Wesley House, Cambridge; Asst Tutor Handsworth Coll. 1957–59; ordained Methodist Minister 1960; Circuit Minister, Suffolk 1959–62; St Paul's United Theological Coll., Limuru, Kenya 1962–68; Tutor Wesley House, Cambridge 1968–80, Prin. 1980–84; Sec. Methodist Conf. of GB 1984–98, Pres. 1993–94; Co.-Chair. Oxford Inst. of Methodist Theological Studies 1976–2002; Sec. E African Church Union Consultation Worship and Liturgy Cttee 1963–68; mem. World Methodist Council 1966–71, 1981–98; Visiting Prof., Wesley Theological Seminary, Washington, DC 1999. *Publications:* Reading the New Testament Today 1977, Christian Character in the Gospel of Luke 1989, Gospel Insights 1998; Exploring Methodism's Heritage 2004; (contrib. to) Christian Belief, A Catholic-Methodist Statement 1970, Unity the Next Step? 1972, Suffering and Martyrdom in the New Testament 1981, Community-Unity-Communion 1998, Rethinking Wesley's Theology 1998, Managing the Church? 2000, Apostolicity and Unity 2002, Reflections on Ministry 2004, Unmasking Methodist Theology 2004, and articles in theological journals. *Leisure interests:* walking, cross-stitch, DIY. *Address:* 26 Hurrell Road, Cambridge, CB4 3RH, England (home). *Telephone:* (1223) 312260 (home). *Fax:* (1223) 312260 (home).

BECK, Sir (Edgar) Philip, Kt, MA; British business executive; b. 9 Aug. 1934; s. of the late Sir Edgar Charles Beck and of Mary Agnes Sorapure; m. 1st Thomasina Joanna Jeal 1957 (divorced); two s.; m. 2nd Bridget Alexandra Heathcoat Amory 1991; ed Jesus Coll., Cambridge; Chair. John Mowlem and Co. PLC 1979–95 (Dir 1963–95), Railtrack 1999–2001; fmr Dir numerous assoc. cos; Chair. Fed. of Civil Eng. Contractors 1982–83; Dir (non-exec.) Invensys PLC 1991– (Interim Chair. 1998, Deputy Chair. 1998–99), Delta PLC 1994–2004, Yorks. Electricity Group PLC 1995–97, Railtrack Group 1999–2001 (non-exec. Dir 1995–99). *Leisure interest:* sailing. *Address:* Lower Park House, Westholme, Pilton, Somerset, BA4 4EN, England (home). *Telephone:* (1749) 899491 (home). *E-mail:* philipbeck98@aol.com (home).

BECK, John C., MD, CM, MACP, FRCP; American professor of medicine; *Director Emeritus, Multicampus Program in Geriatrics and Gerontology, University of California at Los Angeles;* b. 4 Jan. 1924, Audubon, Ia; s. of Wilhelm Beck and Marie Beck; one s.; ed McGill Univ.; Physician-in-Chief, Royal Victoria Hosp. 1964–74, Sr Physician, Dept of Medicine 1974–81; Prof. of Medicine, Univ. of Calif., San Francisco 1974–79; Visiting Prof., UCLA 1978–79, Dir Multicampus Div. of Geriatric Medicine, School of Medicine, UCLA 1979–93, Prof. of Medicine 1979–, Dir Multicampus Program in Geriatrics and Gerontology 1987–93, Dir Emer. 1993–; numerous other professional appointments; Hon. PhD (Ben-Gurion Univ., Israel) 1981; Hon. DSc (McGill Univ., Canada) 1994; Ronald V. Christie Award, Canadian Asscn of Profs of Medicine 1987, Duncan Graham Award, Royal Coll. of Physicians and Surgeons 1990, Distinguished Service Recognition Award, Asscn for Gerontology in Higher Educ. 2001, Donald P. Kent Award, Gerontological Soc. of America 2001, Philips Award, American Coll. of Physicians/American Soc. of Internal Medicine 2003, Chaikin Oration, Australian Acad. of Technological Sciences & Eng 2004. *Publications:* more than 300 articles in professional journals and book chapters. *Address:* 1562 Casale Road, Pacific Palisades, CA 90272, USA (home). *Telephone:* (310) 459-5927 (office). *Fax:* (310) 454-1944 (office). *E-mail:* egebjcb@ucla.edu (office).

BECK, Kurt; German politician; b. 5 Feb. 1949, Bad Bergzabern; m. Roswitha Beck 1968; one s.; apprenticeship as mechanic, specializing in electronics; mem. ÖTV (Public Employees' Union) 1969; mem. SPD 1972–; mem. Rhineland-Palatinate State Ass. 1979–, Whip of SPD Parl. Group 1985–91, Chair. 1991–94; Chair. Rhineland-Palatinate SPD 1993–, Deputy Chair. SPD Party (Germany) 2003–06, Chair. 2006–08; Minister-Pres. of Rhineland-Palatinate 1994–; Chair. Bundesrat 2000–01; Mayor of Steinfeld 1989–94; Chair. Broadcasting Comm. of Fed. States' Minister-Pres.'s 1994–; responsible for cultural matters under German-French co-operation agreement 1999–; Chair. Bd Dirs Zweites Deutsches Fernsehen (ZDF) 1999–. *Address:* Peter-Altmeier-Allee 1, 55116 Mainz, Germany (office). *Telephone:* (6131) 164700 (office). *Fax:* (6131) 164702 (office). *E-mail:* poststelle@stk.rlp.de (office). *Website:* www.rlp.de (office).

BECKE, Axel Dieter, PhD, FRSC; German chemist and academic; *Professor of Chemistry, Queen's University;* b. 6 Oct. 1953, Esslingen; ed Queen's Univ., Kingston, Ont. and McMaster Univ., Hamilton, Ont., Canada; NSERC Postdoctoral Fellow, Dalhousie Univ., Halifax, NS 1981–83, E.B. Eastburn Postdoctoral Fellow 1983–84; NSERC Univ. Research Fellow, Queen's Univ., Kingston, Ont. 1984–94, Prof. of Chem. 1994–; mem. Int. Acad. of Quantum Molecular Science; Fellow, Chemical Inst. of Canada, World Asscn of Theoretically Oriented Chemists; Medal of Int. Acad. of Quantum Molecular Science 1991, Noranda Lecture Award, Canadian Soc. for Chem. 1994, Prize for Excellence in Research, Queen's Univ., Kingston, Ont. 1999, Schroedinger Medal, World Asscn of Theoretically Oriented Chemists 2000. *Publications:* more than 50 articles in scientific journals. *Address:* Department of Chemistry, Queen's University, Chernoff Hall, Room 310, Kingston, Ont. K7L 3N6, Canada (office). *Telephone:* (613) 533-2634 (office). *Fax:* (613) 533-6669 (office). *E-mail:* becke@chem.queensu.ca (office). *Website:* www.chem.queensu.ca (office).

BECKENBAUER, Franz; German professional football manager and sports administrator; b. 11 Sept. 1945, Munich; s. of the late Franz Beckenbauer Sr and of Antonia Beckenbauer; m. Brigitte Wittmann; three s.; ed Northern Coll. of Insurance Studies; played for Bayern Munich, Hanover and New York Cosmos football clubs; won West German Cup (with Bayern Munich) 1966, 1967, 1969, 1971, West German Championship 1972, 1974, European Cup Winners 1967, European Cup 1974–76, World Club Championship 1976; won European Nations Cup (with West German Nat. Team) 1972, World Cup (only man to have won the World Cup both as Capt. and manager) 1974; won North American Championship (with New York Cosmos) 1977, 1978–80; retd. 1984; Man. West German Nat. Team 1984–90; briefly coach for Marseilles; Pres. FC Bayern Munich 1994–2002; Vice-Pres. Deutscher Fussball-Bund 1998–; Pres. 2006 World Cup Organizing Cttee; f. Franz Beckenbauer Foundation 1982; Adviser Mitsubishi Mrawa Football Club 1992–; mem. Exec. Cttee, FIFA 2007–; West German Footballer of the Year 1966, European Footballer of the Year 1972, 1976, Bayern Verdienstorden 1982, Order of FIFA (Int. Football Fed.) 1984, Bundesverdienstkreuz. *Publication:* Einer wie ich (Someone like Me) 1975, Franz Beckenbauer's Soccer Power 1978. *Address:* c/o FIFA, Hitziweg 11, PO Box 85, 8030, Zurich, 30, Switzerland (office). *Website:* www.fifa.com (office); www.dfb.de.

BECKER, Boris; German fmr professional tennis player; b. 22 Nov. 1967, Leimen, nr Heidelberg; s. of the late Karl-Heinz Becker and of Elvira Becker; m. Barbara Feltus (divorced 2001); two s. one d.; started playing tennis aged three, later joined Blau-Weiss Club, Leimen; won West German Jr Championship 1983; subsequently runner-up US Jr Championship; turned professional and coached by Ion Tiriac since 1984; quarter-finalist, Australian Championship, Winner Young Masters Tournament, Birmingham, England 1985, Grand Prix Tournament, Queen's 1985; won Men's Singles Championship, Wimbledon 1985 (youngest ever winner and finalist; beat Kevin Curren), also won 1986, 1989, finalist 1988, 1990, 1991, 1995; finalist, Benson and Hedges Championship, Wembley, London 1985; Masters Champion 1988, finalist 1989; US Open Champion 1989; Semi-finalist French Open 1989; Winner Davis Cup for Germany 1989, Australian Open Championships 1991, 1996, IBM/ATP Tour Championship 1992, 1995, Grand Slam Cup 1996; named World Champion 1991, 64 career titles (49 singles, 15 doubles); Gold Medal (with Michael Stich), Olympic Games, Barcelona 1992; retd from professional tennis 1999; mem. Bd Bayern Munich Football Club 2001–; Co-founder Boris Becker & Co., Völkl GmbH; Partner, DaimlerChrysler; owner of three car dealerships; Chair. Laureus Sports for Good Foundation 2002–, Tennis Masters Hamburg Rothenbaum; commentator for BBC TV, Premiere channel (Germany); columnist, The Times, Handelsblatt (Germany), Blick (Switzerland); Founder Cleven-Becker-Stiftung; Amb. for German AIDS Foundation; mem. Bd Elton John AIDS Foundation; convicted of tax evasion, given a two-year suspended sentence Oct. 2002; Hon. Citizen Leimen 1986; Sportsman of the Year 1985. *Publications:* The Player (autobiog.) 2004. *Leisure interests:* football, basketball, chess, backgammon. *Address:* Boris Becker & Co., Grafenauweg 4, 6300 Zug, Switzerland (office). *Telephone:* (41) 724-65-11 (office). *Fax:* (41) 724-65-05 (office).

BECKER, Gary Stanley, PhD; American economist and academic; *University Professor of Economics, School of Business, University of Chicago;* b. 2 Dec. 1930, Pottsville, Pa; s. of Louis William and Anna Siskind Becker; m. 1st Doria Slote 1954 (deceased); m. 2nd Guity Nashat 1979; two s. two d.; ed Princeton Univ., Univ. of Chicago; Asst Prof., Univ. of Chicago 1954–57; Asst and Assoc. Prof. of Econs Columbia Univ. 1957–60, Prof. of Econs 1960, Arthur Lehman Prof. of Econs 1968–69; Ford Foundation Visiting Prof. of Econs, Univ. of Chicago 1969–70, Univ. Prof., Dept of Econs, 1970–83, Depts of Econs and Sociology 1983–, Chair. Dept of Econs 1984–85; Research Assoc., Econs Research Center, NORC 1980–; Univ. Prof., Grad. School of Business, Univ. of Chicago 2002–; mem. NAS, Int. Union for the Scientific Study of Population, American Philosophical Soc. and American Econ. Asscn (Pres. 1987), Mont Pelerin Soc. (Dir 1985–, Pres. 1990–92); Fellow, American Statistical Asscn, Econometric Soc., Nat. Acad. of Educ., American Acad. of Arts and Sciences; mem. Bd of Dirs UNext.com 1999–; affil. Lexecon Corpn 1990–2002; columnist Business Week 1985–; hon. degrees from Hebrew Univ. of Jerusalem 1985, Knox Coll., Galesburg, Ill. 1985, Univ. of Ill., Chicago 1988, State Univ. of New York 1990, Princeton Univ. 1991, Univs of Palermo and Buenos Aires 1993, Columbia Univ. 1993, Warsaw School of Econs 1995, Univ. of Econs, Prague 1995, Univ. of Miami 1995, Univ. of Rochester 1995, Hofstra Univ. 1997, Univ. d'Aix-Marseille 1999, Univ. of Athens 2002; W. S. Woytinsky Award (Univ. of Mich.) 1964, John Bates Clark Medal (American Econ. Asscn) 1967, Frank E. Seidman Distinguished Award in Political Econ. 1985, Merit Award (Nat. Insts. of Health) 1986, John R. Commons Award, Nobel Prize for Economic Sciences 1992, Lord Foundation Award 1995, Irene Tauber Award 1997, Nat. Medal of Science 2000, Phoenix Prize, Univ. of Chicago 2000, American Acad. of Achievement 2001, Presidential Medal of Freedom 2007. *Publications:* The Economics of Discrimination 1957, Human Capital 1964, Human Capital and the Personal Distribution of Income: Analytical Approach 1967, Economic Theory 1971, Essays in the Economics of Crime and Punishment (ed. with William M. Landes) 1974, The Allocation of Time and Goods over the Life Cycle (with Gilbert Ghez) 1975, The Economic Approach to Human Behavior 1976, A Treatise on the Family 1991, Accounting for Tastes 1996, The Economics of Life 1996, Social Economics 2000; Family, Society and State (in German) 1996, L'Approccio Economico al Comportamento Umano 1998; numerous articles in professional journals. *Leisure interests:* swimming, tennis. *Address:* Department of Economics, University of Chicago, 1126 East 59th Street, Chicago, IL 60637 (office); 1308 E 58th Street, Chicago, IL 60637, USA (home). *Telephone:* (312) 702-8168 (office). *Fax:* (773) 702-8496 (office); (312) 702-8490 (office). *E-mail:* sw47@midway.uchicago.edu (office). *Website:* www.src.uchicago.edu/users/gsb1 (office).

BECKER, Gert O.; German business executive; b. 21 Aug. 1933, Kronberg; s. of Otto Becker and Henriette (née Syring); m. Margrit Bruns 1960; one s. one d.; ed Akad. für Welthandel, Frankfurt; Sales Dept, Degussa, Frankfurt 1956; with rep. office in Tehran, Iran 1960, with subsidiary in São Paulo, Brazil 1963, Div. Man., Frankfurt 1966, Dir 1971, Man. Dir Degussa, Frankfurt 1977–96, Chair. Supervisory Bd 1996–2001; fmr Pres. and CEO; Pres. Asscn of Chemical Industries 1994–95. *Leisure interests:* literature, book collecting, golf.

BECKER, Jürgen; German writer and editor; b. 10 July 1932, Cologne; s. of Robert Becker and Else (née Schuchardt) Becker; m. 1st Mare Becker 1954 (divorced 1965); one s.; m. 2nd Rango Bohne 1965; one step-s. one step-d.; ed Univ. of Cologne; various jobs until 1959; freelance writer and contributor to W German Radio 1959–64; Reader at Rowohlt Verlag 1964–65; freelance writer; living in Cologne, Berlin, Hamburg and Rome; Dir Suhrkamp-Theaterverlag 1974; Head of Drama Dept, Deutschlandfunk Cologne; Writer in Residence, Warwick Univ. 1988; mem. Akademie der Künste Berlin, Deutsche Akademie für Sprache und Dichtung Darmstadt, PEN Club; Förderpreis des Landes Niedersachsen 1964, Stipendium Deutsche Akad. Villa Massimo, Rome 1965, 1966, Group 47 Prize 1967, Literaturpreis der Stadt Cologne 1968, Literaturpreis, Bavarian Acad. of Arts 1980, Kritikerpreis 1981, Bremer Literaturpreis 1986, Peter Huchel Prize 1994, Heinrich Böll Prize 1995, Rhein Literary Prize 1998, Uwe Johnson Prize 2001. *Publications:* Felder (short stories) 1964; Ränder (short stories) 1968, Bilder, Häuser (Radio Play) 1969, Umgebungen (short stories) 1970, Schnee (poems) 1971, Das Ende der Landschaftsmalerei (poems) 1974, Erzähl mir nichts vom Krieg (poems) 1977, In der verbleibenden Zeit (poems) 1979, Erzählen bis Ostende (short stories) 1981, Fenster und Stimmen (poems with Rango Bohne) 1982, Odenthals Küste (poems) 1986, Das Gedicht von der wiedervereinigten Landschaft (poem) 1988, Das Englische Fenster (poems) 1990, Frauen mit dem Rücken zum Betrachter (short stories with Rango Bohne) 1989, Foxtrott im Erfurter Stadion 1993, Korrespondenzen mit Landschaft (poems with pictures from Rango Bohne) 1996, Der fehlende Rest 1997, Aus der Geschichte der Trennungen (novel) 1999, Schnee in den Ardennen (novel) 2003; Ed. Happenings (documentary with Wolf Vostell) 1965. *Address:* Am Klausenberg 84, 51109 Cologne, Germany (home). *Telephone:* 841139 (home).

BECKER, Tom; American business executive; *CEO, Thom Browne;* fmrly with American Express Co.; Vice-Pres. and Sr Strategy Man. Treasury Services New Business Devt Group, J.P. Morgan –2007; CEO Thom Browne (fashion co.), New York 2007–. *Address:* Thom Browne, 100 Hudson Street, New York, NY 10013-2809, USA (office). *Telephone:* (212) 633-1197 (office). *E-mail:* info@thombrowne.com (office). *Website:* www.thombrowne.com (office).

BECKERS, Pierre-Olivier, BA, MBA; Belgian retail executive; *Group President, Director and CEO, Delhaize Group;* ed IAG Louvain-La-Neuve, Harvard Business School; joined Delhaize Group 1983, positions include store man., buyer, Dir of Purchasing, mem. Exec. Cttee 1990–, later Exec. Vice-Pres. responsible for int. activities, Dir Delhaize Group 1995–, Pres. and CEO 1999–, Chair. Delhaize America 2002–; Dir Food Marketing Inst.; Chair. CIES–The Food Business Forum 2002–; Manager of the Year, Trends/Tendances magazine 2000. *Address:* Office of the President, Delhaize, rue Osseghemstraat 53, Molenbeek-St-Jean, 1080 Brussels, Belgium (office). *Telephone:* (2) 412-21-11 (office). *Fax:* (2) 412-21-94 (office). *E-mail:* info@delhaizegroup.com (office). *Website:* www.delhaizegroup.com (office).

BECKETT, Rt Hon. Margaret (Mary), PC; British politician; *Minister of State for Housing and Planning;* b. 15 Jan. 1943, Ashton-under-Lyne, Lancs.; d. of Cyril Jackson and Winifred Jackson; m. Leo Beckett 1979; two step-s.; ed Notre Dame High School, Manchester and Norwich, Manchester Coll. of Science and Tech., John Dalton Polytechnic; eng apprentice (metallurgy), Associated Electrical Industries Ltd, Manchester, subsequently Experimental Officer, Univ. of Manchester; Sec. Trades Council and Labour Party 1968–70; researcher (Industrial Policy), Labour Party HQ 1970–74; Political Adviser to Minister of Overseas Devt Feb.–Oct. 1974; MP (Labour) for Lincoln 1974–79, for Derby S 1983–; Parl. Pvt. Sec., Minister for Overseas Devt 1974–75; Asst Govt Whip 1975–76; Minister, Dept of Educ. 1976–79; Prin. Researcher, Granada TV 1979–83; Opposition Spokeswoman with responsibility for Social Security 1984–89; Shadow Chief Sec. 1989–92; Shadow Leader of House, Campaigns Co-ordinator, Deputy Leader of Opposition 1992–94, Leader of

Opposition May–July 1994; Shadow Sec. of State for Health 1994–95; Shadow Pres. Bd of Trade 1995–97, Pres. Bd of Trade and Sec. of State for Trade and Industry 1997–98; Pres. of Council and Leader House of Commons 1998–2001; Sec. of State for Environment, Food and Rural Affairs 2001–06, for Foreign and Commonwealth Affairs 2006–07; Chair. Intelligence and Security Cttee 2008–; Minister of State for Housing and Planning, Dept for Communities and Local Govt 2008–; Ministerial visits and trade missions to USA, Japan, Mexico, Netherlands, Australia, Paris, Brussels, Singapore, China, Hong Kong and Pakistan, India 1997–2001; mem. Labour Party 1963–, Nat. Exec. Cttee 1980–81, 1985–86, 1988–97, Transport & General Workers Union 1964–, T&GWU Parl. Labour Party Group; mem. Nat. Union of Journalists, BECTU, Fabian Soc., Anti-Apartheid Movt, Tribune Group, Socialist Educ. Cttee, Labour Women's Action Cttee, Derby Co-op Party, Socialist Environment & Resources Asscn, Amnesty Int., Council of St George's Coll., Windsor 1976–82; Privy Councillor 1993–; Hon. Pres. Labour Friends of India; ranked 29th by Forbes magazine amongst 100 Most Powerful Women 2006. *Publications:* Vision for Growth – A New Industrial Strategy for Britain 1996, Renewing the NHS 1995, relevant sections of Labour's Programme 1972, 1973, The Nationalisation of Shipbuilding, Ship Repair and Marine Engineering, The National Enterprise Board, The Need for Consumer Protection. *Leisure interests:* cooking, reading, caravanning. *Address:* Department for Communities and Local Government, Eland House, Bressenden Place, London SW1E 5DU (office); House of Commons, Westminster, London, SW1A 2NE, England (office). *Telephone:* (20) 7944-4400 (office); (20) 7219-3000 (office); (1332) 345636 (constituency office) (office). *Fax:* (20) 7944-4101 (office); www.parliament.uk (office). *E-mail:* contactus@communities.gsi.gov.uk (office). *Website:* www.communities.gov.uk (office).

BECKETT, Sir Terence (Norman), KBE, DL, BSc (Econ), FREng, FIMechE; British business executive; b. 13 Dec. 1923, Walsall, Staffs.; s. of Horace Norman Beckett and Clarice Lillian Beckett (née Allsop); m. Sylvia Gladys Asprey 1950; one d.; ed Wolverhampton and S Staffs. Tech. Coll., London School of Econs; Capt., Royal Electrical and Mechanical Eng, served in Britain, India and Malaya 1945–48; joined Ford Motor Co. as Man. Trainee 1950, Styling Man., Briggs Motor Bodies Ltd (Ford subsidiary) 1954, Admin. Man., Engineer, then Man. Product Staff 1955, Gen. Planning Man., Product Planning Staff 1961, Man. Marketing Staff 1963, Dir, Car Div., Ford Motor Co. Ltd 1964, Exec. Dir 1966, Dir of Sales 1968, Vice-Pres. European and Overseas Sales Operations, Ford of Europe 1969–73; Man. Dir, Chief Exec., Ford Motor Co. Ltd 1974–80, Chair. 1976–80; fmr Chair. Ford Motor Credit Co. Ltd; Dir (non-exec.) CEGB 1987–90, Deputy Chair. 1990; Pro-Chancellor Univ. of Essex 1989–98 (Chair. 1989–95); fmr Dir ICI, Ford Nederland NV, Ford Lusitana SARL, Portugal, Henry Ford & Son Ltd, Ireland, Ford Motor Co. A/S, Denmark, Ford Motor Co. AB, Sweden, Automotive Finance Ltd; fmr mem. of Council CBI, Dir-Gen. 1980–87, mem. Council and Exec. Cttee Soc. of Motor Mfrs and Traders; mem. NEDC 1980–87; mem. Court and Council Essex Univ. 1985–98, Top Salaries Review Body 1987–92; Chair. Governing Body of London Business School, London Business School Trust Co. Ltd 1979–86, Council of Motor Cycle Trades Benevolent Fund; Gov., Cranfield Inst. of Tech., Nat. Inst. of Econ. and Social Research, London School of Econs; Patron, Manpower Services Comm. Award Scheme for Disabled People; Hon. mem. REME Inst. 1990; Hon. Fellow Sidney Sussex Coll., Cambridge 1981–, London Business School 1987–, LSE 1995–; Hon. DSc (Cranfield Inst. of Tech.) 1977, (Heriot-Watt) 1981; Hon. DScEcon (London) 1982; Hon. DTech (Brunel) 1991, (Wolverhampton) 1995; Hon. DUniv (Essex) 1995; Hon. DLitt (Anglia) 1998; Hambro Businessman of the Year Award 1978, BIM Gold Medal 1980. *Leisure interests:* travel, music. *Address:* c/o Barclays Bank PLC, 74 High Street, Ingatestone, Essex, England.

BECKETT, Wendy, (Sister Wendy), MA; British art writer and nun; b. 25 Feb. 1930, Johannesburg, SA; ed Univ. of Oxford; mem. Sacred Heart teaching order, currently living in solitude on the grounds of a Carmelite Monastery. *Television:* several series for BBC and Public Broadcasting Service including Sister Wendy's Grand Tour, Sister Wendy's Story of Painting. *Publications:* A Thousand Masterpieces, The Story of Painting, Meditations, My Favourite Things, Sister Wendy's American Collection 2000, Living the Lord's Prayer (with Rowan Williams) 2007. *Address:* Toby Eady Associates Ltd, Third Floor, 9 Orme Court, London, W2 4RL, England (office). *Telephone:* (20) 7792-0092 (office). *Fax:* (20) 7792-0879 (office). *E-mail:* toby@tobyeady.demon.co.uk (office). *Website:* www.tobyeadyassociates.co.uk (office).

BECKHAM, David Robert Joseph, OBE; British professional football player; b. 2 May 1975, Leytonstone; m. Victoria Beckham (née Adams) (q.v.) 1999; three s.; player with Manchester United –2003, trainee 1991, team debut 1992, on loan at Preston North End 1995, League debut 1995, 386 appearances for Manchester United, 80 goals; player with Real Madrid 2003–07, with Los Angeles Galaxy (Major League Soccer, USA) 2007–; seven caps for England Under-21s, rep. England 1996–2006, Capt. 2000–06; five Premiership medals, two Football Asscn Cup medals, European Cup medal, two Charity Shield winner medals; Bobby Charlton Skills Award 1987, Manchester United Player of the Year 1996–97, Young Player of the Year Professional Football Asscn 1996–97, Sky Football Personality of the Year 1997. *Publications:* David Beckham: My World 2001, David Beckham: My Side 2003. *Address:* c/o Simon Fuller, 19 Entertainment, Unit 33 Ransomes Dock Business Centre, 35-37 Parkgate Road, London SW11 4NP, England; c/o Los Angeles Galaxy, The Home Depot Center, 18400 Avalon Boulevard, Suite 200, Carson, CA 90746, USA (office). *Telephone:* (877) 342-5299 (office). *Fax:* (310) 630-2250 (office). *Website:* www.lagalaxy.com (office).

BECKHAM, Victoria; British singer; b. (Victoria Adams), 17 April 1974, Cuffley, England; d. of Tony Adams and Jackie Adams; m. David Beckham (q.v.) 1999; three s.; ed Jason Theatre School, Laine Arts Theatre Coll.; mem. Touch, later renamed The Spice Girls 1993–2001, as 'Posh Spice', reunion tour 2007–08; solo artist 2000–; two Ivor Novello songwriting awards 1997, Smash Hits Award for Best Band 1997, BRIT Awards for Best Single (for Wannabe) 1997, for Best Video (for Say You"ll Be There) 1997, three American Music Awards 1998, Special BRIT Award for Int. Sales 1998. *Film:* Spiceworld: The Movie 1997. *Recordings include:* albums: with The Spice Girls: Spice 1996, Spiceworld 1997, Forever 2000, Greatest Hits 2007; solo: Victoria Beckham 2001, Not Such An Innocent Girl 2004. *Publication:* Learning to Fly (autobiog.) 2001, That Extra Half an Inch 2006. *Leisure interest:* shopping. *Address:* 19 Entertainment, Unit 33, Ransomes Dock, 35–37 Parkgate, London, SW11 4NP, England (office). *Website:* www.dvbstyle.com.

BECKINSALE, Kate; British actress; b. 26 July 1973; d. of the late Richard Beckinsale and of Judy Loe; one d. (with Michael Sheen); m. Len Wiseman 2004; ed Godolphin and Latymer School, London and New Coll., Oxford. *Films:* Much Ado About Nothing 1993, Prince of Jutland 1994, Uncovered 1994, Haunted 1995, Marie-Louise ou la permission 1995, Shooting Fish 1997, The Last Days of Disco 1998, Brokedown Palace 1999, The Golden Bowl 2000, Pearl Harbor 2001, Serendipity 2001, Laurel Canyon 2002, Underworld 2003, Tiptoes 2003, Van Helsing 2004, The Aviator 2004, Underworld Evolution 2005, Click 2006, Snow Angels 2007, Vacancy 2007, Winged Creatures 2008, Nothing But the Truth 2008, Underworld: Rise of the Lycans 2009. *Play:* The Seagull 1995. *Television:* Devices and Desires (series) 1991, One Against the Wind 1991, Rachel's Dream 1992, Cold Comfort Farm 1994, Emma 1996, Alice Through the Looking Glass 1998. *Address:* International Creative Management, Oxford House, 76 Oxford Street, London, W1N 0AX, England (office). *Telephone:* (20) 7636-6565 (office).

BECKWITH, Athelstan Laurence Johnson, AO, DPhil, FAA, FRS; Australian chemist and academic; *Professor Emeritus of Organic Chemistry, Australian National University;* b. 20 Feb. 1930, Perth, WA; s. of Laurence A. Beckwith and Doris G. Beckwith; m. Phyllis Kaye Marshall 1953; one s. two d.; ed Univ. of Western Australia and Balliol Coll., Univ. of Oxford; Research Scientist, CSIRO, Melbourne 1957–58; Lecturer in Chem., Univ. of Adelaide 1958–62, Prof. of Organic Chem., 1965–81; Lecturer, Imperial Coll., Univ. of London 1962–63; Visiting Prof., Univ. of York 1968; Prof. of Organic Chem., ANU 1981–96, Prof. Emer. 1997–, Dean 1989–91; Pres. Royal Australian Chemical Inst. 1984–85; Vice-Pres. Australian Acad. of Science 1985–86; Chair. Editorial Bd Australian Journals of Science 1988–94; Syntex Pacific Coast Lecturer 1986, Rayson Huang Lecturer 1989, Kharasch Lecturer 1990, Centenary Lecturer 1991; Rennie Memorial Medal 1960, Centenary Medal 1991, Organic Chem. Medal 1992, Carnegie Fellow 1968, H. G. Smith Memorial Medal 1980, Leighton Medal 1997, Federation Medal 2001. *Publications:* numerous scientific papers and reviews in chem. journals, etc. *Leisure interests:* reading, performing music, model-making, golf. *Address:* Research School of Chemistry, Australian National University, Canberra, ACT 0200 (office); 3/9 Crisp Circuit, Bruce, ACT 2617, Australia (home). *Telephone:* (2) 6253-0696 (home). *E-mail:* beckwith@rsc.anu.edu.au (office).

BEDDALL, David; Australian politician and business executive; *Chairman, GPS Online Limited;* b. 27 Nov. 1948, Manchester, UK; s. of G. A. Beddall; m. Helen Beddall; one d.; two s. from previous marriage; mem. staff Commonwealth Banking Corpn 1967–78; Loans Officer, Australian Guarantee Corpn Ltd 1978–83; commercial finance consultant 1979–83; mem. House of Reps for Fadden, Queensland 1983, for Rankin 1984–; Minister for Small Business and Customs 1990–93, for Communications 1993, for Resources 1993–96; Chair. Jt Standing Cttee on Foreign Affairs and Defence 1984–87, House of Reps Standing Cttee on Industry, Science and Tech. 1987–93; currently Chair. GPS Online Ltd. *Address:* GPS Online Limited, Centenary Technology Park, 532 Seventeen Mile Rocks Road, Sinnamon Park, Brisbane (office); Inala Plaza, Corsair Avenue, Inala, Queensland 4077, Australia. *Telephone:* (7) 3725-5400 (office). *Fax:* (7) 3376-6702 (office). *Website:* www.gpsonline.com.au (office).

BEDFORD, David, FRAM, ARAM, FTCL; British composer; b. 4 Aug. 1937, London; s. of L. H. Bedford and L. F. K. Duff; m. 1st M. Parsonage 1958 (divorced); two d.; m. 2nd S. Pilgrim 1969 (divorced); two d.; m. 3rd Allison Powell 1994; one s. two d.; ed Lancing Coll. and Royal Acad. of Music; teacher of music, Whitefield School, Hendon, London 1966–69, Queen's Coll., Harley Street, London 1969–80; Assoc. Visiting Composer, Gordonstoun School 1980–81; Youth Music Dir English Sinfonia 1986–93, Composer in Asscn English Sinfonia 1993–; Patron Barnet Schools Music Asscn 1987; since 1980 freelance composer and arranger; Deputy Chair. Performing Right Soc. 1999, Chair. 2002; Licentiate of Trinity Coll. of Music. *Compositions:* Music for Albion Moonlight 1965, Star Clusters 1971, The Golden Wine 1974, Star's End 1974, The Rime of the Ancient Mariner 1978, The Death of Baldur 1979, Sun Paints Rainbows 1982, Symphony No. 1 1983, Symphony No. 2 1985, some music for film The Killing Fields 1984, Absolute Beginners 1985, The Mission 1986, Into Thy Wondrous House 1986, Ma non Sempere 1987, Gere Curam Mei Nobis (for Katherine) 1987, A Charm of Blessings 1996, String Quartet No. 2 1998, Oboe Concerto 1999, The Sultan's Turret 1999, The City and the Stars 2001, Like a Strand of Scarlet 2002, The Soft Stars that Shine at Night 2006, Wake into the Sun 2008, The Sinking of the Titanic 2009. *Leisure interests:* squash, film, cricket, tennis. *Address:* 12 Oakwood Road, Bristol, BS9 4NR, England (home). *Telephone:* (117) 962-4202 (home). *E-mail:* dvbmus@aol.com (office). *Website:* www.impulse-music.co.uk/davidbedford (office).

BEDFORD, Steuart John Rudolf, BA, FRCO, FRAM; British conductor; b. 31 July 1939, London; s. of L. H. Bedford and Lesley Bedford (née Duff); m. 1st Norma Burrowes 1969 (divorced 1980); m. 2nd Celia Harding 1980; two d.; ed Lancing Coll., Sussex, Univ. of Oxford, Royal Acad. of Music; operatic training as repetiteur, Asst Conductor, Glyndebourne Festival 1965–67; English Opera Group (later English Music Theatre), Aldeburgh and London 1967–73; Co-

Artistic Dir, English Musical Theatre 1976–80, Artistic Dir English Sinfonia 1981–90, Artistic Dir (also Exec. Artistic Dir) Aldeburgh Festival 1987–98; freelance conductor, numerous performances with ENO, Welsh Nat. Opera, Metropolitan Opera, New York (operas include Death in Venice, The Marriage of Figaro), Royal Danish Opera; also at Royal Opera House, Covent Garden (operas include Owen Wingrave, Death in Venice, Così fan tutte) Santa Fe Opera, Teatro Colón, Buenos Aires, Lyon, Garsington Opera, Opéra de Toulon, San Diego Opera, Boston Lyric Opera, Opera Theatre of St Louis etc.; conductor for Orchestre Philharmonique de Montpellier, Mahler Chamber Orchestra, Southern Sinfonia; Medal of the Worshipful Co. of Musicians. *Recordings include:* Death in Venice, Phaedra, Beggar's Opera, Collins Britten series. *Leisure interests:* golf, skiing. *Address:* Harrison Parrott, 5–6 Albion Court, London, W6 0QT, England (office); 76 Cromwell Avenue, London, N6 5HQ, England (home). *Telephone:* (20) 7229-9166 (office). *E-mail:* info@harrisonparrott.co.uk (office). *Website:* www.harrisonparrott.com (office).

BEDI, Bishan Singh, BA; Indian fmr professional cricketer; b. 25 Sept. 1946, Amritsar; s. of the late Gyan Singh Bedi and Rajinder Kaur Bedi; m. 1st Glenith Jill Bedi 1969; one s. one d.; m. 2nd Inderjit Bedi 1980; ed Punjab Univ.; fmr employee Steel Authority of India, New Delhi; slow left-arm bowler; played for Northern Punjab 1961–62 to 1966–67, Delhi 1968–69 to 1980–81, Northamptonshire 1972–77; played in 67 Tests for India (1967–68 to 1979), 22 as Capt., taking 266 wickets (average 28.7); took 1,560 first-class wickets; toured England 1971, 1974, 1976 and 1975 (World Cup); Hon. Life mem. MCC 1981; fmr nat. selector; Padma Shri Award 1969, Arjuna Award 1971. *Leisure interests:* reading, photography, swimming and letter-writing. *Address:* Ispat Bhawan, Lodhi Rd, New Delhi 3, India. *Telephone:* 43133.

BEDI, Kiran; Indian police professional (retd); b. 1949, Amritsar; d. of Prakash Peshawaria and Prem Peshawaria; m. Brij Bedi; one d.; ed Sacred Heart School, Amritsar, Govt Coll. for Women, Amritsar, Punjab Univ., Chandigarh, Delhi Univ. and Indian Inst. of Tech., Delhi; joined Indian Police Service 1972, held various assignments including Dist Police, Delhi Traffic Police, Special Traffic, Goa, Narcotics Control Bureau; f. Navjyoti (residential community-based therapeutic treatment centre) 1987, India Vision Foundation 1994; fmr Deputy Insp.-Gen., Mizoram; fmr Insp.-Gen. of Prisons, of Tihar Jails, Delhi; fmr Special Sec. to Lt Gov. of Delhi; fmr Jt Commr, Delhi Police; fmr Insp.-Gen. of Police, Chandigarh; fmr Jt Commr of Police (Training), Delhi; UN Civilian Police Adviser 2003; f. website www.saferindia.com 2007; Jawaharlal Nehru Fellowship; Police Medal for Gallantry, Int. Org. of Good Templars Asia-Region Award, Ramon Magsaysay Peace Award for Govt Service 1994, Joseph Beuys Foundation Award for Holistic and Innovative Man., Asscns of Christian Colls and Univs Int. Award, American Fed. of Muslims from India Pride of India Award 1999, Serge Sotiroff Memorial Award (for Navjyoti Centre) 1999, State Award (for Navjyoti Centre), Indian Inst. of Tech. Alumni Asscn Award 2000, Western Soc. of Criminology USA Tom Gitchoff Award 2001, Blue Drop Group Man. Cultural and Artistic Asscn (Italy) Woman of the Year Award 2002; fmr Nat. Jr, Sr and Asian Tennis Champion and Rep. India abroad. *Film:* Real Salute 2001. *Publications include:* It's Always Possible, Government@net (jtly with Sandeep Srivastava); writes a fortnightly column 'What Went Wrong' in Times of India and Navbharat Times (compilation of 37 of these articles published in book form, also Hindi trans. Galti Kiski). *Leisure interest:* community work. *Address:* India Vision Foundation, 56 Uday Park (Basement), New Delhi 1100049, India. *Telephone:* (11) 26525741. *E-mail:* kiran@saferindia.com. *Website:* www.saferindia.com/kiranbedi; www.indiavisionfoundation.org; www.kiranbedi.com.

BEDIE, Henri Konan, LenD; Côte d'Ivoirian politician; b. 1934, Dadiekro; m. Henriette Koinzan Bomo 1958; two s. two d.; ed Univ. of Poitiers; Asst Dir Caisse de Sécurité de la Côte d'Ivoire 1959–60; Counsellor, French Embassy, Washington, DC March–Aug. 1960; mem. Perm. Mission to UN 1960; Chargé d'Affaires, Embassy of Côte d'Ivoire, Washington, DC Aug.–Dec. 1960; Amb. to USA 1960–66; Minister-Del. for Econ. and Financial Affairs 1966–68; Minister of Economy and Finance 1968–75; Special Adviser, IFC 1976–80; re-elected Deputy, Nat. Ass. 1980; Pres. Nat. Ass. 1980, re-elected 1985, 1986; mem. Political Bureau, Parti Démocratique de la Côte d'Ivoire (PDCI); Pres. Office Africain et Malgache de la Propriété Industrielle; Pres. of Côte d'Ivoire 1993–2000.

BEDJAOUI, Mohammed; Algerian judge and diplomatist; b. 21 Sept. 1929, Sidi-Bel-Abbès; s. of Benali Bedjaoui and Fatima Oukili; m. Leila Francis 1962; two d.; ed Univ. of Grenoble and Institut d'Etudes Politiques, Grenoble; Lawyer, Court of Appeal, Grenoble 1951; research worker at CNRS, Paris 1955; Legal Counsellor of the Arab League in Geneva 1959–62; Legal Counsellor Provisional Republican Govt of Algeria in Exile 1958–61; Dir Office of the Pres. of Nat. Constituent Ass. 1962; mem. Del. to UN 1957, 1962, 1977, 1978–82; Sec.-Gen. Council of Ministers, Algiers 1962–63; Pres. Soc. Nat. des Chemins de Fer Algériens (SNCFA) 1964; Dean of the Faculty of Law, Algiers Univ. 1964; Minister of Justice and Keeper of the Seals 1964–70; mem., special reporter, Int. Law Comm. 1965–82; Amb. to France 1970–79; Perm. Rep. to UNESCO 1971–79, to UN 1979–82; Vice-Pres. UN Council on Namibia 1979–82; mem. UN Comm. of Inquiry (Iran) 1980; Pres. Group of 77 1981–82; Judge Int. Court of Justice 1982–2001 (Pres. 1994–97); Minister of State for Foreign Affairs 2005–07; fmr Pres. African Soc. of Int. and Comparative Law; Head Algerian Del. to UN Conf. on Law of the Sea 1976–80; mem. Int. Inst. of Law; Carnegie Endowment for Int. Peace 1956; Ordre du Mérite Alaouite, Morocco, Order of the Repub., Egypt, Commdr Légion d'honneur (France), Ordre de la Résistance (Algeria). *Publications:* International Civil Service 1956, Fonction publique internationale et influences nationales 1958, La révolution algérienne et le droit 1961, Succession d'états 1970, Terra nullius, droits historiques et autodétermination 1975, Non-alignment et droit international 1976, Pour un nouvel ordre économique international 1979, Droit international: bilan et perspectives 1992. *Address:* c/o Ministry of Foreign Affairs, place Mohamed Seddik Benyahia, el-Mouradia, Algiers (office); 39 rue des Pins, Hydra, Algiers, Algeria. *Telephone:* (2) 60-30-89.

BEDNARSKI, Krzysztof; Polish sculptor, performer and graphic designer; b. 25 July 1953, Kraków; m. Marina Fabbri; two s.; ed Acad. of Fine Arts, Warsaw; worked for Laboratorium Theatre of Jerzy Grotowski, Wrocław 1976–82; Artist-in-Residence, OMI Foundation, New York 1995; Guest Teacher, studio of Prof. Grzegorz Kowalski, Sculpture Dept, Acad. of Fine Arts, Warsaw 1996–97; Artist-in-Residence, Art Foundation by Daniel Spoerri 'The Garden', Tuscany, Italy 1998–99; contrib. to European project "Global Village Garden" (Germany) 2002–03; has participated in more than 300 exhbns world-wide; Grant from Leube Foundation, Salzburg, Austria 2003, K. Kobro Award, Łódź 2004, 'Exit-New Art in Poland' Award 2004. *Works include:* created series of posters for productions including Vigil 1976–77, Project Mountain 1977, Project Earth 1977–79, Human Tree 1979, and others; installations such as Total Portrait of Karl Marx 1978 (realised in many versions up to 1999, such as The Collected Works of Karl Marx 1988), In Memory of Jan Szeliga 1980, sculptures such as Victoria Victoria 1983, Moby Dick (Best Polish Sculpture 1987) 1987, The Xram Lrak Burial Mound 1988, Moby Dick – Mask 1989, La Rivoluzione siamo Noi 1989, Finite Column 1991, Unsichtbar 1993, Missing Lenin's Hand 1995; monument of Federico Fellini in Rimini under construction 1994 and Krzysztof Kieślowski's tomb in Warsaw 1997, Vision & Prayer 1998–; artwork in Light Art Collection, Targetti Group, Florence, Italy 2005; works in numerous collections in Poland, Italy and elsewhere. *Publications:* Linda Nochlin, The Body in Pieces, The Fragment as a Metaphor of Modernity 1994, Moby Dick Museum of Art 1994, Dictionary of Contemporary Artists 2001, Achille Bonito-Oliva, Oggetti di turno. Dall'arte alla critica 1997, Stownik Sztuki xx wieku 1998. *Address:* Via Dei Banchi Vecchi 134, 00-186 Rome, Italy (home). *Telephone:* 3486529476 (Italy; mobile) (office); 504653975 (Poland; mobile) (office); (06) 6896068 (home). *Fax:* (06) 6896068 (home). *E-mail:* k.bednarski@fastwebnet.it (home); kmbednarski@neostrada.pl (home). *Website:* www.bednarski.art.pl (office); www.myartspace.com (office).

BEDNORZ, George, PhD; German physicist; b. 16 May 1950; ed Swiss Federal Inst. of Tech., Zürich; with IBM Research Lab., Rüschlikon, Zürich 1982–; shared Nobel Prize for Physics for discovery of new super-conducting materials 1987. *Address:* IBM Zürich Research Laboratory, Säumerstrasse 4, 8803 Rüschlikon, Zürich, Switzerland. *Telephone:* (1) 7248111.

BEDREGAL GUTIÉRREZ, Guillermo; Bolivian writer, diplomatist and politician; b. 16 Oct. 1926; La Paz; Minister of Foreign Affairs 1979, 1986–89; fmr Amb. to Spain; unsuccessful cand. for Vice-Pres. (Movimiento Nacionalista Revolucionario) 2005; fmr Pres. UN Conference for the Adoption of a Convention Against Illicit Traffic in Narcotic Drugs Psychotropic Substances. *Address:* c/o Movimiento Nacionalista Revolucionario (MNR), Calle Nicolás Acosta 574, La Paz, Bolivia.

BEDSER, Sir Alec Victor, Kt, CBE; British fmr cricketer and company director; b. 4 July 1918, Reading; s. of the late Arthur Bedser and Florence Beatrice Bedser; ed Monument Hill Secondary School, Woking; served in RAF 1939–46; right-arm fast-medium bowler and right-hand lower-order batsman; played for Surrey 1939–60; played in 51 Tests for England 1946–55, taking then record 236 wickets (average 24.8) including 104 against Australia; took 1,924 first-class wickets; toured Australia 1946–47, 1950–51 and 1954–55; mem. England Cricket Selection Cttee of Test and County Cricket Bd 1962–83, Chair. 1968–81; Asst Man. (to the late Duke of Norfolk) MCC tour to Australia 1962–63, Man. MCC tour to Australia 1974–75, to Australia and India 1979–80; Pres. Surrey Co. Cricket Club 1987–88, fmr Vice-Pres. and Cttee mem., Hon. Life Vice-Pres.; started office equipment firm in partnership with twin brother, the late Eric A. Bedser 1955; Pres. West Hill Golf Club; Freeman City of London 1968; Hon. Life mem. Surrey Cricket Club, Western Prov. Cricket Club, SA 2002, West Hill Golf Club, East India and Devonshire Club, Melbourne Cricket Club, Australia; Hon. Life Vice-Pres. MCC 1999; selected in 'England's Greatest Post-War XI' by The Wisden Cricketer 2004. *Publications:* Our Cricket Story (with Eric A. Bedser) 1951, Bowling 1952, Following On (with Eric A. Bedser) 1954, May's Men in Australia 1959, Cricket Choice 1981, Twin Ambitions (autobiog. with Alex Bannister) 1986. *Leisure interests:* cricket, golf, gardening, charities. *Address:* c/o Surrey County Cricket Club, Kennington Oval, London, SE11 5SS (office); The Coppice, Carlton Road, Woking, Surrey, GU21 4HQ, England (home). *Telephone:* (1483) 773018 (home).

BEEBE, Michael Dale (Mike), BA; American lawyer, politician and state official; *Governor of Arkansas;* b. 28 Dec. 1946, Amagon, Jackson Co., Ark.; m. Ginger Beebe; three c.; ed Newport High School, Arkansas State Univ., Univ. of Arkansas at Fayetteville; family lived in Detroit, St Louis, Chicago, Houston and Alamagordo, NM before moving back to Ark.; served in US Army Reserve; practised law in Searcy, Ark. for 10 years after graduating from law school; Ark. State Senator 1983–2002; Ark. Attorney Gen. 2003–06; Gov. of Ark. 2007–; Democrat. *Address:* Office of the Governor, Room 250, State Capitol, Little Rock, AR 72201, USA (office). *Telephone:* (501) 682-2345 (office). *Fax:* (501) 682-3597 (office). *Website:* www.arkansas.gov/governor (office); www.mikebeebe.com (office).

BEEBEEJAUN, Ahmed Rashid, FRCP; Mauritian politician; *Deputy Prime Minister and Minister of Renewable Energy and Public Utilities;* b. 22 Dec. 1934; m.; ed Univ. of Birmingham, UK; Child Health Consultant 1971–93; mem. Mouvement Militant Mauricien (MMM) 1993–97; mem. Mauritius

Labour Party 2000–, Deputy Leader –2004; mem. Nat. Ass. 2005–; Deputy Prime Minister 2005–, Minister of Public Infrastructure, Land Transport and Shipping 2005–08, of Renewable Energy and Public Utilities 2008–. *Leisure interests:* music, theatre. *Address:* Ministry of Public Utilities, Medcor Building, 10th Floor, John F. Kennedy Street, Port Louis, Mauritius (office). *Telephone:* 210-3994 (office). *Fax:* 208-6497 (office). *E-mail:* minpuuti@intnet.mu (office). *Website:* publicutilities.gov.mu (office).

BEEBY, Thomas Hall; American architect and academic; *Partner, Hammond Beeby Rupert Ainge;* b. 12 Oct. 1941, Oak Park, Ill.; m. 1st Marcia D. Greenlease 1960 (divorced 1973); one s. one d.; m. 2nd Kirsten Peltzer 1975; two s.; ed Lower Merion High School, Ardmore, Pa, Gresham's School, Holt (UK), Cornell and Yale Univs; Assoc. C.F. Murphy Assocs. Chicago 1965–71; partner, Hammond Beeby & Assocs. Chicago 1971–76; partner, Hammond Beeby & Babka (now Hammond Beeby Rupert Ainge), Chicago 1976–; Assoc. Prof. Dept of Architecture, Ill. Inst. of Tech., Chicago 1973–80; Dir School of Arch. Univ. of Ill. at Chicago 1980–85; Dean, Prof. School of Arch. Yale Univ. 1985–91, Adjunct Prof. 1992–; mem. Advisory Bd, Dept of Architecture, Illinois Inst. of Tech. 1993–, Trustee 1997–; work includes office bldgs, shopping centres, housing, libraries, museums, public bldgs etc.; contributor to numerous exhbns of architecture and design in USA and Europe including Venice Biennale 1980; Distinguished Building Award, American Inst. of Architects, Chicago Chapter (numerous times); Nat. Design Award 1984, 1987, 1989, 1991, 1993. *Publications:* articles in professional journals. *Address:* Hammond Beeby Rupert Ainge Inc., 440 N Wells Street, Chicago, IL 60610, USA. *Telephone:* (312) 527-3200 (office). *Fax:* (312) 527-1256 (office). *E-mail:* tbeeby@hbra-arch.com (office).

BEERING, Steven Claus, MD; American physician, academic and university administrator; *President Emeritus, Purdue University;* b. 20 Aug. 1932, Berlin, Germany; s. of Steven and Alice Friedrichs Beering; m. Jane Pickering 1956; three s.; ed Univ. of Pittsburgh; Prof. of Medicine 1969–; Asst Dean, Indiana Univ. School of Medicine 1969–70, Assoc. Dean 1970–74, Dean 1974–83, Dir Indiana Univ. Medical Center 1974–83; Pres. Purdue Univ. and Purdue Univ. Research Foundation 1983–2000, Pres. Emer. 2000–; Hon. ScD (Indiana) 1988, Hon. LLD; numerous awards and prizes. *Publications:* numerous articles in professional journals. *Leisure interests:* music, photography, reading, travel. *Address:* Purdue University, Purdue Memorial Union, Room 218, West Lafayette, IN 47906-3584 (office); 10487 Windemere Drive, Carmel, IN 46032, USA (home). *Telephone:* (765) 496-7555 (office); (317) 581-1414 (home). *Fax:* (765) 496-7561 (office). *E-mail:* scb@purdue.edu (office); sbeering@indy.rr.com (home). *Website:* www.purdue.edu (office).

BEEVERS, Harry, PhD; American biologist and academic; *Professor Emeritus of Biology, University of California, Santa Cruz;* b. 10 Jan. 1924, Shildon, England; s. of Norman Beevers and Olive Beevers; m. Jean Sykes 1949; one s.; ed Univ. of Durham; postdoctoral research, Univ. of Oxford 1946–50; Asst Prof. of Biology, Purdue Univ. 1950–53, Assoc. Prof. 1953–58, Prof. 1958–69; Prof. of Biology, Univ. of Calif., Santa Cruz 1969–90, Prof. Emer. 1990–; Pres. American Soc. of Plant Physiologists 1961; Sr US Scientist, Alexander von Humboldt Foundation 1986; Fellow Crown Coll., Univ. of Calif. Santa Cruz 1969; mem. NAS; Fellow American Acad. of Arts and Sciences 1973; mem. Deutsche Botanische Gesellschaft 1982, Academia Nazionale dei Lincei 1991; Foreign mem. Academia Europaea; Hon. DSc (Purdue Univ.) 1971, (Univ. of Newcastle-upon-Tyne) 1974, (Nagoya Univ.) 1986; Sigma Xi Research Award, Purdue Univ. 1958, McCoy Research Award 1968, Stephen Hales Award, American Soc. of Plant Physiologists 1970, Barnes Award 1998. *Publications:* Respiratory Metabolism in Plants 1961; 200 articles on plant metabolism in scientific journals. *Leisure interest:* gardening. *Address:* Biology Department, University of California, Santa Cruz, CA 95064 (office); 57 Del Mesa Carmel, Carmel, CA 93923, USA (home). *E-mail:* hbeevers@webtv.net (home).

BEFFA, Jean-Louis Guy Henri; French business executive; *Chairman, Compagnie de Saint-Gobain;* b. 11 Aug. 1941, Nice; s. of Edmond Beffa and Marguerite Feursinger; m. Marie-Madeleine Brunel-Grasset 1967; two s. one d.; ed Lycée Masséna, Nice, Ecole Nat. Supérieure des Mines and Inst. d'Etudes Politiques, Paris; mining engineer, Clermont-Ferrand 1967, motor fuel man. 1967–74, head of refinery service 1970–73, Asst to Dir 1973–74, Chief Mining Eng 1974; Dir of Planning, Pont-à-Mousson (subsidiary of Saint-Gobain Group) 1975–77, Dir-Gen. 1978, Pres. Dir-Gen. 1979–82, Deputy Dir (Pipelines) Saint-Gobain-Pont-à-Mousson 1978, Dir 1979–82, Dir-Gen. Cie de Saint-Gobain 1982–86, CEO 1982, Chair. and CEO 1986–2007, Chair. 2007–, also Chair. Saint-Gobain Centre for Econ. Research 2000–; Pres. Inst. de L'Histoire de L'Industrie (Idni) 1992–98; Pres. Supervisory Bd Poliet 1996–; Vice-Pres. Compagnie Générale des Eaux 1998–; Vice-Pres. Admin. Bd BNP Paribas 2000–; mem. Int. Consultative Cttee, Chase Manhattan Bank 1986–, AT&T 1987; mem. Admin. Council Ecole Polytechnique 1993–; Admin. Banque Nat. de Paris, Cie Gen. des Eaux, Cie de Suez et de Petrofina; mem. Bd Dirs Gaz de France, Group Bruxelles Lambert; Officier Légion d'honneur, Officier Ordre nat. du Mérite, Officier des Arts es Lettres, Commdr du Mérite (FRG); CBE (Foreign mem.) (UK). *Leisure interests:* swimming, golf. *Address:* Compagnie de Saint-Gobain, Les Miroirs, 18 Avenue d'Alsace, 92096 Paris la Défense Cedex, France (office). *Telephone:* 1-47-62-30-00 (office). *Fax:* 1-47-78-45-03 (office). *E-mail:* info@saint-gobain.com (office). *Website:* www.saint-gobain.com (office).

BEG, Gen. (retd) Mirza Aslam, BA, MSc; Pakistani army officer (retd) and politician; b. 2 Aug. 1931, Azamgarh, Uttar Pradesh, India; s. of Mirza Murtuza Beg; m.; one s. two d.; ed Shibli Coll., Azamgarh, Aligarh Univ., India, Command and Staff Coll., Quetta and Nat. Defence Coll., Quaid-Azam Univ., Rawalpindi; commissioned 1952; served in Baluch (Infantry) Regt; joined Special Service Group (Commandos) 1961; Brig. Maj. of an Infantry Brigade during India–Pakistan war 1965; Lt-Col 1969; in command, Infantry Bn, India–Pakistan war 1971; Brig. in command of Infantry Brigade 1974; Maj.-Gen. in command of Infantry Div. 1978; Chief of Gen. Staff 1980–85; Lt-Gen. 1984; Corps Commdr 1985; Gen. and Vice-Chief of Army Staff 1987; Chief of Army Staff 1987–91; Founder, Pres. and Chair. Awami Qiyadat Party; Sitara-e-Basalat 1981, Hilal-e-Imtiaz (Mil.) 1982, Nishan-e-Imtiaz (Mil.) 1988, Tongil (First Class) Medal (S Korea) 1988, US Legion of Merit 1989, Bintang Yudha Dharm (Indonesia) 1990, Kt Grand Cross (First Class) (Thailand) 1991. *Publications:* articles in journals and nat. and int. newspapers. *Address:* 88 Race Course Scheme Street 3, Rawalpindi Cantt (office); No. 1, National Park Road, Rawalpindi, Pakistan (home). *Telephone:* (51) 5563309 (office); (51) 5567637 (home). *Fax:* (51) 5564244 (office); (51) 5521219 (home).

BEGG, David, MPhil, PhD, FRSE; British economist and academic; *Principal of Business School and Professor of Economics, Imperial College London;* b. 1951; ed Univ. of Cambridge, Univ. of Oxford, Massachusetts Inst. of Tech., USA; Fellow and Lecturer, Worcester Coll., Univ. of Oxford 1976–86; Research Fellow, Centre for Econ. Policy Research 1983–; Prof. of Econs, Birkbeck Coll., Univ. of London 1986–2003; Prin. of Business School and Prof. of Econs, Imperial Coll., London 2003–; Econ. Policy Adviser to Bank of England 1986–, also Adviser on monetary policy to IMF, HM Treasury; commissioned to provide econs training to Govt of Czechoslavakia 1991, to Nat. Bank of Hungary 1998–99; Chair. Begg Comm. 1999–2005; fmr Research Dir, Centre for Econ. Forecasting, London Business School; mem. Bellagio Group 1999–, Keynes Seminar (convened quarterly by UK Chancellor of the Exchequer) 1999–; mem. HM Treasury Academic Panel 1981–96; mem. Research Awards Advisory Cttee, Leverhulme Trust 1986–93; Founding Man. Ed. Economic Policy 1984–2000. *Publications include:* The Rational Expectations Revolution in Macroeconomics, Economics 2000, Foundations of Economics 2002, The Making of Monetary Union 2005, Emu: Getting The Endgame Right 2005. *Address:* Office of the Principal, Business School, Imperial College, South Kensington Campus, London, SW7 2AZ, England (office). *Telephone:* (20) 7594-9100 (office). *Fax:* (20) 7823-7685 (office). *E-mail:* d.begg@imperial.ac.uk (office). *Website:* www3.imperial.ac.uk/business-school (office).

BEGGS, Jean Duthie, CBE, PhD, FRS, FRSE; British molecular biologist and academic; *Royal Society Darwin Trust Research Professor, University of Edinburgh;* b. 16 April 1950; d. of William Renfrew Lancaster and Jean Crawford Lancaster (née Duthie); m. Ian Beggs 1972; two s.; ed Univ. of Glasgow; Postdoctoral Fellow, Dept of Molecular Biology, Univ. of Edin. 1974–77; Plant Breeding Inst., Cambridge 1977–79; Beit Memorial Fellow for Medical Research 1976–79; Lecturer in Biochemistry, Imperial Coll., London Univ. 1979–85; Univ. Research Fellow, Dept of Molecular Biology, Univ. of Edin. 1985–89, Professorial Research Fellow 1994–99, Prof. of Molecular Biology 1999–, Royal Soc. Darwin Trust Research Prof. 2005–; Royal Soc. Gabor Medal 2003, UK Biochemical Soc. Novartis Medal 2004. *Leisure interests:* walking, scuba diving. *Address:* Wellcome Trust Centre for Cell Biology, University of Edinburgh, King's Buildings, Mayfield Road, Edin. , EH9 3JR, Scotland (office). *Telephone:* (131) 650-5351 (office). *E-mail:* j.beggs@ed.ac.uk (office). *Website:* www.wcb.ed.ac.uk/beggs.htm (office).

BEGICH, Mark P.; American politician; *Senator from Alaska;* b. 31 March 1962, Anchorage; s. of the late Nick Begich and of Pegge Begich; m. Deborah Bonito 1990; one s.; ed Steller Secondary School,; mem. Anchorage Ass. 1988–98, Chair. 1996–98; Mayor of Anchorage 2003–09; Senator from Alaska 2009–; Owner, Carson Hot Springs Resort, Carson City, Nev., also owner of vending machine and property rental cos in Anchorage; mem. Bd of Dirs Boys and Girls Club, Spirit of Youth Foundation, Family Resource Center; mem. Air Force Asscn, Nat. Rifle Asscn; fmr Chair. Alaska Student Loan Corpn; f. Making a Difference Program for first time juvenile offenders; Democrat; named Friend of Educ. by Anchorage Educ. Asscn, voted Alaska's top state official by municipal officials 1997, 2004. *Address:* Office of Senator Mark P. Begich, US Senate, Washington, DC 20510, USA (office). *Telephone:* (202) 224-3121 (office). *Website:* www.senate.gov (office).

BEGLEY, Charlene T., BS; American business executive; *President and CEO, GE Enterprise Solutions;* m.; three d.; ed Univ. of Vermont; began her career at General Electric (GE) 1988, held a variety of leadership roles including Vice-Pres. Operations, GE Capital Mortgage Services, Quality Leader, GE Transportation Systems 1995, Chief Financial Officer 1997, Dir of Finance, GE Plastics-Europe 1998–99, Vice-Pres. Corp. Audit Staff 1999, CEO GE Fanuc Automation North America, Inc. 2001–03, Pres. and CEO GE Rail 2003–05, Pres. and CEO GE Plastics, Pittsfield, Mass 2005–07 (first woman Sr Vice-Pres. in GE history), Pres. and CEO GE Enterprise Solutions; spent a year as Acting CEO Casablanca Fan Co.; mem. Bd of Dirs Nat. Asscn of Mfrs; serves on World Econ. Forum's Young Global Leaders, Business Advisory Council of Univ. of Vermont; ranked by Fortune magazine amongst 50 Most Powerful Women in Business in the US (20th) 2005, (22nd) 2006, (26th) 2007. *Address:* GE Enterprise Solutions, 1 Plastics Avenue, Pittsfield, MA 01201-3662, USA (office). *Telephone:* (413) 448-7110 (office). *E-mail:* Christopher.Tessier@ge.com (office). *Website:* www.geplastics.com (office).

BÉGUIN, Bernard, LèsL; Swiss journalist; b. 14 Feb. 1923, Sion, Valais; s. of Bernard Béguin and Clemence Welten; m. Antoinette Waelbroeck 1948; two s. two d.; ed Geneva High School, Geneva Univ. and Graduate Inst. of Int. Studies; Swiss Sec. World Student Relief 1945–46; corresp. at UN European Headquarters; Journal de Geneva 1946–70, Foreign Ed. 1947, Ed.-in-Chief 1959–70; Diplomatic Commentator, Swiss Broadcasting System 1954–59, Swiss TV 1959–70; Head of Programmes, Swiss French-speaking TV 1970–73; Deputy Dir Radio and TV 1973–86; Cen. Pres. Swiss Press Asscn 1958–60, Hon. mem. 1974–; Visiting Prof. in Professional Ethics, Univ. of Neuchâtel 1984–88; Pres. Swiss Press Council 1985–90; Pres. Swiss Ind. Authority on

Complaints concerning Broadcasting Programmes 1991–92; consultant with UNESCO (assessment of the media environment), Belarus 1994; mem. Fed. Comm. on Cartels 1964–80; mem. Bd, Swiss Telegraphic Agency 1968–71. *Publication:* Journaliste, qui t'a fait roi? Les médias entre droit et liberté, 1988. *Leisure interests:* sailing, camping. *Address:* 41 avenue de Budé, 1202 Geneva 1, Switzerland. *Telephone:* (22) 733-75-30. *Fax:* (22) 733-75-30 (home). *E-mail:* beguinb@worldcom.ch (home).

BEHAJAINA, Maj.-Gen. Petera; Malagasy politician and army officer; ed Asia-Pacific Center for Security Studies; Chief of Staff of Madagascar Army 2003; Minister of Defence 2004–07. *Address:* c/o Ministry of Defence, BP 08, Ampahibe, 101 Antananarivo, Madagascar (office).

BEHBEHANI, Kazem, PhD, FRCPath; Kuwaiti international organization official; *Envoy, World Health Organization;* ed Univs of Liverpool and London, UK; fmr Deputy Dir Gen. Kuwait Inst. for Scientific Research; Prof. Kuwait Medical Faculty; Vice-Rector for Research, Kuwait Univ.; Programme Man., Special Programme for Research and Training, Tropical Diseases, WHO 1991–94, Dir of Tropical Diseases 1994–99, Dir Eastern Mediterranean Liaison Office and in charge of Resource Mobilization for the Eastern Mediterranean Region 1999–2003, Asst Dir Gen. WHO 2003–05, now Envoy; Visiting Prof./Scholar, Harvard Medical School, USA, currently Co-Chair. Scientific Advisory Bd for the Environment and Public Health; mem. British Soc. of Parasitology, American Soc. for Tropical Medicine and Hygiene, Electron Microscopy Soc. of America and European Acad. of Arts, Science and the Humanities; Fellow Islamic Acad. of Sciences; Award for Research in Medicine, Kuwait Foundation for the Advancement of Sciences. *Publications:* a book on science and tech. and more than 100 scientific papers. *Address:* Kuwait Mission, Geneva, Switzerland (office). *Telephone:* (22) 918-01-00 (office). *E-mail:* albader@kuwaitmission.ch (office). *Website:* www.kazembehbehani.com.

BEHMEN, Alija, PhD; Bosnia and Herzegovina politician and economist; b. 25 Dec. 1940, Split, Croatia; m.; two s.; ed Univ. of Sarajevo; worked at Inst. of Econs, Sarajevo; mem. staff Railways Enterprise ŽTO Sarajevo, Deputy Pres., Pres. Exec. Bd 1970–78; Pres. Exec. Bd INTERŠPED 1978–80; Assoc. Prof., Faculty of Transportation and Communications 1980–; Vice-Pres. Social Democratic Party of Bosnia and Herzegovina; mem. Ass. of Sarajevo Canton; Deputy Chair. Parl. of Bosnia and Herzegovina 1998–2001; Prime Minister of the Fed. of Bosnia and Herzegovina 2001–03. *Address:* Social Democratic Party of Bosnia and Herzegovina, Alipašina 41, 71000 Sarajevo, Bosnia and Herzegovina (office). *Telephone:* (33) 663750 (office); (33) 663753 (office). *Fax:* (33) 213675 (office). *Website:* www.sdp-bih.org.ba (office).

BEHNISCH, Günter; German architect; b. 12 June 1922, Dresden; ed Tech. Univ., Stuttgart; architect with Rolf Gutbrod, Stuttgart 1951–52; own practice Behnisch & Partner 1952–; partner Behnisch Behnisch & Partner 1979–; Prof. of Design, Industrial Bldg and Dir of Bldg Form, Inst. for Bldg Standards, Tech. Univ. Darmstadt 1967–87, Prof. Emer. 1987–; Heinrich Hertz Prof. Tech. Univ. Karlsruhe 1994; mem. Berlin Acad. of Arts 1982–, Int. Acad. of Architecture, Sofia 1994–, Bavarian Acad. of Fine Arts 1999–; Founding mem. Saxon Acad. of Fine Arts, Dresden 1996–; Hon. FRIBA; Hon. mem. Royal Incorporation of Architecture, Edin.; Order of Merit 1997; Dr hc (Tech. Univ. Stuttgart) 1984; Int. Olympic Cttee Hon. Prize 1992, Gold Medal, Acad. d'Architecture, Paris 1992, Hans Molfenter Prize, Stuttgart 1993, Hon. Award, Lithuanian Architecture Asscn 1994, Fritz Schumacher Prize, Alfred Toepfer Foundation 1998, Wolfgang Hirsch Award, Chamber of Architects Rheinland-Pfalz 2001. *Publications include:* Plenary Complex of the German Bundestag 1994, Architecture for Nature 1998, Das Bristol Projekt – The Harbourside Centre for Performing Arts 1999; over 1,200 articles in brochures and magazines. *Address:* Behnisch & Partner, Gorch-Fock-Strasse 30, 70619 Stuttgart, Germany (office). *Telephone:* (711) 476560 (office). *Fax:* (711) 4765656 (office). *E-mail:* bp@behnisch.com (office). *Website:* www.behnisch.com (office).

BEHNISCH, Stefan, Dipl.Ing; German architect; *Principal Partner, Behnisch Architekten;* b. 1 June 1957, Stuttgart; m. Petra Behnisch; two s.; with Behnisch & Pnr 1987–; f. Buero Innenstadt 1989, Prin. 1990–, co. became ind. 1991, later renamed Behnisch Architekten; teaches at various univs; also Visiting Prof. at several American univs and External Examiner at several European univs; frequent lecturer at architectural symposia in Germany and abroad; awards include several RIBA awards, Architectural Record/Business Week Awards, Trophée Sommet de la terre et bâtiment (France) 2002. *Address:* Behnisch Architekten, 163A Rotebühlstraße, 70197 Stuttgart, Germany (office); 1517 Park Row, Venice, CA 90291, USA (office); 344 Boylston Street, Boston, MA 02116, USA (office). *Telephone:* (711) 607720 (Stuttgart) (office); (310) 399-9003 (Los Angeles) (office); (617) 522-9808 (Boston) (office). *Fax:* (711) 6077299 (Stuttgart) (office); (310) 399-9677 (Los Angeles) (office); (617) 522-9812 (Boston) (office). *E-mail:* buero@behnisch.com (office); BBPLA@behnisch.com (home); StudioEast@behnisch.com (home). *Website:* www.behnisch.com (office).

BEHRENS, Hildegard; German singer (soprano); b. 9 Feb. 1937, Varel, nr Oldenburg; m. Seth Schneidmann; ed Freiburg Music Conservatory; opera debut in Freiburg 1971; resident mem. Deutsche Oper am Rhein, Düsseldorf; has appeared with Frankfurt Opera, Teatro Nacional de San Carlo, Lisbon, Vienna State Opera, Metropolitan Opera, New York; soloist, Chicago Symphony Orchestra 1984; appeared in Jenufa, Salzburg Festival 2001; Bundesverdienstkreuz (Order of the Merit Cross of the Federal Republic) 1986; Bayerische Kammersängerin 1986, Bayerischer Verdienstorden 1994, Artist of the Year, Circle of Buenos Aires Art Critics 1995, Österreichische Kammersängerin (Austria) 1995, Léonie Sonning Music Prize 1998, Prix Herbert von Karajan 2003. *Address:* Opera-Connection Alste & Mödersheim, Leibnizstrasse 94, 10625 Berlin, Germany (office). *Telephone:* (30) 3199-6688 (office). *Fax:* (30) 3180-9739 (office). *E-mail:* info@opera-connection.com (office). *Website:* www.opera-connection.com (office); www.hildegardbehrens.com.

BEHRMAN, Richard Elliot, MD, JD; American professor of pediatrics and consultant; *Executive Director, Non-Profit Healthcare and Educational Consultants to Medical Institutions;* b. 13 Dec. 1931, Philadelphia, Pa; s. of Robert Behrman and Vivian Keegan; m. Ann Nelson 1954; one s. three d.; ed Amherst Coll., Harvard Univ., Univ. of Rochester and Johns Hopkins Univ.; Oregon Regional Primate Research Center and Univ. of Oregon Medical School 1965–68; Prof. of Pediatrics and Dir Neonatal Intensive Care Unit and Nurseries, Univ. of Ill. Coll. of Medicine 1968–71; Prof. and Chair. Dept of Pediatrics and Dir Babies Hospital, Columbia Univ. Coll. of Physicians and Surgeons 1971–76; Prof. and Chair. Dept of Pediatrics and Dir Dept of Pediatrics, Rainbow Babies and Children's Hosp. Case Western Reserve Univ. School of Medicine 1976–82; Dean, School of Medicine, Case Western Reserve Univ. 1980–89, Vice-Pres. Medical Affairs 1987–89; Dir Center for Future of Children, David and Lucile Packard Foundation 1989–99; Clinical Prof. Stanford Univ. and UCSF 1989; Chair. Bd of Dirs, Lucile Packard Foundation for Children 1997–99, Sr Vice-Pres. Medical Affairs 1999–2002; Exec. Chair. Fed. of Pediatric Orgs 2002; currently Exec. Dir Non-Profit Healthcare and Educational Consultants to Medical Insts, Santa Barbara, Calif.; mem. Bd of Dirs, UCSF Stanford Health Care 1997, Children's Hospices and Palliative Care Coalition, Teddy Bear Cancer Foundation 2007–; Fellow, American Acad. of Pediatrics; mem. Inst. Medicine, NAS; mem. Medical Advisory Bd iMetrikus, Inc;; Hon. DSc (Medical Coll., WI) 2000. *Publications:* The Future of Children (Ed.) 1990–, Essentials of Paediatrics (Ed.) 2002, Nelson Textbook of Paediatrics (Ed.) 2003. *Leisure interests:* running, hiking, reading. *Address:* c/o Board of Directors, Children's Hospices and Palliative Care Coalition, 65 Nielson Street, #108, Watsonville, CA 95076, USA. *E-mail:* behrmannon-profitconsult@nphec.org. *Website:* www.nphec.org.

BEHURIA, Sarthak, BA, MBA; Indian oil industry executive; *Chairman, Indian Oil Corporation Ltd;* b. 2 March 1952, Chatrapur, Orissa; s. of Nrusingha Behuria and Suvarnalata Behuria; one s. one d.; ed St Stephen's Coll., Delhi, Indian Inst. of Man., Ahmedabad; traineeship with Burmah-Shell (later renamed Bharat Petroleum Corpn Ltd) 1973, held various positions including Dir of Operations, Oil Coordination Cttee, Exec. Dir of Sales 1995–98, Dir of Marketing 1998–2002, Chair. and Man. Dir 2002–05; Chair. Indian Oil Corpn 2005–, also Chair. (part-time) group cos Chennai Petroleum Corpn Ltd, Bongaigaon Refinery & Petrochemicals Ltd; Head of Indian Oiltanking Ltd (jt venture); Chair. Petroleum Fed. of India (PetroFed) 2003–, Standing Conf. of Public Enterprises (SCOPE) 2006–, Council of Indian Employers; First Vice-Pres. Bd World LPGas Asscn 006–; Hon. Fellow, Energy Inst., UK; named by Upstream journal amongst the 10 Most Influential Oilmen in India, Udyog Ratna Award, Progress, Harmony and Devt Chamber of Commerce and Industry 2006, SCOPE Award for Excellence and Outstanding Contrib. to Public Sector Man. (Individual Category) 2006–07. *Address:* Indian Oil Corporation Ltd, 3079/3, JB Tito Marg, Sadiq Nagar, New Delhi 110049, India (office). *Telephone:* (11) 26851524 (home); (11) 26260101 (office). *Fax:* (11) 26511410 (home); (11) 26260100 (office). *E-mail:* behurias@iocl.co.in (office). *Website:* www.iocl.com (office).

BEHZAD, Mohamed Ben Yousef, BBA, MS (Econ); Qatari economist and international organization executive; *Director-General, Arab Industrial Development and Mining Organization;* b. 30 June 1954, Doha; ed Cairo Univ., Egypt, California State Polytechnic Univ., Pomona, USA; Econs Researcher, Econs Dept, Qatar Petroleum 1979–88, Economist and Planning Engineer, Tech. Dept 1988–89, Planning Dept 1989–91; Planning Economist, Industrial Studies Dept, Gulf Org. for Industrial Consulting, Qatar 1992–93; Sr Economist and Head of Econ. Planning Dept, Supreme Council for Planning Doha Jan.–Oct. 1994; Financial Economist, OPEC, Vienna, Austria 1998–2006; Dir-Gen. Arab Industrial Devt and Mining Org. 2006–. *Address:* Arab Industrial Development and Mining Organization, rue France, Zanagat al-Khatawat, PO Box 8019, Rabat, Agdal, Morocco (office). *Telephone:* (37) 772600 (office). *Fax:* (37) 772188 (office). *E-mail:* aidmo@arifonet.org.ma (office). *Website:* www.arifonet.org.ma (office).

BEI, Shizhang, Dr rer. nat; Chinese biologist and academic; *Honorary Director, Institute of Biophysics, Chinese Academy of Sciences;* b. 10 Oct. 1903, Ningpo; s. of Bei Qingyang and Chen Ahua; m. Cheng Ihming 1931; two s. two d.; ed Tongji Medical and Eng School, Shanghai and Univ. of Freiburg i. Breisgau, Univ. of Munich, Univ. of Tübingen; Asst Inst. of Zoology, Univ. Tübingen 1928–29; returned home 1929; Assoc. Prof., Prof. and Chair. of Dept of Biology, Univ. of Zhejiang 1930–50, Dean of Science Faculty 1949–50; Dir Inst. of Experimental Biology, Chinese Acad. of Sciences 1950–58; Chair. Dept of Biophysics, Univ. of Science and Tech., China 1958–64; Dir Inst. of Biophysics, Chinese Acad. of Sciences 1958–83, Hon. Dir 1985–; Pres. Chinese Zoological Soc. 1978–83, Chinese Biophysical Soc. 1980–83 (Hon. Pres. 1983–86); Deputy Ed.-in-Chief Scientia Sinica 1958–83, Encyclopedia of China 1984–; Ed.-in-Chief Acta Biophysica Sinica 1985–91; mem. Div. of Biological Sciences, Chinese Acad. of Sciences; mem. 1st NPC 1954–59, 2nd NPC 1959–64, 3rd NPC 1964–75, 4th NPC 1975–78, 5th NPC 1978–83 and 6th NPC 1983–88. *Achievements:* asteroid 31065 Beishizhang named in his honour on his 100th birthday. *Publications:* Cell Reformation, Series 1 (24 papers) 1988, Series 2 (18 papers) in preparation; other studies on cell reformation, chromatin, DNA and histones in yolk granules; several articles in Science Record and Scientia Sinica. *Address:* Institute of Biophysics, Chinese Academy of Sciences, Da Tun Road 15, Chao Yang District, 100101 Beijing, People's Republic of China (office). *Telephone:* 6202-2029 (office); 6255-1064; 6255-4575. *Fax:* 6202-7837 (office).

BEILIN, Yossi, PhD; Israeli politician; b. 1948, Israel; m.; two c.; ed Tel-Aviv Univ.; fmr journalist and mem. Editorial Bd of Davar; Spokesman for Labour Party 1977–84; Cabinet Sec. 1984–86; Dir Gen. for Political Affairs of Foreign Ministry 1986–88; mem. Knesset 1988–99, 2004–; Deputy Minister of Finance 1988–90; mem. Knesset Foreign Affairs and Defense, Immigration and Absorption and Constitution, Law and Justice Cttees 1990–92; Deputy Minister of Foreign Affairs 1992–95; Minister of Econs and Planning July–Nov. 1995; Minister without Portfolio 1995–96; mem. Knesset Foreign Affairs and Defense, Constitution, Law and Justice, Advancement of the Status of Women Cttees 1996–99; Minister of Justice 1999–2001; Founder and Leader Meretz-Yahad (Social Democratic) Party 2002–04, Chair. 2004–08; Dr hc (Univ. of Paris 13); Int. Activist Award, The Gleitsman Foundation 1999, Seligmann Prize 2004. *Publications:* Sons in the Shadow of their Fathers, The Price of Unity, Industry in Israel, Touching Peace, His Brother's Keeper, Israel, A Concise Political History, Touching Peace 1997, The Manual for Leaving Lebanon 1998, From Socialism to Social Liberalism 1999, His Brother's Keeper 2000, Manual for a Wounded Dove 2001, The Path to Geneva: The Quest for a Permanent Agreement. *Telephone:* (2) 747786 (office). *E-mail:* beilin@myparty.org.il (office).

BEINEIX, Jean-Jacques; French film director; b. 8 Oct. 1946, Paris; several films as Asst Dir 1970–77; Founder Cargo Films; numerous prizes and awards at film festivals. *Films include:* Le Chien de Monsieur Michel 1971, Diva 1981, La Lune dans le caniveau (The Moon in the Gutter) 1983, 37.2° le matin (Betty Blue) 1986, Roselyne and the Lions 1989, IP5 1992, Mortel Transfert 2001, Loft Paradoxe (TV) 2002. *Publications:* Diva 1991, L'île aux pachydermes 1992. *Address:* Cargo Films, 9 rue Ambroise Thomas, 75009 Paris, France (office). *Telephone:* 1-53-34-13-80 (office). *Fax:* 1-53-34-13-81 (office). *E-mail:* cargo@cargofilms.com (office). *Website:* www.cargofilms.com.

BEIT-ARIÉ, Malachi, MA, MLS, PhD; Israeli palaeographer and academic; *Ludwig Jesselson Professor of Codicology and Palaeography, Hebrew University;* b. 20 May 1937, Petah-Tiqva; s. of Meir Beit-Arié and Esther (née Elpiner) Beit-Arié; one s. two d.; ed Hebrew Univ., Jerusalem; Dir The Hebrew Palaeography Project, Israel Acad. of Sciences and Humanities 1965–, Inst. of Microfilmed Hebrew Manuscripts 1970–78; Sr Lecturer in Codicology and Palaeography, Hebrew Univ. 1975–78, Assoc. Prof. 1979–83, Prof. 1984–, currently Ludwig Jesselson Professor of Codicology and Palaeography; Dir Nat. and Univ. Library 1979–90; Chair. Int. Advisory Council Jewish Nat. Library 1991–; Visiting Fellow Wolfson Coll., Oxford 1984–85; Visiting Researcher IRHT (CNRS) Paris 1991; Visiting Scholar Harvard Univ. 1992; Fellow Center for Advanced Judaic Studies, Univ. of Pennsylvania 1996, 1999–2000; currently Head of Hebrew Palaeography Project of Israel Academy of Sciences and Humanities; Anne Frank Awards for poetry 1961. *Publications:* These Streets, Those Mountains (lyrics) 1963, The Hills of Jerusalem and All the Pain (poems) 1967, Manuscrits médiévaux en caractères hébraiques (with C. Sirat), Parts I–III 1972–86, Hebrew Codicology 1977, The Only Dated Medieval MS Written in England 1985, Medieval Specimens of Hebrew Scripts 1987, The Makings of the Medieval Hebrew Book 1993, Hebrew Manuscripts of East and West: Towards Comparative Codicology 1993, Catalogue of the Hebrew MSS in the Bodleian Library (Supplement) 1994, Codices Lebraicis litteris exarati quo tempore scripti fuerint exhibentes I–II (with C. Sirat and M. Glalzer) 1997–99, Hebrew Manuscripts in the Biblioteca Palatina in Parma (with B. Richler) 2001. *Leisure interest:* classical music. *Address:* PO Box 34165, Jerusalem 91341 (office); 11C Alkalai Street, Jerusalem 92223, Israel (home). *Telephone:* 2-5619270 (office); 2-5633940 (home). *Fax:* 2-6511771.

BEITZ, Berthold; German industrialist; b. 26 Sept. 1913, Zemmin, West Pomerania; m. Dr Else Hochheim 1939; three d.; ed secondary school; bank apprentice 1934–39; mem. commercial staff, Shell AG, Hamburg; mem. commercial staff, Beskiden-Erdöl AG, Jaslo/Poland 1939; Commercial Man. Karpaten-Oel AG, Boryslaw/Poland 1941; mil. service 1944–45; Deputy Chair. British Zonal Insurance Control Dept, Hamburg 1946; Gen. Man. Iduna Germania Insurance Co. 1949–53; Personal Chief Exec. to Dr Alfried Krupp von Bohlen and Halbach 1953–67; Chair. Bd of Trustees Alfried Krupp von Bohlen und Halbach Foundation 1968, Chair. Supervisory Bd Friedrich Krupp GmbH 1970–89, Hon. Chair. 1989– (ThyssenKrupp AG since 1999, Hon. Chair. 1999–); Chair. Bd of Trustees Max-Grundig Foundation; Founder and Chair. Exec. Cttee Ruhr Arts Trust (Kulturstiftung Ruhr); mem. Bd of Trustees 'pro Ruhrgebiet', Zollverein Foundation; Direktorium der Univ. Witten-Herdecke; Pres. Olympic Museum Foundation, Lausanne, Switzerland; Hon. Chair. Inst. for East–West Security Studies, New York; Hon. Gov. Ernst-Moritz-Arndt Univ. (Greifswald); Hon. mem. Nat. Olympic Cttee, IOC, Univ. of Essen 1983; Hon. Patron German Acad. of Natural Scientists, Leopoldina in Halle 1987; Hon. Prof., State of North Rhine-Westphalia 1988; Hon. Senator Ernst Moritz Arndt Univ., Greifswald; Hon. Citizen of Hanseatic City of Greifswald 1995; Hon. Citizen of City of Kiel 2003; Hon. DrMed (Ernst Moritz Arndt Univ.) 1983; Hon. DPhil (Jagiellonian Univ., Kraków) 1993 (Weizmann Inst., Rehovot, Israel) 1996, (Ruhr Univ., Bochum) 1999; Grosses Bundesverdienstkreuz mit Stern 1973, Commandorium with Star of Order of Merit (Poland) 1974, Grosses Bundesverdienstkreuz mit Stern und Schulterband 1979, Order of Merit of North Rhine-Wesphalia 1986, Grosskreuz des Verdienstordens der Bundesrepublik Deutschland 1987, First Class Order of Madara Reiter (Bulgaria), Ehrenbürger der Hanestadt Greifswald, Medal for Services to German Foundations 1987, Order of Cultural Merit, Repub. of Korea 2001; numerous other honours including Plaque of Honour, City of Essen 1971, Righteous Among the Nations Medal, Yad Vashem, Israel 1973, Ring of Honour of the City of Essen 1983, Inclusion in Scroll of Honour of the Jewish People 1984, Merentibus Medal, Jagellonian Univ., B'nai B'rith Medal for Humanitarianism 1991, Grand Gold Badge of Honour with Star, Austria 1991, Josef Neuberger Medal, Düsseldorf Jewish Community (jtly with Dr Else Beitz) 1997, Leo Baeck Prize, Central Council of Jews in Germany (jtly with Dr Else Beitz) 2000, Leibniz Medal, Berlin-Brandenburg Acad. of Sciences and Humanity 2000, Jewish Museum of Berlin Award 2002, Gold Medal and Jubilee Medal, Univ. of Wrocław 2003, Pomerania Nostra Prize, Univs of Greifswald and Szczecin 2003. *Leisure interests:* sailing, jazz, modern art. *Address:* Alfred Krupp von Bohlen und Halbach Foundation, Hügel 15, 45133 Essen, Germany. *Telephone:* (201) 1881. *Fax:* (201) 412587.

BEKELE, Kenenisa; Ethiopian athlete; b. 13 June 1982, Bekoji; ran first competitive race aged 15; set world jr record for 3,000m 2001; won long and short races at World Cross Country Championships 2002, became first to repeat in consecutive years 2003, won both events again 2004; primarily competes in 5,000m and 10,000m events; won Golden League 5,000m in Oslo 2003; gold medal 10,000m, bronze medal 10,000m World Championships 2003; gold medal 10,000m, silver medal 5,000m Olympic Games, Athens 2004; gold medal 10,000m, gold medal 5,000m Olympic Games, Beijing 2008; holds world records at 5,000m (set in Hengelo, Netherlands 2004) and 10,000m (set in Ostrava, Czech Repub. 2004); based in Njimegen, Netherlands; Goodwill Amb. for UNICEF 2004–; Int. Asscn of Athletics Feds World Athlete of the Year 2004. *Address:* PO Box 3241, Addis Ababa, Ethiopia. *Telephone:* (1) 152495. *E-mail:* athletics@ethiosports.com. *Website:* www.ethiosports.com.

BEKRI, Tahar, PhD; Tunisian poet; *Maître de conférences, University of Paris X-Nanterre;* b. 7 July 1951, Gabès; m. Annick Le Thoër 1987; ed Univ. of Tunisia, Sorbonne, Univ. of Paris; Maître de conférences, Univ. of Paris X-Nanterre; mem. Soc. des Gens de Lettres de France, Maison des Ecrivains; Officier, Mérite Culturel, Tunisia 1993; Prix Tunisie-France 2006. *Publications:* Poèmes bilingues 1978, Exils 1979, Le laboureur du soleil 1983, Les lignes sont des arbres 1984, Le chant du roi errant 1985, Malek Haddad 1986, Le coeur rompu aux océans 1988, Poèmes à Selma 1989, La sève des jours 1991, Les chapelets d'attache 1993, Littératures de Tunisie et du Maghreb 1994, Les songes impatients 1997, Journal de neige et de feu 1997, Le pêcheur de lunes 1998, Inconnues saisons (translated as Unknown Seasons) 1999, De la littérature tunisienne et maghrébine 1999, Marcher sur l'oubli 2000, L'horizon incendié 2002, La brûlante rumeur de la mer 2004, Le vent sans abri 2005, Dernières nouvelles de l'été 2005, Si la musique doit mourir 2006, Le livre du souvenir 2007; contrib. to various publs. *Address:* 32 rue Pierre Nicole, 75005 Paris, France (home). *Telephone:* 1-43-29-33-39 (home). *Fax:* 1-43-29-33-39 (home); 1-40-97-71-51 (office). *E-mail:* taharbekri@wanadoo.fr (home); tahar.bekri@u_paris10.fr (office). *Website:* tahar.bekri.free.fr.

BELAFONTE, Harry; American singer; b. 1 March 1927, New York; s. of Harold George Belafonte Sr and Malvene Love Wright; m. 2nd Julie Robinson 1957; one s. three d.; ed George Washington High School, New York; in Jamaica 1935–39; service with US Navy 1943–45; American Negro Theater; student at Manhattan New School for Social Research Dramatic Workshop 1946–48; first engagement at the Vanguard, Greenwich Village; European tours 1958, 1976, 1981, 1983, 1988; Pres. Belafonte Enterprises Inc.; Goodwill Amb. for UNICEF 1987; Host Nelson Mandela Birthday Concert, Wembley 1988; Broadway appearances in Three For Tonight, Almanac, Belafonte At The Palace and in films Bright Road, Carmen Jones 1952, Island in the Sun 1957, The World, the Flesh and the Devil 1958, Odds Against Tomorrow 1959, The Angel Levine (also producer) 1969, Grambling's White Tiger 1981, White Man's Burden; produced with Sidney Poitier Buck and the Preacher 1971 (also acted), Uptown Saturday Night 1974; Emmy Television Award for Tonight with Belafonte 1960; Producer Strolling '20s 1965, A Time for Laughter 1967, Harry and Lena 1970, Beat Street 1984; concerts in USA, Europe 1989, Canada 1990, USA and Canada 1991, N America, Europe and Far East 1996; mem. Bd NY State Martin Luther King Jr Inst. for Nonviolence 1989–; Hon. DHumLitt (Park Coll., Mo.) 1968; Hon. Dr Arts, New School of Social Research, New York 1968; Hon. DCL (Newcastle) 1997, numerous other hon. doctorates; Golden Acord Award, Bronx Community Coll. 1989, Mandela Courage Award 1990, Nat. Medal of the Arts 1994, NY Arts and Business Council Award 1997, Distinguished American Award, John F. Kennedy Library, Boston 2002, BET Humanitarian Award 2006. *Films include:* Bright Road 1953, Carmen Jones 1954, Island in the Sun 1957, The World, the Flesh and the Devil 1959, Odds Against Tomorrow 1959, The Angel Levine 1970, Buck and the Preacher 1972, Uptown Saturday Night 1974, White Man's Burden 1995, Kansas City 1996, Bobby 2006. *Leisure interests:* photography, water skiing, recording. *Address:* c/o William Morris Agency, 1 William Morris Place, Beverly Hills, CA 90212, USA. *Telephone:* (310) 859-4000. *Fax:* (310) 859-4462. *Website:* www.wma.com.

BELAIZ, Tayeb, LenD; Algerian politician and fmr judge; *Minister of Justice;* b. 21 Aug. 1948, Maghnia; ed Univ. of Oran; early positions at Ministry of the Interior; fmr judge and Pres. of the Chamber, Court of Oran, also fmr Pres. Court of Saida, Court of Sidi-Bel-Abbès and adviser to Supreme Court Judge; Minister of Labour and Social Security 2002–03, of Justice 2003–; mem. Nat. Comm. for Judicial Reform 1999. *Address:* Ministry of Justice, 8 place Bir Hakem, el-Biar, Algiers, Algeria (office). *Telephone:* (21) 92-41-83 (office). *Fax:* (21) 92-17-01 (office). *E-mail:* belaiztayeb@mjustice.dz (office). *Website:* www.mjustice.dz (office).

BÉLANGER, Gerard, MA, MSocSc, RSC; Canadian economist and academic; *Professor of Economics, Université Laval;* b. 23 Oct. 1940, St Hyacinthe; s. of Georges Bélanger and Cécile Girard; m. Michèle Potvin 1964; one d.; ed Princeton and Laval Univs; Prof., Dept of Econs, Laval Univ. 1967–, Prof. of Econs 1977–; Research Co-ordinator, Howe Inst., Montreal 1977–79; mem. Task Force on Urbanization, Govt of Québec 1974–76; Sec. Acad. of Letters and Social Sciences, RSC 1985–88; Woodrow Wilson Fellow. *Publications:* The Price of Health 1972, Le financement municipal au Québec 1976, Taxes and Expenditures in Québec and Ontario 1978, Le prix du transport au Québec 1978, L'économique du secteur public 1981, Croissance du Secteur Public et

Fédéralisme 1988, L'Économique de la santé et l'État providence 2005. *Address:* Department of Economics, Pavillon J.-A.-DeSève, local 2256, Université Laval, Québec, PQ G1V 0A6, Canada (office). *Telephone:* (418) 656-5363 (office); (418) 681-3075 (home). *Fax:* (418) 656-2707 (office). *E-mail:* gebe@ecn.ulaval.ca (office); Gerard.Belanger@ecn.ulaval.ca (office). *Website:* www.ulaval.ca/Al/bienvenueanglais.html (office).

BÉLAVAL, Philippe Marie; French library executive and civil servant; *President, Cour administrative d'appel de Versailles;* b. 21 Aug. 1955, Toulouse; s. of Jacques Bélaval and Marie-Thérèse (née Chazarenc) Bélaval; ed Faculté des Sciences Sociales de Toulouse, Inst. d'études politiques de Toulouse; trainee at École nationale d'admin. 1977–79, auditor 1979; technical adviser Conseil d'Etat 1983–84, counsel 1984, rep. of Sec. of State for Budget and Consumption 1984–86; Asst Dir Office of Minister of Public Affairs and Admin. Reform 1988–89, Dir 1989–90; Dir-Gen. Théâtre nationale de l'Opéra de Paris 1990–92; Dir-Gen. Bibliothèque nationale de France 1994–98; Dir-Gen. Archives de France 1998–2000; Pres. Admin. Council Groupe vocal de France 1985–90; Pres. Cour administrative d'appel, Bordeaux 2001, currently Pres. Cour administrative d'appel de Versailles; Council of State 1996; mem. Admin. Council of École des chartes; Sr lecturer Inst. d'études politiques de Paris; Chevalier Légion d'honneur, Chevalier Ordre nat. du Mérite, Commdr des Arts et des Lettres. *Address:* Cour Administrative d'appel de Versailles, C.P. 1102, 2, esplanade Grand Siècle, 78011 Versailles (office); Conseil d'État, place du Palais Royal, 75100 Paris, France. *Telephone:* 1-30-84-47-00 (office). *Fax:* 1-30-84-47-04 (office).

BELDA, Alain J. P.; French business executive; *Chairman, Alcoa Inc.;* b. 1943; Pres. Alcoa Aluminio SA, Brazil 1979–94, Exec. Vice-Pres., Alcoa Inc. 1994–95, Vice-Chair. 1995–97, Pres. and COO 1997–99, Pres. and CEO 1999–2001, Chair. and CEO 2001–08, Chair. 2008–; Dir Citigroup Inc., E. I. du Pont de Nemours and Co., The Ford Foundation; Trustee, The Conference Bd. *Address:* Alcoa Inc., 201 Isabella Street, Pittsburgh, PA 15212-5858, USA (office). *Telephone:* (412) 553-4545 (office). *Fax:* (412) 553-4498 (office). *E-mail:* info@alcoa.com (office). *Website:* www.alcoa.com (office).

BELENKOV, Yuri N., Dr Med.; Russian neurophysiologist; *Director, Myasnikov Institute of Cardiology;* b. 9 Feb. 1948, Leningrad; s. of Nikita Yu. Belenkov and Marina T. Koval; m. Natalia V. Belenkova; one s.; ed Leningrad State Univ.; jr researcher, sr researcher, head of laboratory, Deputy Dir Myasnikov Inst. of Cardiology 1975–91, Dir 1991–; Chief Cardiologist of Russian Ministry of Public Health; Ed.-in-Chief journal Kardiologya; mem. editorial bds Int. Journal of Medical Practice, Circulation, European Journal of Heart Failure; mem. Presidium Russian Soc. of Cardiologists, Russian Acad. of Medical Sciences (corresp. mem. 1993–99); Hon. mem. Acad. of Medicine of Columbia 1989; USSR State Prize, Lenin Komsomol Prize. *Publications include:* more than 460 scientific papers on ultrasonic diagnostics, magnetic resonance tomography and cardiology; 11 monographs, including Ultrasound Diagnostics in cardiology 1981, Practical Echocardiography 1982, Clinical Application of Magnetic Resonance Tomography 1996, Magnetic Resonance Tomography of Heart and Vessels 1997, Primary Lung Hypertension 1999, Principles of Rational Treatment of Cardiac Insufficiency 2000. *Leisure interests:* driving, classical music, jazz. *Address:* Myasnikov Institute of Cardiology, Russian Academy of Medical Sciences, 3d Cherenkovskaya str. 15a, Moscow 121552, Russia (office). *Telephone:* (495) 415-13-47 (office).

BELEZA, Miguel, PhD; Portuguese economist and banker; *Member of the Advisory Board, Banco de Portugal;* b. 28 April 1950, Porto; ed MIT; Minister of Finance 1990–91; Dir (non-exec.) Siemens Portugal; fmr adviser, Banco Comercial Português; fmr Asst Prof., then Assoc. Prof., Faculty of Econs, Univ. Nova de Lisboa; fmr adviser, IMF; econ. advisor and consultant Bank of Portugal 1979-87, mem. Bd 1987-90, Gov. 1992-94, mem. Advisory Bd 1994–; fmr Visiting Prof., Brown Univ., Univ. dos Açores, INSEAD, Fontainebleau; Dir Banco Expresso Atlântico Lisbon; consultant and Ed. Economia journal (Univ. Católica Portuguesa); Grand Cross, Nat. Order, Cross of the South (Brazil), Grand Cross, Order of Merit. *Publications:* numerous articles in journals. *Address:* c/o Advisory Board, Banco de Portugal, Rua do Ouro 27, 1100-150 Lisbon, Portugal (office). *Telephone:* (21) 3213200 (office). *Fax:* (21) 3464843 (office). *E-mail:* info@bportugal.pt (office). *Website:* www.bportugal.pt (office).

BELICHICK, Bill, BEcons; American football coach; b. 16 April 1952, Nashville, Tenn.; s. of Steve Belichick; m. Debby Belichick; one d. two s.; ed Annapolis High School, Phillips Acad., Andover, Mass, Wesleyan Univ., Middletown, Conn.; Special Asst to Head Coach Ted Marchibroda, Baltimore Colts 1975–76; Asst Special Teams Coach, Tight Ends and Receivers Coach, Detroit Lions 1976–78; Asst Special Teams Coach and Asst to Defensive Coordinator Joe Collier, Denver Broncos 1978–79; Defensive Asst and Special Teams Coach, New York Giants 1979–86, Defensive Coordinator 1986–90; Head Coach, Cleveland Browns 1991–95; Asst Head Coach and Defensive Asst, New England Patriots 1996; Asst Head Coach, New York Jets 1997–2000; Head Coach New England Patriots 2000–; only head coach in league history to win three Super Bowl championships in a four-year span (2001, 2003, 2004); inducted into Annapolis High School Hall of Fame, named one of 100 Most Powerful and Influential People in the World, Time Magazine 2004. *Address:* New England Patriots, 1 Patriot Place, Foxborough, MA 02035-1388, USA (office). *Telephone:* (508) 543-8200 (office). *Fax:* (508) 543-0285 (office). *Website:* www.patriots.com (office).

BELIGAN, Radu; Romanian actor; b. 14 Dec. 1918, Galbeni, Bacău Co.; m.; four c.; ed Bucharest Conservatoire; started career at Muncă şi Lumină (Work and Light) Theatre in Bucharest, then played at Alhambra and Nat. Theatre; Prof. Inst. of Drama and Film Art Bucharest 1960–68; Dir Teatrul de Comedie 1960–68; Dir Nat. Theatre 1969–90; Chair. Int. Theatre Inst.; mem. Cen. Cttee Romanian CP 1969–89; mem. Exec. Bureau Nat. Council Front of Socialist Democracy and Unity 1980–89; performances in classic and modern Romanian plays and int. repertoire (Shakespeare, Gogol, Chekhov, Albee, Dürrenmatt and others); Hon. Citizen of Bucharest, Iasi and Bacau Municipalities; Grand Officer, Nat. Order for Faithful Service (Romania) 2001; Dr hc (Acad. of Arts George Enescu, Bucharest); Merited Artist 1953, People's Artist 1962, Prize of Acad. Le Muse, Florence 1980, Prize of UNITER Gala (Trophy Dionysis) 1995–96, Prize of Romanian Acad. 1997, Prize of Tofan Foundation 1998, Prize "14 Juillet", Ministry of Foreign Affairs of France 1998, Trophy Eugene Ionesco 1999, Prize of Flacara Revue 2000. *Films include:* Cuibul salamandrelor 1976, Bratele Afroditei 1978, Reteaua 'S' 1980, Iancu Jianu, zapciul 1980, Intoarcerea la dragostea dintîi 1981, Horea 1984, Trahir 1993, L'Après-midi d'un tortionnaire 2001, Al matale, Caragiale (TV) 2002. *Publications:* Pretexte şi subtexte (Pretexts and Understatements) (essays) 1968, Luni, marţi, miercuri (Monday, Tuesday, Wednesday) (essays) 1978, Memoirs 1978, Note de insomniac (Notes of an Insomniac) (essays) 2000. *Address:* Str. Spătarului 36, 70241 Bucharest, Romania.

BELINGA-EBOUTOU, Martin; Cameroonian diplomatist and international organization official; *Special Advisor to the President;* b. 17 Feb. 1940, Nkilzok; m.; six c.; ed Catholic Univ., Lavanium-Kinshasa, Univ. of Paris; joined Ministry of Foreign Affairs 1968; Chargé d'Affaires, Congo 1970–74; Chief Regional Orgs Unit 1974–85; Head Econ. Mission of Cameroon, Paris, Rome, Tunis, Rabat 1985–89; Dir then Chief of State Protocol, Office of Pres. 1989–97, Dir Civil Cabinet 1996–97; Perm. Rep. to UN, New York and Geneva and Amb. to Jamaica 1998–2007; Pres. ECOSOC 2001, Pres. UN Security Council Oct. 2002, Chair. Third Cttee of Gen. Ass. (Social, Humanitarian and Cultural Cttee) 2003; Special Advisor to Pres. of Cameroon 2007–; Assoc. Prof., Inst. of Int. Relations 1974–76. *Address:* Office of the President, Palais de l'Unité, Yaoundé, Cameroon (office). *Telephone:* 2223-4025 (office).

BELIZ, Gustavo, LLD; Argentine politician; b. 1962, Buenos Aires; ed Univ. of Buenos Aires, LSE, London; sports journalist, El Gráfico magazine 1979–85; political journalist and head of editorial dept, La Razón 1985–89; sec. of public functions to the presidency and speechwriter for Pres. Carlos Menem 1989–93, Minister of the Interior 1992–93; consultant and researcher, ECLAC 1994–95; private consultant and researcher 1996–97; f. Nueva Dirigencia (political party) 1996; legislator, Ciudad Autónomica de Buenos Aires 1996–2003, Senator and head of city govt 1999–2003; Minister of Justice, Human Rights and Internal Security 2003–04; mem. Opus Dei; chosen as one of ten outstanding young talents in Argentina, Cámara Junior de Buenos Aires 1992. *Address:* c/o Ministry of Justice, Human Rights and Internal Security, Sarmiento 329, Buenos Aires, 1041 Argentina (office).

BELKA, Marek, MA, PhD; Polish politician, economist, academic and UN official; *Director, European Department, International Monetary Fund;* b. 9 Jan. 1952, Łódź; m.; two c.; ed Łódź Univ., Univ. of Chicago, USA, LSE, UK; Master of Econs and Sociology Faculty, Łódź Univ. 1972, Asst Prof., then Prof. of Econs 1973–96; Visiting Scholar, Columbia Univ. (Fulbright Foundation), USA 1978–79; American Council of Scholarly Socs, Univ. of Chicago 1985–86; LSE 1990; Asst Prof., Inst. of Econs, Polish Acad. of Sciences (PAN) 1986–97, Dir 1993–97; adviser and consultant Finance Ministry, Privatisation Ministry and Cen. Planning Office 1990–96; Deputy Chair. Govt Council of Socio-Econ. Strategy 1994–96; Econ. Adviser to the Pres. of Poland 1996–97, 1997–2001; consultant to World Bank 1990–96; adviser to JP Morgan Chase; Deputy Prime Minister and Minister of Finance 1997, 2001–02; Head Coalition Council for Int. Co-ordination in Iraq 2003; Dir in charge of econ. policy, Coalition Provisional Authority 2003–04; Prime Minister of Poland 2004–05; Exec. Sec. UN Econ. Comm. for Europe (UNECE) 2005–08; Dir European Dept, IMF 2008–. *Publications:* around a dozen books and over 100 articles in Polish and foreign press on anti-inflation policy in developed countries, the Milton Friedman socio-econ. doctrine and macroecon. policy in transition periods. *Leisure interests:* travelling, basketball, music. *Address:* European Department, International Monetary Fund, 700 19th Street, NW, Washington, DC 20431, USA (office). *Telephone:* (202) 623-7000 (office). *Fax:* (202) 623-4661 (office). *E-mail:* publicaffairs@imf.org (office). *Website:* www.imf.org (office).

BELKEZIZ, Abdelouahed, DrIur; Moroccan international organization official, lawyer and diplomatist; b. 5 July 1939, Marrakesh; ed Sidi Mohammed Coll., Marrakesh, Faculty of Law, Rabat, Univ. of Rennes, France; Dean Faculty of Juridical, Econ. and Social Sciences, Moroccan Univ., Rabat 1966, Hassan II Univ., Casablanca 1985, Univ. of Ibn Tofail, Kenitra 1992, Univ. Muhammad V, Rabat 1997–2000; Pres. High Studies Reform Comm. 1969; mem. Perm. Royal Comm. for Judicial Reforms, Trade Codification, Penal and Civil Procedures 1971; Juridical Adviser, Moroccan Del. to UN 1976–77; Amb. to Iraq 1977–79; Minister of Information 1979–81, of Information, Youth and Sports 1981–83, of Foreign Affairs 1983–85; Pres. Exec. Cttee of Islamic World Univs Fed., Council of Maghreb Univs 1997–2000; Chair. Nat. Conf. of Moroccan Univ. Deans 1997–2000; Sec.-Gen. OIC 2001–04; mem. Moroccan Award Comm. for Social Sciences 1968–74, Nat. Council for Youth and Future 1985; mem. American Asscn of Comparative Law 1970–; King Abdulaziz Decoration of the Second Rank 1979, Great Spanish Civil Merit Cordon 1979, Commdr of the Civil Div., Order of the British Empire 1980, Great Officer of the Merit Order, Senegal 1981, Grand Officier, Ordre nat. du Mérite 1983, Great Cross of the Order of Rio Branco, Brazil 1984, Commdr of the Throne Order 1994. *Address:* c/o General Secretariat, Organization of the Islamic Conference, Kilo 6, Mecca Road, PO Box 178, Jeddah 21411, Saudi Arabia.

BELKHADEM, Abdelaziz; Algerian politician; *Minister of State and Personal Representative to the Head of State;* b. 8 Nov. 1945, Aflou; Deputy Dir of Int. Relations, Office of the Pres. 1972–77; Rapporteur, Planning and

Finance Comm. 1978–87; mem. Front de Libération Nationale (FLN) 1977–, mem. Bureau Politique 1991–97, currently Sec.-Gen.; Deputy for Sougueur to Assemblée Populaire Nationale (APN) 1977–92, Vice-Pres. 1988–90, Pres. 1990–91, Pres. Educ., Training and Scientific Research Comm. 1987; Minister of State for Foreign Affairs 2000–05; Minister of State and Special Rep. of the Pres. 2005–06; Prime Minister 2006–08; Minister of State and Personal Rep. to Head of State 2008–. *Address:* Front de libération nationale (FLN), 7 rue du Stade, Hydra, Algiers, Algeria (office). *Telephone:* (21) 69-42-81 (office). *Fax:* (21) 69-47-07 (office). *E-mail:* pfln@wissal.dz (office). *Website:* www.pfln.dz (office).

BELL, (Alexander) Scott, CBE; British financial executive; b. 4 Dec. 1941; s. of the late William Scott Bell and Irene Bell; m. Veronica Jane Simpson 1965; two s. one d.; ed Daniel Stewart's Coll., Edin.; Asst Actuary for Canada, Standard Life Assurance Co. 1967, Deputy Actuary 1972, South Region Man. 1974, Asst Gen. Man. (Finance) 1979, Gen. Man. (Finance) 1985–88, Group Man. Dir 1988–2001; Dir Bank of Scotland 1988–96, Hammerson PLC (fmrly Hammerson Property and Devt Corpn) 1988–98, Scottish Financial Enterprise 1989–95, Prosperity SA 1993–, Standard Life Healthcare 1994–2001, Prime Health Ltd 1994–, Standard Life Bank 1997–2001, Standard Life Investments 1998–2001; Dir Asscn of British Insurers 1999–; Chair. Assoc. Scottish Life Offices 1994–96; Dir Univs Superannuation Scheme Ltd 1996–; Hon. Canadian Consul in Scotland 1994–; Hon. DLitt (Herriot-Watt Univ.) 1997; Fellow, Pensions Man. Inst. *Leisure interests:* golf, reading, travel.

BELL, Christopher, BA; British business executive; *CEO, Ladbrokes plc;* ed Wolverhampton Polytechnic; joined Allied Brewers as Grad. Trainee, then Marketing Man. eastern coast pub co., Co. Dir Allied Beer Brands 1986–88, Marketing Dir Victoria Wine 1988–91; joined Ladbrokes plc as Marketing Dir 1991–93, Man. Dir Ladbroke Racing 1995–99, CEO 2000–. *Address:* Ladbrokes plc, Imperial House, Imperial Drive, Rayners Lane, Harrow HA2 7JW, England (office). *Telephone:* (20) 8868-8899 (office). *Fax:* (20) 8868-8767 (office). *Website:* www.ladbrokesplc.com (office).

BELL, Edward; British publisher; *Partner, Bell Lomax Literary and Sport Agency;* b. 2 Aug. 1949; s. of Eddie Bell and Jean Bell; m. Junette Bannatyne 1969; one s. two d.; ed Airdrie High School; with Hodder & Stoughton 1970–85; Man. Dir Collins Gen. Div. 1985–89; launched Harper Paperbacks in USA 1989; Deputy Chief Exec., HarperCollins UK 1990–91, Chief Exec. 1991–92, Chair. 1992–2000; Chair. HarperCollins India 1994–2000; Dir (non-exec.) Haynes Publishing 2001, Be Cogent Ltd, Management Diagnostics Ltd; Chair. (non-exec.) OAG Worldwide Ltd 2001; Chair. Those Who Can Ltd 2001; Pnr, Bell Lomax Literary and Sport Agency 2002–; Gov. Kent and Surrey Inst. of Art and Design. *Leisure interests:* golf, supporting Arsenal, collecting old books. *Address:* The Bell Lomax Agency, James House, 1 Babmaes Street, London, SW1Y 6HF, England (office). *Telephone:* (20) 7930-4447 (office). *Fax:* (20) 7925-0118 (office). *E-mail:* eddie@bell-lomax.co.uk.

BELL, Geoffrey Lakin, BSc (Econ); British international banker; *President, Geoffrey Bell & Co. Ltd;* b. 8 Nov. 1939, Grimsby; s. of the late Walter Lakin Bell and of Anne Bell; m. Joan Rosine Abel 1973; one d.; ed Grimsby Tech. High School and LSE; HM Treasury 1961–63; Visiting Economist, Fed. Reserve System 1963–64; HM Treasury and Lecturer, LSE 1964–66; adviser, British Embassy, Washington, DC 1966–69; joined J. Henry Schroder Wagg and Co. Ltd 1969, Asst to Chair. 1969–72; Dir and Exec. Vice-Pres. Schroder Int. Ltd; Dir Schroder Bermuda Ltd; Exec. Sec. Group of Thirty 1978–; Pres. Geoffrey Bell & Co. Ltd 1982–; Chair. Guinness Mahon Holdings 1987–93; mem. Court of Govs LSE 1994–; Companion of Honour of Barbados. *Publication:* The Euro-Dollar Market and the International Financial System 1973, contrib. The Times and numerous academic and other publs. *Address:* 780 Third Avenue, 7th Floor, New York, NY 10017-2024, USA (office). *Telephone:* (212) 888-3700 (office).

BELL, Graeme I., PhD; Canadian biologist and academic; *Louis Block Professor, Department of Biochemistry and Molecular Biology, University of Chicago;* b. Victoria, BC; ed Univ. of Calgary, Alberta and Univ. of California, San Francisco, USA; Postgraduate Research Biochemist, Dept of Biochemistry and Biophysics, Univ. of California, San Francisco 1977–78, Asst Research Biochemist 1978–81, Asst Adjunct Prof. 1981–84, Asst Adjunct Prof., Metabolic Research Unit 1984–86; also worked as sr scientist Chiron Corpn 1981–86; Assoc. Prof., Dept of Biochemistry and Molecular Biology, Univ. of Chicago 1986–90, Assoc. Prof., Dept of Medicine 1987–90, Prof., Depts of Biochemistry and Molecular Biology, and Medicine 1990–94, Louis Block Prof., Depts of Biochemistry and Molecular Biology, and Medicine 1994–98, Louis Block Prof., Depts of Biochemistry and Molecular Biology, Medicine, and Human Genetics 1998–; Assoc. Investigator, Howard Hughes Medical Inst., Chevy Chase, Md 1986–90, Investigator 1990–; mem. NAS 1998, Inst. of Medicine 1998; Hon. Foreign mem. La Sociedad Artina de Diabetes 2000; Elliot P. Joslin Research and Devt Award, American Diabetes Asscn (ADA) 1980–82, Rolf Luft Award, Swedish Medical Soc. 1989, Mary Jane Kugel Award, Juvenile Diabetes Foundation Int. (JDFI) 1989, Outstanding Scientific Achievement Award by an Investigator (Lilly Award), ADA 1990, William C. Stadie Award, Greater Philadelphia Affiliate of ADA 1990, Distinguished Alumni Award, Univ. of Calgary 1991, Gerold and Kayla Grodsky Basic Research Scientist Award, JDFI 1995, Naomi Berrie Award for Outstanding Achievement in Diabetes Research, Columbia Univ., New York 2000, Benjamin F. Stapleton, Jr Lecturer, Univ. of Colorado Health Science Center 2002, J. Allyn Taylor Int. Prize in Medicine for Diabetes 2002. *Address:* Department of Biochemistry and Molecular Biology, University of Chicago, 5841 S Maryland Avenue, AMB N237, MC1028, Chicago, IL 60637-1028, USA (office). *Telephone:* (773) 702-9116 (office). *Fax:* (773) 702-9237 (office). *E-mail:* g-bell@uchicago.edu (office). *Website:* bmb.bsd.uchicago.edu (office).

BELL, John Anthony, OBE, AM; Australian theatre director and actor; *Artistic Director, The Bell Shakespeare Company;* b. 1 Nov. 1940, Newcastle; s. of Albert Bell and Joyce Feeney; m. Anna Volska 1965; two d.; ed Maitland Marist Brothers High School, NSW and Univ. of Sydney; actor with Old Tote Theatre Co. 1963–64, with RSC, UK 1964–69; co-founder, Nimrod Theatre Co. 1970–85; Founder and Artistic Dir Bell Shakespeare Co. 1990–; roles include King Lear, Macbeth, Shylock, Malvolio and Richard III, Prospero; Hon. DLitt (Newcastle) 1994, (Sydney) 1996, (NSW) 2006; Australia Nat. Living Treasure, Nat. Trust of Australia 1997, Dame Elisabeth Murdoch Cultural Leadership Award, Australian Business Arts Foundation 2003. *Publication:* The Time of My Life (autobiog.) 2002. *Leisure interests:* reading, music, painting. *Address:* The Bell Shakespeare Company, PO Box 10, Millers Point, Sydney NSW 2000, Australia (office). *Telephone:* (2) 8298-9000 (office). *Fax:* (2) 9241-4643 (office). *E-mail:* mail@bellshakespeare.com.au (office). *Website:* www.bellshakespeare.com.au (office).

BELL, Sir John Irving, Kt, DM, PMedSci, FRCP; Canadian medical scientist and academic; *Regius Professor of Medicine, University of Oxford; President, Academy of Medical Sciences;* b. 1 July 1952; ed Ridley Coll., Ont., Univ. of Alberta, Magdalen Coll., Oxford; Clinical Fellow, Dept of Medicine, Stanford Univ., Calif. 1982–87; Wellcome Sr Clinical Fellow and Hon. Consultant, Radcliffe Hosp., Oxford 1987–89, Lecturer, Nuffield Dept of Clinical Medicine, Oxford Univ. 1989–92, Nuffield Prof. of Clinical Medicine 1992–2002, Regius Prof. of Medicine 2002–; f. Wellcome Trust Centre for Human Genetics 1993; Founder Fellow, Acad. of Medical Sciences 1998, Pres. 2006–; mem. Bd of Dirs Roche AG 2001–; mem. Scientific Advisory Bd AstraZeneca 1997–2000, Roche Palo Alto 1998–; fmr mem. Oxford Univ. Council, MRC Council; Chair. Oxford Health Alliance. *Address:* The Offices of the Regius Professor, Level 4, Academic Centre, John Radcliffe Hospital, Headley Way, Headington, Oxford, OX3 9DU, England (office). *Telephone:* (1865) 221340 (office). *Fax:* (1865) 220993 (office). *E-mail:* regius@medsci.ox.ac.uk (office). *Website:* www.medsci.ox.ac.uk (office).

BELL, Joshua; American violinist; b. 9 Dec. 1967, Indiana; ed Indiana Univ.; youngest guest soloist at a Philadelphia Orchestra Subscription concert 1982; European tour with St Louis Symphony 1985; German tour with Indianapolis Symphony 1987; European tour with Dallas Symphony 1997; European tours with Nat. Symphony Orchestra 2002, Minnesota Orchestra 2003; guest soloist with numerous orchestras in USA, Canada, Europe; has also appeared in USA and Europe as a recitalist; played premiere of violin concerto by Nicholas Maw, written for him, with Philharmonia Orchestra 1993; Visiting Prof. at RAM, London; Artistic Partner, St. Paul Chamber Orchestra; Gramophone Award for Best Concerto Recording 1998 (for Barber Concerto), Mercury Music Award 2000, Acad. Award for Best Soundtrack (for Red Violin), Grammy Award 2001, Avery Fisher Prize 2007, named Young Global Leader by World Econ. Forum 2007. *Recordings:* Mendelssohn and Bruch concertos with the Academy of St Martin-in-the-Fields and Sir Neville Marriner, Tchaikovsky and Wieniawski concertos with the Cleveland Orchestra and Vladimir Ashkenazy, recital album of Brahms, Paganini, Sarasate and Wieniawski with Samuel Sanders, Lalo Symphonie Espagnole and Saint-Saëns Concerto with Montreal Symphony Orchestra and Charles Dutoit, Franck, Fauré and Débussy, Chausson Concerto for violin, piano and string quartet with Thibaudet and Isserlis, Poème with Royal Philharmonic Orchestra and Andrew Litton, Mozart Concertos Nos 3 and 5 with the English Chamber Orchestra and Peter Maag, Prokofiev violin concertos with Montréal Symphony Orchestra and Charles Dutoit, Barber and Walton concertos and Bloch Baal Shem with Baltimore Symphony Orchestra and David Zinman, recital disc with Olli Mustonen, Gershwin Fantasy with London Symphony Orchestra and John Williams, Short Trip Home with Edgar Meyer, The Red Violin film soundtrack with Philharmonia Orchestra, Sibelius Goldmark Concertos with Los Angeles Philharmonic Orchestra and Esa-Pekka Salonen, Maw Concerto for violin with London Philharmonic Orchestra and Roger Norrington, Bernstein Serenade and West Side Story Suite with Philharmonia Orchestra and David Zinman, Beethoven and Mendelssohn concertos with Camerata Salzburg and Sir Roger Norrington, Irish film soundtrack, Romance of the Violin 2003, Tchaikovsky Violin Concerto 2005, Voice of the Violin 2006, The Red Violin Concerto 2007, Vivaldi: The Four Seasons 2008. *Leisure interests:* chess, computers, golf. *Address:* c/o Elizabeth Sobol Gomez, IMG Artists, Carnegie Hall Tower, 152 West 57th Street, 5th Floor, New York, NY 10019, USA (office). *Telephone:* (212) 994-3541 (office). *Fax:* (212) 994-3550 (office). *E-mail:* esobol-gomez@imgartists.com (office); heidi@joshuabell.com (office); jb@joshuabell.com (office). *Website:* www.imgartists.com (office); www.joshuabell.com.

BELL, Marian, BA, MSc, CBE; British economist; *Consultant, Bank of England;* b. 28 Oct. 1957, London; d. of Joseph Denis Milburn Bell and Wilhelmenia Maxwell Bell (née Miller); m. Richard Adkin; two d.; ed Hertford Coll. Oxford, Birkbeck Coll., Univ. of London; Econ. Adviser, HM Treasury 1989–91; Sr Treasury Economist, Head of Research, Treasury and Capital Markets, Royal Bank of Scotland 1991–2000; consultant, Alpha Economics 2000–02; External Mem. Monetary Policy Cttee, Bank of England 2002–05, Consultant 2005–; Gov. Contemporary Dance Trust, The Place 2005–; Deputy Chair. Forum for Global Health Protection 2006–; mem. Int. Advisory Council, Zurich Financial Services 2007–; Eucharistic Asst, Cathedral and Abbey Church of St Albans. *Leisure interests:* contemporary dance, art. *Address:* c/o Bank of England, Threadneedle Street, London, EC2R 8AH, England.

BELL, Martin, OBE, MA; British broadcaster and politician; *Humanitarian Ambassador, Children's Fund, United Nations;* b. 31 Aug. 1938; s. of the late Adrian Bell and Marjorie Bell (née Gibson); m. 1st Nelly Gourdon 1971 (divorced); two d.; m. 2nd Rebecca Sobel 1985 (divorced 1993); m. 3rd Fiona Goddard 1998; ed The Leys School, Cambridge, King's Coll., Cambridge;

joined BBC 1962, news Asst, Norwich 1962–64, gen. reporter, London and overseas 1964–76, Diplomatic Corresp. 1976–77, Chief N American Corresp. 1977–89, Berlin Corresp. BBC TV News 1989–93, Vienna Corresp. 1993–94, Foreign Affairs Corresp. 1994–96, Special Corresp., Nine O'Clock News 1997; has reported from over 70 countries and has covered wars in Vietnam, Middle East 1967, 1973, Angola, Rhodesia, Biafra, El Salvador, Gulf 1991, Nicaragua, Croatia, Bosnia; MP (Ind.) for Tatton 1997–2001; Humanitarian Amb. for UNICEF 2001–; Dr hc (Derby) 1996; Hon. MA (E Anglia) 1997, (Aberdeen) 1998; Royal TV Soc. Reporter of the Year 1976, 1992, TV and Radio Industries Club Newscaster of the Year 1995, Inst. of Public Relations Pres.'s Medal 1996. *Publications:* In Harm's Way 1995, An Accidental MP 2000, Through Gates of Fire 2003, The Truth That Sticks: New Labour's Breach of Trust 2007. *Address:* 71 Denman Drive, London, NW11 6RA, England (home).

BELL, Baron (Life Peer), cr. 1998, of Belgravia in the City of Westminster; **Timothy John Leigh Bell,** Kt, FIPA; British public relations executive; b. 18 Oct. 1941; s. of Arthur Leigh Bell and Greta Mary Bell (née Findlay); m. Virginia Wallis Hornbrook 1988; one s. one d.; ed Queen Elizabeth's Grammar School, Barnet, Herts.; with ABC Television 1959–61, Colman Prentis & Varley 1961–63, Hobson Bates 1963–66, Geers Gross 1966–70; Man. Dir Saatchi & Saatchi 1970–75, Chair. and Man. Dir Saatchi & Saatchi Compton 1975–85; Group Chief Exec. Lowe Howard-Spink Campbell Ewald 1985–87, Deputy Chair. Lowe Howard-Spink & Bell PLC 1987–89; Chair. Lowe-Bell Communications 1987–89, Chime Communications 1994–; f. Lowe-Bell Govt Relations 1993–; arranged man. buy-out of Lowe-Bell Communications 1989; Special Adviser to Chair. Nat. Coal Bd 1984–86; mem. South Bank Bd 1985–86; Chair. Charity Projects 1984–93, Pres. 1993–; Dir Centre for Policy Studies; mem. Industry Cttee SCF, Public Relations Cttee Greater London Fund for the Blind 1979–86, Council Royal Opera House 1982–85, Public Affairs Cttee, Worldwide Fund for Nature 1985–88; Creative Leaders' Network Gov. British Film Inst. 1983–86. *Leisure interests:* golf, politics. *Address:* Chime Communications PLC, 14 Curzon Street, London, W1J 5HN, England (office). *Telephone:* (20) 7495-4044. *Fax:* (20) 7491-9860 (office).

BELL BURNELL, Dame S(usan) Jocelyn, DBE, PhD, FRS; British astrophysicist and fmr university administrator; *Visiting Professor, University of Oxford;* b. 15 July 1943; d. of (George) Philip Bell and (Margaret) Allison Bell (née Kennedy); m. (divorced); one s.; ed Univs of Glasgow and Cambridge; Lecturer, Univ. of Southampton 1968–73; part-time with Mullard Space Lab., Univ. Coll. London 1974–82; part-time with Royal Observatory, Edin. 1982–91; Chair. Physics Dept Open Univ. 1991–99; Dean of Science, Univ. of Bath 2001–04; Visiting Prof. for Distinguished Teaching, Princeton Univ. 1999–2000; Visiting Prof., Univ. of Oxford 2004–; Pres. Royal Astronomical Soc. 2002–04; Fellow Royal Soc. of Edin. 2004; Pres. Inst. of Physics 2008–(10); Foreign Assoc. US Acad. of Sciences 2005; discovered the first four pulsars; frequent radio and TV broadcaster on science, on being a woman in science and on science and religion; Hon. Fellow New Hall, Cambridge 1996, British Acad. 2006, Singapore Inst. of Physics 2008; 21 hon. doctorates, including Univs of Cambridge, London, Michigan and Harvard; Joseph Black Medal and Cowie Book Prize, Glasgow Univ. 1962, Michelson Medal, Franklin Inst., USA 1973, J. Robert Oppenheimer Memorial Prize, Center for Theoretical Studies, Fla 1978, Beatrice M. Tinsley Prize, American Astronomical Soc. (first recipient) 1987, Herschel Medal, Royal Astronomical Soc., London 1989, Edinburgh Medal 1999, Magellanic Premium, American Philosophical Soc. 2000, Joseph Priestly Award, Dickinson Coll., Pa 2002, Robinson Medal, Armagh Observatory 2004, Kelvin Medal 2007. *Publications:* three books, three chapters in books, approximately 70 scientific papers and 35 Quaker publs; Dark Matter: Poems of Space (co-ed.) 2008. *Leisure interests:* popularizing astronomy, walking, Quaker activities, listening to choral music, gardening. *Address:* University of Oxford, Astrophysics, Denys Wilkinson Building, Keble Road, Oxford, OX1 3RH, England (office). *Telephone:* (1865) 273306 (office). *Fax:* (1865) 273390 (office).

BELL LEMUS, Gustavo; Colombian academic, journalist and fmr politician; *Director, El Heraldo;* b. 1 Feb. 1957, Barranquilla; ed Javeriana Univ. of Bogotá, Andes Univ. and Univ. of Oxford, UK; fmr Prof., Univ. del Norte e del Atlantico; fmr Man. Nat. Industrial Asscn (Andi), Barranquilla; fmr Gov. of Atlantico; Vice-Pres. of Colombia 1998–2002, Minister of Nat. Defence 2001–02; Dir El Heraldo (newspaper), Barranquilla, Atlantico. *Address:* c/o El Heraldo, Calle 53b, No 46-25, Barranquilla, Atlántico, Colombia (office). *Telephone:* (5) 371-5000 (office). *Fax:* (5) 371-5091 (office). *Website:* www.elheraldo.com.co (office).

BELLAL, Mohamed Vall Ould; Mauritanian politician; b. 1949, Maghtaa Lahjar (Brakna); ed Univ. of Dakar; civil admin. 1965; Head of Mission, Ministry of State for Nat. Orientation 1976–77, Sec.-Gen. 1977–78; Prefect, then Cen. Gov. 1979–81; political analyst, Paris 1993–95; mem. Parl. for Maghtaa Lahjar 1996–2003; Minister of Foreign Affairs and Co-operation 2003–07. *Address:* c/o Ministry of Foreign Affairs and Co-operation, BP 230, Nouakchott, Mauritania (office).

BELLAMY, Carol, JD; American international organization official; *President, School for International Training and President and CEO, World Learning;* b. 1942, Plainfield, NJ; ed Gettysburg Coll. and New York Univ.; Peace Corps Volunteer, Guatemala 1963–65; Assoc., Cravath, Swaine & Moore, New York 1968–71; spent 13 years as elected public official including term as mem. New York State Senate 1973–77; Pres. New York City Council (first woman) 1978–85; Prin., Morgan Stanley and Co. 1986–90; Man. Dir Bear Stearns & Co. 1990–93; Prin. Morgan Stanley & Co. New York; Dir Peace Corps, Washington, DC 1993–95; Exec. Dir UNICEF 1995–2005; Pres. School for Int. Training and CEO World Learning 2005–; Chair. Bd of Dirs Fair Labor Foundation 2007–; fmr Fellow, Inst. of Politics, Kennedy School of Govt, Harvard Univ.; Hon. mem. Phi Alpha Alpha, the US Nat. Honor Soc. for

Accomplishment and Scholarship in Public Affairs and Admin; Hon. LHD (Bates Coll.) 2003; ranked 95th by Forbes magazine amongst 100 Most Powerful Women 2004. *Address:* World Learning, PO Box 676, Kipling Road, Brattleboro, VT 05302-0676, USA (office). *Telephone:* (802) 258-3101 (office). *Fax:* (802) 258-3248 (office). *E-mail:* carol.bellamy@worldlearning.org (office). *Website:* ourworld.worldlearning.org (office).

BELLAMY, Sir Christopher (William), Kt, MA, QC; British barrister and consultant; *Senior Consultant, Linklaters;* b. 25 April 1946, Waddesdon, Bucks.; s. of the late William Albert Bellamy and Vyvienne Hilda Bellamy (née Meyrick); m. Deirdre Patricia Turner; one s. two d.; ed Tonbridge School, Brasenose Coll., Oxford; called to the Bar, Middle Temple 1968 (Bencher 1994), in full-time practice 1970–92, QC 1986, Asst Recorder 1989–92; Judge of Court of First Instance of the EC 1992–99; Pres. of Appeal Tribunals, Competition Comm. (now Competition Appeal Tribunal) 1999–2007; Deputy High Court Judge 2000–; Judge of Employment Appeal Tribunal 2000–07; mem. Council, British Inst. of Int. and Comparative Law 2000–06, Advisory Bd 2007–; Recorder, Crown Court 2001–07; Sr Consultant, Linklaters, London (law firm); Gov. Ravensbourne Coll. of Design and Communication 1988–92. *Publication:* European Community Law of Competition (6th edn) (ed. P. Roth and V. Rose) 2007. *Leisure interests:* family life, walking, history. *Address:* Linklaters, 1 Silk Street, London, EC2Y 8HA, England (office). *Telephone:* (20) 7456-3457 (office). *E-mail:* christopher.bellamy@linklaters.com (office). *Website:* www.linklaters.com (office).

BELLAMY, David James, OBE, PhD, CBiol, FIBiol; British botanist, writer, broadcaster and environmental organization administrator; b. 18 Jan. 1933, London; s. of Thomas Bellamy and Winifred Green; m. Rosemary Froy 1959; two s. three d.; ed Sutton County Grammar School, Chelsea Coll. of Science and Tech., Bedford Coll., Univ. of London; Lecturer, then Sr Lecturer, Dept of Botany, Univ. of Durham 1960–80, Hon. Prof. of Adult and Continuing Educ. 1980–82; Visiting Prof., Massey Univ., NZ 1988–89; Special Prof. of Botany, Univ. of Nottingham 1987–; TV and radio presenter and scriptwriter; Founder Dir Conservation Foundation; Pres. WATCH 1982, Youth Hostels Asscn 1983, Population Concern 1988–, Nat. Asscn of Environmental Educ. 1989–, Plantlife 1990–2005, Wildlife Trust's Partnership 1996–2005, British Inst. of Cleaning Science 1997–, Council Zoological Soc. of London 1991–94, BH&HPA 2000–, Camping and Caravanning Club 2002–; Vice-Pres. BTCV, Fauna and Flora International, Marine Conservation Soc., Australian Marine Conservation Soc.; Chair. Int. Cttee for the Tourism for Tomorrow Awards; Dir David Bellamy Assocs (environmental consultants) 1988–97, Bellamy & Nevard Environmental Consultants 2003–; Trustee, Living Landscape Trust, World Land Trust 1992–2002; Patron Project AWARE Foundation, The Space Theatre, Dundee; has been reported as holding controversial views on climate change and global warming; Hon. Fellow, Chartered Inst. of Water and Environmental Man.; Hon. FLS; Hon. Prof., Central Queensland Univ.; Hon. mem. BSES Expeditions; Dutch Order of the Golden Ark 1989; Hon. DSc (Bournemouth); Hon. DUniv; Dr hc (CNAA) 1990; UNEP Global 500 Award 1990, Busk Medal, Royal Geographical Soc., Duke of Edinburgh's Award for Underwater Research, BAFTA Richard Dimbleby Award, BSAC Diver of the Year Award. *Television series includes:* Life in Our Sea 1970, Bellamy on Botany 1973, Bellamy's Britain 1975, Bellamy's Europe 1977, Botanic Man 1978, Up a Gum Tree 1980, Backyard Safari 1981, The Great Seasons 1982, Bellamy's New World 1983, End of the Rainbow Show 1986, S.W.A.L.L.O.W. 1986, Turning the Tide 1986, Bellamy's Bugle 1986, 1987, 1988, Bellamy on Top of the World 1987, Bellamy's Journey to the Centre of the World 1987, Bellamy's Bird's Eye View 1989, Wheat Today What Tomorrow? 1989, Moa's Ark 1990, Bellamy Rides Again 1992, Blooming Bellamy 1993, 1994, Routes of Wisdom 1993, The Peak 1994, Bellamy's Border Raids 1996, Westwatch 1997, A Welsh Herbal 1998, Salt Solutions 1999, The Challenge 1999. *Publications include:* more than 45 books, including Bellamy on Botany 1972, Peatlands 1974, Bellamy's Britain 1974, Life Giving Sea 1975, Green Worlds 1975, The World of Plants 1975, It's Life 1976, Bellamy's Europe 1976, Botanic Action 1978, Botanic Man 1978, Half of Paradise 1979, Forces of Life 1979, Bellamy's Backyard Safari 1981, The Great Seasons (with Sheila Mackie, illustrator) 1981, Il Libro Verde 1981, Discovering the Countryside with David Bellamy (Vols I, II) 1982, (Vols III, IV) 1983, The Mouse Book 1983, Bellamy's New World 1983, The Queen's Hidden Garden 1984, I Spy 1985, Bellamy's Bugle 1986, Bellamy's Ireland 1986, Turning The Tide 1986, Bellamy's Changing Countryside (four vols) 1987, England's Last Wilderness 1989, England's Lost Wilderness 1990, Wetlands 1990, Wilderness Britain 1990, Moa's Ark 1990, How Green Are You? 1991, Tomorrow's Earth 1992, World Medicine: Plants, Patients and People 1992, Blooming Bellamy 1993, Trees of the World 1993, Poo, You and the Poteroo's Loo 1997, Bellamy's Changing Countryside 1998, The Glorious Trees of Great Britain 2002, Jolly Green Giant (autobiog.) 2002, A Natural Life (autobiog.) 2002, The Bellamy Herbal 2003, Conflicts in the Countryside: The New Battle for Britain 2005, and books connected with TV series; Consultant Ed. and contrib. for series published by Hamlyn in conjunction with Royal Soc. for Nature Conservation: Coastal Walks 1982, Woodland Walks 1982, Waterside Walks 1983, Grassland Walks 1983. *Leisure interests:* children and ballet. *Address:* The Mill House, Bedburn, Bishop Auckland, Co. Durham, DL13 3NN, England (home).

BELLANY, John, CBE, RA; British artist; b. 18 June 1942, Port Seton, Scotland; s. of Richard Weatherhead Bellany and Agnes Maltman Bellany; m. 1st Helen Margaret Percy 1965 (remarried 1986); two s. one d.; m. 2nd Juliet Gray (née Lister) 1979 (died 1985); ed Cockenzie Public School, Preston Lodge, Prestonpans, Edinburgh Coll. of Art, Royal Coll. of Art, London; Lecturer in Fine Art, Winchester School of Art 1969–73; Head of Faculty of Painting, Croydon Coll. of Art 1973–78; Visiting Lecturer in Painting, RCA 1975–85; Lecturer in Fine Art, Goldsmiths Coll., Univ. of London 1978–84; Fellow Commoner, Trinity Hall, Cambridge 1988, Sr Fellow, RCA 1999; Hon. RSA;

Dr hc (Edin.) 1996; Hon. DLit (Edin.) 1998; Arts Council Award 1981, Jt 1st Prize, Athena Int. Award 1985, Chevalier Medal, Florence, Italy 2001, The Freedom of East Lothian Award 2005. *Radio:* regular contributor to Kaleidoscope (BBC Radio 4), Night Waves (BBC Radio 3); John Bellany 30 min. programme (BBC Radio 3) with Judith Bumphus –1995. *Television:* John Bellany (BBC TV) 1972, John Bellany – Artist with a New Liver (BBC TV) 1989. *Publications:* Scottish National Galleries 1986, National Portrait Gallery, London 1986. *Leisure interests:* opera, motoring. *Address:* The Clock House, Shortgrove Hall, Newport, Saffron Walden, Essex, CB11 3TX, England (home); 19 Great Stuart Street, Edinburgh, EH2 7TP, Scotland (home). *Telephone:* (1799) 542442 (Saffron Walden) (office). *Fax:* (1799) 542442 (Saffron Walden) (home). *E-mail:* info@bellany.com. *Website:* www.bellany.com (office).

BELLEN, Heinz, DPhil; German professor of ancient history; b. 1 Aug. 1927, Neuss/Rhein; s. of Heinrich Bellen and Elisabeth Hussmann; m. Agnes Meuters 1958; two d.; secondary school teacher, Düsseldorf 1957–62; Asst Prof. Cologne 1962–68, Lecturer, 1968–73; Prof. of Ancient History, Univ. of Mainz 1974–93; mem. Mainz Acad. 1975–. *Publications:* Studien zur Sklavenflucht im römischen Kaiserreich 1971, Die germanische Leibwache der römischen Kaiser 1981, Metus Gallicus-Metus Punicus 1985, Grundzüge der römischen Geschichte (Vol. I) 1994, (Vol. II) 1998, Politik-Recht-Gesellschaft 1997; Ed.: Forschungen zur antiken Sklaverei 1978–. *Address:* Institüt für Alte Geschichte, Johannes Gütenberg-Universität, Saarstrasse 21, 55099 Mainz (office); Alfred-Nobel Strasse 23, 55124 Mainz, Germany (home). *Telephone:* (6131) 472919.

BELLENS, Didier; Belgian media executive; *CEO, Belgacom SA;* b. 9 June 1955; m.; two c.; ed Ecole de Commerce Solvay, Univ. Libre de Bruxelles; Deputy Gen. Man. Pargesa Holding SA, Geneva –1992; Man. Dir Groupe Bruxelles Lambert SA, Brussels 1992–2000; CEO CLT-UFA, Luxembourg 2000 (merged with Pearson TV to become RTL Group 2000); CEO RTL Group (owns 24 TV and 17 radio stations), Luxembourg 2000–03; CEO Belgacom SA, Brussels 2003–. *Leisure interests:* hikes in the Libyan desert, Morocco and Namibia. *Address:* Belgacom, Boulevard Roi Albert II 27, 1030 Brussels, Belgium (office). *Telephone:* (2) 202-69-30 (office). *Fax:* (2) 217-99-66 (office). *E-mail:* about@belgacom.be (office). *Website:* www.belgacom.be (office).

BELLINGHAM, Alastair John, CBE, FRCP, FRCPE, FRCPath; British professor of haematology; *Chairman, National Health Service Information Authority;* b. 27 March 1938, London; m. 1st Valerie Jill Morford 1963 (died 1997); three s.; m. 2nd Julia d'Q. Willott 2002; ed Tiffin Boys' School, Univ. Coll. Hosp. Medical School, London; Sr Lecturer, Hon. Consultant Haematology Dept, Univ. Coll. Hosp. Medical School 1971; Prof. of Haematology, Univ. of Liverpool 1974, King's Coll., London 1984–97; Pres. British Soc. for Haematology 1992–93, Royal Coll. of Pathologists 1993–96; Chair. Nat. Health Service Information Authority 1999–. *Publications:* numerous publs on red cell physiology and biochemistry, inherited red cell abnormalities, sickle cell disease. *Leisure interests:* photography, wine and viticulture. *Address:* NHS Information Authority, Aqueous II, Aston Cross, Rocky Lane, Birmingham B6 5RQ (office); Broadstones, The Street, Teffont Magna, Salisbury, Wilts., SP3 5QP, England (home). *Telephone:* (121) 333-0104 (office); (1722) 716267 (home). *Fax:* (121) 333-0334 (office). *E-mail:* information@nhsia.nhs.uk (office); savage@teffont.freeservcer.co.uk (home). *Website:* www.nhsia.nhs.uk (office).

BELLINI, Mario; Italian architect; fmrly designer for Olivetti office machines; comms include: Tokyo Design Centre, Sakurada Dori Dist, Villa Erba Int. Congress and Exhbn Centre, Cernobbio on Lake Como, Exhbn Bldgs for Milan Trade Fair. *Address:* c/o Architecture Centre, 66 Portland Place, London W1, England.

BELLOCH JULBE, Juan Alberto; Spanish politician; *Mayor of Zaragoza;* b. 3 Feb. 1950, Mora de Rubielos (Teruel); m.; one s.; mem. Democratic Justice; Founder Asscn of Judges for Democracy, Asscn des Magistrats Européens pour la démocratie et les libertés; Founder and Pres. Asscn for the Human Rights of the Basque Country; Judge, La Gomera, Berga Vic y Alcoy from 1975; Magistrate and Pres. Court of Justice of Biscay 1981–90; mem. Gen. Council of Judiciary 1990–93; Minister of Justice 1993–96, of the Interior 1994–96; Mayor of Zaragoza 2003–. *Address:* c/o PSOE, Ferraz 68 y 70, 28008 Madrid, Spain. *Telephone:* (91) 5820444. *Fax:* (91) 5820422.

BELLOCHIO, Marco; Italian director, actor, writer and producer; b. 9 Nov. 1939, Piacenza, Emilia-Romagna; retrospective at Locarno Int. Film Festival 1998; mem. Jury, Venice Film Festival 1999, Cannes Film Festival 2007; Bronze Leopard for his complete works, Locarno Int. Film Festival 1976, Jury Distinction for his artistic contrib. to the art of cinema, Montréal World Film Festival 1988, Silver St George for Contrib. to World Cinema, Moscow Int. Film Festival 1999, Career Award (Cinema), Flaiano Int. Prizes 2002, Pietro Bianchi Award, Venice Film Festival 2006, Sergei Parajanov Lifetime Achievement Award, Yerevan Int. Film Festival 2006. *Film roles in:* Francesco d'Assisi (Francis of Assisi) 1966, Sbatti il mostro in prima pagina (Slap the Monster on Page One) 1972, Pianeta Venere (Planet Venus) 1974, Salò o le 120 giornate di Sodoma (Salo, or the 120 Days of Sodom) (voice; uncredited) 1975, Vacanze in Val Trebbia (Vacation in Val Tribbia) 1980, L'ora di religione (Il sorriso di mia madre) (The Religion Hour (My Mother's Smile)) 2002, Buongiorno, notte (Good Morning, Night) (uncredited) 2003. *Films directed:* Ginepro fatto uomo 1962, La colpa e la pena 1965, I pugni in tasca (Fists in the Pocket) (Silver Sail, Locarno Int. Film Festival 1965, Silver Ribbon for Best Original Story, Italian Nat. Syndicate of Film Journalists 1966) 1965, La Cina è vicina (China is Near) (FIPRESCI Prize and Special Jury Prize, Venice Film Festival 1967, Silver Ribbon for Best Original Story, Italian Nat. Syndicate of Film Journalists 1968) 1967, Amore e rabbia (Love and Anger; segment 'Discutiamo, discutiamo') 1969, Nel nome del padre (In the Name of the Father) 1972, Sbatti il mostro in prima pagina (Slap the Monster on Page One) 1972, Matti da slegare (Fit to be Untied) (OCIC Award and FIPRESCI Prize – Recommendation, Berlin Int. Film Festival 1975) 1975, Marcia trionfale (Victory March) 1976, Vacanze in Val Trebbia (Vacation in Val Tribbia) 1980, Salto nel vuoto (Leap into the Void) (David di Donatello Award for Best Dir 1980) 1980, Gli occhi, la bocca (Those Eyes, That Mouth) 1982, Enrico IV (Henry IV) 1984, Il diavolo in corpo (Devil in the Flesh) 1986, La visione del Sabba 1988, La condanna (The Conviction) (Silver Berlin Bear, Berlin Int. Film Festival 1991) 1991, Il sogno della farfalla (The Butterfly's Dream) 1994, Sogni infranti (Broken Dreams) 1995, Elena 1997, Il Principe di Homburg (The Prince of Homburg) 1997, La religione della storia 1998, La balia (The Nanny) 1999, L'Affresco 2000, Un altro mondo è possibile (Another World is Possible) 2001, L'ora di religione (Il sorriso di mia madre) (The Religion Hour (My Mother's Smile)) (also producer) (Prize of the Ecumenical Jury – Special Mention, Cannes Film Festival 2002, Best Film, Flaiano Film Festival 2002, Silver Ribbon for Best Dir, Italian Nat. Syndicate of Film Journalists 2002) 2002, Buongiorno, notte (Good Morning, Night) (also producer) (FIPRESCI Prize, European Film Awards 2003, CinemAvvenire Award for Best Film, Little Golden Lion Award and Outstanding Individual Contrib. Award, Venice Film Festival 2003) 2003, Il regista di matrimoni (The Wedding Director) (also producer) 2006, Sorelle 2006. *Television:* Il gabbiano 1977, La macchina cinema (The Cinema Machine, USA) (FIPRESCI Prize, Berlin Int. Film Festival 1979) 1979, L'uomo dal fiore in bocca 1992, . . .Addio del passato. . . (also producer) 2002.

BELLON, Pierre; French business executive; *Chairman, Sodexo Alliance;* b. 24 Jan. 1930, Marseille; m.; four c.; ed Ecole des Hautes Etudes Commerciales; began career with family's ship chandlery business, Marseille 1950s; Asst Man. Soc. d'Exploitations Hôtelières, Aériennes et Terrestres 1958, later Man. Dir, Chair. and CEO; f. Sodexho SA, food and management services co., Marseille 1966 (Sodexho Alliance SA from 1997), CEO 1966–2005, Chair. 1974–, co. renamed Sodexo 2008; Chair. and CEO Bellon SA, Chair. Exec. Bd 1996–2002, Chair. Supervisory Bd 2002–; Nat. Pres. Center for Young Company Managers 1968–70; Pres. Nat. Fed. of Hotel and Restaurant Chains 1972–75; Vice-Chair. MEDEF (French business confed.) 1981–2005; Founder, Association Progrès du Management 1986; mem. Econ. and Social Council 1969–79; Commdr, Légion d'honneur, Ordre nat. du Mérite, Chevalier, Ordre du Mérite Agricole, Commdr, Order of Rio Branco (Brazil). *Address:* Sodexo, 255 Quai de la Bataille de Stalingrad, 92130 Issy les Moulineaux, France (office). *E-mail:* pierre.bellon@sodexo.com (office). *Website:* www.sodexo.com (office).

BELLUCCI, Monica; Italian fashion model and actress; b. 30 Sept. 1964, Città di Castello, Perugia; m. Vincent Cassel 1999; ed Univ. of Perugia; model Elite Model Man., Milan 1988–90, appeared in advertising campaigns for Dolce & Gabbana; began taking acting lessons 1989; debut in TV film Vita Coi Figli (Life With the Sons) 1990. *Films include:* Briganti 1990, La riffa 1991, Bram Stoker's Dracula 1992, Ostinato destino 1992, I mitici 1994, Palla di neve 1995, Il cielo è sempre più blu 1995, L'appartement 1996, Come mi vuoi 1996, Dobermann 1997, Mauvais genre 1997, L'ultimo capodanno dell'umanità (Best Actress, Globo d'Oro) 1998, A los que aman 1998, Méditerranées 1998, Comme un poisson hors de l'eau 1999, Under Suspicion 2000, Franck Spadone 2000, Malèna 2000, Il patto dei lupi 2000, Astérix et Obélix: Mission Cléopâtre 2001, Irreversible 2002, Ricordati di me 2002, The Matrix Reloaded 2003, Tears of the Sun 2003, She Hate Me 2004, The Passion of the Christ 2004, The Brothers Grimm 2005, Combien tu m'aimes? 2005, Sheitan 2006, N (Io e Napoleone) 2006, Le Concile de pierre 2006, Manuale d'amore 2 (Capitoli successivi) 2007, Shoot 'Em Up 2007, Le Deuxième Souffle 2007, Sanguepazzo 2008, L'Uomo che ama 2008, The Private Lives of Pippa Lee 2009. *Address:* c/o Carol Levi, Via G. Pisanelli 2, 00196 Rome, Italy (office); Agence Intertalent, 5 rue Clement-Marot, Paris 75008, France (office). *Telephone:* (06) 36002430 (Italy) (office).

BELLUGI, Piero; Italian conductor; *Principal Conductor, Orchestra Sinfonica di Sanremo;* b. 14 July 1924, Florence; s. of Mario Bellugi and Giulia Favilli; m. Ursula Herzberger 1954 (divorced); five c.; ed Conservatorio Cherubini, Florence, Accad. Chigiana, Siena, Akad. des Mozarteums, Salzburg and Tanglewood, Mass., USA; Musical Dir Oakland (Calif.) and Portland (Ore.) Symphony Orchestras 1955–61; Perm. Conductor Radio Symphony Orchestras, Turin 1967; Prin. Conductor Orchestra Sinfonica di Sanremo; Prof. courses for orchestral players and conductor, Italian Youth Orchestra 1981–; Guest Conductor, La Scala, Milan (debut 1961), Vienna State Opera, Rome Opera, Aix-en-Provence Festival, Berlin Radio, Paris, Rome S. Cecilia, Chicago, San Francisco Operas etc.; Musical Dir Teatro Massimo, Palermo; Hon. mem. Nat. Acad. Luigi Cherubini of Music, Letters and Arts, Nat. Acad. Santa Cecilia, Rome. *Address:* Via Santa Reparata 11, 50129 Florence, Italy (home). *Telephone:* (55) 216492 (home). *Fax:* (55) 216492 (home). *E-mail:* pierobellugi@tin.it (home). *Website:* www.pierobellugi.com (home).

BELMONDO, Jean-Paul; French actor; b. 9 April 1933, Neuilly-sur-Seine; s. of Paul Belmondo and Madeline Rainaud-Richard; m. 1959 (divorced 1967); one s. two d. (one deceased); m. 2nd Natty Tardivel 2002; ed Ecole Alsacienne, Paris, Cours Pascal and Conservatoire nat. d'art dramatique; started career on the stage; mainly film actor since 1957; Pres. French Union of Actors 1963–66; Pres. Annabel Productions 1981–; Dir Théâtre des Variétés 1991; Officier Légion d'honneur, Chevalier, Ordre nat. du Mérite, des Arts et des Lettres; Prix Citron 1972. *Plays acted in include:* L'hôtel du libre-échange, Oscar, Trésor-Party, Médée, La mégère apprivoisée, Kean 1987, Cyrano de Bergerac 1990, Tailleur pour Dames 1993, La Puce à l'oreille 1996, Frédérick ou le boulevard du crime 1998. *Films acted in include:* Sois belle et tais-toi, A pied, à cheval et en voiture, les Tricheurs, Charlotte et son Jules, Drôle de dimanche 1958, Les Copains du dimanche, Mademoiselle Ange, A double tour, Classe tous risques, Au bout de souffle, L'Amour, La Novice, La Ciociara, Moderato Cantabile, Léon Morin Prêtre, Le Doulos 1962, Dragées au poivre, L'Aîné des Ferchaux, Peau de banane, 100,000 dollars au soleil 1963, Two Women, The Man From Rio, Echappement libre 1964, Les tribulations d'un Chinois en Chine, Pierrot le Fou 1965, Paris, brûle-t-il? 1966, Le Voleur 1966, Casino Royale 1967, The Brain 1969, La Sirène du Mississippi 1969, Un Homme qui me plaît 1970, Borsalino 1970, The Burglars 1972, La Scoumoune 1972, L'Héritier 1972, Le Magnifique 1973, Stavisky 1974, Peur sur la ville 1975, L'Incorrigible 1975, L'Alpageur, Le corps de mon ennemi 1976, L'Animal 1977, Flic ou Voyou 1979, L'As de as (also produced) 1982, Le Marginal 1983, Joyeuses Pâques, Les Morfalous 1984, Hold-up 1985, Le Solitaire 1987, Itinéraire d'un enfant gâté (César for Best Actor 1988), L'Inconnu dans la Maison 1992, Les Cent et une Nuits 1995, Les Misérables 1995, Désiré 1996, Une chance sur deux 1998, Peut-être 1999, Les Acteurs 2000, Amazone 2000, L'Aîné des Ferchaux (TV) 2001. *Publication:* 30 Ans et 25 Films (autobiog.) 1963. *Address:* Artmédia, 20 avenue Ropp, 75007 Paris (office); Théâtre des Variétés, 7 blvd Montmartre, 75002 Paris, France.

BELMONT, Joseph; Seychelles politician; *Vice-President, Minister of Tourism and Minister of Public Administration and Internal Affairs;* mem. Seychelles People's Progressive Front; apptd Minister of Manpower and Social Services 1982, subsequently held several ministerial positions, including Minister of Industry and Int. Business –1999, of Housing and Land Use 1999–2004, of Tourism Jan.–April 2004; Vice-Pres., Minister of Tourism and Minister of Public Admin and Internal Affairs 2004–. *Address:* Office of the Vice-President, State House, PO Box 1303, Victoria, Seychelles (office). *Telephone:* 225509 (office). *Fax:* 225152 (office). *E-mail:* jbelmont@statehouse.gov.sc (office). *Website:* www.statehouse.gov.sc (office).

BELNAP, Nuel, PhD; American philosopher and academic; *Alan Ross Anderson Distinguished Professor of Philosophy, University of Pittsburgh;* b. 1 May 1930, Evanston, Ill.; s. of Nuel Dinsmore and Elizabeth Belnap (née Dafter); m. 1st Joan Gohde 1953; m. 2nd Gillian Hirth 1982; four c.; m. 3rd Birgit Herbeck 1997; ed Univ. of Illinois, Yale Univ.; instructor in Philosophy, then Asst Prof., Yale Univ. 1958–63; Assoc. Prof. of Philosophy, Univ. of Pittsburgh 1963–66, Prof. 1966–, Alan Ross Anderson Distinguished Prof. of Philosophy 1984–, Prof. of Sociology 1967–80, of History and Philosophy of Science 1971, of Intelligent Systems 1988–93; Visiting Prof. of Philosophy, Univ. of Calif. at Irvine 1973; Visiting Fellow, Australian Nat. Univ., Canberra 1976; Visiting Oscar R. Ewing Prof. of Philosophy, Indiana Univ. 1977, 1978, 1979; Visiting Leibniz-Prof., Zentrum für Höhere Studien 1996; mem. several editorial bds; Sterling Jr Fellow 1955–56; Fulbright Fellow 1957–58; Morse Research Fellow 1962–63; Guggenheim Fellow 1975–76; Fellow Center for Advanced Studies in Behavioral Science 1982–83; Hon. DPhil (Leipzig) 2000. *Publications:* Computer Programs Bindex Tester 1976; The Logic of Questions and Answers (co-author) 1976, Entailment: The Logic of Relevance and Necessity (co-author) (Vol. I) 1975, (Vol. II) 1992, The Revision Theory of Truth (co-author) 1993, Facing the Future: Agents and Choices in Our Indeterministic World (co-author) 2001. *Address:* Department of Philosophy, University of Pittsburgh, Fifth Avenue, Pittsburgh, PA 15260 (office); 5803 Ferree Street, Pittsburgh, PA 15217, USA (home). *Telephone:* (412) 624-5777 (office); (412) 521-3897 (home). *Fax:* (412) 624-5377 (office). *E-mail:* belnap@pitt.edu (office). *Website:* www.pitt.edu/~belnap (office).

BĚLOHLÁVEK, Jiří; Czech musician and conductor; *Chief Conductor, BBC Symphony Orchestra;* b. 24 Feb. 1946, Prague; m. Anna Fejérová 1971; two d.; ed Acad. of Performing Arts, Prague with Sergiu Celibidache; Conductor Orchestra Puellarum Pragensis (chamber orchestra), Prague 1967–72; Asst Conductor Czech Philharmonic Orchestra 1970–71; Conductor Brno State Philharmonic Orchestra 1971–77; Chief Conductor Prague Symphony Orchestra 1977–90; Conductor Czech Philharmonic Orchestra 1981–90, Prin. Conductor and Music Dir 1990–92; Conductor Int. Philharmonic Youth Orchestra, Prague 1987–; founder and Music Dir Prague Philharmonia 1994–; Principal Guest Conductor BBC Symphony Orchestra 1995–2000, Chief Conductor 2006–; Prof. Acad. of Music, Prague 1995–; Principal Guest Conductor Nat. Theatre Prague 1998; guest appearances with numerous orchestras, including USSR State Symphony Orchestra, BBC Philharmonic, BBC Nat. Orchestra of Wales, Scottish Nat. Orchestra, Royal Liverpool Philharmonic, City of Birmingham Symphony, Berlin Philharmonic, Vienna Symphony Orchestra, Leipzig Gewandhaus, Stockholm Philharmonic, Bavarian Radio Orchestra, Dresden Philharmonic, Deutsche Kammerphilharmonie, Tonhalle (Zürich) Orchestra, New York Philharmonic, Boston Symphony Orchestra, St Louis Orchestra, Washington Nat. Orchestra, Montréal Symphony Orchestra, NHK Philharmonic (Tokyo); Supraphon Prize 1977, Artist of Merit 1986, Supraphon Golden Disc 1986, 1987, 1994, 1999, Diapason d'Or 1992, Barclay Theatre Award 2000, Medal for Merit, Prague 2001, Gramophone Award for Best Opera Recording (for The Excursions of Mr Broucek, with BBC Symphony Orchestra) 2008. *Leisure interests:* gardening, hiking. *Address:* IMG Artists, The Light Box, 111 Power Road, London, W4 5PY, England (office); c/o BBC Symphony Orchestra, BBC Maida Vale Studios, Delaware Road, London, W9 2LG, England (office). *Telephone:* (20) 7957-5800 (office); (20) 7765-2956 (office). *Fax:* (20) 7957-5801 (office); (20) 7286-3251 (office). *E-mail:* rtighe@imgartists.com (office); bbcso@bbc.co.uk (office). *Website:* www.imgartists.com (office); www.bbc.co.uk/orchestras/symphonyorchestra (office).

BELOTSERKOVSKY, Oleg Mikhailovich; Russian mathematician; *Director, Institute for Computer-Aided Design, Russian Academy of Sciences;* b. 29 Aug. 1925, Livni, Orlov Region; m.; two c.; ed Lomonosov Moscow State Univ.; Sr Researcher, Applied Math. Div. and Computing Centre, USSR (now Russian) Acad. of Sciences 1953–76, Head of Computer Centre 1976; Rector Moscow Inst. of Physics and Tech. 1962–87; Corresp. mem. USSR (now Russian) Acad. of Sciences 1972, mem. 1979, Chair. Scientific Council on Cybernetics; Dir Inst. of Computer-Aided Design 1987–; mem. Int. Acad. of Astronautic Fed.; Order of the Red Banner of Labour 1965, 1975, 1981, Order of the October Revolution 1971, Order of Lenin 1985, Order of Merit to the Fatherland (3rd Degree) 1999; N. Zhukovsky Prize and Gold Medal for the Best Work on the Theory of Aviation 1962, Lenin Prize 1966, S. Korolev Medal 1978, S. I. Vavilov Medal. *Publications include:* Flow Past Blunt in Supersonic Flow—Theoretical and Experimental Results 1967, Numerical Methods in Fluid Dynamics 1976, The 'Coarse-Particle' Method in Gas Dynamics 1982, Numerical Modelling in Mechanics of Continuous Media 1984, Computational Mechanics: Contemporary Problems and Results 1991, Mathematical Modelling of Myocardial Infarction 1993, Computational Experiment in Turbulence: From Order to Chaos 1997, Turbulence and Instabilities 1999, Modern Solution Methods for Nonlinear Multidimensional Problems: Mathematics, Mechanics, Turbulence 2000. *Leisure interests:* tennis, swimming. *Address:* Institute for Computer-Aided Design, Russian Academy of Sciences, 2 Brestskaya str. 19/18, 123056 Moscow, Russia. *Telephone:* (495) 250-02-62 (office). *Fax:* (495) 250-95-54. *E-mail:* icad.ran@g23.relcom.ru.

BELOUS, Oleg Nikolayevich; Russian diplomatist; *Director, First European Department, Ministry of Foreign Affairs;* b. 18 Aug. 1951; ed Moscow Inst. of Int. Relations; on staff USSR (later Russian) Ministry of Foreign Affairs 1973–, Deputy Dir First European Dept 1994–96, Dir Dept of All-European Co-operation 1996–98, Dir First European Dept (Belgium, Vatican City, Italy, Spain, Luxembourg, Malta, Monaco, The Netherlands, Portugal, France) 2001–; Counsellor, Russian Embassy to Belgium 1991–94; Perm. Rep. of Russia to OSCE, Vienna 1998–2001. *Address:* First European Department, Ministry of Foreign Affairs, Smolenskaya-Sennaya pl 32/34, Moscow 119200 Russia (office). *Telephone:* (495) 244-41-62 (office). *Fax:* (495) 244-31-87 (office). *E-mail:* ministry@mid.ru (office). *Website:* www.mid.ru (office).

BELOV, Vasiliy Ivanovich; Russian writer; b. 23 Oct. 1932, Timonikha, Vologda; m.; one d.; ed Gorky Inst.; fmr mem. CPSU and USSR Union of Writers; worked on kolkhoz, received industrial training at a FZO school, then as a joiner and mechanic; served in Soviet Army; staff writer on regional newspaper 'Kommunar' in Gryazovets (Vologda) 1950s; secondary ed. (evening classes) 1956–59; Ed. Literary Inst. of Union of Writers 1959–64; People's Deputy of USSR 1989–91, mem. USSR Supreme Soviet 1989–91; Order 'Honour of Fatherland'; USSR State Prize 1981, Russian State Prize 2003. *Films:* Aricanych, The Carpenter Stories, According to the 206, Everything is Behind, Alexander Nevsky, Above the Light Waters. *Publications include:* My Village in the Forest 1961, Hot Summer 1963, Tisha and Grisha 1966, Carpenter Stories 1968 (English trans. 1969), An Ordinary Affair 1969, Village Tales 1971, Day After Day 1972, The Hills 1973, Looks Can Kiss 1975, On the Eve 1972–87, The Way of Rural Life 1985, All is Ahead 1986, Vologda Funny Stories 1988, The Eve 1989, Year of the Great Change 1994, Past Five 1999, Honeymoon 2000, A Story of One Village 2001, Irrevocable Years 2001, Plays 2005. *Leisure Interests:* painting. *Address:* Oktyabrskaya Street 10, Flat 4, Vologda, Russia (home). *Telephone:* (81722) 2-94-65.

BELSHAW, Cyril Shirley, PhD, FRSC; Canadian anthropologist, writer and publisher; b. 3 Dec. 1921, Waddington, NZ; s. of Horace Belshaw and Marion L. S. Belshaw (née McHardie); m. Betty J. Sweetman 1943 (deceased); one s. one d.; ed Auckland Univ. Coll. and Victoria Coll., Wellington (Univ. of New Zealand), London School of Econs; Dist Officer and Deputy Commr for Western Pacific, British Solomon Islands 1943–46; Sr Research Fellow, Australian Nat. Univ. 1950–53; Prof. Univ. of British Columbia 1953–86, Prof. Emer. 1986–; Dir Regional Training Centre for UN Fellows, Van. 1961–62; Ed. Current Anthropology 1974–84; mem. numerous UNESCO comms, working parties and consultancy groups; Pres. Int. Union of Anthropological and Ethnological Sciences 1978–83, XIth Int. Congress of Anthropological and Ethnological Sciences 1983; Exec. American Anthropological Assoc. 1969–70; Chair. Standing Cttee Social Sciences and Humanities Pacific Science Asscn 1968–76; Ed. The Anthroglobe Journal 1998–2000, 2004–06; Propr Webzines of Vancouver; Man. Ed. Adam's Vancouver Dining Guide 1997–2007, www.anthropologising.ca 2001–; Hon. Life Fellow, Royal Anthropological Inst., Pacific Science Asscn, Asscn for the Social Anthropology of Oceania; Hon. Life mem. Royal Anthropological Inst. 1978, Pacific Science Asscn 1981; World Utopian Champion 2005. *Publications:* Island Administration in the South West Pacific 1950, Changing Melanesia 1954, In Search of Wealth 1955, The Great Village 1957, The Indians of British Columbia (with others) 1958, Under the Ivi Tree 1964, Anatomy of a University 1964, Traditional Exchange and Modern Markets 1965, The Conditions of Social Performance 1970, Towers Besieged 1974, The Sorcerer's Apprentice 1976, The Complete Good Dining Guide to Restaurants in Greater Vancouver 1984, Choosing Our Destiny 2006. *Leisure interests:* gardening, photography, travel, restaurants. *Address:* Suite 2901, 969 Richards Street, Vancouver, BC, V6B 1A8, Canada (home). *Telephone:* (604) 739-8130 (home). *E-mail:* cyril@anthropologising.ca (home). *Website:* www.anthropologising.ca (home).

BELTRÃO, Alexandre Fontana; Brazilian coffee executive; b. 28 April 1924, Curitiba, Paraná; s. of the late Alexandre Beltrão and of Zilda Fontana Beltrão; m. Anna Emilia Beltrão 1964; two c.; ed Instituto Santa Maria, Curitiba, Univ. de São Paulo, Escola Nacional de Engenharia, Rio de Janeiro; asst engineer 1944; army officer 1945–46; Asst Engineer, Dept of Soil Mechanics, Inst. de Pesquisas Tecnológicas, São Paulo 1948; trained in regional planning at Inst. Nat. d'Aerophotogrametrie, Ministère de la Reconstruction, Paris and at Ministry of Works, London 1950–51; Founder and Dir of SPL (Planning Services Ltd) 1954–; observer, Govt of State of Paraná to UN Int. Coffee Conf. 1962; special adviser to Pres. Brazilian Coffee

Inst. 1964; Chief Brazilian Coffee Inst. Bureau, NY 1965–67; Pres. World Coffee Promotion Cttee of Int. Coffee Org. 1965–67; Exec. Dir Int. Coffee Org. 1968–94; Sec. of Science and Tech., Paraná 1994–; Commdr Order of Rio Branco. *Publications:* Paraná and the Coffee Economy 1963, essay on Economy of States of Paraná, Pará and Ceará (Brazil) 1958.

BELYAEV, Spartak Timofeyevich, PhD, DrSc; Russian physicist; *Head of Research, Nanotechnology and Information Faculty, Moscow Physico-Technology Institute;* b. 27 Oct. 1923, Moscow; m.; two c.; ed Moscow State Univ.; mil. service 1941–46; jr researcher, sr researcher, Kurchatov Inst. 1952–62; Research Scientist (on leave), Niels Bohr Inst., Copenhagen, Denmark 1957–58; Head of Lab., Novosibirsk Inst. of Nuclear Physics 1962–78; Rector, Novosibirsk State Univ. 1965–78; Head of Lab. and Dir Inst. for Nuclear and Gen. Physics (RRC Kurchatov Inst.) 1978–2006, Head of Research, Nanotechnology and Information Faculty, Moscow Physico-Technology Inst. 2006–; Corresp. mem. USSR (now Russian) Acad. of Sciences 1964–68, mem. 1968–; mem. CPSU 1943–91; L.D. Landau Gold Medal, Russian Acad. of Sciences 1998, Eugene Feenberg Medal in Many-Body Physics 2004. *Publications:* scientific works in field of theory of atomic nucleus, particle movement in cyclotron, physics of relativistic plasma, statistic physics of quantum, many body systems. *Address:* 4 Maksimova st, Moscow, Russian Federation (office). *Telephone:* (499) 196-7203 (office). *E-mail:* fnti-mipt@kiae.ru (office). *Website:* www.fnti.kiae.ru (office).

BELYAKOV, Rostislav Apollosovich, DTechSci; Russian design engineer; *Honourary General and Designer of MiG Aircraft;* b. 4 March 1919, Murom, Vladimirskaya region; m. Lyudmila Nikolayevna Shvernik; one s.; ed Ordzhonikidze Aviation Inst., Moscow; mem. CPSU 1944–91; design engineer 1941–57, Deputy Chief Designer 1957–62, First Deputy General Designer 1962–70, Gen. Designer 1971–97, Gen. Dir/Advisor ANPK MiG 1997–99, Hon. Gen. and Designer of MiG Aircraft 1999–; Corresp. mem. of USSR (now Russian) Acad. of Sciences 1974, mem. 1981–; Deputy to USSR Supreme Soviet 1974–89; 8 Orders of the USSR, one Order of Russian Fed. A.N. Tupolev Gold Medal; Hero of Socialist Labour 1971, 1982, USSR State Prize 1952, 1989, Lenin Prize 1972. *Publications:* papers on aircraft construction. *Address:* RSK "MiG", Leningradskoye Sh. 6, 125299 Moscow, Russia. *Telephone:* (495) 155-23-10. *Fax:* (495) 943-00-27.

BELZA, Svyatoslav Igorevich; Russian literary and music critic; b. 26 April 1942, Chelyabinsk; s. of Igor Belza and Zoya Gulinskaya; divorced; two s.; ed Moscow State Univ.; researcher, Inst. of World Literature USSR (now Russian) Acad. of Sciences 1965–; founder and reviewer TV programme Music on TV 1988–97, Man. and Artistic Dir 1995–97; actively works as literary critic and TV broadcaster; mem. Russian Union of Writers; mem. Acad. of Russian Art, Acad. of Russian TV; Officer Cross of Merit (Poland) 1998, Order of St Nicholas (Ukraine) 1998, Order of Friendship (Russia) 2001; Merited Master of Arts of Russia 1994, of Ukraine 2004, Golden Sign of Honour 1999, Irina Arkhipova Foundation Prize 2001, Prize of Moscow 2002, People's Artist of Russia 2006. *Publications include:* Homo legens 1983, 1990 and over 300 literary works and reviews. *Leisure interests:* reading, travel. *Address:* Stroiteley str. 4, korp. 7, Apt 9, Moscow 119311, Russia (home). *Telephone:* (495) 930-36-61 (home). *Fax:* (495) 930-36-61 (home).

BEM, Pavel, MD; Czech politician; *Mayor of Prague;* b. 18 July 1963; m. Radmila Bem; two s.; ed Faculty of Medicine, Charles Univ., Prague and post-grad. studies in psychiatry, John Hopkins Univ., Baltimore, Florida State Univ. and Univ. of California, San Diego, USA, Mediterranean Inst. for Research and Training in Physiotherapy and Psychiatry, Italy; specialized in psychiatry working with drug addicts; House Officer, Psychiatric Clinic Kosmonosy, Mlada Boleslav 1987; House Officer, Detoxification Ward, Psychiatric Clinic, Charles Univ. 1988–90, Chief Psychiatrist, Outpatient Treatment Centre for Drug Addicts, Faculty Hosp. 1990–91; Man. Dir Filia Foundation for the Support of Mentally Disabled and Drug Dependent Persons 1992–94; Dir and Chief Psychiatrist (Outreach Programme), Contact Centre, Prague 1994; Sec.-Gen. (Anti-Drug Policy Implementation), Nat. Drug Comm., Office of Govt of Czech Repub. 1994–95, Exec. Sec. (Coordination of entire Drug Policy), Nat. Drug Comm., Cabinet of Prime Minister 1997–98; Adviser on Law Enforcement Aspects and Legislation), Minister of the Interior 1996; mem. Civic Democratic Party (ODS); Mayor of Municipal Dist of Prague 6 1998–2002, Mayor of Prague 2002–; mem. Exec. Bd Soc. of Addictive Disorders of Czech Medical Asscn; mem. Advisory Bd to Ministry of Health on Drug Matters 1993–95, Addiction Abstracts; mem. Soc. for Psychotherapy and Family Therapy of Czech Medical Asscn, Chamber of Physicians of Czech Repub., Int. Council on Alcohol and Addiction, Euro – Methwork. *Publications:* Risks of HIV Transmission among IVDU's in the Czech Republic, Minimum Standards and Criteria of Effective Primary Prevention, Methodological Guidelines for School Based Primary Prevention – Manual, Teaching the Teachers Didactics, Risk Behaviour Among Drug Users in Prague, Extent of Substance Abuse in the Czech Republic, Drugs and AIDS – Parents' Guide, Methodological Guide for Community Based Prevention, Organization and Management of Drug Problems at Local Level. *Leisure interests:* hiking, cycling, tennis, diving, classical music, rock, jazz, travel. *Address:* Office of the Mayor of the City of Prague, Mariánské náměstí 2, 110 00 Prague 1 – Staré Město, Czech Republic (office). *Telephone:* (2) 24482633 (office). *Website:* www.pavelbem.cz (office).

BEMBAMBA, Lucien Marie-Noël; Burkinabé economist and politician; *Minister of the Economy and Finance;* b. 8 Jan. 1957; m.; three c.; Finance Admin. Cen. Bank of West African States 1982–93; Gen.-Dir Treasury and Public Accounting Dept, Ministry of Economy and Finance 1993–2007, Del. in Charge of the Budget 2007–08, Minister of Economy and Finance 2008–; Alt. Gov. IMF 2006; Chair. Nat. Public Debt Cttee 2006. *Address:* Ministry of the Economy and Finance, 03 BP 7050, Ouagadougou, Burkina Faso (office).

Telephone: 50-32-42-11 (office). *Fax:* 50-31-27-15 (office). *Website:* www.finances.gov.bf (office).

BEMENT, Arden L., Jr, DrIng; American organization official, engineer and academic; *Director, National Science Foundation;* b. 22 May 1932, Pittsburg; ed Colo School of Mines, Univ. of Idaho, Univ. of Mich.; Sr Research Assoc., Gen. Electric Co. 1954–65; Man. of Fuels and Materials Dept and Metallurgy Research Dept, Battelle Northwest Labs 1965–70; Prof. of Nuclear Materials, MIT 1970–76; Dir Office of Materials Science, Defense Advanced Research Projects Agency (DARPA) 1976–79; Deputy Under-Sec. of Defence for Research and Eng Dept of Defence 1979–80; Vice-Pres. of Tech. Resources and of Science and Tech., TRW Inc. 1980–92; Dir Midwest Superconductivity Consortium and Basil S. Turner Distinguished Prof. of Eng, Purdue Univ. 1993–98, Head of School of Engineering and David A. Ross Distinguished Prof. of Nuclear Eng 1998–2001; Dir Nat. Inst. of Standards and Tech. (NIST) Dept of Commerce 2001–04; Acting Dir NSF 2004, Dir 2004–; with US Nat. Science Board 1990–94, Head NIST's Advanced Tech. Program Advisory Cttee 1999–, with US Nat. Comm. for UNESCO, and Vice Coordinator of the Natural Sciences and Eng Cttee 2004–, with G-8 Heads of Research Councils 2004–; has given over 100 invited lectures and presentations; Lt Col (retd) Corps of Engineers US Army Reserve; mem. Nat. Acad. of Eng, Fellow, American Asscn for the Advancement of Science, American Inst. of Chemists, American Nuclear Soc., ASM Int; Hon. Fellow, American Acad. of Arts and Sciences, Hon. Prof. Chinese Acad. of Sciences Graduate School; Hon. PhD (Cleveland State Univ.) 1989, (Case Western Reserve Univ.) 2000, (Colorado School of Mines) 2004; Distinguished Civilian Service Medal of the Dept of Defence, American Nuclear Soc. Outstanding Achievement Award 2004, Washington Acad. of Science Award for Distinguished Career in Science 2006, American Chemical Soc. Public Service Award 2006. *Publications:* materials sciences and engineering courses; books and monographs on chemistry, engineering, and metals and alloys; reports of the Atomic Energy Comm.; research articles in prof. journals; science policy articles in trade journals. *Leisure interests:* philately, history, biography. *Address:* National Science Foundation, 4201 Wilson Boulevard, Arlington, VA 22230, USA (office). *Telephone:* (703) 292-8000 (office). *Website:* www.nsf.gov (office).

BEN-AMI, Shlomo, BA, MA, PhD; Israeli academic and fmr politician; *Vice-President, Toledo International Centre for Peace;* b. 1943, Morocco; m.; three c.; ed Tel-Aviv Univ., Univ. of Oxford, UK; Visiting Fellow, St Antony's Coll., Oxford 1980–82; Head, Grad. School of History, Tel-Aviv Univ. 1982–86, Elias Sourasky Chair for Spanish and Latin American Studies.1986–, Founder and Head, Curiel Center for Int. Studies 1993–96; Amb. to Spain 1987–91; mem. Knesset 1996–2001; Head of Israel Del. to the Multilateral Talks on Refugees, Ottawa 1992; participated at the Camp David Summit for Israel and Palestine Peace 2000; leader of Israel Del. at the Taba Peace Talks 2001; fmr mem. Foreign Affairs and Defense Cttee; Minister of Public Security 1999–2001; Minister of Foreign Affairs 2000–01; currently Vice-Pres. Toledo International Centre for Peace (TICpax), Spain; mem. Bd of Dirs Int. Crisis Group 2006–. *Publications include:* Quel avenir pour Israel? 2001, A Front Without a Rearguard: A Voyage to the Boundaries of the Peace Process 2004, Scars of War, Wounds of Peace. The Arab-Israeli Tragedy 2006. *Address:* Toledo International Centre for Peace, Felipe IV, 5 Bajo Izq., 28014 Madrid, Spain (office). *Telephone:* (91) 5237452 (office). *Fax:* (91) 5227301 (office). *Website:* www.toledopax.org (home).

BEN BELLA, Mohammed; Algerian politician; b. 1916; Warrant Officer in Moroccan regt during Second World War (decorated); Chief OAS rebel mil. group in Algeria 1947; imprisoned 1949–52 (escaped); directed Algerian nat. movement from exile in Libya 1952–56; arrested Oct. 1956; held in France 1959–62; Vice-Premier Algerian Nationalist Provisional Govt, Tunis 1962, Leader, Algerian Political Bureau, Algeria 1962, Premier of Algeria 1962–65, Pres. of Algeria 1963–65; detained 1965–80; restricted residence, Msila 1979–80; freed 1981; returned from exile Sept. 1990; Chair. Int. Islamic Comm. for Human Rights, London 1982–; Pres. Int. Campaign Against Aggression on Iraq 2003; Lenin Peace Prize 1964.

BEN-DAVID, Zadok; British-Israeli sculptor; b. 1949, Bayhan, Yemen; s. of Moshe Ben-David and Hana Ben-David; ed Bezalel Acad. of Art and Design, Jerusalem, Reading Univ. and St Martin's School of Art, London; emigrated to Israel 1945; Sculpture Teacher at St Martin's School of Art 1977–82, Ravensbourne Coll. of Art and Design, Bromley 1982–85; first solo show at Air Gallery, London 1980. *Publications:* (catalogues) Zadok Ben-David 1987, The Israeli Pavilion: The Venice Biennale 1988, De Circasia et al 2007. *Address:* 65 Warwick Avenue, London, W9 2PP, England (home). *Telephone:* (20) 7266-0536 (home); (20) 7328-6857 (office). *Fax:* (20) 7266-3892 (home); (20) 7328-6857 (office). *E-mail:* zadokbd@yahoo.com (home); zadokstudio@gmail.com (office). *Website:* www.zadokbendavid.com (home).

BEN-ELIEZER, Benjamin (Fuad); Israeli politician and army officer; *Minister of National Infrastructure;* b. 1936, Iraq; ed Israel Nat. Defence Coll.; emigrated to Israel 1949; career officer Israel Defence Forces (IDF), Commdr Six Day War 1967, served on IDF Mil. Mission to Singapore 1970–73, Commdr Yom Kippur War 1973, First CO Southern Lebanon 1977–78, Commdr Judea and Samaria 1978–81; Govt Co-ordinator of Activities in the Administered Areas 1983–84; Minister of Housing and Construction 1992–96; mem. Knesset 1984–, served on Foreign Affairs Cttee 1988–92; mem. Israel Labour Party, Chair. –2002; Deputy Prime Minister and Minister of Communications 1999–2001, Minister of Defence 2001–02, of Nat. Infrastructure 2006–. *Address:* Ministry of National Infrastructure, Ala Building, 216 Jaffa Street, Jerusalem, Israel (office). *Telephone:* 2-5006777 (office). *Fax:* 2-5006888 (office). *E-mail:* pniot@mni.gov.il (office). *Website:* www.mni.gov.il (office).

BEN JELLOUN, Tahar; Moroccan writer and poet; b. 1 Dec. 1944, Fès; m. Aicha Ben Jelloun 1986; two s. two d.; ed Lycée Regnault de Tanger, Faculté de Lettres de Rabat and Univ. of Paris; columnist Le Monde 1973–, La Repubblica (Italy) and La Vanguardia (Spain); mem. Conseil supérieur de la langue française; UN Goodwill Amb. for Human Rights; Dr hc (Montréal); Chevalier Ordre des Arts et Lettres, Légion d'honneur; Prix de l'Amitié Franco-Arabe 1976, Médaille du Mérite Nat. (Morocco), Prix Goncourt 1987, Prix des Hemisphere 1991, UN Global Tolerance Award 1998, Int. IMPAC Dublin Literary Award 2004. *Publications:* fiction: Harrouda 1973, La Réclusion solitaire 1976 (trans. as Solitaire 1988), Moha le fou, Moha le sage 1978, La Prière de l'absent 1980, Muha al-ma'twah, Muha al-hakim 1982, L'Écrivain public 1983, L'Enfant de sable 1985 (trans. as The Sand Child 1987), La Nuit sacrée 1987 (trans. as The Sacred Night 1989), Jour de silence à Tanger 1990 (trans. as Silent Day in Tangier 1991), Les Yeux baissés 1991, L'Ange aveugle 1992, L'Homme rompu 1994, Corruption 1995, Le Premier amour est toujours le dernier 1995, Les Raisins de la galère 1995, La Soudure fraternelle 1995, La Nuit de l'erreur 1997, L'Auberge des pauvres 1999, Labyrinthe des Sentiments 1999, Cette aveuglante absence de lumière (trans. as This Blinding Absence of Light) (Impac Dublin Literary Award 2004) 2001, Amours sorcières 2003, Le Dernier Ami (trans. as The Last Friend) 2004, Partir 2005, L'ecole perdue 2006, Sur ma mère 2008, Au pays 2009; poems: Hommes sous linceul de silence 1970, Cicatrice du soleil 1972, Le Discours du chameau 1974, La Mémoire future: Anthologie de la nouvelle poésie du Maroc 1976, Les Amandiers sont morts de leurs blessures 1976, A l'insu du souvenir 1980, Sahara 1987, La Remontée des cendres 1991, Poésie Complète (1966–95) 1995; plays: Chronique d'une solitude 1976, Entretien avec Monsieur Said Hammadi, ouvrier algérien 1982, La Fiancée de l'eau 1984; non-fiction: La Plus haute des solitudes: Misère sexuelle d'émigrés nord-africains 1977, Haut Atlas: L'Exil de pierres 1982, Hospitalité française: Racisme et immigration maghrebine 1984, Marseille, comme un matin d'insomnie 1986, Giacometti 1991, Le Racisme expliqué à ma fille 1998, L'islam expliqué aux enfants 2002. *Address:* c/o Éditions Gallimard, 5 rue Sébastien-Bottin, 75328 Paris Cedex 07, France. *E-mail:* tbjweb@gmail.com (office). *Website:* www.taharbenjelloun.org (office).

BEN-NATAN, Asher; Israeli diplomatist; *Chairman, Ben-Gurion Foundation;* b. 15 Feb. 1921, Vienna; s. of Nahum Natan and Berta Natan; m. Erika (Rut) Frucht 1940; one s. one d.; ed Z. P. Hayut Hebrew Coll., Vienna and Institut des Hautes Etudes Internationales, Geneva; Co-Founder and mem. Kibbutz Mederot-Zeraim 1938–44, latterly Sec. and Treas.; Political Dept, Jewish Agency 1944–45; on mission to Europe to organize rescue of Jews and illegal immigration to Palestine: attached to office of Head of Jewish Agency 1945–47; Ministry of Foreign Affairs 1948–51; studies in Geneva 1951–53; Govt Rep. on Bd of Red Sea Inkodeh Co. 1953–56, Gen. Man. 1955–56; Rep. of Ministry of Defence in Europe 1956–58; Dir-Gen. Ministry of Defence 1959–65; Amb. to FRG 1965–70, to France 1970–75; Political Adviser to Minister of Defence 1975–78; Adviser to Prime Minister on Special Affairs 1985; Amb. on Special Mission 1993; Chair. Ben-Gurion Foundation 1983–; Pres. Israel-German Asscn 1973–; Officier Légion d'honneur, Commdr Ordre nat. (Ivory Coast), Commdr Ordre de l'Etoile équatoriale (Gabon), Grosses Bundesverdienstorden (Germany) 2000; Grosses Verdienstkreuz mit Mand (Germany); Dr hc (Ben Gurion Univ.) 1990; Hon. DPhil (Ben Gurion Univ.) 1997; Louis Waiss Peace Prize 1974, Heinz Galinski Prize (Berlin) 1992. *Publications:* Briefe an den Botschafter 1970, Dialogue avec des Allemands 1973, Die Chuzpe zu Leben 2004, Broecken Baden aber Nicht Vergessen 2004, Die Bricha 2005, The Audacity To Live (autobiog.) 2007. *Address:* 6 Wilson Street, Tel-Aviv 65220, Israel (office); 89 Haim Levanon Street, Tel-Aviv 69345, Israel (home). *Telephone:* (3) 561-3483 (office); (3) 641-3398 (home). *Fax:* (3) 561-3491 (office). *E-mail:* asherbn@u13.net (home).

BEN YAHIA, Habib; Tunisian politician; *Secretary General, Arab Maghreb Union;* b. 30 July 1938, Tunis; m. Naget Ben Yahia; one s. one d.; ed Univ. of Tunis, Columbia Univ., New York, USA; fmr Dir African Div., Ministry of Foreign Affairs, then Dir Econ. Co-operation with the United States Div.; fmr Econ. Counsellor, Embassies of Tunisia, Paris and Washington, DC; fmr Chief of Staff, Ministry of Foreign Affairs; Amb. to UAE, Japan and Belgium –1981, apptd Amb. to USA 1981; Minister of Foreign Affairs 1991–97, of Defence and Foreign Affairs 1999–2004; Sec. Gen. Arab Maghreb Union 2006–. *Address:* Union du Maghreb Arabe, 14 Rue Zalagh Agdal, Rabat, Morocco (office). *Telephone:* (3) 7671274 (office); (3) 7671280 (office). *Fax:* (3) 7671253 (office). *E-mail:* sg.uma@maghrebarabe.org (office). *Website:* www.maghrebarabe.org (office).

BENACERRAF, Baruj; American (b. Venezuelan) pathologist and scientist; *Fabyan Professor Emeritus of Comparative Pathology, Harvard Medical School;* b. 29 Oct. 1920, Caracas, Venezuela; m. Annette Dreyfus 1943; one d.; ed Lycée Janson, Paris, Columbia Univ., New York, Medical Coll. of Virginia; intern, Queens General Hosp., New York 1945–46; army service 1946–48; Research Fellow, Dept of Microbiology, Coll. of Physicians and Surgeons, Columbia Univ. 1948–50; Chargé de Recherches, CNRS, Hôpital Broussais, Paris 1950–56; Asst Prof. of Pathology, New York Univ. School of Medicine 1956–58, Assoc. Prof. of Pathology 1958–60, Prof. of Pathology 1960–68; Chief, Lab. of Immunology, Nat. Inst. of Allergy and Infectious Diseases, NIH, Bethesda, Md 1968–70; Fabyan Prof. of Comparative Pathology and Chair. Dept of Pathology, Harvard Medical School, Boston, Mass. 1970–91, now Prof. Emer.; mem. Immunology "A" Study Section, NIH 1965–69; Scientific Advisor World Health Org. for Immunology; Trustee and mem. Scientific Advisory Bd Trudeau Foundation 1970–77; mem. Scientific Advisory Bd Mass. General Hosp. 1971–74; mem. Bd of Govs Weizmann Inst. of Science; Chair. Scientific Advisory Cttee, Centre d'Immunologie de Marseille, CNRS-INSERM; Pres. American Asscn of Immunologists 1973–74; Pres. Fed. of American Socs for Experimental Biology 1974–75; Pres. Dana-Farber Cancer Inst., Boston, Mass. 1980–92, now Pres. Emer.; Pres. Int. Union of Immunological Socs; Fellow, American Acad. of Arts and Sciences; mem. American Asscn of Immunologists, American Asscn of Pathologists and Bacteriologists, American Soc. for Experimental Pathology, Soc. for Experimental Biology and Medicine, British Asscn for Immunology, French Soc. of Biological Chemistry, Harvey Soc., New York Acad. of Sciences, American Acad. of Sciences, Inst. of Medicine; Rabbi Shai Shacknai Prize in Immunology and Cancer Research (Hebrew Univ. of Jerusalem) 1974, T. Duckett Jones Memorial Award, Helen Hay Whitney Foundation 1976, Nobel Prize for Physiology or Medicine 1980, Nat. Medal of Science 1990. *Address:* 111 Perkins Street, Boston, MA 02130, USA (office). *Telephone:* (617) 632-3636 (office). *Fax:* (617) 632-3637 (office).

BENACHENHOU, Abdellatif; Algerian economist and government official; fmr financial consultant; worked for UNESCO; fmr econ. consultant for World Bank and UNEP; fmr chief consultant for Mediterranean Comm. on Sustainable Devt Working Group on Trade and Environment; Minister of Finance 1999–2001, 2003–05, currently econ. adviser to Pres. of Algeria. *Address:* c/o Office of the President, Présidence de la République, el-Mouradia, Algiers, Algeria. *Telephone:* (21) 69-15-15. *Fax:* (21) 69-15-95. *Website:* www.el-mouradia.dz.

BENACHENHOU, Mourad, MEcon, DSoc; Algerian economist and politician; b. 30 July 1938, Tlemcen; s. of the late Mohammed Benachenhou and Rostane Hiba; m. Norya Berbar 1962; two s. one d.; ed Univ. D'Alger, Univ. de Bordeaux, Univ. of Maryland; officer, Nat. Liberation Army 1956–62; adviser, Ministry of Agric. 1965–66; Dir Nat. Agronomic Inst., Algiers 1966–78; Dir Higher Ed. 1971–78; Dir Centre of Research on Agronomy 1978–82; Perm. Sec. Ministry of Finance 1982–90; int. consultant 1990–93; Minister of Econ. Affairs 1993–94, of Industrial Restructuring and Participation 1994–96, of Industry 1996; Exec. Dir World Bank 1982; Médaille de la Résistance. *Publications:* Higher Education in Algeria 1976, The Future of the University 1979, Debt and Democracy 1992, Inflation and Devaluation 1993. *Leisure interests:* tennis, chess, computers, reading, writing. *Address:* c/o Ministry of Industry, Le Colisée, Rue Roccas, Algiers, Algeria.

BENAÏSSA, Muhammad, BA; Moroccan politician; b. 3 Jan. 1937, Asilah; m. Laila Hajoun-Benaissa; five c.; ed Univ. of Minnesota, Columbia Univ., USA; Press Attaché, Perm. Mission of Morocco to UN, New York 1964–65; Information Officer, UN Dept of Information, 1965–67; Regional Information Adviser, FAO, Rome 1967–71, Head of Devt Support Communication 1971–73, Asst to Dir of Information 1973–74, Dir of Information Div. 1974–76; Asst Sec.-Gen. of UN, World Food Conf. 1975; elected to City Council of Asilah 1976–83, elected Mayor 1992; mem. Moroccan Parl. 1977–83; Co-Founder and Exec. mem. Moroccan Social Democratic Party (Rassemblement Nat. des Independents) 1978; consultant, UNDP, IFAD, UNFPA 1978–85; Chief Ed. Al-Mithak Al-Watani and Al-Maghrab publs 1980–85; apptd Amb. to USA 1993; Minister of Foreign Affairs and Co-operation 1999–2007. *Publications include:* Grains de Peau 1974. *Address:* Rassemblement national des indépendants (RNI), 6 rue Laos, ave Hassan II, Rabat, Morocco (office). *Telephone:* (3) 7721420 (office). *Fax:* (3) 7733824 (office).

BÉNARD, André Pierre Jacques; French business executive; b. 19 Aug. 1922, Draveil, Essone; s. of Marcel Bénard and Lucie Thalmann; m. Jacqueline Preiss 1946; one s.; ed Lycée Janson-de-Sailly, Lycée Georges Clémenceau, Nantes, Lycée Thiers, Marseilles, Ecole Polytechnique, Paris; joined Royal Dutch/Shell Group 1946; with Société Anonyme des Pétroles Jupiter 1946–49; Shell Petroleum Co. Ltd, London 1949–50; Head of Bitumen Services, Société des Pétroles Shell Berre 1950–58, Head Nat. Activities Dept 1958–59; Asst Dir-Gen. Société pour l'Utilisation Rationnelle des Gaz 1960–61, Pres. Dir-Gen. 1962–64; Marketing Man. Shell Française 1964–67, Pres. Man. Dir 1967–70; Regional Co-ordinator Europe 1970; Dir Shell Petroleum NV 1970; Dir The Shell Petroleum Co. Ltd 1970, Barclays Bank SA, Paris 1989–; Man. Dir Royal Dutch Petroleum Co. 1971–83, mem. Supervisory Bd 1983–; Admin. Royal Dutch 1983–, INSEAD 1983–, La Radiotechnique 1983–; Hon. Pres., French Chamber of Commerce and Industry, in the Netherlands 1980–; Jt Chair. Eurotunnel 1986–90, Pres. Admin. Council 1990–94; Chevalier de l'Ordre nat. du Mérite, Commdr Légion d'honneur, Commdr Order of Orange Nassau, Chevalier du Mérite agricole; Hon. KBE; Prix Descartes 1982, Médaille des Evadés, Médaille de la Résistance. *Leisure interest:* golf.

BÉNASSY, Jean-Pascal, PhD; French economist and researcher; *Director of Research, Centre National de la Recherche Scientifique;* b. 30 Dec. 1948, Paris; s. of Jean Bénassy and Jeannine Bénassy; ed Ecole Normale Supérieure, Paris, Univ. of Berkeley, California, USA; Research Assoc., CEPREMAP 1973–, Dir of Research CNRS 1981–; Dir Laboratoire d'Economie Politique, Ecole Normale Supérieure 1984–88; Dept of Econs Ecole Polytechnique 1987–2002; Fellow, Econometric Soc. 1981, mem. Council 1990–92; Guido Zerilli Marimo Prize, Acad. des Sciences Morales et Politiques 1990. *Publications:* The Economics of Market Disequilibrium 1982, Macroéconomie et théorie du déséquilibre 1984, Macroeconomics: An Introduction to the Non-Walrasian Approach 1986, Macroeconomics and Imperfect Competition 1995, The Macroeconomics of Imperfect Competition and Nonclearing Markets: A Dynamic General Equilibrium Approach 2002, Imperfect Competition – Nonclearing Markets and Business Cycles 2006, Money, Interest and Policy 2007; numerous articles in specialized journals. *Address:* CEPREMAP-ENS, 48 boulevard Jourdan, Bâtiment E, 75014 Paris, France (office). *Telephone:* 1-43-13-43-38 (office). *Fax:* 1-43-13-62-32 (office). *E-mail:* benassy@ (office).

BENAUD, Richard (Richie), OBE; Australian sports commentator and fmr cricketer; b. 6 Oct. 1930; s. of Louis Richard and Irene Benaud; m. Daphne Elizabeth Surfleet 1967; two s. by previous marriage; ed Parramatta High

School; right-hand middle-order batsman and right-arm leg-break and googly bowler; played for New South Wales 1948–49 to 1963–64 (Capt. 1958–59 to 1963); played in 63 Tests for Australia 1951–52 to 1963–64, 28 as Capt., scoring 2,201 runs (average 24.4) including 3 hundreds, taking 248 wickets (average 27.0); first to score 2,000 runs and take 200 wickets in Tests; scored 11,719 runs (23 hundreds) and took 945 wickets in first-class cricket; toured England 1953, 1956 and 1961; int. sports consultant; TV Commentator, BBC 1960–99, Channel Nine 1977–, Channel 4 1999–; Wisden Cricketer of the Year 1962. *Publications:* Way of Cricket 1960, Tale of Two Tests 1962, Spin Me a Spinner 1963, The New Champions 1965, Willow Patterns 1972, Benaud on Reflection 1984, The Appeal of Cricket 1995, Anything But... An Autobiography 1998, My Spin on Cricket 2005. *Leisure interest:* golf. *Address:* 19/178 Beach Street, Coogee, NSW 2034, Australia. *Telephone:* 9664-1124.

BENAVIDES GANOZA, Roque; Peruvian business executive; *President, National Confederation of Private Business Institutes;* b. 1954; Exec. Compañía de Minas Buenaventura S.A.A. 1978–85, Chief Financial Officer 1985–2000, Pres. and C.E.O. 2000–; Pres. Nat. Confed. of Pvt. Business Insts. (Confiep) 1999–. *Address:* Compañía de Minas Buenaventura S.A.A., Avenida Carlos Villarán 790, Lima 13, Peru (office). *Website:* www.buenaventura.com .pe (office).

BENBITOUR, Ahmed, MBA, PhD; Algerian economist, academic and fmr politician; b. 20 June 1946, Ghardaia; m.; four c.; ed Univ. of Algiers, Univ. of Montreal, Canada; fmr CEO Nat. Co. of Studies and Processing, Nat. Co. of Juice and Tinned Fruits of Algeria; fmr Prof. of Business Man.; fmr mem. Parl., Chair.Econ. and Finance Comm. at Council of the Nation (Senate); fmr consultant at World Bank and IMF; fmr Minister of Finance, of Energy, of Treasury; Prime Minister of Algeria 1999–2000; currently Lecturer, African Inst. for Econ. Devt and Planning, Dakar, Senegal. *Publications:* several publs on econ. reforms and finance. *Address:* African Institute for Economic Development and Planning, POBox 3186, 18524 Dakar, Senegal (office). *Telephone:* 823-10-20 (office). *Fax:* 822-29-64 (office). *E-mail:* idep@unidep.org (office). *Website:* www.unidep.org (office).

BENDER, Sir Brian Geoffrey, Kt, KCB, PhD; British civil servant; *Permanent Secretary, Department for Business, Enterprise and Regulatory Reform;* b. 25 Feb. 1949, Sheffield; s. of the late Prof. Arnold Eric Bender; m. Penelope Clark 1974; one s. one d.; ed Imperial Coll., London; joined Dept of Trade and Industry 1973; Pvt. Sec. to Sec. of State for Trade 1976–77; First Sec., Office of Perm. Rep. to EC 1977–82; Prin., Dept of Trade and Industry 1982–84; Counsellor, Office of Perm. Rep. to EC 1985–89; UnderSec. and Deputy Head of European Secr., Cabinet Office 1990–93; Head of Regulation Devt Div., Dept of Trade and Industry 1993–94; Deputy Sec. and Head of European Secr., Cabinet Office 1994–98; Head of Public Service Delivery, Cabinet Office 1998–99; Perm. Sec. Cabinet Office 1999–2000, Ministry of Agric., Fisheries and Food 2000–01, Dept for Environment, Food and Rural Affairs 2001–05, Dept of Trade and Industry 2005–07, Perm. Sec., Dept for Business, Enterprise and Regulatory Reform 2007–. *Address:* Department for Business, Enterprise and Regulatory Reform, 1 Victoria Street, London, SW1H 0ET, England (office). *Telephone:* (20) 7215-5000 (office). *Fax:* (20) 7215-0105 (office). *E-mail:* enquiries@berr.gsi.gov.uk (office). *Website:* www.berr.gov.uk (office).

BENDJEDID, Col Chadli (see Chadli, Col Bendjedid).

BENDTSEN, Bendt; Danish politician; b. 25 March 1954; ed agricultural school, Danish Police Acad.; farm hand 1971–75; police constable 1980, Detective, Odense Criminal Investigation Dept 1984; mem. Bd local Conservative constituency org. 1982; his draft proposal for Party's official policy on legal issues approved by Conservative Nat. Congress 1987; mem. Odense City Council 1989, subsequently Political Spokesman; Deputy Chair. Odense Criminal Investigation Asscn 1989–92; parl. cand. (Conservative) 1990, 1992, 2001; substitute mem. Parl. April 1994, mem. Parl. Sept. 1994–; Leader, Conservative Party and Conservative Group in Danish Parl. 1999–08 (resgnd); Minister for Econ. and Business Affairs 2001–08 (resgnd), Minister for Nordic Cooperation 2001–02. *Address:* c/o Det Konservative Folkeparti (Conservative People's Party), Nyhavn 4, 1051 Copenhagen K, Denmark.

BENDUKIDZE, Kakha Avtandilovich, BSc; Georgian business executive, government official and scientist; b. 20 April 1956, Tbilisi; ed Tbilisi State Univ., Lomonosov State Univ., Moscow, Russia; Sr Lab. Asst and Scientific Research Asst, USSR Acad. of Sciences Inst. of Biochemistry and Physiology of Microorganisms 1981–85; Head, Molecular Genetics Lab., Scientific Research Inst. of Biotechnology 1985–92; f. Bioprocess Asscn 1988, Dir 1990–92; Chair. Bd of Dirs Promtorgbank (Industrial and Trade Bank) 1992–93; Chief Dir NIPEK (Nat. Oil Investment Corpn) 1993–95; co-f. Russian Business Round Table 1993; Chair. Uralmash-Izhora Group 1995–98, CEO 1998–2004; Prof., Higher School of Econs, Moscow 2002–; Minister of Econ. Devt June–Dec. 2004, State Minister, responsible for Econ. Reforms Dec. 2004–2007; Head, Chancellery of the Govt 2008–09. *Address:* c/o Chancellery of the Government, 0105 Tbilisi, P. Ingorovka 7, Georgia. *Telephone:* (32) 92-26-87.

BENEDEK, János, LLM; Hungarian business executive; *Chairman and CEO, Hungarian Investment and Asset Management Inc.;* b. 1 March 1953, Budapest; m.; two c.; ed Eötvös Loraád Univ., Budapest; Legal Adviser, Chemimas Engineering Co., Budapest 1976–79; Legal Adviser, State Construction Enterprise No. 43, Budapest 1979; Civil Servant, Ministry of Construction and Urban Devt 1989; Man., State Devt Inst. 1989–91; Man., Hungarian Investment and Devt Co. Ltd 1991–93, Man. Dir 1993–97; Deputy CEO, Hungarian Devt Bank Ltd 1997–99; Deputy CEO, Hungarian State Railways Ltd 1999–2003; CEO and Chair., Hungarian Investment and Asset Man. Inc. 2003–. *Address:* Hungarian Investment and Asset Management Inc., Széchenyi u. 5, 2040 Budaörs, Hungary (office). *Telephone:* (23) 414031 (office). *E-mail:* benedek@mbv.hu (office). *Website:* www.mbv.hu (office).

BENEDETTI, Mario; Uruguayan writer and poet; b. 14 Sept. 1920, Paso de los Toros, Tacuarembo; s. of Brenno Benedetti and Matilde Farrugia; m. Luz López; ed Colegio Alemán; journalist on Marcha (weekly) and literary, film and theatre critic on El Diario, Tribuna Popular and La Mañana. *Publications include:* fiction: Esta mañana 1949, El último viaje y otros cuentos 1951, Quién de nosotros 1953, Montevideanos 1959, La Tregua 1963, Gracias por el Fuego 1965, La muerte y otras sorpresas 1968, Con o sin nostalgia 1977, Vientos del exilio 1981, Geografías 1984, Las soledades de Babel 1991, La borra del café 1993, El amor, las mujeres y la vida 1995, Andamios 1996, El porvenir de mi pasado 2003; plays: Ustedes por ejemplo 1953, El Reportaje 1958, Ida y vuelta 1958; poetry: La víspera indeleble 1945, Sólo mientras tanto 1950, Poemas de la oficina 1956, Poemas del hoyporhoy 1965, Inventario 1965, Contra los puentes levadizos 1966, A ras de sueño 1967, La casa y el ladrillo 1977, El amor, las mujeres y la vida 1996, La vida ese parentesis 1997, Rincón de Haikus 1999, El mundo que respiro 2001, Insomnios y Duermevelas 2002, Inventario tres 2003, Existir todavía 2003, Defensa propia 2004, Memoria y esperanza 2004, Adioses y bienvenidas 2005, Canciones del que no canta 2006; essays: Peripecia y novela 1948, Marcel Proust y otros ensayos 1951, Literatura uruguaya siglo XX 1963, Letras del continente mestizo 1967, Sobre artes y oficios 1968. *Leisure interests:* reading, football.

BENEDICT XVI, His Holiness Pope (Joseph Alois Ratzinger); German ecclesiastic; b. 16 April 1927, Marktl am Inn, Bavaria; s. of Joseph Ratzinger and Maria Peintner; ed Univ. of Munich; ordained Chaplain 1951; Prof. of Theology, Freising 1958, Bonn 1959–63, Münster 1963–66, Tübingen 1966–69, Regensburg 1969; co-f. Communio (theological journal) 1972; apptd Archbishop of Munich-Freising 1977–82; cr. Cardinal of Munich by Pope Paul VI 1977; Cardinal Bishop of the Episcopal See of Velletri-Segni 1993; fmr Chair. Bavarian Bishops' Conf.; Prefect, Sacred Congregation for the Doctrine of the Faith 1981–2005; Vice-Dean Coll. of Cardinals 1998–2002, Dean 2002–05; Titular Bishop of Ostia 2002; presided over funeral of Pope John Paul II and the Conclave which elected him April 2005; elected Pope 19 April 2005; Pres. Int. Theological Comm., Pontifical Biblical Comm.; mem. of the Congregations for the Oriental Churches, for the Divine Worship and the Discipline of the Sacrament, for the Bishops, for the Evangelization of Reapers, for Catholic Educ.; mem. Pontifical Council for the Promotion of Christian Unity; Dr hc (Navarra) 1998, numerous hon. doctorates. *Publications:* books and articles on theological matters including Without Roots (with Marcello Pera) 2006. *Address:* Palazzo Apostolico Vaticano, 00120 Città del Vaticano, Rome, Italy. *Website:* www.vatican.va.

BENEGAL, Shyam; Indian film director and screenwriter; b. 14 Dec. 1934, Aliwal, Hyderabad. *Films:* Dir: Gher Betha Ganga 1962, Close to Nature 1967, A Child of the Streets 1967, Indian Youth: An Exploration 1968, Flower Garden 1969, Quest for a Nation 1970, The Pulsating Giant 1971, Raga and Melody 1972, Power to the People 1972, Suhani Sadak 1973, Violence: What Price? Who Pays? 1974, The Quiet Revolution 1974, Bal Sansar 1974, Hero 1975, Bhumika 1976, Kondura 1978, Pashu Palan 1979, Jawaharlal Nehru 1982, Arohan 1982, Mandi 1983, Vardan 1985, Festival of India 1985, Nature Symphony 1990, Antarnaad 1991, Suraj Ka Satvan Ghoda 1993, Mammo 1994, Sardari Begum 1996, Hari-Bhari 2000, Zubeidaa 2001, Bose: The Forgotten Hero 2004; Writer: Ankur 1974, Manthan 1976, Bhumika 1976, Junoon 1978, Anugraham 1978, Kalyug 1980, Trikal 1985; Producer: Susman 1987, Powaqqatsi 1988, Sardari Begum 1996.

BENETTON, Alessandro, BS, MBA; Italian business executive; *Chairman and Managing Director, 21 Investimenti SpA;* b. 2 March 1964, Treviso; s. of Luciano Benetton (q.v.) and Maria Teresa Benetton; m.; c.; ed Boston Univ., Harvard Business School, USA; early position as Analyst, Global Finance Dept, Goldman Sachs, London; Founder, Chair. and Man. Dir. 21 Investimenti SpA (investment bank) 1993–; Deputy Chair. Benetton Group 2004–; mem. Bd of Dirs Edizione Holding SpA, Autogrill SpA, Permasteelisa SpA, Industrie Zignago Santa Margherita SpA, Sirti SpA; Chair. 21 Pnrs S.G.R. SpA, 21 Investimenti Pnrs SpA; Vice Chair. Nordest Marchant SpA; Sole Dir. Saibot S.r.l.; mem. Supervisory Bd 21 Centrale Pnrs SA; mem. Advisory Cttee Robert Bosch Internationale Beteiligungen; mem. Council, Confindustria. *Address:* 21 Investimenti SpA, Via G. Felissent, 90, 31100 Treviso, Italy (office). *Telephone:* (0422) 316611 (office). *Fax:* (0422) 316600 (office). *E-mail:* info@21investimenti.it (home). *Website:* www.21investimenti.it (office).

BENETTON, Carlo; Italian business executive; b. 26 Dec. 1943; four c.; Co-founder (with brothers) Benetton Group 1965, responsible for production; currently Deputy Chair. Edizione Holding and Benetton Group. *Address:* Benetton Group SpA, Villa Minelli, 3150 Ponzano, Treviso, Italy (office). *Telephone:* (422) 519111 (office). *Fax:* (422) 969501 (office). *E-mail:* info@ benetton.it (office). *Website:* www.benettongroup.com (office).

BENETTON, Luciano; Italian business executive; *Chairman, Benetton Group SpA;* b. 13 May 1935, Treviso; s. of Leone and Rosa Benetton; m. Maria-Teresa Benetton (separated); four c.; Co-founder (with three brothers) Benetton 1963, now Chair. Benetton Group SpA; mem. Bd of Dirs Edizione Holding (family-owned financial holding co.); mem. Italian Senate 1992–94; Hon. MBA (Instituto de Empresa, Madrid) 1992; Hon. JD (Boston Univ.) 1994; Hon. Laurea in Economia Aziendale (Università ca' Foscari di Venezia) 1995; Civiltà Veneta 1986, Premio Creatività 1992. *Address:* Benetton Group SpA, Via Minelli, 31050 Ponzano (Treviso), Italy (home). *Telephone:* (0422) 519111 (office). *Fax:* (0422) 969501 (office). *Website:* www.benetton.com (home).

BENGOA ALBIZU, Vicente, BSc; Dominican Republic economist; *Secretary of State for Finance;* ed Univ. of Chile; Prof. of Econs and Public Finance, Univ. of Santo Domingo 1973–94, Dir Econs Dept, Technological Inst. 1978–82;

Superintendent of Banking 1997–2000; Deputy in Nat. Ass. 1982–86; Sec. of State for Finance 2004–. *Address:* Secretariat of State for Finance, Avenida México 45, esq. Leopoldo Navarro, Apdo. 1478, Santo Domingo, DN, Dominican Republic (office). *Telephone:* 687-5131 (office). *Fax:* 682-0498 (office). *E-mail:* webmaster@finanzas.gov.do (office). *Website:* www.finanzas.gov.do (office).

BENGSTON, Billy Al, (Moon Doggie, Moondoggy, Moontang, Two Moons); American artist and designer; b. 7 June 1934, Dodge City, Kan.; m. Wendy Al; one d.; ed Los Angeles City Coll., Calif. Coll. of Arts and Crafts, Oakland and Otis Art Inst.; instructor, Chouinard Art Inst. Los Angeles 1961; Lecturer, UCLA 1962–63; Guest Artist, Univ. of Oklahoma 1967; Guest Prof., Univ. of Colorado 1969; Guest Lecturer, Univ. of California, Irvine 1973; Dir Pelican Club Productions Los Angeles 1981–84; Exec. Dir Westfall Arts 1995–98; numerous solo exhbns; works in numerous public collections including Museum of Modern Art, New York, Whitney Museum of American Art, New York, Solomon R. Guggenheim Museum, New York, San Francisco Museum of Art, The Beaubourg, Paris; Nat. Foundation for the Arts Grant 1967; Tamarind Fellow 1968, 1982, 1987; Guggenheim Fellowship 1975; various comms and other awards. *Publications:* contribs to Art in America, Art Forum, Paris Review. *Address:* 110 Mildred Avenue, Venice, CA 90291, USA (office). *Telephone:* (310) 822-2201 (office). *E-mail:* studio@billyalbengston.com (office). *Website:* www.billyalbengston.com (office).

BENGU, Sibusiso Mandlenkosi Emmanuel, PhD; South African politician, diplomatist and academic; *Chancellor, University of Fort Hare;* b. 8 May 1934, Kranskop; s. of Rev. Jackonia Bengu and Augusta Bengu; m. Ethel Funeka 1961; one s. four d.; Prin. Dlangezwa High School 1968–76; Publicity Sec. Natal African Teachers' Asscn 1969–71; Dir Students' Advisory Services, Univ. of Zululand 1977–78; Exec. Sec. for Research and Social Action, Lutheran World Fed., Geneva 1978–91; Rector and Vice-Chancellor Univ. of Fort Hare 1991–94, currently Chancellor and Head of History Writing Project 2004–; Minister of Educ. Govt of Nat. Unity 1994–99; Pres. Intergovernmental Cttee, Ministers of Educ. of Africa (MINEDAF) 1998–99; Amb. to Germany 2000–04; First Gen. Sec. Inkatha Freedom Party, now mem. ANC; Hon. Fellowship of the Coll. of Perceptors (Manchester Univ.) 1997; Hon. DD (Wartburg Theological Seminary, Dubuque Univ.) 1986; Hon. LLD (California State Univ.) 1996; Hon. PhD in Political Science (Univ. of Fort Hare) 2001; Gamaliel Chair for Peace and Justice, Lutheran Campus Ministry, Univ. of Wisconsin in Milwaukee 1985; Distinguished Int. Educator Award, American Council of Education 1998;. *Publications:* African Cultural Identity and International Relations 1975, Chasing Gods Not our Own 1975, Mirror or Model. *Leisure interests:* listening to music, watching sports, reading, research. *Address:* University of Fort Hare, Private Bag X1314, Alice 5700, South Africa (office). *Telephone:* (31) 5731952 (office). *Fax:* (31) 5731552 (office). *Website:* www.ufh.ac.za (office).

BENHABIB, Seyla, MA, PhD; American political scientist, philosopher and academic; *Eugene Meyer Professor of Political Science and Professor of Philosophy, Yale University;* b. Istanbul, Turkey; m. James A. Sleeper; one d.; ed American Coll. for Girls, Istanbul, Brandeis and Yale Univs, USA; Prof., New School for Social Research 1991–93; Prof., Dept of Govt and Sr Research Fellow, Center for European Studies, Harvard Univ. 1993–2000; Ed.-in-Chief Constellations: An International Journal of Critical and Democratic Theory 1993–97; Visiting Sr Fellow, Institut für Wissenschaft vom Menschen, Vienna, Austria 1996; Eugene Meyer Prof. of Political Science and Prof. of Philosophy, Yale Univ. 2000–; Baruch de Spinoza Distinguished Professorship, Univ. of Amsterdam 2000; Russell Sage Foundation Fellow 2000–01; Seeley Lectures, Cambridge 2002, Tanner Lectures, Berkeley 2004; Dr hc (Univ. of Utrecht) 2004. *Publications include:* Critique, Norm and Utopia: A Study of the Foundations of Critical Theory 1986, Situating the Self: Gender, Community and Postmodernism in Contemporary Ethics 1992, The Reluctant Modernism of Hannah Arendt 1996, Feminist Contentions: A Philosophical Exchange 1996; (as ed.): Feminism as Critique: Essays on the Politics of Gender in Late-Capitalist Societies 1987, The Communicative Ethics Controversy (co-ed with Fred Dallmayr) 1990, On Max Horkheimer (co-ed. with Wolfgang Bonss and John McCole) 1993, The Philosophical Discourses of Modernity 1996, Democracy and Difference: Changes Boundaries of the Political 1996, Transformation of Citizenship – Dilemmas of the Nation-State in the Era of Globalization 2000, The Claims of Culture – Equality and Diversity in the Global Era 2002, The Rights of Others: The John Seeley Lectures 2004, Another Cosmopolitanism, with Responses by Jeremy Waldron, Bonnie Honig and Will Kymlicka; (trans.): Hegel's Ontology and the Theory of Historicity by Herbert Marcuse 1987; more than 100 articles on social and political thought, feminist theory and the history of modern political theory. *Address:* Room 211, Department of Political Science, Yale University, PO Box 208301, 124 Prospect Street, New Haven, CT 06520-8301, USA (office). *Telephone:* (203) 436-3693 (office). *Fax:* (203) 432-6196 (office). *E-mail:* seyla.benhabib@yale.edu (office). *Website:* www.yale.edu/polisci/people/sbenhabib.html (office).

BENHAMOUDA, Boualem, DIur; Algerian politician and lexicographer; b. (Boualem Benhamouda), 8 March 1933, Cherchell; m.; two s. one d.; ed Algiers Univ.; served with Army of Nat. Liberation 1956–62; mem. Parl. 1962–65; Minister of Ex-Combatants 1965–70, of Justice 1970–77, of Public Works 1977–80, of the Interior 1980–82, of Finance 1982–86; responsible for Inst. of Global Studies of Strategy 1986–90; mem. Political Bureau of Nat. Liberation Front (FLN) 1979–, Chair. FLN Cttee on Educ. Training and Culture 1979–80, Gen. Sec. FLN 1995–2001, currently mem. Exec. Organ; Medal of Liberation. *Publications:* The Keys of Arabic Language 1991, The Arabic Origin of Some Spanish Words 1991, The Democratic Practice of Power (Between Theory and Reality) 1992, Spanish-Arabic Pocket Dictionary 1993, The Arabic Origin of About 1000 French Words, General French-Arabic Dictionary 1996, General Arabic-French Dictionary 2000, 2001, Citizenship and Power 2006, Read and Understand The Coran 2006. *Leisure interests:* reading, studying, cultural travel, philosophy, science, languages. *Address:* Siege du Parti du FLN, Rue du Stade, Hydra, Algiers (office); 5 Rue de Frère Zennouch, El-Biar, Algiers, Algeria (home). *Telephone:* (21) 694701 (office). *Fax:* (21) 923538 (home).

BENIGNI, Roberto; Italian actor, director and writer; b. 27 Oct. 1952, Misericordia, Tuscany; Dr hc (Bologna) 2002. *Films include:* Belingua ti voglio bene (actor, writer) 1977, Down by Law (actor) 1986, Tutto Benigni (actor, writer) 1986, Johnny Stecchino (dir, actor, writer), Night on Earth (actor) 1992, Son of the Pink Panther (acted) 1993, Mostro (dir, actor, writer), Life is Beautiful (dir, actor, writer, Acad. Award for Best Actor and Best Foreign Film) 1998, Asterisk and Obelisk (actor) 1998, Pinocchio 2002, Coffee and Cigarettes 2003, The Tiger and the Snow (dir) 2006.

BENING, Annette; American actress; b. 29 May 1958, Topeka, Kan.; m. 1st Steven White (divorced); m. 2nd Warren Beatty (q.v.) 1992; four c.; ed San Francisco State Univ.; stage appearances in works by Ibsen, Chekhov and Shakespeare in San Diego and San Francisco; other stage roles in Coastal Disturbances, The Great Outdoors; European Achievement in World Cinema Award 2000. *Films:* The Great Outdoors 1988, Valmont 1989, Postcards from the Edge 1990, The Grifters 1990, Guilty by Suspicion 1991, Regarding Henry 1991, Bugsy 1991, Love Affair 1994, Richard III 1995, The American President 1995, Mars Attacks! 1996, The Siege 1998, In Dreams 1999, American Beauty 1999, What Planet Are You From? 2000, Open Range 2003, Being Julia (Best Actress Award, Nat. Bd of Review, Best Actress in a Musical or Comedy, Golden Globe Awards 2005) 2004, Running with Scissors 2006, The Women 2008. *Television includes:* Mrs. Harris 2005. *Address:* c/o Kevin Huvane, CAA, 2000 Avenue of the Stars, Los Angeles, CA 90067, USA. *Telephone:* (424) 288-2000. *Fax:* (424) 288-2900.

BENIZRI, Shlomo; Israeli politician; b. 1961, Haifa; m.; seven c.; army service; ordained as a rabbi at Or Hachaim Talmudic Coll., Jerusalem; currently Head of Talmudic Coll.; mem. Knesset 1992–; mem. Finance and Anti-Drug Abuse Cttees 1992–96; fmr Head of Shas Knesset Faction; Deputy Minister of Health 1996–99, Minister of Health 1999–2001; Minister of Labour and Social Welfare 2001–02. *Publication:* The Sky is Talking (astrology). *Leisure interests:* sports, computers, nature. *Address:* 2 Kaplan Street, Jerusalem (office); c/o Ministry of Labour and Social Welfare, PO Box 915, 2 Rehov Kaplan, Kiryat Ben-Gurion, Jerusalem 91008, Israel.

BENJAMIN, George William John, FRCM; British composer, conductor, pianist and teacher; b. 31 Jan. 1960, London; s. of William Benjamin and Susan Benjamin (née Bendon); ed Westminster School, Paris Conservatoire, King's Coll., Cambridge, Institut de recherche et coordination acoustique/musique, Paris; first London orchestral performance, BBC Proms 1980; Prince Consort Prof. of Composition, RCM 1984–2001; Henry Purcell Prof. of Composition, King's Coll. London 2001–; has conducted widely in GB, Europe, USA, Australia and Far East; Prin. Guest Artist, Hallé Orchestra 1993–96; operatic conducting debut Pelléas et Mélisande, La Monnaie, Brussels 1999; Carte Blanche at Opéra Bastille, Paris 1992; founding Artistic Dir Wet Ink Festival, San Francisco Symphony Orchestra 1992, Meltdown Festival, South Bank 1993; Featured Composer, 75th Salzburg Festival 1995, Tanglewood Festival 1999, 2000, 2003, Deutsches Symphonie Orchester 2004–05, Strasbourg Musica Festival 2005, Spanish Nat. Orchestra 2005; London Symphony Orchestra Retrospective 'By George', Barbican, London 2002–03; Artistic Consultant BBC Sounding the Century 1996–99; mem. Bavarian Acad. of Fine Arts 2000; Hon. RAM; Chevalier, Ordre des Arts et des Lettres 1996; Lili Boulanger Award, USA 1985, Koussevitzky Int. Record Award 1987, Grand Prix du Disque de l'Académie Charles Cros 1987, Gramophone Contemporary Award 1990, Edison Award 1998, Schönberg Prize, Deutsche Sinfonie Berlin 2002; Royal Philharmonic Soc. Award 2003, 2004. *Publications:* orchestral works: Ringed by the Flat Horizon 1980, A Mind of Winter 1981, At First Light 1982, Jubilation 1985, Antara 1987, Sudden Time 1993, Three Inventions for Chamber Orchestra 1995, Sometime Voices 1996, Palimpsests 2002, Dance Figures 2004, Récit de tierce en taille 2004; chamber music: Piano Sonata 1978, Octet 1978, Flight 1979, Sortilèges 1981, Three Studies for Piano 1985, Upon Silence 1990, Viola, Viola 1997, Shadowlines (for solo piano) 2001, Three Miniatures for violin 2001, Olicantus 2002, Piano Figures 2004; stage works: Into the Little Hill 2006. *Address:* Askonas Holt, Lincoln House, 300 High Holborn, London, WC1V 7JH, England (office); c/o Faber Music, 74–77 Great Russell Street, London, WC1B 3DA, England (office). *Telephone:* (20) 7400-1700 (office); (20) 7908-5310 (office). *Fax:* (20) 7400-1799 (office); (20) 7908-5339 (office). *E-mail:* info@askonasholt.co.uk (office); information@fabermusic.com (office). *Website:* www.askonasholt.co.uk (office); www.fabermusic.com (office).

BENJAMIN, John Oponjo; Sierra Leonean politician; b. 29 Nov. 1952, Segbwema; Chief Sec. of State, Nat. Provisional Ruling Council (NPRC) 1992; Sec.-Gen. NPRC Govt 1993; Interim Chair. Nat. Unity Party 1997; Minister of Finance 2005–07; Exec. Dir African Information Tech. Holdings. *Address:* c/o Ministry of Finance, Secretariat Building, George Street, Freetown, Sierra Leone (office).

BENJAMIN, Raymond; French international civil aviation official; *Secretary General, International Civil Aviation Organization;* began career in civil aviation with French Civil Aviation Admin in 1976, with Human Resources Div. 1976–77, responsible for negotiating bilateral air transport agreements on behalf of Admin 1977–82; Air Transport Officer, European Civil Aviation Conf. 1982–83, Deputy Sec. 1983–89, Exec. Sec. 1994–2007; Chief of Aviation Security Br., ICAO 1989–94, also served as Sec. Aviation Security Panel and Group of Experts for the Detection of Plastic Explosives, Sec. Gen. ICAO

2009–; Special Adviser to Jt Aviation Authorities Training Org. (JAA/TO) and to European Aviation Security Training Inst. 2007–. *Address:* International Civil Aviation Organization, 999 University Street, Montréal, PQ H3C 5H7, Canada (office). *Telephone:* (514) 954-8220 (office). *Fax:* (514) 954-6376 (office). *E-mail:* icaohq@icao.int (office); ray.benjamin@hotmail.com. *Website:* www .icao.int (office).

BENKOVIC, Stephen J., BS, PhD; American chemist and academic; *Eberly Chair in Chemistry, Pennsylvania State University;* b. Orange, NJ; ed Lehigh Univ., Cornell Univ.; Post-Doctoral Research Assoc., Univ. of Calif., Santa Barbara 1964–65; joined Dept of Chemistry, PA State Univ. 1965, Prof. of Chemistry 1970, Evan Pugh Prof. 1977–, Eberly Chair in Chemistry 1986–; Scientific Partner, RhO Ventures; co-founder Anacor Pharmaceuticals; Head, Scientific Advisory Bd, Glaxo SmithKline; mem. NAS 1985–, Inst. of Medicine 1994–, American Philosophical Soc. 2002–; Fellow American Acad. of Arts and Sciences 1984; Hon. DSc (Lehigh Univ.) 1995 Pfizer Award in Enzyme Chemistry, Gowland Hopkins Award 1986, Arthur C. Scope Scolar Award 1988, Repligen Award 1989, Alfred Bader Award 1995, Nakanishi Prize 2004. *Address:* Department of Chemistry, 104 Chemistry Building, University Park, PA 16802, USA (office). *Telephone:* (814) 865-6553 (office). *E-mail:* sjb1@psu .edu (office). *Website:* www.psu.edu/profs/benkovic.html (office).

BENMAKHLOUF, Alexandre; French lawyer; b. 9 Sept. 1939, Oran, Algeria; s. of Tahar Benmakhlouf and Sylviane Jan; m. Gabrielle Steinmann 1965; one s. one d.; Deputy Public Prosecutor, Meaux 1970, Versailles 1972; seconded to Chancellery 1974–84; Pres. Nanterre Magistrates' Court 1984–86; Deputy Sec.-Gen. Professional Asscn of Magistrates 1984–86; Adviser to Prime Minister Jacques Chirac 1986–89; Legal Adviser to Jacques Chirac, Mayor of Paris 1989–91; Pres. Court of Appeal, Versailles 1991–93; Dir of Civil Affairs and Dir of Cabinet of Guardian of the Seal, Ministry of Justice 1993–96; Attorney-Gen., Court of Appeal 1996–97, Solicitor-Gen. 1997–2000, First Counsel for the Prosecution 2001–; Chevalier Légion d'honneur, Ordre des Palmes académiques. *Leisure interests:* reading, travelling, cinema. *Address:* Cour de Cassation, 5 quai de l'Horloge, 75055 Paris RP, France (office).

BENMOSCHE, Robert (Bob) H., BA; American insurance industry executive; ed Alfred Univ.; US Army Signal Corps 1966–68, rank of Lt; Chase Manhattan Bank –1982; joined Paine Webber 1982, Sr Vice-Pres., Marketing 1984–86, Chief Financial Officer, Retail Div. 1986–87, Dir Securities Operations 1988, responsible for tech. org. 1990, for human resources 1992, later Exec. Vice-Pres. and mem. Bd of Dirs –1995; Exec. Vice-Pres. MetLife Inc. 1995–97, Exec. Vice-Pres. for Individual Business 1996, Pres. and COO 1997–98, Dir Metropolitan Life Insurance Co. 1997, Metlife Inc. 1999–, Chair., Pres. and CEO Metropolitan Life Insurance Co. 1998–2006, Chair. MetLife Inc. 1999–2006; Dir Nat. Securities Clearing Corpn 1990–94, Chicago Stock Exchange 1994–95, Crédit Suisse Group, New England Financial, NY Philharmonic; Trustee Alfred Univ.; mem. Int. Business Leaders' Advisory Council for Mayor of Beijing 2002–. *Address:* c/o MetLife Inc., One Madison Avenue, New York, NY 10010-3690, USA (office).

BENN, Rt Hon. Anthony (Tony) Neil Wedgwood, PC, MA; British politician, writer and broadcaster; b. 3 April 1925, London; s. of William Wedgwood Benn (1st Viscount Stansgate), PC and Margaret Eadie (née Holmes); m. Caroline de Camp 1949 (died 2000); three s. one d.; ed Westminster School and New Coll., Oxford; RAF pilot 1943–45; Univ. of Oxford 1946–49; Producer, BBC 1949–50; Labour MP for Bristol SE 1950–60, compelled to leave House of Commons on inheriting peerage 1960, re-elected and unseated 1961, renounced peerage and re-elected 1963, contested and lost Bristol E seat in 1983, re-elected as mem. for Chesterfield 1984–2001; Nat. Exec. Labour Party 1959–94; Chair. Fabian Soc. 1964; Postmaster-Gen. 1964–66; Minister of Tech. 1966–70, of Power 1969–70; Shadow Minister of Trade and Industry 1970–74; Sec. of State for Industry and Minister of Posts and Telecommunications 1974–75; Sec. of State for Energy 1975–79; Vice-Chair. Labour Party 1970, Chair. 1971–72; Chair. Labour Party Home Policy Cttee 1974–82; cand. for Leadership of Labour Party 1976, 1988, for Deputy Leadership 1971, 1981; Pres. Socialist Campaign Group of Labour MPs, EEC Energy Council 1977, Labour Action for Peace 1997–2007, currently Pres. Stop the War Coalition; Visiting Prof. of Politics, LSE 2001–02; fmr mem. Bureau Confed. of Socialist Parties of the European Community; numerous TV and radio broadcasts; Freeman of the City of Bristol 2003; Hon. Fellow, New Coll. Oxford 2005; Hon. LLD (Strathclyde, Williams Coll., USA, Brunel, Bristol, Univ. of West of England, Univ. of N London); Hon. DTech (Bradford); Hon. DSc (Aston); Dr hc (Paisley). *Television:* Speaking Up in Parliament 1993, Westminster Behind Closed Doors 1995, New Labour in Focus 1998, Tony Benn Speaks 2001. *Recordings:* The BBC Benn Tapes 1994, 1995, Writings on the Wall (with Roy Bailey) 1996, Tony Benn's Greatest Hits 2003, An Audience with Tony Benn 2003. *Publications:* The Privy Council as a Second Chamber 1957, The Regeneration of Britain 1964, The New Politics 1970, Speeches by Tony Benn 1974, Arguments for Socialism 1979, Arguments for Democracy 1981, Parliament, People and Power 1982, The Sizewell Syndrome 1984, Writings on the Wall: A Radical and Socialist Anthology 1215–1984 (ed.) 1984, Out of the Wilderness: Diaries 1963–67 1987, Office Without Power: Diaries 1968–72 1988, Fighting Back: Speaking Out for Socialism in the Eighties 1988, Against the Tide: Diaries 1973–76 1989, Conflicts of Interest: Diaries 1977–80 1990, A Future for Socialism 1991, End of an Era: Diaries 1980–90 1992, Common Sense: A New Constitution for Britain (with Andrew Hood) 1993, Years of Hope: Diaries 1940–1962 1994, The Benn Diaries 1940–1990 1995, Free at Last: Diaries 1991–2001 2002, Free Radical: New Century Essays 2003, Dare to be a Daniel (memoir) 2004, More Time for Politics: Diaries 2001–07 2007. *Leisure interests:* political archives. *Address:* 12 Holland Park Avenue, London, W11 3QU, England

(office). *Telephone:* (20) 7229-0779 (office). *E-mail:* tony@tbenn.fsnet.co.uk (office).

BENN, Rt Hon. Hilary James Wedgwood, BA; British politician; *Secretary of State for Environment, Food and Rural Affairs;* b. 26 Nov. 1953, Hammersmith, London; s. of Tony Benn (q.v.) and Caroline Benn; m. 1st Rosalind Retey (died 1979); m. 2nd Sally Christina Clark 1982; three s. one d.; ed Holland Park School, Univ. of Sussex; Research Officer, ASTMS, rose to become Head of Policy for Manufacturing Science and Finance; Council Deputy Leader and Chair of Educ. in Ealing, W London 1986–90; Labour cand. for Ealing North in Gen. Elections 1983, 1987; fmr Head of Policy and Communications, MSF; Special Adviser to David Blunkett MP, Sec. of State for Educ. and Employment 1997–99; MP (Labour) for Leeds Cen. 1999–; fmr mem. Environment, Transport and Regions Select Cttee; with Dept for Int. Devt 2001–02; Home Office Minister 2002–03; cand. for Deputy Leadership of Labour Party June 2007; Sec. of State for Int. Devt 2003–07, for Environment, Food and Rural Affairs 2007–; Patron Holbeck Elderly Aid, Leeds, Faith Together, Leeds, Caring Together, Woodhouse and Little London. *Leisure interests:* gardening, watching sport. *Address:* Department for Environment, Food and Rural Affairs, Nobel House, 17 Smith Square, London, SW1P 3JR (office); 2 Blenheim Terrace, Leeds, West Yorkshire, LS2 9JG, England (office). *Telephone:* (20) 7238-6000 (office); (113) 244-1097 (constituency office) (office). *Fax:* (20) 7238-6609 (office). *E-mail:* helpline@defra.gsi.gov.uk (office); bennh@parliament.uk (office). *Website:* www.defra.gov.uk (office); www .hilarybenn.org.

BENNACK, Frank Anthony, Jr; American publishing executive; *Vice-Chairman of the Board and Chairman, Executive Committee, Hearst Corporation;* b. 12 Feb. 1933, San Antonio; s. of Frank Bennack and Lula Connally; m. Luella Smith 1951; five d.; ed Univ. of Maryland and St Mary's Univ.; advertising account exec. San Antonio Light 1950–53, 1956–58, Advertising Man. 1961–65, Asst Publr 1965–67, Publr 1967–74; Gen. Man. (newspapers), Hearst Corpn New York 1974–76, Exec. Vice-Pres. and COO 1975–78, Pres. and CEO 1978–2002, Vice-Chair. Bd, Chair. Exec. Cttee 2002–; Chair. Museum of TV and Radio, NY City 1991–; Pres. Tex. Daily Newspaper Asscn 1973–; mem. Bd of Dirs J.P. Morgan Chase & Co., Wyeth, Polo Ralph Lauren Corpn, Metropolitan Opera of New York; Dir, Vice-Chair. Lincoln Center for the Performing Arts; Dir Newspaper Asscn of American (fmrly American Newspaper Publrs Asscn), Chair. 1992–93; Gov., Vice-Chair. New York Presbyterian Hosp.; mem. Bd of Dirs Mfrs Hanover Trust Co., New York. *Address:* Hearst Corporation, 959 8th Avenue, New York, NY 10019, USA (office). *Telephone:* (212) 649-2000 (office). *Fax:* (212) 649-2108 (office). *Website:* www.hearstcorp.com (office).

BENNET, Douglas J., Jr, PhD; American academic administrator and fmr government official; *President, Wesleyan University;* b. 23 June 1938, Orange, NJ; s. of Douglas Bennet and Phoebe Bennet; m. 1st Susanne Klejman 1959 (divorced 1995); m. 2nd Midge Bowen Ramsey 1996; two s. one d.; ed Wesleyan Univ., Middletown, Conn., Univ. of Calif. (Berkeley) and Harvard Univ.; Asst to Econ. Adviser (Dr C.E. Lindblom), Agency for Int. Devt, New Delhi 1963–64; Special Asst to Amb. Chester Bowles, US Embassy, New Delhi 1964–66; Asst to Vice-Pres. Hubert Humphrey 1967–69; Admin. Asst to Senator T. F. Eagleton 1969–73, to Senator A. Ribicoff 1973–74; Staff Dir Senate Budget Cttee 1974–77; Asst Sec. of State, Congressional Relations 1977–79; Admin. U.S. Agency for Int. Devt 1979–81; Pres. Roosevelt Center for American Policy Studies 1981–83; Pres., CEO Nat. Public Radio (NPR) 1983–93; Asst Sec. of State, Int. Organizational Affairs, Dept of State 1993–95; Pres. Wesleyan Univ. 1995–; mem. Council of Foreign Relations, North South Round Table, Soc. for Int. Devt, Carnegie Endowment Study on Organizing Int. Financial Co-operation in 1980s, Rockfall Foundation; Dir Overseas Educ. Fund, KTI Corpn, Salzburg Seminar, Middlesex Co. Chamber of Commerce. *Publications:* articles in newspapers and journals. *Leisure interests:* sailing, skiing. *Address:* Office of the President, Wesleyan University, 229 High Street, Middletown, CT 06457 (office); 269 High Street, Middletown, CT 06457, USA (home). *Telephone:* (202) 822-2010 (office). *Website:* www.wesleyan.edu/administration/president (office).

BENNETT, Alan, BA; British playwright and actor; b. 9 May 1934, Leeds; s. of Walter Bennett and Lilian Mary Peel; ed Leeds Modern School, Exeter Coll., Oxford; Jr Lecturer, Modern History, Magdalen Coll., Oxford 1960–62; co-author and actor Beyond the Fringe, Edin. 1960, London 1961, New York 1962; Trustee Nat. Gallery 1993–98; Hon. Fellow, Royal Acad. 2000; Hon. Fellow, Exeter Coll., Oxford; Hon. DLitt (Leeds); Evening Standard Award 1961, 1969, Hawthornden Prize 1988, two Olivier Awards 1993, Evening Standard Film Award 1996, Lifetime Achievement Award, British Book Awards 2003, Evening Standard Best Play Award 2004, Olivier Award for outstanding contribution to British theatre 2005, British Book Awards Reader's Digest Author of the Year 2006, Bodley Medal 2008. *Plays:* On the Margin (TV series, author and actor) 1966, Forty Years On (author and actor) 1968, Getting On 1971, Habeas Corpus 1973, The Old Country 1977, Enjoy 1980, Kafka's Dick 1986, Single Spies 1988, The Wind in the Willows (adapted for Nat. Theatre) 1990, The Madness of George III 1991, The Lady in the Van 1999, The History Boys (Royal Nat. Theatre, London) (Evening Standard Award for Best Play 2004, Critics Circle Theatre Award for Best New Play 2005, Olivier Award for Best New Play 2005, New York Drama Critics' Circle Play of the Year 2006, Drama Desk Award for Best Play 2006, Tony Award for Best Play 2006) 2004, The Habit of Art 2009. *Radio:* The Last of the Sun 2004. *Television scripts:* A Day Out (film) 1972, Sunset Across the Bay (TV film) 1975, A Little Outing, A Visit from Miss Prothero (plays) 1977, Doris and Doreen, The Old Crowd, Me! I'm Afraid of Virginia Woolf, All Day on the Sands, Afternoon Off, One Fine Day 1978–79, Intensive Care, Our Winnie, A Woman of No Importance, Rolling Home, Marks, Say Something Happened,

An Englishman Abroad 1982, The Insurance Man 1986, Talking Heads (Olivier Award) 1992, 102 Boulevard Haussmann 1991, A Question of Attribution 1991, Talking Heads 2 1998. *Films:* A Private Function 1984, Prick Up Your Ears 1987, The Madness of King George 1994, The History Boys 2006. *Television documentaries:* Dinner at Noon 1988, Poetry in Motion 1990, Portrait or Bust 1994, The Abbey 1995, Telling Tales 1999. *Publications:* Beyond the Fringe (with Peter Cook, Jonathan Miller and Dudley Moore) 1962, Forty Years On 1969, Getting On 1972, Habeas Corpus 1973, The Old Country 1978, Enjoy 1980, Office Suite 1981, Objects of Affection 1982, The Writer in Disguise 1985, Two Kafka Plays 1987, Talking Heads 1988, Single Spies 1989, Poetry in Motion 1990, The Lady in the Van 1991, The Wind in the Willows (adaptation) 1991, The Madness of George III 1992, Writing Home (autobiog.) 1994, Diaries 1997, The Clothes They Stood Up In 1998, Talking Heads 2 1998, The Complete Talking Heads 1998, A Box of Alan Bennett 2000, Father, Father! Burning Bright 2000, The Laying on of Hands 2001, The History Boys 2004, Untold Stories 2005, The Uncommon Reader 2007; regular contrib. to London Review of Books. *Address:* Chatto & Linnit, 123A Kings Road, London, SW3 4PL, England (office). *Telephone:* (20) 7352-7722 (office).

BENNETT, Charles L., BS, PhD; American astronomer and academic; *Professor of Physics and Astronomy, Johns Hopkins University;* ed Univ. of Maryland, Carnegie Inst. of Washington, Massachusetts Inst. of Tech.; astrophysicist, NASA Goddard Space Flight Center (GSFC) 1984–2004, Acting Head, Infrared Astrophysics Br. April–Aug. 1993, April–Aug. 1994, Head 1994–2000, Sr Scientist for Experimental Cosmology 2004; Prof. of Physics and Astronomy, Johns Hopkins Univ. 2005–; fmr Deputy Prin. Investigator, Differential Microwave Radiometers (DMR) instrument and mem. Science Team of Cosmic Background Explorer (COBE) mission; Leader and Prin. Investigator, Wilkinson Microwave Anisotropy Probe (WMAP) mission; mem. NAS 2005–, American Acad. of Arts and Sciences 2004–, American Astronomical Soc., American Inst. of Physics, Int. Astronomical Union; Fellow, American Physical Soc. 1999–, AAAS 2003–; NASA Outstanding Performance 1985, 1994, GSFC Group Achievement Award for COBE 1988, NASA/GSFC Performance Award 1989, NASA Group Achievement Award for COBE 1990, NASA Exceptional Scientific Achievement Medal for COBE 1992, GSFC Group Award for MAP Proposal 1996, NASA/GSFC Performance Award 1996, 1998, 2002, NASA MIDEX Group Award 1997, NASA/GSFC Leadership Award 1999, Institutional Support 'Vision' Award for Spacecraft Operations Risk Assessment 2000, Popular Science 'Best of What's New' Award in Aviation and Space for WMAP 2001, ISI Highly Cited Researchers 2002, Sr Scientist for Experimental Cosmology 2002, NASA/GSFC Center of Excellence Group Achievement Award for MAP 2002, NASA/GSFC Group Achievement Award for MAP 2002, Distinguished Alumnus of the Year, Univ. of Maryland 2003, John C. Lindsay Memorial Award for Space Science 2003, NASA Outstanding Leadership Medal 2003, NASA Performance Award 2003, NASA/GSFC WMAP Cosmology Outreach Team 2003, Science Magazine Breakthrough of the Year for WMAP/Sloan proof of Dark Energy 2003, NASA Group Achievement Award to WMAP Science Team 2004, NASA Exceptional Scientific Achievement Medal for WMAP 2004, Rotary Nat. Award for Space Achievement Mid-Career Stellar Award 2005, NAS Henry Draper Medal 2005, Gruber Foundation Cosmology Prize (as mem. COBE Team) 2006, Harvey Prize, Technion – Israel Inst. of Tech. 2006. *Publications:* After The First Three Minutes, AIP Conference Procedings 222 (co-author) 1991, Dark Matter, AIP Conference Procedings 336 (co-author) 1995; more than 140 scientific papers in professional journals. *Address:* Bloomberg 209, Department of Physics and Astronomy, The Johns Hopkins University, 3400 North Charles Street, Baltimore, MD 21218, USA (office). *Telephone:* (410) 516-6177 (office). *Fax:* (410) 516-7239 (office). *E-mail:* cbennett@jhu.edu (office). *Website:* cosmos.pha.jhu.edu/bennett (office).

BENNETT, Emmett Leslie, Jr, PhD; American classical scholar; *Professor Emeritus, Department of Classics, University of Wisconsin;* b. 12 July 1918, Minneapolis, Minn.; s. of Emmett Leslie Bennett, Sr and Mary C. Buzzelle; m. Marja Adams 1942; five c.; ed Univ. of Cincinnati; Research Analyst, US War Dept 1942–45; taught in Dept of Classics, Yale Univ. 1947–58; Fulbright Research Scholar, Athens 1953–54, Cambridge 1965; mem. Inst. for Advanced Study, Guggenheim Fellow, Visiting Lecturer in Greek, Bryn Mawr Coll. 1955–56; Dept of Classical Languages, Univ. of Texas 1958–59; Univ. of Wis. Inst. for Research Humanities 1959–, Acting Dir 1968–69, 1972–75, Dept of Classics 1960–, Moses S. Slaughter Prof. of Classical Studies 1978–88, Prof. Emer. 1988–; Visiting Scholar, Univ. of Texas 1989–; Visiting Prof., Univ. of Colorado 1967, of Cincinnati 1972; Elizabeth A. Whitehead Prof., American School of Classical Studies 1986–87; Adjunct Prof., Dept of Classics, Univ. of Texas-Austin 1992–93, 1995; Ed. Nestor 1957–77, etc.; Corresp. mem. German Archaeological Inst.; mem. Comité Int. Permanent des Etudes Mycéniennes, Archaeological Inst. of America, American Philological Asscn; Hon. Councillor Archaeological Soc. of Athens; Gold Cross (Greece) 1991, McMicken Arts & Sciences Distinguished Alumnus Award 1997, Gold Medal, Archaeological Inst. of America 2001. *Publications:* The Pylos Tablets 1951 and 1956, The Mycenae Tablets 1953 and 1958, Mycenaean Studies 1964. *Address:* 3106 Bluff Street, #2, Madison, WI 53705-3459 (home); Classics Department, Van Hise, 1220 Linden Drive, University of Wisconsin, Madison, WI 53706, USA (office). *Telephone:* (608) 233-2681 (home). *Fax:* (608) 265-4173 (office); (608) 262-8570 (office).

BENNETT, Hywel Thomas; British actor and director; b. 8 April 1944, Garnant, S. Wales; s. of Gorden Bennett and Sarah Gwen Lewis; m. 1st Cathy McGowan 1967 (divorced 1988); one d.; m. 2nd Sandra Layne Fulford 1998; ed Henry Thornton Grammar School, Clapham, London and Royal Acad. of Dramatic Art; London stage debut as Ophelia in Youth Theatre's Hamlet, Queen's Theatre 1959; played in repertory, Salisbury and Leatherhead 1965; Fellow, Welsh Coll. of Music & Drama; Hon. Fellow, Univ. of Wales, Cardiff

1997. *Stage roles include:* Puck in A Midsummer Night's Dream, Edinburgh Festival 1967; Prince Hal in Henry IV (Parts I and II), Mermaid 1970; Antony in Julius Caesar, Young Vic 1972; Stanley in The Birthday Party, Gardner Cen., Brighton 1973; Hamlet (touring S. Africa) 1974; Danny in Night Must Fall, Sherman, Cardiff 1974 and Shaw, 1975; Jimmy Porter in Look Back in Anger, Belgrade, Coventry 1974; Konstantin in the Seagull (on tour), Birmingham Repertory Co. 1974, Otherwise Engaged, Comedy Theatre 1978, Terra Nova, Chichester 1979, The Case of the Oily Levantine, Her Majesty's 1980, She Stoops to Conquer, Nat. Theatre 1984–85; Andrey in Elijah Moshinksy's production of The Three Sisters, Albery Theatre 1987, Treasure Island 1990; has directed several plays including Rosencrantz and Guildenstern are Dead, Leatherhead 1975, A Man for All Seasons, Birmingham 1976, I Have Been Here Before, Sherman Theatre, Cardiff 1976, Otherwise Engaged, Library Theatre, Manchester 1978, What the Butler Saw, Theatre of Wales, Cardiff 1980, Fly Away Home (also producer), Hammersmith 1983. *Films include:* The Family Way 1966, Twisted Nerve 1968, The Virgin Soldiers 1969, Loot 1970, Percy 1971, Alice in Wonderland 1972, Endless Night 1972, Murder Elite, War Zone, Frankie and Johnnie 1985, The Twilight Zone, Checkpoint Chiswick, Age Unknown, Married to Malcolm 1997, Misery Harbour 1998, Nasty Neighbours, Vatel, Jesus and Mary 2000, One for the Road 2003. *Radio:* No Telegrams No Thunder, Dialogues on a Broken Sphere, Dracula, Witness for the Prosecution, Night Must Fall. *TV appearances include:* Romeo and Juliet, The Idiot, Unman, Wittering and Zigo, A Month in the Country, Malice Aforethought (serial), Shelley (two series), Tinker, Tailor, Soldier, Spy (serial) 1979, Coming Out, Pennies From Heaven, Artemis '81, The Critic, The Consultant, Absent Friends, Checkpoint Chiswick, The Secret Agent, A Mind to Kill, Casualty, Virtual Murder, The Other Side of Paradise, Trust Me, Frontiers, Karaoke, Harpur and Isles, Hospital, Neverwhere, Dirty Work, Eastenders 2003, The Second Quest 2004, The Final Quest 2004; many voice-overs and narrations; radio plays. *Leisure interests:* fishing, cooking, golf, painting, walking, swimming, reading and solitude. *Address:* c/o Gavin Barker, 2D Wimpole Street, London W1G 0EB, England.

BENNETT, Jana Eve, OBE, BA, MSc, FRTS; British broadcasting executive; *Director, BBC Vision;* b. 6 Nov. 1956, Cooperstown, USA; d. of Gordon Willard Bennett and Elizabeth Bennett (née Cushing); m. Richard Clemmow 1996; one s. one d.; ed Bognor Comprehensive School, St Anne's Coll., Oxford, London School of Econs; News trainee BBC 1979, fmrly Asst Producer The Money Programme, Producer Newsnight, Producer/Dir Panorama, Series Producer Antenna, Ed. Horizon, Head of BBC Science; Dir of Production and Deputy Chief Exec. BBC 1997–99, Dir of TV 2002–06, Dir BBC Vision 2006–; Exec. Vice-Pres. Learning Channel, US Discovery Communications Inc. 1999–2002; Golden Nymph Award (Panorama), BAFTA, Emmy, Prix Italia (Horizon). *Publication:* The Disappeared: Argentina's Dirty War 1986 (jtly). *Leisure interests:* mountaineering, music, skiing, children, travel. *Address:* BBC TV Centre, Wood Lane, London, W12 7RJ, England (office). *Telephone:* (20) 8225-8483 (office). *Fax:* (20) 8225-8485 (office). *E-mail:* jana.bennett@bbc.co.uk (office). *Website:* www.bbc.co.uk (office).

BENNETT, Martin Arthur, PhD, DSc, FRS, FAA, FRSC; British/Australian chemist and academic; *Professor Emeritus, Australian National University;* b. 11 Aug. 1935, Harrow; s. of Arthur Edward Charles Bennett and Dorothy Ivy Bennett; m. Rae Elizabeth Mathews 1964; two s.; ed Haberdashers' Aske's Hampstead School, Imperial Coll. of Science and Tech., London; Postdoctoral Fellow, Univ. of Southern California 1960–61; Turner and Newall Fellow, Univ. Coll. London 1961–63, Lecturer 1963–67; Fellow, Research School of Chemistry, ANU 1967–70, Sr Fellow 1970–79, Professorial Fellow 1979–91, Prof. 1991–2000, Prof. Emer. 2001–; Adjunct Prof., Royal Melbourne Inst. of Tech. Univ. 2000–; various professorial and visiting fellowships in Canada, Germany, USA, NZ and Japan; mem. Int. Advisory Bd for Dictionary of Organometallic Compounds 1984 and Dictionary of Inorganic Compounds 1988; Corresp. mem. Bavarian Acad. of Sciences 2005; H. G. Smith Medal, Royal Australian Chem. Inst. 1977, RSC Award 1981, G. J. Burrows Award, Royal Australian Chem. Inst. 1987, Nyholm Medal, RSC 1991, Max Planck Soc. Research Award 1994. *Publications:* chapters on ruthenium in Comprehensive Organometallic Chemistry; over 250 papers in journals. *Leisure interests:* golf, reading, foreign languages. *Address:* Research School of Chemistry, Australian National University, Canberra, ACT 0200 (office); 21 Black Street, Yarralumla, ACT 2600, Australia (home). *Telephone:* (2) 6125-3639 (office); (2) 6282-4154 (home). *Fax:* (2) 6125-3216 (office). *E-mail:* bennett@rsc.anu.edu.au (office). *Website:* rsc.anu.edu.au/index.php (office).

BENNETT, Maxwell Richard, AO, BEng, DSc, FAA; Australian physiologist and academic; *Professor of Neuroscience and Head, Neurobiology Laboratory, University of Sydney;* b. 19 Feb. 1939, Melbourne; s. of Herman Adler Bennett (Bercovici) and Ivy G. Arthur; m. Gillian R. Bennett 1965; one s. one d.; ed Christian Brothers Coll., St Kilda, Melbourne and Univ. of Melbourne; John & Alan Gilmour Research Fellow, Univ. of Melbourne 1965; Lecturer in Physiology, Univ. of Sydney 1969, Reader 1973, Prof. of Physiology 1982–2000, Dir Neurobiology Research Centre 1982–90, Prof. of Neuroscience 2000–, also Head, Neurobiology Laboratory; Convener Sydney Inst. of Biomedical Research 1995; Founder Fed. Australian Scientific and Tech. Socs 1985; Co-Founder Australian Neural Networks Soc. 1990; Pres. Australian Neuroscience Soc. 1989–92; Pres. Int. Soc. for Autonomic Neuroscience 2001–03; mem. Council Int. Brain Research Org. 1995–; First Univ. Chair., Univ. of Sydney 2000; Fellow Australian Acad. of Science 1981–; Dir Neuroscience Australia 2002, Brain & Mind Research Inst. 2003, Brain Foundation 2004, Brain & Mind Research Foundation 2004; mem. Council of Mental Health Research Inst. 2003, Mental Health Council of Australia; Opening Plenary Lecture, World Congress of Neuroscience 1995, Goddard Research Prize Nat. Heart Foundation 1996, Ramaciotti Medal for Excellence in Biomedical Research 1996, Renenessin Research Prize Nat. Heart Foundation 1998, Almigren Research Prize, Nat. Heart Foundation 1999, Burnet Medal and Lecture Australian Acad. of Science 1999, Neuroscience Distinguished Achievement Medallion 2001; Ophthalmologica Internationalis Award 2002, Tall Poppy for Excellence in Science Prize 2002, Centenary Medal 2003. *Publications:* Autonomic Neuromuscular Transmission 1972, Development of Neuromuscular Synapses 1983, Optimising Research and Development 1985, The Idea of Consciousness 1997, History of the Synapse 2001, Philosophical Foundations of Neuroscience 2003; 350 papers on neuroscience. *Leisure interests:* history and philosophy of science, science policy. *Address:* Department of Physiology, Anderson Stuart Building F13, University of Sydney, NSW 2006, Australia (office). *Telephone:* (2) 9351-2034 (office). *Website:* www.physiol.usyd.edu.au/research/labs/nrc (office).

BENNETT, Michael Vander Laan, BS, DPhil; American neuroscientist and academic; *Sylvia and Robert S. Olnick Professor of Neuroscience and Distinguished Professor, Albert Einstein College of Medicine;* b. 7 Jan. 1931, Madison, Wis.; s. of Martin Toscan Bennett and Cornelia Vander Laan Bennett; m. 1st Ruth Berman 1963 (divorced 1993); one s. one d.; m. 2nd Ruth Suzanne Zukin 1998; ed Yale Univ., Univ. of Oxford, UK; research worker, Dept of Neurology, Coll. of Physicians and Surgeons, Columbia Univ. 1957–58, Research Assoc. 1958–59; Asst Prof. of Neurology, Columbia Univ. 1959–61, Assoc. Prof. 1961–66; Prof. of Anatomy, Albert Einstein Coll. of Medicine, Yeshiva Univ. 1967–74, Co-Dir Neurobiology Course, Marine Biological Lab. 1970–74, Prof. of Neuroscience 1974–, Dir Div. of Cellular Neurobiology 1974–, Chair. Dept of Neuroscience 1982–96, Sylvia and Robert S. Olnick Prof. 1986–; Rhodes Scholar 1952; Sr Research Fellowship, NIH 1960–62; mem. Editorial Bds Brain Research 1975–, Journal of Cell Biology 1983–85, Journal of Neurobiology 1969–95 (Assoc. Ed. 1979–93), Journal of Neurocytology 1980–82, Journal of Neuroscience (Section Ed. 1981–85); mem. NAS 1982, American Asscn of Anatomists, American Physiological Soc., American Soc. for Cell Biology, American Soc. of Zoologists, Biophysical Soc., Soc. for Neuroscience, Soc. of Gen. Physiologists; Fellow, Nat. Neurological Research Foundation 1958–60, New York Acad. of Sciences, AAAS. *Publications:* more than 300 papers in scholarly books and journals. *Leisure interests:* running, hiking, skiing and scuba. *Address:* Albert Einstein College of Medicine, Department of Neuroscience, Rose F. Kennedy Center, 1410 Pelham Parkway South, Room 704, Bronx, NY 10461, USA (office). *Telephone:* (718) 430-2536 (office). *Fax:* (718) 430-8944 (office). *E-mail:* mbennett@aecom.yu.edu (office). *Website:* www.aecom.yu.edu/phd/facProfile.asp?id=8219&k= (office).

BENNETT, Sir Richard Rodney, Kt, CBE, FRAM; British composer; b. 29 March 1936, Broadstairs, Kent; s. of H. Rodney Bennett and Joan Esther Bennett; ed Leighton Park School, Reading, Royal Acad. of Music, London and under Pierre Boulez, Paris; commissioned to write two operas by Sadler's Wells 1962; Prof. of Composition, RAM 1963–65, Visiting Prof. 1995–; Vice-Pres. RCM 1983–; mem. Gen. Council, Performing Right Soc. 1975–; Arnold Bax Soc. Prize for Commonwealth Composers 1964; Anthony Asquith Memorial Award for Murder on the Orient Express film music, Soc. of Film and TV Awards 1974. *Compositions:* The Approaches of Sleep 1959, Journal, Calendar, Winter Music 1960, The Ledge, Suite Française, Oboe Sonata 1961, Nocturnes, London Pastoral, Fantasy 1962, Aubade, Jazz Calendar, String Quartet No. 4, Five Studies 1964, The Mines of Sulphur (opera) 1964, Symphony No. 1 1965, A Penny for a Song (opera) 1966, Epithalamion 1966, Symphony No. 2 1967, Wind Quintet, Piano Concerto 1968, Victory (opera) 1969, All the King's Men (children's opera) 1969, Jazz Pastoral 1969, Oboe Concerto 1970, Guitar Concerto 1971, Viola Concerto 1973, Commedia I–IV 1972–73, Spells (choral) 1975, Serenade for Youth Orchestra 1977, Isadora (ballet) 1981, Dream Songs 1986, Marimba Concerto 1988, Diversions 1989, Concerto for Stan Getz 1990, Partita 1995, Reflections on a 16th-Century Tune 1999, Seven Country Dances 2000, The Glory and the Dream 2000, Reflections on a Scottish Folksong 2006. *Film music:* Indiscreet, Devil's Disciple, Blind Date, The Mark, Only Two Can Play, Wrong Arm of the Law, Heavens Above, Billy Liar, One Way Pendulum, The Nanny, The Witches, Far from the Madding Crowd, Billion Dollar Brain, The Buttercup Chain, Secret Ceremony, Figures in a Landscape, Nicholas and Alexandra, Lady Caroline Lamb, Voices, Murder on the Orient Express, Equus, Sherlock Holmes in New York, L'Imprecateur, The Brinks Job, Yanks, Return of the Soldier, Four Weddings and a Funeral, Swann. *Television music includes:* Hereward the Wake, The Christians, The Ebony Tower, Poor Little Rich Girl, Gormenghast. *Recordings include:* When Lights Are Low (with Claire Martin) 2005. *Leisure interests:* cinema, modern jazz, art. *Address:* c/o Alice Gribbin, Clarion/Seven Muses, 47 Whitehall Park, London, N19 3TW, England (office). *Website:* www.c7m.co.uk (office).

BENNETT, Robert F. (Bob), BA; American politician and business executive; *Senator from Utah;* b. 18 Sept. 1933, Salt Lake City, Utah; s. of Wallace Bennett; m. Joyce McKay; six c.; ed Univ. of Utah; served in USAF 1951–57; Propr Bennett Paint & Glass Co.; Congressional liaison official for Transportation Dept, Washington, DC 1968–70; became lobbyist after acquiring Robert Mullen's public relations firm 1970; CEO Franklin Quest 1984–91; Adviser to fmr US Senator Wallace Bennett 1962; Senator from Utah 1993–; Republican. *Address:* 431 Dirksen Senate Office, Washington, DC 20510-0001, USA. *Telephone:* (202) 224-5444 (office). *Website:* bennett.senate.gov (office).

BENNETT, Tony, MusD; American singer and entertainer; b. (Anthony Dominick Benedetto), 3 Aug. 1926, Astoria; s. of John Benedetto and Anna Suraci; m. 1st Patricia Beech 1952 (divorced 1971); two c.; m. 2nd Sandra Grant 1971 (divorced 1984); two d.; ed American Theatre Wing, NY and Univ. of Berkeley; frequent appearances on TV and in concert; owner and recording artist with Improv Records; paintings exhibited at Butler Inst. of American Art, Youngstown, Ohio 1994; Grammy Award for Best Traditional Pop Vocal Performer 1998, Kennedy Center Honor 2005, Billboard Century Award 2006, Grammy Award for Best Pop Collaboration with Vocals (with Stevie Wonder) 2007, Ronnie Scott Lifetime Achievement Award 2007. *Recordings include:* The Art of Excellence 1986, Bennett/Berlin 1988, Astoria: Portrait of the Artist 1990, Perfectly Frank 1992 (Grammy Award for Best Traditional Vocal Performance), Steppin' Out 1993 (Grammy Award for Best Traditional Pop Vocal), The Essence of Tony Bennett 1993, MTV Unplugged 1994 (Grammy Award for Album of the Year, Best Traditional Pop Vocal), Here's to the Ladies 1995, The Playground 1998, Cool (Grammy Award) 1999, The Ultimate Tony 2000, A Wonderful World (with kd lang) (Grammy Award for Best Traditional Pop Vocal Album 2004) 2003, The Art of Romance (Grammy Award for Best Traditional Pop Vocal Album 2006) 2005, Duets: An American Classic (Grammy Award for Best Traditional Pop Vocal Album 2007) 2006, Tony Bennett Sings the Ultimate American Songbook, Vol. 1 2007, A Swingin Christmas 2008. *Publication:* The Good Life: The Autobiography of Tony Bennett. *Address:* 130 West 57th Street, Apartment 9D, New York, NY 10019, USA. *Website:* www.tonybennett.net.

BENNOUNA, Mohamed, DIntLaw; Moroccan diplomatist, academic, lawyer and international judge; *Judge, International Court of Justice;* b. 29 April 1943, Marrakech; m.; three c.; ed Univ. of Nancy, Sorbonne Univ., Paris, France and The Hague Acad. of Int. Law, Netherlands; Prof. of Public Law and Political Science, Univ. of the Sorbonne, Paris 1972–75; Prof., Faculty of Law, Mohammed V Univ. of Rabat and Casablanca 1975–79, Dean 1979–85; Dir-Gen. Arab World Inst. 1991–98; Judge, Int. Criminal Tribunal for the fmr Yugoslavia 1998–2001; Perm. Rep. of Morocco to UN, New York 1985–89, 2001–05; Judge, Int. Court of Justice 2006–, Judge ad hoc for dispute between Benin and Niger 2002; Chair. UN Compensation Comm., Geneva 1992–95, Group of 77 and China, UN 2003; mem. UNESCO Int. Panel on Democracy and Devt 1997–, UNESCO World Comm. on Ethics of Scientific Knowledge and Tech. (COMEST) 2002–, UNESCO Int. Bioethics Cttee 1992–98, UN Int. Law Comm., Geneva 1992–95; Nat. Prize for Culture, Morocco, Medal for Culture, Yemen; Chevalier de l'Ordre National de la Légion d'honneur. *Publications:* numerous books, essays and articles on Int. Law. *Address:* International Court of Justice, Peace Palace, 2517 KJ The Hague, Netherlands (office). *Telephone:* (70) 3022323 (office). *Fax:* (70) 3022409 (office). *Website:* www.icj-cij.org (office).

BENOIST, Gilles, LenD; French insurance industry executive; *CEO, CNP Assurances;* b. 1947; ed Institut d'Etudes Politiques, Ecole Nat. d'Admin; began his career with French Interior Ministry, first as Dir Office of the Prefect of Oise Dept 1974–76, then Sec. Gen. Ariège Dept 1976–78; Prin. Pvt. Sec. to Dir Gen. of Local Authorities at Ministry of the Interior 1978–81, Prin. Pvt. Sec. to Minister of the Economy, Finance and Budget 1981–83; Public Auditor, Cour des Comptes (Court of State Auditors) 1983, served successively as rapporteur on Budget and Finance Disciplinary Court and rapporteur to MODAC governmental org. project, seconded to Caisse des Dépôts et Consignations as adviser to Deputy CEO 1987, mem. Exec. Bd and Corp. Sec. Crédit Local de France, promoted to Sr Public Auditor at Cour des Comptes 1989–91, Dir of Cen. Services, Caisse des Dépôts et Consignations 1991–95, mem. Exec. Cttee 1993–98, Group Corp. Sec. and Dir of Human Resources, Caisse des Dépôts Group 1995–96, Chief Advisor, Cour des Comptes 1996–98; Pres. CNP Assurances Executive Board 1998–, currently CEO, mem. Bd Dirs 2007–; Chevalier, Légion d'honneur. *Address:* CNP Assurances, 4 place Raoul Dautry, 75716 Paris, France (office). *Telephone:* 1-42-18-88-88 (office). *Fax:* 1-42-18-86-55 (office). *E-mail:* info@cnp.fr (office). *Website:* www.cnp.fr (office).

BENOÎT DE COIGNAC, Henri Elie Marie; French diplomatist (retd) and international consultant; b. 3 Oct. 1935, Rodez (Aveyron); s. of Emile Benoit de Coignac and Madeleine Bonnefous; m. Nadine Vimont 1966; two s. one d.; ed Collège Saint-Joseph, Sarlat, Lycée Henry IV, Lycée Louis-le-Grand, Faculté de Droit, Univ. of Paris; Asst, Staff Dept, Ministry of Foreign Affairs, Paris 1963–65, Second Sec., Mexico 1965–67, Second Sec. then First Sec., Washington, DC 1967–71, First Sec. Tunis and Chief of Press and Information Service 1971–74, Counsellor in charge of Political Affairs 1974, Cultural Counsellor and Counsellor for Tech. and Scientific Co-operation in India 1975–77, Diplomatic Adviser to Nat. Defence Gen. Sec. and Auditeur, Nat. Defence Inst. for Higher Studies (IHEDN) 1978–79, First Counsellor, Buenos Aires 1979–82, Rep. of Pres. of France (Viguier) in Andorra 1982–84, Chief of Protocol in Paris 1984–88, Minister Plenipotentiary 1986, Amb. to Spain 1988–93, to Morocco 1993–95, to Ireland 1997–2001; Diplomatic Adviser to French Govt 1996–97; special envoy of France for peace process in Sudan 2004–; Chevalier Ordre nat. du Mérite, Officier Légion d'honneur, Grand Coirx Ordre d'Isabelle la Catholique. *Leisure interests:* tennis, golf. *Address:* 26 rue des Boulangers, 75005 Paris (home); Domaine de Farinières, Saint-Germain des Prés, 81700 Puylaurens, France (home). *Telephone:* (5) 63-75-47-68 (office); 1-46-34-21-16 (home). *Fax:* (6) 68-42-47-97 (office). *E-mail:* nethdecoignac@yahoo.fr (office); hdecoignac@yahoo.es (home).

BENSON, Andrew Alm, PhD; American biochemist, plant physiologist and academic; *Professor Emeritus of Biology, Scripps Institution of Oceanography, University of California, San Diego;* b. 24 Sept. 1917, Modesto, Calif.; s. of Carl B. Benson MD and Emma C. Alm; m. 1st Ruth Carkeek 1942 (divorced 1969); m. 2nd Dorothy Dorgan Neri 1971; one s. (deceased) three d. (one deceased); ed Modesto High School, Univ. of California, Berkeley and California Inst. of Tech.; Instructor, Univ. of California, Berkeley 1942–43, Asst Dir Bioorganic Group, Radiation Lab. 1946–54; Research Assoc., Stanford Univ. 1944–45; Assoc. Prof. of Agricultural Biological Chem., Pennsylvania State Univ. 1955–60, Prof. 1960–61; Prof.-in-Residence, Physiological Chem. and Biophysics, UCLA 1961–62; Prof., Scripps Inst. of Oceanography, Univ. of California,

San Diego 1962–88, Prof. Emer. 1988–, Assoc. Dir 1966–70, Dir Physiology Research Lab. 1970–77; Sr Queen's Fellow in Oceanography, Australia 1979; mem. advisory Bd Marine Biotech. Inst. Co. Ltd, Tokyo 1990–, NAS, AAAS, American Acad. of Arts and Sciences, Royal Norwegian Soc. of Sciences and Letters 1984–; Hon. mem. Inst. of Marine Biology, Far East Br., Russian Acad. of Sciences 1992; Dr hc (Université Pierre et Marie Curie, Paris) 1986; Phil. D. hc (Oslo); Sugar Research Foundation Award 1950, California Scientist of the Year 1961, Ernest Orlando Lawrence Award, US Atomic Energy Admin 1962, Stephen Hales Award 1972, AmOil Chemists' Soc./Supelco Research Award 1987, Riken Distinguished Scientist 1995. *Publications:* Path of Carbon in Photosynthesis 1947–55, Wax in Oceanic Food Chains 1975, Arsenic Metabolism, a Way of Life in the Sea 1984, Methanol Metabolism and Plant Growth, Paving the Path 2002; 280 articles in scientific journals, five patents. *Leisure interests:* philately, gardening, starfinder development, nutritional biochemistry, marine and farmed fish fat content and metabolism, collecting honey, preparing memoirs. *Address:* Scripps Institution of Oceanography, La Jolla, CA 92093-0202 (office); 6044 Folsom Drive, La Jolla, CA 92037, USA (home). *Telephone:* (858) 534-4300 (office); (858) 459-3711 (home). *Fax:* (858) 534-7313 (office); (858) 459-1010 (home). *E-mail:* abenson@ucsd.edu (office). *Website:* sio.ucsd.edu (office).

BENSON, Bruce D., BSc; American business executive and university administrator; *President, University of Colorado;* b. 4 Aug. 1938, Chicago; m. Marcy Benson; three c.; ed Univ. of Colorado; f. Benson Mineral Group 1965; Chair. Colo Comm. on Higher Educ. 1986–89; Chair. Colo Republican Party 1987–93, 2002–03; Chair. Gov.'s Blue Ribbon Panel for Higher Educ. for 21st Century 2001–03; Chair. Metropolitan State Coll. Bd of Trustees 2002–07; Pres. Univ. of Colorado 2008–, also Exec. in Residence and Prof. Attendant, Univ. of Colorado Business School; fmr mem. Bd of Dirs US Exploration Inc., American Land Lease Corpn, Asset Investors Corpn; mem. Smith Coll. Bd of Trustees 1990–95; Hon. DHumLitt (Colo) 2004 Univ. of Colorado Medal 1999, Ira C. Rothgerber Award 2003. *Address:* Office of the President, University of Colorado, 1800 Grant Street, Suite 800, Denver, CO 80203, USA. *Telephone:* (303) 860-5600 (office). *Fax:* (303) 860-5610 (office). *E-mail:* OfficeofthePresident@cu.edu (office). *Website:* www.cu.edu (office).

BENSON, Sir Christopher John, Kt, FRICS, JP, DL; British business executive and chartered surveyor; *Chairman, Stratford (East London) Renaissance Partnerships;* b. 20 July 1933, Wheaton Aston; s. of Charles Woodburn Benson and Catherine Clara Bishton; m. Margaret Josephine Bundy 1960; two s.; ed Worcester Cathedral King's School, Thames Nautical Training Coll. HMS Worcester; Midshipman RNR 1949–52; Sub-Lt RNVR 1952–53; worked as chartered surveyor and agricultural auctioneer 1953–64; Dir Arndale Devts Ltd 1965–69; Chair. Dolphin Devts Ltd 1969–71, Dolphin Farms Ltd 1969–, Dolphin Property (Man.) Ltd 1969–; Asst Man. Dir The Law Land Co. Ltd 1972–74; Dir Sun Alliance and London Insurance Group 1978–84, Chair. Sun Alliance Insurance Group PLC 1993–96 (Dir 1988, Vice-Chair. 1991, Deputy Chair. 1992), Chair. Royal and Sun Alliance Insurance Group PLC 1996–97; Advisor to British Petroleum Pension Fund 1979–84; Underwriting Mem. of Lloyd's 1979–97; mem. Council CBI 1979–97; Pres. British Property Fed. 1981–83; Dir House of Fraser PLC 1982–86; Chair. London Docklands Devt Corpn 1984–88; Chair. Reedpack Ltd 1989–90; Man. Dir MEPC PLC 1976–88, Chair. 1988–93; Chair. Housing Corpn; Chair. Boots Co. PLC 1990–94 (Dir 1989); Chair. Costain Group PLC 1993–96; Chair. Funding Agency for Schools 1994–97; Deputy Chair. Thorn Lighting Group PLC 1994–98; Chair. Albright and Wilson PLC 1995–; Chair. Devt Bd Macmillan Cancer Relief 1995–2001, Cross London Rail Links 2001–05, Stratford (East London) Renaissance Partnerships; Gov. Inns of Court School of Law 1996–2000, Prin. 2000–02; Pres. London Chamber of Commerce and Industry 2000–02, Nat. Deaf Children's Soc. 1995–; Vice-Pres. RSA 1992–97; High Sheriff of Wilts. 2002–03; mem. Advisory Bd Hawkpoint Partners Ltd 1999–2001; Master Worshipful Co. of Watermen and Lightermen of the River Thames 2004–05; Chair. and Trustee Coram Family 2005–; Liveryman of Guild of Air Pilots and Air Navigators; Lay Canon, Salisbury Cathedral; Trustee, Magna Carta Trust, Salisbury Cathedral, Marine Soc. and Sea Cadets 2002–, Royal Flying Doctor Service of Australia Friends in the UK 2005–; Patron Changing Faces; Friend, Royal Coll. of Physicians; numerous other public and charitable interests; Hon. Vice-Pres. Nat. Fed. of Housing Asscns 1994–; Hon. Fellow, Wolfson Coll. Cambridge 1990, Chartered Inst. of Bldg 1992–, Royal Coll. of Pathologists 1992–; Hon. Bencher Hon. Soc. of Middle Temple 1984–; Hon. DSc (City), (Bradford). *Leisure interests:* opera, ballet, farming in Wiltshire, flying, swimming. *Address:* Pauls Dene House, Castle Road, Salisbury, SP1 3RY (home); Flat 2, 50 South Audley Street, London, W1K 2QE, England. *Telephone:* (20) 7629-2398 (office). *Fax:* (20) 7493-1334 (office); (1722) 336980 (home). *E-mail:* sircjbenson@btconnect.com (office).

BENSON, Sidney William, AB, PhD, FAAS; American chemist and academic; *Distinguished Professor Emeritus of Chemistry, University of Southern California;* b. 26 Sept. 1918, New York; s. of Julius Benson and Dora Cohen; m. Anna Bruni 1986; one s. one d.; ed Stuyvesant High School, Columbia Coll. and Harvard Univ.; Postdoctoral Research Fellow, Harvard Univ. 1941–42; Instructor in Chem., Coll. of City of New York 1942–43, Group Leader, Manhattan Project 1943; Asst Prof., Univ. of Southern Calif. 1943–48, Assoc. Prof. 1948–51, Prof. of Chemistry 1951–64, 1976–91, Distinguished Prof. Emer. 1989–; Scientific Co-Director, Loker Hydrocarbon Research Inst. 1977–90, Emer. 1991–; Chair. Dept of Kinetics and Thermochemistry, Stanford Research Inst. 1963–76; mem. Int. Editorial Bd, Elsevier Publishing Co., Amsterdam, Netherlands 1965–; Founder and Ed.-in-Chief Int. Journal of Chemical Kinetics 1967–83, Ed. Emer. 1983–; G. N. Lewis Lecturer, Univ. of Calif., Berkeley 1989; mem. Editorial Bd Journal of Physical Chem. 1981–84; mem. ACS, NAS; Foreign mem. Indian Acad. Science 1989; Guggenheim

Fellow, Chemical Kinetics and Fulbright Fellow to France 1950–51; NSF Sr Research Fellow 1957–58, in France 1971–72; Fellow, American Physical Soc.; Dr hc (Univ. of Nancy) 1989; Certificate of Merit for work during WWII, NRC-Div. 9 1943–46, ACS Award in Petroleum Chem. 1977, Tolman Medal 1978, Fellowship Award of the Japanese Soc. for Promotion of Science 1980, Irving Langmuir Award in Chemical Physics, ACS 1986, Polanyi Medal for Work in Chemical Kinetics (Royal Soc.) 1986, ACS Award, Orange Co. 1986, USC Award, Presidential Medallion 1986, Emer. Faculty Award, Univ. of SC 1990, Kapitsa Gold Medal Award, Russian Acad. of Nat. Science 1997, Citation Index for one of ten most cited papers in 25 years, Chemical Reviews Centennial Citation for two of most cited papers in Chemical Reviews. *Leisure interests:* skiing, swimming and tennis. *Address:* University of Southern California, University Park, MC-1661 Los Angeles, CA 90089-1661 (office); 1110 North Bundy Drive, Los Angeles, CA 90049, USA (home). *Telephone:* (213) 740-5964 (office); (310) 471-5841 (home). *Fax:* (213) 740-6679 (office). *E-mail:* benson@mizar.usc.edu (office).

BENTALL, Richard, PhD; British psychologist and academic; *Professor of Experimental Clinical Psychology, University of Manchester;* b. 1956, Sheffield, Yorks.; pnr Aisling; one s. one d.; ed Uppingham School, Rutland, High Storrs School, Sheffield, Univ. Coll. of North Wales, Bangor, Univ. of Liverpool and Univ. Coll., Swansea; worked as forensic clinical psychologist in Nat. Health Service 1986; Lecturer, Univ. of Liverpool 1986–94, Prof. of Clinical Psychology 1994–99; Prof. of Experimental Clinical Psychology, Univ. of Manchester 1999–; Fellow, British Psychological Soc.; May Davidson Award, British Psychological Soc. 1989, British Psychological Society Book Award 2005. *Publications:* Sensory Deception: A Scientific Analysis of Hallucination (co-author) 1988, Reconstructing Schizophrenia (co-author) 1992, Madness Explained: Psychosis and Human Nature 2003; numerous book chapters and articles in scientific journals on psychiatric classification and methodology in psychopathology, cognitive-behavioural therapy, subjective appraisal of neuroleptic drugs and the treatment of chronic fatigue syndrome. *Address:* Room 1.2, Coupland 1 Building, School of Psychological Sciences, Department of Psychology, University of Manchester, Oxford Road, Manchester, M13 9PL, England (office). *Telephone:* (161) 275-2575 (office). *Fax:* (161) 275-2588 (office). *E-mail:* richard.bentall@manchester.ac.uk (office). *Website:* www.psych-sci.manchester.ac.uk/staff/RichardBentall (office).

BENTÉGEAT, Gen. Henri; French army officer and diplomatist; *Chairman, Military Committee, European Union;* b. 27 May 1946, Talence; m.; four c.; ed Mil. Acad. of St Cyr, Institut d'Études Politiques de Paris; jr officer in French Armed Forces, serving in Germany, Senegal, France and Djibouti 1968–73; as field grade officer, served in Army Public Information Service, Chief Operations of 9th Marine Div., Commdr Marine Infantry and Armoured Bn 1988–90; Asst Defence Attaché, Embassy in Washington, DC 1990–92; Asst to Chief of Mil. Staff of Pres. of Repub. 1993–96; Commdr French Forces in West Indies 1996–98; Asst to Dir for Strategic Affairs, Ministry of Defence 1998–99; Chief of Mil. Staff of Pres. of Repub. 1999–2002; Chief of Defence Staff 2002–06; Chair. EU Mil. Cttee 2006–; apptd Maj.-Gen. 1998, Lt-Gen. 1999, Gen. 2001; Commandeur, Ordre nat. du Mérit, Grand officier, Légion d'honneur 2006. *Leisure interest:* reading. *Address:* EU Military Committee, rue de la loi 175, 1048 Brussels, Belgium (office). *Telephone:* 22-81-96-92 (office). *Fax:* 22-81-59-28 (office). *E-mail:* henri.bentegeat@consilium.europa.eu (office). *Website:* www.consilium.europa.eu (office).

BENTHAM, Richard Walker, BA, LLB, FRSA; British professor of law; *Professor Emeritus, University of Dundee;* b. 26 June 1930; s. of Richard H. Bentham and Ellen W. Fisher; m. Stella W. Matthews 1957; one d.; ed Trinity Coll., Dublin and Middle Temple, London; called to Bar 1955; Lecturer in Law, Univ. of Tasmania 1955–57, Univ. of Sydney 1957–61; Legal Dept British Petroleum Co. PLC 1961–83, Deputy Legal Adviser 1979–83; Prof. of Petroleum and Mineral Law and Dir Centre for Petroleum and Mineral Law Studies, Univ. of Dundee 1983–90, Prof. Emer. 1991–; Russian Petroleum Legislation Project (Univ. of Houston, World Bank, ODA) 1991–96; mem. Council ICC Inst. of Int. Business Law and Practice 1988–95; British nominated mem. panel arbitrators IEA Dispute Settlement Centre; mem. Bd Scottish Council for Int. Arbitration 1988–98; mem. Int. Law Asscn, Int. Bar Asscn; Julian Prize, Trinity Coll. Dublin 1952. *Publications:* publications in learned journals in the UK and overseas. *Leisure interests:* cricket, military history. *Address:* Earlham, 41 Trumlands Road, St Marychurch, Torquay, Devon, TQ1 4RN, England. *Telephone:* (1803) 314315. *Fax:* (1803) 314315.

BENTLEY, (Charles) Fred, OC, MSc, PhD, FAAS, FRSC; Canadian soil scientist and academic; b. 14 March 1914, Mass., USA; s. of Charles F. Bentley and Lavina A. (née MacKenzie) Bentley; m. Helen S. Petersen 1943; one s. one d.; ed Univ. of Alberta and Minnesota; Instructor in Soil Science Univ. of Minn. 1942–43; Instructor and Asst Prof. Soil Science Univ. of Sask. 1943–46; Faculty mem. Soil Science Univ. of Alberta 1946–79, Dean Faculty of Agric. 1959–68, Prof. Emer. 1979–; Special Adviser, Agric., Canadian Int. Devt Agency 1968–69; mem. Bd of Govs Int. Devt Research Centre 1970–74; Chair. of Bd Int. Crops Research Inst. for Semi-Arid Tropics, Hyderabad, India 1972–82, Int. Bd for Soil Research and Man., Bangkok, Thailand 1983–87; Consulting Agrologist, Int. Devt Volunteer 1979; Hon. DSc (Guelph) 1984, Alberta 1990; Fellow Agric. Inst. of Canada, Canadian Soc. of Soil Science, American Soc. of Soil Science, American Soc. of Agronomy, Nat. Acad. of India; Pres. Int. Soc. of Soil Science 1975; Queen's Silver Jubilee Medal; Alberta Order of Excellence 1987, M. H. Bennett Award, Soil and Water Conservation Soc. 1989, Conf. Centre of ICRIS, India named C. Fred Bentley Conference Centre 2001; numerous other awards and distinctions. *Publications:* over 100 scientific reports and papers. *Leisure interests:* world devt, int. affairs, agriculture and human welfare, the population problem and planned parenthood, environmentally friendly agricultural practices. *Address:* 13103-66

Avenue NW, Edmonton, Alberta, T6H 1Y6, Canada. *Telephone:* (780) 435-6523.

BENTLEY, Gerald Eades, Jr, DPhil, DLitt, FRSC; American/Canadian fmr professor of English; b. 23 Aug. 1930, Chicago, Ill.; s. of Gerald Eades Bentley and Esther Felt Bentley; m. Elizabeth Budd 1952; two d.; ed Princeton Univ. and Univ. of Oxford, UK; Instructor, Dept of English, Univ. of Chicago 1956–60; Asst, later full Prof. of English, Univ. of Toronto, Canada 1960–96; Fulbright Lecturer, Univ. of Algiers 1967–68, Univ. of Poona, India 1975–76, Fudan Univ., Shanghai, People's Repub. of China 1982–83; Visiting Fellow, Univ. Coll., Swansea 1985, Univ. of Hyderabad, India 1988, Fudan Univ., China 1988; Guggenheim Fellow, London 1958–59; Fellow of Canada Council and successor Social Science and Humanities Research Council of Canada 1963–64, 1970–71, 1977–78, 1984–85, 1991–94, 1995–98; Harold White Fellow, Nat. Library of Australia 1989, Connaught Fellow 1991–92; Rockefeller Research Fellow, Bellaggio, Italy 1991; Prof. and Visiting Research Fellow, Princeton Univ. 1992, Merton Coll. Oxford 1993, Hatfield Coll., Durham 1996; Visiting Lecturer, Australian Defence Force Acad. 1997; Co-Founder Conf. on Editorial Problems 1964–, Occasional Chair.; Jenkins Award for Bibliography 1978. *Publications include:* William Blake (ed.), Vala, or The Four Zoas 1963, The Early Engravings of Flaxman's Classical Designs 1964, Blake Records 1969, A Bibliography of George Cumberland 1975, Editing Eighteenth Century Novels (ed.) 1975, William Blake's Writings (two vols) (ed.) 1978, Blake Books 1977, Blake Records Supplement 1988, George Cumberland, the Captive of the Castle of Sennaar (ed.) 1991, Blake Studies in Japan 1994, Blake Books Supplement 1995, The Stranger from Paradise: A Biography of William Blake 2001, Blake Records (2nd edn), Paul Mellon Centre for studies in British Art 2004, William Blake: Selected Poems (ed.) 2006, William Blake's Conversations 2008. *Leisure interest:* travel. *Address:* 246 MacPherson Avenue, Toronto, ON M4V 1A2, Canada (home); Dutch Boys Landing, Mears, MI 49436, USA (May–Sept.) (home). *Telephone:* (416) 922-5613 (home).

BENTON, Fletcher Chapman, II, BFA; American artist, painter and sculptor; b. 25 Feb. 1931, Jackson, Ohio; m. Roberta Lee 1964; one s. one d.; ed Miami Univ.; mem. Faculty, Calif. Coll. of Arts and Crafts 1959, San Francisco Art Inst. 1964–67; Prof. of Art Calif. State Univ., San José 1967–86; American Acad. of Arts and Letters Award for Distinguished Service to the Arts 1979, President's Scholar Award, Calif. State Univ. San José 1980, San Francisco Arts. Comm. Award of Honor for Outstanding Achievement in Sculpture 1982; Hon. DFA (Miami Univ.) 1993, (Columbus Univ. of Rio Grande, Rio Grande, Ohio) 1994. *E-mail:* bstudio@penn.com (office). *Website:* www.fletcherbenton.com (office).

BENTON, Peter Faulkner, MA, CCMI; British science and economic consultant; b. 6 Oct. 1934, London; s. of the late S. Faulkner Benton and Hilda Benton; m. Ruth S. Cobb 1959; two s. three d.; ed Oundle School and Queens' Coll. Cambridge; Jr man. positions in Unilever, Shell Chemicals and Berger, Jenson and Nicholson 1959–64; consultant, McKinsey & Co., London and Chicago 1964–71; Dir Gallaher Ltd 1971–77, also Chair. subsids; Man. Dir Post Office Telecommunications 1978–81; Deputy Chair. British Telecom 1981–83; Special Adviser to EEC 1983–84; Chair. European Practice, Nolan, Norton & Co. 1984–87, Enfield Dist Health Authority 1986–92; Vice-Pres. European Council of Man. 1989–92; Dir Singer & Friedlander Ltd 1983–89, Tandata Holdings PLC 1983–89, Turing Inst. 1985–95, Woodside Communications Ltd 1995–96; Dir Gen. British Inst. of Man. 1987–92; Chair. Enterprise Support Group 1993–96; Chair. Visiting Group Inst. for Systems, Eng and Informatics, Italy 1993–94, Visiting Group Inst. for Systems, Informatics and Safety, Italy 1996–99; Adviser to Arthur Andersen 1992–98; mem. Int. Advisory Bd for Science and Tech. to Govt of Portugal 1996–2002, Industrial Devt Advisory Bd (DTI) 1988–94; Adviser to Stern Stewart Inc. 1995–2001; gave lectures at Univ. of Pennsylvania 2002–05; mem. Exec. Cttee Athenaeum 1997–2002; Chair. Ditchley Conf. on Information Tech. 1980, North London Hospice 1985–89, World Bank Confs on Catastrophe 1988, 1989, Chair. Delhi Conf. on Indian Infrastructure 1998; Adam Smith Lecturer 1991; Pres. Highgate Literary and Scientific Inst. 1981–88; Treas. Harington Scheme, London 1983–93; Gov. Molecule Theatre, London 1985–91; Ind. mem. British Library Advisory Council 1988–93; IEE Award 1994. *Achievements include:* led reorganization of UK gas industry 1966–71. *Publication:* Riding the Whirlwind 1990. *Leisure interests:* reading, conversation, sailing, early music. *Address:* Northgate House, Highgate Hill, London, N6 5HD (home); Dolphins, Polruan-by-Fowey, Cornwall, PL23 1PP, England (home). *Telephone:* (20) 8341-1122 (London) (home). *Fax:* (20) 8341-1122 (London) (home).

BENYON, Margaret, MBE, PhD, BFA; British/Australian artist; *Honorary Professorial Visiting Fellow, College of Fine Art, University of New South Wales;* b. 29 April 1940, Birmingham; m. William Rodwell 1974; one s. one d.; ed Kenya High School, Slade School of Fine Art, Univ. Coll. London, Royal Coll. of Art, London; Visiting Tutor, Coventry Coll. of Art 1966–68, Trent Polytechnic, Nottingham 1968–71, Holography Unit, RCA 1985–89; Fellow in Fine Art, Univ. of Nottingham 1968–71; Leverhulme Sr Art Fellow, Univ. of Strathclyde 1971–73; Co-ordinator Graphic Investigation, Canberra School of Art, Australia 1977–80; Creative Arts Fellow ANU, Canberra 1978; Artist-in-Residence, Museum of Holography, New York 1981, Center for Holographic Arts, New York 1999; Hon. Professorial Visiting Fellow, Coll. of Fine Arts, Univ. of NSW, Australia 2006–; pioneered holography as an art medium 1968; works in public collections including Australian Nat. Gallery, Nat. Gallery of Vic., Australia, MIT Museum Boston, USA, Calouste Gulbenkian Foundation, Portugal, Victoria and Albert Museum, London; over 100 exhbns to date, including London, Vienna, New York, Frankfurt, Lisbon, Madrid, Nagoya, Liverpool, Bradford, Berlin, Boston, Tokyo, Australia; Hon. FRPS 2001; Audrey Mellon Prize 1964, Carnegie Trust Award 1972, Kodak Photographic Bursary 1982, Calouste Gulbenkian Holography Award 1982, Agfa 'Best of Exhibition' Award (USA) 1985, Shearwater Foundation Holography Award (USA) 1987, Lifetime Achievement Award, Art in Holography International Symposium (UK) 1996, Shearwater Foundation Holography Purchase Award (USA) 2002. *Publications:* articles in more than 100 publs. *Address:* 18 Burra Close, Mount Colah, NSW 2079, Australia (office). *E-mail:* mbenyon@optusnet.com.au (office). *Website:* www.mbenyon.com (office).

BENZ, Edward J., Jr, MD, MA; American professor of medicine, paediatrics and pathology, physician and hospital administrator; *President and CEO, Dana-Farber Cancer Institute;* b. 22 May 1946, Pittsburgh; m. Margaret A. Vettese; one s. one d.; ed Allentown Cen. Catholic High School, Princeton Univ., Harvard Medical School, Yale Univ.; research fellowships Princeton and Boston Univs. 1967–71; Jr Asst Health Services Officer US Public Health Service, N.J.H., NHLBI 1972–73, Sr Asst Surgeon 1973–75; intern Peter Bent Brigham Hosp., Boston 1973–74, Asst Resident Physician 1974–75; Clinical Fellow Harvard Medical School 1973–75; Fellow in Medicine (Hematology) Children's Hosp. Medical Center, Boston 1974–75; Research Assoc. Molecular Hematology Br. NHLBI, NIH, Bethesda, Md 1975–78; Fellow in Hematology Yale Univ. School of Medicine 1978–80; Assoc. Attending in Medicine Yale-New Haven Hosp. 1979–81, Attending Physician 1981–93; Asst Prof. of Medicine Hematology Section, Dept of Internal Medicine, Yale Univ. School of Medicine 1979–82, Assoc. Prof. of Medicine 1982–84, Assoc. Prof. of Human Genetics (Jt) 1983–87, Assoc. Prof. of Internal Medicine 1984–87, Prof. of Internal Medicine and Genetics 1987–93, Chief Hematology Section, Dept of Internal Medicine 1987–93, Assoc. Chair. for Academic Affairs 1988–90, Vice Chair. 1990–93; Jack D. Myers Prof. and Chair. Dept of Medicine, Univ. of Pittsburgh School of Medicine 1993–95, Prof. of Molecular Genetics and Biochem. (Jt) 1993–95; Adjunct Prof. of Biological Sciences, Carnegie Mellon Univ., Pittsburgh 1993–95; Chief Medicine Service, Univ. of Pittsburgh Medical Center 1993–95; Sir William Osler Prof. and Dir Dept of Medicine, Johns Hopkins Univ. School of Medicine 1995–2000, Prof. of Molecular Biology and Genetics 1995–2000; Physician-in-Chief Johns Hopkins Hosp. 1995–2000; Pres. and CEO Dana-Farber Cancer Inst., Harvard Univ. 2000–, CEO Dana-Farber/Partners Cancer Care 2000–, Dir Dana-Farber/Harvard Cancer Center, mem. Governing Bd Dana-Farber/Children's Center; Richard and Susan Smith Prof. of Medicine, Prof. of Pediatrics, Prof. of Pathology, Faculty Dean for Oncology, Harvard Medical School 2000–; numerous visiting professorships and lectures in US, UK, Canada and France; Chair. Red Cells and Hemoglobin Sub-Cttee, American Soc. of Hematology 1983, 1989, Molecular Genetics Educ. Panel 1984–87, Hematology I Study Section, NIH Research 1993–95; Pres. American Soc. of Clinical Investigation 1992, Scientific Affairs Cttee 1992, Educ. Program 1994; mem. Exec. Cttee American Soc. of Hematology 1994–, (Vice-Pres. 1998, Pres. 2000–), Scientific Advisory Bd Inst. of Molecular Medicine, Oxford Univ. 1998; mem. AAAS Asscn of American Physicians, Inst. of Medicine and many other socs concerned with biology, medicine and genetics; mem. Editorial Bd American Journal of Hematology 1985–, Int. Journal of Hematology, Tokyo 1990–99, American Journal of Medicine 1994–; Adviser in Medicine Oxford Univ. Press 1994–; Consulting Ed. Journal of Clinical Investigation 1998–; Assoc. Ed. New England Journal of Medicine 2001–; Fellow American Asscn of Physicians 1992; Basil O'Connor Award, March of Dimes, Nat. Foundation 1980, NIH Research Career Devt Award 1982, Scientific Research Award, American Asscn of Blood Banks 1986, Inst. of Medicine Award and other awards. *Publications:* Molecular Genetics (Methods in Hematology series) (ed.) 1989, Hematology: Principles and Practice (jt ed.) 1990, Oxford Textbook of Medicine (co-ed.) 1997 and around 200 articles in professional journals. *Leisure interests:* tennis, reading, travel, hiking. *Address:* Dana-Farber Cancer Institute, Room D1628, 44 Binney Street, Boston, MA 02115 (office); 28 Chestnut Hill Terrace, Chestnut Hill, MA 02467, USA (home). *Telephone:* (617) 632-4266 (office); (617) 916-5345 (home). *Fax:* (617) 632-2161 (office); (617) 916-5681 (home). *E-mail:* edward_benz@dfci.harvard.edu (office); ebenz@comcast.net (home). *Website:* www.dfci.org (office).

BENZI, Roberto; Italian/French conductor; b. 12 Dec. 1937, Marseille; s. of the late Giuseppe Benzi and the late Maria Pastorino; m. Jane Rhodes 1966; ed Sorbonne, Paris; studied conducting with Andre Cluytens; debut as conductor, France 1948; tours in Europe and S America 1949–52; opera conducting debut 1954; conducted Carmen, Paris Opera 1959, Faust, Met 1971–72; guest conductor Europe, Japan, China, Israel, Mexico, Canada, USA, S Africa and main music festivals; Music Dir Bordeaux-Aquitaine Orchestra 1973–87, Arnhem Philharmonic 1989–98, Dutch Nat. Youth Orchestra 1991–96; Chevalier, Légion d'honneur, Ordre Nat. du Mérite, Ordre des Palmes Académiques, Order of Orange-Nassau. *Publications:* orchestrations of Brahms op. 23 Schumann Variations 1970, Brahms op. 24 Variations and Fugue on a theme by Handel 1973, Rossini Prélude, Thème et Variations 1978, Erik Satie Je te veux, valse 1987. *Leisure interests:* wildlife, astronomy, cycling. *Address:* 12 Villa Ste-Foy, 92200 Neuilly-sur-Seine, France (home). *Telephone:* 1-46-24-27-85 (home). *Fax:* 1-46-24-55-73 (home). *Website:* robertobenzi.com.

BÉRARD, Jean-Luc; French insurance industry executive; *Director-General, Union Nationale pour l'Emploi dans l'Industrie et le Commerce (UNEDIC);* b. 1959; m.; two c.; began career as lawyer Groupement des Industries Métallurgiques d'Île de France 1983–86; Dir Groupe Esys-Montenay (Compagnie Générale des Eaux) 1986–92; Human Resources Dir Union Nationale pour l'Emploi dans l'Industrie et le Commerce (UNEDIC) (nat. unemployment insurance scheme) 1992–97, Dir-Gen. 2007–; Labour Relations Dir Snecma Moteurs 2003–07. *Address:* UNEDIC, 80 rue de Reuilly, 75012 Paris, France (office). *Website:* www.assedic.fr (office).

BERARDI, Antonio, BA; British fashion designer; b. 21 Dec. 1968, Grantham; ed Cen. St Martin's School of Art and Design; career launched when graduation collection was purchased by Liberty and A la Mode; first Spring/Summer own label collection also bought by Liberty and A la Mode 1995; designs featured in New Generation catwalk promotion sponsored by Marks and Spencer 1996; joined Italian Mfrs Givuesse 1996; launched Autumn/Winter label 1997; apptd design consultant Ruffo leather and suede mfrs 1997; Best New Designer, VHI Awards (USA) 1997. *Address:* Show-Room Gibo-Co SpA, via Orobia 34, 20139 Milan, Italy; St Martin's House, 59 St Martin's Lane, London, WC2N 4JS, England. *Website:* www.antonioberardi .com.

BERARDI, Fabio, BSc; San Marino geologist and politician; b. 26 May 1959, Borgo Maggiore; m. Emanuele Bollini; two s.; ed Liceo Classico, Univ. of Bologna; began career with Sotecsa SA (Studio di Geologia Tecnica), San Marino 1984–86; mem. Council Borgo Maggiore 1984–89, 1995–98; Consultant, Studio Geotecnico Italiano, Milan 1986–89; pvt. practice as geologist 1989–95; Co-ordinator Dept of Territory, Environment and Agric. 1995–98; Pres. Admin. Council Azienda Autonoma di Stato per i Servizi Pubblici 1997–98; mem. Consiglio Grande Generale (Parl.) 1998–, Sec. of State for Territory, Environment and Agric. 2001–03, for Foreign and Political Affairs and Econ. Planning 2003–06; mem. Partito Socialista Sammarinese (PSS), mem. PSS Secr. 1999–; fmr Pres. Order of San Marino Geologists. *Address:* c/o Secretariat of State for Foreign and Political Affairs and Economic Planning, Palazzo Begni, Contrada Omerelli, 47890 San Marino, San Marino (office).

BERDENNIKOV, Grigory Vitalievich; Russian diplomatist; b. 24 Dec. 1950, Moscow; m.; one d.; ed Moscow Inst. of Int. Relations; diplomatic service 1973–, sec., attachè Mission in UN, New York 1973–78, Sec. of Div. USSR Ministry of Foreign Affairs 1978–81, Second then First Sec. Mission to UN, Geneva 1981–86, Counsellor, Chief of Div., Deputy Chief Dept of Armament Reduction and Disarmament, USSR (now Russian) Ministry of Foreign Affairs 1986–92, Deputy Minister of Foreign Affairs of Russia 1992–94, 1999–2001, Dir Dept of Security and Disarmament 1998–99; Perm. Rep. to Disarmament Conf. Geneva 1994–98; Perm. Rep. of Russia at Int. Orgs in Vienna 2001–06; Amb.-at-Large, Ministry of Foreign Affairs 2006–; Order of Friendship 1997, 850th Anniversary of Moscow Medal 1998, Presidential Letter of Gratitude 2000. *Address:* Ministry of Foreign Affairs, 119200 Moscow, Smolenskaya-Sennaya pl. 32/34, Russia (office). *Telephone:* (495) 244-16-06 (office). *Fax:* (495) 230-21-30 (office). *E-mail:* ministry@mid.ru (office). *Website:* www.mid .ru (office).

BERDIYEV, Yalym; Turkmenistani politician; *Minister of Defence;* Deputy Chair. State Customs Service –2006, Chair. 2006–09; Minister of Defence and Sec. State Security Council of Turkmenistan 2009–. *Address:* Ministry of Defence, 744000 Aşgabat, ul. Galkynyş 4, Turkmenistan (office). *Telephone:* (12) 35-22-59 (office).

BERDYEV, Batyr Atayevich; Turkmenistani philologist; b. 3 Oct. 1960, Ashgabat, Turkmenistan; ed Turkmen State Univ.; Corresp., Head of Div., Deputy Ed., Ed. Komsomolets Turkmenistana (newspaper) 1982–90; Consultant Int. Div. of Turkmen Presidency 1992–; Deputy Minister of Foreign Relations Turkmenistan 1992–94; Amb. to Austria (also accred to Slovakia and Czech Repub.) 1996–2000; Minister of Foreign Relations and Amb. to OSCE 2000; arrested and sentenced to 25 years' imprisonment in connection with 25 Nov. 2002 attack on Pres. of Turkmenistan 2003; Order of Galkynysh, Order of Bitaraplyk. *Address:* c/o Government House, Ministry of Foreign Affairs, Ashgabat, Turkmenistan (office). *Telephone:* (2) 266211 (office). *Fax:* (2) 253583 (office).

BERDYMUKHAMMEDOV, Gurbanguly Myalikgulyyevich, PhD; Turkmenistani politician and head of state; *President and Prime Minister;* b. 29 June 1957, Babarab, Ahal Prov.; ed Turkmen State Medical Inst.; mem. Dentistry Faculty, Turkmen State Medical Inst. 1979–97, Assoc. Prof. and Dean 1995–97; Head of Dentistry Centre, Ministry of Health 1995–97; Minister of Health 1997–2001; Deputy Prime Minister 2001–06; Acting Pres. (following death of Saparmurat Niyazov) 2006–07, Pres. and Prime Minister 2007–; Chair. Nat. Olympic Cttee 2007–. *Address:* Office of the President and the Council of Ministers, 744000 Aşgabat, Presidential Palace, Turkmenistan (office). *Telephone:* (12) 35-45-34 (office). *Fax:* (12) 35-51-12 (office). *Website:* www.turkmenistan.gov.tm (office).

BEREND, T. Ivan, PhD, DEcon; American economic historian and academic; *Professor of History, University of California, Los Angeles;* b. 11 Dec. 1930, Budapest; s. of Mihály Berend and Elvira Gellei; two d.; ed Univ. of Economics and Univ. of Sciences, Faculty of Philosophy, Budapest; Asst Lecturer, Karl Marx Univ. of Economics 1953, Sr Lecturer 1960, Prof. of Econ. History 1964–, Head of Dept 1967–85, Rector 1973–79; Prof. of History, UCLA 1990–, Dir Center for European and Eurasian Studies 1993–2005; Gen. Sec. Hungarian Historical Soc. 1966–72, Pres. 1975–79; Corresp. mem. Hungarian Acad. of Sciences 1973–79, mem. 1979–, Pres. 1985–90; Fellowship, Ford Foundation, New York 1966–67; Visiting Fellow, St Antony's Coll., Oxford 1972–73; Visiting Prof., Univ. of Calif., Berkeley 1978; Visiting Fellow, All Souls Coll., Oxford 1980; Fellow, Woodrow Wilson Int. Center for Scholars, Washington, DC 1982–83; Co-Chair. Bd of Dirs Inst. for East–West Security Studies 1986; mem. Exec. Cttee of Int. Econ. Soc. 1982–86, Vice-Pres. 1986–1994; First Vice-Pres. Int. Cttee of Historial Sciences 1990–95, Pres. 1995–2000; Corresp. mem. Royal Historical Soc. 1981, Academia Europaea 1987, Bulgarian Acad. of Sciences 1988, British Acad. 1989, Austrian Acad. of Sciences 1989, Czechoslovak Acad. of Sciences 1988; Hon. DLitt (St John's Univ., New York) 1986, (Glasgow) 1990, (Janus Pannonius Univ., Pécs) 1994; Kossuth Prize 1961, State Prize 1985. *Publications:* (with György Ránki): Magyarország gyáripara 1900–1914 1955, Magyarország gyáripara a II. világháboru elött és

a háboru idöszakában 1933–1944 1958, Magyarország a fasiszta Németország "életterében" 1960, Magyarország gazdasága az I. világháboru után 1919–1929 1966, Economic Development in East-Central Europe in the 19th and 20th Centuries 1974, Hungary—A Century of Economic Development, Underdevelopment and Economic Growth, The European Periphery and Industrialization 1780–1914 1982, The Hungarian Economy in the Twentieth Century 1985, The European Economy in the Nineteenth Century 1987; (as sole author): Ujjáépítés és a nagytöke elleni harc Magyarországon 1945–1948 1962, Gazdaságpolitika az elsö ötéves terv meginditásakor 1948–1950 1964, Öt elöadás gazdaságról és oktatásról 1978, Napjaink a történelemben 1980, Válságos évtizedek 1982, Gazdasági utkeresés 1983, The Crisis Zone of Europe 1986, Szocializmus és reform 1986, The Hungarian Economic Reforms 1990, Central and Eastern Europe 1944–93 – Detour from the Periphery to the Periphery 1996, Decades of Crisis: Central and Eastern Europe Before World War II 1998, History Derailed: Central and Eastern Europe in the 'Long' 19th Century 2003, An Economic History of 20th Century Europe 2006, From the Soviet Bloc to the European Union: The Economic and Social Transformation of Central and Eastern Europe since 1973 2008. *Leisure interests:* walking, swimming. *Address:* Department of History, UCLA, 405 Hildgard Avenue, Los Angeles, CA 90096, USA (office). *Telephone:* (310) 825-1178 (office). *Fax:* (310) 206-3556 (office); (310) 206-3556 (home). *E-mail:* iberend@history.ucla.edu (office). *Website:* www.history.ucla.edu/berend (office).

BERENDT, John Lawrence, BA; American writer and journalist; b. 5 Dec. 1939, Syracuse, NY; s. of Ralph Berendt and Carol Berendt (née Deschere); ed Nottingham High School, Syracuse, Harvard Univ.; Assoc. Ed. Esquire 1961–69, columnist 1982–94; Ed. New York magazine 1977–82; freelance writer 1982–; mem. PEN, The Century Asscn. *Publications:* Midnight in the Garden of Good and Evil 1994, The City of Falling Angels 2005. *Address:* c/o The Penguin Press, 375 Hudson Street, New York, NY 10014, USA (office); c/o Hodder & Stoughton, 338 Euston Road, London, NW1 3BH, England.

BÉRENGER, Paul Raymond, BA; Mauritian politician; *Leader, Mouvement Militant Mauricien;* b. 26 March 1945, Quatre Bornes; m. Arline Perrier 1971; one s. one d.; ed Collège du Saint Esprit, Univ. of Wales and Sorbonne, Paris; Gen. Sec. Mouvement Militant Mauricien 1969–82, currently Leader; MP 1976–87, 1991–; Minister of Finance 1982–83, of Foreign Affairs 1991; Deputy Prime Minister and Minister of Foreign Affairs and Int. and Regional Co-operation 1995; Deputy Prime Minister and Minister of Finance Sept. 2000–03; Prime Minister, Minister of Defence and Home Affairs and of External Communications Sept. 2003–05; Gov. IMF, African Devt Bank/ African Devt Fund. *Leisure interests:* reading, swimming. *Address:* Mouvement Militant Mauricien (MMM), 21 Poudrière Street, Port Louis, Mauritius (office). *Telephone:* 212-6553 (office). *Fax:* 208-9939 (office). *Website:* mmm .mmmonline.org (office).

BERENGER, Tom; American actor; b. 31 May 1950, Chicago; ed Univ. of Missouri; stage appearances in regional theatre and off-Broadway including The Rose Tattoo, Electra, A Streetcar Named Desire, End as a Man. *Films:* Beyond the Door 1975, Sentinel, Looking for Mr Goodbar, In Praise of Older Women, Butch and Sundance: The Early Days, The Dogs of War, The Big Chill, Eddie and the Cruisers, Fear City, Firstborn, Rustler's Rhapsody, Platoon, Someone to Watch Over Me, Shoot to Kill, Betrayed, Last Rites, Major League, Love at Large, The Field, Shattered, Chasers, Sniper 1993, Sliver 1993, Major League 2 1994, Last of the Dogmen 1994, Gettysburg 1994, The Substitute 1996, An Occasional Hell 1996, The Gingerbread Man 1997, Takedown 2000, One Man's Hero (also producer) 1999, Diplomatic Siege 1999, A Murder of Crows 1999, The Hollywood Sign 2000, Fear of Flying 2000, Training Day 2001, Watchtower 2001, Eye See You 2001, D-Tox 2002. *TV appearances include:* One Life to Live (series), Johnny We Hardly Knew Ye, Flesh and Blood, If Tomorrow Comes, Johnson County War 2002, Junction Boys 2002, Sniper 2 2002, Peacemakers 2003, Capital City 2004, The Detective 2005, Into the West (miniseries) 2005, Amy Coyne 2006, Nightmares and Dreamscapes: From the Stories of Stephen King (miniseries) 2006, October Road (series) 2006–07. *Address:* c/o ICM Los Angeles, 8942 Wilshire Boulevard, Beverly Hills, CA 90211, USA.

BERENGO GARDIN, Gianni; Italian photographer; b. 10 Oct. 1930, Santa Margherita Ligure; s. of Alberto Berengo Gardin and Carmen Maffei Berengo Gardin; m. Caterina Stiffoni 1957; one s. one d.; began working as photographer 1954; has lived and worked in Switzerland, Rome, Venice; living in Milan 1965–; photographs originally published by Il Mondo magazine, now published by major magazines in Italy and world-wide; photographs in perm. collections of Museum of Modern Art, New York, Bibliothèque Nationale Paris, Eastman House, Rochester, NY, Musée de l'Elysée, Lausanne, Museum of Aesthetic Art, Beijing, Maison Européene de la Photographie, Paris; Mois de la Photo Brassaï Award, Paris 1990, Leica Oskar Barnack Award, Arles 1995, Oscar Goldoni Award 1998, Werner Biscof Award 2006. *Publications:* over 210 photographic books. *Leisure interests:* photography, farming, his little dog Nina. *Address:* Via S. Michele del Carso 21, 20144 Milan, Italy (home). *Telephone:* (02) 4692877. *Fax:* (02) 4692877.

BERESFORD, Bruce; Australian film director; b. 16 Aug. 1940, Sydney; s. of Leslie Beresford and Lona Beresford; m. 1st Rhoisin Beresford 1965; two s. one d.; m. 2nd Virginia Duigan 1989; one d.; ed Univ. of Sydney; worked in advertising; worked for Australian Broadcasting Comm.; went to England 1961; odd jobs including teaching; film ed. Nigeria 1964–66; Sec. to British Film Inst.'s Production Bd 1966; feature film Dir 1971–; directed many short films 1960–75. *Films directed:* The Adventures of Barry Mackenzie 1972, Barry Mackenzie Holds His Own 1974, Side by Side 1975, Don's Party 1976, The Getting of Wisdom 1977, Money Movers 1979, Breaker Morant 1980, Puberty Blues 1981, The Club 1981, Tender Mercies 1983, King David 1984, Crimes of the Heart 1986, Fringe Dwellers 1986, Aria (segment) 1987, Her

Alibi 1988, Driving Miss Daisy 1989 (Acad. Award Best Film 1990), Mr. Johnson 1990, Black Robe 1990, Rich in Love 1993, A Good Man in Africa 1993, Silent Fall 1994, The Last Dance 1995, Paradise Road 1996, Double Jeopardy 1998, Rigoletto (opera) 2000, Bride of the Wind 2001, Evelyn 2002, And Starring Pancho Villa as Himself 2003 (tv), Orpheus (tv) 2006, The Contract 2006. *Address:* c/o Anthony A. Williams, P.O. Box 1379, Darlinghurst, NSW 2010, Australia.

BEREWA, Solomon; Sierra Leonean politician; Attorney-Gen., Sierra Leone 1996–97, 1998–2002; Vice-Pres. 2002–07. *Address:* c/o Office of the Vice-President, State House, Freetown, Sierra Leone (office).

BEREZOVSKII, Boris Abramovich, DrMathSc; Russian mathematician, business executive and fmr politician; b. 23 Jan. 1946, Moscow; s. of Abram Markovich Berezovskii and Anna Gelman; m. four times; six c.; ed Moscow Inst. of Wood Tech., Moscow State Univ.; engineer, Research Inst. of Testing Machines, Equipment and Measurement Devices 1968–69; engineer, Hydrometeorological Research Cen. 1969; engineer, researcher, head of div., Inst. of Problems of Man. 1969–87; supervisor of introduction of automatization on Tolyatti Car Works (VAZ) 1973–91; Co-founder and Dir-Gen. LOGOVAZ Co. 1991–96, 1997–; Dir-Gen. All-Union Automobile Alliance (AVVA) 1993–96; Deputy Chair. Bd of Dirs Public Russian TV 1995–96; Deputy Sec. Security Council of Russian Fed. 1996–97; Exec. Sec. CIS 1998–99; elected to State Duma Dec. 1999, resgnd July 2000; f. Charity Foundation Triumph 1994; f. non-governmental Int. Foundation for Civil Liberties 2000; Co-f. Liberal Russia political party 2001, expelled from party after offering funding to CP of Russian Fed.; survived assassination attempt unharmed 1994; granted asylum in UK 2003; found guilty in absentia by Moscow court of charges of embezzlement in 1990s from Russian airline carrier Aeroflot 2007, sentenced to six years in jail and ordered to repay $9 million; Corresp. mem. Russian Acad. of Sciences 1991. *Publications include:* more than 100 scientific articles on applied math. and theory of man. *Address:* c/o International Foundation for Civil Liberties, 1230 Avenue of the Americas, 7th Floor, New York, NY 10020, USA. *Telephone:* (212) 397-2974.

BEREZOVSKY, Boris Vadimovich; Russian pianist; b. 4 Jan. 1969, Moscow; m. 1989; ed Moscow Conservatoire; London début Wigmore Hall 1988; appeared with Soviet Festival Orchestra, London 1990; recitals in New York, Washington, London, Amsterdam, Salzburg, Moscow, Leningrad, Tokyo, Osaka, etc.; appearances with orchestras including Philharmonia, New York Philharmonic, Philadelphia Orchestra, NDR Hamburg and Danish Nat. Radio Symphony Orchestra; winner Prize of Hope competition, City of Ufa 1985, Gold Medal Int. Tchaikovsky Piano Competition, Moscow 1990. *Recordings:* Chopin Godowsky Etudes 2005. *Telephone:* (495) 241-74-87 (home).

BERG, Adrian, MA, RA, ARCA; British artist; b. 12 March 1929, London; s. of Charles Berg, MD, DPM and Sarah Berg (née Sorby); ed Charterhouse, Gonville and Caius Coll. Cambridge, Trinity Coll., Dublin, St Martin's School of Art, Chelsea School of Art and Royal Coll. of Art; Nat. Service 1947–49; taught at various art schools, especially Central School of Art and Design and Camberwell School of Arts and Crafts 1961–78; Sr Tutor, RCA 1987–88; Hon. Fellow, RCA 1994; several awards and prizes including Gold Medal, Florence Biennale 1973, Lorne Scholarship 1979–80, Major Prize, Third Tolly Cobbold Eastern Arts Asscn Nat. Exhbn 1981 and Third Prize, John Moores Liverpool Exhbns 1980, 1982, First Nat. Trust Foundation for Art Award 1987, First Prize RWS Open Exhbn 2001. *Leisure interests:* imaginative reading, criticism. *Address:* c/o Royal Academy of Arts, Piccadilly, London, W1J 0BD, England. *Telephone:* (20) 7629-2875.

BERG, Christian, DPhil; Danish mathematician and academic; *Professor of Mathematics, University of Copenhagen;* b. 2 June 1944, Haarslev; m. Margrete Vergmann 1967; one s. one d.; ed Univ. of Copenhagen; Assoc. Prof., Univ. of Copenhagen 1972, Prof. of Math. 1978–, Chair. Math. Dept 1996–97, Dir Inst. for Math. Sciences 1997–2002; Pres. Danish Mathematical Soc. 1994–98; mem. Danish Natural Sciences Research Council 1985–92, Royal Danish Acad. of Sciences and Letters 1982– (Vice-Pres. 1999–2005); Gold Medal Univ. of Copenhagen 1970. *Publications:* research monographs: Potential Theory on Locally Compact Abelian Groups (with Forst) 1975, Harmonic Analysis on Semigroups (with Christensen and Ressel) 1984, research papers on potential theory and mathematical analysis. *Address:* Department of Mathematics, Universitetsparken 5, 2100 Copenhagen Ø, Denmark (office). *Telephone:* 35-32-07-28 (office). *Fax:* 35-32-07-04 (office). *E-mail:* berg@math.ku.dk (office). *Website:* www.math.ku.dk/~berg (office).

BERG, Eivinn; Norwegian diplomatist; b. 31 July 1931, Sandefjord; s. of Morten Berg and Ester Christoffersen; m. Unni Berg 1957; one s. two d.; ed Norwegian Coll. of Econs and Business Admin., Bergen, Norway; entered Foreign Service 1957; Attaché and Vice-Consul, Chicago 1957–60; Ministry of Foreign Affairs 1960–63, 1968–70; First Sec. Norwegian Perm. Del. to EFTA/GATT, UN Office, Geneva 1963–66, Head of Dept, EFTA 1966–68; Counsellor of Embassy, Brussels and Norway's Mission to EEC 1970–73; Dir Int. Affairs Norwegian Shipowners Asscn, Oslo 1973–78; Deputy Dir-Gen. Ministry of Foreign Affairs (Dept of External Econ. Affairs) 1978–80, Dir-Gen. 1980–81, State Sec., Ministry of Foreign Affairs 1984–88; Amb. and Perm. Rep. of Norway to NATO 1984–88, to European Union 1989–96; Chief Negotiator European Economic Area 1990–92, for possible accession of Norway to EU 1993–94, for Schengen Agreement 1995–96; Sr Adviser on int. and European affairs to Statoil, Norske Skog, Statkraft; Commdr, Order of the Crown, Belgium 1974, Commdr, Henrique Infante, Portugal 1980, Caballero Gran Cruz al Mérito Civil, Spain 1982, Grand Lion Order of the Lion, Finland 1983, Grand Officier, Order Nat. du Mérite, France 1984, Commdr, Royal Order of St Olav, Norway 1987. *Leisure interests:* golf, sailing, mountain hiking. *Address:* Aasstubben 64, 0381 Oslo, Norway (home). *Telephone:* 22-52-50-08 (home). *Fax:* 22-52-51-88 (home). *E-mail:* eivinnbe@online.no (office).

BERG, Jeffrey (Jeff) Spencer, BA; American arts management agent; *Chairman and CEO, International Creative Management, Inc.;* b. 26 May 1947, LA; ed Univ. of Calif., Berkeley; fmrly Head, Literature Div., Creative Man. Assocs, fmrly Vice-Pres.; Vice-Pres. Motion Picture Dept, Int. Creative Man. Inc. 1975–80, Pres. 1980–85, Chair. and CEO 1985–; mem. Bd of Dirs Oracle Corpn 1997–, Leapfrog Enterprises, Inc., Josephson Int. Inc., Marshall McLuhan Center of Global Communication; Pres. Letters and Science Exec. Bd Univ. of Calif., Berkeley; Co-Chair., Calif. Information Tech. Council; Trustee Univ. of Berkeley Foundation, UCLA Anderson School of Man. *Address:* International Creative Management Inc., 8942 Wilshire Boulevard, Beverly Hills, CA 90211, USA (office). *Telephone:* (310) 550-4000 (office). *Fax:* (310) 550-4100 (office). *Website:* www.icmtalent.com (office).

BERG, Paul, PhD, FAAS; American biochemist and academic; *Robert W.and Vivian K. Cahill Professor Emeritus of Cancer Research, School of Medicine, Stanford University;* b. 30 June 1926, New York; s. of Harry Berg and Sarah Brodsky; m. Mildred Levy 1947; one s.; ed Pennsylvania State Univ. and Western Reserve Univ.; Postdoctoral Fellow, Copenhagen Univ., Denmark 1952–53; Postdoctoral Fellow, Wash. Univ., St Louis, Mo. 1953–54, Scholar in Cancer Research 1954–57, Asst to Assoc. Prof. of Microbiology 1955–59; Prof. of Biochemistry, Stanford Univ. School of Medicine, Stanford, Calif. 1959, Willson Prof. of Biochemistry 1970–94, Chair Dept 1969–74, Dir Beckman Center for Molecular and Genetic Medicine 1985–2001, Robert W.and Vivian K. Cahill Prof. of Cancer Research 1994–2000, now Prof. Emer.; Dir Nat. Biomedical Research Foundation 1994–; Chair. Nat. Advisory Cttee Human Genome Project 1990–92; Dir several cos; Sr Post-Doctoral Fellow of NSF 1961–68; Non-resident Fellow Salk Inst. 1973–83; Foreign mem. Académie des Sciences, France 1981; mem. Inst. Medicine, NAS and several other professional bodies; Pres. American Soc. of Biological Chemists 1974–75; Eli Lilly Prize in Biochemistry 1959, Calif. Scientist of the Year 1963, V. D. Mattia Award 1972, shared Nobel Prize for Chem. 1980, Nat. Medal of Science and other awards and prizes. *Publications:* Genes and Genomes 1991, Dealing with Genes. The Language of Heredity 1992, Exploring Genetic Mechanisms 1997. *Leisure interests:* travel, art and sports. *Address:* Stanford University School of Medicine, Beckman Center, B-062, Stanford, CA 94305, USA (office). *Telephone:* (415) 723-6170 (office). *E-mail:* pberg@cmgm.stanford.edu (office). *Website:* biochemistry.stanford.edu (office).

BERGANT, Boris; Slovenian journalist and broadcasting executive; *Adviser to the Director-General for International Relations and Projects, RTV Slovenija;* b. 19 April 1948, Maribor; s. of Evgen Bergant and Marija Bergant; m. Verena Bergant 1969; one s.; ed Univ. of Ljubljana, Kenyon Coll., USA; fmrly Ed. Foreign Affairs, Ed.-in-Chief of News TV Slovenia; fmr radio journalist; fmr Deputy Dir-Gen. Int. Relations and Programme Cooperation RTV Slovenija, Deputy Dir-Gen. RTV Slovenija 1992–2006, Adviser to Dir-Gen. for Int. Relations and Projects 2006–; mem. Asscn of Journalists of Slovenia (Pres. 1987–91), CIRCOM Regional (Pres. 1990–92, Sec.-Gen. 1993–); mem. Admin. Council European Broadcasting Union 1990–92, 1996–, Vice-Chair. TV Programme Cttee 1993–98, mem. Radio Cttee 1993, Vice-Pres. of Union 1999–; mem. European Inst. for the Media; Tomšičeva Nagrada Prize for Best Journalistic Achievement in Slovenia, awards at Monte Carlo, New York and Leipzig TV festivals. *Leisure interests:* tennis, golf. *Address:* Radio-televizija Slovenija, Kolodvorska 2–4, 1550 Ljubljana (office); Abramova Ulica 8, 1000 Ljubljana, Slovenia (home). *Telephone:* (1) 475-21-51 (office); (1) 256-15-58 (home). *Fax:* (1) 475-21-50 (office); (1) 256-15-58 (home). *E-mail:* boris.bergant@rtvslo.si (office); bergantb@siol.net (home). *Website:* www.rtvslo.si (office).

BERGANZA, Teresa; Spanish singer (mezzo-soprano); b. 16 March 1935, Madrid; d. of Guillermo Berganza and Ascensión Berganza; m. 1st Felix Lavilla 1957; one s. two d; m. 2nd José Rifa 1986; début in Aix-en-Provence 1957, in England, Glyndebourne 1958; has sung at La Scala, Milan, Opera Rome, Metropolitan, New York, Chicago Opera House, San Francisco Opera, Covent Garden, etc.; has appeared at festivals in Edinburgh, Holland, Glyndebourne; concerts in France, Belgium, Holland, Italy, Germany, Spain, Austria, Portugal, Scandinavia, Israel, Mexico, Buenos Aires, USA, Canada, etc.; appeared as Rosina in Il Barbiere di Siviglia, Covent Garden 1967; sung Carmen, at opening ceremony of Expo 92, Seville, also at opening ceremonies Barcelona Olympics 1992, mem. Real Academia de Bellas Artes de San Fernando, Spanish Royal Acad. of Arts 1994; Premio Lucrezia Arana, Premio Extraordinario del Conservatorio de Madrid, Grande Cruz, Isabel la Católica, Harriet Cohen Award, Int. Critic Award 1988; Commdr, Ordre des Arts et des Lettres, Grand Prix de Disque (six times), Grand Prix Rossini. *Film:* Don Giovanni. *Publication:* Flor de Soledad y Silencio 1984. *Leisure interests:* art, music, reading. *Address:* c/o Javier Lavilla, Apartado 118, 28200 San Lorenzo del Escorial, Madrid, Spain (office). *Telephone:* (67) 0237485 (office). *Fax:* (67) 0237489 (office). *E-mail:* info@teresaberganza.com (office). *Website:* www.teresaberganza.com.

BERGARECHE BUSQUET, Santiago, LicenDer; Spanish business executive; *Chairman and CEO, Compañía Española de Petróleos SA (CEPSA);* ed Univ. of Deusto, Bilbao; held several man. positions until becoming Gen. Man. and mem. Exec. Man. Cttee BBVA, apptd Chair. Metrovacesa; Chair. Agromán (following acquisition by Ferrovial Group), later Chair. Ferrovial, subsequently CEO, currently ind. Vice-Chair. Ferrovial Group, mem. Bd of Dirs Gamesa and Vocento and Chair. (non-exec.) Dinamia Ferrovial Group; Chair. (non-exec.) Compañía Española de Petróleos SA (CEPSA) 2008–. *Address:* Compañía Española de Petróleos SA, Campo de las Naciones, Avenida del Partenón 12, 28042 Madrid, Spain (office). *Telephone:* (91)

3376000 (office). *Fax:* (91) 7211613 (office). *E-mail:* webcepsa@cepsa.com (office). *Website:* www.cepsa.com (office).

BERGÉ, Pierre Vital Georges; French business executive; *CEO, Fondation Pierre Bergé Yves Saint Laurent;* b. 14 Nov. 1930, l'Ile d'Oléron; s. of Pierre Bergé and Christiane Bergé (née Sicard); ed Lycée Eugène-Fromentin, La Rochelle; Dir and Ed.-in-Chief La Patrie Mondiale 1949–61; Co-founder and Dir-Gen. Yves Saint Laurent 1961, Pres. 1971–2002, Pres. Yves Saint Laurent of America Inc., New York 1971–2002, Pres., Dir-Gen. Yves Saint Laurent Parfums (merged with Elf-Sanofi) 1987–93; Co-f. Fondation (now Fondaton Pierre Bergé Yves Saint Laurent) 2002, currently CEO; Chair. Asscn of Theatres of the Paris Opera 1988–94, Hon. Pres. 1994–; Pres. Chambre Syndicale du Prêt-à-Porter Des Couturiers et des Créateurs de Mode 1988–93; Goodwill Amb. for UNESCO 1993; Dir Lundis Musicaux de l'Athénée 1977; Admin. Cttee for the Devt and Promotion of Textile and Design, Fondation Cartier Parsons School of Design 1985–, Pres. 1991–; Pres. Inst. Français de la Mode 1985–; Pres. Asscn des Amis de l'Institut François Mitterand 1999–, Médiathèque Musicale Mahler 2000–; Commdr Légion d'honneur, des Arts et des Lettres, Officier Ordre Nat. du Mérite, Order of Orange-Nassau (Netherlands). *Publications:* Bernard Buffet 1957, Liberté, j'écris ton nom 1991, l'Affaire Clovis 1996, l'Inventaire Mitterand 2001, Studies on Pierre Mac-Orlan, Henry de Montherlant, Jean Anouilh, Francis Carco and Jean Giono. *Leisure interest:* modern art. *Address:* c/o Fondation Pierre Bergé Yves Saint Laurent, 5 avenue Marceau, 75116 Paris (office); c/o Médiathèque Musicale Mahler, 11 Bis Rue de Vézelay, 75008 Paris (office); 5 rue Bonaparte, 75006 Paris, France (home). *Telephone:* 1-53-89-09-10 (office). *Fax:* 1-43-59-70-22 (office). *Website:* www.ysl-hautecouture.com; www.bgm.org.

BERGEN, André, MEconSc; Belgian banking executive; *President of the Executive Committee, Executive Director and Group CEO, KBC Group;* b. 1950, Sint-Truiden; ed Univ. of Louvain; joined Econs Research Dept, Kredietbank NV 1977, Foreign Exchange and Treasury Dept, Kredietbank, NY 1979; with Foreign Exchange Advisory Service, Chemical Bank, NY 1980–82; joined Generale Bank, Belgium 1982, mem. Exec. Cttee, Generale (Fortis) Bank 1993–2000; Vice-Pres., Chief Financial and Admin. Officer, Agfa-Gevaert NV, Belgium 2000–01, Deputy Chair. Man. Bd 2001–03; CEO KBC Bank 2003–, also Deputy CEO KBC Group 2003–05, Man. Dir and Deputy CEO 2005–06, Pres. Exec. Cttee, Exec. Dir and Group CEO KBC Group 2006–, mem. Agenda Cttee, Nomination Cttee, mem. Bd Dirs KBC Bank, KBC Insurance; mem. Flemish Architecture Inst. *Address:* KBC Group, Havenlaan 2, 1080 Brussels, Belgium (office). *Telephone:* (2) 429-71-11 (office). *Fax:* (2) 429-44-16 (office). *E-mail:* info@kbc.com (office). *Website:* www.kbc .com (office).

BERGEN, Candice Patricia; American actress and photojournalist; b. 9 May 1946, Beverly Hills; d. of Edgar Bergen and Frances Bergen (née Westerman); m. 1st Louis Malle 1980 (died 1995); one d.; m. 2nd Marshall Rose 2000; ed Westlake School for Girls, Univ. of Pennsylvania; photojournalist work has appeared in Vogue, Cosmopolitan, Life and Esquire. *Films include:* The Group 1966, The Sand Pebbles 1966, The Day the Fish Came Out 1967, Vivre Pour Vivre 1967, The Magus 1968, Getting Straight 1970, Soldier Blue 1970, The Adventurers 1970, Carnal Knowledge 1971, The Hunting Party 1971, T. R. Baskin 1972, 11 Harrowhouse 1974, Bite the Bullet 1975, The Wind and the Lion 1976, The Domino Principle 1977, A Night Full of Rain 1977, Oliver's Story, 1978, Starting Over 1979, Rich and Famous 1981, Gandhi 1982, Stick 1985, Au Revoir les Enfants (Co-Dir) 1987, Miss Congeniality 2000, Sweet Home Alabama 2002, View from the Top 2003, The In-Laws 2003, Sex and the City 2008, The Women 2008. *Television appearances include:* Murphy Brown (series) 1988–98, (Emmy Award 1989, 1990), Mary and Tim 1996, Footsteps 2003, Boston Legal (series) 2005–07. *Publications:* The Freezer (in Best Short Plays of 1968), Knock Wood (autobiog.) 1984. *Address:* c/o William Morris Agency, 1 William Morris Place, Beverly Hills, CA 90212, USA. *Telephone:* (310) 859-4000. *Fax:* (310) 859-4462. *Website:* www.wma.com.

BERGEN SCHMIDT, Ernst Ferdinand; Paraguayan government official and business executive; b. 5 Oct. 1963, Colonia Fernheim (Chaco paraguayo); m. Lucía Ruth Giesbrecht; three c.; has held positions with Tecnoservice SAECA, Inverfin SAECA, Century System SRL, IMAG SRL, Mercotec SRL; fmr Pres. Récord Electric; Minister of Industry and Commerce –2005, of Finance 2005–07, Econ. Adviser to Pres. of Paraguay 2007–. *Address:* Office of the President, Asunción, Paraguay.

BERGER, Albert, LLB; German lawyer and university administrator; *Chancellor, Technische Universität München (TUM);* b. 1962, Munich; ed Ludwig-Maximilians-Universität, Munich; civil servant, Legal Div., Munich Regional High Court 1989–92; Lecturer, Deutsche Privat Finanzakademie AG 1991–92; Prof. of Public Law, Inst. of Law, Armed Forces Univ., Munich 1992–93; lawyer in Personnel and Org. Div., Technischen Universität München (TUM) 1994–95, Head of Personnel Div. 1995–98, Admin Dir Weihenstephan Life and Food Sciences Centre 1998–2003, Chancellor TUM 2006–; Chancellor Rosenheim Univ. of Applied Science 2003–06. *Address:* Office of the Chancellor, Technische Universität München, Arcisstrasse 21, 80333 Munich, Germany (office). *Telephone:* (89) 289-01 (office). *Fax:* (89) 289-22000 (office). *E-mail:* eckenweber@zv.tum.de (office). *Website:* portal.mytum .de (office).

BERGER, Geneviève, PhD, MD; French physician, medical researcher and academic; *Chief Research and Development Officer, Unilever PLC;* b. 1955, Moselle; ed Ecole normale supérieure, Cachan, University of Paris; mem. Scientific Bd Dept of Eng, CNRS 1991–98, Scientific Sec., Treatment and Drugs, Design and Resources Section, CNRS Nat. Cttee Scientific Research 1991–95, Chair. 1995–98, Founder and Researcher Parametric Imaging Lab.

1991–, Dir 1991–2000; Dir-Gen. CNRS 2000–03; Prof. and Hosp. MD, Univ. Pierre et Marie Curie–Paris VI 1996–2008; Head, Dept Biophysics and Nuclear Medicine, Hôtel-Dieu Hosp. 1997–2000; Dir Dept of Bio-Eng, Drugs and Agri-Food, Ministry of Educ., Research and Tech. 1998–2000; Pres. Consultative Cttee Tech. Devt 1999–2000; Pres. Bd of Dirs CNRS Diffusion Soc. 2000–03; Pres. INIST-Diffusion Soc. 2000–03; Pres. FIST Soc. 2000–03; Prof. and Hosp. Practitioner, La Pitié-Salpétrière Teaching Hosp. 2003–08; Chair. Health Advisory Group, EC 2006–08; mem. Bd of Dirs Unilever PLC 2007–08, Chief Research and Devt Officer 2008–; mem. Tech. Programme Cttee IEEE 1990–, Conseil de l'ordre des Palmes académiques 2000, French Research Inst. for Sea Expolitation 2000; Govt Commr Office of Geological and Mining Research 2000; Chair. Health Advisory Bd for Commr of Research, EU 2006–; Hon. Fellow, American Inst. of Ultrasound in Medicine 2006; Chevalier, Légion d'honneur 1988, Commdr des Palmes académiques 2000; CNRS Silver Medal 1994, Yves Rocard Prize 1997, European Grand Prix for Innovation Award 2001. *Address:* Unilever PLC, Unilever House, 100 Victoria Embankment, London, EC4Y 0DY, England (office). *Telephone:* (20) 7822-5252 (office). *Fax:* (20) 7822-5951 (office). *Website:* www.unilever.com (office).

BERGER, Helmut; Austrian actor; b. 1942, Salzburg; ed Feldkirk Coll., Univ. of Perugia, Italy; first film role in Luchino Visconti's Le Streghe 1966. *Films include:* The Young Tigers, The Damned, Do You Know What Stalin Did To Women?, The Garden of the Finzi-Continis, The Picture of Dorian Gray, A Butterfly with Bloody Wings, The Greedy Ones, The Strange Love Affair, Ludwig, Ash Wednesday, Conversation Piece, The Romantic Englishwoman, Orders to Kill, Madame Kitty, Merry-Go-Round, Code Name: Emerald, The Glass Heaven, Faceless, The Betrothed, The Godfather Part III, Once Arizona, Still Waters, Unter den Palmen, Die Haupter Meiner, Honey Baby. *Publication:* Ich (autobiog.) 1998.

BERGER, John; British author and art critic; b. 5 Nov. 1926, London; s. of the late S. J. D. Berger and Miriam Berger (née Branson); ed Cen. School of Art and Chelsea School of Art, London; began career as painter and teacher of drawing; exhbns at Wildenstein, Redfern and Leicester Galleries, London; Art Critic Tribune, New Statesman; Visiting Fellow BFI 1990–; numerous TV appearances including Monitor, two series for Granada; Scenario: La Salamandre (with Alain Tanner), Le Milieu du Monde, Jonas (New York Critics Prize for Best Scenario of Year 1976); George Orwell Memorial Prize 1977. *Plays:* The Three Lives of Lucy Cabrol (with Simon McBurney) 1994, Isabelle (with Nella Bielski) 1998. *Radio:* Will It Be A Likeness? 1996. *Publications:* fiction: A Painter of Our Time 1958, The Foot of Clive 1962, Corker's Freedom 1964, G (Booker Prize, James Tait Black Memorial Prize) 1972, Pig Earth 1979, Once in Europa 1989, Lilac and Flag 1991, To The Wedding 1995, Photocopies 1996, King: A Street Story 1999, Here is Where we Meet 2005, From A to X: A Story in Letters 2008; theatre: Question of Geography (with Nella Bielski) 1984 (staged in Marseille, Paris and by RSC, Stratford), Francisco Goya's Last Portrait (with Nella Bielski) 1989, I Send You This Cadmium Red (with John Christie) 2000; non-fiction: Marcel Frishman 1958, Permanent Red 1960, The Success and Failure of Picasso 1965, A Fortunate Man: The Story of a Country Doctor (with J. Mohr) 1967, Art and Revolution, Moments of Cubism and Other Essays 1969, The Look of Things, Ways of Seeing 1972, The Seventh Man 1975 (Prize for Best Reportage, Union of Journalists and Writers, Paris 1977), About Looking 1980, Another Way of Telling (with J. Mohr) 1982, And Our Faces, My Heart, Brief as Photos 1984, The White Bird 1985 (USA as The Sense of Sight 1985), Keeping a Rendezvous (essays and poems) 1992, Titian: Nymph and Shepherd (with Katya Berger) 1996, Steps Towards a Small Theory of the Visible 1996, The Shape of a Pocket 2001, John Berger Selected Essays (ed. by Geoff Dyer) 2001, Hold Everything Dear: Dispatches on Survival and Resistance 2008; poetry: Pages of the Wound: Poems, Drawings, Photographs 1956–96 1996; translations: (with A. Bostock): Poems on the Theatre by B. Brecht 1960, Return to My Native Land by Aimé Césaire 1969; Oranges for the Son of Alexander Levy by Nella Bielski (with Lisa Appignanesi) 1982. *Address:* Quincy, Mieussy, 74440 Taninges, France (home). *Telephone:* 4-50-43-03-36 (home).

BERGER, Samuel R., BA, JD; American lawyer and fmr government official; *Chairman, Stonebridge International LLC;* b. 28 Oct. 1945, Sharon, Conn.; m. Susan Berger; three c.; ed Cornell Univ., Harvard Univ. Law School; mem. Bar, DC 1971; Legis. Asst to Senator Harold E. Hughes 1971–72, Congressman Joseph Resnick (NY); Special Asst to Mayor John V. Lindsay, New York 1972; Deputy Dir Policy Planning Staff, Dept of State 1977–80; Partner, Hogan & Hartson 1981–97; Asst Dir Nat. Security Presidential Transitional Team 1992; Deputy Asst to Pres. for Nat. Security Affairs 1993–96, Asst 1996–97, Nat. Security Advisor 1997–2001; now Chair. Stonebridge International LLC; Sr Advisor, Lehman Brothers; Int. Strategic Advisor, Hogan and Hartson. *Publications:* Dollar Harvest 1971; numerous articles on int. affairs. *Address:* Stonebridge International LLC, Suite 300 West, 555 13th Street, NW, Washington, DC 20004-1109, USA (office). *Telephone:* (202) 637-8600 (office). *Fax:* (202) 637-8615 (office). *Website:* www.stonebridge -international.com (office).

BERGER, Thomas Louis, BA; American writer; b. 20 July 1924, Cincinnati, OH; s. of Thomas C. Berger and Mildred Berger; m. Jeanne Redpath 1950; ed Univ. of Cincinnati and Columbia Univ. Grad. School; mil. service 1943–46; Assoc. Ed., Popular Science Monthly 1952–53; Distinguished Visiting Prof. Southampton Univ. 1975–76; Visiting Lecturer, Yale Univ. 1981, 1982; Regents Lecturer, Univ. of Calif. at Davis 1982; Dial Fellow 1962; Hon. LittD (Long Island) 1986; Rosenthal Award, Nat. Inst. of Arts and Letters 1965, Western Heritage Award 1965, Ohiona Book Award 1982. *Play:* Other People 1970. *Publications:* Crazy in Berlin 1958, Reinhart in Love 1962, Little Big Man 1964, Killing Time 1967, Vital Parts 1970, Regiment of Women 1973,

Sneaky People 1975, Who is Teddy Villanova? 1977, Arthur Rex 1978, Neighbors 1980, Reinhart's Women 1981, The Feud 1983, Nowhere 1985, Being Invisible 1987, The Houseguest 1988, Changing the Past 1989, Orrie's Story 1990, Meeting Evil 1992, Robert Crews 1994, Suspects 1996, The Return of Little Big Man 1999, Best Friends 2003, Adventures of the Artificial Woman 2004. *Leisure interest:* cooking. *Address:* Don Congdon Associates, 156 Fifth Avenue, Suite 625, New York, NY 10010-7002 (office); 80 Rive Road, Nyack, NY 10960-4902, USA (home). *Telephone:* (212) 645-1229 (office). *Fax:* (212) 727-2688 (office). *E-mail:* doncongdon@aol.com (office).

BERGER PERDOMO, Oscar José Rafael, LLD; Guatemalan politician, business executive, lawyer and fmr head of state; b. 11 Aug. 1946, Guatemala City; m. Wendy Widmann 1967; three s. two d.; ed Liceo Javier, Univ. Rafael Landívar; Founder-mem. Partido de Avanzada Nacional (PAN) 1984; Councillor, Guatemala City 1984–89, Mayor 1990–99; fmr Pres. Federación de Municipios de Centroamérica y Panamá (FEMUCAP), Pres. Asociación Nacional de Municipalidades (ANAM) 1991–93, Pres. Federación de Municipios del Istmo Centroamericano (FEMICA) 1996–97; defeated in presidential elections 1999; left PAN 1999, rejoined 2002, selected as PAN presidential cand. Nov. 2002, won primary elections at head of Gran Alianza Nacional (Gana) Nov. 2003, President 2003–08. *Address:* c/o Partido de Avanzada Nacional (PAN), 7a Avda 10–38, Zona 9 Guatemala City, Guatemala.

BERGGREN, Bo Erik Gunnar; Swedish company executive; b. 11 Aug. 1936, Falun; s. of Tage Berggren and Elsa Höglund; m. Gunbritt Haglund 1962; two s. two d.; ed Royal Inst. of Tech.; metallurgical research and Devt, STORA Kopparbergs Bergslags AB (now STORA), Domnarvet 1962–68, Mill Man., Söderfors 1968–74, Exec. Vice-Pres., Falun 1975–78, Pres. 1984–92, CEO 1984–94, apptd Chair. Bd 1992, Chair. Bd STORA Stockholm 1995–98; Pres. Incentive AB, Stockholm 1978–84; mem. Prime Minister's Special Industry Advisory Cttee 1994–; Chair. Astra; fmr Chair. SAS (Sweden), SAS (Sverige) AB; Vice-Chair. Investor, Fed. of Swedish Industries, Skandinaviska Enskilda Banken; mem. Bd Telefonaktiebolaget L. M. Ericsson, Danisco A/S, Royal Inst. of Tech.; mem. Bd of Dirs Marcus Wallenberg Prize; mem. Int. Council J. P. Morgan & Co. Inc., Robert Bosch Internationale Beteiligungen Advisory Cttee, Royal Swedish Acad. of Eng Sciences, of Forestry and Agric.; Dr hc (Royal Inst. of Tech., Stockholm) (Dalhousie Univ.) 1996; King's Medal 12th Dimension with Ribbon of Order of the Seraphim 1987. *Leisure interests:* the arts, family, music. *Address:* Marcus Wallenberg Foundation, S-791 80, Falun, Sweden.

BERGGREN, Thommy; Swedish actor; b. 12 Aug. 1937; ed The Pickwick Club (pvt. dramatic school), Atelierteatern, Stockholm and Gothenburg Theatre; Gothenburg Theatre 1959–63; Royal Dramatic Theatre, Stockholm 1963. *Plays acted in include:* Gengangaren (Ibsen) 1962, Romeo and Juliet 1962, Chembalo 1962, Who's Afraid of Virginia Woolf? 1964. *Films acted in include:* Pärlemor 1961, Barnvagnen (The Pram) 1962, Kvarteret Korpen (Ravens End) 1963, En söndag i september (A Sunday in September) 1963, Karlek 65 (Love 65) 1965, Elvira Madigan 1967, The Black Palm Trees 1969, The Ballad of Joe Hill 1971, Kristoffers hus 1979, Brusten himmel 1982, Berget på månens baksida (A Hill on the Dark Side of the Moon) 1983, La Sposa americana (The American Bride) 1986, Söndagsbarn 1992, Stora och små män 1995, Glasblåsarns barn 1998, Kontorstid 2003. *Address:* c/o Swedish Film Institute, PO Box 27126, 10252 Stockholm, Sweden.

BERGH, Birger, DPhil; Swedish academic; *Professor Emeritus of Latin, Lund University;* b. 25 June 1935, Luleå; s. of Elsa Bergh and Ragnar Bergh; m. Gunilla Åselius 1958 (divorced 1987); two s. one d.; ed Uppsala Univ.; Asst Prof. of Latin, Uppsala Univ. 1968–75; Prof. of Latin, Lund Univ. 1975–2000, Prof. Emer. 2000–. *Publications:* Critical Editions of St Bridget's Revelations, (Book VII) 1967, (Book V) 1972, (Book VI) 1991, (Book II) 2000, of Mathias Lincopensis' Testa Nucis and Poetria 1996; works on Latin linguistics, studies in Swedish neo-Latin. *Leisure interest:* music. *Address:* Kunt den stores gata 7, 22221 Lund, Sweden (home). *Telephone:* (46) 15-25-06 (home). *E-mail:* birger.bergh@e-bostad.net (home).

BERGKAMP, Dennis; Dutch professional football player (retd); b. 10 May 1969, Amsterdam; m. Henrita Ruizendaal; one s. one d.; striker; played for Ajax Amsterdam 1986–92, Inter Milan 1992–95, Arsenal, London, UK 1995–206, Premiership winner 1998, 2002, 2004, Football Asscn Cup winner 1998, 2002, 2003; player for Holland 1990–2000; fmr all-time leading scorer for Holland; Dutch Player of the Year 1992, 1993, English Player of the Year 1998, English Football Writers' Player of the Year 1998. *Leisure interests:* snooker, golf, reading, films, basketball. *Address:* c/o Arsenal Football Club, Arsenal Stadium, Avenell Road, London, N5 1BU, England.

BERGKAMP, Ger, MA, PhD; Dutch environmental scientist, hydrologist and international organization administrator; *General Director, World Water Council;* ed Amsterdam Univ.; has worked in environmental sciences, hydrology, irrigation and drainage, and soil and water conservation throughout Latin America, the Mediterranean, Africa and S and SE Asia and at int. level since late 1980s; Freshwater Man. Advisor, Wetlands and Water Resources Programme, Int. Union for Conservation of Nature (IUCN—The World Conservation Union) 1997–2008; Gen. Dir World Water Council 2008–. *Address:* World Water Council, Espace Gaymard, 2–4 place d'Arvieux, 13002 Marseille, France (office). *Telephone:* (4) 91-99-41-00 (office). *Fax:* (4) 91-99-41-01 (office). *E-mail:* s.nooij@worldwatercouncil.org (office). *Website:* www.worldwatercouncil.org (office).

BERGLUND, Paavo Allan Engelbert; Finnish conductor; b. 14 April 1929, Helsinki; s. of Hjalmar Berglund and Siiri (Loiri) Berglund; m. Kirsti Kivekäs 1958; one s. two d.; ed Sibelius Acad., Helsinki; violinist, Finnish Radio Symphony Orchestra 1949–56, Conductor 1956–62, Prin. Conductor 1962–71; Prin. Conductor Bournemouth Symphony Orchestra 1972–79, Helsinki

Philharmonic Orchestra 1975–79; Prin. Conductor Royal Stockholm Philharmonic Orchestra 1987–91, Royal Danish Orchestra 1993–96, London Philharmonic 1997; State Award for Music 1972; Hon. OBE. *Recordings:* complete Sibelius symphonies including first recording of Kullervo Symphony 1971–77, Má Vlast (Smetana), Shostakovich Symphonies Nos. 5, 6, 7, 10, 11, many other recordings. *Publication:* A Comparative Study of the Printed Score and the Manuscript of the Seventh Symphony of Sibelius 1970. *Address:* Opus 3 Artists, 470 Park Avenue South, 9th Floor North, New York, NY 10016, USA (office). *Telephone:* (212) 584-7500 (office). *Fax:* (646) 300-8200 (office). *E-mail:* info@opus3artists.com (office). *Website:* www.opus3artists.com (office).

BERGMANN, Barbara Rose, MA, PhD; American economist and academic; *Professor Emerita of Economics, American University;* b. 20 July 1927, New York; d. of Martin Berman and Nellie Wallenstein; m. Fred H. Bergmann 1965; one s. one d.; ed Cornell and Harvard Univs; economist, US Bureau of Statistics, New York 1949–53, New York Metropolitan Regional Study 1957–61; Instructor, Harvard Univ. 1958–61; Sr Research Assoc., Harvard Econ. Research Project 1960–61; Sr Staff Economist, Council of Econ. Advisers, Washington, DC 1961–62; Assoc. Prof., Brandeis Univ. 1962–64; mem. sr staff, Brookings Inst. Washington, DC 1963–65; Sr Econ. Adviser, AID, Washington, DC 1966–67; Prof. of Econs, Univ. of Maryland College Park 1971–88; Distinguished Prof. of Econs, American Univ. Washington, DC 1988–97, Prof. Emer. 1997–; Vice-Pres. American Econ. Asscn 1976; columnist on econ. affairs New York Times 1981–82, Los Angeles Times 1983–; Pres. American Asscn of Univ. Profs 1990–92, Int. Asscn for Feminist Economists 1999; Hon. PhD (De Montford Univ., UK) 1996, (Muhlenberg Coll.) 2000 Carolyn Shaw Bell Award 2004. *Publications:* Projection of a Metropolis (co-author) 1961, The Impact of Highway Investment on Development (co-author), A Microsimulated Transactions Model of the U.S. Economy (co-author) 1985, The Economic Emergence of Women 1986, Saving Our Children from Poverty: What the United States Can Learn From France 1995, In Defense of Affirmative Action 1996, Is Social Security Broke? A Cartoon Guide to the Issues 1999, America's Child Care Problem: The Way Out (co-author) 2002. *E-mail:* bberg@american.edu (office). *Website:* www.american.edu/cas/econ/faculty/bergmann.htm (office).

BERGNER, Christoph, DrAgrar; German politician; *Parliamentary Under-Secretary of State, Federal Ministry of the Interior;* b. 24 Nov. 1948, Zwickau; m.; three c.; ed Univs of Jena and Halle; mem. CDU without office in fmr GDR 1971; Research Asst Inst. of Biochemistry of Plants, Univ. of Halle 1974; mem. Landtag (State Parl.) of Saxony-Anhalt 1990; Vice-Chair. Saxony-Anhalt CDU Asscn 1991–94; Chair. CDU Parl. Party in Landtag 1991–93, 1994–2001; Minister-Pres. of Saxony-Anhalt 1993–94; mem. Bundestag (Fed. Ass.) 2002–; Parl. Under-Sec. of State, Fed. Ministry of the Interior 2005–. *Address:* Deutscher Bundestag, Platz der Republik, 11011 Berlin, Germany (office). *Website:* www.christophbergner.de.

BERGOGLIO, HE Cardinal Jorge Mario; Argentine ecclesiastic; *Archbishop of Buenos Aires;* b. 17 Dec. 1936, Buenos Aires; ordained priest 1969; Bishop 1992; Coadjutor 1997; Archbishop of Buenos Aires 1998–; cr. Cardinal 2001. *Address:* Arzobispado, Rivadavia 415, 1002 Buenos Aires, Argentina (office). *Telephone:* (11) 4343-3925 (office). *Fax:* (11) 4334-8373 (office). *E-mail:* arzobispado@arzbaires.org.ar (office).

BERGONZI, Carlo; Italian singer (tenor); b. 13 July 1924, Busseto, Parma; m. Adele; two c.; ed Parma Conservatory; debut (as baritone) as Figaro (Il Barbiere di Siviglia) at Lecce 1948; debut (as tenor) in title role of Andrea Chénier, Teatro Petruzzelli, Bari 1951; subsequently appeared at various Italian opera houses including La Scala, Milan; US debut in Il Tabarro and Cavalleria Rusticana, Lyric Opera, Chicago 1955; appeared at Metropolitan Opera, New York in Aida (as Radames) and Il Trovatore (as Manrico) 1955–56; appeared at all the maj. opera houses in Europe and also in USA and S America; retd 1994 with occasional appearances thereafter; vocal coach; Midem Classical Lifetime Achievement Award 2009. *Address:* International Creative Management, 10250 Constellation Boulevard, Los Angeles, CA 90067, USA (office); The Decca Music Group, 364–366 Kensington High Street, London W14 8NS, England (office). *Telephone:* (310) 550-4000 (office). *Website:* www.icmtalent.com (office); www.deccaclassics.com (office).

BERGQUIST, Dame Patricia Rose, DBE, PhD, DSc, FRSNZ; New Zealand zoologist and academic; *Professor Emerita of Zoology and Honorary Professor of Anatomy, University of Auckland;* b. 10 March 1933, Auckland; d. of William Smyth and Bertha E. Smyth; m. Peter L. Bergquist 1958; one d.; ed Takapuna Grammar School and Univ. of Auckland; Lecturer in Zoology, Auckland Univ. 1958, Prof. of Zoology (Personal Chair.), 1981, Head of Dept 1986, Asst Vice-Chancellor (Academic) 1989–96, Deputy Vice-Chancellor 1996, Special Asst to Vice-Chancellor 1997–98, Prof. Emer. of Zoology and Hon. Prof. of Anatomy 1999–; Post-doctoral research, Yale Univ. 1961–64; career concentrated on sponge biology, chemistry, chemo-taxonomy; pioneered application of chem. and pharmacology of marine sponges to resolving major questions of sponge phylogeny and relationships; int. consultant in marine sponge taxonomy and marine ecology; Hector Medal, Royal Soc. of NZ 1988. *Publications:* more than 150 articles in professional journals. *Leisure interests:* fishing, classical music. *Address:* 3A Pukerangi Crescent, Ellersie, Auckland 5 (home); Department of Anatomy, University of Auckland, Private Bag 92019, Auckland 1, New Zealand. *Telephone:* (9) 3737599 (office); (9) 5796291 (home). *Fax:* (9) 5796293 (home). *E-mail:* pr.bergquist@auckland.ac.nz (office).

BERGSAGEL, John Dagfinn, PhD; Danish (b. Canadian) musicologist; b. 19 April 1928, Outlook, Sask.; s. of Rev. Dr Knut Bergsagel and Alma Josephine Bergsagel (née Anderson); m. 1st Sondra Rubin 1953 (divorced); 2nd Ingrid Charlotte Sørensen 1965; three s. one d.; ed Gordon Bell High School,

Winnipeg, Man., Univ. of Man., St Olaf Coll., Minn., USA, Cornell Univ., USA, Magdalen Coll. Oxford, UK, RAM, London, UK; Lecturer, Concordia Coll., Minn. 1954–55; Assoc. Prof., Ohio Univ. 1955–59, Exec. Ed. Early English Church Music, Oxford, UK 1961–76; Tutor in History of Music, Oxford Univ. 1962–67, Lecturer, New Coll. 1966–67; Sr Lecturer in Musicology, Manchester Univ. 1967–70; Lecturer in History and Theory of Music, Univ. of Copenhagen 1970–81, Prof. of Musicology 1981–98; Dir Monumenta Musicae Byzantinae, Exec. Bd Foundation for Publishing of Works of Niels W. Gade; Sr Arts Fellow of Canada Council 1959; Gulbenkian Foundation Grant 1961; Fellow, Royal Danish Acad. of Sciences and Letters, Norwegian Acad. of Science and Letters, Academia Europaea (Chair. Musicology Section, mem. Council); Order of Dannebrog. *Publications:* The Collected Works of Nicholas Ludford 1963, Early Tudor Masses I–II 1963, 1976, Engelske Anthems fra det 16. århundrede 1973, Musikk i Norge i Middelalder og Renessanse 1982, Music in Denmark at the Time of Christian IV: Vol. 2, Music for Instrumental Ensemble 1988, Vol. 6, Anonymous Mass and Occasional Motets (with H. Glahn) 1988; numerous articles, contribs to encyclopaedias, translations of many scholarly works. *Address:* Strandvejen 63, 2100 Copenhagen Ø, Denmark. *Telephone:* 39-20-02-02. *E-mail:* jberg@hum.ku.dk (home).

BERGSTEN, C. Fred, MA, PhD; American economist and research institute director; *Director, Peterson Institute for International Economics;* b. 23 April 1941, New York, NY; s. of Dr Carl Bergsten and Halkaline Bergsten; m. Virginia W. Bergsten; one s.; ed Cen Methodist Coll, Fayette, Mo., Fletcher School of Law and Diplomacy, Boston, Mass; Asst for Int. Econ. Affairs, US Nat. Security Council 1969–71; Asst Sec. for Int. Econ. Affairs, US Treasury 1977–81; Dir Inst. for Int. Econs (now Peterson Inst. for Int. Econs) 1981–; Chair. Competitiveness Policy Council 1991–95, Asia-Pacific Econ. Cooperation (APEC) Eminent Persons Group 1993–95; mem. Ind. Task Force on the Future Int. Financial Architecture 2000, Int. Financial Insts Advisory Comm. 2000; Sr Fellow, Council on Foreign Relations 1967–68, Brookings Inst. 1972–76, Carnegie Endowment for Int. Peace 1981; Hon. Fellow, Chinese Acad. of Social Sciences 1997; Chevalier Légion d'honneur 1985; Dept of State Meritorious Honor Award 1965, Dept of Treasury Exceptional Service Award 1981. *Publications include:* America in the World Economy: A Strategy for the 1990s 1988, Pacific Dynamism and the International Economic System (with M. Noland) 1993, Reconcilable Differences? United States-Japan Economic Conflict (with M. Noland) 1993, The Dilemmas of the Dollar (second edn) 1996, Global Economic Leadership and the Group of Seven 1996; Whither APEC? The Progress to Date and Agenda for the Future 1997, No More Bashing: Building a New Japan-United States Economic Relationship 2001, The Korean Diaspora in the World Economy 2003, Dollar Overvaluation and the World Economy 2003, Dollar Adjustment: How Far? Against What? 2004, The United States and the World Economy (ed.) 2005, China: The Balance Sheet 2006; numerous other books and journal articles. *Leisure interests:* photography, basketball, snorkelling. *Address:* Peterson Institute for International Economics, 1750 Massachusetts Avenue, NW, Washington, DC 20036-1903 (office); 4106 Sleepy Hollow Road, Annandale, VA 22003, USA (home). *Telephone:* (202) 328-9000 (office); (703) 256-3802 (home). *Fax:* (202) 659-3225 (office). *E-mail:* kkeenan@petersoninstitute.org (office). *Website:* www.iie.com (office).

BERGSTRÖM, Lars, PhD; Swedish academic; *Professor Emeritus of Practical Philosophy, Stockholm University;* b. 17 July 1935, Stockholm; m. Ulla von Heland 1960; one s.; ed Stockholm Univ.; Assoc. Prof., Lecturer in Philosophy, Stockholm Univ. 1967–74; Prof. of Practical Philosophy, Uppsala Univ. 1974–87; Prof. of Practical Philosophy, Stockholm Univ. 1987–2001, Prof. Emer. 2001–; mem. Royal Swedish Acad. of Sciences 1998–. *Publications:* The Alternatives and Consequences of Actions 1966, Objektivitet 1972, Grundbok i Värdeteori 1990, Döden, Livet och Verkligheten 2004. *Leisure interests:* music, tennis. *Address:* Department of Philosophy, Stockholm University, 106 91 Stockholm (office); Telegrafgränd 1B, 111 30 Stockholm, Sweden (home). *Telephone:* (8) 164209 (office); (8) 6698899 (home). *E-mail:* lars.bergstrom@philosophy.su.se (office). *Website:* www.philosophy.su.se/personal/bergstrom.htm (office).

BERISHA, Kolë; Kosovo politician; b. 26 Oct. 1947, Dobërdol; m.; two c.; fmr high school teacher in Klina; fmrly Sec., Democratic League of Kosovo (LDK), Vice-Pres. 1998–; Pres., Ass. of Kosovo 2006–07; mem. Parl. Group of LDK, Cttee for Rules of Procedure of Ass. *Address:* Kodra e Diellit, Rruga Sali Nivica, 10000 Priština; c/o Office for Media and Publications, Assembly of Kosovo, Rruga Nëna Terezë, Kosovo, 10000 Priština, Serbia. *Telephone:* (38) 211186.

BERISHA, Sali, PhD; Albanian cardiologist and politician; *Prime Minister;* b. 15 Oct. 1944, Tropojë; m.; two c.; ed Univ. of Tirana and studies in Paris, France; worked as cardiologist in Tirana Cardiology Clinic; taught at Univ. of Tirana 1980–90; fmr mem. Albanian Workers' Party; co-f. Democratic Party of Albania (Partia Demokratike e Shqipërisë), Leader 1991–97, Chair. 1991–; mem. Kuvendi Popullor (People's Ass.) 1991–; Pres. of Albania 1992–97; Prime Minister 2005–; mem. Nat. Medical Research Cttee, European Cttee on Medical Scientific Research 1968–. *Publications:* has published several textbooks and scientific articles on cardiology; numerous political articles in newspapers and magazines. *Address:* Office of the Prime Minister, Office of the Council of Ministers, Bulevardi Dëshmorët e Kombit, Tirana, Albania (office). *Telephone:* (4) 229980 (office). *Fax:* (4) 234818 (office). *E-mail:* kryeministri@km.gov.al (office). *Website:* www.keshilliministrave.al (office).

BERKELEY, Michael Fitzhardinge, FRAM, FRWCMD; British composer; b. 29 May 1948, London; s. of the late Sir Lennox Berkeley and of Elizabeth Freda Berkeley (née Bernstein); m. Deborah Jane Coltman-Rogers 1979; one d.; ed Westminster Cathedral Choir School, The Oratory School, Royal Acad. of Music; writer on music and arts for the Observer, Vogue and The Listener 1970–75; presents music programmes (including Proms) for BBC TV 1975–; BBC Radio 3 announcer 1974–79; Dir Britten-Pears Foundation 1996–; mem. Exec. Cttee Asscn of Professional Composers 1982–84, Cen. Music Advisory Cttee, BBC 1986–90; Music Panel Adviser to Arts Council 1986–90; Visiting Prof. Huddersfield Univ. (fmrly Polytechnic) 1991–94; Artistic Dir Cheltenham Int. Festival 1995–2005; Co-Dir Spitalfields Festival 1994–97; Dir Royal Opera House, Covent Garden 1996–2000 (mem. 1994–98, Chair. Opera Bd 1998); Chair. Bd of Govs Royal Ballet 2003–; Composer-in-Asscn BBC Nat. Orchestra of Wales, Welsh Coll. of Music and Drama 2002–; has also composed music for film, TV and radio; The Guinness Prize for Composition 1977, Silver Medal, Worshipful Co. of Musicians 2003. *Major works include:* Meditations for Strings, Oboe Concerto, Fantasia Concertante, Gregorian Variations (orchestra), For The Savage Messiah (piano quintet), Or Shall We Die? (oratorio to text by Ian McEwan), 4 String quartets, Piano Trio, Songs of Awakening Love, Entertaining Master Punch, Clarinet Concerto, Speaking Silence, Baa Baa Black Sheep (opera), Jane Eyre (opera), Viola Concerto, Catch Me If You Can (chamber), Dark Sleep (keyboard), Tristessa (orchestra), The Garden of Earthly Delights (orchestra), Magnetic Field (string quartet), Winter Fragments, Secret Garden (orchestra), Odd Man Out, Entertaining Master Punch, Abstract Mirror (string quartet), Gethsemane (for tenor and ensemble), For You (opera, libretto by Ian McEwan), Gabriel's Lament for orchestra, Piano Quintet. *Publication:* The Music Pack 1994; numerous articles in newspapers and magazines. *Leisure interests:* walking, farming, reading, contemporary painting. *Address:* c/o Oxford University Press, Repertoire Promotion Department, Great Clarendon Street, Oxford, OX2 6DP, England (office). *E-mail:* repertoire.promotion.uk@oup.com (office). *Website:* www.oup.co.uk/music/repprom/berkeley/ (office).

BERKELMAN, Karl, BS, PhD; American physicist and academic; *Professor, Department of Physics, Cornell University;* b. 7 June 1933, Lewiston, ME; s. of Robert and Yvonne Berkelman; m. Mary Hobbie; three s.; ed Univ. of Rochester and Cornell Univ., NY; Research Assoc., Cornell Univ. 1959–60, Asst Prof. 1961–63, Assoc. Prof. 1963–67, Prof. 1967–, Dir Cornell Lab. of Nuclear Studies 1985–2000; NSF Postdoctoral Fellow, Instituto Superiore di Sanita, Rome 1960–61; Visiting Staff Scientist, CERN, Geneva 1967–68, 1981–82, 1991–92, 2000–01; Visiting Staff Scientist, Deutsches Elektronen Synchroton (German Synchrotron Research Centre, DESY), Hamburg 1974–75; Fellow American Physical Soc.; mem. numerous int. scientific cttees at CERN, DESY, Stanford Linear Accelerator Center (SLAC), High Energy Accelerator Research Org. (KEK), Japan. *Publications:* A Personal History of CESR and CLEO 2004; numerous specialist publs on high energy particle physics. *Address:* Department of Physics, Cornell University, 210 Newman Laboratory, Ithaca, NY 14853-2501, USA (office). *Telephone:* (607) 255-4198 (office). *Fax:* (607) 254-4552 (office). *E-mail:* kb25@cornell.edu (office). *Website:* www.physics.cornell.edu/profpages/Berkelman.html (office).

BERKOFF, Steven; British actor, writer and director; b. 3 Aug. 1937, Stepney, London; s. of Alfred Berkoff and Pauline Berkoff; m. 1st Alison Minto 1970; m. 2nd Shelley Lee 1976 (divorced); ed Hackney Downs Grammar School, Webber-Douglas School of Drama. *Films include:* Octopussy, First Blood 2, Beverly Hills Cop, Absolute Beginners, War and Remembrance (TV) 1988, The Krays 1990, Decadence 1994, Rancid Aluminium 2000, Head in the Clouds 2004, Brides 2004, Forest of the Gods 2005. *Plays/Productions include:* Agamemnon (London) 1973, The House of Usher 1974, The Trial 1976, East 1978, Hamlet 1980, 2001, Greek 1980, Decadence 1981, Agamemnon (USA) 1984, Harry's Xmas 1985, Kvetch 1986, 1991 (Evening Standard Award for Comedy of the Year 1991), Sink the Belgrano 1987, Coriolanus 1988, Metamorphosis 1988, Salome 1989, The Trial 1991, Brighton Beach Scumbags 1994; Dir West (London) 1983, Acapulco (LA) 1990, One Man (London) 1993, Coriolanus 1996, Mermaid 1996, Massage (LA and Edinburgh) 1997, Shakespeare's Villains 1998, Messiah 2000 (London 2003), Dir Sit and Shiver (Los Angeles) 2004, Dir Richard II (Ludlow Festival) 2005, Sit and Shiver (London) 2006. *Publications:* America 1988, I am Hamlet 1989, A Prisoner in Rio 1989, The Theatre of Steven Berkoff (photographic) 1992, Coriolanus in Deutschland 1992, Overview (collected essays) 1994, Free Association (autobiog.) 1996, Graft: Tales of an Actor 1998, Shopping in the Santa Monica Mall, Ritual in Blood, Messiah 2000 (Glasgow Herald Golden Angel Award, Edinburgh Festival Fringe First), Oedipus 2000, The Secret Love Life of Ophelia 2001 (Glasgow Herald Golden Angel Award), Tough Acts 2003, My Life in Food 2008. *Leisure interests:* photography, travelling, table tennis, eating. *Website:* www.stevenberkoff.com.

BERLUSCONI, Marina; Italian business executive; *Chairman, Fininvest SpA;* b. ((Maria Elvira Berlusconi)), 10 Aug. 1966, Milan; d. of Silvio Berlusconi; m. Giulio Tassera; one s. and one s. by Maurizio Vanadia; worked in London boutique aged 18; Deputy Chair. Fininvest SpA, Rome 1996–2005, Chair. 2005–; Chair. Arnoldo Mondadori SpA (Italy's largest publishing co.) 2003–; Pres. and mem. Bd Dirs Medusa Film 2001–, Mediobanca SpA 2008–; mem. Bd of Dirs Mediaset SpA, Medusa SpA, 21 Investimenti SpA; ranked by Fortune magazine amongst 50 Most Powerful Women in Business outside the US (ninth) 2001, (ninth) 2002, (seventh) 2003, (ninth) 2004, (sixth) 2005, (seventh) 2006, (seventh) 2007, ranked by Forbes magazine amongst 100 Most Powerful Women (36th) 2004, (74th) 2005, (42nd) 2006, (33rd) 2007, (34th) 2008. *Address:* Fininvest SpA, Via Paleocapa 3, 20121 Milan, Italy (office). *Telephone:* (02) 85411 (office). *Website:* www.fininvest.com (office); www.mondadori.it (office).

BERLUSCONI, Silvio; Italian politician and business executive; *Prime Minister;* b. 29 Sept. 1936, Milan; m. 1st; one d. one s.; m. 2nd Veronica Lari; three c.; ed Univ. of Milan; started building and property devt business aged 26; f. Elinord construction co. 1962; built up Fininvest, major conglomerate with interests in commercial TV, printed media, publishing, advertising, insurance and financial services, retailing and football; worked on Milan 2 Housing project 1969; Canale 5 network began broadcasting 1980; bought Italia 1 TV network 1983, Rete 4 TV network 1984; took stake in La Cinq commercial TV network 1985, Chain, Cinema 5 (largest in Italy); bought Estudios Roma 1986; Milan AC Football Club 1986; La Standa (Italy's largest Dept store chain) 1988; Chair. Arnoldo Mondadori Editore SpA Jan.–July 1990, (half-share) 1991; Founder and Pres. Forza Italia political movt 1993, began full-time political career 1994, declaring he had stepped down from exec. posts in Fininvest, owned 51% of Mediaset (Italy's largest pvt. TV network operator) through Fininvest, reduced stake by one-third 2005; led Forza Italia to win general elections in alliance with Lega Nord and Alleanza Nazionale parties 1994; Prime Minister of Italy April–Dec. 1994, 2001–06, 2008–, also Minister of Foreign Affairs 2002; Founder and Pres. Casa delle Libertà (House of Freedoms) 2002–07, replaced by Popolo della Libertà 2007–; Pres. EU Council July–Sept. 2003; MEP 1999. *Recording:* Meglio 'ne Canzone (album) 2003. *Address:* Office of the Prime Minister, Palazzo Chigi, Piazza Colonna 370, 00187 Rome (office); Fininvest Spa, Via Paleocapa 3, 20121 Milan, Italy. *Telephone:* (06) 67791; (02) 85411. *Fax:* (06) 6788255 (office). *E-mail:* redazione.web@governo.it (office). *Website:* www.governo.it (office); www.fininvest.it; www.casadelleliberta.net.

BERMAN, Gail, BA; American media executive; b. 17 Aug. 1956, Long Island, NY; m. Bill Masters; two c.; ed Univ. of Maryland Coll. of Arts and Humanities; co-produced with Susan Rose first US production of Andrew Lloyd Webber's Joseph and the Amazing Technicolour Dreamcoat, Broadway, New York 1982–83; Supervisor Original Production, HBO's Comedy Channel (precursor of Comedy Central) late 1980s; Head of Sandollar Television, Southern Calif. early 1990s; Pres. and Partner, Regency Television Inc. 1998–2000; Pres. of Entertainment, Fox Broadcasting Co. 2000–05; Pres. Paramount Pictures Corpn 2005–07; ranked by Fortune magazine amongst 50 Most Powerful Women in Business in the US (25th) 2003, (25th) 2004, named No. 5 on Power 100 List, Women in Entertainment Report 2003, Women in Film Lucy Award 2003, ranked by Forbes magazine amongst 100 Most Powerful Women (49th) 2004, (69th) 2005, (90th) 2006. *Plays produced:* Almost an Eagle 1982, Hurlyburly 1984, Blood Knot (co-producer) 1985–86, The Nerd 1987–88. *Television:* Exec. Producer: Someone Like Me 1994, All-American Girl 1994, Social Studies 1997, Buffy the Vampire Slayer 1997, Angel 1999, Firefly 2002, American Idol, 24, That 70s Show. *Address:* c/o Paramount Studios, 5555 Melrose Avenue, Hollywood, CA 90038, USA (office).

BERMAN, Jason (Jay); American music industry executive; fmr Rep. for Warner Music, Recording Industry Asscn of America (RIAA) Bd –1987, Pres. RIAA 1987–92, Chair. 1992–98; Chair. and CEO Int. Federation for the Phonographic Industry (IFPI) 1998–2004; established anti-piracy consultancy, Berman Rosen Global Strategies 2006–.

BERMÚDEZ AMADO, Brig. Gen. Francisco; Guatemalan military officer, government official and diplomatist; *Ambassador to Taiwan;* fmr Brig. Gen., Guatemalan Armed Forces; Minister of Nat. Defence 2006–07; Amb. to Taiwan 2007–. *Address:* Embassy of Guatemala 3/F, 9-1 Lane 62, Tien Mou West Rd, Taipei 11156, Taiwan (office). *Telephone:* (2) 28756952 (office). *Fax:* (2) 28740699 (office). *E-mail:* embaguat.tw@iname.com (office). *Website:* www.geocities.com/WallStreet/Floor/8227 (office).

BERMÚDEZ MERIZALDE, Jaime, PhD; Colombian lawyer, politician and diplomatist; *Minister of Foreign Affairs;* b. 1966, Bogotá; m.; two c.; ed Univ. de los Andes, Univ. of Oxford, UK; with Human Rights Advisory Office 1991–93; Adviser to Minister of Foreign Affairs 1993–94, also coordinator Neighborhood Commissions; pvt communications consultant –2002; Dir Asociación Primero Colombia (political asscn) 2002–06; communications adviser during presidential election campaign of Alvaro Uribe 2002, Presidential Adviser in Communications 2002–06; Amb. to Argentina 2006–07; Minister of Foreign Affairs 2008–; served as UN observer during South African presidential elections 1994. *Address:* Ministry of Foreign Affairs, Palacio de San Carlos, Calle 10a, No 5-51, Bogotá, DC Colombia (office). *Telephone:* (1) 282-7811 (office). *Fax:* (1) 341-6777 (office). *Website:* www.minrelext.gov.co (office).

BERN, Howard Alan, PhD; American biologist and research endocrinologist (cancer); *Professor Emeritus of Integrative Biology, University of California, Berkeley;* b. 30 Jan. 1920, Montreal, Canada; s. of Simeon Bern and Ethel Bern; m. Estelle Bruck 1946; one s. one d.; ed Univ. of California, Los Angeles; mil. service 1942–46; Nat. Research Council Predoctoral Fellow in Biology, UCLA 1946–48; Instructor in Zoology, Univ. of Calif., Berkeley 1948–50, Asst Prof. 1950–56, Assoc. Prof. 1956–60, Prof. of Zoology 1960–89, Prof. of Integrative Biology 1989–90, Prof. Emer. 1990–, Research Endocrinologist, Cancer Research Lab. 1960–; research interests: comparative endocrinology of prolactin, control of prolactin secretion, mammary gland biology, long-term effect of perinatal exposure to hormones; hormones and genital epithelial cell growth, developmental endocrinology and growth of fishes; neurosecretion; Fellow, American Acad. of Arts and Sciences; Foreign Fellow, Indian Nat. Science Acad., Accad. Nazionale dei Lincei (Italy), Acad. of Sciences of Naples; Assoc., Nat. Museum of Natural History, Paris; mem. NAS, American Soc. of Zoologists (Pres. 1967), Int. Soc. of Neuroendocrinology, Endocrine Soc., American Physiological Soc., American Fisheries Soc.; Visiting Prof. at numerous univs; Howard A. Bern Distinguished Lectureship in Comparative Endocrinology, Soc. of Integrative and Comparative Biology 2002–; Hon. mem. Japan Soc. of Comparative Endocrinology, Japan Soc. of Zootechnical Science; Guest of Honor, Int. Symposium on Amphibian and Reptilian Endocrinology, Camerono 2001, Jeju, S Korea 2003; Hon. LLD (Hokkaido) 1994; Hon. PhD (Yokohama) 1997; Hon. DSc (Toho) 2001; Dr hc (Rouen) 1996; Distinguished Teaching Award, Univ. of California, Berkeley 1972, Transatlantic Medal, British Soc. for Endocrinology 1980, Huang-Chan Medal, Hong Kong 1985, Distinguished Service Award, Soc. for the Advancement of Chicanos and Native Americans 1990, Berkeley Citation, Univ. of California, Berkeley 1990, Award of Excellence, Physiology Section, American Fisheries Soc. 1996, Hatai Medal 1998, Beverton Medal 2001, Outstanding Achievement Award, American Inst. of Fisheries Research Biology 2004. *Publications:* A Textbook of Comparative Endocrinology (with A. Gorbman) 1962; co-ed. of six books and author of numerous other publs. *Leisure interests:* collection of art and antiquities. *Address:* Department of Integrative Biology, University of California, Berkeley, CA 94720-3140 (office); 1010 Shattuck Avenue, Berkeley, CA 94707, USA (home). *Telephone:* (510) 642-2940 (office); (510) 524-3480 (home). *Fax:* (510) 643-6264 (office). *E-mail:* bern@berkeley.edu (office).

BERNABÈ, Franco; Italian business executive; *CEO, Telecom Italia SpA;* b. 18 Sept. 1948, Vipiteno/Sterzing (Bozen); s. of Bruno Bernabe and Clara Frigerio; m. Maria Grazia Curtetto; one s. one d.; ed Univ. of Turin; postgraduate fellow, Einaudi Foundation and Prof. of Econs, Univ. of Turin 1973; Sr Economist, Dept of Econs and Statistics, OECD, Paris 1976–78; Chief Economist, FIAT, Turin 1978–83; Asst to Chair. ENI SpA 1983–86, Head of Corp. Planning, Financial Control and Corp. Devt 1986–92, CEO ENI SpA 1992–98; Chair. Telecom Italia SpA 1998–99, CEO 2007–; f. FB Group (investment co.) 1999, Vice-Chair. Rothschild Europe (following merger of financial advisory activities of FB Group with Rothschild Group) 2004–; Ind. Dir (non-exec.) PetroChina 2000–; fmr mem. Bd Dirs Fiat, TNT; apptd by Prime Minister as special rep. of Italian Govt for the reconstruction of Kosovo 1999; Chair. La Biennale di Venezia 2001–03, Mart (Italian museum of modern art) 2004–; mem. Bd Peres Center for Peace, Advisory Bd of Observatoire Méditérranéen de l'Énergie; fmr mem. Advisory Bd Council on Foreign Relations. *Publications include:* Financial Structure and Economic Policy in Italy 1975, Labour Market and Unemployment (with A. Boltho) 1982, Industrial Policies and Industrialization: The Case of the Automobile Industry 1982. *Address:* Telecom Italia SpA, Piazza degli Affari 2, 20123 Milan, Italy (office). *Telephone:* (02) 85951 (office). *Fax:* (02) 85954018 (office). *E-mail:* info@telecomitalia.it (office). *Website:* www.telecomitalia.it (office).

BERNANKE, Ben S., PhD; American economist, academic and government official; *Chairman of the Board of Governors, Federal Reserve System;* b. 21 June 1953, Augusta, Ga; m. Anna; two c.; ed Harvard Univ., Massachusetts Inst. of Tech.; Prof. of Econs and Public Affairs, Princeton Univ. 1985–96, Howard Harrison and Gabrielle Snyder Beck Prof. of Econs and Public Affairs and Chair Econs Dept 1996–2002; fmr Dir Monetary Econs Program, Nat. Bureau of Econ. Research (NBER), fmr mem. Business Cycling Dating Cttee; mem. Bd of Govs, Fed. Reserve System –2005, Chair. 2006–; Chair. Pres.'s Council of Econ. Advisers 2005–06; fmr mem. Montgomery Township Bd of Educ.; Fellow, Econometric Soc., American Acad. of Arts and Sciences; Guggenheim Fellowship, Sloan Fellowship. *Publications:* Principles of Microeconomics (co-author), Principles of Economics (co-author), Macroeconomics (co-author); numerous articles. *Address:* Board of Governors of the Federal Reserve, 20th Street and Constitution Avenue, NW, Washington, DC 20551, USA (office). *Telephone:* (202) 452-3000 (office). *Fax:* (202) 452-3819 (office). *Website:* www.federalreserve.gov (office).

BERNARD, Claire Marie Anne; French violinist; b. 31 March 1947, Rouen; d. of Yvan Bernard and Marie Chouquet; ed Conservatoire Régional de Musique, Rouen and Conservatoire Nat. Supérieur de Musique (CNSM), Paris; began professional career as solo violinist 1965; mem. jury, Tchaikovsky Int. Competition, Moscow 1974; Prof. of Violin at state-run conservatoires and music schools in France; Asst Conservatoire nat. supérieur de musique, Lyon 1990–; mem. contemporary music ensemble "Les Temps Modernes" 1993–; Prof. CNR, CNSM; recordings include works by Khatchaturian, Prokofiev, Barber, Milhaud, Mozart, Haydn and Sarasate; Chevalier, Ordre Nat. du Mérite; First Prize George Enesco Int. Competition 1964 and other awards and prizes. *Leisure interests:* painting, gymnastics, swimming. *Address:* 53 rue Rabelais, 69003 Lyon, France (home).

BERNARD, Daniel; French business executive; *Deputy Chairman, Kingfisher plc;* b. 1946; began career in retail industry; Dir Mammouth and Delta (hypermarket chains) 1975–81; Man. Dir Metro France 1981–89, apptd to Bd of Dirs Metro Int. (Switzerland) 1989; CEO Carrefour SA 1992–98, Chair. and CEO 1998–2005; Founder and currently Pres. Provestis (investment co.); mem. Bd of Dirs Alcatel (ADR) 1997–, Cap Gemini, Compagnie de St Gobain –2006; Chair. Presicarre; Vice-Chair. DIA SA; Deputy Chair. Kingfisher PLC 2006–. *Address:* Kingfisher plc, 3 Sheldon Square, Paddington, London W2 6PX England (office). *Telephone:* (20) 7372-8008 (office). *Fax:* (20) 7644-1001 (office). *Website:* www.kingfisher.co.uk (office).

BERNARD, Desiree Patricia, LLB (Hons); Guyanese attorney-at-law and judge; *Judge of the Caribbean Court of Justice;* b. 2 March 1939, Georgetown; d. of William Bernard and Maude Bernard; one d.; ed Bishops' High School, Georgetown, Univ. of London, UK; solicitor 1963–1979; magistrate 1979–80; Judge (first woman), High Court of Guyana 1980–92; Justice of Appeal 1992–96; Chief Justice (first woman) 1996–2001; Chancellor of the Judiciary (first woman) 2001–05; Judge of the Caribbean Court of Justice (first woman) 2005–; involved in writing laws on equal rights of women and children, property rights of women, discrimination and domestic violence; Founding Pres. Guyana Asscn of Women Lawyers; Founding mem. Conf. on the Affairs and Status of Women in Guyana; Sec. Caribbean Women's Asscn (CARIWA) 1973; fmr Chair. UN Cttee for Convention on Elimination of All Forms of Discrimination Against Women (CEDAW); Chair. Georgetown Legal Aid Clinic 1994, Family Matters and Maintenance Cttee 1996–97; Chancellor of Anglican Diocese 1994; mem. Commonwealth Magistrates and Judges Asscn, Int. Asscn of Women Judges, Commonwealth Lawyers Asscn; Cacique Crown of Honour 1985, Order of Roraima 2002; Hon. LLD (Univ. of the West Indies) 2007; Univ. of Guyana Award for Achievements in Law 1989, Caribbean

Women's Asscn Award 1991, Guild of Grads of Univ. of the West Indies Award, New York Chapter 1992, Bishops' High School Alumni Achievement Award 1999, Caribbean Bar Asscn Award 2001, CARICOM Triennial Award for Women 2005. *Leisure interests:* travel, cricket, promoting women's rights. *Address:* Caribbean Court of Justice, 134 Henry Street, Port-of-Spain (office); 9 Barbados Road, Federation Park, Port-of-Spain, Trinidad & Tobago (home). *Telephone:* 623-9254 (office); 622-3588 (home). *Fax:* 627-8674 (office); 622-4814 (home). *E-mail:* dbernard@caribbeancourtofjustice.org (office). *Website:* www.caribbeancourtofjustice.org (office).

BERNAUER, David W., BPharm; American pharmaceutical industry executive; ed North Dakota State Univ.; joined Walgreen Co. in 1966, Dist Man. 1979–87, Regional Vice-Pres. 1987–90, Vice-Pres. and Treasurer 1990–92, Vice-Pres. of Purchasing 1992–95, Vice-Pres. 1995, Sr Vice-Pres. 1996–99, Pres. and COO 1999–2002, CEO 2002–06, Chair. 2003–07; mem. Bd of Dirs Nat. Asscn of Chain Drug Stores (now Vice-Chair.), Office Depot, Students in Free Enterprise; mem. Bd of Trustees Field Museum, Chicago; Co-Chair. North Dakota State Univ. Coll. of Pharmacy Devt Fund; Hon. DPharm (North Dakota State Univ.); North Dakota State Univ. Distinguished Alumni Award. *Address:* c/o Walgreen Co., 200 Wilmot Road, Deerfield, IL 60015, USA (office).

BERNERD, Elliott; British property developer; *Executive Chairman, Chelsfield Partners LLP;* b. 23 May 1945; s. of the late Geoffrey Bernerd and of Trudie Malawer (née Melzack); m. 1st Susan Elizabeth Lynton 1968 (divorced 1989); two d.; m. 2nd Sonia Ramsay (née Ramalho) 1992; Exec. Chair. Chelsfield PLC (now Chelsfield Pnrs) 1987–, Chair. Duelguide PLC (after taking Chelsfied PLC pvt.) 2004–; Chair. London Philharmonic Trust 1987–94, Wentworth Group Holdings Ltd 1990–, South Bank Foundation 1996–2002, South Bank Bd Ltd 1998–2002, CancerBACUP Benefactor's Scheme 2003–; mem. Bd of Dirs Investment Property Databank (IPD) 2005–. *Leisure interests:* tennis, skiing. *Address:* Chelsfield Partners LLP, 67 Brook Street, London, W1K 4NJ, England (office). *Telephone:* (20) 7290-2388 (office). *E-mail:* ebernerd@chelsfield.com (office). *Website:* www.chelsfield.com (office).

BERNERS-LEE, Sir Timothy John, Kt, OM, OBE, KBE, BA, FRS, FREng; British computer scientist and academic; *Senior Research Scientist and Director of World Wide Web Consortium, Laboratory for Computer Science and Artificial Intelligence, Massachusetts Institute of Technology;* ed Emanuel School, London, Queen's Coll., Oxford; with Plessey Telecommunications Ltd 1976–78; software engineer D.G. Nash Ltd 1978; consultant software engineer CERN June–Dec. 1980, fellowship to work on distributed real-time systems for scientific data acquisition and system control 1984; with Image Computer Systems Ltd, responsible for tech. design 1981–84; began work on global hypertext project (now known as World Wide Web) 1989, launched within CERN 1990, on Internet 1991; joined Lab. for Computer Science (now Lab. for Computer Science and Artificial Intelligence), MIT 1994–, 3Com Founders Chair 1999–; Dir World Wide Web Consortium; Distinguished Fellow British Computer Soc.; Hon. FIEE; Hon. DFA (Parsons School of Design, New York) 1996; Hon. DSc (Southampton Univ.) 1996; Hon. DUniv (Essex Univ.) 1998, (Southern Cross) 1998; Dr hc (Oxford) 2001; Young Innovator of the Year (Kilby Foundation) 1995, ACM Software Systems Award (jtly) 1995, ACM Kobayashi Award 1996, IEEE Computer Soc. Wallace McDowell Award 1996, Computers and Communication Award (jtly) 1996, Duddell Medal, Inst. of Physics 1997, Charles Babbage Award 1998, Mountbatten Medal, Nat. Electronics Council 1998, Royal C Medal 2000, Greatest Briton Award 2004, Millennium Tech. Prize 2004, Charles Stark Draper Prize 2007 and numerous other awards. *Publication:* Weaving the Web: The Original Design and Ultimate Destiny of the World Wide Web by its Inventor 2000. *Address:* Laboratory for Computer Science and Artificial Intelligence, Massachusetts Institute of Technology, Stata Center, Building 32, 32 Vassar Street, Cambridge, MA 02139, USA (office). *Telephone:* (617) 253-5702 (office). *Fax:* (617) 258-5999 (office). *Website:* www.w3.org (office).

BERNES, Thomas Anthony, BA; Canadian international organization official; *Director, Independent Evaluation Office, International Monetary Fund;* b. 21 March 1946, Winnipeg; m. Ann Boyd 1974 (divorced 1997); one s. one d.; ed Univ. of Manitoba; Dir Gen. Trade Policy, Dept of Industry, Trade and Commerce 1981–82, Economic Policy Planning Secr. 1982–83; Head Gen. Trade Policy Div., OECD 1983–85; Dir GATT Affairs, Dept of Foreign Affairs and Int. Trade, Govt of Canada 1985–87; Dir Internal Econ. Relations, Dept of Finance 1987–88, Gen. Dir Int. Trade and Finance Br. 1988–91, Exec. Dir Coordinating Secr. on Canadian Unity, Office of the Deputy Minister 1991–92, Asst Deputy Minister, Int. Trade and Finance Br. 1992–95; G7 Finance Deputy 1995–96; Alt. Gov. for Canada, IMF, Asia Devt Bank, African Devt Bank and Inter-American Devt Bank 1996; Dir Canadian Export Devt Corpn 1996; Exec. Dir IMF 1996–2001; Exec. Sec., Devt Cttee of Int. Bank for Reconstruction and Devt (World Bank) and IMF 2001–05, Dir Ind. Evaluation Office, IMF 2005–. *Address:* Independent Evaluation Office, International Monetary Fund, 700 19th Street, NW, Washington, DC 20431, USA (office). *Telephone:* (202) 623-9980 (office). *Fax:* (202) 623-9990 (office). *E-mail:* tbernes@imf.org (office). *Website:* www.ieo-imf.org (office).

BERNHARD, Sandra; American actress, comedienne and singer; b. 6 June 1955, Flint, Mich.; d. of Jerome Bernhard and Jeanette Bernhard; stand-up comedienne in nightclubs in Beverly Hills 1974–78; Dir HGOCo initiative, Houston Grand Opera 2007–. *Films include:* Cheech and Chong's Nice Dreams 1981, The King of Comedy 1983 (Nat. Soc. Film Critics Award), The House of God 1984, Sesame Street Presents: Follow That Bird 1985, Track 29 1988, Hudson Hawk 1991, Truth or Dare 1991, Inside Monkey Zetterland 1992, Dallas Doll 1994, Museum of Love 1996, The Apocalypse 1997, Plump Fiction 1997, Lover Girl 1997, Exposé 1998, An Alan Smithee Film: Burn Hollywood Burn 1998, Somewhere in the City 1998, Wrongfully Accused 1998, I Woke Up Early the Day I Died 1998, Hercules: Zero to Hero (voice) 1999,

Dinner Rush 2000, Playing Mona Lisa 2000, Zoolander 2001, The Third Date 2003, The Easter Egg Adventure (voice) 2004, Twenty Dollar Drinks 2006, Dare 2009. *Stage appearances (solo):* Without You I'm Nothing 1988, Giving Till It Hurts 1992, I'm Still Here...Damn It! 1998, Everything Bad and Beautiful 2006. *TV appearances:* Without You I'm Nothing 1990, Roseanne (series) 1991–97, Sandra Bernhard: I'm Still Here... Damn It! 1999, The Sandra Bernhard Experience 2001, Silver Lake 2004, The L Word (series) 2005. *Recordings:* albums: I'm Your Woman (co-author 8 songs) 1985, Without You I'm Nothing 1989, Excuses For Bad Behavior (Part One) 1991. *Publications include:* Confessions of a Pretty Lady 1988, Love Love and Love 1993, May I Kiss You on the Lips, Miss Sandra? 1998. *Telephone:* (516) 303-6019. *E-mail:* kennethhartung@comcast.net. *Website:* www.sandrabernhard.com.

BERNHARD, Wolfgang, MSc, MBA, PhD; German automobile industry executive; b. ((Wolfgang Ayerle)), Sept. 1960, Böhen, Landkreis Unterallgäu; ed Maristenkolleg, Mindelheim, Tech. Univ. of Darmstadt, Columbia Univ., NY, USA, Johann Wolfgang Goethe Univ., Frankfurt; Man. Consultant, Mercedes-Benz AG 1990–92, Project Man. 1992–94, Man. for S-Class Ass., Sindelfingen Plant 1994–99, CEO Mercedes-AMG GmbH 1999–2000; Deputy mem. Bd of Man. Daimler-Chrysler AG 2000–02, mem. 2002–04, COO Chrysler Group 2000–04; mem. Bd of Man. and Chair. Volkswagen AG 2005–07; adviser, Cerberus Capital Management LP 2007–. *Address:* Cerberus Capital Management LP, 299 Park Avenue, New York, NY 10171, USA (office). *Telephone:* (212) 891-2100 (office); (212) 891-1558 (office). *Fax:* (212) 891-1540 (office). *E-mail:* media@cerberuscapital.com (office). *Website:* www.cerberuscapital.com (office).

BERNHEIM, Antoine, LèsSc, DenD; French business executive and banker; *Chairman, Assicurazioni Generali SpA;* b. 4 Sept. 1924, Paris; s. of Léonce Bernheim and Renée-Marcelle Schwob d'Héricourt; m. Francine Bernard 1947; one s. one d.; ed Lycée Janson-de-Sailly, Univs of Paris and Grenoble; partner 1954, later Pres., Dir-Gen. Soc. française générale immobilière (fmrly Bernheim Frères et Fils) 1967–72; Man. Partner Lazard Frères et Cie 1967–, Gen. Partner and mem. Exec. Bd Lazard Partners 1984–99, Assoc. Lazard LLC 2000–; mem. Bd of Dirs 1967, Pres., Dir-Gen. La France IARD et Vie 1972; Pres. and Dir-Gen. La France SA 1974–; Pres. and Dir-Gen. Euromarché 1981–91; Vice-Pres. and Dir-Gen. Eurafrance 1984–, Partner 1973–, mem. Supervisory Cttee 1976, Vice-Pres. 1982–95, Pres. 1995–96; Vice-Pres. Generali France Holding 1990–95, 2001–02, Pres. and Dir-Gen. 1996–99; Pres. Euralux 1973–2001; mem. Supervisory Bd then Vice-Pres. Printemps SA 1972; Dir and Vice-Pres. Mediobanca 1988–; mem. Supervisory Bd 1988–, Dir then Vice-Pres. Bd of Dirs LVMH (Louis Vuitton Moët Hennessy) 1992–; mem. Supervisory Bd 1981, Vice-Pres. Pinault-Printemps 1992–93; Pres. Assicurazioni Generali SpA 1995–99, Chair. 2002–; Grand Officier, Légion d'honneur. *Address:* Assicurazioni Generali SpA, Piazza Duca degli Abruzzi 2, 34132 Trieste, Italy (office); 64 avenue Henri-Martin, 75116 Paris, France (home). *Telephone:* (04) 067-1111 (office). *Fax:* (04) 067-1600 (office). *Website:* www.generali.com (office).

BERNIER, Maxime, BCom; Canadian politician and lawyer; b. 18 Jan. 1963, Beauce; s. of Gilles Bernier and Doris Bernier; ed Univ. of Québec, Univ. of Ottawa; called to Québec Bar 1990; fmr Legis. Asst Office of the Deputy Premier of Quebec; Vice-Pres. Standard Life of Canada 2003–05; Man. Corp. and Int. Relations, Comm. des valeurs mobilières du Québec 2003–05; MP 2006–, Minister of Industry 2006–07, of Foreign Affairs 2007–08 (resgnd); mem. Conservative Party of Canada; fmr mem. Bd Montreal Econ. Inst. *Address:* Conservative Party of Canada, 130 Albert St, Suite 1204, Ottawa, ON K1P 5G4, Canada (office). *Telephone:* (613) 755-2000 (office). *Fax:* (613) 755-2001 (office). *Website:* www.conservative.ca (office).

BERNIK, France, PhD; Slovenian academic; b. 13 May 1927, Ljubljana; s. of Franc Bernik and Cecilija Bernik (née Smole); m. Marija Kanc 1956; one d.; ed Univ. of Ljubljana; teaching asst in Slovene Literature, Univ. of Ljubljana 1951–57; Ed., Sec. Slovenska Matica, Ljubljana 1961–71; affiliated with Slovenian Acad. of Sciences and Arts Research Centre 1972–99; Scientific Adviser Inst. for Slovene Literature and Literary Sciences 1977–99, Assoc. mem. 1983, mem. 1987, Pres. Slovenian Acad. of Sciences and Arts 1992–2002; lecturer, Visiting Prof. at various univs; Soc. for Slovene Studies, Bloomington, USA 1992, mem., Senator Academia Scientiarum et Artium Europaea, Salzburg 1993; mem. Croatian Acad. of Sciences and Arts 1994, Int. Acad. of Energy 1997, L'Accad. del Mediterraneo 1999, numerous editorial bds; Hon. mem. Slovenian Acad. of Sciences and Arts 2003; Eques commendator Ordinis sancti Gregorii Magni 1997, Golden Hon. Decoration of Freedom of Repub. of Slovenia 1997, Maréchal Ordre de Saint Fortunat 2001; Dr hc (Maribor) 2000; Int. Cultural Diploma of Honour 1996, Zois Award of Repub. of Slovenia 1999. *Publications:* The Lyrics of Simon Jenko 1962, Cankar's Early Prose 1976, Simon Jenko 1979, Problems of Slovene Literature 1980, Typology of Cankar's Prose 1983, Ivan Cankar: A Monograph 1987, Slovene War Prose 1941–80 1988, Studies on Slovene Poetry 1993, Slowenische Literatur im europäischen Kontext 1993, Ivan Cankar: Ein slowenischer Schriftsteller des europäischen Symbolismus 1997, Horizons of Slovenian Literature 1999, Ed.-in-Chief Collected Works of Slovene Poets and Writers 1981–. *Address:* c/o Slovenian Academy of Sciences and Arts, Novi trg 3, 1000 Ljubljana (office); Zidovska 1, 1000 Ljubljana, Slovenia (home). *Telephone:* (1) 4706151 (office); (1) 4250365 (home). *Fax:* (1) 4253423 (office). *E-mail:* jerka.kern@sazu.si (office). *Website:* www.sazu.si (office).

BERNINI, Giorgio; Italian politician, lawyer and university lecturer; b. 9 Nov. 1928, Bologna; ed Univ. of Bologna; Lecturer in Commercial Law, Univ. of Bologna; fmr adviser to EC (now EU) and Italian Govt on questions of int. commercial law, customs tariffs and tech. transfer; entered politics 1994, Forza Italia Senator 1994–; Minister for Foreign Trade 1994–95; Chair. Int. Council for Arbitration. *Publications:* articles in specialized journals and in daily newspapers. *Address:* c/o Forza Italia, Via dell'Umiltà 48, 00187, Rome, Italy.

BERNSTEIN, Baron (Life Peer), cr. 2000, of Craigweil in the County of West Sussex; **Alexander Bernstein;** British business executive; b. 15 March 1936; s. of the late Cecil Bernstein and of Myra Ella Lesser; m. 1st Vanessa Anne Mills 1962 (divorced 1993); one s. one d.; m. 2nd Angela Mary Serota 1995; ed Stowe School, St John's Coll. Cambridge; Man. Dir Granada TV Rental Ltd 1964–68, Chair. 1977–86; Jt Man. Dir Granada TV Ltd 1971–75; Chair. Granada Group PLC 1979–96 (Dir 1964–96); acquired Forte PLC 1996; Dir Waddington Galleries 1966–; Trustee Civic Trust for the North-West 1964–86, Granada Foundation 1968–, Theatres Trust 1996–2000, Trusthouse Charitable Foundation 1996–; Chair. Royal Exchange Theatre 1983–94 (Deputy Chair. 1980–83), Old Vic Theatre Trust 1998–2002; mem. Nat. Theatre Devt Council 1996–98; mem. of Court, Univ. of Salford 1976–87, Univ. of Manchester 1983–98; Hon. DLitt (Salford) 1981; Hon. LLD (Manchester) 1996. *Leisure interests:* looking at paintings, reading, skiing, gardening. *Address:* c/o House of Lords, London, SW1A 0PW, England.

BERNSTEIN, Carl, LLD; American journalist and author; b. 14 Feb. 1944, Washington; s. of Alfred Bernstein and Sylvia Walker; m. Nora Ephron 1976 (divorced); two s.; ed Univ. of Maryland and Boston Univ.; copyboy, reporter, Washington Star 1960–65; reporter Elizabeth (NJ) Journal 1965–66, Washington Post 1966–77; Washington bureau chief, ABC 1979–81; corresp. ABC News, New York 1981–84; Corresp., contrib. Time Magazine 1990–91; Visiting Prof. New York Univ. 1992–93; Exec. Vice-Pres. and Exec. Dir Voter.com –2001; contributing ed. Vanity Fair 1997–; frequent political commentator on network TV; fmr rock and music critic for the Washington Post; Drew Pearson Prize for investigative reporting of Watergate 1972, George Polk Memorial Award and other awards for journalism. *Publications:* All the President's Men (with Bob Woodward) (Pulitzer Prize 1977) 1974, The Final Days (with Bob Woodward) 1976, Loyalties: A Son's Memoir 1989, His Holiness: John Paul II and the Hidden History of Our Time (with Marco Politi) 1996, A Woman in Charge: the Life of Hillary Rodham Clinton 2007; numerous articles in The New Republic, Rolling Stone, The New York Times, Newsweek and Der Spiegel. *Address:* c/o Knopf Publishing/Author Mail, 1745 Broadway, New York, NY 10019, USA (office). *Website:* www.randomhouse.com/knopf (office).

BERNSTEIN, Robert Louis; American publisher; b. 5 Jan. 1923, New York, NY; s. of Alfred Bernstein and Sylvia Bernstein; m. Helen Walter 1950; three s.; ed Harvard Univ.; US Army Air Force 1943–46; with Simon & Schuster (book publrs) 1946–57, Gen. Sales Man. 1950–57; Random House Inc. 1958–61, Vice-Pres. (Sales) 1961–63, First Vice-Pres. 1963–65, Pres. and CEO 1966–89, Chair. 1975–89; Publr at Large, Adviser John Wiley & Sons Inc. 1991–98; Vice-Chair. Asscn of American Publrs 1970–72, Chair. 1972–73; Chair. Asscn of American Publrs Cttee on Soviet-American Publishing Relations 1973–74, on Int. Freedom to Publish 1975; Chair. US Helsinki Watch Cttee, New York, 1979–92, Founding Chair. 1992; Chair. Fund for Free Expression 1975–90, Founding Chair. 1990; Founding Chair. Human Rights Watch 1975–, now Emer. Bd Mem.; Co-Chair. Human Rights in China 1999–; fmr mem. Council on Foreign Relations, Nat. Advisory Cttee Amnesty Int.; mem. Americas Watch, Asia Watch, Middle East Watch, Africa Watch, Advisory Cttee Carter-Menil Human Rights Foundation, Advisory Bd Robert F. Kennedy Foundation Human Rights Award, Int. Liberal Education Bd Bard Coll.; Vice-Pres. Bd of Dirs Aaron Diamond Foundation, The Century Asscn; Hon. LLD (New School for Social Research) 1991, (Hofstra) 1998; Human Rights Award (Lawyers' Cttee for Human Rights) 1987, Spirit of Liberty Award for the American Way 1989, Barnard Medal of Distinction, Barnard Coll. 1990, Liberty Award, Brandeis Univ. 1994, Eleanor Roosevelt Human Rights Award 1998 and other awards. *Leisure interests:* skiing, tennis, swimming. *Address:* 277 Park Avenue, 49th Floor, New York, NY 10172-0003, USA (office). *E-mail:* r.l.bernstein@att.net (home).

BERNSTEN, Thorbjørn; Norwegian politician and trade union official; b. 15 April 1935, Oslo; m. Adda Bernsten; ed Tech. Coll., Officers' Training School; with Nylands Shipyard 1951–66; Information Sec. Norwegian Union of Iron and Metalworkers, Leader 1965–66; Leader Akers mek. Verksted AS 1962–64; Chair., later Deputy Chair. Oslo Municipal Consultative Cttee for Trade and Industry 1969–83; Deputy Chair. Labour Party 1989; Minister of the Environment 1990–97; mem. Cttee of Reps Oslo Labour Party 1962 (Chair. 1976–82), Standing Cttee on Local Govt and the Environment 1973– (Chair. 1989–90), Storting (Parl.) 1977–. *Address:* c/o Det Norske Arbeiderpartei, Youngstorget 2, P.O. Box 8743, 0028 Oslo, Norway.

BERRESFORD, Susan Vail; American foundation executive; b. 1943, New York, NY; ed The Brearley School, Vassar Coll., Radcliffe Coll.; Program Officer, Neighborhood Youth Corps 1965–67; Manpower Career Devt Agency 1967–68; Project Asst Div. of Nat. Affairs, Ford Foundation 1970–72, Program Officer 1972–80, Officer in charge of Women's Programs 1980–81, Vice-Pres. US and Int. Affairs Programs 1981, Vice-Pres. Program Div. in charge of Worldwide Programming, then Exec. Vice-Pres. and COO, Pres. and mem. Bd of Trustees 1996–2007; Visiting Philanthropist, New York Community Trust 2008–; fmr mem. Bd of Dirs Council on Foundations, Chase Manhattan Bank, Chase Manhattan Corpn, Hermine and Robert Popper Foundation; mem. American Acad. Arts and Sciences, Council on Foreign Relations, N American Cttee Trilateral Comm.; Leadership for Equity and Diversity (LEAD) Award 1997, ranked by Forbes magazine amongst 100 Most Powerful Women (72nd) 2004, (93rd) 2005, (77th) 2006, Work Life Legacy Award 2005. *Address:* New York Community Trust, 909 Third Avenue, 22nd Floor, New York, NY 10022, USA (office). *Telephone:* (212) 686-0010 (office). *Website:* www.nycommunitytrust.org (office).

BERRI, Nabih, BA, LLM; Lebanese politician; *President of Majlis Alnwab;* b. 28 Jan. 1938, Freetown, Sierra Leone; s. of Mustaha Berri; m. 1st; six c.; m. 2nd; ed Ecole de la Sagesse, Beirut, Lebanese Univ., Faculte de Droit, Sorbonne, Paris, France; Pres. Nat. Fed. of Lebanese Students (UNUL), Sorbonne, Paris 1963; lawyer, Court of Appeals, Beirut 1963; joined resistance movt of Imam Moussa Al-Sadr against Israeli occupation of S Lebanon 1975; Head of Amal Movt (militia) 1984–; Minister for Reconstruction of S Lebanon 1984–85; exile in Syria 1986; Minister of Justice, of Hydraulic and Electric Energy Resources, of Housing and Cooperatives 1989–92; Pres. Majlis Alnwab (Nat. Ass.) 1992–. *Address:* Majlis Alnwab, Beirut, Lebanon (office). *E-mail:* nberri@lp.gov.lb (office). *Website:* www.lp.gov.lb (office).

BERRIDGE, Sir Michael (John), Kt, PhD, FRS; British biologist and academic; *Head, Signalling Programme, Babraham Institute, University of Cambridge;* b. 22 Oct. 1938, Gatooma, Rhodesia (now Zimbabwe); s. of George Kirton Berridge and Stella Elaine Hards; m. Susan Graham Winter 1965; one s. one d.; ed Univ. Coll. of Rhodesia and Nyasaland, Univ. of Cambridge; Post-doctoral Fellow, Univ. of Virginia 1965–66; Post-doctoral Fellow, Case Western Reserve Univ. 1966–67, Research Assoc. 1967–69; Sr Scientific Officer, Unit of Invertebrate Chemistry and Physiology, Univ. of Cambridge 1969–72, Prin. Scientific Officer 1972–78, Sr Prin. Scientific Officer, Unit of Insect Neurophysiology and Pharmacology 1978–90, Hon. Prof. of Cell Signalling 1994–; Deputy Chief Scientific Officer, Lab. of Molecular Signalling, Babraham Inst., Cambridge 1990–, Head of Signalling Programme 1996–; mem. Soc. of Gen. Physiologists, Acad. Europaea 1989–, European Molecular Biology Org. 1991–; Acad. of Medical Sciences 1998; Hon. mem. Japanese Biochemical Soc.; Hon. Life mem. Soc. for Experimental Biology; Hon. mem. American Physiological Soc. 1992; mem. NAS 1999; Foreign Hon. mem. American Acad. of Arts and Science 1999; mem. numerous editorial bds including Biochemical Journal 1987–, Journal of Endocrinology 1989–, Molecular Biology of the Cell 1989–, Advances in Second Messenger and Phosphoprotein Research 1990–, Journal of Basic and Clinical Physiology and Pharmacology 1990–, Journal of Experimental Biology 1993–; Advisory Ed. BioEssays 1994–; Foreign Corresp., Acad. Royale de Médecine de Belgique 1994–; Fellow Trinity Coll. Cambridge 1972–; Hon. Fellow Gonville and Caius Coll. Cambridge 1998; Trustee, Isaac Newton Trust 1991–2000; has given numerous memorial lectures; Gov. Strangeways Research Lab. 1987–98; main area of research concerns the mode of action of hormones and neurotransmitters at the cellular level; Dr hc (Limburgs Universitaire Centrum, Belgium) 1993; numerous prizes, awards and medals including Feldberg Prize 1984, King Faisal Int. Prize in Science 1986, Louis Jeantet Prize in Medicine 1986, William Bate Hardy Prize, Cambridge Philosophical Soc. 1987, Gairdner Foundation Int. Award 1988, Baly Medal, Royal Coll. of Physicians 1989, Albert Lasker Basic Medical Research Award 1989, Royal Medal, Royal Soc. 1991, Dr H.P. Heineken Prize for Biochemistry and Biophysics 1994, Wolf Foundation Prize in Medicine, Israel 1995, Massry Prize, USA 1996, Ernst Schering Prize 1999. *Publications:* more than 100 scientific papers. *Leisure interests:* gardening, golf. *Address:* Laboratory of Molecular Signalling, The Babraham Institute, Babraham Hall, Babraham, Cambridge, CB2 4AT, England (office). *Telephone:* (1223) 496621 (office); (1223) 496033. *E-mail:* michael.berridge@bbsrc.ac.uk (office). *Website:* www.babraham.ac.uk.

BERROU, Claude; French electrical engineer and academic; *Professor, Electronics Department, École Nationale Supérieure des Télécommunications de Bretagne;* b. 23 Sept. 1951, Penmarc'h; joined École Nationale Supérieure des Télécommunications de Bretagne (now Telecom Bretagne) 1978, currently Prof., Electronics Dept; mem. Acad. des sciences 2007; Fellow, IEEE 2008; SEE Médaille Ampère 1997, IEEE (Information Theory) Golden Jubilee Award for Technological Innovation 1998, IEEE Richard W. Hamming Medal 2003, Grand Prix France Télécom de l'Acad. des sciences 2005, Marconi Prize, Marconi Foundation 2005. *Achievements include:* co-inventor with Alain Glavieux in 1991 (and Punya Thitimajshima who developed later similar methods published in a doctorate thesis when he was a student in the same research lab) of groundbreaking quasi-optimal error-correcting coding scheme called Turbo codes. *Publications:* Codage de canal – des bases théoriques aux turbocodes (Channel encoding – from theoretical grounds to turbocodes; co-author) 2005, Codes et turbocodes (Codes and turbocodes; co-author) 2007; several book chapters and more than 80 scientific papers in professional journals on algorithm/silicon interaction, electronics and digital communications at large, error correction codes, turbo codes and iterative processing, soft-in/soft-out (probabilistic) decoders; author or co-author of eight registered patents. *Address:* École Nationale Supérieure des Télécommunications de Bretagne, CS 83818, 29238 Brest Cedex 3, France (office). *Telephone:* (2) 29-00-13-06 (office). *Fax:* (2) 29-00-11-84 (office). *E-mail:* claude.berrou@telecom-bretagne.eu (office). *Website:* www.telecom-bretagne.eu (office); perso.enst-bretagne.fr/claudeberrou (office).

BERRUGA FILLOY, Enrique, BA, MA; Mexican business executive, writer and fmr diplomatist; *Vice-President of Corporate Affairs and Communication, Grupo Modelo;* ed El Colegio de México, Johns Hopkins Univ., USA, Instituto Tecnológico Autónomo de México; began career in Foreign Service 1984; Press Attaché, Mexican Embassy, Washington DC 1986–89; Sec., Political Affairs, Mexican Embassy in UK 1989–90; Chargé d'affaires ad hoc in Embassy in Ireland 1991; Sec. Gen., Mexican Comm. UNESCO 1993; Chief of Staff to Minister of Foreign Affairs 1993–97; Dir –Gen. Int. Affairs Div., Ministry of Educ. 1994; Personal Rep. of Pres. Mexico for Reform of UN 1995–97; Amb. to Costa Rica 1997–99; Exec. Dir Mexican Inst. Int. Cooperation 1999–2000; Undersecretary of Foreign Affairs 2000–03; Perm. Rep. to UN, New York 2003–07; Vice-Pres. of Corp. Affairs and Communication, Grupo Modelo 2007–; columnist El Universal (daily newspaper). *Publications include:* novels: Destino los Pinos 1982, El Martes del Silencio 1995, Propiedad Ajena

2000 (translated as Foreign Property 2003); numerous articles and papers. *Address:* Grupo Modelo, Campos Elíseos #400, 8th Floor, Colonia Lomas de Chapultepec 11000 México, D.F., Mexico (office). *Telephone:* (55) 5283-3600 (office). *Fax:* (55) 5280-6718 (office). *Website:* www.gmodelo.com.mx (office).

BERRUTI, Azucena; Uruguayan lawyer, human rights advocate and politician; b. 1929; Sec.-Gen. City Admin of Montevideo 1980s; mem. Partido del Sol (PS); Minister of Nat. Defence 2005–08. *Address:* c/o Ministry of National Defence, Edif. General Artigas, Avda 8 de Octubre 2628, Montevideo, Uruguay (office).

BERRY, Lord of Hastingleigh Brian Joe Lobley, BSc, MA, PhD, FBA, FAAS; American/British geographer, academic, political economist and policy analyst; *Lloyd Viel Berkner Regental Professor and Professor of Political Economy, University of Texas at Dallas;* b. 16 Feb. 1934, Sedgley, Staffs., UK; s. of Joe Berry and Gwendoline Alice Berry (née Lobley); m. Janet E. Shapley 1958; one s. two d.; ed Univ. Coll., London and Univ. of Washington; Asst Prof., then Prof. Univ. of Chicago 1958–76; Faculty mem. Brookings Inst. 1966–76; Prof. Harvard Univ. 1976–81; Prof. and Dean, School of Urban and Public Affairs, Carnegie Mellon Univ. 1981–86; Prof. Univ. of Tex. at Dallas 1986–, Lloyd Viel Berkner Regental Prof. and Prof. of Political Economy 1991–; mem. NAS (mem. Council 1999–2002), Asscn of American Geographers (Pres. 1978–79), American Inst. of Certified Planners, Regional Science Asscn Int.; founding mem. Acad. of Medicine, Eng and Science of Texas; Fellow, Univ. Coll. London 1983, American Acad. of Arts and Sciences, American Asscn for Advanced Science, Texas Acad. of Medicine, Engineering and Science, Weimar School of Land Econs, Inst. of British Geographers, Royal Geographical Soc.; Hon. AM (Harvard) 1976; Anderson Medal, Asscn of American Geographers 1987, Victoria Medal, Royal Geographical Soc. 1988, Rockefeller Prize 1991, and others. *Publications:* more than 500 books, articles and other professional publs. *Leisure interests:* family history, genealogy, travel, pseudonymous novelist. *Address:* School of Social Sciences GR31, University of Texas-Dallas, PO Box 83-0688, Richardson, TX 75083 (office); 2404 Forest Ct., McKinney, TX 75070, USA (home). *Telephone:* (972) 883-2041 (office); (972) 562-1058 (home). *Fax:* (972) 883-6297 (office); (972) 562-1058 (home). *E-mail:* brian.berry@utdallas.edu (office). *Website:* www.utdallas.edu/dept/socsci/faculty/bberry.html (office).

BERRY, Charles (Chuck) Edward Anderson; American singer and composer; b. 18 Oct. 1926, St Louis; m. Thermetta Suggs 1948; four c.; popular artiste in rock and roll, plays guitar, saxophone, piano; concert and TV appearances 1955–; Grammy Award for Life Achievement 1984. *Albums:* After School Sessions 1958, One Dozen Berrys 1958, New Juke Box Hits 1960, Chuck Berry 1960, More Chuck Berry 1960, On Stage 1960, You Can Never Tell 1964, Greatest Hits 1964, Two Great Guitars 1964, Chuck Berry in London 1965, Fresh Berrys 1965, St Louis to Liverpool 1966, Golden Hits 1967, At the Fillmore 1967, Medley 1967, In Memphis 1967, Concerto in B Goods 1969, Home Again 1971, The London Sessions 1972, Golden Decade 1972, St Louis to Frisco to Memphis 1972, Let the Good Times Roll 1973, Golden Decade (Vol. II) 1973, (Vol. V) 1974, Bio 1973, Back in the USA 1973, I'm a Rocker 1975, Chuck Berry 75 1975, Motorvatin' 1976, Rockit 1979, Chess Masters 1983, The Chess Box 1989, Missing Berries 1990, Rarities 1990, On the Blues Side 1993, Anthology 2000. *Films:* Go, Johnny Go, Rock, Rock, Rock 1956, Jazz on a Summer's Day 1960, Let the Good Times Roll 1973, Hail! Hail! Rock 'n' Roll 1987. *Publication:* Chuck Berry: The Autobiography 1987. *Website:* www.chuckberry.com.

BERRY, Halle; American actress and model; b. 14 Aug. 1966, Cleveland, Ohio; d. of Jerome Berry and Judith Berry (née Hawkins); m. 1st David Justice 1993 (divorced 1996); m. 2nd Eric Benet 2001(divorced 2005); pnr Gabriel Aubry; one d.; ed Cuyahoga Community Coll., Cleveland; began competing in formal beauty contests 1980s, won title Miss Ohio 1986; mem. Nat. Breast Cancer Coalition; Harvard Foundation for Intercultural and Race Relations Award. *Films:* Strictly Business 1991, Jungle Fever 1991, The Last Boy Scout 1991, Boomerang 1992, Father Hood 1993, Alex Haley's Queen 1993, The Program 1993, The Flintstones 1994, Losing Isaiah 1995, The Rich Man's Wife 1996, Executive Decision 1996, Race the Sun 1996, Girl 6 1996, B.A.P.S. 1997, Why Do Fools Fall in Love 1998, The Wedding 1998, Bulworth 1998, Victims of Fashion 1999, Ringside 1999, Introducing Dorothy Dandridge (also producer) (Golden Globe for Best Actress, Screen Actors' Guild Award) 1999, X-Men 2000, Swordfish 2001, Monster's Ball (Acad. Award for Best Actress 2002) 2001, James Bond: Die Another Day (Nat. Asscn for the Advancement of Colored People–NAACP Award for Best Supporting Actress 2003) 2002, X-Men 2 2003, Gothika 2003, Catwoman 2004, Robots (voice) 2005, X-Men: The Last Stand 2006, Perfect Stranger 2007, Things We Lost in the Fire 2007. *Television:* TV debut with sitcom Living Dolls 1989, Knots Landing 1991–92, Their Eyes Were Watching God 2005. *Address:* c/o Vincent Cirrincione Associates, 8721 Sunset Blvd., Suite 205, Los Angeles, CA 90069 (office); c/o ICM, 8942 Wilshire Blvd, Beverly Hills, CA 90211, USA (office). *Telephone:* (310) 854-0533 (office). *Fax:* (310) 854-0558 (office). *E-mail:* info@vincentcirrincione.com (office).

BERRY, L(eonard) Michael; Canadian diplomatist; *Director, Pacific Pilotage Authority;* b. 28 Sept. 1937, Bolton, UK; s. of Leonard Berry and Margaret (née Wynne) Berry; m. 1st Linda Kathleen Randal 1963 (deceased); one s. two d.; m. 2nd Anna Sumanti Gill 2002; ed McGill Univ.; entered Canadian Dept of External Affairs 1964, served in Berlin 1966–68 and London 1971–75; High Commr in Singapore 1979–82; Amb. to OECD 1988–91; High Commr in Australia 1991–95; Canadian Special Co-ordinator for the Reconstruction of Former Yugoslavia 1995–97; Diplomat-in-Residence Malaspina Univ., BC 1997–99; Int. Adviser, Berry Assocs 1999–; Dir Port of Nanaimo Authority 2002–05, Pacific Pilotage Authority 2005–; mem. Bd British Columbia Centre for Int. Educ. *Leisure interests:* skiing, golf, cricket, music, investment. *Address:* 541 St Andrew's Road, Qualicum Beach, BC V9K 1L5, Canada. *Telephone:* (250) 752-9360 (office); (250) 752-9360 (home). *Fax:* (250) 752-9372 (office); (250) 752-9360 (home). *E-mail:* lmichaelberry@shaw.ca (office); michaelberry541@hotmail.com (home).

BERRY, Mary Frances, PhD; American lawyer, historian and academic; *Geraldine R. Segal Professor of American Social Thought and Professor of History, University of Pennsylvania;* b. 17 Feb. 1938, Nashville; d. of George Ford and Frances Southall; ed ed. Howard Univ., Univ. of Michigan; Asst Prof. of History, Cen. Mich. Univ., Mount Pleasant 1966–68; Asst Prof. Eastern Mich. Univ., Ypsilanti 1968–69, Assoc. Prof. 1969–70; Acting Dir Afro-American Studies, Univ. of Md 1970–72, Dir 1972–74, Acting Chair. Div. of Behavioural and Social Sciences 1973–74, Provost 1973–76; Prof. of Law, Univ. of Colo 1976–80, Chancellor 1976–77; Asst Sec. for Educ. US Dept of Health, Educ. and Welfare 1977–80; Prof. of History and Law, Howard Univ., Washington 1980–; Geraldine R. Segal Prof. of American Social Thought and Prof. of History, Univ. of Pa 1987–; Vice-Chair. US Comm. on Civil Rights 1980–82, Chair. 1982–2004; mem. Advisory Bd Feminist Press 1980–, Inst. for Higher Educ. Law and Governance, Univ. of Houston; mem. Council UN Univ. 1986–; numerous awards and hon. degrees. *Publications:* Black Resistance/White Law 1971, Military Necessity and Civil Rights Policy 1977, Stability, Security and Continuity, Mr Justice Burton and Decision-Making in the Supreme Court 1945–58 1978, Long Memory: The Black Experience in America 1982 (jtly), The Pig Farmer's Daughter and Other Tales of American Justice: Episodes of Racism and Sexism in the Courts from 1865 to the Present 1999, And Justice for All: The United States Commission on Civil Rights and the Continuing Struggle for Freedom in America 2009. *Address:* Department of History, University of Pennsylvania, 208 College Hall, Philadelphia, PA 19104-6379, USA (office). *Telephone:* (215) 898-9587 (Univ.); (202) 337-0382 (office). *E-mail:* mfb@maryfrancesberry.com (office); mfberry@sas.upenn.edu (office). *Website:* www.maryfrancesberry.com (office); www.history.upenn.edu/faculty/berry.htm.

BERRY, Sir Michael Victor, Kt, BSc, PhD, FRS, FRSA; British physicist and academic; *Melville Wills Professor of Physics, Bristol University;* b. 14 March 1941, Surrey; ed Exeter Univ., St Andrews Univ.; Dept of Scientific and Industrial Research Fellow, Dept of Physics, Bristol Univ. 1965–67, Lecturer 1967–74, Reader in Physics 1974–79, Prof. of Physics 1979–88, Royal Soc. Research Prof. 1988–, currently Melville Wills Prof. of Physics; visiting lecturer at numerous int. univs; mem. Council BAAS 2002–; mem. Bd of Govs, Weizmann Inst., Israel 2000–; mem. Editorial Bd several journals including Journal of Physics A 1994–; mem. Royal Soc. of Sciences, Uppsala 1986–, European Acad. 1989–, Indian Acad. of Sciences 1990–, London Mathematical Soc. 1995–; foreign mem. NAS (USA) 1995–, Royal Netherlands Acad. of Arts and Sciences 2000–; Fellow Royal Inst. 1983–; Hon. Prof., Wuhan Univ. 1994, Hon. Fellow, Inst. of Physics 1999–; DSc hc (Trinity Coll. Dublin) 1996, (Open Univ.) 1997, (St Andrews Univ.) 1998, (Univ. of Warwick) 1998, (Univ. of Ulm) 2001, (Weizmann Inst.) 2003; Inst. of Physics Maxwell Medal 1978, American Physical Soc. Julius Edgar Lilienfeld Prize 1990, Inst. of Physics Paul Dirac Medal 1990, Royal Soc. Royal Medal 1990, London Mathematical Soc. Naylor Prize 1993, Louis-Vuitton Moët-Hennessey 'Science for Art' Prize 1994, Hewlett-Packard Europhysics Prize 1995, Int. Centre for Theoretical Physics (Trieste) Dirac Medal 1996, Russian Acad. of Sciences Kapitsa Medal 1997, Wolf Prize in Physics 1998, Ig Nobel Prize in Physics 2000, Norwegian Tech. Univ. (Trondheim) Onsager Medal 2001, Novartis/Daily Telegraph Visions of Science Prize 2002, Polya Prize, London Mathematical Soc. 2005, Chancellor's Medal, Bristol Univ. 2005. *Publications:* over 400 research papers. *Address:* H H Wills Physics Laboratory, Royal Fort, Tyndall Avenue, Bristol BS8 1TL, England (office). *Telephone:* (117) 928-8778 (office). *Fax:* (117) 925-5624 (office). *Website:* www.phy.bris.ac/people/berry_mv/index.html (office).

BERRY, Richard Stephen, AM, PhD, FAAS; American chemist and academic; *James Franck Distinguished Service Professor Emeritus of Chemistry, University of Chicago;* b. 9 April 1931, Denver, Colo; s. of Morris Berry and Ethel (Alpert) Berry; m. Carla Lamport Friedman 1955; one s. two d.; ed Harvard Univ.; Instructor, Univ. of Mich. 1957–60; Asst Prof. Yale Univ. 1960–64; Assoc. Prof. Univ. of Chicago 1964–67, Prof. Dept of Chem., James Franck Inst. 1967–89, James Franck Distinguished Service Prof. 1989–, now Prof. Emer.; Gaest Prof. Univ. of Copenhagen 1967, 1979; Consultant Argonne Nat. Lab. 1976–, Los Alamos Science Lab. 1975–; Visiting Prof., Univ. de Paris-Sud 1979–80; Hinshelwood Lecturer, Oxford 1980; Chair., Numerical Data Advisory Bd, National Research Council 1978–84; Newton Abraham Prof., Oxford Univ., England 1986–87; mem. Visiting Comm. of Applied Physics, Harvard Univ. 1977–81; mem. NAS (Home Sec. 1999–2003); mem. numerous cttees and orgs; Foreign mem. Royal Danish Acad. of Sciences; Fellow American Acad. of Arts and Sciences (Vice-Pres. 1995–98); MacArthur Prize Fellow 1983; Alexander von Humboldt Preistraeger 1993; J. Heyrosky Medal 1997. *Publications:* (with L. Gaines and T. V. Long II) TOSCA: The Social Costs of Coal and Nuclear Power 1979, (with S. A. Rice and J. Ross) Physical Chemistry 1980, Understanding Energy: Energy, Entropy and Thermodynamics for Everyman 1991, (with others) Optimization Methods in Finite Time Thermodynamics 1999; approximately 450 scientific papers in specialist journals. *Leisure interests:* music, skiing, hiking and climbing, photography, fly-fishing. *Address:* Department of Chemistry, SCL 101, University of Chicago, 5735 S. Ellis Avenue, Chicago, IL 60637 (office); 5317 S. University Ave., Chicago, IL 60615, USA (home). *Telephone:* (773) 702-7021 (office). *Fax:* (773) 702-0805 (office); (773) 834-4049 (office). *E-mail:* berry@uchicago.edu (office). *Website:* berrygroup.uchicago.edu (office); chemistry.uchicago.edu/fac/berry.shtml (office).

BERRY, Wendell, MA; American writer; b. 5 Aug. 1934, Henry County, Ky; m. Tanya Amyx 1957; one s. one d.; ed Univ. of Kentucky; mem. Faculty, Univ.

of Kentucky 1964–77, 1987, Distinguished Prof. of English 1971–72. *Publications:* novels: Nathan Coulter 1962, A Place on Earth 1967, The Memory of Old Jack 1974, Remembering 1988, The Discovery of Kentucky 1991, Fidelity 1992, A Consent 1993, Watch With Me 1994, A World Lost 1996, Jayber Crow 2001; short stories: The Wild Birds 1986; poetry: The Broken Ground 1964, Openings 1968, Findings 1969, Farming: A Handbook 1970, The Country of Marriage 1973, Clearing 1977, A Part 1980, The Wheel 1982, Collected Poems 1985, Sabbaths 1987, Sayings and Doings and an Eastward Look 1990, Entries 1994, The Farm 1995, A Timbered Choir: The Sabbath Poems 1979–1997 1999; essays: The Long-Legged House 1969, The Hidden Wound 1970, The Unforseen Wilderness 1971, A Continuous Harmony 1972, The Unsettling of America 1977, Recollected Essays 1965–80 1981, The Gift of Good Land 1981, Standing by Words 1985, Life is a Miracle: An Essay Against Modern Superstition 2000; co-ed. Meeting the Expectations of the Land 1985, Home Economics 1987, What Are People For? 1990, Harland Hubbard: Life and Work 1990, Standing on Earth 1991, Another Turn of the Crank. *Address:* Lanes Landing Farm, Port Royal, KY 40058, USA.

BERSELLINI, Anita, PhD; French physicist, academic and university administrator; b. 10 Jan. 1943, Nice; m.; one c.; ed Université Paris-Sud XI; researcher, Laboratoire d'Infrarouge, Université Paris-Sud XI 1965–76, Lecturer, 1966–76, Asst Prof. 1976–87, Full Prof. 2nd Class 1987–91, Head NFI Optronics Eng Degree 1991–2000, Full Prof. 1st Class 1992–99, Full Prof. Exceptional Class 1999–, Vice-Pres. 1998–2004, Pres. 2004–09; Researcher, Laboratoire de Photophysique Moléculaire, CNRS 1977–. *Address:* c/o Présidence, Bâtiment 300, Université Paris-Sud XI, 91405 Orsay Cedex, France.

BERSON, Jerome Abraham, BS, MA, PhD; American chemist and academic; *Sterling Professor Emeritus of Chemistry, Yale University;* b. 10 May 1924, Sanford, Fla; s. of Joseph Berson and Rebecca Bernicker Berson; m. Bella Zevitovsky 1946; two s. one d.; ed City Coll. of New York, Columbia and Harvard Univs; NRC Postdoctoral Fellow, Harvard Univ. 1949–50; Asst Prof., Univ. of Southern Calif. 1950–53, Assoc. Prof. 1953–58, Prof. 1958–63; Prof., Univ. of Wis. 1963–69, Yale Univ. 1969–79, Irénée duPont Prof. 1979–92, Sterling Prof. of Chemistry 1992–94, Sterling Prof. Emer. 1994–; Chair. Dept of Chem., Yale Univ. 1971–74; Dir Div. of Physical Sciences and Eng 1983–90; Sherman Fairchild Distinguished Scholar, Calif. Inst. of Tech. 1974–75; Nat. Research Council Postdoctoral Fellow; mem. NAS; Fellow, American Acad. of Arts and Sciences; ACS (Calif. Section) Award 1963, James Flack Norris Award in Physical Organic Chem. 1978, Sr US Scientist Award, Alexander von Humboldt Foundation 1980, Townsend Harris Medal 1984, William H. Nichols Medal 1985, Roger Adams Award 1987, NIH Merit Award 1989, Arthur C. Cope Scholar Award 1992, Oesper Award 1998, Literature Prize, German Chemical Industry Asscn 2000. *Publications:* Chemical Creativity 1999, Chemical Discovery and the Logicians' Program: A Problematic Pairing 2003; scientific papers on organic chem. published mostly in Journal of the American Chemical Soc. *Address:* Department of Chemistry, Yale University, Box 208107, New Haven, CT 06520-8107, USA (office). *E-mail:* jerome.berson@yale.edu (office). *Website:* www.chem.yale.edu/faculty/berson.html (office).

BERTARELLI, Ernesto, BA, MBA; Swiss entrepreneur; b. 22 Sept. 1965, Rome, Italy; m. Kirsty Roper; three c.; ed Babson Coll., Boston, Harvard Business School, USA; began career with Serono SA (family-owned biotechnology co.) 1985, several positions in Sales and Marketing 1985–90, Deputy CEO 1990–95, Vice-Chair. Bd of Dirs 1991–2006, CEO and Chair. Exec. Cttee 1996–2006 (Serono acquired by Merck 2006); mem. Bd (Compensation Cttee), UBS 2002–09; mem. Strategic Advisory Bd, École Polytéchnique Fédérale de Lausanne (EPFL); Pres. Fondation Bertarelli; Légion d'Honneur, Cavaliere di Gran Croce; five times winner Bol d'Or (Lake Geneva) 1997, 2000, 2001, 2002, 2003, winner 12-Metre and Farr 40 Championships 2001, winner America's Cup with Alinghi 2003, 2007; Paolo Venanzangeli Sailing Award 2008. *Leisure interest:* yachting. *Address:* c/o Alinghi, Port America's Cup, 46024 Valencia, Spain (office).

BERTHELOT, Yves M.; French statistician and economist; *Co-director, United Nations Intellectual History Project;* b. 15 Sept. 1937, Paris; m. Dosithée Yeatman 1961; three s. one d.; ed Ecole Polytechnique and Ecole Nationale de la Statistique et de l'Admin Economique; Dir of Studies in the Ministry of Planning, Ivory Coast 1965–68; Chief of the Study of Enterprises Div., then Chief of Service of Programmes of INSEE (Institut Nat. de la Statistique et des Etudes Economiques) 1971–75; Chief, Service des Etudes et Questions Int., French Ministry of Co-operation 1976–78; Dir of Research, Devt Centre of OECD, Paris 1978–81; Dir CEPII (Prospective Studies and Int. Information Centre) 1981–85; Deputy Sec.-Gen. of UNCTAD 1985–93; Exec. Sec. UN Econ. Comm. for Europe 1993–2000; Vice–Pres. Fondation Européenne pour le Développement durable des Régions 1996–; Sr Research Fellow and Head, Geneva Liaison Office, City Univ. of New York Grad. Center 2000–, Co-dir UN Intellectual History Project, Geneva 2000–; mem. High Comm. Int. Co-operation 2001–; Pres. Comité Français de Solidarité Internationale 2002–, Political and Ethical Knowledge on Economic Activities 2003–; Chevalier Ordre Nat. du Mérite, Officier Ordre Nat. (Côte d'Ivoire). *Publications:* numerous articles on economics. *Leisure interests:* sailing, skiing. *Address:* United Nations Intellectual History Project, Geneva Liaison Office, Palais des Nations, B 148, 1211 Geneva 10, Switzerland (office); City University of New York, 365 Fifth Avenue, New York, NY 10021, USA. *Telephone:* (22) 9072290 (office). *E-mail:* yberthelot@bluewin.ch (office); berthelotyd@wanadoo.fr. *Website:* www.unhistory.org (office).

BERTHELSEN, Asger, DPhil; Danish geologist and academic; b. 30 April 1928, Århus; s. of O. V. Berthelsen and Charlotte Berthelsen (neé Jensen); m. 1st Suoma I. Påhlman-Carlsson 1954 (died 1971); one d.; m. 2nd Mona D. Hansen (died 1979); m. 3rd Inge Halberg 1984 (died 2003); ed Copenhagen and Neuchatel Univs; State Geologist 1959; Prof. of Geology, Århus Univ. 1961, Copenhagen Univ. 1966–92; mem. Royal Danish Acad. of Science, Academia Europaea; Order of Dannebrog (First Class); Denmark Geology Prize 1993. *Publications:* On the Geology of the Rupshu District 1953, Geology of Tovqussap Nuna 1960, Precambrian of Greenland 1965, Geological Map of Ivigtut 1975, Geologi pa Rösnäs 1975, Den lille Tektoniker 1976, The EUGENO-S Project 1988, A Continent Revealed: The European Geotraverse Project (co-author) 1992, Rejsen til den blaa Sø 1998. *Leisure interest:* oil painting. *Address:* Fredensvej 14, I, 2920, Charlottenlund, Denmark (home). *Telephone:* 39-90-26-24 (home). *E-mail:* geogalskab@tdcadsl.dk (home).

BERTHOIN, Georges Paul, LenD, LèsL; French civil servant; b. 17 May 1925, Nérac; s. of Jean Berthoin and Germaine Mourgnot; m. 1st Anne W. Whittlesey (deceased); m. 2nd Pamela Jenkins 1965; two s. four d.; ed Univ. of Grenoble, Ecole des Sciences Politiques, Univ. of Paris, Harvard Univ., USA and McGill Univ., Canada; Pvt. Sec. to Minister of Finance 1948–50; Head of Staff, Prefecture of Alsace-Lorraine-Champagne 1950–52; Prin. Pvt. Sec. M. Jean Monnet, Pres. of ECSC 1952–55; Counsellor for Information, ECSC 1955–56; Deputy Chief Rep. of ECSC in UK 1956; Acting Chief Rep. of Comm. of EEC 1967–68, Deputy Chief Rep. 1968–71, Chief Rep. 1971–73; Exec. mem. Trilateral Comm. 1973–75, European Chair. 1975–92, Hon. Chair. 1993–; Int. Chair of European Movement 1978–81; Dir Int. Peace Acad., New York; Bd mem. Aspen-Berlin Inst.; mem. Int. Advisory Bd Johns Hopkins Univ., Bologna, Nine Wise Men Group on Africa; Aspen Inst. Distinguished Fellow; Hon. Chair. Jean Monnet Asscn; Officier, Légion d'honneur; Médaille Militaire; Croix de Guerre; Médaille de la Résistance. *Leisure interests:* art, theatre, walking, collecting objects. *Address:* 67 avenue Niel, 75017 Paris, France.

BERTI, Luciano; Italian art historian; b. 28 Jan. 1922, Florence; s. of Ferdinando Berti and Ines Berti; m. Anna Maria Tinacci 1959; ed Univ. of Florence; attached to Superintendency of Florence 1949; arranged new museums of Casa Vasari, Arezzo 1950, Palazzo Davanzati 1955, Il Museo di Arezzo 1958, Il Museo di S. Giovanni Valdarno 1959, Museum of Verna 1961, Museum of Santa Croce, Florence 1962; Dir Museums of Arezzo, San Marco and Acad., Florence; Dir Museo Nazionale del Bargello; Dir Uffizi Gallery, Florence 1969–87; Dir Monuments, Pisa Gallery 1973–74; Dir of Galleries, Florence 1974–87; mem. Consiglio Superiore 1976–80; Pres. Casa Buonarroti 1990–; Gold Medal, Ministry of Cultural Heritage, Dottore Laurea in Lettere, Libera docenza in Storia dell'Arte, Accademico Emerito Arti del Disegno. *Publications:* Filippino Lippi 1957, Masaccio 1964, Pontormo 1964, Pontormo disegni 1965, Il Principe dello Studiolo 1967, Il Museo tra Thanatos ed Eros 1973–74, Catalogue to the Uffizi Gallery 1979, I Disegni di Michelangelo in Casa Buonarroti 1985, Pontormo e il suo Tempo 1993, Il Portico (novel) 1998; various articles and catalogues. *Leisure interests:* history of art, museology. *Address:* Casa Buonarroti, Via Ghibellina 70, 50122 Florence (office); Via Giusti 6, Florence, Italy (home). *Telephone:* 244938 (home).

BERTINI, Hon. ; **Catherine Ann,** BA; American international organization official and academic; *Professor of Public Administration, Maxwell School of Citizenship and Public Affairs, Syracuse University;* b. 30 March 1950, Syracuse, New York; d. of Fulvio Bertini and Ann Vino Bertini; ed Cortland High School, NY, State Univ. of New York at Albany; Youth Dir, New York Republican State Cttee 1971–74, Republican Nat. Cttee 1975–76; Man., Public Policy, Container Corpn of America 1977–87; Dir Office of Family Assistance, US Dept of Health and Human Services 1987–89; Acting Asst Sec., US Dept of Health and Human Services 1989, Asst Sec. US Dept of Agric. 1989–92; Exec. Dir World Food Programme of UN, Rome 1992–2002; mem. UN Sec.-Gen.'s Panel of High-Level Personalities on African Devt 1992–95; UN Sec.-Gen.'s Special Envoy on Drought in the Horn of Africa 2000–01; UN Sec.-Gen.'s Personal Humanitarian Envoy to Middle East 2002; Chair. UN System Standing Cttee on Nutrition 2002–06; UN Under-Sec.-Gen. for Man. 2002–05; Prof. of Public Admin, Maxwell School of Citizenship and Public Affairs, Syracuse Univ. 2005–; Fellow, Inst. of Politics, Harvard Univ. 1986; Commr Ill. State Scholarship Comm. 1979–84, Ill. Human Rights Comm. 1985–87; Towsley Foundation Policy Maker in Residence, Gerald R. Ford School of Public Policy, Univ. of Michigan 2002; Sr Fellow, Bill & Melinda Gates Foundation 2007–; Order of Merit (Italy) 2002; Hon. DSc (McGill Univ., Montreal) 1997, (Pine Major Coll.) 2000; Hon. DHL (State Univ. of New York, Cortland) 1999, (American Univ., Rome) 2001, (Loyola Univ., Chicago) 2002, (Dakota Wesleyan Univ., Mitchell, SDak) 2003; (Univ. of S Carolina, Spartanburg) 2003, (Colgate Univ.) 2004, Dr hc (Slovak Agricultural Univ., Nitra) 1999, Hon. DPS (John Cabot Univ., Rome) 2001; Leadership in Human Services Award, American Public Welfare Asscn 1990, Excellence in Public Service Award, American Acad. of Pediatrics 1991, Leadership Award, Nat. Asscn of WIC Dirs 1992, Quality of Life Award, Auburn School of Human Sciences 1996, Building World Citizenship Award, World Asscn of Girl Guides/Scouts 2001, Prize of Excellence, Asscn of African Journalists 2002, World Food Prize Laureate 2003, Univ. of Albany Medallion 2002, Leadership Award, Chicago Council on Foreign Relations 2004, Life Time Achievement in Child Nutrition Award, School Nutrition Asscn 2007. *Leisure interest:* music, including playing clarinet. *Address:* Department of Public Administration, 351 Eggers Hall, The Maxwell School of Syracuse University, Syracuse, NY 13244, USA (office). *Telephone:* (315) 443-1341 (office). *Fax:* (315) 443-9085 (office). *E-mail:* cbertini@maxwell.syr.edu (office). *Website:* www.maxwell.syr.edu (office).

BERTINOTTI, Fausto; Italian politician; b. 22 March 1940, Milan; joined Gen. Confed. of Italian Labour 1964, Regional Sec. in Piedmont 1975–85; joined Italian Communist Party (PCI) 1972, left to join Partito della Rifondazione Comunista (PRC) (Party of Communist Refoundation), Nat.

Sec. 1994–; mem. Camera dei Deputati 1994–2004, Pres. Camera dei Deputati 2006–08; Dir Rivista Binestrale Alternative il Socialism; mem. European Parl. 1999–2006. *Publications:* La camera dei lavori 1987, Verso la democrazia autoritaria 1991, Tutti i colori del rosso 1995, Le due sinistre (co-author) 1997, Pensare il '68 (co-author) 1998, Le idee che non muoiono (co–author) 2000, Per una pace infinita (co-author) 2002, Analisi collettiva (co–author) 2004, Non violenza – Le ragioni del pacifismo 2004, Il ragazzo con la maglietta a strisee 2005, La città degli uomini: Cinque riflessioni in un mondo che cambia 2007, Devi augurarti che la strada sia lunga 2009, L'Europa delle passioni forti (co-author), Io ci provo (co-author). *Address:* Camera dei Deputati, Palazzo Theodoli, Piazza del Parlamento 19, 00186 Rome, Italy (office). *Telephone:* (06) 67606018 (office). *Fax:* (06) 67603186 (office). *E-mail:* bertinotti_f@camera.it (office). *Website:* www.faustobertinotti.it.

BERTMAN, Dmitry Aleksandrovich; Russian theatre director; *Artistic Director, Helikon Opera Theatre;* b. 17 Oct. 1967, Moscow; ed Lunacharsky State Inst. of Theatre Arts; started career as Dir in theatres in Moscow, Tver, Odessa, Syktyvkar; founder and Artistic Dir Helikon Opera Theatre, Moscow 1990–; has also directed productions abroad, including in Vienna and Klagenfurt, Austria; docent Russian Acad. of Theatre Arts; awarded The Maltese Cross and title Count of Sovereign Military and Hospitaller Order of St. John of Jerusalem of Rhodes and of Malta 2003; Officier des Palmes Academiques (France) 2003; Honored Art Worker of Russia 1997; People's Artist of Russia 2005; Golden Mask Nat. Prize 1998, 1999, 2001. *Stage productions include:* Lady Macbeth of Mtsensk, Eugene Onegin, La Traviata, Falstaff, Aida, The Rake's Progress, Lulu. *Address:* Helikon Opera, B. Nikitskaya str. 19, 103009 Moscow, Russia (office). *Telephone:* (495) 290-28-88 (office); (495) 290-64-19 (home). *Fax:* (495) 291-13-23 (office). *E-mail:* helikon@helikon.ru (office). *Website:* www.helikon.ru (office).

BERTOLINI, Mark T., BS, MBA; American business executive; *President, Aetna Inc.;* b. 1957; ed Wayne State Univ., Cornell Univ.; COO, later CEO SelectCare Inc. 1992–95; fmr Exec. Vice-Pres. NYLCare Health Plans; Exec. Vice-Pres. Cigna HealthCare 2000–02, Sr Vice-Pres., Regional & Middle Market 2002–03; joined Aetna Inc. 2003, Head of Specialty Products 2003–05, Sr Vice-Pres. Specialty Group 2005, Sr Vice-Pres. Regional Business 2005–06, Exec. Vice-Pres. Regional Business 2006–07, Exec. Vice-Pres. and Head of Business Operations 2007, Pres. Aetna Inc. 2007–; Chair. Operations Cttee, Asscn of Health Insurance Plans; mem. Bd Dirs Univ. of Connecticut Health Center, Connecticut Business and Industry Asscn; mem. Advisory Bd Cornell Univ. School of Human Ecology; National Gay and Lesbian Chamber of Commerce Healthcare Leadership Award 2007. *Address:* Aetna Inc., 151 Farmington Avenue, Hartford, CT 06156, USA (office). *Telephone:* (860) 273-0123 (office). *Fax:* (860) 273-3971 (office). *E-mail:* info@aetna.com (office). *Website:* www.aetna.com (office).

BERTOLUCCI, Bernardo; Italian film director; b. 16 March 1941, Parma; s. of Attilio Bertolucci; m. Clare Peploe 1978; worked with Pier Paolo Pasolini on Accattone; Dr hc (Turin) 2000; European Film Award 1988, nine Acad. Awards, Hon. Golden Lion Award, Venice Film Festival 2007. *Films directed:* La Commare Secca 1962, Prima della Rivoluzione 1964, Agonia in Aurore e Rabbia 1967, Partner 1968, La Strategia del Ragno 1970, Il Conformista 1970, Last Tango in Paris 1972, 1900 1976, La Luna 1979, Tragedy of a Ridiculous Man 1981, The Last Emperor 1987 (Acad. Awards 1988 for Best Dir and Best Screenwriter), The Sheltering Sky 1989, Little Buddha 1993, Stealing Beauty 1995, I Dance Alone 1996, Besieged (Globo D'Oro Award for Best Film 1999) 1998, Ten Minutes Older: The Cello (segment) 2002, The Dreamers 2003. *Publications:* In cerca del mistero (poems) 1962 (Viareggio Prize 1962), Paradiso e inferno (poems) 1999. *Address:* c/o Recorded Picture Company, 24 Hanway Street, London, W1P 9DD, England; c/o Jeff Berg, ICM, 8942 Wilshire Boulevard, Beverly Hills, CA 90211, USA; c/o Carol Levi and Co., 2 Via Pisanelli, 00196 Rome, Italy.

BERTONE, HE Cardinal Tarcisio, DCnL; Italian ecclesiastic and professor of canon law; *Secretary of State, Roman Curia;* b. 2 Dec. 1934, Romano Canavese; ed Oratorio di Valdocco, Turin, Salesian novitiate of Monte Oliveto, Pinerolo, Pontifical Salesian Athenaeum (now Univ.), Rome; entered Soc. of St Francis and St John (Salesian Order); made religious profession 1950; ordained priest by Albino Mensa, Bishop of Ivrea 1960; Prof. of Special Moral Theology, Pontifical Salesian Univ. 1967, Dir of Theologians 1974–76, Prof. of Canon Law 1976–91, Dean Faculty of Canon Law 1979–85, Vice-Rector 1987–89, apptd Rector 1989; Guest Prof. of Public Ecclesiastical Law, Pontifical Lateran Univ. 1978; collaborated in drafting revision of Code of Canon Law; Archbishop of Vercelli 1991–95; Sec. of Congregation of Doctrine of Faith 1995–2002; entrusted with publ. of third secret of Fatima by Pope John Paul II 2000; Archbishop of Genoa 2002–06; Sec. of State, Roman Curia 2006–; cr. Cardinal Priest of S. Maria Ausiliatrice in via Tuscolana 2003–; consultant to several dicasteries of Roman Curia; Hon. PhD (Catholic Univ. of Salta, Argentina) 2005. *Address:* Office of the Secretary of State, 00120, Città del Vaticano, Italy (office). *Telephone:* (06) 69883913 (office). *Fax:* (06) 69885255 (office). *Website:* www.vatican.va/roman_curia/secretariat_state/index.htm (office).

BERTRAND, Françoise, BA; Canadian business executive; *President, Fédération des chambres de commerce du Québec;* b. 1948, Montréal; ed Collège Ste-Marie, Univ. of Montréal, York Univ.; Dir Soc. des Jeux du Québec 1976–78; Project Man. SORECOM Inc. 1978–80; Asst Vice-Pres. (Academic and Research) Univ. of Quebec, Montréal 1980–82, Asst Dean Research Man. 1983–84, Dean 1984–88; CEO Soc. de radio-télévision du Québec 1988–95; Sr Dir Communications Practices, KPMG Consulting 1995–96; Chair. CRTC 1996–2000; Pnr, Secor Consulting 2001; currently Pres. Fédération des chambres de commerce du Québec (Quebec Fed. of Chambers of Commerce); Chair. Bd Théâtre Populaire du Québec 1990–96; mem. Bd of Dirs Asscn for Tele-Educ. in Canada (ATEC), (Chair. 1993–94), TV5 Quebec Canada 1988–95; Vice-Chair. Bd TV5 Latin America 1993–95; one of three Commrs on Fed. Water Policy Comm. 1984–85; mem. Bd of Govs and Exec. Cttee Univ. of Quebec 1990–96; mem. various bds and research orgs involved in educ. and social and community orgs. *Address:* Fédération des chambres de commerce du Québec, 555, boul. René-Lévesque West, 19th Floor, Montréal, PQ H2Z 1B1, Canada (office). *Telephone:* (514) 844-9571 (office). *Fax:* (514) 844-0226 (office). *E-mail:* info@fccq.ca (office). *Website:* www.fccq.ca (office).

BERTRAND, Xavier, PhD; French politician; *Minister for Labour, Labour Relations and Solidarity;* b. 21 March 1965, Châlons-sur-Marne, Marne; mem. Union pour un Mouvement Populaire, Sec.-Gen. March–Dec. 2008, Acting Sec.-Gen. Dec. 2008–; Deputy in Nat. Ass. 2002–04; Sec. of State for Health Insurance, Ministry of Health and Social Welfare 2004–05; Minister of Health and Social Protection 2005–07 (resgnd), for Labour, Labour Relations and Solidarity 2007–; Spokesman for Nicolas Sarkozy's presidential campaign 2007. *Address:* Ministry for Labour, Labour Relations and Solidarity, 127 rue de Grenelle, 75007 Paris, France (office). *Telephone:* 1-44-38-38-38 (office). *Fax:* 1-44-38-20-10 (office). *Website:* www.cohesionsociale.gouv.fr (office).

BERTRANOU, Armando Victorio; Argentine professor of agricultural economics; b. 14 May 1942, Mendoza; s. of Pablo Luis Bertranou and Susana Angélica Saligari; m. Clara Alicia Jalif 1965; two s. two d.; ed Universidad Nacional de Cuyo, Univ. of California, Davis; Titular Prof., Faculty of Agricultural Sciences, Universidad Nacional de Cuyo, Rector 1988–; mem. Bd Nat. Parks Admin. *Publications:* many articles and papers on irrigation and water man. *Leisure interests:* aerobics, rugby, rowing. *Address:* Universidad Nacional de Cuyo, Centro Universitario, Parque General San Martín, 5500 Mendoza; Paso de los Andes 966, 5500 Mendoza; Casilla de Correo 589, 5500 Mendoza, Argentina. *Telephone:* 2-52152; 2-53219; 2-31352.

BERTUCCELLI, Jean-Louis Augusto; French film director; b. 3 June 1942, Paris; s. of Louis Bertuccelli and Charlotte Feral; one d.; ed Conservatoire Régional de Musique de Nice and Faculté des Sciences, Marseille; musician, then sound engineer 1964–66; film producer 1966–; TV corresp. reporting on Japan, Thailand, Hong Kong, Bolivia, Mexico, South Africa, Senegal, USA and Spain 1968–73; Chevalier des Arts et Lettres. *Films include:* Janine ou l'amour 1967, Oaxaca 1967, La Mélodie du Malheur 1967, Remparts d'argile (Prix Jean Vigo) 1968, Tricot 1969, Paulina 1980 1972, On s'est trompé d'histoire d'amour 1974, Docteur Françoise Gailland 1975, L'Imprécateur 1977, Interdit aux moins de treize ans 1982, Stress 1984, Mélies 1988, Aujourd'hui Peut-être 1991, L'homme qui.2003. *Television includes:* La Lettre perdue 1987, Souris noire (series) 1987, Méliès 88: Le rêve du radja 1988, Pognon sur rue 1991, Dis maman, tu m'aimes? 1992, Momo 1992, L'Institut 1993, Le Serment d'Hippocrate 1995, Docteur Sylvestre (series) 1995, Sur un air de mambo 1996, Louis Page (series) 1997, Maître Da Costa (series) 1997, Mauvaises affaires 1997, Marie Marmaille 2002, Papa maman s'ront jamais grands 2003, Depuis qu'Otar est parti..2003, Des bleus à l'âme 2005, Un rebelle dans la famille 2006, Une juge sous influence 2006. *Leisure interests:* music, tennis, piano, flute. *Address:* 9 rue Bénard, 75014 Paris, France. *E-mail:* uccelli@noos.fr. *Website:* www.jean-louis-bertuccelli.com.

BĒRZIŅŠ, Andris; Latvian politician and historian; b. 4 Aug. 1951, Riga; m.; two c.; ed Latvian State Univ.; teacher and admin. in several schools 1975–82; Head, Div. of Personnel Training Cttee for Vocational and Tech. Training 1982–86; Head, Div. State Cttee for Labour and Social Affairs 1986–90; Head, Div., Deputy Dir Welfare Dept Ministry of Econs 1990–92; Deputy Minister, concurrently Head, Labour Dept Ministry of Welfare 1992–93; State Minister of Labour 1993–94; Deputy Prime Minister, Minister of Welfare 1994–95; Minister of Labour 1995–97; Chair. Riga City Council 1997–2000; Prime Minister of Latvia 2000–02; Chair. Latvian Way (Latvijas ceļš) 2000–03; Strategic consultant for UNDP, Latvia 2004–. *Address:* Latvijas ceļš, Terbatas jela 4-9, 1001 Rīga (office); UNDP, 6 A/1 Ogres, 2015 Burmala, Latvia. *Telephone:* (2) 6728-5539 (office); 6781-1462. *Fax:* (2) 6728-1121 (office); 6703-5751. *E-mail:* lc@lc.lv (office); abkonsultants@apollo.lv. *Website:* www.lc.lv (office).

BĒRZIŅŠ, Indulis; Latvian politician and diplomatist; *Ambassador to UK;* b. 4 Dec. 1957, Madona; m. 1st Inese Bērziņš; one s. one d.; m. 2nd Ilze Gelnere; ed Latvian State Univ.; Lecturer, Latvian State Univ. and Latvian Inst. of Agric. 1984–90; TV broadcaster 1988–89; Founder-mem. People's Front Movt for independence 1989; Deputy, Supreme Soviet Latvian Repub., Deputy Chair. Cttee on Foreign Affairs 1990–93, later Chair.; Dir Latvijas Ceļš Union 1993–; mem. People's Front of Latvia 1992–93, Latvia's Way Party 1993–; mem. Latvian del. to NATO 1993–95, Latvian Nat. Group to European Parl. 1995–97, 1998–99; Deputy Speaker of Saeima (Parl.) 1998–99; Minister of Foreign Affairs 1999–2002; Amb., State Sec.'s Bureau, Ministry of Foreign Affairs 2002–03; Amb. to Denmark 2003–05, to UK 2005–; Commdr, Ordre nat. du Mérite 1997, Commdr of the Three Stars Order (Latvia) 2000. *Address:* Embassy of Latvia, 45 Nottingham Place, London, W1U 5LY, England (office). *Telephone:* (20) 7312-0040 (office). *Fax:* (20) 7312-0042 (office). *E-mail:* embassy.uk@mfa.gov.lv (office). *Website:* www.london.mfa.gov.lv (office).

BESCH, Werner Walter, DPhil; German professor of German; *Professor Emeritus, University of Bonn;* b. 4 May 1928, Erdmannsweiler, Schwarzwald; s. of Matthias and Elisabeth Besch (née Fuss); m. Katharina Müller 1957; one s. two d.; Prof. of German Language and Early German Literature, Ruhr Univ., Bochum 1965–70, Univ. of Bonn 1970–93, Prof. Emer. 1993–; Rector, Univ. of Bonn 1981–83, Pro-Rector 1983–85; mem. Wiss-Rat., Inst. für Deutsche Sprache, Mannheim 1976–93; Corresp. mem. Heidelberg Akad. der Wissenschaften; mem. Nordrhein-Westfälische Akad. der Wissenschaften; Corresp. mem. Inst. of Germanic Studies, Univ. of London; Mitglied der

Kommission zur Herausgabe der Deutschen Schriften Martin Bucers, Heidelberg Akademie 1968–2008; Mitglied des Rates für Deutsche Rechtschreibung 2004; Wolfgang Paul Medaille, Univ. of Bonn, Ehrenmitglied der Internationalen Gesellschaft für Dialecktologie des Deutschen 2003, Ehrenmitglied der Gesellschaft Ungarischer Germanisten 2005. *Publications:* Lautgeographie u. Lautgeschichte im obersten Neckar-u. Donaugebiet 1961, Sprachlandschaften u. Sprachausgleich im 15. Jahrhundert 1967, Dialekt/Hochsprache-Kontrastiv 1977, Handbuch Dialektologie 1983, 1984 (co-ed.), Handbuch Sprachgeschichte 1985, (2nd edn) (co-ed.) 1998–2004, Duzen, Siezen, Titulieren. Zur Anrede im Deutschen heute und gestern (2nd edn) 1998, Zur Rolle Luthers in der deutschen Sprachgeschichte 1999, Zeitschrift für deutsche Philologie, Grundlagen der Germanistik (co-ed.), Deutsche Sprache im Wandel 2003, Deutscher Bibelwortschatz in der frühen Neuzeit, Auswahl-Abwahl-Veralten 1989–2007, 2008. *Address:* Römerstrasse 118, 53117 Bonn, Germany (home).

BESHEAR, Steven L.; American lawyer, politician and business executive; *Governor of Kentucky;* b. 21 Sept. 1944, Dawson Springs, Hopkins County, Ky; m. Jane Beshear; two s.; ed Dawson Springs High School, Univ. of Kentucky; elected Pres. Student Body during his third undergraduate year; served in US Army Reserve 1969–75, intelligence analyst, also carried out certain Judge Advocate Gen. duties; elected to Kentucky House of Reps for 76th Dist 1974–79; Attorney Gen. of Kentucky 1980–84, Lt Gov. 1983–87, cr. and headed Kentucky Tomorrow Comm.; cand. in election for Gov. of Kentucky 1987; practised law in Lexington, Kentucky, sr exec. of multi-state law firm; was the Democratic nominee for US Senate 1996; Gov. of Kentucky 2007–; mem. Commerce Lexington, Inc., Kentucky Horse Park Foundation, God's Pantry Food Bank, Bluegrass Tomorrow, Kentucky World Trade Center, Univ. of Kentucky Coll. of Law Visiting Cttee; Democrat. *Address:* 700 Capital Avenue, Suite 100, Frankfort, KY 40601, USA (office). *Telephone:* (502) 564-2611 (office). *Fax:* (502) 564-2517 (office). *E-mail:* info@stevebeshear.com (office); info@governor.ky.gov (office). *Website:* governor.ky.gov (office); www.stevebeshear.com (office).

BESSÉ, Albert; Central African Republic politician; *Minister of Finance and the Budget;* fmr Chargé de Mission des Banques et Institutions Financières, Ministry of Finance and Budget, Minister of Finance and the Budget 2009–; Gen. Treas. CIDEL (Center for Integrated Devt of Ethics and Leadership). *Address:* Ministry of Finance and the Budget, BP 696, Bangui, Central African Republic (office).

BESSER, Gordon Michael, MB, MD, DSc, FRCP, FMedSci; British physician, professor of endocrinology and professor of medicine (retd); *Professor Emeritus, St. Bartholomew's and Royal London School of Medicine and Dentistry;* b. 22 Jan. 1936, London; ed Medical Coll. of St Bartholomew's Hosp., Univ. of London; Sr Lecturer in Medicine, St Bartholomew's Hosp. Medical Coll. 1970–74, Head of Endocrinology and Hon. Consultant Physician 1970–95, Prof. of Endocrinology 1974–92, Prof. of Medicine 1992–2001; Prof. of Medicine and Head of Endocrinology, St Bartholomew's and Royal London School of Medicine and Dentistry 1995–2001, Prof. Emer. 2001–; Civilian Consultant in Endocrinology, RN 1989–97, to the Triservice Medical Service 1997–2004; Visiting Consultant Endocrinologist to Govt of Malta 1989–2002; Chief Exec. Barts NHS Trust 1992–94; currently consultant Endocrinologist, The London Clinic Centre for Endocrinology; Lecturer to Royal Coll. of Physicians: Goulstonian 1974, Lumlean 1993, Simms 1999, Soc. for Endocrinology; Fellow Queen Mary Univ. of London 2005, Hon. Fellow Royal Soc. of Medicine 2008; Hon. MD (Turin) 1985; Jubilee Medalist and Lecturer 2002, William Julius Mickle Fellowship for the Advancement of Medical Science, Univ. of London 1976, Medal of Soc. for Endocrinology 1978, Clinical Endocrinology Prize 1986, Medal of European Neuroendocrinology Asscn 1999. *Publications:* Clinical Endocrinology 1984, DeGroot's Endocrinology (section ed.) 1985, 26 textbooks in gen. medicine and endocrinology and over 500 articles in journals of basic and clinical endocrinology and medicine. *Leisure interests:* early Chinese ceramics, physical fitness, opera, ballet. *Address:* The London Clinic Centre for Endocrinology, 5 Devonshire Place, London, W1G 5HL (office); Department of Endocrinology, St Bartholomew's & Royal London School of Medicine, London, EC1A 7BE (office); White Cottage, 61A Marlborough Place, London, NW8 0PT, England (home). *Telephone:* (20) 7935-4444 (office); (20) 7034-6215 (office). *Fax:* (20) 7616-7791 (office). *E-mail:* endo@thelondonclinic.co.uk (office).

BESSMERTNYKH, Aleksandr Aleksandrovich, CandJurSc; Russian diplomatist; *President, International Foreign Policy Association;* b. 10 Nov. 1933, Biisk; s. of Aleksandr Bessmertnykh and Maria Bessmertnykh; m.; one s. one d.; ed Moscow State Inst. of Int. Relations; joined Diplomatic Service 1957, with Embassy, Washington, DC 1970–83; fmr arms control negotiator; First Deputy Foreign Minister (with special responsibility for N America and the Middle East) 1987–90, Deputy 1986; Amb. to USA 1990–91; Minister of Foreign Affairs Jan.–Aug. 1991; mem. CP Cen. Cttee 1990–91; Head Policy Analysis Centre Soviet (now Russian) Foreign Policy Asscn 1991–92; Pres. Int. Foreign Policy Asscn 1992–, Chair. World Council of Fmr Foreign Ministers 1993–; Chair. Supervisory Bd Advanced Tech. Research Programs Foundation; Prof. Moscow Univ.; mem. Acad. of Social Sciences of Russian Fed.; Corresp. mem. Chilean Acad. of Social and Political Sciences; Order of Friendship of Peoples, Order of Peter the Great, Order of Lomonosov; Badge of Honour, various medals. *Publications:* numerous articles on foreign policy, diplomacy and military strategy. *Leisure interests:* literature, classical music, tennis. *Address:* International Foreign Policy Association, Yakovo-Apostolski per. 10, 105064 Moscow, Russia (office). *Telephone:* (495) 975-21-67 (office); (495) 698-50-08 (office). *Fax:* (495) 975-21-90 (office). *E-mail:* fpa.moscow@public.mtu.ru (office). *Website:* www.forpolicy.ru (office).

BESSON, Luc; French film director, producer and screenwriter; b. 18 March 1959, Paris; s. of Claude Besson and Danièle Plane; one d. with Anne Parillaud; worked as an Asst on films in Paris and Hollywood; first Asst for several advertising films; two features (Homme libre and Les Bidasses aux grandes manoeuvres) and four shorts; f. Les Films du Loup 1982. *Films directed include:* L'Avant dernier 1981, Le Dernier Combat 1983, Subway 1985, The Big Blue 1988, Nikita 1990, Atlantis 1991, Leon 1994, The Fifth Element 1997, The Messenger: The Story of Joan of Arc 1999, Angel-A 2006, Arthur and the Invisibles 2006. *Publications:* Arthur and the Minimoys (juvenile) 2005. *Address:* Leeloo Productions, 53 rue Boissée, 91540 Mennecy (office); c/o CBC, 11 rue de la Croix Boissée, 91540 Mennecy, France. *E-mail:* lucbesson@luc-besson.com (office).

BESTUZHEV-LADA, Igor Vassilyevich, PhD, DHist; Russian sociologist and historian; *Chairman, Russian Pedagogical Society;* b. 12 Jan. 1927, Lada, Penza Region; m.; one s. one d.; ed Inst. of Int. Relations, Inst. of History; researcher, Inst. of History, USSR Acad of Sciences 1954–66; Head Dept of Social Forecasting, Inst. of Sociology, USSR (now Russian) Acad. of Sciences 1967–2000, Prof. Emer. 2001–; Prof., Moscow State Univ. 1969–2000; Academician Sec., Russian Acad. of Education 1993–2002; Pres. Russian Future Studies Acad. 1997–, Int. Future Research Acad. 1999–; Vice Pres. Future Research Cttee, Soviet Sociological Asscn 1967–91, Int. Sociological Asscn 1970–96; Pres. Moscow Humanitarian Prognostic Univ. 2000–; Chair. Presidium Russian Pedagogical Soc. 1989–; Hon. mem. World Future Studies Fed. 1984; Order of St Daniel 1998, Order of Friendship 2003. *Publications:* Exploratory Social Forecasting, Normative Social Forecasting, Forecasting Grounding Social Innovations, Alternative Civilization, Anthology of Classics in Future Studies 1952–82, Memories, Vols 1–5, 2004. *Leisure interests:* classic literature, book design. *Address:* Russian Pedagogical Society, 1st Cadashev pez 11/5-1, 115035, Moscow; Russian Future Studies Academy, Bol. Cheremuskinskaya str. 34, 117218 Moscow (office); Shipilovsky proezd 49/1, apt 364, 115551 Moscow, Russia (home). *Telephone:* (495) 953-2170 (office); (495) 343-0852 (home). *Fax:* (495) 128-1710 (office); (495) 953 9912. *E-mail:* lada@imce.ru (office); pedobsh@online.ru. *Website:* www.pedobsh.ru.

BETANCUR CUARTAS, Belisario; Colombian politician and lawyer; *President, Fundación Santillana;* b. 4 Feb. 1923, Amagá, Antioquia; s. of Rosendo Betancur and Ana Otilia Cuartos; m. Rosa Helena Álvarez; one s. two d.; ed Univ. Bolivariana de Medellín; mem. House of Reps, later Senator; Conservative Party presidential cand. 1962, 1970, 1978; Minister of Labour 1963; Amb. to Spain 1974; Pres. of Colombia 1982–86; mem. Pontifical Acad. of Social Sciences 1994; currently Pres. Fundación Santillana para Iberoamérica, Columbia; Hon. Mem. Bd of Dirs Due Process of Law Foundation. *Address:* Fundación Santillana, calle 80, No 9-75, Apartado Aéreo 3974, Santa Fe de Bogotá, Colombia (office). *Website:* www.fundacionsantillana.org (office).

BÉTEILLE, André Marie, MSc, PhD; Indian sociologist and academic; *Chairman, Indian Council of Social Science Research;* b. 30 Sept. 1934, Chandannagar; s. of the late Maurice Béteille and Renuka Béteille (née Mukherjee); m. Esha Ghoshal; two d.; ed Univs of Calcutta and Delhi; Research Assoc. Indian Statistical Inst. 1958–59; Lecturer in Sociology Delhi School of Econs 1959–64, Reader 1964–72, Prof. 1972–99, Prof. Emer. 1999–; currently Nat. Research Prof. and Chancellor North-Eastern Hill Univ., Shillong; Chair. Indian Council of Social Science Research (ICSSR) 2005–; Corresp. Fellow, British Acad. 1992–; Trustee Sameeksha Trust, Nat. Foundation for India, New India Foundation; Hon. Fellow, Royal Anthropological Inst. 2002–; Hon. DSc (Vidyasagar Univ.) 2004, Hon. DLitt (Kolkata) 2006; Padma Bhushan Award 2005. *Publications:* Caste, Class and Power: Changing Patterns of Stratification in a Tanjore Village 1965, Castes: Old and New, Essays in Social Structure and Social Stratification 1969, Studies in Agrarian Social Structure 1974, Six Essays in Comparative Sociology 1974, Inequality Among Men 1977, The Idea of Natural Inequality and Other Essays 1983, Society and Politics in India: Essays in a Comparative Perspective 1991, Antinomies of Society: Essays on Ideologies and Institutions 2000, Chronicles of Our Time 2000, Sociology: Essays on Approach and Method 2002, Equality and Universality: Essays in Social and Political Theory 2003, Anti-Utopia: Essential Writings of André Béteille (ed. by Dipankar Gupta) 2005, Ideology and Social Science 2006, Marxism and Class Analysis 2007; numerous articles in professional journals. *Address:* Indian Council of Social Science Research, Aruna Asaf, Ali Marg, New Delhi 110 067 (office); 69 Jor Bagh, New Delhi 110 003, India (home). *Telephone:* (11) 26179679 (office); (11) 24645172 (home). *Fax:* (11) 26179836 (office). *E-mail:* chairman@icssr.org (office). *Website:* www.icssr.org (office).

BETHKE, Siegfried, PhD; German physicist and academic; *Managing Director, Max-Planck-Institute for Physics;* b. 15 April 1954, Ludwigshafen; ed Univ. of Heidelberg; Asst, Univ. of Heidelberg 1983–86; Feodor-Lynen Fellow, Univ. of Calif., Berkeley Lab., USA 1988–89; Prof. of Physics, Rheinisch-Westfälische Technische Hochschule (RWTH), Aachen 1993–96; Dir Max-Planck-Inst. for Physics, Munich 1999–, Man. Dir 2000–; Heisenberg Fellow, CERN, Geneva 1989–93; Co-Ed. European Physical Journal C 1994–; mem. numerous specialist cttees including High Energy Physics Referee Bd, Ministry of Science, Research, Tech. and Educ. 1995–2002; mem. Editorial Bd, Journal of Physics G 1997–; mem. German Physical Soc.; Scientific mem., Max-Planck Soc. 1999–; Chair. CERN LHC (Large Hadron Collider) Computing Review 2000–01; mem. Deutsches Elektronen Synchroton (German Synchrotron Research Centre, DESY) Scientific Council, Hamburg 2000–, Chair. 2002–; Gottfried Wilhelm Leibniz Prize 1995. *Publications:* numerous specialist publs. *Address:* Max-Planck-Institute for Physics, Foehringer Ring 6, Room 219, 80805 Munich, Germany (office). *Telephone:* (89) 32354-381 (office). *Fax:* (89) 32354-305 (office). *E-mail:* bethke@mppmu.mpg.de (office). *Website:* www.mppmu.mpg.de/common/members/bethke.html (office).

BETT, Sir Michael, Kt, CBE, MA; British business executive; *Chairman, Pensions Protection Investment Accreditation Board (PPIAB);* b. 18 Jan. 1935; s. of Arthur Bett and Nina Daniells; m. Christine Angela Reid 1959; one s. two d.; ed Aldenham School, Pembroke Coll., Cambridge; Dir Industrial Relations, Energy Employers Fed. 1970–72; Personnel Dir General Electric Co. Ltd 1972–77; Personnel Dir BBC 1977–81; Bd Mem. for Personnel British Telecom (BT) 1981–84, Corporate Dir, Personnel and Corporate Services 1984–85, Man. Dir Local Communications Services 1985–87, Man. Dir UK Communications 1987–88, Man. Dir BT UK 1988–91, Man. Dir BT 1988–91, Deputy Chair. 1991–94, Dir (non-Exec.) 1994–96; Chair. Nurses' Pay Review Body 1990–95; Chair. Save the Children Fund 1992–97; Pres. Chartered Inst. of Personnel and Devt 1992–98; Chair. Cellnet Group 1991–99; Pro-Chancellor Aston Univ. 1993–; Chair. Review of Armed Forces' Manpower and Pay 1994–95; Chair. Inspectorate of the Security Industry 1994–2000, Nat. Security Inspectorate 2000–; First Commr for the Civil Service 1995–2000; Chair. Pensions Protection Investment Accreditation Board (PPIAB) 2000–; Chair. (non-Exec.) Pace Micro Technology PLC 2000–; Chair. J2C PLC 2000–; Dir English Shakespeare Co. 1988–95; mem. numerous official Cttees; Hon. DSc (Aston) 1996. *Leisure interests:* theatre, music, gardening. *Address:* 48 London Road, Sevenoaks, Kent, TN13 1AS, England (office).

BETTENCOURT, Liliane; French business executive; *President, Fondation Bettencourt Schueller;* b. 21 Oct. 1922; d. of Eugène Schueller (founder of L'Oréal); m. André Bettencourt 1950; one d.; inherited L'Oréal fortune from her father 1957, prin. shareholder, Chair. Man. and Remuneration Cttee, L'Oréal; Founder and Pres. Bettencourt Schueller Foundation 1987–; ranked by Forbes magazine amongst 100 Most Powerful Women (79th) 2004, (39th) 2005. *Leisure interest:* wine. *Address:* Fondation Bettencourt Schueller, 16 Place Vendôme, 75001 Paris, France (office). *Website:* www.fondationbs.org (office); www.loreal.com (office).

BETTENCOURT SANTOS, Humberto; Cape Verde business executive and fmr diplomatist; *Chairman, Cabo Verde Telecom S.A;* b. 17 Feb. 1940, Santo Antão Island; s. of Severino Santos and Inacia Santos; m.; two c.; ed Catholic Univ. of Louvain, Belgium; mem. del. in negotiations on colonial dispute with Portugal 1975; elected Deputy to Nat. Ass. 1975, re-elected 1980; Dir-Gen. Fisheries 1975–82; Amb. to EC and to Nordic and Benelux countries 1982–87; Perm. Rep. of Cape Verde to UN 1987–91; mem. Nat. Comm. on Law of the Sea 1979–82; int. consultant; dir of pvt. computer training centre; pvt. consultant in econ. and fisheries for FAO and UNDP 1991; currently Chair. Cabo Verde Telecom S.A. *Leisure interests:* music (guitar), tennis, golf. *Address:* Rua Cabo Verde Telecom, Várzea, CP 220, Praia, Santiago, Cape Verde (office). *Telephone:* 2609200 (office). *Fax:* 2613725 (office). *E-mail:* cvtelecom@cvtelecom.cv (office). *Website:* www.nave.cv (office).

BETTINI, Paolo; Italian road cyclist; b. 1 April 1974, Cecina; m.; one d.; known as 'Il Grillo'; Tuscany Prov. Champion 1994; professional debut 1997; mem. Nat. Team, World Championships, Valkenburg 1998; winner Liège-Bastogne-Liège 2000, 2002, Championship of Zürich 2001, 2005, Milan-San Remo 2003, HEW Cyclassics 2003, Clásica de San Sebastián 2003, Tour of Lombardy 2005; Silver Medal World Championships, Lisbon 2001; winner Union Cycliste Internationale (UCI) World Cup 2002–04; Gold Medal Road Race, Athens Olympics 2004; first in UCI Ranking 2003, second 2004; fmrly with Mapei-Quick Step Cycling Team (now Quick Step-Innergetic Cycling Team). *Address:* Quick Step-Innergetic Cycling Team, Kouterstraat 14, 8560 Wevelgem, Belgium (office). *Telephone:* (56) 40-45-00 (office). *Fax:* (56) 40-45-01 (office). *E-mail:* info@paolobettini.it. *Website:* www.quickstepcycling.com (office); www.paolobettini.it.

BETTS, Donald Drysdale, MSc, PhD, FRSC; Canadian physicist and academic; *Professor Emeritus of Physics, Dalhousie University;* b. 16 May 1929, Montreal; s. of Wallace Havelock Betts and Mary Drysdale Betts; m. 1st Vilma Mapp 1954 (divorced 1981); m. 2nd Patricia Giles McWilliams 1986; three s. one d. two step-s.; ed Queen Elizabeth High School, Halifax, Dalhousie Univ., Halifax and McGill Univ., Montreal; Nat. Research Council Fellow Univ. of Alberta, Edmonton 1955–56, Asst Prof. of Physics 1956–61, Assoc. Prof. 1961–66, Prof. 1966–80; Dean of Arts and Science Dalhousie Univ. 1980–88, of Science 1988–90, Prof. Emer. 1994–; Adjunct Prof., St Francis Xavier Univ., Antigonish, NS 2002– Visiting Prof. of Physics King's Coll., London 1970–71, of Chemistry and Physics Cornell Univ., New York Jan.–June 1975, Univ. of NSW 1991, 1993; Gordon Godfrey Visiting Research Prof. of Theoretical Physics, Univ. of NSW 1995–2000; Dir Theoretical Physics Inst. Univ. of Alberta 1972–78; Ed. Canadian Journal of Physics 1992–; Pres. Canadian Asscn of Physicists 1969–70; Fellow Japan Soc. for Promotion of Science 1982; NATO Science Fellowship 1963–64; Nuffield Fellowship 1970; Peter Kirkby Medal for Outstanding Service to Canadian Physics (Canadian Asscn of Physicists) 1996, 2002 Queen Elizabeth Gold Medal for Outstanding Service to the Royal Soc. of Canada 2003. *Publications:* some 90 refereed articles in physics journals. *Leisure interests:* game of Go, hiking, gardening, badminton and swimming. *Address:* Department of Physics, Dalhousie University, Halifax, NS, B3H 3J5 (office); 8 Simcoe Place, Halifax, NS, B3M 1H3 (home); 14153 Sunrise Trail, Wallace, NS, B0K 1Y0, Canada. *Telephone:* (902) 494-5124 (office); (902) 443-3916 (home); (902) 257-2370. *Fax:* (902) 494-5191 (office); (902) 494-2835. *E-mail:* dbetts@is.dal.ca (office). *Website:* fizz.phys.dal.ca/people/dbetts.html (office).

BEVAN, Tim; British film producer; b. 1958, Queenstown, NZ; m. 1st Joely Richardson (q.v.) 1992; one d.; m. 2nd Amy Gadney; one s. one d.; began career as a runner for John Cleese's Video Arts; f. Aldabra (music video production co.) with Sarah Radclyffe; formed Working Title (film production co.) with Eric Fellner (q.v.) 1984, now Co-Chair.; Empire Film Award for outstanding contribution to British cinema (jtly) 2005. *Films include:* My Beautiful Laundrette, Personal Services, Wish You Were Here, Caravaggio, Pascali's Island, The Tall Guy, The Rachel Papers, Hidden Agenda, Dakota Road, Map of the Human Heart, Bob Roberts, Posse, Romeo is Bleeding, The Hudsucker Proxy, Four Weddings and a Funeral, Dead Man Walking, Elizabeth, Notting Hill, High Fidelity, Fargo, O Brother, Where Art Thou?, Captain Corelli's Mandolin, The Big Lebowski, Plunkett & Macleane, Man Who Cried, Bridget Jones' Diary, Man Who Wasn't There, Long Time Dead, 40 Days and 40 Nights, Ali G. Indahouse, About a Boy, Guru, My Little Eye, Thirteen, Shape of Things, Ned Kelly, Johnny English, Italian Job, Gettin' Square, Love Actually, Shaun of the Dead, The Calcium Kid, Thunderbirds 2003, Wimbledon 2004, Bridget Jones: The Edge of Reason 2004, Mickybo and Me, United 93 (Best British Producer, London Film Critics' Circle Awards 2007) 2006, Hot Fuzz 2007, The Boat that Rocked 2008, Wild Child 2008. *TV includes:* Tales of the City, The Borrowers, High Fidelity. *Address:* Working Title Films, Oxford House, 76 Oxford Street, London, W1D 1BS, England (office). *Website:* www.workingtitlefilms.com (office).

BEVAN, Sir Timothy (Hugh), Kt; British banker; b. 24 May 1927, London; s. of the late Hugh Bevan and Pleasance Bevan (née Scrutton); m. Pamela Murray (née Smith) 1952; two s. two d.; ed Eton Coll.; called to the Bar, Middle Temple 1950; joined Barclays Bank Ltd (now Barclays Bank PLC) 1950, Dir 1966–93, Vice-Chair. 1968–73, Deputy Chair. 1973–81, Chair. 1981–87; Dir Barclays Int. Ltd 1971; Dir BET Public Ltd Co. 1987–92, Chair. 1988–91; Dir Foreign and Colonial Investment Trust PLC 1988–98 (Deputy Chair. 1993–98); fmr Dir Soc. Financière Européenne 1967, Commercial Union Assurance Co. Ltd, Union Discount Co. of London Ltd; Chair. Cttee of London Clearing Bankers 1983–85; Chair. City Communications Centre 1982–83. *Leisure interests:* sailing, gardening. *Address:* c/o Barclays Bank PLC, 54 Lombard Street, London, EC3V 9EX, England.

BEVANDA, Vjekoslav; Bosnia and Herzegovina politician; currently Deputy Prime Minister and Minister of Finance, Fed. of Bosnia and Herzegovina. *Address:* Ministry of Finance, Sarajevo, Mehmeda Spahe 5, Bosnia and Herzegovina (office). *Telephone:* (33) 203147 (office). *Fax:* (33) 203152 (office). *E-mail:* info@fmf.gov.ba (office). *Website:* www.fmf.gov.ba (office).

BEWKES, Jeffrey (Jeff) L., BA, MBA; American broadcasting executive; *Chairman and CEO, Time Warner Inc.;* b. 25 May 1952, Paterson, NJ; s. of Eugene Garrett Bewkes, Jr; m. Margaret (Peggy) Brim; one c.; ed Yale Univ., Stanford Univ. Grad. School of Business; early career as Operations Dir Sonoma Vineyards, Calif.; Accountant Officer, Citibank, New York 1984–86; Exec. Vice-Pres. and Chief Financial Officer Home Box Office Inc. 1986–91, Pres. and COO 1991–95, Chair. and CEO 1995–2002; Chair. Entertainment and Network Group, AOL Time Warner Inc. (now Time Warner Inc.) 2002–05, Pres. Time Warner Inc. 2005–08, also COO 2005–07, mem. Bd of Dirs 2007–, CEO 2008–, Chair. 2009–; mem. Bd of Dirs Nixon Center; mem. Advisory Bd Stanford Univ. Grad. School of Business, American Museum of Natural History, Museum of Television and Radio, The Creative Coalition, Paley Center for Media; Trustee, Yale Univ., Museum of the Moving Image; mem. Council on Foreign Relations. *Address:* Time Warner Inc., 1 Time Warner Center, New York, NY 10019, USA (office). *Telephone:* (212) 484-8000 (office). *Fax:* (212) 489-6183 (office). *E-mail:* info@timewarner.com (office). *Website:* www.timewarner.com (office).

BEWLEY, Thomas Henry, MA, MD, FRCP, FRCPI; Irish consultant psychiatrist; b. 8 July 1926, Dublin; s. of Geoffrey Bewley and Victoria Jane Wilson; m. Beulah Knox 1955; one s. four d.; ed St Columba's Coll., Dublin, Trinity Coll., Dublin; trained at St Patrick's Hosp., Dublin, Maudsley Hosp., London and Univ. of Cincinnati, USA; Consultant Psychiatrist, Tooting Bec and St Thomas' Hosps, London 1961–88; Emer. Consultant St Thomas' Hosp.; mem. Standing Advisory Cttee on Drug Dependence 1966–71, Advisory Council on Misuse of Drugs 1972–84; Consultant Adviser on Drug Dependence to Dept of Health and Social Security 1972–81; Consultant WHO 1969–78; Hon. Sr Lecturer, St George's Hosp. Medical School, Univ. of London 1974–96; Pres. Royal Coll. of Psychiatrists 1984–87 (Dean 1977–82); Jt Founder and mem. Council, Inst. for the Study of Drug Dependence 1967–96; Hon. FRCPsych, Hon. CBE. *Publications:* Handbook for Inceptors and Trainees in Psychiatry 1976, Madness to Mental Illness 2008; papers on drug dependence, medical manpower and side effects of drugs. *Leisure interest:* Irish Georgian Society (London Chapter). *Address:* 4 Grosvenor Gardens Mews North, London, SW1W 0JP, England. *Telephone:* (20) 7730-9592 (home).

BEXELL, Göran Bertil David, PhD; Swedish academic and university administrator; *Professor of Ethics, Lund University;* b. 24 Dec. 1943, Högsby; Prof., Dept of Theology, Lund Univ. 1990–, Dean, Theology Faculty 1995–99, Vice-Chancellor Lund Univ. 2003–08; Ed. Svensk Teologisk Kvartalskrift 1990–97; fmr Pres. Asscn of Swedish Higher Educ. *Publications:* Teologisk etik: en introduktion (co-author), Universal Ethics: Perspectives and Proposals from Scandinavian Scholars (co-ed. with Dan-Erik Andersson) 2002. *Address:* Department of Theology, Lund University, PO Box 117, 221 00 Lund, Sweden (office). *Telephone:* (222) 00-00 (office). *Fax:* (222) 47-20 (office). *E-mail:* Goran.Bexell@rektor.lu.se (office). *Website:* www.lu.se (office).

BEYENE, Tekie, BA; Eritrean central banker; *Governor, Bank of Eritrea;* b. 15 June 1941, Asmara; m. Maaza Haile; ed Univ. of Asmara. *Publications:* contribs to magazine Hewyet (Recovery). *Leisure interest:* writing. *Address:* Bank of Eritrea, PO Box 849, 21 Victory Avenue, Asmara, Eritrea (office); Tiro Alvolo Street 702, No. 14–16, Asmara, Eritrea (home). *Telephone:* (1) 123036 (office); (1) 184351 (home). *Fax:* (1) 122091 (office). *E-mail:* tekieb@boe.gov.er (office).

BEYNON, John David Emrys, PhD, FREng; British professor of electronics and college principal; b. 11 March 1939, Risca, Gwent; s. of John Emrys Beynon and Elvira Beynon; m. Hazel Janet Hurley 1964; two s. one d.; ed Univ. of Wales and Univ. of Southampton; Scientific Officer, Radio Research

Station, Slough 1962–64; Lecturer, Sr Lecturer, then Reader, Univ. of Southampton 1964–67; Prof. of Electronics, Univ. of Wales Inst. of Science and Tech., Cardiff 1977–79; Head Dept of Electronic and Electrical Eng, Univ. of Surrey 1979–83, Pro Vice-Chancellor 1983–87, Sr Pro Vice-Chancellor 1987–90; Prin. King's Coll., Univ. of London 1990–92, Fellow 1990; Hon. Fellow Univ. Coll. of Swansea 1990; mem. British Library Advisory Council 1994–99, Ind. TV Comm. 1995–2000; Chair. Westminster Christian Council 1999–2000; Sec., Bloomsbury Central Baptist Church, London 2000–. *Publications:* Charge-coupled Devices and Their Applications (with D. R. Lamb) 1980; papers on plasma physics, semi-conductor devices and integrated circuits and Eng educ. *Leisure interests:* music, photography, travel. *Address:* Chalkdene, 13 Great Quarry, Guildford, Surrey, GU1 3XN, England (home). *Telephone:* (1483) 503458 (home).

BEYNON, John Herbert, BSc, DSc, CChem, FRSC, CPhys, FInstP, CSci, FRS; British chemist and academic (retd); *Professor Emeritus, University of Wales;* b. 29 Dec. 1923, Ystalyfera, Wales; s. of Leslie Ewart and Phyllis Beynon (née Gibbon); m. Yvonne Lilian Fryer 1947; Scientific Officer, Tank Armament Research 1943–47; Man. and Sr Research Assoc., Physical Chem. Research, ICI Dyestuffs Div. 1952–74; Prof. of Chem. and Dir Mass Spectrometry Center, Purdue Univ., USA 1969–75; Assoc. Prof. of Molecular Sciences, Univ. of Warwick 1972–74; Visiting Prof., Univ. of Essex 1982–; Univ. Prof. and Royal Soc. Research Prof., Univ. of Wales, Swansea 1974–86, Research Prof. 1987–, Prof. Emer. 1991–; Chair. Science Curriculum Devt Cttee, Cttee for Wales 1983–88; Pres. Asscn for Science Educ., Wales 1985–86; Ed. Int. Journal of Mass Spectrometry and Ion Processes 1983–85; Founder and Ed.-in-Chief Rapid Communications in Mass Spectrometry 1987–97; mem. Editorial Bd Organic Mass Spectrometry 1967–88, 1992–94, Int. Journal of Mass Spectrometry and Ion Processes 1967–97, Mass Spectrometry Reviews 1984–2003, Biological Mass Spectrometry 1992–94, J. Mass Spectrometry 1995–; Chair. Swansea Sports Club 1988–92; Dir Swansea Cricket and Football Club 1991–92; Founder Pres. European Mass Spectrometry Soc. 1993–96; Assoc. Inst. Jožef Stefan, Yugoslavia; Fellow, Univ. of Wales Swansea 1988–; Hon. mem. mass spectrometry socs of Japan, China, Italy and Yugoslavia; Hon. Fellow, Serbian Chem. Soc. 1982–;; Hon. DSc (Purdue Univ., USA) 1995, (Babeş-Bolyai Univ., Romania) 1997; 3M-Boomer Award 1965, Hasler Award for Spectroscopy 1979, Jan Marc Marci Medal 1984, Gold Medal of the Int. Mass Spectrometry Soc. 1985, Frank H. Field and Joe L. Franklin Award of the American Chemical Soc. 1987, Aston Medal of British Mass Spectrometry Soc. 1990, Gold Medal, Italian Chemical Soc. 1992. *Publications:* 10 books and over 400 scientific papers. *Leisure interests:* photography, golf, rugby. *Address:* 5 Willow Court, Clyne Common, Swansea, SA3 3JB, Wales (home). *Telephone:* (1792) 235205 (home).

BEYONCÉ; American singer, songwriter and producer; b. (Beyoncé Knowles), 4 Sept. 1981, Houston, TX; d. of Mathew Knowles and Tina Knowles; m. Jay-Z (Shawn Carter) 2008; founding mem., GirlsTyme (with Kelly Rowland, later joined by LaTavia Roberson and LeToya Luckett), group renamed Something Fresh, then The Dolls before settling on Destiny's Child 1989–2005; numerous live performances, tours; solo artist 2001–; established clothing label Touch of Couture; (with Destiny's Child) Billboard Award for Artist of the Year, Group of the Year, Hot 100 Singles Artist of the Year, Hot 100 Group of the Year 2000, Grammy Award for Best R&B Song, Best R&B Performance by a Duo or Group with Vocal (for Say My Name) 2001, NAACP Image Award for Outstanding Duo or Group (for Say My Name) 2001, MTV Video Award for Best R&B Video (for Say My Name) 2001, American Music Award for Favorite Soul/R&B Group 2001, Soul Train Sammy Davis Jr Award for Entertainer of the Year 2001, American Music Award for Favorite Pop/ Rock Band, Duo or Group 2002, BRIT Award for Best Int. Group 2002, MOBO Award for Best Gospel Act 2002, World Music Award for World's Best Pop Group 2005, Lady of Soul Award for Best Group Single (for Soldier) 2005, American Music Award for Favorite Soul/R & B Band, Duo or Group 2005; (solo) Billboard Awards for New Female Artist of the Year, New R&B Artist, Hot 200 Female Artist 2003, BRIT Awards for Best Int. Female Solo Artist 2004, Billboard R&B/Hip Hop Awards for Top Female Artist, New Artist 2004, Grammy Award for Best R&B Song, Best Rap/Sung Collaboration (for Crazy in Love, with Jay-Z) 2004, Grammy Award for Best R&B performance by a duo or group (for The Closer I Get To You, with Luther Vandross) 2004, Grammy Award for Best Female R&B Vocal Performance (for Dangerously In Love) 2004, Billboard Music Award for R&B/Hip-Hop Group of the Year 2005, Grammy Award for Best R&B Performance by a Duo or Group with Vocals (for So Amazing, with Stevie Wonder) 2006, MOBO Awards for Best Song and Best Video (both for Deja Vu), for Best Int. Female 2006, Soul Train Award for Best Single by a Female (for Irreplaceable) 2007, BET Award for Best R&B Female 2007, for Video of the Year (for Irreplaceable) 2007, MTV Video Music Award for Best Collaboration (for Beautiful Liar with Shakira) 2007. *Recordings include:* albums: with Destiny's Child: Destiny's Child 1998, The Writing's On The Wall 1999, Survivor (American Music Award for Favorite Pop/Rock Album 2002) 2001, Eight Days Of Christmas 2001, Destiny Fulfilled (Lady of Soul Award for Best Group Album 2005, American Music Award for Favorite Soul/R&B Album 2005) 2004; solo: Soul Survivors 2002, Dangerously in Love (Grammy Award for Best Contemporary R&B Album 2004) 2003, Live At Wembley 2004, B-Day (Grammy Award for Best Contemporary R&B Album 2007) 2006, I Am... Sasha Fierce 2008. *Film appearances:* Carmen: A Hip Hopera (TV) 2001, Austin Powers in Goldmember 2002, The Fighting Temptations 2003, The Pink Panther 2006, Dreamgirls 2006, Cadillac Records 2008. *Address:* Music World Entertainment, 9898 Bissonnet, Suite 625, Houston, TX 77036, USA (office). *Website:* www.beyonceonline.com; www .destinyschild.com

BEZHUASHVILI, Gela, LLM, MPA; Georgian politician, diplomatist and lawyer; *Head of Special Service, Intelligence Service;* b. 1 March 1967,

Tetritskaro Region; m.; two s. one d.; ed Kyiv State Univ., Ukraine, Southern Methodist Univ. Law School and John F. Kennedy School of Govt, Harvard Univ., USA; positions at Ministry of Foreign Affairs including Second Sec. of Int. Law Problems Div., Deputy Head of Dept then Deputy Head of Int. Law Bd 1991–93; Envoy, Embassy in Kazakhstan 1993–96; Dir Int. Law Dept 1997–2000; Deputy Minister of Defence 2000–04, Minister of Defence 2004; Asst to Pres. of Georgia on Nat. Security Issues and Sec. Nat. Security Council 2004–05; Minister of Foreign Affairs 2005–08; Head of Special Service, Intelligence Service 2008–; mem. Cttee on Int. Law, Cttee Against Corruption and Sub-Cttee on Protection of Nat. Minorities, European Council; Rep. of Georgia, Baku-Tbilisi-Ceyhan Law Documentation Package 1999–2000; Order of Merit, First Class (Ukraine) 2006, Order of Maarjamaa Rist III Class 2007; winner Edmund Mask Programe Nat. Competition (USA) 1995. *Publications:* International Law Aspects of the Foreign Policy of Georgia 2003; articles in professional journals of int. law, nat. minorities and self-determination. *Address:* Intelligence Special Service, 4 Kekelidze Street Tbilisi, Georgia (office). *Telephone:* (32) 93-46-69 (ext. 101) (office). *Fax:* (32) 93-46-69 (office). *E-mail:* dir.int@fiss.gov.ge (office).

BEZOS, Jeffrey (Jeff) Preston, BS; American online retail executive; *Chairman, President and CEO, Amazon.com, Inc.;* b. 12 Jan. 1964, Albuquerque, NM; m. Mackenzie Bezos; two s.; ed Princeton Univ.; with Bankers Trust Co. 1988–90; joined D. E. Shaw & Co. 1990, Sr Vice-Pres. 1992–94; f. Amazon.com Inc., Seattle 1994, Chair., Pres. and CEO 1995–; f. Blue Origin LLC (aerospace co.) 2000; f. Bezos Expeditions (investment co.); Time Magazine Person of the Year 1999. *Address:* Amazon.com Inc., 1200 12th Avenue, South, Suite 1200, Seattle, WA 98144-2734, USA (office). *Telephone:* (206) 266-1000 (office). *Fax:* (206) 266-1821 (office). *Website:* www.amazon.com (office); public.blueorigin.com/index.html.

BHABHA, J. J. (Jamshed Jehangir), BA; Indian business executive; *Chairman, National Centre for the Performing Arts;* b. 21 Aug. 1914, Bombay; ed Cathedral High School, Bombay, Gonville and Caius Coll., Cambridge, Lincoln's Inn, London; Chair. Tata Services Ltd, Tata McGraw-Hill Publishing Co. Ltd, Associated Bldg Co. Ltd; Dir Tata & Sons Ltd, Indian Hotels Co. Ltd, Tata Ltd, London, RDI Print and Publishing Pvt. Ltd, Titan Industries Ltd, Stewarts and Lloyds of India Ltd, Tata Press Ltd; Chair. and Trustee-in-Charge Nat. Centre for the Performing Arts; Vice-Chair. and Man. Trustee Sir Dorabji Tata Trust; Trustee Lady Tata Memorial Trust, J.H. Bhabha Memorial Trust, Prince of Wales Museum of Western India, etc.; Chair. Governing Bd Tata Inst. of Social Sciences; mem. Council Nat. Inst. Advanced Studies, Tata Memorial Centre for Cancer Research and Treatment; mem. numerous public insts; Pres. Nat. Soc. of the Friends of Trees; Vice-Pres. Nat. Soc. for Clean Cities; Kt Commdr of the Order of Merit (Italy) 1976, Commdr's Cross of the Order of Merit (FRG) 1978, Commdr's Cross of the Order of the Crown, Belgium 1979; Austria Award of Honour 1984. *Address:* National Centre for the Performing Arts, Nariman Point, Mumbai 400 021; Tata Sons Ltd, Bombay House, 24 Homi Mody Street, Mumbai 400 001 (office); 12 Little Gibbs Road, Malabar Hill, Mumbai 400 006, India (home). *Telephone:* (22) 2283-3737 (office).

BHADESHIA, Harshad Kumar Dharamshi Hansraj, BSc, PhD, FRS, FREng, FInstP, FIM, CEng, CPhys; British metallurgist and academic; b. 27 Nov. 1953, Nairobi, Kenya; s. of Dharamshi Hansraj Bhadeshia and Narmda Dharamshi Bhadeshia; m. 1978 (divorced 1992); two d.; ed City of London Polytechnic, Univ. of Cambridge; Science Research Council Research Fellow, Univ. of Cambridge 1979–81, demonstrator 1981–85, lecturer 1985–94, Reader in Physical Metallurgy 1994–99, Prof. of Physical Metallurgy 1999–; Distinguished Adjunct Prof., Graduate Inst. of Ferrous Tech., POSTECH, South Korea 2005; Vice-Pres. Industrial Trust; mem. European Acad. of Sciences; Founding Ed. Science and Technology of Welding and Joining 1996–; mem. Editorial Bd Australasian Journal of Welding 2000–, Material Transactions of JIM 2000–, Science and Technology of Advanced Materials 2001–, Materials Science and Technology 2002–, Current Opinion: Solid-State and Materials Science 2002–; Fellow Darwin Coll. 1985–; Fellow Inst. of Materials 1998–, Royal Society 1998–, Royal Acad. of Eng 2002–; Foreign Fellow, Indian Nat. Acad. of Eng 2004–; Royal Charter Prize 1976, Pfeil Medal and Prize 1979, 1991, Larke Medal 1992, Hume-Rothery Prize 1992, Rosenhain Medal and Prize 1994, CBMM Charles-Hatchett Medal and Award, Brazil, 1996, Royal Society Armourers and Brasiers' Company Award 1997, Medal and Rose Bowl 2000, Reaumur Medal 2001, 5th Tendolkar Memorial Lecture India 2002, 37th John Player Memorial lecture 2002, Brooker Medal 2003, Sawamura Award 2003, Comfort A. Adams Award Lecture 2004, 52nd Hatfield Lecture 2004, 17th Hume-Rothery Lecture 2005. *Publications include:* Geometry of Crystals 1987, Bainite in Steels 1992, (jtly) Steels 1995. *Leisure interest:* television, squash. *Address:* University of Cambridge, Department of Materials Science and Metallurgy, Phase Transformations and Complex Properties Research Group, Pembroke Street, Cambridge, CB2 3QZ (office); 57 Barrons Way, Comberton, Cambridge, CB3 7EQ, England (home). *Telephone:* (1223) 334301 (office). *Fax:* (1223) 334567 (office). *E-mail:* hkdb@cus.cam.ac.uk (office). *Website:* www.msm.cam.ac.uk/phase-trans (office).

BHAGWANDAS, Rana, LLB, LLM, MA; Pakistani judge; b. 20 Dec. 1942, Naseerabad, Larkana Dist (now Qamber Shahdadkot Dist), Sindh; called to the Bar 1965, practised law 1965–67; joined Pakistani Judicial System 1967, later became a sessions judge, subsequently judge of Sindh High Court 1994, apptd to superior judiciary 1999, appointment challenged by a constitutional petition, subsequently rejected, claiming that only Muslims can be apptd to superior judiciary; Judge of Supreme Court 2000–, has served as Acting Chief Justice in 2005 while Chief Justice Iftikhar Muhammad Chaudhry was on a ten-day trip to People's Repub. of China, during the latter's period of suspension, March–July 2007; first Hindu and second non-Muslim to serve in this post; honoured with 'Siropa' (robe of honour) during visit to Harimandir Sahib, Amritsar, India 2005. *Address:* Supreme Court of Pakistan, Constitution Avenue, Islamabad, Pakistan (office). *Telephone:* (51) 9220581 (office). *Fax:* (51) 9213452 (office). *Website:* www.supremecourt.gov.pk (office).

BHAI, Aziz Mohammad; Bangladeshi pharmaceuticals executive; Founding Chair. and Man. Dir Ambee Pharmaceuticals Ltd 1976–. *Address:* Ambee Pharmaceuticals Ltd, House No. 1, Road No. 71, Gulshan 2, Dhaka 1212, Bangladesh (office). *Telephone:* (2) 8813991 (office). *Fax:* (2) 8827777 (office). *E-mail:* info@ambeepharma.com (office). *Website:* www.ambeepharma.com (office).

BHAN, Suraj, MA, LLB; Indian politician; *Chairman, National Commission for Scheduled Castes and Scheduled Tribes;* b. 1 Oct. 1928, Mahlan Wali; s. of Garibu Ram; m. Chameli Devi; three s. four d.; ed Punjab and Kurukshetra Univ., Haryana; Founder Pres. Punjab Scheduled Castes Student's Fed. 1947–49; f. Punjab Scheduled Castes Welfare Asscn 1950, Pres. 1950–66; mem. All-India Working Cttee of Bharatiya Jan Sangh 1970–73; Head of Harijan Wing and Sec. of Haryana Jan Sangh 1973–76; mem. Lok Sabha 1967–70, 1977–79, 1980–84, 1996; Pres. Haryana Bharatiya Janata Party (BJP); Sec. All India BJP; Pres. All India BJP Scheduled Castes Cell; mem. Legis. Ass. from Mullana 1987–; Minister for Revenue 1987–89; Deputy Speaker Lok Sabha 1996–98; apptd Gov. of Uttar Pradesh 1998; Chair. Nat. Comm. for Schedule Castes 2004–. *Address:* National Commission for Scheduled Castes and Scheduled Tribes, V th Floor, Lok Nayak Bhavan, New Delhi, India.

BHANDARE, Murlidhar Chandrakant, BSc, LLB; Indian lawyer and politician; *Governor of Orissa;* b. 10 Dec. 1928, Bombay (now Mumbai); s. of Chandrakant Laxmikant Bhandare and Sunanda Bhandare; m.; one s. one d.; Sr Advocate in Supreme Court of India, Pres. Supreme Court Bar Asscn for two terms; mem. Rajya Sabha 1980–; Chair. UN Sub-Comm. for Prevention of Discrimination and Protection of Minority 1984–89, Chair. UNESCO's Appeals Body 1990–2003; Chair. Indira Gandhi Nat. Integration Award Cttee; visited UK, USA, USSR, Germany and other countries; Gov. of Orissa 2007–; active in supporting empowerment of women and protection of rights of children and physically handicapped. *Publications:* The World of Gender Justice (ed.); articles on law, human rights, population control, gender parity and justice published in leading magazines and journals. *Address:* Raj Bhavan, Bhubaneswar, Orissa, India (office). *E-mail:* info@rajbhavanorissa.gov.in (office). *Website:* rajbhavanorissa.gov.in (office).

BHANDIT, Rittakol; Thai film director; b. 1951, Ayutthaya; ed Assumption Coll., Si Racha, Assumption Commercial Coll., Bangkok; news reporter The Nation; became film critic and screenplay writer 1975, directorial debut 1983. *Films:* Boonchu, The Seed (Thai Best Picture award) 1987, Classmates (Best Picture, Best Dir, Best Screenplay) 1990, Miss You (Best Picture, Best Dir, Best Screenplay) 1993, Once Upon a Time (Best Dir, Best Screenplay) 1995, Satang 2000, 14 tula, songkram prachachon (Moon Hunter) (also co-writer) 2001, Chue chop chuan ha reung 2003. *Address:* c/o Five Star Production Co. Ltd, 61/1 Soi Thaweemitr 2, Rama 9 Rd, Huaykwang, Bangkok, Thailand (office). *Telephone:* 246 9025-9 (office). *Fax:* 246 2105 (office). *E-mail:* info@fivestarent.com (office). *Website:* www.fivestarent.com (office).

BHARDWAJ, H. R., LLB, MA; Indian politician and lawyer; *Minister of Law and Justice;* b. 17 May 1937, Garhi village, Rohtak Dist; s. of Jagan Nath Prasad Sharma and Sarti Devi; m. Prafulata Bhardwaj 1960; one s. two d.; ed B.M. Coll., Shimla, Agra Univ. and Panjab Univ., Chandigarh; mem. Nat. Exec., Indian Youth Congress 1957; Public Prosecutor, Delhi High Court 1972–77; Sr Standing Counsel for Uttar Pradesh, Supreme Court of India 1980–82; mem. Rajya Sabha 1982–, mem. Home Affairs Cttee 1998–2004; Minister of State for Law and Justice 1984–89, 1992–96; Sr Vice-Pres., Inst. of Constitutional and Parl. Studies, New Delhi 1988–90; Minister of State for Planning and Programme Implementation 1991–96; Minister of Law and Justice 2004–; mem. Advisory Council, Delhi Devt Cttee 2000–. *Address:* Ministry of Law and Justice, 'A' Wing, Shastri Bhavan, Dr Rajendra Prasad Road, New Delhi 110 001 (office); E-7/19, Charimili, Bhopal, Madhya Pradesh, India (home). *Telephone:* (11) 23384777 (office). *Fax:* (11) 23387259 (office). *E-mail:* lawmin@caselaw.delhi.nic.in (office); hansrajb@sansad.nic.in (office). *Website:* www.lawmin.nic.in (office).

BHARGAVA, Manjul, AB, PhD; Canadian mathematician and academic; *Professor of Mathematics, Princeton University;* b. 1974, Hamilton, Ont.; ed Harvard Univ., Mass, Princeton Univ., NJ; grew up in Long Island, NY; with Nat. Security Agency, Summer 1994; Duluth Summer Research Program, Summer 1995; Center for Communications Research, Princeton, Summer 1996; AT&T Labs Research, Florham Park, NJ, Summer 1997; Clay Research Fellowship (first recipient), Clay Math. Inst., Cambridge, Mass 2000–05; Visiting Mathematician, Princeton Univ. 2001–02; Visiting Asst Prof., Harvard Univ., Spring 2003; Prof. of Math., Princeton Univ. (hired at rank of full prof. with tenure just two years after finishing grad. school) 2003–; fmr Co-Pres. Harvard Math Club; Winner of NY State Science Talent Search 1992, Detur Prize for Outstanding Academic Achievement, Harvard Univ. 1993, Derek Bok Award for Excellence in Teaching, Harvard Univ. 1993, 1994, 1995, Hoopes Prize for Excellence in Scholarly Work and Research, Harvard Univ. 1996, Hertz Foundation Grad. Fellowship in Math. 1996–2000, AMS-MAA-SIAM Frank and Brennie Morgan Prize 1997, named one of Popular Science Magazine's "Brilliant 10" 2002, Hasse Prize for Exposition, Math. Asscn of America 2003, Packard Foundation Fellowship in Science and Eng 2004, Leonard M. and Eleanor B. Blumenthal Award for the Advancement of Research in Pure Math. 2005, Clay Research Award, Clay Math. Inst. (co-recipient) 2005, SASTRA Ramanujan Prize (co-recipient) 2005, MS Frank Nelson Cole Prize in Number Theory, American Math. Soc. 2008. *Achievements:* 13 new Gauss composition laws, including quartic and quintic degree cases; proof of 15 theorem, including extension of theorem to other number sets such as prime numbers; proof of 290 theorem; novel generalization of factorial function, resolving decades-old conjecture by George Pólya. *Publications:* several papers in professional journals on algebraic number theory, combinatorics and representation theory. *Leisure interests:* tabla player (studied under Zakir Hussain), linguistics and its various connections to math. and music. *Address:* 1206 Fine Hall, Department of Mathematics, Princeton University, Princeton, NJ 08544, USA (office). *Telephone:* (609) 258-4192 (office). *Fax:* (609) 258-1367 (office). *E-mail:* bhargava@math.princeton.edu (office). *Website:* www.math.princeton.edu (office).

BHARGAVA, Pushpa Mittra, PhD; Indian scientist, writer and consultant; b. 22 Feb. 1928, Ajmer, Rajasthan; s. of Dr. Ram Chandra Bhargava and Gayatri Devi Bhargava; m. Edith Manorama Patrick 1958; one s. one d.; ed Lucknow Univ.; lecturer, Dept of Chemistry, Osmania Univ., Hyderabad, then mem. staff Cen. Labs. Hyderabad; Post-doctoral Fellow, Univ. of Madison 1953–56; at Nat. Inst. for Medical Research, UK 1957–58; joined Regional Research Lab. (now Indian Inst. of Chemical Tech.) 1958–77; Dir Centre for Cellular and Molecular Biology, Hyderabad 1977–90; CSIR Distinguished Fellow 1990–93; Visiting Prof., Collège de France, Paris; Scientific adviser in several industries; has worked by invitation at McArdle Lab. for Cancer Research, USA, Nat. Inst. for Medical Research, UK, Institut du Radium, France, Max-Planck Institut für Biophysikalische Chemie, Germany; fmr Vice-Chair. Nat. Knowledge Comm.; has given over 250 lectures to int. meetings worldwide; Founder Guha Research Conf.; Founder-mem. Soc. for Study of Reproduction (USA); Past-Pres. Soc. of Biological Chemists; mem. numerous other Indian and int. professional socs and standing or ad hoc cttees of Int. Cell Research Org. and other int. orgs; fmr or current mem. several editorial bds of scientific journals; Fellow, Indian Nat. Science Acad., Indian Acad. of Sciences, Nat. Acad. of Sciences (India), Nat. Acad. of Medical Sciences (India), World Acad. of Arts and Sciences, Indian Acad. of Social Sciences; Corresp. mem. American Asscn for Cancer Research and other bodies; mem. Nat. Security Advisory Bd, 2006–; Life Fellow, Clare Hall, Cambridge, UK; Légion d'honneur 1998; Hon. DSc (Univ. of Burdwan); numerous prizes and awards, including Nat. Citizens Award 1988; Padma Bhushan conferred by Pres. of India 1986. *Publications:* several books, including Proteins of Seminal Plasma 1989, The Saga of Indian Science Since Independence 2003, Angels, Devil and Science 2007; numerous articles. *Leisure interests:* fine arts, reading, current affairs, sports, music, films, photography. *Address:* Anveshna, Furqan Cottage, 12-13-100 Lane 1, Street No. 3, Tarnaka, Hyderabad 500 017 (office); 12-5-27 Vijayapuri, Tarnaka, Hyderabad 500 017, India (home). *Telephone:* (40) 27017789 (office); (40) 27003517 (home). *Fax:* (40) 27017857 (office). *E-mail:* pmb1928@yahoo.co.in (office); bhargava.pm@gmail.com (home).

BHARTIA, Shobhana; Indian newspaper executive; *Vice-Chair and Editorial Director, The Hindustani Times;* b. 4 Jan. 1957, Calcutta (now Kolkata); d. of Birla and Manorama Devi; m. Shyam Sunder Bhartia 1974; two s.; ed Loreto House, Calcutta; Exec. Dir The Hindustani Times Ltd 1986–, Vice-Chair. and Editorial Dir; Dir Press Trust of India Ltd 1987, Indian Airlines, New Delhi 1988–90, Air Travel Bureau Pvt. Ltd 1989; Chair. and Treas. Bd of Govs, Delhi Coll. of Arts and Commerce 1988–90; Chair. HT Vision Ltd 1990–; Chair. Bd of Govs Shyama Prasad Mukherjee Coll. (for Women) 1992; mem. Sri Mata Vaishnu Devi Shrine Bd, Katra 1991; Pres. FICCI (women's org.), Leader dels to Australia, NZ, the Philippines and to World Congress of Women Conf. (Moscow, fmr USSR) 1987–88; Int. Cultural Devt Org. Award 1989, Mahila Shiromani Award 1990, Lok Shri Award, Inst. of Econ. Studies 1990, Vijaya Shri Award, Int. Friendship Soc. of India 1991, Delhi Chamber of Commerce Outstanding Businesswoman Award 2001, Padma Shri 2005. *Leisure interests:* reading, music. *Address:* Hindustani Times House, 18–20 Kasturba Gandhi Marg, New Delhi, 110 065, India. *Telephone:* (11) 3317955 (office); (11) 6830260 (home). *Fax:* (11) 3319021 (office). *Website:* www.htmedia.in (office).

BHATIA, Mick, BSc, PhD; Canadian biologist and academic; *Scientific Director, Stem Cell and Cancer Research Institute, McMaster University;* b. 1970; ed McMaster Univ., Univ. of Guelph; worked for Dept of Human Biology, Univ. of Guelph; Postdoctoral Fellow, Hosp. for Sick Children, Univ. of Toronto; Canadian Research Chair and Dir Krembil Centre for Stem Cell Biology, Robarts Research Inst., Univ. of Western Ont., London –2005; Prof. of Biochemistry and Biomedical Sciences, Professorial Chair in Cancer and Stem Cell Biology, Sr Canadian Research Chair and Scientific Dir, Stem Cell and Cancer Research Inst., McMaster Univ. 2006–; Canada Research Chair in Stem Cell Biology and Regenerative Medicine 2002–07; Postdoctoral Fellowship, Nat. Cancer Inst. of Canada 1995–97; Krembil Foundation Research Chair in Stem Cell Biology and Regenerative Medicine 2003; Annual Trainee Award, American Soc. of Dermatology 1997, Young Scientist Scholarship Award, Medical Research Council 1999–2002, Premiers' Research Excellence Award, Ministry of Energy, Science and Tech. 2000–05, Canada's Top 40 Under 40 2002. *Publications:* numerous articles in professional journals. *Address:* c/o Michael G. DeGroote Centre for Learning and Discovery, 1200 Main Street West, Hamilton, ON L8N 3Z5, Canada (office). *Telephone:* (905) 525-9140. *Fax:* (905) 522-7772. *E-mail:* mbhatia@mcmaster.ca.

BHATIA, Raghunanthanlal, LLB; Indian politician; *Governor of Bihar;* b. 3 July 1921, Amritsar, Punjab; s. of the late Arooramal Bhatia and Lal Devi Bhatia; m. Sarala Bhatia; one s. one d.; ed Punjab Univ., Univ. at Lahore; fmr Pres. Students' Union; mem. Local Body of Amritsar for nine years; mem. Lok Sabha for Amritsar Constituency 1972–, Chair. Cttee on Petitions 1983, fmr mem. Select Cttee for the Amendment of the Constitution 1992, mem. several consultative parl. cttees, including Ministry of Home Affairs, Educ., Railways,

Information and Broadcasting, Law and Justice and Company Affairs, represented India as a del. to UN, del. to 7th NAM Summit, Delhi 1983, Commonwealth Heads of Govt Meeting, New Delhi 1983, 6th SAARC Summit, Colombo 1991, 5th Meeting of Coordinating Countries of the Action Programme for Econ. Cooperation of Non-aligned Countries, Delhi 1986; mem. Exec. Cttee Congress Parl. Party 1975–77; Pres. Punjab Pradesh Congress Cttee 1982–84; mem. India Council for Cultural Relations 1983–84; Gen. Sec. AICC 1991; Union Minister of State for External Affairs July 1992; Gov. of Kerala 2004–08, of Bihar 2008–; Chair. India Bulgaria Friendship Soc. 1983–90, India GDR Friendship Asscn 1983–90; Co-Chair. All India Peace and Solidarity Org. 1981–83; Vice-Pres. Friends of the Soviet Union 1983–84; leader or mem. del. of AICC to People's Repub. of China, USSR, Poland, Bulgaria, Czechoslovakia, USA, Cambodia, Viet Nam, Afghanistan, Japan, UK. *Leisure interests:* reading, gardening. *Address:* 44 Kamalpushpa, Congress Nagar, Amravati 444 601, Maharashtra, India (office). *Telephone:* (612) 2226207 (office). *E-mail:* governorbihar@nic.in (office). *Website:* gov.bih.nic.in (office).

BHATT, Om P.; Indian central banker; *Chairman, State Bank of India;* joined State Bank of India (SBI) as probationary office 1972, held several positions including Scheme Coordinator of br. computerization at Cen. Office of SBI, Regional Man. with Jaipur Zone, Gen. Man. with Lucknow Zone and Chief Gen. Man. with North Zone, Man. Dir State Bank of Travancore, Man. Dir and Group Exec. SBI April–Oct. 2006, Chair. 2006–. *Address:* State Bank of India, Corporate Centre, Madame Cama Road, PO Box 10121, Mumbai 400 021, India (office). *Telephone:* (22) 22022799 (office). *Fax:* (22) 22851391 (office). *E-mail:* sbiid@boms.vsnl.net.in (office). *Website:* www.statebankofindia.com (office); www.sbi.co.in (office).

BHATTACHARYA, Buddhadev, BA; Indian politician; *Chief Minister of West Bengal;* b. 1 March 1944, Kolkata; m.; one d.; ed Sailendra Sarkar Vidyalaya and Presidency Coll., Kolkata; mem. Communist Party of India—Marxist Secr., Cen. Cttee, mem. of Politburo; Minister-in-Charge, W Bengal Information and Public Relations Dept 1977–1982, Dept of Information and Cultural Affairs 1987–1999, Dept of Local Govt, Dept of Urban Devt and Metropolitan Devt 1987–1991, Dept of Information and Cultural Affairs 1991–93, 1994, 1996, Dept of Urban Devt and Municipal Affairs 1991–93, Dept of Home Affairs and Dept of Information Tech. 1996–99, Deputy Chief Minister of West Bengal 1999–2000, Chief Minister 2000–. *Publication:* collection of poems and plays. *Address:* Office of the Chief Minister, Government of West Bengal, Writers' Buildings, Kolkata 700 001, India (office). *Telephone:* (33) 22145555 (office). *Fax:* (33) 22145480 (office). *E-mail:* cm@wb.gov.in (office). *Website:* www.wbgov.com.

BHATTACHARYA, Tara Shankar; Indian banking executive; *Managing Director and Group Executive (Corporate Banking), State Bank of India;* fmr Man. Dir State Bank of India, Mumbai, later Chief Gen. Man. State Bank of India, currently Man. Dir and Group Exec. (Corp. Banking); Certified Assoc. Indian Inst. of Bankers. *Address:* State Bank of India, Corporate Centre, Madame Cama Road, PO Box 10121, Mumbai 400 021, India (office). *Telephone:* (22) 22022799 (office). *Fax:* (22) 22851391 (office). *E-mail:* sbiid@boms.vsnl.net.in (office). *Website:* www.statebankofindia.com (office); www.sbi.co.in (office).

BHATTACHARYYA, S. K.; Indian banking executive; *Managing Director and Chief Credit and Risk Officer, State Bank of India;* held position as Man. Dir SBI International (Mauritius) Ltd, Mauritius, Chief Gen. Man. Hyderabad Circle and Deputy Gen. Man. (Vigilance), Chennai Circle of the Bank, Man. Dir State Bank of Bikaner & Jaipur –2007, Man. Dir and Chief Credit and Risk Officer, State Bank of India 2007–. *Address:* State Bank of India, Corporate Centre, Madame Cama Road, PO Box 10121, Mumbai 400 021, India (office). *Telephone:* (22) 22022799 (office). *Fax:* (22) 22851391 (office). *E-mail:* sbiid@boms.vsnl.net.in (office). *Website:* www.statebankofindia.com (office); www.sbi.co.in (office).

BHATTARAI, Baburam; Nepalese politician and fmr guerrilla leader; *Minister of Finance;* ed Chandigarh Univ.; Leader, Communist Party of Nepal (Maoist), fmr commdr of rebel army, Sr mem. Standing Cttee of the Politburo; Minister of Finance 2008–. *Address:* Ministry of Finance, Singha Durbar, Kathmandu, Nepal (office). *Telephone:* (1) 4211809 (office). *Fax:* (1) 4211831 (office). *E-mail:* admindivision@mof.gov.np (office). *Website:* www.mof.gov.np (office).

BHATTARAI, Bijaya Nath, BCom, MCom, MA (Econs); Nepalese central banker; b. 9 Nov. 1949; m.; two c.; ed Tribhuvan Univ., Vanderbilt Univ., USA; Asst Research Officer, Research Dept, Nepal Rastra Bank (Cen. Bank) 1972–81, Research Officer 1981–92, Econ. Advisor 1992–95, Chief Controller, Foreign Exchange Dept 1995–98, Chief Accountant, Accounts and Expenditure Dept 1998–2000, Deputy Gov. and mem. Bd of Dirs 2000–05, Gov. and Chair. 2005–07 (suspended on charges of corruption); Chair. Asian Clearing Union 2005–; fmr Chair. Rural Self-Reliance Fund; fmr mem. Bd of Dirs Environment Protection Fund, Nepal Inter-modal Transport Devt Bd, Poverty Alleviation Fund, Nepal Bangladesh Bank 1993–97, Agricultural Devt Bank 1998–2000. *Publications:* articles and contribs to various bank publs. *Address:* Nepal Rastra Bank, Central Office, Baluwatar, PO Box 73, Kathmandu (office); Kha-1, 964 Kalimati, Kathmandu 4, Nepal (home). *Telephone:* (1) 4410386 (office); (1) 4271148 (home); (1) 4271829 (home). *Fax:* (1) 4410159 (office). *E-mail:* ofg@nrb.org.np (office). *Website:* www.nrb.org.np (office).

BHATTARAI, Krishna Prasad; Nepalese politician; b. 24 Dec. 1924, Banaras, India; s. of the late Sankata Prasad Bhattarai and Lalita Devi; served 14 years' imprisonment for opposition to absolute monarchy in Nepal; Pres. Nepali Congress Party (banned for 29 years until 1990); Prime Minister of Nepal (presiding over interim multiparty Govt) 1990–91, 1999–2000, also

Minister of Royal Palace Affairs, of Home Affairs, of Foreign Affairs, of Defence and of Women and Social Welfare. *Address:* c/o Office of the Prime Minister, Central Secretariat, Singha Durbar, Kathmandu, Nepal.

BHAVSAR, Natvar, BA, AM, MFA; American (b. Indian) artist; b. 7 April 1934, Gothava; s. of Prahladji Bhavsar and Babuben Bhavsar; m. Janet Brosious Bhavsar; three c.; ed Gujarat Univ., Univ. of Pennsylvania, USA; art instructor Univ. of Rhode Island, Kingston, USA; numerous solo exhbns including ART Cologne, ACP Viviane Ehrli Gallery 1998, 1999; recent group exhbns include: Galleria Civica d'Arte, Italy (Il Sud del Mondo. L'Altra Arte Contemporanea) 1991, Viviane Ehrli Gallery, Switzerland 1997, Dialectica, NY 2000, Sundaram Tagore Gallery 2001, 2002, ACP Viviane Ehrli Gallery, Zurich, Switzerland 2003–04, Galleria Pardo, Milan, Italy 2004, The Dimensions of Color: 40–year Retrospective, Jane Voorhees Zimmerli Art Museum, New Brunswick, NJ, USA 2007, The Third Mind, American Artists Contemplate Asia 1860–1989, Guggenheim Museum, New York 2009; work in public collections including: Australian Nat. Gallery, Boston Museum of Fine Arts, Solomon R. Guggenheim Museum, Metropolitan Museum of Art, MIT, Philadelphia Museum of Art; work in numerous pvt. collections; John D. Rockefeller 3rd Fund Fellowship 1965–66, John Simon Guggenheim Fellowship 1975–76, Aspen Inst. Fellowship 1980, 1983; Vishva Gurjari, Gujarat, India 1987, Cultural Reader, World Econ. Forum 2000, 2002. *Publication:* Monogram 1998. *Leisure interests:* travel, reading. *Address:* 131 Greene Street, New York, NY 10012, USA. *Telephone:* (212) 674-1293.

BHOSLE, Asha; Indian singer and composer; b. 8 Sept. 1933, Sangli, Maharashtra; d. of Dinanath Mangeshkar; Indian film playback singer; has recorded over 12,000 songs in 18 languages; first film Chunaria 1948; first solo in Raat Ki Rani 1949; sang in styles influenced by Latin American and American Big Band Jazz; worked extensively with Kishore Kumar 1970s; numerous tours and performances world-wide; Filmfare Award 1967, 1968, 1971, 1972, 1973, 1974, 1977, 1996, Nat. Award 1981, 1986, Nightingale of Asia 1987, Lata Mangeshkar Award, Madhya Pradesh Govt 1989, Maharashtra Govt 1999, Filmfare Special Award, Rangeela Re 1996, Screen Videocon Award 1997, MTV Contribution to Music Award 1997, five Channel V Awards, Singer of the Millennium, Dubai 2000, Kolhapuri Bhushan Award 2000, Sangli Bhushan Award 2000, Omega Excellence Lifetime Achievement Award 2000, Filmfare Lifetime Achievement Award 2001, Dada Saheb Phalke Award 2001, Dayawati Modi Award 2001, BBC Mega Mela Lifetime Achievement Award 2002. *Recordings include:* albums (soundtracks): Dus Lakh 1967, Shikhar 1968, Hare Rama Hare Krishna 1972, Naina 1973, Pran Jaye Par Vachan Na Jaye 1974, Don 1977, Umrao Jaan 1981, Ijazat 1986, Dilwale Dulhania Le Jayeng 1995, Rangeela 1996; solo: Songs of My Soul – Rare and Classic Vols 1 and 2 2001, You've Stolen My Heart (with the Kronos Quartet) 2005, 75 Years of Asha 2008.

BHUMIBOL ADULYADEJ, HM King of Thailand (King Rama IX); b. 5 Dec. 1927, Cambridge, Mass., USA; youngest s. of Their Royal Highnesses Prince and Princess Mahidol of Songkla; m. Mom Rajawongse Sirikit Kitiyakara 1950; one s., Crown Prince Maha Vajiralongkorn, b. 28 July 1952; three d., Princess Ubol Ratana, b. 5 April 1951, Princess Maha Chakri Sirindhorn, b. 2 April 1955, Princess Chulabhorn, b. 4 July 1957; ed Bangkok and Lausanne, Switzerland; succeeded his brother, King Ananda Mahidol, 9 June 1946; formal coronation 5 May 1950. *Address:* Chitralada Villa, Bangkok, Thailand.

BHUTTO ZARDARI, Bilawal; Pakistani politician; *Co-Chairman, Pakistan People's Party;* b. 21 Sept. 1988; s. of Asif Ali Zardari and the late Benazir Bhutto, fmr Prime Minister; grandson of fmr Prime Minister Zulfiqar Ali Bhutto; ed Karachi Grammar School, Froebels Int. School, Islamabad, Rashid School for Boys, Dubai, Univ. of Oxford, UK; has spent most of his life outside Pakistan, travelling with his mother who went into self-imposed exile in 1999, moving between London and Dubai; fmr Vice-Pres. Student Council, Rashid School for Boys, Dubai; Co-Chair. (with his father) Pakistan People's Party following assassination of his mother Benazir Bhutto Dec. 2007–; currently studying history at Christ Church, Univ. of Oxford. *Leisure interests:* cricket, shooting, horse-riding, black belt in Taekwondo. *Address:* Pakistan People's Party, 8 Street 19, F-8/2, Islamabad Karachi, Pakistan (office). *Telephone:* (51) 2255264 (office). *Fax:* (51) 2282741 (office). *E-mail:* ppp@comsats.net.pk (office). *Website:* www.ppp.org.pk (office).

BIANCHERI, Boris, BL, GCVO; Italian diplomatist; *President, Istituto per gli Studi di Politica Internazionale;* b. 3 Nov. 1930, Rome; m.; one s. one d.; ed Univ. of Rome; entered diplomatic service 1956, Office of the Sec. of State, Ministry of Foreign Affairs 1956–58; Italian Embassy, Athens 1959; Econ. Affairs Dept, Ministry of Foreign Affairs 1964–67, Counsellor 1967–71; Sec.-Gen. of Govt Comm. for 1970 Universal Osaka Exhbn 1968; Political Counsellor, Italian Embassy, London 1972–75; Head of Office of Sec.-Gen. Ministry of Foreign Affairs 1975–78, Chef de Cabinet, Sec. of State for Foreign Affairs 1978, Minister Plenipotentiary 1979; Amb. to Japan 1980–84; Dir-Gen. Personnel and Admin., Ministry of Foreign Affairs 1984, Dir-Gen. Political Affairs 1985; Amb. to UK 1987–91, to USA 1991–95, Sec.-Gen. Ministry of Foreign Affairs 1995–97; Chair. Italian News Agency (Agenzia Nazionale Stampa Associata—ANSA) 1997–, MARSH (Gruppo MMC) 2001; Pres. Federazione Italiana Editori Giornali (Italian Fed. of Newspaper Publrs) 2004–; Pres. Istituto per gli Studi di Politica Internazionale (Inst. for Int. Studies) (ISPI), Milan 1997–; mem. Bd of Dirs M100 Sanssouci-Colloquium; Hon. LLD (St John, NY). *Leisure interests:* gardening, boating, swimming. *Address:* Istituto per gli Studi di Politica Internazionale, Palazzo Clerici, Via Clerici 5, 20121 Milan, Italy (office). *Telephone:* (02) 8633131 (office). *Fax:* (02) 8692055 (office). *Website:* www.ispionline.it (office).

BIANCHERI, Franck; Monegasque government official; *Government Counsellor for External Relations;* m.; two c.; ed Ecole Supérieure de Commerce de Paris; Diplôme d'Expertise Comptable Supérieure (chartered accountancy qualification); Franco-German and British Chambers of Commerce Diplomas; Man. Boulogne-Billancourt Group, Credit Lyonnais 1983–90, responsible for product line for small- and medium-sized firms, Marcel Sembat Agency 1983–90, Channel Man. for product line for cos, Boulogne-Billancourt 1985–88; Dir Aeronautic Dept, Faugère & Jutheau/Groupe Marsh & McLennan 1990–95; Dir Gen. Dept of Finance and the Economy, Principality of Monaco 1995–2000, Rep. Dept of Finance and the Economy within Asscns Sportel and Festival de Télévision de Monte-Carlo 1995–2000; Govt Counsellor for Finance and the Economy 2000–05; Official Rep. to Cabinet of HSH the Prince while retaining the functions of Govt Counsellor for Finance and the Economy 2003–05; Govt Counsellor for External Relations and Int. Econ. and Financial Dossiers 2008–; Dir TMC, RMC, Monaco Telecom 1995–2000. *Address:* Department of External Relations, Ministère d'Etat, Place de la Visitation, MC 98015, Monaco (office). *Telephone:* 98-98-89-04 (office). *Fax:* 98-98-85-54 (office). *E-mail:* relext@gouv.mc (office). *Website:* www.diplomatie.gouv.mc (office).

BIANCHI, Andrés, MA, PhD; Chilean diplomatist and banking executive; b. 12 Sept. 1935, Valdivia; m. Lily Urdinola; two s. one d.; ed Univ. of Chile, Yale Univ., USA; Dir Int. Labor Office Regional Employment Program of Latin America and the Caribbean 1971–73; Visiting Research Assoc. Woodrow Wilson School of Public and Int. Affairs, Princeton Univ. 1973–75; Visiting Prof. Center for Latin American Devt Studies, Boston Univ. 1978; Dir Econ. Devt Div., UN Econ. Comm. for Latin America and the Caribbean 1981–88, Deputy Exec. Sec 1988–89; Gov. Cen. Bank of Chile 1989–91; Chair. Credit Lyonnais Chile 1992–96, Dresdner Banque Nationale de Paris, Chile 1996–2000; mem. External Advisory Group, Latin America and Caribbean Regional Office, World Bank 1994–2000; mem. Pres. of Chile's Nat. Savings Comm. 1997–98; Amb. to USA 2000–06; fmr adviser to cen. banks of Bolivia, Colombia, Mexico and Venezuela. *Leisure interests:* tennis, travel, classical music. *Address:* Ministry of Foreign Affairs, Catedral 1158, Santiago, Chile. *Telephone:* (2) 679-4200. *Fax:* (2) 699-4202. *Website:* www.minrel.gov.cl.

BIANCHI, Tancredi; Italian professor of banking economics; *President, Centrobanca;* ed Bocconi Univ., Milan; Prof. of Banking Econs, Bocconi Univ., Milan 1979; Pres. Associazione Bancaria Italiana (ABI) 1991–2001; Pres. Centrobanca—Banca di Credito Finanziario e Mobiliare SpA 2001–; Hon. Pres. Foundation Ente Luigi Einaudi. *Address:* Centrobanca, Corso Europa 16, 20122 Milan, Italy (office). *Telephone:* (02) 77811 (office). *Fax:* (02) 77814509 (office). *E-mail:* comunica@centrobanca.it (office). *Website:* www .centrobanca.it (office).

BIANCO, Jean-Louis; French civil servant; *President, Regional Council of Alpes-de-Haut-Provence;* b. 12 Jan. 1943, Neuilly-sur-Seine; s. of Louis Bianco and Gabrielle (née Vandries) Bianco; m. Martine Letoublon 1971; three s.; ed Lycée Janson-de-Sailly and Inst. d'études politiques, Paris; auditor, Conseil d'Etat 1971; Official Rep. Groupe central des villes nouvelles 1973–74; attached to Ministry of Health 1976–79; Counsel, Conseil d'Etat 1976; Official Rep. Syndicat intercommunal de Devt Durance-Bléone 1979–81; Official Rep. to the advisers of the Pres. 1981; Sec.-Gen. to the Pres. 1982–91; Minister of Social Affairs and Integration 1991–92, of Equipment, Transport and Housing 1992–93; mem. Regional Council of Alpes-de-Haute-Provence 1992–, Pres. 1998–; Mayor of Digne-les-Bains (Alpes de Haute Provence) 1995–2001, First Deputy Mayor 2001–; Deputy from Alpes de Haute-Provence (Socialist) June 1997–; Pres. François Mitterrand Inst. 1999–2002; Pres. High Council for Int. Co-operation 1999–2002; campaign dir for Ségolène Royal during Presidential elections 2007. *Address:* Conseil d'Etat, Palais Royal, 75100 Paris RP (office); Conseil général des Alpes de Haute-Provence, 13 rue du Docteur Romieu, 04000 Digne-les-Bains, France. *Telephone:* 1-40-63-68-33 (office). *E-mail:* jlbianco@assemblee-nationale.fr. *Website:* www.jean-louis-bianco.com (office).

BIAOU, Rogatien, (Assika Oyinlola), CEPE, BEPC, DUEG, DEA; Benin (b. Niger) politician and diplomatist; *Member of Ministry Cabinet, Ministry of Foreign Affairs;* b. 19 May 1952, Niamey, Niger; s. of the late Joseph Yaï Biaou and of Jeanette Thiakou Afouda; m. Justine Kaoui Atioukpe 1987; four c.; ed Cours Secondaire Protestant de Cotonou, Lycée Mathieu Bouké de Parakou, Nat. Univ. of Benin, Abomey-Calavi, Centre de Formation Admin. et de Perfectionnement, Cotonou, Institut Int. d'Admin Publique (IIAP), Paris, France, Institut des Nations Unies pour la Formation et le Recherche (UNITAR); Université Libre de Bruxelles, Brussels, Belgium; Asst to Gen. Man., Ministry of Higher Educ. and Scientific Research 1980–82; Head of France Div., Direction Europe, Ministry of Foreign Affairs and Cooperation 1982–85, Head of Service, Western European Countries 1985–87, Head of Service, African Countries S of the Sahara, Direction Africa and Arab Countries 1987–90; First Counsellor, Perm. Mission of Benin to UN, New York 1990–93, Minister Counsellor 1993–97; Amb. and Deputy Dir of Cabinet, Ministry of Foreign Affairs 1997–98, Amb. and Dir of Europe Dept 1998–2000, mem. Cabinet, Ministry of Foreign Affairs 2006–; Amb. and Sec.-Gen., Ministry of Foreign Affairs and African Integration 2000–03, Minister for Foreign Affairs and African Integration 2003–06;; Chevalier de l'Ordre Nat. du Bénin. *Publications:* Les Moyens de Communication de Masse et La Politique d'Information au Benin 1980, La Grève de la Faim en Ulster: Conséquences Biologiques et Politiques 1981, Essai d'Analyse du Code de la Citoyenneté de la CEDEAO 1982, An X du Plan d'Action de Lagos 1990, The Challenge of Poverty Eradication in Africa 1996; numerous articles on politics, econs and devt issues. *Leisure interests:* literature, Scrabble, music, sport, cinema. *Address:* c/o Zone Résidentielle, route de l'Aéroport, BP 318, Cotonou 06 (office); 03 BP 2752, Cotonou, Benin (home). *Telephone:* 21-36-08-96 (home); 90-94-80-93 (home). *E-mail:* rogasbiaou@yahoo.fr (home).

BICHARD, Sir Michael (George), KCB, LLB, MScS, FIPD, CCMI, FRSA; British civil servant; *Rector, University of the Arts, London;* b. 31 Jan. 1947, Southampton; s. of the late George Bichard and Nora Reeves; m. Christine Bichard; one s. two d.; ed Univ. of Manchester, Univ. of Birmingham; articled clerk, solicitor, Sr Solicitor Reading Borough Council 1969–73; Co. Liaison Officer, Berks. Co. Council 1973–77; Head of Chief Exec.'s Office, Lambeth Borough Council 1977–80; Chief Exec. Brent Borough Council 1980–86, Glos. Co. Council 1986–90, Social Security Benefits Agency 1990–95; Jt Perm. Sec. Dept for Educ. and Employment July–Dec. 1995, Perm. Sec. 1996–2002; Rector, The London Inst. (now Univ. of the Arts London) 2001–; mem. Econ. and Social Research Council 1989–92, Prince's Trust Volunteers Nat. Bd 1992–97; mem. Bd of Dirs Industrial Soc. 1997–2001, British Council 1996–2001, River and Rowing Museum Foundation 2002–, Council, Dyslexia Inst. 2003–06; Reed plc 2002–04; mem. ESRC 1989–92; Fellow Chartered Inst. of Personnel and Devt, Birmingham Inst. of Local Govt Studies; Chair. Rathbone Training Ltd 2001–, RSe Consulting 2003–, ARTIS, 2003–, Legal Services Comm. 2005–; Chair. and Trustee CNAA Art Collection Trust; mem. NESTA Creative Pioneer Programme Cttee; Gov. Henley Man. Coll. 2002–; mem. Bd of Companions, Inst. of Man.; mem. Guild of Educators; apptd by UK Home Office to chair Soham/Bichard Inquiry Jan. 2004; Ed. Solace Foundation, Chair. Film Clubhouse 2006–; Hon. Fellow Inst. of Local Govt Studies (Birmingham Univ.); Hon. DUniv (Leeds Metropolitan) 1992, (Middlesex) 2001; Hon. LLD (Birmingham) 1999; Dr hc (Bradford) 2004, (Solent). *Address:* University of the Arts, London, 65 Davies Street, London, W1K 5DA, England (office). *Telephone:* (20) 7514-6002 (office). *Fax:* (20) 7514-6236 (office). *E-mail:* m.bichard@arts.ac.uk (office). *Website:* www.arts.ac.uk.

BIČKAUSKAS, Egidijuš; Lithuanian politician and lawyer; b. 29 May 1955, Prienai; m. Jurate Bičkauskienė; ed Vilnius Univ.; investigator, special cases investigator Procurator Gen.'s Office 1978–89; joined People's Front Movt Sajudis 1988; Deputy of USSR Supreme Soviet 1989–90; elected to Parl. Restoration Seimas of Repub. of Lithuania 1990–92, signatory of the Lithuanian Repub. Independence Restoration Act 1990; Head Lithuanian diplomatic mission to Moscow 1990–96; mem. Parl. (Seimas) of Repub. of Lithuania, Deputy Chair. 1992–96, head of faction of Centre Party in Seimas of Lithuania 1996–2000; Vice-Chair. Presidium of Baltic Ass. *Address:* Laurų 35, 2046 Vilnius, Lithuania. *Telephone:* (3702) 225493 (home); (8698) 88761. *E-mail:* info@bickauskas.lt. *Website:* www.bickauskas.lt.

BIDAYA, Thanong, MA, PhD; Thai government official and business executive; b. 28 July 1947, Supanburi Prov.; ed Yokohama Nat. Univ., Japan, Northwestern Univ., USA; fmr positions include Pres. Thai Mil. Bank Public Co., Chair. Thai Airways Int. Public Co., Commercial Union Insurance (Thailand) Co., N.C.C. Man. & Devt Co., Dir Thai Asia Pacific Brewery Co., Bangkok Intercontinental Hotel Co., Thai Life Insurance Group, Shinawatra Computer and Communications Co., Metropolitan Electricity Authority of Thailand, Thanapol Finance and Securities Co., Team Consulting Engineer Co.; fmr Dean Graduate School Business MBA Program, Assumption Univ., Business Admin Dept, Nat. Inst. of Devt Admin; fmr Researcher Devt Econs Dept, World Bank, Washington, DC, USA; Minister of Finance 1997, 2005–06; Minister of Commerce –2005; hon. mem. Suphanburi Chamber of Commerce; Commdr (Third Class) of the Most Noble Order of the Crown of Thailand, Grand Cordon of the Order of the Rising Sun; Dr hc (Yokohama Nat. Univ.). *Address:* c/o Ministry of Finance, Thanon Rama VI, Samsennai, Phaya Thai, Rajatevi, Bangkok 10400, Thailand (office).

BIDDISS, Michael Denis, MA, PhD, FRHistS; British academic and writer; *Professor Emeritus of History, University of Reading;* b. 15 April 1942, Farnborough, Kent; s. of Daniel Biddiss and Eileen Biddiss (née Jones); m. Ruth Margaret Cartwright 1967; four d.; ed Queens' Coll., Cambridge, Centre des Hautes Etudes Européennes, Univ. of Strasbourg, France; Fellow in History, Downing Coll., Cambridge and Dir of Studies in History, Social and Political Sciences 1966–73; lecturer, then Reader in History, Univ. of Leicester 1973–79; Prof. of History, Univ. of Reading 1979–2004, Prof. Emer. 2004–, Dean Faculty of Letters and Social Sciences 1982–85; Visiting Prof., Univ. of Victoria, Canada 1973, Univ. of Cape Town 1976, 1978, Univ. of Cairo 1985, Monash Univ., Australia 1989, Univ. of Nanjing, China 1997; Chair. History at the Univs Defence Group 1984–87; mem. Council, The Historical Asscn 1985– (Pres. 1991–94), Vice-Pres. Royal Historical Soc. 1995–99 (mem. Council 1988–92); Lister Lecturer, BAAS 1975; Hon. Fellow, Faculty of the History of Medicine (Pres. 1994–98), Soc. of Apothecaries 1986–; Osler Medallist, Soc. of Apothecaries of London 1989, Locke Medallist, Soc. of Apothecaries of London 1996, Sydenham Medallist, Soc. of Apothecaries of London 2000. *Publications:* Father of Racist Ideology 1970, Gobineau: Selected Political Writings (ed.) 1970, Disease and History (co-author) 1972, The Age of the Masses 1977, Images of Race (ed.) 1979, Thatcherism (co-ed.) 1987, The Nuremberg Trial and the Third Reich (co-author) 1992, The Uses and Abuses of Antiquity (co-ed.) 1999, The Humanities in the New Millennium (co-ed) 2000. *Leisure interests:* cricket, music and opera, mountain walking, art, travel. *Address:* c/o School of History, University of Reading, Whiteknights, Reading, RG6 6AA, England (office).

BIDDLE, Martin, OBE, MA, FBA, FSA, FRHistS; British archaeologist and academic; *Astor Senior Research Fellow, Hertford College and Professor of Medieval Archaeology, University of Oxford;* b. 4 June 1937, North Harrow, Middx; s. of Reginald Samuel Biddle and Gwladys Florence Biddle (née Baker); m. Birthe Kjølbye 1966; two d. and two d. by previous m.; ed Merchant Taylors' School and Pembroke Coll. Cambridge; Asst Insp. of Ancient Monuments, Ministry of Public Building and Works 1961–63; Lecturer in Medieval Archaeology, Univ. of Exeter 1963–67; Visiting Fellow, All Souls Coll. Oxford 1967–68; Dir Winchester Research Unit. 1968–; Dir Univ. Museum and Prof. of Anthropology and History of Art, Univ. of Pa 1977–81;

Lecturer of The House, Christ Church, Oxford 1983–86; Astor Sr Research Fellow in Medieval Archaeology, Hertford Coll. Oxford 1989–; Prof. of Medieval Archaeology, Univ. of Oxford 1997–; Dir excavations and investigations at Nonsuch Palace 1959–60, Winchester 1961–71, Repton (with wife) 1974–88, 1993, St Alban's Abbey (with wife) 1978, 1982–84, 1991, 1994–95, Holy Sepulchre, Jerusalem (with wife) 1989–90, 1992, 1993, 1998, Qasr Ibrim, Egypt (with wife) 1990, 1992, 1995, 2000; archaeological consultant to Canterbury Cathedral, St Alban's Abbey, Eurotunnel, etc.; mem. Royal Comm. on Historical Monuments for England 1984–95; Trevelyan Lecturer, Univ. of Cambridge 1991; Pres. Soc. for Medieval Archaeology 1995–98; Frend Medal, Soc. of Antiquaries (with Birthe Kjølbye-Biddle) 1986. *Publications:* The Future of London's Past (with C. Heighway) 1973, Winchester in the Early Middle Ages (with others) 1976, The History of the King's Works, Vol. IV, Part 2 (with others) 1982, King Arthur's Round Table 2000, Approaches in Urban Archaeology 1990, Object and Economy in Medieval Winchester 1990, Das Grab-Christi 1998, Nonsuch Palace: The Domestic Materials 1998, The Tomb of Christ 1999, King Arthur's Round Table 2000, The Church of the Holy Sepulchre 2000; papers in learned journals. *Leisure interests:* travel, especially Hellenic travel, architecture, Renaissance art. *Address:* Hertford College, Oxford, OX1 3BW (office); Knight Ayton Management, 114 St. Martin's Lane, London, WC2N 4BE; 19 Hamilton Road, Oxford, OX2 7PY, England (home). *Telephone:* (1865) 513056; (1865) 559017 (office). *Fax:* (1865) 559017; (1865) 559017 (office). *E-mail:* martin.biddle@hertford.ox.ac.uk (office).

BIDEN, Joseph (Joe) Robinette, Jr, JD; American politician; *Vice President of the United States;* b. 20 Nov. 1942, Scranton, Pa; s. of Joseph R. Biden and Jean F. Biden; m. 1st Neilia Hunter (deceased); two s. one d. (deceased); m. 2nd Jill Tracy Jacobs 1977; one d.; ed Univ. of Delaware, Newark and Syracuse Univ. Coll. of Law, NY; Trial Attorney in the Public Defender's Office, Del. 1968; Founder Biden & Walsh Law Firm, Wilmington 1968–72; mem. New Castle Co. Council 1970–72; Senator from Delaware 1972–2008, mem. Foreign Relations Cttee 1987–2008 (fmr Chair.), Judiciary Cttee 1987– (Chair. 1987–95, fmr Chair. Subcommittee on Crime and Drugs), Chair. Senate Caucus on Int. Narcotics Control, Co-Chair. Senate NATO Observer Group, Senate Nat. Security Working Group, Congressional Fireman's Caucus, Congressional Int. Anti-Piracy Caucus, mem. Democratic Steering and Coordinating Cttee, Nat. Guard Caucus, Senate Auto Caucus, Senate Biotechnology Caucus, Congressional Port Security Caucus, Congressional Air Force Caucus; Vice Chair. NATO Parl. Ass.; cand. for Democratic nomination for US Pres. 2007; Vice Pres. of the US 2009–; Adjunct Prof., Widener Univ. School of Law 1991–; mem. Del. Bar Asscn, ABA, American Trial Lawyers' Asscn; Democrat. *Leisure interests:* sports, history, public speaking, American architecture. *Address:* Office of the Vice President, Eisenhower Executive Office Building, 1650 Pennsylvania Ave, NW, Washington, DC 20502, USA (office). *Telephone:* (202) 456-1414 (office). *Fax:* (202) 456-2461 (office). *Website:* www.whitehouse.gov/administration/vice_president_biden (office).

BIDWELL, Charles Edward, PhD, FAAS; American academic; *William Claude Reavis Professor Emeritus of Sociology and Education, University of Chicago;* b. 24 Jan. 1932, Chicago; s. of Charles L. Bidwell and Eugenia Campbell Bidwell; m. Helen Claxton Lewis 1959; one s.; ed Univ. of Chicago; Lecturer in Sociology, Harvard Univ. 1959–61, then to Univ. of Chicago, Assoc. Prof. 1965–70, Prof. of Educ. and Sociology 1970–85, Reavis Prof. Educ. and Sociology 1985–2001, Prof. Emer. 2001–; Chair. Dept of Educ. 1978–88; Chair. Dept of Sociology 1988–94; Dir Ogburn-Stouffer Center 1988–94; Guggenheim Fellow 1971–72; mem. Nat. Acad. of Educ. *Publications:* The School as a Formal Organization, in Handbook of Organizations (Ed. J. March) 1965, The Organization and its Ecosystem (with J. D. Kasarda) 1985, The Collegial Focus: Teaching Fields, Colleague Relationships, and Instructional Practice in American High Schools in Sociology of Education (with J. Yasumoto) 1999. *Leisure interests:* skiing and reading. *Address:* Department of Sociology, 5848 S University Avenue, Chicago, IL 60637, USA. *Telephone:* (773) 702-0388 (office). *Fax:* (773) 702-4617 (office). *E-mail:* c-bidwell@uchicago.edu (office).

BIEBER, Owen F.; American fmr labour official; b. 28 Dec. 1929, North Dorr, Mich.; s. of Albert F. Bieber and Minnie Schwartz Bieber; m. Shirley M. Van Woerkom 1950; three s. two d.; ed High School; elected Regional Dir, United Auto Workers (UAW, now United Automobile, Aerospace and Agricultural Implement Workers of America) Region 1D 1974–80, Vice-Pres. Int. Union 1980–83, Pres. 1983–95; Hon. DHum (Grand Valley Coll.); Hon. DrSc (Ferris State Coll.); Owen Bieber Social Activist Award, UAW 2005.

BIEDENKOPF, Kurt Hans, DJur; German politician and lawyer; b. 28 Jan. 1930, Ludwigshafen; s. of Wilhelm Biedenkopf and Agathe Biedenkopf (née Schmidt); m. Ingrid Ries 1979; Prof. of Law, Ruhr Univ., Bochum 1964–70, Rector 1967–69; Chair. Govt Comm. on Co-determination 1968–70; Gen. Sec. Christian Democratic Party (CDU) 1973–77, Vice-Pres. 1977–83; Pres. CDU Regional Asscn, North Rhine-Westphalia 1980–84; mem. Bundestag 1976–80, 1987–90; Prime Minister of Saxony 1990–2002; Chair. Kuratorium Trust of Devt and Peace; mem. Exec. Bd Henkel Corpn, Düsseldorf 1971–73; mem. Bd Inst. for Econ. and Social Policy, Bonn 1977–; mem. Bd German Nat. Trust; mem. Landtag of North Rhine-Westphalia 1980–88; mem. Senate Max Planck Gesellschaft; Hon. DrJur (Davidson Coll.) 1974, (Georgetown) 1978, (New School for Social Research, New York) 1993, (Katholic Univ., Brussels) 1994. *Publications:* Vertragliche Wettbewerbsbeschränkung und Wirtschaftsverfassung 1958, Grenzen der Tarifautonomie 1964, Fortschritt in Freiheit 1974, Die programmierte Krise–Alternativen zur staatlichen Schuldenpolitik 1979, Die neue Sicht der Dinge 1985, Zeitsignale–Parteienlandschaft im Umbruch 1989, Einheit und Erneuerung 1994, Ordnungspolitik in einer Zeit des Umbruchs 1998, Ein deutsches Tagebuch 1989–90 2000. *Leisure interests:* skiing, sailing. *Address:* Sächsischer Landtag, Bernh.v.Lindenau-Pl. 1, 01067 Dresden, Germany. *Telephone:* (351) 4935506.

BIEGMAN, Nicolaas H., PhD; Dutch diplomatist and writer; *Chairman, Board of Trustees, East West Parliamentary Practice Project;* b. 23 Sept. 1936, Apeldoorn; s. of Nicolaas Biegman and Aukje de Boer; m. Mirjana Cibilic; two s.; ed Univ. of Leiden; Lecturer in Turkish and Persian, Univ. of Leiden 1960–62; various posts in Netherlands Foreign Service 1963–84; Amb. to Egypt 1984–88; Dir-Gen. for Int. Cooperation, Ministry of Foreign Affairs 1988–92; Perm. Rep. to UN 1992–97; Perm. Rep. to NATO 1998–2001 (retd from Dutch Foreign Service); Sr Civilian Rep. of NATO in Macedonia, Skopje 2002–04; currently Chair. Bd of Trustees East West Parl. Practice Project, Amsterdam; fmr mem. Bd of Dirs Int. Peace Acad.; Order of The Netherlands Lion, Order of Merit, UAR. *Publications:* The Turco-Ragusan Relationship 1967, Egypt-Moulids, Saints, Sufis 1990, Egypt's Sideshows 1992, An Island of Bliss 1993, Mainly Manhattan 1997, God's Lovers 2006. *Leisure interest:* photography. *Address:* c/o Board of Trustees, East West Parliamentary Practice Project, Roemer Visscherstraat 18-2, 1054 EX, Amsterdam, Netherlands. *Telephone:* (20) 6623664. *Fax:* (20) 6160892. *E-mail:* ewppp@ewppp.org. *Website:* www.ewppp.org.

BIELECKI, Jan Krzysztof, MSc; Polish politician and economist; *President and CEO, Bank Pekao SA;* b. 3 May 1951, Bydgoszcz; s. of Anastazy Bielecki and Janina Bielecka; m. Barbara Bielecka 1976; one s. one d.; ed Economics Coll., Sopot, Gdańsk Univ.; Asst Lecturer, Gdańsk Univ. 1973–81 (lost his job for his alleged anti-Communist political activities); Head of Research Unit, Centre for Training Managerial Staff, Ministry of Trade and Ministry of Machine Industry 1972–82; trade union and workers' rights activist, expert for econ. affairs, Solidarity Trade Union 1980–81; continued union activity under martial law as assoc. of underground regional and nat. authorities; lorry driver 1982–85; Man. Doradca consulting co-operative, Sopot 1985–91; Deputy to Sejm (Parl.) 1989–93 (mem. Civic Parl. Caucus 1989–91, Leader Parl. Liberal-Democratic Congress Caucus); Prime Minister of Poland Jan.–Dec. 1991; Minister for Poland–EU Relations 1992–93; mem. Liberal-Democratic Congress (mem. Provisional Bd Presidium) 1989–94; apptd by Polish Govt to Bd of Dirs EBRD, London 1993–2003; Pres. and CEO Bank Pekao SA 2003–; currently Exec. Dir European Bank. *Publications:* Histoire de l'Europe 1997; numerous articles in nat. and int. specialist newspapers and magazines. *Leisure interests:* horse riding, tennis, football. *Address:* Bank Pekao SA, ul. Grzybowska 53–57, 00-950 Warsaw, Poland (office). *Website:* www.pekao.com.pl/bank1.xml?/lang=US/201131-720306-08610 (office).

BIELSA, Rafael; Argentine politician; b. 15 Feb. 1953, Rosario, Santa Fe; m. Andrea DArza; two c. from previous m.; ed Univ. de Rosario; Asst Fed. Tribunals of Rosario 1974–78; various positions at Ministry of Justice, Ministry of Educ. and Office of the Presidency; Minister of Foreign Affairs, International Trade and Worship 2003–05; mem. Chamber of Deputies for Buenos Aires 2005–07; mem. Partido Justicialista. *Address:* Partido Justicialista, Domingo Matheu 130, 1082 Buenos Aires, Argentina (office). *Telephone:* (11) 4954-2450 (office). *Fax:* (11) 4954-2421 (office). *E-mail:* contacto@pj.org.ar. *Website:* www.pj.org.ar (office).

BIEMANN, Klaus, PhD; Austrian/American chemist and academic; *Professor Emeritus of Chemistry, Massachusetts Institute of Technology;* b. 1926, Innsbruck, Austria; ed Univ. of Innsbruck; joined MIT 1955, fmr Prof. of Chem., now Prof. Emer.; mem. NAS 1993–; Fellow, American Acad. of Arts and Sciences 1966; Stas Medal, Belgian Chemical Soc. 1962, Powers Award 1973, NASA Exceptional Scientific Achievement Medal 1977, Fritz Pregl Medal, Austrian Microchemical Soc. 1977, Newcomb-Cleveland Prize 1978, first ACS Frank H. Field and Joe L. Franklin Award in applied Mass Spectrometry 1986, Thomson Medal 1991, Pehr Edman Award 1992, ACS Analytical Chem. Award 200, Benjamin Franklin Medal, The Franklin Inst. 2007. *Achievements include:* sent miniaturized mass spectrometer to Mars as part of Viking Mission to look for organic compounds at surface of Red Planet 1976; has been called "the father of organic mass spectrometry". *Publications:* Mass Spectrometry: Organic Chemical Applications 1962; more than 350 publs on devt of mass spectrometry as chemical analysis tool to determine structure of complex molecules of biological and medical interest. *Address:* Room 18-297, Department of Chemistry, Massachusetts Institute of Technology, 77 Massachusetts Avenue, Cambridge, MA 02139-4307, USA (office). *Telephone:* (617) 253-7221 (office). *Fax:* (617) 258-9344 (office). *E-mail:* kbiemann@mit.edu (office). *Website:* web.mit.edu/chemistry (office).

BIENEN, Henry S., BA, MA, PhD; American university administrator and political scientist; *President, Northwestern University;* m. Leigh Bienen; three d.; ed Cornell Univ. and Univ. of Chicago; Asst Prof., Princeton Univ. 1966–69, Assoc. Prof. of Politics and Int. Affairs 1969–72, Prof. of Politics and Int. Affairs 1972–81, William Stewart Tod Prof. of Politics and Int. Affairs 1981–85, James S. McDonnell Distinguished Univ. Prof. and Dean of the Woodrow Wilson School of Public and Int. Affairs 1985–94; Pres. Northwestern Univ. 1995–; Visiting Prof., Makerere Coll., Kampala, Uganda 1963–65, Univ. Coll., Nairobi, Kenya 1968–69, Columbia Univ. 1971–72, Univ. of Ibadan, Nigeria 1972–73; Fellow, Center for Advanced Studies in Behavioral Sciences, Stanford Univ. 1976–77; Polsky Fellow, Aspen Inst. 1982–83; mem. Inst. for Advanced Studies, Princeton 1984–85; consultant to US Dept of State 1972–88, Nat. Security Council 1978–79, Agency for Int. Devt 1980–81, CIA 1982–88 (mem. Sr Review Panel late 1980s), World Bank 1981–89, Hambrecht and Quist Investment Co., Boeing Corpn, Carnegie Corpn, Ford Foundation, Rockefeller Foundation, John D. and Catherine T. MacArthur Foundation; mem. Bd Dirs The Bear Stearns Cos Inc., Deltak edu., Inc., Council on Foreign Relations (Chair. Nominating and Governance Cttee and mem. Exec. Cttee), Chicago Council on Foreign Relations (mem. Exec.

www.worldwhoswho.com

Cttee); mem. Bd Govs Argonne Nat. Lab., mem. Exec. and Nominating Cttees; mem. Exec. Cttee Asscn of American Univs; mem. Cttee on Roles of Academic Health Centers in the 21st Century, Nat. Acads' Inst. of Medicine; mem. Bd Univ. Corpn for Advanced Internet Devt (Internet 2) 1998–2002; other bd and trustee mems include JSTOR, John G. Shedd Aquarium, Steppenwolf Theatre, Alain Locke Charter School; mem. American Political Science Asscn; Univ. of Chicago Professional Achievement Alumni Award 2000, Carnegie Corpn Academic Leadership Award for innovative leadership in higher educ. *Address:* Office of the President, Northwestern University, 633 Clark Street, Evanston, IL 60208, USA (office). *Telephone:* (847) 491-7456 (office). *E-mail:* nu-president@northwestern.edu (office). *Website:* www.northwestern.edu (office).

BIERRING, Ole, LLM; Danish diplomatist; b. 9 Nov. 1926, Copenhagen; s. of Knud Bierring and Ester M. Bierring (née Lorck); m. Bodil E Kisbye 1960; one s. three d.; ed Univ. of Copenhagen and Princeton Univ., USA; joined Ministry of Foreign Affairs 1951; served in Washington, DC 1956–58, Vienna 1960–63, Brussels (NATO) 1968–72; Under-Sec. for Political Affairs 1976–80, Deputy Perm. Under-Sec. 1980; Amb. to France 1980–84; Amb. and Perm. Rep. to UN 1984–88, Rep. on the Security Council 1985–86; Amb. to NATO 1988–95; Observer to WEU 1993–95; Amb.-at-Large 1995–96; Commdr Order of Dannebrog (1st class) and other decorations. *Leisure interests:* music, sailing. *Address:* Rysensteensgade 6, 5 tv, 1564 Copenhagen V, Denmark (home). *Telephone:* 33-91-66-36 (home).

BIESHU, Mariya Lukyanovna; Moldovan singer (soprano); b. 3 Aug. 1935, Moldova; d. of Luca Bieshu and Tatiana Bieshu; m. Arcady Rodomsky 1965; ed Kishinev Conservatoire; soloist with Moldovan Folk Orchestra 1958–60; with Moldovan Opera and Ballet 1961–; postgraduate studies at La Scala, Milan 1965–67; Prof. Kishinev Conservatoire 1980–; Chair. Musicians' Union of Moldova 1986–; Vice-Pres. Int. Union of Musicians; Hon. mem. Acad. of Sciences; awards include: 1st Prize Int. Puccini Competition, Tokyo 1967, People's Artist of USSR 1970, Lenin Prize 1982. *Roles include:* Tosca 1962, Desdemona in Othello 1967, Leonora in Il Trovatore 1969, Zemphira in Aleko 1973, Mimi in La Bohème 1977, Turandot 1979, Iolanta 1979, Elizabeth of Valois in Don Carlos 1985, Amelia in A Masked Ball 1989, Abigail in Nabucco 1991. *Leisure interests:* dogs, open country. *Address:* 24 Pushkin Str., Chişinău 2012, Moldova (home).

BIFFI, HE Cardinal Giacomo; Italian ecclesiastic; b. 13 June 1928, Milan; ordained 1950; consecrated Bishop (Titular Church of Fidene) 1975; Archbishop of Bologna 1984–2003, Archbishop Emer. 2003–; cr. Cardinal Priest of SS Giovanni Evangelista e Petronio 1985. *Address:* c/o Arcivescovado, Via Altabella 6, 40126 Bologna, Italy. *Telephone:* (51) 238202. *Website:* www.bologna.chiesacattolica.it.

BIG BOI; American rap artist; b. (Antoine Patton), 1 Feb. 1975, Savannah, GA; ed Tri-City High School, Atlanta; mem., Outkast (with Andre 3000, aka Dré) 1992–, signed to LaFace Records; designed Outkast Clothing line; Source Award for Best New Rap Group of the Year 1995, American Music Awards for Best Hip Hop/R&B Group 2003, 2004, Grammy Award for best urban/alternative performance 2004, World Music Awards for Best Group, Best Pop Group, Best Rap/Hip-Hop Artist 2004, MTV Europe Best Group Award 2004, Best Song Award, Best Video Award (both for Hey Ya) 2004. *Recordings include:* albums: Southernplayalisticadillacmuzik 1994, ATLiens 1996, Aquemini 1998, Stankonia 2000, Big Boi And Dre Present… 2002, Speakerboxxx/The Love Below (Grammy Awards for Album of the Year, Best Rap Album 2004, American Music Award for Best Rap/Hip-Hop Album 2004) 2003, My Life In Idlewild 2005, Idlewild 2006. *Address:* William Morris Agency, 1325 Avenue of the Americas, New York, NY 10019, USA (office); c/o LaFace Records, A&R Department, 1 Capital City Plaza, 3350 Peachtree Road, Suite 1500, Atlanta, GA 30326, USA. *Telephone:* (212) 586-5100 (office). *Fax:* (212) 246-3583 (office). *Website:* www.outkast.com.

BIGELEISEN, Jacob, AB, MS, PhD; American chemist and academic; *Distinguished Professor Emeritus of Chemistry, State University of New York, Stony Brook;* b. 2 May 1919, Paterson, NJ; s. of Harry Bigeleisen and Ida Bigeleisen (née Slomowitz); m. Grace Alice Simon 1945; three s.; ed New York Univ., Washington State Univ. and Univ. of California, Berkeley; SAM Labs, Columbia Univ. (Manhattan Dist) 1943–45; Ohio State Univ. 1945–46; Univ. of Chicago 1946–48; Assoc. to Sr Chemist, Brookhaven Nat. Laboratory 1948–68; Sr Postdoctoral Fellow, NSF 1962–63; Gilbert N. Lewis Lecturer, Univ. of California 1963; Prof. of Chem., Univ. of Rochester 1968–78, Chair. Dept of Chem. 1970–75, Tracy H. Harris Prof., Coll. of Arts and Sciences 1973–78, Leading Prof. of Chem., State Univ. of New York (Stony Brook) 1978–89, Distinguished Prof. Emer. 1989–, Vice-Pres. for Research 1978–80, Dean of Grad. Studies 1978–80; Visiting Prof., Cornell Univ. 1953; Hon. Visiting Prof., ETH, Zurich 1962–63; Visiting Distinguished Prof., State Univ. of New York, Buffalo 1966; Guggenheim Fellow 1974–75; mem. NAS, ACS; Chair. Ass. of Math. and Physical Science 1976–80, Councilor 1982–85; mem. NAS 1966–; Fellow, American Acad. of Arts and Sciences, American Physical Soc., AAAS; Samuel F. B. Morse Medal 1939, ACS Nuclear Applications to Chem. Award 1958, E. O. Lawrence Memorial Award and Presidential Citation 1964, Meliora Award, Univ. of Rochester 1978, Distinguished Alumnus Award, Washington State Univ. 1983. *Publications:* Calculation of Equilibrium Constants of Isotopic Exchange Reactions 1947, Relative Reaction Velocities of Isotopic Molecules 1949, The Significance of the Product and Sum Rules to Isotope Fractionation Studies 1957, Statistical Mechanics of Isotope Effects in Condensed Systems 1961, Quantum Mechanical Foundations of Isotope Chemistry 1974, and numerous publs on ionization of strong electrolytes, organic photochemistry, semiquinones, acids and bases and particularly theoretical and experimental studies on the chemistry of isotopes. *Address:* 900 North Taylor Street, Apartment 1817, Arlington, VA 22203, USA (home). *Telephone:* (703) 528-7828 (home). *E-mail:* Jacob_Bigeleisen@comcast.net (home). *Website:* www.sunysb.edu/chemistry/faculty/jbigeleisen.htm (office).

BIGELOW, Kathryn; American film director; b. 1952, San Carlos; m. James Cameron (q.v.) 1989 (divorced 1991); ed San Francisco Art Inst. and Columbia Univ., New York; worked with Art and Language performance group, UK; awarded scholarship to Ind. Study Program, Whitney Museum, New York. *Films include:* Set Up (short), The Loveless 1982, Near Dark 1987, Blue Steel 1990, Point Break 1991, Strange Days 1995, Weight of Water 2000, K-19: The Widowmaker 2002, Mission Zero 2007. *Television includes:* Wild Palms (miniseries) 1993. *Address:* c/o Ken Stovitz, CAA, 9830 Wilshire Boulevard, Beverly Hills, CA 90210, USA (office).

BIGGAM, Sir Robin Adair, Kt; British business executive and chartered accountant; b. 8 July 1938, Carluke; s. of Thomas Biggam and Eileen Biggam; m. Elizabeth McArthur (née McDougall) Biggam 1962; one s. two d.; ed Lanark Grammar School; CA Peat Marwick Mitchell 1960–63, ICI 1964–81; ICL Finance Dir 1981–84; Exec. Dir Dunlop 1984–85; Chair. Cadcentre Ltd 1983–86; Non Exec. Dir Chloride Group PLC 1985–87, Lloyds Abbey Life PLC (fmrly Abbey Life Group) 1985–90, Redland Group PLC 1991–97, British Aerospace PLC 1994–2003; Man. Dir BICC PLC 1986–87, CEO 1987–91, Deputy Chair. 1991–, Chair. 1992–96; Dir Fairey Group PLC 1995– (Chair. 1996–2001); Chair. Ind. TV Comm. 1997–2003; Dir (non-exec.) British Energy 1996–2002 (Deputy Chair. 2001–02); Chair. Macquarie European Infrastructure 2000–05; Chancellor, Univ. of Luton (now Univ. of Bedfordshire) 2001–; mem. Inst. of Chartered Accountants of Scotland. *Leisure interests:* golf, gardening, swimming, watching TV, fishing. *Address:* University of Bedfordshire, Park Square, Luton, Beds., LU1 3JU, England (office). *Telephone:* (1234) 400400 (office). *Website:* www.beds.ac.uk (office).

BIGGS, Barton Michael, MBA; American business executive; *Managing Partner, Traxis Partners;* b. 26 Nov. 1932, New York; s. of William Richardson and Georgene Biggs; m. Judith Anne Lund 1959; one s. two d.; ed Yale and New York Univs; First Lt US Marine Corps 1955–59; research analyst E. M. Hutton & Co. 1961–65, Asst to Chair. 1962–65, pnr 1965; co-f. Fairfield Pnrs 1965, Man. Pnr 1965–73; pnr and Man. Dir Morgan Stanley & Co. 1973–, Man. Research Dept 1973–79, 1991–93; Chair. and CEO Morgan Stanley Asset Man. Co. 1980–2003, mem. Man. Cttee 1987–2003, mem. Exec. Cttee Bd of Dirs 1991; Chair. Morgan Stanley Funds; Dir Rand McNally & Co.; Man. Pnr, Traxis Partners 2003–. *Publications:* Diary Of A Hedge Hog 2004, Hedge Hogging 2006. *Address:* c/o John Wiley & Sons, Inc., 111 River Street, Hoboken, NJ 07030, USA.

BIGGS, Peter Martin, CBE, DSc, FRS, FRCVS, FRCPath, CBiol, FIBiol, FMedSci; British veterinary scientist and academic; b. 13 Aug. 1926, Petersfield; s. of Ronald Biggs and Cecile Biggs (née Player); m. Alison Janet Molteno 1950; two s. one d.; ed Bedales School, Petersfield, Cambridge School, Mass., Royal Veterinary Coll., London, Univ. of Bristol; with RAF 1944–48; with Royal Veterinary Coll., London 1948–53; Research Asst, Dept of Veterinary Anatomy, Univ. of Bristol 1953–55; Lecturer in Veterinary Clinical Pathology, Dept of Veterinary Medicine 1955–59; Prin. Scientific Officer, Houghton Poultry Research Station 1959–66, Sr Prin. Scientific Officer 1966–1971, Deputy Dir 1971–74, Dir 1974–86; Dir Inst. for Animal Health 1986–88; Chief Scientific Officer 1981–88; Visiting Prof. of Veterinary Microbiology, Royal Veterinary Coll. London 1982–88, Hon. Prof. of Veterinary Microbiology 2009–, Vice-Chair. of Council 2002–08; Andrew D. White Prof.-at-Large, Cornell Univ., USA 1988–94; Vice-Pres. British Veterinary Asscn 1996–98; Fellow Inst. of Biology 1973, Pres. 1990–92; Fellow, Royal Coll. of Pathologists 1978, Royal Coll. of Veterinary Surgeons 1979, Royal Veterinary Coll. 1983; Hon. Fellow, Royal Agricultural Soc. of England 1986; Hon. Dr of Veterinary Medicine (Ludwig-Maximilians Univ., Munich); Dr hc (Univ. of Liège) and numerous others; Wolf Foundation Prize in Agric. 1989; Dalrymple-Champneys Cup and Medal of the British Veterinary Asscn 1973, Chiron Award, British Veterinary Asscn 1999. *Publications:* more than 100 scientific papers. *Leisure interests:* music making, natural history. *Address:* 'Willows', London Road, St Ives, PE27 5ES, England (home). *Telephone:* (1480) 463471 (home). *Fax:* (1480) 463471 (home). *E-mail:* peter.biggs@bigfoot.com (home). *Website:* www.rvc.ac.uk (office).

BIGOT, Charles André Marie; French aviation engineer; b. 29 July 1932, Angers; s. of Charles Bigot and Marcelle Pousset; m. Marie-Odile Lambert 1959; one s. three d.; ed Ecole Sainte-Geneviève, Versailles, Ecole Nat. Supérieure de l'Aéronautique, Ecole Polytechnique and Cranfield Coll. of Aeronautics, Centre de Perfectionnement Affaires; aeronautical engineer 1957–61; Tech. Dir of Aeronautical Services, Ministry of Aeronautics, CNRS 1961–63; Dir of launch vehicle div., Centre Nat. des Etudes Spatiales (CNES) 1963–70; Deputy Dir Centre Spatial de Brétigny 1970–71; Dir of Devt Air Inter 1971–75; Soc. d'Etudes et de Réalisations Industrielles (Seri-Renault Eng), Dir-Gen. 1975–80; Commercial Dir Soc. Nat. Industrielle Aérospatiale (Snias) 1980–82; Dir-Gen. Arianespace 1982–90, Pres.-Dir-Gen. 1990–98, Hon. Chair. 1998–; mem. Bd of Dirs Ellipso 1998–; mem. Int. Acad. of Astronautics, Acad. Nat. de l'Air et de l'Espace; Chevalier, Légion d'honneur, Commdr, Ordre Nat. du Mérite; Médaille de Vermeil (CNES). *Address:* Arianespace, Bd de l'Europe, BP 117, 91006 Evry Cédex (office); 16 rue de la Chancellerie, 78000 Versailles, France (home). *Telephone:* 1-39-20-01-45.

BIGUM, Jens, MSc; Danish business executive and university administrator; *Chairman, Aarhus University;* b. 28 Aug. 1938; ed Royal Veterinary and Agricultural Univ., Copenhagen; Admin. Officer Oxexport 1965–70; Financial Man. Mejeriselskabet Danmark amba 1970–72, Financial Dir 1972; Dir MD Foods amba 1987–92, Man. Dir 1992–2000 (renamed Arla Foods), Man. Dir Arla Foods amba 2000–04, also Dir and Deputy Chair. Arla Foods UK PLC

2003; Chair. Chr. Hansen Holding A/S 2005–06; currently Chair. Aarhus Univ.; Dir Carlsberg Breweries A/S 1997–, Chair. 2002–, Deputy Chair. Carlsberg A/S 2002–;. *Address:* Office of the Chairman, Aarhus University, 8000 Aarhus, Denmark (office). *Telephone:* 8938-1000 (office). *E-mail:* jens.bigum@arlafoods.com (office). *Website:* www.au.dk (office).

BÍLÁ, Lucie; Czech singer; b. (Hana Zaňáková), 7 April 1966, Otvovice; d. of Josef Zaňák; fmr pnr Petr Kratochvíl; one s.; m. Vaclav Noid Barta; co-owner Theatre Ta Fantastika, Prague; has toured throughout Western Europe; has performed in charity concerts in Czech Repub.; numerous awards including Czech Grammy Prize 1992–96, Most Popular Singer (Czech Repub.) 1994–2007, Czech Musical Acad. Prize 1997, Czech Nightingale Trophy 1996–2004, 2007–08. *Recordings include:* albums: Missariel 1993, Lucie Bílá 1994, Hvezdy jako hvezdy (Stars as Stars) 1998, Uplne naha (Totally naked) 1999, Jampadampa 2003, Laska je laska (Love is love - Best Of) 2004, Koncert (Concert) 2006, Woman 2007. *Theatre includes:* Les Misérables 1992, Dracula 1995, Rat-Catcher 1996, Joan of Arc (Thalia Prize) 2000, Love is Love 2004, Elixir Zivota 2006, Carmen 2008. *Film:* Horká kaše 1988, Divoká srdce 1989, Volná noha 1989, Praákům, těm je hej 1990, Zkoušové období 1990, Fontána pro Zuzanu 2 1993, Princezna ze miejna 1994, King Ubu 1996, Čas dluhů 1998. *Publication:* Nyní ji to vim (Now I Know It Already) 1999, Jen kratka navsteva potesi (Just short visit delights) 2007. *Leisure interest:* family. *Telephone:* (603) 548530 (home). *E-mail:* produkce@luciebila.com (office). *Website:* www.luciebila.com.

BILALI, Mohamed Gharib; Tanzanian politician; fmr govt official; Chief Minister Supreme Revolutionary Council of Zanzibar 1995–2001; mem. CCM (Party for Democracy and Progress). *Address:* c/o Office of the Chief Minister, Supreme Revolutionary Council of Zanzibar, Zanzibar, Tanzania.

BILBY, Bruce Alexander, PhD, FRS; British scientist, academic and consultant; *Professor Emeritus of the Theory of Materials, University of Sheffield;* b. 3 Sept. 1922, London; s. of the late George Alexander Bilby and Dorothy Jean Bilby (née Telfer); m. 1st Hazel Joyce Casken 1946 (divorced 1964); two s. one d.; m. 2nd Lorette Wendela Thomas 1966; two s.; ed Dover Grammar School, Peterhouse, Cambridge, Univ. of Birmingham; Admiralty 1943–46; Research, Birmingham 1946–51; Royal Soc. Sorby Research Fellow, Univ. of Sheffield 1951–57, J. H. Andrew Research Fellow 1957–58, Reader in Theoretical Metallurgy 1958–62, Prof. of Theoretical Metallurgy 1962–66, Prof. of the Theory of Materials 1966–84, Prof. Emer. 1984–; Rosenhain Medal 1963, Griffith Medal 1994. *Publications:* scientific papers in learned journals. *Leisure interest:* sailing. *Address:* Department of Engineering Materials, University of Sheffield, Mappin Street, Sheffield, S1 3JD (office); 32 Devonshire Road, Totley, Sheffield, S17 3NT, England (home). *Telephone:* (114) 222-7713 (office); (114) 236-1086 (home). *E-mail:* B.Bilby@sheffield.ac.uk (office). *Website:* www.shef.ac.uk/materials (office).

BILDT, Carl; Swedish politician and diplomatist; *Minister of Foreign Affairs;* b. 15 July 1949, Halmstad; m. Mia Bohman 1984; one s. one d.; ed Univ. of Stockholm; Chair. Confed. of Liberal and Conservative Students 1973–74, European Democrat Students 1974–76; mem. Stockholm Co. Council 1974–77; Political Advisor on Policy Co-ordination Ministry of Econ. Affairs 1976–78; Under-Sec. of State for Co-ordination and Planning at the Cabinet Office 1979–81; mem. Parl. 1979–2001; mem. Exec. Cttee Moderate Party 1981, Leader 1986–99; mem. Advisory Council on Foreign Affairs 1982–99; mem. Submarine Defence Comm. 1982–83; mem. 1984 Defence Policy Comm. 1984–87; Prime Minister of Sweden 1991–94; EU Peace Envoy in Fmr Yugoslavia 1995; High Rep. of the Int. Community in Bosnia and Herzegovina 1995–97; Vice-Chair. Int. Democrat Union 1989–92, Chair. 1992–99; Special Envoy of Sec.-Gen. of the UN to the Balkans 1999–2001; Chair. At-Large-Membership Study Cttee Internet Corpn for Assigned Names and Numbers (ICANN) 2001–02; currently Chair. Bd of Dirs Kreab Group (public affairs and strategic communication cos), Nordic Venture Network, Teleoptimering AB; Minister of Foreign Affairs 2006–; mem. Bd of Dirs Centre for European Reform, Vostok Nafta, Lundin Petroleum, HiQ, Öhmans; Trustee RAND Corpn; Fellow, Inst. for the Study of Terrorism and Political Violence, Univ. of St Andrews, Scotland; mem. IISS, London. *Publications:* Landet som steg ut i kylan (The Country that Stepped Out into the Cold) 1972, Framtid i frihet (A Future in Freedom) 1976, Hallanning, svensk, europe (A Citizen of Holland, Sweden and Europe) 1991, Peace Journey 1997. *Address:* Ministry for Foreign Affairs, Gustav Adolfs torg 1, 103 39 Stockholm, Sweden (office). *Telephone:* (8) 405-10-00 (office). *Fax:* (8) 723-11-76 (office). *E-mail:* registrator@foreign.ministry.se (office); carl@bildt.net. *Website:* utrikes.regeringen.se (office); www.bildt.net.

BILE, Pastor Micha Ondo, MSc; Equatorial Guinean diplomatist and mining engineer; *Minister of Foreign Affairs, International Co-operation and Francophone Affairs;* b. 2 Dec. 1952, Nsinik-Esawong; m.; six c.; ed Inst. of Mining, Krivoi-Rog Univ.; engineer, Mines and Quarries Section, Dept of Mines and Hydrocarbons, Ministry of Mines and Energy 1982, Chief of Section 1983–84, Dir-Gen. Dept 1984–94, Sec.-Gen. Ministry 1994–95; Perm. Rep. to UN 1995–2001; currently Minister of Foreign Affairs, International Co-operation and Francophone Affairs; Kt (Second Class), Order of Independence. *Address:* Ministry of Foreign Affairs, International Co-operation and Francophone Affairs, Malabo, Equatorial Guinea (office). *Telephone:* (09) 32-20. *Fax:* (09) 31-32.

BILLAUD, Bernard; French civil servant; b. 3 Sept. 1942, Béziers; s. of Bernard Billaud and Raymonde Mazet; m. Claude Devitry 1967; two s. one d.; ed Inst. d'études politiques de Paris and Ecole nat. d'admin, Faculté de droit de Paris; obtained Diplôme de Inst. d'études politiques de Paris and Diplôme d'études supérieures de droit public; auditor 1968, Public Auditor Cour des Comptes 1976, Conseiller maître 1989; Adviser to French Embassy, Holy See 1974–76; Official Rep. to the Prime Minister 1976; Sr Lecturer Inst. d'études politiques de Paris 1977–92; Dir of Staff, Mayor of Paris 1979–83; mem. comm. Vieux Paris 1983–; Pres. comm. on historical works of Ville de Paris 1983–2009; Dir-Gen. Int. Relations, Paris 1983–84; Gen. Commr of the French Language 1987–89; Prime Minister's Rep. of Admin. Council of AFP 1993–98, France 3 1995–98; Vice-Pres. organizing Cttee for 'de la Gaule à la France' 1996; Pres. du conseil d'admin de l'Ecole nationale des chartes 2004–07; Officier, Légion d'honneur, Officier, Ordre nat. du Mérite, Grand Croix Ordre de Saint-Grégoire-le-Grand. *Publications:* L'aide de l'Etat à l'enseignement privé 1966, Georges Bidault – Les éditoriaux de "l'aube" (1938–1940) 2001, D'un Chirac l'autre 2005. *Leisure interest:* history. *Address:* Cour des comptes, 13 rue Cambon, 75001 Paris (office); 12 rue des Jardins Saint Paul, 75004 Paris, France (home). *Telephone:* 1-42-98-99-10 (office); 1-48-87-91-68 (home).

BILLINGTON, James Hadley, PhD; American historian, academic and librarian; *Librarian of Congress;* b. 1 June 1929, Bryn Mawr, Pa; s. of Nelson Billington and Jane Coolbaugh; m. Marjorie A. Brennan 1957; two s. two d.; ed Princeton Univ. and Univ. of Oxford; army service 1953–56; Instructor in History, Harvard Univ. 1957–58, Fellow Russian Research Center 1958–59, Asst Prof. of History 1958–61; Assoc. Prof. of History, Princeton Univ. 1962–64, Prof. 1964–73; Dir Woodrow Wilson Int. Center for Scholars, Washington, DC 1973–87; Librarian of Congress, Library of Congress, Washington, DC 1987–; Visiting Research Prof. Inst. of History of USSR Acad. of Sciences 1966–67, Univ. of Helsinki 1960–61, Ecole des Hautes Etudes en Sciences Sociales, Paris 1985, 1988; visiting lecturer to various univs in Europe and Asia, etc.; Guggenheim Fellow 1960–61; mem. American Acad. of Arts and Sciences, American Philosophical Soc.; Chair. Bd of Foreign Scholarships (Fulbright Program) 1971–73; writer/host The Face of Russia (TV series) 1998; Chevalier Ordre des Arts et des Lettres; Kt Commdr's Cross of the Order of Merit (Germany) 1996; 22 hon. degrees; Gwangha Medal (Repub. of Korea), Woodrow Wilson Award 1992, Pushkin Medal 1999, Univ. of Calif. at LA Medal 2000. *Publications:* Mikhailovsky and Russian Populism 1958, The Icon and the Axe: An Interpretive History of Russian Culture 1966, Fire in the Minds of Men: Origins of the Revolutionary Faith 1980, Russia Transformed: Breakthrough to Hope 1992, The Face of Russia 1998, Russia in Search of Itself 2004; contribs to books and journals. *Address:* Library of Congress, 101 Independence Avenue, SE Washington, DC 20540-0002, USA (office). *Telephone:* (202) 707-5000 (office). *Fax:* (202) 707-1714 (office). *Website:* www.loc.gov (office).

BILLINGTON, Kevin, BA, DipMus; British film, theatre and television director; b. 12 June 1934; s. of Richard Billington and Margaret Billington; m. Lady Rachel Mary Pakenham 1967; two s. two d.; ed Bryanston School and Queens' Coll., Cambridge; film dir BBC programme Tonight 1960–63; documentary film dir, BBC 1963–67; freelance film, theatre and TV dir 1967–; Chair. BAFTA 1989–90, 1990–91; Screenwriters' Guild Award 1966, 1967, Guild of TV Producers and Directors Award 1966, 1967. *Feature films:* Interlude 1967, The Rise and Rise of Michael Rimmer 1969, The Light at the Edge of the World 1970, Voices 1974, Reflections 1984. *Scripts:* Looking For Love 1997, Loving Attitudes 1998, Bodily Harm 2000. *Television films:* And No One Can Save Her 1973, Once Upon a Time is Now (documentary) 1978, The Music Will Never Stop (documentary) 1979, Henry VIII 1979, The Jail Diary of Albie Sachs 1980, The Good Soldier 1981, Outside Edge 1982, The Sonnets of William Shakespeare 1984, The Deliberate Death of a Polish Priest 1986, Heartland 1989, A Time to Dance 1991. *Plays directed:* Find Your Way Home 1970, Me 1973, The Birthday Party 1974, The Caretaker 1975, Bloody Neighbours 1974, Emigrés 1976, The Homecoming 1978, Quartermaine's Terms 1982, The Deliberate Death of a Polish Priest 1985, The Philanthropist 1986, The Lover and A Slight Ache (double bill) 1987, The Breadwinner 1989, Veterans' Day 1989, Quartermaine's Terms 1993, Old Times 1994, Six Characters in Search of an Author 1999, Our Country's Good 1999, Victory 2000, Wild Honey 2002. *Leisure interests:* swimming, football (Queen's Park Rangers). *Address:* c/o Judy Daish Associates, 2 St Charles Place, London, W10 6EG, England (office). *Telephone:* (20) 8964-8811 (office). *Fax:* (20) 8964-8966 (office). *E-mail:* kevin.billington@btinternet.com (office).

BILLINGTON, Michael Keith, BA; British drama critic and author; b. 16 Nov. 1939, Leamington Spa; s. of Alfred R. Billington and Patricia Bradshaw; m. Jeanine Bradlaugh 1977; one d.; ed Warwick School and St Catherine's Coll., Oxford; Public Liaison Officer, Theatre Royal, Lincoln 1962–64; writer on theatre, film and cinema, The Times 1965–71; Drama Critic, The Guardian 1971–, Country Life 1988–; presenter of various BBC Radio arts programmes including Options, Kaleidoscope, Meridian, etc. 1971–91; writer on London arts scene for The New York Times 1984–94; writer and presenter of TV profiles of Peter Hall, Alan Ayckbourn, Peggy Ashcroft 1988–90; IPC Critic of the Year 1974, Theatre Critic of the Year 1993, 1995, 1997. *Publications:* The Modern Actor 1973, Alan Ayckbourn 1983, Tom Stoppard 1987, Peggy Ashcroft 1988, One Night Stands 1993, The Life and Work of Harold Pinter 1996, Stage and Screen Lives (Ed.) 2001, State of the Nation (Theatre Book Prize 2007) 2007. *Leisure interests:* cricket, opera, travel. *Address:* 15 Hearne Road, London, W4 3NJ, England. *Telephone:* (20) 8995-0455. *Fax:* (20) 8742-3496 (home). *E-mail:* michael.billington@guardian.co.uk (office).

BILONOG, Yuriy; Ukrainian shot putter; b. 9 April 1974, Belopol'ye; m.; began shot putting at age nine; World Jr Champion 1992; winner World Indoor Championships, Paris 1997, Golden League, Monaco 2000, Grand Prix, Seville 2003, Helsinki 2003; Bronze Medal World Championships, St-Denis 2003; Gold Medal Athens Olympics 2004; mem. Dynamo Club. *Leisure interests:* music. *Address:* c/o National Olympic Committee of Ukraine, Esplanadna St. 42, 01023 Kiev, Ukraine (office). *Telephone:* (44) 2466426 (office). *Fax:* (44) 2466233 (office). *E-mail:* info@noc-ukr.org (office). *Website:* www.noc-ukr.org (office).

BIN LADEN, Osama; Saudi Arabia-born guerrilla leader; b. Jeddah; s. of the late Mohammad bin Laden; m. five wives including Najua Ghanem; three c.; Amal al-Sadah; one d.; (divorced from one wife); more than 20 c.; ed King Abdul-Aziz Univ., Jeddah; funded and joined troops fighting against Soviet Union in Afghanistan 1979; co-f. group to send aid to Afghan resistance and establish recruitment centres mid-1980s; f. org. to support Islamist opposition movts 1988; expelled from Saudi Arabia for anti-govt activities 1991, Saudi Arabian citizenship removed for 'irresponsible activities' 1994; moved to Sudan 1991, expelled following pressure from USA and UN 1996; continued to support Islamist extremist activities from Afghanistan; as head of the al-Qa'ida org. believed to have masterminded attacks on World Trade Center, New York, and Pentagon, Washington, DC on 11 Sept. 2001.

BINAISA, Godfrey Lukwongwa, LLB; Ugandan politician and lawyer; b. 30 May 1920, Kampala; m. 1st (died 2003); m. 2nd Ms Yamamoto 2004; ed King's Coll., Budo, Makerere Univ., King's Coll., London, Lincoln's Inn, London; in pvt. legal practice 1956–62, 1967–79; mem. of Uganda Nat. Congress, later of Uganda People's Congress; Attorney-Gen. 1962–67; Pres. Uganda Law Soc., Chair. Law Devt Centre 1968; mem. Uganda Judicial Service Comm. 1970; Chair. Organizing Cttee for Commonwealth Lawyers' Conf., 1972; went into exile; in legal practice in New York; returned to Uganda 1979 after fall of Govt of Pres. Idi Amin Dada; Pres. of Uganda 1979–80, also Minister of Foreign Affairs June–July 1979, Minister of Defence; Chancellor, Makerere Univ. 1979–80; under house arrest 1980–81; left Uganda Jan. 1981, returned 2001.

BINCHY, Maeve, BA; Irish writer; b. 28 May 1940, Dalkey, Co Dublin; d. of William Binchy and Maureen Blackmore; m. Gordon Thomas Snell 1977; ed Univ. Coll. Dublin; teacher of history and French, Pembroke School, Dublin 1961–68; columnist, Irish Times 1968–2000; Hon. DLit (Nat. Univ. of Ireland) 1990, (Queen's Belfast) 1998; Int. Television Festival Golden Prague Award, Czech TV 1979, Jacobs Award 1979, WHSmith Fiction Award 2001, Irish PEN/A T Cross Award for Literature 2007. *Publications:* short story collections: Central Line 1978, Victoria Line 1980, Dublin Four 1982, Victoria Line/ Central Line (revised edn of two earlier titles, aka London Transports) 1983, This Year it Will be Different 1996, Return Journey 1998; novels: Silver Wedding 1979, Light a Penny Candle 1982, The Lilac Bus 1984, Echoes 1985, Firefly Summer 1987, Circle of Friends 1990, The Copper Beech 1992, The Glass Lake 1994, Evening Class 1996, Tara Road 1999, Scarlet Feather 2000, Quentins 2002, Nights of Rain and Stars 2004, Whitethorn Woods 2006, This Year it Will be Different 2007; non-fiction: Aches and Pains 2000; other: several plays. *Address:* Christine Green, 6 Whitehorse Mews, Westminster Bridge Road, London, SE1 7QD, England (office); PO Box 6737, Dun Laoghaire, Co Dublin, Ireland. *E-mail:* info@christinegreen.co.uk (office). *Website:* www.christinegreen.co.uk (office); www.maevebinchy.com.

BINDING, Günther, DrIng, DPhil; German professor of art and architecture; *Emeritus Professor, University of Cologne;* b. 6 March 1936, Koblenz; s. of Kurt Binding and Margot (née Masur); m. Elisabeth Dietz 1969; one s. two d.; ed gymnasium in Arnsberg and Cologne, Technische Hochschule, Aachen and Univs of Cologne and Bonn; Dir Lower Rhine section, Rheinisches Land-esmuseum, Bonn 1964–70; Prof., Univ. of Cologne 1970–2000, Rector 1981–83, Pro-Rector 1983–85, now Prof. Emer.; Vice-Pres. W German Rectors' Conf. 1982–84; mem. Sächsische Akad. der Wissenschaften 1999, Wissenschaftliche Gesellschaft an der Universität Frankfurt; Ruhrpreis für Kunst und Wissenschaft 1966, Josef-Humar-Preis 1986, Rheinland-Taler 1987. *Publications:* 40 books and 320 articles about European architecture and history of art. *Address:* Albertus-Magnus-Platz, 50923 Cologne (office); Wingertsheide 65, 51427 Berg.-Gladbach, Germany (home). *Telephone:* (221) 470-4440 (office); (2204) 64956 (home). *E-mail:* guenther.binding@uni-koeln .de. *Website:* www.guenther-binding.de.

BINGAMAN, Jeff, JD; American politician and lawyer; *Senator from New Mexico;* b. 3 Oct. 1943, Silver City, NM; s. of Jesse Bingaman and Beth Ball; m. Ann Kovacovich 1968; one s.; ed Harvard and Stanford Univs; admitted to NM Bar 1968; partner Campbell, Bingaman & Black, Santa Fe 1972–78; Attorney-Gen., NM 1979–82; Senator from New Mexico 1983–; Chair. Energy Cttee 2001; Democrat. *Address:* 703 Hart Senate Building, Washington, DC 20510-0001 (office); PO Box 5775 Santa Fe, NM 87502-5775, USA (home). *Telephone:* (202) 224-5521 (office). *E-mail:* senator_bingaman@bingaman.senate.gov (office). *Website:* bingaman.senate.gov (office).

BINGHAM, H. Raymond, BS, MBA; Singaporean business executive; *Chairman, Flextronics International Ltd;* ed Weber State Univ., Harvard Business School; held sr man. positions at Marriott Corpn, Red Lion Hotels and Inns, Agrico Overseas Investment Co. and N-ReN International; Exec. Vice-Pres. and Chief Financial Officer Cadence Design Systems, Inc. 1993–99, mem. Bd of Dirs 1997–2004, Pres. and CEO 1999–2004, Exec. Chair. 2004–05; Man. Dir General Atlantic LLC (pvt. equity firm) 2006–, also Co-head of Palo Alto, Calif. office; mem. Bd of Dirs Flextronics International Ltd 2005–, Chair. 2008–; mem. Bd of Dirs Freescale Semiconductor, Inc., KLA Tencor Corpn, Oracle Corpn, STMicroelectronics NV; Co-founder and Dir Silicon Valley Educ. Foundation; mem. Bd of Dirs Nat. Parks Conservation Asscn. *Address:* General Atlantic LLC, 228 Hamilton Ave., Palo Alto, CA 94301, USA (office); Flextronics International Ltd, 2 Changi South Lane, 486123, Singapore (office). *Telephone:* (650) 251-7800 (Palo Alto) (office); 6299-8888 (office). *Fax:* (650) 251-9672 (Palo Alto) (office); 6543-1888 (office). *E-mail:* board@ flextronics.com (office). *Website:* www.generalatlantic.com (office); www .flextronics.com (office).

BINGHAM, John, CBE, FRS; British scientist; b. 19 June 1930; s. of Thomas Frederick Bingham and Emma Maud Lusher; m. Jadwiga Anna Siedlecka

1983; one s.; mem. staff Plant Breeding Inst. of Cambridge (subsequently Plant Breeding Int. Cambridge Ltd) 1954–86, Deputy Chief Scientific Officer 1981–91; research in plant breeding, culminating in production of improved winter wheat varieties for British agric.; Pres. Royal Norfolk Agric. Asscn 1991; Hon. Fellow Royal Agric. Soc. of England 1983; Mullard Medal of Royal Soc. 1975, Royal Agric. Soc. of England Research Medal 1975, Massey Ferguson Nat. Award for Services to UK Agric. 1984. *Leisure interests:* farming and wildlife conservation. *Address:* Hereward Barn, Church Lane, Mattishall Burgh, Dereham, Norfolk, NR20 3QZ, England. *Telephone:* (1362) 858354.

BINGHAM OF CORNHILL, Baron (Life Peer) cr. 1996, of Boughrood in the County of Powys; **Thomas (Henry) Bingham,** Kt, PC, MA, KG; British judge; b. 13 Oct. 1933; s. of the late Dr T. H. Bingham and Dr C. Bingham; m. Elizabeth Loxley 1963; two s. one d.; ed Sedbergh School, Balliol Coll. Oxford; called to Bar, Gray's Inn 1959, Bencher 1979; Standing Jr Counsel to Dept of Employment 1968–72; QC 1972; Recorder of Crown Court 1975–80; Judge, High Court of Justice, Queen's Bench Div. and Judge, Commercial Court 1980–86; a Lord Justice of Appeal 1986–92; Master of the Rolls 1992–96; Lord Chief Justice of England and Wales 1996–2000; Sr Law Lord June 2000–; Leader, Investigation into supply of petroleum and petroleum products to Rhodesia 1977–78; Chair. Inquiry into the Supervision of BCCI 1991–92; Commr Interception of Communications 1985, 1992–94; Chair. numerous other comms; Special Trustee St Mary's Hosp. 1985–92 (Chair. 1988–92). *Publications:* Chitty on Contracts (Asst Ed.) (22nd edn 1961), The Business of Judging 2000. *Address:* House of Lords, Westminster, London, SW1 0PA, England (office).

BINMORE, Kenneth George, CBE, PhD, FBA; British economist and academic; *Professor Emeritus of Economics and Research Fellow, University College London;* b. 27 Sept. 1940, London; s. of Ernest Binmore and Maud Binmore (née Holland); m. Josephine Ann Lee 1972; two s. two d.; ed Imperial Coll., London; Prof. of Math., LSE 1974–88; Prof. of Econs, Univ. of Mich. 1988–93, Univ. Coll. London 1991–2003, Prof. Emer. and Research Fellow 2003–; Dir Centre for Econ. Learning and Social Evolution 1994–2003; Fellow Econometric Soc., American Acad. of Arts and Sciences. *Publications include:* 11 books, including Mathematical Analysis 1977, Economics of Bargaining 1986, Fun and Games 1992, Playing Fair: Game Theory and the Social Contract I 1994, Just Playing: Game Theory and the Social Contract II 1998, Natural Justice 2004; 77 published papers. *Leisure interest:* philosophy. *Address:* Department of Economics, University College London, Gower Street, London, WC1E 6BT, England (office); Newmills, Whitebrook, Monmouth, Gwent, NP25 4TY, Wales (home). *Telephone:* (20) 7504-5864 (office); (1600) 860691 (home). *Fax:* (20) 7916-2774 (office); (1600) 860691 (home). *E-mail:* k.binmore@ucl.ac.uk (office). *Website:* else.econ.ucl.ac.uk/newweb/ displayProfile.php?key=2 (office).

BINNIG, Gerd; German physicist; b. 20 July 1947, Frankfurt am Main; m. 1st Lore Wagler 1969; one s. one d.; m. 2nd Renate Binnig 2003; ed Univ. of Frankfurt; mem. Physics Group, IBM Zürich Research Lab., Rüschlikon 1978–2005, Group Leader 1984–2005; Assignment to IBM Almaden Research Centre, San José, Calif., collaboration with Stanford Univ. 1985–86, 1987; IBM Fellow 1986; Visiting Prof., Stanford Univ. 1986–; Foreign Assoc. mem. Acad. of Sciences, Washington, DC 1987; mem. IBM Acad. 1989, Bd Mercedes Automobil Holding AG 1989–93, Bd Daimler Benz Holding 1990–; consultant and mem. Advisory Bd Definiens AG 1994–; Hon. Prof., Univ. of Munich 1986–; Hon. Fellow, Royal Microscopical Soc. 1988; OM (FRG) 1987; shared Nobel Prize for Physics (with E. Ruska and H. Rohrer) 1986, Physics Prize of German Physical Soc. 1982, Otto Klung Prize 1983, shared King Faisal Int. Prize for Physics and Hewlett Packard Europhysics Prize 1984, Eliot Cresson Medal (Franklin Inst., Phila) 1987, Distinguished Service Medal, Minnie Rosen Award (Ross Univ., NY) 1988, Bayerischer Verdienstorden 1992. *Leisure interests:* music, sports. *Address:* Definiens AG, Trappentoen str. 1, 80339 Munich, Germany (office). *Website:* www.definiens.com.

BINNS, Malcolm, ARCM; British pianist; b. 29 Jan. 1936, Nottingham; s. of Douglas Priestley Binns and May Walker; ed Bradford Grammar School, Royal Coll. of Music; soloist with numerous leading orchestras and conductors around the world (including Boulez, Boult, Dorati, Haitink and Rattle) 1960–; toured with Scottish Nat. Orchestra and Limbourg Orchestra 1987–88; regular performer at Wigmore Hall 1958–, the Promenade Concerts 1962–; concerts at Aldeburgh, Leeds, Three Choirs and Canterbury Festivals; solo and concerto performances are broadcast regularly on BBC; Chappell Medal 1956, Medal of Worshipful Co. of Musicians 1956. *Recordings:* more than 30 recordings, including piano sonatas by Bax, Ireland and Bridge for the British Music Soc. 2007, Balakirev Piano Concerti 1 and 2, Rimsky-Korsakov Piano Concerto (English Northern Philharmonia) 1992. *Leisure interests:* gardening, collecting antique gramophone records. *Address:* c/o Michael Harrold Artist Management, 13 Clinton Road, Leatherhead, Surrey KT22 8NU, England (office); 233 Court Road, Orpington, Kent BR6 9BY, England (home). *Telephone:* (1372) 375728 (office); (1689) 831056 (home). *E-mail:* management@angelus.co.uk (office). *Website:* www.angelus.co.uk (office).

BINNS, Hon. Patrick (Pat) George, MA; Canadian politician; b. 8 Oct. 1948, Sask.; s. of Stan and Phyllis Binns; m. Carol Binns; four c.; ed Univ. of Alberta; worked with PEI Rural Devt Council 1972–78; mem. Legis. Ass. representing 4th Kings Dist 1978–88, fmr Minister of Industry, Municipal Affairs, Fisheries, Environment, Labour, Housing, responsibilities for Econ. Devt; mem. House of Commons representing Cardigan 1984–88; Pres. Island Bean Ltd and Pat Binns & Assocs 1988–96; Leader, Progressive Conservative Party of PEI 1996–, MLA for Dist 5, Murray River-Gaspereaux 1996–, Premier, Pres. of Exec. Council, Minister Responsible for Intergovernmental Affairs 1996–2007, Minister of Agric., Fisheries and Aquaculture 2006–07.

Address: c/o Progressive Conservative Party of PEI, 390 University Avenue, Charlottetown, PEI C1A 4N5, Canada (office). *Telephone:* (902) 620-0060. *Fax:* (902) 628-6428. *E-mail:* info@pcparty.pe.ca. *Website:* www.pcparty.pe.ca; www.patbinns.ca.

BINOCHE, Juliette; French actress; b. 9 March 1964, Paris; d. of Jean-Marie Binoche and Monique Stalens; one s. by André Halle; ed Nat. Conservatory of Drama and private theatrical studies. *Films include:* Les nanas, La vie de famille, Rouge Baiser, Rendez-Vous, Mon beau-frère a tué ma soeur, Mauvais Sang, Un tour de manège, Les amants du Pont-Neuf, The Unbearable Lightness of Being, Wuthering Heights 1992, Damage 1992, Trois Couleurs: Bleu 1993, Le Hussard sur le Toit 1995, The English Patient (Acad. Award for Best Supporting Actress 1996, Berlin Film Festival Award 1996, BAFTA Award 1997), Alice et Martin 1999, Les Enfants du Siècle (Children of the Century) 1999, La Veuve de Saint-Pierre 2000, Chocolat 2001, Code Unknown 2001, Décalage horaire (Jet Lag) 2002, Caché 2005, Country of My Skull 2004, Bee Season 2005, Mary 2005, Paris, je t'aime 2006, A Few Days in September 2006, Breaking and Entering 2006, Le Voyage du ballon rouge 2007, Désengagement 2007, Dan in Real Life 2007, Paris 2007, Summer Hours 2008. *Play:* Naked (Almeida, London) 1998. *Address:* c/o UTA, 9560 Wilshire Boulevard, Floor 5, Beverly Hills, CA 90212, USA.

BIO, Brig.-Gen. Julius Maada; Sierra Leonean army officer; fmr Vice-Chair. Supreme Council of State; Chair. Sierra Leone Nat. Provisional Ruling Council Jan.–June 1996.

BIO-TCHANÉ, Abdoulaye, MA; Benin international organization official and economist; *President, West African Development Bank;* ed Univ. of Dijon, France, Centre Ouest-Africain de Formation et d'Etudes, Dakar, Senegal; economist, Cen. Bank for W African Countries (BCEAO), Dir Econ. and Monetary Survey Dept –1998; Minister of Finances and Economy 1998–2002; Dir IMF African Dept 2002–08; Pres. West African Devt Bank 2008–. *Address:* West African Development Bank, 68, Avenue de la Libération, BP 1172, Lomé, Togo (office). *Telephone:* 221-59-06 (office). *Fax:* 221-52-67 (office). *E-mail:* boadsiege@boad.org (office). *Website:* www.boad.org (office).

BIOKE MALABO, Capt. Cristino Seriche; Equatorial Guinean politician and army officer; Second Vice-Pres. and Minister of Health 1981–82; Prime Minister of Equatorial Guinea 1982–91; Minister of Govt Co-ordination, Planning, Economic Devt and Finance 1982–86, of Health 1986, now in Charge of Political and Admin. Co-ordination. *Address:* c/o Oficina del Primer Ministro, Malabo, Equatorial Guinea.

BIONDI, Alfredo; Italian politician and lawyer; b. 29 June 1928, Pisa; m. Giovanna Susak; two c.; fmr mem. Liberal Party (PLI), Nat. Sec. 1985–86; PLI Deputy 1968–92; Unione di Centro (Libertà) Deputy 1992–94, Forza Italia Deputy 1994–2006; Minister of Justice 1994–95, Vice-Chair. Chamber of Deputies 2001–06; mem. Senate 2006–08. *Address:* c/o Forza Italia, Via dell'Umiltà 36, 00187 Rome (office); Camera dei Deputat, Palazzo di Montecitorio, Rome, Italy (office). *Telephone:* (06) 67311 (office). *Fax:* (06) 6788255 (office). *E-mail:* lettere@forza-italia.it (office). *Website:* www.camera.it (office); www.forza-italia.it (office).

BIONDI, Frank J., Jr, BA, MBA; American business executive; *Senior Managing Director, Waterview Advisors LLC;* b. 9 Jan. 1945, New York; s. of Frank Biondi and Virginia Willis; m. Carol Oughton 1974; two d.; ed Princeton and Harvard Univs; Assoc. corporate finance, Prudential Securities, New York 1969, Shearson-Lehman Inc. New York 1970–71; Prin. Frank Biondi & Assocs, New York 1972; Dir business analysis, Teleprompter Corpn New York 1972–73; Asst Treas., Assoc. Dir Business Affairs, Children's TV Workshop, New York 1974–78; Dir Entertainment Planning, HBO, New York 1978, Vice-Pres. programming operations 1979–82, Exec. Vice-Pres. Planning and Admin. 1982–83, Pres. and CEO 1983, Chair. and CEO 1984; Exec. Vice-Pres. entertainment business sector, The Coca-Cola Co. 1985; Chair. and CEO Coca-Cola TV 1986; Pres., CEO and Dir Viacom Int. Inc. New York 1987–96; Pres., CEO and Dir Viacom Inc. 1987–96; Chair., CEO Universal Studios Inc. 1996–98; mem. Bd of Dirs Bank of New York, Amgen, Hasbro, Harrah's Entertainment, Cablevision Systems, The Museum of Television and Radio; Pres. Biondi Reiss Capital Man., New York 1998; Sr Man. Dir Waterview Advisors LLC (private equity fund) 1999–. *Address:* Waterview Advisors LLC, 2425 Olympic Boulevard, Suite 4050, West Santa Monica, CA 90404, USA.

BIONDI, Matt, MA; American fmr swimmer; b. 8 Oct. 1965, Moraga, Calif.; m. Kirsten Biondi 1995; one s.; ed Berkeley Univ., Lewis & Clarke Coll.; mem. USA Water Polo Team, then became freestyle swimmer; career highlights: Olympic Games – 50m freestyle 1st (1988), 2nd (1992); 100m freestyle 1st (1988); 200m freestyle 3rd (1988); 100m butterfly 2nd (1988); 4x100m freestyle 1st (1984, 1988, 1992); 4x200m freestyle 1st (1988); 400m medley 1st (1988, 1992); World Championships – 100m freestyle 1st (1986, 1991); world records: 50m freestyle 22.14 (Seoul 1988), 100m freestyle 48.42 (Austin 1988), 400m medley 3:34.84 (Atlanta 1996), 4x100m freestyle 3:16.53 (Seoul 1988); spokesman Olympic Movt; mem. Int. Hall of Fame Selection Cttee; now a successful motivational speaker; Int. Swimming Hall of Fame 1997, World Swimmer of the Year 1998. *Address:* USA Swimming, 1 Olympic Plaza, Colorado Springs, CO 80909, USA (office).

BIRCH, Bryan John, PhD, FRS; British mathematician and academic; *Professor Emeritus of Mathematics, University of Oxford;* b. 25 Sept. 1931, Burton-on-Trent; s. of Arthur Jack Birch and Mary Edith Birch; m. Gina Margaret Christ 1961; two s. one d.; ed Shrewsbury School and Trinity Coll., Cambridge; Research Fellow, Trinity Coll. 1956–60; Harkness Fellow, Princeton 1957–58; Fellow, Churchill Coll., Cambridge 1960–62; Sr Lecturer, later Reader, Univ. of Manchester 1962–65; Reader in Math., Univ. of Oxford 1966–85, Prof. of Arithmetic 1985–98, Prof. Emer. 1998–, Fellow of Brasenose

Coll. 1966–98, Emer. Fellow 1998–; Del. of Oxford Univ. Press 1988–98; Ed. Proc. London Math. Soc. 2001–03; Senior Whitehead Prize 1993, De Morgan Medal 2007. *Publications:* scholarly articles, particularly on number theory. *Leisure interests:* theoretical gardening, opera, watching marmots and mathematics. *Address:* Mathematical Institute, 24–29 St Giles, Oxford, OX1 3LB (office); Green Cottage, Boars Hill, Oxford, OX1 5DQ, England (home). *Telephone:* (1865) 735367 (home). *Fax:* (1865) 273583 (office); (1865) 730687 (home). *E-mail:* birch@maths.ox.ac.uk (office). *Website:* www.maths.ox.ac.uk (office).

BIRCH, L. Charles, BAgrSc, DSc; Australian biologist and academic; *Professor Emeritus of Biology, University of Sydney;* b. 8 Feb. 1918, Melbourne; s. of Harry Milton Birch and Honoria Eleanor Hogan; ed Scotch Coll., Melbourne, Univs of Melbourne and Adelaide; Research Fellow, Waite Agricultural Research Inst., Adelaide 1939–46; Sr Overseas Research Scholar, Zoology Dept, Univ. of Chicago, USA 1946, Univ. of Oxford, UK 1947; Sr Lecturer in Zoology, Univ. of Sydney 1948–54, Reader in Zoology 1954–60; Challis Prof. of Biology 1960–83, Prof. Emer. 1984–; Fulbright Research Scholar, Zoology Dept, Columbia Univ., New York, USA 1954; Visiting Prof., Univ. of Minnesota 1958; Visiting Prof. of Genetics, Univ. of California, Berkeley 1967; mem. Club of Rome; Fellow, Australian Acad. of Science; David Syme Prize, Univ. of Melbourne 1954, Eminent Ecologist Award, Ecological Soc. America 1988, Gold Medal, Ecological Soc. Australia 1988, Templeton Prize 1990. *Publications:* Nature and God 1965, Confronting the Future 1976; (Co-author) The Distribution and Abundance of Animals 1954, Genetics and the Quality of Life 1975, The Liberation of Life 1981, The Ecological Web 1984, On Purpose 1990, Liberating Life 1990, Regaining Compassion 1993, Feelings 1995, Living with the Animals 1997, Biology and the Riddle of Life 1999, Life and Work 2003. *Leisure interests:* surfing, music (organ). *Address:* 5A/73 Yarranabbe Road, Darling Point, NSW 2027, Australia. *Telephone:* (2) 9362-3788. *Fax:* (2) 9362-3551 (home).

BIRCH, Peter Gibbs, CBE; British business executive; b. 4 Dec. 1937; m. Gillian Benge 1962; three s. one d.; ed Allhallows School, Devon; served Royal West Kent Regt 1957–58; with Nestlé Co. 1958–65; Sales Man., Gillette 1965, Gen. Sales Man. Gillette Australia 1969, Man. Dir Gillette NZ 1971, Gen. Man. Gillette South East Asia 1973, Group Gen. Man. Gillette, Africa, Middle East, Eastern Europe 1975, Man. Dir Gillette UK 1981; Dir Abbey Nat. (fmrly Abbey Nat. Bldg Soc.) 1984–98, Chief Exec. 1984–88, Chief Exec. Abbey Nat. PLC 1988–98; Dir Hoskyns Group 1988–93, Argos 1990–98, Scottish Mutual 1992–98, Dalgety 1993–98, N. M. Rothschild and Sons 1998–, Sainsbury's Bank PLC 2002–; Sr Dir (non-exec.) Trinity Mirror PLC 1999–; Dir (non-exec.) Travelex 1999–; mem. Bd Land Securities PLC 1997– (Chair. 1998–), Dah Sing Financial Holdings 1997–; Chair. Trinity PLC 1998–99, Legal Services Comm. 2000–03, Kensington Group PLC 2000–, UCTX Ltd 2001; Chair. Council of Mortgage Lenders 1991–92; Pres. Middx Asscn of Boys' Clubs 1988–. *Leisure interests:* active holidays, swimming. *Address:* N. M. Rothschild and Sons Ltd, New Court, St Swithin's Lane, London, EC4P 4DU, England (office). *Telephone:* (20) 7280-5482 (office). *Fax:* (20) 7280-5562 (office). *E-mail:* peter.birch@rothschild.co.uk (office). *Website:* www.rothschild.com (office).

BIRD, Adrian Peter, CBE, PhD, FRS, FRSE, FMedSci; British geneticist and academic; *Director, Wellcome Trust Centre for Cell Biology, University of Edinburgh;* b. 3 July 1947; s. of Kenneth George Bird and Aileen Mary Bird; m. 1st 1976; one s. one d.; m. 2nd Catherine Mary Abbott 1993; one s. one d.; ed Univ. of Sussex, Univ. of Edin.; Damon Runyon Fellow, Yale 1972–73; Postdoctoral Fellowship, Univ. of Zurich 1974–87, Medical Research Council, Edin.; mem. scientific staff Mammalian Genome Unit; Sr Scientist Inst. for Molecular Pathology, Vienna 1988–90; Buchanan Prof. of Genetics, Edin. Univ. 1990–; Dir Wellcome Trust Centre for Cell Biology, Edin. Univ. 1999–; Gov. Wellcome Trust 2000–; Louis Jeantet Prize for Medical Research 1999, Gabor Medal, Royal Soc. 1999. *Publications:* numerous papers in scientific journals. *Address:* Wellcome Trust Centre for Cell Biology, University of Edinburgh, King's Buildings, Mayfield Road, Edinburgh, EH9 3JR, Scotland (office). *Telephone:* (131) 650-5670 (office). *Fax:* (131) 650-5379 (office). *E-mail:* a.bird@ed.ac.uk (office).

BIRD, Phillip Bradley (Brad); American director, writer, actor and producer; b. 11 Sept. 1957, Kalispell, Mont.; m. Elizabeth Canney 1988; three c.; ed Corvallis High School, Ore.; trained as a Disney animator; first person to receive a solo writing credit on a feature-length film (The Incredibles) from Pixar Animation Studios; provided voices of Don Carlo in Doctor of Doom 1979, Edna Mode in The Incredibles 2004 and Ambrister Minion in Ratatouille 2007; ranked 23rd on EW's The 50 Smartest People in Hollywood 2007. *Films directed:* Amazing Stories: Book Two (segment 'Family Dog'; also writer) 1992, The Iron Giant 1999, The Incredibles (also writer) 2004, Jack-Jack Attack (also writer) 2005, One-Man Band (producer) 2005, Ratatouille (also screenplay) 2007. *Animator:* Animalympics 1980, The Plague Dogs 1982. *Television directed:* Amazing Stories (aka Steven Spielberg's Amazing Stories) (episode: Family Dog (also writer)) 1987, The Simpsons (two episodes: Krusty Gets Busted 1990, Like Father, Like Clown 1991) 1990–91. *Address:* c/o Jake Bloom, Bloom Hergott Diemer Rosenthal LaViolette & Feldman, LLP, 150 South Rodeo Drive, Third Floor, Beverly Hills, CA 90212; c/o Pixar Animation Studios, 1200 Park Avenue, Emeryville, CA 94608, USA. *Telephone:* (510) 922-3000 (Pixar). *Fax:* (510) 922-3151. *E-mail:* info@pixar.com. *Website:* www.pixar.com.

BIRD, Harold Dennis (Dickie), MBE; British fmr international umpire and fmr cricketer; b. 19 April 1933, Barnsley, Yorks.; s. of James Harold Bird and the late Ethel Bird (née Smith); ed Raley Secondary Modern School, Barnsley; right-hand batsman and right-arm medium-fast bowler; played for Yorks. Co. Cricket Club 1956–59, Leicestershire Co. Cricket Club 1960–64; scored 3,314 runs (average 20.71) with 2 hundreds; highest first-class score 181 not out 1959; First-Class Umpire 1970–98; umpired 68 Test matches (world record 1973–96), 69 limited-overs internationals (1973–95), including 1975, 1979, 1983 and 1987–88 World Cups (officiating in the first three finals), 92 one-day int. matches and seven Sharjah (UAE) tournaments; only person to umpire both men's and women's World Cup Finals; served on Int. Umpires Panel 1994–96; MCC Advanced Cricket Coach; f. Dickie Bird Foundation (for less privileged children) 2004; Hon. Life mem. MCC, Yorks. Co. Cricket Club, Leics. Co. Cricket Club, Barnsley Football Club; Freeman Borough of Barnsley 2000; Hon. DUniv (Sheffield Hallam) 1996; Hon. LLD (Leeds) 1997; Hon. DCL (Huddersfield) 2008; Yorks. Personality of the Year 1977, Rose Bowl, Barnsley Council 1988, Variety Club of GB Yorkshire Award 1988, Carlsberg-Tetley Yorkshireman of the Year 1996, People of the Year Award 1996, Radar Abbey Nat. 1996, Special Sporting Award, Variety Club of GB 1997, Lifelong Achievement Award 1998, Professional Cricketers Asscn Special Merit Award 1998, Yorkshire Co. Cricket Club 50 Years Service Award 1998, The Barnsley Millennium Award of Merit for outstanding services to the community and to cricket and in particular for the promotion of the image and civic pride of the Borough 2000, England and Wales Cricket Bd 30 Years of Service Award, Anglo-American Sporting Club Award for services to cricket, BBC TV Sports Awards, Yorkshire Hall of Fame 2006; statue erected in his honour, Barnsley 2008. *Radio:* Down Your Way with Brian Johnston 1975, Harry Carpenter Show (BBC) 1975, Desert Island Discs with Sue Lawley 1996. *Television appearances include:* The Terry Wogan Show (BBC) 1988, This is Your Life (ITV) 1992, BBC Grandstand 1996, Newsnight (BBC 2) 1996, A Question of Sport (six times) 1999, The Clive Anderson Show 1998, Through the Keyhole (three times), Breakfast with Frost and Songs of Praise (BBC), The Gloria Hunniford Show (ITV, four times), Ready Steady Cook (BBC 2), They Think It's All Over (BBC 1). *Publications:* Not Out 1978, That's Out 1985, From the Pavilion End 1988, Dickie Bird – My Autobiography (best-selling sports autobiog. in history) 1997, White Cap and Bails 1999, Dickie Bird's Britain 2002. *Leisure interest:* watching football. *Address:* White Rose Cottage, 40 Paddock Road, Staincross, Barnsley, Yorks., S75 6LE, England. *Telephone:* (1226) 384491 (home).

BIRD, Lester Bryant, BA; Antiguan politician; *Leader, Antigua Labour Party;* b. 21 Feb. 1938; m.; one s. four d.; ed Antigua Grammar School, Univ. of Mich, USA and Gray's Inn, UK; lawyer in pvt. practice 1969–76; Leader, Antigua Labour Party (ALP) 1971–; Senator, Upper House of Parl. and Leader of Opposition in Senate 1971–76; mem. Parl. 1976–; Deputy Premier and Minister of Econ. Devt, Tourism and Energy 1976–81; Deputy Prime Minister and Minister of Foreign Affairs, Econ. Devt, Tourism and Energy 1981–91; Minister of External Affairs, Planning and Trade 1991–94; Prime Minister of Antigua and Barbuda 1994–2004, Minister of External Affairs, Planning, Social Services and Information 1994, of Communications, Civil Aviation and Int. Transport 1996–98, of Foreign Affairs, Social Services, Civil Aviation and Int. Transport and Information 1998–99, of Foreign Affairs, Caribbean Community Affairs, Defence and Security and Merchant Shipping 1999–2001, of Justice and Legal Affairs 2001–04; del. to numerous Caribbean and int. confs. *Address:* Antigua Labour Party (ALP), S46 North Street, POB 948, St John's, Antigua, West Indies (office). *Telephone:* 462-2235 (office). *E-mail:* alp@antigualabourparty.net (office). *Website:* www.antigualabourparty.net (office).

BIRDSALL, Nancy, MA, PhD; American research institute director; *President, Center for Global Development;* ed Newton Coll. of the Sacred Heart, Paul H. Nitze School of Advanced Int. Studies (SAIS), Johns Hopkins Univ., Yale Univ.; joined World Bank (IBRD) 1979, various positions in research, policy and man. including Head of Team preparing World Devt Report 1983–84, Chief of Social Programs Operations in Brazil, Chief of Environmental Operations in Latin America, Dir Policy Research Dept –1993; Exec. Vice-Pres. IDB 1993–98; Sr Assoc. and Dir, Econ. Reform Project, Carnegie Endowment for Int. Peace 1998–2001; Sr Fellow (non-resident) Brookings Inst. 1998–; Founder and Pres. Center for Global Devt, Washington, DC 2001–; Teacher SAIS, Johns Hopkins Univ.; fmr Adviser to Admin. of UNDP Rockefeller Foundation; fmr Consultant to Asia Soc., AAAS, UN Fund for Population Activities; fmr Chair. Int. Center for Research on Women; mem. Bd of Dir Population Council; fmr mem. Bd Social Science Research Council, Overseas Devt Council, cttees and working groups of Nat. Acad. of Sciences. *Publications include:* Population Growth and Economic Development 1986, Financing Health in Developing Countries: An Agenda for Reform (co-author) 1987, Unfair Advantage: Labor Market Discrimination in Developing Countries (co-ed.) 1991, The East Asian Miracle: Economic Growth and Public Policy (co-ed.) 1993, Opportunity Forgone: Education in Brazil (co-ed.) 1996, Pathways to Growth: Comparing East Asia and Latin America (co-ed.) 1997, Beyond Tradeoffs: Market Reform and Equitable Growth in Latin America (co-ed.) 1998, Population Matters: Demographic Change, Economic Growth and Poverty in the Developing World (co-author) 1999, Distributive Justice and Economic Development (co-ed.) 2000, New Markets, New Opportunities? Economic and Social Mobility in a Changing World 2000, Washington Contentious: Economic Policies for Social Equity in Latin American (co-author) 2001, Delivering on Debt Relief: From IMF Gold to a New Aid Architecture (co-author) 2002, Financing Development: The Power of Regionalism (co-ed.) 2004, Reality Check: The Distributional Impact of Privatization in Developing Countries (co-ed.) 2005; more than 75 articles in scholarly journals and chapters in books. *Address:* Center for Global Development, 1776 Massachusetts Avenue, NW, Suite 301, Washington, DC 20036, USA (office). *Telephone:* (202) 416-0700 (office). *Fax:* (202) 416-0750 (office). *E-mail:* cgd@cgdev.org (office). *Website:* www.cgdev.org (office).

BIRGENEAU, Robert J., PhD, FRS, FInstP, FAAS, FRSC; Canadian physicist, academic and university administrator; *Chancellor and Professor of Physics, University of California, Berkeley;* b. 25 March 1942, Toronto; m. Mary Catherine Birgeneau; ed Univ. of Toronto and Yale Univ., USA; instructor, Yale Univ. 1966–67; Nat. Research Council of Canada Postdoctoral Fellow, Univ. of Oxford, UK 1967–68; mem. tech. staff, Bell Labs 1968–74, Research Head, Scattering and Low Energy Physics 1975; Prof. of Physics, MIT 1975–82, Cecil and Ida Green Prof. of Physics 1982–2000, Assoc. Dir, Research Lab. of Electronics 1983–86, Head, Condensed Matter, Atomic and Plasma Physics 1987–88, Head, Dept of Physics 1988–91; Dean of Science, Univ. of Toronto 1991–2000, Pres. Univ. of Toronto 2000–04; Chancellor and Prof. of Physics, also Prof. of Materials Science and Eng, Univ. of California, Berkeley 2004–; mem. Advisory Bd World Premier Research Center, Tohoku Univ., Japan 2007; Fellow, American Physical Soc., American Acad. of Arts and Sciences 1987, American Philosophical Soc. 2006, AAAS; Foreign Assoc. NAS 2004; Fellow, Neutron Scattering Soc. of America 2008; Morris Loeb Lecturer, Harvard Univ. 1986, H.L. Welsh Lecturer, Univ. of Toronto 1994, A.W. Scott Lecturer, Cambridge Univ. 2000, Tercentennial Lecturer, Yale Univ. 2001; Dr hc (Tsinghua Univ.) 2007, Hon. DEng (Colo School of Mines) 2007, numerous awards including Yale Science and Eng Alumni Achievement Award 1981, Wilbur Lucius Cross Medal, Yale Univ. 1986, Oliver E. Buckley Prize for Condensed Matter Physics, APS 1987, Bertram Eugene Warren Award, ACA 1988, DOE Materials Science Outstanding Accomplishment Award 1988, IUPAP Magnetism Award 1997, J.E. Lilienfeld Award, APS 2000, American Acad. of Arts and Sciences Founders Award 2006, Level Playing Field Inst. Lux Award 2007, Carnegie Corpn Academic Leadership Award 2008. *Address:* Office of the Chancellor, 200 California Hall, #1500, Berkeley, CA 94720-1500, USA (office). *Telephone:* (510) 642-7464 (office). *Fax:* (510) 643-5499 (office). *E-mail:* chancellor@berkeley.edu (office). *Website:* cio.chance.berkeley.edu/chancellor/birgeneau/home.htm (office).

BIRIDO, Omer Yousif, MA; Sudanese diplomatist; b. 1939; m. 1966; five c.; ed Univ. of Khartoum and Delhi Univ., India; Third Sec., Sudan Embassy, New Delhi 1963–66, Second Sec., London 1966–69; Deputy Dir, Consular Dept, Ministry of Foreign Affairs 1969–71; Counsellor Sudan Embassy, Kampala 1971–73; Minister Plenipotentiary, Perm. Mission of Sudan to the UN, New York 1973–76; Dir Dept of Int. Orgs, Ministry of Foreign Affairs 1976–77, Dir Dept of African Affairs 1977–78; Perm. Rep. to UN, Geneva and Vienna, also mem. Sudan Del. and Rep. to Second Cttee at UN Gen. Ass. 1979–83; Perm. Rep. to UN 1984–86; Amb. to Saudi Arabia 1989–96. *Address:* c/o Ministry of Foreign Affairs, Nasseriya Street, Riyadh 11124, Saudi Arabia.

BIRKAVS, Valdis, PhD, DrIur; Latvian politician and lawyer; *Chairman, Strategic Partnership of Construction Development;* b. 28 July 1942, Riga; s. of Voldemars Birkavs and Veronika Birkavs (née Zihelmane); one s.; ed Riga Industrial Polytech. School, Univ. of Latvia; expert, Sr Researcher, Head of Div., Latvian Research Lab. of Forensic Medicine and Criminology 1969–86; Lecturer, Univ. of Latvia 1969–86, Deputy Dean Law Faculty 1986–89; Founder and Pres. Latvian Bar Asscn 1988–; Deputy to Supreme Council of Latvian Repub. from Popular Front of Latvia 1990–93, Deputy Chair. Legis. Cttee, Deputy Chair. Supreme Council of Latvian Repub. 1992–93; Prime Minister of Latvian Repub. 1993–94; Minister of Foreign Affairs 1994–99; Minister of Justice 1999–2000; currently Chair. Latvian Cttee, Business Software Alliance; Chair. Strategic Partnership of Construction Development; mem. Club of Madrid; Royal Order of the Polar Start (Sweden) 1995, Dannebrog Order (Denmark) 1997, Norwegian Royal Order 1998, Légion d'honneur 1997, Grand Master Three Star Order of Latvia 1999, Medal of the Order of Malta 2002, Order of Lithuania 2003. *Publications:* contrib. of more than 200 articles. *Leisure interests:* tennis, yachting, reading, downhill skiing. *Address:* c/o Strategic Partnership of Construction Development, Rīga LV 1010, Latvia (office). *Telephone:* (2) 6949-8195 (office). *Fax:* (2) 6745-1099 (office). *E-mail:* valdis.birkavs@gmail.com (office). *Website:* www.bsa.lv (office).

BIRKE, Adolf Mathias, PhD, FRHistS; German historian and academic; b. 12 Oct. 1939, Wellingholzhausen; s. of Matthias Birke and Maria Birke (née Enewoldsen); m. 1st Linde D. Birn 1968; m. 2nd Sabine Volk 1988; one s. two d.; ed Univ. of Berlin; Prof. of Modern History, Free Univ. of Berlin 1979; Visiting Prof. of German and European Studies, Trinity Coll., Univ. of Toronto, Canada 1980–81; Asst St Antony's Coll., Oxford; Prof. of Modern History, Univ. of Bayreuth 1982–85, Univ. of Munich 1995–2000; Dir German Historical Inst., London 1985–94; Chair. Prince Albert Soc. 1983–95; Cusanuswerk Grant 1962; Heisenberg Fellow 1979; Fed. Cross of Merit 1996. *Publications:* Bischof Ketteler und der deutsche Liberalismus 1971, Pluralismus und Gewerkschaftsautonomie 1978, Britain and Germany 1987, Nation ohne Haus. Deutschland 1945–1961 1989, (4th edn) 1998, Prince Albert Studies (ed.) Vols I–XIII 1983–95, Die Herausforderung des europäischen Staatensystems 1989, Princes, Patronage and the Nobility (ed with R. Asch) 1991, The Quest for Stability (ed. with R. Ahmann and M. Howard) 1992, Control Commission for Germany (British Element) (11 vols) Inventory (with H. Booms and O. Merker) 1993, Die Bundesrepublik Deutschland. Verfassung: Parlament und Parteien 1997, Deutschland und Grossbritannien 1999, An Anglo-German Dialogue (co-ed. with Magnus Brechtken and Alaric Searle) 2000; numerous articles on 19th- and 20th-century German and English history. *Leisure interests:* music, walking. *Address:* Friedenstr. 16, 06114 Halle, Germany (home).

BIRKERTS, Gunnar, FAIA; Latvian architect; *President, Gunnar Birkerts and Associates Inc.;* b. 17 Jan. 1925, Riga, Latvia; s. of the late Peter Birkerts and of Merija Shop Birkerts; m. Sylvia Zvirbulis 1950; two s. one d.; ed Technische Hochschule, Stuttgart, Germany; went to USA 1949; est. own practice 1959, Pres. Gunnar Birkerts and Assocs Inc. 1963–; Prof. of Architecture, Univ. of Mich. 1959–90, Prof. Emer. 1990–; numerous guest lectureships USA, Canada, Mexico and Europe; Architect in Residence,

American Acad. in Rome 1976; Fellow Latvian Architects' Asscn; mem. Latvian Acad. of Sciences; work exhibited USA, Italy, Brazil, Latvia, Estonia, Yugoslavia; Order of Three Stars, Latvia; Dr hc (Riga Tech. Univ., Latvia) 1990; over 50 awards for projects, including American Acad. of Arts and Letters Brunner Memorial Prize in Architecture, Latvian Acad. of Sciences Great Medal. *Major projects include:* Lincoln Elementary School, Columbus, Ind., Fed. Reserve Bank of Minneapolis, Contemporary Arts Museum, Houston, Tex., IBM Corpn Computer Center, Sterling Forest, New York, Corning Museum of Glass, New York, Law Library Addition, Univ. of Mich., Ann Arbor, Coll. of Law Bldg, Univ. of Iowa, St Peter's Lutheran Church, Columbus, Ind., Domino's World HQ Bldg, Ann Arbor, Mich., Law School, Ohio State Univ., Columbus, Cen. Library Addition, Univ. of Calif. at San Diego, Kemper Museum of Contemporary Art, Kan. City, Mo., US Embassy, Caracas, School of Law Addition, Duke Univ., Durham, NC; Library, Univ. of Mich. –Flint; Cathedral of Blessed Sacrament, Addition, Detroit, Mich. *In progress:* Sports Centre, Venice, Italy, Novoli Multi-Use Centre, Florence, Italy, Nat. Library, Riga, Latvia, Univ. of Turin, Italy, Performing Arts Center, Mich. Technological Univ., Houghton; Marriott Library Expansion, Univ. of Utah, Market Master Plan, Riga, Latvia, City/Univ. Library, San Jose, CA. *Leisure interests:* tennis, swimming, music. *Address:* PO Box 812115, Wellesley, MA 02482-0013, USA. *Telephone:* (781) 235-4091. *Fax:* (781) 235-4167. *E-mail:* gunnarbirk@aol.com (office). *Website:* www.gunnarbirkerts.com (office).

BIRKIN, Jane, OBE; French (b. British) actress and singer; b. 14 Dec. 1946, London; d. of David Birkin and Judy Campbell; m. John Barry (divorced); one d.; one d. with the late Serge Gainsbourg (Charlotte Gainsbourg); one s. with Jacques Doillon; Chevalier des Arts et des Lettres; Gold Leaf Award Canada 1968, Triomphe du cinéma 1969, 1973, Victoire de la musique (for best female singer) 1992. *Theatre includes:* Carving a Statue 1964, Passion Flower Hotel 1965, La Fausse suivante 1985, L'Aide-Mémoire 1993, Créatrice et Interprète de Oh! pardon tu dormais 1999, Electra by Sophocles. *Films include:* The Knack 1965, Blow Up 1966, Les Chemins de Katmandou 1969, Je t'aime moi non plus 1976, Mort sur le Nil 1978, Jane B par Agnès V 1988, Noir comme le souvenir 1995, La fille d'un soldat ne pleure jamais 1999, The Last September 2000, Ceci est mon corps 2001, Reines d'un jour 2001, Merci Docteur Rey 2002, Mariées mais pas trop 2003, Boxes (actor and dir) 2007. *Recordings include:* albums: Je T'aime (Beautiful Love) 1970, Lolita Go Home 1975, Ex Fan des Sixties 1978, Baby Alone in Babylone 1983, Lost Song 1987, Au Bataclan 1987, Je Suis Venue Te Dire Que Je M'en Vais 1992, Jane B., Vol. 1 1993, Concert Integral a l'Olympia 1997, Je T'aime Moi Non Plus 1998, Quoi Generique TV 1998, Jane Birkin Coffret 1998, Ballade de Johnny 1998, A la Legere 1998, Jane en Concert au Japan 2001, Jane Birkin et Serge Gainsbourg 2001, Arabesque 2003, Rendez-Vous 2004, Fictions 2006, Enfants d'Hiver 2008; singles: (songs by Serge Gainsbourg) C'est la vie qui veut ça, La Baigneuse de Brighton, Je t'aime moi non plus (Le Métier trophy 1970), Di doo dah, Le Canari est sur le balcon, Baby Song, Si ça peut te consoler, Tu n'es pas le premier garçon, Lolita Go Home, Love for Sale, La Ballade, Ex-fan des sixties, Baby Alone in Babylone (Grand Prix du disque, Acad. Charles-Cros). *Address:* VMA, 20 avenue Rapp, 75007 Paris, France (office). *Telephone:* 1-44-93-02-02 (office). *Fax:* 1-44-93-04-40 (office). *E-mail:* david@visiteurdusoir.com (office).

BIRKIN, Sir (John) Derek, Kt, TD, CBIM; British business executive; b. 30 Sept. 1929; s. of Noah Birkin and Rebecca Birkin (née Stranks); m. Sadie Smith 1952; one s. one d.; ed Hemsworth Grammar School; Man. Dir Velmar Ltd 1966–67, Nairn Williamson Ltd 1967–70; Deputy Chair. and Man. Dir Tunnel Holdings Ltd 1970–75, Chair. and Man. Dir 1975–82; Dir Rio Tinto-Zinc (then RTZ) Corpn 1982–96, Deputy Chief Exec. 1983–85, Chief Exec. and Deputy Chair. 1985–91, Chair. 1991–96; Chair. Watmoughs (Holdings) PLC 1996–98; Dir Smiths Industries Ltd 1977–84, British Gas Corpn 1982–85, George Wimpey PLC 1984–92, CRA Ltd (Australia) 1985–94, Rio Algom Ltd (Canada) 1985–92, The Merchants Trust PLC 1986–99, British Steel PLC (formerly British Steel Corpn) 1986–92, Barclays Bank PLC and Barclays PLC 1990–95, Merck & Co. Inc. (USA) 1992–2000, Carlton Communications PLC 1992–2001, Unilever PLC 1993–2000; mem. Council, Industrial Soc. 1985–97, UK Top Salaries Review Body 1986–89; Trustee Royal Opera House 1990–93, Dir 1993–97; Hon. LLD (Bath) 1998. *Leisure interests:* opera, rugby, cricket. *Address:* 21 Manchester Square, London, W1M 5AP, England.

BIRLA, Basant Kumar; Indian business executive; *Chairman, Century Textiles and Industries Ltd;* b. 16 Feb. 1921; s. of G. D. Birla and Mahadevi; m.; one s. two d.; Chair. Century Textiles and Industries Ltd, Century Enka Ltd, Jay Shree Tea & Industries Ltd, Kesoram Industries & Cotton Mills Ltd, Bharat Commerce & Industries Ltd; Gov. Birla Inst. of Tech. *Address:* Century Textiles and Industries Ltd, Century Bhavan, Dr Annie Besant Road, Worli, Mumbai, 400 030, India (office). *Telephone:* (22) 24957000 (office). *Fax:* (22) 24309491 (office). *E-mail:* centextho@centurytext.com (office). *Website:* www.centurytext.com (office).

BIRLA, Kumar Mangalam, MBA; Indian business executive; *Chairman, Aditya Birla Group;* b. 14 June 1967; m. Neerja Birla; three c.; ed London Business School, UK; Chair. Aditya Birla Group 1997–; apptd mem. Governing Bd Securities and Exchange Bd of India 1998, also served as Chair. Cttees on Corporate Governance and Insider Trading; mem. Bd Tata Iron and Steel Co., Larsen and Toubro, Maruti Udyog Ltd; mem. Bd G. D. Birla Medical Research and Educ. Foundation; mem. Bd Govs Birla Inst. of Tech. and Science, Indian Inst. of Man.; mem. London Business School's Asia Pacific Advisory Bd; has served on various professional and regulatory bds including Prime Minister's Advisory Council on Trade and Industry, Nat. Council of Confed. of Indian Industry, Apex Advisory Council of Associated Chambers of Commerce and Industry of India, Govt of UP's High Powered Investment Task Force; Hon. Fellow, London Business School; Hon. DLitt (Banaras Hindu Univ.); Mumbai Pradesh Youth Congress's Rajiv Gandhi Award for Business Excellence and Contribution to the Country, named as one of World Econ. Forum's Young Global Leaders 2004, Ernst & Young Indian Entrepreneur of the Year 2005, awards from Inst. of Dirs, The Hindustan Times, Giants Int., Amity Business School, Nat. Inst. of Industrial Eng, The Economic Times, Business India. *Address:* Aditya Birla Centre, S. K. Ahire Marg, Worli, Mumbai 400 025, India (office). *Telephone:* (22) 56525000 (office). *Fax:* (22) 56525750 (office). *E-mail:* pragnya.ram@adityabirla.com (office). *Website:* www.adityabirla.com (office).

BIRLA, Sudershan Kumar; Indian business executive; Chair. Mysore Cement Ltd –2007, Birla Eastern Ltd, Birla Metals Ltd; Dir Century Textiles and Industries Ltd –2006, Birla Brothers Pvt. Ltd. *Address:* Birla House, 7, Tees January Marg, New Delhi, 110 011, India (office).

BIRLE, James R., BS; American insurance industry executive; *Lead Director, Massachusetts Mutual Life Insurance Company;* ed Villanova Univ.; numerous positions for over 30 years at General Electric Co. –1988, including Sr Vice-Pres. and Group Exec.; Gen. Pnr Blackstone Group 1988; Founder and Chair. Resolute Pnrs LLC (pvt. investment firm); mem. Bd of Dirs Mass Mutual Life Insurance Co. 1992–, Chair. 2005–07, Lead Dir 2007–; mem. Bd of Dirs IKON Office Solutions, Conn. Health and Educ. Facilities Authority, Transparency Int.; Trustee Villanova Univ. *Address:* Massachusetts Mutual Life Insurance Company, 1295 State Street, Springfield, MA 01111-0001, USA (office). *Telephone:* (413) 744-1000 (office). *Fax:* (413) 744-6005 (office). *Website:* www.massmutual.com (office).

BIRNBAUM, Daniel, PhD; Swedish author, art critic, philosopher, teacher and curator; *Rector, Städelschule Art Academy, Frankfurt am Main;* b. 1963, Stockholm; ed Stockholm Univ.; spent childhood and youth in Geneva, Vienna, Boston and Stockholm; art critic at Expressen and Dagens Nyheter daily newspapers, Stockholm 1988; Lecturer in Philosophy, Stockholm Univ. 1990–95; Lecturer in Art Theory, Univ. Coll. of Art, Craft and Design, Stockholm 1995–97; Founding mem. Artnode Stockholm (internet site for art and theory and venue for art and tech.) 1996; Dir IASPIS (Int. Artists Studio Programme in Sweden) 1997–2000; Contributing Ed., Artforum, New York 1999; Rector Städelschule Art Acad., Frankfurt am Main, Germany 2001–; Dir Kunsthalle Portikus, Frankfurt am Main 2001–; Int. Bd mem. Yokohama Triennial of Contemporary Art 2001–, Manifesta Foundation, Amsterdam 2002–. *Address:* Staatliche Hochschule für Bildende Künste, Städelschule, Dürerstrasse 10, 60596 Frankfurt am Main, Germany (office). *Telephone:* (69) 605008-0 (office). *E-mail:* info@staedelschule.com (office). *Website:* www.staedelschule.com (office).

BIRRELL, Sir James Drake, Kt, FCA, FCBSI; British building society executive; b. 18 Aug. 1933; s. of James R. Birrell and Edith M. Drake; m. Margaret A. Pattison 1958; two d.; ed Belle Vue Grammar School, Bradford; articled clerk, Boyce Welch & Co. 1949–55; Pilot Officer RAF 1955–57; chartered accountant, Price Waterhouse 1957–60; accountant, ADA Halifax 1960–61; man. accountant, Empire Stores 1961–64; Dir and Co. Sec. John Gladstone & Co., 1964–68; with Halifax Bldg Soc. 1968–93, Chief Exec. 1988–93; Dir (non-exec.) Securicor 1993–2002, Wesleyan Gen. Assurance Soc. 1993–2004; mem. Bldg Soc.'s Comm. 1994–2001. *Leisure interests:* golf, gardening, archaeology, local history. *Address:* 4 Marlin End, Berkhamsted, Hertfordshire, HP4 3GB, England.

BIRT, Baron (Life Peer) cr. 2000, of Liverpool in the County of Merseyside; **John Birt,** Kt, MA, FRTS; British business executive; *Adviser, Terra Firma;* b. 10 Dec. 1944, Liverpool; s. of Leo Vincent and Ida Birt; m. 1st Jane Frances Lake 1965 (divorced 2006); one s. one d.; m. 2nd Eithne Victoria Wallis 2006; ed St Mary's Coll., Liverpool, St Catherine's Coll., Oxford; Television Producer of Nice Time 1968–69, Jt Editor World in Action 1969–70, Producer of The Frost Programme 1971–72, Exec. Producer of Weekend World 1972–74, Head of Current Affairs, London Weekend Television (LWT) 1974–77, Co-Producer of The Nixon Interviews 1977, Controller of Features and Current Affairs, LWT 1977–81, Dir of Programmes 1982–87; Deputy Dir-Gen. BBC 1987–92, Dir-Gen. 1992–2000; Vice-Pres. Royal TV Soc. 1994–2000 (Fellow 1989); mem. Media Law Group 1983–94, Working Party on New Techs. 1981–83, Broadcasting Research Unit, Exec. Cttee 1983–87, Int. Museum of TV and Radio, New York 1994–2000, Opportunity 2000 Target Team, Business in the Community 1991–98; Adviser to Prime Minister on criminal justice 2000–01, Strategy Adviser 2001–05; Adviser to McKinsey and Co. Inc. 2000–05; Adviser, Terra Firma (pvt. equity firm) 2005–, Capgemini UK plc 2006–; Chair. Lynx Capital Ventures 2000–04; Chair. WRG Holdings 2006, Chair. Infinis Ltd 2006–07 (after sale of WRG waste disposal business); mem. Bd of Dirs (non-exec.) PayPal (Europe) Ltd 2004–, Eutelsat 2006–, Maltby Capital Ltd 2007–; Visiting Fellow, Nuffield Coll., Oxford 1991–99; Hon. Fellow, Univ. of Wales, Cardiff 1997, St Catherine's Coll., Oxford 1992; Hon. DLitt (Liverpool John Moores) 1992, (City) 1998, (Bradford) 1999; Emmy Award US Nat. Acad. of Television, Arts and Sciences. *Publication:* The Harder Path – The Autobiography. *Leisure interest:* walking, football, cinema. *Address:* House of Lords, London, SW1A 0PW, England.

BIRTWISTLE, Sir Harrison, Kt, CH; British composer; b. 1934, Accrington, Lancs.; m. Sheila Birtwistle 1958; three s.; ed Royal Manchester Coll. of Music and Royal Acad. of Music, London; Dir of Music, Cranborne Chase School 1962–65; Visiting Fellow Princeton Univ. (Harkness Int. Fellowship) 1966; Cornell visiting Prof. of Music, Swarthmore Coll., Pa 1973–74; Slee Visiting Prof., New York State Univ., Buffalo, NY 1975; Assoc. Dir Nat. Theatre 1975–88; Composer-in-Residence London Philharmonic Orchestra 1993–98; Henry Purcell Prof. of Composition King's Coll., London Univ. 1994–2001; Visiting Prof., Univ. of Ala at Tuscaloosa 2001–02; Hon. Fellow Royal Northern Coll. of Music 1990; Dir of Contemporary Music, RAM 1996–2001;

works have been widely performed at the major festivals in Europe including the Venice Biennale, the Int. Soc. of Contemporary Music Festivals in Vienna and Copenhagen, the Warsaw Autumn Festival and at Aldeburgh, Cheltenham and Edinburgh; formed, with Sir Peter Maxwell Davies, The Pierrot Players; Chevalier, Ordre des Arts et des Lettres; Siemens Prize 1995; Grawemeyer Award (Univ. of Louisville, KY) 1987, Ivor Novello Award for Classical Music 2006. *Operatic and dramatic works:* The Mark of the Goat (cantata) 1965, Punch and Judy (one-act opera) 1966, The Visions of Francesco Petrarca (sonnets for baritone and orchestra) 1966, Monodrama for soprano, speaker, ensemble 1967, Down by the Greenwood Side (dramatic pastoral) 1969, The Mask of Orpheus 1973, Ballet, Frames, Pulses and Interruptions 1977, Bow Down 1977, Yan Tan Tethera 1983, Gawain 1988, The Second Mrs Kong 1992, The Last Supper 1999. *Orchestral works:* Chorales for Orchestra 1962, Three Movements with Fanfares 1964, Nomos 1968, An Imaginary Landscape 1971, The Triumph of Time 1970, Grimethorpe Aria for Brass Band 1973, Melencolia I 1976, Silbury Air for small orchestra 1977, Still Movement for 13 solo strings 1984, Earth Dances 1985, Endless Parade for trumpet, vibraphone, strings 1987, Ritual Fragment 1990, Antiphonies for piano and orchestra 1992, The Cry of Anubis for tuba and orchestra 1994, Panic 1995, Night's Black Bird (British Composer Award British Acad. of Composers and Songwriters 2005). *Choral works and narration:* Monody for Corpus Christi for soprano and ensemble 1959, A Description of the Passing Year for chorus 1963, Entr'actes and Sappho Fragments for soprano and ensemble 1964, Carmen Paschale for chorus and organ 1965, Ring a Dumb Clarion for soprano, clarinet, percussion 1965, Cantata for soprano and ensemble 1969, Nenia on the Death of Orpheus for soprano and ensemble 1970, The Fields of Sorrow for 2 sopranos, chorus, ensemble 1971, Meridian for mezzo, chorus, ensemble 1970, Epilogue: Full Fathom Five for baritone and ensemble 1972, agm. for 16 solo voices and 3 instruments 1979, On the Sheer Threshold of the Night for 4 solo voices and 12-part chorus 1980, White and Light for soprano and ensemble 1989, Four Poems by Jaan Kaplinski for soprano and ensemble 1991, The Woman and the Hare, for soprano, reciter and ensemble 1999, Ring Dance of the Nazarene (British Composer Award British Acad. of Composers and Songwriters 2005). *Instrumental works:* Refrains and Choruses for wind quintet 1957, The World is Discovered for ensemble 1960, Tragoedia for ensemble 1965, Three Lessons in a Frame 1967, Chorales from a Toyshop 1967, Verses for Ensembles 1969, Ut heremita solus, arr of Ockeghem 1969, Hoquetus David, arr of Machaut 1969, Medusa for ensemble 1970, Chronometer for 8-track tape 1971, For O For O the Hobby Horse is Forgot for 6 percussion 1976, Carmen Arcadiae Mechanicae Perpetuum for ensemble 1977, Pulse Sampler 1980, Clarinet Quintet 1980, Secret Theatre 1984, Words Overheard 1985, Fanfare for Will 1987, Salford Toccata for brass band and bass drum 1988, Nine Movements for string quartet 1991, An Uninterrupted Endless Melody for oboe and piano 1991, Five Distances for five instruments 1992, Tenebrae for soprano and ensemble 1992, Night for soprano and ensemble 1992, Movement for string quartet 1992, Slow Frieze for piano and 13 instruments 1996, Pulse, Shadows 1997, Harrison's Clocks for piano 1998, The Silk House Tattoo for 2 trumpets and percussion 1998, Three Niedecker Verses for soprano and cello 1998, Exody 1998, The Axe Manual 2000, The Shadow of Night 2001, Theseus Game 2002, The Io Passion 2004, Night's Black Bird 2004, Orpheus Elegies 2004, The Tree of Strings 2007, The Minotaur 2008. *Theatre:* music for Hamlet, Nat. Theatre 1975, The Oresteia, Nat. Theatre 1986, The Bacchae, Nat. Theatre 2002. *Address:* Allied Artists Agency, 42 Montpelier Square, London, SW7 1JZ, England (office).

BIRULÉS Y BERTRÁN, Ana Maria, PhD; Spanish politician and fmr business executive; ed Univ. of Barcelona, Univ. of California, Berkeley; worked for regional Govt of Catalonia; with Banco Sabadell 1990–97, negotiated acquisition of Banco NatWest 1996; Man. Dir Retevisión 1997–2000; Minister of Science and Tech. 2000–04. *Address:* c/o Ministry of Science and Technology, Paseo de la Castellana 160, 28071 Madrid, Spain (office). *Telephone:* (91) 3494976 (office). *Fax:* (91) 4578066 (office). *E-mail:* info@mcyt.es (office). *Website:* www.mcyt.es (office).

BISCHOFF, Manfred, Dr rer. pol; German business executive; *Chairman, European Aeronautic Defence and Space Company (EADS);* b. 22 April 1942, Calw; ed Univs of Tübingen and Heidelberg; Asst Prof. of Econ. Politics and Int. Trade, Alfred-Weber-Inst., Univ. of Heidelberg 1968–76; joined Daimler-Benz AG 1976, Project Co-ordinator for Mercedes Benz Cross Country Cars, Corp. Subsidiaries, M&A Dept 1976–81, Int. Products, M&A, Finance Dept 1981–88 (Vice-Pres. Finance Cos and Corp. Subsidiaries), mem. Bd of Man. and Chief Financial Officer Mercedes do Brazil, São Paulo 1988–89, Deutsche Aerospace AG (later Daimler-Benz Aerospace AG) 1989–95, mem. Bd of Man. Daimler-Benz AG (later DaimlerChrysler AG then Daimler AG) 1995–2003, Chair. Supervisory Bd 2007–, also Chair. Presidential Cttee; mem. Bd of Man., Pres. and CEO DASA (now European Aeronautic Defence and Space Co. (EADS)) 1995–2000, Chair. EADS 2000–; mem. Bd of Man. Mitsubishi Motors Corpn 2000–03; Chair. Supervisory Bd MTU Aero Engines, Munich 2000–03; Pres. European Asscn of Aerospace Industries 1995–96, Fed. of German Aerospace Industries 1996–2000; mem. several supervisory bds in the industry. *Address:* European Aeronautic Defence and Space Co., 81663 Munich, Germany (office). *Telephone:* (89) 607-34300 (office). *Fax:* (89) 607-34306 (office). *Website:* www.eads.net (office).

BISCHOFF, Sir Winfried Franz Wilhelm (Win), Kt, BCom; British/German investment banker; *Chairman, Citigroup;* b. 10 May 1941, Aachen, Germany; s. of the late Paul Helmut Bischoff and Hildegard Bischoff (née Kühne); m. Rosemary Elizabeth Leathers 1972; two s.; ed Marist Brothers, Johannesburg and Univ. of the Witwatersrand; with Int. Dept, Chase Manhattan Bank 1962–63; joined Company Finance Div., J. Henry Schroder & Co. Ltd, London 1966, Man. Dir Schroders Asia Ltd, Hong Kong 1971–82, Dir J. Henry Schroder & Co. Ltd 1978–94 (Chair. 1983–94), Dir Schroders PLC 1983 (Group Chief Exec. 1984–95), Chair. Schroders PLC 1995–2000, then Citigroup Europe (after acquisition of Schroders by Citigroup) 2000–07, interim CEO Citigroup Nov.–Dec. 2007, Chair. Citigroup 2007–; Dir (non-exec.) Cable and Wireless PLC 1991– (Deputy Chair. 1995–2003), The McGraw Hill Cos 1999–, Land Securities PLC 1999–2008, Eli Lilly and Co., Indianapolis 2000–, IFIL, Finanziaria di Partecipazioni SpA, Italy 2001–04, Siemens Holdings PLC 2001–03, AkBank, Turkey 2007–08; Johnson Hon. Fellow, St Anne's Coll. Oxford 2001; Dr hc (City Univ.) 2000. *Leisure interests:* opera, music, golf. *Address:* Citigroup Europe, Citigroup Centre, 33 Canada Square, Canary Wharf, London, E14 5LB, England (office). *Telephone:* (20) 7986 2600 (office); (7770) 496565 (mobile) (office). *Fax:* (20) 7986 2599 (office). *E-mail:* win.bischoff@citigroup.com (office). *Website:* www.citigroup.com (office).

BISH-JONES, Trevor, BSc; British business executive; b. 23 April 1960; m. Amanda Bish-Jones 1991; two d.; ed Varndean Grammar School, Portsmouth School of Pharmacy; research chemist, The Tosco Corpn, Colo 1980–81; Store Man. Boots PLC 1981, rising to Sr Man. position –1994; various man. positions with Dixons Group 1994–2002, including Commercial Dir PC World 1994–95, Marketing Dir Dixons PLC 1995, Man. Dir The Link, Man. Dir Dixons, Dir Currys 2000–02; CEO Woolworths Group PLC 2002–08. *Leisure interests:* horseriding, motorbikes. *Address:* c/o Woolworths Group PLC, 242 Marylebone Road, London, NW1 6JL, England (office).

BISHER, Ilmar, DrSclur; Latvian politician and lawyer; b. 1 Nov. 1930, Riga, Latvia; m. 1st Benita Samuilova 1958 (divorced 1975); m. 2nd Aina Bullite 1975; two s.; ed Latvia Univ.; Prof. of Law, Latvia Univ.; mem. Latvian Popular Front 1989–92; USSR People's Deputy (representing Latvian constituency) 1989–91; Deputy Chair. USSR Supreme Soviet Council of Nationalities 1989–90; First Vice-Chair. Council of Ministers of Latvia 1990–91, Counsellor to Prime Minister 1991–93; barrister, Chair. Bišers & Partneri 1993–; Pres. Latvian Certificate Fund 1994–95, Asscn of Securities Market Participants 1994–95; mem. Council, Democratic Party of Latvia 1992–, Parl. 1995–98. *Address:* Antonijas Iela 9, 1010 Rīga (office); Sporta St 1, Apt 3, 1013 Rīga, Latvia. *Telephone:* 6733-8882 (office); 6727-4310 (home). *Fax:* 6733-8878 (office). *E-mail:* bisers@apollo.lv (office).

BISHOP, James Drew, BA; British journalist; b. 18 June 1929, London; s. of the late Sir Patrick Bishop and Vera Drew; m. Brenda Pearson 1959; two s.; ed Haileybury Coll., Hertford and Corpus Christi Coll., Cambridge; reporter, Northampton Chronicle 1953; editorial staff of The Times (London) 1954–70, Foreign Corresp. 1957–64, Foreign News Ed. 1964–66, Features Ed. 1966–70; Ed. The Illustrated London News 1971–87, Newsweek Int. Diary 1977–88; Dir Int. Thomson Publishing Co. 1980–85; Editorial Dir Orient Express, Connections and Natural World Magazines 1981–94; Ed.-in-Chief Illustrated London News Publs 1987–94; contrib. to The Annual Register 1960–88, mem. Advisory Bd 1970–; Chair. Editorial Bd Natural World 1981–97, Asscn of British Eds 1987–95; Chair. Nat. Heritage 1998– (Trustee 1994–). *Publications:* A Social History of Edwardian Britain 1977, Social History of the First World War 1982, The Story of The Times (with O. Woods) 1983, Illustrated Counties of England (ed.) 1985, The Sedgwick Story 1998. *Leisure interests:* reading, walking. *Address:* Black Fen, Stoke by Nayland, Suffolk, CO6 4QD, England (home). *Telephone:* (1206) 262315 (office). *Fax:* (1206) 262876 (office). *E-mail:* jamesbishop3@compuserve.com (home).

BISHOP, John Michael, MD; American scientist, academic and university administrator; *Chancellor, University of California, San Francisco;* b. 22 Feb. 1936; m. 1959; two c.; ed Gettysburg Coll. and Harvard Univ.; intern in internal medicine Mass. Gen. Hosp., Boston 1962–63, Resident 1963–64; Research Assoc. in Virology, NIH, Washington, DC 1964–66, Sr Investigator 1966–68, Asst Prof. to Assoc. Prof. 1968–72; Prof. of Microbiology and Immunology, Univ. of Calif. Medical Center, San Francisco 1972–, Prof. of Biochemistry and Biophysics 1982–, Univ. Prof. 1994–2000, Chancellor 1998–, Dir G. W. Hooper Research Foundation 1981–;; Gairdner Foundation Int. Award 1984, Medal of Honor, American Cancer Soc. 1984, Nobel Prize for Physiology or Medicine 1989, and many other awards and distinctions. *Address:* Office of the Chancellor, University of California, San Francisco, 513 Parnassus Avenue, S-126, San Francisco, CA 94143-0402, USA (office). *Telephone:* (415) 476-2401 (office). *Fax:* (415) 476-9634 (office). *Website:* chancellor.ucsf.edu (office).

BISHOP, Sir Michael (David), Kt, CBE; British business executive; *Chairman, British Midland PLC;* b. 10 Feb. 1942, Bowdon, Cheshire; s. of Clive Leonard Bishop; ed Mill Hill School; joined Mercury Airlines, Manchester 1963, British Midland Airways Ltd 1964–; Chair. British Midland PLC 1978–, Manx Airlines 1982–2001, British Regional Airlines Group PLC 1982–2001, Deputy Chair. Channel 4 TV Corpn 1991–93, Chair. 1993–97; Chair. D'Oyly Carte Opera Trust Ltd 1989–; Deputy Chair. Airtours PLC 1996– (Dir 1987–2001); Dir Williams PLC 1993–2000, Kidde PLC 2000–02; Hon. DTech (Loughborough Univ. of Tech.) 1989; Hon. DLitt (Salford) 1991; Hon. LLD (Nottingham) 1993; Hon. DUniv (Cent. England) 1993; Hon. DLitt (Coventry) 1994. *Address:* Donington Hall, Castle Donington, nr Derby, DE74 2SB, England. *Telephone:* (1332) 854000 (office).

BISHOP-KOVACEVICH, Stephen (see Kovacevich, Stephen).

BISIGNANI, Giovanni, LLM; Italian airline executive; *Director-General and CEO, International Air Transport Association (IATA);* b. 1946, Rome; m.; one d.; ed Univ. of Rome and Harvard Business School; Sr Asst Prof. in Public Law, Univ. of Rome 1969; with First Nat. City Bank, New York 1970; research and econ. planning, EFIM, Rome 1973–76; Asst to Pres. ENI, Rome 1976–79; Chief of Staff, IRI, Rome 1979–89, Corp. Sr Vice-Pres. (Foreign Affairs) 1981–83, Corp. Exec. Vice-Pres. and Head of Foreign Affairs 1983–89, IRI Rep. on Bd of FINSIDER, ITALSTAT, SME, FINCANTIERI 1979–89; Man.

Dir and CEO Alitalia 1989–94; Pres. Tirrenia di Navigazione SpA 1994–98; Man. Dir and CEO SM Logistics–Gruppo Serra Merzario SpA 1998–2000; CEO Opodo (European airline-owned online travel agency) 2001–02; founding mem. Exec. Cttee Int. Air Transport Asscn (IATA) 1989–94, Dir-Gen. and CEO 2002–; Chair. Asscn of European Airlines 1992, Chair. Galileo Int. (global computer reservation system group) 1993–94; mem. Advisory Bd United Technologies 1998–2001; mem. Bd Assolombarda, Milan 1998–2000, NATS Holding Ltd 2002, Galileo Distribution System Ltd, ILVA (IRI steel co.), Italo-German Chamber of Commerce, Inst. for Int. Affairs; Hon. DSc (Cranfield Univ.). *Publications:* articles on law, economic and financial subjects in professional publs. *Leisure interests:* golf, tennis, riding. *Address:* IATA, 33 Route de l'Aeroport, PO Box 416, Geneva 15 Airport, Switzerland (office). *Telephone:* (22) 770-2903 (office). *Fax:* (22) 770-2680 (office). *E-mail:* iata.dg.ceo@iata.org. *Website:* www.iata.org.

BIŠKUPIĆ, Božo, LLB, MA; Croatian lawyer and politician; *Minister of Culture;* b. 26 April 1938, Mala Mlaka; m.; one d.; f. Biškupić Collection 1964; worked as lawyer in Zagreb 1974–80; collated and ed monographs in the Graphics Inst. in Zagreb and fine art in the Nat. and Univ. Library; f. Vukovar Museum in Exile and project on contemporary Croatian art for the Museum of Croatian Art, Mostar; mem. Croatian Democratic Union (HDZ) 1990–; Dir Republican Fund for Culture, Ministry of Culture 1990–92; Asst Minister of Culture and Educ. 1993–83; Deputy Mayor of Zagreb 1993–95; Minister of Culture 1995–2000, 2003–; mem. Parl. 2000–; Vladimir Nazor Award 1993. *Leisure interests:* music, chess. *Address:* Ministry of Culture, 10000 Zagreb, Runjaninova 2, Croatia (office). *Telephone:* (1) 4866666 (office). *Fax:* (1) 4866280 (office). *E-mail:* bozo.biskupic@min-kulture.hr (office). *Website:* www.min-kulture.hr (office).

BISOGNIERO, Claudio, BSc; Italian diplomatist; *Deputy Secretary-General, NATO;* b. 2 Aug. 1954, Rome; m. Laura Denise Noce Benigni Olivieri; one s. one d.; ed Univ. of Rome; served in Italian army 1976–77; joined Foreign Service 1978, First Sec. for Econ. and Commercial Affairs, Embassy in Beijing 1981–84, Counsellor, Perm. Mission to NATO, Brussels 1984–89, with Office of Diplomatic Adviser to Pres., Rome 1989–92, First Counsellor for Econ. and Commercial Affairs, Embassy in Washington DC 1992–96, at Perm. Mission to UN, New York 1996–99, with Personnel Dept, Foreign Service 1999, with Office of Sec.-Gen., Ministry of Foreign Affairs 1999–2002, Deputy Dir-Gen. for Political Multilateral Affairs (Deputy Political Dir) 2002–05, Dir-Gen. for Americas 2005–07, Deputy Sec.-Gen. NATO 2007–. *Leisure interests:* classical music, reading, sailing, flying. *Address:* Office of the Deputy Secretary-General, North Atlantic Treaty Organization (NATO), blvd Léopold III, 1110 Brussels, Belgium (office). *Telephone:* (2) 707-41-11 (office). *Fax:* (2) 707-45-79 (office). *E-mail:* natodoc@hq.nato.int (office). *Website:* www.nato.int (office).

BISSET, Jacqueline; British actress; b. 13 Sept. 1944, Weybridge; ed French Lycée, London; film début in The Knack 1965. *Other films include:* Two for the Road 1967, Casino Royale 1967, The Sweet Ride 1968, The Detective 1968, Bullitt 1968, The First Time 1969, Airport 1970, The Grasshopper 1970, The Mephisto Waltz 1971, Believe in Me 1971, The Life and Times of Judge Roy Bean 1972, Stand Up and Be Counted 1972, The Thief Who Came to Dinner 1973, Day for Night 1973, Murder on the Orient Express 1974, The Spiral Staircase 1974, End of the Game 1974, St Ives 1975, The Deep 1976, Le Magnifique 1977, Sunday Woman 1977, The Greek Tycoon 1978, Secrets 1978, Too Many Chefs 1978, I Love You, I Love You Not 1979, When Time Ran Out 1980, Rich and Famous 1981, Inchon 1981, Class 1982, Under the Volcano 1983, Forbidden 1986, Choices 1986, High Season 1988, Scenes from the Class Struggle in Beverly Hills 1989, Wild Orchid 1989, La Cérémonie 1995, The Maid, A Judgement in Stone, Once You Meet a Stranger 1996, The Honest Courtesan 1996, Let the Devil Wear Black 1998, Dangerous Beauty 1998, Joan of Arc 1999, In the Beginning 2000, Jesus 2000, Britannic 2000, The Sleepy Time Gal 2001, Sundance Holiday Gift Pack 2003, Latter Days 2003, Swing 2004, Fascination 2004, Domino 2005, Save the Last Dance 2 2006, Death in Love 2008. *Address:* c/o William Morris Agency, One William Morris Place, Beverly Hills, CA 90212, USA; VMA, 10 avenue George V, 75008 Paris, France.

BISSINGER, Frederick Lewis, ME, MS, JD; American chemical executive; b. 11 Jan. 1911, New York; s. of Jacob Frederick Bissinger and Rosel Bissinger (née Ensslin); m. 1st Julia E. Stork 1935 (deceased); one s. one d.; m. 2nd Barbara S. Simmonds 1993; ed Stevens Inst. of Tech. and Fordham Univ.; Chemistry Instructor, Stevens Inst. of Tech. 1933–36; lawyer, Pennie, Davis, Marvin & Edmonds 1936–42; various exec. positions, including Pres. Industrial Rayon Corpn 1942–61; Group Vice-Pres. Midland-Ross Corpn 1961–62; Vice-Pres. and Dir Stauffer Chem. Corpn 1962–65; Vice-Pres. Allied Chemical Corpn 1965–66, Dir 1966–76, Exec. Vice-Pres. 1966–69, Pres. 1969–74, Vice-Chair. 1974–76; Counsel to Pennie & Edmonds 1976–; Chair. Bd Trustees, Stevens Inst. of Tech. 1971–83, Chair. Emer. 1983–; Trustee Fordham Univ. 1970–75, Trustee Emer. 1985–; fmr Dir Selas Corpn, Mid-Atlantic Nat. Bank, Nat. Starch and Chemical Corpn, Neptune Int. Corpn, Otis Elevator Corpn, Rheingold Corpn; mem. Bar NY, Dist of Colo, Ohio, Supreme Court; Hon. DEng (Stevens Inst. of Tech.) 1973. *Address:* 9 West Irving Street, Chevy Chase, MD 20815, USA. *Telephone:* (301) 657-8373.

BISSON, Thomas Noel, PhD; American historian and academic; *Henry Charles Lea Professor of Medieval History, Harvard University;* b. 30 March 1931, New York; s. of Thomas A. Bisson and Faith W. Bisson; m. Margaretta C. Webb 1962; two d.; ed Port Washington High School, New York, Haverford Coll., Univ. of Calif., Berkeley and Princeton Univ.; Instructor in History, Amherst Coll. 1957–60; Asst Prof., Brown Univ. 1960–65; Assoc. Prof., Swarthmore Coll. 1965–67; Assoc. Prof., Univ. of California, Berkeley 1967–69, Prof. 1969–87; Prof., Harvard Univ. 1986–, Henry Charles Lea Prof. of Medieval History 1988–, Chair. Dept of History 1991–95; mem. American Philosophical Soc.; Fellow, Medieval Acad. of America (Pres. 1994–95), Royal Historical Soc., British Acad. etc.; Creu de Sant Jordi (Generalitat of Catalonia) 2001; Dr hc (Barcelona) 1991; Guggenheim Fellow 1964–65. *Publications:* Assemblies and Representation in Languedoc in the Thirteenth Century 1964, Medieval Representative Institutions: Their Origins and Nature 1973, Conservation of Coinage: Monetary Exploitation and its Restraint in France, Catalonia and Aragon (c. AD 1000–c. AD 1225) 1979, Fiscal Accounts of Catalonia under the Early Count-Kings 1151–1213 (two vols) 1985, The Medieval Crown of Aragon: a Short History 1986, Medieval France and her Pyrenean Neighbors 1989, Tormented Voices: Power, Crisis and Humanity in Rural Catalonia 1140–1200 1998, The Crisis of the Twelfth Century 2009; articles in journals. *Leisure interests:* classical music, English literature. *Address:* 21 Hammond Street, Cambridge, MA 02138, USA (home). *Telephone:* (617) 354 0178 (home). *E-mail:* tnbisson@fas.harvard.edu (office). *Website:* www.fas.harvard.edu/~history (office).

BISTA, Kirti Nidhi, MA; Nepalese politician; b. 1927; ed Tri-Chandra Coll., Kathmandu and Lucknow Univ.; Asst Minister for Educ. 1961–62, Minister for Educ. 1962–64, for Foreign Affairs 1964; Vice-Chair. Council of Ministers and Minister for Foreign Affairs and Educ. 1964–66; Vice-Chair. Council of Ministers and Minister for Foreign Affairs and Econ. Planning 1966–67; Deputy Prime Minister and Minister for Foreign Affairs and Educ. 1967–68, Perm. Rep. to UN 1968–69; Prime Minister 1969–70, 1971–73, 1977–79, Minister of Finance, Gen. Admin. and Palace Affairs 1969–73, of Finance, Palace Affairs and Defence 1978–79; Vice-Chair. Council of Ministers and Minister of Industry, Commerce and Supplies, of Population, of Physical Planning and Works, and of Health 2005; mem. Royal Advisory Cttee 1969–70; Leader Nepalese dels to UN Gen. Assemblies 1964, 1965, 1966 and to UNESCO Gen. Confs 1962, 1964, 1966 and to various other confs; accompanied HM the King on many state visits; Order of the Right Hand of Gurkhas (First Class), Fed. German Order of Merit, Chevalier de la Légion d'honneur. *Address:* c/o Ministry of Industry, Commerce and Supplies, Singha Durbar, Kathmandu; Gyaneshwor, Kathmandu, Nepal (home).

BISWAS, Abdul Rahman; Bangladeshi politician and fmr head of state; fmr Speaker, House of Ass.; Pres. of Bangladesh 1991–96; now retd. *Address:* c/o Residence Dhonmondi, Dhaka, Bangladesh.

BITARAF, Habibollah, MS; Iranian government official; b. 1956, Yazd; m. Zahra Mansurie; three d.; ed Tehran Univ.; Deputy Minister for Energy 1991–95, Exec. Man. of Karon 3 and 4 (dam and energy plant) project 1995–97, Minister of Energy 1997–2006; currently Head, Jt Staff of Reformist Groups; mem. Bd of Govs Yazd Univ. *Publication:* Fluid Mechanics. *Leisure interests:* studying, mountaineering, table tennis, pilgrimage, travelling. *Address:* c/o Ministry of Energy, North Palestine Street, Tehran, Iran.

BITEO BORICO, Miguel Abia; Equatorial Guinean politician; Prime Minister and Head of Govt 2004–06; mem. Partido Democrático de Guinea Ecuatorial (PDGE). *Address:* c/o Partido Democrático de Guinea Ecuatorial (PDGE), Malabo, Equatorial Guinea.

BITI, Tendai Laxton; Zimbabwean lawyer and politician; *Minister of Finance;* b. 6 Aug. 1966, Dzivarasekwa, Harare; ed Goromonzi High School, Univ. of Zimbabwe Law School; joined Honey and Blackenberg (law firm), Pnr 1992; co-f. Movt for Democratic Change 1999, Sec.-Gen. 2000–05; MP for Harare E 2000–, mem. Cttee on Budget, Finance and Econ. Devt, fmr mem. Parl. Portfolio Cttee on Lands, Agric., Water Devt, Rural Resources and Resettlement, Cttee on Defence and Home Affairs; Minister of Finance 2009–. *Address:* Ministry of Finance, Private Bag 7703, Causeway, Harare, Zimbabwe (office). *Telephone:* (263) 738603 (office). *Fax:* (263) 792750 (office). *Website:* www.mofed.gov.zw (office).

BITOV, Andrei Georgevich; Russian writer; b. 27 May 1937, Leningrad (St. Petersburg); m. Inga Petkevich; one d.; ed Leningrad Mining Inst.; evacuated 1939–44; worked as stevedore and lathe-operator 1958–62; researcher, Leningrad Mining Inst. 1962; started writing 1960; mem. of 'Young Prose' group in 1960s with Vasiliy Aksyonov (q.v.) and Anatoliy Gladilin (q.v.); contrib. to Metropol 1979; Pres. Russian PEN Centre 1992–; Hon. Doctor, Yerevan State Univ. 1997–, Hon. Citizen of Yerevan; Ordre des Arts et des Lettres (France) 1993; Andrey Bely Prize (Russia) 1990, Pushkin Prize (Germany). *Publications include:* The Big Balloon 1963, Such a Long Childhood 1965, A Summer Place 1967, Apothecary Island 1968, Way of Life 1972, Seven Journeys 1976, Days of Man 1976, Pushkin House (Best Foreign Book Prize, Paris 1990) 1978, Sunday (short stories) 1980, A Man in the Landscape 1987, The Flying Monakhov (Russian State Prize 1992) 1990, We Woke Up in a Strange Country 1991, Awaiting Monkeys 1993, The Possessed (Russian State Prize 1997, Northern Palmira Prize 1997) 1995, Empire in Four Dimensions (collected works), (Vols 1–4) 1996, Inevitability of Non-Written 1998, Life in Windy Weather 2000. *Address:* Krasnoprudnaya str. 30/34, Apt 14, 107140 Moscow, Russia. *Telephone:* (495) 209-45-89 (office); (495) 264-12-93 (home).

BITSCH, Hans-Ullrich; German architect, industrial designer and academic; *Professor of Architecture, Düsseldorf University;* b. 13 June 1946, Essen; s. of Prof. Heinz W. and Lore L. (née Falldorf) Bitsch; m. Evelyn R. Koch 1981; two s.; ed High School, Saarbrücken, State Coll. of Art, Saarbrücken and Illinois Inst. of Tech.; architect, Univ. of Saarbrücken 1968; Instructor Int. Inst. of Design, Washington, DC 1969; Visiting Lecturer, Harrington Inst., Chicago, Ill. 1970–71; Prof. Dept of Architecture, Düsseldorf Univ. 1972–; Pres. German Inst. of Interior Architects 1977–82; Visiting Prof., Univ. of Texas 1981; Prof. Univ. of Naples 1997–; Pres. Professor Bitsch & Assocs (design and architectural office), Düsseldorf; work represented in Smithsonian Inst., Design Collection, Stuttgart and Stiftung Preussischer Kulturbesitz; several awards for architecture and design. *Publications:*

www.worldwhoswho.com

Menschengerechte Gestaltung des Kassenarbeitsplatzes 1978, Farbe und Industrie-Design 1982, Design und Formentwicklung von Stuhlen 1988, Visuelle Wahrnehmung in Architektur und Design 1989, Projekt Hotel 1992, Architectural Visions for Europe 1994, Stilströmungen 1998, Studien aus dem Architekturbüro 1999. *Leisure interests:* skiing, sailing, photography. *Address:* Kaiser-Wilhelm-Ring 23, Rive Gauche, 40545 Düsseldorf Oberkassel, Germany. *Telephone:* (211) 95449000. *Fax:* (211) 553814 (office).

BITTERLICH, Joachim; German business executive and diplomatist; *Executive Vice-President for International Affairs, Veolia Environnement;* b. 10 July 1948, Saarbrücken-Dudweiler; m. 1969; two s. one d.; ed Univ. of Saarbrücken, Ecole Nat. d'Admin.; entered Foreign Office 1976; posted to Algiers 1978–81; Perm. Rep. to EC, Brussels 1981–85; Adviser, Pvt. Office of the Minister of Foreign Affairs 1985–87; Head of European Policy Dept, Fed. Chancellor's Office 1987–93; Dir of Foreign Policy, Econ. Co-operation and External Security, Fed. Chancellor's Office and Foreign and Security Policy Adviser to Fed. Chancellor 1993–98; Amb. and Perm. Rep. to N Atlantic Council, Brussels 1998–99; Amb. to Spain 1999–2003; currently Exec. Vice-Pres. for Int. Affairs, Veolia Environnement, Paris; mem. Bd of Admin, Veolia Properté, Veolia Transport, ENA, MEDEF International; Vice-Pres. France-China Cttee; mem. Supervisory Bd DEKRA eV, Stuttgart; mem. Bd of Trustees, Friends of Europe; Vice-Pres. Notre Europe; mem. Deutsche Gesellschaft für Auswärtige Politik; Assoc. mem. IISS, London; numerous decorations and awards including Hon. CBE 1992, Grosses Silbernes Ehrenzeichen mit Stern (Austria) 1994, Grande Oficial do Ordem de Rio Branco (Brazil) 1995, Officier de al Légion d'honneur 1996, Grande Ufficiale nell Ordine al Merito (Italy) 1997, Orden do Infante Don Enrique (Portugal) 1998, Gran Cruz de la Orden del Mérito Civil (Spain) 1998. *Publications:* EU and EC Treaty: A Commentary (co-author) 1999, Europe: Mission Impossible? 2005; numerous articles in newspapers and journals. *Address:* Veolia Environnement Head Office, 36–38 avenue Kléber, 75116 Paris, France (office). *Telephone:* 1-71-75-01-42 (office). *Fax:* 1-71-75-10-04 (office). *E-mail:* joachim.bitterlich@veolia.com (office). *Website:* www.veolia.com (office).

BIWOTT, Nicholas, BA; Kenyan politician; *Chairman, Kenya African National Union (KANU);* b. 1934, Keiyo Dist; m.; ed Kapsabet Govt African School and Univ. of Melbourne, Australia; served in Ministry of Information and Broadcasting 1959–60; several positions in Cen. Govt 1965–79, including Dist Officer, Ministry of Home Affairs, Asst Sec., Sr Asst Sec., UnderSec. and Deputy Sec.; mem. Parl. 1979–, Minister of Regional Devt, Science and Tech. 1979–82, Minister of Energy 1982–91, Minister of State in the Office of the Pres. 1997, Minister of E African and Regional Co-operation 1998–99, Minister of Tourism, Commerce, and Industry 1999–2001, Minister of Trade and Industry 2001–02; Chair. Kenya African Nat. Union (KANU) 2006–. *Address:* Kenya African National Union (KANU), KICC POB 72394, Nairobi, Kenya (office). *Telephone:* (20) 332383 (office).

BIYA, Paul, LenD; Cameroonian politician and head of state; *President;* b. 13 Feb. 1933, Mvomeka'a; m. 1st Jeanne (née Atyam) Biya (deceased); one c.; m. 2nd Chantal Biya 1994; ed Ndem Mission School, Edea and Akono Seminaries, Lycée Leclerc, Yaoundé, Univ. of Paris, Inst. d'Etudes Politiques, Inst. des Hautes Etudes d'Outre-Mer, Paris; Head of Dept of Foreign Devt Aid 1962–63; Dir of Cabinet in Ministry of Nat. Educ., Youth and Culture 1964–65; on goodwill mission to Ghana and Nigeria 1965; Sec.-Gen. in Ministry of Educ., Youth and Culture 1965–67; Dir of Civil Cabinet of Head of State 1967–68; Minister of State, Sec.-Gen. to Pres. 1968–75; Prime Minister 1975–82; Pres. of Cameroon 1982–; Second Vice-Pres., Central Cttee, mem. Union Nationale Camerounaise (UNC), Pres. 1983–85; Pres. Rassemblement Démocratique du Peuple Camerounais (RDPC) 1985–; mem. Politbureau; Hon. Prof. (Univ. of Beijing); Commdr de l'Ordre de la Valeur Camerounaise, Commdr of Nat. Order of FRG and of Tunisia, Great Commdr of the Medal of St George UK, Great Commdr of Order of Nigeria, Grand Cross of Nat. Order of Merit of Senegal, Grand Officier, Légion d'honneur, Grand Collier of the Ordre of Ouissam Mohammadi, Morocco; Dr hc (Univ. of Maryland); Peace Laureate, Centre European Peace Studies 1988. *Publication:* Communal Liberalism 1987. *Address:* Office of the President, Palais de l'Unité, Yaoundé, Cameroon (office). *Telephone:* 2223-4025 (office). *Website:* www.camnet.cm/celcom/homepr.htm (office).

BIZIMUNGU, Pasteur; Rwandan politician; mem. Front patriotique rwandais (FPR); Pres. of Rwanda 1994–2000 (resgnd); arrested in Angola Aug. 2002; sentenced to 15 years' imprisonment for embezzlement, inciting violence and associating with criminals June 2004.

BJARNASON, Björn, cand. jur.; Icelandic journalist and politician; b. 14 Nov. 1944, Reykjavik; s. of Bjarni Benediktsson and Sigríður Björnsdóttir; m. Rut Ingólfsdóttir; two c.; ed Univ. of Iceland; Ed. Almenna bókafélagið (book publr) 1971–74; Foreign News Ed. Vísir 1974; Div. Chief, Prime Minister's Office 1974, Deputy Sec.-Gen. 1975–79; journalist, Morgunblaðið 1979–84, Asst Ed. 1984–91; mem. Parl. (Independence Party) for Reykjavik 1991–; Minister of Educ., Science and Culture 1995–2002, of Justice and Ecclesiastical Affairs 2003–09 (resgnd); mem. Reykjavik City Council 2002–06; mem. IISS, London. *Publications:* The Security of Iceland, Five Roads to Nordic Security 1973, Icelands Security Policy, Strategic Factors in the North Atlantic 1977, No Other Option in Security Affairs: The Resurgence of Liberalism 1979, Iceland and Nuclear Weapons, Nuclear Weapons Policy in the North, Copenhagen 1982, From the Prime Ministry to Morgunbladid 1983, Iceland's Security Policy: Vulnerability and Responsibility 1985, Í hita kalda stríðsins (In the Heat of the Cold War) 2001, Hvað er Íslandi fyrir bestu? (What is best for Iceland?) 2009; numerous articles. *Address:* Althingi, Parliament of Iceland, 105 Reykjavík, Iceland (office). *Telephone:* 5630500 (office). *E-mail:* bjorn@bjorn.is (home). *Website:* www.bjorn.is (home).

BJARNASON, Gudmundur; Icelandic administrator and fmr politician; *General Manager, Housing Financing Fund;* b. 9 Oct. 1944, Húsavík; s. of Bjarni Stéfánsson and Jakobina Jónsdóttir; m. Vigdís Gunnarsdóttir; three d.; ed Húsavík Secondary School and Co-operative Coll.; with Co-operative Soc., Húsavík 1963–67; Húsavík Br. Co-operative Bank of Iceland 1967–77, Br. Dir 1977–80; elected mem. Húsavík Town Council 1970, Chair. 1974; mem. Althing 1979–99; Minister of Health and Social Security 1987–91, of Environment and Agric. 1995–99; mem. Althing Appropriation Cttee 1979–87 and 1991–95, Vice-Chair 1983–87; Chair. Cttee on Housing Affairs; mem. Jt Cttee on public projects; Gen. Man. Housing Financing Fund 1999–; Bd Research Council; mem. Icelandic del. to Parl. Ass. of Council of Europe 1991–95. *Address:* Housing Financing Fund, Borgartin 21, 105 R, Reykjavik (office); Kirkjusandur 5, 105 Reykjavik, Iceland (home). *Telephone:* 569-6900 (office); 553-9898 (home). *Fax:* 569-6820 (office). *E-mail:* gudmundur@ils.is (office). *Website:* www.ils.is (office).

BJERREGAARD, Ritt; Danish politician; b. 19 May 1941, Copenhagen; d. of Gudmund Bjerregaard and Rita Bjerregaard; m. Søren Mørch 1966; mem. Parl. 1971–95, 2001–; Minister of Educ. 1973, 1975–78, for Social Affairs 1979–81; Chair. Parl. Group, Social Democratic Party (SDP) 1981–92, 1987–92, Deputy Chair. 1982–87; Chair. Parl. Cttee on Public Accounts 1990–95; mem. Parl. Ass. of Council of Europe 1990–95; Pres. Danish European Movt 1992–94; Vice-Pres. Parl. Ass. of CSCE 1992–95; Vice-Pres. Socialist Int. Women 1992–94; EU Commr for Environment 1995–99; Minister of Food, Agric. and Fisheries 2000–01; mem. Trilateral Comm., Centre for European Policy Studies. *Publications:* several books on politics in general and the role of women in politics. *Leisure interests:* her apple farm, organic farming, the environment. *Address:* c/o Folketing, Christiansborg, 1240 Copenhagen K (office); Jens Juels Gade 4, 2100 Copenhagen Ø, Denmark (home). *Telephone:* 33334007 (office); 35430897 (home). *Fax:* 33375209 (office). *E-mail:* sribj@ft.dk (office). *Website:* www.ritt.dk (office).

BJØERNDALEN, Ole Einar; Norwegian biathlete; b. 27 Jan. 1974, Drammen; ed Norwegian Ski Gymnas; winner of six Olympic medals (two Gold Medals (Sprint, Relay) in Nagano, Japan 1998, four Gold Medals (Sprint, Pursuit, Individual, Relay) in Salt Lake City, USA 2002 (became third Olympian to win four gold medals at a single Winter Games); winner of four World Championship medals (Bronze in Pursuit, Osrblie, Slovakia 1997, Bronze in Relay, Kontiolahti, Finland 1999, Bronze in Mass, Holmenkollen, Norway 2000, Silver in Mass, Pokljuka, Slovenia 2001); winner of overall World Cup title, Salt Lake City 2000–01. *Leisure interests:* motorbikes, climbing, off-road. *Address:* Skavelandsvei 12E, Trondheim 7022, Norway (office). *Telephone:* 926 15691 (office).

BJÖRCK, Anders; Swedish politician; *First Deputy Speaker of Parliament;* b. 19 Sept. 1944, Nässjö; m. Py-Lotte Björck; one d.; Nat. Pres. Swedish Young Moderates 1966–71; MP 1968–; mem. Parl. Ass. Council of Europe 1976–91, Pres. (Speaker) 1989–91; Minister of Defence 1991–94; First Deputy Speaker of Swedish Parl. 1994–; mem. Bd Swedish Broadcasting Co. 1978–91, Swedish TV Co. 1979–91; mem. numerous govt comms dealing with constitutional matters, the mass media, environmental protection. *Publications:* various articles on defence, foreign policy and constitutional issues. *Address:* Riksdagen, 100 12 Stockholm (office); Bashult, 555 92 Jönköping, Sweden (home). *Telephone:* (8) 786-4031 (office); (36) 17-40-17 (home). *Fax:* (8) 213-525 (office).

BJÖRK; Icelandic singer and songwriter; b. (Björk Guðmundsdóttir), 21 Nov. 1965, Reykjavík; m. Thór Eldon (divorced); one s.; solo release aged 11; fmr singer for various Icelandic groups, including Exodus, Tappi Tikarras; singer, Kukl, later renamed The Sugarcubes 1986–92; solo artist 1992–; BRIT Award for Best Int. Newcomer 1994, MTV European Music Award for Best Int. Female Artist 1994, 1996, 1997, Q Inspiration Award 2005. *Film* Dancer in the Dark 2000. *Recordings include:* albums: with The Sugarcubes: Life's Too Good 1988, Here Today, Tomorrow Next Week 1989, Stick Around For Joy 1992, It's It 1992; solo: Björk 1977, Debut 1993, Post 1995, Telegram 1996, Homogenic 1997, Selmasongs 2000, Vespertine 2001, Dancer in the Dark 2001, Greatest Hits 2002, Family Tree 2002, Medúlla 2004, Army of Me: Remixes and Covers (charity album) 2005, Drawing Restraint 9 (OST) 2005, Volta 2007, Voltaic 2009. *Address:* c/o One Little Indian Records, 34 Trinity Crescent, London, SW17 7AE, England; Quest Management, 36 Warple Way, Unit 1D, London, W3 0RG, England (office). *Telephone:* (20) 8749-0088 (office). *Fax:* (20) 8749-0080 (office). *E-mail:* info@quest-management.com (office). *Website:* www.bjork.com.

BJÖRK, Anita; Swedish actress; b. 25 April 1923, Tällberg Dalecarlia; m. Stig Dagerman (deceased); one s. two d.; ed Royal Dramatic Theatre School, Stockholm; has toured around USA, Canada, UK and France; O'Neill Prize, Merito Cultural (Portugal), Swedish Critics' Award 1990 and many other Swedish awards. *Films acted in include:* Himlaspelet 1942, Räkna de lyckliga stunderna blott (Count Your Blessings) 1944, Hundra dragspel och en flicka (One Hundred Concertinas and a Girl) 1946, Ingen väg tillbaka (No Return) 1947, Kvinna utan ansikte 1947, Det kom en gäst (There Came a Guest) 1947, Pa dessa skuldror (On these Shoulders) 1948, Människors rike (The Realm of Men and Women) 1949, Kvartetten som sprängdes (The Quartet that was Broken) 1950, Fröken Julie 1950–51 (First Prize, Cannes Film Festival), Han glömde henne aldrig 1952, Night People 1953, Die Hexe 1954, Giftas 1955, Der Cornet 1955, Moln över Hellesta (Dark Clouds over Hellesta) 1956, Sängen om den eldröda blommen 1956, Gäst i eget hus (Guest in One's Own House) 1957, Mannekäng i rött 1958, Tärningen är kastad 1960, Goda vänner trogna grannar 1960, Vita frun 1962, Älskande par 1964, Mother and Daughter 1990, Den Goda viljan 1992, Sanna ögonblick 1998, Bildmakarna (TV) 2000. *Stage appearances at:* more than 80 roles at Royal Dramatic Theatre, Stockholm, including Miss Julie 1951, Agnes (Brand, Ibsen), Celia (The Cocktail Party,

Eliot), Rosalind (As You Like It, Shakespeare), Juliet (Romeo and Juliet, Shakespeare), Eliza (Pygmalion, Shaw), Solange (Les Bonnes, Genet), the girl (Look Back in Anger, Osborne), Johanna (Les séquestrés d'Altona, Sartre), Siri von Essen (Night of The Tribades, P. O. Enquist), Madame Arkadina (The Seagull, Chekhov) 1982-83, Hanna Luise Heiberg (Life of the Rainsnakes, Enquist), Christa Wolf (Kassandra), Yukio Mishima (La Marquise de Sade), Celestina 1998, The Image Maker 1999, Copenhagen (Michael Frayn (q.v.)) 2000, Love Letters by A.R. Gurney, Teater Brunnsgatan Fyra, Stockholm 2008–09. *Address:* Baggensgatan 9, 111 31 Stockholm, Sweden (office). *Telephone:* (8) 209747.

BJÖRK, Claes; Swedish business executive; joined Skanska AB 1967, moved to USA 1971, responsible for Skanska's construction operations in USA 1983, Pres. Skanska (USA) Inc. 1987, Sr Vice-Pres. Skanska AB, Head Skanska USA Operations –1997, mem. Group Man. Skanska AB 1995–, Pres., Group CEO 1997–2002; with Schering-Plough AB 2002–; Chair. Swedish-American Chamber of Commerce 1992–95; mem. Bd Banister Foundation 1990–. *Address:* Schering-Plough AB, PO Box 27190, 102 52 Stockholm, Sweden (office). *E-mail:* claes.bjork@spcorp.com (office).

BJORKEN, James Daniel, BS, PhD; American physicist and academic; *Professor Emeritus, Stanford University;* ed MIT, Stanford Univ.; Research Assoc., then Asst Prof., Stanford Univ. 1959–62, Assoc. Prof., then Prof., Stanford Linear Accelerator Center (SLAC) 1962–79, Theoretical Physicist 1989–98, Prof. Emer. 1998–; Theoretical Physicist and Assoc. Dir for Physics, Fermi Lab. 1979–89; Eastman Prof., Univ. of Oxford, UK 1995–96; mem. NAS, American Acad. of Arts and Sciences; Foreign mem. Swedish Acad. of Sciences; Hon. PhD (Univ. of Turin, Italy) Dannie Heinemann Prize in Math. Physics, American Physical Soc., Ernest Orlando Lawrence Medal, Dept for Energy, Dirac Medal, Abdus Salam Int. Centre for Theoretical Physics 2004. *Address:* c/o Stanford Linear Accelerator Center (SLAC), 2575 Sand Hill Road, Menlo Park, CA 94025, USA (office).

BJÖRKLUND, Leni, BA; Swedish politician; b. 5 July 1944; ed Uppsala Univ.; Research Asst, Dept of Pedagogical Studies, Stockholm Inst. of Educ. 1969–71; Educ. Consultant, Nat. Bd of Educ. 1971–74; Expert, Dept for Cultural Affairs, Ministry of Educ. and Science 1974–76; Municipal Commr Municipality of Järfälla 1977–79; Co. Council Commr Stockholm Co. Council 1980–98; Man. Dir of Planning and Rationalisation, Inst. for Health and Social Services 1989–99; Sec.-Gen. Church of Sweden 1999–2002; Minister of Defence 2002–06; mem. SDP, numerous positions including mem. and Vice-Chair. Exec. Cttee Stockholm Co. SDP; currently Chair. Expert Group on Public Finance (ESO); mem. Bd Nat. Heritage Bd, Mid-Sweden Univ.; fmr Chair. Swedish Medical Research Council; fmr Vice-Chair. Stockholm Co. Admin Bd; fmr mem. Foundation of Strategic Research; Hon. DrMed (Karolinska Institutet). *Address:* c/o Sveriges Socialdemokratiska Arbetareparti (SAP) (Swedish Social Democratic Party) Sveavägen 68, 105 60 Stockholm, Sweden.

BJÖRKMAN, Olle Erik, PhD, DSc, FAAS; American (b. Swedish) professor of plant biology; *Member of Faculty, Carnegie Institution of Washington Department of Plant Biology;* b. 29 July 1933, Jönköping, Sweden; s. of Erik Gustaf Björkman and Dagmar Kristina Björkman (Svensson); m. Monika Birgit Waldinger 1955; two s.; ed Univs of Stockholm and Uppsala; Research Fellow, Swedish Natural Science Research Council, Univ. of Uppsala 1961–63; Postdoctoral Fellow, Carnegie Inst. of Washington Dept. of Plant Biology, Stanford, Calif. 1964–65, Faculty mem. 1966–, Prof. of Biology by courtesy, Stanford Univ. 1977–; mem. Cttee on Carbon Dioxide Effects, US Dept of Energy 1977–82, Cttee on Bioscience Research in Agric. 1984–85; Scientific Adviser, Desert Research Inst., Nevada 1980–81; mem. Editorial Bd Planta 1993–96; mem. NAS; Fellow American Acad. of Arts and Sciences; Corresp. (Foreign) mem. Australian Acad. of Sciences, Foreign mem. Royal Swedish Acad. of Sciences; Linnaeus Prize, Royal Swedish Physiographic Soc. 1977, The Stephen Hale's Award, American Soc. of Plant Physiologists 1986, The Selby Award, Australian Acad. of Sciences 1987, The Barnes Life Membership Award, American Soc. of Plant Biologists 2001. *Publications:* Experimental Studies on the Nature of Species V (co-author) 1971, Physiological Processes in Plant Ecology 1980, more than 170 articles in scientific journals. *Leisure interest:* opera. *Address:* Carnegie Institution of Washington Department of Plant Biology, 260 Panama Street, Stanford, CA 94305 (office); 3040 Greer Road, Palo Alto, CA 94303, USA (home). *Telephone:* (650) 858-0880 (home). *E-mail:* olle_bjorkman@msn.com (home). *Website:* carnegiedpb.stanford.edu (office).

BJORKMAN, Pamela J., BA, PhD; American biologist and academic; *Max Delbrück Professor of Biology and Investigator, Howard Hughes Medical Institute, California Institute of Technology;* b. Portland, Ore.; m. Kai Zinn; two c.; ed Univ. of Oregon and Harvard Univ.; Post-doctoral Researcher, Harvard Univ. 1984–87, Stanford Univ. 1987–88; Asst Prof., California Inst. of Tech. 1988–95, Assoc. Prof. 1995–98, Prof. 1998–2004, Max Delbrück Prof. of Biology 2004–, Asst Investigator, Howard Hughes Medical Inst. Div. of Biology 1989–95, Assoc. Investigator 1995–98, Investigator 1988–99, 2005–, Full Investigator 2000–05, Exec. Officer for Biology 2000–; fmr Pew Scholar in the Biomedical Sciences; fmr American Cancer Soc. Post-doctoral Fellow; fmr American Soc. of Histocompatibility and Immunogenetics Young Investigator; mem. NAS 2001–; William B. Coley Award for Distinguished Research in Fundamental Immunology, Gairdner Foundation Int. Award (co-author) 1994, AAI-PharMingen Investigator Award 1996, Paul Ehrlich and Ludwig Darmstaedter Award, L'Oréal-UNESCO Women in Science Award 2006. *Publications:* numerous papers in scientific journals on the structures of proteins mediating the immune response and on protein crystallography. *Address:* Howard Hughes Medical Institute Division of Biology, Office 361 Broad, MC 114-96, California Institute of Technology, 1200 E California Blvd, Pasadena, CA 91125, USA (office). *Telephone:* (626) 395-8350 (office). *Fax:* (626) 792-3683 (office). *E-mail:* bjorkman@caltech.edu (office). *Website:* www.its.caltech.edu/~bjorker (office).

BJØRNHOLM, Sven, DPhil; Danish physicist; b. 8 Sept. 1927, Tønder; s. of Lt-Col H. L. Bjørnholm and Inger Hillerup; m. Iran Park 1957; two s. one d.; ed Tech. Univ. of Denmark, Sorbonne, Paris and Univ. of Copenhagen; Research Asst, Niels Bohr Inst., Copenhagen 1955–68; Assoc. Prof., Univ. of Copenhagen 1968–96; visiting scientist at research insts in France, USSR, USA, Germany and Brazil 1951–97; mem. Bd Int. Fed. of Insts of Advanced Study 1972–77, Danish Natural Science Research Council 1973–79, Danish Energy Policy Council 1976–86, IUPAP Comm. on Nuclear Physics 1978–84, EC Comm. on Research and Devt 1980–82; Pres. Danish Physical Soc. 1978–80; mem. Royal Danish Acad., Danish Acad. of Tech. Sciences, Royal Physiographical Soc. of Lund, Sweden, Danish Pugwash Cttee; Officier, Ordre des Palmes Académiques; Ole Rømer Award 1965, Ulrich Brinch Award 1973. *Publications:* Energy in Denmark 1990–2005 1976; and articles on the structure and reactions of atomic nuclei and metal clusters, including fission, in professional journals. *Address:* The Niels Bohr Institute, Blegdamsvej 17, 2100 Copenhagen Ø (office); Fuglevangsvej 6B, 1962 Frederiksberg C, Denmark (home). *Telephone:* 35-32-52-94 (office); 33-22-48-85 (home).

BJURSTRÖM, Per Gunnar, PhD; Swedish academic; b. 28 March 1928, Stockholm; s. of Gunnar Bjurström and Claire Bjurström (née Hellgård); m. 1st Eva Gunnars 1957 (divorced 1983); two d.; m. 2nd Görel Cavalli-Björkman; Asst curator, Nat. Museum 1950–68, curator of prints and drawings 1968–79; Dir Nat. Swedish Art Museums 1980–89; Guest Prof., Yale Univ. 1968; Prof., Nat. Gallery of Art, Washington, DC 1990–91; mem. Bd Gen. Art Asscn of Sweden 1964–, Prince Eugen's Waldemarsudde 1980–89; Vice-Chair. Soc. of Art History 1965–91; Chair. Int. Cttee of Museums of Fine Art 1983–88; mem. Royal Acad. of Letters, History and Antiquities and Royal Acad. of Fine Art, Ateneo Veneto, Venice. *Publications:* Giacomo Torelli and Baroque Stage Design 1961, Stage Design in Sweden 1964, Feast and Theatre in Queen Christina's Rome 1966, German Drawings in Swedish Public Collections 1972, French Drawings in Swedish Public Collections 1–3 1976, 1982, 1986, Italian Drawings in Swedish Public Collections 1–4 1979, Johan Tobias Sergel 1975, Three Decades of Swedish Graphic Art 1946–1976, Roman Baroque Scenery 1977, Philip von Schantz 1979, Claude Lorrain Sketchbook 1984, Nationalmuseum 1792–1991 1992, Karl Axel Pehrson 1992, I, Alexander Roslin 1993, Nicola Pio as a Collector of Drawings 1994, Art at the Karolinska Hospital 1997, Evert Lundquist Grafiker 2004, Kännare (On Connoisseurship) 2005. *Address:* Folkungagatan 142, 116 30 Stockholm, Sweden (home). *Telephone:* (8) 641-7093 (home). *E-mail:* per.bjurstrom@tele2.se (home).

BLACK, Dame Carol M., DBE, FRCP, FMedSci, FACP, MD; British physician and academic; *Professor of Rheumatology, Centre for Rheumatology, Royal Free and University College Medical School;* Consultant Rheumatologist and Medical Dir Royal Free Hospital, London 2000–02, currently Prof. of Rheumatology, Centre for Rheumatology, Royal Free and Univ. Coll. Medical School; elected to Royal Coll. of Physicians 1996, Clinical Vice-Pres. 1999–2002, Pres. 2002–06; also Nat. Dir for Health and Work and Chair. Nuffield Trust; Pres. Scleroderma Soc. UK, Raynaud's and Scleroderma Asscn UK; mem. Acad. of Medical Science Council; fmr Bd mem. Nat. Health Service (NHS) Modernisation, Academic Bd NHS Univ.; mem. Imperial Cancer Research Fund Council, Nat. Specialist Commissioning Advisory Group, Postgraduate Medical Educ. and Training Bd; Chair. Acad. of Medical Royal Colls; fmr Adviser Dept of Health; fmr mem. Nat. Inst. for Health and Clinical Excellence (NICE) Appraisal Cttee; Master, American Coll. of Physicians; Companion, Chartered Man. Inst.; mem. Bd of Dirs NHS Inst. for Innovation and Improvement 2006–; mem. Bd of Govs. The Health Foundation; Fellow, Acad. of Medical Science; Foreign Assoc. Inst. of Medicine, Washington, DC; Fellowship of Univ. Coll. London; Hon. MD (Univ. of Nottingham); Hon. DrSc (Bristol, Leicester, Sheffield, Hertfordshire, Exeter, Glasgow, Southampton). *Leisure interests:* long distance walking, running, music (especially opera), reading and travel. *Address:* Centre for Rheumatology and Connective Tissue Disease, Centre for Rheumatology, Department of Medicine, Royal Free Hospital, Pond Street, London, NW3 2QG, England (office). *Telephone:* (20) 7794-0432 (office). *Fax:* (20) 7935-1174 (office). *Website:* www.ucl.ac.uk/medicine/rheumatology-RF/index.html (office).

BLACK, Cathleen P.; American publishing executive; *President, Hearst Magazines;* b. 1944, Chicago; m. Thomas E. Harvey 1982; two c.; ed Trinity Coll., Washington, DC; sold advertising for magazines such as Holiday and Travel & Leisure; joined New York magazine in 1970, Publr 1979; helped launch Ms. magazine 1972, Assoc. Publr; Pres. and Publr USA Today 1983–91, mem. Bd Dirs and Exec. Vice-Pres. Marketing, Gannett Co. Inc. (parent-co.) 1985–91; Pres. and CEO Newspaper Asscn of America 1991–95; Pres. Hearst Magazines, New York 1996–, mem. Bd of Dirs Hearst Corpn 1996–; mem. Bd of Dirs International Business Machines Corpn (IBM) 1995–, Coca-Cola Co. 1990–91, Women.com Networks Inc. 1999–, Advertising Council; Chair. Magazine Publishers of America 1999–2001; Trustee Univ. of Notre Dame; mem. Council on Foreign Relations; eight hon. degrees; Woman of the Year Award Financial Women's Asscn 1986–87, Advertising Age Publishing Executive of the Year 2000, named by Crain's New York Business one of its 100 Most Influential Business Leaders 2002, ranked by Fortune magazine amongst 50 Most Powerful Women in Business in the US 1998–2001, (24th) 2002, (26th) 2003, (30th) 2004, (34th) 2005, (38th) 2006, (43rd) 2007, ranked by Forbes magazine amongst 100 Most Powerful Women (91st) 2005, (92nd) 2006, (94th) 2007, Lifetime Achievement Award, Magazine Publrs of America 2005, named Corp. Publr of the Year, The Delaney Report 2006, Prism Award, New York Univ. 2007. *Publication:* Basic Black: The Essential Guide for Getting Ahead at Work (and in Life) 2007. *Address:*

Hearst Magazines, 959 8th Avenue, New York, NY 10019, USA (office). *Telephone:* (212) 649-2000 (office). *Fax:* (212) 765-3528 (office). *Website:* www.hearstcorp.com/magazines (office).

BLACK, Guy Vaughan, MA, FRSA, MCIPR; British public relations executive; *Corporate Affairs Director, Telegraph Media Group;* b. 6 Aug. 1964, Chelmsford, Essex; s. of Monica Black and Thomas Black; Civil Partner, Mark Bolland; ed Brentwood School, Essex, Peterhouse, Cambridge; Grad. Trainee, Corp. Banking Div., BZW 1985–86; Desk Officer, Conservative Party Research Dept 1986–89; Special Adviser to Sec. of State for Energy 1989–92; Account Dir, Westminster Strategy 1992–94; Assoc. Dir, Lowe Bell Good Relations 1994–96; Dir Press Complaints Comm. 1996–2003; Dir of Communications, Conservative Party 2004–05; Corp. Affairs Dir, Telegraph Media Group 2005–; Dir Advertising Standards Bd of Finance 2005–, Press Standards Bd of Finance 2007–; Conservative mem. Brentwood Dist Council 1988–92; Trustee, Sir Edward Heath Charitable Foundation 2006–, Imperial War Museum 2007–; Chair. Commonwealth Press Union Training and Educ. Trust 2009–; Sir Herbert Butterfield Prize for History, Univ. of Cambridge 1985. *Publication:* The Eclipse of Socialism (with Tim Collins) 1988. *Leisure interests:* reading, music, playing the piano, cats. *Address:* Telegraph Media Group, 111 Buckingham Palace Road, London SW1A 0DT, England (office). *Telephone:* (20) 7931-3806 (office). *E-mail:* guy.black@telegraph.co.uk (office). *Website:* www.telegraph.co.uk (office).

BLACK, J. Cofer, BA, MA; American fmr diplomatist; *Vice Chairman, Blackwater USA;* b. Stamford, Conn.; ed Univ. of Southern Calif.; held various positions in CIA 1974–2002, including Dir's Special Asst for Counterterrorism and Nat. Intelligence Officer for Counterterrorism; Dir of Operations and Task Force Chief, Near East and S Asia Div. 1995, Deputy Chief, Latin America Div. 1998–99, Dir Counterterrorist Center 1999–2002, Coordinator, Office Coordinator for Counterterrorism, State Dept 2002–04, Amb. at Large 2002–04; mem. Counterterrorism Security Group; Vice-Chair. Blackwater USA (pvt. security co.) 2005–; Distinguished Intelligence Medal, George H. Bush Medal for Excellence, Exceptional Collector Award 1994. *Address:* Blackwater USA, POB 1029, Moyock, NC 27958, USA (office). *Telephone:* (252) 435-2488 (office). *Fax:* (252) 435-6388 (office). *E-mail:* webmaster@blackwaterusa.com (office). *Website:* www.blackwaterusa.com (office).

BLACK, Sir James (Whyte), Kt, OM, FRCP, FRS; British pharmacologist and academic; *Emeritus Professor of Analytical Pharmacology, University of London;* b. 14 June 1924; m. Rona McLeod Mackie 1994; ed Beath High School, Cowdenbeath and Univ. of St Andrews; Asst Lecturer in Physiology, Univ. of St Andrews 1946; Lecturer in Physiology, Univ. of Malaya 1947–50; Sr Lecturer Univ. of Glasgow Veterinary School 1950–58; with ICI Pharmaceuticals Ltd 1958–64, Head of Biological Research and Deputy Research Dir Smith, Kline & French, Welwyn Garden City 1964–73; Prof. and Head of Dept of Pharmacology, Univ. College, London 1973–77; Prof. of Analytical Pharmacology, King's Coll. Hosp. Medical School, Univ. of London 1984–93, now Emer.; Chancellor Dundee Univ. 1992–; Dir Therapeutic Research, Wellcome Research Labs 1978–84; mem. British Pharmacological Soc. 1961–; Hon. Fellow RSC 1989; Hon. Assoc. mem. Royal Coll. of Veterinary Surgeons 1990; Hon. MD (Edinburgh) 1989; Hon. DSc (Glasgow) 1989, (Oxford) 1996; Mullard Award, Royal Soc. 1978, (jtly) Nobel Prize for Physiology or Medicine 1988. *Address:* Analytical Pharmacology Unit, Rayne Institute, 123 Cold Harbour Lane, London, SE5 9WU (office); James Black Foundation, 68 Half Moon Lane, London, SE24 9JE, England; University of Dundee, Dundee, DD1 4HN, Scotland. *Telephone:* (20) 7274-7437.

BLACK, Kent March; American business executive; b. 25 Oct. 1939, Carrollton, Ill.; s. of Kenneth Wilbur Black and Alta Jane (March) Black; m. Karen Anne Jones 1960; two d.; ed Univ. of Illinois; joined Rockwell Int. 1962, various posts to Exec. Vice-Pres. and COO 1989; mem. Advisory Cttee Nat. Security Telecom 1989–; CEO United Space Alliance 1995–97; mem. NASA task force examining budget and man. of Int. Space Station program 2001; mem. Int. Acad. of Astronautics. *Address:* c/o United Space Alliance, 1150 Gemini, Houston, TX 77058, USA.

BLACK, Robert Lincoln, MD, FAAP; American pediatrician and academic; *Voluntary Clinical Professor of Pediatrics, Stanford University;* b. 25 Aug. 1930, Los Angeles; s. of Harold Black and Kathryn Stone; m. Jean Wilmott McGuire 1953; two s. one d.; ed Stanford Univ., Kings County Hosp., Brooklyn, Stanford Univ. Hosp., Palo Alto; Capt. USAF Medical Corps 1956–58; Asst Clinical Prof., Stanford Univ., Clinical Prof. 1962–, Assoc. Prof. 1968–79, Prof. of Pediatrics 1980, currently Voluntary Clinical Prof. of Pediatrics; mem. Bd of Educ. Monterey Peninsula Unified School Dist 1965–73; mem. Bd of Dirs Lyceum of Monterey Peninsula 1973–; mem. Bd Mid Coast Health System Agency 1975–81; mem. various cttees of American Acad., of Pediatrics 1962–, Alt. Chapter Chair. 1984–87; Consultant, State of Calif. Dept of Health Service 1962– and of Office of Statewide Health Planning 1975–81; mem. State Maternal, Child, Adolescent Health Care Bd 1984–93; mem. Inst. of Medicine, NAS, Calif. State Maternal, Child, Adolescent Health Bd; Fellow, American Acad. of Pediatrics (FAAP); Martin Gershman Award for Child Advocacy, American Acad. of Pediatrics 1996, Physician of the Year, Monterey County Medical Soc. 2001, Child Advocacy Award, American Acad. of Pediatrics 2003. *Publications:* California Health Plan for Children, California's Use of Health Statistics in Child Health Planning. *Leisure interests:* music, hiking, travel, photography. *Address:* Suite 110, 1900 Garden Road, Monterey, CA 93940, USA (office). *Telephone:* (831) 372-5841 (office). *Fax:* (831) 372-4820 (office). *E-mail:* rblack@chomp.org (office).

BLACK, Shirley Temple; American actress and diplomatist; b. 23 April 1928, Santa Monica, Calif.; d. of George F. Temple and Gertrude Temple; m. 1st John Agar, Jr 1945 (divorced 1949); one d.; m. 2nd Charles A. Black 1950; one s. one d.; ed privately and Westlake School for Girls; career as film actress commenced at 3½ years; first full-length film was Stand Up and Cheer; narrator/actress in TV series Shirley Temple Storybook 1958; hostess/actress Shirley Temple Show 1960; Del. to UN, New York 1969–70; Amb. to Ghana 1974–76, to Czechoslovakia 1989–92; White House Chief of Protocol 1976–77; mem. US Comm. for UNESCO 1973–; mem. US Del. on African Refugee Problems, Geneva 1981; Dir Nat. Multiple Sclerosis Soc.; Dame, Order of Knights of Malta (Paris) 1968; numerous state decorations; American Exemplar Medal 1979, Gandhi Memorial Int. Foundation Award 1988, Screen Actors Guild Lifetime Achievement Award 2006. *Films include:* Little Miss Marker, Baby Take a Bow, Bright Eyes, Our Little Girl, The Little Colonel, Curly Top, The Littlest Rebel, Captain January, Poor Little Rich Girl, Dimples, Stowaway, Wee Willie Winkie, Heidi, Rebecca of Sunnybrook Farm, Little Miss Broadway, Just Around the Corner, The Little Princess, Susannah of the Mounties, The Blue Bird, Kathleen, Miss Annie Rooney, Since You Went Away, Kiss and Tell, That Hagen Girl, War Party, The Bachelor and the Bobby-Soxer, Honeymoon. *Publication:* Child Star (autobiog) 1988. *Address:* 101 Lakeview Drive, Woodside, CA 94062, USA.

BLACK OF CROSSHARBOUR, Baron (Life Peer), cr. 2001, of Crossharbour in the London Borough of Tower Hamlets; **Conrad M. Black,** Kt, PC, OC, LittD, LLD; British (b. Canadian) publisher and business executive; b. 25 Aug. 1944, Montreal, Québec; s. of George Montegu and Jean Elizabeth Black (née Riley); m. 1st Joanna Catherine Louise Black 1978 (divorced 1991); two s. one d.; m. 2nd Barbara Amiel 1992; ed Carleton, Laval, McGill Univs; Chair. and CEO Ravelston Corpn Ltd; Chair. Hollinger Int. 1985–2004, acquired Daily Telegraph newspaper group 1985, Chair. Telegraph Group –2004; CEO Chair. Argus Corpn 1978–2005; Chair. Conrad Black Capital Corpn; Patron The Malcolm Muggeridge Foundation; mem. Advisory Bd, The Nat. Interest, Washington, DC; sentenced to three and a half years' imprisonment on three counts of fraud 2007; Hon. LLD (St Francis Xavier) 1979, (McMaster) 1979. *Publications:* Duplessis 1977, A Life in Progress (autobiog.) 1994, Franklin D. Roosevelt: Champion of Freedom 2003, Richard Milhous Nixon: The Invincible Quest 2007. *Address:* 3044 Bloor Street West, Suite 296, Toronto, ON M8X 2Y8, Canada; c/o 9 Montague Gardens, London, W3 9PT, England.

BLACKADDER, Dame Elizabeth Violet, DBE, MA, RA, RSA; British artist; b. 24 Sept. 1931, Falkirk, Scotland; m. John Houston 1956; ed Falkirk High School, Edinburgh Coll. of Art and Univ. of Edinburgh; teacher of art, St Thomas of Aquinas School, Edin. 1958–59; Librarian, Fine Art Dept, Univ. of Edin. 1959–61; teacher, Edin. Coll of Art 1962–86; Scottish Arts Council retrospective Exhbn Edin., Sheffield, Aberdeen, Liverpool, Cardiff 1981–82; participant in numerous group shows in UK, USA, Canada etc. British Painting 1952–77; Royal Acad., London 1977; HM Painter and Limner in Scotland 2000–; work includes drawings and watercolours (especially botanical), prints, lithographs, portraits, tapestries and stained glass (window commissioned by Nat. Library of Scotland 1987); Hon. FRSE; Hon. DLitt (Heriot-Watt) 1989, (Strathclyde) 1998; Dr hc (Edin.) 1990, (Stirling, St Andrews, London); Hon. LLD (Aberdeen) 1997, (Glasgow) 2001; Jt Winner, Watercolour Foundation Award, RA Summer Exhbn 1988. *Publication:* Favourite Flowers (with Deborah Kellaway) 1994. *Address:* 57 Fountainhall Road, Edinburgh, EH9 2LH; c/o Royal Scottish Academy, The Mound, Edinburgh, EH2 2EL, Scotland. *Telephone:* (131) 667-3687 (home).

BLACKBOURN, David Gordon, PhD, FRHistS; British historian and academic; *Coolidge Professor of History and Director, Minda de Gunzburg Center for European Studies, Harvard University;* b. 1 Nov. 1949, Spilsby, Lincs.; s. of Harry Blackbourn and Pamela Jean Blackbourn; m. Deborah Frances Langton; one s. one d.; ed Leeds Modern Grammar School, Christ's Coll., Cambridge; Research Fellow, Jesus Coll., Cambridge 1973–76; Lecturer in History, Queen Mary Coll., Univ. of London 1976–79, Birkbeck Coll. 1979–85, Reader in Modern History 1985–89, Prof. of Modern European History 1989–92; Coolidge Prof. of History, Harvard Univ., USA 1992–, Dir Minda de Gunzburg Center for European Studies 2007–; lectures and contribs to confs in UK, Ireland, Germany, France, Italy, Yugoslavia, USA and Canada 1973–; Fellow, Inst. for European History, Mainz, FRG 1974–75; Research Fellow, Alexander von Humboldt Foundation, Bonn-Bad Godesberg, FRG 1984–85, 1994–95; Visiting Kratter Prof. of German History, Stanford Univ., Calif., USA 1989–90; Fellow, Guggenheim Foundation, New York 1994–95; Sec. German History Soc. 1978–81, mem. Cttee 1981–86; mem. Acad. Man. Cttee, German Historical Inst., London 1983–92; mem. Editorial Bd Past and Present 1988–; mem. European Sub-cttee of Labour Party Nat. Exec. Cttee 1978–80, Academic Man. Cttee, Inst. for European History, Mainz, Germany 1995–2005, Cttee on Hon. Foreign mems, American Historical Asscn 2000–02; Pres. Conf. Group on Cen. European History, American Historical Asscn 2003–04; mem. Advisory Bd, Edmund Spevack Memorial Foundation, 2003–, mem. Academic Bd, Friends of the German Historical Inst., Washington, DC 2004–; Ed. Penguin Custom Editions: The Western World Database 2000–; consultant to SMASH/The History Channel, USA; Fellow, American Acad. of Arts and Sciences 2007; gave Annual Lecture of German Historical Inst., London 1998, Malcolm Wynn Lecture, Stetson Univ., Florida 2002, George C. Windell Memorial Lecture, Univ. of New Orleans 2006, Crayenborgh Lecture, Leiden Univ., Netherlands 2007; American Historical Asscn Book Prize 1996, Walter Channing Cabot Fellow, Harvard Univ. 2003–04, George L. Mosse Prize, American Historical Asscn 2007, Charles A. Weyerhaeuser Prize, Forest History Soc. 2007. *Publications:* Class, Religion and Local Politics in Wilhelmine Germany 1980, The Peculiarities of German History (with Geoff Eley) 1984, Populists and Patricians: Essays in Modern German History 1987, Volksfrömmigkeit und Fortschrittsglaube im Kulturkampf 1988, The German Bourgeoisie (co-ed. with Richard J. Evans) 1991, Marpingen: Apparitions of the Virgin Mary in Bismarckian Germany 1993, The Fontana History of Germany: the Long Nineteenth Century, 1780–1918 1997, The Conquest of

Nature: Water, Landscape and the Making of Modern Germany 2006; scholarly articles in English, German, French, Serbo-Croat, Japanese and Italian; contribs to several magazines and the BBC. *Leisure interests:* family, reading, music, sport, politics. *Address:* Minda de Gunzburg Center for European Studies, Harvard University, 27 Kirkland Street, Cambridge, MA 02138, USA (office). *Telephone:* (617) 495-4303, ext. 228 (office). *Fax:* (617) 495-8509 (office). *E-mail:* dgblackb@fas.harvard.edu (office). *Website:* www.fas.harvard.edu/~history (office).

BLACKBURN, Elizabeth Helen, BSc, MSc, PhD, FRS; Australian/American biochemist and academic; *Morris Herzstein Professor of Biology, Department of Biochemistry and Biophysics, University of California, San Francisco;* b. 26 Nov. 1948, Hobart, Australia; d. of Harold Stewart Blackburn and Marcia Constance Jack; m. John Sedat 1975; one s.; ed Univ. of Melbourne, Australia and Univ. of Cambridge, UK; Researcher, Molecular Biology Lab., Univ. of Cambridge 1971–74; Post grad. Researcher, Yale Univ., USA 1975–77; mem. Faculty Univ. of California, Berkeley 1978–90; Prof., Dept of Microbiology and Immunology, Univ. of California, San Francisco 1990, Dept Chair. 1993–99, currently Morris Herzstein Prof. of Biology and Physiology, Dept of Biochemistry and Biophysics; Non-Resident Fellow, Salk Inst.; Pres. American Soc. for Cell Biology 1998; Memorial Sloan-Kettering Cancer Center Katharine Berkan Judd Award Lectureship 2001; Travelling Gowrie Research Scholar 1971–73; Anna Fuller Fund Fellowship 1975–77; Steven and Michele Kirsch Foundation Investigator Fellowship 2000; Foreign Assoc. NAS 1993–; Fellow, American Acad. of Arts and Sciences 1991, American Acad. of Microbiology 1993, AAAS 2000; mem. Pres.'s Council on Bioethics 2001–04; mem. American Acad. of Excellence 2000, Inst. of Medicine 2000; Hon. DSc (Yale) 1991; Australian Soc. for Microbiology Prize 1967, Eli Lilly Research Award for Microbiology and Immunology 1988, NAS Award in Molecular Biology 1990, Gairdner Foundation Award 1998, Australia Prize 1998, California Scientist of the Year 1999, Novartis-Drew Award for Biomedical Science 1999, Feodor Lynen Award 2000, Dickson Prize in Medicine 2000, American Cancer Soc. Medal of Honor 2000, American Asscn for Cancer Research–Pezcoller Foundation Int. Award for Cancer Research 2001, General Motors Cancer Research Foundation Alfred P. Sloan Award 2001, Bristol-Meyers Squibb Award for Distinguished Achievement in Cancer Research 2003, Dr A.H. Heineken Prize for Medicine 2004, American Soc. for Cell Biology Public Service Award 2004, Benjamin Franklin Medal in Life Science 2005, Albert Lasker Award for Basic Medical Research (with Carol W. Greider and Jack W. Szostak) 2006, Genetics Prize, Peter Gruber Foundation 2006, Vanderbilt Prize in Biomedical Science 2007, L'Oréal-UNESCO Award for Women in Science 2008. *Publications include:* numerous articles in scientific journals. *Leisure interest:* music. *Address:* University of California, Department of Biochemistry and Biophysics, San Francisco, CA 94143-2200, USA (office). *Telephone:* (415) 476-4912 (office). *Fax:* (415) 514-2913 (office). *E-mail:* telomer@itsa.ucsf.edu (office). *Website:* biochemistry.ucsf.edu/labs/blackburn (office).

BLACKBURN, Jean-Pierre, BBA, MA; Canadian politician and business executive; *Minister of National Revenue;* b. 6 July 1948; ed Université du Québec, Chicoutimi; MP (Jonquière) 1984–93, 2006–; fmr Parl. Sec. to Minister of Nat. Defence; fmr Pres. Blackburn Communication Inc.; Minister of Labour and Minister of the Econ. Devt Agency of Canada for the Regions of Quebec 2006–08, of Nat. Revenue 2008–. *Address:* Canada Revenue Agency, Office of the Minister of National Revenue, 7th Floor, 555 McKenzie Avenue, Ottawa,, ON K1A 0L5, Canada (office). *Telephone:* (613) 952-9184 (office). *Website:* www.cra-arc.gc.ca (office).

BLACKBURN, (Jeffrey) Michael, FCIB, FRSA; British business executive; b. 16 Dec. 1941, Manchester; s. of Jeffrey Blackburn and Renee Blackburn; m. 2nd Louise Clair Jouny 1987; two s.; one s. one d. from previous m.; ed Northgate Grammar School, Ipswich; Chief Man. Business Advisory Service, Lloyds Bank 1979–83; Dir and CEO Jt Credit Card Co. Ltd (Access) 1983–87, Leeds Perm. Bldg Soc. 1987–93; CEO Halifax Bldg Soc. (now Halifax PLC) 1993–98; Dir DFS Furniture PLC 1999–, George Wimpey PLC 1999–, Town Centre Securities PLC 1999–2003; Pres. Chartered Inst. of Bankers 1998–99; mem. court, Leeds Univ. 1989–2000; Companion, Chartered Man. Inst.; Gov. Nat. Youth Orchestra 1999–; Trustee Duke of Edin.'s Award 1998–; Hon. DUniv (Leeds Metropolitan) 1998; Hon. DLitt (Huddersfield) 1998. *Leisure interest:* the arts. *Address:* George Wimpey PLC, Gate House, Turnpike Road, High Wycombe, HP12 3NR, England (office). *Telephone:* (1494) 558–323 (office).

BLACKBURN, Simon W., PhD, DPhil, FBA; British academic; *Professor of Philosophy, University of Cambridge;* b. 12 July 1944, Bristol; s. of Cuthbert Blackburn and Edna Blackburn; m. Angela Bowles 1968; one s. one d.; ed Clifton Coll. Bristol and Trinity Coll., Cambridge; Research Fellow, Churchill Coll. Cambridge 1967–69; Fellow and Tutor in Philosophy, Pembroke Coll. Oxford 1969–90; Ed. Mind 1984–90; Edna J. Koury Distinguished Prof. of Philosophy, Univ. of NC 1990–2000; Adjunct Prof., ANU 1993–; Prof. of Philosophy, Univ. of Cambridge 2001–; Foreign mem. American Acad. of Arts and Sciences; Hon. LLD (Sunderland). *Publications:* Reason and Prediction 1970, Spreading the Word 1984, Essays in Quasi-Realism 1993, Oxford Dictionary of Philosophy 1994, Ruling Passions 1998, Think 1999, Being Good 2001, Lust 2004, Truth: A Guide for the Perplexed 2005, Plato's Republic: A Biography 2006, How to Read Hume 2008. *Leisure interests:* walking, photography, sailing. *Address:* Faculty of Philosophy, University of Cambridge, Sidgwick Avenue, Cambridge, CB3 9DA (office); 141 Thornton Road, Cambridge, CB3 0NE, England (home). *Telephone:* (1223) 528278 (office). *E-mail:* swb24@cam.ac.uk (office). *Website:* www.phil.cam.ac.uk/~swb24/ (office).

BLACKER, Coit D., A, MS, PhD; American political scientist, academic, research institute director and international relations consultant; *Director and Senior Fellow, Freeman Spogli Institute for International Studies, Stanford University;* ed Occidental Coll., Fletcher School of Law and Diplomacy, Tufts Univ.; Professor Stanford Univ. 1978–, and succession of other positions at Stanford, including Dir of Studies, Center for Int. Security and Arms Control, co-Chair. Int. Relations and Int. Policy Studies Programs, Olivier Nomellini Family Univ. Fellow in Undergraduate Educ., Deputy Dir, Freeman Spogli Inst. for Int. Studies, now Dir and Sr Fellow; Assoc. Prof. School of Int. Relations, Univ. of Southern Calif., Dir ad interim Peace and Conflict Studies Program; Special Asst for Nat. Security Affairs to US Senator Gary Hart, then to Pres. Clinton during first admin.; Sr Dir Russian, Ukrainian and Eurasian Affairs, Nat. Security Council; co-Dir Aspen Inst. US-Russia Dialogue 1998–2003; mem. study group US Comm. on Nat. Security in the 21st Century; mem. Council on Foreign Relations; mem. Bd of Dirs Int. Research and Exchanges Bd, Washington, DC; Chair. Exec. Cttee of the Int. Initiative 2005–; mem. Stanford Bd of Trustees Cttee on Devt 2004–07; Dr hc (Russian Acad. of Sciences Inst. of Far Eastern Studies) 1993; Laurance and Naomi Carpenter Hoagland Prize for Undergraduate Teaching 2001. *Publications include:* International Arms Control: Issues and Agreements (co-Ed.) 1984, Reluctant Warriors: the United States, The Soviet Union and Arms Control 1987, Hostage to Revolution: Gorbachev and Soviet Security Policy, 1985–91 1993, NATO After Madrid: Looking to the Future (Vol I) (co-Ed.) 1999, Belarus and the Flight from Sovereignty 2001, Arms Control 2002. *Address:* Freeman Spogli Institute for International Studies, Stanford University, Encina Hall, C137, Stanford, CA 94305-6055, USA (office). *Telephone:* (650) 725-5368 (office). *Fax:* (650) 725-3435 (office). *E-mail:* cblacker@stanford.edu (office). *Website:* www.iis-db.stanford.edu (office).

BLACKMAN, Honor; British actress; b. 22 Aug. 1926, London; film début in Fame is the Spur 1947. *Films include:* Green Grow the Rushes 1951, Come Die My Love 1952, The Rainbow Jacket 1953, The Glass Cage 1954, Dead Man's Evidence 1955, A Matter of Who 1961, Goldfinger 1964, Life at the Top 1965, Twist of Sand 1967, The Virgin and the Gipsy 1970, To the Devil a Daughter 1975, Summer Rain 1976, The Cat and the Canary 1977, Talos—The Mummy, To Walk With Lions, Bridget Jones's Diary 2001, Jack Brown and the Curse of the Crown 2001, Colour Me Kubrick: A Trueish Story 2005, Summer Solstice 2005. *Plays include:* Mademoiselle Colombe 2000, Cabaret 2007. *TV appearances include:* Four Just Men 1959, Man of Honour 1960, Ghost Squad 1961, Top Secret 1962, The Avengers 1962–64, The Explorer 1968, Visit from a Stranger 1970, Out Damned Spot 1972, Wind of Change 1977, Robin's Nest 1982, Never the Twain 1982, The Secret Adversary 1983, Lace 1985, The First Modern Olympics 1986, Minder on the Orient Express 1986, Dr. Who 1986, William Tell 1986, The Upper Hand (TV series), Jack and the Beanstalk: The Real Story 2001, Revolver 2001, Midsomer Murders 2003, The Royal 2003, Coronation Street 2004. *Address:* c/o Jean Diamond, London Management, 2–4 Noel Street, London, W1V 3RB, England.

BLACKMORE, Rayburn; Dominican politician; *Minister of National Security, Immigration and Labour;* MP (Dominica Labour Party—DLP) for Mahaut; fmr Parl. Sec., later Minister of State in Prime Minister's Office with responsibility for Security; Minister of Nat. Security, Immigration and Labour 2007–; Chair. Nat. Symposium on Crime 2003; Chair. Regional Security System –2008. *Address:* Ministry of National Security, Immigration and Labour, Government Headquarters, Kennedy Avenue, Roseau, Dominica (office). *Telephone:* 4482401 (office). *Fax:* 4488960 (office). *E-mail:* burnray@hotmail.com (office).

BLACKSTAD, Theodor Wilhelm, MD; Norwegian professor of anatomy; *Professor Emeritus of Medicine, University of Oslo;* b. 29 July 1925, Iveland; s. of Leif Blackstad and Alfhild (née Holmsen); m. Ebba Helene Dietrichson 1952; two d.; ed Univ. of Oslo; anatomy teacher, Univ. of Oslo 1953, Prof. of Medicine, Univ. of Århus, Denmark 1967–77, Univ. of Oslo 1977–91, Prof. Emer. 1991–; Sr Research Fellow Norwegian Research Council 1991–95; Monrad-Krohn and Nansen prizes. *Publications:* (recently) articles on computer-based analysis of brain morphology. *Address:* Department of Anatomy, Inst. of Basic Medical Sciences, Sognsvannsveien 9, PO Box 1105 Blindern, 0317 Oslo (office); Jernbaneveien 83, 1369 Stabekk, Norway (home). *Telephone:* 22851271 (office); 67532885 (home). *Fax:* 22851278 (office); 22851278. *E-mail:* t.w.blackstad@basalmed.uio.no (office); t.w.blackstad@basalmed.uio.no (home).

BLACKSTONE, Baroness (Life Peer), cr. 1987, of Stoke Newington in Greater London; **Rt Hon. Tessa Ann Vosper Blackstone,** PC, BSc, PhD; British politician and university vice-chancellor; *Vice-Chancellor, University of Greenwich;* b. 27 Sept. 1942, London; d. of the late Geoffrey Vaughan Blackstone, CBE, GM and of Joanna Blackstone; m. Tom Evans 1963 (divorced, died 1985); one s. one d.; ed Ware Grammar School, London School of Econs, Univ. of London; Assoc. Lecturer, Enfield Coll. 1965–66; Asst Lecturer, then Lecturer, Dept of Social Admin., LSE 1966–75; Fellow, Centre for Studies in Social Policy 1972–74; Adviser, Cen. Policy Review Staff, Cabinet Office 1975–78; Prof. of Educational Admin., Univ. of London Inst. of Educ. 1978–83; Deputy Educ. Officer (Resources), then Clerk and Dir of Educ., Inner London Educ. Authority 1983–87; Master, Birkbeck Coll., Univ. of London 1987–97; Opposition Spokesperson on Educ. and Science, House of Lords 1990–92, on Foreign Affairs 1992–97; Minister of State in Dept of Educ. and Employment 1997–2001; Minister of State for the Arts, Dept for Culture, Media and Sport 2001–03; Dir Royal Opera House 1987–97; Chair. General Advisory Council BBC 1987–91, RIBA Trust 2003–, Great Ormond Street Hosp. Trust 2009–; Chair. Bd of Trustees, Inst. for Public Policy Research 1988–97; Trustee British Museum (Natural History) 1992–97; mem. Bd of Dirs Thames TV 1991–92, Rover Learning Business Bd 1991–97, Granada Learning 2003–07,

VT Group 2004–, Teachers TV 2004–09, Mott MacDonald 2005–08; Visiting Prof., LSE 2003–; Vice-Chancellor, Univ. of Greenwich 2004–; Hon. Fellow LSE 1995, Birkbeck Coll. 1998; Hon. DLitt (Bradford) 1990, (Bristol Polytechnic) 1991; Hon. DUniv (Middx) 1993, (Strathclyde) 1996, (Leeds Metropolitan) 1996; Hon. LLD (Aberdeen) 1994, (St Andrews) 1995; Dr hc (Dauphine, Sorbonne, Paris) 1998, (University of Rome Roma 3) 2005. *Publications:* A Fair Start 1971, Education and Day Care for Young Children in Need 1973, Social Policy and Administration in Britain 1975; co-author: Students in Conflict 1970, The Academic Labour Market 1974, Disadvantage and Education 1982, Education Policy and Educational Inequality 1982, Response to Adversity 1983, Testing Children 1983, Inside the Think Tank: Advising the Cabinet 1971–83, 1988, Prisons and Penal Reform 1990, Race Relations in Britain 1997. *Leisure interests:* tennis, walking, ballet, opera. *Address:* House of Lords, Westminster, London, SW1A 0PW, England (office). *Telephone:* (20) 7219-5409 (office); (20) 8331-8880 (office). *E-mail:* vcmail@gre.ac.uk (office). *Website:* www.greenwich.ac.uk (office).

BLACKWELL, Julian Toby; British bookseller; b. 10 Jan. 1929; s. of the late Sir Basil Henry Blackwell and Marion Christine Soans; m. Jennifer Jocelyn Darley Wykeham 1953; two s. one d.; ed Winchester Coll. and Trinity Coll., Oxford; served 5th Royal Tank Regt 1947–49; 21st SAS (TA) 1950–59; Dir and Chair. various Blackwell cos 1956–; Chair. The Blackwell Group Ltd 1980–94; Pres. Blackwell Ltd 1995–, Chair. 1996–99; Chair. Council, ASLIB 1966–68; Pres. Booksellers' Asscn 1980–82; Chair. Thames Business Advice Centre 1986–97, Heart of England TEC 1989–94, Fox FM 1989–98, Cottontail Ltd 1990–; Chair. Son White Memorial Trust 1991–, Milestone Group; DL (Oxfordshire) 1988; Hon. DLitt (Robert Gordon) 1997, DUniv (Sheffield Hallam) 1998. *Leisure interests:* sawing firewood, sailing. *Address:* c/o Blackwell UK, Beaver House, Hythe Bridge Street, Oxford, OX1 2ET, England (office). *Telephone:* (1865) 792792 (office). *Website:* www.bookshop.blackwell.co.uk (office).

BLACKWELL, Baron (Life Peer), cr. 1997, of Woodcote in the County of Surrey; **Norman Roy Blackwell,** MA, PhD, MBA; British business executive and fmr civil servant; *Chairman, Centre for Policy Studies;* b. 29 July 1952, London; s. of Albert Edward Blackwell and Frances Evelyn Blackwell (née Lutman); m. Brenda Clucas 1974; three s. two d.; ed Latymer Upper School, Trinity Coll., Cambridge, Wharton Business School, Univ. of Pa (Thouron Scholar); Jr Exhibitioner RAM 1963–69; Chair. Cambridge Univ. Conservative Asscn 1973; with Strategic Planning Unit, Plessey Co. 1976–78, McKinsey & Co. 1978–86, 1988–95 (partner 1984), Prime Minister's Policy Unit 1986–88, Head 1995–97; Dir of Group Devt NatWest Group 1997–2000; Dir Dixons Group 2000–03; Special Adviser KPMG Corp. Finance 2000–; Dir Corp. Services Group 2000–06, Slough Estates 2001–, Smartstream Technologies Group 2001–06, Standard Life 2003–; Chair. Interserve plc 2006–; Deputy Chair. British Urban Regeneration Asscn 1991–92; Chair. Centre for Policy Studies 2000–; mem. Bd Office of Fair Trading 2003–. *Leisure interests:* classical music, walking. *Address:* c/o House of Lords, London, SW1A 0PW; Centre For Policy Studies, 57 Tufton Street, London, SW1P 3QL, England (office). *Telephone:* (20) 7311-4997; (20) 7222-4488 (CPS) (office). *Fax:* (20) 7222-4388 (CPS) (office). *E-mail:* blackwelln@parliament.uk. *Website:* www.cps.org.uk (office).

BLAGOJEVICH, Rod R., BA, JD; American state official; b. 10 Dec. 1956, Chicago; s. of Rade Blagojevich and Millie Blagojevich (née Govedarica); m. Patricia Blagojevich; two d.; ed Northwestern Univ., Pepperdine Univ.; est. pvt. law practice, Chicago 1983; Asst State Attorney, Cook Co. 1983–92; mem. Ill. Gen. Ass. 1992–96; mem. US House of Reps, Washington, DC 1997–2003; Gov. of Ill. 2003–09 (impeached and removed from office); Democrat; Library Man of the Year, American Library Asscn, Friends of Libraries USA, Whitehouse Conf. on Libraries. *Address:* c/o Office of the Governor, 207 State House, Springfield, IL 62706, USA (office).

BLAH, Moses; Liberian politician; b. 18 April 1947, Toweh Town, Nimba County; m. Nettie Blah; several c.; ed Tappeta Public School, Tajura Military Coll., Libya; mem. Nat. Patriotic Front 1989–, later Insp.-Gen., Adj.-Gen. and special envoy; Amb. to Libya and Tunisia 1997–2000; Vice-Pres. 2000–03, under house arrest June 2003, later reinstated, interim Pres. August–Oct. 2003. *Leisure interests:* sport, photography. *Address:* c/o Office of the President, Executive Mansion, POB 10-9001, 1000 Monrovia 10, Liberia (office).

BLAHNIK, Manolo; Spanish couturier; b. 28 Nov. 1943, Santa Cruz, The Canary Islands; ed Univ. of Geneva; architecture and literature but left univ. and travelled to Paris 1968; moved to London and worked briefly as photographer for Sunday Times 1970; cr. first shoe collection 1972; founder and Dir Manolo Blahnik Int. Ltd; opened shop in Chelsea, London 1973, USA 1981; biannual collections in London and New York; Fashion Council of America Award 1988, 1991, 1997, American Leather New York Award 1991, British Fashion Award 1992, Nieman Marcus Award 1993, Accessory Designer of the Year, British Fashion Council 1990, 1999; Dr hc (Royal London Coll. of Art), (Royal Soc. of Arts of Britain). *Publications:* various int. publs on fashion. *Leisure interests:* painting, reading. *Address:* 49–51 Old Church Street, London, SW3 5BS, England; 15 West 55th Street, New York, NY 10019, USA. *Telephone:* (20) 7352-8622.

BLAINEY, Geoffrey Norman, AC; Australian historian and author; b. 11 March 1930, Melbourne, Vic.; s. of Rev. Samuel C. Blainey and Hilda Blainey; m. Ann Heriot 1957; one d.; ed Ballarat High School, Wesley Coll., Univ. of Melbourne; freelance historian 1951–61; Reader in Econ. History, Univ. of Melbourne 1963–68, Prof. 1968–76, Ernest Scott Prof. of History 1977–88, Dean of Faculty of Arts 1982–87; Prof. of Australian Studies, Harvard Univ. 1982–83; columnist in daily newspapers 1974–; Commr Australian Heritage Comm. 1976–77, Chair. Australia Council 1977–81, Chair., Fed. Govt's Australia-China Council 1979–84, Chair. Commonwealth Literary Fund 1971–73; Pres. Council, Queen's Coll., Univ. of Melbourne 1971–89; Chair. Australian Selection Cttee Commonwealth Fund (Harkness) Fellowships 1983–90; Chancellor Univ. of Ballarat 1994–98; Dir Royal Humane Soc. 1996–2004; Gov. Ian Potter Foundation 1991–; Councillor Australian War Memorial 1997–2004; Del. to Australian Constitutional Convention 1998; Councillor Nat. Council for the Centenary of Fed. 1997–2002 (Chair. 2001–02); Hon. LLD (Melbourne, Ballarat); Gold Medal, Australian Literature Soc. 1963, Capt. Cook Bicentenary Literary Award 1970, Britannica Award for dissemination of learning, New York 1988, Dublin Prize 1986, Australian Author's Soc. Book of the Year 2000. *Publications include:* The Peaks of Lyell 1954, Centenary History of the University of Melbourne 1957, Gold and Paper: a History of the National Bank 1958, Mines in the Spinifex 1960, The Rush That Never Ended 1963, A History of Camberwell 1965, If I Remember Rightly: The Memoirs of W. S. Robinson 1966, The Tyranny of Distance 1966, Wesley College: The First Hundred Years (co-author and ed.) 1967, Across a Red World 1968, The Rise of Broken Hill 1968, The Steel Master 1971, The Causes of War 1973, Triumph of the Nomads: A History of Ancient Australia 1975, A Land Half Won 1980, Our Side of the Country 1984, All for Australia 1984, The Great Seesaw 1988, A Game of Our Own 1990, Eye on Australia 1991, Odd Fellows 1992, The Golden Mile 1993, Jumping over the Wheel 1993, A Shorter History of Australia 1994, White Gold 1997, A History of AMP 1999, In Our Time 1999, A Short History of the World 2000, This Land is all Horizons 2001, Black Kettle and Full Moon: Daily Life in a Vanished Australia 2003, A Very Short History of the World 2004, A Short History of the Twentieth Century 2005, A History of Victoria 2006. *Leisure interests:* travel, wood-chopping, Australian football. *Address:* PO Box 257, East Melbourne, Vic. 3002, Australia (home). *Telephone:* (3) 9417-7782 (home). *E-mail:* ablainey@netlink.com.au (home).

BLAIR, Rt Hon. Anthony (Tony) Charles Lynton, BA, PC; British barrister, consultant and fmr politician; *Special Envoy, Quartet on the Middle East;* b. 6 May 1953, Edinburgh; s. of Leo Blair and the late Hazel Blair; m. Cherie Booth (q.v.) 1980; three s. one d.; ed Fettes Coll., Edinburgh, St John's Coll., Oxford; barrister, specializing in trade union and employment law; MP for Sedgefield 1983–2007; Shadow Spokesman on the Treasury 1984–87, on Trade and Industry 1987–88, on Energy 1988–89, on Employment 1989–92, on Home Affairs 1992–94; Leader of the Labour Party 1994–2007; Prime Minister, First Lord of the Treasury and Minister for the Civil Service 1997–2007 (re-elected 2001, 2005); Special Envoy to Middle East on behalf of Quartet (USA, Russia, EU and UN) 2007–; mem. Bd of Dirs World Econ. Forum Foundation Bd 2007–; f. Tony Blair Sports Foundation 2007, Tony Blair Faith Foundation; Sr Adviser JP Morgan Chase & Co. 2008–; Adviser Zurich Financial Services working on int. politics and climate change 2008–; Howland Distinguished Fellow, Yale Univ. 2008–09; Hon. Bencher, Lincoln's Inn 1994; Hon. LLD (Northumbria) 1995; numerous awards including Charlemagne Prize 1999, Ellis Island Medal of Honor for Int. Leadership 2003, US Congressional Gold Medal of Honor 2003, Polio Eradication Champion, Rotary Int. 2006, US Presidential Medal of Freedom 2009. *Publications:* New Britain: My Vision of a Young Country 1996, The Third Way 1998. *Address:* The Office of Tony Blair, PO Box 60519, London, W2 7JU (office); Myrobella, Trimdon Station, Co. Durham, TS29 6DU, England. *E-mail:* info@tonyblairoffice.org (office). *Website:* www.tonyblairoffice.org (office); tonyblairfaithfoundation.org (office); tonyblairsportsfoundation.org (office).

BLAIR, Bruce G., PhD, BS; American research institute director and academic; *President, World Security Insitute;* ed Univ. of Ill., Yale Univ.; joined USAF, served as Minuteman ICBM launch control officer and support officer for the Strategic Air Command 1970–74; project dir Congressional Office of Tech. Assessment; Sr Fellow, Foreign Policy Studies Program, Brookings Inst. 1987–2000; Pres. World Security Inst. (fmly Center for Defense Information) 2000–; Visiting Prof. in security studies at Yale and Princeton Univs; MacArthur Fellowship Prize 1999. *Publications include:* Strategic Command and Control: Redefining the Nuclear Threat 1985, Crisis Stability and Nuclearwar (co-Ed.) 1988, The Logic of Accidental Nuclear War 1993, Global Zero Alert for Nuclear Forces 1995, De-Alerting Strategic Forces 2000; numerous articles in newspapers and journals. *Address:* World Security Institute, 1779 Massachusetts Avenue, NW, Suite 615, Washington, DC 20036, USA (office). *Telephone:* (202) 332-0900 (office). *Fax:* (202) 462-4559 (office). *E-mail:* info@worldsecurityinstitute.org (office). *Website:* www.worldsecurityinstitute.org (office).

BLAIR, Cherie (see BOOTH, Cherie).

BLAIR, Dennis Cutler, BA; American naval officer (retd) and government official; *Director Of National Intelligence;* m. Diane Blair; one s. one d.; ed US Naval Acad., Annapolis, Md, Univ. of Oxford, UK; commissioned as ensign in USN; rank of Vice-Adm.; Commdr USS Cochrane 1984–86, mem. Naval Staff, Pearl Harbor 1988–89, Kittyhawk Battlegroup 1993–95; Assoc. Dir Mil. Support, CIA 1995–96, also mem. Nat. Security Council; Dir Jt Staff 1996–99; C-in-C US Pacific Command, Hawaii 1999–2002 (retd); Sr Fellow, Inst. for Defense Analyses 2002–03, Pres. 2003–07, then consultant; US Dir of Nat. Intelligence, Washington, DC 2009–; mem. IISS Council; White House Fellow, Naval Operations Fellow; Legion of Merit with three gold stars, Service Medal with two oak leaf clusters. *Address:* Office of the Director of National Intelligence, Washington, DC 20511, USA (office). *Telephone:* 703-733-8600 (office). *Website:* www.dni.gov (office).

BLAIR, Gordon Purves, CBE, PhD, DSc, FREng, FIMechE,; British engineer and academic; *Professor Emeritus of Mechanical Engineering, Queen's University Belfast;* b. 29 April 1937, Larne, Northern Ireland; s. of Gordon Blair and Mary

H. J. Blair; m. Norma Margaret Millar 1964; two d.; ed Larne Grammar School and Queen's Univ. of Belfast; Asst Prof., Mechanical Eng, New Mexico State Univ., USA 1962–64; Lecturer in Mechanical Eng, Queen's Univ. Belfast 1964–71, Sr Lecturer 1971–73, Reader 1973–76, Prof. of Mechanical Eng 1976–96, Prof. Emer. 1996–, Prof. and Head of Dept of Mechanical and Industrial Eng 1982–88, Dean of Faculty 1985–88, Pro-Vice-Chancellor 1989–94; consultant to many industries world-wide on engine design; Fellow, SAE; Colwell Technical Merit Award (SAE), Crompton Lanchester Medal (IMechE), Trident TV Award (IBA). *Publications:* The Basic Design of Two-Stroke Engines 1990, The Design and Simulation of Two-Stroke Engines 1996, The Design and Simulation of Four Stroke Engines 1999; more than 100 tech. papers in int. journals. *Leisure interests:* golf, fishing, motorcycling. *Address:* Ashby Building, The Queen's University of Belfast, Belfast, BT9 5AH (office); 9 Ben Madigan Park South, Newtonabbey, Co. Antrim, BT36 7PX, Northern Ireland (home). *Telephone:* (28) 9037-0368 (home). *Fax:* (28) 9037-0372 (home). *E-mail:* gpb@profblairandassociates.com (office); g.p.blair@qub.ac.uk (home). *Website:* www.profblairandassociates.com (office).

BLAIS, Marie-Claire, CC; Canadian writer; b. 5 Oct. 1939, Québec City; d. of Fernando Blais and Veronique Nolin; ed studied in Québec, Paris, France and USA; Guggenheim Foundation Fellowship, New York 1963, 1964; Hon. Prof. Calgary Univ. 1978; mem. Royal Soc. of Canada, Acad. Royale de Belgique, Acad. des Lettres françaises; Hon. mem. Boivin Center of French Language and Culture, Univ. of Massachusetts, USA; Chevalier, Légion d'honneur; Dr hc (York Univ., Toronto) 1975, (Lyon) 2003, (Ottawa) 2004, (Lyon) 2005; Prix de la langue française 1961, Prix France-Québec 1964, Prix Médicis 1966, Prix de l'Acad. Française 1983, Prix Athanase-David (Québec) 1983, Prix Nessim Habif (Acad. Royale de Belgique) 1991, Prix de la Fondation Prince Pierre de Monaco, Prix du Gouverneur Général (Canada) (three times), Prix Gilles Corbeil 2006 and others. *Publications:* La belle bête 1959, Tête blanche 1960, Le jour est noir 1962, Existences (poems), Pays voilés (poems) 1964, Une saison dans la vie d'Emmanuel 1965, L'insoumise 1966, Les voyageurs sacrés 1966, David Sterne 1967, L'océan 1967, L'exécution 1968, Manuscrits de Pauline Archange 1968, Vivre, vivre 1969, Les apparences 1970, Le loup 1972, Un Joualonais sa Joualonie 1973, Theatre radiophonique 1974, Fièvre 1974, Une liaison parisienne 1976, La nef des sorcières 1976, Les nuits de l'underground 1978, Le sourd dans la ville 1980, Visions d'Anna 1982, Pierre 1984, Sommeil d'hiver 1985, Fière 1985, L'île 1988 (plays), L'ange de la solitude (novel) 1989, Un jardin dans la tempête (play) 1990, Parcours d'un Ecrivain: Notes Americaines (essay) 1993, L'Exile (short stories) 1993, Soifs (novel) 1995, Dans la foudre et la lumière (novel), Théatre (Ed.), Des Rencontres Humaines 2002, Dans la foudre et la lumière 2002 (novel), Noces à midi au-dessus de l'abîme (play) 2004, Augustino et le choeur de la destruction (novel) 2007, Naissance de Rebecca à l'ère des Tourments (Gov. Gen's Award for Fiction) 2008. *Leisure interests:* painting and drawing, cycling, handwriting analysis, travel. *Address:* Agence Goodwin, 839 Sherbrooke Estate, Suite 2, Montréal, H26 1K6, Canada (office); 717 Windsor Lane, Key West, FL 33040, USA (home). *Telephone:* (514) 598-5252 (office); (305) 292-9450 (home). *Fax:* (514) 598-1878 (office). *E-mail:* goodleim@qc.aira.com (office).

BLAIS, Pierre, BA, LLL, PC; Canadian politician; b. 30 Dec. 1948, Berthier-sur-Mer, Québec; m. Chantal Fournier; two s. two d.; ed Laval Univ.; pnr, Montmagny law practice 1976–84; Prof., Univ. du Québec à Rimouski 1982; Prof., Laval Univ. 1982–84; Parl. Sec. to Minister of Agric. 1984–86, to Deputy Prime Minister 1987–87; Minister of State (Agric.) 1987–93, Solicitor-Gen. of Canada 1989–90 Minister of Consumer and Corp. Affairs 1990–93; Minister of Justice and Attorney-Gen. 1993; Justice of the Fed. Court of Canada, Trial Division, ex officio mem. Court of Appeal and Judge, Court Martial Appeal Court of Canada 1998–, Judge of Fed. Court 2003–; Privy Council Pres. 1993. *Leisure interests:* skiing, reading, swimming. *Address:* Federal Court, Ottawa, Ontario K1A 0H9, Canada (office). *Website:* www.fct-cf.gc.ca (office).

BLAKE, Francis (Frank) S., BA, JD; American lawyer and business executive; *Chairman and CEO, The Home Depot Inc.;* b. 30 Aug. 1949, Boston; s. of George Baty Blake and Rosemary Blake (née Shaw); m. Anne McChristian 1977; one s. one d.; ed Harvard Coll., Columbia Univ. School of Law; Legis. Aide, Jt Cttee on Social Welfare, Mass Legislature, Boston 1971–73; law clerk, US Court of Appeals, NY 1976–77, US Supreme Court, Washington, DC 1976–78; Assoc., Leva, Hawes, Symington, Martin & Oppenheimer 1978–81; Deputy Counsel to Vice-Pres. George Bush, The White House 1981–83; Partner, Swidler Berlin & Strelw 1983–85; Gen. Counsel, US Environmental Protection Agency 1985–88; Vice-Pres. and Gen. Counsel, GE Power Systems 1991–95, Vice-Pres. Business Devt & Alliances 1995–98, Pres. Business Devt 1998–2000, Sr Vice-Pres. Corp. Business Devt and Gen. Counsel 2000–01; Deputy Sec. US Dept of Energy 2001–02; Exec. Vice-Pres. Business Devt and Corp. Operations, The Home Depot Inc. 2002–07, Vice Chair. and Exec. Vice-Pres. 2006–07, Chair. and CEO 2007–; mem. Bd Dirs Southern Co., Atlanta 2004–, Hudson Inst., Washington, DC. *Address:* The Home Depot Inc., 2455 Paces Ferry Road, NW, Atlanta, GA 30339-4024, USA (office). *Telephone:* (770) 433-821 (office). *Fax:* (770) 384-2356 (office). *E-mail:* info@homedepot.com (office). *Website:* www.homedepot.com (office).

BLAKE, John Clemens, MA, RCA; American artist; b. 11 Jan. 1945, Providence, RI; s. of John Holland Blake and Elizabeth Clemens (now Romano); ed Carnegie Inst. of Tech. (now Carnegie-Mellon Univ.), Yale Univ., Royal Coll. of Art, London; freelance visual artist in various media including drawing, installations, photographic constructions, film and time-based works, etc.; teaching positions include Hull Polytechnic 1975–76, London Coll. of Printing 1978–82, S Glamorgan Inst. of Higher Educ., S Wales 1983–84, W. de Kooning Academie, Rotterdam 1988–; residencies include

Hokkaido Fellowship, Japan 1984, Banff Centre for the Arts, Canada 1992, Bemis Center for the Arts, Omaha, Neb., USA 2000; Fulbright Fellow 1967–69; Nat. Endowment (USA) 1977; has lived and worked in London and Amsterdam/Woerden 1967–; Nat. Endowment for the Arts 1977, Arts Council Award (UK) 1979, Hokkaido Foundation Award (Japan) 1984. *Works in public collections:* Stedelijk Museum, Amsterdam, Museum Fodor, Amsterdam, Rijksmuseum Kroller-Muller, Otterlo, British Council, London, Eastern Arts Asscn, Cambridge, Musée de Toulon, France, Nat. Gallery of Australia, Melbourne, Stadhuis Middelburg, Netherlands, Tate Gallery, London, Museum Sztucki, Łódź, Arts Council of GB, London, Frans Hals Museum, Haarlem, Victoria & Albert Museum, London, Haagsgemeentemuseum, The Hague, Rijksdienst Collectie, Netherlands, Stadhuis Almere, Netherlands, Muzeum Narodowe, Warsaw, Van Reekum Museum, Apeldoorn, Netherlands, New Museum of Contemporary Art, Warsaw. *Commissioned works and works in public spaces include:* photo-construction installation (outdoor) for Entrepotdok (residential and business complex), Amsterdam 1987, Verpleeghuis 'De Vijf Havens' (jtly), Zevenkamp 1989, Light Trap (jtly) for St Jacobus Ziekenhuis, Zwijndrecht 1990, Veurs Coll., Leideschedam, Netherlands 1991, Haags Montessori Lyceum, The Hague 1991, photo-construction for 'De Cascade', Prov. Archive Offices, Groningen 1998, Dukaat/De Aker (residential and business complex, in collaboration with Tangram Architekten), Osdorp, Amsterdam 2000, outdoor installation incorporating two tram shelters and related object for Kunsthalte With de Withstraat – 'De hals', Museum Quarter/Westersingel, Rotterdam 2000. *Publications:* catalogue of ICA, London 1980, De Vleeshal in De Vleeshal – Their Eves/Hun Ogen (two catalogues) (co-author) 1983, 600 Eyes for Krzysztofory (text and photos) 1987, River – A Work in Almere (text and photos) 1991, Guard 1991, River 1991, John Blake on Aleph 1993, On the Ideal Place 1994, Remember Wtedy i Teraz – Teraz i Wtedy: John Blake's Works in Poland 1980–1994 1995, John Blake: Bunker – München 1996, De Hals: Kunsthalte witte de Withstraat 2000, S-P-I-N-E (with Peter Mason) 2002. *Address:* J.P. Blonk (agent), Gedempte Binnengracht 19A, 3441 AE Woerden, Netherlands. *Telephone:* (348) 481-850. *Fax:* (348) 482-554. *E-mail:* Jb@studiojohnblake.com (office). *Website:* www.studiojohnblake.com (office).

BLAKE, Sir Peter Thomas, Kt, CBE, RA, ARCA, RDI; British artist; b. 25 June 1932, Dartford, Kent; s. of Kenneth William Blake; m. 1st Jann Haworth 1963 (divorced 1982); two d.; m. 2nd Chrissy Wilson 1987; one d.; ed Gravesend Tech. Coll., Gravesend School of Art, Royal Coll. of Art; third assoc. artist of Nat. Gallery, London 1994–96; works exhibited in Inst. of Contemporary Art 1958, 1960, Guggenheim Competition 1958, Cambridge 1959, Royal Acad. 1960, Musée d'Art Moderne, Paris 1963; works in perm. collections, Trinity Coll., Cambridge, Carlisle City Gallery, Tate Gallery, Arts Council of GB, Museum of Modern Art, New York, Victoria and Albert Museum, other maj. galleries; designed cover of Beatles' album Sgt Pepper's Lonely Hearts Club Band 1967; Dr hc (RCA). *Publications:* illustrations for Oxford Illustrated Old Testament 1968, several Arden Shakespeares and in various periodicals and magazines. *Leisure interests:* sculpture, wining and dining, going to rock and roll concerts. *Address:* c/o Waddington Galleries Ltd, 11 Cork Street, London, W1X 2LT, England; Michel Soskine Inc., 900 Park Avenue, New York, NY 10021, USA.

BLAKE, Quentin Saxby, OBE, CBE, RDI, MA, FCSD; British artist, writer, illustrator and teacher; b. 16 Dec. 1932, Sidcup, Kent; s. of William Blake and Evelyn Blake; ed Downing Coll., Cambridge, London Inst. of Educ., Chelsea School of Art; freelance illustrator 1957–; Tutor, Royal Coll. of Art 1965–86, Head of Illustration Dept 1978–86, Visiting Prof. 1989–; first British Children's Laureate 1999–2001; Sr Fellow RCA 1988; Hon. Fellow, Univ. of Brighton 1996, Downing Coll. Cambridge 2000, Cardiff Univ. 2006, Hon. RA; Companion, Guild of George; Officier, Ordre des Arts et des Lettres 2002; Dr hc (London Inst.) 2000, (Northumbria) 2001, (RCA) 2001, (Open Univ.) 2006, (Loughborough) 2007, (Anglia Ruskin Univ.); Hon. DLitt (Cambridge) 2004. *Publications include:* Patrick 1968, Angelo 1970, Mister Magnolia 1980, Quentin Blake's Nursery Rhyme Book 1983, The Story of the Dancing Frog 1984, Mrs Armitage on Wheels 1987, Mrs Armitage Queen of the Road, Quentin Blake's ABC 1989, All Join In 1992, Cockatoos 1992, Simpkin 1993, La Vie de la Page 1995, The Puffin Book of Nonsense Verse 1996, Mrs Armitage and the Big Wave 1997, The Green Ship 1998, Clown 1998, Drawing for the Artistically Undiscovered (with John Cassidy) 1999, Fantastic Daisy Artichoke 1999, Words and Pictures 2000, The Laureate's Party 2000, Zagazoo 2000, Tell Me a Picture 2001, Loveykins 2002, A Sailing Boat in the Sky 2002, Laureate's Progress 2002, Angel Pavement 2004, The Life of Birds 2005; illustrations for over 250 works for children and adults, including collaborations with Roald Dahl, Russell Hoban, Joan Aiken, Michael Rosen, John Yeoman, Michael Morpurgo. *Address:* c/o AP Watt Ltd, 20 John Street, London, WC1N 2DR, England (office); Flat 8, 30 Bramham Gardens, London, SW5 0HF, England (home). *Telephone:* (20) 7405-6774 (office). *Fax:* (20) 7831-2154 (office). *E-mail:* apw@apwatt.co.uk (office). *Website:* www.apwatt.co.uk (office); www.quentinblake.com.

BLAKEMORE, Colin (Brian), PhD, ScD, DSc, FRS, FMedSci, CBiol; British neuroscientist and academic; *Professor of Neuroscience, Universities of Oxford and Warwick;* b. 1 June 1944, Stratford-upon-Avon; s. of Cedric Norman and Beryl Ann Blakemore; m. Andrée Elizabeth Washbourne 1965; three d.; ed King Henry VIII School, Coventry, Corpus Christi Coll., Cambridge, Univ. of California, Berkeley, USA; Harkness Fellowship, Univ. of California, Berkeley 1965–67; Univ. Demonstrator, Physiological Lab., Univ. of Cambridge 1968–72, Lecturer in Physiology 1972–79, Fellow and Dir of Medical Studies, Downing Coll. Cambridge 1971–79; Visiting Prof., New York Univ. 1970, MIT 1971, Univ. of Toronto 1984, McMaster Univ. 1992, Univ. of California, Davis 1980, 1995–97; Visiting Scientist, Salk Inst., San Diego 1982–83, 1992; Locke Research Fellow, Royal Soc. 1976–79; Waynflete Prof. of

Physiology, Univ. of Oxford 1979–2007; Prof. of Physiology, Univ. of Warwick; Professorial Fellow, Magdalen Coll. Oxford 1979–; Vice-Chair. European Dana Alliance for the Brain 1996–; CEO MRC 2003–07; Vice-Pres. BAAS 1990–97, 1998–2001, Pres. 1997–98, Chair. 2001–03; Pres. British Neuroscience Asscn 1997–2000, Physiological Soc. 2001–03, Biosciences Fed. 2002–04; Dir McDonnell-Pew Centre for Cognitive Neuroscience, Oxford 1990–2003, MRC Interdisciplinary Research Centre for Cognitive Neuroscience, Oxford 1996–2003; Assoc. Dir MRC Research Centre in Brain and Behaviour, Oxford 1990–96; Commr UK Drug Policy Comm. 2006–; mem. Advisory Council Asscn of the British Pharmaceutical Industry 2007–; Chair. Gen. Advisory Cttee on Science, Food Standards Agency 2007–, A*STAR – Duke-NUS Grad. Medical School Partnership in Neuroscience, Singapore 2007–; Dir (non-exec.) Harkness Fellows Asscn and Transatlantic Trust 2001–, Physiological Soc. 2001–, SANE 2001–, Biosciences Fed. 2002–, Coalition for Medical Progress, British Technology Group plc 2007–; Assoc. Ed. NeuroReport 1989–2003; Ed.-in-Chief IBRO News 1986–2000; mem. Editorial Bd Perception 1971, Behavioral and Brain Sciences 1977, Journal of Developmental Physiology 1978–86, Experimental Brain Research 1979–89, Language and Communication 1979, Reviews in the Neurosciences 1984–, News in Physiological Sciences 1985, Clinical Vision Sciences 1986, Chinese Journal of Physiological Sciences 1988, Advances in Neuroscience 1989–, Vision Research 1993–, Int. Review of Neurobiology 1996–, EuroBrain 1998, American Journal of Bioethics 2006–; Leverhulme Fellowship 1974–75; Lethaby Prof., RCA, London 1978; Storer Lecturer, Univ. of California, Davis 1980, Regents' Prof. 1995–96; Macallum Lecturer, Univ. of Toronto 1984; Fellow, World Econ. Forum 1994–98; Founder Fellow, Acad. of Medical Sciences 1998–; Foreign mem. Royal Netherlands Acad. of Arts and Sciences 1993; mem. Experimental Psychology Soc. 1968–, Research Defence Soc. (Chair. of Council 2007–) 1969–, European Brain and Behaviour Soc. 1972–, Int. Brain Research Org. 1973–, Cambridge Philosophical Soc. 1975–, Soc. foe Neuroscience 1981–, Oxford Medical Soc. 1986–, Child Vision Research Soc. 1986–, British Asscn for the Advancement of Science (Pres. 1997–98, Chair. 2001–03) 1989–, Int. Soc. for Myochemistry 1989–, European Biomedical Research Asscn (founder mem.) 1994–, Inst. of Biology 1996–, Worshipful Co. of Spectacle Makers (mem. Livery 1998–) 1997–, Fed. of European Neuroscience Socs 2000–; Patron and mem. Professional Advisory Panel Headway (Nat. Head Injuries Asscn) 1997–; Patron Asscn for Art, Science, Eng and Tech. (ASCENT) 1997–; Freeman of the City of London 1997; Hon. Pres. World Cultural Council 1983–; Hon. Prof., Peking Union Medical Coll. 2005; Hon. Fellow, Corpus Christi Coll. Cambridge 1994, Cardiff, Univ. of Wales 1998, Downing Coll. Cambridge 1999; Hon. FRCP 2004; Hon. Fellow, BAAS 2001, Inst. of Biology 2004, Indian Acad. of Neurosciences 2007, British Pharmacological Soc. 2007; Hon. mem. Chelsea Arts Club 1992, Alpha Omega Alpha Honor Medical Soc. 1996, Physiological Soc. 1998, Maverick Club 1999, Motor Neurone Disease Asscn; Hon. Assoc. Rationalist Press Asscn 1986, Rationalist Int. 2000, Cambridge Union Soc. 2003; Hon. DSc (Aston) 1992, (Salford) 1994, (Manchester) 2005, (Aberdeen) 2005, (King's Coll. London) 2007; Hon. DM (Nottingham) 2008; Robert Bing Prize, Swiss Acad. of Medical Sciences 1975, Man of the Year, Royal Soc. for Disability and Rehabilitation 1978, John Locke Medal, Worshipful Soc. of Apothecaries 1983, Netter Prize, Acad. Nat. de Médecine, Paris 1984, Bertram Louis Abrahams Lecture, Royal Coll. of Physicians 1986, Cairns Memorial Lecture and Medal, Soc. of British Neurological Surgeons 1986, Norman McAllister Gregg Lecture and Medal, Royal Australian Coll. of Ophthalmologists 1988, Royal Soc. Michael Faraday Medal 1989, Robert Doyne Medal, Oxford Ophthalmology Congress 1989, John P. McGovern Science and Soc. Lecture and Medal 1990, Montgomery Medal 1991, Sir Douglas Robb Lectures, Univ. of Auckland 1991, Osler Medal, Royal Coll. of Physicians 1993, Ellison-Cliffe Medal, Royal Soc. of Medicine 1993, Charles F. Prentice Award, American Acad. of Optometry 1994, Annual Review Prize Lecture, Physiological Soc. 1995, Centenary Lecture, Univ. of Salford 1996, Alcon Prize 1996, Newton Lecture 1997, Cockcroft Lecture, UMIST 1997, Memorial Medal, Charles Univ., Prague 1998, Alfred Meyer Award, British Neuropathological Soc. 2001, Inst. of Biology Charter Award and Medal 2001, Baly Medal, Royal Coll. of Physicians (Dyster Trust) 2001, British Neuroscience Asscn Outstanding Contrib. to Neuroscience 2001, Menzies Medal, Menzies Foundation, Melbourne 2001, Bioindustry Asscn Award for Outstanding Personal Contrib. to Bioscience 2004, Lord Crook Gold Medal, Worshipful Co. of Spectacle Makers 2004, Edinburgh Medal, City of Edinburgh 2005, Science Educator Award, Soc. for Neuroscience 2005, Kenneth Myer Medal, Howard Florey Inst., Univ. of Melbourne 2006. *Films:* several educational films on neuroscience (Silver Award, BMA Film Competition 1972, Silver Award, Padua Int. Film Festival 1973, BMA Certificate of Educational Commendation 1974). *Radio:* The Reith Lectures (BBC Radio 4) 1976, Machines with Minds (five-part series) 1983. *Television:* Royal Inst. Christmas Lectures 1983, The Mind Machine (13-part series) 1988. *Publications:* Handbook of Psychobiology (ed.) 1975, Mechanics of the Mind 1977, Mindwaves (ed.) 1987, The Mind Machine 1988, Images and Understanding (ed.) 1990, Vision: Coding and Efficiency 1990, Sex and Society 1999, Oxford Companion to the Body 2001, The Physiology of Cognitive Processes (co-ed.) 2003, The Roots of Visual Awareness (co-ed.) 2003; contribs to Constraints on Learning 1973, Illusion in Art and Nature 1973, The Neurosciences Third Study Program 1974 and to professional journals and to nat. newspapers and magazines. *Leisure interests:* running and the arts. *Address:* Room 5609, Nuffield Department of Clinical Medicine, University of Oxford, John Radcliffe Hospital, Oxford, OX3 9DU, England (office). *Telephone:* (1865) 228964 (office). *Fax:* (1865) 222901 (office). *E-mail:* colin.blakemore@ndm.ox.ac.uk (office). *Website:* www.dpag.ox.ac.uk (office).

BLAKEMORE, Michael Howell, AO, OBE; Australian theatre and film director; b. 18 June 1928, Sydney; s. of Conrad Blakemore and Una Mary (née Litchfield) Blakemore; m. 1st Shirley Bush 1960; one s.; m. 2nd Tanya McCallin 1986; two d.; ed The King's School, NSW, Sydney Univ., Royal Acad. of Dramatic Art, UK; actor with Birmingham Repertory Theatre, Shakespeare Memorial Theatre etc. 1952–66; Co-Dir Glasgow Citizens' Theatre 1966–68 (first production The Investigation); Assoc. Artistic Dir Nat. Theatre, London 1971–76; Dir Players, New York, USA 1978; Resident Dir Lyric Theatre, Hammersmith, London 1980; Best Dir, London Critics 1972, Drama Desk Award 1982, Outer Critics' Circle Awards 1982, 1989, Hollywood Dramalogue Award 1983, Drama League Award 1997, Standard Film Award 1982, Film Critics' Award 1994, two Tony Awards 2000, three Drama Desk Awards 1984, 2000, Helpman Award 2002. *Films include:* A Personal History of the Australian Surf (writer and dir) 1981, Privates on Parade (dir) 1983, Country Life (writer and dir) 1994. *Productions include:* A Day in the Death of Joe Egg 1967, Arturo Ui 1969, The National Health 1969, Long Day's Journey into Night 1971, The Front Page, Macbeth 1972, The Cherry Orchard 1973, Design for Living 1973, Separate Tables 1976, Plunder 1976, Privates on Parade 1977, Candida 1977, Make and Break 1980, Travelling North 1980, The Wild Duck 1980, All My Sons 1981, Noises Off 1982 (Drama Desk Award, New York 1983–84), Benefactors 1984, Lettice and Lovage 1987, Uncle Vanya 1988, City of Angels 1989, Lettice and Lovage 1990, After the Fall 1990, The Ride Down Mount Morgan 1991, Tosca (Welsh Nat. Opera) 1992, The Sisters Rosensweig 1994, Death Defying Acts 1995, The Life 1997, Copenhagen 1998, Kiss Me Kate 1999, Three Sisters 2003, Democracy 2003, Is He Dead (Broadway) 2007, Blithe Spirit (Broadway) 2009. *Television productions include:* Long Day's Journey into Night 1972, Hay Fever (Denmark) 1978, Tales from the Hollywood Hills (USA) 1988. *Publications:* Next Season (novel) 1969, Australia Fair? (anthology) 1985, Arguments With England (autobiog.) 2004. *Leisure interest:* surfing. *Address:* 47 Ridgmount Gardens, London, WC1E 7AT, England (home). *Telephone:* (20) 7209-0608 (home). *Fax:* (20) 7209-0141 (home).

BLAKENEY, Allan Emrys, PC, OC, QC, LLB, MA, FRSC; Canadian politician (retd) and academic; *Visiting Scholar, University of Saskatchewan;* b. 7 Sept. 1925, Bridgewater, Nova Scotia; s. of John Cline Blakeney and Bertha May Davies; m. 1st Mary Elizabeth Schwartz 1950 (died 1957); one s. one d.; m. 2nd Anne Louise Gorham 1959; one s. one d.; ed Dalhousie Univ. and Univ. of Oxford, UK; Sec. and legal adviser to Crown Corpn, Govt of Sask. 1950–55; Chair. Sask. Securities Comm. 1955–58; Pnr Davidson, Davidson & Blakeney (law firm) 1958–60; mem. Legis. Ass. 1960–88 (retd); Govt of Sask. Minister of Educ. 1960–61, Prov. Treas. 1961–62, Minister of Health 1962–64, Leader of the Opposition 1970–71, 1982–87, Premier 1971–82; mem. Senate, Univ. of Sask. 1960–62; Chair. of Wascana Centre Authority 1962–64; Pnr Griffin, Blakeney, Beke (law firm) 1964–70; Pres. New Democratic Party of Canada 1969–71; Laskin Prof. of Constitutional Law, Osgoode Hall Law School, York Univ. 1988–90; Law Foundation Prof. of Public Law, Univ. of Sask. 1990–92, Visiting Scholar 1992–; Dr hc (Mount Allison Univ.) 1980, (Dalhousie) 1980, (York) 1991, (Univ. of Western Ont.) 1991, (Univ. of Regina) 1993, (Univ. of Sask.) 1995. *Publications:* Political Management in Canada (with S. Borins) (2nd edn) 1998; articles on public affairs. *Address:* Room 107, College of Law, 15 Campus Drive, University of Saskatchewan, Saskatoon, Saskatchewan, S7N 5A6 (office); 1752 Prince of Wales Avenue, Saskatoon, Saskatchewan, S7K 3E5, Canada (home). *Telephone:* (306) 966-5881 (office); (306) 934-0626 (home). *Fax:* (306) 966-5900 (office). *E-mail:* blakeney@duke.usask.ca (office); annebl2002@yahoo.ca (home).

BLAKENHAM, 2nd Viscount (cr. 1963), of Little Blakenham; **Michael John Hare,** PC, OBE, DL; British business executive; b. 25 Jan. 1938, London; s. of the late 1st Viscount Blakenham and Hon. Beryl Nancy Pearson; m. Marcia P. Hare 1965; one s. two d.; ed Eton Coll. and Harvard Univ.; nat. service 1956–57; with English Electric Co. 1958; Lazard Brothers 1961–63; Standard Industrial Group 1963–71; Royal Doulton 1972–77; Chief Exec. Pearson PLC 1978–90, Chair. 1983–97; Chair. Financial Times 1983–93; Partner Lazard Partners 1984–97 (Dir Lazard Bros. 1975–97); Dir Sotheby's Holdings Inc. 1987–, MEPC PLC 1990–98 (Chair. 1993–98); mem. Int. Advisory Bd Lafarge 1979–97 (Dir 1997–); mem. Int. Advisory Group Toshiba 1997–; Dir UK–Japan 2000 Group 1990–; Chair. Royal Soc. for Protection of Birds 1981–86; Pres. Sussex Wildlife Trust 1983–, Bristol Trust for Ornithology 2001–; mem. House of Lords Select Cttee on Science and Tech. 1984–88, Nature Conservancy Council 1986–90; Trustee The Royal Botanic Gardens, Kew 1991– (Chair. 1997–); Conservative. *Address:* House of Lords, London, SW1A 0PW; 1 St Leonard's Studio, London, SW3 4EN, England (home).

BLAKERS, Andrew, PhD; Australian scientist and academic; *Director, Centre for Sustainable Energy Systems and Director, Australian Research Council (ARC) Centre for Solar Energy Systems, Australian National University;* currently Dir Centre for Sustainable Energy Systems and Dir Australian Research Council (ARC) Centre for Solar Energy Systems, ANU; fmr Humboldt Fellow; has held ARC QEII and Sr Research Fellowships; Fellow, Acad. of Technological Sciences and Eng, Inst. of Energy, Inst. of Physics; Walsh Medal, Australian Inst. of Physics (co-recipient). *Achievements include:* co-invented, with Dr Klaus Weber, sliver cell photovoltaic tech. which uses one tenth of the silicon used in conventional solar panels, with similar power, performance and efficiency. *Publications:* more than 200 scientific papers in professional journals on photovoltaic and solar energy systems, particularly advanced thin film silicon solar cell tech. and solar concentrator cells, components and systems; 12 patents. *Address:* RoomE224, Department of Engineering (Bldg 32), Australian National University, Canberra, ACT 0200, Australia (office). *Telephone:* (2) 6125-5905 (office). *Fax:* (2) 6125-0506 (office). *E-mail:* andrew.blakers@anu.edu.au (office). *Website:* solar.anu.edu.au (office).

BLANC, Christian; French business executive and politician; b. 17 May 1942, Talence, Gironde; s. of Marcel Blanc and Emcarma Miranda; m. Asa

Hagglund 1973; two d.; ed Ecole Montgolfier, Bordeaux, Lycée Montesquieu, Bordeaux and Inst. d'Etudes Politiques, Bordeaux; Asst Dir Sopexa-Scandinavie 1969; Société centrale d'équipement du territoire 1970–74; Chef du bureau, State Secr. for Youth and Sport 1974–76; Asst Del.-Gen. Agence technique interministérielle pour les loisirs et le plein air 1976–80; Dir du Cabinet to Edgard Pisani, mem. of Comm. of EC, Brussels 1981–83; Prefect, Commr, République des Hautes-Pyrénées 1983–84; special Govt assignment, New Caledonia 1985; Prefect for Seine-et-Marne 1985–89; Special Prefect 1989; Chair. and CEO RATP 1989–93; Chair. and CEO Air France (Admin. Council) 1993–97; Dir Middle E Airlines 1998–99, Marceau Investissements 1998–; Chair. Merrill Lynch France SA 2000–02; Presidential cand. 2002; Dir Action contre la Faim 1998–, Chancellery Univs Paris 1991–2001; Pres. Karaval 2001–; f. L'Ami Public; mem. Assemblee Nationale for Yvelines 2002–; Founder and Chair. Énergies démocrates 2002–; Chevalier, Légion d'honneur, Officier Ordre Nat. du Mérite. *Publication:* Le Lièvre et La Tortue (jtly) 1994, La Croissance ou le chaos 2006. *Address:* Assemblée nationale, 126 rue de l'Université, 75355 Paris Cedex 07 (office); Constituency Office, 18 Avenue de Bellevue, 78150 Le Chesnay, France (office). *Telephone:* 1-39-54-46-00 (office). *Fax:* 1-39-66-02-00 (office). *E-mail:* cblanc@assemblee-nationale.fr (office); cblanc@christian-blanc.net. *Website:* www.assemblee-nationale.fr (office); www.christian-blanc.net.

BLANC, Georges; French chef, author and business executive; b. 2 Jan. 1943, Bourg-en-Bresse; s. of Jean Blanc and Paule Blanc (née Tisserand); m. Jacqueline Masson 1966; two s. one d.; ed Ecole Hôtelière de Thonon-les-Bains; worked at Réserve de Beaulieu and Grand Hôtel de Divonne; mil. service as chef to Adm. Vedel on the Foch and the Clémenceau; returned to work in family business 1965, became head of firm 1968; Man. Dir Georges Blanc SA; Maître Cuisinier de France 1975; finalist in Meilleur Ouvrier de France competition 1976; has organized numerous events abroad to promote French cuisine; Founder mem., Second Vice-Pres. Chambre Syndicale de la Haute Cuisine Française 1986; Muncipal Councillor, Vonnas 1989; Officier, Ordre nat. du Mérite, Légion d'honneur, Commdr du Mérite agricole, des Arts et des Lettres, Chevalier des Palmes Académiques. *Publications:* Mes recettes 1981, La cuisine de Bourgogne (co-author), La nature dans l'assiette 1987, Le livre blanc des quatre saisons 1988, Les Blanc (jtly) 1989, Le Grand Livre de la Volaille (jtly) 1991, De la vigne à l'assiette 1995, la Cuisine de nos mères 2000, Cuisine de la vigne à la Carte 2000, Plat du jour 2003, Fêtes des Saveurs 2004, La Vie en Blanc 2008. *Leisure interests:* skiing, tennis. *Address:* Le Mère Blanc, 01540 Vonnas (Ain), France. *Telephone:* (4) 74-50-90-90. *Fax:* (4) 74-50-08-80. *E-mail:* gblanc@georgesblanc.com. *Website:* www.georgesblanc.com.

BLANC, Pierre-Louis, MenD, MèsL; French diplomatist; *President, Council of Francophone Affairs;* b. 18 Jan. 1926; s. of Lucien Blanc and Renée Blanc; m. 1st (wife deceased); one s. two d.; m. 2nd Jutta Freifrau von Cramm 1988; ed Univ. of Paris, Paris Inst. of Political Studies and Ecole Nat. d'Admin; served French embassies in Rabat 1956, Tokyo 1962, Madrid 1965; served Office of Pres. of Repub. 1967–69; pvt. staff of Gen. de Gaulle 1969–70; Acting Deputy Dir for Asia/Oceania, Govt of France 1969–71; Cultural Counsellor, London 1971–75; Deputy Dir for Personnel and Gen. Admin. Ministry of Foreign Affairs 1975; Dir Ecole Nat. d'Admin. 1975–82; Amb. to Sweden 1982–85, to Greece 1985–87; Perm. Rep. to UN 1987–91; Pres. Council of Francophone Affairs 1992–; Vice-Pres. Soc. des Amis des Archives de France 1994–2000; Commdr Légion d'honneur 1992. *Publication:* De Gaulle au soir de sa vie 1990, Valise Diplomatique 2004. *Leisure interest:* writing. *Address:* Quartier de Gergouven, 84560 Ménerbes, France. *Telephone:* 4-90-72-26-52 (home).

BLANC, Raymond René Alfred; French chef; b. 19 Nov. 1949, Besançon; s. of Maurice Blanc and Anne-Marie Blanc; two s.; ed Besançon Tech. Coll.; various positions 1968–76, mil. service 1970–71; Man. and Chef de cuisine, Bleu, Blanc, Rouge, Oxford 1976–77; opening of Les Quat'Saisons, Oxford as Chef Proprietor 1977; opening of Maison Blanc, patisserie and boulangerie 1978, Dir and Chair. 1978–88; opening of Le Manoir aux Quat'Saisons 1984; opening of Le Petit Blanc in Oxford 1996, in Cheltenham 1998, in Birmingham 1999 in Manchester 2000; weekly recipe column in the Observer newspaper 1988–90; mem. Acad. Culinaire de France, British Gastronomic Acad., Restaurateurs' Asscn of GB; rep. GB at Grand Final of Wedgwood World Master of Culinary Arts, Paris 2002; Hon. DBA (Oxford Brookes Univ.) 1999; European Chef of the Year 1989, Personalité de l'Année 1990, Craft Guild of Chefs Special Award 2002, AA Restaurant Guide Chef of the Year 2004, many awards for both the restaurant and hotel; Hon. OBE. *Television:* Blanc Mange (series) 1994, Passion for Perfection (series, Carlton TV) 2002, The Restaurant (series, BBC2) 2007–. *Publications:* Recipes from Le Manoir aux Quat'Saisons 1989, Cooking for Friends 1991, Blanc Mange 1994, Best A Blanc Christmas 1996; contrib. to Take Six Cooks 1986, Taste of Health 1987, Restaurants of Great Britain 1989, Gourmet Garden 1990, European Chefs 1990, Masterchefs of Europe 1998, Blanc Vite 1998, Foolproof French Cooking 2002, A Taste of My Life 2008. *Leisure interests:* classical music, opera, swimming, tennis, sailing. *Address:* Le Manoir aux Quat'Saisons, Church Road, Great Milton, Oxford, OX44 7PD, England (home). *Telephone:* (1844) 278881 (office). *Fax:* (1844) 278847 (home); (1844) 277212 (office). *E-mail:* raymond.blanc@blanc.co.uk (office). *Website:* www.manoir.com.

BLANCHARD, Francis, LLB; French international civil servant; b. 21 July 1916, Paris; s. of Antoine and Marie Blanchard (née Séris); m. Marie Claire Boué 1940 (deceased); two s. (one deceased); ed Univ. of Paris; French Ministry of the Interior 1942–47; Int. Org. for Refugees, Geneva 1947–51; Int. Labour Office, Geneva 1951; Asst Dir-Gen. 1956–68, Deputy Dir-Gen. 1968–74, Dir-Gen. 1974–89; Préfet 1956, Hon. Préfet 1977; mem. French Econ. and Social Council 1989–94; mem. council Centre d'étude des revenus et des coûts 1989–, de la population et de la famille 1990–; Commdr, Légion d'honneur; Dr hc (Brussels, Manila, Seoul, Cairo). *Publications:* L'Organisation Internationale du Travail 2004, De la guerre froide à un nouvel ordre mondial 2004. *Leisure interests:* skiing, tennis. *Address:* Prébailly, 01170 Gex (Ain), France (home). *Telephone:* (4) 50-41-51-70 (home).

BLANCHARD, James J., BA, MBA, JD; American fmr politician, lawyer and diplomatist; *Partner, DLA Piper US LLP;* b. 8 Aug. 1942, Detroit, Mich.; m. 2nd Janet Eifert; one s.; ed Michigan State Univ. and Univ. of Minnesota; admitted to Mich. Bar 1968; Legal Aid, elections bureau, Office of the Sec. of State, Mich. 1968–69; Asst Attorney-Gen., Mich. 1969–74, Admin. Asst to Attorney-Gen. 1970–71, Asst Deputy Attorney-Gen. 1971–72; mem. House of Reps 1975–83; Gov. of Mich. 1983–91; Pnr, Verner, Liipfert, Bernhard, McPherson and Hand 1991–93; Amb. to Canada 1993–96; Pnr, DLA Piper US LLP, Washington DC 1996–; admitted to DC Bar 2000; fmr mem. Pres.'s Comm. on Holocaust; several honorary degrees; Foreign Affairs Award for Public Service 1996, numerous other awards. *Publication:* Behind the Embassy Door 1998. *Address:* DLA Piper US LLP, 500 8thStreet, NW, Washington, DC 2004, USA (office). *Telephone:* (202) 799-4303 (office). *Fax:* (202) 799-5303 (office). *E-mail:* james.blanchard@dlapiper.com (office). *Website:* www.dlapiper.com/us/people/biodetail.aspx?id=9491 (office).

BLANCHARD, Olivier Jean, PhD; French economist and academic; *Economic Counsellor and Director of Research Department, International Monetary Fund;* b. 27 Dec. 1948, Amiens; m. Noelle Golinelli 1973; three d.; ed Univ. of Paris and Massachusetts Inst. of Tech.; Asst Prof., Harvard Univ., USA 1977–81, Assoc. Prof. 1981–83; Assoc. Prof., MIT, Cambridge, Mass, USA 1983–85, Prof. of Econs 1985–, Class of 1941 Prof. 1994–, Chair. Econs Dept 1998–2003; Econ. Counsellor and Dir Dept of Research, IMF 2008–; Vice-Pres. American Econ. Asscn 1995–96; Fellow, Econometric Soc.; mem. American Acad. of Arts and Sciences. *Publications:* Lectures on Macroeconomics (with S. Fischer) 1989, Reform in Eastern Europe 1991, Pour l'Emploi et Cohésion Sociale 1994, Spanish Unemployment: Is There a Solution? 1994, The Economics of Transition 1996, Macroeconomics 1997. *Leisure interest:* tennis. *Address:* International Monetary Fund, 700 19th Street, N.W., Washington DC, 20431; Department of Economics, E52-357, Massachusetts Institute of Technology, Cambridge, MA 02139, USA (office). *Telephone:* (202) 623-7000 (office); (617) 253-8891 (office). *Fax:* (202) 623-4661 (office); (617) 258-8112 (office). *E-mail:* publicaffairs@imf.org (office); blanchar@mit.edu (office). *Website:* www.imf.org (office); econ-www.mit.edu (office).

BLANCHEMAISON, Claude Marie, LenD; French diplomatist; b. 6 March 1944, Loches, Indre et Loire; s. of Roger Blanchemaison and Louise Blanchemaison (née Lacour); ed Faculté de Droit et de Sciences Economiques, Paris; First Sec., then Counsellor to Perm. Rep. at EC 1978–82; Asst Gen. Sec. to the Interministerial Cttee for Questions of European Econ. Cooperation 1982–85; Chargé d'Affaires, SA 1985–86; Deputy Dir Centre Admin., Ministry of Foreign Affairs 1986–89; Amb. to Vietnam 1989–92; Dir for Europe, Ministry of Foreign Affairs 1992–93, for Asia and Oceania 1993–96; Amb. to India 1996–2000, to Russia 2000–04, to Spain 2005–07; Sec.-Gen. Presidency of the EU 2007–08; Chevalier Legion d'honneur, Ordre nat. du Mérite, Ordre du Mérite agricole. *Address:* Ministry of Foreign and European Affairs, 37 quai d'Orsay, 75351 Paris Cedex 07, France (office). *Telephone:* 1-43-17-53-53 (office). *Fax:* 1-43-17-52-03 (office). *Website:* www.diplomatie.gouv.fr (office).

BLANCHETT, Cate; Australian actress; b. 14 May 1969, Melbourne; m. Andrew Upton 1997; three s.; ed Melbourne Univ., Nat. Inst. of Dramatic Art; Co-Artistic Dir Sydney Theatre Co. 2008–; BAFTA Award for Best Actress 1999, Best Actress, Nat. Bd of Review 2001, Golden Camera Award 2001, Career Achievement Award, Palm Springs Int. Film Festival 2007. *Plays include:* Top Girls, Kafka Dances (1993 Newcomer Award), Oleanna (Rosemont Best Actress Award), Hamlet, Sweet Phoebe, The Tempest, The Blind Giant is Dancing, Plenty. *Films include:* Police Rescue 1994, Parklands 1996, Paradise Road 1997, Thank God He Met Lizzie 1997, Oscar and Lucinda 1997, Elizabeth 1998 (Golden Globe Award), Dreamtime Alice (also co-producer), Bangers 1999, The Talented Mr Ripley 1999, An Ideal Husband 1999, Pushing Tin 1999, Bandit 2000, The Man Who Cried 2000, The Gift 2000, Bandits 2000, The Lord of the Rings: The Fellowship of the Ring 2001, Charlotte Gray 2001, The Shipping News 2002, The Lord of the Rings: The Two Towers 2002, Heaven 2002, Veronica Guerin 2003, The Lord of the Rings: The Return of the King 2003, Coffee and Cigarettes 2003, The Aviator (Best Supporting Actress, Screen Actors Guild Awards 2005, Best Actress in a Supporting Role, BAFTA Awards 2005, Best Supporting Actress, Acad. Awards 2005) 2004, The Life Aquatic 2004, Stories of Lost Souls 2005, Little Fish 2005, Babel 2006, The Good German 2006, Notes on a Scandal (Best Supporting Actress, Toronto Film Critics Association) 2006, I'm Not There (Best Actress, Venice Film Festival 2007, Golden Globe for Best Supporting Actress 2008) 2007, Elizabeth: The Golden Age 2007, Indiana Jones and the Kingdom of the Crystal Skull 2008, The Curious Case of Benjamin Button 2008. *TV includes:* Heartland (miniseries) 1994, Bordertown (miniseries) 1995. *Address:* c/o Hylda Queally, Creative Artists Agency, 9830 Wilshire Boulevard, Beverly Hills, CA 90212-1825, USA (office); c/o Robyn Gardiner, PO Box 128, Surry Hill, 2010 NSW, Australia. *Telephone:* (310) 288-4545 (office). *Fax:* (310) 288-4800 (office). *Website:* www.caa.com (office).

BLANCHFLOWER, David G., BA, MSc, PhD; American economist and academic; *Bruce V. Rauner 1978 Professor of Economics, Dartmouth College;* b. 2 March 1952; ed Univ. of Leicester, UK, Univ. of Wales, Univ. of London (Queen Mary Coll.); Research Officer, Inst. for Employment Research, Univ. of Warwick 1984–86; Lecturer, Dept of Econs, Univ. of Surrey 1986–89; Assoc. Prof., Dept of Econs, Dartmouth Coll. 1989–93, Prof. 1993–, Bruce V. Rauner 1978 Prof. of Econs 2002–, Dept Chair. 1998–2000, Assoc. Dean of Faculty of Social Sciences 2000–01; Research Assoc., Nat. Bureau of Econ. Research (NBER); Research Fellow, CESifo, Center for Econ. Studies, Univ. of Munich, Germany; Research Fellow, Inst. for the Study of Labor (IZA), Univ. of Bonn;

mem. Monetary Policy Cttee, Bank of England 2006–09; mem. Editorial Bd Small Business Econs, Scottish Journal of Political Economy, Industrial and Labor Relations Review; Richard A. Lester Prize, Princeton Univ. 1994. *Publications:* numerous articles in professional journals. *Address:* Department of Economics, Dartmouth College, 6106 Rockefeller Hall, Hanover, NH 03755, USA. *Telephone:* (603) 646-2536. *Fax:* 603) 646-2122. *E-mail:* blanchflower@dartmouth.edu. *Website:* www.dartmouth.edu/~economic; www.dartmouth.edu/~blnchflr.

BLANCO, Serge; French fmr rugby union player; b. 31 Aug. 1958, Caracas, Venezuela; m. Lilianne Blanco; two s.; fmr fitter, Dassault aeronautical factory; played for Biarritz Olympique; first B cap, France v. Wales 1978, first full cap, France v. S Africa 1980; retd from int. rugby with 93 caps (233 test points) 1991; Chair. Ligue Nationale de Rugby (Nat. Rugby Union League) 1998–; business interests include the Serge Blanco Hotel and Health Spa on the Basque coast of France. *Address:* Complexe Hôtelies et Thalass-therapie Serge Blanco, 125 blvd. de la mer, BP517, 64705 Hendaye, Cedex, France. *Telephone:* 5-59-51-35-35. *Fax:* 5-59-51-36-00. *E-mail:* info@thalassoblanco.com. *Website:* www.thalassoblanco.com; www.lnr.fr.

BLANCO-CERVANTES, Raúl; Costa Rican politician and physician; b. 1903, San José; s. of Macedonio Blanco Alvarez and Dolores Cervantes Castro; m. Dora Martín Chavarría 1939; one s. four d.; ed Liceo de Costa Rica and Ludwig-Maximilians-Univ. Munich; Medical Dir, Sanatorio Carlos Durán 1933–67; Dir of Anti-Tuberculosis Dept, Ministry of Public Health 1937–67; Minister of Public Health 1948–49; Pres. Coll. of Physicians and Surgeons of Costa Rica 1946, 1947; Dir-Gen. of Assistance, Ministry of Public Health 1950, 1951; First Vice-Pres. of Costa Rica 1953–58, 1962–66; Acting Pres. of Costa Rica 1955; Dir Hospital Nacional para Tuberculosis 1958–; Pres. Colegio de Médicos y Cirujanos de Costa Rica 1946–47; mem. WHO Expert Advisory Panel on tuberculosis 1954–71; Gov. American Thoracic Soc., American Coll. of Chest Physicians –1966; First Pres. and Founder Sociedad Centroamericana de Tisiología; Hon. mem. Sociedad Mexicana de Tisiología. *Leisure interests:* reading, gardening. *Address:* Apdo 918, San José, Costa Rica. *Telephone:* 21-20-82.

BLAND, Sir (Francis) Christopher (Buchan), Kt; British business executive; b. 29 May 1938, Japan; s. of James Franklin MacMahon Bland and Jess Buchan Bland (née Brodie); m. Jennifer Mary, Viscountess Enfield 1981; one s. two step-s. two step-d.; ed Sedbergh and Queen's Coll., Oxford; 2nd Lt 5th Royal Inniskilling Dragoon Guards 1956–58; Lt, Northern Irish Horse (TA) 1958–69; Dir NI Finance Corpn 1972–76; Deputy Chair., IBA 1972–80; Chair., Sir Joseph Causton & Sons 1977–85, LWT (Holdings) 1984–94, Century Hutchinson Group 1984–89, Life Sciences Int. (fmrly Philicom) PLC 1987–97, NFC 1994–2000; Chair., British Telecommunications PLC (now BT Group) 2001–07; Dir, Nat. Provident Inst. 1977–88, Storehouse PLC 1988–93; mem. for Lewisham, GLC 1967–70; mem. Burnham Cttee 1970; Chair. Bow Group 1969–70; Ed., Crossbow 1971–72; mem. Prime Minister's Advisory Panel on Citizen's Charter 1991–94; Chair., NHS Review Group on Nat. Training Council and Nat. Staff Cttees 1982, Hammersmith and Queen Charlotte's Hosps (fmrly Hammersmith) SHA 1982–94, Hammersmith Hosps NHS Trust 1994–96, BBC Bd of Govs 1996–2001; Chair. RSC 2004–; Hon. LLD (South Bank) 1994. *Leisure interests:* fishing, skiing. *Address:* Blissamore Hall, Clanville, Andover, Hants., SP11 9HL; 10 Catherine Place, London, SW1E 6HF, England. *Telephone:* (20) 7834-0021; (1264) 772274 (Andover).

BLANDY, John Peter, CBE, MA, DM, MCh, FRCS, FACS; British professor of urology and surgeon; *Consulting Surgeon, London Hospital;* b. 11 Sept. 1927, Calcutta, India; s. of Sir E. Nicolas Blandy and Dorothy Kathleen Blandy, (née Marshall); m. Anne Mathias 1953; four d.; ed Clifton Coll., Balliol Coll., Oxford, London Hosp. Medical Coll.; House Physician and House Surgeon, London Hosp. 1952, Surgical Registrar and Lecturer in Surgery 1956–60, Sr Lecturer 1961, Consultant Surgeon 1964–92, now Consulting Surgeon; served RAMC 1953–55; Exchange Fellow, Presbyterian St Luke's Hosp., Chicago, USA 1960–61; Resident Surgical Officer, St Paul's Hosp. 1963–64; Consultant Surgeon, St Peter's Hosp. for the Stone 1969–92, now Consulting Surgeon; Prof. of Urology, Univ. of London 1969–92, Prof. Emer. 1992–; mem. BMA, Royal Soc. of Medicine (Hon. Fellow 1995), Council, Royal Coll. of Surgeons 1982–94 (Vice-Pres. 1992–94), Int. Soc. of Pediatric Urology Surgeons, Int. Soc. of Urological Surgeons, British Asscn of Urological Surgeons (Pres. 1984–86), European Asscn of Urology (Pres. 1986–88); Pres. European Bd of Urology 1991–92; Fellow Asscn of Surgeons; Hon. Fellow Balliol Coll. Oxford; Hon. Fellow Royal Coll. of Surgeons, Ireland 1992, Urological Soc. of Australasia, Mexican Coll. of Urology, American, Dutch, Canadian, Romanian and Danish Urological Asscns etc.; Hon. Freeman Worshipful Soc. of Barbers 2000; St Peter's Medal, Freyer Medal, Diaz Medal 1988, Grégoir Medal 2001. *Publications:* Tumours of the Testicle (with A. D. Dayan and H. F. Hope-Stone) 1970, Transurethral Resection 1971, Urology (ed.) 1976, Lecture Notes on Urology 1976, Operative Urology 1978, The Prostate (co-ed. with B. Lytton) 1986, Urology for Nurses (with J. Moors) 1989, Urological and Genital Cancer (co-ed. with R. T. D. Oliver and H. F. Hope-Stone) 1989, Urology (with C. G. Fowler) 1995, The Royal College of Surgeons of England (co-ed. with J. P. S. Lumley) 2000; papers in scientific journals. *Leisure interests:* painting and sculpture. *Address:* 362 Shakespeare Tower, Barbican, London, EC2Y 8NJ, England. *Telephone:* (20) 7638-4095. *E-mail:* john@blandy.net (home).

BLANK, Sir (Maurice) Victor, Kt, MA; British business executive; *Chairman, Lloyds TSB Group;* b. 9 Nov. 1942; s. of Joseph Blank and Ruth Blank (née Levey); m. Sylvia Helen Richford 1977; two s. one d.; ed Stockport Grammar School, St Catherine's Coll., Oxford; solicitor Supreme Court; joined Clifford-Turner as articled clerk 1964, solicitor 1966, partner 1969; Dir and Head Corp. Finance Charterhouse Bank 1981, Chief Exec. 1985–96, Chair. 1985–97, Chief Exec. Charterhouse PLC 1985–96, Chair. 1991–97, Dir Charterhouse Europe Holding 1993–, Chair. 1993–97; Chair. Wellbeing 1989–; Deputy Chair. Great Universal Stores (renamed GUS PLC) 1996–2000, Chair. 2000–06 (Dir 1993–2006); Founding Chair. Trinity Mirror 1999–2006; Chair. Lloyds TSB Group plc 2006–; Dir (non-exec.) Coats Ltd (fmrly Coats Viyella PLC), Chubb PLC (fmrly Williams PLC); Chair. Industrial Devt Advisory Bd; mem. Financial Reporting Council 2002–07; mem. Council, Univ. of Oxford 2000–07; Sr Adviser, Texas Pacific Group; Chair. Wellbeing of Women, UJS Hillel, Council of Univ. Coll. School. *Publication:* Weinberg and Blank on Take-overs and Mergers (jtly) 1971. *Leisure interests:* cricket, family, tennis, theatre. *Address:* Lloyds TSB Group plc, 25 Gresham Street, London, EC2V 7HN (office). *Telephone:* (20) 7626-1500 (home). *Fax:* (20) 7489-3484 (office). *E-mail:* info@lloydstsb.com (office). *Website:* www.lloydstsb.com (office).

BLANKFEIN, Lloyd Craig, BA, JD; American lawyer and business executive; *Chairman and CEO, Goldman Sachs;* b. 1954, The Bronx, New York City; m. Laura Susan Jacobs 1983; three c.; ed Harvard Univ. and Harvard Univ. Law School; corp. tax lawyer, Donovan, Leisure, Newton & Irvine 1978–81; joined J. Aron div. of Goldman Sachs as a gold bar and coin salesman 1981, Head or Co-head Currency and Commodities Div. 1994–97, Co-head Fixed Income, Currency and Commodities Division (FICC) 1997–2002, Vice-Chair. Goldman Sachs, with man. responsibility for FICC and Equities Div. 2002–04, mem. Bd of Dirs Goldman Sachs 2003–, Pres. and COO 2004–06, Chair. and CEO 2006–; mem. Harvard Univ. Cttee on Univ. Resources; mem. Bd of Dirs Partnership for New York City, The Robin Hood Foundation; mem. Bd of Overseers, Weill Medical Coll., Cornell Univ.; Trustee, New York Historical Soc. *Address:* The Goldman Sachs Group, 85 Broad Street, 17th Floor, New York, NY 10004, USA (office). *Telephone:* (212) 902-1000 (office). *Fax:* (212) 902-3000 (office). *E-mail:* info@gs.com (office). *Website:* www.goldmansachs.com (office).

BLANNING, Timothy Charles William, LittD, FBA; British academic; *Professor of Modern European History, University of Cambridge;* b. 21 April 1942, Wells, Somerset; s. of Thomas Walter Blanning and Gwendolen Marchant-Jones; m. Nicky Susan Jones 1988; one s. one d.; ed King's School, Bruton, Somerset, Sidney Sussex Coll., Cambridge; Research Fellow, Sidney Sussex Coll. 1965–68, Fellow 1968–, Asst Lecturer in History, Cambridge Univ. 1972–76, lecturer 1976–87, Reader in Modern European History 1987–92, Prof. of Modern European History 1992–. *Publications:* Joseph II and Enlightened Despotism 1970, Reform and Revolution in Mainz 1743–1803 1974, The French Revolution in Germany 1983, The Origins of the French Revolutionary Wars 1986, The French Revolution: Aristocrats versus Bourgeois? 1987, Joseph II 1994, The French Revolutionary Wars 1787–1802 1996, The French Revolution: Class War or Culture Clash? 1998, The Culture of Power and the Power of Culture 2002, The Pursuit of Glory: Europe 1648–1815 2007; Ed.: The Oxford Illustrated History of Modern Europe 1996, The Rise and Fall of the French Revolution 1996, History and Biography: Essays in Honour of Derek Beales (with Peter Wende), Reform in Great Britain and Germany 1750–1850 1999, The Short Oxford History of Europe: The Eighteenth Century 2000, The Short Oxford History of Europe: The Nineteenth Century 2000, Unity and Diversity in European Culture *c.* 1800 2006, The Triumph of Music 2008. *Leisure interests:* music, gardening, dog-walking. *Address:* Sidney Sussex College, Cambridge, CB2 3HU, England (office). *Telephone:* (1223) 335308 (office). *Fax:* (1223) 335968 (office). *E-mail:* tcb1000@cam.ac.uk (office).

BLASHFORD-SNELL, Col John Nicholas, OBE, FRGS, FRSGS; British explorer, writer and broadcaster; *Chairman, Scientific Exploration Society;* b. 22 Oct. 1936, Hereford; s. of the late Rev. Prebendary Leland John Blashford-Snell and Gwendolen Ives Blatshford-Snell (née Sadler); m. Judith Frances Sherman 1960; two d.; ed Victoria Coll., Jersey, RMA, Sandhurst; commissioned, Royal Engineers 1957; Commdr Operation Aphrodite (Expedition), Cyprus 1959–61; Instructor, Jr Leaders Regt Royal Engineers 1962–63; Instructor, RMA, Sandhurst 1963–66; Adjt, 3rd Div. Engineers 1966–67; Commdr The Great Abbai Expedition (Blue Nile) 1968; attended Staff Coll., Camberley 1969; Chair. Scientific Exploration Soc. 1969–; Commdr Dahlak Quest Expedition 1969–70, British Trans-Americas Expedition (Darien Gap) 1971–72; Officer Commdg 48th Field Squadron, Royal Engineers 1972–74; Commdr, Zaire River Expedition 1974–75; CO, Jr Leaders Regt, Royal Engineers 1976–78; Dir of Operations, Operation Drake 1978–81; Staff Officer, Ministry of Defence 1978–91, Consultant 1992–; Commdr, Fort George Volunteers 1982; Operations Dir, Operation Raleigh 1982–88, Dir-Gen. 1989–91; Dir SES Tibet Expedition 1987; Leader, Kalahari Quest Expedition 1990, Karnali Quest Expedition 1991, Karnali Gorges Expedition 1992, numerous exploration projects thereafter; Trustee, Operation New World 1995–; Chair. Just a Drop Charity 2001–04, Pres. 2004–, The Liverpool Construction-Crafts Guild 2003–05, Pres. 2005–; Pres. The British Travel Health Asscn 2006–; Freeman of the City of Hereford, Hon. Pres. The Vole Club 1996–; Hon. Life Pres. The Centre for Fortean Zoology 2003–; Hon. DSc (Durham); Hon. DEng (Bournemouth) 1997; The Livingstone Medal, The Darien Medal (Colombia) 1972, The Segrave Trophy, Paul Harris Fellow (Rotary Int.), Royal Geographical Soc. Patrons' Medal 1993, Gold Medal (Inst. of Royal Engineers) 1994, La Paz Medal (Bolivia) 2000. *Publications:* Weapons and Tactics (with T. Wintringham) 1970, The Expedition Organiser's Guide (with Richard Snailham) 1970, Where the Trails Run Out 1974, In the Steps of Stanley 1975, Expeditions the Experts' Way (with A. Ballantine) 1977, A Taste for Adventure 1978, Operation Drake (with M. Cable) 1981, In the Wake of Drake (with M. Cable) 1982, Mysteries: Encounters with the Unexplained 1983, Operation Raleigh, The Start of an Adventure 1987, Operation Raleigh, Adventure Challenge (with Ann Tweedy) 1988, Operation Raleigh, Adventure Unlimited (with Ann Tweedy) 1990, Something Lost Behind the Ranges 1994,

Mammoth Hunt (with Rula Lenska) 1996, Kota Mama: Retracing the Lost Trade Routes of Ancient South American Peoples (with Richard Snailham) 2000, East to the Amazon (with Richard Snailham) 2002. *Leisure interests:* motoring, shooting, food, wine, cryptozoology. *Address:* c/o Scientific Exploration Society, Expedition Base, Motcombe, nr Shaftesbury, Dorset SP7 9PB, England. *Telephone:* (1747) 854456 (office). *Fax:* (1747) 851351 (office). *E-mail:* jbs@ses-explore.org (office). *Website:* www.ses-explore.org (office).

BLATHERWICK, Sir David (Elliott Spiby), KCMG, OBE, MA; British diplomatist (retd); *Chairman, Egyptian–British Chamber of Commerce;* b. 13 July 1941, Lincoln; s. of Edward S. Blatherwick; m. (Margaret) Clare Crompton 1964; one s. one d.; ed Lincoln School and Wadham Coll. Oxford; Foreign Office 1964; Second Sec., Kuwait 1968–70; First Sec. Dublin 1970–73; FCO 1973–77; Head of Chancery, Cairo 1977–80; NI Office, Belfast 1981–83; FCO 1983–85; sabbatical, Stanford Univ., USA 1985–86; Head of Chancery, Perm. Mission to UN, New York 1986–89; Prin. Finance Officer and Chief Insp., FCO 1989–91; Amb. to Ireland 1991–95, to Egypt 1995–99; Chair. Egyptian–British Chamber of Commerce 1999–; Jt Chair. Anglo-Irish Encounter 2003–08. *Publication:* The Politics of International Telecommunications 1987. *Leisure interests:* walking, sailing, music. *Address:* Egyptian–British Chamber of Commerce, PO Box 4EG, 299 Oxford Street, London, W1A 4EG, England (office). *Telephone:* (20) 7499-3100 (office). *Fax:* (20) 7499-1070 (office). *E-mail:* info@theebcc.com (office). *Website:* www.theebcc.com (office).

BLATTER, Johann W. (Gianni), PhD; Swiss physicist and academic; *Professor of Theoretical Physics, Institute of Theoretical Physics, ETH Zürich;* b. 10 Nov. 1955; ed Eidgenössische Technische Hochschule Zürich (ETH Zürich); Researcher, Brown Boveri Co. (later Asea Brown Boveri), Baden, Switzerland 1983, 1987–93; fmr Post-Doctoral Researcher, Cornell Univ., Ithaca, NY, USA; Assoc. Prof., Inst. of Theoretical Physics, ETH Zürich 1993–96, Prof. of Theoretical Physics 1996–. *Address:* Institute of Theoretical Physics, HPZ G 10, Schafmattstr. 32, Hönggerberg, 8093 Zürich, Switzerland (office). *Telephone:* (44) 633-2568 (office). *Fax:* (44) 633-2570 (office). *E-mail:* blatterj@itp.phys.ethz.ch (office). *Website:* www.ethz.ch (office).

BLATTER, Joseph Sepp, BBA; Swiss international organization official and sports administrator; *President, Fédération Internationale de Football Association;* b. 10 March 1936, Visp, Viège; one d.; ed Sion and St Maurice Colls, Univ. de Lausanne; footballer (played for Swiss amateur league in top div.) 1948–71; mem. Bd Xamax Neuchâtel Football Club 1970–75; fmr Sec. Tourist Office, Valais; Sec.-Gen. Swiss Fed. of Ice-Hockey 1964; pursued journalistic and public relations activities in the fields of sport and pvt. industry; fmr Dir of Sports Timing and Public Relations, Longines SA; Tech. Dir of Devt Programmes, FIFA 1975–81, Gen. Sec. 1981–90, CEO 1990–98, Pres. 1998–; mem IOC 1999–; mem. Swiss Asscn of Sportswriters, Panathlon Club; Hon. mem. Swiss Football Asscn; Olympic Order, knighthood (with title of Dato') from Sultanate of Pahang, Order of Good Hope (South Africa), Order of Independence (First Class) (Jordan), Grand Cordon du Wissam Alaouite (Morocco), Medalla al Mérito Deportivo (Bolivia), Grand Cordon de l'Ordre de la République Tunisienne, Rank of Grand Officer of Wissam Al Arch (Morocco), Order of Merit in Diamond, Union of European Football Asscns (UEFA), Award of Merit (Yemen), Chevalier de la Légion d'honneur, Order of the Two Niles (Sudan), Commdr de l'Ordre Nat. du 27 Juin 1977 (Djibouti), Supreme Companion of Tambo (South Africa), Ordre de la Médaille de la Reconnaissance (Commdr Grade) (Cen. African Repub.), Commdr's Cross with Star of the Order of Merit (Hungary) 2006, Commdr de l'Ordre Nat. du Lion (Senegal) 2006, 1st Grau da Ordem do Dragoeiro (Cape Verde) 2006, Das Grosse Verdienstkreuz (Germany) 2006, Collar Estrella del Centenario de la Asociación de Fútbol (Paraguay) 2006, Danaker (Kyrgyzstan) 2006; Hon. DArts (De Montfort Univ.), Hon. PhD (Nelson Mandela Metropolitan Univ., SA) 2006; 'Int. Humanitarian of the Year' and 'Golden Charter of Peace and Humanitarianism' Int. Humanitarian League for Peace and Tolerance, American Global Award for Peace, Asian Football Conf. Diamond of Asia Award 2006, numerous awards from clubs, nat. asscns and confeds. *Address:* FIFA, FIFA-Strasse 20, PO Box 8044, Zürich, Switzerland (office). *Telephone:* (43) 222-7777 (office). *Fax:* (43) 222-7878 (office). *Website:* www.fifa.com.

BLATTMANN, René, LicIurU; Bolivian judge; *Second Vice-President, International Criminal Court;* b. 28 Jan. 1948, La Paz; m. Marianne Blattmann; one s. two d.; ed Bolivian Univ., La Paz, Univ. of Basle, Switzerland, Acad. of American and Int. Law, Dallas, TX, USA, Int. Faculty of Comparative Law, France and Italy; Prof. of Criminal Law, San Andrés State Univ., La Paz 1973–94, Bolivian Catholic Univ., La Paz 1993–94; Attorney at Law 1975–93; Minister of Justice and Human Rights 1994–97; Chief of Human Rights and Justice Area, UN Human Rights Verification Mission in Guatemala 1998–2000; Dir Andrean Jurists Comm. (CAJ) 1997–2002; Judge, Int. Criminal Court 2003–, Second Vice-Pres. 2006–; mem. La Paz Bar Asscn, Bolivian Bar Asscn, Andrean Jurists Comm.; Hon. Life mem. Wilshire Bar Asscn, LA, USA 1977–; Hon. mem. Experts Asscn on Criminal Law of Bogota and Cundinamarca, Colombia 1995; Bundesverdienstkreuz 2005; Dr hc (Univ. of Basle) 1998; Robert J. Storey Int. Award of Leadership, Southwestern Legal Foundation, Univ. of Texas at Dallas 1995, Diosa Temis Medal, Nat. Foundation Fora and Interdisciplinary Studies of Colombia 1995, Monseñor Leonidas Proaño Latin American Prize of Human Rights, Latin American Asscn of Human Rights (ALDHU) 1995, Carl Bertelsmann Int. Prize 2001; distinctions from Bolivian Nat. Police 1995, Journalists Asscn of La Paz 1996, Superior Court of Justice of Santa Cruz 1997, Superior Court of Justice of Tarija 1997, Nat. Chamber of Commerce 1997, City Council of La Paz 2000. *Address:* International Criminal Court, Maanweg 174, 2516 AB The Hague, Netherlands (office). *Telephone:* (70) 515-85-15 (office). *Fax:* (70) 515-87-89 (office). *E-mail:* pio@icc-cpi.int (office). *Website:* www.icc-cpi.int (office).

BLATTY, William Peter, MA, DHumLitt; American writer and screenwriter; b. 7 Jan. 1928, New York, NY; s. of Peter Blatty and Mary (née Mouakad) Blatty; m. Julie Alicia Witbrodt 1983; three s. three d.; ed Georgetown Univ., George Washington Univ. and Seattle Univ.; served in USAF 1951–54; ed. with US Information Agency 1955–57; Publicity Dir Univ. Southern Calif. 1957–58; Public Relations Dir Loyola Univ., Los Angeles 1959–60; Acad. Award of Acad. Motion Picture, Arts and Sciences 1973, Acad. of Fantasy, Science Fiction and Horror award 1980, Stoker Award for Lifetime Achievement 1998. *Screenplays:* The Man from the Diner's Club 1961, Promise Her Anything 1962, John Goldfarb, Please Come Home 1963, A Shot in the Dark 1964, The Great Bank Robbery 1967, What Did You Do in the War, Daddy? 1965, Gunn 1967, Darling Lili 1968, Twinkle, Twinkle, 'Killer' Kane (Golden Globe for Best Movie Screenplay) 1973, Mastermind 1976, The Ninth Configuration (also dir) 1978, The Exorcist (Golden Globe for Best Movie Screenplay 1980) 1973, The Exorcist III 1990, Exorcist: The Beginning 2004. *Writing for television:* Watts Made Out of Thread (series episode) (American Film Festival Blue Ribbon and Gabriel Award). *Publications:* Which Way to Mecca, Jack? 1959, John Goldfarb, Please Come Home 1963, I, Billy Shakespeare 1965, Twinkle, Twinkle, 'Killer' Kane 1966, The Exorcist 1970, I'll Tell Them I Remember You (autobiog.) 1973, The Exorcist: From Novel to Film 1974, The Ninth Configuration 1978, Legion 1983, Demons Five, Exorcists Nothing 1996, Elsewhere 1999.

BLAVATNIK, Leonard (Len), MS, MBA, PhD; American (b. Russian) business executive; *Chairman and President, Access Industries, Inc.;* b. (Leonid Valentinovich Blavatnik), 14 June 1957, Russia; m. Emily Blavatnik; ed Moscow Inst. of Transport Eng, Columbia Univ., New York and Harvard Business School, USA; emigrated with his family from Russia to USA 1978; f. Access Industries industrial group, New York 1986, Chair. and Pres. 1986–; Co-founder Renova and AAR investment cos; mem. Bd of Dirs TNK-BP, Warner Music Group, UC RUSAL, Basell Holdings, Eurasia Group; Chair. Supervisory Bd LyondellBasell Industries 2007–; Vice-Chair. Kennan Council, Woodrow Wilson Center, Washington, DC; mem. Global Advisory Bd Centre for Int. Business and Man., Univ. of Cambridge, Bd of Dean's Advisors, Harvard Business School, Academic Bd, Tel-Aviv Univ.; mem. Bd of Dirs 92nd Street Y, The White Nights Foundation of America, The Center for Jewish History in New York, Eurasia Group, New York. *Address:* Access Industries Inc., 730 5th Avenue, 20th Floor, New York, NY 10019-4105, USA (office). *Telephone:* (212) 247-6400 (office). *E-mail:* info@accessindustries.com (office). *Website:* www.accessindustries.com (office).

BLEARS, Rt Hon Hazel Anne, BA; British politician; *Secretary of State for Communities and Local Government;* b. 14 May 1956; d. of Arthur Blears and Dorothy Blears; m. Michael Halsall 1989; ed Wardley Grammar School, Trent Polytechnic; trainee solicitor, Salford Council 1978–80; in pvt. practice 1980–81; solicitor, Rossendale Council 1981–83, Wigan Council 1983–85; Prin. Solicitor, Manchester City Council 1985–97; MP (Labour) for Salford 1997–; Parl. Under-Sec. of State, Dept of Health 2001–03; Minister of State, Home Office 2003–06; Minister without Portfolio, Chair. of the Labour Party 2006–07; Sec. of State for Communities and Local Govt 2007–. *Publications:* Communities in Control 2003, The Politics of Decency 2004. *Leisure interests:* dance, motorcycling. *Address:* Department for Communities and Local Government, Eland House, Bressenden Place, London, SW1E 5DU (office); Jubilee House, 51 The Crescent, Salford, M5 4WX, England (office). *Telephone:* (20) 7944-4400 (office); (161) 925-0705 (constituency) (office). *Fax:* (20) 7944-4101 (office); (161) 743-9173 (constituency) (office). *E-mail:* blearsh@parliament.uk (office); contactus@communities.gsi.gov.uk (office). *Website:* www.hazelblears.co.uk (home); www.communities.gov.uk (office).

BLEASDALE, Alan; British playwright and novelist; b. 23 March 1946; s. of George Bleasdale and Margaret Bleasdale; m. Julia Moses 1970; two s. one d.; ed Wade Deacon Grammar School, Widnes, Padgate Teachers Training Coll.; schoolteacher 1967–75; Hon. DLitt (Liverpool Polytechnic) 1991; BAFTA Writers Award 1982, Royal TV Soc. Writer of the Year 1982; Best Writer Monte Carlo Int. TV Festival 1996 (for Jake's Progress). *Publications:* Scully 1975, Who's Been Sleeping in My Bed? 1977, No More Sitting on the Old School Bench 1979, Boys from the Blackstuff 1982, Are You Lonesome Tonight? (Best Musical, Evening Standard Drama Awards 1985) 1985, No Surrender (film script) 1986, Having a Ball 1986, It's a Madhouse 1986, The Monocled Mutineer (televised 1986) 1986, GBH (TV series) 1991, On the Ledge 1993, Jake's Progress (TV) 1995, Oliver Twist 1999 (Best Drama Series, TV and Radio Industries Club 2000). *Leisure interest:* rowing. *Address:* c/o The Agency, 24 Pottery Lane, Holland Park, London, W11 4LZ, England. *Telephone:* (20) 7727-1346. *E-mail:* info@theagency.co.uk. *Website:* www.theagency.co.uk.

BLECHA, Karl; Austrian politician; *President, Society for Austro-Arab Relations;* b. 16 April 1933, Vienna; s. of Karl Matthias Blecha and Rosa Blecha; m. 1st Ilse Steinhauser 1965; m. 2nd Burgunde Teuber 1982; two d.; m. 3rd Rosi Bahmüller 1999; one d.; ed Univ. of Vienna; vocational adviser in Vienna Employment Exchange and later reader in publishing firm; founder, Dir Inst. for Empiric Social Research 1963–75; mem. Lower Austrian SPÖ (Austrian Socialist Party) Exec. 1964–90; mem. Nationalrat 1970–89; Gen. Sec. SPÖ HQ 1976–81, Vice-Chair. SPÖ 1981–89; Federal Minister of the Interior 1983–89; Dir Mitropa Inst. for Econ. and Social Research, Vienna 1989–; fmr Chair. Socialist Student Movt, Socialist Young Generation, Austrian Asscn for Cultural Affairs; Pres. Austrian Soc. for Promotion of Research 1994–; Pres. Austrian Union of Pensioners 1999–; Pres. Council of Sr in Austria 1999–; Pres. Society for Austro-Arab Relations. *Address:* Society for Austro-Arab Relations, Stutterheimstraße 16-18/2/5, 1150 Vienna, Austria (office). *Telephone:* (1) 526-78-10 (office). *Fax:* (1) 526-77-95 (office). *Website:* www.saar.at (office).

BLEGEN, Judith; American singer (soprano); b. Lexington, KY; d. of Dr Halward Martin Blegen and Dorothy Mae (Anderson) Blegen; m. 1st Peter Singher 1967 (divorced 1975); one s.; m. 2nd Raymond Gniewek 1977; ed Curtis Inst. of Music, Philadelphia, Pa, Music Acad. of the West, Santa Barbara, Calif.; leading soprano, Nuremberg Opera, FRG 1965–68, Staatsoper, Vienna, Austria 1968–70, Metropolitan Opera, New York 1970–84; Vienna roles include Zerbinetta in Ariadne auf Naxos, Rosina in The Barber of Seville, Aennchen in Der Freischütz, Norina in Don Pasquale; numerous performances at Metropolitan include Marzelline in Fidelio, Sophie in Werther, Mélisande in Pelléas et Mélisande, Sophie in Der Rosenkavalier, Adina in L'Elisir d'amore, Juliette in Roméo et Juliette, Susanna in The Marriage of Figaro; other appearances include title role in Manon, Tulsa Opera, Gilda in Rigoletto, Chicago, Despina in Così fan tutte, Covent Garden, Blondchen in The Abduction from the Seraglio, Salzburg Festival, Mélisande in Pélleas et Mélisande, Spoleto Festival, Susanna in The Marriage of Figaro, Edinburgh Festival, Sophie, Paris Opera; Fulbright Scholarship; Artistic Advisor, Opera Naples; Grammy Awards. *Recordings include:* La Bohème, Carmina Burana, Symphony No. 4, Harmonienmesse, The Marriage of Figaro, A Midsummer Night's Dream, Nelson Mass, Gloria, Peer Gynt Suite, Lieder recital (Richard Strauss and Hugo Wolf), baroque music recital. *Address:* c/o Opera Naples, 6017 Pine Ridge Road, PO Box 386, Naples, FL 34119, USA. *Website:* www.operanaples.com.

BLEICKEN, Jochen, DPhil; German academic; *Professor Emeritus of History, Göttingen University;* b. 3 Sept. 1926, Westerland-Sylt; s. of Max Bleicken and Marie (née Jensen) Bleicken; ed Univs of Kiel and Frankfurt am Main; Asst Althistorische Seminar, Göttingen 1955–62, Teacher in Early History 1961; Prof. in Ancient History, Hamburg 1962–67, Frankfurt a. M. 1967–77, Göttingen 1977–91; Prof. Emer. 1991–; mem. Wissenschaftliche Geschichte, Johann Wolfgang Goethe Univ., Frankfurt 1967–, Deutsches Archäologisches Institut (DAI) 1976–, Akad. der Wissenschaften in Göttingen 1978. *Publications:* Das Volkstribunat der klassische Republik 1955, Staatliche Ordnung und Freiheit in der Römische Republik 1972, Lex Publica: Studien zu Gesetz und Recht in der Römische Republik 1975, Verfassung und Sozialgeschichte der Römische Kaiserzeit 1981, Geschichte der Römische Republik 1982, Die Athenische Demokratie 1985, Die Verfassung der Römische Republik 1985, Augustus: Eine Biographie 1998. *Leisure interest:* numismatics. *Address:* Obernjesaer Strasse 8, 37133 Friedland, Germany. *Telephone:* (5504) 381.

BLENDON, Robert J., ScD, MPH, MBA; American academic; *Professor, Department of Health Policy and Politicial Analysis, School of Public Health, Harvard University;* b. 19 Dec. 1942, Philadelphia, Pa; s. of Edward G. Blendon and Theresa M. Blendon; m. Marie C. McCormick 1977; ed Marietta Coll., Univ. of Chicago and Johns Hopkins Univ.; Instructor Johns Hopkins Univ. School of Hygiene and Public Health, Baltimore 1969, Asst to Assoc. Dean (Health Care Programs) 1969–70, Asst Prof. 1970–71, Asst Dir for Planning and Devt, Office of Health Care Programs 1970–71; Special Asst for Health Affairs to Deputy Under-Sec. for Policy Co-ordination, Dept of Health Educ. and Welfare 1971–72, Special Asst for Policy Devt to Asst Sec. for Health and Scientific Affairs 1971–72; Visiting Lecturer, Princeton Univ. 1972–80, Co-ordinator, Medicine in Modern America Course 1980–; Sr Vice-Pres. The Robert Wood Johnson Foundation 1980–87; Prof. Dept of Health Policy and Political Analysis, Harvard Univ. School of Public Health 1987–, Chair. 1987–96; Prof. Kennedy School of Govt 1987– and numerous other professional appointments; Distinguished Investigator Award, AHSR 2000. *Publications:* numerous articles in professional journals. *Address:* Harvard University School of Public Health, Kresge Building, Room 402, 677 Huntington Avenue, Boston, MA 02115 (office); 478 Quinobequin Road, Waban, MA 02468-2127, USA (home). *Telephone:* (617) 432-4502 (office); (617) 965-8279 (home). *E-mail:* rblendon@hsph.harvard.edu (office). *Website:* www.hsph.harvard.edu/faculty/RobertBlendon.

BLEOU, Martin; Côte d'Ivoirian politician, professor and human rights activist; fmr Prof. of Law, Univ. of Abidjan; Minister of Security 2003–06; Pres. Ligue Ivoirienne des droits de l'homme (LIDHO). *Address:* c/o Bloc Ministériel, boulevard Angoulvand, BP V121, Abidjan, Côte d'Ivoire (office).

BLESSED, Brian; British actor; b. 9 Oct. 1936, Mexborough, S Yorks.; s. of William Blessed and Hilda Wall; m. Hildegard Zimmermann 1978; one d.; ed Bolton-on-Dearne Secondary Modern School; studied at Bristol Old Vic; subsequently worked in repertory cos, mainly Nottingham and later Birmingham Repertory Co.; appeared with RSC as Claudius in Hamlet, Hastings in Richard III, Exeter in Henry V; appearance with Nat. Theatre include State of Revolution; also appeared in Metropolis, Cats, The Lion in Winter, Hard Times; one-man show An Evening with Brian Blessed; Pres. Council for Nat. Parks; Hon. DLitt (Bradford), (Sheffield). *Films:* Flash Gordon, Return to Treasure Island, Trojan Women, Man of La Mancha, Henry V, War and Remembrance, Robin Hood Prince of Thieves, Prisoners of Honour, Much Ado About Nothing, Hamlet, King Lear, Tarzan, Star Wars – The Phantom Menace, Mumbo Jumbo, Alexander, Kingdom Hearts, Devil's Harvest, Day of Wrath, The Conclave, As You Like It 2006. *Theatre:* Chitty Chitty Bang Bang, London Palladium 2002–03, The Relapse, Royal Nat. Theatre. *Television appearances include:* role of Fancy Smith in Z Cars and roles in BBC serializations of The Three Musketeers, I, Claudius, My Family and Other Animals, Black Adder, Tom Jones, Winter Solstice, Galahad of Everest 1991, The Legend of the Tamworth Two 2004. *Publications:* The Turquoise Mountain, The Dynamite Kid, Nothing's Impossible, Blessed Everest, Quest to the Lost World. *Leisure interests:* mountaineering, judo (black belt), Koi Carp and animal welfare. *Address:* c/o Stephen Gittins, A.I.M., Fairfax House, Fulwood Place, London, WC1V 6HU, England (office). *Telephone:* (20) 7831-9709 (office). *Fax:* (20) 7242-0810 (office). *E-mail:* email@aimagents.com (office). *Website:* www.aimagents.com (office).

BLESSING, Martin, MBA; German banker; *Chairman, Board of Managing Directors, Commerzbank AG;* b. 6 July 1963, Bremen; m.; three d.; ed Univ. of Frankfurt, Univ. of St Gallen, Switzerland, Univ. of Chicago, USA; apprenticeship at Dresdner Bank AG, Frankfurt 1983–84, Jt Man. Pvt. Customers 1997–2000; univ. studies 1984–88; Frankfurt and New York consultant, McKinsey 1989–96, Pnr 1994; Chair. Advance Bank AG, Munich 2000–01; mem. Bd of Man. Dirs Commerzbank AG, Frankfurt 2001– (responsible for retail banking div. 2001–04, for Information Tech. and Transaction Banking and for Mittelstand Banking Depts of Corp. Banking and Financial Insts 2004–07), Chair. 2007–; mem. Supervisory Bd AMB Generali, Heidelberger Druckmaschinen, ThyssenKrupp Services. *Leisure interests:* jogging, skiing, running the marathon. *Address:* Commerzbank AG, 60261 Frankfurt am Main, Germany (office). *Telephone:* (69) 13620 (office). *Fax:* (69) 285389 (office). *E-mail:* info@commerzbank.com (office). *Website:* www.commerzbank.com (office).

BLETHYN, Brenda Anne, OBE; British actress; b. 20 Feb. 1946, Ramsgate, Kent; d. of William Charles Bottle and Louisa Kathleen Bottle; partner Michael Mayhew 1977; ed St Augustine's RC School, Ramsgate, Thanet Tech. Coll., Guildford School of Acting; with Nat. Theatre (now Royal Nat. Theatre) 1975–90; mem. Poetry Soc. 1976–; Hon. DLitt (Kent) 1999, (Surrey) 2006; numerous awards including Boston Film Critics' Award 1997, LA Film Critics' Award 1997, Golden Globe 1997, London Film Critics' Award 1997, BAFTA 1997. *Theatre appearances include:* for Royal Nat. Theatre: A Midsummer Night's Dream, Troilus and Cressida, Bedroom Farce, Tales From the Vienna Woods, The Guardsman, Fruits of Enlightenment, Madras House, The Provoked Wife, Strife, Force of Habit, Tamburlaine, Plunder (also Old Vic), Camilla Ringbinder Show, Bloody Neighbours (at ICA), The Mysteries 1979, The Double Dealer 1982, Dalliance 1987, The Beaux Stratagem 1989; for Comedy Theatre, London: Steaming (Theatre Critics' Best Supporting Actress Award) 1981; for Vaudeville Theatre, London: Benefactors 1984; for Royal Exchange Theatre, Manchester: A Doll's House 1987, Born Yesterday 1988, An Ideal Husband 1992; for RSC: Wildest Dreams 1993; for Bush Theatre, London: Crimes of the Heart; for Almeida Theatre, London: The Bed Before Yesterday 1994; for Donmar Theatre, London, Habeas Corpus 1996; for Nuffield Theatre, Southampton: The Dramatic Attitudes of Miss Fanny Kemble; for Manhattan Theater Club, New York: Absent Friends (Theatre World Award for Outstanding New Talent 1996) 1996; Mrs Warren's Profession (West End, London) 2002–03. *Films:* Witches, A River Runs Through It 1992, Secrets and Lies (Golden Globe Best Actress 1996, Best Actress Award, Cannes Film Festival 1996, London Film Critics' Circle Best Actress of the Year Award 1996, Boston Critics' Circle Best Actress Award 1996, LA Critics' Circle Best Actress Award 1996, British Acad. Award: Best Actress 1997, Premier Magazine Best Actress Award 1997) 1996, Remember Me 1996, Music From Another Room 1997, Girls' Night 1997, Little Voice (Dallas Fort Worth Critics' Asscn Best Supporting Actress 1999) 1999, Saving Grace (Sundance Film Festival Audience Award 2000, Variety Club of Great Britain Best Screen Actress Award 2001) 1999, On the Nose, In the Winter Dark, Night Train 1999, Daddy and Them 1999, RKO 281 1999, The Sleeping Dictionary 2000, Yellow Bird, Pumpkin 2000, Anne Frank – The Whole Story 2001, Lovely and Amazing 2001, Plots with a View 2002, Sonny 2002, Blizzard 2002, Beyond the Sea 2004, A Way of Life 2004, On a Clear Day 2005, Pride and Prejudice 2006, Atonement 2007, Clubland 2007. *Television includes:* Mona, All Good Things, Grown Ups, The Imitation Game, That Uncertain Feeling, Floating Off, Claws, Sheppey, Yes Minister, Alas Smith and Jones, King Lear, The Shawl, Rumpole, Maigret, Bedroom Farce, The Double Dealer, Death of an Expert Witness, The Storyteller, The Richest Woman in the World, The RNT Mysteries, Henry VI (Part I) 1981, King Lear 1983, Chance in a Million 1983–85, The Labours of Erica 1987, The Bullion Boys 1993, The Buddha of Suburbia 1993, Sleeping with Mickey 1993, Outside Edge (Television's Best Comedy Actress Award) 1994–96, First Signs of Madness 1996, Between the Sheets 2003, Belonging 2004, Mysterious Creatures 2006, War and Peace 2007. *Publications:* Mixed Fancies (memoir) 2006. *Leisure interests:* reading, swimming, cryptic crosswords, running. *Address:* c/o Independent, Oxford House, 76 Oxford Street, London, W1D 1BS, England. *Telephone:* (20) 7636-6565. *Fax:* (20) 7323-0101. *E-mail:* info@independenttalent.com. *Website:* www.independenttalent.com.

BLEWETT, Neal, AC, MA, DPhil, FRHistS, FASSA; Australian politician; b. 24 Oct. 1933, Sydney; s. of James Blewett and Phyllis Blewett (née Kerrison); m. Jill Myford 1962 (died 1988); one s. one d.; ed Launceston High School, Tasmania, Univ. of Tasmania, Oxford Univ.; Lecturer, Oxford Univ. 1959–64; Prof., Dept of Political Theory and Insts, Flinders Univ. 1974–77; MP for Bonython, S. Australia 1977–94; Minister for Health 1983–87, for Community Services and Health 1987–90, for Trade and Overseas Devt 1990–91, Minister for Social Security 1991–93; High Commr in UK 1994–98; Pres. Australian Inst. of Int. Affairs 1998–2006; Pres. Alcohol and Other Drugs Council of Australia 2002–; mem. Exec. Bd WHO 1995–98; Visiting Prof., Faculty of Medicine Sydney Univ. 1999–; Hon. Fellow, Jesus Coll. (Oxford); Hon. DLit (Hull), Hon. LLD (Tasmania, ANU). *Publications:* Playford to Dunstan: The Politics of Transition (with Dean Jaensch) 1971, The Peers, the Parties and the People 1972, A Cabinet Diary 1999. *Leisure interests:* reading, bush walking, cinema. *Address:* 32 Fitzroy Street, Leura, New South Wales 2780, Australia. *Telephone:* (2) 4784-3478 (home). *Fax:* (2) 4784-3478 (home). *E-mail:* nealb@med.usyd.edu.au.

BLEY, Carla Borg; American jazz composer; b. 11 May 1938, Oakland, Calif.; d. of Emil Carl Borg and Arlene Anderson; m. 1st Paul Bley 1959 (divorced 1967); m. 2nd Michael Mantler 1967 (divorced 1992); one d.;

freelance composer 1956–; pianist, Jazz Composers Orchestra, New York 1964–; European concert tours with Jazz Realities 1965–66; founder, WATT 1973–; toured Europe with Jack Bruce Band 1975; leader, Carla Bley Band, touring USA and Europe 1977–; Cultural Council Foundation grantee 1971, 1979; Guggenheim Fellow 1972; Nat. Endowment for Arts grantee 1973; winner, int. jazz critics' poll, Down Beat magazine seven times (1966, 1971, 1972, 1978, 1979, 1980, 1983), Best Composer of Year, Down Beat readers' poll 1984 and Composer/Arranger of Year 1985–92, Best in Field Jazz Times critics' poll 1990, Prix Jazz Moderne for The Very Big Carla Bley Band (Acad. du Jazz) 1992, Best Arranger Down Beat critics' poll 1993, 1994. *Music:* composed and recorded: A Genuine Tong Funeral 1967, Escalator Over the Hill (opera) 1970–71 (Oscar du Disque de Jazz 1973), Tropic Appetites 1973; composed chamber orchestra 3/4 1974–75, Mortelle Rautonnée (film score) 1983; recordings include: Dinner Music 1976, The Carla Bley Band–European Tour 1977, Music Mecanique 1979, Fictitious Sports 1980, Social Studies 1980, Carla Bley Live! 1981, Heavy Heart 1984, I Hate to Sing 1984, Night Glo 1985, Sextet 1987, Live 1987, Duets 1988, Fleur Carnivore 1989, The Very Big Carla Bley Band 1991, Go Together 1993, Big Band Theory 1993, Songs with Legs 1995, Goes to Church 1996, Fancy Chamber Music 1998, Are We There Yet? 1999, 4×4 2000, Looking for America 2003, The Lost Chords 2004, The Lost Chords find Paolo Fresu 2008, Appearing Nightly 2008. *Leisure interests:* gardening, cooking. *Address:* c/o Watt Works, PO Box 67, Willow, NY 12495, USA (office). *Website:* www.wattxtrawatt.com (office).

BLIER, Bertrand; French film director and screenwriter; b. 14 March 1939, Paris; s. of the late Bernard Blier and of Gisèle Brunet; m. Catherine Florin 1973; one d.; also one s. by Anouk Grinberg; ed Lycée Claude Bernard, Paris; worked as asst to several film dirs; Grand Prix Nat. du Cinema 1989. *Films include:* Hitler, connais pas 1963, Si j'étais un espion (Breakdown) 1967, Les valseuses (Making It) 1974, Calmos 1975, Préparez vos mouchoirs (Oscar for Best Foreign Film) 1977, Buffet froid (three Césars) 1979, Beau-père 1981, La femme de mon pote (My Best Friend's Girl) 1983, Notre histoire (Separate Rooms) 1984, Tenue de soirée 1986, Trop belle pour toi (Cannes Special Jury Prize 1989) 1988, Merci la vie 1991, Tango 1992, Un deux trois – soleil 1993, Mon homme 1996, Les acteurs 2000, Les côtelettes 2003, Combien tu m'aimes? 2005. *Publications:* several novels and film scripts. *Address:* c/o Artmédia, 10 avenue Georges V, 75008 Paris (office); 11 rue Margueritte, 75017 Paris, France (home).

BLIGE, Mary J.; American singer and songwriter; b. 11 Jan. 1971, New York; m. Kendu Isaacs 2003; solo artist; numerous tours and live appearances; has collaborated with musicians, including George Michael, Lauryn Hill; American Music Award for Favorite Female Hip-Hop/R&B Artist 2003, for Favorite Female Soul/R&B Artist 2006, Grammy Award for Best Pop Collaboration with Vocals (jtly) 2004, BET Award for Best Female R&B Artist 2006, nine Billboard Awards 2006, Grammy Award for Best Female R&B Vocal Performance (for Be Without You) 2007. *Recordings include:* albums: What's The 411? 1992, My Life 1994, Mary Jane 1995, Share My World 1997, The Tour 1998, Mary 1999, No More Drama 2001, Ballads 2001, Love & Life 2003, The Breakthrough (American Music Award for Favorite Soul/R&B Album 2006, Grammy Award for Best R&B Album 2007, Best R&B/Soul Album by a Female Artist, Soul Train Awards 2007) 2005, Growing Pains (Grammy Award for Best Contemporary R&B Album 2009) 2007. *Address:* Steve Lucas Associates, 156 W 56th Street, New York, NY 10019, USA (office). *Website:* www.mjblige.com.

BLIKLE, Andrzej, PhD; Polish mathematician, confectioner and academic; *Professor, Institute of Computer Science, Polish Academy of Sciences;* b. 24 Sept. 1939, Warsaw; s. of Jerzy Blikle and Aniela Blikle; m.; one s.; ed Warsaw Univ.; master of confectioner's trade 1975; scientific worker, Inst. of Math., Polish Acad. of Sciences 1963–71, Computational Centre, Polish Acad. of Sciences 1971–77, Prof. Inst. of Computer Science, Polish Acad. of Sciences 1977–; Chair. and CEO A. Blikle Ltd 1991–; Pres. Polish Fed. of Food Producers; mem. Polish Math. Soc. 1962–, Polish Information Processing Soc. 1981– (Pres. 1987), Asscn for Theoretical Computer Science 1982–, Academia Europaea 1993; Patron Polish Econ. and Business Asscn. *Publication:* MetaSoft Primer – Towards a Metalanguage for Applied Denotational Semantics Series: Lecture Notes in Computer Science (Vol. 288) (co-ed.) 1987. *Leisure interests:* skiing, windsurfing, films, history. *Address:* ul. Nowy Świat 35, 00-029 Warsaw (office); ul. Czarnieckiego 82, 01-541 Warsaw, Poland (home). *Telephone:* (22) 8430621 (office); (22) 8396365 (home). *Fax:* (22) 8430601 (office). *E-mail:* blikle@medianet.com.pl (office).

BLINDER, Alan Stuart, AB, MSc, PhD; American economist and academic; *Professor of Economics and Public Affairs and Co-Director, Center for Economic Policy Studies, Princeton University;* b. 14 Oct. 1945, Brooklyn, New York; s. of Morris Blinder and Shirley Blinder; m. Madeline Schwartz 1967; two s.; ed Princeton Univ., LSE, MIT; Deputy Asst Dir US Congressional Budget Office 1975; Gordon S. Rentschler Memorial Prof. of Econs and Public Affairs, Princeton Univ., NJ 1982–, Dir Center for Econ. Policy Studies 1989–93, Co.-Dir 1996–; mem. Council of Econ. Advisers to Pres. Clinton 1993–94; Vice-Chair. Bd of Govs, Fed. Reserve System 1994–96; Vice-Chair., G7 Group 1997–; Fellow, American Acad. of Arts and Sciences 1991–; mem. American Philosophical Soc. 1996–; Pnr, Promotory Financial Group 2000–. *Publications include:* Growing Together: An Alternative Economic Strategy for the 1990s 1991, Central Banking in Theory and Practice 1998, Asking About Prices: A New Approach to Understanding Price Stickiness (jtly) 1998, Economics, Principles and Policy (jtly) 2000, The Fabulous Decade: Macroeconomic Lessons from the 1990s (jtly) 2001. *Address:* Department of Economics, Princeton University, 105 Fisher Hall, Princeton, NJ 08544, USA (office). *Telephone:* (609) 258-4023 (office). *Fax:* (609) 258-5398 (office).

E-mail: blinder@princeton.edu (office). *Website:* www.princeton.edu/blinder (office).

BLISS, John William Michael, CM, PhD, FRSC; Canadian historian, academic and writer; *University Professor of History, University of Toronto;* b. 18 Jan. 1941, Kingsville, Ont.; s. of Quartus Bliss and Anne L. Crow; m. Elizabeth J. Haslam 1963; one s. two d.; ed Kingsville Dist High School and Univ. of Toronto; Teaching Asst Harvard Univ. 1967–68; Dept of History, Univ. of Toronto 1968–72, Prof. 1975–99, Univ. Prof. 1999–; Hon. DLitt (McGill) 2001; numerous awards including Tyrrell Medal, Royal Soc. of Canada 1988. *Publications:* A Living Profit 1974, A Canadian Millionaire: The Life of Sir Joseph Flavelle 1978, The Discovery of Insulin 1982, Banting: A Biography 1984, Northern Enterprise: Five Centuries of Canadian Business 1987, Plague: A Story of Smallpox in Montreal 1991, Right Honourable Men: The Descent of Canadian Politics from Macdonald to Mulroney 1994, William Osler: A Life in Medicine 1999. *Address:* Department of History, University of Toronto, Sidney Smith Hall, 100 St. George Street, Toronto, Ont. M5S 3G3, Canada (office). *Telephone:* (416) 978-8480 (office). *Fax:* (416) 971-2160. *E-mail:* m.bliss@sympatico.ca (office). *Website:* www.chass.utoronto.ca/history/index.htm (office).

BLISS, Timothy Vivian Pelham, PhD, FRS, FMedSci; British neuroscientist and academic; *Visiting Worker, Division of Neurophysiology, National Institute for Medical Research;* b. 27 July 1940, Weymouth; s. of Pelham Marryat Bliss and Elizabeth Bliss (née Sproule); m. 1st Virginia Catherine Morton-Evans 1975; one step-s. two step-d.; m. 2nd Isabel Frances Vasseur; two step-s.; one d. by Katherine Clough; ed McGill Univ., Montreal; mem. of scientific staff MRC at Nat. Inst. for Medical Research 1967–, Head, Div. of Neurophysiology 1988–2006, Visiting Worker 2006–, Head, Neurosciences Group 1996–2006; Visiting Prof., Dept of Physiology, Univ. Coll. London 1993–; Bristol Myers Squibb Prize for Neuroscience 1991, Feldberg Prize 1994, British Neuroscience Asscn Award for outstanding contribution to British neuroscience 2003. *Publications:* more than 100 papers in scientific journals relating to the neural basis of learning and memory. *Leisure interests:* architecture, food, wine, naval history, travelling. *Address:* National Institute for Medical Research, Mill Hill, London, NW7 1AA, England (office). *Telephone:* (20) 8816-2382 (office); (20) 8341-1215 (home). *Fax:* (20) 8906-4477 (office). *E-mail:* tbliss@nimr.mrc.ac.uk (office). *Website:* www.nimr.mrc .ac.uk/neuroscience (office).

BLIX, Hans Martin, LLD, PhD; Swedish lawyer and international official (retd); b. 28 June 1928, Uppsala; s. of Gunnar Blix and Hertha Blix (née Wiberg); m. Eva Kettis 1962; two s.; ed Uppsala Univ., Univ. of Cambridge, UK, Columbia Univ., New York, USA, Univ. of Stockholm; Asst Prof. of Int. Law, Univ. of Stockholm 1960–63; Legal Consultant on Int. Law, Foreign Ministry 1963–76; Under-Sec. of State for Int. Devt Co-operation, Foreign Ministry 1976–78, 1979–81; Minister for Foreign Affairs 1978–79; Dir-Gen. IAEA, Vienna 1981–97; mem. Swedish del. to UN Gen. Ass. 1961–81; mem. del. to Conf. on Disarmament, Geneva 1962–78; Exec. Chair. UN Monitoring, Verification and Inspection Comm. for Iraq 2000–03; Hon. Chair. World Nuclear Asscn; Commdr, Légion d'honneur 2004; Dr hc (Moscow State Univ.) 1987, (several other univs); Henry de Wolf Smyth Award 1988, Gold Medal, Uranium Inst. (now World Nuclear Asscn) 1997, Olof Palme Prize 2003. *Publications:* Treaty-Making Power (dissertation), Statsmyndigheternas Internationella Förbindelser (monograph) 1964, Sovereignty, Aggression and Neutrality 1970, The Treaty-Maker's Handbook 1973, Disarming Iraq: The Search for Weapons of Mass Destruction 2004; numerous articles in scientific journals. *Leisure interests:* Oriental rugs, hiking, art.

BLIZNAKOV, Vesselin Vitanov; Bulgarian scientist and politician; b. 18 June 1944, Straldga, Yambol Dist; m.; ed Vassil Kkaragyizov High School, Yambol, Medical Acad., Sofia; began career in general practice, Bourgas Dist 1972–75; Researcher Assoc. and Head of Lab., Nat. Centre for Radio-Biology and Radiation Protection, Sofia 1976–86, Head, Radiation Protection Dept 1986–99; Chair. Bulgarian Nuclear Soc. 1999–2001; fmr mem. Civil Cttee for Protection of Nuclear Power Plant Kozloduy; co-owner Dr. Atanas Shterev's Clinic; mem. Nat. Ass. for Vratsa 2001–05, for Haskovo 2005–, Chair. Energy Cttee 2001–05, mem. Foreign Policy, Defence and Security Cttees 2001–05; Deputy Chair. Parl. Group of Simeon II Nat. Movt 2001–03; mem. Del. to Jt Bulgarian-EU Parl. Cttee 2001; Minister of Defence 2005–08; mem. Governing Council, European Nuclear Soc. 1999–2001. *Address:* c/o Ministry of Defence, 1000 Sofia, ul. Dyakon Ignatiy 3, Bulgaria. *Telephone:* (2) 922-09-22.

BLOBEL, Günter, MD, PhD; American (b. German) cell biologist and academic; *Professor, Rockefeller University;* b. 21 May 1936, Waltersdorf, Silesia (now Poland); m. Laura Maioglio-Blobel; ed Tübingen and Wisconsin Univs; emigrated to USA 1960 (now naturalized citizen); internship in various German hosps 1960–62; joined cell biology lab. of George Palade, Rockefeller Univ., New York, Asst Prof. 1969–73, Assoc. Prof. 1973–76, Prof. 1976–; continued and developed Palade's work, now Head Cell Biology Lab.; Investigator Howard Hughes Medical Inst., Rockefeller Univ. 1986–; Nobel Prize in Physiology or Medicine for work on signal and transport mechanisms of proteins 1999, Ellis Island Medal of Hon. 2000. *Leisure interests:* architecture, classical music, landscapes. *Address:* Rockefeller University Cell Biology Laboratory, 66th and York Avenue, New York, NY 10021 (office); The Howard Hughes Medical Institute, The Rockefeller University, 1230 York Avenue, New York, NY 10021 (office); 1100 Park Avenue, Apt 10D, New York, NY 10128, USA (home). *Telephone:* (212) 327-8096 (office); (212) 369-3552 (home). *Fax:* (212) 327-7880 (office); (212) 534-5556 (home). *E-mail:* blobel@rockvax .rockefeller.edu (office). *Website:* www.rockefeller.edu/labheads/blobel/blobel -lab.html (office); www.rockefeller.edu (home).

BLOCHER, Christoph; Swiss politician and business executive; *Vice-President, Swiss People's Party;* b. 11 Oct. 1940; m. Sylvia Blocher; one s. three d.; ed attended univ. in Zürich, Montpellier and Paris; joined legal dept Ems-Chemie AG 1969, acquired co. 1983, Pres. and Rep to the Bd ems–Chemie Holding AG 1984–; mem. Meilen Dist Council 1974–78; mem. Zürich Canton Council 1975–80; Pres. Swiss People's Party (Schweizerische Volkspartei), Zürich Canton 1977–; mem. Nat. Ass. 1979–; Founder and Pres. Aktion für eine unabhängige und neutrale Schweiz (AUNS) 1986–; mem. Swiss Fed. Council 2003–07, Minister of Justice and Police Affairs 2004–07; Vice-Pres., Swiss People's Party 2008–. *Address:* Federal Council, Federal Palace, West Wing, 3003 Bern; Schweizerische Volkspartei, Brückfelderstr. 18, 3000 Bern, Switzerland (office). *Telephone:* (31) 3005858 (office). *Fax:* (31) 3005859 (office). *E-mail:* christoph@blocher.ch (office). *Website:* www.svp.ch (office); www.blocher.ch.

BLOCK, Gene D., AB, PhD; American biologist, academic and university administrator; *Chancellor, University of California, Los Angeles;* b. 1948, New York; m. Carol Block; two c.; ed Stanford Univ., Univ. of Oregon; postdoctoral work, Stanford Univ. 1975–78; joined faculty at Univ. of Virginia 1978, Vice Provost for Research 1993–98, Vice-Pres. for Research and Public Service 1998–2001, Pres. and Provost 2001–07; Chancellor Univ. Calif., LA (UCLA) 2007–; Fellow, AAAS; Commonwealth of Va Outstanding Public Service Award 1998. *Address:* Office of the Chancellor, University of California, Los Angeles, Box 951405, 2147 Murphy Hall, Los Angeles, CA 90095-1405, USA (office). *Telephone:* (310) 825-2151 (office). *Fax:* (310) 206-6030 (office). *E-mail:* chancellor@ucla.edu (office). *Website:* www.chancellor.ucla.edu (office).

BLOCK, Ned Joel, PhD; American academic; *Silver Professor, Departments of Philosophy, Psychology and Center for Neural Science, New York University;* b. 22 Aug. 1942, Chicago; s. of Eli Block and Blanche Rabinowitz; m. Susan Carey 1970; one d.; ed Massachusetts Inst. of Tech., St John's Coll., Oxford, UK, Harvard Univ.; Asst Prof., MIT 1971–77, Assoc. Prof. 1977–83, Prof. of Philosophy, Dept of Linguistics and Philosophy 1983–96, Chair. of Philosophy 1989–95; Prof. of Philosophy, New York Univ. 1996–, Silver Prof., Depts of Philosophy, Psychology and Center for Neural Science 2005–; Visiting Prof., Harvard Univ. 2002–03; Pres. Soc. for Philosophy and Psychology 1978–79, Association for the Scientific Study of Consciousness; Chair. MIT Press Cognitive Science Bd 1992–95; Fellow, American Council of Learned Socs, Center for Study of Language and Information, American Acad. of Arts and Sciences 2004–; Guggenheim Fellow, NSF Fellow 1985–86, 1988–89; Nat. Endowment for the Humanities Fellow 2006–07; Robert A. Muh Alumni Award in the Humanities, Arts and Social Sciences, MIT 2005; Petrus Hispanus Lecturer, Univ. of Lisbon; Jack Burstyn Memorial Lecturer, Manhattan Marymount; Francis W. Gramlich Lecturer, Dartmouth; Burman Lecturer, Univ. of Umea, Sweden; Lone Star Tourist; Distinguished Visiting Prof., Univ. of Hong Kong; Townsend Visitor, Berkeley; Smart Lecturer, ANU; Josiah Royce Lectures, Brown Univ. *Publications:* The IQ Controversy (with G. Dworkin) 1976, Readings in Philosophy of Psychology (Vol. 1) 1980, (Vol. 2) 1981, Imagery 1981, The Nature of Consciousness (with O. Flanagan and G. Güzeldere), Functionalism, Consciousness and Representation – Collected Papers (Vol. 1) 2007; articles chosen for The Philosophers' Annual 1983, 1990, 1995, 2002. *Address:* Department of Philosophy, New York University, Room 405, 5 Washington Place, New York, NY 10003 (office); 37 Washington Square West, New York, NY 10011, USA (home). *Telephone:* (212) 998-8322 (office). *Fax:* (212) 995-4179 (office). *E-mail:* ned.block@nyu.edu (office). *Website:* www .nyu.edu/gsas/dept/philo/faculty/block (office).

BLOEMBERGEN, Nicolaas, DPhil; American (b. Dutch) scientist and academic; *Professor of Optical Sciences, University of Arizona;* b. 11 March 1920, Dordrecht, Netherlands; s. of Auke Bloembergen and Sophia M. Quint; m. Huberta D. Brink 1950; one s. two d.; ed Univs of Utrecht and Leiden; Research Fellow, Leiden Univ. 1947–49; Soc. of Fellows, Harvard Univ. 1949–51, Gordon McKay Assoc. Prof. 1951–57, apptd Prof. of Applied Physics 1957, Rumford Prof. of Physics 1974–80, Gerhard Gade Univ. Prof. 1980–90, Prof. Emer. 1990–; Prof. of Optical Sciences, Univ. of Arizona 2001–; Guggenheim Fellow 1957; Lorentz Guest Prof., Leiden 1973; Raman Visiting Prof., Bangalore Univ. 1979; Visiting Prof., Coll. de France 1980; mem. NAS (USA); Corresp. mem. Royal Dutch Acad. of Sciences; Foreign mem. Indian Acad. of Sciences, Akad. Leopoldina (GDR), Royal Norwegian Inst. of Science; Foreign Assoc. mem. Acad. des Sciences, Inst. de France 1981–; Commdr, Order of Orange 1988; Hon. DSc (Laval Univ.), Québec, Univ. of Conn., Hartford Univ., Univ. of Mass., Univ. of Cen. Fla); Hon. DSc (Moscow State Univ.) 1997, (N Carolina State Univ.) 1998, (Harvard Univ.) 2000; Buckley Prize, American Physical Soc., Liebmann Prize, Inst. of Radio Engineers, Ballantine Medal, Franklin Inst., Royal Dutch Acad. of Arts and Sciences, Half Moon Trophy, Netherland Club of New York, Nat. Medal of Science 1974, Lorentz Medal, Royal Dutch Acad. of Sciences 1978, Frederick Ives Medal, Optical Soc. of America 1979, Alexander von Humboldt Sr US Scientist Award, Munich 1980, shared Nobel Prize in Physics 1981 for contrib. to development of laser spectroscopy, Medal of Honor, IEEE 1983, Byvoet Medal, Univ. of Utrecht 2001. *Publications:* Nuclear Magnetic Relaxation 1961, Nonlinear Optics 1965, Encounters in Magnetic Resonance 1996, Encounters in Nonlinear Optics 1996; over 300 papers in professional journals. *Leisure interests:* travel, skiing, tennis. *Address:* Optical Sciences Center, University of Arizona, 1630 East University Boulevard, Tucson, AZ 85747, USA (office). *Telephone:* (520) 626-3479 (office); (520) 647-3772 (home). *Fax:* (520) 621-5300 (office). *E-mail:* nbloembergen@optics.arizona.edu (office). *Website:* www .optics.arizona.edu/faculty/Resumes/Bloembergen.htm (office).

BLOKHIN, Alexander Victorovich; Russian politician and engineer; *Ambassador to Australia;* b. 12 Jan. 1951, Ivanovo, Russia; m.; one d.; ed Ivanovo Inst. of Energy; sr engineer, deputy head of workshop, deputy chief energy expert factory Fizpribor, Leningrad 1974–77; with USSR Ministry of Defence in Mongolia 1977–78; chief mechanic, garment factory Ivanovo 1978–80; chief energy expert, State Schelkovo Biological Co., Moscow Region 1983–90; Chair. Sub-cttee, Sec. Cttee of Supreme Soviet on Devt of Self-govt, Moscow 1990–92; Counsellor of Minister of Foreign Affairs, Russian Fed. 1992–93; Dir Dept Ministry of Foreign Affairs, Russian Fed. 1993–95; Amb. for special missions 1995; Amb. to Azerbaijan 1995–2000; Minister for Nationalities and Regional Policy 2000–02; Amb. to Belarus 2002–05, to Australia 2005–. *Address:* Embassy of the Russian Federation, 78 Canberra Avenue, Griffith, ACT 2603, Australia (office). *Telephone:* (2) 6295-9033 (office). *Fax:* (2) 6295-1847 (office). *E-mail:* rusembassy.australia@rambler.ru (office). *Website:* www.australia.mid.ru (office).

BLOKHIN, Oleg Vladimirovich; Ukrainian fmr football player, politician and football coach; b. 5 Nov. 1952, Kiev; s. of Volodimir Ivanovich Blokhin and Katerina Zakharivna Adamenko (fmr sprint hurdler); m. Irina Ivomovna Deryugina; one d.; ed Kiev Physical Culture Inst. and Kiev Univ.; played for Dinamo Kiev 1969–88; played 432 matches in USSR Championships, 109 matches for USSR team (record); scored over 200 career goals; fmr coach Greek clubs Olympiaos, PAOK Saloniki (twice), AEK and Ionikos (twice); Chair. Oleg Blokhin Int. Fund 1994–; Ukraine People's Deputy 1998, mem. Cttee on Problems of Youth Policy and Sport; mem. Batkishchina faction 1999–, CP faction 2002–; Coach Ukrainian nat. football team 2003–; Golden Boot Award 1975; European Footballer of the Year 1975, Best Footballer of USSR 1973–75, seven times Champion USSR, five times winner USSR Cup, winner Cup Winners' Cup 1975, winner Supercup 1975. *Address:* c/o Ministry of Youth and Sport, Espladra 42, 252023 Kiev, Ukraine (office). *Telephone:* 220-02-00.

BLOM-COOPER, Sir Louis Jacques, Kt, LLB, DrIur, QC, FRSA; British lawyer and writer; *Associate Tenant, Doughty Street Chambers;* b. 27 March 1926; s. of Alfred Blom-Cooper and Ella Flesseman; m. 1st 1952 (dissolved 1970); two s. one d.; m. 2nd Jane E Smither 1970; one s. two d.; ed Seaford Coll., King's Coll., London, Municipal Univ. of Amsterdam and Fitzwilliam Coll., Cambridge; army service 1944–47; called to Bar, Middle Temple 1952, Bencher 1978; mem. Home Sec.'s Advisory Council on the Penal System 1966–78; Chair. Howard League for Penal Reform 1973–84, Vice-Pres. 1984–; Chair. Panel of Inquiry into death of Jasmine Beckford 1985; on several comms of inquiry 1986–87; academic appointment, Univ. of London 1962–84; Judge Court of Appeal, Jersey and Guernsey 1989–96; Ind. Commr for the Holding Centres, NI 1993–2000; Chair. Mental Health Act Comm. 1987–94, Press Council 1989–90, Nat. Asscn for Victim Support Schemes (NASS) 1994–97; currently Assoc. Tenant, Doughty Street Chambers, London; Dr hc (Ulster) 1995; Hon. LittD (E Anglia) 1997; Hon. LLD (Loughborough), (Ulster), (Univ. of East Anglia). *Publications:* Bankruptcy in Private International Law 1954, The Law as Literature 1962, The A6 Murder (A Semblance of Truth) 1963, A Calendar of Murder (with T. P. Morris) 1964, Language of the Law 1965, Separated Spouses (with O. R. McGregor and C. Gibson) 1970, Final Appeal: A Study of the House of Lords in its Judicial Capacity (with G. Drewry) 1972; ed. Progress in Penal Reform 1975, Law and Morality (with G. Drewry) 1976, The Falling Shadow (jtly) 1995, The Birmingham Six and Other Cases 1997, With Malice Aforethought (with T. Morris) 2004. *Leisure interests:* watching and reporting on Association football, reading, music, writing, broadcasting. *Address:* Doughty Street Chambers, 10-11 Doughty Street, London WC1N 2PL (office); 1 Southgate Road, London, N1 3JP, (home); Southminster Hall, Southminster, Essex CM0 1EH, England (home). *Telephone:* (20) 7404-1313 (office); (20) 7704-1514 (London) (home). *Fax:* (20) 7226-5457 (London) (home). *E-mail:* l.blom-cooper@doughtystreet.co.uk (office); blomcooper@aol.com (home). *Website:* www.doughtystreet.co.uk (office).

BLOMSTEDT, Herbert Thorsson; Swedish conductor; b. 11 July 1927, Springfield, Mass, USA; s. of Adolphe Blomstedt and Alida Armintha Thorson; m. Waltraud Regina Peterson 1955 (died 2003); four d.; ed Royal Acad. of Music, Stockholm, Uppsala Univ., Mozarteum, Salzburg, Austria, Schola Cantorum, Basel, Switzerland, Juilliard School, New York, USA, Tanglewood, Mass; Music Dir, Norrköping Symphony Orchestra 1954–61; Prof. of Conducting, Swedish Royal Acad. of Music 1961–70; Perm. Conductor, Oslo Philharmonic 1962–68; Music Dir of Danish Radio Symphony Orchestra 1967–77, of Dresden Staatskapelle Orchestra 1975–85, of Swedish Radio Symphony Orchestra 1977–82; Music Dir and Conductor, San Francisco Symphony Orchestra 1985–95, Conductor Laureate 1995–; Music Dir NDR Symphony Orchestra, Hamburg 1996–98, Leipzig Gewandhaus Orchestra 1998–2005; mem. Royal Acad. of Music, Stockholm 1965;; Hon. Conductor NHK Symphony, Tokyo 1985, The Bamberg Symphony Orchestra 2006, Danish Nat. Symphony Orchestra 2006, Swedish Radio Symphony Orchestra 2006; Kt Royal Order of the North Star (Sweden); Kt Royal Order of Dannebrog (Denmark); Grosses Verdienstkreuz der Bundesrepublik Deutschland 2003; Hon. DMus (Andrews), Hon. PhD (Gothenburg) 1999, Dr hc (Southwestern-Adventist Univ., TX) 1993; Jenny Lind Scholarship, Swedish Royal Acad. of Music, Litteris et Artibus, Gold Medal (Sweden), Deutscher Schallplattenpreis 1978, Golden Reward Prize, Tokyo 1984, Grand Prix du Disque 1989, Gramophone Award, London 1990, Record Acad. of Japan Award 1991, Ditson Award for Distinguished Services to American Music, Columbia Univ., New York 1992, Grammy Awards 1993, 1996, Schallplattenpreis der Deutschen Musikkritik 1994, Ehrenpräsident der Stiftung Musikforschung Zentralschweiz 2001, Anton-Bruckner-Preis der Betil-Östbo-Bruckner-Stiftung, Linz 2001, Haederpris, Carl Nielsen Soc., Denmark 2002. *Publications:* Till Kennedomen om Johann Christian Bachs Symfonies 1951, Lars-Erik Larsson och Lars Convertinor (co-author) 1957, Berwald: Sinfonie Singulière 1965. *Leisure interests:* hiking, history, philosophy, literature, art. *Address:* c/o KuenstlepSekretariat am Gasteig, Rosenheimer Strasse 52,

81669 Munich, Germany (office). *Telephone:* (89) 444-8879-0 (office). *Fax:* (89) 444-9522 (office).

BLÖNDAL, Halldór; Icelandic politician; b. 24 Aug. 1938, Reykjavík; m. Kristrún Eymundsdóttir; ed Akureyri High School; teacher and journalist, Morgunbladid 1959–80; mem. staff Authorised Public Accountant office, Akureyri 1976–78; Chief Surveyor of the State Account 1976–87; mem. Bd Dirs Regional Devt Inst. 1983–91, Agric. Bank of Iceland 1985–91; mem. Independence Party, Vice-Chair. Parl. Group 1983–91; mem. Parl. for Northeastern Dist 1979–; Rep. to UN Gen. Ass. 1983; mem. Icelandic Del. to Council of Europe 1984–86, Minister of Communications and Agric. 1991–95; Speaker of the Althingi (Parl.) 1999–2005; Chair. Cttee on Foreign Affairs 2005–; Chair. Icelandic Del. to West Nordic Council 2005–. *Address:* Althingi, v/Austurvöll, 150 Reykjavík, Iceland (office). *Telephone:* 5630500 (office). *Fax:* 5630910 (office). *E-mail:* halldorb@althingi.is (office). *Website:* www.althingi.is (office).

BLOOM, Barry R., BS, DrSc, MA, PhD; American immunologist, academic and university administrator; *Joan L. and Julius H. Jacobson Professor of Public Health, School of Public Health, Harvard University;* ed Amherst Coll., Harvard Univ., Rockefeller Univ.; consultant to White House on Int. Health Policy 1977–78; joined faculty Albert Einstein Coll. of Medicine 1964, Prof. 1973–90, Chair. Dept of Microbiology and Immunology, 1978–90; Dean of Faculty, Harvard School of Public Health 1998–, Joan L. and Julius H. Jacobson Prof. of Public Health 1998–; Investigator, Howard Hughes Medical Inst. 1990–98; Chair. Tech. and Research Advisory Cttee to Global Programme on Malaria, WHO; Founding Chair., Bd of Trustees, Int. Vaccine Inst., South Korea; fmr Chair. Advisory Cttee on Health Research, Leprosy Research and Tuberculosis Research Cttees, WHO, Scientific and Tech. Advisory Cttees, UNDP/World Bank/WHO Special Programme for Research and Training, Vaccine Advisory Cttee on UNAIDS; mem. Ellison Medical Foundation Scientific Advisory Bd; mem. Wellcome Trust Pathogens, Immunology and Population Health Strategy Cttee; mem. Nat. Advisory Bd, Howard Hughes Medical Inst. 1990–98; mem. Scientific Advisory Bd Earth Inst., Columbia Univ.; mem. Advisory Council, Paul G. Rogers Soc. for Global Health Research; fmr Pres. Fed. of American Socs for Experimental Biology; fmr mem. US AIDS Research Cttee, Nat. Advisory Council, Nat. Inst. for Allergy and Infectious Diseases; fmr mem. Scientific Advisory Bd Nat. Center for Infectious Diseases for Disease Control and Prevention; fmr mem. Nat. Advisory Bd Fogarty Int. Center, NIH; fmr mem. Governing Bd Inst. of Medicine; Fellow, American Acad. of Arts and Sciences; mem. NAS, Inst. of Medicine, AAAS, American Asscn of Immunologists (Pres. 1984), American Philosophical Soc.; Bristol-Myers Squib Award for Distinguished Research in Infectious Diseases, Novartis Award in Immunology (jtly) 1998; Robert Koch Gold Medal 1999. *Address:* Department of Immunology and Infectious Diseases, Harvard School of Public Health, Building 1, Room 813, Boston, MA 02115, USA (office). *Telephone:* (617) 432-7684 (office). *E-mail:* bbloom@hsph.harvard.edu (office). *Website:* www.hsph.harvard.edu (office).

BLOOM, Claire; British actress; b. 15 Feb. 1931, London; d. of Edward Bloom and Elizabeth Grew; m. 1st Rod Steiger 1959 (divorced 1969, died 2002); m. 2nd Philip Roth 1990 (divorced 1995); ed London, Bristol and New York; Oxford Repertory Theatre 1946, Stratford-on-Avon 1948; first major stage appearances in The Lady's Not For Burning 1949, Ring Around the Moon 1950; at Old Vic 1951–53; Fellow Guildhall School of Music and Drama 1975. *Other stage performances include:* Duel of Angels 1956, 1967, Andromache in The Trojan Women 1964, Sascha in Ivanov, London 1966, Nora in A Doll's House, New York 1971, London 1973, Hedda Gabler in Hedda Gabler, New York 1971, Mary Queen of Scots in Vivat, Vivat Regina!, New York 1972, A Streetcar Named Desire, London (Evening Standard Drama Award for Best Actress) 1974, The Innocents, USA 1976, Rosmersholm, London 1977, The Cherry Orchard, Chichester Festival 1981, When We Dead Awaken 1990, The Cherry Orchard, USA 1994, Long Day's Journey into Night, USA 1996, Electra, New York 1998, Conversations after a Burial, London 2000, A Little Night Music 2003, Whispering Psyche 2004, Six Dance Lessons in Six Weeks 2006–07. *Films include:* Limelight, Man Between, Richard III, Alexander the Great, Brothers Karamazov, Buccaneer, Look Back in Anger, Three Steps to Freedom 1960, The Brothers Grimm, The Chapman Report 1962, The Haunting 1963, 80,000 Suspects 1963, Alta Infedeltà 1963, Il Maestro di Vigevano 1963, The Outrage 1964, Spy Who Came in from the Cold 1965, Charly 1966, Three into Two Won't Go 1967, Illustrated Man 1968, Red Sky at Morning 1970, A Doll's House 1973, Islands in the Stream 1975, The Clash of the Titans 1979, Always 1984, Sammy and Rosie Get Laid 1987, Brothers 1988, Crimes and Misdemeanours 1989, Daylight 1995, Shakespeare's Women and Claire Bloom, The Book of Eve 2001, Imagining Argentina 2002, Daniel and the Superdogs 2003. *Television appearances:* A Legacy 1975, The Oresteia 1978, Henry VIII 1979, Brideshead Revisited 1979, Hamlet 1980, Cymbeline 1982, Separate Tables 1982, The Ghost Writer 1982, King John 1983, Time and the Conways 1984, Shadowlands (BAFTA Award for Best Actress) 1985, Promises to Keep 1985, Oedipus the King 1985, Lightning Always Strikes Twice 1985; miniseries in USA: Ellis Island 1984, Florence Nightingale 1984, Liberty 1985, Anastasia 1986, Queenie 1986, The Belle of Amherst 1986, Intimate Contact 1987, A Shadow on the Sun 1988, The Camomile Lawn 1991, The Mirror Crack'd from Side to Side 1992, Remember 1993, A Village Affair 1994, Family Money 1996, The Lady in Question, Love and Murder, Yesterday's Children, Law and Order; also performs her one-woman shows Enter the Actress and These are Women, A Portrait of Shakespeare's Heroines, throughout the USA. *Publications:* Limelight and After 1982, Leaving a Doll's House 1996. *Leisure interests:* walking, music. *Address:* c/o Jeremy Conway, 18–21 Jermyn Street, London, SW1Y 6HB, England. *Telephone:* (20) 7287-0077. *Fax:* (20) 7287-1940.

BLOOM, Floyd Elliott, AB, DSc, MD, FAAS; American physician, research scientist and academic; *Chairman, Chief Scientific Officer and Founding Chief Executive Officer, Neurome Inc.;* b. 8 Oct. 1936, Minneapolis; m. 1st D'Nell Bingham 1956 (died 1973); two c.; m. 2nd Jody Patricia Corey 1980; ed S Methodist Univ., Washington Univ., Hahnemann Univ., Univ. of Rochester, Mount Sinai Univ. Medical School, Thomas Jefferson Univ.; intern, Barnes Hosp., St Louis 1960–61, resident internal medicine 1961–62; Research Assoc., Nat. Inst. of Mental Health (NIMH), Washington, DC 1962–64; Fellow Depts of Pharmacology, Psychiatry and Anatomy, Yale School of Medicine 1964–66, Asst Prof. 1966–67, Assoc. Prof. 1968; Chief Lab. of Neuropharmacology, NIMH 1968–75, Acting Dir, Div. of Special Mental Health 1973–75; Commissioned Officer, Public Health Service 1974–75; Prof. Salk Inst., La Jolla, Calif. 1975–83; Dir Div. of Preclinical Neuroscience and Endocrinology, Scripps Research Inst., La Jolla 1983–89, Chair. Dept of Neuropharmacology 1989–2005, Emer. Prof., Dept of Molecular and Integrative Neuroscience 2005–; Ed.-in-Chief, Science Magazine 1995–2000; Founding CEO, Chief Scientific Officer and Chair. Neurome, Inc. 2000–, Chair. of Bd 2002–; mem. Nat. Advisory Mental Health Council 1976–80, Comm. on Alcoholism 1980–81; mem. Scientific Advisory Bd Neurocrine Inc. 1993–2000, Neurobiological Tech. Inc. 1994–98, Healthcare Ventures Inc. 1998–2000, Advancis Pharmaceuticals 1999–, SafeMed 2003–, Saegis Pharmaceuticals 2004–; Trustee Wash. Univ., St Louis 1998–; Chair. Nat. Medical Council 2000–; currently Chair. AAAS; mem. NAS, Inst. of Medicine, American Philosophical Soc., Acad. of Arts and Sciences, Swedish Acad. of Sciences; A. Cressy Morrison Award, NY Acad. of Sciences 1971, Mathilde Solowey Award 1973, McAlpin Research Achievement Award, Mental Health Asscn 1980, Steven Beering Medal 1985, Janssen Award, World Psychiatry Asscn 1989, Herman von Helmholtz Award 1991, Meritorious Achievement Award, Council of Biology Eds 1999, Distinguished Service Award, American Psychiatric Asscn 2000, Walsh McDermott Award, Inst. of Medicine 2004, Bernard and Rhoda Sarnat Award for Mental Health Research, Inst. of Medicine 2005. *Publications include:* Biochemical Basis of Neuropharmacology (with J. R. Cooper and R. H. Roth) 1971, Brain, Mind and Behavior (with Lazerson and Hofstadter) 1984, Brain Browser (with W. Young and Y. Kim) 1989; Ed. Peptides: Integrators of Cell and Tissue Function 1980, Neuro-Psychopharmacology: The Fourth Generation of Progress 1994, Handbook of Chemical Neuroanatomy 1997, The Primate Nervous System 1997, Funding Health Sciences Research (with M. Randolph) 1990. *Leisure interests:* cruise travel, fine food and wine, abstract art. *Address:* Neurome, Inc., 11149 North Torrey Pines Road, La Jolla, CA 92037 (office); Scripps Research Institute, 10550 North Torrey Pines Road, La Jolla, CA 92037-1000 (office); 628 Pacific View Drive, San Diego, CA 92109, USA (home). *Telephone:* (858) 677-0466 (office); (858) 784-9730 (office). *Fax:* (858) 677-0458 (office); (858) 784-8851 (office). *E-mail:* fbloom@neurome.com; fbloom@scripps.edu (office). *Website:* www.neurome.com; www.scripps.edu/np (office).

BLOOM, Harold, PhD; American academic and writer; *Sterling Professor of Humanities and English, Yale University;* b. 11 July 1930, New York; s. of William Bloom and Paula Lev; m. Jeanne Gould 1958; two s.; ed Cornell and Yale Univs, Pembroke Coll., Univ. of Cambridge, UK; mem. Faculty, Yale Univ. 1955–, Prof. of English 1965–77, DeVane Prof. of Humanities 1974–77, Prof. of Humanities 1977–, Sterling Prof. of Humanities and English 1983–; Visiting Prof., Hebrew Univ. Jerusalem 1959, Breadloaf Summer School 1965–66, Soc. for Humanities, Cornell Univ. 1968–69; Visiting Univ. Prof., New School of Social Research, New York 1982–84; Charles Eliot Norton Prof. of Poetry, Harvard Univ. 1987–88; Berg Visiting Prof. of English, New York Univ. 1988–2004; mem. American Acad. and Inst. of Arts and Letters, American Philosophical Soc.; Fulbright Fellow 1955, Guggenheim Fellow 1962; Dr hc (St Michael's Coll.), (Univ. of Rome), (Univ. of Bologna), (Univ. of Coimbra), (Boston Coll.), (Yeshiva Univ.), (Univ. of Mass. at Dartmouth), (Univ. of Buenos Aires); Newton Arvin Award 1967; Melville Cane Award, Poetry Soc. of America 1970; Zabel Prize, American Inst. of Arts and Letters 1982; MacArthur Foundation Fellowship 1985; Christian Gauss Prize 1989, Gold Medal for Criticism, American Acad. of Arts and Letters 1999, Int. Prize of Catalonia 2002, Alfonso Reyes Prize (Mexico) 2003, Hans Christian Anderson Bicentennial Prize (Denmark) 2005. *Publications:* Shelley's Mythmaking 1959, The Visionary Company 1961, Blake's Apocalypse 1963, Commentary to Blake 1965, Yeats 1970, The Ringers in the Tower 1971, The Anxiety of Influence 1973, Wallace Stevens: The Poems of Our Climate 1977, A Map of Misreading 1975, Kabbalah and Criticism 1975, Poetry and Repression 1976, Figures of Capable Imagination 1976, The Flight to Lucifer: A Gnostic Fantasy 1979, Agon: Towards a Theory of Revisionism 1981, The Breaking of the Vessels 1981, The Strong Light of the Canonical 1987, Freud: Transference and Authority 1988, Poetics of Influence: New and Selected Criticism 1988, Ruin the Sacred Truths 1989, The Book of J 1990, The American Religion 1991, The Western Canon 1994, Omens of Millennium 1996, Shakespeare: The Invention of the Human 1998, How to Read and Why 2000, Stories and Poems for Extremely Intelligent Children of All Ages 2000, Genius: A Mosaic of One Hundred Exemplary Creative Minds 2002, Hamlet: Poem Unlimited 2003, Best Poems of the English Language: Chaucer to Hart Crane 2003, Where Shall Wisdom be Found? 2004, The Names Divine: Jesus and Yahweh 2005, Yetziat: Fallen Angels, Demons and Devils 2006. *Leisure interest:* reading. *Address:* Department of English, WHC 202, Yale University, 63 High Street, POB 208302, New Haven, CT 06520-8302, USA (office). *Telephone:* (203) 432-0029 (office). *E-mail:* harold.bloom@yale.edu (office). *Website:* www.yale.edu/english (office).

BLOOM, Myer, PhD, FRSC; Canadian physicist and academic; *Professor Emeritus of Physics, University of British Columbia;* b. 7 Dec. 1928, Montreal; s. of Israel Bloom and Leah Ram; m. Margaret P. Holmes 1954; one s. one d.; ed Baron Byng High School, McGill Univ. and Univ. of Illinois at Urbana; NRC

Travelling Postdoctoral Fellow, Univ. of Leiden, Netherlands 1954–56; Research Assoc., Univ. of BC 1956–57, Asst Prof. 1957–60, Assoc. Prof. 1960–63, Prof. of Physics 1963–94; Prof. Emer. 1995–; Visiting Prof., Harvard Univ. 1964–65, Kyoto Univ. 1965, Univ. de Paris Sud 1971–72, 1978–79, Univ. of Rome 1986, Danish Tech. Univ. 1986; mem. Canadian Asscn of Physicists; Alfred P. Sloan Fellow 1961–65; Fellow, American Physical Soc., Canadian Inst. for Advanced Research 1991–2000; Hon. DTech (Tech. Univ. of Denmark) 1994; Hon. DIur (Concordia Univ., Montreal) 1995; Hon. DSc (British Columbia) 2000; Steacie Prize 1967, Biely Prize 1969; Canadian Asscn of Physicists Gold Medal 1973; Science Council of BC Chair.'s Award for Career Achievements 1992, Izaak Walton Killam Memorial Prize for Natural Sciences 1995. *Publications:* numerous research and review articles. *Leisure interests:* hiking, skiing, squash, wine-making. *Address:* c/o David Bloom, 1616 McLean Drive, Vancouver, BC V5L 3P3, Canada (home). *E-mail:* bloom@physics.ubc.ca (office).

BLOOM, Stephen Robert, MA, MD, DSc, FRCP, FRCPath, FMedSci; British physician, academic and biomedical researcher; *Head of Division of Investigative Science, Imperial College London;* b. 24 Oct. 1942, Maidstone, Kent; s. of Arnold Bloom and Edith Nancy Bloom (née Fox); m. Margaret Janet Sturrock 1965; two s. two d.; ed Univ. of Cambridge; Medical Unit Registrar, Middx Hosp., London 1970–72; MRC Clinical Research Fellow 1972–74; Sr Lecturer, Royal Postgraduate Medical School, Hammersmith Hosp. 1974–78, Reader in Medicine 1978–82, Prof. of Endocrinology 1982–, Head Dept of Endocrinology and Metabolic Medicine, Dir of Pathology and Therapy Services, Hammersmith Hosps NHS Trust 1996–; Prof. of Medicine, Imperial Coll. School of Medicine (ICSM) (fmrly Royal Postgraduate Medical School) 1982–, Dir of Metabolic Medicine and Chief of Service for Chemical Pathology 1994–,; Chair. Div. of Investigative Science, ICSM 1997–; Vice-Pres. (Sr Censor) Royal Coll. of Physicians 1999–2001; Sec. Soc. for Endocrinology 1999–2001, Chair. 2001–. *Publications:* Gut Hormones (ed.) 1978, Endocrine Tumours 1985, Surgical Endocrinology 1992. *Leisure interests:* jogging, classical music, computing. *Address:* Department of Metabolic Medicine, Division of Investigative Science, Imperial College London at Hammersmith Hospital, 6th Floor, Commonwealth Building, Du Cane Road, London, W12 0NN, England (office). *Telephone:* (20) 8383-3242 (office). *Fax:* (20) 8383-3142 (office). *E-mail:* s.bloom@imperial.ac.uk (office). *Website:* www1.imperial.ac.uk/medicine/about/keypeople/people/s.bloom.html (office).

BLOOMBERG, Michael Rubens, MBA; American politician; *Mayor of New York;* b. 14 Feb. 1942, Medford, Mass; m. (divorced); two c.; ed Johns Hopkins Univ., Harvard Univ.; with Salomon Brothers (investment bank) 1966–81, made Pnr 1972; Founder, Chief Exec., Chair. Bloomberg Financial Markets 1981–, Founder, Pres. Bloomberg LP 1982–; Publr Bloomberg Business News, Bloomberg Magazine, Bloomberg Personal Magazine; Gen. Man. Bloomberg Television, Bloomberg Radio WBBR-AM 1130; Mayor of New York 2001–; Chair. Bd of Trustees Johns Hopkins Univ. –2002; Trustee Big Apple Circus, mem. Bd Lincoln Center for Performing Arts, Jewish Museum, NY, Police and Fire Widow's and Children's Fund, Metropolitan Museum of Art and numerous other bodies. *Publication:* Bloomberg by Bloomberg (autobiog.) 1998. *Address:* Office of the Mayor, City Hall, New York, NY 10007 (office). *Telephone:* (212) 788–3000 (office). *Website:* www.nyc.gov (office).

BLOOMER, Jonathan, BSc, ARCS, FCA, CIMgt; British insurance executive; b. 23 March 1954; m. Judy Bloomer (née May); one s. two d.; ed Imperial Coll., London; joined Arthur Andersen 1974, Man. Partner of European Insurance Practice –1994; Group Finance Dir Prudential PLC 1995–2000, Group CEO 2000–05, mem. Bd of Dirs; Dir Railtrack PLC 1999–2002; Deputy Chair. Financial Services Practitioner Panel 2001–03, Chair. 2003–; mem. Bd Asscn of British Insurers 2001–. *Leisure interests:* rugby, boats.

BLOOMFIELD, Sir Kenneth Percy, KCB, MA; British public servant; *Chairman, Northern Ireland Legal Services Commission;* b. 15 April 1931, Belfast; s. of the late Harry Percy Bloomfield and Doris Bloomfield; m. Mary E. Ramsey 1960; one s. one d.; ed Royal Belfast Academical Inst. and St Peter's Coll., Oxford; joined N Ireland Civil Service 1952; Private Sec. to Ministers of Finance 1956–60; Deputy Dir British Industrial Devt Office, New York 1960–63; Asst later Deputy Sec. to Cabinet, N Ireland 1963–72; Under-Sec. N Ireland Office 1972–74; Perm. Sec. Office of Exec. N Ireland 1974–75; Perm. Sec. Dept of Environment, N Ireland 1975–81, Dept of Econ. Devt 1981–84; Head, N Ireland Civil Service and Second Perm. Under-Sec. of State, N Ireland Office 1984–91; Nat. Gov., Chair. Broadcasting Council for N Ireland, BBC 1991–99; Chair. Children in Need Trust 1992–98, N Ireland Higher Educ. Council 1993–2001, N Ireland Victims Commr 1997–98, Bangor and Holywood Town Centre Man. Ltd 2001, BBC Audit Cttee, N Ireland Chief Execs Forum, Higher Educ. Council for N Ireland, N Ireland Legal Services Comm. 2003–; Pres. Ulster People's Coll. 1996–; mem. N Ireland Advisory Bd Bank of Ireland 1991–2001, Green Park Trust 1996–2001; Hon. Fellow St Peter's Coll. Oxford; numerous other appointments; Hon. LLD (Belfast); Hon. DUniv (Open Univ.) 2000; Hon. DLitt (Univ. of Ulster) 2002; Northern Ireland Chamber of Commerce Award for Personal or Corporate Excellence 1990. *Publication:* Stormont in Crisis (a memoir) 1994. *Leisure interests:* reading history and biographies, writing, swimming. *Address:* Northern Ireland Legal Services Commission, 2nd Floor, Waterfront Plaza, 8 Laganbank Road, Belfast, BT1 3BN (office); 16 Larch Hill, Holywood, Co. Down, BT18 0JN, Northern Ireland (home). *Telephone:* (28) 9040-8801 (office); (28) 9042-8340 (home). *Fax:* (28) 9040-8995 (office); (28) 9042-8340 (home). *E-mail:* kenbloomfield@tiscali.co.uk (home).

BLUM, Brad, BA, MBA; American business executive; m.; two step-s.; ed Denison Univ., Granville, OH, Northwestern Univ. J. L. Kellogg Business School, Evanston, IL; joined General Mills as Asst Product Man. Big G (Cereal) Div. 1978, 16 years in marketing, Gen. Man., becoming Vice Pres. of Marketing, Cereal Partners Worldwide (CPW), Morges, Switzerland 1990–94; Sr Vice Pres. of Marketing, Olive Garden Div., Darden Restaurants June–Dec. 1994, Pres. Dec. 1994–1997, Exec. Vice Pres. and Dir, Darden Restaurants 1997–2002, Vice Chair. March–Dec. 2002; Chief Exec. Burger King Corpn Jan. 2003–2004 (resgnd); f. Blum Enterprises LLC (restaurant industry consultancy) 2005; Chair. Econ. Devt Bd, City of Winter Park, FL; mem. Bd of Trustees Atlantic Center for the Arts; mem. Advisory Bd Sun Trust Bank; Multi-unit Foodservice Operators (MUFSO) Operator of the Year 2000. *Leisure interests:* tennis, skiing, motor racing. *Address:* Blum Enterprises, Winter Park FL, USA (office).

BLÜM, Norbert, DPhil; German politician; b. 21 July 1935, Rüsselsheim; s. of Christian Blüm and Margarete (née Beck) Blüm; m. Marita Binger 1964; one s. two d.; ed Volksschule; apprentice, Opel AG, Rüsselsheim, 1949–53, toolmaker 1953–57; worked in building trade and as lorry driver while studying evenings 1957–61; univ. student in Cologne and Bonn 1961–67; Ed. Soziale Ordnung 1966–68; Chief Man. Social Comm. of Christian Democrat employees' Asscn 1968–75, Regional Chair. Rhineland-Palatinate 1974–77, Fed. Chair. 1977–87; mem. Fed. Exec. CDU 1969–; mem. Bundestag 1969–; Deputy Chair. CDU 1981–2000; Senator for Fed. Affairs for Berlin 1981; Minister of Labour and Social Affairs 1982–98; Regional Chair. CDU North Rhine-Westphalia 1987–98; mem. IG Metall; Karl-Valentin-Orden 1987, Heinrich-Brauns Preis 1990 and numerous other awards and prizes. *Publications:* Reform oder Reaktion–Wohin geht die CDU 1972, Gewerkschaften zwischen Allmacht und Ohnmacht 1979, Werkstücke 1980, Die Arbeit geht weiter–zur Krise der Erwerbsgesellschaft 1983, 40 Jahre Socialstaat Bundesrepublik Deutschland 1989, Politikals Balanceakt 1993, Dann Willichs mal probieren–Geschichten vom Lachen und Weinen 1994, Sommerfrische-Regentage inclusive 1995, Die Glücksmargerite–Geschichten zum Vorlesen 1997, Diesseits und Jenseits der Politik 1998. *Leisure interests:* reading, walking. *Address:* Platz der Republik, 11011 Berlin, Germany.

BLUM, Yehuda Z., MJur, PhD; Israeli diplomatist, lawyer and academic; *Hersch Lauterpacht Professor of International Law, Hebrew University of Jerusalem;* b. 2 Oct. 1931, Bratislava; m. Moriah Rabinovitz-Teomim; two s. one d.; ed Hebrew Univ., Jerusalem, Univ. of London; detained in Nazi concentration camp of Bergen-Belsen 1944; Asst to Judge Advocate-Gen. of Israel Defence Forces 1956–59; Sr Asst to Legal Adviser, Ministry for Foreign Affairs 1962–65; UNESCO Fellow, Univ. of Sydney July–Aug. 1968; Office of UN Legal Counsel Sept.–Dec. 1968; Sr Research Scholar, Univ. of Mich. Law School 1969; Visiting Prof., School of Law, Univ. of Tex. 1971, New York Univ. 1975–76, Univ. of Mich. Law School 1985, Cardozo School of Law, New York 1991, 2000, Univ. of Southern Calif., Los Angeles 1991–92, Tulane Univ., New Orleans 1994, 2003, Univ. of Miami 1999, Univ. of Calif., Berkeley 2002; Hersch Lauterpacht Prof. of Int. Law, Hebrew Univ. of Jerusalem 1991–; mem. Israeli del., Third UN Conf. on Law of the Sea 1973, 31st Session of UN Gen. Ass. 1976; Perm. Rep. to UN 1978–84; Law Ed. Encyclopedia Hebraica 1973–78; Hon. DJur (Yeshiva Univ.) 1981; Jabotinsky Prize 1984. *Publications:* Historic Titles in International Law 1965, Secure Boundaries and Middle East Peace 1971, For Zion's Sake 1987, Eroding the UN Charter 1993. *Address:* Faculty of Law, Hebrew University, Mount Scopus, Jerusalem 91905, Israel (office). *Telephone:* 2-5882562 (office). *Fax:* 2-5823042 (home). *E-mail:* msblumy@mscc.huji.ac.il (office). *Website:* law.mscc.huji.ac.il/law1/newsite/hebrew.html (office).

BLUMBERG, Baruch Samuel, MD, PhD, FRCP; American research physician; *Fox Chase Distinguished Scientist and Senior Adviser to the President, Fox Chase Cancer Center;* b. 28 July 1925, New York; s. of late Meyer Blumberg and of Ida Blumberg (née Simonoff); m. Jean Liebesman 1954; two s. two d.; ed Union Coll., Schenectady, Columbia Univ. Coll. of Physicians and Surgeons, Balliol Coll., Oxford; served USN 1943–46; Intern and resident, First (Columbia) Div., Bellevue Hosp., New York 1951–57; Ship's Surgeon 1952; Fellow in Medicine, Presbyterian Hosp., New York 1953–55; Dept of Biochem., Oxford Univ., UK 1955–57; Chief of Geographic Medicine and Genetics Section, NIH, Bethesda, Md 1957–64; Assoc. Dir for Clinical Research, Inst. for Cancer Research, Philadelphia 1964–86, Vice-Pres. for Population Oncology, Fox Chase Cancer Center 1986–89, Fox Chase Distinguished Scientist and Sr Adviser to Pres. 1989–; Univ. Prof. of Medicine and Anthropology, Univ. of Pennsylvania 1977–; George Eastman Visiting Prof., Univ. of Oxford 1983–84, Raman Visiting Prof., Indian Acad. of Sciences, Bangalore, India Jan.–April 1986; Ashland Visiting Prof., Univ. of Ky 1986–87; Master Balliol Coll., Oxford 1989–94; Dir NASA Astrobiology Inst., Ames Research Center, Moffett Field, Calif. 1999–2002; attending physician, Pa Hosp., Hosp. of Univ. of Pennsylvania; admin. NASA HQ, Washington 2000–2002; mem. Asscn of American Physicians, various other medical socs; Fellow, NAS; Hon. Fellow Balliol Coll., Oxford 1976; numerous hon. degees; Bernstein Award, Medical Soc. of New York, 1969, Passano Award 1974, Modern Medicine Distinguished Achievement Award 1975, Karl Landsteiner Award 1975, Showa Emperor Memorial Award, Japan, 1994, shared Nobel Prize in Physiology or Medicine for discoveries concerning new mechanisms for origin and dissemination of infectious diseases 1976, and numerous other awards. *Publications:* Australia Antigen and the Biology of Hepatitis B 1977, Hepatitis B: The Hunt for a Killer Virus 2004; numerous papers to scientific journals. *Leisure interests:* canoeing, mountain walking, cycling, kayaking. *Address:* Fox Chase Cancer Center, 333 Cottman Avenue, Fox Chase, Philadelphia, PA 19111, USA (office). *Telephone:* (215) 728-3164 (office). *Fax:* (215) 728-5310 (office). *E-mail:* baruch.blumberg@fccc.edu (office). *Website:* www.fccc.edu.

BLUME, Judy, BS; American writer; b. 12 Feb. 1938, Elizabeth, NJ; d. of Rudolph and Esther (née Rosenfeld) Sussman; m. 1st John M. Blume 1959 (divorced 1975); one s. one d.; m. 2nd George Cooper 1987; one step-d.; ed New

York Univ.; founder and Trustee The Kids Fund 1981; mem. PEN Club, Authors' Guild, Nat. Coalition Against Censorship, Soc. of Children's Book Writers; Hon. LHD (Kean Coll) 1987; Chicago Public Library Carl Sandburg Freedom to Read Award 1984, American Civil Liberties Union Award 1986, American Library Asscn Margaret A. Edwards Award for Lifetime Achievement 1996; Nat. Book Foundation Medal for Distinguished Contribution to American Letters 2004. *Publications:* juvenile fiction: The One in the Middle Is the Green Kangaroo 1969, Iggie's House 1970, Are You There God? It's Me, Margaret (Outstanding Children's Book) 1970, Then Again, Maybe I Won't 1971, Freckle Juice 1971, It's Not the End of the World 1972, Tales of a Fourth Grade Nothing 1972, Otherwise Known as Sheila the Great 1972, Deenie 1973, Blubber 1974, Forever 1975, Starring Sally J. Freedman as Herself 1977, Superfudge 1980, Tiger Eyes 1981, The Pain and the Great One 1984, Just As Long As We're Together 1987, Fudge-a-mania 1990, Here's to You, Rachel Robinson 1993, Summer Sisters 1998, Places I Never Meant To Be (ed.) 1999, Double Fudge 2002, The Pain and the Great One: Soupy Saturdays 2008; adult fiction: Wifey 1978, Smart Women 1983; non-fiction: Letters to Judy: What Kids Wish They Could Tell You 1986, The Judy Blume Memory Book 1988. *Address:* Harold Ober Associates, 425 Madison Avenue, New York, NY 10017-1110, USA (office). *Website:* www.judyblume.com.

BLUMENTHAL, W(erner) Michael, PhD; American business executive; *Director, Jewish Museum Berlin;* b. 3 Jan. 1926, Germany; s. of Ewald Blumenthal and Rose Valerie (Markt) Blumenthal; ed Univ. of California at Berkeley and Princeton Univ.; went to US 1947, naturalized 1952; Research Assoc., Princeton Univ. 1954–57; Vice-Pres., Dir Crown Cork Int. Corpn 1957–61; Deputy Asst Sec. of State for Econ. Affairs, Dept of State 1961–63; also served as USA Rep. to UN Comm. on Int. Commodity Trade; President's Deputy Special Rep. for Trade Negotiations (with rank of Amb.) 1963–67; Chair. US Del. to Kennedy Round tariff talks in Geneva; Pres. Bendix Int. 1967–70; Dir Bendix Corpn 1967–77, Vice-Chair. June–Dec. 1970, Pres. and Chief Operating Officer 1971–72, Chair. and CEO 1972–77; Sec. of the Treasury 1977–79; Dir Burroughs Corpn (now Unisys) 1979–90, Vice-Chair. 1980, CEO 1981–90, Chair. 1990; Sr Advisor Lazard Frères & Co. 1990–96; Dir, Jewish Museum Berlin 1997–; mem. Council on Foreign Relations; Charter Trustee Emer., Princeton Univ.; Große Verdienstkreuz; Dr h.c. *Publications:* The Invisible Wall 1998. *Leisure interests:* tennis, skiing. *Address:* 227 Ridgeview Road, Princeton, NJ 08540, USA (office). *Telephone:* (609) 497-7676 (office). *Fax:* (609) 497-1888 (office).

BLUMGART, Leslie Harold, BDS, MD, FACS, FRCS (Glas.), FRCSE, FRCPS; British academic and surgeon; *Enid A. Haupt Professor of Surgery, Memorial Sloan-Kettering Cancer Center;* b. 7 Dec. 1931, South Africa; s. of Harold Herman Blumgart and Hilda Blumgart; m. 1st Pearl Navias 1955 (deceased); m. 2nd Sarah Raybould Bowen 1968; two s. two d.; ed Jeppe High School, Johannesburg, Univ. of Witwatersrand, Johannesburg, Univ. of Sheffield, England; Sr Lecturer and Deputy Dir, Dept of Surgery, Welsh Nat. School of Medicine, Cardiff 1970–72; St Mungo Prof. of Surgery, Univ. of Glasgow, Hon. Consultant Surgeon, Glasgow Royal Infirmary 1972–79; Prof. of Surgery and Dir Dept of Surgery, Royal Postgraduate Medical School, Univ. of London and Hon. Consultant, Hammersmith Hosp., London 1979–86; Prof. of Visceral and Transplantion Surgery, Univ. of Bern and Inselspital Bern, Switzerland 1986–91; Enid A. Haupt Prof. of Surgery, Memorial Sloan-Kettering Cancer Center, New York 1991–, Chief of Section of Hepato-Biliary Surgery and Dir Hepato-Biliary Program 1995–2007; Prof. of Surgery, Cornell Univ. Medical Coll. 1993, American Surgery Soc.; Moynihan Fellowship, Asscn of Surgeons of GB and Ireland 1972; mem. Hong Kong Surgical Soc., Hellenic Surgical Soc., LA Surgical Soc.; Pres. Int. Biliary Asscn 1986; Hon. Fellow Royal Coll. of Surgeons in Ireland; Hon. mem. Soc. for Surgery of the Alimentary Tract, USA, Danish Surgical Soc. 1988, Asscn Française de Chirurgie, Yugoslav Soc. of Surgery, Soc. Italiana di Chirurgia 2002, Austrian Soc. of Surgery 2007, French Acad. of Surgery 2008; Order of Prasidda Prabala Gorkha-Dakshin Bahu (Nepal) 1984; Hon. DSc (Sheffield) 1998. *Publications include:* Essentials of Medicine and Surgery for Dental Students (with A. C. Kennedy) 4th Edn 1982, The Biliary Tract, in Clinical Surgery Int., Vol. 5 1982, Liver Surgery, in Clinical Surgery Int., Vol. 12 (with S. Bengmark) 1986, Difficult Problems in General Surgery 1989, Surgery of the Liver and Biliary Tract, Vols 1 and 2 (3rd edn) 2000, Surgery of the Liver, Biliary Tract and Pancreas, Vols 1 and 2 (4th edn); numerous publs concerned with medical educ., gastrointestinal surgery and aspects of oncology with particular interest in surgery of the liver, pancreas and biliary tract. *Leisure interests:* watercolour painting, wood carving. *Address:* Memorial Sloan-Kettering Cancer Center, 1275 York Avenue, New York, NY 10021 (office); 447 East 57th Street, 3E, New York, NY 10022, USA (home). *Telephone:* (212) 639-5526 (office); (212) 755-0836 (home). *Fax:* (212) 794-5852 (office). *E-mail:* blumgarl@mskcc.org (office). *Website:* www.mskcc.org (office).

BLUNDELL, Pamela; British fashion designer; b. 23 Feb. 1969; ed Southampton Univ., Epsom School of Art & Design; worked on samples, design and marketing with late John Flett; numerous freelance clients including English Nat. Opera, Liberty of London; fmr lecturer St Martin's School of Art, London; formed Copperwheat Blundell with Lee Copperwheat (q.v.) 1993; Visiting Lecturer Cen. St Martin's School of Art, Univ. of Nottingham, Brighton Polytechnic 1991–95; winner Courtauld's knitwear competition; Smirnoff Fashion Award for Best Young Designer 1987; Young Designer of the Year 1994 (with Lee Copperwheat). *Address:* Copperwheat Blundell, 14 Cheshire Street, London, E2 6EH, England. *Telephone:* (20) 7613-0651. *Fax:* (20) 7729-8600.

BLUNDELL, Sir Tom Leon, Kt, DPhil, FRS, FMedSci; British biochemist and academic; *Chairman, School of Biological Sciences, University of Cambridge;* b. 7 July 1942, Brighton; s. of Horace Leon Blundell and Marjorie Blundell; m.

Bancinyane Lynn Sibanda 1987; one s. two d.; ed Steyning Grammar School and Brasenose Coll., Oxford; Jr research fellow in molecular physics, Linacre Coll. 1968–70; lecturer, Hertford Coll., Oxford 1970–72; lecturer in Biological Sciences, Sussex Univ. 1973–76; Prof. of Crystallography, Birkbeck Coll., London Univ. 1976–90; Dir-Gen. Agricultural and Food Research Council 1991–94; Chief Exec. Biotechnology and Biological Sciences Research Council 1994–96; Sir William Dunn Prof. of Biochemistry, Univ. of Cambridge 1995–, Fellow Sidney Sussex Coll. 1995–, Head Dept of Biochem., 1996–, Chair. School of Biological Sciences 2003–; Dir Int. School of Crystallography 1982–; Chair. Scientific Advisory Bd Bioprocessing Ltd 1996–99; Dir (non-exec.) Celltech 1997– 2004 (Chair. Scientific Advisory Bd 1998–2004); Scientific Adviser Oxford Molecular Ltd 1996–99; mem. R&D Bd SmithKline Beecham 1997–99, Bd Babraham Inst., Cambridge 1996–2003; Hon. Dir of Imperial Cancer Research Fund Unit of Structural Molecular Biology 1989–96; Chair. Biological Sciences, Science and Eng Research Council (SERC) Council 1983–87, SERC Council 1989–90, AFRC Council and Food Cttee 1985–90, Advisory Council on Science and Tech. 1988–90, Royal Comm. on Environmental Pollution 1998–2005, Science Advisory Bd 2000–; Co-founder and Dir (non-exec.) Astex Tech. 1999–; Consultant, Pfizer 1983–90; mem. Academia Europaea 1993, Council, Royal Soc. 1997–99; Fellow, EMBO 1985–; Fellow Birkbeck Coll. London 1997, Sidney Sussex Coll. Cambridge; Foreign Fellow, Indian Nat. Science Acad. 1994; Trustee Daphne Jackson Trust 1996–, Lawes Trust 1996; mem. Bd Parl. Office of Science and Tech. 1998–; Hon. Fellow, Royal Agricultural Soc. of England 1993, Brasenose Coll., Oxford 1989–, Linacre Coll., Oxford 1991–; Dr hc (Stirling) 2000, (Sussex) 2001, (Pavia) 2002; Hon. DSc (London Univ.) 2003 and numerous other hon. degrees; Gold Medal, Inst. of Biotechnologies 1987, Sir Hans Krebs Medal 1987, CIBA Medal 1988, Feldberg Prize 1988, Medal of Soc. for Chemical Industry 1995, Nat. Equal Opportunities Award 1996, Pfizer European Prize for Innovation 1998. *Publications include:* Protein Crystallography 1976, Progress in Biophysics and Molecular Biology (Ed.) 1980–; various publs in Nature, Journal of Molecular Biology. *Leisure interests:* opera, playing jazz, foreign travel, walking. *Address:* Department of Biochemistry, 80 Tennis Court Road, University of Cambridge, Cambridge, CB2 1GA, England (office). *Telephone:* (1223) 333628 (office). *Fax:* (1223) 766082 (office). *E-mail:* tom@cryst.bioc.cam .ac.uk (home). *Website:* www.bio.cam.ac.uk (office).

BLUNDEN, Sir George, Kt, MA; British central banker (retd); b. 31 Dec. 1922, Sutton, Surrey; s. of George Blunden and Florence Holder; m. Anne Bulford 1949; two s. one d.; ed City of London School, Univ. Coll., Oxford; war service, Royal Sussex Regt 1941–45; Bank of England 1947–55; economist, Balance of Payments Div., IMF 1955–58; various posts, Bank of England 1958–65, Deputy Principal, Discount Office 1965–67, seconded to Monopolies Comm. 1968, Deputy Chief Cashier 1968–73, Chief of Man. Services 1973–74, responsible for banking supervision with rank of Head of Dept 1974–76, Exec. Dir 1976–84, non-exec. Dir 1984–85, Deputy Gov. 1986–90; Chair., Group of Ten Cttees on banking supervision 1975–77 and on payments systems 1981–83; Chair., London Pensions Fund Authority 1990–92; Jt Deputy Chair., Leopold Joseph Holdings 1984–85, 1990–94; Pres. Inst. of Business Ethics 1994–96; Chair. Centre for Study of Financial Innovation 1995–98; Adviser, Union Bank of Switzerland (London br.) 1990–94. *Address:* Ashdale, Gunthorpe, Melton Constable, Norfolk, NR24 2NS, England (home). *Telephone:* (1263) 860359 (home).

BLUNKETT, Rt Hon. David, PC, BA; British politician; b. 6 June 1947; m. (divorced); four s.; ed Sheffield Univ.; worked for E Midlands Gas Bd before entering univ.; subsequently taught industrial relations and politics at Barnsley Coll. of Tech.; joined Labour Party 1963; mem. Sheffield City Council 1970–87, Leader 1980–87; mem. S. Yorks. Co. Council 1973–77; MP for Sheffield Brightside 1987–; elected to Nat. Exec. Cttee (NEC) of Labour Party 1983, Chair. NEC Local Govt Cttee 1984; Local Govt Front Bench Spokesman in Opposition's Environment Team 1988–92; Shadow Sec. of State for Health 1992–94, for Educ. 1994–95, for Educ. and Employment 1995–97; Sec. of State for Educ. and Employment 1997–2001, for the Home Dept 2001–04 (resgnd); Sec. of State for Work and Pensions 2005 (resgnd); Vice-Chair. Labour Party 1992–93, Chair. 1993–94. *Publications:* On a Clear Day (autobiog.) 1995; co-author: Local Enterprise and Workers' Plans 1981, Building from the Bottom: the Sheffield Experience 1983, Democracy in Crisis: the Town Halls Respond 1987, Politics and Progress 2001, The Blunkett Tapes: My Life In The Bearpit (autobiog.) 2006. *Leisure interests:* walking, sailing, poetry. *Address:* House of Commons, London, SW1A 0AA, England (office). *Telephone:* (20) 7219-4043 (office); (114) 273-5987 (constituency office) (office). *Fax:* (20) 7219-5903 (office).

BLUNT, Charles William, BEcons, CPA; Australian politician and business executive; *CEO, American Chamber of Commerce in Australia;* b. 19 Jan. 1961; s. of the late R. S. G. Blunt; mem. House of Reps (for Richmond, NSW) 1984–90, Shadow Minister for Community Service 1987; Exec. Dir Nat. Party 1980–84, Leader 1989–90; CEO American Chamber of Commerce in Australia 1990–; Chair. Maxis Ltd, Permo-Drive Technologies Ltd, Pacific Star Resorts Ltd, Capital Policy and Trade Pty Ltd, Palamedia Ltd; Man. Dir American Business Services Pty Ltd. *Leisure interests:* tennis, squash, golf, motor racing, travel, trekking. *Address:* Suite 4, Gloucester Walk, 88 Cumberland Street, Sydney, NSW 2000, Australia.

BLUNT, Matt Roy, BA; American politician; b. 20 Nov. 1970, Strafford, Mo.; s. of Roy Blunt; m. Melanie Blunt 1997; ed Jefferson City's public high school, US Naval Acad., Annapolis, Md; spent five years on active duty with USN as Eng Officer aboard USS Jack Williams (FFG-24) and then as Navigator and Admin. Officer aboard USS Peterson (DD-969), currently Lt-Commdr, USNR; mem. Mo. State House of Reps for 139th Legis. Dist 1998–2000; Sec. of State for Mo. 2000–04; Gov. of Mo. 2005–2009 (announced he would not seek a second term); mem. State Historical Soc. of Mo., American Legion, Mo. Farm Bureau; Republican; four USN and Marine Corps Achievement Medals and Humanitarian Service Medal. *Address:* Republican National Committee, 310 First Street, SE, Washington, DC 20003, USA (office). *Telephone:* (202) 863-8500 (office). *Fax:* (202) 863-8820 (office). *E-mail:* info@gop.com (office). *Website:* www.rnc.org (office); mattblunt.com (office).

BLY, Robert Elwood, MA; American writer and poet; b. 23 Dec. 1926, Madison, Minn.; s. of Jacob Thomas Bly and Alice Bly (née Aws); m. 1st Carolyn McLean 1955 (divorced 1979); m. 2nd Ruth Counsell 1980; five c.; ed Harvard Univ. and Univ. of Iowa; served USN 1944–46; founder and Ed. The Fifties 1958–, later The Sixties and Seventies Press; f. American Writers Against the Vietnam War 1966; Fulbright Award 1956–57, Amy Lowell Fellow 1964–65, Guggenheim Fellow 1965–66, Rockefeller Foundation Fellow 1967, Nat. Book Award in Poetry 1968. *Publications include:* poems: Silence in the Snowy Fields 1962, The Light Around the Body 1967, Chrysanthemums 1967, Ducks 1968, The Morning Glory: Another Thing That Will Never Be My Friend 1969, The Teeth Mother Naked at Last 1971, Poems for Tennessee (with William Stafford and William Matthews) 1971, Christmas Eve Service at Midnight at St Michael's 1972, Water Under the Earth 1972, The Dead Seal Near McClure's Beach 1973, Sleepers Joining Hands 1973, Jumping out of Bed 1973, The Hockey Poem 1974, Point Reyes Poems 1974, Old Man Rubbing his Eyes 1975, The Loon 1977, Visiting Emily Dickinson's Grave and Other Poems 1979, This Tree Will Be Here for a Thousand Years 1979, Finding an Old Ant Mansion 1981, The Man in the Black Coat Turns 1982, Four Ramages 1983, The Whole Moisty Night 1983, Out of the Rollling Ocean 1984, Mirabai Versions 1984, In the Month of May 1985, A Love of Minute Particulars 1985, Loving a Woman in Two Worlds 1985, Selected Poems (ed.) 1986, The Moon on the Fencepost 1988, The Apple Found in the Plowing 1989, What Have I Ever Lost By Dying?: Collected Prose Poems 1993, Gratitude to Old Teachers 1993, Meditations on the Insatiable Soul 1994, Morning Poems 1997, Eating the Honey of Words: New and Selected Poems 1999, The Best American Poetry (ed.) 1999, The Night Abraham Called to the Stars 2001, My Sentence was a Thousand Years of Joy 2005; prose poems: The Morning Glory 1973, This Body is Made of Camphor and Gopherwood 1977, This Body is Made of Eating the Honey of Words: New and Selected Poems 1999, The Best American Poetry (ed.) 1999; prose: Iron John 1990; criticism: A Poetry Reading Against the Vietnam War 1966, The Sea and the Honeycomb 1966, Forty Poems Touching on Recent American History (ed.) 1967, Leaping Poetry 1975, The Soul is Here for its Own Joy 1995; trans. of vols of poetry from Swedish, Norwegian, German, Spanish and Hindi. *Address:* 1904 Girard Avenue South, Minneapolis, MN 55403, USA.

BLYTH OF ROWINGTON, Baron (Life Peer), cr. 1995, of Rowington in the County of Warwickshire; **James Blyth,** Kt, MA, FRSA; British business executive; *Chairman, Diageo PLC;* b. 8 May 1940; s. of Daniel Blyth and Jane Power Carlton; m. Pamela Anne Campbell Dixon 1967; one d. (one s. deceased); ed Spiers School, Univ. of Glasgow; with Mobil Oil Co. 1963–69, Gen. Foods Ltd 1969–71, Mars Ltd 1971–74; Dir and Gen. Man. Lucas Batteries Ltd 1974–77, Lucas Aerospace Ltd 1977–81; Dir Joseph Lucas Ltd 1977–81; Head of Defence Sales, Ministry of Defence 1981–85; Man. Dir Plessey Electronic Systems 1985–86; CEO Plessey Co. PLC 1986–87; CEO Boots Co. PLC 1987–98, Deputy Chair. 1994–98, Chair. 1998–2000; Dir (non-exec.) Imperial Group PLC 1984–86, Cadbury-Schweppes PLC 1986–90, British Aerospace 1990–94, Anixter Int. Inc. 1995–, NatWest Group 1998–2000; Dir Diageo PLC 1998– (Chair. 2000–); Vice-Chair. Greenhill & Co. 2000–; mem. Council, Soc. of British Aerospace Cos 1977–81; Gov. London Business School 1987–96 (Hon. Fellow 1997); Pres. ME Asscn 1988–93; Chair. Advisory Panel on Citizen's Charter 1991–97; Patron Combined Services Winter Sports Asscn 1997–2002; Liveryman, Coachmakers' and Coach Harness Makers' Co.; Hon. LLD (Nottingham) 1992. *Leisure interests:* skiing, tennis, paintings, theatre. *Address:* Diageo PLC, 8 Henrietta Place, London, W1G 0NB, England (office). *Telephone:* (20) 7927-5993 (office). *Fax:* (20) 7927-4794 (office). *Website:* www.diageo.com (office).

BO, Jørgen; Danish architect; b. 8 April 1919, Copenhagen; s. of Alf Bo and Anne Marie Bo; m. Gerda Bennike 1941 (divorced 1966); two s. two d.; ed Royal Danish Acad. of Fine Arts; own firm since 1943; tech. consultant for Soc. for Preservation of Natural Amenities of Denmark 1944–52; mem. Danish Nature Conservancy Bd 1952–61; mem. Charlottenborg Adjudicating Bd 1958–61; mem. Slotsholm Cttee 1961–63; mem. San Cataldo Council, Italy 1966; consultant planner for Danish Nat. Museum; mem. of various int. juries; Fellow, Royal Danish Acad. of Fine Arts, Prof. 1960–89; Fellow, Royal Danish Acad. in Rome 1968–70; Kt of the Dannebrog. *Works include:* domestic housing 1945–58, the Louisiana Museum 1956–58, Educ. Centre, Monastir, Tunisia 1960, Museum of Music History 1965, IBM HQ in Denmark 1968–73, Danish Embassy in Brasília 1968–73, IBM Int. Educ. Centre, Belgium 1969–75, Ny Carlsberg Glyptotek 1971–78, restoration work for Carlsberg Foundation and Royal Danish Acad. 1973–76, Extension of Louisiana Museum, Art Museum, Bochum and offices and housing in Baghdad 1978–83, Lübcke Museum, Hamm, FRG 1984–, Weisbord Pavilion, Israel Museum, Jerusalem 1987–88, 20th Century Art Pavilion, Israel Museum 1988. *Address:* Lindevangsvej 22, 3460 Birkerød, Denmark.

BO, Xilai, MA; Chinese politician; *Secretary, Chongqing Municipal Committee, Chinese Communist Party;* b. June 1949, Dingxiang, Shanxi Prov.; s. of Bo Yibo; ed Peking Univ., Graduate School, Chinese Acad. of Social Sciences; worked in hardware factory, No. 2 Light Industry Bureau, Beijing 1968; joined CCP 1980; fmrly cadre, Research Dept of Secr. of CCP Cen. Cttee and Gen. Office of CCP Cen. Cttee; Vice-Sec. then Sec. CCP Cttee of Dalian Econ. and Technological Devt Zone; Sec. CCP Jinzhou Dist Cttee; Deputy Mayor (also Acting Mayor) of Dalian, Liaoning Prov. 1992–93, Mayor 1993–2000; Deputy

Sec. CCP Dalian City Cttee 1995–99, Sec. 1999–2000; mem. CCP Prov. Cttee Standing Cttee, Liaoning Prov. 1999, Deputy Sec. CCP Prov. Cttee 2001–04; Vice-Gov. Gov. Liaoning Prov. 2001 (also Acting Gov.), Gov. 2001–04; mem. 16th CCP Cen. Cttee 2002–07; Minister of Commerce 2004–07; Sec. ., CCP Chongqing Municipal Cttee 2007–; mem. 17th CCP Cen. Cttee 2007–, mem. Politburo 2007–; Nat. Model for Respecting the Aged 1995. *Address:* c/o Ministry of Commerce, No. 2 Dong Chang'an Avenue, East Beijing 100731, People's Republic of China (office). *Website:* www.cq.gov.cn.

BOADEN, Helen, BA,; British broadcasting executive; *Director, BBC News;* b. 1 March 1956, Colchester, Essex; d. of William John Boaden and Barbara Mary Boaden; m. Stephen Burley 1994; ed Univ. of Sussex; Care Asst, Hackney Social Services, London 1978; Reporter, Radio WBAI, NY, USA 1979, Radio Tees and Radio Aire 1980–83; Producer, BBC Radio Leeds 1983–85; Reporter, File on 4, Radio 4 1985–91, Brass Tacks, BBC 2 1985–91; Presenter, Woman's Hour, Radio 4 1985–91, Verdict, Channel 4 1991–; Ed., File on 4, Radio 4 1991–94; Head of Network Current Affairs, BBC Manchester (first woman in position) 1994–97; Head of Business Programmes, BBC News 1997, Head of Current Affairs and Business Programmes 1998–2000; Controller, BBC Radio 4 2000–04, BBC 7 2002–04; Dir BBC News 2004–; Fellow Radio Acad., Chair. 2003–; Hon. doctorates (E Anglia, Sussex, York); Sony Gold Award (File on 4 investigation into AIDS in Africa in 1987, Sony Gold Award for File on 4 investigation into bullying in Feltham Young Offenders Inst. 1993, Radio Station of the Year 2003, 2004. *Leisure interests:* walking, food, travel. *Address:* BBC, Television Centre, Wood Lane, London, W12 7RJ, England (office). *Telephone:* (20) 8743-8000 (office). *Website:* www.bbc.co.uk (office).

BOAGIU, Anca Daniela; Romanian engineer and politician; *Vice-President of the Senate (Senatul);* b. 30 Nov. 1968, Constanta; one c.; ed Ovidius Univ., Constanta; Asst to Dir Gen., S.E.Co.L SpA 1994–95, Construction Site Man. 1995–96; Dir Dept of External Financing Programmes, Nat. Admin of Roads 1996–97; Dir Dept for External Financial Relations, Ministry of Transport 1997–99; Dir Programme for Industrial Restructuring and Professional Conversion (RICOP) 1999–2000; Admin. of External Financing Projects, Programme for the Restructuring the Pvt. Sector 1999–2000; Minister of Transport June–Dec. 2000; Deputy of Romanian Parl. 2000–; mem. Cttee for Industries and Services 2000–04, Sec. 2004–; Sec., Cttee for European Integration Sept.–Dec. 2001, Vice-Pres. Feb.–July 2003; Coordinator Sub-cttee for Equal Opportunities 2001–02; Vice-Pres. of Parl. Cttee for European Integration 2004–05; Minister of European Integration 2005–07; Vice-Pres. of Senatul 2008–; mem. friendship parl. groups with Italy, Tunisia and Germany; mem. Romania-EU Jt Parl. Cttee; mem. European Parl. Network; Rep. Democrat Party (PD) within the working group of mems of European Parl.; mem. and Exec. Sec., PD (Democrat Party). *Address:* Senatul, 050711 Bucharest 5, Calea 13 Septembrie 1–3, Romania (office). *Telephone:* (21) 4021111 (office). *Fax:* (21) 3121184 (office). *E-mail:* csava@senat.ro (office). *Website:* www.senat.ro (office).

BOARDMAN, Christopher (Chris) Miles, MBE, MSc; British fmr professional cyclist; b. 26 Aug. 1968; s. of Keith Boardman and Carole Boardman; m. Sally-Anne Edwards 1988; three s. one d; ed Hilbre Secondary School and Withens Coll.; has competed in nine world championships; holder of various nat. records and 20 nat. titles; bronze medal, Commonwealth Games, Edinburgh 1986; two bronze medals, Commonwealth Games, Auckland 1990; gold medal, 4,000m individual pursuit, Olympic Games, Barcelona 1992, Double World Champion (pursuit and time trial) 1994; winner Tour de France Prologue and holder Yellow Jersey 1994, 1997, 1998; World Record for distance cycled in one hour 1993 and 1996; won World 4,000m cycling championships, broke his own world record Sept. 1996; retd Oct. 2001; Co. Dir; mem. English Sports Council (now Sport England) 1996–; expert adviser to British cycling team 2004 Olympic Games; Hon. DSc (Brighton) 1997; Hon. MSc (Liverpool); Man of Year Award, Cheshire Life magazine 1997. *Publication:* Chris Boardman's Complete Book of Cycling. *Leisure interests:* carpentry, swimming, family. *Address:* c/o Beyond Level Four Ltd, Lindfield House, Station Approach, Meols, Wirral, L47 8XA, England.

BOARDMAN, Sir John, Kt, MA, FSA, FBA; British archaeologist and academic; *Professor Emeritus of Classical Archaeology and Art, University of Oxford;* b. 20 Aug. 1927; s. of the late Frederick Boardman and Clare Wells; m. Sheila Stanford 1952; one s. one d.; ed Chigwell School and Magdalene Coll., Cambridge; Asst Dir British School, Athens 1952–55; Asst Keeper, Ashmolean Museum, Oxford 1955–59; Reader in Classical Archaeology, Univ. of Oxford 1959–78, Lincoln Prof. of Classical Archaeology and Art 1978–94, Hon. Fellow 1995, now Prof. Emer.; Fellow, Merton Coll. Oxford 1973–78, Hon. Fellow 1978–, Sub-Warden 1975–78; Prof. of Ancient History, Royal Acad. of Arts 1989–; conducted excavations on Chios 1953–55, Crete 1964–65, in Tocra, Libya 1964–65; Visiting Prof., Columbia Univ. 1965; Geddes-Harrower Prof., Univ. of Aberdeen 1974; Fellow, Inst. of Etruscan Studies, Florence 1983, Austrian and German Archaeological Insts; Foreign mem. Royal Danish Acad.; Assoc. mem. Acad. des Inscriptions et des Belles Lettres, Institut de France; Corresp. mem. Bavarian Acad. of Sciences; Foreign mem. American Philosophical Soc., Accad. dei Lincei, Rome, Russian Acad. of Sciences; Hon. RA; Hon. MRIA; Dr hc (Athens) 1991, (Sorbonne) 1994; Kenyon Medal (British Acad.) 1995. *Publications include:* Cretan Collection in Oxford 1961, Island Gems 1963, Archaic Greek Gems 1968, Athenian Black Figure Vases 1974, Escarabeos de Piedra de Ibiza 1984, The Oxford History of the Classical World (with others) 1986, Athenian Red Figure Vases: Classical period 1989, Oxford History of Classical Art 1993, The Diffusion of Classical Art in Antiquity 1994, Greek Sculpture, Later Classical 1995, Runciman Prioxe 1995, Early Greek Vase Painting 1997, Persia and the West 2000, The History of Greek Vases 2001, Greek Gems and Finger Rings 2001, The

Archaeology of Nostalgia 2002, Classical Phoenician Scarabs 2003, The World of Ancient Art 2006; articles in learned journals. *Address:* 11 Park Street, Woodstock, Oxford, OX20 1SJ (home); Beazley Archive, Classics Centre, Oxford, OX1 3LU, England. *Telephone:* (1993) 811259 (home); (1865) 278084. *Fax:* (1865) 610237 (office). *E-mail:* john.boardman@ashmus.ox.ac.uk (office).

BOARDMAN, Norman Keith, AO, PhD, ScD, FAA, FRS, FTSE; Australian biochemist and academic; b. 16 Aug. 1926, Geelong, Vic.; s. of William R. Boardman and Margaret Boardman; m. Mary C. Shepherd 1952; two s. five d.; ed Melbourne Univ. and St John's Coll., Cambridge; Research Officer, Wool Research Section, CSIRO 1949–51; Sr Research Scientist, Div. of Plant Industry, CSIRO 1956–61, Prin. Research Scientist 1961–64; Fulbright Scholar, UCLA 1964–65; Sr Prin. Research Scientist, Div. of Plant Industry, CSIRO 1966–68, Chief Research Scientist 1968–77, mem. of Exec., CSIRO 1977–85, Chair. and Chief Exec. 1985–86, CEO 1986–90, post-retirement Fellow 1990–97; Pres. Australian Biochem. Soc. 1976–78; fmr Chair. Nat. Science and Industry Forum; Treas. Australian Acad. of Science 1978–81; Dir Sirotech Ltd 1986–90, Landcare Australia Ltd 1990–98; Sec. for Science Policy, Australian Acad. of Science 1993–97; mem. Australian Research Grants Cttee 1971–75, ANU Council 1979–89, 1990–91, Australian Centre for Int. Agric. Research (ACIAR) 1982–88, CRA Scientific Advisory Bd 1983–98, Prime Minister's Scientific Council 1989–90; Fellow, Australian Acad. of Tech. Sciences and Eng, Foreign mem. Korean Acad. of Science and Tech.; David Syme Research Prize, Melbourne Univ. 1967; Lemberg Medal, Australian Biochem. Soc. 1969. *Publications:* scientific papers on plant biochemistry, particularly photosynthesis and structure, function and biogenesis of chloroplasts. *Leisure interests:* listening to music, reading, walking. *Address:* 6 Somers Crescent, Forrest, ACT 2603, Australia (home). *Telephone:* (2) 6295-1746 (home). *Fax:* (2) 6260-6889 (home). *E-mail:* kboardman@netspeed.com.au (home).

BOASE, Martin, MA; British advertising and marketing executive; *Chairman, Jupiter Dividend and Growth Trust PLC;* b. 14 July 1932, Sheffield; s. of Alan Boase and Elizabeth Grizelle Boase (née Forster); m. 1st Terry Ann Moir 1960 (divorced 1971); one s. one d.; m. 2nd Pauline Valerie Brownrigg 1974; one s. one d.; ed Rendcomb Coll., New Coll., Oxford; with Pritchard Wood and Partners 1961–68; Pnr, The Boase Massimi Pollitt Partnership (subsequently Boase Massimi Pollitt PLC, now part of Omnicom UK PLC), Chair. 1977–89; Chair. Omnicom UK PLC 1989–95, Predator Three PLC 1990–97; Chair. Advertising Asscn 1987–92, Kiss 100 FM 1993–2000, Maiden Outdoor 1993–, British TV Advertising Awards Ltd 1993–2000, Herald Investment Trust 1994–, Investment Trust of Investment Trusts 1995–, Heal's 1997–2002, Jupiter Dividend and Growth Investment Trust PLC, 1999–, Global Professional Media PLC 1999–2005, New Star Investment Trust 2000–, New Media Industries PLC 2001–05; Dir Omnicom Group Inc. 1989–93, EMAP PLC 1991–2000, Taunton Cider PLC 1993–97, Matthew Clark PLC 1995–98. *Leisure interest:* the Turf. *Address:* Jupiter Dividend and Growth Trust PLC, 1 Grosvenor Place, London, SW1X 7JJ, England (office). *Telephone:* (20) 7412-0703 (office). *Fax:* (20) 7412-0705 (office). *Website:* www.jupiteronline.co.uk (office).

BOATENG, Ozwald, OBE; British fashion designer; m. Gyunel; two c.; has designed for Pierce Brosnan, Mick Jagger, Will Smith, Stephen Baldwin, Laurence Fishburne, Billy Zane and others; signed exclusive licensing deal with Marchpole Holdings to produce new formal and casual wear ranges 2002–; Creative Dir of Menswear, Givenchy 2003–07; British Menswear Designer of the Year Award 2001. *Address:* 30 Savile Row, London, W1S 3PTL, England (office). *Telephone:* (20) 7440-5231 (office). *E-mail:* tiffany@bespokecoutureltd.co.uk (office). *Website:* www.ozwaldboateng.co.uk.

BOATENG, Paul (Yaw), PC, LLB; British diplomatist, politician, lawyer and broadcaster; *High Commissioner to South Africa;* b. 14 June 1951, Hackney, London; s. of Kwaku Boateng and Eleanor Boateng; m. Janet Alleyne 1980; two s. three d.; ed Ghana Int. School, Accra Acad., Apsley Grammar School and Univ. of Bristol; solicitor, Paddington Law Centre 1976–79; solicitor and pnr, B. M. Birnberg & Co. 1979–87; called to Bar, Gray's Inn 1989; Legal Adviser, Scrap Sus Campaign 1977–81; mem. GLC (Labour) for Walthamstow 1981–86, Chair. Police Cttee 1981–86, Vice-Chair. Ethnic Minorities Cttee 1981–86; MP (Labour) for Brent S 1987–2005; Home Office mem. House of Commons Environment Cttee 1987–89; Opposition Frontbench Spokesman on Treasury and Econ. Affairs 1989–92, on Legal Affairs, Lord Chancellor's Dept 1992–97; Parl. Under-Sec. of State, Dept of Health 1997–98; Minister of State 1998–2001, Deputy Home Sec. 1999–2001; Minister for Young People 2000–01; Financial Sec. to HM Treasury 2001–02, Chief Sec. 2002–05; High Commr to S Africa 2005–; Chair. Afro-Caribbean Educ. Resource Project 1978–86, Westminster CRC 1979–81; Gov. Police Staff Coll., Bramshill 1981–84; mem. Home Sec.'s Advisory Council on Race Relations 1981–86, WCC Comm. on Programme to Combat Racism 1984–91, Police Training Council 1981–85; Exec. Nat. Council for Civil Liberties 1980–86; mem. Court of Univ. of Bristol 1994–; mem. Bd ENO 1984–97; Hon. LLD (Lincoln Univ., Pa) (Bristol). *Television work includes:* Behind the Hardlines (BBC), Nothing but the Truth (Channel 4). *Publications include:* Reclaiming the Ground (contrib.) 1993, Introduction to Sense and Sensibility, The Complete Jane Austen 1993. *Leisure Interests include:* Opera, Swimming, Art History. *Address:* British High Commission, 255 Hill Street, Arcadia, Pretoria 0002, South Africa (office). *Telephone:* (12) 4217500 (office). *Fax:* (12) 4217555 (office). *E-mail:* media.pretoria@fco.gov.uk (office). *Website:* www.britain.org.za (office).

BOATSWAIN, Anthony; Grenadian politician; *Minister of Economic Development and Planning;* elected MP for St Patrick W 1999, re-elected 2003; currently Minister of Finance and Planning 2003–07, of Econ. Devt and Planning 2007–; mem. NNP. *Address:* Ministry of Economic Development and Planning, Building 3, Financial Complex, The Carenage, St George's, Grenada (office). *Telephone:* 440-2214 (office). *Fax:* 440-0775 (office). *E-mail:* finance@gov.gd (office); director@economicaffairs.grenada.gd (office). *Website:* economicaffairs.grenada.gd (office).

BOAZ, A. A., PhD; Indian scientist, environmentalist and academic; *Director-General, South Asia Co-operative Environment Programme;* with Indian Forestry Service 1979–2005, held several sr posts, including Dir Medicinal Plants Task Force, MP, Dir Tourism, Culture, Archaeology, Archives and Museums, Chhattisgarh, Man. Dir Chhattisgarh Tourism Bd, Gen. Man. MP Minor Forest Produce Fed., Exec. Dir Forest Devt Corpn, Conservator of Forests, Forest Dept, MP 1993–2001, Chief Conservator, Project Formulation, Research and Extension, Forest Dept, Chhattisgarh 2001–05; has also worked as consultant for several int. orgs, including FAO, Int. Devt Research Org., Canada, Centre for Int. Forestry Research, Indonesia and Winrock International; Dir-Gen. South Asia Co-operative Environment Programme 2005–; Mem. Sec. South Asia Coral Reef Task Force. *Publications:* several books; numerous research papers in the areas of forestry, medicinal plants, sustainable land use, rural devt and forest tribal interface. *Address:* South Asia Co-operative Environment Programme, 10 Anderson Road, Colombo 05, Sri Lanka (office). *Telephone:* (11) 2589787 (office). *Fax:* (11) 2589369 (office). *E-mail:* info@sacep.org (office); draboaz@yahoo.com (office). *Website:* www.sacep.org (office).

BOBBITT, Philip Chase, JD, PhD; American academic and government official; *A. W. Walker Centennial Chair in Law, University of Texas;* b. 22 July 1948, Temple, Tex.; ed Princeton Univ., Yale Univ., Univ. of Oxford, UK; Asst Prof. of Law, Univ. of Texas School of Law 1976–79, Prof. 1979–, A. W. Walker Centennial Chair 1996–; Jr Research Fellow, Nuffield Coll., Univ. of Oxford 1982–84, Research Fellow 1984–85, Anderson Sr Research Fellow 1985–91, mem. Modern History Faculty 1984–91; Sr Research Fellow, War Studies Dept, Kings Coll. London, UK 1994–97; Assoc. Counsel to Pres. of USA for Intelligence and Int. Security 1980–81; Legal Counsel to US Senate Intra-Contra Cttee 1987–88; Counsellor on Int. Law, US State Dept 1990–93; Dir for Intelligence, Nat. Security Council 1997–98, Sr Dir of Critical Infrastructure 1998–99, Sr Dir for Strategic Planning 1999; mem. American Law Inst., Council on Foreign Relations, Pacific Council on Int. Policy, Int. Inst. for Strategic Studies; fmr Trustee, Princeton Univ. *Publications include:* Tragic Choices (co-author) 1978, Constitutional Fate 1982, Democracy and Deterrence 1987, US Nuclear Strategy (co-author) 1989, Constitutional Interpretation 1991, The Shield of Achilles: War, Peace and the Course of History 2002, Terror and Consent: The Wars for the Twenty-First Century 2008. *Address:* The University of Texas School of Law, TNH4.107, D1800, 727 East Dean Keeton Street, Austin, TX 78712, USA (office). *Telephone:* (512) 232-1376 (office); (512) 474-6460 (home). *Fax:* (512) 471-6988 (office). *E-mail:* pbobbitt@mail.law.utexas.edu (office). *Website:* www.utexas.edu (office).

BOBINAC, Franjo, BEcons, MSc, MBA; Slovenian business executive; *President and CEO, Gorenje gospodinjski aparati d.d.;* b. 1958, Celje; ed Univ. of Ljubljana, Ecole Supérieure de Commerce, Paris, France; began career with Emo Celje 1983–86; Asst to Dir of Export, Gorenje gospodinjski aparati d.d. 1986–91, Marketing Dir 1991–93, Gen. Dir, Gorenje Sidex France 1993–98, mem., Man. Bd, Gorenje d.d. 1998–, later Pres. and CEO; Pres., Man.'s Asscn of Slovenia; Vice-Pres., Man. Cttee, Savinjsko Saleška Regional Chamber of Commerce and Industry; fmr Pres., BIO 19 Organising Cttee; mem. Supervisory Bd, ETI Izlake; mem. Man. Cttee, Chamber of Commerce and Industry of Slovenia; mem. Council, IECD (Bled School of Man.); mem. Council, Slovenian Philharmonic Ljubljana; mem. UNICEF Econ. Cttee. *Address:* Gorenje gospodinjski aparati d.d., Partizanska 12, 3503 Velenje, Slovenia (office). *Telephone:* (3) 8991000 (office). *Fax:* (3) 8992800 (office). *E-mail:* franjo.bobinac@gorenje.si. *Website:* www.gorenje.com (office).

BOBROW, Martin, CBE, DScMed, FRS, FRCP, FRCPath, FMedSci; British medical scientist, geneticist and academic; b. 6 Feb. 1938, Johannesburg, South Africa; s. of Joe Bobrow and Bessie Bobrow; m. Lynda Strauss; three d.; ed Univ. of Witwatersrand, S Africa; Prof. of Human Genetics, Univ. of Amsterdam 1981–82; Prince Philip Prof. of Paediatric Research, United Medical and Dental Schools of Guy's and St Thomas' Hosps, London, 1982–95; Prof. and Head, Dept of Medical Genetics, Univ. of Cambridge 1995–2005, Dir (non-exec.) Addenbrooke's Hosp.; mem. Black Advisory Group on possible increased incidence of cancer in W Cumbria 1983–84, Cttee to examine ethical implications of gene therapy 1989–93, NHS Cen. R&D Cttee, Dept of Health 1991–97, Gene Therapy Advisory Cttee 1993–94, Lewisham NHS Trust Bd 1994–95, Nuffield Council on Bioethics 1996–2003 (fmr Deputy Chair.), Human Genetics Advisory Comm. 1997–99; fmr mem. MRC; Gov. Wellcome Trust 1996–2007, Deputy Chair. 2004–07; Chair. Muscular Dystrophy Campaign; fmr Chair. ULTRA (Unrelated Living Transplant Regulating Authority), COMARE (Dept of Health Advisory Cttee on Radiation in the Environment); Founder Acad. of Medical Sciences 1998. *Publications:* papers in science books and journals 1967–. *Address:* Department of Medical Genetics, Cambridge Institute for Medical Research, Wellcome/MRC Building, Addenbrooke's Hospital, Cambridge, CB2 2XY, England (office). *Telephone:* (1223) 331154 (office). *Fax:* (1223) 331206 (office). *E-mail:* lms28@cam.ac.uk (office). *Website:* www.cimr.cam.ac.uk/medgen (office).

BOBUȚAC, Valeriu; Moldovan politician and diplomatist; *Ambassador to Hungary;* b. 13 March 1945, Khankaun; m. Maria Bobutac; two c.; ed Lvov Trade-Econ. Inst., Ukraine, Higher CP School, Kiev, Ukraine; worked in Comsomol, First-Sec. Cen. Cttee then Sec. Cen. Cttee Moldovan CP; Deputy Minister of Econs and Reforms; Amb. to Russia 1997–99, 2001; Prime Minister of Moldova 1999–2000; at Ministry of Foreign Affairs 2002–05; Amb. to Hungary (also accred. to Slovenia, Croatia, Bosnia and Herzegovina, Holy See) 2005–, also Rep. to Danube Comm. 2005–. *Address:* Embassy of Hungary,

1024 Budapest, Ady Endre u. 16, Hungary (office). *Telephone:* (1) 336-3450 (office). *Fax:* (1) 209-1195 (office). *E-mail:* budapesta@mfa.md (office). *Website:* www.moldovaembassy.hu (office).

BOCCARDO, Mgr Renato; Italian ecclesiastic; *Secretary of the Governorate of the Vatican City State;* b. 21 Dec. 1952, Sant'Ambrogio; ordained priest 1977; Titular Bishop of Aquipendium 2003–; Sec. Pontifical Council for Social Communications 2003–; Sec. Governorate of the Vatican City State 2005–. *Address:* Palazzo del Governatorato, 00120 Vatican City State, Italy (office). *Telephone:* (06) 69885720 (office). *Fax:* (06) 69885720 (office). *Website:* www.vaticanstate.va/EN/State_and_Government/Structure_Governorate/Organizational_Chart/Governorate.htm (office).

BOCELLI, Andrea; Italian singer (tenor); b. 22 Sept. 1958, Lajatico, Pisa; two c.; fmr lawyer. *Recordings include:* albums: various music: Bocelli 1995, Romanza 1997, Sogno 1999, Cieli di Toscana 2001, MW 2006; opera: Viaggio Italiano 1995, Aria 1998, Sacred Arias 1999, Verdi 2000, La Bohème 2000, Verdi Requiem 2001, Sentimento (Classical BRIT Award for Best Album 2003) 2002, Tosca 2003, Aria: The Opera Album 2005, Vivere 2007, Incanto 2008. *Address:* Michele Torpedine, MT Opera and Blues Production and Management, via Irnerio 16, 40126 Bologna, Italy (office). *Telephone:* (51) 251117 (office). *Fax:* (51) 251123 (office). *E-mail:* mtorped@tin.it (office). *Website:* www.mit-operaandblues.it (office); www.andreabocelli.org (office).

BOCEVSKI, Ivica, BJur; Macedonian politician; *Deputy Prime Minister, responsible for European Integration;* b. 15 June 1977, Skopje; m.; one c.; ed Sts Cyril and Methodius Univ., Skopje, Univ. of Pittsburgh, USA; fmr columnist, Utrinski Vesnik; Co-founder and fmr Exec. Dir Inst. for Democracy, Skopje; fmrly worked in Ministry of Foreign Affairs; Spokesperson, Govt of Repub. of Macedonia 2007–08; Deputy Prime Minister, responsible for European Integration 2008–. *Address:* Office of the Prime Minister, 1000 Skopje, Ilindenska bb, Macedonia (office). *Telephone:* (2) 3115455 (office). *Fax:* (2) 3112561 (office). *Website:* www.vlada.mk (office).

BOCHARNIKOV, Mikhail Nikolayevich; Russian diplomatist; *Ambassador to Kazakhstan;* b. 6 March 1948, Moscow; m.; one d.; ed Moscow Inst. of Int. Relations; mem. staff Ministry of Foreign Affairs –1992; Amb. to Zambia 1992–96; Dir Dept of African Countries, Ministry of Foreign Affairs 1996–99; Amb. to Greece 1999–2003; Amb. for Special Missions of the Ministry of Foreign Affairs (Regulation of the Conflict between Abkhazia and Georgia); Amb. to Kazakhstan 2006–. *Address:* Embassy of the Russian Federation, Barayev 4, Astana 010000, Kazakhstan. *Telephone:* (3272) 22-17-14 (office). *Fax:* (3172) 22-38-49 (office). *E-mail:* rfe@nursat.kz (office). *Website:* www.rfembassy.kz (office).

BOCHEŃSKI, Jacek; Polish writer, journalist and translator; b. 29 July 1926, Lvov; m.; one d.; ed State Coll. of Theatrical Arts, Warsaw; Co-Founder and Ed. Zapis (first Polish underground periodical) 1977–81; Pres. Polish PEN Club 1996–99; Polish PEN Club Parandowski Prize 2006. *Radio:* Caprices of an Old Gentleman (weekly five-minute slot) 2001–02. *Television and stage plays:* Taboo, After the Collapse. *Publications include:* novels: Farewell to Miss Syngilu 1960, Divine Julius – Notes of an Antiquary (also translated into German) 1961, Taboo 1965, Naso Poet 1969, After the Collapse (Solidarity Prize 1987) 1987, Caprices of an Old Gentleman 2004; stories: Violets Are Unlucky 1949, Bloody Italian Rarities 1982, Retro 1990; travel book: Farewell to Miss Syngilu or the Elephant and the Polish Question; essay: Thirteen European Exercises 2005; trans.: Tabu 1960, Der Täter heißt Ovid 1975, État de Pesanteur 1995; several essays and contribs to magazines on media ethics and the civic responsibilities of cultural figures. *Address:* ul. Sonaty 6 m. 801, 02-744 Warsaw, Poland (home). *Telephone:* (22) 8435853 (home). *E-mail:* jacek.bochenski@poczta.gazeta.pl (home).

BOCHNIARZ, Henryka Teodora, PhD; Polish economist and politician; *President, Polish Confederation of Private Employers;* b. 29 Oct. 1947, Świebodzin; m. Zbigniew Bochniarz 1969; one s. one d.; ed Warsaw School of Econs and Foreign Trade Research Inst.; Asst, Deputy Head Agric. Div., Foreign Trade Research Inst., Warsaw 1976–80, Asst Prof., Lecturer 1980–84, Dir Agric. Div. and Negotiator 1984–90; Research Asst, Int. Inst. of Socialist Econ. Systems, Moscow, USSR (now Russian Fed.) 1978; Visiting Asst Prof., Vienna Inst. for Comparative Econ. Systems 1983–84; Sr Fulbright Scholar and Visiting Prof., Dept of Agric. and Applied Econs, Univ. of Minn., USA 1985–87; Dir Proexim Ltd 1988–90; Pres. Nicom Consulting Ltd, Warsaw 1990–91, 1992–, Asscn of Econ. Consultants in Poland 1991–; Minister of Industry and Trade 1991–92; Pres. Polish Business Roundtable 1996–99, Polish Confed. of Pvt. Employers 1999–; Co-Chair. (with Leszek Balcerowicz q.v.) Cttee on Deregulation of the Polish Economy 1998–; currently Exec. Pres. Polish Business Council; mem. Bd Dirs TVN SA, Computerland SA, ITI SA; mem. Polish Del. to UN Cttee on Agric., Econ. Comm. for Europe, Geneva, Switzerland 1976–85; Visiting Prof., Dept of Agricultural and Applied Econs, Univ. of Minnesota, USA 1985–87; mem. Negotiating Group on Agric., Uruguay Round GATT talks 1987. *Publications include:* Polish Agricultural Trade (annual reports) 1975–90, Poland: The Impact of Foreign Trade Policy on Self-Sufficiency in Agriculture 1987; numerous papers and contribs to professional journals. *Leisure interests:* skiing, volleyball, theatre. *Address:* Polskej Konfederacji Pracodawców Prywatnych Lewiatan (Polish Confederation of Private Employers), ul. Klonowa 6, 00-591 Warsaw (office); c/o Nicom Consulting Ltd, 10 Inwalidów Square, 01-552 Warsaw, Poland. *Telephone:* (22) 845-95-50 (office). *Fax:* (22) 845-95-51 (office). *E-mail:* pkpp@prywatni.pl (office). *Website:* www.prywatni.pl (office); www.nicom.pl; www.bochniarz.pl.

BOCK, Hans, PhD, DHabil; German chemist and academic; *Professor and Director, Johann Wolfgang Goethe University;* b. 5 Oct. 1928, Hamburg; s. of Paul Bock and Hedwig (née Lis) Bock; m. Dr Luise (née Eisenreich) Bock 1954; two s. three d.; ed Ludwigs Maximilians Univ., Munich, ETH, Zürich; Visiting Scientist, Fed. Inst. of Tech., Zürich 1965–68; Prof. and Dir Johann Wolfgang Goethe Univ., Frankfurt 1969–; Adjunct Prof. Univ. of Michigan, Ann Arbor, USA 1983–2001; External Scientific mem. Max Planck Soc. 1977–; mem. Acad. of Science, Mainz 1984–; Corresp. mem. Acad. of Science, Göttingen 1986, Acad. of Natural Scientists Leopoldina, Halle 1991, Bavarian Acad. of Sciences 1994; Dr hc (Hamburg) 1988, (Montpellier) 1993; Chemistry Award, Acad. of Science, Göttingen 1969, Frederic Stanley Kipping Award, ACS 1974, Wilhelm Klemm Award of the German Chemical Soc. 1987, Hieber Award 1993, Heyrovsky Medal, Prague Acad. of Science 1996, Hieber Lectureship, Wacker AG 2001. *Publications:* The HMO Model and its Application, (three vols, with Edgar Heilbronner) 1965–68; more than 500 scientific publs in int. journals. *Leisure interests:* Norman art, philately. *Address:* c/o Institut für Anorganische Chemie der J. W. Goethe-Universität, Marie-Curie-Str. 11, 60439 Frankfurt am Main (office); Rombergweg 1A, 61462 Königstein, Germany (home). *Telephone:* (69) 79829180 (office); (6174) 931016 (home). *Fax:* (69) 79829188 (office); (6174) 931017 (home).

BOCK, Jerrold (Jerry) Lewis; American composer; b. 23 Nov. 1928, New Haven, CT; s. of George Bock and Rebecca (Alpert) Bock; m. Patricia Faggen 1950; one s. one d.; ed Univ. of Wisconsin; wrote scores for high school and coll. musicals; author of sketches for television 1951–54; mem. NY Bd Educiradio broadcasts 1961–; mem. Wilderness Soc., Horticultural Soc., New York, BMI, American Civil Liberties Union; Johnny Mercer Award, Songwriters Hall of Fame 1990, Theatre Hall of Fame 1990. *Compositions for film:* Wonders of Manhattan 1956. *Compositions for theatre:* Mr Wonderful 1956, The Body Beautiful (with Sheldon Harnick q.v.) 1958, Fiorello (Pulitzer Prize, Antoinette Perry (Tony) Awards) 1959, Tenderloin 1960, She Loves Me (Olivier Award for Best Musical Revival 1994) 1963, Fiddler on the Roof 1964, The Apple Tree 1966, The Rothschilds 1970, Jerome Robbins Broadway 1989, A Stranger Among Us 1992.

BOCKERIA, Leo Antonovich, DrMedSci; Russian cardio-vascular surgeon; *Chairman and Head, A. Bakulev Scientific Centre for Cardiovascular Surgery;* b. 22 Dec. 1939; m.; two d.; ed I. M. Sechenov 1st Medical Inst. (now Sechenov Medical Acad.) Moscow; with A. Bakulev Scientific Centre for Cardiovascular Surgery (SCCVS) 1968–, Dir 1991, now Chair. and Head; Dir, Prof. Burakovsky Research Inst. of Cardiosurgery at SCCVS; mem. Russian Acad. of Medical Sciences 1994–; main research in cardiovascular surgery, hyperbaric oxygenation, treatment of cardiopulse violation problems; apptd mem. Public Chamber of the Russian Fed. 2005, Chair. Comm. for the Formation of a Healthy Lifestyle 2006; Lenin Prize 1976, USSR State Prize 1986, Russian Fed. State Prize 2002. *Publications:* numerous articles on cardiosurgery. *Leisure interests:* painting, collecting encyclopaedias and dictionaries. *Address:* Bakulev Scientific Centre for Cardiovascular Surgery, 135 Rublevskoye shosse, 121552 Moscow, Russia (office). *Telephone:* (495) 414-75-71 (office). *Fax:* (495) 414-78-67 (office). *E-mail:* leoan@heart-house.ru (office). *Website:* www.bakulev.ru (office).

BOCLET, Franck; French fashion designer; *Chief Men's Designer, Emanuel Ungaro;* Artistic Dir for Francesco Smalto –2007; Chief Men's Designer for Emanuel Ungaro 2007–. *Address:* Emanuel Ungaro, 2 avenue Montaigne, 75008 Paris, France (office). *Telephone:* 1-53-57-00-00 (office). *Fax:* 1-47-23-82-31 (office). *E-mail:* info@ungaro.com (office). *Website:* www.ungaro.com (office).

BOCUSE, Paul; French restaurateur; b. 11 Feb. 1926, Collonges-au-Mont-d'Or (Rhône); s. of Georges Bocuse and Irma Roulier; m. Raymonde Duvert 1946; one s. one d.; ed Ecole primaire, Collonges-au-Mont-d'Or and Pensionnat Saint-Louis, Lyons; restaurateur (in business passing from father to son since 1765), Collonges-Mont-d'Or; restaurateur, French Pavilion, Disneyworld, Orlando, Fla, USA; Pres. Asscn Eurotoques 1989–, L'Ecole des Arts Culinaires et de l'Hôtellerie Ecully 1991–95; Pres. Meilleur Ouvrier de France: Section Cuisine-Restauration 1991–; founder and Hon. Pres. Paul Bocuse Inst., Lyon; mem. Asscn des maître-cuisiniers de France; Officier, Légion d'honneur, Ordre nat. du Mérite, Chevalier des Palmes académiques, Officier du Mérite agricole. *Publications:* La Cuisine du marché 1976, Bocuse dans votre cuisine 1982, La cuisine du gibier (in collaboration) 1984, Bon appétit 1989, Cuisine de France 1990, La bonne chère 1995. *Leisure interest:* underwater fishing. *Address:* Paul Bocuse Institute, Château du Vivier, BP 25, 69131 Ecully Cedex (office); Restaurant Paul Bocuse, 40 rue de la Plage, 69660 Collonges-au-Mont d'Or, France (office). *Telephone:* (4) 72-18-02-20 (office). *Fax:* (4) 78-43-33-51 (office). *E-mail:* info@institutpaulbocuse.com (office); paul.bocuse@bocuse.fr (office). *Website:* www.bocuse.fr (office); www.institutpaulbocuse.com (office).

BOD, Péter Ákos, PhD; Hungarian economist, politician and academic; *Professor of Economic Policy, Budapest Corvinus University;* b. 28 July 1951, Szigetvár; s. of Andor Bod and Rózsa Nagy; divorced; one d.; ed high school, Miskolc, Univ. of Econ., Budapest; worked as researcher, later Dept head, Inst. for Econ. Planning; UNDP adviser in Ghana; mem. of Parl. (Hungarian Democratic Forum) 1990–91; Minister of Industry and Trade 1990–91; Pres. Nat. Bank of Hungary 1991–94; mem. Bd EBRD, London 1995–97; Prof. of Econ. Policy and Dept Chair., Budapest Corvinus Univ. 2001–; Personal Econ. Adviser to Pres. of the Repub. 2001–05; Medal of Merit, Pres. of the Repub. 2005. *Publications:* The Entrepreneurial State in the Contemporary Market Economy 1987, Foundations of Economic Theory and Policy 1999, The World of Money – The Money of the World 2001, Economic Policy 2002. *Leisure interests:* tennis, music, history. *Address:* Fövam tér 8, Budapest Corvinus University, 1093 Budapest, Hungary (office). *Telephone:* (1) 482-5370 (office). *Fax:* (1) 482-5034 (office). *E-mail:* petera.bod@uni-corvinus.hu (office). *Website:* www.corvinus.hu (office).

BODE, Ridvan, MSc; Albanian economist and politician; *Minister of Finance;* b. 26 May 1959, Korcë; s. of Vait Bode; ed Higher Agricultural Inst., Tirana,

Mediterranean Agricultural Inst. (DSPU), Montpellier, France; Head, Finance Division, Perrenjas, Librazhd 1983–89; Lecturer on Financial Analysis and Accountability, Tirana Agrarian Univ. 1991–95; Dir-Gen. Albanian Customs Gen. Dept 1995–96; elected MP (Democratic Party—DP) for Devoli Dist 1996, Minister of Finance 1996–97, 2005–; mem. DP Nat. Council and Presidency 1997, Gen.-Sec. 1997–; Visiting Lecturer, Faculty of Econs, Tirana Univ. 2002–. *Publications:* numerous papers on financial analysis. *Address:* Ministry of Finance, Bulevardi Dëshmorët e Kombit, Tirana, Albania (office). *Telephone:* (4) 267654 (office). *Fax:* (4) 226111 (office). *E-mail:* hvako@minfin.gov.al (office); secretary.minister@minfin.gov.al (office). *Website:* www.minfin.gov.al (office).

BODE, Thilo, PhD; German business executive and consultant; *Executive Director, Foodwatch;* b. 1947, nr Munich; ed Munich and Regensburg Univs; int. consultant, Lahmeyer Int., Frankfurt; Project Man. German Bank for Reconstruction and Devt 1978–81; ind. consultant for int. orgs, govts and businesses 1981; Special Asst to Chief Exec. of int. pvt. corpn 1986; Exec. Dir Greenpeace Germany 1989–95, Greenpeace Int. 1995–2001, Foodwatch 2002–. *Publications:* Die Demokratic verrät ihre Kinder 2003. *Address:* Foodwatch, Brunnenstrasse 181, 10119 Berlin, Germany (office). *Telephone:* (30) 2404760 (office). *Fax:* (30) 240476-26 (office). *E-mail:* bode@foodwatch.de (office). *Website:* www.foodwatch.de (office).

BODEK, Arie, BS, PhD; American (b. Israeli) physicist and academic; *Professor of Physics, University of Rochester;* b. 5 Nov. 1947, Tel-Aviv, Israel; ed Massachusetts Inst. of Tech.; Research Assoc., Lab. for Nuclear Science, MIT 1972–74; Milkan Fellow, Calif. Inst. of Tech. 1974–76; Asst Prof. of Physics, Univ. of Rochester, NY 1977–80, Assoc. Prof. 1980–87, Prof. 1987–, Assoc. Chair., Dept of Physics and Astronomy 1995–98, Chair. 1998–; mem. Editorial Bd several journals including European Physics Journal 1992–; Fellow, American Physical Soc. 1985, Japan Soc. for the Promotion of Science 1986–87; American Physical Soc. Panofsky Prize in Particle Physics 2004, Grad. Teaching Award, Univ. of Rochester 2004. *Publications:* more than 700 articles in scientific journals. *Address:* Department of Physics and Astronomy, University of Rochester, Bausch & Lomb 206, Rochester, NY 14627, USA (office). *Telephone:* (585) 275-4344 (office). *Fax:* (585) 273-3237 (office). *E-mail:* bodek@pas.rochester.edu (office). *Website:* spider.pas.rochester.edu/mainFrame/people/pages/Bodek.html (office).

BODEN, Margaret Ann, OBE, ScD, PhD, FBA; British cognitive scientist and academic; *Research Professor of Cognitive Science, University of Sussex;* b. 26 Nov. 1936, London; d. of Leonard F. Boden and Violet Dorothy Boden (née Dawson); m. John R. Spiers 1967 (divorced 1981); one s. one d.; ed Newnham Coll., Cambridge (Major Scholar) and Harvard Grad. School (Harkness Fellow); Lecturer in Philosophy, Univ. of Birmingham 1959–65; Lecturer, then Reader in Philosophy and Psychology, Univ. of Sussex 1965–80, Prof. 1980–, Founding Dean School of Cognitive and Computing Sciences 1987, Research Prof. of Cognitive Science 2002–; Curator Univ. of London Inst. for Advanced Study 1995–; co-founder, Harvester Press Ltd 1970, Dir 1970–85; Vice-Pres. British Acad. 1989–91, Royal Inst. of GB 1993–95, Chair. of Council 1993–95, mem. of Council 1992–95; mem. Advisory Bd for the Research Councils 1989–90, Academia Europaea 1993–, Animal Procedures Cttee 1995–99; Fellow, American Asscn for Artificial Intelligence 1993–, European Coordinating Cttee for Artificial Intelligence 1999–; Hon. DSc (Sussex) 2001, (Bristol) 2002, Hon. DUniv (Open) 2004. *Publications:* Purposive Explanation in Psychology 1972, Artificial Intelligence and Natural Man 1977, Piaget 1979, Minds and Mechanisms 1981, Computer Models of Mind 1988, Artificial Intelligence in Psychology 1989, The Philosophy of Artificial Intelligence (ed.) 1990, Dimensions of Creativity (ed.) 1994, Artificial Intelligence and the Mind (co-ed.) 1994, The Philosophy of Artificial Life (ed.) 1996, Artificial Intelligence (ed.) 1996, The Creative Mind (2nd edn) 2004, Mind as Machine 2006. *Leisure interests:* dressmaking, travelling, passion for India and Polynesia. *Address:* c/o Centre for Research in Cognitive Science, University of Sussex, Falmer, Brighton, BN1 9QJ, England (office). *Telephone:* (1273) 678386 (office). *Fax:* (1273) 671320 (office). *E-mail:* maggieb@cogs.susx.ac.uk (office). *Website:* www.cogs.susx.ac.uk (office).

BODEWIG, Kurt; German politician; *Chairman, Baltic Sea Forum;* b. 26 April 1955, Rheinberg; m.; two s.; ed commercial coll.; joined SPD 1973, mem. Nat. Exec. Cttee 2000–05; held various party posts 1982–98; mem. Bundestag 1998–; Minister of Transport, Building and Housing 2000–02; Chair. Baltic Sea Forum e.V., Bd Trustees German-Lithuanian-Forum; Deputy Chair. Cttee on the Affairs of the EU; Pres. Deutsche Verkehrswacht e.V.; mem. European Council and Parl. Ass., Baltic Sea Parl. Conf.; Deputy mem. NATO Parl. Ass. *Address:* Bundestag, Platz der Republik 1, 11011 Berlin, Germany (office). *Telephone:* (30) 22775313 (office). *Fax:* (30) 22776313 (office). *E-mail:* kurt.bodewig@bundestag.de (office). *Website:* www.kurt-bodewig.de.

BODEWITZ, Hendrik Wilhelm, PhD; Dutch professor of Sanskrit (retd); b. 13 Oct. 1939, Gramsbergen; s. of Johan Adriaan Bodewitz and Jennigjen Lenters; m. Janneke van Uchelen 1964; one s. one d.; ed Lyceum Coevorden, Univ. of Utrecht; lecturer in Sanskrit, Utrecht Univ. 1966–68, Prof. 1976–92, Dean of Faculty 1980–82 and 1984–86; Sr Lecturer, Leiden Univ. 1969–76, Prof. 1992–2002; mem. Netherlands Royal Acad.; founding mem. Academia Europaea. *Publications:* Jaiminīya Brāhmaṇa I, 1-65, with a study of the Agnihotra and the Prāṇāgnihotra 1973, The daily evening and morning offering according to the Brāhmaṇas 1976, The Jyotiṣṭoma Ritual: Jaiminīya Brāhmaṇa I, 66-364 1990, Kauṣitaki Upaniṣad 2002; articles: Venic aghm: evil or sin, distress or death? 2007, The Vedric Concepts āgas and enas 2007, Sins and Vices, their Enumerations and Specifications in the Veda 2008, The Special Meanings of śrama and other derivations of the root śram in the Veda 2008, The refrain kasmai deva ya havisa vidhema 2009. *Address:* Stolberglaan 29, 3583 XL Utrecht, Netherlands (home). *Telephone:* (30) 2510047 (home).

BODIN, Manfred; German banker; b. 14 Nov. 1939, Münster; m.; Stadtsparkasse, Münster 1960–64; Stadtsparkasse, Witten 1964–70; mem. Man. Bd Kreissparkasse Recklinghausen 1970–75, Chair. Man. Bd 1976–83; Chair. Man. Bd Sparkasse Essen 1984–91; Chair. Man. Bd NORD/LB 1991–; Dr hc (Tech. Univ. Braunschweig). *Address:* Norddeutsche Landesbank Girozentrale, Georgsplatz 1, 30159 Hannover, Germany. *Telephone:* (511) 361-0. *Fax:* (511) 361-5242. *Website:* www.nordlb.de (office).

BODINE, Barbara K., BA MA; American diplomatist, academic and university administrator; *Diplomat In Residence and Lecturer of Public Affairs, Woodrow Wilson School of Public and International Affairs, Princeton University;* b. 1948, St Louis, Mo.; ed Univ. of California, Santa Barbara, Fletcher School of Law and Diplomacy, Chinese Univ. of Hong Kong; career mem. Foreign Service, initial tours Hong Kong and Bangkok; Country Officer then Political-Mil. Officer, Bureau of Nr East Affairs, Office of Arabian Peninsula Affairs, later Deputy Office Dir; Congressional Fellow, Office of US Senator Robert Dole; Deputy Prin. Officer in Baghdad, US State Dept. 1980s, Deputy Chief of Mission in Kuwait (held captive by Iraqi invading forces for 137 days) 1990, Assoc. Co-ordinator for Operations early 1990s, Acting Co-ordinator for Counterterrorism 1990s; Dean of Professional Studies, Foreign Service Inst., US State Dept, later Dir of East African Affairs, Amb. to Yemen (arranged release of captured Americans) 1999–2001, US Co-ordinator for Cen. Iraq April–May 2003, Sr Advisor Bureau of Political-Mil. Affairs 2003; fmr Sr Research Fellow and Dir of the Governance Initiative in the Middle East, Kennedy School, Harvard Univ., also fmr Fellow at Center for Public Leadership and Inst. of Politics; fmr Robert Wilhelm Fellow, MIT Center for Int. Studies; currently Diplomat In Residence and Lecturer of Public Affairs, Woodrow Wilson School of Public and Int. Affairs, Princeton Univ.; Treasurer, Alumni Asscns, Univ. Calif., Santa Barbara; Diplomat-in-Residence, Global and Int. Studies Program, Univ. Calif., Santa Barbara 2001–02; Regent-desig. Univ. of Calif. 2002–03, ex-officio Regent 2003–04, Vice-Pres. Alumni Asscns of the Univ. of Calif. 2004–; US Sec. of State Award for Valor (for work in occupied Kuwait) 1990, Univ. Calif., Santa Barbara Distinguished Alumni Award 1991, US Dept of State Distinguished Honor Award (for work in Yemen) 2001. *Address:* Woodrow Wilson School of Public and International Affairs, Princeton University, 432 Robertson Hall, Princeton, NJ 08544-1013, USA (office). *Telephone:* (609) 258-7765 (office). *Fax:* (609) 258-2809 (office). *E-mail:* bbodine@princeton.edu (office). *Website:* wws.princeton.edu (office).

BODMAN, Samuel Wright, III, ScD; American academic, business executive and fmr government official; b. 26 Nov. 1938, Chicago, Ill.; s. of Samuel W. Bodman Jr and Lina B. Bodman; m. 1st Lynda Schubert 1984; three c.; m. 2nd Diane Barber 1997; ed Cornell Univ. and Massachusetts Inst. of Tech.; Instructor, MIT 1964, Asst Prof. 1964–68, Assoc. Prof. 1968–70, Dir School of Chemical Eng Practice, American Cyanamid Co. 1965–67; Tech. Dir American Research and Devt Corpn 1964–70; Founding Pnr, Fidelity Ventures Ltd 1970–86, Vice-Pres. Commercial Devt 1971–75, Pres. Fidelity Man. and Research Co. 1976–86, Pres. and COO FMR Corpn (parent holding co. of Fidelity Investments) 1982–86, Exec. Vice-Pres. and Dir Fidelity Group of Mutual Funds 1980–86; Pres. and COO Cabot Corpn 1987–88, Chair., CEO 1988–2002; US Deputy Sec. of Commerce 2002–04; US Sec. of Energy, Washington, DC 2004–09; Dir Cabot Corpn, Bank of Boston Corpn, Westvaco Inc., Continental Cablevision Inc., Index Tech. Corpn, John Hancock Financial Services, Thermo Electron Corpn, Security Capital Group Inc.; Trustee Mitre Corpn, Babson Coll., Isabella Stewart Gardner Museum, New England Aquarium; mem. Corpn, MIT, Chair. Chemical Eng Visiting Cttee; mem. American Acad. of Arts and Sciences. *Address:* c/o Department of Energy, Forrestal Building, 1000 Independence Avenue, SW, Washington, DC 20585, USA.

BODMER, Sir Walter Fred, Kt, PhD, FRS, FRCPath, FMedSci; British research scientist, academic and university administrator; *Head, Cancer and Immunogenetics Laboratory, Weatherall Institute of Molecular Medicine, ,University of Oxford;* b. 10 Jan. 1936, Frankfurt am Main, Germany; s. of the late Ernest Julius Bodmer and Sylvia Emily Bodmer; m. Julia Gwynaeth Pilkington 1956 (died 2001); two s. one d.; ed Manchester Grammar School and Clare Coll., Cambridge; Research Fellow, Clare Coll., Cambridge 1958–60, Fellow 1961, Hon. Fellow 1989; Demonstrator, Dept of Genetics, Univ. of Cambridge 1960–61; Fellow, Visiting Asst Prof., Dept of Genetics, Stanford Univ. 1961–62, Asst Prof. 1962–66, Assoc. Prof. 1966–68, Prof. 1968–70; Prof. of Genetics, Univ. of Oxford 1970–79; Vice-Pres. Royal Inst. 1981–82; Pres. Royal Statistical Soc. 1984–85; Pres. British Asscn for Advancement of Science 1987–88, Chair. of Council 1996–2003; mem. Advisory Bd for the Research Councils 1983–88; Chair. BBC Science Consultative Group 1981–87; mem. BBC Gen. Advisory Council; Chair. Bd of Trustees, British Museum (Natural History) 1989–93; Pres. Human Genome Org. 1990–92; Dir-Gen. Imperial Cancer Research Fund 1991–96 (Dir of Research 1979–91); Chancellor Univ. of Salford 1995–2005; Prin. Hertford Coll., Oxford 1995–2005, currently Head Cancer and Immunogenetics Lab., Weatherall Inst. of Molecular Medicine; Chair. Cttee on the Public Understanding of Science (COPUS) 1990–94; Pres. Int. Fed. of Asscns for the Advancement of Science and Tech. 1992–94; Dir non-exec. Fisons PLC 1990–96; Chair. UK Nat. Radiological Protection Bd 1998–2003, Leukaemia Research Fund Medical and Scientific Panel 2003–; Pres. British Assoc. for Cancer Research 1998–2002; Foreign Assoc. NAS; Hon. Vice-Pres. Research Defence Soc. 1990–; Hon. Fellow, Green Coll., Oxford, Keble Coll., Oxford, Hertford Coll., Oxford, Clare Coll., Cambridge, Royal Soc. of Medicine; Hon. FRCP; Hon. FRCS; Hon. FRSE; Foreign Hon. mem. American Acad. of Arts and Sciences, American Asscn of Immunologists; Hon. MD (Bologna, Birmingham); Hon. DSc (Bath), (Oxford), (Hull), (Edin.) 1990, (Aberdeen) 1994, (Lancaster) 1994, (London), (Plymouth), (Salford) 1996, (UMIST) 1997; Hon. DUniv (Surrey) 1990; William Allan Memorial Award (American Soc. of

Human Genetics) 1980, Conway Evans Prize (Royal Coll. of Physicians/Royal Soc.) 1982, Rabbi Shai Shacknai Memorial Prize Lectureship in Immunology and Cancer Research 1983, John Alexander Memorial Prize and Lectureship (Univ. of Pa Medical School) 1984, Rose Payne Distinguished Scientist Lectureship 1985, Ellison Cliffe Lecture and Medal 1987, Neil Hamilton-Fairley Medal, Royal Coll. of Physicians 1990, Faraday Award, Royal Soc. 1994, Dalton Medal, Manchester Literary and Philosophical Soc. 2002, D.K. Ludwig Award 2002, Seroussi Research Award 2003. *Publications:* co-author: The Genetics of Human Populations 1971, Our Future Inheritance – Choice or Chance? 1974, Genetics, Evolution and Man 1976, The Book of Man 1994; papers in scientific and medical journals. *Leisure interests:* playing piano, riding, swimming, scuba diving. *Address:* Weatherall Institute of Molecular Medicine, University of Oxford, John Radcliffe Hospital, Oxford OX3 9DS, England (office). *Telephone:* (1865) 222356 (office). *Fax:* (1865) 22243 (office). *E-mail:* walter.bodmer@hertford.ox.ac.uk (office). *Website:* www.imm.ox.ac.uk (office).

BODROV, Sergey Vladimirovich; Russian screenwriter and film director; b. 28 July 1948, Khabarovsk; m. (divorced); ed All-Union Inst. of Cinematography. *Films directed include:* Golosa voyny 1974, Balamut (writer) 1978, Lyubimaya zhenshchina mekhanika Gavrilova (writer) 1981, Molodye lyudi (writer) 1983, Sladkiy sok vnutri travy (also writer) 1984), Yurka - syn komandira (writer) 1984, Ochen vazhnaya persona (writer) 1984, Neprofessionaly (also writer) 1985, Ne khodite, devki, zamuzh (writer) 1985, Ya tebya nenavizhu (also writer) (TV) 1986, Moy dom na zelyonykh kholmakh (writer) 1986, Na pomoshch, brattsy! (writer) 1988, Frantsuz (writer) 1988, S.E.R. - Svoboda eto rai (also writer) 1989, Krejzi 1989, Katala (also writer) 1989, ...I vsya lyubov (writer) 1989, Nash chelovek v San-Remo (writer) 1990, Ya khotela uvidet angelov (also writer) 1992, Belyy korol, krasnaya koroleva (Russkie) (also writer) 1992, Somebody to Love (writer) 1994, Kavkazskiy plennik (also writer) 1996, Est - Ouest (writer) 1999, Running Free 1999, Syostry (story) 2001, The Quickie (also writer) 2001, Bear's Kiss (also writer) 2002, Shiza (writer) 2004, Nomad 2004, Mongol: Part One (also writer) 2007. *Address:* Leninsky prosp. 129, korp. 3, Apt 20, 117513 Moscow, Russia. *Telephone:* (495) 438-38-04.

BOECKMANN, Alan L., BEng; American construction industry executive; *Chairman and CEO, Fluor Corporation;* ed Univ. of Arizona; joined Fluor Corpn as engineer 1974, various man. positions in Calif., Tex., SC, S Africa and Venezuela, becoming Vice-Pres., DuPont Alliance and Head of Eng Div., also Pres. and CEO Fluor Daniel, Pres. and CEO Fluor Corpn 2001–02, Chair. and CEO 2002–; Chair. Eng and Construction Govs, World Econ. Forum; mem. Bd Dirs American Petroleum Inst., Archer Daniels Midland Co., Burlington Northern Santa Fe, Nat. Petroleum Council, Boys and Girls Clubs of America, Southern Methodist Univ.'s Cox School of Business; mem. Business Roundtable, World Econ. Forum, Univ. of Arizona's Coll. of Eng's Industry Advisory Council. *Address:* Fluor Corpn, 6700 Las Colinas Blvd, Irving, TX 75039, USA (office). *Telephone:* (469) 398-7000 (office). *Fax:* (469) 398-7255 (office). *E-mail:* info@fluor.com (office). *Website:* www.fluor.com (office).

BOEDIONO, MEcons, PhD; Indonesian academic, government official and central banker; *Governor, Bank Indonesia;* b. 25 Feb. 1943, Blitar, Jawa Timur; ed Univ. of Western Australia, Monash Univ., Melbourne, Australia, Wharton School, Univ. of Penn., USA; fmr Lecturer, Faculty of Econs, Gajah Mada Univ., Togyakarta; Deputy Gov. Bank Indonesia in charge of fiscal monetary policy 1997–98; State Minister for Nat. Planning and Devt 1998–99; Minister of Finance and State Enterprises Devt 2001–04; Coordinating Minister for the Economy –2008; Gov. Bank Indonesia 2008–. *Address:* Bank Indonesia, Jalan M. H. Thamrin 2, Jakarta Pusat 10350, Indonesia (office). *Telephone:* (21) 3817187 (office). *Fax:* (21) 3501867 (office). *E-mail:* humasbi@bi.go.id (office). *Website:* www.bi.go.id (office).

BOEHM, Gottfried Karl, DPhil; German art historian and academic; *Professor of Art History, University of Basel;* b. 19 Sept. 1942, Braunau, Bohemia; s. of Karl Boehm and Olga Boehm; m. Margaret Hunold 1980; one d.; ed Univs of Cologne, Vienna and Heidelberg; Lecturer in History of Art, Ruhr Univ. Bochum 1975–79, Prof. 1977; Prof. of History of Art, Justus Liebig Univ., Giessen 1979–86, Univ. of Basel 1986–; Dir Nat. Centre of Competence in Research; Perm. Fellow, Inst. für die Wissenschaften vom Menschen, Vienna 1981–; Fellow, Wissenschaftskolleg, Berlin 2001–02; Corresp. mem. Heidelberger Acad. of Sciences 2006–; Ehrenkreuz für Wissenschaft und Kunst (First Class) (Austria). *Publications:* Studien zur Perspektivität, Philosophie und Kunst in der frühen Neuzeit 1969, Zur Dialektik der ästhetischen Grenze 1973, Philosophische Hermeneutik 1976, Die Hermeneutik und die Wissenschaften 1978, Bildnis und Individuum, Über den Ursprung der Porträtmalerei in der italienischen Renaissance 1985, Paul Cézanne, Montagne Sainte-Victoire 1988, Konrad Fiedler, Schriften zur Kunst 1991, Was ist ein Bild? 1994, Beschreibungskunst-Kunstbeschreibung. Ekphrasis von der Antike bis zut Gegenwart 1995, Canto d'amore. Klassizistische Moderne in Musik und bildender Kunst 1996, Paul Cézanne und die Moderne 1999, Der Maler Max Weiler. Das Geistige in der Natur 2001, Homo Pictor 2001, Zwischen-Räume. Malerei, Relief und Skulptur im Werk von Ellsworth Kelly 2002, Der Topos des Lebendigen: Bildgeschichte und ästhetische Erfahrung (in Dimensionen ästhetische Erfahrung) 2003, Mit durchdringendem Blick 2003, Die Härte der Grossen Dinge: Arp und Schwitters in ihren frühen Jahren 2004, Jenseits der Sprache? Anmerkungen zur Logik der Bilder (in Iconic Turn: Die Neue Macht der Bilder) 2004, Ausdruck und Dekoration: Henri Matisse auf dem Weg zu sich selbst 2005, Zeit-Räume. Zum Begriff des plastischen Raumes. Im Schatten von Lessings 'Laokoon' 2006, Das Ende als Anfang – Eine Reflexionsfigur der modernen Kunst, in: End of Art – Endings in Art / La fin de l'art – Les fins dans les arts / Ende der Kunst – Enden in der Kunst 2006, Unbestimmtheit. Zur Logik des Bildes, in: Bild und Einbildungskraft 2006, Wie Bilder Sinn erzeugen 2007. *Address:* Kunstgeschichtliches Seminar, St Alban-Graben-8, 4051 Basel (office); Sevogelplatz 1, 4051 Basel, Switzerland (home). *Telephone:* (61) 2066292 (office); (61) 3116241 (home). *Fax:* (61) 2066297 (office). *E-mail:* gottfried.boehm@unibas.ch (office). *Website:* www.unibas.ch/kunsthist (office); www.eikones.ch (home).

BOEHNER, John, BA; American politician; *House Minority Leader;* b. Nov. 1949, Cincinnati; m. Debbie Boehner; two d.; ed Xavier Univ., Cincinnati; early career as Sale Rep. then Pres. Nucite Sales; Trustee Union Township, Ohio 1982–84; Rep. Ohio State Legislature 1984–90; mem. US House of Reps 1990–, Chair. House Cttee on Educ. and the Workforce 2001–, fmr mem. House Agric. Cttee, House Majority Leader 2007, House Minority Leader 2007–. *Address:* 1011 Longworth H.O.B., Washington, DC 20515, USA (office). *Telephone:* (202) 225-6205 (office). *Fax:* (202) 225-0704 (office). *Website:* johnboehner.house.gov (office).

BOEL, (Else) Mariann Fischer; Danish politician; *Commissioner for Agriculture and Rural Development, European Commission;* b. 15 April 1943, Aasum, Funen; d. of Hans Boel and Valborg Boel; Man. Sec. at export co., Copenhagen 1965–67, Finance Man. 1967–71; mem. Munkebo Municipal Council 1982–91, 1994–97, Second Deputy Mayor 1986–90; Chair. Liberal Party Kerteminde constituency 1987–89; mem. Folketing for Funen Co. 1990–, Chair. Food, Agric. and Fisheries Cttee 1994–98, Trade and Industry Cttee 1998–99, Fiscal Affairs Cttee 1998–99; Minister of Food, Agric. and Fisheries 2001–04; EU Commr for Agric. and Rural Devt 2004–; mem. Cen. Bd, Liberal Party 1990–, mem. Man. Cttee Parl. Liberal Party 1990–; Chair. High Schools' Secr. 1993–; mem. Nat. Assessment Council 1994–98, Nat. Tax Tribunal 1998–2001; mem. Cttee of Reps Østifterne 1991–; mem. Bd of Govs Boel Fund 1992–. *Address:* European Commission, 200 rue de la Loi, 1049 Brussels, Belgium (office); Dr. Tværgade 59, 3. sal, 1302 Copenhagen K, Denmark. *Telephone:* (2) 299-11-11 (office). *Fax:* (2) 295-01-38 (office). *Website:* ec.europa.eu/commission_barroso/fischer-boel (office).

BOESAK, Rev. Allan; South African clergyman; b. 23 Feb. 1946, Kakamas; s. of Andreas Boesak and Sarah Helena Boesak; m. 1st Dorothy Rose Martin 1969; one s. three d.; m. 2nd Elna Botha 1991; two d.; ed Univ. of Western Cape, Theological Univ., Kampen, Netherlands, Union Theological Seminary; prominent anti-apartheid campaigner; elected Pres. World Alliance of Reformed Churches, Ottawa 1982; Pres. Asscn of Christian Students in SA 1984–90; Vice-Pres. South African Council of Churches 1984–87; fmr mem. Dutch Reformed Mission Church; Leader African Nat. Congress (ANC) in Western Cape 1991; Dir Foundation for Peace and Justice 1991; faced 32 theft and corruption charges 1997; on trial for fraud Aug. 1998; sentenced to six years' imprisonment March 1999, sentence halved on appeal May 2000; conviction for misuse of aid money set aside, conviction for theft upheld 2000; released on parole June 2001; granted presidential pardon 2005; co-f. United Democratic Front 1983; Hon. DD (Victoria) 1983, (Yale) 1984, (Interdenominational Theological Center, Atlanta) 1985; Hon. DIur (Warwick) 1989; Third World Prize 1989, numerous other awards and hon. degrees. *Publications:* Farewell to Innocence 1976, Black and Reformed 1984, Walking on Thorns 1984, A Call for an End to Unjust Rule 1986, If This is Treason, I am Guilty (Speeches) 1988, Comfort and Protest 1988, Shadows of the Light 1996, Tot Sterwens Toe (poems) 2001. *Leisure interests:* reading, walking, sports, music. *Address:* 16 Villa Bellini, Constantia Street, Strand 7140, South Africa (home). *Telephone:* (21) 854-4937 (home). *E-mail:* boesak@mweb.co.za (home).

BOETSCH, Wolfgang, DJur; German politician; b. 8 Sept. 1938, Bad Kreuznach; m.; two c.; ed Univ. of Würzburg and Verwaltungshochschule, Speyer; municipal lawyer, Kitzingen 1968–74; legal adviser to Govt of Lower Franconia 1974; mem. Christian Social Union (CSU) 1960–; mem. Würzburg City Council 1972–76; mem. Bavarian Parl. 1974–76; Chair. of CSU, Würzburg 1973–91, also mem. Presidium of CSU; mem. Bundestag 1976–2005; Minister for Posts and Telecommunications 1993–97. *Address:* Waltherstrasse 5A, 97074 Würzburg, Germany. *Telephone:* (931) 83080. *Fax:* (931) 14-8872.

BOFF, Leonardo Genezio Darci, DPhil, DTheol; Brazilian academic, writer and editor; b. 14 Dec. 1938, Concórdia, SC; s. of Mansueto Boff and Regina Fontana Boff; ed Inst. Teológico Franciscano, Petrópolis and Nat. Univ. of Rio de Janeiro; Prof. of Systematic Theology and of Franciscan Spirituality, Inst. Teológico Franciscano, Petrópolis, Rio de Janeiro 1971–92, also Prof. of Theology of Liberation; Adviser to Latin American Conf. of Religions (CLAR) 1971–80, to Nat. Conf. of Brazilian Bishops (CNBB) 1971–80; mem. Editorial Bd of Revista Eclesiástica Brasileira 1971–92; mem. Bd of Dirs Vozes publishing house 1971–92; Pres. Bd of Eds, Theology and Liberation collection 1985–; mem. Editorial Bd Concilium; ordered by Roman Curia to begin unspecified period of 'obedient silence' 1985; Dr hc (Turin, Lund); Paz y Justicia Award, Barcelona, Menschenrechte in der Kirche Award, Herbert Haag Foundation, FRG and Switzerland, Right Livelihood Award, Stockholm 2001. *Publications:* Jesus Christ Liberator 1971, Die Kirche als Sakrament im Horizont der Welterfahrung 1972, Theology of Captivity and Liberation 1972, Ecclesiogenesis 1977, The Maternal Face of God 1979, Church: Charisma and Power 1980, Theology Listening to People 1981, St Francis: A Model for Human Liberation 1984, Trinity and Society 1988, The Gospel of the Cosmic Christ 1989, The New Evangelization: The Perspective of the Oppressed 1990, Ecology and Spirituality 1991, Mística e Espiritualidade 1994, Nova Era: a Consciência Planetária 1994. *Leisure interests:* gardening, social work at the 'favelas', child minding. *Address:* Pr. Martins Leão 12/204, Alto Vale Encantado, 20531-350 Rio de Janeiro, Brazil. *Telephone:* (21) 326-5293. *Fax:* (21) 326-5293.

BOFFO, Dino; Italian journalist and editor; currently Ed.-in-Chief and Man. Dir Avvenire (daily newspaper) and News Ed. SAT 2000 satellite TV network; Sec.-Gen. Azione Cattolica Italiana; taught course on communications and citizenship at Catholic Univ. of the Sacred Heart, Milan 2002–03. *Address:* Avvenire, Piazza Carbonari 3, 20125 Milan, Italy (office). *Telephone:* (02) 67801 (office). *Fax:* (02) 6780208 (office). *E-mail:* info@avvenire.it (office). *Website:* www.avvenire.it (office).

BOFILL, Ricardo; Spanish architect; b. 5 Dec. 1939, Barcelona; s. of Emilio Bofill and Maria Levi; two s.; ed Ecole Française, Barcelona, architectural studies in Geneva; founder mem. and leader, Taller de Arquitectura, Paris, Barcelona; Dr hc (Univ. of Hamburg, Germany) 1968, (Metz Univ., France) 1995; Hon. Fellow, FAIA 1985, Bund Deutscher Architekter (BDA) Bonn, Germany 1996; Associació de Disseny Industrial del Foment de les Arts Decoratives (ADI-FAD) Award in Architecture for building on calle Nicaragua 99, Barcelona, Spain 1963, American Soc. of Interior Designers Int. Prize, New York, 1978, Architecte Agrée Degree Ordre National des Architectes, Paris, France 1979, Ciudad de Barcelona Prize of Architecture 1980, Architect in Belgium, Ordre des Architectes Conseil du Brabant, Brussels 1989, Chicago Architecture Award, Ill. Council/American Inst. of Architects/Architectural Record, Chicago 1989, Académie Internationale de Philosophie de lArt, Bern, Switzerland 1989; Officier de l'Ordre des Arts et des Lettres Degree, Ministry of Culture, Paris, France 1984. *Works include:* Les Espaces d'Abraxas, Marne-la-Vallée, Les Echelles du Baroque, Paris, Antigone, Montpellier, Le Lac and Le Viaduc, Versailles, airports (Barcelona), theatres (Metz and Barcelona), offices, wine cellars Congress Palace, Madrid, Christian Dior Corpn HQ, Paris, Shepherd School of Music, Houston, Tex., USA, 77 West Wacker office tower, Chicago, Ill., USA, Harajuku United Arrows shopping centre, Tokyo. *Address:* Taller de Arquitectura, 14 Avenue Industria, 08960 Saint Just Desvern, Barcelona, Spain (office). *Telephone:* (3) 4999900 (office). *Fax:* (3) 4999950 (office). *E-mail:* rbofill@bofill.com (office). *Website:* www.bofill.com (office).

BOFINGER, Helge; German architect and academic; *Professor of Design and Building Theory, Faculty of Architecture, University of Dortmund;* b. 30 March 1940, Stettin/Pommern; s. of Christa Bofinger and Hans Ullrich Bofinger; m. Margret Schreib Schmitz-Mathies 1965; ed Ratsgymnasium Goslar, Tech. Univ. of Brunswick; Scientific Asst, Tech. Univ. of Brunswick 1968–69; est. own office Bofinger and partner with Margret Bofinger, Brunswick 1969–81, Berlin 1974–, Wiesbaden 1978–; Asst Prof., Univ. of Dortmund 1979–81, Prof. of Design and Bldg Theory, Faculty of Architecture 1986–; Hon. Prof., Univ. of Buenos Aires, Argentina 1985; Visiting Prof. and Lecturer, Venice, Amsterdam, Rotterdam, Buenos Aires, São Paulo, Brasília, Curitiba, Shanghai 1984–91; rep. in numerous exhbns Germany, USA, Canada, Israel, Italy, Argentina, UK, France, USSR 1979–90; Hon. Prof. (Tbilisi) 1995; Deubau Special Prize 1979, German Architectural Prize 1983, Hon. Prize, Transcaucasian Biennale, Tbilisi 1988, Renault Traffic Award 2002. *Works include:* Castle Park, Brunswick 1972–74, Unitéhabitation, Göttingen 1972–74, Piazza Ledenhof, Osnabrück 1976–77, school, Friedland 1977–79, Villa S. Kronberg 1980–82, German Cinema Museum 1979–84, Frankfurt Fair Tower 1984, IBA Berlin, Wilhemstr., Stresemannstr. 1981, 1988–89, Telecommunications Bldg, German Post/Telecom 1987–90, Commerzbank, Frankfurt 1991, Willy-Brandt-Haus (SPD HQ), Berlin 1996, town hall extension, Saarbrücken 1998, Center Sauerland, Wiesbaden 1998, Central Bus Station and Piazza, Osnabrück 2000, Ministry of Econs, Saarbrücken 2004. *Publications:* Architecture in Germany 1979, Young Architects in Europe 1983, Helmut Jacoby – Master of Architectural Drawing (ed.); numerous contribs to German and int. architectural magazines. *Leisure interest:* architecture. *Address:* Biebricher Allee 49, 65187 Wiesbaden, Germany (office). *Telephone:* (611) 87094 (office). *Fax:* (611) 87095 (office). *E-mail:* bofinger@bofinger-partner.de (office). *Website:* www.bofinger-partner.de (office).

BOGAERS, Petrus Clemens Wilhelmus Maria, DrsEcon; Dutch politician and trade union official; b. 2 July 1924, Cuyk a/d Maas; s. of Petrus P. M. J. Bogaers and Henrica Maria Hermans; m. 1st Femmigje Visscher 1950 (divorced 1980); m. 2nd Yvonne M. H. L. Bogaers 1981 (divorced 1986); m. 3rd Ida Heyne 1994; four s. three d.; ed Episcopal Coll. Grammar School, Roermond and Tilburg School of Econs; official Red Cross Army 1945; Asst to Prof. van den Brink 1947; Econ. Adviser to Roman Catholic Workers' Union 1948, Head Scientific Advisory Section 1957–63; mem. Socio-Econ. Council 1954; mem. EEC Econ. and Social Cttee 1958; mem. Second Chamber, Netherlands Parl. 1959; Minister of Housing and Building 1963–65; Minister of Housing and Physical Planning 1965–66; Pres. Gooiland Region 1968–74, Netherlands Asthma Foundation 1976–89 (Hon. mem. 1989); mem. Supervisory Bds various Dutch cos 1976–95; Sec. Employee Participation Foundation BERGEYK 1986–96; mem. Supervisory Bd Dutch Employee Participation Inst. 1994–96; Officer Order of Orange-Nassau 1963, Commdr Order of Orange-Nassau 1966; Dutch Efficiency Prize 1963, Queens House Medal of Orange-Nassau 1965. *Publications:* Memories of Pieter Bogaers, Minister of Housing and Physical Planning (with Reinhilde van der Kroef) 2004. *Leisure interests:* reading, tennis, open-air life. *Address:* Volta Street 53, Amersfoort, Netherlands. *Telephone:* (33) 4615093.

BOGAN, Sir Nagora Y., MBE, KBE, LLB; Papua New Guinea diplomatist and business executive; b. Sept. 1956, Lae; m. Lady Nohoranie; two c.; ed Univ. of Papau New Guinea; fmr Sr Civil Servant, Internal Revenue Service; Oceania Del. to Commonwealth Asscn of Tax Admin (CATA) 1988–91; Chair. Policy Working Group on Tax and Customs, Govt of Papua New Guinea 1988–91, Chair. Man. Cttee 1991–95, First Commr Gen. Internal Revenue Comm. 1992–95; apptd Amb. to USA (also accred. to Mexico and Canada) 1995; High Commr to Canada –2003; Chair. Bd of Dirs Public Officers Superannuation Fund (POSF) (public sector pension fund) 2002–. *Address:* Public Officers Superannuation Fund (POSF), POB 483, Port Moresby, NCD, Papua New Guinea (office). *Telephone:* 3095200 (office). *Fax:* 3214406 (office). *E-mail:* posfpom@posf.com.pg (office). *Website:* www.posf.com.pg (office).

BOGATIKOV, Oleg A., Dr Geol.; Russian geologist; *Head, Zavaritski Laboratory of General Petrography;* b. 15 Dec. 1934; m.; two d.; ed Moscow Inst. of Geological Survey; jr, sr researcher, scientific sec., leading researcher Institute of Geology of Ore Deposits, Petrography, Mineralogy and Geochemistry (IGEM) 1957–; Head Zavaritski Laboratory of General Petrography 1975-; mem. Russian Acad. of Sciences (sec. 2002); State Prize of the Russian Federation 1997, Prize of the Govt of the Russian Federation 1999. *Publications include:* numerous scientific articles and monographs. *Leisure interests:* travelling. *Address:* Russian Academy of Sciences, Leninsky pr. 14, Moscow, Russia (office). *Telephone:* (495) 938-09-40 (office). *E-mail:* oleg@igem.ru (office).

BOGDANCHIKOV, Sergey, DSc; Russian petroleum industry executive; *President, Rosneft Oil Company;* b. 10 Aug. 1957; ed Buguruslansky Oil Tech. School, Ufa Petroleum Inst.; began career in oil and gas industry, Sakhalin Island 1981; joined Sakhalinmorneftegaz 1988, Gen. Dir 1993–97; mem. Bd Dirs Rosneft Oil Co. 1995–, Vice-Pres. 1997–98, Pres. 1998–. *Address:* Rosneft Oil Co., 26/1, Sofiyskaya Embankment, 1, GSP-8, Moscow 115998, Russia (office). *Telephone:* (495) 777-44-22 (office). *Fax:* (495) 777-44-44 (office). *E-mail:* postman@rosneft.ru (office). *Website:* www.rosneft.ru (office).

BOGDANOR, Vernon, CBE, MA, FRSA, FBA; British academic; *Professor of Government, University of Oxford;* b. 16 July 1943, London; s. of Harry Bogdanor and Rosa Weinger; m. Judith Beckett 1972 (divorced 2000); two s.; ed Queen's Coll. and Nuffield Coll. Oxford; Fellow, Brasenose Coll. Oxford 1966–, Sr Tutor 1979–85, 1996–97; mem. Council of Hansard Soc. for Parl. Govt 1981–97; Special Adviser, House of Lords Select Cttee on European Communities 1982–83; adviser to Govts of Czech Repub., Slovakia, Hungary and Israel on constitutional and electoral matters 1988–; Reader in Govt Univ. of Oxford 1989–96, Prof. of Govt 1996–; Special Adviser, House of Commons Public Service Cttee 1996; Gresham Prof. of Law, Gresham Coll., London 2004–07; mem. UK del. to CSCE Conf. Oslo 1991; Mishcon Lecturer 1994; Magna Carta Lecturer 2006; Hon. Fellow, Soc. for Advanced Legal Studies 1997. *Publications:* Devolution 1979, The People and the Party System 1981, Multi-party Politics and the Constitution 1983, What is Proportional Representation? 1984, The Blackwell Encyclopaedia of Political Institutions (ed.) 1987, Comparing Constitutions (co-author) 1995, The Monarchy and the Constitution 1995, Politics and the Constitution 1996, Power and the People 1997, Devolution in the United Kingdom 1999, The British Constitution in the Twentieth Century (ed.) 2003, Joined-Up Government (ed.) 2005, The New British Constitution 2009. *Leisure interests:* music, walking, talking. *Address:* Brasenose College, Oxford, OX1 4AJ, England. *Telephone:* (1865) 277830. *Fax:* (1865) 277822.

BOGDANOV, Aleksey Alekseyevich; Russian biochemist and academic; b. 11 Oct. 1935; s. of Aleksey Bogdanov and Irina Bogdanova; m. Suzanna Bogdanova; two s.; ed Moscow State Univ.; Jr, Sr researcher, docent Moscow State Univ. 1958–69, head of Dept 1969–, Prof. 1973–; corresp. mem. USSR (now Russian) Acad. of Sciences 1984, mem. 1994; research in bioorganic chem. and molecular biology; USSR State Prize. *Publications include:* Chemistry of Nucleic Acids and their Components 1978, Advanced Organic Chemistry of Nucleic Acids (VCH) 1994; numerous articles in scientific journals. *Leisure interest:* classical music. *Address:* Moscow State University, Vorobyevy gory, 119899 Moscow, Russia (office). *Telephone:* (495) 939-31-43 (office).

BOGDANOV, Michael, MA; British theatre, film and television director and writer; *Artistic Director, Wales Theatre Company;* b. 15 Dec. 1938, London; s. of Francis Bogdin and Rhoda Rees; m. 1st Patricia Ann Warwick 1966; two s. one d.; m. 2nd Ulrike Engelbrecht 2000; one d. one s.; ed Trinity Coll., Dublin, Munich Univ., Sorbonne; trained as Producer/Dir BBC 1966; Producer/Dir Radio Telefis Eireann 1966–69; Asst Dir RSC 1970–71; Assoc. Dir Tyneside Theatre Co. 1971–73; Assoc. Dir Leicester Haymarket Theatre 1973, also Artistic Dir Phoenix Theatre 1973–77; Dir Young Vic Theatre 1978–80; Assoc. Dir Royal Nat. Theatre 1980–88; f. (with Michael Pennington) English Shakespeare Co. 1986, Artistic Dir 1986–98; Intendant Deutsches Schauspielhaus, Hamburg 1988–92; Artistic Dir, Wales Theatre Co. 2003–; Sr Fellow, De Montfort Univ. 1992; Assoc. Dir Peter Brook (q.v.) 's production of A Midsummer Night's Dream, RSC 1971; Producer/Dir UK Holocaust Memorial Day Even, Cardiff 2006; Vice-Chair. Dirs Guild of GB; Chair. Welsh Arts Awards; mem. Academi, Wales; Hon. Prof., Univ. of Wales 1993; Hon. Fellow, Welsh Coll. of Music and Drama 1994; Hon. Fellow, in Drama, Trinity Coll., Univ. of Dublin 1997; Hon. Prof., Univ. of Sunderland 1997; Dr hc, Trinity Coll., Univ. of Dublin 2005. *Plays include:* Two Gentlemen of Verona, Teatro Escobar, São Paulo, Brazil, Rabelais (Jean-Louis Barrault) 1971, Sir Gawain and the Green Knight 1977, Hunchback of Notre Dame, Nat. Theatre 1977, The Taming of the Shrew, RSC, Hamlet, Stuttgart and Düsseldorf 1978–79 (Soc. of West End Theatres Dir of the Year 1979), Shadow of a Gunman, Knight of the Burning Pestle, RSC, The Seagull, Tokyo 1980, The Romans in Britain, Mayor of Zalamea, The Hypochondriac, A Spanish Tragedy, Uncle Vanya, all for Nat. Theatre; Hiawatha (Nat. Theatre Christmas production) 1980, 1981, 1982; Lorenzaccio, You Can't Take it With You, National Theatre 1983; Hamlet, Dublin Abbey Theatre 1983, Romeo and Juliet, Tokyo Imperial Theatre 1983 (Japan Critics Circle Dir of the Year 1983); The Story of a Horse, Ancient Mariner, both for Nat. Theatre 1984; The Mayor of Zalamea, Washington 1984, Measure for Measure, Stratford, Ont. 1985 (Toronto Critics Dir of the Year Award 1985), Mutiny, London 1985, Donnerstag aus Licht, Covent Garden 1985, Romeo and Juliet, Royal Shakespeare Co. 1986, Julius

Caesar, Hamburg 1986, Henry IV (parts I and II), Henry V, UK, Europe, Canada, USA 1986–87, Reineke Fuchs, Hamburg 1987, The Wars of the Roses (7-play history cycle) 1987–89 (Dir of the Year, Laurence Olivier Award 1989); Montag aus Licht, (Stockhausen) La Scala 1988; Coriolanus, The Winter's Tale, Macbeth, The Tempest, The Venetian Twins, RSC 1993, 1998, 1999, Hair, Old Vic 1993, Peer Gynt 1995, 1999, Faust 1996, Macbeth 1997, Timon of Athens 1997, Troilus and Cressida 2000, The Merry Wives of Windsor 2001, Ludlow Festival 2002–04, A Servant of Two Masters, Hamburg 2003, Under Milk Wood (50th Anniversary production for Wales Theatre Co.) 2003–04, Lady Hamilton, Hamburg 2004, Twelfth Night, Cymbeline and The Merchant of Venice, Wales Theatre Co. 2004, Lone Star Love (The Merry Wives of Texas), New York 2004, Amazing Grace and Hamlet, Wales Theatre Co. 2005, Der Garderobier (The Dresser), Hamburg 2006, Fiddler on the Roof, Aberystwyth 2006, A Child's Christmas in Wales 2006, Waiting for Godot, Hamburg 2007 (Rolf Mares Prize for Best Dir 2006, Pegasus Prize Best Production 2007), Salto Mortale, Hamburg 2007, Valuing Freedom, Cardiff 2007, Contender, West Side Story, The Servant of Two Masters (all Wales Theatre Co.) 2007. *Television includes:* Channel 4 series Shakespeare Lives, also for Channel 4, Hiawatha, Macbeth (Channel 4), The Tempest in Bute Town (BBC Wales) 1996, A Light in the Valley (BBC) (Royal TV Soc. Best Regional Film 1999), A Light on the Hill (BBC), A Light in the City (BBC), Killing Time (BBC). *Film:* Shakespeare on the Estate 1995 (BAFTA Award), A Light in the Valley (RST Award), The Tempest in Britain (BBC), Macbeth (Granada/Channel 4), The Welsh in Shakespeare (BBC Wales). *Publications:* Hiawatha 1981, The Magic Drum 1983, Ancient Mariner, Reineke Fuchs 1988, The English Shakespeare Company (jtly) 1992, Shakespeare, the Director's Cut 2004. *Leisure interests:* cricket, reading, music, wine, Celtic history. *Address:* Dogo Cymru Ltd, 21 Dogo Street, Pontcanna, Cardiff, CF11 9JJ (office); 21 Dogo Street, Cardiff, CF11 9JJ, Wales (home). *Telephone:* (29) 2064-0069 (office); (29) 2022-1502 (home). *Fax:* (29) 2064-0069 (office). *E-mail:* michael@walestheatrecompany.com (office); michael@bogdanov.freeserve.co.uk (home). *Website:* www.walestheatrecompany.com (office).

BOGDANOV, Vladimir Leonidovich, DEcon; Russian energy industry executive; *Director-General, OJSC Surgutneftegas;* b. 28 May 1951, Suyerka, Tyumen Oblast; m.; one d.; ed Tiumen Industrial Inst., Acad. of Nat. Economy; worked for Nizhnevartovsk Drilling Admin as Driller Asst, Driller, Sr Engineer, Chief Deputy Technological Dept, Chief of Shift 1973–76; Chief, Sr Technologist, Sr Engineer Surgut Drilling Works Administration No. 2, Industrial Asscn (Surgutneftegas) 1976–78; Chief Deputy Drilling Dept, Deputy CEO, Deputy, Head of Drilling Dept Industrial Asscn (Uganskneftegas) 1978–80; Deputy CEO for Northern regions and Head of Drilling Dept Surgutneftegas 1980–83; Deputy Drilling Chief Glavtyumenneftegas 1983–84; CEO Surgutneftegas (now OJSC Surgutneftegas) 1984–, Chair. and CEO 1990, now Dir-Gen.; Delegate Tyumen Regional Council from Surgut 1985–90; mem. Bd of Dirs Kirishinefteproduct 1994–, Lennefteproduct 1994–, Bulk Plant (Ruchi) 1994–, Red Oiler (Krasnyi Neftyanik) 1994–, Onegoneft 1994–, Mosbusinessbank 1996–, ONEXIM Bank 1996–, Nafta Moscow 1997–, AKB Rosbank 2002–; mem. Issuer Council, Fed. Comm. on Securities Market 1999–, Industrial Council 2000–, Steering Cttee, Delovaya Rossiya 2001–; mem. Acad. of Mining Sciences, Acad. of Natural Sciences, Nat. Council on Corp. Governance; Corresp. mem. Acad. of Technological Sciences; Trustee, Global Energy Int. Prize; Entrepreneur of the Year, Russian Union of Industrialists and Entrepreneurs 2000. *Address:* OJSC Surgutneftegas, ul. Kukuyevitskogo 1, Surgut 628415, Tyumen, Russia (office). *Telephone:* (3462) 42-61-33 (office). *Fax:* (3462) 33-32-35 (office). *E-mail:* secret_b@surgutneftegas.ru (office). *Website:* www.surgutneftegas.ru (office).

BOGDANOV, Vsevolod Leonidovich; Russian journalist; *President, International Confederation of Journalists' Unions;* b. 6 Feb. 1944, Arkhangelsk Region; m.; three d.; ed Leningrad State Univ.; corresp., ed. in newspapers, radio and TV Magadan 1961–76; Head Chief Dept of Periodicals State Cttee of Publs 1976–89; Dir-Gen. TV programmes State Radio and TV Cttee 1989–92; Chair. Russian Union of Journalists 1992–; Pres. Nat. Journalist Trade Union 1999–; Pres. Int. Confed. of Journalists' Unions 1999–. *Leisure interests:* book rarities, fishing, hunting, Russian cuisine, music. *Address:* Union of Journalists, Zubovsky blvd 4, 119021 Moscow, Russia (office). *Telephone:* (495) 201-51-01 (office). *E-mail:* ruj@ruj.ru (office). *Website:* www.ruj.ru (office).

BOGDANOVICH, Peter; American film director, writer, producer and actor; b. 30 July 1939, Kingston, NY; s. of Borislav Bogdanovich and Herma (Robinson) Bogdanovich; m. 1st Polly Platt 1962 (divorced 1970); two d.; m. 2nd L. B. Straten 1988; Actor, American Shakespeare Festival, Stratford, Conn. 1956, NY Shakespeare Festival 1958; Dir, Producer off-Broadway plays The Big Knife 1959, Camino Real, Ten Little Indians, Rocket to the Moon 1961, Once in a Lifetime 1964; film feature-writer for Esquire, New York Times, Village Voice, Cahiers du Cinéma, Los Angeles Times, New York Magazine, Vogue, Variety etc. 1961–; owner The Holly Moon Co. Inc. 1992–; mem. Dirs Guild of America, Writers' Guild of America, Acad. of Motion Picture Arts and Sciences; NY Film Critics' Award (1971) and BAFTA Award for Best Screenplay (The Last Picture Show) 1971, Writers' Guild of America Award for Best Screenplay (What's Up, Doc?) 1972, Pasinetti Award, Critics' Prize, Venice Festival (Saint Jack) 1979 and other awards and prizes. *Films include:* The Wild Angels (2nd unit dir, co-writer, actor) 1966, Targets (dir, co-writer, producer, actor) 1968, The Last Picture Show (dir, co-writer) 1971, Directed by John Ford (dir, writer) 1971, What's Up Doc? (dir, co-writer, producer) 1972, Paper Moon (dir, producer) 1973, Daisy Miller (dir, producer) 1974, At Long Last Love (dir, writer, producer) 1975, Nickelodeon (dir, co-writer) 1976, Saint Jack (dir, co-writer, actor) 1979, They All Laughed (dir, writer) 1981, Mask (dir) 1985, Illegally Yours (dir, producer) 1988, Texasville (dir, producer, writer) 1990, Noises Off (dir, exec. producer) 1992, The Thing Called Love (dir) 1993, Who The Devil Made It (dir) 1997, Mr Jealousy (actor) 1997, Highball (actor) 1997, Coming Soon (actor) 1999, Rated X (actor) 2000, The Independent (actor) 2000, The Cat's Meow (dir) 2003, Scene Stealers (actor) 2003, Infamous (actor) 2006, The Doorman (actor) 2007, Broken English (actor) 2007, Dedication (actor) 2007. *Television:* The Great Professional: Howard Hawks (co-dir, wrote), BBC 1967; dir: Saintly Switch 1999, The Sopranos 1999, Hustle 2004, The Mystery of Natalie Wood 2004; regular commentator for CBS This Morning 1987–89; actor: Northern Exposure, CBS 1993, Fallen Angels 1995, Painted Word 1995, To Sir With Love II 1996, Naked City: A Killer Christmas 1998. *Publications:* The Cinema of Orson Welles 1961, The Cinema of Howard Hawks 1962, The Cinema of Alfred Hitchcock 1963, John Ford 1968, Fritz Lang in America 1969, Allan Dwan, the Last Pioneer 1971, Pieces of Time, Peter Bogdanovich on the Movies 1961–85, The Killing of the Unicorn: Dorothy Stratten (1960–80) 1984, A Year and a Day Calendar (ed.) 1991, This is Orson Welles (with Orson Welles) 1992, Who the Devil Made It 1997, Who the Hell's In It? 2004. *Address:* c/o William Pfeiffer, 30 Lane of Acres, Haddonfield, NJ 08033; c/o CAA, 9830 Wilshire Boulevard, Beverly Hills, CA 90212-1804, USA (office).

BOGIANCKINO, Massimo, PhD; Italian opera director; b. 10 Nov. 1922, Rome; s. of Edoardo T. Bogianckino and Fiorangela Liberi; m. Judith Matthias 1950; ed Conservatory of Music and Acad. Santa Cecilia, Rome and Univ. of Rome; fmr musicologist and concert pianist; Dir Enciclopedia dello Spettacolo 1957–62; Dir Accademia Filarmonica, Rome 1960–63; Dir Teatro dell' Opera, Rome 1963–68; Artistic Dir Festival of Two Worlds, Spoleto 1968–71; Dir of Concert Programs, Accad. Santa Cecilia, Rome 1970–71; Artistic Dir La Scala, Milan 1971–74; Gen. Man. Teatro Comunale, Florence 1974–82; Admin. Gen. Paris Opera 1982–85; apptd Mayor of Florence 1985; Grosses Bundesverdienstkreuz (FRG). *Publications:* L'arte clavicembalistica di D. Scarlatti 1956 (English version 1968), Aspetti del teatro musicale in Italia e in Francia nell' età Barocca 1968, Le canzonette e i madrigali di V. Cossa 1981. *Address:* c/o Palazzo Vecchio, 50122 Florence, Italy (office).

BOGLE, Ellen Gray; Jamaican diplomatist and government official (retd); b. 9 Oct. 1941, St Andrew; d. of Victor Gray Williams and Eileen Averil (née Rampie); one s. one d.; ed St Andrew High School, Univ. of the West Indies; Dir Foreign Trade Div., Ministry of Foreign Affairs, with responsibility for formulation of Jamaica's Foreign Trade policy 1978–81; fmr Dir Jamaica Nat. Export Corpn; High Commr in Trinidad & Tobago 1981–89; High Commr in UK 1989–94; fmr Amb., Ministry of Foreign Affairs and Foreign Trade; Amb. and Special Envoy to the Asscn of Caribbean States and CARICOM 1997; fmr Under-Sec. Bilateral and Regional Affairs, Ministry of Foreign Affairs and Foreign Trade; represented Jamaica at numerous int. confs; Commdr Order of Distinction 1987. *Leisure interests:* gardening, reading, cooking, table tennis. *Address:* c/o Ministry of Foreign Affairs and Foreign Trade, 21 Dominica Drive, Kingston 5, Jamaica (office).

BOGNER, Willy, Jr.; German business executive and film director; *Chairman and Managing Director, Willy Bogner GmbH & Co. KGaA;* b. 23 Jan. 1942, Munich; s. of the late Willy Bogner Sr and Maria Bogner; m. Sonia Ribeiro 1973; ed Altes Realgymnasium, Munich and business and technical studies in Munich and Hohenstein; Chair. and Man. Dir Willy Bogner GmbH & Co. KGaA (sportswear co. f. in 1932 by Willy Bogner Sr); Man. Willy Bogner Film GmbH, Munich; mem. German Nat. Olympic Cttee; dir of documentary, advertising, sports (especially skiing) films; several times German ski champion and participated in Winter Olympics, Squaw Valley 1960, Innsbruck 1964 and World Ski Championships, Chamonix 1962, Portillo (Chile) 1966. *Films include:* Skivision 1974, 1975, 1979, Skifaszination, Ski Fantasie 1981, Crystal Dreams 1982, Feuer und Eis 1986, Feuer, Eis und Dynamit 1990, White Magic 1994, Mountain Magic 1999, Ski to the Max 2001; directed ski scene sequences in On Her Majesty's Secret Service 1969, Snow Job 1972, The Spy Who Loved Me 1977, For Your Eyes Only 1981, A View to a Kill 1985. *Leisure interests:* sport (tennis, skiing, golf), sailing, flying, filming and photography. *Address:* Willy Bogner GmbH & Co. KGaA, Sankt-Veit-Strasse 4, 81673 Munich, Germany (office). *Telephone:* (89) 436060 (office). *Fax:* (89) 43606429 (office). *E-mail:* communication@bogner.com (office). *Website:* www.bogner.com (office).

BOGOLEPOV, Nikolai Nikolayevich, DrMed; Russian physiologist; b. 30 Nov. 1933, Moscow; m. Lidia Nikolayevna Rybina; two d.; ed Moscow Inst. of Medicine; corresp. mem. Russian Acad. of Medical Sciences 1988–; researcher, Research Inst. of the Brain, Russian Acad. of Medical Sciences 1957–, fmr head of lab., Dir; mem. Scientific Soc. of Anatomy, Histology; mem. Int. Brain Research Org.; main research in morphology and structure of brain. *Publications include:* 8 books and over 200 scientific papers and articles. *Address:* Institute of the Brain, Russian Academy of Natural Sciences, Obukha str. 5, 107120 Moscow, Russia (office). *Telephone:* (495) 917-80-07 (office). *Website:* www.ihb.spb.ru (office).

BOGOLLAGAMA, Rohitha; Sri Lankan lawyer and politician; *Minister of Foreign Affairs;* b. 5 Aug. 1954, Nikaweratiya; m.; two c.; ed Ananda Coll. and Sri Lanka Law Coll.; apptd attorney 1976; fmr Chair. Sri Lanka Cement Corpn, Sathosa Printers; fmr Dir Foreign Employment Bureau; Legal and Political Adviser to Voice of America project in Sri Lanka 1991–99; Chair. and Dir-Gen. Bd of Investment of Sri Lanka 1993–2000; mem. Parl. (United National Party—UNP) 2000–, served on Parl. Consultative Cttees on Finance, Foreign Affairs, Defence, Industrial Devt and Investment Promotion and Power and Energy 2000–05, Chair. Cttee on Public Enterprises 2005–07, Minister of Industrial Devt 2001–04, of Enterprise Devt and Investment Promotion 2004–07, of Foreign Affairs 2007–. *Address:* Ministry of Foreign Affairs, Republic Building, Colombo 1, Sri Lanka (office). *Telephone:* (11) 2325371 (office). *Fax:* (11) 2446091 (office). *E-mail:* cypher@formin.gov.lk (office). *Website:* www.slmfa.gov.lk (office).

BOGOLUBOV, Hennady; Ukrainian business executive and philanthropist; *Co-Owner, Privat Group;* m.; two c.; Co-owner of Privat business group; first made his fortune in 1990 trading in computer parts, then est. one of Ukraine's first privately owned banks, PrivatBank; group now owns stake in oil drilling co. Ukrnafta and has interests in two western Ukrainian oil refineries and ore pits, also controls ferroalloy plants in Ukraine, Romania, Russia, Poland and USA; Pres. Dnipropetrovsk Jewish Philanthropic Fund; The Yad Vashem Soc. in Ukraine Award in recognition of his activity on behalf of Yad Vashem 2005. *Leisure interest:* enjoys sports. *Address:* PrivatBank, 50 Naberezhnaya Pobedy Street, Dnepropetrovsk, Ukraine (office). *Telephone:* (0562) 390000 (office). *Fax:* (0562) 390271 (office). *E-mail:* hotline@pbank.com.ua (office). *Website:* www.privatbank.ua/info/index3.stm (office).

BOGOLYUBOV, Mikhail Nikolayevich, DPhilSci; Russian philologist; b. 24 Jan. 1918, Kiev; m.; two s.; ed Leningrad Univ.; service in the army 1941–45; lecturer and researcher Leningrad Univ. 1944–60, Prof. of Iranian Studies 1959–, Dean Oriental Dept 1960–95, Hon. Dean 1995–; Corresp. mem. USSR (now Russian) Acad. of Sciences 1966–, mem. 1990; research interests include etymological and dialectological research of the languages of Asia and Africa, interpreting annotated translations of ancient texts in Eastern languages; ed. Russian trans. of Mahabharata 1987. *Publications:* over 150 books and articles on oriental philology and history. *Address:* St Petersburg State Univ., Oriental Faculty, 11 Universitetskaya Naberezhnaya, St Petersburg, Russia. *Telephone:* (812) 328-77-32 (office); (812) 448-51-46 (home). *E-mail:* mnb@mnb .usr.pu.ru (office); mb@mb1018.spb.edu (home). *Website:* www.spbu.ru (office).

BOGOMOLOV, Oleg Timofeyevich, DEcon; Russian economist; *Honorary Director, Institute of International Economic and Political Studies;* b. 20 Aug. 1927, Moscow; s. of T. I. Bogomolov and K. P. Zhelybaeva; m. 1st Larisa Sokolova (died 1962), one s.; m. 2nd Inna Yermakova 1966 (divorced 1977); m. 3rd Tatyana Yarikova 1978; ed Moscow Inst. of Foreign Trade; Ministry of Foreign Trade 1949–50; with CMEA 1954–56; Scientific Inst. for Economical Researches of State Cttee for Planning 1956–62; mem. CPSU 1950–90, Head of Advisors Group (Cen. Cttee) 1962–69; Section Chief, Econ. Research Inst., State Planning Cttee 1958–62; lecturer, then Prof. Moscow Univ. 1967–77; Dir Inst. of Econs of the World Socialist System of Acad. of Sciences (now Inst. of Int. Econ. and Political Studies) 1969–97, Hon. Dir 1997–; Pres. Int. Econ. Asscn 1992–, Council of Ministers Cttee for Mutual Cooperation with Socialist Countries 1970–86; People's Deputy of USSR 1989–91; Deputy, State Duma (Parl.) 1993–95; adviser to Pres. 1998–; mem. USSR (now Russian) Acad. of Sciences 1981, Exec. Cttee of Int. Social Science Council, UNESCO 1996–2003; decorations include Order of October Revolution, Order of Red Banner (twice), Orders of Merit to Fatherland (third and fourth degree). *Publications:* Socialism between Past and Future 1990, Russia and the Commonwealth of Independent States, Trends and Risks of Post-Soviet Development; Europe in Global Change 1993, Market Transformation in Russia: Prospects Still Uncertain, Economics in a Changing World of the Tenth Congress of the IEA 1994, Reformy glazami amerikanskikh i rossiyskikh ucheynykh 1996, Reforms in the Mirror of International Comparison 1998, My Chronicle of Transition Time 2000, Reflections About the Past and the Actualities 2007, World Economy in the Era of Globalization 2007. *Leisure interests:* photography, music, tennis. *Address:* Institute of International Economic and Political Studies, Novo-Cheremushkinskaya 46, 117418 Moscow, Russia. *Telephone:* (495) 120-82-00 (office). *Fax:* (495) 120-83-71 (office).

BOGOSIAN, Eric, BA; American actor and writer; b. 24 April 1953, Woburn, Mass; s. of Henry Bogosian and Edwina Bogosian; m. Jo Anne Bonney 1990; two c.; ed Univ. of Chicago and Oberlin Coll.; Obie Award 1986, 1990, 1994, Drama Critics' Circle Award, Berlin Film Festival Silver Bear Award 1988. *Films include:* Born in Flames 1983, Special Effects 1984, Chasing the Dragon 1987, Arena Brains 1988, Talk Radio 1988, Suffering Bastards 1989, Dolores Claiborne 1995, Under Siege 2: Dark Territory 1995, The Substance of Fire 1996, Beavis and Butt-Head Do America (voice) 1996, Deconstructing Harry 1997, In the Weeds 2000, Wake Up and Smell the Coffee 2001, Ararat 2002, Igby Goes Down 2002, Charlie's Angels: Full Throttle 2003, Wonderland 2003, King of the Corner 2004, Heights 2004, Blade: Trinity 2004. *Television includes:* The Caine Mutiny Court-Martial 1988, Last Flight Out 1990, Witch Hunt 1994, High Incident 1995, A Bright Shining Lie 1998, Blonde 2001, Shot in the Heart 2001, Love Monkey (series) 2006, Law & Order: Criminal Intent (series) 2006. *Plays include:* The New World, Men Inside, The Ricky Paul Show, Funhouse, Talk Radio, subUrbia, Griller, Drinking in America, Pounding Nails in the Floor with My Forehead, Sex, Drugs, Rock & Roll, Wake Up and Smell the Coffee, Red Angel, Humpty Dumpty, This is Now!. *Publications:* Mall 2000, Wasted Beauty 2005. *Address:* c/o George Lane, Creative Artists Agency, 162 5th Avenue, 6th Floor, New York, NY 10010, USA. *Telephone:* (212) 277-9000. *Fax:* (212) 277-9099. *Website:* www .ericbogosian.com.

BOGUSLAVSKY, Mark Moiseyevich, DJur; Russian professor of law; b. 8 June 1924, Moscow; m. 1st Iren Gorodetskaya 1960; m. 2nd Valentina Mazourova 1993; ed Inst. of Foreign Trade; prof. and Sr researcher, USSR (now Russian) Academy of Sciences Inst. of State and Law, Head of Int. Pvt. Law Sector 1985–2007; Dir Inst. für Osteuropäisches Recht, Kiel 1998, Lecturer 1998–, Arbiter Int. Commercial Court of Arbitration at Moscow; specialist in pvt. and econ. int. law, intellectual property and foreign investment legislation; mem. Bd Russian Asscn of Int. Law. *Publications:* International Private Law (textbook, translated into 19 languages) 1989; over 400 publications on pvt. international law. *Address:* Institute of State and Law, Russian Academy of Sciences, Znamenka str. 10, 119991 Moscow,

Russia. *Telephone:* (495) 291-33-81 (office); (495) 118-85-71 (home). *Fax:* (495) 291-85-74. *E-mail:* isl_ran@rinet.ru (office). *Website:* www.igpran.ru (office).

BOHAN, Marc; French couturier; b. 22 Aug. 1926, Paris; s. of Alfred Bohan and Geneviève Baudoux; m. Huguette Rinjonneau (deceased); one d.; ed Lycée Lakanal, Sceaux; Asst with Piguet 1945, later with Molyneux and Patou; Dior org.; London 1958, later Paris; Artistic Dir Soc. Christian Dior 1960–89; Artistic Dir Hartnell, London 1990–92; designed costumes for numerous films 1961–89, for Athens Opera 1992–96; Chevalier, Légion d'honneur; Ordre de Saint-Charles (Monaco); Medaille de la Ville de Paris. *Leisure interests:* classical music, theatre, reading, antiques. *Address:* 35 rue du Bourg à Mont, 21400 Châtillon-sur-Seine, France (home).

BOHATYROVA, Raisa Vasylivna; Ukrainian gynaecologist and politician; *Chairman, National Security and Defence Council;* fmr Minister of Health; mem. Verkhovna Rada (Parl.) 2002–, mem. Party of Regions, fmr Leader Parl. faction; Chair. Nat. Security and Defence Council 2008–. *Address:* National Security and Defence Council (RNBU), 01601 Kyiv, vul. Komandarma Kameneva 8, Ukraine (office). *Telephone:* (44) 255-05-36 (office). *Fax:* (44) 255-05-36 (office). *E-mail:* public@rainbow.gov.ua (office). *Website:* www .rainbow.gov.ua (office).

BOHIGAS GUARDIOLA, Oriol, DArch; Spanish architect; b. 20 Dec. 1925, Barcelona; s. of Pere Bohigas and María Guardiola; m. Isabel Arnau 1957; five c.; ed Escuela Técnica Superior de Arquitectura, Barcelona; Founder-mem. of Grupo R; partnership with Josep Martorell 1951– and with David Mackay 1962–, forming MBM Arquitectes; Chair. of Composition, Escuela Técnica Superior de Arquitectura, Barcelona (ETSAB) 1971–, Head of ETSAB 1977–80; Head of Urban Planning Dept, Barcelona City Council 1980–84; Councillor of Culture 1991–94; mem. Colegio de Arquitectas de Venezuela 1976, Foundation Européenne des Sciences, des Arts et de la Culture 1983; Academician Accad. Nazionale di San Luca 1981; Foreign mem. Royal Swedish Acad. of Eng Sciences (IVA) 1991; Corresp. mem. Acad. d'Architecture de Paris 1991; Hon. Prof. Universidad Politécnica de Barcelona) 1995; Hon. mem. Sociedad Colombiana de Arquitectos 1982, Asscn of Architects of Bulgaria 1987, Die Bund Deutscher Architecten 1990; Hon. FAIA 1993, FRIBA 1996; Dr hc (Darmstadt) 1992, (Menéndez y Pelayo) 1995; Gold Medal for Artistic Merits, City of Barcelona 1986, Sikkens Award, Rotterdam 1989, Gold Medal for Architecture, Consejo Superior de Arquitectas de España, Madrid 1990, Volker Stevin Innovatieprijs Award, Rotterdam 1992, RIBA Royal Gold Medal to City of Barcelona (with others) 1999; firm awarded First Prize in many architectural competitions including Foment de les Arts Decoratives for best bldg in Barcelona 1959, 1962, 1966, 1976, 1979, 1984, 1991, Delta de Plata (industrial design) 1966, First Prize, Internationale Bauhausstellung Berlin 1981, 'Un Progetto per Siena', Italy 1990, 'Operations Sextius Mirabeau', Aix-en-Provence, France 1990, 'Cardiff Bay', Wales 1993, Eric Lyons Housing Award for bldg in Olympic Village, Barcelona 1994, 'Mission Perrache-Confluent', Lyon, France 1997, 'London's Arc of Opportunity', UK 1999, 'Programma di riqualificazione urbana dell'area De-Cecco', Pescara, Italy 2000, Prize of Barcelona City for the bldg of Pompeu Fabra Univ. 2001, Int. Competition for Arts and Crafts, Barcelona 2001, Canfranch railway station transformation, Huesca, Spain 2001, Urban Design, Dublin, Ireland 2001. *Major works include:* urban design for the Olympic Village and Port, Barcelona 1986–92, hotel in Puerto Vallarto, Mexico 1990, urban projects in Aix-en-Provence 1990, new city plan for Salerno, Italy 1991, Pavilion of the Future, Expo '92, Seville 1992, housing in Berlin 1993, urban design of waterfront, Rio de Janeiro, Brazil 1997, urban design in Newham, London, UK 1998, school in the Olympic Village, Barcelona 1999, apartments and student housing in Aix-en-Provence 1999, housing in Kleine Circus, Maastricht, the Netherlands 1999, refurbishment of Roger de Llúria Barracks, Barcelona 2001, Gymnasium Sartre, Berlin 2001. *Publications include:* Barcelona entre el plà Cerdà i el barraquisme 1963, Arquitectura modernista 1968, Contra una arquitectura adjetivada 1969, La arquitectura española de la Segunda República 1970, Polemica d'arquitectura catalana 1970, Reseña y catálogo de la arquitectura modernista 1972, Proceso y erótica del diseño 1972, Once arquitectos 1976, Reconstrucció de Barcelona 1985, Combat d'incerteses. Dietari de records 1989, Dit o fet. Dietari de records II 1992, Gràcies i desgràcies de Barcelona 1993, el Present des del Futur. Epistolari Públic 1994–1995 1996, Del dubte a la Revolució. Epistolari públic 1995–1997 1998, Modernidad en la arquitectura de la España Republicana 1998. *Address:* MBM Arquitectes, Plaça Reial 18, 08002 Barcelona, Spain (office). *Telephone:* (93) 3170061 (office); (93) 4124771 (home). *Fax:* (93) 3177266 (office). *E-mail:* mbm@mbmarquitectes.com (office). *Website:* www.mbmarquitectes.com (office).

BOHL, Heinrich Friedrich; German politician and lawyer; *General Representative, Deutscher Vermögensberatung AG;* b. 5 March 1945, Rosdorf, Göttingen; s. of Heinrich Bohl and Gerda Heyden; m. Elisabeth Bocking; two s. two d.; ed Univ. of Marburg; lawyer 1972–, notary 1976–; mem. CDU and Jungen Union (JU) 1963–; local Chair. JU Marburg-Biedenkopf 1964–70; Dist Chair. JU Mittelhessen 1969–73; mem. Prov. Parl. Hessen 1970–80, Chair. Legal Cttee 1974–78; Acting Chair. CDU Landtagsfraktion 1978–80; Chair. CDU Kreistagsfraktion Marburg-Biedenkopf 1974–90; mem. Fed. German Parl. 1980–, Parl. Man. CDU/CSU Bundestagsfraktion 1984–91; Fed. Minister for Special Tasks and Head of Fed. Chancellery 1991–98; Head of Press and Information, Fed. Govt 1998; now Gen. Rep. Deutscher Vermögensberatung AG; Bundesverdienstkreuz (1st Class) 1987. *Address:* Deutscher Vermögensberatung AG, Querstr. 1, 60322 Frankfurt am Main (office); Finkenstrasse 11, 35043 Marburg Cappel, Germany (home). *Telephone:* 41333 (home).

BOHR, Aage Niels, DPhil, DSc; Danish physicist; b. 19 June 1922, Copenhagen; s. of the late Prof. Niels Bohr and Margrethe Nørlund; m. 1st

Marietta Bettina (née Soffer) (died 1978); two s. one d.; m. 2nd Bente Scharff (née Meyer) 1981; ed Univ. of Copenhagen; Assoc. Dept of Scientific and Industrial Research, London 1943–45; Research Asst, Inst. of Theoretical Physics, Copenhagen 1946; Prof. of Physics, Univ. of Copenhagen 1956; Dir Niels Bohr Inst. 1963–70, Nordita 1975–81; mem. Danish, Norwegian, Pontifical, Swedish, Polish, Finnish, Yugoslav Acads of Science, Nat. Acad. of Sciences, USA, American Acad. of Arts and Sciences, American Philosophical Soc., Royal Physiograph Soc., Lund, Sweden, Acad. of Tech. Sciences, Copenhagen, Deutsche Akad. der Naturforscher Leopoldina, Kungl. Vetenskaps-Societeten, Uppsala, Sweden; Hon. PhD (Oslo, Heidelberg, Trondheim, Manchester, Uppsala); Dannie Heineman Prize 1960, Pius XI Medal 1963, Atoms for Peace Award 1969, Ørsted Medal 1970, Rutherford Medal 1972, John Price Wetherill Medal 1974, Nobel Prize for Physics 1975, Ole Rømer Medal 1976. *Publications:* Rotational States of Atomic Nuclei 1954, Nuclear Structure Vol. I 1969, Vol. II 1975 (with Ben R. Mottelson), Genuine Fortuitousness—Where Did That Click Come From? (with Ole Ulfbeck) 2001, The Principle Underlying Quantum Mechanics (with Ben R. Mottelson and Ole Ulfbeck) 2004. *Address:* c/o Niels Bohr Institute, Blegdamsvej 15–17, 2100 Copenhagen, Denmark.

BOHRER, Karl Heinz, PhD, Dr. habil.; German academic; *Professor Emeritus of Modern Literature, University of Bielefeld;* b. 26 Sept. 1932, Cologne; m. Undine Gruenter 1991; one s. one d.; ed Univ. of Göttingen, Univ. of Heidelberg; Prof. of History of Modern Literature, Univ. of Bielefeld 1982–1997, Prof. Emer. 1997–; Visiting Prof. of Comparative Literature, Stanford Univ. 2003–; Ed. Merkur; J.H. Merck Prize 1978, Lessing Prize 2000, Gadamer Prize 2001, Prize of the Bavarian Acad. of Arts 2005, Prize of the Berlin Acad. of Arts 2007. *Publications:* Die gefährdete Phantasie oder Surrealismus und Terror 1970, Der Lauf des Freitag – Die lädierte Utopie und der Dichter 1973, Die Ästhetik des Schreckens 1978, Plötzlichkeit. Der Augenblick des ästhetischen Scheins 1981, Mythos und Moderne 1983, Der romantische Brief, Die Entstehung aesthetischer Subjektivität 1987, Nach der Natur, Über Politik und Ästhetik 1988, Die Kritik der Romantik 1989, Das absolute Präsens. Die Semantik ästhetischer Zeit 1994, Der Abschied. Theorie der Trauer 1996, Die Grenzen des Aesthetischen 1998, Ästhetische Negativität 2002, Ekstasen der Zeit: Augenblick, Gegenwart, Erinnerung 2003, Imaginationen des Bösen 2004, Groβer Stil 2007, Das Tragische: Erscheinung, Pathos, Klage 2009. *Address:* 110 Lansdowne Way, London, SW8 2EP, England (home); Universität Bielefeld, Fakultät für Linguistik und Literaturwissenschaft, 33501 Bielefeld (office); Franziskastr. 9, Cologne, Germany. *Telephone:* (20) 7162-2386 (home). *Fax:* (20) 7501-0067 (home).

BOIDEVAIX, Serge Marie-Germain, LèsL, LenD; French diplomatist; b. 15 Aug. 1928, Aurillac, Cantal; s. of Jean Boidevaix and Hélène Orcibal; m. Francine Savard 1966; two d.; ed Lycée d'Aurillac, Lycée Louis-le-Grand, Faculté de Droit and Faculté des Lettres, Paris and Ecole Nat. d'Admin; joined Ministry of Foreign Affairs 1954; served Vienna, Washington, DC and Bonn; Adviser, Pvt. Office of Minister of Defence 1969–73; Dir Office of Minister of Foreign Affairs 1973–74; Adviser on int. affairs and cooperation, Office of Prime Minister 1974–76; Amb. to Poland 1977–80, to India 1982–85, to Germany 1986–92; Deputy Sec.-Gen. Ministry of Foreign Affairs 1985–86; Sec. Gen. 1992–93; Sr mem. Council of State 1993–97; Chair. SB Consultants 1997–; Pres. Franco-Arab Chamber of Commerce 2002–06; Commdr, Légion d'honneur, Ordre Nat. du Mérite. *Address:* 5, Rue des Eaux, 75116 Paris, France (home).

BOISARD, Marcel, PhD; Swiss diplomatist and UN official; b. 14 July 1939, Geneva; ed Univ. of Geneva, Inst. of World Affairs, USA and Grad. Inst. of Int. Affairs, Geneva; postgrad. studies in Hamburg, Germany and Cairo, Egypt; fmr. head of research project on Egyptian rural economy; fmr dir research and teaching programme on inter-cultural relations (CSCE–Helsinki Act, Third Basket); fmr Program Officer, Tech. Co-operation Directorate, Dept. of Foreign Affairs; fmr Econ. Adviser to Govt of Burundi; Pres. Experts of African Countries associated with ECE, Brussels 1996; fmr Chief of Del. of Int. Cttee of the Red Cross (ICRC) in Middle East; Dir UNITAR European Office 1983, Exec. Dir UNITAR 1992–2007; mem. numerous int. learned socs; Special Fellow, UN Inst. for Training and Research (UNITAR) 1980. *Publications include:* over 40 books and articles on int. cross-cultural relations, the Arab and Muslim world and multilateral negotiation and intergovt. orgs. *Address:* c/o UNITAR, Palais des Nations, 1211 Geneva 10, Switzerland (office).

BOISCLAIR, André, MA; Canadian politician; b. 14 April 1966, Montréal; s. of Marc-André Boisclair; ed Jean-de-Brébeuf Coll., Montréal, Univ. of Montréal, Harvard Univ., USA; elected to Quebec Nat. Ass. representing Gouin riding 1989 (youngest mem. ever elected), Minister of Immigration and Citizens 1996–98; Minister of Social Solidarity 1998–2001, Govt House Leader 2001–04 (resgnd to attend John F. Kennedy School of Govt, Harvard Univ.); Leader, Parti Québécois 2005–07 (resgnd). *Address:* c/o Parti Québécois, 1200 Avenue Papineau, bureau 150, Montréal, PQ, Canada (office). *Telephone:* (514) 526-0020 (office). *Fax:* (514) 526-0272 (office). *Website:* www.pq.org (office).

BOISSET, Yves; French author and film director; b. 14 March 1939, Paris; s. of Raymond Boisset and Germaine Bonnet; m. Micheline Paintault 1964; two s.; ed Lycée Louis-le-Grand, Faculté des Lettres, Paris and Inst. des Hautes Etudes Cinématographiques; journalist on Cinéma, Paris-Jour etc. 1958–63; Asst Dir to Yves Ciampi 1959, to Jean-Pierre Melville 1962, Claude Sautet and Antoine Bourseiller 1964, Vittorio de Sica and René Clément 1965, Ricardo Freda 1966; television and film dir 1967–; Chevalier des Arts et des Lettres. *Films include:* Coplan sauve sa peau 1968, Cran d'arrêt 1969, Un condé 1970, Le Saut de l'ange 1971, L'Attentat (Grand Prix, Moscow Film Festival 1972) 1972, R.A.S. 1973, Dupont Lajoie (Silver Bear, Berlin Film Festival 1974) 1974, Folle à tuer 1975, Le Juge Fayard dit le Sheriff 1976 (Prix Louis Delluc 1977), Un taxi mauve 1977, La Clé sur la porte 1978, La Femme flic (Award for Best Dir, Karlov Vivary Festival 1979) 1979, Allons z'enfants 1981, Espion lève-toi 1982, Le Prix du danger 1983, Canicule 1984, Bleu comme l'Enfer 1986, La Travestie 1988, Radio Corbeau 1989, La Tribu 1991. *Television includes:* La Fée carabine 1987, Le Suspect 1989, Double Identity (1990), Les Carnassiers 1991, Morlock 1993, L'Affaire Seznec (Best Film, Best Screenplay, Best Dir Dir, 7 D'Or Awards 1993) 1993, L'Affaire Dreyfus (Silver Prize, Monte Carlo TV Festival 1995) 1995, Morlock: Le tunnel 1996, Les Amants de rivière rouge (miniseries) 1996, La Fine équipe 1997, Une leçon particulière 1997, Le Pantalon (Best Film, Best Dir 1997) 1997, Sam 1999, Dormir avec le diable 2001, Cazas 2001, Jean Moulin 2002, Le Blues des Medias 2003, Ils Veulent Cloner le Christ 2004, Lew Mysteres Sanglants de l'Ots 2005, La Bataiile D'Alger 2006, Salengro: Execution d'un Ministre 2007, Douze balles dans la peau pour Pierre Laval 2009. *Publication:* 20 ans de cinéma américain 1962. *Leisure interests:* athletics, basketball, tennis. *Address:* 61 boulevard Inkerman, 92200 Neuilly-sur-Seine (office); 88 Boulevard Victor Hugo, 92200 Neuilly-sur-Seine, France (home). *Telephone:* (1) 47-47-52-05 (home). *E-mail:* yves,baisset@yahoo.fr (home).

BOISSIER, Patrick Marie René; French business executive; *Vice-President, Supervisory Board, Vallourec;* b. 18 Feb. 1950, Versailles; s. of Pierre Boissier and Françoise Boissier (née Hennebicque); m. Isabelle Joly 1972; two s. one d.; ed Ecole Polytechnique, Harvard Business School, USA; engineer, Cegedur Rhenalu 1973–75, Forges de Crans 1976–79, Asst Factory Man. Cegedur 1980–83, Man. Pipes Div. 1984–87, Gen. Man. 1987–90; Deputy Chair. and CEO Tréfimétaux 1990–93; Dept Head Péchiney 1994; Gen. Man. Heating and Air-Conditioning Div., Elfi 1994–97; Chair. and CEO Technibel 1994–97; Gen. Man., then Chair. and CEO Chantiers d'Atlantique 1997–2006; CEO GEC Alsthom Leroux Naval (later Alstom Leroux Naval) 1997–2006; Chair. Alstom Marine 1998–2006; mem. Supervisory Bd Vallourec 2000-, Vice-Pres. 2005–; Chair. European Shipbuilders Asscn Cttee 2004–; mem. Acad. des Technologies; Chevalier, Ordre nat. du Mérite, Légion d'honneur. *Leisure interest:* sailing. *Address:* Supervisory Board, Vallourec, 27 Avenue du Général Leclerc, 92100 Boulogne-Billancourt, France (office). *Telephone:* 1-49-09-38-00 (office). *Fax:* 1-49-09-36-94 (office). *E-mail:* boissier@academie-technologies.fr (office). *Website:* www.vallourec.fr (office).

BOISSON, Jacques-Louis, PhD, LLD; Monegasque diplomatist; b. 8 Jan. 1940, Monaco; m. Carmen Gómez Parejo; one s.; ed Institut d'Etudes Politiques, Institut de Droit Int., Paris, Faculté de Droit et de Sciences Economiques, Aix-en-Provence; int. civil servant (responsible for training, research and protection of human rights) UNESCO 1968–83; Amb. to France 1984–93; Perm. Rep. to UN, New York 1993–2003; Commdr Ordre de Grimaldi; Officier Ordre de St Charles. *Publications:* Le Particularisme Institutionnel de la Principalité de Monaco 1966, Le Droit de la Nationalité Monégasque 1968, La Protection Internationale des Minorités, Vers un Enseignement Universel des Droits de l'Homme, L'Autorité internationale des Fouds Marin 2001; numerous articles on the protection and promotion of int. human rights 1971–99. *Leisure interests:* baroque music, opera, philosophy, poetry. *Address:* c/o Ministry of State, place de la Visitation, 98000 (office); 48 blvd du Jardin Exotique, 98000 Monaco. *Telephone:* 93-25-59-64.

BØJER, Jørgen R.H.; Danish diplomatist; *Chairman, Danish Centre for International Studies and Human Rights;* b. 5 March 1940, Hjørring; s. of Svend Rud Hansen Bøjer and Ingeborg Bøjer (née Frederiksen); m. Lone Heilskov 1964; two d.; ed Univ. of Århus, Institut d'Etudes Politiques, Paris; Foreign Service Officer 1967; Sec. of Embassy, Prague 1971; Head of Section, Ministry of Foreign Affairs, Copenhagen 1973, Dir 1982, Deputy Under-Sec. 1992; Visiting Fellow, Stanford Univ. 1978; Counsellor, Embassy, Washington, DC 1979; Amb. to Egypt (also accred to Sudan and Somalia), then to Austria, Slovenia, Bosnia and Herzegovina; Perm. Rep. to Int. Orgs in Vienna 1993; Perm. Rep. to UN, New York 1997–2001, Co-Chair. UN Int. Conf. on Financing for Devt 2001; Amb. to Czech Repub. 2001–07; Chair. Danish Centre for International Studies and Human Rights 2006–. *Address:* Danish Centre for International Studies and Human Rights, Strandgade 56, 1401 Copenhagen K, Denmark. *Telephone:* 32-69-86-86 (office). *Fax:* 32-69-86-00 (office). *E-mail:* dcism@dcism.dk (office). *Website:* www.dcism.dk (office).

BOJINOV, Bojidar; Bulgarian lawyer and legal adviser; *President, Bulgarian Chamber of Commerce and Industry;* b. 30 Jan. 1939, Pleven City; s. of Boris Bojinov and Nina Bojinova; m. Fani Vladimorova; one s. two d.; ed Charles Univ., Prague; lawyer, Pleven 1967–72; Legal Adviser to Bulgarian Chamber of Commerce and Industry (BCCI), Sofia 1972–77, Dir Patent and Trade Marks Div. 1977–85, Vice-Pres. BCCI 1985–93, Pres. 1993–; Arbitrator at BCCI Court of Arbitration 1975–2004; mem. Advisory Council to Pres. of Repub. on Foreign Investments, Nat. Council for Tripartite Cooperation, Council of Econ. Growth 2002–; fmr Pres. Asscn of Black Sea Zone Chambers of Commerce and Industry, Asscn of Balkan Chambers, Bulgarian Nat. Group of AIPP. *Leisure interests:* music, art, skiing, tennis. *Address:* Office of the President, Bulgarian Chamber of Commerce and Industry, 42 Parchevich Street, 1058 Sofia (office); Patents and Trademarks Bureau, Bojinov & Bojinov Ltd, 38 Alabin Street, PO Box 728, 1000 Sofia (office). *Telephone:* (2) 9872528 (office); (2) 9862974 (office). *Fax:* (2) 9873209 (office); (2) 9863508 (office). *E-mail:* ptmbojinov@bcci.bg (office). *Website:* www.bcci.bg (office).

BOK, Derek, MA, JD; American legal scholar, university administrator and academic; *300th Anniversary University President Emeritus, Professor Emeritus and Faculty Chair, Hauser Center for Non-Profit Organizations, Harvard University;* b. 22 March 1930, Bryn Mawr, Pa; s. of late Curtis Bok and Margaret Plummer (now Mrs. W. S. Kiskadden); m. Sissela Ann Myrdal (d Karl Gunnar and Alva Myrdal) 1955; one s. two d.; ed Univs of S Harvard, George Washington and Inst. of Political Science, I served US Army 1956–58; Asst Prof. of Law, Harvard Univ. 1958–61, Prof. 1961–, Dean 1968–71, 300th Anniversary Univ. Prof. 1991–, now Emer.; Pres. Harvard Univ. 1971–91, now Pres. Emer., Interim Pres. 2006–; Dir, Nat. Chair. Common Cause 1999–; Chair. Spencer Foundation 2002–; Faculty Chair. Hauser Center for Non-Profit Orgs 2002–. *Publications include:* The First Three Years of the Schuman Plan, Cases and Materials on Labor Law (with Archibald Cox), Labor and the American Community (with John Dunlop), The Federal Government and the University, Beyond the Ivory Tower: Social Responsibilities of the Modern University 1982, Higher Learning 1986, Universities and the Future of America 1990, The Cost of Talent 1993, The State of the Nation 1997, The Shape of the River (jtly) 1998, The Trouble with Government 2001, Universities in the Marketplace: the commercialization of higher education 2004. *Leisure interests:* gardening, tennis, swimming. *Address:* Hauser Center for Nonprofit Organizations, 5 Bennett Street, Cambridge, MA 02138 (office); John F. Kennedy School of Government, Harvard University, 79 John F. Kennedy Street, Cambridge, MA 02138, USA (office). *Telephone:* (617) 495-1199 (office). *Fax:* (617) 496-6886 (office). *E-mail:* derek_bok@harvard.edu (office). *Website:* www.ksg.harvard.edu/hauser (office).

BOKROS, Lajos, PhD; Hungarian economist, banker and academic; *Professor of Economics and Public Policy, Central European University;* b. 26 June 1954, Budapest; s. of Lajos Bokros and Irén Szarka; m. Maria Gyetuai; one s. one d.; ed Univ. of Econs, Budapest, Univ. of Panama; Research Fellow, Financial Research Inst., Hungarian Ministry of Finance, Budapest 1980–86, Chief of Public Finance Div. 1986–87; Deputy Gen. Man. Econ. Dept, Nat. Bank of Hungary 1987–89, Man. Dir 1989, Dir Capital Market Dept 1989–91; Chair. Budapest Stock Exchange 1990–95; Chair. and CEO Budapest Bank 1991–95; Chair. Budapest Stock Exchange early 1990s; Minister of Finance 1995–96; Sr Advisor, Financial Sector Devt, IBRD 1996–97, Dir Pvt. and Financial Sector Devt, ECA 1997–99, Dir Financial Advisory Services, Europe and Cen. Asia 1999–2004; Prof. of Econs and Public Policy, Cen. European Univ. 2004–, also Sr Vice-Pres. for Research and Int. Projects and COO; Chief Econ. Adviser to Prime Minister of Croatia 2002–, to Deputy Prime Minister of Poland 2001–; mem. Bd of Dirs State Property Agency 1990–91. *Publications:* Development Commodity Production, Market Economy 1984, Market and Money in the Modern Economy 1985, Public Finance Reform during Transition – The Experience of Hungary (co-author) 1998, Visegrad Twins' Diverging Path to Relative Prosperity – Finance a Uver 2000, Financial Transition in Europe and Central Asia – The World Bank (co-author) 2001, Competition and Solidarity – Comparative Economic Studies 2004. *Address:* Department of Public Policy, Central European University, 1051 Budapest, Nador utca 9-11, Hungary. *Telephone:* (1) 328-3434 (office). *E-mail:* bokrosl@ceu.hu (office). *Website:* www.ceu.hu/dpp/people/bokros.htm (office).

BOKSENBERG, Alexander, CBE, PhD, FRS, FInstP, FRAS; British astronomer and academic; *Honorary Professor of Experimental Astronomy, University of Cambridge;* b. 18 March 1936; s. of Julius Boksenberg and Ernestina Steinberg; m. Adella Coren 1960; one s. one d.; ed Stationers' Co.'s School, Univ. of London, Univ. of Cambridge; SRC Research Asst, Dept of Physics and Astronomy, Univ. Coll. London 1960–65, Lecturer in Physics 1965–75, Head of Optical and Ultraviolet Astronomy Research Group 1969–81, Reader in Physics 1975–78, SRC Sr Fellow 1976–81, Prof. of Physics and Astronomy 1978–81; Sherman Fairchild Distinguished Scholar Calif. Inst. of Tech. 1981–82; Dir Royal Greenwich Observatory 1981–93, Royal Observatories (Royal Greenwich Observatory, Royal Observatory, Edin., Isaac Newton Group of Optical Telescopes, Canary Islands, Jt Astronomy Centre, Hawaii) 1993–96; Hon. Prof. of Experimental Astronomy, Univ. of Cambridge 1991–; Research Prof. Inst. of Astronomy Univ. of Cambridge and PPARC Sr Research Fellow Univs of Cambridge and London 1996–99; Extraordinary Fellow Churchill Coll., Cambridge 1996–, mem. Council 1998–2003; Visiting Prof., Dept of Physics and Astronomy, Univ. Coll. London 1981–, Astronomy Centre, Univ. of Sussex 1981–89; Exec. Ed. Experimental Astronomy 1995–; Hon. Pres. Astronomical Soc. of Glasgow 1995–; Chair. New Industrial Concepts Ltd 1969–81; Pres. West London Astronomical Soc. 1978–; Chair. SRC Astronomy Cttee 1980–81 and numerous other cttees on astronomy 1980–; mem. ESA Hubble Space Telescope Instrument Definition Team 1973–95, S African Astronomical Observatory Advisory Cttee 1978–85, British Council Science Advisory Cttee 1987–91, Anglo-Australian Telescope Bd 1989–91 (Deputy Chair. 1991–92), Fachbeirat of Max Planck Institut für Astronomie 1991–95, European Southern Observatory Vis. Cttee 1993–95, Council and Trustee Royal Soc. 1995–97 (Technical Steering Group 1997–98, Chair. Int. Exchangaes Far East Panel 2000–), Int. Astronomical Union Finance Cttee 1997–2000, UK-Japan N+N Bd on Cooperation in Astronomy 1997–, PPARC VISTA Review Bd 1999–2000, Foundation Cttee UK Nat. Comm. for UNESCO (Chair. Science Cttee 2000–03, mem. Council 2000–03, Chair. Steering Cttee UK Nat. Comm. for UNESCO Campaign Group 2003–04; past mem. of over 40 other councils, bds, cttees etc. 1970–; Fellow Royal Soc. 1978–, Univ. Coll. London 1991–; Asteroid (3205) named Boksenberg 1988; 37th Herstmonceux Conf. The Hubble Space Telescope and the High Redshift Universe in honour of Alec Boksenberg 1996; lecture tours: Royal Soc./Russian Acad. of Sciences 1989, Royal Soc./Chinese Acad. of Sciences 1995, British Council India 1999 and Royal Soc./Japan Acad. 1999; Freeman Clockmakers Co. 1984; Liveryman 1989; Dr hc (l'Observatoire de Paris) 1982; Hon. DSc (Sussex) 1991; Hannah Jackson Medal and Gift 1998, Royal Soc. Hughes Medal 1999, Glazebrook Medal and Prize 2000. *Publications:* Modern Technology and its Influence on Astronomy 1990 (ed.); 220 contribs to learned journals. *Leisure interest:* skiing. *Address:* University of Cambridge, Institute of Astronomy, The Observatories, Madingley Road, Cambridge, CB3 0HA, England. *Telephone:* (1223) 339909. *Fax:* (1223) 339910. *E-mail:* boksy@ast.cam.ac.uk (office). *Website:* www.ast.cam.ac.uk/IoA (office).

BOLAÑOS GEYER, Enrique; Nicaraguan fmr head of state and business executive; b. 13 May 1928, Masaya, nr Managua; s. of Nicolás Bolaños Cortés and Amanda Geyer; m. Lila T. Abaunza; four s. (one deceased) one d.; ed Colegio Centro-América, Granada, St Louis Univ., USA, Instituto Centroamericano de Administración de Empresas, Managua; farmer 1952–59; Gen. Man. Fábrica de Calzados Lorena SA, Masaya 1956–59; Spanish teacher Berlitz School of Languages, St Louis, Mo., USA 1960–62; Gen. Man. Cía. Leonesa de Productos Lácteos SA, León 1962–64; Chair. Bd Impresora Serigráfica SA, Managua 1967–73; Founder and Chair. numerous cos in Grupo Bolaños-SAIMSA; Head COSEP pvt. business Asscn 1979–90; Vice-Pres. of Nicaragua 1997–2000; Pres. of Nicaragua 2002–06; mem. Partido Liberal Constitucionalista (PLC). *Address:* Partido Liberal Constitucionalista (PLC), Semáforos Country Club 100 m al este, Apartado 4569, Managua, Nicaragua (office). *Telephone:* (2) 78-8705. *Fax:* (2) 78-1800. *Website:* www.plc.org.ni.

BOLD, Luvsanvandangiin; Mongolian politician; *Minister of Defence;* b. 1961, Ulaanbaatar; Vice-Chair. and Sec.-Gen. Mongolian Students' Asscn 1989–91; Chair. Center of Youth and Students of Mongol Origin 1992–93; mem. Parl. 1996–2000; Minister of Defence 2008–; mem. Mongolian Social-Democratic Party. *Address:* Ministry of Defence, Government Building 7, Dandaryn Gudamj 51, Bayanzürkh District, Ulan Bator, Mongolia (office). *Telephone:* (11) 458495 (office). *Fax:* (11) 451727 (office). *E-mail:* mdef@mdef.pmis.gov.mn (office). *Website:* www.mdef.pmis.gov.mn (office).

BOLDON, Ato; Trinidadian athlete; b. 30 Dec. 1973, Port of Spain; ed Univ. of Calif. at LA; resident in USA since 1988; coached by John Smith; Cen. American and Caribbean record-holder at 60m indoors (6.49 seconds), 100m (9.86 seconds) and 200m (19.77 seconds); gold medal World Jr Championships 100m and 200m 1992; fourth Commonwealth Games 100m 1994; bronze medal World Championships 100m 1995; gold medal NCAA Championships 100m 1996; bronze medals Olympic Games 100m and 200m 1996; 100m World Champion 1997, 1999; gold medal World Championships 200m 1997; gold medal Goodwill Games, New York 200m 1998; gold medal Commonwealth Games 100m 1998; silver medal Olympic Games 100m 2000, bronze medal 200m; youngest sprinter ever to run under 10 seconds in the 100m and under 20 seconds in the 200m;*Website:* www.atoboldon.com (office).

BOLDYREV, Yuri Yuryevich; Russian politician; b. 29 May 1960, Leningrad; m. 1990; one s.; ed Leningrad Electrotech. Inst., Leningrad Inst. of Finance and Econs; worked as engineer Cen. Research Inst. of Vessel Electronics and Tech. 1983–89; mem. CPSU 1987–90; USSR People's Deputy 1989–91; del. of 28 CPSU Congress; left CPSU 1990; mem. Council of Reps, then of Co-ordination Council of Democratic Russia Movt 1990–91; mem. Higher Advisory Council to Chair. of Russian Supreme Soviet (later to Pres. of Russian Fed.) 1990–92; consultant Russian Govt Feb.–March 1992; Chief State Inspector of Russian Fed., Chief Control Man. of Admin. of Presidency 1992–93; mem. Centre of Econ. and Political Research (Epicentre) 1993–94; mem. Duma (Parl.) 1993–95; Founder-mem. and Deputy Chair. Yabloko Movt 1993–95, left Party Sept. 1995; Deputy Chair. Accountant Chamber of Russian Fed. 1995–2001; Head of St Petersburg electoral candidates, Spravedlivaya Rossiya party (Fair Russia) 2007. *Address:* c/o B. Dmitrovka St 32/1, Moscow 107031, Russia (office). *Telephone:* (495) 650-38-80 (office). *E-mail:* info@spravedlivo.ru (office). *Website:* www.spravedlivo.ru (office).

BOLGER, Dermot; Irish writer, dramatist and poet; b. 6 Feb. 1959, Finglas, Dublin; s. of Roger Bolger and the late Bridie Flanagan; m. Bernadette Clifton 1988; two s.; ed St Canice's BNS, Finglas and Benevin Coll. Finglas; worked as factory hand, library asst and professional author; founder and Ed. Raven Arts Press 1979–92; founder and Exec. Ed. New Island Books, Dublin 1992–; mem. Arts Council of Ireland 1989–93; elected mem. Aosdána 1991–; Playwright in Association, The Abbey (Nat.) Theatre 1997; Writer Fellow, Trinity Coll., Dublin 2003; Writer in Residence, Farmleigh House, Dublin 2008; A. E. Memorial Prize 1986, Macauley Fellowship 1987, A. Z. Whitehead Prize 1987, Samuel Beckett Award 1991, Edinburgh Fringe First Awards 1991, 1995, Stewart Parker BBC Award 1991, The Hennessy Irish Literature Hall of Fame Award 2003, Irish Times/EBS Prize for Best New Irish Play of 2004, Worldplay Int. Radio Prize for Best Script 2005. *Plays:* The Lament for Arthur Cleary 1989, Blinded by the Light 1990, In High Germany 1990, The Holy Ground 1990, One Last White Horse 1991, A Dublin Bloom 1994, April Bright 1995, The Passion of Jerome 1999, Consenting Adults 2000, From These Green Heights 2004, The Townlands of Brazil 2006, Walking the Road 2007, The Consequences of Lightning 2008. *Radio:* The Woman's Daughter 2005, Hunger Again 2006, The Fortunestown Kid 2006, The Night Manager 2007, The Kerlogue 2007, Moving In 2008. *Television screenplay:* Edward No Hands 1996. *Publications:* novels: Night Shift 1985, The Woman's Daughter 1987, The Journey Home 1990, Emily's Shoes 1992, A Second Life 1994, Father's Music 1997, Finbar's Hotel (co-author) 1997, Ladies Night at Finbar's Hotel (co-author) 1999, Temptation 2000, The Valparaiso Voyage 2001, The Family on Paradise Pier 2005, The Journey Home 2008; poetry: The Habit of Flesh 1979, Finglas Lilies 1980, No Waiting America 1981, Internal Exile 1986, Leinster Street Ghosts 1989, Taking My Letters Back, New and Selected Poems 1998, The Chosen Moment 2004; editor: The Dolmen Book of Irish Christmas Stories 1986, The Bright Wave: Poetry in Irish Now 1986, 16 on 16: Irish Writers on the Easter Rising 1988, Invisible Cities: The New Dubliners: A Journey through Unofficial Dublin 1988, Invisible Dublin: A Journey through its Writers 1992, The Picador Book of Contemporary Irish Fiction 1993, 12 Bar Blues (with Aidan Murphy) 1993, The New Picador Book of Contemporary Irish Fiction 2000, Druids, Dudes and Beauty Queens: The Changing Face of Irish Theatre 2001, The Ledwidge Treasury 2007, Night &

Day: 24 Hours in the life of Dublin 2008, External Affairs 2008. *Leisure interests:* soccer, golf. *Address:* c/o AP Watt Ltd, 20 John Street, London, WC1N 2DR, England (office). *Telephone:* (20) 7405-6774 (office). *Fax:* (20) 7831-2154 (office). *E-mail:* apw@apwatt.co.uk (office). *Website:* www.apwatt.co.uk (office).

BOLGER, James Brendan, PC, ONZ; New Zealand politician, diplomatist and business executive; *Chairman, New Zealand Post Ltd.;* b. 31 May 1935, Taranaki; s. of Daniel Bolger and Cecilia Bolger (née Doyle); m. Joan Maureen Riddell 1963; six s. three d.; ed Opunake High School; farmer of sheep and beef cattle, Te Kuiti 1965–72; mem. Parl. 1972–98; Parl. Under-Sec. to Minister of Agric. and Fisheries, Minister of Maori Affairs, Minister in Charge of Rural Banking and Finance Corpn 1975–77; Minister of Fisheries and Assoc. Minister of Agric. 1977–78; Minister of Labour 1978–84, of Immigration 1978–81; Prime Minister of New Zealand and Minister in Charge of Security Intelligence Service 1990–97; Leader Nat. Party 1986–98; Leader Opposition 1986–90; Amb. to USA 1998–2002; Chair. Kiwibank 2001–, New Zealand Post Ltd 2002–, Ian Axford Foundation 2002–; mem. Advisory Bd World Agricultural Forum 2002–, Gas Industry 2004–, Express Couriers Ltd 2004–; Pres. ILO 1983; Hon. DSc (Khon Kaen Univ., Thailand) 1994; Hon. DLitt (Massey Univ.) 2002; Queen's Silver Jubilee Medal 1977, NZ Commemoration Medal 1990, NZ Suffrage Centennial Medal 1993. *Publication:* A View from the Top (political autobiog.). *Leisure interests:* hiking, reading, politics. *Address:* New Zealand Post Ltd, Private Bag 39990, Wellington (office); Sommeville Road, PO Box 406, Te Kuiti, New Zealand (home). *Telephone:* (4) 496-4391 (office); (7) 8786-213 (home). *Fax:* (4) 496-4418 (office); (7) 8786-215 (home). *E-mail:* jimbolger@nzpost.co.nz (office). *Website:* www.nzpost.co.nz (office).

BOLING, Edward J., MS, EdD; American academic; *President Emeritus, University of Tennessee;* b. 19 Feb. 1922, Sevier Co., Tenn.; s. of Sam R. Boling and Nerissa Boling (née Clark); m. Carolyn Pierce 1950; three s.; ed Univ. of Tennessee and George Peabody Coll.; with Union Carbide Corpn of Oak Ridge, Tenn. 1951–54; State Budget Dir 1954–58; Commr of Finance and Admin. 1958–61; Vice-Pres. for Devt and Admin., Univ. of Tenn. 1961–70, Pres. Univ. of Tenn. 1970–88, Pres. Emer. 1988–; Univ. Prof. 1988–92; mem. Educ. Comm. of States 1970–92, mem. Southern Regional Educ. Bd 1957–61, 1970–81, 1983–90, 1992–96; Chair. Tenn. Resource Valley 1991–92, fmr Corpn Bd mem. Magnavox, The Signal Co., Philips Electronics, Allied Signal, Home Fed. Bank and numerous others. *Publications:* Forecasting University Enrolment (with D. A. Gardiner) 1952, Methods of Objectifying the Allocation of Tax Funds to Tennessee State Colleges 1961. *Leisure interests:* boating, tennis, skiing, travel. *Address:* Suite 731, Andy Holt Tower, University of Tennessee, Knoxville, TN 37996 (office); 4911 Westover Terrace, Knoxville, TN 37914, USA (home). *Telephone:* (865) 974-3500 (office); (865) 523-6882 (home). *E-mail:* ejb@utk.edu (home).

BOLKESTEIN, Frederik (Frits), MPh, LLM; Dutch politician; b. 1933; m.; three c.; ed Oregon State Univ., Gemeentelijke Univ. Amsterdam, Univ. of London, Univ. of Leiden; with Shell Group 1960–76; Dir Shell Chimie, Paris 1973–76; Mem. of Parl. for VVD (Liberals) 1978–82, 1986–88, 1989–99; Minister for Foreign Trade 1982–86; Chair. Atlantic Comm., Netherlands 1986–88; Minister of Defence 1988–89; Chair. VVD Parl. Group 1990–98; Pres. Liberal Internationale 1996–99; EU Commr for Internal Market, Financial Services, Customs and Taxation 1999–2004; mem. Royal Inst. of Int. Affairs. *Play:* Floris Count of Holland. *Leisure interest:* tennis. *Address:* c/o Commission of the European Communities, 200 rue de la Loi, 1049 Brussels, Belgium (office).

BOLKHOVITINOV, Nikolai Nikolaevich, DHist; Russian historian; *Director, Centre for North American Studies, Institute of World History, Russian Academy of Sciences;* b. 26 Oct. 1930, Moscow; s. of Nikolai Feodosievich Bolkhovitinov and Lidiia Bolkhovitinova (née Komarova); m. Ludmila Bolkhovitinova (née Povel'nenko)1965; ed Moscow Inst. of Int. Relations; on staff, Dept of History of Diplomacy USSR Ministry of Foreign Affairs 1957–58; Jr, Sr Researcher, Inst. of History 1958–68, Sr Leading Researcher, Head Dept of History of USA and Canada, Dir Centre for North American Studies, Inst. of World History USSR (now Russian) Acad. of Sciences 1968–; Corresp. mem. USSR (now Russian) Acad. of Sciences 1987, full mem. 1992; research in history of USA and history of int. relations in 18th–19th centuries, Russian-American relations and foreign policy of Russia, geographic discoveries on N Pacific and in N America; mem. Russian Geographical Soc., New York Acad. of Sciences, Vargas Historical Centre, Venezuela; Hon. Foreign mem. American Historical Asscn 2005; Koontz Memorial Award, American Historical Asscn, State Prize of Russian Fed. 1997, N. I. Kareev Prize, Russian Acad. of Sciences 2003. *Publications include:* Monroe's Doctrine 1959, USA: Problems of History and Contemporary Historiography 1980, History of Russian America 1732–1867 (3 Vols) 1997–99; series of monographs on history of Russian–American relations 1966–96, and numerous articles, including Beginnings of Russian–American Relations 1775–1815 1966, Russia and the American Revolution 1976, Russia and the United States 1986, Russian–American Relations and the Sale of Alaska 1834–1867 1990, A Russian-American Company and the Study of the Pacific North 1815–1841 (co-ed.) 2005, Russian Scholar-Emigrants (G. V. Vernadskii, M. M. Karpovich, M. T. Florinskii) and the State of Russian Studies in the USA 2006. *Leisure interest:* tennis. *Address:* Institute of World History, Russian Academy of Sciences, Leninskii pr. 32A, 117334 Moscow (office); Timiriazevskaya str. 33/11, 125422 Moscow, Russia (home). *Telephone:* (095) 938-55-86 (office); (495) 977-85-07 (home). *Fax:* (495) 938-22-86 (office). *E-mail:* amercenter@pochtamt.ru (office); bolkhovitinovn@mail.ru (home). *Website:* www.igh.ru/struct/srt_cnt_23.html (office).

BOLKIAH, HRH Prince Haji Jefri; Brunei politician; brother of Sultan Haji Hassanal Bolkiah Mu'izuddin Waddaulah of Brunei; fmrly Minister of Culture, Youth and Sports, Deputy Minister of Finance; Minister of Finance 1988–97; fmr Chair. Royal Brunei Airlines, Brunei Investment Agency; fmr Propr Asprey & Garrad.

BOLKIAH, HRH Prince Mohamed; Brunei politician; *Minister of Foreign Affairs;* b. 27 Aug. 1947, brother of Sultan Haji Hassanal Bolkiah Mu'izuddin Waddaulah of Brunei; ed Royal Mil. Acad., Sandhurst, UK; Minister of Foreign Affairs 1984–. *Address:* Ministry of Foreign Affairs, Jalan Subok, Bandar Seri Begawan (office); Hijau Baiduri, Bukit Kayangan, Jalan Tutong, Bandar Seri Begawan BD 2710, Brunei (home). *Telephone:* (2) 261177 (office); (2) 244101 (office). *Fax:* (2) 261709 (office); (2) 244659 (office).

BOLKIAH MU'IZUDDIN WADDAULAH, HM Sultan and Yang di-Pertuan of Brunei Darussalam, Haji Hassanal, DK, PSPNB, PSLI, SPBM, PANB; *Head of State, Prime Minister, Minister of Defence and Minister of Finance;* b. 15 July 1946; s. of Sultan Haji Omar 'Ali Saifuddien Sa'adul Khairi Waddien, KCMG AND PENGIRAN RAJA ISTERI PENGIRAN ANAK DAMIT; m. HM Raja Isteri Pengiran Anak Hajah Saleha 1965; two s. (including HRH Prince Haji al-Muhtadee Billah) four d.; also m. Mariam Abd Aziz 1981 (divorced 2003); two s. two d.; also m. HRH Pengiran Isteri Azrinaz Mazhar Hakim 2005; one s.; ed privately and Victoria Inst., Kuala Lumpur, Malaysia and Royal Mil. Acad., Sandhurst, UK; appointed Crown Prince and Heir Apparent 1961; Ruler of State of Brunei Oct. 1967–; Prime Minister of Brunei Jan. 1984–, Minister of Finance and Home Affairs 1984–86, of Defence Oct. 1986–, also of Finance; Hon. Marshal RAF 1992; Sovereign and Chief of Royal Orders instituted by Sultans of Brunei; Head Dept of Islamic Religious Faith and Royal Custom and Tradition. *Address:* Istana Nurul Iman, Bandar Seri Begawan, BA 1000, Brunei (office). *Telephone:* (2) 229988 (office). *Fax:* (2) 241717 (office). *E-mail:* info@jpm.gov.bn (office). *Website:* www.pmo.gov.bn.

BOLLAÍN, Icíar; Spanish actress and screenwriter; b. (María Icíar Bollaín Pérez-Míínguez), 12 June 1967, Madrid; two c.; film debut in El Sur (The South) 1983; Pnr, La Iguana (film production co.) 1991–; writer and dir of feature film Hola, ¿estás sola? (Best New Dir Award and Audience Award, Valladolid Int. Film Festival) 1995. *Film appearances include:* El Sur 1983, Al acecho 1987, Malaventura 1988, Sublet 1991, Un Paraguas para tres 1992, Entretiempo 1992, Dime una mentira 1993, Jardines colgantes 1993, Land and Freedom 1995, El techo del mundo 1995, Subjudice 1998, Leo 2000, La balsa de piedra (The Stone Raft) 2002, Nos miran 2002, La Noche del hermano 2005. *Films written include:* Los amigos del muerto 1993, Hola, ¿estás sola? 1995, Flores de otro mundo (co-written with Julio Llamazares, Best Film in Int. Critics' Week, Cannes Film Festival) 1999, Amores que matan 2000, Poniente 2000, Te doy mis ojos 2003. *Films directed include:* Baja corazón 1992, Los amigos del muerto 1993, Hola, ¿estás sola? 1995, Flores de otro mundo (co-written with Julio Llamazares, Best Film in Int. Critics' Week, Cannes Film Festival) 1999, Amores que matan 2000, Te doy mis ojos 2003, Hay motivo 2004, Mataharis 2007. *Address:* Producciones La Iguana S.L., Jardín de San Federico, 15–1D, 28009 Madrid, Spain (office). *Telephone:* (91) 4010254 (office). *Fax:* (91) 3095008 (office). *E-mail:* iguana@la-iguana.com (office). *Website:* www.la-iguana.com (office).

BOLLAND, Marc; Dutch business executive; *CEO, William Morrison Supermarkets PLC;* ed Groningen Univ., London Business School, Institut Européen d'Admin des Affaires (INSEAD); worked at Heineken NV for over 20 years, fmr COO and mem. Bd of Dirs; CEO William Morrison Supermarkets PLC 2006–; Dir (non-exec.) Manpower Inc. 2004–; Chair. Supervisory Bd Hotel de l'Europe, Amsterdam; mem. Dutch Centre for Trade Devt, American Chamber of Commerce, Netherlands. *Address:* William Morrison Supermarkets PLC, Hilmore House, Gain Lane, Bradford, BD3 7DL, England (office). *Telephone:* (845) 611-5000 (office). *Website:* www.morrisons.co.uk (office).

BOLLIGER, Herbert, MBA; Swiss business executive; *Chairman, Federation of Migros Cooperatives;* b. 23 Nov. 1953; m. Beatrice Bolliger; two c.; ed Univ. of Zurich; with Bayer AG, Zurich 1980–83; joined Fed. of Migros Cooperatives 1983, Controller 1983–86, Vice-Dir Schonbuhl 1987–93, Dir Zurich 1994–97, Chair. Migros 2005–, also Chair. Migrosbank AG; Del. to Nat. Climate Forum, Thun Sept. 2007. *Address:* Federation of Migros Cooperatives, Limmatstrasse 152, 8031 Zurich, Switzerland (office). *Telephone:* (44) 277-2111 (office). *Fax:* (44) 277-25-25 (office). *E-mail:* media@migros.ch (office). *Website:* www.migros.ch (office).

BOLLING, Claude; French jazz pianist, composer and band leader; b. 10 April 1930, Cannes; s. of Harry Bolling and Geneviève Brannens; m. Irène Dervize-Sadyker 1959; two s.; ed studied with pvt. music teachers, including Bob Colin, Earl Hines, Maurice Duruflé, Willie 'The Lion' Smith, André Hodeir; worked with Dizzy Gillespie, Stéphane Grappelli, Rex Stewart, Roy Eldridge, Sidney Bechet, Albert Nicholas, Lionel Hampton, The Ellingtonians, Carmen McRae, Jo Williams; formed groups Les Parisiennes, Claude Bolling Big Band; performed in many jazz and variety shows; Hon. Citizen of Los Angeles; Commdr, Ordre des Arts et Lettres 2006; Chevalier, Ordre nat. du Mérite, Légion d'honneur; Médaille d'or Maurice Ravel, SACEM Gold Medal and Grand Prix 1984. *Compositions include:* piano solos, duos, trios and all instrumental combinations, including jazz, big band and symphony orchestra; written and recorded with Jean-Pierre Rampal (Suite for Flute), Alexandre Lagoya (Guitar Concerto), Maurice André (Toot Suite), Pinchas Zukerman (Suite for Violin), Yo-Yo Ma (Suite for Cello). *Compositions for film:* more than 100 film soundtrack scores, including The Awakening, Le Jour et l'Heure, Borsalino, Lucky Luke, Le Magnifique, Willie and Phil, California Suite, La Mandarine, L'Homme en Colère, Flic Story, Le Mur de l'Atlantique, On ne meurt que deux fois, Netchaiev est de retour. *Compositions for television:* Jazz Memories, Les Brigades du Tigre, Chantecler; many jazz and variety shows. *Leisure interests:* ecology, model railroading. *Address:* 20 avenue de Lorraine, 92380 Garches, France (office). *Telephone:* 1-47-41-41-84 (office). *Fax:* 1-47-01-

03-63 (office). *E-mail:* claude@claude-bolling.com (home). *Website:* www.claude-bolling.com (home).

BOLLINGER, Lee C.; American university administrator; *President, Columbia University;* b. 1946, Santa Rosa, Calif.; m. Jean Magnano Bollinger; one s. one d.; ed Univ. of Oregon, Columbia Law School; began career as law clerk, US Court of Appeal 1971–72, US Supreme Court 1972–73; Faculty mem. Univ. of Mich. Law School 1973–94, Dean 1987–94; Provost and Prof. of Govt Dartmouth Coll. 1994–96; Pres. Univ. of Mich. 1996–2002; Pres. Columbia Univ. 2002–; Fellow, American Acad. of Arts and Sciences; mem. Bd Gerald R. Ford Foundation, RSC; Clark Kerr Award for Distinguished Leadership in Higher Education 2005. *Publications:* The Tolerant Society: Freedom of Speech and Extremist Speech in America 1986, Images of a Free Press 1991, Eternally Vigilant: Free Speech in the Modern Era 2002; numerous books, articles and essays in scholarly journals. *Address:* Office of the President, Columbia University, 535 West 116th Street, 202 Low Library, New York, NY 10027, USA (office). *Telephone:* (212) 854-9970 (office). *Fax:* (212) 854-9973 (office). *Website:* www.columbia.edu (office).

BOLLORÉ, Vincent Marie, LLB; French financial investor; *Chairman and CEO, Groupe Bolloré;* b. 1 April 1952, Boulogne-sur-Seine; s. of Michel Bolloré and Monique Bolloré (née Follot); m. Sophie Fossorier 1977; three s. one d.; ed Lycée Janson-de-Sailly, Faculté de droit de Paris; with EIB 1970–75; Deputy Man. Cie financière Rothschild 1976–81; Chair. and CEO Groupe Bolloré and Bolloré Papermills 1981–, Bolloré, Inc., USA 1981–, Banque Rivaud 1996–; mem. Bd of Dirs Banque de France 1988–; mem. Supervisory Bd Vallourec 2004–07; mem. Bd Dirs then Chair. Havas 2005–; mem. Bd of Dirs Natexis Banques Populaires 2006–, Médiamétrie 2007–, Mediobanca, Financière Moncey; mem. Exec. Cttee Conseil nat. du patronat français (CNPF) 1987–96; Chair. Cen. Cttee Armateurs de France 1993–95, Fondation de la deuxième chance 1998; f. Direct8 (TV channel) 2005, DirectSoir (first free evening newspaper in France) 2006; Chevalier, Légion d'honneur, Grand Officier, Ordre du Lion (Senegal), Légion d'honneur (Côte d'Ivoire); Entrepreneur de l'année 1986, Man. de l'année 1987. *Address:* Groupe Bolloré, Tour Bolloré, 31–32 quai Dion Bouton, 92811 Puteaux (office); Havas, 2 alle de Longchamp, 92281 Suresnes Cedex, France (office). *Telephone:* 1-58-47-90-00 (office). *Fax:* 1-58-47-99-99 (office). *Website:* www.bollore.com (office); www.havas.com (office).

BOLLOYEV, Taimuraz Kazbekovich; Russian/Ossetian business executive; b. 23 Feb. 1953, N Ossetia; m.; ed Moscow Inst. of Food Industry; mechanic, then head of beer production Stepan Razin factory, Leningrad, chief technologist 1987–91; Dir Industrial Union, Vsevolzhsk, Leningrad Region 1984–87; Dir-Gen. Baltika (beer manufacturer) 1991–2004; acquired St. Petersburg Clothing Factory (FOSP) and Trud Factory (uniform manufacturer) 2005; est. Real Estate Investment Trust (REIT) Baltika 2005; Order of Honour. *Leisure interests:* classical music, football, Russian baths, wrestling. *Address:* c/o St. Petersburg Clothing Factory (FOSP), 75 nab. Moika, St Petersburg, Russia (office). *Telephone:* (812) 315-1873 (office).

BOLSHAKOV, Aleksey Alekseyevich; Russian politician and radio engineer; *Chairman of Board of Trustees for Development of North and North-West Territories;* b. 17 Dec. 1939, Dno, Pskov Dist; m.; two s.; ed M. Bonch-Bruyevich Electromechanical Inst. of Telecommunications, Leningrad; worked as engineer in factories of Leningrad; Dir-Gen. production union Dalnaya Svyaz; First Deputy Chair. Leningrad City Exec. Cttee, Chair. Planning Comm. 1988–91; Dir-Gen. Jt-Stock Co. Vysokoskorostnye Linii 1991–94; one of initiators of construction of high-speed St Petersburg–Moscow highway; Chair. Intergovernmental Cttee of CIS 1994–; Deputy Chair. Russian Council of Ministers 1994–96, First Deputy Chair. 1996–97; Chair. Bd of Dirs Polimetal 1998–; Chair. Bd of Trustees Fund for Devt of North and North-West Territories 1998–; mem. Bd of Trustees Fund for Devt of St Petersburg and North West Region of Russia 1999–, Chair. 2000–. *Address:* Fund for Development of St Petersburg and North-West Region of Russia, Smolny, 193060 St Petersburg (office); Polimetal, Narodnogo opolcheniya Prosp. 2, 198216 St Petersburg, Russia (office). *Telephone:* (812) 377-38-21 (office). *Fax:* (812) 376-65-20 (office). *E-mail:* info@polymetal.ru (office).

BOLSHOV, Leonid Aleksandrovich, DS; Russian physicist; *Director, Institute of Nuclear Safety (IBRAE), Russian Academy of Sciences;* b. 23 July 1946, Moscow; m.; three c.; ed Moscow State Univ.; engineer, Jr then Sr Researcher, later Head of Lab., Moscow Kurchatov Inst. of Atomic Energy (Troisk Br.) 1970–91; Dir Inst. of Nuclear Safety (IBRAE), Russian Acad. of Sciences 1991–; participated in mitigation of consequences of Chernobyl nuclear accident 1986; mem. Scientific Council, Ministry of Emergency Affairs, Ministry of Atomic Energy; mem. nuclear safety group Eurobank; Corresp. mem. Russian Acad. of Sciences 1997; mem. Ed. Bd journal Atomnaya Energetika; Order of Courage 1997, Order of Honour 2006; USSR State Prize 1988. *Publications:* over 300 scientific publs and monographs on physics of solid surfaces, non-linear optics, physics of laser thermonuclear synthesis and problems of nuclear power safety. *Address:* Institute of Nuclear Safety, Russian Academy of Sciences, B. Tulskaya str. 52, Moscow, Russia (office). *Telephone:* (495) 952-24-21 (office). *Fax:* (495) 958-00-40 (office). *E-mail:* bolshov@ibrae.ac.ru (office). *Website:* www.ibrae.ac.ru (office).

BOLT, Usain; Jamaican athlete; b. 21 Aug. 1986, Trelawny; s. of Wellesley Bolt and Jennifer Bolt; ed William Knibb Memorial High School; holds Olympic and world records for 100m at 9.69 seconds, 200m at 19.30 seconds and, as mem. Jamaican team, the 4×100m relay at 37.10 seconds, all set at Olympic Games, Beijing 2008; first man to win all three events at a single Olympics since Carl Lewis in 1984, and first man in history to set world records in all three at a single Olympics; made first appearance on world stage at Int. Asscn of Athletics Feds (IAAF) World Youth Championships, Debrecen, Hungary 2001 (set new personal best of 21.73 seconds in 200m); moved to Kingston to train with Jamaica Amateur Athletic Asscn at Univ. of Tech.; Gold Medal, 200m,World Jr Championships (youngest-ever gold medallist), Kingston 2002, 200m, World Youth Championships, Sherbrooke 2003; Silver Medal, 4×100m and 4×400m relays, World Jr Championships, Kingston 2002; first jr sprinter to run 200m in under 20 seconds with time of 19.93 seconds at CARIFTA Games 2004; turned professional 2004; missed most of his first two seasons due to injuries; eliminated in first round of 200m heats at Athens Olympics 2004; beat Don Quarrie's 200m Jamaican nat. record with time of 19.75 seconds in 2007; set his first 100m world record with time of 9.72 seconds at Reebok Grand Prix, New York City, May 2007; Gold Medal, 100m and 200m, Olympic Games, Beijing 2008; Silver Medal, 200m and 4×100m relay, World Championships, Osaka 2007; IAAF Rising Star Award 2002, 2003. *Address:* c/o Jamaica Amateur Athletic Association Ltd, PO Box 272, Kingston 5, Jamaica. *Telephone:* 929-6623. *Fax:* 920-4801. *E-mail:* athleticsja@jamweb.net. *Website:* www.jaaaltd.com.

BOLTANSKI, Christian; French artist; b. 6 Sept. 1944, Paris; s. of Etienne Boltanski and Marie-Elise Ilari-Guérin; participant in numerous group exhbns in Europe, USA, Canada and Australia; Prof. Ecole Nationale Supérieure des Beaux Arts 1986; Grand Prix nat. de la Sculpture 1990. *Publications:* L'Album de la Famille B. 1971, Les Compositions Photographiques 1976, Murales 1977. *Address:* 146 boulevard Carmélina, 92240 Malakoff, France. *Telephone:* 1-46-57-63-71.

BOLTEN, Joshua (Josh) B., BA, JD; American lawyer and government official; ed Princeton Univ., Stanford Law School; fmr Ed. Stanford Law Review; law clerk, US Dist Court, San Francisco 1980; Int. Trade Counsel to US Finance Cttee 1985–89, fmr Gen. Counsel to US Trade Rep.; Exec. Dir for Legal and Govt Affairs, Goldman Sachs Int., London 1994–99; Policy Dir Bush-Cheney presidential campaign 1999–2000; Asst to Pres., Deputy Chief of Staff for Policy 2001–03, Dir Office of Man. and Budget (OMB) 2003–06; White House Chief of Staff 2006–09; Republican.

BOLTON, John Robert, BA, JD; American lawyer, academic, fmr government official and fmr diplomatist; *Senior Fellow, American Enterprise Institute for Public Policy Research (AEI);* b. 20 Nov. 1948, Baltimore, Md; s. of Edward Jackson Bolton and Virginia Bolton (née Godfrey); m. Gretchen Brainerd 1986; one d.; ed Yale Univ.; Assoc., Covington & Burling (law firm), Washington, DC 1974–81, Pnr 1983–85; Gen. Counsel, USAID 1981–82, Asst Admin. for Program and Policy Coordination 1982–83; Asst Attorney-Gen. for Legis. Affairs, US Dept of Justice 1985–88, Asst Attorney-Gen., Civil Div. 1988–89; Asst Sec. for Int. Org. Affairs, US State Dept 1989–93; Pnr, Lerner, Reed, Bolton & McManus LLP (law firm), Washington, DC 1993–99; Of Counsel, Kutak Rock 1999–2001; Sr Vice-Pres. American Enterprise Inst. (AEI), Washington, DC 1999–2001, Sr Fellow 2007–; Under-Sec. of State for Arms Control and Int. Security, US State Dept 2001–05; Perm. Rep. to UN, New York (recess appointment) 2005–06; Sr Adviser Kirkland & Ellis (law firm) 2008–; Sr Fellow, Manhattan Inst. 1993; Adjunct Prof., George Mason Univ. Law School 1994–2001; Pres. Nat. Policy Forum 1995–96; mem. US Comm. on Int. Religious Freedom 1999–2001. *Publication:* Surrender is Not an Option: Defending America at the United Nations and Abroad 2008. *Address:* American Enterprise Institute, 1150 Seventeenth Street, NW, Washington, DC 20036, USA (office). *Telephone:* (202) 862-5892 (office). *Fax:* (202) 862-7192 (office). *E-mail:* christine.samuelian@aei.org (office). *Website:* www.aei.org (office).

BOLY, Yéro; Burkinabè politician; *Minister of Defence;* b. 1954, Komki-Ipala; m.; ed Ecole Nat. d'Admin; subprefect, Dori region 1978–80, l'Oudalan region 1980; civil servant, Ministry of the Interior 1983; Sec.-Gen. Namentenga Prov. and Prefect, Boulsa region 1983–84; Hiigh Commr, Gnagna Prov. 1984–86; Amb. to Côte-d'Ivoire 1986–88, to Libya 1988–95, to Iran 1990–92; Minister for Regional Affairs and Security 1995–2000; Head of Presidential Staff 2000–04; Minister of Defence 2004–; Grand Officier Ordre Nat. de Côte d'Ivoire 1988, Officier Ordre du Mérite (France) 2004, Commdr Ordre Nat. du Burkina Faso 2004; Médaille d'Honneur des Sapeurs Pompiers 2000, Médaille d'Honneur de la Police Nationale 2005. *Address:* Ministry of Defence, 01 BP 496, Ouagadougou 01, Burkina Faso (office). *Telephone:* 50-30-72-14 (office). *Fax:* 50-31-36-10 (office). *E-mail:* yeo_boly@yahoo.fr (office). *Website:* www.defense.gov.bf.

BOMBIERI, Enrico, PhD; American (b. Italian) mathematician and academic; *IBM von Neumann Professor of Mathematics, Institute for Advanced Study;* b. 26 Nov. 1940, Milan; ed Univ. of Milan, Trinity Coll., Cambridge, UK; Prof. of Math., Univ. of Pisa 1966–73; Prof. of Math., Scuola Normale Superiore, Pisa 1974–; Visiting mem. Inst. for Advanced Study, Princeton, NJ, USA 1977, currently IBM von Neumann Prof. of Math.; mem. Exec. Cttee Int. Math. Union 1979–82; mem. NAS, American Acad. of Arts and Sciences, Accad. Nazionale dei Quaranta, Rome, Accad. Nazionale dei Lincei, European Acad. of Sciences, Arts and Humanities; Foreign mem. Acad. des Sciences, Paris 1984, Royal Swedish Acad., Academia Europaea; Fields Medal, Int. Congress of Mathematicians, Vancouver 1974, Balzan Int. Prize 1980, Feltrinelli Prize. *Publications:* Geometric Measure Theory and Minimal Surfaces 1973, Le Grand Crible dans la théorie analytique des nombres (The Large Sieve in Analytic Number Theory) 1974, Seminar on Minimal Submanifolds 1983, An Introduction to Minimal Currents and Parametric Variational Problems 1985, Number Theory, Trace Formulas, and Discrete Groups 1989. *Address:* Simonyi Hall 213, School of Mathematics, Institute for Advanced Study, Einstein Drive, Princeton, NJ 08540, USA (office). *Telephone:* (609) 734-8397 (office). *Fax:* (609) 924-8399 (office). *E-mail:* gustafss@ias.edu (home). *Website:* www.math.ias.edu (office).

BON, Michel; French business executive; *Senior Adviser, Dome Close Brothers;* b. 5 July 1943, Grenoble; s. of Emmanuel Bon and Mathilde Bon (née Aussedat); m. Catherine Brunet de Sairigné; four c.; ed Ecole Supérieure Sciences Economiques et Commerciales, Paris Inst. of Political Studies, Ecole Nationale d'Admin., Stanford Business School; auditor Ministry of Finance 1971–75; banker Crédit Nat. 1975–78; joined Crédit Agricole 1978, Head of Commitments, Chair. and Deputy CEO Unicrédit –1985; Chair. then CEO Carrefour 1985–92; Head Nat. Job Placement Agency 1993–95; Chair. France Télécom 1995–2002, Hon. Chair. 2002–; Chair. (non-exec.) Orange (after merger with France Télécom) 2001–02; Sr Adviser, Dome Close Brothers 2002–; Chair. Editions du Cerf 1997–; fmr mem. Advisory Bd Banque de France; Chair. Supervisory Council Ecole Supérieure Sciences Economiques et Commerciales, Inst. Pasteur, Institut de l'Entreprise; Officier, Légion d'honneur; Chevalier du Mérite agricole; Officier, Ordre nat. du Mérite; Man. of the Year 1991, 1992, 1998. *Address:* Dome Close Brothers, 12 rue Leon Jost, 75017, Paris (office); 4 avenue de Camoëns, 75116 Paris, France (home). *Telephone:* 1-42-12-49-01 (office); 1-42-88-84-90 (home). *Fax:* 1-42-12-49-49 (office); 1-42-88-91-11 (home). *E-mail:* michel.bon@wanadoo.fr (office).

BON JOVI, Jon; American singer, songwriter, musician (guitar) and actor; b. (John Francis Bongiovi Jr), 2 March 1962, Perth Amboy, NJ; m. Dorothea Hurley 1989; four c.; singer in local bands Raze, Atlantic City Expressway; founder mem. and lead singer rock group Bon Jovi 1983–88, 92–; solo artist 1988–; numerous tours, television, radio and live appearances worldwide; owner management co. BJM; owner record label Jambco; owner Philadelphia Soul American football team 2003–; American Music Awards for Favorite Pop/Rock Band 1988, for Favorite Pop/Rock Single 1991, Nordoff-Robbins Music Therapy Silver Clef 1990, Golden Globe Award for Best Original Song from a Motion Picture (for Blaze of Glory) 1991, BRIT Award for Best Int. Group (with band) 1995, VH-1 Award for Favorite Video (for It's My Life) 2000, Grammy Award for Best Country Collaboration with Vocals (with Jennifer Nettles) 2007. *Films:* Young Guns II 1990, Moonlight and Valentino (Motion Picture Club Premier Performance Award) 1995, The Leading Man 1996, Little City 1997, Destination Anywhere 1997, No Looking Back 1998, Homegrown 1998, Row Your Boat 1998, U-571 2000, Pay It Forward 2000, Vampires: Los Muertos 2002, Cry_Wolf 2005. *Television appearances:* Unsolved Mysteries 1988, Sex and the City 1998, Ally McBeal 1997. *Recordings include:* albums: with Bon Jovi: Bon Jovi 1984, 7800° Fahrenheit 1985, Slippery When Wet 1986, Bon Jovi Live 1987, New Jersey 1988, Keep The Faith 1991, Cross Road 1994, These Days 1995, Crush 2000, One Wild Night 1985–2001 2001, Bounce 2002, Distance 2003, This Left Feels Right 2003, Have a Nice Day 2005, Lost Highway 2007; solo: Young Guns II: Blaze of Glory 1990, Destination Anywhere 1997. *Address:* Bon Jovi Management, PO Box 237040, New York, NY 10023, USA (office). *Telephone:* (212) 336-9413 (office). *Fax:* (212) 336-5385 (office). *Website:* www.bonjovi.com.

BONCODIN, Hon. Emilia T., MPA; Philippine academic and fmr government official; *Professor, National College of Public Administration and Governance, University of the Philippines;* b. Iriga City; ed Iriga Cen. Pilot School, St Anthony Coll., Univ. of the Philippines, Kennedy School of Govt Harvard Univ. Cambridge, USA; Sr Fiscal Planning Specialist, Dept of Budget and Man. 1978, then Div. Chief, Officer-in-Charge, Govt Corpns Budget Bureau, Asst Sec. of Budget and Man. 1989–91, Under-Sec. 1991–98, Sec. 1998–2005; currently Prof., Nat. Coll. of Public Admin and Governance, Univ. of the Philippines; mem. Bd of Dirs Petron Corpn; mem. Cttee of Experts in Public Admin, UN, New York; Trustee Int. Center for Tropical Agric.; fmr Exec. Dir Ramos Peace and Devt Foundation; Dwight Eisenhower Fellow for the Philippines 1996, Edward S. Mason Fellow, Harvard Univ.; Most Outstanding Tech. Employee 1978, Most Outstanding Div. Chief 1981, Outstanding Alumna, Coll. of Business Admin, UP 1992, Outstanding Women in Nation's Service Award 1995. *Address:* National College of Public Administration and Governance, 303J, University of the Philippines, Diliman, Quezon City 1101, Philippines (office). *Website:* www.up-ncpag.org (office).

BOND, Alan, AO; Australian business executive; b. 22 April 1938, London, England; s. of Frank Bond and Kathleen Bond; m. 1st Eileen Hughes 1956 (divorced); two s. two d.; m. 2nd Diana Bliss 1995; ed Perivale School, London and Fremantle Boys' School, WA; f. and Exec. Chair. Bond Corpn Holdings Ltd 1969–90, now consultant; interests in brewing, property, oil and gas, electronic media, minerals, airships; declared bankrupt April 1992; sentenced to 2¹/²years' imprisonment for dishonesty but found not guilty after retrial Nov. 1992; sentenced to three years' imprisonment for fraud 1996; sentenced to four years' imprisonment for fraud Feb. 1997; sentence extended to seven years Aug. 1997; released March 2000; Syndicate Head Americas Cup Challenge 1983 Ltd; with Money Centre 2000–; Australia Winners of 1983 Americas Cup Challenge; named Australian of the Year 1977. *Leisure interest:* yachting.

BOND, Alan Maxwell, PhD, DSc, FAA, FRACI, FRSC; Australian chemist and academic; *R.L. Martin Distinguished Professor of Chemistry and Federation Fellow, Monash University;* b. 17 Aug. 1946, Cobden, Vic.; s. of the late Ian T. Bond and Joyce M. Bond; m. Tunde-Maria Bond 1969; two s.; ed Univ. of Melbourne; Sr Demonstrator, Dept of Inorganic Chem., Univ. of Melbourne 1970–73, Research Fellow 1973–78; Foundation Prof. of Chem., Deakin Univ. 1978–90; Prof. of Chem., La Trobe Univ. 1990–95, Deputy Head Dept of Chem. 1996, 1997, 1999; Prof. of Chem., Monash Univ. 1995–, Deputy Head Dept of Chem. 1996–97, 1999, Head, School of Chem. 2000–02, R.L. Martin Distinguished Prof. of Chem., Fed. Fellow 2004–; 150th Anniversary Royal Soc. of Chem., Robert Boyle Fellow in Analytical Chem., Univ. of Oxford 1991, Hinshelwood Lecturer 1998, Vallee Visiting Prof. 2004–; mem. Chem. Panel, Australian Research Council 1993–95, Council Australian Acad. of Science 1993–96, Vice-Pres. 1995–96, ACS, USA Electrochemical Soc.; Fulbright

Fellow 1972; Fellow, Japan Soc. for Promotion of Science 1990, IUPAC, Royal Australian Chemical Inst.; Erskine Fellowship 1993; Christensen Fellowship, St Catherine's Coll., Oxford 1998; Fed. of Asian Chemical Socs Foundation Lectureship 1993; mem. numerous editorial bds, including Reviews in Analytical Chem. 1971–, Bulletin of Electrochemistry 1987–, Inorganica Chimica Acta 1988–, Journal of Electroanalytical Chem. 1997–, Green Chem. 1999, Encyclopedia of Analytical Science (second edn) 2001–; Rennie Medal 1975, David Syme Prize 1978, Australian Analytical Chem. Medal 1989, Stokes Medal 1992, Liversidge Award, Australian and NZ AAS 1992, Australian Research Council Special Investigator Award 1997–99, Royal Soc. of Chem. (London) Electrochemistry Group Medal 1997, Royal Australian Chemical Inst. H.G. Smith Medal 1998, Royal Soc. of Vic. Medal 1999, Burrows Medal 2000, Faraday Medal, Royal Soc. of Chem. 2000 Gov.-Gen.'s Centenary Medal for Service to Australian Soc. and Science in Electrochemistry 2003, Craig Medal Australian Acad. of Science 2004, Reilley Award 2005. *Publications:* Modern Polarographic Methods in Analytical Chemistry 1981, Broadening Electrochemical Horizons 2002; more than 600 publs on different aspects of electrochemistry. *Leisure interest:* cricket. *Address:* School of Chemistry, Monash University, Clayton, Vic. 3800, Australia (office). *Telephone:* (3) 9905-1338 (office). *Fax:* (3) 9905-4597 (office). *E-mail:* alan.bond@sci.monash.edu.au (office). *Website:* www.chem.monash.edu.au/staff/bond.html (office).

BOND, Christopher Samuel (Kit), BA, LLB; American politician and lawyer; *Senator from Missouri;* b. 6 March 1939, St Louis; s. of Arthur Doerr and Elizabeth Green Bond; m. Carolyn Reid 1967; one s.; ed Deerfield Acad., Mass., Woodrow Wilson School of Public and Int. Affairs, Princeton Univ., Univ. of Virginia; Clerk, Fifth Circuit, US Court of Appeals 1963–64; with law firm, Covington and Burling, Washington, DC 1964–67; private practice 1968; Asst Attorney-Gen., Chief Counsel of Consumer Protection Div. 1969–70; State Auditor, Missouri 1970–72; Gov. of Missouri 1973–77, 1981–84; Chair. Republican Govs' Asscn 1974–75, Midwestern Govs' Conf. 1976; Exec. Cttee Nat. Govs' Conf. 1974–75; Chair. NGA Cttee on Econ. Devt 1981-82; Pres. Great Plains Legal Foundation, Kansas City, Mo. 1977–81; partner, law firm Gage and Tucker, Kansas City and St Louis 1981–87; Senator from Missouri Jan. 1987–; Republican; Hon. LLD (Westminster and William Jewell Colls, Mo.) 1973; Hon. DLitt (Drury Coll., Springfield, Mo.) 1976. *Address:* 274 Russell Senate Building, Room 293, Washington, DC 20510 (office); 14 S. Jefferson Road, Mexico, MO 65265, USA (home). *Telephone:* (202) 224-5721 (office). *Website:* bond.senate.gov (office).

BOND, Edward; British playwright, director and poet; b. 18 July 1934, London; m. Elisabeth Pablé 1971; Northern Arts Literary Fellowship 1977–79; resident theatre writer, Univ. of Essex 1982–83; City of Lyon Medal 2007; Hon. DLitt (Yale) 1977; George Devine Award 1968, John Whiting Award 1968, Obie Award 1976. *Publications:* plays: The Pope's Wedding 1962, Saved 1965, Narrow Road to the Deep North 1968, Early Morning 1968, Passion 1971, Black Mass 1971, Lear 1972, The Sea 1973, Bingo 1974, The Fool 1976, A-A-America! (Grandma Faust and The Swing) 1976, Stone 1976, The Bundle 1978, The Woman 1979, The Worlds 1980, The Activist Papers 1980, Restoration 1981, Summer: A Play for Europe 1982, Derek 1983, Human Cannon 1985, The War Plays (Red Black and Ignorant, The Tin Can People, Great Peace) 1985, Jackets 1989, In the Company of Men 1990, September 1990, Olly's Prison 1993, Tuesday 1993, Coffee: A Tragedy 1994, At the Inland Sea (A Play for Young People) 1996, Eleven Vests (A Play for Young People) 1997, The Crime of the Twenty-first Century 1999, The Children (A Play for Two Adults and Sixteen Children) 2000, Chair 2000, Have I None 2000, Existence 2002, Born 2004, The Balancing Act 2004, The Short Electra 2004, My Day (Song Cycle for Children) 2005, The Under Room 2006, Arcade 2006, June 2007, People 2007, Collected Plays (eight vols) 1977–2007 2007; short stories: Fables 1982; opera librettos of music by Hans Werner Henze: We Come to the River 1977, The English Cat 1983; ballet libretto of music by Henze: Orpheus 1982; translations: Chekhov's The Three Sisters 1967, Wedekind's Spring Awakening 1974, Wedekind's Lulu: A Monster Tragedy (with Elisabeth Bond-Pablé) 1992; other: Theatre Poems and Songs 1978, Collected Poems 1978–1985 1987, Notes on Post-Modernism 1990, Letters (five vols) 1994–2001, Notes on Imagination 1995, Selected Notebooks Vol. 1 2000, Vol. 2 2001, The Hidden Plot: Notes on Theatre and the State 2000. *Address:* c/o Casarotto Ramsay, Waverley House, 7–12 Noel Street, London, W1F 8GQ, England (office). *Telephone:* (20) 7287-4450 (office). *Fax:* (20) 7287-9128 (office). *E-mail:* agents@casarotto.uk.com (office). *Website:* www.casarotto.uk.com (office).

BOND, Sir John Reginald Hartnell, Kt; British business executive; *Chairman, Vodafone Group plc;* b. 24 July 1941, Oxford; s. of the late Capt. R. H. A. Bond and of E. C. A. Bond; m. Elizabeth Caroline Parker 1968; one s. two d.; ed Tonbridge School, Kent, Cate School, California, USA; joined The Hongkong and Shanghai Banking Corpn (later became HSBC) 1961; worked in Hong Kong, Thailand, Singapore, Indonesia and USA; Chief Exec. Wardley Ltd (Merchant Banking) 1984–87; Chair. Hongkong Bank of Canada 1987–98; Exec. Dir Hongkong and Shanghai Banking Corpn (responsible for the Americas) 1988–89, Commercial Banking, Hong Kong 1990–91; Pres. and CEO Marine Midland Bank, Inc., Buffalo, USA (subsidiary of HSBC Holdings PLC) 1991–92, Chair. HSBC Americas Inc. 1997; Deputy Chair. HSBC Bank PLC (fmrly Midland Bank) 1996–98 (Dir 1993), Chair. 1998–2006; Chair. HSBC Bank Middle East (fmrly British Bank of the Middle East) 1998–2006; Group CEO HSBC Holdings PLC 1993–98, Group Chair. 1998–2006 (Dir 1990–); Dir (non-exec.) Vodafone Group plc, Chair. 2006–; Dir Hang Seng Bank Ltd 1990–96, Bank of England 2001–; Sr Adviser Kohlberg Kravis Roberts 2006–; Dir (non-exec.) London Stock Exchange 1994–99, British Steel 1994–98, Orange PLC 1996–99, Ford Motor Co. 2000– (adviser to Exec. Chair. 2006–); Chair. Inst. of Int. Finance, Washington, DC 1998–2003; Gov. The

English-Speaking Union 1997–; Hon. Fellow, London Business School 2003; Hon. DEcon (Richmond American Univ., London) 1998; Hon. DLit (Loughborough) 2000, (Sheffield) 2002; Hon. LLD (South Bank) 2001; Foreign Policy Asscn Medal, New York 2003, Magnolia Gold Award, Shanghai Municipal People's Govt 2003. *Leisure interests:* golf, skiing, reading biographies. *Address:* Vodafone Group plc, Vodafone House, The Connection, Newbury, West Berks., RG14 2FN, England (office). *Telephone:* (1635) 33251 (office). *Fax:* (1635) 45713 (office). *E-mail:* info@vodafone.com (office). *Website:* www.vodafone.com (office).

BOND, Julian; American civil rights leader and academic; *Professor, Department of History, University of Virginia;* b. 14 Jan. 1940; s. of Horace Mann Bond and Julia Agnes (née Washington); m. 1st Alice Louise Clopton 1961 (divorced 1989); three s. two d.; m. 2nd Pamela Sue Horowitz 1990; ed Morehouse Coll.; Co-founder Cttee on Appeal for Human Rights, Atlanta Univ. 1960; Co-founder Student Non-violent Co-ordinating Cttee 1960, Communications Dir 1961–66; reporter, feature writer Atlanta Inquirer 1960–61, Man. Ed. 1963; mem. Ga House of Reps 1966–75, excluded 1966 by House for criticizing US involvement in Viet Nam, exclusion overruled in Supreme Court; mem. Ga Senate 1975–87; Prof. Drexel Univ. 1988–89; Pappas Fellow, Univ. of Pennsylvania 1989; Visiting Prof. Harvard Univ. 1989, 1991, Univ. of Virginia 1990; Distinguished Prof. in Residence, American Univ. 1991–; Teacher, Nat Endowment for Humanities Seminar, Harvard Univ. 1996–2001; Prof., Univ. of Virginia 1998–; Chair. Bd, Southern Elections Fund, Nat. Asscn for the Advancement of Colored People (NAACP) 1998–; Pres. Emer. Southern Poverty Law Center; Pres. Inst. of Southern Studies; mem. Bd of Dirs Delta Ministry Project of Nat. Council of Churches, Robert F. Kennedy Memorial Fund, Martin Luther King Jr Center for Social Change, Center for Community Change, Southern Regional Council, New Democratic Coalition and other bodies; mem. Nat. Advisory Council of American Civil Liberties Union, Southern Correspondents Reporting Racial Equality Wars; hon. degrees from 24 colls and univs. *Publications:* A Time to Speak, A Time to Act, Gonna Sit at the Welcome Table; poems and articles in books and periodicals. *Address:* 4805 Mt Hope Drive, Baltimore, MD 21215 (office); 5435 41st Place, NW, Washington, DC 20015, USA. *Telephone:* (410) 486-9100 (office); (202) 244-1213 (home). *Fax:* (434) 924-7891 (office). *E-mail:* Julian_Bond@msn.com (office). *Website:* www.virginia.edu/history/files/faculty/bond.html (office); www.naacp.org/about/chairmancorner/index.htm.

BOND, Richard L. (Dick); American food industry executive; ed Elizabethtown Coll.; mem. Bd of Dirs IBP Inc. 1995–2001, Pres. and COO 1997–2001, Co-COO and Group Pres., Fresh Meats and Retail, Tyson Foods Inc. (after acquisition of IBP by Tyson Foods) 2001–03, Pres. and COO Tyson Foods Inc. 2003–06, Pres. and CEO 2006–09 (resgnd); Chair. American Meat Inst. *Address:* c/o Tyson Foods Inc., 2210 West Oaklawn Drive, Springdale, AR 72762-6999, USA (office).

BONDARENKO, Vitaly Mikhailovich; Russian architect; *Professor, Moscow Institute of Communal Industry;* b. 22 June 1925; m.; ed Kharkov Inst. of Eng and Construction; fmr master constructor Zaporozhstal Factory; chief engineer Div. of Mining Construction and Towns, Donbass 1952–62; Head, then Pro-Rector Kharkov Inst. of Eng and Construction 1962–72; Dir All-Union Research Inst. Giproniiselkhoz, Moscow 1972–76; Head of Dept, Prof. Moscow Inst. of Communal Econs and Construction (now Communal Industry) 1976–94, 1999–; Vice-Pres. Russian Acad. of Architecture and Construction Sciences 1994–; mem. Nat. Bd of Dirs. Chamber of Cultural and Historical Heritage of Russia, Russian Acad. of Eng, Int. Acad. of Eng, Int. Acad. of Ecological Reconstruction, British Inst. of Civil Eng; Foreign mem. Ukraine Acad. of Construction; numerous awards and prizes. *Publications:* ten books and over 200 tech. publs. *Leisure interest:* 20th-century Russian history. *Address:* Moscow Institute of Communal Industry, Srednaya Kalitnikovskaya str. 30, 109807 Moscow, Russia (office). *Telephone:* (495) 157-75-07 (office); (495) 202-48-66 (home).

BONDAREV, Yuriy Vasiliyevich; Russian writer; *Chairman, International Committee, Mikhail Sholokhov Prize;* b. 15 March 1924, Orsk; s. of Vasili Vasilevich Bondarev and Claudia Iosifovna Bondareva; m. Valentina Nikitichna Mosina 1950; two d.; ed Gor'kiy Inst., Moscow 1951; writer 1949–; mem. CPSU 1944–91; First Deputy Chair. of RSFSR Writers' Union, Chair. of Bd 1990–93; Pres. Yedineniye (Unity) Asscn 1995–; served in Soviet Army 1941–45; Deputy to Supreme Soviet 1975–80 and Deputy Chair.; Chair., Int. Cttee, Mikhail Sholokhov Prize; Co-Chair., Int. Community of Writers' Unions; mem. Int. Slavian Acad., Acad. of Literature, Peter the Great Acad., Russian Acad.; Hon. mem. Pushkin Acad.; Hon. Citizen of Volgograd, Hon. Prof. of Moscow State Teachers, Univ. of Mikhail Sholokhov; , Order of Honour of Transdniestrian Repub.; Hero of Socialist Labour 1984, two State prizes, Lenin Prize, RSFSR Prize, Tolstoy Prize 1993, Sholokhov Prize 1994, Vladimir Dal Prize 2002, Alexander Nevsky Prize. *Film:* screenplay for epic film Liberation 1964–70. *Play:* The Turnover 1994. *Publications include:* novels: On the Big River 1953, Young Commanders 1956, Fire for the Battalions 1957, Last Salute 1959, Silence 1962, Relatives 1965, Hot Snow 1969, The Shore 1975, A Choice 1980, The Game 1984, Temptation 1991, Instants (essays) 1981–87 and 1987–94, 2001, Collected Works (eight vols) 1993–94, Non-Resistance to Evil 1994, The Bermuda Triangle 2000, Without Mercy 2004. *Leisure interest:* collecting painting albums. *Address:* Lomonosovsky Prospekt N19, Apt 148, 117311 Moscow, Russia. *Telephone:* (495) 334-59-92.

BONDEVIK, Kjell Magne; Norwegian politician and diplomatist; *Secretary-General's Special Humanitarian Envoy to the Horn of Africa, United Nations;* b. 3 Sept. 1947, Molde; s. of Margit Bondevik and Johs Bondevik; m. Björg Bondevik 1970; two s. one d.; ed Free Faculty of Theology, Univ. of Oslo; ordained minister 1979; Deputy Chair. Christian Democratic Youth Asscn 1968–70, Chair. 1970–73; Deputy mem. Storting 1969–73, mem. 1973–; Political Vice-Chair. Christian Democratic Party 1975–83, Chair. 1983–95; Minister of Church and Educ. 1983–86, Deputy Prime Minister 1985–86, Minister of Foreign Affairs 1989–90; Chair. Christian Democratic Party's Parl. Group 1981–83, 1986–89, 1993–97; Prime Minister of Norway 1997–2000, 2002–2005; UN Sec.-Gen.'s Special Humanitarian Envoy for the Horn of Africa 2006–; Founder and Pres. Oslo Center for Peace and Human Rights 2006–; mem. Club of Madrid; Hon. DTech (Brunel) 1997; Dr hc (Suffolk) 2000, (Wonkurang) 2000; Wittenberg Award, Luther Inst. 2000. *Publication:* Et liv i spenning 2006. *Address:* Oslo Center for Peace and Human Rights, Postboks 2753 Solli, 0204 Oslo, Gange Rolvsgate 5, Norway (office). *Telephone:* 23-13-66-70 (office). *Fax:* 23-13-66-77 (office). *E-mail:* post@oslocenter.no (office). *Website:* www.oslocenter.no (office).

BONDS, Barry Lamar; American professional baseball player; b. 24 July 1964, Riverside, Calif.; s. of the late Bobby Bonds (fmr San Francisco Giants player); m.; three c.; ed Serra High School, San Mateo, Calif., Arizona State Univ.; outfielder; drafted by Pittsburgh Pirates in first round (6th pick) 1985 amateur draft, played with Pirates 1985–92, signed as free agent San Francisco Giants 1992–2007, filed for free agency status Oct. 2007; hit 73 home runs 2001 (single-season major league baseball home run record); hit 756th home run on 7 Aug. 2007 to set record of most career home runs; National League Most Valuable Player 1990, 1992, 1993, 2001, 2002, 2003, 2004; National League batting champion 2002 (.370 avg.), 2004 (.362 avg.); f. Bonds Family Foundation; Most Valuable Player (Nat. League), Baseball Writers' Asscn of America 1990, 1992, 1993, 2001, 2002, 2003, 2004, Maj. League Player of Year, Sporting News 1990, 2001, 2004, Nat. League Player of Year, Sporting News 1990, 1992, 1993, 2001, 2002, 2003, 2004. Gold Glove Award 1990–98, Silver Slugger Award 1990–94, 1996–97, 2000–04, 13 All-Star appearances. *Address:* c/o San Francisco Giants, Pacific Bell Park, 24 Willie Mays Plaza, San Francisco, CA 94107, USA (office). *Website:* www.barrybonds.com.

BONDURANT, Amy L., BA, JD; American diplomatist, lawyer and business executive; *Managing Director, Bozman Partners Ltd;* b. Union City, Tenn.; d. of Judge John C. Bondurant; m. David E. Dunn III; one s.; ed Univ. of Ky, American Univ., Washington DC; legis. aide to Senator Wendell Ford 1975; Counsel, then Sr Counsel, Senate Cttee on Commerce, Science and Transportation; pvt. practice with law firm 1987–; Chair. Commercial Space Transportation Advisory Cttee 1993; Perm. Rep. to OECD 1997–2001; Sec.-Treas. and mem. Bd Vice-Pres.'s Residence Foundation 1993–97; currently Man. Dir Bozman Pnrs Ltd (pvt. investment fund); mem. American, DC, Ky Bar Asscns; mem. Founding Cttee of Forum 21 Conf. on Trans-Atlantic Dialogue 2001; mem. Bd of Dirs, Rolls-Royce Group plc 2003–06, American Hosp., Paris; mem. Council on Foreign Relations, Council of American Ambs. *Publication:* Physician Heal Thyself: Can International Organisations Reform? 2001. *Address:* c/o Council of American Ambassadors, 888 17th Street, NW, Suite 306, Washington, DC 20006-3312, USA.

BONDURANT, Stuart, BS, MD; American physician, academic and university administrator; *Interim Executive Vice President and Executive Dean, Georgetown University Medical Center;* b. 9 Sept. 1929, Winston-Salem, NC; m. 1st Margaret Fortescue 1954 (divorced); one s. two d.; m. 2nd Susan Haughton Ehringhaus 1991; ed Univ. of North Carolina at Chapel Hill, Duke Univ. School of Medicine, Durham, NC; Assoc. Dir Indiana Univ. Cardiovascular Research Center, Indiana Univ. Medical Center, Indianapolis, Ind. 1961–67; Chief, Medical Br. Artificial Heart-Myocardial Infarction Program, Nat. Health Inst., NIH 1966–67; Prof. and Chair., Dept of Medicine, Albany Medical Coll., Physician-in-Chief, Albany Medical Center Hosp., New York 1967–74, Pres. and Dean 1974–79; Prof. of Medicine, Univ. of NC 1979–, Dean, Univ. of NC School of Medicine 1979–94, now Dean Emer.; Interim Exec. Vice Pres. and Exec. Dean, Georgetown Univ. Medical Center 2003–; Dir Center for Urban Epidemiology Studies, NY Acad of Medicine 1994–96; Hon. FRCPE; Hon. DSc (Indiana 1980); Thomas Jefferson Award, Univ. of NC 1998. *Address:* Georgetown University Medical Center, 120 Building D, 37th and O Street, NW, Washington, DC 20057, USA (office). *Telephone:* (202) 687-4600 (office). *Website:* gumc.georgetown.edu (office).

BONE, Sir Roger, KCMG, BA; British diplomatist and business executive; *President, Boeing UK Ltd;* ed Palmer's School, Grays, Essex, Univ. of Oxford; career diplomat, FCO; overseas assignments in Moscow, Washington, DC, and with UK Rep. to EU, Brussels; Pvt. Sec. to Foreign Sec. 1982–84; Visiting Fellow in Int. Relations, Harvard Univ., USA 1984–85; Asst Under-Sec. of State, FCO 1991–95; Amb. to Sweden 1995–99, to Brazil 1999–2004; Pres. Boeing UK Ltd 2005–. *Address:* Boeing UK Ltd,16 St James Street, London, SW1A 1ER, England (office). *Telephone:* (20) 7930-5000 (office). *Fax:* (20) 7739-9190 (office). *Website:* www.boeing.com (office).

BONELL, Carlos Antonio; British musician, teacher, guitarist and composer; b. 23 July 1949, London; s. of Carlos Bonell and Ana Bravo; m. Pinuccia Rossetti 1975; two s.; ed William Ellis School, Highgate and Royal Coll. of Music, under John Williams (q.v.); solo début as solo guitarist, Wigmore Hall, London 1971; concerto début with Royal Philharmonic Orchestra 1975; American début, Avery Fisher Hall, New York 1978; concert appearances with all the prin. British orchestras; appearances with John Williams (q.v.), Teresa Berganza (q.v.), Pinchas Zukerman (q.v.) 1975–; formed Carlos Bonell Ensemble 1983; Prof. Royal Coll. of Music 1972–, London Coll. of Music 1983–; Hon. ARCM. *Recordings include:* Guitar Music of Spain 1975, Guitar Music of the Baroque 1976, Showpieces 1981, Rodrigo Concerto 1981, Paganini Trios and Quartets 1983, Twentieth Century Music for Guitar 1987, Once Upon a Time, with Xer-Wai (violin) 1992, Walton Bagatelles and Anon in Love 1993, Britten Folksongs (with Philip Langridge) 1994, The Sea in Spring 1997, The Private Collection 1998, Kinkachoo I Love You (Millenium Guitar, The First 1000 Years) 2000, Trinity Coll. Grade pieces 2003,

Carlos Bonell plays Gordon Mizzi 2003, Guitar Classics 2004. *Publications:* 20 First Pieces 1982, Tarrega: Fantasia on "La Traviata", 3 Spanish Folk Songs, Purcell: Music from the Fairy Queen, Fantasy for 3 Guitars 1995, Technique Builder 1997, Millennium Guitar, The First 1000 Years 2000. *Leisure interests:* reading, walking, snooker, films. *Address:* c/o Upbeat Classical Management, POB 479, Uxbridge UB8 2ZH, England (office). *Telephone:* (1895) 259441 (office). *Fax:* (1895) 259341 (office). *E-mail:* info@upbeatclassical.co.uk (office); carlos@carlosbonell.com (home). *Website:* www.upbeatclassical.co.uk (office); www.carlosbonell.com.

BONELLO DU PUIS, George, LLD, KOM; Maltese politician, diplomatist and notary; b. 24 Jan. 1928; m. Iris Gauci Maistre; two s. one d.; ed St Catherine's High School, Sliema, the Lyceum and Univ. of Malta; practising notary 1952; MP 1971–96; mem. Nationalist Party, Spokesman on Finance, State Industry, Tourism, Trade and Industry; Minister of Finance 1987–92, for Economic Services 1992–95; fmr Chair. Parl. Standing Cttee on Foreign Affairs, EU Malta Jt Parl. Cttee; High Commr to UK 1999–2005; Companion of the Nat. Order of Merit. *Address:* The Park, Antonio Nani Street, Ta'Xbiex, Malta.

BONET, Pep; Spanish architect and designer; b. 19 Nov. 1941, Barcelona; m. Marta Monné 1964; three s.; ed High School of Architecture, Barcelona; f. Studio Per architectural practice, with Cristian Cirici, Lluis Clotet and Oscar Tusquets 1965; began producing furniture and bldg components, co-f. BD Ediciones de Diseño 1972; taught at School of Architecture, Barcelona 1975–78, Washington School of Architecture, St Louis, Mo., USA 1981; Deltas ADI-FAD Award 1967, 1976, 1986, 1990, 1991, Azulejo de Oro Award 1970, Nat. Restoration Award 1980, FAD Award for Architecture 1965, 1970, 1972, 1987, Architecture and Town Planning award 1987 for Triángulo de Oro Sports Centre, Madrid. *Major works include:* (Feria de Barcelona) Plaza Universo 1983–85, Rius i Taulet pavilion 1987, Iberia pavilion 1987, Lleida-Parallel pavilion 1989; Triángulo de Oro Sports Centre 1985, Canillejas civic centre 1985 (Madrid); Granollers Olympic sports centre, COOB-92. *Leisure interest:* playing jazz (tenor saxophone). *Address:* C/Pujades 63, 08005 Barcelona, Spain. *Telephone:* (93) 4855494. *Fax:* (93) 3091472.

BONETTI, Mattia; Swiss designer, decorator and artist; b. 2 May 1952, Lugano; s. of Giorgio Bonetti and Stella Frossard; m. Isabelle Forestier 1990; two d.; ed Centro Scolastico Industrie Artistiche, Lugano; decorated Bernard Picasso's Boisgeloup Castle 1987, Christian Lacroix Showroom and Graphics 1987–88; designs for cafeteria, Schloss Regensburg Thurn und Taxis Museum, Germany 1990; Banque Bruxelles-Lambert, Geneva 1991; packaging for Nina Ricci Cosmetics 1992, 1994; Water Carafe design for Ricard 1995; designed tramway for city of Montpellier 1998, designed 2nd tramway 2006; Venetian Renaissance Glass show installation, Musée des Arts Décoratifs, Paris 2003; Emile Gallé show installation, Musée d'Orsay, Paris 2004; designed choir for Metz Cathedral 2006; Hon. Citizen City of Villeurbanne; Chevalier, Ordre des Arts et des Lettres 1995; 'Créateurs de l'Année 1991' (France). *Publications:* Mattia Bonetti and Elizabeth Garouste 1990, Garouste and Bonetti 1996, 1998, Elizabeth Garouste and Mattia Bonetti 1981–2001, Mattia Bonetti Drawings (monograph) 2005, Mattia Bonetti (monograph) 2009. *Leisure interests:* swimming, photography. *Address:* 10 rue Rochebrune, 75011 Paris (office); 1 rue Oberkampf, 75011 Paris, France (home). *Telephone:* 1-48-05-61-21 (office); 1-48-05-86-51 (home). *Fax:* 1-48-05-61-29 (office); 1-48-05-86-51 (home).

BONFIELD, Sir Peter (Leahy), Kt, CBE, FREng, FIEE, FRSA; British business executive; b. 3 June 1944; s. of George Bonfield and Patricia Bonfield; m. Josephine Houghton 1968; ed Hitchin Boys' Grammar School and Univ. of Loughborough; Div. Dir Texas Instruments Inc. Dallas, TX, USA 1966–81; Group Exec. Dir Worldwide Operations, ICL 1981–84, Man. Dir 1984, Chair. and CEO ICL PLC 1987–97, Deputy Chair. 1997–2000; Deputy Chief Exec. STC PLC 1987–90; Chair. and CEO British Telecommunications PLC 1996–2002; Dir BICC PLC 1992–96, AstraZeneca 1995– (Sr Dir 2002–), MCI Inc. 1996–98, Ericsson 2002–, Mentor Graphics Corpn 2002–, TSMC 2002–; Vice-Pres. British Quality Foundation 1993–; mem. CS Coll. Advisory Council 1993–97, European Round Table 1996–2002, EU–Japan Business Dialogue Round Table 1999–2002, Citigroup Int. Advisory Bd 1999–; Amb. for British Business; Liveryman, Information Technologists' Co. 1992; Trustee Cutty Sark Trust 2002–; Fellow British Computer Soc. 1990, Chartered Inst. of Marketing 1990; Freeman, City of London 1990, Hon. Citizen, Dallas, TX; Commdr, Order of the Lion (Finland) 1995; Dr hc (Open Univ.) 1997; Hon. DTech (Loughborough) 1988, (Brunel) 1997, (Nottingham) 1998, (Northumbria) 1999, (Royal Holloway) 2001, (Cranfield) 2001, (Essex) 2001; Nat. Electronics Council Mountbatten Medal 1995, Inst. of Man. Gold Medal 1996. *Leisure interests:* music, sailing, skiing. *Address:* PO Box 129, Shepperton, Middlesex, TW17 9WL, England.

BONGARD-LEVIN, Grigory Maximovich; Russian historian; *Chief Researcher, Institute of Oriental Studies, Russian Academy of Sciences;* b. 26 Aug. 1933, Moscow; s. of Maxim Bongard-Levin and Lussy Bongard-Levin; m. Irina Bongard-Levin (deceased) 1956; one s.; ed Moscow State Univ.; Jr, Sr researcher, head of div. Inst. of Oriental Studies, USSR (now Russian) Acad. of Sciences 1956–87, chief researcher 1987–, corresp. mem. 1987, mem. 1990; Ed.-in-Chief Vestnik Drevnei Istorii; mem. Nat. Cttee of History of Russia; head Comm. on Sanskrit Studies at Asscn of Oriental Studies; foreign mem., French Acad. of the Belles-Lettres 1999, foreign mem., Swedish Royal Acad. of History, Literature and Antiquities 2004; Hon. Fellow Royal Asiatic Soc., London 1997; Chevalier, Ordre des Arts et des Lettres (France), Chevalier, Légion d'honneur; Dr hc (Sarnath Tibetan Inst.) 1991; Nehru Prize 1975, Asiatic Soc. of Bengal gold medal 1979; USSR State Prize 1988, Int. Prize of St Mark, Venice 1990, Russian Govt Prize 2001, Int. Prize Sicily Italy 2002, Triumph Prize 2003. *Publications:* works on culture and ethnogenesis of peoples of Asia, of old civilizations of Orient and West, including books Ancient India 1969, India of the Epoch of Mauryas 1974, Ancient Indian Civilization 1980, From India to Scythia 1983, India in Ancient Times, Indian Texts from Central Asia (three vols) 1985–2004, Scythian Novel 1997, Parthian Shot 2003, India 2004. *Leisure interests:* paintings, literature, antique furniture. *Address:* Institute of Oriental Studies, Rozhdestvenka 12, 103777 Moscow (office); Leninsky Prospekt 2, R. 1503, VDI, 117334 Moscow, Russia (home). *Telephone:* (495) 938-52-28 (office); (495) 245-46-96 (home). *Fax:* (495) 938-19-12 (office). *E-mail:* vdi@igh.ras.ru (office).

BONGO, Martin; Gabonese politician; b. 4 July 1940, Lekei; ed Ecole Normale de Mitzic; fmrly school dir in Franceville, then Insp. for Primary Instruction for Upper-Ogooué Region; fmr Dir of Cabinet to the Vice-Pres.; Deputy Dir of Cabinet to the Pres. 1968–69; Commr-Gen. for Information April–Dec. 1969; Sec. of State to the Presidency, for Penitentiary Services 1969–70, for Nat. Educ. in charge of Special Missions 1970–72, Head of State's Personal Rep. 1972–73; Minister of Educ. and Scientific Research 1973–75, of Nat. Educ. 1975–76, of Foreign Affairs and Co-operation 1976–81, of State for Foreign Affairs and Co-operation 1981–89; Commdr Order of the Equatorial Star, Grand Officer, Nat. Order of Merit (Mauritania), Grand Officer, Order of Merit (Italy), Commdr Ordre nat. du Mérite. *Address:* c/o Ministère des Affaires Etrangères et de la Coopération, Libreville, Gabon.

BONGO ONDIMBA, Ali; Gabonese politician; *Minister of National Defence;* b. 9 Feb. 1959, Brazzaville, Repub. of Congo; s. of Omar Bongo and Patience Dabany; Foreign Minister in 1989–91 (resgnd); mem. Parl. (Parti démocratique gabonais) 1998–2003; Minister of Nat. Defence 1999–. *Address:* Ministry of National Defence, BP 13493, Libreville, Gabon (office). *Telephone:* 77-86-96 (office).

BONGO ONDIMBA, El Hadj Omar (Albert-Bernard); Gabonese politician and head of state; *President;* b. 30 Dec. 1935, Lewai, Franceville; m.; three c.; ed primary school at Bacongo (Congo–Brazzaville) and technical coll., Brazzaville; civil servant; served in Air Force 1958–60; entered Ministry of Foreign Affairs 1960; Dir of Private Office of Pres. Léon Mba 1962, in charge of Information 1963–64, Nat. Defence 1964–65; Minister-Del. to Presidency in charge of Nat. Defence and Co-ordination, Information and Tourism 1965–66; Vice-Pres. of Govt, in charge of Co-ordination, Nat. Defence Planning, Information and Tourism 1966–67; Vice-Pres. of Gabon March–Nov. 1967, Pres. 1967–, Minister of Defence 1967–81, of Information 1967–80, of Planning 1967–77, Prime Minister 1967–75, Minister of the Interior 1967–70, of Devt 1970–77, of Women's Affairs 1976–77 and numerous other portfolios; Pres. UDEAC 1981; Founder and Sec.-Gen. Parti Démocratique Gabonais 1968; High Chancellor, Ordre Nat. de l'Etoile Equatoriale; decorations from the Ivory Coast, Niger, Chad, Cameroon, Central African Republic, Mauritius, Togo, Taiwan, Zaïre, France, UK and Guinea. *Address:* Présidence de la République, Boîte Postale 546, Libreville, Gabon (office).

BONHAM CARTER, Helena; British actress; b. 26 May 1966; d. of the late Hon. Raymond Bonham Carter and of Elena Bonham Carter; (great grand-daughter of British Prime Minister Lord Asquith); pnr Tim Burton; one s. one d. *Plays include:* The Barber of Seville 1992, Trelawny of the "Wells" 1992. *Films include:* Lady Jane, A Room with a View, Maurice, Francesco, The Mask, Getting it Right, Hamlet, Where Angels Fear to Tread, Howard's End 1991, Mary Shelley's Frankenstein 1994, The Glace Bay Miners' Museum 1994, A Little Loving 1995, Mighty Aphrodite 1995, Twelfth Night 1996, Margaret's Museum 1996, Parti Chinois 1996, The Theory of Flight 1997, Keep the Aspidistra Flying 1997, The Wings of the Dove 1998, The Revengers' Comedies 1998, Women Talking Dirty 1999, Fight Club 1999, Until Human Voices Wake Us 2000, Planet of the Apes 2001, The Heart of Me 2002, Novocaine 2002, Till Human Voices Wake Us 2003, Big Fish 2003, Charlie and the Chocolate Factory 2005, Corpse Bride (voice) 2005, Conversations with Other Women 2005, Wallace & Gromit in the Curse of the Were-rabbit (voice) 2005, Sixty Six 2006, Harry Potter and the Order of the Phoenix 2007, Sweeney Todd 2007. *Television appearances include:* A Pattern of Roses, Miami Vice, A Hazard of Hearts, The Vision, Arms and the Man, Beatrix Potter, A Dark Adapted Eye, Live from Baghdad 2002, Henry VIII 2003. *Address:* c/o Conway van Gelder Limited, 18/21 Jermyn Street, London, SW1Y 6HP, England. *Telephone:* (20) 7287-0077.

BONHOEFFER, Tobias, PhD; German/American neurobiologist; *Director, Max Planck Institute of Neurobiology;* b. 9 Jan. 1960, Berkeley, Calif., USA; ed Max Planck Inst. for Biological Cybernetics, Tübingen; Rockefeller Univ., New York, USA 1989–90; Max Planck Inst. for Brain Research, Frankfurt 1991–93, Max Planck Inst. of Psychiatry, Martinsried nr Munich 1993–98, Dir and Scientific Mem., Max Planck Inst. of Neurobiology 1998–; Assoc. Neuroscience Research Program, Neuroscience Inst.; mem. Soc. for Neuroscience (USA), German Neuroscience Soc., Faculty 1000, Academia Europaea, EMBO; Attempto Prize for Young Neuroscientists, Tübingen Univ., Ernst Jung Prize 2004. *Publications:* numerous articles on visual system, cerebral cortex devt, neuronal plasticity and optical imaging. *Address:* Max Planck Institute of Neurobiology, Am Klopferspitz 18, 82152 Munich -Martinsried, Germany (office). *Telephone:* (89) 8578-3751 (office). *Fax:* (89) 8578-2481 (office). *E-mail:* tobias.bonhoeffer@neuro.mpg.de (office). *Website:* www.neuro.mpg.de (office).

BONI, Yayi, PhD; Benin economist, banker and head of state; *President;* b. 1952, Tchaourou; m.; five c.; ed Nat. Univ. of Benin, Univ. of Dakar, Senegal, Univ. of Orleans and Paris Univ., France; worked for Cen. Bank of the States of West Africa (BCEAO) becoming Deputy Dir 1980–88; Deputy Dir for Professional Devt, West African Centre for Banking Studies, Dakar 1988; worked in office of Pres. of Benin in charge of monetary and banking policies 1992–94; Pres. West African Devt Bank 1994–2006; Pres. of Benin 2006–; Chevalier de l'Ordre national de Mérite (France), Officier de l'Ordre National

www.worldwhoswho.com

(Burkina Faso), Commdr, Ordre National of Benin, of Mali, of Niger, of Senegal. *Address:* Office of the President, BP 1288, Cotonou, Benin (office). *Telephone:* 21-30-00-90 (office). *Fax:* 21-30-06-36 (office). *Website:* www.gouv.bj (office).

BONILLA, Manuel Acosta; Honduran diplomatist and lawyer; b. 13 Jan. 1929, El Progreso, Yoro; Dr Isidoro Acosta, Prof. Adela Bonilla de Acosta; m. Dr Anna Lucia Marchetti de Acosta; four c.; ed Universidad Autónoma de Mexico, Universidad Autónoma de Honduras; Head Int. Relations, Civil Aviation Authority 1953–54; Dir Gen. Welfare, Legal Adviser, Ministry Labour and Social Security 1954–56; Chair. Nat. Electoral Council 1964–65; Minister of Econ. Affairs and Finance 1965–71; Minister of Finance and Public Credit 1972–75; Minister and Adviser, Pres. and Nat. Coordinator, State Modernization Programme 1990–94; mem. Cen. American Parl. 1991, First Vice-Chair., Chair., Human Rights Cttee; Perm. Rep. to UN, New York 2002–06; Deputy Chair. Fundación Iras Ulargui (youth scholarship and children's home); mem. Nat. Law Acad. *Publications:* numerous articles, chapters, and co-authored works. *Address:* c/o Ministry of Foreign Affairs, Centro Cívico Gubernamental, Antigua Casa Presidencial, Blvd Kuwait, Contiguo a la Corte Suprema de Justicia, Tegucigalpa, Honduras.

BONIN, Bernard, DenSc(Econ), FRSC; Canadian economist; *President, Association des Économistes Québécois;* b. 29 Sept. 1936, Joliette; s. of Georges Bonin and Thérèse Racette; m. Andrée Gregoire 1960; one s. one d.; ed Ecole des Hautes Etudes Commerciales, Montreal and Univ. of Paris; Prof. of Econs, Ecole des Hautes Etudes Commerciales, Montreal 1962–74; Asst Deputy Minister for Immigration, Govt of Québec 1974–77, for Intergovernmental Affairs 1977–81; Prof. of Econs, Ecole Nat. d'Admin Publique, Montreal 1979–88; Deputy Gov. Bank of Canada 1988–94, Sr Deputy Gov. 1994–99; currently Pres. Asscn des Économistes Québécois, Université de Montréal. *Publications:* L'investissement étranger à long terme au Canada 1967, A propos de l'association économique Canada-Québec 1980, L'entreprise multinationale et l'état 1984, Innovation industrielle et analyse économique 1988. *Leisure interests:* music, reading, sport. *Address:* Association des Économistes Québécois, CP 6128, succursale Centre-Ville, Montréal, Québec, H3C 3J7, Canada (office). *Telephone:* (514) 342–7537. *Fax:* (514) 342–3967. *E-mail:* national@asdeq.org. *Website:* www.asdeq.org.

BONINGTON, Sir Christian John Storey (Chris), CBE; British mountaineer, writer and photographer; *Chancellor, University of Lancaster;* b. 6 Aug. 1934, Hampstead, London; s. of the late Charles Bonington and Helen Anne Bonington (née Storey); m. Muriel Wendy Marchant 1962; three s. (one s. deceased); ed Univ. Coll. School, Hampstead, Royal Mil. Acad., Sandhurst; commissioned in Royal Tank Regt 1956–59; Instructor Army Outward Bound School 1959–61; man. trainee Unilever 1961–62; writer and photographer 1962–; Vice-Pres. Army Mountaineering Asscn 1980–; Pres. LEPRA 1985–, British Orienteering Fed. 1986– (now Hon. Pres.), British Mountaineering Council 1988–91 (Vice-Pres. 1976–79, 1985–88, now Patron), Council for Nat. Parks 1992–2000, The Alpine Club 1995–99, Chair. (non-exec.) Berghaus 1998–; Chair. Mountain Heritage Trust 2000–; Chancellor Univ. of Lancaster 2005–; 19 expeditions to the Himalayas, including four to Mount Everest and first ascent of south face of Annapurna 1970, British Everest Expedition 1972, Brammah, Himalayas 1973, Changabang, Himalayas 1974, British Everest Expedition (first ascent, SW Face) 1975, Mount Vinson, Antarctica 1983, Panch chuli II, Himalayas (first ascent, W Ridge) 1992, Maslin, Greenland (first ascent) 1993, Rangrik Rang, India (first ascent) 1994, Drangnag-Ri, Nepal (first ascent) 1995, Danga II 2000; reached Everest summit 1985; motivational/after-dinner speaker; Hon. Fellow, UMIST, Lancs. Polytechnic; Hon. Pres. Hiking Club; Hon. MA (Salford); Hon. DSc (Sheffield) 1976, (Lancaster) 1983; Hon. DCL (Northumbria) 1996; Hon. DUniv (Sheffield Hallam) 1998; Hon. DLitt (Bradford) 2002; Founders Medal, Royal Geographical Soc. 1971, Lawrence of Arabia Medal 1986, Livingstone Medal 1991, David Livingstone Medal, Royal Scottish Geographical Soc. 1991. *Publications include:* I Chose to Climb (autobiog.) 1966, Annapurna South Face 1970, The Next Horizon (autobiog.) 1973, Everest South West Face 1973, Changabang 1974, Everest the Hard Way 1976, Quest for Adventure 1981, Kongur: China's Elusive Summit 1982, Everest: The Unclimbed Ridge (with Dr Charles Clarke) 1983, The Everest Years 1986, Mountaineer 1989, The Climbers 1992, Sea, Ice and Rock (with Robin Knox-Johnston) 1992, Great Climbs (co-ed. with Audrey Salkeld) 1994, Tibet's Secret Mountain –The Triumph of Sepu Kangri (with Dr Charles Clarke) 1999, Boundless Horizons 2000, Chris Bonington's Everest 2002, Mountaineer – Thirty Years of Climbing on the World's Great Peaks 2007. *Leisure interests:* mountaineering, orienteering. *Address:* Badger Hill, Hesket Newmarket, Wigton, Cumbria, CA7 8LA, England. *Telephone:* (16974) 78286. *Fax:* (16974) 78238. *E-mail:* chris@bonington.com. *Website:* www.bonington.com.

BONINO, Emma, PhD; Italian politician; *Vice President, Senate;* b. 9 March 1948, Bra, Turin; ed Bocconi Univ., Milan; mem. Camera dei Deputati (Chamber of Deputies) 1976–1983, re-elected 1986, 1992, 1994, 2006; Pres. Parl. Group, Radical Party 1981; mem. European Parl. 1979–2006; Founder, Centro Informazione Sterilizzazione e Aborto 1975, No Peace without Justice; Pres. Transnat. Radical Party 1991–93, Sec. 1993–94; EC Commr for Consumer Policy, EC Humanitarian Office and Fisheries 1995–99; Leader, Rosa nel Pungo party; cand. in presidential elections 1999; presented own list in general elections 2001; mem. Bd of Dirs Int. Crisis Group; Distinguished Visiting Prof., American Univ. of Cairo; Minister for EU Policies 2006–08; Vice-Pres. Senate 2008–; Gran Cruz de la Orden de Mayo (Argentina) 1995, Order of the Prince Branimir (Croatia) 2002; European Personality of the Year 1996, European Communicator of the Year 1997, Premio Principe de Asturias (Spain) 1998, Gonfalone d'Argento Award 2002, Premio Presidente della Repubblica 2003, Premio Campione 2003, Prix Femmes d'Europe 2004, Open Soc. Prize 2004, Premio Galileo 2005. *Leisure interests:* sailing, diving. *Address:* Senate, Piazza Madama, 00186 Rome (office); Radicali Italiani, Via di Torre Argentina 76, 00186 Rome, Italy (office). *Telephone:* (06) 67061 (office); (06) 689791 (office). *Fax:* (06) 68805396 (office). *E-mail:* bonino_e@posta.senato.it (office); segreteria.roma@radicali.it (office). *Website:* www.senato.it (home); www.radicali.it (office).

BONNAIRE, Sandrine; French film actress; b. 31 May 1967, Gannat, Auvergne; m. Guillaume Laurant 2003; two d.; film debut in La Boum 1980; Chevalier des Art et Lettres; Venice Film Festival Award 1995, Grand prix nat. du cinéma, Ministry of Culture 1987, Cesar Award 1983, Best Actress Award 1986. *Plays include:* The Good Person of Sechuan 1989. *Films include:* A Nos Amours (César Award 1983) 1983, Le Meilleur de la Vie 1983, Vagabond (Best Actress Award 1986) 1985, La Puritaine 1986, Sous le Soleil de Satan 1987, Jaune Revolver 1987, Monsieur Hire 1989, Dans la Soinée 1990, Joan of Arc 1992, La Cérémonie 1995, Judgment in Stone, Circle of Passion 1996, Secret défense 1998, The Colour of Lies 1999, East–West 2000, Mademoiselle 2001, Femme fatale 2002, C'est la vie 2002, Confidences trop intimes 2003, L'equipier 2003, Le Cou de la Girafe 2003, Quelques jours avec moi, Des innocents a l'Echine, Peaux de vaches, Le ciel de Paris, L'Équipier 2004, Je crois que je l'aime 2007, Demandez la permission aux enfants 2007, Elle s'appelle Sabine 2007 (dir). *Television includes:* Une femme en blanc 1996, La maison des enfants 2002, Le Procès de Bobigny 2006. *Publications:* Elle s'appelle Sabine 2007. *Address:* c/o Intertalent, 5 rue Clément Marot, 75008 Paris, France (office). *Telephone:* 1-47-23-40-00.

BONNEFOY, Yves Jean, LèsL; French writer and poet; b. 24 June 1923, Tours; s. of Elie Bonnefoy and Hélène Maury; m. Lucille Vines 1968; one d.; ed Lycée Descartes, Tours, Faculté des Sciences, Poitiers and Faculté des Lettres, Paris; Prof. Collège de France 1981; contrib. to Mercure de France, Critique, Encounter, L'Ephémère, La Nouvelle Revue Française etc.; has travelled in Europe, Asia and N America; lectures or seminars at Brandeis, Johns Hopkins, Princeton, Williams Coll., Calif., Geneva, Nice, Yale, CUNY, NY and other univs; Commdr des Arts et des Lettres; Hon. DHumLitt (American Coll., Paris, Univ. of Chicago, Univ. of Neuchâtel, Trinity Coll., Dublin, Rome, Edin., Siena); Prix Montaigne 1980, Grand Prix de poésie (Acad. Française) 1981, Prix Florence Gould 1987, Grand Prix national 1993, Prix de la Fondation Cino-del-Duca 1995, Prix Balzan 1995, Prix Prince Louis de Polignac 1998, American Acad. of Arts and Letters Award, Franz Kafka Prize 2007, and numerous other prizes. *Publications:* poems: Du mouvement et de l'immobilité de Douve 1953 (English 1968), Hier régnant désert 1958, Pierre écrite 1964 (English 1976), Selected Poems 1968, Dans le leurre du seuil 1975, Poèmes (1947–1975) 1978, Ce qui fut sans lumière 1987, Entretiens sur la Poesie 1990, Début et fin de la neige 1991, Les planches courbes 2001; essays: L'Improbable 1959, Arthur Rimbaud 1961 (English trans. 1973), Un rêve fait à Mantoue 1967, Le nuage rouge 1977, Rue traversière 1977; on art: Peintures murales de la France Gothique 1954, Miró 1963, Rome 1630 1969, L'Arrière-Pays 1972, Entretiens sur la poésie 1981, La Présence et l'Image 1983, Récits en rêve 1987, La Vérité de Parole 1988, Alberto Giacometti 1991, La vie errante 1993, Remarques sur le dessin 1993, Dessin, couleur et lumière 1995, Théâtre et poésie: Shakespeare et Yeats, l'Encore aveugle 1998, Zao-Wou-ki (jtly) 1998, Lieux et destins de l'image 1999, La Communauté des traducteurs 2000, Baudelaire: Le Tentation de l'oubli 2000, Keats et Léopardi 2000, Sous l'Horizon du Langage 2001, Remarques sur le regard 2001, Breton à l'avant de soi 2001, Poésie et architecture 2001, L'Enseignement de Léopardi 2001, Le poète et le flot mouvant des multitudes 2003, Le sommeil de personne 2004, La stratégie de l'énigme 2006, L'imaginaire métaphysique 2006, Goya: les peintures noires 2006, Dans un débris de miroir 2006; co-ed. L'Ephémère, trans. of Shakespeare, W. B. Yeats, Keats, Léopardi. *Address:* Collège de France, 11 place Marcelin Berthelot, 75005 Paris, France. *E-mail:* yves.bonnefoy@college-de-france.fr (office).

BONNELAME, Emile Patrick Jérémie; Seychelles politician and diplomatist; b. 24 Oct. 1938, Mahe; ed Inst. Catholique de Paris, Inst. Ecuménique pour les Développement des Peuples, Paris, France, Sion School of Theology, Lucerne School of Theology, Switzerland, Univ. of Québec in Montréal, Canada; teacher, Modern Secondary School of Seychelles 1967–75; Dir-Gen. of Information 1978–79; Prin.-Sec., Ministry of Educ. 1979–80, of External Relations 1981–83, of Educ. and Information 1983–86; Minister of Manpower 1986–88, of Transport 1988–89, of Agric. and Fisheries 1989–93, of Foreign Affairs 1997; Sec.-Gen. Indian Ocean Comm. 1993–97; Perm. Rep. to UN, New York 1997–2007, Amb. to USA 2005–07; Ed.-in-Chief L'Echo des Iles; Pres. Ministerial Council, Tuna Asscn; Co-ordinator Western Indian Ocean Tuna Org. (WIOTO); Gov. Int. Fund for Agricultural Devt; Head of Del. of Seychelles to numerous int. meetings of UN, OAU, ECA, FAO, UNESCO, EU, UNDP. *Leisure interests:* reading, fishing. *Address:* Ministry of Foreign Affairs, Maison Queau de Quincy, PO Box 656, Mont Fleuri, Seychelles (office). *Telephone:* 283500 (office). *Fax:* 225398 (office). *E-mail:* dazemia@mfa.gov.sc (office). *Website:* seychelles.diplomacy.edu (office).

BONNEMAIN, François; French broadcasting executive and fmr journalist; *CEO, TV5 Monde;* b. 9 Oct. 1942; s. of Georges Bonnemain and Renée Charpentier; ed Centre de formation des journalistes de Paris; with Associated Press (AP), Agence France-Presse (AFP), then France-Soir; joined TF 1 TV channel, in charge of political news 1972; Ed. in Chief TF 1 1977; apptd Ed. FR 3 TV channel 1981; Dir News and Current Affairs, France-Inter 1982; Political Ed. Hebdo (weekly magazine); Tech. Adviser to Prime Minister (Jacques Chirac (q.v.)) on Audiovisual Information 1986–88, to Mayor of Paris (Chirac) 1988–94; Man. Dir Radio-Télévision française d'outre-mer (RFO) 1994–95; mem. Conseil Supérieur de l'audiovisuel (CSA) 1996–99; Dir Chaîne Parl.-Sénat 2000–; Dir Human Resources, France Télévision 2000–02; Adviser

www.worldwhoswho.com

to Prime Minister Jean-Pierre Raffarin 2004–5; CEO TV5 Monde 2006–. *Leisure interest:* fine cuisine. *Address:* TV5 Monde, Avenue de Wagram, 75017 Paris (office); Chaîne Parlementaire-Sénat, 15 rue de Vaugirard, 75291 Paris Cedex 06, France (home). *Website:* www.tv5.org (office).

BONNER, Elena Georgievna; Russian human rights activist and writer; b. 25 Feb. 1923, Turkmenistan; m. 2nd Andrei Sakharov 1972 (died 1989); one s. one d.; ed First Leningrad Medical Inst.; active as nurse 1941–45; partially blinded; Lt 1945; doctor 1953–83; f. Moscow group to monitor observation of 1975 Helsinki accords; regular visitor to Sakharov during latter's exile in Gorky 1980–84; sentenced to five years' exile 1984, released 1986; political activist after husband's death; Chair. Comm. for perpetuation of Andrei Sakharov's memory; numerous hon. doctorates; Rafto Prize for Freedom of the Press 1993, Laureat prize, Raoul Wallenberg Int. Fund. *Publications:* Alone Together (memoirs) 1986, A Book on Exile to Gorky 1988, Mothers and Daughters (memoir) 1991. *Address:* A. D. Sakharova Museum, 107120 Moscow, Zemlyanoy val 57, Bldg 6, Russia.

BONNER, Gerald, MA, FSA; British academic (retd); *Reader Emeritus, University of Durham;* b. 18 June 1926, London; s. of Frederick J. Bonner and Constance E. Hatch; m. Priscilla J. Hodgson 1967; one s. one d.; ed The Stationers' Co.'s School, London and Wadham Coll. Oxford; mil. service 1944–48; Asst Keeper, Dept of Manuscripts, British Museum 1953–64; Lecturer in Theology, Univ. of Durham 1964, promoted to personal Readership 1969, Reader Emer. 1989–; Convener and Sec. Bedan Conf. Durham 1973; Distinguished Prof. of Early Christian Studies, Catholic Univ. of America 1991–94; delivered Cathedral Lecture, Durham 1970, Augustine Lecture, Villanova Univ. Pa, 1970, Otts Lectures, Davidson Coll., NC 1992; Visiting Prof. in Augustinian Studies, Villanova Univ. 1999; Johannes Quasten Medal 1994. *Publications:* The Warfare of Christ 1962, St Augustine of Hippo: Life and Controversies 1963, Famulus Christi: Essays in Commemoration of the Thirteenth Centenary of the Venerable Bede (ed.) 1976, God's Decree and Man's Destiny 1987, St Cuthbert, His Cult and His Community (ed. with D. Rollason and C. Stancliffe), Church and Faith in the Patristic Tradition: Augustine, Pelagianism and Early Christian Northumbria 1996, Augustine of Hippo: The Monastic Rules 2004, Freedom and Necessity: St Augustine's Teaching on Divine Power and Human Freedom 2007; articles in the Augustinus-Lexikon (Basle) 1986– and other learned journals. *Leisure interests:* reading, antiquarianism, (moderate) wine-drinking and any sort of history. *Address:* 7 Victoria Terrace, Durham, DH1 4RW, England (home). *Telephone:* (191) 386-3407.

BONNER, John Tyler, PhD; American biologist and academic; *George M. Moffett Professor Emeritus, Department of Ecology and Evolutionary Biology, Princeton University;* b. 12 May 1920, New York; s. of Paul Hyde Bonner and Lilly Marguerite Stehli; m. Ruth Ann Graham 1942 (deceased); three s. one d.; ed Harvard Univ.; US Air Corps 1942–46; Asst Prof., then Prof., Princeton Univ., NJ 1947–58, George M. Moffett Prof. 1966–90, George M. Moffett Prof. Emer. 1990–, Chair. Dept of Biology 1965–77, 1983–84, 1987–88; Bernard Visiting Prof., Williams Coll. 1989; Raman Visiting Prof., Indian Acad. of Sciences 1990; Sheldon Travelling Fellow, Panama, Cuba 1941; Rockefeller Travelling Fellow, Paris 1953; Guggenheim Fellow, Edin. 1958, 1971–72; NSF Sr Postdoctoral Fellow, Univ. of Cambridge 1963; Commonwealth Foundation Book Fund Fellow, Edin. 1971, 1984–85; Josiah Macy Jr Foundation Book Fund Fellow, Edin. 1978; Fellow, American Acad. of Arts and Sciences; mem. American Philosophical Soc., NAS; mem. Oxford Surveys in Evolutionary Biology 1982–93; fmr mem. Editorial Bd American Naturalist, American Scientist and other publs; Hon. Fellow, Indian Acad. of Sciences 1992; Hon. DSc (Middlebury Coll.) 1970, (Princeton Univ.) 2006; Hon. LLD (Concordia Univ.) 2003; Hon. DLitt (Univ. Coll. of Cape Breton) 2004. *Achievement:* pioneer in use of cellular slime moulds to understand evolution and devt. *Television:* Professor Bonner and the Slime Moulds (BBC Horizon programme) 1984. *Publications:* Morphogenesis: An Essay on Development 1952, Cells and Societies 1955, The Evolution of Development 1958, The Cellular Slime Molds 1959, The Ideas of Biology 1962 (several edns in trans.), Size and Cycle 1965, The Scale of Nature 1969, On Development: The Biology of Form 1974, The Evolution of Culture in Animals 1980 (several edns in trans.), On Size and Life 1983, The Evolution of Complexity 1988, Life Cycles 1993, Sixty Years of Biology: Essays on Evolution and Development 1996, First Signals: The Evolution of Multicellular Development 2000, Lives of a Biologist: Adventures in a Century of Extraordinary Science (ForeWord Magazine Book of the Year Award 2002) 2002, Why Size Matters 2006, The Social Amoebae: The Biology of the Cellular Slime Molds 2009; Ed. abridged edn of Growth and Form (D'Arcy Thompson) 1961; more than 230 articles and book reviews. *Leisure interests:* fishing, walking. *Address:* Department of Ecology and Evolutionary Biology, 305 Guyot Hall, Princeton University, Princeton, NJ 08544 (office); 52A Patton Avenue, Princeton, NJ 08540, USA (home). *Telephone:* (609) 258-3841 (office); (609) 924-1255 (home). *Fax:* (609) 258-1712 (office); (609) 258-7892 (office). *E-mail:* jtbonner@princeton.edu (office). *Website:* www.eeb.princeton.edu/FACULTY/Bonner/Bonner.html (office).

BONNER, Paul Max, OBE, FRTS; British television executive (retd); b. 30 Nov. 1934, Banstead, Surrey; s. of Frank Bonner and Jill Bonner; m. Jenifer Hubbard 1956; two s. one d.; ed Felsted School; with Longmans Green & Co., Publrs 1952; trainee reporter, Southend Standard 1953; Nat. Service 1953–55; Asst Press Officer, E. K. Cole Ltd 1955; freelance work for Evening Standard 1955; Trainee Studio Asst, BBC, Bristol 1955–56, Studio Man. 1956–58, Acting Asst Producer, Talks Dept, West Region 1958–59, Production Asst, Talks Dept, TV 1961–65, Sr Producer, Travel and Features Programmes 1965–74, Ed. BBC Community Programmes 1974–77, Special Asst to Controller BBC2 1977, Chair. Small Integrated Multi-Role Production Unit Study Group 1977, Head of Science and Features Dept, TV 1978–81; Channel Controller, Channel Four TV Co. Ltd 1981–83, Controller of Programmes and Exec. Dir 1983–87; Dir of Programme Planning Secr. ITV Asscn 1987–92, Dir ITV Network Centre Secr. 1993–94; Dir House of Commons Broadcasting Unit Ltd 1989–94; Chair. Edin. TV Festival 1979; a Man., Royal Inst. 1982–85; Gov. of Nat. Film and TV School 1981–88; Bd mem. Broadcasting Support Services 1981–93; Chair. Media Group, Cttee on Public Understanding of Science 1981–93. *Television documentaries include:* Climb up to Hell 1967, The Search for the Real Che Guevara 1971, Who Sank the Lusitania? 1972. *Publications:* The Third Age of Broadcasting 1983, Ind. TV in Britain (Vol. 5: ITV and IBA 1981–92) 1998, (Vol. 6: C4, TV-am, Cable & Satellite 1981–92) 2002. *Leisure interests:* photography, music. *Address:* 5 North View, Wimbledon Common, London, SW19 4UJ, England. *Telephone:* (20) 8947-6635.

BONNET, Christian, DenD; French politician and business executive; b. 14 June 1921, Paris; s. of Pierre Bonnet and Suzanne Delebecque; m. Christiane Mertian 1943 (died 1999); five c. (one s. deceased); ed Univ. of Paris and Ecole des sciences politiques; Pres. Les Grandes Marques de la conserve 1952–61, Del. Conseil supérieur de la conserve; MRP Deputy for Morbihan 1956–58; Deputy for the second constituency of Morbihan 1956–83; Gen. Councillor, Belle-Ile 1958–2001; Mayor of Carnac 1964; fmr Sec.-Gen. Républicains Indépendants; Chair. Cttee on the Merchant Marine budget; Pres. Supervisory Council, Caisse des dépots et consignations; Sec. of State for Supply, Housing and Territorial Devt 1972–74; Minister of Agric. 1974–77, of the Interior 1977–81; Senator for Morbihan 1983–2001. *Address:* 56340 Carnac, France (home).

BONNEY, Barbara; American singer (soprano); b. 14 April 1956, Montclair, NJ; d. of Alfred Bonney III and Janet Gates; m. 1st Håkan Hagegård 1989; m. 2nd Maurice Whittaker; ed Univ. of New Hampshire and Mozarteum, Salzburg; chorus mem. Darmstadt City Opera 1979–83; with Frankfurt Opera 1983–84; maj. early appearances include Der Rosenkavalier, Covent Garden 1984, Metropolitan Opera, New York 1990, Die Zauberflöte, La Scala 1985, Falstaff, Metropolitan Opera 1990, The Marriage of Figaro, Covent Garden 1995, Zurich Opera, Metropolitan Opera 1998, 1999, Les Boréades, Salzburg Festival 1999, Idomeneo, San Francisco 1999; noted especially for Mozart and Strauss interpretations; appeared regularly as recitalist accompanied by Geoffrey Parsons; Visiting Prof., RAM; mem. Swedish Acad. of Music; Dr hc (New Hampshire), (Bowdoin Coll.), (Royal Acad. of Music). *Recordings include:* Le Nozze di Figaro, Don Giovanni, Die Zauberflöte, Die Fledermaus, Fidelio, Hansel und Gretel, The Merry Widow, Vocalise, Miss Sallie Chisum Remembers Billy The Kid, Emily Dickinson Songs, Samuel Barber's Hermit Songs, Six Elizabethan Songs, Frauenliebe und-leben, Les mamelles de Tirésias, Diamonds in the Snow (Gramophone Award for Best Solo Vocal Recording), While I Dream. *Leisure interests:* textiles, interior decorating, calligraphy. *Address:* Michael Storrs Music Ltd., 11 Maiden Lane, London, WC2E 7NA, England (office). *Telephone:* (20) 7078-1440 (office). *Fax:* (20) 7078-1456 (office). *E-mail:* info@michaelstorrsmusic.co.uk (office). *Website:* www.michaelstorrsmusic.co.uk (office).

BONNICI, Carmelo Mifsud (see Mifsud Bonnici, Carmelo).

BONNICI, Josef, MA, PhD; Maltese economist and fmr politician; *Member, European Court of Auditors;* b. 15 April 1953, Birzebbuga; m. Rita Oliva; two c.; ed Univ. of Malta and Simon Fraser Univ., Canada; Sr Lecturer in Econs, Deakin Univ., Australia 1980–88; Visiting Prof., Univ. of Malta 1988, Prof. of Econs 1988–2004; Econ. Adviser to Prime Minister 1988–92; appointed adviser to Council of Europe in Co-ordinated Social Research Programme 1992; mem. Parl. 1992–2004; Parl. Sec. Ministry of Finance 1993–95; Minister of Econ. Services 1995–96; Shadow Minister and Opposition Spokesman for Econ. Devt 1996–98; Minister for Econ. Services 1998–2003; mem. European Court of Auditors 2004–, responsible for Court's Statement of Assurance DAS, CEAD Group 2006–, Dean CEAD Group 2008–; mem. Del. to OSCE, to Council of Europe, Jt Malta EU Parl. Cttee; mem. Nat. Comm. for Higher Educ. in Malta 2006–; mem. Nationalist Party; Dr hc (Rikkyo) 1996. *Publications:* Macroeconomics 1992; articles on econs in Malta and in professional econ. journals. *Address:* European Court of Auditors, 12, rue Alcide De Gasperi, 1615 Luxembourg Ville, Luxembourg (office). *Telephone:* 4398-47231 (office). *Fax:* 4398-46233 (office). *E-mail:* jbonnici@waldonet.net.mt (office); josef.bonnici@eca.europa.eu (office). *Website:* eca.europa.eu (office); www.josefbonnici.com (office).

BONNICI, Ugo Mifsud (see Mifsud Bonnici, Ugo).

BONNIN, Didier; French business executive; *CEO, Sergio Rossi, Gucci Group NV;* began career at Arthur Andersen; held several sr positions with Louis Vuitton; CEO Céline Production, Florence –2003; Industrial Dir Bottega Veneta, Gucci Group NV 2003–07, CEO Sergio Rossi 2007–. *Address:* Sergio Rossi, Via Monte Napoleone, 20121 Milan, Italy (office). *Telephone:* (02) 7632081 (office). *Fax:* (02) 76320833 (office). *E-mail:* press.office@sergiorossi.it (office). *Website:* www.sergiorossi.com (office).

BONO; Irish rock singer and songwriter; b. (Paul Hewson), 10 May 1960, Dublin; m. Alison Stewart 1982; ed Mount Temple School; founder mem. and lead singer, the Feedback 1976, renamed the Hype, finally renamed U2 1978–; numerous concerts, including Live Aid Wembley 1985, Self Aid Dublin, A Conspiracy of Hope (Amnesty Int. Tour) 1986, Smile Jamaica (hurricane relief fundraiser) 1988, Very Special Arts Festival, White House, Washington, DC 1988; numerous tours worldwide; Portuguese Order of Liberty 2005, Hon. KBE 2007; Grammy Award for Best Rock Performance by a Duo or Group with Vocal (for Desire) 1988, BRIT Awards for Best Int. Act 1988–90, 1992, 1998, 2001, Best Live Act 1993, Outstanding Contribution to the British Music Industry 2001, JUNO Award 1993, World Music Award 1993, Grammy Award for Song of the Year, Record of the Year, Best Rock Performance by a Duo or Group with Vocal (all for Beautiful Day) 2000, Grammy Awards for Best Pop

Performance by a Duo or Group with Vocal (for Stuck In A Moment You Can't Get Out Of), for Record of the Year (for Walk On), for Best Rock Performance by a Duo or Group with Vocal (for Elevation) 2001, American Music Award for Favorite Internet Artist of the Year 2002, Ivor Novello Award for Best Song Musically and Lyrically (for Walk On) 2002, Golden Globe for Best Original Song (for The Hands That Built America, from film Gangs of New York) 2003, Grammy Awards for Best Rock Performance by a Duo or Group with Vocal, Best Rock Song, Best Short Form Music Video (all for Vertigo) 2004, TED Prize 2004, Nordoff-Robbins Silver Clef Award for lifetime achievement 2005, Q Award for Best Live Act 2005, Digital Music Award for Favourite Download Single (for Vertigo) 2005, Meteor Ireland Music Award for Best Irish Band, Best Live Performance 2006, Grammy Awards for Song of the Year, for Best Rock Performance by a Duo or Group with Vocal (both for Sometimes You Can't Make it on Your Own), for Best Rock Song (for City of Blinding Lights) 2006, Amnesty Int. Ambassadors of Conscience Award 2006, Liberty Medal 2007. *Films:* Rattle and Hum 1988, The Million Dollar Hotel (co-writer) 2000. *Recordings:* albums: Boy 1980, October 1981, War 1983, Under a Blood Red Sky 1983, The Unforgettable Fire 1984, Wide Awake In America 1985, The Joshua Tree (Grammy Award for Album of the Year, Best Rock Performance by a Duo or Group with Vocal) 1987, Rattle and Hum 1988, Achtung Baby (Grammy Award for Best Rock Performance by a Duo or Group with Vocal 1992) 1991, Zooropa (Grammy Award for Best Alternative Music Album) 1993, Passengers (film soundtrack with Brian Eno) 1995, Pop 1997, The Best Of 1980–90 1998, All That You Can't Leave Behind (Grammy Award for Best Rock Album 2001) 2000, The Best Of 1990–2000 2002, How To Dismantle An Atomic Bomb (Meteor Ireland Music Award for Best Irish Album 2006, Grammy Awards for Album of the Year, for Best Rock Album 2006) 2004, No Line on the Horizon 2009. *Address:* Principle Management, 30–32 Sir John Rogersons Quay, Dublin 2, Ireland (office). *E-mail:* candida@numb.ie (office). *Website:* www.u2.com.

BONO MARTÍNEZ, José; Spanish politician; b. 14 Dec. 1950, Salobre; m.; four c.; ed Colegio de la Inmaculada, Alicante, Univ. of Deusto (ICADE); lawyer –1979; fmr Prof. of Political Law, Universidad Complutense de Madrid; Pres. Castilla-La Mancha region 1983–; Minister of Defence 2004–06. *Address:* c/o Ministry of Defence, Paseo de la Castellana 109, 28071 Madrid, Spain (office).

BONYNGE, Richard, AO, CBE; Australian conductor; b. 29 Sept. 1930, Sydney, NSW; s. of C. A. Bonynge; m. Dame Joan Sutherland (q.v.) 1954; one s.; ed NSW Conservatorium of Music, Royal Coll. of Music, London; trained as a pianist; debut as conductor with Santa Cecilia Orchestra, Rome 1962; conducted first opera Faust, Vancouver 1963; Musical Dir Sutherland/Williamson Grand Opera Co., Australia 1965; Artistic Dir Vancouver Opera 1974–77; Musical Dir Australian Opera 1976–86; has conducted La Sonnambula, La Traviata, Faust, Eugene Onegin, L'Elisir d'amore, Orfeo, Semiramide, Giulio Cesare, Lucia di Lammermoor, Norma, The Tales of Hoffmann and many more; has revived many operas not in the repertoire, including Les Huguenots, La Fille du Régiment, Maria Stuarda, Lucrezia Borgia and Thérèse; Hon. Assoc. Accademia Filarmonica di Bologna 2007; Commdr, Ordre Nat. des Arts et des Lettres 1989. *Videos include:* Les Huguenots, La Fille du Régiment, The Merry Widow, Norma, Die Fledermans and The Magic Flute. *Recordings include:* opera: Alcina, La Sonnambula, Norma, Beatrice di Tenda, I Puritani, Faust, Semiramide, Lakmé, La Fille du Régiment, Messiah, Don Giovanni, Les Huguenots, L'Elisir d'amore, Lucia di Lammermoor, Rigoletto, Les Contes d'Hoffmann, Thérèse, Le Toréador, The Land of Smiles and Giuditta, Lucrezia Borgia, Maria Stuarda, Giulio Cesare, Merry Widow, L'Oracolo, Esclarmonde, Le Roi de Lahore, Suor Angelica, Die Fledermaus, Hamlet, I Masnadieri, La Traviata, Il Trovatore; ballet: Le Diable à Quatre, Giselle, Marco Spada, La Péri, Les Sylphides, Coppélia, Sylvia, Le Carillon, La Cigale, Le Papillon, La Boutique Fantastique, Aschenbrödel, The Nutcracker, Sleeping Beauty, Swan Lake, La Sonnambula; recitals: Tchaikovsky and Grieg Piano Concertos, Kalmans Die Herzogin von Chicago, Die Czardasfurstin. *Recordings include:* recordings with Pavarotti, Tebaldi, Sumi Jo, Jerry Hadley, Deborah Riedel, Rosamund Illing, Yvonne Kenny, Cheryl Barker. *Publications:* The Joan Sutherland Album (with Dame Joan Sutherland) 1986, A Collector's Guide to Theatrical Postcards 1988. *Address:* Ingpen & Williams Ltd, 7 St George's Court, 131 Putney Bridge Road, London, SW15 2PA, England (office).

BOOLELL, Arvin, LLM, MB, BCH, BAO, MRCP, MRCS; Mauritian physician and politician; *Minister of Foreign Affairs, Regional Integration and International Trade;* b. 26 May 1953; s. of the late Sir Satcam Boolell; ed Nat. Univ. of Ireland, Royal Coll. of Surgeons, Ireland; fmr medical practitioner; mem. Nat. Ass. 1987–; Minister of Agric. and Nat. Resources 1995–2000, of Agro-Industry and Fisheries 2005–08, of Foreign Affairs, Regional Integration and Int. Trade 2008–. *Address:* Ministry of Foreign Affairs, International Trade and Co-operation, New Government Centre, 5th Floor, Port Louis, Mauritius (office). *Telephone:* 201-1648 (office). *Fax:* 208-8087 (office). *E-mail:* mfa@mail.gov.mu (office). *Website:* foreign.gov.mu (office).

BOON, David Clarence, MBE; Australian fmr professional cricketer; b. 29 Dec. 1960, Launceston; s. of Clarence Leonard Boon and Lesley Mary Boon; m. Philippa Louise Wright 1983; one s. two d.; ed Launceston Church Grammar School; right-hand batsman; teams: Tasmania 1978–79 to 1998–99 (Capt. 1992–93 to 1998–99), Durham, England (Capt.) 1997–99, for Australia played 107 Test matches 1984–96, scoring 7,422 runs (average 43.6) including 21 hundreds and holding 99 catches; toured England 1985, 1989 and 1993; scored more than 23,000 first-class runs (68 hundreds); 181 limited-overs internationals; Marketing Man. Trust Bank Australia 1991–; Marketing and Special Events Co-ordinator 1999; Australian selector 2000–; Patron Road Trauma Support Group, World Vision; Int. Cricketer of the Year 1987–88, Wisden Cricketer of the Year 1994. *Publications:* In the Firing Line (with A. Mark Thomas), Under the Southern Cross (autobiog.) 1996. *Leisure interests:* gardening, golf, music. *Address:* Tasmanian Cricket Association, Bellerive Oval, Bellerive, Tasmania 7018; c/o Australian Cricket Board, 90 Jollimont Street, Vic. 3002, Australia.

BOONSITHI, Chokwatana, PhD; Thai business executive; Chair. Saha Group (consumer goods conglomerate); mem. Advisory Cttee Thai-Japanese Asscn; mem. Bd of Dirs Champ Ace Co. Ltd; Chair. Waseda Education (Thailand) Co. Ltd; Order of the Sacred Treasure, Gold Rays with Neck Ribbon (Govt of Japan) 2002. *Address:* Saha Group, 2156 New Petchburi Road, Bangkapi, Huay Kwang, Bangkok 10320, Thailand (office). *Website:* www.sahagroup.thailand.com (office).

BOORMAN, John, CBE; British film director, producer and screenwriter; b. 18 Jan. 1933; s. of George Boorman and Ivy Boorman (née Chapman); m. 1st Christel Kruse 1956; one s. three d.; m. 2nd Isabella Weibrecht 1994; one s. two d.; ed Salesian Coll., Chertsey; Broadcaster and critic, BBC Radio, also contributor to Manchester Guardian and magazines 1950–54; army service 1951–53; Film Editor, ITN London 1955–58; Dir and Producer Southern TV 1958–60; Head of Documentaries, Bristol, BBC TV; left BBC to work as film director; Chair. Nat. Film Studios of Ireland 1975–85; Gov. British Film Inst. 1983–94, co-f. Merlin Films Group 1989; f. magazine Day by Day; Chevalier de l'Ordre des Arts et Lettres 1985; Best Director Prize, Cannes Festival 1970, 1998; BAFTA Fellowship Award 2004, numerous film awards. *Television:* Dir Citizen 1963, The Newcomers 1960–64. *Films:* Catch us if you Can 1965, Point Blank 1967, Hell in the Pacific 1968, Leo the Last 1969, Deliverance 1970, Zardoz 1973, The Heretic 1976, Excalibur 1981, The Emerald Forest 1985, Hope and Glory 1987 (Golden Globe Award 1988), Where the Heart Is 1989, I Dreamt I Woke Up 1991, Beyond Rangoon 1994, Two Nudes Bathing 1995, The General 1998, The Tailor of Panama 2001, In My Country 2005, The Tiger's Tail 2006. *Publications:* The Legend of Zardoz 1973 (novel), Money into Light 1985, Hope and Glory 1987, Projections 1 1992, Projections 2 1993, Projections 3 1994, Projections $4^1/_2$ (co-ed.) 1995, Projections 5 1996, Projections 6 1997, Projections 7 1997, Projections 8 1998; co-ed. A Year in Film 1993, Adventures of a Suburban Boy (autobiography) 2003. *Leisure interests:* hacking the Wicklow Hills, losing gracefully at tennis, planting trees. *Address:* Merlin Films Group, 16 Upper Pembroke Street, Dublin 2, Ireland. *Telephone:* (1) 6764373. *Fax:* (1) 6764368. *E-mail:* info@merlinfilms.com. *Website:* www.merlinfilms.com.

BOOS, Georgy Valentinovich, CandTechSc; Russian politician; b. 22 Jan. 1963, Moscow; m.; one d.; ed Moscow Energy Inst.; Sr Engineer, All-Union Research Inst. of Light Tech., also teacher of math., secondary school 1986–91; Founder, Dir-Gen., then Pres., Svetoservis Co. 1991–96; mem. State Duma 1996–98; Head, State Taxation Service of Russian Fed. Sept.–Dec. 1998; Minister of Revenue Dec. 1998–May 1999; Head, pre-election staff "Otechestvo-Vsya Rossiya" Movt; mem. State Duma 1999–, re-elected 2003 Yedinaya Rossiya party; Deputy Chair. 2000–; joined Yedinstvo and Otechestvo Union (later Yedibaya Rossiya) 2000–; Pres., Nat. Soc. of Light Tech.; designer of architectural illumination of Moscow 1996; State Prize 1996. *Address:* State Duma, Okhotny Ryad 1, 103265 Moscow, Russia (office). *Telephone:* (495) 292-62-40 (office). *Fax:* (495) 292-80-07 (office).

BOOTH, Cherie, QC, LLD, FRSA; British barrister; *Queen's Counsel, Matrix Chambers;* b. 23 Sept. 1954, Bury, Lancs.; d. of Anthony Booth and Gale Booth (née Smith); m. Anthony Charles Lynton Blair, (Tony Blair (q.v.)) 1980; three s. one d.; ed Seafield Grammar School, Crosby, Liverpool, London School of Econs; called to Bar (Lincoln's Inn) 1976, Asst Recorder 1996–99, Recorder 1999–, Bencher 1999–; pupillage with Alexander Irvine, (now Lord Irvine of Lairg q.v.) 1976–77; Tenant New Court Chambers 1977–91, 4/5 Gray's Inn Square, London 1991–2000, Matrix Chambers 2000–; parl. cand. for Thanet 1983; apptd QC 1995; Gov. London School of Econs 1998–; Chancellor John Moores Univ., Liverpool 1998–, Hon. Fellow; Pres. Comm. of Inquiry into UK Prison and Penal System 2007–; Pres. Barnardo's; Vice-Pres. Kids Club Network, Family Mediators Asscn; Amb., Weston Spirit, London 2012; Patron Refuge, The Citizenship Foundation, CLIC-Sargeant (Cancer Care for Children), Breast Cancer Care 1997–, Islington Music Centre 1999–, Victim Support London, Education for SCOPE, Greater London Fund for the Blind, Home Start Islington, Mary Ward Legal Centre, Noah's Ark, NOJOS Awards, Downside Up, Age Exchange, The Merlyn Trust; Fellow, Int. Soc. of Lawyers for Public Service, Howard League for Penal Reform; Hon. Bencher King's Inn, Dublin 2002; Hon. Fellow, LSE 2003, Open Univ., Inst. of Advanced Legal Studies, Hon. Pres. Plater Coll.; Hon. Patron Genesis Appeal; Hon. DUniv (Open) 1999, Hon. LLD (Westminster), (Liverpool) 2003, Hon. DLitt (UMIST) 2003; ranked by Forbes magazine amongst 100 Most Powerful Women (12th) 2004, (62nd) 2005. *Publications:* The Goldfish Bowl 2004, The Negligence Liabilty of Public Authorities 2005, Speaking For Myself 2008. *Leisure interests:* family, reading, the arts, keeping fit. *Address:* Matrix Chambers, Griffin Building, Gray's Inn, London, WC1R 5LN (office); 29 Connaught Square, London W2 2HL, England (home). *Telephone:* (20) 7404-3447 (office); (20) 7298-0830 (home). *Fax:* (20) 7404-3448 (office). *E-mail:* boothc@matrixlaw.co.uk (office). *Website:* www.matrixlaw.co.uk (office).

BOOTH, Chris; New Zealand sculptor; b. 30 Dec. 1948, Kerikeri, Bay of Islands; m.; two s. one d.; ed Ilam School of Fine Arts, Univ. of Canterbury, Christchurch; undertook specialist sculpture studies with Barbara Hepworth, Denis Mitchell, John Milne and Quinto Ghermandi 1968–70; numerous solo and collective exhbns; represented in public and pvt. collections including Int. Land Art Collections; Frances Hodgkins Fellowship, Univ. of Otago 1982; int. mem. Royal Soc. of British Sculptors 1990–, Int. Sculpture Centre, USA; elected for Art in Motion Biennale, Bos van Ypeij, Netherlands 2003; Christchurch/Seattle Sister City Comm. Award 1996, Greenham Common

Trust Prize 1998, 10th Millfield Int. Sculpture Comm., Somerset 1998, Artists in Industry Project, Vic., Australia 1998–99, Hanover 2000 Expo, Steinbergen, Germany 2000, Kinetic Art Org. Int. Competition, USA 2002. *Major commissions:* Gateway, Albert Park, Auckland 1990, Rainbow Warrior Memorial, Matauri Bay 1990, Tuuram Cairn, Deakin Univ., Warrnambool, Australia 1996, In Celebration of a Tor, Grizedale, Cumbria, UK 1993, Cave, Takahanga Marae, Kaikoura 1996, Wiyung Tchellungnai-Najil, Evandale Sculpture Walk, Gold Coast, Australia 1997, Tranekaer-Vader, Tickon, Langeland, Denmark 1998, Wairau Strata, Seresin Estate, Marlborough 2000, Bukker Tillibul, Swinburne Univ., Lilydale, Melbourne 2001, Waka and Wave (collaboration with Te Warihi Hetaraka), Whangarei District Council, NZ 2003, Kroller-Muller Museum Sculpture Garden, Netherlands 2003–05, Nga Uri O Hinetuparimaunga, Hamilton Gardens Entrance Sculpture (collaboration with Diggeress Te Kanawa), Hamilton City Council, NZ 2004–05, Echo van de Veluwe, Kröller-Müller Museum (Sculpture Park), Otterlo, Netherlands 2004–05, Subterranean Living Sculpture System, Eden Project, Cornwall, UK 2006–, Ciclo, San Miguel de Allende, Mexico 2007–. *Television documentaries include:* When a Warrior Dies 1991, documentary on bombing of Greenpeace ship Rainbow Warrior and the creation of the memorial to the ship and its crew 1995, Sculpture in the Park 1996, 20-minute documentary on Kröller-Müller Museum Sculpture, New in Netherlands, AVRO Television, The Netherlands. *Publications include:* Chris Booth Sculpture 1993, Balanced Stone 1998, Chris Booth: Sculpture in Europe, Australia and New Zealand 2001, Woven Stone: The Sculpture of Chris Booth 2007. *Address:* PO Box 816, Kerikeri, 0245, New Zealand (office). *Telephone:* (9) 407-1331 (home). *Fax:* (9) 401-7413 (office). *E-mail:* chris@chrisbooth.co.nz (office). *Website:* www .chrisbooth.co.nz (office).

BOOTH, Lewis W. K., BEng; British automotive industry executive; *President and CEO, Mazda Motor Corporation;* b. 7 Nov. 1948, Liverpool; ed Liverpool Univ.; joined Ford Motor Co. 1978 as Financial Analysis Coordinator, Product Devt Div., later various man. positions with Ford Europe 1980–1992, Finance Dept, Ford USA 1992–96, Group Man. Dir South Africa Motor Corpn (SAMCOR) 1997–2000; Pres. Ford Asia Pacific, Africa and Tech. Staffs 2000–02; Sr Advisor for Corp. Strategy, Mazda Motor Corpn 2002, Pres. and CEO 2002–. *Address:* Mazda Motor Corporation, Head Office, 3-1 Shinchi, Fucho-cho, Aki-gun, Hiroshima 730-8670, Japan (office). *Telephone:* (82) 282-1111 (office). *Fax:* (82) 287-5190 (office). *Website:* www.mazda.com (office).

BOOTHROYD, Baroness (Life Peer), cr. 2000, of Sandwell in the County of West Midlands; **Rt Hon. Betty Boothroyd,** OM, PC; British parliamentarian; b. 8 Oct. 1929, Dewsbury, Yorks.; d. of Archibald Boothroyd and Mary Boothroyd; ed Dewsbury Coll. of Commerce and Art; sec., Labour Party HQ 1955–60; legis. asst to US congressman, Washington, DC 1960–62; sec. and personal asst to various sr Labour politicians 1962–73; mem. Hammersmith Borough Council 1965–68; contested various elections and by-elections 1957–70; MP (Labour) for W Bromwich 1973, for W Bromwich West 1974–92; Asst Govt Whip 1974–76; mem. Labour Party Nat. Exec. 1981–87; Deputy Speaker 1987–92; Speaker of the House of Commons 1992–2000; currently Ind. Cross Bencher; Chancellor Open Univ. 1994–2006; several hon. degrees from British univs including Hon. LLD (Cambridge) 1994, Hon. DCL (Oxford) 1995, (St Andrews) 2002; Parliamentarian of the Year 1992, Personality of the Year, Communicator of the Year. *Publication:* Betty Boothroyd – The Autobiography 2001. *Address:* House of Lords, Westminster, London, SW1A 0PW, England. *Telephone:* (20) 7219-8673 (office).

BOR, Naci; Turkish professor of physiology; *Professor Emeritus, Medical Faculty, Hacettepe University;* b. 20 Feb. 1928, Bor; s. of Cemal Bor and Zekiye Bor; m. Sema Bor; two d.; ed Istanbul Univ.; researcher in cardiac physiology, Emory Univ., Atlanta 1958–61; est. research in foetal physiology, Philadelphia Presbyterian Hosp.; lecturer Univ. of Pa; Founding Dir of Physiology, Hacettepe Univ. Medical School 1963, f. Medical and Surgical Research Centre 1976, Chair. 1976–, Prof. of Physiology, Hacettepe Univ. Medical Faculty, Prof. Emer. 1995–; Prof. of Physiology, East Mediterranean Univ. Medical Faculty; Chair. Anadolu Health and Research Foundation; fmr Chair. Research Centre, Hacettepe Univ.; mem. Science Council, Turkish Scientific and Tech. Nat. Research Council; Founder and Ed. Doga (scientific journal), Turkish Journal for Medical Sciences; Founding Fellow Islamic Acad. of Sciences (IAS), mem. Council 1994–, Founding Ed. IAS Journal 1988, Medical Journal of IAS; numerous TV and radio broadcasts on health and health research; American Heart Asscn Research Award 1958, Turkish Scientific and Tech. Research Council Prize for Lifetime Medical Research 1992. *Leisure interest:* essentials of Sofism. *Address:* Mithatpasa Caddesi, 66/5 06420 Kizilay, Ankara (office); Cevizli Dere Caddesi, No. 130/7, Yeni Oran, Ankara, Turkey (home). *Telephone:* (312) 4250319 (office); (312) 4762914 (home). *Fax:* (312) 4259487 (office). *E-mail:* nacibor@bir.net.tr (office). *Website:* www .medicaljournal-ias.org (office).

BORCHERDS, Richard Ewen, PhD, FRS; British mathematician and academic; *Professor, Department of Mathematics, University of California, Berkeley;* b. 29 Nov. 1959, South Africa; s. of Dr Peter Howard Borcherds and Margaret Elizabeth Borcherds (née Greenfield); m. Ursula Gritsch; ed Trinity Coll., Cambridge; Research Fellow, Trinity Coll. 1983–87; Morrey Asst Prof., Univ. of Calif. at Berkeley 1987–88, Prof. of Math. 1993–96, 1999–; Royal Soc. Univ. Residential Fellow, Univ. of Cambridge 1988–92, lecturer 1992–93, Royal Soc. Prof., Dept of Math. 1996–99; Jr Whitehead Prize 1992, Prize of the City of Paris 1992, Fields Medal 1998. *Publications:* numerous papers in mathematical journals. *Leisure interest:* films. *Address:* Department of Mathematics, 927 Evans Hall #3840, University of California, Berkeley, CA 94720-3840, USA (office). *Telephone:* (510) 642-8464 (office). *Fax:* (510) 642-8204 (office). *E-mail:* reb@math.berkeley.edu (office). *Website:* math.berkeley .edu/~reb (office).

BORCHERT, Jochen; German politician; b. 25 April 1940, Nahrstedt, Kreis Stendal; m.; two c.; ed studies in agric. and econs; mem. Christian Democratic Union (CDU) 1965–; mem. Bochum City Council 1976–80; mem. Bundestag 1980–2002, Vice-Pres. Farmers' Asscn, Westfalen-Lippe; Chair. Absatzforderungsfonds der Deutschen Land- und Ernährungswirtschaft 1989–93; CDU/CSU Spokesman on Budgetary Policy in Bundestag; Minister of Agric. Food and Forestry 1993–98; Fed. Chair. Protestant Working Group CDU/CSU, mem. Fed. Bd CDU. *Address:* c/o Bundesministerium für Ernährung, Landwirtschaft und Forsten, Rochusstrasse 1, 53123 Bonn, Germany.

BORD, André; French politician; b. 30 Nov. 1922, Strasbourg; s. of Alphonse Bord and Marie-Anne Sigrist; m. 1st Germaine Fend (deceased); two s.; m. 2nd Francine Heisserer 1981; ed St-Etienne Coll., Strasbourg; mem. of Nat. Ass. 1958–81; mem. Municipal Council, Strasbourg 1959–71, 1977–89, Deputy Mayor 1959–65; mem. Conseil Général, Strasbourg-Est and Hun Neudorf 1961–79; Pres. Conseil-Général du Bas-Rhin 1967–79; Pres. Groupe de l'Union démocratique européenne, European Parl. 1961–66, mem. European Parl. 1982–84; Sec. of State for Interior 1966–72, for Ex-Servicemen and War Victims 1972–76, for Relations with Parl. 1976–78; Sec.-Gen. UDR 1975–76; founder and Pres. Asscn for Industrial Devt, Alsace 1967; Pres. Regional Council of Alsace 1973–77, Comm. Interministérielle de Coopération France–République Fédérale d'Allemagne 1986; Médaille militaire, Médaille de la France libre, Médaille de la Résistance; Croix de guerre avec palme; Grand Officer, Order of Orange-Nassau (Netherlands), Order of Polonia Restituta (Poland), Commdr Légion d'honneur and others. *Address:* 27 route de Wolfisheim, 67810 Holtzheim, France (home). *Telephone:* (3) 88-23-44-50 (home). *Fax:* (3) 88-22-48-14 (home).

BORDA, Dionisio, MA, PhD; Paraguayan politician and economist; *Minister of Finance;* b. San Juan, Misiones; ed Univs of Wisconsin and Massachusetts, USA; Prof. of Econs, Universidad Nacional de Asunción; Adviser to Nat. Congress 1994–96; Minister of Finance 2003–05 (resgnd), 2008–; Founder and Dir Center of Analysis and Dissemination of the Paraguayan Economy (CADEP); fmr Visiting Prof., Univ. of Indiana. *Publications:* Presupuesto, Política Fiscal y Desempeño Económico en la Transición 2001, Globalización y Crisis fiscal (Ed.) 2003, Seguridad Social (Ed.) 2003. *Address:* Ministry of Finance, Chile 128 esq. Palmas, Asunción, Paraguay (office). *Telephone:* (21) 44-0010 (office). *E-mail:* info@hacienda.gov.py (office). *Website:* www.hacienda .gov.py (office).

BORDABERRY AROCENA, Juan María; Uruguayan politician; b. 17 June 1928, Montevideo; s. of Domingo Bordaberry and Elisa Arocena de Bordaberry; m. Josefina Herrán Puig; seven s. one d.; ed Univ. Montevideo; Chair., Nat. Meat Bd 1959; mem. Hon. Comm. for Agric. Devt Plan 1960; mem. Nat. Wool Bd 1960–62; Chair. Comm. Against Foot and Mouth Disease 1962; mem. Senate 1962–64; Chair. Liga Federal de Acción Ruralista 1964; Minister of Agric. 1969–72; Pres. of Uruguay 1972–76 (deposed). *Address:* Joaquín Suárez 2868, Montevideo, Uruguay. *Telephone:* 20-14-12.

BORDER, Allan Robert, AO; Australian fmr professional cricketer; b. 27 July 1955, Cremorne, Sydney; s. of John Border and Sheila Border; m. Jane Hiscox 1980; two c.; ed Mosman Primary School, N Sydney Tech. School, N Sydney Boys' High School; fmr clerk; work in motor trade; left-hand middle-order batsman, left-arm slow bowler; teams: NSW 1976–80, Glos., England 1977 (1 match), Queensland 1980–96 (Capt. 1983–89), Essex, England 1986–88; Capt. Australian Nat. Team 1984–94; 156 (record) Tests for Australia 1978–94, including record unbroken sequence of 153 matches, record 93 (unbroken sequence 1984–94) as Capt., scoring 11,174 runs (average 50.5) including 27 hundreds and then holding record 156 catches; scored 27,131 first-class runs (70 hundreds); toured England 1979 (World Cup), 1980, 1981, 1983 (World Cup), 1985, 1989, 1993 (last three as Capt.); then record 273 limited-overs internationals, record 178 as Capt.; with Ronald McConnell Holdings 1980–84; with Castlemaine Perkins 1984–; mem. Nat. Cricket Selection Panel 1998–, Queensland Cricket Bd 2001–; Int. Cricket Council (ICC) Amb. to developing regions, mem. ICC Cttee; Wisden Cricketer of the Year 1982. *Publication:* A Peep at the Poms 1986. *Leisure interests:* golf, tennis, reading. *Address:* c/o Australian Cricket Board, 90 Jolimont Street, Jolimont, Vic. 3002, Australia.

BORDIER, Roger; French writer; b. 5 March 1923, Blois; s. of Robert Bordier and Valentine Jeufraux; m. Jacqueline Bouchaud; ed secondary school; journalist in the provinces, later in Paris; contrib. to Nouvelles Littéraires and Aujourd'hui; radio and TV writer; Officier, Ordre des Artes et Lettres; Prix Renaudot 1961. *Publications:* poems: Les épicentres 1951; novels: La cinquième saison 1959, Les blés 1961, Le mime 1963, L'entracte 1965, Un âge d'or 1967, Le tour de ville 1969, Les éventails 1971, L'océan 1974, Meeting 1976, Demain l'été 1977; plays: Les somnambules 1963, Les visiteurs 1972; essays: L'objet contre l'art 1972, Le progrès: Pour qui? 1973, L'art moderne et l'objet 1978; novels: La grande vie 1981, Les temps heureux 1983, La longue file 1984, 36 La fête 1985, La belle de mai 1986, Les saltimbanques de la Révolution 1989, Vel d'hib 1989, Les fusils du 1er Mai 1991, Chroniques de la Cité Joyeuse 1995, L'interrogatoire, dialogue 1998, Le Zouave du Pont de l'Alma 2001, A la recherche de Paris (essay) 2004. *Address:* Editions Albin Michel, 22 rue Huyghens, 75014 Paris, (office); 8 rue Geoffroy St Hilaire, 75005 Paris, France.

BORDYUZHA, Gen. Nikolai Nikolayevich; Russian fmr army officer, politician and diplomatist; *Secretary General, Collective Security Treaty Organization (CSTO);* b. 22 Oct. 1949, Orel; m.; one s.; ed Perm Military Eng School, Moscow Inst. of Political Science, Military Acad. of the Gen. Staff of Armed Forces of the Russian Fed., Diplomatic Acad. of the Russian Fed.; service in army and state security forces 1972–91; Deputy Head, Personnel Dept, Fed. Agency of Govt Communications and Information of Russian

Presidency 1991–92; Deputy Commdr, Frontier Forces 1992–94; Deputy Dir, Fed. Frontier Service 1995–98, Dir 1998; Chief of Staff of Presidential Exec. Office and Sec., Russian Fed. Security Council 1998–99; Head, State Customs Cttee 1999; Amb. to Denmark 2000–03; Sec. Gen. Collective Security Treaty Organization (CSTO) 2003–; Order of Services to the Motherland, Fourth Class (Russia), of Courage (Russia), of Friendship (Russia), of Friendship of Peoples (Belarus), Dostyk (Kazakhstan), Danaker (Kyrgyzstan), numerous medals. *Leisure interest:* fishing. *Address:* Collective Security Treaty Organization (CSTO), 7 Varvarka, 103012 Moscow, Russia (office). *Telephone:* (495) 606-97-71 (office). *Fax:* (495) 625-76-20 (office). *E-mail:* odkb.gov.ru (office). *Website:* www.odkb.gov.ru (office).

BOREL, Jacques Paul; French restaurant and hotel executive; b. 9 April 1927, Courbevoie; s. of William Borel and Marie (née Le Monnier) Borel; m. Christiane Roubit 1949; two s. one d.; ed Lycées Condorcet and Carnot, Paris, Ecole des Hautes Etudes Commerciales; mem. Sales Force, IBM France 1950–57, Man. Saigon (Viet Nam) Br. Office, IBM; Founder Restaurant Chain Jacques Borel 1957, became Compagnie des Restaurants Jacques Borel (CRJB) 1960, then Jacques Borel Int. (J.B. Int.) 1970, Pres., Dir-Gen. –1977; Pres. J.B. Enterprises Soc. 1977; Dir Sofitel Jacques Borel, Jacques Borel Belgie NV-Belgique SA, Jacques Borel Do Brasil, Jacques Borel Deutschland, Jacques Borel Italia, Jacques Borel Nederland, Jacques Borel Iran, Jacques Borel Misr (Egypt), Jacques Borel Venezuela, Hoteles Jacques Borel (Barcelona), Farah Maghreb (Casablanca); Founder Syndicat Nat. des Restaurants Economiques (now Syndicat Nat. des Chaînes d'Hôtels et de Restaurants de Tourisme et d'Entreprise) 1966; Pres. Groupement HEC Tourisme-Hôtellerie; f. Club TVA (group campaigning for the reduction of VAT in the hotel and restaurant industry) 2000. *Leisure interests:* music, painting, sailing. *Address:* 100 avenue du Président Kennedy, 75016 Paris, France.

BOREN, David Lyle, MA, JD; American politician, lawyer and university administrator; *President, University of Oklahoma;* b. 21 April 1941, Washington, DC; s. of Lyle H. Boren and Christine (McKown) Boren; m. 1st; one s. one d.; m. 2nd Molly W Shi 1977; ed Yale, Oxford and Okla Univs; mem. Okla House of Reps 1966–74; Chair. Govt Dept, Okla Baptist Univ. 1969–74; Gov. of Okla 1975–79; Senator from Okla 1979–94; Pres. Univ. of Okla 1994–; Rhodes Scholar 1965. *Leisure interests:* family, reading, rowing, tennis. *Address:* Office of the President, University of Oklahoma, 660 Parrington Oval, Norman, OK 73019 (office); 750 West Boyd, Norman, OK 73019, USA (home). *Telephone:* (405) 325-3916 (office). *Fax:* (405) 325-7605 (office). *Website:* www.ou.edu (office).

BORG, Alan Charles Nelson, CBE, PhD, FSA; British museum director; b. 21 Jan. 1942; s. of the late Charles J. N. Borg and Frances M. O. Hughes; m. 1st Anne Blackmore 1964 (divorced); one s. one d.; m. 2nd Lady Caroline Hill 1976; two d.; ed Westminster School, Brasenose Coll., Oxford and Courtauld Inst. of Art, London; Lecteur d'anglais, Univ. d'Aix-Marseille 1964–65; Lecturer, History of Art, Indiana Univ. 1967–69; Asst Prof. of History of Art, Princeton Univ. 1969–70; Asst Keeper of the Armouries, HM Tower of London 1970–78; Keeper, Sainsbury Centre for Visual Arts, Univ. of E Anglia 1978–82; Dir-Gen. Imperial War Museum 1982–95; Chair. Nat. Inventory of War Memorials 1988–95, Advisory Cttee on Public Records 1993, Founding Museum 2006–; Dir Vic. and Albert Museum 1995–2000; Pres. Elizabethan Club 1994–2000; Librarian, St John's Gate 2007–; Hon. Fellow, RIBA 2001; Dr hc (Sheffield Hallam) 2000. *Publications include:* Architectural Sculpture in Romanesque Provence 1972, European Swords and Daggers in the Tower of London 1974, Torture and Punishment 1975, Heads and Horses 1976, Arms and Armour in Britain 1979, The Vanishing Past 1981, War Memorials 1991, History of the Painter-Stainers Company 2002; articles in learned journals. *Leisure interests:* fencing, music, travel. *Address:* Telegraph House, 36 West Square, London, SE11 4SP, England.

BORG, Anders E.; Swedish economist and politician; *Minister of Finance;* b. 11 Jan. 1968, Stockholm; m. Sanna Borg; three c.; ed De Geer School, local authority adult secondary educ., Norrköping, Uppsala and Stockholm Univs; Chair. Uppsala Univ. Student Union 1989, Föreningen Heimdal 1989; leader writer, Svenska Dagbladet 1990–91; Political Adviser, Prime Minister's Office, Coordination Secr., with responsibility for coordination of Ministry of Health and Social Affairs, Ministry of Public Admin, Ministry of Culture and Ministry of Educ. and Science 1991–93; Political Adviser to Carl Bildt at Prime Minister's Office 1993–93; Chief Economist, Transferator Alfred Berg 1995–98; Chief Economist, ABN Amro Bank, Stockholm 1998–99; Head of Econ. Analysis Dept, Skandinaviska Enskilda Banken (SEB) 1999–2001; adviser on monetary policy issues to Exec. Bd Riksbank (Swedish Cen. Bank) 2001–02; Chief Economist and Admin. Dir Moderate Party 2002–06; Minister of Finance 2006–; mem. Expert Group on Public Finance 1992–96, Bd Swedish Labour Market Admin 2005. *Address:* Ministry of Finance, Drottninggatan 21, 103 33 Stockholm, Sweden (office). *Telephone:* (8) 405-10-00 (office). *Fax:* (8) 21-73-86 (office). *E-mail:* registrator@finance.ministry.se (office). *Website:* finans.regeringen.se (office).

BORG, Björn Rune; Swedish business executive and fmr professional tennis player; b. 6 June 1956, Stockholm; s. of Rune Borg; m. 1st Mariana Simionescu 1980 (divorced 1984); one s. by Jannike Bjorling; m. 2nd Loredana Berte 1989 (divorced 1992); ed Blombacka School; professional player since 1972; Italian Champion 1974, 1978; French Champion 1974, 1975, 1978, 1979, 1980, 1981; Wimbledon Champion 1976, 1977, 1978, 1979, 1980 (runner-up 1981); WCT Champion 1976; four times runner-up in U.S. Open; Grand Prix Masters Champion 1980, 1981; World Champion 1979, 1980; played Davis Cup for Sweden 1972, 1973, 1974, 1975, 1976, 1977, 1978, 1979, 1980; Winner Stockholm Open 1980; announced retirement from tennis Jan. 1983, two brief comebacks 1984, 1992; later played in srs tour; f. Björn Borg Enterprises Ltd;

Sweden's Sportsperson of the Century, voted second-best tennis player ever by Sports Illustrated and l'Equipe newspaper. *Publication:* Bjorn Borg – My Life and Game (with Eugene Scott) 1980. *Leisure interest:* fishing. *Address:* c/o International Management Group, The Pier House, Strand on the Green, Chiswick, London W4 3NN, England.

BORG, Joseph (Joe), LLD; Maltese politician and lawyer; *Commissioner for Fisheries and Maritime Affairs, European Commission;* b. 19 March 1952; m. Isabelle Agius; one s. one d.; ed Lyceum, Univ. of Malta, Univ. of Wales; practising lawyer 1976–; legal adviser to cos and corpns in Malta and abroad; Lecturer, Univ. of Malta 1979–88, Sr Lecturer 1988; adviser on EU matters to Minister of Foreign Affairs 1989–95; mem. Bd of Govs Malta Int. Business Authority 1989–92, Bd of Dirs of Cen. Bank 1992–95; MP 1995–2004; Shadow Minister for Industry and EU Impact on Malta 1996–98; mem. Foreign Affairs Parl. Cttee, EU-Malta Jt Cttee 1996–98; Parl. Sec., Ministry of Foreign Affairs 1998–99; Minister of Foreign Affairs 1999–2004; EU Commr without Portfolio 2004, for Fisheries and Maritime Affairs 2004–; Hon. LLM (Wales). *Address:* European Commission, Rue de la Loi 200, 1049 Brussels, Belgium (office). *Telephone:* (2) 299-11-11 (office). *Fax:* (2) 295-01-38 (office). *Website:* http://ec .europa.eu/commission_barroso/borg/index_en.htm (office).

BORG, Per O.; Swedish business executive and civil servant; b. 27 Sept. 1943; m. Kerstin Borg Wallin; two c.; ed Univ. of Gothenburg; served Ministry of Finance 1969–71, Ministry of Commerce 1971–78, of Defence 1978–81; Man. Dir IMPOD 1981–82; Under-Sec. of Defence 1982–88; Dir-Gen. FMV 1988–. *Leisure interests:* opera, sailing, skiing. *Address:* FMV, 115 88 Stockholm, Sweden. *Telephone:* (8) 782-63-50.

BORG, Tonio, LLD; Maltese politician and lawyer; *Deputy Prime Minister and Minister for Foreign Affairs;* b. 12 May 1957; s. of Carmelo Borg and Maria Gemma Zarb; m. Adele Galea 1982; one s. two d.; ed St Aloysius Coll. and Univ. of Malta; Lecturer in Public Law, Univ. of Malta; exec. mem. of European Union Young Christian Democrats 1983–85; Dir Mid-Med Bank 1987–92; Pres. of Nationalist Party Gen. Council 1988–95; mem. of European Cttee for Prevention of Torture and Inhuman or Degrading Punishment or Treatment 1990–95; MP 1992–; mem. Planning Authority 1992–95; mem. of Council of Europe Ass. 1992–95; mem. Jt Parl. Cttee of the European Parl. and Maltese House of Reps 1992–95, 1996–98; Minister for Home Affairs 1995–96, 1998–2003, for Justice and Home Affairs 2003–08, for Foreign Affairs and Deputy Prime Minister 2008–; Nationalist Party. *Leisure interests:* reading, cycling. *Address:* Ministry for Foreign Affairs, Palazzo Parisio, Merchants Street, Valletta, VLT 2000, Malta (office). *Telephone:* 22957000 (office). *Fax:* 22957348 (office). *E-mail:* mjha@gov.mt (office). *Website:* www.mjha.gov.mt (office).

BORGE MARTÍNEZ, Tomás; Nicaraguan politician, writer, poet and journalist; b. 13 Aug. 1930, Matagalpa; s. of Tomás Borge Delgado and Ana Martínez Rivera; m. 1st Yelba Mayorga (assassinated by Nat. Guard 1979); m. 2nd Josefina Cerda; eight d.; ed Nat. Univ. León and Granada; first took part in activities against Somoza 1943, sentenced to eight years in prison 1956, escaped 1958, founder Frente Sandinista de Liberación Nacional (FSLN) 1961, guerrilla leader in Río Coco-Bocay, Pancasán and in clandestine struggle in the cities, captured by Somoza's agents 1976 and sentenced to 180 years of imprisonment, suffered torture and thirty months isolation, liberated in 1978 after attack on Nat. Palace; mem. Nat. Directorate FSLN 1978–; Minister of the Interior 1979–90, Adjoint Commdr Armed Forces, First Vice-Pres. Perm. Conference of Political Parties in Latin America (COPP-PAL); founder Espartaco (magazine) 1946 and El Universitario (newspaper) 1950; jury mem. Festival of New Latin American Film 1990, House of Americas Award 1991; Dr hc Autonomous Univ. of Puebla, Mexico 1981. *Publications:* Carlos, el Amanecer ya no es una Tentación 1979, Los Primeros Pasos 1981, Estamos Creando una Nueva Sociedad 1981, La Mujer en la Revolución 1983, La Revolución Combate Contra la Teología de la Muerte 1983, El Axioma de la Esperanza 1984, Nicaragua: Justicia y Revolución 1986, Cristianismo y Revolución 1987, Una Relación Mágica 1989, La Paciente Impaciencia (House of America Award) 1989, La Ceremonia Esperada 1990. *Leisure interest:* film. *Address:* Apartado 1229, Managua, Nicaragua. *Telephone:* 43853-52.

BORGEAUD, Pierre, DiplEng; Swiss business executive; b. 31 March 1934; m.; three c.; ed Swiss Fed. Inst. of Tech.; Research Dept of Sulzer Bros Ltd 1959–73, Man. of Sulzer Eng Works and of Swiss Locomotive and Machine Works, Winterthur 1973–75, Gen. Man., Sulzer Bros. Ltd (now Sulzer Man. Ltd) 1975–81, Pres., CEO 1981–88 (Chair. 1988–2000, Del. 1999), fmr mem. Bd of Dirs; Chair. Presidential Bd of Swiss Fed. of Commerce and Industry 1987–93; Vice-Chair. Clariant Ltd 2000–03; fmr mem. Bd of Dirs Swiss Bank Corpn, Bühler Ltd, Pirelli Int. Ltd, Winterthur Insurance Co.

BORGES, Jacobo; Venezuelan painter; b. 28 Nov. 1931, Caracas; ed Escuela de Artes Plásticas Cristóbal Rojas, Caracas and Ecole des Beaux Arts, Paris; mem. of Young Painters' Group and illustrator of magazines and record covers while in Paris 1951–56, also exhibited in French Nat. Exhbns; Prof. of Scenography and Plastic Analysis, Escuela de Artes Plásticas Cristóbal Rojas, Caracas 1958–65; Prof. of Scenography, Theatre School of Valencia and Dir Experimental Art Centre, Univ. Cent. de Venezuela 1966–; has taught at Int. Summer Acad., Salzburg, Austria 1995–96, 98–99, 2000–04; Int. Exhbns at Guggenheim Museum, New York 1964, 1965; Artist in Residence, Mexico City 1993; Museo Jacobo Borges created to house his work 1995; Nat. Painting Prize 1963, Armando Reverón Bienal Prize 1965. *Major works:* La Lámpara y la Silla 1951, La Pesca 1957, Sala de Espera 1960, Todos a la Fiesta 1962, Ha Comenzado el Espectáculo 1964, Altas Finanzas 1965; series of Las Jugadoras and Las Comedoras de Helados 1965–66. *Address:* c/o Museo Jacobo Borges, Catia, Caracas, Venezuela. *Website:* www.museojacoboborges.org.ve.

BORGNINE, Ernest; American actor; b. 24 Jan. 1917, Hamden, Conn.; s. of Charles B. Borgnine and Anna Borgnine (née Baselli); m. Tova Newman 1972; ed New Haven public schools, Randall School of Dramatic Arts, Hartford. *Films include:* China Corsair 1951, The Whistle at Eaton Falls 1951, The Mob 1951, From Here to Eternity 1953, The Stranger Wore a Gun 1953, Vera Cruz 1954, The Bounty Hunter 1954, Demetrius and the Gladiators 1954, Johnny Guitar 1954, Bad Day at Black Rock 1955, Marty (Acad. Award for Best Performance 1956) 1955, Run for Cover 1955, Violent Saturday 1955, The Last Command 1955, Square Jungle 1955, The Best Things in Life Are Free 1956, The Catered Affair 1956, Jubal 1956, Three Brave Men 1956, Hell Below, Summer of the Seventeenth Doll 1959, Torpedo Run 1958, The Badlanders 1958, The Vikings 1958, The Rabbit Trap 1959, Man on String 1960, Il giudizio universale 1961, Go Naked in the World 1961, I briganti italiani 1961 Il re di Poggioreale 1961, Pay or Die 1960, Barabbas 1962, McHale's Navy 1964, Flight of the Phoenix 1966, The Oscar 1966, The Dirty Dozen 1967, Chuka 1967, The Legend of Lylah Clare 1968, The Split 1968, Ice Station Zebra 1968, The Wild Bunch 1969, Los Desesperados 1969, The Adventurers 1970, Suppose They Gave a War and Nobody Came? 1970, Rain for a Dusty Summer 1971, Willard 1971, Bunny O'Hare 1971, Hannie Caulder 1971, The Revengers 1972, L'uomo dalla pelle dura 1972, The Poseidon Adventure 1972, Emperor of the North Pole 1973, The Neptune Factor 1973, Sunday in the Country 1974, Law and Disorder 1974, Vengeance Is Mine 1974, Hustle 1975, The Devil's Rain 1975, Shoot 1976, The Greatest 1977, Crossed Swords 1977, Convoy 1978, Ravagers 1979, The Double McGuffin 1979, Goin' South 1979, The Black Hole 1979, When Time Ran Out... 1980, Poliziotto superpiù 1980, High Risk 1981, Deadly Blessing 1981, Escape from New York 1981, Young Warriors 1983, Code Name: Wild Geese 1984, Cane arrabbiato 1985, Skeleton Coast 1987, Qualcuno pagherà? 1987, The Big Turnaround 1988, Bersaglio sull'autostrada 1988, Any Man's Death 1988, Spike of Bensonhurst 1988, Gummibärchen küßt man nicht (Real Men Don't Eat Gummi Bears) 1989, L'ultima partita (The Last Match) 1990, Tides of War 1990, Laser Mission 1990, Mistress 1992, The Outlaws: Legend of O.B. Taggart 1994, Spirit of the Season (video) 1994, Captiva Island 1995, Merlin's Shop of Mystical Wonders 1996, All Dogs Go to Heaven 2 (voice) 1996, McHale's Navy 1997, Gattaca 1997, 12 Bucks 1998, Small Soldiers (voice) 1998, BASEketball 1998, Mel 1998, An All Dogs Christmas Carol (voice) 1998, The Last Great Ride 1999, Abilene 1999, The Lost Treasure of Sawtooth Island 1999, The Kiss of Debt 2000, Castlerock 2000, Hoover (also exec. producer) 2000, SpongeBob SquarePants: SuperSponge (video game, voice) 2001, Whiplash 2002, 11'09"01 – September 11 2002, Barn Red 2003, The Long Ride Home 2003, Crimebusters 2003, Blueberry 2004, 3 Below (video) 2005, Rail Kings (video) 2005, La cura del gorilla 2005, Oliviero Rising 2006. *Television includes:* McHale's Navy (series) 1962, Sam Hill: Who Killed Mr. Foster? 1971, The Trackers 1971, Legend in Granite 1973, Twice in a Lifetime 1974, Little House on the Prairie 1974, Natale in casa d'appuntamento (Christmas Time in a Brothel) 1976, Future Cop 1976, Jesus of Nazareth (mini-series) 1977, Fire! 1977, Future Cop (series) 1977, The Ghost of Flight 401 1978, Cops and Robin 1978, All Quiet on the Western Front 1979, Love Boat 1982, Carpool 1983, Blood Feud 1983, Masquerade 1983, Love Leads the Way: A True Story 1984, Airwolf (also series) 1984, The Last Days of Pompeii (mini–series) 1984, Dirty Dozen: The Next Mission 1985, Alice in Wonderland 1985, L'isola del tesoro (mini-series) 1987, The Dirty Dozen: The Deadly Mission 1987, The Dirty Dozen: The Fatal Mission 1988, Oceano (mini-series) 1989, Jake Spanner, Private Eye 1989, Appearances 1990, Mountain of Diamonds 1991, Tierärztin Christine 1993, Der Blaue Diaman (Hunt for the Blue Diamond) 1993, Tierärztin Christine II: Die Versuchung 1995, The Single Guy (series) 1995, All Dogs Go to Heaven: The Series (voice) 1996, The Blue Light 2004, The Trail to Hope Rose 2004. *Leisure interest:* golf. *Address:* 3055 Lake Glen Drive, Beverly Hills, CA 90210, USA.

BORGO BUSTAMANTE, Enrique, JD, MA; Salvadorean business executive, lawyer, politician and diplomatist; *Ambassador to Spain;* b. 1928; ed Universidad de El Salvador, Rome Univ., Italy; Judge, First Instance Criminal Court, San Vicente 1955–57; attorney: Salvadoran Social Security Inst. 1957–60; attorney Cen. Bank of El Salvador 1961–63; Dir Banco Cuscatlán 1975–79; Legal Adviseor, Taca Int. Airlines 1975–80, CEO 1981–94; Vice-Pres. of El Salvador 1994–99; Congressman, Cen. American Congress 1999–2000; Amb. to Spain 2004–. *Address:* Embassy of El Salvador, General Oraá 9, 5° dcha, 28006 Madrid, Spain (office). *Telephone:* (91) 5628002 (office). *Fax:* (91) 5630584 (office). *E-mail:* embasalvamadrid@yahoo .com (office). *Website:* www.embasalva.com (office).

BORGOMEO, Rev. Pasquale, SJ, DLit; Italian ecclesiastic; *Director General, Vatican Radio;* b. 20 March 1933, Naples; s. of Vincenzo Borgomeo and Letizia De Meo; ed Pontano Coll., Naples, Univ. of Naples, Univ. of the Sorbonne, Paris, France; entered Soc. of Jesus 1948; ordained priest 1963; Ed.-in-Chief Vatican Radio 1970–78, Programme Dir 1978–83, Asst Dir Gen. 1983–85, Dir Gen. 1985–; mem. Bureau Univ. Radiophonique et Télévisuelle Int., Paris 1976–98, Bd of Dirs Centro Televisivo Vaticano 1983–97; Pres. Int. Broadcasting Working Party of European Broadcasting Union 1983–93; Consultant to Pontifical Council for Social Communications 1989–, Unione Cattolica Stampa Italiana 1997–; Chevalier, Légion d'honneur 1994. *Publication:* L'Eglise de ce temps dans la prédication de Saint Augustin 1972. *Leisure interests:* photography, motoring. *Address:* Vatican Radio, Palazzo Pio, Piazza Pia 3, 00193 Rome (office); Via dei Penitenzieri, 20, 00193 Rome, Italy (home). *Telephone:* (06) 6988-3945 (office); (06) 6897-7240 (home). *Fax:* (06) 6988-3237 (office). *E-mail:* borgomeo@vatiradio.va (office). *Website:* www.radiovaticana .org (office).

BORIES, Christel; French business executive; *President and CEO, Engineered Products Group, Rio Tinto Alcan Inc.;* b. 1964; ed Hautes Etudes Commerciales School of Management, Paris; worked for Booz Allen & Hamilton; Man. Corporate Value Assocs; joined Pechiney 1993, later Head of Packaging Div., Pres. and CEO Alcan Packaging and Sr Vice-Pres. Alcan Inc. (following takeover of Pechiney by Alcan) 2003–, Pres. and CEO Engineered Products Group (now Rio Tinto Alcan Engineered Products Group) 2006–; Chair. Exec. Cttee European Aluminium Asscn 2007–08; mem. Bd of Dirs Atlas Copco AB 2008–; ranked 24th by the Financial Times amongst Top 25 Businesswomen in Europe 2005. *Address:* Rio Tinto Alcan France S.A.S., 7, place du Chancelier Adenauer, 75218 Paris Cedex 16; 87, avenue Raymond Poincare, 75116 Paris, France. *Telephone:* 1-56-28-20-00 (office). *Website:* www.alcan.com (office).

BORISEVICH, Nikolai Aleksandrovich; Belarusian physicist; *Head of Laboratory, Lebedev Institute of Physics;* b. 21 Sept. 1923, Luchnoy Most, Beresinsky Dist; m. Irina Pavlovna Borisevich 1949; two s.; ed Byelorussian State Univ., Minsk; guerilla, then served in Soviet Red Army 1941–45; Deputy Dir Inst. of Physics, Byelorussian Acad. of Sciences 1955–69 (Head of Lab. 1957–); Head of Lab., Lebedev Inst. of Physics, USSR (now Russian) Acad. of Sciences 1987–; Deputy to USSR Supreme Soviet 1969–89; mem. Byelorussian (Belarus) Acad. of Sciences 1969 (Pres. 1969–87, Hon. Pres. 1992–); Corresp. mem. USSR (now Russian) Acad. of Sciences 1972–81, mem. 1981–; Foreign mem. Czechoslovakian Acad. 1977, Slovenian Acad. of Sciences and Arts 1981; titular mem. European Acad. of Arts, Sciences and Humanities 1991; Order of Red Star 1944, 1945; Order of Patriotic War (First Degree) 1945, (Second Degree) 1985; Order of Red Banner of Labour 1967; Order of Lenin 1971, 1975, 1978, 1983; Order of October Revolution 1973; Order of Friendship 2001; Order of F. Skariny 2003; Hon. PhD (Jena) 1985; USSR State Prize 1973, Hero of Socialist Labour 1978, Lenin Prize 1980, Gold Medal, Czechoslovak Acad. 1983, Slovenian Acad. 1983, Belarus State Prize 1998. *Publications:* Exited States of Complex Molecules in Gas Phase 1967, Infrared Filters 1977; over 270 scientific articles. *Address:* P. N. Lebedev Institute of Physics, B-333, Leninski Prospekt 53, 117924 Moscow, Russia (office); 66 Skariny Avenue, 220072 Minsk (office); 7, Apt 20, Y. Kupala str. 220030 Minsk, Belarus (home). *Telephone:* (095) 135-75-98 (Moscow) (office); (17) 232-1401 (Minsk) (office); (17) 227-4559 (Minsk) (home). *Fax:* (17) 284-0030 (Minsk) (office). *E-mail:* lirp@imaph.bas-net.by (office).

BORISOV, Lt Gen. Boyko Metodiev, DS; Bulgarian politician; *Mayor of Sofia;* b. 13 June 1959, Bankya; ed Higher Specialized School, Ministry of the Interior; early career as police officer, Sofia 1978, Platoon Commdr 1982, later Co. Commdr; Lecturer, Higher Inst. for Officer Training and Scientific Research, Ministry of the Interior 1985–90; f. WON-1 Ltd (security co.) 1991; Sec.-Gen., Ministry of the Interior 2001–05; Mayor of Sofia 2005–; f. GERB (Citizens for the European Devt of Bulgaria) party 2006; fmr Coach, Bulgarian Nat. Karate Team; Founder and Leader Grazhdani za evropeysko razvitie na Balgariya—GERB (Citizens for European Devt of Bulgaria party) 2006–; mem. World Org. of Security Co.; Sign of Honour (Second Degree), Bulgaria 2003, Cross for Police Contrib. with Red Star, Spain 2003, Medal of Honour of the French Police, Medal for Operational Friendship and Co-operation, Russia, Commdr, Order of the Star of Italian Solidarity 2006. *Address:* Office of the Mayor, 1000 Sofia, ul. Moskovska 33, Bulgaria (office). *E-mail:* info@ sofia.bg (office). *Website:* www.sofia.bg (office).

BORITH, Ouch; Cambodian diplomatist; *Secretary of State, Ministry of Foreign Affairs and International Cooperation;* b. 2 Nov. 1957, Phnom-Penh; m.; five c.; ed Medical Faculty, Phnom-Penh, Inst. of Sociology, Moscow; French trans., Ministry of Foreign Affairs 1979–80, Dir Dept UN Humanitarian Org., Ministry of Foreign Affairs 1980–83, Dir Dept of Asia and Pacific Affairs 1987–90; Counsellor in charge of Political Affairs, Embassy, Moscow 1983–87; Amb. to Viet Nam 1990–92; Chargé d'affaires, Perm. Mission to UN 1992–93, Deputy Perm. Rep. 1993–97, Perm. Rep. 1998; currently Sec. of State, Ministry of Foreign Affairs and Int. Cooperation. *Address:* Ministry of Foreign Affairs and International Cooperation, 3 rue Samdech Hun Sen, Khan Chamkarmon, Phnom-Penh, Cambodia (office). *Telephone:* (23) 214441 (office). *Fax:* (23) 216144 (office). *E-mail:* mfaicasean@online.com.kh (office). *Website:* www.mfaic.gov.kh (office).

BORJA CEVALLOS, Rodrigo, PhD, DJur; Ecuadorean politician and academic; b. 19 June 1937, Quito; s. of Luis Felipe Borja de Alcázar and Aurelia Cevallos; m. Carmen Calisto de Borja; one s. three d.; ed Cen. Univ. of Ecuador; Deputy in Nat. Congress 1962–82; founder and fmr Leader Partido Izquierda Democrática; Prof. of Political Sciences, Cen. Univ. of Ecuador 1963–88; Pres. of Ecuador 1988–92; presidential candidate 2002; Pres. Law School Asscn, Cen. Univ. of Ecuador 1958; mem. Special Comm. of Lawyers on Ecuador's Political Constitution 1966; Hon. Mem. Charles Darwin Foundation. *Publications:* Political Constitutional Law (2 vols) 1964, 1971, Democratic Socialism 1983, Diplomatic Asylum in the Americas, Democracy in Latin America, A Political Dictionary; numerous essays. *Address:* c/o Izquierda Democrática, Polonia 161, entre Vancouver y Eloy Alfaro, Quito, Ecuador.

BORK, Robert Heron, JD; American judge (retd) and lawyer; *Professor of Law, Ave Maria School of Law;* b. 1 March 1927, Pittsburgh; s. of Harry Philip Bork and Elizabeth Kunkle; m. 1st Claire Davidson 1952 (died 1980); two s. one d.; m. 2nd Mary Ellen Pohl 1982; ed Univ. of Chicago; admitted to Ill. Bar 1953; Assoc. Kirkland, Ellis, Hodson, Chaffetz & Masters (law firm) 1955–62; Assoc. Prof., Yale Law School 1962–65, Prof. of Law 1965–73, Chancellor Kent Prof. of Law 1977–79, Alexander M. Bickel Prof. of Public Law 1979–81; US Solicitor-Gen. 1973–77; Acting US Attorney-Gen. 1973–74; mem. Kirkland & Ellis (law firm), Washington, DC 1981–82; Circuit Judge for DC Circuit 1982–88; nominated as Assoc. Justice of US Supreme Court and rejected by Senate 1987; Resident Scholar, American Enterprise Inst., Washington, DC 1977, Adjunct Scholar 1977–82 John M. Olin Scholar in Legal Studies 1988–99, Sr Fellow 2000–; Prof. of Law, Ave Maria School of Law, Ann Arbor,

Mich. 2000–; Distinguished Sr Fellow, Hudson Inst.; Tad and Dianne Taube Distinguished Visiting Fellow, Hoover Inst.; Co-Chair. Bd of Trustees Federalist Soc.; mem. Perm. Cttee, Oliver Wendell Holmes Devise 1989; Fellow, American Acad. of Arts and Sciences; Hon. LLD (Creighton Univ.) 1975, (Notre-Dame) 1982; Hon. DHumLitt (Wilkes-Barre Coll.) 1976; Hon. JurDr (Brooklyn Law School) 1984; Francis Boyer Award, American Enterprise Inst. 1984, Shelby Cullom Davis Award 1989. *Publication:* The Antitrust Paradox: A Policy at War with Itself 1978, The Tempting of America: The Political Seduction of the Law 1990, Slouching Towards Gomorrah 1996, Coercing Virtue: The Worldwide Rule of Judges 2002. *Address:* Ave Maria School of Law, 3475 Plymouth Road, Ann Arbor, MI 48105 (office); 5171 Palisade Lane, NW, Washington, DC 20016, USA (home). *Telephone:* (734) 827-8040 (office). *E-mail:* webadmin@avemarialaw.edu (office); rbork@aei.org (office). *Website:* www.avemarialaw.edu (office).

BORKO, Yuri Antonovich, DEcon; Russian economist; *Head, Centre of European Documentation, Institute of Europe, Russian Academy of Sciences;* b. 6 Feb. 1929, Rostov-on-Don; m. Yelena Borisovna Borko; two s.; ed Moscow State Univ.; researcher, Inst. of World Econ. and Int. Relations USSR (now Russian) Acad. of Sciences 1962–63; Ed. and mem. of Bd journal World Econ. and Int. Relations 1963–69; Head of Div. Inst. of Information on Social Sciences, USSR (now Russian) Acad. of Sciences 1970–90; Head of Div., Deputy Dir, Head of Research Centre of European Integration, Head of Centre of European Documentation, Prof., Inst. of Europe, Russian Acad. of Sciences 1990–, Jean Monnet Chairholder 2001–; Pres. Asscn of European Studies 1992–. *Publications include:* works on problems of European integration, European Community policy and int. relations between Russia and European Community. *Leisure interests:* skiing, books, music. *Address:* Institute of Europe, Mokhovaya str. 11, stroenye 3B, 103873 Moscow (office); Sovetskoy Armii str. 13–43, 127018 Moscow, Russia (home). *Telephone:* (495) 292-10-23 (office); (495) 289-21-66 (home). *Fax:* (495) 200-42-98 (office). *E-mail:* aes@aes .org.ru (office), aes@centro.ru (office), yborko@aes.org.ru (home). *Website:* www.ieras.ru (office); www.aes.org.ru (office).

BORLAUG, Norman Ernest, PhD; American agricultural scientist and academic; *Distinguished Professor of International Agriculture, Texas A&M University;* b. 25 March 1914, Cresco, Ia; s. of Henry O Borlaug and Clara (Vaala) Borlaug; m. Margaret G. Gibson 1937; one s. one d.; ed Univ. of Minnesota; with US Forest Service 1935–38; Instructor, Univ. of Minn. 1941; Microbiologist, E. I. DuPont de Nemours Foundation 1942–44; Research Scientist, Wheat Rockefeller Foundation, Mexico 1944–60, Centro Internacional de Mejoramiento de Maíz y Trigo (Int. Maize and Wheat Improvement Center), Mexico 1964–79; Leonard L. Klinck Lecturer, Agric. Inst. of Canada 1966; mem. Citizens' Comm. on Science, Law and Food Supply 1973, Comm. on Critical Choices for America 1973, Council of Agric. Science and Tech. 1973–; Assoc. Dir Rockefeller Found. 1960–63, Life Fellow 1983–, Consultant 1983; A. D. White Distinguished Prof. at Large, Cornell Univ. 1983–85; Distinguished Prof. of Int. Agriculture, Texas A&M Univ. 1984–; Sr Consultant (Agriculture), Carter Center, Atlanta; mem. NAS; Foreign mem. Royal Swedish Acad. of Agric. and Forestry 1971, Indian Nat. Science Acad. 1973; Pres. Sasakawa Africa Asscn (SAA); Hon. Foreign mem. Acad. Nacional de Agronomía y Veterinaria de Argentina, N. I. Vavilovi Acad. (USSR); Hon. Fellow Indian Soc. of Genetics and Plant Breeding 1968; Life Fellow Rockefeller Foundation 1983–; Hon. DSc (Punjab Agric. Univ.) 1969, (Royal Norwegian Agric. Coll.) 1970, (Mich. State Univ.) 1971, (Univ. of Florida) 1973, (Columbia) 1980, (Tulsa) 1991, (De Montfort) 1997 and many others; Nobel Peace Prize 1970, Medal of Freedom 1977, Nat. Medal of Science 2006, Congressional Gold Medal 2007, and numerous other awards. *Leisure interests:* hunting, fishing, baseball, wrestling, football, golf. *Address:* Texas A&M University System, Department of Soil and Crop Sciences, College Station, TX 77843-2474, USA (office); CIMMYT, Apartado Postal 6-641, 06600 Mexico, DF, Mexico (home). *Telephone:* (979) 845-8247 (Texas) (office); 5804-7508 (Mexico) (office). *Fax:* (979) 845-0456 (Texas) (office); 5804-7558/59 (Mexico) (office). *Website:* coals.tamu.edu.

BORLOO, Jean-Louis, MBA; French politician and lawyer; *Minister for Ecology, Energy, Sustainable Development and Spatial Planning;* b. 7 April 1951, Paris; m. Béatrice Schönberg 2005; ed Ecole des Hautes Etudes Commerciales-Institut Supérieur des Affaires (HEC-ISA), Univ. of Manchester, UK; began career as finance lawyer, Paris; set up own law firm; fmr teacher of Financial Analysis, HEC-ISA; Mayor of Valenciennes 1989–2002; mem. European Parl. 1989–92; Regional Counselor for Nord-Pas-de-Calais 1992–93, 1998; mem. Assemblée Nationale 1993–2002, 2007–; Spokesman, Union pour la Démocratie Française (UDF) 2001–02; joined Union pour la majorité présidentielle (now Union pour un Mouvement Populaire—UMP) 2002; Minister-Del. of Towns and Urban Redevelopment, attached to Minister of Social Affairs, Labour and Solidarity 2002–04; Minister of Employment, Labour and Social Cohesion 2004–05, of Employment, Social Cohesion and Housing 2005–07, of the Economy, Finance and Employment May–June 2007, for Ecology, Energy, Sustainable Devt and Spatial Planning June 2007–; Pres. Parti Radical (assoc. party of UMP) 2005–. *Publications:* Un Homme en colère 2002, L'Architecte et l'Horologer 2007. *Address:* Ministry of Ecology, Energy, Sustainable Development and Spatial Planning, Grande Arche, Tour Pascal A et B, 92055 La Défense Cedex, France (office). *Telephone:* 1-40-81-21-22 (office). *E-mail:* ministre@ecologie.gouv.fr (office). *Website:* www .developpement-durable.gouv.fr (office).

BORMAN, Frank; American business executive and fmr astronaut; *Chairman and CEO, Patlex Corporation;* b. 14 March 1928, Gary, Ind.; s. of Edwin Borman and late Marjorie Borman; m. Susan Bugbee 1950; two s.; ed US Mil. Acad., Calif. Inst. of Tech.; pilot training, Williams Air Force Base, Arizona; assigned to various fighter squadrons in US and Philippines; Instructor in

Thermodynamics and Fluid Mechanics, US Mil. Acad. 1957; Master's degree from Calif. Inst. of Tech. 1957; graduated from USAF Aerospace Research Pilots' School 1960; Instructor 1960–62; selected by NASA as astronaut Sept. 1962; Command Pilot Gemini VII 1965; Commdr Apollo VIII spacecraft which made flight round the moon Dec. 1968; Deputy Dir for Flight Operations, NASA, until May 1969; Field Dir of a NASA Space Station Task Group 1969–70; Vice-Pres. Eastern Airlines Inc. 1970–74, Vice-Pres. for Eastern Operations 1974–75, Pres. 1975–85, CEO 1975–86, Chair. of Bd 1976–86; Vice-Chair., mem. Bd of Dirs Texas Air Corp. 1986–92; now Chair. Bd Autofinance Group Inc., Chair., CEO, Dir Patlex Corp. 1992–; Dir Continental Airlines Holdings, Inc. 1992–; NASA Exceptional Service Medal, Harmon Int. Aviation Trophy 1966, Gold Space Medal, Int. Aeronautics 1969, Encyclopedia Britannica Achievement in Life Award 1980. *Leisure interests:* restoring aeroplanes, building model aeroplanes. *Address:* Patlex Corporation, 745 Leonard Bryran Alley, Las Cruces, NM 88005 (office); Autofinance Group Inc., Suite 350, Oakmont Circle 1, 601 Oakmont Lane, Westmont, IL 60559 (office); 4530 Blue Lake Drive, Boca Raton, FL 33431, USA (home). *Telephone:* (505) 523-8081 (Las Cruces). *Fax:* (505) 524-4050 (Las Cruces).

BORMANN, F. Herbert, BS, PhD; American ecologist and academic; *Oastler Professor Emeritus of Forest Ecology, Yale University;* ed Rutgers Univ., Duke Univ.; began researching the New England forest ecosystems in 1950s; began teaching at Yale Univ. 1966, now Oastler Prof. Emer. of Forest Ecology; Adjunct Prof., Rubenstein School of Environment and Natural Resources, Univ. of Vermont, Founding mem. Rubenstein School's Bd of Advisors; est. Hubbard Brook Ecosystem Study in NH; Pres. Ecological Soc. of America 1970–71; mem. American Acad. of Arts and Sciences 1972, NAS 1973; Hon. Lifetime mem. Int. Asscn for Ecology 2005; Hon. DSc (Univ of Vermont) 2005; Tyler Prize 1993, World Prize for Environmental Achievement, Eminent Ecologist Award, Blue Planet Prize, Japanese Asahi Glass Foundation 2003. *Achievements include:* pioneered, with Gene Likens, at Dartmouth 'small watershed technique' to study the biogeochemistry of whole forest ecosystems 1961. *Publications:* author or co-author of eight books, including: Pattern and Process in a Forest Ecosystem: Disturbance, Development, and the Steady State Based on the Hubbard Brook Ecosystem Study (with Gene E. Likens) 1978, Ecology, Economics, Ethics: The Broken Circle (co-ed.) 1992, Redesigning the American Lawn: A Search for Environmental Harmony 1993, Biogeochemistry of a Forested Ecosystem (with Gene E. Likens) 1995; more than 200 scientific papers in professional journals. *Address:* School of Forestry and Environmental Studies, Yale University, 205 Prospect Street, New Haven, CT 06511-2106, USA (office). *Telephone:* (203) 432-5150 (office). *E-mail:* fesinfo@yale.edu (office). *Website:* environment.yale.edu (office).

BORN, Adolf; Czech artist; b. 12 June 1930, České Velenice; m. Emilie Košáková; one d.; ed Pedagogical Faculty of Charles Univ., Prague School of Applied Art, Acad. of Graphic and Plastic Arts; illustration, animated cartoons, film co-operation with Jiří Brdečka 1955–; illustrated 250 children's books including Robinson Crusoe 1971, The Isle of Penguins, La Fontaine's Fables; author of 45 cartoon films for children; Chevalier dans l'Ordre des Arts et des Lettres (France); Gold Medal for Brecht's Mother Courage, Leipzig 1965, Premio preferri di Imperie, Italy 1965, Dattero d'Oro 1966, Albatross Prize for Lifelong Work, Prague 2000. *Films:* co-dir. (with Macourek and Doubrava) of films The Life of Birds, The Life of Children. *Television:* serial Mach and Šebestová. *Leisure interests:* travel, animals.

BORN, Gustav Victor Rudolf, MB, ChB, DPhil, FRS, FRCP; British professor of pharmacology; *Research Professor, William Harvey Research Institute, St Bartholomew's Hospital Medical College;* b. 29 July 1921; s. of the late Prof. Max Born (jt winner 1954 Nobel Prize for Physics); m. 1st Wilfrida Ann Plowden-Wardlaw 1950 (divorced 1961); two s. one d.; m. 2nd Dr Faith Elizabeth Maurice-Williams 1962; one s. one d.; ed Oberrealschule, Göttingen, Germany, Perse School, Cambridge, Edinburgh Acad. and Univs of Edinburgh and Oxford; Medical Officer, RAMC 1943–47; Research Asst, Graham Research Lab., Univ. Coll. Hosp. Medical School, London 1947–49; studentship, training in research methods of MRC 1949–52; mem. scientific staff, Toxicology Research Unit, MRC 1952–53; Sr Research Officer Nuffield Inst. for Medical Research and Medical Lecturer St Peter's Coll., Oxford 1953–60; Vandervell Prof. of Pharmacology, Royal Coll. of Surgeons and London Univ. 1960–73; Sheild Prof. of Pharmacology, Cambridge Univ. and Fellow, Gonville and Caius Coll. Cambridge 1973–78; Prof of Pharmacology, King's Coll., London Univ. 1978–86, Prof. Emer. 1986–, Research Prof., William Harvey Research Inst., St Bartholomew's Hospital Medical Coll. 1988–; fmr mem. Council of the Int. Soc. of Thrombosis and Haemostasis (Pres. 1977–79), Cttee of British Pharmacological Soc., Working Party on Antihaemophilic Globulin of MRC, Official Cttee of Enquiry into Relationship of Pharmaceutical Industry with Nat. Health Service, Medical Advisory Bd, British Council and numerous other cttees and bds; mem. Akad. Leopoldina; Hon. Fellow St Peter's Coll., Oxford; Hon. FRCS; Hon. Life mem. New York Acad. of Sciences, and other hon. memberships; Chevalier, Ordre nat. du Mérite; Hon. DSc (Bordeaux, Paris, Brown Univ.); Hon. MD (Münster, Leuven, Edinburgh, Munich, Loyola Univ., Chicago, Düsseldorf); Royal Soc. Royal Medal, Paul Morawitz Prize, Robert Pfleger Prize, Alexander von Humboldt Award 1995, Gold Medal for Medicine, Jung Foundation. *Publications:* more than 300 scientific publs. *Leisure interests:* music, history. *Address:* The William Harvey Research Institute, St Bartholomew's and the Royal London School of Medicine and Dentistry, Charterhouse Square, London, EC1M 6BQ (office); 5 Walden Lodge, 48 Wood Lane, London, N6 5UU, England (home). *Telephone:* (20) 7882-6070 (office). *Fax:* (20) 7882-6071 (office). *E-mail:* g.v.born@qmul.ac .uk (office).

BORNER, Silvio, Prof.Dr; Swiss economist and academic; *Professor of Political Economics, University of Basle;* b. 24 April 1941; s. of Walter Borner and Meta Borner; m. Verena Barth 1966; two d.; ed St Gall Grad. School and Yale Univ., USA; Prof. of Econs, Univ. of St Gallen 1974–78, of Political Econs, Univ. of Basle 1978–. *Publications:* Die 'sechste Schweiz'—überleben auf dem Weltmarkt, New Forms of Internationalization: An Assessment, Einführung in die Volkswirtschaftslehre, International Finance and Trade in a Polycentric World. *Leisure interests:* sports (active) and culture. *Address:* WWZ der Universität Basel, Abteilung Wirtschaft und Politik, Peter Merian-Weg 6 Postfach, 4002 Basle, Switzerland (office). *Telephone:* (61) 267-33-46 (office). *Fax:* (61) 267-33-40 (office). *E-mail:* silvio.borner@unibas.ch (office).

BORODIN, Pavel Pavlovich; Russian politician and economist; *State Secretary, Union of Russia and Belarus;* b. 25 Oct. 1946, Shakhudya, Nizhnii-Novgorod region; m. Valentina Borodina; one d. three adopted s.; ed Higher CPSU School, Moscow Inst. of Chemical Machine Construction, Ulyanovsk Inst. of Agric.; joined Yakutskgeologiya co. as economist 1978, Deputy Dir-Gen. until 1990; Mayor of Yakutsk 1993; Russian Soviet Federated Socialist Repub. People's Deputy, mem. Cttee on Problems of Women, Family Protection and Childhood 1990–93; moved to Moscow 1993; mem., then Man., then Chair. of Presidential Admin. 1993–2000; State Sec. Union of Russia and Belarus Jan. 2000–; detained in USA on request of Swiss Govt Prosecutor, extradited to Switzerland, found guilty of money laundering 2002; Leader, Great Russia—Eurasian Union electoral bloc, State Duma elections 2003; Order for Service to Motherland; State Prize of Russian Fed. *Leisure interests:* football, pets. *Address:* Executive Committee of Russia and Belarus, Union. Kirova str. 17, 220000 Minsk, Belarus (office). *Telephone:* (17) 229-34-34 (office). *Website:* www.belarus.mid.ru/rusbel.html (office).

BORODIN, Stanislav Vladimirovich; Russian jurist; b. 18 Sept. 1924; m.; two s.; ed Moscow Juridical Inst.; mem. Supreme Court RSFSR 1952–61; Head of Higher School, Ministry of Internal Affairs 1961–65, Deputy Head, then Head All-Union Research Inst. 1965–79, Rector of Acad., Ministry of Internal Affairs 1979–83; Sr researcher, then leading researcher, then chief researcher Inst. of State and Law 1983–; mem. Higher Attestation Comm., Scientific Council, Supreme Court of Russian Fed. *Address:* Institute of State and Law, Znamenka str. 10, 119841 Moscow, Russia (office). *Telephone:* (495) 291-87-92 (office).

BORODINA, Olga Vladimirovna; Russian singer (mezzo-soprano); b. 29 July 1963, Leningrad; d. of Vladimir Nikolaevich and Galina Fedorovna Borodin; m. Ildar Abdrazakov; three s.; ed Leningrad Conservatory (student of Irina Bogacheva); soloist of Kirov (now Mariinsky) Theatre of Opera and Ballet 1987–; debut as Delilah in Samson and Delilah at Royal Opera House, Covent Garden with Placido Domingo 1992; leading roles in operas including Marfa in Khovanshchina, Konchakovna in Prince Igor, Poline in Queen of Spades, Lubava in Sadko, Marina Mnichek in Boris Godunov, Cinderella in La Cenerentola, Carmen, Amneris in Aida, Eboli in Don Carlos, Isabella in The Italian Girl in Algiers; regular performances in all major opera houses as well as recitals and concerts around the world; winner of First Prizes: All-Union Glinka Competition 1987, Int. Rosa Poncell Competition (New York) 1987, Int. Francisco Vignas Competition (Barcelona) 1989, People's Artist of Russia 2002, State Prize of Russia 2007. *Leisure interest:* fishing. *Address:* c/o NFBM Ltd, 28 Smalley Close, London, N16 7LE, England (office). *Telephone:* (20) 7254-9606 (office). *Fax:* (870) 094-1600 (office). *E-mail:* nicola-fee@nfbm.com (office). *Website:* www.nfbm.com (office).

BOROSS, Péter, PhD; Hungarian lawyer and politician; *Senior Counsellor and Adviser to Prime Minister;* b. 27 Aug. 1928, Nagybajom; m.; two c.; ed Eötvös Loránd Univ. of Budapest; with Budapest Metropolitan Council 1951–56; dismissed for membership of revolutionary cttee and revolutionary council 1956; kept under police surveillance until 1959; employed as unskilled worker 1964; organized catering and tourist coll. training; catering chain dir 1971; mem. Council Coll. of Trade and Catering; mem. Hungarian League of Human Rights, Hungarian Chamber of Economy; Founder Nation Bldg Foundation 1988; Minister of State for the Office of Information and the Office of Nat. Security 1990–94; Minister of the Interior 1990–93; Prime Minister of Hungary 1993–94; mem. Parl. (Hungarian Democratic Forum—MDF) 1994–98; Chair. Nat. Security Cttee of Parl. 1994–96; Sr Counsellor and Adviser to Prime Minister 1998–; mem. Hungarian Democratic Forum Nat. Presidium 1993–. *Address:* Kossuth Lajos tér 1–3, 1055 Budapest, Hungary. *Telephone:* (1) 441-3000. *Fax:* (1) 441-4888.

BOROVKOV, Aleksandr Alekseyevich; Russian mathematician and academic; *Professor, Sobolev Institute of Mathematics, Novosibirsk University;* b. 6 March 1931, Moscow; s. of Aleksey and Klaudia Borovkov; m. Svetlana Borovkov 1975; two s.; ed Moscow Univ.; Postgraduate, Research Assoc. Steclev Math. Inst. 1954–60; Head of Dept Inst. of Math., Siberian Branch USSR (now Russian) Acad. of Sciences 1960–, Deputy Dir 1981–91; Prof., Sobolev Institute of Mathematics, Novosibirsk Univ. 1965–; Corresp. mem. USSR (now Russian) Acad. of Sciences 1966–90, full mem. 1990–; mem. Int. Statistical Inst. and Bernulli Soc.; Order Merit to Fatherland, Fourth Degree 2002; Badge of Honours 1975, State Prize 1979, Friendship of Nations 1981, Russian Fed. Govt Prize in Educ. 2003, Russian Acad. of Science Markov Prize 2003. *Publications:* Stochastic Processes in Queuing Theory 1976, Wahrscheinlichkeitstheorie 1976, Asymptotic Methods in Queuing Theory 1980, Statistique Mathématique 1987, Ergodicity and Stability of Stochastic Processes, 1998, Probability Theory 1998, Mathematical Statistics 1998; works on contiguous problems of theory probabilities and mathematical statistics. *Address:* Sobolev Institute of Mathematics, Novosibirsk University, Koptyng prospekt 4, Novosibirsk 630090, Russia. *Telephone:* (3832) 33-34-98 (office); (3832) 30-23-53 (home). *Fax:* (3832) 33-25-98 (office). *E-mail:* borovkov@math.nsc.ru (office). *Website:* www.math.nsc.ru (office).

BOROVOI, Konstantin Natanovich, CTechSc; Russian politician and business executive; *Chairman of Export Council, Russian Stock Exchange;* b. 30 June 1948, Moscow; m. twice; two d.; ed Moscow Inst. of Railway Eng, Moscow State Univ.; worked in field of applied math., taught in Moscow State Univ. and Inst. of Land Utilization 1975–87, business activities since 1987–; publishes journal We and Computer 1988–90; Co-Founder and Pres. Russian Stock and Raw Materials Exchange 1990–92; Pres. Agency of Econ. News 1990; Chair. Bd of All-Russian Nat. Commercial Bank 1990–; Pres. Russian Investment Co. Rinako 1991–; mem. Council of Businessmen of Pres. of Russia 1991–; Co-Chair. Foundation of External Policy of Russia 1992–; Founder Commercial TV Co. 1992–; Founder and Co-Chair. Party of Econ. Freedom 1992–; mem. State Duma 1995–99; Pres. Borovoi Trust Co. 1995–; Chair. Export Council, Russian Stock Exchange 1998–. *Publications:* Tsena svobody (The Price of Freedom) 1993, Dvenadtsat samykh uspeshnykh: Kak stat bogatym (The Twelve Most Successful People: How to Become Rich) 2003; numerous articles. *Leisure interests:* tennis, computer graphics. *Address:* Economic Freedom Party, Novoslobolskaya, str. 9, Korp. 3, 103030 Moscow, Russia. *Telephone:* (495) 973-12-18 (office); (495) 250-95-02 (home).

BOROVSKI, David L.; Russian theatre artist; b. 2 July 1934, Odessa; s. of Lev. D. Borovski-Brodsky and Berta M. Borovskaya-Brodskaya; m.; one s.; ed Kiev School of Fine Art; theatre artist Kiev Theatre of Russian drama 1956–66; chief theatre artist Moscow Stanislavsky Drama Theatre 1966–67, Moscow Taganka Theatre 1967–; People's Artist of Russia; State Prize of the Russian Federation 1998, Independent Nat. Triumph Prize 1994, numerous int. prizes, Gold Medal of PQ 1971, Grand Prix 1975. *Theatre productions include:* with Yuri Lyubimov in Taganka theatre: Exchange, Alive, Mother, Hamlet, Vysotsky, etc., also over 120 stage productions with with other famous stage dirs. incl. G. Tovstonogov, A. Efros, V. Fokin, O. Yefremov, O. Tabakov, G. Volchek, L. Dodin, M. Levitin and others abroad in Italy, Germany, Hungary, France, USA, Finland.

BOROWSKI, Marek Stefan; Polish politician; *Leader, Polish Social Democracy;* b. 4 Jan. 1946, Warsaw; m.; one s.; ed Main School of Planning and Statistics (now Warsaw School of Econs), Warsaw; Sr Economist, Centrum Dept stores, Warsaw 1968–82; Ministry of Nat. Economy 1982–91, Deputy Minister 1989; deputy to Sejm (Parl.) 1991–2001; Deputy Prime Minister, Minister of Finance and Head Econ. Cttee of Council of Ministers 1993–94; Minister/Head Council of Ministers Office 1995–96; Vice-Marshal of Sejm 1996–2001, Marshal 2001–04; mem. Polish United Workers' Party (PZPR) 1967–68, 1975–90; mem. Social Democracy of Polish Repub. 1990–99, Democratic Left Alliance 1999–2004 (Vice-Chair.); Leader, Polish Social Democracy Party (Socjaldemokracja Polska—SDPL) 2004–. *Leisure interests:* brain teasers, bowling, board and card games, classical and light music, science fiction books by Stanislaw Lem. *Address:* Socjaldemokracja Polska, ul. Mokotowska 29A, 00-560 Warsaw, Poland (office). *Telephone:* (22) 621-36-40 (office). *Fax:* (22) 621-53-42 (office). *E-mail:* sdpl@sdpl.pl (office). *Website:* www.sdpl.pl (office); www.borowski.pl (home).

BORRELL FONTELLES, Josep, MA, DEconSci; Spanish politician; b. 24 April 1947, Pobla Segur, Lérida; divorced; two c.; ed Polytechnic Univ. and Complutense Univ. Madrid, Institut français du Pétrole, Paris, France, Stanford Univ., USA; engineer and Dir Dept of Systems, CESPA (Compañía Española de Petróleos) 1972–81, elected as trade-union rep.; mem. Socialist Workers' Party (PSOE) Madrid 1975–, mem. Partit dels Socialistes de Catalunya Nat. Exec. 1992–2004, mem. PSOE Fed. Exec. 1997–2004, won PSOE's primary elections to become party cand. for office of Prime Minister 1998; elected as councillor in Spain's first democratic municipal elections 1979; Deputy, Treasury and Econ. Planning for Prov. Del. Madrid 1979–82; Under-Sec. Budget and Public Spending 1982–84, Sec. of State for the Treasury 1984–91, Deputy for Barcelona in Legis. Ass. 1986–91; Minister of Public Works and Transport 1991–96, of the Environment 1993–96; Chair. Parl. Cttee on European Affairs 1999–2004; Pres. European Parl. 2004–07, Chair. European Parl. Devt Cttee 2007–; mem. European Convention 2002–03; Grand Cross, Order of Charles III. *Address:* European Parliament, 60 rue Wiertz, 1047 Brussels, Belgium (office). *Telephone:* (2) 284-73-41 (office). *Fax:* (2) 284-93-41 (office). *Website:* www.europarl.eu.int (office).

BORRIE, Baron (Life Peer), cr. 1995, of Abbots Morton in the County of Hereford and Worcester; **Gordon Johnson,** Kt, QC, FRSA; British lawyer; *Chairman, Advertising Standards Authority;* b. 13 March 1931; s. of Stanley Borrie; m. Dorene Toland 1960; ed John Bright Grammar School, Llandudno and Univ. of Manchester; called to Bar, Middle Temple 1952; Bencher 1980; Barrister, London 1954–57; Lecturer, later Sr Lecturer in Law, Coll. of Law 1957–64, Univ. of Birmingham 1965–68, Prof. of English Law and Dir Inst. of Judicial Admin. 1969–76, Dean Faculty of Law 1974–76; Dir-Gen. Office of Fair Trading 1976–92; Dir (non-exec.) Woolwich Bldg Soc. 1992–2000, Three Valleys Water Services 1992–2003, Mirror Group Newspapers 1993–99, Telewest Communications 1994–2001, General Utilities 1998–2003; Chair. Accountancy Foundation 2000–03, Advertising Standards Authority 2001–; mem. Parole Bd for England and Wales 1971–74, Consumer Protection Advisory Cttee 1973–76, Equal Opportunities Comm. 1975–76; Pres. Inst. of Trading Standards Admin. 1992–97; Chair. Comm. on Social Justice 1992–94, Money Advice Trust 1993–95; mem. Council of Ombudsman for Corp. Estate Agents 1992–98; Labour cand. Croydon 1955, Ilford 1959; Gov. Birmingham Coll. of Commerce 1966–70; Hon. LLD (City of London Polytechnic) 1989, (Manchester Univ.) 1990, (Hull Univ.) 1991, (Dundee Univ.) 1993, (Nottingham Trent Univ.) 1996, (Univ. of the West of England) 1997, (Nottingham Univ.) 2005. *Publications:* Commercial Law 1962, The Consumer, Society and the Law (with Prof. A. L. Diamond) 1963, Law of Contempt (with N. V. Lowe) 1973, The Development of Consumer Law and Policy 1984. *Leisure interests:* gastronomy, piano playing, travel. *Address:* Advertising Standards Authority,

Mid City Place, 71 High Holborn, London, WC1E 6QT (office); 4 Brick Court, Temple, London, EC4Y 9AD (office); Manor Farm, Abbots Morton, Worcestershire, WR7 4NA, England (home). *Telephone:* (20) 7492-2200 (office); (20) 7353-4434; (1386) 792330. *Fax:* (20) 7583-6148 (home). *Website:* www.asa.org.uk (office).

BÖRSIG, Clemens, PhD; German banker; *Chairman of the Supervisory Board and Director, Deutsche Bank AG;* ed Univ. of Mannheim; Asst Prof. at Univs of Mannheim and Munich 1973–77; held several positions at Mannesmann Group, Dusseldorf 1977–85, including Head of Corp. Planning at Mannesmann-Kienzle GmbH and Chief Financial and Admin. Officer at Mannesmann-Tally; Head of Corp. Planning and Controlling, Robert Bosch GmbH, Stuttgart 1985–97, mem. Man. Bd 1990–97; Chief Financial Officer and mem. Man. Bd RWE AG, Essen 1997–99; Chief Financial Officer Deutsche Bank AG 1999–2006, mem. Man. Bd 2001–06, also Chief Risk Officer responsible for corp. governance, mem. Supervisory Bd 2006–, Chair. 2006–; Deputy Chair. Supervisory Bd EUROHYPO AG –2005; mem. Supervisory Bd Heidelberger Druckmaschinen AG, Bayer AG, Deutsche Lufthansa AG, Foreign & Colonial Eurotrust PLC, Linde Group 2006–, Daimlerchrysler AG (now Daimler AG) 2007–. *Address:* Deutsche Bank AG, Taunusanlage 12, 60262 Frankfurt am Main, Germany (office). *Telephone:* (69) 910-00 (office). *Fax:* (69) 910-34225 (office). *E-mail:* webmaster@db.com (office). *Website:* www.db.com (office).

BORSIK, János, DJur; Hungarian trade union official; *President, Autonomous Trade Union Confederation;* b. 22 June 1946; m.; two s.; ed Janus Pannonius Univ. of Sciences, Pécs; locomotive fitter 1964–88; locomotive driver 1968–86; trade union officer 1986–; consultant on labour law; Pres. Autonomous Trade Union Confed. (Autonóm Szakszervezetek Szövetsége—ASZSZ) 2000–; Vice-Pres. Mozdonyvezetok Szakszervezet (MoSZ) 2000. *Leisure interests:* literature, theatre, sports. *Address:* ASZSZ, Benczúr utca 45, 1068 Budapest (office); Oktogon 3, 1066 Budapest, Hungary (home). *Telephone:* (1) 351-1882 (office); (1) 342-1775 (office); (1) 342-1778 (office). *Fax:* (1) 351-1882 (office). *E-mail:* autonom@euroweb.hu (office).

BORST, Piet, MD, PhD; Dutch biochemist; *staff member, Netherlands Cancer Institute;* b. 5 July 1934, Amsterdam; s. of Prof. J. Borst and A. Borst-de Geus; m. Jinke C. S. Houwing 1957; two s. one d.; ed Gymnasium, Amsterdam, Univ. of Amsterdam; Research Asst, Lab. of Biochemistry, Univ. of Amsterdam 1958–61; Post-doctoral Research Fellow, Dept of Biochemistry, New York Univ. 1963–64; Prof. of Biochemistry and Molecular Biology, Univ. of Amsterdam 1965–83, Head of Section for Medical Enzymology, Lab. of Biochemistry 1966–83, Dir Inst. of Animal Physiology 1972–80, Extraordinary Prof. of Clinical Biochemistry 1983–; Dir of Research Netherlands Cancer Inst., Amsterdam 1983–99, staff mem. 1999–; mem. European Molecular Biology Org. 1974, Royal Netherlands Acad. of Arts and Sciences 1978, Hollandsche Maatschappij der Wetenschappen 1983, Academia Europaea 1989; Foreign mem. Royal Soc. 1986, Foreign Assoc. NAS 1991; Foreign Hon. mem. American Acad. of Arts and Sciences 1995; Commdr Order of the Dutch Lion 1999; Dr hc (Leiden) 2003; Royal Dutch/Shell Prize for the Life Sciences 1981, Federatie van Medisch Wetenschappelijke Verenigingen Prize 1984, Paul-Ehrlich and Ludwig-Darmstaedter Prize (jtly) 1984, Ricketts Award of Univ. of Chicago 1989, Dr G. Wander Award of the Wander Foundation, Berne 1990, Gold Medal of the Genootschap voor Natuur-, Genees- en Heelkunde, Amsterdam 1990, Dr H.P. Heineken Prize for Biochem. and Biophysics, Amsterdam 1992, Gold Medal of the Koch Foundation, Bonn 1992, Hamilton Fairley Award for Clinical Research, ESMO 2000. *Publications:* over 300 scientific articles in biochemistry, molecular biology and cell biology. *Leisure interests:* tennis, windsurfing, skiing, cello, bridge. *Address:* Netherlands Cancer Institute, Plesmanlaan 121, 1066 Amsterdam CX (office); Meentweg 87, 1406 Bussum KE, Netherlands (home). *Telephone:* (20) 5122880 (office); (35) 6914453 (home). *Fax:* (20) 6691383 (office). *E-mail:* p.borst@nki.nl (office).

BORTNIKOV, Lt-Gen. Aleksander Vasilyevich; Russian government official; *Head, Federal Security Service (FSB);* b. 1951, Perm Oblast; m.; one s.; ed Leningrad Inst. for Railway Eng; joined Leningrad KGB 1975, Deputy Head, Fed. Security Service (FSB) Directorate for St Petersburg and Leningrad Oblast in charge of counter-intelligence operations –2003, Head of Directorate 2003–04, Deputy Dir FSB and Head of Econ. Security Service 2004–08, Head of FSB 2008–; mem. Bd of Dirs Sovkomflot. *Address:* Federal Security Service (FSB), 103031 Moscow, Bolshaya Lubyanka, Building 1/3, Russia (office). *Telephone:* (495) 914-43-69 (office). *E-mail:* fsb@fsb.ru (office). *Website:* www.fsb.ru (office).

BORUBAYEV, Altai; Kyrgyzstani mathematician and politician; *Chairman (Speaker) of People's Assembly (Parliament);* b. 1950, Kara-oy, Kyrgyzia; ed Kyrgyz State Univ.; teacher, Frunze Polytechnic Inst. 1975–76; teacher, Sr Teacher, Head of Chair., Dean, Pro-Rector Kyrgyz State Univ. 1976–92, Rector 1998–2000; Rector Kyrgyz State Pedagogical Inst. 1994–98; First Deputy Minister of Educ. 1992–94; Chair. (Speaker) Ass. of People's Reps Chamber of Zhogorku Kenesh (Parl.) 2000–; mem. Nat. Acad. of Sciences 2000, Russian Acad. of Social and Pedagogical Sciences. *Publications:* three monographs, over 100 articles. *Address:* Zhogorku Kenesh, Assembly of People's Representatives, 720003 Bishkek, Kyrgyzstan (office). *Telephone:* (312) 27-17-19 (office).

BORZAKOVSKIY, Yuriy; Russian middle distance runner; b. 12 April 1981, Kratovo; m. Irina; one s.; winner 800m., European Cup Super League, Paris 1999, Annecy 2002; Gold Medal 800m., World Youth Games, Moscow 1998, European Jr Championships, Riga 1999, European Indoor Championships, Gent 2000, World Indoor Championships, Lisbon 2001, Athens Olympics 2004; Gold Medal 400m. European U23 Championships, Amsterdam 2001; Silver Medal 800m., IAAF Grand Prix Final, Melbourne 2001, IAAF World Championships, Paris 2003, Helsinki 2005; Silver Medal 4 x 400m. European Championships, Munich 2002, Bronze Medal IAAF World Indoor Championships Moscow 2006, Bronze Medal IAAF World Championships Osaka 2007. *Address:* c/o Elite Ltd, Tölgyfa u. 27, 2089 Telki, Hungary (office). *Telephone:* (30) 942-6417 (office). *Fax:* (26) 572-109 (office). *E-mail:* spiriev@axelero.hu (office). *Website:* www.elite-athletics.hu/athletics/yuriy/index.html (office).

BORZOV, Valeriy Filippovich; Ukrainian sports administrator, politician and fmr athlete; b. 20 Oct. 1949, Sambor, Lvov Region, Ukraine; s. of Philipp Petrovich Borzov and Valentina Georgiyevna Borzova; m. Lyudmila Turishcheva 1978 (divorced); one d.; ed Kiev State Inst. of Physical Culture; competed Olympic Games Munich 1972, winning gold medals at 100m and 200m; bronze medal at 100m, Montreal 1976; European Junior Champion 100m and 200m 1968; European Champion 100m 1969; 100m and 200m 1971, 100m 1974; European Indoor Champion 60m 1970, 1971, 1972, 50m 1974, 1975, 1976; held European record at 100m and 200m and world record at 60m; Minister of Sport and Youth Ukrainian Repub. 1990–; Chair. State Cttee for Physical Culture and Sport 1996–97; Chair. Nat. Olympic Cttee of Ukraine 1990–; mem. Int. Olympic Cttee, Jt Asscn of Summer Olympic Sports 1994–; f. Nat. Olympic Acad. of Ukraine; Merited Master of Sport. *Leisure interests:* fishing, hunting. *Address:* c/o National Olympic Committee of Ukraine, Esplanadna Street 42, 252023 Kiev, Ukraine (office). *Telephone:* (44) 220-05-50. *Fax:* (44) 220-05-09.

BOS, Caroline Elisabeth, BA; Dutch art historian; *Founder and Director, UNStudio;* b. 17 June 1959, Rotterdam; d. of Peter Bos and Ellen Guibal; ed Birkbeck Coll., Univ. of London; freelance journalist 1982–88; Co-founder (with Ben van Berkel) and Dir Van Berkel & Bos Architectur Bureau 1988–99; Co-founder and Dir UNStudio (network of specialists in architecture, urban devt and infrastructure), Amsterdam 1998–; has lectured at Princeton Univ., Berlage Inst., Amsterdam, Acad. of Fine Arts, Vienna, Acad. of Architecture, Arnhem, Vienna; Chair. Sikkens Foundation; Eileen Gray Award 1983, British Council Fellowship 1986, Charlotte Köhler Prize 1991; winning entry for Police HQ, Berlin 1995, Museum Het Valkof 1995, Music Theatre, Graz 1998, La Defense Offices Almere (Netherlands) 1999, Restructuring Harbour Ponte Parodi, Genoa 2000, Mercedes-Benz Museum, Stuttgart 2002, Agora Theater, Lelystad 2003, Te Papa Museum, Wellington Waterfront, Waitangi, NZ 2005, Charles Jencks Award 2007. *Projects include:* switching substation, Amersfoort 1989–93, Erasmus Bridge, Rotterdam 1990–96, Villa Wilbrink, Amersfoort 1992–94, Möbius House, 't Gooi 1993–98, Rijksmuseum Twente, conversion and extension, Enschede 1992–96, Museum Het Valkhof, Nijmegen 1995–99, Masterplan of station area, Arnhem 1996–2005, Willemstunnel, Arnhem 1996–99, City Hall and Theatre, Ijsselstein 1996–2000, Lab. for NMR facilities, Utrecht 1996–2000, Switching station, Innsbruck 1998–2001, Music Faculty, Graz 1998–2002, Mercedes-Benz Museum 2006, VilLA NM 2007, Theatre Agora 2007; current projects include the restructuring of the station area of Arnhem, a music theatre for Graz and the conversion of a pier in the harbour of Genoa. *Address:* UNStudio, Stadhouderskade 113, 1073 AX Amsterdam, The Netherlands (office). *Telephone:* (20) 5702040 (office). *Fax:* (20) 5702041 (office). *E-mail:* info@unstudio.com (office). *Website:* www.unstudio.com (office).

BOS, Wouter Jacob; Dutch politician; *Deputy Prime Minister and Minister of Finance;* b. 14 July 1963, Vlaardingen; ed Grammar School, Zeist and Free Univ. of Amsterdam; Man. Consultant, Shell Netherlands Refinery BV 1988–90, Policy Adviser, Rotterdam 1990–92, Gen. Affairs Man. Shell Romania Exploration BV, Bucharest 1992–93, Staff Planning and Devt Man., Shell Cos in China, Hong Kong 1993–96, Consultant, New Markets, Shell Int. Oil Products, London 1996–98; mem. Parl. (Partij van de Arbeid) 1998–, Sec. of State for Finance (Taxes) 2002–02; Parl. Leader Partij van de Arbeid (PvdA) 2002–, Deputy Prime Minister and Minister of Finance 2007–. *Address:* Ministry of Finance, Prinses Beatrixlaan 512, PO Box 20201, 2500 EE The Hague, Netherlands (office). *Telephone:* (70) 3428000 (office). *Fax:* 3427900 (office). *E-mail:* webmaster@minfin.nl (office). *Website:* www.minfin.nl (office).

BOSHOFF, Carel Willem Hendrik, MA, DD; South African theologian; b. 9 Nov. 1927, Nylstroom; s. of W.S. Boshoff and A.M. Boshoff; m. Anna Verwoerd, d. of late Hendrik Verwoerd (Prime Minister of SA 1958–66) 1954; five s. two d.; ed Nylstroom High School, Pretoria Univ.; Missionary Dutch Reformed Church 1953–63, Sec. of Missions 1963–66; Prof. and Head of Dept of Theology, Missiology and Science of Religion, Univ. of Pretoria 1967–88, Dean, Theology Faculty 1978–80; Chair. SA Bureau of Racial Affairs (SABRA) 1972–99; Chair. N. G. Kerkboekhandel 1976–88; Chair. Afrikaner Broederbond 1980–83; Chair. Afrikaner Volkswag Cultural Org. 1984–99, Council of Inst. for Missiological Research 1978–88; Exec. Chair. Afrikaner Vryheidstigting 1988–2008; Chair., Dir Orania Bestuurdienste Ltd 1990–; Leader, Die Voortrekkers 1981–89; mem. numerous theological and scholarly cttees; Pres. Burger Council Afrikaner Vryheidstigting 1994–2008; Provincial Leader, Freedom Front of Northern Cape 1994–2003; mem. legislature, Prov. of Northern Cape 1994–2001; mem. S African Akad. vir Wekenskap en Kuns. *Publications:* Die Begin van die Evangelie van Jesus Christus 1963, Uit God Gebore 1968, Die Nuwe Sendingsituasie 1978, Swart Teologie van Amerika Tot in Suid-Afrika 1980; numerous articles in various journals. *Leisure interests:* small farming, breeding Nooitgedacht ponies, hiking, reading. *Address:* PO Box 199, Orania 8752; 26 Jaspis Street, Orania 8752, South Africa (home). *Telephone:* (53) 207-0068 (office); (53) 207-0008 (home); (82) 802-1999 (Mobile). *Fax:* (53) 207-0061.

BOSKIN, Michael Jay, MA, PhD; American economist, government official, academic and consultant; *Tim Friedman Professor of Economics and Hoover Institution Senior Fellow, Stanford University;* b. 23 Sept. 1945, New York; s. of Irving Boskin and Jean Boskin; m. Chris Dornin 1981; ed Univ. of

California, Berkeley; Asst Prof., Stanford Univ., Calif. 1970–75, Assoc. Prof. 1976–78, Prof. 1978–, Tim Friedman Prof. of Econs and Hoover Inst. Sr Fellow 1993–; Dir, Centre for Econ. Policy Research 1986–89; Wohlford Prof. of Econs 1987–89; Chair. Pres.'s Council of Econ. Advisers 1989–93; Chair. Congressional Comm. on the Consumer Price Index; Pres., Boskin & Co., Calif. 1993–; Research Assoc., Nat. Bureau of Econ. Research 1976–; Visiting Prof., Harvard Univ., Mass. 1977–78; Faculty Research Fellow, Mellon Foundation 1973; Distinguished Faculty Fellow, Yale Univ. 1993; Scholar, American Enterprise Inst.; mem. Bd of Dirs ExxonMobil Corpn (following merging of Exxon Corpn and Mobil Corpn), Oracle Corpn, Shinsei Bank; several prizes and awards including Stanford's Distinguished Teaching Award 1987, Adam Smith Prize for Contribs to Econs 1998. *Publications:* Too Many Promises: The Uncertain Future of Social Security 1986, Reagan and the Economy: Successes, Failures, Unfinished Agenda 1987, Frontiers of Tax Reform 1996, Capital Technology and Growth 1996, Toward a More Accurate Measure of the Cost of Living 1996; contrib. articles in various professional journals. *Leisure interests:* tennis, skiing, reading, theatre. *Address:* Stanford University, 213 HHMB, Stanford, CA 94305, USA (office). *Telephone:* (650) 723-6482 (office). *Fax:* (650) 723-6494 (office). *E-mail:* boskin@stanford.edu (office). *Website:* www-hoover.stanford.edu/bios/boskin.html (office).

BOSNICH, Brice, PhD, FRS; Australian chemist and academic; *Professor, Department of Chemistry, University of Chicago;* b. 1936, Queensland; ed Univ. of Sydney, Australian Nat. Univ.; Dept of Industrial and Scientific Research Postdoctoral Fellow, Univ. Coll., London 1962–63; ICI Fellow, 1963–66; Lecturer, Univ. of Toronto 1966–69, Assoc. Prof. 1970–75, Prof. 1975–87; Prof., Univ. of Chicago 1987–; Killam Fellow, Univ. of Toronto 1979–91; Noranda Award in Inorganic Chem., Canadian Inst. of Chem. 1978, Organometallic Medal, Royal Soc. of Chem. 1994, Nyholm Award Medal, Royal Soc. of Chem. 1995, ACS Award in Inorganic Chem. 1998. *Address:* University of Chicago, Department of Chemisty, 5735 South Ellis Avenue, Chicago, IL 60637, USA (office). *Telephone:* (773) 702-0287 (office). *Fax:* (773) 702-0805 (office). *E-mail:* bos5@uchicago.edu (office). *Website:* chemistry .uchicago.edu (office).

BOSSANO, Hon. Joseph J., BSc (Econ), BA; Gibraltarian politician; *Leader, Gibraltar Socialist Labour Party;* b. 10 June 1939; m. 1st Judith Baker 1967 (divorced 1988); three s. one d.; m. 2nd Rose Torilla 1988; ed Gibraltar Grammar School, Birmingham Univ., Univ. of London; factory worker 1958–60; merchant seaman 1960–64; Sec. Integration with Britain Movt 1964; mem. Man. Cttee Tottenham Constituency Labour Party 1965–68; fmr mem. IWBP Exec. Cttee; Leader Gibraltar Socialist Labour Party 1977–; Leader of the Opposition 1984–88, 1996–; Sec. Gibraltar Br. Commonwealth Parl. Asscn 1980–88; Br. Officer TGWU (Gibraltar) 1974–88; Chief Minister of Gibraltar, with responsibility for Information 1988–96. *Leisure interests:* carpentry, fishing, thinking and linguistics. *Address:* 2 Gowland's Ramp, Gibraltar (home); Gibraltar Socialist Labour Party, Suite 16, Watergardens 3, Gibraltar (office). *Telephone:* 50700 (office). *Fax:* 78983 (office). *E-mail:* hqgslp@gibtelecom.net (home). *Website:* www.gslp.gi (office).

BOSSARD, André, DIur; French international police official (retd); b. 18 June 1926, St Ouen; s. of Charles and Aline Bossard (née Sirugue); m. Francine Agen 1956; two d.; ed Lycée Louis le Grand, Paris Univ.; called to bar 1949; joined police service with rank of Commissaire 1950, Commissaire Prin. 1958, Commissaire Divisionnaire 1968; Tech. Adviser at Police Judiciaire HQ 1970; Head of a Div. Int. Criminal Police Org. (INTERPOL) 1971–77; Contrôleur Gén. de la Police Nat. 1977; Sec.-Gen. INTERPOL 1978–85; Visiting Adjunct Prof., Univ. of Ill., USA 1988–91, 1998; Hon. Research Fellow, Univ. of Exeter, UK 1991; Chevalier, Légion d'honneur. *Publications:* Transnational Crime and Criminal Law 1987, Law Enforcement in Europe 1993, Carrefours de la grande truanderie 1998. *Leisure interest:* painting. *Address:* 228 rue de la Convention, 75015 Paris, France (home). *Telephone:* 1-48-28-21-45 (home). *E-mail:* andrebossard@wanadoo.fr (home).

BOSSE, Stine, LLM; Danish lawyer and insurance industry executive; *CEO, TrygVesta;* b. 1960; four c.; ed Univ. of Copenhagen; Univ. of Pa USA; joined TrygVesta 1987, Head of Claims Dept 1988–90, Head of Underwriting Dept 1990–91, Deputy Functional Man. responsible for product and concept devt, Claims and Underwriting Dept 1991–93, Personnel Man. 1993–95, Human Resource Dir 1995–99, Dir 1999–2001; currently Group CEO TrygVesta, CEO Tryg; Chair. Danish Insurance Asscn; Chair. Hjertebarnsfonden; mem. Bd of Dirs Grundfos Man. A/S, Poul Due Jensen Foundation, Nordea, Amlin plc; mem. Welfare Cttee; mem. Supervisory Bd Forsikring & Pension (F&P), TDC; Chair. Supervisory Bds of several intra-group cos; ranked by the Financial Times amongst Top 25 Businesswomen in Europe (15th) 2005, (11th) 2006, (13th) 2007. *Address:* TrygVesta, Klausdalsbrovej 601, 2750 Ballerup, Denmark (office). *Telephone:* 70-11-20-20 (office). *Fax:* 44-20-67-00 (office). *E-mail:* trygvesta@trygvesta.com (office). *Website:* www.trygvesta.com (office).

BOSSI, Umberto; Italian politician; *Secretary, Federation of Northern League Movements;* b. 19 Sept. 1941, Cassano Magnago, Varese; m.; four c. (two by Manuela Marrone); ed Pavia Univ.; f. Lombard Autonomy League 1982; Leader, Lombard League 1984–; Senator 1987; Sec. Fed. of Northern League Movts 1989–; sentenced to five months' imprisonment for libel and eight months for illegal financing of his party Nov. 1995; elected Deputy for Div. III (Lombardy 1), Dist 3, Milan 2001; Minister without Portfolio, responsible for Reforms and Devolution 2001–04 (resgnd); Minister for Reforms 2008–. *Address:* Lega Nord, via C. Bellerio 41, 20161 Milan, Italy (office). *Telephone:* (02) 662341 (office). *Fax:* (02) 66234266 (office). *E-mail:* webmaster@leganord.org (office). *Website:* www.leganord.org (office).

BOSSIDY, Lawrence Arthur, BA; American business executive and writer; b. 5 March 1935, Pittsfield, Mass.; m. Nancy Bossidy 1956; three s. six d.; ed Colgate Univ.; joined Gen. Electric Co. 1957, Vice-Chair. 1984–91; Chair., CEO Allied Signal Inc. 1991–2000; Chair. Honeywell Inc. (after merger of Allied Signal and Honeywell 1999) 2001–02; fmr Chair. and Dir Gen. Electric Credit Corpn New York; mem. Bd of Dirs Merck & Co. 1992–2007, Champion Int. Corpn, J.P. Morgan & Co. Inc., Berkshire Hills Bancorp Inc.; CEO of the Year, Financial World magazine 1994, Chief Executive of the Year, CEO Magazine 1998. *Publications:* Execution: The Discipline of Getting Things Done 2002, Confronting Reality: Doing What Matters to Get Things Right (with Ram Charan) 2004. *Address:* c/o The Leigh Bureau, 92 East Main Street, Suite 400, Somerville, NJ 08876, USA. *Telephone:* (908) 253-8600. *Fax:* (908) 253-8601. *E-mail:* info@leighbureau.com.

BOSSON, Bernard; French lawyer and politician; b. 25 Feb. 1948, Annecy; s. of Charles Bosson and Claire Bosson; m. Danielle Blaise 1976; one d.; ed Coll. Saint-Michel and Faculté de Droit de Lyon; barrister, Annecy 1976–; Mayor of Annecy 1983–2007; Deputy Nat. Ass. 1986–93, 1995–2007; Sec. of State, Ministry of the Interior 1986, Del. Minister, Ministry of Foreign Affairs 1986–88; Minister of Public Transport and Tourism 1993–95; Deputy Vice-Pres. Del. for EC 1988; Vice-Pres. Mouvement européen 1990–97; Sec.-Gen. Centre des Démocrates sociaux 1991; mem. Union pour la démocratie française, Vice-Pres. 1998–. *Address:* c/o Mairie, place de l'Hôtel de Ville, BP 2305, 74001 Annecy cedex, France. *Telephone:* 4-50-63-48-49. *Fax:* 4-50-45-86-37. *Website:* www.bernard-bosson.fr.

BOSTRIDGE, Ian Charles, CBE, MA, DPhil; British singer (tenor); b. 1965, London; s. of the late Leslie John Bostridge and of Lilian Winifred (née Clark); m. Lucasta Miller 1992; one s.; ed Westminster School, Univs of Oxford and Cambridge; debut recital performance in Wigmore Hall, London 1993; operatic debut in Edin. Festival 1994; has since performed at Carnegie Hall and Lincoln Center, New York, Salzburg Festival, Théâtre du Châtelet, Philharmonie, Berlin etc.; annual lieder recitals Munich Opera Festival; Hon. Fellow Corpus Christi Coll., Oxford; Hon. DMus (St Andrews); awards include Gramophone Solo Vocal Awards 1996, 1998, Time Out Classical Music Award 1999, Edison Award 1999, 2002, Grammy Award (opera) 1999, Critics' Choice Classical Brit Award (for The English Songbook) 2000, Preis der Deutschen Schallplattenkritik 2001, Acad. Charles Cros, Grand Prix du Disque 2001. *Television:* Winterreise (Channel 4) 1997, Britten Serenade (BBC) 1999, The South Bank Show (ITV) 2000, Janacek documentary (BBC 4) 2004. *Opera:* A Midsummer Night's Dream, Edin. Festival 1994, The Magic Flute, ENO 1996, The Turn of the Screw, Royal Opera House 1997, 2002, The Bartered Bride, Sadler's Wells 1998, L'incoronazione di Poppea, Munich Festival 1998, The Diary of One Who Vanished, Munich and New York 1999, The Rake's Progress, Munich Festival 2002, Don Giovanni, Royal Opera House, Covent Garden 2003, Ades and The Tempest, Covent Garden 2004, The Rape of Lucretia, Munich 2004. *Recordings include:* Britten 2005. *Publication:* Witchcraft and its Transformations 1650–1750 1997. *Leisure interests:* reading, cooking, looking at pictures. *Address:* c/o Askonas Holt Ltd, Lincoln House, 300 High Holborn, London, WC1V 7JH, England (office). *Telephone:* (20) 7400-1700 (office). *Fax:* (20) 7400-1799 (office). *E-mail:* info@askonasholt .co.uk (office). *Website:* www.askonasholt.co.uk (office).

BOSTRÖM, Rolf Gustav, PhD; Swedish physicist and academic; *Professor Emeritus, Swedish Institute of Space Physics;* b. 15 April 1936, Kalmar; s. of Gustav Boström and Greta Boström (née Bergström); m. Barbro Karlsson 1962; one s.; ed Royal Inst. of Tech.; Research Assoc., Dept of Plasma Physics, Royal Inst. of Tech. 1961–71, Sr Physicist 1971–75, Assoc. Prof. 1975–76; Prof., Uppsala Div. of Swedish Inst. of Space Physics (fmrly Uppsala Ionospheric Observatory) 1976–2002, Prof. Emer. 2002–; Head Dept of Space Physics, Uppsala Univ. 1988–96; mem. Royal Swedish Acad. of Sciences. *Publications:* scientific papers on space plasma physics. *Leisure interests:* hiking, angling. *Address:* Klippvägen 22, 756 52 Uppsala, Sweden (home); Ångström Laboratory, Swedish Institute of Space Physics, Box 537, 751 21 Uppsala (office). *Telephone:* (18) 32-02-61 (home); (18) 471-59-10 (office). *Fax:* (18) 471-59-05 (office).

BOSWORTH, Stephen Warren; American diplomatist; *Dean, The Fletcher School of Law and Diplomacy, Tufts University;* b. 4 Dec. 1939, Conn.; s. of Warren Charles Bosworth and Mina Bosworth; m. Christine Bosworth; two s. two d.; ed Dartmouth Coll. and George Washington Univ.; joined Foreign Service 1962, assignments in Paris, Madrid and Panama City, later Amb. to Tunisia 1979–81, the Philippines 1984–87, Repub. of Korea 1997–2001; various positions with Dept of State including Deputy Asst Sec. for Econ. Affairs and for Inter-American Affairs, Dir of Policy Planning and Head Office of Fuels and Energy; Pres. US-Japan Foundation 1988–96; Exec. Dir Korean Peninsula Energy Devt Corpn 1995–97; Dean, The Fletcher School of Law and Diplomacy, Tufts Univ. 2001–; Adjunct Prof., School of Int. and Public Affairs, Columbia Univ. 1990–94; Order of Rising Sun, Gold and Silver Star (Japan) 2006; Distinguished Service Award, Dept of State 1976, 1986, Distinguished Service Award, Dept of Energy 1979. *Publications:* articles: Why Do They Hate Us? The Reasons are Many, The History Long, Because We are Big, So Powerful, The Boston Globe 2001, Adjusting to the New Asia (with Morton Abramowitz), Foreign Affairs 2003. *Address:* The Fletcher School of Law and Diplomacy, 160 Packard Avenue, Tufts University, Medford, MA 02155, USA (office). *Telephone:* (617) 627-3050 (office). *Fax:* (617) 627-3508 (office). *E-mail:* stephen.bosworth@tufts.edu (office). *Website:* www.fletcher.tufts.edu (office).

BOT, Bernard Rudolf (Ben), DJur; Dutch diplomatist and politician; b. 21 Nov. 1937, Jakarta, Indonesia; s. of Th. H. Bot and E. W. van Hal; m. Christine Bot-Pathy 1962 (deceased); three c.; ed St Aloysius Coll., The Hague, Univ. of Leiden, Acad. of Int. Law, The Hague and Harvard Law School, USA; Deputy Perm. Rep. of Netherlands to North Atlantic Council, Brussels 1982–86; Amb. to Turkey 1986–89; Sec.-Gen. Ministry of Foreign Affairs 1989–92; apptd Perm. Rep. to EU 1992; Minister of Foreign Affairs 2003–07; currently Pres.

www.worldwhoswho.com

Netherlands Inst. of Int. Relations (Clingendael); Kt, Order of Netherlands Lion and other decorations. *Publications:* Non-recognition and Treaty Relations 1968; numerous articles on the Common Market, European political co-operation, NATO and other political matters. *Leisure interests:* cycling, painting, skiing. *Address:* Clingendael, POB 93080, 2509 AB The Hague (office); c/o Ministry of Foreign Affairs, Bezuidenhoutseweg 67, POB 20061, 2500 EB The Hague, The Netherlands. *E-mail:* info@clingendael.nl (office). *Website:* www.clingendael.nl (office).

BOTELHO, João; Portuguese film director; b. 11 May 1949, Lamego; m. Leonor Pinhão; three c.; ed Nat. Conservatory Film School, Lisbon; involved in film socs in Coimbra and Oporto; film critic for newspapers; f. film magazine M. *Films include:* Alexandre e Rosa (short, co-Dir) 1978, Conversa acabada (The Other One) 1980, Um adeus português (A Portuguese Goodbye) 1985, Tempos difíceis (Hard Times) 1987, No dia dos meus anos (On my Birthday) 1992, Aqui na Terra (Here on Earth) 1993, Três Palmeiras (Three Palm Trees) 1994, Tráfico (Traffic) 1998, Se a Memória Existe (If Memories Exist) 1999, Quem és tu? (Who are you?) (Mimmo Rotella Foundation Prize, Venice Film Festival) 2001, O Fatalista 2005. *Address:* c/o Associação Portuguesa de Realizadores, Rua de Palmeira 7, r/c, 1200 Lisbon, Portugal.

BOTELHO, Maurício; Brazilian business executive; Pres. and CEO Empresa Brasileira de Aeronautica SA; BACCF Excellence Award 1999. *Address:* EMBRAER, Av. Brig. Faria Lima 2170, Putim 12227-901, S. Jose dos Campos, São Paulo, Brazil (office). *Telephone:* (12) 345-1000 (office). *Fax:* (12) 321-8238 (office).

BOTERO, Fernando; Colombian artist; b. 19 April 1932, Medellín; s. of David Botero and Flora Botero; m. Cecilia Botero 1964; four c.; first group exhbn, Medellín 1948; first one-man exhbn, Galería Leo Matiz, Bogotá 1951; studied at Acad. San Fernando and El Prado Museum, Madrid 1952; visited Paris and Italy and studied art history with Roberto Longhi, Univ. of Florence 1953–54; lived in Mexico 1956; one-man exhbn Pan American Union, Washington, DC 1957, Colombia 1958–59; lived in New York 1960–; first one-man exhbn in Europe, Baden-Baden and Munich 1966; visited Italy and Germany 1967, studied work of Dürer; travelling retrospective exhbn of 80 paintings in five German museums 1970; one-man exhbn Hannover Gallery, London 1970; moved to Paris 1973; concentrated on Sculpture 1976–77, first one-man exhbn of sculpture, Foire Int. d'Art Contemporain, Paris 1977; retrospective exhbn, Hirshorn Museum and Sculpture Garden, Washington, DC 1979; first one-man exhbn in Japan, Tokyo, Osaka 1981; outdoor sculpture exhbn, Chicago 1994; paintings in public collections in Belgium, Finland, Germany, Israel, Italy, S. America, Spain and USA; Guggenheim Nat. Prize for Colombia 1960.

BOTHA, Roelof Frederik (Pik), BA, LLB; South African politician; b. 27 April 1932, Rustenburg; m. 1st Helena Bosman 1953; two s. two d.; m. 2nd Ina Joubert 1998; ed Volkskool, Potchefstroom, Univ. of Pretoria; joined Dept of Foreign Affairs 1953; served with diplomatic missions in Europe 1956–66; mem. S African legal team in SW Africa case, Int. Court of Justice, The Hague 1963–66, 1970–71; Agent of S African Govt, Int. Court of Justice 1965–66; Legal Adviser Dept of Foreign Affairs 1966–68, Under-Sec. and Head SW Africa and UN sections 1968–70; mem. Parl. for Wonderboom 1970–74, for Westdene 1977–94, re-elected 1994–96, served on various select parl. cttees 1970–74; Sec. Foreign Affairs Study Group of Nat. Party's mems of Parl. 1974; Amb. and Perm. Rep. to UN 1974–77; Amb. to USA 1975–77; Minister of Foreign Affairs 1977–94, of Mineral and Energy Affairs 1994–96, for Information 1980–86; mem. S African Del. to UN Gen. Assembly 1967–69, 1971, 1973–74; Leader Nat. Party in Transvaal 1992–96; Grand Cross, Order of Good Hope, Decoration for Meritorious Service (SA), Grand Cordon, Order of the Brilliant Star (Taiwan). *Leisure interests:* hunting and fishing. *Address:* PO Box 16176, Pretoria North 0116, South Africa.

BOTHAM, Sir Ian Terence, Kt; British fmr professional cricketer; *Chairman, Mission Sports Management;* b. 24 Nov. 1955; s. of Leslie Botham and Marie Botham; m. Kathryn Waller 1976; one s. two d.; ed Buckler's Mead Secondary School, Yeovil; right-hand batsman, right-hand, fast-medium bowler; teams: Somerset 1974–86 (Capt. 1984–85), Worcs. 1987–91, Queensland 1987–88, Durham 1992–93; 102 Tests for England 1977–92, 12 as Capt., scoring 5,200 runs (average 33.5) including 14 hundreds, taking 383 wickets (average 28.4) and holding 120 catches; scored 1,673 runs and took 148 wickets v. Australia; became first player to score a century and take 8 wickets in an innings in a Test match, v. Pakistan (Lord's) 1978; took 100th wicket in Test cricket in record time of 2 years 9 days 1979; achieved double of 1,000 runs and 100 wickets in Tests to create world record of fewest Tests (21) and English records of shortest time (2 years 33 days) and at youngest age (23 years 279 days) 1979; became first player to have scored 3,000 runs and taken 250 wickets in Tests (55) Nov. 1982; first player to score a century and take 10 wickets in a Test match, v. India; scored 19,399 runs (38 hundreds) and took 1,172 wickets in first-class cricket; toured Australia 1978–79, 1979–80, 1982–83 and 1986–87; has also played soccer for Scunthorpe United and Yeovil; mem. Sky cricket commentary team 1995–; Tech. Advisor, England Cricket Team 1996; Chair. Mission Sports Man. 2000–, mem. MCC Cricket Cttee 1995, Sports Council 1995–, Laureus World Sports Acad.; Columnist, Daily Mirror; Hon. MSc (UMIST); Wisden Cricketer of the Year 1978, Lifetime Achievement Award, BBC Sports Personality of the Year 2004. *Publications include:* It Sort of Clicks 1986, Cricket My Way 1989, Botham: My Autobiography 1994, The Botham Report (with Peter Hayter) 1997, Head On: The Autobiography 2007. *Leisure interests:* shooting, golf, flying, fishing. *Address:* Mission Sports Management, Park House, Northfields, London, SW18 1DD, England (office). *Telephone:* (20) 8704-4165 (office). *Fax:* (20) 8704-4169 (office). *E-mail:* adam@missionsportsmanagement.com (office). *Website:* www.missionsportsmanagement.com (office).

BOTHWELL, Thomas Hamilton, DSc, MD, FRCP, FRSSA; South African physician and professor of medicine; *Honorary Professorial Research Fellow, University of the Witwatersrand;* b. 27 Feb. 1926; s. of Robert Cooper Bothwell and Jessie Isobel Bothwell (née Hamilton); m. Alexandrine Moorman Butterworth 1957; one s. two d.; ed St John's Coll., Johannesburg, Univ. of Witwatersrand and Univs of Oxford, UK and Washington, USA; physician, later Sr Physician Dept of Medicine, Univ. of the Witwatersrand 1956–67, Prof. of Medicine and Head Dept of Medicine 1967–91; Chief Physician Johannesburg Hosp. 1967–91; Dir MRC Iron and Red Cell Metabolism Research Unit, Univ. of the Witwatersrand 1969–91, Dean of Medicine 1992–93, Hon. Professorial Research Fellow 1993–; Hon. FCP (SA); Hon. FACP; Dr hc (Univs of Cape Town, Natal, Witwatersrand); Gold Medal, SA Medical Research Council 1987; Medal of the SA Asscn for the Advancement of Science 1980, Biennial Award of the Nutrition Soc. of Southern Africa 1988, John F. W. Herschel Medal of the Royal Soc. of SA 1993, William D. Davis Award, Hemochromatosis Research Foundation 1993, Science-for-Society Gold Medal, Acad. of Science of SA 2005. *Publications:* more than 260 articles in the field of iron metabolism, 55 chapters, seven monographs and two books: Iron Metabolism 1962, Iron Metabolism in Man 1979. *Leisure interests:* reading, walking, dogs. *Address:* Department of Medicine, University of the Witwatersrand, Medical School, 7 York Road, Parktown 2193, Johannesburg, South Africa (office). *Telephone:* (11) 488-3623 (office); (11) 728-2180 (home). *Fax:* (11) 643-8777 (office); (11) 728-2180 (home). *E-mail:* zockja@medicine.wits.ac.za (office).

BOTÍN, Ana Patricia; Spanish banking executive; *Chairman, Banco Banesto;* d. of Emilio Botín; three c.; began career with JP Morgan, New York and Madrid 1981, various positions in Latin American Div. including Vice-Pres. –1988; CEO Banco Santander de Negocios and Exec. Vice-Pres. Banco Santander 1994–99; Founder, Chair. and CEO Suala Capital Advisers 1999–2002; Jt Pres. Banco Santander Central Hispano (BSCH), Chair. of subsidiary Banco Banesto, Madrid 2002–; Chair. coverlink.com; Exec. Chair. Razona (tech. consulting and systems integrations co.) 1999–; mem. Foro Iberoamerica, Trilateral Comm.; mem. Int. Advisory Bd J. E. Robert Cos (int. real estate investment and asset man. firm) 2002–; ranked by Fortune magazine amongst 50 Most Powerful Women in Business outside the US (20th) 2003, (sixth) 2004, (eighth) 2005, (ninth) 2006, (ninth) 2007, ranked by Forbes magazine amongst 100 Most Powerful Women (94th) 2004, (99th) 2005, (73rd) 2006, (40th) 2007, (51st) 2008, ranked by the Financial Times amongst Top 25 Businesswomen in Europe (first) 2005, (first) 2006, (fourth) 2007. *Leisure interest:* golf. *Address:* Banco Español de Crédito (Banesto), Gran Vía de Hortaleza 3, 28043 Madrid, Spain (office). *Telephone:* (91) 3383100 (office). *Fax:* (91) 3381883 (office). *E-mail:* uninternac@banesto.es (office). *Website:* www.banesto.es (office).

BOTÍN-SANZ DE SAUTUOLA Y GARCÍA DE LOS RÍOS, Emilio; Spanish banker; *Chairman, Banco Santander Central Hispano SA;* b. 1934, Santander; m. Paloma O'Shea; six c.; ed Univ. of Duesto, Bilbao; appointed a Dir of the bank 1960, inherited Banco de Santander 1986, Pres. 1986–99 (absorbed Banesto 1993), Co-Pres. Banco Santander Central Hispano SA (following merger of Banco de Santander with Banco Hispano Americano and Banco Central 1999) 1999–2002, Exec. Dir and Chair. 2002–, also Chair. Exec. Cttee, Int. Cttee, Tech., Productivity and Quality Cttee; Dir (non-exec.) Shinsei Bank Ltd. *Leisure interests:* hunting, fishing, golf, the arts. *Address:* Banco Santander Central Hispano SA, Paseo de la Castellana 75, Edificio Azca – Planta 12, 28046 Madrid, Spain (office). *Telephone:* (91) 3423175 (office). *Fax:* (91) 3423177 (office). *E-mail:* info@santander.com (office). *Website:* www.santander.com (office).

BOTNARU, Ion, PhD; Moldovan diplomatist; *Ambassador to Turkey;* b. 19 Aug. 1954, Chişinău; s. of Toma Botnaru and Tatiana Sheremet; m. 1979; one s. one d.; ed Inst. of Oriental Studies, Moscow, Moscow State Univ.; fmr translator and interpreter of Turkish and English; Sr Researcher, Inst. of History Studies, Nat. Acad. of Science, Chişinău 1983–84; Prof. of Contemporary History of Asia and Africa, Chişinău State Univ. 1987–89; Deputy Dir-Gen. Dept of Protocol, Ministry of Foreign Affairs 1989–90, Dir-Gen. Dept of Political Affairs 1990–92, Deputy Minister 1992–93, Minister 1993–94; Amb. to Turkey (also accred to Kuwait and Egypt) 1994–98; Perm. Rep. to UN, New York 1998–2002; Amb. to Turkey 2002–; mem. Moldovan del. to UN Gen. Ass. 1992; Head Moldovan del. to UN World Conf. on Human Rights 1993; mem. Asscn of Orientalists 1985–. *Publications:* The Army and Politics in Turkey 1986, Islam and Political Parties in Turkey 1989, The Process of Democratisation in Moldova—Political Aspects 1993; numerous papers and articles. *Address:* Embassy of Moldova, Kaptanpaşa Sok 49, Ankara, Turkey (office). *Telephone:* (312) 4465527 (office). *Fax:* (312) 4465816 (office).

BOTT, Martin Harold Phillips, MA, PhD, FRS; British earth scientist; *Professor Emeritus of Geophysics, University of Durham;* b. 12 July 1926, Stoke-on-Trent; s. of Harold Bott and Dorothy Bott (née Phillips); m. Joyce Cynthia Hughes 1961; two s. one d.; ed Clayesmore School, Dorset, Keble Coll. Oxford (army short course) and Magdalene Coll. Cambridge; Nat. Service in army (Royal Signals) 1945–48, rank of Lt; Turner & Newall Research Fellow, Univ. of Durham 1954–56, Lecturer in Geophysics 1956–63, Reader 1963–66, Prof. 1966–88, Research Prof. in Geophysics 1988–91, Prof. Emer. 1991–; Head of Dept of Geological Sciences 1970–73, 1976–82; Chair. British Nat. Cttee for Geodesy and Geophysics 1985–89; Murchison Medal, Geological Soc. of London 1977, Clough Medal, Geological Soc. of Edinburgh 1979, Sorby Medal, Yorks. Geological Soc. 1981, Wollaston Medal, Geological Soc. of London 1992. *Achievements:* completed climbing the Scottish Munros at age of 76 Sept. 2002. *Publications:* The Interior of the Earth (revised edn) 1982, Structure and Development of the Greenland–Scotland Ridge: new methods and concepts (co-ed.) 1983, Sedimentary Basins of Continental Margins and

Cratons (ed.) 1976 and many scientific papers in journals. *Leisure interests:* Reader Emer. (Anglican Church), mountain walking, garden slavery, etc. *Address:* 11 St Mary's Close, Shincliffe, Durham, DH1 2ND, England (home).

BOTTAI, Bruno; Italian diplomatist; *President, Società Dante Alighieri;* b. 10 July 1930, Rome; ed Univ. of Rome; entered Ministry of Foreign Affairs 1954, served abroad in Tunis, Brussels, London and Holy See and Ministry of Foreign Affairs 1955–76; Amb. to the Holy See and the Sovereign Mil. Order of Malta 1979; Dir-Gen. of Political Affairs, Ministry of Foreign Affairs 1981–85; Amb. to UK 1985–87; Sec.-Gen. Ministry of Foreign Affairs 1987–94; Amb. to the Holy See 1994–97; Chair. Int. Balzan Foundation; Pres. Società Dante Alighieri 1995–; Foundation-Milan Pres. Balzan Prize 1999. *Leisure interest:* modern paintings. *Address:* Palazzo Firenze, Piazza Firenze 27, 00186 Rome, Italy. *Telephone:* (06) 6873692/4/5 (office); (06) 6786427 (home). *Fax:* (06) 6873692 (office). *E-mail:* presidente@ladante.it (office). *Website:* www.ladante.it (office).

BOTTOMLEY, Baroness (Life Peer), cr. 2005, of Nettlestone; **Rt Hon. Virginia (Hilda Brunette Maxwell) Bottomley,** PC, BA, MSc,; British politician; *Chancellor, University of Hull;* b. 12 March 1948; d. of the late W. John Garnett and of Barbara Garnett (née Rutherford-Smith); m. Peter Bottomley, MP; one s. two d.; ed Putney High School, Univ. of Essex, London School of Econs; Behavioural Scientist 1971–84; Vice-Chair. Nat. Council of Carers and their Elderly Dependants 1982–88; Dir Mid Southern Water Co. 1987–88; mem. MRC 1987–88; MP Surrey South-West 1984–; Parl. Pvt. Sec. to Minister of State for Educ. and Science 1985–86, to Minister for Overseas Devt 1986–87, to Sec. of State for Foreign and Commonwealth Affairs 1987–88; Parl. Under-Sec. of State Dept for the Environment 1988–89; Sec. Conservative Backbench Employment Cttee 1985; Fellow, Industry Parl. Trust 1987; Minister of State (Minister for Health) 1989–92; Sec. of State for Health 1992–95; Sec. of State for Nat. Heritage 1995–97; Pnr, Odgers Ray & Berndtson Int. 2000–; mem. Supervisory Bd Akzo Nobel 2000–; Nat. Pres. Abbeyfield Soc. 2003–; Co-Chair. Women's Nat. Comm. 1991–92; mem. Court of Govs LSE 1985–, British Council 1997–2001, House of Commons Select Cttee on Foreign Affairs 1997–99; Gov. Ditchley Foundation 1991–, London Univ. of the Arts 1999–; JP Inner London 1975 (Chair. Lambeth Juvenile Court 1981–84); Lay Canon Guildford Cathedral; Pro-Chancellor, Univ. of Surrey 2005–; Chancellor, Univ. of Hull 2006–; Pres. Farnham Castle Centre for Int. Briefing; Trustee The Economist; Hon. LLD (Portsmouth) 1992. *Leisure interest:* family. *Address:* Odgers, Ray & Berndtson, 11 Hanover Square, London, W1S 1JJ (office); House of Lords, Westminster, London, SW1A 0PW, England. *Telephone:* (20) 7219-1060 (office). *Fax:* (20) 7219-1212 (office). *E-mail:* bottomley@parliament.uk.

BOTWIN, Will; American music executive; *President and CEO, Red Light Management;* founder, Side One Management 1982–97; Gen. Man., then Exec. Vice-Pres. Columbia Records 1998–2001; Pres. Columbia Records Group 2002–06; Pres. and CEO Red Light Management and ATO Records 2006–. *Address:* Red Light Management, 44 Wall Street, 22nd Floor, New York, NY 10005, USA (office). *E-mail:* info@redlightmanagement.com (office). *Website:* www.redlightmanagement.com (office).

BOUABRÉ BOHOUN, Paul-Antoine; Côte d'Ivoirian politician; fmr Minister of State, Economy and Finance. *Address:* c/o Ministry of the Economy and Finance, 16e étage, Immeuble SCIAM, avenue Marchand, BP V163, Abidjan, Côte d'Ivoire.

BOUASONE, Bouphavanh; Laotian politician; *Prime Minister;* b. 1954, Salavan Province; ed in USSR; student activist in 1970s; fmr Pres. State Planning Cttee; fmr Third Deputy Prime Minister, First Deputy Prime Minister 2003–06, Prime Minister 2006–. *Address:* Office of the Prime Minister, Ban Sisavat, Vientiane, Laos (office). *Telephone:* (21) 213653 (office). *Fax:* (21) 213560 (office).

BOUBLIL, Alain Albert; French writer and dramatist; b. 5 March 1941, Tunis; four s.; wrote libretto and lyrics for: La Révolution Française 1973, Les Misérables 1980, Abbacadabra 1984, Miss Saigon 1989, Martin Guerre 1996; Le Journal d'Adam et Eve (play) 1994; two Tony Awards, Two Grammy Awards, two Victoire de la Musique Awards, Molière Award (all for Les Misérables), Evening Standard Drama Award (for Miss Saigon), Laurence Olivier Award (for Martin Guerre). *Leisure interests:* theatre, opera, cinema, tennis.

BOUCHAIN, Patrick; French architect; b. 31 May 1945, Paris; Prof. of Drawing and Architecture, École Camondo, Paris 1972–74, École des Beaux-Arts de Bourges 1974–81, École de Création industrielle, Paris 1981–83; adviser to Jack Lang at Ministry of Culture, then to Pres. Établissement public du Grand Louvre 1992–94; Dir Atelier public d'architecture et d'urbanisme, Blois 1990–93. *Works include:* Magasin, Grenoble 1985, Zingaro Theatre, Aubervilliers 1988, Dromesko Birdcage, Lausanne 1991, Admin. and Tech. Centre, Valeo à La Verrière 1995, registered office of Thomson Multimédia, Boulogne-Billancourt 1997, transformation of the old LU factories in Nantes for CRDC 1999, Musée int. des Arts modestes, Sète 2000; has collaborated with numerous contemporary artists, including Daniel Buren ('Les deux plateaux', court of the Palais Royal 1986), Sarkis, Ange Leccia, Bartabas (Celebration of the battle of Valmy 1989), Joseph Kosuth (Figeac 1989), Claes Oldenbourg ('Le vélo enseveli', Parc de la Villette 1990), Jean-Luc Vilmouth ('Comme deux tours', Châtellerault 1994); architectural installations 'L'amour de l'art' for first Biennale d'art contemporain de Lyon 1991, 'Tous, ils changent le monde', Lyon Bienniale 1993; leader, spectacle of the Grandes Roues on Champs-Elysées in Paris as part of the Millennium celebrations 1999–2000. *Address:* c/o Institut Français d'Architecture, ZA Les Portes du Vexin, 1 chemin de la Chapelle St Antoine, 95300 Ennery, France. *Telephone:* 1-46-33-90-36. *Fax:* 1-34-43-83-81. *Website:* www.ifa.fr.

BOUCHARD, Benoît, BA; Canadian fmr politician and fmr diplomatist; b. 16 April 1940, Roberval, Québec; m. Jeannine Lavoie; three c.; ed Laval Univ.; teacher, Coll. Classique, Coll. Notre-Dame, then Prin. Coll. Notre-Dame and Villa étudiante, Roberval; Dir-Gen. St Félicien CEGEP 1979; alderman, Roberval 1973–80; MP for Roberval, Quebec 1984–93, served as Minister of State (Transport) 1984–85, Minister of Communications 1985–86, of Employment and Immigration 1986–88, of Transport 1988–90, of Industry, Science and Tech. 1990–91, of Nat. Health and Welfare 1991–93; Amb. to France 1993–96; Chair. Transportation Safety Bd of Canada 1996–2001; currently mem. Bd of Dirs Bennett Environmental Inc. *Address:* c/o Board of Directors, Bennett Environmental Inc, 1540 Cornwall Road, Suite 208, Oakville, ON L6J 7W5, Canada.

BOUCHARD, Lucien, BA, BSc; Canadian politician; b. 22 Dec. 1938, Saint-Coeur-de-Marie, Lac Saint-Jean, Québec; s. of Philippe Bouchard and Alice Simard; m. Audrey Best; two s.; ed Laval Univ.; admitted Québec Bar 1964; pvt law practice in Chicoutimi until 1985; mem. numerous comms and orgs connected with labour relations, both in public and pvt. sectors; Pres. Saguenay Bar 1978; Amb. to France 1985–88; Sec. of State of Canada 1988; MP 1988–2001; Minister of the Environment 1989–90; resgnd from Conservative Party 1990 to lead Bloc Québécois; Chair. and Leader, Bloc Québécois 1991–96; Leader Parti Québécois 1996–2001; Leader of Opposition, House of Commons 1993–95; Prime Minister of Québec 1996–2001. *Publications:* À visage découvert 1992; articles in legal and labour relations journals. *Address:* c/o Parti Québécois, 1200 avenue Papineau, Bureau 150, Montreal, Québec, H2K 4R5, Canada (office).

BOUCHÈNE, Abderrahmane; Algerian publisher; b. 1941, Algiers; m.; four c.; ed Algeria and Lausanne Univs; worked in family clothing shop; admin. posts at Société nat. d'édition et de diffusion, Entreprise nat. du livre and Ministry of Culture; f. Editions Bouchène publishing house, Kouba, in late 1980s; by 1990 owner of two bookshops in Algiers, one in Riad-El-Feth; forced to flee Algeria and close business 1994; exile in Tunisia 1994–96; moved to Paris and set up new co. specializing in Algerian historical texts and historical anthropology of Maghreb socs. *Address:* Editions Bouchène, 113–115 rue Danielle Casanova, 93200 Saint-Denis, Paris, France (office). *Telephone:* 1-48-20-93-75 (office). *Fax:* 1-48-20-20-78 (office). *E-mail:* edbouchene@wanadoo.fr (office). *Website:* www.bouchene.com (office).

BOUCHER, Carlston B., BSc, MA; Barbadian diplomatist and international civil servant; b. 18 May 1933; m.; ed Univs of London and Sussex, UK; govt appointments 1957–72; Research Economist, Econ. Programmes Dept, World Bank 1972–74, Country Economist for SA, Botswana, Lesotho and Swaziland, Africa Regional Dept 1974–78, Deputy Special Rep. of World Bank to UN 1978–83, Sr Economist, Strategic Planning and Review Dept 1983–87, Adviser, External Relations Dept 1987–90, Prin. Econ. Affairs Officer, Operations Policy Dept, Int. Econs Div. 1990–93, Special Rep. to UN, New York and Geneva 1993–95; Perm. Rep. to UN 1995–2001. *Address:* c/o Ministry of Foreign Affairs and Foreign Trade, 1 Culloden Road, St Michael, Barbados (office).

BOUCHIER, Ian Arthur Dennis, CBE, MB, ChB, MD, FRCP, FRCPE, FRSA, FRSE, FFPHM, FIBiol, FMedSci; British professor of medicine (retd); b. 7 Sept. 1932, Cape Town, S Africa; s. of E. A. Bouchier and May Bouchier; m. Patricia N. Henshilwood 1959; two s.; ed Rondebosch Boys' High School and Univ. of Cape Town; jr staff positions, Groote Schuur Hosp., Cape Town 1955–60; Registrar, Lecturer, Royal Free Hosp., London 1961–63; Research Fellow, Boston Univ. 1963–65; Sr Lecturer, Univ. of London 1965–70, Reader in Medicine 1970–73; Prof. of Medicine, Univ. of Dundee 1973–86, Univ. of Edin. 1986–97; Sec.-Gen. World Org. of Gastroenterology 1982–90, Pres. 1990–98; Chief Scientist for Scotland 1992–97; mem. Chief Scientist Cttee; Visiting Prof., Univ. of Michigan 1979, Madras Medical Coll. 1981, McGill Univ. 1983, Royal Postgraduate Medical School 1984, Univ. of Hong Kong 1988, China Medical Univ. 1988, Univ. of Dunedin 1989, Keio Univ. 1991; mem. Council British Soc. of Gastroenterology 1987–90 (Pres. 1994–95); mem. Council, Royal Soc. of Edin. 1986–89, British Soc. of Gastroenterology 1992–; Corresp. mem. Italian Soc. of Gastroenterology, Royal Catalonian Acad. of Medicine; mem. numerous editorial bds; Hon. FCP (SA); Hon. mem. South African Soc. of Gastroenterology, Japanese Soc. of Gastroenterology; Hon. MD (Iasi). *Publications:* 28 textbooks and 600 articles mainly on gastroenterological topics. *Leisure interests:* music of Berlioz, history of whaling, cooking. *Address:* 8A Merchiston Park, Edinburgh, EH10 4PN, Scotland.

BOUDART, Michel, MA, PhD; American chemical engineer and academic; *Professor Emeritus of Chemical Engineering, Stanford University;* b. 18 June 1924, Brussels, Belgium; s. of François Boudart and Marguerite Swolfs; m. Marina M. D'Haese 1948; three s. one d.; ed Princeton Univ., Univ. of Louvain; Asst then Assoc. Prof. Princeton Univ. 1954–61; Prof. Univ. of Calif. (Berkeley) 1961–64, adjunct Prof. of Chemical Eng 1994–; Prof. of Chemical Eng and Chemistry Stanford Univ. 1964–80, William M. Keck Prof. 1980–94, Prof. Emer. 1994–; mem. tech. advisory Bd British Petroleum 1992–98, Nova 1997–, numerous editorial bds; Co-Founder and Dir Catalytica Inc. 1973; mem. NAS, Nat. Acad. of Eng, American Acad. of Arts and Sciences, Calif. Acad. of Sciences, Royal Belgian Acad. of Sciences, Acad. Nat. de Pharmacie. *Publications include:* Kinetics of Chemical Processes 1968, Kinetics of Heterogeneous Catalytic Reactions 1984 (with G. Djéga-Mariadassou), co-author (with J. R. Anderson) Catalysis: Science and Technology, 11 vols 1981–96, (with Marina Boudart and René Bryssinck) Modern Belgium 1990. *Leisure interest:* travel. *Address:* Department of Chemical Engineering, Keck Science Building, Room 177, Stanford University, Stanford, CA 94305-5025 (office); 228 Oak Grove Avenue, Atherton, CA 94027, USA (home). *Telephone:* (650) 723-0385 (office); (650) 723-4748 (office). *Fax:* (650) 723-9780 (office). *E-mail:* michel.boudart@stanford.edu (office); lindi@chemeng.stanford.edu

www.worldwhoswho.com

(office). *Website:* chemeng.stanford.edu/01About_the_Department/03Faculty/Boudart/Boudart.html (office).

BOUDRIA, Don, PC, BA; Canadian fmr politician; b. 30 Aug. 1949, Hull, Québec; m. Mary Ann Morris 1971; one s. one d.; ed Eastview High School, Univ. of Waterloo; entered Fed. Govt 1966, held various positions including Chief Purchasing Agent –1981; Councillor, Cumberland Township 1976–80, fmr mem. Cumberland Township Housing Corpn; mem. Ontario Legis. (mem. Prov. Parl. for Prescott-Russell) 1981–84, Opposition Critic of Govt Services 1981–82, of Community and Social Services 1982–83, of Consumer and Commercial Relations 1983–84; mem. Parl. for Glengarry-Prescott-Russell 1984–2005 (retd); Opposition Critic on Fed. Supply and Services; mem. Standing Cttee on Agriculture 1984; mem. Ont. Liberal Caucus 1984, Chair. 1985–87; Opposition Critic on Public Works 1985, Govt Operations 1987, Canada Post and Govt Operations 1988; Deputy Opposition Whip 1989; Asst House Leader for the Official Opposition and Govt Operations Critic 1990–93; Deputy Govt Whip 1994; Minister of Int. Co-operation and Francophonie 1996–97; Minister of State and Leader of Govt in House of Commons 1997–2002; Minister of Public Works and Govt Services Jan.–May 2002; Minister of State and Leader of the Govt in House of Commons 2002–03; Founding Pres. Ont. Section, Int. Asscn of French-speaking Parliamentarians; Founding mem. Sarsfield Knights of Columbus; currently Chair. Canadian Section FIPA. *Publications:* Busboy: From Kitchen to Cabinet 2005. *Leisure interests:* history, music, downhill skiing. *Address:* 3455 Dessaint Crescent, Sarsfield, Ont., K0A 3E0, Canada (home).

BOUGIE, Jacques, OC; Canadian business executive; b. 1947, Montreal; ed Univ. de Montréal; joined Alcan 1979, Man. Beauharnois Works, then various positions in Winnipeg, Toronto and Montreal in major project devt, planning and gen. man., responsible for fabricating operations in N America, Pres., COO Alcan Aluminium Ltd 1989–93, Pres., CEO 1993–2001; fmr Vice-Chair. Business Council on Nat. Issues; mem. Bd Dirs Abitibi-Consolidated Inc., Nova Chemicals Inc. 2001–, McCain Foods Ltd, Rona Inc.; Chair. Int. Advisory Council, CGI Group Inc. 2004–. *Address:* c/o International Advisory Council, CGI Group Inc., 1130 Sherbrooke Street West, 5th Floor, Montreal, Quebec H3A 2M8, Canada.

BOUH, Yacin Elmi; Djibouti politician; *Minister of the Interior and Decentralization;* b. 4 June 1962; ed Univ. of Nantes, France; Minister of the Economy, Finance and Planning, in charge of privatization 1997–2005; fmr mem. Bd of Govs Islamic Devt Bank; currently Minister of Interior and Decentralization. *Address:* Ministry of the Interior and Decentralization, BP 33, Djibouti, Djibouti (office). *Telephone:* 352542 (office). *Fax:* 354862 (home). *Website:* www.elec.dj (office).

BOUHAFS, Abdelhak; Algerian economist and government official; b. 15 Aug. 1945; m.; one c.; ed Algiers and Grenoble Univs; with Sonatrach 1974, Asst to Vice-Pres. and responsible for devt and for valorization of hydrocarbons 1974–80, Co-ordinator of Energy Studies 1980–83; joined Ministry of Energy and Petrochemical Industries 1983; Dir-Gen. of Energy Coordination and of Commercialization 1984–86; responsible for Studies and Synthesis in sphere of Int. Relations 1986–88; Chef de Cabinet to Minister of Energy and Petrochemical Industries 1988–89; Man. Dir Sonatrach in 1990's then return as Chair. 2000–01; Pres. Association Algérienne de l'Industrie du Gaz 2003. *Address:* c/o Association Algérienne de l'Industrie du Gaz, 121 rue Didouche Mourad, Algiers, Algeria.

BOUHAMED CHAABOUNI, Habiba, DèsSc; Tunisian medical geneticist and academic; ed Faculty of Medicine, Tunis; est. first genetic counselling service and launched epidemiological studies on consanguinity in northern Tunisia 1981, set up medical genetics and consultation service to carry out antenatal diagnostic tests 1993; fmr Prof. of Medical Genetics, Univ. of Tunis, Head of Dept of Congenital and Hereditary Diseases, Charles Nicolle Hosp., Tunisia, Dir Human Genetics Research Lab. and Faculty of Medicine, Tunis; fmr mem. Tech. Comm. of Arab League for Genetic Diseases Prevention and Genetic Counselling, represented Tunisia in Cttee of Governmental Experts to prepare UNESCO draft declaration on the Human Genome; mem. Soc. Tunisienne des Sciences Médicales, Soc. Tunisienne de Pédiatrie, American Soc. of Human Genetics, European Soc. of Cytogenetics; L'Oréal-UNESCO Women in Science Award 2006. *Publications:* more than 100 scientific papers on the analysis and prevention of hereditary disorders. *Address:* University of Tunis El Mar, BP 94, Tunis 1068, Tunisia (office).

BOUHIA, (Haya) Hynd, SM, MA, PhD; Moroccan economist and business executive; *Director-General, Casablanca Stock Exchange;* b. 21 Oct. 1972, Casablanca; m. Khalid Zerouali; one s.; ed Ecole Centrale, Paris, France, Johns Hopkins School for Advanced Int. Studies and Harvard Univ., USA; joined World Bank Young Professional Program, Washington, DC 1996, worked on Bank's lending operations 1996–2001, worked as Water and Environmental Economist in Middle East and N Africa (MENA) Region, in Latin America Region on water sector strategy for Argentina and water quality control in Brazil and SE Asia Region, Special Asst to Vice-Pres. for MENA Region –2001, Sr Financial Officer in Capital Market Operations unit of Banking, Capital Markets and Financial Eng Dept, World Bank Treasury 2001–04; econ. adviser to Prime Minister of Morocco 2004–08; Dir-Gen. Casablanca Stock Exchange 2008–; mem. Washington Conservatory of Music (performs classical piano); Hon. Prize of Casablanca Conservatory of Music for Piano performances; ranked by Forbes magazine amongst 100 Most Powerful Women (29th) 2008. *Publications:* Water in the Macro Economy: Application of an Integrated Analytical Model 2001; several academic papers and book chapters. *Leisure interest:* athletic and fitness activities. *Address:* 57 Avenue du Phare-Bourgogne, 20 000, Casablanca, Morocco (office). *Telephone:* (22) 364214/364216 (office). *Fax:* (22) 364210 (office). *E-mail:* hbouhia@hotmail.com (office). *Website:* www.casablanca-bourse.com/homeen.html (office).

BOUKPESSI, Payadowa; Togolese government official; Minister of the Economy, Finance and Privatization 2005–. *Address:* Ministry of the Economy, Finance and Privatization, CASEF, ave Sarakawa, BP 387, Lomé, Togo (office). *Telephone:* 221-00-37 (office). *Fax:* 221-25-48 (office). *E-mail:* eco@republicoftogo.com (office).

BOULANGER, Daniel; French writer; b. 24 Jan. 1922, Compiègne, Oise; s. of Michel Boulanger and Hélène Bayart; m. 2nd Clémence Dufour; four s. three d.; ed Petit Séminaire Saint-Charles, Chauny; sub-ed., Affaires économiques 1946–48; writer 1948–; wrote scripts or screenplays for over 100 films, including Cartouche 1962, L'Homme de Rio 1963, Les Tribulations d'un Chinois en Chine 1965, La Vie de Château 1966, Le Voleur 1967, Le Diable par la Queue 1968, Le Roi de Coeur (Prix Louis-Delluc) 1969, Les Maries de l'An II 1971, L'Affaire Dominici 1973, Police Python 1975, Une femme fidèle 1976, La Menace 1976, Cheval d'Orgueil 1980, Chouans 1988, La Révolution Française 1989; numerous plays; mem. Acad. Goncourt 1983–2008; Officier Légion d'honneur, Officier Ordre nat. du Mérite, Commdr des Arts et Lettres; Prix Pierre de Monaco for complete body of work 1979, Prix Kléber Haedens 1983. *Publications include:* novellas: Les Noces du Merle 1963 (Prix de la Nouvelle 1963), L'été des Femmes 1964, Fête Ste. Beuve 1966, Le Chemin des Caracoles 1966, Memoire de la Ville 1970, Vessies et Lanternes 1971 (Prix de l'Académie française 1971), Fouette Cocher 1974 (Prix Goncourt de la Nouvelle 1974); novels: La Confession d'Omer 1991, Ursacq 1992, Le Retable Wasserfall 1994, Caporal Supérieur 1994, Le Miroittier 1995, Tombeau d'Héraldine 1997, Talbard 1998, Le Ciel de Bargetal 1999, Clémence et Auguste 2000, Les Mouches et l'âne 2001, Cache-Cache 2002, Du temps qu'on plaisantait 2003, La Poste de Nuit 2004; poems: Tchadiennes 1969, Le Jardin d'Armidère Touches 1969 (Prix Max Jacob 1970), Jules Bouc 1987, Un Eté à la diable 1992, A la courte paille 1993, Etiquettes 1994, Taciturnes 1995, Fenêtre mon navire 2008. *Address:* 22 rue du Heaume, 60300 Senlis, France.

BOULARÈS, Mohamed Habib; Tunisian politician, writer and journalist; b. 29 July 1933, Tunis; s. of Sadok Ben Mohamed and Zoubeida Bent Abdelkader Aziz; m. Line Poinsignon 1966; one d.; ed Collège Sadiki, Tunis; mem. staff exec. office, Parti Destourien 1955; Deputy Ed. daily Essabah 1956; in charge of publications, Ministry of Information 1957; Ed. Nat. Radio news service 1958; Ed. Al Amal (Parti Destourien daily newspaper) 1960; first Man. Dir Tunis Afrique Presse news agency 1961; Dir Radio Télévision Tunisienne, Dir of Information, Ministry of Cultural Affairs and Information 1962; mem. Econ. and Social Council 1964–70; Minister of Cultural Affairs and Information 1970; Dir Ecole Internationale de Bordeaux, France 1972–73; teacher, Institut de Langues Orientales, Paris for four years; mem. Parl. 1981–86, 1989–94, 1994–; Amb. to Egypt 1988; Minister of Culture 1988–89, of Culture and Information 1989–90, of Foreign Affairs 1990–91, of Nat. Defence Feb.–Oct. 1991; Special Adviser to Pres. of Repub. March 1990; Pres. Nat. Ass. 1991–94; Sec.-Gen., Arab Maghreb Union 2002–06; Grand Officier Ordre de l'Indépendance, Grand Cordon Ordre de la République, Commdr Ordre du 7 Novembre, numerous foreign decorations. *Publications:* L'Islam, la peur et l'espérance (trans. in English); several other non-fiction works and plays. *Address:* c/o L'Union du Maghreb Arabe, 14, rue Zelagh Agdal, Rabat, Morocco (office).

BOULEZ, Pierre; French composer and conductor; b. 26 March 1925, Montbrison; s. of Léon Boulez and Marcelle Calabre; ed Paris Conservatoire; studied with Messiaen, Vaurabourg-Honegger and Leibowitz; Dir of Music to Jean-Louis Barrault theatre co. 1948; aided by Barrault and Madeleine Renaud Barrault he founded the Concert Marigny which later became the Domaine Musical, Paris; Prin. Guest Conductor Cleveland Symphony Orchestra 1968; Prin. Conductor BBC Symphony Orchestra 1971–75; Musical Dir New York Philharmonic 1971–77; Dir Inst. de Recherches et de Coordination Acoustique/Musique (IRCAM) 1975–91, Hon. Dir 1992–; Founder and Pres. Ensemble Intercontinental 1977–98; Prof. Collège de France 1976–95; Prin. Guest Conductor Chicago Symphony Orchestra 1995–2006, Conductor Emer. 2006–; conducted the centenary production of Wagner's Ring, Bayreuth 1976–80; Hon. Conductor Staatskapelle Berlin 2005, Vienna Philharmonic 2005, Fellow British Acad. of Composers and Songwriters 2005, Distinguished Musician Award Inc. Soc. of Musicians 2006–07; Hon. CBE; Dr hc (Cambridge) 1980, (Bâle) 1980, (Los Angeles) 1984, (Oxford) 1987, (Brussels) 1988; Prize of the Siemens Foundation 1979, Praemium Imperiale, Japan Art Asscn 1989, Polar Music Prize, Sweden 1996, Wolf Foundation Prize in Arts 2000, Grawemeyer Award 2001, Inc. Soc. of Musicians Distinguished Musician Award 2005. *Compositions include:* First Piano Sonata 1946, Sonatina for Flute and Piano 1946, Le Visage nuptial (5 poems of René Char for 2 solo voices, female choir and orch.) 1946–50, Second Piano Sonata 1948, Le Soleil des eaux (2 poems of René Char for voice and orch.) 1948, Livre pour Quatuor (string quartet) 1949, Le Marteau sans maître (cantata for voice and instruments to texts by René Char, also ballet 1965) 1955, Structures (2 pianos) 1964, Third Piano Sonata 1957–58, Improvisations sur Mallarmé (soprano and chamber ensemble) 1958, Doubles (orch.) 1958, Poésie pour pouvoir (orch.) 1958, Tombeau (soprano and orch.) 1959, Pli selon Pli 1958–62, Figures–Doubles-Prismes 1964/74, Eclat and Eclat/Multiples 1965, Domaines 1968–69, cummings ist der dichter 1970, explosante-fixe for 8 solo instruments 1973, Rituel 1974, Messagesquisse 1977, Notations 1979, Répons 1981–86, Dérive 1984, Dialogue de l'ombre double 1984, Mémoriale 1985, le Visage nuptial 1989, . . . explosante-fixe . . . for Midi-flute, 2 solo flutes, ensemble and electronics 1993, Anthèmes 2 1997, sur Incises 1998, Notations VII 1999, Dérive 2 2002–05. *Publications:* Penser la musique aujourd'hui 1966, Relevés d'apprenti (essays) 1967, Par volonté et par hasard 1975, Points de repère 1981, Le pays fertile: Paul Klee 1989, Orientations: Collected

Writings 1986. *Address:* IRCAM, 1 place Igor Stravinsky, 75004 Paris, France (office). *Telephone:* 1-42-77-95-01 (office). *Fax:* 1-44-78-15-40 (office). *E-mail:* secretariat.pierre.boulez@ircam.fr (office).

BOULUD, Daniel; French chef and restaurateur; b. 25 March 1955, St Pierre de Chandieu, Rhône; began career as apprentice chef at age 14; spent two years as chef in Copenhagen; chef, European Comm., Washington DC 1981; opened first restaurants, The Polo Lounge, Westbury Hotel, and Le Régence, Hotel Plaza Athenée, New York; Exec. Chef Le Cirque, New York 1986–92; opened Daniel restaurant 1993 (Gourmet Magazine Top Table Award), Café Boulud, New York Sept. 1998, DB Bistro Moderne June 2001, Café Boulud, Florida 2003; Founding Pnr Payard Patisserie & Bistro –2000; Owner Feast & Fêtes Catering and Daniel Boulud CONNOISSEUR (direct mail co.); mem. Bd of Dirs Citymeals-on-Wheels 1999–; contrib. Elle Décor; Bon Appétit Magazine Chef of the Year, Outstanding Restaurateur, James Beard Foundation 2006. *Publications include:* Cooking with Daniel Boulud 1993, Daniel Boulud's Café Boulud Cookbook 1999, Chef Daniel Boulud Cooking in New York City 2002, Letters to a Young Chef (jt author) 2003, Daniel's Dish: Entertaining at Home with a Four-Star Chef 2003, Braise: A Journey through International Cuisine 2006; Easy Cooking with Great Chefs (Ed.) monthly newsletter. *Address:* c/o Daniel, 60 East 65th Street, New York NY 10021, USA (office). *Telephone:* (212) 288 0033 (office). *Fax:* (212) 396 9014 (office). *Website:* www.danielnyc.com (office).

BOUMA, Johannes, PhD; Dutch soil scientist and academic; b. 29 Oct. 1940, 't Bildt; s. of S. Bouma and J. Bouma (née Werff); m. Marianne Wiebols 1969; one s. one d.; ed Agricultural Univ., Wageningen, Univ. of Wisconsin, Madison; Asst Prof. Soils Dept, Univ. of Wis., Madison 1969–73, Assoc. Prof. 1973–75; Head of Soil Physics Dept, Netherlands Soil Survey Inst., Wageningen 1975–82, Deputy Dir in charge of research 1982–86; Prof. of Soil Science, Agricultural Univ. of Wageningen 1986–2002, Scientific Dir Environmental Sciences Group Research Centre 2002–04; mem. Netherlands Scientific Council for Govt Policy 1998–2003; mem. Royal Dutch Acad. of Sciences 1989; Corresp. mem. German Soil Science Asscn 1982; Fellow Soil Science Soc. of America 1985; Officer of the Order of Orange-Nassau 2001. *Publications:* several books and various articles in tech. journals. *Leisure interests:* jogging, cycling. *Address:* Alterra, PO Box 47, 6700 AA Wageningen (office); Spoorbaanweg 35, 3911 CA Rhenen, Netherlands (home). *Telephone:* (317) 613469 (home). *E-mail:* johan.bouma@wur.nl (office); johan.bouma@planet.nl (home).

BOUNGNANG, Volachit; Laotian politician and army officer; *Vice President;* b. 1936; m. Keosaychay Sayasone; fmr army officer; fmr Gov. Savannaket, then Mayor Vientiane Municipality; apptd mem. Politburo 1996; Minister of Finance and Deputy Prime Minister 1999–2001; Prime Minister of Laos 2001–06; Vice Pres. 2006–. *Address:* Office of the Vice President, rue Lane Xang, Vientiane, Laos. *Telephone:* (21) 214200 (office). *Fax:* (21) 214208 (office).

BOUQUET, Carole; French actress; b. 18 Aug. 1957, Neuilly-sur-Seine; m. 1st Jean-Pierre Rassam (deceased); two s.; fmr Face of Chanel No. 5. *Films include:* Cet Obscur Objet du Désir 1977, Buffet Froid 1979, Le Manteau d'Astrakan 1979, For Your Eyes Only 1981, Le Jour des Idiots 1981, Bingo Bango 1982, Dream One 1983, Mystère 1983, Dagobert 1984, Rive droite, Rive gauche 1984, Double Messieurs 1985, Special Police 1985, Le Mal d'Aimer 1986, Jenatsch 1986, On se dépêche d'en rire 1987, Bunker Palace Hotel 1988, Trop Belle pour toi (César for Best Actress) 1990, Grosse Fatigue 1994, A Business Affair 1994, Lucie Aubrac 1997, In All Innocence, The Bridge, Tango 1993, En plein cœur 1998, Un pont entre deux rives 1999, Le Pique-nique de Lulu Kreutz 2000, Embrassez qui vous voudrez 2002, Blanche 2002, Bienvenue chez les Rozes 2003, Feux Rouges 2004, Les Fautes d'orthographe 2004, Nordeste 2005, Travaux, on sait quand ça commence 2005, L'Enfer 2005, Aurore 2006, Un ami parfait 2006, Si c'était lui 2007, Les Enfants de Timpelbach 2007, Les Hauts murs 2008. *Television:* Ruy Blas 2002. *Plays include:* Phèdre, Théâtre Dejazet, Paris 2002. *Address:* c/o Intertalent, 5 rue Clément-Marot, 75008 Paris, France (office).

BOURDAIS DE CHARBONNIÈRE, Eric; French automobile executive; *Chairman of the Supervisory Board, Compagnie Générale des Établissements Michelin;* b. 1939; began career with JP Morgan 1965, various positions including commercial banker, Controller and Treasurer, NY and Paris 1965–81, Chair. and CEO JP Morgan (France) 1981–85, Sr Vice-Pres. JP Morgan Continental Europe 1985–87, Exec. Vice-Pres. JP Morgan Europe 1987–90; Chief Financial Officer, Compagnie Générale des Établissements Michelin 1990–2000, Chair. of Supervisory Bd 2000–; mem. Bd Dirs Thomson 2003–, also Chair. Audit Cttee; mem. Supervisory Bd ING Group 2004–. *Address:* Compagnie Générale des Établissements Michelin, 12 cours Sablon, 63000 Clermont-Ferrand, France (office). *Telephone:* 4-73-98-59-00 (office). *Fax:* 4-73-98-59-04 (office). *Website:* www.michelin.com (office).

BOURDEAU, Philippe François, PhD, FAAS; Belgian fmr European Community official and university professor; b. 25 Nov. 1926, Rabat, Morocco; s. of Michel Bourdeau and Lucienne Imbrecht; m. Flora Gorirossi 1954; three d.; ed Gembloux, Belgium and Duke Univ. USA; Asst Prof., State Univ. of NC 1954–56, Yale Univ. 1956–58, 1960–62; Prof., Univ. of Belgian Congo 1958–60; Head, Radiobiology Dept EURATOM, Jt Research Centre, Ispra, Italy 1962–71; Head of Div. then Dir research programmes in environment and in non-nuclear energy, Comm. of EC, Brussels 1971–91; Prof., Univ. Libre de Bruxelles 1972–96; Head, European Environment Agency Task Force 1991; Chair. Scientific Cttee, European Environmental Agency (EEA); mem. Belgian Royal Acad. of Applied Sciences. *Publications:* scientific papers in the fields of environment policy, ecophysiology, ecotoxicology. *Leisure interests:* reading, sport. *Address:* ULB, CP 130/02, 50 avenue F. D. Roosevelt, 1050 Brussels, Belgium (office). *E-mail:* bourdeau@ulb.ac.be (office).

BOURGAIN, Jean, PhD; Belgian mathematician and academic; *Professor, School of Mathematics, Institute for Advanced Study;* b. 28 Feb. 1954, Ostend; ed Free Univ. of Brussels; Research Fellowship, NSF (NFWO), Belgium 1975–81; Prof., Free Univ. of Brussels 1981–85; J.L. Doob Prof. of Math., Univ. of Illinois, USA 1985–; Prof., IHES, France 1985–95; Lady Davis Prof. of Math., Hebrew Univ. of Jerusalem, Israel 198; Fairchild Distinguished Prof., Calif. Inst. of Tech. 1991; Prof., Inst. for Advanced Study, Princeton, NJ 1994–; mem. Editorial Bd Annals of Mathematics, Journal de l'Institut de Mathématique de Jussieu, Publications Mathématiques de l'IHES, Duke Math Journal, International Mathematical Research Notices, Geometrical and Functional Analysis, Journal d'Analyse de Jérusalem, Discrete and Continuous Dynamical Systems; foreign mem. Acad. des Sciences, Paris, Polish Acad.; Dr hc (Université Marne-la-Vallée, France) 1994, (Hebrew Univ. of Jerusalem) 1991, (Free Univ. of Brussels) 1995; Alumni Prize, Belgium NSF 1979, Empain Prize, Belgium NSF 1983, Salem Prize 1983, Damry-Deleeuw-Bourlart Prize, Belgian NSF 1985, Langevin Prize, Acad. française 1985, E. Cartan Prize, Acad. française 1990, Ostrowski Prize, Ostrowski Foundation (Basel, Switzerland) 1991, Fields Medal, ICM Zurich 1994. *Address:* Simonyi Hall 203, School of Mathematics, Institute for Advanced Study, Princeton, NJ 08540, USA (office). *Telephone:* (609) 734-8397 (office). *Fax:* (609) 951-4459 (office). *E-mail:* bourgain@ias.edu (office). *Website:* www.math.ias.edu (office).

BOURGES, Hervé; French administrator and journalist; *President, Union Internationale des Journalistes at de la Presse de Langue Française;* b. 2 May 1933, Rennes, Ile-et-Vilaine; s. of Joseph Bourges and Marie-Magdeleine Desjeux; m. Marie-Thérèse Lapouille 1966; ed Lycée de Biarritz, Coll. Saint-Joseph, Reims, École supérieure de journalisme; Ed. then Ed.-in-Chief Témoignage Chrétien 1956–62; attached to the Keeper of the Seals 1959–62, Dir Algerian Ministry of Youth and Popular Education, attached to Ministry of Information; Asst Lecturer Univ. de Paris II 1967–; Founder and Dir École supérieure de journalisme de Yaoundé, Cameroun 1970–76; Dir then Pres. Admin. Council École nat. supérieure de journalisme de Lille 1976–80; Dir Information Service and Dir-Gen.'s Messenger UNESCO 1980–81, Amb. to UNESCO 1994–95; Dir then Dir-Gen. Radio France Int. 1981–83; Chair. Dir-Gen. TV Française 1 (TF1) 1983–87, Hon. Pres. 1987–93; Hon. Pres. Admin. Council, Ecole Supérieure de Journalisme de Lille 1992–; Dir-Gen. Radio Monte Carlo (RMC) 1988; Pres., Dir-Gen. Société financière de radiodiffusion (Sofirad) 1989–91; Pres. Canal Horizon 1990–91, Conseil Supérieur de L'Audio-Visuel (CSA) 1995–2001; Pres. L'Union internationale des journalistes et de la presse de langue française (UIJPLF) 2001–; Docteur d'état en sciences politiques; Chevalier, Légion d'honneur; Croix de la Valeur Militaire. *Publications:* L'Algérie à l'épreuve du pouvoir 1967, La Révolte étudiante 1968, Décoloniser l'information 1978, Les cinquante Afriques (jtly) 1979, Le village planétaire (jtly) 1986, Une Chaîne sur les bras 1987, Un amour de télévision (jtly) 1989, La Télévision du Public 1993, De mémoire d'éléphant (autobiog.) 2000, Le règne de la terreur sacrée (with Liess Boukra) 2001, Entretiens (with Jean-Michel Djian) 2003, Léopold Sédar Senghor, lumière noire 2006, Ma rue Montmartre 2006. *Address:* UIJPLF, 3 cité Bergère, 74009 Paris (office); 12 rue Magellan, 75008 Paris, France. *Telephone:* 1-47-70-02-80 (office); 1-45-68-10-00. *Fax:* 1-48-24-26-32 (office); 1-45-67-16-90. *E-mail:* union@presse-francophone.org (office). *Website:* www.presse-francophone.org (office).

BOURGUIBA, Habib, Jr, LèsD; Tunisian diplomatist (retd); b. 9 April 1927, Paris, France; s. of the late Pres. Habib Bourguiba; m. Neila Zouiten 1954; two s. one d.; ed Collège Sadiki, Law School, France; collaborated in nat. liberation movt, especially 1951–54; Counsellor, Tunisian Embassy, Washington 1956–57; Amb. to Italy 1957–58, to France 1958–61, to USA 1961–63, to Canada 1961–62, to Mexico 1962–63; Perm. Rep. to UN 1961–62; Sec.-Gen., Govt of Repub. 1963–64; in charge of Dept of Youth and Sports, Dept of Tourism, Nat. office of Artisanship and Information Dept 1963–64; elected mem. Nat. Assembly Nov. 1964; Sec. of State for Foreign Affairs 1964–70; Special Adviser to the Pres. 1977–86; Pres., Gen. Man. Banque de Développement de l'Economie de la Tunisie 1971–88; consultant 1988–; many Tunisian and foreign decorations. *Leisure interests:* staying home with family, computers, golf. *Address:* Dar Essalam, 14 rue Chedli Zouiten, La Marsa 2070, Tunisia (home). *Telephone:* 71-74-85-09 (home). *Fax:* 71-74-26-66 (home). *E-mail:* hb.jr@planet.tu (home).

BOURGUIGNON, François, DEcon, PhD; French economist; *Chief Economist and Senior Vice President, World Bank;* b. 22 May 1945; ed Ecole Nationale de la Statistique at des Analyses Economique (ENSEA), Univ. of Paris VI, Univ. of Western ON, Canada, Univ. of Orléans; Asst Prof. Univ. of Chile 1968–70, of Toronto 1975–77; Researcher, OECD Devt Center 1971–72, CNRS, Paris 1978–84; Prof. of Econs, Ecole des Hautes Etudes en Sciences Sociales (EHESS); mem. Conseil d'Analyse Economique (advisory group to prime minister), Paris; Visiting Prof. Concordia Univ. 1979, Birkbeck Coll. 1984, Univ. of Geneva 1989–90, Univ. Bocconi, Milan 1992–95; Chief Economist and Sr Vice–Pres. World Bank 2003–; Dir Devt Research Group, Devt Econs Vice-Pres. 2003; Ed. World Bank Economic Review, European Economic Review; fmr consultant UN, EC, ILO; Pres. European Soc. for Population Econs 1995; Fellow Econometrics Soc. 1985; Dr hc (Univ. de Quebec) 2002, (Univ. de Genève) 2005 El Fasi Award, CNRS Bronze Medal 1984, Silver Medal 1997. *Publications include:* Handbook of Income Distribution (jt author); contributions to numerous specialist journals. *Address:* The World Bank, 1818 H Street NW, Washington DC 20433, USA (office). *Telephone:* (202) 473-1000 (office). *Fax:* (202) 477-6391 (office). *Website:* web.worldbank.org (office).

BOURGUIGNON, Philippe Etienne, MScEcon, MBA; French business executive; *Vice-Chairman, Revolution Places Group;* b. 11 Jan. 1948, Salins les Bains; s. of Jacques Bourguignon and Paule Clément; m. Martine Lemardeley 1977; one s. one d.; ed Univ. of Aix; analyst, Synthèse Documentaire, Paris 1971–72; Project Man. Systembau, Munich 1973; Vice-Pres. Devt Accor, Novotel Asia, Middle East 1974–79; Exec. Vice-Pres. Accor North America, New York 1979–84; Pres. and CEO Accor Asia Pacific, Los Angeles 1984–88; Sr Vice-Pres. Real Estate Devt Euro Disney, Paris 1989–92; Pres. Euro Disney SA, Paris 1992, Chair. and CEO 1993–97; Exec. Vice-Pres. for Europe Walt Disney Co. 1996–97; Chair. Bd of Dirs Club Méditerranée 1997–2002; Pres. Exec. Comm. for Paris' bid for Olympic Games 2008 1998; Man. Dir World Econ. Forum Aug.–Oct. 2003, co-CEO 2003–04; Chair. Aegis Media France 2004–06; Vice-Chair. Revolution Resorts (div. of Revolution LLC) 2006–07, Vice Chair Revolution Places Group and CEO Revolution Places Devt 2007–; Pres. Young Pres. Org. 1990; mem. Bd of Dirs eBay Inc 1999–, American Chamber of Commerce in France; mem. Econ. Council Confed. of French Industries and Services; Chair. YPO French Chapter 1990; Chevalier, Légion d'honneur, Officier Ordre nat. du Mérite. *Leisure interests:* sailing, reading, tennis, skiing. *Address:* c/o Revolution LLC, 1717 Rhode Island Avenue, NW, Washington, DC 20036-3023, USA (office). *Telephone:* (202) 776-1400. *Website:* www.revolution.com.

BOURHANE, Ali; Comoran international civil servant; *Senior Adviser, African Development Bank;* b. 2 April 1946; m. Neila Bourhane; one s. one d.; ed Univ. of Bordeaux, Ecole Nationale d'Administration, Paris and Univ. of Toulouse; Research Fellow, Univ. of Toulouse 1971; Prof. of Math., Comoros 1972–75; civil servant 1980–85; Sr Economist, IMF, Washington, DC 1985–90; Alt. Exec. Dir IBRD 1990–94, Exec. Dir 1994–99; currently Sr Adviser African Devt Bank, Tunis. *Leisure interests:* reading (religion, African history and anthropology, Devt Econs), tennis, running. *Address:* African Development Bank, Angle des Trois Rues: Avenue du Ghana, Rue Pierre de Coubertin, Rue Hedi Nouira, POB 323, 1002 Tunis (office); Apartment A41, Venus, Rue Hedi Novira, Ennassa 2, 2037 Tunis, Tunisia (home). *Telephone:* (71) 102-686 (office); (71) 816-152 (home). *E-mail:* a.bourhane@afdb.org (office); alboucom@hotmail.com (home).

BOURHANE, Nourdine; Comoran politician; Prime Minister of Comoros 1997–98. *Address:* BP 551, Moroni, Comoros. *Telephone:* 73-07-83.

BOURJAILY, Vance, BA, DLit; American novelist and academic; b. 17 Sept. 1922, Cleveland; s. of Monte Ferris Bourjaily and Barbara Webb Bourjaily; m. 1st Bettina Yensen 1946; one s. two d.; m. 2nd Yasmin Mogul 1985; one s.; ed Handley High School, Va and Bowdoin Coll., Maine; American Field Service 1942–44; US Army 1944–46; Publisher, Record, New Castle, Va 1947–48; Staff Writer, San Francisco Chronicle 1949–50; Ed. Discovery 1951–53; Instructor, Mexico City Coll. 1953; Dramatic Critic, The Village Voice 1955–56; freelance TV writer 1956–57; Visiting Lecturer, Univ. of Iowa 1957–59, Prof. 1961; Specialist, US State Dept 1960; Boyd Prof. of English, La. State Univ. 1989, now Prof. Emer.; Acad. Award in Literature, American Acad. of Arts and Letters 1993. *Publications:* novels: The End of My Life 1947, The Hound of Earth 1953, The Violated 1957, Confessions of a Spent Youth 1960, The Man Who Knew Kennedy 1967, Brill Among the Ruins 1970, Now Playing at Canterbury 1976, The Great Fake Book 1986, Old Soldier 1990, Fishing by Mail: The Outdoor Life of a Father and Son 1993; non-fiction: The Unnatural Enemy 1963, Country Matters 1973; plays: Time is a Dancer 1950, The Quick Years 1956, Confessions 1971. *Leisure interests:* politics, mycology, conservation. *Address:* c/o Department of English, 260 Allen Hall, Louisiana State University, Baton Rouge 70803, USA.

BOURJINI, Salah Amara, MA (Econs), PhD; Tunisian UN official; *Resident Representative and Co-ordinator for Libya, Development Programme, United Nations;* b. 17 Jan. 1938, Lekef; m. 1967; one s. two d.; engineer in planning and statistics, Tunis 1963–67; Lecturer in Econs, Univ. of Kansas, USA 1969–72; Prof., Univ. of Tunis 1972–80; Adviser to Minister of Economy 1972–76; Deputy Dir-Gen. Ministry of Foreign Affairs 1976–80; Deputy UN Resident Rep. and UN Co-ordinator, Algeria 1980–82; Chief, Div. for Regional Programme, Arab States, UNDP, New York 1982–87, UN Resident Rep. and UN Co-ordinator, Iraq 1987–92, UN Resident Rep. and UN Co-ordinator, Libya 1992–; Chevalier de la République; various UN service awards. *Publications:* Human Capital Investment and Economic Growth 1974, New International Economic Order 1978; articles on devt, educ. and trade. *Leisure interests:* tennis, swimming, music. *Address:* United Nations Development Programme, PO Box 358, Tripoli, Libya (office). *Telephone:* (21) 3330855 (office). *Fax:* (21) 3330856 (office).

BOURNE, Larry Stuart, PhD, DèsS, FRSC, MCIP, RPP; Canadian geographer and academic; *Professor of Geography and Planning and Research Associate, Centre for Urban and Community Studies and Global Cities Program, University of Toronto;* b. 24 Dec. 1939, London, Ont.; s. of Stuart H. Bourne and Florence Bourne; m. Paula T. O'Neill 1967; one s. one d.; ed Univs of Western Ontario, Alberta and Chicago; Asst Prof. of Geography, Univ. of Toronto 1967–69, Assoc. Prof. and Assoc. Dir, Centre for Urban and Community Studies (CUCS) 1969–82, Prof. and Dir 1973–78, 1979–84, Prof. of Geography and Planning, Co-ordinator of Grad. Studies 1985–89, 1991–94; Dir Grad. Planning Program 1996–98, 1999–2002, 2004–06, currently Prof. of Geography and Planning; Research Assoc., Centre for Urban and Community Studies and Global Cities Program; Visiting Scholar, Univ. of Monash, Australia and LSE, UK 1972–73, Centre for Environmental Studies, London, UK 1978–79; Visiting Prof., Univ. of Alberta, Univ. of Tex., USA 1984, Marburg (W Germany) 1985, Melbourne 1988, Meiji Univ., Tokyo 1991, Univ. of Tokyo 1996, Ben Gurion Univ. 1998, Seoul Nat. Univ. 1999; Chair. Comm. on Urban Systems and Devt, Int. Geographical Union 1988–92; consultant to local, nat. and int. agencies; Pres. Canadian Asscn of Geographers 1993–94, North American Regional Science Council 1994–95; Dr hc (Waterloo) 1999; Award for Scholarly Distinction, Canadian Asscn of Geographers 1985, Honors Award, Asscn of American Geographers 1985, Elected to Royal Soc. of Canada 1986, Award for Service to Geography (Ont. Div. Canadian Asscn of Geographers) 1990, Teaching Award, Univ. of Toronto 1999, Massey Medal, Royal Canadian Geographical Society, 2004. *Publications:* 19 books, including Urban Systems: Strategies for Regulation 1975, The Geography of Housing 1981, Internal Structure of the City 1982, Urbanization and Settlement Systems 1984, Urban Systems in Transition 1986, The Changing Geography of Urban Systems 1989, Urbanization and Urban Growth 1991, Changing Social Geography of Canadian Cities 1993, People and Places 2000; over 230 articles in journals and professional reports. *Address:* Department of Geography, University of Toronto, 100 St George Street, Toronto, Ont., M5S 3G3 (office); 26 Anderson Avenue, Toronto, Ont., M5P 1H4, Canada (home). *Telephone:* (416) 978-3375 (office); (416) 486-7819 (home). *Fax:* (416) 946-3886 (office); (416) 978-6729 (home). *E-mail:* bourne@geog.utoronto.ca (office); larry.bourne@utoronto.ca (home). *Website:* www.geog.utoronto.ca/info/facweb/lsb (office).

BOURNE, Matthew Christopher, OBE, BA; British dancer and choreographer; b. 13 Jan. 1960, London; s. of Harold Jeffrey (Jim) Bourne and June Lillian Bourne (née Handley); ed Laban Centre for Movt and Dance, London; f. Adventures in Motion Pictures 1987; Dir Spitfire Trust 1996–; Founding Dir New Adventures 2002–; mem. Hon. Cttee Dance Cares 1995–; Hon. Fellow of the Laban Centre 1997 (mem. Bd 1999–); Assoc. Artist, Sadler's Wells Theatre 2005–; Tony Award 1999, Astaire Award 1999, numerous other dance awards and prizes. *Dance:* Overlap Lovers 1987, Town and Country 1991, Nutcracker 1992, 2002, Highland Fling 1994, Swan Lake 1995, Cinderella 1997, The Car Man 2000–01 (also televised Channel 4), My Fair Lady (Olivier Award for Best Theatre Choreographer 2002) 2001, South Pacific 2002, Play Without Words (Olivier Awards for Best Entertainment and Best Theatre Choreographer 2003) 2002, Mary Poppins (with Stephen Mear) (Olivier Award for Best Theatre Choreographer 2005) 2004, Edward Scissorhands 2006, Dorian Gray 2008. *Publication:* Matthew Bourne & His Adventures in Motion Pictures 1999. *Leisure interests:* theatre, cinema, music. *Address:* c/o Duncan Heath, ICM, Oxford House, 76 Oxford Street, London, W1N 0AX (office); 21 Stamford Road, London, N1 4JP, England (home). *Telephone:* (20) 7636-6565 (office). *Fax:* (20) 7323-0701 (office). *E-mail:* matthewatamp@hotmail.com (office).

BOURNE, Stephen Robert Richard, MA, FCA, FRSA; British publisher; *CEO, Cambridge University Press;* b. 20 March 1952, Kampala, Uganda; s. of Colyn M. Bourne and Kathleen Bourne; m. Stephanie Ann Bickford 1978; one s. one d.; ed Berkhamsted School, Univ. of Edinburgh; with Deloitte Haskins and Sells, London and Hong Kong 1974–80; with Exxon Chemical Asia-Pacific, Hong Kong 1980–86; Financial Dir Asia, Dow Jones Telerate, London and Hong Kong 1986–89, Gen. Man. Northern Europe 1989–94; Man. Dir, Financial Printing Div., St Ives PLC, London 1994–96; Devt Dir, Cambridge Univ. Press 1997–2000, Chair. of Printing Div. 2000–, CEO 2002–; mem. Bd Britten Sinfonia, The Wine Soc., CBI East, Univ. of the Arts London; mem. Publishing Studies Advisory Bd, Univ. Coll. London, City Univ., London Coll. of Communication; Fellow, Clare Hall, Cambridge, Inst. of Printing; Liveryman and Chair. Trade and Industry Forum, The Stationers' Co. *Leisure interests:* fine wines, performing arts, cricket, skiing, Real Tennis. *Address:* Cambridge University Press, The Edinburgh Building, Shaftesbury Road, Cambridge, CB2 8RU (office); Falmouth Lodge, Snailwell Road, Newmarket, CB8 7DN, England (home). *Telephone:* (1223) 325184 (office). *Fax:* (1223) 325701 (office). *E-mail:* sbourne@cambridge.org (office). *Website:* www.cambridge.org (office).

BOURSEILLER, Antoine; French theatre director and producer; b. 8 July 1930, Paris; s. of Marcel Edouard Bourseiller and Denise Fisteberg; m. Chantal Darget 1966 (deceased); one s. one d.; Dir of Theatre, Studio des Champs-Elysées 1960–63, Poche 1964–66, Centre Dramatique National de Marseille 1966–75, Recamier 1975–78, Orléans 1980–82; Dir-Gen. Opéra-Théâtre de Nancy et de Lorraine 1982–96; Artistic Adviser, Théâtre de Tarascon 2003–05; Chevalier, Légion d'honneur; Commdr des Arts et Lettres. *Operas directed:* La Clémence de Titus (Aix-en-Provence Festival) 1973, Le Barbier de Seville (Théâtre Lyrique du Sud) 1979, Mireille (Geneva) 1981, (London) 1983, Carmen (Nancy) 1981, Woyzeck (Angers) 1982; Boulevard Solitude 1984, Cantate d'Octobre, Erwartung 1986, Donna Abbandonata 1987, King Priam 1988 (all at Nancy); Lulu (Nantes), Lady Macbeth de Mtsensk (Nancy) 1989; La Noche Triste 1989, Lohengrin L'Homme de Mancha (Brussels-Liège) 1994, 1998, Voyage à Reims (Liège) 2000. *Films:* Cleo de 5 à 7, 2 places pour le 26, Masculin Feminin, La Guerre est finie. *Plays directed:* Va donc chez Torpe 1961, Axel 1963, L'Amérique 1964, Metro Fantôme 1965, Striptease 1965, Silence, l'arbre… 1967, Les Brigands 1972, Jean Harlow 1972, Leuco 1974, Kennedy's Children 1975, La Tour 1976, S.T. 1979, The Idiot 2005, Le Bagne 2006, Hamlet/Lorenzo 2006, Lorenzaccio 2007, parution chez Actes Sud. Artes du livre Sans Relâche 2008, Figures de l'enrol amoureux l'Ane d'Or, Festival Avignon 2009, Corrida, theatre du Rond-Point du Champs-Elysees 2009. *Address:* 55 quai des Grands Augustins, 75006 Paris, France (home). *Telephone:* 1-46-33-05-27 (home).

BOUSNINA, Mongi; Tunisian diplomatist and international organization executive; *Director-General, Arab League Educational, Cultural and Scientific Organization (ALECSO);* fmr Minister of Culture; fmr Amb. to Morocco, to France; Gen. Co-ordinator for the Arab Participation Programme at the Frankfurt Book Fair 2004; Dir-Gen. Arab League Educational, Cultural and Scientific Org. (ALECSO) 2001–. *Address:* Arab League Educational, Cultural and Scientific Organization (ALECSO), avenue Mohamed V, PO Box 1120, Tunis, Tunisia (office). *Telephone:* (71) 784-466 (office). *Fax:* (71) 784-496 (office). *E-mail:* alecso@email.ati.tn (office). *Website:* www.alecso.org.tn (office).

BOUSQUET, Jean; French politician and couturier; *CEO, Cacharel;* b. 29 March 1932, Nîmes; s. of Célestin Bousquet and Rosa Pyronnet; m. Dominique Sarrut 1965; one s. one d.; ed Ecole Tech. de Nîmes; dress cutter, Jean Jourdan, Paris 1955–57; Founder and CEO Soc. Jean Cacharel 1964–, of subsidiaries abroad 1972–; Mayor of Nîmes 1983–95; Deputy (UDF) for Gard, Assemblée Nat. 1986–97; mem. Radical Party 1993–96; Oscar for export achievement 1969, Man of the Year, Jeune Chambre économique française 1985. *Leisure interests:* travel, football, golf, skiing. *Address:* Cacharel, 36 rue Tronchet, 75009 Paris, France. *Telephone:* 1-42-68-38-88 (office). *Fax:* 1-42-68-38-77 (office). *E-mail:* jeanbousquet@cacharel.fr (office). *Website:* www.cacharel.fr (office).

BOUSQUET, Rufus; Saint Lucia politician; mem. House of Ass. (Parl.) for Choiseul 2006–, Minister for External Affairs, Int. Financial Services, Information and Broadcasting 2006–07; mem. United Workers Party (UWP), fmr Deputy Leader and Chair. Public Relations Cttee. *Address:* House of Assembly, Greaham Louisy Administrative Building, Waterfront, Castries, Saint Lucia (office). *Telephone:* 468-2116 (office). *Fax:* 453-1614 (office). *E-mail:* info@dis.gov.lc (office).

BOUTALEB, Abdelhadi, BA; Moroccan politician and academic; b. 28 Dec. 1923, Fez; m. Touria Chraïbi 1946; two s. one d.; ed Al Qarawiyin Univ.; Prof. of Arabic History and Literature and Tutor to Prince Moulay Hassan and Prince Moulay Abdallah; Founder-mem. Democratic Party of Independence 1944–51, Shura and Istiqlal Party 1948, mem. Politburo –1959; campaigned, through the Party, for Moroccan independence and for this purpose attended UN Session, Paris 1951 and Negotiating Conf. at Aix-les-Bains 1955; Minister of Labour and Social Affairs 1956; Chief Ed. of journal Al-Rai-Alaam 1956–61; Amb. to Syria 1962; Sec. of State, Ministry of Information Nov. 1962, Ministry of Information, Youth and Sports Jan. 1963; Interim Minister in Charge of Mauritania and Sahara Nov. 1963; Minister of Justice 1964–67, of Nat. Educ. and Fine Arts 1967; Minister of State 1968; Minister of Foreign Affairs 1969–70; Pres. Chamber of Reps 1970–71; Lecturer in Constitutional Law and Political Insts, Rabat Law Univ. 1974, in Constitutional Law and Political Insts 1979–; Amb. to USA, 1974–76, to Mexico 1976; Adviser to HM Hassan II 1977–78, 1992–96, Tutor to Crown Prince Sidi Mohamed 1978; Minister of State in Charge of Information 1978; Dir-Gen. Islamic Educ., Scientific and Cultural Org., Rabat May 1982; Vice-Pres. Int. Comm. for the Presentation of Int. Cultural Heritage 1983–; mem. Royal Acad. for Islamic Civilization Research, Royal Acad. of Morocco 1982, Hon. Cttee of Pascual de Gayancos Arab-Spanish Foundation 1985, Consulting Council of Human Rights 1994; Adviser to His Majesty King Hassan II 1991–; Commdr of the Throne of Morocco, Grand Cordon of the Repub. of UAR, Supreme Distinction of Merit of the Kingdom of Morocco 1990, and other decorations. *Publications:* many cultural and literary works. *Leisure interests:* sports, music, reading. *Address:* 100 rue des Oudayas, 20300 Casablanca, Morocco. *Telephone:* (2) 61-82-85. *Fax:* (2) 62-11-95. *E-mail:* contact@abdelhadiboutaleb.com. *Website:* www.abdelhadiboutaleb.com.

BOUTEFLIKA, Abdul Aziz; Algerian head of state; *President and Minister of Defence;* b. 2 March 1937, Oujda; ed Morocco; Maj., Nat. Liberation Army and Sec. of Gen. Staff; mem. Parl. for Tlemcen 1962; Minister of Youth, Sports and Tourism 1962–63, of Foreign Affairs 1963–79; Counsellor to the Pres. March 1979–80; Pres. of Algeria and Minister of Defence 1999–; mem. FLN Political Bureau 1964–81, mem. Cen. Cttee 1989; mem. Revolutionary Council 1965–79; led negotiations with France 1963, 1966, for nationalization of hydrocarbons 1971; leader of dels to many confs of Arab League, OAU 1968, Group of 1977 1967, Non-aligned Countries 1973, Pres. Seventh Special Session of UN Gen. Ass. 1975, Int. Conf. on Econ. Co-operation, Paris 1975–76; Pres. 29th UN Gen. Ass. 1974; mem. Nat. Council Moujahidin (Nat. Liberation Army) 1990–. *Address:* Office of the President, el-Mouradia, Algiers (office); 138 Chemin Bachir Brahimi, El Biar, Algiers, Algeria. *Telephone:* (21) 69-15-15 (office); (21) 60-34-59 (home). *Fax:* (21) 69-15-95 (office). *Website:* www.el-mouradia.dz (office).

BOUTERSE, Col Désiré Delano; Suriname politician; *President, Nationale Democratische Partij;* b. 13 Oct. 1945, Paramaribo; led mil. coup 1980, Chair. Nat. Mil. Council (de facto Leader) 1980–88 (resgnd); Pres. 1982; led mil. coup 1990, Chief of Army 1990–92 (resgnd); Pres. Nationale Democratische Partij 1992–99, 2006–; political adviser to Pres. 1996–99; convicted of drug trafficking in absentia, Netherlands 1999; mem. Parl. 2005–; unsuccessful cand. in presidential election 2005. *Address:* Nationale Democratische Partij, dr H.D. Benjaminstraat 38, Paramaribo, Suriname (office). *Telephone:* 499183 (office). *Fax:* 432174 (office). *E-mail:* ndpsur@sr.net (office). *Website:* www.ndp.sr (office).

BOUTIN, Bernard Louis, PhB; American management consultant; b. 2 July 1923, Belmont, NH; s. of Joseph L. Boutin and Annie E. (Laflam) Boutin; m. Alice M. Boucher 1945; six s. five d.; ed St Michael's Coll., Winooski, Vt and Catholic Univ. of America, Washington, DC; Pres. and Treas., Boutin Insurance Agency Inc., Laconia, NH 1948–63; Proprietor, Boutin Real Estate Co., Laconia 1955–63; Mayor of Laconia 1955–59; Deputy Admin. Gen. Services Admin. (GSA), Washington DC Feb.–Nov. 1961; Admin. GSA 1961–64; Exec. Vice-Pres. Nat. Assen Home Builders 1964–65; Admin. of Small Business Admin. 1966–67; Deputy Dir Office of Econ. Opportunity 1965–66; Exec. Sanders Assoc. Inc. 1967–69; Chair. NH State Bd of Educ. 1968–69; mem. Nat. Highway Safety Comm. 1969–70; Democratic Candidate for Gov. of NH 1958, 1960; Pres. St Michael's Coll. 1969–75; Exec. Vice-Pres. Burlington Savings Bank (Vt) 1975–76, Pres., Treas., Trustee 1976–80; Treas. and Trustee Medical Center Hospital of Vermont 1978–80; Dir New England College Fund 1979–80; Dir First Deposit Nat. Bank 1991–94; numerous decorations including Kt of the Equestrian Order of the Holy Sepulchre of Jerusalem; Hon. LLD (St Michael's Coll.); Hon. LHD (Plymouth Coll. of the Univ. of New Hampshire); Hon. HHD (Franklyn Pierce Coll.); charter member, St Michael's Coll., Academic Hall of Fame. *Publication:* Echoes of Me 1991. *Leisure interests:* reading, use of my computer. *Address:* 631 Benton Drive, Laconia, NH 03241, USA (home). *Telephone:* (603) 528-1014. *E-mail:* bboutin34612@earthlinkl.net (home).

BOUTON, Daniel; French business executive; b. 1950; ed Ecole nat. d'Admin; Insp. of Finance, Ministry of Finance 1973–76, Budget Dept, Ministry of Finance 1977–86, Chief of Staff to Alain Juppé, Deputy Minister in charge of the Budget 1986–88; Exec. Vice-Pres. Société Générale 1991, CEO 1993–2008, Chair. 1997–2009 (resgnd); mem. Bd of Dirs Total, Veolia; Chevalier, Légion d'honneur, Ordre nat. du Mérite. *Address:* c/o Société Générale, 189 rue d'Aubervilliers, 75886 Paris Cedex 18, France (office).

BOUTROS, Fouad; Lebanese politician and lawyer; b. Nov. 1917, Beirut; m. Tania Shehade 1953; one s. two d.; ed Coll. des Frères, Beirut, St Joseph Univ. Law School; clerk, Mixed Appeal Court, Beirut 1939; Judge, Civil Court of Mount Lebanon 1942; Judge, Mixed Civil and Commercial Tribunal of Beirut 1944–46; Head, State Legal Dept 1946–47; Examining Magistrate, Mil. Court 1944–47; attorney at law 1947–; Minister of Educ. and Planning 1959–60; mem. Chamber of Deputies 1960–68; Deputy Speaker (Vice-Pres.), Chamber of Deputies 1960–61; Minister of Justice 1961–64; Vice-Pres., Council of Ministers, Minister of Educ. and Defence April–Dec. 1966; Vice-Pres., Council of Ministers, Minister of Foreign Affairs and Tourism Feb.–Oct. 1968; Vice-Pres., Council of Ministers, Minister of Foreign Affairs 1976–82, and of Defence 1976–78; numerous decorations including Grand Cross of the Order of Gregory the Great 1997. *Publications:* Ecrits politiques 1997, Memories of Fouad Boutros 2009; numerous lectures and political articles in the press, in Arabic and French. *Leisure interests:* reading, walking. *Address:* Hazmieh, Gardenia Street, Ghaleb Center, Beirut POB 45-224 (office); Sursock Street, Fouad Boutros Building, Beirut, Lebanon (home). *Telephone:* (5) 459411 (office); (1) 201500 (home). *Fax:* (5) 457992 (office); (5) 458933 (office); (1) 217216 (home). *E-mail:* tboutros@dm.net.lb (home).

BOUTROS GHALI, Boutros, LLB, PhD; Egyptian international civil servant and politician; *Secretary-General, Organisation Internationale de la Francophonie;* b. 14 Nov. 1922, Cairo; m. Leia Nadler; ed Cairo Univ. and Paris Univ.; fmr Prof. of Int. Law and Int. Relations and Head Dept of Political Sciences, Cairo Univ. 1949–77; fmr mem. Cen. Cttee Arab Socialist Union; Pres. Cen. of Political and Strategic Studies; f. Al Ahram Al Iktisadi, Ed. 1960–75, f. Al-Siyassa Ad-Dawlya, Ed.; Minister of State for Foreign Affairs 1977–91, Deputy Prime Minister for Foreign Affairs 1991–92; Sec.-Gen. of UN 1992–96; Sec.-Gen. Org. Int. de la Francophonie 1997–; Vice-Pres. Egyptian Soc. of Int. Law 1965–; mem. Cttee on Application of Conventions and Recommendations of Int. Labour Org. 1971–79; Pres. Centre of Political and Strategic Studies (Al-Ahram) 1975–; mem. Int. Comm. of Jurists, Geneva and Council and Exec. Cttee of Int. Inst. of Human Rights, Strasbourg; mem. UN Comm. of Int. Law 1979–92, Secretariat Nat. Democratic Party 1980–92, Parl. 1987–92; Onassis Foundation Prize 1995, recipient of honorary titles and awards from 24 countries. *Publications include:* Contribution à l'étude des ententes régionales 1949, Cours de diplomatie et de droit diplomatique et consulaire 1951, Le principe d'égalité des états et les organisations internationales 1961, Foreign Policies in World Change 1963, L'Organisation de l'unité africaine 1969, La ligue des états arabes 1972, Les Conflits des frontières en Afrique 1973; also numerous books in Arabic and contribs to periodicals. *Leisure interests:* the works of Matisse, collecting old pens from the Ottoman Empire. *Address:* 2 avenue Epnipgiza, Cairo, Egypt (home).

BOUTROS-GHALI, Yousuf, BA, PhD; Egyptian economist and politician; *Minister of Finance;* ed Cairo Univ., Massachusetts Inst. of Tech., USA; Sr Economist, IMF 1981–86; Econ. Adviser to Prime Minister and Gov. of Cen. Bank of Egypt 1986–93; Minister of State for Int. Cooperation 1993–95, Minister of State at Council of Ministers 1993–95; Minister of State for Econ. Affairs 1996–97, Minister of Economy 1997–99, Minister of Economy and Foreign Trade 1999–2001, of Foreign Trade 2001–2004, of Finance 2004–; fmr Lecturer of Econs, American Univ. in Cairo and MIT, Assoc. Prof. of Econs, Cairo Univ.; fmr Dir Centre for Econ. Analysis, Council of Ministers; mem. Bd of Dirs Nat. Bank of Egypt 1991–93. *Publications:* 22 papers and books on devt and theoretical issues in field of econs. *Address:* Ministry of Finance, Ministry of Finance Towers Cairo (Nasr City), Egypt. *Telephone:* (2) 3428886 (office). *Fax:* (2) 6861861 (office). *E-mail:* finance@mof.gov.eg (office). *Website:* www.mof.gov.eg (office).

BOUVET, Jean-Christophe; French actor, director and screenwriter; b. 24 March 1947, Paris. *Film appearances include:* La philosophie dans le boudoir 1969, Change pas de main 1975, Le pendule 1976, Les pornocrates 1976, Le théâtre des matières 1977, Le borgne 1980, C'est la vie 1981, Loin de Manhattan 1982, L'archipel des amours 1983, En haut des marches 1983, Sous le soleil de Satan 1987, Les dents de ma mère 1991, J'embarassa pas 1991, Krapatchouk 1992, Bouvet son texte 1992, Les nuits fauves 1992, Terre sainte 1994, Dadou 1994, La cité de la peur 1994, L'eau froide 1994, J'aime beaucoup ce que vous faites 1995, Dialogue au sommet 1996, Des progrès en amour 1996, Le complexe de Toulon 1996, Le rocher d'Acapulco 1996, L'@mour est à réinventer 1996, Vicious Circles 1997, Un arrangement 1997, Le passager 1997, Le Plaisir (et ses petits tracas) 1998, Pain au chocolat 1998, Le comte de Monte Cristo 1998, L'examen de minuit 1998, Out! 1999, Le domaine 1999, Glória 1999, Les passagers 1999, Recto/Verso 1999, Lovers 1999, Une rue dans sa longeur 2000, Taxi 2 2000, Cosmocrator 2000, Lise et André 2000, La chambre obscure 2000, Effraction 2001, Le chien, le chat et le cibachrome 2001, La boîte 2001, Being Light 2001, Jojo la frite 2002, Le nouveau Jean-Claude 2002, La sirène rouge 2002, Le cou de Clarisse 2003, Taxi 3 2003, Saltimbank 2003, En famille 2003, Notre musique 2004, Mensonges et trahisons 2004, Prisonnier 2004, Comme un frère 2005, Journal IV 2005, Il sera une fois 2005, La comédie du pouvoir 2005, Marie-Antoinette 2006, Les brigades du tigre 2006. *Films directed and written include:* Le troisiéme wagon 1981, En veux-tu, en voilà (TV) 1982, Peinture à l'eau (TV) 1983, En voilà 2 (TV) 1983, Et de trois (TV) 1988, Les dents de ma mère 1991, Bouvet et son texte 1992. *Address:* Agence Artistique Terenga, 32, rue Yves Toudic, Paris 75010, France (office). *Telephone:* 1-53-36-72-91 (office). *Fax:* 1-53-36-71-85 (office). *E-mail:* terenga@noos.fr (office). *Website:* www.terenga.com (office).

BOUYGUES, Martin; French business executive; *Chairman and CEO, Bouygues SA;* b. 3 May 1952; s. of Francis Bouygues; three c.; ed Univ. of Paris Dauphine; joined Bouygues Group 1974, site supervisor for Les Halles shopping complex, Paris 1974–78, f. Maison Bouygues 1978, Chair. and CEO Saur 1986, mem. Bd of Dirs Bouygues SA 1982–, Vice-Chair. 1987–89, Chair. and CEO 1989–; Chair. SCDM; mem. Bd of Dirs TF1, Sodeci, CIE; mem. Supervisory Bd Paris-Orléans; Chevalier, Légion d'honneur, Ordre nat. du Mérite. *Leisure interests:* hunting, boating. *Address:* Bouygues Headquarters, 32 avenue Hoche, 75378 Paris Cedex 08, France (office). *Telephone:* (1) 44-20-10-00 (office). *Fax:* (1) 44-20-14-99 (office). *E-mail:* presse@bouygues.com (office). *Website:* www.bouygues.com (office).

BOVENDER, Jack O., Jr, BSc; American healthcare industry executive; *Chairman and CEO, HCA Inc.;* ed Duke Univ., Durham, NC; Navy Service Medical Corps, rank of Lt; fmr Asst Admin., Community Gen. Hosp., Thomasville, NC; joined HCA Inc., CEO Medical Center Hosp., Largo, FL and W FL Regional Medical Center, Pensacola, later several man. positions 1985–92, including Vice-Pres. HCA Atlanta Div., Pres. HCA Eastern Group Operations, Exec. Vice-Pres. and COO HCA 1992–94, 1997–2001, Pres. and CEO 2001–02, Chair. and CEO 2002–; Dir Quorum Health Group Inc. 1994–97, American Retirement Corpn 1994–97, Nashville Electric Service 1994–97; mem. Bd of Govs, American Coll. of Healthcare Execs (ACHE) 2003–; Dir Nashville Community Foundation, Frist Foundation, Tennessee Performing Arts Center, Center for Non-Profit Man.; fmr Dir Nashville Healthcare Council, American Hosp. Asscn, Fed. of American Healthcare Systems, FL League of Hosps; mem. Bd of Visitors, Duke Univ. Fuqua School of Business; mem. Exec. Cttee, Duke Univ. Annual Fund; Hon. mem. Bd of Visitors, Duke Univ. Divinity School. *Address:* HCA Inc., One Park Plaza, Nashville, TN 37203, USA (office). *Telephone:* (615) 344-9551 (office). *Fax:* (615) 344-2266 (office). *E-mail:* info@hcahealthcare.com (office). *Website:* www.hcahealthcare.com (office).

BOWE, Riddick Lamont; American professional boxer; b. 1967, Brooklyn; s. of Dorothy Bowe; m. 1st Judy Bowe 1986 (divorced); one s. two d.; 2nd Terri Bowe; amateur boxer 1982–89, professional boxer 1989–, won World Boxing Asscn, World Boxing Confed., Int. Boxing Fed. titles 1992, World Boxing Asscn, Int. Boxing Fed. titles 1993, World Boxing Org. title 1995, defeating two challengers in that year to retain title; Silver Medal Super Heavyweight Div., Olympic Games, Seoul, 1988; ranked Undisputed Heavyweight Champion 1992–93, 1995; retd from boxing 1996; briefly with US Marine Corps; pleaded guilty to fed. charge of abduction June 1998, served 18 months, released 2004; announced resumption of boxing career 2004; 42 wins and 1 loss, with 1 no-contest, and 33 knockouts.

BOWEN, Gregory, BEng (Mech), MEng; Grenadian politician; *Deputy Prime Minister and Minister of Agriculture, Lands, Forestry and Fisheries, Public Utilities, Energy and The Marketing and National Importing Board;* m.; five c.; ed Presentation Brothers Coll., Univ. of the West Indies, Univ. of Saskatchewan, Canada; several diplomas and certificates in Financial Man., Eng Man. and Business; taught at Presentation Brothers Coll. and Anglican High School; Lecturer, Inst. for Further Educ. 1980–81; Planning and Devt Engineer, Grenada Electricity Services Ltd 1983, later Man.; Senator and Minister for Communications, Works, Public Utilities, Energy and Transport 1995–2003; mem. Parl. for St George South East 1999–; Deputy Prime Minister and Minister of Agric., Lands, Forestry and Fisheries, Public Utilities, Energy and The Marketing and Nat. Importing Bd 2003–; mem. ASME, Inst. of Diesel and Gas Turbine Engineers, Grenada Inst. of Professional Engineers, American Soc. of Agricultural Engineers. *Leisure interest:* guitar playing. *Address:* Ministry of Agriculture, Lands, Forestry and Fisheries, Ministerial Complex, 2nd and 3rd Floors, St George's, Grenada (office). *Telephone:* 440-2708 (office). *Fax:* 440-4191 (office). *E-mail:* grenfish@caribsurf.com (office).

BOWEN, Most Rev. Michael George, STL, PhL; British ecclesiastic; *Archbishop Emeritus of Southwark;* b. 23 April 1930, Gibraltar; s. of Maj. C. L. J. Bowen and Mary J. Pedley; ed Downside Abbey School, Trinity Coll., Cambridge and Gregorian Univ., Rome; army service 1948–49; in the wine trade 1951–52; Venerable English Coll., Rome 1952–59; ordained RC priest 1958; curate, Earlsfield and Walworth, Diocese of Southwark 1959–63; teacher of Theology, Pontifical Beda Coll., Rome 1963–66; Chancellor, Diocese of Arundel and Brighton 1966–70, Coadjutor Bishop 1970–71, Bishop of Arundel and Brighton 1971–77; Archbishop and Metropolitan, Diocese of Southwark 1977–2003, Archbishop Emer. 2003–; Vice-Pres. Catholic Bishops' Conf. England and Wales 1996–99; Pres. 1999–2000; Freeman City of London 1984. *Leisure interests:* golf, tennis. *Address:* c/o Archbishop's House, 150 St George's Road, London, SE1 6HX, England. *Telephone:* (20) 7928-2495. *Fax:* (20) 7928-7833.

BOWEN, Ray M., PhD; American engineer, academic and university administrator; *Professor, Department of Mechanical Engineering and President Emeritus, Texas A&M University;* b. 30 March 1936, Fort Worth, Tex.; s. of Winfred Herbert Bowen and Elizabeth Williams Bowen; m. Sara Elizabeth Gibbons Bowen 1958; one s. one d.; ed Texas A&M Univ., California Inst. Tech.; Assoc. Prof. Mechanical Eng, Louisiana State Univ. 1965–67; Prof. Mechanical Eng, Rice Univ. 1967–83, Chair. Dept Mechanical Eng 1972–77; Div. Dir NSF 1982–83, Acting Asst Dir Eng to Dep. Asst Dir 1990–91; Prof. and Dean of Eng, Univ. of Ky 1983–89; Vice-Pres. Academic Affairs, Okla State Univ. 1991–93, Interim Pres. 1993–94; Pres. Tex. A&M Univ. 1994–2002, Pres. Emer. and Prof., Dept of Mechanical Eng and Sara and John H. Lindsey '44 Chair 2002–; mem. Nat. Science Bd 2002–08, Soc. of Scholars, Johns Hopkins Univ., ASEE Fellows. *Publications:* Introduction to Continuum Mechanics for Engineers; Introduction to Vectors and Tensors (co-author); Rational Thermodynamics (contrib.); contrib. numerous articles in professional journals. *Leisure interests:* travelling, opera. *Address:* Department of Mechanical Engineering, Texas A&M University, 3.252C Evans, Library Annex, College Station, TX 77843, USA (office). *Telephone:* (979) 862-2955 (office). *Fax:* (979) 862-2956 (office). *E-mail:* rbowen@tamu.edu (office). *Website:* www.mengr.tamu.edu (office).

BOWEN, Tim; British music industry executive; Head of Business Affairs Sony Music UK; Head Sony Music Publishing Int., New York 1982–86; Man. Dir CBS/Columbia Records UK 1986–91; Sr Vice-Pres. Marketing and Business Affairs, Universal Music Int. 1994–99, Exec. Vice-Pres. 1999–2001; COO BMG Europe 2002–03, Chair. BMG Entertainment, UK and Ireland 2003–04, Chair. Sony BMG UK & Ireland, Canada, Australia, New Zealand, South Africa 2004–06, COO Sony BMG 2006–08. *Address:* c/o Sony BMG Music Entertainment, 550 Madison Avenue, New York, NY 10022-3211, USA (office).

BOWEN, William Gordon, PhD; American academic; b. 6 Oct. 1933, Cincinnati, Ohio; s. of Albert A. Bowen and Bernice Pomert; m. Mary Ellen Maxwell 1956; one s. one d.; ed Denison and Princeton Univs; Asst Prof. of Econs, Princeton Univ. 1958–61, Assoc. Prof. 1961–65, Prof. 1965–87; Dir of Graduate Studies, Woodrow Wilson School of Public and Int. Affairs, Princeton Univ. 1964–66; Provost, Princeton Univ. 1967–72, Pres. 1972–88; lecturer Oxford Univ. 2000; Pres. Andrew W. Mellon Foundation, New York 1988, now Trustee; Dir NCR Corpn 1975–91; Regent Smithsonian Inst. 1980, now Regent Emer.; Trustee, Denison Univ. 1966–75, 1992–2000, Center for Advanced Study in the Behavioral Sciences 1973–84, 1986–92, Reader's Digest 1985–97, American Express 1988–, ISTOR 1995–, Merck and Co. 1986–, Ithaka Harbors, Inc., Univ. Corpn for Advanced Internet Devt 1998–; mem. Bd of Overseers Teachers Insurance and Annuity Asscn and Coll. Retirement Equities Fund 1995–; Dr hc. (Oxford) 2001; Joseph Henry Medal, Smithsonian Inst. 1996, Grawemeyer Award in Educ., Univ. of Louisville 2001. *Publications:* The Wage-Price Issue: A Theoretical Analysis 1960, Performing Arts: The Economic Dilemma (with W. J. Baumol) 1966, The Economics of Labor Force Participation (with T. A. Finegan) 1969, Ever the Teacher 1987, Prospects for Faculty in the Arts and Sciences 1989 (with J. A. Sosa), In Pursuit of the PhD 1992 (with Neil L. Rudenstine), Inside the Boardroom: Governance by Directors and Trustees 1994, (with T. Nygren, S. Turner and E. Duffy) The Charitable Nonprofts 1994, Universities and Their Leaderships (ed. Harold Shapiro) 1998, The Shape of the River: Long-Term Consequences of Considering Race in College and University Admissions (with Derek Bok) 1998, The Game of Life: College Sports and Educational Values 2001, At a Slight Angle to the Universe (also Romanes Lecture, Univ. of Oxford) 2001, Reclaiming the Game: College Sports and Educational Values (with Sarah A. Levin) 2003. *Address:* c/o Andrew W. Mellon Foundation, 140 East 62nd Street, New York, NY 10021, USA (office).

BOWER, Gordon H., MS, PhD; American psychologist and academic; *Albert Ray Lang Professor Emeritus of Psychology, Stanford University;* b. 30 Dec. 1932, Scio, Ohio; s. of Clyde W. Bower and Mabelle Bosart Bower; m. Sharon Anthony 1957; one s. two d.; ed Western Reserve (now Case Western Reserve) and Yale Univs; Asst Prof., Stanford Univ. 1959–63, Assoc. Prof. 1963–65, Prof. 1965–75, Albert Ray Lang Prof. of Psychology 1975–2005, Prof. Emer. 2005–, Chair. Dept of Psychology 1978–82, Assoc. Dean, Stanford Univ. 1983–86; Ed. The Psychology of Learning and Motivation 1964–92; Pres. Western Psychological Asscn 2004–05; mem. NAS, American Acad. of Arts and Sciences, Soc. of Experimental Psychologists, American Philosophical Soc.; hon. degrees from Univ. of Chicago, Indiana State Univ.; Distinguished Scientist Contrib. Award, American Psychology Asscn 1979, Warren Medal, Soc. of Experimental Psychologists, Wilbur Cross Medal, Yale Univ., Nat. Medal of Science 2005. *Publications:* co-author of five books and more than 250 scientific papers. *Leisure interests:* reading, sport. *Address:* Department of Psychology, Jordan Hall, Building 420, Stanford University, 450 Serra Mall, Stanford, CA 94305, USA (office). *Telephone:* (650) 725-2400 (office). *Fax:* (650) 725-5699 (office). *E-mail:* gordon@psych.stanford.edu (office). *Website:* www-psych.stanford.edu (office).

BOWERING, George Henry, OC, MA; Canadian writer, poet and lecturer; b. 1 Dec. 1936, Penticton, BC; s. of Ewart Bowering and Pearl Bowering (née Brinson); m. Angela Luoma 1962 (died 1999); one d.; ed Victoria Coll., Univ. of British Columbia, Univ. of Western Ontario; served as Royal Canadian Air Force photographer 1954–57; Lecturer, Univ. of Calgary 1963–66; Writer-in-Residence, Sir George Williams Univ., Montreal 1967–68, Lecturer 1968–71; Lecturer, Simon Fraser Univ., Burnaby, BC 1972–2001; Parl. Poet Laureate 2002–04; Hon. DLit (British Columbia) 1997, (Western Ontario) 2003; Order of BC 2005; Gov.-Gen.'s Award for poetry 1967, for fiction 1980, bp Nichol Chapbook Awards for Poetry 1991, 1992, Canadian Authors' Asscn Award for Poetry 1993. *Play:* The Home for Heroes 1962. *Radio plays:* George Vancouver (CBC) 1972, Sitting in Mexico (CBC) 1973, Music in the Park (CBC) 1986, The Great Grandchildren of Bill Bissett's Mice (CBC) 1989. *Television play:* What Does Eddie Williams Want? (CBC) 1966. *Publications:* poetry collections: Sticks & Stones 1963, Points on the Grid 1964, The Man in Yellow Boots/El hombre de las botas amarillas 1965, The Silver Wire 1966, Rocky Mountain Foot 1969, The Gangs of Kosmos 1969, Touch: Selected Poems 1960–1969 1971, In the Flesh 1974, The Catch 1976, Poem & Other Baseballs 1976, The

Concrete Island 1977, Another Mouth 1979, Particular Accidents: Selected Poems 1981, West Window: Selected Poetry 1982, Smoking Poetry 1982, Smoking Mirrow 1982, Seventy-One Poems for People 1985, Delayed Mercy & Other Poems 1986, Urban Snow 1992, George Bowering Selected: Poems 1961–1992 1993; chapbooks: How I Hear Howl 1967, Two Police Poems 1969, The Sensible 1972, Layers 1–13 1973, In Answer 1977, Uncle Louis 1980, Spencer & Groulx 1985, Quarters 1991, Do Sink 1992, Sweetly 1992, Blondes on Bikes 1997, A, You're Adorable 1998, 6 Little Poems in Alphabetical Order 2000, Some Writers 2001, Joining the Lost Generation 2002; long poems: Sitting in Mexico 1965, George,Vancouver 1970, Geneve 1971, Autobiology 1972, Curious 1973, At War With the U.S. 1974, Allophanes 1976, Ear Reach 1982, Kerrisdale Elegies 1984, His Life: A Poem 2000, Baseball: A poem in the magic number 9 2003; novels: Mirror on the Floor 1967, A Short Sad Book 1977, Burning Water 1980, En eaux troubles 1982, Caprice 1987, Harry's Fragments 1990, Shoot! 1994, Parents from Space 1994, Piccolo Mondo 1998, Diamondback Dog 1998; short story collections: Flycatcher & Other Stories 1974, Concentric Circles 1977, Protective Footwear 1978, A Place to Die 1983, The Rain Barrel 1994, Standing on Richards 2004; non-fiction: Al Purdy 1970, Three Vancouver Writers 1979, A Way with Words 1982, The Mask in Place 1983, Craft Slices 1985, Errata 1988, Imaginary Hand 1988, The Moustache: Memories of Greg Curnoe (memoir) 1993, Bowering's B.C. 1996, Egotists and Autocrats – the Prime Ministers of Canada 1999, A Magpie Life (memoir) 2001, Cars (memoir) 2002, Stone Country 2003, Standing on Richards (stories) 2004. *Leisure interests:* baseball, fastball. *Address:* 303 Fielden Avenue, Port Colborne, ON L3K 4T5, Canada (home). *Telephone:* (905) 834-0642 (home). *E-mail:* bowering@sfu.ca (home).

BOWERS-BROADBENT, Christopher Joseph, FRAM; British organist and composer; *Organist and Choirmaster of Gray's Inn and Organist of the West London Synagogue;* b. 13 Jan. 1945, Hemel Hempstead; s. of Henry W. Bowers-Broadbent and Doris E Mizen; m. Deirdre Cape 1970; one s. one d.; ed King's Coll. Cambridge, Berkhamsted School and Royal Acad. of Music; Organist and Choirmaster of St Pancras Parish Church 1965–88; Organist of West London Synagogue 1973–; Organist and Choirmaster of Gray's Inn 1983–; debut organ recital, Camden Festival 1966; Prof. of Organ, Royal Acad. of Music 1976–92; Recordings include: Trivium, O Domina Nostra, Meditations Sur, Mattins Music, Duets and Canons; Three Choirs Festival Composers' Competition Prize 1978. *Operas include:* The Pied Piper 1972, The Seacock Bane 1979, The Last Man 1983–2000. *Leisure interests:* sketching, silence. *Address:* 94 Colney Hatch Lane, Muswell Hill, London, N10 1EA, England (home). *Telephone:* (20) 8883-1933 (home). *Fax:* (20) 8883-8434 (home); (20) 8888-8434 (home). *E-mail:* chris@christopherbowers-broadbent.com (home). *Website:* www.christopherbowers-broadbent.com.

BOWIE, David; British singer and actor; b. (David Robert Jones), 8 Jan. 1947, Brixton, London; s. of Hayward Stenton Jones and of the late Margaret Mary Jones (née Burns); m. 1st Angela Barnett 1970 (divorced 1980); one s.; m. 2nd Iman Abdul Majid 1992; one d.; solo singer and songwriter 1966–; numerous tours, live and TV appearances; film actor 1967–; mem. and lead singer, Tin Machine 1989–91; founded online art dealer, Bowieart.com; guest curator of arts event, High Line Festival, New York 2007; Silver Clef Award for Outstanding Achievement 1987, Ivor Novello Award for Outstanding Contribution to British Music 1990, BRIT Award for Outstanding Contribution to Music 1996; Commdr, Ordre des Arts et des Lettres. *Films:* The Image 1967, The Virgin Soldiers 1969, Love You Till Tuesday 1969, The Man Who Fell to Earth 1976, Schöner Gigolo, armer Gigolo (trans. as Just a Gigolo) 1979, Christiane F 1980, Cat People 1982, The Hunger 1983, Merry Christmas Mr Lawrence 1983, Yellowbeard 1983, Ziggy Stardust and the Spiders from Mars 1983, Into the Night 1985, Absolute Beginners 1986, Labyrinth 1986, The Last Temptation of Christ 1988, The Linguini Incident 1990, Twin Peaks: Fire Walk with Me 1992, Basquiat 1996, Trainspotting 1996, Il Mio West 1998, Everybody Loves Sunshine 1999, Mr Rice's Secret 2000, The Prestige 2006, Arthur and the Invisibles (voice) 2006. *Television:* The Pistol Shot (film) 1968, Baal (film) 1982, The Hunger (series) 1999–2000. *Play:* The Elephant Man (New York) 1980. *Compositions include:* When the Wind Blows (theme) 1986, The Buddha of Suburbia (music, BBC series) 1993. *Recordings include:* albums: solo: David Bowie 1969, The Man Who Sold The World 1971, Hunky Dory 1971, The Rise And Fall Of Ziggy Stardust And The Spiders From Mars 1972, Aladdin Sane 1973, Pin-Ups 1973, Diamond Dogs 1974, David Live 1974, Young Americans 1975, Station To Station 1976, Low 1977, Heroes 1977, Lodger (with Brian Eno) 1979, Scary Monsters and Super Creeps 1980, Let's Dance 1983, Tonight 1984, Never Let Me Down 1987, Black Tie White Noise 1993, Outside 1995, Earthling 1997, Hours 1999, Bowie At The Beeb (radio sessions and concerts) 2000, Heathen 2002, Reality 2003, Club Bowie 2004; with Tin Machine: Tin Machine 1989, Tin Machine II 1991. *Leisure interests:* boxing, martial arts instruction, listening to Polish and Chinese Communist music. *Address:* Isolar Enterprises, 641 Fifth Avenue, Suite 22Q, New York, NY 10022, USA (office). *Website:* www.davidbowie.com.

BOWLES, Erskine; American investment banker, university administrator and fmr government official; *President, University of North Carolina;* b. 1945, Greensboro, NC; s. of Hargrove "Skipper" Bowles; m. Crandall Bowles 1971; three c.; ed Univ. of NC, Columbia Univ. Grad. School of Business; with Morgan Stanley & Co. New York; Bowles Hollowell Conner & Co. Charlotte, NC 1975–93; Admin. Small Business Admin. Washington, DC 1993–94; Deputy Chief of Staff to Pres., The White House, Washington, DC 1994–97, Chief of Staff 1997–99; Pnr Forstmann Little & Co., Charlotte 1999–2001; unsuccessful campaigns for US Senate from NC 2002, 2004; Pres. Univ. of NC 2006–; mem. Bd of Dirs General Motors, Cousins Properties, NC Mutual Life Insurance Co.; apptd UN Deputy Special Envoy to tsunami affected countries in SE Asia 2005; fmr Pres. Juvenile Diabetes Foundation; fmr Trustee Duke Endowment, Golden LEAF Foundation; fmr Chair. Rural Prosperity Task Force, NC; co-founder Dogwood Equity, NC; eight hon. degrees from US univs. *Address:* Office of the President, The University of North Carolina, 910 Raleigh Road, POB 2688, Chapel Hill, NC 27515, USA (office). *Telephone:* (919) 962-1000 (office). *Website:* www.northcarolina.edu (office).

BOWMAN, Philip; Australian business executive; *CEO, Smiths Group plc;* b. Melbourne; ed Univ. of Cambridge, UK; served in accountancy positions in venture devt in Iran, Australia and USA; fmr CEO and Chair. Bass Taverns; Dir of Finance and Admin Coles Myer Ltd, Australia 1995–98; Finance Dir Allied Domecq 1998–99, CEO 1999; fmr non-exec. Chair. (non-exec.) Liberty plc; CEO Scottish Power plc 2006–07; CEO Smiths Group plc 2007–; mem. Bd of Dirs Scottish & Newcastle plc, Burberry plc. *Address:* Smiths Group plc, 765 Finchley Road, London NW11 8DS, England (office). *Telephone:* (20) 8458-3232 (office). *Fax:* (20) 8458-0680 (office). *E-mail:* plc@smith-group.com (office). *Website:* www.smiths-group.com (office).

BOWMAN, William Scott (Scotty); Canadian fmr professional ice hockey coach and sports executive; *Senior Advisor, Chicago Blackhawk Hockey Team, Inc.;* b. 18 Sept. 1933, Verdun, PQ; m. Suella; three s. two d.; early and short career as player then minor league coach in Montréal Canadiens system; began Nat. Hockey League (NHL) coaching career as Coach St Louis Blues 1967–71, then Montréal Canadiens 1971–79, winning Stanley Cups 1973, 1976–79; Coach and Gen. Man. Buffalo Sabres 1979–87; left NHL and worked as analyst for CBCs 'Hockey Night in Canada' TV programme 1987; returned to NHL as Dir of Player Personnel Pittsburgh Penguins 1987–91, then Coach 1991–93, winning Stanley Cup 1992; Coach Detroit Red Wings 1993–2002, winning Stanley Cup 1997, 1998, 2002; records include winning nine Stanley Cups, coaching 1,244 NHL regular-season wins (next highest total is 781), 223 post-season wins; retd at end of 2002 season, consultant, Detroit Red Wings 2002–08; Sr Advisor, Chicago Black Hawks 2008–; NHL Jack Adams Award for Outstanding Coach 1977, 1996, NHL Lester Patrick Award for outstanding service to hockey in the United States 2001; mem. Hockey Hall of Fame 1991, Mich. Sports Hall of Fame 1999, Greater Buffalo Sports Hall of Fame in 2000; Canada Walk of Fame 2003. *Address:* Chicago Blackhawk Hockey Team, Inc., 1901 West Madison Street, Chicago, IL 60612, USA (office). *Telephone:* (312) 455-7000 (office). *Fax:* (312) 455-7041 (office). *Website:* www.chicagoblackhawks.com (office).

BOWN, Jane Hope, CBE; British photographer; b. 13 March 1925, Ledbury; d. of Charles Wentworth Bell and Daisy Bown; m. Martin Grenville Moss, CBE 1954 (died 2007); two s. one d.; ed William Gibbs School for Girls, Faversham, Kent; photographer for the Observer 1950–; Hon. DLitt (Bradford) 1986; Gerald Barry Award 1994, What the Papers Say Lifetime Achievement Award. *Publications:* The Gentle Eye 1980, Women of Consequence 1985, Men of Consequence 1986, The Singular Cat 1988, Pillars of the Church 1991, Jane Bown Observer 1996, Faces 2000, Rock 2003, Unknown Bown 2007. *Leisure interests:* animals, the country, antiques. *Address:* 3–7 Herbal Hill, London, EC1R 5EJ, England (office). *Telephone:* (7713) 4275 (mobile) (office).

BOWNESS, Sir Alan, Kt, CBE; British art historian; b. 11 Jan. 1928; s. of George Bowness and Kathleen Bowness (née Benton); m. Sarah Hepworth-Nicholson 1957; one s. one d.; ed Univ. Coll. School, Downing Coll., Cambridge, Courtauld Inst. of Art, Univ. of London; with Friends' Ambulance Unit and Friends' Service Council 1946–50; Regional Art Officer, Arts Council of GB 1955–57; Courtauld Inst. 1957–79, Deputy Dir 1978–79; Reader, Univ. of London 1967–78, Prof. of History of Art 1978–79; Visiting Prof. Humanities Seminar, Johns Hopkins Univ., Baltimore 1969; Dir Tate Gallery 1980–88, Henry Moore Foundation 1988–94 (Trustee 1984–88, 1994–2003); mem. Arts Council 1973–75, 1978–80, Art Panel 1960–80 (Vice-Chair. 1973–75, Chair. 1978–80), Arts Film Cttee 1968–77 (Chair. 1972–75); mem. Fine Arts Cttee, British Council 1960–69, 1970–93 (Chair. 1981–93); mem. Exec. Cttee, Contemporary Art Soc. 1961–69, 1970–86, Cultural Advisory Cttee, UK Nat. Comm. for UNESCO 1973–82; Gov. Chelsea School of Art and London Inst. 1965–88; Hon. Sec. Assen of Art Historians 1973–76; Dir Barbara Hepworth Museum, St Ives, Cornwall 1976–88; mem. Council Royal Coll. of Art 1978–99; Trustee Yorkshire Sculpture Park 1979–, Handel House Museum 1994–2001 (Chair. 1997–2001); mem. int. juries for Premio Di Tella, Buenos Aires 1965, São Paulo Bienal 1967, Lehmbruck Prize, Duisburg 1970, Rembrandt Prize 1982, Venice Biennale 1986, Heiliger Prize 1998; Hon. Fellow Downing Coll., Cambridge 1980, UWE Bristol 1980, Courtauld Inst. of Art 1985; Chevalier, Ordre des Arts et Lettres 1973; Hon. DLitt (Liverpool) 1988, (Leeds) 1995, (Exeter) 1996. *Publications:* William Scott Paintings 1964, Impressionists and Post Impressionists 1965, Henry Moore: Complete Sculpture 1955–64 1965, Modern Sculpture 1965, Barbara Hepworth Drawings 1966, Alan Davie 1967, Recent British Painting 1968, Gauguin 1971, Barbara Hepworth: complete sculpture 1960–69 1971, Modern European Art 1972, Ivon Hitchens 1973, Picasso 1881–1973 (contrib.) 1973, The Genius of British Painting (contrib.) 1975, Henry Moore: Complete Sculpture 1964–73 1977, Henry Moore: Complete Sculpture 1974–80 1983, Henry Moore: Complete Sculpture 1981–86 1988, The Conditions of Success 1989, British Contemporary Art 1910–1990 (contrib.) 1991, Bernard Meadows 1995. *Leisure interests:* going to concerts, opera, theatre. *Address:* 91 Castelnau, London, SW13 9EL; 16 Piazza, St Ives, Cornwall, TR26 1NQ, England. *Telephone:* (20) 8846-8520 (London); (1736) 795444 (St Ives).

BOWRING, Peter, CBE, FID, FRSA, FZS; British company director; b. 22 April 1923, Bromborough; s. of Frederick Clive Bowring and Agnes Walker Bowring (née Cairns); m. Barbara Ekaterina Brewis 1946 (divorced); one s. one d.; m. 2nd Carol Gillian Hutchings 1979 (divorced); m. 3rd Carole Mary Dear 1986; ed Shrewsbury School; commissioned, Rifle Brigade 1942, served in Egypt, North Africa, Italy and Austria (mentioned in despatches); Dir C.T. Bowring & Co. Ltd 1956; Chair. C.T. Bowring Trading (Holdings) Ltd 1967; Deputy Chair. C.T. Bowring and Co. Ltd 1973; Chair. Bowmaker (Plant) Ltd 1972–83,

Bowmaker Ltd 1978–82, C.T. Bowring & Co. Ltd 1978–82; Dir Marsh and McLennan Companies Inc. 1980–85, Vice-Chair. 1982–84; Dir Aldeburgh Foundation 1975–90, Chair. 1982–89, Vice-Pres. 1991–; Chair. Help the Aged Ltd 1977–87, Pres. 1987–2000; Chair. Inter-Action Social Enterprise Trust Ltd 1989–91; Chair. Wakefield (Tower Hill, Trinity Square) Trust 2002–05; Master Worshipful Co. of World Traders 1989–90; mem. Lloyds 1968–98, Worshipful Co. of Insurers, Co. of Watermen and Lightermen, Bd Govs St Dunstan's Educational Foundation 1974–94, Chair. 1977–90 (Companion 1998), Bd Govs Shrewsbury School 1969–97; Dir Independent Primary and Secondary Educ. Trust 1986–2002, Centre for Policy Studies 1983–88, City Arts Trust 1984–94 (Chair. 1987–94), Int. Human Assistance Programs Inc. 1985–89, Rhein Chemie Holding GmbH 1968–; Trustee, Zoological Soc. Devt Trust 1987–90, Ironbridge Gorge Museum Devt Trust 1987–93 (Companion 1993), Upper Severn Navigation Trust (now Spry Trust Ltd) 1987–; Freeman City of London. *Publication:* The Last Minute 2000, A Thicket of Business 2007. *Leisure interests:* travel, photography, motoring, music, cooking. *Address:* Flat 79, New Concordia Wharf, Mill Street, London, SE1 2BB, England (home). *Telephone:* (20) 7237-0818 (home). *Fax:* (20) 7237-0818 (home). *E-mail:* saloptrumpeter@aol.com (office).

BOWYER, (Arthur) William, RA, RP, RWS; British artist; b. 25 May 1926, Leek, Staffs.; s. of Arthur Bowyer and Emma Bowyer; m. Vera Mary Small 1951; two s. one d.; ed Burslem School of Art, Royal Coll. of Art; Head of Fine Art, Maidstone Coll. of Art 1971–82; Hon. Sec. New English Art Club 1968–98; mem. Royal Soc. of Painters in Watercolour. *Leisure interests:* cricket, snooker. *Address:* 12 Cleveland Avenue, Chiswick, London, W4 1SN, England. *Telephone:* (20) 8994-0346.

BOXER, Barbara, BA; American politician; *Senator from California;* b. 11 Nov. 1940, Brooklyn, New York; d. of Ira Levy and Sophie Levy (née Silvershein); m. Stewart Boxer 1962; one s. one d.; ed Brooklyn Coll.; stockbroker, New York 1962–65; journalist then Assoc. Ed. Pacific Sun 1972–74; Congressional Aide, Democratic 5th Congressional Dist, San Francisco 1974–76; mem. Marin Co. Bd of Supervisors, San Rafael, Calif. 1976–82, Pres. 1980–81; mem. US House of Reps from 6th Calif. Dist, Washington, DC 1982–93; Senator from California 1993–, mem. Foreign Relations Cttee, Chair. Environment and Public Works Cttee, Chair. Subcttee on Near Eastern and S Asian Affairs, Chief Deputy Whip in Majority 2007–; mem. Bd of Dirs Golden Gate Bridge Highway and Transport Dist, San Francisco 1978–82; Pres. Democratic New Mems Caucus 1983–; Democrat; numerous awards. *Address:* 112 Hart Senate Office Building, Washington, DC 20510-0001, USA. *Telephone:* (202) 224-3553 (office). *Website:* boxer.senate .gov (office).

BOXSHALL, Geoffrey Allan, PhD, FRS; British/Canadian zoologist; *Deputy Chief Scientific Officer, Natural History Museum (UK);* b. 13 June 1950, Oyen, Alberta; s. of John Edward Boxshall and Sybil Irene Baker; m. Roberta Gabriel Smith 1972; one s. three d.; ed Churcher's Coll., Univ. of Leeds; joined Natural History Museum 1974, Deputy Chief Scientific Officer 1997–; Scientific Medal of the Zoological Soc. of London 1986, Linnean Soc. Medal for Zoology 2004. *Publications:* co-author: Dictionary of Ecology, Evolution and Systematics, Illustrated Dictionary of Natural History, Copepod Evolution, An Introduction to Copepod Diversity. *Leisure interests:* travel, tennis, lexicography. *Address:* Natural History Museum, Cromwell Road, London, SW7 5BD, England (office). *Telephone:* (20) 7942-5749 (office). *Fax:* (20) 7942-5054 (office). *E-mail:* g.boxshall@nhm.ac.uk (office). *Website:* www.nhm.ac.uk/ science (office).

BOYARCHIKOV, Nikolai Nikolayevich; Russian choreographer; *Artistic Director, Mussorgsky Academic Opera and Ballet Theatre;* b. 27 Sept. 1935, Leningrad; s. of Maria Boyarchikova; m. Larissa Klimova; ed Leningrad Vaganova School of Choreography, Leningrad State Conservatory; soloist Mussorgsky Academic Opera and Ballet Theatre (fmrly Leningrad Maly State Academic Opera and Ballet Theatre) 1954–71, Artistic Dir 1977–; chief choreographer Perm Opera and Ballet Theatre 1971–77; Glinka Prize 1977, People's Artist of Russia 1985, State Prize of Russian Fed., Order of Friendship 1996. *Theatre productions include:* Romeo and Juliet 1972, Tsar Boris 1975, Robber 1982, Quiet Don 1988. *Address:* Mussorgsky Theatre, 1 Arts Square, 191011 St Petersburg, Russia. *Telephone:* (812) 219-19-78.

BOYARCHUK, Aleksander Alekseyevich; Russian astrophysicist; *Academic Secretary, Department of General Physics and Astronomy;* b. 21 June 1931, Grozny; s. of Aleksei Boyarchuk and Maria Boyarchuk; m. Margarita Yevgenyevna Boyarchuk (née Kropotova) 1955; one s.; ed Leningrad State Univ.; researcher, Deputy Dir Crimea Astrophysical Observatory USSR Acad. of Sciences 1953–87; Dir Inst. of Astronomy 1987–; mem. USSR (now Russian) Acad. of Sciences 1987; Acad.-Sec. Dept of Gen. Physics and Astronomy 1996–; published over 200 works on astrospectroscopy, physics of star atmospheres, construction of astronomic equipment, cosmic studies, Ed.-in-Chief Astronomical journal, Pres. Int. Astronomical Union 1991–94; mem. Int. Astronomical Acad., Royal Astronomical Soc. of UK, American Astronomical Soc., American Physical Soc.; USSR State Prize. *Address:* Institute of Astronomy, Pyatnitskaya str. 48, 109017 Moscow, Russia. *Telephone:* (495) 951-54-61 (Institute) (office); (495) 938-16-95 (Academy) (office); (495)-951-09-24 (office). *Fax:* (495) 230-20-81 (office); (495)-951-55-57 (office). *E-mail:* aboyar@inasan .rssi.ru (office). *Website:* www.inasan.rssi.ru (office).

BOYARSKY, Mikhail Sergeyevich; Russian actor and singer; *Artistic Director, Benefice Theatre;* b. 26 Dec. 1949, Leningrad; s. of the late Sergei Boyarsky; m. Larisa Luppian; one s. one d.; ed Leningrad Inst. of Theatre, Music and Cinematography; fmrly with Lensovet Theatre, appeared in musicals Interview in Buenos Aires, Troubadour and His Friends; cinema debut 1974, more than 60 roles; Artistic Dir Benefice Theatre; People's Actor of Russian Fed. 1984, People's Artist of Russia 1995. *Films include:* Starshiy syn 1975, Sentimentalnyy roman 1976, Ma-ma 1976, Kak Ivanushka-durachok za chudom khodil 1976, Dikiy Gavrila 1976, Poka bezumstvuyet mechta 1978, Komissiya po rassledovaniyu 1978, Nesravnennyy Nakonechnikov 1981, Kuda on denetsya! 1981, Dusha 1981, Tamozhnya 1982, Lishniy bilet 1983, Geroy eyo romana 1984, Gum-gam 1985, Chelovek s bulvara Kaputsinov 1987, Uznik zamka If 1988, Iskusstvo zhit v Odesse 1989, Vivat, gardemariny! 1991, Choknute 1991, Mushketyory 20 let spustya 1992, Tayna korolevy Anny ili mushketyory 30 let spustya 1993, Plachu vperyod! 2001, Klyuchi ot smerti (Keys to Death 2) 2002, Novogodnyye muzhchiny (New Year's Men) 2004, Schastlivyi (Happy) 2005, Vy ne ostavte menya (Don't Leave Me) 2006. *Television includes:* Don Sezar de Bazan 1989, Tartyuf 1992, Koroleva Margo (series) 1996, Zal ozhidaniya (series) 1998, Idiot (miniseries) 2003. *Address:* Naberezhnaya Moiki 31, Apt. 2, 191186 St Petersburg; c/o Benefice Theatre, 24 Moyki reki nab, St. Petersburg, Russia. *Telephone:* (812) 311-37-97.

BOYCE, Adm. The Lord Michael (Cecil), GCB, KStJ, OBE, DL; British naval officer; *Lord Warden and Admiral of the Cinque Ports and Constable of Dover Castle;* b. 2 April 1943, Cape Town, SA; s. of the late Commdr Hugh Boyce and of the late Madeline Boyce (née Manley); m. 1st Harriette Gail Fletcher 1971 (divorced 2005); one s. one d.; m. 2nd Fleur Margaret Ann Rutherford (née Smith); ed Hurstpierpoint Coll., Royal Naval Coll., Dartmouth Royal Coll. of Defence Studies; joined RN 1961; qualified submariner 1965, TAS 1970, served in HM submarines Anchorite, Valiant and Conqueror 1965–72, commanded HM submarines Oberon 1973–74, Opossum 1974–75, Superb 1979–81, frigate HMS Brilliant 1983–84, Capt. (SM) Submarine Sea Training 1984–86; Royal Coll. Defence Staff 1988; Sr Naval Officer ME 1989; Dir Naval Staff Duties 1989–91; Flag Officer, Sea Training 1991–92, Surface Flotilla 1992–95; Commdr Anti-Submarine Warfare Striking Force 1992–94; Second Sea Lord and C-in-C Naval Home Command 1995–97; Flag ADC to the Queen 1995–97; C-in-C Fleet, C-in-C Eastern Atlantic Area and Commdr Naval Forces NW Europe 1997–98; First Sea Lord 1998–2001; Chief of Defence Staff 2001–03; First and Prin. Naval ADC to the Queen 1998–2001, ADC 2001–03; Lord Warden and Adm. of the Cinque Ports and Constable of Dover Castle 2004–; Gov. Alleyn's School 1995–2005; mem. Bd Dirs W S Atkins 2004–, VT Group PLC 2004–; Pres. Officers Asscn 2003–, London Dist St John Ambulance 2003–, Submarine Museum 2005–; Patron Sail4Cancer 2003–, Submarine Asscn 2003–; mem. Council White Ensign Asscn 2003– (Chair. 2007–), Royal Nat. Lifeboat Inst. 2004– (Vice-Chair. 2006–); Trustee, Nat. Maritime Museum 2004–; Freeman City of London 1999, Younger Brother Trinity House 1999–2006, Elder Brother 2006–, DL Greater London 2003–, Hon. Freeman Drapers' Co. 2005; Commdr, Legion of Merit (USA) 1999, Bronze Oak Leaf (USA) 2003; Hon. LLD (Portsmouth) 2005. *Leisure interests:* squash, tennis, real tennis, sailing, windsurfing, opera, ballet. *Address:* House of Lords, Westminster, London, SW1A 0PW, England (office).

BOYCE, Ralph, BA, MPA; American diplomatist; b. 1 Feb. 1952, Washington, DC; m. Kathryn Sligh; two c.; ed George Washington Univ., Princeton Univ.; joined Foreign Service 1976, Staff Asst to Amb., Tehran 1977–79, Commercial Attaché, Tunis 1979–81, Financial Economist, Islamabad 1981–84, Special Asst, then Adviser to Deputy Sec. of State, State Dept 1984–88, Political Counsellor, Bangkok 1988–92, Deputy Chief of Mission, Singapore 1992–93, Chargé d'affaires a.i. 1993–94, Deputy Chief of Mission, Bangkok 1994–98, Deputy Asst Sec. for E Asia and Pacific Affairs 1998–2001, Amb. to Indonesia 2001–04, to Thailand 2004–07. *Address:* US Department of State, 2201 C Street NW, Washington, DC 20520, USA (office). *Telephone:* (202) 647-4000 (office). *Fax:* (202) 647-6738 (office). *Website:* www.state.gov (office).

BOYCOTT, Geoffrey, OBE; British sports commentator and fmr professional cricketer; b. 21 Oct. 1940, Fitzwilliam, Yorks.; s. of the late Thomas Wilfred Boycott and Jane Boycott; m. Rachael Swinglehurst 2003; one d.; ed Kinsley Modern School and Hemsworth Grammar School; fmrly in civil service; right-hand opening batsman; teams: Yorkshire 1962–86 (Capt. 1971–78), Northern Transvaal 1971–72; 108 Tests for England 1964–82, 4 as Capt., scoring then record 8,114 runs (average 47.7) including 22 hundreds; scored 48,426 first-class runs (151 hundreds); completed 100 hundreds for Yorkshire 1985, 7th batsman to achieve this for a county; toured Australia 1965–66, 1970–71, 1978–79 and 1979–80; only Englishman to achieve average of 100 in English County season 1971; repeated this achievement in 1979; scored 100th hundred, England v. Australia, Headingly, Leeds Aug. 1977; became 18th batsman in history of game to score 100 hundreds and the first to achieve this in a Test match; mem. Gen. Cttee; served as coach for Pakistan's Nat. Acad. 2001; cricket commentator for BBC and Sky –1998, for Channel 4 2004–; Wisden Cricketer of the Year 1965. *Publications:* Geoff Boycott's Book for Young Cricketers 1976, Put to the Test: Ashes Series in Australia 1978/79 1979, Geoff Boycott's Cricket Quiz 1979, Boycott on Batting 1980, Opening Up 1980, In the Fast Lane 1981, Master Class 1982, Boycott – The Autobiography 1987, Boycott on Cricket 1990, Geoffrey Boycott on Cricket 1999, The Best XI 2008. *Leisure interest:* golf. *Address:* Channel 4 Television, 124 Horseferry Road, London, SW1P 2TX, England (office). *Telephone:* (20) 7396-4444 (office). *E-mail:* email@cricket4.com (office). *Website:* www.channel4.com (office).

BOYCOTT, Rosie; British journalist and author; b. 13 May 1951; d. of Charles Boycott and Betty Boycott; m. 1st David Leitch (divorced); one d.; m. 2nd Charles Howard 1999; ed Cheltenham Ladies Coll., Kent Univ.; f. Spare Rib 1972; est. Virago Books 1973; worked on Village Voice (magazine), New York; subsequently edited Arabic women's magazine in Kuwait; Features Ed. Honey; Deputy Ed. Daily Mail's Male and Femail pages; Ed. Discount Traveller; Commissioning Ed. The Sunday Telegraph; Deputy Ed. Harpers & Queen 1989; Deputy Ed. and Features Ed. (British) Esquire 1991, Ed. 1992–96, of Ind. on Sunday 1996–98, of the Ind. 1998, of the Express 1998–2001, of the Express on Sunday 1998–2001; Chair., Panel of Judges,

Orange Prize for Fiction 2001; mem. Exec. Cttee English PEN. *Publications:* A Nice Girl Like Me (autobiog.) 1983, All For Love 1985, Our Farm: A Year in the Life of a Smallholding 2007. *Address:* c/o Bloomsbury Publishing Plc, 36 Soho Square, London, W1D 3QY, England (office).

BOYD, Sir John Dixon Iklé, KCMG, MA; British fmr diplomatist and fmr university administrator; b. 17 Jan. 1936, Cambridge; s. of the late Prof. James Dixon Boyd and of Amélie Lowenthal; m. 1st Gunilla Kristina Ingregerd Rönngren 1968 (divorced 1977); one s. one d.; m. 2nd Julia Daphne Raynsford 1977; three d.; ed Westminster School, Clare Coll., Cambridge, Yale Univ., USA; joined HM Foreign Service 1962; in Hong Kong 1962–64, Beijing (Third Sec.) 1965–67; at FCO 1967–69, Asst Under-Sec. of State 1984, Deputy Under-Sec. of State 1987–89, Chief Clerk 1989–92; with Embassy, Washington 1969–73; First Sec. Embassy, Beijing 1973–75; on secondment to Treasury 1976; Econ. Counsellor Embassy, Bonn 1977–81; Counsellor (Econ. and Social Affairs) Perm. Mission to UN 1981–84; Political Adviser, Hong Kong 1985–87; Amb. to Japan 1992–96; Master Churchill Coll., Cambridge 1996–2006; Chair. Bd of Govs Bedales School 1966–2001, David Davies Memorial Inst. 1997–2001; Co-Chair. Nuffield Languages Inquiry 1998–2000; Vice-Chair. Yehudi Menuhin Int. Violin Trust Ltd 1996–; Dir UK-Japan 21st Century Group 2006–; Dir (non-exec.) British Nuclear Fuels PLC 1997–2000; Adviser, East Asia Inst., Univ. of Cambridge 1998–2005; mem. ASEM (Asia-Europe Meeting) "Vision Group" 1998–2000, ANA Advisory Group 2003–; Trustee British Museum 1996–2006 (Chair. 2002–06), Sir Winston Churchill Archive Trust 1996–2006, Cambridge Union (also Chair.) 1997–2006, Margaret Thatcher Archive Trust 1997–2006, Cambridge Foundation 1997–2005, The Wordsworth Trust 1997–, Great Britain-Sasakawa Foundation 2001–, Council of Senate Cambridge Univ. 2001–04, Huang Hsing Foundation 2001–, RAND (Europe) UK 2001–, Joseph Needham Research Inst. 2005–; Syndic Fitzwilliam Museum 1997–2002; Gov. RSC 1996–2005; Hon. Fellow Clare Coll., Cambridge 1994, Westminster School 2003, Life Fellow Churchill Coll., Cambridge 2006. *Publications:* contrib. articles to Asian Affairs and others. *Leisure interests:* music, books, sheep farming, fly-fishing. *Address:* 87 Elizabeth Street, London, SW1W 9PG, England. *Telephone:* (20) 7730-8389. *E-mail:* jul.boyd@gmail.com.

BOYD, Joseph Aubrey, MS, PhD, FAAS, FIEEE; American business executive (retd); b. 25 March 1921, Oscar, Ky; s. of Joseph R. Boyd and Relda J. Myatt; m. Edith A. Atkins 1942; two s.; ed Univs of Kentucky and Michigan; Instr., Asst Prof. of Electrical Eng Univ. of Ky 1947–49; mem. Faculty, Univ. of Mich. 1949–62, Prof. of Electrical Eng 1958–62, Dir Willow Run Labs 1958–62, Dir Inst. of Science and Tech. 1960–62; Exec. Vice-Pres. Radiation Inc., Melbourne, Fla 1962–63, Pres. 1963–72; Exec. Vice-Pres. Electronics, Harris Corpn Cleveland (now in Melbourne, Fla) 1967–71, Exec. Vice-Pres. Operations 1971–72, Dir 1972–87, Chair. Exec. Cttee 1987–, Pres. 1972–85; Chair., CEO Fairchild Space and Defense Corpn 1992–94, Fairchild Controls 1994; Consultant, Inst. for Defense Analyses 1956, Nat. Security Agency 1957–62; Special Consultant to Army Combat Surveillance Agency 1958–62; Chair. Advisory Group, Electronic Warfare, Office of Dir of Defense Research, Dept of Defense 1959–61, Consultant 1959–. *Publications:* articles in professional journals.

BOYD, Joseph Walker, BA; American music industry executive and film producer; b. 5 Aug. 1942, Boston; s. of Joseph M. Boyd and Elizabeth Walker Boyd; ed Harvard Univ.; Gen. Man. Elektra Records UK 1965–66; Man. Dir Witchseason Productions Ltd 1966–71; Dir Music Services, Warner Bros. Films 1971–73; Man. Dir Osiris Films 1976–79; Vice-Pres. Broadway Pictures, New York 1979–80; Man. Dir Hannibal Records Ltd 1980–91; Vice-Pres. A & R Rykodisc Inc. 1991–98; A & R Dir Hannibal/Ryko Latino Labels 1999; Grammy Award 1974. *Publication:* White Bicycles: Making Music in the 1960s 2007. *Leisure interests:* history, tennis. *Address:* c/o Serpents Tail Press, 3a Exmouth House, Pine Street, London, EC1R 0JH, England (office). *Telephone:* (20) 7841-6300 (office). *E-mail:* rebecca@serpentstail.com (office). *Website:* www.serpentstail.com (office); www.joeboyd.co.uk.

BOYD, Michael, MA; British theatre director; *Artistic Director, Royal Shakespeare Company;* b. 6 July 1955, Belfast, Northern Ireland; s. of John Truesdale Boyd and Sheila Boyd; partner Caroline Hall; one d.; one s. one d. by previous partner; ed Latymer Upper School, London, Daniel Stewart's Coll., Edin. and Univ. of Edin.; Trainee Dir Malaya Bronnaya Theatre, Moscow; Trainee Asst Dir Belgrade Theatre, Coventry, Asst Dir 1980–82; Assoc. Dir Crucible Theatre, Sheffield 1982–84; Founding Artistic Dir Tron Theatre, Glasgow 1985–96; Assoc. Dir RSC 1996–2003, Artistic Dir 2003–. *Productions include:* for Tron Theatre: The Trick is to Keep Breathing, Macbeth, Good, The Real World, Crow, Century's End, Salvation, The Baby, Clyde Nouveau, The Guid Sisters; for the RSC: The Broken Heart 1994–95, Measure for Measure 1996–97, The Spanish Tragedy, Much Ado About Nothing 1997–98, Troilus and Cressida 1998–99, A Midsummer Night's Dream 1999–2000, Romeo and Juliet 2000–01, Henry VI, Parts I, II and III and Richard III (Olivier Award for Best Dir) 2000–01, The Tempest 2002, Hamlet 2004, Twelfth Night 2005, The Histories (eight play cycle) 2006–08; other theatre productions include: Miss Julie (Haymarket Theatre, West End) 1999, Commedia (Lyric Hammersmith) 1983, Othello 1984, Hard to Get (Traverse Theatre, Edin.), Hedda Gabler (Leicester Haymarket), The Alchemist (Cambridge Theatre Co.). *Leisure interests:* walking, reading, music, cooking. *Address:* Royal Shakespeare Company, Royal Shakespeare Theatre, Waterside, Stratford-upon-Avon, Warwickshire, CV37 6BB, England (office). *Telephone:* (1789) 296655 (office). *Fax:* (1789) 412610 (office). *E-mail:* info@rsc.org.uk (office). *Website:* www.rsc .org.uk (office).

BOYD, Sir Robert, Kt, MA, MB, BChir, FRCP, FFPHM, FRCPCH, FMedSci; British paediatrician; b. 14 May 1938, Cambridge; s. of James Dixon Boyd and Amélie Boyd; m. Meriel Cornelia Talbot 1966; one s. two d.; ed Ley's School, Clare

Coll., Cambridge, Univ. Coll. Hosp., London; jr posts, Hosp. for Sick Children, Great Ormond Street, Brompton Hosp., Univ. Coll. Hosp. (UCH), London 1962–65; Sir Stuart Halley Research Fellow and Sr Registrar, UCH 1966–71; Goldsmiths MRC Travelling Fellow, Univ. of Colo Medical Center, USA 1971–72; Sr Lecturer and Hon. Consultant UCH Medical School 1972–80; Sec. Academic Bd, British Paediatric Asscn 1976–79, Chair. 1987–90; Asst Registrar Royal Coll. of Physicians 1980–81; Prof. of Paediatrics, Univ. of Manchester 1981–96, Dean 1989–93, Visiting Prof. 2003–; Prin. St George's Hosp. Medical School and Prof. of Paediatrics 1996–2003, Pro-Vice-Chancellor for Medicine, Univ. of London 2000–03, Deputy Vice-Chancellor 2002–03; Chair. Manchester Health Authority 1994–96, Nat. Primary Care R&D Centre, Univs of Manchester, Salford and York 1994–96, Dir Nat. Health Service (NHS) Research and Devt, Greater Manchester 2004–08; Chair., Council of Heads of UK Medical Schools 2001–03, Lloyds TSB Foundation for England and Wales 2003–; Chair. Council for Assisting Refugee Academics 2004–; Ed. Placenta 1989–95; mem. Health Cttee Universities UK 1997–2003, Asscn of Medical Research Charities Scientific Advisory Cttee 1996–2002, Task Force 'Supporting Research & Devt in the NHS' 1994; mem. Council, Royal Veterinary Coll. 1999–2003; Gov. Kingston Univ. 1998–2003, Univ. of Manchester 2004–; Hon. Consultant St Mary's Hosp., Manchester and Booth Hall Children's Hosp., Manchester 1981–96, St George's Healthcare Nat. Health Service Trust, London 1996–2003; Hon. Fellow American Pediatric Soc.; Hon. DSc (Kingston, Keele). *Publications:* Paediatric Problems in General Practice (jtly) 1982; contribs to Placental and Fetal Physiology and Paediatrics and Health Administration. *Leisure interests:* cooking, reading, holidays. *Address:* The Stone House, Skellorn Green, Adlington, Macclesfield, Cheshire, SK10 4NU, England (home). *Telephone:* (1625) 872400 (home). *E-mail:* rboyd@doctors.org.uk (home).

BOYD, William Andrew Murray, CBE, MA, FRSL; British writer; b. 7 March 1952, Ghana; s. of Dr Alexander Murray Boyd and Evelyn Boyd; m. Susan Anne Boyd (née Wilson) 1975; ed Gordonstoun School, Glasgow Univ., Jesus Coll., Oxford; lecturer in English, St Hilda's Coll., Oxford 1980–83; TV critic, New Statesman 1981–83; Officier, Ordre des Arts et des Lettres; Hon. DLitt (St Andrews), (Glasgow), (Stirling). *Film appearance:* Rabbit Fever 2006. *Publications include:* A Good Man in Africa (Whitbread Prize 1981, Somerset Maugham Award 1982) 1981 (screenplay 1994), On the Yankee Station 1981, An Ice-Cream War (John Llewellyn Rhys Prize) 1982, Stars and Bars 1984 (screenplay 1988), School Ties 1985, The New Confessions 1987, Scoop (screenplay) 1987, Brazzaville Beach (McVities Prize and James Tait Black Memorial Prize) 1990, Aunt Julia and the Scriptwriter (screenplay) 1990, Mr Johnson (screenplay) 1990, Chaplin (screenplay) 1992, The Blue Afternoon (novel) 1993, A Good Man in Africa (screenplay) 1994, The Destiny of Nathalie 'X' 1995, Armadillo 1998 (screenplay 2001), Nat Tate: An American Artist 1998, The Trench (screenplay, also dir) 1999, Sword of Honour (screenplay) 2001, Any Human Heart 2002, Fascination 2004, Bamboo (collection of literary reviews) 2005, A Waste of Shame (screenplay) 2005, Restless (novel) (Costa Book Award for Novel of the Year, Yorkshire Post Book of the Year 2007) 2006, Granta 100 (Ed.) 2008, The Dream Lover (short stories) 2008. *Leisure interests:* tennis, strolling. *Address:* The Agency, 24 Pottery Lane, Holland Park, London, W11 4LZ, England (office).

BOYD OF DUNCANSBY, Baron (Life Peer), cr. 2006, of Duncansby in the County of Caithness Colin Boyd, PC, QC, BA (Econ), LLB, FRSA, LARTPI; British lawyer; b. 7 June 1953, Falkirk; s. of David Hugh Aird Boyd and Betty Meldrum Boyd; two s. one d.; ed Wick High School, George Watson's Coll., Edinburgh, Univ. of Manchester and Univ. of Edinburgh; qualified as solicitor 1978; called to Bar 1983; Legal Assoc. Royal Town Planning Inst. 1990; Advocate Depute (prosecutor) 1993–95; QC 1995; Solicitor-Gen. for Scotland, UK Govt 1997; Solicitor-Gen., Scottish Exec. 1999–2000; Lord Advocate of Scotland 2000–06; Hon. Fellow, Inst. of Advanced Legal Studies 2001. *Leisure interests:* reading, walking, watching rugby. *Address:* House of Lords, London, SW1A 0PW, England (office). *Telephone:* (20) 7219-3000 (office). *E-mail:* boydcd@parliament.uk (office).

BOYD OF MERTON, 2nd Viscount (cr. 1960) of Merton-in-Penninghame, Co. Wigtown; **Simon Donald Rupert Neville Lennox-Boyd,** MA; British business executive (retd); b. 7 Dec. 1939, London; s. of the late Alan Lennox-Boyd (1st Viscount Boyd of Merton) and of Lady Patricia Guinness; m. Alice Mary Clive 1962; two s. two d.; ed Eton Coll., Christ Church, Oxford; Deputy Chair. Arthur Guinness & Sons 1981–86; Vice-Chair. Save the Children Fund 1979–82, Chair. 1987–93; Chair. Stonham Housing Asscn 1992–98, Trustee, Guinness Trust 1974–; Dir The Iveagh Trustees Ltd. *Leisure interest:* forestry. *Address:* Ince Castle, Saltash, Cornwall, PL12 4QZ, England. *Telephone:* (1752) 842672. *Fax:* (1752) 847134 (home). *E-mail:* boydince@aol.com (home).

BOYE, Mame Madior; Senegalese politician and lawyer; b. 1940; ed Faculty of Legal and Econ. Sciences, Dakar, Centre Nat. d'Etudes Judiciaires, Paris; fmr Deputy Procurator of Repub.; Judge, First Vice-Pres. First Class Regional Court, Dakar; fmr Pres. Dakar Court of Appeal; Minister of Justice and Keeper of the Seals 2000–01; Prime Minister of Senegal 2001–02; Special Rep. for the Promotion of the Protection of Civilians in Armed Conflicts, African Union 2004–; mem. Parti Démocratique Sénégalais. *Address:* Siege de L'Union Africaine, PO Box 3243, Addis Ababa, Ethiopia (office). *Telephone:* (1) 517700 (office). *Fax:* (1) 517844 (office). *Website:* www.africa-union.org (office).

BOYER, Paul Delos, PhD; American biochemist and academic; *Professor Emeritus of Biochemistry, UCLA;* b. 31 July 1918, Provo, Utah; s. of Dell Delos Boyer and Grace Guymon; m. Lynda Wicker 1939; one s. two d.; ed Brigham Young Univ. and Univ. of Wisconsin; Research Asst, Univ. of Wis. 1939–43; Instructor, Stanford Univ. 1943–45; Assoc. Prof., Univ. of Minn. 1947–53, Prof. 1953–56, Hill Prof. of Biochem. 1956–63; Prof. of Biochemistry, Univ. of

Calif. at Los Angeles 1963–89, Dir Molecular Biology Inst. 1965–83, Biotechnology Program 1985–89, Prof. Emer. 1989–; mem. Nat. Acad. of Sciences; Fellow American Acad. of Arts and Sciences, Vice-Pres. Biological Sciences 1985–87; Pres. American Soc. of Biol. Chemists 1969–70; Guggenheim Fellowship 1955; Ed. Annual Biochemistry Review 1964–89, Ed. Biochemical and Biophysical Research Communications 1968–80, The Enzymes 1970–; Dr hc (Stockholm) 1974, (Minn.) 1996, (Wis.) 1998; ACS Award 1955, Tolman Medal 1981, Rose Award (American Soc. of Biochemistry and Molecular Biology) 1989; shared Nobel Prize for Chem. 1997. *Publications:* author or co-author of over 200 scientific papers in biochemistry and molecular biology. *Leisure interest:* tennis. *Address:* Department of Chemistry and Biochemistry, UCLA, 639A MBT Building, 607 Charles B. Young Drive East, Los Angeles, CA 90095-0001 (office); 1033 Somera Road, Los Angeles, CA 90077-2625, USA (home). *E-mail:* pdboyer@ucla.edu (office). *Website:* www.chem.ucla.edu/dept/Faculty/boyer.html (office).

BOYER, Yves, PhD; French research institute director; *Deputy Director, Fondation pour la Recherche Stratégique;* b. 9 Oct. 1950, Blois; m. Isabelle Kraft 1978; one s. one d.; ed Inst. d'Etudes Politiques, Paris and Paris-Panthéon Univ.; Deputy Gen. Sec. SOFRESA, Paris 1978–80; Bureau des Etudes Stratégiques et des Négociations Internationales, Secr. Gén. de la Défense Nationale 1980–82; Defence Consultant and Research Assoc., IISS, London 1982–83; Sr Researcher, Inst. Français des Relations Internationales 1983–88; Research Fellow, Woodrow Wilson Center 1986; fmr Deputy Dir CREST, Ecole Polytechnique; Prof., Army Acad. 1986–, Staff Coll. 1992–; currently Deputy Dir Fondation pour la Recherche Stratégique; Assoc. Prof., Institut d'Études Politiques de Paris, École Polytechnique; Chair. French Soc. for Mil. Studies (SFEM), Working Groups for the French Ministry of Defence's Scientific Advisers; mem. Editorial Bd, Annuaire Français de Relations Internationales; Chevalier, Ordre des Palmes Académiques. *Address:* Fondation pour la Recherche Stratégique, 27 rue Damesme, 75013 Paris (office); 2 rue de Haut Bourg, 41000 Blois, France (home). *Telephone:* (1) 43-13-77-66 (office). *Fax:* (1) 43-13-77-78 (office). *E-mail:* y.boyer@frstrategie.org (office).

BOYER SALVADOR, Miguel; Spanish politician; b. 5 Feb. 1939, San Juan de Luz, France; m. 1st Elena Arnedo; two s.; m. 2nd Isabel Preysler 1988; joined Spanish Socialist Workers' Party 1960, imprisoned for 6 months for political activities; fmr economist, Studies Group of Banco de España; Dir Studies, Nat. Industrial Inst., Strategic Planning Group, Explosivos Río Tinto SA, Strategic Planning, Nat. Hydrocarbons Inst.; Minister of Economy, Finance and Commerce 1982–85; Chair. Banco Exterior de España 1985–88, Cartera Central, Grueyersa 1989–93; Vice-Chair. FCC Construcción 1993; Chair. Compania Logistica de Hidrocarburos CLH, SA –2005; Gov. IBRD; Rep. to IDB 1983–85. *Address:* Capitán Haya nr 41, 28020 Madrid, Spain. *Telephone:* (1) 556-70-00. *Fax:* (1) 556-90-07.

BOYLE, Danny; British film director; b. 20 Oct. 1956, Bury, Lancs.; Artistic Dir Royal Court Theatre 1982–87; Golden Ephebe Award 1997. *Films:* Shallow Grave 1994, Trainspotting 1996, A Life Less Ordinary 1996, Twin Town (exec. producer) 1996, The Beach 1999, Alien Love Triangle 1999, 28 Days Later 2002, Alien Love Triangle 2002, Millions 2004, Sunshine 2007, Slumdog Millionaire (Best Film Nat. Bd of Review 2008, Golden Globe Award for Best Dir 2009, BAFTA Award for Best Dir 2009, Acad. Award for Best Picture 2009, Acad. Award for Best Dir 2009) 2008. *Television:* Elephant (producer) 1989, The Greater Good (dir, series) 1991, Mr Wroe's Virgins (dir) 1993, Not Even God is Wise Enough (dir) 1993. *Address:* c/o Robert Newman, The Endeavor Agency, 9601 Wilshire Blvd., 10th Floor, Beverly Hills, CA 90212; c/o D6A, 7920 West Sunset Boulevard, Los Angeles, CA 90046, USA (office).

BOYLE, Thomas Coraghessan (T. C.), BA, MFA, PhD; American academic and writer; *Professor, Department of English, University of Southern California;* b. 2 Dec. 1948, Peekskill, NY; m. Karen Kvashay 1974; two s. one d.; ed SUNY at Potsdam, Univ. of Iowa; Founder-Dir, Creative Writing Program 1978–86, Asst Prof. of English 1978–82, Assoc. Prof. of English 1982–86, Prof. of English 1986–, Univ. of Southern California; mem. Nat. Endowment of the Arts literature panel 1986–87; Nat. Endowment for the Arts grants 1977, 1983; Guggenheim Fellowship 1988, mem. American Acad. of Arts and Letters 2009–; Hon. DHumLitt (SUNY) 1991; PEN/Faulkner Award 1988, Commonwealth Club of California Gold Medal for Literature 1988, O. Henry Short Story Awards 1988, 1989, Prix Passion Publishers' Prize, France 1989, Eds' Choice, New York Times Book Review 1989, Harold D. Vursell Memorial Award, American Acad. of Arts and Letters 1993, Prix Médicis Étranger 1997. *Publications:* Descent of Man 1979, Water Music 1982, Budding Prospects 1984, Greasy Lake 1985, World's End 1987, If the River was Whiskey 1989, East is East 1990, The Road to Wellville 1993, Without a Hero 1994, The Tortilla Curtain 1995, Riven Rock 1998, T.C. Boyle Stories 1998, A Friend of the Earth 2000, After the Plague 2001, Drop City 2003, The Inner Circle 2004, Tooth and Claw 2006, Talk Talk 2006, The Women 2009; contrib. to numerous anthologies and periodicals. *Address:* Department of English, University of Southern California, Los Angeles, CA 90089, USA (office). *Telephone:* (213) 740-3734 (office). *E-mail:* tcb@tcboyle.com (office). *Website:* www.tcboyle.com.

BOYLE, Willard S., BSc, MSc, PhD; Canadian physicist (retd); b. 19 Aug. 1924, Amherst, NS; ed McGill Univ.; served in Fleet Air Arm of Royal Canadian Navy during World War II but did not see active service; Post-doctoral Fellow, Radiation Lab., McGill Univ. 1950–51; Asst Prof., Royal Mil. Coll. 1951–53; mem. research staff, Bell Laboratories 1953–79, held positions in New Jersey, Washington and Pennsylvania, Dir Space Science and Exploratory Studies, Bell Labs subsidiary Bellcomm 1962, returned to Bell Labs 1964, later Exec. Dir Device Devt, Exec. Dir Communication Science Div. 1975–79; mem. Research Council, Canadian Inst. of Advanced Research 1979–, Science

Council, Prov. of NS 1979–; Fellow, American Physical Soc., IEEE; mem. Nat. Acad. of Eng; Hon. LLD (Dalhousie); jtly for co-invention with George E. Smith of the charge-coupled device (CCD): Stuart Ballentine Medal, Franklin Inst. 1973, IEEE Morris N. Liebmann Memorial Award 1974, Progress Medal, Photographic Soc. of America 1986, IEEE Device Research Conf. Breakthrough Award 1999, C&C Prize (Computer and Communications), NEC Foundation, Tokyo 1999, Edwin H. Land Medal, Soc. for Imaging Science and Tech. 2001, Charles Stark Draper Prize (co-recipient) 2006. *Address:* c/o Research Council, Canadian Institute for Advanced Research, 180 Dundas Street West, Suite 1400, Toronto, ON M5G 1Z8, Canada.

BOYNTON, Robert Merrill, PhD, FAAS; American psychologist and academic; *Professor Emeritus of Psychology, University of California, San Diego;* b. 28 Oct. 1924, Evanston, Ill.; s. of Merrill Holmes Boynton and Eleanor Matthews Boynton; m. 1st Alice Neiley 1947 (died 1996); three s. one d.; m. 2nd Sheleah Maloney 1998; ed Amherst Coll. and Brown Univ.; Asst Prof., Univ. of Rochester 1952–57, Assoc. Prof. 1957–61, Prof. 1961–74, Dir and Founder, Center for Visual Science 1963–71, Chair. Dept of Psychology 1971–74; Prof., Dept of Psychology, Univ. of Calif. at San Diego 1974–91, Emer. Prof. 1991–; Assoc. Dean, Graduate Studies and Research 1987–91; Chair. Visual Sciences B Study Section, NIH 1972–75; Chair. Bd of Eds Vision Research 1982–85; mem. NAS; Godlove Award, Inter-society Color Council 1982, Tillyer Medal, Optical Soc. of America 1972, Ives Medal and Quinn Prize, Optical Soc. of America 1995, Prentice Award, American Acad. of Optometry 1997, Distinguished Achievement Award (Brown Univ.) 1986; Snaker Heights High School Hall of Fame 1996. *Publications:* Human Color Vision 1979 (2nd edition, with Peter Kaiser); 150 scientific articles and 12 articles on baseball. *Leisure interest:* baseball research. *Address:* 376 Bellaire Street, Del Mar, CA 92014, USA (home). *Telephone:* (858) 481-0263 (home). *E-mail:* rboynton@ucsd.edu (office).

BOZANGA, Simon-Narcisse; Central African Republic politician and lawyer; *Adviser, Transitional Constitutional Court;* b. 26 Dec. 1942, Bangassou; Dir of Legal Studies, Ministry of Foreign Affairs 1972–74, Sec.-Gen. 1974–78; Amb. to Gabon 1978–79; Sec.-Gen. to Govt 1979–80; Minister of Justice 1980–81; Prime Minister and Head of Govt April–Sept. 1981 (deposed by mil. coup); Dir-Gen. Société Centrafricaine des Hydrocarbures (CentraHydro) 1982; Adviser, Transitional Constitutional Court 2004–. *Address:* Transitional Constitutional Court, Bangui, Central African Republic.

BOZANIĆ, HE Cardinal Josip, MTS, LLM; Croatian ecclesiastic; *Archbishop of Zagreb;* b. 20 March 1949, Rijeka; s. of Ivan Bosanić and Dinka Valković; ed Lower Seminary of Pazin, Faculties of Theology, Rijeka and Zagreb, Pontifical Gregorian Univ. and Pontifical Lateran Univ., Rome; ordained priest by Bishop of Krk, Karmelo Zazinović 1975; Sec. to Bishop of Krk 1975–76; Parish Priest 1976–78; Chancellor of Diocesan Curia in Krk 1986–87; Gen. Priest 1987–89; Prof. of Canon Law and Theology, Seminary of Rijeka 1988–97; elected Bishop of Krk 1989; consecrated by Cardinal Franjo Kuharić 1989; Admin. of Archdiocese of Rijeka-Senj 1996; Archbishop of Metropolitan See of Zagreb 1997–; Pres. Croatian Conf. of Bishops; Vice-Pres. Council of European Bishops' Confs; cr. Cardinal Priest of Saint Jerome of the Croatians 2003–; del. to Special Ass. for Europe, World Synod of Bishops, Vatican 1999. *Address:* Archdiocese of Zagreb, Kaptol 31, p.p. 553, 10001 Zagreb, Hrvatska, Croatia (office). *Telephone:* 4894802 (office). *Fax:* 4816104 (office). *E-mail:* Josip.Bozanic@hbk.hr (office). *Website:* zagreb.hbk.hr (office).

BOZER, Ali Husrev; Turkish academic, judge and government official; *Professor of Law, Çankaya University;* b. 28 July 1925, Ankara; s. of Mustafa Fevzi Bozer and Zehra Bozer; m.; three s.; ed Ankara and Neuchâtel Univs and Harvard Law School; Asst judge, Ankara 1951; Asst, Faculty of Law, Ankara Univ. 1952–60, Agrégé 1955–60, Head of Dept 1961, apptd Prof. of Commercial Law 1965; Prof. of Law Çankaya Univ. 1992–; lawyer at bar, Ankara 1952–; Dir Inst. de Recherche sur le Droit commercial et bancaire 1960–; Judge, European Court of Human Rights 1974–76; mem. Admin. Council, Turkish Radio-TV Corpn 1968–71, Vice-Pres. 1971–73; Minister of Customs and Monopolies 1981–83, of State for Relations with EEC 1986–90; Deputy Prime Minister and Minister of State 1989–90; Minister of Foreign Affairs Feb.–Oct. 1990; fmr Pres., now Hon. Pres. European Asscn of Former Parliamentarians of the Member Countries of the European Council or the EU; mem. Bd AxA OYAK; Officier Légion d'honneur 1993; Merite Européan 1992. *Publications:* Les droits d'administration et de jouissance de père et mère sur les biens de l'enfant, Nantissement commercial, Aperçu général sur le droit des assurances sociales en droit turc, Droit commercial pour les employés de banques, Papiers valeurs pour les employés de banques, Droits des Assurances, Droit des Obligations, Insurance Law, Contracts Law, Negotiable Instruments; monographs and articles in several reviews in Turkish and French. *Leisure interest:* theatre, music, sport, tennis, swimming. *Address:* Ahmet Rasim sok. 35/5, Çankaya, Ankara, Turkey. *Telephone:* (312) 4424112 (office). *Fax:* (312) 4424113 (office).

BOZIZÉ, Jean Francis; Central African Republic government official; *Minister of National Defence, War Veterans, War Victims, Disarmament and the Restructuring of the Armed Forces;* s. of Pres. François Bozizé Yangovounda; has served in several positions in the Ministry of National Defence, War Veterans, War Victims, Disarmament and the Restructuring of the Armed Forces, including Chief of Staff to the Minister, Deputy Minister, Minister of Nat. Defence, War Veterans, War Victims, Disarmament and the Restructuring of the Armed Forces 2008–. *Address:* Ministry of National Defence, War Veterans, War Victims, Disarmament and the Restructuring of the Armed Forces, Bangui, Central African Republic (office).

BOZIZE YANGOVOUNDA, Gen. François; Central African Republic army officer and head of state; *President;* opposition leader 1981–93, led unsuccessful coup 1983; spent many years in exile in Togo; presidential cand. 1993; supported Pres. Ange-Felix Patasse in suppressing coups 1996–97; sacked as Army Chief; participated in unsuccessful coup against Pres. 2001, took control of N Bangui before escaping to Chad with 300 supporters; launched several rebel attacks from base in Chad 2001–02; led successful coup March 2003, suspended constitution and dissolved Parl.; self-proclaimed Pres. of Cen. African Repub. 2003–05, elected 2005–, Minister of Defence 2005–08. *Address:* Office of the President, Palais de la Renaissance, Bangui, Central African Republic (office). *Telephone:* 61-46-63 (office).

BOŽOVIĆ, Radoman, PhD; Serbian politician and economist; b. 1953, Sipcan, nr Niksic, Montenegro; m.; two c.; ed Belgrade Univ.; academic 1976–89; fmr deputy to Vojvodina Ass., later head of provincial Govt; mem. Socialist Party of Serbia (SPS) (fmrly League of Communists of Yugoslavia—LCY); Deputy, Serbian Ass. 1990–, Head SPS Parl. Group; Prime Minister of Serbia 1991–93; Chair. Council of Citizens, Fed. Ass. 1992–97; f. Bancor Group Sept. 1997; Prof., Univ. Subotica. *Publications:* numerous books and articles including Political Economy (two vols), Accumulation and Economic Development, Types of Prosperity in Socialism, Problems of Economic System Reform in Yugoslavia.

BRABECK-LETMATHE, Peter, BA; Austrian business executive; *Chairman, Nestlé SA;* b. 13 Nov. 1944, Villach; ed Univ. of World Trade, Vienna; fmrly with Findus Austria; joined Nestlé Group as new products specialist 1968, Nat. Sales Man. 1970, later Head of Marketing, Savory (Chile), frozen food and ice-cream specialist, Nestlé HQ 1975, Marketing and Sales Div. Man., Chiprodal (Chile) 1976, Asst to Regional Man. for S America, Nestlé HQ 1980, Man. Dir Nestlé Ecuador 1981, Nestlé Venezuela 1983, Sr Vice-Pres. and Head of Culinary Products Div., Nestlé SA, Vevey 1987, Exec. Vice-Pres. and Head of Strategic Business Group 2 1992, Group CEO (desig.) Nestlé SA, Vevey 1995–97, Group CEO 1997–2008, Vice-Chair. 2001–05, Chair. 2005–, also Chair. Chairman's and Corp. Governance Cttee, Nomination Cttee; Vice-Chair. L'Oréal, Crédit Suisse Group; mem. Bd of Dirs Roche Holding SA, Delta Topco Ltd; Deputy Chair. The Prince of Wales Int. Business Leaders' Forum; mem. European Round Table of Industrialists, Int. Asscn for the Promotion and Protection of Pvt. Foreign Investments; mem. Foundation Bds World Econ. Forum, Foundation for the Int. Fed. of Red Cross and Red Crescent Socs. *Address:* Nestlé, Avenue Nestlé 55, 1800 Vevey, Switzerland (office). *Telephone:* (21) 924-21-11 (office). *Fax:* (21) 921-18-85 (office). *E-mail:* info@nestle.com (office). *Website:* www.nestle.com (office).

BRABHAM, Sir John Arthur (Jack), Kt, OBE; Australian fmr racing driver; b. 2 April 1926, Sydney, Australia; s. of C. T. Brabham; m. 1st Betty Evelyn (divorced); three s.; m. 2nd Margaret Brabham; ed Hurstville Tech. Coll., Sydney; served in RAAF 1944–46; started own engineering business 1946; Midget Speedway racing 1946–53; numerous wins driving a Cooper-Bristol, Australia 1953–54; went to Europe 1955; Australian Grand Prix 1955, 1963; World Champion, Formula II 1958, 1966; Formula II Champion of France 1964; World Champion Driver 1959–60, 1960–61, 1966; came first in Monaco and UK Grandes Epreuves 1959; won Grand Prix of Netherlands, Belgium, France, UK, Portugal, Denmark 1960, Belgium 1961, France 1966, 1967, UK 1966; began building own cars 1961; winner Formula 1 Mfrs Championship 1966, 1967; fmr Chair. Jack Brabham (Ewell) Ltd; fmr Dir Engine Developments Ltd; Ferodo Trophy 1964, 1966; Australian of the Year 1966; BRDC Gold Star 1966, BARC Gold Medal 1959, 1966, 1967. *Publications:* Jack Brabham's Book of Motor Racing 1960, When the Flag Drops 1971, The Jack Brabham Story 2004. *Leisure interests:* flying, scuba diving, water skiing, cruising. *Address:* c/o Lady Brabham, Suite 404, Bag No. 1, Robina Town Centre, Queensland, 4230, Australia. *Telephone:* (7) 5564-7072 (office). *Fax:* (7) 5564-9872 (office).

BRACHER, Karl Dietrich, DPhil; German historian, political scientist and academic; *Professor Emeritus, University of Bonn;* b. 13 March 1922, Stuttgart; s. of Theodor Bracher and Gertrud Zimmermann; m. Dorothee Schleicher (niece of Dietrich Bonhoeffer) 1951; one s. one d.; ed Gymnasium, Stuttgart, Univ. of Tübingen and Harvard Univ., USA; Research Asst and Head of Dept, Inst. of Political Science, Berlin 1950–58; Lecturer, German Hochschule für Politik, Berlin; Privatdozent and Prof., Free Univ., Berlin 1955–58; Prof. of Political Science and Contemporary History, Univ. of Bonn 1959–, now Prof. Emer.; Pres. Comm. for History of Parl. and Political Parties, Bonn 1962–68; Fellow, Center for Advanced Study in the Behavioral Sciences, Stanford, USA 1963–64; Chair. German Asscn of Political Science 1965–67; mem. Inst. for Advanced Study, Princeton, USA 1967–68, 1974–75; mem. Wilson Center, Washington, DC, USA 1980–81; Chair. Bd, Inst. für Zeitgeschichte, Munich 1980–88, German Asscn of Foreign Policy, German PEN Centre; Visiting Prof., Sweden 1962, Univ. of Oxford 1971, Tel-Aviv Univ. 1974, Japan 1975, European Univ. Inst., Florence 1975–76, Seattle 1984; Corresp. Fellow, British Acad., American Philosophical Soc., Austrian Akad. der Wissenschaften; mem. Deutsche Akad. für Sprache und Dichtung, Rhenish-Westfalian Acad. of Sciences; Ed. Vierteljahrshefte für Zeitgeschichte; mem. Editorial Bd, Politische Vierteljahresschrift until 1970, Neue Politische Literatur, Bonner Historische Forschungen, Journal of Contemporary History, Government and Opposition, Societas, Zeitschrift für Politik, Tempo Presente, Risorgimento, European Journal of Int. Affairs, History of the Twentieth Century, Bonner Schriften zur Politik und Zeitgeschichte, Quellen zur Geschichte des Parliamentarismus, Dokumente zur Deutschlandpolitik; Hon. mem. American Acad. of Arts and Sciences; Ordre of Merit for Sciences and Arts 1992–; Hon. DHumLitt (Florida); Hon. DJur (Graz); Hon. Dr rer. pol (Berlin); Dr hc (Paris); Premio Storia Acqui 1973, Bentinck-Preis 1981, Curtius-Preis 1994. *Publications:* Conscience in Revolt (with others) 1954, Die Auflösung der Weimarer Republik 1955, Staat und Politik (with E. Fraenkel) 1957, Die Nationalsozialistische Machtergreifung (with others) 1960, Propyläen Weltgeschichte (vol. nine) (Dutch trans.) 1960, The Foreign Policy of the Federal Republic of Germany 1963, Problems of Parliamentary Democracy in Europe 1964, Adolf Hitler 1964, Deutschland zwischen Demokratie und Diktatur 1964, Theodor Heuss 1965, Modern Constitutionalism and Democracy (co-ed. two vols) 1966, Internationale Beziehungen (with E. Fraenkel) 1969, The German Dictatorship (English, Italian, Spanish, French, Japanese, Hebrew trans.) 1970, Nach 25 Jahren (ed.) 1970, Das deutsche Dilemma 1971 (English trans. 1974), Western Europe (in Times History of Our Times) 1971, Democracy (in Europe Tomorrow) 1972, Zeitgeschichtliche Kontroversen 1976, Die Krise Europas seit 1917 1976 and 1992 (Italian trans.), Schlüsselwörter in der Geschichte 1978, Geschichte und Gewalt 1981, Bibliographie zur Politik (co-ed.) 1970, 1976, 1982, Zeit der Ideologien 1982 (English, Spanish and Italian trans. 1985), Nationalsozialistische Diktatur 1983, Das Gewissen steht auf 1984, Die totalitäre Erfahrung 1987, Geschichte der BR Deutschland 1981–87, Verfall und Fortschritt im Denken der frühen römischen Kaiserzeit 1987, Die Weimarer Republik 1998, Deutschland zwischen Krieg und Frieden 1991, Staat und Parteien (co-ed.) 1992, Wendezeiten der Geschichte 1992, Deutschland 1933–1945 1993, Hitler et la dictature allemande 1995, Turning Points in Modern Times 1995, Geschichte als Erfahrung 2001. *Leisure interest:* playing piano and chamber music, mountain walking. *Address:* Stationsweg 17, 53127 Bonn, Germany. *Telephone:* 284358.

BRACHES, Dr Ernst; Dutch academic (retd); b. 8 Oct. 1930, Padang, Indonesia; s. of Godfried Daniel Ernst Braches and Zeni Jansz; m. Maartje van Hoorn 1961; three s., one foster s.; ed Univ. of Amsterdam; asst, Univ. of Amsterdam 1957–65; Keeper, Western Printed Books, Univ. Library, Leiden 1965–73; Dir Rijksmuseum Meermanno-Westreenianum, The Hague 1973–77; Librarian, Univ. of Amsterdam 1977–88; Prof. of History of the Printed Book, Univ. of Amsterdam; Hon. mem. Soc. de la Reliure Originale, Paris. *Publications include:* Henry James: Engel en Afgrond 1983, Lord Peter Whimsey as a Book Lover 1989, The Scheffers Type 1990, Gutenberg's Scriptorium 1991, The Steadfast Tin Soldier of Joh Enschede en Zonen 1992, Alle nieuwe kunst wordt eerst niet begrepen… 2003, Nieuwe Kunst en het boek 2003, Nieuwe Kunst Documentatie 2006, Der Tod in Venedig: Kommentar zum ersten Kapitel 2007, Der Tod in Venedig: Thomas Manns Arbeitsnotizen 2008. *Address:* Vrijburglaan 53, 2051 LB Overveen, Netherlands (home). *Telephone:* (23) 5253246 (home). *Fax:* (23) 5253246 (home).

BRACKEN, Richard M., BSc, MSc; American healthcare services executive; *President and COO, HCA Healthcare Inc.;* b. 14 Sept. 1952; m. Judith Bracken, four c.; ed San Diego State Univ., Medical Coll. of Virginia; joined HCA Healthcare 1981, has held numerous man. positions including CEO Green Hospital, Scripps Clinic and Research Foundation, San Diego, Centennial Medical Center, Nashville, Pres. Pacific Div. 1995–97, Pres. Western Group 1997–2001, COO 2001–, Pres. 2002–, mem. Bd of Dirs 2002–; fmr mem. Bd of Dirs Calif. Hospital Asscn, Fed. of American Hospitals, St. Luke's Community Center, United Way of Metropolitan Nashville; mem. American Soc. of Corporate Execs. *Address:* HCA Healthcare Inc., 1 Park Plaza, Nashville, TN 37203, USA (office). *Telephone:* (615) 344-9551 (office). *Fax:* (615) 344-2266 (office). *Website:* www.hcahealthcare.com (office).

BRACKS, Hon. Stephen (Steve) Phillip, DipBusStudies, GradDipEduc; Australian politician; b. 15 Oct. 1954, Ballarat; m.; two s. one d.; ed Ballarat Univ.; secondary commerce teacher 1976–81; employment project worker and municipal recreation officer 1981–85; Exec. Dir Ballarat Educ. Centre 1985–89; Statewide Man. Victoria's Employment Programmes 1989–1993; Adviser to Premier of Vic. 1990; Prin. Adviser to Fed. Parl. Sec. for Transport and Communications 1993; Exec. Dir Victorian Printing Industry Training Bd 1993–94; mem. Parl. (Labour) 1994–; Deputy Chair. Public Accounts and Estimates Cttee 1996–99; Shadow Minister for Employment, Industrial Relations and Tourism 1994–96; Shadow Treas., Shadow Minister for Finance and Industrial Relations 1996–99; Premier of Vic., Minister for Multicultural Affairs 1999–2007, Treas. of Vic. 1999–2000, Minister for Veterans' Affairs 2004–07; Adviser to Prime Minister of Timor-Leste (East Timor) Xanana Gusmao 2007–; Chair. United Super Pty Ltd (Cbus) 2008–; Ind., Chair. Australian Subscription TV and Radio Asscn (ASTRA) 2008–; Sr Adviser KPMG 2007–, Nat. Australia Bank (NAB) 2008–; mem. Bd Jardine Lloyd Thompson Pty Ltd 2007–; Hon. Chair. 2010 Road World Cycling Championship. *Leisure interests:* camping, distance swimming, tennis. *Address:* Old Treasury Building, 20 Spring Street, Melbourne, Vic. 3000, Australia (office). *Telephone:* (3) 9651-2223 (office). *Fax:* (3) 9651-5453 (office). *E-mail:* info@stevebracks.com.au (office). *Website:* www.stevebracks.com.au (office).

BRADBEER, Sir (John) Derek (Richardson), Kt, MA, OBE, TD; British lawyer; b. 29 Oct. 1931; s. of the late William Bertram Bradbeer and Winifred Bradbeer (née Richardson); m. Margaret Elizabeth Chantler 1962; one s. one d.; ed Canford School, Sidney Sussex Coll. Cambridge; admitted solicitor 1959; Partner, Wilkinson Maughan (fmrly Wilkinson Marshall Clayton & Gibson) 1961–97; mem. Criminal Injuries Compensation Bd 1988–2000, Criminal Injuries Compensation Appeals Panel 1996–; mem. Disciplinary Cttee Inst. of Actuaries 1989–96, Insurance Brokers Registration Council 1992–96; mem. Council, Law Soc. 1973–94, Vice-Pres. 1986–87, Pres. 1987–88; Pres. Newcastle-upon-Tyne Inc. Law Soc. 1982–83; Gov. Coll. of Law 1983–2002 (Chair. 1990–99); Dir Newcastle and Gateshead Water PLC 1978–90, Sunderland and South Shields Water PLC 1990–2002; Chair. North East Water 1992–2002; Deputy Chair. Northumbrian Water Group 1996–2002; UK Vice-Pres. Union Int. des Avocats 1988–92; Vice-Chair. N of England Territorial Auxiliary and Volunteer Reserve Asscn 1988–90, Chair. 1990–96; DL Tyne and Wear 1988; Hon. DUniv (Open Univ.) 2000. *Leisure interests:* reading, gardening, sport. *Address:* Forge Cottage, Shilvington, Newcastle-upon-Tyne, NE20 0AP (home); Criminal Injuries Compensation

Appeals Panel, 11th Floor, Cardinal Tower, Farringdon Road, London, EC1M 3HS, England (office). *Telephone:* (1670) 775214 (home). *Fax:* (1670) 775214 (home). *E-mail:* bradbeer4@aol.com (home).

BRADBURY, Ray Douglas; American writer, poet and dramatist; b. 22 Aug. 1920, Waukegan, Ill.; s. of Leonard Bradbury and Esther Bradbury; m. Marguerite Susan McClure 1947; four d.; ed public schools; mem. SFWA (pres. 1951–53), Screen Writers' Guild of America (bd of dirs 1957–61); O. Henry Prizes 1947, 1948, Nat. Inst. of Arts and Letters Award 1954, Writers' Club Award 1974, Balrog Award for Best Poet 1979, PEN Body of Work Award 1985, Nat. Book Foundation Hon. Medal 2000, Pulitzer Prize Special Citation 2007. *Plays:* The Meadow 1948, Way in the Middle of the Air 1962, The Anthem Sprinters and Other Antics 1963, The World of Ray Bradbury 1964, The Wonderful Ice-Cream Suit 1965, Leviathan 99 1966, The Day it Rained Forever (play of novel A Medicine for Melancholy) 1966, The Pedestrian 1966, Christus Apollo 1969, Madrigals for the Space Age 1972, Pillars of Fire and Other Plays for Today, Tomorrow, and Beyond Tomorrow 1975, That Ghost, That Bride of Time: Excerpts from a Play-in-Progress 1976, The Martian Chronicles 1977, A Device Out of Time 1986, Falling Upward 1988. *Screenplays:* It Came from Outer Space 1952, Moby Dick 1954, Icarus Montgolfier Wright 1961, The Picasso Summer 1968; TV scripts include Alfred Hitchcock Show, Twilight Zone. *Publications:* fiction: The Martian Chronicles 1950, Fahrenheit 451 1953, Switch on the Night 1955, Dandelion Wine 1957, Something Wicked This Way Comes 1962, R is for Rocket 1962, S is for Space 1966, The Halloween Tree 1972, Death is a Lonely Business 1985, A Graveyard for Lunatics 1990, Green Shadows, White Whale 1992; short story collections: Dark Carnival 1947, The Illustrated Man 1951, The Golden Apples of the Sun 1953, The October Country 1955, A Medicine for Melancholy 1959, The Ghoul Keepers 1961, The Small Assassin 1962, The Machineries of Joy 1964, The Vintage Bradbury 1965, The Autumn People 1965, Tomorrow Midnight 1966, Twice Twenty-Two 1966, I Sing the Body Electric! 1969, Bloch and Bradbury: Ten Masterpieces of Science Fiction (with Robert Bloch) 1969, Whispers From Beyond (with Robert Bloch) 1972, Harrap 1975, Long After Midnight 1976, To Sing Strange Songs 1979, The Stories of Ray Bradbury 1980, The Dinosaur Tales 1983, A Memory of Murder 1984, The Toynbee Convector 1988, Kaleidoscope 1994, Quicker Than the Eye 1996, Driving Blind 1997, Now and Forever 2008, Marionettes Inc. 2009; non-fiction: Teacher's Guide: Science Fiction 1968, Zen and the Art of Writing 1973, Mars and the Mind of Man 1973, The Mummies of Guanajuato 1978, Beyond 1984: Remembrance of Things Future 1979, Los Angeles 1984, Orange County 1985, Yestermorrow: Obvious Answers to Impossible Futures 1991, Ray Bradbury on Stage: A Chrestomathy of his Plays 1991, Journey to Far Metaphor: Further Essays on Creativity, Writing, Literature and the Arts 1994, The First Book of Dichotomy, The Second Book of Symbiosis 1995, Bradbury Speaks: Too Soon from the Cave, Too Far from the Stars 2005; poetry: Old Ahab's Friend, and Friend to Noah, Speaks his Piece: A Celebration 1971, When Elephants Last in the Dooryard Bloomed 1972, That Son of Richard III: A Birth Announcement 1974, Where Robot Mice and Robot Men Run Round in Robot Towns 1977, Twin Hieroglyphs That Swim the River Dust 1978, The Bike Repairman 1978, The Author Considers his Resources 1979, The Aqueduct 1979, The Attic Where the Meadow Greens 1979, The Last Circus 1980, The Ghosts of Forever 1980, The Haunted Computer and the Android Pope 1981, The Complete Poems of Ray Bradbury 1982, The Love Affair 1983, Forever and the Earth 1984, Death Has Lost its Charm for Me 1987. *Leisure interests:* oil painting, ceramics, collecting native masks. *Address:* c/o Bantam Doubleday Dell, 1540 Broadway, New York, NY 10036 (office); c/o Avon Books, 1350 Avenue of the Americas, New York, NY 10019 (office); 10265 Cheviot Drive, Los Angeles, CA 90064, USA (home).

BRADEMAS, John, DPhil; American fmr politician and university administrator; *President Emeritus, New York University;* b. 2 March 1927, Mishawaka, Ind.; s. of Stephen J. Brademas and Beatrice Goble; m. Mary Ellen Briggs 1977; ed Harvard Univ. and Univ. of Oxford; Legis. Asst to Senator Pat McNamara; Admin. Asst to Rep. Thomas L. Ashley 1955; Exec. Asst to presidential nominee Stevenson 1955–56; Asst Prof. of Political Science, St Mary's Coll. Notre Dame, Ind. 1957–58; mem. 86th–96th Congresses from 3rd Ind. Dist; Chief Deputy Majority Whip 93rd–94th Congresses; Majority Whip 95th–96th Congresses; Pres. New York Univ. 1981–92, Pres. Emer. 1992–, currently Pres. King Juan Carlos I of Spain Center, New York Univ. Foundation; Chair. Pres.'s Comm. on the Arts and Humanities 1994; fmr mem. Bd Dirs and Chair. American Ditchley Foundation, currently a Gov. The Ditchley Foundation; fmr Chair. Fed. Reserve Bank of New York, Nat. Endowment for Democracy 1993–2001; Dir RCA/NBC, Scholastic Inc., New York Stock Exchange, Rockefeller Foundation; Founder John Brademas Center for the Study of Congress, New York Univ.; fmr mem. Cen. Comm. WCC, Trilateral Comm., Bd Aspen Inst., Overseers of Harvard, New York Stock Exchange, Rockefeller Foundation, Univ. of Notre Dame; Trustee, New York Univ., World Conf. of Religions for Peace; mem. Nat. Acad. of Educ., Acad. of Athens, Nat. Acad. of Educ. of Argentina, European Acad. of Sciences and Arts; Fellow, American Acad. of Arts and Sciences; Hon. Fellow, Brasenose Coll. Oxford; Gran Cruz de la Orden de Alfonso X el Sabio (Spain) 1997, Grand Cross of the Order of Makarios the III (Cyprus) 2007; hon. degrees from 51 colls and univs; Annual Gold Medal of Spanish Inst. 1984, Public Leadership in the Arts Awards 2004, and many other awards and distinctions. *Publications:* Anarcosindicalismo y revolución en España, 1930–37 1974, Washington, DC to Washington Square 1986, The Politics of Education: Conflict and Consensus on Capitol Hill 1987. *Leisure interests:* reading, travel. *Address:* Office of the President Emeritus, New York University King Juan Carlos I Center, 53 Washington Square South, New York, NY 10012, USA (office). *Telephone:* (22) 998-3636 (office). *Fax:* (212) 995-4810 (office). *E-mail:* jb1@nyu.edu (office). *Website:* www.nyu.edu (office).

BRADFORD, Barbara Taylor, OBE; British writer and journalist; b. Leeds, England; d. of Winston Taylor and Freda Walker; m. Robert Bradford 1963; reporter, Yorkshire Evening Post 1949–51, Women's Ed. 1951–53; Fashion Ed. Woman's Own 1953–54; columnist, London Evening News 1955–57; Exec. Ed. London American 1959–62; Ed. Nat. Design Center Magazine 1965–69; syndicated columnist, Newsday Specials, Long Island 1968–70; nat. syndicated columnist, Chicago Tribune-New York (News Syndicate), New York 1970–75, Los Angeles Times Syndicate 1975–81; Dir Library of Congress, DL; mem. Bd American Heritage Dictionary, Police Athletic League, Author's Guild Foundation 1989–; Girls Inc.; Hon. DLit (Leeds) 1990, (Bradford) 1995; Hon. DHumLit (Teikyo Post Univ.) 1996; numerous awards and prizes. *Television:* ten novels adapted into TV mini-series. *Publications:* Complete Encyclopaedia of Homemaking Ideas 1968, A Garland of Children's Verse 1968, How to be the Perfect Wife 1969, Easy Steps to Successful Decorating 1971, How to Solve your Decorating Problems 1976, Decorating Ideas for Casual Living 1977, Making Space Grow 1979, A Woman of Substance (novel) 1979, Luxury Designs for Apartment Living 1981, Voice of the Heart 1983, Hold the Dream 1985, Act of Will (novel) 1986, To Be The Best 1988, The Women in his Life (novel) 1990, Remember (novel) 1991, Angel (novel) 1993, Everything to Gain (novel) 1994, Dangerous to Know (novel) 1995, Love in Another Town (novel) 1995, Her Own Rules 1996, A Secret Affair 1996, Power of a Woman 1997, A Sudden Change of Heart 1998, Where You Belong 2000, The Triumph of Katie Byrne 2001, Three Weeks in Paris 2002, Emma's Secret 2003, Just Rewards 2006, The Ravenscar Dynasty 2007, Heirs of Ravenscar 2007. *Leisure interests:* boating, travelling, art collecting. *Address:* Bradford Enterprises, 450 Park Avenue, New York, NY 10022, USA. *Telephone:* (212) 308-7390. *Fax:* (212) 935-1636. *Website:* www.barbarataylorbradford.com.

BRADFORD, Max, MCom; New Zealand politician and economist; b. 1942, Christchurch; s. of Robert Bradford and Ella Bradford; m. 1st Janet Grieve (divorced); m. 2nd Rosemary Bradford; two step-d.; ed Univ. of Canterbury, NZ; fmr mem. staff of Treasury and of IMF, Washington, DC, Chief Exec. NZ Bankers' Assen; econ. and financial consultant; Nat. Party MP for Tarawera (now for Rotorua) 1990–; Minister of Labour, Energy, Immigration and Business Devt 1996–98, of Labour, Energy, Defence, Enterprise and Commerce 1998–99, of Tertiary Educ. 1999; fmr Chief Exec. Nat. Party. *Leisure interests:* fishing, music, reading, sailing. *Address:* Parliament Buildings, Wellington, New Zealand (office). *Telephone:* (4) 471-9577 (office); (4) 971-1011 (office). *Fax:* (4) 472-4169 (office). *E-mail:* max.bradford@parliament.govt.nz (office). *Website:* www.maxbradford.co.nz (home).

BRADFORD, William E.; Canadian insurance industry executive; b. 14 Oct. 1933, Montreal; s. of the late Elwood Joseph Bradford and Jessie (née Murray) Bradford; m. Dolores MacDonnell 1954; three s. four d.; ed Concordia Univ., Montreal; with Northern Electric Co. Ltd 1950–59, Canada Iron Foundries Ltd 1959–62; Asst Controller, Reynolds Extrusion Co. Ltd 1962–66; Vice-Pres. and Controller, Churchill Falls (Labrador) Corpn Ltd 1967–70; Vice-Pres. and Sr Financial Officer, Brinco 1970–74; Exec. Vice-Pres. for Finance, Bank of Montreal 1975, for Finance and Admin. 1976, Exec. Vice-Pres. and Deputy Gen. Man. Domestic Banking 1978, also Gen. Man. 1979, Exec. Vice-Pres., Chief Gen. Man. Bank of Montreal 1980, Pres. 1981–83, Deputy Chair. 1983–87; Pres. and CEO N American Life Assurance Co. (now Manulife Financial) 1987–93, Deputy Chair. and CEO 1993–94; Fellow Certified Gen. Accountants' Assen of Ont., Financial Execs Inst. *Leisure interests:* tennis, squash, golf, skiing, hunting, fishing. *Address:* 1333 Watersedge Road, Mississauga, ON L5J 1A3, Canada (home).

BRADLEE, Benjamin Crowninshield, AB; American newspaper editor; *Vice-President at Large, Washington Post;* b. 26 Aug. 1921, Boston; s. of Frederick Bradlee and Josephine de Gersdorff; m. 1st Jean Saltonstall 1942; one s.; m. 2nd Antoinette Pinchot 1956; one s. one d.; m. 3rd Sally Quinn 1978, one s.; ed Harvard Univ.; reporter, NH Sunday News, Manchester 1946–48, Washington Post 1948–51; Press Attaché, US Embassy, Paris 1951–53; European corresp. Newsweek, Paris 1953–57; reporter, Washington Bureau, Newsweek 1957–61, Sr Ed. and Chief of Bureau 1961–65; Man. Ed. Washington Post 1965–68, Vice-Pres. and Exec. Ed. 1968–91, Vice-Pres. at Large 1991–; Chair. History of St Mary's City Comm. 1992–; Burton Benjamin Award 1995. *Publications:* That Special Grace 1964, Conversations with Kennedy 1975, A Good Life: Newspapering and Other Adventures (autobiog.) 1995. *Address:* 1150 15th Street, NW, Washington, DC 20071-0001, USA (home). *Telephone:* (202) 334-7510 (home).

BRADLEY, Bill, MA; American business executive, fmr politician and fmr professional basketball player; *Managing Director, Allen & Company LLC;* b. 28 July 1943, Crystal City, Mo.; s. of Warren W. Bradley and Susan Crowe; m. Ernestine Schlant 1974; one d.; ed Princeton and Oxford Univs; served in USAF Reserve 1967; after Princeton, attended Univ. of Oxford as Rhodes Scholar; returned to USA to play professional basketball with New York Knickerbockers of Nat. Basketball Assen (NBA) 1967–77; Senator from New Jersey 1979–96; Payne Dist Prof., Inst. for Int. Studies, Stanford Univ., Calif. 1997–98; fmr Chief Outside Advisor to McKinsey & Co.'s non-profit practice; fmr Sr Advisor and Vice Chair. of Int. Council, J.P. Morgan & Co.; unsuccessful bid for Democratic Party nomination for President 2000; currently Man. Dir Allen & Company LLC (investment bank); mem. Bd of Dirs Seagate Tech., Starbucks Coffee Co., Willis Group Holdings Ltd, Quinstreet Inc. 2004–; mem. Advisory Bd Hakluyt & Co. (UK) 2005–; fmr Visiting Prof. Stanford Univ., Notre Dame Univ., Univ. of Maryland; Hon. DCL (Univ. of Oxford) 2003; elected mem. Basketball Hall of Fame. *Publications:* Life on the Run 1976, The Fair Tax 1984, Time Present, Time Past 1996, Values of the Game 1998, The New American Story 2007. *Address:* c/o Allen & Company LLC, 711 Fifth Avenue, 9th Floor, New York, NY 10022 (office); 1661 Page Mill Road, Palo Alto, CA 94304, USA (home). *Telephone:* (212) 832-8000 (office). *Fax:* (212) 832-8023 (office).

BRADLEY, Clive, CBE, MA; British publishing and media executive and barrister; *Convenor, Confederation of Information Communication Industries;* b. 25 July 1934, London; s. of the late Alfred Bradley and Annie Kathleen. Bradley; ed Felsted School, Essex, Clare Coll., Cambridge and Yale Univ., USA; barrister (Middle Temple); with BBC 1961–63; Broadcasting Officer, Labour Party 1963–65; Political Ed., The Statist 1965–67; Group Labour Adviser, Int. Publishing Corpn and Deputy Gen. Man. Mirror Group Newspapers 1967–73; Dir The Observer 1973–75; Chief Exec. The Publishers Asscn 1976–97; Convenor Confed. of Information Communication Industries 1984–; Chair. Central London Valuation Tribunal, Richmond upon Thames Arts Council 2003–; Deputy Chair. Age Concern, Richmond 2001–03; Gov. Felsted School. *Publications:* many articles and broadcasts on politics, econs, industrial relations, industry media and current affairs. *Leisure interests:* politics, reading, walking. *Address:* 8 Northumberland Place, Richmond-upon-Thames, Surrey TW10 6TS, England (home). *Telephone:* (20) 8940-7172 (home). *Fax:* (20) 8940-7603 (home). *E-mail:* bradley_clive@btopenworld.com (home).

BRADLEY, Daniel Joseph, PhD, FRS, FIEEE, FInstP, MRIA; Irish physicist and academic; *Emeritus Fellow, Physics Department, Trinity College, Dublin;* b. 18 Jan. 1928; s. of late John Bradley and Margaret Bradley; m. Winefride M. T. O'Connor 1958; four s. one d.; ed St Columb's Coll., Derry, St Mary's Training Coll., Belfast, Birkbeck and Royal Holloway Colls, London; primary school teacher, Londonderry 1947–53, secondary school teacher, London area 1953–57; Asst Lecturer, Royal Holloway Coll. 1957–60; lecturer, Imperial Coll. of Science and Tech. 1960–64; Reader, Royal Holloway Coll. 1964–66; Prof. and Head of Dept of Pure and Applied Physics, Queen's Univ., Belfast 1966–73; Prof. of Optics, Imperial Coll. 1973–80, Head, Dept of Physics 1976–80, Emer. Prof. London Univ. 1980–; Prof. of Optical Electronics, Trinity Coll., Dublin 1980–, Emer. Fellow 1983–; Visiting Scientist, MIT 1965; Consultant, Harvard Observatory 1966; Chair. Laser Facility Cttee SRC 1976–79, British Nat. Cttee for Physics 1979–80, Quantum Electronics Comm. IUPAP 1982; mem. Rutherford Lab. Establishment Cttee SRC 1977–79, Science Bd, SRC 1977–80; mem. Council, Royal Soc. 1979–80; Fellow, Optical Soc. of America; Fellow, Trinity Coll., Dublin; Hon. DSc (New Univ., Ulster) 1983, (Belfast) 1986; Thomas Young Medal, Inst. of Physics 1975; Royal Medal, Royal Soc. 1983, Charles Hard Townes Award of Optical Soc. of America 1989, Cunningham Medal, Royal Irish Acad. 2001. *Publications:* papers on optics, lasers, spectroscopy, chronoscopy and astronomy in learned journals. *Leisure interests:* television. *Address:* c/o Physics Department, Trinity College, College Green, Dublin 2, Ireland. *Telephone:* (1) 6772941.

BRADLEY, David John, MA, DM, FRCP, FRCPath, FFPHM, FIBiol, FMedSci; British medical scientist and academic; *Ross Professor Emeritus, Ross Institute of Tropical Hygiene, London School of Hygiene and Tropical Medicine;* b. 12 Jan. 1937; s. of the late Harold Robert Bradley and of Mona Bradley; m. Lorne Marie Farquhar 1961 (divorced 1989); two s. two d.; ed Wyggeston Grammar School, Leicester, Selwyn Coll. Cambridge and Univ. Coll. Hosp. Medical School, London; Univ. Coll. Hosp. 1960–61; Medical Research Officer, Ross Inst. Bilharzia Research Unit, Mwanza, Tanzania 1961–64; lecturer, Makerere Medical School, Univ. of E Africa 1964–66; Sr lecturer in Preventive Medicine 1966–69; Royal Soc. Tropical Research Fellow 1969–73; Sr Research Fellow, Staines Medical Fellow, Exeter Coll. Oxford 1971–74; Clinical Reader in Pathology, Univ. of Oxford Clinical Medical School 1973–74; Prof. of Tropical Hygiene, Univ. of London, Dir and Head of Dept Ross Inst. of Tropical Hygiene, London School of Hygiene and Tropical Medicine 1974–2000, Ross Prof. Emer. 2000–, Chair. Div. of Communicable and Tropical Diseases 1982–88; Visiting Prof. Univ. of Wales Coll. of Medicine 1995–; numerous professional appointments, consultancies to int. orgs etc.; corresp. mem. German Tropenmedizingesellschaft; foreign corresp. mem. Royal Belgian Acad. of Medicine; numerous awards and distinctions. *Publications:* five books and more than 150 papers on tropical medicine and related topics. *Leisure interests:* natural history, landscape gardens, travel. *Address:* Ross Institute, London School of Hygiene and Tropical Medicine, Keppel Street, London, WC1E 7HT (office); Flat 3, 1 Taviton Street, London, WC1H 0BT, England (home). *Telephone:* (20) 7927-2216 (office); (20) 7383-0228 (home). *Fax:* (20) 7580-9075 (office). *E-mail:* David.Bradley@lshtm.ac.uk. *Website:* www.lshtm.ac.uk.

BRADLEY, Donald Charlton, PhD, DSc, FRSC, FRSA, FRS; British inorganic chemist and academic; *Professor Emeritus, Queen Mary College, University of London;* b. 7 Nov. 1924, London; m. 1st Constance Joy Hazeldean 1948 (died 1985); one s.; m. 2nd Ann Levy (née MacDonald) 1990; ed Hove Co. School for Boys, Birkbeck Coll., Univ. of London; Research Asst, British Electrical and Allied Industries Research Asscn 1941–47; Asst Lecturer in Chem., Birkbeck Coll. 1949–52, Lecturer 1952–59; Prof. of Chem., Univ. of Western Ont. 1959–64; Prof. of Inorganic Chem., Queen Mary Coll., Univ. of London 1965–87, Emer. Prof. 1988–, Head of Chem. Dept 1978–82, Fellow 1988; Chair. Bd of Studies in Chem. and Chemical Industries, Univ. of London 1977–79; mem. Senate, London Univ. 1981–87; Pres. Dalton Div. Royal Soc. Chem.; MRI (mem. Council 1987–93, Hon. Sec. 1988–93); Exec. Ed. Polyhedron 1982–97; Fellow Royal Soc. 1980; Freeman City of London 1996; Ludwig Mond Medal and Lectureship, Royal Soc. Chem. 1987, Royal (Queen's) Medal, Royal Soc. 1998. *Publications:* Metal Alkoxides (jt author) 1978, Alkoxo and Aryloxo Derivatives of Metals (jt author) 2001; over 260 scientific papers. *Leisure interests:* travelling, gardening, music, archaeology. *Address:* Department of Chemistry, Queen Mary College, University of London, Mile End Road, London, E1 4NS (office); 171 Shakespeare Tower, Barbican, London, EC2Y 8DR, England (home). *Telephone:* (20) 7882-5025 (office); (20) 7638-

2054 (home). *E-mail:* d.c.bradley@qmul.ac.uk (office); don@bradleyhome.net (home). *Website:* www.chem.qmul.ac.uk (office).

BRADLEY, Michael Carl, MBE; British trade union official; *General Secretary, General Federation of Trade Unions;* b. 17 Feb. 1951, Birmingham; s. of Ronald William Bradley and Doris Florence Bradley (née Hill); m. Janice Bradley (née Holmes) 1973; ed Aldridge Grammar School, Brooklyn Coll., Birmingham; Exec. Officer, Inland Revenue 1971–74; Payroll Admin. Smedley H.P. Foods 1974–80; Researcher Transport and Gen. Workers Union (TGWU) 1980–82; Staff Section Organizer Nat. Union of Lock and Metal Workers 1982–87, Gen. Sec. 1988–92; Gen. Sec. Gen. Fed. of Trade Unions 1993–; mem. Unity Trust Advisory Cttee 1986–, Social Security Appeals Tribunal 1986–98, Governing Council, Ruskin Coll. Oxford 1994–, Trade Union Labour Party Liaison Cttee 1996–; Chair. Trade Union Co-ordinating Cttee 2003–; Gov. The Northern Coll., Barnsley 2000–; Trustee, Trade Union Unit Charitable Trust 2000–; Hon. Fellow, Oxford Brookes Univ. 2006. *Leisure interests:* sport, reading, music. *Address:* General Federation of Trade Unions, Central House, Upper Woburn Place, London, WC1H 0HY, England (office). *Telephone:* (20) 7388-0852 (office). *Fax:* (20) 7383-0820 (office). *E-mail:* mike@gftu.org.uk (office). *Website:* www.gftu.org.uk (office).

BRADLEY, Stephen Edward; British diplomatist; *Consul General, Hong Kong Special Administrative Region;* b. 4 April 1958; m. Elizabeth Bradley; one s. one d.; ed Balliol Coll., Oxford, Fudan Univ., Shanghai; joined FCO 1981, Afghan/Pakistan Desk, S Asian Dept 1981–83; Second Sec., Econ., later First Sec., Chancery, British Embassy, Tokyo 1983–87; Deputy Political Adviser to Hong Kong Govt 1988–93; FCO French Desk, W European Dept 1995; Deputy Head of Near East and N Africa FCO Dept 1996–97; Head of W Indian Atlantic Dept 1997–98; Dir of Trade and Investment Promotion, British Embassy, Paris 1999–2002; Minister, Deputy Head of Mission and Consul Gen., British Embassy, Beijing 2002; Consul-Gen., Hong Kong Special Admin. Region 2003–; Marketing Dir, Guinness Peat Aviation, Hong Kong 1987–88, Assoc. Dir, Lloyd George Investment Man., Hong Kong 1993–95, New Millennium Experience Co. 1998–99. *Leisure interests:* books, gardens, travel, hiking. *Address:* British Consulate-General, 1 Supreme Court Road, Hong Kong (office). *Telephone:* 29013000 (office). *Fax:* 29013066 (office).

BRADMAN, Godfrey Michael, FCA; British business executive; b. 9 Sept. 1936; s. of William I. Bradman and Anne Bradman (née Goldsweig); m. Susan Bennett 1975; two s. three d.; Sr Pnr, Godfrey Bradman & Co. (chartered accountants) 1961; Chair. Bankers London Mercantile Corpn 1969; Jt Chair. Broadgate Devts 1984–91; Chair. European Land and Property Corpn PLC 1992–2003, Ashpost Finance Ltd 1993–2004, Vic. Quay 1993–2000, Pond-bridge Europe Ltd 1994–2000; Deputy Chair. Kyp Holdings PLC 2003–; Founder CLEAR (Campaign for Lead-Free Air) 1981–91; Jt Founder and Pres. Campaign for Freedom of Information 1983–, Founder and Chair. Citizen Action and European Citizen Action 1983–91; Chair. Friends of the Earth Trust 1983–91; Founder and Dir AIDS Policy Unit 1987–90; Pres. Soc. for the Protection of Unborn Children Educational Research Trust 1987–2006; mem. Bd of Dirs Property and Land Investment Corpn 2001–, Midatech Ltd 2004–, Metropolitan and Suburban Ltd 2006–; mem. Council UN Int. Year of Shelter for the Homeless 1987; mem. governing body London School of Hygiene and Tropical Medicine 1988–91; Founder and Jt Chair. Parents Against Tobacco Campaign; Founder Opren Victims Campaign; Trustee Right to Life Charitable Trust; Wilkins Fellow, Cambridge 1999; Hon. Fellow, King's Coll. London, Downing Coll., Cambridge; Hon. DSc (Salford). *Leisure interests:* reading. *Address:* 1 Berkeley Street, London, W1J 8DJ, England. *Telephone:* (20) 7706-0189. *E-mail:* gb@godfreybradman.com.

BRADSHAW, Peter, BA, FRS; American (b. British) professor of aerodynamics; *Professor Emeritus of Engineering, Stanford University;* b. 26 Dec. 1935, Torquay; s. of J. W. N. Bradshaw and F. W. G. Bradshaw (née Finch); m. Sheila Dorothy Brown 1968; ed Torquay Grammar School, St John's Coll., Cambridge; Scientific Officer, Aerodynamics Div., Nat. Physical Lab., Teddington 1957–69; Sr Lecturer, Dept of Aeronautics, Imperial Coll., Univ. of London 1969–71, Reader 1971–78, Prof. of Experimental Aerodynamics 1978–88; Thomas V. Jones Prof. of Eng, Dept of Mechanical Eng, Stanford Univ. 1988–95, Prof. Emer. 1996–; Hon. DSc (Exeter) 1990; Royal Aeronautical Soc. Bronze Medal 1971, Royal Aeronautical Soc. Busk Prize 1972, AIAA Fluid Dynamics Award 1994. *Publications include:* Experimental Fluid Mechanics 1964, An Introduction to Turbulence 1971, Momentum Transfer in Boundary Layers (with T. Cebeci) 1977, Engineering Calculation Methods for Turbulent Flow (with T. Cebeci and J. H. Whitelaw) 1981, Convective Heat Transfer (with T. Cebeci) 1984. *Leisure interests:* ancient history, walking. *Address:* Thermosciences Division, Department of Mechanical Engineering, Stanford University, Stanford, CA 94305-3032, USA (office). *Telephone:* (650) 725-0704 (office). *Fax:* (650) 725-4862 (office). *E-mail:* bradshaw@stanford.edu (office). *Website:* www.stanford.edu/~bradshaw (office).

BRADY, Conor, BA, MA; Irish journalist and academic; *Commissioner, Garda Síochána Ombudsman Commission;* b. 24 April 1949, Dublin; s. of Conor Brady and Amy MacCarthy; m. Ann Byron 1971; two s.; ed Mount St Joseph Cistercian Abbey, Univ. Coll. Dublin; reporter Irish Times 1969–73, Asst Ed. 1977–81, Dir and Deputy Ed. 1984–86, Ed. and Group Editorial Dir 1986–2002, Ed. Emer. 2002–; Ed. Garda Review 1973–74; Tutor, Dept of Politics, Univ. Coll. Dublin 1973–74 Presenter/Reporter RTE News At One and This Week 1974–75; Ed. The Sunday Tribune 1981–82; Chair. Bd of Counsellors, European Journalism Centre, Maastricht 1993–98; Pres. World Eds' Forum, Paris 1995–2000; mem. Bd of Dirs World Press Freedom Cttee, Federation International des Editeurs de Journeaux 1995–2000; Commr, Garda Síochána Ombudsman Comm. 2006–; Visiting Prof., John Jay Coll., CUNY; Sr Teaching Fellow, Michael Smurfit Grad. School of Business, Univ. Coll. Dublin; Chair. British-Irish Asscn; Cttee Mem. UNESCO Int. Press

Freedom; Award for Outstanding Work in Irish Journalism 1979. *Publications:* Guardian of the Peace 1974, Up With The Times 2005. *Leisure interests:* travel, reading, swimming. *Address:* Garda Síochána Ombudsman Commission, 150 Abbey Street Upper, Dublin 1, Ireland (office). *Telephone:* (1) 8716727 (office); 89-0600800 (mobile). *Fax:* (1) 8147023 (office). *E-mail:* info@gsoc.ie (office). *Website:* www.gardaombudsman.ie (office).

BRADY, James S., BS; American fmr government official and lawyer; *Trustee, Brady Center to Prevent Gun Violence;* b. 29 Aug. 1940, Centralia, Ill.; m. Sarah Kemp; one s., one d.; ed Univ of Ill.; staff member Minority Leader US Senate Everett Dirksen 1961–62; Honor Intern US Dept of Justice 1962 then returned to Ill.; mem. faculty Southern Ill. Univ. 1964–65; Asst Nat. Sales Man. and Exec. Man. to Pres. Lear-Seigler 1965–66; Dir Legislation and Public Affairs Ill. State Medical Soc. 1966–68; Chicago Office Man. Whitaker and Baxter 1968–69; Exec. Vice-Pres. James and Thomas Advertising and Public Relations 1969–73; Communications Consultant 1973 then Special Asst US Sec. Housing and Urban Devt Washington DC 1973–75; Special Asst Dir US Office of Man. and Budget 1975–76; Asst US Sec. of Defense 1976–77; joined staff of Senator William V. Roth Jr. (R-DE) 1977–79; Press Sec. presential candidate John Connally 1979; Dir Public Affairs Reagan-Bush Cttee and Spokesperson Office of Pres.-Elect 1980; Asst to Pres. Ronald Reagan and White House Press Sec. 1981–88; gunshot wound to head during attempt to assassinate Pres. Reagan March 1981; lobby group Brady Campaign to Prevent Gun Violence (fmrly Handgun Control) 1988–; Bd Trustees Brady Center to Prevent Handgun Violence (fmrly Center to Prevent Handgun Violence); Vice-Chair. Nat. Head Injury Foundation, Nat. Org. on Disability; numerous awards including Robert A. Taft Award for Outstanding Service to Republican Party, Significant Sigma Chi Award, Distringuished Eagle Award from Boy Scouts of America, Lincoln Award; with wife awards include Advancement Communications Award, Lenore and George W. Romney Citizen Volunteer Award, John W. Gardner Leadership Award, Margaret Chase Smith Award, Jules Cohen Memorial Award; White House Press Briefing Room officially named James S. Brady Briefing Room 2000. *Address:* Brady Center to Prevent Gun Violence, 1225 Eye Street, NW, Washington, DC 20005 (office). *Telephone:* (202) 289-7319 (office). *Fax:* (202) 408-1851 (office). *Website:* www.bradycenter.org (office).

BRADY, Nicholas F.; American fmr government official, investment banker and financial executive; *Chairman, Darby Overseas Investment Ltd.;* b. 11 April 1930, New York; s. of James C. Brady and Eliot Brady; m. Katherine Douglas 1952; three s. one d.; ed Yale and Harvard Univs; with Dillon, Read and Co. Ltd 1954–82, fmr Chair., CEO 1982–88; Chair. Purolater Inc. 1971–87; US Treasury Sec. 1988–93; appointee to US Senate from NJ 1982; Chair. Templeton Latin American Investment Trust 1994–, est. Darby Overseas Investments 1994–; Dir Amerada Hess Corpn, Christiana Cos, H. J. Heinz Co.; Dir/Trustee US Templeton Funds; served on five Presidential comms including Chair. Presidential Task Force on Market Mechanisms (known as Brady Comm.), mem. Scowcroft Comm. on Strategic Forces, Kissinger Comm. on Cen. America, Packard Comm. on Defense Man.; fmr Chair. Jockey Club, New York. *Address:* Darby Overseas Investments Ltd 1133 Connecticut Avenue, NW Suite 400, Washington, DC 20036, USA (office). *Telephone:* (202) 872-0500 (office). *Fax:* (202) 872-1816 (office). *E-mail:* contact@doil.com (office). *Website:* www.darbyoverseas.com (office).

BRADY, Roscoe Owen, MD; American medical research scientist and academic; *Scientist Emeritus, National Institutes of Health;* b. 11 Oct. 1923, Philadelphia, Pa; s. of Roscoe O. Brady and Martha Roberts Brady; m. Bennett Carden Manning 1972; two s.; ed Pennsylvania State Univ., Harvard Medical School and Univ. of Pennsylvania; Thyroid Clinic Assoc., Mass Gen. Hosp., Boston; Nat. Research Council Fellow, Dept of Biochemistry, Univ. of Pa School of Medicine 1948–50, also US Public Health Special Research Fellow and Fellow in Clinical Medicine; Officer-in-Charge, Dept of Chem., US Naval Medical School 1952–54; Section Chief, Nat. Inst. of Neurological Diseases and Blindness (now Nat. Inst. of Neurological Disorders and Stroke), NIH 1954–67, Acting Chief, Lab. of Neurochemistry 1967–68, Asst Chief 1969–71, Chief, Developmental and Metabolic Neurology Br. 1972–2006, now Scientist Emer., NIH; Professorial Lecturer, Dept of Biochemistry, George Washington Univ. School of Medicine 1963–73; Adjunct Prof. of Biochemistry, Dept of Biochemistry, Georgetown Univ. School of Medicine 1965–; mem. of medical staff Children's Hosp., Wash., DC 1992–; mem. Inst. of Medicine, NAS; Dr hc (Uppsala) 2005; Gairdner Foundation Int. Award 1973, Cotzias Award, American Acad. of Neurology 1980, Passano Foundation Award 1982, Lasker Foundation Award 1982, Kovalenko Medal, NAS 1991, Alpert Foundation Prize, Harvard Medical School 1992, US Nat. Medal of Tech. and Innovation 2007. *Publications:* Neurochemistry of Nucleotides and Amino Acids (ed. with D. B. Tower) 1960, The Basic Neurosciences (ed.) 1975, The Molecular Basis of Lysosomal Storage Disorders (ed. with J. A. Barranger) 1984; and more than 440 scientific publs. *Leisure interests:* piano, cycling. *Address:* Building 10, Room 3D04, National Institutes of Health, 9000 Rockville Pike, Bethesda, MD 20892-1260, USA (office). *Telephone:* (301) 496-3286 (office); (301) 881-3474 (home). *Fax:* (301) 496-9480 (office). *E-mail:* bradyr@ninds.nih.gov (office); bradyroscoe@yahoo.com (home). *Website:* www.neuroscience.nih.gov (office).

BRADY, HE Cardinal Seán Baptist, DCL; Irish ecclesiastic; *Archbishop of Armagh and Primate of All Ireland;* b. 16 Aug. 1939, Laragh, Co. Cavan; s. of the late Andrew Brady and Teresa Smith; ed Caulfield Nat. School, St Patrick's Coll., Cavan, St Patrick's Coll., Maynooth, Irish Coll., Rome and Lateran Univ.; ordained priest 1964; language teacher, St Patrick's Coll. Cavan 1967–80; Diocesan Sec., Kilmore 1973–80; Vice-Rector Irish Coll., Rome 1980, Rector 1987–94; Parish Priest, Ballyhaise, Co. Cavan 1994; Coadjutor Archbishop of Armagh 1995–96, Archbishop of Armagh and Primate of All Ireland 1996–; cr. Cardinal (Cardinal-Priest of Ss. Quirico e Giulitta) 2007; served on Cavan Co. Bd of Gaelic Athletic Asscn. *Leisure interest:* Gaelic football. *Address:* Ara Coeli, Armagh, BT61 7QY, Northern Ireland. *Telephone:* (28) 37522045. *Fax:* (28) 37526182. *E-mail:* admin@aracoeli.com (office). *Website:* www.armagharchdiocese.org.

BRADY, Thomas Edward Patrick, Jr. (Tom); American football player; b. 3 Aug. 1977, San Mateo, CA; s. of Tom Brady, Sr and Galynn Johnson-Brady; m. Gisele Bündchen 2009; ed Junipero Serra High School, Univ. of Mich.; quarterback, New England Patriots 2000–; set Univ. of Mich. record completing 214 of 350 passes and 15 touchdowns 1999; drafted by New England Patriots of Nat. Football League (NFL) 2000; became youngest quarterback to win a Super Bowl 2001 season, won second Super Bowl 2003, third 2005; picked in 1995 Major League Baseball draft in 18th round as a catcher by the Montreal Expos; Superbowl Most Valuable Player (MVP) 2001 (third youngest player to win award), 2003 (fourth player to win multiple MVP awards). *Leisure interests:* golf, reading. *Address:* New England Patriots, 1 Patriot Place, Foxborough, MA 02035-1388, USA. *Website:* www.patriots.com.

BRAGG, Baron (Life Peer), cr. 1998, of Wigton in the County of Cumbria; **Melvyn Bragg,** MA, FRSL, FRTS; British author and television presenter; *Controller of Arts and Features, London Weekend TV;* b. 6 Oct. 1939, Carlisle; s. of Stanley Bragg and Mary E. Park; m. 1st Marie-Elisabeth Roche 1961 (deceased); one d.; m. 2nd Catherine M. Haste 1973; one s. one d.; ed Nelson-Thomlinson Grammar School, Wigton and Wadham Coll., Oxford; BBC Radio and TV Producer 1961–67; TV Presenter and Ed. The South Bank Show for ITV 1978–(2010); Head of Arts, London Weekend TV 1982–90, Controller of Arts and Features 1990–(2010); Deputy Chair. Border TV 1985–90, Chair. 1990–96; novelist 1965–; writer and broadcaster 1967–, writer and presenter of BBC Radio Four's Start the Week 1988–98, In Our Time 1998–, Routes of English 1999–, The Adventure of English 2001; mem. Arts Council and Chair. Literature Panel of Arts Council 1977–80; Pres. Cumbrians for Peace 1982–, Northern Arts 1983–87, Nat. Campaign for the Arts 1986–; Gov. LSE 1997–; Chancellor Leeds Univ. 1999–; mem. Bd Really Useful Co. 1989–90; Pres. Nat. Acad. of Writing; Pres. MIND; Appeal Chair. Royal Nat. Inst. for the Blind Talking Books Appeal 1998–2005; Hon. Fellow, Lancashire Polytechnic 1987, The Library Asscn 1994, Wadham Coll. Oxford 1995, Univ. of Wales, Cardiff 1996; Domus Fellow, St Catherine's Coll., Oxford 1990; Hon. DLitt (Liverpool) 1986, (CNAA) 1990, (Lancaster) 1990, (South Bank) 1997, (Leeds) 2000, (Bradford) 2000; Hon. DUniv (Open Univ.) 1988; Hon. DCL (Northumbria) 1994; Hon. DSc (UMIST) 1998, (Brunel) 2000; Dr hc (St. Andrews) 1993, (Sunderland) 2001; John Llewellyn-Rhys Memorial Award 1968, PEN Award for Fiction 1970, Richard Dimbleby Award for Outstanding Contribution to Television 1987, Ivor Novello Award for Best Musical 1985, VLV Award 2000, WHSmith Literary Award 2000, four Prix Italia awards, various BAFTA Awards. *Plays:* Mardi Gras 1976, Orion 1977, The Hired Man 1985, King Lear in New York 1992. *Screenplays:* Isadora, The Music Lovers, Jesus Christ Superstar, A Time to Dance. *Publications:* novels: For Want of a Nail 1965, The Second Inheritance 1966, Without a City Wall 1968, The Hired Man 1969, A Place in England 1970, The Nerve 1971, The Hunt 1972, Josh Lawton 1972, The Silken Net 1974, A Christmas Child 1976, Autumn Manoeuvres 1978, Kingdom Come 1980, Love and Glory 1983, The Cumbrian Trilogy 1984, The Maid of Buttermere 1987, A Time to Dance (televised 1992) 1990, Crystal Rooms 1992, Credo 1996, The Sword and the Miracle 1997, The Soldier's Return 1999, A Son of War 2001, Remember Me 2008; non-fiction: Speak for England 1976, Land of the Lakes 1983, Laurence Olivier 1984, Rich, The Life of Richard Burton 1988, The Seventh Seal: A Study on Ingmar Bergman 1993, On Giants' Shoulders 1998, The Adventure of English 2003, Crossing the Lines 2004, Twelve British Books That Changed the World 2006. *Leisure interests:* walking, watching football. *Address:* 12 Hampstead Hill Gardens, London, NW3 2PL, England (office). *Telephone:* (20) 7261-3128 (office). *Fax:* (20) 7261-3299 (office). *E-mail:* melvyn.bragg@granadamedia.com (office).

BRAGHIŞ, Dumitru; Moldovan politician and business executive; *Co-Leader, Moldova Noastra Alliance;* b. 28 Dec. 1957, Grătieşti; ed Institutul Politehnic din Chişinău; First Sec. Komsomol, Moldovan SSR 1989–91; Dir-Gen. Dept Foreign Econ. Relations, Ministry of the Economy and Reform 1995; First Deputy Minister of Economy and Reform 1997–99; Prime Minister of Moldova 1999–2001; mem. Parl. 2000–; Leader Social-Democratic Alliance 2001–03; Co-Leader Moldova Noastra (AMN–Our Moldova) Alliance, following merger of Social-Democratic Alliance and two other centrist parties 2003–. *Address:* Alianţa Moldova Noastra, str. Puşkin A, Chişinău, Moldova (office). *Telephone:* (2) 54-85-38. *E-mail:* vitalia@ch.moldpac.md. *Website:* www.amn.md.

BRAHAM, Allan John Witney, PhD; British fmr gallery curator and author; b. 19 Aug. 1937, Croydon; s. of Dudley Braham and Florence Mears; m. Helen Clare Butterworth 1963 (divorced 2004); two d.; ed Dulwich Coll., Courtauld Inst. and London Univ.; Asst Keeper Nat. Gallery 1962, Deputy Keeper 1973, Keeper and Deputy Dir 1978–88; Hitchcock Medal, Bannister Fletcher Prize for writings 1980. *Publications include:* François Mansart (with Peter Smith) 1973, Carlo Fontana: The Drawings at Windsor (with Hellmut Hager) 1977, The Architecture of the French Enlightenment 1980, El Greco to Goya 1981, Italian Paintings of the Sixteenth Century 1985. *Leisure interest:* history of architecture. *Address:* Catherine Lodge, 40 Woodside Park Rd, London, N12 8RP, England (home).

BRAHIC, André; French astronomer and astrophysicist; *Director, Laboratory Gamma-gravitation, Commissariat a l'Energie Atomique;* b. 1942, Paris; Prof., Université de Paris VII Denis Diderot, Dir Lab. Gamma-gravitation, Commissariat a l'Energie Atomique; worked with Évry Schatzman and Michel Hénon on supernovas, chaos theory, the dynamics of galaxies, planetary rings and the formation of the Solar System; specialist in exploration of Solar System by space probes; developed one of main models for rings of Saturn

1974; mem. Voyager spacecraft Imaging Team 1981; co-discoverer, with Bruno Sicardy and William Hubbard, of the rings of Neptune (five years before photographic confirmation by Voyager) 1984; mem. Cassini spacecraft Imaging Team 2004; Carl Sagan Medal for Excellence in Public Communication in Planetary Science, Div. for Planetary Sciences 2001, Prix Jean-Perrin 2006. *Publications include:* Enfants du Soleil (Children of the Sun) 1999, Planètes et Satellites 2001, Lumières d'étoiles – Les couleurs de l'invisible (with Isabelle Grenier) 2008; chapter: Saturn's Rings Seen by Cassini Spacecraft: Discoveries, Questions and New Problems, in, Traffic and Granular Flow (co-ed. Schadschneider, Poschel, Kuhne and Schreckenberg) 2005; numerous scientific papers in professional journals. *Address:* CEA/Saclay, 91191 Gif-sur-Yvette Cedex, France (office). *Telephone:* 1-69-08-60-00 (office). *E-mail:* brahic@cea.fr (office). *Website:* www.cea.fr (office); www-centre-saclay.cea.fr (office).

BRAHIMI, Abdelhamid, DEcon; Algerian politician and academic; *Director-General, Centre for Maghreb Studies;* b. 2 April 1936, Constantine; m.; one c.; officer, Nat. Liberation Army 1956–62; Wali of Annaba (Govt Rep. in province of Annaba) 1963–65; Dir OCI (Algerian-French Bd for promotion of industrial co-operation) 1968–70; Prof. of Econs, Univ. of Algiers 1970–75; Chair. SONATRACH Inc., USA 1976–78; Minister of Planning and Regional Devt 1979–83; Prime Minister of Algeria 1984–88; fled to UK after assasination attempt 1990s; currently Dir-Gen., Centre for Maghreb Studies, London. *Publications include:* Dimensions et perspectives du monde arabe 1977, Stratégies de développement pour l'Algérie (1962-1991) 1992, Justice sociale et développement en économie islamique 1993, Le Maghreb à la croisée des chemins à l'ombre des transformations mondiales (1956-1995) 1996, Aux origines de la tragédie algérienne (1958-2000) 2000.

BRAHIMI, Lakhdar, Algerian UN official (retd), diplomatist and politician; b. 1 Jan. 1934; m.; three c.; ed in Algeria and France; FLN Rep. in SE Asia 1956–61; Perm. Rep. to Arab League, Cairo 1963–70; Amb. to UK 1971–79, to Egypt and Sudan; Diplomatic Adviser to Pres. of Algeria 1982–84; Under-Sec.-Gen., League of Arab States 1984–91, Special Envoy Arab League Tripartite Cttee to Lebanon 1989–91; Minister of Foreign Affairs 1991–93; Rapporteur, UN Conf. on Environment and Devt (Earth Summit) 1992; Special Rep. of UN Sec.-Gen. in SA –1994, in Haiti 1994–96; Under-Sec.-Gen. for Special Assignments in Support of Preventive and Peacemaking Efforts of the Sec.-Gen. 1997; Special Envoy of UN Sec.-Gen. in Afghanistan, UN Special Mission to Afghanistan (UNSMA) 1997–99, Special Rep. 2001–04; Special Envoy of UN Sec.-Gen. in Angola 1998; Special Adviser to UN Sec.-Gen. 2004–05 (retd); Chair. UN panel for evaluation of peace-keeping operations March–Aug. 2000; other special missions to Zaïre (now Democratic Repub. of the Congo), Yemen, Liberia, and Iraq; Special Rep. of the UN Sec.-Gen. for Afghanistan and Head, UN Assistance Mission in Afghanistan 2001–03; Dir Visitor Inst. for Advanced Study, Princeton 2007; mem. Comm. on Legal Empowerment of the Poor (UNDP); Chair. Ind. Panel on Safety and Security of UN Personnel and Premises 2007–; Harvard Law School Great Negotiator Award 2002, Dag Hammarskjöld Hon. Medal, German UN Asscn 2004. *Address:* c/o Executive Office of the Secretary-General, Room 5-3860, United Nations, United Nations Plaza, New York, NY 10017, USA (office).

BRAHMS, Hero Heinrich, B. Dipl.-Kfm; German business executive; *Chairman, Supervisory Board, Arcandor AG;* b. 6 July 1941, Munster; s. of Johannes Brahms and Ursula Brahams (née Stuhlmann); ed Univ. Munster; fmrly with SKET Schwermaschinenbau Magdeburg and Deutsche Waggonbau AG; joined Hoesch AG, Dortmund 1969, becoming Man. Dir 1981–91; Vice-Chair. Treuhandanstalt (privatization agency), Berlin 1991–94; Chief Financial Officer Kaufhof Holding AG, Cologne 1994–95; Chair. Supervisory Bd Bremer Vulkan (shipyard) 1995; mem. Exec. Cttee and Chief Financial Officer Linde AG 1996–2003; mem. Supervisory Bd Karstadtquelle AG (renamed Arcandor AG 2007), Chair. 2005–; fmr mem. Supervisory Bd Deutsche Post AG –2004, Wincor Nixdorf, Morgan Stanley AG, M.M. Warburg; Sr Adviser SG Corporate & Investment Banking (SG CIB) 2004. *Address:* Arcandor AG, Theodor-Althoff-Strasse 2, 45133 Essen, Germany (office). *Telephone:* (201) 7271 (office). *Fax:* (201) 7275216 (office). *Website:* www.arcandor.com (office).

BRAITHWAITE, Sir Rodric Quentin, GCMG; British fmr diplomatist; *Senior Consultant in Global Investment Banking, Deutsche Bank;* b. 17 May 1932, London; s. of Henry Warwick Braithwaite and Lorna Constance Davies; m. Gillian Mary Robinson 1961; four s. (one deceased) one d.; ed Bedales School, Christ's Coll., Cambridge; mil. service 1950–52; joined Foreign Service 1955; Third Sec., Jakarta 1957–58; Second Sec., Warsaw 1959–61; Foreign Office 1961–63; First Sec. (Commercial), Moscow 1963–66; First Sec., Rome 1966–69; FCO 1969–72, Head of European Integration Dept (External) 1973–75, Head of Planning Staff 1979–80, Asst Under-Sec. of State 1981, Deputy Under-Sec. of State 1984–88; Head of Chancery, Office of Perm. Rep. to EEC, Brussels 1975–78; Minister, Commercial, Washington 1982–84; Amb. to Soviet Union 1988–92; Foreign Policy Adviser to Prime Minister 1992–93; Chair. Jt Intelligence Cttee 1992–93; currently Sr Consultant in Global Investment Banking, Deutsche Bank AG, London; Chair. Britain Russia Centre 1994–2000, Moscow School of Political Studies 1998–; mem. European Strategy Bd ICL 1994–2000, Supervisory Bd Deutsche Bank Moscow 1998–99, Bd Ural Mash Zavody (Moscow and Ekaterinburg) 1998–99; mem. Advisory Bd Sirocco Aerospace 2000–; mem. RAM 1993–2002 (Chair. of Govs 1998–2002); Visiting Fellow All Souls Coll. Oxford 1972–73; Hon. Fellow Christ's Coll. Cambridge; Hon. FRAM; Hon. Prof. (Birmingham) 2000; Dr hc (Birmingham) 1998. *Publications:* Engaging Russia (with Blackwill and Tanaka) 1995, Russia in Europe 1999, NATO at Fifty: Perspectives of the Future of the Atlantic Alliance (jtly) 1999, Across the Moscow River 2002, Moscow 1941 2006. *Leisure interests:* chamber music (viola), sailing, Russia.

Address: Deutsche Bank AG, 6th Floor, Winchester House, Great Winchester Street, London, EC2N 2DB, England (office). *Telephone:* (20) 7545-8000 (office). *Fax:* (20) 7545-4577 (office).

BRAKS, Gerrit J. M., MAgr; Dutch politician; b. 23 May 1933, Odiliapeel; s. of Theodorus H. Braks and Helena Johanna Kroef; m. Frens Bardoel 1965 (died 2000); two s. three d.; ed Agricultural Univ., Wageningen; worked on parents' farm –1955; Asst Govt Agricultural Advisory Service, Eindhoven 1955–58; Directorate for Int. Econ. Co-operation, Ministry of Agric. and Fisheries 1965–66; Deputy Agricultural Attaché, Perm. Mission of Netherlands to EEC, Brussels 1966–67; Sec. North Brabant Christian Farmers' Union (NCB), Tilburg 1967–69; Agricultural Counsellor, Perm. Mission of Netherlands to EEC 1969–77; mem. Second Chamber of Parl. 1977–80, 1981–82; Chair. Standing Cttee on Agric., Second Chamber 1979–80 parl. year; Minister of Agric. and Fisheries 1980–81, 1982–90; mem. First Chamber of Parl. (Christian Democratic Appeal—CDA) 1991–; Pres. Catholic Broadcasting Org. 1991–96; Chair. and Pres. Céhavé Farmers Cooperative 1995–; mem. Interparl. Benelux Council 1996–2001; Pres. of Senate 2001–03; Govt Commr 'Floriade 2002'; currently ind. adviser; Commdr, Order of Netherlands Lion and other decorations. *Leisure interests:* gardening and golf. *Address:* Ruwenbergstraat 4, 5271 Sint-Michielsgestel AG, Netherlands. *Telephone:* (73) 5514759; (6) 52303360. *E-mail:* g.braks@planet.nl (home).

BRALY, Angela Fick, BA, JD; American lawyer and business executive; *President and CEO, WellPoint, Inc.;* b. 2 July 1962, Dallas, Tex.; m.; three c.; ed Texas Tech. Univ., Southern Methodist Univ. School of Law; Partner, Lewis, Rice and Fingersh LC (law firm), St Louis 1987–99; joined Right-CHOICE Managed Care Inc. (now Blue Cross Blue Shield of Mo., an operating subsidiary of WellPoint Inc.) as Gen. Counsel 1999, Pres. and CEO 2003–05, Exec. Vice-Pres., Gen. Counsel and Chief Public Affairs Officer WellPoint, Inc. 2005–07, Pres. and CEO 2007–; mem. United Way Women's Initiative Cttee, Cen. Ind., ABA, American Health Lawyers Asscn; named one of Modern Healthcare magazine's Top 25 Women in Healthcare 2007, named by The Wall Street Journal No. 1 on list of Women to Watch 2007, ranked by Fortune magazine amongst 50 Most Powerful Women in Business in the US (fourth) 2007, ranked by Forbes magazine amongst 100 Most Powerful Women (16th) 2007, (fourth) 2008. *Address:* WellPoint, Inc., 120 Monument Circle, Indianapolis, IN 46204, USA (office). *Telephone:* (317) 532-6000 (office). *Fax:* (317) 488-6028 (office). *E-mail:* info@wellpoint.com (office). *Website:* www.wellpoint.com (office).

BRAMALL, Baron (Life Peer), cr. 1987, of Bushfield in the County of Hampshire; **Field Marshal The Lord Edwin Noel Westby Bramall,** KG, GCB, OBE, MC, KStJ; British army officer (retd); b. 18 Dec. 1923, Tunbridge Wells, England; s. of the late Maj. Edmund Haselden Bramall and Katherine Bridget Bramall (née Westby); m. Dorothy Avril Wentworth Vernon 1949; one s. one d.; ed Eton Coll.; commissioned in King's Royal Rifle Corps 1943, served in North-west Europe 1944–45, occupation of Japan 1946–47; Instructor, School of Infantry 1949–51; served Middle East 1953–58; Instructor, Army Staff Coll. 1958–61; on staff of Lord Mountbatten with special responsibility for reorg. of Ministry of Defence 1963–64; CO 2nd Green Jackets (King's Royal Rifle Corps) 1965–66; Commdr 5th Airportable Brigade 1967–69; GOC 1st Div. BAOR 1972–73; rank of Lt-Gen. 1973; Commdr British Forces Hong Kong 1973–76; Col Commdt 3rd Royal Green Jackets 1973–84; Col 2nd Gurkhas 1976–86; rank of Gen. 1976; C-in-C UK Land Forces 1976–78; Vice-Chief of Defence Staff (Personnel and Logistics) 1978–79; Chief of Gen. Staff and ADC Gen. to HM The Queen 1979–82; rank of Field Marshal 1982; Chief of Defence Staff 1982–85; Lord Lt of Greater London 1986–98; Pres. of MCC 1988–89; Trustee Imperial War Museum 1983–, Chair. 1989–98; JP London 1986; KStJ 1986; Golden Medallion for Service to Christian-Jewish Dialogue 2001. *Publication:* The Chiefs: The Story of the United Kingdom Chiefs of Staff (co-author) 1993. *Leisure interests:* cricket, painting, travel, tennis. *Address:* House of Lords, London, SW1A 0PW, England.

BRAMMERTZ, Serge; Belgian lawyer and author; *Prosecutor, International Criminal Tribunal for the former Yugoslavia (ICTY);* b. 17 Feb. 1962, Eupen; Deputy Prosecutor, then Chief Deputy Prosecutor, Court of First Instance, Eupen 1996–97, before becoming Deputy to the Prosecutor-Gen., Liège Court of Appeal; Fed. Prosecutor of the Kingdom of Belgium 1997–2002; Scientific Asst, then Prof. of Law, Univ. of Liège –2002; Deputy Prosecutor of Int. Criminal Court in charge of Investigations Div. of Office of the Prosecutor 2003–07; Commr Int. Ind. Investigation Comm. into the murder of fmr Lebanese Prime Minister Rafiq Hariri 2006–07; Prosecutor, Int. Criminal Tribunal for the fmr Yugoslavia (ICTY) 2008–; assisted Council of Europe as expert on organized crime; also served on Justice and Internal Affairs Cttee of EC and as adviser for Int. Org. for Migration, leading major research studies on cases of cross-border corruption and trafficking in human beings in Cen. Europe and the Balkans. *Publications:* has published extensively in int. academic journals on global terrorism, organized crime and corruption. *Address:* Office of the Prosecutor, International Criminal Tribunal for the former Yugoslavia, Churchillplein 1, 2517 JW The Hague, Netherlands (office). *Telephone:* (70) 512-53-60 (office). *Fax:* (70) 512-53-58 (office). *E-mail:* brammertz@un.org (office). *Website:* www.un.org/icty (office).

BRANAGH, Kenneth; British actor and director; b. 10 Dec. 1960, Belfast; s. of William Branagh and Frances Branagh; m. 1st Emma Thompson 1989 (divorced 1998); m. 2nd Lindsay Brunnock 2003; ed Meadway Comprehensive School, Reading, Royal Acad. of Dramatic Art (RADA); f. Renaissance Theatre Co. 1987 (resgnd 1994), Renaissance Films PLC 1988 (resgnd 1994), Shakespeare Film Co. 1999; mem. Bd BFI 1993–97; Officier des Arts et des Lettres; Hon. DLitt (Queen's Univ., Belfast) 1990, (Univ. of Birmingham) 2001; Bancroft Gold Medal RADA 1982; BAFTA Award (best dir) 1990. *Theatre:* Another Country 1982 (Soc. of W End Theatres Award for Most

Promising Newcomer), The Madness 1983, Francis, Henry V, Hamlet, Love's Labour's Lost, Golden Girls, Tell Me Honestly (writer and dir) 1986, Romeo and Juliet (producer and dir) 1986, Public Enemy (writer, actor) 1986, Napoleon (dir) 1987, Twelfth Night (dir) 1987, Much Ado About Nothing, As You Like It, Hamlet, Look Back in Anger 1989, Napoleon: The American Story (dir) 1989, King Lear (actor, dir) 1989, Midsummer Night's Dream (actor, dir) 1989, Uncle Vanya (co-dir) 1991, Coriolanus (actor), Hamlet (actor, RSC) 1992, The Play What I Wrote (dir) 2001–03, Richard III (actor) 2002, Edmond (actor, Royal Nat. Theatre) 2003, Ducktastic (Albery Theatre, London, dir) 2005, Ivanov (actor, Wyndham's Theatre) 2008. *Television:* The Boy in the Bush, Billy (Trilogy), To the Lighthouse, Maybury, Derek, Coming Through, Ghosts, Fortunes of War, Strange Interlude, The Lady's Not for Burning, Shadow of a Gunman, Conspiracy (Emmy Award for Best Actor 2001), Shackleton 2002, Warm Springs 2004, Wallander 2008. *Radio:* Hamlet (actor, dir) 1992, Romeo and Juliet (actor, dir) 1993, King Lear (actor) 1994, Bequest to the Nation 2005. *Films:* High Season, A Month in the Country, Henry V (actor, dir, writer) (Evening Standard Best Film, NY Film Critics' Circle Best Dir Award) 1989, Dead Again (actor, dir) 1991, Peter's Friends (actor, dir, producer) 1992, Swing Kids (actor) 1992, Swan Song (dir) 1992, Much Ado about Nothing (actor, dir, producer) 1993, Mary Shelley's Frankenstein (actor, dir), Othello (actor) 1995, In the Bleak Midwinter (dir, writer) 1995, Hamlet (actor, dir, producer) 1996, The Theory of Flight 1997, The Proposition 1997, The Gingerbread Man 1997, Celebrity 1998, Wild, Wild West 1998, Love's Labour's Lost (actor, dir, producer) 2000, How to Kill Your Neighbor's Dog 2002, Rabbit Proof Fence 2002, Harry Potter and the Chamber of Secrets 2002, Five Children and It 2004, The Magic Flute (dir) 2006, As You Like It (dir) 2006, Sleuth (dir) 2007, Valkyrie 2008, The Boat That Rocked 2009. *Publications:* Public Enemy (play) 1988, Beginning (memoirs) 1989; The Making of Mary Shelley's Frankenstein 1994, In the Bleak Midwinter 1995, screenplays for Henry V, Much Ado About Nothing, Hamlet. *Address:* Shepperton Studios, Studio Road, Shepperton, Middx, TW17 0QD, England.

BRANCO, Joaquim Rafael; São Tome and Príncipe politician; *Prime Minister;* b. 1953; Minister of Foreign Affairs 2000–01, of Public Works 2003; Prime Minister 2008–; Pres. Movt for the Liberation of São Tomé and Príncipe–Social Democratic Party. *Address:* Office of the Prime Minister, Rua do Município, CP 302, São Tomé, São Tomé and Príncipe (office). *Telephone:* 223913 (office). *Fax:* 224679 (office). *E-mail:* gpm@cstome.net (office).

BRAND, Stewart, BS; American editor, writer and publisher; *President, The Long Now Foundation;* b. 14 Dec. 1938, Rockford, Ill.; m. 1st Lois Jennings 1966 (divorced 1972); m. 2nd Ryan Phelan 1983; one s. from a previous relationship; ed Phillips Exeter Acad., Stanford Univ.; served in US Army 1960–62; fmrly with Merry Pranksters; consultant to Gov. of Calif. 1976–78; research scientist Media Lab., MIT 1986; Visiting Scholar Royal Dutch/Shell 1986; f. America Needs Indians, Whole Earth Review 1985, Point Foundation, Hacker's Conf.; co-f., The Well (Whole Earth 'Lectronic Link—Internet bulletin bd) 1985–, Global Business Network consultancy 1988–, The Long Now Foundation 1996– (also Pres.), All Species project 2000–; Trustee, Santa Fe Inst. 1989–. *Television:* How Buildings Learn (writer and presenter) 1997. *Publications:* Two Cybernetic Frontiers 1974, The Media Lab: Inventing the Future at MIT 1987, How Buildings Learn 1994, The Clock of the Long Now 1999; Ed. (or Co-Ed.) and Publr: The Last Whole Earth Catalog 1968–72 (Nat. Book Award), Whole Earth Epilog 1974, Whole Earth Epilog: Access to Tools 1974, The Co-Evolution Quarterly 1974–85, The Next Whole Earth Catalog 1980–81, The (Updated) Last Whole Earth Catalog: Access to Tools (16th edn) 1975, Space Colonies, Whole Earth Catalog 1977, Soft-Tech 1978, The Next Whole Earth Catalog: Access to Tools 1980, (revised 2nd edn) 1981, Whole Earth Software Catalog (Ed.-in-Chief) 1983–85, Whole Earth Software Catalog for 1986, '2.0 edition' of above title (Ed.-in-Chief) 1985, News That Stayed News 1974–1984: Ten Years of CoEvolution Quarterly 1986. *Address:* 3E Gate 5 Road, Sausalito, CA 94965 (home); The Long Now Foundation, PO Box 29462, Presidio of San Francisco, CA 94129-0462, USA (office). *Telephone:* (415) 561-6582 (office). *Fax:* (415) 561-6297 (office). *E-mail:* sb@gbn.org (home). *Website:* sb.longnow.org (office).

BRANDÃO, Lázaro de Mello; Brazilian banking executive; *Chairman, Banco Bradesco SA;* joined Casa Bancária Almeida 1942, (later Banco Brasileiro de Descontos 1943, then Banco Bradesco SA), Officer Banco Bradesco SA 1963–77, Vice-Pres. 1977–81, Pres. 1981–99, Vice-Chair. 1982–90, Chair. 1990–; mem. Bd of Dirs Banking Asscn of the states of São Paulo, Paraná, Mato Grosso and Mato Grosso do Sul 1966–83, Chair. 1974–83; Vice-Pres. Bd of Dirs Nat. Fed. of Banks (FENABAN) 1971–76, 1980–83; Pres. Bd of Dirs Companhia Brasileira de Securitização 1997–99; Pres. Fundo Garantidor de Créditos 1999–2001; Pres. Fundacao Bradesco; Chair. Bd of Dirs Bradespar; mem. Man. Bd Banco Espírito Santo SA, Portugal;. *Address:* Banco Bradesco SA, Cidade de Deus, Prédio Novo, Osasco 06029-900 São Paulo, Brazil (office). *Telephone:* (11) 3684-9229 (office). *Fax:* (11) 3684-4570 (office). *Website:* www.bradesco.com.br (office).

BRANDAUER, Klaus Maria; Austrian actor; b. 6 Feb. 1944, Bad Aussee; m. Karin Brandauer 1965; ed Acad. of Music and Dramatic Arts, Stuttgart; mem. Burgtheater, Vienna; extensive stage repertoire; Cannes Film Festival Prize for film Mephisto 1981; appeared as Jedermann at Salzburg Festival 1983, as Speer, Almeida Theatre, London 1999; Acad. Award (Oscar) for title role in film Mephisto 1982. *Films include:* Mephisto 1980, Colonel Redl 1985, Out of Africa 1985, Burning Secret 1988, Hannussen 1988, Russia House, Angel in Hell 1989, Streets of Gold 1989, The French Revolution 1989, The Artisan (also dir), Becoming Colette 1991, White Fang 1991, The Resurrected, Seven Minutes (also dir), Felidae (voice), Marco and the Magician (also dir), Die Wand (dir), Rembrandt, Introducing Dorothy Dandridge 1999, Druids 2001, Jedermanns Fest 2002, Between Strangers 2002, Poem - Ich setzte den Fuss in die Luft, und sie trug 2003. *Television includes:* Quo Vadis?, Perlasca, un eroe italiano 2002, Die Entführung aus dem Serail 2003. *Address:* Bartensteingasse 8/9, 1010 Vienna, Austria.

BRANDT, Elmar, DPhil; German cultural institute director; b. 18 Nov. 1936, Berlin; s. of Arthur Brandt and Anna Maria Brandt (née Monscheuer); m. Holle Behncke 1983; one d. one step-s.; ed Univs of Frankfurt Main, Berlin and Munich; Dir Goethe-Institut, Yaoundé, Cameroon 1965–68, Deputy Dir Goethe-Institut, Tokyo 1968–70, Dir Goethe-Institut Osaka, Japan 1970–77, Head, Media Dept, Goethe-Institut Head Office, Munich 1977–83, Dir Goethe-Institut, São Paulo, Brazil 1983–89, London 1989–95, Rome 1995–. *Publications include:* Fundamentals of a Theory of Meaning 1963–64, Current Problems of Consumer Protection 1978, The Woman in the Twentieth Century 1988, New Strategies of Urban Planning 1992. *Leisure interests:* gardening, photography, painting.

BRANKOVIĆ, Nedžad, MSc, PhD; Bosnia and Herzegovina engineer and politician; *Prime Minister, Federation of Bosnia and Herzegovina;* b. 28 Dec. 1962, Višegrad; m.; two c.; ed Univ. of Sarajevo; served with Bosnia-Herzegovina Army then apptd to head logistics team attached to Gen. Staff; with IPSI (Inst. for Transport and Communications), Sarajevo 1987–92; Dir-Gen. BiH Railways 1993–98; Dir-Gen. Energoinvest Co. (eng firm) 1998–2002; Sr Teaching Asst, Faculty for Transport and Communications, Univ. of Sarajevo; Minister of Transport and Communications, Fed. of Bosnia and Herzegovina 2003–07, Prime Minister 2007–; mem. Party of Democratic Action (SDA). *Address:* Office of the Prime Minister of the Federation of Bosnia and Herzegovina, 71000 Sarajevo, Alipašina 41, Bosnia and Herzegovina (office). *Telephone:* (33) 656679 (office). *Fax:* (33) 444718 (office). *E-mail:* kabprem@fbihvlada.gov.ba (office). *Website:* www.fbihvlada.gov.ba (office).

BRANSCOMB, Lewis McAdory, MS, PhD; American physicist and academic; *AETNA Professor Emeritus of Public Policy and Corporate Management and Director Emeritus, Public Policy Program, John F. Kennedy School of Government, Harvard University;* b. 17 Aug. 1926, Asheville, NC; s. of Bennett Harvie Branscomb and Margaret Vaughn Branscomb; m. 1st Anne Wells 1951 (died 1998); one s. one d.; m. 2nd Constance Hammond Mullin 2005; ed Duke and Harvard Univs; Instructor in Physics, Harvard Univ. 1950; Lecturer in Physics, Univ. of Maryland 1950–51; Chief, Atomic Physics Section, Nat. Bureau of Standards, Washington, DC 1954–60, Chief Atomic Physics Div. 1960–62; Chair. Jt Inst. for Lab. Astrophysics 1962–65, 1968–70; Chief, Lab. Astrophysics Div., Nat. Bureau of Standards, Boulder, Colo 1962–69; Dir Nat. Bureau of Standards 1969–72; Chief Scientist, Vice-Pres. IBM Corpn 1972–86; Prof., Dir Public Policy Program Kennedy School of Govt, Harvard Univ. 1986–96, now Dir Emer., AETNA Prof. of Public Policy and Corp. Man. 1988–96, Prof. Emer. 1996–; Adjunct Prof., Univ. of California San Diego School of Int. Relations and Pacific Studies, Distinguished Research Fellow, Inst. for Global Conflict and Cooperation, Univ. of California; Visiting Prof., Vanderbilt Univ. 1999–2000; mem. tech. assessment advisory council, Office of Tech. Assessment, US Congress 1990–95; mem. Bd, Mobil Corpn, MITRE Corpn; mem. Nat. Acad. of Sciences (mem. Council 1972–75, 1998–), Inst. of Medicine, Nat. Acad. of Eng; Fellow, American Acad. of Arts and Sciences, American Philosophical Soc.; mem. Nat. Acad. of Public Admin, Harvard Univ. Bd of Overseers, Comm. on Global Information/Infrastructure 1995–; Trustee, Carnegie Inst. of Washington 1973–90, Vanderbilt Univ., Nat. Geographic Soc., Woods Hole Oceanographic Inst., LASPAU 1999–2004; 16 hon. degrees; several awards. *Publications:* Empowering Technology 1993, Confessions of a Technophile 1994, Korea at the Turning Point 1996, Investing in Innovation 1998, Taking Technical Risks 2000; numerous articles in professional journals. *Leisure interests:* skiing, sailing. *Address:* John F. Kennedy School of Government, Harvard University, 79 John F. Kennedy Street, Cambridge, MA 02138-5801 (office); 1600 Ludington Lane, La Jolla, CA 92037, USA (home). *Telephone:* (858) 454-6871 (office); (858) 454-6871 (home). *Fax:* (858) 456-1752 (home). *E-mail:* lewis_branscomb@harvard.edu (office); lbranscomb@branscomb.org (home). *Website:* ksgfaculty.harvard.edu/Lewis_Branscomb (office); www.branscomb.org (home).

BRANSON, Sir Richard Charles Nicholas, Kt; British business executive; *Chairman, Virgin Group Ltd;* b. 18 July 1950, Blackheath, London; s. of Edward James Branson; m. 1st Kristen Tomassi 1969 (divorced 1979); m. 2nd Joan Templeman 1989; one s. one d.; ed Stowe School; set up Student Advisory Centre (now Help) 1970; f. Virgin mail-order co. 1969, first Virgin record shop 1971, recording co. 1973, nightclub (The Venue) 1976, Virgin Atlantic Airlines 1984; f. and Chair. Virgin Retail Group, Virgin Communications, Virgin Travel Group, Voyager Group; took Virgin Music Group public 1986, bought back shares 1988 (rotating chairmanship 1991, Chair. 1991–92, now Life Pres. after sale of shares 1992); Group also includes publishing, broadcasting, construction, heating systems, holidays; Chair. UK 2000 1986–88, Pres. 1988–; Dir Intourist Moscow Ltd 1988–90; f. The Healthcare Foundation 1987, Virgin Books 1989 (sold to Random House 2007), Virgin Radio 1993, Virgin Rail Group Ltd 1996, Virgin Express 1996 (merged with SN Brussels Airlines forming Brussels Airlines 2006), V2 Records 1997 (sold to Universal Music Group 2007), Virgin Mobile (sold to NTL/NTL:Telewest 2006 and re-launched as Virgin Media 2007) 1999, Virgin Blue (Australia) 2000, Virgin Galactic (space tourism co.) 2004, Virgin Comics 2006, Virgin Animation 2006, Virgin Health Bank 2007, Virgin Nigeria 2007, Virgin America 2007, Virgin Fuels 2009; launched Virgin Cola (drink) 1994, Babylon (restaurant) 2001, Virgin Vodka (drink); crossed Pacific in hot air balloon with Per Lindstrand 1991; world record for fastest crossing of the Channel in amphibious vehicle 2004; made unsuccessful attempt with his children at eastbound record crossing of Atlantic Ocean under sail in 99ft (30m) sloop, Virgin Money (also known as Speedboat) 2008; Chair. jury of first Picnic Green Challenge 2007; set up global science and tech. prize, The Virgin Earth Challenge 2007; hosted environmental gathering at his pvt. island, Necker Island (part of British Virgin Islands) in Caribbean with several prominent entrepreneurs, celebrities and world leaders to discuss global warming-related problems March 2008; Patron Int. Rescue Corps, Prisoners Abroad; Hon. DTech (Loughborough) 1993; Blue Riband Title for Fastest Atlantic Crossing 1986, Segrave Trophy 1987, ranked No. 85 on list of 100 Greatest Britons (BBC) 2002, ranked No. 86 on list of 100 Worst Britons (Channel 4) 2003, ranked by Time Magazine amongst Top 100 Most Influential People in the World 2007, UN Correspondents Asscn Citizen of the World Award 2007. *Film and TV appearances:* Friends, Baywatch, Birds of a Feather, Only Fools and Horses, The Day Today, Goodness Gracious Me, Tripping Over, Live & Kicking, The Rebel Billionaire 2004, Around the World in 80 Days 2004, Casino Royale 2006, Superman Returns 2006, Rabbit Fever 2006. *Publication:* Losing My Virginity (autobiog.) 1998, Screw It, Let's Do It 2006, Business Stripped Bare: Adventures of a Global Entrepreneur 2008. *Leisure interest:* sailing. *Address:* Virgin Group Ltd, 120 Campden Hill Road, London, W8 7AR, England (office). *Telephone:* (20) 7229-1282 (office). *Fax:* (20) 7727-8200 (office). *E-mail:* info@virgin.com (office). *Website:* www.virgin.com (office); entrepreneur.virgin.com (office).

BRANSTAD, Terry Edward, BA, JD; American university administrator and fmr state governor; *President, Des Moines University;* b. 17 Nov. 1946, Leland, Iowa; s. of Edward Arnold Branstad and Rita Garland; m. Christine Ann Johnson 1972; two s. one d.; ed Univ. of Iowa and Drake Univ.; served in US Army 1969–71; admitted to Iowa Bar; sold interest in Branstad/Schwarm, Lake Mills, Iowa; farmer, Lake Mills; mem. Iowa House of Reps 1972–78; Lt-Gov. of Iowa 1979–82, Gov. of Iowa 1983–99; Pres. Des Moines Univ. 2002–; mem. Bd of Dirs Iowa Health System, Cementech, Featherlite, Liberty Bank, Living History Farms, Advanced Analytical Technologies, Inc., American Inst. of Certified Public Accountants; Republican. *Address:* Office of the President, Des Moines University, 3200 Grand Avenue, Des Moines, IA 50312-4198, USA (office). *Telephone:* (515) 271-1500 (office). *Fax:* (515) 271-1532 (office). *E-mail:* terry.branstad@dmu.edu (office). *Website:* www.dmu.edu/about/president (office).

BRAR, D. S.; Indian business executive; Pres. Ranbaxy Laboratories Ltd 1996–99, CEO, Man. Dir 1999–2004; Dir Central Bd Reserve Bank of India. *Address:* c/o Ranbaxy Laboratories Ltd, 19 New Place, New Delhi, 110 019, India.

BRASH, Donald Thomas, MA, PhD; New Zealand banker and politician; b. 24 Sept. 1940, Wanganui; s. of Rev. Dr Alan A. Brash and Mrs Brash; m. 1st Erica Beatty 1964; m. 2nd Je Lan Lee 1989; two s. one d.; ed Christchurch Boys' High School, Canterbury Univ. and Australian Nat. Univ.; Gen. Man. Broadbank Corpn Ltd 1971–81; Gen. Man. Finance and Computer Sector, Fletcher Challenge Ltd 1981–82; Man. Dir NZ Kiwifruit Authority 1982–86; Man. Dir Trust Bank Group 1986–88; Gov. Reserve Bank of New Zealand 1988–2002; mem. NZ Monetary and Econ. Council 1974–78, NZ Planning Council 1977–80; mem. Nat. Party; mem. Parl. (Nat. Party) 2002–; Nat. Spokesperson (Opposition) on Finance 2002–03; Leader, Nat. Party and Parl. Opposition 2003–06; Dr hc (Canterbury) 1999; NZIER-QANTAS Econs Award 1999. *Publications:* New Zealand's Debt Servicing Capacity 1964, American Investment in Australian Industry 1966. *Leisure interest:* kiwifruit growing. *Address:* New Zealand National Party, Willbank House, 14th Floor, 57 Willis St, POB 1155 Wellington, 60015 New Zealand (office). *Telephone:* (4) 472-5211 (office). *Fax:* (4) 478-1622 (office). *E-mail:* info@donbrash.com (office). *Website:* www.donbrash.com (office).

BRASSEUR, Claude; French actor; b. 15 June 1936, Paris (as Claude Espinasse); s. of the late Pierre Espinasse (known as Pierre Brasseur) and of Odette Joyeux; m. 2nd Michèle Cambon 1970; one s.; ed René Girard and René Simon drama schools, Paris; Beatrix Dussane Trophy 1974, César Awards for Best Supporting Actor in Un éléphant ça trompe énormément 1976, Best Actor in La guerre des polices 1980; Chevalier, Ordre Nat. du Mérite. *Plays include:* Un ange passe, L'enfant du dimanche, Match 1964, La calèche 1966, Britannicus 1966, Du côté de chez l'autre 1971, Les jeux de la nuit 1974, George Dandin 1987, Le Souper 1989, Dîner de cons 1993, La Dernière salve 1995, À torts et à raisons 1999. *Films include:* Rue des prairies, Les yeux sans visage 1959, Le noeud de vipères, La verte moisson, Pierrot la tendresse 1960, Le caporal épinglé, La bride sur le cou 1961, Germinal 1962, Dragées au poivre, Peau de banane 1963, Bande à part, Lucky Joe 1964, L'enfer (unfinished), Le chien fou, Du rififi à Paname 1966, Un homme de trop, Caroline chérie 1967, La chasse royale, Catherine ou il suffit d'un amour 1968, Le viager, Le portrait de Marianne, Un cave 1971, Une belle fille comme moi 1972, Bel ordure 1973, Les seins de glace 1974, Il faut vivre dangereusement, L'agression 1975, Attention les yeux 1976, Barocco, Le grand Escogriffe, Un éléphant ça trompe énormément 1976, Monsieur papa, Nous irons au paradis, L'état sauvage 1977, L'argent des autres, Une histoire simple 1978, La guerre des polices 1979, La boume 1980, Une langouste au petit déjeuner, Une robe noire pour un tueur, L'ombre rouge, Une affaire d'hommes 1981, Josepha, Guy de Maupassant 1982, Légitime violence 1982, T'es heureuse? Moi toujours 1983, la Crime 1983, Signes extérieurs de richesse 1983, Souvenir, Le Léopard 1984, Palace 1985, Les loups entre eux 1985, La gitane 1986, Taxi Boy 1986, Descente aux enfers 1986, George Dandin 1988, Radio Corbeau 1989, l'Union sacrée 1989, l'Orchestre Rouge 1989, Dancing Machine 1990, Sale comme un Ange 1991, Le Bal des Casse-Pieds 1992, Le Souper 1992, le Fil de L'Horizon 1993, Le plus beau pays du monde et fait d'hiver 1999, Fait d'hiver 1999, La Taule 2000, Toreros et les Acteurs 2000, Malabar Princess 2004, L'Amour aux trousses 2005, Les Parrains (voice) 2005, Camping 2006, J'invente rien 2006, Les Petites Vacances 2006, Le Héros de la famille 2006, Fauteuils d'orchestre 2006. *Television appearances include:* Le paysan parvenu, La misère et la gloire, Don Juan, Le mystère de la chambre jaune (as Rouletabille), Les eaux mêlées, Vidocq, Les nouvelles aventures de Vidocq, l'Équipe, l'Argent, Véga 1999, Soraya 2003, Franck Keller 2003. *Leisure interests:* boxing, swimming, football, bobsleighing, skiing. *Address:* c/o Artmédia, 20 avenue Rapp, 75007 Paris, France.

BRATHWAITE, Rt Hon. Sir Nicholas, Kt, OBE, PC, BEd; Grenadian educationalist, administrator and politician (retd); b. 8 July 1925, Carriacou; s. of Charles Brathwaite and Sophia Brathwaite; m.; three s. one d.; ed Univ. of West Indies; fmr teacher, Sr Tutor, Prin. Teachers' Coll.; fmrly Chief Educ. Officer; fmr Minister of Social Affairs; fmr Commonwealth official; Chair. Interim Council set up after US invasion of Grenada and deposition of fmr mil. Govt 1983–84; leader Nat. Democratic Congress (NDC) 1989–94; Prime Minister 1990–95, also fmr Minister of Home Affairs, Nat. Security, Foreign Affairs, Finance, Personnel and Man. and Carriacou and Petit Martinique Affairs. *Address:* Villa 'A', St George's, Grenada (home).

BRAUCHLI, Marcus, BA; American journalist; *Executive Editor, The Washington Post;* b. 19 June 1961, Boulder, Colo; s. of Christopher R. Brauchli and Margot L. Brauchli; m. Maggie Farley; ed Columbia Univ.; began career as copyreader for AP-Dow Jones 1984; foreign correspondent in Hong Kong, Dow Jones Newswires 1984–87, in Scandinavia 1987–88, in Japan 1988–95, Head, China Bureau 1995–99; News Ed. Wall Street Journal 1999–2000, Nat. News Ed. 2000–03, Global News Ed. 2003–05, Deputy Man. Ed. 2005–07, Man. Ed. 2007–08 (resgnd); Exec. Ed., The Washington Post 2008–. *Address:* The Washington Post, 1150 15 St. NW, Washington, DC 20071, USA (office). *Telephone:* (202) 334-6000 (office). *E-mail:* letters@washpost.com (office). *Website:* www.washintonpost.com (office).

BRAUER, Arik; Austrian artist; b. 4 Jan. 1929, Vienna; s. of Simon Moses Brauer and Hermine Brauer; m. Naomi Dahabani 1957; three d.; ed Wiener Kunstakademie; underground, Vienna 1942–45; after studies in Vienna travelled in Africa, France, Spain, Austria, Greece and Israel 1950–58, USA, E Africa, Ethiopia, Japan 1965–74; Prof. Acad. of Fine Arts Vienna 1986; one-man exhbns 1956–, in Austria, Germany, Switzerland, France, Denmark, Liechtenstein, Italy, Canada, Sweden, Yugoslavia, Bulgaria, Norway, Japan, Israel and USA; world travelling exhbn 1979–; group exhbns, including travelling exhbns with Wiener Schule des Phantastischen Realismus 1962–, in W Europe, USA, S. America, Poland, Yugoslavia, Israel, Iran, Turkey, Japan; Scenery for The Seven Mortal Sins (Vienna 1972), Bomarzo (Zürich 1970); scenery and costumes for Medea (Vienna 1972), The Magic Flute (Paris 1977); book, design and costumes for Sieben auf einen Streich (Vienna 1978); mural design for Univ. of Haifa, Israel 1982–; designer Brauerhaus, Vienna 1983–95; Guest Lecturer, Int. Summer Acad. for Fine Arts, Salzburg 1982, 83; two gold records for Erich Brauer LP (poetry, music and songs) 1971. *Publications:* Zigeunerziege 1976, Runde Fliegt 1983. *Leisure interests:* alpinism, skiing, windsurfing. *Address:* c/o Arts Directory GmbH, Sandstr. 33, 80335 Munich, Germany. *Website:* www.arikbrauer.com.

BRAUER, Stephen Franklin, BEcons; American business executive and diplomatist; *President and CEO, Hunter Engineering Company;* b. 3 Sept. 1945, St Louis, MO; m. Camilla Thompson Bauer 1971; three c.; ed Westminster Coll.; First Lt, US Army Corps of Engineers 1967–70, tour of duty in Viet Nam; joined Hunter Engineering Co. 1971, Exec. Vice-Pres. and COO 1978–81, Pres. and CEO 1981–2001; Amb. to Belgium 2001–03; Hon. Consul of Belgium in Missouri state 1987–2001; pnr and part-owner of St Louis Cardinals professional baseball team; Trustee St Louis Art Museum, Missouri Botanical Garden (Pres. Bd Trustees), Smithsonian Inst., Washington, DC, Washington Univ. *Leisure interest:* baseball. *Address:* Hunter Engineering Company, 11250 Hunter Drive, Bridgeton, MO 63044 USA (office). *Telephone:* (314) 731-3020 (office). *Fax:* (314) 731-1776 (office). *Website:* www.hunter.com (office).

BRAUMAN, John I., PhD; American chemist and academic; *J.G. Jackson-C.J. Wood Professor of Chemistry, Stanford University;* b. 7 Sept. 1937, Pittsburgh, Pa; s. of Milton Brauman and Freda S. Brauman; m. Sharon Lea Kruse 1964; one d.; ed MIT and Univ. of California (Berkeley and Los Angeles); Asst Prof., Stanford Univ. 1963–69, Assoc. Prof. 1969–72, Prof. 1972–80, J. G. Jackson-C. J. Wood Prof. 1980–, Chair. 1979–83, 1995–96; Deputy Ed. Science 1985–2000, Chair. Sr Editorial Bd 2000–; mem. editorial bds several journals including Nouveau Journal de Chimie 1977–85, Chemical Physics Letters 1982–85, Chemical and Engineering News 1982–84, Journal of Physical Chemistry 1985–87; mem. Nat. Research Council Bd on Chemical Sciences and Tech., advisory panels of NASA, Nat. Science Found., Atomic Energy Comm.; mem. NAS and AAAS; Award in Pure Chemistry and Harrison-Howe Award, American Chemical Soc., James Flack Norris Award in Physical Organic Chemistry, Arthur C. Cope Scholar Award, NAS Award in Chemical Sciences 2001. *Publications:* over 270 publs in scientific journals. *Address:* Department of Chemistry, Stanford University, Stanford, CA 94305-5080 (office); 849 Tolman Drive, Palo Alto, CA 94305, USA (home). *Telephone:* (415) 723-3023 (office); (415) 493-1378 (home). *Fax:* (650) 725-0259 (office). *E-mail:* brauman@stanford.edu (office). *Website:* www.stanford.edu/dept/chemistry/faculty/brauman (office).

BRAUN, Carol Moseley (see Moseley-Braun, Carol).

BRAUN, Ewa, MA; Polish costume designer, production decorator and art director; *Lecturer, Polish National Film, Television and Theatre School;* b. 2 Aug. 1944, Kraków; ed Warsaw Univ.; costume designer, Documentary Film Producers 1967–72; interior decorator, Art Dir, Film Production Agency 1972–99; mem. Polish Film Makers 1994–; Lecturer, Polish Film, Television and Theatre School, Łódź 1999–. *Films:* interior decorations and designs in over 60 films including Illumination 1972, Jealousy and Medicine 1973, Hotel Pacific 1975, Camouflage 1977, Career of Nikodem Dyzma 1979, Queen Bona 1980, C.K. Dezerterzy 1985, Young Magician (Gdańsk Bronze Lions 1987)

1986, Europe, Europe 1990, Eminent Domain 1991, Coupable d'innocence 1992, The Silent Touch 1992, Schindler's List (Acad. Award for Art Direction/ Set Decoration 1994) 1993, Les Milles 1995, Holy Week 1995, Bandit 1996, Palais de la Santé 1997, Brother of Our God 1997, Jacob the Liar 1997, Gold Deserts 1998. *Leisure interests:* movies, travels, music, literature. *Address:* Polish National Film, Television and Theatre School, ul. Targowa 61/ 63, 90-323 Łódź, Poland (office). *Telephone:* (42) 6749494 (office); (22) 6428153 (home). *Fax:* (42) 6748153 (office). *E-mail:* braunewa@hotmail.com (home); ebraun@parta.onet.pl (home). *Website:* www.filmschool.lodz.pl.

BRAUN, Pinkas; Swiss actor and director; b. 7 Jan. 1923, Zürich; s. of Chaja and Nathan Braun; m. (divorced); one s. two d.; partner Ingrid Resch; ed drama school, Zürich; mem. of co. of Schauspielhaus Zürich 1945–50, 1952–56; own co. 1950–51; freelance 1957–; has undertaken theatre work as actor and dir in Germany, Austria and Israel and TV and cinema work in Germany, Austria, France, Italy and UK. *Roles include:* Woyzeck, Baron (in Nachtasyl), Pelegrin (in Santa Cruz), Salieri (in Amadeus), Shylock (in The Merchant of Venice), Iago (in Othello), Otto Frank (in The Diary of Anne Frank), George Bernard Shaw (in The Best of Friends). *Films include:* Rätsel der roten Orchidee, Das (The Puzzle of the Red Orchid) 1962, Das Feuerschiff (The Lightship) 1963, Clint el solitario (Clint the Stranger) 1967, Die Zeit danach 1992, Komiker (Comedian) 2000, Hilfe, ich bin ein Junge (Help, I'm a Boy!) 2002. *Television includes:* Grenzenloses Himmelblau 1985, Die Katze von Kensington 1996, Annas Fluch - Tödliche Gedanken 1998, Edelweiss 2001, Singapur-Express–Geheimnis einer Liebe 2002. *Dance:* The Last Escape, Dog Eat Dog, Tout Feu, Tout Flamme, K, Das Feuerschiff, Das Wunder des Malachias, Wir Wunderkinder etc. *Publications:* trans. into German of most of Edward Albee's plays. *Address:* Lamontstr. 1 (III), 81679 Munich, Germany (home). *Telephone:* (89) 473734 (home). *Fax:* (89) 473734 (home). *E-mail:* ip.resch-brown@bluewin.ch (home).

BRAUN, Volker; German poet and playwright; b. 7 May 1939, Dresden; ed Univ. of Leipzig; Asst Dir Deutsches Theater, Berlin 1972–77, Berlin Ensemble 1979–90; mem. Akad. der Künste, Berlin; Heinrich Mann Prize 1980, Bremen Literature Prize 1986, Nat. Prize, First Class 1988, Berlin Prize 1989, Schiller Commemorative Prize 1992, Büchner Prize 2000. *Plays:* Die Kipper 1965, Grosser Frieden 1979, Dmitri 1982, Die Ubergangsgesellschaft 1987, Lenins Tod 1988, Transit Europa: Der Ausflug der Toten 1988, Böhmen am Meer 1992. *Publications:* poetry: Provokation für mich 1965, Vorläufiges 1966, Wir und nicht sie 1970, Gegen die symmetrische Welt 1974, Training des aufrechten Gangs 1979, Langsamer knirschender Morgen 1987, Der Stoff zum Leben 1990, Lustgarten Preussen 1996; prose: KriegsErklärung 1967, Gedichte 1972, Es genügt nicht die einfache Wahrheit 1975, Unvollendete Geschichte 1977, Hinze-Kunze-Roman 1985, Bodenloser Satz 1990, Der Wendehals: Eine Enterhaltung 1995, Lustgarten Preußen 1996, Wir befinden uns soweit wohl. Wir sind erst einmal am Ende 1998, Tumulus 1999, Das Wirklichgewollte 2000, Das unbesetzte Gebiet 2004, Das Mittagsmahl 2007; essays: Verheerende Folgen magnelnden Anscheins innerbetrieblicher Demokratie 1988. *Address:* Wolfshagenerstrasse 68, 13187 Berlin, Germany (home).

BRAUNFELS, Michael; German composer, pianist and teacher; b. 3 April 1917, Munich; s. of Walter Braunfels and Bertele Braunfels (née von Hildebrand); m. Mechthild Russel 1954; two s. three d.; studied piano in Basle under Paul Baumgartner and composition with Frank Martin; concert pianist in all West European music centres, Near East, Asia and Africa 1949–; Prof. of Piano, Cologne Music Coll. 1954–. *Compositions include:* two piano concertos, Cembaloconcerto 1956, Oboe concerto 1960, Symphony for 12 celli 1975, Concerto for cello and piano with orchestra 1976, Concerto for string trio and string orchestra 1978, Das Parlament (variations for orchestra) 1982, Sinfonietta serena seria 1984, The King's Messenger (musical for children), chamber music, lieder and piano music. *Leisure interest:* history. *Address:* Dransdorferstrasse 40, 50968 Cologne, Germany. *Telephone:* (221) 383660 (home). *Fax:* (221) 383660 (home).

BRAUNGART, Michael, PhD; German chemist and academic; *Professor of Process Engineering, University of Lüneburg;* ed Univs of Darmstadt, Konstanz and Hannover; fmr Greenpeace activist, led formation of Chem. Section of Greenpeace International, Leader of Greenpeace Chem. 1985; now Prof. of Process Eng, Univ. of Lüneburg 1994–, also Dir interdisciplinary materials flow man. Masters programme; Founder and Scientific Dir Environmental Protection Encouragement Agency International Umweltforschung GmbH, Hamburg 1987–; Co-founder and Prin. McDonough Braungart Design Chemistry, Charlottesville, Va, USA; Co-founder and Scientific Dir HUI Hamburger Umweltinstitut eV 1989; Visiting Prof., Darden School of Business. *Publications:* Hannover Principles of Design: Design for Sustainability 2000, Cradle to Cradle: Remaking the Way We Make Things 2002. *Address:* Trostbrücke 4, 20457 Hamburg, Germany (office). *Telephone:* (40) 879762-0 (office). *Fax:* (40) 879762-26 (office). *E-mail:* braungart@braungart.com (office). *Website:* www.braungart.com (office).

BRAUNWALD, Eugene, MD; American physician and academic; *Hersey Distinguished Professor of Theory and Practice of Physical Medicine, Harvard University;* b. 15 Aug. 1929, Vienna, Austria; m. 1st Nina Starr 1952 (deceased); three d.; m. 2nd Elaine Smith 1994; ed New York Univ.; successively Chief of Section of Cardiology, Clinic of Surgery, Cardiology Br. and Clinical Dir Nat. Heart, Lung & Blood Inst. 1958–68; Prof. and Chair. Dept of Medicine, Univ. of Calif. San Diego School of Medicine 1968–72; Hersey Prof. of Theory and Practice of Physical Medicine, Harvard Medical School 1972–96, Hersey Distinguished Prof. of Theory and Practice of Physical Medicine 1996–, Faculty Dean for Academic Programs 1996–2003; Sr Consultant in Medicine Mass. Gen. Hosp. 1994–; Vice-Pres. Academic Programs Partners Healthcare System 1996–2003; Herrmann Blumgart Prof. of Medicine 1980–89; Chair. Dept of Medicine, Peter Bent Brigham Hosp. (now Brigham & Women's Hosp.) 1972–96; Chair. TIMI Study Group, Brigham & Women's Hosp. 1984–; 14 hon. degrees; J. Allyn Taylor Int. Prize in Medicine 1993, and many other awards. *Publications:* over 1,200 articles, reviews and book chapters. *Address:* TIMI Study Group, 350 Longwood Avenue, Boston, MA 02215, USA (office). *Telephone:* (617) 732-8989 (office). *Fax:* (617) 975-0955 (office). *E-mail:* ebraunwald@partners.org (office). *Website:* www.timi.org (office).

BRÄUTIGAM, Hans Otto, DJur, LLM; German fmr diplomatist and fmr politician; b. 6 Feb. 1931, Völklingen, Saar; s. of Maximilian Bräutigam and Margarethe Sauerwald; m. Dr Hildegard Becker 1961; two s.; ed Bonn Univ. and Harvard Law School, USA; Research Asst in Int. Law, Heidelberg 1958–62; served in foreign service of FRG 1962–74; Deputy Head, Perm. Representation of FRG to GDR 1974–77, Dir Fed. Chancellor's Office, Bonn 1977–80; Foreign Office, Bonn 1980–82, Perm. Rep. to GDR 1982–89; Perm. Rep. of FRG to UN 1989–90; Brandenburg Minister of Justice 1990–99; mem. Bd Dirs Foundation for Remembrance, Responsibility and Future, Berlin 2000–02, Chair. 2004–06; Grosses Verdienstkreuz mit Stern der Bundesrepublik Deutschland. *Leisure interests:* arts, literature. *Address:* Eichenallee 37, 14050 Berlin, Germany (home). *Telephone:* (30) 3048037 (home). *Fax:* (30) 3048037 (home). *E-mail:* hobraeutigam@gmx.de (home).

BRAVO, Rose Marie; American retail executive; *Vice-Chairman, Burberry Ltd;* ed Bronx High School of Science and Fordham Univ., Bronx, New York; began retailing career at Abraham & Strauss 1971–74; joined R. H. Macy and Co., New York as assoc. buyer 1974, various positions 1974–87, Chair. and CEO I. Magnin Specialty Div. 1987–92; Pres. Saks Fifth Avenue, New York 1992–97; CEO Burberry Ltd, London, UK 1997–2006, Vice-Chair. 2006–, mem. Bd Burberry Group PLC 1997–; mem. Bd Tiffany & Co., The Estee Lauder Cos, Inc., Nat. Italian American Foundation; Vice-Chair. Kennedy Center's Corp. Fund Bd; mem Advisory Bd Fashion Group International, The Fashion Inst. of Tech., New York; Trustee Fordham Univ.; honoured for excellence in retailing by Nat. Italian American Foundation, March of Dimes, City of Hope, Eleanor Lambeth Award, Council of Fashion Design Awards, New York 2003, ranked by Fortune magazine amongst 50 Most Powerful Women in Business outside the US (29th) 2003, (13th) 2004, (13th) 2005, ranked by Forbes magazine amongst 100 Most Powerful Women (63rd) 2005, ranked by the Financial Times amongst Top 25 Businesswomen in Europe (ninth) 2005. *Address:* Burberry Ltd, 18–22 Haymarket, London, SW1 4DQ, England (office). *Telephone:* (20) 7968-0412 (office). *Fax:* (20) 7318-2666 (office). *Website:* www.burberry.com (office).

BRAYBROOKE, David, PhD, FRSC; Canadian/American philosopher, academic and author; *Professor of Government, Professor of Philosophy and Centennial Commission Chair in the Liberal Arts, University of Texas at Austin;* b. 18 Oct. 1924, Hackettstown, NJ; s. of Walter Leonard Braybrooke and Netta Rose Braybrooke (née Foyle); m. 1st Alice Boyd Noble 1948 (divorced 1982); two s. one d.; m. 2nd Margaret Eva Odell 1984 (divorced 1994); m. 3rd Gomyo Michiko 1994; ed Hobart Coll., New School for Social Research, Downing Coll., Cambridge, UK, Columbia Univ., Harvard and Cornell Univs, USA, New Coll., Oxford, UK; Instructor, History and Literature, Hobart and William Smith Colls 1948–50; Teaching Fellow, Econ., Cornell Univ. 1950–52; Instructor, Philosophy, Univ. of Mich., USA 1953–54, Bowdoin Coll. 1954–56; Asst Prof. of Philosophy, Yale Univ., USA 1956–63; Assoc. Prof. of Philosophy and Politics, Dalhousie Univ., Halifax 1963–65, Prof. 1965–88, McCulloch Prof. of Philosophy and Politics 1988–90, Prof. Emer. 1990–; Prof. of Govt, Prof. of Philosophy and Centennial Comm. Chair in the Liberal Arts Univ. of Texas at Austin 1990–; Visiting Fellow, Wolfson Coll., Cambridge, UK 1985–86; Fellowships of Canada Council and Social Sciences and Humanities Research Council, Canada; Fellowship, American Council of Learned Socs 1952–53, Rockefeller Foundation Grant 1959–60, Guggenheim Fellow 1962–63. *Publications:* A Strategy of Decision: Policy Evaluation as a Social Process (with C. E. Lindblom) 1963, Philosophical Problems of the Social Sciences 1965, Three Tests for Democracy 1968, Traffic Congestion Goes through the Issue-Machine 1974, Ethics in the World of Business 1983, Philosophy of Social Science 1987, Meeting Needs 1987, Logic on the Track of Social Change (with B. Bryson and P. K. Schotch) 1995, Social Rules (co-author) 1996, Moral Objectives, Rules and the Forms of Social Change 1998, Natural Law Modernized 2001, Utilitarianism: Resorations, Repairs, Renovations 2004, Analytical Political Philosophy 2006. *Leisure interests:* reading (poetry, fiction, history), listening to music, walking. *Address:* Department of Government, University of Texas at Austin, Austin, TX 78712, USA (office); Department of Philosophy, Dalhousie University, Halifax, NS B3H 3J5, Canada (office); 1500 Scenic Drive, 300, Austin, TX 78703, USA (home); 1 Prince Street 510, Dartmouth, NS, B2Y 4L3, Canada (home). *Telephone:* (902) 494-3810 (Canada) (office); (902) 466-3660 (Canada) (home); (512) 479-8963 (USA) (home); (512) 471-5121 (USA) (office). *E-mail:* braybrookedb@yahoo.com (office). *Website:* www.utexas.edu/cola/depts/government (office).

BRAYFIELD, Celia Frances; British author and journalist; *Senior Lecturer in Creative Writing, Brunel University, London;* b. 21 Aug. 1945, Wembley Park; d. of the late Felix Brayfield and Ada Ellen Brayfield (née Jakeman); one d.; ed St. Paul's Girls' School, Universitaire de Grenoble; feature writer, Daily Mail 1969–71, TV critic, Evening Standard 1974–82, The Times 1983–88; columnist, Sunday Telegraph 1989–90, The Times 1998–; contrib. to numerous other media; Dir Nat. Acad. of Writing 1999–2003; Sr Lecturer in Creative Writing, Brunel Univ., London 2005–; Trustee One Parent Families 1988–; mem. Soc. of Authors. *Publications:* The Body Show Book 1981, Glitter: The Truth About Fame 1985, Pearls 1987, The Prince 1990, White Ice 1993, Harvest 1995, Bestseller 1996, Getting Home 1998, Sunset 1999, Heartswap

2000, Mr Fabulous and Friends 2003, Wild Weekend 2004, Deep France 2004; contrib. various journals, magazines and newspapers. *Leisure interests:* family life, the arts. *Address:* Curtis Brown Ltd, Haymarket House, 28–29 Haymarket, London, SW1Y 4SP, England (office). *Telephone:* (20) 7393-4400 (office). *Fax:* (20) 7393-4401 (office). *E-mail:* celia@celiabrayfield.com (office). *Website:* www.celiabrayfield.com.

BRAZAUSKAS, Algirdas Mykolas, DEcon; Lithuanian politician; b. 22 Sept. 1932, Rokiškis; s. of Kazimieras Brazauskienė and Zofija Brazauskas; m. Kristina Brazauskienė; ed Kaunas Polytechnical Inst.; Sr Engineer, Kaunas Hydroelectric Power Station 1956–57; Head Petrašiūnai Construction and Ass. Bd Energy Construction Trust 1958–61; Dir of Construction, Kaunas Reinforced Concrete Structures Plant 1961; Head Construction Board of Kaunas Construction Trust 1961–62; Head Building Materials Bd, People's Econ. Council of Lithuanian SSR 1962–65; Minister for the Construction Materials Industry of Lithuanian SSR 1965–66; First Deputy Chair. of State Planning Cttee, Lithuanian SSR 1966–77; Deputy, Supreme Council of Lithuania 1967–90; cand. mem. Cen. Cttee of Lithuanian CP 1966–76, mem. 1976–92, Sec. for Industry and Economy, Cen. Cttee of Lithuanian CP 1977–88, First Sec. 1988–90; Chair. Democratic Labour Party 1990–93; Chair. Presidium Lithuanian SSR 1990; mem. Reconstituent Seimas (Supreme Council) for Kaišiadorys 1990–92, mem. Seimas 1992–, Speaker 1992; Deputy Chair. USSR Supreme Soviet 1990; Deputy Premier of Lithuania 1990–91; Acting Pres. of Lithuania 1992; Pres. of Lithuania 1993–98; Chair. Lithuanian Social Democratic Party (LSDP) (Lietuvos Socialdemokratų Partija) 2000–07; Prime Minister of Lithuania 2001–06 (resgnd); Grand Cross of the Order of Vytautas the Great, Order of Vytautas the Great with the Golden Chain 2003; Lithuanian Independence Medal. *Publications:* A Strategy of Developing a Building Complex on the Example of the Lithuanian SSR (with V. Matulaitis) 1988, An Interview for the Lithuanian Radio: 14 Jan 1989–24 Nov 1989 (co-author) 1990, Lithuanian Divorce 1992, Five Years as the President 2000, Self-Determination: 1988–1991 2004, Lithuania's Power: Works Accomplished and Thoughts about the Future 2004, Even Then We Worked for the Benefit of Lithuania 2007; numerous articles. *Leisure interest:* yachting. *Address:* Lithuanian Social Democratic Party (LSDP) (Lietuvos Socialdemokratų Partija), Barboros Radvilaites g. 1, Vilnius 01124 (office); Turniškių 30, Vilnius 2016, Lithuania (home). *Telephone:* (5) 261-3907 (office). *Fax:* (5) 261-5420 (office). *E-mail:* info@lsdp.lt (office). *Website:* www.lsdp.lt (office).

BREAM, Julian, CBE, FRCM, FRNCM; British classical guitarist and lutenist; b. 15 July 1933, London; s. of Henry G. Bream; m. 1st Margaret Williamson; one adopted s.; m. 2nd Isobel Sanchez 1980 (divorced); ed Royal Coll. of Music; began professional career Cheltenham 1947, London debut, Wigmore Hall 1950; has made many transcriptions for guitar of Romantic and Baroque works; commissioned new works from Britten, Walton, Henze and Arnold; tours throughout the world, giving recitals as soloist and with the Julian Bream Consort (f. 1960); many recitals with Sir Peter Pears and Robert Tear, and as guitar duo with John Williams; 60th Birthday Concert, Wigmore Hall, London 1993; Hon. DUniv (Surrey) 1968, Hon. DMus (Leeds) 1984; Villa-Lobos Gold Medal 1976, Gramophone Award for Best DVD (for My Life in Music) 2007, numerous recording awards. *Leisure interests:* playing the guitar, cricket, table tennis, gardening, backgammon. *Address:* c/o Hazard Chase Limited, 25 City Road, Cambridge CB1 1DP, England (office). *Telephone:* (1223) 312400 (office). *Fax:* (1223) 460827 (office). *E-mail:* info@hazardchase.co.uk (office). *Website:* www.hazardchase.co.uk (office).

BREARLEY, John Michael, OBE; British psychoanalyst and fmr professional cricketer; b. 28 April 1942, Harrow, Middlesex; s. of Horace Brearley and of the late Midge Brearley; pnr Mana Sarabhai; two c.; ed City of London School and St John's Coll., Cambridge; right-hand opening batsman, occasional wicket-keeper; played for Cambridge Univ. 1961–64, captained Cambridge Univ. 1963, 1964; awarded county cap (Middx) 1964; Capt. of Middx (winning County Championships four times and Gillette Cup twice) 1971–82; Test debut 1976; Capt. of England 1977–81 (39 Tests in all); went on tours of South Africa 1964–65, Pakistan 1967, India, Sri Lanka and Australia 1976–77, Pakistan 1977–78, Australia 1978–79, Australia and India 1979–80; holds record for most runs scored at Cambridge Univ. (4,310 at an average of 38.48) 1964; scored 312 not out for MCC under-25 v. North Zone, Peshawar 1967; Lecturer in Philosophy, University of Newcastle-upon-Tyne 1968–71; Assoc. mem. British Psycho-Analytical Soc. 1985, Full mem. 1990; occasional cricket journalism and speaking; Hon. DCL (Lancaster) 1999; Wisden Cricketer of the Year 1977. *Publications:* (with Dudley Doust) The Return of the Ashes 1978, The Ashes Retained (with Dudley Doust) 1979, Phoenix: the Series that Rose from the Ashes 1982, The Art of Captaincy 1985, 2001, Arlott in Conversation with Mike Brearley (with John Arlott) 1986. *Address:* c/o Middlesex County Cricket Club, Lord's Cricket Ground, St John's Wood Road, London, NW8 8QN, England. *Telephone:* (20) 7289-1300.

BREAUX, John B., JD; American business executive and fmr politician; *Senior Managing Director, Clinton Group Inc.;* b. 1 March 1944, Crowley, La; s. of Ezra Breaux and Katie Breaux; m. Lois Gail Daigle 1964; two s. two d.; ed Southwestern Univ. and State Univ. of Louisiana; called to La Bar 1967; Partner Brown, McKernan, Ingram and Breaux 1967–68; Legislative Asst to US Congressman 1968–69; Dist Asst 1969–72; mem. 92nd–99th Congresses from 7th Dist, La 1971–87; Senator from Louisiana 1987–2005 (retd); mem. House Policy and Steering Cttee, Finance Cttee 1990–2005, Chief Deputy Whip 1993–2005; mem. Senate Cttee on Commerce, Science and Transportation, on Environment and Public Works, Special Cttee on Aging, Democratic Leadership Council; Chair. Nuclear Regulation Sub cttee, Democratic Senatorial Campaign Cttee, Nat. Water Alliance 1987–88; Sr Man. Dir Clinton Group, Inc. (investment firm) 2005–; Sr Counsel Patton Boggs LLP 2005–; Sr Advisor Riverstone Holdings LLC 2005–; mem. Bd of Dirs Managed Funds Asscn (MFA) 2005–; apptd by Pres. Bush as Vice-Chair. nat. comm. to make recommendations or changes to current US tax laws 2005; Co-Chair. Nat. Bipartisan Comm. on Future of Medicare 1998–99; American Legion Award, Neptune Award, American Oceanic Org. 1980. *Address:* Clinton Group Inc., 9 West 57 Street, 26th Floor, New York, NY 10019, USA (office). *Telephone:* (212) 825-0400 (office). *Fax:* (212) 825-0079 (office). *Website:* www.clinton.com (office).

BRECHER, Michael, PhD, FRSC; Canadian political scientist and academic; *R. B. Angus Professor of Political Science, McGill University;* b. 14 March 1925, Montreal; s. of Nathan Brecher and Gisela Hopmeyer; m. Eva Danon 1950; three d.; ed McGill and Yale Univs; mem. Faculty, McGill Univ. 1952–, R. B. Angus Prof. of Political Science 1993–; Pres. Int. Studies Asscn 1999–2000; Visiting Prof., Univ. of Chicago 1963, Hebrew Univ., Jerusalem 1970–75, Univ. of Calif., Berkeley 1979, Stanford Univ. 1980; Nuffield Fellow 1955–56; Rockefeller Fellow 1964–65; Guggenheim Fellow 1965–66; f. Shashtri Indo-Canadian Inst. 1968 (Pres. 1969–71); Watumull Prize (American Hist. Asscn) 1960, Killam Awards (Canada Council) 1970–74, 1976–79, Woodrow Wilson Award (American Political Science Asscn) 1973, Fieldhouse Award for Distinguished Teaching (McGill Univ.) 1986, Distinguished Scholar Award (Int. Studies Asscn) 1995, Léon-Gérin Quebec Prize 2000, Award for High Distinction in Research, McGill Univ. 2000. *Publications:* The Struggle for Kashmir 1953, Nehru: A Political Biography 1959, The New States of Asia 1963, Succession in India 1966, India and World Politics 1968, Political Leadership in India 1969, The Foreign Policy System of Israel 1972, Israel, the Korean War and China 1974, Decisions in Israel's Foreign Policy 1975, Studies in Crisis Behavior 1979, Decisions in Crisis 1980, Crisis and Change in World Politics 1986, Crises in the 20th Century (Vols I, II) 1988, Crisis, Conflict and Instability 1989, Crises in World Politics 1993, A Study of Crisis 1997, 2000, Millennial Reflections on International Studies (Vols 1–5) 2002, International Political Earthquakes 2008; over 85 articles in journals. *Address:* Department of Political Science, McGill University, 855 Sherbrooke Street West, Montreal, PQ H3A 2T7, Canada (office); PO Box 4438, Jerusalem 91043, Israel (home). *Telephone:* (514) 398-4816 (office). *Fax:* (514) 398-1770 (office). *E-mail:* michael.brecher@mcgill.ca (office). *Website:* www.mcgill.ca/politicalscience (office).

BRÉCHIGNAC, Catherine, DSc; French physicist; *Executive President, Centre National de la Recherche Scientifique (National Center for Scientific Research) (CNRS);* b. (Catherine Teillac), 12 June 1946, Paris; d. of Jean Teillac and Andrée Teillac (née Kerleguer); m. Philippe Bréchignac 1969; two s. one d.; ed Ecole Normale Supérieure, Fontenay-aux-Roses; research asst CNRS 1971–78, supervisor 1978–85, Dir of Research 1985–91, Del. to the Scientific Dir, Dept of Physical and Math. Sciences 1985–89, Dir of Aimé Cotton Lab. 1989–95, Scientific Dir, Dept of Physical and Math. Sciences 1995–97, Dir-Gen., CNRS 1997–2000, Exec. Pres. 2006–; Assoc. Researcher Institut d'astrophysique d'Ottawa, Canada 1979–80; Visiting Prof. Ecole Polytechnique de Lausanne 1987–; Adjunct Prof. then Distinguished Visiting Scholar, Georgia-Tech Univ. 2001–; Pres. Int. Council for Science (ICSU) 2008–; corresp. mem. French Acad. des Sciences 1997, mem. 2005; mem. French Acad. Tech. 2000; corresp. mem. American Acad. of Arts and Sciences; Officier de la Légion d'honneur, Ordre nat. du mérite; Dr hc (Univ. of Berlin, Georgia Tech. Inst., Atlanta, Ecole polytechnique fédérale de Lausanne); French Academy of Science Prize 1991, Acad. des Sciences Prize 1991, CNRS Silver Medal 1994, Holweck Prize and Medal 2003;. *Leisure interests:* opera, painting, literature. *Address:* Centre National de la Recherche Scientifique (CNRS), 3 rue Michel Ange, 75794 Paris cedex 16, France (office). *Telephone:* 1-44-96-44-71 (office). *Fax:* 1-44-96-49-65 (office). *E-mail:* catherine.brechignac@cnrs-dir.fr (office). *Website:* www.cnrs.fr (office).

BRÉCHOT, Christian, PhD; French medical researcher and professor of cell biology; b. 23 July 1952, Paris; s. of Claude Bréchot and Marie-Louise Bréchot (née Tisne); m. 1 st (divorced); one s. two d.; m. 2 nd Patrizia Paterlini; two s.; ed Lycée Montaigne, Paris, Lycée Louis le Grand, Paris, Univ. of Paris VII, Inst. Pasteur; Prof. of Cell Biology, Necker-Enfants Malades Faculty of Medicine, Univ. of Paris V 1989–2001; Head Hybridotest Lab., Inst. Pasteur 1990–98; Head Institut nat. de la santé et de la recherche médicale (INSERM) Research Unit U.370, Necker Hosp., Paris 1993–2001, Head Liver Unit, Necker Hosp. 1997–2001, Head Nat. Reference Centre on the molecular epidemiology of viral hepatitis, Inst. Pasteur and INSERM U.370 1998–2001, Dir-Gen. INSERM 2001–07 (resgnd); WHO study co-ordinator for standardization of PCR in diagnosis of HIV infections 1988–91; mem. Scientific Cttee, Asscn pour la Recherche sur le Cancer 1988–2001, Agence Française du Sang 1993–96; mem. Inst. Universitaire de France 1992–, European Asscn for Virological Diagnosis, American Asscn for the Study of Liver Diseases, French Asscn for the Study of the Liver, European Asscn for the Study of the Liver (Sec. 1993–97); Biotrol Award 1982, Fondation pour la Recherche Médicale Award 1982, Abott Award for research on viral hepatitis 1983, Ligue Française contre le cancer Paris Award for research on liver cancer and hepatitis B virus 1985, APMS Award for research on prevention of transmissible diseases 1987, French Medical Soc., René Fauvert Award 1987, French Acad. of Medicine Award 1996, Fondation de France Jean Valade Award 2000. *Leisure interests:* paintings, tennis, rugby. *Address:* c/o Institut National de la Santé de la Recherche Médicale (INSERM), 101 rue de Tolbiac, 75654 Paris Cédex 13, France (office).

BRECKENRIDGE, Sir Alasdair Muir, Kt, CBE, MD, MSc, FRCP, FRCPE, FRSE; British scientist and academic; *Chairman, Medicines and Healthcare Products Regulatory Agency (MHRA);* b. 7 May 1937, Arbroath, Scotland; s. of Thomas Breckenridge and Jane Breckenridge; m. Jean M. Boyle 1967; two s.; ed Bell-Baxter School, Cupar, Fife and Univ. of St Andrews; House Physician and Surgeon, Dundee Royal Infirmary 1961–62; House Physician, Registrar,

www.worldwhoswho.com

Lecturer, Sr Lecturer, Hammersmith Hosp. and Royal Postgraduate Medical School 1963–74; Prof. of Clinical Pharmacology, Univ. of Liverpool 1974–2002, Prof. Emer. 2002–; mem. Cttee on Safety of Medicines 1981, Chair. 1999–2003; Chair. Medicines and Healthcare Products Regulatory Agency (MHRA) 2003–; Councillor Int. Union of Pharmacology 1981–87; Foreign Sec. British Pharmacological Soc. 1983–91, Dir Research and Devt, Mersey Region 1992–96; Vice-Chair. Advisory Cttee on Drugs 1985–98; mem. Council Royal Coll. of Physicians 1983–86, Panel of Tropical Diseases, Wellcome Trust 1984–88, WHO Steering Cttee on Chemotherapy of Malaria 1987–91, MRC Physiological Systems and Disorders Bd 1987–91, Council MRC 1992–96, Cen. Research and Devt Cttee, Nat. Health Service 1991–95; Chair. NW Regional Office of the Nat. Health Service 1996–99; Chair. Jt Medical Advisory Cttee of Higher Educ. Funding Councils of the UK 1998–2002;; Goulstonian Lecturer, Royal Coll. of Physicians 1975; Paul Martini Prize for Clinical Pharmacology 1974, Poulson Medal (Norwegian Pharmacological Soc.) 1988, Lilly Prize (British Pharmacological Soc.) 1993. *Publications:* articles in scientific and medical journals. *Leisure interest:* golf. *Address:* Medicines and Healthcare Products Regulatory Agency, Market Towers, 1 Nine Elms Lane, London, SW8 5NQ (office); Cree Cottage, Feather Lane, Wirral, L69 3BX, England (home). *Telephone:* (20) 7084-2534 (office); (151) 342-1096 (home). *Website:* www.mhra.gov.uk/index.htm (office).

BREDESEN, Philip Norman, AB; American state official; *Governor of Tennessee;* b. 21 Nov. 1943, New York; s. of Phillip Norman Bredesen, Sr and Norma Bredesen (née Walborn); m. 1st Susan Cleaves 1968 (divorced 1974); m. 2nd Andrea Conte 1974; one s.; ed Red Jacket Cen. School, NY, Harvard Univ.; computer programmer Itek Corpn, Mass. 1967–70; Dir of Systems Devt G.D. Seale & Co. 1971–73, Div. Man. 1973–75; Dir of Special Projects Hosp. Affiliates Int. Nashville 1976–80; f. Healthplans Corpn (later HealthAmerica Corpn) 1980, Chair., CEO 1980–86 (sold co.); co-f. Coventry Corpn 1986, Chair. 1986–90; co-f. Clinical Pharmaceuticals 1986, Chair. 1986–93; Mayor of Nashville 1991–99; Pres. Bredex Corpn 2000–02; Gov. of Tenn. 2003–; f. Nashville's Table 1989, mem. Bd of Dirs 1989–91; f. Land Trust for Tenn. 1999, Chair. 1999–2001; mem. Bd of Dirs. Tenn. State Univ. Foundation, Nashville Publrs' Library Foundation 1997–; mem. Bd of Trustees Frist Center for Visual Arts 1998–; Democrat. *Leisure interests:* oil painting, flying glider planes, jogging, hunting, fishing, skiing, hiking. *Address:* Office of the Governor, State Capitol Building, Nashville, TN 37243-0001 (office); 1724 Chickering Road, Nashville, TN 37215-4908, USA (home). *Telephone:* (615) 741-200 (office). *E-mail:* Phil.Bredesen@state.tn.us (office). *Website:* www.tennessee.gov/governor (office).

BREDIN, Frédérique Marie Denise Colette; French politician and media executive; b. 2 Nov. 1956, Paris; d. of Jean-Denis Bredin (q.v.) and Danièle Hervier; m. Jean-Pascal Beaufret 1985; two c.; ed Inst. d'Etudes Politiques, Paris and Ecole Nat. d'Admin; Insp. Gen. of Finance 1980–84; special assignment to Minister of Culture 1984–86, to Pres. of Repub. 1986–88; Socialist Deputy to Nat. Ass. 1988–91, 1995–, to European Parl. 1994–96; Mayor of Fécamp 1989–95; Minister of Youth and Sport 1991–93; Nat. Sec. Socialist Party, with responsibility for Culture and Media 1996–2000; Dir of Strategies and Devt, Lagardère Médias Group 2000, Vice-Pres. New Markets, Hachette Filipacchi Médias (subsidiary of Lagardère) 2004–; Dir Etudes Marketing, Press Magazine France 2004–; Publr Journal du Dimanche 2004–. *Address:* Hachette Filipacchi Médias, Hachette Livre 43, quai de Grenelle, 75905 Paris Cedex 15, France (office). *E-mail:* webmaster@hachette-livre.fr. *Website:* www.hachette.com.

BREDIN, Jean-Denis, LèsL; French lawyer; b. 17 May 1929, Paris; m. Danièle Hervier; two c. (including Frédérique Bredin q.v.); ed Lycée Charlemagne and Facultés de Droit et des Lettres, Paris; called to the Bar 1950–; Prof. Faculté de Droit, Rennes 1958, Lille 1967; Adviser to Council for Higher Educ. 1968–69; Prof. of Pvt. Law, Univ. of Paris-Dauphine 1969; Prof. Univ. of Paris I 1971–93, Prof. Emer. 1993–; worked with Edgar Faure on higher educ. reform 1968; Vice-Pres. Mouvement des radicaux de gauche 1976–80; Pres. Man. Bd Bibliothèque Nationale 1983–88; Vice-Pres. Comm. Moinot 1981; Pres. Comm. for Reform of Cinema 1982; Adviser on Audiovisual Matters to Prime Minister 1985; mem. Acad. Française 1989–; Prix Gobert 1984. *Publications include:* Traité de droit commercial international 1967, La République de Monsieur Pompidou 1974, Les Français au pouvoir 1977, Eclats 1976, Joseph Cailleux 1980, L'Affaire 1983, Un coupable 1985, L'Absence 1986, La Tâche 1988, Weisbuch 1989, Un enfant sage 1990, Battements de coeur 1991, Bernard Lazare 1992, Comédie des Apparences 1994, Encore un peu de temps 1996, Convaincre, dialogues sur l'éloquence 1997, L'Affaire 1998, Une singulière famille 1999, Rien ne va plus 2000, Lettre à Dieu le fils 2001, Un tribunal au garde-à-vous 2002, Et des amours desquelles nous parlons 2004, Mots et pas perdus: images du Palais 2004, On ne meurt qu'une fois: Charlotte Corday 2006. *Address:* 130 rue du Faubourg Saint-Honoré, 75008 Paris; Institut de France, 23 quai de Conti, 75006 Paris, France. *Telephone:* 1-44-35-35-35 (office).

BREEDON, Tim, MA, MSc; British insurance industry executive; *Group Chief Executive, Legal and General Group Plc;* m.; three c.; ed Calthorpe Comprehensive School, Fleet, Hampshire, Farnborough Coll., Worcester Coll. Oxford, London Business School; began career with Standard Chartered Bank 1981–85; joined Legal & General Investment Man. Ltd 1987, Man. Quantitative Products and Index Funds 1987, Dir Index Funds 1994, Man.-Dir (Index Funds) 2000–02, mem. Bd of Dirs and Group Dir (Investments) 2002–05, Deputy Group Chief Exec. Legal & General Group Plc 2005–06, Group Chief Exec. 2006–, mem. Group Risk and Compliance Cttee, Corp. Social Responsibility Cttee, Group Capital Cttee, Group Insurance Risk Cttee, Group Investment and Market Risk Cttee; mem. Bd of Dirs Asscn of British Insurers. *Address:* Legal & General Group Plc, One Coleman Street, London, EC2R 5AA, England (office). *Telephone:* (20) 3124-2000 (office). *Fax:* (20) 7528-6222 (office). *E-mail:* info@legalandgeneralgroup.com (office). *Website:* www.legalandgeneralgroup.com (office).

BREEN, Edward D., Jr, BS; American business executive; *Chairman and CEO, Tyco International Inc.;* m.; three c.; ed Grove City Coll., Pa; joined General Instrument (GI) Corpn 1978, Sr Vice-Pres. of Sales 1988–94, Pres. GI Broadband Networks Group 1994–97, Chair., Pres. and CEO GI 1997–2000; Vice-Pres. Motorola 2000–02, Pres. Motorola Broadband Communications Sector 2000–01, Pres. Motorola Networks Sector 2001–02, Pres. and COO Motorola Jan.–July 2002; Chair. and CEO Tyco International Inc. July 2002–; mem. Bd Dirs Comcast Corpn; Vanguard Award, Nat. Cable TV Asscn 1998, ranked by CableFAX magazine as one of the top 15 of the 100 most influential people in cable 1999. *Address:* Tyco International Inc., 9 Roszel Road, Princeton, NJ 08540, USA (office). *Telephone:* (609) 720-4200 (office). *E-mail:* directors@tyco.com (office). *Website:* www.tyco.com (office).

BREGGIN, Peter R., BA, MD; American psychiatrist; b. 5 Nov. 1936, New York; m. 3rd Ginger Ross 1984; one c. (and three c. from two previous marriages); ed Harvard Coll., Case Western Reserve School of Medicine, State Univ. of New York, Upstate Medical Center, Massachusetts Mental Health Centre; consultant Nat. Inst. of Mental Health 1966–68; psychiatrist in pvt. practice 1968–; Founder and Dir Int. Center for Study of Psychiatry and Psychology 1972–2002, Dir Emer. 2002–; Adjunct Prof. of Conflict Resolution George Mason Univ. 1990–96; Faculty Assoc. Dept of Counselling Johns Hopkins Univ. 1996–99; Ed. numerous journals, including Journal of Mind and Behaviour, Int. Journal of Risk and Society in Medicine, The Humanistic Psychologist, Review of Existential Psychology and Psychiatry; Founding Ed. Ethical Human Sciences and Services 1999–; Ludwig von Mises Award of Merit 1987, Minn. Mental Health Asscn Advocacy Award 1990, honours from Harvard Coll. *Publications:* Toxic Psychiatry 1991, Talking Back to Prozac (with Ginger Breggin) 1994, Brain-Disabling Treatments in Psychiatry 1997, The Heart of Being Helpful 1997, The War Against Children of Color (with Ginger Breggin) 1998, Talking Back to Ritalin 1998, Your Drug May Be Your Problem (with David Cohen) 1999, Reclaiming Our Children 2000, The Ritalin Fact Book 2001, The Antidepressant Fact Book 2002. *Address:* 101 East State Street, PMB 112, Ithaca, NY 14850, USA. *Telephone:* (607) 272-5328. *Fax:* (607) 272-5329. *Website:* www.breggin.com (office).

BRÉGIER, Fabrice; French aeronautics industry executive; *COO, Airbus S.A.S.;* b. 16 July 1961; m.; three c.; ed École Polytechnique and École des Mines; test engineer, Creys-Malville nuclear power station 1983–84; Sales Man. Pechiney, Japan 1984–86; Directions Régionales de l'Industrie de la Recherche et de l'Environnement (Ministry of Industry), Alsace 1986–89; Dir Econ. and Financial Affairs, Ministry of Agric. 1989–90; Tech. Advisor to Minister of Foreign Trade 1990–91, to Minister of Post and Telecommunications 1991–93; Chair. Apache MAW GIE and Eurodrone GIE, Matra Défense (later Matra BAe Dynamics) 1993–96, Dir of Stand-Off Activities 1996–98, CEO 1998–2001; CEO MBDA (European Missile Systems Company) 2001–03; Pres. and CEO Eurocopter, European Aeronautic Defence and Space Co. (EADS) 2003–06, mem. Exec. Cttee EADS 2005–, COO Airbus S.A.S. 2006–. *Address:* Airbus S.A.S.1, Rond point Maurice Bellonte, 31707 Blagnac Cedex, France (office). *Telephone:* (5) 61-93-33-33. *Fax:* (5) 61-93-49-55. *Website:* www.airbus.com (office).

BREGU, Majlinda Enver, PhD; Albanian politician; *Minister of European Integration;* b. 19 May 1974, Tirana; ed Sami Frashëri Gymnasium, Univ. of Tirana and Univ. of Urbino, Italy; worked for Albanian Radio-TV 1992–2002; Lecturer on Social Sciences and Gender Issues, Univ. of Tirana 1996–; Visiting Prof., McGill Univ., Canada 2000; mem. (Kuvendi Popullor (Parl.) (Democratic Party of Albania—Partia Demokratike e Shqipërisë) 2005–, Head Parl. Del. to European Parl. 2005, Chair. Parl. Sub-comm. for Juveniles and Equal Opportunities (in cooperation with Children's Human Rights Centre of Albania) 2006; Minister of European Integration 2007–. *Publications:* co-author: Qualitative Research for Social Sciences 2003, Media Monitoring on Domestic Violence 2003, Domestic Violence and Judiciary System 2005, Assesment of Health Care Workers 2006, National Strategy for Gender Equality 2006; ed.: Prostitute. Ci passerano davanto nel Regno dei Cieli 2004. *Address:* Ministry of European Integration, Bulevardi Dëshmoret e Kombit, Tirana, Albania (office). *Telephone:* (4) 228645 (office). *Fax:* (4) 228645 (office). *E-mail:* m.bregu@k-o-p.org (office); majlindabregu@yahoo.com (home). *Website:* www.mie.gov.al (office).

BREGVADZE, Nani Georgievna; Georgian singer; b. 21 July 1938; ed Tbilisi Conservatoire (pianoforte class under Machutadze); soloist with Georgian State Philharmonia 1959–, with Georgian popular orchestra 'Rero' 1959–64, with 'Orera' 1964–80; specializes in Georgian music and Russian romances; has toured abroad on numerous occasions; People's Artist of USSR 1983, Hon. Citizen of Tbilisi 1995, Order of Honour 1995, People's Artist of Georgia 1996, State Prize of Georgia 1997. *Address:* Irakly Abashidze str. 18A, Apt. 10, 380079 Tbilisi, Georgia. *Telephone:* (32) 22-37-22.

BREIEN, Anja; Norwegian film director; ed Inst. des hautes études cinématiques, France; Dir of short films and feature films 1967–; mem. European Film Acad.; Hon. Amanda 2005. *Short films include:* 17. Mai: en film om ritualer 1969, Ansikter 1971, Murer rundt fengslet 1972, Herbergister 1973, Mine Søsken, goddag 1974, Gamle 1975, Solvorn 1997, Å se en båt med seil (To see a boat in sail; UIP/EFA Prize, Berlin Film Festival, Best Short Feature, Toronto) 2001, Untitled (Sans titre) 2005. *Feature films include:* Vokse opp (Part 1 of Dager fra 100 år) 1967, Voldtekt (Rape) 1971, Hustruer (Wives) 1975, Den Allvarsamme Leken (Games of Love and Loneliness) 1977 (Silver Hugo Award, Chicago 1977), The Swedish (Guldbogga) 1978, Arven (Next of Kin/The Inheritance) 1979, Forfølgelsen (Witch Hunt) 1981,

Papirfuglen (Paper Bird) 1984 (Silver Hugo Award, Chicago 1984), Hustruer: ti år etter (Wives: Ten Years After) (Norwegian Film Prize Amanda) 1985, Smykketyven (Twice upon a Time) 1990, Hustruer III (Wives III) 1996, Solvorn 1997, Å se en båt med seil 2000; has also written script for film Trollsyn (Second Sight), Dir Ola Solum 1994. *Publications:* Forfølgelsen (script) 1981, Trollsyn (script) 1995. *Leisure interest:* skiing. *Address:* Norwegian Film Institute, Dronningens 6T. 16, 0152 Oslo, Norway (office). *Telephone:* 22-82-24-00. *E-mail:* anja@mfu.no (office).

BREILLAT, Catherine; French film director, screenwriter and novelist; *Professor of Auteur Cinema, European Graduate School;* b. 1948, Bressuire; Prof. of Auteur Cinema, European Grad. School, Switzerland. *Film roles include:* Last Tango in Paris 1972, Dracula Père et Fils 1977. *Films directed include:* Une vraie jeune fille (A Real Young Girl) 1975 (released 2000), Tapage nocturne (Nocturnal Uproar) 1979, 36 Fillette (Virgin) 1988, Sale comme un ange (Dirty Like an Angel) 1990, Parfait Amour (Perfect Love, jtly) 1996, Romance 1999, À ma soeur! (Fat Girl) 2001, Brève traversée (Brief Crossing) 2001, Scènes intimes 2002, Sex is Comedy 2002, Anatomie de l'enfer 2004, Une Vieille Maîtresse (The Last Mistress) 2007. *Publications include:* L'homme facile (novel), Tapage nocturne 1979, Romance 1999, Le livre du plaisir 1999, Une vraie jeune fille 2000, À ma soeur! 2001, Pornocratie 2001, Ein Mädchen 2001. *Screenplays include:* Catherine et Cie (Catherine & Co., jtly) 1975, Bilitis 1977, La peau (The Skin) 1981, Et la nave va (And the Ship Sails On) 1983, L'araignée de satin (The Satin Spider) 1984, Police 1985, Milan noir (Black Milan, jtly) 1987, Zanzibar (jtly) 1988, La nuit de l'océan (The Night of the Ocean, jtly) 1988, Aventure de Catherine C. (The Adventure of Catherine C., jtly) 1990, Le diable au corps 1990, La Thune (Money, jtly) 1991, Couples et amants (Couples and Lovers, jtly) 1994, Viens jouer dans la cour des grands (TV) 1997, Selon Matthieu 2000. *Address:* c/o European Graduate School, Ringacker, 3953 Leuk-Stadt, Switzerland (office). *Telephone:* (27) 474 9917 (office). *Fax:* (27) 474 9969 (office).

BREIMER, Douwe Durk, PhD; Dutch fmr university rector, pharmacologist and academic; b. 24 Nov. 1943, Gaasterland; m. Joan Breimer; four d.; ed Univs of Groningen and Nijmegen; apptd Prof. of Pharmacology, Leiden Univ. 1975, mem. Bd, Rector Magnificus and Pres. Exec. Bd Leiden Univ. 2001–07; Foreign Assoc. mem. Inst. of Medicine of NAS, Nat. Innovation Platform; Knight of the Order of the Dutch Lion; Dr hc (Ghent Univ., Uppsala Univ., Semmelweis Univ. (Budapest), Univ. of Navarra, Hoshi Univ. (Tokyo), Univ. of London, Université de Montréal). *Publications:* more than 500 scientific papers on pharmacokinetics, pharmacodynamics and drug metabolism. *Address:* c/o Office of the President, Leiden University, LACDR, PO Box 9502, 2300 RA Leiden, Netherlands (office). *Telephone:* (71) 5274707 (office); (71) 5176410 (home). *Fax:* (71) 5176420 (office). *E-mail:* ddbreimer@lacdr.leidenuniv.nl (office).

BREITENSTEIN, (Fredrik) Wilhelm, LLM; Finnish diplomatist (retd); b. 17 May 1933, Tampere; s. of B. Rafael Breitenstein and Ebba Huikarinen; m. 1st Dorrit I. Martin (divorced 1977); one s. three d.; m. 2nd Satu Marjatta Lefkowitz (née Nuorvala) 1978; one d.; ed Univ. of Helsinki; intern, UN Secr. New York 1957–58; Ministry of Foreign Affairs 1960–62, 1966–68, 1978–83; Attaché and Sec. of Embassy, Perm. Mission to UN, New York 1962–66; Deputy Perm. Rep. to EFTA and Int. Orgs Geneva 1968–72, Perm. Mission to UN, New York 1972–78; Gov. Asian Devt Bank 1978–83, African Devt Bank 1978–83; Alt. Gov. Inter-American Devt Bank 1978–83; Perm. Rep. to OECD and UNESCO 1983–91, Vice-Pres. UNESCO Gen. Conf. 1986, Chair. Head Comm. UNESCO 1986–88, Chair. Advisory Bd for Devt Centre, OECD 1989–90; Perm. Rep. to UN 1991–98; Pres. Gov. Council UNDP 1993, Co-Chair. Open-ended Work Group of Gen. Ass. for Reform of UN Security Council 1994–98; Vice-Pres. Preparatory Comm. for 50th Anniversary of UN; mem. Exec. Bd. Int. Asscn of Perm. Reps to UN; del. to numerous UN and other int. confs. *Leisure interests:* art and antiques. *Address:* c/o Ministry of Foreign Affairs, Merikasarmi, PO Box 176, 00161 Helsinki, Finland (office).

BREJON DE LAVERGNÉE, Arnauld, DenL; French museum curator; *Director, Mobilier National;* b. 25 May 1945, Rennes; s. of Jacques Brejon de Lavergnèe and Monique Perquis; m. Barbara Mercillon 1977; four c.; ed Univ. of Sorbonne, Paris; trainee curator, Louvre Museum, Museums of Cluny and Dijon 1969–70; Visiting Fellow Acad. of France in Rome 1971–72; Curator Museum of Cluny 1973–76; Curator Dept of Painting, Louvre Museum 1976–87; Gen. Curator of Heritage 1987; Curator Museum of Fine Arts, Lille 1987–2003 (oversaw 220 million French franc restoration project 1992–97); Dir Mobilier National 2003–; Corresp. mem. Acad. of Fine Arts 1993–, Acad. of Bologne; Fotillon Fellow, Yale Univ. 1977; Getty Center Art History Grant 1984; Chevalier, Légion d'honneur, Ordre nat. du Mérite, Ordre nat. des Arts et Lettres; Prix nat. de Muséographie 1987. *Publications include:* L'art italien dans les collections françaises, La collection du Bailli de Breteuil, Une monographie sur Simon Vouet, La collection des tapissiers de Louis XIV. *Address:* Mobilier National, 1, rue Berbier du Mets, 75013 Paris, France (office). *Telephone:* 1-44-08-52-00 (office). *E-mail:* communication.mobilier@culture.gouv.fr (office). *Website:* www.mobiliernational.culture.gouv.fr.

BREMAN, Jan; Dutch professor of comparative sociology; b. 24 July 1936, Amsterdam; Dir Centre of Asian Studies, Univ. of Amsterdam; Prof. Inst. of Social Studies, The Hague; extensive anthropological research in India and Indonesia 1962–; devt consultant on social policies in Asia; mem. Nat. Advisory Council on Devt Cooperation in the Netherlands; mem. Royal Netherlands Acad. of Sciences. *Publications:* Of Patronage and Exploitation 1974, Landless Labour in Colonial Java 1984, Of Peasants, Migrants and Workers 1985, Taming the Coolie Beast 1989, Beyond Patronage and Exploitation 1993, Wage Hunters and Gatherers 1994, Footloose Labour: Working India's Informal Economy (Edgar Graham Prize 1998) 1996. *Address:* Oude Hoogstraat 24, 1012 CE Amsterdam, Netherlands. *Telephone:* (20) 5252745. *Fax:* (20) 525 2446.

BREMER, Kåre, PhD; Swedish botanist, academic and university administrator; *Vice-Chancellor, Stockholm University;* b. 17 Jan. 1948, Lidingö; m. Birgitta Bremer; one s. one d.; ed Stockholm Univ.; Asst Prof., later Assoc. Prof. of Systematic Botany, Stockholm Univ. 1972–75, 1976–80, Vice Chancellor (Rector) 2004–; Head of Curator Dept of Phanerogamic Botany, Swedish Museum of Natural History 1980–89; Research Assoc. and B. A. Krukoff Curator of African Botany, Mo. Botanical Garden, USA 1985–86; Prof. of Systematic Botany, Uppsala Univ. 1989–2004, Dean of Biology 1993–99; Fellow, Royal Swedish Acad. of Sciences; Foreign Mem. Linnean Soc. of London 1998; Lund Royal Physiographic Soc. Linnaeus Prize 1999. *Publications:* numerous papers in learned journals. *Address:* Office of the Vice Chancellor, Stockholm University, 106 91 Stockholm, Sweden (office). *Telephone:* (8) 162271 (office). *E-mail:* rektor@su.se (office). *Website:* www.systbot.uu.se/staff/k_bremer/k_bremer.html (office).

BREMER, L. Paul, III, BA, MBA; American business executive, fmr diplomatist and fmr government official; *Chairman, Board of Advisors, Global Secure Corporation;* ed Yale Univ., Institut d'études politiques, Paris, Harvard Grad. School of Business Admin; joined US State Dept, Special Asst to six Secs of State, service at US Embassies in Afghanistan and Malawi; fmr Deputy Chief of Mission, US Embassy, Norway; Amb. to Netherlands 1983–86; fmr Exec. Sec., State Dept and Amb. at Large for Counter Terrorism; Presidential Envoy to Iraq and Admin. Coalition Provisional Authority 2003–04; currently Chair. Bd of Advisors, Global Secure Corpn; Man. Dir Kissinger Assocs 1989–2000; Chair. Nat. Comm. on Terrorism 1999; fmr Chair. and Chief Exec. Marsh Crisis Consulting Co.; fmr Dir Air Products and Chemicals Inc., Akzo Nobel NV, Harvard Business School Club of New York, Netherland-America Foundation; fmr Trustee Econ. Club of New York; Founder and Pres. Lincoln/Douglass Scholarship Foundation; mem. Pres.'s Homeland Security Advisory Council 2002–; mem. IISS, Council on Foreign Relations; fmr mem. NAS Comm. on Science and Tech.; State Dept Superior Honor Award, two Presidential Meritorious Service Awards, Distinguished Honor Award, Presidential Medal of Freedom 2004. *Publications:* My Year in Iraq 2006. *Address:* Global Secure Corporation, 2600 Virginia Avenue, Suite 600, Washington, DC 20037, USA (office). *Telephone:* (202) 333-8400 (office). *Fax:* (202) 333-0082 (office). *E-mail:* info@globalsecurecorp.com (office). *Website:* www.globalsecurecorp.com (office).

BREMI, Ulrich; Swiss business executive and politician; b. 6 Nov. 1929, Zürich; s. of Heinrich Bremi-Sennhauser and Johanna Bremi-Sennhauser; m. Anja Bremi-Forrer; two d.; ed School of Mechanical Eng, Winterthur and Swiss Fed. Inst. of Tech., Zürich; CEO Kaba Holding Ltd Zürich 1962–90; Chair. Bd Neue Zürcher Zeitung 1988–99, Georg Fischer AG 1989–98, Swiss Reinsurance Co. 1992–2000, Flughafen-Immobilien-Gesellschaft 1992–2000; mem. Swiss Nat. Parl. 1975–91, Chair. 1990–91; Hon. Senator St Gallen Univ. 2000. *Address:* Swiss Reinsurance Company, Mythenquai 50/60, PO Box 8022, Zürich, Switzerland (office). *Telephone:* (1) 2853553. *Fax:* (1) 2854180 (office). *E-mail:* ulrich_Bremi@swissre.com (office).

BREN, Donald L., BA; American real estate investment industry executive; *Chairman, The Irvine Company Inc.;* b. Los Angeles; m.; four c.; ed Univ. of Wash.; served as officer in US Marine Corps; f. Bren Co. to build homes in Orange County, Calif. 1958, later renamed Calif. Pacific Homes; Founder and Pres. Mission Viejo Co., Orange County 1963, sold his interest in co. 1967; purchased The Irvine Co. from The Irvine Foundation with others 1977, later mem. Exec. Cttee and Vice-Chair., bought out pnrs and elected Chair. 1983–, sole shareholder 1996–; f. Donald Bren Foundation; mem. Bd of Trustees Chapman Univ., Calif. Inst. of Tech. (Caltech), LA County Museum of Art, Orange County Museum of Art; Univ. of Calif. Presidential Medal 2004. *Leisure interests:* skiing, tennis, sailing, windsurfing. *Address:* The Irvine Company Inc., 550 Newport Center Drive, Newport Beach, CA 92660, USA (office). *Telephone:* (949) 720-2000 (office). *Fax:* (949) 720–2218 (office). *Website:* www.irvinecompany.com (office).

BRENCIU, Marius; Romanian singer (tenor); b. 11 Nov. 1973, Braşov; s. of Radu Brenciu and Maria-Elena Brenciu; m.; ed Andrei Saguna High School, Univ. of Music, Bucharest; began singing in choir of local Orthodox church aged 12; teaching asst, Univ. of Music, Bucharest 1997–2000; debut as Don Ottavio in Mozart's Don Giovanni at Bucharest Opera 1997; Perm. Leading Singer, Romanian Nat. Opera, Bucharest; Second Prize and Opera Prize, Queen Elizabeth Competition, Brussels 1999, First Prize, Young Artists Int. Auditions, New York 2001, Winner Cardiff Singer of the World (also Song Prize) 2001. *Operatic roles include:* Lenski (Eugene Onegin), Steva (Jenůfa), Alfredo (La Traviata), Idomeneo (Idomeneo). *Other repertoire includes:* Requiem (Verdi), Mass in C Minor (Mozart), Messa di Gloria (Puccini), Messe Solennelle (Gounod), A Child of our Time (Tippett). *Leisure interests:* literature, foreign languages, history, surfing the net. *Address:* c/o Young Concert Artists, Inc., 250 West 57th Street, Suite 1222, New York, NY 10107, USA (office). *Telephone:* (212) 307-6655 (office). *Fax:* (212) 581-8894 (office). *E-mail:* yca@yca.org (office). *Website:* www.yca.org (office).

BRENDEL, Alfred; Austrian pianist and writer; b. 5 Jan. 1931, Wiesenberg; s. of Ing. Albert and Ida Brendel (née Wieltschnig); m. 1st Iris Heymann-Gonzala 1960 (divorced 1972); one d.; m. 2nd Irene Semler 1975; one s. two d.; studied piano under Sofija Deželić (Zagreb), Ludovika v. Kaan (Graz), Edwin Fischer (Lucerne), Paul Baumgartner (Basel), Edward Steuermann (Salzburg); studied composition under A. Michl (Graz) and harmony under Franjo Dugan (Zagreb); first piano recital Musikverein Graz 1948; concert tours through Europe, Latin America, North America 1963–2008, Australia 1963, 1966, 1969, 1976; has appeared at many music festivals, including Salzburg

1960–2008, Vienna, Edinburgh, Aldeburgh, Athens, Granada, Lucerne, Puerto Rico, London Proms and has performed with most of the major orchestras of Europe and USA, etc.; mem. American Acad. of Arts and Sciences; Hon. RAM; Hon. RCM; Hon. Fellow, Exeter Coll. Oxford 1987; Commdr, Ordre des Arts et des Lettres 1985, Hon. KBE 1989, Ordre pour le Mérite (Germany) 1991; Hon. DMus (London) 1978, (Oxford) 1983, (Warwick) 1991, (Yale) 1992, (Exeter) 1998, (Southampton) 2002, Hon. DLitt (Sussex) 1981, Dr hc (Cologne) 1995; Premio Città de Bolzano, Concorso Busoni 1949, Grand Prix du Disque 1965, Edison Prize (five times 1973–87), Grand Prix des Disquaires de France 1975, Deutscher Schallplattenpreis (four times 1976–84, 1992), Wiener Flötenuhr (six times 1976–87), Gramophone Award (six times 1977–83), Japanese Record Acad. Award (five times 1977–84, with Scottish Symphony Orchestra/Sir Charles Mackerras 2002), Japanese Grand Prix 1978, Franz Liszt Prize (four times 1979–83), Frankfurt Music Prize 1984, Diapason D'Or Award 1992, Heidsieck Award for Writing on Music 1990, Hans von Bülow-Medaille, Kameradschaft der Berliner Philharmoniker eV, 1992, Cannes Classical Award 1998, Ehrenmitgliedschaft der Wiener Philharmoniker 1998, Léonie Sonnings Musikpris, Denmark 2002, Ernst von Siemens Musikpreis 2004, Prix Venezia 2007. *Recordings:* extensive repertoire; Beethoven's Complete Piano Works, Beethoven Sonatas, three sets of Beethoven Concertos (with Vienna Philharmonic Orchestra and Simon Rattle) 1998. *Publications:* essays on music and musicians in Phono, Fono Forum, Österreichische Musikzeitschrift, Music and Musicians, Hi-Fi Stereophonie, New York Review of Books, Die Zeit, Frankfurter Allgemeine Zeitung, Musical Thoughts and Afterthoughts 1976, Nachdenken über Musik 1977, Music Sounded Out (essays) 1990, Musik beim Wort genommen 1992, Fingerzeig 1996, Störendes Lachen während des Jaworts 1997, One Finger Too Many 1998, Kleine Teufel 1999, Collected Essays on Music 2001, Augerechnet Ich (aka The Veil of Order: In Conversation with Martin Meyer) 2001, Spiegelbild und Schwarzer Spuk (poems) 2003, Cursing Bagels (poems) 2004, Alfred Brendel über Musik 2005. *Leisure interests:* books, theatre, the visual arts, films, baroque and romanesque architecture, unintentional humour, kitsch. *Address:* c/o Ingpen & Williams, 7 St George's Court, 131 Putney Bridge Road, London, SW15 2PA, England (office). *Telephone:* (20) 8874-3222 (office). *Fax:* (20) 8877-3113 (office). *E-mail:* info@ingpen.co.uk (office).

BRENDISH, Clayton (Clay), CBE, BSc, MSc, CEng, FBCS, FIMgt; British business executive; *Chairman, Beacon Investment Trust;* co-f. Admiral PLC 1979, Exec. Chair. 1979–2000; Exec. Deputy Chair. CMG PLC (following CMG's merger with Admiral) 2000–01; fmr Chair. Exec. Bd Inst. of Man., Pres. 2001–, Chair. Information Tech. Task Group, mem. Remuneration Cttee; fmr Adviser to Chancellor of Duchy of Lancaster and Parl. Sec., Office of Public Services; Dir (non-exec.) Ordnance Survey 1993–96, Elexon Ltd, Defence Logistics Org., Herald Investment Trust PLC, QinetiQ; Chair. (non-exec.) Beacon Investment Trust 1995–; external mem. Defence Meteorological Bd 1995–; mem. Ind. TV Comm. 2000–, Council City Univ., London 2000–; Trustee, Economist Newspapers Ltd. *Address:* Institute of Management, 2 Savoy Court, Strand, London, WC2R 0EZ, England (office). *Telephone:* (20) 7497-0580 (office). *Fax:* (20) 7592-0463 (office). *Website:* www.inst-mgt.org.uk (office).

BRENNAN, David R., BBA; American pharmaceutical industry executive; *CEO, AstraZeneca PLC;* m.; four c.; ed Gettysburg Coll.; joined Merck as sales rep. 1975, Gen. Man. Chibret Int. (French subsidiary) 1990–92; joined AstraMerck 1992, was responsible for business planning and devt at Astra Pharmaceuticals, Sr Vice-Pres. of Commercial Operations, AstraZeneca Pharmaceuticals LP (N America) 1999–2001, Pres. and CEO AstraZeneca LP (N America) 2001–06, Exec. Bd Dir AstraZeneca 2005–, CEO AstraZeneca PLC 2006–; mem. Exec. Bd Pharmaceutical Research and Mfrs of America, European Fed. of Pharmaceutical Industries and Asscns; fmr Chair. Southeastern Pennsylvania Chapter, American Heart Asscn; Commr UK Comm. for Employment and Skills 2007–; Hon. mem. Bd of Dirs CEO Roundtable on Cancer. *Leisure interests:* scuba diving, cycling, amateur photography. *Address:* AstraZeneca PLC, 15 Stanhope Gate, London, W1K 1LN, England (office). *Telephone:* (20) 7304-5000 (office). *Fax:* (20) 7304-5151 (office). *E-mail:* info@astrazeneca.com (office). *Website:* www.astrazeneca.com (office).

BRENNAN, Hon. Sir (Francis) Gerard, Kt, AC, KBE, LLB, QC; Australian judge (retd); b. 22 May 1928, Rockhampton, Queensland; s. of Hon. Mr. Justice Frank T. Brennan and Gertrude Brennan; m. Dr Patricia O'Hara 1953; three s. four d.; ed Christian Brothers' Coll., Rockhampton, Downlands Coll., Toowoomba and Univ. of Queensland, Brisbane; admitted to Bar 1951, QC 1965; Pres. Bar Asscn of Queensland 1974–76, Australian Bar Asscn 1975–76, Admin. Review Council 1976–79, Admin. Appeals Tribunal 1976–79; mem. Exec. Law Council of Australia 1975–76, Australian Law Reform Comm. 1975–77; Additional Judge, Supreme Court of ACT 1976–81; Judge, Australian Industrial Court 1976–81, Fed. Court of Australia 1977–81; Justice, High Court of Australia 1981–95; Chief Justice of Australia 1995–98; External Judge, Supreme Court of Fiji 1999–2000; Non-permanent Judge, Court of Final Appeal of Hong Kong 2000–; Foundation Scientia Prof. of Law, Univ. of NSW 1998; Chancellor, Univ. of Tech., Sydney 1998–2004; Hon. LLD (Univ. of Dublin Trinity Coll.) 1988, (Univ. of Queensland) 1996, (ANU) 1996, (Melbourne Univ., Univ. of Tech., Sydney) 1998, (Univ. of NSW) 2005; Hon. DLitt (Central Queensland Univ.) 1996; Hon. DUniv (Griffiths Univ.) 1996, (Univ. of Tech., Sydney) 2005. *Address:* c/o Suite 3003, Piccadilly Tower, 133 Castlereagh Street, Sydney, NSW 2000, Australia. *Telephone:* (2) 9261-8704 (office). *Fax:* (2) 9261-8113 (office).

BRENNAN, John J., AB, MBA; American business executive; *Chairman and CEO, Vanguard Group Inc.;* b. 1954, Boston; m. Catherine Brennan; one d. two s.; ed Dartmouth Coll., Harvard Business School; Assoc., New York Bank for Savings 1976–78; Planning Assoc., S. C. Johnson & Son 1980–82; joined Vanguard Group Inc. 1982, Asst to Chair. 1982–85, Chief Financial Officer 1985–89, Pres. 1989–96, CEO 1996–98, Chair. and CEO 1998–; mem. Bd of Trustees, Vanguard Funds. *Address:* The Vanguard Group Inc., 100 Vanguard Boulevard, Malvern, PA 19355, USA (office). *Telephone:* (610) 648-6000 (office). *Fax:* (610) 669-6605 (office). *Website:* www.vanguard.com (office).

BRENNEMAN, Ronald A., MSc; Canadian petroleum industry executive; *President and CEO, Petro-Canada;* ed Univ. of Toronto, Univ. of Manchester, Sr Exec. Program, Sloan School of Business, Massachusetts Inst. of Tech.; joined Imperial Oil Ltd 1969, Operations Man. 1977, various man. roles 1978–83, with Exxon Corpn (parent co.), NY 1983–86, becoming Vice-Pres. then Pres. Imperial Oil Ltd 1992–94, CEO Esso Benelux 1994–97, Gen. Man. of Corp. Planning, Exxon, Dallas 1997–99; mem. Bd of Dirs, Pres. and CEO Petro-Canada 2000–; Trustee, United Way of Greater Toronto, Hosp. for Sick Children. *Address:* Petro-Canada, 150 6th Avenue, SW, Calgary, Alberta, T2P 3E3, Canada (office). *Telephone:* (403) 296-8000 (office). *Fax:* (403) 296-3030 (office). *E-mail:* info@petro-canada.ca (office). *Website:* www.petro-canada.ca (office).

BRENNER, Sydney, CH, MB, DPhil, FRS, FRCP; British scientist and academic; *Distinguished Research Professor, Salk Institute for Biological Studies;* b. 13 Jan. 1927, Germiston, South Africa; s. of Morris Brenner and Lena Brenner (née Blacher); m. May Woolf Balkind; two s. (one step-s.) two d.; ed Univ. of the Witwatersrand, Johannesburg and Oxford Univ.; Lecturer in Physiology, Univ. of Witwatersrand 1955–57; mem. Scientific Staff, MRC 1957–92, Dir MRC Lab. of Molecular Biology, Cambridge 1979–86, Dir Molecular Genetics Unit, Cambridge 1986–92; mem. Scripps Inst., La Jolla, Calif. 1992–94; Dir Molecular Sciences Inst., Berkeley, Calif. 1996–2001; Distinguished Research Prof. Salk Inst. for Biological Studies, La Jolla, Calif., USA 2001–; mem. MRC 1978–82, 1986–90; Fellow, King's Coll., Cambridge 1959–; Hon. Prof. of Genetic Medicine, Univ. of Cambridge Clinical School 1981–87; Foreign Assoc., NAS 1977; Foreign mem., American Philosophical Soc. 1979; Foreign Assoc., Royal Soc. of S. Africa 1983; Foreign mem. Real Academia de Ciencias 1985; External Scientific mem. Max Planck Soc. 1988; mem. Academia Europaea 1989; Corresp. Scientifique Emérite de l'INSERM, Associé Etranger Académie des Sciences, France, Fellow American Acad. of Microbiology; Foreign Hon. mem. American Acad. of Arts and Sciences 1965, Hon. mem. Deutsche Akademie der Natursforscher Leopoldina 1975, Soc. for Biological Chemists 1975, Hon. FRSE, Hon. Fellow, Exeter Coll. 1985, Hon. Fellow, Indian Acad. of Sciences 1989, Hon. mem. Chinese Soc. of Genetics 1989, Hon. Fellow, Royal Coll. of Pathologists 1990, Hon. Fellow, Acad. Medical Sciences 1999, Hon. mem. Assoc. of Physicians of GB and Ireland 1991; Hon. DSc (Dublin, Witwatersrand, Chicago, London, Leicester, Oxford, La Trobe); Hon. LLD (Glasgow) 1981, (Cambridge) 2001; Hon. DLitt (Singapore); Hon. Dr rer. nat (Jena); Warren Triennial Prize 1968, William Bate Hardy Prize, Cambridge Philosophical Soc. 1969, Gregor Mendel Medal of German Acad. of Science Leopoldina 1970, Albert Lasker Medical Research Award 1971, Gairdner Foundation Annual Award (Canada) 1978; Royal Medal of Royal Soc. 1974, Prix Charles Leopold Mayer, French Acad. 1975, Krebs Medal, Fed. of European Biochemical Socs 1980, Ciba Medal, Biochemical Soc. 1981, Feldberg Foundation Prize 1983, Neil Hamilton Fairley Medal, Royal Coll. of Physicians 1985, Croonian Lecturer Royal Soc. of London 1986, Rosenstiel Award, Brandeis Univ. 1986, Prix Louis Jeantet de Médecine (Switzerland) 1987, Genetics Soc. of America Medal 1987, Harvey Prize, Israel Inst. of Tech. 1987, Hughlings Jackson Medal, Royal Soc. of Medicine 1987, Waterford Bio-Medical Science Award (The Research Inst. of Scripps Clinic) 1988, Kyoto Prize (Inamori Foundation) 1990, Gairdner Foundation Award (Canada) 1991, Copley Medal (Royal Soc.) 1991, King Faisal Int. Prize for Science (King Faisal Foundation) 1992, Bristol-Myers Squibb Award for Distinguished Achievement in Neuroscience Research 1992, Albert Lasker Award for Special Achievement 2000, Nobel Prize for Physiology or Medicine 2002, Dan David Prize 2002. *Leisure interest:* rumination. *Address:* Brenner Laboratory, Salk Institute for Biological Studies, 10010 North Torrey Pines Road, La Jolla, CA 92186-5800 (office); 22 Black Hill, Ely, Cambs. CB7 2BZ, England (home). *Telephone:* (858) 453-4100 (office). *E-mail:* sbrenner@salk.edu (office). *Website:* www.salk.edu (office).

BRENT, Richard Peirce, PhD, DSc, FAA, FIEEE; Australian computer scientist, mathematician and academic; *Australian Research Council Federation Fellow, Australian National University;* b. 20 April 1946, Melbourne, Vic.; s. of Oscar Brent and Nancy Brent; m. Erin O'Connor 1969 (died 2005), two s.; m. Judy-anne Osborn 2007; ed Melbourne Grammar School, Monash Univ., Stanford Univ., USA; Research Scientist, IBM T.J. Watson Research Center, Yorktown Heights, New York, USA 1971–72; Research Fellow etc., ANU, Canberra 1972–78, Prof. of Computer Sciences 1978–98, Australian Research Council Fed Fellow and Prof., Math. Sciences Inst. 2005–; Prof. of Computing Science, Univ. of Oxford 1998–2005, Fellow, St Hugh's Coll. 1998–2005; Fellow, Inst. for Electrical and Electronic Engineers (USA), Inst. of Math. and its Applications, Asscn for Computing Machinery (USA), Australian Math. Soc.; Australian Math. Soc. Medal 1984, Forsythe Memorial Lecturer 1990, Hannan Medal 2005. *Publications:* Algorithms for Minimization without Derivatives 1973, Topics in Computational Complexity and the Analysis of Algorithms 1980, Modern Computer Arithmetic (with Paul Zimmermann) 2009. *Leisure interests:* music, chess, bridge, farming. *Address:* Mathematical Sciences Institute, Australian National University, Canberra, ACT 0200, Australia (office). *Telephone:* (2) 6125-3873 (office). *E-mail:* richard.brent@maths.anu.edu.au (office).

BRENTON, Anthony; British diplomatist; b. 1 Jan. 1950; m. Susan Mary Penrose 1982; one s. two d.; joined FCO 1975, Far Eastern Dept 1975–76, language training (UK and Middle Eastern Centre for Arabic Studies)

1976–78, Second, later First Sec., Chancery, Cairo 1978–81, EC Dept, FCO 1981–85, First Sec. (Energy) and UK Rep., Brussels 1985–86, secondment to EC 1986–89, Counsellor (Head of UN Dept), FCO 1989–92, Career Devt Attachment, Harvard Univ. 1992–93, Counsellor (Econ., Aid and Scientific), Moscow 1994–98, Dir (Global Issues), FCO 1998–2001, Minister and Deputy Head of Mission, Washington, DC 2001–04, Amb. to Russia 2004–2008. *Address:* Foreign and Commonwealth Office, King Charles St, London, SW1A 2AH, England (office). *Telephone:* (20) 7008-1500 (office). *Website:* www.fco .gov.uk (office).

BRENTON, Howard, BA; British playwright; b. 13 Dec. 1942, Portsmouth; s. of Donald Henry Brenton and Rose Lilian Brenton (née Lewis); m. Jane Fry 1970; two s.; ed Chichester High School for Boys and St Catharine's Coll., Cambridge; resident writer, Royal Court Theatre, London 1972–73; writer-in-residence, Warwick Univ. 1978–79; Granada Artist in Residence, Univ. of Calif. at Davis 1997; Arts and Humanities Research Bd Fellowship, Birmingham Univ. 2000; Hon. Dr of Arts (Univ. of N London) 1996; John Whiting Award 1970, Standard Best Play of the Year Award 1976, Standard Best Play of the Year (jtly with David Hare) 1985. *Publications:* Notes from a Psychotic Journal and Other Poems 1969, Revenge 1969, Christie in Love (plays) 1969, Scott of the Antarctic (or what God didn't see) 1970, Lay By (co-author) 1972, Plays for Public Places 1972, Hitler Dances 1972, Magnificence 1973, Brassneck (with David Hare) 1973, The Churchill Play 1974, Government Property 1975, The Saliva Milkshake 1975, Weapons of Happiness 1976, The Paradise Run (TV play) 1976, Sore Throats 1979, Plays for the Poor Theatre 1980, The Romans in Britain 1980, Thirteenth Night 1981, The Genius 1983, Desert of Lies (TV play) 1983, Sleeping Policemen (with Tunde Ikoli) 1983, Bloody Poetry 1984, Pravda (with David Hare) 1985, Dead Head 1986, Greenland 1988, Diving for Pearls (novel) 1989, Iranian Nights (with Tariq Ali) 1989, Hess is Dead 1990, Moscow Gold (with Tariq Ali) 1990, Berlin Bertie 1992, Hot Irons (Essays and Diaries) 1995, Playing Away (opera) 1994, Goethe's Faust, Parts I and II (adaptation) 1995, Plays I 1996, Plays II 1996, in Extremis 1997, Ugly Rumours (with Tariq Ali) 1998, Collateral Damage (with Tariq Ali and Andy de la Tour), Nasser's Eden (play for radio) 1999, Snogging Ken (with Tariq Ali and Andy de la Tour) 2000, Kit's Play 2000, Spooks (TV series) 2002–05, Paul (play) 2005, In Extremis (play) 2006, Never So Good (play) 2007. *Leisure interest:* painting. *Address:* c/o Cassarotto Ramsay Ltd, 60/66 National House, Wardour Street, London, W1V 4ND, England. *Telephone:* (20) 7287-4450. *Fax:* (20) 7287-9128.

BRESLOW, Lester, BA, MD, MPH, ScD; American physician and academic; *Professor Emeritus of Health Services and Dean Emeritus, School of Public Health, UCLA;* b. 17 March 1915, Bismarck, ND; s. of Joseph Breslow and Mayme Danziger; m. Devra Miller 1967; three s.; ed Univ. of Minnesota; Dist Health Officer, Minn. 1941–43; US Army 1943–46; Chief, Bureau of Chronic Diseases, Calif. Dept of Public Health 1946–60, Div. of Preventative Medicine 1960–65; Dir Calif. Dept of Public Health 1965–68; Prof. School of Public Health, UCLA 1968–, now Prof. Emer., Dean 1972–80, now Dean Emer.; Dir for Cancer Control Research, Jonsson Comprehensive Cancer Center 1982–86; Dir Health Promotion Center 1986–91; Pres. Int. Epidemiological Asscn 1967–68; Pres. American Public Health Asscn 1968–69; Pres. Asscn of Schools of Public Health 1973–75; mem. Inst. of Medicine 1975–; Founding Ed. Annual Review of Public Health 1980–90; Lasker Award 1960, Sedwick Medal 1977, American Public Health Asscn, Dana Award 1988, Healthtrac Prize 1995, Lienhard Award, Inst. of Medicine 1997, The Porter Prize 1998, Stephen Smith Award, NY Acad. of Medicine 2005. *Publications:* Health and Ways of Living: The Alameda County Study 1983, A Life in Public Health: An Insider's Retrospective 2004. *Leisure interest:* gardening. *Address:* School of Public Health, UCLA, 650 South Young Drive, Los Angeles, CA 90095, USA (office). *Telephone:* (310) 825-1388 (office). *Fax:* (310) 825-3317 (office). *E-mail:* breslow@ph.ucla.edu (office). *Website:* www.ph.ucla.edu.

BRESLOW, Ronald Charles, PhD; American chemist and academic; *University Professor of Chemistry, Columbia University;* b. 14 March 1931, Rahway, NJ; s. of Alexander Breslow and Gladys Fellows; m. Esther Greenberg 1956; two d.; ed Harvard Univ.; Instructor, Columbia Univ. 1956–59, Assoc. Prof. 1959–62, Prof. 1962–67, Mitchill Prof. of Chem. 1966–, Univ. Prof. 1992–; Ed. Benjamin Inc. 1962–; Sloan Fellowship 1961–63; Fellow AAAS 1986; mem. Nat. Acad. of Sciences, American Acad. of Arts and Sciences, American Philosophical Soc., Exec. Cttee of Organic Div. of American Chemical Soc.; mem. Ed. Bd Organic Syntheses 1965–, Bd of Eds Journal of Organic Chem. 1968, Tetrahedron, Tetrahedron Letters 1977, Chemical Eng News 1980–83; Hon. mem. Korean Chemical Soc. 1996, Royal Soc. of Chem. (UK) 1996; Procurator, NAS 1984; Trustee, American-Swiss Foundation for Scientific Exchange Inc. 1969–71; Chair. Div. of Organic Chem., American Chemical Soc. 1970–71, Pres. of Soc. 1996; Chair. Div. of Chem., NAS 1974; Chair. Dept of Chem., Columbia Univ. 1976–; mem. Advisory Bd, Chemical and Engineering News 1980; Foreign mem. Royal Soc.; Chair. Bd of Scientific Advisers, Sloan Foundation 1981–; mem. Bd of Scientific Advisers, Gen. Motors 1982–; Centenary Lecturer, London Chemical Soc. 1972; Trustee, Rockefeller Univ. 1981–; A. R. Todd Visiting Prof., Univ. of Cambridge 1982; Foreign Fellow Indian Acad. of Science 1992; Annual Ciba Foundation Lecturer, London 1982; mem. European Acad. of Science 2004; Hon. mem. Japan Chemical Soc. 2002; Foreign Hon. mem. Royal Soc. 2000; ACS Award in Pure Chem. 1966, Fresinius Award 1966, Mark van Doren Award 1969, Baekeland Medal 1969, Harrison Howe Award 1974, Remsen Medal 1977, Roussel Prize 1978, American Chemical Soc. James Flack Norris Award in Physical Organic Chem. 1980, Richards Medal in Chem. 1984, Arthur Cope Award 1987, George Kenner Award 1988, Nichols Medal 1989, Nat. Acad. of Sciences Chem. Medal 1989, Paracelsus Medal, Swiss Chemical Soc. 1990, US Nat. Medal of Science 1991, Priestley Medal, ACS 1999, New York City Mayor's Award in Science 2002, ACS Bader Award in Bioorganic Chem. 2002, Esselen Award for Chem. in the Public Interest 2002, Robert A. Welch Award in Chem. 2003, Willard Gibbs Medal, ACS 2004. *Publications:* Organic Reaction Mechanisms 1965, Chemistry Today and Tomorrow 1996; over 400 scientific papers. *Leisure interest:* piano performance. *Address:* Department of Chemistry, Columbia University, 3000 Broadway, mail code 3105, New York, NY 10027 (office); 44 West 77th Street, New York, NY 10024, USA (home). *Telephone:* (212) 854-2170 (office). *Fax:* (212) 854-2755 (office). *E-mail:* rb33@columbia.edu (office). *Website:* www.columbia .edu/cu/chemistry/breslow (office); www.columbia.edu/cu/chemistry (office).

BRESSANI, Ricardo, PhD; Guatemalan biochemist; *Head, Food Science and Technology Center, Research Institute, Universidad de Valle;* b. 28 Sept. 1926, Guatemala; s. of César Bressani and Primina Castignoli de Bressani; m. Alicia Herman 1949; five s. two d.; ed Univ. of Dayton, Iowa State Univ. and Purdue Univ.; Visiting Prof. MIT, Rutgers Univ.; Ed.-in-Chief, Archivos Latinoamericanos de Nutrición; Head and Research Dir, Div. of Agric. and Food Sciences, Inst. of Nutrition of Cen. America and Panama (INCAP) 1988–; Head Food Science and Tech. Center, Research Inst. Univ. de Valle; mem. Directive Cttee Agroindustrial Rural Devt (PRODAR) Costa Rica 1991–; Corresp. Academic mem., Acad. of Medical, Physical and Natural Sciences of Guatemala 1990–; Foreign mem. NAS; mem. American Inst. of Food Technologists, Acad. of Science of the Int. Union for Food Science and Tech.; Orden del Quetzal en el Grado de Gran Cruz 1999; Dr hc (Purdue), (Universidad del Valle de Guatemala); Babcock Hart Award 1970, McCollum Award 1976, World Science Award 'Albert Einstein' 1984, Abraham Horowitz Award 1990, Ibero-American Prize in Science and Technology, Mexico 2001, Danone Int. Prize of Nutrition 2003. *Publications:* over 500 scientific publications in related professional fields including books, monographs and articles in scientific journals. *Leisure interests:* swimming, horseback riding, agricultural conservation. *Address:* Institute of Nutrition of Central America and Panama, Calzada Roosevelt zona 11, 01011 Guatemala City (office); Centro de Ciencia y Tecnología de Alimentos, Instituto de Investigaciones, Universidad del Valle de Guatemala, 18 avenida 11-95 zona 15, Vista Hermosa III, 01015 Guatemala City (office); 6a calle 'A' 7-74 zona 9, Guatemala City, 01009 Guatemala (home). *Telephone:* (502) 332-6125 (home); (502) 472-3762 (Inst. of Nutrition); (502) 364-0336 (University). *Fax:* (502) 473-6529 (Inst. of Nutrition) (office); (502) 364-0212 (University) (office). *E-mail:* bressani@incap.org.gt (office); bressani@incap.ops-oms.org (office); bressani@uvg.edu.gt (office). *Website:* www.incap.org.gt (Inst.of Nutrition) (office); www.uvg.edu.gt (University) (office).

BRETH, Andrea; German theatre director; *Director-in-Residence, Vienna Burgtheater;* b. 31 Oct. 1952, Rieden, Allgau; d. of Prof. Herbert Breth and Maria Breth (née Noether); ed Darmstadt, Heidelberg; Dir Bremen, Hamburg, Berlin 1976, Zürich, Bochum 1980, Freiburg (Bernarda Albas Haus, Lorca) 1984, Schauspielhaus Bochum (Le Sud, Green; The Last, Gorki) 1986–90, Burgtheater, Vienna (Zerbrochener Krug, Kleist) 1990, Schaubuhne Berlin (Einsamer Weg, Schnitzler) 1991 and (Nachtasyl, Gorki) 1992, Burgtheater Vienna (End of the Beginning, O'Casey) 1991, Tschulimsk, Wampilow (Letzten Sommer) 1992, Kaiser (Von morgens bis mitternachts) 1993, (Hedda Gabler) 1993, (Orestes) 1995, (Die Möwe) 1995; Art Dir Berliner Schaubühne am Leniner Platz 1992–97; Dir-in-Residence, Vienna Burgtheater 1997–; mem. der Darstellenden Künste, Frankfurt, Akademie der Künste Berlin; Fritz-Kortner-Prize 1987, Nestroy-Award 2003, and other awards. *Leisure interests:* literature, music, paintings, theatre. *Address:* Burgtheater, Dr. Karl-Lueger-Ring 2, 1010 Vienna, Austria (office). *Telephone:* (1) 51444-4140 (office). *Fax:* (1) 51444-4440 (office). *Website:* www.burgtheater.at (office).

BRETON, Thierry; French government official and business executive; *CEO and Chairman of the Management Board, Atos Origin;* b. 15 Jan. 1955; m.; three c.; ed Lycée Louis Le Grand, Supelec Electrical Eng . School, Paris and French Inst. for Nat. Defence Studies (IHEDN); nat. mil. service as teacher of information tech. and math., French Lycée, New York 1979–81; Chair. and CEO Forma Systèmes 1981–86; Chief Adviser of Minister for Information and New Technologies, Ministry of Educ. and Research 1986–88; CEO Futuroscope de Poitiers (science and tech. theme park) and CEO Futuroscope Telecommunications Platform 1986–90; CEO CGI Group 1990–93; CEO and Vice-Chair. Bd Dirs Bull Group 1993–97; Chair. and CEO Thomson SA and Thomson Multimedia 1997–2002; Chair. and CEO France Telecom SA 2002–05; Minister of the Economy, Finance and Industry 2005–07; CEO and Chair. Man. Bd Atos Origin 2008–; mem. Bd of Dirs Carrefour SA 2008–; Chevalier, Légion d'honneur, Commdr, Ordre nat. du Mérite. *Publications:* Softwar 1984, Vatican III 1985, Netwar 1987, La Dimension Invisible 1991, La Fin des Illusions 1992, Le Lievre et la Tortue 1994. *Address:* Atos Origin, Tour les Miroirs–Bat C, 18 avenue d'Alsace, 92926 Paris, La Défense 3 Cedex, France (office). *Telephone:* 1-55-91-20-00 (office). *Fax:* 1-55-91-20-05 (office). *Website:* www.atosorigin.com (office).

BRETSCHER, Mark Steven, MA, PhD, FRS; British/Swiss research scientist; *Visitor, MRC Laboratory of Molecular Biology;* b. 8 Jan. 1940, Cambridge; s. of Hanni Bretscher (née Greminger) and Egon Bretscher; m. Barbara M. F. Pearse 1978; one s. one d.; ed Abingdon School, Gonville and Caius Coll., Cambridge; research student, Gonville and Caius Coll., Cambridge 1961–64; Scientific Staff mem. MRC, Lab. of Molecular Biology, Cambridge 1965–2005, now Visitor, Head, Div. of Cell Biology 1984–95; Visiting Prof. Harvard Coll., USA 1974–75, Stanford Univ., USA 1984–85; Friedrich-Miescher Prize 1979. *Television:* Bags of Life (Horizon), BBC 1974. *Publications:* scientific papers in professional journals. *Leisure interest:* silviculture. *Address:* Medical Research Council, Laboratory of Molecular Biology, Hills Road, Cambridge, CB2 2QH (office); Ram Cottage, Commercial End, Swaffham Bulbeck, Cambridgeshire, CB5 0ND, England (home). *Telephone:* (1223) 248011 (office); (1223) 811276 (home). *Fax:* (1223) 412142 (home). *E-mail:* msb@mrc

-lmb.cam.ac.uk (office). *Website:* www2.mrc-lmb.cam.ac.uk/personal/bretscher/msb_home.html (office).

BREUER, Michael; German accountant and politician; *Chairman, Rheinische Sparkassen- und Giroverband (Rheinische Savings Bank and Giro Association);* b. 2 Oct. 1965, Brühl, North Rhine-Westphalia; ed Abitur in Lechenich, Univ. of Bonn; grew up in Erftstadt-Ahrem; mil. service in Munster and Lüneburg; mem. CDU 1983–, co. and dist chair. Jungen Union, mem. North Rhine-Westphalia State Parl. and mem. Bd CDU Parl. Group Cttee 1995–, Spokesman for Budgetary Control 1995–2005; Dist Chair. CDU Cen. Rhine (Cologne, Bonn, Leverkusen, Rhine Erft) 1999–, mem. regional-level Party Council of CDU North-Rhine-Westphalia; Minister for Fed., European and Int. Affairs, State of North Rhine-Westphalia 2005–07; worked for KPMG German trust 1993–2004; ind. certified public accountant and tax adviser 2004–05; Chair. Rheinische Sparkassen- und Giroverband (Rheinische Savings Bank and Giro Asscn), Düsseldorf 2008–. *Address:* Rheinischer Sparkassen- und Giroverband, Kirchfeldstraße 60, 40217 Düsseldorf, Germany (office). *Telephone:* (211) 3892-01 (office). *Fax:* (211) 3892-240 (office). *E-mail:* info@rsgv.de (office). *Website:* www.rsgv.de (office).

BREUER, Rolf-Ernst, DJur; German banker; b. 1937; ed Univs of Lausanne, Munich and Bonn; Spokesman, Bd of Man. Dirs and Chair., Group Exec. Cttee, Deutsche Bank AG, Frankfurt 1997–2002, Chair. Supervisory Bd 2002–06 (resgnd); numerous other commercial appointments. *Address:* c/o Deutsche Bank, 60262 Frankfurt am Main, Germany (office).

BREWER, Richard George, PhD; American atomic physicist and academic; *Consulting Professor in Applied Physics, Stanford University;* b. 8 Dec. 1928, Los Angeles, Calif.; s. of Louis Ludwig and Elise Brewer; m. Lillian Magidow 1954; one s. two d.; ed California Inst. of Technology and Univ. of California, Berkeley; Instructor, Harvard Univ. 1958–60; Asst Prof., Univ. of Calif., Los Angeles 1960–63; IBM Research Staff mem., San José, Calif. 1963–73, 1973–94, Fellow Emer. 1994–; Consulting Prof., Applied Physics, Stanford Univ. 1977–; IBM Fellow; mem. NAS 1980; Fellow, American Physical Soc., Optical Soc. of America; Albert A. Michelson Gold Medal, Franklin Inst. 1979, Distinguished Alumni Award, CIT 1994, Charles H. Townes Silver Medal, Optical Soc. of America 2000. *Publications:* more than 150 papers in scientific journals. *Leisure interests:* growing magnolias, classical music, reading Italian literature. *Address:* Department of Applied Physics, Stanford University, Main Office, Varian Physics Room 108, 382 Via Pueblo Mall, Stanford, CA 94305-4060 (office). *Telephone:* (650) 723-4344 (office). *E-mail:* rgbrewer1@sbcglobal.net (home). *Website:* www.stanford.edu/dept/physics (office).

BREYER, Stephen, AB, BA, LLB; American lawyer, academic and judge; *Associate Justice, Supreme Court;* b. 15 Aug. 1938, San Francisco, Calif.; s. of Irving Breyer and Anne Breyer; m. Joanna Hare 1967; one s. two d.; ed Stanford Univ., Magdalen Coll. Oxford Univ. and Harvard Univ. Law School; law clerk to Mr Justice Arthur Goldberg, US Supreme Court 1964–65; Special Asst to Asst US Attorney-Gen., Antitrust Div. US Dept of Justice 1965–67; Asst Prof. of Law, Harvard Univ. 1967–70; Prof. of Law, Harvard Law School 1970–80; Prof., Kennedy School of Govt Harvard Univ. 1977–80; Lecturer, Harvard Law School 1981–; Asst Special Prosecutor, Watergate Special Prosecution Force 1973; Special Counsel, Admin. Practices Subcttee, US Senate Judiciary Cttee 1974–75, Chief Counsel, Senate Judiciary Cttee 1979–80; Circuit Judge, US Court of Appeals for the First Circuit 1980–94, Chief Judge 1990–94; mem. US Sentencing Comm. 1985–89; Judicial Conference of the US 1990–94; Assoc. Justice, US Supreme Court 1994–; Visiting Lecturer, Coll. of Law, Sydney, Australia 1975; Visiting Prof., Univ. of Rome 1993; Fellow, American Acad. of Arts and Sciences. *Publications:* The Federal Power Commission and the Regulation of Energy (with P. MacAvoy) 1974, Administrative Law and Regulatory Policy (with R. Stewart) 1979, Regulation and Its Reform 1982, Breaking the Vicious Circle: Towards Effective Risk Regulation 1993; numerous articles and book chapters. *Address:* United States Supreme Court, One First Street, NE, Washington, DC 20543, USA (office). *Telephone:* (202) 479-2977 (office). *Fax:* (202) 479-2963 (office). *Website:* www.supremecourtus.gov (office).

BREYTENBACH, Breyten; South African poet and writer; b. 16 Sept. 1939, Bonnievale; m. Hoang Lien 1962; ed Univ. of Cape Town; taught at Univ. of Natal, Princeton Univ.; Visiting Prof., Univ. of Cape Town 2000–02; Hertzog Prize 1984, 1999, Rapport Prize 1986, Alan Paton Award 1994. *Publications include:* Katastrofes 1964, Die Ysterkoei Moet Sweet 1964, A Season in Paradise 1976, Voetskrif 1976, Sinking Ship Blues 1977, And Death White as Words: Anthology 1978, In Africa Even the Flies Are Happy: Selected Poems 1964–77 1978, Vingermaan 1980, Mouroir: Mirrornotes of a Novel 1983, True Confessions of an Albino Terrorist 1985, Return to Paradise 1993, The Memory of Birds in Times of Revolution (essays) 1996, Papierblom 1998, Boklied 1998, Dog Heart 1999, Lady One 2001, Windcatcher: New and Selected Poems 1964–2006 2007.

BREZIGAR, Barbara; Slovenian lawyer and government official; *State Prosecutor General;* b. 1 Dec. 1953, Ljubljana; m.; two c.; ed Univ. of Ljubljana; Dist State Prosecutor, Ljubljana Public Prosecutor's Office 1980, Vice-Pres. 1994, Head of Office 1995, apptd head of special team of prosecutors dealing with organized crime 1996–99; Supreme State Prosecutor 1998–2000, 2000–05; Minister of Justice in caretaker Govt of Andrej Bajuk 2000; presidential cand. 2002; Nat. mem. for Slovenia at Eurojust 2004–05; State Prosecutor Gen., Repub. of Slovenia 2005–. *Address:* Office of the State Prosecutor General, Trg OF 13, 1000 Ljubljana, Slovenia (office). *Telephone:* (1) 434-1900 (office). *Fax:* (1) 434-1936 (office). *E-mail:* bbrezigar@dt-rs.si (office). *Website:* www.dt-rs.si (office).

BREZIS, Haim; French academic; *Professor of Mathematics, Institut Universitaire de France;* b. 1 June 1944, Riom-ès-Montagnes; s. of Jacob Brezis and Rebecca Brezis; m. Michal Govrin 1982; two d.; ed Univ. of Paris; Prof. Pierre et Marie Curie Univ. 1974–, Inst. Universitaire de France 1997–; Visiting Prof. New York Univ., Univ. of Chicago, Princeton Univ., MIT, Hebrew Univ.; Visiting Distinguished Prof. Rutgers Univ., Technion (Haifa); mem. Acad. des Sciences, Academia Europaea; Foreign Hon. Mem. Nat. Acad. of Sciences, USA, Foreign Hon. Mem. American Acad. of Arts and Sciences; Hon. mem. Romanian Acad., Hon. mem. Real Academia Madrid, Royal Acad. of Belgium; numerous hon. degrees; Prix. Ampère 1985. *Publications:* Analyse Fonctionnelle 1983, Ginzburg-Landau vortices 1994, Un mathématicien juif 1999. *Leisure interest:* Hebraic studies. *Address:* Analyse Numérique, Université Pierre et Marie Curie, 4 place Jussieu, 75252 Paris Cedex 05 (office); 18 rue de la Glacière, 75013 Paris Cedex 13, France (home). *Telephone:* 1-44-27-42-98 (office); 1-43-36-15-10 (home). *Fax:* 1-44-27-72-00 (office). *E-mail:* brezis@ccr.jussieu.fr (office).

BRIANÇON, Pierre, LLM; French journalist; b. 3 Aug. 1954, Tunis, Tunisia; s. of Claude Briançon and Geneviève Pochard; three c.; ed Université Paris II, Institut d'Etudes Politiques, Paris; journalist, Forum International 1979; Econs and Business Ed. Libération 1981–88, Moscow Corresp. 1988–91, USA Bureau Chief, Washington 1992–95, Ed.-in-Chief 1996–98; contrib. France Inter radio 1982–86; Asst Editorial Dir L'expansion 1998–2000; Chief Dow Jones Newswire Paris Bureau 2003–06; Paris corresp. Breaking-Views.com 2006–; Dir Startup Avenue (econ. information site) 2000–; fmr CEO and Chair. B to B Avenue.com. *Publications:* A Droite en sortant de la gauche? 1986, Héritiers du désastre 1992, Messier Story 2002. *Address:* c/o Breaking Views Ltd, First Floor, 16 St Helen's Place, London, EC3A 6DF, England (office). *Telephone:* (20) 7256-9333 (office). *Fax:* (20) 7256-5880 (office). *E-mail:* pierre.briancon@breakingviews.com (office). *Website:* www.breakingviews.com.

BRICEÑO, Hon. John, BBA; Belizean politician; b. 17 July 1960, Orange Walk Town; m. Rossana Briceño; three s.; ed Muffles High School, St John's Coll., Belize City, Univ. of Texas at Austin, USA; mem. Parl. for Orange Walk Cen. Div. (People's United Party) 1993–, currently Deputy Leader; Deputy Prime Minister 1998–2007, also Minister of Natural Resources and the Environment 1998–2007, of Commerce Trade and Industry 1999–2007, of Local Govt 2005–07. *Leisure interests:* reading, music, cinema. *Address:* People's United Party (PUP), 3 Queen Street, Belize City, Belize (office). *Telephone:* 223-2428 (office). *Fax:* 223-3476 (office). *Website:* www.pupbelize.bz (office).

BRIDGEMAN, John Stuart, CBE, TD, DL, BSc, CIMgt, FRSA, FRGS, FID; British business executive; *Chairman, Direct Marketing Authority;* b. 5 Oct. 1944; s. of the late James Alfred George Bridgeman and Edith Celia Bridgeman (née Watkins); m. Lindy Jane Fillmore 1967; three d.; ed Whitchurch School, Cardiff, Univ. Coll., Swansea, McGill Univ., Montreal; with Alcan Industries 1966–69, Aluminium Co. of Canada 1969–70, Alcan Australia 1970, Commercial Dir Alcan UK 1977–80, Vice-Pres. (Europe) Alcan Basic Raw Materials 1978–82, Man. Dir Extrusion Div. British Alcan Aluminium PLC 1983–87, British Alcan Enterprises 1987–91, Dir Corp. Planning Alcan Aluminium Ltd, Montreal 1992–93, Man. Dir British Alcan Aluminium PLC 1993–95, Monopolies and Mergers Comm. 1990–95; Dir-Gen. of Fair Trading 1995–2000; Dir Regulatory Impact Unit, Cardew & Co. Corp. Financial Advisers 2000–; Chair. Dir Marketing Authority 2000–; Oxford Psychologists Press; Consultant with law firm Norton Rose; Chair. Standards Cttee Worcs. Co. Council; Visiting Prof. of Man. Keele Univ. 1992–, Imperial Coll. London 2001–; Chair. N Oxon. Business Group 1984–92, Enterprise Cherwell Ltd 1985–91, N Oxon Coll. 1989; Vice-Pres. Aluminium Fed. 1995, UK–Canada Chamber of Commerce 1995–96 (Pres. 1997–98); Gov. N Oxon Coll. 1985–98; Deputy Chair. Heart of England Trading and Enterprise Council 1989–; Chair. 2000–; Chair. Oxfordshire Econ. Partnership 2000–; Commissioned TA and Reserve Forces 1978, Queen's Own Yeomanry 1981–84, Maj. REME (V) 1985–94, Staff Coll. 1986, mem. Territorial Auxiliary and Volunteer Reserve Asscn Oxon. and E Wessex 1985–2000; mem. British Airways NE Consumer Council 1978–81, Defence Science Advisory Council 1991–94, Nat. Employer Liaison Cttee for Reserve Forces 1992– (Chair. 1997–), UK–Canada Colloquium 1993–2000; Fellow Univ. of Wales, Swansea 1997; numerous trusteeships; High Sheriff, Oxon. 1995–96; DL (Oxon.) 1989; Dr hc (Sheffield Hallam) 1996; US Aluminum Asscn Prize 1988. *Leisure interests:* education, gardening, public affairs, shooting, skiing. *Address:* Regulatory Impact Unit, Cardew & Co., 12 Suffolk Street, London, SW1Y 4HQ (office); The Reform Club, 104 Piccadilly, London, SW1Y 5EW, England. *Telephone:* (20) 7930-0777 (office). *Fax:* (20) 7925-0646 (office). *E-mail:* john@cardew.co.uk (office). *Website:* www.cardew.co.uk (office).

BRIDGEMAN, Viscountess Victoria Harriet Lucy, (Harriet Bridgeman), MA, FRSA; British fine arts specialist, library executive, art historian and editor; *Chairman, The Bridgeman Art Library;* b. (Victoria Harriet Lucy Turton), 30 March 1942, Co. Durham; d. of Ralph Meredyth Turton and Mary Blanche Turton (née Chetwynd Stapylton); m. Viscount Bridgeman 1966; four s. (one deceased); ed St Mary's School, Wantage, Trinity Coll., Dublin; worked as an editorial trainee with The Lady magazine; Exec. Ed. The Masters 1965–69; Ed. Discovering Antiques 1970–72; est. own co. producing books and articles on fine and decorative arts; Founder and Chair. The Bridgeman Art Library 1971–; Cttee mem. British Asscn of Picture Libraries and Agencies; Founder Artists' Collecting Soc. 2006; European Woman of the Year (Arts Section) Award 1997, Int. Business Woman of the Year 2005. *Publications:* Encyclopaedia of Victoriana, Needlework: An Illustrated History, The British Eccentric 1975, Society Scandals 1977, Beside the Seaside 1977, Guide to the Gardens of Europe 1980, The Last Word 1982 (all jtly with Elizabeth Drury), eight titles in Connoisseur's Library series. *Leisure interests:* reading, family, travel. *Address:* The Bridgeman Art Library, 17–19 Garway Road, London,

W2 4PH, England (office); 19 Chepstow Road, London, W2 5BP (home); Watley House, Sparsholt, nr Winchester, Hants., SO21 2LU, England (home). *Telephone:* (20) 7727-4065 (London) (office); (20) 7727-5400 (London) (home); (1962) 776297 (Winchester) (home). *Fax:* (20) 7792-8509 (London) (office); (20) 7792-9178 (London) (home); (1962) 776297 (Winchester) (home). *E-mail:* harriet.bridgeman@bridgemanart.co.uk (office). *Website:* www.bridgemanart.com (office).

BRIDGES, Alan; British film director; b. 28 Sept. 1927, Liverpool; m. Eileen Middleton 1954; one s. one d.; Dir of numerous films and dramas for TV including The Intrigue, The Ballad of Peckham Rye, Alarm Call: Z Cars, The Brothers Karamazov, The Idiot, Days to Come, Great Expectations, Les Miserables, Dear Brutus, Army Captain (376285); Palme d'Or, Cannes Film Festival, Golden Globe, Emmy Award, Moscow Film Festival Award. *Films include:* Act of Murder, Invasion, The Lie (BAFTA for Best Drama 1970), The Wild Duck, Shelley, The Hireling (Palme d'Or, Best Film, Cannes Festival 1973), Brief Encounter, Out of Season, Summer Rain, The Girl in Blue Velvet, Very Like a Whale, Rain on the Roof, The Return of the Soldier, The Shooting Party, Displaced Persons, Apt Pupil, Secret Places of the Heart, Fire Princess, Pig Robinson. *Leisure interests:* reading, music, sport, theatre. *Address:* 29 Nursery Gardens, Sunbury-on-Thames, Middx, TW16 6LQ, England.

BRIDGES, Jeff; American actor; b. 4 Dec. 1949, Los Angeles; s. of the late Lloyd Bridges and of Dorothy Bridges; m. Susan Bridges; three d.; acting début at the age of 8; Career Achievement Award, Nat. Bd of Review 2004. *Films include:* Halls of Anger 1970, The Last Picture Show 1971, Fat City 1971, Bad Company 1972, The Last American Hero 1973, The Iceman Cometh 1973, Thunderbolt and Lightfoot 1974, Hearts of the West 1975, Rancho Deluxe 1975, King Kong 1976, Stay Hungry 1976, Somebody Killed her Husband 1978, Winter Kills 1979, The American Success Company 1980, Heaven's Gate 1980, Cutter's Way 1981, Tron 1982, Kiss Me Goodbye 1982, The Last Unicorn 1982, Starman 1984, Against All Odds 1984, Jagged Edge 1985, 8 Million Ways to Die 1986, The Morning After 1986, Nadine 1987, Tucker, the Man and his Dream 1988, See You in the Morning 1990, Texasville 1990, The Fabulous Baker Boys 1990, The Fisher King 1991, American Heart, The Vanishing, Blown Away 1994, Fearless 1994, Wild Bill, White Squall 1995, The Mirror Has Two Faces 1996, The Big Lebowski 1997, Arlington Road 1998, Simpatico 1999, The Muse 1999, The Contender 2000, K-Pax 2002, Lost in La Mancha (voice) 2002, Seabiscuit 2003, The Door in the Floor 2004, The Moguls 2005, Tideland 2005, Stick It 2006, Surf's Up (voice) 2007, How to Lose Friends & Alienate People 2008, Iron Man 2008. *Television:* Raising the Hammoth (voice) 2000, National Geographic: Lewis and Clark – Great Journey West 2002. *Address:* c/o Rick Nicita, Creative Artists Agency, 9830 Wilshire Boulevard, Beverly Hills, CA 90212, USA.

BRIDGES, 2nd Baron; **Thomas Edward Bridges,** GCMG, MA; British diplomatist (retd); b. 27 Nov. 1927, London; s. of Edward, 1st Baron Bridges, KG, and Hon. Katharine D. Farrer; m. Rachel M. Bunbury 1953 (died 2005); two s. one d.; ed Eton Coll. and New Coll., Oxford; joined diplomatic service 1951, served in Bonn, Berlin, Rio de Janeiro, Athens and Moscow; Asst Pvt. Sec. to Foreign Sec. 1963–66; Pvt. Sec. (Overseas Affairs) to Prime Minister 1972–74; Commercial Minister, Washington, DC 1976–79; Deputy Sec. (for int. econ. affairs), FCO 1979–83; Amb. to Italy 1983–87; Dir Consolidated Gold Fields PLC 1988–89; mem. Select Cttee on the European Communities, House of Lords 1988–92, 1994–98; Chair. UK Nat. Cttee of UNICEF 1989–97; Ind. Bd mem. Securities and Futures Authority Ltd 1989–97, Pres. Dolmetsch Foundation; Trustee Rayne Foundation. *Address:* 56 Church Street, Orford, Woodbridge, Suffolk, IP12 2NT, England. *Telephone:* (1394) 450235. *Fax:* (1394) 450235.

BRIERLEY, Sir Ronald Alfred; New Zealand business executive; b. 2 Aug. 1937, Wellington; s. of J.R. Brierley; ed Wellington Coll.; Chair. Brierley Investments Ltd 1961–89 (Founder 1961, Founder Pres. 1990–); Deputy Chair. Bank of NZ 1987–89; Chair. Industrial Equity Pacific Ltd 1966–90, Guinness Peat Group PLC 1990–, Tozer Kemsley & Millbourn Holdings PLC 1986, The Citizens & Graziers Life Assurance Co. Ltd 1990–91; Dir Ariadne Australia Ltd 1989–91, The Australian Gas Light Co. 1987–, Australian Oil & Gas Corpn Ltd, Mid-East Minerals Ltd 1992–, Metals Exploration Ltd 1992–, Tyndall Australia Ltd 1992–, Advance Bank Australia 1990–; mem. NZ Cricket Council, NZ Cricket Foundation; Dir Sydney Cricket & Sports Ground Trust. *Leisure interests:* cricket, ballet, stamp collecting, chess. *Address:* Guinness Peat Group PLC, First Floor, Times Place, 45 Pall Mall, London, SW1Y 5GP, England.

BRIERS, Richard David, CBE; British actor; b. 14 Jan. 1934, Merton; s. of Joseph Briers and Morna Richardson; m. Ann Davies 1957; two d.; ed Rokeby Prep. School, Wimbledon, Ridgeway School, Wimbledon and Royal Acad. of Dramatic Art; Hon. DLit (South Bank Univ.); Royal TV Soc. Hall of Fame 1996, Comic Heritage Lifetime Achievement Award 2000. *Films:* Henry V 1988, Much Ado About Nothing 1992, Swan Song 1993, Mary Shelley's Frankenstein 1995, In the Bleak Midwinter 1995, Hamlet 1996, Love's Labours Lost 1999, Peter Pan 2003, As You Like It 2006. *Stage roles include:* Gilt and Gingerbread 1956, Arsenic and Old Lace 1965, Relatively Speaking 1966, The Real Inspector Hound 1968, Cat Among the Pigeons 1969, The Two of Us 1970, Butley 1972, Absurd Person Singular 1973, Absent Friends 1975, Middle Age Spread 1979, The Wild Duck 1980, Arms and the Man 1981, Run for Your Wife 1983, Why Me? 1985, The Relapse 1986, Twelfth Night 1987, King Lear 1990, Midsummer Night's Dream 1990, Coriolanus 1991, Uncle Vanya 1991, Home 1994, A Christmas Carol 1996, The Chairs 1997, Spike 1999, Bedroom Farce 2002, The Tempest 2003. *Television series include:* Brothers-in-Law, Marriage Lines, The Good Life, OneUpManShip, the Other One, Norman Conquests, Ever-Decreasing Circles, All in Good Faith, Monarch of the Glen. *Publications:* Natter Natter 1981, Coward and Company 1987, A Little Light Weeding 1993, A Taste of the Good Life 1995. *Leisure interests:* gardening, reading. *Address:* Hamilton Hodell Management, 5th Floor, 66–68 Margaret Street, London, W1W 8SR, England. *Telephone:* (20) 7636-1221.

BRIGGS, Baron (Life Peer), cr. 1976, of Lewes in the County of Sussex; **Asa Briggs,** BSc, MA, FBA; British historian; b. 7 May 1921, Keighley, Yorks.; s. of William Walker Briggs and Jane Briggs; m. Susan Anne Banwell 1955; two s. two d.; ed Keighley Grammar School and Sidney Sussex Coll., Cambridge; Cryptographer, Bletchley Park 1942–45; Fellow, Worcester Coll., Oxford 1945–55, Reader in Recent Social and Econ. History, Univ. of Oxford 1950–55; Prof. of Modern History, Leeds Univ. 1955–61; Prof. of History, Univ. of Sussex 1961–76, Dean of Social Studies 1961–65, Pro-Vice-Chancellor 1961–67, Vice-Chancellor 1967–76; Provost Worcester Coll., Oxford 1976–91; Chancellor, Open Univ. 1979–94; Pres. Workers Educational Asscn 1958–67; Chair. Appts Comm. Press Council 1972–88; mem. Univ. Grants Cttee 1959–67; Trustee, Int. Broadcast Inst. 1968–86, Hon. Trustee 1990–; Gov. British Film Inst. 1970–76; Chair. European Inst. of Educ. 1974–84; mem. Council of UN Univ. 1974–80; Chair. Cttee on Nursing 1970–72, Heritage Educ. Group 1976–86, Commonwealth of Learning 1988–93; Pres. Social History Soc. 1976–, Ephemera Soc. 1984–, Victorian Soc. 1983–; Vice-Pres. Historical Asscn 1986–; Vice-Chair. of Council, UN Univ. 1974–80; Hon. mem. American Acad. of Arts and Sciences 1970–; Hon. LLD, Hon. DLitt, Hon. DSc; Marconi Medal for Services to Study of Broadcasting 1975, Medal of French Acad. for Architecture 1982, Wolfson History Prize 2001. *Publications:* Patterns of Peacemaking (with D. Thomson and E. Meyer) 1945, History of Birmingham, 1865–1938 1952, Victorian People 1954, Friends of the People 1956, The Age of Improvement 1959 (revised edn 2000), Ed. Chartist Studies 1959, History of Broadcasting in the United Kingdom, Vol. I 1961, Vol. II 1965, Vol. III 1970, Vol. IV 1979, Vol. V 1995, Victorian Cities 1963, The Nineteenth Century (ed.) 1970, Cap and Bell (with Susan Briggs) 1972, Essays in the History of Publishing (ed.) 1974, Essays in Labour History 1918–1939 1977, Governing the BBC 1979, From Coalbrookdale to the Crystal Palace 1980, The Power of Steam 1982, Marx in London 1982, A Social History of England 1983 (Haut-Brion: An Illustrious Lineage 1994), The BBC—The First Fifty Years 1985, The Collected Essays of Asa Briggs, (Vol. 1, 2, 3), The Franchise Affair (with Joanna Spicer) 1986, Victorian Things 1988, The Longman Encyclopedia (ed.) 1989, Haut-Brion: An Illustrious Lineage 1994, The Channel Islands: Occupation and Liberation 1940–45 1995, Fins de Siècle (co-ed.) 1996; co-author Modern Europe 1789–1989 1996, The History of Bethlem 1997, Chartism 1998, Go to It! War: Working for Victory on the Home Front, 1939–45 2000, Michael Young: Social Entrepreneur 2000, A Social History of the Media (with Peter Burke) 2002, A History of Longmans and Their Books, 1724-1990: Longevity in Publishing 2008. *Leisure interest:* travel. *Address:* 26 Oakmede Way, Ringmer, East Sussex, BN8 5JL (office); The Caprons, Keere Street, Lewes, Sussex, BN7 1TY, England (home). *Telephone:* (1273) 474704 (home). *Fax:* (1273) 474704 (home). *E-mail:* pat.spencer@ukgateway.net (office).

BRIGGS, Raymond Redvers, NDD, DFA, FSCD, FRSL; British writer, illustrator and cartoonist; b. 18 Jan. 1934, Wimbledon, London; s. of Ernest R. Briggs and Ethel Bowyer; m. Jean Taprell Clark 1963 (died 1973); ed Rutlish School, Merton, Wimbledon School of Art and Slade School of Fine Art, London; freelance illustrator 1957–; part-time lecturer in illustration Brighton School of Art 1961–87; children's author 1961–; mem. Soc. of Authors; awards include Kate Greenaway Medal 1966, 1973, BAFTA Award, Francis Williams Illustration Award (Victoria & Albert Museum) 1982, Broadcasting Press Guild Radio Award 1983, Children's Author of the Year 1992, Kurt Maschler Award 1992, Illustrated Book of the Year Award 1998, Smarties Silver Award 2001. *Radio play:* When the Wind Blows. *Publications:* The Strange House 1961, Midnight Adventure 1961, Ring-a-Ring o' Roses 1962, Sledges to the Rescue 1963, The White Land 1963, Fee Fi Fo Fum 1964, The Mother Goose Treasury 1966, Jim and the Beanstalk 1970, The Fairy Tale Treasury 1972, Father Christmas 1973 (also film version), Father Christmas Goes on Holiday 1975, Fungus the Bogeyman 1977, The Snowman 1978 (also film version), Gentleman Jim 1980 (also stage version), When the Wind Blows 1982 (stage and radio versions 1983, animated film version 1987), The Tinpot Foreign General and the Old Iron Woman 1984, The Snowman Pop-Up 1986, Unlucky Wally 1987, Unlucky Wally Twenty Years On 1989, The Man 1992, The Bear 1994 (also film version), Ethel and Ernest 1998, UG 2001, Blooming Books (with Nicolette Jones) 2003, The Puddleman 2004. *Leisure interests:* second-hand books, walking, gardening, fishing. *Address:* Weston, Underhill Lane, Westmeston, nr Hassocks, Sussex, BN6 8XG, England.

BRIGGS, Winslow Russell, MA, PhD; American biologist and academic (retd); *Professor Emeritus, Carnegie Institution of Washington;* b. 29 April 1928, St Paul, Minn.; s. of John Briggs and Marjorie (Winslow) Briggs; m. Ann Morrill 1955; three d.; ed Harvard Univ.; Instructor in Biological Sciences, Stanford Univ. 1955–57, Asst Prof. 1957–62, Assoc. Prof. 1962–66, Prof. 1966–67, 1973–93, Dir Dept of Plant Biology, Carnegie Inst. of Washington, Stanford 1973–93, now Prof. Emer.; Prof. of Biology, Harvard Univ. 1967–73; Guggenheim Fellow 1973–74; mem. Nat. Acad. of Sciences; Dr. hc (Univ. of Freiburg, Germany) 2002; Stephen Hales Award American Society of Plant Physiologists 1994, Sterling Hendricks Award, ACS and US Dept of Agric. 1995; Philip C. Hamm Award (Minn.) 1999; Anton Lang Memorial Lecturer, Mich. State Univ. 1999, Finsen Medal, Asscn Int. de Photobiologie. *Publications:* Life on Earth (with others) 1973; over 250 articles in professional journals and books. *Leisure interests:* hiking, Chinese cooking, park volunteer. *Address:* Department of Plant Biology, Carnegie Institution of Washington, 260 Panama Street, Palo Alto, CA 94305 (office); 480 Hale Street, Palo Alto, CA 94301-2207, USA (home). *Telephone:* (650) 325-1521 ext 207 (office); (650)

www.worldwhoswho.com

324-1455 (home). *Fax:* (650) 325-6857 (office). *E-mail:* briggs@stanford.edu (office). *Website:* carnegiedpb.stanford.edu/research/research_briggs.php (office).

BRIGHTMAN, Sarah; British actress and singer; d. of Grenville Brightman and Pauline Brightman (née Hall); m. Andrew Lloyd Webber (q.v.) 1984 (divorced 1990); pnr Frank Peterson; fmr mem. Pan's People and Hot Gossip groups; concerts world-wide. *Performances include:* Cats, Requiem, The Phantom of the Opera, Aspects of Love (music all by Andrew Lloyd Webber), I and Albert, The Nightingale, The Merry Widow, Trelawney of the Wells, Relative Values, Dangerous Obsession, The Innocents. *Recordings:* albums include: As I Came of Age 1990, Sarah Sings the Music of Andrew Lloyd Webber 1992, Dive 1993, Surrender 1995, Fly 1995, Timeless 1997, Eden 1999, La Luna 2000, Classics 2001, Harem 2003, Diva 2006, Symphony 2008, A Winter Symphony 2008. *Address:* c/o Claudia Dorrell, Dorrell Management, 2nd Floor, Lyme Wharf, 191 Royal College Street, London, NW1 OSG, England (office). *Telephone:* (870) 420-5088 (office). *Fax:* (870) 420-5188 (office). *E-mail:* claudia@dorrellmanagement.com (office). *Website:* www .sarah-brightman.com.

BRIGHTY, (Anthony) David, CMG, CVO; British diplomatist (retd); *Chairman, Co-ordinating Committee on Remuneration;* b. 7 Feb. 1939; m. 1st Diana Porteous 1963 (divorced 1979, died 1993); two s. two d.; m. 2nd Jane Docherty 1982 (divorced 1996); m. 3rd Susan Olivier 1997; ed Clare Coll., Cambridge; joined FCO 1961; Third Sec. Brussels 1962–64; Third Sec. Havana 1964–66, Second Sec. 1966–67; FCO 1967–69; Asst Man. S.G. Warburg & Co. 1969–71; FCO 1971–73; Head of Chancery, Saigon 1973–75; First Sec. UK Mission, New York 1975–78; Royal Coll. of Defence Studies 1979; FCO 1979–83; Counsellor, Lisbon 1983–86; Dir of Cabinet of Sec.-Gen. to NATO, FCO 1986–87; Amb. to Cuba 1989–91; Amb. to Czech Repub. and Slovakia (non-resident) 1991–94; Amb. to Spain and Andorra (non-resident) 1994–98; Dir (non-exec.) EFG Pvt. Bank 1999–2006; Chair. Co-ordinating Cttee on Remuneration (NATO, OECD, etc.) 1999–2006; Dir (non-exec.) Henderson European Microcap Trust 2000–04; Chair. Anglo-Spanish Soc. 2001–07, Friends of the British Library 2004–07, Canada Blanch Foundation (UK; Robin Humphries Fellow, ILAS, Univ. of London 2003. *Address:* 15 Provost Road, London, NW3 4ST, England.

BRILLINGER, David Ross, PhD, FRSC; Canadian academic; *Professor of Statistics, University of California, Berkeley;* b. 27 Oct. 1937, Toronto; s. of Austin C. Brillinger and Winnifred E. Simpson; m. Lorie Silber 1961; two s.; ed Univ. of Toronto and Princeton Univ.; Lecturer in Math. Princeton Univ., concurrently mem. tech. staff, Bell Telephone Labs 1962–64; lecturer, then Reader, LSE 1964–69; Prof. of Statistics, Univ. of Calif. Berkeley 1969–; International Statistical Review 1987–9; Guggenheim Fellow 1975–76, 1982–83; Fellow American Acad. of Arts and Sciences 1993; Wald Lecturer 1983; R. A. Fisher Award 1991, Gold Medal, Statistical Soc. of Canada 1992. *Publications:* Time Series: Data Analysis and Theory 1975, Directions in Time Series 1980. *Address:* Department of Statistics, University of California, Berkeley, CA 94720, USA (office). *Telephone:* (510) 642-0611 (office). *Fax:* (510) 642-7892 (office). *E-mail:* brill@stat.berkeley.edu (office). *Website:* stat -www.berkeley.edu/users/brill (office).

BRIM, Orville Gilbert, Jr., PhD; American foundation administrator and author; b. 7 April 1923, Elmira, New York; s. of Orville Gilbert and Helen Whittier Brim; m. Kathleen J. Vigneron 1944; two s. two d.; ed Yale Univ.; Instructor in Sociology, Univ. of Wis. 1952–53, Asst Prof., Sociology 1953–55; Sociologist, Russell Sage Foundation, New York 1955–60, Asst Sec. 1960–64, Pres. 1964–72; author and consultant 1972–74; Pres. Foundation for Child Devt 1974–85; Chair., Bd of Dirs, Automation Eng Lab. 1959–67, Special Comm. on the Social Sciences, Nat. Science Foundation 1968–69; mem. Drug Research Bd, NAS 1964–65; Vice-Chair., Bd of Trustees, American Insts for Research 1971–88, Chair. 1988–90; MacArthur Foundation Research Program on Successful Aging 1986–89; Dir McArthur Foundation Research Network on Successful Midlife Devt 1989–2002; Pres. Life Trends Inc. 1991–2002; Interim Pres. Social Science Research Council 1998–99; Kurt Lewin Memorial Award 1979, Soc. Research in Child Devt Award for Distinguished Scientific Contributions to Child Devt Research 1985. *Publications:* Sociology and the Field of Education 1958, Education for Child Rearing 1959, Personality and Decision Processes 1962, Intelligence: Perspectives 1965, Socialization after Childhood: Two Essays 1966, American Beliefs and Attitudes Toward Intelligence 1969, The Dying Patient 1970; ed.: Lifespan Development and Behavior, Vols II–VI 1979–84, Constancy and Change in Human Development 1980, Ambition: How we manage success and failure throughout our lives 1992, How Healthy Are We?: A National Study of Well-being at Midlife 2004. *Leisure interests:* sports and world ocean beaches. *Address:* 503 River Drive, Vero Beach, FL 32963, USA (home). *Telephone:* (772) 231-3329 (home). *Fax:* (772) 234-8559 (home).

BRIN, Sergey Mihailovich, BS, MSc; American (b. Russian) internet industry executive; *Co-Founder and President, Technology, Google Inc.;* b. 21 Aug. 1973, Moscow; s. of Michael Brin and Genia Brin; m. Anne Wojcicki 2007; one s.; ed Univ. of Maryland, Stanford Univ.; co-f. Google Inc. with Larry Page (q.v.), Pres. 1998–2001, Pres., Tech. 2001–; Fellow, NSF; Hon. MBA (Instituto de Empresa); Marconi Award (with Larry Page) 2004, Economist Innovation Award (with Larry Page) 2005; named one of the World's Most Influential People by Time Magazine 2005, one of 50 Most Important People on the Web, PC World 2007, one of 25 Most Powerful People in Business, Fortune Magazine 2007. *Publications:* more than a dozen academic papers including Extracting Patterns and Relations from the World Wide Web, Dynamic Data Mining: A New Architecture for Data with High Dimensionality (with Larry Page), Scalable Techniques for Mining Casual Structures, Dynamic Itemset Counting and Implication Rules for Market Basket Data, Beyond Market Baskets: Generalizing Association Rules to Correlations. *Address:* Google Inc., 2400 Bayshore Parkway, Mountain View, CA 94043, USA (office). *Telephone:* (650) 623-4000 (office). *Fax:* (650) 618-1499 (office). *Website:* www.google.com (office).

BRINDLE, Ian, FCA, BA; British business executive; b. 17 Aug. 1943; s. of John Brindle and Mabel Brindle (née Walsh); m. Frances Elisabeth Moseby 1967; two s. one d.; ed Blundells School, Manchester Univ.; articled Price Waterhouse London 1965, Toronto 1975, partner 1976–2001, mem. Supervisory Cttee 1988–98, Dir Auditing and Business Advisory Services 1990–91, Sr Partner 1991–98; Chair. PricewaterhouseCoopers UK (following merger with Coopers and Lybrand) 1998–2001, Sr Partner UK 1991–98; mem. Auditing Practices Cttee Consultancy Cttee of Accounting Bodies 1986–90, Chair. 1990; mem. Accounting Standards Bd 1993–2001; mem. Council Inst. of Chartered Accountants in England and Wales 1994–97; mem. Financial Reporting Council 1995–; Deputy Chair. Financial Reporting Review Panel 2001–. *Leisure interests:* tennis, golf, classical music. *Address:* 5th Floor, Aldwych House, 71–91 Aldwych, London, WC2B 4HN (office); Milestones, Packhorse Road, Bessels Green, Sevenoaks, Kent, TN13 2QP, England (home). *Website:* www.frrp.org.uk/committee.

BRINDLEY, Giles Skey, MA, MD, FRCP, FRS; British physiologist and academic; *Professor Emeritus, University of London Institute of Psychiatry;* b. (Giles Skey), 30 April 1926, Woking, Surrey; s. of the late Arthur James Benet Skey and Dr Margaret Beatrice Marion Skey (née Dewhurst), later Brindley; m. 1st Lucy Dunk Bennell 1959 (divorced); m. 2nd Dr Hilary Richards 1964; one s. one d.; ed Leyton Co. High School, Downing Coll., Cambridge, London Hosp. Medical School; clinical and research posts 1950–54; Russian Language Abstractor, British Abstracts of Medical Sciences 1953–56; Demonstrator, then Lecturer and Reader in Physiology, Univ. of Cambridge 1954–68; Prof. of Physiology, Univ. of London Inst. of Psychiatry 1968–91, Prof. Emer. 1991–; Hon. Dir MRC Neurological Prostheses Unit 1968–92; partner Brindley Surgical Implants 1991–2001; Hon. Consultant Physician Maudsley Hosp. 1971–92; Fellow King's Coll., Cambridge 1959–62, Trinity Coll., Cambridge 1963–68; Chair. Editorial Bd Journal of Physiology 1964–66; Visiting Prof., Univ. of Calif., Berkeley 1968; Hon. FRCS 1988; Hon. FRCSE 2000; Liebrecht-Franceschetti Prize, German Ophthalmological Soc. 1971, Feldberg Prize, Feldberg Foundation 1974, St Peter's Medal, British Asscn of Urological Surgeons 1987. *Compositions:* Tyrolean Suite for wind quintet 1999, The Waterman's Daughter for soprano and woodwind quartet 2001. *Publications:* Physiology of the Retina and Visual Pathway 1960, numerous scientific papers. *Leisure interests:* designing and playing musical instruments, composing chamber music. *Address:* 102 Ferndene Road, London, SE24 0AA, England (home). *Telephone:* (20) 7274-2598 (home). *E-mail:* gsbrindley@rcsed.ac.uk (home).

BRINDLEY, Dame Lynne Janie, DBE, MA, FLA, FRSA, CCMI; British librarian; *Chief Executive, The British Library;* b. 2 July 1950, London; d. of Ivan Blowers and Janie Blowers (née Williams); adopted d. of Ronald Williams and Elaine Williams (née Chapman); m. Timothy Stuart Brindley 1972; ed Truro High School, Univ. of Reading, Univ. Coll. London; Head of Marketing and of Chief Exec.'s Office, British Library 1979–85, Chief Exec. British Library 2000–; Dir of Library and Information Services, also Pro-Vice Chancellor, Aston Univ. 1985–90; Prin. Consultant, KPMG 1990–92; Librarian and Dir of Information Services, LSE 1992–97; Librarian and Pro-Vice Chancellor, Univ. of Leeds 1997–2000, Visiting Prof. of Knowledge Man., 2000–; Visiting Prof. of Information Man., Leeds Metropolitan Univ. 2000–03; mem. Int. Cttee on Social Science Information, UNESCO 1992–97, Lord Chancellor's Advisory Cttee on Public Records 1992–98, Stanford Univ. Advisory Council for Libraries and Information Resources 1999–, Resource Bd 2002–, Eng and Physical Sciences Research Council User Panel 2002–04, Ithaka Bd; Trustee, Thackray Medical Museum, Leeds 1999–2001; Fellow, Univ. Coll. London 2002; Freeman, City of London 1989; Liveryman, Goldsmiths' Co. 1993; Hon. DLitt (Nottingham Trent) 2001, (Oxford) 2002, (Leicester) 2002, (Sheffield) 2004, (Reading) 2004; Hon. DPhil (London Guildhall) 2002; Hon. DSc (City) 2005. *Publications:* numerous articles on electronic libraries and information man. *Leisure interests:* classical music, theatre, modern art, hill walking. *Address:* The British Library, 96 Euston Road, London, NW1 2DB, England (office). *Telephone:* (20) 7412-7273 (office). *Fax:* (20) 7412-7268 (office). *E-mail:* chief-executive@bl.uk (office). *Website:* www.bl.uk (office).

BRINK, André Philippus, MA; South African writer and academic; *Honorary Professor, Department of English Language and Literature, University of Cape Town;* b. 29 May 1935, Vrede; s. of Daniel and Aletta (née Wolmarans) Brink; three s. one d.; ed Lydenburg High School, Potchefstroom Univ., Sorbonne, Paris; began writing at an early age; first novel (Afrikaans) published 1958; on return from Paris became mem. and spokesman of young Afrikaans writers' group Sestigers; returned to Paris 1968; went back to South Africa to resist apartheid through writing; novel Kennis van die Aand banned 1973 (first Afrikaans novel to be banned); began to write in English as well; Dir several plays, but abandoned theatre owing to censorship; resumed playwriting 1996; Founder-mem. Afrikaans Writers' Guild; Prof. of Afrikaans and Dutch Literature, Rhodes Univ. (previously lecturer) 1980–89; Prof. of English, Univ. of Cape Town 1991–2000, now Hon. Prof.; Chevalier Légion d'honneur 1983; Commdr Ordre des Arts et des Lettres 1992; Hon. DLitt (Witwatersrand) 1985, (Univ. of Free State) 1997, (Montpellier) 1998, (Rhodes) 2001, (Pretoria) 2003; Reina Prinsen Geerlings Prize 1964, CNA Award for Literature, South Africa 1965, 1978 and 1982, Martin Luther King Memorial Prize 1979, Prix Médicis Etranger, France 1979, Biannual Freedom of Speech Prize by Monismanien Foundation, Univ. of Uppsala 1991, Premio Mondello (Italy) 1997, Commonwealth Prize for Literature (Africa) 2003, Sunday Times Fiction Award 2004. *Publications include:* File on a Diplomat

1966, Looking on Darkness (novel) 1974, An Instant in the Wind (novel) 1976, Rumours of Rain (novel) 1978, A Dry White Season (novel) 1979, A Chain of Voices (novel) 1982, Mapmakers (essays) 1983, The Wall of the Plague (novel) 1984, The Ambassador (novel) 1985, A Land Apart (co-ed with J M Coetzee) 1986, States of Emergency (novel) 1988, An Act of Terror (novel) 1991, The First Life of Adamastor (novel) 1993, On the Contrary (novel) 1993, Imaginings of Sand (novel) 1996, Reinventing a Continent (essays) 1996, Devil's Valley (novel) 1998, The Rights of Desire (novel) 2000, The Other Side of Silence (novel) 2002, Before I Forget (novel) 2004, Praying Mantis 2004, Other Lives: A Novel in Three Parts 2008, A Fork in the Sand (auto-biog.) 2009; several plays 1965–75, The Jogger 1997. *Address:* Department of English Language and Literature, University of Cape Town, Rondebosch 7701, South Africa (office). *Fax:* (21) 685-3945 (home). *Website:* web.uct.ac.za/depts/english.

BRINK, Andries Jacob, MD, DSc, FRCP, FACC; South African professor of medicine; *Editor-in-Chief, Cardiovascular Journal of South Africa;* b. 29 Aug. 1923, Potchefstroom; s. of Andries J. Brink and Petronella J. Havenga; m. Maria Ruskovich 1949; two s. two d.; ed Jeppe High School, Univs of Witwatersrand, Pretoria and Stellenbosch, Johns Hopkins Univ., Baltimore, USA, Postgraduate Medical School, London, UK; Postgraduate Medical School, Hammersmith Hosp., London 1951; Fellow in Paediatrics, Johns Hopkins Hosp., USA 1952; Internist, Sr Lecturer, Univ. of Pretoria 1953–56; Founder Prof. Dept of Medicine, Univ. of Stellenbosch 1956, Chief Cardiologist and Founder, Dept of Cardiology 1956–78, Dean, Faculty of Medicine 1971–83; Dir Molecular and Cellular Cardiac Research Unit, MRC 1956–69; Pres. (part-time) SA Medical Research Council 1969–83, Full-time Pres. 1984–89; Man. Dir Clinics Cardive Publishing Co. 1990–, Nat. Dir MC Research Pty Ltd 1998–2000; mem. Bd Scientific Advisory Council 1972–83, 1990–94, SA Medical and Dental Council 1971–83, World Asscn of Medical Eds 2002–; Founder Heart Foundation of SA; Founder, Ed.-in-Chief Cardiovascular Journal of South Africa 1989–; Founder, Ed. South African Journal of Diabetes and Vascular Disease; wine producer (Galleon Wines); Hon. DSc (Natal) 1976, (Potchefstroom) 1985; Hon. MD (Stellenbosch) 1989; nearly 40 major awards and prizes, including Recht Malan Award, (for Dictionary of Afrikaans Medical Terms), Merit Awards (Gold), S African Medical Research Council 1986; Decoration for Meritorious Service (Gold) 1981. *Publications:* 150 scientific and general medical publs, including 10 books and a medical dictionary. *Leisure interests:* reading, music, cycling, painting, oenology, viticulture. *Address:* PO Box 62, Durbanville 7551 (office); 15 La Verona, Durbanville 1550, South Africa (home). *Telephone:* (21) 976-8129 (office); (21) 976-1786 (home). *Fax:* (21) 976-8984 (office); (21) 976-1786 (home). *E-mail:* andries.medcon@absamail.co.za (home). *Website:* www.cvjsa.co.za (office).

BRINKHORST, Laurens Jan, MA; Dutch politician and academic; *Professor of International and European Law and Governance, University of Leiden;* b. 18 March 1937, Zwolle; ed Leiden Univ. and Columbia Univ., New York, USA; worked for Shearman & Sterling law firm, New York; worked at Europe Inst., Leiden Univ., Dir Europe Inst. and Sr Lecturer in the Law of Int. Orgs 1965, later Extraordinary Prof. of Int. Environmental Law; Chair of European Law, Groningen Univ. 1967–73; State Sec. for Foreign Affairs with European Affairs portfolio 1973–77; mem. House of Reps of States Gen. 1977–82; mem. Democraten 66 (D66), Leader Parl. Party 1981–82, now Hon. mem.; Head, Del. of Comm. of European Communities in Japan 1982; Dir-Gen. of Environment, Consumer Protection and Nuclear Safety, EC 1987–89, of Environment, Nuclear Safety and Civil Protection 1989; mem. European Parl. 1994–99; Minister of Agric., Nature Man. and Fisheries 1999–2002; European Affairs Adviser, NautaDutilh law firm, Brussels 2002; Minister of Economic Affairs 2003–04; Deputy Prime Minister and Minister of Econ. Affairs 2004–06 (resgnd); mem. Bd of Dirs Salzburg Seminar, Int. Inst. of Sustainable Devt; currently Prof. of Int. and European Law and Governance, Univ. of Leiden; Coordinator EC for the Project No. 6 Trans-eur. Network; Dr hc (Sofia). *Address:* Lange Voorhut 82, 2514 EJ The Hague, Netherlands (office). *Telephone:* (70) 30-20-165. *Fax:* (70) 42-77-345 (office). *E-mail:* l.j.brinkhorst@gmail.com (office); office@voorhout82.nl (office).

BRINKHUES, Josef; German ecclesiastic; b. 21 June 1913, Aachen; s. of Heinrich Brinkhues and Cläre Brinkhues (neé Führen); m. Dr Ilse Volckmar 1946; one s. one d.; ed Frankfurt and Bonn; ordained priest 1937; consecrated Bishop 1966; mem. Int. Old Catholics Bishops' Conf. of Utrecht Union 1966–1986; Bishop Emer. of Old-Catholic Church in Germany. *Leisure interest:* music. *Address:* Oberdorf 18, 53347 Impekoven Alfter, Germany. *Telephone:* (228) 643301.

BRINKLEY, Alan, BA, PhD; American historian and academic; *Provost and Allan Nevins Professor of History, Columbia University;* b. 2 June 1949, Washington, DC; s. of the late David Brinkley; m. Evangeline Morphos 1989; one d.; ed Princeton and Harvard Univs; Asst Prof. of History, MIT 1978–82; visiting position, Harvard Univ. 1980, Dunwalke Assoc. Prof. of American History 1982–88; Prof. of History, Grad. School and Univ. Center, CUNY 1988–91; visiting positions, Princeton Univ. 1991, Univ. of Turin 1992, New York Univ. 1993, École des Hautes Études en Sciences Sociales, Paris 1996; Prof. of History, Columbia Univ. 1991–98, Allan Nevins Prof. of History 1998–, Provost 2003–; Harmsworth Prof. of American History, Univ. of Oxford 1998–99; Fellow, Soc. of American Historians 1984– (Exec. Bd mem. 1989–); mem. American Historical Assen, Org. of American Historians (Exec. Bd mem. 1990–93), Century Foundation (Trustee 1995–, Chair. 1999–), Nat. Humanities Center (Trustee 2004–), American Acad. of Arts and Sciences; Nat. Endowment for the Humanities Fellowship 1972–73, American Council of Learned Socs Fellowship 1981, Robert L. Brown Prize, Louisiana Historical Asscn 1982, Nat. Book Award for History 1983, Guggenheim Fellowship 1984–85, Woodrow Wilson Center for Int. Scholars Fellowship 1985, Joseph R. Levenson Memorial Teaching Prize, Harvard Univ. 1987, Nat. Humanities Center Fellowship 1988–89, Media Studies Center Fellowship 1993–94, Russell Sage Foundation Fellowship 1996–97, Great Teacher Award, Columbia Univ. 2003. *Publications:* Voices of Protest: Huey Long, Father Coughlin, and the Great Depression 1982, American History: A Survey 1983, The Unfinished Nation: A Concise History of the American People 1993, The End of Reform: New Deal Liberalism in Recession and War 1995, Eyes of the Nation: A Visual History of the United States (with others) 1997, New Federalist Papers (with Kathleen Sullivan and Nelson Polsby) 1997, Liberalism and Its Discontents 1998, The Chicago Handbook for Teachers (co-ed.) 1999, The Reader's Companion to the American Presidency (co-ed.) 2000; contribs to scholarly books and journals. *Address:* Office of the Provost, 205 Low Library, Columbia University, New York, NY 10027, USA (office). *Telephone:* (212) 854-2403 (office). *E-mail:* ab65@columbia.edu (office). *Website:* www.columbia.edu/cu/history (office).

BRINKLEY, Amy Woods; American banking executive; *Global Risk Executive, Bank of America;* ed Univ. of N Carolina at Chapel Hill; began her career as man. trainee in Commercial Credit Department Dept, Bank of America 1978, later Corp. Banking Officer, Asia Pacific Area of Int. Div., later Commercial Banker in Greensboro, NC, Exec. Vice-Pres. and Sr Consumer Credit Policy Exec. 1990, Marketing Group Exec. 1993–99, Pres. Consumer Products 1999–2001, Chair. Credit Policy and Deputy Corp. Risk Man. Exec. 2001–02, Global Risk Exec., mem. Risk and Capital Cttee and Man. Operating Cttee 2002–; mem. Bd Carolinas HealthCare System, Private Export Funding Co. (PEFCO); mem. Bd of Advisors, Partners in Out-of-School Time, N Carolina Dance Theatre (fmr Chair. Bd of Trustees); fmr mem. Univ. of N Carolina Bd of Visitors; Trustee Princeton Theological Seminary; ranked by Fortune magazine amongst 50 Most Powerful Women in Business in the US (22nd) 2003, (19th) 2004, (25th) 2005, (23rd) 2006, (23rd) 2007, named by US Banker magazine amongst Most Powerful Women in Banking (first) 2005, ranked by Forbes magazine amongst 100 Most Powerful Women (48th) 2008. *Address:* Bank of America Corpn, Corporate Center, 100 N Tryon Street, Charlotte, NC 28255, USA (office). *Telephone:* (800) 432-1000 (office). *Fax:* (704) 386-6699 (office). *Website:* www.bankofamerica.com (office).

BRINKLEY, Robert Edward, MA; British diplomatist; *High Commissioner to Pakistan;* b. 21 Jan. 1954; m. Mary Brinkley; three s.; ed Stonyhurst Coll., Lancs., Corpus Christi Coll., Oxford; joined FCO, London 1977, mem. staff 1982–88, 1992–96; mem. UK Del. to Comprehensive Test Ban Negotiations, Geneva 1978; assigned to Embassy in Moscow 1979–82, 1996–99, to Embassy in Bonn 1988–92; with FCO/Home Office Jt Entry Clearance Unit 2000–02; Amb. to Ukraine 2002–06; High Commr to Pakistan 2006–. *Leisure interests:* reading, walking, music (violin). *Address:* High Commission of the United Kingdom, Diplomatic Enclave, Ramna 5, POB 1122, Islamabad, Pakistan (office). *Telephone:* (51) 2012000 (office). *Fax:* (51) 2823439 (office). *E-mail:* bhcmedia@isb.comsats.net.pk (office). *Website:* www.britainonline.org.pk (office).

BRINKMAN, Leonard Cornelis (Eelco), Dr rer. pol; Dutch politician and national organization official; *President, Het Nederlandse Rode Kruis (Netherlands Red Cross);* b. 5 Feb. 1948, Dirksland; m. J. Salentijn; three c.; ed Gymnasium, Dordrecht, Free Univ., Amsterdam; research post in the Public Admin. Dept, Free Univ. 1969–74; mem. Co-ordination Office for North of West Holland conurbation 1974–75; Head of Office of Sec.-Gen., Ministry of Home Affairs 1976–79, Dir-Gen. 1980–82; Minister for Welfare, Health and Cultural Affairs 1982–89; Pres. Het Nederlandse Rode Kruis (Netherlands Red Cross) 2001–; Christian Democratic Alliance. *Publications:* articles on public admin. in specialist journals. *Address:* Het Nederlandse Rode Kruis, Postbus 28120, 2502 KC The Hauge, Netherlands (office). *Telephone:* (70) 4455666 (office). *Fax:* (70) 4455777 (office). *E-mail:* info@redcross.nl (office). *Website:* www.rodekruis.nl (office).

BRINSTER, Ralph L., VMD, PhD; American physiologist and academic; *Richard King Mellon Professor of Reproductive Physiology, University of Pennsylvania;* b. Montclair, NJ; ed School of Agric., Rutgers Univ., New Brunswick, NJ, School of Veterinary Medicine and Grad. School of Arts and Sciences, Univ. of Pennsylvania; Postdoctoral Fellow, Jackson Lab., Bar Harbor, ME 1960, Marine Biological Lab., Woods Hole, Mass 1962; Teaching Fellow, Dept of Physiology, School of Medicine, Univ. of Pennsylvania 1960–64, Instructor 1964–65, Asst Prof. of Physiology, School of Veterinary Medicine 1965–66, Assoc. Prof. of Physiology, Dept of Animal Biology 1966–70, Program Dir, Reproductive Physiology Training Program 1968–83, Program Dir, Veterinary Medical Scientist Training Program 1969–84, Prof. of Physiology, School of Veterinary Medicine and Grad. School of Arts and Sciences and Grad. Faculty 1970–, Richard King Mellon Prof. of Reproductive Physiology, School of Veterinary Medicine and Grad. School 1975–; mem. Inst. of Medicine (NAS) 1986, NAS 1987, American Veterinary Medical Asscn, American Physiological Soc., American Soc. of Cell Biology, Soc. for the Study of Fertility (GB), Soc. for the Study of Reproduction; Fellow, American Acad. of Arts and Science 1986, AAAS 1989, American Acad. of Microbiology 1992; Hon. MD (Univ. of the Basque Country) 1994; Hon. DSc (Rutgers Univ.) 2000; Distinguished Service Award, US Dept of Agric. 1989, Pioneer Award, Int. Embryo Transfer 1992, Charles-Leopold Mayer Prize, Acad. des Sciences (France) 1994, Alumni Award of Merit, Univ. of Pennsylvania School of Veterinary Medicine 1995, Prize in Developmental Biology, March of Dimes 1996, John Scott Award for Scientific Achievement, City Trusts of Philadelphia 1997, Bower Award and Prize for Achievement in Science, Franklin Inst. 1997, Carl Hartman Award, Soc. for the Study of Reproduction 1997, honoured by Special Festschrift Issue, International Journal of Developmental Biology 1998, Pioneer in Reproduction Research Award, Nat. Inst. of Child

Health and Human Devt (NICHHD) 1998, George Hammel Cook Distinguished Alumni Award, Rutgers Univ. 1999, Charlton Lecturer, Tufts Univ. School of Medicine 2000, Ernst W. Bertner Award, Univ. of Texas M.D. Anderson Cancer Center 2001, selected for Hall of Honor, NICHHD 2003, Wolf Prize in Medicine (Israel) 2003, Gairdner Foundation Int. Award 2006. *Publications:* more than 360 articles in scientific journals. *Address:* School of Veterinary Medicine, University of Pennsylvania, 3850 Baltimore Avenue, Philadelphia, PA 19104, USA (office). *Telephone:* (215) 898-8805 (office). *Fax:* (215) 898-0667 (office). *Website:* www2.vet.upenn.edu (office).

BRIQUET MARMOL, Armando; Venezuelan politician; *Secretary-General, Primero Justicia;* b. 1970, Caracas; m. Teresa Saavedra de Briquet; one s.; ed Universidad Central de Venezuela, Universidad Católica Andrés Bello; Gen. Man. for Health and Social Issues, Caracas City Council 1996–98; Man. Dir Municipality of Baruta 1998–2002; Man. Dir Office of Pres. of Nat. Congress 1999; Sec.-Gen. Primero Justicia opposition party 2002–; Head Inter-Governmental Affairs, Baruta 2003. *Address:* Primero Justicia, Planta de Oficianas, Centro Comercial Chacaito, Chacaito, Caracas, Venezuela (office). *Telephone:* (212) 952-9733 (office). *Website:* www.primerojusticia.org.ve.

BRISVILLE, Jean-Claude Gabriel; French writer; b. 28 May 1922, Bois-Colombes/Hauts-de-Seine; s. of Maurice Brisville and Geneviève Gineste; m. 2nd Irène Kalaschnikowa 1963; one s. one d. by first m.; ed Lycée Jacques Decour, Paris; literary journalist 1946–; Reader, Hachette 1951–58; Sec. to Albert Camus 1957–59; Deputy Literary Dir Juilliard 1959–64, Literary Dir 1964–70; Head of Drama Video Section, ORTF 1971–75; Literary Dir Livre de poche 1976–81; Chevalier, Légion d'honneur, Chevalier, Ordre des Arts et des Lettres; Prix du Théâtre de la Société des Auteurs et Compositeurs Dramatiques (SACD). *Publications:* narrative works: Prologue 1948, D'un amour (Prix Sainte-Beuve) 1954, La Fuite au Danemark 1962, La Zone d'ombre 1976; plays: Le Fauteuil à bascule (Prix Ibsen, Prix de la meilleure création dramatique) 1982, Le Bonheur à Romorantin, L'entretien de M. Descartes avec M. Pascal le jeune, La Villa bleue, Les Liaisons dangereuses (adaptation), Le Souper (Prix du Théâtre, Acad. Française) 1990, L'Officier de la Garde 1990, L'Antichambre 1991, Contre-jour 1993, Dernière Salve 1995; essays; stories for children. *Address:* SACD, 12 rue Ballu, 75009 Paris, France.

BRITO, Carlos, MBA; Brazilian business executive; *CEO, InBev;* b. 1960; ed Fed. Univ. of Rio de Janeiro, Stanford Univ., USA; worked for Shell Oil and Daimler Benz –1989; Financial Analyst, Brahma, AmBev (now InBev) 1989–91, Plant Man. 1991–92, Head Softdrink Div. 1992–96, Head Beer Sales 1997–2001, Head Operations 2002–03, CEO Ambev Jan.–Aug. 2004, Zone President for N America (after merger with Interbrew) 2004–05, CEO InBev 2005–. *Address:* InBev, Brouwerijplein 1, Leuven 3000, Belgium (office). *Telephone:* (16) 24-71-11 (office). *Fax:* (16) 24-74-07 (office). *E-mail:* info@inbev.com (office). *Website:* www.inbev.com (office).

BRITTAN, Sir Samuel, Kt, MA; British writer and journalist; *Columnist, Financial Times;* b. 29 Dec. 1933, London; brother of Lord Brittan of Spennithorne; ed Kilburn Grammar School, Jesus Coll., Cambridge; journalist on The Financial Times 1955–61, prin. economic commentator 1966–, Asst Ed. 1978–95; Econs Ed. The Observer 1961–64; Adviser, Dept of Econ. Affairs 1965; Research Fellow, Nuffield Coll., Oxford 1973–74, Visiting Fellow 1974–82; Visiting Prof., Chicago Law School, USA 1978; mem. Peacock Cttee on Finance of the BBC 1985–86; Hon. Prof. of Politics Univ. of Warwick 1987–92; Hon. Fellow Jesus Coll., Cambridge 1988; Chevalier, Légion d'honneur 1993; Hon. DLitt (Heriot-Watt) 1985; Hon. DUniv (Essex) 1995; first winner Sr Harold Wincott Award for financial journalists 1971, George Orwell Prize for political journalism 1980, Ludwig Erhard Prize 1987. *Publications:* Steering the Economy (3rd edn 1970), Left or Right: The Bogus Dilemma 1968, The Price of Economic Freedom: A Guide to Flexible Rates 1970, Is There an Economic Consensus? 1973, Capitalism and the Permissive Society 1973 (new edn A Restatement of Economic Liberalism 1988), The Delusion of Incomes Policy (with Peter Lilley) 1977, The Economic Consequences of Democracy 1977, How to End the 'Monetarist' Controversy 1981, Role and Limits of Government: Essays in Political Economy 1983, There Is No Such Thing As Society 1993, Capitalism with a Human Face 1995, Essays, Moral, Political and Economic 1998, Against the Flow 2005. *Address:* The Financial Times, Number 1 Southwark Bridge, London, SE1 9HL, England (office). *Telephone:* (20) 7873-3000 (office). *Fax:* (20) 7873-4343 (office). *E-mail:* samuel.brittan@ft.com (office). *Website:* www.samuelbrittan.co.uk (home).

BRITTAN OF SPENNITHORNE, Baron (Life Peer), cr. 2000, of Spennithorne in the County of North Yorkshire; **Rt Hon. Leon Brittan,** Kt, PC, QC, DL; British politician, barrister and investment banker; *Vice-Chairman, UBS Investment Bank;* b. 25 Sept. 1939, London; s. of the late Dr Joseph Brittan and of Rebecca Brittan; brother of Sir Samuel Brittan; m. Diana Peterson 1980; two step-d.; ed Haberdashers' Aske's School, Trinity Coll., Cambridge, Yale Univ.; Chair. Cambridge Univ. Conservative Asscn 1960; Pres. Cambridge Union 1960, debating tour of USA 1961; called to Bar, Inner Temple 1962 (Bencher 1983); Chair. Bow Group 1964–65; contested N Kensington seat 1966, 1970; Ed. Crossbow 1966–68; mem. Political Cttee Carlton Club, Cttee of the British Atlantic Group of Young Politicians 1970–78; Vice-Chair. of Govs of Isaac Newton School 1968–71; MP for Cleveland and Whitby 1974–83, for Richmond (N Yorks.) 1983–88; QC 1978; Vice-Chair. Parl. Conservative Party Employment Cttee 1974–76; Opposition Spokesman on Devolution and House of Commons Affairs 1976–78, on Devolution and Employment 1978–79; Minister of State, Home Office 1979–81; Chief Sec. to the Treasury 1981–83, Home Sec. 1983–85; Sec. of State for Trade and Industry 1985–86; Commr with responsibility for Competition Policy and Financial Insts, Comm. of the European Communities (EC) 1989–92, for Econ. Relations 1993–94, for External Trade and Relations with N America and parts of Asia 1995–99, a Vice-Pres. 1989–99; consultant, Herbert Smith 2000–06; Vice-Chair. UBS Investment Bank 2000–; Advisory Dir Unilever 2000–04, Dir (non-exec. 2004–; Chair. Lotis group of Int. Financial Services London (IFSL) 2001–06; Distinguished Visiting Fellow Inst. of Policy Studies 1988; Hersch Lauterpacht Memorial Lecturer, Univ. of Cambridge 1990; Chair. Soc. of Conservative Lawyers 1986–89; Vice-Chair. Nat. Asscn of School Govs and Mans 1970–78; Chancellor Univ. of Teesside 1993–2005; Deputy Lt, Co. of N Yorks. 2001–; Hon. DCL (Newcastle) 1990, (Durham) 1992; Hon. LLD (Hull) 1990, (Bath) 1995; Hon. DL (Bradford) 1992; Hon. DEcon (Korea Univ.); Dr hc (Edin.) 1991. *Publications:* The Conservative Opportunity (contrib.), Millstones for the Sixties (co-author), Rough Justice, Infancy and the Law, How to Save your Schools, A New Deal for Health Care 1988, Defence and Arms Control in a Changing Era 1988, Discussions on Policy 1989, Monetary Union: the Issues and the Impact 1989, Europe: Our Sort of Community (Granada Guildhall Lecture) 1989, Hersch Lauterpacht Memorial Lectures (Univ. of Cambridge) 1990, European Competition Policy 1992, Europe: The Europe We Need 1994, A Diet of Brussels 2000. *Leisure interests:* walking, cricket, opera. *Address:* 1 Finsbury Avenue, London, EC2M 2PP (office); House of Lords, Westminster, London, SW1A 0PW, England. *Telephone:* (20) 7568-6305 (office). *Fax:* (20) 7568-6520 (office). *E-mail:* leon .brittan@ubs.com (office). *Website:* www.ubs.com (office).

BRITTEN, Roy John, PhD; American biophysicist and molecular biologist; *Distinguished Carnegie Senior Research Associate in Biology Emeritus, California Institute of Technology;* b. 1 Oct. 1919, Washington, DC; s. of Rollo H. Britten and Marion Britten (née Hale); m. (divorced); two s.; m. 2nd Jacqueline Aymar Reid 1986 (died 2001); ed Univ. of Virginia, Johns Hopkins and Princeton Univs; staff mem. Biophysics Group, Dept of Terrestrial Magnetism, Carnegie Inst. of Washington 1951–71; inventor, quadrupole focusing of energetic beams; discoverer, repeated DNA sequences in genomes of higher organisms; Visiting Assoc. Calif. Inst. of Tech. and staff mem. Dept of Terrestrial Magnetism, Carnegie Inst. of Washington 1971–73; Sr Research Assoc. Calif. Inst. of Tech. and staff mem. Carnegie Inst. of Washington 1973–81; Distinguished Carnegie Sr Research Assoc. in Biology, Calif. Inst. of Tech. and staff mem. Carnegie Inst. of Washington 1981–89; Distinguished Carnegie Sr Research Assoc. in Biology, Calif. Inst. of Tech. 1989–99; Distinguished Carnegie Sr Research Assoc. in Biology Emer., Calif. Inst. of Tech. 1999–; Adjunct Prof. Univ. of Calif., Irvine 1991–; mem. NAS, Acad. Arts and Sciences. *Publications:* articles in professional journals. *Leisure interests:* inventing, sailing, music, painting. *Address:* Kerckhoff Marine Laboratory, California Institute of Technology, 101 Dahlia Avenue, Corona del Mar, CA 92625-2814, USA (office). *Telephone:* (949) 675-2159 (office).

BRITZ, Robert, BSc; American financial executive; b. 1951; ed Manhattan Coll., Harvard Business School; joined New York Stock Exchange (NYSE) 1972, various man. posts in corp. marketing, then Man. Dir Corp. Business Devt, Vice-Pres. New Listings and Client Service, Sr Vice-Pres., Exec. Vice-Pres., Group Exec. Vice-Pres. overseeing operation of NYSE market, tech. and information products, mem. Office of Chair. 1995–2001, Co-COO, Pres. and Exec. Vice-Chair. 2001–05 (retd); fmr mem. Bd of Dirs The Stanley Works, Securities Industry Automation Corpn (SIAC), Sector Inc. *Address:* c/o New York Stock Exchange, 11 Wall Street, 6th Floor, New York, NY 10005, USA (office).

BRIXNER, Ulrich, Dr rer. pol; German banker; b. 1941, Munich; ed Univ. of Mannheim; fmrly CEO GZ Bank; Chair. and CEO DZ BANK AG (formed by merger of GZ Bank and DG Bank Deutsche Genossenschaftsbank) 2001–07; mem. Supervisory Bd Südzucker AG. *Address:* c/o DZ BANK AG, Deutsche Zentral-Genossenschaftsbank, Platz der Republik, 60265 Frankfurt am Main, Germany (office).

BRIZ ABULARACH, Jorge; Guatemalan politician and business executive; b. 27 Sept. 1955, Guatemala City; m.; ed Univ. Rafael Landívar de Guatemala; trained as lawyer; Dir Chamber of Commerce 1985–86, Vice-Pres. 1987–88, Pres. 1989–91, 1995–99, 2001–03; Leader Partido Movimento Reformador (MR–Movt. for Reform Party) 2002–; elected mem. of Parl. 2003–; Minister of Foreign Affairs 2004–06; Pres. Coordinating Cttee, Asscn of Agric., Commerce, Industry and Finance (CACIF) 1990–96, Dir 2000–03; Pres. Perm. Secr. of Latin American Chambers of Commerce and Industry (CAMACOL) 1997–98; fmr Dir Fed. of Chambers of Commerce of Cen. America (CAMACOL); mem. Financial Bd of Guatemala 1992–2002; del. to IMF, World Bank, Inter-American Devt Bank and EU; Gran Oficial, Orden al Mérito Bernardo O'Higgins (Chile) 1997, Orden José Cecilio del Valle (Guatemala) 1999. *Address:* c/o Ministry of Foreign Affairs, 2a Avda La Reforma 4–47, Zona 10, Guatemala City, Guatemala (office).

BRIZUELA DE AVILA, María Eugenia; Salvadorean lawyer and politician; b. 31 Oct. 1945, San Salvador; m. Ricardo Antonio Avila Araujo; three c.; ed Geneva Univ., Switzerland, Sorbonne Univ., Paris, France, Dr. José Matías Delgado Univ. of El Salvador, Cen. American Inst. of Business (INCAE), Nicaragua; Pres. Admin. Council for Int. Insurance, Salvadorean Asscn for the Study of Insurance Rights (AIDA) 1995–98, Salvador Foundation for the Devt of Women 1995–98; mem. Bd of Dirs Banco Salvadoreño; Co-ordinator 'The New Alliance', Govt of El Salvador 1999–; Minister of Foreign Affairs 1999–2004; mem. El Salvador Lawyers' Asscn 1985–, Chamber of Arbitration and Conciliation, Inst. of Notary Rights 1985–, Juridicial Studies Centre 1989–; Exec. mem. Social Security Inst. 1994, Social Investment Fund 1995. *Address:* c/o Ministry of Foreign Affairs, 5500 Alameda Dr Manuel Enrique Araújo, Km 6, Carretera a Santa Tecla, San Salvador, El Salvador (office).

BROAD, Eli, BA, CPA; American business executive; *Chairman, AIG SunAmerica Inc.;* b. 6 June 1933, New York; s. of Leon Broad and Rebecca Broad (née Jacobson); m. Edythe Lois Lawson 1954; two s.; ed Michigan State Univ.; Asst Prof. Detroit Inst. of Tech. 1956; Co-Founder, Chair., Pres. and

CEO AIG SunAmerica Life Insurance Co. (fmrly Kaufman & Broad, Inc.), LA 1957–2001, Chair. 2001–; Chair. of numerous cos including CalAmerica Life Insurance Co., KB Home (fmrly Kaufman & Broad Home Corpn) 1989–93, Stanford Ranch Co.; mem. Exec. Cttee Fed. Nat. Mortgage Asscn 1972–73; mem. Calif. Business Roundtable 1986–2000; co-owner Sacramento Kings and Arco Arena 1992–99; Dir LA World Affairs Council 1988– (Chair. 1994–99), DARE America 1989–95 (Hon. Dir 1995–); Chair. Mayor's Housing Policy Comm. 1974–75; mem. Advisory Council, Town Hall of Calif. 1985–87; mem. Contemporary Art Comm., Harvard Univ. Art Museum 1992–; mem. Bd of Overseers, Univ. of Southern Calif. Keck School of Medicine 1999–, Bd of Dirs EdVoice 2001–; Fellow American Acad. of Arts and Sciences 2001–; Trustee Pitzer Coll., Claremont, CA 1970–82 (Chair. Bd of Trustees 1973–79, Life Trustee 1982–), Haifa Univ., Israel 1972–80, Windward School, Santa Monica, CA 1972–77, Calif. State Univ. 1978–82 (Vice Chair. Bd of Trustees 1979–80, Trustee Emer. 1982–), Museum of Contemporary Art, LA 1980–93, Univ. of Calif. at LA (UCLA) Foundation 1986–, Caltech 1993–, Trustee Comm. for Econ. Devt 1993–95; Founder and Trustee The Broad Foundation 1999–; numerous philanthropic donations including funds to build the Frank Gehry-designed Walt Disney Concert Hall 2003; Chevalier, Légion d'honneur; Golden Plate Award, American Acad. of Achievement 1971, Humanitarian Award, NCCJ 1977, Public Affairs Award, Coro Foundation 1987, KCET-Los Angeles Visionary Award 1999, Julius Award, Univ. of Southern Calif. 2001, Teach for America Educational Leadership Award 2001, United Way Alexis de Tocqueville Award 2002, Exemplary Leadership in Man. Award, Anderson School, Univ. of Calif., Los Angeles 2002; ranked 6th in ArtReview magazine's Power 100 list 2005. *Address:* AIG SunAmerica Inc., 1 SunAmerica Center, Century City, Los Angeles, CA 90067-6022, USA (office). *Telephone:* (310) 772-6000 (office). *Fax:* (310) 772-6564 (office). *Website:* www.sunamerica.com (office).

BROADBENT, Jim; British actor and writer; b. 24 May 1949, s. of the late Roy Broadbent and Dee Broadbent; m. Anastasia Lewis 1987; two step-s.; ed Leighton Park School, Reading, Hammersmith Coll. of Art, London Acad. of Music and Dramatic Arts (LAMDA); actor 1972–; mem. Nat. Theatre and RSC; wrote and appeared in short film A Sense of History (Clermont-Ferrand Int. Film Festival Award). *Theatre:* The Recruiting Officer, A Winter's Tale, The Government Inspector, A Flea in Her Ear, Goose Pimples, Our Friends in the North, Habeas Corpus. *Films include:* The Shout, Breaking Glass, The Dogs of War, The Good Father, Superman IV, Life is Sweet, Enchanted April, The Crying Game, Widow's Peak, Princess Caraboo, Richard III, The Borrowers, Little Voice, The Avengers, Topsy Turvy 1999, Moulin Rouge (Acad. Award for Best Supporting Actor 2002, BAFTA Award for Best Supporting Actor 2002) 2001, Bridget Jones's Diary 2001, Iris (Golden Globe for Best Supporting Actor) 2001, Gangs of New York 2002, Nicholas Nickleby 2002, Bright Young Things 2003, Around the World in Eighty Days 2004, Vanity Fair 2004, Vera Drake 2004, Bridget Jones: The Edge of Reason 2004, The Chronicles of Narnia: The Lion, the Witch and the Wardrobe 2005, Art School Confidential 2006, Free Jimmy (voice) 2006, Hot Fuzz 2007, And When Did You Last See Your Father? 2007, Indiana Jones and the Kingdom of the Crystal Skull 2008. *Television includes:* Not the Nine O'Clock News, Sense of History (also writer), Murder Most Horrid, Only Fools and Horses, The Victoria Wood Show, Silas Marner, Blackadder, Birth of a Nation, Gone to the Dogs, Gone to Seed, The Peter Principle, The Gathering Storm, The Young Visitors, Spider-Plant Man 2005, Longford (BAFTA Award for Best Actor 2007) 2006. *Address:* c/o Harriet Robinson, ICM, 76 Oxford Street, London W1D 1BS, England. *Telephone:* (20) 7636-6565.

BROADBENT, Hon. John Edward (Ed), OC, CC, PhD; Canadian politician and professor; b. 21 March 1936, Oshawa, Ont.; s. of Percy E. Broadbent and Mary A. Welsh; m. Lucille Munroe 1971; one s. one d.; ed High School in Oshawa, Univ. of Toronto, London School of Econs and Political Science; Prof. of Political Science, York Univ., Ont. 1965–68; mem. House of Commons 1968–89; Co-Chair. Policy Review Cttee for New Democratic Party Fed. Convention 1969; Chair. Fed. Caucus 1972–74, Parl. Leader of Fed. Caucus 1974–75; Nat. Leader of New Democratic Party (NDP) 1975–89; Vice-Pres. Socialist Int. 1978–90, Hon. Pres. 1991–; Pres. Int. Centre for Human Rights and Democratic Devt 1990–96; J. S. Woodsworth Chair. Inst. for the Humanities, Simon Fraser Univ. 1997–99; Skelton-Clark Fellow, Queen's Univ. 1999–2000; MP representing riding of Ottawa Centre 2004–05; LLD hc (Dalhousie Univ.) 1990, (York Univ.) 1991, DLitt (Trinity Coll., Oxford) 1990, (Toronto Univ.) 1990; Nation Builder of the Year, Globe and Mail 2005. *Publication:* The Liberal Rip-Off 1970. *Leisure interests:* reading contemporary fiction, listening to music, skiing. *Address:* New Democratic Party of Canada, 279 Laurier Avenue West, Suite 300, Ottawa, ON K1P 5J9, Canada.

BROCK, Gunnar, MBA; Swedish business executive; *President and Chief Executive, Atlas Copco Group;* b. 1950; ed Stockholm School of Econs; various positions with Tetra Pak including Man. Dir, Pres. Tetra Pak Europe and Exec. Vice Pres. Tetra Pak Group 1974–92, Pres. and CEO 1994–2000; Pres. and CEO Alfa Laval Group 1992–94; CEO Thule International 2001–02; Pres. and CEO Atlas Copco Group July 2002–; Dir OM-Gruppen, Lego AS, Denmark; mem. Royal Swedish Acad. of Eng Sciences (IVA). *Address:* Atlas Copco Group Center, Atlas Copco AB, 105 23 Stockholm, Sweden (office). *Telephone:* (8) 743-80-00 (office). *Fax:* (8) 644-90-45 (office). *Website:* www.atlascopco-group.com (office).

BROCK, John F.; American business executive; *Chairman and CEO, Coca-Cola Enterprises Inc.;* b. 1948; with Procter & Gamble Inc. 1972–83; joined Cadbury Schweppes North America 1983, various sr positions, becoming mem. Bd and Man. Dir, Global Beverages Div. 1996, COO 1999–2002; CEO Interbrew (later InBev SA following merger with AmBev 2004) 2003–05; Pres. and CEO Coca-Cola Enterprises 2006–08, Chair. and CEO 2008–; Dir (non-

Exec.) Reed Elsevier PLC; Dir Georgia Inst. of Tech. Presidential Advisory Bd; USA Beverage Industry Exec. of the Year 2000. *Address:* Coca-Cola Enterprises Inc., 2500 Windy Ridge Parkway, Atlanta, GA 30339, USA (office). *Telephone:* (770) 989-3000 (office). *Fax:* (770) 989-3788 (office). *E-mail:* info@cokecce.com (office). *Website:* www.cokecce.com (office).

BROCKES, Jeremy Patrick, PhD, FRS; British biologist and academic; *MRC Research Professor, University College London;* b. 29 Feb. 1948, Haslemere; s. of Bernard Brockes and Edna Heaney; ed St John's Coll., Cambridge, Edinburgh Univ.; Asst, then Assoc. Prof. of Biology Caltech 1978–83; mem. MRC Biophysics Unit, King's Coll., London 1983–88; mem. Ludwig Inst. for Cancer Research 1988–97; Prof. of Cell Biology Univ. Coll. London 1992–97, MRC Research Prof. Dept of Biochemistry 1997–. *Publication:* Amphibian Limb Regeneration: Rebuilding a Complex Structure 1997, Plasticity and Reprogramming of Differentiated Cells in Amphibian Regeneration 2002. *Leisure interest:* soprano saxophone. *Address:* Department of Biochemistry and Molecular Biology, Room 417, Darwin Building, University College London, Gower Street, London, WC1E 6BT, England (office). *Telephone:* (20) 7679-4483 (office). *E-mail:* j.brockes@ucl.ac.uk (office). *Website:* www.biochem.ucl.ac.uk/research/brockes/brockes.htm (office).

BROCKINGTON, Ian Fraser, MPhil, MD, FRCP, FRCPsych; British psychiatrist and academic; *Professor Emeritus of Psychiatry, University of Birmingham;* b. 12 Dec. 1935, Chillington, Devon; s. of Fraser Brockington and Joyce Brockington; m. Diana Hilary Pink 1969; two s. two d.; ed Winchester Coll., Univ. of Cambridge, Univ. of Manchester Medical School; Wellcome Research Fellow, Royal Postgraduate Medical School and Univ. of Ibadan, Nigeria 1966–69; Visiting Prof., Univ. of Chicago, USA 1980–81, Washington Univ., St Louis, USA 1981; Prof. of Psychiatry, Univ. of Birmingham 1983–2002, Prof. Emer. 2002–; Visiting Prof., Univ. of Nagoya, Japan 2002, Univ. of Kumamoto, Japan 2003; Pres. The Marcé Society 1982–84; Founder and first Pres. Women's Mental Health section, World Psychiatric Asscn; est. Eyry Press 2002; Cottman Fellow, Monash Univ. 1988. *Publications:* papers on African heart diseases 1966–80, on schizoaffective psychosis, methods of clinical psychiatric research, pregnancy-related psychiatric disorders; Motherhood and Mental Health 1996. *Leisure interests:* family activities, choral singing, French, Italian and German literature, publishing, distance running. *Address:* Lower Brockington Farm, Bredenbury, Bromyard, Herefordshire, HR7 4TE, England (home). *Telephone:* (1885) 3245 (home). *E-mail:* i.f.brockington@bham.ac.uk.

BRÖDER, Ernst-Günther, DEcon; German banker, economist and international consultant; b. 6 Jan. 1927, Cologne; ed Univs of Cologne, Mainz, Freiburg and Paris; mem. Corpn staff, Bayer AG, Leverkusen 1956–61; Projects Dept World Bank (IBRD) 1961–64; joined KfW-Bankengruppe (fmrly Kreditanstalt für Wiederaufbau) 1964, Deputy Man. 1968–69, Man. 1969–75, mem. Man. Bd 1975–84, Man. Bd Spokesman 1980–84; Dir European Investment Bank (EIB) 1980–84, Pres. and Chair. Bd of Dirs 1984–93, Hon. Pres. 1993–; Chair. Inspection Panel, IBRD 1994–96, 1998–99, mem. 1997–98; mem. Supervisory Bd DEG Deutsche Finanzierungsgesellschaft für Beteiligungen in Entwicklungsländern GmbH 1980–84; mem. Panel of Conciliators, Int. Centre for Settlement of Investment Disputes 1976–, Special Advisory Group, Asian Devt Bank 1981–82; high decorations in Germany, Belgium, Italy and Luxembourg.

BRODER, Samuel, BS, MD; American physician; *Chief Medical Officer, Celera Genomics;* b. 24 Feb. 1945, Łódź, Poland; m. Gail Broder; two d.; moved to USA 1949; ed Univ. of Michigan and Stanford Univ.; clinical assoc. Nat. Cancer Inst. (NCI), Bethesda, Md 1972, investigator, medicine br. 1975, Sr investigator, metabolism br. 1976, in charge of lab. overseeing new drug trials 1981–89; Dir NCI 1989–95; Sr Vice-Pres. for Research and Devt IVAX Corpn 1995–98; Chief Medical Officer, Celera Genomics 1998–; mem. Inst. of Medicine. *Publications:* AIDS: Modern Concepts and Therapeutic Challenges (ed.) 1987; more than 300 scholarly articles. *Leisure interests:* long walks, playing cards, cinema, dinner with friends. *Address:* Celera Genomics, 45 West Gude Road, Rockville, MD 20850, USA (office). *Telephone:* (240) 453-3000 (office). *Fax:* (240) 453-4000 (office). *Website:* www.celera.com.

BRODERICK, Matthew; American actor; b. 21 March 1962, New York City; s. of James Broderick and Patricia Broderick; m. Sarah Jessica Parker (q.v.) 1997; one s. *Theatre includes:* Valentine's Day (workshop production), Torch Song Trilogy, Brighton Beach Memoirs (Tony Award), Biloxi Blues,The Widow Claire, How to Succeed in Business Without Really Trying (Tony Award), The Producers, The Odd Couple 2005. *Films include:* War Games, Ladyhawke, 1918, On Valentine's Day, Ferris Bueller's Day Off, Project X, Biloxi Blues, Torch Song Trilogy, Glory, Family Business, The Freshman, Lay This Laurel, Glory, Out on a Limb, The Night We Never Met, The Lion King (voice), Road to Welville, Mrs Parker and the Vicious Circle, Infinity (also dir), The Cable Guy, Addicted to Love, The Lion King II: Simba's Pride (voice), Godzilla, Election, Inspector Gadget 1999, Walking to the Waterline 1999, You Can Count on Me 2000, Suspicious Minds 2001, Good Boy! (voice) 2003, Marie and Bruce 2004, Lion King 1 1/2 (voice) 2004, Stepford Wives 2004, Last Shot 2004, Strangers with Candy 2005, The Producers: The Movie Musical 2005, Deck the Halls 2006, Then She Found Me 2007, Bee Movie (voice) 2007, Margaret 2007. *Television includes:* Master Harold . . . and the Boys, Cinderella, Jazz 2001, The Music Man 2003. *Address:* c/o CAA, 9830 Wilshire Boulevard, Beverly Hills, CA 90212, USA.

BRODHEAD, Richard H., PhD; American university administrator and writer; *President, Duke University;* b. Dayton, OH; m. Cynthia Brodhead; one s.; ed Yale Univ.; mem. Faculty, Yale Univ. 1972–2004, later A. Bartlett Giamatti Prof. of English and American Studies –2004, served as Chair. Dept of English for six years, Dean of Yale Coll. 1993–2004; Prof. of English and

Pres. Duke Univ., Durham, NC 2004–; spent eight summers teaching high school teachers at Bread Loaf School, Middlebury, Vt; has lectured widely in univs at home and in Europe and Asia; mem. Business-Higher Educ. Forum; Trustee Carnegie Corpn of New York; fmr Pres. J. William Fulbright Foreign Scholarship Bd; mem. American Acad. of Arts and Sciences; DeVane Medal for Outstanding Teaching, Yale Univ. *Publications:* The Good of This Place: Values and Challenges in College Education; has written or ed more than a dozen books on Nathaniel Hawthorne, Herman Melville, Charles W. Chestnutt, William Faulkner, Harriet Beecher Stowe, Louisa May Alcott, Richard Wright and Eudora Welty, among others. *Address:* Office of the President, Duke University, 207 Allen Building, Box 90001, Durham, NC 27708-0001, USA (office). *Telephone:* 919) 684-2424 (office). *Fax:* (919) 684-3050 (office). *E-mail:* president@duke.edu (office). *Website:* www.duke.edu (office).

BRODIE, Harlow Keith Hammond, MD, FRSM; American academic; *James B. Duke Professor of Psychiatry and Professor of Law, Duke University;* b. 24 Aug. 1939, Stamford, Conn.; s. of Lawrence Sheldon and Elizabeth Hammond Brodie; m. Brenda Ann Barrowclough 1967; three s. one d.; ed Princeton Univ. and Columbia Univ. College of Physicians and Surgeons; Internship, Ochsner Foundation Hosp., New Orleans 1965–66; Asst Resident in Psychiatry, Columbia-Presbyterian Medical Center, New York 1966–68; Clinical Asscn, Sec. on Psychiatry, Lab. of Clinical Science, Nat. Inst. of Mental Health 1968–70; Asst Prof., Dept of Psychiatry, Stanford Univ. School of Medicine 1970–74; Program Dir, Gen. Clinical Research Center, Stanford Univ. School of Medicine 1973–74; Prof. and Chair., Dept of Psychiatry, Duke Univ. School of Medicine 1974–82; Chief, Psychiatry Service, Duke Univ. Hosp. 1974–82; Chancellor Duke Univ. 1982–85, Acting Provost 1982–83, Pres. 1985–93, Pres. Emer. 1993–; James B. Duke Prof. of Psychiatry and Behavioral Sciences 1981–; Prof. Dept of Psychology, Prof. Law 1980–; Chair. Cttee on Substance Abuse and Mental Health Issues in AIDS Research 1992–95; mem. Coll. of Physicians and Surgeons of Columbia Univ. Asscn of Alumni Gold Medal 1985, Carnegie Council on Adolescent Devt 1986–97, Nat. Review and Advisory Panel for Improving Campus Race Relations, Ford Foundation 1990–94; Hon. LLD (Richmond) 1987; Strecker Award, Inst. of Pennsylvania Hosp. 1980, Distinguished Alumnus Award, Ochsner Foundation Hosp. 1984, Distinguished Medical Alumni Award, Columbia Univ. 1985, NC Award for Science 1990, William C. Menninger Memorial Award 1994. *Publications:* The Importance of Mental Health Services to General Health Care 1979, co-author Modern Clinical Psychiatry 1982, co-ed. American Handbook of Psychiatry (Vol. 6 1975, Vol. 7 1981, Vol. 8 1986), co-Critical Problems in Psychiatry 1982, Signs and Symptoms in Psychiatry 1983, Aids and Behavior: An Integrated Approach 1994, Keeping an Open Door: Passages in a University Presidency 1996, The Research University Presidency in the Late Twentieth Century 2005; also numerous articles. *Leisure interests:* tennis, reading, hiking. *Address:* 3211 Shannon Road, Suite 603, Durham, NC 27707 (office); 63 Beverly Drive, Durham, NC 27707, USA (home). *Telephone:* (919) 403-8070 (office). *Fax:* (919) 493-3628 (office). *E-mail:* brodie@duke.edu (office).

BRODIE, James William, OBE, MSc, FRSNZ; New Zealand marine scientist; b. 7 Oct. 1920, Bebington, Cheshire, UK; s. of James Thomas Fielding Brodie and Isabella Garner; m. Audrey Jacobsen 1945; two s.; ed Napier Boys' High School, Victoria Coll., Univ. of New Zealand; with NZ Lands and Survey Dept 1937–45; staff of Head Office, NZ Dept of Scientific and Industrial Research 1945–49, Geophysics Div. 1949–54, Dir NZ Oceanographic Inst. 1954–1977; Dir Fisheries Research Div., NZ Marine Dept 1964–67; Consultant on Marine Sciences, UNESCO; SE Asia, Paris, Indonesia 1965–79, Marine Science Adviser for SE Asia, Jakarta, Indonesia 1978–79, Chair. West Pacific Oceanographic Workshop, Tokyo 1979; Chair. Tech. Advisory Group, S Pacific Offshore Prospecting, ESCAP 1975, 1976, 1978, Chair. Marine Geoscience Symposium, Suva, Fiji 1976; Pres. Geological Soc. of NZ 1960–61, NZ Marine Sciences Soc. 1966–67; Hon. Librarian Royal Soc. of NZ 1965–78, Home Sec. 1983–87, Vice-Pres. 1986–87; Ed. NZ Stamp Collector 1980–85; mem. Bd of Trustees, Nat. Art Gallery and Museum 1982–92, Project Devt Bd, Museum of NZ 1988–92; Marsden Medal, NZ Asscn of Scientists 1978; NZ Marine Sciences Soc. Award 1985, Fellow Royal Philatelic Soc. of NZ 1978, Rhodes Medal 1988. *Publications:* Bathymetry of the NZ Region 1964, Terawhiti and the Goldfields 1986, The First Seven Thousand: A Jubilee History of Scots College 1991; Ed. (with Audrey Brodie) Haddenham Quaker History 1988, NZ Journeys of Lucy Violet Hodgkin 1989, Seeking a New Land: Quakers in New Zealand 1993, Go Anywhere, Do Anything: New Zealanders in the Friends' Ambulance Unit in China 1945–1951 1996, Keeping Touch: the Quaker Population in Nineteenth Century New Zealand 1999, Remembrance of Friends Past: Lives of New Zealand Quakers 1843–1998 1999, A View of the Bay: From the Journals of Lucy Violet Holdsworth 1922–24 2000, John Holdsworth and the House Called Swarthmoor 2001; contribs to Dictionary of New Zealand Biography 1993–2000; papers on geological, marine science and local history topics; philatelic monographs. *Leisure interests:* archaeology, historical research. *Address:* 1 Fettes Crescent, Wellington 3, New Zealand. *Telephone:* (4) 388-6894.

BRODY, Alexander, BA; American advertising executive; b. 28 Jan. 1933, Budapest, Hungary; s. of John Brody and Lilly Pollatschek; ed Princeton Univ.; with Young & Rubicam Inc. 1953–83; Vice-Pres., Man. Young & Rubicam Inc., Frankfurt, Germany 1965–70; Sr Vice-Pres., Head, European Operations, Young & Rubicam Inc. 1967–70; Int. Pres. Young & Rubicam Inc., Brussels and New York 1970–82; Pres. and CEO DYR Worldwide, New York 1984–87; Pres. Int. Ogilvy & Mather Worldwide 1987–93, consultant 1993–, now Pres. and CEO Int. Operations. *Address:* Ogilvy & Mather Worldwide, Worldwide Plaza, 309 W 49th Street, New York, NY 10019, USA.

BRODY, Jane Ellen, MS; American journalist and author; *Personal Health Columnist, New York Times;* b. 19 May 1941, Brooklyn; d. of Sidney Brody and Lillian Kellner; m. Richard Engquist 1966; twin s.; ed New York State Coll. of Agric., Cornell Univ. and Univ. of Wisconsin; reporter, Minn. Tribune 1963–65; science writer, personal health columnist, New York Times 1965–; mem. Advisory Council, New York State Coll. of Agric. 1971–77; numerous awards including Howard Blakeslee Award, American Heart Asscn 1971, Science Writers' Award, ADA 1978, J.C. Penney–Univ. of Missouri Journalism Award 1978, Lifeline Award, American Health Foundation 1978. *Publications:* Secrets of Good Health (with R. Engquist) 1970, You Can Fight Cancer and Win (with A. Holleb) 1977, Jane Brody's Nutrition Book 1981, Jane Brody's New York Times Guide to Personal Health 1982, Jane Brody's Good Food Book 1985, Jane Brody's Good Food Gourmet 1990, Jane Brody's Good Seafood Book (with Richard Flaste) 1994, Jane Brody's Cold and Flu Fighter 1995, Jane Brody's Allergy Fighter 1997, The New York Times Book of Health 1997, The New York Times Book of Women's Health 2000, The New York Times Book of Alternative Medicine 2001, Jane Brody's Guide to the Great Beyond 2009. *Address:* New York Times, 620 Eighth Avenue, New York, NY 10018, USA (office). *E-mail:* engquist@nytimes.com (office). *Website:* www .nytimes.com (office); janebrody.net.

BRODY, William R., BS, MS, PhD, MD; American physician, biomedical engineer, research institute director and fmr university administrator; *President, Salk Institute for Biological Studies;* b. 4 Jan. 1944, Stockton, Calif.; m. Wendy Brody; two c.; ed Massachusetts Inst. of Tech. and Stanford Univ., Univ. of California, San Francisco; Fellow, Dept of Cardiovascular Surgery, Stanford Univ. School of Medicine 1970–71, Intern, Dept of Surgery 1971–72, Resident, Dept of Cardiovascular Surgery 1972–73; Clinical Assoc., Surgery Br., Nat. Heart, Lung, and Blood Inst., Bethesda, Md 1973–75; Resident, Dept of Radiology, Univ. of California, San Francisco 1975–77; Assoc. Prof. of Radiology and, by courtesy, Electrical Eng, Stanford Univ. School of Medicine 1977–82, Dir of Research Labs, Div. of Diagnostic Radiology 1977–84, Dir Advanced Imaging Techniques Lab., Dept of Radiology 1978–84, Prof. of Radiology and, by courtesy, Electrical Eng 1982–86, on unpaid leave of absence 1984–86; Martin Donner Prof. and Dir Dept of Radiology, The Johns Hopkins Univ. School of Medicine 1987–94, Prof. of Biomedical Eng 1987–94, Prof. of Electrical and Computer Eng 1987–94, Radiologist-in-Chief, The Johns Hopkins Hosp. 1987–94, Pres. The Johns Hopkins Univ. 1996–2008; Prof. of Radiology, Univ. of Minnesota 1994–96, Provost, Academic Health Center 1994–96; Pres. The Salk Inst., La Jolla, Calif. 2009–; Founder and Consultant, Resonex, Inc. 1983–84, Pres. 1984–86, Pres. and CEO 1986–87, Chair. 1987–89; mem. Bd of Dirs Mercantile Bankshares Corpn 1997–, Medtronic Inc. 1998–, AEGON USA 2000–; mem. Selection Cttee Goldseker Foundation 1996–, Int. Academic Advisory Cttee, Singapore 1997–, Governing Cttee Whitaker Foundation 1997–, Exec. Cttee Council on Competitiveness 1998–, Bd Dirs The Commonwealth Fund 2000–, CareFirst Inc. 2004–, FBI's Nat. Security Higher Educ. Advisory Bd 2005–; mem. Pres.'s Foreign Intelligence Advisory Bd 2003–05; fmr mem. Bd Minnesota Orchestra Asscn, Corpn of Massachusetts Inst. of Tech.; mem. Nat. Acad. of Eng, Inst. of Medicine, NAS, AAAS; Fellow, IEEE, American Coll. of Radiology, American Coll. of Cardiology, American Heart Asscn, Int. Soc. of Magnetic Resonance in Medicine, American Inst. of Biomedical Eng, American Acad. of Arts and Sciences; Founding Fellow, American Inst. of Medical and Biological Eng; Trustee Baltimore Museum of Art 1997–, Baltimore Community Foundation 2004–; Hon. mem. Canadian Asscn of Radiologists; Prize Manuscript Award, Western Thoracic Surgical Soc. 1974, Established Investigator Award, American Heart Asscn 1980–84, Outstanding Alumnus Award, Univ. of California, San Francisco 1994. *Publications:* Digital Radiography: Proceedings of the Stanford Conference on Digital Radiography. Society for Photooptical Instrumentation Engineers (SPIE). Proceedings Vol. 315 (ed.) 1981, Digital Radiography 1984, Computer Applications to Assist Radiology. Proceedings of the 11th S/CAR Symposium (co-ed.) 1992; more than 120 publs and one patent (US Patent No. 4,445,226, 1984) in the field of medical imaging; bimonthly columns for Diagnostic Imaging 1990–94. *Address:* Salk Institute for Biological Studies, P.O. Box 85800, San Diego, CA 92186-5800, USA (office). *Telephone:* (858) 453-4100 (office). *Fax:* (858) 453-8534 (office). *E-mail:* communications@salk.edu (office). *Website:* www.salk.edu (office).

BROECKER, Wallace (Wally) Smith, BA, MA, PhD; American geophysicist and academic; *Newberry Professor, Department of Earth and Environmental Sciences and Scientist, Lamont-Doherty Earth Observatory, Columbia University;* b. 1931; ed Wheaton Coll.; transferred to Columbia Univ., worked at Lamont Geological Observatory, currently Newberry Prof., Dept of Earth and Environmental Sciences and Scientist, Lamont-Doherty Earth Observatory; mem. American Acad. of Arts and Sciences, NAS; Fellow, American Geophysical Union, European Geophysical Union; Crafoord Prize in Geosciences, Royal Swedish Acad. of Sciences 2006, Nat. Medal of Science, Maurice W. Ewing Medal, American Geophysical Union, NAS Alexander Agassiz Medal, Urey Medal, European Asscn for Geochemistry, V.M. Goldschmidt Award, Geochemical Soc., Vetlesen Prize, G. Unger Vetlesen Foundation, Wollaston Medal, Geological Soc. of London, Roger Revelle Medal, American Geophysical Union, Tyler Prize for Environmental Achievement, Univ. of Southern California, Blue Planet Prize, The Asahi Glass Foundation, Benjamin Franklin Medal in Earth and Environmental Science, The Franklin Inst. 2008, Balzan Prize 2008. *Achievements include:* best known for discovery of role played by ocean in triggering abrupt climate changes that punctuated glacial time, in particular, development and popularization of idea of global 'conveyor belt' linking circulation of global ocean; inadvertently coined phrase 'global warming' when he published paper entitled: Climate Change: Are We on the Brink of a Pronounced Global Warming? 1975. *Publications:* Chemical

Equilibria in the Earth (co-author) 1971, Chemical Oceanography 1974, Tracers in the Sea 1982, How to Build a Habitable Planet 1988, Greenhouse Puzzles 1993, The Glacial World According to Wally 1995, Greenhouse Puzzles: Keeling's World, Martin's World, Walker's World 1998, Fixing Climate: What Past Climate Changes Reveal About the Current Threat – And How to Counter It (co-author) 2008; more than 400 scientific papers in professional journals on Pleistocene geochronology, radiocarbon dating and chemical oceanography, including oceanic mixing based on stable and radioisotope distribution. *Address:* Lamont-Doherty Earth Observatory, Columbia University, PO Box 1000, 301 Comer 61, Route 9W, Palisades, NY 10964-8000, USA (office). *Telephone:* (845) 365-8413 (office). *E-mail:* broecker@ldeo.columbia.edu (office). *Website:* www.ldeo.columbia.edu (office).

BROERS, Baron (Life Peer), cr. 2004, of Cambridge in the County of Cambridgeshire; **Alec Nigel Broers,** ScD, FRS, FREng; British electrical engineer and academic; *President, Royal Academy of Engineering;* b. 17 Sept. 1938, Calcutta; s. of the late Alec W. Broers and of Constance A. Broers (née Cox); m. Mary T. Phelan 1964; two s.; ed Geelong Grammar School, Melbourne Univ. and Gonville & Caius Coll. Cambridge; mem. research staff and man. of photon and electron optics groups, IBM Thomas Watson Research Center 1965–80; Man., Semiconductor Lithography and Process Devt and Advanced Devt, IBM East Fishkill Lab. 1981–84; mem. Corp. Tech. Cttee, IBM Corp. HQ 1984; Prof. of Electrical Eng, Univ. of Cambridge 1984–96, Prof. Emer. 1996–; Head, Electrical Div. 1984–92, of Dept of Eng 1992–96; Dir (non-exec.) Vodafone Group 1998–2000, Vodafone PLC 2000–, Lucas Industries Group 1995–96, R.J. Mears 2003–; Adviser, Warburg Pincus 2003–; Chair. House of Lords Select Cttee on Science and Tech. 2004–; Fellow, Trinity Coll., Cambridge 1984–90; Master, Churchill Coll., Cambridge 1990–96, Fellow 1996–; Vice-Chancellor, Univ. of Cambridge 1996–2003; Pres. Royal Acad. of Eng 2001–; Foreign Assoc. Nat. Acad. of Eng (USA); IBM Fellow 1977; Hon. Fellow, Gonville and Caius Coll. Cambridge 1996–, Trinity Coll. Cambridge 1999–, Univ. of Wales, Cardiff 2001–, St Edmund's Coll. Cambridge 2004–, Imperial Coll. London 2004–; Hon. DEng (Glasgow) 1996; Hon. DSc (Warwick) 1997; Hon. LLD (Melbourne) 2000; Hon. DUniv (Anglia Polytechnic) 2000; Dr hc (Greenwich) 2000, (UMIST) 2002, (Peking) 2002; Prize for Industrial Applications of Physics, American Inst. of Physics 1982, Cledo Brunetti Award, Inst. of Electrical and Electronic Engineers 1985. *Publications:* patents, papers and book chapters on electron microscopy, electron beam lithography and integrated circuit fabrication. *Leisure interests:* music, sailing, skiing. *Address:* The Royal Academy of Engineering, 29 Great Peter Street, London, SW1P 3LW, England (office). *Telephone:* (20) 7227-0511 (office). *Fax:* (20) 7233-0054 (office). *E-mail:* president@raeng.co.uk (office). *Website:* www.raeng.org.uk (office).

BROKAW, Thomas (Tom) John, BA; American broadcast journalist and writer; b. 6 Feb. 1940, Webster, S Dakota; s. of Anthony O. Brokaw and Eugenia Conley; m. Meredith Lynn Auld 1962; three d.; ed Univ. of South Dakota; morning news KMTV, Omaha 1962–65; news ed., anchorman, WSB-TV, Atlanta 1965–66; reporter, corresp., anchorman KNBC-TV, Los Angeles 1966–73; White House corresp. NBC, Washington, DC 1973–76; anchorman, Saturday Night News, New York 1973–76; host, Today Show, New York 1976–82; anchor and Man. Ed., NBC Nightly News 1982–2004 (retd), Special Corresp. NBC News 2005–; mem. Bd of Dirs Council on Foreign Relations, Cttee to Protect Journalists, Int. Rescue Cttee; mem. advisory cttee Reporters Cttee for Freedom of Press, Gannett Journalism Center, Columbia Univ.; Trustee, Norton Simon Museum of Art, Pasadena, Calif.; mem. American Acad. of Arts and Sciences; Dr hc (Univ. of South Dakota), (Washington Univ., St. Louis), (Syracuse Univ.), (Hofstra Univ.), (Boston Coll.), (Emerson Coll.), (Simpson Coll.), (Duke Univ.) 1991, (Notre Dame Univ.) 1993; Hon. DHL (Dartmouth Coll.) 2005; two Dupont Awards, Peabody Award, Alfred I. duPont-Columbia Univ. Award for Excellence in Broadcast Journalism 1997, ten Emmy Awards including Emmy for Outstanding Interview 2003, Records of Achievement Award, Foundation for the Nat. Archives 2005, George Catlett Marshall Medal, Asscn of the US Army 2005, Edward R. Murrow Award for Lifetime Achievement in Broadcasting, Wash. State Univ. 2006, Sylvanus Thayer Award, US Military Acad. at West Point 2006, Walter Cronkite Award for Journalism Excellence, Ariz. State Univ. 2006; elected to TV Hall of Fame 1997. *Publications:* The Greatest Generation 1998, The Greatest Generation Speaks 1999, An Album of Memories 2001, A Long Way from Home 2002, Boom! Voices of the Sixties 2007. *Address:* c/o Board of Directors, Council on Foreign Relations, The Harold Pratt House, 58 East 68th Street, New York, NY 10021, USA.

BROLIN, Josh; American actor; b. 12 Feb. 1968, Santa Monica, Calif.; s. of James Brolin and Jane Cameron Agee; m. 1st Alice Adair, two c.; m. 2nd Diane Lane. *Films include:* The Goonies 1985, Thrashin' 1986, Bed of Roses 1996, Flirting with Disaster 1996, Nightwatch 1997, Best Laid Plans 1999, Hollow Man 2000, Slow Burn 2000, Melinda and Melinda 2004, Into the Blue 2005, The Dead Girl 2006, Grindhouse - Planet Terror 2007, In the Valley of Elah 2007, No Country for Old Men 2007, American Gangster 2007, W. 2008, Milk 2008. *Television includes:* Picnic 2000, Mister Sterling 2003, Into the West 2005. *Address:* William Morris Agency, One William Morris Place, Beverly Hills, CA 90212, USA (office). *Telephone:* (310) 859-4000 (office). *Fax:* (310) 859-4462 (office). *E-mail:* michael.cooper@wma.com (office). *Website:* www .wma.com (office).

BRON, Eleanor, BA; British actress and author; b. 14 March 1938, Stanmore; d. of Sydney Bron and Fagah Bron; ed North London Collegiate School and Newnham Coll. Cambridge; started at Establishment Night Club, toured USA 1961; TV satire, Not So Much a Programme, More a Way of Life; co-wrote and appeared in TV series Where was Spring?, After That This, Beyond A Joke; Dir Actors' Centre 1982–93, Soho Theatre Co. 1993–2000. *Stage appearances include:* Private Lives, Hedda Gabler, Antony and Cleopatra, Madwoman of Chaillot, Hamlet; appeared at Royal Exchange in Uncle Vanya, Heartbreak House, Oedipus, The Prime of Miss Jean Brodie, Present Laughter; appeared at Nat. Theatre in The Duchess of Malfi, The Cherry Orchard, The Real Inspector Hound, The Miser, The White Devil, Desdemona – If You Had Only Spoken! (one-woman show), Dona Rosita The Spinster, A Delicate Balance, Be My Baby, Making Noise Quietly, Twopence to Cross the Mersey 2005, The Clean House 2006, In Extremis 2007. *Television:* appearances in Rumpole, Dr Who, French & Saunders, Absolutely Fabulous, Vanity Fair; BBC TV Play for Today: Nina, A Month in the Country, The Hour of the Lynx, The Blue Boy, Ted and Alice, Fat Friends. *Films:* Help!, Alfie, Two for the Road, Bedazzled, Women in Love, The National Health, Turtle Diary, Little Dorritt, The Attic, Deadly Advice 1994, Black Beauty 1993, A Little Princess 1994, The House of Mirth 2000, Iris 2001, The Heart of Me 2002, Love's Brother 2003, Wimbledon 2004. *Concert appearances (as narrator) include:* Façade, Carnival des Animaux, Peter and the Wolf, Bernstein's Symphony No. 3 with BBC Symphony Orchestra. *Publications include:* Song Cycle (with John Dankworth) 1973; verses for Saint-Saëns Carnival of the Animals 1975; Is Your Marriage Really Necessary? (with John Fortune) 1972, Life and Other Punctures 1978, The Pillow Book of Eleanor Bron 1985, Desdemona—If You Had Only Spoken! (translation of original by Christine Brückner) 1992, Double Take (novel) 1996. *Address:* c/o Rebecca Blond, 69A King's Road, London, SW3 4NX, England. *Telephone:* (20) 7351-4100. *Fax:* (20) 7351-4600.

BRON, Zakhar; Russian violinist and academic; *Professor of Violin, Hochschule für Musik Köln;* b. 1947, Uralsk; ed Stoliarski School of Music, Odessa, Gnessin Conservatoire, Moscow, Tchaikovsky Conservatoire; studied with Boris Goldstein and Igor Oistrakh; has taught at Musikhochschule, Lübeck, Glinka Conservatoire, Novosibirsk, RAM, London, Rotterdam Conservatoire, Reina Sofia School, Madrid; currently Prof. of Violin, Hochschule für Musik, Cologne; lectures and gives masterclasses in many countries; has performed with many maj. int. orchestras; prizewinner Wieniawski Int. Violin Competition, Poznań, Queen Elizabeth Competition, Brussels; Verdienstkreutz am Bande (Germany). *Address:* Hochschule für Musik Köln, Dagobertstr. 38, 50668 Cologne, Germany. *Telephone:* (221) 9128180. *Fax:* (221) 131204. *E-mail:* zakharbron@web.de (home). *Website:* www.zakharbron.com (home).

BRONEVOY, Leonid Sergeyevich; Russian actor; b. 17 Dec. 1928, Kiev, Ukraine; m.; one d.; ed Tashkent Inst. of Theatre Art, Studio School, Moscow Art Theatre; with Malaya Bronnaya Theatre 1961–88, with Moscow Lenkom Theatre 1998–; USSR People's Artist, State Prize of Russian Fed. *Films include:* Lebedev protiv Lebedeva 1965, Ispolnyayushchiy obyazannosti 1973, Vracha vyzyvali? 1974, Proshu slova 1975, Klop 75 ili Mayakovskiy smeyotsya 1975, Vooruzhyon i ochen opasen 1977, Pokhishchenie 'Savoi' 1979, Agoniya 1981, Vozvrashcheniye rezidenta 1982, Konets operatsii Rezident 1986, Chicherin 1986, Zagadochnyy naslednik 1987, Nebesa obetovannyye 1991, Italyanskiy kontrakt 1993, Shizofreniya 2001, Prostyye veshchi 2006. *Theatre includes:* Capulet in Romeo and Juliet, Don Louis in Don Juan, Shpigelsky in A Month in the Country, Krutitsky in Wizard, Dr Dorn in The Seagull. *TV includes:* Povinnuyu golovu 1971, Semnadtsat mgnoveniy vesny (miniseries) 1973, Tanya 1974, Tot samyy Myunkhgauzen 1979, Pokrovskiye vorota 1982, Yesli verit Lopotukhinu 1983, Formula lyubvi 1984, Bolshaya igra (miniseries) 1988. *Address:* Lenkom Theatre, 6 Malaya Dmitrovka Street, Moscow 127006 (office); Tverskoy blvd 3, Apt 22, 103104 Moscow, Russia. *Telephone:* (495) 291-73-46. *Website:* www.lenkom.ru (office).

BRONFMAN, Charles Rosner, PC, CC; Canadian business executive; b. 27 June 1931, Montreal, Québec; s. of the late Samuel Bronfman and Saidye Bronfman (née Rosner); m. 2nd Andrea Morrison 1982 (died 2006); one s. one d. from previous m.; ed Selwyn House School, Montreal, PQ, Trinity Coll., Port Hope, Ont., McGill Univ., Montreal; joined The Seagram Co. Ltd 1951, Pres. and Co.-Chair. 1986–2000 9 co. sold to Vivendi); Chair., prin. owner Montreal Expos 1968–90; fmr Chair. Koor Industries Ltd; Chair. The Jerusalem Report, Andrea and Charles Bronfman Philanthropies, Claridge Israel LLC, The CRB Foundation, United Jewish Communities; mem. Int. Advisory Corpn of Canada; Hon. Pres. United Israel Appeal of Canada; mem. of Bd Washington Inst. for Near E Policy, The Kravis Center for Performing Arts, Fla; Co-founder and Co-Chair. Birthright Israel; Chair. (non-exec.) The Nat. Jewish Center for Learning and Leadership; Hon. DPhil (Hebrew Univ. of Jerusalem), Hon. DL (McGill Univ., Montreal), (Concordia Univ., Montreal), (Univ. of Waterloo), (Univ. of Toronto), Hon. DHumLitt (Branders). *Leisure interests:* tennis, golf. *Address:* c/o The Andrea and Charles Bronfman Philanthropies, 275 Park Avenue, 6th Floor, New York, NY 10152, USA (office). *Telephone:* (212) 572-7715 (NY) (office); (514) 987-5200 (NY) (office).

BRONFMAN, Edgar Miles, BA; American business executive; b. 20 June 1929, Montreal, Québec; s. of the late Samuel Bronfman and Saidye (Rosner) Bronfman; m. Jan Aronson; four s. three d.; ed Trinity Coll. School, Port Hope, Ont., Williams Coll., Williamstown, Mass. and McGill Univ., Montreal; joined Distillers Corpn-Seagrams Ltd (renamed The Seagram Co. Ltd 1975) 1951, Pres. 1971–75, Chair. 1975–2000, CEO 1975–94 (Seagram Co. Ltd merged with Vivendi and CANAL+ to form Vivendi Universal Dec. 2000), Dir Vivendi Universal 2000–2003; Dir Int. Exec. Service Corps, American Technion Soc.; Chair. Clevepak Corpn; Pres. World Jewish Congress 1979–2007; Dir E.I. duPont de Nemours & Co., United Negro Coll. Fund, Weizmann Inst. of Science, American Cttee; Trustee Salk Inst. for Biological Studies, Mt Sinai Hosp. and School of Medicine; mem. Bd of Dirs Inter-racial Council for Business Opportunity; mem. Foreign Policy Asscn, Center for Inter-American Relations Inc., Cttee for Econ. Devt, Dir US–USSR Trade and Econ. Council, Inc.; Chevalier Légion d'honneur; Hon. DHumLitt (Pace) 1982, (Rochester) 1999; Hon. LLD (Williams Coll.) 1986, (Tulane Univ. Freeman Business

School) 1995; Hon. DCS (New York) 1997; Hon. PhD (Hebrew Univ. of Jerusalem) 1997; Brandeis Award, Zionist Org. of America 1986. *Publications:* The Making of a Jew 1996, Good Spirits: The Making of a Businessman 1998. *Address:* c/o World Jewish Congress, PO Box 90400, Washington, DC, 20090, USA (office).

BRONFMAN, Edgar Miles, Jr; American business executive; *Chairman and CEO, Warner Music Group;* b. 16 May 1955, Montreal; s. of Edgar Miles Bronfman; m. 1st Sherri Brewer 1979 (divorced 1991); three c.; m. 2nd Clarissa Alcock 1994; three c.; began career working in British and US film industries as producer; joined family firm Seagram as Asst to Pres. 1982, Man. Dir Seagram Europe in London 1982–84, Pres. House of Seagram 1984–88, Exec. Vice-Pres. US Operations 1988–89; Pres. and COO J.E. Seagram Corpn New York 1989–94; Pres. and CEO Seagram Co. Ltd 1994–2000 (after merger with Vivendi to form Vivendi Universal), Vice-Chair. Bd of Dirs Vivendi Universal 2000–03; attempted to buy back Seagram assets in 2003 but failed; Chair. and CEO Lexa Pnrs LLC, then with Thomas H. Lee Pnrs acquired Warner Music Group, Chair. and CEO 2004–; fmr Acting Pres. MCA Inc.; mem. Bd of Dirs French & Associates 2001–; Chair. Bd of Dirs Endeavor; Gen. Pnr, Accretive Tech. Pnrs LLC (venture capital firm); Chair. Governing Bd, World Jewish Congress 2007–. *Address:* Warner Music Group, 75 Rockefeller Plaza, New York, NY 10019, USA (office). *Telephone:* (212) 484-8000 (office). *Fax:* (212) 333-3987 (office). *Website:* www.wmg.com (office).

BRONIAREK, Zygmunt; Polish journalist and broadcaster (retd); *Columnist, Trybuna;* b. 27 Aug. 1925, Warsaw; s. of Wacław Broniarek and Marianna Broniarek; m. Elzbieta Sarcewicz 1972; ed Warsaw School of Econs; radiotelegraphic operator and stenographer, Czytelnik publrs, Warsaw 1945–48; Corresp. Trybuna Ludu 1950–90, Perm. Corresp. in USA 1985; in USA 1955, 1958, 1974, Latin America 1956, Paris 1959–60, 1969–73, Washington 1960–67, East Africa 1975, West Africa 1976, Nordic countries 1977–82; mem. Polish United Workers' Party (PZPR) 1956–90; Corresp., Polish Radio and TV, for Finland and Sweden; Chair. Polish Asscn of Int. Journalists and Writers 1974–77; mem. Bd of Foreign Press Asscn, Stockholm 1979–81; mem. Presidium of Journalists' Asscn Polish People's Repub. 1983–85; Vice-Pres. Polish Club of Int. Journalism 1984–85, 1991–; Corresp. Trybuna Ludu, LA Olympic Games 1984; Special Corresp. in Australia 1984; Corresp. Trybuna Ludu, USA 1985–90; presenter The Guests of Mr. Broniarek (TV), The Inner History of the Great Policy (TV) 1983, Behind the Scenes of Int. Politics (TV) 1983–85; retd 1990; columnist, Trybuna 1996–, Rynki Zagraniczne 1998–, Swiat Elit 2005–, Biznes Trendy 2006–; Gold Cross of Merit, Order of Banner of Labour (Second Class) 1984, Commdr's Cross with Star of Infante Dom Henrique the Navigator (Portugal), Commdr's Cross with Star of Polonia Restituta 2002; Int. Journalists Club of Polish Journalistic Asscn Prize 1978, Golden Screen Award of Weekly Ekran 1984, Victor Prize (TV) 1985, Polish Club of Int. Journalism (1st Prize) 1990, Bolesław Prus Award, First Class (SD PRL) 1984, Hon. Silver Ace of Polish Promotion Corpn 1995, City of Warsaw Award of Merit 2000, Gold Medal, Polish Acad. of Success 2000, Leader of Polish Journalism 2005. *Publications:* Od Hustonu do Mississipi 1956, Gorące dni Manhattanu 1960, Walka o Pałac Elizejski 1974, Kto się boi rewolucji (co-author) 1975, Angola zrodzona w walce 1977, Od Kissingera do Brzezińskiego 1980, Szaleństwo zbrojeń (co-author) 1982, Źródła spirali zbrojeń (co-author) 1985, Szczeble do Białego Domu 1986, Tajemnice Nagrody Nobla 1987, Ronald Reagan w Białym Domu 1989, Jak nauczyłem się ośmiu języków 1991, Biały Dom i Jego Prezydenci 1992, Wesoła spowiedź 1993, Książę Karol w Polsce 1994, Sekrety korespondenta zagranicznego 1995, Okiem światowca 1999, Kronika towarzyska Warszawy 2002, 365 dni z angielskim 2002, Kulisy polityki 2003, Papiez Pius X, syn Polaka a Pasja Mela Gibsona 2004, Broniarek o sobie, inni o Broniarku 2005, TVN Series Kulisy Slawy (Hall of Fame) 2008. *Leisure interests:* good company, good food. *Address:* ul. Gałczyńskiego 12 m. 9, 00-362 Warsaw, Poland (office). *Telephone:* (22) 8263304 (office). *Fax:* (22) 8276202 (home).

BRONSTEIN, Alexander Semenovich, DrMed; Russian therapist (internist); *Director-General, Centre of Endosurgery and Lithotripsy;* b. 19 Sept. 1938, Khmelnitsky, Ukraine; s. of Semen Bronstein and Rebecca Yangarber; m. Inna Vladimirovna Kunina 1939; two d.; ed Moscow Sechenov Inst. of Med.; gen. practitioner of polyclinic, therapist, Moscow hosp.; Intern, Jr, then Sr Researcher, Inst. of Proctology 1964–76; Head, Div. of Gastroenterology, Moscow clinic 1976–90; Pres., Dir-Gen. Centre of Endosurgery and Lithotripsy 1993–; Prof., Moscow Sechenov Acad. of Medicine; mem. Editorial Bd International Medical Journal; Academician, Russian Acad. of Nat. Sciences; Order of St Constantine the Great; Merited Dr of Russian Fed. *Publications:* Clinical Medicine (two vols) and more than 150 scientific works. *Leisure interests:* classical music, tennis, singing. *Address:* Centre for Endosurgery and Lythotripsy, Entusiastov shosse 62, 111125 Moscow (office); Petrovsko-Razumovskaya Allea 20, Apt 18, Moscow, Russia (home). *Telephone:* (495) 305-15-83 (office). *Fax:* (495) 305-22-09 (office). *E-mail:* bronshtein@celt.ru (office). *Website:* www.celt.ru (office).

BROOK, Adrian G., PhD; Canadian chemist and academic; *University Professor Emeritus, Department of Chemistry, University of Toronto;* b. 21 May 1924, Toronto; s. of Frank A. Brook and Beatrice M. Wellington; m. Margaret E. Dunn 1954; two s. one d.; ed Lawrence Park Collegiate and Univ. of Toronto; Lecturer in Chem., Univ. of Toronto 1953–56, Asst Prof. 1956–60, Assoc. Prof. 1960–62, Prof. 1962–89, Acting Chair. Dept of Chem. 1969–71, Chair. 1971–74, Chair. Univ. of Toronto Research Bd 1976–81, Univ. Prof. 1987–89, Univ. Prof. Emer. 1989–; Nuffield Fellow 1950–51; ACS Stanley Kipping Award 1973; CIC Medal (Chem. Inst. of Canada) 1986, Killam Prize (Canada Council) 1994. *Publications:* over 140 papers on aspects of organic chem. *Leisure interest:* computers. *Address:* Department of Chemistry, University of Toronto, 80 Saint George Street, Toronto, ON M5S 3H6 (office); 7 Thornwood Road, Apt 202, Toronto, ON M4W 2R8, Canada (home). *Telephone:* (416) 978-3573 (office); (416) 920-8383 (home). *Fax:* (416) 978-8775 (office). *E-mail:* abrook@chem.utoronto.ca (office). *Website:* www.chem.utoronto.ca (office).

BROOK, Peter Stephen Paul, CH, CBE, MA; British theatre director, film director and writer; *Director, Bouffes du Nord Theatre, Paris;* b. 21 March 1925; s. of Simon Brook; m. Natasha Parry 1951; one s. one d.; ed Westminster and Gresham's Schools and Magdalen Coll., Oxford; joined RSC 1962; Producer, Co-Dir Royal Shakespeare Theatre; f. Centre for Theatre Research, Paris 1970, opened Théâtre des Bouffes du Nord, Paris 1974–(2010); Dir Int. Centre for Theatre Creations; Officier des Arts et Lettres; Légion d'honneur; Praemium Imperiale; Hon. DLitt (Birmingham), (Strathclyde) 1990; Freiherr von Stein Foundation, Shakespeare Award 1973, Wexner Prize (Ohio State Univ.) 1991, Onassis Int. Award 1993, Times Award 1994, Dan David Prize, 2005. *Films include:* The Beggar's Opera 1952, Moderato Cantabile 1959, Lord of the Flies 1963, Marat/Sade 1967, Tell Me Lies 1967, King Lear 1969, Meetings With Remarkable Men 1976–77, La Tragédie de Carmen 1983, The Mahabharata 1989, The Tragedy of Hamlet 2002. *Productions include:* Dr. Faustus 1943, Pygmalion, King John, Lady from the Sea 1945, Romeo and Juliet (at Stratford) 1947, Dir of Productions at Covent Garden Opera 1949–50, Faust (at Metropolitan Opera, New York) 1953, The Dark is Light Enough (London) 1954, House of Flowers (New York) 1954, Cat on a Hot Tin Roof (Paris) 1956, Eugene Onegin (New York) 1958, View from the Bridge (Paris) 1958, The Fighting Cock (New York) 1959, Irma la Douce 1960, King Lear 1963, The Physicists (New York) 1964, The Marat/Sade (New York) 1965, Oedipus (Seneca) 1968, A Midsummer Night's Dream 1970, The Conference of the Birds 1973, Timon of Athens (Paris) 1974, The Ik (Paris) 1975, (London) 1976, (USA) 1976, Ubu (Paris) 1977, Meetings with Remarkable Men (film, also dir screenplay) 1977, Antony and Cleopatra (Stratford and London) 1978, Measure for Measure (Paris) 1978, Conference of the Birds, L'os (Festival Avignon and Paris) 1979, (New York) 1980, The Cherry Orchard (Paris) 1981, (New York) 1988, (Moscow) 1989, La Tragédie de Carmen (opera) (Paris) 1981, (film) 1983, Le Mahabharata (Avignon and Paris) 1985, (World tour) 1988, Woza Albert! (Paris) 1989, The Mahabharata (film) 1989, La Tempête (Paris) 1990, Impressions de Pelléas (opera) 1992, L'Homme Qui (Paris) 1993, 1997, The Man Who 1994, Oh! Les Beaux Jours (Lausanne) 1995, (Paris) 1996, Don Giovanni (opera) 1998, Je suis un phénomène (Paris) 1998, Le Costume (Paris) 1999, The Tragedy of Hamlet (Paris) 2000, Far Away (Paris) 2002, La Tragédie d'Hamlet (Paris) 2002, La Mort de Krishna (Paris) 2002, Ta Main Dans La Mienne (Paris) 2003, Tierno Bokar (Paris) 2004, Le Grand Inquisiteur (Paris) 2004. *Publications:* The Empty Space 1968, The Shifting Point: Forty years of theatrical exploration 1946–87, 1987, There Are No Secrets 1993 (appeared in USA as The Open Door: Thoughts on Acting and the Theatre), Threads of Time (autobiog.) 1998, Evoking Shakespeare 1999. *Leisure interests:* painting, playing the piano, air travel. *Address:* Théâtre des Bouffes du Nord, 37 bis boulevard de La Chapelle, 75010 Paris, France (office). *E-mail:* cict@bouffesdunord.com (office).

BROOK, Robert Henry, MD, ScD, FACP; American physician and professor of medicine; *Director, Health Program and Vice-President, RAND Corporation;* b. 3 July 1943, New York; s. of Benjamin N. Brook and Elizabeth Berg; m. 1st Susan Weiss 1966; m. 2nd Jacqueline Kosecoff 1981; one s. three d.; ed Univ. of Arizona, Johns Hopkins Medical School, Johns Hopkins School of Hygiene and Public Health; mil. service, US Public Health Services 1972–74; Dir Health Program, RAND Corpn 1990–, Vice-Pres. 1998–; Prof. of Medicine and Public Health, UCLA Center for Health Sciences 1974–; Dir Robert Wood Johnson Clinical Scholars Program 1974–; mem. Inst. of Medicine, NAS, American Soc. of Clinical Investigation, American Asscn of Physicians; Commendation Medal Richard and Hinda Rosenthal Foundation Award Baxter Health Services Research Prize 1988 Sonneborn Distinguished Lecturer, Univ. of Pa, Distinguished Health Services Researcher, Asscn of Health Services Research Robert J. Glaser Award of Soc. of Gen. Internal Medicine, Johns Hopkins Soc. of Scholars Hollister Univ. Lecturer, Northwestern Univ. Nat. Cttee for Quality Assurance Health Quality Award 2001, Research America 2000 Advocacy Award for Sustained Leadership 2001, Inst. of Medicine Gustav O. Lienhard Medal 2005, American Asscn of Medical Colls David Rogers Award 2007. *Publications:* over 300 articles on quality of medical care. *Leisure interests:* tennis, swimming, golf. *Address:* The RAND Corporation, PO Box 2138, 1776 Main Street, Santa Monica, CA 90401-3297 (office); 1474 Bienvenida Avenue, Pacific Palisades, CA 90272-2346, USA (home). *Telephone:* (310) 393-0411 (office); (310) 454-0766 (home). *Fax:* (310) 451-6917 (office); (310) 454-2797 (home). *E-mail:* brook@rand.org (office). *Website:* www.rand.org (office).

BROOKE, Beth A., BS; American business executive; *Global Vice-Chairman, Strategy, Ernst & Young LLP;* ed Purdue Univ.; served as Tax Services Coordinator, Ernst & Young, later Nat. Dir Tax Consulting Services and Man. Pnr Nat. Tax Dept, currently Global Vice-Chair., Strategy, Ernst & Young LLP, mem. Ernst & Young's Americas Exec. Bd; left Ernst & Young to join Clinton Admin 1993, responsible for all tax policy matters related to insurance and managed care; mem. Bd of Dirs TechnoServe, Inc., Atlantic Council of the United States, March of Dimes Public Policy Advisory Council, Nat. Women's Hall of Fame Advisory Council; mem. Committee of 200; Henry Crown Fellow, Aspen Inst.; ranked by Forbes magazine amongst 100 Most Powerful Women (41st) 2006, (70th) 2007, (79th) 2008. *Address:* Ernst & Young International, 5 Times Square, New York, NY 10036, USA (office). *Telephone:* (212) 773-3000 (office). *Fax:* (212) 773-6350 (office). *Website:* www.eyi.com (office).

BROOKE, Christopher Nugent Lawrence, CBE, MA, LittD, FBA, FRHistS, FSA; British historian and academic; *Professor Emeritus, University of Cambridge;* b. 23 June 1927, Cambridge; s. of Zachary Nugent Brooke and

Rosa Grace Brooke (née Stanton); m. Rosalind Beckford Clark 1951; three s. (one deceased); ed Winchester Coll., Gonville and Caius Coll., Cambridge; Asst Lecturer, Univ. of Cambridge 1953–54, Lecturer 1954–56; Prof. of Medieval History, Univ. of Liverpool 1956–67; Prof. of History, Westfield Coll., London 1967–77; Dixie Prof. of Ecclesiastical History, Univ. of Cambridge 1977–94, Prof. Emer. 1994–; Pres. Soc. of Antiquaries 1981–84; Fellow, Gonville and Caius Coll. Cambridge 1949–56, 1977–; Corresp. Fellow, Medieval Acad. of America; corresp. mem. Monumenta Germaniae Historica, Bavarian Acad. of Sciences; Fellow, Società Internazionale di Studi Francescani; mem. Royal Comm. on Historical Monuments 1977–83, Reviewing Comm. on Export of Works of Art 1979–82; Hon. DUniv (York) 1984; Lord Mayor's Midsummer Prize City of London 1981. *Publications:* The Letters of John of Salisbury vol. I (ed.) 1955, The Dullness of the Past 1957, Carte Nativorum (ed.) 1960, From Alfred to Henry III 1961, The Saxon and Norman Kings 1963, Europe in the Central Middle Ages 1964, Gilbert Foliot and his Letters (with A. Morey) 1965, The Letters and Charters of Gilbert Foliot (ed. with A. Morey) 1967, Time the Archsatirist 1968, The Twelfth Century Renaissance 1969, Structure of Medieval Society 1971, Medieval Church and Society (selected papers) 1971, Heads of Religious Houses, England and Wales 940–1216 (ed. with D. Knowles and V. London) 1972, The Monastic World (with Wim Swaan) 1974, London 800–1216 (with G. Keir) 1975, Marriage in Christian History 1977, The Letters of John of Salisbury vol. II (ed.) 1979, Oxford (fmrly Nelson's) Medieval Texts (gen. ed.) 1979–87, Nelson's History of England (gen. ed.), Councils and Synods Vol. I (ed. with D. Whitelock and M. Brett) 1981, Popular Religion in the Middle Ages, 1000–1300 (with Rosalind Brooke) 1984, A History of Gonville and Caius College 1985, The Church and the Welsh Border in the Central Middle Ages 1986, Oxford and Cambridge (with Roger Highfield and Wim Swaan) 1988, A History of the University of Cambridge (four vols) 1988–2004, The Medieval Idea of Marriage 1989, David Knowles Remembered (with R. Lovatt, D. Luscombe and A. Sillem) 1991, Churches and Churchmen in Medieval Europe (with R. B. Brooke) 1999, Jane Austen: Illusion and Reality 1999, A History of Emmanuel College, Cambridge (with S. Bendall and P. Collinson) 1999, The Age of the Cloister 2001; contrib. articles and reviews to professional journals. *Address:* Gonville and Caius College, Cambridge, CB2 1TA, England.

BROOKE, Edward William, LLD, LLM; American politician and lawyer; b. 26 Oct. 1919, Washington, DC; s. of Edward Brooke and Helen Brooke; m. 2nd Anne Fleming 1979; ed Howard Univ. and Boston Univ.; Capt., US Army, World War II; admitted to Mass Bar 1948; Chair. Finance Comm., Boston 1961–62; Attorney-Gen. of Mass 1963–67; US Senator from Mass (first African-American to be elected by popular vote to US Senate) 1967–79; Chair. Boston Opera Co.; fmr Pnr, O'Connor & Hannan, Washington, DC; Chair. Nat. Low-Income Housing Coalition 1979–; Counsel, Csaplar & Bok, Boston 1979–; Ltd Pnr, Bear Stearns, New York 1979; Fellow, ABA, American Acad. of Arts and Sciences; Republican; 34 hon. degrees; Presidential Medal of Freedom 2004. *Publication:* The Challenge of Change 1966, Bridging the Divide: My Life 2006. *Address:* 808 Brickell Key Drive, #3101, Miami, FL 33131, USA.

BROOKE OF SUTTON MANDEVILLE, Baron (Life Peer), cr. 2001, of Sutton Mandeville in the County of Wiltshire; **Peter Leonard Brooke,** CH, PC, MA, MBA, FSA; British politician; *Chairman, Association of Conservative Peers; Chairman and Pro-Chancellor, University of London Council;* b. 3 March 1934, London; s. of Lord Brooke of Cumnor, CH, PC and Baroness Brooke of Ystradfellte, DBE; m. 1st Joan Smith 1964 (died 1985); four s. (one deceased); m. 2nd Lindsay Allinson 1991; ed Marlborough Coll., Balliol Coll., Oxford, Harvard Business School, USA; Research Asst, Inst. pour l'Etude des Méthodes de Direction de l'Entreprise (IMEDE), Lausanne and Swiss Corresp. of Financial Times 1960–61; Spencer Stuart Man. Consultants 1961–79, Chair. of parent co. 1974–79; MP for City of London and Westminster S. 1977–97, for Cities of London and Westminster 1997–2001; Govt Whips' Office 1979–83; Dept of Educ. and Science Parl. Under-Sec. 1983–85; Minister of State, HM Treasury 1985–87, Paymaster Gen. 1987–89; Chair. Conservative Party 1987–89; Sec. of State for NI 1989–92, for Nat. Heritage 1992–94; Chair. Commons Select Cttee on NI 1997–2001; mem. House of Lords 2001–; Chair. Asscn of Conservative Peers 2004–; lay mem. Univ. of London Council 1994–, Deputy Chair. 2001–02, Chair. and Pro-Chancellor 2002–; Pres. British Antique Dealers Asscn 1995–, British Art Market Fed. 1996–; Trustee Wordsworth Trust 1974–2001, Cusichaca Project 1978–98; Lay Adviser, St Paul's Cathedral 1980–99; Chair. Churches Conservation Trust 1995–98; Sr Fellow, RCA 1987, Presentation Fellow, King's Coll. London 1989, Hon. Fellow, Queen Mary and Westfield Coll. 1996; Hon. DLitt (Westminster) 1999, (London Guildhall Univ.) 2001. *Leisure interests:* churches, conservation, cricket, visual arts. *Address:* House of Lords, London, SW1A 0PW, England (office). *Telephone:* (20) 7219-2150 (office). *Fax:* (20) 7219-8602 (office). *E-mail:* brookep@parliament.uk (office).

BROOKNER, Anita, CBE, BA, PhD, FRSL; British academic, writer and art historian; b. 16 July 1928, London; d. of Newson Brookner and Maude Brookner; ed James Allen's Girls' School, King's Coll., London, Courtauld Inst. and Paris; Visiting Lecturer in Art History, Univ. of Reading 1959–64; Lecturer, Courtauld Inst. of Art 1964–77, Reader in Art History 1977–87; Slade Prof., Univ. of Cambridge 1967–68; Fellow, New Hall Cambridge, King's Coll. London; Commdr, Ordre des Arts et Lettres 2002; Hon. DLitt (Loughborough Univ. of Tech.) 1990; Dr hc (Smith Coll., USA). *Publications:* fiction: A Start in Life 1981, Providence 1982, Look at Me 1983, Hôtel du Lac (Booker Prize) 1984, Family and Friends 1985, A Misalliance 1986, A Friend from England 1987, Latecomers 1988, Lewis Percy 1989, Brief Lives 1990, A Closed Eye 1991, Fraud 1992, A Family Romance 1993, A Private View 1994, Incidents in the rue Laugier 1995, Altered States 1996, Soundings 1997, Visitors 1997, Falling Slowly 1998, Undue Influence 1999, The Bay of Angels 2000, The Next Big Thing 2002, The Rules of Engagement 2003, Leaving Home 2005, Strangers 2009; non-fiction: An Iconography of Cecil Rhodes 1956, J. A. Dominique Ingres 1965, Watteau 1968, The Genius of the Future: Studies in French Art Criticism 1971, Greuze: The Rise and Fall of an Eighteenth-Century Phenomenon 1972, Jacques-Louis David, a Personal Interpretation: Lecture on Aspects of Art 1974, Jacques-Louis David 1980; editor: The Stories of Edith Wharton (two vols) 1988, 1988; contrib. to books and periodicals, including Burlington Magazine. *Address:* 68 Elm Park Gardens, London, SW10 9PB, England. *Telephone:* (20) 7352-6894.

BROOKS, Albert; American actor, writer and director; b. (Albert Einstein), 22 July 1947, Beverly Hills, Calif.; s. of Harry Brooks and Thelma (Leeds) Einstein; began career with several successful comedy albums then directing short comedy films for TV shown on Great American Dream Machine (PBS) and Saturday Night Live (NBC). *Films include:* (actor) Taxi Driver 1976, Private Benjamin 1980, Twilight Zone: The Movie 1983, Unfaithfully Yours 1983, Terms of Endearment 1983, Broadcast News 1987, I'll Do Anything 1994, The Scout 1994, Critical Care 1997, Out of Sight 1998, Dr Dolittle (voice) 1998, The Muse 1999; (dir, writer and actor) Real Life 1979, Modern Romance 1982, Lost in America 1985, Defending Your Life 1991, Mother 1996 (NY Soc. of Film Critics' Award, Nat. Soc. of Film Critics' Award for Best Screenplay), The Muse 1999, My First Mister 2000, Finding Nemo (voice) 2003, The In-Laws 2003, Looking for Comedy in the Muslim World 2006, The Simpsons Movie (voice) 2007. *Television includes:* The Simpsons (voice) 1990–2005; dir, writer short films Saturday Night Live 1975–76. *Recordings include:* Comedy Minus One, A Star is Bought. *Address:* c/o Toni Howard, International Creative Management Inc. (ICM), 8942 Wilshire Blvd., Beverly Hills, CA 90211; 1880 Century Drive Park East, #900, Los Angeles, CA 90067-1609, USA.

BROOKS, (Troyal) Garth, BS; American country singer, songwriter and musician (guitar); b. 7 Feb. 1962, Tulsa, OK; s. of Troyal Raymond and Colleen Carroll Brooks; m. 1st Sandra Mahl 1986; three c.; m. 2nd Trisha Yearwood 2005; ed Oklahoma State Univ.; mem. ASCAP, CMA, ACM; Acad. of Country Music Entertainer of the Year 1991, 1992, 1993, 1994, Male Vocalist of the Year Award 1991, Horizon Award 1991, Country Music Asscn Entertainer of the Year award 1991, 1992, Grammy Award for Best Male Country Vocalist 1992, Best Male Country Music Performer 1992, 1993, Best Male Musical Performer, People's Choice Awards 1992–95, Country Music Award for Artist of the Decade 1999, American Music Award for Favorite Country Artist 2000, Special Award of Merit 2002. *Recordings:* albums: Garth Brooks 1989, No Fences (Acad. of Country Music Album of the Year 1991, CMA Award for Best Album 1991) 1990, Ropin' The Wind 1991, Beyond The Season 1992, The Chase 1992, In Pieces 1993, The Hits 1994, Fresh Horses 1995, Sevens 1997, In The Life Of Chris Gaines 1999, Garth Brooks & The Magic Of Christmas 1999, Double Live (American Music Award for Favorite Country Album 2001) 2000, Scarecrow 2001; singles: If Tomorrow Never Comes 1989, The Dance (Acad. Country Music Song of Year, CMA Award for Best Single) 1991, Friends in Low Places (Acad. Country Music Single Record of Year) 1991, If Tomorrow Never Comes (American Music Country Song of Year) 1991, Tour EP 1994, To Make You Feel My Love 1998, One Heart At A Time 1998, Lost In You 1999, Call Me Claus 2001, The Thunder Rolls, We Shall Be Free, Somewhere Other Than The Night, Learning to Live Again. *Television specials:* This is Garth Brooks 1992, This is Garth Brooks Too 1994, Garth Brooks: The Hits 1995, Garth Brooks Live in Cen. Park 1997. *Address:* Scott Stern, G. B. Management Inc., 1111 17th Avenue S, Nashville, TN 37212, USA (office).

BROOKS, James L.; American screenwriter, director and producer; b. 9 May 1940, North Bergen, NJ; s. of Edward M. Brooks and Dorothy Helen Sheinheit; m. 1st Marianne Catherine Morrissey 1964 (divorced); one d.; m. 2nd Holly Beth Holmbert 1978; one s. one d.; ed New York Univ.; writer CBS News, New York 1964–66; writer-producer documentaries Wolper Productions, LA 1966–67; founder and owner Gracie Films 1984; mem. Guild of America, Writers' Guild of America, TV Acad. of Arts and Sciences, Acad. of Motion Picture Arts and Sciences. *TV series include:* creator Room 222 1968–69 (Emmy Award for Outstanding New Series); co-creator, producer Mary Tyler Moore Show 1970–77 (Emmy Awards for Comedy Writing, Outstanding Comedy Series, Peabody Award, Writers' Guild of America Award, Humanitas Award and others); writer, producer Paul Sand in Friends and Lovers 1974; co-creator, co-exec. producer series Rhoda Show 1974–75 (Emmy and Humanitas Awards); co-creator, exec. producer Taxi 1978–80 (Emmy, Film Critics' Circle, Golden Globe and Humanitas Awards); co-exec. producer, co-writer Cindy 1978; co-creator, exec. producer The Associates 1979; exec. producer, co-exec. producer, co-creator The Tracey Ullman Show 1986–90 (3 Emmy Awards for Outstanding Variety or Comedy Series, 2 Emmy Awards Outstanding Writing Variety or Music Show), The Simpsons 1990– (3 Emmy Awards), The Critic (exec. producer) 2000, What About Joan (exec. producer) 2001. *Films include:* producer, writer, dir Terms of Endearment 1983 (Golden Globe Best Screenplay and Best Picture Awards, Acad. Awards for Best Film, Best Dir, Best Screenplay, Dirs' Guild of America Award for Best Dir), Spanglish 2004; writer, dir, producer Broadcast News 1987 (New York Film Critics' Awards for Best Picture, Best Dir, Best Screenplay); exec. producer Big 1988, The War of the Roses 1989; producer Jerry Maguire 1996, As Good As It Gets 1997, Riding in Cars With Boys 2001. *Address:* Gracie Films, c/o Sony Film Corporation, 10202 West Washington Boulevard, Culver City, CA 90232, USA (office). *Telephone:* (310) 244-4222 (office). *Fax:* (310) 244-1530 (office). *Website:* www.graciefilms.com (office).

BROOKS, Mel; American actor, writer, producer and director; b. (Melvin Kaminsky Brooks), 28 June 1926, Brooklyn, New York, NY; m. 1st Florence Baum; two s. one d.; m. 2nd Anne Bancroft 1964 (died 2005); one s.; script writer for TV series Your Show of Shows 1950–54, Caesar's Hour 1954–57, Get Smart 1965; set up feature film production co. Brooksfilms. *Television:* Get Smart (writer) 1965–70, The Nutt House (writer) 1989, Mad About You (Emmy Award for Outstanding Guest Actor in a Comedy Series 1997, 1998, 1999),. *Films include:* The Critic (writer, cartoon) (Academy Award 1964) 1963, The Producers (writer, dir) (Acad. Award for Best Screenplay) 1968, The Twelve Chairs (writer, dir, actor) 1970, Shinbone Alley (writer) 1971, Blazing Saddles (writer, dir, actor) 1974, Young Frankenstein (writer, dir) 1974, Silent Movie (writer, dir, actor) 1976, High Anxiety (writer, dir, actor, producer) 1977, The Muppet Movie (actor) 1979, The Elephant Man (exec. producer) 1980, History of the World Part I (writer, dir, actor, producer) 1981, My Favourite Year 1982, To Be or Not to Be (actor, producer) 1983, The Doctor and the Devils (exec. producer) 1985, Solarbabies (exec. producer) 1986, Fly I 1986, Spaceballs (writer, dir, actor, producer) 1987, 84 Charing Cross Road (exec. producer) 1987, Fly II 1989, Life Stinks (writer, dir, actor, producer) 1991, The Vagrant (exec. producer) 1992, Robin Hood: Men in Tights (writer, dir, actor, producer) 1993, The Little Rascals (actor) 1994, Dracula: Dead and Loving It (writer, dir, actor, producer) 1995, Svitati (actor) 1999, The Producers: The Movie Musical 2005. *Musical:* The Producers (producer, co-writer, composer) (Tony Awards for Best Book, Best Score, Best Musical 2001, Evening Standard Award for Best Musical 2004, Critics Circle Theatre Award for Best Musical 2005) 2001, Young Frankenstein 2007. *Address:* c/o The Culver Studios, 9336 W Washington Boulevard, Culver City, CA 90232, USA.

BROOME, David McPherson, CBE; British professional show jumper and farmer; b. 1 March 1940, Cardiff; s. of Fred Broome and Amelia Broome; brother of veteran show jumper Liz Edgar; m. Elizabeth Fletcher 1976; three s.; ed Monmouth Grammar School for Boys; European show jumping champion, riding Sunsalve, Aachen 1961, riding Mr Softee, Rotterdam 1967 and Hickstead 1969; world champion, riding Beethoven, La Baule (France) 1970; professional world champion, riding Sportsman and Philco, Cardiff 1974; mem. of six British Olympic teams (including Barcelona 1992); Master of Foxhounds. *Publications:* Jump-Off 1970, Horsemanship (with S. Hadley) 1983. *Leisure interests:* hunting, shooting, golf. *Address:* Mount Ballan Manor, Crick, Caldicot, Monmouthshire, NP26 5XP, Wales. *Telephone:* (1291) 420778.

BROSNAN, Pierce; Irish actor; b. 16 May 1953, Navan, Co. Meath; s. of Tom Brosnan and May Smith; m. Cassandra Harris (died 1991); one s.; m. Keely Shaye Smith 2001; two s.; ed Drama Center; London stage appearances include Wait Until Dark, The Red Devil Battery Sign (cast in role of McCabe in British premiere by Tennessee Williams), Filumenia; co-f. (with Beau St. Clair) Irish Dreamtime (production co.) 1996. *Films include:* The Mirror Crack'd 1980, The Long Good Friday, Nomads, The Fourth Protocol, Taffin, The Deceivers, Mister Johnson, The Lawnmower Man, Mrs Doubtfire 1993, Love Affair 1994, Robinson Crusoe 1995, Mars Attacks! 1996, The Mirror Has Two Faces 1996, Dante's Peak 1997, The Nephew 1998, The Thomas Crown Affair 1999, Grey Owl 2000, The Tailor of Panama 2001, Laws of Attraction 2004, After the Sunset 2004, The Matador 2005, Seraphim Falls 2006, Mamma Mia! 2008; role of James Bond in Goldeneye 1994, Tomorrow Never Dies 1997, The World is Not Enough 1999, Die Another Day 2002, Married Life 2007. *TV appearances include:* role of detective in Remington Steele (series), Noble House (NBC mini-series), Nancy Astor, Around the World in Eighty Days, The Heist, Murder 101, Victim of Love, Live Wire, Death Train, Robinson Crusoe 1994, The James Bond Story 1999. *Address:* Irish Dreamtime, 3110 Main Street, Suite 200, Santa Monica, CA 90405; c/o Guttman Associates, 118 South Beverly Drive, Suite 201, Beverly Hills, CA 90212, USA (office). *Telephone:* (310) 449-3411 (Irish Dreamtime). *Fax:* (310) 586-8138 (Irish Dreamtime). *Website:* www.piercebrosnan.com.

BROTMAN, Jeffrey (Jeff) H., BA, JD; American retail executive; *Chairman, Costco Wholesale Corporation;* m. Susan Brotman; two c.; ed Univ. of Washington; Founding Chair. Costco Wholesale Corpn 1983–93, Vice-Chair. 1993–94, Chair. 1994–; Dir Starbucks Coffee 1988–99, Garden Botanika 1989–98, Seattle-First Nat. Bank 1990–99, The Sweet Factory Inc. 1992–98; Regent Univ. of Wash. 1998–, Vice-Pres. Bd of Regents 2002–03, Pres. 2004–; Co-Chair. King County United Way Campaign Bd 1997–; Trustee, Seattle Art Museum 1990–, Seattle Foundation 1991–, Univ. of Washington Medical Center Bd 1991–. *Address:* Costco Wholesale Corporation, 999 Lake Drive, Issaquah, WA 98027, USA (office). *Telephone:* (425) 313-8100 (office). *Fax:* (425) 313-8103 (office). *E-mail:* info@costco.com (office). *Website:* www.costco.com (office).

BROTODININGRAT, Soemadi Djoko Moerdjono; Indonesian diplomatist; b. 13 June 1941, Solo, Cen. Javan Prov.; m.; one s. one d.; ed Gadjah Mada Univ. and Int. Inst. of Public Admin, France; with Dept of Foreign Affairs 1965–, Head of Section (and later of Staff), Directorate of Information 1965–71; Third then Second Sec., Embassy in Brussels 1971–75; Deputy Dir of Social and Cultural Relations, Dept of Foreign Affairs 1975–78; First Sec., Counsellor, Perm. Mission to UN, New York 1978–82, Minister Counsellor 1984–88; Deputy Dir, Directorate of Multilateral Econ. Cooperation, Dept of Foreign Affairs 1982–84, Dir 1988–91; Perm. Rep. to UN, Geneva 1991–95; Dir-Gen. for Foreign Econ. Relations, Dept of Foreign Affairs 1995–98; Amb. to Japan and Federated States of Micronesia 1998–2002, to USA (also attributed to Grenada, St Lucia, St Vincent and Dominica) 2002–05; Head of Indonesian Delegation to Indonesia–Japan Econ. Partnership 2005–. *Address:* c/o Ministry of Foreign Affairs, Jalan Taman Pejambon 6, 10th Floor, Jakarta 10110, Indonesia (office). *Telephone:* (21) 3858052 (office).

BROUGHTON, Martin Faulkner, FCA; British business executive and chartered accountant; *Chairman, British Airways PLC;* b. 15 April 1947, London; s. of Edward Broughton and Laura Faulkner; m. Jocelyn Mary Rodgers 1974; one s. one d.; ed Westminster City Grammar School; joined British-American Tobacco Co. (BAT) 1971, with group's Brazilian subsidiary Souza Cruz 1980–85, Finance Dir BAT Industries 1988–93, Group Chief Exec. and Deputy Chair. 1993–98, Chair. BAT PLC (following demerger) 1998–2004; Finance Dir Eagle Star 1985–88, Chair. 1992–93, Chair. Wiggins Teape Group 1989–90; Dir (non-exec.) Whitbread 1993–2000; Dir (non-exec.) British Airways PLC 2000–, Deputy Chair. (non-exec.) 2003–04, Chair. (non-exec.) 2004–, Chair. Nominations Cttee; Pres. CBI 2007–; Ind. Dir British Horseracing Bd 1999–2004, Chair. 2004–07; Co-Chair. Transatlantic Business Dialogue 2006–08, currently European Chair.; mem. Financial Reporting Council 1998–, European Round Table of Industrialists. *Leisure interests:* golf, football, horse racing, the theatre. *Address:* British Airways PLC, Waterside, Harmondsworth, London, UB7 0GB, England (office). *Telephone:* (844) 493-0787 (office). *Fax:* (20) 8738-9801 (office). *E-mail:* info@britishairways.com (office). *Website:* www.britishairways.com (office).

BROUT, Robert H., AB, PhD; Belgian physicist and academic; *Professor of Physics, Université Libre de Bruxelles;* b. 14 June 1928, New York, USA; s. of Samuel Brout and Ruth Brout; m. Martine Feut-Brout (deceased); two s. one d.; ed New York Univ., Colombia Univ., New York; Guggenheim Fellow 1961; currently Prof. of Physics, Université Libre de Bruxelles; Dr hc (Mons) 1984; Gravity Research Foundation First Award, Europhysics High Energy Prize 1997, Wolf Prize in Physics 2004. *Leisure interests:* gardening, poetry, music. *Address:* Université Libre de Bruxelles, Campus de la Plaine, CP 225, Boulevard du Triomphe, 1050 Brussels (office); Drène Marissal 20, 1630 Linkebeek, Belgium (home). *Telephone:* (2) 650-55-82 (office); (2) 380-64-65 (home). *Fax:* (2) 650-59-51 (office). *E-mail:* physth@ulb.ac.be (office); Robert.Brout@ulb.ac.be (home). *Website:* www.ulb.ac.be/sciences/physth (office).

BROWALDH, Tore, BA, LLM, DEng, DEcon; Swedish banker; *Honorary Chairman, Svenska Handelsbanken;* b. 23 Aug. 1917, Västerås; s. of Ernfrid Browaldh and Ingrid (née Gezelius) Browaldh; m. Gunnel Ericson 1942; three s. one d.; Financial Attaché Swedish Legation, Washington, DC 1943; Asst Sec. Swedish Royal Cttee of Post-War Econ. Planning 1944–45: Admin. Sec. Swedish Industrial Inst. for Econ. and Social Research 1944–45; Sec. Bd of Man., Svenska Handelsbanken 1946–49, Chief Gen. Man. 1955–66, Chair. 1966–78, Vice-Chair. 1978–88, Hon. Chair. 1988–; Dir Econ., Social, Cultural and Refugee Dept, Sec.-Gen. Council of Europe 1949–51; Exec. Vice-Pres. Confed. of Swedish Employers 1951–54; mem. Bd Swedish Bankers Asscn, Chair. 1959–61; Chair. AB Industrivärden 1966–88, Svenska Cellulosa AB 1960–88, Swedish IBM 1960–88, Swedish Unilever AB 1968–; Deputy Chair. Nobel Foundation 1966–88, AB Volvo; mem. Bd IBM World Trade Corpn 1976–88; mem. Advisory Bd Unilever, Rotterdam 1976–88; mem. Bd Dag Hammarskjöld Foundation 1961–63, Swedish Govt Research Advisory Bd 1966–70, Swedish Govt Industrial Policy Comm. 1968–70, Swedish Govt Econ. Planning Comm. 1962–80; Special Adviser to Int. Fed. of Insts for Advanced Studies; mem. UN Group to Study Multinational Corpns.; mem. Swedish Royal Acad. of Sciences 1980, Swedish Acad. of Eng Sciences 1961–, Royal Acad. of Arts and Sciences, Uppsala; St Erik Medal, Commdr Order of Vasa, Commdr Grand Cross Order of the Northern Star. *Publications:* Management and Society 1961, The Pilgrimage of a Journeyman 1976, The Road Ahead 1980, Ascent and Tailwind 1984. *Leisure interests:* playing jazz on piano, golf, computer technology. *Address:* c/o Svenska Handelsbanken, Kungsträdgårdsgatan 2, 106 70 Stockholm (office); 14 Sturegatan, 114 36 Stockholm, Sweden (home). *Telephone:* (8) 661-96-43 (home).

BROWDER, Felix Earl, MA, PhD; American mathematician, academic and university administrator; *University Professor of Mathematics, Rutgers University;* b. 31 July 1927, Moscow, Russia; s. of Earl Browder and Raissa Berkmann; m. Eva Tislowitz 1949; two s.; ed Yonkers High School and Princeton Univ.; CLE Moore Instructor in Math. MIT 1948–51; Instructor in Math. Boston Univ. 1951–53; US Army 1953–55; Asst Prof. of Math. Brandeis Univ. 1955–56; Asst Prof. then Prof. Yale Univ. 1956–63; Prof. of Math. Univ. of Chicago 1963–72, Louis Block Prof. of Math. 1972–82, Max Mason Distinguished Service Prof. 1982–87, Chair. Math. Dept 1971–76, 1979–85; Visiting Prof. MIT 1961–62, 1977–78; Vice-Pres. for Research Rutgers Univ. 1986–91, Univ. Prof. 1986–; Pres. American Mathematical Soc. 1999–2001; ed. numerous journals; mem. NAS (mem. Council 1992–95, Governing Bd Nat. Research Council 1994–95); Fellow, American Acad. of Arts and Sciences; Dr hc (Paris) 1990; Nat. Medal of Science 1999. *Publications:* Problèmes non-linéaires 1966, Functional Analysis and Related Fields 1970, Nonlinear Functional Analysis (2 Vols) 1970, 1976, Mathematical Heritage of Henri Poincaré 1984, Nonlinear functional analysis and its applications (2 Vols) 1985; numerous papers in mathematical journals. *Leisure interests:* reading, especially in philosophy, history and classics. *Address:* Department of Mathematics, Hill Center-Busch Campus, Rutgers University, 110 Frelinghuysen Road, Rutgers University, Piscataway, NJ 08854-8019, USA. *Telephone:* (732) 445-2393 (office); (732) 297-6040 (home). *E-mail:* browder@math.rutgers.edu (office). *Website:* www.math.rutgers.edu (office).

BROWN, Adriane M., BSc, MA; American automotive industry executive; *President and CEO, Transportation Systems, Honeywell International Inc.;* ed Old Dominion Univ., Norfolk, Va, Massachusetts Inst. of Tech. (Sloan Fellow); Vice-Pres. and Gen. Man. Environmental Products Div., Corning Inc. 1980–94, Vice-Pres. and Gen. Man. Automotive Products business 1994–99; Vice-Pres. and Gen. Man. Aircraft Landing Systems, Honeywell Aerospace 1999, later Vice-Pres. and Gen. Man. Engine Systems and Accessories, Pres. and CEO Transportation Systems, Honeywell International Inc., Torrance, Calif. 2005–; mem. Bd of Dirs Jobs for America's Graduates; mem. Exec. Leadership Council, Arizona Women's Forum; named one of Top 100 Leading Women in the Automotive Industry 2005. *Address:* Honeywell Transportation Systems, 23326 Hawthorne Blvd, # 200, Torrance, CA 90505, USA (office). *Telephone:* (310) 791-9101 (office). *Website:* www.honeywell.com (office).

BROWN, Alexander Claude, PhD, DSc, FRSSA; South African zoologist and academic; *Professor Emeritus of Zoology, University of Cape Town;* b. 19 Aug. 1931, Cape Town; s. of Alexander John Brown and Doris Hilda Brown (née Todd); m. Rosalind Jane Roberts 1957; three s.; ed Rhodes Univ. and Univ. of Cape Town; Lecturer in Zoology, Rhodes Univ. 1954; Research Officer Council for Scientific and Industrial Research 1954–57; Lecturer and Sr Lecturer, Univ. of Cape Town 1957–74, Prof. and Head, Dept of Zoology 1975–96, Prof. Emer. 1997–; Dir Univ. Centre for Marine Studies 1997–2000; Deputy Dean, Faculty of Music 1970–80; worked at the Univs of London, Manchester, Cambridge and Plymouth Marine Lab.; expeditions to Chile and Antarctica; Ed. Transactions of the Royal Soc. of South Africa 1968–82; mem. Ed. Bd Journal of Experimental Marine Biology and Ecology; Past Pres. Royal Soc. of South Africa; Life Fellow Univ. of Cape Town; Gold Medal, Zoological Soc. of Southern Africa, Gilchrist Medal for Outstanding Marine Research. *Publications:* A History of Scientific Endeavour in South Africa (ed.), Ecology of Sandy Shores (with A. McLachlan) 1990; several textbooks and about 200 research papers on the ecophysiology of sandy beach animals and marine pollution. *Leisure interests:* music, musicological research. *Address:* Department of Zoology, University of Cape Town, Rondebosch 7701 (office); 10 Monroe Road, Rondebosch 7708, South Africa (home). *Telephone:* (21) 6503628 (office); (21) 6713504 (home). *Fax:* (21) 6503301 (office). *E-mail:* acbrown@botzoo.uct.ac.za (office). *Website:* web.uct.ac.za/depts/zoology (office).

BROWN, Cedric Harold, FREng, FICE; British business executive; b. 7 March 1935; s. of the late William Herbert Brown and Constance Dorothy Brown (née Frances); m. Joan Hendry 1956; one s. three d.; ed Sheffield, Rotherham and Derby Colls of Tech.; East Midlands Gas Bd 1953–59; Eng Asst Tunbridge Wells Borough Council 1959–60; Eng posts, East Midlands Gas Bd 1960–75; Dir of Eng East Midlands Gas 1975–78; joined British Gas Corpn (now British Gas PLC) 1978; Dir Morecambe Bay Project 1980–87; Regional Chair. British Gas West Midlands 1987–89; Dir and Man. Dir Exploration and Production 1989; Man. Regional Services 1989–91; Sr Man. Dir 1991; Chief Exec. British Gas PLC 1992–96; Chair. CB Consultants 1996–, Intellihome PLC 1997–, Atlantic Caspian Resources PLC 1999–, Business Champions-East Midlands Devt Agency 2001–, Lachesis Investment Advisory Cttee 2002–; Pres. Institution of Gas Engineers 1996–97, Fellow; Dir Bow Valley Industries 1988–92, Orb Estates 2000–; mem. Advisory Council on Business and the Environment 1993–95. *Publications:* tech. papers. *Leisure interests:* sport, countryside, places of historic interest. *Address:* CB Consultants Limited, 1 Great Cumberland Place, London, W1H 7AL, England.

BROWN, Dan; American writer; b. 1965, Exeter, NH; m. Blythe Newlon 1997; ed Phillips Exeter Acad., Amherst Coll.; English teacher 1986–1996. *Publications:* 187 Men to Avoid (as Danielle Brown) 1995, Digital Fortress 1998, Angels and Demons 2001, Deception Point 2002, The Da Vinci Code (British Book Award for Book of the Year 2005) 2003, The Lost Symbol 2009. *Address:* Heide Lange, Sandford J. Greenburger Associates Inc., 55 Fifth Avenue, New York, NY 10003, USA (office). *Telephone:* (212) 206-5600 (office). *Fax:* (212) 463-8718 (office). *E-mail:* queryHL@sjga.com (office). *Website:* www.greenburger.com (office); www.danbrown.com.

BROWN, David, AB, MS; American film producer; b. 28 July 1916, New York City; m. Helen Gurley Brown (q.v.) 1959; ed Stanford Univ. and Columbia School of Journalism; early career as reporter, wrote numerous short stories, rose to Man. Ed. Cosmopolitan; moved to Hollywood as story ed. at Twentieth Century-Fox 1953, formed partnership with Richard D. Zanuck when the latter was apptd Production Head, est. Zanuck-Brown Productions, split amicably 1988; fmr ed. at New American Library; Irving G. Thalberg Memorial Award (jtly with Richard D. Zanuck), Acad. of Motion Picture Arts and Sciences for their achievements in producing 1990. *Theatre includes:* numerous Broadway musicals, including Sweet Smell of Success: The Musical 2002, Dirty Rotten Scoundrels 2005, and the off-Broadway Jerry Herman musical revue Showtune 2003. *Films include:* SSSSSSS (exec. producer) (aka SSSSnake, UK) 1973, Willie Dynamite 1974, The Sugarland Express 1974, The Black Windmill (exec. producer) 1974, The Girl from Petrovka 1974, The Eiger Sanction (exec. producer) 1975, Jaws 1975, MacArthur (exec. producer) 1977, Jaws 2 1978, The Island 1980, Neighbors 1981, The Verdict 1982, Cocoon 1985, Target 1985, Cocoon: The Return 1988, Driving Miss Daisy (exec. producer) 1989, The Player 1992, A Few Good Men 1992, The Cemetery Club (aka Looking for a Live One) 1993, Rich in Love (co-producer) 1993, Watch It (exec. producer) 1993, Canadian Bacon 1995, The Saint 1997, Kiss the Girls 1997, Deep Impact 1998, Angela's Ashes 1999, Chocolat (also uncredited appearance) 2000, Along Came a Spider 2001. *Television includes:* Women & Men 2: In Love There Are No Rules (aka The Art of Seduction, UK: DVD box title) 1991, A Season in Purgatory (exec. producer) 1996, Framed (exec. producer) 2002. *Publication:* Brown's Guide to Growing Grey 1987, Let Me Entertain You 1990, The Rest of Your Life is the Best of Your Life 1991, Brown's Guide to the Good Life Without Tears, Fears or Boredom 2006. *Address:* 1775 Broadway, suite 410, New York, NY 10019 (office); 1 West 81st Street, 22D, New York, NY 10024, USA (home). *Telephone:* (212) 258-2541 (office); (212) 799-8202 (home). *Fax:* (212) 258-2546 (office). *Website:* www.barricadebooks.com.

BROWN, David Arthur, PhD, DSc, MRIA; British chemist and academic; *Professor Emeritus, Department of Chemistry, University College Dublin;* b. 5 June 1929, High Wycombe; s. of Arthur Percy Brown and Fanny Catherine Brown (née Withell); m. Rita Brown; two s. four d.; ed Watford Grammar School, Queen Mary Coll., King's Coll., Cambridge; lecturer, Univ. Coll. Dublin 1959, Prof. of Inorganic Chem. 1964, Head of Dept 1974–77, 1983–86, 1989, Dean of Faculty of Science 1984–87, mem. of Governing Body 1979–81, 1985–87, now Prof. Emer.; Pres. Inst. of Chem. of Ireland 1976–77; Wheeler Lecturer 1999; Boyle-Higgins Medal 1996. *Publications:* over 200 publs on organo-metallic chem., bioinorganic chem. and theoretical chem. *Leisure interests:* walking, travelling, reading, music. *Address:* c/o Department of Chemistry, University College, Belfield, Dublin 4, Ireland.

BROWN, Donald David, MS, MD; American biologist and academic; *Member of Staff, Department of Embryology, Carnegie Institution and Adjunct Professor, Department of Biology, Johns Hopkins University;* b. 30 Dec. 1931, Cincinnati, Ohio; s. of Albert L. Brown and Louise R. Brown; m. Linda Weil 1957; one s. two d.; ed Walnut Hills High School, Cinn., Dartmouth Coll and Univ. of Chicago; Intern, Charity Hosp., New Orleans 1956–57, Sr Asst Surgeon, US Public Health Service, Bethesda 1957–59; Postdoctoral Fellow, Pasteur Inst. 1959–60, Dept of Embryology, Carnegie Inst. of Washington, Baltimore 1960–62, staff mem. 1963–, Dir 1976–94; Adjunct Prof., Dept of Biology, Johns Hopkins Univ. 1968–; Pres. Life Sciences Research Foundation 1981–; Pres. American Soc. of Cell Biology 1992; US Steel Award in Molecular Biology 1973, V. D. Mattia Award 1976, Boris Pregel Award, New York Acad. of Science 1977, Ross Harrison-ISDB Award 1981, Ernst W. Bertner Award, Texas Univ. Cancer Center 1982, Louisa Gross Horwitz Award, Columbia Univ. 1985, Rosensteil Award 1985, Feodor Lynen Medal, Miami Winter Symposium 1987, E. B. Wilson Award 1996. *Address:* Carnegie Institution, Department of Embryology, 3520 San Martin Drive, Baltimore, MD 21218 (office); 6511 Abbey View Way, Baltimore, MD 21212, USA (home). *Telephone:* (410) 246-3052 (office); (410) 377-0812 (home). *Fax:* (410) 243-6311 (office). *E-mail:* brown@ciwemb.edu (office). *Website:* www.ciwemb.edu/labs/brown/index.php (office); www.bio.jhu.edu/directory/faculty/brown/default.html (office).

BROWN, Edmund Gerald (Jerry), Jr, AB, JD; American politician and lawyer; *Attorney General of California;* b. 7 April 1938, San Francisco; s. of Edmund G. Brown and Bernice Layne; m. Anne Gust 2005; ed Univ. of Calif., Berkeley, Yale Law School; Research Attorney, Calif. Supreme Court 1964–65, Attorney, Los Angeles 1966–69; Calif. Sec. of State 1971–74; Gov. of Calif. 1975–83; Chair. Calif. State Democratic Party 1989–90; unsuccessful Democratic Presidential cand. 1992; Mayor of Oakland, Calif. 1999–2006; Attorney Gen. of Calif. 2006–; fmr Pnr Reavis and McGarth; Trustee, Los Angeles Community Colls 1969. *Publication:* Dialogues 1988. *Address:* Attorney General's Office, California Department of Justice, Attn: Public Inquiry Unit, PO Box 944255, Sacramento, CA 94244-2550, USA (office). *Telephone:* (916) 322-3360 (office). *Fax:* (916) 323-5341 (office). *Website:* ag.ca.gov (office); www.jerrybrown.org.

BROWN, Hon. Ewart Frederick, Jr, BSc, MD, MPH, JP; Bermudian physician and politician; *Premier and Minister of Transport and Tourism;* b. 1946, Bermuda; s. of Ewart Brown and Helene Brown; m. Wanda Henton Brown; four s. from previous m.; ed Berkeley Inst., Howard Univ., Washington DC, USA, Howard Coll. of Medicine, UCLA; represented Bermuda at Commonwealth Games, Kingston, Jamaica, where he ran the 400m and 1600m relay 1966; spent many years practising medicine in USA, including at Vermont-Century Medical Clinic, Los Angeles –1993; Medical Dir Bermuda HealthCare Services Ltd; MP for Warwick West 1993–98, for Warwick South Cen. 1998–; Minister of Transport 1998–2003; Deputy Premier and Minister of Transport 2003–04; Deputy Premier and Minister of Transport and Tourism 2004–06; Premier and Minister of Transport and Tourism 2006–; Leader Bermuda Progressive Labour Party 2006–; certified Diplomat of American Bd of Family Practice; Diplomat of American Bd of Quality Assurance and Utilization Review Physicians; fmr Vice-Pres. Union of American Physicians and Dentists; fmr Asst Prof., Dept of Family Practice, Charles R. Drew Univ. of Medicine and Science; fmr Dir, Marcus Garvey School, Los Angeles; fmr mem. Bd Union of American Physicians and Dentists (California Fed.); fmr mem. Editorial Bd Feeling Good magazine; fmr mem. Bd Dirs Marina Hills Hosp., Los Angeles; fmr physician consultant of Rev. Jesse Jackson (1988 US presidential cand.); fmr mem. California State Comm. on Maternal, Child and Adolescent Health; founding Commr Bd of Prevention Commrs for South Cen. Los Angeles Regional Centre for Devt Disabilities; Founder and Chair. Western Park Hosp., Calif.; fmr Dir of Quality Assurance, Los Angeles Doctor's Hosp.; fmr Student Body Pres., Howard Univ.; fmr Chair. Minority Group Affairs, Student American Medical Asscn; fmr Coordinator Summer Health Task Force, Nat. Urban Coalition, Washington, DC; fmr Chair. Utilization Review Cttee, West Adams Hosp., Los Angeles; fmr Sec. Charles R. Drew Medical Soc., Los Angeles; mem. Nat. Medical Asscn, American Coll. of Utilization Review Physicians, Golden State Medical Asscn, American Medical Asscn, American Acad. of Family Physicians, American Public Health Asscn, Charles R. Drew Medical Soc.; fmr Trustee Howard Univ., Charles R. Drew Univ. of Medicine and Science; Howard Univ. Service Awards 1968, 1972, Physician's Recognition Award, American Medical Asscn 1977, Sons of Watts Grassroots Health Award 1979, Community Leadership Award, DuBois Academic Inst. 1982, Pacesetter Award, Nat. Asscn for the Advancement of Coloured People 1984, Humanitarian of the Year Award, Marcus Garvey School, Los Angeles 1991, Scroll Award, Union of American Physicians and Dentists 1993. *Leisure interests:* travel, exercising, golf. *Address:* Progressive Labour Party, Alaska Hall, 16 Court Street, Hamilton, HM 17, Bermuda (office). *Telephone:* 292-2264 (office). *Fax:* 295-7890 (office). *E-mail:* info@plp.bm (office). *Website:* www.plp.bm/leadership/leader (office).

BROWN, Gavin, AO, MA, PhD; Australian mathematician, academic and university administrator; *Director, Royal Institution of Australia (RiAus);* b. 27 Feb. 1942, Fife, Scotland; s. of Frank Brown and Alexandria Duncanson; m. 1st Barbara Routh (died 2001); one s. one d.; 2nd Diané Ranck 2004; ed Madras Coll., St Andrews, Univ. of St Andrews, Univ. of Newcastle upon Tyne; Asst Lecturer, Lecturer, Sr Lecturer Univ. of Liverpool 1966–75; Visiting Prof., Univ. of Paris 1975, Univ. of York 1979, Univ. of Cambridge 1986; Prof. of Pure Math., Univ. of NSW 1976–92, Dean Faculty of Science

1989–92; Deputy Vice-Chancellor Univ. of Adelaide 1992–93, Vice-Chancellor 1994–96; Vice-Chancellor and Prin. Univ. of Sydney 1996–2008; Dir Royal Inst. of Australia (RiAus) 2009–; Fellow, Australian Acad. of Science 1981; Corresp. FRSE; Hon. LLD (St Andrews Univ.) 1998, (Univ. of Dundee) 2004; Australian Math. Soc. Medal 1982. *Publications:* numerous publs in math. journals. *Leisure interest:* racing. *Address:* Ri Australia, Adelaide Stock Exchange Building, PO Box 3652, Rundle Mall, Adelaide, SA 5000, Australia (office). *Telephone:* (8) 8226-5377 (office). *Fax:* (8) 8463-6622 (office). *Website:* www.riaustralia.org.au (office).

BROWN, Rt Hon. (James) Gordon, PC, MA, PhD; British politician; *Prime Minister;* b. 20 Feb. 1951, Glasgow; s. of the late Rev. Dr J. Brown and of the late J. Elizabeth Brown; m. Sarah Macaulay 2000; one d. (deceased) two s.; ed Kirkcaldy High School and Univ. of Edinburgh; Rector, Univ. of Edinburgh 1972–75, Temporary Lecturer 1976; Lecturer, Glasgow Coll. of Tech. 1976–80; journalist and Current Affairs Ed., Scottish TV 1980–83; MP (Labour) for Dunfermline East 1983–; Chair. Labour Party Scottish Council 1983–84; Opposition Chief Sec. to the Treasury 1987–89; Shadow Sec. of State for Trade and Industry 1989–92; Shadow Chancellor of the Exchequer 1992–97; Chancellor of the Exchequer 1997–07; Prime Minister 2007–; Leader, Labour Party 2007–; mem. Chair. Interim Cttee IMF 1999–; mem. Transport and Gen. Workers' Union; Hon. DCL (Newcastle) 2007. *Publications:* The Red Paper on Scotland (ed.) 1975, The Politics of Nationalism and Devolution (with H. M. Drucker) 1980, Scotland: The Real Divide (ed.) 1983, Maxton 1986, Where There is Greed 1989, John Smith: Life and Soul of the Party (with J. Naughtie) 1994, Values, Visions and Voices (with T. Wright) 1995, Speeches 1997–2006 2006, Courage: Eight Portraits 2007. *Leisure interests:* reading, writing, football and tennis. *Address:* Office of the Prime Minister, 10 Downing Street, London, SW1A 2AA, England (office). *Telephone:* (20) 7270-3000 (office); (1383) 611702 (Dunfermline East constituency) (office). *Fax:* (20) 7295-0918 (office). *Website:* www.number-10.gov.uk (office).

BROWN, Gregory Q., BA; American business executive; *President and Co-CEO, Motorola, Inc.;* b. 14 Aug. 1960; ed Rutgers Univ.; held several sales and marketing positions with AT&T 1983–87; joined Ameritech 1987, Pres. Custom Business Services and Ameritech New Media, Inc. 1994–96; Chair. and CEO Micromuse, Inc., San Francisco 1999–2003; joined Motorola 2003, held several exec. positions including Exec. Vice-Pres., CEO Commercial, Govt and Industrial Solutions 2003–05, Exec. Vice-Pres. Networks and Enterprise 2005–07, mem. Bd Dirs 2007–, Pres. and COO March–Dec. 2007, Pres. and Co-CEO 2008–, CEO Broadband Mobility Solutions; apptd by White House to serve on Nat. Security Telecommunications Advisory Cttee 2004–; mem. Bd Dirs Commercial Club of Chicago, World Business Chicago, Northwestern Memorial Hosp.; mem. US-China Business Council, US-Brazil CEO Forum, Tech. CEO Council, 2016 Chicago Olympic Cttee; mem. Bd of Overseers, Rutgers Univ. *Address:* Motorola, Inc., 1303 East Algonquin Road, Schaumburg, IL 60196, USA (office). *Telephone:* (847) 576-5000 (office). *Fax:* (847) 576-5372 (office). *E-mail:* info@motorola.com (office). *Website:* www .motorola.com (office).

BROWN, Hank, JD, LLM, CPA; American university administrator, lawyer and fmr politician; b. 12 Feb. 1940, Denver, Colo; s. of Harry W. Brown and Anna M. Hanks; m. Nana Morrison 1967; one s. two d.; ed Univ. of Colo and George Washington Univ.; Lt USN 1962–66; tax accountant, Arthur Andersen 1967–78; admitted Colo Bar 1969; Asst to Pres. Monfort of Colo Inc., Greeley 1969–70, Corp. Counsel 1970–71, Vice-Pres. Monfort Food Distributing 1971–72, Vice-Pres. Corp. Devt 1973–75, Int. Operations 1975–78, Lamb Div. 1978–80; mem. US House of Reps (97th–101st) Congresses from Colo 4th Dist; mem. Colo State Senate 1972–76, Asst Majority Leader 1974–76; US Senator from Colorado (102nd Congress) 1991–97; mem. Senate Judiciary, Budget and Foreign Affairs Cttees 1991–97; Pres. Univ. of N Colo 1998–2002; Pres. and CEO Daniels Fund 2002–05; Pres. Univ. of Colo 2005–08; Republican; Order of Merit, Poland, Grand Cordon of the Order of the Brilliant Star, Repub. of China, Nishan-I-Quaid-I-Azam, Pakistan; Hungarian Presidential Gold Medal, Air Medal, Viet Nam Service Medal, Nat. Western Stock Show Citizen of the West Award 2008. *Leisure interest:* skiing. *Address:* c/o University of Colorado, 35 SYS, 914 Broadway, Boulder, CO 80309-0035, USA (home).

BROWN, Harold, PhD; American fmr government official and physicist; *Counsellor, Center for Strategic and International Studies;* b. 19 Sept. 1927, New York City; s. of A. H. Brown and Gertrude Cohen; m. Colene McDowell 1953; two d.; ed New York City public schools and Columbia Univ.; Lecturer in Physics, Columbia Univ. 1947–48, Stevens Inst. of Tech. 1949–50; Univ. of Calif. Radiation Laboratory, Berkeley 1950–52; Livermore Radiation Laboratory, 1952–61, Dir 1960–61; mem. Polaris Steering Cttee, Dept of Defense 1956–58; Consultant to Air Force Scientific Advisory Bd 1956–57; mem. Scientific Advisory Cttee on Ballistic Missiles to Sec. of Defense 1958–61; mem. President's Science Advisory Cttee 1961; Sec. of Air Force 1965–69; Pres. Calif. Inst. of Tech. 1969–77; US Sec. of Defense 1977–81; Distinguished Visiting Prof. of Nat. Security Affairs, School of Advanced Int. Studies, Johns Hopkins Univ. 1981–84, Chair. Johns Hopkins Univ. Foreign Policy Inst. 1984–92; business consultant 1981–; Dir Philip Morris, Evergreen Holdings Inc., Mattel; Pnr Warburg, Pincus and Co. 1990–; Counsellor, Center for Strategic and Int. Studies 1992–; mem. Del. to Strategic Arms Limitation Talks 1969; mem. NAS; Hon. DEng (Stevens Inst. of Tech.); Hon. LLD (Long Island Univ., Gettysburg Coll., Occidental Coll., Univ. of Calif., Univ. of S Carolina, Franklin and Marshall Coll., Univ. of the Pacific, Brown Univ.); Hon. DSc (Univ. of Rochester); Presidential Medal of Freedom 1981, Fermi Award 1993. *Publications:* Thinking About National Security: Defense and Foreign Policy in a Dangerous World 1983, The Strategic Defense Initiative: Shield or Snare? (ed.) 1987. *Leisure interests:* tennis, swimming, reading.

Address: Center for Strategic and International Studies, 1800 K Street, Suite 400, NW, Washington, DC 20006, USA (office). *Telephone:* (202) 887-0200 (office). *Fax:* (202) 775-3199 (office). *E-mail:* webmaster@csis.org (office). *Website:* www.csis.org (office).

BROWN, Helen Gurley (see Gurley Brown, Helen).

BROWN, James (Jim) Nathaniel; American fmr football player and actor; b. 17 Feb. 1936, St. Simons Island, Ga; m. Sue Jones; two s. one d.; ed Manhasset High School Long Island, Syracuse Univ.; All-American running back and lacrosse player at Syracuse Univ.; fullback for Cleveland Browns 1957–65; played in nine straight NFL (Nat. Football League) Pro Bowls; NFL's leading rusher in eight of his nine seasons; NFL Most Valuable Player—MVP 1958, 1963, 1965; All-NFL 1957–61, 1963–65; career totals include: 118 games played, 12,312 rushing yards, 262 receptions, 15,459 combined net yards, 756 points scored, 126 touchdowns, 106 rushing touchdowns, average 104 yards per game, 5.2 yards per carry; retd from football to pursue acting career 1966; co-f. Negro Industrial Economic Union (NIEU) 1966; works with Coor Golden Door, Barriers and Vital Issues inmates and ex-convicts training programmes 1980–; Founder and Pres. Amer-I-Can Program Inc. 1988–, Chair. Amer-I-Can Foundation for Social Change 1993–; mem. Bd Rebuild LA Project 1992–; Syracuse All-America 1956, NFL Rookie of the Year 1957, Jim Thorpe Trophy 1965; elected to Pro Football Hall of Fame 1971 (second youngest ever, at 35), to Lacrosse Hall of Fame 1984, to Coll. Football Hall of Fame 1995; Walter Camp All-Century Team. *Films include:* Rio Conchos 1964, Dirty Dozen 1967, Mercenaries 1968, Ice Station Zebra 1968, The Split 1968, Riot 1969, Kenner 1969, 100 Rifles 1969, tick...tick...tick 1970, Grasshopper 1970, Slaughter 1972, Black Gunn 1972, Slaughter's Big Rip-Off 1973, Slams 1973, I Escaped from Devil's Island 1973, Three the Hard Way 1975, Kid Vengeance 1977, Fingers 1978, Pacific Inferno 1979, One Down, Two to Go 1982, Running Man 1987, I'm Gonna Git You Sucka 1988, Crack House 1989, L.A. Heat 1989, Twisted Justice 1990, Killing American Style 1990, Divine Enforcer 1991, Original Gangstas 1996, Mars Attacks! 1996, He Got Game 1998, Any Given Sunday 1999, New Jersey Turnpikes 1999, On the Edge 2002, She Hate Me 2004, Dream Street 2005. *Address:* The Amer–I–Can Program, 269 South Beverly Drive, #1048, Los Angeles, CA 90212, USA. *Telephone:* (310) 652-7884. *Fax:* (310) 652-9353. *E-mail:* info@amer-i-can.org. *Website:* www.amer-i-can.org.

BROWN, John Joseph, AO; Australian politician; *Emeritus Chairman, Tourism Task Force Ltd;* b. 19 Dec. 1931, Sydney; s. of Norman Leslie Brown and Eva May Spencer; m. Jan Murray 1963; four s. one d.; ed St Patrick's Coll., Strathfield and Sydney Univ.; worked as distributor and co. dir in wholesale meat business; Alderman, Parramatta City Council 1970–77; MP for Parramatta, NSW 1977–90; Minister for Sport, Recreation and Tourism 1983–87 (also Minister assisting the Minister for Defence), for Admin. Services 1983–84; Chair. NSW Wholesale Meat Traders' Asscn 1974–76, Tourism Task Force Ltd 1989–, Environmental Choice 1992–94, London/ Sydney Air Race; Dir Tourism Assets Ltd 1992–98, Sea World Man. Ltd 1993–98, Duty Free Operators Accreditation Bd 1998–, Sport Industry Australia, Macquarie Tourism and Leisure, Canterbury Bankstown Leagues Club; mem. Australasian Meat Industry Employees' Union, Sport and Tourism, Advisory Council of the Australian Opera, Advertising Standards Council; Labor Party; Patron Les Clefs d'Or; Olympic Silver Order of Merit 1986; "Australian of the Year" 1986, Gold Award, Australian Inst. of Marketing, Distinguished Service Award, US Sports Acad., Australian Sport Medal 2000. *Leisure interests:* golf, jogging, horse racing, theatre, opera, gardening. *Address:* Tourism Task Force Ltd., Level 10, Westfield Towers, 100 William Street, Sydney, NSW 2011, Australia (office). *Telephone:* (2) 9368-1500. *Fax:* (2) 9810 5344. *E-mail:* jbrown@ttf.org.au (office); jj.brown@bigpond .com (home). *Website:* www.ttf.org.au.

BROWN, Lawrence (Larry); American basketball coach and fmr basketball player; *Head Coach, Charlotte Bobcats;* b. Brooklyn, NY; m. Shelly Brown; one s. four d.; ed Long Beach High School, NY; Univ. of North Carolina; played college basketball Univ. of NC 1960–63, asst coach 1965–67; played for Akron, OH (AAU) 1964–65, then began professional career in American Basketball Asscn (ABA) with New Orleans Buccaneers 1967–68, Oakland Oaks 1968–69, Washington Capitols 1969–70, Virginia Squires 1970–71, Denver Nuggets 1971–72; mem. gold-medal winning US Olympic basketball team 1964; ABA All-Star team 1968–70, Most Valuable Player ABA All-Star Game 1968; won ABA Championship with Oakland 1969; began coaching career as head coach Carolina Cougars 1973–74, then Denver Rockets 1975–76, Denver Nuggets 1977–79 (all ABA), three time ABA coach of the year 1973, 1975, 1976; switched to college coaching UCLA 1979–81, led team to NCAA championship game 1980; returned to professional ranks with Nat. Basketball Asscn (NBA) New Jersey Nets 1981–83; returned to college coaching Univ. of Kansas 1983–88, won Nat. Collegiate Athletic Asscn (NCAA) Championship 1988; returned to professional coaching NBA San Antonio Spurs 1988–93, Los Angeles Clippers 1991–93, Indiana Pacers 1993–97, Philadelphia 76ers 1997–2003, Detroit Pistons 2003–05 (won NBA championship 2004), New York Knicks 2005–06; Exec. Vice President Philadelphia 76ers 2007–08; Head Coach, Charlotte Bobcats 2008–; won 900th NBA game 2003–04 (seventh coach to win 900 games); in 22 seasons as NBA coach has record of 987 wins and 741 losses (.571), ranking fourth all-time among NBA coaches and first amongst active coaches; only coach in NBA history to take seven different teams to play-offs; Asst Coach of gold-medal winning Team USA Olympic Games, Sydney 2000, Head Coach bronze-medal winning Team USA Olympic Games, Athens 2004; winning Head Coach NBA All-Star Game 2001; NBA coach of the year 2001; elected Naismith Memorial Hall of Fame. *Leisure interests:* golf. *Address:* Bobcats Basketball Holdings, LLC, 333 East Trade

Street., Suite 700, Charlotte, NC 28202, USA. *Telephone:* (704) 424-4120. *Fax:* (704) 388-8734. *Website:* www.nba.com/bobcats.

BROWN, Lawrence Michael, MA, PhD, DSc, FRS; British/Canadian physicist and academic; *Professor Emeritus of Physics, University of Cambridge;* b. 18 March 1936, Windsor, Ont.; s. of B. W. and Edith Brown; m. Susan Drucker 1965; one s. two d.; ed Univ. of Toronto, Univ. of Birmingham, UK; work in Cambridge 1960–, Fellow Gonville and Caius Coll. 1963–77, Univ. Demonstrator in Physics 1966, Reader in Structure and Properties of Materials, Dept of Physics 1983–89, Prof. of Physics 1989–2001, Prof. Emer. 2001–; Fellow Robinson Coll. 1977–; Rosenhain Medal, Inst. of Metals 1980, Robert Franklin Mehl Award, TMS 1991, Van Horn Distinguished Lecturer, Case Western Reserve Univ. 1994, Guthrie Medal and Prize, Inst. of Physics 2000, Frontiers of Electron Microscopy and Materials Science (FEMMS) Prize Lecture 2007. *Publications:* many papers in Philosophical Magazine and Acta Metallurgica (now Acta Materialia). *Leisure interests:* reading, gardening. *Address:* Cavendish Laboratory, J. J. Thomson Avenue, Cambridge, CB3 0HE; 74 Alpha Road, Cambridge, CB4 3DG, England (home). *Telephone:* (1223) 337076 (office); (1223) 362987 (home). *E-mail:* lmb12@cam.ac.uk (office).

BROWN, Melanie Janice; British singer; b. 29 May 1975, Leeds, England; m. 1st Jimmy Gulzar 1998 (divorced); two d.; m. 2nd Stephen Belafonte 2007; mem. Touch, later renamed The Spice Girls 1993–2001, as Melanie B (later Melanie G) or 'Scary Spice', reunion tour 2007–08; numerous tours, concerts, television and radio appearances; world tours include UK, Europe, India, USA; solo artist 1998–; two Ivor Novello songwriting awards 1997, Smash Hits Award for Best Band 1997, BRIT Awards for Best Single (for Wannabe), for Best Video (for Say You"ll Be There) 1997, three American Music Awards 1998, Special BRIT Award for Int. Sales 1998. *Film:* Spiceworld: The Movie 1997. *Television:* presenter This is My Moment (ITV 1) 2001. *Recordings include:* albums: with The Spice Girls: Spice 1996, Spiceworld 1997, Forever 2000, Greatest Hits 2007; solo: Hot 2003, LA State of Mind 2005. *Address:* c/o Virgin Records Ltd, 553–79 Harrow Road, London, W10 4RH, England. *Website:* www.melaniebrown.com; www.spicegirlsforever.co.uk.

BROWN, Michael Stuart, BA, MD; American geneticist and academic; *Paul J. Thomas Professor of Genetics and Director, Center of Genetic Diseases, Southwestern Medical School, University of Texas;* b. 13 April 1941, New York; s. of Harvey Brown and Evelyn Katz; m. Alice Lapin 1964; two d.; ed Univ. of Pennsylvania; Intern, then Resident, Mass. Gen. Hosp. Boston 1966–68; served with US Public Health Service 1968–70; Clinical Assoc. Nat. Inst. of Health 1968–71; Asst Prof. Univ. of Texas Southwestern Medical School, Dallas 1971–74, Paul J. Thomas, Prof. of Genetics and Dir Center of Genetic Diseases 1977–; mem. NAS and other scientific socs; numerous hon. degrees; ACS Pfizer Award 1976; Lounsbery Award (NAS) 1979, Lita Annenberg Hazen Award 1982, Albert Lasker Medical Research Award 1985, Nobel Prize in Medicine or Physiology 1985, Nat. Medal of Science USA 1988. *Address:* University of Texas Health Science Center, Department of Molecular Genetics, 5323 Harry Hines Boulevard, Dallas, TX 75390-9046, USA. *Telephone:* (214) 648-2179 (office). *E-mail:* mike.brown@ut-southwestern.edu (office). *Website:* www8.utsouthwestern.edu.

BROWN, Rt Hon. Nicholas (Hugh), PC, BA; British politician; *Chief Whip and Parliamentary Secretary to the Treasury;* b. 13 June 1950; s. of the late R. C. Brown and G. K. Brown (née Tester); ed Swatenden Secondary Modern School, Tunbridge Wells Tech. High School, Univ. of Manchester; trade union officer Gen. and Municipal Workers' Union, Northern Region 1978–83; mem. Newcastle-upon-Tyne City Council 1980–83; MP (Labour) for Newcastle-upon-Tyne E 1983–97, for Newcastle-upon-Tyne E and Wallsend 1997–; Labour spokesman on Legal Affairs 1987–92, on Treasury Affairs 1988–94, on Health 1994–95; Deputy Chief Opposition Whip 1995–97; Chief Whip and Parl. Sec. to the Treasury 1997–98, 2008–, Sec. of State for Agric., Fisheries and Food 1998–2001; Minister of State for Work, Dept for Work and Pensions 2001–03. *Address:* Chief Whip's Office, 9 Downing Street, London, SW1A 2AG, England (office). *Telephone:* (20) 7276-2020 (office). *Fax:* (20) 7276-2015. *E-mail:* ministers@hm-treasury.gov.uk (office). *Website:* www.hm-treasury.gov.uk (office).

BROWN, Richard H. (Dick), BSc; American business executive; *Chairman and Chief Executive Officer, Electronic Data Systems;* b. 3 June 1947, New Brunswick, NJ; ed Ohio Univ.; began working in telecommunications industry 1974–; fmr. Vice-Pres. Sprint Corpn.; Vice-Chair., mem. Bd. of Dirs. and largest subsidiary of Ameritech Corpn. 1993; C.E.O. Illinois Bell; fmr. Pres. and C.E.O. H & R Block Inc. 1995; C.E.O. and mem. Bd. Dirs. Cable & Wireless (C & W) PLC, London; Chair. and C.E.O. Electronic Data Systems (EDS) Co. Dec. 1998–; mem. Bd. Dirs. Vivendi Universal, The Home Depot Inc., DuPont; mem. Business Roundtable (BRT), Business Council, Pres.'s Advisory Cttee. on Trade and Policy Negotiations (ACTPN), U.S.–Japan Business Council; French–American Business Council, Pres.'s Nat. Security Telecommunications Advisory Cttee. (NSTAC); Hon. Dr.Iur. (Ohio Univ.); Hon. Ph.D. (James Madison Univ.). *Address:* Electronic Data Systems, 5400 Legacy Drive, Plano, TX 75024-3199, U.S.A. (office). *Telephone:* (972) 605-6000 (office). *E-mail:* dick.brown@eds.com (office). *Website:* www.eds.com (office).

BROWN, Robert A., BS, MS, PhD; American engineer, academic and university administrator; *President, Boston University;* b. 1951; m. Beverly Brown; two s.; ed Univ. of Texas at Austin; Instructor, Dept of Chemical Eng and Material Science, Univ. of Minnesota 1978; Asst Prof. of Chemical Eng, Massachusetts Inst. of Tech. (MIT) 1979–82, Assoc. Prof. 1982–84, Prof. 1984–2005, Arthur Dehun Little Prof. of Chemical Eng 1986–92, Warren K. Lewis Prof. 1992–2005, Dean of Eng 1996–98, Provost 1998–2005; Pres. Boston Univ. 2005–; Exec. Ed. Journal of Chemical Engineering Science 1991–2004; mem. Pres.'s Council of Advisors on Science and Tech. 2006; mem. American Acad. of Arts and Sciences, Nat. Acad. of Eng, NAS; Chair. Singapore Ministry of Educ. Academic Research Council; fmr Dir Singapore Nat. Research Foundation; Dir DuPont Co. 2007–; Hon. Citizen of Singapore. *Publications:* over 250 papers in areas related to mathematical modelling of transport phenomena in materials. *Address:* Office of the President, University of Boston, 8th Floor, 1 Silber Way, Boston MA 02215, USA (office). *Telephone:* (617) 353-2200 (office). *Fax:* (617) 353-3278 (office). *Website:* www.bu.edu/president (office).

BROWN, Robert James (Bob), MB BS; Australian physician and politician; *Senator for Tasmania;* b. 27 Dec. 1944, Oberon, NSW; pnr, Paul Thomas 1996; ed Blacktown Boys High School, Univ. of Sydney; elected School Capt. in sr year; medical practice, Canberra, London, Sydney, Perth, Launceston 1969–80; moved to Tasmania to work in Launceston gen. practice 1972; cand. for United Tasmania Group 1975; Dir The Wilderness Soc. 1979–84; emerged as leader of campaign to prevent construction of Franklin Dam late 1970s, spent 19 days in Hobart's Risdon Prison 1983; elected to Tasmanian House of Ass. 1983–93, Leader of five Green inds, formed accord with Labor Party 1989–92; unsuccessful cand. for Fed. House of Reps 1993; extensive tours of Australian cities and towns as Australian Greens Nat. Spokesperson 1994–96; Senator for Tasmania (first Australian Greens Senator) 1996–, re-elected 2001, 2007; hosted first Global Greens Conf., Canberra 2001; Leader, Australian Greens 2005–; elected first Fed. Parl. Leader of The Greens 2005–; Founding Pres. Australian Bush Heritage Fund (now Bush Heritage Australia) 1990–96; Australian of the Year, The Australian newspaper 1983, UNEP Global 500 Award 1987, Goldman Environmental Prize (USA) 1990, World's Most Inspiring Politician, BBC Wildlife magazine 1996, Nat. Trust Australian Nat. Treasure 1998, Rainforest Action Network Environmental Hero 2006. *Publications:* several books, including Wild Rivers 1983, Lake Pedder 1986, Tarkine Trails 1994, The Greens (with Peter Singer) 1996, Memo for a Saner World 2004, Tasmania's Recherche Bay 2005. *Leisure interests:* photography, bushwalking, poetry, philosophy. *Address:* GPO Box 404, Hobart, TAS 7001 (office); Parliament House, Canberra, ACT, Australia (office). *Telephone:* (3) 6224-3222 (Hobart) (office); (2) 6277-3170 (Canberra) (office). *Fax:* (3) 6224-2999 (Hobart) (office); (2) 6277-3185 (Canberra) (office). *E-mail:* senator.bob.brown@aph.gov.au (office). *Website:* www.bobbrown.org.au (office); www.aph.gov.au/senate/senators/homepages/s-qd4.htm (office).

BROWN, Ronald Drayton, AM, PhD, FAA; Australian chemist and academic; *Professor Emeritus of Chemistry, Monash University;* b. 14 Oct. 1927, Melbourne; s. of William Harrison Brown and Linda Grace Drayton; m. Florence Catherine Mary Stringer 1950; two s. one d.; ed Wesley Coll., Melbourne, Univ. of Melbourne and Univ. of London, UK; Lecturer, Univ. Coll., London, Univ. of Melbourne; Prof. of Chem., Monash Univ. 1960–93, Head Chem. Dept 1959–92, Prof. Emer. 1993–; current research interests cover theoretical chem., spectroscopy, galactochemistry and life in space; past Pres. Comm. 51 (Bioastronomy) of Int. Astronomical Union; fmr mem. of Exec. Cttee and Bureau, Int. Union of Pure and Applied Chem.; Fellow Australian Acad. of Science (fmr mem. Council, Vice-Pres. and Sec. of Physical Sciences); Matthew Flinders Lecturer 1988; Masson Medal, Royal Chemical Inst. 1948, Rennie Medal 1951, Smith Medal 1959, David Syme Prize for Research, Univ. of Melbourne 1959, Edgeworth-David Medal, Royal Soc. of NSW 1961, Royal Soc. Medal of Victoria 1977, Matthew Flinders Medal (Australian Acad. of Science) 1988. *Publications:* Manual of Elementary Practical Chemistry (co-author), Atomic Structure and the Theory of Valency, The ABZ of Valency, Valency; more than 300 research papers in int. journals. *Leisure interest:* tennis. *Address:* 3 Moonya Road, Glen Iris, Vic. 3146 (home); School of Chemistry, Monash University, Wellington Road, Clayton, Vic. 3168, Australia (office). *Telephone:* (3) 9885-4069 (home); (3) 9905-4550 (office). *E-mail:* rbro6153@bigpond.net.au (home); ronald.brown@sci.monash.edu.au (office). *Website:* web.chem.monash.edu.au/Department/HomePage (office).

BROWN, Sarah; British charity administrator and fmr public relations executive; b. 31 Oct. 1963, Bucks.; d. of Iain Macaulay and Pauline Macaulay; m. Prime Minister Gordon Brown 2000; two s. one d. (deceased); ed Camden High School for Girls, Bristol Univ.; spent much of her early childhood in Tanzania; began professional career at Wolff Olins public relations agency; Founding Pnr, Hobsbawm Macaulay Communications (public relations co.) –2001; Founder and Pres. PiggyBankKids (charity); Founder Jennifer Brown Research Fund 2002; Patron Women's Aid, Maggie's Cancer Caring Centre, Shine, First Women Awards; Dr hc (Wolverhampton) 2007. *Publication:* Magic (co-ed.) 2002. *Address:* 10 Downing Street, London, SW1A 2AA; PiggyBankKids Projects Limited, 5 Montague Close, Minerva House, London, England. *Telephone:* (20) 7556-6855 (PiggyBankKids). *Fax:* (20) 7925-0918. *Website:* www.number-10.gov.uk; www.piggybankkids.org.

BROWN, Sherrod, BA, MA; American politician; *Senator from Ohio;* b. 9 Nov. 1952, Mansfield, Ohio; m. Connie Schultz; two d. one step-s. one step-d.; ed Yale Univ. and Ohio State Univ.; taught at Mansfield br. campus, Ohio State Univ. 1979–81; Ohio State Rep. 1975–82; Ohio Sec. of State 1982–91; mem. US House of Reps 1993–2006, ranking minority mem. on House Energy and Commerce Cttee's Health Sub-cttee, also served on Sub-cttee on Telecommunications and the Internet and Sub-cttee on Commerce, Trade and Consumer Protection, mem. House Int. Relations Cttee, Sub-cttee on Asia and the Pacific; Senator from Ohio 2007–; mem. Congressional Progressive Caucus; Democrat; American Public Health Asscn Distinguished Public Health Legislator of 2002, Congressional Leadership Award, Nat. Asscn of Public Hosps and Health 2005, Congressional Leadership Award, American Coll. of Emergency Physicians 2002, Paul G. Rogers Award, Asscn of Academic Health Centers 2002, recognized by Acad. of Medicine of Cleveland and Northern Ohio Medical Asscn. *Publications:* Congress from the Inside:

Observations from the Majority and the Minority, Myths of Free Trade: Why American Trade Policy Has Failed. Address: 455 Russell Senate Office Bldg, Washington, DC 20510, USA (office). *Telephone:* (202) 224-2315 (office). *Fax:* (202) 228-6321 (office). *Website:* brown.senate.gov (office); www.sherrodbrown.com (office).

BROWN, Shona L., PhD; American business executive; *Senior Vice-President of Business Operations, Google Inc.;* ed Carleton Univ., Canada, Univ. of Oxford, UK (Rhodes Scholar), Stanford Univ.; has taught in Dept of Industrial Eng and Grad. School of Business, Stanford Univ. and within McKinsey's mini-MBA programme; Pnr, McKinsey & Co., worked with tech. clients in Toronto and Los Angeles and Leader, Global Strategy Practice 1995–2003; Vice-Pres. Business Operations, Google Inc. 2003–06, Sr Vice-Pres. Business Operations 2006–. *Publications:* Competing on the Edge: Strategy as Structured Chaos (co-author) 1998; numerous articles in both applied and academic journals. *Address:* Google Headquarters, 1600 Amphitheatre Parkway, Mountain View, CA 94043, USA (office). *Telephone:* (650) 253-0000 (office). *Fax:* (650) 253-0001 (office). *Website:* www.google.com (office).

BROWN, Christina Hambley (Tina), MA, CBE; British writer and magazine editor; b. 21 Nov. 1953, Maidenhead; d. of the late George Hambley Brown and Bettina Iris Mary Brown (née Kohr); m. Harold Matthew Evans 1981; one s. one d.; ed Univ. of Oxford; columnist, Punch magazine 1978; Ed.-in-Chief Tatler Magazine 1979–83, of Vanity Fair Magazine, New York 1984–92, London 1991–92; Ed. The New Yorker 1992–98, Talk magazine 1999–2002; Partner and Chair. Talk Media 1998–2002, Talk Miramax Books 1998–2002; columnist, Washington Post 2003–; Founder and Ed. The Daily Beast (internet news site) 2008–; Most Promising Female Journalist, Katherine Pakenham Prize Sunday Times 1973, Young Journalist of the Year 1978, Univ. of Southern Calif. Distinguished Achievement in Journalism Award 1994. *Publications:* Under the Bamboo Tree (play) (Sunday Times Drama Award) 1973, Happy Yellow (play) 1977, Loose Talk 1979, Life as a Party 1983, The Icarus Complex 2005, The Diana Chronicles 2007. *Address:* The Daily Beast, IAC Headquarters, 555 West 18th Street, New York, NY 10011, USA (office). *E-mail:* editorial@thedailybeast.com (office). *Website:* www.thedailybeast.com.

BROWN, Trisha, BA; American choreographer; *Artistic Director, Trisha Brown Dance Company;* b. 25 Nov. 1936, Aberdeen, Wash.; ed Mills Coll., Calif.; with Judson Dance Theater 1960s; Founder and Artistic Dir Trisha Brown Dance Co. 1970–; mem. Nat. Council on the Arts 1994–97; Hon. mem. American Acad. of Arts and Letters; Officier des Arts et Lettres 2000; numerous hon. doctorates; Nat. Endowment for the Arts Fellowship in Choreography (five times), John Simon Guggenheim Memorial Foundation Fellowship in Choreography (twice), MacArthur Foundation Fellowship Award 1991, Samuel H. Scripps American Dance Festival Award 1994, Prix de la Danse de la Soc. des Auteurs et Compositeurs Dramatiques 1996, NY State Gov.'s Arts Award 1999. *Dance:* has choreographed numerous dances for alternative spaces including rooftops and walls 1961–; Opal Loop/Cloud Installation 1980, Son of Gone Fishin' 1981, Set and Reset 1982, Lateral Pass 1985, Carmen (opera) 1986, Newark 1987, Astral Convertible 1989, Foray Forêt 1990, Astral Converted (50") 1991, For M.G.: The Movie 1991, One Story as in Falling 1992, Another Story as in Falling 1993, Yet Another Story 1994, Long and Dream 1994, If You Couldn't See Me 1994, You Can See Us 1995, M.O. 1995, Twelve Ton Rose 1996, Canto/Pianto 1997, L'Orfeo (opera) 1998, Five Part Weather Invention 1999, Rapture to Leon James 2000. *Address:* Trisha Brown Dance Company, 625 West 55th Street, 2nd Floor, New York, NY 10019, USA (office). *Telephone:* (212) 582-0040 (office), (212) 977-5365 (office). *Website:* www.trishabrowncompany.org (office).

BROWN, William Charles Langdon, CBE; British banker (retd); b. 9 Sept. 1931, London; s. of Charles Leonard Brown and Kathleen May Tizzard; m. Nachiko Sagawa 1959; one s. two d.; ed John Ruskin School, Croydon, Ashbourne Grammar School, Derbyshire; with Chartered Bank of India, Australia and China, serving throughout Far East 1954–75, Area Gen. Man., Hong Kong 1975–87, Sr Gen. Man. (London) for Asia Pacific Region 1987; Exec. Dir Standard Chartered Bank PLC (SCB) 1987, Man. Dir 1988, Deputy Group Chief Exec. 1988, Group Deputy Chair. 1989–91, Dir (non-exec.) 1991–94; Dir and Treasurer Royal Commonwealth Soc. 1991–95, Commonwealth Trust 1991–95; Dir HongKong Investment Trust PLC 1991–97; Dir (non-exec.) Kexim Bank UK Ltd 1992–2003, Arbuthnot Latham & Co. Ltd 1993–99; Chair. (non-exec.) Atlantis Japan Growth Fund Ltd 1996–2002; Unofficial mem. Legis. Council of Hong Kong 1980–85; Hon. DScS (Chinese Univ., Hong Kong) 1987. *Leisure interests:* mountain walking, yoga, skiing, philately, photography, classical music. *Address:* Penthouse B, 15 Portman Square, London, W1H 6LJ (home); Appleshaw, 11 Central Avenue, Findon Valley, Worthing, Sussex, BN14 0DS, England (home). *Telephone:* (20) 7487-5741 (home); (1903) 873175 (home). *Fax:* (20) 7486-3005 (home). *E-mail:* wclbrown@yahoo.co.uk (home).

BROWNBACK, Sam, BS, JD; American politician; *Senator from Kansas;* b. Parker, Kan.; m. Mary Brownback; three c.; ed Kan. State Univ. and Univ. of Kan.; Pnr, law firm in New York; Instructor in Law, Kan. State Univ.; City Attorney, Ogden and Leonardville, Kan.; mem. 104th Congress 1994–97; Senator from Kan. 1996–, mem. Foreign Relations Cttee, Chair. Sub-Cttee on E Asian and Pacific Affairs; Republican; unsuccessful campaign for Republican nomination for Pres. of US 2007. *Address:* 303 Hart Senate Office Building, Washington, DC 20510-0001, USA. *Telephone:* (202) 224-6521 (office). *Website:* brownback.senate.gov (office).

BROWNE, Rt Hon. Des, PC, LLB; British politician and lawyer; b. 22 March 1952, Ayrshire; m.; two s.; ed St Michael's Acad., Kilwinning, Univ. of Glasgow; admitted as solicitor 1976; joined Ross, Harper and Murphy (law firm), Kilmarnock; Co-founder McCluskey Browne (law firm) –1993; unsuccessful cand. for MP for Argyll and Bute 1992; called to the Bar 1993, served as specialist child law advocate; MP for Kilmarnock and Loudoun 1997–2005, for New Kilmarnock and Loudoun 2005–; Parl. Pvt. Sec. to Sec. of State for Scotland Donald Dewar 1998–99, for Adam Ingram 2000; Parl. Under-Sec. of State, NI Office 2001–03; Minister of State, Dept for Work and Pensions (Work) 2003–04; Minister of State, Home Office (Citizenship, Immigration and Nationality) 2004–05; Chief Sec. to Treasury 2005–06; Sec. of State for Defence 2006–08, for Scotland 2007–08; Prime Minister's Special Envoy for Sri Lanka 2009–; Sec. Scottish Labour Party Working Party on Prison System 1988–90; mem. Commons Select Cttees on NI Affairs 1997–98, Public Admin 1999–2000, Jt Cttee on Human rights 2001; mem. Labour Party Departmental Cttees for NI, Treasury, Civil Liberties Group 1997–2001; Hon. Sec. Labour Party Departmental Cttee for Social Security 1997–2001. *Address:* 32 Grange Street, Kilmarnock, KA1 2DD, Scotland (office); House of Commons, London, SW1A 0AA, England (office). *Telephone:* (1563) 520267 (constituency) (office). *Fax:* (1563) 539439 (constituency) (office). *E-mail:* browned@parliament.uk (office). *Website:* www.kilmarnockandloudoun.co.uk (office).

BROWNE, Michael (Mike); Saint Vincent and the Grenadines government official; Minister of Educ., Youth and Sport –2005, of Foreign Affairs and of Commerce and Trade May–Dec. 2005. *Address:* c/o Ministry of Foreign Affairs, Administrative Centre, Kingstown, Saint Vincent and the Grenadines (office).

BROWNE OF MADINGLEY, Baron (Life Peer), cr. 2001, of Madingley in the County of Cambridgeshire, **(Edmund) John (Philip) Browne,** BSc, MS, FRS, FREng, FInstP, FInstPet, CIMgt; British business executive; *Managing Director and Managing Partner, Riverstone Europe;* b. 20 Feb. 1948, Hamburg, Germany; ed Univ. of Cambridge, Stanford Univ., Calif., USA; joined BP 1966; various exploration and production posts Anchorage, New York, San Francisco, London and Canada 1969–83; Group Treas. and Chief Exec. BP Finance Int. 1984–86; Exec. Vice-Pres. and Chief Financial Officer The Standard Oil Co., Cleveland, Ohio 1986–87, BP America and CEO Standard Oil Production Co. (following BP/Standard merger) 1987–89; Man. Dir and CEO BP Exploration, London 1989–91; Man. Dir The British Petroleum Co. PLC 1991–95, Group CEO 1995–98, Group CEO BP Amoco (now BP PLC) 1998–2007 (resgnd); Man. Dir and Man. Pnr, Riverstone Europe 2007–; mem. Bd of Dirs (non-exec.) Foster + Pnrs 2007–, Goldman Sachs 1999–2007, SmithKline Beecham 1996–99, Intel Corpn 1997–2006; mem. Supervisory Bd Daimler Chrysler AG 1998–2001, Chair.'s Council 2001–04; Chair. Advisory Bd Cambridge Business School; Chair. Emer. Advisory Bd, Stanford Grad. School of Business; Pres. Royal Acad. of Eng; Vice-Pres. Prince of Wales Business Leaders Forum; mem. British-American Business Council (also fmr Chair.), Cambridge Consultative Cttee and Chem. Appeal (also fmr Chair.), Guild of Cambridge Benefactors, Council of the Foundation for Science and Tech., Bd of Catalyst, School of Econs and Man., Tsinghua Univ. (Chair. Advisory Bd); Chair. Advisory Bd Apax Pnrs Worldwide 2006–07; Trustee, British Museum 1995–2005, Tate Gallery 2007– (Chair. 2009–); Global Counsellor, Conference Bd, Inc.; Fellow, Inst. of Mining and Metallurgy; Sr Mem. St Anthony's Coll. Oxford; Hon. Fellow, St John's Coll. Cambridge; Hon. FIChemE; Hon. FGS; Hon. FIMechE; Hon. FRSC; Hon. Trustee, Chicago Symphony Orchestra; Hon. DEng (Heriot Watt, Colorado School of Mines, Belfast); Hon. DTech (Robert Gordon); Hon. LLD (Dundee, Thunderbird, Notre Dame); Hon. DUniv (Sheffield Hallam); Hon. DSc (Cranfield, Hull, Leuven, Warwick, Mendeleyev University of Chemical Technology—Moscow, Buckingham); Hon. DLitt (Arizona State Univ.); Prince Philip Medal, Royal Acad. of Eng 1999, Henry Shaw Medal, Missouri Botanical Gardens, Gold Medal, Inst. of Man., Ernest C. Arbuckle Award, Stanford Business School Alumni Asscn 2001, Soc. of Petroleum Engineers Public Service Award 2002. *Address:* RiverStone Management, 2nd Floor, Mint House, 77, Mansell Street, London, E1 8AF, England (office). *Telephone:* (20) 7977-1600 (office). *Website:* www.rsml.co.uk (office).

BROWNE-WILKINSON, Baron (Life Peer), cr. 1991, of Camden, in the London Borough of Camden; **Nicolas Christopher Henry Browne-Wilkinson,** PC, QC, BA; British judge; *Chairman, Financial Markets Law Committee, Bank of England;* b. 30 March 1930, London; s. of the late Canon A. R. Browne-Wilkinson and Molly Browne-Wilkinson; m. 1st Ursula de Lacy Bacon 1955 (died 1987); three s. two d.; m. 2nd Hilary Tuckwell 1990; ed Lancing Coll., Magdalen Coll., Oxford; called to Bar, Lincoln's Inn 1953, Bencher 1977; QC 1972; Jr Counsel to Registrar of Restrictive Trading Agreements 1964–66, to Attorney-Gen. in Charity Matters 1966–72, in bankruptcy, to Dept of Trade and Industry 1966–72; a Judge of the Courts of Appeal of Jersey and Guernsey 1976–77; Judge of the High Court, Chancery Div. 1977–83; a Lord Justice of Appeal 1983–85; Vice-Chancellor of the Supreme Court 1985–91; Lord of Appeal in Ordinary 1991–2000, Sr Law Lord 1998–2000; currently Chair. Financial Markets Law Cttee, Bank of England; Pres. Employment Appeal Tribunal 1981–83, Senate of the Inns of Court and the Bar 1984–86; Fellow, St Edmund Hall, Oxford 1986, Magdalen Coll. 1993, American Coll. of Trial Lawyers, American Law Inst. *Leisure interests:* gardening, music. *Address:* House of Lords, London, SW1A 0PW (office); Financial Markets Law Committee, c/o Bank of England, Threadneedle Street, London, EC2R 8AH, England. *Telephone:* (20) 7219-3202 (office). *Website:* www.bankofengland.co.uk.

BROWNER, Carol Martha, BA, JD; American lawyer and government official; *White House Coordinator for Energy and Climate;* b. 16 Dec. 1955, Miami, Fla; d. of Michael Browner and Isabella Browner (née Hugues); m. 1st Michael Podhorzer (divorced); one s.; m. 2nd Thomas Joseph Downey 2007; two step-c.; ed Univ. of Florida; gen. counsel of a Cttee of Fla Legis. 1979–83; Assoc. Dir Citizen Action, Washington, DC 1983–86; mem. staff Senator

Lawton Chiles 1986–89; mem. staff Senate Cttee on Energy and Natural Resources 1989; Legis. Dir on staff of Senator Al Gore 1989–90; Head of Dept of Environmental Regulation, State of Fla 1990–93; Admin. Environmental Protection Agency 1993–2001, Co-founder and Prin. The Albright Group LLC (consulting firm), Washington, DC 2001–08, also Prin. Albright Capital Management (investment advisory firm); Coordinator for Energy and Climate, The White House, Washington, DC 2009–; fmr mem. Bd of Dirs Audubon Soc., League of Conservation Voters, Alliance for Climate Protection; Outstanding Mother of the Year, Nat. Mother's Day Cttee 1997, Woman of the Year, Glamour magazine 1998, Guy M. Bradley Lifetime Achievement Award, S Florida Chapter of Audubon Soc., Lifetime Environmental Achievement Award, New York State Bar Asscn. *Address:* The White House Office, 1600 Pennsylvania Avenue, NW, Washington, DC 20500, USA (office). *Telephone:* (202) 456-1414 (office). *Fax:* (202) 456-2461 (office). *Website:* www.whitehouse.gov (office).

BROWNING, Keith Anthony, BSc, PhD, DIC, FRS, ARCS; British meteorologist and academic; *Professor Emeritus, Department of Meteorology, University of Reading;* b. 31 July 1938, Sunderland; s. of the late James Anthony Browning and Amy Hilda Greenwood; m. Ann Baish 1962; one s. two d.; ed Imperial Coll. of Science and Tech., Univ. of London; Research Atmospheric Physicist, Air Force Cambridge Research Labs, Mass, USA 1962–66; Prin. then Chief Meteorological Officer, Meteorological Office Radar Research Lab., Royal Signals and Radar Establishment, Malvern, Worcs. 1966–74, 1975–85; Chief Scientist, Nat. Hail Research Experiment, Nat. Center for Atmospheric Research, Boulder, Colo, USA 1974–75; Deputy Dir (Physical Research), Meteorological Office, Bracknell, Berks. 1985–89, Dir of Research 1989–91; Visiting Prof., Dept of Meteorology, Univ. of Reading 1988–94; Visiting Scientist, Jt Centre for Mesoscale Meteorology, Univ. of Reading 1991–92, Dir 1992–2003; Prof. in Dept of Meteorology, Univ. of Reading 1995–2003, Prof. Emer. 2003–; Visiting Prof. of Atmospheric Science, School of Earth and Environment, Univ. of Leeds 2006–2009; Dir Univs Weather Research Network 2000–03; Dir Univs Facility for Atmospheric Measurements 2001–03; Chair. Meteorology & Atmospheric Physics Sub-Cttee of British Cttee for Geodesy and Geophysics 1985–89; mem. Natural Environment Research Council 1984–87; Pres. Royal Meteorological Soc. 1988–90; mem. Scientific Steering Group, Global Energy and Water Cycle Experiment 1988–97; Jt Scientific Cttee, World Climate Research Programme 1990–94; mem. Scientific Steering Cttee, World Weather Research Programme 1996–2005; mem. Academia Europaea 1989–; Foreign Assoc., Nat. Acad. of Eng (USA) 1992–; Fellow, American Meteorological Soc. 1975–; Fellow, Royal Soc. 1978–; Chartered Meteorologist and Fellow, Royal Meteorological Soc., Hon. mem. 2006–,; Ministry of Defence L. G. Groves Memorial Prize 1969, Inst. of Physics Charles Chree Medal 1981, Symons Gold Medal 2001 and three other awards from Royal Meteorological Soc., Carl Gustaf Rossby Medal 2003 and two other awards from American Meteorological Soc. *Publications:* about 200 articles on meteorology since 1962. *Leisure interests:* home and garden. *Address:* High Croft, Under Loughrigg, Ambleside LA22 9LJ, England (home). *Telephone:* (153) 9433615 (home). *E-mail:* annandkeith@vodafone.net (home).

BROWNLIE, Ian, CBE, QC, DCL, FBA; British international law practitioner, barrister and arbitrator; *Queen's Counsel, Blackstone Chambers;* b. 19 Sept. 1932, Liverpool; s. of Amy Isabella Atherton and John Nason Brownlie; m. 1st Jocelyn Gale 1957; one s. two d.; m. 2nd Christine Apperley, 1978; ed Alsop High School, Liverpool, Hertford Coll. Oxford and King's Coll., Cambridge; called to Bar (Gray's Inn) 1958; in practice 1967–; QC 1979; mem. Blackstone Chambers; Bencher of Gray's Inn 1988; Fellow, Wadham Coll. Oxford 1963–76; Prof. of Int. Law, London Univ. (attached to LSE) 1976–80; Chichele Prof. of Public Int. Law, Oxford and Fellow of All Souls 1980–99; Dir of Studies, Int. Law Asscn 1982–91; Lecturer, Hague Acad. of Int. Law 1995; Judge, European Nuclear Energy Tribunal 1995–2000, Pres. 1996–2000; mem. Inst. of Int. Law 1983, mem. Int. Law Comm. of UN 1997–2008 (Chair. 2007–08); Distinguished Fellow, All Souls Coll. Oxford 2004; Hon. Mem. American Soc. of Int. Law 2004, Indian Soc. of Int. Law 2009; Commdr, Order of Merit of the Norwegian Crown. *Publications:* International Law and the Use of Force by States 1963, Principles of Public International Law 1966, Encyclopaedia of African Boundaries 1979, State Responsibility, Part I 1983, Liber Amicorum for Lord Wilberforce 1987; British Year Book of International Law (co-ed.) 1974–99. *Leisure interests:* travel, book collecting, maps. *Address:* Blackstone Chambers, Temple, London, EC4Y 9BW, England (office). *Telephone:* (20) 7583-1770 (office). *Fax:* (20) 7822-7350 (office). *Website:* www.blackstonechambers.com (office).

BROWNLOW, Kevin; British film historian and television director; b. 2 June 1938, Crowborough, Sussex; s. of Robert Thomas Brownlow and Niña Fortnum; m. Virginia Keane 1969; one d.; ed Univ. Coll. School, Hampstead; joined World Wide Pictures 1955; became film ed., then co-dir 1964; with Thames TV 1975–90. *Films include:* It Happened Here 1964, Winstanley 1975 (both with Andrew Mollo). *Television includes:* 13-part series Hollywood 1980, three-part Unknown Chaplin 1983, three-part British Cinema 1986, three-part Buster Keaton: A Hard Act to Follow 1987, two-part Harold Lloyd 1988, three-part D. W. Griffith 1993, six-part Cinema Europe: The Other Hollywood 1995 (all with David Gill), Universal Horror 1998, Lon Chaney: A Thousand Faces 2000, The Tramp and the Dictator (with Michael Kloft) 2002, Cecil B. De Mille: American Epic 2003; with Christopher Bird: Buster Keaton: So Funny It Hurt 2004, Garbo 2005, I'm King Kong: The Exploits of Merion C. Cooper 2005. *Publications:* Parade's Gone By 1968, The War, the West and the Wilderness 1978, Napoleon (Abel Gance's Classic Film) 1983, Behind the Mask of Innocence 1990, David Lean: A Biography 1996, Mary Pickford Rediscovered 1999. *Address:* c/o Photoplay Productions, 21 Princess Road, London, NW1 8JR, England (office). *Telephone:* (20) 7722-2500.

BROWSE, Sir Norman Leslie, Kt, MD, FRCP, FRCS; British government official and surgeon (retd); *President, States of Alderney, Channel Islands;* b. 1 Dec. 1931, London; s. of Reginald Browse and Margaret Browse; m. Jeanne Menage 1957; one s. one d.; ed St Bartholomew's Hosp. Medical Coll. and Univ. of Bristol; Capt. RAMC 1957–59; Sr House Officer and Registrar, Bristol 1959–62; Lecturer in Surgery, Westminster Hosp. 1962–65; Harkness Fellow, Research Assoc. Mayo Clinic, Rochester, Minn. 1964–65; Reader in Surgery and Consultant Surgeon, St Thomas' Hosp. 1965–72, Prof. of Vascular Surgery 1972–81, Prof. of Surgery 1981–96, Consulting Surgeon 1996–; Hon. Consultant to Army and RAF 1980–96; Prof. of Surgery, United Medical and Dental Schools 1981–96; Prof. Emer. Univ. of London 1996–; Pres. States of Alderney, CI 2002–; Pres. Royal Coll. of Surgeons of England 1992–95; Chair., Jt Consultants Cttee 1994–98, Lord Brock Memorial Trust 1994–2001; Vice-Chair. British Vascular Foundation 1997–; Visiting Prof. and Lecturer, Cape Town, Johannesburg, Perth, Sydney, Melbourne, Brisbane, Boston, Ann Arbor, San Diego, Los Angeles, Vancouver, Seattle, Singapore, Hong Kong, Madras, Sri Lanka, Delhi, Kuwait, Paris, Marseille, Barcelona, Amsterdam, Copenhagen, Stockholm, Helsinki; mem. Council Marlborough Coll. 1990–2001; Gov. American Coll. of Surgeons 1997–2003; Fellow, King's Coll., London 2000–; Patron HOPE 2002–; Hon. Fellow Royal Coll. of Physicians and Surgeons (Glasgow) 1993; Hon. FRACS 1994; Hon. Fellow in Dental Surgery 1994; Hon. Fellow Royal Coll. of Surgeons in Ireland 1995; Hon. FACS 1995; Hon. Fellow Faculty of Accident and Emergency Medicine 1995; Hon. FRCSE 1996; Hon. Fellow Coll. of Medicine of S Africa 1996; Distinguished Alumnus, Mayo Clinic 1993; Hon. Freeman Worshipful Co. of Barbers 1997; Arris and Gale Medal 1968, Abraham Colles Medal 1990, Kinmouth Medal 1991, Vicary Medal 2000. *Publications:* Physiology and Pathology of Bed Rest 1964, Symptoms and Signs of Surgical Disease 1978, Reducing Operation for Lymphoedema 1986, Diseases of the Veins 1989, Diseases of the Lymphatics (co-author) 2003. *Leisure interests:* marine art, medieval history, sailing. *Address:* Corbet House, Butes Lane, Alderney, GY9 3UW, Channel Islands (home). *E-mail:* norman.browse@virgin.net (home).

BROYLES, William Dodson, Jr, MA; American journalist; b. 8 Oct. 1944, Houston; s. of William Dodson and Elizabeth (née Bills) Broyles; m. Sybil Ann Newman 1973; one s. one d.; ed Rice Univ., Houston, Oxford Univ.; US Marine Corps Reserve 1969–71; teacher Philosophy US Naval Acad. 1970–71; Asst Supt Houston Public Schools 1971–72; Ed.-in-Chief Texas Monthly 1972–82; Ed.-in-Chief California Magazine 1980–82; Ed.-in-Chief Newsweek Magazine 1982–84; Columnist, US News and World Report 1986; Co-producer, exec. consultant China Beach (TV programme) 1988–; screenwriter Apollo 13 1995; Bronze Star.

BRUBECK, David (Dave) Warren, BA; American musician; b. 6 Dec. 1920, Concord, Calif.; s. of Howard P. Brubeck and Elizabeth Ivey; m. Iola Whitlock 1942; five s. one d.; ed Pacific and Mills Colls; Leader Dave Brubeck Octet, Trio and Quartet 1946–; formed Dave Brubeck Quartet 1951; numerous tours and recordings; Duke Ellington Fellow, Yale Univ.; composer of 250 jazz pieces and songs; mem. American Jazz Hall of Fame 1995; f. Brubeck Inst., Univ. of the Pacific 2000; Hon. PhD (Univ. of Pacific, Fairfield Univ., Univ. of Bridgeport, Mills Coll., Niagara Univ., Kalamazoo Coll.); Jazz Pioneer Award, BMI 1985, Compostela Humanitarian Award 1986, Connecticut Arts Award 1987, American Eagle Award, Nat. Music Council 1988, Gerard Manley Hopkins Award 1991, Nat. Medal of the Arts 1994, Lifetime Achievement Award, Nat. Acad. of Recording Arts and Sciences 1996, Univ. of Notre Dame Laetare Medal 2006, BBC Jazz Lifetime Achievement Award 2007; many awards from trade magazines including Metronome, Downbeat, Billboard, Melodymaker. *Recordings include:* Dave Brubeck - Jazz At Storyville 1951, Jazz Goes to College 1954, Jazz Impressions of USA 1956, Dave Digs Disney 1957, The Riddle 1959, Brubeck a la Mode 1960, Jingle Bell Jazz 1962, Time Changes 1963, Bravo! Brubeck! 1967, The Gates of Justice 1969, All the Things We Are 1973, A Cut Above 1978, Back Home 1979, Paper Moon 1981, Moscow Night 1987, Quiet as the Moon 1988, Nightshift 1993, Just You, Just Me 1994, So What's New 1997, The Crossing 2001. *Extended works:* ballets: Points on Jazz 1962, Glances 1976; orchestral: Elementals 1963, They All Sang Yankee Doodle 1976; flute and guitar: Tritonis 1979; piano: Reminiscences of the Cattle Country 1946, Four by Four 1946; Oratorios: The Light in the Wilderness 1968, Beloved Son 1978, Voice of the Holy Spirit 1985; cantatas: Gates of Justice 1969, Truth is Fallen 1971, La Fiesta de la Posada 1975, In Praise of Mary 1989; chorus and orchestra: Pange Lingua Variations 1983, Upon this Rock Chorale and Fugue 1987, Lenten Triptych 1988, Joy in the Morning 1991; Mass: To Hope! A Celebration 1980; SATB Chorus: I See, Satie 1987, Four New England Pieces 1988; Earth is our Mother 1992, To Hope! A Celebration, a Mass 1996, Regret 2001, Chromatic Fantasy Sonata 2002. *Address:* The Brubeck Institute, University of the Pacific, 3601 Pacific Avenue, Stockton, CA 95211; c/o Sutton Artists Corporation, 20 West Park Avenue, Suite 305, Long Beach, NY 11561; Box 216, Wilton, CT 06897, USA.

BRUCE, Christopher, CBE; British ballet dancer and choreographer; b. 3 Oct. 1945, Leicester; s. of Alexander Bruce and Ethel Parker; m. Marian Meadowcroft 1967; two s. one d.; ed Rambert School, London; dancer, Ballet Rambert, London 1963–80, Assoc. Dir 1975–79, Assoc. Choreographer 1979–87, Artistic Dir Rambert Dance Co. 1994–2003; Assoc. Choreographer, English Nat. Ballet (fmrly London Festival Ballet), London 1986–91; Assoc. Choreographer, Houston Ballet 1989–; choreographer for Kent Opera, Nederlands Dans Theater, Ballet du Grand Théâtre de Genève, etc; Dr hc (De Montfort) 2000; Hon. DLitt (Exeter) 2001; Evening Standard Inaugural Dance Award 1974, Int. Theatre Inst. Award 1993, Evening Standard Ballet Award 1996. *Ballets include:* George Frideric 1969, For Those Who Die as Cattle 1971, There Was a Time 1972, Weekend 1974, Ancient Voices of Children 1975, Black Angels 1976, Cruel Garden 1977, Night with Waning Moon 1979, Dancing Day 1981, Ghost Dances 1981, Berlin Requiem 1982,

Concertino 1983, Intimate Pages 1984, Ceremonies 1986, Swansong 1987, Symphony in Three Movements 1989, Waiting 1993, Crossing 1994, Meeting Point 1995 (for 'United We Dance' Int. Festival celebrating 50 years of UN), Quicksilver (tribute to Marie Rambert to celebrate Rambert Dance Co.'s 70th anniversary) 1996, Stream 1996, Four Scenes 1998, God's Plenty 1999, Hurricane 2000, Grinning in Your Face 2001, 3 Songs, 2 Voices 2005, A Steel Garden 2005, Hush 2006, Shift 2007, Dance at the Crossroads 2007. *Address:* c/o Rambert Dance Company, 94 Chiswick High Road, London, W4 1SH, England; c/o Houston Ballet, 1921 West Bell Street, Houston, TX 77019, USA. *Website:* www.rambert.org.uk; www.houstonballet.org.

BRUCKHEIMER, Jerry, BA,; American film and TV producer; b. 1945, Detroit, Mich.; m. Linda Bruckheimer; ed Univ. of Arizona; fmr producer of TV commercials; formed Don Simpson/Jerry Bruckheimer Productions with the late Don Simpson 1983; formed Jerry Bruckheimer Films 1996; Hon. DFA Univ. of Arizona Coll. of Fine Arts; ShoWest Producer of the Year 1999, David O. Selznick Lifetime Achievement Award 2000, Emmy Award 2004, 2005, 2006, Nat. Bd of Review Producers Award 2004, Variety Showman of the Year 2006, Salute to Excellence, Museum of TV and Radio 2006, Norman Lear Achievement in TV Award 2007. *Films include:* (assoc. producer) Culpepper Cattle Company 1972, Rafferty and the Gold Dust Twins 1975, (producer) Farewell My Lovely 1975, March or Die 1977, Defiance 1980, American Gigolo 1980, Thief 1981, Cat People 1982, Young Doctors in Love 1982, Flashdance 1983, Beverly Hills Cop 1984, Thief of Hearts 1984, Top Gun 1986, Beverly Hills Cop II 1987, Days of Thunder 1990, The Ref (exec. producer) 1994, Dangerous Minds 1995, Bad Boys 1995, Crimson Tide 1995, The Rock 1996, Con Air 1997, Enemy of the State 1998, Armageddon 1998, Gone in 60 Seconds 2000, Coyote Ugly 2000, Remember the Titans 2000, Pearl Harbor 2001, Black Hawk Down 2002, Bad Company 2002, Kangaroo Jack 2003, Pirates of the Caribbean 2003, Bad Boys 2003, Veronica Guerin 2003, King Arthur 2004, National Treasure 2004, Pirates of the Caribbean: Dead Man's Chest 2006, Glory Road 2006, Deja Vu 2006, Pirates of the Caribbean: At World's End 2007, National Treasure: Book of Secrets 2007, Confessions of a Shopaholic 2009, G-Force 2009, Prince of Persia: The Sands of Time 2010, The Sorcerer's Apprentice 2010. *Television:* exec. producer CSI: Crime Scene Investigation, The Amazing Race, CSI: Miami, Without a Trace, Cold Case, CSI: New York, Eleventh Hour, The Line. *Leisure interest:* ice hockey. *Address:* c/o Jerry Bruckheimer Films Inc., 1631 10th Street, Santa Monica, CA 90404, USA (office). *Telephone:* (310) 664-6260 (office). *Fax:* (310) 664-6261 (office). *Website:* www.jbfilms.com (office).

BRUCKMANN, Gerhart, PhD; Austrian politician and statistician; b. 9 Jan. 1932, Vienna; s. of Friedrich Bruckmann and Anny Bruckmann (née Pötzl); m. Hilde Bartl 1961; two s.; ed Univ. of Graz, Vienna and Rome, Antioch Coll., USA; with Austrian Fed. Chamber of Commerce 1957–67; Prof. of Statistics, Univ. of Linz 1967–68, Univ. of Vienna 1968–92; Dir Inst. for Advanced Studies 1968–73; Consultant Int. Inst. for Applied Systems Analysis 1973–83, Council mem. 1983–86; mem. Parl. 1986–94, 1999–2002; Bd mem. Austrian Sr Citizens' Union 1998–; Exec. Officer European Sr Citizens' Union 1998–2001; mem. Austrian Acad. of Sciences; Hon. PhD (Linz) 1998. *Publications:* Auswege in die Zukunft 1974, Sonnenkraft statt Atomenergie 1978, Groping in the Dark (with D. Meadows and J. Richardson) 1982, Megatrends für Österreich 1988, Österreicher wer bist du? 1989. *Leisure interest:* collecting anchor building blocks. *Address:* Österr. Seniorenbund, Lichtenfelsgasse 7, 1010 Vienna (office); Zehenthofgasse 11, 1190 Vienna, Austria (home). *Telephone:* (431) 40126-151 (office). *Fax:* (431) 4066-266 (office).

BRUCKNER, Pascal, DèsSc, PhD; French writer and lecturer; b. 15 Dec. 1948, Paris; s. of René Bruckner and Monique Bruckner; m. Violaine Barret 1970 (divorced 1973); one s.; also one d. by Caroline Thompson; ed Lycée Henri IV, Univs de Paris I (Sorbonne), Paris VII (Jussieu); annual travels in Asia 1977–90; Lecturer, Inst. d'Etudes Politiques, Paris 1990–94; Visiting Prof., Univ. of San Diego and New York Univ. 1986–95; mem. Bd of Dirs Action contre la faim 1983–88; mem. Cercle de l'Oratoire (French think tank) 2001–; Chevalier des Arts et des Lettres, Légion d'honneur 2002. *Theatre:* many of his books have been played on stage throughout Europe and in India. *Publications:* Le Nouveau Désordre Amoureux 1977, Lune de Fiel 1982 (adapted for screen by Roman Polanski under the title Bitter Moon 1992), Le sanglot de l'homme blanc 1983, Le palais des claques 1986, Le Divin Enfant 1992, La Tentation de l'Innocence (Prix Médicis) 1995, Les Voleurs de Beauté (Prix Renaudot) 1997, Les ogres anonymes 1998, L' Euphorie perpétuelle, essai sur Le devóir de bonheur 2000, Misère de la prospérité. La religion marchande et ses ennemis (Sénat Prix du Livre d'économie) 2002, Au secours, le Père Noël revient 2003, L'amour du prochain 2006, La Tyrannie de la pénitence: Essai sur le masochisme en Occident 2006; translations in 25 countries. *Leisure interests:* piano, sports, fantasy films. *Address:* 8 rue Marie Stuart, 75002 Paris,; c/o Editions Denoel, 9 Rue de Cherche-Midi, 75248 Paris, France (office). *Telephone:* 1-40-26-68-79. *Fax:* 1-40-56-34-37. *E-mail:* bruckner@wanadoo.fr (home); contact@lemeilleurdesmondes.org (office). *Website:* www.lemeilleurdesmondes.org.

BRUECKNER, Keith Allan, MA, PhD; American professor of physics (retd); b. 19 March 1924, Minneapolis, Minn.; s. of Leo John and Agnes Holland Brueckner; m. Bonnie Brueckner; two s. one d.; ed Univs of Minnesota and California (Berkeley), Inst. for Advanced Study, Princeton; Asst Prof. Indiana Univ. 1951–54, Assoc. Prof. 1954–55; Physicist, Brookhaven Nat. Lab. (NY) 1955–56; Prof. of Physics, Univ. of Pennsylvania 1956–59; Prof. of Physics, Univ. of Calif. (San Diego) 1959– (now retd); Vice-Pres. and Dir of Research, Inst. for Defense Analyses, Wash., DC 1961–62; Tech. Dir KMS Tech. Center, San Diego 1968–71; Exec. Vice-Pres. and Tech. Dir KMS Fusion Inc., Ann Arbor 1971–74; Consulting Ed., Pure and Applied Physics Series, Academic Press 1964–; mem. NAS; Hon. DSc (Indiana) 1976; Dannie Heinemann Prize for Mathematical Physics 1963. *Publications:* numerous articles in scientific journals. *Leisure interests:* mountain climbing, skiing, sailing, surfing. *Address:* c/o Department of Physics, University of California at San Diego, La Jolla, CA 92093 (office); 3120 Almahurst Row, La Jolla, CA 92037, USA. *Telephone:* (619) 452-2892 (office).

BRUEL, Jean-Marc André; French business executive; *Chairman, Firmenich SA;* b. 18 Feb. 1936, Akbou, Algeria; s. of René Bruel and Jeanine Poirson; m. Anne-Mary Barthod 1962; two s. two d.; ed Ecole Centrale des Arts et Manufactures; Head of Tech. Services, Rhodiaceta, Brazil 1964; Dir nylon polyester factory, Rhône-Poulenc, Brazil 1968; Deputy Dir-Gen. of Textile Poduction Rhône-Poulenc, Brazil 1971; Deputy Dir-Gen. Div. of Plant Hygiene, Groupe Rhône-Poulenc 1975, Dir-Gen. 1976; Asst to Pres. and mem. Exec. Cttee Rhône-Poulenc 1979–80, Deputy Dir-Gen. 1980, Dir-Gen. 1982–84; mem. Exec. Cttee Sandoz, Basle 1985–87; Dir-Gen. Rhône Poulenc 1987–92, Vice-Pres. 1992–99; Pres. Rhône Poulenc Chimie 1987–92; Vice-Pres. European Council of Fed. of Chemical Industry (Cefic) 1988; Pres. Soc. of Chemical Industry 1993–94, Villette Enterprises 1995–2005, Institut Curie 1998–2002; mem. Supervisory Bd Sanofi-Aventis 1999–2004, ind. dir 2004–; Chair. Firmenich SA, Geneva 2000–; mem. Bd of Dirs Rhodia 2002–05; Chevalier Légion d'honneur, Officier Ordre nat. du Mérite. *Leisure interests:* tennis, sailing. *Address:* Firmenich SA, Route de La Plaine 125, 1283 La Plaine, Geneva, Switzerland (office); 105 bis rue de Longchamp, 92200 Neuilly-sur-Seine, France (home). *Telephone:* (22) 780-22-11 (office). *Fax:* (22) 754-14-73 (office). *Website:* www.firmenich.com (office).

BRUFAU NIUBÓ, Antonio, MBA; Spanish business executive; *Chairman and CEO, Repsol YPF SA;* b. 1948, Mollerussa, Lérida; ed Univ. of Barcelona, IESE Business School, Univ. of Navarra; fmr Partner and Head of Audit Div., Arthur Andersen; Asst Gen. Man. La Caixa 1998, Man. Dir La Caixa Group 1999–2004; mem. Bd of Dirs Repsol YPF SA 1996–, Chair. and CEO 2004–, Chair. Man. Cttee, mem. Global E & P Cttee, Global Downstream Cttee, Human Resources Cttee; Chair. Gas Natural SDG 1997–2004, Vice-Chair. 2004–; Chair. Comupet Madrid 2008, S.L., Fundation Repsol YPF; Pres. Círculo de Economía de Barcelona 2002–05; fmr mem. Bd of Dirs Enagás, Abertis, Aguas de Barcelona, Colonial, Suez, Caixa Holding, CaixaBank France, CaixaBank Andorra; mem. Exec. Cttee ICC. *Address:* Repsol YPF SA, Paseo de la Castellana 278, 28046 Madrid, Spain (office). *Telephone:* (91) 3488000 (office). *Fax:* (91) 3482821 (office). *E-mail:* info@repsol.com (office). *Website:* www.repsol.com (office).

BRUGUERA, Sergi; Spanish fmr professional tennis player; b. 16 Jan. 1971, Barcelona; s. of Luis Bruguera; coached by his father; Nat. Jr Champion 1987; turned professional 1988; winner French Open 1993, 1994, finalist 1997; Olympic silver medal, Atlanta, USA 1996; winner of 17 titles (three doubles); retd 2002; currently plays Delta Tour of Champions. *Address:* Delta Tour of Champions, ATP Tennis International Headquarters, 201 ATP Boulevard, Ponte Vedra Beach, FL 32082, USA. *Telephone:* (904) 285-8000. *Fax:* (904) 285-5966. *Website:* www.atptennis.com/championstour/default.asp.

BRUININKS, Robert H., BA, MA, PhD; American university administrator, psychologist and academic; *President, University of Minnesota;* m. Dr Susan Andrea Hagstrum; three s.; ed Western Michigan Univ., George Peabody Coll. (now part of Vanderbilt Univ.; Asst Prof., Dept of Educational Psychology, Univ. of Minnesota 1968, later Prof., Dean, Exec. Vice-Pres. and Provost Univ. of Minnesota, Pres. 2002–; Fellow, American Asscn on Mental Retardation, American Psychological Asscn, American Psychological Soc.; named by Minnesota Monthly magazine Minnesotan of the Year 2004. *Publications:* more than 90 journal articles and 70 book chapters, as well as training materials and several nationally standardized tests. *Address:* Office of the President, University of Minnesota, 202 Morrill Hall, 100 Church Street SE, Minneapolis, MN 55455, USA (office). *Telephone:* (612) 626-1616 (office). *Fax:* (612) 625-3875 (office). *E-mail:* UPres@umn.edu (office). *Website:* www1.umn.edu (office).

BRUMMELL, Paul, BA; British diplomatist; *Ambassador to Kazakhstan and Non-Resident Ambassador to Kyrgyzstan;* b. 28 Aug. 1965, Harpenden; s. of Robert George Brummell and June Brummell (née Rawlins); ed St Albans School, St Catharine's Coll., Cambridge; joined HM Diplomatic Service 1987; Third Sec., later Second Sec., Islamabad 1989–92; with FCO, London 1993–94; First Sec., Rome 1995–2000; Deputy Head Eastern Dept, FCO 2000–01; Amb. to Turkmenistan 2002–05, to Kazakhstan (and non-resident to Kyrgyzstan) 2005–. *Publications:* Turkmenistan: The Bradt Travel Guide 2005. *Address:* Embassy of the United Kingdom, 480062 Almaty, Furmanova 173, Kazakhstan (office); c/o Foreign and Commonwealth Office (Almaty), King Charles Street, London, SW1A 2AH, England (office). *Telephone:* (3272) 50-61-91 (office). *Fax:* (3272) 50-62-60 (office). *E-mail:* british-embassy@nursat.kz (office); paul.brummell@fco.gov.uk (office). *Website:* www.britishembassy.gov.uk/kazakhstan (office).

BRUNDIN, Clark Lannerdahl, BS, PhD; American/British university administrator, engineer and academic; *Councillor, Oxford City Council;* b. 21 March 1931, Los Angeles, Calif.; s. of the late Ernest Brundin and Elinor Brundin (née Clark); m. Judith Anne Maloney 1959; two s. two d.; ed Whittier High School, Calif. Inst. of Tech. and Univ. of Calif., Berkeley; electronics petty officer, USN 1951–55; Assoc. in Mech. Eng, Univ. of Calif., Berkeley 1956–57, Research Engineer, Inst. of Eng Research 1959–63; Demonstrator, Dept of Eng Science, Univ. of Oxford 1957–58, Lecturer 1963–85; Vice-Chair. Gen. Bd of Faculties, Univ. of Oxford 1984–85; Fellow and Tutor in Eng, Jesus Coll., Oxford 1964–85, Sr Tutor 1974–77, Estates Bursar 1978–84, Hon. Fellow 1985–; Gov. Oxford Polytechnic 1978–83, Cokethorpe School 1983–96, Magdalen Coll. School 1987–99, Coventry School Foundation; Vice-Chancellor Univ. of Warwick 1985–92; Visiting Prof., Univ. of Calif., Santa Barbara 1978;

Visiting Scholar, Center for Higher Educ. Studies, Univ. of Calif., Berkeley 1997–2004; Lib Dem City Councillor, Oxford 2004–; Chair. Anchor Housing Asscn 1985–91; Dir Blackwell Science Ltd 1990–98; Dir Heritage Projects (Oxford) 1986–97, Oxford Univ. School of Man. Studies 1992–96, Finsbury Growth Trust PLC 1995–2000, Charities Aid Foundation America 1997–2000 (Pres. 1998–2000); Pres. Templeton Coll., Oxford 1992–96; mem. Eng Bd, CNAA 1976–82; Hon. LLD (Warwick) 2005. *Publications:* articles on rarefied gas dynamics and education. *Leisure interests:* sailing, mending old machinery, all types of music. *Address:* Jesus College, Oxford, OX1 3DW, England (office).

BRUNDTLAND, Gro Harlem, Cand. med, MPH; Norwegian politician, diplomatist, physician and international organization official; *Secretary-General's Special Envoy on Climate Change, United Nations;* b. 20 April 1939, Oslo; d. of Gudmund Harlem and Inga Harlem; m. Arne Olav Brundtland 1960; three s. (one deceased) one d.; ed Oslo Univ. and Harvard Univ., USA; Consultant, Ministry of Health and Social Affairs 1965–67; Medical Officer, Oslo City Health Dept 1968–69; Deputy Dir School Health Services, Oslo 1969; Minister for Environmental Affairs 1974–79; Deputy Leader Labour Party 1975–81, Leader Labour Parl. Group 1981–92; Prime Minister of Norway Feb.–Oct. 1981, 1986–89, 1990–96; mem. Parl. Standing Cttee on Foreign Affairs, fmr mem. Parl. Standing Cttee on Finance; mem. of Storting (Parl.) 1977–97; Dir-Gen. WHO 1998–2003; Chair. UN World Comm. on Environment and Devt 2003–05; UN Sec.-Gen.'s Special Envoy on Climate Change 2007–; consultant, Pepsi Co.; fmr Vice-Chair. Sr Secondary Schools' Socialist Asscn, Students' Asscn of Labour Party; mem. Council of Women World Leaders, Club of Madrid; Founding mem. The Elders group, Johannesburg, S Africa 2007; Dr hc (Oxford) 2001; Third World Prize for Work on Environmental Issues 1989, Indira Gandhi Prize 1990, Onassis Foundation Award 1992, Scientific American Policy Leader of the Year Award 2003, Thomas Jefferson Foundation Medal in Architecture 2008. *Publications:* articles on preventive medicine, school health and growth studies. *Leisure interest:* cross-country skiing. *Address:* United Nations, New York NY, 10017, USA (office). *Telephone:* (212) 963-1234 (office). *Fax:* (212) 963-4879 (office). *Website:* www.un.org (office).

BRUNER, Jerome Seymour, BA, PhD; American psychologist, academic and professor of law; *University Professor, School of Law, New York University;* b. 1 Oct. 1915, New York; s. of Herman Bruner and Rose Bruner; m. 1st Katherine Frost 1940 (divorced 1956); one s. one d.; m. 2nd Blanche Marshall McLane 1960 (divorced 1984); m. 3rd Carol Fleisher Feldman; ed Duke and Harvard Univs; US Intelligence 1941–42; Assoc. Dir Office of Public Opinion Research, Princeton 1942–44; Political Intelligence, France 1943; Research, Harvard Univ. 1945–72, Prof. of Psychology 1952–72, Dir Center for Cognitive Studies 1961–72; Ed. Public Opinion Quarterly 1943–44; Lecturer, Salzburg Seminar 1952; Bacon Prof., Univ. of Aix-en-Provence 1965; Watts Prof. of Psychology, Oxford Univ. 1972–80; Univ. Prof., New School for Social Research, New York 1981–88; Research Prof. of Psychology, New York Univ. 1988–96, Sr Researcher Fellow, Law School 1991–96, Univ. Prof. 1996–; Fellow, New York Inst. for the Humanities; mem. American Acad. of Arts and Sciences; Hon. DSc (Northwestern) 1965, (Sheffield) 1970, (Bristol) 1965, (Columbia) 1991; Hon. MA (Oxford) 1972; Hon. LLD (Temple) 1965, (Cincinnati) 1966, (New Brunswick) 1969, (Yale) 1978; Hon. DLitt (N Mich.) 1969, (Duke) 1969, (York Univ.) 1993; Dr hc (Sorbonne) 1974, (Leuven) 1976, (Ghent) 1977, (Madrid) 1986, (Free Univ. of Berlin) 1988, (Rome) 1992, (Harvard) 1996, (Bologna) 1996, (Salerno) 2001, (Crete) 2002; Int. Balzan Foundation Prize 1987. *Publications:* Mandate from the People 1944, A Study of Thinking 1956, The Process of Education 1960, On Knowing: Essays for the Left Hand 1962, Toward a Theory of Instruction 1966, Processes of Cognitive Growth: Infancy, (Vol. III) 1968, The Relevance of Education 1971, Under Five in Britain 1980, Communication as a Language 1982, In Search of Mind 1983, Child's Talk 1983, Actual Minds, Possible Worlds 1986, Acts of Meaning 1990, The Culture of Education 1996, Minding the Law 2000, Making Stories 2002; also co-author of several books. *Leisure interests:* sailing, drama. *Address:* New York University School of Law, 40 Washington Square South, New York, NY 10012, USA (office). *Telephone:* (212) 998-6463 (office); (212) 674-7816 (home). *Fax:* (212) 995-4881 (office); (212) 673-6118 (home). *E-mail:* brunerj@juris.law.nyu.edu (office); jerome.bruner@nyu.edu (home). *Website:* www.law.nyu.edu/faculty/profiles/affiliated/brunerj.html (office).

BRUNET, Michel, LèsSc, PhD, DSc; French palaeontologist and academic; *Professor of Vertebrate Palaeontology, University of Poiters;* b. 1940, Vienne (Poitou); ed Univs of Paris and Poitiers; formed with colleague Emile Heintz a team to search for extinct apes in Afghanistan 1970s, expedition was unsuccessful; moved to Africa 1980s, described a new Chadian hominid species, *Australopithecus bahrelghazali* (nicknamed Abel), dated around 3.5 Ma 1995, published in Nature an almost complete cranium of claimed oldest human ancestor: *Sahelanthropus tchadensis* (nicknamed Toumai) discovered in Chad in 2001 2002; Founder and current Head of int. transdisciplinary team MPFT (Mission Paléoanthropologique Franco-Tchadienne), a scientific collaboration between Univs of Poitiers, N'Djamena and Centre Nationale d'Appui à la Recherche; currently Prof. of Vertebrate Paleontology, Univ. of Poiters; Dan David Prize 2003. *Address:* Laboratoire de Géobiologie, Biochronologie et Paléontologie Humaine (LGBPH) UMR 6046, Université de Poitiers, 40 avenue du Recteur Pineau, Bâtiment Sciences Naturelles, 86022 Poitiers Cedex, France (office). *Telephone:* (5) 49-45-37-53 (office). *Fax:* (5) 49-45-40-17 (office). *E-mail:* michel.brunet@univ-poitiers.fr (office). *Website:* www.univ-poitiers.fr (office).

BRUNETTA, Renato; Italian politician, labour economist, academic and government official; *Minister for Public Administration and Innovation;* b. 26 May 1950, Venice; ed Marco Foscarini Liceo Classico, Venice and Univs of Padua, Cambridge, UK and Rotterdam, Netherlands; researcher in political sciences, Univ. of Padua 1975–77, Prof. of Labour Econs 1978–82; Gen. Sec. Fondazione G. Brodolini, Rome 1980–; Chief Consultant, Econ. Adviser to Ministry of Labour 1983–88; Sec., Italian Asscn of Labour Economists 1985–87; Vice-Pres., OECD Manpower and Social Affairs Cttee 1985–89; Prof. of Labour Econs, Rome Univ. II 'Tor Vergata' 1990–; mem. Scientific Cttee on European Integration, Ministry of Foreign Affairs 1990–92, Taskforce for Programming and Econ. Policy, Ministry of the Budget 1990–; mem. European Parl. 1999–; Econ. Adviser to Prime Minister 2004–06; Minister for Public Administration and Innovation 2008–; Ed. Economia & Lavoro (quarterly review), Rome 1980–; Founder and Ed. Labour (4-monthly journal) 1987–; Pres. Comm. on Information for CNEL (Nat. Council of Economy and Labour) 1989–94, Councillor 1995; mem. European Asscn of Labour Economists 1989–93, ASPEN-Italy 1989–; fmr Vice-Pres. Cttee on Industry, External Trade, Research and Energy; Premio St Vincent (for Econs) 1988, Premio Tarantelli (for Econs) 1993, Scanno Prize 1994, Rodolfo Valentino Int. Prize 2000. *Publications:* Economia del Lavoro 1981, Multi-localizzazione produttiva come strategia d'impresa 1983, Squilibri, conflitto, piena occupazione 1983, Spesa pubblica e conflitto 1987, Microeconomia del lavoro: Teorie e analisi empiriche 1987, Labour Relations and Economic Performance (ed.) 1990, Il Modello Italia 1991, Economics for the New Europe 1991, Il conflitto e le relazioni di lavoro negli anni '90 1992, Disoccupazione, Isteresi, Irreversibilità 1992, Retribuzione, costo del lavoro. Regolazione e deregolazione; il capital umano; la destrutturazione del mercato (ed.) 1992, La fine della società dei salariati 1994, Sud: Alcune idee perché il Mezzogiorno non resti com'è 1995, Venezia XXI, Cronache di una transizione difficile 2004, Quindici piu Direci: Il difficile camminodell'integrazaione europea (jt author) 2004, Il coraggio e la paura, Scritti de economia e politica 1999–2003 2004; articles and essays on labour econs and industrial relations; Columnist, Il Sole 24 ore, Il Giornale. *Leisure interests:* photography, history of Venice, gastronomy. *Address:* Via dell'Umilta 36, 00187 Rome, Italy (office); Palais de l'Europe Louise Weiss, 67070 Strasbourg, France (office). *Telephone:* (66) 731234 (Italy) (office); (3) 88-17-53-93 (France) (office). *Fax:* (66) 731362 (Italy) (office); (3) 88-17-93-93 (France) (office). *E-mail:* rbrunetta@europarl.eu.int. *Website:* www.renatobrunetta.it.

BRUNETTI, Wayne H., BSc; American energy industry executive (retd); ed Univ. of Fla, Harvard Business School; fmr Exec. Vice-Pres. Fla Power & Light Co.; fmr Pres. and CEO, Man. Systems Int.; Chair., Pres. and CEO, New Century Energies –2000; joined Public Service Co. of Colo 1994, Pres. and CEO 1994, later Chair., Pres. and CEO; Chair., Pres. and CEO, Southwestern Public Service Co., Cheyenne Light, Fuel and Power Co.; Chair., Pres. and CEO, Xcel Energy Inc., 2001–03, Chair. and CEO 2003–05 (retd); fmr Chair. Colo Asscn of Commerce and Industry, 2000 Mile High United Way Campaign; Dir Capital City Partnership, Minn. Orchestral Asscn, Juran Center for Leadership and Quality, Labour Relations Cttee, Chamber of Commerce of the USA; mem. Nat. Petroleum Council, Minn. Business Partnership, Colo Renewable Energy Task Force; fmr Cttee mem., Electric Power Research Inst., Edison Electrical Inst. (EEI), also EEI First Vice- Chair. *Publications:* Achieving Total Quality in Integrated Business Strategy and Customer Needs. *Address:* c/o Xcel Energy, 414 Nicollet Mall, Minneapolis, MN 55401-1993, USA (office).

BRUNO, Franklin (Frank) Roy, MBE; British fmr professional boxer; b. 16 Nov. 1961, London; s. of the late Robert Bruno and of Lynette Bruno (née Campbell); m. Laura Frances Mooney 1990 (divorced 2001); one s. three d.; ed Oak Hall School, Sussex; began boxing with Wandsworth Boys' Club, London 1970; mem. Sir Philip Game Amateur Boxing Club 1977–80; won 20 out of 21 contests as amateur; professional career 1982–96; won 38 out of 42 contests as professional 1982–89; European heavyweight champion 1985–86 (relinquished title), world heavyweight title challenges against Tim Witherspoon 1986, Mike Tyson 1989; staged comeback, won first contest 1991; lost 4th world title challenge against Lennox Lewis Oct. 1993; WBC heavyweight champion 1995–96, lost title to Mike Tyson 1996; announced retirement Aug. 1996; numerous appearances in pantomimes; fmr presenter, BBC TV; SOS Sports Personality of the Year 1990; TV Times Sports Personality of the Year 1990, Lifetime Achievement Award, BBC Sports Personality of the Year Awards 1996. *Publications:* Personality: From Zero to Hero (with Norman Giller) 1996, Frank (autobiog., with Kevin Mitchell) (Sky Sports Autobiography of the Year 2006) 2005. *Leisure interests:* music, training, swimming. *Address:* Little Billington, Leighton Buzzard, Beds., LU7, England.

BRUNTON, Sir Gordon Charles, Kt; British business executive; *Chairman, Communications and General Consultants Ltd;* b. 27 Dec. 1921, London; s. of Charles A. Brunton and Hylda Pritchard; m. 1st Nadine Sohr 1946 (divorced 1965); one s. (one s. deceased) two d.; m. 2nd Gillian A. Kirk 1966; one s. one d.; ed Cranleigh School and London School of Econs; war service 1942–46; joined Tothill Press 1947, Exec. Dir 1956; Man. Dir Tower Press Group 1958; Exec. Dir Odhams Press 1961; joined Thomson Org. 1961, Dir 1963, Man. Dir and CEO Int. Thomson Org. PLC (fmrly Thomson British Holdings) and Thomson Org. Ltd 1968–84; Man. Dir Thomson Publications 1961; Chair. Thomson Travel 1965–68; Pres. Int. Thomson Org. Ltd 1978–84; Dir Times Newspapers Ltd 1967–81, Bemrose Corpn 1974 (Chair. 1978–91), Sotheby Parke Bernet Group PLC 1978–85, Cable and Wireless PLC 1981–91, Yattendon Investment Trust PLC 1985–2001; fmr non-exec. Dir Cable and Wireless PLC, South Bank Bd (Arts Council); Pres. Periodical Publishers' Asscn 1972–74, 1981–82, Nat. Advertising Benevolent Soc. 1973–75; Chair. Econ. Devt Council for Civil Eng 1978–84, Appeals Cttee, Ind. Adoption Soc., Communications and Gen. Consultants Ltd 1985–, Mercury Communications Ltd 1986–90, Cavendish Shops 1985–93, Community Industry Ltd 1985–92, The Racing Post PLC 1985–97, Ingersoll Publications 1988–91, Verity Group PLC (fmrly Wharfedale PLC) 1991–97, Green Field Leisure Group Ltd 1992–,

PhoneLink PLC (now Telme.com PLC) 1993–2001, Galahad Gold PLC 2003–07, Euram Consulting Ltd, Focus Investments Ltd, Cavendish Retail, Racing Int. Ltd and other limited cos; Gov. and Fellow LSE, Henley Man. Coll. 1983–86; Pres. The History of Advertising Trust 1981–84; mem. Council, Templeton Coll. (fmrly Oxford Cen. for Man. Studies); mem. South Bank Bd, Arts Council 1985–92. *Leisure interests:* books, breeding horses. *Address:* North Munstead Stud Farm, North Munstead Lane, Godalming, Surrey, GU8 4AX, England. *Telephone:* (1483) 424181 (office); (1483) 416313 (home). *Fax:* (1483) 426043 (office).

BRUS, Louis E.; American chemist and academic; *Thomas Alva Edison Professor and Scientific Head, Columbia University;* Lt, USN, US Naval Research Lab., Washington, DC 1969–73; Mem. Tech. Staff, AT&T Bell Laboratories, Murray Hill, NJ 1973–84, Distinguished Mem. Tech. Staff 1984–96; Prof. of Chemistry, Columbia Univ. 1996–, Prof. of Chemical Eng and Applied Chemistry 1997–, Thomas Alva Edison Prof. and Scientific Head 2001–; Visiting Lecturer at numerous univs; Vice Chair. Gordon Research Confs 1997, Chair. 1998; mem. Editorial Bd several journals including Journal of Chemical Physics 1988–91, Journal of Physical Chemistry 1990–93, Journal of the American Chemical Soc. 1990–96, Nano Letters 2000–; mem. numerous review cttees; mem. NAS 2004–; Fellow American Physical Soc. 1980–, American Acad. of Arts and Sciences 1998–; Univ. of Chicago Herman Bloch Award 1995, American Physical Soc. Irving Langmuir Prize in Chemical Physics 2001, American Chemical Soc. E. I. Pont de Nemours & Co. Award in the Chemistry of Materials 2005. *Address:* Department of Chemistry, Columbia University, Havemeyer Hall, MC 3125, 3000 Broadway, New York, NY 10027, USA (office). *Telephone:* (212) 854-4041 (office). *Fax:* (212) 932-1289 (office). *E-mail:* brus@chem.columbia.edu (office). *Website:* www.columbia.edu/cu/chemistry/faculty/leb.html (office).

BRUSENDORFF, Anne Christine; Finnish lawyer and international organization official; *Executive Secretary, Helsinki Commission (HELCOM) – Baltic Marine Environment Protection Commission;* currently Exec. Sec. Helsinki Comm. (HELCOM) – Baltic Marine Environment Protection Comm.; Visiting Prof. of Int. Environmental Law, Queen Mary Univ. of London. *Address:* Helsinki Commission (HELCOM), Katajanokanlaituri 6 B, 00160 Helsinki, Finland (office). *Telephone:* (207) 412628 (office). *Fax:* (207) 412628 (office); (207) 412639 (office). *E-mail:* anne.brusendorff@helcom.fi (office); anne.christine.brusendorff@helcom.fi (office). *Website:* www.helcom.fi (office).

BRUSKIN, Grisha (Brouskine Grigori); Russian artist; b. 21 Oct. 1945, Moscow; s. of David Brouskin and Bassia Strunina; m. 1st Ludmila Dmitrieva 1975 (divorced 1978); m. 2nd Alexandra Makarova 1982; one d. one adopted s.; ed Art High School, Moscow, Moscow Textile Inst.; mem. Soviet Artists' Union 1968; work includes paintings, gouaches, drawings, sculptures, performances; work included in first Sotheby's auction in Moscow, designed poster for Chicago Art Exhbn 1988; now lives and works in New York; solo exhbns in Moscow 1976, 1984, Vilnius, Lithuania 1983, Marlborough Gallery, New York 1990; numerous group exhbns including The Painter and Modernism, Moscow 1987, 100 Years of Russian Art, Barbican, London and in Chicago, Berne, Seoul, Cologne, Chicago, New York, Barcelona, Paris, Munich, Düsseldorf, Lisbon, Brussels, Berlin, Copenhagen 1988–; works in Art Inst. of Chicago, Jewish Museum, New York, Museum of Modern Art, New York, Nat. Museum of Israel, Jerusalem etc. *Leisure interests:* literature, music. *Address:* c/o Marlborough Galleries, 40 West 57th Street, New York, NY 10019, USA.

BRUSTEIN, Robert Sanford, MA, PhD; American drama critic, actor and producer; *Founding Director and Creative Consultant, American Repertory Theatre;* b. 21 April 1927, New York, NY; m. 1st Norma Cates 1962 (deceased 1979); one s. one step-s; m. 2nd Doreen Beinart 1996; two step-c.; ed Amherst Coll., Yale Univ. Drama School, Columbia Univ.; played about 70 roles in theatre groups and TV plays 1950–; Instructor, Cornell Univ. 1955–56, Vassar Coll. 1956–57; Llecturer, Columbia Univ. 1957–58, Asst Prof. 1958–63, Assoc. Prof. 1963–65, Prof. 1965–66; Prof. of English, Yale Univ., Dean of Yale Drama School, Artistic Dir and founder Yale Repertory Theatre 1966–79; founder and Artistic Dir American Repertory Theatre, Loeb Drama Center, Cambridge, Mass. 1979–2002, Founding Dir and Creative Consultant 2002–; Prof. of English, Harvard Univ. 1979–2002; Drama Critic, The New Republic 1959–67, 1978–, Contributing Ed. 1959–79; host and writer, The Opposition Theatre (Net TV) 1966; regular contrib. to New York Times 1972–; Advisory Ed., Theatre Quarterly 1967–; Guest Critic, The Observer, UK 1972–73, 1978–, Contributing Ed. 1959–; Trustee, Sarah Lawrence Coll. 1973–77; panel mem. Nat. Endowment for the Arts 1970–72, 1981–84; mem. Nat. Acad. Arts and Sciences; Fulbright Fellow 1953–55, Guggenheim Fellow 1961–62, Ford Fellow 1964–65; Hon. LittD (Lawrence Univ.) 1968, (Amherst Coll.) 1972; Hon. LHD (Beloit Coll.) 1975; Hon. Dr of Arts (Bard Coll.) 1981; George G. Nathan Prize in Criticism 1962, George Polk Memorial Award in Criticism 1964, Jersey City Journal Award in Theatre Criticism 1967, Eliot Norton Award for Theatre, New England Theatre Conf. Award for Excellence in Theme, Award, Outstanding Achievement in American Theater, New England Theater Council 1985, Tiffany Award for Excellence in Theater, Soc. for Performing Arts Administrators 1987, American Acad. of Arts and Letters Distinguished Services to Arts Award 1995, ATHE Award for Lifetime Achievement in the Theater 2000. *Publications:* Introduction to The Plays of Chekhov 1964; Ed. The Plays of Strindberg 1964; author: The Theatre of Revolt 1964, Seasons of Discontent 1965, The Third Theatre 1969, Revolution as Theatre 1971, The Culture Watch 1975, The Plays and Prose of Strindberg (ed.), Critical Moments 1980, Making Scenes 1981, Who Needs Theatre 1987, Reimagining American Theatre 1991, Dumbocracy in America 1994, Demons 1995 (play), Nobody Dies on Friday 1996 (play), Culturak Calisthenics 1998, Poker Face 1999, The Face Lift 1999, Chekhov on Ice 2000, Three Farces and a Funeral 2000, Divestiture 2001, The Siege of the Arts 2001. *Address:*

American Repertory Theatre, Loeb Drama Center, Harvard University, 64 Brattle Street, Cambridge, MA 02138, USA. *Telephone:* (617) 495-2668. *Website:* www.amrep.org.

BRUTON, John Gerard, BA, BL; Irish politician, barrister and farmer; *European Union Ambassador and Head, European Commission Delegation to USA;* b. 18 May 1947, Dublin; s. of Matthew Joseph Bruton and Doris Mary Delany; m. Finola Gill 1981; one s. three d.; ed Clongowes Wood Coll., Univ. Coll., Dublin, King's Inn, Dublin; mem. Dáil Éireann (House of Reps) 1969–2004; Fine Gael Spokesman on Agric. 1972–73; Parl. Sec. to Minister for Educ. 1973–77, to Minister for Industry and Commerce 1975–77; Fine Gael Spokesman on Agric. 1977–81, on Finance Jan.–June 1981; Minister of Finance 1981–82, of Industry, Trade, Commerce and Tourism 1982–86, of Finance 1986–87; Deputy Leader of Fine Gael 1987–90, Leader 1990–2001, Fine Gael Spokesman on Industry and Commerce 1987–89, on Educ. 1989–90; mem. Parl. Ass., Council of Europe 1989–91, British-Irish Parl. Body 1993–94, Parl. Ass., WEU 1997–; Prime Minister of Ireland 1994–97; Leader of Opposition 1997–2001; EU Amb. and Head, EC Del. to USA 2004–; mem. Fine Gael Front Bench 2002; Gov. Ditchley Foundation 1999–; Hon. Citizen, Sioux City, Iowa, USA; Hon. LLD (Memorial Univ., St John's, Newfoundland), (Nat. Univ. of Ireland); Commdr, Grand Cross of the Royal Order of the Polar Star (Sweden). *Publications:* Reform of the Dail 1980, A Better Way to Plan the Nation's Finances 1981. *Leisure interests:* history, folk music, tennis. *Address:* European Union, Delegation of the European Commission to the United States, 2300 M Street, NW, Washington, DC 20037, USA (office); Cornelstown, Dunboyne, Co. Meath, Ireland (home). *Telephone:* (202) 862-9500 (office). *Fax:* (202) 429-1766 (office). *E-mail:* john.bruton@ec.europa.eu (office). *Website:* www.eurunion.org (office).

BRUTUS, Dennis, BA; South African academic and poet; *Professor Emeritus of Africana Studies, University of Pittsburgh;* b. 28 Nov. 1924, Salisbury, S Rhodesia (now Harare, Zimbabwe); s. of Francis Henry Brutus and Margaret Winifred Brutus (née Bloemetjie); m. May Jaggers 1950; four s. four d.; ed Paterson High School, Port Elizabeth, Fort Hare and Witwatersrand Univs; language teacher, Paterson High School, Cen. Indian High School; office boy and law student, Witwatersrand Univ.; imprisoned for opposition to apartheid 1964–65, exiled 1966, political asylum in USA 1983; Dir World Campaign for Release of S African Political Prisoners; worked for Int. Defence and Aid Fund, fmrly UN Rep.; Visiting Prof. Denver Univ.; Prof. of English, Northwestern Univ., Evanston, Ill.; Visiting Prof., English Dept, African and Afro-American Studies and Research Center, Univ. Tex. 1974–75; Visiting Prof., Dept of English, Amherst Coll., Mass. 1982–83, Dartmouth Coll., NH 1983; Adjunct Prof., Northeastern Univ., Boston, Mass. 1984; Prof., Dept of Africana Studies, Univ. of Pittsburgh, now Prof. Emer.; Pres. S African Non-Racial Olympic Cttee (SAN-ROC); Chair. Int. Campaign Against Racism in Sport (ICARIS), Africa Network from 1984; Dir Program on African and African-American Writing in Africa and the Diaspora from 1989; Interport lecturer Univ. of Pittsburgh; Founding Chair., Exec. mem. African Literature Asscn, fmr Chair. ARENA (Inst. for Study of Sport and Social Issues); mem. of Bd, Black Arts Celebration, Vice-Pres. Union of Writers of the African People; mem. Bd of Dirs UN Asscn of Chicago and Ill., Editorial Bd Africa Today; Dir Troubadour Press; Fellow, Int. Poetry Soc.; mem. Modern Language Asscn 1972, Int. Platform Asscn 1979–; Dr hc (Univ. of Mass., Amherst), (Northeastern Univ., Boston), (Univ. of the District of Columbia); Hon. HLD (Worcester State Coll.) 1982; Mbari Prize for Poetry in Africa, Chancellor's Prize for Bilingualism (Univ. of S Africa), Freedom Writers' Award, Kenneth David Kaunda Humanism Award, Int. Jury Books Abroad Award 1976, Nat. Council for Black Studies Academic Excellence Award 1982, UN Human Rights Day Award 1983, Paul Robeson Award, Langston Hughes Award. *Publications:* Sirens, Knuckles, Boots 1963, Letters to Martha and Other Poems from a South African Prison 1968, Poems from Algiers 1970, Thoughts Abroad (as John Bruin) 1971, A Simple Lust 1973, China Poems 1975, Strains 1975, Stubborn Hope 1978, 1979, 1983, Salutes and Censures 1980, Airs and Tributes 1988, Still the Sirens 1993. *Leisure interests:* sport, music, chess. *Address:* c/o Department of Africana Studies, 4140 Wesley W. Posvar Hall, University of Pittsburgh, 230 South Bouquet Street, Pittsburgh, PA 15260, USA (office).

BRYAN, Sir Arthur, Kt, KStJ; British fmr business executive; b. 4 March 1923, Stoke-on-Trent; s. of William Woodall Bryan and Isobel Alan (née Tweedie); m. Betty Ratford 1947; one s. one d.; ed Longton High School; served with RAFVR 1941–45; joined Wedgwood Ltd 1947, sales rep. 1949, Asst London Man. 1950–53, London Man. and Gen. Man. of Wedgwood Rooms 1953–59, Gen. Sales Man. 1959–60; Dir and Pres. Josiah Wedgwood & Sons Inc. of America 1960–62; Man. Dir Wedgwood PLC 1963–85, Chair. 1968–86; Pres. Waterford Wedgwood Holdings PLC 1986–88; Dir Waterford Glass Group PLC 1986–88; Chair. Wedgwood Museum Trust –2005; Dir Friends' Provident Life Asscn 1985–92, UK Fund Inc. 1987–2001, Dartington Crystal Group 1995–2001; Pres. British Ceramic Mfrs Fed. 1970–71; mem. Court, Univ. of Keele; Chair. Consumer Market Advisory Cttee, Dept of Trade and Industry 1988–; Companion, British Inst. of Man. 1968; Fellow, Inst. of Marketing, Royal Soc. of Arts 1964; Companion, Inst. Ceramics; Lord Lt for Staffs. 1968–93. *Leisure interests:* walking, reading. *Address:* Parkfields Cottage, Tittensor, Stoke-on-Trent, Staffs., ST12 9HQ, England (home).

BRYAN, John Henry, BA; American business executive; b. 5 Oct. 1936, West Point, Miss.; s. of John H. Bryan, Sr; m. Neville Frierson Bryan 1958; two s. two d.; ed Southwestern Univ. (now Rhodes Coll.), Memphis; joined Bryan Packing Co. 1960, Pres., CEO 1968–74; Exec. Vice-Pres., Dir Sara Lee Corpn March–Oct. 1974, Pres. 1974–75, CEO 1975 then, Chair. 1976–2001, now consulant to corpn; mem. Bd of Dirs BP plc, Gen. Motors 1993–, Goldman Sachs Group, Inc.; fmr mem. Bd of Dirs Amoco Corpn, First Chicago Corpn,

The First Nat. Bank of Chicago; fmr Chair. and mem. Bd of Dirs of Grocery Mfrs of America, Inc.; mem. Business Roundtable, Bds Catalyst, Nat. Women's Econ. Alliance, Art Inst. of Chicago; Dir Business Cttee for Arts; Prin. of Chicago United; Trustee Rush-Presbyterian-St Luke's Medical Center, Univ. of Chicago; Trustee Cttee for Econ. Devt; fmr Chair. and current mem. Chicago Council on Foreign Relations; Légion d'honneur, Order of Orange Nassau (Netherlands); Order of Lincoln Medallion. *Address:* c/o Board of Directors, Goldman Sachs Group, Inc., 85 Broad Street, New York, NY 10004, USA (office).

BRYAN, Richard H., LLB; American lawyer and fmr politician; *Partner, Lionel Sawyer & Collins;* b. 16 July 1937, Washington, DC; m. Bonnie Fairchild; three c.; ed Univ. of Nev. and Hastings Coll. of Law, Univ. of Calif.; admitted to Nev. Bar 1963, US Supreme Court Bar 1967; Deputy Dist Attorney, Clark Co., Nev. 1964–66; Public Defender, Clark Co. 1966–68; Counsel, Clark Co. Juvenile Court 1968–69; mem. Nev. Ass. 1969–71; Nev. Senate 1973–77; Attorney-Gen., Nev. 1979–83; Gov. of Nev. 1983–89; Senator from Nev. 1989–2001; Pnr and mem. Exec. Cttee Lionel, Sawyer & Collins (law firm) 2001–; mem. Bd of Trustees Nev. Devt Authority 2001–, Econ. Devt Authority of Western Nev. (EDAWN), Las Vegas Chamber of Commerce; mem. Bd of Dirs Las Vegas Performing Arts Center; mem. City of Las Vegas Centennial Cttee; Chair. Preserve Nevada; mem. Order of the Coif; rated in The Best Lawyers in America 2008. *Address:* Lionel Sawyer & Collins, 1700 Bank America Plaza, 300 South Fourth Street, Las Vegas, NV 89101, USA (office). *Telephone:* (702) 383-8916 (office). *Fax:* (702) 383-8845 (office). *E-mail:* rbryan@lionelsawyer.com (office). *Website:* www.lionelsawyer.com (office).

BRYANT, Gyude, BEcons; Liberian politician and business executive; b. 17 Jan. 1949; m.; three c.; Founder, Chair. Liberia Machinery and Supply Co. 1977–; co-f. Liberian Action Party (LAP) 1984, Chair. 1992–; Chair. Nat. Transitional Govt Oct. 2003–Jan. 2006; charged with graft by govt 2007. *Address:* c/o Liberian Action Party, Monrovia, Liberia (office).

BRYANT, John; British journalist; *Chairman, Press Association Trust;* trainee journalist The Scotsman; fmr Exec. Ed. The Daily Mail; fmr Managing Ed. The Times 1986, then Deputy Ed.; fmr Ed. The Sunday Correspondent 1990, The European; Consulting Ed. The Daily Mail –2005; Ed.-in-Chief Telegraph Newspapers 2005–, acting Ed. The Daily Telegraph 2005; Chair. Press Asscn Trust 2008–; Chair. Editorial Bd, London Evening Standard 2009–. *Publications:* non-fiction: 3:59.4 2005, The London Marathon 2006. *Address:* London Evening Standard, Northcliffe House, 2 Derry Street, London, W8 5TT, England (office). *Website:* www.standard.co.uk (office).

BRYANT, John Martin, MA, CEng, FIM, FREng; British business executive; b. 28 Sept. 1943, Cardiff; s. of William George Bryant and Doris Bryant; m. Andrea Irene Emmons 1965; two s. one d.; ed W Monmouth School, Pontypool, St Catharine's Coll., Cambridge; grad. trainee Steel Co. of Wales 1965–68; various tech., production, personnel positions British Steel 1968–78, Works Man. Hot Rolled Products 1978–87, Dir Coated Products 1987–90, Dir Tinplate 1990–92, Man. Dir Strip Products 1995–99, Exec. Dir 1996–98, Chief Exec. 1999; Chief Exec. Corus PLC 1999–2001; Dir ASW PLC 1993–95, Bank of Wales PLC 1996–2001, Welsh Water PLC 2001–, Glas Cymru Ltd 2001–, Costain Group PLC 2002–; Hon. DSc (Wales) 2000. *Leisure interests:* all sports, particularly squash and rugby, family. *Address:* Broadway Farm, 24 Roger Lane, Laleston, Bridgend, CF32 0LA, Wales (home). *Telephone:* (1656) 647558 (home). *Fax:* (1656) 664348 (home). *E-mail:* drjmbryant@aol .com (home).

BRYANT, Kobe; American professional basketball player; b. 23 Aug. 1978, Philadelphia, Pa; s. of Joe 'Jellybean' Bryant and Pam Bryant; m. Vanessa Bryant (née Laine) 2001; two d.; ed Lower Merion High School, Pa; position: guard; moved with family to Italy where he lived until 1992; selected from high school by Charlotte Hornets in first round (13th pick overall) 1996 Nat. Basketball Asscn (NBA) draft, draft rights traded to LA Lakers; youngest-ever NBA all-star starter at 19 years of age 1998; three times NBA champion with Lakers (2000, 2001, 2002); played in gold medal-winning US Nat. Team at FIBA Americas Championships, Las Vegas 2007; played in gold medal-winning Team USA ('Redeem Team') at Olympic Games, Beijing 2008; 10-time NBA All-Star 1998, 2000–08, NBA Most Valuable Player in All-Star Game 2002, 2007, NBA Scoring Champion 2005–06, 2006–07, NBA Most Valuable Player 2008. *Address:* Los Angeles Lakers, 555 North Nash Street, El Segundo, CA 90245, USA. *Telephone:* (310) 426-6031. *Website:* www.nba.com/ lakers; www.kb24.com.

BRYANT, Thomas Edward, MD, JD; American physician and attorney; *Chairman, Nonprofit Management Inc.;* b. 17 Jan. 1936, Ala; s. of Howard Edward Bryant and Alibel Nettles Bryant; m. Lucie Elizabeth Thrasher 1961 (divorced); one s. one d.; ed Emory Univ., Atlanta; Dir of Health Affairs, US Office of Econ. Opportunity 1969–70; Pres. Nat. Drug Abuse Council 1970–78; Chair. Pres. Comm. on Mental Health 1977–78; Dir Children of Alcoholics Foundation 1983–; mem. Inst. of Medicine, NAS 1972; Chair. The Public Cttee on Mental Health 1977–79, Council for Understanding Mental Illnesses 1983–87, Aspirin Foundation of America 1987–; founder and Chair. Nonprofit Man. Inc. 1989–; Exec. Dir Co. Behavioral Health Inst. 1997–; Practising Attorney specializing in Health Law with Webster and Sheffield 1980–84; Chair. The Rosalynn Carter Inst. 1986–; Pres. The Friends of the Nat. Library of Medicine 1985–; Emory Outstanding Alumnus Medal 1987. *Address:* Nonprofit Management Inc., 1555 Connecticut Avenue, NW, Suite 200, Washington, DC 20036, USA (office). *Telephone:* (202) 462-9600 (office). *E-mail:* tom@nonprofitmgt.com (office). *Website:* www.nonprofitmgt.com (office).

BRYANTSEV, Dmitri Aleksandrovich; Russian choreographer; *Artistic Director, Moscow Stanislavsky Ballet;* b. 18 Feb. 1947, Leningrad; ed Leningrad Higher School of Choreography, Moscow State Inst. of Theatre; soloist Moscow Choreographic Ensemble Classical Ballet 1966–77; ballet master and choreographer since 1975; Artistic Dir Moscow Stanislavsky Ballet 1985–; staged numerous productions including Choreographic Miniatures (Kirov Theatre), Hussars' Ballad by T. Khrennikov (Kirov and Bolshoi Theatres 1979, 1980), Othello, Corsair, Optimistic Tragedy, Hunchback Horse; author of TV ballet productions Galatea, Old Tango; staged dances in opera productions including Dead Souls by R. Shchedrin (Bolshoi Theatre) and drama productions (Turandot, Taganka Theatre); People's Artist of Russia 1989. *Address:* Musical Theatre, Bolshaya Dmitrovka 17, 103009 Moscow, Russia. *Telephone:* (495) 229-28-35 (office).

BRYARS, Gavin, BA; British composer and academic; *Associate Research Fellow, Dartington College of Arts;* b. 16 Jan. 1943, Goole, Yorks.; s. of Walter Joseph Bryars and Miriam Eleanor Bryars; m. 1st Angela Margaret Bigley 1971 (divorced 1993); two d.; m. 2nd Anna Tchernakova 1999; one s. one step d.; ed Goole Grammar School, Sheffield Univ., Northern School of Music and pvt composition study with Cyril Ramsey, George Linstead and Benjamin Johnston; freelance double bassist 1963–66; Lecturer in Liberal Studies, Northampton Coll. of Technology 1966–67; freelance composer/performer 1968–70; Lecturer in Music, Portsmouth Polytechnic 1969–70; Sr Lecturer School of Fine Art, Leicester Polytechnic 1970–78, Sr Lecturer and Head of Music, School of Performing Arts 1978–85; Prof. of Music, De Montfort Univ. 1985–96; currently Assoc. Research Fellow Dartington Coll. of Arts; collaborations with artists, including Aphex Twin, John Cage, Brian Eno, Tom Waits; mem. Collège de Pataphysique, France 1974–; Ed. Experimental Music Catalogue 1972–81; British Rep. Int. Soc. for Contemporary Music Festival 1977; Visiting Prof., Univ. of Herts.; Arts Council Comms 1970, 1980, 1982, Bursary 1982; Dr hc (Plymouth) 2006. *Films:* Sea and Stars (Nat. Film Bd of Canada) 2003. *Radio:* I Send You This Cadmium Rec (BBC Radio 3, with John Berger and John Christie) 2002, Egil's Last Days (BBC Radio 3) 2004. *Television:* Last Summer (CBC TV, Dir Anna Tchernakova) 2000. *Compositions include:* The Sinking of the Titanic 1969, Jesus' Blood Never Failed Me Yet 1971, Out of Zaleski's Gazebo 1977, The Vespertine Park 1980, Medea (opera with Robert Wilson) 1982, My First Homage for two pianos 1978, Effarene 1984, String Quartet No. 1 1985, Pico's Flight 1986, By the Vaar for double bass and ensemble 1987, The Invention of Tradition 1988, Glorious Hill 1988, Cadman Requiem 1989, String Quartet No. 2 1990, Four Elements (dance piece) 1990, The Black River for soprano and organ 1991, The White Lodge 1991, The War in Heaven for chorus and orchestra 1993, Epilogue from 'Wonderlawn' for four players 1994, Three Elegies for Nine Clarinets 1994, The North Shore for solo viola and small orchestra 1994, After Handel's Vesper 1995, Cello Concerto 1995, The Adnan Songbook 1996, Doctor Ox's Experiment (opera) 1997, String Quartet No. 3 1998, The Porazzi Fragment for strings 1998, Biped (ballet) 1999, First Book of Madrigals 2000, Violin Concerto 2000, G (opera) 2001, Second Book of Madrigals 2001, Double Bass Concerto 2002, Book of Laude 2003, Writings on Water (ballet) 2003, Third Book of Madrigals 2003, Eight Irish Madrigals 2004, New York (percussion concerto) 2004, From Egil's Saga 2004, Creamer Etudes 2005, New York 2005, Paper Nautilus 2006, The Stones of the Arch 2006, Nothing Like the Sun 2007, Nine Irish Madrigals 2007. *Publications:* contrib. to Music and Musicians, Studio International, Art and Artists, Contact, The Guardian. *Leisure interests:* cricket (mem. Yorks. Co. Cricket Club), football, Dalmatians. *Address:* Schott and Co. Ltd, 48 Great Marlborough Street, London, W1F 7BB, England (office). *Telephone:* (20) 7534-0750 (office). *Fax:* (20) 7534-0759 (office). *E-mail:* sally.groves@schott-music.com (office); questions@ gavinbryars.com (office). *Website:* www.schott-music.com (office); www .gavinbryars.com (office).

BRYCE ECHENIQUE, Alfredo; Peruvian writer; b. 19 Feb. 1939, Lima; Premio Nacional de Literatura de Perú 1972, Premio Passion, France 1983, Encomienda de Isabel la Católica, Spain 1993, Premio Nacional de Narrativa, Spain 1998, Encomienda de Alfonso X El Sabio, Spain 2000, Premio Grinzane Cavour, Piemonte, Italy 2002, Premio Planeta, Spain 2002; Commdr, Ordre des Arts et des Lettres 2000. *Publications:* Huerto cerrado (short stories) 1968, Un mundo para Julius (novel) 1970, La felicidad ja ja (short stories) 1974, Tantas veces Pedro (novel) 1977, A vuelo de buen cubero y otras crónicas (non-fiction) 1977, La vida exagerada de Martín Romaña (novel) 1981, El hombre que hablaba de Octavia de Cádiz 1984, Magdalena peruana y otros cuentos (short stories) 1986, Crónicas personales 1986, La última mudanza de Felipe Carrillo (novel) 1988, Dos señoras conversan (novella) 1990, Permiso para vivir (Antimemorias) (memoir) 1993, No me esperen en abril (novel) 1995, A trancas y barrancas (articles) 1997, Reo de nocturnidad (novel) 1997, Guía triste de París (short stories) 1999, La amigdalitis de Tarzán (novel) 1999, El huerto de mi amada 2002. *Address:* c/o Alfaguara, Avenida San Felipe 731, Jesús María, Lima, Peru.

BRYDEN, Alan, Dip in Nuclear Physics; British/French international organization executive; *Secretary-General, International Organization for Standardization Policy;* b. 1945; m. Laurence Bryden; three c.; ed Ecole Polytechnique, Paris, Ecole des Mines, Paris and Univ. d'Orsay, France; began career in metrology with Nat. Bureau of Standards (now Nat. Inst. of Standards and Tech.), USA; Dir-Gen. Laboratoire Nat. d'Essais 1981–99; f. Eurolab (European Fed. of Measurement, Testing and Analytical Labs), Pres. 1990–96; Dir-Gen. AFNOR (French nat. standardization inst.) 1999–2003; mem. Council Int. Org. for Standardization (ISO) 1999–2003, Sec.-Gen. 2003–; fmr Vice-Pres. European Cttee for Standardization Policy; fmr Vice-Pres. Cttee on Tech. Barriers to Trade in GATT (now WTO); fmr Chair. Labs Cttee of Int. Lab. Accreditation Co-operation; Ordre nat. du Mérite 1988, Chevalier, Légion d'honneur 1995. *Leisure interests:* riding, sailing. *Address:* International Organization for Standardization, Case Postale 56, 1211 Geneva 20,

Switzerland (office). *Telephone:* (22) 7490217 (office). *Fax:* (22) 7333440 (office). *E-mail:* bryden@iso.org (office). *Website:* www.iso.org (office).

BRYDON, Donald Hood, CBE; British investment executive; *Chairman and Chief Executive Officer, AXA Investment Managers;* b. 25 May 1945, Stirling, Scotland; s. of James Hood Brydon and Mary Duncanson Brydon (née Young); m. 1st Joan Victoria Brydon 1971 (divorced 1995), one s. one d.; m. 2nd Corinne Susan Jane Green 1996; ed George Watson's Coll., Edinburgh, Univ. of Edinburgh; with Econs Dept Univ. of Edinburgh 1967–70; with British Airways Pensions Fund 1970–77; Barclays Investment Man.'s Office 1977–81, Deputy Man. Dir Barclays Investment Man. Ltd 1981–86; Dir BZW Investment Man. 1986–88, Man. Dir 1988–91, Chair., CEO BZW Asset Man. Ltd 1991–94, Chair. (non-exec.) 1994–95, Deputy Chief Exec. Barclays de Zoete Wedd 1994–96, Acting CEO 1996; Chair., CEO AXA Investment Managers 1997–; Chair. Smiths Group 2004–; Pres. European Asset Man. Asscn 1999–2001; Dir Stock Exchange 1991–98; Dir Edinburgh Inca Investment Trust 1996–2002, Allied Domecq 1997–, AXA UK (fmrly Sun Life and Provincial Holdings) 1997–, Amersham 1997–2004, Scottish Power 2003–; Chair. European Children's Trust 1999–2001, Fund Man. Asscn 1999–2001, Financial Services Practitioner Panel 2001–03. *Publications:* Economics of Technical Information Services (jtly) 1972. *Address:* AXA Investment Managers Ltd, 7 Newgate Street, London, EC1A 7NX, England (office). *Telephone:* (20) 7003-1500 (office). *Fax:* (20) 7003-1507 (office). *E-mail:* donald.brydon@axa-im.com (office).

BRYMER, Charles; American business executive; fmrly with BBDO Inc. Houston and New York; joined Interbrand Group (int. consultancy specializing in brands and branding) 1985, later CEO. *Address:* Interbrand Schechter Inc., 437 Madison Avenue, New York, NY 10022, USA. *Telephone:* (212) 752-4400. *Fax:* (212) 752-4503.

BRYN, Kåre; Norwegian diplomatist; *Secretary-General, European Free Trade Association;* b. 12 March 1944; m.; four c.; ed Norwegian School of Econs and Business Admin; Trainee Ministry of Foreign Affairs 1969, Attaché/Second Sec. Norwegian Embassy, London 1971–74, First Sec., Belgrade 1974–76, Exec. Officer Ministry of Foreign Affairs 1976–79, First Sec., later Counsellor, Perm. Mission of Norway, Geneva 1979–84, Head of Div., Ministry of Foreign Affairs 1984, Asst Dir-Gen. 1985–89, Dir-Gen. Dept for Natural Resources and Environmental Affairs 1989–99, Norwegian Rep. to Int. Whaling Comm. (IWC) 1995–99, Amb. and Perm. Rep. to European Free Trade Asscn (EFTA) and WTO, Geneva 1999–2003 (Chair. WTO Gen. Council 2000–01), Amb. to the Netherlands 2003–06; Sec.-Gen. EFTA 2006–. *Address:* European Free Trade Association (EFTA), 9–11 rue de Varembé, 1211 Geneva 20, Switzerland (office). *Telephone:* 223322626 (office). *Fax:* 223322677 (office). *E-mail:* mail.gva@efta.int (office). *Website:* www.efta.int (office).

BRYNGDAHL, Olof; Swedish scientist and academic; *Professor, University of Essen;* b. 26 Sept. 1933, Stockholm; s. of Carl Olof Bryngdahl and Ingeborg M. Pihlgren; m. Margaretha Schraut 1959; ed Royal Inst. of Tech. Stockholm; Research Assoc. Inst. for Optical Research, Stockholm 1956–64; staff mem. Xerox Research Lab. Rochester, NY 1964–65; Man. IBM Research Lab. San José, Calif. 1966–69; Sr scientist, IBM Research Lab. Yorktown Heights NY 1970; Prin. Scientist, Xerox Research Lab., Palo Alto, Calif. 1970–77; Prof., Inst. d'Optique, Univ. of Paris 1975–76; Prof., Univ. of Essen 1977–; Fellow, Optical Soc. of America. *Publications:* more than 200 scientific articles; 14 patents in optics. *Address:* University of Essen, 45117 Essen, Universitätsstrasse 2, Germany (office). *Telephone:* (201) 1832562 (office). *E-mail:* olof.bryngdahl@uni-due.de (office).

BRYNTSALOV, Vladimir Alekseyevich; Russian business executive; b. 23 Nov. 1946, Cherkessk; m. 1st; one d.; m. 2nd Natalya Bryntsalova; one s. one d.; ed Inst. of Construction and Eng; engineer, then Head Construction Dept in Stavropol 1970–80; expelled from CPSU for 'petty bourgeois inclination'; pvt. enterprise activities started late 1980s; f. co-operative Pchelka (Bee) 1987; bought stock shares of pharmaceutical factories, f. Co. Ferein 1992– (produces over one third of all medicaments in Russia) (Hon. Pres. 1996–); mem. State Duma (Parl.) 1995–1999 (joined Our Home–Russia faction 1997); f. Russian Socialist Party 1998; re-elected as ind. cand. 1999–; Deputy Chair. Yedinstvo i Otechestvo party; cand. for Presidency of Russia 1996. *Address:* Ferein, Nagatinskaya str. 1, 117105 Moscow, Russia. *Telephone:* (499) 611-13-20 (office); (495) 111-00-79 (office). *E-mail:* info@ferain.ru (office). *Website:* www.ferain.ru (office).

BRYSON, Bill; American writer; b. 1951, Des Moines, IA; m.; four c.; ed Drake Univ.; travelled to England and worked as orderly in mental hosp. 1973; worked as journalist for The Times and the Independent; returned with his family to USA 1993; apptd to selection panel, Book of the Month Club 2001; Commissioner for English Heritage; Chancellor Univ. of Durham 2005–; Pres. Campaign to Protect Rural England 2007–; Hon. DCL (Durham) 2004, Hon. OBE 2006. *Publications:* Penguin Dictionary of Troublesome Words (reprinted as Bryson's Dictionary of Troublesome Words) 1985, The Lost Continent 1987, The Mother Tongue: English and How It Got That Way, Made in America 1994, Neither Here Nor There: Travels in Europe 1995, Notes From a Small Island 1995, A Walk in the Woods 1998, I'm a Stranger Here Myself (essays, aka Notes From a Big Country) 1999, In a Sunburned Country (aka Down Under) 2000, The Best American Travel Writing (ed.), African Diary 2002, A Short History of Nearly Everything (Aventis Prize 2004, Descartes Science Communication Prize 2005) 2003, The Life and Times of the Thunderbolt Kid (memoirs) 2006, Shakespeare: A Short Life (biog.) 2007. *Address:* The Marsh Agency, 11 Dover Street, London, W1S 4LJ, England (office); c/o Publicity Department, Transworld Publishers, 61–63 Uxbridge Road, London, W5 5SA, England. *Telephone:* (20) 7399-2800 (office). *Fax:* (20) 7399-2801 (office). *Website:* www.marsh-agency.co.uk (office); www.cpre.org.uk.

BRYSON, John E., LLB, JD; American energy industry executive; *Chairman, President and CEO, Edison International;* b. 1944; ed Stanford Univ., Yale Law School; Dir Edison Int. 1990–, Chair. and CEO 1990–99, Chair., Pres. and CEO 2000–, Dir Southern Calif. Edison (subsidiary) 1990–99, Jan. 2003–, Chair. and CEO 1990–99, Chair. Jan. 2003–, Chair., Edison Mission Energy (subsidiary) 2000–02; mem. Bd of Dirs The Boeing Co., Pacific American Income Shares Inc., Western Asset Funds Inc., The Walt Disney Co., W. M. Keck Foundation; Trustee Calif. Inst. of Tech.; fmr Chair. Calif. Business Roundtable; fmr Trustee Stanford Univ. *Address:* Edison International, 2244 Walnut Grove Avenue, POB 999, Rosemead, CA 91770, USA (office). *Telephone:* (626) 302-1212 (office). *Fax:* (626) 302-2517 (office). *Website:* www.edison.com (office).

BRZEZINSKI, Zbigniew Kazimierz, PhD; American academic and fmr government official; *Counsellor, Center for Strategic and International Studies;* b. 28 March 1928, Warsaw, Poland; s. of Tadeusz Brzezinski and Leonia Roman; m. Emilie Anna (Muska) Benes 1955; two s. one d.; ed McGill and Harvard Univs; settled in N America 1938; Instructor in Govt and Research Fellow, Russian Research Center, Harvard Univ. 1953–56; Asst Prof. of Govt, Research Assoc. of Russian Research Center and of Center for Int. Affairs, Harvard Univ. 1956–60; Assoc. Prof. of Public Law and Govt, Columbia Univ. 1960–62, Prof. 1962–89 (on leave 1966–68, 1977–81) and Dir Research Inst. on Communist Affairs 1961–77 (on leave 1966–68); mem. Policy Planning Council, Dept of State 1966–68; mem. Hon. Steering Cttee, Young Citizens for Johnson 1964; Dir Foreign Policy Task Force for Vice-Pres. Humphrey 1968; Asst to the Pres. for Nat. Security Affairs 1977–81; mem. Nat. Security Council 1977–81; Counsellor, Center for Strategic and Int. Studies, Washington, DC 1981–; Robert E. Osgood Prof. of American Foreign Policy, Paul Nitze School of Advanced Int. Studies, Johns Hopkins Univ. 1989–; Fellow, American Acad. of Arts and Sciences 1969–; mem. Council on Foreign Relations, New York, Bd of Trustees, Freedom House; Guggenheim Fellowship 1960, Ford Fellowship 1970; Dr hc (Alliance Coll.) 1966, (Coll. of the Holy Cross) 1971, (Fordham Univ.) 1979, (Williams Coll.) 1986, (Georgetown Univ.) 1987, (Catholic Univ. of Lublin) 1990, (Warsaw Univ.) 1991; Presidential Medal of Freedom 1981, Order of White Eagle (Poland) 1995, Order of Merit (Ukraine) 1996, Masaryk Order 1998, Gedymim Order 1998. *Publications include:* Political Controls in the Soviet Army 1954, The Permanent Purge–Politics in Soviet Totalitarianism 1956, Totalitarian Dictatorship and Autocracy (with Carl Joachim Friedrich) 1957, The Soviet Bloc–Unity and Conflict 1960, Ideology and Power in Soviet Politics 1962, Africa and the Communist World (ed. and contrib.) 1963, Political Power: USA/USSR (with Samuel P. Huntington) 1964, Alternative to Partition: For a Broader Conception of America's Role in Europe 1965, Dilemmas of Change in Soviet Politics (ed. and contrib.) 1969, Between Two Ages: America's Role in the Technetronic Era 1970, The Fragile Blossom: Crisis and Change in Japan 1972, The Relevance of Liberalism 1977, Power and Principle: Memoirs of the National Security Adviser 1977–1981 1983, Game Plan: A Geostrategic Framework for the Conduct of the US-Soviet Contest 1986, In Quest of National Security 1988, The Grand Failure: The Birth and Death of Communism in the 20th Century 1989, Out of Control: Global Turmoil on the Eve of the Twenty-First Century 1993, The Grand Chessboard: American Primacy and its Geostrategic Imperatives 1996, The Geostrategic Triad: Living with China, Europe, and Russia 2000, The Choice: Global Domination or Global Leadership 2004, Second Chance: Three Presidents and the Crisis of American Superpower 2007, America and the World: Conversations on the Future of American Foreign Policy 2008 (with Brent Scowcroft); contrib. to many publications, journals and periodicals. *Address:* Center for Strategic and International Studies, 1800 K Street NW, Washington, DC 20006, USA (office). *Telephone:* (202) 833-2408 (office). *Fax:* (202) 833-2409 (office). *E-mail:* zb@csis.org (office). *Website:* www.csis.org (office).

BU HE, (Yun Shuguang); Chinese party and government official; b. 24 March 1926, Inner Mongolia; s. of the late Ulanfu and Yun Ting; m. Zhulanqiqige 1947; one s. two d.; ed Yan'an Inst. for Nationalities, Nationalities Coll. of Yan'an Univ.; joined CCP 1942; Lecturer and Deputy Dir Political Dept of Nei Mongol Autonomous Coll. in Chifeng 1946; CCP Br. Sec. and Dir of Nei Mongol Art Troupe 1947–53; Leading Party Group Sec. and Deputy Dir Nei Mongol Cultural Bureau 1954–64; Acting mem. Standing Cttee of CCP Cttee, Nei Mongol and Sec. and Dir of CCP Cttee of Cultural and Educ. Comm., Nei Mongol 1966; Sec. Municipal Party Cttee of Baotou 1974–77; Dir Propaganda Dept of CCP Cttee, Nei Mongol 1978; Deputy Dir State Nationalities Affairs Comm. 1978–81; Sec. CCP Cttee and Mayor of Huhhot City 1978–81; Deputy Sec. CCP Cttee, Nei Mongol 1981–82; mem. of 12th CCP Central Cttee 1982–87; Deputy Sec. CCP Cttee and Chair. Provincial Govt, Nei Mongol 1983; mem. 13th CCP Cen. Cttee 1987–92; Vice-Chair. 8th NPC Standing Cttee 1993–98, 9th NPC 1998–2003; Chair. Regional Fed. of Literary and Art Circles 1954–65; mem. 2nd, 3rd, 4th Council of Chinese Fed. of Literary and Art Circles. *Publications:* The Basic Knowledge of Autonomy in the Nationalities Region, the Nationalities Theory of Marxism and the Party's Nationalities Policies, The Animal Husbandry in Inner Mongolia Today, In the Sea of Poems (poetry collection), Bu He's Collection of Theses in Literature and Art. *Leisure interests:* calligraphy, literature and art-writing. *Address:* c/o Office of the Regional Governor, Hohhot, Nei Mongol, People's Republic of China.

BUALLAY, Yassim Muhammad, BBA; Bahraini diplomatist; *Ambassador to Tunisia;* b. 15 March 1942, Muharraq; s. of Muhammad Buallay and Balkees Buallay; m. Satia Buallay 1969; two s. two d.; ed American Univ. of Beirut, Long Island Univ., NY; Supervisor, Bursaries Section, Ministry of Educ.

1963–69; int. civil servant, UNESCO, Paris 1970–74; Amb. to France 1974–79, to Tunisia 1987–94, 2004–; Perm. Rep. to UN 1994–2004; Dir of Econ. Affairs, Ministry of Foreign Affairs, Bahrain 1979–87; Ordre nat. du Mérite, France, decorations of Morocco (Alawite, First Class) 1994 and Tunisia 1994 (First Class). *Leisure interests:* reading, theatre, music, tennis, gastronomy. *Address:* Embassy of Bahrain, 72 rue Mouaouia ibn Soufiane, al-Menzah VI, Tunis, Tunisia (office). *Telephone:* (71) 750-865 (office).

BUBALO, Predrag, LLM, LLD; Serbian politician; *Minister of Trade and Services;* b. 14 Oct. 1954, Vladicin Han; m.; one s. one d.; ed Faculty of Law, University of Novi Sad; joined Livnica Kikinda (foundry co.) as Adviser to Gen. Man. 1977, Eng Man. 1981–90, Financial Man. 1991–94, Head, office in Beijing 1994–2000, Man. AUTO-KUCA (Livnica Kikinda subsidiary) 2000–02, Gen. Man. Livnica Kikinda 2002–04; Minister of International Economic Relations March–Oct. 2004, Coordinator, Ministry of Economy July–Oct. 2004, Minister of the Economy 2004–06, of Trade and Services 2007–; mem. Democratic Party of Serbia (DPS). *Address:* Ministry of Trade and Services, 11000 Belgrade, Nemanjina 22–26, Serbia (office). *Telephone:* (11) 3618852 (office). *Fax:* (11) 3610258 (office). *E-mail:* kabinet@minttu.sr.gov.yu (office). *Website:* www.minttu.sr.gov.yu (office).

BUBKA, Sergey Nazarovich; Ukrainian politician, sports official and fmr athlete; b. 4 Dec. 1963, Voroshilovgrad (now Lugansk); s. of Nazar Bubka and Valentina Bubka; m. Lilya Tioutiounik 1983; two s.; former pole vaulter; set 17 world records outdoors and 10 indoors; cleared 6m or better in more than 44 competitions; first man to clear 20 feet both indoors and out 1991; holder of indoors and outdoors world records (Dec. 2002); 6-time world champion 1983, 1987, 1991, 1993, 1995, 1997; winner Olympic gold medal, Seoul, South Korea 1988; mem. IOC Exec. Bd, IOC Evaluation Comm. for 2008, IOC Athletes' Comm., IAAF Council 2001–; Nat. Olympic Cttee Bd; Chair. IOC Athletes' Comm.; Pres. S. Bubka Sports Club; elected to Parl. (United Union faction) 2002–; L'Equipe Sportsman of the Year 1997, Track and Field Best Pole Vaulter of the Last Half-Century. *Address:* c/o State Committee of Physical Culture and Sport, 42 Esplanadnaya, 252023 Kiev, Ukraine (office). *Telephone:* (44) 220-02-43. *Fax:* (44) 220-02-94.

BUCHACHENKO, Anatoly Leonidovich, DrChemSc; Russian chemical physicist; b. 7 Sept. 1935, Arkhangelsk region; s. of L. P. Buchachenko and A. S. Buchachenko; m. M. S. Buchachenko 1960; one s. one d.; ed Gorky Univ.; post grad., Jr then Sr scientific Asst 1958–68; Head of Lab. of USSR (now Russian) Acad. of Sciences Inst. of Chemical Physics 1970–, Vice-Dir 1989–94, Dir 1994–96; Head of Dept 1996; Head of Dept of Chemical Kinetics, Moscow State Univ. 1988–; Prof. 1975–; mem. USSR (now Russian) Acad. of Sciences 1987; State Prize 1977, Lenin Prize 1986. *Publications:* works on the physical chemistry of free radicals, chemical reactions, spin chemistry, molecular ferromagnets. *Leisure interests:* wood architecture modelling. *Address:* N. N. Semenov Institute of Chemical Physics of the Russian Academy of Sciences, 1 Academyya Semenova Prospect, Chernogolovka, Noginskyy Region, Moscow oblast 142432, Russia (office). *Telephone:* (495) 993-57-07 (office); (495) 331-31-70 (home). *Fax:* (496) 515-54-20 (office). *Website:* www.icp.ac.ru (office).

BUCHANAN, Isobel Wilson; British singer (soprano); b. 15 March 1954, Glasgow; d. of Stewart Buchanan and Mary Buchanan; m. Jonathan Stephen Geoffrey King (actor Jonathan Hyde) 1980; two d.; ed Cumbernauld Comprehensive High School and Royal Scottish Acad. of Music and Drama; professional début in Sydney, Australia with Richard Bonynge and Joan Sutherland 1976–78; British début, Glyndebourne 1978; US and German débuts 1979; Vienna Staatsoper début 1979; ENO début 1985, Paris Opera début 1986; now freelance artist working with all major opera cos and orchestras; also Leader and tutor, The Samling Foundation. *Recordings:* Beethoven's Ninth Symphony, Werther, Mozart Arias and Duets. *Leisure interests:* cooking, reading, gardening, yoga, knitting. *Address:* The Samling Foundation, Community Centre, Gilesgate, Hexham, Northumberland, NE46 3NP, England (office). *Telephone:* (1434) 602885 (office). *E-mail:* enquiries@samlingfoundation.org (office). *Website:* www.samlingfoundation.co.uk (office).

BUCHANAN, J. Robert, MD; American medical scientist and academic; *Professor of Medicine, School of Medicine, Harvard University;* b. 8 March 1928, Newark, NJ; m. Susan Carver; one s. one d.; ed Amherst Coll. and Cornell Univ. Medical School; Intern, then Asst Resident Physician, New York Hosp. 1954–58, Research Fellow in Medicine 1956–57; Research Fellow in Endocrinology, Cornell Univ. Medical Coll., New York 1960–61; WHO Travelling Fellow 1963; Instructor in Medicine, Cornell Univ. Medical Coll. 1961–63, Asst Prof. 1963–67, Asst to Chair. Dept of Medicine 1964–65, Assoc. Dean 1965–69, Clinical Assoc. Prof. 1967–69, Assoc. Prof. 1969–71, Prof. 1971–76, Acting Dean, then Dean 1969–76; Prof. of Medicine, Univ. of Chicago, Ill. 1977–82; Assoc. Dean, Pritzker School of Medicine, Chicago 1978–82; Prof. of Medicine, Harvard Medical School, Boston, Mass. 1982–; Gen. Dir, Mass. Gen. Hosp. 1982–94; Gen. Dir Emer. 1994–; physician at hosps in New York, Chicago and Boston 1956–; mem. Admin. Bd, Council of Teaching Hosps 1984–89, mem. Exec. Council 1985–; Dir Mass. Div., American Cancer Soc. 1984–; Bd of Dirs Bank of New England 1986–91, AMI Holdings 1991–, Exec. Cttee Mass. Hosp. Asscn 1987– (Chair. 1990–91), Charles River Labs; Chair. Council of Teaching Hosps, Asscn of American Medical Colls 1988–89; mem. NAS Cttee to review Inst. of Medicine, American Cancer Soc., Mass. Div., Soc. of Medical Admins; Chair. Educ. Comm. for Foreign Medical Grads 1994–; Fellow, American Coll. of Physicians; Founding Trustee, Aga Khan Univ.; Hon. ScD (Amherst Coll.); Hon. LHD (Rush Univ.); Hon. MD (Peking Union Medical Coll., Beijing, China). *Publications:* numerous papers and articles in journals. *Leisure interests:* boating, gardening. *Address:* 5 Chestnut Hill Road, POB 669, Killingworth, CT 06419, USA (office). *Telephone:* (860) 663-2637 (home). *Fax:* (860) 663-3058 (home). *E-mail:*

jrobertbuchan@aol.com (home). *Website:* hms.harvard.edu/hms/home.asp (office).

BUCHANAN, James McGill, MA, PhD; American academic; *Professor Emeritus of Economics, Center for the Study of Public Choice, George Mason University;* b. 3 Oct. 1919, Murfreesboro, Tenn.; s. of James Buchanan and Lila Scott; m. Anne Bakke 1945; ed Middle Tenn. State Coll. and Univs of Tenn. and Chicago; Prof. of Econs Univ. of Tenn. 1950–51, Fla State Univ. 1951–56, Univ. of Va 1956–62; Paul. G. McIntyre Prof. of Econs Univ. of Va 1962–68; Prof. of Econs Univ. of Calif. Los Angeles 1968–69; Univ. Distinguished Prof. of Econs Va Polytechnic Inst. 1969–83, Dir Center for Study of Public Choice 1969–88, Advisory Gen. Dir 1988–, Prof. Emer. 2000–; Univ. Distinguished Prof. of Econs George Mason Univ. 1983–99, Prof. Emer. 1999–; Fulbright Research Scholar, Italy 1955–56; Ford Faculty Research Fellow 1959–60; Fulbright Visiting Prof. Univ. of Cambridge 1961–62; Assoc. Prof. Francesco Marroquin Univ., Guatemala 2001–; Fellow, American Acad. of Arts and Sciences; Distinguished Fellow, American Econ. Asscn; Dr hc (Giessen) 1982, (Zürich) 1984, (Valencia) 1987, (Lisbon) 1987, (Fairfax) 1987, (London) 1988, (Rome) 1993, (Bucharest) 1994, (Catania) 1994, (Valladolid) 1996; American Econ. Asscn Seidman Award 1984, Nobel Prize for Econs 1986. *Publications:* author and co-author of numerous books on financial policy and other econ. matters; articles in professional journals. *Address:* Center for the Study of Public Choice, George Mason University, Buchanan House Mail Stop 1 E6, Fairfax, VA 22030-4443 (office); PO Box G, Blacksburg, VA 24063-1021, USA (home).

BUCHANAN, John Machlin, PhD, DSc; American biochemist and academic; *Professor Emeritus of Biology, Massachusetts Institute of Technology;* b. 29 Sept. 1917, Winamac Ind.; s. of Harry J. Buchanan and Eunice B. Buchanan (née Miller); m. Elsa Nilsby 1948; two s. two d.; ed De Pauw Univ., Univ. of Michigan and Harvard Univ.; Instructor, Dept of Physiological Chem., School of Medicine, Univ. of Pa 1943–46, Asst Prof. 1946–49, Assoc. Prof. 1949–50, Prof. 1950–53; Nat. Research Council Fellow in Medicine, Nobel Inst., Stockholm 1946–48; Prof., Head, Div. of Biochemistry, Dept of Biology, MIT 1953–67, Wilson Prof. of Biochemistry 1967–88, Prof. Emer. 1988–; mem. Medical Fellowship Bd 1954–; mem. NAS, American Soc. of Biological Chemists, ACS, Int. Union of Biochemists, American Acad. of Arts and Sciences; Fellow, Guggenheim Memorial Foundation; Hon. DSc (De Pauw) 1975, (Michigan) 1961; ACS Eli Lilly Award in Biological Chem. 1951. *Leisure interests:* golf, reading. *Address:* Room 68-333B, Department of Biology, Massachusetts Institute of Technology, Cambridge, MA 02139 (office); 56 Meriam Street, Lexington, MA 02420-3622, USA (home). *Telephone:* (617) 253-3702 (office); (781) 862-1066 (home). *Fax:* (617) 253-8699 (office). *Website:* mit.edu/biology/www (office).

BUCHANAN, Patrick (Pat) Joseph, MS; American journalist and fmr government official; b. 2 Nov. 1938, Washington; s. of William Buchanan and Catherine Crum; m. Shelley A. Scarney 1971; ed Georgetown and Columbia Univs; editorial writer, St Louis Globe Democrat 1962–64, asst editorial writer 1964–66; Exec. Asst to Richard Nixon 1966–69; Special Asst to Pres. Nixon 1969–73; consultant to Pres. Nixon and Pres. Ford 1973–74; Asst to Pres., Dir of Communications, White House, Washington, DC 1985–87; syndicated columnist, political commentator, New York Times special features 1975–78, Chicago Tribune-New York News Syndicate 1978–85, Tribune Media Services 1987–91, 1993–95; commentator, NBC Radio Network 1978–82; co-host Crossfire (TV Show) Cable News Network 1982–85, 1987–91, 1993–95, 1997–; appeared as host and panellist in TV shows 1978–; Ed.-in-Chief PJB—From the Right (newsletter) 1990–91; moderator Capital Gang TV show CNN 1988–92; Chair. The American Cause 1993–95, 1997–, Pat Buchanan & Co., Mutual Broadcasting System 1993–95; Cand. for Republican Presidential nomination 1992, 1996; Republican. *Publications:* The New Majority 1973, Conservative Votes, Liberal Victories 1975, Right from the Beginning 1988, Barry Goldwater, The Conscience of A Conservative 1990, The Great Betrayal 1998, A Republic, not an Empire 2000, State of Emergency 2006, Day of Reckoning 2008. *Address:* The American Cause, 501 Church Street, Suite 217, Vienna, VA 22180 (office); 1017 Savile Lane, McLean, VA 22101, USA. *Telephone:* (703) 255-2632 (office). *Fax:* (703) 255-2219 (office). *E-mail:* webmaster@theamericancause.org (office). *Website:* www.theamericancause.org (office).

BUCHANAN, Robin William Turnbull, MBA, FCA, FRSA; American/British business executive and academic administrator; *Dean, London Business School;* b. 2 April 1952; s. of Iain Buchanan and Gillian Pamela Buchanan (née Hughes-Hallett); m. Diana Tei Tanaka 1986; one s. one d.; ed Harvard Business School (Baker Scholar); with Mann Judd Landau (now Deloitte & Touche) 1970–77; with American Express Int. . Banking Corpn 1979–82; with Bain & Co. Inc. 1982–, Bain Capital 1982–84, Man. Pnr, London 1990–96, Sr Pnr, London 1996–2007, Sr Adviser 2007–; Dean London Business School 2007–; Dir (non-exec.) Liberty International plc 1997–, Shire plc (fmrly Shire Pharmaceuticals Group plc) 2003–. *Address:* Office of the Dean, London Business School, Regent's Park, London, NW1 4SA, England (office). *Telephone:* (20) 7700-7014 (office). *Fax:* (20) 7000-7011 (office). *E-mail:* press@london.edu (office). *Website:* www.london.edu (office).

BUCHWALD, Christoph; German publishing executive; fmrly Ed. Hanser, Munich; fmrly Publr Luchterhand Literaturverlag; now with Suhrkamp Verlag KG, Frankfurt 1998–. *Address:* Suhrkamp Verlag KG, Frankfurt a.M., Postfach 101945, Germany (office). *Telephone:* (69) 756010 (office). *Fax:* (69) 75601522 (office). *Website:* www.suhrkamp.de (office).

BUCK, Linda B., PhD; American physiologist and academic; *Affiliate Professor of Physiology and Biophysics, University of Washington;* ed Univ. of Wash., Univ. of Tex. Southwestern Medical Center, Dallas; Postdoctoral

Fellow, Columbia Univ. Coll. of Physicians and Surgeons 1980-84; Assoc., Howard Hughes Medical Inst., Columbia Univ. 1984–91; Asst Prof., Dept of Neurobiology, Harvard Medical School 1991–96, Assoc. Prof. 1996–2001, Prof. 2001–02; Asst Investigator Howard Hughes Medical Inst. (HHMI) 1994–97, Assoc. Investigator, 1997–2000, Full Investigator 2001–; Affiliate Prof. of Physiology and Biophysics, Univ. of Wash. 2003–; Full Mem. Basic Sciences Div., Fred Hutchinson Cancer Research Center 2002–; Fellow, AAAS, American Acad. of Arts and Sciences; mem. NAS; mem. Bd of Dirs International Flavors and Fragrances Inc. 2007–; Lewis S. Rosenstiel Award, Unilever Science Award, Perl/UNC Neuroscience Prize, Gairdner Foundation Int. Award, Nobel Prize in Physiology or Medicine (jtly with Richard Axel) 2004. *Publications:* numerous articles in professional publs; books include The Human Olfactory Receptor Gene Family (co-author) 2004, The Mouse Olfactory Receptor Gene Family (co-author) 2004. *Address:* Fred Hutchinson Cancer Research Center, 1100 Fairview Avenue North, POB 19024, Seattle, WA 98109-1024 (office); Howard Hughes Medical Institute, 4000 Jones Bridge Road, Chevy Chase, MD, 20815-689, USA (office). *Telephone:* (206) 667-6316 (office); (301) 215-8500 (office). *Fax:* (206) 667-1031 (office). *E-mail:* lbuck@ fhcrc.org (office); webmaster@hhmi.org (office). *Website:* www.fhcrc.org (office); www.hhmi.org (office).

BUCKINGHAM, Amyand David, CBE, FRS, FRSC, FInstP; Australian chemist and academic; *Professor Emeritus of Chemistry, University of Cambridge;* b. 28 Jan. 1930, Sydney; s. of the late Reginald Joslin Buckingham and Florence Grace Buckingham; m. Jillian Bowles 1965; one. s. two d.; ed Barker Coll., Hornsby, NSW, Univ. of Sydney, Corpus Christi Coll., Cambridge; Lecturer, then Student and Tutor, Christ Church, Univ. of Oxford 1955–65, Univ. Lecturer in Inorganic Chem. 1958–65; Prof. of Theoretical Chem., Univ. of Bristol 1965–69; Prof. of Chem., Univ. of Cambridge 1969–97, Fellow, Pembroke Coll., Cambridge 1970–97, Prof. Emer. 1997–; Pres. Faraday Div. of Royal Soc. of Chem. 1987–89, Cambridge Univ. Cricket Club 1990–; Foreign mem. American Acad. of Arts and Sciences; Foreign Assoc. (US) NAS; Foreign mem. Royal Swedish Acad. of Sciences; Fellow, Royal Australian Chemical Inst., American Physical Soc., Optical Soc. of America; mem. ACS, mem. Council Royal Soc. 1999–2001; Harrie Massey Medal, Inst. of Physics 1995, Hughes Medal, Royal Soc. 1996, Faraday Medal, RSC 1998, Townes Medal, Optical Soc. of America 2001, Inaugural Ahmed Zewail Prize 2007. *Achievement:* Cricket Blue, Univ. of Sydney 1953. *Publications:* over 320 papers in scientific journals, The Laws and Applications of Thermodynamics 1964, Organic Liquids: Structure, Dynamics and Chemical Properties 1978, The Principles of Molecular Recognition 1993. *Leisure interests:* cricket, woodwork, travel, walking. *Address:* Department of Chemistry, University of Cambridge, Cambridge, CB2 1EW (office); Crossways, 23 The Avenue, Newmarket, CB8 9AA, England (home). *Telephone:* (1223) 336458 (office); (1638) 663799 (home). *Fax:* (1223) 336362 (office). *E-mail:* adb1000@cam.ac.uk (office). *Website:* www.ch.cam.ac.uk/CUCL/staff/adb.html (office).

BUCKLAND, David John; British artist and theatre director; *Director, Cape Farewell;* b. 15 June 1949, London; s. of Denis Buckland and Valarie Buckland; partner, Siobhan Davies 1978; one s. one d.; ed Dorchester Secondary Modern School, Dorset, Hardye's Grammar School, Dorchester, Deep River High School, Ottawa and London Coll. of Printing; has participated in group exhbns and work appears in public collections in London, New York, Chicago, Los Angeles, Paris etc; Artistic Dir Siobhan Davies Dance Co.; Lecturer, RCA, London Coll. of Printing, Chicago Art Inst.; 21 set and costume designs for dance including Rambert Dance Co., Siobhan Davies Dance Co., English Nat. Ballet and work for TV; Northern Arts Fellow 1972–73; Kodak Bursary 1978; founder and dir Cape Farewell environmental project 2000–; Minn. First Bank Award 1988–90. *Leisure interests:* multi-hull sailor, arts, theatre, travel, hill walking. *Address:* Cape Farewell, 239 Royal College Street, London, NW1 9LT, England (office). *Telephone:* (20) 7209-0610 (office). *E-mail:* davidbuckland@capefarewell.com (office). *Website:* www.capefarewell .com (office).

BUCKLAND, Sir Ross, Kt, FCIS; Australian business executive; b. 19 Dec. 1942, Sydney; s. of William Buckland and Elizabeth Buckland; m. Patricia Bubb 1966; two s.; ed Sydney Boys' High School; various positions in banking, Eng and food industries 1958–66; Dir Finance and Admin. Elizabeth Arden Pty Ltd 1966–73; Kellogg (Australia) Pty Ltd 1973–77, 1978; Man. Dir Kellogg Salada Canada Inc., Pres. and Chief Exec. 1979–80; Chair. Kellogg Co. of GB Ltd, Dir European Operations and Vice-Pres. Kellogg Co. USA 1981–90; Chief Exec. Unigate (now Uniq) PLC 1990–2001; Dir Allied Domecq 1998–2004, Mayne Group 2001–2004 (resgnd) Goodman Fielder –2003, Clayton Utz; Co-Group Chair., The CEO Circle Pty Ltd, Sydney; Pres. Nat. Australia Bank Europe 1999; Fellow, Inst. of Grocery Distribution, Chartered Inst. of Secs and Admins, Australian Soc. of Certified Practising Accountants; mem. MRC 1998–. *Leisure interest:* walking. *Address:* c/o The CEO Circle Pty Ltd, Suite 11, 15 Terminus Street, Castle Hill, NSW 2154, Australia. *Telephone:* (2) 9659-1288. *Fax:* (2) 9659-1388. *E-mail:* ceo@ceocircle.com.au. *Website:* www .theceocircle.com.

BUCKLEY, George W., BSc, PhD; British business executive; *Chairman, President and CEO, 3M Company;* ed Univs of Southampton and Huddersfield; fmr Man. Dir Cen. Services Div., British Railways Bd, UK; fmr Pres. Electric Motors Div. and Automotive and Precision Motors Div., Emerson Electric Co., St Louis, Mo., USA; joined Brunswick Corpn 1997, Chair. and CEO 2000–05; Chair., Pres. and CEO 3M Company 2005–; mem. Bd of Dirs Black and Decker, Archer-Daniels-Midland Co.; Trustee, St Thomas Univ., St Paul, Minn.; Hon. DSc (Huddersfield). *Address:* 3M Corporate Headquarters, 3M Center, St Paul, MN 55144-1000, USA (office). *Telephone:* (651) 733-1110 (office). *Fax:* (651) 733-9973 (office). *E-mail:* info@mmm.com (office). *Website:* www.mmm.com (office).

BUCKLEY, James Lane, LLB; American fmr politician and judge (retd); b. 9 March 1923, New York, NY; s. of William F. Buckley and Aloise Steiner Buckley; m. Ann F. Cooley 1953; five s. one d.; ed Yale Univ.; served US Navy 1943–46; Senator from New York 1971–77; Under-Sec. of State for Security Assistance 1981–82; Pres. Radio Free Europe–Radio Liberty 1982–85; Circuit Judge, US Court of Appeals, DC Circuit 1985–2001, Sr Judge, retd 2001; Co-Chair. US Del. to UN Conf. on Environment, Nairobi 1982; Chair. US Del. to UN Conf. on Population, Mexico City 1984; Republican. *Publication:* If Men Were Angels 1975. *Leisure interests:* natural history, American History. *Address:* PO Box 597, Sharon, CT, 06069, USA (office).

BUCKLEY, Michael; Irish banker; *Group Chief Executive Officer, Allied Irish Bank PLC;* b. Cork; m. Anne Buckley; fmr stockbroker and civil servant in Ireland and EU; joined Allied Irish Bank PLC (AIB) 1991, Exec. Dir 1995–2001, Man. Dir Capital Markets Div. 1994–99, Head Polish Div. 1999–2001, Group Chief Exec. 2001–. *Address:* AIB Bankcentre, PO Box 452, Ballsbridge, Dublin 4, Ireland (office). *Telephone:* (1) 6600311 (office). *Website:* www.aibgroup.com (office).

BUCKLEY, Stephen, MFA; British artist and university professor; b. 5 April 1944, Leicester; s. of Nancy Throsby and Leslie Buckley; m. Stephanie James 1973; one s. one d.; ed Univs of Newcastle-upon-Tyne and Reading; taught at Canterbury Coll. of Art 1969, Leeds Coll. of Art 1970, Chelsea School of Art 1971–80; Artist in Residence, King's Coll., Cambridge 1972–74; Prof. of Fine Art, Univ. of Reading 1994–2009; over 40 solo exhbns throughout world including Museum of Modern Art, Oxford 1985, Yale Center for British Art, New Haven, Conn., USA 1986, Tate Britain 1997; worked with Rambert Dance Co., London 1987–88; works in public collections in Chile, Sweden, UK, Venezuela, USA, NZ, Australia; comms include Neal Street Restaurant 1972, mural painting for Penguin Books 1972, Leith's Restaurant 1973; prizewinner, John Moores Exhbn 1974, 1985, Chichester National Art Exhbn 1975, Tolly-Cobbold Exhbn 1977. *Address:* c/o Department of Fine Art, University of Reading, 1 Earley Gate, Whiteknights Road, Reading, RG6 6AT, England. *Telephone:* (118) 378-8050 (office). *Fax:* (118) 926-2667 (office). *E-mail:* contact@stephenbuckley.com (office). *Website:* www.stephenbuckley.com (office).

BUCKOVSKI, Vlado, PhD; Macedonian politician; *Chairman, Socijaldemokratski Sojuz na Makedonije—SDSM (Social Democratic Alliance of Macedonia);* b. 2 Dec. 1962, Skopje; ed Univ. of Skopje; expert legal collaborator for Parl. 1987–88; Jr Teaching Asst of Roman Law, Univ. of Skopje 1988–91, Sr Teaching Asst 1992–99, Docent 1999–, Assoc. Prof., Faculty of Law 2004–; mem. State Election Comm. 1998–2000; Party Spokesman Socijaldemokratski Sojuz na Makedonije—SDSM (Social Democratic Alliance of Macedonia) 1999–2001, Vice-Pres. SDSM 1999–2004, Chair. 2004–; Chair. Council of Skopje 2000–01; Minister of Defence May–Nov. 2001, Oct. 2002–04; Prime Minister of Fmr Yugoslav Repub. of Macedonia 2004–06. *Publications include:* academic papers on public law. *Address:* Socijaldemokratski Sojuz na Makedonije—SDSM (Social Democratic Alliance of Macedonia), 1000 Skopje, Bihačka 8, Macedonia (office). *Telephone:* (2) 3135380 (office). *Fax:* (2) 3120462 (office). *E-mail:* contact@sdsm.org.mk (office). *Website:* www.sdsm.org.mk (office).

BUCKSTEIN, Mark Aaron, JD, BS; American lawyer; b. 1 July 1939, New York; s. of Henry Buckstein and Minnie Buckstein; m. Rochelle J. Buchman 1960; one s. one d.; ed New York Univ. Law School and City Coll. of New York; Sr Partner, Baer, Marks & Upham (law firm), New York 1968–86; Special Prof. of Law, Hofstra Univ. School of Law 1981–93; Adjunct Prof. of Law, Rutgers Univ. Law School 1993–96; Sr Vice-Pres. and Gen. Counsel, Trans World Airlines Inc. 1986; Exec. Vice-Pres., Gen. Counsel GAF and Int. Speciality Products, NJ 1993–96; Dir Bayswater Realty and Capital Corpn, Travel Channel Inc., TWA; Counsel, Greenberg, Traurig, Fort Lauderdale, Fla 1996–99, Professional Dispute Resolution Inc., Boca Raton 1999–; mem. nat. arbitration and mediation cttee NASD 1998–2001. *Leisure interests:* tennis, puzzles, reading, music. *Address:* Professional Dispute Resolution, 1200 North Federal Highway, Boca Raton, FL 33432–2803 (office); 5832 Waterford, Boca Raton, FL 33496, USA (home). *Telephone:* (561) 447-8215 (office); (561) 994-6067 (home). *Fax:* mabresolve@aol.com (office).

BUDAKIAN, Raffi, BS, MS, PhD; American physicist and academic; *Professor of Physics, University of Illinois at Urbana-Champaign;* ed Univ. of California, Los Angeles; fmr Researcher, Physics Dept, UCLA; currently Prof. of Physics, Univ. of Illinois at Urbana-Champaign; Visiting Scientist, IBM Almaden Research Center, San Jose, Calif. 2002–05; Edwin Pauly Merit Fellowship, UCLA 1994–98, E. Lee Kinsey Award in Physics, UCLA 1994, IBM Research Div. Award for Single Spin Detection 2004, World Tech. Award in Materials, The World Tech. Network (co-recipient) 2005. *Achievements include:* part of team that made first demonstrations of magnetic resonance force microscopy (MRFM) 1992, work reached key milestone with manipulation and detection of individual electron spin 2004. *Publications:* numerous scientific papers in professional journals on experimental condensed matter physics, magnetic resonance force microscopy, ultra-sensitive force/displacement detection, design and fabrication of micro- and nanomechanical devices. *Address:* Room 106 MRL, Department of Physics, University of Illinois at Urbana-Champaign, 1110 West Green Street, Urbana, IL 61801-3080, USA (office). *Telephone:* (217) 333-3065 (office). *Fax:* (217) 244-8544 (office). *E-mail:* budakian@illinois.edu (office). *Website:* physics.illinois.edu (office).

BUDD, Sir Alan Peter, Kt, PhD; British economist and academic; *Provost, The Queen's College, University of Oxford;* b. 16 Nov. 1937, Kent; s. of Ernest Budd and Elsie Budd; m. Susan Millott 1964; three s.; ed Oundle School, London School of Economics, Cambridge Univ.; Lecturer in Econs, Southampton Univ. 1966–69; Ford Foundation Visiting Prof., Carnegie-Mellon

Univ., USA 1969–70; Sr Econ. Adviser, HM Treasury 1970–74; Sr Research Fellow, London Business School 1974–81, Prof. of Econs 1981–88, Fellow 1997; Econ. Adviser, Barclays Bank 1988–91; Chief Econ. Adviser to HM Treasury 1991–97; Provost, The Queen's Coll. Oxford 1999–; mem. Bank of England Monetary Policy Cttee 1997–99; Visiting Prof., Univ. of NSW, Australia 1983; Grocers' Co. Scholarship; Leverhulme Undergraduate Scholarship; Chair. Gambling Review Body 2000–01; Gov. Nat. Inst. of Econ. and Social Research 1998–; Chair. (non-exec.) Oxford Biosensors Ltd 2001–02. *Publication:* Politics of Economic Planning 1978. *Leisure interests:* music, gardening, reading. *Address:* The Queen's College, Oxford, OX1 4AW, England (office). *Telephone:* (1865) 279125 (office). *Website:* www.queens.ox.ac.uk (office).

BUDIŠA, Dražen; Croatian fmr politician and linguist; *Editor, Školska Knjiga;* b. 25 July 1948, Drniš; m. Nada Budiša; three s.; ed Zagreb Univ.; Pres. of Students' League of Zagreb 1971; Pres. Croatian Social-Liberal Party (Hrvatska socijalno-liberalna stranka—HSLS) 1990–96, 2002–04; Minister in Croatian Govt 1991–92; mem. House of Reps (Parl.) of Croatia 1992, 1995–2003; presidential cand. 2000; currently Ed., Školska Knjiga. *Publications:* Beginning of Printing in Europe 1984, Heritage of Croatian Reformers in Custody of the National and University Library 1985, Humanism in Croatia 1988, Croatian Books Published in Venice from 15th to 18th Centuries 1990. *Leisure interest:* gardening. *Address:* Školska Knjiga, 28, 10000 Zagreb, Croatia (office). *Website:* www.skolska.com.hr (office).

BUDOWSKI, Gerardo, MS, PhD; Venezuelan agronomist and forester; *Emeritus Professor, Tropical Agricultural Research and Training Centre, Costa Rica;* b. (Gert Budowski), 10 June 1925, Berlin, Germany; s. of Dr Issar Budowski and Marguerite Wolffgang; m. Thelma T. Palma 1958; two d.; ed Univ. Central de Venezuela, Inter-American Inst. of Agricultural Sciences, Turrialba, Costa Rica and Yale Univ. School of Forestry; Div. of Research, Ministry of Agriculture Forestry Service 1947–49, Head 1949–52; Head of Renewable Resources, Inter-American Inst. of Agricultural Sciences 1953–67; Visiting Prof. of Geography and Forestry, Univ. of Calif., Berkeley 1967; Programme Specialist for Ecology and Conservation, UNESCO, Paris 1967–70; Dir-Gen. Int. Union for Conservation of Nature and Nat. Resources (UICN) 1970–76; Head, Renewable Natural Resources Dept, Tropical Agricultural Research and Training Centre (CATIE), Costa Rica 1976–86, Prof. Emer. 1996–; Dir Natural Resources, Univ. for Peace, Costa Rica 1986–2001, Vice-Rector 2000–01, now Prof. Emer.; Int. Co-ordinator for Agroforestry, UN Univ. (Tokyo) 1978–; Special Adviser to Worldwide Fund for Nature (WWF) 1995–; Pres. The Ecotourism Soc. 1993–97, Life mem. 2000–; mem. Tech. Advisory Cttee, Consultative Group on Int. Agricultural Research 1989–93, Earth Council Advisory Cttee 1992–, Deputy Dir 1997–99; Hon. mem. Int. Union for Conservation of Nature and Natural Resources, Int. World Wide Fund for Nature, Soc. of American Foresters; Order of the Golden Ark (Netherlands) 1976, Order Henry Pittier, 1st Class (Venezuela) 1979, Order Semper Virens (Nicaragua) 1994; IUCN Fred Packard Award 1991. *Publications:* La Conservación como instrumento para el desarrollo 1985 and more than 250 articles. *Leisure interest:* chess (champion of Venezuela and mem. of Olympic team). *Address:* PO Box 198, 2300 Curridabat, San José, Costa Rica (home); University for Peace, 138–6100 Ciudad Colón, San José (office). *Telephone:* (506) 205-9000 (office); (506) 2253008 (home). *Fax:* (506) 249-1929 (office); (506) 253-4227 (home). *E-mail:* gbudowski@upeace.org (office). *Website:* www.upeace.org (office).

BUERGENTHAL, Thomas, LLM, JD, SJD; American judge and academic; *Judge, International Court of Justice;* b. 11 May 1934, Lubochna, Slovakia; s. of Mundek Buergenthal and Gerda Buergenthal; m. 2nd Marjorie Julia Buergenthal (née Bell); three s. from previous m.; ed Bethany Coll., W Va, New York Univ. Law School (Root Tilden Scholar), Harvard Law School; became US citizen 1957; mem. (Judge, then Pres.) Inter-American Court on Human Rights 1979–91; mem. (Judge, then Pres.) Admin. Tribunal, IDB 1989–94; mem. UN Human Rights Comm. 1995–99; mem. Claims Resolution Tribunal for Dormant Accounts, Switzerland 1998–99, Vice-Chair. 1999; Judge, Int. Court of Justice 2000–; Lobingier Prof. Emer. of Int. and Comparative Law, George Washington Univ. Law School, Washington, DC; Dr hc (Bethany Coll.) 1981, (Heidelberg Univ.) 1986, (Free Univ. of Brussels) 1994, (State Univ. of New York) 2000, (American Univ., Washington, DC) 2002, (Univ. of Minnesota) 2003, (George Washington Univ.) 2004; Manley O. Hudson Medal, American Soc. of Int. Law 2002, and numerous other awards. *Publications include:* Law-Making in the International Civil Aviation Organization 1969, International Protection of Human Rights (with L. B. Sohn) 1973, Protecting Human Rights in the Americas (with D. Shelton, fourth edn) 1995, International Human Rights (with D. Shelton and D. Stewart, third edn) 2002, Public International Law (with S. Murphy, third edn) 2002. *Address:* International Court of Justice, Peace Palace, Carnegieplein 2, 2517 KJ The Hague, Netherlands (office). *Telephone:* (70) 3022408 (office). *Fax:* (70) 3022464 (office). *E-mail:* t.buergenthalon@icj-cij.org (office).

BUFE, Uwe-Ernst, PhD; German business executive and chemist; b. 22 May 1944, Teschen; m.; two c.; ed Technische Universität, Munich; with Spang and Co. 1971–74; Product Man. Degussa Frankfurt 1974, Corp. Devt and Inorganic Chemicals 1981, mem. Bd Degussa AG 1987, Corp. Devt Degussa Corpn 1977, Exec. Vice-Pres. Chemical Group 1985, Chair. Bd, CEO 1996–99, Chair. Degussa-Hüls AG 1999–. *Address:* Degussa-Hüls AG, 60287 Frankfurt am Main, Germany. *Telephone:* (69) 21801. *Fax:* (69) 2183218.

BUFFET, Marie-George; French politician; *National Secretary, Parti Communiste Français;* b. 7 May 1949, Sceaux (Hauts-de-Seine); d. of Paul Kossellek and Raymonde Rayer; m. Jean-Pierre Buffet 1972; two c.; joined Parti Communiste Français (PCF) 1969, elected to PCF Cen. Cttee 1987, mem. Nat. Bureau 1994, Head Nat. Women's Cttee 1996, elected to Nat. Secr. 1997, Nat. Sec. 2001–; municipal councillor, then Deputy Mayor Châtenay-Malabry (Hautes-de-Seine) 1977–83; Nat. Ass. Deputy for Seine-Saint-Denis 1997–; Minister for Youth and Sport 1997–2002. *Address:* Parti Communiste Français, 2 place du Colonel Fabien, 75019 Paris, France (office). *Telephone:* 1-40-40-12-12 (office). *Fax:* 1-40-40-13-56 (office). *E-mail:* pcf@pcf.fr (office). *Website:* www.pcf.fr (office).

BUFFETT, Warren Edward; American financier and investor; *Chairman and CEO, Berkshire Hathaway Inc.;* b. 30 Aug. 1930, Omaha, Neb.; s. of Howard Homan Buffett and Leila Stahl; m. 1st Susan Thompson 1952 (died 2004); two s. one d.; m. 2nd Astrid Menks 2006; ed Wharton Business School Univ. of Pennsylvania, Univ. of Neb., Columbia Univ. Business School; worked as investment salesman for father's brokerage firm 1951–54; Graham-Newman Corpn New York City 1954–56; formed Buffett Partnership, Omaha 1956–69; Chair. and CEO Berkshire Hathaway (investment co.), Omaha, Neb. 1969–, Nat. Indemnity Co., Buffalo Evening News; mem. Bd of Dirs Salomon Brothers 1987–, interim Chair. and CEO 1991–92; mem. Bd of Dirs Coca-Cola Co. (second largest stockholder in co.) 1989–2006; f. Buffet Foundation. *Address:* Berkshire Hathaway Inc., 1440 Kiewit Plaza, Omaha, NE 68131, USA (office). *Telephone:* (402) 346-1400 (office). *Fax:* (402) 346-3375 (office). *E-mail:* info@berkshirehathaway.com (office). *Website:* www.berkshirehathaway.com (office).

BUFI, Ylli; Albanian politician; b. 25 May 1948, Tiranë; m. Zana Bufi 1978; two d.; Minister of Foodstuff Industry 1990–91, of Food and Light Industry Feb.–May 1991, of Nutrition May–June 1991; Prime Minister of Albania June–Dec. 1991; Minister of the Public Economy and Privatization –2000; mem. Leading Cttee of Socialist Party; mem. Parl., Chair. Cttee on Industry, Energetics, Transport and Telecommunications, Cttee on Economy, Finance and Privatization 2002–. *Address:* c/o Ministry of the Public Economy and Privatization, c/o Këshilli i Ministrave, Tirana, Albania. *E-mail:* ybufi@hotmail.com.

BUHARI, Maj.-Gen. Muhammadu; Nigerian government official and army officer (retd); b. 17 Dec. 1942, Daura, Katsina Prov. of Kaduna; m. Safinatu Yusuf 1971; two d.; ed Katsina Prov. Secondary School, Nigerian Mil. Training Coll., Mons Officers' Cadet School, Aldershot, England; joined Army 1962; commissioned 1963; served 2nd Bn in Congo (now Zaire) 1963–64; Army Service Corps 1964–66; staff and command appointments in 1st and 3rd Infantry Divs; Defence Service Staff Coll., Wellington, India 1972–73; Acting Dir of Supply and Transport, Nigerian Army 1974–75; Mil. Gov. of North Eastern State (divided into three States Feb. 1976) 1975–76, of Borno State Feb.–March 1976; Fed. Commr for Petroleum 1976–78; Chair. Nigerian Nat. Petroleum Corpn 1976–80; Mil. Sec. Nigerian Army 1978; mem. Supreme Mil. Council 1976–77; overthrew Govt of Shehu Shagari (q.v.); Head of State, Chair. Supreme Mil. Council and C-in-C of Armed Forces 1983–85; detained 1985–88, released 1988; mem. All Nigeria's People's Party (ANPP), presidential cand. 2003, 2007; Chair. Special Trust Fund 1994–. *Leisure interests:* tennis, squash, golf. *Address:* c/o All Nigeria People's Party, Plot 274, Central Area, Behind NICON Plaza, Abuja; GRA, Daura, Katsina State, Nigeria.

BUHL RASMUSSEN, Jørgen, BEcons, MBA; Danish business executive; *President and CEO, Carlsberg A/S;* b. 18 Aug. 1955; ed Copenhagen School of Econs and Business Admin; Research Man. and Consultant IFH Research Int. (Unilever), Denmark 1979–82; Product Group Man. A/S Lagerman, Slagelse 1982–85; Marketing Man. Pet Food, MasterFoods Denmark 1985–87; Nordic Marketing Dir Duracell Denmark 1987–88, Gen. Man. Duracell Denmark and Finland 1988–93, Gen. Man. Duracell UK and Ireland 1993–95, Area Dir Duracell N Europe 1995–97; Pres. Gillette Group N Europe 1997–99, Pres. Gillette Group AMEE (Africa, Middle East, E Europe) 2001–06; mem. Exec. Bd Carlsberg A/S 2006–, Exec. Vice-Pres. 2006–07, Pres. and CEO 2007–. *Address:* Carlsberg A/S, 100 Ny Carlsberg Vej, 1760 Copenhagen V, Denmark (office). *Telephone:* 33-27-33-00 (office). *Fax:* 33-27-48-08 (office). *Website:* www.carlsberggroup.com (office).

BUICAN, Denis, DèsScNat, DèsL et ScHum; Romanian/French academic, biologist and philosopher of biology; *Honorary Professor, Université de Paris X Nanterre;* b. 21 Dec. 1934, Bucharest; s. of Dumitru Peligrad and Elena Buican; ed Bucharest Univ., Faculté des Sciences de Paris, Univ. de Paris I-Sorbonne; teaching asst, Bucharest Univ. 1956–57, Prin. Scientific Researcher 1957–60, Course Leader Gen. Biology and Genetics with History of Science course 1960–69, Invited Prof. 1990–; Invited Prof. First Class, History of Sciences, Faculté des Sciences, Univ. de Paris 1969–70, Univ. de Paris-Sorbonne 1970–74, Assoc. Prof., History and Philosophy of Science 1970–74; Assoc. Prof., History and Philosophy of Science, Univ. of Dijon 1974–80; Assoc. Prof., History of Sciences, Univ. de Paris I Panthéon-Sorbonne 1980–83; Assoc. Prof. First Class, History of Sciences, Univ. de Paris X 1983–86; Invited Prof. Collège de France 1984, 1993; Prof. First Class, Univ. de Paris X Nanterre 1986–2003, Hon. Prof. 2003–; Hon. Citizen of Saliste (Romania) 2003; Grand Prix, Acad. Française 1989. *Achievements:* developed new synergetic theory of evolution and Biognoseology theory of knowledge. *Publications include:* Histoire de la génétique et de l'évolutionnisme en France 1984, La Génétique et l'évolution 1986, Génétique et pensée évolutionniste 1987, Darwin et le darwinisme 1987, Lyssenko et le lyssenkisme 1988, L'Evolution et les évolutionnismes 1989, La Révolution de l'évolution 1989, L'Explosion biologique, du néant au Sur-être 1991, Dracula et ses avatars de Vlad l'Empaleur à Staline et Ceausescu 1991, Charles Darwin 1992, Mendel et la génétique d'hier et d'aujourd'hui 1993, Les Métamorphoses de Dracula 1993, Biognoséologie: Evolution et révolution de la connaissance 1993, Jean Rostand 1994, Histoire de la Biologie 1994, Evolution de la pensée biologique 1995, L'Evolution aujourd'hui 1995, L'Evolution: la grande aventure de la vie 1995, Ethologie comparée 1996, Dictionnaire de Biologie 1997, L'Evolution et les théories évolutionnistes

1997, L'Epopée du vivant, L'Evolution de la biosphère et les avatars de l'Homme 2003, Le Darwinisme et les évolutionnismes 2005, Memorii 2007, L'Odyssée de l'Evolution 2008, Darwin dans l'histoire de la pensée biologique 2008, Mendal dans l'histoire de la génétique 2008; poetry books: Arbre seul 1974, Lumière aveugle 1976, Mamura 1993, Spice (poèmes anciens et nouveaux) 2006, Margaritare negre (Perles noires) 2008, Roue de torture-Roue de lumière 2009. *Leisure interests:* literature and the arts. *Address:* 15 rue Poliveau, 75005 Paris, France (home). *Telephone:* 1-43-36-33-97 (home).

BUIJNSTERS, Piet J.; Dutch academic; *Professor of Dutch Literature, University of Nijmegen;* b. 18 Oct. 1933, Breda; s. of Adriaan Buijnsters and Johanna Wirken; m. Leontine Smets 1961; two s. two d.; ed Univs of Nijmegen and Tübingen; f. Werkgroep 18e Eeuw (with CM Geerars) 1968; Prof. of Dutch Literature, Univ. of Nijmegen 1971–; mem. Royal Netherlands Acad. of Arts and Sciences; Anne Frank Foundation Prize 1964, Jan Campbert Stiching Prize 1974, Menno Hertzberg Prize 1981. *Publications:* Tussen twee werelden: Rhijnvis Feith als dichter van 'Het Graf' 1963, Hieronymus van Alphen 1746–1803 1973, Nederlandse literatuur van de acht-tiende eeuw 1984, Wolff en Deken, een biografie 1984, Briefwisseling van Betje Wolff en Aagje Deken 1987, Het verzamelen van boeken 1985. *Leisure interest:* book collecting. *Address:* University of Nijmegen, Department of Language and Literature, Erasmusplein 1, 6525 GG Nijmegen (office); Witsenburgselaan 35, 6524 TE Nijmegen, Netherlands (home). *Telephone:* (80) 512888 (office); (80) 225466 (home).

BUIRA, Ariel, MA; Mexican economist; *Professor of Economics, Universidad Iberoamericana, Mexico, DF;* b. 20 Sept. 1940, Chihuahua; s. of Antonio Buira and Enriqueta Seira de Buira; m. Janet Clark 1965; two s.; ed Univ. of Manchester, UK; Lecturer, Centre for Econ. and Demographic Studies, El Colegio de México 1966–68; Prof. of Econs, Grad. School of Business, Instituto Tecnológico de Monterrey 1968–70; Economist, IMF 1970–74; Econ. Adviser to Gov., Man. for Int. Research, Banco de México, SA 1975–78, Deputy Dir then Dir for Int. Orgs and Agreements 1982–94, then Deputy Gov. and mem. Bd of Govs; Del. to Conf. on Int. Econ. Co-operation (CIEC) (Financial Affairs Comm.) 1976–77; Alt. Exec. Dir, IMF 1978–80, Exec. Dir for Mexico, Spain, Venezuela, Cen. America 1980–82; Chair. Bd of Dirs BLADEX 1985–94; mem. Bd of Govs Bank of Mexico 1994–96; Amb. to Greece 1998–2001; Sr mem., St Antony's Coll., Oxford 2001–02; Special Envoy of the Pres. of Mexico and Chair. of the Panel, UN Int. Conf. on Financing for Devt 2002; Dir Secretariat, Intergovernmental Group of Twenty Four on Int. Monetary Affairs and Devt (G–24) 2002–06; currently Prof. of Econs, Univ. Iberoamericana, Mexico, DF; Order of the Phoenix (Greece) 2001; First Prize, Course on Econ. Integration, Coll. Européen des Sciences Sociales et Economiques 1963, Medal of the City of Athens 2001. *Publications:* 50 Años de Banca Central (jtly) 1976, LDC External Debt and the World Economy 1978, Directions for Reform – The Future of the International Monetary System (jtly) 1984, México: Crisis Financiera y Programa de Ajuste in América Latina: Deuda, Crisis y Perspectivas 1984; Is There a Need for Reform? 1984; contrib.: Politics and Economics of External Debt Crisis – The Latin American Experience 1985, Incomes Policy (ed. V. L. Urquidi) 1987, Money and Finance Vol. I (R. Tandon) 1987, Adjustment with Growth and the Role of the IMF 1987, La Economía Mundial: Evolución y Perspectivas 1989, Una Evalución de la Estrategia de la Deuda 1989, Los Determinantes del Ahorro en México 1990, Evolución de la Estrategia de la Deuda 1990, International Liquidity and the Needs of the World Economy (Vol. IV) 1994, Reflections on the International Monetary System 1995, Can Currency Crises be Prevented or Better Managed? (co-ed. Jan Joost Teunissen) 1996, The Potential of the SDR for Improving the International Monetary System 1996, Reflections on the Mexican Crisis of 1994 1996; and numerous articles and essays; as ed.: The IMF and the World Bank at Sixty 2005, Introduction (in The IMF and the World at Sixty) 2005, The IMF at Sixty: An Unfulfilled Potential? (in The IMF and the World at Sixty) 2005, Reforming the Governance of the IMF and the World Bank 2005, The Bretton Woods Institutions: Governance Without Legitimacy? (in Reforming the Governance of the IMF and the World Bank) 2005; as contrib. and ed.: The Governance of the IMF in a Global Economy, An Analysis of IMF Conditionality (in Challenges to the World Bank and the IMF: Developing Country Perspectives) 2003; as contrib.: Curbing the Impact of Shocks (in Protecting the Poor; ed. Jan Joost Teunissen and Age Akkerman) 2005, Does the IMF Need More Financial Resources? (in Reform of the IMF for the 21st Century; ed. Edwin M. Truman) 2006. *Leisure interests:* music, literature. *Address:* Ruben Dario 45, piso 9, Col. Ricon del Bosque, México, DF 11560, Mexico (home). *Telephone:* (55) 5250-1711 (home). *Fax:* (202) 623-6000 (office). *E-mail:* abuiras@yahoo.com.mx (home).

BUITER, Willem Hendrik, CBE, PhD, FBA; American/British professor of economics; *Chief Economist and Special Counsellor to the President, European Bank for Reconstruction and Development;* b. 26 Sept. 1949, The Hague, Netherlands; s. of Hendrien Buiter van Schooten and Harm Geert Buiter; m. 1st Jean Archer 1988; two c.; m. 2nd Anne C. Sibert 1998; ed Univ. of Cambridge, Yale Univ.; Asst Prof. of Econs and Int. Affairs, Woodrow Wilson School, Princeton Univ. 1975–79; Prof. of Econs, Univ. of Bristol 1980–82; Cassel Prof. of Econs with Special Reference to Money and Banking, LSE 1982–85; Prof. of Econs, Yale Univ. 1985–94, Juan T. Trippe Prof. of Int. Econs 1990–94; Prof. of Int. Macroeconomics, Univ. of Cambridge 1994–; mem. Monetary Policy Cttee, Bank of England 1997–2000; Chief Economist and Special Counsellor to the Pres., EBRD 2000–; Consultant IMF, IBRD, IDB 1979–; Adviser House of Commons Treasury Select Cttee, UK 1980–82, Netherlands Ministry of Educ. 1985–86, EC, DGII 1982–85; Corresp. mem. Royal Netherlands Acad. of Sciences 1995–, Research Assoc. Nat. Bureau of Econ. Research, Research Fellow Centre for Econ. Policy Research; N. G. Pierson Medal (Netherlands) 2000. *Publications:* Temporary and Long-run Equilibrium 1979, Budgetary Policy, International and Intertemporal Trade in the Global Economy 1989, Macroeconomic Theory and Stabilization Policy 1989, Principles of Budgetary and Financial Policy 1990, International Macroeconomics 1990, Financial Markets and European Monetary Cooperation: The Lessons of the 92–93 ERM crisis (with Giancarlo Corsetti and Paolo Pesenti) 1997. *Leisure interests:* tennis, theatre, westerns, science fiction and fantasy novels, poetry. *Address:* European Bank for Reconstruction and Development, One Exchange Square, London, EC2A 2JN (office); 2 St David's Square, London, E14 3WA, England (home). *Telephone:* (20) 7338-6805 (office); (20) 7517-9289 (home); (20) 7338-6037. *Fax:* (20) 7338-6110 (office). *E-mail:* buiterw@ebrd.com (office); willembuiter@whsmithnet.co.uk (home). *Website:* ebrdnet.ebrd.com (office); www.nber.org/wbuiter (home).

BUJAK, Zbigniew; Polish politician and trade union official; b. 29 Nov. 1954, Łopuszno; ed Warsaw Univ.; worked in Polfa Pharmaceutical plant, Grodzisk Mazowiecki, then Ursus Mechanical Works 1973–81; nat. service in airborne commando div. 1974–76; organizer of strike in Ursus Works in July 1980; assoc. Workers' Cttee for solidarity with striking coastal workers Aug. 1980; Chair. Founding Cttee Solidarity Trade Union, Mazowsze Region 1980; mem. Nat. Consultative Comm. of Solidarity, took part in negotiations with Govt 1981; under martial law in hiding, continued union activity 1981–86; Chair. Bd Mazowsze Region in Provisional Exec. Comm. of Solidarity 1982–86; arrested May 1986, pardoned Sept. 1986; mem. Nat. Exec. Comm. of Solidarity 1987–90; Chair. Citizens' Cttee of Solidarity 1988–90; took part in Round Table debates in Groups for Political Reform and for Economy and Social Policy Feb.–April 1989; Chair. Council of Warsaw Agreement of Citizens' Cttees 1990–91; one of founders and leaders Citizens' Movt–Democratic Action (ROAD) 1990–91; Deputy to Sejm (Parl.) 1991–97, Chair. Sejm Comm. of Admin. and Internal Affairs 1993–97; Chair. Cen. Bd of Customs 1999–2001; Chair. of Democratic-Social Movt 1991; Co-Founder and Vice-Chair. Union of Labour (UP) 1992–98; mem. Freedom Union (UW) Party 1998–; fmr mem. Socialist Rural Youth Union; Robert F. Kennedy Human Rights Award 1988. *Publication:* Przepraszam za Solidarność 1991. *Address:* Główny Urząd Ceł, ul. Świętokrzyska 12, 00-916 Warsaw, Poland. *Telephone:* (22) 6944946 (office). *E-mail:* gabinet_prezesa_guc@guc.gov.pl (office). *Website:* www.guc.gov.pl (office).

BUJOLD, Genevieve; Canadian actress; b. 1 July 1942, Montréal; m. Paul Almond 1967 (divorced); one s.; ed Montréal Conservatory of Drama; fmr cinema usherette in Montréal. *Films include:* La guerre est finie, La fleur de l'age, Entre la mer et l'eau douce, King of Hearts, The Thief of Paris, Isabel, Anne of the Thousand Days, The Act of the Heart, The Trojan Women, The Journey, Earthquake, Alex and the Gypsy, Kamouraska, Obsession, Swashbuckler, Another Man Another Chance, Coma, Murder by Decree, Final Assignment, The Last Flight of Noah's Ark, Monsignor, Tightrope, Choose Me, Trouble in Mind, The Moderns, Dead Ringers, False Identity, Secret Places of the Heart, A Paper Wedding, Star Trek: Generations, An Ambush of Ghosts, Mon Ami Max, Dead Innocent 1996, The House of Yes 1997, Last Night 1998, Eye of the Beholder 1999, Alex in Wonder 2001, La Turbulence des fluides 2002, Jericho Mansions 2003, Finding Home 2003, Downtown: A Street Tale 2004, Mon petit doigt m'a dit 2005, Disappearances 2006, Délivrez-moi 2006. *Stage appearances include:* The Barber of Seville, A Midsummer Night's Dream, A House... A Day. *TV appearances include:* St Joan, Antony and Cleopatra, Mistress of Paradise, Red Earth, White Earth, Star Trek. *Address:* c/o William Morris Agency, One William Morris Place, Beverly Hills, CA 90212, USA (office).

BUJON DE L'ESTANG, François; French diplomatist and business executive; *Chairman, Citigroup France;* b. 21 Aug. 1940, Neuilly-sur-Seine, Hauts-de-Seine; s. of Henry Bujon de l'Estang and Vera Markels; m. Anne Jacquin de Margerie 1963; four c.; ed Institut Politique de Paris, Ecole Nat. d'Admin, Harvard Grad. School of Business Admin; Office of Perm. Rep., Ministry of Foreign Affairs 1966; Special Adviser on staff of Pres. of Repub. 1966, Deputy to Pres.'s Diplomatic Adviser –1969; Second, then First Sec., Embassy in Washington, DC 1969–73; First Sec. and Second Counsellor in London 1973–75; Adviser on Int. Affairs to Del. Gen. for Energy, Ministry of Industry 1975–77; Dir for Int. Relations, Atomic Energy Commissariat 1978–79, Chief of Staff 1980–81; French Rep. on Bd of Govs IAEA 1979; f. COGEMA Inc., Washington, DC 1982, Pres. and CEO 1982–86; apptd Amb. to Mexico 1986 (did not take up post); Sr Adviser to Pres. Chirac for Diplomatic Affairs, Defence and Co-operation 1986–88; Amb. to Canada 1989–91, to USA 1995–2002, rank of Amb. of France 1999; mem. Bd Dirs Sofratome, Technicatome and Eurodif 1979–80, Copperweld Corpn (Imetal Group) 1982–86; Sr Vice-Pres. Compagnie de Navigation Mixte and Via Banque 1991–92; Chair. and CEO SFIM 1991–92, mem. Bd Dirs 1991–93; f. FBE International Consultants 1992; mem. Bd Dirs Banque Indosuez 1993–95, CNES 2003–, Institut Pasteur 2003–05, Tembec Inc. 2005–07, Thales 2003–, IFRI 2003–; mem. Int. Advisory Bd TOTAL 2004–; Chair. Citigroup France 2003–; Vice-Chair. French-American Foundation, NY 2003–; Pres. Harvard Business School Club of France 1992–95; Officier, Legion d'honneur, Commdr, Ordre nat. du Mérite. *Address:* Citigroup France, 1–5 rue Paul Cezanne, 75008 Paris, France (office); FBE International Consultants, 38 rue Marbeuf, 75008 Paris, France (office). *Telephone:* 1-70-75-50-81 (office); 1-42-25-55-53 (office). *Fax:* 1-70-75-50-82 (office); 1-42-25-55-56 (office). *E-mail:* francois .bujondelestang@citigroup.com (office); francois.bujondelestang@wanadoo.fr (office). *Website:* www.citibank.fr (office).

BUKAR, Muftah Abd as-Salam; Libyan politician; currently Sec. for Security Affairs. *Address:* General Secretariat of the General People's Congress, Tripoli, Libya (office).

BUKAYEV, Gennadii Ivanovich; Russian politician and engineer; b. 15 Sept. 1947, Stepnoye, Orenburg Region; m.; one s.; ed Ufa Inst. Oil., Sverdlovsk Higher CPSU School; Sr Engineer 1972–75; Head of Div. Ufa

Inst. of Oil 1975–77; Deputy Chair. Ufa Regional Exec. Cttee 1977–78; Instructor Bashkiria Regional Exec. CPSU Cttee 1980–85; Chair. Belebelyevo City CP Exec. Cttee. 1985–90; Head Div. of Trade Council of Ministers Bashkiria Autonomous Repub. 1990–92; Head State Taxation Inspection Repub. of Bashkortostan 1992–99; mem. Exec. Bd Ministry of Taxes and Levies of Russian Fed. 1999–2000, Minister 2000–04; Presidential Aide 2004–. *Address:* c/o Office of the President, Kremlin, 103073 Moscow, Russia (office).

BUKEJLOVIĆ, Pero, MEng; Bosnia and Herzegovina politician and engineer; b. 9 Aug. 1946, Bušletic, Doboj municipality; m.; one s.; ed Univ. of Sarajevo, Univ. of Zagreb; various positions as engineer; Gen. Man. Trudbenik Co.; Minister of Industry and Tech. 2001–03; Prime Minister of Republika Srpska 2003–06. *Address:* c/o Office of the Prime Minister, 78000 Banja Luka, Vuka Karadžica 4, Bosnia and Herzegovina (office).

BUKENYA, Gilbert Balibaseka, MSc, MD, PhD; Ugandan politician and professor of public health; *Vice-President;* b. May 1949, Wakiso Dist; m.; three c.; ed Makerere Univ. Medical School, Royal Inst. of Public Health and Hygiene, London, UK, Ross Inst., London School of Hygiene and Tropical Medicine, Univ. of Queensland, Australia; internship in Uganda; following studies in public health in London returned to Uganda in 1983; Lecturer, Inst. of Public Health, Makerere Univ. 1983–84, Dir 1989, Assoc. Prof. 1993, Dean Faculty of Medicine 1995; Lecturer, Dept of Community Medicine, Univ. of Papua New Guinea 1984–87, Head of Dept 1987–89; Assoc. Prof., Tulane Univ. School of Public Health, New Orleans, La, USA 1995–; Adjunct Prof. of Int. Health, Case Western Reserve Univ., Cleveland, OH, USA 2004–; MP for Busiro North 1996–, Chair. Movement Caucus; Minister of State for Trade and Minister in charge of the Presidency; Vice-Pres. of Uganda 2003–; Chair. Nat. Advisory Cttee on Environmental Health and Maternal and Child Health, Papua New Guinea 1985–91, Bd of Examiners, Coll. of Allied Health Sciences Health Inspectors' Programme 1985–91; Vice-Chair. Network of African Postgraduate Public Health Training Schools, WHO-Afro Region 1992–94, Chair. 1994–96. *Address:* c/o Office of the President, Parliament Building, POB 7168, Kampala, Uganda (office). *Telephone:* (41) 258441 (office). *Fax:* (41) 256143 (office). *E-mail:* vp@statehouse.go.ug (office). *Website:* www.statehouse.go.up (office).

BUKHARY, Tan Sri Syed Mokhtar al-; Malaysian business executive; *Executive Chairman, Al-Bukhary Foundation;* b. 1952, Alor Star; m. Puan Sri Sharifah Zarah Al-Bukhary; five c.; began career in meat and later rice trading; f. transport business 1973; owns stakes in numerous cos in Malaysia and abroad, including Malaysian Mining Corpn (MMC), Johor Port Bhd, Malakoff (ind. power producer), Gas Malaysia; investment interests include plantations, property devt, construction, power generation, retailing, information tech., infrastructure and ports; f. Syarikat Impian Teladan Sendirian Bhd; Owner SKS Ventures; Exec. Chair Al-Bukhary Foundation; mem. Bd Syarikat Bina Puri Holdings Berhad; mem. United Malays Nat. Org.; Panglima Setia Mahkota, Dato' Setia Mahkota Kedah, announced and awarded Tokoh Ma'al Hijrah by The Yang Di Pertuan Agong of Malaysia in recognition of his contrib. to nation building 2008. *Address:* Al-Bukhary Foundation, Kuala Lumpur, Malaysia (office).

BUKOVAC, Martin J., PhD; American scientist and academic; *Distinguished Professor Emeritus, Department of Horticulture, Michigan State University;* b. 12 Nov. 1929, Johnston City, Ill.; s. of John Bukovac and Sadie Fak; m. Judith A. Kelley 1956; one d.; ed Mich. State Univ.; Asst Prof., Dept of Horticulture, Mich. State Univ. 1957–61, Assoc. Prof. 1961–63, Prof. 1963–92, Univ. Distinguished Prof. 1992–, now Distinguished Prof. Emer.; Biological Science Collaborator, USDA/Agricultural Research Service 1982–2003; Postdoctoral Fellow, Univs of Oxford and Bristol, UK 1965–66; Dir Mich. State Univ. Press 1983–91; Adviser, Eli Lilly Co. 1971–88; Pres. Martin J. Bukovac Inc. 1996–; Fellow, AAAS, American Soc. of Horticultural Science; mem. NAS, Editorial Advisory Bd Horticultural Abstracts 1990–2003, Editorial Bd Encyclopedia of Agricultural Science 1991–96, Int. Editorial Bd, Horticultural Science, Kertészetic Tudomány, Budapest 1989–2003; mem. Int. Advisory Bd, Life Sciences Div., Center for Nuclear Sciences, Grenoble 1993–2000; Hon. DrAgr (Bonn) 1995; Alexander von Humboldt Award for Sr Scientist 1995, Gold Veitch Memorial Medal, Hall of Fame, American Soc. for Horticultural Science 2001, Royal Horticultural Soc. 2003, Spiridon Brusina Medal, Croatian Soc. of Natural Sciences 2004. *Publications:* over 350 research articles. *Leisure interests:* photography, sports. *Address:* A390B Plant and Soil Sciences, Michigan State University, East Lansing, MI 48824-1325 (office); 4428 Seneca Drive, Okemos, MI 48864-2946, USA (home). *Telephone:* (517) 355-5191, ext 393 (office); (517) 349-1952 (home). *Fax:* (517) 353-0890 (office). *E-mail:* bukovacm@msu.edu (office). *Website:* www.hrt.msu.edu/faculty/bukovac.htm (office).

BUKOVSKY, Vladimir Konstantinovich, MA; Russian writer and scientist; b. 30 Dec. 1942, Belebey; s. of Konstantin Bukovsky and Nina Bukovsky; ed Moscow State Univ., Univ. of Cambridge; worked at Moscow Centre of Cybernetics; arrested for possessing banned literature 1963, confined to Leningrad Psychiatric Prison Hosp. for 15 months; arrested for demonstration on behalf of Soviet writers 1965, confined for eight months in psychiatric institutions; arrested for civil rights work 1967, on trial Sept. 1967 and sentenced to three years' corrective labour; arrested for delivering information on psychiatric abuse to the West 1971, on trial 1972 and sentenced to two years in prison, five in a labour camp and five in exile; after world-wide campaign for his release, was exchanged for Chilean Communist Party leader Luis Corvalán in Zürich Dec. 1976; citizenship restored 1992; research work, Stanford Univ., Calif. 1982–90; f. Centre for Democracy in Support of New Russia, New York; co-founder political group 'Committee 2008' 2004 (aimed to promote free and fair 2008 presidential elections; last meeting 2005); nominated candidate 2008 presidential elections 2007; hon. mem. several human rights orgs, several PEN clubs; lives in England; Konrad Adenauer Freedom and Literature Prize 1984. *Publications:* short stories in Russia's Other Writers 1970 and in Grani, Opposition–Eine neue Geisteskrankheit in der USSR (German edn) 1972, A Manual on Psychiatry for Dissenters (with Semyon Gluzman) 1974, To Build a Castle: My Life as a Dissenter (in English; trans. in Swedish, Italian, Spanish, French and German) 1978, Cette lancinante douleur de la liberté 1981, The Peace Movement and the Soviet Union 1982. *Leisure interests:* the arts, architecture. *Website:* bukovsky.org/official/ (office).

BUL-BUL, Polad Oğlu, PhD; Azerbaijani composer, singer and film actor; b. 4 Feb. 1945, Baku; s. of Bul-Bul; ed Azerbaijan State Conservatory; head of pop-music ensembles 1975–87; Head Azerbaijan State Philharmonic 1987–88; Minister of Culture 1988–; mem. Milli-Medjlis 1995–; Dir-Gen. Int. Org. TURKSOI 1994; Hon. Prof., Azerbaijan Univ. of Culture and Arts; Prof. Int. Humanitarian Acad.; People's Artist of Azerbaijan. *Music:* symphonic works, chamber and instrumental music, musical, vocal cycles, incidental music, pop-songs. *Address:* Ministry of Culture, Azadliq meydani1, 1016 Baku (office); Fioletova str. 6/8, Apt 53, Baku, Azerbaijan (home). *Telephone:* (12) 4934398 (office); (12) 4932177 (home). *Fax:* (12) 4935605 (office).

BULAI, Igor Borisovich, CandHist; Russian diplomatist; b. 17 May 1947, Moscow; m.; two c.; ed Moscow State Inst. of Int. Relations, Inst. of USA and Canada Acad. of Sciences; Jr Researcher, Inst. of USA and Canada 1973–79; Instructor, Div. of Information Cen. Cttee CPSU 1979–85; Counsellor, Embassy in Washington, DC, USA 1985–91; with Dept of Information, USSR Ministry of Foreign Affairs 1991–92; Head, Dept of Information and Press, Ministry of Foreign Affairs of Russia 1992–98; Consul-Gen. in Edin. 1998–2001; mem. staff, Dept for Information and Press and Head, Press Centre, Ministry of Foreign Affairs 2001–05. *Address:* c/o Press Centre, Ministry of Foreign Affairs, Sadoraya-Sennaya 32/34, 119200 Moscow, Russia (office). *Telephone:* (495) 244-16-06 (office). *Fax:* (495) 230-21-30 (office). *E-mail:* ministry@mid.ru (office). *Website:* www.mid.ru (office).

BULATOVIĆ, Momir, CandEconSc; Montenegrin politician; b. 21 Sept. 1956, Belgrade; ed Titograd Univ.; fmr mem. League of Communists of Montenegro, then leader Republican League of Communists; Chair. Democratic Party of Socialists (DPS) 1990–98; Chair. Socialist People's Party of Montenegro (SNP) 1998–2001; Pres. of Montenegro 1990–98; Prime Minister of Yugoslavia 1998–2001. *Address:* Socialist People's Party of Montenegro, Podgorica, Montenegro (office).

BULATOVIĆ, Predrag; Montenegrin politician; b. 16 July 1956, Kolašin; m.; three d.; ed Faculty of Mechanical Eng, Univ. of Montenegro, Podgorica; various admin., teaching and exec. positions, Univ. of Montenegro 1975–80; Sec. of Montenegro Youth Org. and Socialist Fed. Repub. of Yugoslavia Youth Org. 1982–84; worked for Radoje Dakić Factory, Podgorica 1985–89; began career as professional politician 1989–; elected to Ass. of Repub. 1990–; elected to Fed. Ass. of Fmr Yugoslavia 2001–02, Chair. Foreign Policy Cttee 2000–03; Pres. Parliamentary Group of Democratic Party of Socialists (DPS) 1992–97; Vice-Pres. Socialist People's Party of Montenegro (SSPM–following division of DPS 1997) 1997–2001, Pres. 2001–02; Vice-Pres. Parl. Group of SSPM 1997–2001; mem. Montenegro Ass. 2006–, mem. Cttee for Int. Relation and European Integration; several Awards and Prizes from Univ. of Montenegro. *Address:* 13 Jula No. 49, Podgorica (home); Vaka Djurovica No. 5, Podgorica, Montenegro (office). *Telephone:* (20)-272 421 (office). *Fax:* (20) 272-421 (office). *Website:* www.snp.cg.yu (office).

BULCKE, Paul; Belgian business executive; *CEO, Nestlé SA;* b. 1954, Roeselare; m.; three c.; ed Univs of Louvain and Ghent, Belgium, Program for Exec. Devt, IMD Business School, Switzerland; financial analyst, Scott Graphics International, Bornem, Belgium 1977–79; with Nestlé Group, Vevey, Switzerland 1979–, marketing trainee, Nestlé SA (Switzerland, Spain, Belgium) 1979–80, Marketing, Sales and Div. functions, Nestlé Peru, Nestlé Ecuador and Nestlé Chile 1980–96, Man. Dir Nestlé Portugal 1996–98, Man. Dir Nestlé Czech and Slovak Repubs 1998–2000, Man. Dir Nestlé Germany, Frankfurt am Main 2000–03, Exec. Vice-Pres. responsible for Zone Americas: USA, Canada, Latin America, Caribbean 2004–08, CEO Designate and mem. designate Bd Nestlé SA 2007–08, mem. Bd Dirs and CEO 2008–; Co-Chair. Supervisory Bd Cereal Partners Worldwide; mem. Bd Alcon Inc. (Switzerland). *Address:* Nestlé SA, 1800 Vevey, Switzerland (office). *Telephone:* (21) 924-21-11 (office). *Fax:* (21) 921-18-85 (office). *E-mail:* webmaster@nestle.com (office). *Website:* www.nestle.com (office).

BULDAKOV, Aleksey Ivanovich; Russian actor; b. 26 March 1951, Makarovka, Altai Territory; m.; ed Pavlodar Drama Theatre Studio; worked in theatres in Pavlodar, Ryazan, Karaganda, Moscow. *Films include:* Through Fire 1982, Semen Dezhnev, Two Steps From Elysium, Sign of Trouble, Burn, Peculiarities of Russian Hunting, Quiet Investigation, Moonzund, Hey, Fools. *Address:* Kastanayevskaya str. 23, korp. 4, Apt 27, 121096 Moscow, Russia. *Telephone:* (495) 144-02-73.

BULGAK, Vladimir Borisovich, CandTechSc, DEconSc; Russian politician and business executive; b. 9 May 1941, Moscow; m.; one d.; ed Moscow Electrotech. Inst. of Communications, Inst. of Man. of Nat. Econ., USSR State Cttee on Science and Tech.; instructor, then sec. Moscow City Komsomol Cttee 1963–68; for 15 years worked in Moscow radio trans. network; head of depts USSR Ministry of Telecommunications 1983–90; Minister 1990–91; Minister of Telecommunications Russian Fed. 1991–97; Deputy Chair. Govt of Russian Fed. 1997–98, 1998–99; Minister of Science and Tech. April–Sept. 1998; Chair. TV-Holding Svyazinvest 1999–2001, Comincom-Combellga group 1999–2003; fmr Chair. Insurance Group Nasta; mem. Council of Dirs Sovintel (operating company of Golden Telecom) 2004–; mem. Int. Acad. of Informatization, Russian Acad. of Tech. Sciences, Russian Acad. of Natural Sciences; USSR

State Prize. *Publications:* several textbooks on communication techniques; over 100 articles and papers. *Address:* Golden Telecom, 1 Kozhevnicheskii prospect, 115114 Moscow, Russia (office). *Telephone:* (495) 787-10-00 (office). *E-mail:* info@goldentelecom.ru (office). *Website:* www.goldentelecom.ru (office).

BULGURLU, Bülent, MS, PhD; Turkish business executive; *CEO, Koç Holding AŞ;* b. 1947, Ankara; m.; three c.; ed Ankara Eng and Architectural Faculty, Norwegian Tech. Univ.; Construction Engineer, Elliot Strömme A/S, Oslo 1972; Asst Lecturer and Researcher, Norveç Tech. Univ. 1972–77; Project Man., Intes San. ve Tic. AŞ 1977–79; Construction Engineer, Garanti Insaat AŞ Oct.–Dec. 1979, Planning and Construction Man. 1979–81, Site Coordination Construction Man. 1981–82, Asst Gen. Man. 1982–84, Asst Gen. Man. (Tech.) 1984–86, Asst Gen. Man. (Production) Tech. Processes (by proxy) 1986–88, Gen. Man. 1988–90, Gen. Man. Garanti Koza Insaat AŞ 1990–96; Vice-Pres. Tourism and Services Group, Koç Holding AŞ 1996–2000, Pres. Tourism and Services Group 2000–01, Pres. Tourism and Construction Group 2001–03, Pres. Durable Goods and Construction Group 2004–07, mem. Bd of Dirs and CEO 2007–; mem. Turkish Industrialists' and Businessmen's Asscn (TÜSIAD), Altunizade Rotary Club, T.E.D. Club, Anatolian Club, Turkish Marine Environment Protection Asscn, Turkish Tourism Investors Asscn, Chaîne de Rotisseurs. *Address:* Koç Holding AŞ, Nakkaştepe Aziz Bey Sok. 1, Kuzguncuk, 34674 Istanbul, Turkey (office). *Telephone:* (216) 5310000 (office). *Fax:* (216) 5310099 (office). *E-mail:* info@koc.com.tr (office). *Website:* www.koc.com.tr (office); www.rmk-museum.org.tr (office).

BULIN, Gen. René Henri; French aeronautical engineer; b. 8 Aug. 1920, Langres; s. of Louis Bulin and Louise Bulin (née Walter); m. 1st Claudine Prostot 1955 (deceased); m. 2nd Catherine Tambuscio 1982; ed Ecole Polytechnique Paris, Ecole Nationale Supérieure de l'Aéronautique; engineer responsible for setting up Centre d'Essais des Propulseurs (Fort de Villeras) 1946–53; French Air Force pilot 1947; Head Operations Dept and Instructor, Ecole Nationale de l'Aviation Civile 1953–56; Deputy Dir, then Dir Air Navigation Secrétariat Général de l'Aviation Civile, France 1956–61; first Dir-Gen. European Org. for the Safety of Air Navigation (EUROCONTROL) 1961–78, responsible for having set up the Air Traffic Services Agency, Brussels and the EUROCONTROL Experimental Centre, Brétigny-sur-Orge and for establishing the Upper Area Control Centres, Maastricht, Netherlands, Karlsruhe, Germany, Shannon, Ireland, the EUROCONTROL Inst. of Air Navigation Services, Luxembourg and the Users Charge Service, Brussels; Adviser Thomson-CSF 1978–83; Special Adviser to EC Aeronautical Comm.; Commdr, Légion d'honneur; Grand Croix du Mérite (Germany); Grand Croix du Mérite Aeronautique (Spain); Commdr (Portugal, Austria, Belgium, Luxembourg); Officier (Ethiopia). *Address:* Altirama, 23 avenue Frédéric Mistral, 06130 Grasse, France (home). *Telephone:* (4) 93-70-60-58 (home). *E-mail:* renebulin1@libertysurf.fr (home).

BULL, Deborah Clare, CBE; British ballerina, writer, broadcaster and artistic director; *Creative Director, Royal Opera House;* b. 22 March 1963, Derby; d. of Rev. Michael John Bull and Doreen Audrey Franklin Bull (née Plumb); ed Royal Ballet School; joined Royal Ballet 1981, Prin. Dancer 1992–2001; teacher of Nutrition, Royal Ballet School 1996–99; Dir Clore Studio Upstairs, Royal Opera House 1999–2001, Creative Dir, ROH2, Royal Opera House 2002–08, Creative Dir, Royal Opera House 2008–; mem. Dance Panel, Arts Council 1996–98, Arts Council 1998–2005; Gov. South Bank Centre 1997–2003, BBC 2003–06; columnist, The Telegraph 1999–2002; Patron Nat. Osteoporosis Soc., Foundation for Community Dance; Dr hc (Derby) 1998, (Sheffield) 2001, (Open Univ.) 2005; Prix de Lausanne 1980, Dancer of the Year, Sunday Express and The Independent on Sunday 1996, Overall Prize Dancescreen Monaco 2002. *Dance:* appearances with Royal Ballet include leading roles in La Bayadère (Gamzatti), Swan Lake (Odette/Odile), The Sleeping Beauty (Aurora), Don Quixote (Kitri), Steptext (cr. for her by William Forsythe) 1995; appeared in Harrogate Int. Festival 1993, 1995, An Evening of British Ballet, Sintra Festival, Portugal 1994, 1995, Diamonds of World Ballet Gala, Kremlin Palace, Moscow 1996, Rite of Spring, Teatro dell'Opera, Rome 2001–02. *Radio:* regular contrib. to BBC Radio 4 including Breaking the Law 2001, Law in Order 2002, A Dance Through Time 2002, Hothouse Kids 2009. *Television:* Dance Ballerina Dance (writer, presenter) 1998, Travels with my Tutu (writer, presenter) 2000, Coppélia, Royal Ballet (live broadcast), Rambert Dance Co., Sadler's Wells (live broadcast), The Dancer's Body (writer, presenter) 2002, Saved for the Nation (presenter) 2006. *Publications:* The Vitality Plan 1998, Dancing Away 1998; The Faber Guide to Classical Ballets (with Luke Jennings) 2004; numerous articles and reviews in newspapers and dance magazines. *Leisure interests:* reading, writing, walking, dancing, talking, neurology, psychology, fitness. *Address:* Royal Opera House, Covent Garden, London, WC2E 9DD, England (office). *Telephone:* (20) 7240-1200 (office). *Website:* www.roh.org.uk (office).

BULL, Sir George, Kt; British business executive; *Chairman, J Sainsbury PLC;* b. 16 July 1936, London; s. of Michael Bull and Hon. Noreen Hennessy; m. Tessa Freeland 1960; four s. one d.; ed Ampleforth Coll.; Coldstream Guards 1954–57; joined Twiss Browning & Hallowes 1958; Gilbey Vintners Ltd 1970; Dir Int. Distillers and Vintners (IDV) 1973; Man. Dir IDV Europe 1977; Deputy Man. Dir IDV Ltd 1982; Dir Grand Metropolitan Ltd 1985; Chief Exec. IDV Ltd 1987; Chair. and CEO IDV Ltd (Drinks Sector of Grand Metropolitan PLC) 1988; Chair. and CEO Grand Met Food Sector 1992; Group Chief Exec. Grand Metropolitan PLC 1993, Chair. Grand Metropolitan PLC 1996–97; Co.-Chair. Diageo (after merger with Guinness PLC) 1997–98; Chair. J Sainsbury PLC 1998–; Dir (non-exec.) BNP Paribas UK Holdings 2000–, The Maersk Co. Ltd 2001–; mem. Advisory Bd Marakon Assocs 2002–; Chevalier, Légion d'honneur 1994. *Leisure interests:* golf, photography. *Address:* J Sainsbury PLC, Stamford House, Stamford Street, London, SE1

9LL (office); The Old Vicarage, Arkesden, Saffron Walden, Essex, CB11 4HB, England (home). *Telephone:* (20) 7695-6000 (office); (1799) 550445 (home). *Fax:* (20) 7695-0320 (office).

BULL, William V. S., MA; Liberian diplomatist; b. 1946, Monrovia; ed Univ. of Liberia, Univ. of Pittsburgh, USA; joined Bureau of African and Asian Affairs, Ministry of Foreign Affairs 1972; Counsellor and Deputy Chief of Mission, Washington, DC 1976, Chargé d'affaires 1980; Asst Minister for American Affairs, Monrovia 1981, for African and Asian Affairs 1982–86, Prin. Deputy to Minister of Foreign Affairs 1987–90; Amb. and Perm. Rep. to UN, New York 1990–98; Amb. to UK 1998–2000, to USA 2000–03. *Address:* c/o Embassy of Liberia, 5201 16th Street, NW, Washington, DC 20011, USA (office).

BULLARD, Robert D., PhD; American sociologist and academic; *Edmund Asa Ware Distinguished Professor of Sociology and Director, Environmental Justice Resource Center, Clark Atlanta University;* b. 1946; ed Iowa State Univ.; currently Edmund Asa Ware Distinguished Prof. of Sociology, Clark Atlanta Univ., Founder and Dir Environmental Justice Resource Center 1994–; featured in CNN People You Should Know, Bullard: Green Issue is Black and White July 2007, named by Newsweek magazine as one of 13 Environmental Leaders of the Century 2008. *Publications:* Invisible Houston: The Black Experience in Boom and Bust 1987, In Search of the New South: The Black Urban Experience in the 1970s and 1980s 1989, Houston: Growth and Decline in a Sunbelt Boomtown (co-author) 1989, Dumping in Dixie: Race, Class and Environmental Quality, 1990, Confronting Environmental Racism: Voices From the Grassroots (ed.) 1993, Unequal Protection: Environmental Justice and Communities of Color (ed.) 1994, Residential Apartheid: The American Legacy (co-ed.) 1994, Just Transportation: Dismantling Race and Class Barriers to Mobility (co-ed.) 1997, People of Color Environmental Groups Directory 2000, 2000, Sprawl City: Race, Politics and Planning in Atlanta, Washington, DC (co-ed.) 2000, Just Sustainabilities: Development in an Unequal World (co-author) 2003, Highway Robbery: Transportation Racism and New Routes to Equity (co-author) 2004, The Quest for Environmental Justice: Human Rights and the Politics of Pollution 2005, In the Wake of the Storm: Environment, Disaster and Race After Katrina (co-author) 2006, Toxic Wastes and Race at Twenty: 1987–2007 2007, Growing Smarter: Achieving Livable Communities, Environmental Justice, and Regional Equity 2007, The Black Metropolis in the Twenty-First Century: Race, Power, and the Politics of Place 2007, Deadly Waiting Game Beyond Hurricane Katrina: Government Response, Unnatural Disasters, and African Americans 2009, Race, Place and Environmental Justice After Hurricane Katrina: Struggles to Reclaim, Rebuild, and Revitalize New Orleans and the Gulf Coast 2009. *Address:* Environmental Justice Resource Center, Clark Atlanta University, 223 James P. Brawley Drive, Atlanta, GA 30314, USA (office). *Telephone:* (404) 880-6911 (office). *Fax:* (404) 880-6909 (office). *E-mail:* ejrc@cau.edu (office). *Website:* www.ejrc.cau.edu (office).

BULLER, Arthur John, BA, MB, BSc, PhD, FRCP, FIBiol, FRSA; British physiologist and academic; *Professor Emeritus, Faculty of Medicine, University of Bristol;* b. 16 Oct. 1923; s. of Thomas Alfred Buller and Edith May Buller (née Wager); m. Helena Joan Pearson 1946; one s. two d. (one deceased); ed Duke of York's Royal Mil. School, Dover, St Thomas's Hosp. Medical School; Kitchener Scholar 1941–45; Lecturer in Physiology St Thomas' Hosp. 1946–49; Maj. RAMC, Specialist in Physiology, Jr Sec. Mil. Personnel Research Cttee 1949–53; Lecturer in Medicine, St Thomas' Hosp. 1953–57; Reader in Physiology, King's Coll., London 1961–65; Gresham Prof. of Physic 1963–65; Prof. of Physiology, Univ. of Bristol 1965–82, Dean Faculty of Medicine 1976–78, Prof. Emer. 1982–; Chief Scientist (on secondment) Dept of Health and Social Security 1978–81; Visiting Prof., Monash Univ., Australia 1972; Royal Soc. Commonwealth Fellow, Canberra, Australia 1958–59; mem. Bd of Govs Bristol Royal Infirmary 1968–74, Avon Health Authority 1974–78, MRC 1975–81; Chair. Neurosciences and Mental Health Bd, MRC 1975–77; External Scientific Adviser, Rayne Inst. St Thomas' Hosp. 1979–85; Research Devt Dir, Muscular Dystrophy Group of GB and NI 1982–90; mem. BBC, IBA Cen. Appeals Advice Cttee 1983–88; Hon. Consultant in Clinical Physiology, Bristol Dist Hospital 1970–85; Emergency Reserve Decoration (Army); Long Fox Memorial Lecturer, Univ. of Bristol 1978, Milroy Lecturer, Royal Coll. of Physicians 1983. *Publications:* articles in books and journals on normal and abnormal physiology. *Leisure interests:* clarets and conversation. *Address:* Flat 13, Turnpike Court, Hett Close, Ardingly, Haywards Heath, RH17 6GQ, England. *Telephone:* (1444) 891903 (home).

BULLOCK, Sandra; American actress; b. 26 July 1964, Arlington, VA; d. of John Bullock and Helga Bullock; m. Jesse James 2005; ed East Carolina Univ.; grew up in Germany and Washington, DC; frequent appearances on European stage with opera-singer mother; appeared in off-Broadway productions including No Time Flat (WPA Theatre); f. Fortis Films (production co.). *Films include:* Love Potion Number Nine 1992, When the Party's Over 1992, The Vanishing 1993, The Thing Called Love 1993, Fire on the Amazon 1993, Demolition Man 1993, Wrestling Ernest Hemingway 1993, Speed 1994, While You Were Sleeping 1995, The Net 1995, Two If By Sea 1996, Moll Flanders, A Time to Kill 1996, In Love and War 1996, Practical Magic 1998, Forces of Nature 1999, Gun Shy 1999, Making Sandwiches 1996 (also writer), Speed 2 1997, Hope Floats (also exec. producer) 1998, Prince of Egypt (voice only) 1998, 28 Days 2000, Famous 2000, Miss Congeniality 2000, Murder by Numbers 2001, Exactly 3:30 2001, Divine Secrets of the Ya-Ya Sisterhood 2002, Two Weeks' Notice 2002, Crash 2005, Loverboy 2005, Miss Congeniality 2: Armed and Fabulous 2005, The Lake House 2006, Infamous 2006, Premonition 2007. *Television includes:* The Preppy Murder (film), Lucky Chances (miniseries), Working Girl (NBC series). *Address:* c/o CAA, 9830 Wilshire Boulevard, Beverly Hills, CA 90212; Fortis Films, 8581 Santa

Monica Blvd, Suite1, West Hollywood, CA 90069, USA. *Telephone:* (310) 659-4533 (Fortis).

BULLOCK, Theodore Holmes, PhD; American professor of neurosciences; *Professor Emeritus of Medicine, University of California, San Diego;* b. 16 May 1915, Nanking, China; s. of A. Archibald Bullock and Ruth Beckwith Bullock; m. Martha Runquist 1937; one s. one d.; ed Univ. of California, Berkeley; Sterling Fellow, Yale Univ. 1940–41; Rockefeller Fellow 1941–42; Instructor in Neuroanatomy, Yale Univ. 1942–44; Asst Prof. of Anatomy, Univ. of Missouri 1944–46; Instructor and sometime Head, Invertebrate Zoology, Marine Biol. Lab., Woods Hole, Mass.; Asst Prof., Assoc. Prof., Prof. of Zoology, Univ. of Calif., Los Angeles 1946–66; Prof. of Neurosciences, Univ. of Calif. San Diego School of Medicine 1966–82, Prof. Emer. 1982–; Head of Neurobiology Unit, Scripps Inst. of Oceanography; mem. American Acad. Arts and Sciences, NAS, American Phil. Soc., Int. Soc. for Neuroethology; fmr Pres. American Soc. of Zoology, Soc. for Neuroscience; Dr hc (Frankfurt) 1988; Hon. DSc (Loyola Univ., Chicago) 2001; Lashley Prize, American Philosophical Soc. 1968, Gerard Prize, Soc. for Neuroscience 1984. *Publications:* Structure and Function in the Nervous Systems of Invertebrates (with G. A. Horridge) 1965, Introduction to Nervous Systems (with R. Orkand and A. D. Grinnell) 1977, Electroreception (with W. Heiligenberg) 1986, Brain Dynamics (with E. Basar) 1989, Induced Rhythms in the Brain (with E. Basar) 1992, How Do Brains Work? 1993. *Address:* Department of Neurosciences, University of California, San Diego, La Jolla, CA 92093, USA. *Telephone:* (858) 534-3636. *Fax:* (858) 534-3919 (office). *E-mail:* tbullock@ucsd.edu (office). *Website:* cogprints.soton.ac.uk (office).

BULMAHN, Edelgard, BA; German politician; b. 4 March 1951, Minden; m.; ed Petershagen Aufbaugymnasium and Hanover Univ.; secondary school teacher for seven years; joined SPD party 1969; mem. Bundestag (SPD) 1987–, mem. Exec. Cttee SPD Parl. Group 1991–98, Exec. Cttee SPD 1993–; Deputy Spokesman on Research and Tech. SPD Parl. Group 1990–94; Chair. Cttee on Educ., Science, Research, Tech. and Tech. Assessment 1995–96; spokesman on Educ. and Research SPD Parl. Group 1996–98; Fed. Minister of Educ. and Research 1998–2005; Chair. European Space Agency (ESA) at ministerial level 2001–. *Address:* c/o Sozialdemokratische Partei Deutschlands (SPD), Wilhelmstr. 141, 10963 Berlin, Germany.

BULMER-THOMAS, Victor Gerald, OBE, MA, DPhil; British economist, academic and international consultant; *Visiting Professor, Department of History, Florida International University;* b. 23 March 1948, London; s. of the late Ivor Bulmer-Thomas and of Joan Bulmer; m. Barbara Swasey 1970; two s. one d.; ed Westminster School, New Coll. and St Antony's Coll., Oxford; Research Fellow, Fraser of Allander Inst. 1975–78; Lecturer in Econs, Queen Mary Coll., Univ. of London 1978–87, Reader 1987–90, Prof. of Latin American Econs 1990–98, Prof. Emer. 1998–, Dir Inst. of Latin American Studies 1992–98, Sr Research Fellow 1998–2001; Dir Chatham House (Royal Inst. of Int. Affairs) 2001–06; Visiting Prof., Fla Int. Univ., Miami 2007–; Dir Schroders Emerging Countries Fund 1996–2003, Deutsche Latin America Companies Trust 2004, New India Investment Trust 2004–; fmr Dir Gartmore Latin America New Growth Fund SA; fmr consultant for EC, IDB; Order of San Carlos (Colombia) 1998, Order of the Southern Cross (Brazil) 1998. *Publications:* Input-Output Analysis for Developing Countries 1982, The Political Economy of Central America since 1920 1987, Studies in the Economics of Central America 1988, Britain and Latin America: A Changing Relationship (ed.) 1989, The Economic History of Latin America Since Independence 1994, The New Economic Model in Latin America and Its Impact on Income Distribution and Poverty (ed.) 1996, Thirty Years of Latin American Studies in the UK 1997, United States and Latin America: The New Agenda (ed.) 1999, Regional Integration in Latin America and the Caribbean: The Political Economy of Open Regionalism (ed.) 2001, The Cambridge Economic History of Latin America, Vol. I: The Colonial Era and the Short Nineteenth Century, Vol. II The Long Twentieth Century (co-ed.) 2005. *Leisure interests:* music (viola), tennis, walking, canoeing, underwater photography. *Address:* Department of History, Florida International University, University Park (DM-397), Miami, FL 33199, USA (office). *Telephone:* (305) 348-3883 (office). *Fax:* (305) 348-3561 (office). *Website:* www.fiu.edu/~history (office).

BUMAYA HABIB, André; Rwandan politician; *Leader, Parti démocratique idéal (PDI);* fmr Minister of Labour and Public Service; Minister of Foreign Affairs and Regional Co-operation 2000–02; Leader, Parti démocratique idéal (PDI) (fmrly Parti démocratique islamique). *Address:* Parti démocratique idéal (PDI), Kigali, Rwanda (office).

BUMPERS, Dale Leon, LLD; American lawyer and fmr politician; *Counsel, Arent Fox Kintner Plotkin & Kahn;* b. 12 Aug. 1925, Charleston, Ark.; s. of William Rufus Bumpers and Lattie (née Jones) Bumpers; m. Betty Flanagan 1949; two s. one d.; ed Univ. of Arkansas and Northwestern Law School; Propr Charleston Hardware and Furniture Co. 1951–66, Angus Breeding Farm 1966–70; Attorney, Charleston, Ark. 1951–70; Gov. of Arkansas 1971–74; Senator from Arkansas 1975–99; fmr Dir Center for Defense Information; Counsel, Arent Fox Kintner Plotkin & Kahn, Washington, DC 2000–. *Leisure interests:* reading, tennis, hunting. *Address:* Arent Fox Kintner Plotkin & Kahn, 1050 Connecticut Avenue, NW, Washington, DC 20036-5339, USA (office). *Telephone:* (202) 857-8951 (office). *Fax:* (202) 857-6395 (office). *E-mail:* bumpers.dale@arentfox.com (office). *Website:* www.arentfox.com (office).

BUND, Karlheinz, DrIng, Dr rer. pol; German business executive; b. 18 March 1925, Saarlouis; m. Anni Kronenberger; ed Technische Hochschule, Darmstadt; Chair. Bd of Ruhrkohle AG 1973–85; Chair. EVG and Chair. Advisory Bd INNOTEC 1985, ENRO Energie und Rohstoff GmbH; mem. Supervisory Bd ASEA Brown, Boveri, Deutsche Babcock Anlagen AG; Pres. World Coal Inst. (WCI); Chair. ENRO GmbH; Grosses Bundesverdienstkreuz 1975. *Address:* Huyssenallee 86–88, 45128 Essen, Germany. *Telephone:* (201) 245 360. *Fax:* (201) 245 3639.

BÜNDCHEN, Gisele; Brazilian fashion model; b. 20 July 1980, Horizontina; d. of Valdir Bündchen and Vânia Bündchen; m. Tom Brady 2009; has participated in modelling campaigns for Valentino, Tommy Hilfiger, Chloe, Celine, Versace, Christian Dior, Michael Kors, Ralph Lauren, Victoria's Secret, Louis Vuitton and Dolce & Gabbana; VH1/Vogue Model of the Year Award 1999. *Films:* Taxi 2004, The Devil Wears Prada 2006. *Address:* c/o img models NY, 304 Park Ave South, 12 Floor, New York NY 10010, USA (office). *Website:* www.imgmodels.com (office); www.giselebundchen.com.br.

BUNDHUN, Raouf; Mauritian politician and diplomatist; *Vice-President;* fmr Amb. to France; Vice-Pres. of Mauritius 2002–; Officier, Ordre nationale du Mérite; Officier, Ordre de la Pleiade (Ordre de la Francophonie). *Address:* Office of the Vice-President, State House, Port Louis, Mauritius (office). *Telephone:* 454-3021 (office). *Fax:* 564-5370 (office). *E-mail:* statepas@intnet.mu (office). *Website:* ncb.intnet.mu/president.htm (office).

BUNDU, Abass, PhD; Sierra Leonean diplomatist and lawyer; *Leader, People's Progressive Party;* b. 3 June 1948; s. of Isatu Kallay Bundu and Pa Santigie; m. Khadija Allie 1976; two s. three d.; ed Australian Nat. Univ., Canberra, Univ. of Cambridge, UK; Asst Dir, Commonwealth Secr., London 1975–82; mem. of Parl. for Port Loko NE 1982–90; Minister of Agric., Natural Resources and Forestry 1982–85; Exec. Sec., Econ. Community of W African States (ECOWAS) 1989–93; Sec. of State for Foreign Affairs and Int. Co-operation 1993–95; presidential cand., People's Progressive Party 1996, currently Leader; Yorke Award, Univ. of Cambridge. *Leisure interests:* tennis, swimming. *Address:* c/o Department of Foreign Affairs, Gloucester Street, Freetown, Sierra Leone.

BUNDY, Colin James, BA, DPhil; British historian, academic and university administrator; *Warden, Green College, Oxford;* m.; two c.; ed Univ. of Natal, Univ. of Witwatersrand, Merton Coll. Oxford; Research Fellow, Queen Elizabeth House, Oxford 1979–80, Dept for External Studies, Oxford 1980–84; fmr Sr Lecturer, Manchester Polytechnic; Dir Inst. for Historical Research, Univ. of the W Cape 1992–94, Vice-Rector 1994–97; Vice-Chancellor and Prin. Univ. of Witwatersrand 1997–2001; Dir and Prin. School of Oriental and African Studies (SOAS), London 2001–06; Deputy Vice-Chancellor Univ. of London 2003–06; Warden, Green Coll., Oxford 2006–; Hon. Fellow, Kellogg Coll., Oxford. *Publications:* History, Revolution and South Africa 1987, Remaking the Past: New Perspectives in South African History 1987, Hidden Struggles in Rural South Africa: Politics & Popular Movements in the Transkei & Eastern Cape 1890–1930 (co-author) 1987, The History of the South African Communist Party 1991. *Leisure interests:* cricket, chess, music and hiking. *Address:* Office of the Warden, Green College, Radcliffe Observatory, Woodstock Road, Oxford, OX2 6HG, England (office). *Telephone:* (1865) 274770 (office). *Fax:* (1865) 274796 (office). *E-mail:* colin.bundy@green.ox.ac.uk. *Website:* www.green.ox.ac.uk (office).

BUNDY, James Abbott, AB, MFA; American theatre director and academic; *Dean, School of Drama, Yale Univesity;* b. 8 May 1959, Boston; s. of McGeorge Bundy and Mary L. Bundy; m. Anne Tofflemire 1988; two d.; ed Harvard Coll., London Acad. of Music and Dramatic Art, Yale School of Drama; Man. Dir Cornerstone Theater Co., New York 1989–91; Assoc. Producing Dir The Acting Company 1996–98; Artistic Dir Great Lakes Theater Festival, Cleveland 1998–2002; Adjunct Prof. of Theatre, Case Western Reserve Univ., Cleveland –2002; Artistic Dir Yale Repertory Theatre, New Haven, Conn. 2002–, Prof. of Drama, Yale School of Drama 2002–, Dean 2002–; mem. Bd of Dirs Theatre Communications Group 2007–; fmr Dir Calif. Shakespeare Festival, Ala Shakespeare Festival, Lincoln Center Theater Dirs Lab, Juilliard School Drama Div.; Trustee Groton School 2003–; Tom Killen Award, Conn. Critics Circle 2007. *Address:* Yale School of Drama, 222 York Street, New Haven, CT 06520 (office); Yale Repertory Theatre, PO Box 208244, New Haven, CT 06505, USA (office). *Telephone:* (203) 432-1234 (office). *Fax:* (203) 432-1521 (office). *E-mail:* james.bundy@yale.edu (office). *Website:* drama.yale.edu (office); www.yalerep.org (office).

BUNE, Poseci Wagalevu; Fijian politician and diplomatist; *Minister for Public Service and Public Sector Reform;* ed Queen Victoria School, Royal Coll. of Public Admin., London; joined Public Service Dept 1966, apptd Sr Admin. Officer 1972, attached to Australian Embassy, Bangkok 1973, joined Perm. Mission to UN, New York 1973, apptd First Sec. 1973, Counsellor, Mission to EEC 1976–80; Western Divisional Commr, Ministry of Rural Devt 1981–85; Amb. to EEC (also accred to Belgium, Luxembourg, Netherlands, France and Italy) 1985–87; Perm. Sec. for Public Service 1987–95, Perm. Sec. to Govt and for Public Service 1990–95; Perm. Rep. to UN 1995–2000; mem. Parl. for Macuata 2001–; Leader, Veitokani ni Lewenivanua Vakarisito (Christian Democratic Alliance); Minister for Public Service and Public Sector Reform 2007–. *Address:* Ministry of Public Service and Public Sector Reform, PO Box 2278, Government Buildings, Suva, Fiji (office). *Telephone:* 3314588 (office). *Fax:* 3302570 (office). *Website:* www.psc.gov.fj (office).

BUNGEI, Wilfred Kipkemboi; Kenyan athlete; b. 24 July 1980, Kabirirsang, nr Kapsabet; second cousin of Kenyan-born Danish fmr athlete Wilson Kipketer; ed Samoei High School; middle distance runner; ranked World No. 1 over 800m in 2002 and 2003; set personal best of 1:42.34 in Rieti 2002; part of 4×800m relay team that holds world record 2008; Silver Medal, World Jr Championships, Annecy, France 1998, World Championships, Edmonton 2001; Bronze Medal, African Championships, Radès 2002, World Indoor Championships, Birmingham 2003; finished first at Int. Asscn of Athletics Feds (IAAF) World Athletics Final, Monaco 2003, fifth at Olympic Games, Athens 2004, fourth at World Championships, Helsinki 2005, first at IAAF

World Athletics Final, Monaco 2005; Gold Medal, World Indoor Championships, Moscow 2006; Bronze Medal, IAAF World Athletics Final, Stuttgart 2006; finished first at World Championships, Osaka 2007; Gold Medal, Olympic Games, Beijing 2008. *Address:* c/o Kenya Athletics Federation, PO Box 46722, Aerodrome Road, Riadha House, 00100 Nairobi West, Kenya. *Telephone:* (2) 605021. *Fax:* (2) 605020. *E-mail:* athleticskenya@gt.co.ke. *Website:* www.athleticskenya.org.

BUNGEY, Michael, BSc (Econs); British advertising executive; b. 18 Jan. 1940; s. of William Frederick George Bungey and Irene Edith Bungey; m. Darleen Penelope Cecilia Brooks 1976; one s. two d.; ed St Clement Danes Grammar School and London School of Econs; marketing with Nestlé 1961–65; Assoc. Dir Crawfords Advertising 1965–68; Account Dir S.H. Benson Advertising 1968–71; Chair. Michael Bungey DFS Ltd 1972–84; Chair., CEO DFS Dorland 1987, Bates Dorland 1988, Bates Europe 1989; Deputy Chair. Dorland Advertising (now Bates Dorland Advertising Ltd) 1984, Chair. 1987–96, CEO 1987; Chair., CEO Bates Worldwide (fmrly BSB Worldwide) 1994–; Chair. Backer Spielvogel Bates Europe 1988–, Pres., COO Backer Spielvogel Bates Worldwide 1993–94, CEO 1994–; Chair., CEO Bates Worldwide 1994–; CEO Cordiant Communications Group PLC 1997–2003; Dir Cordiant PLC (fmrly Saatchi & Saatchi) 1995. *Address:* c/o Bates UK, 121–141 Westbourne Terrace, London, W2 6JR, England. *Website:* www.batesww.com.

BUNIN, Igor Mikhailovich; Russian political commentator; *Director-General, Political Technologies Centre;* b. 25 Feb. 1946, Moscow; m.; one d.; ed Moscow State Univ.; Sr Researcher, Inst. of World Econs and Int. Relations, USSR Acad. of Sciences 1973–82; Chief Researcher, Inst. of Int. Workers' Movt 1982–92; Chief Scientific Expert, Int. Foundation of Socio-Econ. and Political Studies (Gorbachev Foundation) 1992–93; Dir Centre of Business Initiatives, Ekspertiza 1992–93; Dir-Gen. Political Technologies Centre 1993–; Dir-Gen. Ind. Information Site of Political Comments (www.politcom.ru) 2001–. *Publications include:* Socialists and Political Struggle in France in the 1980s 1989, New Russian Businessmen and Myths of Post-Communist Mentality 1993, Businessmen of Russia: 40 Stories of Success 1994, Experience of Formation 1994, Financial and Industrial Groups and Conglomerates in Economics and Politics of Russia 1997, Political Processes in the Regions of Russia 1998, The '99 Elections: Results and Lessons 2000, Political Prognosis as the Art of the Possible: Contemporary Russian Politics, A Course of Lectures 2003. *Address:* Political Technologies Centre, Bolshoi Zlatoustovsky per. 8/7 office 73–95, 101000 Moscow, Russian Federation (office). *Telephone:* (495) 206-80-30 (office). *Fax:* (495) 20682-58 (office). *E-mail:* info@cpt.ru (office). *Website:* www.cpt.ru (office).

BUNKIN, Fedor Vasilyevich, DrPhysMathSc; Russian physicist; *Director, Wave Research Center, General Physics Institute, Russian Academy of Sciences;* b. 17 Jan. 1929; m.; two c.; ed Moscow State Univ.; Jr, Sr researcher, head of sector, head of lab. Physical Inst. USSR (now Russian) Acad. of Sciences 1955–82; Deputy Dir Inst. of Gen. Physics USSR Acad. of Sciences 1982–98; currently Dir Wave Research Center, Gen. Physics Inst., Russian Acad. of Sciences; corresp. mem. USSR Acad. of Sciences 1976, mem. 1992–; main research in quantum physics, electronics, nonlinear optics, acoustics; mem. Co-ordination Council on problem Coherent and Nonlinear Optics Russian Acad. of Sciences; USSR State Prize. *Publications include:* 6 books; numerous articles in scientific journals. *Address:* Wave Research Center of Gen. Physics Institute, Vavilova str. 38, 119991, Moscow, Russia (office). *Telephone:* (495) 135-82-34 (office); (495) 331-32-62 (home). *E-mail:* wrc@kapella.gpi.ru. *Website:* www.gpi.ru/wrc.

BUNNAG, Marut; Thai politician; b. 21 Aug. 1925, Bangkok; s. of Phra Sutthikarnvinijchai and Mrs Phongsri; m. Phantipha Bunnag; two c.; ed Thammasat Univ.; with Ministry of Justice –1952; Marut Bunnag Int. Law Office law practice 1952–; Minister of Justice 1979; mem. Parl. (Democratic Party) 1983–; Minister of Public Health 1983–86, Sept.–Dec. 1990; Minister of Educ. 1988; Deputy Leader, Democrat Party, Sr Adviser. *Address:* c/o Marut Bunnag International Law Office, Forum Tower, 22nd Floor, 184/130–136 Patchadaphisek Road, Huaykwang, Bangkok, 10320 (office); 45/1 Pradipat Road, Kwaeng Samsane-nai, Khet Phyathai, Bangkok 10400, Thailand (home); c/o House of Representatives, Bangkok. *Telephone:* (2) 645-2556 (office); (2) 271-1081 (home). *Fax:* (2) 645-2568 (office). *E-mail:* marut@loxinfo.co.uk. *Website:* www.marut.th.com (office).

BUNNING, Jim, BS; American politician and fmr professional baseball player; *Senator from Kentucky;* b. 23 Oct. 1931, Southgate, Ky; m. Mary Bunning; nine c.; ed Xavier Univ.; professional baseball player 1955–71; with Detroit Tigers 1955–63, Phila Phillies 1964–67, 1970–71, Pittsburgh Pirates 1968–69, LA Dodgers 1969; retd 1971; mem. Ky State Senate 1979–83; mem. 100th–104th Congresses from 4th Ky Dist 1987–99; Senator from Kentucky 1998–; mem. Senate Finance Cttee 2002–; Republican; Nat. Baseball Hall of Fame 1996. *Address:* US Senate, 316 Hart Senate Office Building, Washington, DC 20510, USA (office). *Telephone:* (202) 224-4343 (office). *Website:* bunning.senate.gov (office).

BUNROD, Gen. Somtad; Thai government official and army officer (retd); *Minister of Defence;* served in special warfare unit of Thai army; fmr Army Jt Chief of Staff; Minister of Defence 2006–. *Address:* Ministry of Defence, Thanon Sanamchai, Bangkok 10200, Thailand (office). *Telephone:* (2) 222-1121 (office). *Fax:* (2) 226-3117 (office). *E-mail:* webmaster@mod.go.th (office). *Website:* www.mod.go.th (office).

BUNSUMPUN, Prasert, BEng, MBA; Thai energy executive; *President and CEO, PTT Public Company Ltd;* b. 20 Feb. 1952; ed Churalongkorn Univ., Utah State Univ., Harvard Univ. and Nat. Defense Coll., USA, King Prajadhipoks Inst.; Dir Dept of Petroleum Procurements & Contracts, Petroleum Authority of Thailand (PTT) 1986–91, Asst Gov. of Marketing 1991–92, Sr Vice-Pres., Marketing Downstream Oil Business 1992–96, Pres. PTT Oil 1996–99, Pres. PTT Gas Business Group 2000–01, Sr Exec. Vice-Pres. PTT Gas Business Group 2001–03, Pres. and CEO PTT Public Co. Ltd 2003–; mem. Bd Dirs PTT Exploration and Production PLC, Trans Thai-Malaysia (Thailand) Co. Ltd, PTT Natural Gas Distribution Co. Ltd, Thai Olefin Public Co. Ltd, Thai Petroleum Pipeline Co. Ltd, Nat. Petrochemical PLC, Thaioil Co. Ltd, Thaioil Power Co. Ltd, Ind. Power (Thailand) Co. Ltd; Pres. Utah Univ. Alumni, USA; Chair. Community Enterprise Inst., Churalongkorn Univ. Eng Alumni. *Address:* PTT Public Co. Ltd, 555 Vibhavadi Rangsit Road, Chatuchak, Bangkok 10900, Thailand (office). *Telephone:* 2537-2000 (office). *Fax:* 2537-3499 (office). *E-mail:* info@pttplc.com (office). *Website:* www.pttplc.com (office).

BUORA, Carlo Orazio; Italian business equipment and telecommunications executive; *Joint CEO, Olivetti SpA; CEO and Managing Director, Telecom Italia SpA;* b. 1945; m.; two s.; Dir Pirelli SpA 1999–; Jt CEO Olivetti SpA 2001–; apptd Chair. Telecom Italia Mobile (TIM) SpA Sept. 2002, currently CEO and Man. Dir Telecom Italia SpA. *Address:* Olivetti SpA, Via Jervis 77, 10015 Ivrea, Turin, Italy (office). *Telephone:* (011) 255200 (office). *Fax:* (011) 25522524 (office). *Website:* www.olivetti.com (office).

BURBIDGE, (Eleanor) Margaret Peachey, PhD, FRS; American (b. British) astronomer and academic; *Professor Emerita of Physics, University of California, San Diego;* b. 12 Aug. 1919, Davenport, England; d. of Stanley John Peachey and Marjorie Peachey, (née Stott); m. Geoffrey Burbidge (q.v.) 1948; one d.; ed Frances Holland School, London and Univ. Coll., London; Second Asst, Asst Dir and acting Dir Univ. of London Observatory 1946–51; Research Fellow, Yerkes Observatory, Harvard Coll. Observatory 1951–53, Calif. Inst. of Technology 1955–57; Research Fellow and Assoc. Prof. Univ. of Chicago 1957–62; Assoc. Research Physicist, Univ. of Calif., San Diego 1962–64, Prof. 1964–, Univ. Prof. 1984–91, Prof. Emer. 1991–, Research Prof., Dept of Physics 1990–, Dir Center for Astrophysics and Space Sciences 1979–88; Dir Royal Greenwich Observatory 1971–73; Ed. Observatory 1948–51; mem. Editorial Bd Astronomy and Astrophysics 1969–85; Lindsay Memorial Lecture, NASA 1985; mem. Royal Astronomical Soc., American Astronomical Soc. (Pres. 1978), American Acad. of Arts and Science, NAS, AAAS (Fellow 1981, Pres. 1982), American Philosophical Soc., Soc. Royale des Sciences de Liège, Astronomical Soc. of the Pacific, New York Acad. of Sciences; Fellow, Univ. Coll., London, Lucy Cavendish Coll., Cambridge, Girton Coll., Cambridge; Hon. DSc (Smith Coll., Mass, Rensselaer Political Inst. and Univs of Sussex, Leicester, Bristol, Chicago, Mich., Mass, City Univ., London, Notre Dame, London and Williams Coll.); numerous prizes and awards including Helen B. Warner Prize (jtly with Geoffrey Burbidge) 1959, Karl G. Jansky Lectureship, Nat. Radio Astronomy Observatory 1977, Bruce Gold Medal, Astronomical Soc. of the Pacific 1982, Nat. Medal of Science, USA 1983, Einstein Medal 1988, Gold Medal, Royal Astronomical Soc. (jtly with Geoffrey Burbidge) 2005. *Publications:* Quasi-Stellar Objects (with Geoffrey Burbidge) 1967; numerous articles in scientific journals. *Address:* Center for Astrophysics and Space Sciences, University of California, Mail Code #0424, La Jolla, CA 92093, USA (office). *Telephone:* (858) 534-4477. *Fax:* (858) 554-7051 (office). *E-mail:* mburbidge@ucsd.edu (office). *Website:* casswww.ucsd .edu (office).

BURBIDGE, Geoffrey, PhD, FRS; British physicist and academic; *Professor of Physics, University of California, San Diego;* b. 24 Sept. 1925, Chipping Norton, England; s. of Leslie and Eveline Burbidge; m. Margaret Peachey, (q.v.) 1948; one d.; ed Bristol Univ. and Univ. Coll., London; Asst Lecturer, Univ. Coll. London 1950–51; Agassiz Fellow, Harvard Univ. 1951–52; Research Fellow, Cavendish Lab., Cambridge 1953–55; Carnegie Fellow, Mount Wilson and Palomar Observatories 1955–57; Asst Prof., Dept of Astronomy, Univ. of Chicago 1957–58; Assoc. Prof. 1958–62; Assoc. Prof., Univ. of Calif., San Diego 1962–63, Prof. 1963–84, Prof. Emer. 1984–88; Prof. 1988–; Dir Kitt Peak Nat. Observatory 1978–84; Phillips Visiting Prof., Harvard Univ. 1968; Pres. Astronomical Soc. of the Pacific 1974–76; Dir Associated Univs for Research in Astronomy 1971–74; Fellow, Univ. Coll., London; Ed., Annual Review of Astronomy and Astrophysics 1973–, Scientific Ed., Astrophysical Journal 1996–2002; Trustee, Associated Univs Inc. 1973–82; Helen B. Warner Prize (jtly with Margaret Burbidge) 1959, Bruce Gold Medal, Astronomical Soc. of the Pacific 1999. *Publications:* Quasi-Stellar Objects, (with Margaret Burbidge) 1967, A Different Approach to Cosmology (with F. Hoyle and J. V. Narlikar) 2000; more than 400 astrophysics papers in scientific journals. *Address:* Department of Physics, Center for Astrophysics and Space Sciences, 0424, University of California, San Diego, La Jolla, CA 92093, USA (office). *Telephone:* (858) 534-6626 (office). *E-mail:* gburbidge@UCSD.EDU (office). *Website:* www-physics.ucsd.edu/fac_staff/profiles/bg.html (office).

BURBULIS, Gennady Eduardovich; Russian politician; b. 4 Aug. 1945, Pervouralsk, Sverdlovsk (now Ekaterinburg); s. of Eduard Kazimirovich Burbulis and Valentina Ivanovna Belonogova; m. Natalia Kirsanova; one s.; ed Ural State Univ.; Lecturer Ural Polytechnic Inst. 1974–83; Head of Chair., Deputy Dir Inst. of Non-Ferrous Metals 1983–89; USSR People's Deputy 1989–90; formed Discussion Tribune, Sverdlovsk 1988; elected to Congress of People's Deputies 1989; mem. Inter-Regional Group; Chief of Staff to Boris Yeltsin 1991; State Sec. RSFSR (now Russian Fed.) 1991–92, State Council Sec. 1991–92; First Deputy Chair. Russian Govt 1991–92, Sec. of State May–Nov. 1992, Head of Advisors' Team Nov.–Dec. 1992; Founder and Pres. Int. Humanitarian and Political Cen. Strategy 1993–; mem. State Duma (Parl.) 1993–99, mem. Cttee for Geopolitics; Deputy Gov. Novgorod Region 1999–2001; Chair. Observational Bd Novotrubny factory, Pervouralsk 1997–98; Rep. of Novgorod Region to Council of Fed. 2002–; Chair. Fed. Council Comm. on Methodology of Exercising the Fed. Council's Constitutional Powers 2002–. *Publication:* Profession – Politician 1999. *Leisure interests:* poetry, playing soccer and tennis. *Address:* Council of Federation, B. Dmitrovca 26, 103426 Moscow, Russia (office). *Telephone:* (495) 292-61-23 (office). *Fax:* (495) 926-69-50 (office). *E-mail:* GEBurbulis@council.gov.ru (office).

BURD, Steven A., BSc, MA; American retail executive; *Chairman, President and CEO, Safeway Inc.;* b. 1979, Valley City, ND; m. Chris Burd; two c.; ed Carroll Coll., Univ. of Wisconsin; worked for Arthur D. Little, New York 1981–87; man., Safeway Stores, Kohlberg Kravis Roberts & Co. 1986–91; consultant Stop and Shop Cos, Boston 1988–89; consultant and interim CEO Fred Meyer Inc., Portland, Ore. 1991–92; Pres. Safeway Inc. 1992–, CEO 1993–, Chair. 1998–; mem. US Dept of Homeland Security's Pvt. Sector Sr Advisory Cttee 2003–. *Address:* Safeway Inc., 5918 Stoneridge Mall Road, Pleasanton, CA 94588-3229, USA (office). *Telephone:* (925) 467-3000 (office). *Fax:* (925) 467-3321 (office). *E-mail:* info@safeway.com (office). *Website:* www.safeway.com (office).

BURDA, Hubert, DPhil; German publisher and author; *CEO, Hubert Burda Media;* b. 9 Feb. 1940, Heidelberg; s. of Dr Franz Burda and Aenne Lemminger; ed Univ. of Munich; Man. Bild & Funk 1966–74; partner, Burda GmbH 1974, now CEO, Hubert Burda Media; Co-Publr Elle-Verlag GmbH, Munich; co-f. Europe Online SA, Luxembourg; Publr Anna, Bunte, Burda Moden, Das Haus, Elle, Elle Bistro, Elle Deco, Elle TopModel, Focus, Focus Online, Focus TV, Freundin, Freizeit Revue, Futurekids, Glücks Revue, Haus + Garten, Lisa, Lisa Kochen & Backen, Lisa Wohnen & Dekorieren, Mein schöner Garten, Meine Familie & ich, Norddeutsche Neueste Nachrichten, Schweriner Volkszeitung, Starwatch Navigation, Super Illu, Super TV, TraXXX, Verena; mem. Bd German School of Journalism, Munich; f. Petrarca Prize (for poetry), Bambi (Media-Prize), Corp. Art Prize 1997. *Address:* Hubert Burda Media, Arabellastrasse 23, 81925 Munich, Germany (office). *E-mail:* info@hubert-burda-media.com (office). *Website:* www.hubert-burda-media.com (office); www.hubert-burda.de (office).

BURDETT-COUTTS, William Walter, MA; British artistic director and film and television producer; *Chairman, Riverside Television Studios Ltd;* b. 17 Feb. 1955, Harare, Zimbabwe; s. of William A. F. Burdett-Coutts and Nancy C. Burdett-Coutts (née Gervers); one s., two d.; ed Radley Coll., Oxford, Rhodes Univ., South Africa, Univ. of Essex; Artistic Dir Ass. Rooms Edinburgh 1981–; Festival Dir Mayfest, Glasgow 1987–90; Head of Arts Granada TV 1990–93; Dir Riverside TV Studios Ltd 1993–, Chair. 2002–; Exec. Producer Ass. Film and TV 1994–; Chair. Kiss 102 1993–97, Kiss 105 1996–97; Festival Dir Brighton Comedy Festival 2002–. *Address:* Riverside Studios, Crisp Road, London, W6 9RL, England. *Telephone:* (20) 8237-1075 (office). *Fax:* (20) 8237-1071 (office). *E-mail:* wbc@riversidestudios.co.uk (office). *Website:* www.riversidestudios.co.uk (office).

BUREAU, Jérôme, DHist; French journalist; *Director of Communications, Métropole Télévision 6 (M6);* b. 19 April 1956, Paris; m. Fabienne Pauly 1999; two c. (and two from a previous marriage); journalist with Libération 1978–81; Sr Reporter L'Équipe Magazine 1981–87, Ed.-in-Chief 1989–93; Ed.-in-Chief Le Sport 1987–88; Editorial Dir L'Équipe, L'Équipe-TV 1997–2003, L'Équipe Magazine, Vélo, XL, Tennis de France 1993–2003, lequipe.fr 1999–2003; TV and Radio Producer, Sport FM 2004; Dir of Communications, Métropole Télévision 6 (M6) 2004–. *Publications:* L'Amour-Foot 1986, Les Géants du football 1996, L'année du football 2004, Euro 2004: la grande fête du football 2004, Les champions d'Athènes 2004, Braaasil: Les magiciens du football 2005. *Leisure interests:* cookery, bullfighting. *Address:* Métropole Télévision 6 (M6), 89 avenue Charles de Gaulle, 92575 Neuilly sur Seine cedex (office); 34 bis avenue Bernard Palissy 92, 92210 Saint-Cloud; 102 avenue Denfert-Rochereau, 75014 Paris, France (home). *E-mail:* jereome.bureau6@wanadoo.fr. *Website:* www.m6.fr (office).

BURELLI RIVAS, Miguel Angel, LLB, DrPolSc; Venezuelan diplomatist and lawyer; b. 8 July 1922; ed Univ. de Los Andes, Bogotá, Univ. Cen. de Venezuela y de Ecuador, Univ. Nacional de Bogotá, Univ. de Madrid and Univ. di Firenze; pre-seminary Prof. of Political Sociology and Chief Prof. of Mining and Agrarian Legislation, Faculty of Law, Univ. de Los Andes, Bogotá, Chief Prof. of Humanities I and II, Faculty of Civil Eng, Dir of Univ. Culture, Founder of School of Humanities, Founder-Dir of Univ. reviews, Bibliotheca and Universitas Emeritensis; Political Dir Ministry of the Interior; Dir-Gen. Ministry of Foreign Affairs (nine times Acting Minister); Interim Minister of Foreign Affairs; returned to legal profession 1961; mem. Venezuelan Supreme Electoral Council 1961; Minister of Justice 1964–65; Amb. to Colombia 1965–67, to UK 1967–69; presidential cand. 1968, 1973; Amb. to USA 1974–76; Minister of Foreign Affairs 1994–99; numerous decorations. *Address:* c/o Ministry of Foreign Affairs, Casa Amarilla Biblioteca Central, esq. Principal, Caracas 1010, Venezuela.

BURENGA, Kenneth L.; American publishing executive; b. 30 May 1944, Somerville, NJ; s. of Nicholas Burenga and Louanna Chamberlin; m. Jean Case 1964; one s. one d.; ed Rider Coll.; budget accountant, Dow Jones & Co., S Brunswick, NJ 1966–67, Asst Man. data processing control 1968–69, staff asst for systems devt 1970–71, Man. systems devt and control 1972–76, circulation marketing Man. 1977–78, circulation sales dir 1979–80, Vice-Pres. circulation and circulation dir 1980–86; Chief Financial Officer and Admin. Officer, Dow Jones & Co., New York 1986–88, Exec. Vice-Pres., Gen. Man. 1989–91, Pres. COO 1991, Pres. and CEO –1998 (retd); fmr Gen. Man. Wall Street Journal 1989; mem. Bd of Dirs Dow Jones Courier. *Leisure interest:* cattle farming.

BURG, Avraham, BA; Israeli politician; b. 1955; s. of Dr. Josef Burg; m. Yael Burg; six c.; ed Hebrew Univ., Jerusalem; army service; mem. Knesset 1988–2004, Speaker 1999–2003; mem. Finance and State Control Cttees 1988–92; Chair. Educ. Cttee 1992–95; mem. Cttee for the Advancement of the Status of Women 1992–95; Chair. Jewish Agency for Israel 1995–99; fmr Chair. Zionist Movt, Co-Chair. World Jewish Restitution Organisation 1995–1999, Deputy Chair. World Jewish Congress; mem. int. cttee that negotiated settlement with Swiss banks 1995–1999, mem. Board of Claims Conference 1995–1999. *Publication:* The Holocaust is Over: We Must Rise from its Ashes 2007. *Address:* c/o The Knesset, Kiryat Ben-Gurion, Hakirya, Jerusalem 91950, Israel (office).

BURGEN, Sir Arnold (Stanley Vincent), Kt, MD, FRS; British scientist; b. 20 March 1922, London; s. of the late Peter and Elizabeth Burgen (née Wolfers); m. 1st Judith Browne 1946 (died 1993); two s. one d.; m. 2nd Olga Kennard 1993; ed Christ's Coll., Finchley, London, Middlesex Hosp. Medical School; Demonstrator, later Asst Lecturer, Middlesex Hosp. Medical School 1945–49; Prof. of Physiology, McGill Univ., Montreal 1949–62; Deputy Dir McGill Univ. Clinic, Montreal Gen. Hospital 1957–62; Sheild Prof. of Pharmacology, Univ. of Cambridge 1962–71; Dir Nat. Inst. of Medical Research, London 1971–82; Master Darwin Coll., Cambridge 1982–89; Deputy Vice-Chancellor, Cambridge Univ. 1983–89; mem. Medical Research Council (MRC) 1969–71, 1973–77, Hon. Dir MRC Molecular Pharmacology Unit 1967–72; Pres. Int. Union of Pharmacology 1972–75; Vice-Pres. Royal Soc. 1970–76, Foreign Sec. 1981–86; Fellow Downing Coll., Cambridge 1962–71, Hon. Fellow 1972; mem. Deutsche Akad. der Naturforscher Leopoldina 1984; mem. Bureau, European Science and Tech. Ass. 1994–; Ed. European Review 1993–; Corresp. mem. Royal Acad. of Spain 1984; Foreign Assoc. NAS; Pres. Academia Europaea 1988–94; Academician of Finland; Hon. FRCP, Canada; Hon. DSc (McGill, Leeds, Liverpool); Hon. MD (Zürich) 1983, (Utrecht); Hon. DUniv (Surrey) 1983; Wellcome Gold Medal 1999. *Publications:* papers in journals of pharmacology and physiology. *Leisure interests:* sculpture, music. *Address:* 8A Hills Avenue, Cambridge, CB1 7XA, England. *Telephone:* (1223) 415381. *Fax:* (1223) 363852. *E-mail:* asvb@cam.ac.uk (office).

BURGESS, Ian Glencross, AO, BSc; Australian business executive; b. 26 Nov. 1931, Sydney; m. Barbara J. Hastie 1957; ed The King's School, Parramatta and Univ. of New South Wales; Man. Dir CSR Ltd 1987–93, Chair. 1997–; Chair. AMP Ltd 1994– (Dir 1989–); Dir Western Mining Co., Deputy Chair. 1997–, Chair. 1999–. *Leisure interests:* reading, golf. *Address:* AMP Ltd, Corner Phillip and Alfred Streets, Circular Quay, NSW 2000, Australia. *Telephone:* (2) 9257-7764 (office).

BURGESS, Robert George, PhD; British academic administrator; *Vice-Chancellor, University of Leicester;* b. 23 April 1947; s. of George Burgess and Olive Burgess (née Andrews); m. Hilary Margaret Mary Joyce 1974; ed Univs of Durham and Warwick; Lecturer, Univ. of Warwick 1974–84, Sr Lecturer 1984–88, Dept Chair. 1985–88, Dir Centre for Educational Devt Appraisal and Research 1987–99, Chair. Faculty of Social Sciences 1988–91, Prof. of Sociology 1988–99, Founding Chair. Grad. School 1991–95, Pro-Vice-Chancellor 1995–99; Vice-Chancellor, Univ. of Leicester 1999–; mem. Research Resources Bd, Econ. and Social Research Council 1991–96, mem. Council 1996–2000, Chair. Postgrad. Training Bd 1997–2000 (mem. 1989–93, Vice-Chair. 1996–97); Founding Chair. UK Council for Grad. Educ. 1993–99; Chair. East Midlands Univs Asscn 2001–04; mem. Higher Educ. Funding Council for England (HEFCE) Review of Postgraduate Educ. 1995–96, mem. HEFCE Quality Assessment, Learning and Teaching Cttee 2003–, Bd UCAS 2001– (Chair. 2005–), Jt Equality Steering Group 2001–2003, Bd British Library 2003–; Trustee, Higher Educ. Acad. 2003–; Academician, Acad. of Learned Socs in the Social Sciences 2000–; Chair. Econ. and Social Research Council (ESRC) Teaching and Learning Research Programme 2004–; Hon. DLitt (Staffordshire) 1998, Hon. DUniv (Northampton) 2007. *Publications:* Experiencing Comprehensive Education 1983, In the Field 1984, Education, Schools and Schooling 1985, Sociology, Education and Schools 1986, Implementing In-Service Education (jtly) 1993, Research Methods 1993 and ed. of over 24 books on social research methodology and the sociology of educ. *Leisure interests:* gardening, music, walking. *Address:* Vice-Chancellor's Office, University of Leicester, Leicester, LE1 7RH, England (office). *Telephone:* (116) 252-2322 (office). *Fax:* (116) 255-8691 (office). *E-mail:* vc@le.ac.uk (office). *Website:* www.le.ac.uk.

BURGH, Sir John Charles, KCMG, CB, BSc (Econ), MA, FRCM; British administrator; b. 9 Dec. 1925, Vienna, Austria; m. Ann Sturge 1957; two d.; ed Friends' School, Sibford, LSE; Leverhulme post-intermediate Scholarship, LSE, Pres. of Union 1949; mem. UK Del. to UN Conf. on Trade Devt 1964; Asst Sec., Dept of Econ. Affairs 1964; Prin. Pvt. Sec. to successive First Secs of State and Secs of State for Econ. Affairs 1965–68; Under-Sec., Dept of Employment 1968–71; Deputy Chair. Community Relations Comm. 1971–72; Deputy Sec. Cabinet Office (Cen. Policy Review Staff) 1972–74, Dept of Prices and Consumer Protection 1974–79, Dept of Trade 1979–80; Dir-Gen. British Council 1980–87; Pres. Trinity Coll., Oxford 1987–96; Dir English Shakespeare Co. 1988–94; Gov. LSE 1980–2004, Chair. 1985–87; mem. Exec., Political and Econ. Planning 1972–78, Council, Policy Studies Inst. 1978–85, Council VSO 1980–87, Wilton Park 1984–87; Chair. Assoc. Bd Royal Coll. of Music 1987–94, Nat. Opera Co-ordinating Cttee 1991–2007 (Sec. 1972–91), Oxford Educational Trust for Devt of the Arts 1991–96; Vice-Chair. Int. Student House 1985–86, Chair. 1987–92; Vice-Chair. The Yehudi Menuhin School 1995–; Chair. New Berlioz Edn 1993–; Hon. Fellow, LSE 1983, Trinity Coll. 1997; Hon. mem. Royal Northern Coll. of Music; Hon. LLD (Bath). *Leisure interests:* friends, music, the arts generally. *Address:* 2 Oak Hill Lodge, Oak Hill Park, London, NW3 7LN, England.

BURGHARDT, Günter, PhD, DrJur; German lawyer, academic and fmr diplomatist; *Senior Counsel, Mayer Brown International LLP;* m. Rita Byl; three c.; ed Univs of Hamburg, Paris and Strasbourg; mem. of Legal Service, EC 1970, Desk Officer for External Relations (USA, Canada and Australia), for Devt of EC External Relations Network and Asst to Dir-Gen. Sir Roy Denman 1972–80, Deputy Head of Cabinet to Commr Karl-Heinz Narjes 1981–84, to Pres. Jacques Delors 1985–88, Political Dir, Sec. Gen. of the Comm. under Pres. Delors 1988–93, Dir-Gen. of External Relations (Europe and Newly Ind. States), Common Foreign and Security Policy and External Service under Commr Hans van den Broek 1993–99, Dir-Gen. of External Relations for Commr Chris Patten 1999–2000; Amb. and Head Del. of EC to USA 2000–05; Visiting Prof., European Political and Admin. Studies Dept. and EU Int. Relations and Diplomacy Studies Dept, Coll. of Europe, Bruges 2005–; Sr Counsel Mayer Brown International LLP, Brussels 2005–. *Address:* Mayer Brown International LLP, Avenue des Arts 52, 1000 Brussels (office); Vossenlaan 12, 3080 Tervuren (home); c/o Department of EU International Relations and Diplomacy Studies, College of Europe, Dijver 11, 8000 Bruges, Belgium (office). *Telephone:* (2) 502-55-17 (Mayer Brown) (office); (50) 47-72-51 (office). *Fax:* (2) 502-54-21 (Mayer Brown) (office); (50) 47-72-50 (office). *E-mail:* gburghardt@mayerbrown.com (office); ird.info@coleurop.be (office). *Website:* www.mayerbrown.com (office); www.coleurop.be (office).

BURGIN, Victor, ARCA, MFA; British artist, writer and academic; *Millard Professor of Fine Art, Goldsmiths College, London;* b. 24 July 1941, Sheffield; s. of Samuel Burgin and Gwendolyne A. Crowder; m. 1st Hazel P. Rowbotham 1964 (divorced 1975); m. 2nd Francette Pacteau 1988; two s.; ed Firth Park Grammar School, Sheffield, Sheffield Coll. of Art, Royal Coll. of Art, London and Yale Univ., USA; Sr Lecturer, Trent Polytechnic, Nottingham 1967–73; Prof. of History and Theory of Visual Arts, Faculty of Communication, Polytechnic of Cen. London 1973–; Prof. of Art History, Univ. of Calif., Santa Cruz 1988–95, Prof. of History of Consciousness 1995–2001, Prof. Emer. of History of Consciousness 2001–; Millard Prof. of Fine Art Goldsmiths Coll., Univ. of London 2001–; Deutscher Akademischer Austauschdienst Fellowship 1978–79; Picker Professorship, Colgate Univ., Hamilton, New York 1980; mem. arts advisory panel, Arts Council of Great Britain 1971–76, 1980–81; numerous mixed and solo exhbns at galleries around the world from 1965; Hon. DUniv (Sheffield Hallam). *Publications:* Work and Commentary 1973, Thinking Photography 1982, The End of Art Theory 1986, Between 1986, Passages 1991, In/Different Spaces 1996, Some Cities 1996, Venice 1997, Shadowed 2000, The Remembered Film 2005; contrib. to exhbn catalogues. *Address:* c/o Goldsmiths College, New Cross, London, SE14 6NW, England (office). *Telephone:* (20) 7919-7671 (office). *Fax:* (20) 7919-7673 (office). *E-mail:* v.burgin@gold.ac.uk. *Website:* www.goldsmiths.ac.uk/departments/visual-arts (office).

BURGMANS, Antony, MA; Dutch food and personal care products industries executive; b. 13 Feb. 1947, Rotterdam; m. Jacqueline Burgmans; one s. one d.; ed Nijenrode Univ., Univ. of Stockholm, Sweden, Univ. of Lancaster, England; joined Unilever NV 1972, Marketing Asst, Lever Netherlands and Indonesia, Marketing and Sales Dir, Lever, Netherlands 1982–85, Lever Germany 1985–88, Chair. PT Unilever Indonesia 1988–91, Dir Unilever (Personal Care Products Div.) 1991–94, (Ice Cream and Frozen Foods—Europe) 1994–98, Chair. Unilever European Cttee 1994–98, Vice-Chair. Unilever NV 1998–99, Chair. 1999–2007 (retd); Chair. Supervisory Bd Mauritshuis Museum, The Hague; Co-Chair. Global Commerce Initiative (GCI); mem. Supervisory Bd ABN AMRO Bank, Allianz AG. *Leisure interests:* golf, skiing, Dutch painters, soccer. *Address:* Weena 455, 3013 AL Rotterdam, Netherlands (office).

BURGO, Carlos Duarte de; Cape Verde politician; *Governor, Central Bank of Cape Verde;* b. 5 March 1958, Nova Sintra, Ilha da Brava; ed Univ. of Iowa, USA; Prof. of Econs and Dir Instituto Amílcar Cabral; Pres. Municipal Ass. of Brava; Deputy for Nação; Pres. Special Perm. Comm. for Finance; 2001–03; Minister of Finance, Planning and Regional Devt 2001–03; currently Gov. Central Bank of Cape Verde Islands; mem. Nat. Council and Political Comm. of PAICV. *Address:* Central Bank of Cape Verde, Av.Amilcar Cabral, CP 101, Praia, Cape Verde (office). *Telephone:* 61-55-26 (office). *Website:* www.bcv.cv.

BURGON, Geoffrey; British composer and conductor; b. 15 July 1941, Hambledon; s. of Alan Wybert Burgon and Ada Vera Isom; m. 1st Janice Garwood 1963 (divorced); one s. one d.; m. 2nd Jacqueline Krofchak 1992; one s.; ed Pewley School, Guildford, Guildhall School of Music; freelance trumpeter/composer 1964–71; conductor 1964–; full-time composer 1971–; Ivor Novello Awards 1980, 1981, Gold Disc 1986, BAFTA Awards 2001, 2002. *Compositions include (dramatic works):* Epitaph for Sir Walter Raleigh 1968, Joan of Arc 1970, The Fall of Lucifer 1977, Orpheus 1982, Hard Times (opera) 1990; (*orchestral and solo music*): Concerto for String Orchestra 1963, Gending 1968, Alleluia Nativitas 1970, Paradise Dances (Brass Band) 1994, City Adventures 1997, Singapore Vtns 1997, Fantasia on REX 1997, A Different Dawn 1999; (*with voices*): Acquainted with Night 1965, Think on Dredful Domesday 1969, Canciones del Alma 1975, Requiem 1976, Magnificat and Nunc dimittis 1979, The World Again 1983, Revelations 1984, Title Divine 1986, A Vision 1990, Trumpet concerto 1992, First Was the World 1993, Music's Empire 1993, Merciless Beauty 1997; (*ballet music*): The Golden Fish 1964, The Calm 1974, Running Figures/Goldberg's Dream 1975, Songs, Lamentations and Praises 1979, Mass 1984, Prometheus 1988; (*chamber music*): Four Guitars 1977, Six Studies 1980, Waiting (for solo pianoforte) 1993, Almost Peace 1995, The Wanderer 1998, Recitativo 1998, Dancers in a Landscape 1999; (*with voices*): Hymn to Venus 1966, Five Sonnets of John Donne 1967, Worldës Blissë 1971, Two Love Songs, Lunar Beauty 1986, Nearing the Upper Air 1988, Heavenly Things 2000, Alleluia Psallat 2002; (*choral music*): Three Elegies 1964, Short Mass 1965, Golden Eternity 1970, The Fire of Heaven 1973, Dos Coros 1975, A God and Yet a Man 1984, Prayer to St Richard 1989, Songs of the Creation 1989, The Song of the Creatures 1989, Five Love Songs, The First World 1991, Christ's Love 2000, Magic Words 2000, Three Mysteries 2003, Of Flowers and Emeralds Sheen 2004; (*music for children*): Divertimento 1964, Five Studies 1965, Now Welcome Summer 1966, Beginnings 1969, Shirtless Stephen 2003; (*film music*): Life of Brian 1979, Dogs of War 1980, Turtle Diary 1985, Robin Hood 1991, When Trumpets Fade 1998; (*TV music*): Dr Who 1975, Tinker Tailor Soldier Spy (Ivor Novello Award 1980) 1979, Brideshead Revisited (Ivor Novello Award 1981) 1981, Testament of Youth 1979, How Many Miles to Babylon 1981, Bewitched 1983, The Death of the Heart 1985, Happy Valley 1987, The Old Wives Tale 1988, Sophia and Constance 1988, The Chronicles of Narnia 1988–90, Children of the North 1990, A Foreign Field 1992, Martin Chuzzlewit 1994, Silent Witness 1995, Turning World 1996, Cider with Rosie 1998, Longitude (BAFTA Award 2001) 2000, Labyrinth 2001, The Forsyte Saga (BAFTA Award) 2002, Island at War 2004. *Leisure interests:* cricket, jazz, wasting money on old Bristols. *Address:* c/o Cool Music Ltd, 1A Fishers Lane, Chiswick, London, W4 1RX, England (office). *Telephone:* (20) 8995-7766 (office). *Fax:* (20) 8987-8996 (office). *E-mail:* burgon@argonet.co.uk (home); geoffreyburgon@orpheusmail.co.uk (home). *Website:* www.coolmusicltd.com (office); www.geoffreyburgon.co.uk (home).

BURJANADZE, Nino, JD, PhD; Georgian politician, lawyer and professor of international law; b. 16 July 1964, Kutaisi; d. of Tina Morchadze and Anzor Burjanadze; m. Badri Bitsadze 1960; two c.; ed Akaki Tsereteli School, Kutaisi, Tbilisi State Univ., Moscow Lomonosov State Univ.; Prof. of Int. Relations and Int. Law, Tbilisi State Univ. 1991–; consultant to Ministry of Environmental Protection 1991–92, Parl. Cttee on Foreign Relations 1992–95; mem. Parl. 1995–, Deputy Chair. Cttee on Constitutional Legal Affairs and Rule of Law 1995–98, Chair. 1998–99, Chair. Cttee on Foreign Relations 2000–01, Speaker of Parl. of Georgia 2001–04, 2004–08; Rapporteur Gen. Cttee on Democracy, Human Rights and Humanitarian Issues, OSCE Parl. Ass. 1998–2000, Vice-Pres. OSCE Parl. Ass. 2000–; Pres. Parl. Ass. of Black Sea Econ. Co-operation 2001–02; fmr mem. Citizen's Union of Georgia, initiated efforts to organize opposition alliance of United Democrats, Nat. Movt and New Rights Party 2003; formed Burjanadze Democrats electoral bloc Aug. 2003; Interim Pres. of Georgia Nov. 2003–Jan. 2004, Nov. 2007–Jan. 2008; Chair. Perm. Parl. Del. to UK 1995–98; Co-Chair. EU–Georgian Parl. Co-operation Cttee 1999–2000; Pres. Black Sea Econ. Cooperation Parl. Ass. 2001–02; mem. Young Lawyers Asscn, Int. Justice Asscn, Int. Marine Justice Asscn, US Int. Justice Asscn; participant in numerous int. confs. *Publications include:* Legal Problems of International Organisations of a New Type; more than 40 articles on issues related to int. law and int. relations. *Address:* Sakartvelos Parlamenti, 0118 Tblisi, Rustaveli 8, Georgia (office). *Telephone:* (32) 93-61-70 (office). *Fax:* (32) 99-93-86 (office). *E-mail:* hdstaff@parliament.ge (office). *Website:* www.parliament.ge (office).

BURK, Martha; American psychologist and national organization official; *Chairperson, National Council of Women's Organizations;* ed Univ. of Texas; political psychologist and women's equity expert; fmr Univ. Research Dir, Prof. of Man. and adviser to political campaigns and orgs; Co-Founder and Pres. Center for Advancement of Public Policy, Washington, DC; currently Chair. Nat. Council of Women's Orgs; fmr mem. Comm. for Responsive Democracy, Advisory Cttee of Americans for Workplace Fairness, Sex Equity Caucus of Nat. Asscn for the Educ. of Young Children, Bd Dirs Nat. Org. for Women; mem. Bd Wider Opportunities for Women; Chair. Legislative Task Force for Nat. Cttee on Pay Equity; mem. advisory bd to several other nat. orgs including Univ. of Texas, US Bureau of Indian Affairs, US Dept of Educ., US Dept of State, NSF, Kansas House of Reps Smithsonian Inst., Women's Int. News Gathering Service, Nat. Educ. Asscn, Search for Common Ground and US Information Agency; numerous TV and radio broadcasts and frequent contrib. to major newspapers and magazines on public policy; Ed. Washington Feminist Faxnet. *Address:* National Council of Women's Organizations, 1050 17th Street NW, Suite 250, Washington, DC 20036, USA (office). *Telephone:* (202) 293-4505 (office). *Fax:* (202) 293-4507 (office). *E-mail:* ncworg@aol.com (office). *Website:* www.womensorganizations.org (office).

BURKE, Bernard Flood, PhD; American physicist and astrophysicist; *Professor Emeritus of Astrophysics, Massachusetts Institute of Technology;* b. 7 June 1928, Boston, Mass; s. of Vincent Paul Burke and Clare Aloyse Brine; m. 1st Jane Chapin Pann 1953 (died 1993); three s. one d.; m. 2nd Elizabeth King Platt 1998; ed Massachusetts Inst. of Tech.; mem. of staff, Carnegie Inst. of Washington 1953–65; Chair. Radio Astronomy Section, Carnegie Inst. of Washington, Dept of Terrestrial Magnetism 1962–65; Prof. of Physics, MIT 1965–2000, William Burden Prof. of Astrophysics 1981–2001, Prof. Emer. 2001–; Visiting Prof., Leiden Univ. 1971–72, Manchester Univ. 1992–93; Pres. American Astronomical Soc. 1986–88; Ed. Comments on Astrophysics 1984–87; Trustee Associated Univ. Inc. 1972–90; Trustee and Vice-Chair. NE Radio Observatory Corpn 1973–82, Chair. 1982–95; Oort Lecturer, Leiden Univ. 1993, Karl Jansky Lecturer, Nat. Radio Astronomy Observatory 1998; Visiting Scholar, Carnegie Inst. of Washington 1998; mem. Nat. Science Bd 1990–96; mem. Nat. Acad. of Science, American Acad. of Arts and Sciences; Sr Fellow, Carnegie Inst. of Washington 1997; Fellow, AAAS; Sherman Fairchild Scholar, Calif. Inst. of Tech. 1984–85; Smithsonian Regents Fellow 1985; Helen B. Warner Prize, American Astron. Soc. 1963, Rumford Prize, American Acad. of Arts and Sciences 1971, NASA Achievement Award 1989, 1998, Oort Lecturer, Univ. of Leiden 1997, Karl Jansky Lecturer, Nat. Radio Astronomy Observatory 1997. *Publications:* Microwave Spectroscopy 1953–54, Radio Noise from Jupiter 1955–61, Galactic Structure 1959–, Very Long Baseline Interferometry 1968–, Interstellar Masers 1968–, Gravitational Lenses 1980–, Interferometry in Space 1984–, Introduction to Radio Astronomy (2nd edn) (co-author) 2002; miscellaneous publs in radio astronomy 1955–. *Leisure interests:* skiing, sailing, hiking, chamber music. *Address:* Room 37-641, Massachusetts Institute of Technology, Department of Physics, Cambridge, MA 02139 (office); 34 Bradbury Street, Cambridge, MA, 02138 USA (home). *Telephone:* (617) 253-2572 (office); (617) 354-1209 (home). *Fax:* (617)

253-0861 (office). *E-mail:* bfburke@space.mit.edu (office); bfburke@comcast.net (home).

BURKE, Kathy; British actress and director; b. 13 June 1964, London; ed Anna Scher's Theatre School, London. *Play:* Smaller (dir) 2006. *TV includes:* Harry Enfield and Chums, Absolutely Fabulous, Common as Muck, Mr Wroe's Virgins (Royal TV Soc. Award), Tom Jones, Gimme Gimme Gimme. *Films:* Scrubbers, Nil by Mouth (Best Actress, Cannes Film Festival 1997, Best Actress, British Ind. Film Awards 1998), Elizabeth 1998, This Year's Love 1999, Love, Honour and Obey 2000, The Martins 2001, Once Upon a Time in the Midlands 2002, Anita and Me 2003, Flushed Away (voice) 2006. *Theatre includes:* Mr Thomas, London, Boom Bang-a-Bang, London (Dir). *Address:* c/o Hatton McEwan, POB 37385, London, N1 7XF, England.

BURKE, Nazim; Grenadian lawyer and politician; *Minister of Finance;* ed Concordia Univ., Univ. of Windsor, York Univ., Queen's Univ., Canada; Perm. Sec., Ministry of Trade 1979–83; lawyer, Burke, Sealy-Burke (law firm), Toronto 1992–2000; Founding Pnr Ciboney Chambers Law Firm 2000; mem. Grenada House of Reps 2003–; Minister of Finance 2008–; mem. Nat. Democratic Congress Party, fmr Public Relations Officer. *Address:* Ministry of Finance, Financial Complex, The Carenage, St George's, Grenada (office). *Telephone:* 440-2741 (office). *Fax:* 440-4115 (office). *E-mail:* finance@gov.gd (office). *Website:* finance.gov.gd (office).

BURKE, (Ulick) Peter, MA, FRHistS, FBA; British historian and academic; *Professor Emeritus of Cultural History, University of Cambridge;* b. 16 Aug. 1937, Stanmore; s. of John Burke and Jenny Burke (née Colin); m. 1st Susan Patricia Dell 1972 (divorced 1983); m. 2nd Maria Lucía García Pallares 1989; ed St Ignatius' Coll., Stamford Hill, St John's Coll., Oxford, St Antony's Coll., Oxford; Asst Lecturer, then Lecturer, then Reader in History (later Intellectual History), School of European Studies, Univ. of Sussex 1962–78; Lecturer in History, Univ. of Cambridge 1979–88, Reader in Cultural History 1988–96, Prof. of Cultural History 1996–2004, Prof. Emer. 2004–; Fellow, Emmanuel Coll. Cambridge 1979–; Visiting Prof., Univ. of São Paulo, Brazil 1986, 1987, Nijmegen Univ. 1992–93, Groningen Univ. 1998–99, Heidelberg Univ. 2002; Fellow, Wissenschaftskolleg, Berlin 1989–90, Netherlands Inst. for Advanced Study 2005; Erasmus Prize, Academia Europaea 1999. *Publications:* The Renaissance Sense of the Past 1969, Culture and Society in Renaissance Italy 1972, Venice and Amsterdam 1974, Popular Culture in Early Modern Europe 1978, Sociology and History 1980, Montaigne 1981, Vico 1985, Historical Anthropology of Early Modern Italy 1987, The Renaissance 1987, The French Historical Revolution: The Annales School 1929–1989 1990, The Fabrication of Louis XIV 1992, History and Social Theory 1992, Antwerp: A Metropolis in Europe 1993, The Art of Conversation 1993, The Fortunes of the Courtier 1995, Varieties of Cultural History 1997, The European Renaissance 1998, A Social History of Knowledge 2000, Eyewitnessing 2001, (jtly) A Social History of the Media 2002, Languages and Communities in Early Modern Europe 2004. *Leisure interest:* travel. *Address:* Emmanuel College, Cambridge, CB2 3AP (office); 14 Warkworth Street, Cambridge, CB1 1EG, England (home). *Telephone:* (1223) 334272 (home). *Fax:* (1223) 334426 (office). *E-mail:* upb1000@cam.ac.uk (home). *Website:* www.hist.cam.ac.uk (office).

BURKE, Philip George, CBE, PhD, FInstP, FAPS, MRIA, FRS; British mathematical physicist and academic; *Professor Emeritus, Queen's University, Belfast;* b. 18 Oct. 1932, London; s. of Henry Burke and Frances Mary Burke (née Sprague); m. Valerie Mona Martin 1959; four d.; ed Univ. Coll. of SW of England, Exeter, Univ. Coll., Univ. of London; Research Fellow Univ. Coll., Univ. of London 1956–57, Lecturer Computer Unit 1957–59; Research Physicist, Alvarez Bubble Chamber Group, Theory Group, Lawrence Radiation Lab., Berkeley, Calif. 1959–62; Research Fellow, later Prin. Scientific Officer, then Sr Prin. Scientific Officer, Atomic Energy Research Establishment, Harwell 1962–67; Prof. of Math. Physics, Queen's Univ., Belfast 1967–98, Prof. Emer. 1998–, Head Dept of Applied Math. and Theoretical Physics 1974–77, Dir School of Math. and Physics 1988–90; Chair. Inter-Council High Performance Computing Man. Cttee 1996–98; Head Div. Theory and Computational Science, Science and Eng Research Council, Daresbury Lab., Cheshire 1977–82 (jt appointment with Queen's Univ.); Founding and Prin. Ed., Computer Physics Communications 1969–79, Hon. Ed. 1980–; mem. UK Science and Eng Research Council 1989–94, Chair. Supercomputing Man. Cttee 1991–94; mem. Council Royal Soc. 1990–92; Fellow Univ. Coll., London 1986; Hon. DSc (Exeter) 1981, (Queens Univ., Belfast) 1999; Inst. of Physics' Guthrie Medal and Prize 1994, Sir David Bates Prize 2000. *Publications:* over 350 articles in many specialist journals; author or co-author of seven books. *Leisure interests:* walking, books, music. *Address:* Brook House, Norley Lane, Crowton, Northwich, Cheshire, CW8 2RR, England (home); Department of Applied Mathematics and Theoretical Physics, Queen's University, Belfast, BT7 1NN, Northern Ireland (office). *Telephone:* (2890) 975047 (office); (1928) 788301 (home). *Fax:* (2890) 979182 (office). *E-mail:* p.burke@qub.ac.uk (office).

BURKE, Ray; Irish politician; b. 30 Sept. 1943, Dublin; m. Anne Fassbender; two d.; ed O'Connell's Co. Boys' School, Dublin; mem. Dublin Co. Council 1967–78, Chair. 1985–87; elected mem. Dail 1973; Minister of State, Dept of Industry and Commerce and Energy 1978–80, Minister for Environment 1980–81, 1982, for Energy and Communications 1987–88, for Industry, Commerce and Communications 1988–89, for Justice and for Communications 1989–92, for Foreign Affairs July–Oct. 1997; Fianna Fáil; sentenced to six months' imprisonment for tax offences Jan. 2005. *Address:* c/o Dáil Éireann, Dublin 2; Briargate, Malahide Road, Swords, Co. Dublin, Ireland (home).

BURKE, Richard T.; American business executive; *Chairman, UnitedHealth Group;* b. 1944, Raleigh, NC; m. Jude Burke; five c.; ed Georgia State Univ., Univ. of Virginia; f. UnitedHealth Inc. (later UnitedHealth Group), Dir 1977–, Chair. and CEO 1974–88, Chair. (non-exec.) 2006–; Owner and CEO, Phoenix Coyotes (professional sports franchise of Nat. Hockey League) 1995–2001; Dir First Cash Financial Services Inc. 1993–, Meritage Homes Corpn 2004–. *Address:* UnitedHealth Group, PO Box 1459, Minneapolis, MN 55440-1459, USA (office). *Telephone:* (800) 328-5979 (office). *Website:* www.unitedhealthgroup.com (office).

BURKE, Sir Thomas Kerry, Kt, BA; New Zealand politician; b. 24 March 1942, Christchurch; m. 1st Jennifer Shiel (divorced 1984); two s.; m. 2nd Helen Paske 1984 (died 1989); one s.; ed Univ. of Canterbury, Christchurch Teachers' Coll.; general labourer in Auckland 1965–66, Factory del., Auckland Labourers' Union; teacher, Rangiora High School 1967, Chair. Rangiora Post-Primary Teachers' Asscn 1969–71; MP for Rangiora 1972–75, for West Coast 1978–90; teacher, Greymouth High School 1975–78; Minister of Regional Devt and of Employment and Immigration 1984–87; Speaker, New Zealand Parl. 1987–91. *Leisure interests:* skiing, swimming.

BURKE, Tom, CBE, BA, FRSA; British/Irish environmental policy adviser; *Environmental Policy Adviser, Rio Tinto plc;* b. (David Thomas Burke), 5 Jan. 1947, Cork, Ireland; s. of J. V. Burke and Mary Bradley; ed St Boniface's Coll., Plymouth, Univ. of Liverpool; Great George's Community Arts Project 1969–70; Lecturer, Carlett Park Coll., Cheshire 1970, Old Swan Tech. Coll. 1971–73; Local Groups Co-ordinator, Friends of the Earth 1973–75, Exec. Dir 1975–79, Dir of Special Projects 1979–80, Vice-Chair. 1980–81; Policy Adviser, European Environment Bureau 1978–88, mem. Exec. Cttee 1988–91; Sec.-Gen. Bergen 1990 NGO Conf. 1988–90; Dir The Green Alliance 1982–91 (mem. Exec. Cttee 1979–82, 1997–), Sustainability Ltd 1987–89; Sec. Ecological Studies Inst. 1987–92; Special Adviser to Sec. of State for Environment 1991–97; Environmental Policy Adviser, Rio Tinto plc 1996–, BP PLC 1997–2001; mem. Council English Nature 1999–2005; Adviser, Cen. Policy Group, Office of the Deputy Prime Minister 2002–, Sr Adviser to Special Rep. on Climate Change 2005–; Founding Dir E3G 2003–; Chair. Review of Environmental Governance in NI 2006–07; Chair. Editorial Advisory Bd ENDS 2005–; Visiting Fellow, Cranfield School of Man. 1990–94; Visiting Prof., Imperial Coll. London 1997–, Univ. Coll. London 2003–; mem. Bd of Dirs Earth Resources Research 1975–87, Waste Man. Advisory Council 1976–80, Packaging Council 1978–82, Exec. Cttee Nat. Council for Voluntary Orgs and Chair. Planning and Environment Group 1984–89, UK Nat. Cttee for European Year of the Environment 1986–88, Council, Royal Soc. for Nature Conservation 1993–97; mem. Council Royal Soc. of Arts 1990–92 (mem. Environment Cttee 1989–96), Overseas Cttee, Save the Children Fund 1992–97, Exec. Bd World Energy Council Comm. 1990–93; Dir (non-exec.) Earth Resources Research 1975–88; Fellow Inst. of Energy; mem. Co-operative Insurance Services Environ Trust Advisory Cttee 1990–92, 1997–2001, OECD High Level Advisory Group on the Environment 1996–98; stood as Social Democrat Party cand., Gen. Elections 1983, 1987; mem. Council London Sustainable Devt Comm. 2002–06, American Chem. Council Leadership Dialogue (USA) 2003–07, Advisory Bd Center for Environmental Leadership in Business (USA), Council Inst. of Environmental Man.; Hon. Visiting Fellow, Manchester Business School 1984–86; Hon. Prof., Faculty of Laws, Univ. Coll. London; Royal Humane Soc. Testimonials on Vellum 1966, on Parchment 1968, UNEP Global 500 Laureate 1991. *Publications:* Europe: Environment 1981, Pressure Groups in the Global System (co-author) 1982, Ecology 2000 (co-author) 1984, The Green Capitalists (co-author) 1987, Green Pages (co-author) 1988, Ethics, Environment and the Company (with Julie Hill) 1990. *Leisure interests:* photography, birdwatching. *Address:* c/o Rio Tinto PLC, 6 St James's Square, London, SW1Y 4LD (office); Studio 2, Clink Wharf Studios, Clink Street, London, SE1 9DG, England (home). *Telephone:* (20) 7781-1135 (office); (20) 7357-9146 (home). *E-mail:* tom.burke@riotinto.com (office); tom@tomburke.co.uk (office). *Website:* www.riotinto.com (office); www.tomburke.co.uk.

BURLAND, John Boscawen, CBE, DSc, FRS, FREng, FICE, FIStructE; British scientist, academic and civil engineer; *Professor Emeritus of Soil Mechanics, Imperial College London;* b. 4 March 1936, Little Chalfont; s. of John Whitmore Burland and Margaret Irene Burland (née Boscawen); m. Gillian Margaret Burland (née Miller) 1963; two s. one d.; ed Parktown Boys' High School, Univ. of the Witwatersrand, Johannesburg, Cambridge Univ.; engineer Ove Arup and Pnrs, London 1961–63; Sr Scientific Officer then Prin. Scientific Officer, Bldg Research Station (BRS), Watford 1966–72, Head Geotechnics Div. 1972–79, Asst Dir BRS 1979–80; Prof. of Soil Mechanics, Imperial Coll. of Science, Tech. and Medicine, London Univ. 1980–, now Prof. Emer.; mem. Italian Prime Minister's Cttee for stabilising the Leaning Tower of Pisa; Kt Commdr of the Royal Order of Francis I, Italy; Commendatore Ordine della Stella di Solidarietá Italiana (OSSI); Hon. DEng (Heriot-Watt, Glasgow), Hon. DSc (Nottingham, Warwick), Hon. Fellow (Imperial Coll., London, Emmanuel Coll., Cambridge, Cardiff Univ.), Hon. DSc (Eng) (Univ. of Witwatersrand); Kelvin Medal, Baker Medal, Kevin Nash Gold Medal, Gold Medal, Inst. of Structural Engineers, Gold Medal, Inst. of Civil Engineers, Public Promotion of Engineering Medal, Royal Acad. of Engineering. *Publications:* numerous papers on soil mechanics and civil eng. *Leisure interests:* golf, painting, sailing. *Address:* Department of Civil and Environmental Engineering, Imperial College, South Kensington Campus, London, SW7 2AZ, England (office). *Telephone:* (20) 7594-6079 (office). *Fax:* (20) 7594-5934 (office). *E-mail:* j.burland@imperial.ac.uk (office). *Website:* www.cv.imperial.ac.uk (office).

BURLATSKY, Fedor Mikhailovich, DPhil; Russian journalist, writer and politician; b. 4 Jan. 1927, Kiev; s. of Mikhail Burlatsky and Sofia Burlatsky; m. 1st Seraphyma Burlatsky 1952 (divorced 1974); two s.; m. 2nd Kyra Burlatsky 1974; one d.; ed Tashkent Law Inst.; journalist Tashkent 1948–50; post grad.

at Inst. of State Law, USSR Acad. of Sciences 1950–53; journalist with Kommunist 1953–59; head of section in Cen. Cttee Dept for Liaison with Communist and Workers' Parties of Socialist Countries 1959–65; political observer with Pravda 1965–67; Deputy Dir of USSR Inst. of Sociological studies 1968–72; head of section, USSR Inst. of State and Law (later Chief Scientific Researcher 1990–) and Head of Philosophy Dept, Inst. of Social Science, Cen. Cttee of CPSU 1975–88; Vice-Pres. Soviet Assoc. of Political Science 1976, currently Pres.; USSR People's Deputy 1989–91; Chair. Sub cttee on Humanitarian, Scientific and Cultural Co-operation, Cttee on Foreign Affairs 1989–91; political observer Literaturnaya Gazeta 1983–90, Ed.-in-Chief 1990–91; Chair. of Public Comm. for Int. Co-operation on Humanitarian Problems and Human Rights 1989–90; Dir Public Consultative Council to Chair. of State Duma 1993–96; Chief Scientific Researcher Inst. of State and Law 1992–; Visiting Prof. Heidelberg Univ. 1988, Harvard Univ. 1992, Oxford Univ. 1993; Pres. Euro-Asian Fund for Humanitarian Co-operation 1996–, Int. League for Defence of Culture; Chair., Scientific Council on Politology, Pres. Russian Acad. of Sciences 1995–; Pres. Fund 'International Cultural Co-operation' 2003–, Fund 'Euro-Atlantic State Co-operation' 2003–; mem. Acad. of National Sciences 1993, Acad. of Socio-Political Sciences 1996; Italian Senate Prize 1988. Publications include: Mao Zedong (biography) 1976, The Modern State and Politics 1978, The Legend of Machiavelli 1987, New Thinking 1988, Leaders and Advisers 1990, Khrushchev and the First Russian Spring 1992, The End of the Red Empire 1993, Russian Sovereigns–Age of the Reformation 1996. Leisure interest: tennis. Address: Institute of State and Law, Znamenka str. 10, 119841 Moscow, Russia (office); Novovagankovsky per. 22, Apt 90, 123022 Moscow, Russia (home). Telephone: (495) 291-88-16 (office); (495) 291-85-06 (home). Fax: (495) 291-87-56 (office). E-mail: isl-ran@rinet.ru (office).

BURLEIGH, A. Peter; American diplomatist and government official; Ambassador in Residence and Distinguished Visiting Professor, University of Miami; b. 7 March 1942, Los Angeles; ed Colgate Univ.; Teaching Fellow, Wharton School, Univ. of Pennsylvania; Deputy Asst Sec. of State, Bureau of Near Eastern and South Asian Affairs 1987–89, Prin. Deputy Asst Sec. of State for Intelligence and Research 1989–91; Co-ordinator Office of Counter-Terrorism 1991–92; Prin. Deputy Asst Sec. of State for Personnel 1992–95; Amb. to Sri Lanka (also accred to the Maldives) 1995–97; Deputy Rep. to UN 1997–99, Chargé de Mission 1998–99; Amb. to Repub. of Philippines (also accred to Palau) 1999–2000; currently Amb. in Residence and Distinguished Visiting Prof., Univ. of Miami; Fulbright Scholar; mem. Asia Soc., American Foreign Service Asscn; numerous Dept of State Superior Honor Awards, Sr Foreign Service Presidential Award, Meritorious Service Award, Sec. of State's Distinguished Service Medal 2000, Presidential Distinguished Service Award 2000. Address: Master of Arts in International Administration (MAIA) Program, University of Miami, PO Box 248005, Coral Gables, FL 33124-1610 (office); 2300 Riverlane Terrace, Fort Lauderdale, FL 33312-4762, USA (home). Telephone: (305) 284-2211 (office). E-mail: apburl@bellsouth.net (home). Website: www.miami.edu/maia (office).

BURNET, Alastair (see Burnet, Sir J. W A).

BURNET, Sir James William Alexander (Alastair), Kt; British journalist; b. 12 July 1928, Sheffield, Yorks.; s. of the late Alexander Burnet and Schonaid Burnet; m. Maureen Campbell Sinclair 1958; ed The Leys School, Cambridge and Worcester Coll., Oxford; Sub-Ed. and Leader Writer, Glasgow Herald 1951–58, Leader Writer, The Economist 1958–62; Political Ed., Independent Television News (ITN) 1963–64, with ITN 1976–91, Dir 1982–90, Assoc. Ed. ITN 1981–91; Ed. The Economist 1965–74; Ed. Daily Express 1974–76; Contributor to TV current affairs programmes, This Week, Panorama, News at Ten, etc.; Ind. Dir Times Newspapers Holdings Ltd 1982–2002; mem. Council of the Banking Ombudsman 1985–96; Dir United Racecourses Ltd 1985–94; Hon. Vice-Pres. Inst. of Journalists 1990 Richard Dimbleby Award, BAFTA 1966, 1970, 1979, Royal Television Society Judges' Award 1981, Hall of Fame 1999. Address: 43 Hornton Court, Campden Hill Road, London, W8 7RU, England. Telephone: (20) 7937-7563.

BURNETT, Keith, CBE, BA, DPhil, FRS; British physicist, academic and university administrator; Vice-Chancellor, Sheffield University; b. 1953, Llwynypia, Wales; m. Ann Burnett; one s. one d.; ed Oxford Univ.; began career as Research Assoc., Jt Inst. for Lab. Astrophysics, Colo, USA; fmr Asst Prof. of Physics, Univ. of Colorado; Physics Lecturer, Imperial Coll. 1984–87; Lecturer in Physics and Fellow of St John's Coll. Oxford 1987, becoming Chair. of Physics, Univ. of Oxford, Head of Div. of Math., Physical and Life Sciences 2005–07; Vice-Chancellor Sheffield Univ. 2007–; mem. Univs UK, Yorkshire Univs, Russell Group; Dir Worldwide Univs Network, Sheffield Univ. Enterprises Ltd; Dir Graduate Prospects Ltd, Higher Educ. Careers Service Unit; mem. Science and Tech. Facilities Council; Fellow, Inst. of Physics; Inst. of Physics Thomas Young Medal and Prize 1997, Royal Soc. Wolfson Merit Award 2003. Publications: author or jt author of nearly 200 scientific papers in the fields of atomic, molecular and laser physics; Spectral Line Shapes 1983, Ultracold Atoms and Bose-Einstein-Condensation 1996. Leisure interests: Chinese language and culture. Address: Office of the Vice Chancellor, University of Sheffield, Western Bank, Sheffield, S10 2TN, England (office). Telephone: (114) 222-2000 (office). E-mail: vc@sheffield.ac.uk (office). Website: www.shef.ac.uk/vc (office).

BURNEY, Mohammad Ilyas, MBBS, MCPath, FCPS, FRCPath; Pakistani virologist and academic; Scientist Emeritus, National Institute of Health, Islamabad; b. 1 Jan. 1922, Simla, India; est. first Dept of Virology at Armed Forces Inst. of Pathology, Pakistan 1959, later first Measles and HDC Rabies Vaccine Production Labs in the developing world; isolated Congo virus 1976 and Chlamydia trachomatis and EV-70 and Coxsackie-21 viruses in the course of his career; new species of Phlebotomus named after him in recognition of

pioneering work on viruses; Emer. Prof. Army Medical Coll.; Fellow Islamic Acad. of Sciences, Pakistan Acad. of Sciences, Nat. Acad. of Medical Sciences, Pakistan; Hilal-i-Imtiaz Prize 1982, WHO Shousha Award 1984, Sitara-i-Imtiaz 1991. Publications: seven books/monographs and more than 80 research papers. Address: c/o Islamic Academy of Sciences, PO Box 830036, Amman, Jordan (office); 213/3 Ordinance Road, Rawalpindi, Pakistan (home). Telephone: (51) 9255232 (office); 5583405 (home). Fax: (51) 5518695 (office); (51) 5518695 (home). E-mail: miburney@hotmail.com (home).

BURNEY, Sayed Muzaffir Hussain, MA; Indian politician; b. 14 Aug. 1923, Bulandshahr, Uttar Pradesh; s. of Ejaz Hussain Burney and Imtiazi Burney; m. Sabeeha Burney; three s. two d.; entered Indian Admin. Service; various posts, including Jt Sec., Ministry of Agric. 1965–72, Additional Sec. in Ministry of Petroleum and Chemicals 1973–75, Sec., Ministry of Information and Broadcasting 1975–77, Sec., Ministry of Home Affairs 1980–81; served Orissa Govt as Divisional Commr and Chief Sec. 1979–80; Gov. of Nagaland, Manipur and Tripura, then Haryana 1981–88; Chair. Minorities Comm. 1988–92 and Chancellor Jamia Millia Islamia. Publications: Iqbal Poet – Patriot of India, Collected Letters of Iqbal (in Urdu), Collected Speeches. Address: F-3/17, Vasant Vihar, New Delhi 110057, India.

BURNHAM, Andrew (Andy) Murray, MA; British politician; Secretary of State for Culture, Media and Sport; b. 7 Jan. 1970, Liverpool; m. Marie-France Van Heel 2000; one s. two d.; ed Fitzwilliam Coll., Cambridge; researcher for Tessa Jowell MP 1994–97; researcher, Nat. Health Service Confed. 1997; Special Adviser to Chris Smith MP, Dept for Culture, Media and Sport 1998; MP (Labour) for Leigh 2001–,; mem. Health Select Cttee 2001–03, Parl. Pvt. Sec. to Home Sec. David Blunkett 2003–04, Parl. Under-Sec. State for Immigration, Citizenship and Nationality 2005–06, Minister of State at Dept of Health 2006–07, Chief Sec. to Treasury 2007–08, Sec. of State for Culture, Media and Sport 2008–. Leisure interest: Everton football club. Address: Department for Culture, Media and Sport, 2–4 Cockspur Street, London, SW1Y 5DH (office); 10 Market Street, Leigh, WN7 1DS, England (office). Telephone: (1942) 682353 (Leigh) (office). E-mail: enquiries@culture.gsi.gov.uk (office). Website: www.andyburnham.org (home); www.culture.gov.uk (office).

BURNHAM, Christopher Bancroft, BA, MPA; American international organization executive; Under-Secretary-General for Management, United Nations; b. 1956, New York City; ed Washington & Lee Univ., Harvard Univ., Georgetown Univ. Nat. Security Studies Program; served in US Marine Corps Reserve, veteran of first Gulf War, led one of the first infantry units to reach and liberate Kuwait City in 1991; elected to Conn. House of Reps three times, served as Asst Minority Leader; fmr investment banker with Credit Suisse First Boston and Advest Corp. Finance; Treas. of Conn. 1994; fmr CEO PIMCO's Columbus Circle Investors (asset man. and mutual fund co.), fmr Vice-Chair. PIMCO's mutual fund group; Asst Sec. for Resource Man. and Chief Financial Officer, State Dept 2002–05; UN Under-Sec.-Gen. for Man. 2005–; recipient of several accounting, leadership and civic awards. Address: Office of the Secretary-General, UN Headquarters, First Avenue at 46th Street, New York, NY 10017, USA (office). Telephone: (212) 963-1234 (office). Fax: (212) 963-4879 (office). Website: www.un.org/News/ossg/sg/stories/burnham_bio.asp (office).

BURNHAM, James B., PhD; American banker and academic; Professor of Finance, John F. Donahue Graduate School of Business, Duquesne University; b. 22 Oct. 1939, New York; s. of James Burnham and Marcia Lightner; m. Anne Mullin 1964; two s. two d.; ed Milton Acad., Princeton Univ., Washington Univ., St Louis; economist and Special Asst, Federal Reserve Bd, Washington, DC 1969–71; Sr Economist, Mellon Bank, Pittsburgh, Pa 1971–74, Vice-Pres. 1974–81, Sr Vice-Pres. 1985, Office of Govt Affairs 1979–81, Chair. Country Review Cttee 1977–81; Staff Dir and Special Asst to Chair., Pres.'s Council of Econ. Advisors 1981–82; US Exec. Dir IBRD, Washington, DC 1982–85; John M. Olin Visiting Prof., Center for the Study of American Business, Washington Univ., St. Louis 1989–90; Prof. of Finance, John F. Donahue Graduate School of Business, Duquesne Univ. 1990–; Fulbright Scholar, Univ. of São Paulo, Brazil 1962; Fulbright Sr Research Grant, Turkey 2005; mem. American Econs Asscn, Nat. Asscn of Business Economists. Publications: articles on contemporary economic subjects. Leisure interests: canoeing, bridge. Address: John F. Donahue Graduate School of Business, Duquesne University, 918 Rockwell Hall, Pittsburgh, PA 15282, USA (office). Telephone: (412) 396-5118 (office). Fax: (412) 396-1797 (office). E-mail: burnham@duq.edu (office). Website: www.business.duq.edu/faculty/burnham (office).

BURNS, Conrad Ray; American lobbyist and fmr politician; Senior Advisor, GAGE Business Consulting and Government Affairs; b. 25 Jan. 1935, Gallatin, Mo.; s. of Russell Burns and Mary Frances Burns (née Knight); m. Phyllis Jean Kuhlmann; one s. one d.; ed Univ. of Missouri; Field Rep. Polled Hereford World magazine, Kansas City 1963–69; Public Relations Officer, Billings Livestock Cttee, Mont. 1969–73; Founding Pres. Ag-Network 1975–86; Farm Dir KULR TV 1974; Commr Yellowstone Co. 1987–89; mem. Republican Party; Senator from Montana 1989–2007, Chair. Appropriations Sub-cttee of Mil. Construction, Cttee on Science and Transportation, Sub-cttee of Cttees, Energy and Natural Resources Cttee, mem. Ageing Cttee, Small Business Cttee; Sr Advisor, GAGE Business Consulting and Government Affairs, Washington C 2007–; mem. Nat. Asscn of Farm Broadcasters. Leisure interest: football officiating. Address: GAGE Business Consulting and Government Affairs, 122 C Street, NW, Suite 380, Washington, DC 20001, USA (office). Telephone: (202) 393-4262 (office). Fax: (202) 393-1002 (office). Website: www.gage.cc (home).

BURNS, Duncan Thorburn, BSc, MA, PhD, DSc, CChem, FRSC, MRIA, FRSE,; British chemist and academic; *Professor Emeritus of Analytical Chemistry, Queen's University, Belfast;* b. 30 May 1934, Wolverhampton; s. of James Thorburn Burns and Olive Mary Constance Burns (née Waugh); m. 1st Valerie Mary Vinton 1961 (divorced 1994); one s. two d.; m. 2nd Celia Mary Thorburn-Burns 1994; ed Whitcliffe Mount School and Leeds Univ.; Asst Lecturer in Physical Chem., Medway Coll. of Tech. 1958–59, Lecturer 1959–63; Sr Lecturer in Analytical Chem., Woolwich Polytechnic 1963–66, Loughborough Univ. 1966–71, Reader 1971–75; Prof. of Analytical Chem., Queen's Univ., Belfast 1975–99, Prof. Emer. 1999–; Redwood Lecturer, Royal Soc. of Chem. 1982, Pres. Analytical Div. 1988–90; Fellow, Inst. of Chem. in Ireland, European Chemist; Visiting Prof., Kasetsart Univ., Bangkok; Hon. mem. Pharmaceutical Soc. of NI 2001; Reagents and Reactions Royal Soc. of Chem. Medal and Award 1982, Boyle/Higgens Gold Medal, Inst. of Chem. of Ireland 1990, Ehren Nadel in Gold, Analytical Inst. Technische Univ. Wien 1990, AnalaR Gold Medal, Royal Soc. of Chem. 1990, SAC Gold Medal, Royal Soc. of Chem. 1993, Fritz Pregl Medal, Austrian Chemical Soc. 1993, Tertiary Chemical Educ. Medal and Award, Royal Soc. of Chem. 1995, Sigillum Magnum, Univ. of Bologna 1996, Div. of Analytical Chem. (DAC) Tribute, European Asscn for Chemical and Molecular Sciences 2005. *Publications:* nine books and over 395 papers. *Leisure interest:* history of chemistry. *Address:* Science Library, The Queen's University of Belfast, Belfast BT9 5AG (office); 318 Stranmillis Road, Belfast, BT9 5EB, Northern Ireland (home). *Telephone:* (2890) 975442 (office); (2890) 668567 (home). *Fax:* (2890) 668567 (office). *E-mail:* d.t.burns@qub.ac.uk (office); profburns@chemistry.fsbusiness.co.uk (home).

BURNS, John Fisher; British journalist; *Chief of Bureau for London, New York Times;* b. 4 Oct. 1944, Nottingham, England; s. of Air Cdre R. J. B. Burns and Dorothy Burns (née Fisher); m. 1st Jane Pequegnat 1972 (divorced); m. 2nd Jane Scott-Long 1991; two s. one d.; ed Stowe School, McGill Univ., Canada and Harvard Univ., USA; China correspondent, Globe and Mail, Toronto, Canada; Foreign Corresp. New York Times 1975–80, Soviet Union 1981–84, China 1984–86, Canada 1987–88, Afghanistan 1989–90, Persian Gulf 1990, Balkans 1991–94, India 1994–98, Special Corresp. for Islamic Affairs 1999–2002, Chief of Bureau for Baghdad 2002–07; Chief of Bureau for London 2007–; Chief of Bureau for Pakistan and Afghanistan, Washington Post 2002; Pulitzer Prize for Int. Reporting 1993 (co-winner for reporting from Bosnia), 1997 (for coverage of the Taliban regime in Afghanistan); George Polk Prize for Foreign Correspondence 1978, 1997. *Leisure interests:* golf, music, motor racing. *Address:* The New York Times, 229 West 43rd Street, New York, NY 10036, USA (office). *Telephone:* (212) 556-1234 (office). *Website:* www.nytimes.com (office).

BURNS, Kenneth (Ken) Lauren, BA; American film director and film producer; b. 29 July 1953, Brooklyn, New York; s. of Robert Burns and Lyla Burns; m. 1st Amy Stechler Burns (divorced); two c.; m. 2nd Julie Deborah Brown 2003; ed Ann Arbor Pioneer High School, Mich., Hampshire Coll.; Co-founder Florentine Films; Dr hc (Bowdoin Coll.) 1991, (Amherst Coll.) 1991, (Univ. of New Hampshire), (Franklin Pierce Coll.), Notre Dame Coll.), (Coll. of St Joseph), (Springfield Coll.), (Pace Univ.), (Univ. of NC, Chapel Hill). *Films include:* Brooklyn Bridge 1981, The Shakers: Hands to Work, Hearts to God 1984, The Statue of Liberty 1985, Huey Long 1985, Thomas Hart Benton (TV) 1988, The Congress (TV)) 1988, The Civil War (TV miniseries, more than 40 major film and TV awards including two Emmy Awards, two Grammy Awards, Producer of the Year Award from Producer's Guild, People's Choice Award, Peabody Award, DuPont-Columbia Award, D.W. Griffiths Award, Lincoln Prize) 1990, Empire of the Air: The Men Who Made Radio 1991, Baseball (TV miniseries, numerous awards including Emmy, CINE Golden Eagle Award, Clarion Award, TV Critics Awards for Outstanding Achievement in Sports and Special Programming) 1994, The West (producer, Erik Barnouw Prize) 1996, Thomas Jefferson (TV miniseries) 1997, Lewis & Clark: The Journey of the Corps of Discovery 1997, Frank Lloyd Wright (Peabody Award) 1998, Not for Ourselves Alone: The Story of Elizabeth Cady Stanton and Susan B. Anthony (TV miniseries, Peabody Award) 1999, Jazz (TV miniseries) 2001, Mark Twain (TV, Leon Award for Best Documentary, St Louis Film Festival) 2001, Horatio's Drive: America's First Road Trip (TV) 2003, Unforgivable Blackness: The Rise and Fall of Jack Johnson (three Primetime Emmy Awards) 2004, The War 2007. *Publication:* The Civil War (with Geoffrey C. Ward), Baseball (with Geoffrey C. Ward), Lewis and Clarke: The Journey of the Corps of Discovery (with Dayton Duncan), The War (with Geoffrey C. Ward) 2007. *Address:* Florentine Films, PO Box 613, Walpole, NH 03608, USA (office). *Telephone:* (603) 756-3038 (office). *Fax:* (603) 756-4389 (office). *Website:* www.florentinefilms.com (office).

BURNS, R. Nicholas, MA; American diplomatist; b. 28 Jan. 1956, Buffalo, NY; m. Elizabeth Baylies; three d.; ed Univ. of Paris, Boston Coll., Johns Hopkins School of Advanced Int. Studies; before entering Foreign Service worked in US Embassy in Mauritania and as programme officer for AT Int.; Vice-Consul and Staff Asst to Amb., Cairo 1983–85; political officer, Consulate-Gen., Jerusalem 1985–87; staff officer, Operations Center and Secr., Dept of State 1987–88, Special Asst to Counsellor 1989–90; Adviser to Pres. George Bush on Greece, Turkey and Cyprus and Dir for Soviet (later Russian) Affairs; Special Asst to Pres. Clinton and Sr Dir for Russia, Ukraine and Eurasia Affairs; Spokesman, Dept of State and Acting Asst Sec. for Public Affairs 1995–97; Amb. to Greece 1997–2001; Perm. Rep. to NATO, Brussels 2001–05; UnderSec. Of State for Political Affairs 2005–08 (resgnd); mem. Council on Foreign Relations, Order of St. John, Int. Inst. for Strategic Studies; Order of the Terra Mariana (Estonia); Dr hc (Worcester Polytechnic Inst.) 1997; Superior Honor Award (three times), James Clement Dunn Award for Excellence 1994, Charles E. Cobb Award for Trade Devt by an Amb. 2000, Woodrow Wilson Award for Distinguished Govt Service (Johns Hopkins Univ.) 2002. *Address:* c/o Office of the Under Secretary for Political Affairs, US Department of State, 201 C Street, NW, Washington, DC 20520, USA (office).

BURNS, Sir Robert Andrew, KCMG, MA, FRSA; British diplomatist (retd); *Chairman of the Council, Royal Holloway, University of London;* b. 21 July 1943, London; s. of the late Robert Burns CB, CMG and Mary Burns (née Goodland); m. Sarah Cadogan 1973; two s. one d.; ed Highgate School, Trinity Coll. Cambridge, School of Oriental and African Studies, Univ. of London; joined Diplomatic Service 1965, served in New Delhi 1967–71, FCO, London and UK Del. to CSCE 1971–75, First Sec. and Head of Chancery, Bucharest 1976–78, Pvt. Sec. to Perm. Under-Sec. and Head of Diplomatic Service, FCO 1979–82, Fellow, Center for Int. Affairs, Harvard Univ., USA 1982–83, Counsellor (Information) and Head of British Information Services, Washington, DC and New York 1983–86, Head S Asian Dept, FCO 1986–88, Head News Dept 1988–90, Asst Under-Sec. of State (Asia), FCO 1990–92; Amb. to Israel 1992–95; Deputy Under-Sec. of State (non-Europe, Trade and Investment Promotion) 1995–97; British Consul-Gen., Hong Kong Special Admin. Region and Macao 1997–2000; High Commr in Canada 2000–03; Int. Gov. BBC 2005–06; Dir JP Morgan Chinese Investment Trust 2003–; Chair. Council, Royal Holloway, Univ. of London 2004–, Anglo-Israel Asscn 2004–05, Hestercombe Gardens Trust 2005–, Advisory Council British Expertise 2006–; Vice-Chair. Cttee of Univ. Chairmen 2007–; mem. British North America Cttee 2004–; Fellow, Portland Trust 2004–; Hon. Pres. Canada UK Colloquia 2003–. *Publication:* Diplomacy, War and Parliamentary Democracy 1989. *Leisure interests:* music, theatre, Exmoor. *Address:* Royal Holloway, University of London, Egham, Surrey, TW20 0EX, England (office). *Telephone:* (1784) 443011. *Fax:* (1784) 433619. *E-mail:* andrew.burns@rhul.ac.uk (office). *Website:* www.rhul.ac.uk (office).

BURNS, Stephanie A., PhD; American business executive; *Chairman, President and CEO, Dow Corning Corporation;* ed Iowa State Univ.; postdoctoral research in organic chemistry, Université Montpellier, Sciences et Techniques du Languedoc, France; joined Dow Corning Corpn 1983, Researcher 1983–87, Product Devt Man. for Electronics Industry 1987–94, Dir of Women's Health 1994–97, Science and Tech. Dir for Europe, Brussels, Belgium 1997–99, Industry Dir for Life Sciences in Europe 1999, European Electronics Industry Dir 1999–2000, Exec. Vice-Pres. 2000–03, apptd mem. Bd Dirs 2000, Pres. and COO 2003–04, Pres. and CEO 2004–06, Chair., Pres. and CEO 2006–; mem. Bd of Dirs GlaxoSmithKline plc, Manpower Inc., Michigan Molecular Inst., Chemical Bank Midland Area, American Chem. Council, Dow Corning/Genencor Int. Partnership, The Conference Board; mem. Advisory Bd Chemical and Engineering News; mem. Exec. Cttee Soc. of Chemical Industry; mem. ACS; Trustee Midland Community Center; Michigan Woman Exec. of the Year 2003, ranked by Forbes magazine amongst 100 Most Powerful Women (81st) 2004, (82nd) 2005, (84th) 2006, (86th) 2007, Vanguard Award, Chemical Educ. Foundation 2006. *Address:* Dow Corning Corporation, 2200 West Salzburg Road, Midland, MI 48686, USA (office). *Telephone:* (989) 496-4000 (office). *Fax:* (989) 496-4393 (office). *Website:* www.dowcorning.com (office).

BURNS, Baron (Life Peer), cr. 1998, of Pitshanger in the London Borough of Ealing; **Terence Burns,** GCB, BAEcon; British economist and business executive; *Chairman, Abbey National plc;* b. 13 March 1944, Durham; s. of the late Patrick Owen Burns and of Doris Burns; m. Anne Elizabeth Powell 1969; one s. two d.; ed Houghton-le-Spring Grammar School and Victoria Univ. of Manchester; held various research positions at London Business School 1965–70, Lecturer in Econs 1970–74, Sr Lecturer in Econs 1974–79, Dir Centre for Econ. Forecasting 1976–79, Prof. of Econs 1979; Chief Econ. Adviser to HM Treasury and Head, Govt Econ. Service 1980–91; Perm. Sec. to Treasury 1991–98; Chair. Inquiry into Hunting 1999; Chair. Financial Services and Markets Jt Cttee 1999–, Nat. Lottery Comm. 2000–01, Abbey Nat. plc 2002–; Deputy Chair. Marks & Spencer Group 2005–06, Chair. 2006–08; Dir (non-exec.) Legal and General Group PLC 1999–2001, Pearson 1999–, British Land 2001–05, Banco Santander 2004–; Vice-Pres. Soc. of Business Economists 1985–99, Pres. 1999–; Fellow, London Business School 1989–; mem. Council Royal Econ. Soc. 1986–91, Vice-Pres. 1992–; Visiting Prof., Durham Univ. 1995–; Gov. RAM 1998–; Hon. DScS (Manchester) 1992. *Leisure interests:* Dir Queen's Park Rangers Football team 1996–2001, music and golf. *Address:* Abbey plc, Grupo Santander, The Causeway, Worthing, West Sussex, BN99 6DA (office); House of Lords, London, SW1A 0PW, England (office). *E-mail:* burnst@parliament.uk (office). *Website:* www.abbey.com (office).

BURNS, Ursula M., MSc (MechEng); American business executive; *President, Xerox Corporation;* b. 20 Sept. 1958, New York; m. Lloyd Bean; two c.; ed Brooklyn Polytechnic Inst. of New York and Columbia Univ., New York; mechanical eng summer intern, Xerox Corpn in 1980, Exec. Asst to Chair. and CEO 1991–92, held several positions in eng, including product devt and planning, led several business teams, including office colour and fax business, office network copying business and departmental business unit 1992–2000, Sr Vice-Pres. Corp. Strategic Services 2000–01, Pres. Document Systems and Solutions Group 2001–02, Sr Vice-Pres. and Pres. Business Group Operations 2002–07, mem. Bd Dirs and Pres. Xerox Corpn 2007–; mem. Bd Dirs American Express Corpn, Boston Scientific Corpn, FIRST (For Inspiration and Recognition of Science and Tech.), Nat. Asscn of Manufacturers, PQ Corpn, Univ. of Rochester, The Rochester Business Alliance, CASA – The Nat. Center on Addiction and Substance Abuse at Columbia Univ.; ranked 28th by Fortune magazine amongst Most Powerful Black Executives 2002, ranked by Fortune magazine amongst 50 Most Powerful Women in Business in the US (44th) 2003, (44th) 2004, (48th) 2005, (27th) 2006, (11th) 2007, named by Time/CNN Annual on List of Global Business Influentials 2003, named by U.S. Black Engineering & Information Technology magazine one of 50 Most Important

African-Americans in Tech. 2003, 2004, ranked by Forbes magazine amongst 100 Most Powerful Women (55th) 2008. *Address:* Xerox Corporation, 800 Long Ridge Road, Stamford, CT 06904, USA (office). *Telephone:* (203) 968-3000 (office). *Fax:* 203-968-3218 (office). *Website:* www.xerox.com (office).

BURNS, William Joseph, DPhil; American diplomatist; *Ambassador to Russia;* b. 11 April 1956; m. Lisa Carty; two d.; ed LaSalle Univ., Univ. of Oxford, UK; entered Foreign Service 1982; Political Officer, US Embassy, Amman; mem. staff Bureau of Near East Affairs, Office of Deputy Sec. of State; Special Asst to the Pres., Sr Dir for Near East and S Asian Affairs, Nat. Security Council; Acting Dir and Prin. Deputy Dir State Dept's Policy Planning; Minister-Counsellor for Political Affairs, Moscow; Exec. Sec., State Dept and Special Asst to Sec. of State; Amb. to Jordan 1998–2001; Asst Sec. of State for Near Eastern Affairs 2001–05; Amb. to Russia 2005–; Marshall Scholarship, two Distinguished Honor Awards, James Clement Dunn Award, five Superior Honor Awards, two Presidential Distinguished Service Awards, Robert C. Frasure Memorial Award. *Publication:* Economic Aid and American Policy Toward Egypt, 1955–1981. *Address:* Embassy of the United States, Bolshoy Devyatinskii per. 8, 121099 Moscow, Russia (office). *Telephone:* (495) 728-50-00 (office). *Fax:* (495) 728-50-90 (office). *E-mail:* pamoscow@pd.state .gov (office). *Website:* moscow.usembassy.gov (office).

BURNSTOCK, Geoffrey, PhD, DSc, FRS, FAA, FMedSci; Australian/British scientist and academic; *President, Autonomic Neuroscience Centre, University College London;* b. 10 May 1929, London; s. of James Burnstock and Nancy Green; m. Nomi Hirschfeld 1957; three d.; ed London and Melbourne Univs; Nat. Inst. for Medical Research, London 1956–57; Post-Doctoral Fellow, King's Coll., London 1957; Dept of Pharmacology, Oxford Univ. 1957–59; Dept of Physiology, Illinois Univ. 1959; Sr Lecturer, Dept of Zoology, Melbourne Univ. 1959–62, Reader 1962–64, Prof. and Chair. 1964–75, Assoc. Dean (Biological Sciences) 1969–72, Prof. Emer. 1993–; Visiting Prof., Dept of Pharmacology, Univ. of Calif. 1970; Vice-Dean, Faculty of Medical Sciences, Univ. Coll., London 1980–83, Prof. of Anatomy 1975–, Head of Dept of Anatomy and Developmental Biology 1975–97, Convenor, Centre for Neuroscience 1979–, Fellow 1996, Dir Autonomic Neuroscience Inst., Royal Free and Univ. Coll. Medical School, UCL 1997–, now Pres. Autonomic Neuroscience Centre; Contract Prof., Univ. of Siena 1985–87, Univ. of Milan 1993–94; Visiting Prof., Royal Soc. of Medicine Foundation, New York 1988; Chair. Scientific Advisory Bd, Eisai London Ltd 1990–96; Chair. Bd of Clinical Studies, Royal Nat. Orthopaedic Hosp. Trust 1996; Pres. Int. Soc. for Autonomic Neuroscience 1995–2000, Int. Neurovegetative Soc. 1995–, British Assen (Medical); Founder FMedSci 1998; mem. Academia Europaea 1992; mem. Russian Soc. of Neuropathology 1993; Ed.-in-Chief, Journal of the Autonomic Nervous System 1992–97; mem. Bd of over 30 journals; Fellow, Real Academia Nacional de Farmacia, Spain 2003–; Hon. FRCS; Hon. FRCP; Hon. MRCP 1987; Dr hc (Antwerp) 2002; Royal Soc. of Vic. Silver Medal 1970, Special Award, NIH Conf., Bethesda 1989, Royal Medal, Royal Soc. 2000, Janssen Award for Lifetime Achievement 2000. *Publications:* books: Adrenergic Neurons: Their Organisation, Function and Development in the Peripheral Nervous System 1975, An Atlas of the Fine Structure of Muscle and its Innervation 1976; Ed. Purinergic Receptors 1981, Somatic and Autonomic Nerve-Muscle Interactions 1983, Nonadrenergic Innervation of Blood Vessels 1988, Peptides: A Target for New Drug Development 1991, Nitric Oxide in Health and Disease 1997, Cardiovascular Biology of Purines 1998; series Ed. The Autonomic Nervous System (Vols 1–14) 1992–97, Neural-Endothelial Interactions in the Control of Local Vascular Tone 1993, Nitric Oxide in Health and Disease 1997, Cardiovascular Biology of Purines 1998; also author of over 1,800 publs in scientific and medical journals and books. *Leisure interests:* wood sculpture, tennis. *Address:* Autonomic Neuroscience Centre, Royal Free and University College Medical School, Rowland Hill Street, London, NW3 2PF, England (office). *Telephone:* (20) 7830-2948 (office). *Fax:* (20) 7830-2949 (office). *E-mail:* g.burnstock@ucl.ac.uk (office). *Website:* www.ucl.ac.uk/ani (office).

BURNYEAT, Myles Fredric, CBE, FBA, BA; British academic; *Emeritus Fellow, All Souls College, University of Oxford;* b. 1 Jan. 1939; s. of Peter James Anthony Burnyeat and Cynthia Cherry Warburg; m. 1st Jane Elizabeth Buckley 1971 (divorced 1982); one s. one d.; m. 2nd Ruth Sophia Padel 1984 (divorced 2000); one d.; m. 3rd Heda Segvic 2002 (died 2003); ed Bryanston School and King's Coll., Cambridge; Russian Interpreter, Civil Service 1959; Asst Lecturer in Philosophy, Univ. Coll., London 1964, Lecturer 1965; Lecturer in Classics, Univ. of Cambridge 1978, Lecturer in Philosophy, Robinson Coll. 1978, Fellow 1978–96, Hon. Fellow 2006–; Laurence Prof. of Ancient Philosophy, Cambridge 1984–96, Sr Research Fellow in Philosophy, All Souls Coll., Oxford 1996–06, Emer. Fellow 2006–; Foreign Hon. mem. American Acad. of Arts and Sciences 1992–. *Publications:* Philosophy As It Is (co-ed.) 1979, Doubt and Dogmatism (co-ed.) 1980, Science and Speculation (co-ed.) 1982, The Sceptical Tradition (ed.) 1983, The Theaetetus of Plato 1990, The Original Sceptics (co-ed.) 1997, A Map of Metaphysics Zeta 2001, Aristotle's Divine Intellect 2008. *Leisure interest:* travel. *Address:* Robinson College, Grange Road, Cambridge, CB3 9AN, England (office).

BURR, Richard; American politician; *Senator from North Carolina;* m.; two s.; ed R. J. Reynolds High School, Wake Forest Univ.; various positions with Carswell Distributing 1977–94; elected to US Congress from N Carolina 1994–2005, wrote Food and Drug Admin Modernization Act ("Burr Bill") 1997, Vice-Chair. House Energy and Commerce Cttee 2001, mem. House Select Cttee on Intelligence and Task Force on Terrorism 2001; Senator from N Carolina 2005–; Co-Chair. Partnership for a Drug Free N Carolina; mem. Bd Brenner Children's Hosp., Idealliance. *Address:* 217 Russell Senate Office Building, Washington, DC 20510, USA (office). *Telephone:* (202) 224-3154 (office). *Fax:* (202) 228-2981 (office). *Website:* burr.senate.gov (office).

BURRELL, Leroy; American fmr professional athlete; b. 21 Feb. 1967, Lansdowne, Philadelphia; m. Michelle Finn (fmr Olympic sprinter); two s.; ed Pen Wood High School, Lansdowne and Univ. of Houston, TX; fmr sprinter and long jumper; set world record, 100m in 9.90 seconds at US Championships, New York June 1991; set another world record 100m of 9.85 seconds July 1994; Olympic gold medal 4×100m relay, Barcelona 1992; Head Track and Field Coach, Univ. of Houston 1998–. *Address:* c/o USA Track and Field Press Information Department, 1 RCA Dome, Suite 140, Indianapolis, IN 46225, USA.

BURRINGTON, Ernest; British newspaper executive; b. 13 Dec. 1926; s. of the late Harold Burrington and of Laura Burrington; m. Nancy Crossley 1950; one s. one d.; reporter, Oldham Chronicle 1941–44, reporter and sub-ed. 1947–49; mil. service 1945–47; sub-ed. Bristol Evening World 1950; sub-ed. Daily Herald, Manchester 1950, night ed. 1955, London night 1957; night ed. IPC Sun 1964, Asst ed. 1965; Asst ed. and night News Int. Sun 1969; deputy night ed. Daily Mirror 1970; Deputy Ed. Sunday People 1971, Assoc. Ed. 1972; Ed. The People 1985–88, 1989–90; Dir Mirror Group Newspapers 1985–92, Deputy Chair. and Asst Publr 1988–91, Man. Dir 1989–91, Chair. 1991–92; Chair. Syndication Int. 1989–92; Deputy Chair. Mirror Publishing Co. 1989–91; Dir Mirror Group Magazine and Newsday Ltd 1989–92, Legionstyle Ltd 1991–92, Mirror Colour Print Ltd 1991–92; Dir (non-exec.) Sunday Correspondent 1990, The European 1990–91, IQ Newsgraphics 1990–92, Sygma Picture Agency, Paris 1990–91; Deputy Publr Globe Communications, Montreal, Canada 1993–95, Exec. Vice-Pres. and Assoc. Publr 1995–96; Pres. Atlantic Media 1996–98; Consultant Head of Marketing Harveys PLC, UK 1998–2000; mem. Council Nat. Press Asscn 1988–92, Int. Press Inst. British Exec. 1988–92; Trustee Int. Centre for Child Studies 1986–90; Life mem. NUJ 1960–; Hon. Life mem. NUJ 1996; Hon. Red Devil (Manchester United Football Club) 1985. *Leisure interests:* travel, bridge, Manchester United FC. *Address:* 17499 Tiffany Trace Drive, Boca Raton, FL 33487, USA; South Hall, Dene Park, Shipbourne Road, Tonbridge, TN11 9NS, England. *Telephone:* (561) 995-9897 (USA); (1732) 368517 (England). *Fax:* (561) 995-9897 (USA); (1732) 368517 (England). *E-mail:* burringtone@aol.com (home).

BURRIS, Robert Harza, PhD, DSc; American biochemist and academic; *W. H. Peterson Professor Emeritus of Biochemistry, University of Wisconsin;* b. 13 April 1914, Brookings, SDak; s. of Edward Thomas Burris and Mable Harza Burris; m. Katherine Irene Brusse 1945; one s. two d.; ed S Dakota State Coll. and Univ. of Wis.; Research Asst, Univ. of Wis. 1936–40; Nat. Research Council Postdoctoral Fellow, Columbia Univ. 1940–41; Instructor in Bacteriology, Univ. of Wis. 1941–44, Asst Prof. of Biochemistry 1944–46, Assoc. Prof. 1946–51, W. H. Peterson Prof. of Biochemistry 1951–94, W. H. Peterson Prof. Emer. of Biochemistry 1994–, Chair. Dept of Biochemistry 1958–70; Pres. American Soc. of Plant Physiologists 1960; mem. NAS, American Acad. of Arts and Sciences, American Philosophical Soc.; Foreign Fellow, Indian Nat. Science Acad. 1985; Hon. DSc (S Dakota State Univ.) 1966; Guggenheim Fellow 1954, Merit Award of Botanical Soc. of America 1966, American Soc. of Plant Physiologists Stephen Hales Award 1968, Charles Reid Barnes Award 1977, Soc. for Industrial Microbiology Charles Thom Award 1977, American Soc. of Agronomy Edward W. Browning Award 1978, Nat. Medal of Science 1980, NAS Carty Award 1984, Wolf Award 1985, ACS Spencer Award 1990. *Publications:* Manometric Techniques 1945, Biological Nitrogen Fixation 1992; 350 scientific papers 1936–2001. *Leisure interests:* photography, lapidary, vitreous enamelling. *Address:* Room 237E, Department of Biochemistry, University of Wisconsin, 433 Babcock Drive, Madison, WI 53706 (office); 6225 Mineral Point Road, Apt 96, Madison, WI 53705, USA (home). *Telephone:* (608) 262-3042 (office). *Fax:* (608) 262-3453 (office). *E-mail:* burris@biochem .wisc.edu (office). *Website:* www.biochem.wisc.edu/burris/index.html (office).

BURRIS, Roland Wallace, BA, JD; American attorney, politician and fmr banker; *Senator from Illinois;* b. 3 Aug. 1937, Centralia, Ill.; m. Berlean M. Burris; one s. one d.; ed Centralia High School, Southern Illinois Univ., Carbondale, Univ. of Hamburg, Germany, Howard Univ.; Nat. Bank Examiner, Office of Comptroller, Currency for US Treasury Dept, Washington, DC 1963–64; called to Ill. Bar 1964; worked at Continental Illinois National Bank and Trust Company 1964–73, positions included tax accountant, tax consultant, commercial banking officer, Vice-Pres.; Dir Dept of Central Management Services, State of Ill. 1973–77, Comptroller 1979–91, Attorney-Gen. 1995–98; Nat. Exec. Dir and COO Operation Push Jan.–Oct. 1977; Man. Pnr, Jones Ware & Grenard 1995–98; Of counsel, Buford & Peters LLC (law firm) 1999–2002, Burris, Wright, Slaughter & Tom LLC 2002–07; Sr Counsel, Gonzalez Saggio & Harlan LLP 2007–09; Man. and CEO Burris & Lebed Consulting LLC 2002–09; Senator from Illinois 2009–; fmr Adjunct Prof., MPA Program, Southern Illinois Univ. 1995–98; Chair. Ill. Comm. of African-American Males 1992–94; Chair. Nat. Asscn of Attorneys Gen. Civil Rights Comm. 1993–95; Chair. Ill. State Justice Comm. 1994–96; Pres., Nat. Asscn of State Auditors, Comptrollers and Treasurers 1981–82; Founder and Pres. Nat. Forum on State Leaders 1982–; Trustee, Govt Finance Officers Asscn of US and Canada 1987–91; Trustee, Financial Accounting Foundation Bd 1991–94; served three years on Exec. Bd as Trustee, Govt Finance Office of US and Canada; fmr Vice-Chair. Cttee on Illinois Govt; fmr mem. of Bd Ill. Criminal Justice Authority, Law Enforcement Foundation of Ill., Ill. Supreme Court Cttee for Civil Jury Instructions, mem. Nat. Center for Responsible Gaming 1996–2005, Auditorium Theater of Chicago 2001–06, Better Business Bureau 2008; mem. ABA, Ill. Bar Asscn, Cook Co. Bar Asscn, Chicago Bar Asscn, Nat. Asscn for Advancement of Colored People, Howard Univ. Law School Alumni Asscn, Southern Illinois Univ. Alumni Asscn, Southern Illinois Univ. Foundation, Mental Health Asscn of Greater Chicago, US Jaycees, Chicago Area Council of Boy Scouts of America; Hon. LLD Nat. Louis Univ., Evanston, Ill., Tougaloo Coll., Miss. *Address:* 523 Dirksen Senate Office

Building, Washington, DC 20510, USA (office). *Telephone:* (202) 224-2854 (office). *Website:* burris.senate.gov (office).

BURROW, John Wyon, MA, PhD, FBA, FRHistS; British historian and academic; *Emeritus Fellow, Balliol College, University of Oxford;* b. 4 June 1935, Southsea; s. of Charles Burrow and Alice Burrow (née Vosper); m. Diane Dunnington 1958; one s. one d.; ed Exeter School and Christ's Coll., Cambridge; Research Fellow, Christ's Coll. Cambridge 1959–62; Fellow and Dir of Studies in History, Downing Coll. Cambridge 1962–65; Reader, School of European Studies, Univ. of E Anglia 1965–69; Reader in History, Univ. of Sussex 1969–82, Prof. of Intellectual History 1982–95; Visiting Fellow All Souls Coll. Oxford Univ. 1994–95, Prof. of European Thought and Fellow of Balliol Coll. 1995–2000, Emer. Fellow 2001–; Research Prof. of History, Univ. of Sussex 2000–; Visiting Prof. Univ. of Calif. Berkeley 1981; Visiting Fellow, History of Ideas Unit, ANU 1983; Carlyle Lecturer, Univ. of Oxford 1985; Ed. History of European Ideas 1996–2006; Distinguished Visiting Prof., Ben Gurion Univ. of the Negev 1998; delivered Gauss Seminars, Princeton Univ. 1988; Hon. Dr Political Sciences (Bologna) 1988; Wolfson Prize for History 1981. *Publications:* Evolution and Society 1966, A Liberal Descent 1981, That Noble Science of Politics (with S. Collini and D. Winch) 1983, Gibbon 1985, Whigs and Liberals 1988, The Crisis of Reason 2000, A History of Histories 2007. *Leisure interest:* cooking. *Address:* Balliol College, Oxford, OX1 3BJ; 22 Bridge Street, Witney, Oxon. OX18 2HY, England (home). *Telephone:* (1993) 201396.

BURROW, Sharan Leslie; Australian trade union official; *President, Australian Council of Trade Unions;* b. 1954, Warren, NSW; ed Univ. of New South Wales; fmr Pres. Bathurst TLC; fmr Sr Vice-Pres. NSW Teachers' Fed.; fmr mem. Bd Curriculum Corpn; Vice-Pres. Educ. Int. 1995; Pres. Australian Educ. Union 1993–2000; Pres. Australian Council of Trade Unions (ACTU) 2000–; Pres. (first woman) Int. Confederation of Free Trade Unions (now Int. Trade Union Confederation) 2004–. *Address:* Australian Council of Trade Unions (ACTU), 365 Queen Street, Melbourne, Vic. 3000, Australia (office). *Telephone:* (3) 9664-7333 (office). *Fax:* (3) 9600-0859 (office). *E-mail:* sburrow@actu.asn.au (office). *Website:* www.actu.asn.au (office); www.ituc-csi .org.

BURROWS, Richard; Irish business executive and banker; *Governor, Bank of Ireland;* b. 16 Jan. 1946; m.; four c.; began career as chartered accountant; joined Irish Distillers 1971, Man. Dir Old Bushmills Distillery 1972–76, Gen. Man. Irish Distillers 1976–78, CEO 1978–91, Chair. and CEO Irish Distillers (acquired by Pernod Ricard SA 1988) 1978–2000, Dir-Gen. Pernod Ricard SA 2000, Co-CEO 2000–05, mem. Bd of Dirs 2004–; apptd to Court of Bank of Ireland 2000, Deputy Gov. 2002–05, Sr Ind. Dir 2003–, Gov. 2005–; fmr Pres. Irish Business and Employers Confed.; Dir Cityjet Ltd 2007–; Royal Dublin Soc. Gold Medal Award for Excellence in Industry 2005. *Address:* Bank of Ireland, Lower Baggot Street, Dublin 2, Ireland (office). *Telephone:* (1) 604-3834 (office). *Fax:* (1) 676-7850 (office). *E-mail:* info@bankofireland.com (office). *Website:* www.bankofireland.com (office); www.bankofireland.ie (office).

BURROWS, (James) Stuart, OBE; British singer; b. 7 Feb. 1933, Cilfynydd, S Wales; s. of Albert Burrows and Irene Burrows (née Powell); m. Enid Lewis 1957; one s. one d.; ed Trinity Coll., Carmarthen; school teacher until debut Royal Opera House, Covent Garden 1967; a leading lyric tenor and has sung in world's major opera houses including San Francisco, Vienna, Paris, Buenos Aires (Théâtre Cologne) and Brussels (Théâtre de la Monnaie) as well as Covent Garden and Metropolitan Opera, New York; toured Far East with Royal Opera 1979 and sang with co. at Olympic Festival, Los Angeles 1984; four US tours with Metropolitan Opera; concert appearances throughout Europe and N America, under Solti, Barenboim, Mehta, Ozawa, Bernstein and Ormandy, including two recitals in Brahmssaal, Vienna; BBC TV series Stuart Burrows Sings 1978–85 also radio broadcasts; many recordings, including Die Zauberflöte, Don Giovanni, Die Entführung aus dem Serail, La Clemenza di Tito, La Damnation de Faust, Les Contes d'Hoffmann, Maria Stuarda, Anna Bolena, Eugene Onegin, The Midsummer Marriage, Messiah, Grande Messe des Morts (Berlioz), Les Nuits d'Eté, Das Klagende Lied, Beethoven's 9th (Choral) Symphony and single discs of Mozart arias, Operetta Favourites, German and French songs, popular ballads and Welsh songs; The Stuart Burrows Int. Voice Competition set up in his honour 2006; Pres. Save the Children, Cancer Research; Hon. Freedom of the Borough, Rhondda Cynon Taff, South Wales 2008; Hon. DMus (Wales) 1981, Dr hc (Univ. Coll. of Wales, Aberystwyth). *Leisure interests:* breeding koi carp, gardening, snooker, listening to music. *Address:* 29 Blackwater Grove, Alderholt, Dorset, SP6 3AD, England (office). *E-mail:* stuartburrows@nicholls.f9.co.uk (office). *Website:* www.stuartburrows.f9.co.uk (office).

BURSÍK, Martin, RNDr; Czech politician; *Deputy Prime Minister and Minister for the Environment;* b. 12 Aug. 1959, Prague; ed Faculty of Natural Sciences, Charles Univ., Prague; signatory of civic initiative 'Civil Liberty Movement' 1989; involved in Civic Forum from outset, mem. and subsequently Deputy Chair. following split in party; switched to Free Democrats (Svobodní Demokraté) –2003; Chair. Environmental Protection Cttee, Prague City Ass. 1994–98, specialized in waste man. and transport, mem. Environment Protection Cttee 1998–2002; unsuccessful cand. for Mayor of Prague; later joined Christian and Democratic Union – Czechoslovak People's Party (KDU-ČSL); Minister for the Environment 1998; consultant in field of energy and environmental protection 1998–2005; external energy and environment adviser to Minister for the Environment 2002–05; mem. Strana zelených (Czech Green Party) 2004–, Chair. 2005–; mem. Parl. (Green Party) 2006–; Deputy Prime Minister and Minister for the Environment 2007–; Dir Ecoconsulting s.r.o. *Address:* Ministry of the Environment, Vršovická 65, 100 10 Prague 10, USA (office). *Telephone:* (267) 121111 (office). *Fax:* (267) 310308 (office). *E-mail:* posta@mzp.cz (office). *Website:* www.env.cz (office).

BURSON, Harold, BA; American public relations executive and consultant; *Chairman, Burson-Marsteller;* b. 15 Feb. 1921, Memphis; s. of Maurice Burson and Esther Burson; m. Bette Foster 1947; two s.; ed Univ. of Miss.; Acting Dir Ole Miss News Bureau 1938–40; reporter Memphis Commercial Appeal 1940; Asst to Pres. and Public Relations Dir, H. K. Ferguson Co. 1941–43; operated own public relations firm for six years; Chair. Burson-Marsteller 1953–, CEO 1953–88; Public Relations Adviser to Pres. Reagan 1989–94; Dir World Environmental Center 1998–; Exec. Vice-Pres. Young and Rubicam Inc., mem. Exec. Cttee 1979–85; Garrett Lecturer on Social Responsibility, Columbia Univ., Grad. School of Business 1973; Exec.-in-Residence, Univ. of Ky Coll. Comm. 2000; Visiting Prof., Leeds Univ. 2001; Vice-Pres. and mem. Exec. Cttee, Nat. Safety Council 1964–77; Int. Trustee World Wildlife Fund 1977–81; Trustee and mem. Exec. Cttee Foundation for Public Relations Research and Educ. 1978–84; Founder and Sec. Corporate Fund, John F. Kennedy Centre for the Performing Arts 1977; Dir Kennedy Cen. Productions Inc. 1974–89; presidential appointee to Fine Arts Comm. 1981–85, to Exec. Cttee Young Astronauts Co. 1984–88; mem. Advisory Cttee, Medill School of Journalism, Northwestern Univ. 1985, Grad. School of Business, Emory Univ. 1986; mem. Public Relations Soc. of America, Int. Public Relations Asscn of Business Communicators, Overseas Press Club, NY Soc. of Security Analysts, Exec. Cttee, Catalyst Inc. 1977–88, Public Relations Advisory Cttee, US Information Agency 1981; assoc. mem. NY Acad. of Medicine; Counsellor, Nat. Press Foundation; Trustee The Economic Club of NY, Ray Simon Inst. of Public Relations, Syracuse Univ. 1985; Chair. Jt Council on Econ. Educ., Public Relations Seminar 1983; Hon. Prof. Fudan Univ., Shanghai 1999; Hon. DHumLitt (Boston Univ.) 1988; Public Relations Professional of the Year Award (Public Relations News) 1977, Gold Anvil Award (Public Relations Soc. of America) 1980, Univ. of Miss. Alumni Hall of Fame 1980, Silver Em Award (Miss. Press Asscn) 1982, Arthur Page Award, Univ. of Tex. 1986, Horatio Alger Award 1986, Nat. Public Relations Achievement Award, (Ball State Univ.), Inside PR Life Achievement Award 1993. *Publications include:* The Making of Burson-Marsteller 2004. *Leisure interests:* stamp collection, West Highland White terriers. *Address:* Burson-Marsteller, 230 Park Avenue South, New York, NY 10003-1513, USA. *Telephone:* (212) 614-4444 (office). *Fax:* (212) 598-5679 (office). *E-mail:* harold_burson@nyc.bm.com (office). *Website:* www.bm.com.

BURSTYN, Ellen; American actress; b. 7 Dec. 1932, Detroit, Mich.; d. of John Austin and Coriene Marie (née Hamel) Gillooly; m. 1st William C. Alexander; m. 2nd Paul Roberts; m. 3rd Neil Burstyn; one s.; ed Cass Tech. High School, Detroit, Mich.; Co-Artistic Dir The Actor's Studio, New York 1982–88; Pres. Actors' Equity Asscn 1982–88; Dir Judgement (off Broadway) 1981, Into Thin Air 1985; Best Supporting Actress, The Last Picture Show (New York Film Critics' Award, Nat. Soc. of Film Critics' Award); Best Actress, Alice Doesn't Live Here Anymore (Acad. Award, British Acad. Award); Best Actress, Same Time Next Year (Tony Award, Drama Desk Award, Outer Critics' Circle Award). *Stage Productions include:* Fair Game 1957, Same Time Next Year 1975, 84 Charing Cross Road, Shirley Valentine 1989–90. *Films include:* Goodbye Charlie 1964, For Those Who Think Young 1965, Tropic of Cancer 1969, Alex in Wonderland 1970, The Last Picture Show 1971, The King of Marvin Gardens 1972, Thursday's Game (TV), 1973, The Exorcist 1973, Harry and Tonto 1974, Alice Doesn't Live Here Anymore 1975, Providence 1976, Dream of Passion 1978, Same Time Next Year 1978, Resurrection, Silence of the North 1980, Alamo Bay 1985, Twice in a Lifetime 1985, Hannah's War 1987, When You Remember Me (TV Film), The Colour of Evening 1990, Dying Young 1990, The Cemetery Club 1993, When a Man Loves A Woman 1994, Roommates 1994, How to Make an American Quilt 1995, The Babysitters Club 1995, Deceiver 1997, You Can Thank Me Later 1998, Playing By Heart 1998, Walking Across Egypt 1999, Requiem for a Dream 1999, The Yards 1999, Divine Secrets of the Ya-Ya Sisterhood 2002, Cross the Line 2005, The Wicker Man 2006, The Fountain 2006, 30 Days 2006, Charlotte's Web 2006, W. 2008. *Television films:* Into Thin Air 1985, Getting Out 1994, The Matchmaker 1996, A Will of Their Own 1998, Deceiver 1998, Night Ride Home 1999, Mermaid 2000, Dodson's Journey 2001, Within These Walls 2001, Brush with Fate 2003, The Five People You Meet in Heaven 2004. *Address:* c/o CAA, 9830 Wilshire Blvd, Beverly Hills, CA 90212, USA.

BURT, Sir Peter Alexander, Kt, MA, MBA, FCIBS, FIB (Scot.); British business executive; *Chairman, Gleacher Shacklock LLP;* b. 6 March 1944; s. of Robert W. Burt and May H. Rodger; m. Alison Mackintosh Turner 1971; three s.; ed Merchiston Castle School, Edin., Univs of St Andrews and Pennsylvania; joined Hewlett Packard, Calif. 1968–70; worked for CSL, Edin. 1970–74, then Edward Bates & Sons Ltd 1974; moved to Bank of Scotland 1975, Int. Div. 1975–88 (Head 1985), Asst Gen. Man. 1979–84, Divisional Gen. Man. 1984–85, Jt Gen. Man. 1985–88, Treas. and Chief Gen. Man. 1988–96, mem. Bd of Dirs 1995–03, Chief Exec. 1996–2001, Gov. 2001–03; Exec. Deputy Chair. HBOS (formed after merger of Halifax PLC with Bank of Scotland) 2001–03; non-exec. Chair. ITV PLC (formed by merger of Carlton Communications and Granada) 2004–07; Dir Shell Transport and Trading 2002–, Templeton Emerging Markets Investment Trust plc 2004–; currently Chair. Gleacher Shacklock LLP (investment bank); mem. High Constables and Guard of Honour Holyrood House, Edin. *Leisure interests:* golf, skiing, gardening, reading. *Address:* Auldhame House, Auldhame, North Berwick, EH39 5PW, England (home). *Telephone:* (1620) 893375 (home). *Fax:* (1620) 893375 (home). *Website:* www.gleachershacklock.com.

BURT, Robert Amsterdam, MA, JD; American lawyer and academic; *Alexander M. Bickel Professor of Law, Yale University;* b. 3 Feb. 1939, Philadelphia, Pa; s. of Samuel Mathew Burt and Esther Amsterdam Burt; m.

Linda Gordon Rose 1964; two d.; ed Princeton, Oxford and Yale Univs; Law Clerk, US Court of Appeals, Dist of Columbia Circuit 1964–65; Asst Gen. Counsel, Exec. Office of the Pres. of USA 1965–66; Legis. Asst, US Senate 1966–68; Assoc. Prof. of Law, Chicago Univ. 1968–70; Assoc. Prof. of Law, Univ. of Michigan 1970–72, Prof. of Law 1972–73, Prof. of Law and Prof. of Law in Psychiatry 1973–76; Prof. of Law, Yale Univ. 1976–, Southmayd Prof. of Law 1982–93, Alexander M. Bickel Prof. 1993–; Special Master US Dist Court, Conn. 1987–92; Rockefeller Fellowship in Humanities 1976; mem. Bd of Dirs, Benhaven School for Autistic Persons 1977–, Chair. 1983–96, Mental Health Law Project 1985–, Chair. 1990–2000; Dir Yale Hillel Foundation 1996–; mem. Inst. of Medicine and NAS 1976, Advisory Bd Open Soc. Inst. Project on Death in America 1993–2004; John Simon Guggenheim Fellowship 1997. *Publications:* Taking Care of Strangers: The Rule of Law in Doctor-Patient Relations 1979, Two Jewish Justices: Outcasts in the Promised Land 1987, The Constitution in Conflict 1992, Death is That Man Taking Names 2002. *Leisure interests:* cello, swimming, bicycling. *Address:* Yale Law School, PO Box 208215, 127 Wall Street, New Haven, CT 06520 (office); 66 Dogwood Circle, Woodbridge, CT 06525, USA (home). *Telephone:* (203) 432-4960 (office); (203) 393-3881 (home). *Fax:* (203) 432-4982 (office); (203) 393-1292 (home). *E-mail:* robert.burt@yale.edu (office). *Website:* www.law.yale.edu (office).

BURTON, Ian, (Burtoni), MA, PhD, FRSC; Canadian/British environmental scientist, geographer, scholar and consultant; *Scientist Emeritus, Meteorological Service of Canada;* b. 24 June 1935, Derby, England; s. of Frank Burton and Elsie Victoria Barnes; m. 1st Lydia Demodoff 1962 (divorced 1977); one s. one d.; m. 2nd Anne V. T. Whyte 1977 (divorced 1995); one s. two d.; m. 3rd Elizabeth May; one d.; ed Derby School, Univ. of Birmingham, Univ. of Chicago and Oberlin Coll., Ohio; Lecturer, Indiana Univ. 1960–61, Queen's Univ., Kingston, Ont. 1961; Consultant, Ford Foundation, India 1964–66; Prof., Univ. of Toronto 1968–90, Adjunct Prof. 1990–, Dir Inst. for Environmental Studies 1979–84, now Prof. Emer.; Prof. of Environmental Science, Univ. of East Anglia, UK 1972–73; Sr Adviser, Int. Devt Research Centre, Ottawa 1972–75; Sr Connaught Fellow, École des Hautes Études en Sciences Sociales, Paris 1984–86; Dir Int. Fed. of Insts for Advanced Study 1986–92; Dir Environmental Adaptation Research, Atmospheric Environmental Service, Meteorological Service of Canada 1990–96, Scientist Emer. 1996–; mem. Bd of Dirs Foundation for Int. Training 1994–; mem. Ind. World Comm. on the Oceans 1995–98; mem. Int. Soc. of Biometeorology, Vice-Pres. 1996–2002, Pres. 2002–05; numerous cttee and consultant assignments with UNESCO, WHO, UNEP, Rockefeller Foundation, UNDP, World Bank Global Environment Facility, World Resources Inst., Intergovernmental Panel on Climate Change, European Comm., Ford Foundation, projects in Sudan and Nigeria etc.; mem. Jury, St Francis Environment Prize; Fellow, World Acad. of Art and Sciences; Order of Zvonkova (USSR) 1968. *Publications:* co-author: The Human Ecology of Coastal Flood Hazard in Megalopolis 1968, The Hazardousness of a Place: A Regional Ecology of Damaging Events 1971, The Environment as Hazard 1978; co-ed.: Readings in Resource Management and Conservation 1986, Environmental Risk Assessment 1980, Living with Risk 1982, Geography, Resources and Environment 1986, Climate Change and Adaptation 2007. *Leisure interests:* swimming, hiking, cricket. *Address:* Meteorological Service of Canada, 4905 Dufferin Street, Downsview, ON M3H 5T4 (office); 26 St Anne's Road, Toronto, ON M6J 2C1, Canada (home). *Telephone:* (416) 739-4314 (office); (416) 538-2034 (home). *Fax:* (416) 739-4297 (office). *E-mail:* ian.burton@ec.gc.ca (office); Ianburtonian@aol.com (home). *Website:* www.msc-smc.ec.gc.ca (office).

BURTON, Hon. Mark; New Zealand politician; b. 16 Jan. 1956, Northampton, England; m. Carol Burton; two s. one d.; ed Wanganui Boys' Coll., Univ. of Waikato, Massey Univ., NZ Council of Recreation and Sport; began career in community and social work, adult educ. and recreation; fmr employee Red Cross, Dept of Social Welfare, Palmerston North City Council; fmr Community Educ. Organiser, Cen. N Island; MP for Tongariro 1993–96, for Taupo 1996–; Sr Labour Party Whip 1996–99; Minister of Defence, State-Owned Enterprises and Tourism 1999–2005, also Minister of Internal Affairs and Veterans' Affairs 1999–2002; Deputy Leader of the House 1999–2007; Minister Responsible for Fire Service Comm. 2004–05; Minister of Justice and of Local Govt and in Charge of Treaty of Waitanagi Negotiations and Minister Responsible for Law Comm. 2005–07; Pres. Japan Karate NZ; NZ 1990 Medal. *Address:* Parliament Buildings, PO Box 10–041, Wellington, New Zealand (office). *Telephone:* (4) 817-8134 (office). *E-mail:* Helen.Kennelly@parliament .govt.nz (office). *Website:* www.ps.parliament.govt.nz (office).

BURTON, Richard St John Vladimir, CBE, RIBA; British architect and artist; b. 3 Nov. 1933, London; s. of Percy Basil Harmsworth Burton and Vera (née Poliakoff Russell); m. Mireille Dernbach-Mayen 1956; three s. one d.; ed Bryanston, Architectural Asscn School of Architecture; Dir Ahrends Burton and Koralek 1961–2002; currently artist; founder and Trustee, Makepeace School for Craftsmen in Wood 1977–83; Chair. of numerous cttees including Arts Council of England Architecture Advisory Group, Nat. Steering Cttee Per Cent for Art 1990–92, RIBA Steering Group on Architectural Educ. 1991–93, Health Bldgs for the 21st Century; NHS Estates 1991–93, Patient Care Study 1993, Building a 2020 Vision: Future Heathcare Environments; Chair. NHS Design Brief Working Group 2001–04; mem. ACE Visual Arts Panel 1994–98; Patron, Arts for Health, Axis, Healing Arts, Isle of Wight. *Design projects include:* Chichester Theological Coll. 1964, Trinity Coll. Dublin Library 1967, Templeton Coll., Oxford 1965–96, Hooke Park Coll., Dorset 1983–90, St Mary's Hosp., Isle of Wight 1991, Lawson Practice Primary Care Centre, London 1997, Housing Estates, Basildon, Essex 1974–80, New British Embassy, Moscow 1988–2000. *Publications:* Ahrends Burton and Koralek 1991, (jtly) Collaborations: The Architecture of ABK 2002. *Leisure interests:* building and writing. *Address:* Ahrends Burton and Koralek, Unit 1, 7 Chalcot Road, London, NW1 8LH (office). *Telephone:* (20) 7586-3311 (office). *Fax:* (20)

7722-5445 (office). *E-mail:* abk@abklondon.com (office); rsvb@blueyonder.co .uk (home). *Website:* www.abk.co.uk (office).

BURTON, Tim; American film director and screenwriter; b. 25 Aug. 1958, Burbank, Calif.; pnr Helena Bonham Carter; one s. one d.; ed Calif. Arts Inst.; began career as animator, Walt Disney Studios (projects included The Fox and the Hound and The Black Cauldron); short-length film awards include two from Chicago Film Festival, Golden Lion Lifetime Achievement Award, Venice Int. Film Festival 2007. *Films as director:* Vincent (also animator) 1982, Luau 1982, Hansel and Gretel (TV) 1982, Frankenweenie (short, for Disney) 1984, Pee-Wee's Big Adventure 1985, Alfred Hitchcock Presents (TV episode, The Jar) 1985, Beetlejuice 1988, Batman 1989, Edward Scissorhands (also prod.) 1991, Batman Returns (also prod.) 1992, Ed Wood (also prod.) 1994, Mars Attacks! (also prod.) 1996, Sleepy Hollow 1999, Planet of the Apes 2001, Big Fish 2003, Charlie and the Chocolate Factory 2005, Corpse Bride (also prod.) 2005, Sweeney Todd The Demon Barber of Fleet Street (Best Dir, Nat. Bd of Review 2007, Golden Globe for Best Musical or Comedy 2008) 2007. *Films as producer:* Beetlejuice (TV series) 1993, Family Dog (TV series) 1993, The Nightmare Before Christmas 1993, Cabin Boy 1994, Batman Forever 1996, James and the Giant Peach 1996, Lost in Oz (TV series) 2000. *Film screenplays:* The Island of Doctor Agor 1971, Stalk of the Celery 1979, Vincent 1982, Luau 1982, Beetlejuice (story) 1988, (TV series creator) 1989, Edward Scissorhands (story) 1990, The Nightmare Before Christmas (story) 1993, Lost in Oz (TV pilot episode story) 2000, Point Blank (TV series) 2002. *Publications:* My Art and Films 1993, The Melancholy Death of Oyster Boy and Other Stories 1997, Burton on Burton 2000; various film tie-in books. *Address:* Chapman, Bird & Grey, 1990 South Bundy Drive, Suite 200, Los Angeles, CA 90025, USA (office). *Website:* www.timburton.com (office).

BURWITZ, Nils, BA (Fine Arts); German freelance artist, sculptor and lecturer; b. 16 Oct. 1940, Swinemünde; s. of Ulrich Burwitz and Johanna Lohse; m. Marina Schwezova 1964; two s. one d.; ed Univ. of Witwatersrand and postgrad. studies in London, Fribourg and Salzburg; emigrated to S Africa 1958; settled in Balearic islands 1976; 102 solo exhbns including 36 Exposures 1971 and restrospective exhbn in Sollerich Palace, Palma, Majorca 1985, Pretoria Art Museum, Pretoria 1991, Nat. Gallery 1992, Kunsthalle Munich-Germering 1995; lecturer at Lessinghaus, Herzog Bibliothek, Wolfenbüttel 2002; visual concept for stage works Iconostasis 1967–68, 8 Birds 1969, 8 Beasts 1970, Gentlemen (with R. Kirby) 1972, Mobile (with V. Rodzianko), London 1972, Retalls de l'Ignorancia (with R. Esteras) 1978, Llagrimes del Vienès (with A. Ballester) 1995; stained glass windows in churches of St Philip and St James and Sta Eulalia, Palma de Mallorca, Monastery of Lluch, La Ermita de la Santísima Trinidad, Royal Carthusian Monastery, Valldemossa, Majorca, Cupola for Castillo Hotel Son Vida, Palma de Mallorca, Cathedral, Palma de Mallorca; Founder Libra Press 1984; opened Funda Art Centre, Soweto, SA 1986; works in 89 public collections including: Albertinum, Vienna; Albertinum, Dresden; Fitzwilliam Museum Cambridge, Ludwig Museum, Cologne, Nat. Gallery, Warsaw, Nat. Portrait Gallery, Wash., Museum of Modern Art, Tokyo, Vic. and Albert Museum, London, Sculpture for Plaza de la Concordia sa Pobla; has collaborated in three video documentaries in SA and Namibia; posters for UNHCR 2001, OAU 2001, Max Planck Inst. (Einstein's Legacy) 2005; portfolios: Locust Variations 1967, It's About Time 1973, Tidal Zone 1974, Heads or Tails? 1981, 9 Terraces 1986, The Journey to Dresden 1989, Marinas Terraces 1995, The Invisible Miró 2000; numerous honours and awards including Gold Medal (Design), Johannesburg 1963, African Arts Centre Award, Durban 1971, Art Critics' Award, XI Graphic Biennale, Ljubljana 1975, Prix de la Ville de Monaco 1981, Primer Premio 'Ciutat de Palma' 1982, Merit Award, II Biennale of Painting, Barcelona 1987, Balearic European Citizen Award 1999, Premio Importantes, Diario de Mallorca 2002, Bishop Teodor Ubeda Memorial Award 2004. *Publications:* On the Razor's Edge 1995, Walking the Tightrope 2002. *Leisure interests:* swimming, diving. *Address:* Calle Rosa 22, 07170 Valldemossa, Majorca, Balearic Isles, Spain (home). *Telephone:* (971) 612838 (home). *Fax:* (971) 612839 (home). *E-mail:* nils@burwitz-art.com (home). *Website:* www .burwitz-art.com (office).

BURZAN, Dragiša, MS, PhD; Montenegrin politician and diplomatist; *Ambassador to UK;* b. 1950, Podgorica; m. Vesna Burzan; one s. two d.; ed Univ. of Montenegro, Univ. of Belgrade, Univ. of Essex, UK; mem. staff, Dept of Natural Sciences, Univ. of Montenegro 1976–98; Founder Democratic Alternative 1989; mem. Reform Forces of Fmr Yugoslavia 1991; Co-founder Montenegro Party 1992, Int. Sec. 1992–; mem. Parl. (Montenegro) 1992–96; Deputy Prime Minister of Montenegro with portfolios of Educ., Labour and Welfare, Health, Culture, Sport, Secr. of Information, Secr. for Int. and Science Cooperation, Commissariat for Refugees, etc. 1998–2001; Minister of Labour and Social Welfare 2001–02, of Foreign Affairs 2003–04; Amb. of Serbia and Montenegro to UK 2004–06, Amb. of Montenegro to UK 2007–; Chair. Parl. Comm. investigating abduction of group of Muslims in Bosnia; Vice-Pres. SDP 1996–2000; Co-founder Monitor (weekly). *Publications:* numerous articles on physics in scientific journals. *Address:* Embassy of Montenegro, 5th Floor, Trafalgar House, 11–12 Waterloo Place, London, SW1Y 4AU, England (office). *Telephone:* (20) 7863-8806 (office). *Fax:* (20) 7863-8807 (office). *E-mail:* dragisa_burzan@yahoo.co.uk (office).

BUSAIDI, Sayyid Badr bin Saud bin Hareb al-; Omani politician; currently Minister Responsible for Defence Affairs. *Address:* Ministry of Defence, POB 113, Muscat 113, Oman (office). *Telephone:* 24312605 (office). *Fax:* 24702521 (office).

BUSCEMI, Steve; American actor and film director; b. 13 Dec. 1957, Brooklyn, NY; m. Jo Andres 1987; one s.; ed Valley Stream Cen. High School, NY; moved to Manhattan following high school graduation to study acting with John Strasberg; worked as bartender, ice-cream truck driver, stand-up comedian; NY City Fireman, Engine Co. No. 55, Little Italy Section 1980–84; began writing and performing theatre pieces with Mark Boone, Jr; film debut in The Way It Is 1984; first lead role in Parting Glances 1986; directed several episodes of TV series The Sopranos 1999, appeared in series 2004; currently volunteer fireman, NY. *Film appearances include:* The Way It Is 1984, Tommy's 1985, Parting Glances 1986, Heart 1987, Kiss Daddy Goodnight 1988, Vibes 1988, New York Stories 1989, Slaves of New York 1989, Mystery Train 1989, Coffee and Cigarettes II 1989, Borders 1989, King of New York 1990, Miller's Crossing 1990, Barton Fink 1991, Zandalee 1991, Billy Bathgate 1991, In the Soup 1992, CrissCross 1992, Reservoir Dogs 1992, Who Do I Gotta Kill? 1992, Claude 1993, Rising Sun 1993, Twenty Bucks 1993, Ed and His Dead Mother 1993, Floundering 1994, The Hudsucker Proxy 1994, Airheads 1994, Somebody to Love 1994, Pulp Fiction 1994, Living in Oblivion 1995, Dead Man 1995, Things to Do in Denver When You're Dead 1995, Fargo 1996, Trees Lounge 1996, Kansas City 1996, Escape from L.A. 1996, The Real Blonde 1997, The Wedding Singer 1998, The Big Lebowski 1998, The Impostors 1998, Armageddon 1998, Louis & Frank 1998, Animal Factory 2000, 28 Days 2000, Ghost World 2000, Final Fantasy: The Spirits Within 2001, The Grey Zone 2001, Monsters Inc. 2001, The Laramie Project 2002, Love in the Time of Money 2002, 13 Moons 2002, Mr Deeds 2002, Spy Kids 2: Island of Lost Dreams 2002, Deadrockstar 2002, Spy Kids 3-D: Game Over 2003, Coffee and Cigarettes 2003, Big Fish 2003, Home on the Range 2004, The Sky is Green 2004, Romance & Cigarettes 2005, Art School Confidential 2004, The Island 2005, A License to Steal 2005, Cordless 2005, Delirious 2005, Paris, je t'aime 2006, Monster House 2006, Charlotte's Web (voice) 2006, Interview 2007, I Think I Love My Wife 2007, I Now Pronounce You Chuck and Larry 2007, Igor (voice) 2008. *Films directed include:* What Happened to Pete? 1992, Trees Lounge 1996, Animal Factory 2000, Lonesome Jim 2004, Interview 2007. *Films produced include:* Animal Factory 2000, Lonesome Jim 2004. *Films written include:* What Happened to Pete? 1992, Trees Lounge 1996. *Address:* William Morris Agency, 1 William Morris Place, Beverly Hills, CA 90212; c/o Artists Management Group, 9465 Wilshire Blvd., #419, Beverly Hills, CA 90212, USA (office).

BUSCH, August A., III; American brewery industy executive; *Director, Anheuser-Busch Companies Inc.;* b. 16 June 1937, St Louis, MO; s. of the late August A. Busch, Jr; one s.; ed Univ. of Arizona; began career with family-business Anheuser-Busch Cos Inc. (brewery, theme-park operator and mfr of alumnium cans), mem. Bd of Dirs 1963–, Pres. 1974–2002, CEO 1975–2002, Chair. 1977–2006; mem. Bd of Dirs Emerson Electric Co., SBC Communications Inc.; Beverage Forum Lifetime Achievement Award 2003. *Address:* Anheuser-Busch Companies Inc., 1 Busch Place, St Louis, MO 63118, USA (office). *Telephone:* (314) 577-2000 (office). *Fax:* (314) 577-2900 (office). *Website:* www.anheuser-busch.com (office).

BUSCH, August Adolphus, IV, MBA; American brewing industry executive; *President and CEO, Anheuser-Busch Companies, Inc.;* b. 15 June 1964; s. of August Busch III; m. Kathryn Busch (neé Thatcher) 2006; ed St Louis Univ., Int. Brewing Inst., Berlin; joined Anheuser-Busch as apprentice brewer 1985, Vice-Pres. Brand Man. 1994–96, Vice-Pres. Marketing 1996–2000, Group Vice-Pres. Marketing and Wholesale Operations 2000–02, Pres. 2002–, CEO 2006–, mem. Bd of Dirs 2006–; mem. Bd of Dirs FedEx Corpn; f. Great Rivers Habitat Alliance; Hon. DBA (Webster Univ.) 2006. *Address:* Anheuser-Busch Companies, Inc., 1 Busch Place, St Louis, MO 63118, USA (office). *Telephone:* (314) 577-2000 (office). *Fax:* (314) 577-2900 (office). *Website:* www.anheuser-busch.com (office).

BUSCH, May Chien, MBA; British/American investment banker; *Chief Operating Officer, Morgan Stanley & Co International Ltd;* ed Harvard Coll., Harvard Business School; joined Morgan Stanley Dean Witter 1985, later Head of Debt Capital Markets in Europe for Corporates, later Man. Dir and Co-Head of European Coverage of Global Capital Markets, Morgan Stanley & Co. Int. Ltd 2002–04, Head of Firm Relationship Man. 2004–06, COO 2006–; mem. Council for Industry and Higher Educ., Advisory Bd SEO London UK Internship Programme. *Address:* Morgan Stanley Investment Management Ltd, 25 Cabot Square, Canary Wharf, London, E14 4QA, England (office). *Telephone:* (20) 7425-8000 (office). *Fax:* (20) 7425-7832 (office). *E-mail:* info@morganstanley.com (office). *Website:* www.morganstanley.com (office).

BUSEK, Erhard, DJur; Austrian politician; b. 25 March 1941, Vienna; m. Helga Busek; ed Univ. of Vienna; Second Sec. Parl. Austrian People's Party (ÖVP); joined Fed. Exec. Cttee of Austrian Econ. Fed. 1968, Deputy Sec.-Gen. 1969, Sec.-Gen. 1972–76; Gen. Sec. ÖVP 1975–76; mem. Parl. 1975–78; City Councillor, Vienna City Senate 1976–78, 1987–89; Deputy Mayor of Vienna 1978–87; Deputy Fed. Chair. ÖVP 1983–91, Chair. 1991–95; Pres. Austrian Research Community; Fed. Minister of Science and Research 1989–94, of Educ. and Culture 1994–95, Vice-Chancellor 1992–95; with Instituts für den Donauraum und Mitteleuropa (IDM) 1995–; Co-ordinator for Southeastern European Co-operative Initiative 1996–; Pres. European Forum Alpbach 2000–; Special Co-ordinator Stability Pact for SE Europe 2002–08; Guest Prof., Duke Univ., USA 1995–; Perm. Sr Fellow Centre for Research into European Integration, Bonn; Pres. Gustav Mahler Youth Orchestra, Österreichischen Volksliedwerkes, Stipendienwerkes 'pro scientia'; Jt-Pres. Technologieforums Sloweniens; Dr hc (Univs of Kraków, Bratislava, Czernowitz and Ruse). *Publications:* Projekt Mitteleuropa 1986, Aufbruch nach Mitteleuropa (with G. Wilflinger) 1986, Wissenschaft, Ethik und Politik (with M. Peterlik) 1987, Wissenschaft und Freiheit – Ideen zu Universität und Universalität (with W. Mantl and M. Perterlik) 1989, Heimat – Politik mit sitz im Leben 1994, Mensch im Wort 1994, Mitteleuropa: Eine Spurensicherung 1997, Politik am Gängelband der Medien 1998, Österreich und der Balkan – Vom Umgang mit dem Pulverfass Europas 1999, Eine Reise ins Innere Europas – Protokoll eines Österreichers 2001, Offenes Tor nach Osten 2003, Die Europäische Union auf dem Weg nach Osten 2003. *Address:* Austrian People's Party, Lichtenfelsgasse 7, 1010 Vienna, Austria (office). *Telephone:* (1) 401-26-0 (office). *Fax:* (1) 401-26-10-9 (office). *E-mail:* email@oevp.at (office). *Website:* www.oevp.at (office).

BUSER, Walter Emil, DrIur; Swiss government official; b. 14 April 1926, Lausen; s. of Emil Buser and Martha Buser; m. Renée Vuille 1947; ed Humanistic Gymnasium, Basel, Univs of Basel and Berne; Ed. Sozialdemokratische Bundeshauskorrespondenz 1950–61; Legal Consultant 1962–64; Head, legal and information service, Fed. Dept of Interior 1965–67; Vice-Chancellor of the Swiss Confed. 1968–81, Chancellor 1981–92; Hon. Dozent (Basel). *Publications:* Das Bundesgesetz über die Ordnung des Arbeitsverhaltnisses vom 27.6.19, Die Rolle der Verwaltung und der Interessengruppen im Entscheidungsprozess der Schweiz, Betrachtungen zum schweizerischen Petitionsrecht, Die Organisation der Rechtsetzung, in Hundert Jahre Bundesverfassung 1874–1974, Das Institut der Volksinitiative in rechtlicher und rechtspolitischer Sicht. *Address:* c/o Federal Chancellery, Swiss Confederation, 3003 Berne, Switzerland.

BUSH, Barbara; fmr First Lady; b. 8 June 1925, Rye, NY; d. of Marvin Pierce and Pauline (née Robinson) Pierce; m. George Herbert Walker Bush (q.v.) 1945; four s. including George W. Bush and John Ellis (Jeb) Bush, one d.; ed Smith Coll.; mem. Bd of Dirs, Reading is Fundamental (also Hon. Chair. Advisory Bd), Business Council for Effective Literacy; mem. Advisory Council, Soc. of Memorial Sloan-Kettering Cancer Center; Hon. Chair. Advisory Council, Literacy Volunteers of America; Pres. Ladies of the Senate 1981–88; founder and Hon. Chair. Barbara Bush Foundation for Family Literacy 1989–; numerous hon. degrees; Outstanding Mother of the Year Award 1984, Distinguished Leadership Award, United Negro Coll. Fund 1986, Distinguished American Woman Award, Mt St Joseph Coll. 1987, Free Spirit Award, Freedom Forum 1985. *Publications:* C. Fred's Story, Millie's Book, Barbara Bush: A Memoir 1994. *Address:* c/o Barbara Bush Foundation for Family Literacy, 1201 15th Street, NW, Suite 420, Washington, DC 20005, USA. *Website:* www.barbarabushfoundation.com.

BUSH, George Herbert Walker, BA (Econs); American fmr head of state; b. 12 June 1924, Milton, Mass.; s. of the late Prescott Sheldon Bush and of Dorothy Walker; m. Barbara Bush (née Pierce) (q.v.) 1945; four s. (including George Walker Bush, John Ellis (Jeb) Bush) one d.; ed Phillips Acad., Andover, Mass. and Yale Univ.; naval carrier pilot USN 1942–45; Co-founder, Bush-Overbey Oil Devt Co. 1951; Co-founder, Dir Zapata Petroleum Corpn 1953–59; Founder, Pres. Zapata Offshore Co. 1956–64, Chair. 1964–66; mem. House of Reps for 7th Dist of Texas 1967–71; Perm. Rep. to UN 1971–72; Chair. Republican Nat. Cttee 1973–74; Head US Liaison Office, Peking (now Beijing) 1974–75; Dir CIA 1976–77; Vice-Pres. of USA 1981–89, Pres. of USA 1989–93; Republican; Sr Adviser, Asia Advisory Bd, Carlyle Group 1998–2003; apptd UN Special Envoy in Pakistan and Kashmir earthquake zone 2005; Hon. KBE (UK); DFC, three Air Medals; Hon. GCB 1993; numerous hon. degrees; Churchill Award 1991. *Publications:* Looking Forward: An Autobiography (with Victor Gold) 1988, A World Transformed (with Brent Scowcroft) 1998, All the Best, George Bush 1999. *Leisure interests:* tennis, jogging, boating, fishing, golf. *Address:* Suite 900, 10000 Memorial Drive, Houston, TX 77024-3422, USA (office). *Telephone:* (713) 686-1188 (office).

BUSH, George Walker, BA, MBA; American business executive, politician and fmr head of state; b. 6 July 1946, New Haven, Conn.; s. of George Herbert Bush (q.v.) (fmr Pres. of USA) and Barbara Bush (née Pierce) (q.v.); brother of John Ellis (Jeb) Bush; m. Laura Welch Bush; twin d.; ed Yale Univ. and Harvard Business School; trained as F-102 fighter pilot, Tex. Air Nat. Guard 1968; CEO Bush Exploration, Midland, Tex. 1975–83; Chair. and CEO Spectrum 7 Energy Corpn (merged with Harken Energy Corpn 1986) 1983–87; worked in father's presidential campaign 1988; Man. Gen. Pnr, Tex. Rangers professional baseball team 1989–94; Gov. of Tex. 1995–2000; Pres. of USA 2001–09. *Publication:* A Charge To Keep (with Karen Hughes) 2000. *Address:* c/o The White House, 1600 Pennsylvania Avenue, NW, Washington, DC 20500, USA (office).

BUSH, John Ellis (Jeb), BA; American business executive, politician and fmr state official; b. 11 Feb. 1953, Midland, Tex.; s. of George Herbert Bush (q.v.), fmr Pres. of USA and Barbara Bush (q.v.); brother of George W. Bush (q.v.), Pres. of USA; m. Columba Bush; two s. one d.; ed Univ. of Tex.; co-f. Codina Group (real estate devt co.), Miami, Fla 1981, Pres. and COO; Sec. of Commerce, State of Fla 1987–88; unsuccessful bid for Fla Gov.'s office 1994; f. Foundation for Fla's Future 1995, serving as Chair.; Gov. of Florida 1998–2007; mem. private equity advisory bd, Lehman Brothers 2007–; Republican. *Address:* Lehman Brothers, 745 Seventh Avenue, 30th Floor, New York, NY 10019, USA (office). *E-mail:* CorpCommUS@lehman.com (office). *Website:* www.lehman.com (office).

BUSH, Kate; British singer and songwriter; b. 30 July 1958, Bexleyheath, Kent; pnr Danny McIntosh; one s.; numerous live and TV appearances; Dir Novercia Ltd; BPI Awards for Best Vocalist 1979, 1987, Ivor Novello Award for Outstanding British Lyrics (for The Man With The Child In His Eyes) 1979, BRIT Award for Best Female Artist 1987, Q Magazine Award for Best Classic Songwriter 2001, Ivor Novello Award for Outstanding Contribution to British Music by a Songwriter 2002. *Film:* The Line, The Cross and The Curve (writer, dir and actor) 1993. *Recordings include:* albums: The Kick Inside 1978, Lionheart 1978, Never Forever 1980, The Dreaming 1982, Hounds Of Love 1985, The Whole Story 1986, The Sensual World 1989, This Woman's Work 1990, The Red Shoes 1993, Aerial 2005. *Website:* www.katebush.com.

BUSH, Laura Welch, BA, MLS; American public servant and teacher; b. Midland, Tex.; m. George W. Bush 1977; twin d.; ed Southern Methodist

Univ., Univ. of Tex.; worked as teacher at Longfellow Elementary School, Dallas, Tex. 1968–69; teacher, John F. Kennedy Elementary School 1969–72; librarian, Houston Public Library 1973–74, Dawson Elementary School, Austin, Tex. 1974–77; First Lady of Tex. 1995–2000; First Lady of US 2001–09; ranked by Forbes magazine amongst 100 Most Powerful Women (fourth) 2004, (46th) 2005, (43rd) 2006, (60th) 2007, (44th) 2008. *Address:* c/o Office of the First Lady, 200 East Wing, The White House, 1600 Pennsylvania Avenue, NW, Washington, DC 20500, USA (office).

BUSH, Wesley G., BSc, MSc; American defence industry executive; *President and Chief Operating Officer, Northrop Grumman Corporation;* ed MIT, UCLA; worked at Aerospace Corpn and Comsat Labs; joined TRW as systems engineer 1987, served in several man. positions including Vice-Pres. TRW Ventures, Vice-Pres. and Gen. Man. Telecommunications Programs Div., Pres. and CEO Aeronautical Systems UK; Corp. Vice-Pres. and Pres. of Space Tech., Northrop Grumman Corpn 2002–05, Vice-Pres. and Chief Financial Officer 2005–06, Pres. 2006–, also Chief Financial Officer 2006, COO 2007–. *Address:* Northrop Grumman Corporation, 1840 Century Park East, Los Angeles, CA 90067-2199, USA (office). *Telephone:* (310) 553-6262 (office). *Fax:* (310) 553-2076 (office). *E-mail:* onewebmaster@ngc.com (office). *Website:* www.northropgrumman.com (office).

BUSQUIN, Philippe; Belgian politician; b. 6 Jan. 1941; m.; ed Université Libre de Bruxelles; fmr Prof. of Biology and Physics; Deputy for Hainaut 1977–78, for Charleroi 1978–; Minister of Nat. Educ. 1980–81, of the Interior and Nat. Educ. Feb.–Dec. 1981, for the Budget and Energy (French region) 1982–85, of the Economy and Employment (French region) Feb.–May 1988, of Social Affairs 1988–92; Chair. Parti Socialiste (PS) 1992–99; Vice-Pres. Socialist Int. 1992–, PES 1995–; EU Commr responsible for Science, Research and Devt and the Jt Research Centre 1999–2004. *Address:* c/o European Commission, 200 rue de la Loi, 1049 Brussels, Belgium (office).

BUSSELL, Darcey Andrea, CBE; British ballet dancer; b. 27 April 1969, London; d. of Philip M. Bussell and Andrea Williams; m. Angus Forbes 1997; two d.; ed Arts Educational School and Royal Ballet School; joined Sadler's Wells Royal Ballet (later Birmingham Royal Ballet) 1987; debut with leading role in The Prince of The Pagodas (Kenneth MacMillan) 1988; soloist, Royal Ballet 1988, first soloist 1989, prin. ballerina 1989–2006, guest artist 2006–07; appearances with Royal Ballet include leading roles in The Spirit of Fugue (created for her by David Bintley), first Royal Ballet performances of Balanchine's Rubies and Stravinsky Violin Concerto and leading roles in Agon, Symphony in C, Tchaikovsky pas de deux, Apollo (Terpsichore), Prodigal Son (Siren), Duo Concertante, Ballet Imperial and Serenade, Kenneth Macmillan's The Prince of the Pagodas (role of Princess Rose created for her), Winter Dreams (role of Masha created for her), Manon (title role), Song of the Earth, Elite Syncopations, Raymonda, Romeo and Juliet, Requiem, Mayerling and Anastasia, Frederick Ashton's Cinderella (title role), Monotones II, Les Illuminations (Sacred Love), Birthday Offering, Les Rendezvous, William Forsyth's In the middle, somewhat elevated and Herman Scherman (pas de deux), Glen Tetley's La Ronde (Prostitute), Ninette de Valois' Checkmate (Black Queen), Ashley Page's Bloodlines (creator of leading role) and ...now langourous, now wild..., Twyla Tharp's Push Comes to Shove (co. premiere), Jerome Robbins' The Concert (Ballerina), Antony Tudor's Lilac Garden (Caroline), Roland Petit's Le Jeune Homme et La Mort, Balanchine's The Four Temperaments and Themes and Variations, Alistair Marriot's Kiss; classical repertory includes leading roles in Swan Lake (Odette/Odile), The Sleeping Beauty (Princess Aurora), The Nutcracker (Sugar Plum Fairy), La Bayadère (Nikiya and Gamzatti), Cinderella (title role), Giselle (title role), Raymonda Act III (title role); numerous appearances on TV and abroad as guest with other ballet cos in Paris, St Petersburg, New York, Australian Ballet, La Scala; in Viva La Diva touring production (with Katherine Jenkins) 2007–08; Prix de Lausanne 1989, Dance and Dancers Magazine Dancer of the Year 1990, Variety Club of GB Sir James Garreras Award 1991, Evening Standard Ballet Award 1991, Jt Winner Cosmopolitan Achievement in the Performing Arts Award 1991, Olivier Award 1992. *Publications:* Life in Dance (with Judith Mackrell) 1998, Favourite Ballet Stories, The Young Dancer, Pilates for Life 2005, Darcey Bussell's Dance Body Workout 2007. *Leisure interests:* sketching/painting, arts. *Website:* www.darceybussell.com.

BUSSEREAU, Dominique; French politician; *Secretary of State for Ecology, Energy, Sustainable Development and Spatial Planning, responsible for Transport;* b. 13 July 1952, Tours, Indre-et-Loire; ed Institut d'études politiques, Paris; Conseiller Général, Charente-Maritime 1985–, Pres. Conseil Gen. 2008–; Deputy (4ème circonscription) for Charente-Maritime, Assemblée nationale 1986–88, 1993–2002, 2007–, mem. Comm. des Lois, comité directeur du fonds d'investissement pour le développement économique et social des territoires d'outre-mer (fidestom); Conseiller régional de Poitou-Charentes 1992–93, March–April 2004; Mayor of Saint-Georges-de-Didonne, Charente-Maritime 1989–2002, 1er adjoint au Maire 2002–08, Conseiller municipal 2008–; Sec. of State, Transports et à la Mer 2002–04, for the Budget and Budgetary Reform, Ministry of the Economy, Finances and Industry March–Nov. 2004; Minister of Agric., Food, Fishing and the Countryside 2004–05, of Agric. and Fishing 2005–07, Sec. of State for Ecology, Energy, Sustainable Devt and Spatial Planning, responsible for Transport 2007–; mem. Union pour un Mouvement Populaire (UMP); Pres. Asscn Avenir Transports; Commdr, Ordre du Mérite agricole, Ordre du Mérite maritime, Ordre du Mérite Agricole (Senegal), Grand Cordon, Order of the Rising Sun (Japan). *Address:* Ministry of Ecology, Energy, Sustainable Planning and Regional Development, Grande Arche, Tour Pascal A et B, 92055 La Défense Cedex, France (office). *Telephone:* 1-40-81-21-22 (office). *E-mail:* ministre@ecologie.gouv.fr (office). *Website:* www.developpement-durable.gouv.fr (office).

BUSTAMANTE, Jean-Marc; French artist, sculptor and photographer; b. 1952, Toulouse; conceptual and installation artist, has incorporated ornamental design and architectural space in his works, has also worked with film; with Bernard Bazile operated under jt name BazileBustamante 1983–87; teaches at Rijksakademie, Amsterdam. *Address:* Rijksakademie van beeldende kunsten, Sarphatistraat 470, 1018 GW Amsterdam, Netherlands.

BUSTAMANTE PONCE, Fernando, MPA; Ecuadorean politician; *Minister of Government, Worship, Police and Municipalities;* ed Catholic Univ. of Chile, Harvard Univ.,; fmr Prof., San Francisco Univ., Quito; Minister of Internal and External Security Policy Co-ordination 2007-08, of Govt, Worship, Police and Municipalities 2008–; columnist diario Hoy. *Address:* Ministry of Government, Worship, Police and Municipalities, Espejo y Benalcázar, Quito, Ecuador (office). *Telephone:* (2) 295-5666 (office). *Fax:* (2) 295-8360 (office). *E-mail:* febusta@hoy.com.ec; informacion@mingobierno.gov.ec (office). *Website:* www.mingobierno.gov.ec (office).

BUSTANI, José Mauricio, LLB; Brazilian diplomatist and government official; *Ambassador to France;* b. 5 June 1945, Porto Velho, Rondônia; m. Janine-Monique Bustani; two s. one d.; ed Pontifício Universidade Católica (Law School), Rio de Janeiro, Rio Branco Inst.; joined Ministry of Foreign Relations 1967, Asst to Assoc. Sec.-Gen. for Int. Orgs 1967–70, 1975–77; posted to Brazilian Embassy in Moscow 1970–73, Vienna 1973–75, Brazilian Mission to the UN 1977–84, Embassy in Montevideo 1984–86 Consulate-Gen. Montreal 1987–92; Head Dept for Tech., Financial and Devt Policy, Ministry of Foreign Relations 1992–93; Dir-Gen. Dept for Int. Orgs 1993–97; Dir-Gen. UN OPCW, The Hague 1997–2002; Amb. to UK 2003–08, to France 2008–; del. to numerous int. confs. including UNIDO, Vienna 1973–75, UN Conf. on the Law of the Sea (13 sessions 1974–93), UN Gen. Ass. 1977–83, UN Special Sessions on Disarmament 1978–82, UN Emergency Sessions on Afghanistan 1980, Namibia 1981. *Address:* Embassy of Brazil, 34 cours Albert 1er, 75008 Paris, France (office). *Telephone:* 1-45-61-63-00 (office). *Fax:* 1-42-89-03-45 (office). *E-mail:* imprensa@bresil.org (office). *Website:* www.bresil.org (office).

BUTAGIRA, Francis, LLB, LLM; Ugandan diplomatist; *Permanent Representative and Chairman, General Assembly Third Committee, United Nations;* b. 22 Nov. 1942, Bugamba; m.; seven c.; ed Dar es Sallaam Univ. Coll., Harvard Univ., USA, SOAS, London, UK; State Attorney, Ministry of Justice 1967; Lecturer in Law, Nsamizi Law School 1968; Head, Law Dept, Law Devt Center 1969–70; Chief Magistrate of Buganda Road Law Courts 1973, of Mbarara 1974; High Court Judge 1974–79; mem. Nat. Consultative Council 1979–80; mem. Parl. 1980–85, also served as Pres. Jt. Ass. of the European Econ. Community and the African, Caribbean and Pacific Group of States (EEC/ACP) 1981–83; Chair. Legal and Security Affairs Cttee, Nat. Resistance Council (Parl.) 1989–96; Amb. to Ethiopia and Perm. Rep. to Org. of African Unity (OAU), Addis Ababa 1998; led team of Ugandan negotiators in talks leading to establishment of E African Community 1999; fmr High Commr to Kenya and Perm. Rep. to UNEP and UN-HABITAT, Nairobi; served as mediator in Sudanese peace talks sponsored by Intergovernmental Authority on Devt (IGAD) 2000–03; Perm. Rep. to UN 2003–, Chair UN Gen. Ass. Third Cttee (Social, Humanitarian and Cultural) 2005–; Sr Pnr Butagira and Co. (law firm) 1989–; Uganda Investment Authority Golden Award for Attraction of Investment 2002. *Address:* Permanent Mission of Uganda to the United Nations, 336 East Street, New York NY 10017, USA (office). *Telephone:* (212) 949-0110 (office); (212) 963-5722 (Third Cttee) (office). *Fax:* (212) 687-4517 (office); (212) 963-5935 (Third Cttee) (office). *E-mail:* ugandaunny@un.int (office); 3rdcommittee@un.org (office). *Website:* www.un.int/uganda (office); www.un.org/ga/60/third (office); www.butagiraadvocates.com.

BUTCHER, Hon. David John, BA (Hons); New Zealand economist and consultant; *Consultant, David Butcher and Associates;* b. 19 Sept. 1948, England; s. of Frank George Butcher and Dorothy May Butcher; m. Mary Georgina Hall 1980; two d.; ed Victoria Univ. of Wellington; Research Economist, Dept of Labour 1972–74; Field Officer, Clerical Workers Union and NZ Labourers Union, Hawke's Bay, Wellington 1976–78; mem. Parl. 1978–90; Parl. Under-Sec. to Ministers of Agric., Lands and Forests 1984–87; Minister of Energy, of Regional Devt and Assoc. Minister of Finance 1987–88, of Regional Devt 1987–90, of Commerce 1988–90, of Energy 1989–90; Consultant, David Butcher and Assocs (econ. consultancy) 1992–; Sr Man., Ernst & Young, Wellington 1995–96; mem. Labour Party; Fellow, NZ Inst. of Man.; mem. NZ Asscn of Economists, NZ Soc. of Public Admin, NZ Asscn of Former MPs; Commemorative Medal 1990. *Publications include:* Agriculture in a More Market Economy 1985, Lessons for the Future from the Free Market Economy; contrib. Privatization Yearbook 1993, 1994, 1995, 1999; numerous speeches and articles. *Leisure interests:* tramping, reading, classical music, family history, photography. *Address:* c/o GGI, 2 Solnet House, 70 The Terrace, Wellington (office); PO Box 5279, Wellington, 6145, New Zealand (home). *Telephone:* (4) 476-9001 (office). *Fax:* (4) 386-4909 (office). *E-mail:* david@dba.org.nz (office). *Website:* www.dba.org.nz (office).

BUTCHER, Eugene (Gene) Corning, BS, MD; American immunologist and academic; *Professor of Pathology, Stanford University;* b. 6 Jan. 1950, St Louis, Mo.; ed Massachusetts Inst. of Tech., Washington Univ., St Louis; Residency in Pathology (Anatomic), Dept of Pathology, Stanford Univ., Calif. 1976–77, 1979–80, NIH Postdoctoral Fellowship, Dept of Pathology 1977–79, Sr Fellow, American Cancer Soc., Calif. Div., Dept of Pathology 1980–82, Asst Prof., Dept of Pathology, Stanford Univ. Medical Center 1982–89, Assoc. Prof. 1989–99, Prof. 1999–; Staff Physician, Veterans Admin Palo Alto Health Care System 1982–, Dir Serology and Immunology Section, Veterans Admin Palo Alto Health Care System 1982–; Co-Dir Immunohistologic Diagnosis Service, Surgical Pathology, Stanford 1983–93; Univ. Lecturer, Univ. of Texas Southwest Medical Center 1996; Burroughs-Wellcome Visiting Prof., Univ. of New Mexico 1996; mem. American Asscn of Pathologists, American Asscn of

Immunologists, Asscn of American Physicians 2003, Fed. of American Socs for Experimental Biology, American Soc. for Investigative Pathology, Mars Soc., Planetary Soc.; Eloranta Award 1971, PLU (Hon. Chem. Soc.) 1972, Richard S. Brookings Award for Excellence in Medical Student Research 1976, Scholar, Leukemia Soc. of America 1982–87, Established Investigator, American Heart Asscn 1987–92, Warner-Lambert/Parke-Davis Award for meritorious research in experimental pathology, American Soc. for Investigative Pathology 1989, Marjorie J. Williams Lecturer, Asscn of Veterans Admin Pathologists 1989, AAI-Huang Foundation Meritorious Career Award, American Asscn of Immunologists 1999, William S. Middleton Award (Highest Research Award from Dept of Veterans Affairs) 2001 (presented 2002), Stanford Univ. Outstanding Inventor Award 2004, Crafoord Prize in Polyarthritis, Royal Swedish Acad. of Sciences (co-recipient) 2004, invited to membership of Scientific Advisory Bd, 'SystemsX' (Swiss nat. initiative in systems biology) 2005. *Publications:* 33 reviews and 279 scientific papers in professional journals on the trafficking of white blood cells, including their interactions with the endothelial lining of blood vessels at sites of leukocyte extravasation, and their chemotactic responses in tissues; nine US patents. *Address:* Department of Pathology, Stanford University School of Medicine, Lane Building, Mailcode 5324, Stanford, CA 94305-5324, USA (office). *Telephone:* (650) 852-3369 (office). *Fax:* (650) 858-3986 (office). *E-mail:* ebutcher@stanford.edu (office); marthas1@stanford.edu (office). *Website:* med.stanford.edu/profiles/Eugene_Butcher (office); butcherlab.stanford.edu (office).

BUTCHER, John Charles, PhD, DSc, FRSNZ; New Zealand academic; *Professor of Mathematics, University of Auckland;* b. 31 March 1933, Auckland; s. of Charles Hastings Butcher and Alice Lilac Cornwall (née Richards) Butcher; m. 1st Patricia Frances Nicolas 1957 (divorced 1989); two s. one d.; m. 2nd Jennifer Ann Wright (née Bowman) 1990; ed Dargaville, Taumarunui and Hamilton High Schools, Univ. of New Zealand and Sydney; Lecturer in Applied Math., Univ. of Sydney 1959–61; Sr Lecturer in Math., Univ. of Canterbury 1961–64; computer scientist, Stanford Linear Accelerator Center 1965–66; Prof. of Math., Univ. of Auckland 1966–79 (Head Math. Dept 1967–73), of Computer Science 1980–88 (f. Dept of Computer Science 1980), Head, Applied and Computational Math. Unit 1989–94, 1997–98, Prof. of Math. 1989–98, Hon. Research Prof. and Prof. Emer. 1999–; various visiting lectureships and professorships USA, UK, Sweden, Austria, Germany, USSR, Netherlands 1965–; Fellow Inst. of Math. and its Applications (UK) 1972; Fellow and Past Pres. NZ Math. Soc.; mem. American Math. Soc. 1966; mem. Soc. for Industrial and Applied Math. (Pa, USA), Australian and NZ Industrial and Applied Mathematics; mem. Bd of various journals; Award for Math. Research (NZ Math. Soc.) 1991, Hector Medal (Royal Soc. of NZ) 1996. *Publications:* The Numerical Analysis of Ordinary Differential Equations: Runge-Kutta and General Linear Methods 1987, papers on numerical analysis and other topics. *Leisure interests:* classical music, bridge. *Address:* Department of Mathematics, University of Auckland, Private Bag 92019, Auckland (office); 16 Wallace Street, Herne Bay, Auckland, New Zealand (home). *Telephone:* (9) 3737999 (office); (9) 3762743 (home). *Fax:* (9) 3737457 (office). *E-mail:* butcher@mat.auckland.ac.nz (office).

BUTHELEZI, Rt Rev. Bishop Manas, STM, PhD; South African ecclesiastic; b. 10 Feb. 1935, Mahlabathini; s. of Absalom Buthelezi and Keslinah Mkhabase; m. Grace Mhlungu 1963; two s. two d.; ed St Francis Coll. and Yale and Drew Univs, USA; high school teacher 1957; Visiting Prof., Heidelberg Univ., FRG 1972, Wesley Seminary 1975; Bishop, Cen. Diocese, Evangelical Lutheran Church 1977–2000, Bishop Emer. 2000–; Pres. SA Council of Churches 1984–91; mem. Comm. on Studies, Lutheran World Fed. 1970–77, Comm. on World Mission and Evangelism, WCC 1975–83; mem. Standing Cttee Faith and Order Comm., Pvt. Sector Council on Urbanization, Int. Comm. on Lutheran/Catholic Dialogue, Iliff School of Theology; St John's Visiting Prof., Lutheran Theological Seminary at Phila 2001; several hon. degrees. *Leisure interests:* music and photography. *Address:* PO Box 1210, Roodepoort 1725, South Africa.

BUTHELEZI, Chief Mangosuthu Gatsha, BA; South African politician; b. 27 Aug. 1928, Mahlabatini; s. of the late Chief Mathole Buthelezi and Princess Magogo; m. Irene Audrey Thandekile Mzila 1952; three s. four d.; ed Adams Coll., Fort-Hare Univ.; installed as Chief of Buthelezi Tribe 1953; assisted King Cyprian in admin. of Zulu people 1953–68; elected leader of Zululand territorial authority 1970; Chief Minister of KwaZulu 1976–94; Minister of Home Affairs (in Gov. of Nat. Unity) 1994–2004; Pres. Inkatha Freedom Party; Hon. LLD (Zululand and Cape Town); George Meany Human Rights Award 1982; Kt Commdr Star of Africa (Liberia), Commdr Ordre Nat. du Mérite 1981 and numerous other awards. *Publication:* South Africa: My Vision of the Future 1990. *Address:* c/o Ministry of Home Affairs, Private Bag X741, Pretoria 0001 (office); Inkatha Freedom Party, Albany House North, 4th Floor, Albany Grove, PO Box 443, Durban 4000, South Africa. *Telephone:* (31) 3074962. *Fax:* (12) 3074964. *Website:* www.fp.org.za.

BUTIME, Tom; Ugandan government official; joined Nat. Resistance Army guerillas in 1981; mil. training in Libya 1982; Acting Minister of Foreign Affairs 2004–05, also fmr Minister of State for International Affairs and Second Deputy Prime Minister; Minister of State for Karamoja Affairs 2006 (resgnd). *Address:* c/o Ministry of Foreign Affairs, Embassy House, POB 7048, Kampala, Uganda (office).

BUTKEVIČIUS, Algirdas, MS; Lithuanian politician and engineer; b. 19 Nov. 1958, Paežeriai, Raadviliškis; m. Janina; one s. one d.; ed Vilnius Eng Construction Inst., Lithuanian Acad. of Man., Kaunas Technological Univ.; construction work supt, Vilkaviškis Region Industrial Union 1982–85, Exec. Cttee 1985–90; Head of Dept of Econs and Finance, Deputy Gov. Vilkaviškis Region 1991–95; mem. Seimas (Parl.) 1996–, Chair. Treasury Sub-Cttee 1996–2001, Chair. Budget and Finance Cttee 2001–04; Minister of Finance 2004–05 (resgnd), of Interior –2008; mem. Lithuanian SDP (LSDP), Deputy Chair. 1999–. *Leisure interest:* sports. *Address:* c/o Lithuanian Social Democratic Party (LSDP) (Lietuvos Socialdemokratų Partija) Barboros Radvilaites g. 1, Vilnius 01124; Žircnūnus 38A -31, Vilnius, Lithuania (home). *Telephone:* (5) 261-3907; (6) 984-2492 (home). *Fax:* (5) 261-5420. *E-mail:* info@lsdp.lt. *Website:* www.lsdp.lt.

BUTLER, Basil Richard Ryland, CBE, MA, FREng; British business executive; b. 1 March 1930, Hexham; s. of Hugh Montagu Butler and Annie Isabel Butler (née Wiltshire); m. Lilian Joyce Haswell 1954; one s. two d.; ed Denstone Coll., Staffs., St John's Coll., Cambridge; 2nd Lt, 5th Royal Inniskilling Dragoon Guards; Operations Man. Sinclair and BP Colombian Inc. 1968–70, Operations Man. BP Alaska Inc. 1970–72, Gen. Man. BP Petroleum Devt Ltd 1978–81, Chief Exec. BP Exploration Co. Ltd 1981–86, Dir 1986–89, Man. Dir BP Co. PLC 1986–91; Dir BP Solar Int. 1991–98, Chair. 1991–95; Chair. European Council of Applied Sciences and Eng 1993–98; Dir Brown and Root Ltd 1991–97, Chair. 1993–97; Dir Murphy Oil Corpn 1991–2002; Gen. Man. of Kuwait Oil Co. Ltd 1972–75, of Sullom Voe Devt 1975–78; Chair. KS Biomedix Holdings PLC 1995–2001; Pres. Inst. of Petroleum 1990–92; mem. Council Royal Acad. of Eng 1993–2002, Hon. Sec. Int. Activities 1995–98, Sr Vice-Pres. 1996–99; Commodore, Royal Western Yacht Club of England 2004–; Liveryman Shipwrights' Co. 1988. *Leisure interests:* sailing, music. *Address:* c/o Royal Academy of Engineering, London, SW1P 3LW, England.

BUTLER, David Edgeworth, CBE, MA, DPhil, FBA; British psephologist; b. 1924; s. of the late Prof. Harold E. Butler and Margaret Pollard; m. Marilyn S. Evans (Marilyn Butler (q.v.)) 1962; three s.; ed St Paul's School, Princeton Univ., USA and New Coll., Oxford; J.E. Procter Visiting Fellow, Princeton Univ. 1947–48; student, Nuffield Coll. Oxford 1949–51, Research Fellow 1951–54, Fellow 1954–92, Emer. Fellow 1992–, Dean and Sr Tutor 1956–64; Personal Asst to British Amb. in Washington 1955–56; co-ed. Electoral Studies 1982–92; Hon. DUniv (Paris) 1978, (Essex) 1993; Hon. DSc (Queen's Univ. Belfast) 1985, (Teesside) 1998; Hon. LLD (Plymouth) 1997. *Publications include:* The Study of Political Behaviour 1958, Elections Abroad (ed.) 1959, British Political Facts 1900–1960 (with J. Freeman), Political Change in Britain 1969, The Canberra Model 1973, Coalitions in British Politics (ed.) 1978, Policy and Politics (ed. with A.H. Halsey), Referendums (with A. Ranney) 1978, British Political Facts 1900–79 (with A. Sloman), European Elections and British Politics (with D. Marquand) 1981, Democracy at the Polls (with A. Ranney) 1981, Democracy and Elections (with V. Bogdanor) 1983, Governing without a Majority 1983, A Compendium of Indian Elections 1984, Party Strategies in Britain (with P. Jowett) 1985, British Political Facts 1900–2000 (with G. Butler) 2000, Sovereigns and Surrogates (with A. Low) 1991, Failure in British Government (with others) 1994, India Decides (with P. Roy) 1995, Referendums Around the World (co-ed.) 1995, British Politics and European Elections (with Martin Westlake) 2000, The British General Election of 2001 2001; also numerous books on the British electoral system and British elections since 1945. *Address:* Nuffield College, Oxford, OX1 1NF, England. *Telephone:* (1865) 278500.

BUTLER, Sir James (Jim), Kt, KCB, CBE, FCA; British chartered accountant; b. 15 March 1929, Batheaston; m. Margaret Butler (née Copland); one s. two d.; ed Marlborough Coll., Clare Coll., Cambridge; articled clerk, Peat Marwick (chartered accountants) 1952; negotiated Peat Marwick's merger with Klynveld Main Goerdeler to form KPMG 1986–87; Sr Pnr, Peat Marwick (UK arm of KPMG) 1987–93; Chair. KPMG Int. 1991–93; Dir Camelot PLC 1994–2002 (Deputy Chair. 1995), Royal Opera House 1994–99, Wadworth and Co. Ltd 1994–, Nicholson, Graham & Jones 1994–2005. *Leisure interests:* shooting, bridge. *Address:* Littleton House, Crawley, Winchester, Hants., SO21 2QF, England. *Telephone:* (1962) 880206 (home). *Fax:* (1962) 886177 (home).

BUTLER, James Walter, MBE, RA, RWA, FRBS; British sculptor; b. 25 July 1931, London; s. of the late Rosina Kingman and Walter Arthur Butler; m. Angela Elizabeth Berry 1975; five d.; ed Maidstone Grammar School, Maidstone School of Art, St Martin's School of Art, City & Guilds of London Art School, Royal Coll. of Art; worked as stone carver; taught sculpture and drawing, City & Guilds Art School; professional sculptor working on public and pvt. comms and exhbns; work in various galleries. *Leisure interest:* astronomy. *Address:* Valley Farm Studios, Radway, Warwick, CV35 0UJ, England (office). *Telephone:* (1926) 641938 (office). *Fax:* (1926) 640624 (office). *E-mail:* info@jamesbutler-ra.com (office).

BUTLER, Marilyn Speers, DPhil, FRSL, FRSA; British academic; b. (Marilyn S. Evans), 11 Feb. 1937, Kingston-upon-Thames, Surrey; d. of Trevor Evans and Margaret Evans (née Gribbin); m. David Edgeworth Butler (q.v.) 1962; three s.; ed Wimbledon High School, St Hilda's Coll. Oxford; BBC trainee and producer 1960–62; Jr Research Fellow, St Hilda's Coll. Oxford 1970–73; Fellow and Tutor, St Hugh's Coll. Oxford 1973–86; King Edward VII Prof. of English Literature, Cambridge Univ. 1986–93; Fellow King's Coll. Cambridge 1987–93; Rector Exeter Coll., Oxford 1993–; Titular Prof. of English Language and Literature, Univ. of Oxford 1998–; British Acad. Reader 1982–85; Foreign mem. US Acad. of Arts and Sciences 1999; Hon. Fellow, St Hilda's Coll. Oxford, St Hugh's Coll. Oxford, King's Coll. Cambridge; Hon. LittD (Leicester) 1992, (Birmingham) 1993, (Oxford Brookes) 1994, (Williams Coll., Mass) 1995, (Lancaster, Warwick, Surrey) 1997, (Kingston) 1998, (Open) 2000, (Roehampton) 2000. *Publications:* Maria Edgeworth: A Literary Biography 1972, Jane Austen and the War of Ideas 1975, Peacock Displayed 1979, Romantics, Rebels and Reactionaries 1981, Burke, Paine, Godwin and the Revolution Controversy (ed.) 1984, Collected Works of Wollstonecraft (Ed. with J. Todd) 1989, Edgeworth's Castle Rackrent and Ennui (ed.) 1992, Mary Shelley's Frankenstein (ed.) 1993, Jane Austen's Northanger Abbey (ed.) 1995, Collected Works of Edgeworth (ed. with M. Myers), 12 Vols, 1999. *Leisure interests:* art of all periods, especially political caricature from late 18th century; grandchildren, books they will like, films and theatre from pantomime to Shakespeare; old books, old and new friends; dogs, for walking with. *Address:* 151 Woodstock Road, Oxford, OX2 7NA, England (home). *Telephone:* (1865) 558323 (home). *E-mail:* marilyn.butler@exeter.ox.ac.uk (home).

BUTLER, Sir Michael Dacres, GCMG; British diplomatist (retd); b. 27 Feb. 1927, Nairobi, Kenya; s. of Thomas D. Butler and Beryl M. Butler (née Lambert); m. Ann Clyde 1951; two s. two d.; ed Winchester Coll. and Trinity Coll., Oxford; joined Foreign Office 1950; served at UK Mission to UN 1952–56, Baghdad 1956–58, Paris 1961–65, UK Mission to UN in Geneva 1968–70; sabbatical year at Harvard 1970–71; served in Washington, DC 1971–72; Head of European Integration Dept, FCO 1972–74, Under-Sec. for EC Affairs 1974–76, Deputy Under-Sec. for Econ. Affairs 1976–79; Perm. Rep. to EC 1979–85; Labour Party's Special Envoy on Enlargement 1996–97; Adviser to Robin Cook on Europe 1997–98; mem. Council Britain in Europe 1999–2005, Bd 2001–05; Chair. European Movt Sr Experts Group 2005–; mem. Advisory Council, Foreign Policy Centre 1998–; Adviser to Pres., Honda Motor Europe 1993–; Chair. Guide Phone Ltd 1998–2002; Deputy Chair. Bd of Trustees, Victoria and Albert Museum 1985–97; Chair., Council, RCA 1991–96, Sr Fellow 1997; Dir The Wellcome Foundation, PLC 1985–94; Exec. Dir Hambros Bank 1986–97, Hambros PLC 1986–97, Eurosynergies (France) 1990–98, Incofina (Portugal) 1990–93; Chair. Oriental Art Magazine 1987–94, European Strategy Bd ICL 1988–2001, European Cttee of British Invisibles 1988–93, Editorial Advisory Panel of Treasury Man. Int. 1992–, Business Link Dorset 1994–2001, Halo Ltd 1994–96, Rudolfinia Ltd 1994–2004, Pathway Group Ltd 1995–2000; Knight Grand Cross of Portuguese Order of Merit 1998; Hon. DBA (Bournemouth) 1998; Adolphe-Bentinck Prize 1987. *Publications:* Chinese Porcelain at the End of the Ming (OCS Transactions, Vol. 48) and at the Beginning of the Qing (OCS Transactions, Vol. 49), Europe – More than a Continent 1986, Seventeenth-Century Porcelain from the Butler Family Collection 1990, Shunzhi Porcelain – Treasures of an Unknown Reign 2002, Beauty's Enchantments: 17th Century Chinese Porcelain from the Shanghai Museum and the Butler Collections 2005/06. *Leisure interests:* collecting Chinese porcelain, skiing. *Address:* 54C Lennox Gardens, London, SW1X 0DJ, England (home). *Telephone:* (20) 7584-3367. *Fax:* (20) 7589-6547. *E-mail:* sirmibu@aol.com (office).

BUTLER, Hon. Richard William, AC, DUniv; Australian diplomatist; b. 13 May 1942; s. of H.H. Butler; m. Barbara Evans 1974; three s. one d.; ed Randwick Boys High School, Univ. of Sydney, Australian Nat. Univ.; Second Sec., Embassy and Perm. Mission to UN, Deputy Perm. Rep. IAEA, Vienna 1966–69; First Sec. Mission to UN, New York 1970–73; Deputy High Commr, Singapore, 1975–76; Prin. Pvt. Sec. to Leader of Opposition 1976–77; Counsellor, Bonn Embassy 1978–81; Minister-Del. to OECD, Paris, Amb. and Perm. Rep. to UN (Disarmament Matters), Geneva 1983–88; Amb. to Thailand 1989–92; Amb. and Perm. Rep. to Supreme Nat. Council of Cambodia 1991–92; Amb. and Perm. Rep. to UN, New York 1992–97; Exec. Chair. UN Special Comm. on Iraqi Disarmament 1997–99; Diplomat-in-Residence, Council on Foreign Relations, New York 1999–; Gov. of Tasmania 2003–04 (resgnd). *Publications:* The Greatest Threat 2000, Saddam Defiant 2000. *Leisure interests:* art, music, rugby. *Address:* c/o Government House, Hobart, Tasmania 7000, Australia.

BUTLER, William Elliott, MA, JD, LLM, PhD, LLD, FRSA, FSA; American/ British legal scholar and academic; *John Edward Fowler Distinguished Professor of Law, Dickinson School of Law, Pennsylvania State University;* b. 20 Oct. 1939, Minneapolis, Minn.; s. of the late William E. Butler and of Maxine Swan Elmberg; m. 1st Darlene Johnson (died 1989); two s.; m. 2nd Maryann Gashi 1991; ed Hibbing Jr Coll., The American Univ., Harvard Law School, Russian Acad. of Sciences, Johns Hopkins School of Advanced Int. Studies, Univ. of London; Research Asst, Washington Center for Foreign Policy Research, Johns Hopkins Univ. 1966–68; Research Assoc. in Law and Assoc., Russian Research Center, Harvard Univ. 1968–70; Reader in Comparative Law, Univ. of London 1970–76, Prof. of Comparative Law 1976–2005, Dean, Faculty of Laws 1988–90, Prof. Emer. 2005–; mem. Council, School of Slavonic and E European Studies 1973–93; Dean, Faculty of Laws, Univ. Coll. London 1977–79, Vice-Dean 1979–81; Dir Vinogradoff Inst. Univ. Coll. London 1982–2005; Dean, Faculty of Law and Speranskii Prof. of Int. and Comparative Law, Moscow Higher School of Social and Econ. Sciences 1995–; John Edward Fowler Distinguished Prof. of Law, Dickinson School of Law, Pa State Univ. 2005–, mem. Faculty Council, School of Int. Affairs 2007–, mem. Senate, Pa State Univ. 2008–(2012); Professorial Research Assoc., SOAS, Univ. of London 2006–; Pnr, White & Case 1994–96, Price Waterhouse Coopers 1997–2001; Sr Pnr, Phoenix Law Assocs, Moscow 2002–; Special Counsel, Comm. on Econ. Reform, USSR Council of Ministers 1989–91; consultant, IBRD; adviser and consultant, Russian Fed., Belarus, Ukraine, Kyrgyzstan, Repub. of Kazakhstan, Repub. of Tajikistan, Repub. of Uzbekistan; Legal Adviser, UN Office on Drugs and Crime (UNODC) 2006–08; Visiting Scholar, Moscow State Univ. 1972, 1980, Mongolian State Univ. 1979, Inst. of State and Law, USSR Acad. of Sciences 1976, 1981, 1983, 1984, 1988, Harvard Law School 1982; Visiting Prof., New York Univ. Law School 1978, Ritsumeikan Univ. 1985, Harvard Law School 1986–87, Washington and Lee Univ. 2005; mem. Russian Court of Int. Commercial Arbitration 1995–, Expert Council on Reform of Corp. Man., Ministry of Econ. Devt and Trade of Russian Fed. 2004–06; Academician, Russian Acad. of Natural Sciences, Nat. Acad. of Sciences of Ukraine, Int. Acad. of the Book and Art of the Book, Russian Acad. of Legal Sciences; mem. Sr Common Room, St Antony's Coll., Oxford 2004–; mem. Exec. Council, Russian Asscn of Maritime Law 2008–; G.I.Tunkin Medal 2003, Ivan Fedorov Medal 2004, FISAE

Certificate of Honour. *Publications:* more than 900 books, articles, reviews and translations including Soviet Law 1983, The Non-Use of Force in Int. Law 1989, Perestroika and Int. Law 1990, The History of Int. Law in Russia 1647–1917 1990, Foreign Investment Legislation in the Republics of the Former Soviet Union 1993, Russian Law of Treaties 1997, Russian Legal Texts 1998, Russian Law 1999, 2003, 2009, Constitutional Foundations of the CIS Countries 2000, American Bookplates 2000, Russian Company Law 2000, Russian-English Legal Dictionary 2001, Foreign Investment Laws in the CIS 2002, The Law of Treaties in Russia and the CIS 2002, Civil Code of the Russian Fed. 2003, Russian Co. and Commercial Law 2003, Narcotics and HIV in Russia 2005, Russian Intellectual Property Law (fourth edn) 2005, Russian Foreign Relations and Investment Law 2006, Russian Legal Biography 2007 (with V. A. Tomsinov), Civil Code of Uzbekistan 2007, Civil Code of Kazakhstan 2008, Russia and the Law of Nations in Historical Perspective 2009. *Leisure interests:* book collecting and bookplate collecting. *Address:* 155 Mount Rock Road, Newville, PA 17241 (home); Dickinson School of Law, Penn State University, 150 South College Street, Carlisle, PA 17013, USA (office). *Telephone:* (717) 776-7359 (home); (717) 240-5227 (office). *Fax:* (717) 240-5126 (office). *E-mail:* webakademik@aol.com (home); web15@psu.edu (office). *Website:* www.dsl.psu.edu/faculty/butler (office).

BUTLER, William Joseph; American lawyer; *President, American Association of The International Commission of Jurists;* b. 22 March 1924, Brighton, Mass; s. of Patrick L. Butler and Delia Conley; m. Jane Hays 1945; one s. one d.; ed Harvard Univ. and New York Univ. School of Law; mem. New York Bar 1950; Assoc. Hays, St John, Abramson & Schulman, New York 1949–53; partner Butler, Jablow & Geller, New York 1953–; special counsel American Civil Liberties Union; Attorney for petitioner in Engel v. Vitale (school prayer case, landmark case in history of US constitutional law), US Supreme Court 1962; Lecturer, Practising Law Inst. 1966; Sec., Dir, Cen. Counsel, Walco Nat. Corpn, FAO Schwarz, New York; mem. Comm. on Urban Affairs, American Jewish Congress 1965–70; mem. Bd of Dirs New York Civil Liberties Union, Int. League for Rights of Man; mem. Exec. Cttee League to Abolish Capital Punishment; mem. Standing Cttee on Human Rights, World Peace Through Law Center, Geneva; Chair. Advisory Cttee Morgan Inst. for Human Rights; mem. Int. Comm. of Jurists (Pres. American Asscn for the Int. Comm. of Jurists), American Bar Asscn, Council on Foreign Relations, Int. Law Asscn, American Soc. of Int. Law, etc.; int. legal observer, Int. Human Rights Org. at trials in Greece, Burundi, Iran, Nicaragua, S Korea, Philippines, Uruguay, Israel, at Int. Criminal Tribunal for fmr Yugoslavia, The Hague 1996–; Special Regional Adviser for N America on Human Rights to the UN High Comm. for Human Rights 1998; originator of Princeton Project on Universal Jurisdiction; Hon. DHumLitt (Cincinnati) 1988. *Publications include:* Human Rights and the Legal System in Iran 1976, The Decline of Democracy in the Philippines 1977, Human Rights in United States and United Kingdom Foreign Policy 1977, Guatemala, a New Beginning 1987, Palau: A Challenge to the Rule of Law in Micronesia 1988, The New South Africa – The Dawn of Democracy 1994; contribs to professional journals. *Address:* 280 Madison Avenue, New York, NY 10016 (office); 24 E 10th Street, New York, NY 10003, USA. *E-mail:* wjb@iopener.net (office). *Website:* www.law.uc.edu/archives/index.html (office).

BUTLER, William T., BA, MD; American immunologist, academic, university administrator and petrochemical industry executive; ed Western Reserve Univ., Oberlin Coll.; served as Chief Clinical Assoc., Lab. of Clinical Medicine, Nat. Inst. of Allergy and Infectious Diseases, Washington, DC; joined faculty Baylor Coll. of Medicine, Houston 1966, served in several positions including Prof. of Internal Medicine and Microbiology and Immunology, Assoc. Dean, Dean of Admissions, Exec. Vice Pres. and Dean 1976–79, Pres. and Pres. 1979–96, Chancellor 1996–2004, Chancellor Emer. 2004–; mem. Bd of Dirs Lyondell Chemical Co., Houston 1989–2007, Chair. 1997–2007 (retd); mem. Bd of Dirs Browing-Ferris Industries, C. R. Bard Inc; mem. Inst. of Medicine. *Publications:* numerous publications in the fields of immunology, infectious disease and medical admin. *Address:* c/o Lyondell Chemical Company, 1221 McKinney Street, Suite 700, Houston, TX 77010, USA (office).

BUTLER OF BROCKWELL, Baron (Life Peer), cr. 1998, of Herne Hill in the London Borough of Lambeth; **Frederick Edward Robin Butler,** KG, GCB, CVO, PC; British public servant; b. 3 Jan. 1938, Poole, Dorset; s. of the late Bernard Butler and Nora Butler (née Jones); m. Gillian Lois Galley 1962; one s. two d.; ed Harrow School, University Coll., Oxford; with HM Treasury 1961–69, Pvt. Sec. to the Financial Sec. 1964–65, Sec. Budget Cttee 1965–69; seconded to Cabinet Office as mem. Cen. Policy Review Staff 1971–72; Pvt. Sec. to Prime Minister 1972–74, 1974–75, 1982–85; Head of General Expenditure Policy Group 1977–80; Principal Establishment Officer, HM Treasury 1980–82; Second Perm. Sec., Public Services 1985–87; Sec. to Cabinet and Head of Home Civil Service 1988–98; Master Univ. Coll., Oxford 1998–2008; Chair. Cttee to review intelligence on weapons of mass destruction 2004; Chair. of Govs Dulwich Coll. 1997–2003; Gov. Harrow School 1975–91 (Chair. of Govs 1985–91); mem. Royal Comm. for Lords' Reform 1999; Hon. Fellow, Univ. Coll. Oxford 1989; Hon. DSc (Cranfield) 1994; Hon. LLD (Exeter) 1998; Hon. DCL (London) 1999. *Leisure interests:* competitive games, opera. *Address:* House of Lords, London, SW1A 0PW, England (office). *E-mail:* lord.butler@univ.ox.ac.uk. *Website:* www.univ.ox.ac.uk.

BUTLER-SLOSS, Baroness (Life Peer), cr. 2006, of Marsh Green in the County of Devon; **(Ann) Elizabeth (Oldfield) Butler-Sloss,** DBE, GBE, PC, FRSM; British judge; b. 10 Aug. 1933; d. of the late Sir Cecil Havers and Enid Snelling; m. Joseph William Alexander Butler-Sloss 1958; two s. one d.; ed Wycombe Abbey School; called to Bar, Inner Temple 1955, Bencher 1979; contested Lambeth, Vauxhall as Conservative Cand. 1959; practising barrister 1955–70; Registrar, Prin. Registry of Probate, later Family Div. 1970–79;

Judge, High Court of Justice, Family Div. 1979–87; Lord Justice of Appeal 1988–99; Pres. of Family Div. 1999–2005; Chair. Crown Appointments Comm. 2002–; Lord of Appeal 2006–; a Vice-Pres. Medico-Legal Soc.; Chair. Cleveland Child Abuse Inquiry 1987–88, Advisory Council, St Paul's Cathedral; Pres. Honiton Agricultural Show 1985–86; Treas. Inner Temple 1998; mem. Judicial Studies Bd 1985–89; Hon. Fellow St Hilda's Coll., Oxford 1988, Visiting Fellow 2001–; Fellow, Kings Coll., London 1991, mem. Council 1992–98; Chancellor Univ. of W of England 1993–; Hon. FRCP; Hon. FRCPsych; Hon. FRCPaed; Hon. LLD (Hull) 1989, (Bristol) 1991, (Keele) 1991, (Brunel) 1992, (Exeter) 1992, (Manchester) 1995, (Cambridge) 2000, (Greenwich) 2000, (East Anglia) 2001, (Liverpool) 2001, (Ulster) 2004, (London) 2004; Hon. DLit (Loughborough Univ. of Tech.) 1993; Hon. DUniv (Univ. of Cen. England) 1994. *Publications:* Jt Ed. Phipson on Evidence (10th edn), Corpe on Road Haulage (2nd edn), fmr Ed. Supreme Court Practice 1976, 1976. *Address:* House of Lords, London, SW1A 0PW, England. *Telephone:* (20) 7219-4044.

BUTLER-WHEELHOUSE, Keith Oliver, BComm; British business executive; b. 29 March 1946, Walsall; s. of the late Kenneth Butler-Wheelhouse and May Butler-Wheelhouse; m. Pamela Anne Bosworth Smith 1973; two s.; ed Technicon, Port Elizabeth, Univ. of Witwatersrand and Univ. of Cape Town Grad. School of Business; Ford Motor Co. S Africa 1965–85; Dir of Tech. Operations, Gen. Motors S Africa 1985–86; Chair. and CEO Delta Motor Corpn 1987–92; Pres. and CEO Saab Automobile 1992–96; Chief Exec. Smiths Group (fmrly Smiths Industries) PLC 1996–2007. *Leisure interests:* golf, tennis, shooting, skiing, keeping fit. *Address:* c/o Smiths Group PLC, 765 Finchley Road, London, NW11 8DS, England (office).

BUTLIN, Martin Richard Fletcher, CBE, MA, DLit, FBA; British museum curator and art historian; b. 7 June 1929, Birmingham; s. of K. R. Butlin and Helen M. Butlin (née Fletcher); m. Frances C. Chodzko 1969; ed Trinity Coll., Cambridge and Courtauld Inst. of Art., Univ. of London; Asst Keeper, Tate Gallery, London 1955–67, Keeper of the Historic British Collection 1967–89; consultant to Christie's 1989–; Mitchell Prize (jtly) 1978. *Publications:* A Catalogue of the Works of William Blake in the Tate Gallery 1957, 1971, 1990, Samuel Palmer's Sketchbook of 1824 1962, Turner Watercolours 1962, Turner (with Sir John Rothenstein) 1964, Tate Gallery Catalogues: The Modern British Paintings, Drawings and Sculpture (with Mary Chamot and Dennis Farr) 1964, The Later Works of J. M. W. Turner 1965, William Blake 1966, The Blake-Varley Sketchbook of 1819 1969, The Paintings of J. M. W. Turner (with E. Joll) 1977, 1984, The Paintings and Drawings of William Blake 1981, Aspects of British Painting 1550–1800 1988, Turner at Petworth (with Mollie Luther and Ian Warrell) 1989, The Oxford Companion to J. M. W. Turner ed. (with Evelyn Joll and Luke Herrmann) 2001; catalogues, articles, reviews etc. *Leisure interests:* music, travel. *Address:* 74C Eccleston Square, London, SW1V 1PJ, England (home).

BUTOR, Michel; French writer and lecturer; b. 14 Sept. 1926, Mons-en-Baroeul, Nord; s. of Emile Butor and Anne Brajeux; m. Marie-Josephe Mas 1958; four d.; ed Univ. of Paris; teacher at Sens, France 1950, Minieh, Egypt 1950–51, Manchester, England 1951–53, Salonica, Greece 1954–55, Geneva, Switzerland 1956–57; Visiting Prof. Bryn Mawr and Middlebury, USA 1960, Buffalo, USA 1962, Evanston, USA 1965, Albuquerque, USA 1969–70, 1973–74, Nice and Geneva 1974–75; Assoc. Prof. Vincennes 1969, Nice 1970–73; Prof. of Modern French Literature, Geneva 1975–91; Reader Éditions Gallimard 1958–; Chevalier, Ordre nat. du Mérite, Ordre des Arts et des Lettres; Hon. PhD (Univ. of Mainz) 1995, (Univ. of Massachusetts) 1999, (Univ. of Thessaloniki) 2001; Prix Felix Féneon 1957, Prix Renaudot 1957, Grand prix de la critique littéraire 1960. *Publications:* novels: Passage de Milan 1954, L'emploi du temps 1956, La modification 1957, Degrés 1960, Intervalle 1973; essays: Le Génie du lieu 1958, Répertoire 1960, Histoire extraordinaire 1961, Mobile 1962, Réseau aérien 1963, Description de San Marco 1963, Les oeuvres d'art imaginaires chez Proust 1964, Répertoire II 1964, Portrait de l'artiste en jeune singe 1967, Répertoire III 1968, Essais sur les essais 1968, Les mots dans la peinture 1969, La rose des vents 1970, Le génie du lieu II 1971, Dialogue avec 33 variations de L. van Beethoven 1971, Répertoire IV 1974, Matière de rêves 1975, Second sous-sol 1976, Troisième dessous 1977, Boomerang 1978, Quadruple Fond 1981, Répertoire V 1982; poetry: Illustrations 1964, 6,801.000 litres d'eau par second 1965, Illustrations II 1969, Travaux d'approche 1972, Illustrations III 1973, Illustrations IV 1976, Envois 1980, Brassée d'Avril 1982, Exprès 1983, Herbier Lunaire 1984, Mille et un plis 1985, Le Retour du Boomerang 1988, Improvisations sur Flaubert 1991, Patience, Collation 1991, Transit A, Transit B 1993, Improvisations sur Michael Butor 1994, L'Utilité Poétique 1995, Le Japon depuis la France, un rêve à l'ancre 1995, Curriculum Vitae 1996 (jtly), Gyroscope 1996, Ici et là 1997, Improvisations sur Balzac 1998, Entretiens 1999, M. Butor par M. Butor 2003, Anthologie nomade 2004, L'Horticulteur itinérant 2004, Octogénaire 2006, Seize Lustres 2006, Oeuvres complètes I–IV 2006, V–VI 2007, VII–VIII 2008. *Leisure interest:* teaching. *Address:* à l'Ecart, 216 Place de l'Eglise, 74380 Lucinges, France.

BÚTORA, Martin; Slovak diplomatist, sociologist and author; b. 1944; m.; four c.; Ed.-in-Chief, Bratislava student paper 1966–67, Deputy Ed.-in-Chief 1969; Ed. Kulturny Zivot 1968; Research Asst, Research Inst of Labor and Social Studies 1971–77; sociologist and psychotherapist at outpatient clinic for alcohol and drug addiction, Bratislava 1978; freelance writer and researcher 1988–; Co-founder and Leader Public Against Violence; Adviser to Pres. Havel on Human Rights Issues and Dir Human Rights Section, Office of Pres. of Fed. Repub. 1990–92; Sr Assoc. mem. St Anthony's Coll. 1993; taught at Faculty of Social Sciences, Charles Univ., Prague and Trnava Univ. 1991–98; Amb. to USA 1999–2003; unsuccessful candidate for presidency 2004; German Marshall Fund Fellow 1993, Exec. Educ. Fellow, Woodrow Wilson School of Public and Int. Affairs 1993. *Publications include:* numerous books, journals and magazine articles on post-communist transition, civil society, NGOs, political behaviour, foreign policy issues, ethnicity, nationalism and anti-Semitism. *Address:* c/o Ministry of Foreign Affairs, Hlboká cesta 2, 833 36, Bratislava, Slovakia (office).

BUTROS, Albert Jamil, PhD; Jordanian academic and diplomatist; *Professor Emeritus of English, University of Jordan;* b. 25 March 1934, Jerusalem; s. of Jamil Issa Butros and Virginie Antoine Butros (née Albina); m. Ida Maria Albina 1962; four d.; ed Univs of London and Exeter, UK, Columbia Univ., USA; taught English and Math. in two pvt. schools, Amman 1950–55; instructor, Teachers' Coll., Amman 1958–60; lecturer in English, Hunter Coll., CUNY 1961; Instructor, Miami Univ., Oxford, Ohio 1962–63; Asst Prof. of English, Univ. of Jordan 1963–65, Assoc. Prof. 1965–67, Prof. 1967–79, Acting Chair. Dept of English 1964–67, Chair. 1967–73, 1974–76, Dean Research and Graduate Studies 1973–76, Prof. of English 1985–2004, Prof. Emer. 2004–; Visiting Prof. of English, Ohio Wesleyan Univ., Delaware, Ohio 1971–72, Jordan Univ. for Women, Amman 1995–96; Dir-Gen. and Pres. Royal Scientific Soc., Amman 1976–84; Sr Research Fellow, Int. Devt Research Centre, Ottawa, Canada 1983–84, Gov. 1986–98; Special Adviser to HRH Crown Prince Hassan of Jordan 1984–85; Amb. to UK 1987–91, (also accred to Ireland 1988–91, to Iceland 1990–91); mem. Bd of Trustees, Philadelphia Univ., Amman 1995–; Rapporteur Cttee on the Jordan Incentive State Prize in Trans. 2001, Cttee on Selection for the Shoman Foundation Prize for Young Arab scholars in the Humanities and Social Sciences 2002, Cttee on Selection of Outstanding Researchers in Jordan 2004; Fellow, World Acad. of Art and Science 1986–; mem., Int. Advisory Bd Jordan Journal of Modern Languages and Literature 2007–; Istiqlal Order, First Class 1987, Order of Merit (Grande Ufficiale), Italy 1983, KStJ 1991. *Publications:* Leaders of Arab Thought 1969; several articles in learned journals; several translations including parts of Chaucer into Arabic; long paper on the English language and non-native writers of fiction in English, published 2004. *Leisure interests:* reading, writing, translation, art, world affairs. *Address:* Department of English, University of Jordan, Amman, Jordan (office). *Telephone:* (6) 535-5000 (office); (6) 515-7870 (home). *Fax:* (6) 535-5511 (office); (6) 515-7870 (home). *E-mail:* butros@nol.com.jo (home). *Website:* www.ju.edu.jo (office).

BUTT, Michael Acton, MA, MBA; British business executive; *Chairman, Axis Capital Holdings Limited;* b. 25 May 1942, Thruxton; s. of Leslie Acton Kingsford Butt and Mina Gascoigne Butt; m. 1st Diana Lorraine Brook 1964; two s.; m. 2nd Zoe Benson 1986; ed Rugby School, Magdalen Coll., Oxford and Inst. Européen d'Administration des Affaires (INSEAD), France; joined Bland Welch Group 1964; Dir Bland Payne Holdings 1970; Chair. Sedgwick Ltd 1983–87; Deputy Chair. Sedgwick Group PLC 1985–87; Chair. and CEO Eagle Star Holdings PLC 1987–91; Chair. and CEO Eagle Star Insurance Co. 1987–91; Dir BAT Industries PLC 1987–91, Marceau Investissements SA (France) 1987–94; Dir Phoenix Int. (Bermuda) 1992–97, Bank of N. T. Butterfield & Son Ltd (Bermuda) 1996–2002; Pres. and CEO Mid Ocean Ltd 1993–98, Chair. and CEO Mid Ocean Reinsurance Co. Ltd 1993–98; Dir Exel Capital Ltd 1998–99, XL Capital Ltd 1998–2002; Chair. Axis Capital Holdings Ltd 2002–; Dir Istituto Nazionale delle Assicurazioni (INA) 1994–97; Bd mem. and mem. Int. Advisory Council, INSEAD 1982–. *Leisure interests:* travel, tennis, opera, reading, family, the European movt. *Address:* Axis Capital Holdings Ltd, Axis House, 92 Pitts Bay Road, Pembroke, HM 08, Bermuda (office); Leamington House, 50 Harrington Sound Road, Hamilton Parish, CR O4, Bermuda (home). *Telephone:* 496-2600 (office); 293-1378 (home). *Fax:* 405-2720 (office); 293-8511 (home). *E-mail:* michael.butt@axis.bm (office).

BUTT, Noor Mohammed, PhD, DSc; Pakistani nuclear solid state physicist (retd); *Chairman, Pakistan Science Foundation;* b. 3 June 1936, Sialkot City; s. of the late Ferozuddin Butt and Sardar Begum; m. Gulzar Butt; two s. one d.; ed Punjab Univ., Univ. of Birmingham, UK; fmrly Chief Scientist and Dir Gen., Pakistan Inst. of Nuclear Science and Tech.; fmr Vice-Pres. Crystallography Soc. of Pakistan; Pres. Pakistan Nuclear Soc. 1995–97; Treas. Pakistan Acad. of Sciences 1994–98; Chair. Pakistan Science Foundation 2005–; Visiting Scientist, AERE, Harwell, UK, Univ. of Oxford, ICTP, Trieste, Reactor Inst., Stockholm, Sweden; Chair Nat. Comm. on Nano-Science and Tech.; (NCNST); IAEA nuclear energy consultant; Fellow, Islamic Acad. of Sciences; Open Gold Medal in Physical Sciences, Pakistan Acad. of Sciences 1990, Sitara-I-Imtiaz 1991, 8th Kharazmi Prize (jtly) (Iran) 1995, Scientist Emer., PAEC, Life Title 1996. *Radio and television:* occasional appearances on Pakistan radio and TV. *Publications:* Waves and Oscillations (text book) 1973, International Seminar on Solid State Physics (ed.) 1974, CTBT and its Implications (ed.) 1996; ed. of five books; more than 140 research papers on nuclear solid state physics; journals and conf. proceedings. *Leisure interest:* photography, playing with grandchildren. *Address:* Pakistan Science Foundation, 1 Constitution Avenue, Islamabad, Pakistan (office); H: 155, St 15, Sector E-7, Islamabad (home). *Telephone:* (51) 9204522 (office); (51) 2652242 (home). *Fax:* (51) 9202468 (office). *E-mail:* nmbutt36@yahoo.com (office). *Website:* www.psf.gov.pk.

BUTTERWORTH, David, Eur Ing, BSc (Eng), FREng, FIChemE, FRSA; British chemical engineer; *General Secretary, Aluminium Plate-Fin Heat Exchanger Manufacturers Association;* b. 24 Oct. 1943; m. Pauline Morgan 1966; one s.; ed Univ. Coll. London; Visiting Engineer, MIT, USA 1976–77; Group Leader, UKAEA 1977–89; Man. Dir Heat Transfer and Fluid Flow Service 1989–95, Sr consultant in heat transfer 1995–; Visiting Prof. Bristol Univ. 1993–, Cranfield Univ. 1995–2002, Aston Univ., Birmingham 1996–2001; Pres. UK Heat Transfer Soc. 1988–89; Gen. Sec. Aluminium Plate-Fin Heat Exchanger Mfrs Assen 1995–; AIChE Kern Award 1986. *Publications:* Introduction to Heat Transfer 1977, Two-Phase Flow and Heat Transfer 1977 (Russian trans. 1980), Design and Operation of Heat Exchangers (co-ed.) 1992, New Developments in Heat Exchangers (co-ed.). *Leisure interests:* landscape painting, cooking. *Address:* 29 Clevelands, Abingdon, Oxon., OX14 2EQ, England. *Telephone:* (1235) 525955. *Fax:* (1235) 200906. *E-mail:* davebutterworth@alpema.org (office); davebutterworth@aol.com (home). *Website:* www.alpema.org (office); members.aol.com/davebutterworth (home).

BUTTERWORTH, Ian, CBE, FRS; British physicist and academic; *Professor Emeritus of Physics, Imperial College London;* b. 3 Dec. 1930, Tottington; s. of Harry Butterworth and Beatrice Butterworth; m. Mary Therese Gough, 1964; one d.; ed Bolton County Grammar School, Univ. of Manchester; Scientific Officer, then Sr Scientific Officer UKAEA, Harwell AERE 1954–58; Lecturer in Physics, Imperial Coll., Univ. of London 1958–64, Sr Lecturer 1965–68, Head High Energy Nuclear Physics Group, Univ. Prof. of Physics 1971–91, Head of Physics Dept 1980–83, Prof. Emer. 1991–; Visiting Physicist Lawrence Berkeley Lab., Univ. of Calif. 1964–65; Sr Prin. Scientific Officer Rutherford Lab. 1968–71; Research Dir CERN (on leave of absence from Imperial Coll.) 1983–86; Prin. Queen Mary and Westfield Coll. 1989–91 (of Queen Mary Coll. 1986–89); Pro-Vice-Chancellor for European Affairs, Univ. of London 1989–91; Chair. IOP Publs Ltd 1993–97; Vice-Pres. Inst. of Physics 1993–97; mem. Academia Europaea 1989–, Vice-Pres. 1997–2004; Fellow, Imperial Coll. 1988, Sr Research Fellow 1991–; Dr hc (Soka Univ.) 1989. *Publications:* numerous papers on particle physics in scientific journals. *Leisure interest:* history of art. *Address:* Blackett Laboratory, Imperial College, Prince Consort Road, London, SW7 2BZ (office); 1 Paramount Court, University Street, London, WC1E 6JP, England (home). *Telephone:* (20) 7594-7525 (office). *E-mail:* i.butterworth@imperial.ac.uk (office). *Website:* www.hep.ph.ic.ac.uk (office).

BUTTIGLIONE, Rocco; Italian academic and politician; *Vice-President, Camera dei Deputati;* b. 16 June 1948, Gallipoli, Lecce; m.; four d.; fmr Acting Chancellor, Int. Acad. of Philosophy, Liechtenstein; Prof. of Political Science, Saint Pius V Univ., Rome; Minister of European Union Affairs 2001–05, of Cultural Assets and Activities 2005–06; Sec.-Gen. Partito Popolare Italiano 1994–95, Cristiani Democratici Uniti 1995–2002; Pres. Unione dei Democratici Cristiani e di Centro (UDC) 2002–; Vice-Pres. Camera dei Deputati 2008–; Dr hc (Univ. Cattolica di Lublino, Univ. Francisco Marroquin). *Address:* Camera dei Deputati, Palazzo di Montecitorio, Rome (office); Unione dei Democratici Cristiani e di Centro, Via dei Due Macelli 66, 00182 Rome, Italy (office). *Telephone:* (06) 67603316 (office); (06) 69791001 (office). *Fax:* (06) 6791574 (office). *E-mail:* dlwebmast@camera.it (office); info@udc-italia.it (office). *Website:* www.camera.it (office); www.udc-italia.it (office).

BÜTTNER LIMPRICH, José Ernesto, MA; Paraguayan politician, banker and international organization executive; ed Pontificia Universidad Católica, Santiago de Chile; fmr Vice-Minister of Economy and Integration; fmr Alt. Gov. for Paraguay, IMF; Dir Mercosur Secr. 2006–08. *Address:* c/o Mercosur Secretariat, Edificio Mercosur, Dr Luis Piera 1992 piso 1, CP 11.200, Montevideo, Uruguay. *Telephone:* (2) 412-9024.

BUXTON, Andrew Robert Fowell, CMG, FIB; British banker; b. 5 April 1939, London; m. Jane Margery Grant 1965; two d.; ed Winchester Coll. and Pembroke Coll., Oxford; joined Barclays Bank Ltd 1963; Gen. Man. Barclays Bank PLC 1980, CEO 1992–93, Chair. 1993–99; Deputy Chair. (non-exec.) Xansa PLC 1999–; Chair. Heart of the City; Pres. British Bankers' Asscn 1997–2002; mem. Bd of Dirs Capitaland Ltd; mem. Court, Bank of England 1997–2001, Guild of Int. Bankers 2001, Panel on Takeovers and Mergers 2001; Gov. Imperial Coll. of Science and Technology; Visiting Prof., City Univ.; Hon. DSc (City). *Address:* c/o Board of Directors, Xansa PLC, 420 Thames Valley Park Drive, Thames Valley Park, Reading, Berks., RG6 1PU, England. *Telephone:* (8702) 416181. *Fax:* (8702) 426282. *E-mail:* information@xansa.com. *Website:* www.xansa.com.

BUYOYA, Maj. Pierre; Burundian politician and fmr head of state; *President, Foundation for Unity, Peace and Democracy;* b. 24 Nov. 1949, Mutangaro, Rutovu; m. Sophie Buyoya 1978; one s. three d.; ed Royal Mil. Acad., Brussels, staff coll. in France, war coll. in Germany; degree in social science and mil. affairs; mem. Cen. Cttee UPRONA Party 1979–87; fmr COO Ministry of Nat. Defence; led mil. coup against fmr Pres. Bagaza Sept. 1987; Pres. of Third Repub. and Minister of Nat. Defence 1987–92; Chair. Mil. Cttee for Nat. Salvation 1987–93; Pres. Foundation for Unity, Peace and Democracy 1994–; Pres. of Burundi 1987–93, 1996–2003; mem. Senate 2003–. *Publications:* Building Peace in Burundi – Mission Impossible 1998. *Leisure interests:* reading, football, swimming. *Address:* BP 2006, Bujumbura, Burundi (office). *Telephone:* (2) 20796 (office); (2) 13208 (home). *Fax:* (2) 20816 (office). *E-mail:* fupd2003@yahoo.fr (office).

BUYSSE, Baron Paul; Belgian business executive; *Chairman, NV Bekaert SA;* b. 17 March 1945, Antwerp; m.; five c.; various marketing and sales functions, Ford Motor Co. 1966–76; Gen. Man. Car Sales & Marketing, Deputy Man. Dir British Leyland Belgium NV 1976–79, Exec. Dir Tenneco Belgium 1980–84, Man. Dir J.I. Case Benelux 1980–84, Gen. Man. Europe N, J.I. Case, Int. Harvester and Poclain 1984–88; Group Man. Dir Hansen Transmissions Int. 1988; Group Chief Exec. BTR Automotive & Eng Group (London) 1989, Group Chief Exec. BTR Eng and Dunlop Overseas 1991, Exec. Dir BTR PLC 1992–97; CEO Vickers PLC 1998–2000; Chair. NV Bekaert SA 2000–; Dir (non-exec.) Bd of Generale Bank, Censor Nat. Bank of Belgium; Chair., mem. Exec. Cttee and Dir King Baudouin Foundation; Chair. Prince Filip Foundation; Hon. Pres. Antwerp Chamber of Commerce & Industry; Hon. Dean of Labour; Emer. Hon. Dean of Labour 2003, Hon. Companion, Most Distinguished Order of St Michael and St George 2005; Kt Order of Leopold 1988, Officer Order of Orange-Nassau 1994, Officier Order nat. du mérite 1996, CBE 1997, Commdr in Order of Leopold II 2001, Grand Officer, Order of Leopold II 2005; UNIZO Prize 2003. *Leisure interests:* golf, reading. *Address:* NV Bekaert SA, Diamant Building, Bd. A. Reyers 80, 1030 Brussels, Belgium (office). *Telephone:* (2) 706-84-54 (office). *Fax:* (2) 706-84-60 (office). *E-mail:* paul.buysse@bekaert.com (office). *Website:* www.bekaert.com (office).

BÜYÜKANIT, Gen. (Mehmet) Yaşar; Turkish army officer; *Commander of the Turkish Armed Forces;* b. 1 Sept. 1940, Istanbul; m. Filiz Büyükanit; one d.; ed Mil. Acad., Infantry School, Army Staff Coll., NATO Defence Coll.; served in different units of Land Forces as Platoon and Commando Co. Commdr 1963–70, then numerous leadership positions including Chief of Operations, 6th Infantry Div., Instructor, Army Staff Coll., Intelligence Div. Basic Intelligence Br. Forces and Systems Section Chief, Supreme HQ Allied Powers Europe (SHAPE), Mons, Belgium, Section then Br. Chief of Gen.-Adm. Br. at Turkish Gen. Staff (TGS) HQ, Commdr of Kuleli Mil. High School and of Presidential Guard Regiment; 2nd Armored Brigade Commdr then Chief of Intelligence Dept, AFSOUTH HQ, Naples, Italy; Sec. Gen. of Turkish Gen. Staff then Supt Turkish Army Acad. 1992–96; 7th Army Corps Commdr 1996–98; Chief of Operations TGS 1998–2000, Deputy Chief 2000–03, Commdr of First Army 2003–04; Commdr Turkish Land Forces 2004-06; Commdr Turkish Armed Forces 2006–; Turkish Armed Forces (TAF) Medal of Distinguished Service, TAF Medal of Distinguished Courage and Self-Sacrifice, TAF Medal of Honor, Italian Medal of Honor, USA Legion of Merit, Pakistani Nishan-ı Imtiaz. *Address:* Ministry of National Defence, Milli Savunma Bakanlığı, 06100 Ankara, Turkey (office). *Telephone:* (312) 4254596 (office). *Fax:* (312) 4184737 (office). *E-mail:* meb@meb.gov.tr (office). *Website:* www.msb.gov.tr (office); www.tsk.mil.tr (office).

BUZATU, Gheorghe, DHist; Romanian historian, research institute director and fmr politician; b. 6 June 1939, Sihlea, Vrancea Co., Romania; s. of Ilie Buzatu and Maria Buzatu; m. Constanţa Huiban 1970; one s.; ed Iaşi Univ.; Prof., Ovidius Univ., Constanţa; Prof., Univ. of Craiova, Dir Centre for the Study of Int. Relations; Scientific Researcher and Dir European History and Civilization Centre of Romanian Acad./Filiala Iaşi; Scientific Researcher, Pvt. Inst. for Romanian Studies Constantin C. Giurescu; Vice-Pres. Senate 2000–04; mem. Parl. Ass. of Council of Europe 2003–04; mem. editorial bds Europa XXI, Dosarele Istoriei, Anuarul Muzeului Marinei Române, Saeculum, Orizont XXI, Historia; Dr hc (Univ. of Constanţa); Prizes of the Romanian Acad. 1981, 1983, Prize of Flacăra magazine 1992, Prize of Revista de Istorie Militară 1993, 1995, 1996. *Publications include:* (in Romanian): Files of the World War 1939–45 1979, Romania and the International Oil Trusts up to 1929 1981, From the Secret History of World War II Vols I and II 1988, 1995, Romania and World War II: A Bibliography (with others) 1981, Titulescu and the Strategy of Peace (ed.) 1982, The Romanians in World History Vols 1–138 (ed.) 1986–2008, Marshal Antonescu versus History, Vols I–V (with others) 1990–2002, Forbidden History 1990, Romania with and without Antonescu 1991, The Romanians in the American Archives (ed.) 1992, The Trial of Corneliu Zelea Codreanu (with others) 1994, Geopolitics (Vol. I) (ed.) 1994, N Iorga, The Man and the Word (Vols I–III) 1971–99, Romania and the World War of 1939–1945 1995, The Romanians in the Kremlin's Archives 1995, How the Holocaust against the Romanians Began 1996, The Romanian Right (ed.) 1996, The Secret Archives, Vols I–II (with others) 1998, A History of Romanian Oil 1998, History of the Romanians 1918–1948 (with others) 1999, Stalin (with others) 1999, Romania and the Second World War (with others) 2002, Diplomacy and Romanian Diplomats (Vols 1–2) (with others) 2001–02, Marshal Antonescu at the Judgement of History 2003, Romania and the Great Powers 1939–1947 2003, History of the Romanian Senate (with others) 2004, Parliamentarian Discourses and Debates 1864–2004 (ed.) 2004, Hitler–Stalin–Antonescu I-III, 2005–08, Journal of Marshall Antonescu I 1940–1941, 2008 (ed.) 2005, Romania Under the Empire of Chaos (1939–1945) 2007; (in English): Anglo-Romanian Relations after 1821 (ed.) 1983, N Titulescu and Transylvania 1984, Romania's Options in June 1940 1995, The Oil Policy of Romania until 1918 2004, The Reconstruction of Europe (1944–1947): Romania and the Great Powers 2004, A History of Romanian Oil (Vols I-II) 2004–06; (in Spanish): Breve Historia de Rumania (with others) 1982. *Address:* European History and Civilization Centre of Romanian Academy, Aleea Mihail Sadoveanu, nr. 3, parter, Iaşi 6600 (office); Splai Bahlui, nr 20A, Bloc I/1, Apt 5, Iaşi 6600, Romania (home). *Telephone:* (32) 212441 (Iaşi) (office); (24) 1671448 (Constanţa) (office); (40) 633764 (home). *Fax:* (32) 212441 (Iaşi) (office). *E-mail:* stela_cheptea@yahoo.com (office).

BUZEK, Jerzy Karol; Polish politician and chemical engineer; b. 3 July 1940, Śmiłowice; m. Ludgarda Buzek; one d.; ed Silesian Tech. Univ., Gliwice; Scientific Researcher and Prof., Chemical Eng Inst., Polish Acad. of Sciences, Gliwice 1963–97, Prof. of Tech. Science 1997–; mem. Solidarity Trade Union 1980–; organizer of Solidarity underground structures in Silesia; activist of union's regional and nat. leadership; Chair. 1st, 4th, 5th and 6th Nat. Congresses of Dels; expert and co-author economic program of the Solidarity Election Action (AWS), Chair. Nat. Bd of Social Movt of Solidarity Election Action 1999–2001, Chair. AWS coalition 2001–; Deputy to Sejm (Parl.) 1997–2001; Prime Minister of Poland 1997–2001; Researcher and Pro-Rector Polonia Univ., Częstochowa 2002–; Prof., Mechanical Div., Tech. Univ. of Opole; mem. European Parl. (Silesian Voivodship constituency) (Group of the European People's Party—Christian Democrats and European Democrats) 2004–, mem. Cttee on Industry, Research and Energy, mem. Temp. Cttee on Climate Change, Substitute mem. Cttee on the Environment, Public Health and Food Safety, mem. Del. to EU-Ukraine Parl. Cooperation Cttee, Substitute mem. Del. for Relations with the Countries of Cen. America; f. Family Foundation together with his wife 1998; est. annual Pro Publico Bono Prize for the best national civic initiatives 1999; Dr hc (Seoul, Dortmund); Laureate, Grzegorz Palka Award 1998. *Publications include:* several dozen articles and monographs on mathematical modelling, desulphurization of exhaust gases and optimization of processes. *Leisure interests:* poetry, theatre, horse riding, tennis, yachting. *Address:* European Parliament, Bâtiment Altiero Spinelli,

05F243, 60 rue Wiertz, 1047 Brussels, Belgium (office). *Telephone:* (2) 284-56-31 (office). *E-mail:* jbuzek@europarl.eu.int (office). *Website:* www.buzek.pl (office).

BUZOIANU, Cătălina; Romanian stage director; b. 13 April 1938, Brăila; d. of Roman Buzoianu and Elena Buzoianu; m. Papil Panduru 1963; one s. one d.; ed Bucharest Theatrical and Cinematographic Art Inst.; started career at Nat. Theatre Iaşi with Le Malade Imaginaire (Molière) 1970; at Teatrul Tineretului (Youth Theatre) in Piatra Neamţ; Prin. Dir at Teatrul Mic, Bucharest 1978–85; has directed plays by Chekhov, Strindberg, Bulgakov, Anski, Pirandello, Shepard, Kleist and Goldoni; tours abroad and participation in int. festivals; Prof. Theatre and Cinema Institute; Dean of Theatre Dept, Theatre and Film Acad. 1990–; numerous awards including Salvo Randoni Award for whole career and especially for Pirandello performances, Italy 1995, Prix théâtre vivant, Radio France Int. 1994, Prize for Excellence, Int. Asscn of Critics, Romanian Section. *Publications:* Novele teatrale (essays), Meridiane (Ed.) 1987; articles and essays in various periodicals. *Address:* Bulandra Theatre, 1 Bd Schitu Măgureanu, 70626 Bucharest (office); C. A. Rosetti Str., Et.7, Ap.19, Sect. 1, Bucharest, Romania (home). *Telephone:* (1) 211-00-88 (home). *Fax:* (1) 312-28-97 (office).

BYAM SHAW, Nicholas Glencairn; British publisher; b. 28 March 1934, London; s. of the late Lt-Commdr David Byam Shaw and Clarita Pamela Clarke; m. 1st Joan Elliott 1956 (divorced 1973); two s. one d.; m. 2nd Suzanne Filer (née Rastello) 1974; m. 3rd Constance Mary Wilson (née Clarke) 1987; ed Royal Naval Coll., Dartmouth; served RN, retiring with rank of Lt 1951–56; on staff of Collins (printers and publrs), Sales Man. 1956–64; joined Macmillan Publrs Ltd as Sales Man. 1964, Deputy Man. Dir 1968, Man. Dir 1970–90, Chair. 1990–97, Deputy Chair. 1998–99; Dir St Martin's Press 1980–99 (Deputy Chair. 1997–99), Pan Books Ltd 1983–99 (Chair. 1986–99), Gruppe Georg von Hotzbrinck, Stuttgart, Germany 1996–99; mem. British Council Publrs' Advisory Cttee, Byam Shaw School Council. *Leisure interests:* travel, gardening, reading, music. *Address:* 9 Kensington Park Gardens, London, W11 3HB, England (home). *Telephone:* (20) 7221-4547 (home).

BYAMBASUREN, Dashiyn; Mongolian politician; *Director, Centre for Development Strategy and System Research;* b. 20 June 1942, Binder somon Dist, Hentii Prov.; s. of Lombyn Dash and Tsevegeen Perenlee; m. Sanjeen Dulamlkhand 1968; three s. three d.; ed Inst. of Economics and Statistics, Moscow, USSR; apptd Dept Chief, State Statistics Bd; Deputy Chair., then Chair. State Cttee for Prices and Standardization 1970–76; Chair. Construction and Repair Work Trust for Auto Transport 1984, Chief Research Officer, Research Inst. of Project Drafts for Automated Man. Systems 1985, Dir Manager Training Inst., Council of Ministers 1986; Deputy Chair. Council of Ministers 1989–90, First Deputy Chair. March–Sept. 1990, Prime Minister 1990–92; Pres. Mongolian Devt Foundation, World Mongolian Fed. 1993; fmr mem. Parl; Chair. Mongolian Democratic Renewal Party 1994–; Rector Inst. of Admin. and Man. 1998–2000; Rector Acad. of Man.; Dir Centre for Devt Strategy and System Research 2001–; Prof. and Academician, Nat. Acad. of Science. *Publications:* Orchlongiin hurd, Sergen mandakh ireedui, Uuriin javar. *Address:* GPO Box 248, Ulan Bator, Mongolia (home). *Telephone:* 324167 (office). *Fax:* 320090 (office). *E-mail:* byambasuren@cdssr.mn (office). *Website:* www.cdssr.mn (office).

BYATT, Dame Antonia Susan (A.S.), (Dame Antonia Duffy), DBE, BA, FRSL; British writer; b. 24 Aug. 1936, Sheffield, Yorkshire; d. of His Honour John F. Drabble, QC and the late Kathleen M. Bloor; sister of Margaret Drabble; m. 1st Ian Charles Rayner Byatt (q.v.) 1959 (divorced 1969); one s. (deceased) one d.; m. 2nd Peter John Duffy 1969; two d.; ed Sheffield High School, The Mount School, York, Newnham Coll., Cambridge, Bryn Mawr Coll., PA, USA and Somerville Coll., Oxford; Extra-Mural Lecturer, Univ. of London 1962–71; Lecturer in Literature, Cen. School of Art and Design 1965–69; Lecturer in English, Univ. Coll., London 1972–81, Sr Lecturer 1981–83; Assoc. Newnham Coll., Cambridge 1977–82; mem. BBC Social Effects of TV Advisory Group 1974–77; mem. Bd of Creative and Performing Arts 1985–87, Bd of British Council 1993–98; Kingman Cttee on English Language 1987–88; Man. Cttee Soc. of Authors 1984–88 (Chair. 1986–88); mem. Literature Advisory Panel of the British Council 1990–98; broadcaster, reviewer and judge of literary prizes; Fellow English Asscn; Hon. Fellow, Newnham Coll. Cambridge 1999, London Inst. 2000, Univ. Coll. London 2004, Somerville Coll. Oxford 2005; Chevalier, Ordre des Arts et Lettres 2003; Hon. DLitt (Bradford) 1987, (Durham, York) 1991, (Nottingham) 1992, (Liverpool) 1993, (Portsmouth) 1994, (London) 1995, (Cambridge) 1999, (Sheffield) 2000, (Kent at Canterbury) 2004, (Oxford) 2007, (Winchester) 2007; Premio Malaparte Award, Capri 1995, Toepfer Foundation Shakespeare Prize, Hamburg 2002. *Radio:* dramatisation of quartet of novels (BBC Radio) 2002. *Television:* profile on Scribbling (series, BBC 2) 2002. *Films:* Angels and Insects 1996, Possession 2002. *Publications:* fiction: The Shadow of the Sun 1964, The Game 1967, The Virgin in the Garden 1978, Still Life (PEN/Macmillan Silver Pen for Fiction 1986) 1985, Sugar and Other Stories 1987, Possession: A Romance (Booker Prize 1990, Irish Times-Aer Lingus Int. Fiction Prize 1990, Eurasian Regional Award of the Commonwealth Writers' Prize 1991) 1990 filmed 2002, Angels and Insects (novellas) 1992 filmed 1996, The Matisse Stories 1993, The Djinn in the Nightingale's Eye (Mythopoeic Fantasy Award 1998) 1994, Babel Tower 1996, Elementals, Stories of Fire and Ice 1998, The Biographer's Tale 2000, A Whistling Woman 2002, Little Black Book of Stories 2003, The Children's Book 2009; non-fiction: Degrees of Freedom: The Novels of Iris Murdoch (revised edn as Degrees of Freedom: The Early Novels of Iris Murdoch) 1965, Wordsworth and Coleridge in Their Time (revised edn as Unruly Times: Wordsworth and Coleridge in Their Time) 1970, Iris Murdoch 1976, Passions of the Mind (selected essays) 1991, Imagining Characters: Conversations About Women Writers (with Ignês Sodré) 1995, New Writing 4 (ed. with Alan Hollinghurst) 1995, New Writing 6 (co-ed.) 1997, The Oxford Book of English Short Stories (ed.) 1998, On Histories and Stories (essays) 2000, Portraits in Fiction 2001, Bird Hand Book (with V. Schrager) 2001, Memory (ed., anthology, with Harriet Harvey Wood) 2008; ed. and introduction to numerous works by other writers. *Address:* c/o Rogers Coleridge and White, 20 Powis Mews, London, W11 1JN, England (office). *Telephone:* (20) 7221-3717 (office). *Fax:* (20) 7229-9084 (office). *Website:* www.asbyatt.com.

BYATT, Sir Ian Charles Rayner, Kt, BA, DPhil; British economist and government official; *Senior Associate, Frontier Economics;* b. 11 March 1932, Preston; s. of Charles Rayner Byatt and Enid Marjorie Annie Byatt (née Howat); m. 1st Antonia Susan Drabble 1959 (divorced 1969); one s. (deceased) one d.; m. 2nd Prof. Deirdre Kelly 1997; two step-s.; ed Kirkham Grammar School, St Edmund Hall and Nuffield Coll., Oxford, Harvard Univ.; Lecturer in Econs, Durham Coll., Univ. of Durham 1958–62, LSE 1964–67; Econ. Consultant, HM Treasury 1962–64; Sr Econ. Adviser, Dept of Educ. and Science 1967–69; Dir of Econs, Ministry of Housing and Local Govt (and subsequently Dept of Environment) 1969–72; Under-Sec., HM Treasury 1972–78, Deputy Chief Econ. Adviser 1978–89, Chair. Advisory Cttee to HM Treasury on Accounting for Econ. Costs and Changing Prices 1986, Dir-Gen. of Water Services 1989–2000; Sr Assoc. Frontier Economics 2001–; Pres. Econs and Business Educ. Asscn 1998–2001; mem. Econ. Policy Cttee of EC 1978–89 (Chair. 1982–85), mem. Econ. and Social Research Council 1983–89, Bd of Man., Int. Inst. of Public Finance 1987–90, 2001–, Council, Royal Econ. Soc. 1983–90; adviser to Water Industry Commr for Scotland 2000–; mem. Public Services Productivity Panel, HM Treasury 2000–; mem. Bd of Regulatory Policy Inst. 2001–; Panel of Advisors to NI Govt in reform of water services 2003–; Council of Man., Nat. Inst. of Econ. and Social Research 1996–2002, Advisory Bd Centre for Management Under Regulation, Warwick Business School 1996–, Governing Body of Birkbeck Coll. 1997–, Bd of Advisers, St Edmund Hall 1998–2003, Council Regulatory Policy Inst. 2001–, Int. Advisory Cttee Public Utilities Research Center, Univ. of Florida 2002–; Vice-Pres. Strategic Planning Soc. 1993–; Chair. Friends of Birmingham Cathedral 1999–, mem. Cathedral Council 2003–; Trustee Acad. of Youth, Birmingham 2001–; Hon. DUniv (Brunel) 1994, (Univ. of Cen. England) 2000, (Aston Univ.) 2005; Hon. Prof. (Birmingham Univ.)Freeman, City of London 1995. *Publications:* The British Electrical Industry 1875–1914 1979, Delivering Better Services to Citizens 2001; articles and book chapters on nationalized industries and public utilities; contribs to govt reports on micro-econ. policy. *Leisure interests:* painting, family life. *Address:* Frontier Economics, MidCity Place, 71 High Holborn, London, WC1V 6DA (office); 34 Frederick Road, Birmingham, B15 1JN, England (home). *Telephone:* (20) 7031-7000 (office); (121) 689-7946 (home). *Fax:* (20) 7031-7001 (office); (121) 454 6438 (home). *E-mail:* ianbyatt@blueyonder.co.uk (home); ianbyatt@blueyonder.co.uk (home); ian.byatt@frontier-economics.com (office); ian_byatt@yahoo.co.uk (home). *Website:* www.frontier-economics.com (office).

BYATT, Ronald (Robin) Archer Campbell, CMG; British diplomatist (retd); b. 14 Nov. 1930; s. of the late Sir Horace Byatt and Lady Byatt (née Olga Campbell); m. Ann Brereton Sharpe 1954; one s. one d.; ed Gordonstoun, New Coll., Oxford; joined Diplomatic Service 1959; Foreign Office 1959, 1963; served in Havana 1961, Kampala 1970; with UK Mission to UN, New York 1966, Counsellor and Head of Chancery 1977–79; Head of Rhodesia Dept, FCO 1972–75; Asst Under-Sec. of State for Africa 1979–80; High Commr in Zimbabwe 1980–83; Amb. to Morocco 1985–87, High Commr in NZ (also accred to Western Samoa and Gov. of Pitcairn Island) 1987–90; Visiting Fellow, Glasgow Univ. 1975–76; Civilian Dir Royal Coll. of Defence Studies, London 1983–84; Panel Chair. Civil Service Selection Bd 1992–95; mem. Forestry Comm. Home-Grown Timber Advisory Cttee (Chair. Environment Sub-Cttee) 1993–98; Trustee Beit Trust 1987–, UK Antarctic Heritage Trust 1993–2001; Wissem Alaouite (First Class) (Morocco) 1987. *Leisure interests:* birdwatching, sailing, gardening. *Address:* Drim-na-Vullin, Lochgilphead, Argyll, Scotland (home).

BYCHKOV, Semyon; Russian-born conductor; b. 1952, Leningrad; brother of Yakov Kreizberg; ed Leningrad Conservatory (pupil of Musin); invited to conduct Leningrad Philharmonic Orchestra; left. USSR 1975; debut with Concertgebouw, Amsterdam and Berlin Philharmonic 1984–85; toured Germany with Berlin Philharmonic 1985; Music Dir Grand Rapid Symphony Orchestra 1980, Buffalo Philharmonic Orchestra 1986–87, Orchestre de Paris 1989–98, Semperoper, Dresden 1999–2003; conducted Czech Philharmonic 1989–90; Prin. Guest Conductor Maggio Musicale Fiorentino 1992–; Franco Abbiati Prize 1996. *Recordings:* R. Strauss's Daphne (with Cologne Radio Chorus and Symphony Orchestra) 2005, Elektra (with Chorus and Symphony Orchestra of Westdeutscher Rundfunk, Cologne) 2005. *Address:* c/o Van Walsum Management, 4 Addison Bridge Place, London W14 8XP, England (office). *Telephone:* (20) 7371-4343 (office). *Fax:* (20) 7371-4344 (office). *E-mail:* vwm@vanwalsum.com (office). *Website:* www.vanwalsum.com (office).

BYCZEWSKI, Iwo, DrIur; Polish diplomatist and lawyer; *Ambassador to Belgium;* b. 29 Feb. 1948, Poznań; m.; two d.; ed Adam Mickiewicz Univ., Poznań and Collège d'Europe, Bruges; mem. staff, Ministry of Justice 1977–82; researcher, Inst. of Econ. Sciences, Polish Acad. of Sciences (PAN) 1982–89; Prin. Expert, Sec. Comm. in Senate Chancellery; Ministerial Adviser, Vice-Dir Council of Minister's Office 1989–90; Dir Personnel Dept, Ministry of Foreign Affairs 1990–91, Under-Sec. of State 1991–95; Perm. Rep. to EU 2001–02; Amb. to Belgium and Luxembourg 2002–03, to Belgium 2005–; Chair. Supervisory Bd Alcatel Polska SA 1995–; consultant, Hogan and Hartson (American law firm) 1996–; Chair. Centre of Int. Affairs Foundation 1997–. *Address:* Ambassade de la République de Pologne, Av. des Gaulois 29, 1040 Brussels, Belgium (office). *Telephone:* (2) 73-90-151 (office). *Fax:* (2) 73-

61-881 (office). *E-mail:* polambbxl@skynet.be (office). *Website:* www.polembassy.be (office).

BYDDER, Graeme M., PhD, MD; British radiologist and academic; *Professor of Radiology and Director, Bydder Laboratory, University of California, San Diego;* fmrly with Robert Steiner Magnetic Resonance Unit, MRC Clinical Sciences Centre, Imaging Sciences Dept, Imperial Coll. Faculty of Medicine, Hammersmith Hosp., London, UK, later Prof. and Fellow, Acad. of Medical Sciences; Prof. of Radiology and Dir Bydder Lab., Univ. of Calif. at San Diego 2003–; Taylor Prize, Robarts Research Inst. 1998. *Publications include:* Magnetic Resonance Imaging Atlas of the Brain (co-author) 1989, MRI Atlas of the Brain (co-author) 1990, Advanced MR Imaging Techniques (co-author) 1997. *Address:* Department of Radiology, School of Medicine, University of California, 200 West Arbor Drive, San Diego, CA 92103-8756, USA (office). *Telephone:* (619) 543-3617 (office). *Fax:* (619) 543-3767 (office). *E-mail:* gbydder@ucsd.edu (office). *Website:* www.ucsd.edu (office).

BYERS, Rt Hon. Stephen (John), PC, LLB, FRSA; British politician; b. 13 April 1953, Wolverhampton; s. of the late Robert Byers; ed Chester City Grammar School, Chester Coll., Liverpool Polytech.; Sr Lecturer of Law Newcastle Polytech. 1977–82; Labour Party MP for Wallsend 1992–97, for Tyneside N 1997–; Opposition Whip 1994–95, frontbench spokesman on educ. and employment 1995–97; Minister of State Dept for Educ. and Employment 1997–98; Chief Sec. to the Treasury 1998–99; Sec. of State for Trade and Industry 1999–2001, for Transport, Local Govt and the Regions 2001–02. *Address:* House of Commons, London, SW1A 0AA, England (office).

BYFORD, Mark, LLB; British broadcasting executive; *Deputy Director General, British Broadcasting Corporation (BBC);* b. 13 June 1958, Castleford; s. of Sir Lawrence Byford and Lady Muriel Byford (née Massey); m. Hilary Bleiker 1980; two s. three d.; ed Christ's Hospital School, Lincoln; Univ. of Leeds; joined BBC as Holiday Relief Asst 1979, Controller, Regional Broadcasting 1991–94, Deputy Man. Dir 1994–96, Dir 1996–98; Dir BBC World Service and Global News 1998–2004, Deputy Dir Gen. 2003–; mem. BBC Exec. Cttee; Fellow, Radio Acad. 2000; Royal TV Soc. Journalism Awards 1980, 1982, 1988, Webby Award (World Service) 2001, Sony Radio Special Award (World Service) 2002, One World Special Award (World Service) 2002. *Leisure interests:* family life, soccer, cricket, rock music, being surrounded by children. *Address:* Room MC4A1, The Media Centre, BBC, 201 Wood Lane, London, W12 7QT (office); Bolberry House, 1 Clifton Hill, Winchester, Hants., SO22 5BL, England (home). *Telephone:* (20) 8008-5900 (office); (1962) 860197 (home). *Fax:* (20) 8008-5906 (office). *E-mail:* mark.byford@bbc.co.uk (office). *Website:* bbc.co.uk (office).

BYKOV, Oleg Nikolayevich, DrHist; Russian political scientist; *Counsellor, Russian Academy of Sciences;* b. 15 Oct. 1926, Tula; m.; one d.; ed Moscow State Inst. of Int. Relations; mem. staff Soviet Cttee of Peace 1952–55, Deputy Exec. Sec. 1959–64; mem. staff World Peace Council, Vienna 1953–59; Sr Researcher, Head of Int. Relations Dept, Deputy Dir Inst. of World Econs and Int. Relations, Russian Acad. of Sciences 1964–98, Counsellor, Russian Acad. of Sciences 1998–; mem. UN Consultative Bd on Studies of Disarmament Problems; Govt expert UN Research Group on Measures of Confidence; Ed.-in-Chief Year of the Planet (yearly journal) 1992–; Corresp. Mem. USSR (now Russian) Acad. of Sciences 1987; Soviet Orders of Labour Red Banner (1981, 1986), Russian Fed. Order of Merit 1999; USSR State Prize; four medals. *Publications:* over 600 scientific publs on contemporary int. relations, Russian foreign policy, mil. and political problems; monographs: Russia in the System of International Relations of the Coming 10 Years 1995, Russian and International Stability 1995, National Security of Russia 1997, International Relations: The Global Structure Transformed (two vols) 2003. *Address:* Institute of World Economics and International Relations, Russian Academy of Sciences, Profsoyuznaya str. 23, Moscow 117997, Russia (office). *Telephone:* (495) 120-5236 (office); (495) 120-23-40 (office). *E-mail:* imemoran@imemo.ru (office). *Website:* www.imemo.ru (office).

BYNG, Jamie, BA; British publishing director; *Managing Director, Canongate Books;* b. 1969, Winchester; s. of the Earl of Strafford; m. 1st (divorced); one s. one d.; m. 2nd Elizabeth Sheinkman 2005; ed Edinburgh Univ.; joined Canongate Books as unpaid worker 1992, bought the co. 1994, Man. Dir 1994–, books published include Yann Martel's Life of Pi (winner of Man Booker Prize, over two million copies sold) 2002; Canongate named Publisher of the Year 2003. *Address:* Canongate Books, 14 High Street, Edinburgh EH1 1TE, Scotland (office); Canongate Books, Basement, 151 Chesterton Road, London W10 6ET, England (office). *Telephone:* (131) 557-5111 (office); (20) 8969-6011 (office). *Fax:* (131) 557-5211 (office); (20) 8969-8462 (office). *E-mail:* info@canongate.co.uk (office). *Website:* www.canongate.co.uk (office).

BYRD, Harry Flood, Jr; American newspaper executive and politician; b. 20 Dec. 1914; s. of Harry Flood Byrd, Sr; m. Gretchen B. Thomson 1941 (died 1989); two s. one d.; ed John Marshall High School, Richmond, Virginia Mil. Inst. and Univ. of Virginia; Ed. and writer, Winchester Evening Star 1935, Ed. and Publr 1935–81, Ed. and Publr Harrisonburg Daily News-Record 1937–2000; also active in firm of H. F. Byrd, Inc., apple growers; mem. Va State Senate 1947–65; mem. Democratic State Cen. Cttee 1940–70; served in USNR 1941–46; Dir Associated Press 1950–66; US Senator from Virginia (succeeding his father) 1965–83; Ind. *Address:* Rockingham Publishing Co. Inc., 2 North Kent Street, Winchester, VA 22601 (office); 411 Tennyson Avenue, Winchester, VA 22601, USA (home). *Telephone:* (540) 662-7745 (office). *Fax:* (540) 667-6729 (office).

BYRD, Robert C., JP; American politician; *Senator from West Virginia;* b. 20 Nov. 1917, North Wilkesboro, NC; s. of Cornelius Sale and Ada Byrd; m. Erma O James 1936; two d.; ed George Washington Univ. Law School and Washington Coll. of Law (American Univ.); mem. W Va House of Delegates 1946–50, W Va Senate 1950–52; mem. US House of Reps rep. 6th Dist of W Va 1952–58; Senator from West Virginia 1959–; Asst Democratic Leader in Senate 1971–77, Majority Leader 1977–81, Minority Leader 1981–87, Majority Leader 1987–88; Chair. Appropriations Cttee 2001–; mem. Senate Appropriations, Armed Services and Rules and Admin. Cttees; Democrat. *Publications:* The Senate 1789–1989 (four vols) 1989–94, The Senate of the Roman Republic: Addresses on the History of Roman Constitutionalism 1995, Losing America 2004. *Address:* 311 Hart Senate Office Building, Washington, DC 20510-0001, USA. *Telephone:* (202) 224-3954 (office). *Website:* byrd.senate.gov (office).

BYRNE, David; American musician, songwriter, composer and director; b. 14 May 1952, Dumbarton, Scotland; s. of Thomas Byrne and Emily Anderson (née Brown) Byrne; m. Adele Lutz 1987; one c.; ed Rhode Island School of Design, Maryland Inst. Coll. of Art; founder mem., Talking Heads 1974–92; solo artist, musician, composer, producer 1980–; producer for artists, including B-52s, Fun Boy 3, Margareth Menezes; producer Index Video 1983–; dir videotapes 1981–; designer stage sets, lighting, album covers and posters 1977–; f. Luaka Bop label 1988; Film Critics' Award for Best Documentary 1985, MTV Video Vanguard Award 1985, Music Video Producers Asscn Award 1992. *Compositions for film, television and theatre:* Stop Making Sense 1984, The Knee Plays 1984, Alive from Off Center 1984, Dead End Kids 1986, True Stories 1986, Tribute 1986, The Kitchen Presents Two Moon July 1986, True Stories 1986, The Forest 1986, Something Wild 1986, The Last Emperor (Acad. Award, Golden Globe, Hollywood Foreign Press Asscn Award for Best Original Score) 1987, Married to the Mob 1988, A Rustling of Leaves: Inside the Philippine Revolution 1988, The Catherine Wheel 1988, Magicians of the Earth: The Giant Woman and The Lightning Man (TV) 1990, Magicians of the Earth: A Young Man's Dream and a Woman's Secret (TV) 1990, Blue in the Face 1995, In Spite of Wishing and Wanting 2002, Young Adam 2003; contrib. songs to numerous other films. *Films:* Stop Making Sense (actor) 1984, True Stories (actor, dir and co-screenwriter) 1986, Checking Out 1988. *Recordings include:* albums: with Talking Heads: Talking Heads '77 1977, More Songs About Buildings And Food 1978, Fear Of Music 1979, Remain In Light 1980, The Name Of This Band Is Talking Heads 1982, Speaking In Tongues 1983, Stop Making Sense 1984, Little Creatures 1985, True Stories 1986, Naked 1988, Popular Favourites: Sand In The Vaseline 1992; solo: My Life In The Bush Of Ghosts (with Brian Eno) 1981, The Knee Plays 1985, The Forest 1988, Rei Momo 1989, Uh-Oh 1992, David Byrne 1994, Feelings 1997, Look Into The Eyeball 2001, Grown Backwards 2004, Big Love: Hymnal 2008, Everything that Happens will Happen Today (with Brian Eno) 2008. *Publications:* Stay Up Late 1987, What the Songs Look Like 1987, Strange Ritual 1995. *Address:* Maine Road Management, 195 Chrystie Street, Suite 901F, New York, NY 10002, USA (office). *Telephone:* (212) 979-9004 (office). *Fax:* (212) 979-0985 (office). *E-mail:* mailbox@maineroadmanagement.com (office). *Website:* www.maineroadmanagement.com (office); www.davidbyrne.com.

BYRNE, David, BA, BL, SC, FRCPI; Irish EU official, politician and barrister; b. 26 April 1947; m.; three c.; ed Dominican Coll., Newbridge, Univ. Coll. Dublin, King's Inns, Dublin; called to the Bar 1970; mem. Bar Council 1974–87; mem. Exec. Cttee, Irish Maritime Law Asscn 1974–92; called to Inner Bar 1985; mem. Nat. Cttee ICC 1988–97; mem. Govt Review Body on Social Welfare Law 1989; mem. ICC Int. Court of Arbitration, Paris 1990–97; mem. Constitution Review Group 1995–96; External Examiner for Arbitration and Competition Law, King's Inns 1995–97; Attorney-Gen. 1997–99; mem. Council of State, Cabinet Sub-cttees on Social Inclusion, European Affairs, Child Abuse; EU Commr for Health and Consumer Protection (with particular responsibility for Food Safety, Public Health and Consumer Protection) 1999–2004; mem. Barristers' Professional Practices and Ethics Cttee 1995–97; participated in negotiation of Good Friday Agreement April 1998; Fellow, Chartered Inst. of Arbitrators of England and Ireland 1998–; f. Free Legal Advice Centre, Dublin; Hon. Treasurer, Bar Council 1982–83. *Publications:* numerous papers on legal affairs. *Address:* c/o European Commission, 200 rue de la Loi, 1049 Brussels, Belgium (office).

BYRNE, Edward, AO, MBBS, DSc, FRACP; Australian neuroscientist, academic and university administrator; *Vice-Chancellor, Monash University;* b. 1952; ed Univ. of Tasmania; Muscular Dystrophy Research Fellow, Univ. Coll. London (UCL) Inst. of Neurology 1980–82, Vice Provost (Health), UCL 2007–09; Neurology Registrar, Adelaide Hosp. 1978–83; Dir of Neurology, St Vincent's Hosp., Melbourne 1983; Founding Dir Melbourne Neuromuscular Research Unit, Centre for Neuroscience; fmr Prof. of Experimental Neurology, Univ. of Melbourne; Dean, Faculty of Medicine, Nursing and Health Sciences, Monash Univ. 2003–07, Vice-Chancellor Monash Univ. 2009–; Dir (non-Exec.) Cochlear Pty Ltd 2002–, BUPA 2008–; UCL Queen Square Prize for Neurological Research 1982, Bethlehem Griffith Research Medal 2003, Sir Louis Pyke Award for Contribution to Multiple Sclerosis 2004, John Sands Medal 2005. *Publications:* The Science Wars. *Leisure interests:* fly fishing, classical music. *Address:* Office of the Vice-Chancellor, Monash University, Melbourne, Vic. 3800, Australia (office). *Telephone:* (3) 9902-6000 (office). *Fax:* (3) 9905-4007 (office). *E-mail:* edward.byrne@adm.monash.edu.au (office). *Website:* www.monash.edu.au (office).

BYRNE, Gabriel; Irish actor; b. 12 May 1950, Dublin; m. Ellen Barkin (q.v.) 1988 (separated); two c.; ed Univ. Coll. Dublin; archaeologist, then teacher, began acting in amateur productions; joined an experimental repertory co. 1980; first TV appearance in series The Riordans 1982; first cinema role in Excalibur; moved to New York 1987; f. Plurabelle Films (production co.) 1985. *Theatre:* several roles Nat. Theatre, London; A Touch of the Poet (Broadway) 2005. *Films include:* Hanna K, Gothic, Julia and Julia, Siesta, Miller's Crossing, Hakon Hakenson, Dark Obsession, Cool World, A Dangerous Woman, Little Women, Usual Suspects, Frankie Starlight, Dead Man, Last of the High Kings, Mad Dog Time, Somebody is Waiting 1996, The End of Violence (dir) 1997, This is the Sea 1997, Toby's Story, Polish Wedding 1998, The Man in the Iron Mask 1998, Quest for Camelot (voice) 1998, An Ideal Husband, Enemy of the State 1998, Stigmata 1999, End of Days 1999, Canone inverso – making love 2000, Spider 2002, Virginia's Run 2002, Emmett's Mark 2002, Ghost Ship 2002, Shade 2003, Vanity Fair 2004, P.S. 2004, The Bridge of San Luis Rey 2004, Assault on Precinct 13 2005, Wah-Wah 2005, Played 2006, Jindabyne 2006, Emotional Arithmetic (aka Autumn Hearts: A New Beginning) 2007; co-producer In the Name of the Father. *Television includes:* Madigan Men 2000, Patrick (voice) 2004, Live from Lincoln Center (episode, Camelot) 2008, In Treatment (several episodes) (Golden Globe Award for Best Actor in a TV Series – Drama 2009) 2008–09. *Address:* c/o ICM, 8942 Wilshire Blvd, Beverly Hills, CA 96211, USA (office); Plurabelle Films, 10125 Washington Blvd, #205, Culver City, CA 90232, USA. *Telephone:* (310) 244-6782 (Plurabelle).

BYRNE, John V., MA, PhD, FAAS; American academic; *Professor of Oceanography, Oregon State University;* b. 9 May 1928, Hempstead, NY; m. Shirley O'Connor 1954; one s. three d.; ed Hamilton Coll., Clinton, NY, Columbia Univ. and Univ. of S. Calif., Los Angeles; research geologist, Humble Oil & Refining, Houston, Tex. 1957–60; Assoc. Prof. Oregon State Univ., Corvallis, Ore. 1960–66, Prof. of Oceanography 1966–, Chair, Oceanography 1968–72, Dean, Oceanography 1972–76, Dean, Research 1976–80, Vice-Pres. Research and Grad. Studies 1980–81, Pres. 1984–95; Program Dir Oceanography, Nat. Science Foundation 1966–67; US Commr to Int. Whaling Comm. 1982–85; Exec. Dir Kellogg Comm. on Future of State and Land Grant Univs 1996–2000; Admin. Nat. Oceanic & Atmospheric Admin., Washington, DC 1981–84; Hon. Assoc. of Arts (Lynn-Benton Community Coll., OR); Hon. JD (Hamilton Coll.) 1994; Distinguished Service Award (Oregon State Univ.) 1996. *Leisure interests:* fishing, skiing, music, painting. *Address:* 811 SW Jefferson Avenue, Corvallis, OR 97333, USA (office). *Telephone:* (541) 737-3542. *Fax:* (541) 737-4380. *E-mail:* john.byrne@orst.edu (office).

BYRNE, Liam, MBA; British politician; *Minister for the Cabinet Office and Chancellor of the Duchy of Lancaster;* b. Oct. 1970, Warrington; m.; three c.; ed Manchester Univ., Harvard Business School; early positions at Andersen Consulting and NM Rothschilds; f. e-Government Solutions Ltd 2000; adviser to Labour Party on re-organisation of Millbank and nat. business campaign 1996–97; MP (Labour) for Hodge Hill 2004–; Under-Sec. of State for Care Services, Dept of Health 2005; Minister of State for Borders and Immigration 2006–08; Minister for the Cabinet Office and Chancellor of the Duchy of Lancaster 2008–; mem. Amicus, Christian Socialist Movt, Fabian Soc.; fmr Assoc. Fellow, Social Market Foundation. *Publications:* Local Government Transformed 1996, Information Age Government 1998, Cities of Enterprise 2002, Britain in 2020 2003, Reinventing Government Again (co-author) 2004, Why Labour Won 2005, A Common Place 2007. *Address:* Cabinet Office, 70 Whitehall, London, SW1A 2AS, England (office). *Telephone:* (20) 7276-1234 (office). *E-mail:* mst@cabinet-office.x.gsi.gov.uk (office). *Website:* www .cabinetoffice.gov.uk (office).

BYSTRITSKAYA, Elina Avraamovna; Russian actress; b. 4 April 1928, Kiev, Ukraine; ed Medical School, Nezhin City 1947, Kiev Inst. of Theatre Art 1953; began career in Vilnius Drama Theatre 1953–58; leading actress, Moscow Maly Theatre 1958–; over 50 roles in theatre and films; Prof. Moscow Lunacharsky State Inst. of Theatre Art, Founder and President, Charity supporting Arts and Science 1994, Vice-Pres., Nat. Acad. Cinematographic Arts and Science 2000; People's Artist of the RSFSR 1966, People's Artist of the USSR 1978. *Films include:* Peaceful Days 1951, Quiet Don, Unfinished Story 1951, Volunteers 1958, Seven Days after the Murder 1991, Wild Field 1998. *Plays:* includes Lady Windemere's Fan, Glass of Water, Masquerade, Summer Residents and many leading roles in plays by A. Ostrovsky. *Publications:* Meeting Under the Star of Hope (memoirs); numerous publications in periodicals and newspapers on topics of arts and culture. *Leisure interests:* billiards. *Address:* 103009 Moscow, Leontievski per. 14, Apt 13; Theatralnaia Square, 1/6, Moscow, Russia (office). *Telephone:* (495) 925-9868 (office); (495) 203-2642 (home).

BYZANTINE, Julian Sarkis, ARCM; British classical guitarist; b. 11 June 1945, London; s. of Carl Byzantine and Mavis Harris; ed Royal Coll. of Music, London and Accademia Chigiana, Siena, Italy; studied with John Williams at RCM, subsequently with Julian Bream and with Andrés Segovia and Alirio Diaz in Siena; taught at RAM 1966–68; Sr Lecturer in Guitar, Queensland Conservatorium, Griffith Univ., Australia; London debut Wigmore Hall 1969, New York debut Carnegie Hall 1980; has performed in 76 countries; has given concerts with leading British orchestras including Royal Philharmonic, City of Birmingham Symphony, Scottish Chamber, BBC Symphony; numerous radio and TV appearances; awarded first ARCM for guitar 1966; scholarships to study with Segovia from Vaughan Williams and Gilbert Foyle Trusts. *Recordings include:* four solo albums for Classics for Pleasure, solo album for, recordings with flautist Gerhard Mallon. *Publications:* Arrangements of Six Albéniz Piano Works for Guitar 1984, Guitar Technique Rationalised 2002. *Leisure interests:* collecting oriental art, archaeology, tennis. *Address:* Flat 1, 42 Ennismore Gardens, London, SW7 1AQ, England. *Telephone:* (20) 7584-7486. *E-mail:* j.byzantine@griffith.edu.au. *Website:* www .julianbyzantine.com.

C

CAAMAÑO DOMÍNGUEZ, Francisco, DIur; Spanish politician; *Minister of Justice;* b. 8 Jan. 1963, A Coruña; m.; two d.; ed Univ. de Santiago de Compostela; Adjunct Prof., then Prof. of Constitutional Law, Univ. de Santiago de Compostela; counsel to Constitutional Court 1993–2002; Prof. of Constitutional Law, Univ. of Valencia 2002; Dir Democracy and Local Govt Foundation 2001–04; Sec. of State for Constitutional and Parl. Affairs 2004–09; Minister of Justice 2009–. *Address:* Ministry of Justice, San Bernardo 45, 28015 Madrid, Spain (office). *Telephone:* (91) 3904500 (office). *Website:* www.mjusticia.es (office).

CAAN, James; American actor and director; b. 26 March 1940, Bronx, New York; s. of Arthur and Sophie Caan; m. 1st DeeJay Mathis 1961 (divorced 1966); one d.; m. 2nd Sheila Ryan 1976 (divorced 1977); one s.; m. 3rd Linda O'Gara 1995; two c.; ed Michigan State Univ., Hofstra Coll.; made theatre debut in the off-Broadway production of La Ronde 1960; Broadway debut in Blood Sweat and Stanley Poole, 1961; Outstanding Achievement in Acting, Hollywood Film Festival 1999. *Films include:* Irma La Douce 1963, Lady in a Cage 1964, The Glory Guys 1965, Countdown 1967, Games 1967, Eldorado 1967, Journey to Shiloh 1968, Submarine XI 1968, Man Without Mercy 1969, The Rain People 1969, Rabbit Run 1970, T. R. Baskin 1971, The Godfather 1972, Slither 1973, Cinderella Liberty 1975, Freebie and the Bean 1975, The Gambler 1975, Funny Lady 1975, Rollerball 1975, The Killer Elite 1975, Harry and Walter Go to New York 1976, Silent Movie 1976, A Bridge Too Far 1977, Another Man, Another Chance 1977, Comes a Horseman 1978, Chapter Two 1980, Thief 1982, Kiss Me Goodbye 1983, Bolero 1983, Gardens of Stone 1988, Alien Nation 1989, Dad 1989, Dick Tracy 1990, Misery 1991, For the Boys 1991, Dark Backward 1991, Honeymoon in Vegas 1992, Flesh and Bone 1993, The Program 1994, North Star 1995, Boy Called Hate 1995, Eraser 1996, Bulletproof 1996, Bottle Rocket 1996, This Is My Father 1997, Poodle Springs 1997, Blue Eyes 1998, The Yards 1999, The Way of the Gun 1999, In the Boom Boom Room 2000, Luckytown 2000, Viva Las Nowhere 2000, In the Shadows 2001, Night at the Golden Eagle 2002, City of Ghosts 2002, Dogville 2003, This Thing of Ours 2003, Jericho Mansions 2003, Elf 2003, Get Smart 2008; dir and actor Hide in Plain Sight 1980, dir Violent Streets 1981; starred in television movie, Brian's Song, 1971, The Warden 2000. *Television includes:* Las Vegas (series) 2003 and numerous other TV appearances. *Address:* c/o Fred Specktor, Endeavor, 9701 Wilshire Boulevard, 10th Floor, Beverly Hills, CA 90212, USA (office). *Telephone:* (818) 905-9500.

CABALLÉ, Montserrat; Spanish singer (soprano); b. 12 April 1933, Barcelona; m. Bernabé Marti (tenor) 1964; one s. one d.; ed Conservatorio del Liceo; studied under Eugenia Kemeny, Conchita Badia and Maestro Annovazi; debut as Mimi (La Bohème), State Opera of Basel; N American début in Manon, Mexico City 1964; U.S. debut in Lucrezia Borgia, Carnegie Hall 1965; appeared at Glyndebourne Festival as the Marschallin in Der Rosenkavalier and as the Countess in The Marriage of Figaro 1965; debut at Metropolitan Opera as Marguerite (Faust) Dec. 1965; now appears frequently at the Metropolitan Opera and numerous other opera houses throughout the USA; has performed in most of the leading opera houses of Europe including Gran Teatro del Liceo, Barcelona, La Scala, Milan, Vienna State Opera, Paris and Rome Operas, Bayerische Staatsoper (Munich), etc. and also at Teatro Colón, Buenos Aires; repertoire of over forty roles; apptd UNESCO Goodwill Amb. 1994; Most Excellent and Illustrious Doña and Cross of Isabella the Catholic 1966, Commdr des Arts et des Lettres 1986; Gold Medal, Gran Teatro dek Liceu, Echo Award 2000, Gramophone Lifetime Achievement Award 2007, numerous other awards. *Recordings include:* Lucrezia Borgia, La Traviata, Salomé, Aida, La Canción Romántica Española (Latin Grammy Award for Best Classical Album) 2007. *Address:* Postfach 1462, 26172 Rastede, Germany. *Website:* www.montserratcaballe.com; www.montserrat-caballe.de.

CABALLEROS, Rómulo Alfredo; Guatemalan economist, diplomatist and politician; *Minister of the Economy;* b. 29 March 1941; m. Nora Wellmann de Caballeros; ed Univ. de San Carlos de Guatemala, Centro Interamericano de Enseñanza Estaística (CIENES), Instituto Latinoamericano de Planificación Economica y Social (ILPES), Univ. de Madrid, Spain; worked at Bank of Guatemala 1962–72; consultant to Dept of Gen. Studies, Secr. Gen. of Econ. Planning 1972–73, Dir 1973–75; consultant to UNDP 1975; Econ. Affairs Exec., Econ. Comm. for Latin America and the Caribbean (CEPAL) 1975–79, Deputy Head of Econ. Devt, Int. Trade and Statistics Section 1976–81, Head of Section 1983–90, Deputy Dir CEPAL Satellite Office, Mexico 1990–92, 1994–96, Dir Planning, Programmes and Operations Div. 1996–97, Dir Sub-regional Office, Mexico 1997–2000; Sec.-Gen. of Econ. Planning 1993; Amb. to Mexico 2000–02; consultant to EC, UN, IDB, World Bank 2002–07; Minister of the Economy 2008–; Orden del Águila Azteca (Mexico). *Address:* Ministry of the Economy, 8a Avda 10-43, Zona 1, Guatemala City, Guatemala (office). *Telephone:* 2238-3330 (office). *Fax:* 2238-2413 (office). *E-mail:* racaballeros@mineco.gob.gt (office); racaballeros@gmai.com (office). *Website:* www.mineco.gob.gt (office).

CABANILLAS BUSTAMANTE DE LLANOS DE LA MATA, Mercedes, BA, MA, DrEduc; Peruvian politician; *Minister of the Interior;* b. 22 May 1947; ed Federico Villareal Nat. Univ., Universidad Particular Inca Garcilaso de la Vega; worked as promoter for SINAMOS (agency in charge of organizing popular support for the left-wing Velasco mil. dictatorship) 1972; elected mem. of Congress 1985, Pres. Congressional Cttee for the Family 1985–86, Congressional Cttee for Educ., Culture and Sport 1986–87, elected mem. of Congress 2000– (re-elected 2006), Pres. of Congress 2006–07; Minister of Educ. (first woman) 1987–89, 1989–90; cand. for Mayorship of Lima 1989; Senator 1990–99; Deputy Sec. Socialist Party 1992–2000, Parl. Co-Spokesperson 2000; unsuccessful cand. in presidential elections 1995; Pres. Comm. of Educ., Science, Tech., Culture and Cultural Patrimony 2005–06, Nat. Defence, Internal Order, Alternative Devt and the Fight Against Drugs 2007–08; Minister of the Interior 2009–. *Address:* Ministry of the Interior, Plaza 30 de Agosto 150, San Isidro, Lima 27, Peru (office). *Telephone:* (1) 2242406 (office). *Fax:* (1) 2242405 (office). *E-mail:* ministro@mininter.gob.pe (office). *Website:* www.mininter.gob.pe (office).

CABEZAS MOLINA, Eduardo; Ecuadorean economist, diplomatist and central banker; *Ambassador to UK;* m. Berta Cabezas; ed Universidad Cen. del Ecuador, Queen's Coll., New York, USA; Minister, Embassy in Bonn 1981–84, Amb. to Uruguay 1994, to UK (also accred to Portugal) 2003–06, 2008–; Pres. Cen. Bank of Ecuador 2006–08. *Address:* Embassy of Ecuador, Flat 3B, 3 Hans Crescent, Knightsbridge, London, SW1X 0LS, England (office). *Telephone:* (20) 7584-8084 (office); (20) 7584-2648 (office). *Fax:* (20) 7823-9701 (office). *E-mail:* eecugranbretania@mmrree.gov.ec (office).

CABEZAS MORALES, Rodrigo Eduardo; Venezuelan politician and economist; b. 19 June 1956, Valera, Trujillo state; m.; ed Univ. of Zulia; mem. Faculty, Univ. of Zulia 1982–, currently Prof. and mem. Instituto de Investigaciones; Deputy Congreso de la República 1990–93, 1994–98; Deputy Asamblea Nacional 2000–04, then Vice-Chair. Asamblea Nacional Finance Comm. 2000–01, Chair. 2002–06; Minister of Finance 2007–08; Bd mem. Nat. Council on Culture 2002; mem. Por la Democracia Social (PODEMOS) party. *Address:* Por la Democracia Social (PODEMOS), Caracas, Venezuela (office). *E-mail:* contacto@podemos.org.ve (office). *Website:* www.podemos.org.ve (office).

CABI, Martinho N'Dafa; Guinea-Bissau politician; b. 17 Sept. 1957, Nhacra, Oio Prov.; s. of Cabi Imbitna and Tchambu Insol; belongs to Balanta ethnic group; joined Partido Africano da Independência da Guiné e Cabo Verde (PAIGC) 1974, various roles including Chair. Cttee for Autonomous Region of Guinea-Bissau, mem. Cen. Cttee 1999, Third Vice-Pres. 2002–07; fmr Minister of Energy; Minister of Nat. Defence 2004–05; Prime Minister 2007–08. *Address:* Partido Africano da Independência da Guiné e Cabo Verde (PAIGC), CP 106, Bissau, Guinea-Bissau (office). *Website:* www.paigc.org (office).

CABIBBO, Nicola; Italian professor of elementary particle physics; *President, Pontificia Academia Scientiarum;* b. 30 April 1935, Rome; Prof. of Theoretical Physics 1965–, of Elementary Particle Physics, Univ. of Rome; Pres. Istituto Nazionale di Fisica Nucleare 1983–93, ENEA (Nat. agency for new tech. energy and the environment) 1993–, Pontifical Acad. of Sciences 1993–. *Address:* c/o Pontificia Academia Scientiarum, Casina Pio IV, 00120 Vatican City (office); c/o ENEA, Viale Regina Margherita 125, 00198 Rome, Italy. *Telephone:* (06) 85282214; (06) 69883451 (office). *Fax:* (06) 69885218 (office); (06) 85282313 (office). *E-mail:* nicola.cabibbo@roma1.infn.it (home); academy.sciences@acdscience.va (office). *Website:* www.vatican.va/roman_curia/pontifical_academies/acdscien (office).

CABRAAL, Ajith Nivard; Sri Lankan chartered accountant and central banker; *Governor, Central Bank of Sri Lanka;* est. own man. consultancy before taking up public service 2005; fmr Chair. and/or Dir of several quoted and unquoted public cos; Sec., Ministry of Plan Implementation and Adviser to Pres. on Econ. Affairs –2006, also served as mem. Bd Strategic Enterprises Man. Agency; mem. Govt Team at Geneva Talks with Liberation Tigers of Tamil Eelam Feb. 2006; represented Govt in Millennium Challenge Fund negotiations with US Govt; Gov. Cen. Bank of Sri Lanka 2006–, Chair. Monetary Bd; fmr Eisenhower Fellow; Founder-Chair. Corp. Governance Cttee; fmr Pres. Business Recovery and Insolvency Practitioners Asscn of Sri Lanka; Past Pres. Inst. of Chartered Accountants of Sri Lanka, S Asian Fed. of Accountants, St Peter's Coll. Old Boys Union; fmr mem. Bd Securities and Exchange Comm., Nat. Inst. of Business Man., Postgraduate Inst. of Man., Univ. of Moratuwa. *Publications:* Towards a Sri Lankan Renaissance, Lak Mawata Muthu Potak (A String of Pearls for Mother Lanka, collection of more than 60 short essays submitted to popular nat. newspapers 2003–04). *Address:* Central Bank of Sri Lanka, 30 Janadhipathi Mawatha, PO Box 590, Colombo 1, Sri Lanka (office). *Telephone:* (11) 2477000 (office). *Fax:* (11) 2477712 (office). *E-mail:* cbslgen@cbsl.lk (office). *Website:* www.cbsl.gov.lk (office).

CABRAL, Alfredo Lopes, BSc; Guinea-Bissau diplomatist; *Permanent Representative, United Nations;* b. 1946, Dakar, Senegal; m.; joined Mouvement de Libération Nationale de la Guinée-Bissau 1964; Chef de Cabinet, Foreign Ministry 1973–75, Dir Afro-Asian Div. 1975–79, First Counsellor, Perm. Mission to UN 1979–83, Perm. Rep. 1986–90, 1996–2000, 2003–; Amb. to Algeria 1983–86, to USA (also accred to Canada and Mexico) 1987–96; Sec.-Gen.'s Rep. and Head of UN Civilian Police Mission in Haiti 1999–2001; Dir Gen. Office of Strategic Studies and Policy Planning, Ministry of Foreign Affairs 2001–03. *Address:* Permanent Mission of Guinea Bissau to the United Nations, 211 East 43rd Street, Room 704, New York, NY, 10017, USA. *Telephone:* (212) 338-9394 (office). *Fax:* (212) 293-0264 (office). *E-mail:* guinea-bissau@un.int (office).

CABRAL BARRETO, Ireneu; Portuguese judge; *Judge, European Court of Human Rights;* b. 5 Feb. 1941, Ponta do Sol, Madeira; ed Coimbra Law Univ.; Asst to Dist Attorney for Ourique, S Vicente, Vila Nova de Famalicão, Vila Verde, Portimão and Lisbon 1964–70; Judge, São Jorge co. 1971–72; Asst to

Dist Attorney for Bragança, Évora and Setúbal 1972–75; Deputy Attorney Gen. of Portugal 1975–97; Legal Adviser, Ministry of Trade and Tourism 1975–77; Judge, Supreme Court of Justice 1997–98; mem. European Comm. of Human Rights 1993–99; Judge, European Court of Human Rights 1998–. *Publications:* A Convenção Europeia dos Direitos do Homen (third ed.) 2005; numerous articles in professional journals. *Address:* European Court of Human Rights, Council of Europe, 67075 Strasbourg, France (office). *Website:* www.echr.coe.int (office).

CACCIAVILLAN, HE Cardinal Agostino, DCnL, DCL; Italian ecclesiastic and diplomatist; b. 14 Aug. 1926, Novale; ordained priest of Vicenza 1949; joined Holy See diplomatic service 1959, served in Philippines, Spain, Portugal; Head Documentation and Information Office, Secr. of State, Vatican City 1969–76; Apostolic Pro-Nuncio to Kenya, Apostolic Del. to Seychelles 1976–81; Apostolic Pro-Nuncio to India 1981–90, to Nepal 1985–90, to USA 1990–98; Pres. Admin. Patrimony of the Apostolic See 1998–2002, now Pres. Emer.; mem. Pontifical Comm. for Vatican City State; Perm. Observer to OAS 1990–98; cr. Cardinal 2001, Cardinal-Deacon of Ss Angeli Custodi a Città Giardino; Kt Grand Cross, Order of the Holy Sepulchre. *Address:* c/o Patrimony of the Apostolic See, Palazzo Apostolico, 00120 Vatican City, Italy.

CACOYANNIS, Michael; Greek film and stage director and actor; b. 11 June 1922, Limassol, Cyprus; s. of the late Sir Panayotis Cacoyannis and of Lady Cacoyannis; brother of Stella Soulioti (q.v.); ed Greek Gymnasium and London at Gray's Inn, Cen. School of Dramatic Art and Old Vic School; called to the Bar 1943; producer for BBC Overseas Service 1941–50; screen and stage producer-dir 1950–; Hon. Citizen, Limassol 1965, Dallas 1982; Dr hc (Columbia Coll., Chicago) 1981, (Athens Univ.) 2002, (Cyprus Univ.) 2003, (Aristotelian Univ., Thessalonika) 2005; Order of the Phoenix (Greece) 1965, Commdr des Arts et des Lettres 1987; Special Jury Prize for Electra, Cannes 1962, Grand Prix Special des Amériques, Montreal 1999, Life Achievement Award, Jerusalem Film Festival 2000, Lifetime Achievement Award, Cairo Film Festival 2002. *Stage productions include:* The Trojan Women, Paris 1965, 1995, The Devils, New York 1966, Mourning Becomes Electra, Metropolitan Opera, New York 1967, Romeo and Juliet, Paris 1968, Iphigenia in Aulis, New York 1968, La Bohème, New York 1972, King Oedipus, Dublin 1973, The Bacchae, Comédie Française, Paris 1977, Antony and Cleopatra, Athens 1979, The Bacchae, New York 1980, Zorba (musical), USA 1983, Sophocles' Electra, Epidaurus Festival 1983, Gluck's Iphigenia in Aulis and Iphigenia in Taulis, Frankfurt State Opera 1987, La Clemenza di Tito, Aix-en-Provence Music Festival 1988, Athens 1994, Cherubini's Medea, Athens 1995, The Trojan Women, Epidaurus 1997, Master Class, Athens 1998, Euripdes' Medea, Spain 2001–02, Hamlet, Nat. Theatre, Greece 2003, Coriolanus, Athens Festival 2005. *Stage appearances include:* Wilde's Salomé as Herod 1947, in Camus's Caligula 1949, in Two Dozen Red Roses 1949, others. *Films include:* Windfall in Athens 1953, Stella 1955, A Girl in Black 1957, A Matter of Dignity 1958, Our Last Spring 1959, The Wastrel 1960, Electra 1961, Zorba the Greek 1964 (three Acad. Awards 1964), The Day the Fish Came Out 1967, The Trojan Women 1971, The Story of Jacob and Joseph 1974, Attila 74 1975, Iphigenia 1977 (Prix Femina 1977), Sweet Country 1986, Up, Down and Sideways 1992, The Cherry Orchard 1999. *Publications:* translations into Greek of Shakespeare: Antony and Cleopatra 1980, Hamlet 1985, Coriolanus 1990, The Trojan Women 1995, Othello 2001; into English: The Bacchae 1982; Collected Writings 1991, Stella (screenplay) 1991. *Address:* 15 Mouson Street, Athens 117–41, Greece. *Telephone:* 922-2054. *Fax:* 921-6483. *E-mail:* micaco@ otenet.gr.

CADBURY, Sir (Nicholas) Dominic, Kt, MBA; British business executive; *Chairman, Misys PLC;* b. 12 May 1940; s. of the late Laurence John Cadbury and Joyce Cadbury (née Mathews); m. Cecilia Sarah Symes 1972; three d.; ed Eton Coll., Trinity Coll., Cambridge, Stanford Univ., USA; Chief Exec. Cadbury Schweppes PLC 1984–93, Chair. 1993–2000; Dir Economist Group 1990–2003, Chair. 1994–2003; Jt Deputy Chair. Guinness (now Diageo PLC) 1994–97, Deputy Chair. 1996 (Dir 1991–); Jt Deputy Chair EMI Group PLC 1999–; Chair. The Wellcome Trust 2000–06, Transense Techs 2000–03; Pres. Food and Drink Fed. 1999; Dir (non-exec.) Misys PLC 2000–, interim Chair. 2005, Chair. 2006–; mem. Royal Mint Advisory Cttee 1986–94, Pres.'s Cttee CBI 1989–94, Food Asscn 1989–2000, Stanford Advisory Council 1989–95; Chancellor Univ. of Birmingham 2002–. *Leisure interests:* tennis, golf, shooting. *Address:* Office of the Chairman, Misys PLC, One Kingdom Street, Paddington, London, W2 6BL (office); Office of the Chancellor, University of Birmingham, Edgbaston, Birmingham, B15 2TT, England. *Telephone:* (20) 33200-5000 (office). *Fax:* (20) 3320-1771 (office). *Website:* misys.com (office); www.about.bham.ac.uk.

CADBURY-BROWN, Henry Thomas, OBE, TD, RA, FRIBA; British architect; b. 20 May 1913; s. of Henry William Cadbury Brown and Marion Ethel Sewell; m. Elizabeth Romeyn Elwyn 1953 (died 2002); ed Westminster School, Architectural Asscn School of Architecture; pvt. practice since winning competitition for British Railway Branch Offices 1937; taught at Architectural Asscn School 1946–49; Tutor, Royal Coll. of Art. 1952–61; architect in partnership with John Metcalfe 1962–84; Visiting Critic, School of Architecture, Harvard Univ. 1956; Prof. of Architecture, Royal Acad. 1975–88; mem. group partnership with Eric Lyons, Cunningham partnership for W Chelsea redevt. for Royal Borough of Kensington and Chelsea; mem. RIBA Council 1951–53, British Cttee of Int. Union of Architects 1951–54, Modern Architectural Research group (MARS); Pres. Architectural Asscn 1959–60; Hon. Fellow, RCA, Kent Inst. of Art and Design 1992. *Work includes:* pavilions for 'The Origins of the People, main concourse and fountain display, Festival of Britain; schools, housing, display and interiors; new civic centre, Gravesend; halls of residence, Univ. of Birmingham; new premises for Royal Coll. of Art (with Sir Hugh Casson and Prof. Robert Goodden); lecture halls, Univ. of Essex. *Address:* 3 Church Walk, Aldeburgh, Suffolk, IP15 5DU, England. *Telephone:* (1728) 452591.

ČAĐO, Stanislav; Bosnia and Herzegovina politician; *Minister of Internal Affairs, Republika Srpska;* b. 1961, Bosanska Gradiška; m.; two c.; ed Univ. of Banja Luka; worked for Vuk Karadžić publishing co.; Civil Servant, Dept for Social-Political Orgs, Laktaši Municipal Council; fmr Commercial Man., Sim Prom (import and export co.); fmr Gen. Man. Technogas; Minister of Internal Affairs 2006–. *Address:* Ministry of Internal Affairs of Republika Srpska, 78000 Banja Luka, Desanke Maksimović 4, Bosnia and Herzegovina (office). *Telephone:* (51) 334306 (office). *Fax:* (51) 334304 (office). *E-mail:* mup@mup .vladars.net (office). *Website:* www.mup.vladars.net (office).

CADOGAN, Sir John Ivan George, Kt, CBE, PhD, FRS, FRSE, CChem, FRSC; British chemist, industrialist and academic; *Professorial Fellow, University College of Swansea;* b. 8 Oct. 1930, Pembrey, Carmarthenshire; s. of the late Alfred Cadogan and of Dilys Cadogan; m. 1st Margaret Jeanne Evans 1955 (deceased 1992); one s. one d.; m. 2nd Elizabeth Purnell 1997; ed Grammar School, Swansea and King's Coll., London; research at King's Coll., London 1951–54; Civil Service Research Fellow 1954–56; Lecturer in Chem., King's Coll., London 1956–63; Purdie Prof. of Chem. and Head of Dept, St Salvator's Coll., Univ. of St Andrews 1963–69; Forbes Prof. of Organic Chem., Univ. of Edin. 1969–79; Chief Scientist, BP Research Centre 1979–81; Dir of Research, British Petroleum 1981–92, CEO BP Ventures 1988–92; Dir Gen. Research Council 1994–99; Chair. DNA Research Innovations Ltd 1999–2004; Science Policy Adviser, Science Foundation Ireland 1999-2005; Dir BP Chemicals Int. Ltd, BP Venezuela Ltd; Visiting Prof., Imperial Coll., London 1979–2002; Professorial Fellow, Univ. Coll. of Swansea, Univ. of Wales 1979–; mem. Council, Royal Inst. 1984–87, Royal Comm. on Criminal Justice 1991–93; Past Pres. Royal Soc. of Chem. 1982–84; Gov. Jt Research Centre, EC 1994–; Chair. Fusion Antibodies Ltd 2005–; mem. numerous scientific cttees; Hon. FREng 1992; recipient of 20 fellowships and hon. degrees; several prizes. *Publications:* about 300 papers in professional journals. *Leisure interests:* supporting rugby football, being in France, gardening. *Address:* Department of Chemistry, University of Wales, Singleton Park, Swansea, SA2 8PP, Wales (office). *Telephone:* (1792) 295306 (office). *Website:* www.swan.ac.uk/chemistry (office).

CADOT, Michel François Jacques; French civil servant and administrator; *Minister of Agriculture;* b. 22 May 1954, Suresnes, Seine; s. of Jean Cadot and Elsa Cadot (née Puiatti); m. Catherine Van Luchene 1981; three s. two d.; ed Lycées Charlemagne and Henri IV, Paris, Univ. of Paris II Panthéon, Ecole Nat. d'Admin.; Civil Admin., Ministry of the Interior 1980; Asst. Prefect, Dir. of Cabinet of Prefect of Oise 1980–82 Sec.-Gen. of Prefecture of Cantal 1982–85; Civil Admin., Embassy in Venezuela 1985–88; Asst. Prefect of Saint-Julien-en-Genevois 1988–89; Civil Admin., Elf Aquitaine 1989–93; Sec.-Gen. Elf Trading S.A. 1989–93; Asst. Prefect of Béziers 1993–95; Prefect of Languedoc-Roussillon 1993–95, of Meuse 1998–2000, of Martinique 2000–04; Dir. Office of Sec. of State for Rural Devt. 1995, of Minister for Agric., Food and Fisheries 2004–06, Advisor to Prime Minister Dominique de Villepin 2006–07, Minister of Agric. 2007–; Dir for Man. of Region of Datar 1995–98. *Address:* Ministry of Agriculture, 78 rue de Varenne, 75349 Paris, France (office). *Telephone:* 1-49-55-60-11 (office). *Fax:* 1-49-55-83-55 (office). *E-mail:* info@ agriculture.gouv.fr (office). *Website:* www.agriculture.gouv.fr (office).

CAETANI, Oleg; Swiss conductor; *Chief Conductor and Artistic Director, Melbourne Symphony Orchestra;* b. 1956, Lausanne; ed studied with Nadia Boulanger, Franco Ferrara in Rome, Kyrill Kondrashin in Moscow and Ilia Mussin in Leningrad; Asst to Otmar Suitner, Staatsoper Berlin 1981–84; Deutsche Nationaltheater Weimar 1984–87; Kapellmeister, Städtische Buhnen Frankfurt am Main; Music Dir, Wiesbaden 1992–95, leading the Ring, Tristan und Isolde, La Forza del Destino, Otello, Rimsky's Invisible City of Kitezh and Bluebeard's Castle; guest engagements with Semiramide in Vienna, Les Vêpres Siciliennes in Nice, Lucia di Lammermoor and Tosca at Trieste and Verdi's Falstaff at Stuttgart 1996–97; Zürich Opera with Rigoletto, The Nutcracker, La Bohème and Norma; led Tchaikovsky's Maid of Orleans at Strasbourg 1998; concert repertory includes music by Beethoven, Schubert, Schumann and Shostakovich, with soloists such as Martha Argerich, Viktoria Mullova, Shlomo Mintz and the late Sviatoslav Richter; Music Dir, Chemnitz 1996–2001; Chief Conductor Designate Melbourne Symphony Orchestra 2003–04, Chief Conductor and Artistic Dir 2005–; winner RAI Competition in Turin 1979, prizewinner, Herbert von Karajan Competition 1982. *Address:* Melbourne Symphony Orchestra, GPO Box 9994, Melbourne, Vic. 3001, Australia (office). *E-mail:* olegcaetani@ hotmail.com (home). *Website:* www.olegcaetani.com.

CAFFARELLI, Luis A., MSc, PhD; Argentine/American mathematician and academic; *Sid Richardson Chair, University of Texas;* b. 8 Dec. 1948, Buenos Aires; m. Irene M. Gamba; three s.; ed Univ. of Buenos Aires; expert in free boundary problems for nonlinear partial differential equations; Postdoctoral Researcher, Univ. of Minnesota 1973–74, Asst Prof. 1975–77, Assoc. Prof. 1977–79, Prof. 1979–83; Prof., Courant Inst. of Math. Sciences, New York Univ. 1980–82, 1994–97; Prof., Univ. of Chicago 1983–86; Perm. Faculty Mem. Inst. for Advanced Study, Princeton 1986–96; Prof., Univ. of Texas at Austin 1997–, currently holds Sid Richardson Chair; mem. NAS 1991, American Math. Soc., Union Matematica Argentina, American Acad. of Arts and Sciences, Pontifical Acad. of Sciences; Foreign mem. Accad. Nazionale delle Scienze (dei XL, Italy), Accad. Nazionale dei Lincei (Italy), Academia Nacional de Ciencias, Buenos Aires, Academia Nacional de Ciencias, Cordoba, Insituto Lombardo, Accad. di Scienze e Lettere (Italy); Hon. Prof., Universidad de Buenos Aires, Universidad de Mar del Plata; Dr hc (École Normale Superieure, Paris, Universidad Autónoma de Madrid, Universidad de La Plata, Argentina, Universidad de San Luis, Argentina); Stampacchia Prize (jtly) 1982, Bocher Prize 1984, Pius XI Gold Medal, Pontifical Acad. of Sciences

1988, Premio Konex, Platino y Brillantes (Argentina) 2003, Rolf Schock Prize, Royal Swedish Acad. of Sciences 2005, American Math. Soc. Steele Prize for Lifetime Achievment 2009. *Publications:* numerous articles on partial differential equations and their applications. *Address:* RLM 10.150, Department of Mathematics, University of Texas at Austin, 1 University Station C1200, Austin, TX 78712-0257, USA (office). *Telephone:* (512) 471-3160 (office). *Fax:* (512) 471-9038 (office). *E-mail:* caffarel@math.utexas.edu (office). *Website:* www.ma.utexas.edu (office).

CAFU; Brazilian professional football player; b. (Marcos Evangelista de Moraes), 7 June 1970, São Paulo; defender (right back) São Paulo 1988–93, Zaragoza 1994–95, Palmeiras 1995–97, Roma, Italy 1997–2003, AC Milan, Italy 2003–08; mem. nat. team 1994–2006; 142 int. caps; only player to have played in three World Cup finals; Brazilian record of 16 World Cup appearances. *Address:* Fundação Cafu, Rua Edward Joseph, 122, cj. 85/86 Morumbi, São Paulo, SP 05709-020, Brazil. *Telephone:* (11) 3772-6630. *E-mail:* cafu@fundacaocafu.org.br (office). *Website:* www.fundacaocafu.org.br.

CAGE, Nicolas; American actor and film company executive; b. (Nicolas Coppola), 7 Jan. 1964, Long Beach, Calif.; s. of Prof. August Coppola and Joy Vogelsang; nephew of Francis Ford Coppola (q.v.); m. 1st Patricia Arquette (q.v.) 1995 (divorced 2001); m. 2nd Lisa Marie Presley 2002 (divorced 2004); m. 3rd Alice Kim 2004, one s.; one s. with Christina Fulton; ed studied theatre at Beverly Hills High; changed his name early in his career to make his own reputation; secured bit part in Fast Times at Ridgemont High 1982; took job selling popcorn at Fairfax Theater; then landed role in his uncle's film Rumble Fish 1983 followed by role as punk-rocker in Valley Girl 1983 (released first) which launched his career; f. Saturn Films (production co.); Dr hc (Calif. State, Fullerton); numerous awards including Acad. Award for Best Actor 1996, Golden Globe Award for Best Actor 1996, Lifetime Achievement Award 1996, P. J. Owens Award 1998, Charles A. Crain Desert Palm Award 2001. *Films include:* Fast Times at Ridgemont High 1982, Valley Girl 1983, Rumble Fish 1983, Racing with the Moon 1984, The Cotton Club 1984, Birdy 1984, The Boy in Blue 1986, Peggy Sue Got Married 1986, Raising Arizona 1987, Moonstruck 1987, Never on Tuesday (uncredited) 1988, Vampire's Kiss 1989, Tempo di uccidere (aka Le raccourci, aka The Short Cut, aka Time to Kill) 1989, Fire Birds 1990, Wild at Heart 1990, Zandalee 1991, Red Rock West 1992, Honeymoon in Vegas 1992, Amos & Andrew 1993, Deadfall 1993, Guarding Tess 1994, It Could Happen to You 1994, Trapped in Paradise 1994, Kiss of Death 1995, Leaving Las Vegas (Golden Globe Award for Best Actor 1996, Acad. Award for Best Actor 1996) 1995, The Rock 1996, The Funeral 1996, Con Air 1997, Face/Off 1997, City of Angels 1998, Snake Eyes 1998, 8MM 1999, Bringing Out the Dead 1999, Gone in 60 Seconds 2000, The Family Man 2001, Captain Corelli's Mandolin 2001, Christmas Carol: The Movie (voice) 2001, Windtalkers 2002, Sonny 2002, Adaptation 2003, Matchstick Men 2003, National Treasure 2004, Lord of War 2005, The Weather Man 2005, The Ant Bully (voice) 2006, World Trade Center 2006, The Wicker Man 2006, Ghost Rider 2006, Grindhouse 2007, Next 2007, National Treasure: Book of Secrets 2007, Bangkok Dangerous 2007, Knowing 2009. *Television includes:* Best of Times 1981, Industrial Symphony No. 1: The Dream of the Brokenhearted 1990. *Address:* c/o Creative Artists Agency, 9830 Wilshire Blvd, Beverly Hills, CA 90212-1825, USA (office); Saturn Films, 9000 W Sunset Boulevard, Suite 911, West Hollywood, CA 90069, USA (office). *Telephone:* (310) 288-4545 (office); (310) 887-0900. *Fax:* (310) 288-4800 (office); (310) 248-2965. *Website:* www.caa.com (office); www.saturnfilms.com.

CAGIATI, Andrea, LLB; Italian diplomatist; b. 11 July 1922, Rome; s. of Filippo Cagiati and Germaine Dewies; m. Sigrid von Morgen 1968; one s. one d.; ed Univ. of Siena; entered Foreign Service 1948; Sec., Paris 1950–51; Prin. Pvt. Sec. to Minister of State for Foreign Affairs 1951–53; Vice-Consul-Gen., New York 1953–55; Prin. Pvt. Sec. to Minister of State for Foreign Affairs, then with Dept of Political Affairs 1955–57; Counsellor, Athens 1957–60, Mexico 1960–62; Del. Disarmament Cttee, Geneva March–Dec. 1962; mem. Italian del. to UN June 1962; Head NATO Dept 1962–66; Minister-Counsellor, Madrid 1966–68; Amb. to Colombia 1968–71; Inst. for Diplomatic Studies 1971–72; Diplomatic Adviser to Prime Minister 1972–73; Amb. to Austria 1973–80, to UK 1980–86, to the Vatican 1986–88; Vice-Chair. Alitalia 1989–94 (Dir 1987–94); Pres. Fondazione Cagiati-von Morgen 1990–, Fondazione Aristenza Sanitaria Melitense 1997–; Vice-Pres. Fondazione De Gasperi; Hon. Pres. Circolo Studi Diplomatici, Eurodéfence Italia; Hon. GCVO 1980, Grand Cross of Merit (Italy, Austria, Holy See), Kt, Order of Malta. *Publications:* La Diplomazia 1945, Verso quale avvenire? 1957, I sentieri della vita 1990, Scritti di politica estera (five vols) 1991–2007, Verso l'Europa Unita 2008; and numerous articles on foreign policy and int. affairs. *Leisure interests:* sculpture, golf, shooting. *Address:* 3 Av. degli Astalli, 00186 Rome (office); Largo Olgiata, 15 (49D), 00123 Rome, Italy (home). *Telephone:* (6) 6791052 (office); (6) 30888135 (home). *Fax:* (6) 6781148 (office).

ÇAĞLAYAN, Zafer; Turkish business executive and politician; *Minister of Industry and Trade;* b. 1957, Muş; m.; two c.; ed Gazi Univ., Ankara; Chair. Ankara Chamber of Industry (ASO) 1995–2007; Deputy Chair. Turkish Union of Chambers and Commodities Exchanges (TOBB) 2005–07; mem. Parl. (AKP) 2007–, Minister of Industry and Trade 2007–; Chair. Çağlayanlar Alüminyum Ltd, Akel Alüminyum A.Ş. *Address:* Ministry of Industry and Trade, Sanayi ve Ticaret Bakanliği, Eskişehir yolu üzeri 7 km, Ankara, Turkey (office). *Telephone:* (312) 2860365 (office). *E-mail:* zcaglayanailetin@zafercaglayan.com.tr; akel@akelmetal.com.tr. *Website:* www.sanayi.gov.tr; www.zafercaglayan.com; www.akelmetal.com.tr.

CAHILL, Teresa Mary, LRAM, AGSM; British singer (soprano); b. 30 July 1944, Maidenhead, Berks.; d. of Henry D. Cahill and Florence Cahill (née Dallimore); m. 1st John Anthony Kiernander 1971 (divorced 1978); m. 2nd Dr Robert Saxton 2005; ed Notre Dame High School, Southwark, Guildhall School of Music and Drama and London Opera Centre; debut at Glyndebourne 1969, Covent Garden 1970, La Scala, Milan 1976, Philadelphia Opera 1981; Prof., Trinity Coll. of Music, London; specializes in works of Mozart, Strauss, Mahler, Elgar and Tippett; has given concerts with all the London orchestras, Boston Symphony Orchestra, Chicago Symphony Orchestra, Berlin, Vienna and Bath Festivals and throughout Europe, USA and the Far East; Artistic Adviser Nat. Mozart Competition 1997–; Adjudicator Live Music Now 1988– (Musical Adviser 2000–); Gov. Royal Soc. of Music 2000–04; masterclasses, Dartington Festival 1984, 1986, Hertogenbosch 1988, 2000, Univ. of Oxford 1995–96, Peabody Inst. Baltimore 1999, RAM 2002, Bowdoin Coll., Maine 2004; Worshipful Company of Musicians Silver Medal 1966, John Christie Award 1970. *Recordings include:* works by Elgar, Strauss, Mahler, Mozart, Rachmaninov, Saxton and Lutyens. *Publications:* contrib. to 'Divas in their Own Words', compiled by Andrew Palmer. *Leisure interests:* cinema, theatre, travel, photography, reading and going to sales, from car boots to Sothebys. *Address:* 65 Leyland Road, London, SE12 8DW, England. *Telephone:* (020) 8852-0847 (home). *E-mail:* tessitura@btopenworld.com (office).

CAHUC, Pierre, DEcon; French economist and academic; *Professor of Economics, Ecole Polytechnique;* three c.; ed Ecole polytechnique, Agrégation des Universités en Sciences Economiques; Prof. of Econs, Univ. of Paris I-Panthéon-Sorbonne 1992–2003, Research Fellow, CREST-INSEE Laboratoire de Macroéconomie 2003–; Asst Prof. (Professeur charge de cours), École Polytechnique, Paris 1998–, Prof. of Econs 2007–; Research Fellow, Inst. for the Study of Labor (IZA), Bonn, Germany 1999–, Program Dir 'Labor Markets and Institutions' 2004–; Research Fellow, Centre for Econ. Policy Research 2001–; mem. Comm. Economique de la Nation 2003–, Conseil de l'Emploi des Revenus et de la Cohésion Sociale 2004–, Prime Minister's Econ. Council 2006–; Assoc. Ed. Labour Economics, Journal of Economics/Zeitschrift für Nationalökonomie; mem. Scientific Cttee Problèmes Economiques, Economie et Statistique; Jr mem. Institut Universitaire de France 1998–2003; Chevalier des Palmes Acadèmiques 2004; Prix de thèse, Asscn Française de Science Economique 1989, Prix du 'Meilleur jeune economiste', Le Monde and Le Cercle des Economistes 2001, Prix Risque les Echos 2005, Prix Zerilli-Marimo 2006, Prix du livre d'Economie 2007, Lire magazine Best Essay Prize 2007, Prix du livre des dirigeants, essay section 2007. *Publications:* Les negociations salariales, des fondements microéconomiques aux implications macroéconomiques 1991, La Nouvelle Microéconomie 1993, Economie du travail, La formation des salaires et les déterminants du chômage (with Andre Zylberberg) 1996, La réduction du temps de travail, une solution pour l'emploi? (co-ed.) 1997, Le marché du travail (with Andre Zylberberg) 2001, La microéconomie du marché du travail (with Andre Zylberberg) 2003, Le chômage, fatalité ou nécessité? (with Andre Zylberberg) (Prix Mutation et Travail 2004, Prix Européen du livre d'économie 2004, Prix ManPower 2005 de l'ouvrage de ressources humaines) 2004, Labor Economics (with Andre Zylberberg) 2004; more than 85 articles in professional journals. *Address:* CREST-INSEE, Timbre J 360, 15 Boulevard Gabriel-Peri, 92245 Malakoff, France (office). *Telephone:* 1-41-17-37-17 (office). *E-mail:* cahuc@ensae.fr (office). *Website:* www.crest.fr/pageperso/cahuc/cahuc.htm (office).

CAI, Guo-Qiang; Chinese artist; b. 8 Dec. 1957, Quanzhou City, Fujian Prov.; ed Shanghai Drama Inst., Nat. and Int. Studio Program at P.S. 1, New York; lived in Japan 1986–95; explored properties of gunpowder in his drawings, experimented with explosives including signature explosion events exemplified in his series Projects for Extraterrestrials; has collaborated with specialists and experts from various disciplines including Issey Miyake, Rafael Vinoly, Zaha Hadid, Tan Dun and Tsai Ming-liang among others; has lived in New York since 1995; Dir of Visual and Special Effects for opening and closing ceremonies of Beijing Olympics 2008; Japan Cultural Design Prize, Tokyo 1995, Benesse Prize of Transculture Exhbn, 46th Venice Biennial 1995, Oribe Awards, Gifu (Japan) 1997, 48th Venice Biennial Int. Golden Lion Prize 1999, CalArts/Alpert Award in the Arts (USA) 2001, Hiroshima Art Prize, Hiroshima City Culture Foundation (Japan) 2007; several awards for Best Exhbn and Best Installation from Int. Curators Asscn; repeatedly listed amongst the UK journal ArtReview's Power 100. *Works in permanent collections:* Agnes Gund Collection, New York, Annie Wong Art Foundation, Vancouver, BC, Astrup Fernley Museum of Modern Art, Oslo, Centre Pompidou, Paris, City of New York, City of Iwaki, Japan, City of Mito, Japan, Cleveland Museum of Art, Contemporary Art Gallery, Art Tower Mito, Japan, Dentsu, Caretta Shiodome, Tokyo, Deste Foundation, Athens, Deutsche Bank Collection, Germany Echigo-Tsumari Region, Niigata Prefecture, Japan, Fogg Art Museum, Harvard Univ. Art Museums, Fondation Cartier pour l'art contemporain, Paris, Fonds Nat. d'art Contemporain and Musée d'art contemporain Lyon, Fukuoka Asia Art Museum, Fukuoka, Japan, Glory Fine Arts Museum, Hsinchu, Taiwan, Graphische Sammlung Albertina Wien, Vienna, Guangdong Museum of Art, Guangzhou, China, Hirshhorn Museum and Sculpture Garden, Smithsonian Inst., Washington, DC, Ho-Am Art Museum, Seoul, Issey Miyake Inc., Japan, Iwaki City Art Museum, Japan, The Japan Foundation, Tokyo, Louisiana Museum of Modern Art, Humlebaek, Denmark, Ludwig Foundation, Germany, MARTa Herford, Herford, Germany, Modern Museum, Stockholm, Mori Art Center, Tokyo, Museo Navale di Venezia, Museu de Arte Moderna da Bahia, Bahia, Brazil, Museum of Contemporary Art, Tokyo, Museum of Modern Art, New York, Museum of Modern Art, Saitama, Japan, Naoshima Contemporary Art Museum, Japan, Queensland Art Gallery, Brisbane, Queens Museum of Art, New York, Riiksmuseum, Kroller-Muller, Netherlands, Setagaya Art Museum, Tokyo, Shigaraki Ceramic Cultural Park, Shigaraki, Japan, San Diego Museum of Art, Shiseido Co. Ltd, Tokyo, S.M.A.K.: Museum van Hedendaags Kunst Ghent, Solomon R. Guggenheim Museum, New York, Stadtische Galerie Nordhorn, Germany, Takamatsu City Museum of Art, Japan, Taiwan Museum of Art, Taichung, Tate Collection, London, Toki Messe Art Monument Project, Niigata Prefecture, Japan, among others. *Solo projects include:* Primeval Fireball: The Project for Projects, P3 art and environment, Tokyo 1991, Project to Extend the Great Wall of China by 10,000 Meters, Jiayuguan City 1993, The Century with Mushroom Clouds – Projects for the 20th Century, Nevada, Nuclear Test Site, Salt Lake, New York 1996, Cultural Melting Bath: Projects for the 20th Century, Queens Museum of Art, Queens, New York 1997, APEC Cityscape Fireworks Show, Asia Pacific Econ. Cooperation, Shanghai 2001, Explosion Project for Tate Modern, London 2003, Light Cycle Over Central Park, Asia Soc. and Museum, New York 2003, Explosion Project for Central Park, Creative Time, New York 2003, Kite Project for Siwa, Egypt 2003, Explosion Project for the Festival of China, John F. Kennedy Center for the Performing Arts, Washington, DC 2005, Curator DMoCA, Echigo-Tsumari Triennial, Japan 2006. *Address:* Cai Studio, 40 East First Street, New York, NY 10003, USA (office). *Telephone:* (212) 995-0908 (office). *Fax:* (212) 254-0336 (office). *E-mail:* studio@caiguoqiang.com (office). *Website:* www.caiguoqiang.com (office).

CAI, Wu; Chinese government official; *Minister of Culture;* b. Oct. 1949, Wedu Co., Gansu Prov.; ed Beijing Univ.; joined CCP 1973; mem. Communist Youth League of China (CYLC), Cen. Cttee, Standing Cttee 1983–95; mem. All-China Youth Fed. and Deputy Sec.-Gen. then Prin. 1983–95; Dir Int. Liaison Dept 1983–95, Research Office, then Deputy Sec.-Gen. 1995–97, Vice-Minister Int. Liaison Dept 1997–2005; Dir Information Office, State Council 2005–08; mem. 17th CCP Cen. Cttee 2007–; Minister of Culture 2008–; Prof. of Int. Relations, Beijing Univ. *Address:* Ministry of Culture, 10 Chaoyangmen Bei Jie, Dongcheng Qu, Beijing 100020, People's Republic of China (office). *Telephone:* (10) 65551432 (office). *Fax:* (10) 65551433 (office). *E-mail:* webmaster@whb1.ccnt.com.cn (office). *Website:* www.ccnt.com.cn (office).

CAI, Zhenhua, MA; Chinese fmr table tennis coach and sports official; *Deputy Minister, General Administration of Sport;* b. 3 Sept. 1961, Wuxi, Jiangsu Prov.; ed Hebei Normal Univ.; Head Coach, Chinese Men's Table Tennis Team 1991–97, Chief Coach 1997–2004; Chief Coach, Italian table tennis team 1985–89; Vice-Chair. Chinese Table Tennis Asscn; Deputy Head, Chinese Olympic Del. 2008; Vice-Pres. Chinese Olympic Cttee; Deputy Minister, Gen. Admin of Sports 2007–; fmr Vice-Pres. All-China Youth Fed. *Coaching achievements include:* 2000 Olympic Games: 4 gold medals, 3 silver medals, 1 bronze medal; 2001 World Championships: gold medals, 4 silver medals, 5 bronze medals; 2003 World Championships: 4 gold medals; 2004 World Team Championships: 1st men's/women's. *Address:* c/o State General Administration for Physical Culture and Sports, 9 Tiyuguan Road, Chongwen District, Beijing, 100061 People's Republic of China (office). *Telephone:* (10) 87183505 (office). *Fax:* (10) 67110248 (office).

CAI, Zimin; Chinese politician; b. 1926, Zhanghua City, Taiwan Prov.; ed Waseda Univ., Tokyo, Japan; Ed.-in-Chief, Zhonghua Daily, Beijing 1945–46, Freedom Daily, Taipei, Taiwan 1946–47; took part in Taiwan uprising 28th Feb. 1947; worker, People's Broadcasting Station, Shanghai 1947–48; Dir-Gen. Asscn of Fellow Taiwan Provincials in Shanghai 1947–48; joined CCP 1948; joined Taiwan Democratic Self-Govt League (TDSGL) 1949, later Exec. mem. 3rd Council and Head Propaganda Dept, Chair. Presidium 4th TDSGL 1987–88, Presidium 5th TDSGL 1992–97, Hon. Chair. Cen. Cttee TDSGL 1997–; Deputy Chief East China People's Broadcasting Station, Taiwan Section 1949; Head Cen. People's Broadcasting Station, Taiwan Group 1954; Chief Chinese People's Asscn for Cultural Relations with Foreign Countries, Japan Section 1975–78; Head Asian Group, Chinese People's Asscn for Cultural Relations with Foreign Countries 1975–78; Deputy Dir Relations with Foreign Countries Dept, Ministry of Culture 1975–78; fmr mem. Exec. Council Chinese Inst. of Taiwan Studies, China Overseas Exchanges Asscn; mem. 4th NPC 1975–78, 5th NPC 1978–83, Standing Cttee of 6th NPC 1983–88, Standing Cttee of 7th NPC 1988–93, Standing Cttee of 8th NPC 1993–98, Standing Cttee of 9th CPPCC 1998–2003; Counsellor, Cultural Section, Chinese Embassy, Tokyo 1981–85; Adviser Asscn for Relations across the Taiwan Straits (ARATS) 1991–; Vice-Chair. Cttee for Hong Kong, Macao, Taiwan and Overseas Chinese Affairs; Vice-Pres. China Overseas Friendship Asscn 1997–. *Publication:* Historical Trends in Taiwan. *Address:* c/o National Committee of Chinese People's Political Consultative Conference, 23 Taipingqiao Street, Beijing, People's Republic of China.

CAIN, John, LLB; Australian politician; b. 26 April 1931; s. of the late John Cain; m. Nancye Williams 1955; two s. one d.; ed Northcote High School, Scotch Coll. and Melbourne Univ.; mem. Council Law Inst. of Victoria 1967–76, Exec. Law Council of Australia 1973–76; Vice-Chair. Vic. Br. Australian Labor Party 1973–75; Pres. Law Inst., Vic. 1972–73, Chair. Council 1971–72; mem. Legis. Ass. for Bundoora, Vic. 1976–92; Leader of Opposition 1981–82; Premier of Vic. 1982–90; Professorial Assoc., Dept of Political Science, Melbourne Univ. 1991–; Attorney-Gen. 1982–83; Minister for Fed. Affairs 1982, Minister for Women's Affairs 1982–90, for Ethnic Affairs 1990; Treas. Law Inst., Vic. 1969–70; part-time mem. Law Reform Comm. of Australia 1975–77; mem. Commonwealth Secr. Observer Group, South African elections 1994; mem. Trust, Nat. Tennis Centre, Flinders Park 1990–94; Trustee, Melbourne Cricket Ground 1982–98, 1999–; Pres. Melbourne Univ. Grad. Union 2005–; Chair. Hume Global Village Learning Advisory Bd 2004–; mem. Faculty of Business and Law Academic Advisory Bd, Deakin Univ. 2004–, Melbourne and Olympic Parks Trust 2005–, Library Bd of Vic. 2005– (Pres. 2006–). *Publications:* John Cain's Years: Power, Parties and Politics 1994, On With the Show 1998, Off Course (with John Hewitt) 2004. *Leisure interests:* tennis, swimming, jogging. *Address:* 9 Magnolia Road, Ivanhoe, Vic. 3079, Australia.

CAINE, Sir Michael, Kt, CBE; British actor; b. (Maurice Joseph Micklewhite), 14 March 1933, London; s. of the late Maurice Joseph Micklewhite and of Ellen Frances Marie Micklewhite; m. 1st Patricia Haines 1954 (divorced); one d.; m. 2nd Shakira Khatoon Baksh 1973; one d.; ed Wilson's Grammar School, Peckham; army service, Berlin and Korea 1951–53; worked at repertory theatres, Horsham and Lowestoft 1953–55; Theatre Workshop, London 1955; mem. IBA 1984–; Hon. Fellow, Univ. of London 1994; BAFTA Award 2000. *Films include:* A Hill in Korea 1956, How to Murder a Rich Uncle 1958, Zulu 1964, The Ipcress File 1965, Alfie 1966, The Wrong Box 1966, Gambit 1966, Funeral in Berlin 1966, Billion Dollar Brain 1967, Woman Times Seven 1967, Deadfall 1967, The Magus 1968, Battle of Britain 1968, Play Dirty 1968, The Italian Job 1969, Too Late the Hero 1970, The Last Valley 1970, Kidnapped 1971, Pulp 1971, Get Carter 1971, Zee and Co. 1972, Sleuth 1973, The Black Windmill 1974, The Wilby Conspiracy 1974, The Destructors (also known as The Marseilles Contract) 1974, Peeper (also known as Fat Chance) 1975, The Romantic Englishwoman 1975, The Man Who Would be King 1975, Harry and Walter Go to New York 1976, The Eagle has Landed 1976, A Bridge Too Far, The Silver Bears 1976, The Swarm, California Suite 1977, Ashanti 1978, Beyond the Poseidon Adventure 1979, The Island 1979, Dressed to Kill 1979, Escape to Victory 1979, Deathtrap 1981, The Hand 1981, Educating Rita 1982, Jigsaw Man 1982, The Honorary Consul 1982, Blame it on Rio 1983, Water 1984, The Holcroft Covenant 1984, Sweet Liberty 1985, Mona Lisa 1985, The Whistle Blower 1985, Half Moon Street 1986, The Fourth Protocol 1986, Hannah and Her Sisters (Academy Award for Best Supporting Actor) 1986) 1986, Surrender 1987, Without a Clue 1988, Dirty Rotten Scoundrels 1988, A Shock to the System 1989, Mr. Destiny 1989, Bullseye 1989, Noises Off 1991, Blue Ice 1992, The Muppet Christmas Carol 1992, On Deadly Ground 1993, Bullet to Beijing 1994, Blood and Wine 1995, 20,000 Leagues under the Sea 1996, Mandela and De Klerk 1996, Curtain Call, Shadowrun, Little Voice 1997, The Debtors 1998, The Cider House Rules (Academy Award for Best Supporting Actor 2000) 1999, Quills 1999, Shiner 2000, Last Orders 2000, Quick Sand 2000, The Quiet American 2001, Austin Powers: Gold Member 2002, The Actors 2002, The Quiet American 2002, Secondhand Lions 2003, The Statement 2003, Around the Bend 2004, The Weather Man 2005, Bewitched 2005, Batman Begins 2005, Children of Men 2006, The Prestige (Best British Actor in a Supporting Role, London Film Critics' Circle Award 2007) 2006, Flawless 2007, Sleuth 2007, The Dark Knight 2008. *TV includes:* over 100 TV plays 1957–63, Jack the Ripper (mini-series) (Golden Globe Award 1988) 1988, World War 2: When Lions Roared (NBC TV) 1993. *Plays include:* Next Time I'll Sing to You 1963. *Publications:* Michael Caine's File of Facts 1987, Not Many People Know This 1988, What's It All About? 1992, Acting in Film 1993. *Leisure interests:* gardening, reading. *Address:* c/o Toni Howard, ICM, 8942 Wilshire Blvd, Beverly Hills, CA 90211, USA; c/o Duncan Heath, International Creative Management, Oxford House, 76 Oxford Street, London, W1R 0AX, England.

CAINE, Uri; American jazz pianist and classical composer; b. Philadelphia; ed Univ. of Pennsylvania; began studying piano with Bernard Pfeiffer; played in bands led by Philly Joe Jones, Johnny Coles, Odean Pope, Hank Mobley, Grover Washington, Mikey Roker and Jymmie Merritt during high school; studied music composition with George Crumb and George Rochenberg at univ. and performed with Joe Henderson, Donald Byrd, J. J. Johnson, Stanley Turrentine, Lester Bowie and Freddie Hubbard; recently performed in groups led by Don Byron, Dave Douglas, Terry Gibbs and Buddy DeFranco, Clark Terry, Rashid Ali, Arto Lindsay, Sam Rivers and Barry Altschul, Bobby Watson, Craig Handy, Annie Ross, Arto Lindsay, The Enja Band, Global Theory, The Woody Herman Band, The Master Musicians of Jajouka; performed at What is Jazz? Festival, New York, North Sea Jazz Festival, The Hague, Montréal Jazz Festival, Jazz Across the Borders, Berlin, Texaco Jazz Festival, NY, Umbria Jazz Festival, Gustav Mahler Festival, Toblach, Italy, Vittoria Jazz Festival, San Sebastian Jazz Festival, Newport Jazz Festival, Salzburg Festival, Munich Opera, Holland Festival, Israel Festival, ICRAM and others; Toblacher Komponierhäuschen Award for Best Mahler CD 1997. *Compositions include:* ballet composed for Vienna Volksoper 2000, version of Diabelli Variations for Concerto Köln 2001, Mahler Reimagined, London 2002. *Recordings include:* albums: Sphere Music 1993, Toys 1995, Urlicht/Primal Light 1996, Wagner e Veneza 1997, Blue Wail 1998, Sidewalks of New York 1999, Love Fugue 2000, The Goldberg Variations 2000 (performed by Penn. Ballet 2001), Solitaire 2001, Rio 2001, Bedrock3 2001, Closure (with Mark O'Leary and Ben Perowsky) 2006. *E-mail:* ucaine@verizon.net. *Website:* www.uricaine.com.

CAIO, Francesco, MBA; Italian business executive; *Vice-Chairman, Europe, Investment Banking, Nomura International plc;* b. 23 Aug. 1957; m. Meryl Caio; two c.; ed Politecnico di Milano, INSEAD; consultant with McKinsey, London 1986–1991; CEO Omnitel Pronto Italia (now Vodafone Italy) 1993–96; CEO Merloni (now Indesit) 1997–2000; Founder and CEO Netscalibur (internet service provider) 2000–03; Group CEO Cable & Wireless 2003–06; Vice-Chair., Europe, Lehman Brothers 2006–08, Chair. European Advisory Bd 2008, Vice-Chair., Europe, Investment Banking, Nomura International plc (after acquisition by Nomura of Lehman Brothers' Europe and Middle East investment bank and equities businesses) 2008–; mem. Bd of Dirs Motorola Corpn 2000–03; mem. Int. Advisory Bd, Univ. Bocconi, Milan; head of ind. review on next generation high speed broadband for UK Dept for Business Enterprise and Regulatory Reform 2008; mem. Steering Bd Digital Britain Report 2008–. *Address:* Nomura International plc, 25 Bank Street, London, E14 5LS, England (office). *Telephone:* (20) 7102-1000 (office). *Website:* www.nomura.com (office).

CAIRD, Most Rev. Donald Arthur Richard, BD, MA, DipEd; Irish ecclesiastic; b. 11 Dec. 1925, Dublin; s. of George R. Caird and Emily F. Dreaper; m. Nancy B. Sharpe 1963; one s. two d.; ed Wesley Coll., Dublin and Trinity Coll., Dublin; Curate-Asst, St Mark's, Dundela, Belfast 1950–53, Asst Master and Chaplain The Royal School, Portora 1953–57; Lecturer in Philosophy, Univ. of Wales 1957–60; Rector Rathmichael Parish, Co. Dublin 1960–69; Asst

www.worldwhoswho.com

Lecturer in Philosophy, Trinity Coll. Dublin 1962–63; Dean of Ossary, Kilkenny 1969–1970; Bishop of Limerick, Ardfert and Aghadoe 1970–76, of Meath and Kildare 1976–1985; Archbishop of Dublin, Primate of Ireland and Bishop of Glendalough 1985–96; Chair. Council Alexandra Coll. (Dublin); Chair. Church of Ireland Coll. of Educ.; mem. Bórd na Gaeilge (Govt Bd for Irish Language); Patron Nat. Youth Council of Ireland; Fellow, St Columba's Coll., Dublin; Visiting Prof. of Anglican Studies, Gen. Theological Seminary, New York 1997; Sr Exhibitioner, Foundation Scholar and Sr Moderator, Univ. of Dublin; Life mem. Royal Dublin Soc. 1995–; Hon. DD (Trinity Coll., Dublin) 1988; Hon. LLD (Nat. Univ. of Ireland) 1995; Hon. PhD (Pontifical Univ., Maynooth, Co. Kildare) 2002; Nat. Council for Educational Awards 1993. *Publication:* The Predicament of Natural Theology since the Criticism of Kant, in Directions 1970. *Leisure interests:* walking and swimming. *Address:* 3 Crofton Avenue, Dun Laoghaire, Co. Dublin, Ireland (home). *Telephone:* (1) 2807869 (home). *Fax:* (1) 2301053 (home).

CAIRNCROSS, Frances Anne, BA, MA; British journalist and academic; *Rector, Exeter College, Oxford;* b. 30 Aug. 1944, Otley, Yorks.; d. of Alexander Kirkland Cairncross and Mary Frances Cairncross; m. Hamish McRae 1971, two d.; ed St Anne's Coll., Oxford and Brown Univ., Providence, RI, USA; staff mem. The Times 1967–69, The Banker 1969, The Observer 1969–71; Econs Corresp., The Guardian 1973–81, Women's Ed. 1981–84; Britain Ed., The Economist 1984–89, Public Policy Ed. 1997–2000, Man. Ed. 2000–04; Chair., Econ. and Social Research Council 2001–07; High Sheriff of London 2004–05; elected to Rectorship of Exeter Coll., Oxford 2004–; Pres. BAAS 2005–06; Sr Fellow, School of Public Policy, UCLA; Visiting Fellow, Nuffield Coll.; Hon. Fellow, St Anne's Coll., Oxford, St Peter's Coll., Oxford; Dr hc (Univs of Glasgow, Birmingham, City, Loughborough, Trinity Coll. Dublin, East Anglia). *Publications:* Capital City (with Hamish McRae) 1971, The Second Great Crash 1973, The Guardian Guide to the Economy 1981, Changing Perceptions of Economic Policy 1981, Second Guardian Guide to the Economy 1983, Guide to the Economy 1987, Costing the Earth 1991, Green, Inc. 1995, The Death of Distance 1997, The Company of the Future 2002. *Leisure interest:* winter swimming. *Address:* Exeter College, Oxford, OX1 3DP, England (office). *Telephone:* (1865) 279647 (office). *Website:* www.exeter.ox .ac.uk (office).

CAIRNS, Christopher (Chris) Lance; New Zealand professional cricketer; b. 13 June 1970, Picton, Marlborough; s. of Lance Cairns; right-hand batsman, right-arm fast-medium bowler; teams: Northern Districts, Nottinghamshire 1989–96, 2003, Canterbury, New Zealand; in 62 Tests scored 3,320 runs (average 33.53), 218 wickets (average 29.40); in 199 One Day Ints scored 4,697 runs (average 29.72), 188 wickets (average 31.63); 10,680 first-class runs (average 35.36), 643 wickets (average 28.42) in 216 matches; with father Lance Cairns (former Test Player), the only father and son to have captured 10 wickets in single Test matches; retd from Test cricket 2004; Capt. Chandigarh Lions –2008; currently plays for Nottinghamshire in Twenty20 League; Wisden Cricketer of the Year 2000, PricewaterhouseCoopers No 1 All-rounder in the World 2000, New Zealand Nat. Bank Player of the Year 2001, Redpath Cup for Batting, Windsor Cup for Bowling. *Address:* c/o Nottinghamshire County Cricket Club, Trent Bridge, Nottingham, Notts., NG2 6AG, England.

CAIRNS, David Adam, CBE, MA; British journalist and musicologist; b. 8 June 1926, Loughton, Essex; s. of Sir Hugh William Bell Cairns and Barbara Cairns (née Smith); m. Rosemary Goodwin 1959; three s.; ed Winchester Coll., Oxford, Princeton Univ. Graduate Coll., USA; Library Clerk, House of Commons 1951–53; critic, Record News 1954–56; mem. editorial staff, Times Educational Supplement 1955–58; music critic, Spectator 1958–63, Evening Standard 1958–63; asst music critic, Financial Times 1963–67; music critic, New Statesman 1967–70; mem. staff, Philips Records, London 1968–70; Classic Programme Co-ordinator 1970–73; asst music critic, Sunday Times 1975–84, music critic 1985–92; Leverhulme Research Fellow 1972–74; Distinguished Visiting Prof., Univ. of California, Davis 1985; Distinguished Visiting Scholar, Getty Center for the History of Art and Humanities 1992; Visiting Resident Fellow, Merton Coll., Oxford 1993; Officier, Ordre des Arts et des Lettres 1991; Hon. DLitt (Southampton) 2001; British Acad. Derek Allen Memorial Prize 1990, Royal Philharmonic Soc. Award 1990, 1999, Yorkshire Post Prize 1990. *Publications:* The Memoirs of Hector Berlioz (ed. and trans.) 1969, Responses: Musical Essays and Reviews 1973, The Magic Flute (ENO Opera Guide) 1980, Falstaff (co-author, ENO Opera Guide) 1982, Berlioz: The Making of an Artist 1803–1832 (ASCAP Deems Taylor Award 2001) 1989, Berlioz: Servitude and Greatness 1832–1869 (Whitbread Biog. of the Year 2000, Samuel Johnson Non-Fiction Prize 2000, Prix de l'Academie Charles Croz 2003) 1999, Mozart and his Operas 2006; contrib. to articles on Beethoven and Berlioz, in Viking Opera Guide 1993. *Leisure interests:* conducting, reading, walking, cinema, theatre, cricket. *Address:* 49 Amerland Road, London, SW18 1QA, England. *Telephone:* (20) 8870-4931. *E-mail:* do3 .cairns@zen.co.uk (office).

CAIRNS, 6th Earl; Simon Dallas Cairns, BA, CVO, CBE; British business executive; *Chairman, Charities Aid Foundation;* b. 27 May 1939; s. of 5th Earl Cairns and Barbara Jeanne Harrisson; m. Amanda Mary Heathcoat Amory 1964; three s.; ed Eton, Trinity Coll., Cambridge; Chair. VSO 1981–92 (Treas. 1974–81); mem. City Capital Markets Cttee 1989–95; Dir S.G. Warburg Group PLC (fmrly Mercury Int. Group) 1985–95, Vice-Chair. 1987–91; Jt Chair. S.G. Warburg and Co. 1987–95, CEO, Deputy Chair. 1991–95; Chair. Commonwealth Devt Corpn (CDC Group PLC) 1995–2004, BAT Industries 1996–98 (Deputy Chair. June–Dec. 1995); Chair. Allied Zurich 1998–2000, Actis Capital LLP 2004–05; Vice-Chair. Zurich Allied 1998–2000, Zurich Financial Services 1998–2000; Chair. Commonwealth Business Council 1997–2003, Overseas Devt Inst. 1994–2002; Receiver Gen. Duchy of Cornwall 1990–2000; Dir Fresnillo PLC; mem. Bd of Dirs Celtel Int. BV, now Zain Africa BV 2I 2005– (Chair. 2007–), mem. Bd of Dirs The Mo Ibrahim Foundation. *Address:* c/o Zain Africa BV 2I, 4th Floor, 78 Brook Street, London, W1K 5EF; Bolehyde Manor, Allington, nr Chippenham, Wilts., SN14 6LW, England. *Telephone:* 7499-4555 (office). *E-mail:* Simon.Cairns@zain.com (office).

CALABRESI, Guido, BS, LLB, MA; American judge and professor of law; *Judge, US Court of Appeals (Second Circuit);* b. 18 Oct. 1932, Milan, Italy; s. of Massimo Calabresi and Bianca Maria Finzi-Contini Calabresi; m. Anne Gordon Audubon Tyler 1961; one s. two d.; ed Yale Coll., Magdalen Coll., Oxford, UK and Yale Law School; Asst Instructor, Dept of Econs, Yale Coll. 1955–56; with Thacher & Bartlett (law firm), New York 1957; mem. Conn. Bar 1958; law clerk to Mr Justice Hugo Black, US Supreme Court 1958–59; Asst Prof. of Law, Yale Univ. School of Law 1959–61, Assoc. Prof. 1961–62, Prof. of Law 1962–70; John Thomas Smith Prof. of Law, Yale Univ. 1970–78, Sterling Prof. of Law 1978–95, Sterling Prof. of Law Emer. 1995–, Dean Yale Univ. Law School 1985–94; Judge, US Court of Appeals (Second Circuit) 1994–; Corresp. mem. British Acad.; mem. Royal Acad. of Sweden, Accademia delle Scienze di Torino, Accad. Nazionale dei Lincei, American Acad. of Arts and Sciences, American Philosophical Soc.; Commendatore, Repub. of Italy 1994; awarded more than thirty hon. degrees; awards include Laetare Medal, Univ. of Notre Dame 1985, Thomas Jefferson Medal in Law 2000. *Publications:* The Costs of Accidents: A Legal and Economic Analysis 1970, Tragic Choices (with P. Bobbit) 1978, A Common Law for the Age of Statutes 1982, Ideals, Beliefs, Attitudes and the Law: Private Law Perspectives on a Public Law Problem 1985; more than 80 articles on law and related subjects. *Leisure interests:* walking, reading (especially history), gardening, travel, bridge. *Address:* United States Court of Appeals for the Second Circuit, 157 Church Street, New Haven, CT 06510-2100 (office); 639 Amity Road, Woodbridge, CT 06525-1206, USA (home). *Telephone:* (203) 773-2291 (office); (203) 393-0008 (home). *Fax:* (203) 773-2401 (office); (203) 393-1575 (home). *E-mail:* guido.calabresi@ yale.edu (office).

CALATRAVA VALLS, Santiago, PhD; Spanish architect, artist and civil engineer; *Principal, Santiago Calatrava LLC;* b. 28 July 1953, Benimamet, nr Valencia; m. Robertina Marangoni Calatrava; three s. one d.; ed Escuela Tecnica Superior de Arquitectura, Valencia, Fed. Inst. of Tech. (ETH), Zürich, Switzerland; asst, Fed. Inst. of Tech. (ETH), Zürich 1979; undertook small eng comms. 1980s; est. firm Santiago Calatrava LLC, Zürich, 1983, second office Paris 1989, third office Valencia 1991, fourth office New York 2004; won competitions to design and construct Stadelhofen Station, Zürich 1983, Bach de Roda Bridge (commissioned by Olympic Games), Barcelona 1984, Cathedral of St John the Divine, New York 1991; sculptural works include Shadow Machine (large-scale sculpture with undulating concrete fingers) 1993; recently selected to design the expansion of Museo dell'Opera del Duomo, Florence and Symphony Center for the Atlanta Symphony Orchestra, Georgia; mem. Acad. des Arts et Lettres, Paris; Creu Sant Jordi, Barcelona; twelve hon. doctorates; Gold Medal, Inst. of Structural Engineers (UK), City of Toronto Urban Design Award (Canada), Global Leader for Tomorrow, World Econ. Forum, Davos (Switzerland), Algur H. Meadows Award for Excellence in the Arts, Meadows School of the Arts, Gold Medal, Circolo de Bellas Artes, Valencia, Sir Misha Black Medal, Royal Coll. of Art (UK), Leonardo da Vinci Medal, Société pour les Formations des Ingénieurs (France); Principe de Asturias Art Prize; Eugene McDermott Award in the Arts, MIT, American Inst. of Architects Gold Medal, Gold Medal for Merit in the Fine Arts, Ministry of Culture (Granada). *Architectural works include:* Alamillo Bridge Viaduct, Seville 1987–92, BCE Place Mall, Toronto 1987–92, Campo Volantin Footbridge, Bilbao 1990–97, Alameda Bridge and Underground Station, Valencia 1991–95, Lyon Airport Station, France 1989–94, City of Arts and Sciences, Valencia 1991–, Oriente Railway Station, Lisbon, Portugal 1993–98, Sondica Airport, Bilbao 2000, The Bridge of Europe, Orléans, France 2000, Bodegas Ysios Winery, Laguardia 2001, Milwaukee Art Museum, USA (Time Magazine 'Best of 2001' designation) 2001, Tenerife Auditorium, Santa Cruz, Canary Islands, 2003, Turtle Bay Bridge, Redding, Calif., USA 2004, Athens Olympic Sports Complex, Greece 2004, World Trade Center Transportation Hub, New York 2004–, Valencia Opera House 2005, Petach Tikvah Bridge, Israel 2005, Quarro Ponte sul Canal Grande, Venice, Italy 2005, Turning Torso Tower, Malmö, Sweden 2005. *Address:* Santiago Calatrava LLC, Parkring 11, 8002 Zürich, Switzerland (office). *Telephone:* (1) 2045000 (office). *Fax:* (1) 2045001 (office). *E-mail:* zurich@scsa-mail.com (office). *Website:* www .calatrava.com (office).

CALDER, Elisabeth (Liz) Nicole, BA; British publisher; b. 20 Jan. 1938, New Zealand; d. of Ivor George Baber and Florence Mary Baber; m. 1st Richard Henry Calder 1958 (divorced 1972); one s. one d.; m. 2nd Louis Baum 2000; ed Palmerston North Girls' High School, NZ and Univ. of Canterbury, NZ; catwalk model in Brazil 1965–68; reader Metro-Goldwyn-Mayer Story Dept 1969–70; Publicity Man. Victor Gollancz 1971–74, Editorial Dir 1975–78; Editorial Dir (fiction), Jonathan Cape 1979–86; Founding Publishing Dir Book Div., Bloomsbury Publishing 1986–2008, Ed. 2008–; co-f. Women in Publishing 1979; co-f. Groucho Club, London 1984; f. Parati Int. Literary Festival, Brazil 2003–; Chair. Royal Court Theatre 2001–05, Vice-Chair. 2005–; Order of Merit for services to culture, Brazil 2004. *Address:* Bloomsbury Publishing plc, 38 Soho Square, London, W1V 5DF, England. *Telephone:* (20) 7494-2111. *Website:* www.bloomsbury.com.

CALDER, John Mackenzie; British publisher, critic, playwright and theatre administrator; *Managing Director, Calder Publishers Ltd;* b. 25 Jan. 1927; m. 1st Mary A. Simmonds 1949; one d.; m. 2nd Bettina Jonic 1960 (divorced 1975); one d.; ed Gilling Castle, Yorks., Bishops Coll. School, Canada, McGill Univ., Montreal, Sir George Williams Coll. and Univ. of Zürich, Switzerland; Founder and Man. Dir John Calder (Publishers) Ltd 1950–91, Calder Publishers Ltd 1991–, Calder and Boyars Ltd 1964–75, f.

Calder Bookshop; expanded to Edin. 1971; organized literature confs, Edin. Festival 1962, 1963, Harrogate Festival 1969; f. Ledlanet Nights (music and opera festival) Kinross-shire 1963–74; Pres. Riverrun Press Inc., New York 1978–; Prof. of Literature and Philosophy, Ecole Active Bilingue, Paris 1994–96; Lecturer in History, Univ. of Paris-Nanterre 1995; acquired bookselling business of Better Books, London 1969; Chair. North American Book Clubs 1982–89, Fed. of Scottish Theatres 1972–74; Co-founder Defence of Literature and the Arts Soc.; Dir of other cos associated with opera, publishing etc.; f. Samuel Beckett Theatre, Waterloo, London; Theatre Admin. Godot Co.; Chevalier des Arts et des Lettres; Officier, Ordre nat. du Mérite; Dr hc (Edinburgh, Zurich). *Plays include:* Lorca, The Voice, The Trust. *Publications:* A Samuel Beckett Reader, The Burroughs Reader 1981, New Beckett Reader 1983, Henry Miller Reader 1985, Nouveau Roman Reader 1986, The Defence of Literature 1991, The Garden of Eros 1992, The Philosophy of Samuel Beckett 1998, What's Wrong, What's Right (poetry) 1999, Pursuit (autobiography) 2001. *Leisure interests:* writing, reading, music, theatre, opera, chess, conversation, travelling, promoting good causes, good food and wine. *Address:* Calder Publications Ltd, 51 The Cut, London, SE1 8LF, England (office); Riverrun Press Inc., 100 Newfield Avenue, Edison, NJ 08837, USA (office); 9 rue de Ramainville, 93100 Montreuil, France. *Telephone:* (20) 7633-0599 (UK) (home); 1-49-88-75-12 (France). *Fax:* 1-48-59-66-68 (France). *E-mail:* info@calderpublications.com (office). *Website:* www.calderpublications.com (office).

CALDERA, Louis Edward, BS, MBA, JD; American lawyer, university administrator and government official; *Director, White House Military Office;* b. 1 April 1956, El Paso, Tex.; s. of Benjamin Luis Caldera and Soledad Siqueiros; m. Eva Orlebeke Caldera; ed US Mil. Acad., West Point and Harvard Univ.; called to Bar, Calif. 1987; Commdr 2nd Lt US Army 1978, advanced through ranks to Capt. 1982, resigned comm. 1983; Assoc. O'Melveny & Myers (law firm), LA 1987–89, Buchalter, Nemer, Fields & Younger, LA 1990–91; Deputy Co. Counsel, Co. of LA 1991–92; mem. Calif. State Ass., 46th Dist, LA 1992–97, Chair. Banking and Finance Cttee; Man. Dir and COO Corpn for Nat. Service, Washington, DC 1997–98; Sec. of US Army 1998–2001; Vice-Chancellor for Univ. Advancement, Calif. State Univ. System 2002–03; Pres. Univ. of New Mexico 2003–06, mem. faculty School of Law 2006–08; Dir White House Mil. Office, Washington, DC 2009–; mem. Bd of Dirs IndyMac Bank 2002–08; mem. Bd of Trustees Claremont McKenna Coll., Nat. World War II Museum; mem. Council on Foreign Relations; Democrat; Dr hc (Norwich Univ.) 2000. *Address:* White House Military Office, Executive Office of the President, 1600 Pennsylvania Ave, NW, Washington, DC 20500, USA (office). *Telephone:* (202) 456-1414 (office). *Website:* www.whitehouse.gov/whmo (office).

CALDERA CARDINAL, Norman José, DPhil; Nicaraguan politician, economist and consultant; b. 21 Oct. 1946, Managua; m. Nora Maria Mayorga Arg Üello; one s. two d.; ed Wentworth Mil. Acad., Lexington, Mo., Univ. of Texas, Columbia Univ., USA; fmr Marketing Supervisor, then Product Man. Kimberley Clark Co.; Finance Gen. Empresas Universales SA 1972, Exports Man. 1975, Gen. Man. 1976; consultant to Agricultural Devt of Latin America Investment Co. 1979, to OAS 1979, to UNCTAD/GATT 1980–96, to GUATEXPRO 1980–84 (apptd Chief Adviser 1984); Adjunct Sec.-Gen. SIECA and COMIECO (Cabinet of Integration and Commerce of Cen. America) 1992–95; consultant to IDB 1995–96, UNCTAD 1996; Econ. Adviser to Pres. of Nicaragua 1996–97; Exec. Sec., Cttee to Reform the Public Admin 1997; Minister of Trade, Industry and Commerce 1999–2001, of Foreign Affairs 2002–06. *Address:* c/o Ministry of Foreign Affairs, Del Cine González al Sur sobre Avda Bolivar, Managua, Nicaragua (office).

CALDERA RODRÍGUEZ, Rafael; Venezuelan lawyer and fmr head of state; b. 24 Jan. 1916, San Felipe, Yaracuy; s. of Dr Rafael Caldera and Rosa Sofia R. Caldera; m. Alicia Pietri Montemayor 1941; three s. three d.; Sec., Cen. Council of Soc. of Venezuelan Catholic Youth 1932–34; f. Nat. Union of Students (UNE) 1936; graduated as lawyer 1939; mem. Chamber of Deputies 1941; f. Acción Nacional 1942; Co-founder Partido Social-Cristiano (COPEI) 1946, imprisoned several times during regime of Marcos Pérez Jiménez, which he opposed; unsuccessful presidential cand. for COPEI 1947, 1958, 1963, 1986; Pres. of Chamber of Deputies 1959–61; Pres. of Democratic Christian Org. of America (ODCA) 1964–69; Pres. of Venezuela 1969–74, 1994–99; Senator-for-Life 1974; Pres. Inter-Parl. Council 1980–83; Prof. Emer. of Sociology and Labour Jurisprudence, Univ. Cen. de Venezuela; Fellow, Venezuelan Acad. of Languages, Acad. of Political and Social Sciences 1952, 1983; numerous decorations; Dr hc from more than 20 American and European univs. *Publications:* essays on legal matters, sociology and politics. *Address:* c/o Central Information Office of the Presidency, Palacio de Miraflores, Avenida Urdaneta, Caracas 1010, Venezuela.

CALDERÓN, Sila María, BA, MPA; Puerto Rican politician; b. 23 Sept. 1942, San Juan; three c.; ed Convent of the Sacred Heart, San Juan, Manhattanville Coll., New York, Univ. of Puerto Rico; worked for Sec. of Labour; Special Asst for Econ. Devt and Labour to the Gov. of Puerto Rico 1974, Pres. of Commonwealth Investment Co., Product Man. for Business Devt, Citibank, 1973–84; Chief of Staff 1985, Sec. of State for Gov. of Puerto Rico, 1985–90, Sec. of the Interior, Sec. of State 1988; Mayor of San Juan 1996–2000; Gov. of Puerto Rico 2001–05; fmr Pres. and Leader Partido Popular Democrático (PPD); mem. Bd of Dirs Banco Popular; mem. Sister Isolina Ferré Foundation; Orden Isabel la Católica 1987; Dr hc (Manhattanville Coll., Boston Univ., New School Univ.); Outstanding Woman of the Year, Puerto Rico Chamber of Commerce 1975, 1985, 1987, Puerto Rican Products Assen 1986, Puerto Rica Chapter American Assen of Publishers Works 1988. *Address:* c/o Fundacion Sila M. Calderón, Inc., PO Box 10655, San Juan, PR 00922-0655.

CALDERÓN HINOJOSA, Felipe, MEcon, MPA; Mexican lawyer, politician and head of state; *President;* b. 18 Aug. 1962, Morelia, Michoacan; s. of Luis Calderón Vega and María del Carmen Hinojosa González; m. Margarita Zavala; two s. one d.; ed Escuela Libre de Derecho, Mexico City, Instituto Tecnológico Autónomo de México (ITAM), Kennedy School of Govt, Harvard Univ., USA; Pres. Partido Acción Nacional (PAN) youth group 1986, Sec.-Gen. 1993, Nat. Pres. 1996–99, Leader Parl. Group 2000–03; Rep. to Mexico City Legis. Ass. 1988; mem. Cámara Federal de Diputados Mexico (Fed. Chamber of Deputies) 1991–94, 2000–03; Dir Banobras 2001–03; Sec. of Energy 2003–04 (resgnd); Pres. of Mexico 2006–; unsuccessful cand. for Gov. of Michoacan 1995; named as a Global Leader of Tomorrow, World Econ. Forum 1997. *Publication:* El Hijo Desobediente 2006. *Address:* Office of the President, Los Pinos, Col. San Miguel Chapultepec, 11850 México, DF, Mexico (office). *Telephone:* (55) 5091-1100 (office). *Fax:* (55) 5277-2376 (office). *E-mail:* felipe.calderon@presidencia.gob.mx (office). *Website:* www.presidencia.gob.mx (office).

CALDERÓN MARTÍNEZ, Rafael P.; Dominican Republic politician and sociologist; m.; ed Univ. Autónoma de Santo Domingo; lecturer on sociology at various insts in Dominican Repub. and Cen. America 1975–94; Dir-Gen. Planning and Programs, Dist. Council of Santo Domingo 1994–95, mem. Comm. on Modernisation 1998–2000; Tech. Sec. of the Presidency 2000–03; Sec. of State for Finance 2003–04; Dir Dept of Studies and Programs, Caritas Dominicanas 1970–81; Dir-Gen. Centre of Scientific Investigation and Consultation (CENICC) 1973–2000; Gen. Coordinator for Area of Latin America, Mexico, Panama and the Caribbean, Carita Int. 1978–93; Pres. Dominican Assen of Sociologists 1979–81, Recursos del Futuro Foundation (FUNDARE) 1990–99; Vice-Pres. Amigos de los Niños Foundation 1994–98; currently mem. Chamber of Deputies for Ázua; mem. artido Revolucionario Dominicano (PRD). *Publications:* numerous articles in periodicals and nat. journals. *Address:* c/o Partido Revolucionario Dominicano, Espaillat 118, Santo Domingo, DN, Dominican Republic. *Telephone:* 687-2193. *E-mail:* julio.estevez@prd.partidos.com. *Website:* www.prd.partidos.com.

CALDERÓN SOL, Armando; Salvadorean fmr head of state; b. 24 June 1948, San Salvador; m. Elisabeth Aguirre; three c.; ed Univ. of El Salvador; f. Alianza Republicana Nacionalista (ARENA) 1981, elected leader 1988; deputy 1985–88; Mayor of San Salvador 1988–94; Pres. of El Salvador 1994–99. *Address:* c/o Alianza Republicana Nacionalista, Prolongación Calle Arce 2423, entre 45 y 47 Avda Norte, San Salvador, El Salvador.

CALDICOTT, Dame Fiona, DBE, BM, BChir, MA, FRCP, FRCPsych, FRCPI; British psychiatrist and psychotherapist; *Principal, Somerville College, University of Oxford;* b. 12 Jan. 1941; d. of Joseph Maurice Soesan and Elizabeth Jane Soesan (née Ransley); m. Robert Gordon Woodruff Caldicott 1965; one d. (one s. deceased); ed City of London School for Girls, St Hilda's Coll., Oxford Univ.; House Surgeon and Physician, Coventry Hosps 1966–67; GP, Family Planning and Child Welfare 1968–70; training in psychiatry 1970–76; Sr Registrar in Psychiatry, W Midlands Regional Training Scheme 1977–79; Consultant Psychiatrist, Univ. of Warwick 1979–85; Consultant Psychotherapist, Uffculme Clinic, Birmingham 1979–96; Sr Clinical Lecturer in Psychotherapy, Univ. of Birmingham 1982–96; Unit Gen. Man., Mental Health, Cen. Birmingham 1989–91; Clinical Dir Adult Psychiatric and Psychotherapy Service, Mental Health Unit, S Birmingham 1991–94; Medical Dir S Birmingham Mental Health Nat. Health Service (NHS) Trust 1994–96; mem. Sec. of State's Standing Advisory Cttee on Medical Manpower (now Workforce) Planning 1991–2001, on Postgrad. Medical Educ. 1993–99, Council Univ. of Oxford 1998–; Chair. Monospecialist Cttee for Psychiatry 1995– (Sec. 1991–95); Sec. European Bd of Psychiatry 1992–96; Sub-Dean Royal Coll. of Psychiatrists 1987–90, Dean 1990–93, Pres. 1993–96; Chair. Conf. of Medical Royal Colls. 1995–96; Prin. Somerville Coll., Oxford Univ. 1996–; Pro-Vice-Chancellor Oxford Univ. 2001–02; mem. Union of European Medical Specialists, Broadcasting Standards Council 1996–, Czech Psychiatric Soc. 1994; Fellow Acad. of Medicine, Singapore 1994; Chevalier du Tastevin 1991; Hon. DSc (Warwick) 1997; Hon. MD (Birmingham) 1997. *Publications:* contrib. to Discussing Doctors' Careers (ed. Isobel Allen) 1988; papers in learned journals on psychiatry. *Leisure interests:* family, friends, reading, theatre, wine. *Address:* Somerville College, Oxford, OX2 6HD (office); The Old Rectory, Manor Farm Lane, Balscote, Banbury, OX15 6JJ, England (home). *Telephone:* (1865) 270630 (office); (1295) 730293 (home). *Fax:* (1865) 280623 (office); (1295) 730549 (home). *E-mail:* principals.office@some.ox.ac.uk (office); fiona.caldicott@some.ox.ac.uk (office). *Website:* www.some.ox.ac.uk (office).

CALDWELL, John Bernard, OBE, PhD, DSc, FREng; British professor of naval architecture; *Professor Emeritus, University of Newcastle-upon-Tyne;* b. 26 Sept. 1926, Northampton; s. of John R. Caldwell and Doris Caldwell (née Bolland); m. Jean M. F. Duddridge 1955; two s.; ed Bootham School, York and Univs of Liverpool and Bristol; Prin. Scientific Officer, RN Scientific Service 1957–60; Asst Prof., Royal Naval Coll., Greenwich 1960–66; Visiting Prof., MIT 1962–63; Prof. of Naval Architecture, Univ. of Newcastle-upon-Tyne 1966–91, Prof. Emer. 1991–, Head, Dept of Naval Architecture 1966–83, Head, School of Marine Tech. 1975–80, 1986–88, Dean, Faculty of Eng 1983–86; Pres. Royal Inst. of Naval Architects 1984–87, Fellow; Dir Nat. Maritime Inst. Ltd 1983–85, Marine Design Consultants Ltd 1985–89, Marine Tech. Directorate 1986–90; mem. Eng Council 1988–94; Hon. DSc (Tech. Univ. of Gdansk); Gold Medal of NECIS 1973, Froude Medal of RINA 1984, David Taylor Medal of SNAME (USA) 1987, Pres.'s Award of Eng Council 1995. *Publications:* over 70 papers in various eng and scientific publs. *Leisure interests:* music, walking, reading. *Address:* Barkbooth, Winster, Windermere, Cumbria, LA23 3NZ, England. *Telephone:* (15395) 68222. *E-mail:* caldwell892@btinternet.com (home).

CALDWELL, Philip, MBA; American business executive; b. 27 Jan. 1920, Bourneville, Ohio; s. of Robert Clyde Caldwell and Wilhelmina Caldwell (née

www.worldwhoswho.com

Hemphill); m. Betsey Chinn Clark 1945; one s. two d.; ed Muskingum Coll. and Harvard Univ.; served in USN, later Lt 1942–46; Navy Dept 1946–53, Deputy Dir of Procurement Policy Div. 1948–53; joined Ford Motor Co. 1953, Vice-Pres. 1968–73, Dir 1973–90; Gen. Man. Truck Operations 1968–70; Pres. and Dir Philco-Ford Corpn 1970–71; Vice-Pres. of Mfg Group 1971–72; Chair., CEO and Dir Ford Europe Inc. 1972–73; Exec. Vice-Pres. with responsiblity for int. automotive operations 1973–77, Vice-Chair. and Deputy CEO 1978–79, Pres. of Ford Motor Co. 1978–80, CEO 1979–85, Chair. 1980–85; also Dir Ford of Europe 1972–85, Ford Latin America 1973–85, Ford Asia-Pacific Inc. 1973–85, Ford Mid-East and Africa Inc. 1973–85, Ford of Canada 1977–85, Ford Motor Credit Co. 1977–85; Dir and Sr Man. Dir Lehman Brothers Inc. (and predecessor Shearson Lehman Brothers Holdings Inc.) 1985–98; fmr mem. Bd of Dirs Mettler-Toledo Int. Inc., The Mexico Fund, Russell Reynolds Assocs Inc., Waters Corpn, Chase Manhattan Corpn, Chase Manhattan Bank N.A. 1982–85, Digital Equipment Corpn, Kellogg Co., Federated Dept Stores Inc. 1984–88, Zurich Holding Co. America; mem. Int. Advisory Cttee, Chase Manhattan Bank 1979–85, Business-Higher Educ. Forum, numerous cttees, bds and forums; Trustee, Cttee for Econ. Devt, Muskingum Coll. Policy Comm. Business Roundtable 1980–85; Dir Harvard Business School Assocs 1977–93, INSEAD Int. Council 1978–81; Sec. Motor Vehicle Manufacturers' Asscn; Dir Detroit Symphony Orchestra 1979–85; Hon. DH (Muskingum Coll.) 1974; Hon. DBA (Upper Iowa) 1978; Hon. LLD (Boston Univ. 1979, Eastern Mich. Univ. 1979, Miami Univ. 1980, Davidson Coll. 1982, Lawrence Inst. of Tech. 1984, Ohio Univ. 1984); USN Meritorious Civilian Service Award 1953, 1st William A. Jump Memorial Award 1950, Golden Plate Award, American Acad. of Achievement 1984 and several other awards. *Address:* 174 Rosebrook Road, New Canaan, CT 06840 USA (office).

CALDWELL-MOORE, Sir Patrick Alfred, (R. T. Fishall), Kt, CBE, FRS; English astronomer and writer; b. 4 March 1923, Pinner, Middx; s. of the late Capt. Caldwell-Moore, MC and Gertrude Lilian Moore (née White); ed privately; Officer, Bomber Command, RAF 1940–45; Ed. Year Book of Astronomy 1962–; Dir Armagh Planetarium 1965–68; freelance 1968–; Pres. British Astronomical Asscn 1982–84, then Life Hon. Vice-Pres.; mem. Royal Astronomical Soc. of Canada, Royal Astronomical Soc. of NZ; Hon. DSc (Lancaster) 1974, (Hatfield Polytechnic) 1989, (Birmingham) 1990, (Portsmouth) 1997, (Leicester) 1996; Dr hc (Keele) 1994; Lorimer Gold Medal 1962, Goodacre Medal (British Astronomical Asscn) 1968, Jackson Gwilt Gold Medal (Royal Astronomical Soc.) 1977, Roberts-Klumpke Medal (Astronomical Soc. of the Pacific) 1979, Royal Astronomical Soc. Millennium Award 2000, BAFTA Special Award 2002, Minor Planet No. 2602 is named in his honour; Royal TV Soc. Baird Medal 2007. *Play:* Quintet (Chichester) 2002. *Television includes:* The Sky at Night (BBC) 1957–. *Radio:* frequent broadcaster on radio. *Compositions:* Perseus (opera) 1975, Theseus 1982, Galileo 2003. *Publications include:* The Amateur Astronomer 1970, Atlas of the Universe 1970, Guide to the Planets 1976, Guide to the Moon 1976, Guide to the Stars 1977, Guide to Mars 1977, Out of the Darkness: The Planet Pluto (jtly) 1980, The Unfolding Universe 1982, Travellers in Space and Time 1983, History of Astronomy 1983, The Return of Halley's Comet (with Heather Couper) 1984, The Story of the Earth (with Peter Cattermole) 1985, Patrick Moore's Armchair Astronomy 1985, Stargazing 1985, Exploring the Night Sky with Binoculars 1986, The A–Z of Astronomy 1986, TV Astronomer 1987, Astronomy for the Under Tens 1987, Astronomers' Stars 1987, The Planet Uranus (jtly) 1988, Space Travel for the Under Tens 1988, The Planet Neptune 1989, Mission to the Planets 1990, The Universe for the Under Tens 1990, A Passion for Astronomy 1991, Fireside Astronomy 1992, The Starry Sky 1994, The Great Astronomical Revolution 1994, Stars of the Southern Skies 1994, Guinness Book of Astronomy 1995, Passion for Astronomy 1995, Teach Yourself Astronomy 1995, Eyes on the Universe 1997, Brilliant Stars 1998, Patrick Moore on Mars 1999, Yearbook of Astronomy AD 1000 (with Allan Chapman) 1999, Astronomy Data Book 2000, Eighty Not Out 2003, Stars of Destiny 2004, Venus 2004, Patrick Moore The Autobiography 2004, Patrick Moore on the Moon 2005, Bang! The Complete History of the Universe (with Brian May and Chris Lintott) 2006, Moore on Mercury 2007, Space: The First 50 Years (with HJP Arnold) 2007. *Leisure interests:* music, cricket, chess, tennis. *Address:* Farthings, 39 West Street, Selsey, Sussex, PO20 9AD, England. *Telephone:* (1243) 603668. *Fax:* (1243) 607237 (office); (1243) 607237 (home).

ČALFA, Marián, DrIur; Czech politician and lawyer; b. 1946, Trebišov, Slovakia; m. Jiřina Čalfová; two d.; studied law in Prague, subsequently worked in legal and admin. depts. of official press agency CTK; Minister without portfolio 1988–89; resgnd from CP of Czechoslovakia; Prime Minister of Czechoslovakia 1989–92; Chair. State Defence Council 1990–92; Deputy to House of Nations of Fed. Ass. CSFR 1990–92; official, Fed. Govt of CSFR July–Oct. 1992; Deputy Chair. Civic Democratic Union—Public Against Violence 1991–92; Co-founder CTL Consulting, Prague 1992–95, Čalfa, Bartošík a partneři, Prague 1995–; Chair. Supervisory Bd I. Silas, Deputy Chair. Alia Chem. 1995–; Ed.-in-Chief Legal Adviser 1993–95, Chair. Editorial Bd 1995–99; mem. M. R. Štefánik Foundation 2000–; Grand Cross of the Order of the Crown (Belgium) 1990. *Address:* Čalfa, Bartošík a Partneři, právní kancelář Přemyslovská 28, 130 00 Prague 3, Czech Republic.

CALHEIROS, Renan; Brazilian politician; b. (José Renan Vasconcelos Calheiros), 16 Sept. 1955, Murici; s. of Olavo Calheiros Novais and Ivanilda Vasconcelos Calheiros; m. Verônica Calheiros; three c.; ed Universidade Federal da Alagoas; student Pres., Universidade Federal da Alagoas 1974; State Deputy for Alagoas, Movimento Democrático Brasileiro 1978–80; Leader, Alagoas Legis. Ass. 1980–82; Fed. Deputy, Partido do Movimento Democrático Brasileiro (PMDB) 1982–92, Leader of the House of Deputies 1990–92; Vice Pres. PMDB 1984–85; Senator for Alagoas state 1994–, Minister of State for Justice 1998–99, Leader of PMBD in Fed. Senate 2001–02, Pres. of Fed. Senate 2005–07 (resgnd); Exec. Vice Pres. Petrobras Química 1992–94. *Address:* Ala Senador Teotônio Vilela, Gabinete 22, Senado Federal, Praça dos Três Poderes, 70165-900 Brasília, DF, Brazil (office). *Telephone:* (61) 3311-2261 (office). *Fax:* (61) 3311-1695 (office). *E-mail:* renan.calheiros@senados.gov.br (office). *Website:* www.senado.gov.br/renan (office).

CALIFANO, Joseph Anthony, Jr, AB, LLB; American lawyer, writer, academic and fmr government official; *Chairman, National Center on Addiction and Substance Abuse, Columbia University;* b. 15 May 1931, Brooklyn, New York; s. of Joseph A. Califano and Katherine Gill Califano; m. 2nd Hilary Paley Byers 1983; two s. one d. from previous marriage; one step-s. one step-d.; ed Holy Cross Coll. and Harvard Univ.; admitted to New York Bar 1955; served in USNR 1955–58; attorney, Dewey Ballantine, Bushby, Palmer Wood, New York 1958–61; Special Asst to Gen. Counsel, US Dept of Defense, Washington, DC 1961–62; Special Asst to US Sec. of Army 1962–63, Gen. Counsel, US Dept of Army 1963–64; Special Asst to Sec. and Deputy Sec. of Defense 1964–65; Special Asst to Pres. 1965–69; US Sec. of Health, Educ. and Welfare 1977–79; Special Counsel to US House of Reps Cttee on Standards of Official Conduct 1982–83; admitted to US District Court; US Court of Appeals for 2nd Circuit; US Supreme Court Bar 1966; mem. ABA, Fed. Bar Asscn, American Judicature Soc.; attorney, Arnold & Porter 1969–71, Williams, Connolly & Califano 1971–77, Califano, Ross & Heineman 1980–82, Dewey, Ballantine, Bushby, Palmer & Wood 1983–92; General Counsel, Democratic Nat. Cttee 1971–72; Prof. of Public Health Policy, Schools of Medicine and Public Health, Columbia Univ. 1992–; Founder and Chair. Nat. Center on Addiction and Substance Abuse, Columbia Univ. 1992–; mem. Democratic Party's Nat. Charter Comm. 1972–74; Chair. Inst. for Social Policy in the Middle East, Kennedy School of Govt, Harvard Univ.; mem. Bd of Dirs Midway Games Inc. 2004–, Willis Group Holdings 2004–, CBS Corpn 2006–; fmr mem. Bd of Dirs Viacom Inc. 2003–05, Primerica Corpn, Automatic Data Processing Inc., K-Mart Corpn, True North Communications, Inc., Warnaco; Trustee Urban Inst.; hon. degrees from Coll. of Holy Cross, Coll. of New Rochelle, Univ. of Michigan, Davis and Elkins Coll., Howard Univ., Univ. of Notre Dame, City Coll., New York; Distinguished Civilian Service Medal, Dept of Army 1964, Dept of Defense 1968; Man of Year Award, Justinian Soc. Lawyers 1966. *Publications:* The Student Revolution, A Global Confrontation 1969, A Presidential Nation 1975, The Media and the Law (with Howard Simons) 1976, The Media and Business (with Howard Simons) 1978, Governing America: An Insider's Report from the White House and the Cabinet 1981, Report on Drug Abuse and Alcoholism 1982, America's Health Care Revolution: Who Lives? Who Dies? Who Pays? 1985, High Society: How Substance Abuse Ravages America and What to Do About It 2007; numerous articles for various newspapers and other publications. *Leisure interest:* jogging. *Address:* Center on Addiction and Substance Abuse, Columbia University, 633 Third Avenue, 19th Floor, New York, NY 10017-6706, USA. *Telephone:* (212) 841-5200. *Website:* www.casacolumbia.org.

CALIFF, Robert McKinnon, MD; American cardiologist and academic; *Donald F. Fortin, MD, Professor of Cardiology, Vice-Chancellor for Clinical Research and Director of the Duke Translational Medicine Institute, Duke University;* b. 29 Sept. 1951, Columbia, SC; m. Lydia Carpenter 1974; two s. one d.; ed Duke Univ. and Duke Univ. Medical School, Durham, NC; internship in cardiology, Univ. of Calif., San Francisco 1978–79, Resident 1979–80; fellowship in cardiology, Duke Univ. 1978, 1980–83, Attending Physician 1983–, Donald F. Fortin Prof. of Cardiology and Prof. of Internal Medicine 1995–, Dir Duke Clinical Research Inst. 1995–2006, Dir Translational Medicine Inst. 2006–, Assoc. Vice-Chancellor for Clinical Research 1995–2005, Vice-Chancellor for Clinical Research 2005–; mem. Health Sector Advisory Council The Fuqua School of Business; fmr mem. Cardiorenal Advisory Panel US Food and Drug Admin., Pharmaceutical Roundtable of Inst. of Medicine (IOM), IOM Cttee; Dir Co-ordinating Center for Centers for Educ. and Research in Therapeutics; Ed.-in Chief Mosby's American Heart Journal; Contributing Ed. theheart.org; Fellow, American Coll. of Cardiology 1988. *Publications:* Acute Coronary Care (ed.), Textbook of Cardiovascular Medicine (section ed.); more than 600 articles in medical journals. *Leisure interests:* golf, basketball, listening to music. *Address:* Department of Medicine (Cardiology), Duke Clinical Research Institute, 2400 Pratt Street, Suite 7028, Campus PO Box 3850, Durham, NC 27705, USA (office). *Telephone:* (919) 668-8820 (office). *Fax:* (919) 668-7103 (office). *E-mail:* calif001@mc.duke.edu (office). *Website:* www.mc.duke.edu (office).

CALLADINE, Christopher Reuben, ScD, FRS, FREng; British engineer and academic; *Professor Emeritus of Structural Mechanics, University of Cambridge;* b. 19 Jan. 1935, Derby; s. of Reuben Calladine and Mabel Calladine (née Boam); m. Mary Ruth Howard Webb 1964; two s. one d.; ed Nottingham High School, Peterhouse, Cambridge, Massachusetts Inst. of Tech., USA; Lecturer, Dept of Eng, Univ. of Cambridge 1963–79, Reader 1979–86, Prof. of Structural Mechanics 1986–2002, Prof. Emer. 2002–, Fellow, Peterhouse 1960–92, Sr Fellow 1992–2002, Emer. Fellow 2002–; mem. Gen. Bd Univ. of Cambridge 1984–88; mem. Council The Royal Soc. 2000–02; Hon. DEng (Malaysian Univ. of Tech.) 2002; IMechE Ludwig Mond Prize 1966, ICE James Alfred Ewing Medal 1998, ICE Frederick Palmer Prize 2007. *Publications:* Engineering Plasticity 1969, Theory of Shell Structures 1983, Understanding DNA (with H. R. Drew, B. F. Luisi and A. A. Travers) (3rd edn) 2004; many articles in eng and biological journals. *Leisure interest:* mending toys. *Address:* CRC, Department of Engineering, University of Cambridge, Cambridge, CB2 1PZ (office); 25 Almoners Avenue, Cambridge, CB1 8NZ, England (home). *Telephone:* (1223) 764099 (office). *Fax:* (1223) 332662 (office). *E-mail:* crc@eng.cam.ac.uk (office). *Website:* www-civ.eng.cam.ac.uk/crc/crc_web.htm (office).

CALLAWAY, Howard Hollis (Bo); American public official; *Chairman Emeritus, Ida Cason Cason Callaway Foundation;* b. 2 April 1927, LaGrange, Ga; s. of Cason J. Callaway and Virginia Hand Callaway; m. Elizabeth Walton 1949; three s. two d.; ed US Mil. Acad., West Point; served in US Army infantry, participating in Korean War in Far Eastern Command, later becoming Instructor, Infantry School, Fort Benning, Ga 1949–52; mem. US House of Reps for Third Dist of Ga 1965–66; unsuccessful Republican cand. for Gov. of Ga 1966; Civilian Aide for US Third Army Area 1970–73; US Sec. of the Army, Washington, DC 1973–75; Campaign Man. for President Gerald Ford in 1976 presidential election; fmr Chair. Interfinancial Inc. of Atlanta; Chair. Crested Butte Mountain Resort Inc., GOPAC; Chair. Colorado Republican Party; Dir United Bank of Denver; mem. Regents Univ. System of Ga Nat. 4-H Service Cttee 1953–54, 1966–70, 1993–; mem. Bd of Trustees, Nat. Recreation Asscn; Chair. Emer., Ida Cason Callaway Foundation; Chair. Tourism Cttee, Ga Dept of Industry, Trade and Tourism 2001–03, Ga Chamber of Commerce Tourism Cttee 2004; Dept of Defense Medal 1975. *Leisure interests:* skiing, sailing, tennis, trout fishing. *Address:* PO Box 1326, Pine Mountain, GA 31822, USA (home). *Telephone:* (706) 663-5075 (office); (706) 333-4994 (home). *Fax:* (706) 663-5081 (office). *E-mail:* bocallaway@callawaygardens.com (office). *Website:* www.callawaygardens.com (office).

CALLEJAS, Rafael Leonardo; Honduran politician and economist; *President, Honduran Football Federation;* b. (Rafael Leonardo Callejas Romero), 14 Nov. 1943, Tegucigalpa; s. of Rafael Callejas Valentine and Emma Romero; m. 1st Nan López (divorced); m. 2nd Norma Regina Gaborit; ed Mississippi State Univ., USA; fmr Pres. Cen. Cttee, Partido Nacional; Under-Sec. for Natural Resources 1972–75; Minister for Agric. and Natural Resources 1978–81; unsuccessful cand. for Pres. of Honduras 1985, Pres. of Honduras 1990–93; Pres. Honduran Football Asscn 2002–; Dr hc (Mississippi State 1989, Georgetown 1990, Vermont 1990, Pepperdine 1991, Guadalajara 1998). *Address:* El Hatillo, Calle Principal, Kilometro 9, Tegucigalpa (home); Edificio Palmira, 5 piso, Frente Hotel Honduras Maya, Tegucigalpa (office); c/o Partido Nacional, Tegucigalpa, Honduras. *Telephone:* 239-2875 (office); 211-9359 (home). *Fax:* 239-2059 (office); 211-9173 (home). *E-mail:* rcallejas2001@yahoo.com (home).

CALLEY, John; American film producer; b. 30 June 1930, NJ; m. 1st Olinka Schoberova 1972 (divorced); m. 2nd Meg Tilly 1995 (divorced); four step-c.; Dir of Night-time Programming and Dir Programming Sales NBC, New York 1951–57; Production Exec. and TV Producer, Henry Jaffe Enterprises 1957; Vice-Pres. Radio and TV, Ted Bates Advertising Agency 1958; Exec. Vice-Pres. and film producer, Filmways Inc. 1960–69; with Warner Bros Inc., Burbank, Calif. 1969–87, Exec. Vice-Pres. Worldwide Production 1969–75, Pres. 1975–80, Vice-Chair. Bd 1977–80, consultant 1980–87; ind. film producer 1987–93; Pres. and COO United Artists Pictures 1993–96; Pres. and COO Sony Pictures Entertainment Inc., Culver City, Calif. 1996–98, Pres. and CEO 1998, Chair. and CEO 1998–2003; currently with John Calley Productions (ind. film production co.); fmr mem. Bd American Film Inst.; Career Achievement Award, Los Angeles Film Critics Asscn 2008. *Films produced include:* Face in the Rain 1963, The Wheeler Dealers 1963, The Americanization of Emily 1964, The Sandpiper 1965, The Loved One 1965, The Cincinnati Kid 1965, Eye of the Devil 1966, Don't Make Waves 1967, Castle Keep 1969, Catch-22 1970, Fat Man and Little Boy 1989, Postcards from the Edge 1990, The Remains of the Day 1993, Closer 2004, The Da Vinci Code 2006, The Jane Austen Book Club 2007. *Address:* John Calley Productions, 10202 West Washington Blvd., Lean Bldg., Suite 119, Culver City, CA 90232, USA. *Telephone:* (310) 244-7777. *E-mail:* john_calley@spe.sony.com.

CALLIL, Carmen Thérèse, BA, FRSA; Australian/British publisher and writer; b. 15 July 1938, Melbourne; d. of Lorraine Claire Allen and Frederick Alfred Louis Callil; ed Star of the Sea Convent, Loreto Convent, Melbourne and Melbourne Univ.; settled in England 1963; Buyer's Asst, Marks and Spencer 1963–65; Editorial Asst, Hutchinson Publishing Co. 1965–66, B. T. Batsford 1966–67, Publicity Man., Granada Publishing 1967–70, André Deutsch 1971–72; f. Carmen Callil Ltd, Book Publicity Co. and Virago Press 1972; Chair. and Man. Dir Virago Press 1972–82, Chair. 1982–95, Man. Dir Chatto and Windus, The Hogarth Press 1983–93; Publr-at-Large Random House, UK 1993–94; Ed.-at-Large Knopf, New York 1993–94; mem. Bd Channel 4 1985–91, Random Century Bd 1989–94; Gov. Museum of London 1992–; Chair. Booker Prize for Fiction 1996; Hon. DLitt (Sheffield) 1994, (Oxford Brookes Univ.) 1995; Hon. DUniv (York) 1995, (Open) 1997; Int. Women's Writing Guild Distinguished Service Award. *Publications:* The Modern Library: The 200 Best Novels in England Since 1950 (jtly) 1999, Bad Faith: A Forgotten History of Family and Fatherland 2006. *Leisure interests:* friends, reading, animals, films, gardening, politics, France, Europe. *Address:* c/o Rogers, Coleridge & White Literary Agency, 20 Powis Mews, London, W11 1JN, England (office). *Telephone:* (20) 7221-3717 (office). *Fax:* (20) 7229-9084 (office). *E-mail:* info@rcwlitagency.co.uk (office). *Website:* www.rcwlitagency.co.uk (office).

CALLOW, Simon Philip Hugh, CBE; British actor, director and writer; b. 15 June 1949; s. of Neil Callow and Yvonne Mary Callow; ed London Oratory Grammar School, Queen's Univ., Belfast, Drama Centre; debut Edinburgh Festival 1973; repertory seasons, Lincoln and Traverse Theatre, Edin.; work at the fringe theatre, the Bush, London; joined Joint Stock Theatre Group 1977, Nat. Theatre 1979; regular book reviewer The Guardian; Hon. DLitt (Queen's Univ., Belfast) 1999, (Birmingham) 2000; Evening Standard Patricia Rothermere Award 1999. *Stage appearances include:* Passing By 1975, Plumbers Progress 1975, Arturo Ui 1978, Titus Andronicus 1978, Mary Barnes 1978, As You Like It 1979, Amadeus 1979, Sisterly Feeling 1979, Total Eclipse 1982, Restoration 1982, The Beastly Beatitudes of Balthazar B 1982, The Relapse 1983, On The Spot 1984, Melancholy Jacques 1984, Kiss of the Spider Woman 1985, Faust 1988, Single Spies 1988, 1989, The Destiny of Me 1993, The Alchemist 1996, The Importance of Being Oscar 1997, Chimes at Midnight 1997, The Mystery of Charles Dickens 2000–02, Through the Leaves 2003, The Holy Terror 2004, The Woman in White (Palace Theatre, London) 2005, Aladdin (Richmond Theatre, London) 2005, Present Laughter (tour) 2006. *Films include:* Amadeus 1983, A Room With A View 1984, The Good Father 1985, Maurice 1986, Manifesto 1987, Mr and Mrs Bridge 1991, Postcards from the Edge 1991, Soft Top Hard Shoulder 1992, Four Weddings and A Funeral 1994, Jefferson in Paris 1994, Victory 1994, Le Passager Clandestin 1995, England, My England 1995, Ace Ventura: When Nature Calls 1995, James and the Giant Peach (voice) 1996, The Scarlet Tunic 1996, Woman In White 1997, Bedrooms and Hallways 1997, Shakespeare in Love 1997, No Man's Land 2000, Thunderpants 2001, A Christmas Carol 2001, George and the Dragon 2002, Phantom of the Opera 2004, Rag Tale 2005, Bob The Butler 2005, Chemical Wedding 2008. *TV appearances:* Wings of Song 1977, Instant Enlightenment inc. VAT 1979, La Ronde 1980, Man of Destiny 1982, Chance in a Million 1982–84, Deadhead 1984, Handel 1985, David Copperfield 1986, Cariani and the Courtesan 1987, Old Flames 1989, Patriot Witness 1989, Trial of Oz 1991, Bye Bye Columbus 1992, Femme Fatale 1993, Little Napoleons 1994, An Audience with Charles Dickens 1996, A Christmas Dickens 1997, The Woman in White 1998, Trial-Retribution 1999, 2000, Galileo's Daughter, The Mystery of Charles Dickens 2002, Angels in America 2003, Miss Marple 2004, Midsomer Murders 2006. *Directed:* Loving Reno 1983, Passport 1985, Nicolson Fights Croydon 1986, Amadeus 1986, The Infernal Machine 1986, Così Fan Tutte 1987, Jacques and His Master 1987, Shirley Valentine (theatre production) 1988/89, Die Fledermaus 1989/90, Facades 1988, Single Spies 1988/89, Stevie Wants to Play the Blues 1990, The Ballad of the Sad Café (film) 1991, Carmen Jones (Evening Standard Olivier Award) 1991, My Fair Lady 1992, Shades 1992, The Destiny of Me 1993, Carmen Jones 1994, Il Trittico 1995, Les Enfants du Paradis (RSC) 1996, Stephen Oliver Trilogy 1996, La Calisto 1996, Il Turco in Italia 1997, HRH 1997, The Pajama Game 1999, The Consul 1999, Tomorrow Week (play for radio) 1999, Le Roi Malgré Lui 2003, Everyman 2003, Jus' Like That 2004. *Publications:* Being An Actor 1984 (expanded edn 2004), A Difficult Actor: Charles Laughton 1987, Shooting the Actor, or the Choreography of Confusion (with Dusan Makevejev) 1990 (expanded edn 2004), Acting in Restoration Comedy 1991, Orson Welles: The Road to Xanadu 1995, Les Enfants du Paradis 1996, Snowdon – On Stage 1996, The National 1997, Love is Where it Falls 1999, Shakespeare on Love 2000, Charles Laughton's the Night of the Hunter 2000, Oscar Wilde and His Circle 2000, The Nights of the Hunter 2001, Henry IV Part 1 2002, Henry IV Part 2 2003, Dicken's Christmas 2003, Orson Welles: Hello Americans 2006; translations of works of Cocteau, Kundera, Prévert, Chabrier; weekly column in Sunday Express, Independent, Country Life; contrib. to The Times, The Sunday Times, The Guardian, The Observer, Evening Standard, etc. *Leisure interest:* 'dreaming' the future of the British theatre. *Address:* c/o BAT, 180 Wardour Street, London, W1V 3AA, England. *Telephone:* (20) 7413-0869 (office). *Fax:* (20) 7413-0870 (office). *E-mail:* karen@ichkin.freeserve.co.uk (office).

CALMAN, Sir Kenneth (Charles), DL, MD, PhD, KCB, FRCP, FMedSci, FRCPE, FRCS, FFPHM, FRSE; British chief medical officer and university administrator (retd); b. 25 Dec. 1941; s. of Arthur McIntosh Calman and Grace Douglas Don; m. Ann Wilkie 1967; one s. two d.; ed Allan Glen's School, Glasgow, Univ. of Glasgow; Hall Fellow in Surgery, Western Infirmary, Glasgow 1968; Lecturer in Surgery, Univ. of Glasgow 1969, Prof. of Clinical Oncology 1974, Dean of Postgraduate Medicine and Prof. of Postgraduate Medical Educ. 1984–88; MRC Clinical Research Fellow, Inst. of Cancer Research, London 1972; Chief Medical Officer, Scottish Office Home and Health Dept 1989–91, (at Dept of Health and Social Security) Dept of Educ. and Science (later Dept for Employment, then Dept for Educ. and Employment) 1991–98; Vice-Chancellor and Warden, Univ. of Durham 1998–2007 (retd); mem. Statistics Comm. 2000–; Fellow, Royal Coll. of Surgeons (Glasgow) 1971, Royal Coll. of Gen. Practitioners 1989; Hon. Fellow, Inst. of Cancer Research; Hon. MD (Nottingham) 1994, (Newcastle) 1995, (Birmingham) 1996; Hon. DSc (Strathclyde) 1993, (Westminster) 1995, (Glasgow Caledonian) 1995, (Glasgow) 1996, (Birmingham) 1996, (Brighton) 2000; Hon. DUniv (Stirling) 1992, (Open Univ.) 1996, (Paisley) 1997; Sir Thomas and Lady Dixon Medal, Belfast 1994, Francis Bissett Hawkins Medal, RCP 1995, Crookshanks Medal, RCR 1995, Alexander Hutchinson Medal, Royal Soc. of Medicine (RCS) 1995, Gold Medal, Macmillan Cancer Relief 1996, Heberden (also Orator), British Soc. of Rheumatology 1996, Silver Medal, Royal Coll. of Surgeons in Ireland 1997, Allwyn Smith Medal, Faculty of Public Health Medicine 1998, Bradlaw Medal, RCS Dental Faculty 1999, Thomas Graham Medal, Royal Philosophical Soc., Glasgow 1999. *Publications:* Basic Skills for Clinical Housemen 1971, Basic Principles of Cancer Chemotherapy 1982, Invasion 1984, Healthy Respect 1987, The Potential for Health 1998, Storytelling, Humour & Learning in Medicine 2000. *Leisure interests:* gardening, golf, collecting cartoons, Scottish literature, sundials. *Address:* Old Shire Hall, Durham, DH1 3HP, England.

CALMON DE SÁ, Angelo (see Sá, Angelo Calmon de).

CALMY-REY, Micheline; Swiss politician; *Minister of Foreign Affairs;* b. 8 July 1945, Sion, Valais canton; m. André Calmy; two c.; ed Ecole de commerce, St Maurice, Valais, Grad. Inst. of Int. Studies, Geneva; ran family books business 1977–97; joined Social Democratic Party 1979, Pres. 1986–90; elected Deputy Geneva Grand Council 1981–97, fmr Pres. Finance Comm., fmr Pres. Grand Council; elected to Geneva Conseil d'Etat (Head Dept of Finances) 1997–, Vice-Pres. 2000–01, Pres. 2001–02; elected to Fed. Council 2002–; Minister of Foreign Affairs 2002–; Vice-Pres. of the Swiss Confed. 2006, Pres. 2007; mem. Bd of Dirs Caisse d'épargne, Geneva 1986–93, Geneva Int. Airport 1994–97; Vice-Pres., later Pres. Caisse de la pension des employées de la fonction publique 1998–2002; mem. Bd of Dirs Fonds d'équipement communal 1998–2002, Banque Nat. Suisse 2002–. *Address:* Federal Department of Foreign Affairs, Bundeshaus West, 3003 Bern, Switzerland (office). *Telephone:* (31) 3222111 (office). *Fax:* (31) 334001 (office). *E-mail:* micheline.calmy -rey@etat.ge.ch (office); *Website:* www.eda.admin.ch (office); www.calmy-rey .net (office).

CALNE, Sir Roy Yorke, Kt, MA, MS, FRCP, FRS; British surgeon, academic and artist; b. 30 Dec. 1930; s. of Joseph R. Calne and Eileen Calne; m. Patricia D. Whelan 1956; two s. four d.; ed Lancing Coll. and Guy's Hosp. Medical School, London; with RAMC 1954–56; Departmental Anatomy Demonstrator, Univ. of Oxford 1957–58; Sr House Officer, Nuffield Orthopaedic Centre, Oxford 1958; Surgical Registrar, Royal Free Hosp. 1958–60; Harkness Fellow in Surgery, Peter Bent Brigham Hosp., Harvard Medical School 1960–61; Lecturer in Surgery, St Mary's Hosp. London 1961–62; Sr Lecturer and Consulting Surgeon, Westminster Hosp. 1962–65; Prof. of Surgery, Univ. of Cambridge 1965–98, Prof. Emer. 1998; Ghim Seng Prof. of Surgery, Nat. Univ. of Singapore 1998–2003; Pres. Int. Transplantation Soc. 1992–94; Fellow, Trinity Hall Cambridge 1965–98, Emer. 1998–; mem. Scientific Advisory Bd Tissera, Inc. 2004–; Hon. Consulting Surgeon, Addenbrooke's Hosp., Cambridge 1965–98; Hon. FRCS (Edinburgh) 1992; Grand Officer of the Repub. of Italy 2000; Hon. MD (Oslo) 1986, (Athens) 1990, (Hanover) 1991, (Thailand) 1993, (Belfast) 1994, (Edin.) 2001; Royal Coll. of Surgeons: Hallet Prize, Jacksonian Prize, Hunterian Prof. 1962, Cecil Joll Prize 1966; numerous other honours and awards including Lister Medal 1984, Hunterian Oration 1989, Cameron Prize 1990, Ellison-Cliffe Medal 1990, Ernst-Jung Prize, Gold Medal of Catalan Transplantation Soc. 1996, King Faisal Int. Prize for Medicine 2001, Prince Mahidol Prize for Medicine 2002, Thomas E. Starzl Prize in Surgery & Immunology 2002. *Achievements include:* first surgeon to perform a pancreas transplant in UK 1979 and first to perform an intestinal transplant in UK 1992. *Publications include:* Renal Transplantation 1963, Too Many People 1994, Art, Surgery and Transplantation 1996, The Ultimate Gift 1998; books and scientific papers on renal and liver transplantation and gen. surgery. *Leisure interests:* painting, tennis, squash, sculpture. *Address:* 22 Barrow Road, Cambridge, CB2 2AS; Department of Surgery, Douglas House Annexe, 18 Trumpington Road, Cambridge, CB2 2AH, England (office). *Telephone:* (1223) 361467 (office); (1223) 359831. *Fax:* (1223) 301601 (office). *E-mail:* cpr1000@cam.ac.uk (office).

CALOW, Peter, OBE, PhD, FIBiol, FRSA; British zoologist and academic; *Professor of Zoology, Roskilde University;* b. 23 May 1947; two c.; ed Univ. of Leeds; Lecturer, Reader, Univ. of Glasgow 1972–84, Warden Wolfson Hall 1975–84; Prof. of Zoology, Univ. of Sheffield 1984–, Dir Inst. of Environmental Sciences and Tech. 1991–96; Dir Environmental Businesses Network 1998–2000; Founding Ed. Functional Ecology 1986–1999; Pres. SETAC (Europe) 1990–91; Chair. UK Govt Advisory Cttee on Hazardous Substances 1991–2000; Trustee Health and Environmental Sciences Inst. 1996–2002, Int. Life Sciences Inst. 1999–2001; Dir Danish Nat. Environmental Assessment Inst. 2004–06; Prof. of Zoology, Roskilde Univ., Denmark, 2004–; mem. Council Freshwater Biology Asscn 1995–99, Univ. of Buckingham 1997–2002. *Publications:* author, jt author of 20 books; more than 220 articles in tech. journals. *Leisure interests:* running, reading, writing. *Address:* Department of Environmental, Social and Spatial Change, Roskilde University, 4000 Roskilde, Denmark (office). *Telephone:* 46-36-93-26 (office). *E-mail:* pcalow@ ruc.dk (office). *Website:* www.ruc.dk/enspac_en (office).

CALTAGIRONE, Francesco Gaetano; Italian business executive; *Chairman, Caltagirone SpA;* b. 1943, Rome; m.; three c.; developed family construction firm into large holding co. with interests in cement manufacturing, real estate, media and construction, currently Chair. Caltagirone SpA, also Chair. of subsidiaries Caltagirone Editore SpA, Il Messaggero SpA, Il Gazzettino SpA, Eurostazioni SpA; Vice-Chair. Banca Monte dei Paschi di Siena; mem. Bd of Dirs Grandi Stazioni SpA, Ical SpA; Cavaliere del Lavoro 2006. *Address:* Caltagirone SpA, Via Barberini 28, 00187 Rome, Italy (office). *Telephone:* (6) 4541-2293 (office). *Fax:* (6) 4541-2299 (office). *Website:* caltagironespa.caltanet.it (office).

CALVERT, Rev. Lorne Albert, BA; Canadian politician; *Leader of the Opposition, Saskatchewan Legislative Assembly;* b. Moose Jaw; m. Betty Sluzalo; two c.; ed St Andrew's Coll. Seminary, Saskatoon, Univ. of Regina, Univ. of Sasketchewan; ordained in United Church of Canada 1976 and served congregations in Perdue, Gravelbourg, Bateman, Shamrock, Coderre, Palmer; Minister Zion United Church, Moose Jaw 1979–86; MLA Sask. 1986–; apptd to Cabinet as Assoc. Minister of Health and Minister Responsible for Wakamow Valley Authority 1992; fmr Minister Responsible for SaskPower and SaskEnergy, Minister of Health, Minister of Social Services, Minister Responsible for Public Service Comm., Minister Responsible for Srs, Minister Responsible for Office of Disabilities; Leader New Democratic Party of Sask. 2001–; Premier of Sask. and Pres. Exec. Council 2001–07; Leader of the Opposition, Saskatchewan Legis. Ass. 2007–. *Address:* Saskatchewan New Democratic Party, 1122 Saskatchewan Drive, Regina, Sask. S4P 0C4, Canada (office). *Telephone:* (306) 525-1322 (office). *Fax:* (306) 569-1363 (office). *E-mail:* info@saskndp.com (office). *Website:* www.saskndp.com (office).

CALVERT, Peter Anthony Richard, BA, AM, MA, PhD, FRHistS; British political scientist, writer and academic; *Professor Emeritus of Comparative and International Politics, School of Social Sciences, University of Southampton;* b. 19 Nov. 1936, Islandmagee, Co. Antrim, NI; s. of the late Raymond Calvert and Irene Calvert; m. Susan Ann Milbank 1987; ed Campbell Coll., Belfast, Queens' Coll., Cambridge, Univ. of Michigan, Ann Arbor, USA; Lecturer, Univ. of Southampton 1964–71, Sr Lecturer 1971–74, Reader 1974–83, Prof. of Comparative and Int. Politics 1984–2002, Prof. Emer. 2002–; Research Fellow, Charles Warren Center, Harvard Univ. 1969–70; Visiting

Lecturer/Prof., Birkbeck Coll., London, 1983–84; Co-Ed. Democratization 1996–2007; mem. Royal Historical Soc.; Fulbright Scholar 1960, 1969, Ford Foundation grantee 1984–88. *Publications:* The Mexican Revolution 1910–1914 1968, 2008, A Study of Revolution 1970, The Falklands Crisis 1982, The Concept of Class 1982, Guatemala 1985, The Foreign Policy of New States 1986, Argentina: Political Culture and Instability (with Susan Calvert) 1989, Revolution and Counter Revolution 1990, Latin America in the 20th Century (with Susan Calvert) 1990, 1993, An Introduction to Comparative Politics 1993, International Politics of Latin America 1994, Politics and Society in the Third World (with Susan Calvert) 1995, 2001, Revolution and International Politics 1996, The South, the North and the Environment (with Susan Calvert) 1999, Comparative Politics: An Introduction 2002, A Political and Economic Dictionary of Latin America 2004, Politics and Society in the Developing World (with Susan Calvert) 2007; editor: The Process of Political Succession 1987, The Central American Security System 1988, 2008, Political and Economic Encyclopedia of South America and the Caribbean 1991, The Resilience of Democracy (with Peter Burnell) 1999, Civil Society in Democratization (with Peter Burnell) 2004, Border and Territorial Disputes of the World (fourth edn) 2004. *E-mail:* pcpol@socsci.soton.ac.uk (office); pcpol@soton.ac.uk (office). *Website:* www.soton.ac.uk (office); www.tandf.co .uk/journals/titles/13510347.asp.

CALVET, Jacques, LenD; French business executive and banker (retd); b. 19 Sept. 1931, Boulogne-sur-Seine; s. of Prof. Louis Calvet and Yvonne Olmières; m. Françoise Rondot 1956; two s. one d.; ed Paris Univ. and Nat. School of Admin., Diplomé d'études supérieures d'économie politique et de sciences économiques, Diplomé de l'Institut Politique de Paris; at Cour des Comptes 1957–63; Chargé de mission to office of Valéry Giscard d'Estaing (Sec. of State for Finance) 1959–62, Dir 1962–66; Dir Financial Affairs, Paris Dist 1966–68; Prin. Pvt. Sec. to Minister of Finance 1968–74; Deputy Gen. Man. Banque Nat. de Paris (BNP) 1974–75, Gen. Man. 1975–79, Chair. 1979–82, Hon. Chair. 1997–; Vice-Chair. Peugeot SA 1982–84, Pres. 1984–97; Chair. Automobiles Peugeot 1982–84, Bd Pres. 1984–, Vice-Pres., Dir-Gen. 1984–89, Pres. 1990–97; Pres. Citroën 1983–97; Pres. Conseil d'Admin. de la Publicité Française 1991–97; Dir Petrofina; Chair. European Automobiles Mfrs Asscn 1996; Chair. and Pres. Supervisory Bd Bazar de l'Hôtel de Ville (BHV) 2000–; Vice-Chair. Galeries Lafayette, also Chair. Audit CTTEE; mem. Bd of Dirs Icade (Chair. Audit Cttee), Censor, Société Foncière Lyonnaise, Cottin Frères, Soc. Européenne de Participations Industrielles, Enjoy; mem. Advisory Council Banque de France; Commdr, Légion d'honneur, Officier, Ordre nat. du Mérite, du Mérite agricole,Italian Order of Merit, Chevalier des Palmes académiques. *Publication:* La Grande faillite: Comment l'éviter 1998. *Leisure interest:* tennis, gardening. *Address:* 31 avenue Victor Hugo, 75116 Paris, France (home). *Telephone:* 1-40-67-16-25 (home). *E-mail:* jaccalvet@ wanadoo.fr (office).

CALVOCORESSI, Peter John Ambrose; British lawyer, writer, book publisher and university lecturer; b. 17 Nov. 1912, Karachi, Pakistan; s. of Pandia J. Calvocoressi and Irene Calvocoressi (née Ralli); m. 1st Barbara Dorothy Eden 1938 (died 2004); two s.; m. 2nd Rachel Scott 2006; ed Eton Coll. and Balliol Coll., Oxford; called to Bar 1935; with RAF Intelligence 1940–45; assisted at Trial of Major War Criminals, Nuremberg, Germany 1945–46; on staff, Royal Inst. of Int. Affairs 1949–54; Pnr, Chatto & Windus (publrs) 1955–65; Reader in Int. Relations, Sussex Univ. 1965–71; Editorial Dir Penguin Books 1972, Publr and CEO 1973–76; Chair. Open Univ. Educational Enterprises Ltd 1979–88; mem. UN Sub-comm. on the Prevention of Discrimination 1961–71; Chair. The London Library 1970–73; Hon. DUniv (Open Univ.) 1989. *Publications:* Nuremberg: The Facts, the Law and the Consequences 1947, Survey of International Affairs: vols for 1947–48, 1949–50, 1951, 1952 and 1953, Middle East Crisis (with Guy Wint) 1957, South Africa and World Opinion 1961, World Order and New States 1962, Total War (with Guy Wint) 1972, The British Experience: 1945–75, Top Secret Ultra 1980, A Time for Peace 1987, Who's Who in the Bible 1987, Resilient Europe 1991, Threading My Way 1994, Fall Out: World War II and the Shaping of Postwar Europe 1997, World Politics 1945–2000 2001. *Leisure interest:* music. *Address:* Old Mill Lane Farmhouse, Marnhull, Dorset, DT10 1JX, England. *Telephone:* (1258) 820562.

CALZAGHE, Joe, CBE; British professional super-middleweight boxer (retd); b. Hammersmith, London; s. of Enzo Calzaghe and Jackie Calzaghe; joined Newbridge Boxing Club aged nine; won British Amateur Boxing Asscn (ABA) titles 1991 (welterweight), 1992 (light-middleweight), 1993 (middleweight); 2nd to win three ABA titles in consecutive years; professional debut Oct. 1993; won British Super-Middleweight Championship Oct. 1995; won World Boxing Organization World Super-Middleweight Championship Oct. 1997, Int. Boxing Fed. Championship March 2006; 18 defences; won 41 fights including 30 knock-outs, undefeated since turning professional; retd 2009; Professional Boxing Asscn and the Boxing Writers' Club Young Boxer of the Year 1995, BBC Sports Personality of the Year Award 2007. *Publication:* No Ordinary Joe (auto-biog.) 2007. *E-mail:* joe@joecalzaghe.com. *Website:* www.joecalzaghe .com.

CAMACHO, Felix Perez, BBA; American politician; *Governor of Guam;* b. 30 Oct. 1957, Camp Zama, Japan; s. of fmr Gov. of Guam Carlos Camacho; m. Joann Camacho; three c.; ed Father Duenas Memorial School and Marquette Univ., Wis., USA; fmr Account Admin. IBM Corpn; fmr Insurance Man. Pacific Financial Corpn; served in 22nd, 23rd and 24th Guam Legislatures, Senator 1992–2002, Chair. 26th Guam Legislature's Cttee on Tourism, Transportation and Econ. Devt 2000–02; Gov. of Guam 2003–; fmr mem. and Exec. Dir Civil Service Comm. *Address:* Office of the Governor, POB 2950, Hagåtña, GU 96932, Guam (office). *Telephone:* 472-8931 (office). *Fax:* 477-

4826 (office). *E-mail:* governor@mail.gov.gu (office). *Website:* governor.guam.gov (office).

CAMAÑO, Eduardo Oscar; Argentine politician; fmr Pres. Partido Justicialista de Quilmes; Pres. of Bloc in Consejal 1983–85; Prov. Deputy 1985–87; Municipal Council, Quilmes 1987–91; Deputy to Nat. Ass. 1991–2007, Vice-Pres. Bloc Justicialista 1994–98, Second Vice-Pres. Chamber of Deputies 1999–2001, Pres. 2001–07, Acting Head of Exec. Br. Dec. 2001–Jan. 2002. *Address:* c/o Partido Justicialista, Domingo Matheu 130, C1082ABD Buenos Aires, Argentina.

CAMARA, Almamy Kabèlè; Guinean economist and government official; ed Univ. of Conakry; intern, Ministry of State Supervision 1979; Deputy Dir-Gen. Alimag (supply co.) 1980–85; Dir Commercial Operations SNG (govt maritime transport co.) 1986–97; Deputy Gen. Man. 1997–2000, Dir-Gen. 2000–01; fmr Dir Gen. Port Autonome De Conakry; Minister of Nat. Defence 2008–09; mem. Exec. Cttee Confed. of African Football. *Address:* c/o Ministry of National Defence, Camp Samory-Touré, Conakry, Guinea (office).

CAMARA, Kabèlè Abdoul; Guinean politician and lawyer; fmr lawyer, Court of Appeal, Conakry; Overseer of Senegal elections for Parl. Ass. of Francophone Countries 2000; Pres. Bar Asscn of Guinea 2000–06; Minister of Foreign Affairs, Int. Co-operation, African Integration and Guineans Abroad 2007–08. *Address:* c/o Ministry of Foreign Affairs, face au Port, ex-Primature, BP 2519, Conakry, Guinea (office).

CAMARA, Mady Kaba; Guinean politician; fmr Minister of Trade, Minister of Finance 2004, Minister of the Economy and Finance 2004–07, Gov. for Guinea, IMF Bd of Govs 2006. *Address:* c/o Ministry of the Economy and Finance, face au collège Boulbinet, BP 221, Conakry, Guinea (office).

CAMARA, Gen. Ousmane Arafan; Guinean politician; b. Faranah; fmr personal aide to Pres. Lansana Conté; fmr Deputy Chief-of-Staff of the Armed Forces; Minister of National Defence March–May 2007. *Address:* c/o Ministry of Defence, c/o Office of the President, BP 1000, Boulbinet, Conakry, Guinea (office).

CAMARENA BADÍA, Vicente, PhD; Spanish mathematician and academic; *Professor of Applied Mathematics, University of Zaragoza;* b. 26 Aug. 1941, Xátiva, Valencia; s. of Vicente Camarena and Victoria Badía; m. Carmen Grau; one s. four d.; ed Universidad de Zaragoza; Asst Prof. of Math., Universidad de Zaragoza 1966–81, Prof. 1981–84, Rector 1984–92, Prof. of Applied Math. 1992–; mem. Spanish Asscn of Math., Spanish Soc. of Gen. Systems, American Math. Soc., Soc. for Industries and Applied Math., Int. Astronomical Union. *Publications:* Curso de Mecánica 1977–78, Optimización de Trayectorias y efecto de Trampolín Lunar 1972, Formulación Sistemática de la Teoría de Perturbaciones en el Movimiento Orbital 1976, Determinación del Vector Primer de Lawden en Forma Universal y su Aplicación a Problemas de Optimización 1979–83, Elementos Orbitales y Osculadores en Teoría de Perturbaciones, Uniformización de Métodos Canónicos de Perturbaciones 1984, Números y Cálculo con Números: Del 1 al 0, hasta el ∞ 1999. *Leisure interests:* cycling and swimming. *Address:* Universidad de Zaragoza, Centro Politécnico Superior, MªLuna 3, Zaragoza 50018 (office); Latassa 17, Zaragoza, Spain (home). *E-mail:* camarena@unizar.es (office). *Website:* www.cps.unizar.es (office).

CAMBRELING, Sylvain; French conductor; b. 2 July 1948, Amiens; conducting debut with Orchestre de Lyon 1975; Prin. Guest Conductor, Ensemble Intercontemporain, Paris 1976; subsequent appearances in Paris with Orchestre de Paris, Nat. Orchestra of France and Ensemble Intercontemporain; has worked regularly at Paris Opéra since conducting Chéreau's production of Les Contes d'Hoffmann; Glyndebourne Opera debut (The Barber of Seville) 1981; Musical Dir Nat. Opera, Théâtre Royal de la Monnaie, Brussels 1981–91; Music Dir Frankfurt Opera 1990s; currently Chief Conductor SWR Sinfonieorchester Baden-Baden und Freiburg and Prin. Guest Conductor Klangforum Wien; apptd Prin. Conductor Designate, Yomiuri Nippon Symphony Orchestra 2008–; debut at La Scala (Lucio Silla) 1984, Metropolitan Opera, New York (Romeo et Juliette) 1986; has also appeared at Salzburg, Aix-en-Provence and Bregenz festivals; has worked in UK with Halle and Royal Liverpool Philharmonic orchestras, in Germany with Berlin Philharmonic, Berlin Radio Symphony and other orchestras and in USA. *Address:* c/o Van Walsum Management, The Tower Building, 11 York Road, London SE1 7NX, England (office). *Telephone:* (20) 7902-0520 (office). *Fax:* (20) 7902-0530 (office). *E-mail:* jvw@vanwalsum.com (office). *Website:* www.vanwalsum.com (office); www.sylvaincambreling.com.

CAMDESSUS, Michel Jean; French international civil servant; *Honorary Governor, Banque de France;* b. 1 May 1933, Bayonne; s. of Alfred Camdessus and Madeleine Cassembon; m. Brigitte d'Arcy 1957; two s. four d.; ed Notre Dame Coll., Betharram, Inst. of Political Studies, Paris, Nat. School of Admin.; civil servant, Treasury, Ministry of Finance 1960–66; Chief, Bureau of Industrial Affairs, Treasury, Ministry of Econ. and Finance 1969–70; Chair. 'Investissements' Sub-Cttee of Treasury 1971; Deputy Dir of Treasury 1974–82, Dir 1982–84; Financial Attaché, Perm. Representation, EEC, Brussels 1966–69; mem. Monetary Cttee, EEC 1978, Pres. 1982; Sec. Conseil de Direction du Fonds de Développement Economique et Social 1971; Asst Dir 'Épargne et Crédit' Sub-Cttee 1972; Deputy Gov. Banque de France 1984, Gov. 1984–87, Hon. Gov. 1987–; Man. Dir IMF 1987–2000; Pres. Club de Paris 1978–84; Chair. Centre d'études prospectives et d'informations internationales (CEPII) 2000–04, Semaines Sociales de France 2001–; UN Sec.-Gen. Special Envoy to the Monterrey Conf. 2002; Dir Banque Européenne d'Investissements, Banque Cen. des États de l'Afrique de l'Ouest, Air France, Soc. Nat. des Chemins de fer Français, Crédit Lyonnais (all 1978); Personal Rep. to Africa for French Govt and G8 Heads of State 2002; Commdr, Légion d'honneur; Chevalier, Ordre nat. du Mérite; Croix de la Valeur militaire. *Publications:* Notre foi dans ce siècle (with M. Albert, J. Boissonnat), Eau (with Bertrand Badré, Ivan Chéret, Pierre-Frédéric Tenière-Buchot) 2004, Le Sursaut: Vers une nouvelle croissance pour la France 2004. *Address:* Banque de France, 09-1060, 75049 Paris Cedex 01 (office); 27 rue de Valois, 75001 Paris, France (home). *Telephone:* 1-42-97-73-38 (office). *Fax:* 1-42-97-76-42 (office). *E-mail:* cyliane.huot@banque-france.fr (office).

CAMERON, Dame Averil Millicent, DBE, MA, PhD, FBA, FSA; British historian of late antiquity and Byzantine studies and writer; *Warden, Keble College, University of Oxford;* b. 8 Feb. 1940, Leek, Staffs.; d. of Tom Roy Sutton and Millicent Drew; m. Alan Douglas Edward Cameron 1962 (divorced 1980); one s. one d.; ed Somerville Coll., Oxford, Univ. Coll., London; Asst Lecturer Classics, King's Coll., London 1965, Lecturer 1968, Reader in Ancient History 1970, Prof. 1978–88, Prof. of Late Antique and Byzantine Studies 1988–94, Dir Centre for Hellenic Studies 1989–94, Fellow 1987–; Warden of Keble Coll., Oxford 1994–; Prof. of Late Antique and Byzantine History, Oxford Univ. 1997–; Pro-Vice-Chancellor Univ. of Oxford 2001–; Visiting Prof., Columbia Univ., New York 1967–68; Visiting Mem., Inst. for Advanced Study, Princeton, NJ 1977–78, Distinguished Visitor 1992; Summer Fellow, Dumbarton Oaks 1980; Sather Prof. of Classical Literature, Univ. of Calif., Berkeley 1985–86; Visiting Prof., Coll. de France 1987, Lansdowne Lecturer, Victoria, BC 1992; Ed. Journal of Roman Studies 1985–90; Pres. Soc. for the Promotion of Roman Studies 1995–98, Ecclesiastical History Soc. 2005–06, Council for British Research in the Levant 2005–; Chair. Cathedrals Fabric Comm. for England 1999–2005, Review Group on the Royal Peculiars 1999–2000; Hon. Fellow, Somerville Coll., Oxford; Hon. DLitt (Warwick, St Andrews, Queen's, Belfast, Aberdeen, London); Hon. DTheol (Lund). *Publications:* Procopius 1967, Agathias 1970, Corippus, In laudem Iustini minoris 1976, Images of Women in Antiquity (ed.) 1983, Continuity and Change in Sixth-Century Byzantium 1981, Constantinople in the Eighth Century (ed.) 1984, Procopius and the Sixth Century 1985, 1996, History as Text (ed.) 1989, The Greek Renaissance in the Roman Empire (ed.) 1990, Christianity and the Rhetoric of Empire 1991, The Byzantine and Early Islamic Near East I (ed.) 1992, II (ed.) 1994, III (ed.) 1995, The Later Roman Empire 1993, The Mediterranean World in Late Antiquity A.D. 395–600 1993, Changing Cultures in Early Byzantium (ed.) 1996, Cambridge Ancient History Vol. XIII. The Late Empire (ed.) 1998, Eusebius, Life of Constantine (ed. and trans.) 1999, Cambridge Ancient History Vol. XIV. Late Antiquity: Empire and Successors (ed.) 2000, Fifty Years of Prosopography (ed.) 2003, Cambridge Ancient History Vol. XII. The Crisis of Empire (ed.) 2005. *Address:* Keble College, Oxford, OX1 3PG, England. *Telephone:* (1865) 272700 (office). *Fax:* (1865) 272785 (office). *E-mail:* averil.cameron@keb.ox.ac.uk (office). *Website:* www.keble.ox.ac.uk (office).

CÁMERON, Daniel Omar; Argentine government official; *Minister of Energy;* b. 28 March 1954, Río Gallegos, Santa Cruz Prov.; m.; three c.; ed Colegio Nuestrea Señora de Luján, Universidad Nacional del Sur, Bahía Blanca, Buenos Aires Technological Inst.; fmr Gen. Man. then Dir state-owned SPSE; fmr adviser to state energy bd of Santa Cruz, then chief adviser to state economy minister and public works ministry; Minister of Economy and Public Works, State of Santa Cruz 1991; Rep. for Santa Cruz to Ofephi (fed. org. of hydrocarbon-producing states) 1991–99 (later Exec. Sec.), also Rep. of Ofephi to fed. govt ministries of economy and public works during privatization of state-owned oil co. YPF (mem. Bd 1998–200); mem. govt comm. that drafted basic energy law 1993, fed. electricity comm. 1998–2002, Man. Cttee, Fed. Trust for Electricity 2002; Minister of Energy 2003–. *Address:* Ministry of Energy, av. Paseo Colón 171, Capital Federal – CP (C1063ACB), Argentina (office). *Telephone:* (11) 4349-8069 (office). *E-mail:* energia@minplan.gov.ar (office). *Website:* energia.mecon.gov.ar (office).

CAMERON, Rt Hon David, BA; British politician; *Leader, Conservative Party;* b. Oct. 1966; m. Samantha Cameron; two s. one d.; ed Eton Coll., Brasenose Coll., Oxford; Head of Political Section, Conservative Research Dept 1988–92; Special Adviser to Chancellor of the Exchequer 1992–93, to Home Sec. 1993–94; Dir of Corp. Affairs, mem. Exec. Bd Carlton Communication plc 1994–2001; MP (Witney) 2001–, fmr mem. Home Affairs Select Cttee, Modernisation Cttee, currently Vice-Chair. All Party Cttee on Drugs, All Party Media Cttee; Shadow Deputy Leader of the House of Commons 2003; Deputy Chair. Conservative Party 2003; Front Bench Spokesman on Local Govt Finance 2004; Head of Policy Co-ordination –2005; Shadow Sec. of State for Educ. and Skills 2005; Leader, Conservative Party 2005–; mem. Exec. British–American Parl. Group; mem. Council Royal Inst. for Int. Affairs; Patron St Mary's Church, Witney, Carterton Educational Trust, Oxon., Victoria County History Trust, Mulberry Bush School, Standlake. *Leisure interests:* tennis, riding, country sports, television, cooking. *Address:* Conservative and Unionist Party, 25 Victoria Street, London, SW1H 0DL (office); House of Commons, Westminster, London SW1A 0AA, England (office). *Telephone:* (20) 7219-4410 (office). *E-mail:* camerond@parliament.uk (office). *Website:* www.conservatives.com (office); www.davidcameronmp.com (office).

CAMERON, Ian Rennell, CBE, MA, DM, FRCP, FMedSci; British professor of medicine; b. 20 May 1936, London; s. of James Cameron and Frances Cameron; m. 1st Jayne Bustard 1964 (divorced); one s. one d.; m. 2nd Jennifer Payne 1980; ed Westminster School, Corpus Christi Coll. Oxford and St Thomas's Hosp. Medical School; Jr appointments at. St Thomas's Hosp. 1961–64; Lecturer, St Thomas's Hosp. Medical School 1967, Sr Lecturer 1969, Reader 1975, Prof. of Medicine 1979–94, Dean 1986–89; Research Asst Dept of Physiology, Univ. Coll. London 1966–68; NIH Postdoctoral Fellowship, Cedars-Sinai Medical Center, Los Angeles and Asst Prof. Dept of Physiology, UCLA 1968–69; Prin. United Medical and Dental Schools of Guys and St Thomas's Hosps 1989–92; Dir Research and Devt South-East Thames Health

www.worldwhoswho.com

Authority 1993–94, Bro Taf Health Authority (non-exec.) 1996–; Provost and Vice-Chancellor, Univ. of Wales Coll. of Medicine 1994–2001; mem. and Treas. GMC 1995–2001; mem. Comm. for Health Improvement 1999–2004; Hon. Fellow, King's Coll. London 1998, Corpus Christi Coll., Oxford 2000; Hon. LLD (Univ. of Wales) 2001; Hon. DSc Univ. of Glamorgan) 2001; Hon. PhD (Tokyo Women's Medical Univ., Kobe Gakuin Univ. Japan) 2001. *Publications:* Respiratory Disorders (with N. T. Bateman) 1983; papers in medical and physiological journals. *Leisure interests:* collecting paintings, books and ceramics. *Address:* The Old Mill House, 10 Mill Lane, Middle Barton, Oxon., OX7 7BT, England.

CAMERON, James; Canadian film director and screenwriter; b. 16 Aug. 1954, Kapuskasing, Ont.; m. 1st Sharon Williams (divorced); m. 2nd Gale Anne Hurd (divorced); m. 3rd Kathryn Bigelow (divorced); m. 4th Linda Hamilton 1996 (divorced); one d.; m. 5th Suzy Amis; one d.; ed Fullerton Jr Coll.; formed Lightstorm Entertainment 1990, Head 1992–; CEO Digital Domain 1993–. *Films include:* Piranha II – The Spawning (dir), The Terminator (dir and screenplay) 1984, Rambo – First Blood Part II (co-screenwriter), Aliens (dir and screenplay), The Abyss (dir and screenplay), Terminator 2 – Judgment Day (co-screenwriter, dir and producer) 1991, Point Break (exec. producer) 1994, True Lies 1994, Strange Days (writer) 1995, Titanic (Acad. Award for Best Dir, film won 11 Acad. Awards equalling record) 1997, Solaris 2002, Ghosts of the Abyss (documentary; dir and producer) 2003, Volcanoes of the Deep Sea (exec. producer) 2003, Aliens of the Deep (dir and producer) 2005. *Television includes:* Dark Angel (series) (exec. producer) 2000, Expedition: Bismarck (producer) 2002. *Publication:* Strange Days 1995. *Address:* Lightstorm Entertainment, 919 Santa Monica Boulevard, Santa Monica, CA 90401, USA (office). *Telephone:* (310) 656-6100 (office). *Fax:* (310) 656-6102 (office).

CAMERON, Peter Duncanson, LLB, PhD; British academic; *Professor of International Energy Law and Policy, University of Dundee;* b. 21 June 1952, Glasgow; s. of Stewart Cameron and Margaret Cameron; m. Qiumin Li 2004; one s.; ed Bishop Vesey Grammar School, High School of Stirling and Univ. of Edinburgh; Lecturer in Law, Univ. of Dundee 1977–86; Visiting Research Assoc., Oxford Univ. Centre for Socio-Legal Studies 1980, Visiting Scholar, Stanford Law School 1985; Adviser, UN Centre on Transnational Corpns 1985–86; Dir Int. Inst. of Energy Law, Univ. of Leiden 1986–97; Prof. of Int. Energy Law and Policy, Univ. of Dundee 1997–; Chair. Academic Advisory Group and mem. Council, Int. Bar Assen Section on Energy and Natural Resources Law 1996–2001; Jean Monnet Fellow, European Univ. Inst., Florence, Italy 2001–02, Prof. 2002–05; Adviser UN ESCAP 1988–89; Consultant, World Bank 1990–; Visiting Prof., Univ. Autónoma de Madrid 1997–2000; mem. Editorial Bd Oil and Gas Law and Taxation Review 1989–97; Assoc. Ed. Journal of Energy and Natural Resources Law 1990–97, Jt Ed. 1997–2002; Fellow, Energy Delta Inst., Netherlands 2006–; Research Awards from Assen of Int. Petroleum Negotiators (AIPN) 1996, 2005. *Publications:* Property Rights and Sovereign Rights: The Case of North Sea Oil 1983, Petroleum Licensing 1984, The Oil Supplies Industry: A Comparative Study of Legislative Restrictions and Their Impact 1986, Nuclear Energy Law After Chernobyl (ed.) 1988, The Regulation of Gas in Europe 1995, Gas Regulation in Western and Central Europe 1998, Kyoto: From Principles to Practice (ed.) 2001, Competition in Energy Markets 2002, Legal Aspects of EU Energy Regulation (ed.) 2005. *Leisure interests:* long-distance running (marathons: New York, Stockholm, Amsterdam), travel, cinema. *Address:* Centre for Energy, Petroleum and Mineral Law and Policy, University of Dundee, Park Place, Dundee, DD1 4HN (office); 23 Ainslie Place, Edinburgh, EH3 6AJ, Scotland (home). *Telephone:* (1382) 344388 (office); (131) 226-6536 (home). *Fax:* (1382) 322578 (office); (131) 225-7793 (home). *E-mail:* p.d.cameron@dundee.ac.uk (office); peterdcameron@btinternet.com (home). *Website:* www.cepmlp.org (office).

CAMERON OF LOCHBROOM, Baron (Life Peer), cr. 1984, of Lochbroom in the District of Ross and Cromarty; **Kenneth John Cameron,** LLB, MA, QC, FRSE, FRSA; British lawyer; b. 11 June 1931, Edin.; s. of the late Lord Cameron and Eileen Dorothea Burrell; m. Jean Pamela Murray 1964; two d.; ed The Edinburgh Acad., Corpus Christi Coll., Oxford and Univ. of Edinburgh; called to Bar 1958; QC 1972; Chair. Industrial Tribunals (Scotland) 1966–81; Pres. Pensions Appeal Tribunal (Scotland) 1976–84; Chair. Cttee for Investigation in Scotland of Agricultural Marketing Schemes 1980–84; Advocate Depute 1981–84; Lord Advocate 1984–89; Senator of Coll. of Justice in Scotland 1989–2003; Chair. Royal Fine Art Comm. for Scotland 1994–2005; Pres. Scottish Council for Voluntary Orgs 1989–2001; Chancellor's Assessor, Univ. of Edin. 1997–; Hon. Bencher, Lincoln's Inn, London; Hon. Fellow, Corpus Christi Coll. Oxford, Royal Incorporation of Architects in Scotland, Royal Scottish Acad. *Leisure interest:* fishing. *Address:* Stoneyhill House, Musselburgh, Edinburgh, EH21 6RP, Scotland. *Telephone:* (131) 665-1081.

CAMERON WATT, Donald, MA, DLitt, FBA, FRHistS; British historian and academic; *Professor Emeritus of International History, London School of Economics;* b. 17 May 1928, Rugby; s. of Robert Cameron Watt and Barbara Bidwell; m. 1st Marianne R. Grau 1951 (died 1962); m. 2nd Felicia Cobb Stanley 1962 (died 1997); one s., one step-d.; ed Rugby School and Oriel Coll., Oxford; Asst Ed. (Foreign Office Research Dept), Documents on German Foreign Policy 1918–1945, 1951–54, 1951–59; Asst Lecturer in Political History, LSE 1954–56, Lecturer in Int. History 1957–63, Sr Lecturer 1964–65; Reader in Int. History, Univ. of London 1966–72, Prof. in Int. History 1972–82, Stevenson Prof. of Int. History 1982–93, Prof. Emer. 1993–; Ed. Survey of Int. Affairs, Royal Inst. of Int. Affairs 1962–71; Historian, Cabinet Office Historical Section 1977–94; Rockefeller Fellow in Social Sciences 1960–61; Fellow Polish Acad. of Arts and Sciences, Kraków; fmr FRSA; Sec. Comm. for History of Int. Relations 1982–95, Vice Pres. 1995–; Hon. Fellow Oriel Coll., Oxford 1998; Wolfson Prize for History 1990. *Publications:* Oxford Poetry 1950 (ed.) 1951, Britain and the Suez Canal 1956, Documents on the Suez Crisis 1957, Britain Looks to Germany 1965, Personalities and Policies 1965, A History of the World in the 20th Century 1967, Contemporary History in Europe 1969, Hitler's Mein Kampf (ed.) 1969, 1992, Current British Foreign Policy 1970–72, Too Serious a Business 1975, 1992, Succeeding John Bull, America in Britain's Place 1900–1975 1983, Documents on British Foreign Affairs 1867–1939 1985–97, How War Came 1989, Argentina Between the Great Powers 1990. *Leisure interests:* cats. *Address:* c/o Department of International History, London School of Economics, Aldwych, London, WC2A 2AE, England. *Website:* www.lse.ac.uk/collections/internationalHistory.

CAMILLERI, Louis C., BA; American (b. Egyptian) business executive; *Chairman and CEO, Philip Morris International;* b. 1955, Alexandria, Egypt; m. (divorced); three c.; ed Univ. of Lausanne, Switzerland; business analyst with W. R. Grace & Co., Lausanne –1978; joined Philip Morris Europe as a Business Devt Analyst 1978–82, Dir, Business Devt and Planning 1982–86, Vice-Pres., Eastern Europe, Middle East and Africa (EEMA) Region 1986–90, Vice-Pres., Cen. and Eastern Europe 1990–93, Sr Vice-Pres., EU Region 1993–95, Vice-Pres., Corp. Business Strategy Feb.–Aug. 1995, Sr Vice-Pres., Corp. Planning, Philip Morris Cos Inc. (later Altria Group, Inc.), New York Aug.–Dec. 1995, Sr Vice-Pres. and Chief Financial Officer 1996–2002, Pres. and CEO April–Aug. 2002, Chair. and CEO Aug. 2002–08, Chair. and CEO Philip Morris International (following spin-off from Altria Group, Inc. March 2008) 2008–; Pres. and CEO Kraft Foods Int. 1995–2002, mem. Bd Dirs 2001–07, Chair. 2002–07; Dir (non-exec.) SABMiller 2002–. *Leisure interests:* motorsports, scuba diving. *Address:* Philip Morris International, Avenue de Cour 107, 1171 Lausanne, Switzerland (office). *Telephone:* (21) 618-61-11 (office). *E-mail:* info@pmintl.com (office). *Website:* www.philipmorrisinternational.com (office).

CAMILLERI, Victor; Maltese diplomatist; *Permanent Representative, United Nations, Geneva;* b. 8 Oct. 1942, St Venera; m. Elizabeth B. Heaney 1967; two s.; ed Lyceum, Malta, Univ. of Birmingham, UK, Columbia Univ., USA; fmr teacher, Educ. Dept; joined External Affairs Service, Ministry of Commonwealth and Foreign Affairs 1968; First Sec., Perm. Mission to UN, New York 1974–81; Perm. Rep. to UNIDO and UNESCO 1981–84; apptd Head Multilateral Section, Ministry of Foreign Affairs, Valletta 1984, Acting Sec. 1985–87; Amb. and Head Malta's del. to Stockholm Conf., CSCE on Confidence and Security Building Measures 1984–85; Deputy High Commr in London 1987–90, High Commr (also accred to Sweden) 1991; Chef de Cabinet, Office of Pres. of 45th Session of UN Gen. Ass. 1990; Perm. Rep. to UN, New York 1991–93, 2003–07, to UN, Geneva 2007–; Amb. to Belgium 1997. *Address:* Permanent Mission of Malta to the UN, Parc du Château-Banquet 26, 1202 Geneva, Switzerland (office). *Telephone:* 229010580 (office). *Fax:* 227381120 (home). *E-mail:* malta-un.geneva@gov.mt (office).

CAMILO, Michel; Dominican Republic jazz musician (piano) and composer; b. 4 April 1954, Santo Domingo; m. Sandra Camilo 1975; ed Nat. Conservatory, Santo Domingo, Mannes and Juilliard School of Music, New York; mem. Nat. Symphony Orchestra, Santo Domingo 1970, conductor 1987; moved to New York 1979; debut at Carnegie Hall with trio 1985; Musical Dir Heineken Jazz Festival, Dominican Rep. 1987–92; guest soloist with numerous orchestras 1994–; Co-Artistic Dir Latin-Caribbean Music Festival, Washington, DC 1998; has performed in N America, the Caribbean, Japan, Europe, S America and Israel; Prof. Emer., Univ. Autónoma de Santo Domingo 1992; Dr hc (Univ. Tecnológica de Santiago) 1994, (Berklee Coll. of Music) 2000; mem. AfofM, RMA, American Music Center; Clearwater Jazz Holiday Int. Jazz Award 1993, Emmy Award 1986; Kt Heraldic Order of Christopher Columbus, Silver Cross of the Order of Duarte, Sanchez y Mella 2001. *Recordings include:* albums: The Goodwill Games (theme) (Grammy Award), Calle 54 (OST), Amo mi cama rica (OST) 1970, Why Not! (Grammy Award) 1986, Suntan/Michel Camilo in Trio 1987, Michel Camilo 1988, On Fire 1991, On The Other Hand 1991, Amo tu cama rica (OST) 1992, Rhapsody for two pianos 1992, Rendezvous 1993, Los Peores años de nuestra vida (OST) 1994, One More Once 1994, Two Much (OST) 1996, Hands of Rhythm (with Giovanni Hidalgo) 1997, Thru My Eyes 1997, Piano Concerto and Suite 1998, Spain (with Tomatito) 2000, Calle 54 2001, Triangulo 2002, Concerto for piano and orchestra 2002, Solo 2005, Live at the Blue Note 2005, Rhapsody in Blue 2006, Spain Again (with Tomatito) 2006, Spirit of the Moment 2007. *Address:* c/o Sandra Camilo, Redondo Music & Management Co., PO Box 216, Katonah, NY 10536, USA (office). *Telephone:* (914) 234-6030 (office). *Fax:* (914) 205-3082 (office). *E-mail:* Mijazz@ix.netcom.com (office). *Website:* www.michelcamilo.com.

CAMMARATA, Bernard (Ben); American retail executive; *Chairman, The TJX Companies Inc.;* b. 1941; f. The TJX Cos Inc. (owns TX Maxx, Marshalls, Home Goods and A.J. Wright dept stores) 1976, Pres. –1999, Chair. and CEO –2000, Acting CEO 2005–06, Chair. 2000–; Co-Chair. Inner-City Scholarship Fund, The Catholic Schools Foundation Inc. 2003–04; mem. Bd of Trustees, Bentley Coll. (Trustee Emer. 2004–), Lahey Clinic, Burlington, Mass. *Leisure interest:* golf. *Address:* The TJX Companies Inc., 770 Cochituate Road, Framingham, MA 01701, USA (office). *Telephone:* (508) 390-1000 (office). *Fax:* (508) 390-2828 (office). *E-mail:* info@tjx.com (office). *Website:* www.tjx.com (office).

CAMOYS, 7th Baron (cr. 1264, called out of abeyance 1839); **(Ralph) Thomas Campion George Sherman Stonor,** GCVO, PC; British banker; b. 16 April 1940; s. of 6th Baron Camoys and Mary Jeanne Stourton; m. Elisabeth Mary Hyde Parker 1966; one s. three d.; ed Eton Coll., Balliol Coll., Oxford; Man. Dir Rothschild Intercontinental Bank Ltd 1969–75; with Amex Bank Ltd 1975–78; Man. Dir Barclays Merchant Bank 1978–84, Exec. Vice.-Chair. 1984–86; Dir Barclays Bank PLC 1984–94; Chief Exec. Barclays de

Zoete Wedd Holdings Ltd 1986–87, Deputy Chair. 1987–98; Deputy Chair. Sotheby's Holdings Inc. 1994–97; Dir 3i Group 1991–2002, Perpetual PLC 1994–2000, British Grolux Ltd 1994–; Lord Chamberlain of HM Household 1998–2000; Perm. Lord in Waiting to the Queen 2000–; Pres. River and Rowing Museum, Henley-on-Thames 1998–; mem. Court of Assistants, Fishmongers' Co. 1980–; Consultor Extraordinary Section of Admin. of the Patrimony of the Holy See 1991–2006; Lord-in-Waiting to HM the Queen 1992–98; DL Oxfordshire 1994–; Order of Gorkha Dakshina Bahu, 1st Class (Nepal), Knight Grand Cross of the Order of St Gregory the Great 2006; Hon. DLitt (Sheffield) 2001. *Leisure interests:* the arts, family. *Address:* Stonor Park, Henley-on-Thames, Oxon., RG9 6HF, England. *Telephone:* (1491) 638644. *Fax:* (1491) 639348.

CAMP, Jeffery Bruce, RA; British artist; b. 1923, Oulton Broad, Suffolk; s. of George Camp and Caroline Denny; m. Laetitia Yhap 1963; ed Lowestoft and Ipswich Art Schools and Edin. Coll. of Art (under William Gillies); Andrew Grant Scholarship for travelling and study 1944, 1945, David Murray Bursary for landscape painting 1946; painted altarpiece for St Alban's Church, Norwich 1955; Lecturer, Slade School of Fine Art, London 1963–88; mem. London Group 1961; numerous solo and mixed exhbns 1958–; works in numerous public collections in UK; Athena Art Award 1987. *Publications:* Draw 1981, Paint 1996. *Address:* c/o Browse & Darby, 19 Cork Street, London, W1X 2LP; 27 Stirling Road, London, SW9 9EF, England. *Telephone:* (20) 7734-7984.

CAMPBELL, Alastair John, MA; British civil servant and journalist; b. 25 May 1957; s. of Donald Campbell and Elizabeth Campbell (née Caldwell); pnr Fiona Millar; two s. one d.; ed City of Leicester Boys School, Gonville and Caius Coll., Cambridge; trainee reporter Tavistock Times and Sunday Independent 1980–82; freelance reporter 1982–83; reporter, Daily Mirror 1982–86, Political Ed. 1989–93; News Ed. Sunday Today 1985–86; Political Corresp. Sunday Mirror 1986–87, Political Ed. 1987–89, columnist 1989–91; Asst Ed. and columnist, Today 1993–95; Press Sec. to Leader of the Opposition 1994–97; Press Sec. to Prime Minister 1997–2001, Dir of Communications and Strategy 2001–03, mem. election campaign team 2005; Pres. Keighley Br., Burnley Football Supporters' Club; Visiting Fellow, Inst. of Politics, Harvard Univ. 2004. *Publication:* The Blair Years 2007, All in the Mind (novel) 2008. *Leisure interests:* bagpipes, Burnley Football Club. *Address:* c/o Random House, 20 Vauxhall Bridge Road, London, SW1V 2SA, England.

CAMPBELL, Hon. Alexander Bradshaw, PC, QC, LLD; Canadian lawyer and politician; b. 1 Dec. 1933, Summerside, PEI; s. of the late Thane A. Campbell and Cecilia Bradshaw; m. Marilyn Gilmour 1961; two s. one d.; practised law in Summerside, PEI 1959–66; mem. PEI Legislature 1965–78, Leader of Liberal Party for PEI Dec. 1965–78; Premier of PEI 1966–78; Minister of Devt 1969–72, of Agric. and Forestry 1972–74, Pres. Exec. Council, Minister of Justice, Attorney and Advocate-Gen. 1974–78; Justice, Supreme Court of PEI 1978–94; mem. Privy Council for Canada 1967; mem. and fmr Sec. Summerside Bd of Trade; Past Pres. Y's Men's Club; fmr Vice-Pres. and Exec. mem. PEI Young Liberal Asscn; Pres. Summerside YMCA 1981–91; Elder, United Church, Summerside; Founding Pres. Summerside Area Historical Soc. 1983–88; Founding Chair. Duke of Edinburgh's Awards Cttee (PEI) 1984; Trustee Wyatt Foundation 1990; mem. Heedless Hoarsemen Men's Chorus, Largo, Fla; Co-founder Prince Edward Island Day, Fla; Hon. LLD (McGill, PEI). *Leisure interests:* golf, swimming, gardening. *Address:* Stanley Bridge, Kensington, R.R. #6, Prince Edward Island, C0B 1M0, Canada; 7100 Ulmerton Road, Lot 314, Largo, FL 33771, USA (Winter). *Telephone:* (902) 886-2081 (Summer); (727) 530-9499 (Winter). *E-mail:* alexbcampbell@auracom.com (home).

CAMPBELL, Allan McCulloch, MS, PhD; American biologist and academic; *Professor of Biological Sciences, Stanford University;* b. 27 April 1929, Berkeley, Calif.; s. of Lindsay Campbell and Virginia Campbell; m. Alice Del Campillo 1958; one s. one d.; ed Univ. of Calif. (Berkeley) and Univ. of Ill.; Instructor in Bacteriology, Univ. of Michigan Medical School, Ann Arbor 1953–57; Research Assoc., Carnegie Inst. of Washington, Dept of Genetics 1957–58; Asst Prof. to Prof. of Biology, Univ. of Rochester, 1958–68; Prof. of Biological Sciences, Stanford Univ. 1968–, Barbara Kimball Browning Prof. of Humanities and Sciences 1992–; Fellow, American Acad. of Arts and Sciences; mem. NAS; Hon. DSc (Univ. of Chicago) 1978, (Univ. of Rochester) 1981; Abbott/ASM Lifetime Achivement Award (Microbiology) 2004. *Publications:* Episomes 1969, General Virology 1978. *Address:* Department of Biological Sciences, Stanford University, Stanford, CA 94305 (office); 947 Mears Court, Stanford, CA 94305-1041, USA (home). *Telephone:* (650) 723-1170 (office); (650) 493-6155 (home). *Fax:* (650) 725-1848 (home). *E-mail:* AMC@stanford.edu (office). *Website:* www.stanford.edu/dept/biology (office).

CAMPBELL, Ben Nighthorse, BA; American lawyer and fmr politician; *Senior Policy Advisor, Holland & Knight LLP;* b. 13 April 1933, Auburn, Calif.; m. Linda Price; two c.; ed Univ. of California, San José; educator, Sacramento Law Enforcement Agency; mem. (Democrat) Colo Gen. Ass. 1983–86; mem. US House of Reps 1987–93; Senator from Colo 1993–2005; Sr Policy Advisor Holland & Knight LLP (law firm), Washington, DC 2005–; rancher, jewellery designer; one of 44 chiefs Northern Cheyenne Tribe; mem. American Quarter Horse Asscn, American Indian Educ. Asscn, Aircraft Owners and Pilots Asscn; Ellis Island Medal of Honor 2008. *Address:* Holland & Knight LLP, 2099 Pennsylvania Avenue, NW, Suite 100, Washington, DC 20006, USA (office). *Telephone:* (202) 457-7035 (office). *Fax:* (202) 955-5564 (office). *E-mail:* ben.campbell@hklaw.com (office). *Website:* www.hklaw.com (office).

CAMPBELL, Colin Kydd, FRSC, FRSA, LFIEEE, FEIC; Canadian/British engineer and academic; *Professor Emeritus of Electrical and Computer Engineering, McMaster University;* b. 3 May 1927, St Andrew's, Scotland; s. of David Walker Campbell and Jean Bell Campbell; m. Vivian G. Norval 1954; two s. one d.; ed Madras Coll. St Andrew's, Univ. of St Andrew's and Mass. Inst. of Tech.; mil. service 1944–46; communications engineer, Diplomatic Wireless Service and Foreign Office, London, Washington and New York 1946–48; electronics engineer, Atomic Instrument Co., Cambridge, Mass 1954–57; research scholar, Royal Naval Scientific Service, St Andrew's Univ. 1957–60; Asst Prof. of Electrical Eng, McMaster Univ. 1960–63, Assoc. Prof. 1963–67, Prof. of Electrical and Computer Eng 1967–89, Prof. Emer. 1989–; Visiting Research Fellow, Rand Afrikaans Univ., Johannesburg, S Africa 1995; Invitation Fellow, Japan Soc. for the Promotion of Science 1995; Visiting Research Scholar, Virginia Polytechnic Inst. and State Univ. 2000, 2002; Hon. BSc (Eng) 1951, Hon. SM 1953, Hon. PhD 1960, Hon. DSc 1984; Eadie Medal (RSC) 1983. *Publications:* Surface Acoustic Wave Devices and their Signal Processing Applications 1989, Surface Acoustic Wave Devices for Mobile and Wireless Communications 1998; numerous scientific and eng publs in professional and tech. journals with specialization in surface acoustic wave devices. *Leisure interests:* fishing, travelling. *Address:* 160 Parkview Drive, Ancaster, Ont., L9G 1Z5, Canada (home). *Website:* www3.sympatico.ca/colin.kydd.campbell (home).

CAMPBELL, Sir Colin Murray, Kt, LLB; British academic and university administrator; b. 26 Dec. 1944, Aberdeen; s. of the late Donald Campbell and Isobel Campbell; m. 1st Elaine Carlisle 1974 (divorced 1999); one s. one d.; m. 2nd Maria Day 2002; ed Robert Gordon's Coll. Aberdeen and Univ. of Aberdeen; Lecturer, Faculty of Law, Univ. of Dundee 1967–69, Univ. of Edin. 1969–73; Prof. of Jurisprudence, Queen's Univ., Belfast 1974–88, now Prof. Emer.; Vice-Chancellor Univ. of Nottingham 1988–2008; mem. Council, Soc. for Computers and Law 1973–88, Standing Advisory Comm. on Human Rights 1977–80, Legal Aid Advisory Cttee, NI 1978–82, Mental Health Legislation Review Cttee, NI 1978–82, Nottingham Devt Enterprise 1988–91, Inquiry into Police Responsibilities and Rewards 1992–93; Chair. Ind. Advisory Group on Consumers' Protection in NI 1984, NI Econ. Council 1987–94 (mem. 1985–94), Lace Market Devt Co. 1989–97, Human Fertilisation and Embryology Authority 1990–94, Medical Workforce Standing Advisory Cttee 1991–2001, Food Advisory Cttee 1994–2001, Human Genetics Advisory Comm. 1996–99; Chair. QUBIS Ltd 1983–88, Zeton Ltd 1990; Dir (non-exec.) Swiss Re GB 1999–2005; HM's First Commr for Judicial Appointments 2001–06; Hon. LLD (Aberdeen) 2001. *Publications:* Law and Society 1979 (jtly), Do We Need a Bill of Rights? (ed.) 1980, Data Processing and the Law (ed.) 1984; numerous articles in books and journals. *Leisure interests:* walking, sport, music, reading. *Address:* c/o University of Nottingham, University Park, Nottingham, NG7 2RD, England (office).

CAMPBELL, Finley Alexander, PhD, FRSC; Canadian geologist and academic; *Professor Emeritus, Department of Geology and Geophysics, University of Calgary;* b. 5 Jan. 1927, Kenora, Ont.; s. of Finley McLeod Campbell and Vivian Delve; m. Barbara E. Cromarty 1953; two s. one d.; ed Kenora High School, Portland Univ., Brandon Coll., Univ. of Manitoba, Queen's Univ. Kingston, Ont. and Princeton Univ.; exploration and mine geologist 1950–58; Asst, Assoc. Prof., Univ. of Alberta 1958–65; Prof. and Head, Dept of Geology, Univ. of Calgary 1965–69; Vice-Pres. Capital Resources, Univ. of Calgary 1969–71, Vice-Pres. (Academic) 1971–76, Prof. of Geology 1976–84, Vice-Pres. Priorities and Planning 1984–88, Prof. Emer. Dept of Geology and Geophysics 1988–; Vice-Chair. Bd of Dirs Canadian Energy Research Inst.; Pres. Emer. Asscn, Univ. of Calgary; Queen's Jubilee Medal, Commemorative Medal for 125th Anniversary of Canada, Distinguished Service Award (Brandon Univ.) 1993 and other awards and distinctions. *Publications:* over 50 publs on geological topics. *Leisure interests:* sailing, golf, music, skiing, ballet. *Address:* Department of Geology and Geophysics, University of Calgary, 2500 University Drive NW, Calgary, AB T2N 1N4 (office); 3408 Benton Drive NW, Calgary AB T2L 1W8, Canada (home). *Telephone:* (403) 220-3258 (office). *E-mail:* campbelf@ucalgary.ca (office). *Website:* www.geo.ucalgary.ca (office).

CAMPBELL, Hon. Gordon, BA, MBA; Canadian politician; *Premier of British Columbia;* b. Vancouver; m. Nancy Campbell; two s.; ed Dartmouth Coll., Simon Fraser Univ.; taught secondary school in Yola, Nigeria 1970s; Asst to Vancouver Mayor Art Phillips; Gen. Man. of Devt, Marathon Realty 1976–81; f. Citycore Devt Corpn 1981; mem. Vancouver City Council 1984–86; Mayor of Vancouver 1986–93; Leader BC Liberal Party 1993–; mem. BC Legislature for Vancouver-Quilchena 1994–2001, for Vancouver-Point Grey 2001–; Premier of BC 2001–. *Address:* Office of the Premier, POB 9041, Stn. Prov. Govt., Victoria, BC V8W 9E1, Canada (office). *Telephone:* (250) 387-1715 (office). *Fax:* (250) 387-0087 (office). *E-mail:* premier@gov.bc.ca (office). *Website:* www.gov.bc.ca (office); www.gordoncampbellmla.bc.ca.

CAMPBELL, Gordon Arden, CBE, MA, FIChemE, FREng, CBIM; British chemical engineer and business executive; *Chairman, British Nuclear Fuels PLC;* b. 16 Oct. 1946; s. of the late Hugh Eric Campbell and Jessie Campbell; m. Jennifer Vaughan 1970; two d.; ed Oldershaw Grammar School, Churchill Coll., Cambridge; joined Courtaulds Research 1968; Man. Dir British Celanese Ltd 1980–85, Saiccor (Pty) Ltd, S Africa 1985–87; Dir Courtaulds PLC 1987–98, Chief Exec. 1996–98; Chair. Acordis Group 1999–2000, Babcock Int. Group PLC 2000–; Pres. Inst. of Chemical Engineers 1998; Pres. Comité Int. de Rayonne et Fibres Synthétiques 1995–98; mem. (non-exec.) UKAEA 1993–96; Dir (non-exec.) A.E.A. Tech. 1996–97, Argos PLC 1997–98, British Nuclear Fuels PLC 2000–, (Chair. 2004–), Accysis Technologies PLC 2005–, HSS Holdings PLC 2005–; Chair. Wade-Allied Holdings 1999–2003, Jupiter Split Trust PLC 2001–04, Jupiter Second Split Trust 2004–, ITI Scotland 2003–05; Vice-Pres. Royal Acad. of Eng 2001–04; Visiting Prof., Strathclyde Univ.; mem. British Heart Foundation Council. *Leisure interests:* golf, skiing,

www.worldwhoswho.com

rugby. *Address:* British Nuclear Fuels PLC, 65 Buckingham Gate, London, SW1E 6AP, England (office). *Telephone:* (20) 7202-0865 (office). *Fax:* (20) 799-3224 (office). *Website:* www.bnfl.com (office).

CAMPBELL, Iain Donald, MA, PhD, FRS; British biochemist and academic; *Professor of Structural Biology, Department of Biochemistry, University of Oxford;* b. 24 April 1941, Perth, Scotland; s. of Daniel Campbell and Catherine Campbell (née Lauder); m. Karin C. Wehle 1967; one s. two d.; ed Univs. of St Andrews and Oxford; with Dept of Physics, Univ. of Bradford 1966–67; with Physical Chemistry Lab., Univ. of Oxford 1967–70, Dept of Biochemistry 1970–, Tutor in Biochemistry and Fellow, St John's Coll. 1987–, Prof. of Structural Biology 1992–, Assoc. Head of Dept of Biochemistry 1998–; del. to Oxford Univ. Press 1996–; mem. Wellcome Trust MC Panel 1997–2002, European Molecular Biology Org. 1990–; Trustee EPA Cephalosporin Fund 2004–, EMF Biological Research Trust; Hon. DSc (Portsmouth) 2000;, Hon. DTech (Lund) 2000; BHD Medal (Biochemical Soc.) 1990, Novartis Medal (Biochemical Soc.) 2003, Croonian Medal (Royal Soc.) 2006. *Publications:* papers and reviews in scientific journals. *Address:* St John's College, Oxford OX1 3JP (office); Department of Biochemistry, University of Oxford, South Parks Road, Oxford, OX1 3QU, England (office). *Telephone:* (1865) 275346 (office). *Fax:* (1865) 275253 (office). *E-mail:* iain.campbell@bioch.ox.ac.uk (office). *Website:* www.ocms.ox.ac.uk/idc (office).

CAMPBELL, John F., MA; Irish diplomatist; b. 23 June 1936, Dublin; s. of Ernest Campbell and Bertha Campbell (née Willan); m. Nicole Lafon 1964; two s.; ed Trinity Coll. Dublin, Yale Univ., USA; Amb. to People's Repub. of China 1980–83, to FRG 1983–86, to EC 1986–91, to France 1991–95, Perm. Rep. to UN, New York 1995–98, Amb. to Portugal (also accred to Brazil and Morocco) 1999. *Address:* c/o Department of Foreign Affairs, 80 St Stephen's Green, Dublin 2, Ireland (office).

CAMPBELL, Juliet Jeanne d'Auvergne, CMG, MA; British fmr diplomatist and university administrator (retd); *Life Fellow, Girton College, Cambridge;* b. 23 May 1935, London; d. of Wilfred d'Auvergne Collings and Harriet Nancy Draper Bishop; m. Alexander Elmslie Campbell 1983 (died 2002); ed schools in S Africa, Palestine, Lebanon and UK, Lady Margaret Hall, Oxford; joined Foreign Office, London 1957, Del. to Conf. negotiating Britain's proposed entry to EC 1961–63, Second Sec., Bangkok 1964–67, First Sec. Paris (NATO) 1966, First Sec., FCO News Dept 1967–70, Head of Chancery, The Hague 1970–74, First Sec. then Counsellor FCO 1974–77, Counsellor, Paris 1977–80, Royal Coll. Defence Studies 1981, Counsellor, Jakarta 1982–83, Head, Training Dept 1983–87; Amb. to Luxembourg 1987–91; mem. Wilton Park Acad. Council 1992–2000; Mistress Girton Coll., Cambridge 1992–98, Life Fellow 1998–; Deputy Vice-Chancellor, Cambridge Univ. 1993–98; mem. Council Queen's Coll., Harley St 1992–2002; Gov. Marlborough Coll. 1999–2007; Trustee Cambridge European Trust 1994–98, Kurt Hahn Trust 1995–98, Changing Faces (Charity) 1994–2006, Council Royal Soc. for Asian Affairs 2008–; Hon. Fellow, Lady Margaret Hall, Oxford 1992. *Address:* 3 Belbroughton Road, Oxford, OX2 6UZ, England (home). *Telephone:* (1865) 558685 (home). *E-mail:* jencampbell@aol.com (home).

CAMPBELL, Rt Hon Kim Avril Phaedra, BA, LLB, PC QC; Canadian politician and lawyer; b. 10 March 1947; m. Hershey Felder; ed Univ. of British Columbia, LSE, UK; Lecturer in Science and History, Vancouver Community Coll., in Political Science, Univ. of BC; mem. BC Legis.; elected Progressive Conservative House of Commons 1988, Progressive Conservative leader June–Nov. 1993; Minister of State Affairs and Northern Devt 1989–90, Minister of Justice and Attorney-Gen. of Canada 1990–93; Minister of Defence 1993; Prime Minister (first female) of Canada June–Nov. 1993; mem. Visiting Cttee Center for Int. Affairs, Harvard Univ. 1995; Consul Gen. of Canada in Los Angeles serving states of California, Utah, Nevada, Arizona, Hawaii and territory of Guam; Visiting Prof. of Practice John F. Kennedy School of Govt, Harvard Univ. 2001–2004; Chair. Council of Women World Leaders 1999–2003, Chair. Emer. 2003–; Pres. Int. Women's Forum 2003–; Sec.-Gen. Club of Madrid 2004–06; Sr Fellow, Gorbachev Foundation of North America; mem. Int. Council of Asia Society; Hon. degrees Brock Univ. 1998, Univ. of British Columbia 2000, Mt Holyoke Coll., South Hadley, Mass 2004, DPS Northeastern Univ., Boston 1999; Hon. Fellow LSE 1994. *Publication:* Time and Chance: A Political Memoir of Canada's First Woman Prime Minister 1996. *Address:* c/o American Program Bureau, 313 Washington Street, Suite 225, Newton, MA 02458, USA (office). *Telephone:* (800) 225 4575 (office). *Fax:* (617) 965 6610 (office). *E-mail:* kim_campbell@ksg.harvard.edu. *Website:* www.apbspeakers.com (office).

CAMPBELL, Lewis B., BEng; American transport industry executive; *Chairman, President and CEO, Textron Incorporated;* ed Duke Univ.; 24 years at Gen. Motors, including Gen. Mfg Man., Rochester Products Div., Mfg Man., Chevrolet-Pontiac, Exec. Dir GM/UAW Quality Network, Vice-Pres. Gen. Motors and Gen. Man. Flint Automotive Group 1988–91, Gen. Man. GMC Truck 1991–92; joined Textron Inc. 1992 as Exec. Vice-Pres. and COO, Pres. and COO 1994–98, CEO 1998–, also Chair. 1999– and Pres. 2001–; Dir Bristol-Myers Squibb, Allegheny Energy Inc.; mem. Business Roundtable, Business Council; mem. Bd of Visitors, Fuqua School of Business, Duke Univ. *Address:* 40 Westminster Street, Providence, RI 02903-2596, USA (office). *Telephone:* (401) 421-2800 (office). *Fax:* (401) 421-2878 (office). *Website:* www.textron.com (office).

CAMPBELL, Naomi; British model; b. 1970, London; d. of Valerie Morris; ed Barbara Speake Stage School, Italia Conti; fashion model 1985–. *Film appearances include:* Ready To Wear 1994, Miami Rhapsody 1995, Catwalk 1995, Invasion of Privacy 1996, Beautopia 1996, Prisoner of Love 1999, Destinazione Verna 2000. *Albums:* Baby Woman 1994, Love and Tears 1994. *Publication:* Swan (novel) 1994. *Address:* Women Model Agency, 2nd Floor, 107 Greene Street, New York, 10012, USA. *Telephone:* (20) 7333-0891 (office). *Fax:* (20) 7323-1221 (office).

CAMPBELL, Neve Adrienne; Canadian actress; b. 3 Oct. 1973, Guelph, Ont.; m. Jeff Colt 1995 (divorced 1997); ed Nat. Ballet School, Canada. *Dance includes:* The Phantom of the Opera, The Nutcracker, Sleeping Beauty. *Films include:* Paint Cans 1994, The Dark 1994, Love Child 1995, The Craft 1996, Scream (Saturn Award for Best Actress 1996, MTV Movie Award for Best Female Performance 1996) 1996, A Time to Kill 1996, Simba's Pride 1997, Scream 2 (MTV Movie Award for Best Female Performance 1996, Blockbuster Entertainment Award for Favourite Actress – Horror 1997) 1997, Wild Things 1998, Hairshirt 1998, 54 1998, Three to Tango 1999, Scream 3 2000, Panic 2000, A Lust for Life 2000, Drowning Mona 2000, Last Call 2003, Blind Horizon 2003, Lost Junction 2003, The Company 2003, When Will I Be Loved 2004, Churchill: The Hollywood Years 2004, Partition 2006. *Television includes:* Catwalk 1992–93, Web of Deceit 1993, Baree 1994, The Forget-Me-Not Murders 1994, Party of Five 1994–98, The Canterville Ghost 1996, Reefer Madness: The Movie Musical 2005. *Address:* Creative Artists Agency, 9830 Wilshire Boulevard, Beverly Hills, CA 90212, USA (office).

CAMPBELL, Philip Henry Montgomery, PhD, FInstP, FRAS; British journalist and academic; *Editor-in-Chief, Nature;* b. 19 April 1951; s. of Hugh Campbell and Mary Montgomery Campbell; m. Judie Yelton 1980 (died 1992); two s.; ed Shrewsbury School, Univ. of Bristol, Queen Mary Coll., London, Univ. of Leicester; postdoctoral research asst, Dept of Physics, Univ. of Leicester 1977–79; Asst Ed. Nature journal 1979–82, Physical Sciences Ed. 1982–88, Ed., Nature journal and Ed.-in-Chief Nature journal and Nature publications 1995–, Dir Nature Publishing Group 1997–; Founding Ed. Physics World magazine 1988–95; Trustee Cancer Research UK; Hon. DSc (Leicester) 1999. *Radio:* broadcasts on BBC World Service. *Publications:* numerous papers and articles in journals, magazines and newspapers. *Leisure interest:* music. *Address:* c/o Nature Publishing Group, The Macmillan Building, 4 Crinan Street, London, N1 9XW, England (office). *Telephone:* (20) 7833-4000 (office). *Fax:* (20) 7843-4596 (office). *E-mail:* exec@nature.com (office). *Website:* www.nature.com (office).

CAMPBELL, Roderick Samuel Fisher, AM, PhD, DSc, DVMS, MRCVS, FRSE, FRCPath, FACVSc, FACTM; Australian veterinary scientist and academic; *Professor Emeritus, Australian Institute of Tropical Veterinary and Animal Sciences, James Cook University;* b. 5 June 1924, Glasgow, Scotland; s. of Robert Campbell and Harriet Hodson; m. Barbara M. Morris 1956; three s.; ed Allan Glens School, Glasgow, McLaren High School, Callander and Glasgow Veterinary Coll.; Lecturer in Veterinary Pathology, Univ. of Glasgow 1948, Sr Lecturer 1956–69; Prof. and Head, Grad. School of Tropical Veterinary Science, James Cook Univ. Townsville 1969–87, Prof. Emer. 1987–, Chair. Convocation 1992–94, Dir Anton Breinl Centre for Tropical Health and Medicine, Townsville 1990–91; Visiting Prof., Khartoum Univ. 1964–65, Purdue Univ., USA 1967–68; Deputy Chair. Australian Veterinary Schools Accreditation Cttee 1988–92; Project Man. Balitvet Inst. Project, Bogor, Indonesia 1981–; Consultant, FAO, World Bank, Australian Centre for Int. Agric. Research, Int. Devt Program of Australian Univs, Australian Devt Asst Bureau, Ove Arup; Trustee, Indonesia Int. Animal Science Research and Devt Foundation 1990–93; Fellow Australian Coll. of Veterinary Science, Australian Coll. of Tropical Medicine, Royal Coll. of Pathology; Hon. DSc (James Cook); Hon. Dr Veterinary Medicine and Surgery (Glasgow) 2000; Kesteven Medal for Contrib. to Int. Veterinary Science, Pegasus Medal. *Publications:* numerous scientific papers on infectious diseases, veterinary educ., devt assistance etc. *Leisure interests:* history, music, golf. *Address:* School of Veterinary and Biomedicall Sciences, James Cook University, Townsville, QLD 4811 (office); 4/49 Quinn Street, Townsville, QLD 4812, Australia (home). *Telephone:* 4781-4278 (office); 4728-8192 (home). *Fax:* 4779-1526 (office). *E-mail:* roderick.campbell@jcu.edu.au (office); rsfc@ozemail.com.au (home).

CAMPBELL, Sydney, MA (Econ); Belizean central banker; *Governor and Vice-Chairman, Central Bank of Belize;* ed Florida Int. Univ., USA; joined Cen. Bank of Belize 1981, served in various posts including Deputy Gov. –2003, Gov. and Vice-Chair. 2003–. *Address:* Central Bank of Belize, Gabourel Lane, PO Box 852, Belize City, Belize (office). *Telephone:* 223-6194 (office). *Fax:* 223-6226 (office). *E-mail:* info@centralbank.org.bz (office). *Website:* www.centralbank.org.bz (office).

CAMPBELL, Sir Walter Menzies (Ming), Kt, CBE, QC, MA, LLB, LLD; British politician; b. 22 May 1941; m.; ed Hillhead High School, Univ. of Glasgow, Stanford Univ., USA; ran 200m. at 1964 Tokyo Olympic Games and 1966 Commonwealth Games, Capt. UK Athletics Team 1965–66; called to Scottish Bar as Advocate 1968; Chair. Scottish Liberal Party 1975; MP for Fife North East 1987–, Spokesman on Sport and Defence 1988–94, Shadow Foreign Sec. 1997–2006; Deputy Leader, Liberal Democrat party 2003–06, Leader 2006–07; Chancellor St Andrews Univ. 2006–; Dr hc (Glasgow), (Strathclyde). *Achievements include:* held British 100m. record 1967–74. *Publication:* Menzies Campbell: My Autobiography 2008. *Address:* Liberal Democrats, 4 Cowley Street, London, SW1P 3NB, England (office); North East Fife Liberal Democrats, 16 Millgate, Cupar, Fife, KY15 5EG, Scotland (office). *Telephone:* (20) 7222-7999 (office); (1334) 656361 (office). *Fax:* (20) 7799-2170 (office); (1334) 654045 (office). *E-mail:* westminster_office@mingcampbell.org.uk (office); info@libdems.org.uk (office). *Website:* www.libdems.org.uk (office); www.mingcampbell.org.uk (office).

CAMPBELL-BROWN, Veronica; Jamaican athlete; b. 15 May 1982, Trelawny; d. of Cecil Campbell and Pamella Bailey; m. Omar Brown 2007; ed Vere Tech. High School, Clarendon, Barton Co. Community Coll., Great Bend, Kan. and Univ. of Arkansas, USA; track and field sprint athlete; five-time Olympic medallist, Olympic 200m and World 100m Champion; Gold Medals, 100m and 4×100m, inaugural Int. Asscn of Athletics Feds (IAAF) World Youth Championships 1999; first female to win sprint double at IAAF World Jr Championships 2000; Silver Medal, 4×100m relay, Olympic Games, Sydney 2000; only female athlete to win both 100m and 200m sprints at same World Youth Championships; Silver Medal, 100m, Commonwealth Games, Manchester 2002; Bronze Medal, 100m, Olympic Games, Athens 2004, Gold Medals, 200m and 4×100m; Silver Medals, 100m and 4×100m relay, World Championships, Helsinki 2005; Silver Medal, 200m, Commonwealth Games, Melbourne 2006; Gold Medal, 100m, World Championships, Osaka 2007, Silver Medals, 200m and 4×100m relay; Gold Medal, 200m, Olympic Games, Beijing 2008 (set new personal best time of 21.74 seconds; only second woman in history to win Olympic 200m twice and successfully defend her title). *Address:* c/o Jamaica Amateur Athletic Association Ltd, PO Box 272, Kingston 5, Jamaica. *Telephone:* 929-6623. *Fax:* 920-4801. *E-mail:* athleticsja@jamweb.net. *Website:* www.jaaaltd.com; www.veronicacampbellbrown.com.

CAMPBELL-WHITE, Martin Andrew, FRSA; British business executive; *Joint Chief Executive Officer, Askonas Holt Limited;* b. 11 July 1943; s. of late John Vernon Campbell-White and Hilda Doris Ash; m. Margaret Mary Miles 1969; three s.; ed Dean Close School, Cheltenham, St John's Coll., Oxford, Univ. of Strasbourg, France; with Thomas Skinner & Co. Ltd (Publrs) 1964–66, Ibbs & Tillett Ltd (Concert Agents) 1966–72, Dir 1969–72, Harold Holt Ltd (Concert Agents), subsequently Askonas Holt Ltd 1972–, Dir 1973–, Deputy Chair. 1989–92, Chief Exec. 1992–98, Jt Chief Exec. 1998–; Chair. British Asscn of Concert Agents 1978–81; Council mem. London Sinfonietta 1973–86; Dir Chamber Orchestras of Europe 1983–93; Asst Dir Festival of German Arts 1987; Founding Dir Japan Festival 1991; mem. Bd Première Ensemble 1991–, Riverside Studios 1998–2000; Trustee Abbado Trust for Young Musicians 1987–2006, Salzburg Festival Trust 1996–2000; Exec. Trustee Musicians Benevolent Fund 2006–; Sebetia Ter prize for Culture, Naples, Italy 1999. *Leisure interests:* golf, watching cricket, classical music, travel. *Address:* Askonas Holt Ltd, Lincoln House, 300 High Holborn, London, WC1V 7JH, England (office). *Telephone:* (20) 7400-1700 (office). *Fax:* (20) 7400-1799 (office). *E-mail:* martin.campbell-white@askonasholt.co.uk (office). *Website:* www.askonasholt.co.uk (office).

CAMPESE, David Ian, AM; Australian fmr professional rugby union player; *Managing Director, Goosestep Pty Ltd;* b. 21 Oct. 1962, Queanbeyan, NSW; s. of Tony Campese and Joan Campese; m. Lara Berkenstein 2003; partner Campo's Sports Store; int. debut Australia versus NZ 1982; Capt. Australia team; winner World Cup 1991; world's leading int. try scorer with 64; scored 310 points for Australia; fmrly Australia's most capped player (represented Australia 101 times); Dir David Campese Man. Group 1997–; Man. Dir Goosestep (Co.); Australian Writers Player of the Year 1991, English Rugby Writers Player of the Year 1991, Int. Rugby Hall of Fame 2001, Order of Australia Medal (for services to rugby union) 2002. *Publication:* On a Wing and a Prayer (biog.), My Game, Your Game 1994, Still Entertaining 2003. *Leisure interests:* golf, cooking, music, reading. *Address:* 13 Nicholas Avenue, Concord, Sydney, NSW 2137, Australia (home). *E-mail:* dcampese@bigpond.net.au (office). *Website:* www.goosestep.com.au (office).

CAMPION, Jane, BA; New Zealand film director and writer; b. 30 April 1954, Wellington; d. of Richard Campion and Edith Campion; ed Victoria Univ., Chelsea School of Arts, London, Australian Film, TV and Radio School, Sydney Coll. of the Arts; Adjunct Prof., Sydney Coll. of the Arts, Univ. of Sydney 2000; Pres. Int. Jury of 54th Mostra Internazionale d'Arte Cinematografica Festival, Venice Film Festival; Hon. DLitt (Victoria Univ. of Wellington) 1999; Women in Hollywood Icon Award, Taormina Arte Diamond Award (Italy), Taormina Arte Award for Cinematic Excellence (Italy) 1990, Winner Byron Kennedy Award for Excellence and Contrib. to Australian Cinema. *Films directed include:* Peel (Palme d'Or for Best Short Film, Cannes Film Festival) 1981–82, Girl's Own Story (Best Dir, Best Telemovie, Best Screenplay at Australian Film Inst. (AFI) Awards, Rouben Mamoulian Award for Best Overall Short Film, Sydney Film Festival, Best Direction, Best Screenplay, Best Cinematography, AFI Awards, First Prize, Cinestud (Press Prize), Amsterdam Film Festival, voted Best Film by critics at Cinestud 1985) 1984, Two Friends (Best Dir, Best Telemovie, Best Screenplay, AFI Awards 1987) 1985, Sweetie (also co-writer) 1988, The Piano (more than 30 int. international awards, including the Palme d'Or (only female winner), Cannes Film Festival, three Academy Awards, including Best Screenplay, winner Best Dir, New York Film Critics' Circle, Los Angeles Film Critics' Asscn, Australian Film Critics, winner Best Picture, Australian Film Inst.) 1993, The Portrait of a Lady (Best Film, Venice Film Festival 1996) 1996, Holy Smoke 1999, In the Cut 2003, The Water Diary (short film for UNDP) 2005, The Lady Bug (short) 2006, Bright Star 2008. *Address:* c/o HLA Management Theatrical Agency Australia, PO Box 1536, Strawberry Hills, Sydney, NSW 2012, Australia (office). *Telephone:* (2) 9310-4948 (office). *Fax:* (2) 9310-4113 (office). *E-mail:* kate.richter@hlamgt.com.au (office); hla@hlamgt.com.au (office).

CAMPORINI, Gen. Vincenzo, FRAeS; Italian military officer; *Chief of Defence General Staff;* b. 1946; ed Air Force Acad., NATO Defence Coll., ITAF Air War Coll.; Staff Officer Personnel Div., Air Staff 1982–83, Aide-de Camp to Chief of Staff 1983–85; Commdr Air Force Flight Test Centre and Rep. to Aerospace Application Study Cttee, Advisory Group for Aerospace Research and Devt, NATO 1988; Head of Plans, Operations and Training Div., Air Force Staff 1993–96; Aviation Insp., The Navy 1996–97; Dir Inspectorate for Flight Safety 1997–98; Head of Mil. Policy and Planning Div., Defence Gen. Staff 1998–2001; Deputy Chief of Defence, Gen. Staff 2001–04; Pres. Italian Centre for High Defence Studies 2004–06; Chief of Staff of Air Force 2006–08; Chief of Defence Gen. Staff 2008–; Grand Kt Cross, Order of Merit, Commdr, Ordre Nat. du Mérite (France); Gold Medal for Flying Merit, Command Gold Medal, Gold Cross for Mil. Service, Italian Defence Gen. Staff Medal of Honour, Santos Dumont Medal. *Address:* Ministry of Defence, Palazzo Baracchini, Via XX Settembre 8, 00187 Rome, Italy (office). *Telephone:* (06) 46911 (office). *E-mail:* pi@smd.difesa.it (office). *Website:* www.difesa.it (office).

CAMPOS E CUNHA, Luis; Portuguese economist and fmr government official; b. 1954; m.; three c.; ed Univ. Católica Portuguesa, Columbia Univ., USA; Asst Prof. of Econs, School of Econs, Universidade Nova de Lisboa 1985–91, Assoc. Prof. 1991–95, Prof. 1995–, Dean, School of Econs 2002–04; Vice-Gov. Banco de Portugal 1996–2002; Minister of Finance and Public Admin, Minister of State March–July 2005; mem. Int. Relations Cttee, European Cen. Bank, Frankfurt 1998–2002; mem. Econ. and Finance Cttee, Brussels 1998–2001; mem. Bd of Dirs (non-exec.) Fundação Serralves 2006–. *Address:* c/o Board of Directors, Fundação Serralves, Rua Dom João de Castro, 210, 4150–500 Oporto, Portugal.

CAMUS, Philippe; French business executive; *Senior Managing Director, Evercore Partners;* b. 28 June 1948, Paris; ed Ecole Normale Supérieure, Paris, Institut des Etudes Politiques de Paris; Special Project Man. Caisse des Dépôts et Consignations 1972–82; Dir, Sr Man. Lagardère Groupe, Co-Pres. Chair. Financial Cttee 1993–98, Co-Man Pnr Lagardère SCA 1998–, Chair. and CEO ARCO (gen. pnr Lagardère Group) 1992; Chair. Financial Cttee Matra Group 1982–92; CEO and Chair. Man. Bd Aérospatiale Matra 1999–2000; Co-CEO European Aeronautic Defence and Space Co. (EADS) 2000–05; Chair. Supervisory Bd Banque Arjil 1987–93; Pres. Groupement des Industries Françaises Aéreonautiques et Spatiales (GIFAS) 2001–05; Sr Man. Dir Everscore Pnrs (investment man. co.) 2006–; Chair. Alcatel-Lucent 2008–; mem. Bd of Dirs Crédit Agricole SA, Accor SA, Institut d'Expertise et de Prospective of the Ecole Normale Supérieure, Paris Ueroplace Asscn; Chevalier, Légion d'honneur 2000, Bundesverdienstkreuz 2004; Aviation Week Aerospace Laureate 1989; Prix de la meilleure opération financière 2000. *Address:* Evercore Partners, 10 Hill Street, London, W1J 5NQ, England; Lagardère SCA, 4 Rue de Presbourg, 75016 Paris Cedex 16, France France. *Telephone:* (20) 7268-2700 (London); 1-40-69-16-00 (Paris). *Fax:* (20) 7268-2710 (London); 1-40-69-21-31 (Paris). *Website:* www.evercore.com; www.lagardere.fr.

CANALES CLARIOND, Fernando, MBA; Mexican lawyer, business executive and politician; b. 21 July 1946, Monterrey, Nuevo León; m. Angela Stelzer; two s. two d.; ed Escuela Libre de Derecho, Instituto Tecnológico y de Estudios Superiores de Monterrey, Univ. of the Sorbonne, Paris, France, Instituto de Altos Estudios en La Haya, Holanda; fmr Pres. Grupo IMSA SA de CV, also fmr Man. Dir Corporativo Grupo IMSA, SA de CV; mem. Partido Accion Nacional 1978–; mem. Congress for First Dist of Nuevo León 1979–81; Gov. of Nuevo León 1997–2003; Minister for the Economy 2003–05; Sec. of Energy 2005–06 (by law also Pres. of Bd of PEMEX, CFE and Luz y Fuerza del Centro); currently Pres. Corporación Finestra SA de CV, Monterrey; Pres. Chamber of Commerce of Nuevo León, Monterrey Chamber of Commerce; Vice-Pres. Nat. Confed. of Chambers of Commerce in Mexico; mem. Nuevo Leon Business Council, IMSS Ass., Movimiento de Promocion Rural, AC, Consejo Coordinador Empresarial; mem. Mexico–USA Comm. of the Ford Foundation. *Address:* c/o Partido Acción Nacional, Avda Coyoacán 1546, Col. del Valle, Del. Benito Juárez, 03100 México, DF, Mexico (office).

CANCELA, Walter; Uruguayan economist and central banker; *President, Central Bank of Uruguay;* b. 1950, Montevideo; four c.; ed Universidad de la República; worked at Cen. Bank of Uruguay 1970–78, Centro Cooperativo Uruguayo 1978–85; researcher, Centro Latinoamericano de Economía Humana (CLAEH) 1975–90; Prof., Universidad de la República 1987–2002, Dir Econ. Inst. 2003–; adviser on Uruguay to UN and EC 1990–2000; currently Pres. Cen. Bank of Uruguay. *Address:* Banco Central del Uruguay, Avda Juan P. Fabini 777, Casilla 1467, 11100 Montevideo, Uruguay (office). *Telephone:* (2) 9085629 (office). *Fax:* (2) 9021634 (office). *E-mail:* info@bcu.gub.uy (office). *Website:* www.bcu.gub.uy (office).

CANE, Louis Paul Joseph; French artist; b. 13 Dec. 1943, Beaulieu-sur-Mer; s. of Albert Cane and Andrée Cane (née Pasquier); m. Nicole Rondinella 1970; two d.; ed Collège des Frères Dominicains de Sorèze, Lycée Gassendi de Digne, Ecole Nationale des Arts Décoratifs, Nice, Ecole Nationale Supérieure des Arts Décoratifs, Paris; first exhbn 1970; exhbns at Galerie Yvon, Lambert, Paris 1972, Galerie Templon, Paris, Milan 1973–75, Castelli Gallery, New York 1982, Galerie Beaubourg, Paris (sculptures) 1985–90, Musée de l'Orangerie des Tuileries 1994; regular exhbns in Germany, Sweden, Spain, Belgium, Italy, Australia, Japan, fmr USSR, UK; perm. exhbn at La Galerie 14, Paris; Officier des Arts et Lettres. *Publications:* Louis Cane, artiste-peintre 1967, Toiles découpées 1971, Toiles sol/mur 1972, Annonciations 1982, Déluges 1983, Accouchements 1983, Déjeuners sur l'herbe 1985, Trois graces 1987, 1988, Fleurs et tampons 1989, Nymphéas 1992. *Leisure interests:* 18th-century France, studying 18th-century French bronzes. *Address:* 184 rue Saint Maur, 75010 Paris (office); 37 rue d'Enghien, 75010 Paris, France (home). *Telephone:* 1-42-03-73-31. *Fax:* 1-42-03-01-19.

CANELLA, Guido; Italian architect and academic; *Partner, Canella & Achilli architetti;* b. 19 Jan. 1931, Bucharest, Romania; m. Laura Testori 1960; two s. two d.; ed Polytechnic of Milan; Founding Pnr, Canella & Achilli architetti, Milan 1959–; Prof. of Architectural Composition, Polytechnic of Milan 1970–, Dir Inst. of Architectural Composition 1970–79, Dir Dept of Architectural Design 1979–81; Dir Architecture Section, Triennale of Milan 1978–82; Ed.-in-Chief Hinterland 1977–85, Zodiac 1989–; S. Luca Nat. Acad.; mem. Scientific Cttee Nat. Group of Architecture of Nat. Research Council; Inst. of Architects Prize 1968, Int. Cttee of Architecture Critics Prize 1995. *Major Works:* Segrate Town Hall, Milan 1963, social services and Piazza, Villaggio Incis, Milan 1968; civic centres in Pieve Emanuele, Milan 1971 and

Pioltello, Milan 1976; school centres in Opera, Milan 1974, Cesano Boscone, Milan 1975 and Parma 1985; residential complexes in Bollate, Milan 1974, Peschiera Borromeo, Milan 1983, Milan 2002; Law Courts redevelopment in Ancona 1975; town offices and law courts in Legnano, Milan 1982; social services, housing and Piazza in Monte d'Ago, Ancona 1984; theatre projects in Taranto 1988, Aosta 1989, Varese 1990; Church projects at Casamassima, Bari 1991, Modena 2001; auditorium, church and health complex in Peschiera Borromeo, Milan 1983–91; Italian Embassies' projects in Washington and Berlin 1992; Pescara Airport 1992; city planning projects for Milan 1991, Berlin 1992, Como 1993, Beirut 1994, Bucharest 1996, Pordenone 2001; Cinema multiplex, Milan 1997; Motel Inter-Continental, Asmara, Eritrea 1999; museum, Meina, Novara 1997; New City Hall, offices and car park building, Bari 1998; opera house and theatre, Taranto 1998; City Hall extension, Gorgonzola, Milan 2001; New Theatre of Porta Romana and residential complex, Milan 2002; private residence, Woodland, Houston, Texas 2003; restaurant and bookstore complex, Milan 2003. *Publications:* Il sistema teatrale a Milano 1966, Università: ragione, contesto, tipo 1975; articles in various specialist journals. *Address:* Canella & Achilli architetti, Via Revere 9, 20123 Milan, Italy (office). *Telephone:* (02) 4695222 (office). *Fax:* (02) 4813704 (office). *E-mail:* info@canella-achilli.com (office). *Website:* www.canella-achilli.com (office).

CANEPA, Heliane; Swiss business executive; b. 1948; m.; ed business school at Dornbirn, Austria, West London Coll., UK, Sorbonne, Paris, Foreign Exec. Devt Program, Princeton Univ., USA; joined Schneider Worldwide (medical tech. co.) 1980, CEO 1981–2001; Pres. and CEO Nobel Biocare Holding AB 2001–07, CEO Nobel Biocare Holding AG 2002–07; mem. Bd of Dirs Sonova Holding AG (fmrly Phonak Holding AG) 1999–; Entrepreneur of the Year, Switzerland 1999, 2006, ranked by the Financial Times amongst Top 25 Businesswomen in Europe (sixth) 2005, (seventh) 2006. *Address:* c/o Board of Directors, Sonova Holding AG, Laubisrütistrasse 28, 8712 Stäfa, Switzerland.

CANESTRI, HE Cardinal Giovanni; Italian ecclesiastic (retd); *Archbishop Emeritus of Genoa;* b. 30 Sept. 1918, Castelspina, Alessandria; ordained priest 1941, began his pastoral ministry in Rome; nominated Spiritual Dir Pontifical Major Roman Seminary 1959; mem. Comm. for first Diocesan Synod of Rome; served as Apostolic Examiner of the clergy; consecrated Titular Bishop of Tenedo and Auxiliary of the Cardinal Vicar of Rome 1961; participated in gen. congregations of Second Vatican Council on the themes of ecumenism and religious liberty; transferred to See of Tortona 1971–75; transferred to Titular See of Monterano with personal title of Archbishop and apptd Vice-Regent of Diocese of Rome 1975–84; Archbishop of Cagliari 1984–87, of Genoa 1987–95, Archbishop Emer. of Genoa 1995–; cr. Cardinal-Priest of S. Andrea della Valle 1988. *Address:* c/o Archdiocese of Genoa, Piazza Matteotti 4, 16123 Genoa, Italy. *Telephone:* (010) 27001. *Fax:* (010) 2700220. *Website:* www.diocesi.genova.it.

CANET, Guillaume; French actor and film director; b. 10 April 1973, Boulogne-Billancourt; m. Diane Kruger 2001 (divorced 2006); ed Saint-Louis-Notre-Dame-Du-Bel-Air school, briefly studied at the Cours Florent; was engaged in a circus aged 10; parents were horses breeders, briefly followed a professional career in horse riding until an accident aged 18 forced him to take up acting. *Films:* Fils unique 1995, Barracuda 1997, Sentimental Education 1998, Ceux qui m'aiment prendront le train (Those Who Love Me Can Take the Train) 1998, En plein cœur (In All Innocence) 1998, Trait d'union (short) 1999, Je règle mon pas sur le pas de mon père (Walking in My Father's Footsteps) 1999, J'peux pas dormir… (short) (also dir) 2000, The Beach (La Plage) 2000, La Fidélité 2000, The Day the Ponies Come Back 2000, Les Morsures de l'aube (Love Bites) 2001, Vidocq (aka Dark Portals) 2001, Le Frère du guerrier (The Warrior's Brother) 2002, Mille millièmes (aka The Landlords) 2002, Mon idole (My Idol) (also dir and assoc. producer) 2002, Jeux d'enfants (Love Me if You Dare) 2003, Les Clefs de bagnole (cameo, as himself) 2003, Narco (aka The Secret Adventures of Gustave Klopp) 2004, Joyeux Noël (Merry Christmas) 2005, L'Enfer (Hell) 2005, Un ticket pour l'espace (A Ticket to Space) 2005, Ne le dis à personne (Tell No One) 2006, Cars (French voice of Flash McQueen) 2006, Ensemble, c'est tout (aka Hunting and Gathering) 2007, Darling 2007, La Clef (The Key) 2007, Les Liens du sang (Rivals) 2008; as dir: Sans regrets 1996, Je taim 1998, Ne le dis à personne (Tell No One) (César Award for Best Dir) 2007. *Television:* La colline aux mille enfants 1994, Jeanne 1994, Ils n'ont pas 20 ans 1995, Le juge est une femme (episode Le secret de Marion) 1995, 17 ans et des poussières 1996, Le voyage de Pénélope (The Voyage of Penelope) 1996, Je m'appelle Régine 1996, Le cheval de coeur 1996, Pardaillan 1997, La vocation d'Adrienne (episode Pilot) 1997, Le porteur de destins 1999, Electrochoc 2004; as dir: Scénarios sur la drogue (episode Avalanche) 2000. *Address:* c/o Bertrand de Labbey, VMA, 20 avenue Rapp, 75007 Paris, France. *Telephone:* 1-43-17-37-00. *Fax:* 1-47-20-15-86. *E-mail:* d.leprestre@vma.fr. *Website:* www.vma.fr.

CANGEMI, Joseph P., MS, EdD; American psychologist, academic and consultant; *Professor Emeritus of Psychology, Western Kentucky University;* b. 26 June 1936, Syracuse, NY; s. of Samuel Cangemi and Marion Cangemi; m. Amelia Elena Santalo' 1962; two d.; ed State Univ. of New York, Oswego, Syracuse and Indiana Univs; taught in Syracuse public schools and in Dominican Repub. 1960–64; Chair. and Lecturer in Psychology, State Univ. of NY and Community Coll., Syracuse 1962–65; Supervisor of Educ. and of Training and Devt, US Steel Corpn, Venezuela 1965–68; Teaching Assoc., Indiana Univ., Bloomington 1972, 1973; Asst Prof. to Assoc. Prof., Western Kentucky Univ., Bowling Green 1968–79, Prof. of Psychology and Full mem. Grad. Faculty 1979, now Prof. Emer.; consultant to Firestone, General Motors and numerous cos; Ed. Journal of Human Behavior and Learning 1983–90, Psychology: A Journal of Human Behavior 1977–, Organization Development Journal 1983–88; mem. Editorial Bd Educ. and several other publs; mem. American Psychological Asscn, Inter-American Soc. of Psychology, Int. Registry of Org. Devt Professionals, Psychologists in Man.; mem. Bd of Trustees, William Woods Univ. 1988–; Diplomate in Professional Counselling, Int. Acad. of Behavioural Medicine, Counselling and Psychotherapy 1994; Hon. LLD (William Woods Univ.) 1996; Dr hc (State Univ. of Humanities, Moscow) 2001; Distinguished Public Service Award, Western Kentucky Univ. 1983, Distinguished Alumnus Award, State Univ. of NY 1983, Diplomate American Coll. of Counsellors, American Coll. of Forensic Examiners 1996, Excellence in Productive Teaching Award, Coll. of Educ. and Behavioral Sciences, Western Ky Univ. 1977, 1991, 1999, Excellence in Research/Creativity Award, Western Ky Univ. Coll. of Ed. and Behavioral Sciences 1987. *Publications:* author, ed. or co-ed. of 16 books and monographs in Spanish, Portuguese, Romanian, Russian and Chinese and over 300 papers and articles published in over 80 periodicals, including 31 foreign journals. *Leisure interests:* Latin American music, foreign travel, international exchanges. *Address:* Tate Page Hall 227, Western Kentucky University, 1906 College Heights Blvd, #21030, Bowling Green, KY 42101-1030 (office); Creative Leadership Strategies Inc., 1409 Mt. Ayr Circle, Bowling Green, KY 42103-4708, USA. *Telephone:* (270) 745-2343 (office); (270) 842-3436 (home). *Fax:* (270) 842-0432 (office); (270) 842-0432 (home). *E-mail:* Joseph.Cangemi@wku.edu (office); joseph.camgemi@insight.bb (office). *Website:* edtech.tph.wku.edu (office).

CANI, Shkëlqim, DEcon; Albanian central banker, economist, politician and academic; b. 6 May 1956, Tirana; m.; ed Univ. of Tirana; Credit Officer, State Bank of Albania (SBA), Tirana br. 1979–81, Export-Import Officer, SBA Head Office 1981–83, Chief Economist, Research Div. 1984–85, Dir Overseas Dept, mem. Bd of Dirs Cen. Bank 1985–90; Exec. Gen. Man. Commercial Bank of Albania 1990–91, Deputy Gen. Man. 1991–92; ind. financial adviser 1996–97; Gov. Bank of Albania 1997–2004, also Gov. IMF for Albania; currently Prof., Inst. for Econ. and Juridical Consultations, Univ. of Tirana; Project Man. jt Italian-Albanian project L'aqua e il falcone volano insieme 2008; Chair. Tirana Stock Exchange 1997; mem. People's Ass. 1991–96, July–Aug. 1997, Deputy Prime Minister of Albania 1991; mem. Econ. Policies Comm. *Address:* Faculty of Economics, University of Tirana, Bulevardi Dëshmorët e Kombit, Sheshi Nen Tereza, Tirana, Albania. *Website:* www.unitir.edu.al.

CANIVET, Guy, JD, FBA; French judge and academic; *Member, Conseil constitutionnel;* b. 23 Sept. 1943, Lons-le-Saunier, Jura; s. of Pierre Canivet and Henriette Barthélémy; m. Françoise Beuzit 1981; two s. two d.; ed Univ. of Dijon; judge, Trial Court of Chartres 1972–75; Public Prosecutor, Paris 1975–77; Sec.-Gen., Trial Court of Paris 1977–83, judge 1983–86; Justice, Court of Appeal, Paris 1986–94, Chief Justice 1996–99; Justice, Cour de Cassation 1994–96, Chief Justice 1999–2007; mem. Constitutional Council 2007–; Assoc. Prof., Institut d'études politiques, Paris 2004–; Founder and Pres. Network of the Pres of the Supreme Judicial Courts of the EU 2004–07; Hon. Bencher, Gray's Inn, London, King's Inn, Dublin; Officier, Ordre nat. du Mérite, Palmes académiques, Commdr Légion d'honneur, des Arts et des Lettres; Hon. LLD from several univs. *Publication:* Droit français de la concurrence 1995. *Leisure interests:* music, outdoor recreational activities. *Address:* Conseil constitutionnel, 2 rue de Montpensier, 75001 Paris (office); 8 rue Nicolas Charlet, 75015 Paris, France (home). *Telephone:* 1-40-15-30-03 (office). *Fax:* 1-40-20-93-27 (office). *E-mail:* guy.canivet@conseil-constitutionnel.fr (office). *Website:* www.conseil constitutionnel.fr (office).

CANNADINE, Sir David Nicholas, Kt, DPhil, LittD, FRHistS, FBA, FRSA, FRSL; British historian and academic; *Whitney J. Oates Senior Research Scholar, Princeton University;* b. 7 Sept. 1950; s. of Sydney Douglas Cannadine and Dorothy Mary Hughes; m. Linda Jane Colley (q.v.) 1982; one d. (deceased); ed King Edward's Five Ways School, Birmingham, Clare Coll., Cambridge, St John's Coll., Oxford, Princeton Univ., USA; Resident Fellow, St John's Coll. Cambridge 1975–77, Asst Lecturer in History 1976–80, Lecturer 1980–88; Fellow, Christ's Coll. Cambridge 1977–88, Dir of Studies in History 1977–83, Tutor 1979–81; Prof. of History, Columbia Univ., New York 1988–92, Moore Collegiate Prof. 1992–98; Dir Inst. of Historical Research Univ. of London 1998–2003, Prof. 1998–2003, Queen Elizabeth the Queen Mother Prof. of British History 2003–08, Hon. Fellow 2005–, Consultant, History in Educ. 2008–; Visiting mem., Inst. for Advanced Study, Princeton Univ. 1980–81, NJ, Visiting Fellow, Council of the Humanities 2003–05, Whitney J. Oates Sr Research Scholar 2008–; Visiting Prof., Birkbeck Coll., Univ. of London 1995–97; Visiting Fellow, Whitney Humanities Center, Yale Univ. 1995–96; Visiting Scholar, Pembroke Coll., Cambridge 1997; Pres. Worcs. Historical Soc. 1999–; Vice-Pres. British Records Soc. 1998–, Royal Historical Soc. 1998–2002; Chair. IHR Trust 1999–2003; mem. Advisory Bd Centre for Study of Soc. and Politics, Kingston Univ. 1998–2003, ICBH 1998–2003, Advisory Council Warburg Inst. 1998–2003, Inst. of US Studies 1999–2004, Public Record Office 1999–2004, Inst. of English Studies 2000–03, Inst. of Latin American Studies 2000–04, Kennedy Memorial Trust 2000–, Nat. Trust Eastern Regional Cttee 2000–, Royal Mint Advisory Cttee 2004–, Editorial Bd History of Parliament 2004–, Advisory Council Inst. for the Study of the Americas 2004–; Gov. Ipswich School 1982–88; Fellow, Berkeley Coll., Yale Univ. 1985, J. P. Morgan Library, New York 1992–98; American Council of Learned Socs Fellowship 1990–91; regular radio and TV broadcaster; Ed.-in-Chief Journal of Maritime History 1999–; Gen. Ed. Studies in Modern History 1979–2002, Penguin History of Britain 1989–, Penguin History of Europe 1991–, Historical Research 1998–2003; Trustee Kennedy Memorial Scholarship Fund 1999–, Nat. Portrait Gallery 2000– (Chair. of Trustees 2005–), British Empire and Commonwealth Museum 2003–, Commr English Heritage 2001–; Visiting Fellow, Australian Nat. Univ., Canberra 2005 (Adjunct Prof. 2006), Nat. Humanities Center, North Carolina 2006; Chair. Blue Plaques Panel, English Heritage; Hon. Fellow, Christ's Coll. Cambridge 2005, Hon. Prof., Univ. of London 2008 Hon. DLitt (East Anglia) 2001, (South Bank) 2001,

www.worldwhoswho.com

(Birmingham) 2002; T.S. Ashton Prize (Econ. History Soc.) 1977, Silver Jubilee Prize (Agric. History Soc.) 1977, Lionel Trilling Prize 1991, Governors' Award 1991, Dean's Distinguished Award in the Humanities, Columbia Univ. 1996. *Radio:* A Point of View (BBC Radio 4) 2005–06. *Publications:* Lords and Landlords: The Aristocracy And The Towns 1774–1967 1980, (ed. and contrib.) Patricians, Power and Politics in Nineteenth-Century Towns 1982, (jt and contrib.) H. J. Dyos, Exploring the Urban Past 1982, (jt and contrib.) Rituals of Royalty: Power and Ceremonial in Traditional Societies 1987, The Pleasures of the Past 1989, (ed. and contrib.) Winston Churchill's Famous Speeches 1989, (jt and contrib.) The First Modern Society: Essays in English History in Honour of Lawrence Stone 1989, The Decline and Fall of the British Aristocracy (Lionel Trilling Prize) 1990, G. M. Trevelyan: A Life in History 1992, Aspects of Aristocracy: Grandeur and Decline in Modern Britain 1994, (jt and contrib.) History and Biography: Essays in Honour of Derek Beales 1996, Class in Britain 1998, History in Our Time 1998, Making History Now 1999, Ornamentalism: How the British Saw Their Empire 2001, In Churchill's Shadow: Confronting the Past in Modern Britain 2002, What is History Now? (ed.) 2002, History and the Media (ed.) 2004, Winston Churchill in the 21st Century (co-ed. and contrib.) 2004, Admiral Lord Nelson, his context and legacy (ed.) 2005, Mellon 2006, Trafalgar: A Battle and its Afterlife (ed.) 2006, National Portrait Gallery: A Brief History 2007, Empire, the Sea and Global History: Britain's Maritime World c. 1763–1840 (ed.) 2007, History and Philanthropy: Past Present Future (co-ed. and contrib.) 2008, Making History Now and Then: Discoveries, Controversies and Explanations 2008; numerous contribs to other books and learned journals. *Leisure interests:* life, laughter. *Address:* Institute of Historical Research, Senate House, Malet Street, London, WC1E 7HU, England (office). *Telephone:* (20) 7862-8755 (office). *Fax:* (20) 7862-8754 (office). *E-mail:* jennifer.wallis@sas.ac.uk (office). *Website:* www.history.ac.uk (office).

CANNAVARO, Fabio Mamerto; Italian professional footballer; b. 13 Sept. 1973, Naples; m. Daniela Cannavaro; two s. one d.; centre-back; played for S.S.C. Napoli 1992–95, Parma FC 1995–2002, FC Internazionale Milano 2002–04, Juventus FC 2004–06; Serie A debut at Turin's Stadio Delle Alpi against Juventus 1993; currently playing for Real Madrid in Spanish Primera Divisiòn (wearing No. 5 jersey) 2006–; mem. two European championship-winning Italy Under-21 teams 1992–94, 1994–96; debut for full nat. team 1997, played in World Cup, France 1998; helped Juventus to win Serie A titles 2004/05, 2005/06 (club was stripped of titles and demoted to Serie B by a sports tribunal investigating claims of match-fixing); Capt. FIFA World Cup-winning team, Germany 2006; 105 int. caps for Italy; nicknames: Il muro di Berlino (The Berlin Wall), Il umano bus (The Human Bus); has helped establish charity foundation FCF (Fondazione Cannavaro Ferrara), specialising in the procurement of cancer research equipment and surgery for special cases of cancer for a hosp. in Naples; European Footballer of the Year 2006, Ballon d'Or, France Football magazine 2006. *Address:* Real Madrid C.F., Avenida Coucha, Espina Nr. 1, 28036 Madrid, Spain (office). *Telephone:* (91) 389-43-32 (office). *Fax:* (91) 458-75-78 (office). *E-mail:* fabio@fabiocannavaro.it. *Website:* www.fabiocannavaro.it; www.realmadrid.com (office).

CANNELL, Melvin Gilbert Richard, BSc, PhD, DSc, FRSE; British research scientist; b. 12 Aug. 1944, Bungay; s. of Charles Cannell and Joyce Cannell; m. Maria Rietdijk 1966; two d.; ed Bungay Grammar School and Univ. of Reading; research officer, coffee research station, Kenya 1966–71; NERC Inst. of Tree Biology Edin. 1971–74, NERC Inst. of Terrestrial Ecology (now Centre for Ecology and Hydrology) 1974–87, Dir 1987, Prof. (retd), now consultant; Fellow, Inst. of Chartered Foresters; Founder Bd mem. European Forest Inst. *Publications:* Jt Tree Physiology and Yield Improvement 1976, Trees as Crop Plants 1985; over 100 other scientific publs. *Address:* Centre for Ecology and Hydrology, Bush Estate, Penicuik, Midlothian, EH26 0QB (office); Easter Greyfield, Eddleston Road, Peebles, Tweeddale, EH45 9JB, Scotland (home). *Telephone:* (131) 445-4343 (office); (1721) 720144 (home). *Fax:* (131) 445-3943 (office). *E-mail:* mgrc@ceh.ac.uk (office). *Website:* www.ceh.ac.uk (office).

CANNON, Lawrence, BA, MBA; Canadian politician; *Minister of Foreign Affairs;* b. 6 Dec. 1947; s. of Louis Cannon and Rosemary Power; ed Université de Montréal, Université Laval; Councillor Cap-Rouge 1979–85; mem. Nat. Ass. 1985–94, Deputy Speaker 1989–94; Minister of Communications 1991–94; fmr Parl. Sec. to Minister of External Trade; fmr consultant; City Councillor, Gastineau 2001; Chair. Outaouais Urban Transit Corpn 2001, Strategic Choices Comm., City of Gatineau; Pres. Asscn du transport urbain du Québec 2004; Minister of Transport, Infrastructure and Communities 2006–08, of Foreign Affairs 2008–; fmr Gen. Man., mem. Bd Hull Bicentennial Corpn. *Address:* Foreign Affairs and International Trade Canada, Lester B. Pearson Bldg, 125 Sussex Drive, Ottowa, ON K1A 0G2, Canada (office). *Telephone:* (613) 944-4000 (office). *Fax:* (613) 996-9709 (office). *E-mail:* enqserv@dfait-maeci.gc.ca (office). *Website:* www.international.gc.ca (office); www.lawrencecannon.com.

CANNON, Michael R., BEng; American computer industry executive; *President of Global Operations, Dell Inc.;* b. 1952; ed Michigan State Univ., Harvard Business School; began career with Boeing Corpn, various man. positions in Mfg Research and Devt Group; fmr Man. Imprimis Tech., Singapore; fmr Vice Pres., IBM Personal Storage Systems Div., also becoming Vice Pres. of IBM Product Design and Worldwide Mfg; Pres., Dir and CEO Maxtor Corpn 1997–2003; Pres. and CEO Solectron Corpn 2003–07; Pres. of Global Operations, Dell Inc. 2007–; mem. Bd of Dirs Adobe Systems 2003–, US-China Business Council, Silicon Valley Mfg Group. *Address:* Dell Inc., 1 Dell Way, Round Rock, TX 78682-2222, USA (office). *Telephone:* (512) 338-4400 (office). *Fax:* (512) 283-6161 (office). *Website:* www.dell.com (office).

CANNY, Nicholas Patrick, PhD, FRHistS, MRIA, FBA; Irish historian and academic; *Director, Moore Institute for Research in the Humanities, National University of Ireland, Galway; President, Royal Irish Academy;* b. 4 Jan. 1944, Clifden, Co. Galway; s. of Cecil Canny and Helen Joyce; m. Morwena Denis 1974; one s. one d.; ed St Flannan's Coll., Ennis, Co. Clare, Univ. Coll., Galway, Univ. of London, UK, Univs of Pennsylvania, Harvard and Yale, USA; Lecturer in History, Univ. Coll., Galway (now Nat. Univ. of Ireland, Galway) 1972–79, Prof. of History 1980–; mem. Inst. for Advanced Study, Princeton 1979–80; Fellow, Nat. Humanities Center, NC 1985–86; mem. Irish Manuscripts Comm. 1980–, Nat. Archives Advisory Council 1986–96; Chair. Irish Comm. Historical Sciences 1991–97; Distinguished Visiting Prof., New York Univ. 1995; Dir Moore Inst. for Research in the Humanities, Nat. Univ. of Ireland 2000–; Fellow-in-Residence, Netherlands Inst. for Advanced Study 2000–01; Prof. invité, École des Hautes Études en Sciences Sociales, Paris 2005; Sr Parnell Research Fellow, Magdalene Coll., Univ. of Cambridge 2005–06; Pres., Royal Irish Acad. 2008–; mem. Academia Europaea 1995–; Foreign mem. American Philosophical Soc. 2007–; Irish Historical Research Prize 1976, 2003. *Publications include:* The Elizabethan Conquest of Ireland 1976, The Upstart Earl: The Social and Mental World of Richard Boyle 1982, From Reformation to Restoration: Ireland 1534–1660 1987, Colonial Identity in the Atlantic World 1500–1800 1987, Kingdom and Colony: Ireland in the Atlantic World 1560–1800 1988, Europeans on the Move: Studies on European Migration 1500–1800 1994, The Oxford History of the British Empire (Vol. I): The Origins of Empire 1998, Making Ireland British 1580–1650 2000. *Leisure interests:* reading, walking, music. *Address:* Moore Institute for Research in the Humanities, National University of Ireland, Galway (office); Furramelia West, Barna, Co. Galway, (home); Royal Irish Academy, 19 Dawson Street, Dublin 2, Ireland (office). *Telephone:* (91) 592351 (Galway) (office); (91) 493907 (Galway) (office); (1) 6762570 (Dublin) (office). *Fax:* (91) 495507 (Galway) (office); (1) 6762346 (Dublin) (office). *E-mail:* nicholas.canny@nuigalway.ie (office). *Website:* www.nuigalway.ie/chs (office); www.nuigalway.ie/history/canny (office).

CANO, Alfonso; Colombian rebel leader; *Leader, Fuerzas Armadas Revolucionarias de Colombia—Ejército del Pueblo (FARC–EP);* b. (Guillermo León Saenz-Vargas), 22 July 1948, Bogota; ed Nacional Univ., Bogota; joined Communist Youth at Nacional Univ.; joined Fuerzas Armadas Revolucionarias de Colombia—Ejército del Pueblo (FARC–EP) guerrilla movt 1982, named to Secr. 1984, Leader of FARC—EP (in succession to Manuel Marulanda) 2004–.

CANOGAR, Rafael, BA; Spanish painter; b. 17 May 1935, Toledo; s. of Genaro Rafael Canogar and Alfonsa Canogar; m. 1st Ann Jane McKenzie 1960; m. 2nd Purificación Chaves 1992; six c.; studied under Daniel Vázquez Díaz 1949–54; Founder Mem. El Paso group 1957–60; Visiting Prof., Milles Coll., Oakland, Calif. 1965–66; Artist-in-Residence, DAAD, Berlin 1972, 1974; mem. Exec. Cttee Círculo de Bellas Artes, Madrid 1983–86, Advisory Bd Dept of Fine Arts, Ministry of Culture 1981–82, 1983–84, Bd of Trustees, Museo Nacional de Arte Contemporáneo, Madrid 1983, Admin. Bd Nat. Art Collections 1984–90, Exec. Cttee Fundación de Gremios, Madrid 1984–87; more than 120 solo shows and numerous group exhbns; works in many public art collections world-wide; mem. Real Acad. de Bellas Artes de San Fernando 1998; nominated "Hijo predilecto" of City of Toledo 2001; Chevalier, Ordre des Arts et Lettres 1985, Special Commendation, Orden de Isabel la Católica 1991; Dr hc (Universidad nacional de educación a distancia (UNED), Madrid) 2001; Golden Palette Award, Int. Painting Festival, Cagnes-sur-Mer 1969, Grand Prize, São Paulo Biennale 1971, Special Award, Int. Painting Triennale, Sofia 1982, Premio Nacional de Artes Plásticas, Madrid 1982. *Address:* c/o Bernardino Obregón, 6 Local, 28012 Madrid, Spain (office). *Telephone:* (91) 5287729. *Fax:* (91) 2223589. *E-mail:* info@rafaelcanogar.com (home).

CANTACUZÈNE, Jean Michel, DS; French director of research (retd); b. 15 Dec. 1933, Bucharest, Romania; s. of Dr. Alexandre Cantacuzène and Marianne Cantacuzène (née Labeyrie); m. 1st Anne-Marie Szekely 1956 (divorced); one s. one d.; m. 2nd Danièle Ricard 1971; one s.; ed Ecole Supérieure Chem. Industry, Lyon, Ecole Normale Supérieure, Paris; Asst Prof., Ecole Normale Supérieure, Paris 1960–62, Deputy Dir, Lab. Chimie 1964–67; Scientific attaché, French Embassy, Moscow 1962–64, Counsellor for Science and Tech., Washington, DC 1977–80; Prof. of Organic Chem., Univ. of Paris 1967–73, Titular Prof. 1972–; Counsellor for Scientific Affairs, Ministry of Foreign Affairs, Paris 1971–77; Dir Chem. Scientific Dept, CNRS Paris 1973–77, Sr Counsellor for Industrial Affairs 1988; Scientific Dir Total Co. Française des Pétroles, Paris 1980–90; Chair. Bd SOLEMS 1983–86, AVRIST 1982; mem. Conseil pour l'innovation industrielle 1989–91, Applications cttee, Acad. of Science (Cadas) 1989–2000, exec. cttee groupe Climents français 1990–92; mem. Advisory Comm. for Science and Tech. 1971–75, Chair. Industrial R and D Advisory Cttee, EEC, Brussels 1983–86; mem. Council Nuclear Safety Cttee, 1981–90; Pres. Adit 1992–95; mem. Acad. des Technologies (Paris) 2001–; Officier, Légion d'honneur, Ordre nat. du Mérite; Grand Cross of the Romanian Merit Nat. Order 2000; Le Bel Award of the Chemical Soc. of France 1968. *Publications:* Chimie Organique (three vols) (co-author) 1971–75, America, Science and Technology in the 80s (two vols) 1981, Mille Ans dans les Balkans, Chronique des Cantacuzène dans la Tourmente des Siècles 1992; historical papers in Archiva Genealogica and Biblos and over 100 papers in scientific journals. *Leisure interests:* book collecting, history. *Address:* 52 bis route de Damiette, 91190 Gif-sur-Yvette (home); Académie des Technologies, 28 rue Saint Dominique, 75007 Paris, France (office). *E-mail:* jcantacuzene@wanadoo.fr (home).

CANTARELLA, Paolo; Italian business executive; *Operating Partner, Advent International S.r.l.;* b. 4 Dec. 1944, Varallo Sesia/Vercelli; m. Clara Cantarella; ed Turin Polytechnic; began working in car components industry 1977; Commercial Dir Ages (Fiat Group) 1978; Intersectoral Coordinator and Asst to Man. Dir, Fiat Group 1980; Man. Dir Comau (machine tools) 1983;

Man. of Supplies and Distribution, Fiat Auto SpA 1989; Vice-Chair. Maserati SpA (luxury sports cars), Modena 1989, Chair. 1993–96; Man. Dir and Gen. Man. Fiat Auto SpA 1990–96, Chair. 1996–2002; Pres. and CEO Fiat SpA 1996–2002; Pres. European Automobile Mfrs Asscn (ACEA) 2000–02; Co-Chair. EU–Russia Industrialists' Round Table (IRT) 2001; Chair. IVECO NV, Business Solutions (Fiat Group) 2001–02; Dir Polaroid Holding 2003–08; Operating Pnr, Advent International 2008–; mem. Bd of Dirs Iride, Inpartner (Investitori & Partner Immobiliari); fmr mem. Bd of Dirs Organizing Cttee of the Olympic 2006 Winter Games, Turin; Knight, Order of Labour Merit 1997. *Address:* Advent International S.r.l., Via Marina, 6, 20121 Milan, Italy (office). *Telephone:* (02) 7712981 (office). *Fax:* (02) 77129888 (office). *Website:* www.adventinternational.com (office).

CANTENOT, Jean; French business executive and engineer; b. 19 Sept. 1919, Paris; s. of Joseph Cantenot and Marcelle Cantenot (née Tournay); m. Nicole Berrier 1948; two d. (one deceased); ed Ecole Polytechnique and Ecole des Mines de Paris; with Dept of Iron Smelting, Ministry of Industry 1948–50; Chief Engineer, ARBED factory, Burbach-Saar 1950–57; Chief Engineer, Schneider SA 1957, Asst Dir 1963–68; Man. Dir, then Chair. Droitaumont-Bruville Mining Co. 1957–69; Chair. and Man. Dir Aciéries de Pompey 1968–82; Pres. Asscn pour la gestion du régime d'assurance des créances des salariés (AGS) 1974–2004, Hon. Pres. 2004–; Chair. and Man. Dir SACILOR (steel co.) 1980–83; Pres. Union des industries métallurgiques et minières 1973–85, Hon. Pres. 1985, Lormines 1979–85; Pres. Centre d'Entraide des Ingénieurs (Cedi) 1988, Hon. Pres. 1994; Officier, Légion d'honneur, Officier Ordre nat. du Mérite; Croix de guerre. *Address:* c/o AGS, 3 rue Paul Cézanne, 75008 Paris (office); 1 rue Perronet, 92200 Neuilly-sur-Seine, France (home).

CANTERBURY, Archbishop of (see Williams, Most Rev. and Rt Hon. Rowan Douglas).

CANTO SPERBER, Monique, PhD; French philosopher, academic and university administrator; *Director, École normale supérieure Paris;* b. 14 May 1954, Algeria; m. Dan Sperber (divorced); ed École normale supérieure Paris, Univ. Paris I; Asst, Dept of Philosophy, Univ. de Haute-Normandie 1980–84; Prof., Univ. de Picardie 1984–91; Visiting Researcher, King's Coll. London 1988, Princeton Univ., USA 1989, 1990; Visiting Fellow, Inst. for Advanced Study, Princeton, NJ 1993; Dir of Research, CNRS 1993–95; Visiting Prof., Univ. de Caen 1993–96; Visiting Prof., Institut franco-argentin, Buenos Aires 2000, Stanford Univ. 2001, 2002, 2003; fmr Prof., Ecole des Hautes Etudes en Sciences Sociales; Head of Dir's Office, École normale supérieure Paris 2003–05, Dir 2005–; mem. Centre Nat. des Lettres Philosophy Comm. 1988–91; mem. Editorial Bd European Journal of Philosophy 1993–96; mem. Comité Consultatif Nat. d'Ethique 2001– (Vice-Pres. 2005–). *Publications:* Platon, Menon 1991, Les paradoxes de la connaissance 1991, La Philosophie morale britannique 1994, Dictionaire d'ethique et philosophie morales (ed.) 1996, La Philosophie grecque 1997, Les Ethiques grecques 2001, L'Inquiétude morale et la vie humaine 2001, La philosophie morale 2006, Faut-il sauver le libéralisme? (co-author) 2006. *Address:* Office of the Director, École normale supérieure, 45 rue d'Ulm, 75230 Paris cedex 05, France (office). *Telephone:* 1-44-32-30-00 (office). *Fax:* 1-44-32-20-99 (office). *Website:* www.ens.fr (office).

CANTONA, Eric; French actor and fmr professional football player; b. 24 May 1966, Paris; s. of Albert Cantona and Léonor Raurich; m. 1st Isabelle Ferrer 1987 (divorced 2003); two c.; m. 2nd Rachida Brakni 2007; player, Auxerre 1980–88, Bordeaux, Marseille 1988–89, Montpellier 1989–90, Nîmes 1992; player, Leeds United (League Champions 1992) 1992–93, Manchester United (League Champions 1993, 1994, 1995–96) 1993–97, Capt. 1996–97 (scoring 80 goals in 182 appearances); retd 1997; currently plays in European Pro Beach Soccer League; Player of the Year (Professional Footballers' Asscn) 1994, Footballer of the Year (Football Writers' Asscn) 1996. *Films include:* Le Bonheur est dans le Pré 1995, Elizabeth 1998, Mookie 1998, Les Enfants du Marais 1999, La Grande Vie 2001, L'Outremangeur 2003, Les Clefs de bagnole 2003, Une belle histoire 2005, La Vie est à nous! 2005, Le Deuxième souffle 2007, Jack Says 2007, French Film 2008, Looking for Eric 2009. *Leisure interest:* painting. *Address:* c/o Mikado, 36 rue Montorgueil, 75001 Paris, France (office).

CANTOR, Charles Robert, PhD, FAAS; American molecular biologist and academic; *Chief Scientific Officer, Sequenom Inc.;* b. 26 Aug. 1942, New York; s. of Ida Diane Banks and Louis Cantor; ed Columbia Coll. and Univ. of Calif., Berkeley; Asst Prof. of Chem., Columbia Univ. 1966–69, Assoc. Prof. of Chem. and Biological Sciences 1969–72, Prof. 1972–81, Prof. of Genetics and Devt; Sherman Fairchild Scholar, Calif. Inst. of Tech. 1975–76; Deputy Dir Comprehensive Cancer Center, Coll. of Physicians and Surgeons 1981–89; Dir Human Genome Center, Lawrence Berkeley Lab. 1989–90; Prof. of Molecular Biology, Univ. of Calif., Berkeley 1989–92; Prof. of Biomedical Eng, Boston Univ. 1992–, Chair. 1994–98, Dir Center for Advanced Biotech. 1992–; Prof. of Pharmacology 1995–; Prin. Scientist, Human Genome Project, US Dept of Energy 1990–92; Chief Scientific Officer, Sequenon Inc. 1998–, mem. Bd of Dirs 2000–; Assoc. Ed. Annual Review of Biophysics and Biophysical Chemistry 1983–93; Pres. Americas Human Genome Org. 1991–98; mem. Biophysics and Biophysical Chem. Study Section, NIH 1971–75, Proposal Review Panel Stanford Sychrotron Radiation Lab. 1976–88, Ozone Update Comm., NRC 1983, Research Opportunities in Biology Comm. 1985–89, Comm. on Human Genome 1986–89, Scientific Advisory Bd, Hereditary Disease Foundation 1987–89; mem. Council, Human Genome Org. 1989–92, Vice-Pres. 1990–92, Pres. 1991–98; mem. US Nat. Cttee of Int. Union of Pure and Applied Biophysics 1986–94, Vice-Chair. 1988–91, Chair. 1991–94; Chair. US Dept of Energy Human Genome Coordinating Comm. 1989–92; mem. Advisory Cttee Searle Scholars Program 1987–93, Chair. 1993–94; mem. Advisory Cttee Program in Parasite Biology, MacArthur Foundation 1990–93, Scientific Advisory Council Rosewell Park Cancer Inst. 1992–98, Scientific Advisory Cttee European Molecular Biology Lab. 1989–94, Bd of Scientific Counsellors, Nat. Centre for Biotechnology Information, Nat. Library of Medicine 1990–95; consultant, Incyte Pharmaceuticals Inc. 1992–98, Genelabs Inc. 1988–, Samsung Advanced Inst. Tech. 2000–; mem. Bd of Dirs Applied Biophysics 1993–99, Visiting Cttee for Biology, Brookhaven Nat. Lab. 1986–89; mem. Bd of Dirs and Chair. Scientific Advisory Cttee Avitech Diagnostics Inc. (fmly ATGC Inc.) 1992–97, Nomenclature Cttee IUBMB 1989–; Chair. Advisory Cttee European Bioinformatics Inst. 1993–94; mem. USDA Genome Advisory Cttee 1992–98; Co-Chair. Biotechnology Advisory Cttee Fisher Scientific 1994–, Biology Advisory Cttee Lawrence Livermore Nat. Lab. 1995–, Chair. 2000–04; mem. Scientific Advisory Cttee Aclara Inc. 1996–2003, Caliper Inc. 1996–; mem. Bd of Dirs ExSar Inc. (fmrly Carta Inc.) 1999–2004, SIGA Inc. (fmrly Plexus Inc.), The Molecular Sciences Inst. Selectxpharmaceuticals 2003–2004 (Chair. Scientific Advisory Bd 2003–), Keystone Conferences 1999–2006; mem. Scientific Advisory Cttee Odyssey Inc. 2002–; Pres. Biochemist Inc. 2001–2002; Quest Scholar, Quest Diagnostics Inc. 1997–99; mem. Biotech Council, Dept of Energy 1996–99; mem. Unconventional Pathogen Countermeasures Advisory Cttee 1996–2000; mem. Advisory Cttee Uppsala Bio-X 2004–06; Adjunct Prof. of Biomedical Eng, Univ. of Calif., San Diego 2002–; mem. NAS, American Acad. of Arts and Sciences, Biophysics Soc., American Soc. of Biological Chemists, ACS, Analytical Cytology Soc., Harvey Soc., American Soc. of Human Genetics, Biomedical Eng Soc., Biophysical Soc.; Fellow, Alfred P. Sloan Foundation 1969–71; Hon. mem. Japanese Biochemical Soc.; Fresenius Award 1972, Guggenheim Fellow 1973–74, Eli Lilly Award in Biological Chem., ACS 1978, Nat. Cancer Inst. Outstanding Investigator Grantee 1985, Analytica Prize 1988, ISCO Prize 1989, Sober Prize 1990, Emily Gray Prize 2000. *Publications:* Biophysical Chemistry (3 vols, with Paul Schimmel), Genomics: The Science and Technology behind the Human Genome Project. *Leisure interests:* gastronomy, running, skiing. *Address:* Sequenom Inc., 3595 John Hopkins Court, San Diego, CA 92121 (office); 526 Stratford Court, Apt E, Del Mar, CA 92014-2767, USA (home). *Telephone:* (858) 202-9012 (office). *Fax:* (858) 858-9020 (office). *E-mail:* ccantor@sequenom.com (office). *Website:* www.sequenom.com (office).

CANTWELL, Maria E., BA; American politician; *Senator from Washington;* b. 13 Oct. 1958, Indianapolis, Ind.; d. of Paul Cantwell and Rose Cantwell; ed Univ. of Miami, Ohio; with Cantwell and Assocs (public relations firm) 1981–87; mem. Washington State House of Reps 1987–92; mem. US House of Reps from 1st Congressional Dist 1993–95; Vice-Pres. of Marketing Progressive Networks (now RealNetworks) 1994–97, Sr Vice-Pres. 1997–2000; Senator from Washington 2001–. *Address:* 511 Dirksen Senate Office Building, Washington, DC 20510, USA (office). *Telephone:* (202) 224-3441 (office). *Fax:* (202) 228-0514 (office). *Website:* cantwell.senate.gov (office).

CAO, Bochun; Chinese politician; *Deputy Director, NPC Environment and Resources Protection Committee;* b. Nov. 1941, Zhuzhou City, Hunan Prov.; ed Zhuzhou School of Aeronautical Industry; teacher, Zhuzhou School of Aeronautical Industry 1963; joined CCP 1966; Deputy Chief No. 331 Factory, Aircraft Engine Factory, Political Div., Jiangnan, Zhejiang Prov. 1970–83, Dir No. 331 Factory, Political Dept 1970–83, Deputy Dir No. 331 Factory 1980–83; Deputy Sec. and Head CCP Publicity Dept, Zhuzhou City Cttee 1983, Sec. Zhuzhou City Cttee 1984; Sec. CCP Xiangtan City Cttee 1990; Vice-Gov. Hunan Prov. 1991; Deputy Sec. CCP Liaoning Prov. Cttee 1992–95, Sec. Dalian City Cttee 1992–95; Alt. mem. 14th CCP Cen. Cttee 1992; mem. 15th CCP Cen. Cttee 1997–2002, 16th CCP Cen. Cttee 2002–07 Sec. CCP Guangxi Zhuang Autonomous Regional Cttee 1997–2002; Chair. Standing Cttee Guangxi Zhuang Autonomous Regional People's Congress 2002–06; Deputy Dir NPC Environment and Resources Protection Cttee 2003–. *Address:* Environment and Resources Protection Committee, National People's Congress, Beijing, People's Republic of China.

CAO, Gen. Gangchuan; Chinese politician and army officer; b. Dec. 1935, Wuyang Co., Henan Prov.; ed Third Artillery Tech. School, Zhengzhou City, PLA Russian Tech. School, Dalian, Artillery Mil. Eng Acad. Moscow and PLA Univ. of Nat. Defence; joined PLA 1954; teacher, No. 1 Ordnance Tech. School 1956; mem. CCP 1956–; Asst, PLA Gen. Logistics Dept, Ordinance Dept, Ammunition Div. 1963–69, Gen. Logistics Dept, Mil. Equipment Dept, Munitions Div. 1969–75; Staff Officer and Deputy Dir Gen. Planning Div., Mil. Equipment Dept Gen. Staff HQ 1975–82; Deputy Commdr artillery troops during Sino-Vietnamese border conflict 1979; Deputy Dir Mil. Equipment Dept Gen. Staff HQ 1982–89; Dir Mil. Affairs Dept Gen. Staff HQ 1989–90; Dir Mil. Products Trade Office of Mil. Cttee of Cen. Cttee of CCP 1990–92; Deputy Dir Leading Group for Placement of Demobilized Army Officers; Deputy Sec. Comm. for Disciplinary Inspection; Deputy Chief of Gen. Staff, PLA 1992–96; Minister, State Comm. of Science, Tech. and Industry for Nat. Defence 1996–98; rank of Gen. 1996; Dir PLA Gen. Armaments Dept 1998–; mem. 15th Cen. Cttee CCP 1997–2002, 15th Cen. Cttee CCP Cen. Mil. Comm. 1997–2002, 16th Cen. Cttee CCP 2002–07, 16th Cen. Cttee CCP Politburo 2002–07; Vice-Chair. 16th Cen. Cttee CCP Cen. Mil. Comm. 2002–07; State Councillor 2003–08; Minister of Nat. Defence 2003–08. *Address:* c/o Ministry of National Defence, 20 Jingshanqian Jie, Beijing 100009, People's Republic of China.

CAO, Qingze; Chinese government and party official; b. 1932, Lixian Co., Hunan Prov.; ed No. 3 Br., PLA Mil. and Political Coll., 2nd Field Army; clerical staff, People's Govt Gen. Office, Liangping Co., Sichuan Prov. 1950, CCP Co. Cttee Organization Dept, Liangping Co. 1950; joined CCP 1952; staff mem., CCP Prov. Cttee Agricultural Dept, Sichuan Prov. 1955, CCP Revolutionary Cttee, Sichuan Prov. 1966–76 (Deputy Head Agricultural Group 1978); Deputy Dir Prov. Agricultural Office, Sichuan Prov. 1978; trainee, CCP Cen. Cttee Cen. Party School 1980; Deputy Sec.-Gen. People's Govt, Sichuan

Prov. 1981–85; Deputy Sec. later Sec. Comm. for Discipline Inspection of CCP Sichuan Prov. Cttee 1985–93; mem. Standing Cttee, 14th CCP Cen. Cttee 1992–97; mem. Cen. Comm. for Discipline Inspection 1989–97; Deputy Sec. CCP Cen. Comm. for Inspecting Discipline 1992–2002; Minister of Supervision 1993–98; Hon. Pres. Soc. of Supervision. *Address:* c/o Ministry of Supervision, 35 Huayuanbei Lu, Haidan Qu, Beijing 100083, People's Republic of China.

CAO, Lt-Gen. Shuangming; Chinese army officer (retired) and party official; b. 1929, Linxian Co., Henan Prov.; joined CCP 1946; Deputy Commdr PLA Shengyang Mil. Area Command 1987–92, Commdr PLA Air Force 1992–94; rank of Lt-Gen. 1988; mem. 14th CCP Cen. Cttee 1992–97. *Address:* Shengyang Military Area Command, People's Liberation Army, Shengyang City, Liaoning Province, People's Republic of China.

CAO, Zhi; Chinese politician; b. 1928, Anqiu, Shandong Prov.; joined CCP 1947; Dir Acheng News Report, Acheng Co., Heilongjiang Prov. 1947–48; Sec. CCP Co. Cttee, Acheng Co. 1948–49, Deputy Head CCP Co. Cttee Publicity Dept 1949–51, Head 1951–52; Deputy Section Chief CCP Prov. Cttee Publicity Dept, Heilongjiang Prov. 1952–53, Div. Chief 1953–60, Deputy Dir CCP Prov. Cttee Gen. Office 1960–66; Deputy Sec. CCP Prefectural Cttee, Hejiang Prefecture, Heilongjiang Prov. 1966–70; Vice-Chair. CCP Revolutionary Cttee, Heilongjiang Prov. 1970–77; Leading mem. State Devt and Reform Comm. 1977–78; Head CCP Cen. Cttee Research Office 1978–83; Deputy Head CCP Cen. Cttee Org. Dept 1983–87; Deputy Dir Research Office, Secr. CCP Cen. Cttee 1987–88; Sec.-Gen. 7th Standing Cttee NPC 1988–93, 8th Standing Cttee NPC 1993–98; Vice-Chair. Standing Cttee 9th NPC 1998–2003; Del. 14th CCP Nat. Congress 1992–97, 15th CCP Nat. Congress 1997–2002; Vice-Pres. Cen. Cttee for Comprehensive Man. of Public Security 1993; mem. Hong Kong Special Admin. Region Preparatory Cttee Govt Del. for Hong Kong Hand-Over Ceremony 1997. *Address:* c/o Standing Committee, National People's Congress, Tian'anmen Square, Beijing, People's Republic of China.

CAPECCHI, Mario Renato, PhD; American (b. Italian) geneticist and academic; *Professor and Investigator, Department of Human Genetics, Howard Hughes Medical Institute, University of Utah School of Medicine;* b. 6 Oct. 1937, Verona; m. 1963, 1985, one d.; ed Antioch Coll., Harvard Univ.; Jr Fellow in Biophysics, Harvard Univ. 1966–69, Asst Prof. to Assoc. Prof. of Biochemistry, Medical School 1969–73; Prof. of Biology, Univ. of Utah 1973–88, Prof. of Human Genetics, School of Medicine 1989–, Distinguished Prof. 1993–, Investigator, Howard Hughes Inst., Univ. of Utah 1988–; mem. Bd Scientific Counselors, Nat. Cancer Inst.; mem. NAS, American Biochemial Soc., American Soc. of Microbiology, New York Acad. of Science, Int. Genome Soc., Genetics Soc. of America, AAAS, Soc. for Developmental Biology, European Acad. of Sciences; ACS Biochemistry Award 1969, Bristol-Myers Squibb Award for Distinguished Achievement in Neuroscience Research 1992, Gairdner Foundation Int. 1993, Gen. Motors Corpn Alfred P. Sloan Jr Prize 1994, Kyoto Prize in Basic Sciences 1996, Franklin Medal 1997, Baxter Award 1998, Lasker Award 2001, Nat. Medal of Science 2001, John Scott Medal Award 2002, Pezcoller Foundation-AACR Int. Award 2003, Wolf Prize in Medicine 2002–03, March of Dimes Prize in Developmental Biology 2005, Nobel Prize for Medicine (with Sir Martin Evans and Oliver Smithies) 2007 for the discovery of principles for introducing specific gene modifications in mice by the use of embryonic stem cells; American Heart Asscn Distinguished Scientist Award 2008. *Publications:* Targeted Gene Replacement 1994, The Making of a Scientist (Howard Hughes Medical Inst. Bulletin) 1997, Generating Mice with Targeted Mutations 2001, and a total of 141 peer-reviewed manuscripts, books and book chapters. *Address:* Howard Hughes Medical Institute, University of Utah, 15 N 2030 E, Room 5100, Salt Lake City, UT 84112-5331 (office); 1172 South Bonneville Drive, Salt Lake City, UT 84108, USA (home). *Telephone:* (801) 581-7096 (office). *Fax:* (801) 585-3425 (office). *E-mail:* mario.capecchi@genetics.utah.edu (office). *Website:* capecchi.genetics.utah.edu (office).

CAPELLAS, Michael D., BBA; American business executive; *Chairman and CEO, First Data Corporation;* b. 19 Aug. 1954; m. Marie Capellas; two c.; ed Kent State Univ.; systems analyst, Republic Steel Corpn 1976–81; joined Schlumberger Ltd 1981, holding successive posts as First Corp. Dir for Information Systems, Controller and Treas. of Asia Pacific Operations, Chief Financial Officer Dowell Schlumberger, Operations Man. Schlumberger's Fairchild Semiconductor unit 1981–96; Founder and Man. Pnr, Benchmarking Partners, Cambridge, Mass 1996; Dir of Supply-Chain Man., SAP America 1996–97; Sr Vice-Pres. and Gen. Man. Global Energy Business, Oracle Corpn 1997–98; Chief Information Officer Compaq Computer Corpn 1998–99, Pres. and CEO 1999–2000, Chair. and CEO 2000–02; Pres. Hewlett-Packard Co. (following acquisition of Compaq by Hewlett-Packard) 2002; Chair. and CEO WorldCom (now MCI Group) 2002–04, Pres. and CEO 2004–06; Acting Pres. and CEO Serena Software Inc. 2006–07; Sr Advisor, Silver Lake Partners (investment firm) 2007–; Chair. and CEO First Data Corpn 2007–; mem. Bd of Dirs Cisco Systems Inc. 2006–; Trustee American Univ., Washington, DC. *Leisure interests:* community leadership and charity work, golf. *Address:* First Data Corporation, 6200 South Quebec Street, Greenwood Village, CO 80111, USA (office). *Telephone:* (303) 488-8000 (office). *Website:* www.firstdata.com (office).

CAPELLINO, Ally, BA; British fashion designer; b. (Alison Lloyd), 1956; ed Middlesex Univ.; worked in Courtaulds Cen. Design Studio 1978–79; est. Ally Capellino Little Hat, initially selling hats and accessories 1979; developed clothing line with accessories for Moscow Olympics collection 1979–80; began selling Ally Capellino label to int. markets 1980; launched menswear collection 1986; first London fashion show 1986; opened shop in Soho, London 1988; launched Hearts of Oak sportswear collection 1990, Mini Capellino children's wear 1991; signed promotional and licensing agreement with Coats Viyella PLC 1992; launched 'ao' collection 1996; opened Ally Capellino shop, London 1997; opened flagship store Tokyo, Japan 1998. *Address:* c/o Goodley PR, 41 Dover Street, Mayfair, London, W1S 4NS, England. *Telephone:* (20) 7493-9600 (office). *E-mail:* info@allycapellino.co.uk (office). *Website:* www.allycapellino.co.uk (office).

CAPELLO, Fabio; Italian professional football manager; *Manager, England national football team;* b. 18 June 1946, Pieris, Bisiacheria; s. of Guerrino Capello and Evelina Capello; m. Laura Capello; two c.; fmr football player with Spal, A.S. Roma, Juventus, AC Milan and the Italian nat. team, winning 32 caps for Italy 1962–79; Man. AC Milan (Serie A) 1991–96, 1997–2000, winner four championships and European Cup 1994; Man. Real Madrid 1996–97, winner La Liga; Man. A.S. Roma, 2000–04 (winner Serie A 2000–01); Man. Juventus 2004–06; Man. Real Madrid 2006–07, winner La Liga; Man. England nat. football team 2008–. *Address:* The Football Association, 25 Soho Square, London, W1D 4FA, England (office). *Telephone:* (20) 7262-4542 (office). *Website:* www.thefa.com (office).

CAPITANICH, Jorge Milton; Argentine accountant and politician; *Governor of Chaco Province;* b. 28 Nov. 1964, Roque Saenz Peña; Head of Under-Secr. of Social Planning, Ministry of Social Devt 1998; Senator for Chaco Dec. 2001–07; Acting Minister of Trade 2001; apptd Cabinet Chief of Argentina 2002; Gov. of Chaco Prov. 2007–. *Publications:* Investigación Sobre El Orígen de las Crisis Provinciales, Federalismo Fiscal y Coparticipación, La Sumergida. Chaco, Propuestas para la Integración. *Address:* Marcelo T de Alvear 144, Resistencia, Chaco H3500, Argentina (office). *Telephone:* (3722) 448097 (office). *Website:* portal.chaco.gov.ar (office).

CAPLIN, Mortimer Maxwell, BS, LLB, JSD; American lawyer, government official and academic; *Senior Partner, Caplin & Drysdale Attorneys;* b. 11 July 1916, New York; s. of Daniel Caplin and Lillian Epstein; m. Ruth Sacks 1942; three s. one d.; ed Univ. of Virginia and New York Univ. Law School; law Clerk to US Circuit Judge 1940–41; legal practice with Paul, Weiss, Rifkind, Wharton & Garrison, New York 1941–50; with USNR, Beachmaster in Normandy landings 1942–45; Prof. of Law, Univ. of Virginia 1950–61, Lecturer and Visiting Prof. 1965–87, Prof. Emer. 1988–; Counsel, Perkins, Battle & Minor 1952–61; US Commr of Internal Revenue 1961–64; Founder and Sr Pnr, Caplin & Drysdale, Washington, DC 1964–; Chair. Nat. Civil Service League 1965–80, American Council on Int. Sports 1975–80, Nat. Citizens' Advisory Cttee 1975–80, Asscn of American Medical Colls., Univ. of Virginia Council of the Arts; Dir Fairchild Corpn, Presidential Reality Corpn, Danaher Corpn; mem. Public Review Bd, Arthur Andersen & Co. 1980–88; mem. House of Dels 1980–92, DC and Fed. Bar Asscns, Va and NY State Bars, American Law Inst.; Ed.-in-Chief Virginia Law Review 1939–40; mem. Bd of Trustees, George Washington Univ. 1964, Bd of Visitors, Univ. of Virginia Law School Foundation 1982–; Emer. Trustee Shakespeare Theatre, Wolf Trap Foundation and Arena Stage; Hon. LLD (St Michael Coll.) 1964; Raven Award, Alexander Hamilton Award, Univ. of Virgina/Thomas Jefferson Memorial Foundation Medal in Law 2001 and other awards; Order of the Coif. *Publications:* Doing Business in Other States, Proxies, Annual Meetings and Corporate Democracy; numerous articles on tax and corporate matters. *Leisure interests:* swimming, horseback riding, gardening. *Address:* Caplin and Drysdale, One Thomas Circle, NW, Washington, DC 20005-5802 (office); Apartment 18E, 5610 Wisconsin Avenue, Chevy Chase, MD 20815-4415, USA (home). *Telephone:* (202) 862-5050 (office). *E-mail:* mmc@capdale.com (office). *Website:* www.capdale.com (office).

ČAPLOVIČ, Dušan, DrSci; Slovak politician; *Deputy Prime Minister for Knowledge-Based Society, European Affairs, Human Rights and Minorities;* b. 18 Sept. 1946, Bratislava; ed Comenius Univ.; Sr Researcher and Scientist, Slovak Acad. of Sciences 1980–2002, mem. Presidium 1992–2001, Deputy Pres. 1995–2001; mem. Nat. Council 2002–06; Deputy Prime Minister for Knowledge-Based Soc., European Affairs, Human Rights and Minorities 2006–; mem. Council for Science and Tech. 1992–95; mem. Advisory Bd Ministry of Culture 1995–98. *Address:* Office of the Government, nám. Slobody 1, 813 70 Bratislava, Slovakia (office). *Telephone:* (2) 5729-5111 (office). *Fax:* (2) 5249-7595 (office). *E-mail:* urad@government.gov.sk (office). *Website:* www.government.gov.sk (office).

CAPPE, Mel, MA; Canadian diplomatist and economist; *President and CEO, Institute for Research on Public Policy;* b. 3 Dec. 1948, Toronto; m. Marline (Marni) Cappe (née Pliskin); one s. one d.; ed Univs of Toronto and Western Ontario; joined Canadian public service as a policy analyst 1975; with Treasury Bd 1975–78, Deputy Sec. 1990–94; with Dept of Finance 1978–82; Deputy Dir Investigation and Research, Dept of Consumer and Corp. Affairs 1982–90; Deputy Asst Sec. Dept of Finance 1990, Deputy Sec. Program Br. 1990; fmr Asst Deputy Minister Competition Policy; fmr Asst Deputy Minister Policy Co-ordination; fmr Asst Deputy Minister Corp. Affairs and Legis. Policy; Deputy Minister of the Environment 1994–96; Deputy Minister of Human Resources Devt 1996–99; Chair. Employment Insurance Comm. 1996–99; Deputy Minister of Labour 1996–99; Clerk of the Privy Council, Sec. to Cabinet and Head of the Public Service 1999–2002; Special Adviser to Prime Minister 2002; High Commr to UK 2002–06; Pres. and CEO Inst. for Research on Public Policy, Montreal 2006–; Hon. PhD (Univ. of Western Ontario); Hon. LLD. *Address:* Institute for Research on Public Policy, 1470 Peel Street, Suite 200, Montreal, PQ H3A 1T1, Canada (office). *Telephone:* (514) 985-2461 (office). *Fax:* (514) 985-2559 (office). *E-mail:* irpp@irpp.org (office). *Website:* www.irpp.org (office).

CAPPON, Claudio; Italian broadcasting executive; *Director-General, Radiotelevisione Italiana SpA (RAI);* b. 9 July 1952, Rome; m.; three c.; ed Univ. of Rome; worked for Istituto per la Ricostruzione Industriale for 20 years, specializing in control and man.; Dir of Industrial Activities, Fintecna

1994–96, Dir-Gen. and CEO 1996–98; Deputy Dir-Gen. Radiotelevisione Italiana SpA (RAI) 1998–2001, Dir-Gen. 2001–02, 2006–; CEO Consap (Concessionaria dei servizi assicurativi pubblici) 2002–; Pres. APT (Asscn of TV Producers) 2002–. *Address:* Radiotelevisione Italiana SpA, Viale Mazzini 14, 00195 Rome, Italy (office). *Telephone:* (06) 38781 (office). *E-mail:* info@rai .it (office). *Website:* www.rai.it (office).

CAPPS, Thomas E., BA, JD; American business executive; b. 31 Oct. 1935, Wilmington, North Carolina; s. of Edward S. Capps Jr and Agnes Rhodes; m. 1st Jane Paden 1963; two c.; m. 2nd Sandra Lee Hurley; four c.; ed Univ. of North Carolina; in pvt. legal practice, N Carolina and Fla 1966–70; held positions in legal depts of two electric utilities; joined Dominion Resources Inc. 1984, apptd Pres. 1990, Vice-Chair., Pres. and CEO 2000, Chair., Pres. and CEO 2000–03, Chair. and CEO 2003–06, Chair. 2006–07 (retd); Chair. and Dir Va Electric and Power Co., Consolidated Natural Gas Co.; mem. Bd of Dirs Amerigroup Corpn 2004–, Associated Electric and Gas Insurance Services Ltd, Shaw Group Inc. 2007–; mem. Bd of Visitors Coll. of William and Mary; Trustee Univ. of Richmond, Va Foundation of Ind. Colls. *Address:* c/o Board of Directors, The Shaw Group Inc., 4171 Essen Lane, Baton Rough, LA 70809, USA.

CAPRA, Carlo; Italian historian and academic; b. 14 Nov. 1938, Quartu S. Elena, Cagliari; s. of Agostino Capra and Maria Maxia; m. Maria Grazia Bosi 1964; one s.; ed Università degli Studi, Milan; teacher of English in state secondary schools –1970; Asst Lecturer in History, Università degli Studio di Milano 1970–72, Reader 1972–81, Assoc. Prof. 1981–86, Prof. 1986–2008, Head, Dept of History 1989–92; mem. Scientific Council, Società Italiana di Studi sul XVIII Secolo. *Publications:* Giovanni Ristori da illuminista a funzionario (1755–1830) 1968, Il giornalismo nell'età rivoluzionaria e napoleonica 1976, La Lombardia austriaca nell'età delle riforme 1984, 1987, Cesare Beccaria, Carleggio Vols IV–V of Edizione Nazionale delle Opere (ed.) 1995, I progressi della ragione. Vila di Pietro Verri 2002. *Leisure interests:* music, cinema. *Address:* Corso Garibaldi 71, Milan 20121, Italy (home). *Telephone:* (02) 86461509 (home). *E-mail:* carlo.capra1@unimi.it (home).

CAPRIATI, Jennifer Maria; American professional tennis player; b. 29 March 1976, New York; d. of Stefano Capriati and Denise Capriati; ed Pasco High School, Fla; coached by her father; winner, French Open Jr 1989, US Open Jr 1989, Wimbledon and US Open Jr Doubles 1989; youngest player in Whiteman Cup 1989; youngest player to reach a professional final (aged 13 years and 11 months at Boca Raton 1990); gold medal (Olympic Games of 1992); Wimbledon debut 1990; semi-finalist French Open 1990, 2002, US Open 1991, 2001, 2003, Wimbledon 1991 (youngest Grand Slam semi-finalist in tennis history), 2001; won Australian Open 2001, 2002, French Open 2001; 15 career professional titles in total (one doubles title); Int. Tennis Fed. World Champion 2001; finished 2004 season as world number 10. *Leisure interests:* dancing, golf, music, reading, writing. *Address:* International Management Group, c/o Barbara Perry, 22 East 71st Street, New York, NY 10021, USA.

CAPRON, Alexander Morgan, LLB; American academic and lawyer; *University Professor and Scott H. Bice Chair in Healthcare Law, Policy and Ethics, University of Southern California;* b. 16 Aug. 1944, Hartford, Conn.; s. of William M. Capron and Margaret Capron (née Morgan); m. 1st Barbara A. Brown 1969 (divorced 1985); m. 2nd Kathleen M. West 1989; four c.; ed Palo Alto High School, Swarthmore Coll. and Yale Law School; law clerk to Chief Judge, US Court of Appeals, DC Circuit 1969–70; Lecturer and Research Assoc., Yale Law School 1970–72; Asst Prof. to Prof. of Law and Prof. of Human Genetics, Univ. of Pa 1972–82; Exec. Dir Pres.'s Comm. for Study of Ethical Problems in Medicine and Biomedical and Behavioural Research 1979–83; Prof. of Law, Ethics and Public Policy, Georgetown Univ. 1983–84; Topping Prof. of Law, Medicine and Public Policy, Univ. of Southern Calif. 1985–89, Univ. Prof. of Law and Medicine 1989–, Co-Dir Pacific Center for Health Policy and Ethics 1990–, Henry W. Bruce Prof. of Law 1991–2006, Scott H. Bice Chair in Healthcare Law, Policy and Ethics 2006–; Dir Ethics, Trade, Human Rights and Health Law, WHO 2002–06; Pres. American Soc. of Law and Medicine 1988–89; Pres. Int. Asscn of Bioethics 2005-07; Chair. Biomedical Ethics Advisory Cttee, US Congress 1988–91; mem. Nat. Bioethics Advisory Comm. 1996–2001; mem. Inst. of Medicine, NAS; Fellow, AAAS, Hon. Fellow, American Coll. of Legal Medicine; several honours and awards. *Publications:* books including Catastrophic Diseases: Who Decides What? (with J. Katz) 1975, Law, Science and Medicine (with others) 1984, Treatise on Health Care Law (with others) 1991 and 230 articles in journals and books. *Leisure interests:* gardening, films, travel. *Address:* Gould School of Law, University of Southern California, University Park, MC 0071, Los Angeles, CA 90089-0071, USA (office). *Telephone:* (213) 740-2557 (office). *Fax:* (213) 740-5502 (office). *E-mail:* acapron@law.usc.edu (office). *Website:* lawweb.usc .edu (office).

CAPUÑAY, Juan Carlos, BEcons; Peruvian diplomatist and international organization official; *Executive Director, Asia-Pacific Economic Co-operation (APEC);* b. 1948; ed Nat. Univ. of San Marcos; joined Ministry of Foreign Affairs 1972, Third Sec. Embassy in Tokyo 1973–76, Second Sec. 1976, Second Sec. Perm. Mission to UN, New York 1976–79, First Sec. 1979–82, First Sec. Perm. Mission to OAS 1982–83, Counsellor 1983–86, Minister Counsellor and Alt. Rep. 1986–91, Minister, Embassy in Tokyo and Alt. Rep. to Int. Org. for Tropical Woods 1991–94, Minister, Embassy in Beijing 1994–97, Minister, Chargé d'Affaires to Singapore 1997–98, Amb. to Singapore and Brunei 1998–2003, Amb. and Dir-Gen. Asia-Pacific Econ. Co-operation (APEC) Div., also Sr Official of Peru in APEC Under-Secr. for Asia and Pacific Basin Affairs 2003–07, Amb., Deputy Exec. Dir APEC Secr. 2007, Exec. Dir 2008–; official decorations from Japan, Repub. of Korea and Chile. *Address:* APEC, 35 Heng Mui Keng Terrace, Singapore 119616, Singapore (office). *Telephone:* 67756012

(office). *Fax:* 6775603 (office). *E-mail:* info@apec.org (office). *Website:* www .apec.org (office).

CAPUS, Steve, BA; American media executive; *President, NBC News;* b. 1963; m. Sophia Faskianos; two s. one d.; ed Temple Univ.; with WCAU-TV, Philadelphia 1986; joined KYW-TV, Philadelphia 1987, Exec. Producer 1990–93; joined NBC as Sr Producer NBC Nightside, 1993, Broadcast Producer NBC News Sunrise 1994, Supervising Producer Today Show 1995, Sr Producer MSNBC daytime news 1996–97, Exec. Producer The News with Brian Williams (MSNBC) 1997–2001, Exec. Producer, Nightly News show 2001–05, Sr Vice-Pres., News Division June–Nov. 2005, Pres. NBC News Nov. 2005–; Alfred I. DuPont-Columbia Award, four Emmys, six Edward R. Murrow Awards, six Nat. Headliner Awards. *Address:* NBC News, 30 Rockefeller Plaza, New York, NY 10112, USA (office). *Website:* www.nbc .com/nbc/NBC_News (office).

CAPUTO, Dante; Argentine politician, diplomatist and academic; *Secretary for Political Affairs, Organization of American States;* b. 25 Nov. 1943, Buenos Aires; m. Anne Morel; three s.; ed Salvador Univ. of Buenos Aires, Univ. of Paris, Tufts Univ. and Harvard Univ., USA; secondary school teacher 1962–64; Adjunct Prof. of Political Sociology, Salvador Univ., Buenos Aires 1973–74; Assoc. Prof. of Public Admin, Univ. of Buenos Aires 1973–74, Assoc. Prof. of Admin. Systems 1973–74, Prof. of Int. Relations 2000; Prof. of Int. Relations, Nat. Univ. of Quilmes 1996–97, Universidad Nacional de la Plata 1998–99; Nat. Deputy 1989–92, 1997–99; Sec. of State for Tech., Science and Useful Innovations 1999–2001; Dir Center for Social Investigations on State and Admin. 1976; Adjunct Investigator, Nat. Center for Scientific Investigation, France; Minister of Foreign Affairs and of Worship 1983–89; Pres. UN Gen. Ass. 1988–89; Special Rep. of UN Sec.-Gen. in Haiti 1993–94; Vice-Pres. ASO FREP 1996–2000; Dir UNDP Regional Project on Democratic Devt in Latin America 2001–04; Sec. for Political Affairs, OAS, Washington, DC 2006–; Founder and Dir Bimestre Politico y económico, Buenos Aires 1981–92. *Address:* Organization of American States, 17th St and Constitution Ave, NW, Washington, DC 20006, USA (office). *Telephone:* (202) 458-3000 (office). *Fax:* (202) 458-6319 (office). *E-mail:* pi@oas.org (office). *Website:* www.oas.org (office).

CARAMITRU, Ion; Romanian actor, theatre director and politician; *General Director, National Theatre of Bucharest;* b. 9 March 1942, Bucharest; s. of Aristide Caramitru and Maria Caramitru; m. Michaela Caracas 1975; three s.; ed Theatre and Cinema Art Inst., Bucharest; actor and dir Lucia Sturdza Bulandra Theatre, Bucharest 1965–90, Artistic Dir 1990–93, 1996–2000; Acting Prof., I.L.Caragiale Acad. of Drama and Film, Bucharest 1976–81; mem. Exec. Bureau, Council of Nat. Salvation Front 1989, Pres. of Cultural Cttee 1990; Vice-Pres. of Prov. Council for Nat. Unity (responsibility for cultural and youth problems) Feb.–May 1990; Founder and Pres. ITI Romanian Centre, Romanian Theatre Union (UNITER) 1990–; Minister of Culture 1996–2000; currently Gen. Dir Nat. Theatre of Bucharest; Vice-Pres. PNTCD 2001–06 (resgnd); Hon. OBE 1995, Chevalier des Arts et Lettres 1997; Best Actor of the Year 1975, 1979, 1981, 1985, Cinema magazine FIlm Award 1976, "Special Award of the Jury" for leading part in Luchian, Nat. Film Festival, Costinesti 1984. *Principal roles include:* Romeo, Hamlet, Julius Caesar, Feste, Brutus, Leonce (Büchner), Eugene Marchbanks (Bernard Shaw), Cotrone (Pirandello), Perdican (Musset), Riccardo Fontana (Rolf Hochhuth) etc. *Directed:* Remembrances (Aleksei Arbuzov), Insignificance (Terry Johnson), Dialogues (author's performance), The Third Stake (Marin Sorescu), The Shape of the Table (David Edgar), Home (David Storey); musical theatre: Eminescu (Paul Urmuzescu), My Fair Lady; opera: The Little Sweep (Benjamin Britten), Carmen (Bizet) for Belfast Opera 1993, Eugene Onegin (Tchaikovsky) for Belfast Opera 1994, Bastien and Bastienne (Mozart) for Tăndărică puppet theatre, Bucharest. *Films include:* The Treasure from Old River Bed, The City Blue Gates, Luchian, Oak – Extreme Urgency, The Purse with Dragonflies, High-School Pupils, Civic Education Test-Write, Darkness, Citizen X, Mission Impossible. *Television appearances:* Jude City (BBC serial) 1992, An Exchange of Fire 1993, A Question of Guilt 1993, Two Deaths (BBC TV) 1994. *Leisure interests:* collecting icons, tennis, writing, painted popular eggs. *Address:* National Theatre of Bucharest, 2, Nicolae Bălcescu boulevard, 010051, Sector 1, Bucharest (office); UNITER, 2–4, George Enescu Str., Bucharest; 16, Caderea Bastiliei, Sector 1, Bucharest, Romania (home). *Telephone:* (21) 313 9437 (office); (21) 3113214 (UNITER); (21) 2106337 (home). *Fax:* (21) 3123169 (office); (21) 3120913 (UNITER); (21) 2105783 (home). *E-mail:* contact@tncaragiale.ro (office). *Website:* www.tnb.ro (office).

CARAZO ODIO, Rodrigo; Costa Rican politician; *President Emeritus, University for Peace;* b. 27 Dec. 1926, Cartago; s. of Mario Carazo Paredes and Julieta Odio Cooper; mem. Partido de Liberación Nacional (PLN) until resignation in 1969, posts included Dir Nat. Inst. of Housing and Urbanization 1954–59, Adviser on Housing and Finance, Banco Obrero de Venezuela 1959–63, Dir Banco Cen. de Costa Rica 1963–65; Deputy to Legislative Ass. of Costa Rica 1966, then Pres., Dir Recope (state enterprise controlling distribution of petroleum products); f. Renovación Democrática, taking fourth place in presidential elections 1974; Leader Unidad (coalition of Renovación Democrática, Republicano Calderonista, Unión Popular, Demócrata Cristiano) 1976–82; Pres. of Costa Rica 1978–82; Prof. of Econs, Admin., Econ. Devt and History, visiting lecturer to USA and S America; Founder and Pres. Emer. Univ. of Peace (UPEACE); agricultural, commercial and industrial activities; Hon. DHumLitt (Univ. of South Alabama) 2004. *Address:* University for Peace, Apdo 138-6100, Ciudad Colon, Costa Rica. *Website:* www .upeace.org.

CARBONEZ, Luc, LLD; Belgian diplomatist; *Ambassador to the Netherlands;* b. 1946; m. Marie-Claire Carbonez-deJager; four d.; ed Univ. of Louvain; joined Diplomatic Corps 1978, has served in numerous positions including

Attaché, Embassy in Dublin 1979–80, Embassy Sec., Abidjan 1980–84, Consul, Lille 1984–88, Deputy Head of Mission, Vienna 1988–92; Counsellor for Foreign Affairs, Brussels 1992–94, Minister-Counsellor and Perm. Deputy Rep. of Belgium to EU 1994–97, Amb. to Canada 1997–2002; Dir European Security, Ministry of Foreign Affairs 2002–06; Amb. to Netherlands 2006–, also Perm. Rep. to Org. for the Prohibition of Chemical Weapons (OPCW). *Address:* Embassy of Belgium, Alexanderveld 97, 2585 DB The Hague, Netherlands (office). *Telephone:* (70) 3123456 (office). *Fax:* (70) 3645579 (office). *E-mail:* thehague@diplobel.org (office). *Website:* www.diplomatie.be/thehague (office).

CARCIERI, Donald L.; American state official; *Governor of Rhode Island;* b. 16 Dec. 1942, East Greenwich, RI; s. of Nicola Carcieri and Marguerite Carcieri; m. Suzanne Owren; four c.; ed East Greenwich High School, Brown Univ.; fmr math. teacher; with Old Stone Bank 1971–81, rising to Exec. Vice-Pres.; Head of Catholic Relief Service's West Indies operation, Kingston, Jamaica 1981–83; joined Cookson America 1983, rising to CEO and Jt Man. Dir Cookson Group Worldwide; Gov. of Rhode Island 2003–; co-f. (with wife) Acad. Children's Science Center, East Greenwich; Dir Providence Center; mem. Catholic Relief Services Leadership Council; Republican. *Address:* Office of the Governor, State House, Room 115, Providence, RI 02903–1196, USA (office). *Telephone:* (401) 222-2080 (office). *Fax:* (401) 222-8096 (office). *Website:* www.governor.state.ri.us (office).

CARD, Andrew (Andy) H., Jr, BS; American government official and business executive; b. 10 May 1947, Brockton, Mass.; m. Kathleene Card; three c.; ed USA Merchant Marine Acad., Univ. of South Carolina; served in USN 1965–67; Engineer, Maurice Reidy Engineers, Inc. 1971–72, David M. Berg Inc. 1972–75; mem. Mass. House of Reps 1975–83; Special Asst for Intergovernmental Affairs, The White House, Washington, DC 1983–87, Dir Office of Intergovernmental Affairs 1988, Asst to Pres. George H. W. Bush and Deputy Chief of Staff 1989–92; New Hampshire Campaign Man. for George H. W. Bush 1987–88; Sec. of Transportation 1992–93; Pres. and CEO American Automobile Mfrs Asscn 1993–98; Vice-Pres. for Governmental Relations, Gen. Motors Corpn 1999–2000; Chief of Staff to President George W. Bush 2000–06 (resgnd); mem. Bd of Dirs Union Pacific Corpn 2006–; Dr hc (Univ. of Massachusetts) 2007; named Legislator of the Year by Nat. Republican Legislators Asscn 1982, Mass. Municipal Asscn Distinguished Legislator Award 1982. *Address:* 1207 Buchanan Street, McLean, VA 22101, USA.

CARDEN, Joan Maralyn, AO, OBE; Australian opera singer (soprano); b. 9 Oct. 1937, Richmond, Vic.; d. of the late Frank Carden and of Margaret Carden (née Cooke); m. William Coyne 1962 (divorced 1980); two d.; ed Trinity Coll. of Music, London, Stuyvesant Scholar at London Opera Centre, voice studies with Thea Phillips and Henry Portnoj, Melbourne, Vida Harford, London, and David Harper, UK/Australia; nat. debut: Grisette in Merry Widow with June Bronhill, Melbourne 1960; int. debut, world premiere of Malcolm Williamson's Our Man in Havana, Sadler's Wells 1963; joined Australian Opera (Opera Australia) 1971: Royal Opera, Covent Garden as Gilda in Rigoletto 1974, Glyndebourne as Anna in Don Giovanni 1977, Scottish Opera as Constanze 1977; US debut at Houston as Amenaide in Tancredi 1977; Metropolitan Opera Tour as Anna in Don Giovanni 1978, Kennedy Center 1980, Miami Opera 1981; Singapore Festival 1983; Adelaide Festival 1984; other appearances include Victoria State Opera, Lyric Opera of Queensland, State Opera of South Australia; 56 major roles to 2007 include most Mozart heroines, Liu in Turandot, Marguerite in Faust, Gilda in Rigoletto, four heroines in Contes d'Hoffmann, Natasha in War and Peace, Tatyana in Onegin, Lakme, Leonora in Forza del Destino/Il Trovatore, Violetta in La Traviata, Alice in Falstaff, Mimi, Musetta in La Bohème, Madama Butterfly, Eva in Die Meistersinger, Feldmarschallin in Der Rosenkavalier, Elisabetta in Maria Stuarda, Medee, Tosca, Public Opinion in Orpheus in the Underworld, Mother Abbess in Sound of Music, Ida Straus in Titanic 2006, Mother Superior in Harp on the Willow 2007; concerts with Australian, Sydney, Melbourne, and Queensland Symphony Orchestras and for Australian Broadcasting Corpn, Sydney Univ. Graduates Choir (sponsors of Joan Carden Award, Sydney Conservatorium); repertoire includes Mozart Masses, concert arias, choral works, Vier Letzte Lieder (R. Strauss), works by Australian composers including Moya Henderson, Peter Sculthorpe, Nigel Butterley; soloist at numerous state and fed. occasions, including 1988 Bicentenary, royal and presidential state visits; Hon. DUniv (Swinburne Univ. of Tech., Melbourne) 2000, (Australian Catholic Univ., Sydney); Dame Joan Hammond Award for Outstanding Service to Opera in Australia 1987, Australian Govt Creative Fellowship 1993, Australian Govt Fed. Centenary medal 2001. *Recordings:* Joan Carden Sings Mozart, Great Opera Heroines: Joan Carden, The Australian Opera, Mozart: A Bicentennial Celebration, Stars of The Australian Opera Sing Verdi; Verdi aria in Priscilla, Queen of the Desert, film score. *Leisure interests:* dogs, walking, writing, gardening, reading, history. *Address:* Opera Australia, PO Box 291, Strawberry Hills, NSW 2012, Australia (office). *Telephone:* (2) 9699-1099 (office). *Website:* www.opera-australia.org.au (office).

CARDENAL, Ernesto; Nicaraguan poet, priest and government official; b. 20 Jan. 1925, Granada; s. of Rodolfo Cardenal and Esmerelda Cardenal (née Martinez); ed Univ. of Mexico, Columbia Univ., New York; ordained RC priest 1965–; Minister of Culture 1979–90; Co-founder and Hon. Pres. Casa de los Tres Mundos (literary org.);; Premio de la Paz 1980. *Publications:* Proclama del conquistador 1947, Gethsemani Ky 1960, Hora 0 1960, Epigramas 1961, Poemas 1961, Salmos 1964, Oración por Marilyn Monroe y otros poemas 1965, La voz de un monje en la era nuclear 1965, El estrecho dudoso 1966, Homenaje a los Indios Americanos 1969, Mayapán 1970, Vida en el amor 1971, La hora cero y otros poemas 1971, Canto nacional al F.S.L.N. 1972, Oráculo sobre Managua 1973, El evangelio en solentiname 1975, La santidad de la revolución 1976, Cátulo marcial 1978, Nueva antología poética 1978, Viaje a New York 1980, Nostalgia del futuro 1982, Crónica de un reencuentro 1982, Waslala 1983, Vuelos de victoria 1984, With Walker in Nicaragua and other early poems 1949–54 1984, Quetzalcoatl 1985, Nuevo cielo y tierra nueva 1985, From Nicaragua with Love: Poems 1976–1986 1986, Cántico cósmico 1989, La noche iluminada de palabras 1991, Los ovnis de oro 1991, El telescopio en la noche oscura 1993, Del monasterio al mundo: correspondencia entre Ernesto Cardenal y Thomas Merton 1998, Vida perdida 1999, Los años de Granada 2002, Las ínsulas extrañas 2002, La revolución perdida 2003, Thomas Merton—Ernesto Cardenal: Correspondencia (1959–1968) 2004, Versos del pluriverso 2005. *E-mail:* escritor@ibw.com.ni. *Website:* www.ernestocardenal.org/sitiooficialernestocardenal.

CARDENAS CONDE, Victor Hugo, BA; Bolivian politician and academic; *Leader, Tupac Katari Revolutionary Liberation Movement Party;* b. 4 June 1951, Achica Abajo Aymara Indian community, Omasuyos Prov., Dept of La Paz; m. Lidia Katari 1980; one s. two d.; ed Ayacucho High School, Universidad Mayor de San Andrés; Lecturer, then Prof. in Educ. Sciences, Linguistics and Languages, Faculty of Humanities and Educ., Universidad Mayor de San Andrés 1975–92; Chair. First Nat. Congress for Peasant Unity 1979; consultant on educational issues UNESCO and UNICEF 1990, various other orgs 1992; Prof., Latin American Coll. of Social Sciences 1992–93; Nat. Rep. Tupac Katari Revolutionary Liberation Movt party (MRTKL), Exec. Sec. (Nat. Exec. Cttee) 1993, currently Leader; Pres. Nat. Congress 1993–94, Andean Parl. 1993–94, Science and Tech. Nat. Council 1993–94; Vice-Pres. of Bolivia 1993–97; mem. Culture and Educ. Comm., Bolivian Workers Union 1979, Educ. and Culture Comm., House of Reps 1985–86, political forum of Latin American Inst. for Social Research 1992–93, Exec. Council UNESCO 1995–2000; Fray Bartolomé de las Casas Award (Spain) 1994. *Publications:* articles on culture, educ. and history in local and foreign books, journals and newspapers. *Address:* Movimiento Revolucionario Túpac Katarí de Liberación, Avda Baptista 939, Casilla 9133, La Paz, Bolivia. *Telephone:* (2) 235-4784.

CÁRDENAS SOLÓRZANO, Cuauhtémoc; Mexican politician; *President, Fundación para la democracia;* b. 1 May 1934, Mexico City; s. of Lázaro Cárdenas and Amalia Solórzano; m. Celeste Batel; two s. one d.; ed Escuela Nacional de Ingenieros, Universidad Nacional Autónoma de México; Senator from Michoacán 1976–82; Under-Sec. for Forestry and Wildlife 1976–80; Gov. of Michoacán 1980–86; cand. for presidency (Frente Democrático Nacional) 1988, (Partido de la Revolución Democrática—PRD) 1994, (Allianza por México) 2000; Pres. PRD 1988–93; Pres. Fundación para la democracia—alternativa y debate 1995–; Mayor of Mexico City 1997–99; Vice-Pres. Socialist International 2003–; Grand officier, Ordre nat. du Mérite (France) 1999; Cardenal Cisneros Medal, Universidad Complutense, Madrid (Spain) 1991. *Publications include:* Nuestra lucha a penas comienza 1988, Nace—una esperanza 1990, El proyecto nacional de la Revolució mexicana, un camino a retomar 1990, La esperanza en marcha. Ideario polìtico 1998, Palabras de Cárdenas 1999. *Leisure interests:* reading, travel. *Address:* Fundación para la democracia, Guadalajara No. 88 Col. Roma, 06700 México, DF (office); Edgar Allan Poe No. 28-1102, 11560 México, DF, Mexico (home). *Telephone:* (55) 5286-1114 (office). *Fax:* (55) 5286-1114 (office). *E-mail:* c_cardenas@mexico.com (office).

CARDIN, Benjamin L., BA; American politician; *Senator from Maryland;* b. 5 Oct. 1943; m. Myrna Edelman; one s. (died 1998) one d.; ed Univ. of Pittsburgh and Univ. of Maryland School of Law; served in Md House of Dels 1967–86, Chair. Ways and Means Cttee 1974–79, Speaker 1979–86; mem. US House of Reps for Third Congressional Dist of Md 1987–2006, mem. Ways and Means Cttee, ranking mem. Trade Sub-cttee and mem. Human Resources Sub-cttee 1999–2005, ranking mem. Comm. on Security and Cooperation in Europe (US Helsinki Comm.), Vice-Pres. OSCE Parl. Ass., Co-Chair. Bipartisan Ethics Task Force 1997, also held leadership positions on Org., Study and Review Cttee and Steering Cttee of Democratic Caucus and Senior Democratic Whip; Senator from Md 2007–; Chair. Special Study Comm. on Md Public Ethics Law by Md Gen. Ass.; Chair. Md Legal Services Corp 1988–95; mem. Bd of Visitors, Univ. of Maryland School of Law 1991–, UMBC's Pres.'s Bd of Visitors 1998–; mem. St Mary's Advisory Bd, Center for Study of Democracy 2002–; mem. Bd of Trustees St Mary's Coll. 1988–99, Goucher Coll. 1999–; Trustee Baltimore Council on Foreign Affairs 1999–; Democrat; hon. degrees (Univ. of Baltimore School of Law) 1990, (Univ. of Maryland at Baltimore) 1993, (Baltimore Hebrew Univ.) 1994, (Goucher Coll.) 1996; Congressional Award, Small Business Council of America 1993, 1999, 2005, 'Deficit Hawk' Honor Roll, Concord Coalition 1998, 1999, Dr Nathan Davis Award for Public Service, American Medical Asscn 1999, Congressional Advocate of the Year Award, Child Welfare League of America 2000, Nat. Leadership Award for Service to Children and Families, Casey Family Services 2000, named by Worth Magazine among the top "100 people who have influenced the way Americans think about money" 2001, Congressional Leadership Award, American Coll. of Emergency Physicians 2001, Congressional Champion Award, Nat. Coalition for Cancer Research 2002, Outstanding Leadership Award, American Occupational Therapy Asscn 2003, Congressional Service Award, American Soc. for Gastrointestinal Endoscopy 2003, Public Sector Distinguished Award, Tax Foundation 2003, named to Treasury and Risk Management's list of "100 Most Influential People in Finance" 2004, Public Service Award, Towson Business Asscn 2004, Wall of Fame Award, Maryland's Welfare Advocates 2005. *Address:* 509 Hart Senate Office Building, Washington, DC 20510, USA (office). *Telephone:* (202) 224-4524 (office). *Fax:* (202) 224-1651 (office). *Website:* cardin.senate.gov (office); www.bencardin.com (office).

www.worldwhoswho.com

CARDIN, Pierre; French couturier; b. 2 July 1922, San Biagio di Callatla, Italy; fmrly worked with Christian Dior; f. fashion house 1949; f. Espace Pierre Cardin (theatre group); Dir Ambassadeurs-Pierre Cardin Theatre (now Espace Pierre Cardin Theatre) 1970–; Man. Société Pierre Cardin 1973; Chair. Maxims 1982–; Exhbn at Victoria and Albert Museum 1990; mem. Acad. des Beaux-Arts; Hon. UNESCO Amb. 1991–; Grand Officer, Order of Merit (Italy) 1988; Order of the Sacred Treasure (Gold and Silver Star) 1991; Officier, Légion d'honneur 1997; Fashion Oscar 1985; Council of Fashion Designers of America International Award 2007. *Publications:* Fernand Léger, Sa vie, Son oeuvre, Son rêve 1971, Le Conte du Ver à Soie 1992 (Prix Saint-Exupéry valeurs-jeunesse 1992). *Address:* Haute Couture 14, place Francois-1er, 8e, 75008 Paris (office); 27 avenue Marigny, 75008 Paris, France (office); Pierre Cardin, 7 rue Royale, 75008 Paris (office); Institut de France, 23 quai Conti, 75006 Paris (office). *Website:* www.pierrecardin.com; www.maxims-de-paris.com.

CARDINAL, Douglas Joseph, OC, BArch, FRAIC, RCA; Canadian architect; b. 7 March 1934, Calgary, Alberta; s. of Joseph Treffle Cardinal and Frances Margarete Rach; m. 1st Marilyn Zahar 1973; three s. three d.; m. 2nd Idoia Arana-Beobide 1996; ed Univ. of BC, Univ. of Texas; design architect, Bissell & Halman, Red Deer 1963–64; Prin. Douglas Cardinal Architect, Red Deer 1964–67, Edmonton 1967–76, Douglas J. Cardinal Architect Ltd, Edmonton 1976–1985, Ottawa 1985–; Honour Award, Alberta Asscn of Architects, for St Mary's Church 1969 and Award of Excellence, Canadian Architect Magazine, for Grande Prairie Regional Coll. 1972, Governor General's Award in Visual and Media Arts in March 2001. *Major works include:* St Mary's Church, Red Deer, Alberta, Grande Prairie Regional Coll., Grande Prairie, Alberta, Ponoka Provincial Bldg, Ponoka, Alberta, St Albert Place, St Albert, Alberta, Canadian Museum of Civilization, Hull, Québec, Nat. Museum of the American Indian, Washington, DC. *Publications:* contribs to Of the Spirit 1977 and Human Values: A Primary Motive in Planning 1981. *Address:* Douglas J. Cardinal Architect Ltd., 331 Somerset Street West, Suite #1, Ottawa, ON K2P 0J8, Canada (office). *Telephone:* (613) 234-3377 (office). *Fax:* (613) 233-2462 (office). *E-mail:* info@djcarchitect.com (office). *Website:* www.djcarchitect.com (office).

CARDINALE, Claudia; Italian actress; b. 15 April 1939, Tunis, Tunisia; d. of Franco and Yolanda Cardinale; m. Franco Cristaldi 1966; one s.; ed Lycée Carnot and Collège Paul Cambon, Tunis; made first film 1958; awards include Nastro d'Argento, David di Donatello, Grolla d'Oro; UNESCO Goodwill Amb.; Golden Apple for Contrib. to European Cinema, European Actors' Awards 2003. *Films include:* 8½, The Pink Panther, The Leopard, The Professionals, Once Upon a Time in the West, Fury, The Magnificent Showman, La Scoumoune, Fitzcarraldo 1982, Le Ruffian 1982, History (TV), A Man in Love 1988, The French Revolution 1989, Hiver '54, L'abbé Pierre, Mother, 588 Rue Paradis, Son of the Pink Panther 1993, Women Only Have One Thing On Their Minds, Un café... l'addition 1999, Li chiamarono... briganti! 1999, And Now... Ladies and Gentlemen 2002, Le Démon de midi 2005. *Address:* c/o Carole Levi, Via Pisanelli 2, 00196 Rome, Italy.

CARDONA, Manuel, PhD; Spanish/American physicist and academic; *Emeritus Director, Max-Planck-Institut für Festkörperforschung;* b. 7 Sept. 1934, Barcelona, Spain; s. of Juan Cardona and Angela Castro; m. Inge Hecht 1959; two s. one d.; ed Univs of Barcelona and Madrid and Harvard Univ.; Research Asst, Harvard Univ. 1956–59; mem. tech. staff, RCA Labs Ltd, Zürich 1959–61, Princeton, NJ 1961–64; Assoc. Prof. of Physics, Brown Univ., Providence, RI 1964–66, Prof. 1966–71; Scientific mem. and Founding Dir Max Planck Inst. for Solid State Research, Stuttgart 1971–, now Emer. Dir, Business Man. Dir 1973–74; mem. various advisory bds, professional bodies, etc.; mem. NAS, Academia Europaea, Mexican Acad. of Science 2002–; mem. Comité Nat. d'Evaluation de Recherche (France) 1999–2002; Fellow, American Physical Soc.; A.D. Sloan Fellowship 1965–68; Guggenheim Fellowship 1969–70; Lecturer, Air NZ 2001; Grand Cross of Alfonso X el Sabio; Dr hc (Madrid) 1985, (Barcelona) 1985, (Sherbrook Univ., Canada) 1993, (Regensburg) 1994, (Rome) 1995, (Toulouse) 1998, (Thessaloniki) 2001, (Brno) 2002, (Valencia) 2004, (La Laguna, Canary Islands) 2006; Prince of Asturias Prize 1988, F. Isakson Prize, American Physical Soc. 1988, Italgas Prize 1993, Mateucci Medal Italian Physical Soc. 1994, J. Wheatley Prize, American Physical Soc. 1997, E. Mach Medal (Czech Repub.) 1999, Mott Medal and Award (UK) 2001, Blaise Pascal Medal European Acad. of Science 2004, and numerous other awards and distinctions. *Publications:* Modulation Spectroscopy 1969, Light Scattering in Solids, Vols I–IX 1975–2007, Photoemission in Solids, Vols I–II 1978–81, Fundamentals of Semiconductors 1996 (fourth edn 2009). *Leisure interests:* reading, travel, listening to music. *Address:* Max-Planck-Institut für Festkörperforschung, Heisenbergstrasse 1, 70569 Stuttgart, Germany (office). *Telephone:* (711) 6891710 (office). *Fax:* (711) 6891712 (office). *E-mail:* m.cardona@fkf.mpg.de (office).

CARDOSO, Fernando Henrique, DSc; Brazilian sociologist and fmr head of state; b. 18 June 1931, Rio de Janeiro; m. Ruth Corrêa Leite Cardoso (died 2008); three c.; ed Univs of São Paulo and Paris, France; Prof., Latin American Inst. for Econ. and Social Planning (ILPES/CEPAL), Santiago 1964–67; Prof. of Sociological Theory, Univ. of Paris-Nanterre 1967–68; Prof. of Political Science, Univ. of São Paulo 1968–69; Visiting Prof., Stanford Univ., USA 1972, Inst. for Econ. and Social Devt Univ. of Paris 1977, Univ. of Calif. 1981; Simon Bolivar Prof., Univ. of Cambridge, UK 1976; Assoc. Dir of Studies, Inst. for Higher Studies in Social Sciences, Univ. of Paris 1980–81; Prof., Coll. de France 1981; Prof. at Large, Watson Institute for International Studies, Brown Univ., USA 2003–; Fed. Senator for State of São Paulo 1983–94; fmr Leader, Brazilian Social Democratic Party (PSDB) in Fed. Senate; Govt Leader in Congress 1985–86; Minister of Foreign Affairs 1992–93; Minister of Economy and Finance 1993–94; Pres. of Brazil 1995–2002; Founder, Pres. of Fernando Henrique Cardoso Institute 2004; Co-Pres. Inter-American Dialogue; mem. of consultative Comm. for Institute for Advanced Study, Princeton Univ. and Rockefeller Foundation, New York; Pres. of Fundação Osesp; Foreign Hon. mem. American Acad. of Arts and Sciences;; Grand Cross, Order of Rio Branco; Chevalier, Légion d'honneur; Grand Cross, Order of Merit of Portugal; Dr hc (Rutgers), (Notre Dame, Ill.) 1991, (Santiago) 1993, (Central of Caracas), (Porto and Coimbra), (Sofia, Japan), (Free Univ. of Berlin), (Lumière Lyon 2), (Bologna), (Cambridge), (London); Fulbright Award for International Understanding. *Publications:* (jtly) São Paulo Growth and Poverty 1978, Dependency and Development in Latin America 1979, The New Global Economy in the Information Age 1993, Charting a New Course (co-ed.) 2001, A Arte da Política 2006, Carta a jovem político 2006. *Address:* c/o Watson Institute for International Studies, Brown University, POB 1970, Providence, RI 02912, USA (office). *Website:* www.watsoninstitute.org (office).

CARELL, Steve; American comedian and actor; b. 16 Aug. 1963, Acton, Mass; s. of Edwin A. Carell and Harriet T. Koch; m. Nancy Walls; one s. one d.; ed Denison Univ., Granville, Ohio; fmr mem. Second City, Chicago. *Films include:* Bruce Almighty 2003, Anchorman: The Legend of Ron Burgundy 2004, The 40 Year-Old Virgin 2005 (also co-writer) (MTV Movie Award for Best Comedic Performance 2006), Bewitched 2005, Little Miss Sunshine 2006, Evan Almighty 2007, Dan in Real Life 2007, Horton Hears a Who! (voice) 2008, Get Smart 2008. *Television includes:* The Daily Show 1999–2004, The Office 2005–07 (also co-writer) (2006 Golden Globe Award for Best Actor in Television Comedy).

CARENCO, Jean-François Claude, LL.L.; French administrator; *Prefect of of région Haute-Normandie and Seine-Maritime;* b. 7 July 1952, Talence, Gironde; s. of Guy Carenco and Roselyne Carenco (née Dalmas); m. Magali Serre 1977; two d.; ed Lycée Thiers, Marseilles, Stanislas Coll., Paris and Sorbonne Univ., Ecole Nat. d'Admin.; Councillor of Administrative Tribunal, Marseille 1979–83; Dir.-Gen. of Dist. of Montpellier 1983–88, Sec.-Gen. 1988–90; Sec.-Gen. of New Caledonia 1990–91; Sec.-Gen. of Prefecture of Yvelines 1991–96; Prefect of Saint-Pierre et Miquelon 1996–97, of Tarn-et-Garonne 1997–99, of Guadeloupe 1999–2002, of Haute-Savoie 2002–04, of région Haute-Normandie and Seine-Maritime 2006–; Chief of Staff Minister of Employment, Labour and Social Cohesion, then Employment, Social Cohesion and Housing 2004–06; Chevalier Légion d'honneur, Ordre nat. du Mérite, des Palmes academiques, Chevalier du Mérite de l'Ordre souverain de Malte. *Publications include:* L'Espérance occitane (jtly) 1979. *Address:* Préfecture de la région Haute-Normandie, 7 place de la Madeleine, 76000 Rouen, France (office).

CAREW, David Omashola, BSc (Econ); Sierra Leone chartered accountant and politician; *Minister of Finance and Development;* m.; two c.; ed Univ. of Sierra Leone; joined KPMG accounting and man. consultancy firm as grad. accountant in 1979, seconded to KPMG Nigeria 1979–86, Audit Supervisor in charge of KPMG's clients in banking and financial institutions industry, Kanu, designated Training Man. for three northern states in Nigeria, Asst Man., KPMG, Freetown 1986, acted as Relief Man. during leave of Resident Man. in The Gambia, promoted to Asst Man., then Deputy Man., then Man. and later Sr Man. 1986–88, Pnr, KPMG-Sierra Leone 1989, Pnr, KPMG-Gambia 1991, set up Man. Consulting Services in Sierra Leone and The Gambia, assisted Sr Pnr and was also in charge of forensic work with Govt of Sierra Leone, Man. Pnr for KPMG-Sierra Leone and for delivering KPMG services to clients in The Gambia and Liberia –2007; Minister of Finance and Devt 2007–; Fellow, Inst. of Chartered Accountants (Nigeria); Fellow and Past Pres. Inst. of Chartered Accountants (Sierra Leone). *Leisure interests:* golf, philanthropy. *Address:* Ministry of Finance and Development, Secretariat Bldg, George Street, Freetown, Sierra Leone (office). *Telephone:* (22) 225612 (office). *Fax:* (22) 228472 (office).

CAREY, Chase; American business executive; *President and CEO, The DIRECTV Group, Inc.;* fmr mem. Bd of Dirs, Pres. and CEO Sky Global Networks, Inc.; fmr mem. Bd of Dirs and Co-COO Fox Entertainment Group, Inc., also Chair. and CEO Fox TV; Exec. Dir and Co-COO News Corpn 1996–2002, mem. Bd of Dirs 2004–07; mem. Bd of Dirs, Pres. and CEO The DIRECTV Group, Inc. 2003–; Trustee Emer., Colgate Univ. *Address:* The DIRECTV Group Inc., 2230 East Imperial Highway, El Segundo, CA 90245, USA (office). *Telephone:* (310) 964-5000 (office). *Fax:* (310 535-5225 (office). *E-mail:* investorrelations@directv.com (office). *Website:* www.directv.com (office).

CAREY, John, MA, DPhil, FRSL, FBA; British literary critic and academic; *Merton Professor Emeritus of English Literature, University of Oxford;* b. 5 April 1934; s. of Charles William and Winifred Ethel Carey (née Cook); m. Gillian Mary Florence Booth 1960; two s.; ed Richmond and East Sheen County Grammar School, St John's Coll., Oxford; served in East Surrey Regt 1953–54; Harmsworth Sr Scholar, Merton Coll., Oxford 1957–58; Lecturer, Christ Church, Oxford 1958–59; Andrew Bradley Jr Research Fellow, Balliol Coll., Oxford 1959–60; Tutorial Fellow, Keble Coll., Oxford 1960–64, St John's Coll. 1964–75; Merton Prof. of English Literature, Univ. of Oxford 1976–2001, Prof. Emer. 2001–; Chief Book Reviewer, Sunday Times (London) 1976–; T. S. Eliot Memorial Lecturer, Univ. of Kent 1989; Northcliffe Lecturer, Univ. Coll., London 2004; Chair. Booker Prize Judges 1982, 2003, Int. Booker Prize Judges 2005; Judge, W H Smith Prize 1989–95; Hon. Fellow, St John's Coll. Oxford 1991, Balliol Coll. Oxford 1992; Hon. Prof. Univ. of Liverpool 2004–. *Publications:* The Poems of John Milton (co-ed. with Alastair Fowler) 1968, Milton 1969, The Violent Effigy: A Study of Dickens' Imagination 1973, Thackeray: Prodigal Genius 1977, John Donne: Life, Mind and Art 1981, The Private Memoirs and Confessions of a Justified Sinner, by James Hogg (ed.), William Golding: The Man and His Books (ed.) 1986, Original Copy: Selected Reviews and Journalism 1987, The Faber Book of Reportage (ed.) 1987, John

Donne (Oxford Authors) (ed.) 1990, The Intellectuals and the Masses 1992, The Faber Book of Science (ed.) 1995, The Faber Book of Utopias (ed.) 1999, Pure Pleasure 2000, What Good are the Arts? 2005; articles in Review of English Studies, Modern Language Review, etc. *Address:* Brasenose Cottage, Lyneham, Oxon., OX7 6QL; 57 Stapleton Road, Headington, Oxford, England. *Telephone:* (1865) 764304. *E-mail:* john.carey53@ntlworld.com (home).

CAREY, Mariah; American singer and songwriter; b. 22 March 1970, Long Island, NY; m. 1st Tommy Mottola 1993 (divorced 1998); m. 2nd Nick Cannon 2008; fmr backing singer, Brenda K. Starr, New York 1988; solo artist 1988–; concerts world-wide; f. Crave record label 1997; f. Camp Mariah holiday project for inner-city children; Grammy Awards for Best New Artist, Best New Pop Vocal by a Female Artist 1990, Soul Train Awards for Best New Artist, Best Single by a Female Artist 1990, Rolling Stone Award for Best Female Singer 1991, eight World Music Awards 1991–95, seven Billboard Awards 1991–96, four American Music Awards 1992–96, Int. Dance Music Award for Best Solo Artist 1996, American Music Awards Special Award of Achievement 2000, Lady of Soul Award for Best Solo R&B/Soul Single (for We Belong Together) 2005, Vibe Awards for Artist of the Year, for R&B Voice of the Year, for Best R&B Song (for We Belong Together) 2005, American Music Award for Favorite Female Soul/R&B Artist 2005, Female Billboard 200 Album Artist of the Year 2005, Billboard Music Awards for Hot 100 Song of the Year, Hot 100 Airplay of the Year, Rhythmic Top 40 Title of the Year (all for We Belong Together) 2005, Billboard Music Award for Female R&B/Hip-Hop Artist of the Year 2005, Grammy Award for Best Female R&B Vocal Performance (for We Belong Together) 2006. *Recordings include:* albums: Mariah Carey (Soul Train Award for Best Album by a Female Artist) 1990, Emotions 1991, MTV Unplugged (EP) 1992, Music Box 1993, Merry Christmas 1994, Daydream 1995, Butterfly 1997, #1s 1998, Rainbow 1999, Glitter 2001, Charmbracelet 2002, The Remixes 2003, The Emancipation of Mimi (Lady of Soul Award for Best Solo R&B/Soul Album, Vibe Award for Album of the Year, Grammy Award for Best Contemporary R&B Album 2006, Image Award for Best Album 2006) 2005, E=MC2 2008. *Film:* Glitter (also soundtrack) 2001. *Address:* c/o Island Records, 825 Eighth Avenue, New York, NY 10019, USA (office). *Website:* www.mariahcarey.com.

CAREY, Peter Philip, FRSL; Australian writer and academic; *Director, Creative Writing Program, Hunter College, CUNY;* b. 7 May 1943, Bacchus Marsh, Vic.; m. 2nd Alison Summers 1985 (divorced); two s.; ed Geelong Grammar School and Monash Univ.; fmr Pnr, McSpedden Carey Advertising Consultants, Sydney; writer-in-residence, New York Univ. 1990; fmr teacher Columbia Univ. and Princeton Univ.; currently Dir, Creative Writing Program, Hunter Coll., CUNY; Hon. LittD (Queensland). *Screenplay:* Bliss (jtly), Until the End of the World (jtly). *Publications:* The Fat Man in History (short stories, aka Exotic Pleasures 1981) 1974, War Crimes (short stories) (NSW Premier's Award) 1979, Bliss (novel) (Miles Franklin Award, Nat. Book Council Award, NSW Premier's Award) 1981, Illywhacker (novel) (Age Book of the Year Award, Nat. Book Council Award, Victorian Premier's Award) 1985, Oscar and Lucinda (Booker Prize for Fiction 1988, Miles Franklin Award, Nat. Book Council Award, Adelaide Festival Award, Foundation for Australian Literary Studies Award) 1988, Until the End of the World 1990, The Tax Inspector (novel) 1991, The Unusual Life of Tristan Smith (novel) (Age Book of the Year Award) 1994, Collected Stories 1995, The Big Bazoohley (children's novel) 1995, Jack Maggs 1997, The True History of the Kelly Gang (Booker Prize 2001) 2000, 30 Days in Sydney: A Wildly Distorted Account 2001, My Life as a Fake 2003, Wrong About Japan 2005, Theft: A Love Story 2006, His Illegal Self 2008. *Address:* Department of English, Hunter College, The City University of New York, 695 Park Avenue, New York, NY 10021 (office); c/o Amanda Urban, ICM, 40 West 57th Street, New York, NY 10019, USA (office). *Telephone:* (212) 772-5164 (office). *Fax:* (212) 772-5411 (office). *Website:* sapientia.hunter.cuny.edu/~creativewriting (office); petercareybooks.com (office).

CAREY OF CLIFTON, Baron (Life Peer), cr. 2002, of Clifton in the City and County of Bristol; **Most Rev. and Rt Hon. George Leonard Carey,** RVO, PC, MTh, PhD; British ecclesiastic and university chancellor; *Chancellor, University of Gloucestershire;* b. 13 Nov. 1935, London; s. of George Thomas Carey and Ruby Catherine Carey; m. Eileen Harmsworth Hood 1960; two s. two d.; ed Bifrons Secondary Modern School, Barking, Essex, King's Coll., London Univ.; Nat. Service, RAF 1954–56; univ. studies and theological training 1957–62; Curate St Mary's, Islington 1962–66; lecturer, Oak Hill Theological Coll. 1966–70, St John's Coll., Nottingham 1970–75; Vicar St Nicholas' Church, Durham 1975–82; Prin. Trinity Theological Coll., Bristol 1982–87; Bishop of Bath and Wells 1987–91; Archbishop of Canterbury 1991–2002; Chancellor, Univ. of Gloucestershire 2003–; Patron or Pres. of 300 orgs; Fellow King's Coll., London; Hon. Bencher Inner Temple; Freeman Cities of London and of Wells 1990; Hon. DLitt (Polytechnic of East London) 1991; Hon. DD (Kent) 1991, (Nottingham) 1992, (Bristol) 1992, (Durham) 1994; Hon. LLD (Bath) 1992; several hon. degrees from American univs; Greek, Hebrew and theological prizes. *Publications:* I Believe in Man 1978, The Great Acquittal 1981, The Church in the Market Place 1983, The Meeting of the Waters 1985, The Gate of Glory 1986, The Great God Robbery 1988, I Believe 1991, Spiritual Journey 1994, My Journey Your Journey 1996, Canterbury – Letters to the Future 1998, Jesus 2000, Know The Truth 2004. *Leisure interests:* walking, football, poetry, music. *Address:* House of Lords, Westminster, London, SW1A 0PW, England. *E-mail:* george@glcarey.co.uk (office).

CARL XVI GUSTAF, HM The King of Sweden (Carl Gustaf Folke Hubertus); b. 30 April 1946; s. of Prince Gustaf Adolf and Sibylla, Princess of Saxe-Coburg-Gotha; m. Silvia Sommerlath (HM Queen Silvia) 1976; two d., Crown Princess Victoria Ingrid Alice Désirée b. 14 July 1977, Princess Madeleine Thérèse Amelie Josephine b. 10 June 1982; one s., Prince Carl Philip Edmund Bertil b. 13 May 1979; ed studied in Sigtuna and Univs of Uppsala and Stockholm; cr. Duke of Jämtland; became Crown Prince 1950; succeeded to the throne on death of his grandfather, King Gustaf VI Adolf 15 Sept. 1973; Chair. Swedish Branch, World Wide Fund for Nature; Hon. Pres. World Scout Foundation; Dr hc (Swedish Univ. of Agricultural Sciences, Stockholm Inst. of Tech., Åbo Acad., Finland); US Environmental Protection Agency Award. *Leisure interests:* hunting, sailing and water sports, motor sport, cross-country and downhill skiing, art, music and food. *Address:* The Royal Palace, 111 30 Stockholm, Sweden (office). *Telephone:* (8) 402-60-00 (office). *Fax:* (8) 402-60-05 (office). *E-mail:* info@royalcourt.se (office). *Website:* www.royalcourt.se (office).

CARLESON, Lennart Axel Edvard, PhD; Swedish mathematician and academic; *Professor Emeritus, Mathematics Department, Uppsala University;* b. 18 March 1928, Stockholm; m. Sylvia Elmstedt 1978; one s.; ed Uppsala Univ.; Dir Mittag-Leffler Inst., Djursholm, Stockholm 1968–84; currently Prof. Emer., Math. Dept, Uppsala Univ.; frmly at Royal Inst. of Tech., Stockholm, UCLA, USA; Pres. Int. Math. Union 1978–82; Wolf Prize 1992, Lomonosov Gold Medal 2002, Sylvester Medal 2003, Abel Prize for outstanding work in the field of maths, particularly for his proof of the convergence of the Fourier series 2006. *Publications:* Selected Problems on Exceptional Sets 1967, Complex Dynamics (with T. W. Gamelin) 1993, Matematik för vår tid (Mathematics for Our Time); numerous articles in professional journals on harmonic analysis. *Address:* Svista 22, 186 97 Brottby, Sweden (home). *Telephone:* (8) 51241588 (home). *Fax:* (8) 7231788 (office). *E-mail:* carleson@math.kth.se (office).

CARLIN, John William; American business executive, archivist, academic and fmr state governor; *Visiting Professor/Executive in Residence, School of Leadership Studies, Kansas State University;* b. 3 Aug. 1940, Smolan, Kan.; s. of Jack W. and Hazel L. Carlin (née Johnson); m. 1st Ramona Hawkinson 1962 (divorced 1980); one s. one d.; m. 2nd Lynn Carlin 1997; ed Lindsborg High School, Univ. of Kansas; farmer and dairyman, Smolan, Kan. 1962–80; mem. Kan. House of Reps for 93rd Dist 1970–73, 73rd Dist 1973–79, Minority Leader 1975–77, Speaker 1977–79; Gov. of Kan. 1979–87; Visiting Prof. of Public Admin. and Int. Trade, Wichita State Univ. 1987–88; Visiting Fellow, Univ. of Kansas 1987–88; Pres. Econ. Devt Assocs Inc. 1987–92; Pnr, Carlin and Assocs, Topeka 1989–95; Vice-Chair. and CEO Midwest Superconductivity Inc., Lawrence 1990–94; Pnr, Clark Publishing Inc., Topeka 1991–95; Archivist of the US, Nat. Archives and Records Admin., Washington, DC 1995–2005; Visiting Prof./Exec. in Residence, School of Leadership Studies, Kansas State Univ., also Co-Chair. Advancement Council for School of Leadership Studies; Pres. Econ. Devt Asscn 1987–92, Vice-Chair. Midwest Superconductivity Inc. 1990–94; mem. Kan. Bioscience Authority 2006–; Chair. Nat. Historical Publications and Records Comm. 1995–2005, Nat. Comm. for Industrialized Farm Animal Production 2006–08; fmr Chair. Nat. Govs Asscn, mem. Nat. Govs Asscn (NGA) Exec. Cttee; fmr Chair. Midwestern Govs Conf.; Democrat; Hon. DIur (Kan.). *Leisure interests:* golf, swimming. *Address:* School of Leadership Studies, Kansas State University, 918 North Manhattan Avenue, Manhattan, KS 66502, USA (office). *Telephone:* (785) 532-6346 (office). *E-mail:* jwcarlin@k-state.edu (office). *Website:* www.k-state.edu/leadership (office).

CARLING, William (Will) David Charles, OBE; British sports commentator and fmr rugby union player; b. 12 Dec. 1965, Bradford-on-Avon, Wilts.; m. 1st Julia Carling 1994 (divorced 1996); m. 2nd Lisa Cooke 1999; one s. one step-s. one step-d.; ed Durham Univ.; centre; fmr mem. Durham Univ. Club; mem. Harlequins club; int. debut England versus France 1988; Capt. England team 1988–96; announced retirement from int. rugby 1997 (brief return to the game with Harlequins 1999); played 72 times for England, Capt. 59 times (world record); rugby football commentator 1997–; owner Inspirational Horizons Co., Insights Ltd. *Publications:* Captain's Diary 1991, Will Carling (autobiog.) 1994, The Way to Win (with Robert Heller) 1995, My Autobiography 1998. *Leisure interests:* painting and sketching. *Address:* c/o Mike Burton Management, Bastian House, Brunswick House, Brunswick Road, Gloucester, GL1 1JJ, England (office). *Telephone:* (1542) 419666 (office). *Fax:* (1306) 713605 (office). *E-mail:* will@willcarling.com (office). *Website:* www.willcarling.com.

CARLISLE, Sir James (Beethoven), Kt, GCMG, BDS; Antiguan/British dental surgeon and fmr administrator; b. 5 Aug. 1937; s. of the late James Carlisle and of Jestina Jones; m. 1st Umilta Mercer 1963 (divorced 1973); one s. one d.; m. 2nd Anne Jenkins 1973 (divorced 1984); one d.; m. 3rd Nalda Amelia Meade 1984; one s. one d.; ed Univ. of Dundee; dentist 1972–93; Gov.-Gen. Antigua and Barbuda 1993–2007; Chair. Nat. Parks Authority 1986–90; Chief Scout Antigua and Barbuda 1986–90; mem. American Acad. of Laser Dentistry, Int. Asscn of Laser Dentistry; Hon. Fellow, Dental Surgery Royal Coll. of Surgeons of Edin. 1995; Hon. mem. British Dental Asscn; Kt Grand Cross, Order of Queen of Sheba (Ethiopia) 1995, Kt Grand Collar, Most Distinguished Order of the Nation (Antigua and Barbuda) 2000, Kt of Grace, Kt of Justice, Order of St John; Hon. LLD (Andrews Univ., USA) 1996. *Leisure interests:* gardening, reading, music. *Address:* POB W1644, St John's, Antigua. *Telephone:* (305) 396-3542 (home). *E-mail:* govg@hotmail.com (home).

CARLOS, Roberto; Brazilian singer and songwriter; b. 19 April 1941, Cachoeiro de Itapemirim; s. of Robertino Braga and Laura Moreira Braga; m. 1st Cleonice Rossi 1968 (divorced 1978); one d.; m. 2nd Myrian Rios 1980 (divorced 1989); m. 3rd Maria Rita Simões Braga 1996 (died 1999); two s. one d.; ed Conservatório Musical de Cachoeiro; started performing professionally in 1958; has presented numerous radio and TV programmes; pioneered Jovem Guarda movt in 1970s; influenced by American rock and roll; numerous tours in S America; has performed with Maria Bethânia, Tom Jobim, Chico

Buarque, Caetano Veloso, Dorival Caymmi; First Prize, San Remo Festival 1968, Latin Grammy Award for Best Singer 1989, Latin Grammy Award for Best Brazilian Romantic Album 2005. *Recordings include:* Louco por Você 1961, O Inimitável 1968, À Janela, A Distância e Por Amor 1971, Honestly 1981, Se Diverte e já não Pensa em Mim 1988, Amor sem limite 2000, Pra sempre 2003; over 45 albums including Para Sempre Ao Vivo No Pacaembu (Latin Grammy Award for Best Brazilian Romantic Album), Roberto Carlos 2006 (Latin Grammy Award for Best Brazilian Romantic Album). *Address:* c/o Sony BMG Brasil, Rua Lauro Muller 116, 40° Andar, Conjunto 4001 a 4003, Botafogo, 22290-160 Rio de Janeiro, Brazil. *Telephone:* (21) 2128-0600 (office). *Website:* www.robertocarlos.com.

CARLOS, Roberto (see ROBERTO CARLOS).

CARLOS MOCO, Marcolino José, PhD; Angolan lawyer and politician; b. 19 July 1953, Huamba Prov.; fmr Gov. Bié and Huambo Provs; mem. Assembléia Nacional 1992–; Prime Minister of Angola 1992–96; fmr Minister of Youth and Sports; mem. Movimento Popular de Libertação de Angola (MPLA), fmr Sec.-Gen. *Address:* Assembléia Nacional, CP 1204, Luanda, Angola (office). *Telephone:* 222334021 (office). *Fax:* 222331118 (office). *E-mail:* assembleianacional@parlamento.ebonet.net (office). *Website:* www .parlamento.ao (office).

CARLOT KORMAN, Maxime; Ni-Vanuatu politician; *Leader, Vanuatu Republikan Pati;* fmr Minister of Foreign Affairs, of Public Service, Planning and Statistics, of Media and Language Services; Prime Minister of Vanuatu 1991–95, Feb.–Sept. 1996; fmr Minister of Infrastructure and Public Utilities, Minister of Lands; fmr Leader, Union of Moderate Parties; currently Leader Vanuatu Republikan Pati. *Address:* Vanuatu Republikan Pati, Port Vila, Vanuatu (office).

CARLSON, Arne Helge, BA; American politician and business executive; b. 24 Sept. 1934, New York; s. of Helge William and Kerstin Carlson (née Magnusson); m. 1st Barbara Carlson (divorced); one s. two d.; m. 2nd Joanne (divorced); m. 3rd Susan Shepard 1985; one d.; ed Williams Coll., Univ. of Minnesota; with Control Data, Bloomington, Minn. 1962–64; Councilman Minneapolis City Council 1965–67; in pvt. business, Minneapolis 1968–69; Legislator, Minn. House of Reps, St Paul 1970–78; State Auditor, State of Minn. 1978–90; Sec. Minn. Housing Finance Agency 1979–91; Gov. of Minn. 1991–98; Chair. IDS Mutual Fund Group, Minneapolis 1999; Ind. Chair. American Express Funds (now RiverSource Funds) 1999–2006, mem. Bd 2006–; mem. Bd of Dirs Minn. Land Exchange Bd, Exec. Council St Paul; Trustee Minn. State Bd Investment; several awards including Small Business Guardian Award, Nat. Fed. of Ind. Businesses 1994. *Leisure interests:* reading, squash, Univ. of Minnisota basketball and football games. *Address:* 7570 208th Street North, Forest Lake, MN 55025-9737; RiverSource Funds, 901 Marquette Avenue, Suite 2810, Minneapolis, MN 55402, USA (office). *Website:* www.riversource.com/funds (office).

CARLSON, Lawrence E., BS, MS, DEng; American engineer and academic; *Professor of Mechanical Engineering, University of Colorado;* ed Univ. of Wisconsin, Univ. of California, Berkeley; Lecturer, Dept of Mechanical Eng, Univ. of Illinois at Chicago 1971–74; Lecturer, Dept of Eng Design and Econ. Evaluation, Univ. of Colorado, Boulder 1974–78, Dept of Mechanical Eng 1978–, currently Prof. of Mechanical Eng, Founding Co-Dir Integrated Teaching and Learning Lab. 1997–2007; numerous awards including Soc. of Automotive Engineers Ralph R. Teetor Award 1976, Coll. of Eng and Applied Science Charles Hutchinson Outstanding Teaching Award 2001, John and Mercedes Peebles Innovation in Educ. Award 2004, Nat. Acad. of Eng Bernard M. Gordon Prize (with Jacquelyn Sullivan) 2008. *Address:* University of Colorado, College of Engineering and Applied Science, 1111 Engineering Drive 422, Boulder, CO 80309-0422, USA (office). *Telephone:* (303) 492-5071 (office). *Fax:* (303) 492-2199 (office). *E-mail:* lawrence.carlson@colorado.edu (office). *Website:* engineering.colorado.edu/overview/Profiles/faculty_carlson .htm (office); spot.colorado.edu/~carlsole (office).

CARLSSON, Arvid, MD, PhD; Swedish pharmacologist and academic; *Professor Emeritus of Pharmacology, University of Göteborg;* b. 25 Jan. 1923, Uppsala; physician, Univ. of Lund 1951, Asst Prof. 1951–56, Assoc. Prof. 1956–59; Prof. of Pharmacology, Univ. of Göteborg 1959–89, Prof. Emer. 1989–; co-f. Carlsson Research AB 1998; mem. Scientific Advisory Bd, ACADIA Pharmaceuticals 1999–; mem. Swedish Acad. of Sciences; Foreign Mem. NAS; numerous awards and prizes include: Magnus Blix Prize, Univ. of Lund 1947, Wolf Prize in Medicine, Jerusalem (jt recipient) 1979, Paul Hoch Prize, American Psychopathological Asscn 1990, Japan Prize in Psychology and Psychiatry 1994, Gold Medal and Hon. Diploma, Swedish Parkinson Asscn 1996, Gold Medal, Soc. of Biological Psychiatry, Toronto 1998, Antonio Feltrinelli Int. Award, Accad. Dei Lincei, Rome 1999, Nobel Prize for Medicine (jt recipient) 2000. *Publications:* several hundred specialist articles in journals. *Address:* Carlsson Research AB, Thorild Wulffsgatan 50, 413 19 Göteborg (office); Department of Pharmacology, University of Göteborg, Medicinaregatan 7, Box 431, 405 30 Göteborg, Sweden (office). *Telephone:* (31) 82-90-45 (office). *Fax:* (31) 82-14-34 (office). *E-mail:* arvid.carlsson@pharm.gu .se (office).

CARLSSON, Gunilla; Swedish politician; *Minister for International Development Cooperation;* b. 1963; ed accounting and auditing courses and non-degree courses at Linköping Univ.; mem. Vadstena Municipal Council 1989; accountant 1984–90, accounting man. 1990–94; co-opted to Bd of Moderate Party, mem. Moderate Party Programme Cttee, Political Admin. at Moderate Party Secr. of Riksdag 1994, Vice-Chair. Moderate Party Youth League 1992–95, mem. Bd of Moderate Party 1999–, Second Vice-Chair. Moderate Party 1999–2003, First Vice-Chair. 2003–; Vice-Chair. Nordic Young Conservative Union 1993–94; Vice-Chair. Int. Young Democratic Union 1994–98;

mem. European Parl. (Group of the European People's Party (Christian Democrats) and European Democrats—EPP-ED) 1995–2002, Leader Moderate Party Del., mem. Cttee on Foreign Affairs, Human Rights, Common Security and Defence Policy 1999–2002, mem. Del. to EU-Lithuania Jt Parl. Cttee, Del. to EU-Poland Jt Parl., Substitute mem. Cttee on Industry, External Trade, Research and Energy, Vice-Chair. EPP 2004–06; mem. Parl. (Riksdag) 2002–, mem. War Del. 2002–, mem. Cttee on Educ. 2002–03, Cttee on EU Affairs 2002–04, Cttee on Foreign Affairs 2003–04, Deputy Chair. Cttee on Foreign Affairs 2004–, Deputy mem. Cttee on EU Affairs 2004–, Minister for Int. Devt Cooperation 2006–; Alt. mem. Swedish Del. to Nordic Council 2004–. *Address:* Office of the Minister for International Development Cooperation, Ministry of Foreign Affairs, Gustav Adolfs torg 1, 103 39 Stockholm, Sweden (office). *Telephone:* (8) 405-10-00 (office). *Fax:* (8) 723-11-76 (office). *Website:* www.sweden.gov.se/sb/d/2085 (office).

CARLSSON, Ingvar Gösta, MA; Swedish politician; b. 9 Nov. 1934, Borås; m. Ingrid Melander 1957; two d.; ed Lund Univ. and Northwestern Univ. USA; Sec. in Statsradsberedningen (Prime Minister's Office) 1958–60; Pres. Social Democratic Youth League 1961–67; mem. Parl. 1964–; Under-Sec. of State, Statsradsberedningen 1967–69; Minister of Educ. 1969–73, of Housing and Physical Planning 1973–76, Deputy Prime Minister 1982–86, Minister of the Environment 1985–86, Prime Minister 1986–91, 1994–96; Co-Chair. Comm. on Global Governance 1995–2001, Inter Action Council 2005–; mem. Exec. Cttee Social Democratic Party, Chair. 1972–96. *Publications:* Ur skuggan av Olof Palme 1999, Så tänkte jag 2003. *Address:* c/o Parliament Buildings, 10012 Stockholm, Sweden.

CARLUCCI, Frank Charles; American fmr politician and business executive; *Chairman Emeritus, Carlyle Group;* b. 18 Oct. 1930, Scranton, Pa; s. of Frank Carlucci and Roxann Carlucci; m. 1st Jean Anthony 1954 (divorced 1974); one s. one d.; m. 2nd Marcia Myers Carlucci 1976; one d.; ed Princeton Univ. and Harvard Grad. School of Business Admin.; with Jantzen Co., Portland, Ore. 1955–56; Foreign Service Officer, Dept of State 1956; Vice-Consul, Econ. Officer, Johannesburg 1957–59; Second Sec., Political Officer, Kinshasa 1960–62; Officer in charge of Congolese Political Affairs, Zanzibar 1962–64, Consul-Gen. 1964–65; Counsellor for Political Affairs, Rio de Janeiro 1965–69; Asst Dir for Operations, Office of Econ. Opportunity 1969–70, Dir 1970; Assoc. Dir Office of Man. and Budget 1971–72, Deputy Dir 1972; Under-Sec. Dept of Health, Educ. and Welfare 1972–74; Amb. to Portugal 1974–77; Deputy Dir CIA 1977–81, Deputy Sec. of Defense 1981–82, Sec. 1987–89; Pres. and COO Sears World Trade Inc. 1983–84, Chair. and CEO 1984–86; Nat. Security Adviser to Pres. of USA 1986–87; Vice-Chair. Carlyle Group, Washington 1989–93, Chair. 1993–2003, Chair. Emer. 2003–; Hon. DHum-Litt; Superior Service Award and Superior Honor Award, US Dept of State, Presidential Citizens Award, Distinguished Intelligence Medal and other awards. *Leisure interests:* tennis, swimming. *Address:* The Carlyle Group, 1001 Pennsylvania Avenue, NW, Suite 220 South, Washington, DC 20004-2505, USA (office). *Telephone:* (202) 729-5224 (office). *Fax:* (202) 347-1597 (office). *E-mail:* frank.carlucci@carlyle.com (office). *Website:* www .thecarlyegroup.com (office).

CARLYLE, Joan Hildred; British singer (soprano) and teacher; b. 6 April 1931; d. of the late Edgar J. Carlyle and Margaret M. Carlyle; m.; two d.; ed Howell's School, Denbigh, N Wales; studied singing with Madame Bertha Nichlass Kempner; Prin. Lyric Soprano, Covent Garden 1955; has sung at La Scala Milan, Staatsoper Vienna, Munich, Berlin, Teatro Colón Buenos Aires, San Carlo Naples, Monet Monte Carlo, Nico Milan, Cape Town, Brussels, Geneva, Zurich, Amsterdam, Boston, New York; teaches privately and also in London 2003; gives master classes, promotes young singers and judges prestigious competitions. *Major roles sung in UK include:* Oscar, Un Ballo in Maschera 1957–58, Sophie, Der Rosenkavalier 1958–59, Nedda, Pagliacci (Zeffirelli production) 1959, Mimi, La Bohème 1960, Titania, Midsummer Night's Dream, Britten (Gielgud production) 1960, Pamina, Magic Flute 1962, 1966, Countess, Marriage of Figaro 1963, Zdenka, Arabella (Hartman Production) 1964, Suor Angelica 1965, Desdemona, Othello 1965, Arabella 1967, Marschallin, Der Rosenkavalier 1968, Jenifer, Midsummer Marriage 1969, Donna Anna, Don Giovanni 1970, Reiza, Oberon 1970, Adrianna Lecouvreur 1970, Russalka, Elisabetta, Don Carlos 1975. *Major roles sung abroad include:* Oscar, Nedda, Mimi, Pamina, Zdenka, Micaela, Donna Anna, Arabella, Elisabetta and Desdemona. *Recordings include:* Von Karajan's production of Pagliacci as Nedda, Midsummer Marriage as Jenifer, Medea, Pagliacci from Buenos Aires, Mavra, Purcell Anthology, Voice from the Old House (1/11) 2002, (12/29), (30/42) 2003, Complete versions of Otello, Arabella, Suor Angelica, Highlights from La Bohème 2003, complete versions of Arabella and Adriana Lecouvreur, Rusalka, Oberon, Complete Ballo 1962, 1971, Benevuto Cellini 2004. *Leisure interests:* gardening, travel, preservation of the countryside, interior design, cooking. *Address:* Laundry Cottage, Hanmer, SY13 3DQ, Clywdd, Wales. *Telephone:* (1948) 830265. *E-mail:* joan@ joancarlyle.co.uk (home). *Website:* www.joancarlyle.co.uk (home).

CARLYLE, Robert, OBE; British actor; b. 14 April 1961, Glasgow; s. of Joseph Carlyle and Elizabeth Carlyle; m. Anastasia Shirley 1997; ed N Kelvinside Secondary School, Royal Scottish Acad. of Music and Drama; f. Rain Dog Theatre Co. 1990, productions include: Wasted, One Flew Over the Cuckoo's Nest (Paper Boat Award), Conquest of the South Pole, Macbeth (Paper Boat Award 1992); Scottish BAFTA Award 1995, Royal TV Award 1996, Salerno Film Festival Award 1997, Evening Standard Outstanding British Actor Award 1998, Film Critics' Circle Award for Best Actor 1998, Variety Club Actor of the Year 1998, Bowmore Whisky/Scottish Screen Award for Best Actor 2001, Michael Elliot Award for Best Actor 2001, David Puttnam Patrons Award. *Stage appearances include:* Twelfth Night, Dead Dad Dog, Nae Problem, City, No Mean City, Cuttin' a Rug, Othello. *Television includes:*

The Part of Valour 1981, Hamish Macbeth 1995, Cracker 1994, Safe 1993, The Advocates, Arena, Byrne on Byrne, Taggart, The Bill, Looking After Jo Jo 1998, Hitler: The Rise of Evil 2003, Gunpowder, Treason and Plot 2004, Class of '76 2005, Human Trafficking 2005, Born Equal 2006. *Films include:* Marooned, Riff Raff 1990, Silent Scream 1990, Safe 1993, Being Human 1993, Priest 1994, Go Now 1995, Trainspotting 1996, Carla's Song 1996, Face 1997, The Full Monty (BAFTA Award for Best Actor 1998) 1997, Ravenous 1999, Apprentices, Plunkett and Macleane 1999, The World is Not Enough 1999, Angela's Ashes 2000, The Beach 2000, There's Only One Jimmy Grimble 2000, To End All Wars 2000, 51st State 2001, Once Upon a Time in the Midlands 2002, Black and White 2002, Dead Fish 2004, Marilyn Hotchkiss' Ballroom Dancing and Charm School 2005, The Mighty Celt 2005, Eragon 2006, 28 Weeks Later 2007, Stone of Destiny 2008, Summer 2008. *Address:* c/o ICM, Oxford House, 76 Oxford Street, London, W1D 1BS, England (office).

CARMACK, John; American software industry executive; *Technical Director, id Software;* worked for Softdisk Publishing; co-f. and Technical Dir id Software 1991–, creating influential computer games, including Wolfenstein 3-D, Doom and Quake, notable for enhanced graphic detail and three-dimensional illusion; numerous awards from gaming publs. *Address:* id Software, Town East Tower, Suite 615, 18601 LBJ Freeway, Mesquite, TX 75150, USA (office). *Website:* www.idsoftware.com.

CARMI, Rivka, MD; Israeli paediatrician, geneticist and university administrator; *President, Ben-Gurion University;* ed Hebrew Univ. Medical School, Jerusalem, Harvard Univ., USA; Sr Faculty mem. Faculty of Health Sciences and Soroka Medical Center, Be'ersheva, Dir Clinical Genetics Unit, Soroka Hosp., Prof. and Dean, Faculty of Health Sciences (first woman dean of a faculty of health sciences in Israel) 2000– (fmr Assoc. Dean of Student Affairs), Acting Pres. Ben-Gurion Univ. of the Negev (first woman pres. of Israeli univ.) Feb.–May 2006, Pres. May 2006–; fmr Chair. Selection Cttee Joyce and Irving Goldman Medical School, Instructional Cttee Recanati School for Community Health Professions, Ben-Gurion Univ.; fmr Acting Dir Nat. Inst. for Biotechnology in the Negev; mem. Editorial Bd American Journal for Medical Genetics; mem. and adviser in local and nat. cttees and in int. insts. *Publications:* more than 100 scientific papers on molecular genetics of rare recessive diseases and on community genetics. *Address:* Office of the President, Ben-Gurion University of the Negev, PO Box 653, Be'ersheva 84105, Israel (office). *Telephone:* (8) 6461111 (office). *Fax:* (8) 6479434 (office). *E-mail:* rcarmi@bgumail.bgu.ac.il (office). *Website:* www.bgu.ac.il (office).

CARMONA ESTANGA, Pedro; Venezuelan politician, economist and oil executive; b. 6 June 1941, Barquisimeto; ed Universidad Católica Andrés Bello, Université Libre de Bruxelles, Belgium; with Aditivos Orinoco 1989–93, Química Venoco 1989–2000, Industrias Venoco 1990–2000, Promotora Venoco 2001; First Vice-Pres. Fedecamaras 1999–2001, Pres. 2001–02; Pres. Andean Enterprise Consultative Council 2000–01; also worked for Venezuelan Confed. of Industry–Conindustria, Venezuelan Asscn of the Chemical and Petrochemical Industries, Venezuelan Asscn of Exporters (AVEX), Chamber of Commerce, Venezuelan–Columbian Integration (CAVECOL); fmr mem. Directive Council Instituto de Estudios Superiores de la Administración de Empresas; fmr mem. Junta del Acuerdo de Cartagena, fmr Pres. Venezuelan Del. to Comisión del Acuerdo de Cartagena; fmr mem. Corporación Andina de Fomento; fmr Dir Instituto de Comercio Exterior, Sistema Económico Latinoamericano; fmr adviser to Directorate of Econ. Policy, Ministry of Foreign Affairs; installed by army as interim Pres. of Venezuela 12 April 2002 following anti-govt protests against Pres. Chavez; placed under house arrest 14 April 2002, accused of rebellion and usurping the presidency, later granted asylum by Colombian Govt; Order of the Sun (Peru), Nat. Order of Merit (Colombia), Bernardo O'Higgins Order (Chile).

CARNEGIE, Sir Roderick Howard, Kt, AC, BSc, MA, MBA, FTS; Australian business executive; *Chairman, Pacific Edge Group;* b. 27 Nov. 1932, Melbourne; s. of D. H. Carnegie and Margaret F. Carnegie; m. Carmen Clarke 1959; three s.; ed Trinity Coll., Melbourne, New Coll., Oxford, Harvard Business School; Assoc., McKinsey and Co., Melbourne and New York 1959–64, Prin. Assoc. 1964–68, Dir 1968–70; Dir Conzinc Riotinto of Australia Ltd (now CRA Ltd) 1970, Jt Man. Dir 1971–72, Man. Dir and Chief Exec. 1972–74, Chair. and Man. Dir 1974–83, Chair. and Chief Exec. 1983–86; Dir Comalco Ltd, CRA Ltd, Rio Tinto-Zinc Corpn Ltd; Chair. Consultative Cttee on Relations with Japan 1984–87; Pres. German-Australian Chamber of Industry and Commerce 1985; Pres. Business Council of Australia 1987–88; Chair. Hudson Conway Ltd 1987–2000; currently Chair. Pacific Edge Holdings Pty Ltd and La Trobe Lignite Developments Pty Ltd; Vice-Pres. Australian Mining Industry Council; Chair. Salvation Army Council 1992–, G10 Australia Holdings Ltd 1992–94, Valiant Consolidated Ltd 1993–98, Adacel Techs Ltd 1998–2003, GPT Ltd 1994–, Newcrest Mining Ltd 1994–; Dir Lexmark Holdings Inc. (USA) 1994–; fmr Dir John Fairfax Holdings Pty; Ltd mem. Int. Council Morgan Guaranty Trust, The Asia Soc., The Brookings Inst.; mem. IBM World Trade Asia/Pacific Group Bd; Sr Adviser The Michael Allen Co.; Patron Australian Centre for Blood Diseases; Hon. DSc (Newcastle) 1985. *Address:* Pacific Edge Group, PO Box 7458, St Kilda Road, Melbourne, Vic. 8004, Australia (office). *Telephone:* (3) 9863-7242 (office). *Fax:* (3) 9863-7241 (office). *E-mail:* peta@carboniron.com.au (office).

CARNEY, Mark, BA, MA, PhD; Canadian central banker; *Governor, Bank of Canada;* b. 16 March 1965, Fort Smith, NWT; m.; four c.; ed Harvard Univ., Univ. of Oxford, UK; worked at Goldman Sachs 1988–2001, as analyst in London, later working in Tokyo and New York before becoming Man. Dir Goldman's investment banking div., based in Toronto; Deputy Gov. Bank of Canada, responsible for int. issues 2003–04, Advisor to the Gov. 2007–08, Gov. Bank of Canada (youngest cen. banker among the Group of Seven nations) 2008–; Sr Assoc. Deputy Minister, Dept of Finance 2004–07; served as Canada's Finance Deputy at the G-7, G-20 and the Financial Stability Forum. *Address:* Bank of Canada, 234 Wellington Street, Ottawa, ON K1A 0G9, Canada (office). *Telephone:* (613) 782-8111 (office). *Fax:* (613) 782-7713 (office). *E-mail:* mcarney@bankofcanada.ca (office). *Website:* www.bankofcanada.ca (office).

CARNEY, Rt Hon. Patricia (Pat), BA, PC, MA; Canadian politician and economist; b. 26 May 1935, Shanghai, China; d. of James Carney and Dora Sanders; m. 2nd Paul S. White 1998; one s. one d. from previous marriage; ed Univ. of British Columbia; Adjunct Prof., Univ. of British Columbia; fmrly econ. journalist; f. Gemini North Ltd (consulting firm for socio-econ. impact studies) 1970; first elected MP 1980; Minister of State for Finance, Minister of Finance, Energy, Mines and Resources; Minister of Energy, Mines and Resources 1984–86, of Int. Trade 1986–88; Pres. Treasury Bd April–Oct. 1988; Chair. Cabinet Cttee on Trade; mem. Senate 1990–; fmr Chair. Standing Senate Cttee on Energy, the Environment and Natural Resources; mem. Standing Senate Cttee on Foreign Affairs, Aboriginal Peoples, Fisheries; Adjunct Prof., School of Community and Regional Planning, Univ. of British Columbia; mem. Canadian Inst. of Planners, Asscn of Professional Economists of BC; fmr mem. Econ. Council of Canada; Hon. Fellow, Royal Architectural Inst. of Canada 1989; Hon. LLD (Univ. of British Columbia) 1990, (British Columbia Open Univ.) 1991. *Publications:* Trade Secrets: A Memoir. *Address:* The Senate, Ottawa, ON K1A 0A4, Canada (office). *Telephone:* (613) 943-1433 (office). *Fax:* (613) 943-1503 (office). *E-mail:* carnep@sen.parl.gc.ca (office). *Website:* www.sen.parl.gc.ca/pcarney (office).

CARNLEY, Most Rev. Peter Frederick, AO, DD, PhD; Australian archbishop and theologian; b. 17 Oct. 1937, New Lambton, NSW; s. of F. Carnley; m. Carol Ann Dunstan, 1966; one s. one d.; ed St John's Theological Coll., NSW, Trinity Coll., Melbourne Univ., St John's Coll., Univ. of Cambridge; Deacon 1962; Priest 1964; Chaplain, Mitchell Coll. of Advanced Educ., NSW 1970–72; Research Fellow, St John's Coll., Cambridge 1971–72; Warden St John's Coll., Univ. of Queensland 1973–81; Anglican Archbishop of Perth and Metropolitan of the Province of Western Australia 1981–2005, Primate of the Anglican Church of Australia 2000–05; mem. Archbishop of Canterbury's Comm. on Communion and Women in the Episcopate 1988, Int. Anglican Theological and Doctrinal Comm. 1994; Visiting Prof. of Anglican Studies, Gen. Theological Seminary, New York 1993, 1996, 1999; Anglican Co-Chair. Anglican-Roman Catholic Int. Comm. (ARCIC) 2003–; Adjunct Prof. of Theology, Murdoch Univ. 2004–; Patron, Australian Council of Christians and Jews 2004–; Hon. Fellow, Trinity Coll., Univ. of Melbourne 2000, St John's Coll., Cambridge 2000; Dr hc (Newcastle) 2000, (Western Australia) 2000, (Charles Sturt) 2001, (Queensland) 2002; Hon. Dr of Sacred Theology (Melbourne Coll. of Divinity) 2004. *Publications:* The Structure of Resurrection Belief 1987, The Yellow Wallpaper and Other Sermons 2001, Faithfulness in Fellowship: Reflections on Homosexuality and the Church 2001, Reflections in Glass: Trends and Tensions in the contemporary Anglican Church 2004. *Leisure interests:* gardening, music. *Address:* GPO Box W2067, Perth, WA 6846, Australia.

ČARNOGURSKÝ, Ján, LLD, DJur; Slovak politician and lawyer; b. 1 Jan. 1944, Bratislava; s. of Pavol Čarnogurský and Kristína Fašungová; m. Marta Stachová 1970; two s. two d.; ed Charles Univ., Prague 1966–69; lawyer, Bratislava 1970–81; mem. of Slovak Lawyers' Cen. Office and Czech Lawyers' Cen. Office; banned from legal profession after defence in a political trial 1981; driver, lawyer for a co. Bratislava 1982–86; unemployed, after expulsion from legal profession, continued giving legal advice to members of the political opposition and religious activists 1987–89; held in custody, released and pardoned, Aug.–Nov. 1989; First Deputy Premier, Govt of Czechoslovakia 1989–90, Deputy Premier June 1990; Chair. Legis. Council Feb.–Aug. 1990; Chair. Christian Democratic Movt 1990–2000; First Deputy Premier, Govt of Slovak Repub. 1990–91, Prime Minister of Slovak Govt 1991–92; mem. State Defence Council 1991–92; Deputy to Slovak Nat. Council (Slovak Parl.) for KDH (Christian Democratic Movt) 1992–98; Deputy Chair. Parl. Ass. of CSCE 1993–95; Minister of Justice 1998–2002; advocate in pvt sector 2002–; Trustee Order of the German Kts 1994–; Slovak Literary Fund Prize (Journalists' Section) 1992. *Publications:* The Bratislava Letters (samizdat), Suffered for the Faith 1987, Seen from Danube 1997. *Leisure interests:* history, jogging. *Address:* Kardla Adlera 10, 84102 Bratislava (home); Law Office, Dostojevskēho rad 1, 81109 Bratislava (office); Karola Adlera 10, 84102 Bratislava, Slovakia. *Telephone:* (2) 5263-6954 (office). *Fax:* (2) 5263-6955 (office). *E-mail:* jancarnogursky@slovanet.sk (home); carnogursky@ba.psg.sk.

CARO, Sir Anthony, Kt, OM, CBE, KBE, MA; British sculptor; b. 8 March 1924, London; s. of Alfred Caro and Mary Caro; m. Sheila Girling 1949; two s.; ed Charterhouse School, Christ's Coll., Cambridge, Regent St Polytechnic and Royal Acad. Schools, London; served Fleet Air Arm RN; Asst to Henry Moore 1951–53; part-time Lecturer, St Martin's School of Art, London 1953–79; taught at Bennington Coll. Vermont 1963–65; works in over 200 public collections world-wide; initiated Triangle Summer Workshop, Pine Plains, New York 1982; undertook comm. for new East Bldg, Nat. Gallery of Art, Washington, DC, 1977; mem. Council RCA 1981–83, Slade School of Art 1982–92; Trustee Tate Gallery 1982–89, Fitzwilliam Museum, Cambridge 1984; Hon. Fellow, Christ's Coll. Cambridge 1981, RCA, London 1986, Wolfson Coll., Oxford 1992, RIBA 1997, Royal Soc. of British Sculptors 1997, Glasgow School of Art 19998, Bretton Hall Coll. 1998, Univ. of Arts, London 2004; Hon. mem. American Acad. & Inst. of Arts and Letters 1979, American Acad. of Arts and Sciences 1988, Acad. di Belle Arte di Brera 1992; Hon. Trustee Int. Sculpture Centre 1998; Sr Academician, RA 2004; Order of Merit 2000; Dr hc (RCA, Univs of Alberta, Brandeis, Cambridge, Durham, E Anglia, Florida, Lille, London, Southampton, Surrey, Westminster, Yale, York/Toronto); Sculpture Prize, Paris Biennale 1959, David E. Bright Award, Venice

www.worldwhoswho.com

Biennale 1966, Prize for Sculpture, São Paulo Biennale 1969, presented with Key of City of New York 1976; Henry Moore Grand Prize 1991, Praemium Imperiale 1992, Int. Sculpture Centre Lifetime Achievement Award 1997, Christobal Gabarron Foundation Award for Visual Arts 2004, Julio Gonzales Award 2005; Chevalier des Arts et Lettres (France) 1996. *Leisure interest:* listening to music. *Address:* c/o Barford Sculptures, 38C Georgiana Street, London, NW1 0EB, England (office). *Telephone:* (20) 7482-2871 (office). *Fax:* (20) 7794-9983 (office). *E-mail:* sculpture@barfordsculptures.org (office). *Website:* www.anthonycaro.org (office).

CARO, David Edmund, AO, OBE, MSc, PhD, FInstP, FAIP, FACE; Australian academic and university administrator; *Chairman, Sarou Pty Ltd;* b. 29 June 1922, Melbourne; s. of George Caro and Alice Caro; m. Fiona Macleod 1954; one s. one d.; ed Geelong Grammar School, Univs of Melbourne and Birmingham, UK; war service, RAAF 1941–46; Demonstrator in Physics, Univ. of Melbourne 1947–49, Lecturer 1952, Sr Lecturer 1954, Reader 1958, Prof. of Experimental Physics and Head of Dept of Physics 1961–72, Deputy Vice-Chancellor 1972–77, Vice-Chancellor and Prin. 1982–87; Vice-Chancellor, Univ. of Tasmania 1978–82; Chair. Antarctic Research Policy Advisory Cttee 1979–84, Australian Vice-Chancellors Cttee 1982–83, Melbourne Theatre Co. 1982–87, UniSuper Ltd 1984–94, Sarou Pty Ltd 1991–; mem. Council Asscn of Commonwealth Univs 1982–84, Royal Melbourne Hosp. Cttee of Man. 1982–92; Interim Vice-Chancellor N Territory Univ. 1988–89; mem. Council Victorian Coll. of the Arts 1989–2001, Pres. 1989–92; mem. Council Univ. of S. Australia 1991–94; Chancellor Univ. of Ballarat 1998–2004, mem. Council 1994–2004; Exhbn of 1851 Overseas Research Scholar 1949–51; Hon. LLD (Melbourne) 1978, (Tasmania) 1982; Hon. DSc (Melbourne) 1987, (Ballarat) 2004. *Publication:* Modern Physics (co-author) 1961. *Leisure interests:* skiing, gardening, theatre. *Address:* 17 Fairbairn Road, Toorak, Vic. 3142, Australia. *Telephone:* (3) 9827-2004.

CAROLUS, Cheryl, BA; South African organization executive and diplomatist; *CEO, South African Tourism Board;* m. Graeme Bloch 1989; ed Univ. of the Western Cape; Gen. Sec. Nat. Exec. Cttee United Democratic Front (UDF) 1983–87, Fed. of S African Women (FedSAW) 1987, UDF Western Cape Region 1983; UDF Del. Int. Centre for Swedish Labour Movt 1986; mem. Interim Leadership Group S African Communist Party 1990; mem. Interim Leadership Cttee African Nat. Congress (ANC) 1990, ANC Rep. at talks with Govt at Groote Schur, Cape Town 1990, Deputy Sec.-Gen. ANC 1994; High Commr to UK 1998–2001; CEO South African Tourism Bd (SATOUR) 2001–; mem. Congress of S African Trade Unions, Nat. Educ. Crisis Cttee 1989, OAU, Harare, Bd of Dirs Int. Inst. for Democracy and Electoral Assistance; detained under emergency regulations 1986, 1989. *Address:* South African Tourism Board, 442 Rigel Avenue South, Erasmusrand 0181, Private Bag X164, Pretoria 0001, South Africa (office). *Telephone:* (12) 4826200 (office). *Fax:* (12) 3478753 (office). *E-mail:* jhb@satour.com (office). *Website:* www.za.satour.com (office).

CARON, Leslie Claire Margaret; French actress and ballet dancer; b. 1 July 1931, Boulogne-Billancourt; m. 1st George Hormel; m. 2nd Peter Reginald Frederick Hall (q.v.) 1956 (divorced 1965); one s. one d.; m. 3rd Michael Laughlin 1969 (divorced); ed Convent of the Assumption, Paris and Conservatoire de Danse; with Ballet des Champs Elysées 1947–50, Ballet de Paris 1954; Chevalier Légion d'honneur; Officier Ordre nat. du Mérite. *Films include:* An American in Paris 1951, Man with a Cloak 1951, Glory Alley 1952, Story of Three Loves 1953, Lili 1953, Glass Slipper 1955, Daddy Long Legs 1955, Gaby 1956, Gigi 1958, The Doctor's Dilemma 1958, The Man Who Understood Women 1959, The Subterranean 1960, Austerlitz 1960, Fanny 1961, Guns of Darkness 1962, The L-Shaped Room 1962, Father Goose 1964, A Very Special Favor 1965, Promise Her Anything 1965, Is Paris Burning? 1966, Head of the Family 1969, Madron 1970, Chandler 1971, Purple Night 1972, Surreal Estate 1976, The Man Who Loved Women 1977, Valentino 1977, Nicole 1978, Golden Girl 1979, The Contract 1980, All Stars 1980, Chanel Solitaire 1981, Imperative 1982, Deathly Moves 1983, The Train 1987, Courage Mountain 1990, Guns 1990, Damage 1992, The Genius 1993, Guerriers et Captives 1994, Funny Bones 1995, Let It Be Me 1995, The Reef 1996, Chocolat 2000, Le Divorce 2003. *Television Includes:* The Wild Bird 1959, Les Fables de La Fontaine 1964, Carola 1973, QB VII 1974, Docteur Erika Werner 1978, Run, Rabbit, Run 1982, Tales of the Unexpected 1982, The Unapproachable 1982, Le Château faible 1983, Master of the Game 1984, La Génie du Faux 1984, L'oiseau bleu 1985, Mon meilleur Noël 1985, Falcon Crest 1987, The Man Who Lived at the Ritz 1988, Lenin: The Train 1990, The Ring 1996, The Last of the Blonde Bombshells 2000, Murder on the Orient Express 2001. *Plays include:* Orvet (Jean Renoir), La Sauvage (Anouilh), Gigi (Anita Loos), 13 rue de l'Amour (Feydan), Ondine (Giraudoux), Carola (Renoir), La Répétition (Anouilh), On Your Toes (Rogers and Hart), Apprends-moi Céline (Maria Pacôme) (played in English in USA as One for the Tango 1985), Grand Hotel (Vicky Baum), George Sand (Bruno Villien), Le Martyre de Saint Sébastien (Debussy), Nocturne for Lovers (Villien), Babar the Elephant (Poulenc); toured France in Apprends-moi Céline 1998–99; stage appearances in Paris, London, USA, Germany and Australia; readings of Colette, USA and Australia. *Publication:* Vengeance 1983. *Address:* Merritt Blake Agency, 23441 Malibu Road, Malibu, CA 90265, USA. *Telephone:* (310) 456-2022 (office). *Fax:* (310) 456-9994 (office). *E-mail:* blakeagency@aol.com (office). *Website:* www.theblakeagency.com (office).

CARP, Daniel A., MS, MBA; American business executive; *Chairman, Delta Air Lines, Inc.;* b. Wytheville, Va; ed Ohio Univ., Rochester Inst. of Tech., Sloan School of Man., MIT; with Kodak 1970–, Asst Gen. Man. Latin American Region 1986–88, Vice-Pres., Gen. Man. 1988–90, Gen. Man. European Marketing Cos 1991, Gen. Man. European, African and Middle Eastern Region 1991, Exec. Vice-Pres. and Asst COO Eastman Kodak Co.

1995–97, Dir, Pres. and COO 1997–2000, Chair., Pres. and CEO 2000–01, Chair. and CEO 2001–05; Chair. (non-exec.) Delta Air Lines, Inc. 2007–; mem. Bd Dirs Liz Claiborne Inc., Norfolk Southern Corpn, Texas Instruments Inc.; mem. Business Roundtable, Business Council; Trustee, Nat. Urban League, George Eastman House; Human Relations Award from American Jewish Cttee Photographic Imaging Div. 1997, Photographic and Imaging Manufacturers Asscn Leadership Award 2001, Diversity Best Practices CEO Leadership Award 2003, PhotoImaging Manufacturers and Distributors Asscn Person of the Year Award 2004. *Address:* Delta Air Lines, Inc., PO Box 20706, 1030 Delta Blvd, Atlanta, GA 30320-6001, USA (office). *Telephone:* (404) 715-2600 (office). *Fax:* (404) 715-5042 (office). *E-mail:* info@delta.com (office). *Website:* www.delta.com (office).

CARPENTER, John Howard; American film director and screenwriter; b. 16 Jan. 1948, Carthage, NY; s. of Howard Ralph Carpenter and Milton Jean Carpenter (née Carter); m. 1st Adrienne Barbeau 1979; m. 2nd Sandy King 1990; ed Univ. of Southern California; mem. American Soc. of Composers, Authors and Publrs, Acad. of Motion Picture Arts and Sciences, Dirs Guild of America, West, Writers Guild of America. *Films directed:* The Resurrection of Bronco Billy 1970, Dark Star 1974, Assault on Precinct 13 1976, Halloween 1978, Elvis 1978, The Fog 1979, Escape from New York 1980, The Thing 1982, Christine 1983, Starman 1984, Big Trouble in Little China 1986, Prince of Darkness 1987, They Live 1987, Memoirs of an Invisible Man 1992, In the Mouth of Madness 1995, Village of the Damned 1995, Escape from LA 1996, Vampires 1998, Ghosts of Mars 2001. *Television includes:* Someone's Watching Me! 1978, Elvis 1979, Body Bags 1993, Masters of Horror 2005–06. *Leisure interests:* music, helicopter piloting. *Address:* c/o International Creative Management, 8942 Wilshire Boulevard, Beverly Hills, CA 90211, USA.

CARPENTER, Leslie Arthur; British business executive; b. 26 June 1927; s. of William Carpenter and Rose Carpenter; m. 1st 1952; one d.; m. 2nd Louise Botting 1989; ed Hackney Tech. Coll.; Dir Country Life 1965, George Newnes 1966; Man. Dir Odhams Press Ltd 1968; Dir Int. Publishing Corpn 1972, IPC (America) Inc. 1975; Chair. Reed Holdings Inc. 1977, Reed Publishing Holdings Ltd 1981; Chair. and Chief Exec. IPC Ltd 1974; Dir Reed Int. PLC 1974, CEO 1982–86, Chair. 1985–87; Dir Watmoughs (Holdings) PLC 1988–98. *Leisure interests:* racing, gardening. *Address:* Gable House, High Street, Broadway, Worcs., WR12 7DP, England.

CARPENTIER, Alain F., DenM, DèsSc; French cardiac surgeon; *Head, Department of Cardiovascular Surgery and Organ Transplantation, Hôpital Européen Georges Pompidou;* b. 11 Aug. 1933, Toulouse; Lab. Researcher, CNRS 1963–66; Founder and Dir, Lab. for the Study of Cardiac Grafts and Prostheses 1967–; apptd Lab. Dir, Univ. of Paris VI 1978, now Prof. Emer.; Head of Dept of Cardiovascular Surgery, l'Hôpital Broussais 1982, of Cardiovascular Surgery and Organ Transplantation, Hôpital Européen Georges Pompidou 1999–; Visiting Prof., New York Univ. 1983, 2001–05, Adjunct Prof., Mount Sinai School of Medicine, New York Univ. 2002–; Visiting Prof., Univ. of Oregon 1986, 1989, Univ. of London 1989, 1996–2002, Cleveland Clinic Foundation 1990, Harvard Univ. 1991, 1996, 1999, 2002, 2005, Univ. of Montreal 1991, 2004–6, Baylor Univ. 1992, Univ. of Washington 1994, 2000, Florida Heart Inst. 1996, 1999, Univ. of Padua 1996, Hôtel Dieu de France de Beyrouth 1996, Univ. of Virginia 1997, Univ. of North Carolina 1998, Univ. of Tokyo 1998, 2000, 2003, Univ. of Bangkok 2000, Univ. of Pavia 2000, Univ. of Mexico 2004, Univ. of Delhi 2006; Scientific Advisor, Edwards LifeSciences Research Centre, Calif. 1975–; Founder and Pres. Heart Inst., Ho Chi Minh City 1991–; Pres. Cttee Télémédecine et technologies pour la santé, Ministry of Nat. Educ., Research and Tech. 1999; mem. Conseil Nat. de la Science, 1998–, l'Acad. des Sciences 2000–, Haut Conseil de la science et de la Tech. 2006–, Cardiothoracic Surgery Network, European Asscn for Cardio-Thoracic Surgery, French Soc. for Thoracic and Cardiovascular Surgery, Soc. for Heart Valve Disease, American Asscn for Thoracic Surgery, Western Thoracic Surgical Asscn; mem. Bd of Dirs World Heart Foundation; Hon. mem. Mexican Cardiology Soc. 1978–, American Surgical Asscn 1985–, Soc. of Cardiothoracic Surgeons of GB and Ireland 1986–, American Coll. of Surgeons 1988–, American Coll. of Cardiology 1990, Royal Coll. of Doctors and Surgeons of Canada 1991–, Royal Coll. of Surgeons of England 1992–; Officier de la Légion d'Honneur, Commdr de l'Ordre National du Mérite, du Mérite de l'Ordre de Malte, de l'Ordre du Cèdre (Lebanon), Grand Croix de l'Ordre de Léopold (Belgium); Dr. hc (Univ. of Bucharest, Romania) 2001, (Univ. of Pavia, Italy) 2001; Prix de l'Internat, Médaille d'argent 1965, Bronze Medal, CNRS 1967, Prix de l'Asscn française de chirurgie 1967, Grand Prix, Acad. des Sciences 1986, Prix Médecine-Sciences du Rayonnement français 1990, Grand prix mondial Cino del Duca 1996, Grand Prize, The Foundation for Medical Research 1998, Fifth Scientific Achievement Award, American Asscn for Thoracic Surgery 2005, Prix Lasker 2007. *Publications:* Le Mal Universitaire 1988, La Transplantation d'Organes 1994, Philosophie du Progrès en Cardiologie (jtly) 2002. *Address:* Hôpital Européen Georges Pompidou, 20 rue Leblanc, Paris 75908 Cedex 15, France (office). *Telephone:* 1-56-09-36-01 (office). *Fax:* 1-56-09-36-04 (office). *E-mail:* alain.carpentier@hop.egp.ap-hop-paris.fr (office); prcarpentier@europost.org (office).

CARPENTIER, Jean Claude Gabriel; French aeronautical engineer; *Scientific Adviser, Office Nationale d'études et de recherches aérospatiales (ONERA);* b. 13 April 1926, Haspres; m. Micheline Robinet 1950; ed Ecole Polytechnique, Ecole Nationale Supérieure Aéronautique et Espace; Service technique de l'aéronautique 1950; Direction des recherches et moyens d'essais 1961; Dir Direction des recherches, études et techniques, Ministry of Defence 1977; Pres. Office Nat. d'études et de recherches aérospatiales (ONERA) 1984–91, Sr Consultant 1991–, Scientific Adviser 1991–; Pres. Man. Cttee Nat. Meteorological Bureau 1989–94; Pres. Comité Avion-Ozone 1992–96; Ed. Aerospace Research 1994–; Co-Ed.-in-Chief Aerospace Science and Technology 1997–, Revue Scientifique et Technique de la Défense; mem. Acad. Nat. de l'Air et de l'Espace; Commdr Légion d'honneur, Ordre Nat. du Mérite; Médaille de l'Aéronautique. *Publications:* Flight Mechanics 1952, Autopilots 1953, Inertial Navigation 1962, Recherche Aéronautique et Progrès de l'Aviation 1999. *Leisure interest:* history. *Address:* Office National d'études et de recherches aérospatiales, 29 avenue de la Division Leclerc, PO Box 72, 92322 Chatillon Cedex, France (office). *Telephone:* 1-46-73-40-01 (office). *Fax:* 1-46-73-41-65 (office). *Website:* www.onera.fr (office).

CARPENTIER, Michel André Georges, LenD, LenSc (Econ); French international organization official and international science consultant; b. 23 Oct. 1930, Billy Montigny, Pas de Calais; m. Annick Puget 1956; four s.; ed Ecole des Hautes Etudes Commerciales, Ecole des Sciences Politiques and Univ. of Paris; Commissariat à l'Energie Atomique (CEA) 1958; EURATOM 1959; Head of Dept Industrial, Technological and Scientific Affairs, EC Comm. 1967, Dir-Gen. Environment 1977, Dir-Gen. Energy 1981; Dir-Gen. Task Force for Information Technologies and Telecommunications, EC Comm. 1984; Dir-Gen. Information Technologies and Telecommunications, EC Comm. 1986; Dir-Gen. DG XIII, Telecommunications, Information Markets and Exploitation of Research, EC Comm. 1993–95; Hon. Dir-Gen. and Special Adviser EU Comm. 1996–; industrial adviser 1996–97; Pres. Scientific Cttee Aquitaine Europe Communication 1997; mem. Econ. and Social Cttee, EC Comm., Paris 1995–96; Pres. Centre Informatique Documentaire (CID) 1997–98, Paris, Orientation Cttee, AEC 1998–2004; Vice-Pres. AIACE, Paris; Municipal Councillor for Montcaret 2002–; Hon. mem. IEEE (USA), Royal Swedish Acad. of Eng Science; Chevalier, Légion d'honneur, Ehrenkreuz für Wissenschaft und Forschung (Austria), Commdr, Ordre du Mérite (Luxembourg), Order of the Rising Sun (Japan); Dr hc (Loughborough, Madrid). *Publications:* Telecommunications in Transition (with others) 1992, The French Space Policy 1998. *Leisure interests:* fishing, classical music, opera, reading. *Address:* Domaine de Lespinassat, 24230 Montcaret, France (home). *Telephone:* (5) 53-58-66-05 (home). *Fax:* (5) 53-58-66-05 (home). *E-mail:* m.carpentier@wanadoo.fr.

CARPER, Thomas Richard, BA, MBA; American politician; *Senator from Delaware;* b. 23 Jan. 1947, Beckley, W Va; s. of Wallace Richard Carper and Mary Jean Carper (née Patton); m. Martha Stacy 1986; two s.; ed Ohio State Univ., Univ. of Delaware; Commdr USN 1968–73, Capt., USN Reserve 1973–91; industrial devt specialist, then State Treasurer, State of Del., Dover 1976–83; mem. US House of Reps from Del. 1983–93; Gov. of Delaware 1993–2001; Senator from Delaware 2001–; fmr mem. Nat. Govs Asscn (Vice-Chair. 1997–98, Chair. 1998–99); Hon. Chair. Delaware Special Olympics 1987–. *Leisure interests:* physical fitness, running, weightlifting, tennis, reading, raising two sons. *Address:* 513 Hart Senate Office Building, Washington, DC 20510 (office); 600 West Matson Run Parkway, Wilmington, DE 19802, USA (home). *Telephone:* (202) 224-2441 (office). *Fax:* (202) 228-2190 (office). *E-mail:* carper@senate.gov (office). *Website:* carper.senate.gov (office).

CARR, Jack, DPhil, FRSE; British mathematician and academic; *Professor, Department of Mathematics, Heriot-Watt University;* b. 29 Aug. 1948, Newcastle-upon-Tyne; s. of John George Carr and Elizabeth Eleanor Carr; m. Teresa Nancy Thorpe 1976; one s. two d.; ed Walbottle Secondary School, Univ. of Bath, St Catherine's Coll., Oxford; Lecturer, Heriot-Watt Univ., Edin. 1974–83, Prof. of Math. 1983–; Visiting Prof., Brown Univ., USA 1978–79, Michigan State Univ., USA 1982, Ecole Polytechnique, Lausanne, Switzerland 1983. *Publication:* Applications of Centre Manifolds 1981. *Leisure interest:* cricket. *Address:* Department of Mathematics, School of Mathematical and Computer Sciences, Room CM.G03, Scott Russell Building, Heriot-Watt University, Riccarton, Edinburgh, EH14 4AS (office); 42 Balgreen Avenue, Edinburgh, EH12 5SU, Scotland. *Telephone:* (131) 451-3229 (office). *Fax:* (131) 451-3249 (office). *E-mail:* J.Carr@ma.hw.ac.uk (office). *Website:* www.ma.hw.ac.uk/maths/People/Frontpages/jack.html (office).

CARR, Sir (Albert) Raymond Maillard, Kt, MA, DLitt, FRSL, FRHistS, FBA; British historian; b. 11 April 1919, Bath; s. of Reginald Henry Maillard Carr and Ethel Gertrude Marion Carr; m. Sara Ann Mary Strickland 1950; three s. one d.; ed Brockenhurst School and Christ Church, Oxford; Gladstone Research Exhibitioner, Christ Church 1941; Fellow, All Souls Coll., Oxford 1946–53, New Coll. 1953–64, St Antony's Coll. 1964–; Dir Latin American Centre 1964–68, Chair. Soc. for Latin American Studies 1966–68; Prof. of History of Latin America, Univ. of Oxford 1967–68, Warden St Antony's Coll. 1968–87; mem. Nat. Theatre Bd 1980; Corresp. mem. Royal Acad. of History, Madrid 1968; Hon. Fellow, Christ Church Coll., St Antony's Coll., Oxford; Grand Cross of the Order of Alfonso El Sabio (for services to Spanish history) 1983; Hon. DLitt (Madrid); Prince of Asturias Award in Social Sciences 1999. *Publications:* Spain 1808–1939 1966, Latin American Affairs (ed.) 1969, The Republic and the Civil War in Spain (ed.) 1971, English Fox Hunting 1976, The Spanish Tragedy: The Civil War in Perspective 1977, Spain: Dictatorship to Democracy (co-author) 1979, Modern Spain 1980, Fox-Hunting (with Sara Carr) 1982, Puerto Rico: A Colonial Experiment 1984, The Spanish Civil War (ed.) 1986, The Chances of Death: A Diary of the Spanish Civil War (ed.) 1995, Visiones de fin de siglo 1999, Spain: A History (ed.) 2001; contrib. to scholarly books and journals. *Leisure interest:* foxhunting. *Address:* 58 Fitzgeorge Avenue, London, W14 0SW, England (home). *Telephone:* (20) 7603-6975 (home).

CARR, Roderick (Rod) M., LLB, BCom, MA, MBA, PhD; New Zealand business executive; *Managing Director, Jade Software Corporation Ltd;* b. 26 Nov. 1958; ed Wharton Business School, Univ. of Pennsylvania, Columbia Univ., New York, USA, Otago Univ.; fmr Head of Global Payments, Nat. Australian Bank, Melbourne; Deputy CEO and Deputy Gov. Reserve Bank of New Zealand –2003, fmr Acting Gov.; Man. Dir Jade Software Corpn Ltd 2003–; mem. Otago Business School Bd of Advisers, Univ. of Canterbury Coll. of

Business and Econs; Dir Canterbury Employers' Chamber of Commerce 2006–; Fellow, NZ Inst. of Man.; NZ Hi-Tech Co. Leader of the Year 2006. *Publication:* Productivity and Efficiency in the US Life Insurance Industry. *Leisure interests:* running, swimming, hiking. *Address:* Jade Software Corporation Ltd, 19 Sheffield Crescent, PO Box 20152, Christchurch 8053, New Zealand (office). *Telephone:* (3) 365 2500 (office). *Fax:* (3) 358 7276 (office). *E-mail:* Rcarr@jadeworld.com (office). *Website:* www.jadeworld.com (office).

CARR, Roger M., FRSA; British business executive; *Chairman, Centrica plc;* b. 1947; various sr positions including CEO Williams PLC and Chair. Thames Water PLC 1984–2000; Chair. Chubb PLC 2000–02; mem. Bd Dirs Centrica plc 2001–, Chair. 2004–, also Chair. Nominations Cttee; mem. Bd of Dirs Cadbury-Schweppes plc 2001–, Deputy Chair. 2003–08, Chair. 2008–; Chair. Mitchells & Butlers plc –2008; Dir (non-exec.) Six Continents PLC 2002, Court of the Bank of England; Sr Adviser to Kohlberg Kravis Roberts Co. Ltd; mem. Industrial Devt Advisory Bd, CBI Council. *Address:* Centrica plc, Millstream, Maidenhead Road, Windsor, Berks., SL4 5GD, England (office). *Telephone:* (1753) 494000 (office). *Fax:* (1753) 494001 (office). *E-mail:* info@centrica.co.uk (office). *Website:* www.centrica.co.uk (office).

CARR, Willard Zeller, Jr, BS, JD; American attorney; b. 18 Dec. 1927, Richmond, Ind.; s. of Willard Z. Carr and Susan E Brownell Carr; m. Margaret Paterson Carr 1952; two s.; ed Purdue Univ., Indiana Univ. School of Law; Capt. Judge Advocate Gen.'s Dept USAF 1951–52; Pnr, Gibson, Dunn & Crutcher (law firm), Los Angeles 1952–2007 (retd); fmr Chair. Labor and Employment Practice Group, The Federalist Soc., now Sr Advisor; admitted to practice US Supreme Court 1963; mem. ABA, Los Angeles County Bar Asscn, Calif. State Bar Asscn, Int. Bar Asscn (Chair. Labour Law Cttee 1973–83); mem. Bd of Visitors Southwestern Univ. Law School, Indiana Univ. School of Law; mem. Advisory Council Int. and Comparative Law Center, Southwestern Legal Foundation, Nat. Panel of Arbitrators, American Arbitration Asscn, World Affairs Council, Republican State Cen. Cttee for Calif.; Chair. Calif. Chamber of Commerce;; Jurisprudence Award, Anti-Defamation League 1987. *Publications:* International Handbook on Contracts of Employment 1976, Symposium on Private Investments Abroad: Problems and Solutions in International Business 1982; numerous specialist articles. *Leisure interests:* tennis, travel. *Address:* 2185 Century Hill, Los Angeles, CA 90067-3548, USA.

CARR OF HADLEY, Baron (Life Peer), cr. 1975, of Monken Hadley in Greater London; **(Leonard) Robert Carr,** PC, MA; British fmr politician, company director and metallurgist; b. 11 Nov. 1916, London; s. of the late Ralph Edward and of Katie Elizabeth Carr; m. Joan Kathleen Twining 1943; one s. (deceased) two d.; ed Westminster School and Gonville and Caius Coll., Cambridge; MP 1950–75, Parl. Pvt. Sec. to Sec. of State for Foreign Affairs 1951–55, to Prime Minister April–Dec. 1955, Parl. Sec. Ministry of Labour and Nat. Service 1955–58, Sec. for Tech. Co-operation 1963–64; Sec. of State for Employment 1970–72; Lord Pres. of Council and Leader of House of Commons April–Nov. 1972; Sec. of State Home Dept 1972–74; joined John Dale Ltd 1938, Chief Metallurgist 1945–48, Dir of Research and Development 1948–55, Chair. 1959–63 and 1965–70; Dir Carr, Day & Martin Ltd 1947–55, Isotope Developments Ltd 1950–55; Deputy Chair. and Joint Man. Dir Metal Closures Group Ltd 1960–63, Dir 1965–70; Dir Scottish Union and Nat. Insurance Co. (London) 1958–63; Dir S. Hoffnung and Co. 1963, 1965–70, 1974–80, Securicor Ltd 1965–70, 1974–85; Norwich Union Insurance Group (London) 1965–70, 1974–76; Dir S.G.B. Group Ltd 1974–86; Dir Prudential Assurance Co. 1976–85, Deputy Chair. 1979–80, Co-Chair. 1980–85; Dir Prudential Corpn Ltd 1978–89, Deputy Chair. 1979–80, Chair. 1980–85; Dir Cadbury Schweppes Ltd 1979–87; Chair. Strategy Ventures 1988–2001; mem. Political Honours Scrutiny Cttee 1977–87; Fellow, Imperial Coll., London 1985; Conservative. *Publications:* (Co-author) One Nation 1950, Change is our Ally 1954, The Responsible Society 1958, One Europe 1965. *Leisure interests:* lawn tennis, gardening, music. *Address:* 14 North Court, Great Peter Street, London, SW1P 3LL, England (home); House of Lords, Westminster, London, SW1A 0PW, England (office).

CARRANZA UGARTE, Luis, DEcon; Peruvian economist, banker and government official; *Minister of Economy and Finance;* b. 1967; ed Pontifical Catholic Univ. of Peru, Lima, Univ. of Minnesota, USA; worked as official at IMF for several years 1990s; worked in Dept of Econ. Investigation, US Fed. Reserve Bank of Minneapolis 1990s; apptd Deputy Finance Minister and Dir Cen. Bank by Pres. Alejandro Toledo 2004–05 (resgnd); Chief Economist for Latin America and Emerging Markets, Banco Bilbao Vizcaya Argentaria 2005–06; consultant, IDB; Minister of Economy and Finance 2006–08, 2009–; Visiting Prof., Univ. of Navarra, Spain. *Address:* Ministry of Economy and Finance, Jirón Junín 339, 4°, Circado de Lima, Lima 1, Peru (office). *Telephone:* (1) 3115930 (office). *E-mail:* postmaster@mef.gob.pe (office). *Website:* www.mef.gob.pe (office).

CARRARD, François Denis Etienne, Dr. iur.; Swiss lawyer and international organization official; b. 19 Jan. 1938, Lausanne; ed Lausanne, John Muir High School, Pasadena, Calif., USA, Univ. of Lausanne; with audit co., Lausanne 1962; with law firm, Stockholm, Sweden 1963–64; Attorney, Lausanne 1965–, admitted to bar of Vaud (Swiss bar) 1967, Sr Pnr, Etude Carrard, Paschoud, Heim et Associés (now Carrard & Associés); Dir-Gen. Int. Olympic Cttee 1989–2003, currently Sr Adviser in charge of legal affairs; Chair. Montreux Jazz Festival Foundation, Gabriella Giorgi-Cavaglieri Foundation; Pres. Automobile-Club de Suisse; fmr Vice-Pres. Bd of Vintage Brands of Vaud; fmr mem. Swiss Fed. Comm. of Foreign Indemnities; mem. Ordre des Avocats Vaudois, Fédération Suisse des Avocats, Int. Bar Asscn, Asscn Suisse de l'Arbitrage, Union Internationale des Avocats; Commdr Orden del Mérito Civil (Spain) 1992; Officier Ordre de Saint-Charles (Monaco) 1993. *Address:* Carrard & Associés, PO Box 7191, Place Saint-François 1, 1002 Lausanne, Switzerland (office). *Telephone:* 213491919 (office). *Fax:* 213491920 (office). *E-mail:* fcarrard@carrard-associes.ch (office). *Website:* www.carrard-associes.ch (office).

CARRARO, Franco; Italian sports administrator and business executive; *President, MCC—Mediocredito Centrale SpA;* b. 6 Dec. 1939, Padua; m.; two c.; Pres. Italian Water-skiing Fed. 1962–76, Chair. Tech. Comm. 1963–67; Chair. World Water-skiing Union 1967–73; Chair. football team Milan Calcio 1967–71; fmr Chair. Comm. for Amateur and Professional Football; fmr Chair. Sub-comm. for Professional Football, UEFA, now mem. UEFA Exec. Cttee; Vice-Pres. Italian Nat. Olympic Cttee 1976–78, Pres. 1978–; Vice-Pres. Alitalia 1981–87; Minister of Tourism and Performing Arts 1987–90; Mayor of Rome 1989–93; Chair. Impregilio 1994–99; Pres. MCC—Mediocredito Centrale SpA (bank) 2000–; mem. Int. Olympic Cttee 1982–, Vice-Chair. Comm. for the Olympic Programme 1983–94, Chair. Olympic Programme Working Group 1998–2001, mem. Exec. Bd 2000–04, Chair. Olympic Programme Comm. 2002–; Pres. Italian Football Fed. (Federazione Italiana Gioco Calcio) 1976–78, 2001–06; Chair. Asscn of European Olympic Cttees 1980–87; Chair. Organizing Cttee World Cup Football Championship 1990;. *Achievements include:* fmr champion water skier, Italian jr champion 1953–54, Italian Open champion 1955–60, European champion, slalom and combined 1956 and 1961, European team champion 1958, 1959, 1960; bronze medallist World Championships 1957. *Address:* MCC SpA, Via Piemonte 51, 00187 Rome, Italy (office). *Telephone:* (06) 47911 (office). *Fax:* (06) 47913130 (office). *Website:* www.mcc.it (office).

CARRASQUILLA BARRERA, Alberto, MS, PhD; Colombian politician and economist; b. Bogotá; ed Univ. of Los Andes, Univ. of Ill., USA; Tech. Man., Banco de la República 1993–97; Prin. Economist, Investigation Div., IDB, Washington, DC 1997–99; Econ. Adviser, Gen. Repub. Controllership 1999–2000; fmr Assoc. Teacher, Univ. of Los Andes, Dean Faculty of Econs 2000–02; Deputy Minister of Finance 2002–03, Minister of Finance 2003–07; fmr Assoc. Investigator, Fedesarrollo. *Address:* c/o Ministry of Finance and Public Credit, Carrera 8a, No 6–64, Of. 305, Bogotá, DC, Colombia (office).

CARRELL, Robin Wayne, MA, PhD, DSc, FRS, FRCP, FRSNZ; New Zealand biochemist and academic; *Professor of Haematology, University of Cambridge;* b. 5 April 1936, Christchurch; s. of Ruane George Carrell and Constance Gwendoline Carrell (née Rowe); m. Susan Wyatt Rogers 1962; two s. two d.; ed Christchurch Boys' High School, Univs of Otago, Canterbury and Cambridge; mem. MRC Haemoglobin Unit, Cambridge 1965–68; Dir Clinical Biochemistry, Christchurch Hosp., NZ 1968–75; Lecturer in Clinical Biochemistry, Univ. of Cambridge, UK 1976–78, Prof. of Haematology 1986–; Prof. of Clinical Biochemistry and Dir Molecular Research Lab., Christchurch Clinical School of Medicine, Otago Univ. 1978–86; Commonwealth Fellow, St John's Coll., Cambridge and Visiting Scientist, MRC Lab. of Molecular Biology 1985; Gov. Imperial Coll. London 1997–98, mem. Court 1999–2003; Pres. British Soc. of Thrombosis and Haemostasis 1999; Fellow, Trinity Coll., Cambridge 1987–; Hector Medal, Royal Soc. of NZ 1986. *Publications:* articles in scientific journals on genetic abnormalities of human proteins and new protein family, serpins. *Leisure interests:* gardening, walking. *Address:* 19 Madingley Road, Cambridge, CB3 0EG (home); Haematology Department, University of Cambridge, Cambridge Institute for Medical Research, Hills Road, Cambridge, CB2 2XY, England (office). *Telephone:* (1223) 312970 (office). *Fax:* (1223) 336827 (office). *E-mail:* rwc1000@cam.ac.uk (office). *Website:* www.cimr.cam.ac.uk/people/profiles/carell_robin_profile.html (office).

CARREÑO, Jose Manuel; Cuban ballet dancer; *Principal Dancer, American Ballet Theatre;* b. 25 May 1968, Havana; ed Prov. School of Ballet and Nat. Ballet School, Cuba; with Nat. Ballet of Cuba 1986–90; joined English Nat. Ballet 1990; Prin. Dancer, The Royal Ballet 1993–95; Prin. Dancer, American Ballet Theatre 1995–; numerous appearances in Europe, Latin America, USA and Japan; Gold Medal, NY Int. Ballet Competition 1987, Grand Prix, Int. Ballet Competetition, Jackson, MS 1990, Dance Magazine Award 2004. *Repertoire includes:* (with English Nat. Ballet): Solor in La Bayadère, the Prince in Cinderella, Franz in Coppélia, Albrecht in Giselle, the Prince and the Gopak in The Nutcracker, Romeo in Romeo and Juliet, Petruchio in The Taming of the Shrew, pas de deux in A Stranger I Came, Graduation Ball and Prince Igor; (with The Royal Ballet): Bluebird in The Sleeping Beauty, Basilio in Don Quixiote, Oberon and Puck in The Dream, leading role in Caught Dance and Herman Schmerman; (with American Ballet Theatre): title role in Apollo, leading role in Ballet Imperial, Conrad, Ali, the Slave and Lanckendem in Le Corsaire, third sailor in Fancy Free, Danilo in The Merry Widow, pas de deux in The Nutcracker, leading role in Push Comes to Shove, the Son in Prodigal Son, Romeo and Mercutio in Romeo and Juliet, Prince Desire in The Sleeping Beauty, Misgir in The Snow Maiden, Prince Siegfield in Swan Lake, leading role Études, Themes and Variations, Stepping Stones, Raymonda, Petit Mort. *Films:* Born to be Wild, PBS. *Address:* American Ballet Theatre, 890 Broadway, New York, NY 10003, USA (office). *Telephone:* (212) 477-3030 (office); (646) 912-9380 (home). *Fax:* (646) 912-9380 (home). *E-mail:* jcarreno@aol.com (home). *Website:* www.abt.org (office).

CARRERAS, José; Spanish singer (tenor); b. 5 Dec. 1947, Barcelona; s. of José Carreras and Antonia Carreras; m. Ana Elisa Carreras; one s. one d.; opera debut as Gennaro in Lucrezia Borgia, Liceo Opera House, Barcelona 1970–71 season; appeared in La Bohème, Un Ballo in Maschera and I Lombardi alla Prima Crociata at Teatro Regio, Parma, Italy 1972; US debut as Pinkerton in Madame Butterfly with New York City Opera 1972; debut Metropolitan Opera as Cavaradossi 1974; debut La Scala as Riccardo in Un Ballo in Maschera 1975; has appeared at major opera houses and festivals including Teatro Colón, Buenos Aires, Covent Garden, London, Vienna Staatsoper, Easter Festival and Summer Festival, Salzburg, Lyric Opera of Chicago; recordings include Un Ballo in Maschera, La Battaglia di Legnano, Il Corsaro, Un Giorno di Regno, I Due Foscari, Simone Boccanegra, Macbeth, Don Carlos, Tosca, Thais, Aida, Cavalleria Rusticana, Pagliacci, Lucia di Lammermoor, Turandot, Elisabetta, regina d'Inghilterra, Otello (Rossini); Pres. José Carreras Int. Leukaemia Foundation 1988–; Hon. mem. RAM 1990; Commdr des Arts et Lettres, Chevalier Légion d'honneur; Grammy Award 1991, Sir Lawrence Olivier Award 1993, Gold Medal of City of Barcelona, Albert Schweizer Music Award 1996, ECHO Klassik Lifetime Achievement Award 2008; and numerous other awards and prizes. *Films include:* La Bohème, I Lombardi, Andrea Chenier, Turandot, Carmen, Don Carlos, La Forza del Destino, Fedora, Jerusalem, My Life. *Publication:* Singing from the Soul 1991. *Address:* c/o José Carreras International Leukaemia Foundation, Muntaner 383, 2n, 08021 Barcelona (office). *Telephone:* (90) 2240480 (office). *Fax:* (93) 2010588 (office). *E-mail:* info@fcarreras.es (office); info@josepcarreras.com (office). *Website:* www.fcarreras.es (office); www.josepcarreras.com.

CARRÈRE D'ENCAUSSE, Hélène, DèsSc; French political scientist; *Secretary for Life, Académie Française;* b. 6 July 1929, Paris; d. of Georges Zourabichvili and Nathalie von Pelken; m. Louis Carrère 1952; one s. two d.; ed Univ. of Paris, Sorbonne; fmr Prof., Univ. of Paris (Sorbonne); currently Prof., Inst. d'Etudes Politiques, Paris and Dir of Research, Fondation Nationale des Sciences Politiques; Pres. Radio Sorbonne-Radio France 1984–87; Advisor on Reconstruction and Devt, European Bank 1992; fmr mem. Bd of Dirs East-West Inst. for Security Studies; Visiting Prof. at numerous univs in USA; mem. Acad. Française, Sec. for Life 2000–; Foreign mem. Russian Acad. of Science 2003–, Acad. of Georgia; Assoc. mem. Acad. Royale de Belgique; mem. European Parl. 1994–99; fmr Vice-Pres. Comm. on Foreign Affairs and Defence, on French Diplomatic Archives; mem. Nat. Council for New Devts in Human and Social Sciences 1998; Pres. Statistical Observatory on Immigration and Integration 2004; Hon. mem. Acad. of Georgia; Officier, Légion d'honneur, Commdr Légion d'honneur 2005; Dr hc (Montréal, Louvain); Prix de la Fondation Louis-Weiss 1986, Prix Comenius 1992. *Publications include:* Le marxisme et l'Asie 1965, Réforme et révolution chez les musulmans de l'Empire russe 1966, L'URSS et la Chine devant les révolutions dans les sociétés pré-industrielles 1970, L'Empire éclaté (Prix Aujourd'hui) 1978, Lénine: la révolution et le pouvoir 1979, Staline: l'ordre par la terreur 1979, Le pouvoir confisqué 1982, Le Grand Frère 1983, La déstalinisation commence 1984, Ni paix ni guerre 1986, Le Grand Défi: bolcheviks et nations 1917–30 1987, Le Malheur russe 1988, La Gloire des nations ou la fin de l'Empire soviétique 1991, Victorieuse Russie 1992, Nicholas II: la transition interrompue (Prix des Ambassadeurs) 1996, Lénine 1998, La Russie inachevée 2000, Catherine II 2002, L'Impératrice et l'abbé un duel littéraire ivédit 2003, L'Empire d'Eurasie 2005, La Deuxième Mort de Staline 2006. *Address:* Académie Française, 23 quai Conti, 75006 Paris, France (office). *Telephone:* 1-44-41-43-00 (office). *Fax:* 1-43-29-47-45 (office). *E-mail:* contact@academie-francaise.fr (office). *Website:* www.academie-francaise.fr (office).

CARREY, Jim; Canadian/American film actor; b. 17 Jan. 1962, Newmarket, Ont., Canada; s. of Percy Carrey and Kathleen Carrey; m. 1st Melissa Worner 1986 (divorced); one d.; m. 2nd Lauren Holly 2001; began performing in comedy clubs in Toronto aged 17, before moving to Los Angeles 1979; Star on Hollywood Walk of Fame 2000, American Film Inst. Star Award 2005. *Films:* All in Good Taste 1983, The Sex and Violence Family Hour 1983, Introducing... Janet 1983, Copper Mountain 1983, Finders Keepers 1984, Once Bitten 1985, Peggy Sue Got Married 1986, The Dead Pool 1988, Earth Girls Are Easy 1988, Pink Cadillac 1989, The Itsy Bitsy Spider (voice) 1992, Ace Ventura: Pet Detective (also screenplay) 1994, The Mask 1994, High Strung 1994, Dumb & Dumber 1994, Batman Forever 1995, Ace Ventura: When Nature Calls 1995, The Cable Guy (MTV Movie Award) 1996, Liar Liar (Blockbuster Entertainment Award) 1997, The Truman Show (Golden Globe for Best Performance 1999) 1998, Simon Birch 1998, Man on the Moon (Golden Globe for Best Performance 2000) 1999, Me, Myself & Irene 2000, How the Grinch Stole Christmas 2000, The Majestic 2001, Bruce Almighty 2003, Pecan Pie 2003, Eternal Sunshine of the Spotless Mind 2004, Lemony Snicket's A Series of Unfortunate Events 2004, Fun with Dick and Jane 2005, The Number 23 2007, Horton Hears a Who! (voice) 2008. *Television includes:* The Duck Factory (series) 1984, Mike Hammer: Murder Takes All 1989, In Living Color (series, also writer) 1990–94, Doing Time on Maple Drive 1992. *Address:* c/o Jimmy Miller, 10th Floor, 9200 Sunset Blvd, Los Angeles, CA 90069; Creative Artists Agency, Inc., 9830 Wilshire Blvd, Beverly Hills, CA 90212-1825, USA. *Telephone:* (310) 288-4545 (CAA). *Fax:* (310) 288-4800 (CAA). *Website:* www.caa.com.

CARRICK, Hon. Sir John Leslie, KCMG, AC, BEcons; Australian politician (retd) and educationalist; b. 4 Sept. 1918, Sydney; s. of Arthur James Carrick and Emily Ellen Carrick (née Terry); m. Diana Margaret Hunter 1951; three d.; ed Sydney Tech. High School, Univ. of Sydney; commissioned Univ. of Sydney Regt 1939, served in Australian Imperial Force, Sparrow Force; POW 1942–45; mem. Citizen Mil. Force 1948–51; Gen. Sec. NSW Div. of Liberal Party of Australia 1948–71; mem. Senate 1971–87; mem. Library Cttee 1971–73, Senate Standing Cttee on Educ., Science and the Arts 1971–75, Senate Standing Cttee on Foreign Affairs and Defence 1971–74, Jt Cttee on Foreign Affairs 1971–72, on Foreign Affairs and Defence 1973–75, Senate Standing Cttee on Standing Orders 1978–83, Senate Select Cttee on Human Embryo Experimentation Bill 1985 1985–, Standing Cttee on Regulations and Ordinances 1983–86, Jt Select Cttee on Electoral Reform 1983–87; Opposition Spokesman for Federalism and Intergovernment Relations 1975; Minister for Housing and Construction, for Urban and Regional Devt Nov.–Dec. 1975, for Educ. 1975–79, Minister assisting the Prime Minister in Fed. Affairs 1975–78; Leader of Govt in the Senate 1978–83, Vice-Pres. of Exec. Council 1978–82; Minister for Nat. Devt and Energy 1979–83; Chair. NSW State Govt Cttee Review of Schools 1988–89, Advisory Cttee GERRIC, Univ. of NSW

www.worldwhoswho.com

1997–2006; Pres. Univ. of Sydney Dermatology Research Foundation 1989–2003; Chair. Gas Council of NSW 1990–95; mem. NSW Exec. Cttee, Foundation for Aged Care 1989–2000, Ministerial Advisory Council on Teacher Educ. and Quality of Teaching 1992–95, Advisory Bd Inst. of Early Childhood, Macquarie Univ. 1992–2000; Chair. Inst. of Early Childhood Foundation 2001–; Commonwealth Gov. Roundtable on Indigenous Capacity 2000; Hon. FACE 1994; Hon. DLitt (Sydney) 1988, (Macquarie) 2000, (Univ. of Western Sydney) 2006; Hon. D Educ. (NSW) 2006; Centenary Medal 2000. *Leisure interests:* walking, reading. *Address:* Apt 21, 162E Burwood Road, Concord, NSW 2137, Australia (home). *Telephone:* (2) 9747-8320 (home). *Fax:* (2) 747-8340 (home).

CARRICK, Sir Roger John, Kt, KCMG, LVO; British international consultant and fmr diplomatist; *Chairman, Strategy International Ltd;* b. 13 Oct. 1937, Middx; s. of John Carrick and Florence Carrick; m. Hilary E. Blinman 1962; two s.; ed Isleworth Grammar School, Jt Services School for Linguists and School of Slavonic and E European Studies, Univ. of London; RN 1956–58; joined HM Diplomatic Service 1956; served in Sofia 1962, FCO 1965, Paris 1967, Singapore 1971, FCO 1973–77; Visiting Fellow, Inst. of Int. Affairs, Univ. of Calif., Berkeley 1977–78; Counsellor, Washington, DC 1978; Head, Overseas Estate Dept FCO 1982; Consul-Gen., Chicago 1985–88; Asst Under-Sec. of State (Econ.), FCO 1988–90; Amb. to Indonesia 1990–94; High Commr to Australia 1994–97; Deputy Chair. Britain-Australia Soc. 1998–99, Chair. 1999–2002, Vice-Pres. 2003–, Pres. West Country Br. 2003–; Dir (non-exec.) cmb technologies 2000–02; Chair. (non-exec.) Charteris Mackie & Baillie Ltd 2001–03; Deputy Chair. The D Group 1999–2007; Dir Strategy International Ltd 2001–07, Chair. 2007–; Trustee Chevening Estate 1998–2003, Britain-Australia Bicentennial Trust; Churchill Fellow, Westminster Coll., Mo. 1986; Freeman of the City of London 2002. *Publications:* East-West Technology Transfer in Perspective 1978, RolleroundOz: Reflections on a Journey Around Australia 1998. *Leisure interests:* sailing, reading, music, theatre, travel, public speaking, avoiding gardening. *Address:* c/o Britain-Australia Society, West Country Branch, The Clerk's House, Pound Lane, Martock, TA12 6LU, England (office). *Website:* www.britozwest.org.uk (office).

CARRIER, Hervé, SJ; Canadian sociologist and priest; b. 26 Aug. 1921, Grand-Mère, Québec; s. of Fortunat Carrier and Cora Gélinas; ed Univ. de Montreal, Jesuit Faculty, Montreal, Catholic Univ. of America, Washington, DC and Sorbonne, Paris; Prof. of Sociology, Gregorian Univ. Rome 1959–, Rector 1966–78; Pres. Int. Fed. of Catholic Univs 1970–80, Dir Centre for Coordination of Research 1978–82; Sec. Pontifical Council for Culture, Vatican City 1982–93; mem. Acad. des Lettres et des Sciences Humaines of RSC, European Acad. of Sciences and Arts; Officier, Légion d'honneur; Dr hc (Sogang Univ., Seoul and Fu Jen Univ., Taipei). *Publications:* Psycho-sociology of Religious Belonging 1965, Higher Education facing New Cultures 1982, Cultures: notre avenir 1985, Evangile et cultures 1987, Psico-sociologia dell'appartenenza religiosa 1988, Gospel Message and Human Cultures 1989, The Social Doctrine of the Church Revisited 1990, Evangélisation et Développement des Cultures 1990, Lexique de la Culture 1992, Evangelizing the Culture of Modernity 1993, Diccionario de la Cultura 1994, Guide pour l'inculturation de l'Evangile 1997, Dizionario della cultura 1997, The Gregorian University After Vatican II 2003. *Address:* Maison Bellarmin, 25 rue Jarry ouest, Montréal, PQ H2P 1S6, Canada. *Telephone:* (514) 387-2541. *Fax:* (514) 387-4244. *E-mail:* hcarrier@qc.aira.com (office).

CARRIERE, Berthold, MMus; Canadian composer and music director; *Director of Music, Stratford Festival;* b. 27 Feb. 1940, Ottawa; s. of Rolland and Berthe Carriere (Paradis); m. Nancy Carpenter 1969; ed Univs of Montréal and Western Ontario; Musical Dir, Banff School of Fine Arts 1968–72; Resident Musical Dir, Theatre London 1972–74, Dir of Music 1976–77, Assoc. Dir 1976; Dir of Music, Stratford Festival 1976–83, 1985–; Musical Dir, Talk of Toronto 1980–82; Conductor/Arranger, Dominion Day Celebrations 1967; Man of the Year, City of Ottawa 1967, Guthrie Award, Stratford Shakespearean Festival 1976, Dora Mavor Moore Musical Dir Award 1981, 1982, 1987. *Address:* Stratford Festival, POB 1013, Stratford, Ont., N5A 6W4 (office); Box 1273, St Mary's, Ont., N0M 2V0, Canada (home). *Website:* www.stratford-festival.on.ca (office).

CARRILLO, Santiago; Spanish journalist and politician; b. 18 Jan. 1915, Gijón; s. of Wenceslao Carrillo and Rosalía Carrillo (née Solares); m. Carmen Menéndez; three s.; Sec.-Gen. de la Juventud Socialista Unificada 1936; Councillor of Public Order, Junta de Defensa de Madrid 1936; Sec.-Gen. Partido Comunista de España 1960–82, expelled from CP 1985; mem. Congress of Deputies 1977–86, Deputy for Madrid 1982–86; Co-founder Workers Party of Spain-Communist Unity (PTE-UC) 1986 (subsequently merged with PSOE); Dir Ahora 1984–; Pres. de Unidad Comunista 1985; Dr hc (Autonomous University of Madrid) 2005. *Publications:* Después de Franco, ¿Qué?, Nuevos enfoques a problemas de hoy, Mañana España, Eurocomunismo y Estado, El año de la Constitución, Memoria de la transición 1983, Le communisme malgré tout 1983. *Address:* c/o Plaza & Janés Editores, Travessera de Gràcia 47–49, 08021 Barcelona, Spain.

CARRILLO ZÜRCHER, Federico, LLB; Costa Rican lawyer, banker and fmr government official; *Vice President, Central American Bank for Economic Integration;* b. 29 Sept. 1964, San José; m.; four c.; ed Austin Community Coll. and Univ. of Texas, USA, Univ. of Costa Rica; Fulbright-Hats Scholarship, Northwestern Univ., Evanston, Ill., USA 1990; worked in investment banks in New York 1992–2000, later Exec. Vice-Pres. Lehman Brothers, Inc. and Salomon Brothers; Man. Costa Rican Stock Exchange 2000–04; Dir Tech. Advisory Cttee on Civil Aviation 2004; Minister of Finance 2004–05; Vice-Pres. Cen. American Bank for Econ. Integration 2005–;. *Address:* Central American Bank for Economic Integration, Headquarters Building, Boulevard Suyapa, Tegucigalpa, Honduras (office). *Telephone:* 240-2243 (office). *Fax:* 240-2185/87 (office). *Website:* www.bcie.org (office).

CARRINGTON, Alan, CBE, MA, PhD, FRS; British chemist and academic; b. 6 Jan. 1934, Greenwich; s. of Albert Carrington and Constance Carrington (née Nelson); m. Noreen H. Taylor 1959; one s. two d.; ed Colfe's Grammar School and Univs of Southampton, Oxford and Cambridge; Asst in Research, Univ. of Cambridge 1960, Asst Dir of Research 1963; Fellow, Downing Coll., Cambridge 1960, Hon. Fellow 1999–; Prof. of Chem., Univ. of Southampton 1967, Royal Soc. Research Prof. 1979–84, 1987–99; Royal Soc. Research Prof. and Fellow, Jesus Coll. Oxford 1984–87; Pres. Faraday Div., Royal Soc. of Chem. 1997–99; Foreign Assoc., NAS 1994; Foreign Hon. mem. American Acad. of Arts and Sciences; Hon. DSc; numerous medals and awards. *Publications:* Introduction to Magnetic Resonance (with A. D. McLachlan) 1967, Microwave Spectroscopy of Free Radicals 1974, Rotational Spectroscopy of Diatomic Molecules 2003; papers in learned journals. *Leisure interests:* family, music, fishing. *Address:* 46 Lakewood Road, Chandler's Ford, Hants., SO53 1EX, England. *Telephone:* (23) 8026-5092 (home). *E-mail:* ac@soton.ac.uk (home).

CARRINGTON, Edwin Wilberforce, MSc; Trinidad and Tobago economist and international organization official; *Secretary-General, Caribbean Community and Common Market (CARICOM);* b. 23 June 1938; m.; two s. one d.; ed Univ. of the West Indies, McGill Univ., Montreal, Canada; Admin. Cadet, Cen. Planning Unit, Prime Minister's Office 1964; Chief of Econs and Statistics, Caribbean Community and Common Market (CARICOM) 1973–76, Dir Trade and Integration Div. 1973–76, Sec.-Gen. CARICOM 1992–; Deputy Sec.-Gen. African, Caribbean and Pacific (ACP) states 1976–85, Sec.-Gen. 1985; High Commr to Guyana 1991; Sec.-Gen. Caribbean Forum ACP states; Duarte Sanchez y Mella, Gran Cruz de Plata (Dominican Repub.) 1993, Trinity Cross (Trinidad and Tobago 2005, Chaconia Medal Gold (Trinidad and Tobago) 1987, Order of Distinction (Belize) 2001, Companion of Honour (Barbados) 2002, Order of Jamaica (Jamaica) 2003, Cacique Crown of Honour (Guyana) 2003, Cacique's Crown of Honour (Guyana) 2004; Dr hc (Univ. of the West Indies) 2005, (Medgar Evers Coll., CUNY) 1995; Pinnacle Award Nat. Coalition of Caribbean Affairs. *Publications:* Industrialization by Invitation: The Case of Trinidad and Tobago 1968, The Solution of Economic Problems through Regional Groupings (jtly), Tourism as a Vehicle for Economic Development 1975. *Address:* Caribbean Community and Common Market, Bank of Guyana Building, PO Box 10827, Turkeyen, Greater Georgetown (office); Colgrain House 205 Camp Street, Georgetown, Guyana (home). *Telephone:* (2) 222-0001/75 (office). *Fax:* (2) 222-0171 (office). *E-mail:* osc@caricom.org (office). *Website:* www.caricom.org (office).

CARRINGTON, 6th Baron; **Peter Alexander Rupert Carrington,** KG, GCMG, CH, MC, PC, JP, DL; British politician and international administrator; b. 6 June 1919, London; s. of 5th Baron Carrington and the Hon. Sybil Marion Colville; m. Iona McClean 1942; one s. two d.; ed Eton Coll. and Royal Mil. Coll., Sandhurst; Grenadier Guards 1939, served in NW Europe; Parl. Sec., Ministry of Agric. 1951–54, Ministry of Defence 1954–56; High Commr in Australia 1956–59; First Lord of the Admiralty 1959–63; Minister without Portfolio (at the Foreign Office), Leader of the House of Lords 1963–64; Leader of the Opposition in the House of Lords 1964–70, 1974–79; Sec. of State for Defence 1970–74, also Minister of Aviation Supply 1971–74; Chair. Conservative Party 1972–74; Sec. of State for Energy Jan.–March 1974, for Foreign and Commonwealth Affairs 1979–82, Minister of Overseas Devt 1979–82; Chair. GEC 1983–84; Sec.-Gen. NATO 1984–88; Chair. Christie's Int. PLC 1988–93 (Dir 1988–); sits in the House of Lords as Lord Carrington of Upton 1999–; Dir The Daily Telegraph 1990–2003; EC Negotiating Cttee on Yugoslavia 1991 (resgnd Aug. 1992); Chancellor Univ. of Reading 1992–2007; Sec. for Foreign Correspondence and Hon. mem. Royal Acad. of Arts 1982–; Chair. Bd Trustees, Victoria and Albert Museum 1983–88; Pres. The Pilgrims 1983–2002, VSO 1993–98; mem. Kissinger Assocn 1982–84, 1988–; Pres. Chiltern Open Air Museum 1983–; Hon. Bencher of the Middle Temple 1983; Hon. Fellow, St Antony's Coll., Oxford 1982–; Chancellor, Order of St Michael and St George 1984–94; Order of the Garter 1994–; Grand Officier, Légion d'honneur; Hon. LLD (Cambridge) 1981, (Leeds) 1981, (Univ. of Philippines) 1982, (Univ. of Aberdeen) 1985, (Sussex) 1989, (Nottingham) 1993, (Birmingham) 1993; Hon. DUniv (Essex) 1983; Hon. Dr Laws (Univ. of SC) 1983, (Harvard Univ.) 1986; Hon. DLit (Reading) 1989; Hon. DSc (Cranfield) 1983; Hon. DCL (Oxford) 2003; Dr hc (Buckingham) 1989; Presidential Medal of Freedom 1988, Four Freedoms Award 1992, Freedom from Fear Award (Franklin Delano Inst.) 1992. *Publication:* Reflect on Things Past: The Memoirs of Lord Carrington 1988. *Address:* House of Lords, Westminster, London, SW1A 0PW (office); 32A Ovington Square, London, SW3 1LR; Manor House, Bledlow, Princes Risborough, Bucks., HP27 9PB, England. *Telephone:* (20) 7584-1476 (London); (1844) 343499 (Bucks.). *Fax:* (20) 7823-9051 (London).

CARRIO, Elisa Maria Avelina ('Lilita'); Argentine politician; *Leader, Afirmación para una República Igualitaria;* b. 1956; four c.; ed Universidad Nacional del Nordeste; fmr Prof. of Law, Chaco; mem. Constitutional Convention 1994; mem. Chamber of Deputies for Prov. of Chaco 1995–; Founder Alternativa por una República de Iguales party (now Afirmación para una República Igualitaria), Pres. 2001–; mem. Comm. of Asuntos Constitutionales, Pres. 2000–01; mem. Comm. of Juicio Político; mem. Women's Leadership Conf. of the Americas, Soc. for Int. Devt Emerging Leaders of the Western Hemisphere Conf., Argentinian Asscn of Constitutional Law, Argentinian Soc. of Philosophy, Argentine Soc. of Political Science; Corresp. mem. Inst. of Parl. Law; Premio Parlamentario 1996, 1997, 1998; Dipl. Al mérito 'Konex' 1998, 'Actitud de Vida' Award, Constitutional Convention Gold Medal; Día Internacional de la Mujer Award, NEXO Award 1998. *Publications include:* Interpretando la Constitución, Acerca de la praxis interpretativa Constitucional, Recurso de Inconstitucionalidad Local (jtly); more than 50 articles on law, sociology and political science. *Address:* Afirmación para una República Igualitaria, Avda Callao 143, Buenos Aires, Argentina (office). *E-mail:* arinacional@ari.org.ar (office). *Website:* www.ari.org.ar (office).

CARRIÓN MENA, Francisco, PhD; Ecuadorean diplomatist and academic; b. 8 April 1953, Quito; ed Univ. Cen. del Ecuador, Quito; joined Ecuadorian Foreign Service 1974; Counsellor, Embassy in Paris 1982–88; Diplomatic Adviser to Pres. of Repub. 1988–91; Minister, Embassy in London 1991–96; Under-Sec., Ministry of Foreign Affairs 1996–98; Vice-Minister of Foreign Affairs 1998–2000; Amb. to Spain 2000–05; Minister of Foreign Affairs 2005–07; currently Researcher, Facultad Latinoamericana de Ciencias Sociales (FLACSO); Prof. of Int. Relations and Politics, Univ. Cen. del Ecuador and Diplomatic Acad. of Quito 1988–92; Guest Lecturer, Univ. de Salamanca, Spain 2001, Univ. de Alcalá de Henares 2002; mem. Cttee on Protection of Rights of all Migrant Workers and Mems of their Families, Int. Service for Human Rights 2004–07; columnist, El Comercio newspaper, Quito. *Publications:* articles in scholarly and popular journals. *Address:* c/o Ministry of Foreign Affairs, Avda 10 de Agosto y Carrión, Quito, Ecuador (office).

CARRIZALES RENGIFO, Col Rámon Alonso; Venezuelan army officer (retd) and politician; *Vice-President and Minister of National Defence;* b. 8 Nov. 1952, Zaraza, Guarico; ed Venezuelan Acad. of Mil. Sciences; fmr Col of Venezuelan Armed Forces, retd 1994; Chair. Fondo Nacional de Transporte Urbano (Fontur) 2000–04; Minister of Infrastructure 2004–07, of Housing 2007–08, of Nat. Defence 2009–; Vice-Pres. of Venezuela 2008–. *Address:* Central Information Office of the Presidency, Torre Oeste 18°, Parque Central, Caracas 1010, Venezuela (office). *Telephone:* (2) 572-7110 (office). *Fax:* (2) 572-2675 (office).

CARROLL, Cynthia, MSc, MBA; American metal industry executive; *Chief Executive, Anglo American plc;* ed Univ. of Kansas, Harvard Univ.; fmr Sr Petroleum Geologist, Amoco, USA; joined Rolled Products Group, Alcan 1988, apptd Gen. Man. Foil Products, USA 1991, Man. Dir Aughinish Alumina, Ireland, Pres. Bauxite, Alumina and Speciality Chemicals Group 1998–2002, Pres. and CEO Alcan Primary Metal Group 2002–06, also Officer, Alcan Inc., Montreal; Chief Exec. Anglo American plc 2007–, Chair. Exec. Cttee, Chief Exec.'s Cttee, mem. Safety Cttee, Sustainable Devt Cttee; fmr mem. Bd of Dirs AngloGold Ashanti Ltd, Sara Lee Corpn; Dir (non-exec.) BP plc, Anglo Platinum Ltd, De Beers; ranked by Forbes magazine amongst 100 Most Powerful Women (seventh) 2007, (fifth) 2008, ranked by Fortune Magazine amongst 50 Most Powerful Women in Business outside the US (first) 2007, ranked by the Financial Times amongst Top 25 Businesswomen in Europe (second) 2007. *Address:* Anglo American plc, 20 Carlton House Terrace, London, SW1Y 5AN, England (office). *Telephone:* (20) 7968-8888 (office). *Fax:* (20) 7968-8500 (office). *E-mail:* info@angloamerican.co.uk (office). *Website:* www.angloamerican.co.uk (office).

CARROLL, Philip J., MS; American oil industry executive (retd); b. 1937; m. Charlene Carroll; three c.; ed Loyola Univ., Tulane Univ., New Orleans; began career with Shell Oil Co. as petroleum engineer 1961, held positions in exploration and production business 1970s, Man. Dir Shell Int. Gas and Int. Petroleum, London, UK –1986, Head of Admin, Shell Oil Co., Houston, Tex. 1986–93, Pres. and CEO US Operations, Shell Group 1993–98; Chair. and Fluor (eng and construction firm), Calif. 1998–2002; apptd Chair. and CEO, advisory bd for Iraqi Oil Ministry 2003; Dir Energy Conservation Div., US Dept of Commerce 1971–74; fmr Exec. Dir Nat. Industrial Energy Council; mem. Bd of Dirs Vulcan Materials, BAE Systems PLC, London 2005–; dir numerous petroleum industry asscns, professional eng orgs, educ. insts and philanthropic and civic groups. *Address:* 2001 Kirby, #1004, Houston, TX 77019, USA (office). *Telephone:* (713) 522-6099. *Fax:* (713) 522-6062.

CARRON, René Joseph; French banking executive; *Chairman, Crédit Agricole SA;* b. 13 June 1942, Yenne, Savoie; s. of Albert Carron and Claudine Philippe Carron (née Genoud); m. Françoise Dupasquier 1963; three s. one d.; fmr dairy farmer in Yenne; Pres. Yenne br. Crédit Agricole 1981–, Pres. regional br. in Savoie 1992, all Savoie 1994, mem. Bureau 1995–, Pres. Fédération nationale du crédit agricole 2000–, Dir 1999–, Vice-Pres. Caisse nationale de crédit agricole (CNCA, renamed Crédit Agricole SA 2000) 2000–, mem. Supervisory Council, Crédit Agricole Indosuez 2000–, Chair. Crédit Agricole SA 2002–; Chair. SAS La Boétie 2001–; Pres. Savoie Chamber of Agric. 1983–92, Savoie 92 (asscn to promote Winter Olympics in Albertville 1992) 1988–92, Mission prospective du département de la Savoie 1988–98, Groupe d'étude et de mobilisation Espaces ruraux 1991, Steering Cttee for Savoie Strategic Plan Year 2000 1991–98; Counsellor Banque de France de la Savoie 1991– (mem. 1992–, mem. Perm. Comm. 1992–); Vice-Pres. Conseil géneral of Savoie 1995–98; Mayor of Yenne 1995–; mem. Econ. and Social Council 2000–, Man. Bd. Groupement Européen des Banques Coopératives; Dir Soc. de banque de financement pour le commerce (Sofinco); Chevalier, Légion d'honneur, Chevalier, Ordre nat. du Mérite, Officier du Mérite agricole. *Address:* Crédit Agricole SA, 91–93 boulevard Pasteur, 75015 Paris, France (office). *Telephone:* 1-43-23-52-02 (office). *Fax:* 1-43-23-34-48 (office). *E-mail:* info@credit-agricole-sa.fr (office). *Website:* www.credit-agricole-sa.fr (office).

CARSBERG, Sir Bryan (Victor), Kt, MSc, MA; British public servant and academic; *Chairman, Pensions Compensation Board;* b. 3 Jan. 1939, London; s. of Alfred Victor and Maryllia Ciceley Carsberg (née Collins); m. Margaret Linda Graham 1960; two d.; ed London School of Econs; practice in Calif. 1962–64; Lecturer in Accounting, LSE 1964–68, Arthur Andersen Prof. of Accounting 1981–87, Visiting Prof. 1987–89; Visiting Lecturer, Grad. School of Business, Univ. of Chicago 1968–69; Prof. of Accounting, Univ. of Manchester 1969–78; Visiting Prof. of Business Admin., Univ. of California, Berkeley 1974; Asst Dir Research and Tech. Activities, US Financial Accounting Standards Bd 1978–81; Dir of Research, Inst. of W. B. Peat Medal and Prize (Inst. of Chartered Accountants, England) in England and Wales 1981–87; Dir-Gen. of Telecommunications, Oftel 1984–92; mem. Accounting Standards Bd 1990–94 (Vice-Chair. 1990–92); Dir-Gen. of Fair Trading 1992–95; Sec. Gen. Int. Accounting Standards Cttee 1995–2001; Chair. Pensions Compensation Bd 2001–04; Dir Nynex Cable Communications 1996–97, Cable & Wireless Communications 1997–2000, RM plc 2002–, Philip Allan (publrs); Chair. MLL Telecoms Ltd 1999–; mem. Bd Radio Communications Agency 1990–92; mem. Council Univ. of Surrey 1990–92, Loughborough Univ. 1999– (Chair. 2001–); apptd by Royal Inst. of Chartered Surveyors to review comsumer protection 2004; apptd Chair. of independently run review of UK residential property sector 2007; Hon. Fellow, LSE; Hon. DSc (East Anglia) 1992; Hon. DLitt (Loughborough) 1994; Hon. D Univ. (Essex) 1995; Hon. LLD (Bath) 1990; Dr hc (Nottingham Trent) 2008; Inst. Medal, W. B. Peat Medal and Prize (Inst. of Chartered Accountants, England); Chartered Accountants Founding Socs Centenary Award 1988, Blaew Prize for Telecommunications 1992, Sempier Award, Int. Fed. of Accountants 2002. *Publications:* An Introduction to Mathematical Programming for Accountants 1969, Analysis for Investment Decisions 1974, Economics of Business Decisions 1975 and others. *Leisure interests:* running, theatre, music, opera. *Address:* c/o Royal Institution of Chartered Surveyors, Surveyor Court, Westwood Way, Coventry, CV4 8JE, England. *E-mail:* b.carsberg@ntlworld.com.

CARSON, Anne, BA, MA, PhD; Canadian academic, poet and writer; *Professor, Department of English, University of Michigan;* b. 21 June 1950, Toronto, Ont.; ed St Michael's Coll., Univ. of Toronto, Univ. of St Andrews, Scotland; Prof. of Classics, Univ. of Calgary 1979–80, Princeton Univ. 1980–87, Emory Univ. 1987–88; fmr John MacNaughton Prof. of Classics, McGill Univ. and Dir of Grad. Studies, Classics; currently Prof., Dept of English, Univ. of Michigan; Guggenheim Fellowship 1999; John D. and Catherine T. MacArthur Foundation Fellowship 2001; Anna-Maria Kellen Fellow, American Acad., Berlin, Germany 2007; Lannan Literary Award 1996, Pushcart Prize for Poetry 1997. *Publications include:* Eros the Bittersweet: An Essay 1986, Short Talks 1992, Plainwater 1995, Glass, Irony and God 1995, Autobiography of Red 1998, Economy of the Unlost 1999, Men in the Off Hours (Griffin Poetry Prize 2001) 2000, The Beauty of the Husband (Poetry Book Soc. T. S. Eliot Prize 2001) 2001, Sophocles' Electra 2001, If Not, Winter: Fragments of Sappho (trans.) 2002, Decreation 2005, Grief Lessons: Four Plays by Euripides (trans. 2006; contribs to anthologies and journals. *Address:* Department of English, University of Michigan, 435 South State Street, 3143 Angell Hall, Ann Arbor, MI 48109, USA (office); 5900 Esplanade Avenue, Montréal, PQ H2T 3A3, Canada (home). *Telephone:* (734) 763-2265 (office). *E-mail:* carsona@umich.edu (office); decreation@hotmail.com. *Website:* www.lsa.umich.edu/english (office).

CARSON, William Hunter, OBE; British thoroughbred horse breeder and fmr professional jockey; b. 16 Nov. 1942, Stirling, Scotland; s. of Thomas Whelan and Mary Hay Carson (née Hunter); m. 1st Carole Jane Sutton 1962 (divorced 1979); three s.; m. 2nd Elaine Williams 1982; ed Riverside School, Stirling, Scotland; apprentice with Capt. Gerald Armstrong 1957–62; rode first winner Pinker's Pond at Catterick 1962; first jockey to Lord Derby 1968, to Bernard van Cutsem 1971–75, to Maj. Dick Hern 1977–89, to HM The Queen 1977; champion jockey 1972, 1973, 1978, 1980, 1983; rode the winners of 18 English Classics, eight Irish Classics and 68 English Group One races; rode six winners at one meeting July 1990; best horses ridden Nashwan and Dayjur; bred and rode St Leger winner Minster Son 1988; 3,828 career winners in UK (1997); retd 1997 as fourth-most successful ever UK jockey; racing pundit, BBC 1997–; Owner Minster Stud; Dir Swindon Town Football Club 1997–98, Head of Public Relations 1997–, Chair. 2001–; Dr hc (Stirling). *Publication:* Willie Carson Up Front: A Racing Autobiography 1993. *Leisure interests:* golf, football. *Address:* Minster House, Barnsley, Cirencester, Glos., GL7 5DZ, England. *Telephone:* (1285) 658919. *Fax:* (1285) 885355. *Website:* williecarson.com.

CARSTENS, Agustín, BA, MA, PhD; Mexican economist and government official; *Secretary of Finance and Public Credit;* b. 1958, Mexico City; m. Catherine Mansell; ed Instituto Tecnológico Autónomo de México, Univ. of Chicago, USA; Intern, Banco de México 1983; left for studies in USA; rejoined Banco de México 1986, Treas. 1987, Dir-Gen. Econ. Research and Chief of Staff in Gov.'s office 1991–94, Chief Economist and Research Dir 1994–98; Alt. Gov. for Mexico at IDB and World Bank 1998–2000; Deputy Sec. of Finance 2000–03, organized UN Conf. on Financing for Devt, Monterrey, meetings of Group of 20 2002; Second Deputy Man. Dir IMF 2003–06; Sec. of Finance and Public Credit 2006–. *Publications:* has published articles in collections edited by Fed. Reserve Bank of Boston, Univ. of London, OECD, IMF and World Bank and in journals including Columbia Journal of World Business, American Economic Review, Journal of Asian Economics, Journal of International Finance, Cuadernos Económicos del ICE (Spain) and Gaceta de Economía del ITAM (Mexico). *Address:* Secretariat of State for Finance and Public Credit, Palacio Nacional, Primer Patio Mariano, 3°, Of. 3045, Col. Centro, Del. Cuauhtémoc, 06000 Mexico City, DF, Mexico (office). *Telephone:* (55) 3688-2655 (office). *Fax:* (55) 3688-1142 (office). *E-mail:* secretario@hacienda.gob.mx (office). *Website:* www.hacienda.gob.mx (office).

CARSWELL, Baron (Life Peer), cr. 2004, of Killeen in the County of Down; **Robert Douglas Carswell,** PC; British judge; b. 28 June 1934, Belfast, Northern Ireland; s. of Alan E. Carswell and Nance E. Carswell; m. Romayne Winifred Ferris 1961; two d.; ed Royal Belfast Academical Inst., Pembroke Coll., Oxford, Univ. of Chicago Law School, USA; called to the Bar, NI 1957, to

English Bar, Gray's Inn 1972; Counsel to Attorney-Gen. for NI 1970–71; QC 1971; Sr Crown Counsel for NI 1979–84; Judge High Court of Justice in NI 1984–93; Lord Justice of Appeal, Supreme Court of Judicature 1993–97; Lord Chief Justice of NI 1997–2004; Lord of Appeal in Ordinary 2004–; Chancellor, Dioceses of Armagh and of Down and Dromore 1990–97; Chair. Council of Law Reporting for NI 1987–97, Law Reform Advisory Cttee for NI 1989–97, Distinction and Meritorious Service Awards Cttee, DHSS 1995–97; Pres. NI Scout Council 1993–; Pro-Chancellor, Chair. Council, Univ. of Ulster 1984–94; Hon. DLitt (Ulster) 1994. *Publications:* Trustee Acts (NI) 1964; articles in legal periodicals. *Leisure interests:* golf, hillwalking, music, architecture, antiques and conservation, wildlife. *Address:* House of Lords, Westminster, London, SW1A 0PW, England (office). *Telephone:* (20) 7219-8114 (office).

CARTELLIERI, Ulrich; German lawyer and banker; b. 21 Sept. 1937; ed Univs of Munich and Cologne; joined Deutsche Bank AG, Frankfurt 1970, Man. Dir 1975–77, CEO 1977 82, Chair. Chair. Supervisory Bd European Asian Bank 1982, then Chair. Deutsche Bank (Asia Credit) Ltd, Singapore, DB Finance (Hong Kong) Ltd, Hong Kong; AG 1990–98, mem. Deutsche Bank Man. Bd 1981–97, also served as Deputy Chair. Deutsche Bank North America, mem. Supervisory Bd 1997; mem. Supervisory Bd Robert Bosch GmbH; fmr mem. Supervisory Bd Deutsche Solvay-Werke GmbH, Solingen, Deutsche Telephonwerke und Kabelindustrie AG, Berlin, Euro-Pacific Finance Corpn Ltd, Melbourne, Girmes-Werke AG, Grefrath-Oedt, Th. Goldschmidt AG, Essen, Wilhelm Karmann GmbH, Osnabrück, Thyssen Edelstahlwerke AG, Düsseldorf, G. M. Pfaff AG, Kaiserslautern; mem. Bd of Dirs (non-exec.) BAE Systems; fmr Pres. German Soc. on Foreign Affairs; fmr German Co-Chair. German-Japanese Forum. *Address:* c/o Board of Directors, BAE Systems, Stirling Square, Carlton Gardens, London, SW1Y 5AD, England (office). *Telephone:* (1252) 373232 (office). *Fax:* (1252) 383121 (office). *Website:* www.baesystems.com (office).

CARTER, Ashton B., BA, PhD; American academic; *Co-Director, Preventive Defense Project and Ford Foundation Professor of Science and International Affairs, Harvard University;* b. 24 Sept. 1954, Philadelphia; m. Ava Clayton Spencer 1983; one s. one d.; ed Yale Univ., Univ. of Oxford, UK; early career positions at MIT, US Congressional Office of Tech. Assessment, Rockefeller Univ.; served as Asst Sec. of Defense for Int. Security Policy, US Dept of Defense, Washington, DC 1993–96, responsible for nat. security policy towards states of fmr Soviet Union, US nuclear missile defense programs and int. arms control, nominated for US Under-Sec. of Defense for Acquisition, Tech. and Logistics 2009; currently Co-Dir Preventive Defense Project and Ford Foundation Prof. of Science and Int. Affairs, Harvard Univ.; Sr Pnr, Global Technology Partners; Chair. Advisory Bd MIT Lincoln Labs; Chair. Editorial Bd International Security (journal); mem. Bd of Dirs Mitretek Systems; consultant to US Dept of Defense, Goldman Sachs, Mitre Corpn; mem. Defense Science Bd, Defense Policy Bd, Draper Lab. Corpn, Aspen Strategy Group, Council on Foreign Relations, American Physical Soc., IISS, Nat. Cttee on US-China Relations; Fellow, American Acad. of Arts and Sciences; mem. American Acad. of Diplomacy 2009–; Ten Outstanding Young Americans 1987, US Dept of Defense Distinguished Service Medal (twice), Defense Intelligence Medal. *Publications:* Directed Energy Missile Defense in Space 1984, Ballistic Missile Defense 1984, Managing Nuclear Operations 1987, Soviet Nuclear Fusion: Control of the Nuclear Arsenal in a Disintegrating Soviet Union 1991, Beyond Spinoff: Military and Commercial Technologies in a Changing World 1992, A New Concept of Cooperative Security 1992, Cooperative Denuclearization: From Pledges to Deeds 1993, Preventive Defense (jtly) 1997, Keeping the Edge: Managing Defense for the Future (co-ed.) 2001. *Address:* John F. Kennedy School of Government, Harvard University, Littauer 374, 79 John F. Kennedy Street, Cambridge, MA, 02138, USA (office). *Telephone:* (617) 495-1405 (office). *Fax:* (617) 495-9250 (office). *E-mail:* ashton_carter@harvard.edu (office). *Website:* www.ksg.harvard.edu (office).

CARTER, Brandon, DSc, FRS; British theoretical physicist and academic; *Director of Research, Laboratoire de l'Univers Théorique, Centre National de la Recherche Scientifique (CNRS);* b. 26 May 1942, Sydney, Australia; s. of Harold B. Carter and Mary Brandon-Jones; m. Lucette Defrise 1969; three d.; ed George Watson's Coll., Edinburgh, Univ. of St Andrews, Univ. of Cambridge (Pembroke Coll.); Research Fellow, Pembroke Coll., Cambridge 1967–72; staff mem., Inst. of Astronomy, Cambridge 1968–72; Asst Lecturer, Dept of Applied Math. and Theoretical Physics, Univ. of Cambridge 1973, Lecturer 1974; Maître de Recherche, CNRS, Paris 1975–85, Dir-Adjoint, Group d'Astrophysique Relativiste, Observatoire de Paris-Meudon 1975–82, Dir 1987–2001, Dir of Research, Laboratoire de l'Univers Théorique 2002–. *Publications:* Global Structure of the Kerr Family of Gravitational Fields 1968, Black Hole Equilibrium States 1973, Large Number Coincidences and the Anthropic Principle in Cosmology 1974, The General Theory of the Mechanical Electromagnetic and Thermodynamic Properties of Black Holes 1979, The Anthropic Principle and its Implications for Biological Evolution 1983, Covariant Mechanics of Simple and Conducting Strings and Membranes 1990. *Address:* L.U.T.H., Observatoire de Paris-Meudon, 92195 Meudon (office); 19 rue de la Borne au Diable, 92310 Sèvres, France (home). *Telephone:* 1-45-07-74-34 (office). *Fax:* 1-45-07-79-71 (office). *E-mail:* brandon.carter@obspm.fr (office). *Website:* www.luth.obspm.fr (office).

CARTER, Elliott, AB, AM; American composer; b. 11 Dec. 1908, New York; s. of Elliott Carter and Florence Carter (née Chambers); m. Helen Frost-Jones 1939 (died 2003); one s.; ed Harvard Univ., Ecole Normale de Musique, Paris; Musical Dir Ballet Caravan 1937–39; critic, Modern Music 1937–42; tutor, St John's Coll., Annapolis 1939–41; teacher of composition, Peabody Conservatory 1946–48, Columbia Univ. 1948–50, Queen's Coll. (New York) 1955–56; Prof. of Music, Yale Univ. 1960–61; Prof., Dept of Composition, Juilliard School, New York 1966–82; Andrew White Prof.-at-Large, Cornell Univ. 1967; mem. Bd of Trustees, American Acad., Rome; mem. Int. Soc. for Contemporary Music, Dir 1946–52, Pres. American Section 1952, Nat. Inst. of Arts and Letters; mem. American Acad. of Arts and Sciences; Commdr, Ordre des Arts et des Lettres; hon. degrees from Swarthmore Coll. and Princeton Univ. 1969, Univs of Harvard, Yale and Boston 1970, Univ. of Cambridge, UK 1983; First Prize, Liège Int. Music Competition 1953, Prix de Rome 1953, Sibelius Medal, Harriet Cohen Foundation 1960, Ernst Von Siemens Prize, Munich 1981, Gold Medal, Nat. Inst. of Arts and Letters 1971, Handel Medallion of New York 1978, awarded Nat. Medal of Art by Pres. Reagan 1985, Gold Medal, Royal Philharmonic Soc. 1996. *Works include:* orchestral: Symphony No. 1 1942, Variations for Orchestra 1955, Double Concerto (New York Critics' Circle Award 1961) 1961, Piano Concerto 1965, Concerto for Orchestra 1969, Symphony of Three Orchestras 1977, Oboe Concerto 1987, 3 Occasions for Orchestra 1989, Violin Concerto 1990, Clarinet Concerto 1996, Symphonia 1998, Asko Concerto 2000, Cello Concerto 2001, Boston Concerto 2002; chamber music: Quartet for Four Saxophones (American Composers' Alliance Prize 1943), Elegy 1943, Sonata for Cello and Piano, Woodwind Quintet 1948, Sonata for Flute, Oboe, Cello and Harpsichord 1952, Brass Quintet 1974, five String Quartets (Pulitzer Prize for Second String Quartet, for Third String Quartet 1973) 1951–93, Triple Duo 1982, Penthode 1985, Oboe Quartet for Heinz Holliger 2001; vocal music: A Mirror on Which to Dwell 1975, In Sleep In Thunder 1983, Of Rewaking 2002; choral music: The Defense of Corinth 1949; instrumental music: Piano Sonata 1946, Night Fantasies for piano 1980, A Six-letter Letter for English Horn; stage works: Pocahontas 1939, The Minotaur 1947, What Next? (opera) 1999, and numerous others. *Leisure interests:* literature, art. *Address:* Boosey & Hawkes Inc., 35 East 21st Street, New York, NY 10010, USA (office).

CARTER, (Edward) Graydon; Canadian magazine editor; *Editor-in-Chief, Vanity Fair;* b. 14 July 1949; s. of E. P. Carter and Margaret Ellen Carter; m. Anna Scott 2005; three s. one d.; ed Carleton Univ., Univ. of Ottawa; Ed. The Canadian Review 1973–77; writer, Time 1978–83, Life 1983–86; Founder, Ed. Spy 1986–91; Ed. New York Observer 1991–92; Ed.-in-Chief, Vanity Fair 1992–; Hon. Ed. Harvard Lampoon 1989; Advertising Age Editor of the Year 1996, Nat. Magazine Award for Gen. Excellence 1997, 1999, Nat. Magazine Award for Photography 2000, 2002, Nat. Magazine Award for Reviews and Criticism 2003. *Television as executive producer:* 9/11 (CBS) 2002. *Film as producer:* The Kid Stays in the Picture 2002. *Publications:* Vanity Fair's Hollywood 2000, What We've Lost 2004, Oscar Night: 75 Years of Hollywood Parties 2004, Vanity Fair Portraits 2008. *Leisure interest:* fly fishing. *Address:* Vanity Fair, Condé Nast Building, 4 Times Square, New York, NY 10036-6522, USA (office). *Website:* www.vanityfair.com (office).

CARTER, James (Jimmy) Earl, Jr, BSc; American politician, international political consultant, farmer and fmr head of state; *Chairman, Carter Center;* b. 1 Oct. 1924, Plains, Ga; s. of the late James Earl Carter, Sr and Lillian Gordy; m. Eleanor Rosalynn Smith 1946; three s. one d.; ed Plains High School, Georgia Southwestern Coll., Georgia Inst. of Tech., US Naval Acad., Annapolis, Md, Union Coll., New York State; served in USN 1946–53, attained rank of Lt (submarine service); peanut farmer, warehouseman 1953–77, businesses include Carter Farms, Carter Warehouses, Plains, Ga; State Senator, Ga 1962–66; Gov. of Georgia 1971–74; Pres. of USA 1977–81; Distinguished Prof., Emory Univ., Atlanta 1982–; leader of int. observer teams Panama 1989, Nicaragua 1990, Dominican Repub. 1990, Haiti 1990; hosted peace negotiations in Ethiopia 1989; visited Democratic People's Repub. of Korea (in pvt. capacity) June 1994; negotiator in Haitian crisis Sept. 1994; visit to Bosnia Dec. 1994; f. Carter Presidential Center 1982; est. Jimmy and Rosalynn Carter Work Project for Habitat for Humanity International 1984; Chair. Bd of Trustees, Carter Center Inc. 1986–, Carter-Menil Human Rights Foundation 1986–, Global 2000 Inc. 1986–, Council of Freely Elected Heads of Govt 1986–, Council of Int. Negotiation Network 1991–; mem. Sumter Co., Ga, School Bd 1955–62 (Chair. 1960–62), Americus and Sumter Co. Hosp. Authority 1956–70, Sumter Co. Library Bd 1961; Pres. Plains Devt Corpn 1963; Georgia Planning Asscn 1968; Dir Ga Crop Improvement Asscn 1957–63 (Pres. 1961); Chair. West Cen. Ga Area Planning and Devt Comm. 1964; State Chair. March of Dimes 1968–70; Dist Gov. Lions Club 1968–69; Chair. Congressional Campaign Cttee, Democratic Nat. Cttee 1974; Democrat; several hon. degrees; Ansel Adams Conservation Award, Wilderness Society 1982, World Methodist Peace Award 1984, Albert Schweitzer Prize for Humanitarianism 1987, Onassis Foundation Award 1991, Notre Dame Univ. Award 1992, Matsunaga Medal of Peace 1993, J. William Fulbright Prize for Int. Understanding 1994, shared Houphouët Boigny Peace Prize, UNESCO 1995, UNICEF Int. Child Survival Award (jtly with Rosalynn Carter) 1999, Presidential Medal of Freedom 1999, Eisenhower Medallion 2000, Nobel Peace Prize 2002. *Publications:* Why Not the Best? 1975, A Government as Good as Its People 1977, Keeping Faith: Memoirs of a President 1982, The Blood of Abraham: Insights into the Middle East 1985, Everything to Gain: Making the Most of the Rest of Your Life 1987, An Outdoor Journal 1988, Turning Point: A Candidate, a State and a Nation Come of Age 1992, Always a Reckoning (poems) 1995, Sources of Strength 1997, The Virtues of Ageing 1998, An Hour Before Daylight 2001, The Hornet's Nest (novel) 2003, Our Endangered Values 2005, Palestine: Peace Not Apartheid 2006, We Can Have Peace in the Holy Land: A Plan that Will Work 2009. *Leisure interests:* reading, tennis. *Address:* The Carter Center, 453 Freedom Parkway, 1 Copenhill Avenue NE, Atlanta, GA 30307, USA (office). *Telephone:* (404) 420-5100 (office). *Fax:* (404) 420-5196 (office). *E-mail:* carterweb@emory.edu (office). *Website:* www.cartercenter.org (office).

CARTER, Marshall, BS, MS, MA; American business executive; *Chairman of the Board of Directors, NYSE Group Inc.;* b. 23 April 1940, Newport News, Va; m. Mary Meehan 1964; one s. one d.; ed US Mil. Acad. at West Point, US Naval

Postgraduate School, Monterey, George Washington Univ.; fmr Marine Corps officer; White House Fellow, State Dept and Agency for Int. Devt 1975–76; with Chase Manhattan Bank –1992; Chair. and CEO State Street Bank and Trust Co., State Street Corp. 1992–2001; Fellow, Center for Public Leadership, Kennedy School of Govt, Harvard Univ. 2001–05; Lecturer in leadership and man., Sloan School of Man., MIT; mem. Bd of Dirs New York Stock Exchange 2003–, Chair. 2005–06, Chair. NYSE Group Inc. 2006–; Chair. Bd of Trustees, Boston Medical Center; Fellow, American Acad. of Arts and Sciences 2006; Navy Cross, Bronze Star, Purple Heart. *Address:* NYSE Group Inc., 11 Wall Street, New York, NY 10005, USA (office). *Telephone:* (212) 656-3000 (office). *Website:* www.nyse.com (office).

CARTER, Stephen, LLB; British business executive; *Chief of Strategy and Principal Adviser to Prime Minister;* b. 12 Feb. 1964, Scotland; m. Anna Carter; two c.; ed Currie High School, Edinburgh, Univ. of Aberdeen; began career as trainee, J. Walter Thompson UK (advertising agency), Man.-Dir 1995–97, CEO 1997–2000; Man.-Dir of UK Operations, NTL (cable TV co.) 2000–02; CEO Ofcom 2003–06; CEO Brunswick Group LLP 2006–08 (resgnd); Dir (non-exec.) Royal Mail 2007–08 (resgnd); Chief of Strategy and Prin. Adviser to Prime Minister 2008–; Chair. Ashridge Business School; Gov. Royal Shakespeare Co. *Leisure interest:* running. *Address:* Prime Minister's Office, 10 Downing Street, London, SW1A 2AA, England (office). *Telephone:* (20) 7270-3000 (office). *Fax:* (20) 7295-0918 (office). *Website:* www.number10.gov .uk (home).

CARTER, Stephen Lisle, BA, JD; American academic and lawyer; *William Nelson Cromwell Professor of Law, Yale University;* b. 1954, Washington, DC; m.; c.; ed Stanford and Yale Univs; fmr Note Ed. Yale Law Journal; admitted to Bar, Washington, DC 1981; law clerk, Judge Spottswood W. Robinson III, US Court of Appeal, Washington, DC 1979–80; law clerk, Justice Thurgood Marshall, US Supreme Court 1980–81; Assoc. Shea & Gardner, Washington, DC 1981–82; Asst Prof. of Law, Yale Univ. 1982–84, Assoc. Prof. 1984–85, Prof. 1986–91, William Nelson Cromwell Prof. of Law 1991–; Official Adviser to US Pres. Bill Clinton 1993; Hon. LLD (Univ. of Notre Dame) 1996. *Publications include:* Reflections of an Affirmative Action Baby 1991, The Culture of Disbelief 1993, The Confirmation Mess 1994, Integrity 1996, The Dissent of the Governed 1998, Civility 1998, God's Name in Vain 2000, The Emperor of Ocean Park 2002, New England White 2007, Palace Council 2008, Jericho's Fall 2009. *Address:* Yale Law School, POB 208215, New Haven, CT 06520 (office); c/o Knopf Publishing (Author Mail), 1745 Broadway, New York, NY 10019, USA (office). *E-mail:* stephen.carter@yale.edu (office). *Website:* www.law.yale.edu/outside/html/home/index.htm (office).

CARTIER, Jean-Albert; French theatre director; b. 15 May 1930, Marseille; s. of Albert Cartier and Myriem Bordes; m. Solange Ottavy 1959; two d.; ed Lycée Perier, Marseille and Ecole du Louvre; art critic, Combat and numerous reviews; artistic collaborator, France-Inter; arranged several exhbns for Marseille Museum; participated Paris Biennale 1959, 1961, 1963, 1965; Founder and Dir Asscn technique pour l'action culturelle 1966–72; Creator Ballet-Théâtre contemporain, Centre chorégraphique nat. 1968–72; Dir Centre chorégraphique et lyrique nat. 1972; Dir Angers Municipal Theatre 1972–78; Founder and Dir Anjou Arts Festival 1975–77; Creator and Dir Ballet-Théâtre français de Nancy 1978–87; Dir-Gen. Grand Théâtre de Nancy 1979–81, Dir Théâtre Musical, Paris-Châtelet 1980–88; Dir Festival of Paris 1988, 1989, 1991; Dir Théâtre Nat. de l'Opéra de Paris 1988, Gen. Man. 1989–91; Dir of Music, Radio France 1991–94; Dir-Gen. L'Opéra de Nice 1994–97; Creator and Dir Europa Danse 1999–; Chevalier, Légion d'honneur, des Arts et Lettres; Officier, Ordre nat. du Mérite. *Publication:* L'oeuvre du peintre POUGNY (two vols). *Address:* Europa Danse, 18 rue de l'Hôtel de Ville, 75004 Paris (office); 8 rue Vernier, 06000 Nice; 24 rue Saint-Paul, 75004 Paris, France. *Telephone:* 1-42-77-31-34 (office); 1-44-54-06-48 (home). *Fax:* 1-42-77-32-34 (office).

CARTLEDGE, Sir Bryan George, KCMG; British diplomatist (retd) and college principal; b. 10 June 1931; s. of Eric Cartledge and Phyllis Shaw; m. 1st Ruth Hylton Gass 1960 (dissolved), one s. one d.; m. 2nd Freda Gladys Newcombe 1994 (died 2001); ed Hurstpierpoint and St John's Coll., Cambridge; served Queen's Royal Regt 1950–51; Commonwealth Fund Fellow, Stanford Univ., Calif. 1956–57; Research Fellow, St Antony's Coll., Oxford 1958–59; joined Foreign Service 1960, served Foreign Office 1960–61, British Embassy, Stockholm 1961–63, Moscow 1963–66, Diplomatic Service Admin. Office 1966–68, Tehran 1968–70, Harvard Univ. 1971–72, Counsellor, Moscow 1972–75, Head of E European and Soviet Dept, FCO 1975–77, Pvt. Sec. (Overseas Affairs) to Prime Minister 1977–79, Amb. to Hungary 1980–83, Asst UnderSec. of State, FCO 1983–84, Deputy Sec. of the Cabinet 1984–85, Amb. to USSR 1985–88; Prin. Linacre Coll., Oxford 1988–96; Hon. Fellow, St John's Coll., Cambridge 1985, St Antony's Coll., Oxford 1987, Linacre Coll., Oxford 1996. *Publications:* Monitoring the Environment (ed.) 1992, Energy and the Environment (ed.) 1993, Health and the Environment (ed.) 1994, Population and the Environment (ed.) 1995, Transport and the Environment (ed.) 1996, Mind, Brain and Environment (ed.) 1997. *Address:* 52 Middle Way, Oxford, OX2 7LG, England.

CARTWRIGHT, General James E., MA; American military officer; *Vice-Chairman, Joint Chiefs of Staff;* ed Maxwell Air Command and Staff Coll., Naval War Coll., Newport, RI, MIT; commissioned Second Lt in US Marine Corps 1971, Naval Flight Officer, graduated 1973, Naval Aviator, graduated 1977, operational assignments as an NFO in the F-4 and as a pilot in the F-4, OA-4 and F/A-18, has served in numerous leadership positions including Commdr Marine Aviation Logistics Squadron 12 1989–90, Marine Fighter Attack Squadron 232 1992, Marine Aircraft Group 31 1994–96, Deputy Commanding Gen., Marine Forces Atlantic 1999–2000, Commanding Gen., First Marine Aircraft Wing 2000–02; Commdr US Strategic Command, Offutt Air Force Base, Neb. 2004–07, command areas include full-spectrum global strike, space operations, computer network operations, Dept of Defense information operations, strategic warning, integrated missile defense, combating weapons of mass destruction; staff assignments have included Asst Program Man. for Eng, F/A-18 Naval Air Systems Command 1986–89, Deputy Aviation Plans, Policy and Budgets HQ, US Marine Corps 1993–94, Directorate for Force Structure, Resources and Assessment, J-8 the Jt Chiefs of Staff 1996–99, Dir for Force Structure, Resources and Assessment, J-8 the Jt Chiefs of Staff 2002–04; Vice-Chair. Jt Chiefs of Staff 2007–, Chair. Jt Requirements Oversight Council, Co-Chair Defense Acquisition Bd, mem. Nat. Security Council Deputies Cttee, Nuclear Weapons Council, Missile Defense Exec. Bd; Co-Chair. Deputies Advisory Working Group; Outstanding Carrier Aviator, Asscn of Naval Aviation 1983. *Address:* Office of the Vice-Chairman of the Joint Chiefs of Staff, 400 Joint Staff, Pentagon, Washington, DC 20318-0400, USA (office). *Website:* www.jcs.mil (office).

CARTWRIGHT, Nancy Delaney, PhD, FBA; American/British academic; *Professor of Philosophy, Logic and Scientific Method, London School of Economics;* b. 24 June 1944, Pennsylvania; d. of Claudis Delaney and Eva Delaney; m. 1st Bliss Cartwright 1966 (divorced); m. 2nd Ian Hacking 1974 (divorced); m. 3rd Sir Stuart Hampshire 1985 (died 2004); two d.; ed Univs of Pittsburgh and Illinois; Prof. of Philosophy, Stanford Univ. 1983–91; Prof. of Philosophy, Logic and Scientific Method, LSE 1991–, Dir Centre for the Philosophy of the Natural and Social Sciences 1993–2001; Prof. of Philosophy, Univ. of California, San Diego 1997–; Macarthur Foundation Award 1993, Leopoldina 1999. *Publications:* How the Laws of Physics Lie 1983, Nature's Capacities and Their Measurement 1989, Otto Neurath: Between Science and Politics (with others) 1995, The Dappled World: A Study of the Boundaries of Science 2000. *Address:* Room T203, Department of Philosophy, Logic and Scientific Method, London School of Economics, Houghton Street, London, WC2A 2AE, England (office); Department of Philosophy, University of California, San Diego, 9500 Gilman Drive, La Jolla, CA 92093-0302, USA (office). *Telephone:* (20) 7955-7330 (office). *Fax:* (20) 7242-0392 (office). *E-mail:* N.L.Cartwright@lse.ac.uk. *Website:* www.lse.ac.uk/Depts/Philosophy (office); www.lse.ac.uk/Depts/cpnss (office); personal.lse.ac.uk/cartwrig/Default.htm.

CARTWRIGHT, The Hon. Dame Silvia Rose, DBE, PCNZM, QSO, LLB; New Zealand judge; b. 7 Nov. 1943, Dunedin; d. of Monteith Poulter and Eileen Jane Poulter; m. Peter John Cartwright 1969; ed Univ. of Otago; Pnr, Harkness Henry & Co. barristers and solicitors, Hamilton 1971–81; Dist Court and Family Court Judge 1981–89, Chief Dist Court Judge 1989–93; Judge High Court of NZ 1993–2001; Gov.-Gen. of NZ 2001–06; Judge in Trial Chamber, Extraordinary Chambers in the Courts of Cambodia for the Prosecution of Crimes Committed during the Period of Democratic Kampuchea 2007–; mem. Comm. for the Future 1975–80, Cttee UN Human Rights Convention to eliminate discrimination against women 1992–2000; Chair. Comm. of Inquiry into the Treatment of Cervical Cancer and Other Related Matters, Nat. Women's Hosp. 1987–88; Int. Hon. Mem., Zonta International 2001; Hon. LLD (Otago) 1993, (Waikato) 1994, (Canterbury) 2002; NZ Medal 1990, NZ Suffrage Centennial Medal 1993. *Address:* Extraordinary Chambers in the Courts of Cambodia, National Road 4, Chaom Chau Commune, Dangkao District, Phnom Penh, Cambodia (office). *Telephone:* (23) 219814 (office). *Fax:* (23) 219841 (office). *E-mail:* info@eccc.gov.kh (office). *Website:* www.eccc.gov.kh (office).

CARTY, Donald J., OC; Canadian business executive; *Chairman, Virgin America;* m. Ana Carty; ed Queen's Univ., Kingston, Ont., Harvard Grad. School of Business Admin., USA; various man. positions at Celanese Canada Ltd, Air Canada, Canadian Pacific Railway, American Airlines Inc.; Pres. and CEO CP Air 1985–87; Sr Vice-Pres. (Airline Planning) AMR Corpn 1987–89, Exec. Vice-Pres. (Finance and Planning) AMR Corpn and American Airlines Inc. 1989–95, Pres. AMR Airline Group and American Airlines Inc. 1995–98, Chair., Pres. and CEO AMR Corpn and American Airlines Inc. 1998–2003 (resgnd); Chair. Virgin America Airlines 2006–; Chair. Porter Airlines, Toronto 2006–; mem. Bd of Dirs Dell Computer Inc. 1992–, Vice-Chair. and Chief Financial Officer 2007, Vice-Chair. 2008–; mem. Bd of Dirs CHC Helicopter Corpn, Barrick Gold Corpn, Brinker Int., Canada-US Foundation for Educational Exchange, Hawaiian Holdings Inc.; mem. Nat. Infrastructure Advisory Council 2002–05. *Address:* Virgin America, 555 Airport Blvd., Fl. 2, Burlingame, CA 94010, USA (office). *Telephone:* (650) 762-7000 (office). *Fax:* (650) 762-7001 (office). *Website:* www.virginamerica.com (office).

CARUANA, Peter R., QC; Gibraltarian politician and lawyer; *Chief Minister;* b. 15 Oct. 1956; m.; six c.; ed Christian Brothers School, Grace Dieu Manor, Leicester, Ratcliffe Coll. Leicester, Queen Mary Coll., Univ. of London, Council of Legal Educ., London; joined Triay & Triay (law firm), Gibraltar 1979, Pnr specializing in commercial and shipping law 1990–95; joined Gibraltar Social Democrats 1990, Leader Feb. 1991–; elected in Gibraltar's first-ever by-election to House of Ass. May 1991; Leader of Opposition 1992–96; QC for Gibraltar 1998; Chief Minister of Gibraltar 1996–, (re-elected 2000, 2003, 2007); Hon. Fellow, Queen Mary Coll., Univ. of London. *Leisure interests:* golf, political and current affairs. *Address:* 10/3 Irish Town (home); Office of the Chief Minister, 6 Convent Place, Gibraltar (office). *Telephone:* 20070071 (office). *Fax:* 20076396 (office). *E-mail:* govsec@gibnet.gi (office). *Website:* www.gibraltar.gov.gi/chief_minister (office).

CARUANA LACORTE, Jaime; Spanish central bank governor; *General Manager, Bank for International Settlements, IMF;* b. 14 March 1952, Valencia; ed Univ. Complutense Madrid; fmr telecommunications engineer; various posts with Ministry of Trade 1979–84; Commercial attaché to the Spanish Commercial Office, New York 1984–87; Man. Dir and CEO Renta 4, SA, SVB 1987–91, Pres. 1991–96; Gen. Dir of the Treasury and Financial Policy 1996–99; mem. Bd SEPP (State Holding Co.) 1996–99; mem. EU

www.worldwhoswho.com

Monetary Cttee 1996–99; Pres. SETE (Euro State Co.) 1997–99; Gen. Dir for Supervision, Banco de España 1999–2000, Gov. 2000–06; Counsellor and Dir Monetary and Capital Markets Dept, IMF 2006–09, Gen. Man. BIS 2009–; Chair. Basel Cttee for Banking Supervision 2003–06; mem. Governing Council, European Cen. Bank 2000–, Group of Thirty (G-30) 2003–. *Publications:* numerous articles on the Spanish financial system, the financing of public admins and the man. of public debt. *Address:* Bank for International Settlements, Centralbahnplatz 2, 4002 Basel, Switzerland (office). *Telephone:* 612808080 (office). *Fax:* 612809100 (office). *E-mail:* email@bis.org (office). *Website:* www.bis.org (office).

CARVALHO, Mário Costa Martins de; Portuguese writer, lawyer and academic; *Director of Creative Writing, Instituto Português do Livro e das Bibliotecas (Portuguese Institute for Book and Libraries) (IPLB);* b. 25 Sept. 1944, Lisbon; s. of Domingos Martins Carvalho and Maria Luísa Costa Carvalho; m. Maria Helena Taborda Duarte 1969; two d.; ed Univ. of Lisbon Law School; involved in student resistance to dictatorship; received conviction for political activities; served with Army; in exile in Paris and Lund, Sweden 1973–74; returned to Portugal after revolution of 1974; involved in politics 1974–77; f. law practice 1981; Prof. of Scriptwriting, Cinema School 1999–2001; mem. Bd Portuguese Asscn of Writers; Prof. of Playwriting, Univ. of Lisbon 2000–02; Dir of Creative Writing, Instituto Português do Livro e das Bibliotecas (Portuguese Institute for Book and Libraries) (IPLB) and Portuguese Society of Authors (SPA) 2003–; City of Lisbon Prize, Theatre Prize 1999, several other awards and prizes. *Plays include:* 'Se perguntarem Por Mim, Não Estou', a Rapariga de Varsóvia. *Film:* F.F. Preto e Branco. *Publications:* Contos da Sétima Esfera 1981, O Livro Grande de Terras, Navio e Mariana 1982, A Paixão do Conde de Fróis 1986, Os Alferes 1989, Um Deus Passeando Pela Brisa da Tarde 1995, Era Bom que Trocassemos umas Ideias sobre o Assunto 1995, Fantasia para dois coronéis e uma Piscina 2003. *Address:* R. António Pereira Carrilho 27 R/C, 1000-046 Lisbon (home); Instituto Português do Livro e das Bibliotecas (Portuguese Institute for Book and Libraries) (IPLB), Campo Grande, 83-1°, 1700-088 Lisbon, Portugal (office). *Telephone:* (21) 8460576 (home). *Fax:* (21) 8464227 (home). *E-mail:* advogados.1@netc.pt (office). *Website:* www.iplb.pt (office).

CARVALHO DE ANDRADE, Marcelo, PhD; Brazilian banker and international organization official; *President, Earth Council Alliance;* s. of Atabalipa de Andrade and the late Maria Carvalho de Andrade; m. Lisa Bjornson 1995; ed Univ. Gama Filho, Rio de Janeiro; PNR, T. W. P. Ltd (investment firm), Rio de Janeiro, Earth Capital Partners LLP (responsible for external relations); Co-founder Terra Capital; Founder and Chair. Pro-Natura International (first int. NGO based in Southern Hemisphere to specialize in sustainable devt), Rio de Janeiro 1980s; Advisor (non-exec.), BHP Billiton, DuPont, Shell; mem. Biotechnology Advisory Panel, E. I. du Pont de Nemours & Co. 2004–; Pres. Earth Council Alliance; mem. CONCEC (pvt.-sector advisory panel for Brazilian Govt), Counterpart International, Earth Restoration Corps; George and Cynthia Mitchell Int. Prize for Sustainable Devt 1997. *Address:* Earth Council Alliance, 101 West Broadway, Suite 1980, San Diego, CA 92101, USA (office). *Telephone:* (619) 595-0760 (office). *Fax:* (619) 595-0764 (office). *E-mail:* info@earthcouncilalliance.org (office). *Website:* www .earthcouncilalliance.org (office).

CARVILLE, James; American political consultant; b. 25 Oct. 1944, Fort Benning, Ga; s. of Lucille Carville; m. Mary Matalin 1993; two d.; ed Louisiana State Univ.; litigator Baton Rouge 1973–79; managed first campaign 1982, then managed campaign for Gov. of Texas 1983; subsequent successful campaigns included Robert Casey for Penn. Gov. 1986, Wallace Wilkinson for Ky Gov. 1987, Frank Lautenberg for NJ Sen. 1988, Zell Miller for Ga Lt.-Gov. 1990, Harris Wofford for Penn. Sen. 1991; co-f. Carville and Begala (political consulting co.) 1989; co-managed Clinton Presidential Campaign 1992, later sr political adviser to Pres.; numerous int. political clients 1993–, including successful campaign for Ehud Barak for PM Israel 1999; Co-f. Democracy Corps (consultancy and polling co.); Campaign Man. of the Year 1993. *Films include:* The People vs. Larry Flynt 1996, All the King's Men (exec. producer) 2006. *Publications:* All's Fair: Love, War and Running for President (with Mary Matalin) 1995, We're Right, They're Wrong (with Mary Matalin) 1996, And The Horse He Rode In On: The People v. Ken Starr 1998, Stickin': The Case for Loyalty 2000, Take It Back: Our Party, Our Country, Our Future (with Paul Begala) 2006. *Address:* Democracy Corps, 10 G Street, NE, Suite 400, Washington, DC 20002 (office); Gaslight Inc., 424 South Washington Street, Lower Level, Alexandria, VA 22314, USA (office). *Telephone:* (202) 478-8330 (DC) (office); (703) 739-7777 (office). *Fax:* (202) 289-8648 (DC) (office); (703) 739-7766 (office). *E-mail:* james@carville.info (office). *Website:* www .democracycorps.com (office); www.carville.info (office).

CASADESUS, Jean Claude; French conductor; *Director, Lille National Orchestra;* b. (Jean Claude Probst), 7 Dec. 1935, Paris; s. of Lucien Probst and Gisèle Casadesus; two s. one d.; ed Paris Nat. Conservatoire and Ecole Normale, Paris; solo timpanist, Concert Colonne 1959–68; percussion soloist, Domaine Musical (with Boulez); Conductor, Paris Opéra 1969–71; Co-Dir Orchestre Pays de Loire 1971–76; Founder and Dir Lille Nat. Orchestra 1976–; appears as guest conductor with leading orchestras in UK, USA, France, Germany, Norway, Russia, Czech Repub., int. music festivals etc.; Pres. Musique Nouvelle en Liberté; Musical Dir, Orchestre Français des Jeunes; Commdr Légion d'honneur; Commdr Ordre nat. du Mérite; Commdr des Arts et des Lettres; Chevalier Ordre des Palmes académiques; Commdr Order of Orange Nassau (Netherlands); Officer Order of Léopold (Belgium); Grand Prix de la SACEM and several other prizes and awards for recordings. *Recordings include:* works by Dutilleux (1st Symphony), Berlioz, Mahler, Bizet, Stravinsky, Mozart, Beethoven, Ravel, Debussy, Poulenc, Groupe des Six, Prokofiev, Dukas, Massenet, Milhaud, Honneger, Mussorgsky, Franck, Canteloube—Songs of the Auvergne. *Publications:* Le plus court chemin d'un coeur à un autre 1998, Stock (ed.). *Leisure interests:* yachting, sailing, skiing, tennis. *Address:* Orchestre National de Lille, 30 place Mendès-France, BP 119, 59027 Lille Cedex (office); 2 rue de Steinkerque, 75018 Paris, France (home). *Telephone:* (3) 20-12-82-68 (office). *Fax:* (3) 20-78-29-10 (office).

CASANOVA, Jean-Claude, DEcon; French economist and journalist; *Editor, Commentaire;* b. 11 June 1934, Ajaccio, Corsica; s. of Jean Casanova and Marie-Antoinette Luciani; m. Marie-Thérèse Demargne 1962; two s.; ed Lycée Carnot, Inst. des Hautes Etudes, Tunis, Univ. of Paris, Harvard Univ.; Asst Fondation nat. des sciences politiques 1958; Chief of Staff to Minister of Industry 1958–61; Asst in Law Faculty, Univ. of Dijon 1963; Sr Lecturer then Prof., Faculty of Law and Econ. Sciences, Univ. of Nancy 1964–68; with Univ. of Paris-Nanterre 1968; with Inst. d'Etudes politiques, Paris 1969–; Dir of Studies and Research, Fondation nat. des Sciences politiques 1965–90, Pres. 2007–; Tech. Adviser to Minister of Educ. 1972–74; Adviser to Prime Minister Raymond Barre 1976–81; Ed. Commentaire 1978–; leader writer, L'Express 1985–95; regular contrib. to Le Figaro 1996–2001; mem. Econ. and Social Council 1994–2004, Acad. des Sciences morales et politiques 1996–; columnist, Le Monde 2002–; Officier, Ordre nat. du Mérite 1996, Commdr, Légion d'honneur 2008. *Address:* Commentaire, 116 rue du Bac, 75007 Paris (office); Institut de France, quai Conti, 75270 Paris (office); 11-13, Rue de l'Aude, 75014 Paris, France (home). *Telephone:* 1-45-49-37-82; 1-43-26-51-95. *Fax:* 1-45-44-32-18. *E-mail:* jcc@commentaire.fr (office); jcc-1@wanadoo.fr (home). *Website:* www.commentaire.fr (office).

CASAS-GONZALEZ, Antonio; Venezuelan engineer, business executive and fmr government official; *Principal, Tecnoconsult SA;* b. 24 July 1933, Mérida; m. Carmen Elena Granadino de Casas; five s. one d.; ed George Washington Univ., Georgetown Univ., USA; fmrly Prof. of Econs at various insts; Adviser, Venezuelan Petrochemical Inst. and Asst to Minister of Mines and Hydrocarbons 1957–59; Petroleum and Econ. Counsellor, Embassy in Washington, DC 1959–61; with Interamerican Devt Bank 1961–69; Vice-Minister of Devt 1969; Minister for Nat. Planning Office (CORDIPLAN) 1972; Man. Dir Petróleos de Venezuela (UK) SA 1990–94; Gov. Banco Cen. de Venezuela 1994–99; Vice-Pres. Intergovernmental Group of Twenty-Four on Int. Monetary Affairs 1996–; mem. Bd of Dirs Venezolana de Aviación (VIASA) 1970–73, Corp. Andina de Fomento 1970–73, Banco Cen. de Venezuela 1972–75, Corp. Venezolana de Guyana 1979–82, Petróleos de Venezuela SA 1979–90; currently Prin., Tecnoconsult SA; mem. Int. Council Elliot School of Int. Affairs, George Washington Univ.; sixteen decorations from nine countries. *Publications:* América Latina y los problemas de Desarrollo (co-author) 1974, Venezuela y el CIAP (co-author) 1974, La planificación en América Latina (co-author) 1975, World Development (co-author) 1977; articles for various publs. *Leisure interest:* golf. *Address:* Tecnoconsult SA, Av. Sur 11, Monroy a Puente Victoria, No. 33, Caracas 1050-A, Venezuela (office). *Telephone:* (212) 508-2189 (office). *Fax:* (212) 508-2363 (office). *E-mail:* TCcaracas@tecnoconsult.com (office). *Website:* www.tecnoconsult.com (office).

CASAS REGUEIRO, Lt-Gen. Julio; Cuban military officer and government official; *Vice-President and Minister of the Revolutionary Armed Forces;* b. 16 Feb. 1936, Santiago de Cuba; ed Inst. of Advanced Mil. Studies, Havana; joined II Eastern Front, Oriente Prov. 1958; Officer, Nat. Revolutionary Police 1959–61; Chief of Logistics and Services of Armed Forces 1961–67; mem. Cuba CP 1965–, alt. mem. Cen. Cttee 1975–80, full mem. 1980–, mem. Politburo 1991–; Vice Minister of Armed Forces 1969–72; apptd Brig.-Gen. 1970; served in mil. missions in Africa 1972–75; Div. Gen., Chief of Rear Services (Logistics), Ministry of Revolutionary Armed Forces 1977–80, Chief of Anti-Air Defences and Air Force 1980–87, Deputy Minister in charge of Econ. Activity 1988–90, First Deputy Minister 1990–2008, Vice-President and Minister of Revolutionary Armed Forces 2008–. *Address:* Ministry of the Revolutionary Armed Forces, Plaza de la Revolución, Havana, Cuba (office). *Website:* www.cubagob.cu/otras_info/minfar/far/minfar.htm (office).

CASDIN-SILVER, Harriet, AB; American artist; b. 10 Feb. 1925, Worcester, Mass; d. of Samuel Casdin-Cohen and Rose Fanya Ostroff; m. Simon Silver 1952; two d.; ed Univ. of Vermont, Columbia Univ., New School for Social Research, New York, Cambridge Goddard Grad. School, Mass; Artist-in-Residence, American Optical Research Labs, Framingham, Mass 1968–73, Ukrainian Inst. of Physics, Kiev 1989; Asst Prof. of Physics, Brown Univ., RI 1974–78; Fellow, Center for Advanced Visual Studies, MIT 1976–85; consultant, Rockefeller Foundation Arts Program 1980–81; Visiting Lecturer, RCA, London, UK 1992, also Univ. of Ghent, Belgium; Prof. of Art, Massachusetts Coll. of Art and Design, Boston 1999–; Presenter SKYART Conf., Delphi & Ikaria, Greece 2002; also ind. artist; Rockefeller Foundation Awards 1978–79, 1980–82, Shearwater Foundation Awards for Excellence in Holography 1987, 2001, Lifetime Achievement Award for Art in Holography, Univ. of Nottingham, UK 1996, Visible Repub. Award for Public Art 2001. *Publications include:* My First 10 Years as Artist/Holographer 1989, Holographic Installations: Sculpting with Light 1991, Putting Guts into the Machine (book review, Women's Review of Books) 2004. *Leisure interests:* reading, walking, ocean watching. *Address:* 99 Pond Avenue, D403, Brookline, MA 02445 (home); 51 Melcher Street, 5th Floor, Boston, MA 02210, USA (studio). *Telephone:* (617) 739-6869 (home); (617) 423-4717 (studio). *Fax:* (617) 739-6869 (home). *E-mail:* casdinsilver@hotmail.com (home). *Website:* www .harrietcasdinsilver.com.

CASE, Stephen M., MA; American business executive; *Chairman, Exclusive Resorts LLC;* b. 21 Aug. 1958, Honolulu; m. Joanne Case (divorced); three d.; ed Williams Coll.; worked in marketing dept, Procter & Gamble 1980–82; Man. of New Pizza Devt, Pizza Hut Div., PepsiCo 1982–83; Marketing Asst, Control Video Corpn, Va 1983–85, Marketing Dir Quantum Computer Services (fmrly Control Video then renamed America Online (AOL))

1985–92, CEO AOL 1992–2001, Chair. 1995–2001; Chair. AOL Time Warner (cr. after merger of Time Warner and AOL) 2001–03, Dir with jt responsibility for corp. strategy 2003, mem. Bd of Dirs –2005 (resgnd); prin. investor and Chair. Exclusive Resorts LLC, Denver, Colo 2004–; prin. investor, Maui Land and Pineapple, HI; f. Revolution LLC (health care holding co.) 2005; f. Case Foundation 1997; f. ABC2, Accelerate Brain Cancer Cure 2001; Entrepreneur of the Year, Incorporated Magazine 1994. *Leisure interests:* reading political science and history. *Address:* Exclusive Resorts LLC, 1530 16th Street, Suite 500, Denver, CO 80202, USA (office). *Telephone:* (303) 226-4900 (office). *Website:* www.exclusiveresorts.com (office); www.abc2.org.

CASEY, Robert (Bob) Patrick, Jr, JD; American lawyer and politician; *Senator from Pennsylvania;* b. 13 April 1960, Scranton, Pa; eldest s. of the late Pa Gov. Robert P. Casey and Ellen Casey; m. Terese Foppiano Casey 1985; four d.; ed Coll. of the Holy Cross, Catholic Univ. of America; taught fifth grade and coached eighth grade basketball team for Jesuit Volunteer Corps, Gesu School, Philadelphia 1983; began practising law in Scranton 1988; Pa State Auditor Gen. 1997–2005; cand. for State Gov. 2002; State Treas. 2005–06; Senator from Pa 2007–, mem. Foreign Relations Cttee, Banking, Housing and Urban Affairs Cttee, Agric. Cttee, US Congress Jt Econ. Cttee, Special Cttee on Aging; Democrat. *Address:* 383 Russell Senate Office Building, Washington, DC 20510, USA (office). *Telephone:* (202) 224-6324 (office). *Fax:* (202) 228-0604 (office). *Website:* casey.senate.gov (office); www.bobcasey.com (office).

CASH, Pat; Australian sports commentator, tennis coach and fmr professional tennis player; b. 27 May 1965, Melbourne; s. of Patrick Cussen and Dorothy Hart Cash; m. Emily Cash; four c.; ed Whitefriars Coll.; winner, US Open Jr Championship 1982; mem. winning Australian Davis Cup team 1983; in quarter-finals at Wimbledon 1985; finalist Australian Open 1987, 1988; Wimbledon Champion 1987; retd 1997; plays on Masters Tennis circuit; co-f. Pat Cash Tennis Acad.; currently BBC Wimbledon analyst; Australian Tennis Hall of Fame 2003. *Leisure interests:* music, football. *Address:* c/o Duncan Marsh, Red Baron Enterprises, Day and Co, 88 College Road, Harrow, Middx, HA1 1BQ, England; c/o Pat Cash and Associates, PO Box 2238, Footscray, Vic. 3011, Australia (office). *Telephone:* (7956) 447811. *E-mail:* duncan@patcash.co.uk. *Website:* www.patcash.net; www.patcash.co.uk.

CASHMORE, Roger John, MA, DPhil, FRS, FInstP, CMG; British physicist and academic; *Principal, Brasenose College, Oxford;* b. 22 Aug. 1944, Birmingham; s. of C. J. C. Cashmore and E. M. Cashmore; m. Elizabeth Ann Lindsay 1971; one s.; ed Dudley Grammar School, St John's Coll., Cambridge, Balliol Coll., Oxford; Weir Jr Research Fellow, Univ. Coll., Oxford 1967–69; 1851 Research Fellow 1968; Research Assoc. Stanford Linear Accelerator, Calif. 1969–74; Research Officer Univ. of Oxford 1974–79, Lecturer 1979–90, Reader in Experimental Physics 1990–91, Prof. 1991–98; Research Dir CERN 1999–2003, Deputy Dir CERN 2002–03; Prin. Brasenose Coll., Oxford 2002–; Boys Prize, Inst. of Physics 1983, Humboldt Research Award 1995. *Publications:* contribs to Physics Review. *Leisure interests:* sports, wine. *Address:* Brasenose College, Oxford, OX1 4AJ, England (home). *Telephone:* (1865) 277821 (office). *Fax:* (1865) 277514 (office). *E-mail:* roger.cashmore@bnc.ox.ac.uk (office).

CASIDA, John Edward, MS, PhD, FRS; American entomologist, toxicologist and academic; *Professor of Toxicology and Entomology and Director, Environmental Chemistry and Toxicology Laboratory, University of California, Berkeley;* b. 22 Dec. 1929, Phoenix, Ariz.; s. of Lester Earl Casida and Ruth Casida (née Barnes); m. Katherine Faustine Monson 1956; two s.; ed Univ. of Wisconsin-Madison; served with USAF 1953; Research Asst, Univ. of Wisconsin 1951–53, Asst Prof. then Assoc. Prof. 1954–63, Prof. of Entomology 1959–63; Prof. of Entomology, Univ. of California, Berkeley 1964–, William Muriece Hoskins Chair in Chemical and Molecular Entomology 1996–, Faculty Research Lecturer 1998, Dir Environmental Chem. and Toxicology Lab. 1964–; Scholar-in-Residence, Bellagio Study and Conf. Centre, Rockefeller Foundation, Lake Como, Italy 1978; Messenger Lecturer, Cornell Univ. 1985; Sterling B. Hendicks Lecturer, US DE of Agric. and ACS 1992–; Lecturer in Science, Third World Acad. of Sciences, Univ. of Buenos Aires 1997; mem. NAS, ACS, Entomological Soc. of America, Soc. of Environmental Toxicology and Chem., European Acad. of Sciences 2004–; Haight Travelling Fellow 1958–59; Guggenheim Fellow 1970–71; Fellow, Entomological Soc. of America 1989; Foreign mem. Royal Soc. 1998; Hon. mem. Soc. of Toxicology, Pesticide Science Soc. of Japan; Hon. DUniv (Buenos Aires) 1997; ACS Int. Award for Research in Pesticide Chem. 1970, ACS Spencer Award in Agric. and Food Chem. 1978, Bussart Memorial Award, Entomological Soc. of America 1989, Wolf Prize in Agric. 1993, Founder's Award, Soc. of Environmental Toxicology and Chem. 1994, Kôrô-sho Prize Pesticide Science Soc. (Japan) 1995. *Publications:* numerous papers in scientific journals on pesticide chem. and toxicology, metabolism and mode of action of organic toxicants, and insect biochemistry. *Address:* Department of Environmental Science, Policy and Management, University of California, Berkeley, 114 Wellman Hall, Berkeley, CA 94720 (office); 1570 La Vereda Road, Berkeley, CA 94708, USA (home). *Telephone:* (510) 642-5424 (office). *Fax:* (510) 642-6497 (office). *E-mail:* ectl@nature.berkeley.edu (office). *Website:* espm.berkeley.edu/directory/fac/casida_j.html (office).

CASINI, Pier Ferdinando; Italian politician; *President, Inter-Parliamentary Union;* b. 3 Dec. 1955, Bologna; m. Roberta Lubich (divorced); two d.; partner, Azzurra Caltagirone; one d.; joined Unione dei Democratici Cristiani e di Centro (UDC) 1980; elected Town Councillor, Bologna 1980; mem. Chamber of Deputies 1983–94, Pres. 2001–06; Mem. European Parl. 1994–2001 (PPE-DE Group); Pres. Inter-Parl. Union 2005–; Pres. Centrist Democrat Int. (CDI) (fmrly Christian Democrat Int.) 2006–; fmr Pres. Christian Democratic Centre; Order of Merit from Austria, Brazil, Chile, France, Germany, Hungary, Lithuania, Luxembourg, Malaysia, Malta, Norway, Peru, Poland, San Marino, Spain. *Address:* Unione dei Democratici Cristiani e di Centro (UDC) (Union of Christian and Centre Democrats), Via dei Due Macelli 66, 00182 Roma, Italy (office); Inter-Parliamentary Union 5, chemin du Pommier, Case postale 330, 1218 Le Grand-Saconnex, Geneva, Switzerland (office). *Telephone:* (06) 69791001 (UDC) (office); 229194150 (IPU) (office). *Fax:* (06) 6791574 (UDC) (office); 229194160 (IPU) (office). *E-mail:* info@udc-italia.it (office); postbox@mail.ipu.org (office); pier@pierferdinandocasini.it (office). *Website:* www.udc-italia.it (office); www.ipu.org (office); www.pierferdinandocasini.it (office).

CASORATI, Francesco; Italian artist; b. 2 July 1934, Turin; s. of Felice Casorati and Daphne Maugham; m. Paola Zanetti 1959; three s.; ed Liceo Artistico dell' Accad. di Torino; held first solo show in Milan 1954; has since exhibited at numerous int. exhbns including Pittori Italiani, Moscow, Budapest, Prague, Sofia 1957–58, Expo, Brussels 1958, Venice Biennale, etc.; numerous solo and group shows in various European cities; taught at Liceo Artistico di Torino 1959–75, Accad. Albertina di Torino 1970–75; holder, Chair. of Decorative Art, Accad. Albertina di Torino 1975–84. *Address:* Via Mazzini 52, Turin; C.so Kossuth 19, Turin, Italy (home). *Telephone:* (011) 831491; (011) 894950 (home).

CASPER, William Earl (Billy); American professional golfer; b. 24 June 1931, San Diego, Calif.; m. Shirley Casper (née Franklin); six c., five adopted c.; ed Univ. of Notre Dame; fmr fruit farmer; professional golfer since 1954; winner, US Open 1959, 1966, Masters 1970; played eight times in Ryder Cup 1961–75; winner of 51 tournaments on pro circuit and several more on seniors tour; won Brazilian Open twice, the Lancôme 1974, Italian Open 1975, Mexican Open 1977; Sr Advisor and Consultant Billy Casper Golf LLC; US PGA Player of the Year 1966, 1970, PGA Hall of Fame 1982, Vardon Trophy (lowest scoring average) 1960, 1963, 1965, 1966, 1968. *Address:* Billy Casper Golf LLC, 8300 Boone Boulevard, Suite 350, Vienna, VA 22182, USA (office). *Telephone:* (703) 761-1444 (office). *Fax:* (703) 893-3504 (office). *E-mail:* info@billycaspergolf.com (office). *Website:* www.billycaspergolf.com.

CASPERSEN, Sven Lars, MEcon; Danish academic; b. 30 June 1935, Åabenraa; s. of Jes P. Caspersen and Carla Caspersen; m. Eva Caspersen 1962; three s.; Asst Sec., Danish Cen. Bureau of Statistics 1962–64; Deputy Chief, Cen. Statistical Centre of Danish Insurance Cos at Danish Insurance Asscn 1964–68; Assoc. Prof. of Statistics, Copenhagen School of Econs and Business Admin. 1968–73, Head of Dept of Statistics 1970–73; Dean of Social Sciences, Åalborg Univ. 2004, Rector 1976–2004, Chair. Bd 2004–06; Chair. Bd Copenhagen Stock Exchange 1989–96; Chair. Liaison Cttee of Rectors' Conferences of mem. states of the EC 1992–94; Chair. Govt Advisory Council on EU Matters 1993–2001; Chair. European Capital Markets Inst. 1993–95; Vice-Pres. Fed. of Stock Exchanges of the EC 1993–95, Pres. 1995–96; Pres. Int. Asscn of Univ. Pres.'s 1999–2002; Chair. Bd Åalborg Theatre 1986; Dr hc (Vilnius Tech. Univ.) 1993; recipient, Tribute of Appreciation, US Dept of State 1981. *Leisure interests:* chess, bridge, tennis. *Address:* Duebrødrevej 6, 9000 Aalborg, Denmark (home).

CASS, Sir Geoffrey Arthur, Kt, MA, CCMI; British publishing executive and arts and lawn tennis administrator; b. 11 Aug. 1932, Bishop Auckland; s. of the late Arthur Cass and Jessie Cass (née Simpson); m. Olwen Mary Richards, JP, DL 1957; four d.; ed Queen Elizabeth Grammar School, Darlington and Jesus Coll., Oxford; Nuffield Coll., Oxford 1957–58; RAF 1958–60; ed. Automation 1960–61; Consultant, PA Man. Consultants Ltd 1960–65; Pvt. Man. Consultant, British Communications Corpn and Controls and Communications Ltd 1965; Dir Controls and Communications Ltd 1966–69; Dir George Allen & Unwin 1965–67, Man. Dir 1967–71; Dir Weidenfeld Publrs. 1972–74, Univ. of Chicago Press, UK 1971–86; Chief Exec. Cambridge Univ. Press 1972–92, Consultant 1992–; Sec. Press Syndicate, Univ. of Cambridge 1974–92; Univ. Printer 1982–83, 1991–92; Fellow, Clare Hall, Cambridge 1979–; Trustee Shakespeare Birthplace Trust 1982–94 (Life Trustee 1994–); Chair. Royal Shakespeare Co. 1985–2000 (Deputy Pres. 2000–), Royal Shakespeare Theatre Trust 1983–, British Int. Tennis and Nat. Training 1985–90, Nat. Ranking Cttee; mem. Bd of Man., Lawn Tennis Asscn of GB 1985–90, 1993–2000, Deputy Pres. 1994–96, Pres. 1997–99; Chair. Tennis Foundation 2003–07, Pres. 2007–; mem. Cttee of Man., Wimbledon Championships 1990–2002; Pres., Chair. or mem. numerous other trusts, bds, cttees, charitable appeals and advisory bodies particularly in connection with theatre, sport and medicine; Oxford tennis Blue and badminton; played in Wimbledon Tennis Championships 1954, 1955, 1956, 1959; British Veterans Singles Champion, Wimbledon 1978; Hon. Fellow, Jesus Coll., Oxford 1998; Chevalier, Ordre des Arts et Lettres. *Publications:* articles in professional journals. *Leisure interests:* tennis, theatre. *Address:* Middlefield, Huntingdon Road, Cambridge, CB3 0LH, England. *Website:* www.tennisfoundation.org.uk.

CASSAB, Judy, AO, CBE, DLitt; Australian painter; b. (Judith Kaszab), 15 Aug. 1920, Vienna, Austria; d. of Imre Kaszab and Ilona Kont; m. John Kampfner 1939; two s.; ed Budapest and Prague; mem. Council for the Honours of Australia 1975–79; Trustee, Art Gallery of NSW 1981–88; has held 75 individual exhbns in galleries throughout Australia, in London and Paris since 1953 and works are in all major Australian galleries including Nat. Gallery, Canberra, galleries in UK including Nat. Portrait Gallery, London, in USA and at Nat. Gallery of Budapest, Exhbn in Vasarely Museum, Budapest 2003, Exhbn in Charlemagne Bldg, Brussels 2004 to celebrate Hungary's accession to the EU; Dr hc (Sydney) 1995; several prizes including Archibald Prize 1961, 1967, Sir Charles Lloyd Jones Memorial Prize (four times), The Trustees Watercolour Prize 1994, 2003, Foundation for Australian Literary Studies Prize 1996, Nita Kibble Literary Award (for Judy Cassab Diaries) 1996, two Archibald Prizes 2003, The Pring Prize, The Painters and Sculptors Asscn of Australia Medal 2004. *Publications:* Ten Australian Portraits (lithographs) 1984, Judy Cassab, Places, Faces and Fantasies 1985, Artists and Friends 1988, Judy Cassab Diaries 1995, Judy Cassab, Portraits of Artists and Friend 1998, catalogue to the Vasarely Museum Exhbn 2003, Judy Cassab, Rainbow Valley – The Spirit of the Place. *Leisure interest:* writing my diary. *Address:* 16A Ocean Avenue, Double Bay, Sydney, NSW 2028, Australia. *Telephone:* (9) 326-1348. *E-mail:* jcassab@bigpond.net.au (home). *Website:* www.judycassab.com (office).

CASSEL, Vincent; French actor; b. 23 Nov. 1966, Paris; s. of Jean-Pierre Cassel; m. Monica Bellucci 1999. *Films include* Les Clés du paradis 1991, Hot Chocolate 1992, Café au Lait 1993, Jefferson in Paris 1995, La Haine 1995, Blood of the Hunter 1995, Adultery: A User's Guide 1995, L'Appartement 1996, L'Elève 1996, Come mi vuoi 1996, Dobermann 1997, Compromis 1998, Mediterranée 1998, Le Plaisir (et ses petits tracas) 1998, Elizabeth 1998, Guest House Paradiso 1999, Messenger: The Story of Joan of Arc 1999, Les Rivières pourpres (Crimson Rivers) 2000, Birthday Girl 2000, The Reckoning 2001, Le Pacte des loups (Brotherhood of the Wolf) 2001, Sur mes lèvres 2001, Shrek 2001, Irréversible (also co-producer) 2002, Ice Age 2002, Blueberry 2004, Spy Bound 2004, Ocean's Twelve 2004, Robots (voice) 2005, Derailed 2005, Sheitan 2006, Ocean's Thirteen 2007, Eastern Promises 2007, Sa majesté Minor 2007. *Address:* c/o Adequat, 80 rue d'Amsterdam, 75009 Paris, France; c/o CAA, 9830 Wilshire Boulevard, Beverly Hills, CA 90212, USA. *Telephone:* 1-44-62-69-69. *Fax:* 1-44-62-69-68. *E-mail:* contact@120films.com.

CASSEL-CROCHON, Jean-Pierre; French actor; b. 27 Oct. 1932, Paris; m. 2nd Anne Célérier 1981; two s. one d.; film debut in 1959; frequent TV appearances, regular theatre activity, music hall; Chevalier, Légion d'honneur 2004. *Theatre includes:* Roméo et Juliette, Chorus Line, Little Black Book, Who's Afraid of Virginia Woolf?, The Collection, Elvire, Festen. *Films include:* Les Jeux de l'Amour, Le Caporal Epinglé, Paris brûle-t-il? Those Magnificent Men in Their Flying Machines, Oh What A Lovely War!, Baxter, The Discreet Charm of the Bourgeoisie, The Three Musketeers, Le Mouton Enragé, Murder on the Orient Express, That Lucky Touch, The Twist, Who is Killing the Great Chefs of Europe?, Les Rendezvous d'Anna, From Hell to Victory, The Return of the Musketeers, Mangeclous, La Truite, Chouans, Mr. Frost, Phantom of the Opera, Theo and Vincent, The Favour, The Watch and the Very Big Fish, Amour et Petit Doigt de Pied, Pétain, Thé Noir au Citron, Casque Bleu, Prêt à Porter 1994, La Cérémonie 1995, Sade, La Patinoire, Les Rivières Pourpres 2000, Michel Vaillant 2002, Narco 2003, The Wooden Camera 2003, Virgil 2004, King Kong Paradise 2005. *Television includes:* Love in a Cold Climate, Shillingbury Tales, Liberty, Casanova, Secret of Sahara, Matter of Convenience, Warburg, The Maid, The French Kill, Notorious, Dust and Blood, Young Indy, La 13e Voiture, Printemps de Chien, Le Fils de Paul, Le Président et la Garde Barrière 1996, Un printemps de chien, Les Tiers mondains 1996, Le Coeur et l'epée, Les Montagnes bleues 1998, Le Coup du Lapin, Histoire d'Amour (Crimes en Série) 1999, Rastignac 2000, Pique-Nique chez Osiris 2000, La Chanson du Maison 2001, La maison du canal 2002, La faux 2002, La Mémoire et le Pardon. *Music:* album: Et maintenant 2000; DVD: Je ne veux pas vivre sans amour 2003. *Publications:* A mes amours 2004. *Address:* Art-Ciné, 36 rue de Ponthieu, 75008 Paris, France. *Telephone:* 1-42-56-04-20 (office). *Fax:* 1-42-56-04-19 (home). *E-mail:* cecilpro@noos.fr (home).

CASSELLS, Peter; Irish civil servant and trade union official; *Executive Chairman, National Centre for Partnership and Performance;* b. 20 Oct. 1949, Co. Meath; m. Paula Carey; legislation officer, Irish Congress of Trade Unions 1973–80, Econ. and Social Affairs Officer 1980–85, Asst Gen. Sec. 1985–87, Gen. Sec. 1987–2000; Chair. Nat. Centre for Partnership and Performance 2001–; currently Exec. Dir Peter Cassells Consultants Ltd, also Chair. DHR Communications; Dr hc (Nat. Univ. of Ireland) 2002. *Address:* National Centre for Partnership and Performance, 16 Parnell Square, Dublin 1 (office); Peter Cassells Consultants Ltd., Molyneux House, Bride Street, Dublin 8, Ireland. *Telephone:* (1) 8146391 (office). *Fax:* (1) 8146301 (office). *E-mail:* info@ncpp.ie (office). *Website:* www.ncpp.ie (office).

CASSELS, John William Scott, MA, PhD, FRS, FRSE; British mathematician and academic; *Fellow, Trinity College, University of Cambridge;* b. 11 July 1922, Durham City; s. of the late John William Cassels and Muriel Speakman Cassels (née Lobjoit); m. Constance Mabel Merritt (née Senior) 1949 (died 2000); one s. one d.; ed Neville's Cross Council School, Durham, George Heriot's School, Edinburgh and Univs of Edinburgh and Cambridge; Lecturer, Univ. of Manchester 1949–50; Lecturer, Univ. of Cambridge 1950–65, Reader in Arithmetic 1965–67, Sadleirian Prof. of Pure Mathematics 1967–84, Fellow, Trinity Coll., Cambridge 1949–. *Publications:* An Introduction to Diophantine Approximations 1957, An Introduction to the Geometry of Numbers 1959, Rational Quadratic Forms 1979, Economics for Mathematicians 1981, Local Fields 1986, Lectures on Elliptic Curves 1991, Prolegomena to a middlebrow arithmetic of curves of genus 2 (with E. V. Flynn) 1996. *Leisure interests:* The Higher Arithmetic, gardening. *Address:* c/o Trinity College, Trinity Street, Cambridge, CB2 1TQ (office); 3 Luard Close, Cambridge, CB2 8PL, England (home). *Telephone:* (1223) 338400; (1223) 246108 (home).

CASSELTON, Lorna Ann, PhD, DSc, FRS; British geneticist and academic; *Professor Emerita of Fungal Genetics, University of Oxford;* b. (Lorna Ann Smith), 18 July 1938, Rochford, Essex; d. of William Charles Henry Smith and Cecille Smith (née Bowman); m. 1st Peter John Casselton 1961 (divorced 1978); m. 2nd William Joseph Dennis Tollett 1981; ed Southend High School for Girls, Univ. Coll., London; Asst Lecturer, Royal Holloway Coll. 1966–67, Lecturer 1967–76; Reader Queen Mary Coll. (later Queen Mary and Westfield Coll., now Queen Mary London) 1976–89, Prof. of Genetics 1989–91, Visiting Prof. of Genetics 1997–; Agricultural and Food Research Council (now Biotechnology and Biological Sciences Research Council) Postdoctoral Fellow, Univ. of Oxford 1991–95, Sr Research Fellow 1995–2001, Prof. of Fungal Genetics 1997–2003, Prof. Emer. 2003–; Fellow, St Cross Coll., Oxford 1993–2003; Leverhulme Fellow Emer. 2003–05; Foreign Sec. and Vice-Pres. Royal Soc. 2006–; mem. Academia Europaea; Hon. Fellow, St Hilda's Coll. Oxford 2000; Hon. Mem. British Mycological Soc. 2002–. *Publications:* numerous articles in scientific journals. *Leisure activities:* classical music, travel, reading, walking. *Address:* Department of Plant Sciences, University of Oxford, Oxford, OX1 3RB (office); 83 St Bernards Road, Oxford, OX2 6EJ, England (home). *Telephone:* (1865) 559997 (home). *Fax:* (1865) 275000 (office). *E-mail:* lorna.casselton@plants.ox.ac.uk (office).

CASSESE, Sabino; Italian lawyer, judge and academic; *Judge, Corte costituzionale;* b. 20 Oct. 1935, Atripalda; Prof., Faculté Int. de droit comparé, Luxembourg 1966; Prof. of Public Admin. and Prof. of Govt, Dept of Econs, Univs of Ancona and Naples, Political Science Dept, Univ. of Rome, School for Higher Civil Servants, Rome; Dir Inst. of Public Law, Law Dept, Univ. of Rome 1991–93, Prof. of Admin. Law 1993–; Judge, Corte costituzionale (Constitutional Court) 2005–; Fellow, European Inst. of Public Admin., Maastricht 1985–86; Prof., Univ. de Paris I 1986, 1994; Assoc. Prof., Univ. of Nantes 1987; Visiting Prof., Inst. d'Etudes Politiques, Paris 1991, 2005–07; Visiting Scholar, Law School, Univ. of California, Berkeley 1965, LSE 1969, Law School, Stanford Univ., USA 1970, 1975, 1981, 1986; Guest Scholar, Wilson Int. Center for Scholars, Washington, DC 1983; Visiting Scholar and Jemolo Fellow, Nuffield Coll., Oxford 1987–89, 1995; mem. editorial bds of several journals including Rivista di Diritto Pubblico, International Review of Administrative Sciences, Revue européenne de droit administratif, Western European Politics, Revue française d'administration publique; mem. Prime Minister's policy unit 1988–89; fmr consultant to several Govt ministries and Bank of Italy; Minister for the Public Service 1993–94; Grande Ufficiale della Repubblica Italiana, Cavaliere di Gran Croce, Ordino al Merito della Repubblica Italiana; Campano d'Oro, Associazione Laureati Ateneo Pisano 1994, Premio Tarantelli 1993, Prix Alexis de Tocqueville, Inst. européen d'admin. publique 1997. *Publications:* Lo Stato introvabile 1998, Maggioranza e Minoranza. Il problema della democrazia in Italia 1995, La nuova Costituzione economica 2000, Le basi del diritto amministrativo 2000 and many other books. *Address:* Corte costituzionale, Piazza del Quirinale, 41, 00187 Rome tel. - fax. - (office); Department of Law, University of Rome, Via Orazio Raimondo 00173 Rome, Italy (office). *Telephone:* (06) 46981 (Corte costituzionale) (office); (06) 72591 (office). *Fax:* (06) 4698916 (Corte costituzionale) (office); (06) 7234368 (office). *E-mail:* ccost@cortecostituzionale.it (office). *Website:* www.cortecostituzionale.it (office).

CASSIDY, (Charles) Michael Ardagh, BD, MA; South African evangelist and author; b. 24 Sept. 1936, Johannesburg; s. of Charles Stewart Cassidy and Mary Craufurd Cassidy; m. Carol Bam 1969; one s. two d.; ed Parktown School, Johannesburg, Michaelhouse, Natal, Cambridge Univ., UK, Fuller Theological Seminary, Calif., USA; Founder and Int. Team Leader, interdenominational evangelistic mission team African Enterprise 1962–2002; conducted missions in cities including Cape Town, Johannesburg, Nairobi, Cairo, Lusaka, Gaborone, Monrovia (Liberia), Mbabane (Swaziland); initiated SA Congress on Mission and Evangelism 1973, Pan African Christian Leadership Ass. 1976, SA Christian Leadership Ass. 1979, Nat. Initiative for Reconciliation 1985; speaker at events including Lausanne II conf., Manila, Philippines 1989, Missionsfest 1990, N American Renewal Conf. 1990, UN 50th Anniversary, Dublin Castle, Repub. of Ireland 1995; admitted to Anglican Order of Simon of Cyrene 1983; Hon. HLD (Azusa Pacific Univ., USA) 1993; Paul Harris Fellow, Rotary Award 1997, Michaelhouse St Michael's Award 1997. *Radio:* Daywatch (weekly South African radio programme). *Publications:* Decade of Decisions 1970, Where Are You Taking the World Anyway? 1971, Prisoners of Hope 1974, Relationship Tangle 1974, Bursting the Wineskins 1983, Chasing the Wind 1985, The Passing Summer 1989, The Politics of Love 1991, A Witness For Ever 1995, Window on the Word 1997. *Leisure interests:* music, photography, scrapbooks, sport. *Address:* African Enterprise, PO Box 13140, Cascades 3202, South Africa (office). *Telephone:* (33) 347-1911 (office). *Fax:* (33) 347-1915 (office). *E-mail:* aeusa@ae.org.za (office). *Website:* www.africanenterprise.org.za (office).

CASSIDY, HE Cardinal Edward Idris, DCnL; Australian ecclesiastic (retd); b. 5 July 1924, Sydney; s. of Harold Cassidy and Dorothy Phillips; ed Parramatta High School, Sydney, St Columba's Seminary, Springwood, St Patrick's Coll. Manly, Lateran Univ. Rome and Pontifical Ecclesiastical Acad. Rome; ordained priest 1949; Asst Priest, Yenda, NSW 1950–52; diplomatic service in India 1955–62, Ireland 1962–67, El Salvador 1967–69, Argentina 1969–70; consecrated Archbishop 1970; Titular Archbishop of Amantia 1970; Apostolic Pro-Nuncio in Taiwan 1970–79 (also accred to Bangladesh and Burma 1973–79); Apostolic Del. to Southern Africa and Apostolic Pro-Nuncio to Lesotho 1979–84; Apostolic Pro-Nuncio to the Netherlands 1984–88; Substitute of the Secr. of State 1988–89; Pres. Pontifical Council for Promoting Christian Unity and Comm. for Religious Relations with the Jews 1989–2001; cr. Cardinal 1991; Cavaliere, Gran Croce dell'Ordine al Merito della Repubblica Italiana; decorations from El Salvador, Taiwan, Netherlands, Australia, France, Sweden and Germany. *Publications:* Ecumenism and Interreligious Dialogue 2005. *Leisure interests:* tennis, golf, music. *Address:* 16 Coachwood Drive, Warabrook, NSW 2304, Australia (home). *Telephone:* (2) 4968-9025 (home). *Fax:* (2) 4968-9064 (home). *E-mail:* iecassidy@bigpond.com (home).

CASSIDY, Kathryn A., BA, MBA; American business executive; *Vice-President, Corporate Treasury, General Electric Company;* m.; three c.; ed Univ. of Connecticut, Fordham Univ.; joined General Electric (GE) 1980, serving in several positions including Man. Dir GE Capital Real Estate, led Real Estate Capital Markets 1996–2000, Vice-Pres. and Treas. General Electric Co. 2001–; mem. Bd of Dirs UCONN Foundation, Building with

Books; mem. Treasury Leadership Roundtable, Washington, DC; ranked by Fortune magazine amongst 50 Most Powerful Women in Business in the US (50th) 2005. *Address:* 152 Canyon Road, Wilton, CT 06897-2639; General Electric Company, 3135 Easton Turnpike, Fairfield, CT 06828-0001, USA (office). *Telephone:* (203) 373-2211 (office). *Fax:* (203) 373-3131 (office). *Website:* www.ge.com (office).

CASSIDY, Sheila Anne, BM, BCh, MA; British psychotherapist (retd); b. 18 Aug. 1937, Lincs.; d. of the late Air Vice-Marshal John Reginald Cassidy and of Barbara Margaret Cassidy (née Drew); ed Our Lady of Mercy Coll., Parramatta, NSW, Univ. of Sydney and Oxford Univ.; resident posts, Radcliffe Infirmary, Oxford 1963–68, Leicester Royal Infirmary 1968–70; Medical Asst 1970–71; Asst Surgeon, Asistencia Pública, Santiago, Chile 1971–75; tortured and imprisoned for treating wounded guerrilla Nov.–Dec. 1975; human rights lecturing 1976–77; studied monastic life, Ampleforth Abbey, York 1977–79; novice in Bernardine Cistercian Convent 1979–80; resident in radiotherapy, Plymouth Gen. Hosp. 1980–82, Research Registrar, Dept Radiotherapy 1982; Medical Dir, St Luke's Hospice, Plymouth 1982–93; Palliative Care Physician, Plymouth Gen. Hosp. 1993, Specialist in Psychosocial Oncology, Plymouth Oncology Centre 1996–2002, psychotherapist in pvt. practice 2002–; Lecturer, St Lukes Hospice, Plymouth 2002–; mem. United Kingdom Council for Psychotherapists (UKCP); Hon. DSc (Exeter) 1991, Hon. DLitt (Council for Nat. Academic Awards) 1992; Hon. DM (Univ. Plymouth) 2002; Valiant for Truth Media Award. *Publications:* Audacity to Believe (autobiog.) 1977, Prayer for Pilgrims 1979, Sharing the Darkness 1988, Good Friday People 1991, Light from the Dark Valley 1994, The Loneliest Journey 1995, Creation Story 1996, Faith, Hope and Shopping 2006. *Leisure interests:* writing, broadcasting, drawing, dogs (chows), swimming, knitting, TV. *Address:* 7 The Esplanade, The Hoe, Plymouth, PL1 2PJ, England (home). *Telephone:* (1752) 2658892. *E-mail:* sheila@cassidy5836.freeserve.co.uk (home).

CASSON, Mark Christopher, BA, FRSA; British economist and academic; *Professor of Economics, University of Reading;* b. 17 Dec. 1945, Grappenhall, Cheshire; s. of Stanley Christopher Casson and Dorothy Nowell Barlow; m. Janet Penelope Close 1975; one d.; ed Manchester Grammar School, Univ. of Bristol, Churchill Coll., Cambridge; Lecturer in Econs, Univ. of Reading 1969–77, Reader 1977–81, Prof. 1981–, Head Dept of Econs 1987–94, Dir Centre for Institutional Performance 2003–; Fellow Acad. of Int. Business, Univ. of Leeds 1993, Visiting Prof. of Int. Business 1995–; Visiting Prof. of Man., Univ. of London 2004–; Leverhulme Major Research Fellow 2006–; mem. Council Royal Econ. Soc. 1985–90; Chair. Business Enterprise Heritage Trust 2000–. *Publications:* The Future of the Multinational Enterprise 1976, The Entrepreneur: An Economic Theory 1982, Economics of Unemployment: An Historical Perspective 1983, The Firm and the Market: Studies in Multinational Enterprise and the Scope of the Firm 1987, The Economics of Business Culture: Game Theory, Transaction Costs and Economic Welfare 1981, Entrepreneurship and Business Culture 1995, Information and Organization: A New Perspective on the Theory of the Firm 1997, Economics of International Business 2000, Enterprise and Leadership 2000, Oxford Handbook of Entrepreneurship 2006, Economics of Networks 2008, The World's First Railway System 2009. *Leisure interests:* railway history, Church of England activities, book collecting, drawing in pastel. *Address:* School of Economics, University of Reading, PO Box 218, Reading, Berks., RG6 6AA (office); 6 Wayside Green, Woodcote, Reading, RG8 0QJ, England (home). *Telephone:* (118) 931-8227 (office); (1491) 681483 (home). *Fax:* (118) 975-0236 (office); (1491) 681483 (home). *E-mail:* m.c.casson@reading.ac.uk (office); mark@casson14.freeserve.co.uk (home). *Website:* www.henley.reading.ac.uk/economics/about/staff/m-c-casson (office).

CASTA, Laetitia; French model and actress; b. 11 May 1978, Pont-Audemer; d. of Dominique Casta and Line Casta; one d. (with pnr Stephane Sednaoui); launched by Yves Saint Laurent; first maj. advertising campaign for Guess jeans 1993; model, Victoria's Secret 1996–; appeared in Sports Illustrated 1997, 1998, 1999, on covers of Vogue, Elle, Cosmopolitan, Rolling Stone; contracts with L'Oréal, Galeries Lafayette; chosen to represent Marianne (nat. emblem of France) 2000. *Films include:* Astérix et Obélix contre César 1999, La bicyclette bleue, Les ames fortes (tv miniseries) 2000, Gitano 2000, Rue des plaisirs 2002, Errance 2003, Luisa Sanfelice (tv miniseries) 2004. *Address:* c/o Artmedia, 10 ave Georges V, 75008 Paris, France (office).

CASTAGNA, Vanessa J., BS; American retail executive; ed Purdue Univ., West Lafayette, Ind.; began career with Lazarus (div. of Federated Department Stores) 1972, later Sr Vice-Pres. and Gen. Merchandising Man.; fmr Sr Vice-Pres. and Gen. Merchandising Man. Marshalls Stores (div. of TJX Companies); Vice-Pres. Merchandising—Women's, Target Stores (div. of Dayton Hudson Corpn, now known as Target Corpn) 1985–92; Sr Vice-Pres. and Gen. Merchandising Man., home decor, furniture, crafts and children's apparel, Wal-Mart Stores Div. 1994–96, Sr Vice-Pres. and Gen. Merchandise Man. for women's and children's accessories and apparel 1996–99; Exec. Vice-Pres. and COO JCPenney Stores, Merchandising and Catalog 1999–2001, Exec. Vice-Pres., Pres. and COO JCPenney Stores, Catalog and Internet 2001–03, Exec. Vice-Pres., Chair. and CEO, Stores, Catalog, Internet, J.C. Penney Company, Inc. 2003–04; Sr mem. Cerberus Capital Man. and Exec. Chair. Mervyns' Bd of Dirs 2005–07; mem. Bd of Dirs Levi Strauss & Co. 2007–; Chair. Women's Leadership Council United Way of Metropolitan Dallas; fmr mem. Advisory Bd School of Business at Southern Methodist Univ.; fmr mem. Advisory Bd Nat. Minority Supplier Devt Council, Bd JCPenney Afterschool Fund; ranked by Fortune magazine amongst 50 Most Powerful Women in Business in the US 2001, (46th) 2002, (41st) 2003, (40th) 2004, ranked by Forbes magazine amongst 100 Most Powerful Women (38th) 2004, (64th) 2005, Young Menswear Asscn AMY Award 2006. *Address:* c/o Board of Directors, Levi Strauss & Co., 1155 Battery Street, San Francisco, CA 94111, USA.

CASTANEDA, Jorge G., BA, MA, PhD; Mexican politician, academic and writer; *Global Distinguished Professor of Politics and Latin American and Carribean Studies, New York University;* b. 24 May 1953, Mexico City; s. of the late Jorge Castañeda y Álvarez de la Rosa; ed Princeton Univ., USA, Universite de Paris-I (Pantheon-Sorbonne), Ecole Pratique de Hautes Etudes, Paris I, Univ. of Paris, France; has taught at Nat. Autonomous Univ. of Mexico,Princeton Univ., Univ. of California, Berkeley; Sr Assoc. Carnegie Endowment for Int. Peace 1985–87; Global Distinguished Prof. of Politics and Latin American and Caribben Studies, New York Univ. 1997–; Sec. of State for Foreign Affairs 2000–03; announced campaign for candidacy in 2006 presidential election in 2004, Supreme Court ruled he could not run without support of a registered political party; mem. Bd of Dirs Human Rights Watch; f. San Angel Group 1994; regular columnist for Reforma (Mexican daily newspaper), Los Angeles Times and Newsweek International; John D. and Catherine T. MacArthur Foundation Research and Writing Grant Recipient 1989–91. *Publications include:* 12 books and numerous articles. *Address:* Center for Latin American and Caribbean Studies, King Juan Carlos I of Spain Center, 53 Washington Square South, Floor 4W, New York, NY 10012, USA (office). *Telephone:* (212) 998-8682 (office). *Fax:* (212) 995-4163 (office). *E-mail:* jorge.castaneda@nyu.edu (office). *Website:* www.nyu.edu/gsas/program/latin (office).

CASTEEN, John Thomas. III, BA, MA, PhD; American writer, academic and university administrator; *President, University of Virginia;* b. 11 Dec. 1943, Portsmouth, Va; s. of John T. Casteen, Jr and Naomi Irene Casteen; m. Elizabeth F. Casteen; two s. three d.; ed Univ. of Virginia; Asst Prof. of English, Univ. of California, Berkeley 1970–75; Assoc. Prof. and Dean Univ. of Virginia 1975–81; Prof., Virginia Commonwealth Univ. 1982–85; Sec. of Educ., Commonwealth of Va 1982–85; Pres. and Prof., Univ. of Connecticut 1985–90; Pres. Univ. of Virginia 1990–, also George M. Kaufman Presidential Prof. and Prof. of English 1990–; Chair. Jefferson Science Associates LLC, Universitas 21; mem. Bd of Dirs Wachovia Corpn, U21 Global Pte Ltd, SAGE Publications Inc.; Trustee Chesapeake Bay Foundation; mem. Virginia Univ. Research Partnership Bd; Hon. LLD (Shenandoah Coll.), (Bentley Coll.) 1992, (Piedmont Community Coll.) 1992, (Bridgewater Coll.) 1993, Transylvania Univ.) 1999, Dr hc (Athens) 1996; Raven Award, Univ. of Va, Outstanding Virginian of 1993, American Asscn of Univ. Profs Jackson Davis Award 1993, Gold Medal, Nat. Inst. of Social Sciences 1998, Higher Educ. Center for Alcohol and Other Drug Prevention's Presidents Leadership Group Award 2002, Architecture Medal for Va Service, Va Soc. of the American Inst. of Architects 2004. *Publications:* 16 stories 1982; numerous essays and articles 1970–. *Leisure interest:* sailing, walking. *Address:* Office of the President, University of Virginia, Madison Hall, PO Box 9011, Charlottesville, VA 22906, USA (office). *Telephone:* (434) 924-3337 (office). *Fax:* (434) 924-3792 (office). *E-mail:* jtc@virginia.edu (office). *Website:* www.virginia.edu/president (office).

CASTELLANOS ESCALONA, Diego Luis, PhD; Venezuelan banker and academic; b. 1 Sept. 1930, Caracas; ed Cen. Univ. of Venezuela; Prof., Cen. Univ. of Venezuela 1959–; Dir Advisory Council to SELA (Foundation for the Coordination of Latin American Economies) 1980–82; Sec. of Nat. Econ. Council 1991–98; financial consultant, Industrial Investment Fund (FONCREI) 1984–86; Pres. Banco de Comercia Exterior –2000; Exec. Dir Fundafuturo 1999–2000; Pres. Banco Central de Venezuela 2000–05; Exec. Sec. Venezuelan Council of Industry 1982–83; fmr Perm. Rep. to UN, Geneva. *Publications:* Export: Market Studies Manual 1951, Markets and Commercialization 1963, Principles and Objectives 1972. *Address:* c/o Banco Central de Venezuela, Avda Urdaneta, esq. de Carmelitas, Caracas 1010, Venezuela (office).

CASTELLI, Roberto; Italian engineer and politician; b. 12 July 1946, Lecco, Lombardy; m.; one s.; ed Alessandro Manzoni School, Lecco, Politecnico di Milano; worked as researcher developing technological system of electronic noise reduction; adviser to EC on environmental affairs; joined Lega Nord 1986, elected Deputy for Lecco 1992, 1994, fmr Vice-Pres. of Lega Nord in Chamber of Deputies; elected Senator for Lecco e Bergamo 1996–, Pres. Lega Nord Parl. Group 1999–2001; Minister of Justice 2001–06; Group Leader Transport Cttee; mem. Budget Cttee of Senate, Parl. Cttee for Impeachments; mem. Jt Cttee on Regional Affairs, Supervision over RAI TV and Radio, Investigations over Terrorism and Massacres; fmr mem. Comm. for Regional Affairs, Comm. on Terrorism; voluntary mem. Nat. Alpine and Speleological Rescue Corps; Hon. Pres. Alpe (Asscn of Free Padan Hikers). *Leisure interests:* ski-alpinism, hiking, sailing, reading. *Address:* Senate (Senato), Piazza Madama, 00186 Rome (office); c/o Lega Nord, Via C. Bellerio 41, 20161 Milan, Italy. *Telephone:* (06) 67061 (office). *E-mail:* castelli_r@posta.senato.it (office); sen.robertocastelli@tin.it. *Website:* www.senato.it (office); www.leganord.org.

CASTELLINA, Luciana, LLB; Italian politician and journalist; b. 9 Aug. 1929, Rome; m. (divorced); one s. one d.; ed Univ. of Rome; Ed. Nuova Generazione (weekly) 1958–62, Il Manifesto (daily) 1972–78, Pace e Guerra (weekly) then Liberazione (weekly) 1992–94; elected mem. Parl. 1976, 1979, 1983; elected mem. European Parl. 1979, 1984, 1989, 1994, Chair. Culture and Media Cttee 1994–96, later Chair. External Econ. Relations Cttee; fmr mem. Presidence Italian Women's Union, directorate Italian Communist Party; Pres. Italia Cinema Srl, Cineuropa.org, Europacinema, UCCA (ARCI cine clubs); Vice-Pres. Eurovisioni Bd; lecturer, Pisa State Univ.; mem. Bd of Dirs Associazione di Promozione Sociale, Lelio Basso Foundation; Kt Commdr of the Argentine Repub. *Publications:* Che c'è in America (reports from America) 1972, Family and Society in Marxist Analysis 1974, Il Commino Dei Movimenti 2003, 50 Anni d'Europa 2007, Eurollywood 2009. *Leisure interest:* films. *Address:* Via di San Valentino 32, 00197 Rome (home); c/o Board of

Directors, ARCI, Via dei Monti di Pietralata 16, 00182 Rome, Italy (office). *E-mail:* lcastellina@mclink.it (home).

CASTIGLIONI SORIA, Luis Alberto; Paraguayan politician; b. 31 July 1962, Itacurubí del Rosario; joined Partido Colorado 1979; Perm. Mem. Partido Colorado Nat. Constituent Convention 1991–92; Perm. Mem. Partido Colorado Govt Bd 1992–95; Pres. Capital Sectional Cttee No. 4 1996–2000; Vice-Pres. of Paraguay 2003–07 (resgnd); unsuccessful cand. (Partido Colorado) for Pres. of Paraguay 2008; Gen. Sec. Supreme Council of Int. Parl. for Safety and Peace. *Address:* c/o Asociación Nacional Republicana—Partido Colorado, Casa de los Colorados, 25 de Mayo 842, Asunción, Paraguay (office); International Parliament for Safety and Peace, Via Marchese di Roccaforte, 10, 90143 Palermo, Sicily, Italy. *Telephone:* (21) 44-4137 (office). *Fax:* (21) 49-7857 (office). *Website:* www.anr.org.py (office); www.international-parliament .net.

CASTILLO, Eva; Spanish investment banker; *Head of Global Wealth Management, Europe, Middle East and Africa and President, Merrill Lynch Spain;* b. 1963; ed Universidad Pontificia de Comillas of Madrid; equity researcher, Beta Capital Sociedad de Valores, SA 1987–92; with Goldman Sachs Int., London, UK in Int. Equities Dept 1992–97; Head of Equity Markets for Spain and Portugal, Merrill Lynch Spain, Madrid 1997–99, Gen. Man. for Spain and Portugal 1999–2000, CEO Merrill Lynch Capital Markets Spain 2000, then COO Europe, Middle East and Africa (EMEA) Equity Markets, then Head of Global Markets and Investment Banking in Spain and Portugal 2003, also Pres. Merrill Lynch Spain, currently Head of Global Wealth Man. EMEA, including Merrill Lynch Bank and Int. Trust and Wealth Structuring, mem. Merrill Lynch EMEA Exec. Cttee, Global Wealth Man. Exec. and Operating Cttees; mem. Bd of Dirs Telefonica SA. *Address:* Merrill Lynch Spain, Edificio Torre Picasso, Floors 30 & 40, Plaza Pablo Ruiz Picasso 1, 28020 Madrid, Spain (office). *Telephone:* (91) 5143000 (office). *Fax:* (91) 5143001 (office). *Website:* www.ml.com (office).

CASTILLO, Michel Xavier Janicot del, LèsL, LenP; French writer; b. 2 Aug. 1933, Madrid, Spain; s. of Michel Janicot and Isabelle del Castillo; ed Coll. des jésuites d'Ubeba, Spain, Lycée Janson-de-Sailly, Paris; mem. Soc. des gens de lettres, PEN; Chevalier Légion d'honneur; Commdr des Arts et Lettres; Prix des Magots 1973, Grand Prix des libraires 1973, Prix Chateaubriand 1975, Prix Renaudot 1981, Prix Maurice Genevoix 1994. *Publications:* Tanguy 1956 (Prix des Neufs), La Guitare 1957, Le Colleur d'affiches 1958, Le Manège espagnol 1960, Tara 1962, Gerardo Laïn 1967, Le Vent de la nuit 1972, Le Silence des pierres 1975, Le Sortilège espagnol 1977, Les Cyprès meurent en Italie 1979, Les Louves de l'Escurial 1980, La nuit du décret 1981, La Gloire de Dina 1984, La Halte et Le Chemin 1985, Nos Andalousies 1985, Le Démon de l'oubli 1987, Mort d'un poète 1989, Une Femme en Soi 1991, Andalousie 1991, Le Crime des Pères 1993, Carlos Pradal 1993, Rue des Archives 1994, Mon frère l'idiot 1995 (Prix de l'Ecrit Intime), Le Sortilege Espagnol : Les Officiants De La Mort 1996, La Tunique d'infamie 1997, De père français 1998, Colette, une certaine France (Prix Femina 1999), L'Adieu au siècle 2000, Droit d'auteur 2000, Les Etoiles Froides 2001, Colette En Voyage 2002, Algerie, L'Extase Et Le Sang 2002, Les Portes Du Sang 2003, Le Jour Du Destin 2003, Sortie Des Artistes 2004, Le Dictionnaire Amoureux De L'Espagne (Prix Méditerranée) 2005. *Address:* Editions Stock, 27 rue Cassette, 75006 Paris (office); Le Colombier, 7 avenue Camille Martin, 30190 La Calmette, France (home). *E-mail:* webmaster@micheldelcastillo.com. *Website:* www .micheldelcastillo.com.

CASTILLO DE SOLANO, Azucena; Nicaraguan organization executive and fmr government official; *General Manager, Asociación de Productores y Exportadores de Nicaragua;* Vice-Minister of Economy and Devt 1997–2002; Sec. of the Presidency 2002; Exec. Sec. of Social Emergence Inversion Fund 2002–05; Minister of Devt, Industry and Trade 2005–07; Gen. Man. Asociación de Productores y Exportadores de Nicaragua (Asscn of Producers and Exporters of Nicaragua) 2008–. *Address:* Asociación de Productores y Exportadores de Nicaragua, Barrio Bolonia, Iglesia San Francisco 1/2 c. arriba, Casa #1150, Apdo. 6149, Managua, Nicaragua (office). *E-mail:* apen@ apen.org.ni (office). *Website:* www.apen.org.ni (office).

CASTLE, Michael (Mike) N., BA, LLB; American politician and lawyer; b. 2 July 1939, Wilmington, Del.; s. of J. Manderson and Louisa B. Castle; m. Jane Castle; ed Hamilton Coll. and Georgetown Univ.; called to Del. Bar 1964, DC Bar 1964; Assoc. Connolly, Bove and Lodge (law firm), Wilmington 1964–73, Pnr 1973–75; Deputy Attorney-Gen. State of Del. 1965–66; mem. Del. House of Reps 1966–67; mem. Del. Senate 1968–77; Pnr, Schnee & Castle PA 1975–80; Lt-Gov. State of Del. 1981–85; Gov. of Delaware 1985–93; mem. US House of Reps 1993–; Prin. Michael N. Castle 1981–; Co-founder and mem. Republican Main Street Partnership (fmr Pres.); Republican. *Address:* 1233 Longworth HOB, Washington, DC 20515-0801, USA (office). *Telephone:* (202) 225-4165 (office). *Website:* www.house.gov/castle (office).

CASTON, Geoffrey Kemp, CBE, MA, MPA; British university administrator; b. 17 May 1926, Beckenham, Kent; s. of Reginald Caston and Lilian Caston; m. 1st Sonya Chassell 1956; two s. one d.; m. 2nd Judy Roizen 1983; ed St Dunstan's Coll., Peterhouse, Cambridge, Harvard Univ., USA; Sub-Lt RNVR 1945–47; Colonial Office 1951–58; First-Sec. UK Mission to UN 1958–61; Dept of Tech. Co-operation 1961–64; Asst Sec., Dept of Educ. and Science 1964–66; Sec. Schools Council 1966–70; Under-Sec., Univ. Grants Cttee 1970–72; Registrar of Univ. and Fellow of Merton Coll., Oxford 1972–79; Sec. Gen. Cttee of Vice-Chancellors 1979–83; Vice-Chancellor, Univ. of South Pacific, Fiji 1983–92; Visiting Assoc., Center for Studies in Higher Educ., Univ. of California, Berkeley 1978–; Distinguished Lecturer in Pacific Studies, Univ. of Hawaii 1992; GAP Project Man., S. Pacific 1994–99; Chair. Commonwealth Scholarship Comm. in the UK 1996–2001; mem. or chair. numerous dels and

cttees, nat. and int., including UN Tech. Assistance Cttee 1962–64, Visiting Mission to Trust Territory of Pacific Islands 1961, OECD Workshops on Educational Innovation 1969, 1970, 1971, Nat. Inst. for Careers Educ. and Counselling 1975–83, Exec. Cttee Inter-Univ. Council for Higher Educ. Overseas 1977–83, Library Advisory Council (UK) 1973–78, Council, Univ. of Papua New Guinea; Trustee, Just World Pnrs 1993–; Hon. LLD (Dundee) 1982; Hon. DLitt (Deakin) 1991; George Long Prize for Jurisprudence 1950, Symons Medal for Outstanding Service to Commonwealth Univs 2001. *Publication:* The Management of International Cooperation in Universities 1996. *Address:* 3 Pennsylvania Park, Exeter, EX4 6HB, England. *Telephone:* (1392) 272986.

CASTRESANA FERNÁNDEZ, Carlos; Spanish jurist and international organization official; *Commissioner, Comisión Internacional contra la Impunidad en Guatemala (International Commission against Impunity in Guatemala—CICIG);* ed Universidad Complutense de Madrid, Institut Int. de Droits de l'Homme, Strasbourg, France; taught criminal law at Univ. of San Francisco and Universidad Carlos III, Madrid; served as prosecutor in circuit courts of Madrid and Catalunya, temporarily dist and investigating judge and magistrate of territorial court of Madrid before being assigned to Special Prosecutor's Office against drug smuggling and money laundering 1993–95; Special Anti-Corruption Prosecutor for Spain's nat. court 1995–2005; Public Prosecutor for Spanish Supreme Court 2005–06; began working for the Mexico and Cen. America regional office of UN Office on Drugs and Crime (UNODC) 2006–07; Commr Comisión Internacional contra la Impunidad en Guatemala (Int. Comm. against Impunity in Guatemala—CICIG, body established under agreement between UN and Guatemalan Govt) 2007–; Dr hc (Universidad Central, Chile, Universidad de Guadalajara, Mexico); Human Rights Nat. Prize (Spain) 1997. *Address:* Comisión Internacional contra la Impunidad en Guatemala (CICIG), 5 Avenida 5-55 Zone 14, Torre IV, Nivel 10, Guatemala City, Guatemala.

CASTRILLÓN HOYOS, HE Cardinal Dario; Colombian ecclesiastic; b. 4 July 1929, Medellín; ed Pontifical Gregorian Univ., Univ. of Louvain; ordained priest 1952; consecrated Bishop 1971, Bishop of Pereira 1976, Archbishop of Bucaramanga 1992–96; Pro-Prefect Congregation for the Clergy 1996–98; elevated to Cardinal-Deacon of SS. Nome di Maria al Foro Traiano 1998; Prefect of Clergy, Roman Curia 1998–, Pres. Ecclesia Dei, Roman Curia 2000–. *Address:* Palazzo delle Congregazioni, Piazza Pio XII, 3, 00193 Rome, Italy; c/o Arzobispado, Calle 33, N 21-18, Bucaramanga, Santander, Colombia.

CASTRO, Fidel (see Castro Ruz, Fidel).

CASTRO, Gen. Raúl (see Castro Ruz, Gen. Raúl).

CASTRO CALDAS, Júlio de Lemos de; Portuguese politician and lawyer; *Partner, Almeida Sampaio & Associados;* b. 19 Nov. 1943, Lisbon; s. of Eugénio Queiroz de Castro Caldas and Maria Lusitana Mascarenhas de Lemos de Castro Caldas; m. Ana Cristina Ribeiro Sobral Cid; one s. two d.; ed Classic Univ. of Lisbon; Leader, Students' Asscn, Classic Univ. of Lisbon 1963; mil. service in Portuguese Army 1967–70; f. Associação para o Desenvolvimento Económico e Social (SEDES) 1970, Partido Popular Democrático 1974; Legal Adviser to Pres. of Portugal 1976–78; Democratic Alliance mem. Parl. for Viana do Castelo 1979; Leader Parl. Group of Democratic Alliance 1979–82; Minister of Defence, Socialist Party 1999–2001; currently Pnr, Almeida Sampaio & Associados (law firm), Lisbon' mem. Supreme Council of Public Prosecutor Dept 1980–92; Chair. Bilbao Vizcaya Bank (Portugal) 1995–99; fmr chair. several cos; mem. Portuguese Bar Asscn, Treas. 1988–91, Pres. 1993–99; Pres. European Bar Fed. 1997–99; fmr mem. Bd of Dirs (non-exec.) Companhia le Seguros Global SA, Carrefour SA. *Address:* Almeida Sampaio & Associados, Av. Duque D'Ávila, 66, 1069-075 Lisbon, Portugal (office). *Telephone:* (21) 3536926 (office). *Fax:* (21) 3536927 (office). *E-mail:* castro.caldas@jsc.pt (office). *Website:* www.almeidasampaio-law.com (office).

CASTRO RUZ, Fidel, DIur; Cuban fmr head of state; b. 13 Aug. 1926, brother of Raúl Castro Ruz; m. Mirta Diaz-Bilart 1948 (divorced 1955); one s.; ed Jesuit schools in Santiago and Havana, Univ. de la Habana; law practice in Havana; began active opposition to Batista regime by attack on Moncada barracks at Santiago 26th July 1953; sentenced to 15 years' imprisonment 1953; amnestied 1956; went into exile in Mexico and began to organize armed rebellion; landed in Oriente Province with small force Dec. 1956; carried on armed struggle against Batista regime until flight of Batista Jan. 1959; Prime Minister of Cuba 1959–76; Head of State and Pres. of Council of State 1976–2008 (resgnd), Pres. of Council of Ministers 1976–2008; Chair. Agrarian Reform Inst. 1965; First Sec. Partido Unido de la Revolución Socialista (PURS) 1963–65, Partido Comunista 1965–2008 (mem. Political Bureau 1976–2008), Head Nat. Defence Council 1992–2008; Order of Lenin 1972, 1986, Order of the October Revolution 1976, Somali Order (1st Class) 1977, Order of Jamaica 1977, Gold Star (Vietnam) 1982; Lenin Peace Prize 1961, Hero of the Soviet Union 1963, Dimitrov Prize (Bulgaria) 1980, Muammar Gaddafi Human Rights Prize 1998. *Publications:* Ten Years of Revolution 1964, History Will Absolve Me 1968, Fidel (with Frei Betto) 1987, How Far We Slaves Have Come: South Africa and Cuba in Today's World (with Nelson Mandela) 1991, Fidel Castro (autobiog.) 2007. *Address:* c/o Palacio del Gobierno, Havana, Cuba.

CASTRO RUZ, Gen. Raúl; Cuban politician and head of state; *President, Council of State;* b. 3 June 1931, brother of Fidel Castro Ruz; m. Vilma Espín 1959 (died 2007); one d.; ed Jesuit School of Colegio Dolores, Santiago, Colegio de Belén, Havana; sentenced to 15 years' imprisonment for insurrection 1953; amnestied 1954; assisted his brother's movement in Mexico and in Cuba after Dec. 1956, made Commdt 1957; First Vice-Pres. of the Councils of State and Ministers and Maximum Gen. of the Revolutionary Armed Forces 1959–2008, Acting Pres. Council of State 2006–08, Pres. 2008–; led Cuban mil. in repulsing exiles forces in Bay of Pigs invasion 1961; Second Sec. CP Cen. Cttee 1965; Deputy, Asamblea Nacional del Poder Popular 1976; Order of Lenin 1979, Order of the October Revolution 1981, Orden Máximo Gómez 1998; Medal for Strengthening of Brotherhood in Arms 1977. *Address:* Palicio del Gobierno, Havana, Cuba (office). *Website:* www2.cuba.cu/politica/webpcc (office).

CASULE, Slobodan; Macedonian politician and journalist; b. 27 Sept. 1945, Skopje; ed Pontifical Catholic Univ., Lima, Peru; journalist and interpreter, Skopje TV 1965–67, Ed., Foreign Corresp. 1967–74; Latin America Corresp. Tanjung News Agency 1974–80, Chief Ed. 1980–90; Dir and Chief Ed. Macedonian Radio 1990–94, Ed., Commentator 1994–99; Dir-Gen. Nova Makedonija 1999; govt adviser 2000–; Minister of Foreign Affairs 2001–02; mem. Parl. (VMRO-DPMNE) 2002–06; Founder and mem. Human Rights Forum of Macedonia, Int. Relations Forum; mem. European Inst. of Media, Inst. of East–West Dialogue, Int. Fund for Media, US Democratic Inst., Helsinki Watch, Peace in the Country–Peace in the World Org., Journalists' Asscn of Macedonia, Int. Journalists' Asscn; f. TV Skopje. *Address:* c/o Vnatrešno-Makedonska Revolucionerna Organizacija—Demokratska Partija za Makedonsko Nacionalno Edinstvo, 1000 Skopje, Petar Drapshin br. 36, Macedonia (office).

CATARINO, Pedro Manuel; Portuguese diplomatist; b. 12 May 1941, Lisbon; m. Cheryl A. Steyn 1969; one s. one d.; ed Univ. of Lisbon; joined Foreign Service in 1964, served in Embassy in Pretoria 1967–69, Defence Counsellor, Del. to NATO, Brussels 1974–79, Consul-Gen., Hong Kong 1979–82, mem. int. staff, NATO, Brussels 1983–89, head of del. to negotiations for a new defence and co-operation agreement with USA 1989–92, Pres. Interministerial Comm. of Macao and Head of Portuguese del. to Jt Luso-Chinese Liaison Group, Perm. Rep. to UN 1992–97, Amb. to China 1997–2002, to USA 2002–06; Silver Medal for Distinguished Services. *Leisure interest:* tennis. *Address:* Ministry of Foreign Affairs, Palácio das Necessidades, Largo do Rilvas, 1399-030 Lisbon, Portugal (office). *Telephone:* (21) 3946000 (office). *Fax:* (21) 3946053 (office). *E-mail:* gii@mne.gov.pt (office). *Website:* www.min -nestrangeiros.pt (office).

CATHALA, Thierry Gerard, DenD; French judge; b. 23 Feb. 1925, Bordeaux; s. of Jean Cathala and Juliette Monsion; m. Marie F. Mérimée 1954; two s. one d.; ed Saint-Genes Coll., Lycée Montaigne, Faculté de droit de Bordeaux and Paris; trainee barrister, Bordeaux Bar 1946–48; Deputy Judge, Bordeaux 1948–51, Examining Magistrate 1951–65; Prin. Admin. EEC Comm., Brussels 1965–73; judge, Nanterre and Paris Courts 1974–81; Chief Justice, French Polynesia Court of Appeal 1981–85; Counsellor, Supreme Court of Cassation 1985–94; French Rep., South Pacific Judicial Conf. 1982–84; mem. Supreme Judiciary Council 1987–91; Chair. Ninth South Pacific Judicial Conf., Tahiti 1991; mem. Comm. Informatique et Libertés 1994–99; Chair. Judicial Court, Monaco 1999–; Pres. Asscn of Friends of French Polynesia 1994–; Officier Légion d'honneur, Ordre nat. du Mérite. *Publications:* Le Contrôle de la légalité administrative par les tribunaux judiciaires 1966; numerous articles on law. *Leisure interests:* geography, travelling, religious questions. *Address:* CNIL, 21 rue Saint-Guillaume, 75340 Paris; 8 rue Ploix, 78000 Versailles, France (home); Aybrams, Crampagna, 09120 Varilhes, France. *Telephone:* 39-50-31-98 (home).

CATHCART, (William) Alun; British business executive; *Chairman, Avis Europe;* b. 9 Dec. 1943; mem. Bd of Dirs (non-exec.) Avis Rent A Car Inc. 1980–98, CEO and Deputy Chair. Avis Europe PLC 1999–2003, Chair. (nonexec.) 2004–; Deputy Chair. (non-exec.) Nat. Express Group PLC 1992; Deputy Chair. Belron Int.; Chair. (non-exec.) Selfridges 1998–2003; Chair. (non-exec.) The Rank Group 2001–07; mem. Bd of Dirs Emap plc 2005, Exec. Chair. 2006–08, Chair. (non-exec.) 2008–; Dir Tikkun UK Ltd (charity). *Address:* Avis Europe plc, Avis House, Park Road, Bracknell, Berks., RG12 2EW, England (office). *Telephone:* (1344) 426-644 (office). *Website:* www.avis -europe.com (office).

CATHCART, Kevin James, MA, PhD, MRIA; Irish academic; *Professor Emeritus of Near Eastern Languages, University College, Dublin;* b. 9 Oct. 1939, Derrylin, Co. Fermanagh, N Ireland; s. of Andrew Cathcart and Elizabeth Cathcart (née Flannery); m. Ann McDermott 1968; two s.; ed Salesian Coll., Cheshire, UK, Mellifont Abbey, Co. Louth, Trinity Coll., Dublin, and Pontifical Biblical Inst., Rome, Italy; Lecturer in Hebrew, Pontifical Biblical Inst., Rome 1968; Lecturer in Near Eastern Studies, Univ. of Ottawa, Canada 1968–71, Asst Prof. 1971–73, Assoc. Prof. 1973–74; Sr Lecturer in Semitic Languages and Dept Head, Univ. Coll. Dublin 1974–79, Prof. of Near Eastern Languages and Dept Head 1979–2001, Prof. Emer. of Near Eastern Languages 2001–; Campion Hall, Univ. of Oxford 2001–; Visiting Fellow, St Edmund's Coll., Cambridge 1987–88, 1993–94; Visiting Academic, St Benet's Hall, Oxford 1994; Visiting Prof., Heidelberg 1981, 1986, 1992, Ottawa 1983, Århus 1986, Toronto 1989, Mainz 1992; mem. Bd Electors (Regius Professorship of Hebrew), Univ. of Cambridge 1989–; editorial consultant Journal of Semitic Studies 1991–; mem. Royal Danish Acad.; Trustee, Chester Beatty Library, Dublin 1974–89, Chair. Bd of Trustees 1984–86. *Publications include:* Nahum in the Light of Northwest Semitic 1973, Back to the Sources: Biblical and Near Eastern Studies (with J.F. Healey) 1989, The Targum of the Minor Prophets (with RP Gordon) 1989, The Aramaic Bible (20 vols, co-ed.), The Edward Hincks Bicentenary Lectures 1994, Targumic and Cognate Studies (with M. Maher) 1996, The Letters of Peter le Page Renouf (1822–97) (four vols) 2002–04, The Correspondence of Edward Hincks (1792–1866), Vol. 1 2007. *Leisure interests:* birdwatching, medieval architecture. *Address:* 8 Friarsland Road, Clonskeagh, Dublin 14, Ireland (home). *Telephone:* (1) 2981589 (home). *E-mail:* kevincathcart@yahoo .co.uk (office).

CATHERWOOD, Sir (Henry) Frederick (Ross), Kt; British politician, industrialist and church leader; b. 30 Jan. 1925, Castledawson, Northern Ireland; s. of the late Stuart Catherwood and Jean Catherwood; m. Elizabeth Lloyd-Jones 1954; two s. one d.; ed Shrewsbury School and Clare Coll., Cambridge; Chartered Accountant 1951; Sec., Laws Stores Ltd, Gateshead 1952–54; Sec. and Controller, Richard Costain Ltd 1954–55, Chief Exec. 1955–60; Asst Man. Dir British Aluminium Co. Ltd 1960–62, Man. Dir 1962–64; Chief Industrial Adviser, Dept of Econ. Affairs 1964–66; mem. Nat. Econ. Devt Council (NEDC) 1964–71, Dir Gen. 1966–71; mem. British Nat. Export Council 1965–70; Vice-Chair. British Inst. of Man. 1972–74, Chair. 1974–76, Vice-Pres. 1976–; Chair. British Overseas Trade Bd 1975–79; Chair. Mallinson-Denny Ltd 1976–79 (Dir 1974); mem. Bd of Dirs John Laing Ltd 1971–80 (Group Man. Dir and Chief Exec. 1972–74), Goodyear Tyre and Rubber Co. (GB) Ltd 1975–89; Pres. Fellowship of Ind. Evangelical Churches 1977–78; MEP for Cambridgeshire and Wellingborough 1979–84, for Cambridgeshire and N Bedfordshire 1984–94, Vice-Pres. European Parl. 1989–92 (mem. Del. to US Congress 1983–89, to Hungary 1989, to Canada 1991–94), Chair. Cttee for External Econ. Relations 1979–84, Vice-Pres. European Democratic Group 1983–87, Chair. Land Use and Food Policy Intergroup 1987–92, Vice-Chair. Foreign Affairs Comm. 1992–94); mem. Council Royal Inst. of Int. Affairs 1964–77; Treas., Int. Fellowship Evangelical Students 1979–93, Vice-Pres. 1995–2003; Pres. Evangelical Alliance 1992–2001; Hon. Fellow, Clare Coll., Cambridge 1992; Hon. DSc (Aston) 1972; Hon. DScEcon (Queen's Univ., Belfast) 1973; Hon. DUniv (Surrey) 1979. *Publications:* The Christian in Industrial Society 1964, Britain with the Brakes Off 1966, The Christian Citizen 1969, A Better Way 1975, First Things First 1979, God's Time God's Money 1987, Pro-Europe? 1991, David: Poet, Warrior, King 1993, At the Cutting Edge (memoirs) 1995, Jobs and Justice, Homes and Hope 1997, It Can Be Done 2000, The Creation of Wealth 2002. *Leisure interests:* reading, writing, walking. *Address:* Sutton Hall, Balsham, Cambs., CB1, England. *Telephone:* (1223) 894017. *Fax:* (1223) 894032.

CATLOW, (Charles) Richard Arthur, MA, DPhil, FRS, FRSC, FInstP; British professor of natural philosophy; *Director, David Faraday Research Laboratory, Royal Institution of Great Britain; Head, Department of Chemistry, University College London;* b. 24 April 1947, Simonstone, Lancs.; s. of Rolf M. Catlow and Constance Catlow (née Aldred); m. 1st Carey Anne Chapman 1978; one s.; m. 2nd Nora de Leeuw 2000; ed Clitheroe Royal Grammar School and St John's Coll., Oxford; Grad. Scholar, Jesus Coll., Oxford 1970–73; Research Fellow, St John's Coll., Oxford 1970–76; Lecturer, Univ. Coll., London 1976–85, Head, Dept of Chem. 2002–; Prof. of Chem., Univ. of Keele 1985–89; Wolfson Prof. of Natural Philosophy, Royal Inst. of GB 1989–, Dir Davy Faraday Research Lab. 1998–; Royal Soc. of Chem. Medal (Solid State Chem.) 1992, Royal Soc. of Chem. Award (Interdisciplinary Science) 1992, 1998. *Publications:* jtly: Computer Simulation of Solids 1982, Mass Transport in Solids 1983, Computer Simulation of Fluids, Polymers and Solids 1989, Applications of Synchrotron Radiation 1990; over 800 research papers and several monographs, New Frontiers in Materials Chemistry (jtly) 1997, Microscopic Properties or Processes in Minerals (jtly) 1999, Computational Materials Science (jtly) 2003. *Leisure interests:* reading, walking, music. *Address:* Royal Institution of Great Britain, 21 Albemarle Street, London W1X 4BS (office); Department of Chemistry, University College London, Christopher Ingold Laboratories, 20 Gordon Street, London, WC1H 0AJ, England (office). *Telephone:* (20) 7670-2901 (RI) (office); (20) 7679-2818 (UCL) (office). *Fax:* (20) 7670-2920 (RI) (office); (20) 7679-7463 (UCL) (office). *E-mail:* richard@ri.ac.uk (office); c.r.a.catlow@ucl.ac.uk (office). *Website:* www.ri.ac .uk/DFRL (office); www.chem.ucl.ac.uk/people/catlow (office).

CATMULL, Ed, BS, PhD; American studio executive and computer graphics designer; *President, Pixar Animation Studios;* b. 31 March 1945, Parkersburg, WV; m. Susan Catmull; five c.; ed Univ. of Utah; Vice-Pres. Computer Div., Lucasfilm Ltd 1979–86, managed devt in areas of computer graphics, video editing, video games and digital audio, key developer of RenderMan programme; Co-Founder Pixar Animation Studios 1986, Chief Tech. Officer and exec. mem. 1986–2001, Pres. 2001–, Pres. Pixar and Disney animation studios after acquisition by Walt Disney Co. 2006–; animated films include Toy Story, Toy Story 2, A Bug's Life, Monsters Inc., Finding Nemo, The Incredibles; mem. Acad. of Motion Picture Arts and Sciences, Science and Tech. Awards Cttee; Scientific and Tech. Eng Awards (three), Acad. of Motion Picture Arts and Sciences Award, Coons Award for Lifetime Contrib. to Computer Graphics Industry, Gordon E. Sawyer Award, Acad. of Motion Picture Arts and Sciences 2009. *Address:* Pixar Animation Studios, 1200 Park Avenue, Emeryville, CA 94608, USA (office). *Telephone:* (510) 752-3000 (office). *Fax:* (510) 752-3151 (office). *Website:* www.pixar.com (office).

CATON-JONES, Michael; British film director; b. 15 Oct. 1957, Broxburn, West Lothian, Scotland; m. 1st Beverly Caton (divorced); one d.; m. 2nd Laura Viederman 2000; ed Nat. Film School; worked as stagehand in London West End theatres, wrote and directed first film The Sanatorium and several other short films before being accepted by Nat. Film School; films made while a student include: Liebe Mutter (first prize European film school competition), The Making of Absolute Beginners (for Palace Productions), The Riveter; left School to make serial Brond for Channel 4 TV, then Lucky Sunil (BBC TV). *Films:* Scandal 1989, Memphis Belle 1990, Doc Hollywood 1991, This Boy's Life 1993, Rob Roy 1995, The Jackal 1997, City By The Sea 2002, Shooting Dogs 2005, Basic Instinct 2 2006. *Address:* c/o William Morris Agency (UK) Ltd, 52 Poland Street, London, W1F 7LX, England.

CATTANACH, Bruce MacIntosh, PhD, DSc, FRS; British geneticist (retd); b. 5 Nov. 1932, Glasgow; s. of James Cattanach and Margaretta May Cattanach (née Fyfe); m. 1st Margaret Bouchier Crewe 1966 (died 1996); two d.; m. 2nd Josephine Peters 1999; ed Heaton Grammar School, Newcastle-upon-Tyne,

King's Coll., Univ. of Durham and Univ. of Edinburgh; mem. scientific staff MRC Induced Mutagenesis Unit, Edinburgh 1959–62, 1964–66; NIH Post-Doctoral Research Fellow, Biology Div., Oak Ridge, Tenn., USA 1962–64; Sr Scientist, City of Hope Medical Centre, Duarte, Calif. 1966–69; Sr Scientist, MRC Radiobiology Unit, Chilton, Oxon. 1969–86, Head of Genetics Div. 1987–96; Acting Dir MRC Mammalian Genetics Unit, Harwell, Oxon. 1996–97. *Publications:* numerous papers in scientific journals. *Leisure interests:* control of inherited disease in pedigree dogs; Boxer dog breeding, exhibiting and judging. *Address:* Downs Edge, Reading Road, Harwell, Oxon., OX11 0JJ, England (home). *Telephone:* (1235) 841190 (office); (1235) 835410 (home). *Fax:* (1235) 835691 (office); (1235) 835410 (home). *E-mail:* b.cattanach@har.mrc.ac.uk (office); bcattanach@steynmere.freeserve.co.uk (home).

CATTANEO, Elena, DrSc; Italian professor of pharmaceutical biotechnology; *Professor of Pharmaceutical Biotechnology, University of Milan;* b. 1962, Milan; m.; one s. one d.; ed Univ. of Milan, Massachusetts Inst. of Tech., USA; researcher of neutral stem cells, MIT, USA; joined Dept of Pharmacological Science, Univ. of Milan 1994, currently Prof. of Pharmaceutical Biotechnology, Dir Lab. of Stem Cell Biology and Pharmacology of Neurodegenerative Diseases, Co-founder and Dir UniStem, the Centre for Stem Cell Research; Coalition Investigator, Huntington's Disease Soc. of America 1997–; Coordinator FIRB (Fondo Investimento per la Ricerca di Base) research programme 2002–05; mem. Italian Del., Genomics and Biotechnology Work Programme, EU, Brussels 2002; mem. Bd of Dirs EuroStemCell, NeuroNE; mem. Scientific Advisory Bd Hereditary Disease Foundation, Euro-HD Network; Cavaliere Ufficiale (Knight) of the Italian Repub. 2006; Cure Huntington's Disease Initiative Award, Hereditary Disease Foundation 1997, Le Scienze Prize for Medicine 2001, Presidential Medal, Italy 2001, Marisa Bellisario and Chiara D'Onofrio prizes 2005. *Leisure interest:* cooking. *Address:* Department of Pharmacological Sciences and Centre of Stem Cell Research (UniStem), University of Milan, via Balzaretti 9, 20133 Milan, Italy (office). *Telephone:* 0250318333 (office). *Fax:* 0250318284 (office). *E-mail:* elena.cattaneo@unimi.it (office); cattaneolab@unimi.it. *Website:* users.unimi.it/~spharm/cattaneo.

CATTAUI, Maria Livanos, BA; Swiss international organization official and consultant; *Director, Petroplus Holdings, AG;* b. 25 June 1941, New York, USA; m. Stéphane Cattaui (deceased); two s.; ed Harvard Univ., USA; staff writer and researcher, Encyclopedia Britannica 1965–67; Ed. Time Life Books 1967–69; Dir, then Man. Dir World Econ. Forum 1977–96; Sec.-Gen. ICC 1996–2005; Vice-Chair. Int. Crisis Group, Brussels –2007; currently mem. Bd of Dirs Petroplus Holdings, AG, Switzerland; mem. Bd EastWest Inst., New York, Inst. of Int. Educ., New York, Nat. Bureau of Asian Research (NBR), Int. Youth Foundation, Baltimore, Schulich School of Business, York Univ., Toronto), Elliott School of Int. Affairs, George Washington Univ., Washington, DC; Hon. LLD (York Univ., Toronto).

CATTELAN, Maurizio; Italian artist; b. 1960, Padua; self-taught artist, works include sculpture, multimedia and installations. *Address:* c/o Galerie Emmanuel Perrotin, 5 & 20, rue Louise Weiss, 75013 Paris, France. *Telephone:* 1-42-16-79-79. *Fax:* 1-42-16-79-74. *Website:* www.galerieperrotin.com.

CATTO, Sir Graeme Robertson Dawson, Kt, DSc, MD, FRCP, FRSA, FRSE, FRCPE, FRCPGlas, FRSA, FMedSci; British professor of medicine; *President, General Medical Council;* b. 24 April 1945, Aberdeen, Scotland; s. of William D. Catto and Dora E. Catto (née Spiby); m. Joan Sievewright 1967; one s. one d.; ed Robert Gordon's Coll., Univ. of Aberdeen, Harvard Univ.; House Officer, Aberdeen Royal Infirmary 1969–70, Hon. Consultant Physician and Nephrologist 1977–2000; Research Fellow then Lecturer, Univ. of Aberdeen 1970–75, Sr Lecturer then Reader in Medicine 1977–88, Prof. of Medicine and Therapeutics 1988–2000, Dean, Faculty of Medicine and Medical Sciences 1992–98, Vice-Prin. 1995–2000, Prof. of Medicine 2005–; Chief Scientist, Scottish Exec. (fmrly Scottish Office) Health Dept 1997–2000; Vice-Prin. King's Coll. London 2000–05; Dean, Guy's, King's Coll. and St Thomas' Hosps Medical and Dental School 2000–05, Hon. Nephrologist, Guy's and St Thomas' Hosps NHS Trust 2000–; Pro-Vice-Chancellor Univ. of London 2003–05; Vice-Chair. Aberdeen Royal Hosps NHS Trust 1992–99; mem. Gen. Medical Council (GMC) 1994–, Chair. GMC Educ. Cttee 1999–2002, Pres. GMC 2002–; mem. Scottish Higher Educ. Funding Council 1996–2002, Specialist Training Authority 1999–, Lambeth, Southwark and Lewisham Health Authority 2000–02, South East London Strategic Health Authority 2002–, Council for the Regulation of Healthcare Professionals 2003–; Founder-mem. FMedSci 1998 (Treas. 1998–2001); Chair. Robert Gordon's Coll. Aberdeen 1995–; Treas. Acad. of Medical Sciences 1998–2001; Harkness Fellow, Commonwealth Fund of New York; Fellow in Medicine, Harvard Univ. and Peter Bent Brigham Hosp., Boston 1975–77; Hon. Fellow, Royal Coll. of Gen. Practitioners 2001, Royal Coll. of Surgeons of Edinburgh 2002; Hon. LLD (Aberdeen) 2002; Hon. DSc (St Andrew's) 2003, (Robert Gordon's) 2004; Hon. MD (Southampton) 2004. *Leisure interests:* hills and glens. *Address:* School of Medicine, University of Aberdeen, Polwarth Building, Foresterhill, Aberdeen, AB25 2ZD, Scotland (office); General Medical Council, 178 Great Portland Street, London, W1W 5JE, England (office); Maryfield, Glenbuchat, Strathdon, Aberdeenshire, AB36 8TS, Scotland (home); 4 Woodend Avenue, Aberdeen, AB15 6YL (home). *Telephone:* (1224) 551838 (Aberdeen) (office); (20) 7189-5012 (London) (office); (1975) 641317 (Strathdon) (home); (1224) 310509 (Aberdeen) (home). *Fax:* (20) 7189-5009 (office). *E-mail:* g.catto@abdn.ac.uk (office); graeme.catto@kcl.ac.uk (office); g.catto@doctors.org.uk (home). *Website:* www.abdn.ac.uk/medicine_therapeutics (office); www.kcl.ac.uk (office).

CATTO, Henry Edward, BA; American diplomatist, business executive and academic; *Chairman Emeritus, Atlantic Council of the United States;* b. 6 Dec. 1930, Dallas; s. of Henry Edward Catto and Maureen Catto (née Halsell); m. Jessica Oveta Hobby 1958; two s. two d.; ed Williams Coll.; Pnr, Catto & Catto (insurance brokerage firm), San Antonio 1955–2000; Deputy Rep. OAS 1969–71; Amb. to El Salvador 1971–73; Chief of Protocol, The White House 1974–76; Perm. Rep. to UN, Geneva 1976–77; Asst Sec. of Defense, Pentagon, Washington, DC 1981–83;; Amb. to the UK 1989–91; Dir US Information Agency 1991–93; Adjunct Prof. of Political Science, Univ. of Texas, San Antonio 1993–; mem. Bd of Dirs Cullen-Frost Bankers, San Antonio, Nat. Public Radio; Vice-Chair. Aspen Inst. 1993–, H and C Communications 1983–89; Chair. Atlantic Council of the US 1999–2007, Chair. Emer. 2007–; mem. Int. Advisory Bd Direct Relief International 2001–; mem. Council on Foreign Relations 1979; columnist, San Antonio Light 1985–89; fmr Publr Washington Journalism Review, now Contributing Ed.; Hon. LLD (Aberdeen) 1990. *Publication:* Ambassador at Sea 1999. *Leisure interest:* skiing. *Address:* 4026 Fawnridge Drive, San Antonio, TX 78229, USA (office).

CATTORETTI, Marco; Italian fashion designer and business executive; *CEO, Tuleh LLC;* pnr, Bryan Bradley; moved to New York and co-f. and co-designed, with Luca Mosca, own fashion collection 'Luca+Marco' 1994; Vice-Pres. Malo, Milan –2007; CEO Tuleh LLC fashion co., New York 2007–. *Films:* costume designer: Hostage 1999, Girlfight 2000, Hamlet 2000, Happy Here and Now 2002, When Will I Be Loved 2004. *Television:* costume designer: The Education of Max Bickford (series) 2001. *Address:* Tuleh LLC, 181 Chrystie Street, Apt 2, New York, NY 10002-1280, USA (office). *Telephone:* (212) 979-7888 (office).

CATZ, Safra A.; American business executive; *President, Oracle Corporation;* held various investment banking positions 1986–94; Sr Vice-Pres. Donaldson, Lufkin & Jenrette (global investment bank) 1994–97, Man. Dir 1997–99; Sr Vice-Pres. Oracle Corpn April–Oct. 1999, Exec. Vice-Pres. 1999–2004, mem. Bd of Dirs 2001–, Pres. Oracle Corpn with responsibility for global operations 2004–, Chief Financial Officer 2005–08, mem. Exec. Man. Cttee; ranked by Fortune magazine amongst 50 Most Powerful Women in Business in the US (49th) 2005, ranked by Forbes magazine amongst 100 Most Powerful Women (22nd) 2005, (21st) 2006, 28th (2007), (15th) 2008. *Address:* Oracle Corpn, 500 Oracle Parkway, Redwood City, CA 94065-1675, USA (office). *Telephone:* (650) 506-7000 (office). *Fax:* (650) 506-7200 (office). *E-mail:* info@oracle.com (office). *Website:* www.oracle.com (office).

CAUBET, Marie-Christine; French automotive industry executive; b. 4 Dec. 1950, Salins Les Bains; ed Institut d'Etudes Politiques, Aix-en-Provence, Centre Européen d'Educ. Permanente (CEDEP), Fontainebleau; joined Renault SA as financial analyst in 1973–85, Dir Mantes sales br. 1985–88, Regional Br. Dir 1988–90, Regional Dir Île de France region 1990–93, Marketing Dir for France 1993–97, Regional Dir Renault France Automobiles 1997–2000, Sr Vice-Pres. Market Area France and mem. Renault Man. Cttee 2000–05, Sr Vice-Pres. Market Area Europe 2005–08; ranked by Fortune magazine amongst 50 Most Powerful Women in Business outside the US (40th) 2005, (50th) 2006. *Address:* 50 rue de la Pompe, 75016 Paris, France.

CAUCHON, Hon. Martin, DCL, LLM; Canadian politician and lawyer; *Partner, Gowling Lafleur Henderson LLP;* b. 23 Aug. 1962, La Malbaie, Québec; ed Univ. of Ottawa, Bar School of Québec, Univ. of Exeter, UK, Inst. of Corporate Dirs; practised as civil and commercial lawyer 1985–93; MP for Outremont 1993–2004 (resgnd); apptd Sec. of State responsible for the Econ. Devt Agency of Canada for the Regions of Québec 1996–2002, Minister of Nat. Revenue (responsible for Canada Customs) 1999–2002, Minister of Justice, Attorney-Gen. 2002–03; Pres. Canada-France Inter-parl. Asscn 1994–95; Pres. Liberal Party of Canada (Québec) 1993–95; Vice-Chair. Standing Cttee on Public Accounts 1994; mem. Standing Cttee on Human Resources Devt 1994–96; currently Pnr, Gowling Lafleur Henderson LLP (law firm), Montréal. *Publications:* articles in Revue du Barreau and Bulletin de la Société de droit int. économique. *Address:* Gowling Lafleur Henderson LLP, 1 Place Ville Marie, 37th Floor, Montréal, PQ H3B 3PA, Canada (office). *Telephone:* (514) 392-9529 (office). *Fax:* (514) 878-1450 (office). *E-mail:* martin.cauchon@gowlings.com (office). *Website:* www.gowlings.com (office).

CAUTE, (John) David, MA, DPhil, JP, FRSL; British writer; b. 16 Dec. 1936; m. 1st Catherine Shuckburgh 1961 (divorced 1970); two s.; m. 2nd Martha Bates 1973; two d.; ed Edinburgh Acad., Wellington, Wadham Coll., Oxford; St Antony's Coll. 1959; army service Gold Coast 1955–56; Henry Fellow, Harvard Univ. 1960–61; Fellow, All Souls Coll., Oxford 1959–65; Visiting Prof. New York Univ. and Columbia Univ. 1966–67; Reader in Social and Political Theory, Brunel Univ. 1967–70; Regents' Lecturer, Univ. of California 1974, Visiting Prof. Univ. of Bristol 1985; Literary Ed. New Statesman 1979–80; Co-Chair. Writers' Guild 1982. *Plays:* Songs for an Autumn Rifle 1961, The Demonstration 1969, The Fourth World 1973, Brecht and Company (BBC TV) 1979. *Radio plays:* The Demonstration 1971, Fallout 1972, The Zimbabwe Tapes (BBC Radio) 1983, Henry and the Dogs (BBC Radio) 1986, Sanctions (BBC Radio) 1988, Animal Fun Park (BBC Radio) 1995. *Publications:* At Fever Pitch (novel) (Authors' Club Award 1960, John Llewelyn Rhys Award 1960) 1959, Comrade Jacob (novel) 1961, Communism and the French Intellectuals 1914–1960 1964, The Left in Europe Since 1789 1966, The Decline of the West (novel) 1966, Essential Writings of Karl Marx (ed.) 1967, Fanon 1970, The Confrontation: a trilogy, The Demonstration (play), The Occupation (novel), The Illusion 1971, The Fellow-Travellers 1973, Collisions: Essays and Reviews 1974, Cuba, Yes? 1974, The Great Fear: The Anti-Communist Purge Under Truman and Eisenhower 1978, Under the Skin: the Death of White Rhodesia 1983, The Baby-Sitters (novel, as John Salisbury) 1978, Moscow Gold (novel, as John Salisbury) 1980, The K-Factor (novel) 1983, The Espionage of the Saints 1986, News from Nowhere (novel) 1986, Sixty Eight:

www.worldwhoswho.com

the Year of the Barricades 1988, Veronica or the Two Nations (novel) 1989, The Women's Hour (novel) 1991, Joseph Losey: A Revenge on Life 1994, Dr Orwell and Mr Blair (novel) 1994, Fatima's Scarf (novel) 1998, The Dancer Defects: The Struggle for Cultural Supremacy During the Cold War 2003, Marechera and the Colonel 2009. *Address:* 41 Westcroft Square, London, W6 0TA, England.

CAUTHEN, Stephen Mark (Steve); American fmr professional jockey; b. 1 May 1960, Walton, Ky; s. of Ronald Cauthen and Myra Cauthen; m. Amy Rothfuss 1992; two d.; rode first race 1976, first winner 1976, top jockey, USA with 487 winners 1977; at 18, youngest person to win US racing's Triple Crown; moved to UK 1979; champion jockey 1984, 1985, 1987; won Derby on Slip Anchor 1985, on Reference Point 1987; rode 1,704 winners including 10 classics 1979–93 (retd); only jockey to have won Kentucky, Epsom, Irish, French and Italian Derbys; now works on family farm, Ky and as racing commentator on TV; Vice-Pres. Turfway Racing Asscn, Ky; Seagram Prize 1977, Eclipse Award 1977; youngest person to be elected to Racing Hall of Fame. *Address:* 167 South Main Street, Walton KY 41094, USA.

CAUVIN, Patrick, LèsL; French writer; b. (Claude Klotz), 6 Oct. 1932, Marseille; s. of Joseph Klotz and Victoria Cauvin; m. Evelyne Berrot 1959; two s. one d.; served in Algeria 1958–60; full-time writer 1968–. *Screenplays:* Le Main de la coiffeuse (directed by P. Laconte), L'heure du train (directed by P. Laconte). *Television:* six films for TV. *Publications:* L'Amour aveugle, E=MC²mon amour, Monsieur Papa, Laura Brams, Ville Vanille, Pythagore, je t'adore, Pov chéri 1987, Belles galères 1991, Menteur 1993, Villa vanille 1995, Torrentera 2000, La Reine du Monde 2001, Le sang des Roses 2003, Dictionaire des héros (ed. Plom). *Leisure interest:* football. *Address:* 59 rue Caulaincourt, 75018 Paris, France. *Telephone:* 1-42-79-10-00 (office); 1-42-52-25-41 (home).

CAVACO SILVA, Anibal, PhD; Portuguese politician, economist, academic and head of state; *President;* b. 15 July 1939, Loulé; s. of Teodoro Silva and Maria do Nascimento Cavaco; m. Maria Cavaco Silva 1963; one s. one d.; ed Univ. of York, UK and Inst. of Econ. and Financial Studies; taught Public Econs and Political Economy, Inst. of Econ. and Financial Studies 1965–67, then at Catholic Univ. 1975–2006 and New Univ. of Lisbon 1977–2002; Research Fellow, Calouste Gulbenkian Foundation 1967–77; Dir of Research and Statistical Dept, Bank of Portugal 1977–85; Minister of Finance and Planning 1980–81; Pres. Council for Nat. Planning 1981–84; Leader, PSD 1985–95; Prime Minister of Portugal 1985–95; mem. Real Academia de Ciencias Morales y Políticas, Spain; Econ. Adviser to Bank of Portugal (Cen. Bank) 1995–2004; Pres. of Portugal 2006–; Social Democrat (PSD) mem. Exec. Cttee Club of Madrid in Democratic Transition and Consolidation; Dr hc (Univ. of York, UK, Universidade da Coruña, Spain); Joseph Bech Prize 1991, Max Schmidleinz Foundation Prize, Carl Bertelsmann Prize. *Publications:* Budgetary Policy and Economic Stabilization 1976, Economic Effects of Public Debt 1977, The Economic Policy of Sá Carneiro's Government 1982, Public Finance and Macroeconomic Policy 1992, A Decade of Reforms 1995, Portugal and the Single Currency 1997, European Monetary Union 1999, Political Autobiography 2002; over 20 articles on financial markets, public economics and Portuguese economic policy. *Leisure interests:* golf, gardening. *Address:* Office of the President, Presidência da República, Palácio de Belém, Calçada da Ajuda, 1349-022 Lisbon, Portugal (office). *Telephone:* (21) 3614600 (office). *Fax:* (21) 3614611 (office). *E-mail:* presidente@presidenciarepublica.pt (office). *Website:* www.presidenciarepublica.pt (office).

CAVALIER-SMITH, Thomas (Tom), PhD, FRS, FRSC, FLS, FIBiol; British/Canadian biologist and academic; *Professor of Evolutionary Biology, University of Oxford;* b. 21 Oct. 1942, London; s. of Alan Hailes Spencer Cavalier-Smith and Mary Maude Cavalier-Smith (née Bratt); m. 1st Gillian Glaysher 1967 (divorced); one s. one d.; m. 2nd Ema E-Yung Chao 1991; one d.; ed Norwich School, Gonville and Caius Coll., Cambridge, King's Coll., London; Guest Investigator and Damon Runyon Memorial Fellow, Rockefeller Univ., New York 1967–69; Lecturer in Biophysics, King's Coll., Univ. of London 1969–82, Reader 1982–89; Prof. of Botany, Univ. of British Columbia 1989–99; Natural Environment Research Council Research Prof., Dept of Zoology, Univ. of Oxford 1999–2007, Prof. of Evolutionary Biology 2000–; Pres. British Soc. for Protist Biology; mem. Council of Int. Congress of Systematic and Evolutionary Biology, Advisory Cttee of Canadian Inst. for Advanced Research's Programme on Integrated Microbial Biodiversity; Fellow, Canadian Inst. for Advanced Research Evolutionary Biology Programme 1988–2007; Int. Prize for Biology 2004, Linnean Medal for Zoology 2007, Frink Medal, Zoological Soc. of London 2008. *Publications:* Biology, Society and Choice (ed.) 1982, The Evolution of Genome Size (ed.) 1985; more than 180 scientific papers on cell and genome evolution, large scale phylogeny and the tree of life, understanding major evolutionary transitions, molecular evolution, cell biology, ultrastructure, ecology, and classification of Protozoa. *Leisure interests:* reading, natural history. *Address:* Department of Zoology, University of Oxford, The Tinbergen Building, South Parks Road, Oxford, OX1 3PS (office); 54 Warwick Street, Oxford, Oxon., OX14 1SX, England (home). *Telephone:* (1865) 281065 (office). *Fax:* (1865) 281310 (office). *E-mail:* tom.cavalier-smith@zoo.ox.ac.uk (office). *Website:* evolve.zoo.ox.ac.uk (office).

CAVALLI, Roberto; Italian fashion designer; b. 15 Nov. 1940, Florence; grandson of Giuseppe Rossi; m. (divorced); two c.; m. 2nd Eva Duringer; three c.; ed Accad. di Belle Arti, Florence; first collection, Palazzo Pitti, Florence 1972. *Fashion lines include:* Just Cavalli, Class, Freedom, Timewear, Angels. *Address:* Press Office, Via Gesu 19, Milan, Italy (office). *Telephone:* (02) 784416 (office). *Fax:* (02) 782361 (office). *E-mail:* press@robertocavalli.it (office). *Website:* www.robertocavalli.it (office).

CAVALLI-SFORZA, Luigi Luca, MA, MD; Italian/American geneticist and academic; *Professor Emeritus, School of Medicine, Stanford University;* b. 25 Jan. 1922, Genoa; ed Univs of Pavia and Cambridge, UK; Dir of Research in Microbiology, Istituto Sieroterapico Milanese, Milan 1950–57; Prof. of Genetics, Univ. of Parma 1960–62; Prof. of Genetics, Univ. of Pavia 1962–70, Dir Inst. of Genetics 1962–70; Prof. of Genetics, Stanford Univ. 1970–92, Chair. Dept of Genetics 1986–90, Prof. Emer., School of Medicine 1992–; numerous awards. *Publications:* The History and Geography of Human Genes, Genes 1994, Peoples and Languages 2000, Consanguinity Inbreeding and Drift in Italy 2004. *Address:* Pop. Genetics Laboratory, CNR Institute of Molecular Genetics, 27100 Pavia (office); Via Fatebene Sorelle 18, 20121 Milan, Italy (home). *Telephone:* (02) 36567973 (office). *E-mail:* cavallisforza@gmail.com.

CAVALLO, Domingo Felipe, DEcon, PhD; Argentine politician and economist; b. 21 July 1946, San Francisco, Córdoba; m. Sonia Abrazián; three s.; ed Nat. Univ. of Córdoba and Harvard Univ.; Under-Sec. for Devt . Govt of Prov. of Córdoba 1969–70; Vice-Pres. Bd of Dirs Banco de la Provincia de Córdoba 1971–72; Titular Lecturer, Nat. and Catholic Univs 1970–83; Founding Dir Inst. for Econ. Studies of Mediterranean Foundation 1977–87; fmr Pres., then Gov. Argentine Cen. Bank; mem. Advisory Cttee Inst. for Econ. Devt of World Bank 1988, Nat. Deputy for Córdoba 1987–91; Minister of Foreign Affairs and Worship 1989–91, of the Economy 1991–92, of the Economy and Public Works 1992–96, 2001; Visiting Prof., Stern School of Business, New York Univ. 1996–97; elected Nat. Deputy for Buenos Aires 1997; f. Acción por la República Party 1997; arrested for alleged involvement in arms smuggling April 2002, released June 2002; Robert Kennedy Visiting Prof. in Latin American Studies, Harvard Univ. 2004. *Publications:* Volver a Crecer 1986, El Desafío Federal 1986, Economía en Tiempos de Crisis 1989, La Argentina que pudo ser 1989, El Peso de la Verdad 1997, Pasion por Crear (co-author with Juan Carlos De Pablo), Estanflacion 2008; numerous tech. publs and articles in Argentine and foreign newspapers. *Address:* Hipólito Yrigoyen 250, 1310 Buenos Aires, Argentina. *Website:* www.cavallo.com.ar (office).

ČAVIĆ, Dragan; Bosnia and Herzegovina politician and fmr head of state; *President, Serbian Democratic Party of Bosnia and Herzegovina (SDP) (Srpska Demokratska Stranka Bosne i Hercegovine) (SDS BiH);* b. 10 March 1958, Zenica; m.; two c.; ed Banja Luka Univ.; worked as man. at several state and pvt. enterprises; mem. Parl. 1998–2000; Vice-Pres. Republika Srpska 2000–02, Pres. 2002–06; Deputy Pres. Serbian Democratic Party of Bosnia and Herzegovina (SDP) (Srpska Demokratska Stranka Bosne i Hercegovine) (SDS BiH) 2002–04, Pres. 2004–. *Address:* Serbian Democratic Party of Bosnia and Herzegovina (SDP) (Srpska Demokratska Stranka Bosne i Hercegovine) (SDS BiH), 78000 Banja Luka, Kralja Petra I Karađorđevića, Bosnia and Herzegovina (office). *Telephone:* (51) 212738 (office). *Fax:* (51) 217640 (home).

CAVIEZEL, James (Jim) Patrick; American actor; b. 26 Sept. 1968, Mount Vernon, Wash.; s. of Jim Caviezel and Maggie Caviezel; m. Kerri Browitt 1997; one s. (adopted); ed Mount Vernon High School, O'Dea High School, Burien Kennedy High School, Seattle, Bellevue Community Coll., Univ. of Wash.; moved to LA and worked as waiter between auditions 1992; modelled for The Gap; Spokesperson for Redeem the Vote (Catholic-Conservative counterpart to Rock the Vote); Dr hc (King's Coll., Wilkes-Barre, Pa) 2003. *Films include:* My Own Private Idaho 1991, Diggstown 1992, Wyatt Earp 1994, Ed 1996, The Rock 1996, G.I. Jane 1997, The Thin Red Line 1998, Ride with the Devil 1999, Resurrection 2000, Frequency 2000, Pay It Forward 2000, Madison 2001, Angel Eyes 2001, The Count of Monte Cristo 2002, High Crimes 2002, Highwaymen 2003, I Am David 2003, The Final Cut 2004, The Passion of the Christ 2004, Bobby Jones: Stroke of Genius 2004, Unknown 2006, Deja Vu 2006, Outlander 2008, The Stoning of Soraya M. 2008. *Television includes:* Murder, She Wrote 1984, The Wonder Years 1988, The Prisoner 2009. *Leisure interests:* basketball, Indy car racing. *Address:* c/o United Talent Agency, 9560 Wilshire Boulevard, Suite 500, Beverly Hills, CA 90212, USA (office). *Telephone:* (310) 273-6700 (office). *Fax:* (310) 247-1111 (office).

CAVINESS, Madeline Harrison, BA, MA, PhD, FSA; American medieval art historian and academic; *Mary Richardson Professor Emerita, Department of Art History, Tufts University;* b. 1938, London, UK; d. of Eric Vernon Harrison and Gwendoline Fownes Rigden; m. Verne Strudwick Caviness, Jr 1962; two d.; ed Newnham Coll., Cambridge, Harvard Univ.; Prof. of Medieval Art, Tufts Univ. 1981–2007, Mary Richardson Prof. 1987–2007, Prof. Emer. 2007–; Pres., Int. Acad. Union 1998–2001, Int. Center for Medieval Art 1984–87, Medieval Acad. of America 1993–94, Int. Council for Philosophy and Humanistic Studies 2001–04; Vice-Pres. Corpus Vitrearum Int. Bd 1983–87, Pres. 1987–95, Hon. Pres. 2000–; Vice-Pres. New England Medieval Conference 1985, Pres. 1986; Fellow, Soc. of Antiquaries, London 1980; mem. American Acad. of Arts and Sciences 2007–; Fellow, Medieval Acad. of America 1992–; Hon. Phi Beta Kappa, Radcliffe Coll. 1977; Hon. DLitt (Bristol, UK) 2000; John Nicholas Brown Prize, Medieval Acad. 1981, Haskins Medal, Medieval Acad. 1993, Distinguished Sr Scholar Award, American Asscn of Univ. Women Educational Foundation 2005, Tufts Univ. Award for Distinguished Research and Seymour Simches Award for Teaching and Advising 2005. *Publications include:* Early Stained Glass of Canterbury Cathedral (John Nicholas Brown Prize, Medieval Acad. 1981) 1977, Sumptuous Arts at the Royal Abbeys in Reims and Braine (Charles Homer Haskins Medal, Medieval Acad. of America 1993) 1980, Visualizing Women in the Middle Ages: Sight, Spectacle and Scopic Economy 2001, Medieval Art in the West and its Audience 2001, Reframing Medieval Art: Difference, Margins, Boundaries (e-book) 2001. *Leisure interests:* travel, archaeology, gardens. *Address:* 8 Whittier Place, 24H, Boston MA 02114-1497, USA (home); Department of Art and Art History, Tufts University, 11 Talbot Avenue, Medford, MA 02155, USA (office). *Telephone:* (617) 627-3567 (office); (617)670-

4008 (home). *Fax:* (617) 627-3890 (office). *E-mail:* mhcaviness@comcast.net (office); madeline.caviness@tufts.edu (home). *Website:* ase.tufts.edu/art (office); nils.lib.tufts.edu/Caviness (office).

CAWLEY, Charles M.; American financial services executive (retd); ed Georgetown Univ.; began career in financial services in 1963; joined Maryland Nat. Bank 1972; sr mem. of man. team that est. MBNA America 1982, Pres. 1985–2002, CEO MBNA American Bank 1990–2002, Pres. MBNA Corpn 1991–2003, Chair. and CEO 2002–03 (retd); mem. Bd of Dirs MasterCard Int.; mem. Bd Grand Opera House, Wilmington, Delaware, St Benedict's Preparatory School, George Bush Presidential Library Foundation, Metropolitan Wilmington Urban League; mem. Bd of Trustees Univ. of Del.; mem. Bd of Regents Georgetown Univ., American Architectural Foundation. *Address:* 1111 Berkeley Road, Wilmington, DE 19807, USA (office).

CAWLEY, Evonne Fay Goolagong, AO, MBE; Australian fmr professional tennis player; b. 31 July 1951, Griffith, NSW; d. of the late Kenneth Goolagong and Linda Hamilton; m. Roger Anson Cawley 1975; one s. one d.; ed Willoughby High School, Sydney; professional tennis player 1970–83; Wimbledon Champion 1971, 1980 (singles), 1974 (doubles); Australian Champion 1974, 1975, 1976, 1977; French Champion 1971; Italian Champion 1973; S African Champion 1972; Virginia Slims Circuit Champion 1975, 1976; played Fed. Cup for Australia 1971, 1972, 1973, 1974, 1975, 1976; Capt. Australian Fed. Cup Team 2001–04; consultant to Indigenous Sports Programme; Sports Amb. to Aboriginal and Torres Strait Island Communities 1997–; Amb. and Exec. Dir Evonne Goolagong Sports Trust; f. Evonne Goolagong Getting Started Programme for young girls; Hon. DUniv (Charles Sturt) 2000; Australian of the Year 1982, Int. Tennis Hall of Fame 1988. *Publications:* Evonne Goolagong (with Bud Collins) 1975, Home: The Evonne Goolagong Story (with Phil Jarratt) 1993. *Leisure interests:* fishing, reading, researching Aboriginal heritage, movies, soccer. *Address:* c/o IMG, 281 Clarence Street, Sydney, NSW 2000; PO Box 1347, Noosa Heads, Queensland 4567, Australia. *Telephone:* (7) 5474-0112. *Fax:* (7) 5474-0113.

CAYETANO, Benjamin Jerome, BA, JD; American politician and lawyer; b. 14 Nov. 1939, Honolulu; m. 1st Lorraine Gueco 1958; m. 2nd Vicky Tiu 1997; two s. three d.; ed Farrington High School, Honolulu, Univ. of Calif., Los Angeles and Loyola Law School, Los Angeles; practising lawyer 1971–86; Pnr, Schutter Cayetano Playdon (law firm) 1983–86; mem. Hawaii State Legis. 1975–78, 1979–86; Lt-Gov. of Hawaii 1986–94, Gov. 1994–2002; Chair. W Gov.'s Asscn 1999; Democrat; Hon. LLD (Univ. of the Philippines) 1995, Hon. Dr of Public Service (Loyola Marymount Univ.) 1998; numerous awards for public service including Medal of UCLA 1995, The Aloha Council Boy Scouts of America Harvard Foundation Leadership Award 1996, Distinguished Citizens Award 1997, Edward A. Dickson Alumnus of the Year Award, UCLA 1998, Distinguished Alumnus of the Year, Loyola Law School 2002. *Publication:* Ben: A Memoir, From Street Kid to Governor 2007. *Address:* 1926 Okoa Place, Honolulu, HI 96821-2651, USA (office).

CAYGILL, Hon. David Francis, LLB; New Zealand politician and lawyer; *Chairman, Electricity Commission;* b. 15 Nov. 1948, Christchurch; s. of Bruce Allott Caygill and Gwyneth Mary Caygill; m. Eileen E Boyd 1974; one s. three d.; ed Univ. of Canterbury; practised law in Christchurch legal firm 1974–78; mem. Christchurch City Council 1971–80; mem. House of Reps (Labour) 1978–90; Minister of Trade and Industry, Minister of Nat. Devt, Assoc. Minister of Finance 1984–87, of Health, Trade and Industry 1987–88, Deputy Minister of Finance 1988, Minister of Finance 1988–90, of Revenue 1988–89, Deputy Leader of the Opposition 1994–96; Pnr, Buddle Findlay, Barristers and Solicitors 1996–; Chair. Accident Compensation Corpn 1998–; Chair. Ministerial Inquiry into the Electricity Ind. 2000; Deputy Chair. Commerce Comm. 2004–; Chair. Electricity Comm. 2007–; Chair. Educ. NZ Trust, Advisory Cttee on Official Statistics; mem. Canterbury Regional Planning Authority 1977–80; fmr mem. Bd of Dirs Infratil Ltd. *Leisure interests:* collecting classical music records, science fiction, following American politics. *Address:* Electricity Commission, Level 7, ASB Bank Tower, 2 Hunter Street, PO Box 10041, Wellington, New Zealand (office). *Telephone:* (4) 460-8860 (office). *Fax:* (4) 460-8879 (office). *E-mail:* info@electricitycommission.govt.nz (office). *Website:* www.electricitycommission.govt.nz (office).

CAYNE, James E.; American business executive; b. 14 Feb. 1934, Evanston, Ill.; m. Patricia Cayne; two c.; ed Purdue Univ.; US army service in Japan; worked in scrap iron business; Bond Salesman Lebenthal & Co. 1966–69; Stockbroker Bear Stearns and Co. Inc. 1969–73, Gen. Pnr 1973, later Head of Retail Dept, mem. Office of the Pres. 1985–88, Sr Man. Dir 1985, Pres. 1988–2001, CEO 1993–2008 (resgnd), Chair. 2001–08 (resgnd), mem. Bd of Dirs 2008–. *Leisure interest:* bridge. *Address:* Bear Stearns and Co. Inc., 383 Madison Avenue, New York, NY 10179, USA (office). *Telephone:* (212) 272-2000 (office). *Fax:* (212) 272-4785 (office). *Website:* www.bearstearns.com (office).

CAYROL, Roland; French researcher, opinion pollster and producer; b. 11 Aug. 1941, Rabat, Morocco; m. Annabelle Gomez 1989; two s. two d.; Prof. and Researcher, Nat. Foundation of Political Sciences, Centre de Recherches Politiques de Sciences Po 1968, Research Dir 1978–; Scientific Adviser, Louis Harris France 1977–86; Dir CSA (Opinion polling and market research co.) 1986–98, Dir Gen. CSA Group 1998–2006, Special Adviser 2006–; Special Adviser, Bolloré Group 2006–; Chevalier du Mérite agricole. *Television productions include:* Portrait d'un Président: François Mitterrand (with A. Gaillard) 1985. *Publications:* François Mitterrand 1967, Le Député Français (with J. L. Parodi and C. Ysmal) 1970, La Presse écrite et audiovisuelle 1973, La télévision fait-elle l'élection? (with G. Blumler and G. Thoveron) 1974, La nouvelle communication politique 1986, Les médias 1991, Le grand malentendu, Les Français et la politique 1994, Médias et démocratie: la dérive 1997, Sondages mode d'emploi 2000, La nuit des politiques 2006, La revanche de l'opinion : Médias, sondages, Internet (with Pascal Delannoy) 2007. *Address:* CSA 2 rue de Choiseul, 75002 Paris, France (office). *Telephone:* 1-44-94-59-57 (office). *E-mail:* roland.cayrol@csa.eu (office); roland.cayrol@wanadoo.fr (home). *Website:* www.cevipof.msh-paris.fr (home).

CAZALET, Sir Peter Grenville, Kt, MA; British business executive (retd); b. 26 Feb. 1929, Weymouth; s. of Vice-Adm. Sir Peter Cazalet, KBE, CB, DSO, DSC and Lady (Elise) Cazalet (née Winterbotham); m. Jane Jennifer Rew 1957; three s.; ed Uppingham School and Univ. of Cambridge; Gen. Man. BP Tanker Co. Ltd 1968–70, Regional Co-ordinator, Australasia and Far East, BP Trading Ltd 1970–72, Pres. BP North America Inc. 1972–75, Dir BP Trading Ltd 1975–81, Chair. BP Oil Int. Ltd 1981–89, Man. Dir BP 1981–89, Deputy Chair. 1986–89; Chair. APV PLC 1989–96, Hakluyt & Co. 1998–99, Breamar Seascope Group PLC 2001–02; Chair. Armed Forces Pay Review Body 1989–93; Deputy Chair. (non-exec.) GKN PLC 1989–96; Dir Standard Oil Co., Cleveland, Ohio 1973–76, Peninsular & Oriental Steam Navigation Co. Ltd 1980–99, De La Rue Co. PLC 1983–95, Energy Capital Investment Co. 1995–98, Seascope Shipping Holdings PLC 1997–2001 (Chair. 2000–01); Dir Gen. Maritime Corpn (US) 2000–02; mem. Top Salaries Review Body 1989–94, Lloyds Register of Shipping Bd 1981–86 and Gen. Cttee 1981–99; Vice-Pres. ME Asscn 1982–, China–Britain Trade Group 1993–96 (Pres. 1996–98); Trustee Uppingham School 1976–95; Trustee The Wellcome Trust 1989–92, Gov. The Wellcome Trust Ltd 1992–96; Hon. Sec. King George's Fund for Sailors 1989–2000; Liveryman, Tallow Chandlers' Co. (Master 1991–92), Shipwrights' Co. *Leisure interests:* golf, theatre, fishing. *Address:* c/o 53 Davies Street, London, W1K 5JH, England. *Telephone:* (20) 7496-5821. *Fax:* (20) 7496-4436 (office).

CAZALOT, Clarence P., Jr, BS; American oil industry executive; *President and CEO, Marathon Oil Corporation;* b. 1 Feb. 1951; ed Louisiana State Univ.; joined Texaco Inc. as Geophysicist 1972, becoming Vice-Pres. 1992, also Pres. of Texaco Latin America/W Africa 1992, Pres. Texaco Exploration and Production Inc. 1994–97, Pres. Texaco Int. Marketing and Mfg 1997, Pres. Int. Production 1998, Chair. Texaco Ltd, London 1998–99, Chair. Texaco Worldwide Production 1999–2000; Vice-Chair. USX Corpn 2000, mem. Bd Dirs Marathon Oil Co. (later Corpn) 2000–, Pres. 2000–, CEO 2002–; Chair. Marathon Ashland Petroleum LLC; mem. Bd Dirs Baker Hughes Inc., US-Saudi Arabian Business Council, American Petroleum Inst., Greater Houston Partnership; mem. The Business Council, Advisory Bd of World Affairs Council of Houston; Hon. DHumLitt (Louisiana State Univ.) 2007. *Address:* Marathon Oil Corporation, 5555 San Felipe Road, Houston, TX 77056-2723, USA (office). *Telephone:* (713) 629-6600 (office). *Fax:* (713) 296-2952 (office). *E-mail:* info@marathon.com (office). *Website:* www.marathon.com (office).

CAZENOVE, Christopher de Lerisson; British actor; b. 17 Dec. 1943, Winchester; s. of Brig. Arnold Cazenove and Elizabeth L. Cazenove (née Gurney); m. Angharad M. Rees 1974 (divorced 1993); two s.; ed Dragon School, Oxford and Eton Coll.; trained as actor at Bristol Old Vic Theatre School. *Stage roles include:* The Lionel Touch, My Darling Daisy, The Winslow Boy, Joking Apart, In Praise of Rattigan, The Life and Poetry of T. S. Eliot, The Sound of Music, An Ideal Husband, Goodbye Fidel, Brief Encounter, London Suite, Art, My Fair Lady (tour) 2005–06. *Films:* Zulu Dawn, East of Elephant Rock, Eye of the Needle, Heat and Dust, Until September, Mata Hari, The Fantasist, Souvenir, Hold My Hand I'm Dying, Three Men and a Little Lady, Aces: Iron Eagle III, The Proprietor, Shadow Run, A Knight's Tale, Trance, Beginner's Luck. *Television appearances include:* The Regiment (two series), The Duchess of Duke Street (two series), Jennie: Lady Randolph Churchill, The Riverman, Jenny's War, Dynasty, Hammer's House of Mystery, Lace, Windmills of the Gods, Shades of Love, Souvenir, The Lady and the Highwayman, Tears in the Rain, Ticket to Ride (A Fine Romance), To be the Best, Judge John Deed, Johnson County War, La Femme Musketeer. *Address:* c/o Lesley Duff, Diamond Management, 31 Percy Street, London, W1T 2DD, England (home). *Telephone:* (20) 7631-0400. *E-mail:* agents@diman.co.uk (office).

CEBRIÁN ECHARRI, Juan Luis; Spanish writer and journalist; *CEO, El País;* b. 30 Oct. 1944, Madrid; s. of Vicente Cebrián and Carmen Echarri; m. 1st María Gema Torallas 1966 (divorced); two s. two d.; m. 2nd Teresa Aranda 1988; one s. one d.; ed Univ. of Madrid; Founder-mem. of magazine Cuadernos para el Diálogo, Madrid 1963; Sr Ed. newspapers Pueblo, Madrid 1962–67, Informaciones, Madrid 1967–69; Deputy Ed.-in-Chief, Informaciones 1969–74, 1974–76; Dir News Programming, Spanish TV 1974; Ed.-in-Chief newspaper El País, Madrid 1976–88; CEO Grupo PRISA 1988–, Canal Plus 1989–, Estructura 1989–; Publr, CEO El País 1988–; Vice-Pres. SER 1990–; Pres., Asscn of Spanish Newspaper Editors 2003–04; mem. Int. Press Inst. (Vice-Pres. 1982–86, Chair. 1986–88); Dr hc (Iberoamericana Univ., Santo Domingo) 1988; Control Prize for Outstanding Newspaper Ed. 1976, 1977, 1978, 1979; Víctor de la Serna Prize for Journalism, Press Asscn Fed. 1977; Outstanding Ed. of the Year (World Press Review, New York) 1980, Spanish Nat. Journalism Prize 1983; Freedom of Expression Medal, F. D. Roosevelt Four Freedoms Foundation 1986; Medal of Honor, Univ. of Miss. 1986; Trento Int. Prize for Journalism and Communication 1987; Gold Medal, Spanish Inst. New York 1988. *Publications:* La Prensa y la Calle 1980, La España que bosteza 1980, ¿Qué pasa en el mundo? 1981, Crónicas de mi país 1985, La rusa Alfaguara 1986, El Tamaño del elefante 1987, Red Doll 1987, La isla del viento 1990, El tamaño del elefante 1993, El siglo de las sombras 1994, Cartas a un joven periodista 1997, Exaltación del vino, y de la alegria 1998, La red 1998, La agonía del dragón 2000, Francomomribundia 2003, El Fundamentalismo Democrático 2004. *Leisure interests:* music, literature. *Address:* El País, Miguel Yuste 40, 28037 Madrid, Spain (office). *Telephone:* (91) 3378200 (office). *Fax:* (91) 3377758 (office). *Website:* www.elpais.com (office).

www.worldwhoswho.com

CEBUC, Alexandru, PhD; Romanian art historian and critic; b. 5 April 1932, Păuşeşti-Măglabi; s. of Ion and Ana Cebuc; m. Florica Turcu 1958; one d.; ed Univ. of Bucharest; Head of Dept, Museum of History of City of Bucharest 1957–69; Vice-Pres. Culture Cttee of City of Bucharest 1969–77; Dir Art Museum of Romania 1977–90; Gen. Man. 2000 ARC (publishing and printing firm) 1990–; Order of Cultural Merit, Kt of Italian Repub. *Publications:* The History of the City of Bucharest 1966, The History of Passenger Transportation 1967, Historical and Art Monuments of the City of Bucharest 1968, The Nat. Gallery 1983, Ion Irimescu (monograph) 1983, Etienne Hadju (monograph) 1984, Nicolae Grigorescu (monograph) 1985, H. H. Catargi (monograph) 1987, I. Ianchelevici (monograph) 1989, I. Irimescu – Album Drawings 1994, Encyclopaedia of Plastic Artists in Romania (Vol. I) 1994, Encyclopaedia of Plastic Artists in Romania, (Vol. II) 1999, (Vol. III) 2000. *Leisure interests:* art, music, travelling. *Address:* B. Dul. Carol I, HR 23, Ap. 10, Bucharest (office); Str. Spatarului No. 36, ET. II Ap. 5, Bucharest, Romania. *Telephone:* (1) 3124018 (office). *Fax:* (1) 3124018 (office); (1) 2118617 (home).

CECCATO, Aldo; Italian conductor and music director; b. 18 Feb. 1934, Milan; m. Eliana de Sabata; two s.; ed Milan Conservatory, Hochschule für Musik Berlin; Musical Dir Detroit Symphony Orchestra 1973–77, Hamburg Philharmonic 1974–82; Chief Conductor Hannover Radio Orchestra 1985–, Bergen Symphony 1985–90, Orquesta Nacional de España 1991–94, Brno Philharmonic Orchestra 1995–2002; Musical Dir I Pomeriggi Musicali orchestra 1999–2004, now Dir Emer.; Hon. DMus (Eastern Michigan Univ.). *Leisure interests:* tennis, stamps, books. *Address:* c/o Orchestra I Pomeriggi Musicali, Teatro Dal Verme, via San Giovanni sul Muro 2, 20121 Milan, Italy (office).

CECCHI GORI, Vittorio; Italian film producer and politician; *Head of Gruppo Cecchi Gori;* b. 27 April 1943, Florence, Tuscany; s. of Mario Cecchi Gori; ed Univ. of Rome; began cinematographic career in father's co. Gruppo Cecchi Gori (previously Casa di Produzione Cinematografica); apptd Head of Group 1993, purchased Telemontecarlo and Videomusic (now TMC2) 1995; has produced more than 150 films; fmr Senator (Partido Populare Italiano), mem. Perm. Comm. for Labour and Social Welfare. *Films produced include:* Il bisbetico domato 1980, Asso 1981, Innamorato pazzo 1981, Grand Hotel Excelsior 1982, Attila 1982, La casa stregata 1982, Acqua e Sapone 1983, Softly Softly 1984, Pizza Connection 1985, Joan Lui 1986, Sono un fenomeno paranormale 1985, Scuola di Ladri 1986, Me and My Sister 1987, Il Burbero 1987, Il volpone 1988, La leggenda del santo bevitore (Best Film, Venice Film Festival) 1988, La chiesa 1989, Russicum 1989, La voce della luna 1990, Il segreto 1990, La Femme Nikita 1990, Che ora è? 1990, Il sole buio 1990, La setta 1991, Atlantis 1991, Volere volare 1991, Mediterraneo 1991, Piedipiatti 1991, Miliardi 1991, Johnny Stecchino 1991, Maledetto il giorno che t'ho incontrato 1992, Folks! 1992, Puerto escondido 1992, Man Trouble 1992, Al lupo, al lupo 1992, L'angelo con la pistola 1992, House of Cards 1993, Io speriamo che me la cavo 1993, Caino e Caino 1993, Una pura formalità 1994, Il postino 1994, Occhio Pinocchio 1994, Pisolini, un delitto italiano 1995, Al di là delle nuvole 1995, La scuola 1995, L'uomo delle stelle 1995, Viaggi di nozze 1995, I laureati 1995, Vite strozzate 1996, Tre 1996, Il ciclone 1996, Sono pazzo di Iris Blond 1996, Nirvana 1997, Ovosodo 1997, Le bossu 1997, Naja 1997, I piccoli maestri 1998, La seconda moglie 1998, Viola bacia tittu 1998, La fame e la sete 1999, Canone inverso — Making love 2000, Denti 2000, Faccia di Ricasso 2000, Almost Blue 2000, Commedia sexy 2001, E adesso sesso 2001, Figli 2001, Momo 2001, Imperial Treasures 2001, My Name is Tanino 2002, L'anima gemella 2002, La vita come viene 2003, Opopomoz 2003, L'Amore è eterno finché dura 2004, In questo mondo di ladri 2004, Cose da pazzi 2005, Il Ritorno del Monnezza 2005, Towards the Moon with Fellini 2006, Scusa ma ti chiamo amore 2008. *Address:* c/o Gruppo Cecchi Gori, Via Valadier, 00193 Rome, Italy (office). *Telephone:* (06) 324721 (office). *E-mail:* webmaster@ cecchigori.com (office). *Website:* www.cecchigori.com (office).

CECH, Thomas Robert, PhD; American professor of chemistry and biochemistry; *Distinguished Professor, Department of Chemistry and Biochemistry, University of Colorado;* b. 8 Dec. 1947, Chicago; s. of Robert Franklin Cech and Annette Marie Cech (née Cerveny); m. Carol Lynn Martinson 1970; two d.; ed Grinnell Coll., Univ. of California, Berkeley; Postdoctoral Fellow, Dept of Biology, MIT, Cambridge, Mass. 1975–77; Asst Prof., then Assoc. Prof. of Chem., Univ. of Colorado, Boulder 1978–83, Prof. of Chem. and Biochem. and of Molecular, Cellular and Devt Biology 1983–, Distinguished Prof. 1990–; Research Prof., American Cancer Soc. 1987–; Investigator, Howard Hughes Medical Inst. 1988–99, Pres. 2000–09; Deputy Ed. Science; mem. Editorial Bd Genes and Devt; Nat. Science Foundation Fellow 1970–75; Public Health Service Research Fellow, Nat. Cancer Inst. 1975–77; Guggenheim Fellow 1985–86; mem. American Acad. of Arts and Sciences, NAS 1987–; Hon. DSc (Grinnell Coll.) 1987, (Univ. of Chicago) 1991, (Drury Coll.) 1994, (Colorado Coll.) 1999, (Univ. of Maryland) 2000, (Williams Coll.) 2000, (Charles Univ., Prague) 2002; Medal of American Inst. of Chemists 1970, Research Career Devt Award, Nat. Cancer Inst. 1980–85, Young Scientist Award, Passano Foundation 1984, Harrison Howe Award 1984, Pfizer Award 1985, US Steel Award 1987, V.D. Mattia Award 1987, Heineken Prize 1988, Gairdner Foundation Award 1988, Lasker Award 1988, Warren Triennial Prize 1989, Nobel Prize for Chem. 1989, Rosenstiel Award 1989, Nat. Medal of Science 1995, Gregor Mendel Medal 2002. *Leisure interest:* skiing. *Address:* Cristol Chemistry 334B, Department of Chemistry and Biochemistry, University of Colorado, Boulder, CO 80309-0215, USA (office). *Telephone:* (303) 492-8606 (office). *E-mail:* Thomas.Cech@colorado.edu (office). *Website:* www.colorado .edu/chem (office); cechlab.colorado.edu (office).

CECIL, Henry Richard Amherst; British race horse trainer; b. 11 Jan. 1943; s. of the late Horace Henry Kerr Auchmury Cecil and of Elizabeth Rohays Mary Burnett; m. 1st Julie Murless 1966 (divorced 1990); one s. one d.;

m. 2nd Natalie Payne 1992 (divorced 2002); one s.; ed Canford School; Asst to Sir Cecil Boyd-Rochfort; started training under flat race rules 1969; first trainer to win more than £1 million in a season (1985); leading trainer 1976, 1978, 1979, 1982, 1984, 1985, 1987, 1988, 1990, 1993: won a record 23 classics. *Publication:* On the Level (autobiog.) 1983. *Leisure interest:* gardening. *Address:* Warren Place, Newmarket, Suffolk, CB8 8QQ, England (home). *Telephone:* (1638) 662387 (office). *Fax:* (1638) 669005 (office). *E-mail:* henry .cecil@btconnect.com (office).

CEDAIN, Zhoima; Chinese singer; b. 1 Aug. 1937, Xigaze, Xizang (Tibet); ed Shanghai Music Coll.; joined CCP 1961; performed in USSR 1963; in political disgrace during Proletarian Cultural Revolution 1966–76; rehabilitated 1977; mem. Standing Cttee 5th NPC 1978–83; Vice-Chair. 6th CPPCC Tibet Regional Cttee 1987; Vice-Chair. Chinese Musicians' Asscn 1979–; mem. Standing Cttee 6th NPC 1983–88, 7th CPPCC 1988–92; Exec. Vice-Chair. China Fed. of Literary and Art Circles 1988–. *Address:* Chinese Musicians' Association, Beijing, People's Republic of China.

CEJAS, Paul L., BBA, CPA; American diplomatist and business executive; *Chairman, PLC Investments, Inc.;* b. 4 Jan. 1943, Havana, Cuba; ed Univ. of Miami; Founder, fmr Chair. and CEO CareFlorida Health Systems Inc. –1984; Amb. to Belgium 1998–2001; currently Chair. PLC Investments, Inc., Miami; mem. Bd of Dirs Mellon Financial Corpn, Ivax Corpn; Chair. Dade Co. School Bd; Trustee Univ. of Miami; mem. Nat. Bd Smithsonian Inst.; mem. Latin American Advisory Bd, Tate Museum, London; mem. Bd of Regents, Fla Univ. System 1994; Chair. Post-Summit Cttee, Hemispheric Summit of the Americas 1994, Fla Partnership of the Americas 1994–97; Rep. US Del. to Gen. Ass., OAS 1996; fmr Dir Miami Art Museum of Dade County; fmr Trustee Fla Int. Univ.; Hon. PhD (Florida Int. Univ.) 1988. *Address:* PO Box 191679, Miami, FL 33119, USA.

ČEKANAUSKAS, Vytautas Edmundas; Lithuanian architect; *Professor, Vilnius Academy of Arts;* b. 13 May 1930, Šiauliai; m. Teresa Chekanauskienė; one d.; ed Lithuanian Art Inst., Vilnius; architect, then Sr Architect, Group Man., Sr Projects Architect, Inst. of Urban Planning 1985–90; Prof., Vilnius Acad. of Arts (fmrly Inst. of Arts) 1974–; mem. USSR (now Russian) Acad. of Arts 1988, Int. Architects Asscn; Lenin Prize 1974, People's Architect of USSR 1975. *Major projects:* has designed exhbn pavilion in Vilnius 1967, produced gen. plan of Lazdynai, residential dist in Vilnius 1968–73, and other projects, including Contemporary Art Centre. *Address:* Lithuanian State Arts Academy, Maironio 6, 2600 Vilnius (office); U. Paco 13-9, 2000 Vilnius, Lithuania (home). *Telephone:* (2) 619944 (office); (2) 721711 (home).

ÇEKU, Agim; Kosovo politician and military officer; b. 29 Oct. 1960, Qyshk; m.; two s. one d.; ed Mil. High School, Belgrade and Zadar Mil. Acad.; began career as Platoon Commdr, Yugoslav People's Army 1984; joined newly formed Croatian Army as Capt. 1991, and rose to rank of Brig. Gen. 1995; joined Kosovo Liberation Army (KLA) and apptd Chief of Gen. Staff 1999, oversaw KLA demilitarisation and formation of Kosovo Protection Corps, Commdr 2000–06; Prime Minister 2006–08; nine Croatian army decorations. *Address:* c/o Office of the Prime Minister, 10000 Priština, Government Building, Rruga Nëna Terezë, Kosovo (office). *Telephone:* (38) 211567 (office). *Fax:* (38) 20014612 (office). *E-mail:* info@ks-gov.net (office). *Website:* www.ks -gov.net/pm (office).

ČEKUOLIS, Dalius; Lithuanian diplomatist; *Permanent Representative, United Nations;* b. 29 March 1959, Vilnius; m. Jūraté Čekuoliené; one d.; ed Inst. of Int. Relations, Moscow; Head of Press and Information Dept, Ministry of Foreign Affairs 1990–92; Amb. to Denmark, Norway and Iceland 1992–94, to Belgium, the Netherlands and Luxembourg 1994–98, to Portugal 1999–2004; Rep. to WEU and NATO 1994–98; Head of Cttee of Sr Officials of the Council of the Baltic States 1998–99; Sec., Ministry of Foreign Affairs 2004–06; Perm. Rep. to UN, New York 2006–, Vice-Chair. ECOSOC 2006–07, Pres. 2007–. *Address:* Office of the Permanent Representative of Lithuania, United Nations, 420 Fifth Avenue, 3rd Floor, New York, NY 10018, USA (office). *Telephone:* (212) 354-7820 (office). *Fax:* (212) 354-7833 (office). *E-mail:* lithuania@un.int (office). *Website:* www.un.int/lithuania (office).

CELESTE, Richard F., PhB; American diplomatist, university administrator and fmr state governor; *President, Colorado College;* b. 11 Nov. 1937, Cleveland, Ohio; s. of Frank Celeste; m. 1st Dagmar Braun 1962; three s. three d.; m. 2nd Jacqueline Lundquist; one s.; ed Yale Univ. and Univ. of Oxford, UK; Staff Liaison Officer, US Peace Corps 1963; Special Asst to US Amb. to India 1963–67; Officer with Nat. Housing Consultants, Cleveland 1967–74; mem. Ohio House of Reps 1970–74, Majority Whip 1972–74; Lt-Gov. of Ohio 1975–79, Gov. 1983–91; Dir US Peace Corps, Washington, DC 1979–81; Man. Pnr, Celeste and Sabety Ltd (econ. devt consultancy), Cleveland 1991–97; Amb. to India 1997–2001; Pres. Colorado Coll. 2002–; Chair. Midwestern Govs' Conf. 1987–88; Great Lakes Govs' Asscn 1987–89; Chair. Bd of Trustees Health Effects Inst., Boston; Lifetime Nat. Assoc., The Nat. Acads; Visiting Fellow in Public Policy, Case Western Reserve Univ. 1995–97; mem. Bd of Dirs Nat. Asscn of Ind. Colls and Univs 2006–08, Garden City Co. 2007–; Pres. Colorado Springs Downtown Partnership; Trustee Glimcher Realty Trust 2007–; mem. Advisory Bd Inst. of Int. Educ. 2003–, Leadership Council of ServiceNation 2008–; mem. Council on Foreign Relations; Hatch Prize, Yale Univ. 1959, Delta Sigma Rho-Tau Kappa Alpha Speaker of the Year Award 2006. *Address:* Office of the President, Colorado College, 14 East Cache La Poudre Street, Colorado Springs, CO 80903, USA (office). *Telephone:* (719) 389-6748 (office). *E-mail:* president@ColoradoCollege .edu (office). *Website:* www.coloradocollege.edu/welcome/PresidentsOffice (office).

CELIŃSKI, Andrzej, MA; Polish politician; b. 26 Feb. 1950, Warsaw; m.; three s.; ed Warsaw Univ.; co-f. Underground Soc. for Scholarly Courses; mem.

Workers' Defence Cttee (KOR) and Solidarity Ind. Self-governing Trade Union; mem. Civic Cttee attached to Solidarity leader Lech Wałęsa (q.v.) 1988–90; participant Round Table plenary debates 1989; Senator 1989–93 (mem. Civic Parl. Caucus, then Democratic Union Caucus); Deputy to Sejm (Parl.) 1993–; Vice-Chair. Democratic Union (UD) 1993–94; mem. Freedom Union (UW) 1994–99; Chair. Programme Comm., then Vice-Chair. Democratic Left Alliance (SLD) 1999–; Minister of Culture and Nat. Heritage 2001–02. *Address:* c/o Ministry of Culture and National Heritage, ul. Krakowskie Przedmieście 15/17, 00-071 Warsaw, Poland (office).

CELLUCCI, (Argeo) Paul, BS, JD; American lawyer, diplomatist, business executive and fmr politician; *Special Counsel, McCarter & English, LLP;* b. 24 April 1948, Marlboro, Mass.; s. of Argeo R. Cellucci and Priscilla Rose Cellucci; m. Janet Garnett 1971; two d.; ed Boston Coll.; attorney, Kittredge, Cellucci and Moreira, Hudson, Mass. 1973–90; mem. Charter Comm. Hudson 1970–71, Selectman 1971–77; State Rep. Third Middx Dist, Mass. 1977–84; State Senator Middx and Worcs. Dists, Mass 1985–90; Lt-Gov. of Massachusetts 1991–97, Gov. 1997–2000; Amb. to Canada 2001–05; Exec. Vice-Pres. of Corp. Devt Magna Entertainment Corpn 2005–06; Special Counsel, McCarter & English, LLP, Boston 2006–; Capt., US Army Reserves 1970–78; mem. ABA, Mass Bar Asscn; Republican. *Address:* McCarter & English, LLP, 265 Franklin Street, Boston, MA 02110, USA (office). *Telephone:* (617) 449-6503 (office). *Fax:* (617) 607-9135 (office). *E-mail:* pcellucci@mccarter.com (office). *Website:* www.mccarter.com (office).

CENIĆ, Svetlana; Bosnia and Herzegovina economist, academic and fmr government official; b. 6 Dec. 1960, Sarajevo; m. (divorced); one d.; ed Univ. of Sarajevo, Univ. of Cambridge, UK, European Centre for Peace and Devt; worked for Razvoj-Projekt, Univerzal, and several foreign cos; fmr adviser to Nikola Koljevic; worked as ind. consultant; adviser to Vice-Pres., and then to Pres. of Republika Srpska; Minister of Finance of Republika Srpska –2006; mem. World Network for Sustainable Devt. *Address:* c/o Ministry of Finance, Vuka Karadzica 4, 78000 Banja Luka, Bosnia and Herzegovina (home).

CENTERMAN, Jörgen, MSc; Swedish business executive; *Chairman, Gunnebo Industrier AB;* b. 1951; ed Univ. of Tech. of Lund; joined ABB 1976, worked in Singapore, Sweden, Germany, USA, Switzerland, Head of Automation –2000, Pres. and CEO 2001–02 (resgnd); Chair. HMS Industrial Networks AB 2004–09; Chair. Gunnebo Industrier AB 2008–, also Chair. Dacke PMC, Kemetyl Holding AB; mem. Bd of Dirs Micronic Laser Systems AB 2004–, Telelogic, XPonCard, Segulah Advisor AB; mem. Int. Advisory Group, Blekinge Inst. of Technology. *Address:* Gunnebo Industrier AB, Bruksvägen 3, 590 93 Gunnebo, Sweden (office). *Telephone:* (490) 89-000 (office). *Fax:* (490) 89-198 (office). *E-mail:* info@gunneboindustries.com (office). *Website:* www.gunneboindustries.com (office).

ČEPANIS, Alfreds; Latvian politician; b. 3 Aug. 1943, Kalsnava, Madona Region; m. Ilma Čepane; one d.; ed Jaungolbene School of Agric., Higher CP School in Moscow by correspondence; Comsomol functionary 1968–74; Deputy Chair., Chair. Ventspils District Exec. Cttee 1975–79; Sec. Preili Regional Cttee Latvian CP 1979–84; First Sec. Liepaja regional CP Cttee 1983–88; Deputy Chair. Council of Ministers 1989–90; mem. Supreme Soviet of Latvia 1990–93; mem. Saeima (Parl.), Deputy Speaker 1993–95; mem. faction Demikratiska Partija Samnieks 1995, Speaker 1996–98; now business executive. *Leisure interests:* hunting, literature, theatre. *Address:* c/o Saeima, Jēkaba iela 11, 226811 Rīga, Latvia. *Telephone:* 6708-71-11.

CERF, Vinton (Vint) Gray, MSc, PhD; American computer scientist; *Chief Internet Evangelist, Google Inc.;* b. 23 June 1943, New Haven, Conn.; m. Sigrid Cerf; two s.; ed Van Nuys High School, Stanford Univ., UCLA; began career working for N American Aviation, Rocketdyne, then IBM; Prof. of Computer Science, Stanford Univ. 1972–76, worked on ARPANET (earliest packet switched computer network), authored several RFCs, designed protocol for first internetwork 1974; Head of Research and Devt Program, Advanced Research Projects Agency (DARPA), US Dept of Defense 1976–82; played key role in devt of the internet and TCP/IP protocols; Vice-Pres. MCI Digital Information Services 1982–86, led eng of MCI Mail (first commercial email service on internet), Sr Vice-Pres. of Internet Architecture and Tech. 1994–2005; headed several research projects including digital libraries, Corpn for Nat. Research Initiatives (CNRI) 1986–94; f. Internet Soc. (ISOC) 1992, Pres. 1992–95, Chair. 1999; Chief Internet Evangelist, Google Inc. 2005–; currently consultant on Interplanetary Protocol, Jet Propulsion Lab., NASA; mem. US Presidential Information Tech. Advisory Cttee (PITAC) 1997–2001; mem. Bd Internet Corpn for Assigned Names and Numbers (ICANN) 1999–2007, Chair. –2007; serves on several nat., state and industry cttees focused on cyber-security; mem. Bd of Dirs Endowment for Excellence in Educ., Avanex Corpn, ClearSight Systems Corpn; Fellow, IEEE, ACM, AAAS, American Acad. of Arts and Sciences, Int. Eng Consortium, Computer History Museum, Nat. Acad. of Eng; Hon. Chair. IPv6 Forum; Dr hc (Univ. of Balearic Islands, Swiss Inst. of Tech., Lulea Univ. of Tech., Sweden, Capitol Coll., Gettysburg Coll., George Mason Univ., Rovira i Vergili Univ., Spain, Rensselaer Polytechnic Inst., Univ. of Twente, The Netherlands, Univ. of Pisa, Brooklyn Polytechnic, Beijing Univ. of Posts and Telecommunications); Marconi Fellowship, Prince of Asturias Award for Science and Tech., NEC Computer and Communications Prize, Silver Medal of Int. Telecommunications Union, IEEE Alexander Graham Bell Medal, IEEE Kobi Kobayahsi Award, ACM Software and Systems Award, Yuri Rubinsky Memorial Award 1995, ACM SIGCOMM Award 1996, Legend Award, Computer and Communications Industries Asscn Industry, US Nat. Medal of Tech. 1997, Kilby Award, Lifetime Achievement Award, Yankee Group/Network World/Interop, Strowger Award, Ohio Univ. 2001, George R. Stibitz Award, Werner Wolter Award, Andrew Saks Eng Award, IEEE Third Millennium Medal, Computerworld/Smithsonian Leadership Award, J.D. Edwards Leadership Award, Charles Stark Draper Prize, Nat. Acad. of Eng 2001, Premio Principe de Asturias de Investigacion Cientifica (Spain) 2002, Alexander Graham Bell Asscn for the Deaf and Hard of Hearing Award, World Inst. on Disability Annual Award, Library of Congress Bicentennial Living Legend Medal, ACM Turing Award 2005, US Presidential Medal of Freedom 2005, Medal of Science (Tunisia), St Cyril and St Medodius Medal (Bulgaria). *Publications:* A Protocol for Packet Network Intercommunication (co-author with Bob Kahn) 1974; numerous articles in professional journals. *Leisure interests:* fine wine, gourmet cooking, science fiction. *Address:* Google Inc., 13800 Coppermine Road, Herndon, VA 20171, USA (office). *Telephone:* (703) 234-1823 (office). *Fax:* (703) 234-5822 (office). *E-mail:* vint@google.com (office). *Website:* www.google.com (office).

CERIC, Mustafa, PhD; Bosnia and Herzegovina ecclesiastic; *Grand Mufti of Bosnia-Herzegovina and President, Council of Ulema;* b. 5 Feb. 1952, Veliko Cajno; m.; one s. two d.; ed Medressa, Sarajevo, Al-Azhar Univ., Cairo, Egypt, Univ. of Chicago, USA; returned to Bosnia from Egypt and became an imam; Imam of US Islamic Cultural Center of Greater Chicago 1981–87; Grand Imam of Zagreb, Croatia 1987–, of Sanjak, Croatia and Slovenia; Grand Mufti of Bosnia-Herzegovina 1993–; currently Reis-ul-Ulema (Pres. Council of Ulema); Prof., Int. Inst. of Islamic Thought and Civilization, Kuala Lumpur 1991–92; has delivered numerous lectures and led several workshops on inter-religious and inter-faith issues at local and int. confs; mem. Interreligious Council of Bosnia-Herzegovina, Council of 100 Leaders of the World Econ. Forum, European Council for Fatwas and Research, World Conf. of Religions for Peace, European Council of Religious Leaders 2002–; mem. Exec. Bd Foundation for Srebrenica/Potocari Memorial and Cemetery, Sarajevo; Trustee, International Islamic Univ., Islamabad; co-recipient UNESCO Felix Houphoet Boigny Peace Prize for Contrib. to World Peace 2003, Annual Sir Sternberg Award for Exceptional Contrib. to Inter-faith Understanding, Int. Council of Christians and Jews 2003, Theodor-Heuss-Stiftung Award 2007. *Publications:* several books in Bosnian, including Roots of Synthetic Theology in Islam. *Address:* c/o European Council of Religious Leaders, PO Box 6820, 0130 Oslo, Norway.

CERJACK, Harmodio Arias; Panamanian politician; ed Villanova Univ., PA, USA; Pres. General Masterpack Trading Corpn 1986–1990; Amb. to Ecuador 1990–93; Vice-Minister of Commerce and Industry 1993–94; Vice-Minister of Foreign Affairs 1999–2003, Minister of Foreign Affairs 2003–04. *Address:* c/o Ministry of Foreign Affairs, Altos de Ancón, Complejo Narciso Garay, Panamá 4, Panama (office).

ČERNÁK, Ľudovít, DipTech; Slovak politician and business executive; *President, Sitno Holding a.s.;* b. 12 Oct. 1951, Hliník nad Hronom; m. (divorced); three c.; ed Univ. of Tech., Bratislava; man. training in UK 1990; fmr Chair. Slovak Nat. Party (SNP); Minister of Economy 1992–93, 1998–2000; Vice-Chair. Nat. Council 1993–94; fmr mem. Parl. of Slovakia; fmr Vice-Chair. Democratic Union; mem. Int. Cttee for Econ. Reform and Co-operation 2000; in pvt business (investment, finance, offsets) 2000–, Pres. Sitno Holdings; Pres. Slovak Defence Industry Asscn 2005–; Owner and Pres. Sk Slovan Bratislava Football Club 2005–; Pres., Slovak-Russian Business Council 2006–. *Leisure interests:* family, detective novels, turismus, football. *Address:* Sitno Holding a.s., Kalinčiakova 31, 831 04 Bratislava (office); Buková 8, 811 01 Bratislava, Slovakia (home). *Telephone:* (2) 49405111 (office). *Fax:* (2) 49405110 (office). *E-mail:* lcernak@sitno.sk (office). *Website:* www.sitnobusiness.com (office).

CEROVSKÝ, Gen. Milan, DipEng; Slovak army officer; b. 10 Oct. 1949, Kalinovo; m.; two c.; ed Mil. Acad., Vyškov; Mil. Acad., Brno, Royal Coll. of Defence, London, UK; began career with Hungarian armed forces 1971, positions include platoon and co. Commdr 1971–74; Deputy Chief of Staff 60th Tank Regt, 14th Tank Div., E Mil. Dist, Commdr Tank Battalion; Chief of Staff 63rd Mechanized Regt, 14th Tank Div., Commdr; Chief of Staff 13th Tank Div., Deputy Commdr of Operations, Commdr 1993–94; Commdr 1st Army Corps 1994–98; Chief of Integration and Standardization Admin. of Army Gen. Staff 1998, Chief of Gen. Staff of Army 1998–2002, of Armed Forces 2002–04; rank of Lt-Gen. 1999–2003, Gen. 2003–. *Leisure interest:* sport. *Address:* c/o Ministry of Defence, Kutuzovova 7, 832 28 Bratislava, Slovakia (office). *Telephone:* (2) 4425-0329 (office). *Fax:* (2) 4425-3242 (office). *Website:* www.mod.gov.sk (office).

CÉSAR, Carlos Manuel Martins do Vale; Portuguese politician; *President, Regional Government of the Azores;* b. 30 Oct. 1956, Ponta Delgada; s. of Aurélio Augusto César and Maria Natália Martins do Vale César; m. Luísa Maria Assís Vital Gomes; one s.; ed Antero de Quental High School, Faculty of Law, Lisbon; f. Socialist Youth and Socialist Party 1974, mem. Nat. Exec. Socialist Party 1975–; Asst to State Sec. for Public Admin 1977–78; Deputy, Regional Ass. 1980–96, Vice-Pres. –1996; Pres. Regional Govt of the Azores 1996–; mem. State Council, Higher Nat. Defence Council, Higher Internal Security Council, Cttee of the Regions, Ass. of European Regions, Conf. of Presidents of Ultra-peripheral Regions, Conf. of Peripheral Maritime Regions of Europe, Congress of Local Regional Authorities of Europe. *Address:* Residência do Presidente, Governo Regional, Palácio de Santana, 9500-077 Ponta Delgada, The Azores (office). *Telephone:* (296) 301000 (office). *Fax:* (296) 628890 (office). *E-mail:* presidencia@azores.gov.pt (office). *Website:* www.azores.gov.pt (office).

CESCAU, Patrick Jean-Pierre, MBA; French business executive; b. 27 Sept. 1948, Paris; s. of Pierre Cescau and Louise Cescau; m. Ursula Kadanski; one s. one d.; ed Institut Européen d'Admin des Affaires (INSEAD); joined Unilever France as org. officer 1973, sr consultant –1977, held post at Astra-Calvé and served as Chief Accountant, UDL Germany 1980–84, Commercial mem. Edible Fats and Dairy Co-ordination, Rotterdam, Netherlands 1984–86,

Financial Dir Unilever Indonesia 1986–89, Nat. Man., Unilever Portugal 1989–91, Chair. PT Unilever Indonesia 1991–95, Pres. and CEO Van den Bergh Foods, USA 1995–96, Pres. and CEO Lipton, USA (following merger of Van den Bergh and Lipton) 1997–98, Controller and Deputy Financial Dir Unilever 1998–99, Financial Dir 1999–2000, Head, Bestfoods integration team 2000–01, Dir Unilever Global Foods Div. 2001, Chair. Unilever PLC and mem. Exec. Cttee, Unilever NV 2004–5, Group CEO 2005–08; Chair., Nat. Asscn of Margarine Mfrs 1996–98; mem. Bd of Dirs Pearson PLC 2002–; mem. Exec. Cttee, Tea Council 1997–98; Chevalier, Légion d'honneur 2004. *Leisure interests:* arts, reading, photography, theatre. *Address:* c/o Unilever PLC, Unilever House, 100 Victoria Embankment, London, EC4Y 0DY, England. *Telephone:* (20) 7822-5252. *E-mail:* Press-Office.London@Unilever.com.

ÇETİN, Hikmet; Turkish politician; b. 1937, Diyarbakir; m.; two c.; ed Ankara Univ. Political Sciences Faculty, Williams Coll., USA; Sec.-Gen. Social Democratic Populist Party (SHP) (merged to form Republican People's Party), Chair. 1995; Deputy from Gaziantep; Minister of Foreign Affairs 1991–94; Deputy Prime Minister and Minister of State 1995–96; Speaker, Turkish Parl. 1997–99; Sr Civilian Rep. for Afghanistan, NATO 2003–06. *Address:* Rafet Canitez Cad. No. 3/47, Oran, Ankara, Turkey (home). *Telephone:* (312) 4903696 (home). *E-mail:* hikmetcetin@superonline.com.

CEYER, Sylvia T., AB, PhD; American physical chemist and academic; *John C. Sheehan Professor of Chemistry, Massachusetts Institute of Technology;* b. Chicago, Ill.; ed Hope Coll., Univ. of California, Berkeley; Post-doctoral Fellow, Nat. Bureau of Standards (now Nat. Inst. of Standards and Tech.) 1979–81; joined MIT faculty 1981, Class of 1943 Career Devt Chair 1985–88, tenure 1987, W.M. Keck Foundation Professorship in Energy 1991–96, apptd to Faculty Advisory Cttee to MIT Corpn 2004, Assoc. Head of Dept of Chem. 2005–, John C. Sheehan Prof. of Chem. 2006–; held Chem. Chair of NAS –2006; Fellow, NAS, American Physical Soc., American Acad. of Arts and Sciences; Harold E. Edgerton Award 1988, Baker Memorial Award for Excellence in Undergraduate Teaching 1988, Young Scholar Award, American Asscn of Univ. Women 1988, ACS Nobel Laureate Signature Award 1993, MIT School of Science Teaching Prize 1993, MacVicar Faculty Fellow 1998, ACS Willard Gibbs Award 2007, ACS Langmuir Lectureship, Welch Foundation Lectureship. *Publications:* numerous scientific papers in professional journals on dynamics of interactions of molecules with surfaces of materials. *Address:* Room 6-217, Department of Chemistry, Massachusetts Institute of Technology, 77 Massachusetts Avenue, Cambridge, MA 02139-4307, USA (office). *Telephone:* (617) 253-4537 (office). *Fax:* (617) 253-7030 (office). *E-mail:* stceyer@mit.edu (office). *Website:* ceyer.mit.edu (office).

CHA, Laura M., BA, JD; Chinese politician, lawyer and business executive; *Member, Executive Council, Government of the Hong Kong Special Administrative Region;* b. 1949, China; m.; ed Univ. of Wisconsin and Santa Clara Univ., USA; began career as attorney with Pillsbury, Madison & Sutro, San Francisco, Calif. and Coudert Brothers, Hong Kong 1982–90; joined Securities and Futures Comm. (SFC), Hong Kong 1991, Asst Dir then Sr Dir 1991–94, Exec. Dir 1994–2001, Deputy Chair. 1998–2001; Vice-Chair. China Securities Regulatory Comm. 2001–04, Vice-Chair. Int. Advisory Cttee 2004–; apptd to Exec. Council of Govt of Hong Kong Special Admin. Region (HKSAR) 2004–; mem. Shanghai Int. Financial Advisory Council, Shanghai Municipal Govt 2007–; HKSAR Deputy for 11th NPC, People's Repub. of China 2008–; Standing mem. CPPCC Shanghai Cttee 2008–; Dir (non-exec.) Johnson Electric Holdings Ltd 2004–, The Hong Kong and Shanghai Banking Corpn Ltd 2004–, Baoshan Iron and Steel Co. 2006–, Hong Kong Exchanges and Clearing Ltd 2006–, Bank of Communications 2006–, Tata Consultancy Services Ltd 2006–; Sr Advisor, Investor AB, Sweden 2004–; mem. Int. Advisory Bd, Marsh & McLennan Cos Inc. 2007–; Chair. Univ. Grants Cttee, Hong Kong 2007–, Advisory Cttee on Corruption, Ind. Comm. Against Corruption in Hong Kong 2007–; mem. Advisory Bd, Millstein Center of Corp. Governance and Performance, Yale Univ., USA 2006–; mem. ABA, State Bar of Calif., Int. Council of Asian Soc., New York; JP 1995–2001, 2006; Silver Bauhinia Star Medal 2001. *Address:* 23/F China Merchants Tower, Shun Tak Centre, 168 Connaught Road Central, Hong Kong Special Administrative Region, People's Republic of China (office). *Telephone:* 22381217 (office). *Fax:* 29873538 (office). *E-mail:* anita.yiu@hkri.com (office).

CHAABANE, Sadok; Tunisian professor of law and government official; *President, Conseil Economique et social;* b. (Sadok Chaabane), 23 Feb. 1950, Sfax; s. of Jilani Chaabane; m. Dalenda Nouri 1974; one s. two d.; Prof. of Law, Univ. of Tunis 1973, now Assoc. Prof. of Public Law and Political Science; Dir of Studies, Research and Publ Centre 1975–82; Perm. Sec. of RCD 1988; Sec. of State for Higher Educ. and Scientific Research 1989; Adviser to the Pres. on Political Affairs 1990; Sec. of State for Scientific Research 1991; Prin. Adviser to the Pres. on Human Rights 1991; Minister of Justice 1992–97, of Higher Educ., Scientific Research and Tech. 1999–2004; Minister Counselor to the Pres., responsible for Political Affairs and Human Rights; Pres. Econ. and Social Council (Conseil Economique et social) 2007–; fmr Dir Tunisian Inst. of Strategic Studies; Founder-mem. Int. Acad. of Constitutional Law, Int. Law Asscn; Commdr Order of Nov. 7; Great Cordon of Order of the Repub. *Publications:* The Law of International Institutions 1985, Ben Ali and The Way to Pluralism in Tunisia 1997, The Challenges of Ben Ali 1999, Hannibal Redux: The Renewal of Modern Tunisia 1977. *Address:* Conseil Economique et social, 38, L'Avenue Mohamed V, BP 27, 1002 Tunis (office); 30 Rue Mannoubia Ben Nasr, Manar 3, 2092 Tunis, Tunisia (home). *Telephone:* (71) 830-345 (office); (71) 889-690 (home). *Fax:* (71) 835-225 (office). *E-mail:* saadok .chaabane@ces.org.tn (office). *Website:* www.ces.org.tn (office).

CHABON, Michael, MFA; American writer; b. 1964, Columbia, Md; m. Ayelet Waldman; two s. two d.; ed Univ. of Pittsburgh, Univ. of Calif., Irvine; Publishers Weekly Best Book 1995, New York Times Notable Book 1995, O. Henry Award 1999. *Publications:* The Mysteries of Pittsburgh 1988, A Model World (short stories) 1991, The Wonder Boys 1995, Werewolves in Their Youth (short stories) 1995, The Amazing Adventures of Kavalier & Clay (Pulitzer Prize for fiction 2001) 2000, The Final Solution 2005, The Yiddish Policemen's Union (novel) (Nebula Award for Best Novel 2008, Hugo Award for Best Novel 2008) 2007, Gentlemen of the Road 2007, Maps and Legends: Reading and Writing along the Borderlands 2008; contrib. short stories to several magazines. *Address:* Steven Barclay Agency, 12 Western Avenue, Petaluma, CA 94952, USA (office). *Telephone:* (707) 773-0654 (office). *Fax:* (707) 778-1868 (office). *Website:* www.barclayagency.com (office).

CHABRAJA, Nicholas D., BA, JD; American lawyer and defence industry executive; *Chairman and CEO, General Dynamics Corporation;* b. 6 Nov. 1942, Gary, Ind.; ed Northwestern Univ.; lawyer, Jenner and Block (law firm) 1968–1997, Partner 1984–93; 1986, Special Counsel to US House of Reps 1986; Sr Vice-Pres. and Gen. Counsel, Gen. Dynamics Corpn 1993–94, Exec. Vice-Pres. 1994–96, Vice-Chair. 1996–97, Chair. and CEO 1997–; Dir Ceridian Corpn, Northern Trust Corpn 2007–; mem. Kennedy Center Corp. Fund Bd. *Address:* General Dynamics Corpn, 2941 Fairview Park Drive, Suite 100, Falls Church, VA 22042-4513, USA (office). *Telephone:* (703) 876-3000 (office). *Fax:* (703) 876-3125 (office). *E-mail:* info@gendyn.com (office). *Website:* www .gendyn.com (office).

CHABROL, Claude; French film director and producer; b. 24 June 1930, Paris; s. of Yves Chabrol and Madeleine Delarbre; m. 1st Agnès Goute; two s.; m. 2nd Colette Dacheville (Stéphane Audran (q.v.)); one s.; m. 3rd Aurore Pajot 1983; ed Paris Univ., Ecole Libre des Sciences Politiques; fmrly film critic and Public Relations Officer in Paris for 20th-Century Fox; dir and producer 1958–; Locarno Festival Grand Prix 1958, Berlin Festival Golden Bear 1959. *Films directed include:* Le beau Serge 1957, Les cousins 1958, A double tour 1959, Les bonnes femmes 1959, Les godelureaux 1960, Ophélia 1962, L'oeil du malin 1961, Landru 1962, Les plus belles escroqueries du monde 1963, Le tigre aime la chair fraîche 1964, Le tigre se parfume à la dynamite 1965, Marie-Chantal contre le Docteur Kha 1965, Le scandale 1967, Les biches 1968, La femme infidèle 1968, Que la bête meure 1969, Le boucher 1970, La rupture 1970, Juste avant la nuit 1971, Doctor Popaul 1972, La décade prodigieuse 1972, Les noces rouges 1973, Nada 1973, Une partie de plaisir 1975, Les innocents aux mains sales 1976, Alice ou la dernière fugue 1977, Les liens de sang 1977, Violette Nozière 1978, The Twist, Blood Relations 1979, Le Cheval d'Orgueil 1980, Les fantômes du chapelier 1982, Cop au vin 1985, Inspecteur Lavardin 1986, Masques 1987, Une Affaire des Femmes 1988, Story of Women 1989, Dr. M 1989, Quiet Days in Clichy 1989, Madame Bovary 1991, Betty 1991, L'Enfer 1993, La Cérémonie, Through the Eyes of Vichy, A Judgement in Stone, Rien ne va plus 1997, Merci pour le chocolat 2000, La fleur du mal 2003, La Demoiselle d'honneur 2004, L'Ivresse de pouvoir 2006, La Fille coupée en deux 2007. *Publications:* Alfred Hitchcock (with E. Rohmer), Les Noces rouges, Et pourtant je tourne. *Address:* c/o Artmedia, 10 avenue Georges V, 75008 Paris; 15 Quai Conti, 75006 Paris, France.

CHACÓN PIQUERAS, Carme, LLD; Spanish politician; *Minister of Defence;* b. 13 March 1971, Esplugues de Llobregat, Barcelona; m.; one s.; ed Univ. of Barcelona, Osgoode Hall Law School, Toronto, Univ. of Kingston, Univ. of Montreal, Canada; Prof. of Constitutional Law, Univ. of Girona 1994–2004; Sec. of Educ., Culture and Research, Exec. Comm., Spanish Socialist Workers' Party (PSOE) 2000–04, mem. Fed. Exec. Comm. 2000–; MP (PSOE) for Barcelona 2000–, Vice-Pres. Congress of Deputies (Lower House) 2004–07; Minister of Housing 2007–08, of Defence 2008–. *Address:* Ministry of Defence, Paseo de la Castellana 109, 28071 Madrid, Spain (office). *Telephone:* (91) 3955000 (office). *E-mail:* infodefensa@mde.es (office). *Website:* www.mde.es (office).

CHADERTON MATOS, Roy; Venezuelan politician and diplomatist; *Ambassador to Mexico;* b. 17 Aug. 1942; ed Cen. Univ. of Venezuela, Instituto de Altos Estudios de Defensa Nacional; Second Sec., Embassy in Poland 1969–72; First Sec., Embassy in FRG 1973, Embassy in Canada 1975; at Ministry of Foreign Affairs 1973–75, Counsellor 1979, Minister Counsellor 1979–82, Amb. 1983–85, Gen. Dir of Int. Political Affairs 1990–93, Gen. Dir (Vice-Pres.) 1994–95; Counsellor Embassy in Belgium 1977–78; Counsellor, Perm. Mission to UN, New York 1978–79, Deputy Perm. Rep. 1982–83; Amb. to Gabon 1985–87, to Norway and Iceland 1987–90, to Canada 1993–94, to UK and Ireland 1996–2000, to Colombia 2000–02, to USA 2002, to France 2004–07, to Mexico 2007–; Minister of Foreign Affairs 2002–04; mem. Social Christian Party of Venezuela 1958–, Official Rep. 1994; Caballero de Madara Order (Bulgaria), Francisco de Miranda Order, First Class (Venezuela), Bernardo O'Higgins Order (Chile), Great Cross, May Order (Argentina), Great Cross, San Olav Order (Norway), Great Cross, Cruceiro do Sul National Order (Brazil), Great Cord Libertador Order (Venezuela). *Address:* Embassy of Venezuela, Schiller 326, Col. Chapultepec Morales, Del. Miguel Hidalgo, 11570 México, DF, Mexico (office). *Telephone:* (55) 5203-4233 (office). *Fax:* (55) 5203-5072 (office). *E-mail:* embemve.mxmdf@mre.gob.ve (office).

CHADIRJI, Rifat Kamil, DipArch, FRIBA; Iraqi architect; b. 6 Dec. 1926, Baghdad; s. of Kamil Chadirji; m. Balkis Sharara 1954; ed Hammersmith School of Arts and Crafts, London; Founder and Sr Pnr and Dir Iraq Consult 1952–; Section Head, Baghdad Bldg Dept Waqaf Org. 1954–57; Dir-Gen. of Housing, Ministry of Planning, Baghdad 1958–59, Head of Planning Cttee Ministry of Housing 1959–63; returned to full-time pvt. practice with Iraq Consult 1963–78; apptd Counsellor to Mayoralty of Baghdad 1980–82; mem. Iraqi Tourist Bd 1970–75; Loeb Fellow, Harvard Univ. 1983; Hon. Fellow, RIBA, American Inst. of Architects; numerous awards including First Prize for Council of Ministers Bldg, Baghdad 1975, First Prize New Theatre, Abu Dhabi, UAE 1977, First Prize, Council of Ministers, Abu Dhabi, UAE 1978.

Works include: Council of Ministers Bldg, Baghdad 1975, Cabinet Ministers' Bldg, UAE 1976, Nat. Theatre, Abu Dhabi, UAE 1977, Al-Ain Public Library, UAE 1978. *Leisure interests:* photography, travel. *Address:* 28 Troy Court, Kensington High Street, London, W8, England. *Telephone:* (20) 7937-3715.

CHADLINGTON, Baron (Life Peer), cr. 1996, of Dean in the County of Oxfordshire; **Peter Selwyn Gummer,** MA, FRSA; British business executive; *CEO, Huntsworth plc;* b. 24 Aug. 1942, Bexley; s. of the late Rev. Canon Selwyn Gummer and Sybille Gummer (née Mason); brother of John Selwyn Gummer (q.v.); m. Lucy Rachel Dudley-Hill 1982; one s. three d.; ed King's School, Rochester, Selwyn Coll., Cambridge; with Portsmouth & Sunderland Newspaper Group 1964–65, Viyella Int. 1965–66, Hodgkinson & Partners 1966–67, Industrial & Commercial Finance Corpn (3i Group) 1967–74; Founder, Chair. and Chief Exec. Shandwick PLC 1974–94, Chair. 1994–2000; Dir (non-exec.) CIA Group PLC 1990–94, non-exec. mem. Halifax Bldg Soc. London Bd 1990–94, Dir (non-exec.) Halifax PLC 1994–2001, Black Box Music Ltd 1999–2001, Oxford Resources 1999–2002, Chair. Hotcourses Ltd 2000–04, Britax Childcare Holdings Ltd; CEO Huntsworth PLC 2000–; mem. EU Select Sub-Cttee B (Energy, Ind. and Transport), House of Lords 2000–2003; Chair. Action on Addiction 1999–; mem. Nat. Health Service Policy Bd 1991–95, Chair. Royal Opera House 1996–97; Chair. Understanding Industry Trust 1991–96, Arts Council of England (fmrly GB) 1991–96, Marketing Group of GB 1993–95, Nat. Lottery Advisory Bd for the Arts and Film 1994–96; Int. Public Relations 1998–2000, Guideforlife.com 2000–2002; Dir Walbrook Club 1999–2004; Chair. Chadlington Consultancy; mem. Council, Cheltenham Ladies Coll. 1998–2003, Bd of Trustees, American Univ. 1999–2001; Hon. Fellow Bournemouth Univ. 1999–; Trustee Atlantic Partnership 1999–; Inst. of Public Relations Pres.'s Medal 1988. *Publications:* articles and booklets on public relations and marketing. *Leisure interests:* opera, rugby, cricket. *Address:* House of Lords, London, SW1A 0PW; Huntsworth PLC, 15–17 Huntsworth Mews, London, NW1 6DD (office); Dean Manor, Dean, Chipping Norton, Oxon., OX7 3LD, England (home). *Telephone:* (20) 7219-5172 (House of Lords); (20) 7298-6583 (office); (20) 7219-3000. *Fax:* (20) 7493-3048 (office). *E-mail:* lordchadlington@huntsworth.com (office). *Website:* www.huntsworth.co.uk (office).

CHADWICK, Michael J. (Mike), MA, PhD; British environmental scientist and academic; b. 13 Sept. 1934, Leicester; s. of John Chadwick and Hilda Corman; m. Josephine Worrall 1958; one s. two d.; ed Godalming Co. Grammar School and Univ. Coll. of North Wales, Bangor; Lecturer, Dept of Botany, Univ. of Khartoum, Sudan 1959–62; Univ. Demonstrator, School of Agric., Univ. of Cambridge 1962–66; Lecturer and Prof., Dept of Biology, Univ. of York 1966–91; Dir Stockholm Environment Inst., Stockholm, Sweden 1991–96; Dir LEAD-Europe, Geneva, Switzerland 1996–; Sr Research Assoc., Stockholm Environment Inst.'s York Centre; now works as pvt. consultant on environmental matters, most recently with MISTRA in Sweden, IPCC, EU projects and with Rockefeller Foundation on poverty alleviation and sustainable livelihoods; fmr Sec., British Ecological Soc.; Hon. Visiting Prof., Depts of Environment and Biology, Univ. of York; Award for Contributing to Nobel Peace Prize 2007 given to Intergovernmental Panel on Climate Change. *Publications:* Restoration of Land (with A. D. Bradshaw) 1980, The Relative Sensitivity of Ecosystems in Europe to Acidic Depositions (with J. C. I. Kuylenstierna) 1990, A Perspective on Global Air Pollution Problems (with J. C. I. Kuylenstierna and W.K. Hicks) 2002. *Leisure interests:* music, gardening, travel. *Address:* Stockholm Environment Institute, Grimston House, University of York, Heslington, York, YO10 5DD (office); 3 Skipwith Road, Escrick, York, YO19 6JT, England (home). *Telephone:* (1904) 728025 (office); (1904) 728234 (home). *Fax:* (1904) 728025 (office). *E-mail:* cmjchadwick@aol.com (office).

CHADWICK, (William) Owen, OM, KBE, FBA, FRSE; British historian and academic; b. 20 May 1916, Bromley, Kent; s. of John Chadwick and Edith Chadwick (née Horrocks); m. Ruth Hallward 1949; two s. two d.; ed St John's Coll., Cambridge; Fellow, Trinity Hall, Cambridge 1947–56, Master of Selwyn Coll., Cambridge 1956–83, Fellow 1983–, Dixie Prof. of Ecclesiastical History, Univ. of Cambridge 1958–68, Regius Prof. of Modern History 1968–83; Vice-Chancellor Univ. of Cambridge 1969–71; Pres. British Acad. 1981–85; Chancellor Univ. of East Anglia 1985–94; Chair. of Trustees Nat. Portrait Gallery 1988–94; Hon. mem. American Acad. of Arts and Sciences; Hon. DD (St Andrews) 1960, (Oxford) 1973, (Wales) 1993: Hon. DLitt (Kent) 1970, (Columbia Univ.) 1977, (East Anglia) 1977, (Bristol) 1977, (London) 1983, (Leeds) 1986, (Cambridge) 1987; Hon. LLD (Aberdeen) 1986; Wolfson Literary Award 1981. *Publications:* From Bossuet to Newman 1957, The Victorian Church (two vols) 1966–70, John Cassian (2nd edn) 1968, The Reformation (20th edn) 1986, The Secularization of the European Mind 1976, The Popes and European Revolution 1981, Britain and the Vatican during the Second World War 1987, Michael Ramsey: A Life 1990, The Christian Church in the Cold War 1992, A History of Christianity 1995, A History of the Popes 1830–1914 1998, The Early Reformation on the Continent 2001; numerous articles and reviews in learned journals. *Leisure interests:* music and gardening. *Address:* 67 Grantchester Street, Cambridge, CB3 9HZ, England. *Telephone:* (1223) 314000 (home). *E-mail:* oc207@cam.ac.uk (office).

CHADWICK, Peter, PhD, ScD, FRS; British mathematician and academic; *Professor Emeritus, School of Mathematics, University of East Anglia;* b. 23 March 1931, Huddersfield; s. of Jack Chadwick and Marjorie Chadwick (née Castle); m. Sheila G. Salter 1956 (deceased); two d.; ed Huddersfield Coll., Univ. of Manchester and Pembroke Coll., Cambridge; Scientific Officer, then Sr Scientific Officer, Atomic Weapons Research Establishment, Aldermaston 1955–59; Lecturer, then Sr Lecturer in Applied Math., Univ. of Sheffield 1959–65; Prof. of Math., Univ. of E Anglia 1965–91, Prof. Emer. 1991–, Dean, School of Math. and Physics 1979–82; Visiting Prof., Univ. of Queensland

1972; Leverhulme Emer. Fellow 1991–93; Hon. DSc (Glasgow) 1991. *Publications:* Continuum Mechanics: Concise Theory and Problems 1976, 1999; articles in books and learned journals. *Leisure interests:* walking, music. *Address:* 8 Stratford Crescent, Cringleford, Norwich, NR4 7SF, England.

CHAFEE, Lincoln Davenport, BA; American academic and fmr politician; *Distinguished Visiting Fellow, Watson Institute for International Studies, Brown University;* b. 26 March 1953, Warwick, RI; s. of the late John Chafee; m. Stephanie Chafee; one s. two d.; ed Brown Univ., Montana State Univ. Horseshoeing School, Bozeman; farrier 1977–83; planner, General Dynamics, Quonset Point 1983; Exec. Dir Northeast Corridor Initiative 1980s; began political career as del. to Rhode Island Constitutional Convention 1985–86; with Warwick City Council 1986–92, Mayor of Warwick 1993–99; apptd by Gov. of Rhode Island to fill the unexpired term of his father the late Senator John H. Chafee Nov. 1999, elected Senator from Rhode Island 2000–07, mem. Cttee on the Environment and Public Works, Cttee on Foreign Relations, Chair. Sub-cttee on Near Eastern and South Asian Affairs, Jt Econ. Cttee, Chair. Sub-cttee on Superfund, Waste Control and Risk Assessment, Sub-cttee on Western Hemisphere, Peace Corps, Narcotics and Terrorism; Distinguished Visiting Fellow, Watson Inst. for Int. Studies, Brown Univ. 2007–; mem. Republican Party (resgnd from party 2007); Francis M. Driscoll Award for Leadership, Scholarship and Athletics, Brown Univ. *Publication:* Against the Tide: How a Compliant Congress Empowered a Reckless President 2008. *Leisure interests:* skiing, horseback trail riding. *Address:* Watson Institute, Brown University, 111 Thayer Street, Box 1970, Providence, RI 02912-1970, USA (office). *Telephone:* (401) 863-2809 (office). *Fax:* (401) 863-1270 (office). *Website:* www.watsoninstitute.org (office).

CHAI, Songyue; Chinese politician; b. Nov. 1941, Putuo Co., Zhejiang Prov.; joined CCP 1961; Deputy Sec. CCP Party Cttee, Changguang Coal Mine Co. 1961, later Sec.; Vice-Gov. Zhejiang Prov. 1988–97, Acting Gov. 1997–98, Gov. 1998–2002; mem. CCP Zhejiang Provincial Cttee Standing Cttee 1993–; Deputy Sec. CCP Zhejiang Provincial Cttee 1993–; Alt. mem. 14th CCP Cen. Cttee 1992–97; mem. 15th CCP Cen. Cttee 1997–2002, 16th CCP Cen. Cttee 2002–07; Chair. State Electricity Regulatory Comm. 2002–07. *Address:* c/o China Electricity Regulatory Commission, Chang'an Street 86, Xicheng District, West Beijing 100031 People's Republic of China (office). *Telephone:* (10) 58681803 (office). *E-mail:* manager@serc.gov.cn (office). *Website:* www .serc.gov.cn (office).

CHAI, Zhifang; Chinese nuclear physicist; currently Prof. and Dir Lab. of Nuclear Analytical Techniques, Inst. of High Energy Physics, Chinese Acad. of Sciences; mem. Hevesy Medal Selection Panel 2006; George Hevesy Medal 2005. *Publications:* numerous scientific papers in professional journals. *Address:* Laboratory of Nuclear Analytical Techniques, Institute of High Energy Physics, Chinese Academy of Sciences, PO Box 918, Beijing 100039, People's Republic of China (office). *Telephone:* (10) 88212859 (office). *Fax:* (10) 88212859 (office). *E-mail:* chaizf@ihep.ac.cn (office). *Website:* www.ihep.ac.cn (office).

CHAIGNEAU, Pascal Gérard Joël, DèsSc, DenScPol, DenScEcon, DenD; French academic; *Director, Centre d'Etudes Diplomatiques et Stratégiques;* b. 8 Feb. 1956, Paris; s. of André Chaigneau and Hélène Alexandre; m. Marie-Claude Ratsarazaka-Ratsimandresy 1983; three s.; ed Coll. St Michel de Picpus and Facultés de Droit et des Lettres, Paris; practical work 1974–75; Asst 1976–78, Prof. Ecole des Hautes Etudes Internationales and Ecole Supérieure de Journalisme 1978–, Dir of Studies 1984–85, Dir-Gen. 1985–90, Admin.-Gen. 1990–; Research, Fondation pour les Etudes de Défense Nationale 1980–82; in charge of course, Univ. de Paris II 1982–90; Maître de conférences, Univ. de Paris V 1990–2000, Professeur des universités 2000–;; Sec.-Gen. Centre de Recherches Droit et Défense, Univ. de Paris V 1985–; Founder and Dir Centre d'Etudes Diplomatiques et Stratégiques 1986–; Advocate, Court of Appeal, Paris 1990–; Prof. Centre des Hautes Etudes sur l'Afrique et l'Asie Modernes; Lecturer, Inst. des Hautes Etudes de Défense Nationale; in charge of course, Ecole des Hautes Etudes Commerciales 1990–92, Prof. 1992–; Prof. Collège Interarmes de Défense 1994–; with Bolivian Consulate in France 1994–97; Foreign Trade Counsellor 1995–; many other public appointments; mem. Acad. des Sciences d'Outre-mer, Soc. d'Economie Politique; Chevalier, Légion d'honneur; Officier, Ordre nat. du mérite, Commdr, Ordre des Palmes Académiques; Commdr des Arts et des Lettres; decorations from Bolivia, Burkina Faso, Belgium, Honduras, Chad, Madagascar, Niger, etc.; Hon. LLD (Richmond, USA); Dr hc (Nat. Univ. of Bolivia); Grand Prix de l'Asscn des Ecrivains de Langue Française 1987, Prix de l'Acad. des Sciences Morales et Politiques 1993 and other prizes, awards and distinctions. *Publications:* La Stratégie soviétique 1978, La Politique militaire de la France en Afrique 1984, Rivalités politiques et socialisme à Madagascar 1985, Les Pays de l'Est et l'Afrique 1985, France-océan indien-mer rouge (with others) 1986, Pour une analyse du commerce international 1987, La Guerre du Golfe 1991, Europe: la nouvelle donne stratégique 1993, Les grands Enjeux du monde contemporain 1997, Dictionnaire des Relations Internationales 1998, Gestion des Risques internationaux 2001. *Address:* Centre d'Etudes Diplomatiques et Stratégiques, 54 avenue Marceau, 75008 Paris (office); 68 avenue de Gravelle, 94220 Charenton-le-Pont, France (home). *Telephone:* 1-47-20-57-47 (office). *Fax:* 1-47-20-57-30 (office). *E-mail:* contact@ceds-fr.com (office). *Website:* www.ceds-fr.com.

CHAIKA, Yurii Yakovlevich; Russian lawyer and government official; *Prosecutor-General;* b. 1951, Nikolayevsk-on-Amur, Khabarovsk Krai; m.; two c.; ed Sverdlovsk Inst. of Law; electrician at shipbuilding factory, Nikolayevsk-on-Amur 1970; joined Prosecutor's Office, Irkutsk Region 1976, held several positions including investigator, Deputy Regional Public Prosecutor, Taishetsk Transport Public Prosecutor, Head, Investigative Div. of East Siberian Transport Public Prosecutor's Office 1983–92, Public Prosecutor of

Irkutsk Region 1992–95; instructor, Admin. Div., Irkutsk Regional CPSU Cttee 1984–92; First Deputy Prosecutor-Gen. of Russian Fed. 1995–99, Prosecutor-Gen. April–July 1999, 2006–; Minister of Justice 1999–2006; Hon. Lawyer of the Russian Fed., Hon. Officer, Prosecution Service of the Russian Fed.; Order of Merit for Country, IV Degree, Order of Honour. *Address:* Office of the Prosecutor-General, 125993 Moscow, ul. B. Dmitrovka 15A, Russia (office). *Telephone:* (495) 692-26-82 (office). *Fax:* (495) 292-88-48 (office). *Website:* www.genproc.gov.ru (office).

CHAILLY, Riccardo; Italian conductor; *Chief Conductor, Leipzig Gewandhausorchester;* b. 20 Feb. 1953, Milan; s. of the late Luciano Chailly and of Anna Marie Motta; m. Gabriella Terragni 1987; two s.; ed Giuseppe Verdi and Perugia Conservatories and with Franco Caracciolo and Franco Ferrara; Asst to Claudio Abbado, La Scala, Milan 1972–74; debut as Conductor with Chicago Opera 1974; debut, La Scala 1978, Covent Garden (operatic debut) 1979; concert debut with London Symphony Orchestra and Edin. Festival 1979; American concert debut, Los Angeles Philharmonic, CA 1980; Metropolitan Opera debut 1982; Prin. Guest Conductor, London Philharmonic Orchestra 1982–85; Chief Conductor Radio Symphony Orchestra, Berlin 1982–89; Vienna State Opera debut 1983; appearances Salzburg Festival 1984, 1985, 1986; Japan debut with Royal Philharmonic Orchestra 1984; New York Philharmonic Orchestra debut 1984; Music Dir Bologna Orchestra, Teatro Comunale 1986–93; Chief Conductor Royal Concertgebouw Orchestra, Amsterdam 1988–2004, Conductor Emeritus 2004–; Principal Conductor and Music Dir Giuseppe Verdi Symphony Orchestra, Milan 1999–2005, Conductor Laureate 2005–; Chief Conductor Leipzig Gewandhausorchester 2005–; Music Dir Leipzig Opera 2005–; Hon. mem. Royal Acad. of Music, London; Gramophone Award Artist of the Year 1998, Diapason d'Or Artist of the Year 1999; Grand' Ufficiale della Repubblica Italiana, Knight of Order of Netherlands Lion 1998, Cavaliere di Gran Croce (Italy) 1998, Abrogino d'Oro, Comune Milano (Italy). *Leisure interests:* music, paintings, the arts in general. *Address:* Gewandhausorchester, Opernhaus, Augustusplatz 12, 04109 Leipzig, Netherlands (office). *Telephone:* (341) 1270365 (office). *Website:* www.gewandhaus.de (office).

CHAISANG, Chaturon, MA; Thai politician; b. 1 Jan. 1956, Chachoengsao; ed State Univ. of New York at Buffalo, American Univ., Washington DC; Asst Sec. to Minister of Finance 1986–87; Sec. Econ. Cttee, House of Reps 1986–88; mem. Parl. Chachoengsao 1986–92, 1995–; Sec. Cttee on Finance, Banking and Financial Insts, House of Reps 1988–91 (mem. 1992); Sec. to Minister of Commerce and adviser to Minister of Agric. 1991; adviser Minister of Science, Tech. and Environment 1992, Ministry of Labour and Social Welfare 1995; Spokesman for New Aspiration Party 1992–95, fmr Sec.-Gen.; Deputy Minister of Finance 1996–2001, Minister attached to Prime Minister's Office 2001, Minister of Justice 2002, Deputy Prime Minister 2002–06; fmr Acting Leader Thai Rak Thai party (now banned); fmr Chair. Cttee of Science and Tech., House of Reps; Kt Grand Cross (First Class) of Crown of Thailand. *Address:* 441/12 Supakij Road, Maung, Chachoengsao 24000, Thailand.

CHAKRAVARTY, Pinak Ranjan; Indian diplomatist; *High Commissioner to Bangladesh;* m. Radha Chakravarty; Chief of Protocol, Ministry of Foreign Affairs 2003–05, Jt Sec. 2005; Amb. to the Philippines 2005–06; High Commr to Bangladesh 2007–. *Address:* High Commission of India, House No. 2, Road No. 142, Gulshan-1, Dhaka, Bangladesh (office). *Telephone:* (2) 9889339 (office). *Fax:* (2) 8817487 (office). *E-mail:* hc@hcidhaka.org (office). *Website:* www.hcidhaka.org (office).

CHALABI, Ahmad, PhD; Iraqi politician; *Leader, Iraqi National Congress;* b. 1945, Baghdad; m.; four c.; ed in UK, MIT and Univ. of Chicago, USA; family moved to England following coup d'état and assassination of King of Iraq 1958; fmr Prof. of Math., American Univ. of Beirut; f. Bank of Petra, Jordan 1980, taken over by mil. decree 1989, charged with embezzlement, fraud and misuse of depositor funds by Jordanian court 1991, sentenced in absentia to 22 years' imprisonment 1992; organized conf. of 400 opposition leaders in Northern Iraq 1992; Chair. Exec. Council and Leader, Iraqi Nat. Congress 1992–; survived failed coup 1995; lived in exile in London 1996–2003; returned to Iraq to help establish an interim govt following overthrow of Saddam Hussein's regime April 2003; Deputy Prime Minister 2005–06, Acting Minister of Oil 2005. *Address:* Iraqi National Congress, Baghdad, Iraq (office). *E-mail:* info@inciraq.com (office). *Website:* inciraq.com (office).

CHALANDON, Albin Paul Henri, LèsL; French politician and business executive; b. 11 June 1920, Reyrieux, Ain; s. of Pierre Chalandon and Claire Cambon; m. Princess Salomé Murat 1951; three s.; ed Lycée Condorcet, Paris; Inspecteur des Finances; Dir Banque Nationale pour le Commerce et l'Industrie (Afrique) 1950–51; Admin. and Dir-Gen. Banque Commerciale de Paris 1952–64, Président-Directeur Général 1964–68; mem. Parl. 1967–76; Minister of Industry May 1968, of Public Works, Housing and Urban Devt 1968–72, of Justice 1986–88; Special Asst, Ministry of Foreign Affairs Feb.–Aug. 1974; Treas. Cen. Cttee Union pour la Nouvelle République (now Union des Démocrates pour la République— UDR) 1958–59, Sec.-Gen. 1959, Deputy Sec.-Gen. UDR 1974–75; Pres., Dir-Gen. Soc. Nat. Elf Aquitaine (SNEA) 1976–83; Pres., Dir-Gen. Texmaille 1989–97; mem. Social and Econ. Council 1963–67; Conseil Supérieure du Plan 1962–67; Grand Officier de la Légion d'honneur; Croix de guerre. *Publications:* Le système monétaire international 1966, Les joueurs de flûte 1977, Quitte ou Double 1986. *Leisure interests:* literature, philosophy, politics. *Address:* 12 rue de Lota, 75016 Paris, France (home). *Telephone:* 1-53-67-70-71 (office). *Fax:* 1-53-67-70-71 (office).

CHALAYAN, Hussein, MBE, BA; British fashion designer; ed Cyprus and Cen. St Martin's School of Art, London; student final year collection featured in Brown's window; set up own label; exhbn of first solo collection, West Soho Galleries, London 1994; second collection shown during London Fashion Week and in Kobe and Tokyo; fourth collection received Absolut Vodka's Absolut Creation Sponsorship Award (first recipient) 1996; solo exhbn (key pieces from past collections), The Window Gallery, Prague 1996; exhibited Buried and Path dresses, Jam (style, music and media) exhbn, Barbican Art Gallery 1996; designs selected for Cutting Edge exhbn, Victoria and Albert Museum 1997; invited to exhibit in Challenge of Materials exhbn, Science Museum 1997; talk at Tate Gallery (with Zaha Hadid, Michael Bracewell and Georgina Starr) on parallels between fashion, art and architecture 1997; Creative Dir, Puma 2008–; Designer of the Year, London Fashion Awards 1998, 2000. *Address:* 71 Endell Road, London, WC2 9AJ, England. *Website:* www.husseinchalayan.com.

CHALFIE, Martin, PhD; American biochemist and academic; *William R. Kenan, Jr. Professor of Biological Sciences, Columbia University;* b. 1947; ed Harvard Univ.; teacher, Hamden Hall Country Day School, Conn. 1970–71; post-doctorate research at Lab. of Molecular Biology, Univ. of Cambridge, UK 1977–82; William R. Kenan, Jr. Prof. of Biological Sciences, Columbia Univ. 1982–, also Chair. of Biological Sciences; mem. NAS 2004–; Nobel Prize in Chem. (jtly) 2008. *Publications:* articles in academic journals. *Address:* Columbia University, Biological Sciences, 1018 Fairchild Center, M.C. 2446, New York, NY 10027, USA (office). *Telephone:* (212) 854-8870 (office). *Fax:* (212) 865-8246 (office). *E-mail:* mc21@columbia.edu (office). *Website:* www.columbia.edu/cu/biology/faculty/chalfie (office).

CHALFONT, Baron (Life Peer), cr. 1964, of Llantarnam in the County of Monmouthshire; **(Arthur) Alun Gwynne Jones,** PC, OBE, MC, FRSA; British politician and writer; b. 5 Dec. 1919, Llantarnam, Wales; s. of Arthur Gwynne Jones and Eliza Alice Hardman; m. Dr Mona Mitchell 1948; one d. (deceased); ed West Monmouth School; commissioned into S. Wales Borderers (24th Foot) 1940; served in Burma 1941–44, Malaya 1955–57, Cyprus 1958–59; resgnd comm. 1961; Defence Corresp. The Times, London 1961–64; consultant on foreign affairs to BBC TV, London 1961–64; Minister of State for Foreign Affairs 1964–70, Minister for Disarmament 1964–67, 1969–70, in charge of day-to-day negotiations for Britain's entry into Common Market 1967–69; Perm. Rep. to WEU 1969–70; Foreign Ed. New Statesman 1970–71; Chair. All-Party Defence Group House of Lords 1980–96, Pres. 1996–; Chair. Industrial Cleaning Papers 1979–86, Peter Hamilton Security Consultants Ltd 1984–86, UK Cttee for Free World 1981–89, European Atlantic Group 1983–, VSEL Consortium PLC 1987–93, Marlborough Stirling Group 1994–99; Deputy Chair. IBA 1989–90; Chair. Radio Authority 1991–94; Pres. Hispanic and Luso Brazilian Council 1975–80, Royal Nat. Inst. for Deaf 1980–87, Llangollen Int. Music Festival 1979–90; Chair. Abington Corpn (Consultants) Ltd 1981–, Nottingham Building Soc. 1983–90, Southern Mining Corpn 1997–99; Dir W. S. Atkins Int. 1979–83, IBM UK Ltd 1973–90 (mem. IBM Europe Advisory Council 1973–90), Lazard Brothers and Co. Ltd 1983–90, Shandwick PLC 1985–95, Triangle Holdings 1986–90, TV Corpn PLC 1996–2001; Pres. Freedom in Sport Int.; mem. IISS, Royal Inst.; Hon. Fellow, Univ. Coll. Wales, Aberystwyth 1974. *Publications:* The Sword and the Spirit 1963, The Great Commanders (ed.) 1973, Montgomery of Alamein 1976, Waterloo: Battle of Three Armies (ed.) 1979, Star Wars: Suicide or Survival 1985, Defence of the Realm 1987, By God's Will: A Portrait of the Sultan of Brunei 1989, The Shadow of My Hand (autobiog.) 2000; contrib. to The Times and nat. and professional journals. *Leisure interests:* music, theatre. *Address:* House of Lords, London, SW1A 0PW, England.

CHALIAND, Gérard, PhD; French academic and writer; ed Institut National des Langues et Civilisations Orientales, Univ. of Paris V; f. magazine Partisans during Algerian war;; Prof., Ecole nat. d'admin (ENA), Collège interarmes de défense 1980–89; taught at l'École Supérieure de Guerre 1993–99; Visiting Prof., Harvard Univ., Univ. of Calif., Berkeley, Military Acad., Bogota, Colombia, Univ. of Capetown, SA, Univ. of Salamanca, Spain, Univ. of Manchester, UK; Visiting Fellow, Centre for Conflict and Peace studies; advisor to Centre for Analysis and Planning, Ministry of Foreign Affairs 1984–94; Dir Centre européen d'étude des conflits 1997–2000. *Publications include:* Armed Struggle in Africa 1969, Mythes révolutionnaires du tiers-monde 1977, Atlas stratégique (with J.-P. Rageau) 1987, Anthologie mondiale de la stratégie 1996, Voyage dans le demi-siècle (with Jean Lacouture) 2001, Atlas du nouvel ordre mondial 2003, Histoire du terrorisme: de l'Antiquité à Al-Qaïda 2004, Guerres et civilisations. De l'Assyrie à l'époque contemporaine 2005, L'Amérique en guerre. Irak-Afghanistan 2007. *Address:* 63 Rue Pascal, 75013 Paris, France (home). *Telephone:* 1-43-31-09-12 (home). *E-mail:* gchaliand@aol.com (home).

CHALKER OF WALLASEY, Baroness (Life Peer), cr. 1992, of Leigh-on-Sea in the County of Essex; **Lynda Chalker,** PC; British politician and consultant on business and development in Africa; *Chairman, Africa Matters Ltd;* b. (Lynda Bates), 29 April 1942, Hitchin, Herts.; d. of the late Sidney Henry James Bates and Marjorie Kathleen Randell; m. 1st Eric Robert Chalker 1967 (divorced 1973); m. 2nd Clive Landa 1981 (divorced 2003); ed Heidelberg Univ., Germany, London Univ., Cen. London Polytechnic; statistician with Research Bureau Ltd (Unilever) 1963–69; Deputy Market Research Man., Shell Mex & BP Ltd 1969–72; Chief Exec. Int. Div. of Louis Harris Int. 1972–74; MP for Wallasey 1974–92; Parl. Under-Sec. of State, Dept of Health and Social Security 1979–82, Dept of Transport 1982–83; Minister of State, Dept of Transport 1983–86, FCO 1986–97, Minister for Overseas Devt 1989–97; ind. consultant on Africa and Devt 1997–; Chair. Africa Matters Ltd 1998–; Dir (non-exec.) Capital Shopping Centres 1997–2000, Unilever PLC and NV 1998–2007, Landell Mills Ltd 1999–2001, Ashanti Goldfields Co. 2000–04, Group 5 (Pty) Ltd 2001–, Devt Consultants Int. 2001–05, Equator Exploration Ltd 2005–07; Chair. Greater London Young Conservatives (GLYC) 1969–70; Nat. Vice-Chair. Young Conservatives 1970–71; Chair. London School of Hygiene and Tropical Medicine 1998–2006; Chair. Bd of

Medicines for Malaria Venture 2006–; mem. Advisory Bds Lafarge et Cie 2003–, MerchantBridge Int. 2005–, Renaissance Africa 2008–; mem. BBC Gen. Advisory Cttee 1975–79; Hon. Fellow Queen Mary and Westfield Coll., Hon. Fellow Inst. of Transportation; Dr hc (Bradford) 1995, (Liverpool), (John Moores), (Cranfield), (Warwick), (Westminster), (East London). *Publications:* We Are Richer Than We Think 1978 (co-author), Africa: Turning the Tide 1989. *Leisure interests:* music, cooking, theatre, driving. *Address:* 51 Causton Street, London, SW1P 4AT (office); House of Lords, London, SW1A 0PW, England. *Telephone:* (20) 7976-6850 (office). *Fax:* (20) 7976-4999 (office). *E-mail:* bstendall@africamatters.com (office). *Website:* www.africamatters.com (office).

CHALMERS, Sir Neil Robert, Kt, MA, PhD; British biologist and museum director; *Warden, Wadham College, Oxford;* b. 19 June 1942, Surrey; s. of William King and Irene Margaret Chalmers (née Pemberton); m. Monica Elizabeth Byanjeru Rusoke 1970; two d.; ed King's Coll. School, Wimbledon, Magdalen Coll., Oxford, St John's Coll., Cambridge; Lecturer in Zoology, Makerere Univ. Coll., Kampala, Uganda 1966–69; Scientific Dir Natural Primate Research Centre, Nairobi, Kenya 1969–70; Lecturer, subsequently Sr Lecturer then Reader in Biology, Open Univ. 1970–85, Dean of Science 1985–88; Dir Natural History Museum, London 1988–2004; Warden, Wadham Coll., Oxford 2004–. *Publications:* Social Behaviour in Primates 1979, and other books on animal behaviour; numerous papers in Animal Behaviour and other learned journals. *Leisure interests:* music, golf, swimming. *Address:* Wadham College, Oxford, OX1 3PN, England (office). *Telephone:* (1865) 277931 (office). *E-mail:* warden@wadham.cx.ac.uk (office). *Website:* www.wadham.cx.ac.uk (office).

CHALONER, William Gilbert, PhD, FRS; British botanist and academic; *Professor Emeritus, Royal Holloway, University of London;* b. 22 Nov. 1928; s. of the late Ernest J. Chaloner and L. Chaloner; m. Judith Carroll 1955; one s. two d.; ed Kingston Grammar School and Univ. of Reading; Lecturer and Reader, Univ. Coll. London 1956–72, Visiting Prof. 1995–; Visiting Prof., Pennsylvania State Univ., USA 1961–62; Prof., Univ. of Nigeria 1965–66; Prof. of Botany, Birkbeck Coll. London 1972–79; Hildred Carlile Prof. of Botany and Head of School of Life Sciences, Royal Holloway and Bedford New Coll. 1985–94 (Bedford Coll. 1979–85), Prof. Emer., Geology Dept, Royal Holloway, Univ. of London 1994–; Wilmer D. Barrett (Visiting) Prof. of Botany, Univ. of Massachusetts, USA 1987–91; mem. Bd of Trustees, Royal Botanic Gardens Kew 1983–96; Pres. Linnean Soc. 1985–88; fmr mem. Senate London Univ.; fmr mem. Nat. Environment Research Council; Corresp. mem. Botanical Soc. of America 1987–, Associé Etranger de l'Acad. des Sciences; Hon. Fellow Royal Holloway 2002. *Publications:* papers in scientific journals. *Leisure interests:* swimming, tennis, visiting USA. *Address:* 26 Warren Avenue, Richmond, Surrey, TW10 5DZ, England (home). *E-mail:* w.chaloner@rhul.ac.uk (office).

CHALUPEC, Igor Adam, BEcons; Polish economist and business executive; b. 1966; ed Warsaw School of Econs, Warsaw Univ.; consultant, Polexpert Sp. zo.o 1989–90; consultant, Proexim Sp. zo.o 1990; licensed stockbroker 1991–; Dir Cen. Brokerage House, Bank Pekao SA 1991–95, mem. Man. Bd 1995–2000, Vice-Pres. 2000–03; Under-Sec. of State and Gen. Insp. of Financial Information, Ministry of Finance 2003–04; Pres. and CEO PKN Orlen SA 2004–07; Chair. Supervisory Bd, Unipetrol as, Prague –2007; Chair. Brokerage Houses Asscn 1994–95; mem. Supervisory Bd, Warsaw Stock Exchange 1994–2003; Deputy Chair., Insurance and Pensions Funds Supervisory Comm. 2003–04, Comm. for Banking Supervision 2003–04; mem. European Corp. Governance Forum 2004–, Capital Market Council 2005–. *Leisure interests:* literature, cinema, politics, tennis, bridge. *Address:* c/o PKN Orlen, ul. Chemików 7, 09–411 Płock, Poland (office).

CHAM, Prasidh; Cambodian politician; *Senior Minister and Minister of Commerce;* b. 15 May 1951, Phnom Penh; m. Tep Bopha Prasidh; one s. two d.; ed Lycée Descartes, Phnom Penh; mem. Cambodian People's Party (CPP); currently Sr Minister and Minister of Commerce; Sr Adviser to His Holiness Samdech Preah Sometheatheppadey Tep Vong, Supreme Patriarch of the Mohanjkhay Buddhist Clergy 2004–; Order of the Sowathara, Moha Sereywadaan class, Order of the Kingdom of Cambodia Assarith Class 1998, Thipadin Class 2001, Oknha 2002. *Leisure interests:* golf, tennis, volleyball. *Address:* Ministry of Commerce, 20a–b Norodom blvd, Phnom-Penh, Cambodia (office). *Telephone:* (23) 991708 (office). *Fax:* (23) 213288 (office). *E-mail:* moccabdir@yahoo.com (office). *Website:* www.moc.gov.kh (office).

CHAMBAS, Mohamed Ibn, BA, MA, JD, PhD; Ghanaian lawyer, diplomatist, political scientist and international organization official; *President, Executive Secretariat, Economic Community of West African States (ECOWAS) Commission;* b. 12 July 1950; m.; ed Mfantsipim School, Cape Coast and Govt Secondary School, Tamale, Univ. of Ghana, Legon, Cornell Univ., New York, Case Western Reserve Univ., Cleveland, USA; teacher, Oberlin Coll., Ohio; practised law with Forbes, Forbes and Teamor Legal Practice, Ohio; Deputy Foreign Minister 1987; MP for Bimbilla 1993–96, 2000–; First Deputy Speaker of Parl. 1993–94; Deputy Foreign Minister 1994–, Chair. Foreign Affairs Cttee 1993–94; Deputy Minister of Educ. 1997–2000; Exec. Sec. Econ. Community of West African States (ECOWAS) 2001–06, Pres. Exec. Secr. ECOWAS Comm. (after restructuring of ECOWAS insts) 2007–; fmr Del. to UN Gen. Ass., OAU, Non-aligned Movt, Commonwealth; mem. Nat. Democratic Congress; mem. Cornell Univ. Council 1997–2001, 2003–07. *Leisure interests:* soccer, horse riding. *Address:* ECOWAS Executive Secretariat, 60 Yakubu Gowon Crescent, PMB 401, Asokoro, Abuja, Nigeria (office). *Telephone:* (9) 3147647 (office). *Fax:* (9) 3147646 (office). *E-mail:* info@ecowas.int (office). *Website:* www.ecowas.int (office).

CHAMBERLAIN, (George) Richard; American actor; b. 31 March 1935, Los Angeles; s. of Charles Chamberlain and Elsa Chamberlain; ed Los Angeles Conservatory of Music and drama studies with Jeff Corey. *Films include:* Secret of Purple Reef 1960, Thunder of Drums 1961, Twilight of Honor 1963, Joy in the Morning 1965, Petulia 1968, The Madwoman of Chaillot 1969, The Music Lovers 1971, Julius Caesar 1971, Lady Caroline Lamb 1971, The Three Musketeers 1974, Towering Inferno 1974, The Four Musketeers 1975, The Slipper and the Rose 1977, The Swarm 1978, Murder by Phone 1982, King Solomon's Mines 1985, Alan Quartermain and The Lost City of Gold 1987, The Return of the Musketeers 1989, Bird of Prey 1996, River To Drown In 1997, All the Winters That Have Been 1997, The Pavilion 1999, Strength and Honour 2007, I Now Pronounce You Chuck and Larry 2007, Endless Bummer 2008. *Stage appearances include:* King Lear, Hamlet, Richard II, The Lady's Not for Burning, Night of the Iguana, Cyrano de Bergerac, My Fair Lady. *Television includes:* Dr. Kildare (series) 1961–65, Portrait of a Lady 1968, The Woman I Love 1973, The Count of Monte Cristo 1975, Centennial (miniseries) 1978, The Good Doctor 1978, The Man in the Iron Mask 1978, Shogun 1980 (Golden Globe Award), The Thorn Birds (miniseries) 1983, Cook & Peary: The Race to the Pole 1983, The Miracle 1985, Wallenberg: A Hero's Story 1985, Dream West (miniseries) 1986, Casanova 1987, The Bourne Identity 1988, Ordeal in the Arctic 1993, The Thorn Birds, The Missing Year 1996, The Lost Daughter 1997, All the Winters That Have Been 1997, Too Rich: The Secret Life of Doris Duke 1999, Blackbeard (miniseries) 2006. *Address:* c/o Eric Gardner, Panacea Entertainment Management and Communications, Ltd, 13587 Andalusia Drive, Camarillo, Calif. 93012, USA. *Telephone:* (805) 491-9400.

CHAMBERLIN, Wendy J., MS; American diplomatist, international organization official and fmr UN official; *President, Middle East Institute;* b. 12 Oct. 1948, Bethesda, Md; ed Northwestern, Boston and Harvard Univs; joined Foreign Service, Dept of State, Washington, DC 1975; Consular and Econ. Officer, Vientiane 1976–78; Staff Aide E Asia Bureau, Washington, DC 1978–79; Special Asst to Deputy Sec. of State 1979; Political Officer, Kinshasa 1980–82; Pearson Fellow, US Senate, Washington, DC 1982–83; Political-Mil. Officer, Office of Israel Affairs, Dept of State 1983–85; Dir (acting) Office of Regional Affairs, Bureau of Near East-S Asian Affairs 1985–87; Asst Gen. Service Officer, Rabat 1988–89; Special Asst to Under-Sec. for Political Affairs, Dept of State 1989–90; Dir of Counter-Terrorism, Nat. Security Council, Washington, DC 1990–91; Dir Office of Press–Public Affairs, Bureau of Near East-S Asian Affairs 1991–93; Deputy Chief of Mission, Kuala Lumpur 1993–96; Amb. to Laos 1996–99; Prin. Deputy Asst Bureau of Int. Narcotics and Law Enforcement Programs, Washington, DC 1999–2001; Amb. to Pakistan 2001–02; Asst Admin. for Asia and Near East, USAID 2002–04; Deputy UN High Commr for Refugees 2004–Feb. 2005, June 2005–06, Acting High Commr Feb.–June 2005; Pres. Middle East Inst. 2007–; Nat. Security Fellow 1984; Dr hc (Northwestern Univ.); numerous meritorious awards from US State Dept. *Address:* Middle East Institute, 1761 N Street, NW, Washington, DC 20036-2882, USA (office). *Telephone:* (202) 785-1141 (office). *Fax:* (202) 331-8861 (office). *E-mail:* mideasti@mideasti.org (office). *Website:* www.mideasti.org (office).

CHAMBERS, Anne Cox; American media proprietor and fmr diplomatist; *Co-Director, Cox Enterprises Inc.;* b. 1 Dec. 1919, Ga; d. of the late James M. Cox; sister of Barbara Cox Anthony; m. (divorced); three c.; fmr Dir Fulton Nat. Bank 1973; Amb. to Belgium 1977–81; currently Co-Dir (with sister) Cox Enterprises Inc., parent co. of Cox Radio Inc., Cox Communications Inc., AutoTrader.com LLC, Mannheim Auctions Inc., The Atlanta-Journal Constitution, Atlanta Beat, other enterprises; Chair. Atlanta Newspapers Inc.; Vice-Chair. American Advisory Bd Pasteur Foundation; mem. Bd of Dirs Bank of the South 1977–82, Coca-Cola Co. 1981–91, American Soc. French Legion of Honor, MacDowell Gallery, Cities in Schools, High Museum of Art, Atlanta, Friends of Art and Preservation in Embassies, French American Foundation; Pres. American Friends Int. Lyric Art Festival, Aix-en-Provence; Trustee Int. Council Museum of Modern Art, Nat. Cttee Whitney Museum, Council of American Ambs, Council on Foreign Relations; Ordre de la Couronne, Officier de la Légion d'honneur; YMCA Women of Achievement Award 1985, ranked 67th by Forbes magazine amongst 100 Most Powerful Women 2004. *Address:* Cox Enterprises Inc., 6205 Dunwoody Road, Atlanta, GA 30328, USA (office). *Telephone:* (678) 645-0000 (office). *Fax:* (678) 645-1079 (office). *Website:* www.coxenterprises.com (office).

CHAMBERS, John T., BL, BA, BSc, MBA; American computer industry executive; *Chairman and CEO, Cisco Systems, Inc.;* m. Elaine Chambers; two c.; ed West Virginia Univ., Indiana Univ.; with IBM 1976–82; with Wang Labs 1982–90; Sr Vice-Pres., Worldwide Sales and Operations, Cisco Systems, Inc., San Jose, Calif. 1991–94, Exec. Vice-Pres. 1994–95, Pres. 1995, CEO 1995–, Chair. 2006–; Chair. NetAid 1999–; mem. Bd Dirs Clarify Inc., Arbor Software; co-sponsored Jordan Educ. Initiative in partnership with HM King Abdullah II of Jordan and World Econ. Forum; spearheaded 21st Century Schools initiative in Gulf Coast Region affected by Hurricane Katrina 2005; co-led del. of US business leaders, in partnership with US State Dept, to form the Partnership for Lebanon 2006; formed public-pvt. partnership to help rebuild health care and education models in Sichuan, China following earthquake of May 2008; fmr Vice-Chair. Nat. Infrastructure Advisory Council; also served on Pres. George W. Bush's Transition Team and Educ. Cttee and on Pres. Clinton's Trade Policy Cttee; Award for Lifetime Achievement, PricewaterhouseCoopers 1999, Mr Internet, Top 25 Executives Worldwide, Business Week 1999, Internet Industry Leader Award, US Internet Council 2000, CEO of the Year, Chief Executive Magazine 2000, Top 10 Most Influential Leaders Shaping Technology, Time Digital 2000, Best Boss in America, 20/20 2000, #2 CEO in America, Worth Magazine 2000, Top 100 Best Corporate Citizens, Business Ethics Magazine 2001–06, three-time winner, Best Investor Relations by a CEO, Investor Relations Magazine 2002,

www.worldwhoswho.com

2004, 2007, six-time winner, Best CEO, Telecommunications, Data Networking, Institutional Investor Magazine 2003–08, Scholars of the Smithsonian Inst. 2004, Presidential Award: Ron Brown Award for Corporate Leadership, The Business Council 2004, Award for Corporate Excellence, US State Dept 2005, Excellence in Corporate Philanthropy Award, Cttee to Encourage Corp. Philanthropy 2005, Woodrow Wilson Award for Corporate Citizenship, Woodrow Wilson Center for Excellence in Workplace Volunteer Programs, Points of Light Foundation 2005, Int. Community Service Award, US Chamber of Commerce, Business Civic Leadership Center 2007, Gala Award Honoree, American India Foundation 2007, Clinton Global Citizen Award (pvt. sector), Clinton Global Initiative 2007, Business Leadership Award, NASSCOM (India) 2007–08, 20th Anniversary Leadership Award, City Year 2008, World's 100 Most Influential People, Time Magazine 2008, World's Best CEOs, Barron's top 30 list 2008, 25 Most Powerful People In Business, Fortune 2008, Top 10 CEO Vision Award, InternetNews.com 2008. *Address:* Cisco Systems, Inc., Building 10, 170 West Tasman Drive, San Jose, CA 95134-1706, USA (office). *Telephone:* (408) 526-4000 (office). *Fax:* (408) 526-4100 (office). *E-mail:* jochambe@cisco.com (office). *Website:* www.cisco.com (office).

CHAMBERS, Richard Dickinson, PhD, DSc, FRS; British chemist and academic; *Professor Emeritus of Chemistry, University of Durham;* b. 16 March 1935, West Stanley, Co. Durham; s. of Alfred Chambers and Elizabeth Chambers (née Allsop); m. Anne Boyd 1959; one s. one d.; ed Stanley Grammar School, Univ. of Durham; postdoctoral research at Univ. of British Columbia, Vancouver 1959–60; Lecturer, Univ. of Durham 1960–69, Reader 1969–76, Prof. of Chem. 1976–2003, Chair. and Head of Dept of Chem. 1983–86, Sir Derman Christopherson Research Fellow 1988–89, Research Prof. 2000–03, Prof. Emer. 2003–; Tarrant Visiting Prof., Univ. of Florida, Gainesville 1999; Fulbright Scholar, Case Western Reserve Univ., Ohio 1966–67; Dir (non-exec.) BNFL Fluorochemicals Ltd 1995–2000; ACS Award for Creative Work in Fluorine Chemistry 1991, Moissan Int. Prize 2003. *Publications:* Fluorine in Organic Chemistry 1973, 2004; also numerous articles in scientific journals. *Leisure interests:* opera, golf, watching soccer. *Address:* University of Durham, Department of Chemistry, Science Laboratories, South Road, Durham, DH1 3LE, England. *Telephone:* (191) 374-3120. *Fax:* (191) 384-4737. *E-mail:* r.d.chambers@durham.ac.uk. *Website:* www.dur.ac.uk/chemistry/Staff/rdc/rdc.htm.

CHAMBLISS, Saxby, BA, JD; American lawyer and politician; *Senator from Georgia;* b. 10 Nov. 1943, Warrenton, NC; m. Julianne Chambliss (née Frohbert); ed Univ. of Georgia, Univ. of Tennessee; fmr small businessman and attorney, Moultrie; mem. US House of Reps from 8th Dist of Georgia 1988–2003, mem. House Perm. Select Cttee on Intelligence 2001, Chair. Intelligence Sub-Cttee on Terrorism and Homeland Security, Chair. Agric. Gen. Farm Commodities and Risk-Man. Cttee 2001, mem. Armed Services Cttee (f. Congressional Air Power Cttee); Senator from Georgia 2003–; fmr Chair. Congressional Sportsmen's Caucus; Republican; Friend of the Farmer Award, Georgia Farm Bureau 1995, Distinguished Service Award, Georgia Peanut Comm. 1997, W. Stuart Symington Award, Air Force Asscn; named Fed. Legislator of the Year, Safari Club Int. 1999. *Leisure interests:* Little League baseball volunteer, YMCA basketball coach. *Address:* 416 Russell Senate Office Building, Washington, DC 20510, USA (office). *Telephone:* (202) 224-3521 (office). *Fax:* (202) 224-0103 (office). *Website:* chambliss.senate.gov (office).

CHAMBON, Pierre, LèsSc, MD; French biochemist and academic; *Director, Institut Clinique de la Souris;* b. 7 Feb. 1931, Mulhouse; s. of Henri Chambon and Yvonne Weill; m. Brigitte Andersson 1957; two s. one d.; ed Univ. of Strasbourg; Research Asst, Strasbourg Medical School 1956–61, Assoc. Prof. 1962–66; Sabbatical, Dept of Biochemistry, Stanford Univ. Medical School 1966–67; Prof. of Biochemistry, Inst. de Chimie Biologique, Faculté de Médecine, Strasbourg 1967–91; Prof., Universitaire de France, Faculté de Médecine, Louis Pasteur Univ., Strasbourg 1991–93; Prof., Collège de France 1993–2002, Hon. Prof. 2002–; Dir Lab. de Génétique Moléculaire des Eucaryotes (LGME), CNRS 1977–2002; Dir Unité 184 de Biologie Moléculaire et de Génie Génétique, Inst. Nat. de la Santé et de la Recherche Médicale (INSERM) 1978–2002; Dir Inst. of Genetics and Molecular and Cellular Biology (IGBMC), CNRS 1994–2002, Emer. Dir 2002–; Dir Génopôle de Strasbourg Alsace-Lorraine 1999–; Pres. Scientific Bd, Genome Programme, Ministry of Research 1999–2002; Founder and Dir Inst. Clinique de la Souris (ICS) 2002–; mem. numerous scientific and editorial bds etc.; mem. Acad. des Sciences; Foreign mem. NAS, Royal Swedish Acad.; Corresp. mem. Liège Acad.; hon. mem. Chinese Soc. of Genetics; Foreign Hon. mem. American Acad. of Arts and Science, Acad. Royale de Médecine, Belgium; Officier, Ordre Nat. du Mérite 1987, Commdr 1995, Officier, Ordre Nat. de la Légion d'Honneur 1991; Dr hc (Univ. de Liège, Belgium, Univ. of Sapporo, Japan); Prix Rosen 1976, CNRS Gold Medal 1979, Freeman Foundation Prize of New York Acad. 1981, Lounsbery Prize (NAS and Acad. des Sciences) 1982, Oberling Prize 1986, Prix Griffuel 1987, Prix Harvey, Israeli Inst. of Tech. 1987, Prix Henry et MaryJane Mitjavile, Acad. Nat. de Médecine, Paris 1987, King Faisal Int. Prize 1988, Krebs Medal 1990, Prix Roussel 1990, Prix Louis Jeantet 1991, Grand Prix, Fondation for Medical Research 1996, Robert A. Welch Award in Chem. 1998, Louisa Gross Horwitz Prize 1999, Prix AFRT 1999, Albert Lasker Award for Basic Medical Research (jtly) 2004. *Publications:* 400 articles in scientific reviews. *Address:* Institut Clinique de la Souris, 1 Rue Laurent Fries BP 10142, Parc d'Innovation, 67404 Illkirch Cedex (office); IGBMC, 1 rue Laurent Fries, B.P. 163, 67404 Illkirch Cedex, C.U. Strasbourg, France (office). *Telephone:* 3-88-65-32-15 (office). *Fax:* 3-88-65-32-99 (office). *E-mail:* ics@titus.u-strasbg.fr (office); chambon@igbmc.u-strasbg.fr (office). *Website:* www-mci.u-strasbg.fr (office).

CHAMEAU, Jean-Lou, PhD; French civil engineer, academic and university administrator; *President, California Institute of Technology;* b. 1953; m. Carol Carmichael; ed École Nat. Supérieure d'Arts et Métiers (ENSAM), Stanford Univ.; Prof. of Civil Eng, Purdue Univ. 1980; Dir School of Civil and Environmental Eng, Georgia Inst. of Tech. 1991–94, 1995–2001, Provost 2001–06; Pres. Golder Associates Inc. 1994–95; Pres. California Inst. of Tech. 2006–; ENSAM Prix Nessim Habif, Nat. Science Foundation Presidential Young Investigator Award, American Soc. of Civil Engineers Arthur Casagrande Award, Soc. of Women Engineers Rodney Chipp Memorial Award. *Address:* Office of the President, California Institute of Technology, 1200 E. California Blvd, M/C 204-31, Pasadena, CA 91125, USA (office). *Telephone:* (626) 395-6301 (office). *Fax:* (626) 449-9374 (office). *Website:* president.caltech.edu (office).

CHAMLING, Pawan Kumar; Indian politician, poet and writer; *Chief Minister of Sikkim;* b. 22 Sept. 1950, Yangang Busty, South Sikkim; s. of Shri Ash Bahadur Chamling and Smt. Asharani Chamling; m. Tika Maya Chamling; four s. four d.; began career as ind. farmer; entered politics in 1973; Vice-Pres. Dist Youth Congress 1975; Pres. Sikkim Handicapped Persons Welfare Mission 1976–77; Ed. Nava Jyoti 1976–77, Founder Nirman Prakashan 1977, Ed. Nirman (quarterly literary magazine) 1977–; Gen. Sec. and Vice-Pres. Sikkim Prajatantra Congress 1978–84; Pres. of Yangang Gram Panchayat 1982; mem. Sikkim Legis. Ass. 1985–; Minister for Industries, Printing and Information and Public Relations 1989–92; formed Sikkim Democratic Front Party 1993, Leader 1993–; Chief Minister of Sikkim 1994–; Chair. Sikkim Distilleries Ltd 1985–; Hon. PhD (Manipal Univ.) 2003; numerous awards including Chinton Puraskar 1987, Bharat Shiromani 1996, Man of the Year 1998, The Greenest Chief Minister of India 1998, Man of Dedication 1999, Secular India Harmony Award 1998, Manav Sewa Puraskar 1999, Pride of India Gold Award 1999, Best Citizen of India 1999, Poets' Foundation Award 2001, Nat. Citizens of India Award 2002. *Publications include:* Veer koh Parichaya (poem) 1967, Antahin Sapana Meroh Bipana 1985, Perennial Dreams and My Reality, Prarambhek Kabitaharu 1991, Pratiwad 1992, Damthang Heejah ra Aajah 1992, Ma koh Hun 1992, Prarambheek Kabitaharu 1993, Sikkim ra Narikon Maryadha 1994, Crucified Prashna Aur Anya Kabitaye 1996, Sikkim ra Prajatantra 1996, Democracy Redeemed 1997, Prajatantra koh Mirmireymah 1997, Meroh Sapana Ko Sikkim 2002, Perspectives and Vision 2002. *Leisure interests:* reading, writing. *Address:* CM Secretariat, Tashiling, Gangtok, Sikkim 737 101 (office); Ghurpisay, Namchi, South Sikkim 737 126, India (home). *Telephone:* (3592) 222263 (office); (3592) 228200 (office); (3595) 263748 (home); (3592) 222536 (home). *Fax:* (3592) 222245 (office); (3592) 224710 (home). *E-mail:* cm-skm@nic.in (office). *Website:* sikkim.nic.in (office).

CHAMORRO, Violeta Barrios de (see BARRIOS de CHAMORRO, Violeta).

CHAMORRO BARRIOS, Cristiana; Nicaraguan foundation director and editor; *Director, Fundación Violeta Barrios de Chamorro;* d. of Pedro Joaquin Chamorro Cardenal and Violeta Barrios de Chamorro; Dir Diario La Prensa 1986–91, Chair. Bd Dirs 1991–93, currently Ed. and Dir; Vice-Pres. Comm. for the Freedom of Expression 1987–93; Adviser to Pres. of Nicaragua Violeta Barrios de Chamorro 1991–96; Ed. Servicio Especial de Mujeres (SEM), Costa Rica; Founder, Dir and Sec. Fundación Violeta Barrios de Chamorro (non-profit org. for peace, democracy and freedom of expression). *Address:* Fundación Violeta Barrios de Chamorro, CC. Plaza España, Edificio Málaga Módulo B-9, Managua, Nicaragua (office). *Telephone:* (505) 268-6500 (office). *Fax:* (505) 268-6502 (office). *E-mail:* cristiana.chamorro@ibw.com.ni (office). *Website:* www.violetachamorro.org.ni (office).

CHAN, Agnes, PhD; Japanese singer, academic and international organization official; *Ambassador of the Japan Committee, UNICEF;* b. 1955, Hong Kong; m. Tsutomu Kaneko 1985; three c.; ed Sophia Univ., Univ. of Toronto, Canada, Stanford Univ., USA; debut single Circle Game released in Hong Kong 1969; Japan debut single Hinagesi no Hana released 1972; performed charity concerts for Cambodia in Hong Kong and Japan 1980, Beijing 1985; Lecturer Shinshui and Reitaku Univs 1986; Lecturer on Cross-Cultural Communication, Nagoya Women's Cultural Coll. 1993–7, Prof. 1997–; Asst Prof., Mejiro Univ. 1994–97, Prof. 1997–; Prof., Kyouei Univ. 2001; Amb. of Japan Cttee, UNICEF 1998–, travelled to Vietnam, Cambodia, Thailand, Sudan and Philippines on issues of child prostitution and child soldiers; lobbied the law against child prostitution and won its passage in the diet 1999; named Amb. of Hong Kong and Japan 2001; cr. new clothing line called Dear Agnes 1990; opened Chan's Boutique, Odaiba, Tokyo 2001; mem. Bd of Dirs, Wild Bird Asscn of Japan, Children's Dream Foundation, Children's Earth Club, Blue Sky Foundation, Kaijo Hoan Tomo no Kai; mem. Bd of Trustees, Day of Peace of Tokyo, Yokohama Museum, Sung Kei Ling Foundation, Japan and Chine Goodwill Asscn; TV talk show personality; regular contribs to newspapers and magazines; makes over one hundred concert performances and speech tours throughout Japan each year; Hong Kong Top Ten Singers Award 1971, Japan Records Grand Prize 1973, New Artist Award 1973, Shinjuku Music Award 1973, Best New Artist Award 1974, Golden Arrow Award 1974, Japan Cable Music Award 1974, Int. Year of Youth Award (for essay on world peace) 1984, S. J. Grand Prize Winner, Asscn of Women Working in Broadcasting 1986, Asscn of Japanese Journalists Special Award 1986, Galaxy Award 1986, Most Popular Name of the Year Award 1988, Best Eye Wear Award 1997; numerous gold and platinum discs. *Albums include:* more than one hundred albums and CDs in several different languages. *Publications:* The Road Winds Uphill All the Way: Gender, Work, and the Family in the United States and Japan (co-author with Myra Strober) 1999; over forty books on music, for children, on gender equality in the workplace. *Address:* c/o UNICEF House, 4-6-12 Takanawa, Minato-ku, Tokyo 108-8607, Japan (office). *Website:* www.agneschan.gr.jp (office).

CHAN, Chun-po, BA, MA; Taiwanese politician; *Secretary General of the Presidential Office;* b. 30 Oct. 1941; ed Tunghai Univ., Harvard Univ., USA; fmr Gen. Man. Taiwan TV; fmr Vice-Chair. Kuanghwa Investment Holdings Co.; mem. Nationalist Party of China (KMT), numerous positions included Vice-Chair., Sec.-Gen. Cen. Cttee, Deputy Exec. Dir and Chief Exec. Policy Cttee, Vice-Chair., Chair. and Sec.-Gen. Taipei Municipal Cttee, Deputy Dir Secr., Cen. Cttee, Deputy Dir Dept of Policy Research, Dept of Organizational Affairs, Vice-Chair. Taiwan Prov. Cttee; Sec.-Gen. of Presidential Office 2008–. *Address:* Office of the President, 122 Chongqing South Road, Zhongzheng District, Taipei 100, Taiwan (office). *Telephone:* (2) 23113731 (office). *Fax:* (2) 23311604 (office). *E-mail:* public@mail.oop.gov.tw (office). *Website:* www.president.gov.tw (office).

CHAN, Florinda da Rosa Silva, MBA; Chinese politician; *Secretary for Administration and Justice, Macao Special Administrative Region;* b. June 1954, Macao; ed Int. Open Univ. of Asia (Macao), Univ. of Languages and Culture, Beijing, Nat. Inst. of Public Admin., Beijing; joined Macao Govt 1974, Deputy Dir Macao Economic Services Bureau 1995–98, Dir 1998–99, Sec. for Admin. and Justice, Macao Special Admin. Region 1999–; Medal of Professional Merit 1987, Medal of Dedication 1988. *Address:* Office of the Secretary for Administration and Justice, Headquarters of the Government, Avenida da Praia Grande, Macao Special Administrative Region, People's Republic of China (office). *Telephone:* 89895179 (office). *Fax:* 28726880 (office). *E-mail:* florindachan.saj@raem.gov.mo (office). *Website:* www.gov.mo (office).

CHAN, Heng Chee, MA, PhD; Singaporean diplomatist and professor of political science; *Ambassador to USA;* b. 19 April 1942, Singapore; ed Nat. Univ. of Singapore, Cornell Univ., USA; Asst Lecturer, Nat. Univ. of Singapore 1967–70, Lecturer 1970–75, Sr Lecturer 1976–80, Assoc. Prof. of Political Science 1981–, Head, Dept of Political Science 1985–88, Prof. 1990; Dir Inst. of Policy Studies, Singapore Jan.–Dec. 1988; Perm Rep. to UN 1989–91, Amb. to Mexico 1989–91, High Commr to Canada 1989–91; Exec. Dir Singapore Int. Foundation 1991–96; Amb. to USA 1996–; Dir Inst. of SE Asian Studies 1993; mem. Int. Council of Asia Soc. 1991–, Singapore Nat. Cttee of Council for Security Co-operation in the Asia-Pacific 1993–, IISS Council, Hong Kong, 1995–, Int. Advisory Bd of Council on Foreign Relations, New York 1995–; Hon. DLit (Newcastle, Australia) 1994, (Buckingham, UK) 1998; Nat. Book Award (non-fiction) 1978, 1986, Woman of the Year (Singapore) 1991. *Publications:* The Dynamics of One Party Dominance: The PAP at the Grassroots 1976, A Sensation of Independence 1984, Government and Politics of Singapore (co-ed.), The Prophetic and the Political 1987. *Address:* Embassy of Singapore, 3501 International Place, NW, Washington, DC 20008, USA (office); Singapore International Foundation, 111 Somerset Road, 11-07 Devonshire Wing, Singapore 238164. *Telephone:* (202) 537-3100 (office). *Fax:* (202) 537-0876 (office). *E-mail:* singemb_was@sgmfa.gov.sg (office). *Website:* www.mfa.gov.sg/washington (office).

CHAN, Jackie, MBE; Chinese actor, martial artist, film director and film producer; b. (Chan Kong-Sang), 7 April 1954, Hong Kong; s. of Chi-Ping Chan and Lee-Lee Chan; m. Lin Feng-Jiao 1982; one s.; ed Chinese Opera Research Inst.; attached to Beijing opera troupe at age of six; began film career as stuntman; worked in Australia; returned to Hong Kong, roles as stuntman or extra, Shaw Brothers Studios; signed with Golden Harvest 1980; est. The Jackie Chan Charitable Foundation 1988, The Jackie Chan Civil Aviation Foundation 2006; Amb., Hong Kong Tourism Board 2003–, Asia Pacific Tourism 2006–; UN Goodwill Amb. 2004–; Cultural Amb., People's Repub. of China 2006–; Fellow, Hong Kong Acad. of Performing Arts 1998–; Appeal Patron Save China's Tigers Campaign 2006–; took part in Beijing Olympics closing ceremony 2008; Hon. Prin. Qiannan Normal Coll. for Nationalities, People's Repub. of China; Silver Bauhinia Star (Hong Kong) 1999; Hon. DScS (Baptist Univ. Hong Kong) 1996; numerous awards, including Best Picture Award, Hong Kong Film 1989, Best Actor, Golden Horse Awards (Taiwan) 1992, 1993, MTV Lifetime Achievement Award 1995, Best Action Choreography, Hong Kong Film 1996, 1999, Maverick Tribute Award Cinequest San Jose Film Festival 1998, Third Hollywood Film Festival Actor of the Year 1999, Indian Film Awards Int. Achievement Award 2000, Montreal World Film Festival Grand Prix of the Americas 2001, MTV Movie Awards Best Fight Scene 2002, Golden Horse Best Action Choreography (Taiwan) 2004, Hong Kong Film Award for Professional Achievement 2005, mem. American Red Cross Nat. Celebrity Cabinet 2006, Laureus Friends and Ambs Certificate, Laureus Sport for Good 2006, Goodwill Amb., Beijing Olympics 2008. *Films include:* child roles: Big and Little Wong Tin-Bar 1962, The Lover Eternal 1963, The Story of Qui Xiang Lin 1964, Come Drink with Me 1966, A Touch of Zen 1968; adult roles: Fist of Fury (stuntman) 1971, The Little Tiger of Canton 1971, The Heroine 1971, Not Scared to Die 1973, Enter the Dragon (stuntman) 1973, All in the Family 1975, The Himalayan (stuntman) 1975, Hand of Death 1976, New Fist of Fury 1976, Shaolin Wooden Men 1976, Killer Meteors 1977, To Kill with Intrigue 1977, Snake and Crane Arts of Shaolin 1978, Half a Loaf of Kung Fu 1978, Magnificent Bodyguards 1978, Spiritual Kung Fu 1978, Dragon Fist 1978, Snake in Eagle's Shadow 1978, Drunken Master 1978, Fearless Hyena 1979, Fearless Hyena II 1980, The Young Master (also dir) 1980, Battle Creek Brawl 1980, The Cannonball Run 1980, Dragon Lord (dir and actor) 1982, Fantasy Mission Force (stuntman) 1982, Winners and Sinners 1983, Cannonball Run II 1983, Project A (also dir) 1983, Wheels on Meals 1984, My Lucky Stars 1985, Twinkle, Twinkle, Lucky Stars 1985, The Protector 1985, Heart of Dragon 1985, Police Story (Hong Kong Best Film Award) 1985, Armour of God (also co-dir) 1986, Project A II (also dir and writer) 1987, Dragons Forever 1987, Police Story II (also dir, writer and stunt coordinator) 1988, Miracles: Mr. Canton and Lady Rose (also dir, writer and stunt coordinator) 1989, Armour of God II: Operation Condor (also dir, producer, writer and stunt coordinator) 1990, Island of Fire 1991, Twin Dragons 1991 (also stunt choreographer), Police Story III: Supercop (also exec. producer and stunt coordinator) 1992, City Hunter (also producer and stunt coordinator) 1993, Crime Story (also producer and stunt coordinator) 1993, Drunken Master II (also dir (uncredited), jt stunt coordinator and martial arts dir) 1994, Rumble in the Bronx (also producer, writer, jt stunt coordinator and martial arts dir) 1994, Thunderbolt (also producer and stunt coordinator) 1995, Police Story IV: First Strike (also producer and jt stunt coordinator) 1996, Mr. Nice Guy (also producer) 1997, An Alan Smithee Film: Burn Hollyhood Burn (special appearance) 1997, Who Am I? (also dir, co-producer, co-writer and stunt coordinator) 1998, Rush Hour (also stunt coordinator) 1999, Gorgeous (also co-producer, co-writer and action choreographer) 1999, Shanghai Noon (also co-producer and exec. producer) 2000, Accidental Spy (also co-producer and stunt choreographer) 2001, Rush Hour II (also stunt choreographer) 2001, The Tuxedo 2002, Shanghai Knights (also stunt choreographer) 2003, The Medallion (also exec. producer) 2003, The Twins Effect 2003, Enter the Phoenix (also exec. producer) 2004, Around the World in 80 Days (exec. producer, actor, stunt coordinator) 2004, New Police Story (also exec. producer, stunt choreographer and action dir) 2004, The Huadu Chronicles: Blade of the Rose 2004, Rice Rhapsody (exec. producer) 2005, The Myth (also exec. producer and stunt dir) 2005, Everlasting Regret (co-producer) 2005, Rob-B-Hood (also exec. producer, writer, stunt choreographer and action dir) 2006, Rush Hour 3 2007, Kung Fu Panda (voice) 2008, The Forbidden Kingdom 2008, Shinjuku Incident 2008. *Publications:* I'm Jackie Chan (autobiog.). *Address:* The Jackie Chan Group, 145 Waterloo Road, Kowloon-Tong, Kowloon, Hong Kong Special Administrative Region, People's Republic of China. *Telephone:* 27940388 (office). *Fax:* 23387742 (office). *E-mail:* jcgroup@jackiechan.com (office). *Website:* www.jackiechan.com (office).

CHAN, Rt Hon. Sir Julius, GCL, GCMG, KBE, PC; Papua New Guinea politician; *Governor, New Ireland Province;* b. 29 Aug. 1939, Tanga, New Ireland; s. of Chin Pak and Tingoris Chan; m. Stella Ahmat 1966; one d. three s.; ed Marist Brothers Coll., Ashgrove, Queensland and Univ. of Queensland, Australia; Co-operative Officer, Papua New Guinea Admin. 1960–62; Man. Dir Coastal Shipping Co. Pty Ltd; mem. House of Ass. 1968–75, 1982–97, Deputy Speaker, Vice-Chair. Public Accounts Cttee 1968–72; Parl. Leader, People's Progress Party 1970–97; Minister of Finance and Parl. Leader of Govt Business 1972–77; Deputy Prime Minister and Minister for Primary Industry 1977–78, Prime Minister 1980–82, Deputy Prime Minister 1986–88, Minister of Trade and Industry 1986–88, Deputy Prime Minister 1992–94, Minister for Finance and Planning 1992–94, for Foreign Affairs and Trade 1994–96; Prime Minister 1994–97; mem. Parl. 2007–; Gov. New Ireland Prov. 2007–; Gov. for Papua New Guinea and Vice-Chair. Asian Devt Bank 1975–77; Fellowship mem. Int. Bankers' Asscn Inc., USA 1976; Hon. DEcon (Dankook Univ., Seoul) 1978; Hon. DTech (Univ. of Tech., Papua New Guinea) 1983. *Leisure interests:* boating, swimming, walking. *Address:* Office of the Governor, Kavieng, New Ireland Province, Papua New Guinea.

CHAN, Kwok-Bun, PhD; Canadian sociologist and academic; *Chair Professor, Department of Sociology, Hong Kong Baptist University;* b. 9 April 1950, China; m. Wong Suk-yee; two c.; ed York Univ., Canada; currently Prof. and Head of Dept of Sociology, Hong Kong Baptist Univ.; fmr Dir David C. Lam Inst. for East–West Studies; Sr Lecturer in Sociology, Nat. Univ. of Singapore; mem. Hong Kong Central Policy Unit; Ed. Social Transformation of Chinese Society. *Publications:* Chinese Business Networks: State, Economy and Culture (ed.) 2000, Alternate Identities: the Chinese of Contemporary Thailand (co-ed.) 2001, Past Times: A Social History of Singapore (co-ed.) 2003, Chinese Identities, Ethnicity and Cosmopolitanism 2005, Migration, Ethnic Relations and Chinese Business 2005, Stepping Out: The Making of Chinese Entrepreneurs (jt author) 1995, Conflict and Innovation: Joint Ventures in China (co-ed.) 2006, Work Stress and Coping Among Professionals (ed.) 2007, East-West Identities: Globalization, Localization, and Hybridization (co-ed.) 2007, Circuit Entrepreneurs: A Study of Mobile Chinese Immigrant Entrepreneurs (in Chinese) (jt author) 2007, Our Families, Our Homes: Sociological Studies of Families in Hong Kong and China (in Chinese) (ed.) 2008; several articles in journals, contribs to books. *Address:* Department of Sociology, Hong Kong Baptist University, Kowloon Tong, Hong Kong Special Administrative Region, People's Republic of China (office). *Telephone:* 3411-7130 (office). *Fax:* 3411-7893 (office). *E-mail:* ckb@hkbu.edu.hk (office). *Website:* www.hkbu.edu.hk/~sosc1/soc (office).

CHAN, Laurie; Solomon Islands politician; b. 6 April 1965; mem. Nat. Parl. for W Guadalcanal Constituency 2001–, mem. Bills and Legislation Cttee 2006–, Chair. Foreign Relations Cttee 2008–; Minister of Finance and Treasury 2002, of Foreign Affairs, Commerce and Tourism 2002–06. *Address:* National Parliament Office, POB G19, Honiara, Solomon Islands (office). *Telephone:* 28520 (office). *Fax:* 24272 (office). *Website:* www.parliament.gov.sb (office).

CHAN, Margaret Fung Fu-chun, OBE, MSc, MScPH, MD, DSc, FFPHM; Chinese physician and international organization executive; *Director-General, World Health Organization;* b. 1947, Hong Kong; m.; one s.; ed Northcote Coll. of Educ., Hong Kong, Univ. of Western Ontario, Canada, Nat. Univ. of Singapore, Harvard Business School, USA, Tsinghua Univ., Beijing, Nat. School of Admin, Beijing; Rotating Internship, Victoria Hosp., London, Ont. 1977–78; Medical Officer (Maternal and Child Health Services), Dept of Health, Hong Kong 1978–85, Sr Medical Officer (Family Health Services) 1985–78, Prin. Medical Officer (Health Admin) 1987–89, Asst Dir (Personal Health Services) 1989–92, Deputy Dir 1992–94, Dir Dept of Health, Hong Kong Special Admin. Region 1994–2003; Dir Dept of Protection of the Human Environment, WHO 2003–05, Asst Dir-Gen. of Communicable Diseases and Rep. of Dir-Gen. for Pandemic Influenza 2005–06, Dir-Gen. WHO 2006–, Organizer 43rd Session WHO Regional Cttee for the Western Pacific 1992,

Chair. 49th Session WHO Regional Cttee for the Western Pacific 1998, WHO Guidelines on Methodologies for Research and Evaluation of Traditional Medicine 2000, WHO Int. Conf. for Drug Regulatory Authorities 2001 Planning Cttee 2000–02, Vice-Chair. WHO Working Group on Framework Convention on Tobacco Control 1999–2000, Moderator WHO Western Pacific Region Ministerial Roundtable on Social Safety Net 1999; Prince Mahidol Award in Public Health (Thailand) 1999, ranked by Forbes magazine amongst 100 Most Powerful Women (37th) 2007, (84th) 2008. *Address:* World Health Organization, Ave Appia 20, 1211 Geneva 27, Switzerland (office). *Telephone:* 227912111 (office). *Fax:* 227913111 (office). *E-mail:* info@who.int (office). *Website:* www.who.int (office).

CHAN FANG ON SANG, Hon. Anson, GCMG, CBE, JP, BA; Chinese fmr government official; b. 17 Jan. 1940, Shanghai; d. of Fang Zhaoling; m. Archibald Chan Tai-wing 1963; two c.; ed Hong Kong Univ.; held numerous positions at Govt Secr. including Asst Sec., 1963, 1966, Sec. 1988, Asst Financial Sec. 1970, Prin. Financial Sec. 1972, Deputy Sec. for NT 1975, for Social Services 1976–79, Dir Social Welfare Dept 1980, 1982–84, Sec. for Econ. Services 1987–93, Chief Sec. of Hong Kong 1993–2001 (retd); MP in Hong Kong Parl. for Hong Kong Island 2007–08; Founding mem. UNICEF Hong Kong Cttee; Patron and Hon. Adviser, Children's Cancer Foundation; Patron, Enlighten Hong Kong Ltd, SoulTalk Foundation; Dir Reuters Founders Share Co. Ltd; mem. Salvation Army Advisory Bd; Patron Hong Kong Br. and mem. Bd of Dirs Royal Over-Seas League; Hon. Prof., Jiao Tong Univ. Shanghai, Hon. Fellow, SOAS, London; Grand Bauhinia Medal, Chevalier of the Nat. Order of the Legion d'Honneur; Hon. LLD (Hong Kong, Liverpool, Open Univ. of Hong Kong, Hong Kong Chinese Univ., Sheffield); Hon. DHumLitt (Tufts). *Leisure interests:* music, reading, cooking. *Address:* 13C Queen's Centre, 58-64 Queen's Road East, Wanchai, Hong Kong Special Administrative Region, People's Republic of China (office). *Telephone:* 2849-7766 (home). *Fax:* 2849-4423 (home). *E-mail:* afangchan@biznetvigator.com (office). *Website:* www.yourchoiceyourvoice.org (office).

CHANCE, Britton, MS, PhD, ScD (Cantab.); American biophysicist and academic; *Eldridge Reeves Johnson University Professor Emeritus of Biophysics, Physical Chemistry and Radiologic Physics, University of Pennsylvania;* b. 24 July 1913, Wilkes-Barre, Pa; s. of Edwin M. Chance and Eleanor Chance (née Kent); m. 1st Jane Earle 1938 (divorced); m. 2nd Lilian Streeter Lucas 1955 (divorced); four s. four d., two step-s. two step-d.; ed Univ. of Pennsylvania and Univ. of Cambridge, UK; Acting Dir Johnson Foundation, Univ. of Pennsylvania 1940–41, Dir 1949–83, Asst Prof. of Biophysics and Physical Biochemistry 1941–49, Prof. 1949–77, Chair. of Dept of Biophysics and Physical Biochemistry 1949–75, Eldridge Reeves Johnson Prof. of Biophysics 1964–75, Prof. of Biochemistry and Biophysics 1975–83, Eldridge Reeves Johnson Univ. Prof. Emer. of Biophysics, Physical Chem. and Radiologic Physics 1983–; Investigator Office of Scientific Research and Devt 1941; staff mem. Radiation Lab., MIT 1941–46; Dir Inst. for Functional and Structural Studies, Pa 1982–90, Inst. for Biophysical and Biomedical Research 1990–99; Pres. Medical Diagnostic Research Foundation, Phila 1998–; Guggenheim Fellow, Nobel and Molteno Inst. 1946–48; scientific consultant, research attaché, USN, London 1948; consultant, NSF 1951–56; mem. Pres.'s Scientific Advisory Cttee 1959–60; mem. Council, Nat. Inst. on Alcohol Abuse and Alcoholism 1971–75, Nat. Cancer Inst. Working Group on Molecular Control 1973–; Vice-Pres. Int. Union Pure and Applied Biophysics 1972–75, Pres. 1975–79; mem. NAS, American Acad. of Arts and Sciences, American Philosophical Soc., Royal Acad. of Arts and Sciences, Biophysical Soc., Royal Soc. of Arts, Acad. Leopoldina, etc.; Foreign mem. Max-Planck-Gesellschaft zur Förderung der Wissenschaften, Munich 1974, Royal Soc. of London 1981; Fellow, Pennsylvania Coll. of Physicians 1974; 10 hon. degrees; numerous awards including Presidential Certificate of Merit 1950, Paul Lewis Award in Enzyme Chem., ACS 1950, William J. Morlock Award in biochemical electronics, IEEE 1961, Netherlands Biochemical Soc. Award 1965, Harrison Howe Award, ACS 1966, Franklin Medal 1966, Heineken Medal, Netherlands 1970, Gairdner Award 1972, Festschrift Symposium, Stockholm 1973, Semmelweis Medal 1974, Nat. Medal of Science 1974, DaCosta Oratusi 1976, Philip Morris Lecturer 1978, Gold Medal for Distinguished Service to Medicine, Coll. of Physicians 1987, Benjamin Franklin Medal for Distinguished Achievement in the Sciences, American Philosophical Soc. 1990, Lifetime Achievement Award in Biomedical Optics 2001. *Publications:* Waveforms (with Williams, Hughes, McNichol, Sayre) 1949, Electronic Time Measurements (with Hulsizer, McNichol, Williams) 1949, Enzyme-Substrate Compounds 1951, Enzymes in Action in Living Cells 1955, The Respiratory Chain and Oxidative Phosphorylation 1956, Techniques for Assay of Respiratory Enzymes 1957, Energy-Linked Functions of Mitochondria 1963, Rapid Mixing and Sampling Techniques in Biochemistry 1964, Control of Energy Metabolism 1965, Hemes and Hemoproteins 1966, Probes of Structure and Function of Macromolecules and Enzymes 1972, Alcohol and Aldehyde (three vols), Tunneling in Biological Systems 1979. *Leisure interests:* yacht sailing and cruising, amateur radio. *Address:* 4014 Pine Street, Philadelphia, PA 19104, USA (home).

CHANCELLOR, Alexander Surtees, BA; British journalist; b. 4 Jan. 1940, Ware, Herts.; s. of Sir Christopher Chancellor, CMG and Sylvia Mary Chancellor (née Paget); m. Susanna Elizabeth Debenham 1964; two d.; ed Eton Coll., Trinity Hall, Cambridge; with Reuters News Agency 1964–74, Chief Corresp. in Italy 1968–73; with ITV News 1974–75; Ed. The Spectator 1975–84; Ed. Time and Tide 1984–86; Deputy Ed. Sunday Telegraph 1986; Washington Ed. The Independent 1986–88; Ed. The Independent Magazine 1988–92; The New Yorker (Ed. The Talk of the Town) 1992–93; columnist, The Times 1992–93, The Guardian 1996–, Slate 1997, The Daily Telegraph 1998–2004, Saga Magazine 2002–. *Publication:* Some Times in America 1999. *Address:* The Court House, Stoke Park, Stoke Bruerne, Towcester, NN12 7RZ, England (home). *Telephone:* (1604) 862329 (home). *E-mail:* chancellor@dial.pipex.com.

CHAND, Lokendra Bahadur, BA, LLB; Nepalese politician; b. 15 Feb. 1940, Kurkuriya Village, Bashulinga Village Devt Cttee, Baitadi; s. of Mahavir Chand and Laxmi Chand; m.; seven c.; ed Pithauragarh, India, Tri-Chandra Coll., Kathmandu, DSB Degree Coll., Nainital, India and DAV Post-Grad. Coll., Dehradun, India; Founding mem. Shree Basudev High School, Liskita, served voluntarily as teacher 1961–64; practising advocate 1964–68; Vice-Chair. Lisakita Village Panchayat, Baitadi Dist 1968, Chair. Baitadi Dist Panchayat 1970, Pres. Mahakali Zonal Panchayat 1973, Vice-Chair. and Chair. Rastriya Panchayat (Nat. Ass.) 1974; Founder Rastriya Prajatantra Party (RPP), Chair. 1991, Leader and Pres. Parl. Bd after unification of Thapa and Chand Group 1994; elected mem. Parl. (RPP) for both constituencies of Baitadi Dist 1995, 2008–; Prime Minister of Nepal 1983–85, 1990, 1997, 2002–03; Founding Chair. Mahakali Sewa Samaj 1967; mem. Nepal Red Cross Soc. Cen. Exec. Cttee 1970. *Publications include:* Bahraun Kheladi (Twelfth Player), Visarjan (short stories) (Madan Puruskar Prize), Hiunko Tanna, Indra Dhanush, Aparichit Netako Saathi; also satirical essays, humorous plays and collections of short stories. *Leisure interest:* reading books on contemporary literature. *Address:* Rashtriya Prajatantra Party (RPP), Charumati Bahal, Chabahil, Kathmandu, Nepal. *Telephone:* (1) 4471071. *Fax:* (1) 4423384. *E-mail:* info@rppnepal.com. *Website:* www.rppnepal.org.

CHANDLER, Sir Colin (Michael), Kt, FCMA; British business executive; *Chairman, easyJet plc;* b. 7 Oct. 1939; s. of Henry John Chandler and Mary Martha Chandler (née Bowles); m. Jennifer Mary Crawford 1964; one s. one d.; ed St Joseph's Acad., Hatfield Polytechnic; commercial apprentice, De Havilland Aircraft Co. 1956–61; Contracts Officer, Hawker Siddeley Aviation 1962–66, Commercial Man. 1967–72, Exec. Dir (Commercial) 1973–76, Exec. Dir and Gen. Man. 1977; Div. Man. Dir British Aerospace 1978–82, Group Marketing Dir 1983–85; Head of Defence Export Services, Ministry of Defence 1985–89; Man. Dir Vickers PLC 1990–92, Chief Exec. 1991–96, Deputy Chair. and Chief Exec. 1996, Chair. 1997–99, Chair. Vickers Defence Systems (subsidiary of Rolls-Royce) 2000; Chair. (non-exec.) easyJet plc 2002–; Dir (non-exec.) Siemens Plessey Electronic Systems 1990–95, TI Group (subsequently Smiths Group) (now Deputy Chair.) 1992–, Guardian Royal Exchange 1995–99, Racal Electronics PLC 1999–2000 (Chair. 2000–02), Thaler PLC 2000–, Hoggett Bowers 2000–; mem. Cttee, Dept Trade and Industry Priority Japan Campaign 1992–2001; mem. Nat. Defence Industries Council 1992–2002; Chair. Overseas Project Bd Healthcare Sector Group; Pro-Chancellor Cranfield Univ. 2001–; mem. Bd of Govs Reigate Grammer School 2003–; Trustee Hives Save Lives Africa; Commdr Order of Lion of Finland 1982; Dr hc (Herts) 1999. *Leisure interests:* jogging, playing tennis, reading, listening to music. *Address:* Office of the Chairman, easyJet plc, easyLand, London Luton Airport, Beds., LU2 9LS, England (office). *Telephone:* (1582) 700-000 (office). *Fax:* (1582) 443-355 (office). *Website:* www.easyjet.com (office).

CHANDLER, Sir Geoffrey, Kt, CBE, MA; British international organization official (retd); *Trustee, Environment Foundation;* b. 1922; s. of Dr Frederick George Chandler and Marjorie Chandler (née Raimes); m. Lucy Bertha Buxton 1955; four d.; ed Trinity Coll., Cambridge; mil. service: Political Warfare Exec., Cairo and Special Operations Exec., Greece 1942–46; with BBC Foreign News Service 1949–51; Leader Writer and Features Ed., Financial Times 1951–56; Commonwealth Fund Fellow 1953–54; Man., Econs Div., Shell Int. Petroleum Co. 1957–61, Area Coordinator for West Africa 1961–64; Chair. and Man. Dir Shell Trinidad Ltd 1964–69; Public Affairs Coordinator, Shell Int. Petroleum 1969–78; Dir Shell Petroleum Ltd and Shell Petroleum NV 1976–78; Dir-Gen. Nat. Econ. Devt Office and mem. Council 1978–83; Dir Industry Year 1986, 1984–86; Industry Adviser to RSA and Leader Industry Matters 1987–92; Chair. Amnesty Int. UK Business Group 1992–2001, now Chair. Emer.; Chair. BBC Consultative Group on Industrial and Business Affairs 1984–88; Chair. Consultative Council, Soc. of Educ. Officers School Curriculum Award 1984–97; Assoc., Ashridge Man. Coll. 1984–89; Pres. Asscn of Man. and Business Educ. 1986–90; Chair. Nat. Council for Voluntary Orgs 1989–96; mem. British Overseas Trade Advisory Council 1978–82, Council and Exec. Cttee Voluntary Service Overseas, Inst. of Petroleum (Pres. 1972–74), Trustee, Environment Foundation 2001–; mem. Liberal Democrat Party; Hon. Fellow, Sheffield Hallam Univ., Girton Coll. Cambridge; Hon. DBA (Int. Man. Centre, Buckingham); Hon. DSc (Aston Univ., Bradford Univ., CNAA). *Publications include:* The Divided Land: An Anglo-Greek Tragedy 1959, The State of the Nation: Trinidad and Tobago in the Late 1960s 1969; Industry Year 1986: An Attempt to Change a Culture – Its Allies and Obstacles 2003; Britain's Economic Performance (contrib.) 1994, Human Rights and the Oil Industry 2000; numerous articles on oil, energy, econ. devt and the human rights obligations of cos. *Leisure interests:* music, gardening, observing butterflies. *Address:* Little Gaterounds, Newdigate, Dorking, RH5 5AJ, England (home). *Telephone:* (1306) 631612 (home). *Fax:* (1306) 631361 (home). *E-mail:* geoffchand@aol.com (home).

CHANDLER, Kenneth A.; British journalist and consultant; b. 2 Aug. 1947, Westcliff-on-Sea, Essex; s. of Leonard Gordon Chandler and Beatrix Marie Chandler (née McKenzie); m. Erika Schwartz; five c.; Man. Ed. The New York Post 1978–86, 1993–99, Ed.-in-Chief, then Publr 1999–2002; Ed. Boston Herald 1986–93, Editorial Dir 2004–06; f. ChandlerMedia (media consulting firm), New York 2006, now Chandler Regan Strategies; Exec. Producer Fox TV's A Current Affair 1993; CEO Natural Energy Solutions Corpn 2002–03; mem. Bd of Dirs The Bridge Fund;*Telephone:* (914) 310-0876. *E-mail:* ken@kchandler.com. *Website:* chandlermedia.com (office).

CHANDRA, Subhash; Indian media executive; *Chairman, Essel Group;* b. Hissar; m.; three c.; fmr rice packer in Hissar, Haryana; Founder Chair. Essel

Group 1976, comprising media, packaging, entertainment, tech.-enabled services, infrastructure devt and educ. assets; Group cos include Zee Telefilms Ltd, Essel Propack Ltd, ETC Networks Ltd; fmr jt owner (with Rupert Murdoch q.v.) of Zee Cinema, Zee TV and Zee India TV/Zee News; Chair. Ekal Vidyalaya Foundation of India; est. Transnational Alternate Learning for Emancipation and Empowerment thorough Multimedia (TALEEM) 1996; Trustee Global Vipassana Foundation; fmr Chair. Confed. of Indian Industry; Ernst & Young Entrepreneur of the Year Award 1999, Business Standard's Businessman of the Year 1999, Enterprising CEO of the Year, Int. Brand Summit 1999. *Address:* Essel Group, 135, Continental Building, Dr. Annie Besant Road, Worli, Mumbai 400 018, India (office). *Telephone:* (22) 24903926 (office). *Fax:* (22) 24988728 (office). *E-mail:* feedback@esselgroup.com (office). *Website:* www.esselgroup.com (office).

CHANDRA MUNGRA, Subhas, MA; Suriname diplomatist, international organization official and economist; b. 2 Sept. 1945, Paramaribo; m.; three c.; ed Municipal Univ. of Amsterdam; Lecturer in Finance and Banking, Monetary Theory, Anton de Kom Univ. of Suriname 1976–86; Chair. Nat. Cardboard Industry 1985–86; Dir Nat. Devt Bank 1983; Minister of Foreign Affairs 1991–96, of Finance 1986–90; Chair. Jt Governing Bd of Centre for the Devt of Industry on behalf of the African, Caribbean and Pacific Group in Brussels 1988–90; Perm. Rep. to UN, New York 1997–2001, Vice-Chair. Third UN Conf. on Least Developed Countries 2000, Pres. (Acting) UN Gen. Ass. Jan. 2001. *Publications:* numerous articles on econ. issues. *Address:* c/o Ministry of Foreign Affairs, Lim A. Postraat 25, POB 25, Paramaribo, Suriname. *Telephone:* 471209. *Fax:* 410411. *E-mail:* buza@sr.net.

CHANDRASEKHARAN, Komaravolu, MA, MSc, PhD; Indian mathematician and academic; *Professor Emeritus, Eidgenössische Technische Hochschule (ETH), Zürich;* b. 21 Nov. 1920, Masulipatam, India; m. A. Sarada 1944; two s.; ed Presidency Coll., Madras and Inst. for Advanced Study, Princeton; Head, School of Math., Tata Inst. of Fundamental Research, Bombay 1949–65; Prof., ETH, Zürich 1965–88, Prof. Emer. 1988–; Sec., Int. Math. Union 1961–66, Pres. 1971–74; Vice-Pres. Int. Council of Scientific Unions 1963–66, Sec.-Gen. 1966–70; mem. Scientific Advisory Cttee to Cabinet, Govt of India 1961–66; Fellow, Nat. Inst. of Sciences of India, Indian Acad. of Sciences; Foreign mem. Finnish Acad. of Science and Letters 1975; lectured at more than 50 univs in the USA, USSR, Europe and Asia; Hon. Fellow, Tata Inst. 1970; Hon. mem. Austrian Acad. of Sciences 1996, American Math. Soc. 1998; Padma Shri 1959, Shanti Swarup Bhatnagar Memorial Award for Scientific Research 1959, Ramanujan Medal 1966. *Publications:* Fourier Transforms (with S. Bochner) 1949, Typical Means (with S. Minakshisundaram) 1952, Lectures on the Riemann Zeta-function 1953, Notebooks of Srinivasa Ramanujan (two vols) (ed.) 1957, Collected Papers of Hermann Weyl (four vols) (ed.) 1968, Analytic Number Theory 1968, Arithmetical Functions 1970, Elliptic Functions 1985, Classical Fourier Transforms 1989, Siegel's Lectures on the Geometry of Numbers (ed.) 1989, Lectures on Topological Groups 1996, Integration Theory 1996; more than 70 research papers. *Leisure interests:* painting, English literature, music. *Address:* Rämistrasse 101, Hut D15, Eidgenössische Technische Hochschule, 8092 Zürich (office); Hedwigstrasse 29, 8032 Zürich, Switzerland (home). *Telephone:* (44) 6324199 (office); (44) 3819686 (home).

CHANDY, Oommen, BA, BL; Indian politician; b. 31 Oct. 1943, Kumarakom, Kottayam Dist; s. of Puthupally Karottu Vallakkalil K. O. Chandy and Baby Chandy; m. Mariamma Oommen; one s. two d.; ed St George High School, Puthupally, CMS Kottayam, SB Coll. Changanassery, Law Coll., Ernakulam; State Pres. Kerala Students Union 1967, Youth Congress 1969; mem. Kerala Legis. Ass. 1970–; Minister for Labour 1977–78, for Home Affairs 1981–82, for Finance 1991–94; Convenor United Democratic Front 1991, 2001; Chief Minister of Kerala 2004–05. *Address:* c/o North Block, Secretariat, Thiruvananthapuram, Kerala, India (office). *E-mail:* oommenchandy@niyamasabha .org. *Website:* www.oommenchandy.org.

CHANEY, Frederick Michael, AO, LLB; Australian politician and lawyer; b. 28 Oct. 1941, Perth; s. of the late Frederick Charles Chaney and of Mavis Mary Bond; m. Angela Margaret Clifton 1964; three s.; ed Univ. of Western Australia; public service, Papua New Guinea 1964–66; pvt. law practice 1966–74; Senator from Western Australia 1974–90; Senate Opposition Whip 1975, Govt Whip 1976–78; Minister for Admin. Services 1978, Assisting the Minister for Educ. 1978–79, for Aboriginal Affairs 1978–80, Assisting the Minister for Nat. Devt and Energy 1979–80, for Social Security 1980–83; Leader of Opposition in Senate 1983–90; Shadow Minister for Industrial Relations 1987–88, 1989–90, for the Environment 1990–92; Deputy Leader of the Opposition 1989–90; Chair. Fightback! (Co-ordination and Marketing Group) 1992–93; Researcher, lecturer Grad. School of Man., Univ. of Western Australia 1993–95; Chancellor Murdoch Univ., Western Australia 1995–2003; Chair. Desert Knowledge Australia 2005; mem. House of Reps for Pearce 1990–93; mem. Nat. Native Title Tribunal 1995–2000, Deputy Pres. 2000–07; Co-Chair. Reconciliation Australia 2000–05, mem. Bd of Dirs 2000–; Hon. LLD (Murdoch WA), Hon. DUniv (Australian Catholic Univ.) 2007. *Leisure interests:* swimming, reading. *Address:* 23B Brown Street, Claremont, WA 6010, Australia.

CHANEY, Michael, AO, BSc, MBA; Australian business executive; *Chairman, National Australia Bank Ltd;* ed Univ. of Western Australia and Harvard Business School, USA; fmr adviser on corp. lending and finance, Australian Industry Devt Corpn; worked in finance and petroleum industries in Australia and USA –1983; joined Wesfarmers Ltd 1983, Chief Financial Officer 1984–92, mem. Bd 1988, Man. Dir and CEO 1992–2004, Man. Dir 1992–2005, Dir (non-exec.) 2004–; Dir (non-exec.) National Australia Bank, Chair. 2005–, also Chair. Nomination Cttee; Dir (non-exec.) Woodside Petroleum Ltd 2005–; Chancellor Univ. of Western Australia 2005–; Chair.

Australian Research Alliance for Children and Youth; mem. JP Morgan Int. Council, Council of Nat. Gallery of Australia; Hon. Chair. Gresham Partners Holdings Ltd; Hon. Pres. Business Council of Australia; Hon. LLD (Univ. of Western Australia). *Address:* National Australia Bank, Bourke Street, Melbourne, Vic. 3000, Australia (office). *Telephone:* (8) 9322-7913 (Perth) (office); (3) 8641-3500 (Melbourne) (office). *Fax:* (8) 9322-7913 (Perth) (office); (3) 8641-4912 (Melbourne) (office). *Website:* www.national.com.au (office).

CHANG, Datuk Brian; Singaporean shipping industry executive; *Executive Chairman, Yantai Raffles Shipyard Pte Ltd;* b. South Africa; m. Annie Chang; three c.; ed London School of Engineering; started career with Vosper Thorneycroft, Singapore, then with Far East Levingston Shipbuilding Pte Ltd (now Kepfels) 1967–70; f. Promet Group (civil and marine eng. contractor) 1970, Exec. Chair. –1994; Founder and Exec. Chair. Yantai Raffles Shipyard Pte Ltd 1994– (shipyard located in Yantai, Shandong, People's Repub. of China). *Address:* Yantai Raffles Shipyard Pte Ltd, No. 1 Claymore Drive #08-04, Orchard Towers, Singapore 229594 (office). *Telephone:* 6735-8690 (office). *Fax:* 6734-5449 (office). *E-mail:* enquire@yantai-raffles.com (office). *Website:* www.yantai-raffles.com (office).

CHANG, Chin-chen, PhD, FIEE; Taiwanese computer scientist and academic; *Professor and Dean of Academic Affairs, National Chung Cheng University;* b. 12 Nov. 1954, Taiwan; m. Ling-Hui Hwang 1981; one s. two d.; ed Nat. Tsing Hua Univ., Hsinchu and Nat. Chiao Tung Univ., Hsinchu; Assoc. Prof., Dept of Computer Eng, Nat. Chiao Tung Univ. 1982–83; Assoc. Prof., Dept of Applied Math., Nat. Chung Hsin Univ. 1983–85, Prof. 1985–89; Prof. and Chair. Dept of Computer Eng, Nat. Chung Cheng Univ. 1989–92, Prof. and Dean Coll. of Eng 1992–95, Prof. and Dean of Academic Affairs 1995–, Acting Pres. 1996–99; Ed. Journal of Information Science and Engineering 1988–93, Journal of the Chinese Institute of Engineers 1990–93, Information Science Applications 1994–; Ed.-in-Chief Information and Education 1987–; reviewer for numerous int. journals of information science; Outstanding Talent in Information Science Award of Repub. of China 1984, several Distinguished Research Awards of Nat. Science Council 1986–. *Publications:* more than 300 tech. papers on database design and information security in leading scientific journals and conf. proceedings; 12 books in Chinese on database design, data structures, computer viruses, information security, cryptography etc.; Ed. Advanced Database Research and Development Series (vols 1, 2, 3) 1992. *Address:* Department of Computer Science and Information Engineering, National Chung Cheng University, Chiayi, Taiwan (office). *Telephone:* (5) 272-0411 (office); (4) 325-9100 (home); (5) 272-0405. *Fax:* (5) 272-0839; (4) 327-7423 (home); (5) 272-0404. *E-mail:* ccc@cs.ccu.edu.tw (office). *Website:* www.cs.ccu .edu.tw/-ccc (office).

CHANG, Chun-hsiung, LLB; Taiwanese politician; b. 23 March 1938; m.; three s. one d.; ed Nat. Taiwan Univ.; defence lawyer in mil. trial following Kaohsiung Incident 1980; mem. Legis. Yuan 1983–; a Founder-mem. Democratic Progressive Party (DPP) 1986–, mem. Cen. Standing Cttee and Cen. Exec. Cttee DPP 1986–2000, Exec. Dir DPP Caucus in Legis. Yuan 1987–88, Gen. Convenor 1990, 1998–99, Sec.-Gen. DPP 2002–07; Sec.-Gen. Office of Pres. 2000; Vice-Premier 2000; Premier 2000–02, 2007–08. *Address:* Democratic Progressive Party, 10/F, 30 Beiping East Road, Taipei, 10051, Taiwan (office). *Telephone:* (2) 23929989 (office). *Fax:* (2) 23929989 (office). *E-mail:* foreign@dpp.org.tw (office). *Website:* www.dpp.org.tw (office).

CHANG, Dae-whan, MA, PhD; South Korean politician and business executive; *Chairman, Maeil Business Newspaper and TV;* b. 21 March 1952; m.; two c.; ed Univ. of Rochester, USA, Coll. of Europe, Belgium, George Washington Univ., New York Univ., USA; Instructor and Capt., Korea Air Force Acad. 1977–83; mem. Acad. of Int. Business, USA 1984; Dir Planning Office, Maeil Business Newspaper 1986, mem. Bd of Dirs and Dir of Business Devt HQ 1986, Man. Dir 1987, Exec. Dir 1988, Pres. and Publr 1988–2002, Pres. Maeil Business News TV Co. 1993–2002, currently Chair. Maeil Business Newspaper and TV; Acting Prime Minister of Repub. of Korea Aug. 9–28 2002; Lecturer in Int. Business Man., Grad. School of Seoul Nat. Univ. 1988–97; Auditor IPI Korean Nat. Cttee 1988–2002, PFA Korean Nat. Cttee 1991–2002; Dir Korea Newspapers Asscn 1986–2002, Auditor 1996–2002; Founder Vision Korea Campaign 1997–2002, World Knowledge Forum 1998–2002; Chair. Press Foundation of Asia March–Aug. 2002, New York Univ. Korean Alumni Asscn; mem. Advisory Bd Sungkyunkwan Univ. Grad. School of Business, World Asscn of Newspapers 1986–2002; Order of Civil Merit 1992, Dong-bag Medal 1992. *Publications include:* (in Korean): International Business Negotiation 1989, New Product Millennium (jtly.) 1997. *Address:* Maeil Business Newspaper Building, 51-9, 1-ga, Bil-dong, Jung-gu, Seoul 100-728, Republic of Korea (office). *Telephone:* (2) 2000-2114 (office). *E-mail:* mkmaster@mk.co.kr (office). *Website:* www.mk.co.kr (office).

CHANG, Hsin-kang (H.K.), BS, MS, PhD; Chinese university administrator and academic; *Yeh-Lu Xun Chair Professor in Social Sciences, Peking University;* ed Nat. Taiwan Univ., Stanford and Northwestern Univs, USA; Asst Prof. of Civil Eng, Coll. of Eng and Applied Sciences, State Univ. of New York, Buffalo, USA 1969–75, Assoc. Prof. 1975–76; Assoc. Prof. of Biomedical Eng and Physiology, Faculty of Medicine, McGill Univ., Montreal, Canada 1976–80, Prof. 1980–84, Adjunct Prof. of Chemical Eng 1980–84; Visiting Prof., Faculté de Médecine, Université Paris-Val de Marne, Créteil, France 1981–82; Prof. of Biomedical Eng, School of Eng and Prof. of Physiology and Biophysics, School of Medicine, Univ. of Southern California, Los Angeles, USA 1984–90, Chair. Dept of Biomedical Eng 1985–90; Prof. of Chemical Eng and Founding Dean, School of Eng, Hong Kong Univ. of Science and Tech. 1990–94; Prof. of Chemical Eng and Dean, School of Eng and Prof. of Medicine, School of Medicine, Univ. of Pittsburgh 1994–96; Univ. Prof. and Pres. City Univ. of Hong Kong 1996–2007; Hon. Prof. and Wei Lun Sr Visiting Scholar, Tsinghua Univ. 2007–; Yeh-Lu Xun Chair Prof. in Social Sciences, Peking

Univ. 2007–; Chair. Culture and Heritage Comm., Govt of Hong Kong Special Admin. Region (SAR) 2000–03; Dir (Non-Exec.) Hon Kwok Land Investment Co. Ltd 2007–, PCCW Ltd; mem. Judicial Officers Recommendation Comm., Govt of Hong Kong SAR 1999–2005, Council of Advisors on Innovation and Tech., Govt of Hong Kong SAR 2000–04, CPPCC 2003–; Foreign mem. Royal Acad. of Eng (UK); Gold Bauhinia Star (Hong Kong SAR) 2002; Justice of Peace (Hong Kong SAR) 1999; Chevalier de la Légion d'honneur (France). *Publications:* five books and many articles in Chinese; more than 100 scientific articles, two research monographs and one Canadian patent. *Address:* Department of Sociology, Peking University, Haidian District, Beijing, People's Republic of China (office). *Website:* www.pku.edu.cn (office).

CHANG, John H., BA, MS; Taiwanese politician; b. 2 May 1941, Kiangsi; m. Helen Chang Huang; three c.; ed Soochow Univ., Georgetown Univ.; Third then Second Sec., Embassy in Washington, DC 1974–78; Section Chief Dept of N American Affairs, Ministry of Foreign Affairs 1978, Deputy Dir 1980–81; Sec.-Gen. Coordination Council of N American Affairs (now TECO/TECRO) 1981–82, Dir of Dept 1982–86; Admin. Vice-Minister of Foreign Affairs 1986–90; Dir-Gen. Dept of Overseas Affairs, Kuomintang Cen. Cttee 1990; Political Vice-Minister of Foreign Affairs 1990–93; Minister of Overseas Chinese Affairs Comm. and Minister of State 1993–96; Minister of Foreign Affairs 1996–97, Deputy Prime Minister 1997; Sec.-Gen. Presidential Office 1999–2000; mem. Li-Fa Yuan (Legislative Yuan) 2002–; mem. Kuomintang Cen. Cttee and Cen. Standing Cttee 1993–, fmr Sec.-Gen. *Publication:* Damansky Island Incident. *Address:* c/o Kuomintang (KMT) (Nationalist Party of China), 11 Jongshan South Road, Taipei, Taiwan. *Website:* www.kmt.org.tw.

CHANG, Jung, PhD; British writer; b. 25 March 1952, Yibin, Sichuan Province, China; d. of Chang Shou-Yu and Xia De-Hong; m. Jon Halliday 1991; ed Sichuan Univ., Univ. of York; fmrly worked as a peasant, a 'barefoot doctor', a steelworker and an electrician; Asst Lecturer, Sichuan Univ.; moved to UK to study linguistics 1978; now full-time writer; Dr hc (Buckingham) 1996, (Warwick, York) 1997, (Open Univ.) 1998, (Bowdoin Coll., USA) 2005; Bjørnsonordenen, Den Norske Orden for Literature, Norway 1995. *Publications:* Madame Sun Yet-sen (with Jon Halliday) 1986, Wild Swans: Three Daughters of China (NCR Book Award 1992, UK Writers' Guild Best Non-Fiction Book 1992, Fawcett Soc. Book Award 1992, Book of the Year 1993, Golden Bookmark Award, Belgium 1993, 1994, Best Book Award, Humo, Belgium 1993) 1991, Mao: the Unknown Story (with Jon Halliday) 2005. *Address:* Aitken Alexander Associates Ltd, 18–21 Cavaye Place, London, SW10 9PT, England (office). *Telephone:* (20) 7373-8672 (office). *Fax:* (20) 7373-6002 (office). *E-mail:* reception@aitkenalexander.co.uk (office). *Website:* www.aitkenalexander.co.uk (office).

CHANG, King-yuh, LLM, PhD; Taiwanese government official and academic; *Chairman, Foundation on International and Cross-Strait Studies;* b. 27 April 1937, Hsiangtan County, Hunan; s. of Shao Chu Chang and Hsi-chen Huang; m. Grace Yu 1964; two s.; ed Nat. Taiwan Univ., Nat. Chengchi Univ. and Columbia Univ.; Lecturer, Hofstra Univ., USA 1968–69; Asst Prof., Western Illinois Univ. 1972; Assoc. Prof., Nat. Chengchi Univ. 1972–75, Chair. Dept of Diplomacy 1974–77, Dir Grad. School of Int. Law and Diplomacy 1975–77, Prof. 1975–, Deputy Dir Inst. of Int. Relations 1977–81, Dir 1981–84, Pres. Nat. Chengchi Univ. 1989–94; currently Prof. of Int. Affairs and Strategic Studies, Tamkang Univ.; fmr Chair. Mainland Affairs Council, Exec. Yuan; currently Chair. Foundation on Int. and Cross-Strait Studies; Visiting Fellow, Johns Hopkins Univ. 1976–77; Distinguished Visiting Scholar, Inst. of E Asian Studies, Univ. of California, Berkeley 1983; Dir-Gen. Govt Information Office 1984–87; Dir Inst. of Int. Relations 1987–90; Minister of State, Exec. Yuan 1994–96. *Leisure interests:* reading, mountain climbing and sports. *Address:* Foundation on International and Cross-Strait Studies, 10050 Taipei (office); 1 Chung Hsiao East Road, Sec. 1, Taipei, Taiwan. *Telephone:* (2) 3968760 (office). *Fax:* (2) 3917850 (office). *E-mail:* webfics@gmail.com (office). *Website:* www.fics.org.tw (office).

CHANG, Manuel, MPhil; Mozambican government official; *Minister of Finance;* b. 22 Aug. 1955, Gaza; s. of the late Chang Dai Fão and Angelina Mugabe; m. Lizete Izilda Adriano Simões Maia; three c.; ed Escola Industrial Mouzinho de Albuquerque, Universidade Eduardo Mondlane, Univ. of London, UK; joined Ministry of Finance 1974, Section Head 1977, Section Head, Service Comm. 1979, Acting Head, Dept of the Treasury 1987, Head, Dept of the Treasury 1988–89, Adjunct Nat. Dir of the Treasury 1989–93, Dir of Nat. Budget 1993–96, Vice-Minister of Planning and Finance –2005, Minister of Finance 2005–; mem. Frente de Libertação de Moçambique (Frelimo) party; Vice-Pres. Fund for the Promotion of Fishing; Pres. of audit council Banco de Moçambique; mem. Bd of Dirs Pipeline Mocambique-Zimbabwe; mem. Admin. Council Correios de Moçambique 1994–96, Silos Granoleiros de Matola. *Leisure interests:* playing football, reading and watching television. *Address:* Ministério do Plano e Finanças, Praça da Marinha Popular, CP 272, Maputo, Mozambique. *Telephone:* 21306808. *Fax:* 21306261. *E-mail:* dnpo@dnpo.uem.mz. *Website:* www.mozambique.mz/governo/mpf/dnpo.

CHANG, Michael; American fmr professional tennis player; b. 22 Feb. 1972, Hoboken, NJ; s. of Joe Chang and Betty Chang; m. Amber Liu; ed Biola Univ.; coached by his brother Carl and others; aged 15 was youngest player since 1918 to compete in men's singles at US Open 1987; turned professional 1988; first played at Wimbledon 1988; winner, French Open 1989, becoming youngest player of a Grand Slam tournament; Davis Cup debut 1989; winner Canadian Open 1990; semi-finalist, US Open 1992, finalist 1996; finalist French Open 1995, semi-finalist Australian Open 1995, finalist 1996; won 34 singles titles; retd Aug. 2003; highest singles ranking: 2nd (1996); apptd USA Tennis High Performance Cttee, US Tennis Assen 2005–06; Trustee Biola Univ.; est. Chang Family Foundation 1999; inducted into Int. Tennis Hall of Fame 2008. *Publication:* Holding Serve: Persevering On and Off the Court 2001. *Address:* c/o Chang Family Foundation, 28562 Oso Pkwy, D343, Rancho Santa Margarita, CA 92688; Advantage International, 1751 Pinnacle Drive, Suite 1500, McLean, VA 22102, USA (office). *E-mail:* cffoundation@mchang.com. *Website:* mchang.com (office).

CHANG, Sang, BSc, MDiv, DPhil; South Korean politician, theologist and academic; b. 9 Oct. 1939; ed Ewha Women's Univ., Yonsei Univ., Yale Univ. and Princeton Theological Seminary, USA; Prof. of New Testament Theology, Dept of Christian Studies, Ewha Women's Univ. (EWU) 1977–2002, Dir of Academic Affairs, Grad. School 1980, Chair. Dept of Christian Studies 1988, Dir Korea Cultural Research Inst., EWU 1989, Dean Student Affairs 1990, Dean Coll. of Liberal Arts 1993, Dean Grad. School of Information Science 1995, Vice-Pres. EWU 1996, Pres. 1996–2002; ordained to the Ministry of the Word 1988; mem. Exec. Cttee YWCA Korea 1979–97 (Vice-Pres. 1983–97), Exec. Cttee World Alliance of Reformed Churches (WARC) 1982–89 (Moderator Dept of Co-operation and Witness 1989–97), Exec. Cttee World YWCA 1987–91; mem. Public Official Ethics Cttee, Ministry of Admin. and Home Affairs 1997–99, Women's Policies Cttee 1997–2002; mem. Advisory Council on Korean Unification 1998–2002; Vice-Pres. Advisory Council on Democratic and Peaceful Unification 1998–2002; mem. Presidential Comm. for the New Millennium 1999–2002, Admin. Negotiating Cttee 2000–02; nominated Prime Minister of S. Korea July 2002, appointment vetoed by Parl.; Chair. Press Assen of Pvt. Univs 1999–2002; Vice-Pres. Korean Council for Univ. Educ. 1999–2002; Chair. Korean Council for Pres. of Pvt. Univs 1999–2002; Trustee United Bd for Christian Higher Educ. in Asia 1995–2002, Int. Women's Univ., Hanover, Germany 2000–02, Bd Korea Research Foundation 2000–02, Korea Inst. of Science and Tech. Evaluation and Planning 2001–02; Order of Civil Merit 1999, Moran Medal 1999. *Publications include:* On Interpretation of Paul's Thoughts, Women's Status and Role in First Christian Movement, Paul's Somatic Understanding of Human Beings, The Origin and Development of Feminist Theology, Christianity and World Korean Theology in Transition, Korean Women's Studies, Paul's Understanding of History and Gospel. *Address:* 1901, Samdok Ever Villa, 105-1, Namgajwa-dong, Seodaemun-gu, Seoul, Republic of Korea (home).

CHANG, Shana; Chinese artist; b. 26 March 1931, Lyon, France; d. of Chang Shuhong; one s.; ed Dunhuang, Boston Museum of Fine Art School and New York; returned to China 1950; asst to architect Liang Sicheng, Qinghua Univ. 1951–56; Prof., Cen. Acad. of Arts and Design 1957–85, Deputy Dean 1982–83, Dean 1983–98; Del. 12th CCP Cen. Cttee 1982, 13th CCP Cen. Cttee; mem. New York Students League 1953; mem. Educ., Science, Culture and Public Health Cttee 8th NPC;; mem. Standing Cttee 9th NPC; fmr Vice-Pres. China Artists Assen. *Address:* c/o Central Academy of Arts and Design, 34 North Dong Huan Road, Beijing 100020, People's Republic of China (office).

CHANG, Steve, MSc; Taiwanese software industry executive; *Chairman, Trend Micro Inc.;* ed Fu-Jen Catholic Univ., Taiwan, Lehigh Univ., Pa, USA; fmr engineer, Hewlett-Packard; f. AsiaTek Inc. (UNIX software design co.), Taiwan; Co-founder, Chair. and CEO Trend Micro Inc. (software co. specialising in network virus protection and internet security), Calif., USA (now based in Japan) 1988–2005, Chair. 2005–; mem. Bd of Dirs AsiaInfo Holdings, Inc. 2001–; Business Week Star of Asia Award, Asia Business Leader Award 2004. *Address:* Trend Micro Inc., Shinjuku MAYNDS Tower, 1-1, Yoyogi 2-Chome, Shibuya-ku, Tokyo 151-0053, Japan (office). *Telephone:* (3) 5334-3650 (office). *Fax:* (3) 5334-3651 (office). *Website:* www.trendmicro.com (office).

CHANG, Xiaobing, MBA; Chinese engineer and telecommunications executive; *Executive Director, Chairman and CEO, China United Telecommunications Corporation (China Unicom Group);* b. 1958; ed Nanjing Inst. of Posts and Telecommunications, Tsinghua Univ.; Deputy Dir Nanjing Municipal Posts and Telecommunications (MPT) Bureau, Jiangsu Prov. 1993–96; Deputy Dir-Gen. Dept of Telecommunications Admin, Ministry of Information Industry 1996–2000, Dir 2000–04; Vice-Pres. China Telecom Group –2004, Pres. 2004–; Exec. Dir, Chair. and CEO China United Telecommunications Corpn (China Unicom Group) 2004–, CEO and Chair. China Unicom Ltd, Chair. China United Telecommunications Corpn Ltd. *Address:* China Unicom Ltd 75th Floor, The Center, 99 Queen's Road Central, Hong Kong Special Administrative Region (office); China United Telecommunications Corpn Ltd, No. 133A, Xidan North Street, Xicheng District, Beijing 100032, People's Republic of China (office). *Telephone:* (852) 212-62018 (Hong Kong) (office); (10) 66505588 (Beijing) (office); (21) 52732228 (Beijing) (office). *Fax:* (852) 212-62016 (office). *Website:* www.chinaunicom.com.hk (office); www.chinaunicom.com.cn (office).

CHANG, Yung Ho, BS, MArch; Chinese architect and academic; *Professor and Head of Department of Architecture, Massachusetts Institute of Technology;* b. 1956, Beijing; m. Lijia Lu; ed Najing Inst. of Tech., Beijing, Ball State Univ., USA, Univ. of California, Berkeley; taught at Ball State Univ., Muncie, Ind. 1985–88, Univ. of Michigan (Walter B. Sanders Fellow) 1988–90, Univ. of California, Berkeley 1990–92, Rice Univ. 1993–96; co-f. Atelier Fiechang Jianzhu Architects, Beijing 1993; f. Grad. Centre of Architecture, Peking Univ. 1999, Head and Prof. 2004–05; Kenzo Tange Chair, Harvard Univ. Grad. School of Design 2002–03; Prof. and Head of Dept of Architecture, MIT 2005–; Walter B. Sanders Fellow, Univ. of Michigan 1989–90, Steedman Travelling Fellowship, Washington Univ., St Louis 1992; First Place, Shinkenchiku Residential Design Competition, Japan Architect 1986, First Prize, From Table to Tablescape Design Competition, Formica Corpn 1988, Winner, Young Architects Forum, Architectural League of New York 1992, UNESCO Prize for Promotion of the Arts 2000. *Publications:* Yung Ho Chang/Atelier Feichang Jianzhu: A Chinese Practice (contrib.) 2002. *Address:* Room 7-337D, Department of Architecture, Massachusetts Institute of Technology,

77 Massachusetts Avenue, Cambridge, MA 02139-4307, USA (office); Atelier Fiechang Jianzhu Architects, Yuan Ming Yuan East Gate Nei, Yard No. 1 on northside, Yuan Ming Yuan Dong Lu, Beijing 100084, People's Republic of China (office). *Telephone:* (617) 253-4411 (office). *E-mail:* yungho@mit.edu (office); fcjz@fcjz.com (office). *Website:* architecture.mit.edu (office); www.fcjz .com (office).

CHANG, Zhenming; Chinese banking executive; *President and Vice-Chair, CITIC Group;* b. 1957; joined CITIC Group 1983, Deputy Dir, Capital Dept 1992, seconded to USA as Trader 1992–93, Deputy Man. 1993–94, Deputy Chief Man. in charge of Financial Business 1994–95; apptd Chair. and Pres. CITIC Securities 1995; Dir CITIC Pacific (Hong Kong) Ltd 2000–05; apptd Pres., CEO and Dir CITIC Ka Wah Bank Ltd (CKWB) 2001, Exec. Vice-Chair. 2002–04; Dir and CEO CITIC Int. Financial Holdings Ltd 2002–04, Vice-Chair. 2006–; Dir Capital Market Holdings Ltd; Dir and Exec. Vice-Pres. CITIC Group –2004, Pres. and Vice-Chair. 2006–; Pres. China Construction Bank (CCB) 2004–06. *Address:* CITIC Group, Capital Mansion, 6 Xinuan Nanlu, Beijing 10004, People's Republic of China (office). *Telephone:* (10) 64660088 (office). *Fax:* (10) 64661186 (office). *Website:* www.citic.com.cn (office).

CHANG-HIM, Rt Rev. French Kitchener, LTh; Seychelles ecclesiastic; b. 10 May 1938, Seychelles; s. of Francis Chang-Him and Amelia Zoé; m. Susan Talma 1975 (died 1996); twin d.; ed Seychelles Coll., Lichfield Theological Coll., St Augustine's Coll. Canterbury and Univ. of Trinity Coll. Toronto; primary school teacher 1958; man. of schools 1973–77; Chair. Teacher Training Coll. Bd of Govs 1976–77; Vicar-Gen. Diocese of Seychelles 1973–79; Archdeacon of Seychelles 1973–79; Bishop of Seychelles 1979–2004; Dean, Prov. of Indian Ocean 1983–84, Archbishop 1984–95; Hon. DD (Univ. of Trinity Coll., Toronto) 1991; Rajiv Ghandi Foundation Lifetime Achievement Award 2003. *Publication:* The Seychellois: In Search of an Identity 1975. *Leisure interests:* international affairs, cooking, gardening, reading. *Address:* PO Box 44, Victoria, Seychelles. *Telephone:* 248151. *Fax:* 248151. *E-mail:* changhim@seychelles.sc (office).

CHANGEUX, Jean-Pierre, DèsSc; French medical scientist and academic; *Professor, Laboratoire de Neurobiologie Moléculaire, Institut Pasteur;* b. 6 April 1936, Domont; s. of Marcel Changeux and Jeanne Benoît; m. Annie Dupont 1962; one s.; ed Lycées Montaigne, Louis le Grand and St Louis, Paris and Ecole Normale Supérieure, Ulm; research asst 1958–60; Asst Lecturer, Science Faculty, Univ. of Paris 1960–66; post-doctoral Fellow, Univ. of Calif. 1966, Columbia Univ., New York 1967; Vice-Dir Coll. de France (Chair. of Molecular Biology) 1967; Prof., Laboratoire de Neurobiologie Moléculaire, Institut Pasteur 1974–; Prof., Coll. de France 1975–; Pres. Interministerial Comm. for Preservation of Nat. Artistic Heritage 1989–, Consultative Cttee on Ethics for Life and Medical Sciences 1993–99 (Hon. Pres. 1999–); mem. Soc. Des Amis du Louvre 2004–, Vice-Pres. 2006–; mem. Scientific Bd World Knowledge Dialogue 2007–; Corresp. mem. numerous comms, Turin Acad. of Medicine, Acad. des Sciences, Akad. Leopoldina, Halle, NAS, Swedish and Belgian acads; Commdr, Légion d'honneur, Ordre des Arts et Lettres, Grand Croix, Ordre nat. du Mérite;; Alexandre Joannidès prize (Acad. des Sciences), Gairdner Foundation Award 1978, Lounsbery Prize (NAS) 1982, Co-recipient Wolf Foundation Prize 1982, Céline Prize 1985, F.O. Schmitt Prize (Neurosciences Research Inst., New York) 1985, Fidia Neuroscience Award 1989, Bristol-Myers-Squibb Award in Neuroscience 1990; Carl-Gustav Bernhard Medal (Swedish Acad. of Sciences) 1991, Médaille d'Or (CNRS) 1992, Prix Jeantet (Geneva) 1993, Goodman and Gilman Award 1994, Camillo Golgi medal (Accad. Nazionale dei Lincei, Rome) 1994, Sir Hans Krebs medal (Helsinki) 1994, Grand Prix (Fondation de la Recherche Médicale) 1997, Eli Lilly Award 1999, Langley Award, Washington 2000, Prix Balzan 2001, Biotechnology Study Center Award, NY Univ. 2006. *Publications include:* L'homme neuronal 1983, Matière à pensée 1989 (with Alain Connes), Raison et Plaisir 1994, Conversations on Mind, Matter and Mathematics (with Alain Connes) 1995, La Nature et la Règle (with Paul Ricoeur) 1998, L'Homme de vérité 2002, Les passions de l'âme 2006; author and co-author of several research papers on allosteric proteins, on the acetylcholine receptor and on the devt of the nervous system. *Leisure interests:* baroque paintings, organ music. *Address:* Laboratoire de Neurobiologie Moléculaire, Institut Pasteur, 25 rue du Docteur Roux, 75015 Paris (office); 47 rue du Four, 75006 Paris, France (home). *Telephone:* 1-45-68-88-05 (office); 1-45-48-44-64 (home). *Fax:* 1-45-68-88-36 (office). *E-mail:* changeux@pasteur.fr (office). *Website:* www.pasteur.fr (office).

CHANNING, Carol; American actress; b. 31 Jan. 1923, Seattle, Wash.; d. of George Channing and Carol Glaser; m. 3rd Charles Lowe 1956; one s.; m. 4th Harry Kullijian 2003; Special Tony Award 1968, Lifetime Achievement Tony Award 1995. *Plays include:* No for an Answer, Let's Face It, So Proudly We Hail, Lend an Ear (Critics' Circle Award), Gentlemen Prefer Blondes, Wonderful Town, The Vamp, Hello Dolly (Tony Award, Best Actress, Musical 1964) 1963. *Films include:* Paid in Full (1950, The First Traveling Saleslady 1956, All About People (1967, Thoroughly Modern Millie (Golden Globe Award for Best Supporting Actress 1967) 1967, Skidoo 1968, Sgt. Pepper's Lonely Hearts Club Band 1978, Alice in Wonderland (tv) (1985), Where's Waldo?" (voice) (tv) 1991, Hans Christian Andersen's Thumbelina (voice) 1994, The Brave Little Toaster Goes to Mars (voice) 1998. *Address:* c/o William Morris Agency, 1 William Morris Place, Beverly Hills, CA 90212, USA.

CHANNING, Stockard, BA; American actress; b. (Susan Stockard), 13 Feb. 1944, New York; m. four times; ed Harvard Univ.; performed in experimental drama with Theatre Co. of Boston 1967. *Films include:* Comforts of the Home 1970, The Fortune 1975, Sweet Revenge 1975, The Big Bus 1976, Grease 1978, The Cheap Detective 1978, Boys Life 1978, Without A Trace 1983, Heartburn 1986, Men's Club 1986, Staying Together 1987, Meet the Applegates 1987,

Married to It 1993, Six Degrees of Separation 1993, Bitter Moon 1994, Smoke 1995, Up Close and Personal 1996, Moll Flanders, Edie and Pen, The First Wives Club 1996, Practical Magic 1998, Twilight 1998, Lulu on the Bridge (voice) 1998, The Red Door 1999, Other Voices 1999, Isn't She Great 1999, The Venice Project 1999, Where the Heart Is 2000, The Business of Strangers 2001, Life or Something Like It 2002, Behind the Red Door 2002, Bright Young Things 2003, Le Divorce 2003, Anything Else 2003, Red Mercury 2005, Must Love Dogs 2005, 3 Needles 2005, Sparkle 2007. *Stage appearances include:* Two Gentlemen of Verona, New York, San Francisco, LA 1972–73, No Hard Feelings, New York 1973, Vanities, LA 1976, As You Like It 1978, They're Playing Our Song, Lady and the Clarinet 1983, The Golden Age 1983, A Day in the Death of Joe Egg 1985 (Tony Award for Best Actress), House of Blue Leaves 1986, Woman in Mind 1988, Love Letters 1989, Six Degrees of Separation, New York 1990 (also London stage début, Royal Court Theatre 1992), Four Baboons Adoring the Sun 1992. *Television appearances include:* The Stockard Channing Show 1979–80, The West Wing 1999–2006, Batman Beyond 1999–2000, Out of Practice 2005–06 and various television movies including The Truth About Jane 2000, The Piano Man's Daughter 2000, Confessions of an Ugly Stepsister 2002, Hitler: The Rise of Evil 2003, The Piano Man's Daughter 2003, Jack 2004. *Address:* ICM, c/o Andrea Eastman, 40 W 57th Street, New York, NY 10019, USA.

CHANNON, Rt Hon. (Henry) Paul Guinness (see KELVEDON of ONGAR, Baron.)

CHANTLER, Sir Cyril, Kt; British paediatric nephrologist and healthcare administrator; *Chairman, UCL Partners;* b. 1939; m. Shireen Chantler; Gen. Man. Guy's Hosp. 1985–88, Prin. United Medical and Dental School, Guy's and St Thomas's Hosps 1992–98, also Prof. of Paediatric Nephrology –2000 (retd); Pro-Vice Chancellor, Univ. of London 1997–2000; Chair. Great Ormond Street Hosp. for Children NHS Trust 2001–09; Chair. UCL Partners 2009–; Chair. King's Fund; Chair. Strategic Devt Group for Dulwich Community Hosp.; Chair. Council of Heads of UK Medical Schools and Faculties 1998–99; Chair. Beit Memorial Fellowships Bd; Pres. British Asscn of Medical Mans 1991–97; Medical Dir, Well Child Medical Research Fund; mem. Bd of Govs South Bank Univ.; Trustee, Dunhill Medical Trust; mem. Advisory Panel, Assoc. Parl. Health Group; mem. NHS Policy Bd 1989–96; mem. Gen. Medical Council 1994–2003. *Address:* UCL Partners, University College London, Gower Street, London, WC1E 6BT, England (office). *Telephone:* (20) 7679-2000 (office). *Website:* www.ucl.ac.uk (office).

CHANTURIA, Lado; Georgian lawyer, judge and academic; *Professor, Faculty of Law, University of Bremen;* b. 14 April 1963, Jvari; ed Iv. Javakhishvili Tbilisi State Univ., Moscow Legislation Inst., Göttingen Univ., Germany; Asst Prof., Assoc. Prof., then Prof. Faculty of Law, Tbilisi State Univ. 1995–; co-ordinator Civil and Econ. Law Reform Project 1993–96; Research Fellow, Max Planck Inst. for Foreign and Int. Pvt. Law 1996; mem. Council of Justice 1997; Minister of Justice 1998–99; Chief Justice of the Supreme Court of Georgia 1999–2004; Humbolt Fellow and Prof., Faculty of Law, Univ. of Bremen, Germany 2004–; legal advisor to Pres. Michail Saakaschwili 2004–; mem. Int. Advisory Bd, ABA/CEELI Inst., Prague. *Publications:* over 60 published works. *Leisure interests:* soccer, travel. *Address:* GW1, C 1020, University of Bremen, Faculty of Law, 28353 Bremen, Germany (office); Phanaskerteli st. 9/97, 0110 Tbilisi, Georgia (home). *Telephone:* (421) 2187462 (office); (32) 36-02-08 (home). *E-mail:* lado .chanturia@uni-bremen.de (office); chanturialado@yahoo.com (home). *Website:* www.jura.uni-bremen.de (office).

CHANTURIYA, Valentin Alekseyevich; Russian metallurgist; *Director, Research Institute of Complex Exploitation of Mineral Resources, Russian Academy of Sciences;* b. 15 Oct. 1938; m. 2nd Yelena Leonidovna Chanturiya; two s. two d.; ed Moscow Inst. of Steel and Alloys; Jr, Sr Researcher, Head of Lab. Moscow Inst. of Earth Sciences 1969–74; Sr Researcher, Head of Lab., Inst. for Problems of Complex Exploitation of Mineral Resources, Russian Acad. of Sciences 1974–, Deputy Dir 1993–2003, Dir 2003–; Corresp. mem. Russian (fmrly USSR) Acad. of Sciences 1990, mem. 1994–; research in physical and chemical aspects of processing mineral raw materials; Prize of USSR Council of Ministers, Govt Prize, Russian Fed. 1983, 1990, 1998, Melnikov Gold Medal, Presidium Russian Acad. of Sciences 1992, Prize of Pres. of Russian Fed. in Educ. 2001. *Publications include:* Chemistry of Surfacial Phenomena at Flotation 1983, Electrochemistry of Sulphides 1993, Mining Sciences 1997, Modern Problems of Primary Processing of Minerals in Russia 2004, Nanoparticles in Geological Materials Destruction and Extraction Processes 2006. *Leisure interest:* fishing. *Address:* Research Institute of Complex Exploitation of Mineral Resources (IPKON), Russian Academy of Sciences, 111020 Moscow, Kryukovsky tupic 4, Russia (office). *Telephone:* (495) 360-06-06 (office); (495) 348-93-94 (home). *E-mail:* info@ipkonran.ru (office). *Website:* www.ipkonran.ru (office).

CHAO, Elaine L., BEcons, MBA; American fmr government official; m. Mitch McConnell 1993; ed Mount Holyoke, Harvard Business School, Dartmouth Coll., Columbia Univ.; banker, Citicorp 1979–83; White House Fellow 1983–84; Vice-Pres. Syndications BankAmerica Capital Markets Group, San Francisco 1984–86; Deputy Admin. US Maritime Admin. 1986–88, Chair. Fed. Maritime Comm. 1988–89; Deputy Sec. US Dept of Transportation; Dir Peace Corps, est. first Peace Corps in Baltic nations and newly ind. states of fmr USSR; Pres. and CEO United Way America 1992–96; US Sec. of Labor 2001–09; Fellow, Heritage Foundation, Washington, DC 1996–2001; 31 hon. degrees including Hon. LLD (Villanova Univ. 1989, Sacred Heart Univ. 1991, St John's Univ. 1991, Notre Dame 1998, St Mary's Coll. 2002, N Alabama 2003, Fu-Jen Catholic Univ. 2003), Hon. LHD (Drexel Univ. 1992, Niagara Univ. 1992, Thomas More Coll. 1994, Bellarmine Coll. 1995, Univ. of Toledo 1995, Univ. of Louisville 1996, Goucher Coll. 1996, Centre Coll. 2003);

Outstanding Young Achiever Award, Nat. Council of Women 1986; Harvard Univ. Grad. School of Business Alumni Achievement Award 1994. *Address:* 214 Massachusetts Avenue NE, Washington, DC 200002, USA (office). *Telephone:* (202) 546-4400 (office). *Fax:* (202) 675-1173 (office). *Website:* elainelchao.com.

CHAO, Manu; French singer and songwriter; b. 26 June 1961, Paris; one s.; as teenager played in various bands, including Les Hot Pants; formed Mano Negra 1987, band split 1993; first single earned group contract with Virgin; toured Latin America; moved to Spain 1995; formed 10-mem. Radio Bemba Sound System; spent next few years recording in South and Central America; King of Bongo recording featured on soundtrack to Madonna's The Next Big Thing film; British tour 2002; producer for Amadou and Mariam, Akli D; BBC Radio 3 World Music Innovator award 2002, Latin Grammy Award for Best Alternative Song (for Me Llaman Calle) 2007. *Recordings:* with Mano Negra: Patchanka 1988, Puta's Fever 1989, King Of The Bongo 1991, Hell Of Patchinko 1992, Casa Babylon 1994; solo: Clandestino 1998, Próxima Estación: Esperanza 2001, Sibérie m'áétait contéee 2004, La Radiolina 2007. *Address:* Management Corida, 120 boulevard Rochechouard, 75018 Paris, France (office); Because Music, 173–175 rue de Faubourg, Poissonnière, 75009 Paris, France (office). *Telephone:* 1-42-23-67-04 (office); 1-53-21-53-21 (office). *Fax:* 1-53-20-02-40 (office). *E-mail:* info@because.tv (office). *Website:* www.because.tv (office); www.manuchao.net.

CHAOVARAT, Chanweerakul, BSc; Thai business executive and politician; *Minister of the Interior;* b. 7 June 1936; m. Tassanee Chanrvirakul; three c.; ed Thammasat Univ.; Man. Dir Sino-Thai Eng & Construction PLC 1962–94, Dir and Chair. Advisory Bd 1998–2007; Chair. Bd of Dirs Stp&I PLC 1975–94, 1998–2007; Deputy Minister of Finance 1994–95, 1996–97; Minister of Public Health Feb.–Sept. 2008, Deputy Prime Minister of Thailand Sept.–Nov. 2008, Acting Prime Minister Nov.–Dec. 2008; Minister of the Interior Dec. 2008–; mem. (Fifth Class) of the Most Exalted Order of the White Elephant 1982, Commdr (Third Class) 1992, Kt Grand Cross (First Class) 1996, (Special Class) 2004; Commdr (Third Class) of the Most Noble Order of the Crown of Thailand 1991, Kt Grand Cross (First Class) 1995, Kt Grand Cordon (Special Class) 1997; Hon. PhD (Ramkhamhaeng Univ.) 2006. *Address:* Ministry of the Interior, Thanon Atsadang, Bangkok 10200, Thailand (office). *Telephone:* (2) 222-1141 (office). *Fax:* (2) 223-8851 (office). *E-mail:* webteam@moi.go.th (office). *Website:* www.moi.go.th (office).

CHAPLIN, Geraldine; American actress; b. 3 July 1944, Santa Monica, Calif.; d. of Charles Chaplin and Oona (O'Neill) Chaplin; one s.; ed pvt. schools, Royal Ballet School, London, UK. *Films include:* Doctor Zhivago 1965, Stranger in the House 1967, I Killed Rasputin 1968, The Hawaiians 1970, Innocent Bystanders 1973, Buffalo Bill and the Indians or Sitting Bull's History Lesson, The Three Musketeers 1974, The Four Musketeers, Nashville 1975, Raise Ravens 1975, Welcome to LA Cria, Roseland 1977, Remember My Name, A Wedding 1978, The Mirror Crack'd 1980, Voyage en Douce 1981, Bolero 1982, Corsican Brothers, The Word, L'Amour Par Terre, White Mischief 1988, The Moderns 1988, The Return of the Musketeers, I Want To Go Home, The Children, Chaplin 1992, Jane Eyre, In the Name of God's Poor 1997, Cousin Bette 1998, In the Beginning 2000, Las Caras de la Luna 2001, En la Ciudad sin Límites 2002, Talk to Her 2002, El Puente de San Luis Rey 2004, Without Love 2004, Disappearances 2004, Oculto 2005, Heidi 2005, BloodRayne 2005, Melissa P. 2005, The Orphanage 2006, Miguel and William 2007, Teresa, el cuerpo de Cristo 2007. *Television appearances include:* My Cousin Rachel, A Foreign Field 1994, To Walk With Lions 1999, Dinotopia (series) 2002, Winter Solstice 2003, A Christmas Carol 2004, The Bridge of San Luis Rey 2004, Les Aventuriers des mers du Sud 2006.

CHAPMAN, Dinos, MA; British artist; b. 1962, London; brother of Jake Chapman (q.v.); two d.; ed Ravensbourne Coll. of Art, RCA; studied painting at RCA; teacher of textiles in boys' school; worked as asst to artists Gilbert and George; now works jtly with brother Jake; Charles Wollaston Award (for The Marriage of Reason and Squalor), RA Summer Exhbn 2003. *Address:* c/o White Cube, 48 Hoxton Square, London, N1 6PB, England. *Fax:* (20) 7930-5373. *E-mail:* enquiries@whitecube.com. *Website:* www.whitecube.com/artists/chapman/texts/10.

CHAPMAN, (F.) Ian, CBE, CBIM, FRSA, FFCS; British publisher; *Vice-President, National Academy of Writing;* b. 26 Oct. 1925, St Fergus, Aberdeenshire, Scotland; s. of the late Rev. Peter Chapman and Frances Burdett; m. Marjory Stewart Swinton, MA 1953; one s. one d.; ed Shawlands Acad., Ommer School of Music, Glasgow; served in RAF 1943–44; miner (nat. service) 1945–47; with William Collins Sons & Co. Ltd (fmrly W.M. Collins Holdings PLC, now Harper Collins) 1947, Man. Trainee New York br. 1950–51, Sales Man. London br. 1955; mem. main operating Bd, Group Sales Dir 1959, Jt Man. Dir 1967–76, Deputy Chair. 1976–81, Chair. CEO 1981–89; Deputy Chair. Orion Publishing Group 1993–94, Dir William Collins overseas cos 1968–89: Canada 1968–89, USA 1974–89, S. Africa 1978–89, NZ 1978–89, William Collins Int. Ltd 1975–89; Chair. Scottish Radio Holdings PLC (fmrly Radio Clyde) 1972–96 (Hon. Pres. 1996–2000), Harvill Press 1976–89, Hatchards Ltd 1976–89, William Collins Publrs Ltd 1979–81, The Listener Publs PLC 1988–93, RadioTrust PLC 1997–2001, Guinness Publrs Ltd 1991–98; Dir Pan Books Ltd 1962–84 (Chair. 1973–76), Book Tokens Ltd 1981–94, Ind. Radio News 1984–85, Stanley Botes Ltd 1986–89, Guinness PLC (non-exec.) 1986–91; Pres.-Dir Gen. Guinness Media SAS, Paris 1996–99; f. Chapmans Publrs., Chair. and Man. Dir 1989–94; Trustee Book Trade Benevolent Soc. 1982–2003; Trustee The Publrs Asscn 1989–97; mem. Gov. Council SCOTBIC; mem. Council Publishers Asscn 1962–77, Vice-Pres. 1978, Pres. 1979–81; Chair. Nat. Acad. of Writing 2000–03, Vice-Pres. 2003–; mem. Bd Book Devt Council 1967, Ancient House Bookshop 1972–89, Scottish Opera, Theatre Royal Ltd 1974–79, IRN Ltd 1983–85; Chair. Advisory Bd Strathclyde Univ. Business School 1985–88; Hon. DLitt (Strathclyde Univ.) 1990; Scottish Free Enterprise Award 1985. *Leisure interests:* grandchildren, music, golf, reading. *Address:* Kenmore, 46 The Avenue, Cheam, Surrey, SM2 7QE, England (home). *Telephone:* (20) 8642-1820 (home). *Fax:* (20) 8642-7439 (home). *E-mail:* fic@onetel.net.uk (home).

CHAPMAN, Jake, MA; British artist; b. 1966, Cheltenham; brother of Dinos Chapman (q.v.); ed North East London Polytechnic, RCA; studied sculpture at RCA; now works jtly with brother Dinos; Charles Wollaston Award (for The Marriage of Reason and Squalor), RA Summer Exhbn 2003. *Publications:* articles in Frieze art magazine. *Address:* c/o White Cube, 48 Hoxton Street, London, N1 6PB, England (office). *Telephone:* (20) 7930-5373. *E-mail:* enquiries@whitecube.com. *Website:* www.whitecube.com/artists/chapman/texts/10.

CHAPONDA, George; Malawi lawyer and politician; b. 1 Nov. 1942, Mulanje; m.; ed Univ. of Delhi, India, Univ. of Zambia, Yale Univ., USA; lawyer, UNHCR, positions included Deputy Regional Dir for East and Horn of Africa, Addis Ababa, Ethiopia, also worked in Tanzania, Switzerland, Bangladesh, Thailand, Kenya, Somalia 1984–2002; Chair. Univ. Council, Univ. of Malawi 2003–04; mem. Parl. (United Democratic Front) for Mulanje South West constituency 2004–, Minister of Foreign Affairs 2004–05, of Local Govt and Rural Devt 2005–. *Leisure interests:* jogging, reading and football. *Address:* Ministry of Local Government and Rural Development, POB 30312, Lilongwe 3, Malawi (office). *Telephone:* 1789388 (office). *Fax:* 1788083 (office).

CHAPPELL, Gregory (Greg) Stephen; Australian business executive, fmr professional cricketer and cricket coach; *Managing Director, Greg Chappell Promotions Plc;* b. 7 Aug. 1948, Adelaide; s. of Arthur Martin Chappell and Jeanne Ellen Chappell (née Richardson); grandson of V.Y. Richardson (Australian Cricket Capt. 1935–36); brother of I.M. Chappell (Australian Cricket Capt. 1971–75); m. Judith Elizabeth Donaldson 1971; two s. one d.; ed St Leonard's Primary School and Plympton High School, Adelaide and Prince Alfred Coll., Adelaide; teams: S. Australia 1966–73, Somerset 1968–69, Queensland 1973–84 (Capt. 1973–77, 1979–80); 87 Tests for Australia 1970–84, 48 as Capt., scoring 7,110 runs (average 53.8) including 24 hundreds and holding 122 catches; scored 108 on Test debut v. England, Perth 1970; only player to have scored a century in each innings of 1st Test as capt. (versus West Indies, Brisbane 1975); holds record for most catches in a Test match (7, versus England, Perth 1975); scored 24,535 first-class runs (74 hundreds); toured England 1972, 1975, 1977 and 1980; Man. Dir AD Sports Technologies (fmrly Fundamental Golf and Leisure Ltd) 1993–95 (Dir 1992–), Greg Chappell Sports Marketing 1995–98; mem. Australian Cricket Bd 1984–88; State Man. of Cricket, S. Australian Cricket Asscn 1998–; coach, S. Australian Redbacks 2002; Patron Leukaemia Foundation of SA 1998–, Happi Foundation 2001–2003; Man. Dir Greg Chappell Promotions PLC 2003–; contracted coaching tours in Pakistan 2005–05; coach India nat. team 2005–07; Hon. MBE 1979, Hon. Life mem. MCC 1985 Wisden Cricketer of the Year 1973; Australian Sportsman of the Year 1976; chosen for Australian Team of the Century 2000; elected to Australian Cricket Hall of Fame 2001. *Publications:* Greg Chappell's Health and Fitness Repair Manual 1998, Greg Chappell's Family Health and Fitness Manual 1999. *Leisure interests:* golf, tennis, reading, listening to music. *Address:* c/o South Australian Cricket Association, Adelaide Oval, North Adelaide, SA 5006, Australia.

CHAPPLE, Field Marshal Sir John (Lyon), GCB, CBE, MA, FZS, FLS, FRGS; British army officer (retd); b. 27 May 1931; s. of C. H. Chapple; m. Annabel Hill 1959; one s. three d.; ed Haileybury and Trinity Coll., Cambridge; joined 2nd King Edward's Own Gurkhas 1954, served Malaya, Hong Kong, Borneo; Staff Coll. 1962, Jt Services Staff Coll. 1969; Commdr 1st Bn 2nd Gurkhas 1970–72; Directing Staff, Staff Coll. 1972–73; Commdr 48 Gurkha Infantry Brigade 1976; Gurkha Field Force 1977; Prin. Staff Officer to Chief of Defence Staff 1978–79; Commdr British Forces, Hong Kong and Maj.-Gen. Brigade of Gurkhas 1980–82; Dir of Mil. Operations 1982–84; Deputy Chief of Defence Staff (Programmes and Personnel) 1985–87; Col 2nd Gurkhas 1986–94; C-in-C UK Land Forces 1987–88; Aide-de-Camp Gen. to the Queen 1987–92; Chief of Gen. Staff 1988–92; Gov. and C-in-C Gibraltar 1993–95; Pres. Zoological Soc. of London 1991–94; Vice-Lord Lt of Greater London 1997–; Services Fellow, Fitzwilliam Coll., Cambridge 1973; mem. Council Nat. Army Museum 1980–93; Pres. Combined Services Polo Asscn 1991–, Indian Mil. History Soc. 1991–, Mil. History Soc. 1992–, Soc. for Army Historical Research 1993–, Trekforce 1998–, Sir Oswald Stoll Foundation 1998–, British Schools Exploring Soc. Expeditions 1999–; Trustee World Wide Fund for Nature (UK) 1985–93; mem. Council, Conservation Foundation; mem. Bd of Trustees, King Mahendra Trust for Nature Conservation 1993, currently Chair. King Mahendra United Kingdom Trust for Nature Conservation; Patron, Gap Activity Projects. *Address:* c/o Gap Activity Projects, 44 Queen's Road, Reading, Berks. RG1 4BB, England.

CHAR; Japanese singer and rock guitarist; b. (Takenaka Hisato), 16 June 1955, Tokyo; s.; began taking classical music piano lessons age seven; began playing the guitar age eight; formed first band with friends at school age 11; formed underground music band Smoky Medicine 1973; launched solo career with release of self-titled debut album 1976; formed blues-rock-fusion power band JL&C (renamed Pink Cloud) with Johnny Yoshinaga and Kabe Shogi 1979, disbanded 1994; later formed bands Psychedelix 1991 and Baho (acoustin duo); performs with son who raps in English 1998–. *Albums include:* Char 1976, Have a Win 1977, Thrill 1978, U.S.J. 1981, The Best of Char 1982, Moon Child 1982, Play Back Series 1987, Psych 1987, Psych II 1988, When I Wake Up in the Morning 1989, Black Shoes 1989, Flash Back Memories 1991, Days Went By 1988–1993 1993, Mustang 1995, Character 1996, Char e Doya Collection 1999, All Around Me 1999, Char Psyche 2000, Char Played With and Without 2000, Bamboo Shoots 2001, Sacred Hills 2002, You Set Me Free

2003, Amano Jack 2005, Flying Toys 2007. *Address:* c/o Universal Music Japan, 1-8-4 Ohashi, Megoro-ku, Tokyo 153-8511, Japan (office). *E-mail:* dibs@char-net.com (home). *Website:* www.char-net.com.

CHARA; Japanese singer; b. 13 Jan. 1968, Kawaguchi-shi, Saitama Co.; m. Tadanobu Asano (q.v.) 1994; one d. one s.; began taking piano lessons age 4; signed contract with Epic/Sony Records 1990; first performance debut at Quattro Club, Tokyo 1991; released debut single Heaven and debut album Sweet 1991; TV commercials for Suntory, Shiseido and Marui 1990s; appeared in film Swallowtail Butterfly (Best Actress Award, Japanese Acad. Awards) 1996. *Albums include:* Sweet 1991, Soul Kiss 1992, Violet Blue 1993, Happy Toy 1994, Baby, Baby, Baby XXX 1995, Yen Town Band (soundtrack album for film Swallowtail Butterfly) 1996, Junior Sweet 1997, Strange Fruits 1999, Mood 2000, Caramel Milk 2000, Madrigal 2001, Yokae Mae 2003, Sweet 2004, A Scenery Like Me 2004, Something Blue 2005, Union 2007, Sugar Hunter 2007, Honey 2008, Kiss 2008. *Address:* c/o Universal Music Japan, 30 Minato-ku, Akasaka, Tokyo 107-8583, Japan (office). *Website:* www.charaweb.net.

CHARASSE, Michel Joseph; French politician; *Senator from Puy-de-Dôme;* b. 8 July 1941, Chamalières; s. of Martial Henri Charasse and Lucie Castellani; m. Danièle Bas 1978; ed Lycée Blaise Pascal, Clermont-Ferrand, Institut d'Etudes Politiques and Faculté de Droit de Paris; mem. staff, Ministry of Finance 1965–92; Asst Sec.-Gen. Socialist group in Nat. Ass. 1962–67, 1968–81 and FGDS group 1967–68; Mayor Puy-Guillaume, Puy-de-Dôme 1977–; Regional Councillor, Auvergne 1979–87; Adviser to Pres. of the Repub. 1981–95; Senator from Puy-de-Dôme 1981–88, 1992–; Sec. of Senate 1995–98; Minister-Del. for Budget 1988–92, Minister for Budget April–Oct. 1992; Treas. Asscn of Mayors of France; mem. High Council for Co-operation 2000–. *Publications:* 55 Faubourg St Honoré 1996, Pensées, Répliques et Anecdotes de François Mitterrand 1998. *Leisure interests:* hunting, fishing, reading. *Address:* Mairie, place Jean Jaurès, 63290 Puy-Guillaume; Sénat, 15 rue du Vaugirard, 75921 Paris, cedex 06, France. *Telephone:* 4-73-94-70-49 (Puy-Guillaume); 1-42-34-29-54 (Sénat). *Fax:* 1-42-34-43-43 (office). *Website:* www.senat.fr.

CHARBONNEAU, Hubert, MA, PhD; Canadian demographer and academic; *Professor Emeritus, Department of Demography, University of Montréal;* b. 2 Sept. 1936, Montréal; s. of Léonel Charbonneau and Jeanne Durand; m. Marie-Christiane Hellot 1961; one d.; ed Univs of Montréal and Paris; Sr Lecturer, Univ. of Montréal 1962–68, Asst Prof. 1968–70, Assoc. Prof. 1970–76, Prof. 1976–97, Prof. Emer. 1997–; Visiting Prof., Univ. do Paraná, Brazil 1978, 1980, 1983, Univ. de Buenos Aires 1994, 1997; Killam Sr Research Scholarship 1974, 1975, 1976; J. B. Tyrrell Historical Medal, Royal Soc. of Canada 1990. *Publications:* author and co-author of several books on demographic topics. *Leisure interests:* genealogy, billiards, cross-country skiing. *Address:* Département de démographie, Université de Montréal, CP 6128, succ. "Centre-Ville", Montréal, PQ H3C 3J7 (office); 19 avenue Robert, Outremont, PQ H3S 2P1, Canada (home). *Telephone:* (514) 731-5503 (home). *Fax:* (514) 343-2309 (home). *E-mail:* hubert.charbonneau@umontreal.ca (office); hubert.charbonneau@videotron.ca (home). *Website:* www.125 .umontreal.ca/Pionniers/Charbonneau (office).

CHAREST, The Hon. Jean, PC, LLB; Canadian lawyer and politician; *Premier of Québec;* b. 24 June 1958, Sherbrooke, Québec; m. Michèle Dionne 1980; one s. two d.; ed Université de Sherbrooke; mem. Sherbrooke Legal Aid Office 1981; Assoc. Beauchemin, Dussault et Charest 1981–84; Progressive Conservative MP for Sherbrooke 1984–; Asst Deputy Speaker, House of Commons 1984; Minister of State for Youth 1986–90, for Fitness and Amateur Sport 1988–90; Deputy Govt Leader in House of Commons 1989–90; Minister for the Environment 1991–93; Deputy Prime Minister of Canada and Minister of Industry; Leader Progressive Conservative Party 1993–98; Leader Liberal Party in Québec 1998–, Leader of the Opposition 1998–2002; Premier of Québec 2003–; mem. numerous Cabinet cttees; mem. Québec Bar Asscn, Canadian Bar Asscn. *Leisure interests:* skiing, sailing. *Address:* Office of the Premier, 885 Grande-Allée est, Edif. C, 3e étage, Québec, PQ G1A 1A2, Canada (office). *Telephone:* (418) 643-5321 (office). *Fax:* (418) 643-3924 (office). *E-mail:* premier.ministre@mce.gouv.qc.ca (office). *Website:* www.premier .gouv.qc.ca (office).

CHARETTE DE LA CONTRIE, Hervé Marie Joseph de; French politician; b. 30 July 1938, Paris; s. of Hélion de Charette de la Contrie and Jeanne de Nolhac; m. 2nd Michèle Delor; one c. and three c. by previous m.; ed Ecole des Hautes Etudes Commerciales, Inst. d'Etudes Politiques, Paris and Ecole Nat. d'Admin.; Deputy Sec.-Gen. Council of State 1969–72, Maître des requêtes 1973; Ministry of Labour 1973–78; Pres. Admin. Council, Nat. Immigration Office 1977; Dir Office of Minister of Educ. 1978; Pres. Sonacotra 1980–81; Deputy Sec.-Gen. Parti Républicain 1979; returned to Council of State 1981; Deputy to Nat. Ass. 1986, 1988–93, 1997–; Asst Minister, Office of Prime Minister 1986–88; Mayor of St-Florent-le-Vieil 1989–; Vice-Pres. Union pour la Démocratie Française (UDF) 1991; Vice-Pres. Conseil Régional, Pays de la Loire 1992–; Minister of Housing 1993–95, of Foreign Affairs 1995–97; Pres. Parti populaire pour la démocratie française 1995, convention démocratie 2002. *Publications:* Ouragon sur la République 1995, Lyautey 1997. *Address:* Mairie, 49410 St-Florent-le-Vieil; Assemblée Nationale, 75355 Paris, France.

CHARKIN, Richard Denis Paul, MA; British publishing executive; *Executive Director, Bloomsbury PLC;* b. 17 June 1949, London; s. of Frank Charkin and Mabel Doreen Charkin (née Rosen); m. Susan Mary Poole 1972; one s. two d.; ed Haileybury, Imperial Service Coll., Univ. of Cambridge and Harvard Business School; Science Ed. Harrap & Co. 1972; Sr Publishing Man. Pergamon Press 1973; Medical Ed. Oxford Univ. Press 1974, Head of Science and Medicine 1976, Head of Reference 1980; Man. Dir Academic and Gen.

1984; joined Octopus Publishing Group (Reed Int. Books) 1988; Chief Exec. Reed Consumer Books 1989–94, Exec. Dir Reed Books Int. 1988–96, Chief Exec. 1994–96; CEO Current Science Group 1996–97; CEO Macmillan Ltd 1998–2007; Exec. Dir Bloomsbury PLC 2007–; Non-Exec. Dir, Inst. of Physics Publishing 2009–; Visiting Prof., Univ. of Arts, London 2004–; Visiting Fellow, Green Coll., Oxford 1987; Chair. Common Purpose 1998–2008; mem. man. cttee John Wisden; mem. Publishers Asscn (Vice-Pres. 2004–05, Pres. 2005–06). *Publications:* Charkin Blog: The Archive 2008. *Leisure interests:* music, cricket. *Address:* Bloomsbury Publishing PLC, 36 Soho Square, London, W1D 3QY, England (office). *Telephone:* (20) 7494-2111 (office). *Fax:* (20) 7434-0151 (office). *Website:* www.bloomsbury.com (office).

CHARKVIANI, Gela; Georgian politician and diplomatist; *Ambassador to UK;* b. 1 March 1939, Tbilisi, Georgia; s. of Candide Charkviani and Tamar Djaoshvili; m. Nana Toidze-Charkviani; one s. one d.; ed Tbilisi Inst. of Foreign Languages, Univ. of Mich., USA; teacher Tbilisi Inst. of Foreign Languages; author and narrator TV monthly programme Globe, Georgian TV 1976–94; Vice-Pres. Georgian Soc. for Cultural Relations with Foreign Countries 1984–92; apptd Chief Adviser to Pres. Shevardnadze on Foreign Affairs, Head of Int. Relations Georgian State Chancellery 1992; taught sociology at Tbilisi State Univ. 1982–; Asst to Pres. Saakashvili of Georgia and Presidential Spokesperson 2005–06; Amb. to UK (also accred to Ireland) 2006–; Chair. Presidential Comm. on Peaceful Caucasus; has lectured in Austria, Germany, Sweden, UK and USA; Order of Honour 1998. *Music:* CD of piano miniatures released 2001. *Television:* author and dir of five-part documentary The Georgians in the Kremlin (Rustavi-II TV) 2004. *Publications include:* trans. of King Lear; Georgia, Transcaucasus and Beyond 1996; articles in numerous journals. *Leisure interests:* piano music, exotic cuisines. *Address:* Embassy of Georgia, 4 Russell Gardens, London, W14 8EZ, England (office); Gamsakhurdia str. 14, Tbilisi, Georgia (home). *Telephone:* (20) 7603-7799 (office); (32) 989679 (home). *Fax:* (20) 7603-6682 (office). *E-mail:* embassy@geoemb.plus.com (office). *Website:* www.geoemb.org.uk (office).

CHARLES, Caroline, OBE; British fashion designer; b. 18 May 1942, Cairo, Egypt; d. of Noel St John Fairhurst and Helen T. Williams; m. Malcolm Valentine 1966; one s. one d.; ed Sacred Heart Convent, Woldingham, Surrey, Swindon Art School; f. Caroline Charles 1963; established retail outlet in London selling Caroline Charles Collection 1979; Caroline Charles own shops in ten locations; wholesale business suppliers to leading British shops and stores and exports to USA, Japan, Australia and Europe; Evening Standard Design Award 1983 and other design awards. *Publication:* Weekend Wardrobe. *Leisure interests:* travel, theatre, gardening, tennis, reading. *Address:* 56–57 Beauchamp Place, London, SW3 1NY, England (office). *Telephone:* (20) 7225-3197. *Website:* www.carolinecharles.co.uk.

CHARLES-ROUX, Edmonde; French writer; *President, Académie Goncourt;* b. 17 April 1920, Neuilly-sur-Seine; d. of François Charles-Roux and Sabine Gounelle; m. Gaston Defferre 1973 (deceased); ed Italy; served as nurse, then in Resistance Movt, during Second World War, in which she was twice wounded; reporter, magazine Elle 1947–49; Features Ed., French edn of Vogue 1949–54, Ed.-in-Chief 1954–66; mem. Académie Goncourt 1983–, Pres. 2002–; Croix de guerre 1940–45, Officier, Légion d'honneur 2003; Prix Goncourt 1966, Grand Prix Littéraire de Provence 1977. *Publications:* Oublier Palerme 1966, Elle Adrienne 1971, L'irrégulière ou mon itinéraire Chanel 1974, Le temps Chanel 1979, Stèle pour un bâtard, Don Juan d'Autriche: 1980, Une enfance sicilienne 1981, Un désir d'Orient: La jeunesse d'Isabelle Eberhardt 1988, Nomade j'étais: Les années africaines d'Isabelle Eberhardt 1995, L'homme de Marseille 2001. *Leisure interests:* music, sea and sailing. *Address:* Editions Grasset, 61 rue des Saints-Pères, Paris 75006, France (office). *Website:* www.academie-goncourt.fr.

CHARLESWORTH, Brian, BA, PhD, FRS, FRSE; British biologist and academic; *Professor and Head, Institute of Evolutionary Biology, University of Edinburgh;* b. 29 April 1945, Brighton, Sussex; ed Queens' Coll., Cambridge; Post-doctoral Fellow in Population Biology, Univ. of Chicago 1969–71, Prof. of Ecology and Evolution 1985–92, George Wells Beadle Distinguished Service Prof. of Ecology and Evolution 1992–97; Lecturer in Genetics, Univ. of Liverpool 1971–74; Lecturer in Biology, Univ. of Sussex, Brighton 1974–82, Reader in Biology 1982–84; Royal Soc. Research Professorship, Univ. of Edinburgh 1997–2007, Prof. and Head of Inst. of Evolutionary Biology 2007–; Pres. Genetics Soc. (UK) 2006–; mem. Genetical Soc. of Great Britain 1966– (mem. Cttee 1981–84), Soc. for the Study of Evolution 1985– (Pres. 1999), Genetics Soc. of America 1986–99, Soc. for Molecular Biology and Evolution 1995–97, 2001–, European Soc. for Evolutionary Biology 1997–99, Research Fellowships Cttee Royal Soc. 1999– (mem. Awards Cttee 2001–), Functional Genomics Cttee Wellcome Trust 2000–03, Sectional Cttee A3 Royal Soc. of Edinburgh 2000–03, ERA Initiative Cttee Biotechnology and Biological Sciences Research Council 2001; Assoc. Ed. Current Biology 1992–; mem. Editorial Bd Genetical Research 1996–, Philosophical Transactions of the Royal Soc. 1999–2004; Ed. Biology Letters 2004–; mem. Advisory Bd Journal of Theoretical Biology 1996–2005; Reviewer, Nature, Science, Evolution, Genetics, Genetical Research, Journal of Theoretical Biology, American Naturalist, Molecular Biology and Evolution; Hon. Fellow, American Acad. of Arts and Sciences 1996; Darwin Prize, Univ. of Edinburgh 1994, Darwin Medal, Royal Soc. 2000, Sewall Wright Award, American Soc. of Naturalists 2006, Frink Award, Zoological Soc. of London 2007. *Publications:* more than 240 publs in scientific journals on theoretical population genetics and evolutionary biology. *Leisure interests:* reading, classical music, hill-walking. *Address:* Institute of Cell, Animal and Population Biology, University of Edinburgh, Ashworth Laboratories, West Mains Road, Edinburgh, Midlothian, EH9 3JT, Scotland (office). *Telephone:* (131) 650-5750 (office).

Fax: (131) 650-6564 (office). *E-mail:* brian.charlesworth@ed.ac.uk (office). *Website:* www.biology.ed.ac.uk (office).

CHARLTON, John (Jack), OBE, DL; British fmr professional football player and fmr professional football manager; b. 8 May 1935, Ashington, Northumberland; s. of the late Robert Charlton and of Elizabeth Charlton; brother of Sir Robert Charlton (q.v.); m. Patricia Charlton 1958; two s. one d.; ed Hirst Park School, Ashington; player for Leeds United 1952–73; 35 full England caps 1965–70; played with winning teams League Championship 1969, Football Asscn Cup 1972, League Cup 1968, Fairs Cup 1968, 1971, World Cup (England v. Germany) 1966; Man. Middlesbrough (Div. 2 Champions 1974) 1973–77, Sheffield Wednesday 1977–83, Newcastle United 1984–85, Repub. of Ireland (qualified for European Championships, West Germany 1988, World Cup, Italy 1990, USA 1994) 1986–95; Football Writers' Asscn Footballer of the Year 1967. *Publications:* Jack Charlton's American World Cup Diary 1994, Jack Charlton: The Autobiography 1996. *Leisure interests:* shooting, fishing. *Address:* Cairn Lodge, Dalton, Ponteland, Northumbria, England.

CHARLTON, Sir Robert (Bobby), Kt, CBE; British sports official, fmr professional football player and fmr professional football manager; b. 11 Oct. 1937, Ashington, Northumberland; s. of the late Robert Charlton and of Elizabeth Charlton; brother of Jack Charlton (q.v.); m. Norma Charlton 1961; two d.; ed Bedlington Grammar School, Northumberland; professional footballer with Manchester United 1954–73, played 751 games, scored 245 goals; F.A. Cup winners' medal 1963; First Div. championship medals 1956–57, 1964–65, 1966–67; World Cup winners' medal (with England) 1966; European Cup winners' medal 1968; 106 appearances for England 1957–73, scored record 49 goals; Man. Preston North End 1973–75; Chair. NW Council for Sport and Recreation 1982–; Dir Manchester United Football Club 1984–; mem. Laureus World Sports Acad.; Hon. Fellow, Manchester Polytechnic 1979; Hon. MA (Univ. of Manchester); BBC Sports Personality of the Year Lifetime Achievement Award 2008. *Publications:* My Soccer Life 1965, Forward for England 1967, This Game of Soccer 1967, Book of European Football, Books 1–4 1969–72, My Manchester United Years: The Autobiography 2007. *Leisure interest:* golf.

CHARNLEY, Irene; South African business executive; b. 6 May 1960; m. Clement Charnley; two s. one d.; ed Univ. of the Witwatersrand, Harvard Univ., USA; negotiator and strategist, Nat. Union of Mineworkers 1996; Commercial Dir MTN Group (fmrly M-Cell Ltd) 2001–05, Group Exec. Vice-Pres. 2005–07, mem. Bd of Dirs (non-exec.) 2008–, fmr Exec. Dir Johnnic Holdings, fmr Chair. M-Cell (subsidiary); Chair. Orbicom; mem. Bd of Dirs FirstRand Bank 2004–, Pontso Investment Holdings, Time Media Ltd, Metropolitan Life Ltd, Int. Marketing Council of South Africa, Black Econ. Empowerment Task Team; mem. King Committee on Corp. Governance; Trustee Eskom Pension Fund, Johnnic Ikageng Share Trust, Vaal Reefs Trust; World Econ. Forum Global Leader for Tomorrow, Businesswoman of the Year 2000, ranked 48th by Fortune magazine amongst 50 Most Powerful Women in Business outside the US 2002. *Address:* MTN Group Limited, Innovation Centre, 216 14th Avenue, Fairlands (office); Private Bag X9955, Sandton, Johannesburg 2146, South Africa. *Website:* www.mtn.com (office).

CHARPAK, Georges, PhD; French physicist; b. 1 Aug. 1924, Dabrovica, Poland; s. of Anna Szapiro and Maurice Charpak; m. Dominique Vidal 1953; two s. one d.; ed Ecole des Mines de Paris, Collège de France; prisoner in Dachau 1943–45; physicist, CNRS 1948–59, CERN 1959–94; mem. Bd of Dirs Fimalac 1997–; f. Soc. for Biospace Measurement 1997; mem. Higher Council of Integration 1994–; mem. French Acad. of Sciences 1985, Austrian Acad. of Sciences 1993, Acad. of Sciences Lisbon 1995; Foreign Assoc. NAS 1986; Foreign mem. Russian Acad. of Sciences 1994; Nat. Corresp. mem. French Acad. of Medicine 2002; Hon. mem. Austrian Acad. of Sciences 1993; Mil. Cross 1939–45, Officier, Ordre Nat. du Mérite 1997, Officier, Légion d'honneur 2006; Dr hc (Geneva) 1977, (Thessalonica) 1993, (Brussels) 1994, (Coimbra) 1994, (Ottawa) 1995, (Rio de Janeiro) 1996; Prize of European Physics Soc., Nobel Prize for Physics 1992, and others. *Publications:* La Vie à fil tendu 1993 (jtly), Feu follet et champignon nucléaire (jtly) 1997, Enfants, chercheurs et citoyens 1998, Megawatts and Megatons (jtly) 2001, Devenez sorcier, devenez savant 2002, Soyez savants, devenez prophètes 2004; numerous articles in learned journals. *Leisure interests:* skiing, music, trekking. *Address:* CERN, 1211 Geneva 23, Switzerland (office); 22 rue Pierre at Marie Curie, 75005 Paris, France (home). *Telephone:* (22) 7672144 (office). *Fax:* (22) 7677555 (office). *E-mail:* charpak@emse.fr (office); anne.dirat@cern.ch (office).

CHARPY, Christian; French government official; *Director-General, Agence Nationale Pour l'Emploi;* mem. Conseil d'Orientation pour l'Emploi (Employment Policy Council); currently Dir-Gen. Agence Nationale Pour l'Emploi; Pres. World Asscn of Public Employment Service 2006–. *Address:* Agence Nationale Pour l'Emploi, c/o Ministère du Travail, des Relations Sociales et de la Solidarité, 127 rue de Grenelle, 75007 Paris 07 SP, France (office). *E-mail:* info@anpe.fr (office). *Website:* www.anpe.fr (office).

CHARTIER, Roger; French academic; *Director of Studies, Ecole des Hautes Etudes en Sciences Sociales;* b. 9 Dec. 1945, Lyons; s. of Georges Chartier and Laurence Fonvielle; m. Anne-Marie Trépier 1967; one s. one d.; ed Ecole Normale Supérieure, St Cloud; Prof., Lycée Louis-Le-Grand, Paris 1969–70; Asst Prof., Univ. Paris I, Panthéon-Sorbonne 1970–75; Assoc. Prof., Ecole des Hautes Etudes en Sciences Sociales 1975–83, Dir of Studies 1984–; Prof., Collège de France 2007–; Visiting Prof., Univ. of California, Berkeley 1987, Cornell Univ. 1988, Johns Hopkins Univ. 1992; Annual Award, American Printing History Asscn 1990; Grand Prix d'Histoire, Acad. Française 1992. *Publications include:* L'Education en France du XVIe au XVIIIe siècle (jtly) 1976, La Nouvelle Histoire (co-ed.) 1978, Histoire de l'Edition Française (ed.)

1982–86, Figures de la gueuserie 1982, Représentation et vouloir politique: Autour des Etats Généraux de 1614 (jtly) 1982, Figure della furfanteria, Marginalità e cultura popolare in Francia tra Cinque e Seicento 1984, Pratiques de la lecture (ed.) 1985, The Cultural Uses of Print in Early Modern France 1987, The Culture of Print (ed.) 1987, Cultural History: Between Practices and Representations 1988, The Cultural Origins of the French Revolution 1991, Correspondence: Models of Letter Writing from the Middle Ages to the Nineteenth Century 1991, The Order of Books 1994, Forms and Meanings: Texts, Performances, and Audiences from Codex to Computer 1995, A History of Reading in the West 1995, Culture écrite et société. L'ordre des livres 1996, On the Edge of the Cliff: History, Language, and Practices 1998, Publishing Drama in Early Modern Europe: The Panizzi Lectures 1998, Le Jeu de la règles 2000, Identités d'auteur dans l'Antiquité et la tradition européenne (co-ed.) 2004, Inscrire et effacer: Culture écrite et littérature 2005. *Address:* Ecole des Hautes Etudes en Sciences Sociales, 54 boulevard Raspail, 75006 Paris (office); Collège de France, 11, Place Marcelin Berthelot, 75231 Paris, France (office). *Telephone:* 1-44-27-12-11 (office); 1-49-54-25-25 (office). *E-mail:* webmestre@ehess.fr (office). *Website:* www.ehess.fr.

CHARTRES, Rt Rev. and Rt Hon. Richard John Carew, PC, DD, DLitt, FSA; British ecclesiastic; *The Bishop of London;* b. 11 July 1947; s. of Richard Chartres and Charlotte Chartres; m. Caroline Mary McLintock 1982; two s. two d.; ed Hertford Grammar School, Trinity Coll. Cambridge, Cuddesdon Theological Coll. Oxford and Lincoln Theological Coll.; ordained deacon 1973, priest 1974; Asst Curate, St Andrew's Bedford 1973–75; Domestic Chaplain to Bishop of St Albans 1975–80; Chaplain to Archbishop of Canterbury 1980–84; Vicar, St Stephen with St John, Westminster 1984–92; Dir of Ordinands for London Area 1985–92; Gresham Prof. of Divinity 1986–92; Bishop of Stepney 1992–95, of London 1996–; Dean of the Chapels Royal 1995–; Ecclesiastical Patron Prayer Book Soc.; Prelate of Imperial Soc. of Kt.'s Bachelor; Liveryman Merchant Taylors' Co.; Hon. Freeman Weavers' Co. 1998, Leathersellers' Co. 1999, Woolmen's Co. 2000, Vintners' Co. 2001; Drapers' Co.; Prelate of OBE 1995–; Chair. Churches Main Cttee 1998–2001; Chair. Church Bldgs Div.; Fellow Soc. of Antiquaries 1998; Hon. Bencher, Middle Temple; Hon. DLitt (London Guildhall) 1998, Hon. DD (London) 1999, (City) 1999, (Brunel) 1999. *Publication:* The History of Gresham College 1597–1997 1998, Tree of Knowledge Tree of Life 2005. *Address:* London Diocesan House, 36 Causton Street, London, SW1P 4AU (office); The Old Deanery, Dean's Court, London, EC4V 5AA, England. *Telephone:* (20) 7932-1100 (office); (20) 7248-6233 (home). *Fax:* (20) 7932-1110 (office); (20) 7248-9721 (home). *E-mail:* communications@london.anglican.org (office); bishop@londin.clara.co.uk (office). *Website:* www.london.anglican.org (office).

CHASE, Chevy (Cornelius Crane), MA; American comedian, actor and writer; b. 8 Oct. 1943, New York; s. of Edward Tinsley Chase and Cathalene Crane (née Widdoes) Chase; m. 1st Jacqueline Carlin 1976 (divorced 1980); m. 2nd Jayni Chase; three d.; ed Bard Coll., Inst. of Audio Research, MIT; writer and actor, Channel One (satirical revue), The Great American Dream Machine, co-writer and actor, Lemmings (Nat. Lampoon satirical musical), writer and performer Nat. Lampoon Radio Hour, Saturday Night Live (TV series); writer Mad magazine 1969; mem. American Fed. of Musicians, Stage Actors Guild, Actors Equity, American Fed. of TV and Radio Artists; three Emmy Awards, Writers' Guild of America Award, Man of the Year, Harvard Univ. Theatrical Group 1992. *Films include:* Tunnelvision 1976, Foul Play 1978, Oh Heavenly Dog 1980, Caddyshack 1980, Seems Like Old Times, Under the Rainbow 1981, Modern Problems 1981, Vacation 1983, Deal of the Century 1983, European Vacation 1984, Fletch 1985, Spies Like Us 1985, Follow that Bird 1985, The Three Amigos 1986, Caddyshack II 1988, Funny Farm 1988, Christmas Vacation 1989, Fletch Lives 1989, Memoirs of an Invisible Man 1992, Hero 1992, Last Action Hero 1993, Cops and Robbersons 1994, Man of the House 1995, National Lampoon's Vegas Vacation 1997, Snow Day 1999, Orange County 2002, Bad Meat 2003, Karate Dog (voice) 2004, Goose! 2004, Ellie Parker 2005, Funny Money 2005, Zoom 2006. *Television appearances include:* The Great American Dream Machine, Smothers Brothers Show, Saturday Night Live 1975–77. *Address:* Cornelius Productions, Box 257, Bedford, NY 10506, USA.

CHASE, David, MA; American scriptwriter, television director and producer; b. (David DeCesare), 22 Aug. 1945, Mount Vernon, NY; s. of Henry DeCesare and Norma DeCesare; m. Denise Kelly; one d.; ed Wake Forest Univ., NC, School of Visual Arts, New York, New York Univ., Stanford Univ., Calif.; produced episodes of Northern Exposure and The Rockford Files, among other series; cr. TV series The Sopranos; Mystery Writers of America Special Edgar Award for his entire body of work. *Television includes:* Kolchak: The Night Stalker (series) (writer) 1974–75, The Rockford Files (series) (writer, producer) (Emmy Award 1977) 1976–80, Off the Minnesota Strip (film) (writer, producer) (Emmy Award 1979, Writers Guild of America Award 1980) 1980, Moonlight 1982, Alfred Hitchcock Presents (series) (dir) 1985, Almost Grown (series) (writer, dir) 1988–89, Grave of the Vampire (film) 1972, I'll Fly Away (writer, exec. producer) (Norman Felton Award, Producers Guild of America 1993) 1992–93, Northern Exposure (series) (exec. producer) 1993–95, The Sopranos (series) (writer, exec. producer, dir) (Emmy Award for College episode 1998, Golden Globe Award 1999, Norman Felton Award, Producers Guild of America 2000, Outstanding Directorial Achievement Award, Directors Guild of America 1999, Peabody Award 2000, Drama Series of the Year Award, American Film Inst. 2001, Primetime Emmy for Outstanding Writing for a Drama Series & Outstanding Drama Series, Acad. of TV Arts and Sciences 2007) 1999–2007, The Rockford Files: A Blessing in Disguise (film) (producer) 1995, The Rockford Files: The Punishment and Crime (writer, producer, dir) 1996. *Address:* c/o David Harbert, United Talent Agency, 9560 Wilshire Blvd, Suite 500, Beverly Hills, CA 90212-2401, USA (office).

Telephone: (310) 273-6700 (office). *Fax:* (310) 247-1111 (office). *E-mail:* webmaster@unitedtalent.com (office). *Website:* www.unitedtalent.com (office).

CHASE, Rodney Frank, CBE; business executive; *Chairman, Petrofac Ltd.;* b. 12 May 1943; s. of Norman Maxwell Chase and Barbara Chase; m. Diana Lyle 1968; one s. one d.; with British Petroleum PLC London, joined depts of shipping, refining and marketing, distribution, oil trading, gas; CEO BP Finance, Group Treas.; Chief Financial Officer, fmr Exec. Vice-Pres. BP America Inc., CEO, Chair. 1992–94; CEO BP Exploration Inc. (Western Hemisphere), Man. Dir The British Petroleum Co. PLC (now BP Amoco PLC) 1992–98, Deputy Group Chief Exec. 1998–2003; Deputy Chair. Tesco plc; Chair. Petrofac Ltd 2005–; mem. Bd of Dirs Computer Sciences Corpn, Nalco Co., Tesoro Corpn; fmr Dir (non-exec.) BOC Group PLC, Diageo plc; mem. UK Advisory Cttee on Business and the Environment, UK Roundtable on Sustainable Devt; Bd mem. World Conservation Monitoring Centre; Fellow, Asscn of Corp. Treas. *Leisure interests:* downhill skiing, golf. *Address:* Petrofac Ltd, 117 Jermyn Street, London, SW1 6HH, England (office). *Telephone:* (20) 7811-4900 (office). *Fax:* (20) 7811-4901 (office). *Website:* www.petrofac.com (office).

CHASKALSON, Arthur, SC, BCom, LLB; South African judge; b. 24 Nov. 1931, Johannesburg; s. of Harry Bernard Chaskalson and Mary Dorothea Chaskalson (née Oshry); m. Lorraine Diane Ginsberg 1961; two s.; ed Univ. of Witwatersrand; admitted to Bar 1956, SC 1971; Chair. Johannesburg Bar Council 1976, 1982 (mem. 1967–71, 1973–84); Vice-Chair. Gen. Council of S African Bar 1982–87, Int. Legal Aid Div., Int. Bar Asscn 1983–93; Nat. Dir Legal Resources Centre 1979–93; Hon. Prof. of Law, Univ. of Witwatersrand 1981–95; Visiting Prof., Columbia Univ., New York 1987–88, 2004; Chair. Rhodes Scholarship Selection Cttee for SA 1988–93; consultant to Namibian Constituent Ass. (in relation to the drafting of the Namibian Constitution) 1989–90, to African Nat. Congress (ANC) on drafting S African Constitution 1990–94; mem. Tech. Cttee on Constitutional Issues during the Multi-Party Negotiating Process May–Dec. 1993; Pres. Constitutional Court 1994–; Commr Int. Comm. of Jurists 1995–, Pres. 2001–; Chief Justice 2001–05; mem. Nat. Council of Lawyers for Human Rights 1980–91, Johanneburg Soc. of Advocates, numerous other memberships; Hon. mem. Bar Asscn of New York City 1985, Boston Bar Asscn; Supreme Counsellor of the Baobab (Gold); eight hon. degrees; numerous awards including Human Rights Award (Foundation for Freedom and Human Rights, Switzerland) 1990, Justice Prize, Peter Gruber Foundation 2004. *Address:* 118 Dumbarton Avenue, Athol, Sandton 2196 (home); c/o Constitutional Court, Private Bag X1, Constitutiona Hill, Braamfontein 2017, South Africa. *Telephone:* (11) 359-7425 (office). *Fax:* (11) 403-6063 (office). *E-mail:* chaskalson@concourt.org.za (office).

CHATAH, Mohamad, BA, PhD; Lebanese economist, academic, diplomatist and government official; *Minister of Finance;* b. March 1951, Tripoli; m.; two c.; ed American Univ. of Beirut, Univ. of Texas, USA; Instructor, Dept of Econs, Univ. of Texas 1977–92; advisor to Exec. Dir, IMF 1983–93, advisor on external relations 2000–02, 2003–05, Alt. Exec. Dir 2002–03; Vice-Gov. Cen. Bank of Lebanon 1993–97; Amb. to USA 1997–99; Chief Advisor to Pres. of Council of Ministers 2005–08; Minister of Finance 2008–. *Address:* Ministry of Finance, 4e étage, Immeuble MOF, place Riad es-Solh, Beirut, Lebanon (office). *Telephone:* (1) 981001 (office). *Fax:* (1) 981059 (office). *E-mail:* infocenter@finance.gov.lb (office). *Website:* www.finance.gov.lb (office).

CHATAWAY, Rt Hon. Sir Christopher John, Kt, PC; British fmr politician, fmr athlete and business executive; b. 31 Jan. 1931; m. 1st Anna Lett 1959 (divorced 1975); two s. one d.; m. 2nd Carola Walker 1976; two s.; ed Sherborne School and Magdalen Coll., Oxford; rep. of UK at Olympic Games 1952, 1956, holder of world 5,000m. record 1954; Jr Exec., Arthur Guinness, Son and Co. 1953–55; Staff Reporter, Ind. TV News 1955–56; Current Affairs Commentator, BBC TV 1956–59; mem. London Co. Council 1958–61; MP for Lewisham N 1959–66, for Chichester 1969–74; Parl. Pvt. Sec. to Minister of Power 1961–62; Jt Parl. Under-Sec. of State, Dept of Educ. and Science 1962–64; Leader, Inner London Educ. Authority 1967–69; Minister of Posts and Telecommunications 1970–72, for Industrial Devt 1972–74; Man. Dir Orion Royal Bank 1974–88; Chair. Civil Aviation Authority 1991–96, UK Athletics 1999–2000, Bletchley Park Trust 2000–08; Dir BET PLC 1974–96; Hon. Treas., later Chair., ActionAid 1974–2000; Trustee, Foundation for Sport and the Arts 1991–; Pres. Commonwealth Games Council for England 1992–2009; Hon. DLitt (Loughborough) 1980, (Macquarie Univ., Australia) 2000; Hon. DSc (Cranfield) 1985. *Address:* 21B Warwick Avenue, London, W9 2PS, England. *E-mail:* cjchataway@hotmail.com.

CHATER, Keith Frederick, PhD, FRS; British geneticist and academic; *Emeritus Fellow, Department of Molecular Biology, The John Innes Centre;* b. 23 April 1944, Croydon, Surrey; s. of Frederick Ernest Chater and Marjorie Inez Chater (née Palmer); m. Jean Wallbridge 1966; three s. one d.; ed Trinity School of John Whitgift, Croydon, Univ. of Birmingham; scientist, The John Innes Centre 1969–, Deputy Head, Dept of Genetics 1989–98, Head 1998–2001, Head, Dept of Molecular Microbiology 2001–04, Emer. Fellow 2004–; Hon. Prof., Univ. of East Anglia 1988–, Chinese Acad. of Sciences Inst. of Microbiology, Beijing 1998–, Huazhong Agricultural Univ., Wuhan 2000–; Fred Griffith Review Lecturer, Soc. for Gen. Microbiology 1997, Leeuwenhoek Lecturer, Royal Soc. 2005. *Publications:* Genetic Manipulation of Streptomyces (ed jtly) 1985, Genetics of Bacterial Diversity (jtly) 1989, Practical Streptomyces Genetics 2000. *Leisure interests:* art, birdwatching, gardening, cooking. *Address:* Department of Molecular Microbiology, John Innes Centre, Norwich Research Park, Colney, Norwich, NR4 7UH (office); 6 Coach House Court, Norwich, NR4 7QR, England (home). *Telephone:* (1603) 450297 (office); (1603) 506145 (home). *Fax:* (1603) 450045 (office). *E-mail:* keith.chater@bbsrc

.ac.uk (office); keithchater@yahoo.com (home). *Website:* www.jic.bbsrc.ac.uk/staff/keith-chater.

CHATIKAVANIJ, Korn, BA, MA; Thai investment banker and politician; *Minister of Finance;* b. 19 Feb. 1964; ed Srinakharinwirot Univ., Univ. of Oxford, UK; worked for S.G. Warburg & Co., London 1982–85; Founder and Pres. JF Thanakom Securities Ltd 1985–2000, Pres. J.P. Morgan (Thailand) Ltd (after take–over of JF Thanakom Securities Ltd by J.P. Morgan) 2000–04; mem. Sapha Poothaen Rassadorn (House of Reps) for Bangkok 2005–; Minister of Finance 2008–; mem. Democratic Party, currently Deputy Sec.-Gen. *Address:* Ministry of Finance, Thanon Rama VI, Samsennai, Phaya Thai, Rajatevi, Bangkok 10400 (office); 57 Yen-Arkart Road, Chongnonsi, Yannawa District, Bangkok, Thailand. *Telephone:* (2) 273-9021 (office). *Fax:* (2) 273-9408 (office). *E-mail:* prinya@mof.go.th (office); info@korndemocrat.com. *Website:* www.mof.go.th (office); www.korndemocrat.com.

CHATT, Amares, BSc, MSc, PhD; Canadian (b. Indian) nuclear chemist and academic; *Adjunct Professor, Department of Chemistry, Dalhousie University;* b. (Amares Chattopadhyay), S India; ed Univ. of Calcutta, Indian Inst. of Tech., Roorkee, Univ. of Waterloo, Univ. of Toronto; joined Dept of Chem., Univ. of Dalhousie, Halifax, NS c. 1975, becoming Prof., also Dir Dalhousie Slowpoke-2 Nuclear Research Reactor, Faculty of Science Killam Prof. in Chem. 2001–06, now Adjunct Prof.; fmr Adviser, IAEA, Vienna; Fellow, Chemical Inst. of Canada 1985–, American Nuclear Soc. 1993–; Francis W. Karasek Award 1993, American Nuclear Soc. William D. Ehmann Award 1999, George Hevesy Medal 2001. *Address:* Department of Chemistry, Dalhousie University, Halifax, NS B3H 4J3, Canada (office). *Telephone:* (902) 494-2474 (office). *Fax:* (902) 494-1310 (office). *E-mail:* a.chatt@dal.ca (office). *Website:* chemistry.dal.ca (office); myweb.dal.ca/chatt (office).

CHATTERJEE, Somnath, MA; Indian politician, lawyer and trade union official; *Speaker of Lok Sabha; Leader, Communist Party of India—Marxist;* b. 25 July 1929, Tezpur, Assam; m. Renu Chatterjee; one s. two d.; ed Calcutta (now Kolkata) Univ., Univ. of Cambridge and Middle Temple, UK; mem. Communist Party of India—Marxist (CPI—M) 1968–, currently Leader; mem. Lok Sabha 1971–, Chair. Cttee on Subordinate Legislation 1977–79, 1991–93, Cttee on Privileges 1990–91, Cttee on Railways 1993–96, Cttee on Communications 1996–97, 1998–99, Leader of CPI—M in Lok Sabha 1991–97, Speaker 2004–; Chair. Bengal Table Tennis Asscn, Life Saving Soc., Kolkata; mem. Cricket Asscn of Bengal, India Int. Centre; Outstanding Parliamentarian Award 1996. *Leisure interests:* gardening, reading, sports. *Address:* Speaker's Office, Lok Sabha Secretariat, 17 Parliament House, New Delhi 110 001, India (office). *Telephone:* (11) 23017795 (office). *Fax:* (11) 23792927 (home). *E-mail:* speakerloksabha@sansad.nic.in (office). *Website:* www .speakerloksabha.nic.in (office).

CHATTERJEE, Soumitra, (Soumitra Chattopadhyay); Indian actor; b. 19 Jan. 1935, Padma Bhushan 2004, Rajat Kamal (Silver Lotus Award) for Best Actor, Nat. Film Awards (Govt of India) 2007. *Films include:* Apur Sansar (The World of Apu) 1959, Kshudista Pashan (Hungry Stones) 1960, Devi (The Goddess) 1960, Teen Kanya 1961, Punasha (Over Again) 1961, Atal Jaler Ahwan (1962), Abhijaan (The Expedition) 1962, Saat Pake Bandha 1963, Charulata (The Lonely Wife) 1964, Kapurush (The Coward) 1965, Kanch Kata Hirey 1965, Ek Tuku Basa 1965, Akash Kusum (Up in the Clouds) 1965, Prastar Swakshar 1967, Mahashweta 1967, Baghini 1968, Teen Bhuboner Porey 1969, Parineeta (The Fiancee) 1969, Aparachita 1969, Aranyer Din Ratri (Days and Nights in the Forest, USA) 1970, Malyadaan 1971, KhunjeyBerai 1971, Stree 1972, Ashani Sanket (Distant Thunder, USA) 1973, Basanata Bilap 1973, Jadi Jantem 1974, Sonar Kella (The Golden Fortress, USA) 1974, Sangini 1974, Asati 1974, Sansar Seemantey 1975, Datta 1976, Joi Baba Felunath (The Elephant God) 1978, Ganadevata 1979, Naukadubi 1979, Debdas 1979, Heerak Rajar Deshe (The Kingdom of Diamonds) (TV) 1980, Khelar Putul 1981, Amar Geeti 1983, Ghare-Baire (The Home and the World) 1984, Kony 1984, Shyam Saheb 1986, Ekti Jiban (Portrait of a Life) 1987, La Nuit Bengali (Bengali Night) 1988, Ganashatru (An Enemy of the People, UK) 1989, Shakha Proshakha (Tyhe Branches of the Tree) 1990, Mahaprithivi (World Within, World Without) 1992, Wheel Chair 1994, Uttoran (The Broken Journey) 1994, Sopan 1994, Vrindavan Film Studios 1996, Gaach (The Tree) (as himself) 1998, Asukh (Malaise) 1999, Paromitar Ek Din 2000, Dekha 2001, Saanjhbatir Roopkathara (Strokes and Silhouettes) 2002, Abar Aranye (In the Forest Again) 2003, Patalghar 2003, Nil Sanket (Tryst of Blue) 2004, Schatten der Zeit 2004, Faltu 2005, Nishijapon 2005, 15 Park Avenue 2005, The Bong Connection 2006, Podokkhep 2006.

CHAU, Nguyen Thanh, MA; Vietnamese diplomatist; b. 17 Sept. 1945, Phu Tho; m.; two c.; ed Australian Nat. Univ.; Lecturer, Inst. of Int. Relations, Ministry of Foreign Affairs, Hanoi; Second Sec., Perm. Mission to UN, New York 1983–86; various positions with Viet Nam Comm. for UNESCO including Sec.-Gen. 1987–92; Amb. to Australia (also accred to NZ, Papua New Guinea, Vanuatu and Fiji) 1992–96; Dir Int. Orgs Div., Ministry of Foreign Affairs 1996–2000; Perm. Rep. to UN, New York 2000–04. *Address:* c/o Ministry of Foreign Affairs, 1 Ton That Dam, Ba Dinh District, Hanoi, Viet Nam. *Telephone:* (4) 8452980. *Fax:* (4) 82318725. *E-mail:* banbientap@mofa .gov.vn. *Website:* www.mofa.gov.vn.

CHAUDHRY, Amir Husain; Pakistani lawyer and politician; b. 1942, Jammu, India; mem. Nat. Ass. 1985–2008, Speaker 2002–08; mem. Council, Azad Jammu and Kashmir Council 1985–90; Vice-Pres. Muslim Conf., Azad Jammu 1985–90; mem. Pakistan Muslim League. *Address:* c/o Pakistan Muslim League, PML House, F-7/3, Islamabad, Pakistan (office).

CHAUDHRY, Iftikhar Mohammad, BA, LLB; Pakistani judge; *Chief Justice;* b. 12 Dec. 1948, Quetta; s. of Jan Muhammad Chaudhry; called to Bar 1974;

enrolled as Advocate of the High Court 1976, Advocate of the Supreme Court 1985; Advocate Gen., Balochistan 1989–90; Additional Judge, Balochistan High Court 1990–99, also served as Banking Judge, Judge of Special Court for Speedy Trials, Judge of Customs Appellate Courts and Company Judge; Chief Justice High Court of Balochistan 1999–2000; elevated to Supreme Court 2000, Chief Justice of Pakistan 2005–March 2007, reinstated July–Nov. 2007 (suspended for refusing to ratify Pres. Musharraf's emergency rule), reinstated March 2009; Pres. High Court Bar Asscn, Quetta; Chair. Balochistan Local Council Election Authority 1992–, Prov. Review Bd for Balochistan, Enrolment Cttee of Pakistan Bar Council, Supreme Court Bldg Cttee; fmr Chair. Pakistan Red Crescent Soc., Balochistan; mem. Bar Council; Lawyer of the Year, National Law Journal 2007, Medal of Freedom, Harvard Law School Asscn 2007. *Address:* Supreme Court of Pakistan, Constitution Avenue, Islamabad (office); 54-B Zarghon Road, Quetta, Pakistan (home). *Telephone:* (51) 9220581 (office). *Fax:* (51) 9213452 (office). *Website:* www.supremecourt.gov.pk (office).

CHAUDHRY, Mahendra Pal; Fijian politician; *Secretary General, Fiji Labour Party;* b. 2 Sept. 1942, Ba, Fiji; s. of the late Ram Gopal Chaudhry and Devi Chaudhry (née Nair); two s. one d.; Sr Auditor, Office of the Auditor Gen. 1960–75; Gen. Sec. Nat. Farmers' Union 1978–; Gen. Sec. Fiji Public Service Asscn 1970–99; Nat. Sec. Fiji Trades Union Congress 1988–92; Minister of Finance April–May 1987 (ousted in May 1987 coup), Founding mem. Fiji Labour Party 1985, Parliamentary Leader 1992, Sec.-Gen. 1994–; Prime Minister and Minister of Finance, Public Enterprise, Sugar Industry and Information 1999–2000; ousted in coup by George Speight May 2000; reassumed post of Prime Minister 1 March 2001, dismissed 14 March 2001 by Pres. of Fiji; Leader of the Opposition 2004–; Minister of Finance, National Planning, Public Enterprise and Sugar Reform (in Cdre Josaia Bainimarama's interim govt) Jan. 2007–08 (resgnd); Bharatiya Samman Award, Govt of India 2004. *Leisure interests:* reading, music, gardening, social work. *Address:* Fiji Labour Party, PO Box 2162, Suva (office); 6 Albert Lee Place, Nailuva Road, Suva (office); 3 Hutson Street, Suva, Fiji (home). *Telephone:* 3305811 ext. 405 (office); 301875 (home). *Fax:* 3305317 (office). *E-mail:* flp@connect.com.fj (office); mahendrachaudhry42@hotmail.com (home). *Website:* www.flp.org.fj (office).

CHAUDHRY, Air Vice-Marshal Shahzad Aslam, MSc; Pakistani air force officer (retd) and diplomatist; *High Commissioner to Sri Lanka;* m.; five c.; ed Air Command and Staff Coll., USA, Nat. Defence Coll., Islamabad; served in various command/staff and instructional roles during air force career including Officer Commanding F-16 Squadron 1987–89, Officer Commanding F-16 Wing 1996–97, Base Commdr, Pakistan Air Force Base, Rafiqui 2000–02, Air Officer Commanding Southern Air Command 2003, Deputy Chief of Air Staff (Operations), Pakistan Air Force 2003–06; Air Attaché, Pakistan High Comm., London 1992–96; High Commr to Sri Lanka 2006–; mem. UN Asscn of Sri Lanka; Hilal-e-Imtiaz (Mil.), Sitara-e-Imtiaz (Mil.), Tamgha-e-Basalat, Professional Efficiency Badge. *Address:* High Commission of Pakistan, No. 211 De Saram Place, Colombo 10, Sri Lanka (office). *Telephone:* (11) 2696301 (office). *Fax:* (11) 2695780 (office). *E-mail:* parepcolombo@sltnet.lk (office). *Website:* www.mfa.gov.pk/Green_Book/Srilanka_GB.htm (office).

CHAUHAN, Shivraj Singh, MA; Indian politician; *Chief Minister of Madhya Pradesh;* b. 5 March 1959, Jait village, Sehore Dist; s. of Shri Prem Singh Chouhan and Smt. Sundar Bai Chouhan; m. Smt. Sadhana Singh 1992; two s.; ed Barkatullah Univ., Bhopal; Pres. Model Higher Secondary School Students Union 1975; participated in underground movt against Emergency 1976–77, imprisoned in Bhopal Jail; joined Rashtriya Swayamsevak Sangh (Nat. Volunteers' Union—Hindu nationalist org.) 1977; Organizing Sec. Akhil Bhartiya Vidyarthi Parishad (ABVP) 1977–78, Jt Sec. ABVP 1978–80, Gen. Sec. 1980–83, mem. Nat. Exec. of ABVP 1982–83; Jt Sec. Bhartiya Janta Yuva Morcha (BJYM) 1984–85, Gen. Sec. BJYM, Madhya Pradesh (MP) 1985–88, Pres. BJYM, MP 1988–91, Gen. Sec. All India BJYM 1992–, Nat. Pres. 2000–03; mem. Bharatiya Janata Party (BJP), fmr Pres. MP state party unit, Gen. Sec. BJP, MP 1992–94, 1997–98, later Nat. Sec. BJP, Pres. BJP, MP 2005–; elected to State Ass. from Budhni Constituency 1990–91; a convener of Akhil Bhartiya Keshariya Vahini 1991–92; five-time MP (Lok Sabha—Lower House of Parl.) 1991–, first representing Vidisha, currently represents Budhni, Sehore Dist, MP in State Ass., mem. Cttee, Ministry of Human Resources Devt 1992–96, mem. Cttee on Labour and Welfare 1993–96, mem. Hindi Salahkar Samiti 1994–1996, mem. Cttee on Urban and Rural Devt, mem. Consultative Cttee, Ministry of Human Resources Devt 1996–97, mem. Cttee on Urban and Rural Devt and its Sub-Cttee on Ministry of Rural Areas and Employment 1998–99, mem. Cttee on Agric. 1999–2000, mem. Cttee on Public Undertakings 1999–2001, Chair. House Cttee (Lok Sabha), mem. Consultative Cttee, Ministry of Communications 2000–04, mem. Cttee on Agric. 2004, mem. Jt Cttee on Offices of Profit 2004, Sec. Parl. Bd 2004, Sec. (Cen. Election Cttee), Chair. Housing Cttee 2004, mem. Cttee on Ethics 2004; Chief Minister of MP 2005–; Gold Medal in Philosophy, Barkatullah Univ. *Leisure interests:* music, spiritual literature, debates and discussions with friends, sight-seeing, watching movies, Kabaddi (a team sport originally from S Asia), cricket, volleyball. *Address:* Office of the Chief Minister, Bhopal, Madhya Pradesh (office); 1 Shyamla Hills, Bhopal, Madhya Pradesh, India (home). *Telephone:* (755) 2441581 (office); (755) 2442231 (home). *E-mail:* cm@mp.gov.in (office). *Website:* www.mp.gov.in (office).

CHAUNU, Pierre, DèsL; French academic; *Professor Emeritus of Modern History, Université Paris-Sorbonne;* b. 17 Aug. 1923, Belleville, Meuse; m. Huguette Catella 1947; two s. (one deceased) four d.; ed Lycées de Metz and Rouen, Sorbonne Univ., Ecole des Hautes Etudes Hispaniques, Madrid and Seville; teacher, Bar-le-Duc Lycée 1947; joined School of Advanced Hispanic Studies, Madrid 1948–51; teacher, Michelet de Vanves Lycée 1951–56; researcher CNRS 1956–59, now mem. Directorate; Lecturer Univ. de Caen 1959–71; Prof. of Modern History, Univ. de Paris à la Sorbonne 1971–, now Prof. Emer.; Assoc. Prof., Faculté de Théologie Réformée, Aix-en-Provence 1974; mem. of Section, Conseil Econ. et Social 1976–77; Pres. Conseil Supérieur des Corps Universitaires 1977; Columnist Le Figaro 1982–; mem. Social and Econ. Council 1976–; Vice-Pres. Scientific Cttee (history section), CNRS 1957–1991, numerous other cttees; Pres. Fed. Nat. des syndicats autonomes de l'enseignement supérieur 1988–90; mem. Acad. des Sciences morales et politiques 1982– (Pres. 1993), High Council for Integration 1994–; Commdr, Légion d'honneur 1999, Commdr des Palmes Académiques 1999. *Publications:* forty books including: Seville et l'Atlantique (1504–1650) (12 vols), Le Pacifique des Ibériques, Civilisation de l'Europe classique, Civilisation de l'Europe des lumières, Temps des Réformes, L'Espagne de Charles Quint, La Mort à Paris, Histoire et Prospective, La Mémoire et le sacré, Le refus de la vie, La violence de Dieu, Un futur sans avenir, La mémoire de l'éternité, Le sursis 1979, Histoire et foi, Histoire et imagination 1980, Réforme et contre-réforme, Eglise, Culture et Société, Histoire et Décadence 1981, La France 1982, Ce que je crois 1982, Le chemin des mages 1983, Combats pour l'histoire 1983, L'historien dans tous ses états 1984, L'historien en cet instant 1985, Rétrohistoire, Au coeur religieux de l'histoire, L'aventure de la réforme 1986, Une autre voie (jtly.) 1986, Du Big Bang à l'enfant 1987, L'obscure mémoire de la France 1988, Apologie pour l'histoire 1988, Le grand déclassement 1989, Journal de Jean Héroard 1989, Trois millions d'années, Quatre-vingts millards de destins 1990, Reflets et miroir de l'histoire 1990, Colère contre Colère 1991, Dieu, Apologie 1991, L'Aventure de la Réforme, Le monde de Jean Calvin 1992, Brève histoire de Dieu 1992, l'Axe du temps 1994, l'Instant éclaté 1994, Les Enjeux de la Paix 1995, L'Héritage 1995, Baptême de Clovis, Baptême de la France 1996, Danse avec l'histoire 1998, Le Basculement religieux de Paris 1998, Charles Quint 2000, La Femme et Dieu 2001, Essai de Prospective Démographique 2003, Leçons pour la paix 2006; 120 articles. *Address:* Université Paris-Sorbonne, 1 rue Victor-Cousin, 75230 Paris Cedex 05 (office); 12 rue des Cordeliers, 14000 Caen, France (home). *Telephone:* 2-31-86-61-51 (Caen) (home).

CHAUTALA, Om Prakash; Indian politician; *Leader, Indian National Lok Dal;* b. 1 Jan. 1935; Chief Minister of Haryana 1989, 1990, 1999, 2000–05; Pres. Haryana Unit, Indian Nat. Lok Dal 1999; Pres. Haryana State Janata Dal; Nat. Gen. Sec. Samajwadi Janata Party; Leader, Indian Nat. Lok Dal party (later United National Progressive Alliance, after merger with other regional parties). *Address:* Indian National Lok Dal, 18 Janpath, New Delhi 110 001, India (office). *Telephone:* (11) 23793409 (office).

CHAUVIN, Yves; French chemist; *Honorary Director of Research, Institut Francais du Petrole;* b. 10 Oct. 1930; ed École supérieure de chimie-physique-électronique (CPE), Lyon; Research Engineer, Institut Francais du Petrole 1960, later Head of Research, apptd Dir of Research 1991, currently Hon. Dir of Research; Emer. Dir of Research, École supérieure de chimie-physique-électronique, Lyon; mem. French Acad. of Sciences; Académie des sciences Prix Clavel-Lespiau 1990, German Scientific Soc. for Coal and Petroleum Research Karl Engler Medal 1994, Nobel Prize in Chem. (jtly) 2005. *Publications:* Progress in Polymer Science 1977. *Address:* Institut Francais du Petrole, 1 & 4 avenue de Bois-Préau, 92852 Rueil-Malmaison (office); Laboratoire de Chimie Organométallique de Surface, CPE Lyon, 43 Bd du 11 Novembre 1918, 69622 Villeurbanne cedex, France (office). *Telephone:* 1-47-52-60-00 (office); 4-72-43-17-94 (office). *Fax:* 1-47-52-70-00 (office); 4-72-43-17-95 (office). *Website:* www.cpe.fr/lcoms (office).

CHAUVIRÉ, Yvette; French ballerina; b. 22 April 1917, Paris; d. of Henri Chauviré and Berthe Pinchard; ed Paris Opera Ballet School; joined Paris Opera Ballet 1930, Danseuse Etoile 1941, Prima Ballerina Assoluta; with Monte Carlo Opera Ballet 1946–47; Artistic and Tech. Adviser to Admin. of Paris Opera 1963–68; Dir Acad. int. de danse, Paris 1970; Pres. Europa Danse 1999–; Commdr de la Légion d'honneur; Commdr des Arts et Lettres; Grand Officier, Ordre nat. du Mérite 1994; Grand Croix 1998. *Ballets include:* Istar, Les deux pigeons, Sleeping Beauty, David triomphant, Giselle, Les créatures de Prométhée, Roméo et Juliette, L'écuyère, Les suites romantiques, Lac des cygnes, L'oiseau de feu, Petrouchka, Sylvia, La belle Hélène, Casse-Noisette, Les mirages, Le cygne, La dame aux camélias. *Films include:* Carrousel Napolitain 1953, Le cygne 1984, Une étoile pour l'exemple. *Publications:* Je suis ballerine (autobiog.) 1961. *Leisure interests:* drawings, watercolours, collecting swans. *Address:* c/o Anne Forgeron, 21 rue Chevert, 75007 Paris, France (office). *Telephone:* 1-45-55-66-27 (office). *Fax:* 1-45-51-27-32 (office).

CHAVALIT, Gen. Yongchaiyudh; Thai politician and army officer (retd); b. 15 May 1932, Bangkok; m. Khunying Phankrua Yongchaiyudh; ed Chulachomklao Royal Mil. Acad., Army Command and Gen. Staff Coll., Fort Leavenworth, Kan., USA; Dir of Operations 1981, Chief of Staff 1985, C-in-C 1986–90, Acting Supreme Commdr 1987–90; Deputy Prime Minister and Minister of Defence 30 March–21 June 1990; Opposition Leader May–Sept. 1992; Minister of Interior 1992–94, of Labour and Social Welfare 1993–94; Deputy Prime Minister July–Oct 1994, Deputy Prime Minister and Minister of Defence 1995–96, 2001–02, 2008 (resgnd); Prime Minister and Minister of Defence 1996–97 (resgnd); Deputy Prime Minister 2008 (resgnd); fmr Leader New Aspiration Party (now Muan Chon party). *Address:* c/o Muan Chon, 630/182 Thanon Prapinklao, Bangkok 10700, Thailand (office).

CHAVAN, Ashok Shankarrao, MBA; Indian politician; *Chief Minister of Maharashtra;* b. 28 Oct. 1958, Mumbai; s. of Shankarrao B. Chavan and Kusumtai Chavan; m. Ameeta Ashok Chavan; two d.; MP (Indian Nat. Congress) for Nanded constituency 1987–; MLC from Maharashtra Legis. Ass. Constituency 1992–, Minister of State for Public Works, Urban Devt and Home 1993, Minister for Transport, Ports, Cultural Affairs and Protocol 2003; Minister of Revenue, Maharashtra Region 1999–2004, also Minister of

www.worldwhoswho.com

Cultural Affairs 2004–, of Industries 2004–, of Mines 2004–, of Protocol 2004–, Chief Minister 2008–; Gen. Sec. Maharashtra Pradesh Congress Cttee 1995–99; Pres. Sai Sevabhavi Trust, Nanded. *Address:* Office of the Chief Minister, Government of Maharashtra, Mantralaya, Mumbai 400 032, India (office). *Telephone:* (22) 22025151 (office). *Fax:* (22) 22029214 (office). *E-mail:* chiefminister@maharashtra.gov.in (office). *Website:* maharashtraonline.in (office).

CHAVANAVIRAJ, Saroj, BA, MA; Thai government official and fmr diplomatist; b. 11 May 1942; ed UCLA, Nat. Defence Coll. of Thailand; joined Ministry of Foreign Affairs 1967, Third Sec., Protocol Div. 1967–69, Asst Sec. to Minister, Office of Sec. to the Minister 1969–72; Second Sec., Perm. Mission to UN, New York 1972–76; Chief of East Asian Div., Political Dept, Ministry of Foreign Affairs 1976–77, Asst Sec. to the Minister, Office of the Sec. to the Minister 1977–79, Deputy Dir-Gen. Dept of Political Affairs 1979–80, Dir-Gen. Dept of Int. Orgs 1980–83; Chair. Social Cttee 38th Session of UN Gen Ass., New York 1983; Amb. to Singapore 1983–86; Dir-Gen. Dept of Information, Ministry of Foreign Affairs 1986–88, Dir-Gen. Dept of ASEAN Affairs 1988–90, Dir-Gen. Dept of Political Affairs 1990–92, Deputy Perm. Sec., Office of Perm. Sec. 1992–96, Perm. Sec., Ministry of Foreign Affairs 1996–2000; Amb. to France 2000–02; Advisor to Foreign Minister 2002–08; Minister for Foreign Affairs Sept. 2008; Hon. MBE (UK) 1972, Knight Grand Cordon (Special Class) of the Most Noble Order of the Crown of Thailand 1988, Order of the Sacred Treasure, Gold and Silver Star (Japan) 1991, Knight Grand Cordon (Special Class) of the Most Exalted Order of the White Elephant 1993, Hon. KCMG (UK) 1997, Knight Commander (Second Class, lower grade) of the Most Illustrious Order of Chula Chom Klao 2002. *Address:* c/o Ministry of Foreign Affairs, Thanon Sri Ayudhya, Bangkok 10400, Thailand (office).

CHÁVEZ FRIAS, Adán, BSc, MA; Venezuelan government official; *Governor of Barinas;* b. 1953, Estado de Mérida; brother of Pres. Hugo Chávez Frias; fmr mem. Ruptura political movt; Founding mem. Movimento Bolivariano Revolucionario 2000, Movimento Quinta República 2000 (MVR); Nat. Dir MVR 2001–, also responsible for electoral policy; elected to Nat. Constituent Ass. for Meridá 2001, served as Vice-Pres. Comisión de Disposiciones Transitorias, Pres. Sub-Comm. for Domestic Policy in Comisión Legislativa Nacional, Pvt. Sec. to Pres. Hugo Chávez; Amb. to Cuba –2006; Presidential Chief of Staff 2006–07; Minister of Educ. 2007–08; Gov. of Barinas 2008–; Pres. Inst. Nacional de Tierras 2001. *Address:* Office of the Governor, Barinas, Estado Barinas, Venezuela (office). *Website:* www.barinas.net.ve (office).

CHÁVEZ FRÍAS, Lt-Col Hugo Rafael, MA; Venezuelan politician and head of state; *President;* b. 28 July 1954, Sabaneta, Barinas State; s. of Hugo de los Reyes Chávez and Elena de Chávez; m. 1st (divorced); three d.; m. 2nd María Isabel Rodríguez (divorced); one d.; ed Liceo O'Leary, Barinas State, Mil. Acad., Univ. Simón Bolívar, Caracas; f. Movimiento Bolivariano Revolucionario 1982; Lt-Col Venezuelan Paratroops 1990; led failed mil. coup against Pres. Carlos Pérez 1992; f. Movimiento Revolucionario V República 1998; represents Patriotic Pole coalition; Pres. of Venezuela 1999–12 April 2002, 14 April 2002–; Estrella de Carabobo Cruz de las Fuerzas Terrestres, Orden Militar Francisco de Miranda, Orden Militar Rafael Urdaneta, Orden Militar Libertador V Clase. *Film appearance:* The War on Democracy (documentary) 2007. *Publication:* Cómo salir del Laberinto? (co-author) 1992. *Address:* Central Information Office of the Presidency, Torre Oeste 18°, Parque Central, Caracas 1010, Venezuela. *Telephone:* (2) 572-7110. *Fax:* (2) 572-2675.

CHAVUNDUKA, Gordon Lloyd, MA, PhD; Zimbabwean academic and politician; *Professor Emeritus, University of Zimbabwe;* b. 16 Aug. 1931, Umtali (now Mutare); s. of Solomon and Lillian Chavunduka; m. Rachel Chavunduka 1959; two s. four d.; ed Univ. of California, Los Angeles, Univs of Manchester and London, UK; Lecturer in Sociology, Univ. of Rhodesia, Salisbury 1966–78, Acting Head, Dept of Sociology 1974–75, Head 1978–86; mem. Univ. Senate 1972–96; Dean, Faculty of Social Studies 1978–88, 1991; Pro-Vice-Chancellor, Univ. of Zimbabwe 1991–92, Vice-Chancellor 1992–96; Prof. Emer. 1997–; joined Movt for Democratic Change 1999, fmr mem. Nat. Policy Council and Sec. for Traditional Leaders, mem. Nat. Exec. Cttee 2007–, also Sec. for Nat. Integration; Zimbabwe Govt Commr for Public Enterprises 1988–90; Sec.-Gen. African Nat. Council 1973–76; Pres. Asscn of Univ. Teachers of Rhodesia 1974–, Zimbabwe Nat. Traditional Healers Asscn (Zinatha) 1980–; Chair. Traditional Medical Practitioners Council 1983–. *Publications:* Traditional Healers and the Shona Patient, Professionalisation of African Medicine, Traditional Medicine in Modern Zimbabwe; also papers in the field of sociology and contribs. to INCIDI, The Society of Malawi Journal, etc. *Leisure interests:* gardening, boxing (spectator), football. *Address:* Movement for Democratic Change, Harvest House, 6th Floor, cnr Angwa St and Nelson Mandela Ave, Harare (office); 40 The Chase, Mount Pleasant, Harare, Zimbabwe (home). *Telephone:* 332958. *Website:* www.mdczimbabwe.org (office).

CHAZAL, Gilles; French museum director; *Director, Petit Palais, Paris;* fmr Lecturer in Art History, Catholic Inst. of Paris; Chief Curator, Petit Palais—Musée des Beaux-Arts de la ville de Paris 1979–98, Museum Dir 1998–. *Publications:* Pérou, l'art de Chavín aux Incas (with Patrick Lemasson) 2006, numerous contribs to art journals and books. *Address:* Petit Palais—Musée des Beaux-Arts de la ville de Paris, Avenue Winston Churchill, 75008 Paris, France (office). *Telephone:* 1-53-43-40-00 (office). *E-mail:* gilles.chazal@paris.fr (office). *Website:* www.petitpalais.paris.fr (office).

CHAZOT, Georges-Christian; French business executive; *Chairman, Prosegur France;* b. 19 March 1939, Algiers; s. of Raymond Chazot and Suzanne Monnet; m. Marie-Dominique Tremois 1962; one s. two d.; ed Lycée Bugeaud, Algiers, Ecole Polytechnique, Paris, Harvard Int. Marketing Inst. and MSEE Univ. of Florida; electronic engineer EMR Sarasota, Florida 1962; Man., Space Electronics, Schlumberger 1965–68, Tech. Dir for Industrial Control 1968–70, Commercial Dir for Instruments and Systems 1970–74, Audio-professional Dir-Gen. 1974–76; Dir-Gen. for Alkaline Accumulators, SAFT 1976–80, Dir-Gen. 1981–83, Pres., Dir-Gen. 1983–88, Hon. Pres. and Admin. 1989; Pres., Dir-Gen. Centre d'Etudes et de Services pour le Développement Industriel (CEI) 1983–86; Vice-Pres., Dir-Gen. Télic Alcatel and Opus Alcatel 1989–90; Pres., Dir-Gen. Alcatel Business Systems 1990–91; Pres. Business Systems Group, Vice-Pres. Alcatel NV 1990–92; Pres., Dir-Gen. Adia France 1992–94; Group Man. Dir Eurotunnel 1994–2000, Chair. Eurotunnel Developments Ltd 2002–04; Chair. GCC Consultants 2001–, Prosegur France 2003–; Vice-Pres. French Chamber of Commerce in GB –2000; Chair. Paris Notre-Dame magazine 2001–; Vice-Chair. Radio Notre Dame 2001–; Dir X-PM Transition Partners 2001–, Giat Industries 2002–; Fellow, Chartered Inst. of Transport; Chevalier, Légion d'honneur 1990; Officier, Ordre nat. du Mérite 1996. *Leisure interests:* opera, sailing, skiing. *Address:* 24 rue de Réservoirs, 78000 Versailles (home); Prosegur France, 21 rue Calmette, 78 Jouy en Josas, France (office). *Telephone:* 1-30-67-75-10 (office); 1-30-21-83-14 (home). *Fax:* 1-30-67-74-91 (office); 1-30-21-83-14 (home). *E-mail:* georges.chazot@fr.prosegur.com (office); georges-christian.chazot@wanadoo.fr (home). *Website:* www.prosegur.fr (office).

CHAZOV, Yevgeny Ivanovich, MD, PhD; Russian politician and cardiologist; *General Director, Russian Cardiology Research Complex, Federal Health and Social Development Agency;* b. 10 June 1929, Gorky; ed Kiev Medical Inst.; mem. CPSU 1962–91, mem. Cen. Cttee 1982–90; Sr Scientific Worker, Inst. of Therapy 1959; Deputy Dir Inst. of Therapy, USSR Acad. of Medical Science 1963–65, Dir Inst. of Cardiology 1965–67; Deputy Minister of Public Health 1967–87, Minister 1987–91; mem. Supreme Soviet 1974–89; Gen. Dir Cardiology Research Complex, Fed. Health and Social Devt Agency 1975–; personal physician to Brezhnev, Andropov, Chernenko and Gorbachev; mem. USSR (now Russian) Acad. of Medical Sciences 1971, USSR (now Russian) Acad. of Sciences 1979; Pres. USSR (now Russian) Soc. of Cardiology 1975; Co-Pres. Int. Physicians for Prevention of Nuclear War (IPPNW) 1980–87 (IPPNW awarded Nobel Prize for Peace 1985); mem. acads of USA, Germany, Hungary, Serbia, Mexico, Poland, Romania; Hon. mem. World Albert Schweitzer Medical Acad.; State Prize 1969, 1976, Hero of Socialist Labour 1978, Lenin Prize 1982, UNESCO Peace Prize 1984, State Prize 2004. *Publications:* Myocardial Infarction (with others) 1971, Cardiac Rhythm Disorders 1972, Anti-coagulants and Fibrinolytics 1977, Health and Power (memoirs) and other monographs; over 500 articles on cardiology. *Leisure interests:* hunting, photography. *Address:* Russian Cardiology Research Complex, 121552 Moscow, 3D Cherepkovskaya Street 15A, Russia (office). *Telephone:* (495) 415-00-25 (office). *Fax:* (495) 414-61-13 (office). *E-mail:* Rcardio-Chazov@list.ru (office).

CHE, Yingxin, BA; Chinese banking executive; *Chairman of the Board of Supervisors, Agricultural Bank of China;* b. 1954, Henan Prov.; ed Henan Banking School, Henan CCP Party School; held posts at various local brs of People's Bank of China (PBC), Henan Prov., including Lushi Co. Br. and Luoyang, Sanmenxia and Xinyang Municipal Brs 1980–92, Vice-Pres. Prov. Br., PBC, Henan Prov. 1992–97, Deputy Dir-Gen. Auditing Dept, PBC 1997–98, Dir-Gen. Staff Compliance Dept, PBC 1998–2003, Deputy Disciplinary Officer, Staff Compliance Department 1998–2003; Deputy Dir State Adm. of Foreign Exchange, Prov. Office, Henan Prov. 1992–97; Dir-Gen. Banking Supervision Dept, China Banking Regulatory Comm. 2003–05, Vice-Chair. China Banking Regulatory Comm. 2005–; Chair. Bd of Supervisors, Agricultural Bank of China 2008–. *Address:* Agricultural Bank of China, 69 Jianguomennei, Dong Cheng District, Beijing 100005, People's Republic of China (office). *Telephone:* (10) 85106660 (office). *Fax:* (10) 85106661 (office). *E-mail:* webmaster@intl.abocn.com (office). *Website:* www.abchina.com (office).

CHEA CHANTO, PhD; Cambodian banker and politician; *Governor, National Bank of Cambodia;* b. 9 Oct. 1951, Kompon Thom Prov.; m.; ed secondary school, Kampong Thom, Univ. of Commerce, Phnom Penh, Hanoi Univ., Viet Nam; Dir Phnom Penh Municipality Bank 1979–81; Deputy Gov. Nat. Bank of Cambodia 1981–86, Gov. 1998–, Gov. for IMF 1998–; First Vice-Minister, Ministry of Planning 1986, Minister of Planning 1986–98; mem. Parl. (Kampong Thom Constituency) 1993–98; Resident Adjunct Prof., Univ. of Southern California, USA 1995; Hon. PhD (Univ. of Southern California) 1995. *Publications:* Socio-Economic Rehabilitation Plan, 1994–1995 1994, Socio-Economic Survey of Cambodia, 1993–1994 1995, Survey of Industrial Establishment, 1993 1996, First Five Year Socio-Economic Development Plan, 1996–2000 1997, Cambodian Human Resource Development Report 1997, Law on Banking and Financial Institutions 1999, Financial Sector Blueprint for 2001–2010 2001, Law on Negotiable Instruments and Payment Transactions 2005, Draft Law on Financial Leasing 2006, Draft Law on Anti-Money Laundering and Financial Terrorism 2006. *Address:* National Bank of Cambodia, 22–24 boulevard Preah Norodom, BP 25, Phnom Penh, Cambodia (office). *Telephone:* (23) 722563 (office). *Fax:* (23) 426117 (office). *E-mail:* nbc2@online.com.kh (office).

CHEADLE, Don, BFA; American actor; b. 29 Nov. 1964, Kansas City, Mo.; two c.; ed Calif. Inst. of the Arts. *Films include:* Moving Violations 1985, Punk 1986, Hamburger Hill 1987, Colors 1988, Roadside Prophets 1992, The Meteor Man 1993, Things to Do in Denver When You're Dead 1995, Devil in a Blue Dress 1995, Rosewood 1997, Volcano 1997, Boogie Nights 1997, Bulworth 1998, Out of Sight 1998, Mission to Mars, 2000, The Family Man 2000, Traffic 2000, Things Behind the Sun 2001, Manic, 2001, Swordfish 2001, Ocean's Eleven 2001, The Hire: Ticker 2002, The United States of Leland 2003, The Assassination of Richard Nixon 2004, Crash 2004 (also producer), Hotel

Rwanda 2004, After the Sunset 2004, Ocean's Twelve 2004, Other Side of Simple 2006, The Dog Problem 2006, Reign Over Me 2007, Talk to Me 2007, Ocean's Thirteen 2007, Traitor 2008, Brooklyn's Finest 2009, Hotel for Dogs 2009. *Television includes:* The Golden Palace (series) 1992, Picket Fences (series) 1992, Lush Life 1993, Rebound: The Legend of Earl The Goat Manigault 1996, The Rat Pack 1998, A Lesson Before Dying 1999, Fail Safe 2000. *Publication:* Not On Our Watch (with John Prendergast) 2007. *Address:* c/o Creative Artists Agency, 9830 Wilshire Blvd, Beverly Hills, CA 90212-1852, USA (office). *Telephone:* (310) 288-4545 (office). *Fax:* (310) 288-4800 (office). *Website:* www.caa.com (office).

CHEARAVANONT, Dhanin; Thai business executive; *Chairman and CEO, Charoen Pokphand (CP) Group;* b. Bangkok; m. Vatanalikit Tawee (Khunying); five c.; ed secondary school, Shantou, China and commercial school, Hong Kong; Chair. Charoen Pokphand (CP) Group (conglomerate of 250 cos involved in agribusiness and food, telecommunications, retail and distribution and other industries) and Chia Tai Group 1989–; Chair. True Corpn 1993–; major shareholder BD Bank, Shanghai (first foreign-owned bank with head office in China); adviser to Chinese Govt during Hong Kong negotiations with Britain. *Address:* 18 True Tower, Ratchadapisek Road, Huai Kwang, Bangkok 10320, Thailand (office). *Telephone:* (2) 643-1111 (office). *Fax:* (2) 643-1651 (office). *E-mail:* cp@cpthailand.com (office). *Website:* www.cpthailand.com (office).

CHECA CREMADES, Fernando, DenFil y Letras, LicEnD; Spanish professor of art history, arts administrator and writer; *Professor of Art History, Universidad Complutense de Madrid;* b. 14 May 1952, Madrid; s. of Francisco Checa and Concepción Cremades; Lecturer in Art History, Univ. Complutense de Madrid 1976–, Prof. of Art History –1996, 2002–; Dir Prado Museum 1996–2002; Summer Visiting Prof., Inst. of Advanced Studies, Princeton, NJ 1988; Paul Mellon Sr Fellow, Center of Advanced Studies in Visual Arts, Nat. Gallery of Art, Washington, DC 1989; Fae Norton Prof., Oklahoma State Univ. 1995; fmr mem. Ministerial Comm. for Classification of State Collections; organizer of four major exhbns; Premio Extraordinario de Doctorado 1981, Nat. Prize for History 1993. *Publications include:* Pintura y escultura del Renacimiento en España 1983, La imagen impresa en el Renacimiento y el Manierismo 1987, Carlos V y la imagen del héroe en el Renacimiento 1987, Felipe II: mecenas de las artes 1992 (Nat. History Prize, Spain), Tiziano y la Monarquía Hispánica 1994, El coleccionismo en España (jtly) 1984, Las casas del Rey: Casas reales, cazaderos, jardines. Siglos XVI y XVII (jtly) 1986, Carlos V. La imagen del poder en el Renacimiento 1999. *Address:* Department of Art History, Universidad Complutense de Madrid, Ciudad Universitaria, Avda. Seneca 2, 28040 Madrid, Spain (office). *Website:* www.ucm.es (office).

CHECHELASHVILI, Valeri, PhD; Georgian diplomatist and international organization official; *Secretary General, Organization for Democracy and Economic Development (GUAM);* b. 17 March 1961, Tbilisi; s. of Karlo Chechelashvili and Tina Chechelashvili; m. Marine Neparidze; two s. one d.; ed Kiev State Univ., Ukraine; mem. staff, Foreign Econ. Relations Dept, Ministry of Light Industry 1987–88; Deputy Head of Foreign Econ. Relations section, Jt Stock Co. Gruzkurort 1988–89; First Sec. Dept of Int. Econ. Relations, Ministry of Foreign Affairs 1989–90, Deputy Dir 1990–91, First Deputy Dir 1991–92, Dir 1992–94, Deputy Minister of Foreign Affairs 1998–2000; Amb. to Ukraine 1994–98, to Moldova 1996–98; Sec.-Gen. Black Sea Econ. Co-operation (BSEC) 2000–04; Amb. to Russian Fed. 2004–05; Minister of Finance Feb.–June 2005; Amb. to Switzerland and Perm. Rep. to UN and Other Int. Orgs, Geneva July–Nov. 2005; First Deputy Foreign Minister of Georgia 2005–07; Sec. Gen. Org. for Democracy and Econ. Devt 2007–; Second Degree Order for Service, Ukraine 1998, Order for Merit (1st Degree), Ukraine 2002. *Publications:* several articles on econ. co-operation in learned journals. *Leisure interests:* classical music, fiction, tennis. *Address:* GUAM Secretariat, 1001 Kyiv, Sofiyivska 2-A, Ukraine (office). *Telephone:* (44) 206-37-37 (office). *Fax:* (44) 206-30-06 (office). *E-mail:* secretariat@guam-organization.org (office). *Website:* guam-organization.org (office).

CHECKLAND, Sir Michael, Kt, BA, CCMI, FCMA; British broadcasting executive; b. 13 March 1936, Birmingham; s. of Leslie Checkland and Ivy Florence Checkland; m. 1st Shirley Checkland 1960 (divorced 1983) (deceased); two s. one d.; m. 2nd Sue Zetter 1987; ed King Edward's Grammar School, Five Ways, Birmingham and Wadham Coll., Oxford; accountant, Parkinson Cowan Ltd 1959–62, Thorn Electronics Ltd 1962–64; Sr Cost Accountant, BBC 1964–67, Head, Cen. Finance Unit 1967, Chief Accountant, Cen. Finance Services 1969, Chief Accountant, BBC TV 1971, Controller, Finance 1976, Controller, Planning and Resource Man., BBC TV 1977, Dir of Resources, BBC TV 1982, Deputy Dir-Gen. BBC 1985–87, Dir-Gen. 1987–92, Dir BBC Enterprises 1979–92 (Chair. 1986–87); Dir Visnews 1980–85; Vice-Pres. RTS 1985–94, Fellow 1987–; Trustee Reuters 1994–; Pres. Commonwealth Broadcasting Asscn 1987–88; Vice-Pres. EBU 1991–92; Chair. NCH (fmrly Nat. Children's Home) 1991–2001; Gov. Westminster Coll. Oxford 1992–97, Birkbeck Coll. London 1993–97, Brighton Univ. 1996–97, 2001–; Dir Nat. Youth Music Theatre 1991–2002, Nynex Cablecomms 1995–97, Wales Millennium Centre 2003–; Chair. City of Birmingham Symphony Orchestra 1993–2001, Brighton Int. Festival 1993–2002, Higher Educ. Funding Council for England 1997–2001, Brighton Univ. 2002–; Vice-Pres. Methodist Conf. 1997; mem. Ind. TV Comm. 1997–2003; numerous other appointments; Hon. Fellow Wadham Coll. Oxford 1989; Dr hc (Open Univ.) 1993, (Birmingham) 1999. *Leisure interests:* sport, music, travel. *Address:* Orchard Cottage, Park Lane, Maplehurst, West Sussex, RH13 6LL, England (home).

CHÉDID, Andrée, BA; French writer; b. 20 March 1920, Cairo, Egypt; d. of Selim Saab and Alice K. Haddad; m. Louis A. Chedid 1942; one s. one d.; ed French schools, Cairo and Paris, American Univ. in Cairo; has lived in Paris since 1946; Officier, Légion d'honneur, Commdr des Arts et des Lettres; Prix

Louise Labé 1966, L'aigle d'or de la poésie 1972, Grand Prix des Lettres Françaises de l'Acad. Royale de Belgique 1975, Prix de l'Afrique Méditerranéenne 1975, Prix de l'Acad. Mallarmé 1976, Prix Goncourt for short story 1979, Prix de Poésie (Soc. des Gens de Lettres) 1991, Prix PEN Club Int. 1992, Prix Paul Morand, Acad. Française 1994, Prix Albert Camus 1996, Prix Poésie de la SALEH 1999, Prix Côté Femmes 2001, Prix Louis Jouilloux 2001, Grand Prix Paul Morand 2001. *Publications include:* poetry: Fraternité de la parole 1975, Epreuves du vivant 1983, Textes pour un poème 1949–1970, 1987, Poèmes pour un texte 1970–91, Par delà les mots 1995, Fugitive Suns: Selected Poetry 1999; novels: Le Sommeil délivré 1952, Le Sixième Jour 1960, L'Autre 1969, Nefertiti et le rêve d'Akhnaton 1974, La Maison sans racines 1985, L'Enfant multiple 1989, Lucy: La Femme Verticle 1998, Le Message 2000; plays: Bérénice d'Egypte, Les Nombres, Le Montreur 1981, Echec à la Reine 1984, les saisons de passage 1996; short stories: Les Corps et le temps 1979, Mondes Miroirs Magies 1988, A la Mort, A la Vie 1992, La Femme de Job 1993, Les Saisons de passage 1996, Le Jardin perdu 1997, Territoires du Souffle 1999, Le Cœur demeure 1999, Rythmes 2003; essays, children's books. *Leisure interest:* collages. *Address:* c/o Flammarion, 87, quai Panhard et Levassor, 75647 Paris Cedex 13, France. *Telephone:* 1-40-51-31-00. *Website:* www.andreechedid.com.

CHEE, Soon Juan, PhD; Singaporean neuropsychologist and politician; *Secretary-General, Singapore Democratic Party;* ed Univ. of Georgia, USA; Lecturer in Psychology, Nat. Univ. of Singapore –1993; joined Singapore Democratic Party 1992, currently Sec.-Gen.; Chair. Alliance for Reform and Democracy in Asia; Reagan Fellow, Nat. Endowment for Democracy, Washington, DC; participated in numerous int. orgs, including World Movt for Democracy, Forum of Democratic Leaders in Asia Pacific; participated in Reagan-Fascell Democracy Program at Nat. Endowment for Democracy, Washington, DC 2004; declared a bankrupt by High Court after failing to pay S\$500,000 in damages awarded to Prime Minister Goh Chok Tong and Sr Minister Lee Kuan Yew, not allowed to stand for elections until Feb. 2011; fined S\$6,000 and sentenced to Queenstown Remand Prison for eight days for contempt of court after he criticized independence of Singapore judiciary; Hon. Research Assoc., Monash Asia Inst. 1997, Univ. of Chicago 2001; Defender of Democracy Award, Parliamentarians for Global Action 2003. *Address:* Singapore Democratic Party, 1357A Serangoon Road, Singapore, 328240, Singapore (office). *Telephone:* 63981675 (office). *Fax:* 63981675 (office). *E-mail:* speakup@yoursdp.org (office). *Website:* www.singaporedemocrat.org (office); cheesoonjuan.blogspot.com.

CHEETHAM, Anthony John Valerian, BA; British publisher; b. 12 April 1943; s. of Sir Nicolas John Alexander Cheetham; m. 1st Julia Rollason 1969 (divorced); two s. one d.; m. 2nd Rosemary de Courcy 1979 (divorced); two d.; m. 3rd Georgina Capel 1997; ed Eton Coll., Balliol Coll., Oxford; Editorial Dir Sphere Books 1968; Man. Dir Futura Publs 1973, Macdonald Futura 1979; Chair. Century Publishing 1982–85; Man. Dir Century Hutchinson 1985; Chair. and CEO Random Century Group 1989–91; Founder and CEO Orion Publishing Group (fmrly Orion Books) 1991–2003; Exec. Chair. Quercus Publishing plc 2005–08, Chair. (non-exec.) 2008–09. *Publication:* Richard III 1972. *Leisure interests:* tennis, gardening, trees, medieval history. *Address:* c/o Quercus Publishing plc, 21 Bloomsbury Square, London, WC1A 2QA, England (office). *Website:* www.quercusbooks.co.uk (office).

CHEF, Genia, MA; Russian artist; b. 28 Jan. 1954, Aktyubinsk, Kazakhstan; s. of Vladimir Scheffer and Sinaida Scheffer; m. Elke Schwab 1983; ed Polygraphic Inst., Moscow, Acad. of Fine Arts, Vienna; painter, graphic and computer artist; has provided illustrations for publs including Edgar Allan Poe, Prose and Poetry 1983, American Romantic Tales 1984, Finger World 1993, American Alphabet 1998; numerous appearances on radio and TV in New York, Berlin and Moscow; KStJ 2003; Fueger Gold Prize, Acad. of Fine Arts, Vienna 1993, Delfina Studio Trust Award, New York 1994. *Publications:* Manifesto of Degeneration 1988, Manifesto of Post-Historicism 1989, Viva Canova! 1995, New Computer Renaissance 2002. *Leisure interests:* music, books, collecting insects. *Address:* 'Künstlerhof', Alt Lietzow 12, 10587 Berlin (office); Schustehrusstr. 1, 10585 Berlin, Germany (home). *Telephone:* (30) 3246479 (home); (173) 6162940 (mobile). *E-mail:* geniachef@gmx.de (home). *Website:* www.artnews.info/geniachef.

CHEIFFOU, Amadou; Niger politician and civil servant; *President, Rassemblement social-démocratique–Gaskiya;* fmr regional official of Int. Civil Aviation Org., then Regional Dir Western and Cen. African Office, Dakar; Prime Minister and Minister of Defence 1991–93; fmr Vice-Pres. Convention démocratique et social–Rahama; Founder and Pres. Rassemblement social-démocratique–Gaskiya (RSD) 2004; mem. Assemblée nationale 2004–; unsuccessful cand. for Pres. Niger 2004. *Address:* Rassemblement social-démocratique–Gaskiya, Quartier Poudrière, Niamey, Niger (office). *Telephone:* 20-74-00-90 (office).

CHELI, HE Cardinal Giovanni, MTheol, DCnL; Italian ecclesiastic; *President Emeritus, Pontifical Council for the Pastoral Care of Migrants and Itinerant People;* b. 4 Oct. 1918, Turin; ed Pontifical Lateran Univ., Pontifical Acad. for Diplomacy; ordained priest 1942; Second Sec., Apostolic Nunciature in Guatemala 1952–55, First Sec., Madrid 1955–62; Counsellor, Nunciature in Rome 1962–67; served on Council for Public Affairs of the Church, Vatican City 1967–73; Titular Archbishop of Santa Giusta 1978; Perm. Observer to UN 1978–86; Pro-Prefect Pontifical Council for the Pastoral Care of Migrants and Itinerant People 1986–89, Pres. 1989–98, Pres. Emer. 1998–; cr. Cardinal-Deacon of Ss. Cosma e Damiano 1998; Kt Commdr Orden de Isabel la Católica (Spain), Ordine al Merito della Repubblica Italiana, Verdienstkreuz der Bundesrepublik Deutschland (Germany); Grand Cross 'pro piis meritis' of the Sovereign Order of Malta; High Patron of the Order of St Maurice. *Publication:* L'applicazione delle Riforme Tridentine nella diocesi di Asti

1952. *Leisure interests:* tennis, mountain climbing, reading, listening to classical music. *Address:* Piazza San Calisto 16, 00153 Rome, Italy. *Telephone:* (06) 69887392. *Fax:* (06) 69887137. *E-mail:* mc2927@mclink.it (home).

CHELYSHEV, Yevgeny Petrovich; Russian philologist; *Academic Secretary, Department of Literature and Language, Russian Academy of Sciences;* b. 27 Oct. 1921; m.; two d.; ed Mil. Inst. of Foreign Languages; Head of Chair of Indian Languages Mil. Inst. of Foreign Languages, Head of Sector of Indian Philology, Head Div. of Literature Inst. of Oriental Sciences, USSR (now Russian) Acad. of Sciences, Corresp. mem. USSR (now Russian) Acad. of Sciences 1981, mem. 1987, Acad. Sec. Dept of Literature and Language 1991–; Pres., Soc. for Russian-Indian Cultural Connections; mem. Bureau of Indian Soc. of Philosophy, Asian Soc. in Calcutta; main research in the field of culture, comparative literary criticism, Indian philosophy; Merited Worker of Sciences of Russia, Int. Nehru Prize; Swami Vivekananda Prize. *Publications:* Modern Poetry in Hindi 1967, Contemporary Indian Literature 1981, Indian Literature Today and Yesterday 1989, Complicity in Beauty and Spirit 1991; articles in specialized periodicals. *Leisure interest:* music. *Address:* Department of Literature and Language, Russian Academy of Sciences, 117334 Moscow, Leninsky prosp. 32A, Russia. *Telephone:* (495) 938-19-36 (office); (495) 202-66-25 (home).

CHEMETOV, Paul; French architect and academic; b. 6 Sept. 1928, Paris; s. of Alexandre Chemetoff and Tamara Blumine; m. Christine Soupault 1958; one s. two d.; ed Ecole Nationale Supérieure des Beaux Arts; participated in founding of Atelier d'urbanisme et l'architecture 1961; Prof., Ecole d'architecture, Strasbourg 1968–72; Visiting Prof., UP8 1973; exhibited in the Venice Biennial 1976; Prof. of Architecture, Ecole Nationale des Ponts et Chaussées 1977–89; mem. Directorial Cttee, then Vice-Pres. Plan Construction 1979–87; Visiting Prof., Ecole Polytechnique Fédérale, Lausanne 1993–98; mem. Acad. d'Architecture 1996; Officier, Légion d'honneur, Ordre Nat. du Mérite, Ordre des Arts et des Lettres; Prix d'architecture, Cercle d'études architecturales 1965, Grand Prix Nat. d'architecture 1980; Médaille d'honneur d'Architecture 1991. *Publications:* Architectures – Paris 1848–1914 (jtly.) 1980, Cinq projets 1979–82 (jtly.) 1983, Paris – Banlieue 1919–1939 (with B. Marrey and M. J. Dumont) 1989, La Fabrique des villes 1992, Le Territoire de L'Architecte 1995, Vingt Mille Mots pour la Ville 1996, Un architecte dans le siècle 2002, Mecano-factures (jtly) 2006; numerous articles in professional journals. *Address:* Chemetov, 4 square Masséna, 75013 Paris, France. *Telephone:* 1-45-82-85-48. *Fax:* 1-45-86-89-14. *E-mail:* cplush@compuserve.com (home).

CHEMEZOV, Sergei; Russian business executive; *Director General, Rosoboroneksport (Russian Defence Export) State Corporation;* b. 20 Aug. 1952, Irkutsk; ed Irkutsk Inst. of Nat. Economy; worked in Irkutsk Scientific Research Inst. of Rare and Nonferrous Metals; worked with Experimental-Industrial Asscn Beam, represented Beam in GDR 1983–88; Asst to Gen. Dir Sovintersport 1989–96; Head Dept of Foreign Econ. Relations, Admin of the Pres. of Russian Fed. 1996–99; Dir Gen. FSUE Tehnoexport 1999–2004; Dir Gen. Rosoboroneksport (Russian Defence Export) State Corpn 2004–. *Address:* Rosoboroneksport (Russian Defence Export) State Corporation, 119992 Moscow, Gogolevskii bulvar 21, Russia (office). *Telephone:* (495) 291-81-77 (office). *Fax:* (495) 202-45-94 (office). *E-mail:* glad@post.rusarm.ru (office). *Website:* www.rusarm.ru (office).

CHEN, Ailian; Chinese dancer, academic and choreographer; b. 24 Dec. 1939, Shanghai; d. of Chen Xi Kang and Yu Xiu Ying; m. Wei Dao Ning; two d.; ed First Coll. of Chinese Dancing; teacher, Beijing Coll. of Dancing 1959–63; Chief Actress, China Opera and Dancing House 1963–; now Prof., Arts Dept, Nan Kai Univ., Hainan Univ., Wang Kan Arts Coll.; demonstrations and lectures in Shangdong Prov., Shaanxi Prov., Beijing Univ., Foreign Languages Inst., Post and Telegraph Inst., Light Industry Inst. and Municipal Dancers' Unions; Chief Dancer, Chinese Art Del. to USSR, USA, France, Spain, Belgium, Denmark, Finland, Sweden, Italy, Norway, Hong Kong, Germany, etc.; f. Chen Ailian Artistic Troupe 1989 (first non-governmental performing org. in China); est. Chen Ailian Dancing School, Beijing 1995; mem. CPPCC Nat. Cttee; won four gold medals as a traditional dancer at 8th World Youth Festival in Helsinki 1962; Excellent Performance Award, First Nat. Dance Concert, First Prize Ministry of Culture for Dance Soirée and Princess Wenzhen. *Performances include:* The Peony Pavilion, In the Dusk of Evening, The Oriental Melody, The Lantern Dance, Water, The Sword Dance, Ball Dance, The Song of the Serfs, Women Militia in the Grassland, The Red Silk Dance, A Dream of Red Mansions 2007. *Publications:* I Came From An Orphanage; articles and commentaries on dance. *Leisure interests:* literature, music, traditional opera, travel, mountain climbing. *Address:* Room 101/7, 2 Nanhuadong Street, Hufang Road, Beijing 100050, People's Republic of China. *Telephone:* 3015066.

CHEN, B. L.; Taiwanese oil industry executive; *President, CPC Corporation;* currently Dir and Pres. CPC Corpn, Taiwan (fmrly Chinese Petroleum Corpn).

CHEN, Bangzhu; Chinese politician; *Chairman, Subcommittee of Human Resources and Environment, Chinese People's Political Consultative Conference;* b. Sept. 1934, Jiujiang City, Jiangxi Prov.; ed Chonqing Civil Eng Coll.; engineer, Jilin Chemical Industrial Dist Construction Co. 1954–65; engineer, Chief Engineer, Deputy Man., Man. Ministry of Chemical Industry No. 9 Chemical Industrial Construction Co. 1966–80; joined CCP 1975; Chief Engineer, Man. Jiuhua Bldg Co. 1980–84; Mayor of Yueyang and Deputy Sec. CCP Yueyang City Cttee 1983–84; Vice-Gov. Hunan Prov. 1984–89, Acting Gov. 1989–93, Gov. 1993–95; Minister of Internal Trade 1995–98; Vice-Minister State Econ. and Trade Comm. 1998–2000; Dir State Bureau of Surveying and Mapping 2000–; Alt. mem. 13th CCP Cen. Cttee 1987–92; Deputy Sec. CCP 6th Hunan Provincial Cttee 1989–; mem. 14th CCP Cen. Cttee 1992–97, 15th CCP Cen. Cttee 1997–2002; Vice-Minister State Econ. and Trade Comm. 1998–2000; mem. Macao Special Admin. Region Preparatory Cttee 1998–99, 9th CPPCC Nat. Cttee Standing Cttee 1998–2003 (Chair. CPPCC Sub-cttee on Human Resources and Environement 2003–); Hon. Pres. Chinese Asscn for Materials Circulation 1995–. *Address:* Chinese People's Political Consultative Conference, Beijing, People's Republic of China.

CHEN, Gen. Bingde; Chinese army officer and politician; *Chief of General Staff, People's Liberation Army;* b. July 1941, Nantong City, Jiangsu Prov.; ed Mil. Acad. of the Chinese PLA; joined PLA 1961, then Squadron Leader, Platoon Leader, Staff mem. PLA Services and Arms, Army (or Ground Force), Combat Training Section, Regt Chief of Staff, Div. Deputy Chief of Staff, Div. Chief of Staff 1979–81, Div. Commdr 1981–83, Deputy Commdr PLA Services and Arms, Army (or Ground Force) 1983, Maj.-Gen. 1988–95, Lt-Gen. 1995–2002, Chief of Staff, PLA, Nanjing Mil. Region 1985, C-in-C 1996–99, C-in-C Jinan Mil. Region 1999–2004, Pres. PLA Nanchang Infantry Acad., Gen. 2002–; Dir-Gen. PLA Gen. Armaments Dept 2004–07; joined CCP 1962, Deputy Sec. CCP Party Cttee PLA, Nanjing Mil. Region 1996–99; mem. 15th CCP Cen. Cttee 1997–2002, 16th CCP Cen. Cttee 2002–07, 17th CCP Cen. Cttee 2007–; mem. Cen. Mil. Comm. 2005–. *Address:* PLA General Staff Headquarters, 21, North Andeli Street, Beijing, People's Republic of China.

CHEN, Chao-min; Taiwanese air force officer and government official; *Minister of National Defence;* b. 10 July 1940; ed Armed Forces Univ. (now Nat. Defence Univ.), Repub. of China Air Force Acad.; Dir of Operations, Office of the Deputy Chief of Gen. Staff for Operations, Ministry of Nat. Defence 1986–88, Commdr 443rd Tactical Fighter Wing 1988–89, Dir 4th Dept 1990–91, Dir Operations Div., Air Force Gen. HQ 1991–92, Insp.-Gen. Inspection Office 1992–93, Gen. Commdr Eastern Command 1993–94, Commdr Air Force Operations Command 1995–97, Deputy Commdr Air Force Gen. HQ 1997–98, C-in-C 1998–2002; strategic adviser to Pres. of Taiwan 2002, Deputy Minister for Armaments 2002–04, Minister of Nat. Defence 2008–; Exec. Dir Repub. of China Air Force Acad. 1989–90, Supt 1994–95. *Address:* Ministry of National Defense, 2/F, 164 Po Ai Road, Taipei 10048, Taiwan (office). *Telephone:* (2) 23116117 (office). *Fax:* (2) 23144221 (office). *Website:* www.mnd.gov.tw (office).

CHEN, Char-Nie, OBE, JP, MB, MSc, FHKAM(Psychiatry), FHKCPsych, FRCPsych, FRANZCP, DPM; British physician, academic and college principal; *Chairman, Hong Kong Advisory Council on AIDS;* b. 19 July 1938, Fujian Prov., China; s. of the late Kam-Heng Chen and of Mei-Ai Chen-Hsu; m. Chou-May Chien 1970; one s. two d.; ed Nat. Taiwan Univ. and Univ. Coll., London; Rotating Intern, Nat. Taiwan Univ. Hosp. 1964–65, Resident Physician, Dept of Neurology and Psychiatry 1965–68; Sr House Officer, Morgannwg Hosp., Wales 1968–69; Registrar, St George's Hosp. Medical School, London 1969–71, Lecturer and Hon. Sr Registrar 1971–72, 1973–78, Sr Lecturer and Hon. Consultant Psychiatrist 1978–80; Prof., Dept of Psychiatry, Chinese Univ. of Hong Kong 1981–98, Chair. of Dept 1981–93, mem. Univ. Senate 1981, Head of Shaw Coll. 1987–94, mem. Univ. Council 1987–94; mem. Coll. Council, Hong Kong Baptist Coll. 1984–95; Pres. Hong Kong Psychiatric Asscn 1982–84, Hong Kong Soc. of Neurosciences 1983–84, 1988–89; Exec. Chair. Hong Kong Mental Health Asscn 1983–98; Pres. Pacific Rim Coll. of Psychiatrists 1988–90, Dir 1990–; Chair. Action Comm. Against Narcotics 1992–98, Hong Kong Advisory Council on AIDS; Pres. Hong Kong Coll. of Psychiatrists 1993–98; Fellow, Royal Coll. of Psychiatrists 1985–, Royal Australian and NZ Coll. of Psychiatrists 1983–, Royal Soc. of Medicine 1975–, Hong Kong Acad. of Medicine 1993–, Hong Kong Soc. of Sleep Medicine (Pres. 1993–), Hong Kong Coll. of Psychiatrists (Pres. 1994–98, Chief Examiner 1998–); mem. British Asscn for Psychopharmacology 1974–, European Sleep Research Soc. 1976–, British Medical Asscn 1979–, Collegium Internationale Neuro-psycho-pharmacologium 1981–, Hong Kong Medical Asscn 1981–, Int. Brain Research Org. 1985–, Mental Health Asscn, Hong Kong (Chair. 1983–98, Vice-Pres. 1998–); Corresp. Fellow, American Psychiatric Asscn 1991; Visiting Prof., St George's Hosp. Medical School, London 1984; JP, Hong Kong 1993–; Hon. Fellow, Hong Kong Psychological Soc. 1986–. *Publications:* over 90 scientific papers. *Leisure interests:* reading, travelling, good food. *Address:* Hong Kong Advisory Council on AIDS, 5/F Yaumatei Jockey Club Clinic, 145 Battery Street, Yaumatei, Kowloon, Hong Kong (office); Flat 16B, Block 3, Villa Athena, 600 Sai Sha Road, Ma On Shan, Hong Kong Special Administrative Region, People's Republic of China. *Telephone:* (852) 2633-4192. *Fax:* (852) 2633-3067. *E-mail:* aca@dh.gov.hk (office).

CHEN, Deming, BA, PhD; Chinese government official; *Minister of Commerce;* b. July 1949, Shanghai; ed Jiangxi Communist Labor Univ. (now Jiangxi Agricultural Univ.); began career in 1969 in Jiangxi, working five years for production team; joined CCP 1974; worked for three years for Jiangxi Agricultural Machinery Bureau, then worked for Jiangsu Food Products Corpn; Asst Dir, Gen. Office, Jiangsu Bureau of Commerce 1984, Deputy Dir 1985; fmr Sec.-Gen., Gen. Office, Jiangsu Prov. Govt; Mayor of Suzhou City 1998–2003; Vice-Gov. Shaanxi Prov. 1998–2003, Acting Gov. 2004–05, Gov. 2005–06; Vice-Chair. State Devt and Reform Comm. 2006–07; Vice-Minister of Commerce 2007, Minister of Commerce 2007–; Deputy to 9th NPC 1998–2003, Del. to 16th CCP Cen. Cttee 2002–07, Alt. mem. 17th CCP Cen. Cttee 2007–. *Address:* Ministry of Commerce, 2 Dongchangan Jie, Dongcheng Qu, Beijing 100731, People's Republic of China (office). *Telephone:* (10) 65121919 (office). *Fax:* (10) 65599340 (office). *E-mail:* webmaster@mofcom.gov.cn (office). *Website:* www.mofcom.gov.cn (office).

CHEN, Din Hwa; Chinese business executive; *Chairman, Nan Fung Textiles Consolidated Limited, Nan Fung Development Limited;* b. 1923, Ningbo, Zhejiang Prov.; man. of family business textile business, Shanghai 1945; family moved to Hong Kong 1949; f. Nan Fung Textiles Consolidated Ltd 1954, currently Chair., delisted Nan Fung Textiles 1989, invested in real estate, Chair. Nan Fung Development Ltd, owns stakes in China Aoyuan Property

Group, Singapore, Sino Land; f. D. H. Chen Foundation (charity) 1970; Dr hc (Hong Kong Polytechnic Univ.). *Address:* Nan Fung Textiles, 9th Floor, Central Building, 3 Pedder Street, Central, Hong Kong Special Administrative Region, People's Republic of China (office). *Telephone:* 2521-7417 (office). *Fax:* 2524-1276 (office). *E-mail:* info@nanfung.com (office). *Website:* www .nanfung.com (office).

CHEN, Ding-Shinn, MD; Taiwanese physician and academic; *Dean, College of Medicine, National Taiwan University;* b. 6 July 1943, Yin-Ge; ed Coll. of Medicine, Nat. Taiwan Univ.; Researcher, Nat. Cancer Center Research Inst., Tokyo, Japan 1975; Lecturer, Dept of Internal Medicine, Coll. of Medicine, Nat. Taiwan Univ. 1975, Assoc. Prof. 1978, Prof. 1983, Dean, Coll. of Medicine 2001–; Chair. Taiwanese Govt's Hepatitis Control Cttee; Pres. Taiwan Asscn for the Study of the Liver 1996–98, Gastroenterological Soc. of Taiwan 1997–2003, Formosan Medical Asscn 2001–; Vice-Pres. Int. Asscn for the Study of the Liver 2000; Assoc. Ed. Hepatology, Journal of Biomedical Science; mem. Editorial Bd Journal of Hepatology and other int. journals; mem. NIH 1979–80, Academia Sinica 1992; Foreign Assoc. NAS 2005; Trieste Science Prize (jtly), Acad. of Sciences for the Developing World (Third World Acad. of Sciences) 2006. *Achievements include:* famous for his leading role in uncovering the factors responsible for the transmission of the Hepatitis B virus from mothers to infants and for proving that this viral disease is associated not only with liver cirrhosis but also with liver cancer; leading to a programme of mass vaccination against Hepatitis B. *Publications:* more than 550 articles in scientific journals on internal medicine, gastroenterology, viral hepatitis and liver disease. *Address:* Department of Internal Medicine, National Taiwan University Hospital and National Taiwan University College of Medicine, No. 7 Chung-Shan South Road, Taipei, Taiwan (office). *Telephone:* (2) 23562185 (office). *Fax:* (2) 23224793 (office). *E-mail:* dean@ha.mc.ntu.edu.tw (office). *Website:* ntuh.mc.ntu.edu.tw (office).

CHEN, Dun; Chinese business executive; *President, China Electric Green Technology Group;* b. Dec. 1928, Tianjin City; Vice-Minister for Coal 1985–90; Gen. Man. China Nat. Coal Corpn 1993; currently Pres. China Electric Green Technology Group; mem. 7th CPPCC 1987–92, 8th 1993–97. *Address:* China Electric Green Technology Group, Shanghai, People's Republic of China. *Website:* www.cegt.com.cn (office).

CHEN, Gang; Chinese composer; b. 10 March 1935, Shanghai; s. of Chen Ge-Xin and Jin Jiao-Li; m. (divorced); two d.; ed Shanghai Conservatory of Music; now Prof. of Composition, Shanghai Conservatory of Music; mem. Council of Chinese Musicians' Asscn; Art Dir Shanghai Chamber Orchestra; Guest Prof., USA, France, Canada and Hong Kong; Sec. Chinese Dramatist Asscn 1987–; Golden Record Prize (five times). *Compositions include:* The Butterfly Lovers (with He Zhan Hao), Violin Concerto 1959, The Sun Shines on Tashikuergan, Violin Solo 1973, Morning on the Miao Mountains, Violin Solo 1975; A Moonlight Spring Night on the Flower-surrounded River, Symphonic Picture 1976, Concerto for Oboe 1985, Wang Zhaojun, Violin Concerto 1986, Chamber Music Ensemble 1989, Dragon Symphony 1991. *Leisure interests:* literature, writing. *Address:* Shanghai Conservatory of Music, 20 Fen Yang Road, Shanghai, People's Republic of China (office). *Telephone:* 4370689 (office).

CHEN, Geng; Chinese petroleum industry executive; b. 1947; ed Beijing Econs Inst.; Deputy Dir Changqing Petroleum Exploration Bureau 1983–85; Deputy Dir Labour Dept, Ministry of Petroleum Industry 1985–88; Dir Labour Bureau, China Nat. Petroleum Corpn 1988–93, Asst to Gen. Man. 1993–97, Deputy Gen. Man. 1997–98, Gen. Man. 2004–06, also Pres.; Dir PetroChina 2001–06, Pres. 2002–04, Chair. 2004–06. *Address:* c/o China National Petroleum Corporation, 6 Liupukang Jie, Xicheng District, Beijing 100724, People's Republic of China (office). *Telephone:* (10) 6209-4114 (office). *Fax:* (10) 6209-4806 (office). *E-mail:* master@cnpc.com.cn (office). *Website:* www.cnpc .com.cn (office).

CHEN, Guangyi; Chinese government official; *Chairman, Overseas Chinese Affairs Committee of the National People's Congress;* b. 7 Aug. 1933, Putian City, Fujian Prov.; s. of Chen Zhaohe and Li Muxin; m. Chen Xiuyun 1961; two s. one d.; ed Northeast China Engineering Coll.; joined CCP 1959; Deputy Div. Chief Prov. Heavy Industry Dept, Gansu Prov. 1960–64; Dir Production Office, Northwest China Nonferrous Metallurgical Design Acad. 1964–75; Div. Chief Prov. Metallurgical Bureau, Gansu Prov. 1977–80; Deputy Dir Prov. Planning Cttee, Gansu Prov. 1980–83; Deputy Sec. CCP Prov. Cttee, Gansu Prov. 1983; Gov. of Gansu Prov. 1983–86; Sec. 5th CCP Cttee, Fujian 1986; Chair. CPPCC 6th Fujian Provincial Cttee 1988; Chair. Fujian Prov. People's Congress Standing Committee 1993–94; mem. 12th CCP Cen. Cttee 1982–87, 13th CCP Cen. Cttee 1987–92, 14th CCP Cen. Cttee 1992–97, 15th CCP Cen. Cttee 1997–2002; Party Cttee Sec. and Head Civil Aviation Gen. Admin. of China 1993–98; Chair. Financial and Econ. Cttee of 9th NPC 1998–2003, Overseas Chinese Affairs Cttee of 9th NPC 2003–; Hon. Pres. Nanjing Aerospace Inst. *Address:* c/o Standing Committee of National People's Congress, Beijing, People's Republic of China.

CHEN, Hong; Chinese automotive executive; *President, Shanghai GM Automobile Company Ltd;* ed Tongji Univ., Shanghai; joined Shanghai Tractor and Automobile Co. (later Shanghai Automotive Industry Group Corpn —SAIC) 1984, with Shanghai-Volkswagen Automobile Co. Ltd (S-VW) project, Asst to Exec. Vice-Pres. of Human Resources, S-VW 1985–92, also Dir of Policy Research and Pres. S-VW Engine Factory, with Shanghai General Motors Co. Ltd (Shanghai-GM) Sedan Project 1995–97, Vice-Pres. Shanghai-GM 1997–99, currently Pres. Shanghai-GM Automobile Co. Ltd; Vice-Chair. SAIC; Pres. Shanghai Automotive Co. Ltd 2007–; Chair. SsangYong Motor Co. 2005–. *Address:* Shanghai GM Automobile Co. Ltd, No 489, Wei Hai Road, Shanghai 200041, People's Republic of China (office). *Telephone:* (21) 22011688 (office). *Fax:* (21) 22011188 (office). *E-mail:* info@gmchina.com (office). *Website:* www.gmchina.com (office).

CHEN, Houqun; Chinese geologist; *Research Professor and Chairman of the Academic Committee, Institute of Water Resources and Hydropower Research;* b. 3 May 1932, Wuxi, Jiangsu Prov.; ed Tsinghua Univ., Moscow Power Mechanics Inst., USSR; made original contrib. to the theoretical study of seismic hardening of concrete dams and to solving key problems of seismic resistance in maj. civil eng projects such as Xinfengjiang, Ertan and Xiaolangdi dams; presided over the compiling, editing and revising of many nat. standards, including Standard for the Anti-Seismic Design of Hydraulic Structures; built China's first large-scale three-dimensional and six-free-degree earthquake simulation platform; Chair. Standing Cttee, Dept of Civil Eng, Hydraulic and Constructional Eng, Chinese Acad. of Eng; Sr Engineer and Dir Eng Anti-Seismic Research Centre, China Water Conservancy and Hydroelectric Science Research Inst.; currently Research Prof. and Chair. Acad. Cttee, Institute of Water Resources and Hydropower Research; Fellow Chinese Acad. of Eng; 20 nat., ministerial and provincial awards for science and tech., including Prize of Progress in Science and Technology, Ho Leung Ho Lee Prize 2001. *Publications:* over 150 research papers. *Address:* Institute of Water Resources and Hydropower Research, 20 Chegongzhuang West Road, Beijing 100044, People's Republic of China (office). *Telephone:* (10) 68415522 (office). *Fax:* (10) 68478065 (home). *E-mail:* engach@mail.cae.ac.cn (office). *Website:* www.iwhr.com (office).

CHEN, Huanyou; Chinese administrator; *Chairman, Standing Committee of Jiangsu Provincial People's Congress;* b. 1934, Nantong City, Jiangsu Prov.; ed East China Military and Political Acad., People's Univ. of China; joined PLA, CCP 1954; Lecturer, Jilin Industrial Univ. 1959–65 (also Sec., Teaching Office 1959–65 and Deputy Sec. CCP Gen. Br. 1959–65); Dir Wuxi Diesel Engine Plant, Jiangsu Prov. 1975–81 (also Deputy Sec. and Sec. CCP Party Cttee 1975–81); Deputy Dir Prov. Econ. Cttee and Nat. Defence Industry Cttee, Jiangsu Prov. 1981–83; mem. Standing Cttee of Jiangsu CCP Prov. Cttee 1984, later Chair. People's Armament Cttee; Deputy to 8th NPC Jiangsu Prov.; Vice-Gov. Jiangsu Prov. 1983–84, Exec. Vice-Gov. 1984–89, Gov. 1989–94; Deputy Sec. CCP Jiangsu Prov. Cttee 1986–93, Sec. CCP Jiangsu Prov. Cttee 1993–2000; Del., 13th CCP Nat. Congress 1987–92, 14th CCP Nat. Congress 1992–97, 15th CCP Nat. Congress 1997–2002; Deputy, 7th NPC 1988–92, 8th NPC 1993–98; Chair. Standing Cttee, Jiangsu Prov. People's Congress 1998–; Hon. Pres. Red Cross Soc. of China, Jiangsu Prov. 1994–. *Address:* 70 W Beijing Road, Nanjing 210000, Jiangsu Province, People's Republic of China. *Telephone:* 025-663 5164.

CHEN, Huiguang; Chinese politician; b. 1938, Yulin City, Guangxi Zhuang Autonomous Region; ed Guangxi Inst. of Coal Mining; successively, Engineer, Mining Technician, Head of Production Section, Deputy Head and Head Dongluo Mining Admin, Guangxi Zhuang Autonomous Region 1961–1980 (also Deputy Sec. CCP Party Cttee 1961–80); joined CCP 1965; Deputy Dir Coal Industry Bureau, Guangxi Zhuang Autonomous Region 1980–83; Sec. CCP Municipal Cttee, Nanning 1983–85; Deputy Sec. CCP Cttee, Guangxi Zhuang 1983–85, (Leading) Sec. 1985–88; mem. 12th CCP Cen. Cttee 1982–87, 13th CCP Cen. Cttee 1987–92; Chair. CPPCC Guangxi Zhuang Autonomous Regional Cttee 1983–; Del. 14th CCP Nat. Congress 1992–97, 15th CCP Nat. Congress 1997–2002; mem. 8th CPPCC Nat. Cttee 1993–98, 9th CPPCC Nat. Cttee 1998–2003. *Address:* 1 Minlelu Road, Nanning City, Guangxi, People's Republic of China.

CHEN, Jiaer; Chinese professor of physics; b. 1 Oct. 1934, Shanghai; ed Jilin Univ.; joined CCP 1952; Lecturer in Physics, Peking Univ. 1955 (also Dir Teaching Staff Office and Deputy Dean), later Assoc. Prof., Prof. of Physics and Doctorate Dir 1984–, Vice-Pres. and Pres. Postgraduate School 1984–96, Pres. Beijing Univ. 1996–99, Vice-Pres. Council of Capital Devt Inst. 1999–; Visiting Scholar, Univ. of Oxford, UK 1963–66; fmr Dir Teaching Staff Office, Hanzhong School, Shaanxi Prov.; Visiting Scientist, South Africa 1982–84; Dir Heavy Ion Physics Research Inst. 1986–2001; Deputy Dir Nat. Natural Sciences Foundation of China 1991–99, Dir 1999–2003; Pres. Beijing Asscn of Science and Tech. 1997–, Asscn of Asia Pacific Physical Socs 1998–2001; Bd Dir China Physics Soc. 1996–99; Academician, Chinese Acad. of Sciences 1993– (mem. 4th Presidium of Depts, Chinese Acad. of Sciences 2000–02); Alt. mem. 15th CCP Cen. Cttee 1997–2002; mem. Third World Academy of Sciences 2002; Fellow Inst. of Physics 2001; Hon. SSc (Menlo Coll., Calif.) 1999, (Waseda Univ., Japan) 2000, (Chinese Univ. of Hong Kong) 2000, (Loughborough) 2002; numerous awards including First Grade Prize, State Educ. Comm. for Progress in Science and Tech. 1992, 1995, Zhou Pei-yuan Physics Award 1997, Ho Leung Ho Lee Foundation Award 2001. *Address:* National Natural Science Foundation of China, 83 Shuangqing Road, Haidian District, 100085 Beijing (office); Room 4–501, Bldg 12, Lanqiying, Peking University, Beijing, People's Republic of China (home). *Telephone:* (10) 62326876 (office); (10) 62758868 (home). *Fax:* (10) 62327082 (office); (10) 62758868 (home). *E-mail:* chenjer@rose.nsfc.gov.cn (office); chenje@pku.edu .cn (home). *Website:* www.nsfc.gov.cn (office).

CHEN, Jian; Chinese diplomatist and UN official; *President, United Nations Association of China;* b. 2 Feb. 1942; m.; one d.; ed Fudan Univ., Beijing Foreign Studies Univ.; attaché, Perm. Mission of China to the UN 1972–77, Third, Second then First Sec. 1980–84, Amb. and Deputy Perm. Rep. to UN 1992–94; attaché, Dept of Int. Orgs and Confs, Ministry of Foreign Affairs 1977–80, Dir, Counsellor then Deputy Dir-Gen. 1985–92; Asst, Office of Exec. Dir representing China at IMF 1984–85; Dir-Gen. Dept of Information and Spokesperson Ministry of Foreign Affairs 1994–96; Asst Minister of Foreign Affairs 1996–98; Amb. to Japan 1998–2001; Under-Sec.-Gen. for Gen. Ass. and Conf Man., UN, New York 2001–07; Pres. UN Asscn of China 2007–; fmr Rep. to UN Gen. Ass., Security Council, ECOSOC, UNEP, ESCAP and numerous confs and meetings. *Address:* United Nations Association of China, 71 Nanchizi Street, Beijing, 100006, People's Republic of China. *Website:* www.unachina.org (office).

CHEN, Jiangong; Chinese writer; b. Nov. 1949, Beihai, Guangxi Prov.; ed Peking Univ.; joined Beijing Writers' Asscn 1981; Sec. of Secr., Chinese Writers' Asscn 1995–2001, 2003–, Vice-Chair. 2001–; Dir Nat. National Museum of Modern Chinese Literature, Beijing. *Publications:* The Meandering Stream 1980, the Fluttering Flowered Scarf 1981, A Girl with the Eyes of a Red Phoenix 1981, Selected Novels by Chen Jiangong, No. 9 Huluba Alley, Letting Go, Curly Hair, Previous Offence. *Address:* c/o Beijing Writers' Association, Beijing, People's Republic of China.

CHEN, Jinhua; Chinese government official and business executive; b. 1929, Qingyang, Anhui Prov.; ed People's Univ. of China, Beijing, Beijing Television Univ.; worker, Ministry of Textile Industry, Ministry of Light Industry 1949; fmr Head, Liaoyang Petrochemical Fiber Corpn, Liaoning Prov., Tianjin Petrochemical Corpn; Vice-Mayor of Shanghai Municipality 1977–83; Gen. Man. China Petrochemical Corpn (Sinopec) 1983–90; Minister in charge of State Econ. Restructuring Comm. 1990–93, State Devt and Reform Comm. 1993–98; Head Co-ordination Group for Tertiary Industries 1993–98; mem. 14th Cen. Cttee CPC 1992–97; Vice-Chair. 9th Nat. Cttee of CPPCC 1998–2003. *Address:* c/o National Committee of Chinese People's Political Consultative Conference, 23 Taipingqiao Street, Beijing, People's Republic of China.

CHEN, Jun, PhD; Chinese geochemist, academic and university administrator; *President, Nanjing University;* b. 1954, Yangzhou, Jiangsu Prov.; ed Nanjing Univ.; Prof. of Geochemistry, Dept of Earth Sciences, Nanjing Univ. 1992–, becoming Dean, Dept of Earth Sciences, Vice-Pres. and Exec. Vice-Pres. Nanjing Univ., Pres. 2006–; Standing Dir Chinese Geological Soc., Chinese Soc. for Quaternary Research; Vice-Pres. Chinese Soc. for Mineralogy, Petrology and Geochemistry; mem. Fifth Cttee of Science and Tech., Ministry of Educ.; several Ministry of Educ. prizes for science and tech. *Address:* Office of the President, University of Nanjing, No. 22 Hankou Road, Nanjing, Jiangsu 210093, People's Republic of China (office). *Telephone:* (025) 3593186 (office). *E-mail:* chenjun@nju.edu.cn (office). *Website:* www.nju.edu.cn/cps/site/NJU/njue/profile/profile/president.htm (office).

CHEN, Junsheng; Chinese government official; b. 1927, Huanan Co., Helongjiang Prov.; joined CCP 1947; mem. Standing Cttee of Heilongjiang Prov. CP, Sec.-Gen. 1979–80, Deputy Sec. 1983–84; Sec. Qigihar City CP 1980–82; Sec. of the Fed. of TU, Deputy Chair. Exec. Cttee 1984–85; Vice-Pres. Fed. TU 1985; Sec. Gen. State Council 1985–88; Sec. CCP Cttee of Cen. State Organs 1986–88; Head Leading Group for Econ. Devt in Poor Areas (now Leading Group for Helping the Poor through Devt) 1986–, for Comprehensive Agricultural Devt, for Housing System Reform; Del., 12th CCP Nat. Congress 1982–87, 15th CCP Nat. Congress 1997–2002; Deputy, 6th NPC 1983–88; Vice-Pres. All-China Fed. of Trade Unions 1984; Deputy Dir CCP Cen. Cttee Rural Policy Research Office 1985–88; Sec.-Gen. State Council 1985–88, State Councillor 1988–98; mem. 13th CCP Cen. Cttee 1987–92, 14th CCP Cen. Cttee 1992–97; fmr Dir State Flood-Control and Drought Relief HQ; fmr Vice-Chair. Three Gorges Project Construction Cttee; Chair. Nat. Afforestation Cttee; Chair. Bd of Dirs Nat. Office of Supply and Marketing Co-operatives 1995–98; Vice-Chair. 9th Nat. Cttee of CPPCC 1998–2003. *Address:* c/o National Committee of Chinese People's Political Consultative Conference, 23 Taipingqiao Street, Beijing, People's Republic of China.

CHEN, Kaige; Chinese film director; b. 1954, Beijing; m. Chen Hong; ed Beijing Cinema Coll.; worker, rubber plantation, Yunnan; soldier for four years; Golden Palm Award 1993, New York Film Critics' Best Foreign Film 1993. *Films include:* The Yellow Earth (Best Film, Berlin Film Festival), Life on a String, King of the Children 1988, Farewell My Concubine 1993, The Assassin 1998, The Emperor and the Assassin 1999, Killing Me Softly 2002, He ni zai yi qi (Together with You) 2002, Ten Minutes Older: The Trumpet (segment) 2002, Mo gik (The Promise) 2004, Zhanxiou Village 2007, Mei Lanfang 2008. *Publications:* King of the Children, The New Chinese Cinema (with Tony Raynes) 1989, Bawang bieji 1992. *Address:* William Morris Agency, 151 South El Camino Drive, Beverly Hills, CA 90212 (office); Beijing Cinema College, Beijing, People's Republic of China.

CHEN, Kuiyuan; Chinese party official; *Vice-Chairman, 11th Chinese People's Political Consultative Conference National Committee;* b. 1941; ed Inner Mongolia Teachers' Univ.; joined CCP 1965; fmr mem., Deputy Sec.-Gen., Sec.-Gen. CCP League Cttee Standing Cttee, Hulun Buir League, Inner Mongolia Autonomous Region, Deputy Sec. and Sec. 1983–89; mem. CCP Autonomous Regional Cttee Standing Cttee, Inner Mongolia Autonomous Region 1989–92: Vice-Chair. Inner Mongolia Autonomous Regional People's Congress 1989–92; Deputy Sec. CCP Tibet Autonomous Region Cttee 1992, Sec. 1992–2000; mem. 14th CCP Cen. Cttee 1992–97, 15th CCP Cen. Cttee 1997–2002, 16th CCP Cen. Cttee 2002–07, 17th CCP Cen. Cttee 2007–; apptd First Sec. CCP Party Cttee PLA, Tibet Mil. Region 1996; Sec. CCP Henan Prov. Cttee 2000–02; Pres. Chinese Acad. of Social Sciences 2002–; Vice-Chair. 10th CPPCC Nat. Cttee 2003–08, 11th CPPCC Nat. Cttee 2008–. *Address:* Chinese Academy of Social Sciences, 5 Jianguomennei Dajie, Beijing 100732, People's Republic of China.

CHEN, Liangyu; Chinese politician; b. Oct. 1946, Ningbo, Zhejiang Prov.; ed PLA Logistics Engineering Inst., Tongji Univ., Shanghai, Party School, First Bureau of Electrical Machinery, Univ. of Birmingham, UK; joined PLA 1963, soldier, Services and Arms Group Army Unit No. 6716 1968–70; worker, designer, Deputy Section Chief of Infrastructure, Shanghai Pengpu Machinery Factory 1970–83; joined CCP 1980; designer, Shanghai Pengpu Machine Bldg Factory; Sec. CCP Shanghai Electric Appliances Corpn Cttee; Vice-Dir, then Dir Veteran Cadre Dept, Shanghai Municipal Cttee –1985, Vice-Sec.-Gen., then Vice-Sec. Shanghai Municipal Cttee 1992–96; Vice-Sec., then Dist Magistrate Huangpu Dist Cttee 1985–92; Exec. Vice-Mayor of Shanghai 1996–2001, Acting Mayor 2001–02, Mayor 2002–03; Alt. mem. 15th CCP Cen. Cttee 1997–2002, 16th CCP Cen. Cttee 2002–07, Politburo 2002–07, Sec. CCP Municipal Cttee, Shanghai 2002–06 (sacked for misuse of Shanghai pension fund), expelled from CCP and sentenced to 18 years imprisonment on corruption charges 2008.

CHEN, Lu Yu; Chinese television presenter; b. Beijing; known as "Oriental Oprah"; host of daily chat show A Date with Lu Yu on Hong Kong-based Phoenix Satellite TV station; working with Sina.com to develop new, daily, Oprah Winfrey-style of talk show; China TV Programme Award for the Best Female Presenter of the Year 2000. *Television includes:* Good Morning China, Phoenix Afternoon Express. *Address:* A Date with Lu Yu, Phoenix Satellite TV, Room 306, No. 165 Haidian Road, Haidian District, Beijing, 100080, People's Republic of China (office). *Telephone:* (10) 62510868 (office); (10) 62510511 (office). *Fax:* (10) 62510484 (office). *Website:* www.phoenixtv.com (office).

CHEN, Mingyi; Chinese administrator; *Chairman, Fujian Provincial Committee, Chinese People's Political Consultative Conference;* b. 1940, Fuzhou City, Fujian Prov.; ed Jiaotong Univ., Shanghai; joined CCP 1960; teacher, Jiaotong Univ.; Vice-Gov. Fujian Prov. 1993–94, Gov. 1994–96; Deputy Sec. CCP Fujian Prov. Cttee 1993–95, Sec. 1996–2000; Chair. CPPCC Fujian Prov. Cttee 2001–; Alt. mem. 12th CCP Cen. Cttee 1982–87, 13th CCP Cen. Cttee 1987–92, 14th CCP Cen. Cttee 1992–97, mem. 15th CCP Cen. Cttee 1997–2002; Deputy to 8th NPC 1996. *Address:* Fujian Provincial People's Political Consultative Conference, Fuzhou City, People's Republic of China.

CHEN, Muhua; Chinese politician; *Honorary Chairperson, Bank of China;* b. 1921, Qingtian Co., Zhejiang Prov.; ed Yanan Mil. School; joined CCP 1938; mem. 10th Cen. Cttee of CCP 1973; Minister for Econ. Relations with Foreign Countries 1977–82, also in charge of the State Family Planning Comm. 1981–82, Minister of Foreign Trade 1982–85, a Vice-Premier 1978–82; Pres. People's Bank of China 1985–88, Chair. Council People's Bank of China June 1985, Hon. Chair. People's Bank of China 1985–; Dir State Treasury Aug. 1985–; Alt. mem. Politburo 1977–87; Head Population Census Leading Group 1979–; mem. 12th CCP Cen. Cttee 1982–87, 13th CCP Cen. Cttee 1987–92; mem. 14th CCP Cen. Cttee 1992–97; State Councillor 1982–; Chair. Cen. Patriotic Sanitation Campaign Cttee Cen. Cttee 1981–; Pres. China Greening Foundation; Chinese Gov. World Bank 1985–88, Asian Devt Bank 1986–; Pres. China Women Devt Fund 1988–; Vice-Chair. NPC 7th Standing Cttee 1988–93, 8th Standing Cttee 1993–98; Pres. All-China Women's Fed. 1988–98, Hon. Pres. 1998–; Adviser Nat. Co-ordination Group for Anti-Illiteracy Work 1994–, Chinese Asscn for Promotion of the Population Culture; Hon. Pres. Int. Econ. Co-operation Soc. 1983–, Florists' Asscn 1984–; Hon. Pres. China Asscn of Women Judges 1994–, China Asscn of Women Doctors, Asscn for Import and Export Commodity Inspection. *Address:* All-China Women's Federation, 15 Jian Guo Men Nei Street, 100130 Beijing, People's Republic of China (office). *Telephone:* (10) 65225357 (office). *Fax:* (10) 65136044 (office).

CHEN, Nengkuan, DEng; Chinese physicist; b. 1923, Cili, Hu'nan Prov.; ed Tangshan Eng College, Jiaotong Univ., Yale Univ., USA; fmrly Research Fellow Inst. of Physics and Inst. of Atomic Energy, Chinese Acad. of Sciences; Research Fellow, Chinese Atomic Energy Science Research Inst.; Vice-Dir Science and Tech. Cttee of Ministry of Nuclear Industry; mem. Technological Science Dept, Chinese Acad. of Sciences; Exec. Council mem. Chinese Nuclear Soc.; Meritorious Service Medal for work on the devt of China's atomic and hydrogen bombs and satellites by the CCP Cen. Cttee, the State Council and the Cen. Mil. Comm. 1999. *Address:* Chinese Academy of Sciences, 52 Sanlihe Road, Beijing 100864, People's Republic of China (office).

CHEN, Ningning; Chinese business executive; *Chairman, Pioneer Metals Holdings;* d. of Lu Hui; fmr Exec. Dir and Vice-Chair. China Oriental Group Co. Ltd; Chair. Pioneer Metals Holdings. *Address:* Pioneer Metals Holdings, 5F China Textile Building, No. 19 Jianguomennei Street, Beijing 100005, People's Republic of China (office). *Telephone:* (10) 65129966 (office). *Fax:* (10) 65285085 (office). *E-mail:* webmaster@pioneer-metals.com (office). *Website:* www.pioneer-metals.com (office).

CHEN, Peisi; Chinese comedian and actor; b. 1953, Ningjin, Hebei; s. of Chen Qiang; worked in Nei Monggo Production and Construction Corps 1969–73; with PLA Bayi Film Studio 1973–; comic sketches in collaboration with Zhu Shimao, at successive Chinese New Year Gala Nights on Chinese Cen. TV; took part in Olympic Torch Relay, Nanjing May 2008. *Films:* Look at This Family, Inside and Outside the Law Court, Sunset Boulevard, Erzi Running a Shop, A Stupid Manager, A Chivalrous Ball-Game Star in the Capital, A Young Master's Misfortune, A Millionaire from the South China Sea, Make a Bomb 1993, Sub-Husband 1993, Her Majesty is Fine 1995, Bao lian deng (voice) 2000, The Secret of the Magic Gourd (voice) 2007. *Plays:* A Dou (producer and lead actor) 2008. *Address:* People's Liberation Army Bayi Film Studio, Beijing, People's Republic of China (office).

CHEN, Qingtai, BSc; Chinese politician and business executive; b. 1937, Fengrun, Hebei Prov.; ed Tsinghua Univ., Beijing; joined CCP 1956; Dir Design Dept, Vice-Chief Engineer, Chief Engineer, Gen. Man., then Chair. Aeolus United Automotive Industry Corpn 1962–88, Chair. Aeolus-Citroen Automobile Co. Ltd; Chair. and CEO Dongfeng Peugeot Citroen Automobile Ltd 1985–92; Deputy Dir State Econ. and Trade Comm. 1992–93, Vice-Minister 1993–98; mem. Chinese Monetary Policy Cttee 1997–; Dir Devt Research Centre of the State Council 1993–98, Deputy Dir 1998–2001; mem. 9th CPPCC Nat. Cttee 1998–2003; Dir Sinopec Corpn 2000–06; Dir Bank of Communications Co. Ltd 2005–, Mindray Medical Int. Ltd 2006–; Nat.

Excellent Entrepreneur 1988. *Address:* Development Research Centre of the State Council, Beijing, People's Republic of China (office).

CHEN, Qiqi; Chinese administrator; b. 26 April 1941, Guangdong Prov.; m. Prof. Zheng Sheu Xen; one s.; ed Guangdong Medical School, Medical Coll. of Italy; doctor, Guangdong Leprosy Hosp. 1965–75; teacher, Guangzhou Medical School 1975–81; Vice-Mayor of Guangzhou Municipality 1985; Pres. Guangdong Red Cross; Dir China Red Cross; Vice-Pres. Guangzhou People's Asscn for Friendship with Foreign Countries. *Address:* 1 Fuqian Road, Guangzhou, Guangdong (office); 86 Yue Hwa Road, Guangzhou, Guangdong, People's Republic of China (home). *Telephone:* (20) 330360 (office); (20) 3333100 (home). *Fax:* (20) 340347.

CHEN, Quanxun; Chinese business executive; *Chairman, Supervisory Board, Shanghai Baosteel Group Corporation;* currently Chair. Supervisory Bd Shanghai Baosteel Group Corpn; Dir Sichuan Chuantou Energy Co. Ltd 2008–; Chair. State-Owned Enterprise Supervisory Panel –2008. *Address:* Shanghai Baosteel Group Corporation, Baosteel Tower, Shanghai 200122, People's Republic of China (office). *Telephone:* (21) 58350000 (office). *Fax:* (21) 68404832 (office). *Website:* www.baosteel.com (office).

CHEN, Rongzhen; Chinese business executive (retired); b. Aug. 1938, Feidong, Anhui Prov.; Dir Hefei Washing Machine Gen. Factory (later renamed Rongshida Group) 1986–2002, Chair. and Pres. Rongshida Group –2002 (retd). *Address:* c/o Rongshida Group, 669 Changjian Road, Hefei 230088, Anhui Province, People's Republic of China (office).

CHEN, Shineng; Chinese administrator; b. 1938, Jiaxing Co., Zhejiang Prov.; ed Qinghua Univ.; joined CCP 1962; Vice-Minister of Light Industry 1984–93; Gov., Guizhou Prov. 1993–96; Deputy Sec., CCP 7th Guizhou Prov. Cttee 1993–96, Dir Cttee for Comprehensive Man.; Vice-Minister of Chemical Industry 1996; Vice-Chair. NPC Ethnic Affairs Cttee 2003–. *Address:* Ethnic Affairs Committee, National People's Congress, Beijing 100723, People's Republic of China.

CHEN, Shui-bian, LLB; Taiwanese politician, civil servant and fmr head of state; b. 18 Feb. 1951, Taiwan; s. of the late Chen Sung-ken and of Chen Li Shen; m. Wu Shu-jen 1975; one s. one d.; ed Nat. Taiwan Univ.; attorney-at-law 1974, Chief Attorney-at-Law, Formosa Int. Marine and Commercial Law Office 1976–89; mem. Taipei City Council 1981–85; Publr Free Time serial magazines 1984; Exec. mem. Taiwan Asscn for Human Rights 1984; in jail 1986–87; mem. Democratic Progressive Party (DPP) 1987–2008, Cen. Standing Cttee 1987–89, 1996–2000, Cen. Exec. 1987–89, 1991–96, Chair. 2002–04 (resgnd), 2007–08 (resgnd); mem. Legis. Yuan (Parl.) 1989–94, Exec. Dir DPP Caucus 1990–93, Convener Nat. Defence Cttee 1992–94, Convener Rules Cttee 1993, mem. Judiciary Cttee 1994; Chair. Formosa Foundation 1990–94, 1999–2000; Mayor of Taipei City 1994–98; Pres. of Taiwan 2000–May 2008; arrested and charged with graft Nov. 2008; Hon. DEcons (Plekhanov Russian Acad. of Econs) 1995; Hon. LLD (Kyungnam Univ., Repub. of Korea) 1995; Hon. DPolSc (Yong-In Univ., Repub. of Korea) 2000; Dr hc (Nat. Asuncion Univ., Paraguay 2001, (Nat. Autonomous Univ., Honduras) 2001; Man of the Taiwan Parl. 1993, Newsweek magazine Global Young Leaders for the New Millennium 1994, Asiaweek magazine Asia's 20 Young Political Stars 1999, Prize for Freedom, Liberal International 2001, Int. League for Human Rights Award 2003. *Publications:* National Defense Black Box and White Paper (co-author), Series on Justice (four vols), Conflict, Compromise and Progress, Through the Line Between Life and Death, The Son of Taiwan, The First Voyage of the Century: Reflections on Taiwan's First Alternation of Political Power, Believe in Taiwan: Chen Shui-bian's Report to the People, President A-bian: Up Close and Personal, Taiwan, Young and Vibrant: Journeying Down the Road of Progress, The New Middle Road for Taiwan: A New Political Perspective (speech). *Address:* c/o Democratic Progressive Party, 10/F, 30 Beiping East Road, Taipei 10051, Taiwan (office).

CHEN, Shupeng, (Shijen), MSc; Chinese scientist; *Honorary Director, Institute of Remote Sensing Applications, Chinese Academy of Sciences;* b. (Shijen), 28 Feb. 1920, Jiangxi, Pingshang; s. of Chen Yuoyuan and Lee Manlian; m. Zhang Dihua 1944; one s. one d.; ed Zhejiang Univ., Hanzhou; Research Prof., Geography Science and Resource Research Inst. of Academia Sinica 1978–; Chief Designer China-Brazil Satellite Resources Application 1987–92; Pres. Geographical Soc. of China 1991–94; Hon. Dir Inst. of Remote Sensing Applications, Chinese Acad. of Sciences 1988–, Co-Chair. Space Science Application Cttee 1990–; Chair. Science and Tech. Consultation Cttee, State Environmental Protection Admin; Consultant, Nat. Remote Sensing Centre; Fellow Third World Acad. of Sciences 1992–; Academician, Dept of Earth Sciences, Academia Sinica 1980–, Chinese Acad. of Sciences 1980–, Int. Eurasian Acad. of Science 1992–; mem. China Council for Int. Cooperation on Environment and Devt; Hon. mem. Soc. Geographie, France; Dr hc (Chinese Univ. of Hong Kong) 2006; 30 prizes including Hon. State Prize of Science of China 1988, Jinniu Prize, State Planning Comm. 1992, State Gold Prize for Environmental Science 1993, O. Miller Cartographic Award, American Geographical Soc. 1998, Tan Kah Kee Prize in Earth Science 1999, Award of Natural Science, 1st Class, CAS 2000, Carl Mannerfelt Gold Medal, Int. Cartographic Asscn 2001, Contrib. Award, Int. Karst Asscn 2001, Nat. Award of Science and Tech., 2nd class PRC 2005. *Publications include:* Atlas of China's Landscape in Bird's-eye View 1947, Atlas of Landsat Image Analysis in China 1985, Probe on Geo-Sciences, Vols I–VI 1990–2003, Dictionary of Remote Sensing (Ed.-in-Chief) 1990, Atlas of Multidisciplinary Analysis of Meteorological Satellite Imagery in China (Ed.-in-Chief) 1992, The Start of Remote Sensing and Geo-information Systems in China 1993, Geo-information Science and Digital Earth (in English) 2004. *Leisure interests:* travel, field sketching, Chinese painting, Beijing opera. *Address:* Institute of Remote Sensing Applications, Chinese Academy of Sciences, PO Box 9718, Datun Road, Beijing 100101; No. 1301, Building 801A, Apartment of CAS, Zhongguancun, Beijing 100080, People's Republic of China (home). *Telephone:* (10) 64889547 (office); (10) 82661812 (home). *Fax:* (10) 8488 9630; (10) 82661812 (home). *E-mail:* Chsp@Ireis.ac.cn (office); chsupg@public.bta.net.cn (home).

CHEN, Suzhi; Chinese politician; b. 1931, Shengyang City, Liaoning Prov.; ed Liaoning Univ.; joined the CCP 1949; factory dir 1978; Vice-Gov. Liaoning in charge of industrial work 1982; Alt. mem. 12th CCP Cen. Cttee 1982–87, 13th Cen. Cttee 1987–92; mem. Standing Cttee CCP Prov. Cttee Liaoning 1982; Dir Liaoning Prov. Trade Union Council 1986; Alt. mem. CCP 12th and 13th Cen. Cttee; mem. Standing Cttee 7th CPC Liaoning Provincial Cttee 1985–; Rep. to CCP 13th Nat. Congress; Vice-Gov. Liaoning Prov. 1988–; Deputy to 8th NPC Liaoning Prov.; Vice-Chair. Liaoning Provincial 8th People's Congress Standing Cttee 1992–, Cttee for Comprehensive Man. of Social Security; mem. NPC Internal and Judicial Affairs Cttee. *Address:* Liaoning Trade Union Offices, Shenyang, People's Republic of China.

CHEN, Tan-Sun (Mark), MS, PhD; Taiwanese politician; b. 1935, Tainan County; m. June Chen; three s.; ed Nat. Taiwan Univ., Purdue Univ. and Univ. of Oklahoma, USA; with US Dept of Commerce, Washington, DC 1973–92; mem. Legis. Yuan 1992, 2001–04; Magistrate of Tainan Co. 1993–2001; Minister of Foreign Affairs 2004–06; Sec.-Gen. Office of the Pres. 2006–07; Sec.-Gen. Nat. Security Council 2007; indicted on corruption and forgery charges Sept. 2007; Chair. Taiwanese Asscn of America 1979, World Fed. of Taiwanese Asscns 1979, Formosan Asscn for Public Affairs 1982, Int. Cooperation and Devt Fund 2004; fmr Vice-Chair. Taiwan Foundation for Democracy; mem. Democratic Progressive Party; Dr hc Purdue Univ. 2006. *Leisure interests:* hiking, tennis, swimming, reading, music. *Address:* c/o Democratic Progressive Party, 10/F, 30 Beiping East Rd, Taipei 10051, Taiwan. *Telephone:* (2) 23929989. *Fax:* (2) 23929989. *E-mail:* foreign@dpp.org.tw. *Website:* www.dpp.org.tw.

CHEN, Tian-jy, BSc, PhD; Taiwanese economist, academic and government official; *Minister of the Council for Economic Planning and Development;* ed Nat. Taiwan Univ., Pennsylvania State Univ., USA; Asst Prof., Dept of Econs, Univ. of Mississippi, USA 1983–85, Drexel Univ. 1986–87; Prof., Dept of Econs, Nat. Taiwan Univ. 1995–; Assoc. Research Fellow, Int. Div., Chung-Hua Inst. for Econ. Research 1985–88, Research Fellow 1988–95, Dir 1991–95, Acting Pres. 2002–03, Pres. 2003–05; Minister of the Council for Econ. Planning and Devt, Exec. Yuan 2008–. *Address:* Council for Economic Planning and Development, 3 Baocing Road, Taipei 10020, Taiwan (office). *Telephone:* (2) 23165300 (office). *Fax:* (2) 23700415 (office). *Website:* www.cepd.gov.tw (office).

CHEN, Tonghai; Chinese economist and oil industry executive; b. Sept. 1948, Shandong; s. of Chen Weida; ed Northeastern Petroleum Inst.; Deputy Sec. then Sec. Zhenhai Petroleum and Petrochemical Gen. Plant (subsidiary of fmr China Petrochemical Corpn) 1983–86; Acting Deputy Mayor Ningbo City, Zhejiang Prov. 1986–89, Acting Mayor 1991–92, Mayor 1992–94; Acting Deputy Dir Planning and Econ. Comm. of Zhejiang Prov. 1989–91; Vice-Minister State Devt and Planning Comm. 1994–98; Vice-Pres. China Petrochemical Group Co. (now Sinopec Corpn) 1998–2003, Pres. 2003–06, Dir and Vice-Chair. 2000–03, Dir and Chair. 2003–2007 (resgnd). *Address:* c/o China Petroleum & Chemical Corporation (Sinopec), 6A Huixingdong Street, Chaoyand District, Beijing 100029, People's Republic of China (office).

CHEN, Tsu-Pei, BA; Taiwanese business executive; *President, Cathay Financial Holding Co.;* ed Nat. Chengchi Univ.; Pres. Cathay United Bank, Pres. Cathay Financial Holding Co.; mem. Turnaround Man. Asscn. *Address:* Cathay Financial Group (Cathay Financial Holding Co.), 16th Floor, 296, Sec. 4, Ren Ai Road, Taipei 106, Taiwan (office). *Telephone:* (2) 2708-7698 (office). *Fax:* (2) 2325-2488 (office). *E-mail:* service@cathayholdings.com.tw (office). *Website:* www.cathayholdings.com.tw (office).

CHEN, Wei-jao, MD, MPH, DMSc; Taiwanese surgeon; *Professor of Surgery and Public Health, National Taiwan University;* b. 15 Nov. 1939, Taichung; s. of the late Chen Wen-Chiang and of Chen Wu-Ping; m. Shiang Yang Tang 1970; one s. one d.; ed Coll. of Medicine, Nat. Taiwan Univ., Postgraduate Medical School, Tohoku Univ. Japan and School of Hygiene and Public Health, Johns Hopkins Univ. USA; Resident, Dept of Surgery, Nat. Taiwan Univ. Hosp. 1966–70, Visiting Surgeon (Pediatric Surgery) 1975–, Deputy Dir 1989–91; mem. Faculty, Coll. of Medicine Nat. Taiwan Univ. 1975–, Dean 1991–93, Pres. Nat. Taiwan Univ. 1993–2005, also Prof. of Surgery and Public Health; Fellow in Pediatric Surgery, Tohoku Univ. Japan 1972–75; Visiting Research Assoc. Prof., Univ. of Cincinnati 1981–82; recipient of numerous awards. *Publications:* Story of Separation of Conjoined Twins 1980, Unilateral Occlusion of Duplicated Mullerian Ducts with Renal Anomaly (jtly) 2000, New Advances in Clinical Nutrition; more than 190 scientific papers on surgery, nutrition and public health. *Leisure interest:* hiking. *Address:* 7 Chung-shan South Road, Taipei 100 (office); 1 Roosevelt Road, Sec. 4, Taipei 106 (office); No 15, Sec II, Hsin-Yi Road, Taipei, Taiwan (home). *Telephone:* (2) 2356-2122 (office); (2) 2351-6380 (home). *Fax:* (2) 2341-2969 (office). *E-mail:* chenwj@ntu.edu.tw (office).

CHEN, Wenchi, MS; Taiwanese business executive; *President and CEO, VIA Technologies, Inc.;* m. Cher Wang; two c.; ed Nat. Taiwan Univ., California Inst. of Tech., USA; held positions of Vice-Pres. Sales and Marketing, ULSI Systems Technology and Sr Architect, Intel; Co-founder, Pres. and CEO Symphony Laboratories, Santa Clara, Calif. –1992; Pres. and CEO VIA Technologies, Inc. 1992–; named Top Star in Asia by Business Week 1999, ranked No. 1 Entrepreneur in Asia by Business Week 2001. *Address:* VIA Technologies, Inc., 1F, 531, Chung-Cheng Road, Hsin-Tien, Taipei 231,

Taiwan (office). *Telephone:* (2) 22185452 (office). *Fax:* (2) 22185453 (office). *E-mail:* mkt@via.com.tw (office). *Website:* www.via.com.tw (office).

CHEN, Xianglin; Chinese automobile executive; Pres. Shanghai Automotive Industry Corpn (SAIC) 1983–86, 1995–2006; Dir Shanghai Planning Comm. 1986–93; Vice Party Sec., Shanghai CP Cttee 1993–94. *Address:* c/o Shanghai Automotive Industry Corporation (SAIC), 487 Wei Hai Road, Shanghai 200041, People's Republic of China (office).

CHEN, Xieyang; Chinese conductor; *Music Director and Principal Conductor, Shanghai Symphony Orchestra;* b. 4 May 1939, Shanghai; s. of Chen Dieyi and Liang Peiqiong; m. Wang Jianying 1973; ed Music High School, Shanghai Conservatory; Conductor, Shanghai Ballet 1965–84; studied with Prof. Otto Mueller, Yale Univ., USA 1981–82; Conductor, Aspen Music Festival, Group for Contemporary Music, New York, Brooklyn Philharmonia, Honolulu Symphony, Philippines State Orchestra, Hong Kong Philharmonic, Shanghai Symphony Orchestra, Cen. Philharmonic, Beijing 1981–83, Symphony Orchestra of Vilnius, Kaunas, Novosibirsk, USSR 1985, Tokyo Symphony Orchestra 1986, Orchestre Regional de Cannes 2003; Music Dir and Prin. Conductor Shanghai Symphony Orchestra 1984–; has made recording for Kuklos CBE, France 1983; Dir China Musicians' Asscn; Pres. Shanghai Symphonic Music Lovers' Soc.; Excellent Conducting Prize, Shanghai Music Festival 1986. *Address:* Shanghai Symphony Orchestra, 105 Hunan Road, Shanghai 200031, People's Republic of China. *Telephone:* 64335608 (office); 64672915 (home). *Fax:* 64333752 (office). *E-mail:* shso105@ sh163.net (office). *Website:* www.sh-symphony.com.

CHEN, Yaobang; Chinese politician; b. 1935, Panyu City, Guangdong Prov.; ed Cen. China Agricultural Coll.; Asst. Cen. China Agricultural Coll. 1957–62; Deputy Chief Div. of Cash Crops Bureau, Ministry of Agriculture 1979–82; joined CCP 1982; Deputy Dir Animal Husbandry and Fisheries, Agricultural Bureau, Ministry of Agric. 1982–84, Vice-Minister 1986–88, Vice-Minister of Agric. 1988–93, Minister of Agric. 1998–2003; Deputy Sec. CCP Wuxi City Cttee 1984–86; Del., 13th CCP Nat. Congress 1987–92, 14th CCP Nat. Congress 1992–97; Vice-Minister State Devt and Reform Comm. 1993–97; mem. Science and Tech. Sub-cttee, CPPCC Nat. Cttee 1993–98; Deputy Chief State Flood Control and Drought Relief HQ 1993–98; Deputy Dir Nat. Afforestation Cttee 1993–98, Nat. Cttee on Mineral Reserves 1995–97; Vice-Pres. China Mining Industry Asscn 1997; Deputy Dir Beijing Afforestation Cttee 1997; Minister of Forestry 1997–98; mem. 15th CCP Cen. Cttee 1997–2002. *Address:* c/o Ministry of Agriculture, Nongzhanguan Nan Li, Chaoyang Qu, Beijing 100026, People's Republic of China (office).

CHEN, Yong; Chinese seismologist; b. Dec. 1942, Chongqing; ed Chinese Univ. of Science and Tech.; Assoc. Research Fellow, Research Fellow, Dir Geophysics Research Inst. of Nat. Bureau of Seismology 1965–85, Vice-Dir Nat. Bureau of Seismology 1985–96; Dean, School of Earth and Space Science, Chinese Univ. of Science and Tech. 2005–; mem. Chinese Acad. of Sciences 1993–, also Deputy Dir-Gen., Seismology Div.; fmr Chair. Comm. on Earthquake Prediction and Hazard, Int. Asscn of Seismology and Physics of the Earth's Interior; Exec. Dir Int. Seismological Center –2005; Vice Pres. Chinese Geophysical Soc., Chinese Seismological Soc.; Fellow Third World Acad. of Sciences 2000–; award for Progress in Science and Technology (several times); Holeung Ho Lee Foundation Earth Sciences Prize 2006. *Publications:* seven monographs and over 100 essays; The Great Tangshan Earthquake of 1976. *Address:* National Bureau of Seismology, 61 Fuxing Lu, Beijing 100036, People's Republic of China (office).

CHEN, Yuan, BS, MA; Chinese banker; *Governor, China Development Bank;* b. 13 Jan. 1945, Shanghai; s. of Chen Yun; ed China Acad. of Social Sciences, Tsinghua Univ., Beijing; Sec. CCP Cttee of Xicheng Dist, Beijing 1982–84; Dir-Gen. Dept of Commerce and Trade, Beijing Municipal Govt 1984–88; Vice-Gov. People's Bank of China 1988–98; Gov. China Devt Bank 1998–; mem. Preparatory Cttee of Hong Kong Special Admin. Region, Vice-Pres. Financial Soc.; mem. Securities Comm. of the State Council; Sec. CCP Xicheng Dist Cttee, Beijing; Alt. Mem. 16th CCP Cen. Cttee 2002–07, 17th CCP Cen. Cttee 2007–; Dir Inst. for Int. Econs, USA (mem. Advisory Cttee and the Financial Stability Inst.); Deputy Gov., Dir Business and Trade Activities Dept, and Adviser to Postgraduates, People's Bank of China (also Deputy Sec. CCP Party Cttee). *Publications:* The Underlying Problems and Options in China's Economy, Macroeconomic Management: The Need for Deepening Reform, Collected Works. *Address:* China Development Bank, 29 Fuchengmenwai Lu, Xicheng Qu, Beijing 100037, People's Republic of China (office). *Telephone:* (10) 68307608 (office). *Fax:* (10) 68306541 (office). *Website:* (office).

CHEN, Yun-ti, PhD; Chinese professor of chemistry; *Professor of Chemistry, Nankai University;* b. 7 Nov. 1919, Dianjiang Co., Sichuan Prov.; m. Yang Guangyu 1947; one s. one d.; ed Indiana Univ., USA; researcher, Northwestern Univ. and Chicago Univ. 1952–54; Prof., Nankai Univ. Tianjin 1954–; mem. Chinese Acad. of Sciences 1980–, 7th NPC 1988–93, 8th Standing Cttee 1993–; Vice-Dir Standing Cttee Tianjin People's Congress 1993–; Distinguished Visiting Scholar, NAS 1984; Cornell Distinguished Visiting Prof., Swarthmore Coll., USA 1988; Hon. State Prize of Science of China 1985, 1986, 1987, 1991, 1999; Chugayev Medal and Diploma, USSR Acad. of Sciences 1987. *Publications:* Correlation Analysis in Co-ordination Chemistry 1994; over 300 articles in Chinese and foreign journals. *Leisure interests:* classical music and Beijing Opera. *Address:* Department of Chemistry, Nankai University, Tianjin 300071, People's Republic of China. *Telephone:* (22) 28363645. *Fax:* (22) 22-23502458. *E-mail:* ytchen@sun.nankai.edu.cn (office).

CHEN, Yunlin; Chinese politician; *President, Association for Relations Across the Taiwan Straits;* b. Dec. 1941, Heishan Co., Liaoling Prov.; ed Beijing Agricultural Univ.; joined CCP 1966; technician, Deputy Dir, Dir Yucuntun Chemical Works, Qiqihar City, Heilongjiang Prov. 1960s–70s (also

Deputy Sec. CCP Party Cttee); Deputy Sec. CCP Qiqihar City Cttee 1983; Mayor Qiqihar City 1983; Deputy Sec. CCP Heilongjiang Prov. Cttee 1984 (also mem. Standing Cttee, CCP Prov. Cttee); Dir Comm. for Restructuring the Economy, Heilongjiang Prov. 1984; Vice-Gov. Heilongjiang Prov. 1987–94; Del., 13th CCP Nat. Congress 1987–92; Deputy Dir Cen. Office for Taiwan Affairs of State Council 1999–2003, Dir 2003–08; Pres. Asscn for Relations Across the Taiwan Straits 2008–; Alt. mem. 14th CCP Cen. Cttee 1992–97, mem. 15th CCP Cen. Cttee 1997–2002, 16th CCP Cen. Cttee 2002–07; mem. CCP Qiqihar City Standing Cttee. *Address:* Association for Relations Across the Taiwan Straits, No. 6-1, Guang'anmen Nanjie, Xuanwu District, Beijing, People's Republic of China (office). *Telephone:* (10) 83551779 (office).

CHEN, Zhangliang, PhD; Chinese professor of biology and government official; *Head of Plant Gene Engineering Laboratory, Beijing University;* b. 1961; ed Huanan Tropical Crops Coll., Washington Univ., USA; Prof., Head of Plant Gene Eng Lab., Biology Dept and Vice-Pres. Beijing Univ.; Pres. China Agricultural Univ., Beijing 1987–; Vice-Chair. Guangxi Zhuang Autonomous Region People's Govt 2008–. *Address:* Department of Biology, Beijing University, Haidian District, Beijing, People's Republic of China.

CHEN, Zhili; Chinese politician, academic and fmr physicist; *Vice-Chair, 11th NPC Standing Committee;* b. 21 Nov. 1942, Xianyou Co., Fujian Prov.; ed Fudan Univ., Shanghai Inst. of Ceramics, Chinese Acad. of Sciences; joined CCP 1961; served in People's Liberation Armym No. 6409 Army Unit, Danyang Lake Farm 1968–70; Assoc. Research Fellow, Chinese Acad. of Sciences 1970–80, 1982–84, Deputy Sec., CP Cttee of the Inst. 1982–84; Visiting Scholar, Materials Research Lab., Pa State Univ., USA 1980–82; Deputy Sec. CCP Party Cttee, Shanghai Inst. of Ceramics 1983–84; Deputy Sec. and Sec. Science and Tech. Work Cttee, Shanghai CCP Municipal Cttee 1984–86; Alt. mem. 13th CCP Cen. Cttee 1987–92, 14th CCP Cen. Cttee 1992–97; mem. Standing Cttee, Shanghai CCP Municipal Cttee 1988–89, Head Publicity Dept 1988–91, Deputy Sec. Publicity Dept 1989–91; Deputy Sec. CCP Shanghai Municipal Cttee 1991–97; Vice-Minister and Sec. CCP Leading Party Group, State Educ. Comm. 1997–98; Minister of Educ. 1998–2003; apptd mem. State Steering Group of Science, Tech. and Educ. 1998; apptd Vice-Chair. State Academic Degree Cttee 1999; State Councillor 2003–08; mem. 15th CCP Cen. Cttee 1997–2002, 16th CCP Cen. Cttee 2002–07, 17th CCP Cen. Cttee 2007–; Vice-Chair. 11th NPC Standing Cttee 2008–; Hon. Pres. Shanghai Inst. of Int. Friendship. *Address:* c/o Zhongguo Gongchan Dang (Chinese Communist Party), Beijing, People's Republic of China (office).

CHEN, Zhongshi; Chinese novelist; *Chairman, Shaanxi Provincial Writers' Association;* b. 1942, Xian, Shanxi Prov.; Chair. Shaanxi Prov. Writers' Asscn 1993–; Vice-Chair. Chinese Writers' Asscn 2001; Hon. Dean, Dept of Humanities, Shiyou Univ. 2004; took part as torchbearer in Olympic Flame Relay, Xian 2008. *Publications:* Bai Lu Yuan (White Deer Plain) (Mao Dun Prize for Literature 1997) 1993, Early Summer, Mr. Blue Gown, The Cellar 1994, numerous novellas and short stories. *Address:* Shanxi Provincial Writers' Association, Xian, People's Republic of China.

CHEN, Zhu, PhD; Chinese medical scientist and government official; *Minister of Health;* b. Aug. 1953, Zhenjiang, Jiangsu Prov.; ed Shanghai No. 2 Medical Sciences Univ., St Louis Hosp., Univ. de Paris 7, France; apptd Foreign Resident Doctor, St Louis Hosp., Paris 1984; Research Fellow, Chinese Acad. of Sciences (Div. of Biological Sciences) 1990–; Dir Shanghai Haematology Research Inst. 1995; Deputy Dir Shanghai Research Centre of Life Sciences 1996; Deputy Dir Jt Genetics and Medical Sciences Centre, Shanghai No. 2 Medical Sciences Univ.; undertook over 20 nat. key scientific research projects and int. research projects and achieved results on the treatment of leukaemia with diarsenic trioxide and its molecular mechanism, providing a representative model for cancer research; academician, Chinese Acad. of Sciences 1995–, Vice-Pres. 2000–07; Minister of Health 2007–; Laureate, First Shanghai Honour Award of Medical Science 1994, China Youth Scientists' Prize 1994, Ho Lee and Ho Leung Foundation Prize for Medicine 1996, Shanghai Science Elite Nat. Model Worker 1996, Nat. Outstanding Science and Technology Worker 1996, Yangtze Scholar Awarding Program Top Grade Prize 1999, Outstanding Technician Medal, Ministry of Personnel 1999. *Address:* Ministry of Health, 1 Xizhinenwai Bei Lu, Xicheng Qu, Beijing 100044, People's Republic of China (office). *Telephone:* (10) 68792114 (office). *Fax:* (10) 64012369 (office). *Website:* www.moh.gov.cn (office).

CHEN, Zhuo Lin; Chinese business executive; *Chairman, Agile Property Holdings Ltd;* b. Guangdong Prov.; Pres. Zhongshan Agile Co. 1992–96, Zhongshan Group Co. 1997–; Gen. Man. Zhongshan Dynasty Furniture Factory 1989–92; Co-founder Agile Property brand name, Chair. Agile Property Holdings Ltd 2005–; Vice-Chair. Zhongshan Qiaozi Enterprise Asscn; Hon. Chair. Hong Kong Zhongshan Sanxiang Friendship Asscn. *Address:* Agile Property Holdings Ltd, 20/F, 238 Nathan Road, Kowloon, Hong Kong Special Administrative Region, People's Republic of China (office). *Telephone:* (760) 6686868 (office). *Fax:* (760) 6683913 (office). *Website:* www .agile.com.cn (office).

CHEN, Ziming; Chinese writer and dissident; b. 1952; m. Wang Zhihong; imprisoned for 13 years for role in Tiananmen Square pro-democracy demonstrations 1989, released on medical parole 1994, rearrested for staging hunger strike 1995, released on medical grounds 1996; Cttee to Protect Journalists' Int. Press Freedom Award 1991.

CHEN, Zuohuang, MM, DMA; Chinese/American conductor; *Music Director, Shanghai and Incheon Philharmonic Orchestras;* b. 2 April 1947, Shanghai; s. of Chen Ru Hui and Li He Zhen; m. Zaiyi Wang 1969; one c.; ed Cen. Conservatory of Beijing, Univ. of Michigan, USA; Musical Dir China Film Philharmonic 1974–76; Assoc. Prof., Univ. of Kansas, USA 1985–87; Prin.

Conductor Cen. Philharmonic Orchestra of China 1987–96; Music Dir/Conductor Wichita Symphony Orchestra 1990–2000; Music Dir/Conductor Rhode Island Philharmonic Orchestra 1992–96; Artistic Dir, Conductor China Nat. Symphony Orchestra 1996–2000; Music Dir OFUNAM of Mexico 2002–06; Music Dir Shanghai Philharmonic Orchestra, People's Republic of China 2004–, Incheon Philharmonic Orchestra, Republic of Korea 2006–; Artistic Dir, China Nat. Centre for Performing Arts, Beijing 2007–; guest conductor in over 20 countries with Zürich Tonhalle Orchestra, Vancouver Symphony Orchestra, Budapest Philharmonic Orchestra and State Symphony, Gulbenkian Orchestra, Iceland Symphony Orchestra, Tanglewood Music Festival Orchestra, Colorado Symphony Orchestra, Pacific Symphony Orchestra, Virginia Symphony Orchestra, Alabama Symphony Orchestra, Russian Philharmonic Orchestra, Haifa Symphony, Slovak Radio Symphony Orchestra, Hong Kong Philharmonic Orchestra, Singapore Symphony Orchestra, Pusan Philharmonic Orchestra, Mexico Nat. Symphony Orchestra and Mexico City Philharmonic Orchestra, Taipei Symphony Orchestra.

CHEN, Zuolin; Chinese politician; b. 1923, Wuwei Co., Anhui Prov.; Vice-Chair. Revolutionary Cttee, Zhejiang Prov. 1975–79; Deputy Sec. CCP Cttee, Zhejiang 1976, Sec. 1977–83; Alt. mem. 11th CCP Cen. Cttee 1977, 12th Cen. Cttee 1982; Vice-Gov., Zhejiang 1979–83; Sec.-Gen. Cen. Comm. for Discipline Inspection 1985–87, Deputy Sec. 1987; Deputy Sec. CCP Cen. Discipline Inspection Comm. 1992–; mem. Presidium of 14th CCP Nat. Congress 1992, CCP Standing Cttee, Cen. Leading Group for Party Building Work, Internal and Judicial Affairs Cttee; Deputy to 8th NPC Jiangxi Prov. *Address:* Zhejiang Government Office, 28 Reuminlu Road, Hangzhou, People's Republic of China. *Telephone:* 24911.

CHEN, Zutao; Chinese automobile executive (retired); b. 1928; ed Moscow Baumann Highest Tech. Inst.; joined CCP 1960; First Chief Engineer and Vice Dir for Techniques, Dongfeng Motor Corpn 1965–80; First Chief Engineer, Deputy Man. and Gen. Man., China Nat. Automotive Industry Corpn (CAIC) 1981; Commr, Ministry of Science and Tech. 1989. *Address:* c/o China National Automotive Industry Corporation, 46 Fucheng Lu, Haidián Qu, Beijing 100036, People's Republic of China.

CHEN TIANQIAO, Timothy, BEcons; Chinese business executive; *Chairman and CEO, Shanda Entertainment;* ed Fudan Univ.; various man. positions with Shanghai Lujiazui Group 1994–98; Deputy Dir Office of the Pres. Kinghing Trust & Investment Co. Ltd 1998–99; Co-founder, Chair. and CEO Shanghai Shanda Networking Co. Ltd (now Shanda Entertainment) 1999–, Chair. and CEO Shanda Interactive Entertainment Ltd 1999–; mem. 11th CPPCC Nat. Cttee 2008–; Alt. mem. 15th Chinese Communist Youth League Cen. Cttee; youngest mem. China Top 50, Rising Business Star Award, China Central TV 2003. *Address:* Shanda Entertainment, No. 1 Intelligent Office, Building No. 690, Bibo Road, Shanghai 201203, People's Republic of China (office). *Telephone:* (21) 50504740 (office). *Fax:* (21) 50508088 (office). *E-mail:* info@shanda.com.cn (office). *Website:* www.snda.com (office).

CHENAULT, Kenneth Irvine, BA, JD; American financial services company executive; *Chairman and CEO, American Express Company;* b. 2 June 1951, Long Island, NY; s. of Hortensius Chenault and Anne N. Chenault (née Quick); m. Kathryn Cassell 1977; two s.; ed Waldorf School of Garden City, Bowdoin Coll., Harvard Univ. Law School; called to Bar, Mass 1981; assoc., Rogers & Wells, New York 1977–79; consultant, Bain & Co., Boston 1979–81; Dir Strategic Planning, American Express Co., New York 1981–83, Vice-Pres. American Express Travel Related Services Co. Inc., New York 1983–84, Sr Vice-Pres. 1984–86, Exec. Vice-Pres. Platinum Card/Gold 1986–88, Personal Card Div. 1988–89, Pres. Consumer Card and Financial Services Group 1990–93, Pres. (USA) 1993–95, Vice-Chair. American Express Co., New York 1995–97, Pres. and COO 1997–2000, Chair. and CEO 2001–; mem. Bd of Dirs IBM, Brooklyn Union Gas, Quaker Oats Co., New York Univ. Medical Center; mem. Council of Foreign Relations, New York 1988, ABA; several hon. degrees; listed by Ebony magazine as one of 50 "living pioneers" in the African-American community 1995. *Address:* American Express Company, American Express Tower, World Financial Center, 200 Vesey Street, New York, NY 10285-5104, USA (office). *Telephone:* (212) 640-2000 (office). *E-mail:* info@americanexpress.com (office). *Website:* www.americanexpress.com (home).

CHÊNEVERT, Louis R.; Canadian business executive; *President and CEO, United Technologies Corporation;* b. 25 June 1957; ed Univ. of Montreal; worked at Gen. Motors 1979–93, served as Production Gen. Man., St Therese; Vice-Pres. for Operations, Pratt & Whitney Canada 1993–97, Exec. Vice-Pres. 1998–99, Pres. 1999–2006; mem. Bd of Dirs, Pres. and COO United Techs Corpn 2006–08, Pres. and CEO 2008–; Founding Dir Friends of HEC Montreal; Co-Chair. Yale-New Haven Cancer Hosp. Capital Campaign Cttee; mem. Bd of Overseers Bushnell Center for the Performing Arts, Hartford, Conn.; mem. Yale Cancer Center Dir's Advisory Bd; Fellow, AIAA; Nouveaux Performant, Quebec 1995, Quebec Quality Movement Harrington Medal 1997.

CHENEY, Lynne Vincent, BA, MA, PhD; American academic and writer; *Senior Fellow, American Enterprise Institute for Public Policy Research (AEI);* b. 14 Aug. 1941, Casper, Wyo.; d. of Wayne Vincent and Edna (née Lybyer) Vincent; m. Richard B. Cheney (q.v.) 1964; two d. including Elizabeth Cheney; ed Colorado Coll., Univ. of Colorado, Univ. of Wisconsin; freelance writer 1970–83; Lecturer, George Washington Univ. 1972–77, Univ. of Wyoming 1977–78; researcher and writer Md Public Broadcasting 1982–83; Sr Ed. Washingtonian magazine 1983–86; Chair. Nat. Endowment for Humanities 1986–93; W. H. Brady Fellow, American Enterprise Inst. for Public Policy Research, Washington, DC 1993–95, Sr Fellow 1996–; Commr US Constitution Bicentennial Comm. 1985–87; cr. James Madison Book Award Fund 2003; ranked by Forbes magazine amongst 100 Most Powerful Women (23rd) 2004. *Publications:* Executive Privilege 1978, Sisters 1981, Kings of the Hill (jtly) 1983, The Body Politic 1988, Telling the Truth 1995, America: A Patriotic Primer 2002, A is for Abigail: An Almanac of Amazing American Women 2003. *Address:* American Enterprise Institute, 1150 17th Street, NW, Washington, DC 20036, USA (office). *Telephone:* (202) 862-5800 (office). *Fax:* (202) 862-7177 (office). *Website:* www.aei.org (office).

CHENEY, Richard (Dick) B., BA, MA; American politician and fmr business executive; b. 30 Jan. 1941, Lincoln, Neb.; s. of Richard H. Cheney and Marjorie Dickey Cheney; m. Lynne Vincent Cheney (q.v.); two d.; ed Univ. of Wyoming, Univ. of Wisconsin; engaged on staff of Gov. of Wis.; Special Asst to Dir White House Office of Econ. Opportunity 1969–70; Deputy to White House Presidential Counselor 1970–71; Asst Dir of Operations, White House Cost of Living Council 1971–73; partner, Bradley, Woods & Co. 1973–74; Deputy Asst to the Pres. 1974–75, White House Chief of Staff 1975–77; Congressman, At-large District, Wyoming, 1978–89; Chair. Republican Policy Cttee 1981–87; Chair. House Republican Conf. 1987; House Minority Whip 1988; Sec. of Defense 1989–93; Sr Fellow American Enterprise Inst. 1993–95; Chair. Bd and CEO Halliburton Co., Dallas, Tex. 1995–2000 (Pres. 1997); Vice-Pres. of USA 2001–09; Presidential Medal of Freedom 1991. *Address:* c/o Office of the Vice-President, Eisenhower Executive Office Building, 1650 Pennsylvania Avenue, NW, Washington, DC 20502, USA.

CHENG, Andong; Chinese politician; b. Oct. 1936, Huainan City, Anhui Prov.; ed Hefei Polytechnical Univ.; engineer, Mining Admin, Pingxiang City, Jiangxi Prov. 1965–67, Chief Engineer and Deputy Dir 1977–83; Chief Engineer and Deputy Dir Gaokeng Coal Mine, Jiangxi Prov. 1967–1977; mem. CCP 1980–; Mayor of Pingxiang City and Deputy Sec. CCP City Cttee 1983–84; Mayor of Nanchang City, Jiangxi Prov. 1984–90; Asst to Gov. Jiangxi Prov. 1990; Sec. CCP Xian Municipal Cttee 1990; mem. Standing Cttee CCP Shaanxi Prov. Cttee 1990–94, 1998–, Deputy Secretary Provincial Cttee 1994–; Chair. City People's Congress Standing Cttee, Xi'an City, Shaanxi Prov. 1992; Alt. mem. 14th CCP Cen. Cttee 1992–97, mem. 15th CCP Cen. Cttee 1997–2002; Vice-Gov. Shaanxi Prov. 1994, Gov. 1995–2003; Hon. Pres. Bd Hefei Polytechnical Univ. 1995. *Address:* c/o Office of the Governor, Xi'an City, Shaanxi Province, People's Republic of China.

CHENG, Eva, BA, MBA; Chinese business executive; *Executive Vice-President for Greater China and Southeast Asia, Amway Corporation;* ed Univ. of Hong Kong; govt official in Hong Kong –1977; joined Amway Hong Kong as a sec. 1977, apptd Pres. Amway Hong Kong 1980, Exec. Vice-Pres. Amway, responsible for markets in Greater China (Amway (China) Co. Ltd) and SE Asia 2005–, Chair. Amway China and Exec. Vice-Pres. Amway Corpn (global parent firm); ranked by Forbes magazine amongst 100 Most Powerful Women (88th) 2008. *Leisure interest:* Cantonese opera. *Address:* Amway (China) Co. Ltd, 40 & 41F CITIC Plaza, 233 Tianhe North Road, Guangzhou 510613, Guangdong, People's Republic of China (office). *Telephone:* (20) 3891-1368 (office). *Fax:* (20) 3891-2801 (office). *E-mail:* amway@amwaynet.com.cn (office). *Website:* www.amway.com.cn (office).

CHENG, Lianchang; Chinese government official; b. 14 May 1931, Jilin; m. Huang Shulan; one s. one d.; ed Jilin Industrial School, People's Univ. of China; joined CCP 1950; Vice-Minister of 7th Ministry of Machine Building 1975–82; Vice-Minister, Exec. Vice-Minister of Astronautical Ind. 1982–88; Sr Engineer and Researcher 1988–; Exec. Vice-Minister of Personnel 1988–94; mem. State Educational Comm. 1988–94; Vice-Pres. Nat. School of Admin. 1994–96; Vice-Chair. Steering Cttee for Enterprise; Standing mem. 8th Nat. Cttee CPCCC 1993–97, 9th Nat. Cttee CPPCC 1998–2003; Prof., China People's Univ.; Fellow World Acad. of Productivity Science 2001; First-class Award, Ministry of Astronautical Ind. 1984, State Council Award for Outstanding Contribution in High-energy Physics 1991. *Publications:* Selected Works (two vols), Textbook for State Public Servant Examination (20 vols). *Leisure interest:* swimming. *Address:* Room 1501, No. 13 Building, Cuiwei Xili, Haidian District, Beijing 100036, People's Republic of China (home); c/o Ministry of Personnel, Hepingli Zhongjie, Beijing 100013 (office). *Telephone:* (10) 68462628 (office); (10) 68258072 (home); (10) 11184228. *Fax:* (10) 84223240. *E-mail:* chenglch@tom.com (home).

CHENG, Siwei, MBA; Chinese politician; *Director of Science Management Division, National Natural Science Foundation of China;* b. June 1935, Xiang City, Hunan Prov.; ed East China Chemical Eng Inst., Univ. of California at Los Angeles, USA; worker, Shenyang Chemical Eng Research Inst., Liaoning Prov. 1956–58; engineer, Tianjin Chemical Eng Research Inst. 1958–73, Petrochemical Eng Research Inst. (Petroleum Chem. Div.) 1973–81; Chief Engineer, Ministry of Chemical Industry, Science and Tech. Bureau 1984–93, Vice-Chair. Science and Tech. Research Inst. 1988–93; Deputy Dir Ministry of Chemical Industry 1994–96; Vice-Chair. Cen. Cttee China Democratic Nat. Construction Asscn 1994–96, Chair. 1996–; mem. Standing Cttee 8th CPPCC 1993–98; Vice-Chair. Standing Cttee of 9th NPC 1998–2003, Standing Cttee of 10th NPC 2003–; Dir Science Man. Div., Nat. Natural Science Foundation of China 2003–; Chair. China Soft-Science Research Soc.; Hon. DBA (Hong Kong Polytechnic Univ.) 2000; Globalist of the Year 2008. *Address:* National Natural Science Foundation of China, Beijing, People's Republic of China. *Website:* www.nsfc.gov.cn (office).

CHENG, Weigao; Chinese government official; b. 1933, Suzhou City, Jiangsu Prov.; Dir CCP City Cttee, Student Dept and Juvenile Dept, Changzhou City, Jiangsu Prov. 1949–54, Head of CCP Propaganda Dept 1949–54; joined CCP 1950; worker, People's Govt Gen. Office, Changzhou City 1955–62, Deputy Dir 1962–63, Dir 1963–65; Dir Changzhou Tractor Plant 1965–72 (also Sec. CCP Party Cttee 1965–72); Sec. CCP Party Cttee, Shanghuang Coal Mine, Jiangsu Prov. 1972–77; Vice-Chair. Planning Cttee and Chair. Capital Construction Cttee, Changzhou City 1977–80; Sec. CCP City Cttee, Changzhou 1980–84; Deputy, 6th NPC 1983–88; Sec. CCP City Cttee, Nanjing, Jiangsu Prov.

1984–87; mem. Standing Committee, CCP Prov. Cttee, Jiangsu Prov. 1984–87; Deputy Sec. CCP Prov. Cttee, Henan Prov. 1987–90; Vice-Gov. Henan Prov. 1987–88, Gov. 1988–90; Acting Gov. Hebei Prov. 1990–91, Gov. 1991–93; Deputy Sec. CCP Hebei Prov. Cttee 1990–93, Sec. 1993–98; Chair. Standing Cttee of NPC, Hebei Prov. 1998–99; mem. 13th CCP Cen. Cttee 1987–92, 14th CCP Cen. Cttee 1987–92, 15th CCP Cen. Cttee 1997–2002; Deputy, 9th NPC 1998–2003. *Address:* c/o Hebei Provincial Committee of Chinese Communist Party, Shijiazhuang City, Hebei Province, People's Republic of China.

CHENG, Yanan; Chinese sculptor; b. 15 Jan. 1936, Tianjin; d. of Cheng Goliang and Liuo Shijing; m. Zhang Zuoming 1962 (died 1989); one s. one d.; ed Cen. Acad. of Fine Arts, Beijing; sculptor Beijing Architectural Artistic Sculpture Factory 1961–84, Sculpture Studio, Cen. Acad. of Fine Arts 1984–; mem. China Artists' Asscn. *Address:* 452 New Building of Central Institute of Fine Arts, No 5 Shuaifuyan Lane, East District, Beijing, People's Republic of China.

CHENG, Yu-Tung; Chinese business executive; *Chairman, New World Development Company Ltd;* b. 27 Aug. 1925, Shunde, Guangdong; m.; two c.; Dir New World Development Co. Ltd 1970–, Chair. 1982–; Chair. New World Hotels (Holdings) Ltd, Chow Tai Fook Enterprises Ltd; Chair. (non-exec.) Lifestyle International Holdings Ltd; Dir Cheng Yu-Tung Family (Holdings) Ltd, Centennial Success Ltd; Dir (non-exec.) Shun Tak Holdings Ltd 1982–, Hang Seng Bank Ltd; Hon. Consul for Bhutan; Trustee United Coll., Chinese Univ. of Hong Kong; Hon. LLD (Toronto 1987), Hon. DBA, Hon. DSc (Chinese Univ. of Hong Kong 1993); Grand Bauhinia Medal 2008. *Address:* New World Development Company Limited, 30th Floor, New World Tower 18, Queen's Road, Central Hong Kong Special Administrative Region, People's Republic of China (office). *Telephone:* 25231056 (office). *Fax:* 28104673 (office). *Website:* www.nwd.com.hk (office).

CHEONG, Yip Seng; Singaporean journalist and editor; *Editorial Advisor, Singapore Press Holdings;* b. June 1943; trainee journalist The Straits Times Press 1963, then Ed. The New Nation, then Ed. The Straits Times, Deputy Ed.-in-Chief English/Malay Newspapers Div., Singapore Press Holdings (including The Straits Times, Business Times, Berita Harian and The New Paper) late 1970s–87, Ed.-in-Chief English/Malay Newspapers Div. 1987–2007, Editorial Advisor Singapore Press Holdings 2007–; mem. Bd of Dirs SBS Transit Ltd; mem. Nat. Univ. of Singapore Council 2004–; Founding mem. Singapore Press Club 1971–; ASEAN Award for Information 1997. *Address:* The Straits Times, SPH News Centre, P2, 1000 Toa Payoh North, Singapore City, 318994, Singapore (office). *Telephone:* 6319-5106 (office). *Fax:* 6737-5576 (office). *E-mail:* cheong@sph.com.sg (office). *Website:* www.straitstimes.com (office); www.sph.com.sg (office).

CHEPIK, Sergei; Russian artist; b. 24 June 1953, Kiev; s. of Mikhail Chepik and Ludmilla Sabaneyeva; m. Marie-Aude Albert 1992; two s.; ed Shevchenko Art Inst., Kiev, Repin Art Inst., Leningrad; mem. Young Artists' Union 1978; studied at Mylnikov's Studio, USSR 1978–81; mem. USSR Artists' Union 1981–; moved to Paris 1988; more than 25 solo exhbns, London, Paris, Milan 1988–; Grand Prix, Salon d'Automne, Paris 1988, Monaco City Award 1989. *Art works include:* paintings: The House of the Dead 1979–87, Petrushka 1984–86, Memories 1989, Golgotha 1996, The Way, the Truth, the Life (St Paul's Cathedral, London) 2002–04, The Redemption 2007, The Last Supper 2007; other: illustrations for Bulgakov's The White Guard 2006. *Leisure interests:* literature, ballet, ceramics, sculpture. *Address:* c/o The Catto Gallery, 100 Heath Street, London, NW3 1DP, England (office). *Telephone:* (20) 7435-6660 (London) (office). *Fax:* (20) 7431-5620 (London) (office). *E-mail:* contact@chepik.com (home). *Website:* www.chepik.com (home).

CHEPURIN, Aleksandr Vasilyevich; Russian diplomatist; *Director, Department of Interaction with Compatriots Abroad, Ministry of Foreign Affairs;* b. 1952; ed Moscow Inst. of Int. Relations; on staff Ministry of Foreign Affairs 1975–; various diplomatic posts abroad and in USSR Ministry of Foreign Affairs; Deputy Head, then First Deputy Head of Personnel Service, Ministry of Foreign Affairs 1992–93, Dir Dept of Personnel 1994–96; Amb. to Denmark 1996–99; at Ministry of Foreign Affairs 1999–2005, Dir Dept of Interaction with Compatriots Abroad 2005–. *Leisure interests:* cinema, books, tennis. *Address:* Department of Interaction with Compatriots Abroad, Ministry of Foreign Affairs, 119200 Moscow, Smolenskaya-Sennaya 32/34, Russia (office). *Telephone:* (495) 244-43-51 (office). *Fax:* (495) 244-38-17 (office). *E-mail:* drs@mid.ru (office). *Website:* www.mid.ru (office).

CHER; American singer and actress; b. (Cherilyn Lapierre Sarkisian), 20 May 1946, El Centro, Calif.; d. of John Sarkisian and Georgina Holt; m. 1st Sonny Bono 1964 (divorced 1975, died 1998); one d.; m. 2nd Gregg Allman 1975 (divorced); one s.; formed singing duo 'Sonny & Cher' with Sonny Bono 1964–74, with TV series; solo artist 1964–, with own TV variety series and night club act; VH1 First Music Award for achievements within the music industry 2005. *Theatre:* Come Back to the Five and Dime, Jimmy Dean, Jimmy Dean. *Television:* Sonny & Cher Comedy Hour (CBS) 1971, Sonny & Cher Show (CBS) 1976–75, Cher (CBS) 1975–76. *Films:* Chastity 1969, Come Back To The Five and Dime, Jimmy Dean Jimmy Dean 1982, Silkwood 1983, Mask (Cannes Film Festival Best Actress Award) 1985, The Witches of Eastwick 1987, Suspect 1987, Moonstruck (Acad. Award for Best Actress 1988) 1987, Mermaids 1989, Club Rhino 1990, Faithful 1996, If These Walls Could Talk 1996, Nine 1996, Tea with Mussolini 1999, Stuck on You 2003. *Recordings include:* albums: as Sonny & Cher: Baby Don't Go 1965, Look At Us 1965, The Wondrous World Of Sonny & Cher 1966, Good Times 1967, In Case You're In Love 1967, Sonny & Cher Live 1971, All I Ever Need Is You 1972, Live In Las Vegas 1974, Mama Was A Rock 'N' Roll Singer 1974; solo: All I Really Want To Do 1965, Cher 1966, The Sonny Side Of Cher 1966, With

Love 1967, Backstage 1968, 3614 Jackson Highway 1969, Cher 1971, Gypsies Tramps and Thieves 1971, Foxy Lady 1972, Half Breed 1973, Bittersweet White Light 1974, Dark Lady 1974, Stars 1975, I'd Rather Believe In You 1976, Cherished 1977, Two The Hard Way 1977, This Is Cher 1978, Take Me Home 1979, Prisoner 1982, I Paralyze 1984, Cher 1987, Heart Of Stone 1989, Outrageous 1989, Love Hurts 1991, It's A Man's World 1995, Believe 1998, Black Rose 1999, Not.Com.mercial 2000, Holdin' Out For Love 2001, Believe 2001, Living Proof 2001, Live: The Farewell Tour 2003; singles: as Sonny & Cher: I Got You Babe 1975, Baby Don't Go 1965, Just You 1965, But You're Mine 1965, What Now My Love 1966, Little Man 1966, The Beat Goes On 1967, All I Ever Need Is You 1971, A Cowboy's Work Is Never Done 1972; solo: All I Really Want To Do 1965, Bang Bang 1966, Gypsies Tramps And Thieves 1971, The Way Of Love 1972, Half Breed 1973, Dark Lady 1974, Take Me Home 1979, Dead Ringer For Love (duet with Meatloaf) 1982, I Found Someone 1987, We All Sleep Alone 1988, After All (duet with Peter Cetera, for film Chances Are) 1989, If I Could Turn Back Time 1989, Jesse James 1989, Heart of Stone 1990, The Shoop Shoop Song (for film Mermaids) 1990, Love And Understanding 1991, Save Up All Your Tears 1991, Oh No Not My Baby 1992, Love Can Build A Bridge (with Neneh Cherry and Chrissie Hynde) 1995, Walking In Memphis 1995, One By One 1996, Paradise Is Here 1996, Believe (Grammy Award for Best Dance Recording 2000) 1998, Strong Enough 1999, All Or Nothing 1999, Dov'e l'Amore 1999, The Music's No Good Without You 2001, Alive Again 2002, A Different Kind Of Love 2002, When The Money's Gone 2003. *Address:* ICM, 10250 Constellation Boulevard, Beverly Hills, CA 90067, USA (office). *Website:* www.cher.com.

CHÉREAU, Patrice; French film, theatre and opera director; b. 2 Nov. 1944; s. of Jean-Baptiste Chéreau and Marguerite Pélicier; ed Lycée Louis-le-Grand and Faculté de Lettres, Paris; Co-Dir Théâtre nat. populaire (TNP) 1972–81; Dir Théâtre des Amandiers, Nanterre 1982–90; Chevalier, Légion d'honneur; Officier des Arts et Lettres; numerous prizes. *Theatre productions include:* L'Intervention 1964, L'Affaire de la rue de Lourcine 1966, Les Soldats 1967, La Révolte au Marché noir 1968, Don Juan, Richard II, Splendeur et Mort de Joaquin Murieta 1970, La Finta Serva 1971, Lulu 1972, Massacre à Paris 1972, La Dispute 1973, Lear 1975, Peer Gynt 1981, Les Paravents 1983, Combats de Nègre et de Chiens 1983, La Fausse suivante 1985, Quai Ouest 1986, Dans la solitude des champs de coton 1987, 1995, Hamlet 1988, Le Retour au désert 1988, Le Temps et la Chambre 1991. *Opera productions:* L'Italiana in Algeri 1969, The Tales of Hoffmann 1974, Der Ring des Nibelungen (Bayreuth 1976–80), Lulu 1979, Lucio Silla 1984, Wozzeck 1992, Don Giovanni (Salzburg 1994–96). *Films include:* La Chair de l'Orchidée 1974, Judith Therpauve 1978, L'Homme blessé 1984, Hôtel de France 1987, Le Temps et la Chambre 1993, Queen Margot 1994, Those Who Love Me Can Take The Train 1998 (César Award for Best Dir), Intimacy 2001 (Golden Bear, Berlin Film Festival), Gabrielle 2005. *Address:* c/o Artmédia, 10 avenue Georges V, 75008 Paris, France.

CHERESHNEV, Valery Aleksandrovich, DMed; Russian immunologist and academic; *Director, Institute of Ecology and Microorganism Genetics, Russian Academy of Sciences;* b. 24 Oct. 1944, Khabarovsk; m.; two c.; ed Medical Inst., Perm, Russian Acad. of Sciences; researcher, Medical Inst., Perm State Univ. –1988; Dir Inst. of Ecology and Microorganism Genetics, Russian Acad. of Sciences, Ural, Perm State Univ. 1988–; Corresp. mem. Russian Acad. of Sciences 1990–97, mem. 1997–, elected Vice-Pres. Russian Acad. of Sciences, Ural Br. 1999, now Pres., Chair. The Urals Program; Fellow, World Acad. of Art and Science 2005; Medal for Merits in Labour; Order of Friendship. *Leisure interest:* khatkha yoga. *Address:* Presidium, Ural Branch, Russian Academy of Sciences, Permovmayskaya str., 91, 620219 Yekaterinburg (office); Institute of Ecology and Micro-organism Genetics, Golev str. 13, 614081 Perm Russia (office). *Telephone:* (3432) 74-02-23 (office); (3432) 33-54-54 (home). *E-mail:* chereshnev@prm.uran.ru (office). *Website:* prm.uran.ru (office).

CHÉRIF, Taïeb, MSc, PhD; Algerian aviation official; b. 29 Dec. 1941, Kasr El Boukhari; m.; three c.; ed Univ. of Algiers, Ecole Nationale de l'aviation civile, France, Cranfield Inst. of Tech., UK; Eng Officer, Civil Aviation Directorate, Ministry of Transport, Algiers 1970–71, Deputy Dir of Transport and Aerial Activities 1971–74, Deputy Dir of Air Navigation 1974–75, Dir of Air Transport 1985–87, Dir aeronautical construction project 1987–92; State Sec. for Higher Educ. 1992–94; Algerian Rep., ICAO Council 1998–2003, Sec.-Gen. ICAO 2003–09; Dir Algiers Int. Airport 1975–76; Civil Aviation Consultant 1982–85, 1995–97; Visiting Lecturer, Inst. for Civil Aviation and Meteorology, Algiers 1970–71, Ecole Nationale des Techniciens de l'Aéronautique, Blida 1973–74, Econ. Science Inst., Algiers 1984–85. *Address:* c/o International Civil Aviation Organization, External Relations and Public Information Office, 999 University Street, Montreal, H3C 5H7, Canada (office).

CHERITON, David R., MMath, PhD; Canadian computer scientist and academic; *Professor of Computer Science, Stanford University;* ed Univ. of Waterloo; began career as Asst Prof., Univ. of BC; currently Prof. of Computer Science, Stanford Univ., Leader, Distributed Systems Group; Co-founder Granite Systems and Kealia Inc. (computer networking equipment cos); early investor in Google, Inc.; SIGCOMM Lifetime Achievement Award 2003. *Address:* Computer Science Department, Stanford University, 353 Serra Mall, Stanford, CA 94305-9025, USA (office). *Telephone:* (650) 723-1131 (office). *E-mail:* cheriton@cs.stanford.edu (office). *Website:* www-dsg.stanford.edu (office); www.stanford.edu (office).

CHERKASKY, Michael G., BA, JD; American lawyer and business executive; *CEO, US Investigations Services Inc.;* b. 2 March 1950, Bronx, NY; m. Betsy Cherkasky; four c.; ed Fieldston School, Case Western Reserve Univ.; began career as law clerk in US Dist Court, Northern Dist of Ohio; Asst Dist

Attorney, NY Co. Dist Attorney's Office 1978–85, 1985–93, Deputy Chief of Trial Bureau 40 1983–84, Chief of Trial Bureau 1984–85, Head of Rackets Bureau 1986–90, Chief of Investigations Div. 1990–94; Head of Re-election Campaign of Robert Morgenthau 1985; joined Kroll Assocs 1994, Head of New York Office 1994–96, Head of N America Region 1996–97, COO and Exec. Man.-Dir 1997, Pres. and COO The Kroll-O'Gara Co. (following merger with O'Gara-Hess & Eisenstadt 1997, renamed Kroll Inc. 2001) 1997–2001, Pres. and CEO Kroll Inc. 2001–04, Chair. and CEO Marsh Kroll Inc. (after acqusition of Kroll by March & McLennan Cos) 2004; Pres. and CEO March & McLennan Inc. 2004–08; CEO US Investigations Services Inc., Falls Church, Va 2008–. *Publication:* Forewarned: Why the Government is Failing to Protect Us and What We Must Do to Protect Ourselves 2002. *Address:* US Investigations Services Inc., 7799 Leesburg Pike, Suite 1100 North, Falls Church, VA 22043-2413, USA (office). *Telephone:* (703) 448-0178 (office). *Website:* www.usis.com (office).

CHERKESOV, Col.-Gen. Victor Vasilejvich; Russian security officer and lawyer; *Director, Federal Agency for the Procurement of Military and Special Equipment;* b. 13 July 1950, Leningrad; m. Natalya Sergejvna Cherkesova (née Chaplina); two d.; ed Leningrad State Univ.; investigator Leningrad KGB Dept 1975–; Head Dept of Fed. Security Service St Petersburg and Leningrad Region 1992–98; First Deputy Dir Russian Fed. Security Service 1998–2000; Rep. of Russian Pres. to NW Fed. Dist 2000–2003; mem. Russian Federation Security Council; Dir Fed. Service for Control over Drugs and Psychotropic Substances 2003–08; Dir Fed. Agency for the Procurement of Mil. and Special Equipment 2008–; Order of the Red Star 1985, Order of Honour 2000; 14 medals including Honoured Lawyer of the Russian Fed., Honourable Domestic Intelligence Officer of the Russian Fed., Honourable External Intelligence Officer of the Russian Fed. *Address:* Federal Agency for the Procurement of Military and Special Equipment, c/o Office of the President, 1031324 Moscow, Staraya pl. 4, Russia (office). *Telephone:* (495) 925-35-81 (office). *Fax:* (495) 206-07-66 (office). *E-mail:* president@gov.ru (office). *Website:* www.kremlin.ru (office).

CHERMAYEFF, Peter, AB, MArch, FAIA; American architect; *President, Chermayeff & Poole, Inc.;* b. 4 May 1936, London, England; s. of Serge Ivan Chermayeff and Barbara Chermayeff; m. 1st Clare Brandt (née Scott) 1960; m. 2nd Jane Borden (née Batchelder) 1966, one s. two step-s.; m. 3rd Andrea Petersen 1983, one d.; ed Phillips Acad., Andover, Harvard Coll. College, Harvard Graduate School of Design; Co-founder Cambridge Seven Assocs Inc. 1962, resigned 1998; Co-founder (with Peter Sollogub and Bobby Poole) Chermayeff, Sollogub & Poole, Inc. 1998–2005, continuing as Chermayeff & Poole, Inc. 2005–; Co-founder, Pres. and CEO of affiliated firm International Design for the Environment Assocs (IDEA) Inc. 1990–2009; mem. Mass Council on Arts and Humanities 1969–72, Bd of Advisors School of Visual Arts, Boston Univ. 1976–80, Visiting Cttee Rhode Island School of Design, Providence 1969–75, Bd of Design Consultants, Univ. of Pennsylvania 1976–80; Claude M. Fuess Award "For Distinguished Contribution to the Public Service", Phillips Acad., Andover 1979, AIA Firm of the Year Award (with others at Cambridge Seven Assocs) 1992. *Films include:* producer: Orange and Blue 1962, Cheetah, Zebra, Lion, Elephant & Giraffe (with Jane Borden) 1971, Wildebeest, Rhino, Impala, Gazelle, Baboon & Ostrich (with Andrea Petersen) 1984; exec. producer: Where's Boston? 1975. *Major complete works include:* design: Guidelines and Standards, Mass Bay Transportation Authority 1967, US Exhibition Expo '67 Montreal 1967, New England Aquarium, Boston 1969, 'Where's Boston?' exhbn and show, Boston 1975, San Antonio Museum of Art, San Antonio, Tex. 1981, Nat. Aquarium, Baltimore, Md 1981, 2005, Ring of Fire Aquarium, Osaka, Japan 1990, Tennessee Aquarium, Chattanooga 1992, 2005, Genoa Aquarium, Italy 1992, Nivola Museum, Sardinia 1996, Lisbon Oceanarium, 1998; start-up operations: Genoa Aquarium 1992, Lisbon Oceanarium 1998, Scientific Centre of Kuwait 2000. *Work in progress includes:* New Bedford Aquarium, LA, Child (Rainforest) Cedar Rapids, Mammal Partition, Virginia Marine Science Museum, Oberhausen Aquarium, Germany, Cala Gonone Aquarium, Sardinia, Mindelo Aquarium, São Vicente, Cape Verde. *Address:* Chermayeff & Poole, Inc., 268 Summer Street, Boston, MA 02210, (office); 111 Highland Road, Andover, MA 01810, USA (home). *Telephone:* (617) 357-5000 (office). *Fax:* (617) 357-5011 (office). *E-mail:* pchermayeff@cp-architects.com (office); peter@chermayeff.com (home). *Website:* www.cp-architects.com (office); www.idea-aquariums.com (office).

CHERNIN, Peter F.; American media executive; b. 29 May 1951, Harrison, New York; early career as Assoc. Publicity Dir St Martin's Press and Ed. Warner Books; fmr Vice-Pres. of Devt and Production, David Gerber Co.; fmr Exec. Vice-Pres. of Programming and Marketing, Showtime/The Movie Channel Inc.; Pres. and COO Lorimar Film Entertainment 1988–89; joined Fox Broadcasting Co. 1989, Pres. of Entertainment Group 1989–92, Chair. Twentieth Century Fox Film Corpn (now Fox Filmed Entertainment) 1992–2009, Pres. and COO News Corpn 1996–20009, Chair. and CEO Fox Entertainment Group 1998–; Chair. Malaria No More; mem. Bd of Dirs Gemstar-TV Guide 2002–, DirecTV 2003–, American Express Co. 2006–. *Address:* The News Corporation Limited, 1211 Avenue of the Americas, New York, NY 10036, USA (office). *Telephone:* (212) 852-7017 (office). *Fax:* (212) 852-7145 (office). *Website:* www.newscorp.com (office).

CHERNOBROVKINA, Tatyana Anatolyevna; Russian ballerina; b. 14 Aug. 1965; m. Dmitry Zababurin; one s.; ed Saratov Ballet School; soloist, Saratov Theatre of Opera and Ballet 1983–86; soloist, Stanislavsky and Nemirovich-Danchenko Moscow Academic Music Theatre 1987–; prizewinner, 5th Moscow Int. Competition of Ballet Dancers 1985, Merited Artist of Russia 1994, People's Artist of Russia 1999. *Main ballet roles:* Odette/Odile (Swan Lake), Macha (The Nutcracker), Aurora (Sleeping Beauty), Juliet (Romeo and Juliet), Kitry (Don Quixote), Giselle (Giselle). *Address:* Moscow Academic Music Theatre, 103009 Moscow, B. Dmitrovka str. 17, Russia (office). *Telephone:* (495) 229-19-57 (office); (495) 954-14-26 (home). *Fax:* (495) 954-14-26 (home). *Website:* www.stanislavskymusic.ru (office).

CHERNOFF, Herman, PhD; American mathematician and academic; *Professor Emeritus of Statistics, Harvard University;* b. 1 July 1923, New York, NY; s. of Max Chernoff and Pauline Markowitz; m. Judith Ullman 1947; two d.; ed Townsend Harris High School, City Coll. of New York, Brown and Columbia Univs; Research Assoc., Cowles Comm. for Research in Econs, Univ. of Chicago 1947–49; Asst Prof. of Math., Univ. of Illinois 1949–51, Assoc. Prof. 1951–52; Assoc. Prof. of Statistics, Stanford Univ. 1952–56, Prof. 1956–74; Prof. of Applied Math., MIT 1974–85, now Prof. Emer.; Prof. of Statistics, Harvard Univ. 1985–97, Prof. Emer. 1997–; mem. NAS, American Acad. of Arts and Sciences; Dr hc (Ohio State) 1983, (Technion) 1984, (Univ. of Rome, La Sapienza) 1995, (Athens) 1999; Townsend Harris Prize 1982, Wilks Medal 1987. *Publications:* Elementary Decision Theory (with L. E. Moses) 1959, Sequential Analysis and Optimal Design 1972; numerous articles in scientific journals. *Address:* Department of Statistics, SC711, Harvard University, Cambridge, MA 02138 (office); 75 Crowninshield Road, Brookline, MA 02446, USA (home). *Telephone:* (617) 495-5462 (office); (617) 232-8256 (home). *Fax:* (617) 496-8057 (office). *E-mail:* chernoff@stat.harvard.edu (office). *Website:* www.fas.harvard.edu/~stats (office).

CHERNOMYRDIN, Viktor Stepanovich, CandTechSc; Russian politician and diplomatist; *Ambassador to Ukraine;* b. 9 April 1938, Cherny-Otrog, Orenburg Dist; m.; two s.; ed Kuibyshev Polytechnic Inst., All-Union Correspondence Polytechnic; served in Soviet Army 1957–60; operator in oil refinery 1960–67; mem. CPSU 1961–91 (mem. Cen. Cttee 1986–90); work with Orsk City Cttee 1967–73; deputy chief engineer, Dir of Orenburg gas plant 1973–78; work with CPSU Cen. Cttee 1978–82; USSR Deputy Minister of Gas Industry, Chief of All-Union production unit for gas exploitation in Tyumen Dist 1982–85; USSR Minister of Gas 1985–89; Chair. Bd Gasprom 1989–92, 1999–2000; Deputy Prime Minister, Minister of Fuel and Energy June–Dec. 1992; Chair. Council of Ministers 1992–98; Acting Prime Minister Aug.–Sept. 1998; Deputy to USSR Supreme Soviet 1987–89; Chair. Bd All-Russian Movt Our Home–Russia 1995–2000; apptd Special Rep. of Pres. Yeltsin on Kosovo conflict settlement April 1999; mem. State Duma 1999; joined Yedinstvo (Unity) Movt 2000; Amb. to Ukraine and Special Rep. of Pres. of Russian Fed. for Devt of Trade and Econ. Relations 2001–; mem. Russian Eng Acad.; Hon. Prof. (Moscow State Univ.); numerous orders and medals including Order of October Revolution, Order of Labour Red Banner, Order for Services to the Motherland. *Publications:* Challenge 2004. *Leisure Interests:* hunting, automobiles, playing accordion. *Address:* Embassy of Russia, Povitroflotskyi pr. 27, 03049 Kiev, Ukraine. *Telephone:* (44) 244-09-63 (office). *Fax:* (44) 246-34-69 (office). *E-mail:* embrus@public.icyb.kiev.ua (office). *Website:* www.embrus.org.ua (office).

CHERNOV, Vladimir Kirillovich; Russian singer (baritone) and academic; *Professor of Vocal Studies, University of California, Los Angeles;* b. 1956, Belorechensk; m. Olga Chernova; one s.; ed Moscow Conservatory with Georgy Seleznev and Hugo Titz; winner of All-Union Glinka Competition, int. Competitions: Tchaikovsky (Moscow), Voci Virdiagni (Vercelli), M. Helin (Helsinki); soloist of Kirov (now Mariinsky) Theatre 1990–; debut in USA 1988 (La Bohème, Boston), in UK 1990 (Forza del Destino, Glasgow); perm. soloist of Metropolitan Opera 1990–, Wiener Staatsoper 1991–; guest singer at La Scala, Chicago Lyric Opera, Mariinsky Opera, La Monnaie (Brussels) and other theatres of Europe and America; leading parts in operas Queen of Spades, Boris Godunov, Barber of Seville, La Traviata, Eugene Onegin, Don Carlos, War and Peace, The Masked Ball, Faust, Rigoletto, Falstaff, Hérodiade (Hérod), La Cenerentola (Dandini), Nabucco (title role); in concerts and recitals performs opera arias, song cycles of Mahler, Tchaikovsky, romances; Regents' Lecturer, Voice and Opera, UCLA 2005, Professor of Vocal Studies 2007–; faculty mem. Opera Ischia. *Address:* Askonas Holt Ltd, Lincoln House, 300 High Holborn, London, WC1V 7JH, England (office); Robert Lombardo and Associates, 61 W. 62nd Street, Suite 6F, New York, NY 10023, USA (office); UCLA Department of Music, 2539 Schoenberg Music Building, Box 951616, Los Angeles 90095-1616, USA (office). *Telephone:* (20) 7400-1700 (office); (212) 586-4453 (office); (310) 794-9501 (office). *Fax:* (20) 7400-1799 (office); 212) 581-5771 (office); (310) 206-4738 (office). *E-mail:* info@askonasholt.co.uk (office); robert@robertlombardo.com (office); musicwebmaster@arts.ucla.edu (office). *Website:* www.askonasholt.co.uk (office); www.rlombardo.com (office); www.vchernov.com; www.music.ucla.edu/People/Faculty%20bios/VChernov.html.

CHERNOW, Ron, BA, MA; American writer; b. 3 March 1949, New York, NY; m. Valerie Stearn 1979 (died 2006); ed Yale Coll., Pembroke Coll., Cambridge; fmr freelance journalist; Dir of Financial Policy Studies Twentieth Century Fund (think tank) 1982; book reviewer, essayist, TV and radio commentator; mem. PEN American Center (fmr Sec., Pres. 2006–), Authors' Guild; contrib. to New York Times, Wall Street Journal; United Steelworkers of America Jack London Award 1980, English-Speaking Union of the USA Amb. Book Award 1990. *Publications:* The House of Morgan: An American Banking Dynasty and the Rise of Modern Finance (Nat. Book Award for Nonfiction 1990) 1990, The Warburgs: The Twentieth-Century Odyssey of a Remarkable Jewish Family (George S. Eccles Prize for the best business book 1993) 1993, The Death of the Banker: The Decline and Fall of the Great Financial Dynasties and the Triumph of the Small Investor (essays) 1997, Titan: The Life of John D. Rockefeller Sr 1998, Alexander Hamilton (George Washington Book Prize 2005) 2004. *Address:* c/o PEN American Center, 588 Broadway, Suite 303, New York, NY 10012, USA (office). *E-mail:* pen@pen.org (office).

CHERNUKHIN, Vladimir Anatolyevich; Russian business executive and fmr government official; b. 31 Dec. 1968, Moscow; ed Acad. of Int. Business, Acad. of Finance, Russian Fed. Govt; with Techmashexport Co., Ministry of Foreign Trade 1986–87; with Chimmashexport Co., Ministry of Chemical Machine Construction 1986–87; army service 1987–89; Sr Expert, Technomashimport Ministry of External Econ. Relations 1989–96; Vice-Pres. Dept of Credits, Vnesheconombank 1996, mem. Bd of Dirs Vnesheconombank (Foreign Economic Bank) 1998–2004, Deputy Finance Minister and Vice-Chair. 2000–2002, Chair. 2002–04; acquired 27/35 Poultry, London EC2 for devt 2006; Badge of Honour 2004. *Address:* c/o Vnesheconombank, Adademika Sakharova prosp. 9, 103810 Moscow, Russia.

CHERNY, Gorimir Gorimirovich; Russian scientist; *Head, Department of Aeromechanical and Gas Dynamics, Mechanical-Mathematical Faculty, Moscow State University;* b. 22 Jan. 1923, Kamenets-Podol'sky; s. of the late Gorimir Cherny and Zoja Cherny; m. 1st Augusta Gubarev 1949 (died 1986); m. 2nd Alla Sebik 1989; two d.; ed Moscow Univ.; served in Soviet Army 1941–45; worked for Cen. Inst. of Aircraft Engines 1949–58; mem. CPSU 1954–91; Prof. at Moscow Univ. 1958; Dir Univ. Research Inst. of Mechanics 1960–92; Corresp. mem. USSR (now Russian) Acad. of Sciences 1962–81, mem. 1981, Acad.-Sec., Div. of Eng, Mechanics and Control Processes 1992–97, Scientific Adviser to Presidium 1997–; currently Head, Dept of Aeromechanical and Gas Dynamics, Mechanical-Mathematical Faculty, Moscow State Univ.; Corresp. mem. Int. Acad. of Astronautics 1966, mem. 1969; Foreign mem. Nat. Acad. of Eng, USA 1998; State Prizes 1972, 1978, 1991, nine orders and various medals. *Publications:* author of numerous books and scientific articles on aerodynamics, theory of detonation and combustion, theory of gas-fired machines. *Address:* Department of Aeromechanical and Gas Dynamics, Mechanical-Mathematical Faculty, Moscow State University, 119899 Moscow, Vorobevy gory (office); 123272 Moscow, 1 Kudzinskaja pl., apt 365, Russia (home). *Telephone:* (495) 939-39-49 (office); (495) 247-47-41 (home); (495) 938-14-04. *Fax:* (495) 939-20-90 (office); (495) 939-02-65. *E-mail:* ggcher@inmech.msu.zu (office). *Website:* www.math.msu.su/department/ aeromech (office).

CHERPITEL, Didier J.; French international organization official and investment banker; b. 24 Dec. 1944, Paris; s. of Bernard Cherpitel and Denise Cherpitel (née Lange); m. Nicole Estrangin 1973; one s. two d.; ed Inst. d'Etudes Politiques, Paris, Univ. of Paris; joined JP Morgan/Morgan Guaranty Trust 1972, various posts in Paris 1972–80, Man. Dir of Investment Banking Operations, Morgan Guaranty Pacific, Singapore 1980–83, Head of Commercial Banking Activities, Brussels 1983–84, Exec. Dir and Head of Capital Markets Activities, London 1984–88, Man. Dir Soc. de Bourse JP Morgan SA, Paris 1988–96, mem. Bd JP Morgan Europe 1994–97, Man. Dir of Pvt. Banking Activities Europe, JP Morgan, London 1977–98; mem. Bd French Stock Exchange (CBV) 1991–96; Admin. and Treas. American Chamber of Commerce in France 1991–96; Man. Dir Security Capital Markets Group Ltd, London 1998–99; Admin. Cie générale d'industrie et de participations (CGIP) 1999–; mem. Bd Wendel Investissements 2002–05, mem. Supervisory Bd 2005–; Chair. Atos Origin 2004–; Managers sans Frontières; Treas. François Xavier Bagnoud Int.; Sec.-Gen. Int. Fed. of Red Cross and Red Crescent Socs, Geneva 2000–03. *Leisure interests:* travel, photography, opera, golf. *Address:* c/o Atos Origin, Tour les Miroirs, Bat. C, 18 avenue d'Alsace, 92926 Paris 3 Cedex, France (office).

CHERTOFF, Michael, BA, JD; American judge and fmr government official; b. 28 Nov. 1953, Elizabeth, NJ; ed Harvard Univ.; Summer Assoc., Miller, Cassidy, Larroca & Lewin (law firm) 1978; Law Clerk, Court of Appeals Second Circuit 1978–79, Supreme Court 1979–80; Assoc., Latham & Watkins 1980–83, Pnr 1994–2001; Asst US Attorney, Attorney's Office, Southern Dist of NY 1983–87, First Asst US Attorney, Dist of NJ 1987–90, US Attorney 1990–94; Special Counsel, US Senate Whitewater Cttee 1994–96; Asst Attorney-Gen., Criminal Div., US Dept of Justice 2001–03; Judge, Court of Appeals Third Circuit 2003–05; US Sec. of Homeland Security, Washington, DC 2005–09. *Address:* c/o Department of Homeland Security, Washington, DC 20528, USA.

CHESHIRE, Ian; British retail executive; *Group Chief Executive, Kingfisher plc;* m.; three c.; ed Univ. of Cambridge; worked at Guinness and the Piper Trust; more than 20 years' retail experience, including Group Commercial Dir Sears plc; joined Kingfisher as Group Strategy Dir in 1998, subsequently joined main Bd as Chief Exec. of Kingfisher's e-Commerce Div. 2000–02, CEO Int. and Devt, with responsibility for all retail operations outside the UK and France 2002–05, CEO B&Q UK 2005–08, Group Chief Exec. Kingfisher plc 2008–; Dir (non-exec.) Bradford & Bingley plc; mem. Climate Change Leaders' Group. *Address:* Kingfisher plc, 3 Sheldon Square, Paddington, London, W2 6PX, England (office). *Telephone:* (20) 7372-8008 (office). *Fax:* (20) 7644-1001 (office). *E-mail:* hrenquiries@kingfisher.com (office). *Website:* www.kingfisher .com (office).

CHESHIRE, Air Chief Marshal Sir John (Anthony), KBE, CB, FRAeS; British air force commander and government official; *Chairman, Royal Air Force Charitable Trust;* b. 4 Sept. 1943; m. Shirley Ann Stevens 1964; one s. one d.; ed Ipswich School, Worksop Coll., RAF Coll., Cranwell; specialist in air support, Special Forces until 1980; Commdr Air Wing, Brunei 1980–82, RAF Lyneham 1983–85, Plans Br. HQ Strike Command 1986–87; Defence and Air Attaché, Moscow 1988–90; Deputy Commdt RAF Staff Coll. 1991–92; Asst Chief of Staff for Policy Supreme HQ, Allied Powers, Europe 1992–94; Mil. Rep. to NATO HQ 1995–97; C-in-C Allied Forces NW Europe 1997–2000; Lt-Gov. and C-in-C of Jersey (Channel Islands) 2001–06; Chair. Royal Air Force Charitable Trust, also Pres. Royal Int. Air Tattoo. *Leisure interests:* int. and defence affairs, creative writing, collecting (affordable) antiques, golf, squash, tennis. *Address:* c/o Royal Air Force Charitable Trust Enterprises, Douglas

Bader House, Horcott Hill, Fairford, Glos., GL7 4RB, England (office). *Website:* www.rafcte.com (office).

CHESNAKOV, Aleksei Aleksandrovich, PhD; Russian political scientist; b. 1 Sept. 1970, Baku, Azerbaijan; m.; one d.; ed Moscow State Univ.; Jr, then Sr Researcher, Inst. of Mass Political Movts, Russian-American Univ. 1991–93; Researcher, then Head of Collective of Political Lectures, Centre of Political Conjunction of Russia 1993–97, Dir 1997–; Dir Centre of Social-Political Information, Inst. of Social-Political Studies, Russian Acad. of Sciences 1997; currently Deputy Presidential Domestic Policy Directorate; mem. Presidium Ind. Assoc. Civil Soc. *Publications:* numerous scientific publs on social and political problems; monographs: One Hundred Political Leaders of Russia 1993, Azerbaijan: Political Parties and Organizations 1993, Russia: Power and Elections 1996, Social and Political Situation in Russia in 1996 1997, Russia: New Stage of Neo-liberal Reforms 1998. *Address:* Directorate of Domestic Policy, c/o Office of the President, 103132 Moscow, Staraya pl. 4, Russia. *Telephone:* (495) 925-35-81. *Fax:* (495) 206-07-66. *E-mail:* president@gov.ru. *Website:* www.kremlin.ru.

CHET, Ilan, PhD; Israeli microbiologist, academic and university administrator; *Francis Ariowitsch Chair of Agricultural Biotechnology, Hebrew University of Jerusalem;* b. 12 April 1939, Haifa; m. Ruth Geffen; two s. three d.; ed Hebrew Univ. of Jerusalem; teacher of microbiology (specializing in soil microbiology, fungal physiology and biological control of plant diseases), Faculty of Agric., Hebrew Univ. of Jerusalem 1965–2001, Assoc. Prof. of Microbiology 1975–78, Prof. 1978–2001, Head Dept of Plant Pathology and Microbiology 1981–83, Dean Faculty of Agric. 1986–89, currently Francis Ariowitsch Chair. of Agricultural Biotechnology; mem. Senate, Hebrew Univ. of Jerusalem 1978, mem. Exec. Cttee of Hebrew Univ. 1990–92, Bd of Man. 1990–2001, Vice-Pres. for Research and Devt 1992–2001, Chair. Univ. Authority for Research and Devt 1992–2001; Prof., Dept of Biological Chem., Weizmann Inst., Rehovot 2001–, Pres. Weizmann Inst. 2001–06; Dir Otto Warburg Center of Biotechnology in Agric., Rehovot 1983–86, 1990–92; mem. Bd Scientific Incubators Co. 1992–94, Yissum R&D Co. 1992–2001; Chair. Nat. Cttee for Strategic Infrastructure 1998–2001; Chair. Cttee for Agric. and Biotechnology, Nat. Council of Research and Devt 1984–86; mem. Nat. Cttee for Biotechnology 1985–92, 1996–97, IUPAC Comm. on Biotechnology 1986–92, Editorial Bd, European Journal of Plant Pathology 1995–; Chair. Special Projects Cttee, Int. Soc. for Plant Pathology 1989–93; mem. External Adviser to EU Group 1998–2002; panel mem. NATO 2000–03; numerous visiting professorships and lectureships; mem. Israeli Nat. Acad. of Sciences and Humanities 1998; Fellow American Phytopathological Soc. 1991; Officer's Cross, Order of Merit (Germany) 2001; Dr hc (Lund) 1991; Max-Planck Research Award 1994, Israel Prize for Agricultural Research 1996, Wolf Prize 1998, E.M.T Prize European Acad. of Science & Art 2003, Invited Speaker, World Econ. Forum, Davos, Switzerland 2003 and numerous other prizes. *Publications:* Soil-Plant Interaction (co-ed.) 1986, Innovative Approaches to Plant Disease Control (ed.) 1987, Biotechnology in Plant Disease Control (ed.) 1993; 350 chapters, reviews and articles; 32 patents. *Leisure interests:* antique microscopes and scales. *Address:* Faculty of Agriculture, Hebrew University of Jerusalem, Rehovot 76100, Israel (office). *Telephone:* (8) 9489236 (office); (8) 9342190 (home). *Fax:* (8) 9468785 (office). *E-mail:* chet@huji.ac.il (office).

CHETTIAR, Angidi Verriah; Mauritian politician; *Vice-President;* Vice-Pres. of Mauritius 1997–2002, 2007–, Acting Pres. Feb. 2002 (resgnd). *Address:* Office of the President, State House, Le Réduit, Port Louis, Mauritius (office). *Telephone:* 454-3021 (office). *Fax:* 464-5370 (office). *E-mail:* president@mail.gov.mu (office). *Website:* president.gov.mu (office).

CHEUNG, Maggie; Hong Kong actress; b. 20 Sept. 1964, Hong Kong; m. Olivier Assayas 1998 (divorced 2001); fmr fashion model; actress 1984–; jury mem. Cannes Film Festival 2007. *Films include:* Yuen fan (Behind the Yellow Line) 1984, Ching wa wong ji (Prince Charming) 1984, Ging chaat goo si (Jackie Chan's Police Force) 1985, Xin tiao yi bai (Heartbeat) 1987, Yue liang, xing xing, tai yang (Moon, Stars & Sun) 1988, Wong gok ka moon (As Tears Go By) 1988, Nan bei ma da (Mother vs Mother) 1988, Liu jin sui yue (Golden Years) 1988, Qiu ai ye jing hun (In Between Love) 1989, Xiao xiao xiao jing cha (Little Cop) 1989, Ketu qiuhen (Song of Exile) 1990, Hong chang fei long (Crying Freeman: Dragon from Russia) 1990, Hei xue (Will of Iron) 1990, Gungun hongchen (Red Dust) 1990, A Fei jing juen (Days of Being Wild) 1991, Yuen Ling-yuk (Centre Stage) (Best Actress Award, Berlin Int. Film Festival) 1992, Shuan long hui (Brother vs Brother) 1992, Jia you xi shi 1992, Dung fong saam hap 1993, Wu xia qi gong zhu (Holy Weapon) 1993, Shen Jing Dao yu Fei Tian Mao (Flying Dagger) 1993, Fei yue mi qing (Enigma of Love) 1993, Chai gong 1993, Bai mei gui (Blue Valentine) 1993, Tian mi mi (Comrades: Almost a Love Story) 1996, Irma Vep 1996, Song jia huang chao (The Soong Sisters) 1997, Augustin, roi du Kung-fu 1999, Fa yeung nin wa (In the Mood for Love) 2000, Ying xiong (Hero) 2002, 2046 2004, Clean (Best Actress Award, Cannes Film Festival) 2004, Ashes of Time Redux 2008. *Address:* c/o Golden Harvest, 16/F Peninsula Office Tower, 18 Middle Road, Tsumshatsui/Rowlon, Hong Kong Special Administrative Region, People's Republic of China.

CHEUNG, Yan, (Zhang Nin); Chinese business executive; *Founder and Chairperson, Nine Dragons Paper (Holdings) Ltd;* b. Heilongjiang Prov.; m.; two s.; worked in paper products co. in Shenzhen in early 1980s; moved to Hong Kong 1985, est. waste-paper trading business; moved to Los Angeles 1990, est. paper recycling plant; returned to China 1995, est. Nine Dragons Paper Ltd (packaging manufacturer), currently Chair.; mem. Nat. Cttee CPPCC; Vice Chair. Women's Fed. of Commerce; Hon. Citizen, City of Dongguan. *Address:* Nine Dragons Paper (Holdings) Ltd, 31st Floor, Sun Hung Kai Centre, 30 Harbour Road, Wanchai, Hong Kong Special Administrative Region, People's Republic of China (office). *Telephone:* 25116338 (office). *E-mail:* info@ndpaper.com (office). *Website:* www.ndpaper.com (office).

CHEUNG WING LAM, Linus, JP, BSocSc; Chinese business executive; ed Univ. of Hong Kong; Deputy Man. Dir Cathay Pacific Airways Ltd 1971–94; apptd Exec. Dir Cable & Wireless PLC 1995; Chief Exec. and Exec. Dir Hongkong Telecom (HKT) Ltd 1995–2000; Deputy Chair. and Exec. Dir PCCW Ltd (fmrly Pacific Century CyberWorks Ltd) (merged with Cable & Wireless HKT Ltd 2000) 2000–04; Chair. Companhia de Telecomunicações de Macao 1996; Dir China Unicom Ltd 2004–; Chair. Man. Bd, School of Business, Univ. of Hong Kong; Univ. apptd adviser to Chinese Soc. of Macroeconomics of the State Planning Comm., People's Repub. of China 1995; Adjunct Prof., Chinese Univ. of Hong Kong; mem. Council Univ. of Hong Kong. *Address:* China Unicom Limited, 75th Floor, The Center, 99 Queen's Road, Central, Hong Kong Special Administrative Region, People's Republic of China (office).

CHEVALIER, Roger; French aeronautical engineer; b. 3 May 1922, Marseille; s. of Louis Chevalier and Marie-Louise Assaud; m. Monique Blin 1947; two s.; ed Ecole Polytechnique and Ecole Nationale Supérieure de l'Aéronautique; Head of Dept, Aeronautical Arsenal 1947–53; Chief Engineer, Nord-Aviation 1953–60; Technical Dir Soc. pour l'Etude et la Réalisation d'Engins Balistiques (SEREB) 1960, Dir-Gen. 1967–70; Dir Aérospatiale 1970–74; mem. Admin. Council Onera 1972–; Vice-Pres. Gifas 1977–81; Gen. Man. Soc. Nationale de l'Industrie Aérospatiale (SNIAS), Exec. Sr Vice-Pres. 1976–82, Vice-Chair. 1982–87; Pres. Asscn Aéronautique et Astronautique de France; mem. Int. Astronautical Fed. (IAF) 1980–82, Pres. 1982–83; Vice-Pres. Aero-Club de France 1981; Pres. French Acad. for Aeronautics and Astronautics; Pres. Soc. d'études de réalisation et d'applications techniques (SERAT) 1985–91; mem. Air and Space Acad., Vice-Pres. 1983–86, 1989–91, Pres. 1991–93; Fellow, American Aeronautic and Astronautic Inst.; mem. Int. Acad. of Astronautics, Acad. des Technologies; Commdr Légion d'honneur, Ordre nat. du mérite, Chevalier des Palmes Académiques; Médaille de l'Aéronautique, Prix Galabert 1966, Prix Acad. des Sciences 1967, Allan D. Emil Award 1982; Commdr. *Leisure interests:* tennis, hunting, reading. *Address:* Hespérides des Ternes, 14, rue Gustave Charpentier, 75017 Paris, France (home). *Telephone:* 1-42-27-59-28 (home). *E-mail:* roger.chevalier@academie-technologies.fr (office).

CHEVALIER, Tracy, MA; American writer; b. Oct. 1962, Washington, DC; m.; one s.; ed Oberlin Coll., Univ. of East Anglia, England; moved to London, England 1984; fmr reference book ed. –1993; Barnes & Noble Discover Award 2000. *Publications:* novels: The Virgin Blue 1997, Girl with a Pearl Earring 1999, Falling Angels 2001, The Lady and the Unicorn 2003, Burning Bright 2007. *Address:* c/o Jonny Geller, Curtis Brown, Haymarket House, 28–29 Haymarket, London, SW1Y 4SP, England (office). *Telephone:* (20) 7393-4400 (office). *E-mail:* hello@tchevalier.com (office). *Website:* www.tchevalier.com (office).

CHEVÈNEMENT, Jean-Pierre; French politician; *President, Citizen and Republican Movement;* b. 9 March 1939, Belfort; s. of Pierre Chevènement and Juliette Garessus; m. Nisa Grünberg 1970; two s.; ed Lycée Victor-Hugo, Besançon, Univ. de Paris, Ecole Nationale d'Admin.; joined Section française de l'Int. ouvrière (SFIO) 1964; Commercial Attaché, Ministry of Econ. and Finance 1965–68; Sec.-Gen. Centre d'études, de recherches et d'éducation socialistes (CERES) 1965–71; Commercial Adviser, Jakarta, Indonesia 1969; Political Sec. Fédération socialiste de Paris 1969–70; Dir of Studies, Soc. Eres 1969–71; Co-founder Parti Socialiste (PS) 1971, Nat. Sec. PS 1971–75, 1979–80, mem. Exec. Bureau 1971–81, 1986–93, Steering Cttee 1971–92; Deputy (Belfort) to Nat. Ass. 1973–81, 1986–2002; regional councillor Franche-Comté 1974–88; mem. Bd Dirs Repères magazine; Minister of State, Minister of Research and Tech. 1981–82, of Industry 1982–83, of Nat. Educ. 1984–86, of Defence 1988–91, of the Interior 1997–2000; cand. presidential elections 2002, 2007; First Asst to Mayor of Belfort 1977–83, 1997–2001, Mayor 1983–97, 2001–07; Pres. République Moderne 1983–; Pres. Conseil Régional de Franche-Comté 1981–82, mem. 1986–88, fmr Vice-Pres.; Founder and Pres. Citizens Movt (MDC), 1992–2003, became Citizen and Republican Movement (MRC) 2003, Hon. Pres. MRC 2003–08, Pres. MRC 2008–; mem. Foreign Affairs Comm. Nat. Ass. 1986–88, 1991–93, Finance Comm. 1993–97, 2001–02; Founder Asscn Fondation Res Publica (research foundation) 2004, Pres. 2005–;; Croix de la valeur militaire. *Publications:* (as Jacques Mandrin): L'énarchie ou les mandarins de la société bourgeoise 1967, Socialisme ou socialmédiocratie 1969, Clefs pour le socialisme 1973, Le vieux, la crise, le neuf 1975, Les socialistes, les communistes et les autres, Le service militaire 1977, Etre socialiste aujourd'hui 1979, Apprendre pour entreprendre 1985, Le pari sur l'intelligence 1985, Une certaine idée de la République m'amène à 1992, le Temps des citoyens 1993, Le Vert et Le Noir. Intégrisme, Pétrole, Dollar 1995, France–Allemagne: parlons franc 1996, La République contre les bien-pensants 1999, Défis républicains 2004, Pour l'Europe votez non 2005, La Faute de M. Monnet. La République et l'Europe 2006. *Leisure interest:* chess. *Address:* Citizen and Republican Movement, 9 rue du Faubourg Poissonnière, 75009 Paris (office); Fondation Res Publica, 52 rue de Bourgogne, 75007 Paris, France (office). *Telephone:* 1-44-83-83-00 (MRC) (office); 1-45-50-39-50 (office). *Fax:* 1-45-55-68-73 (office). *E-mail:* contact@mrc-france.org (office); info@fondation-res-publica.org (office). *Website:* www.mrc-france.org (office); www.fondation-res-publica.org (office).

CHEW, Choon Seng, BMechEng, MSc; Singaporean business executive; *CEO, Singapore Airlines Ltd;* ed Univ. of Singapore and Imperial Coll. of Science and Tech., Univ. of London, UK; joined Singapore Airlines 1972, man. assignments in Japan and Italy, regional apppointments as Sr Vice-Pres. SW Pacific, the Americas and Europe, headed of Planning, Marketing and Finance Divs, Sr Exec. Vice-Pres. (Admin) for Corp. Affairs, Auditing and Finance 2001–03, CEO 2003–; Chair. SMRT Corpn Ltd, Singapore Aircraft Leasing Enterprise; mem. Bd of Dirs Singapore Airport Terminal Services Ltd, SIA Engineering Co., Virgin Atlantic Airways. *Address:* Singapore Airlines Ltd, Airline House, 25 Airline Road, 819829, Singapore (office). *Telephone:* 65415880 (office). *Fax:* 65456083 (office). *Website:* www.singaporeair.com (office).

CHEW, Geoffrey Foucar, PhD; American physicist and academic; *Professor Emeritus of Physics, University of California, Berkeley;* b. 5 June 1924, Washington, DC; s. of Arthur Percy Chew and Pauline Lisette Foucar; m. 1st Ruth Elva Wright 1945 (died 1971); one s. one d.; m. 2nd Denyse Mettel 1972; two s. one d.; ed George Washington Univ. and Univ. of Chicago; Research Physicist, Los Alamos Scientific Lab. 1944–46; Research Physicist, Lawrence Radiation Lab. 1948–49, Head of Theoretical Group 1967; Asst Prof. of Physics, Univ. of California, Berkeley 1949–50, Prof. of Physics 1957–91, Prof. Emer. 1991–, Chair. Dept of Physics 1974–78, Dean of Physical Sciences 1986–92; Asst Prof., then Assoc. Prof. of Physics, Univ. of Illinois 1950–55, Prof. 1955–56; Fellow, Inst. for Advanced Study 1956; Overseas Fellow, Churchill Coll., Cambridge 1962–63; Scientific Associate, CERN 1978–79; Prof., Miller Inst. 1981–82; Visiting Prof., Univ. of Paris 1983–84; mem. NAS, American Acad. of Arts and Sciences; Hughes Prize of American Physical Soc. 1962, Lawrence Award of US Atomic Energy Comm. 1969, Berkeley Citation (Univ. of Calif.) 1991. *Publications:* The S-Matrix Theory of Strong Interactions 1961, The Analytic S-Matrix 1966; over 100 scientific articles. *Leisure interests:* gardening, hiking. *Address:* 10 Maybeck Twin Drive, Berkeley, CA 94708, USA (home). *Telephone:* (510) 848-1830 (home). *Fax:* (510) 848-4117 (home). *E-mail:* gfchew@sbcglobal.net (home).

CHEY, Tae-won, BS, MA, PhD; South Korean energy industry executive; *Chairman and CEO, SK Holdings Co. Ltd;* b. 1961; ed Korea Univ., Univ. of Chicago; Man. Business Devt, METRA Co., Calif. –1991; Gen. Man. SK Networks (fmrly SK Global) Co. Ltd 1991–93, with SK Global America Inc. 1993–96, Man. Dir SK Corpn 1996–97, Exec. Vice-Pres. 1997–98, Chair. 1998–2007, mem. Bd Dirs, Chair. and CEO SK Holdings Co. Ltd 2007–, Chair. and CEO SK Energy Co. Ltd 2007–; Exec. Dir Okedongmu; mem. Int. Business Leaders' Advisory Council; Co-Chair. East Asia Econ. Summit in Malaysia, Asian regional forum of WEF; Invited Prof., Seoul Nat. Univ. 2002, PhD program in Econs, Univ. of Chicago; arrested on charges of fraud 2003, jailed for seven months in connection with accounting fraud at affiliate SK Networks; selected one of The Next 100 Leaders, World Econ. Forum 1998, WEF Global Leader for Tomorrow. *Address:* SK Holdings Co. Ltd, 99 Seorin-Dong, Jongru-Gu, Seoul 110-110, Republic of Korea (office). *Telephone:* (2) 2121-5114 (office). *Fax:* (2) 2121-7001 (office). *E-mail:* Byc778@sk.com (office). *Website:* www.sk.com (office); www.skenergy.com (office).

CHEYSSON, Claude; French politician; b. 13 April 1920, Paris; s. of Pierre Cheysson and Sophie Funck-Brentano; m. 3rd Danielle Schwarz 1969; one s. two d. (and three c. from previous m.); ed Ecole Polytechnique and Ecole d'Admin, Paris; escaped from occupied France to Spanish prison 1943; Officer in the Free French Forces 1943–45; entered French Diplomatic Service 1948; attached to UN Mission in Palestine 1948; Head of French liaison office with Fed. German Govt, Bonn 1949–52; adviser to Prime Minister of Vietnam, Saigon 1952–54; Chef de Cabinet to French Prime Minister (Mendès-France) 1954–55; technical adviser to Minister for Moroccan and Tunisian Affairs 1955–56; Sec.-Gen. Comm. for Tech. Co-operation in Africa (CCTA), Lagos 1957–62; Dir-Gen. Sahara Authority (Organisme Saharien), Algiers 1962–65; Amb. to Indonesia 1966–69; Pres. Entreprise minière et chimique and Pres. Dir-Gen. Cie des potasses du Congo 1970–73; mem. Bd Le Monde 1970–81, 1985–92; Commr for Devt Aid, Comm. of EC 1973–81; Minister of External Relations 1981–84; Commr for Mediterranean Policy and North–South Relations, Comm. of EC 1985–88; mem. European Parl. 1989–94; mem. Exec. Bd Socialist Party 1989–94; Pres. Institut Mendès-France 1987–89; Pres. Fondation Arche de la Fraternité 1989–93; Town Councillor, Bargemon, France 1983–89, 1995; Commdr, Légion d'honneur, Croix de guerre, Grand Cross, Grand Officier, Commdr from numerous cos; Dr hc (Louvain); Joseph Bech Prize 1978, Prix Luderitz (Namibia) 1983;. *Leisure interest:* skiing. *Address:* 52 rue de Vaugirard, 75006 Paris; La Belle Bastide, 83830 Bargemon, France. *Telephone:* 1-43-26-46-65 (Paris); 4-94-76-64-62 (Bargemon). *Fax:* 1-43-26-46-65.

CHHABRIA, Vidya M.; Indian business executive; *Chairperson, Jumbo Group;* b. Bangalore; m. Manohar (Manu) Rajaram Chhabria (deceased); three d.; Chair. Jumbo Group 2002–, cos in group include Shaw Wallace & Co., Maharashtra Distilleries, SKOL Breweries, Shaw Wallace Distilleries, Shaw Wallace Breweries, Hindustan Dorr-Oliver, Mather & Platt, Falcon Tyres, Gordon Woodroffe and Shaw Wallace Hedges; Patron-in-Chief Confed. of Indian Alcoholic Beverage Cos 2003; ranked by Fortune magazine amongst 50 Most Powerful Women in Business outside the US (44th) 2002, (38th) 2003, (38th) 2004, (49th) 2005, ranked by Forbes magazine amongst 100 Most Powerful Women (95th) 2006, (97th) 2007. *Address:* Jumbo Group, PO Box 3426, Union Towers, Sheikh Zayed Road, Dubai, United Arab Emirates (office). *Fax:* (4) 343-7397 (office). *E-mail:* chairman@jumbocorp.com (office). *Website:* www.jumbocorp.com (office).

CHHATWAL, Surbir Jit Singh, MPolSc; Indian diplomatist; b. 1 Oct. 1931, Bannu; s. of Datar Singh Chhatwal and Rattan Kaur Chhatwal; m. Neelam Singh 1962; one s. one d.; ed Agra Univ.; joined Foreign Service 1955; Ministry of External Affairs, including one year at Cambridge, UK; Third Sec., Madrid 1958–60; Under-Sec., Ministry of External Affairs, New Delhi 1960–62; First Sec. CDA a.i. Havana, Cuba 1962–64; Deputy Sec. (Co-ordination), Ministry of External Affairs, New Delhi 1964–66; First Sec. and Acting High Commr, Ottawa, Canada 1966–68; First Indian Consul-Gen., Seoul, S Korea 1968–71; Dir Ministry of Foreign Trade, New Delhi 1971–73; Chief of Protocol, Ministry of External Affairs, New Delhi 1973–75; High Commr in Malaysia 1975–79, in Sri Lanka 1982–85, in Canada 1985–90; Amb. to Kuwait 1979–82; Visiting Prof., Jawaharlal Nehru Univ., New Delhi 1990–91; mem. and Chair. Union Public Service Comm. 1991–96; Sec. Asscn of Indian Diplomats 1991–93, Vice-Pres. 1993–94, Pres. 1994–95; mem. Advisory Council of Foundation for Aviation and Sustainable Tourism (NGO) 1993–2001; Nat. Co-Chair. Inst. of Marketing and Man., New Delhi 1994–; Life Trustee, Inst. for World Congress on Human Rights 1999–; mem. Governing Body, Indian Council of World Affairs, New Delhi 2006–. *Leisure interests:* reading, golf. *Address:* S-168, Panch Shila Park, New Delhi 110017, India (office). *Telephone:* (11) 26014488 (office). *Fax:* (11) 26015398 (office).

CHI, Gen. Haotian; Chinese politician and army officer; b. 1929, Zhaoyuan Co., Shandong Prov.; m. Jiang Qingping; ed Anti-Japanese Mil. and Political Coll., Nanjing Mil. Acad., Political Acad. of the Chinese PLA, PLA High Infantry School, Mil. Acad. of the Chinese PLA; joined PLA 1945, CCP 1946; Company Instructor, Field Army, PLA Services and Arms 1946–49; joined Chinese People's Volunteers during Korean War 1951, bn instructor and Deputy Dir PLA Regimental Political Dept; Maj., unit, Nanjing Mil. Region 1958; Deputy Political Commissar, Beijing Mil. Region 1975–77; Deputy Ed.-in-Chief, People's Daily 1977–82; Deputy Chief of Staff PLA 1977–82; Political Commissar, Jinan Mil. Region 1985–87; PLA Chief of Staff 1987–92; Minister of Nat. Defence 1993–1998, 1998–2003, State Councillor 2000–03; Chair. Drafting Cttee for Nat. Defence Law of People's Repub. of China; mem. PRC Cen. Cttee 1992–95, Vice-Chair 1995–2003; rank of Gen. 1988; mem. 14th CCP Cen. Cttee 1992–97, 15th CCP Cen. Cttee 1997–2002; mem. 8th NPC 1993–98, Politburo; State Councillor 1992–95; mem. Macao Special Admin. Region Preparatory Cttee, Govt Del., Macao Hand-Over Ceremony 1999; Hon. Pres. Wrestling Asscn of China; Third-Class People's Hero of East China. *Address:* c/o Ministry of National Defence, Jingshanqian Jie, Beijing 100009, People's Republic of China (office).

CHIABRA LEÓN, Gen. Roberto; Peruvian army officer (retd) and politician; b. 1950, Callao; ed Escuela Militar de Chorrillos, Inst. Int. de Derechos Humanos, Costa Rica, Univ. of Piura; fmr instructor, Escuela Militar de Chorrillos, Escuela Superior de Guerra, Centro de Altos Estudios Militares (CAEM); Commdr-in-Chief, Cenepa conflict 1995 (rank of Col, later Brig.-Gen., Gen. Commdr Second Mil. Region 2002, Commdr Gen. of Armed Forces 2002–03; Minister of Defence 2003–07; numerous mil. awards including Medalla Académica del Ejército (Merit, Honour and Distinction), Peruvian Cross of Merit, Marshal Andrés Avelino Cáceres Medal, Grand Cross of Mil. Order Francisco Bolognesi. *Address:* c/o Ministry of Defence, Avda Arequopa 291, Lima 1, Peru (office).

CHIANG, Antonio; Taiwanese journalist and editor; *Publisher and Editor-in-Chief, Taipei Times;* fmr Ed. and Publr The Eighties magazine; fmr Publr The Journalist (weekly political magazine) 1980s; Co-founder and sr journalist, Taipei Times 1998, later Ed.-in-Chief, currently Publr and Ed.-in-Chief; Deputy Sec.-Gen. Nat. Security Council 2000–04. *Address:* Taipei Times, 14/F, 399 Ruiguang Road, Neihu District, Taipei City 11492, Taiwan (office). *Telephone:* (2) 2656-1000 (office). *Fax:* (2) 2656-1099 (office). *E-mail:* letters@taipeitimes.com (office). *Website:* www.taipeitimes.com (office).

CHIBA, Kazuo, BEcons; Japanese business executive; b. 26 March 1925, Miyagi Pref.; m. Noriko Chiba 1954; two s.; ed Univ. of Tokyo; joined Oji Paper Co. Ltd 1950, Dir 1974, Mill Man. Kasugai Mill 1978, Man. Dir 1981, Sr Man. Dir 1985, Exec. Vice-Pres. 1987, Pres. 1989–; Blue Ribbon Medal 1990. *Leisure interests:* golf, reading. *Address:* Umegaoka 16-32, Midori-ku, Yokohama, 227 Japan. *Telephone:* (45) 9716602.

CHIBESAKUNDA, Hon. Justice Lombe Phyllis, BL; Zambian lawyer, judge and diplomatist; b. 5 May 1944; ed Chipembi Girls' School, Nat. Inst. of Public Admin, Lusaka, Australian Nat. Univ.; called to the Bar, Gray's Inn, UK; State Advocate Ministry of Legal Affairs 1969–77; pvt legal practice with Jacques and Partners 1972–73; mem. Nat. Ass. (Parl.) for Matero 1973–75; Solicitor Gen. and Deputy Minister of Legal Affairs 1973–75; Amb. to Japan 1975–77; High Commr to UK, also accred Amb. to FRG, the Netherlands and the Holy See 1977–82; Chair. Industrial Relations Court 1981–86; Judge, High Court, Lusaka 1986–94; Judge in charge of Copperbelt, Luapula, Northern and Northwestern Provs 1994–97; Supreme Court Judge 1997; Chair. Perm. Human Rights Comm. 1997–2003; Judge Admin. Tribunal of African Devt Bank 1997–, Vice-Pres. 2005–; Assessor of external examinations, Zambia Inst. of Advanced Legal Educ., Lusaka 2005–; Pres. Zambia Asscn of Women Judges 2005–; Chief Zambian Del., UN Law of the Sea Conf. 1974–79; Rep. UN Comm. on the Status of Women 1984–88; Chair. Equality Cttee Sub-Cttee UN Independence Party's Women's League; f. Social Action Charity, Lusaka; Founder-mem. Link Voluntary Org. 1979, Rotary Club 1994–97, Int. Asscn of Women Judges 1994–97; Life mem. Commonwealth Parl. Asscn; Kt Grand Cross of the Order of Pope Pius IX 1979. *Achievements include:* first woman lawyer in Zambia; first woman Solicitor Gen. in Zambia and Africa. *Address:* c/o Zambia Institute of Advanced Legal Education, PO Box 30690, Lusaka, Zambia (office).

CHIBURDANIDZE, Maiya Grigorievna; Georgian chess player; b. 17 Jan. 1961, Kutaisi, Georgia; ed Tbilisi Medical Inst. 1978; Int. Grand Master 1977; Honoured Master of Sport 1978; USSR Champion 1977; World Champion 1978–91 (youngest-ever world champion aged 17); winner of numerous women's int. chess tournaments; Capt. winning Soviet team at 8th Women's Chess Olympics 1978, Georgian winning team at Chess Olympics 1994; Oscar Chess Prize 1984–87. *Address:* Georgian Chess Federation, M. Kostava Str. 37a, 0179 Tbilisi, Georgia.

CHICAGO, Judy, MFA; American artist, author and academic; b. 20 July 1939, Chicago, Ill.; m. 1st Jerry Gerowitz 1961 (died 1962); m. 2nd Lloyd Hamrol 1969; m. 3rd Donald Woodman; ed Univ. of Calif., Los Angeles; taught art at Univ. of Calif. Extension, Los Angeles 1963–69, Univ. of Calif. Inst. Extension, Irvine 1966–69, California State Univ., Fresno (f. art programme for women) 1969–71, Calif. Inst. of the Arts, Valencia (f. first Feminist Art Programme) 1971–73; co-f. Feminist Studio Workshop and Woman's Bldg, Through the Flower Corpn, Los Angeles 1977; Presidential Appt. in Art and Gender Studies, Indiana Univ. 1999; Robb Lecturer, Univ. of Auckland 1999; Visiting Prof., Artist-in-Residence, Duke Univ. and Univ. of N Carolina, Chapel Hill 2000; Prof. in Residence, Western Kentucky Univ., Bowling Green 2001; Hon. DFA (Smith Coll., Northampton, Mass.) 2000, (Duke Univ., Durham, NC) 2003; Hon. DHumLitt (Lehigh Univ., Bethlehem, Pa) 2000; Int. Lion of Judah Conference Award For Pioneering American Women Jewish Artists 2004, Visionary Woman Award Moore Coll. of Art, Philadelphia 2004; numerous other awards. *Publications:* Through the Flower: My Struggle as a Woman Artist 1975, The Dinner Party: A Symbol of Our Heritage 1979, Embroidering Our Heritage: The Dinner Party Needlework 1980, The Birth Project 1985, Holocaust Project: From Darkness into Light 1993, The Dinner Party/Judy Chicago 1996, Beyond the Flower: The Autobiography of a Feminist Artist 1996, Women and Art: Contested Territory 1999, Fragments from the Delta of Venus 2004, Kitty City: a Feline Book of Hours 2005. *Leisure interests:* cats and exercise. *Address:* POBox 1327, Belen, NM 87002, USA (office). *Telephone:* (505) 861-1499 (office). *E-mail:* info@judychicago.com (office). *Website:* www.judychicago.com (office).

CHICO PARDO, Jaime, BEng, MBA; Mexican telecommunications executive; *Vice-Chairman and CEO, Teléfonos de México SA de CV (Telmex);* m.; several c.; ed Universidad Iberoamericana, Univ. of Chicago, USA; spent six years doing M&A work at Banamex Int. Div., later managed operations of cos acquired by bank; then Deputy Man. Dir International Mexican Bank (INTERMEX), London, UK; f. International Financial Engineering (investment bank); Sr Exec. Euzkadi, Gen. Tire de México –1993, Fimbursa –1993; Pres. and CEO Grupo Condumex SA de CV 1993–95; joined Teléfonos de México SA (Telmex) 1995, Vice-Chair. and CEO 1995–; Chair. and CEO Carso Global Telecom 2004–; Co-Chair. IDEAL (Impulsora del Desarrollo y el Empleo en America Latina); Dir America Movil SAB de CV, AT&T, Inc., Grupo Carso, Grupo Financiero Inburso, Honeywell International, Inc., Prodigy Communications Corpn, Mexican Business Advisory Council, Papalote Children's Museum; Distinguished Corp. Alumni Award 2005. *Address:* Teléfonos de México SA de CV, Parque Vía 190, Col Cuahtémoc, 06599 Mexico City (office); Carso Global Telecom SAB de CV, Avenida Insurgentes Sur 3500, Piso 5, Edificio Telmex, Colonia Peña Pobre, 14060 Mexico City, DF, Mexico (office). *Telephone:* (55) 5222-1212 (Telmex) (office); (55) 5244-0802 (Carso) (office). *Fax:* (55) 5545-5550 (Telmex) (office); (55) 5244-0808 (Carso) (office). *E-mail:* info@telmex.com.mx (office); info@cgtelecom.com.mx (office). *Website:* www.telmex.com.mx (office); www.cgtelecom.com.mx (office).

CHIDAMBARAM, Palaniappan, BSc, LLB, MBA; Indian politician; *Minister of Home Affairs;* b. 16 Sept. 1956, Kanadukathan, Tamil Nadu; s. of the late Shri Palaniappan and of Lakshmi Achi; m. Nalini Chidambaram; one c.; ed Presidency Coll., Madras Univ., Harvard Business School, USA; first elected to Parl. 1984; Deputy Minister, Dept of Commerce and Dept of Personnel 1985; Minister of State, Depts of Personnel and Home Affairs 1986–89; Minister of State, Dept of Commerce 1991–92, 1995–96; Minister of Finance 1996–98, 2004–08, of Home Affairs 2008–; Trustee Rajiv Gandhi Foundation, Indian Asscn of Literature. *Address:* Ministry of Home Affairs, North Block, Central Secretariat, New Delhi 110 001, India (office). *Telephone:* (11) 23092011 (office). *Fax:* (11) 23093750 (office). *E-mail:* mhaweb@mhant.delhi.nic.in (office). *Website:* www.mha.nic.in (office).

CHIDYAUSIKU, Godfrey Guwa, LLB; Zimbabwean judge; *Chief Justice, Supreme Court of Zimbabwe;* b. 1 March 1947, Goromonzi; s. of Nyamayaro Chidyausiku and Helen Chidyausiku (née Chogugudza); m. Sheila Chidyausiku; seven s. three d.; ed London Univ., Univ. of Zimbabwe; MP (Ind.) 1974–77, elected Zimbabwe African Nat. Union-Patriotic Front (ZANU-PF) MP 1980; Deputy Minister of Local Govt 1980, of Justice 1981; Attorney-Gen. 1983, apptd High Court Judge 1987, Judge Pres. High Court 1998, Chief Justice of Zimbabwe 2001–; Chair. Constitutional Comm. 1999. *Address:* Chambers of the Chief Justice, Supreme Court of Zimbabwe, CY 870, Causeway, Zimbabwe (office). *Telephone:* (4) 798634-5 (office). *Fax:* (4) 731867 (office).

CHIEN, Eugene Y. H., BS, MS, PhD; Taiwanese politician and professor of engineering; *Chairman, Taiwan Institute for Sustainable Energy;* b. 4 Feb. 1946, Taoyuan Co.; m. Wang Kuei-Jung (Gwendolyn Chien); two s. one d.; ed Nat. Taiwan Univ. and New York Univ., USA; Assoc. Prof., Tamkang Univ. 1973–76, Prof. and Chair. Dept of Aeronautical Eng 1976–78, Prof. and Dean Coll. of Eng 1978–84; mem. Legis. Yuan 1984–87, Chair. Nat. Defense Cttee 1984–85, Educ. Cttee 1986; Minister of State, Environmental Protection Admin. 1987–91; Minister of Transportation and Communications 1991–93; Nat. Policy Adviser to Pres. 1993–96; Rep., Taipei Rep. Office, UK 1993–97; Project Consultant EBRD 1997; Sr Adviser, Nat. Security Council 1997–2000; Deputy Sec.-Gen., Office of the Pres. 2000–02; Minister of Foreign Affairs 2002–04; Chair. Int. Co-operation and Devt Fund 2002–; consultant to various hi-tech cos 2004–; Chair. Taiwan Inst. for Sustainable Energy 2007–; Pres. Chinese Inst. of Environmental Eng 1988–91, Sino-British Cultural and Econ. Asscn 1998–; Prof. Emer., Catholic Univ. of Honduras 2002; Hon. Fellow, Cardiff Univ., UK 1998; Ten Outstanding Young Persons of the World, Jaycees Int. 1985, Chinese Inst. of Environmental Eng Award 1991, Environment Protection Admin Medal 1998. *Publications:* The Asian Regional Economy (co-ed.) 1993. *Leisure interests:* horse riding, reading, swimming, jogging, chess, go chess. *Address:* 5F, No. 35, Kwang Fu N. Road, Taipei,

www.worldwhoswho.com

Taiwan (office); 7F, No. 61 Ching-Chong Street, Taipei 105, Taiwan (home). *Telephone:* (2) 2768-2655 (office); (2) 2718-4172 (home). *Fax:* (2) 2719-0733 (home). *E-mail:* chieneugene@yahoo.com.tw.

CHIEN FU, Fredrick, BA, MA, PhD; Taiwanese politician (retd); *Senior Adviser, Cathay Financial Holdings;* b. 17 Feb. 1935, Beijing; m. Julie Tien; one s. one d.; ed Nat. Taiwan Univ., Yale Univ., USA; Sec. to Premier, Exec. Yuan 1962–63; Visiting Assoc. Prof., Nat. Chengchi Univ. 1962–64; Section Chief, Dept of N American Affairs, Ministry of Foreign Affairs 1964–67, Deputy Dir 1967–69, Dir 1969–72, Dir-Gen. Govt Information Office 1972–75; Visiting Prof., Nat. Taiwan Univ. 1970–72; Admin. Vice-Minister of Foreign Affairs 1975–79, Political Vice-Minister 1979–82; Rep., CCNAA Office in USA 1983–88; Minister of State and Chair. Council for Econ. Planning and Devt, Exec. Yuan 1988–90; Minister of Foreign Affairs 1990–96; apptd. mem. Kuomintang (KMT) Cen. Standing Cttee 1988–98; Speaker, Nat. Ass. 1996–98; Visiting Prof., Law School, Soochow Univ. 1997–98, Nat. Taiwan Univ. 1997–99; Pres. Control Yuan 1999–2005; currently Chair. Cathay Charity Foundation and Sr Adviser Cathay Financial Holdings; Order of Diplomatic Service Merit (Korea) 1972, Order of Kim Grand, Grade of Sac-Lenh (Viet Nam) 1973, Order of Brilliant Star with Grand Cordon (China) 1975, Orden Nacional del Merito en el Grado del Gran Cruz (Paraguay) 1975, Orden del Merito de Duarte, Sanchez y Mella, Grado de Gran Oficial (Dominican Repub.) 1975, Orden del Merito de Duarte en el Grado de Gran Cruz Placa de Plata (Dominican Repub.) 1978, Orden de Jose Cecilio del Valle en el Grado de Gran Cruz de Plata (Honduras) 1979, Orden Nacional Jose Matias Delgado en el Grado de Gran Cruz de Plata (El Salvador) 1979, L'Ordre Nacional Honneur et Merite Grand Officier (Haiti) 1979, Order of Good Hope, Grand Cross Class (SA) 1979, Orden de Vasca Nunez de Balboa (Panama) 1980, Orden de Don Cristobal Colon en el Grado de Gran Cruz de Plata (Dominican Repub.) 1982, Orden Merito en el Grado de Gran Cruz Extraordinario (Paraguay) 1990, Chief Counsellor of the Royal Order of Sobhuza II (Swaziland) 1991, Orden de Morazan, Gran Cruz, Placa de Plata (Honduras) 1991, Ordre du Merite Centrafricain, Grand Officier 1992, Gran Cruz de la Orden Quetzal (Guatemala) 1992, Orden Jose Matias Delgado, Grado de Gran Cruz, Placa de Plata (El Salvador) 1992, Orden de Antonio Jose De Irisari en el Grado de Gran Cruz (Guatemala) 1992, Orden Jose Dolores Estrada, Batalla de San Jacinto, en el Grado de Gran Cruz (Nicaragua) 1993, Orden Nacional Juan Mora Fernandez en el Grado de Gran Cruz de Plata (Costa Rica) 1993, Grand Officier de l'Ordre National du Niger 1994, Officier de l'Ordre National (Burkina Faso) 1994, Orden Manuel Amador Guerrero en el Grado de Gran Cruz (Panama) 1994, Ordem Nacional de Merito de Cooperacao e Desenvolvimento (Guinea Bissau) 1995, Soberano Congreso Nacional en el Grado de Gran Cruz (Guatemala) 1995, Order of Propitious Cloud with Special Grand Cordon (China) 2000, Order of Chung Cheng (China) 2005; Hon. DLit (Wilson Coll.), Hon. LLD (Boston Univ., Idaho State Univ., Sun Kyun Kwan Univ., Caribbean American Univ.), Dr hc (Florida Int.). *Publications:* The Opening of Korea: A Study of Chinese Diplomacy 1876–1885, Speaking as a Friend, More Views of a Friend, Faith and Resilience: The ROC Forges Ahead, Opportunity and Challenge, Memoir of Fredrick F. Chien. *Leisure interests:* reading, golf. *Address:* c/o Cathay Financial Center, 19th Floor, No. 7, Sung Ren Road, Hsin-yi District, Taipei 11073, Taiwan. *Telephone:* (2) 8722-6701. *Fax:* (2) 8789-4242 (office). *E-mail:* fredrickchien@cathaybk.com.tw (office). *Website:* www.cathaybk.com.tw (office).

CH'IEN KUO FUNG, Raymond, CBE, PhD, JP; Chinese business executive; *Chairman, CDC Corporation;* b. 26 Jan. 1952, Tokyo, Japan; m. Whang Hwee Leng; one s. two d.; ed schools in Hong Kong, Rockford Coll., Ill., Univ. of Pennsylvania, USA; Second Vice-Pres. and Economist, Chase Manhattan Bank, NA, New York 1978–81; Vice-Pres. and Dir Spencer Stuart & Assocs, Hong Kong 1981–84; Group Man. Dir Lam Soon Hong Kong Group 1984–97; currently Chair. CDC Corpn, Chair. China.com Inc.; Chair. (non-exec.) MTR Corpn Ltd, HSBC Private Equity (Asia) Ltd; Dir Hongkong and Shanghai Banking Corpn Ltd, Inchcape Pacific Ltd, Convenience Retail Asia Ltd, VTech Holdings Ltd, The Wharf (Holdings) Ltd; Chair. Hong Kong/EU Business Cooperation Cttee; fmr Chair. Fed. of Hong Kong Industries, now Hon. Pres.; mem. Exec. Council 1992–97, Exec. Council Hong Kong Special Admin. Region 1997–2002; Hon. Adviser, China Aerospace Corpn; Hon. Prof., Nanjing Univ.; Gold Bauhinia Star (Hong Kong); Young Industrialist Award, Fed. of Hong Kong Industrialists 1988, Global Leader for Tomorrow, World Econ. Forum 1993. *Leisure interests:* hiking, tennis, scuba diving, Chinese paintings and ceramics. *Address:* CDC Corporation, 33/F Citicorp Centre, 18 Whitfield Road, Causeway Bay, Hong Kong Special Administrative Region, People's Republic of China (office).

CHIEPE, Gaositwe Keagakwa Tibe, MBE, PH, BSc, MA, FRSA; Botswana politician, diplomatist and educationist (retd); b. 20 Oct. 1922, Serowe; d. of the late T. Chiepe and S.T. Chiepe (née Sebina); ed secondary school in Tigerloof, S Africa and Univs of Fort Hare and Bristol; Educ. Officer, Botswana 1948, Sr Educ. Officer 1962, Deputy Dir of Educ. 1965, Dir of Educ. 1968; High Commr in UK and Nigeria 1970–74, concurrently accred to Sweden, Norway, Denmark, FRG, France, Belgium and the EEC; Minister of Commerce and Industry 1974–77, of Mineral Resources and Water Affairs 1977–84, of External Affairs 1984–95, of Educ. 1995–99; Chair. Commonwealth Observer Group to observe elections in Zanzibar 2000; Patron Botswana Forestry Soc., Botswana Soc. for the Arts; Hon. Pres. Kalahari Conservation Soc.; Hon. LLD (Bristol); Hon. DLitt (Chicago) 1994; Hon. DEduc (Fort Hare) 1996. *Leisure interests:* music, gardening. *Address:* PO Box 186, Gaborone, Botswana. *Telephone:* 352796 (home).

CHIHARA, Charles Seiyo, PhD; American academic; *Emeritus Professor of Philosophy, University of California, Berkeley;* b. 19 July 1932, Seattle, Wash.; s. of George Chihara and Mary Chihara; m. Carol Rosen 1964; one d.; ed Seattle and Purdue Univs, Univ. of Washington, Univ. of Oxford, UK; Faculty mem. Univs of Wash. 1961–62, Ill. 1962–63, Calif. at Berkeley 1963–, Prof. 1975–, Prof. Emer. 2000; Mellon Postdoctoral Fellowship 1964–65, Humanities Research Fellowship 1967–68, Nat. Endowment for the Humanities Fellowship 1985–86, 1994–95, Univ. of Calif. Pres.'s Research Fellowship in the Humanities 1996–97. *Publications:* Ontology and the Vicious-Circle Principle 1973, Constructibility and Mathematical Existence 1990, The Worlds of Possibility: Modal Realism and the Semantics of Modal Logic 1998, A Structural Account of Mathematics 2004. *Leisure interests:* tennis, travel. *Address:* Department of Philosophy, University of California, Berkeley, CA 94720 (office); 567 Cragmont Avenue, Berkeley, CA 94708, USA (home). *Telephone:* (510) 525-4023 (home). *Fax:* (510) 642-4164 (home). *E-mail:* charles1@socrates.berkeley.edu (office). *Website:* philosophy.berkeley.edu/chihara/index (office).

CHIK, Tan Sri Sabbaruddin, BA, MPA; Malaysian business executive and fmr politician; *Chairman, Priceworth Wood Products Bhd;* b. 11 Dec. 1941, Temerloh, Penang; ed Abu Bakar Secondary School, Temerloh, Malay Coll., Kuala Kangser, Perak, Univ. of Malaya and Inst. of Social Studies, The Hague; Asst State Sec. Negri Sembilan, Prin. Asst Sec. JPM, Dir Planning, GPU/SERU, Dir Int. Trade, Ministry of Trade and Industry, Deputy State Sec. Selangor 1966–81; Gen. Man. Pernes Trading Sdn. Bhd 1981–82; mem. Parl. for Temerloh 1982–99; Deputy Minister of Finance 1982; Minister of Culture, Arts and Tourism 1987–99; mem. UMNO Supreme Council 1984; mem. Bd of Dirs Priceworth Wood Products Bhd (Chair. 2001–), EDEN Inc. Bhd 2002–. *Address:* Priceworth Wood Products Berhad, Suite 04-01A and 04-01B, 4th Floor, Menara Keck Seng, 203 Jalan Bukit Bintang, 55100 Kuala Lumpur, Malaysia (office). *Telephone:* (3) 21443299 (office). *Website:* www.pwpmalaysia.com.my (office).

CHIKÁN, Attila, PhD; Hungarian politician, economist and academic; *Professor, Corvinus University of Budapest;* b. 4 April 1944, Budapest; m. Márta Nagy; one s. one d.; ed Karl Marx Univ. of Econ. Sciences, Budapest, Grad. School of Business, Stanford Univ.; Prof., Budapest Univ. of Econ. Sciences and Public Admin (now Corvinus Univ. of Budapest) 1968–, Prof. and Chair. 1990, Rector 2000; Minister of Econ. Affairs 1998–99; Chair. Council of Econ. Advisers of the Prime Minister 2000–; First Vice-Pres., Sec.-Gen. Int. Soc. for Inventory Research; Pres. Fed. of European Production and Industrial Man. Societies 1996–; Pres. Int. Fed. of Purchasing Materials and Man. 2000–01; mem. editorial bds Int. Journal of Purchasing and Materials Man., Int. Journal of Logistics 1997–, Int. Journal of Quantitative and Operations Man. 1998–. *Publications:* author or ed. of several books, including Current Trends in Inventory Research: A Selection of Papers Presented at the Sixth International Symposium on Inventories, Budapest, August 1990, Inventory Models (co-ed.) 1991, Erzsebet Czako Zoltay-Paprika 2002. *Leisure interest:* sports. *Address:* Corvinus University of Budapest, 1093 Budapest IX, Fővám tér 8, Hungary (office). *Telephone:* (1) 482-5496 (office). *Fax:* (1) 482-5567 (office). *E-mail:* chikan@uni-corvinus.hu (office). *Website:* www.uni-corvinus.hu (office).

CHIKANE, Rev. Frank, MA; South African ecclesiastic and government official; *Director-General in the Presidency;* b. 3 Jan. 1951, Soweto; s. of James Mashi and Erenia Chikane; m. Kagiso Oglobry; three s.; ed Turfloop Univ. and Univs of S Africa, Durban and Pietermaritzburg; worked with Christ for All Nations 1975–76; ordained Minister 1980; part-time Research Officer, Inst. of Contextual Theology 1981, Gen. Sec. 1983; Gen. Sec. S African Council of Churches 1987–94; Dir-Gen. in Deputy Pres. Office 1994–99, Dir-Gen. in the Office of Presidency 1999–, also Chancellor of Nat. Orders, also Chair. Forum of S Africa's Dirs-Gen.; mem. Nat. Exec. Cttee, African Nat. Congress 1997–; Sr Research Fellow, Univ. of Cape Town 1995–; Hon. DTheol (Groningen); Diakonia Peace Prize 1986; Star Crystal Award 1987, Third World Prize 1989. *Publications:* Doing Theology in a Situation of Conflict 1983, The Incarnation in the Life of People in South Africa 1985, Children in Turmoil: Effect of the Unrest on Township Children 1986, Kairos Document – A Challenge to Churches, No Life of my Own (autobiog.). *Leisure interests:* reading, keeping fit (mentally, spiritually, physically). *Address:* The Presidency, Union Buildings, West Wing, Government Avenue, Private Bag X1000, Pretoria 0001 (office); University of Cape Town, Private Bag, Rondebosch 7700; 310 Zone 7, Pimville 1808, Soweto, South Africa (home); PO Box 4291, Johannesburg 2000. *Telephone:* (12) 3005200 (office). *Fax:* (12) 3238246 (office). *E-mail:* president@po.gov.za (office). *Website:* www.gov.za (office).

CHIKANE, Thenjiwe, BComm, CA (SA); South African business executive; Head, Dept of Finance and Econ. Affairs, Gauteng –2003; CEO MGO Consulting 2003–; Devt Bank of Southern Africa, Mpumalanga Econ. Empowerment Corpn; Dir (non-exec.) and mem. Bd Audit Cttee, Datacentrix May–Sept. 2005; Chair. State Information Tech. Agency 2005–08; mem. Bd of Dirs Telkom Group 2004–06, Nedbank, Ltd 2006–, PetroSA 2007–; mem. Audit Cttee Poslec, Rosslyn Mining Co.; mem. S African Inst. of Chartered Accountants, Asscn of Black Accountants of S Africa; fmr mem. Univ. of S Africa Transformation Forum. *Address:* c/o Board of Directors, Nedbank Ltd, 135 Rivonia Road, Sandown 2196, South Africa (office).

CHIKIN, Valentin Vasilevich; Russian journalist; b. 25 Jan. 1932; ed Moscow Univ.; literary corresp. for Moscow Komsomol newspaper 1951–58; mem. CPSU 1956–91, CP of Russian Fed. 1992–; literary corresp., Deputy Ed., Ed. of Komsomolskaya Pravda 1958–71; Deputy then First Deputy Ed.-in-Chief of Sovietskaya Rossiya 1971–84, Ed.-in-Chief 1986–91; First Deputy Pres. of State Cttee on Publishing, Printing and the Book Trade 1984–86; Sec. of USSR Union of Journalists 1986–90; cand. mem. of CPSU Cen. Cttee 1986–91; mem. State Duma (CP faction) 1993–, re-elected 1995, 1999, 2003, 2007. *Address:* Gosudarstvennaya Duma, 103265 Moscow, Okhotnyi ryad 1 (office); Communist Party of the Russian Federation (Kommunisticheskaya partiya Rossiiskoi Federatsii), 103051 Moscow, per. M. Sukharevskii 3/1, Russia. *Telephone:* (495) 692-80-00 (office); (495) 628-04-90. *Fax:* (495) 203-42-58 (office); (495) 292-90-50. *E-mail:* stateduma@duma.ru (office); kprf2005@yandex.ru. *Website:* www.duma.ru (office); www.kprf.ru.

CHIKVAIDZE, Alexander Davidovich; Georgian diplomatist; b. 19 Jan. 1932, T'bilisi; m.; two s.; ed Moscow State Univ., Acad. of Political Sciences, Diplomatic Acad.; taught int. law, Moscow State Univ., headed youth orgs in Georgian Repub., then Head of Tbilisi Region Cttee of CPSU; Chair. Rep. Cttee for Publishing and Book Trade 1976–79; fmr Vice-Consul (Cultural Affairs), Mumbai, First Sec. (Cultural Dept), Embassy of USSR in London; Consul-Gen., San Francisco 1979–83; Amb. to Kenya and to UNEP and Habitat 1983–85; Head of Sector, CPSU Cen. Cttee 1985–88; USSR Amb. to Netherlands 1988–91, Russian Amb. to the Netherlands 1991–92; Minister of Foreign Affairs of Georgia 1992–95; Amb. to Greece –2003, to Switzerland (also Perm. Rep. to UN Office and Other Int. Orgs) 2003; fmr Chair. USSR Chess Fed.; Lenin Centenary Medal. *Publication:* Western Countries' Foreign Policy on the Eve of the Second World War 1976. *Address:* c/o Ministry of Foreign Affairs, 0108 Tbilisi, Sh. Chitadze 4, Georgia.

CHILADZE, Otar; Georgian writer; b. 20 March 1933, Signakhi, Georgia; s. of Ivane Chiladze and Tamar Chiladze; brother of Tamaz Chiladze; m. Nana Chiladze 1956 (died 1990); one s. one d.; ed Tbilisi State Univ.; professional writer since 1950s; Sh. Rustaveli Prize 1983, State Prize of Georgia for play Labyrinth 1993. *Publications include:* The Trains and Passengers (collection of verses) 1959, Iron Bed, The Other Side, Remember about Life; A Man was Going by the Road (novel) 1973, Each Who Meets Me (novel) 1976, Iron Theatre (novel) 1983, March Cock (novel) 1987, Avelum 1996, Godori (novel) 2003. *Address:* Av. of David Agmashenebeli 181, Apt. 6, 380012 Tbilisi, Georgia. *Telephone:* (32) 34-51-84 (home). *E-mail:* zazachila@yahoo.com (home).

CHILADZE, Tamaz; Georgian writer; b. 5 March 1931, Signakhi; s. of Ivane Chiladze and Tamar Chiladze; brother of Otar Chiladze; ed Univ. of Tbilisi; first published works in 1951; mem. CPSU 1967–89; Chief Ed. Sabchota Khelovneba 1973–89, Mratobi 1997–; Shota Rustaveli Prize 1992, State Prize of Georgia 1997. *Publications include:* Sun Dial (poems) 1961, A Network of Stars 1961, Pony-trek 1963, The First Day 1965, Who Lives on the Stars 1970, White Smoke 1973, Memory (poems) 1978, Martyrdom of St Shushanik (essay) 1978, Herald of Spring (essay) 1985, The Ray of the Setting Sun (novel) 1993, The Cactus Garden (novel) 1993; plays: Shelter on the Ninth Floor, Murder, Role for a Beginner Actress, Bird Fair, The Day of Appointment. *Address:* 22 Simon Chickovani Street, Flat 7, Tbilisi 0171, Georgia. *Telephone:* (32) 33-49-87. *Fax:* (32) 33-40-75. *E-mail:* shalva@sultanishvili.ge.

CHILDS, David M., BA, MArch, FAIA; American architect; *Consulting Partner, Skidmore, Owings and Merrill LLP;* b. 1 April 1941, Princeton, NJ; two c.; ed Yale Univ., Yale School of Art and Architecture; Design Dir Pennsylvania Avenue Comm., Washington, DC 1968–71; joined Skidmore, Owings and Merrill LLP, Washington, DC 1971, moved to New York City office 1984, currently Consulting Design Pnr; Chair. Nat. Capital Planning Comm. 1975–81; Chair. US Comm. of Fine Arts 2003–08; mem. Bd of Dirs Municipal Arts Soc. of New York; Trustee American Acad. in Rome, Museum of Modern Art, Smithsonian Nat. Portrait Gallery, Nat. Bldg Museum; Fellow, AIA. *Completed projects include:* in Washington, DC: Washington Mall master plan and Constitution Gardens, Nat. Geographic HQ, 1300 New York Avenue, Metro Center, US News and World Report HQ, Dulles Airport Extension, Four Seasons, Park Hyatt and Regent hotels; in New York: Worldwide Plaza on 8th Avenue, 450 Lexington Avenue, Bertelsmann Tower, NY Mercantile Exchange, JFK Airport Arrivals Bldg, Bear Stearns HQ, Stuyvesant School Bridge; other projects include Swiss Bank Center, Stamford, Conn., Deerfield Acad. Natatorium, US Courthouse, Charleston, WV, Lester B. Pearson Int. Airport, Toronto, Canada, Ben Gurion Int. Airport, Tel-Aviv, Israel, West Ferry Circus at Canary Wharf, London, England, US Embassy in Ottawa, Canada. *Address:* Skidmore, Owings and Merrill, 14 Wall Street, 24th Floor, New York, NY 10005, USA (office). *Telephone:* (212) 298-9300 (office). *Fax:* (212) 298-9500 (office). *E-mail:* somnewyork@som.com (office). *Website:* www.som.com (office).

CHILINGAROV, Artur Nikolayevich, CandGeoSc; Russian polar explorer and politician; b. 25 Sept. 1939, Leningrad; m.; one s. one d.; ed Adm. Makarov Higher Marine School of Eng; worked as metalworker in Baltic vessel repair plant; First Sec. Regional Comsomol Cttee in Yakutya; headed drifting station N Pole 19, organized station N Pole 22, head Bellingshausen station in Antarctica, head expedition to free scientific vessel Mikhail Somol in Antarctic, expedition on board atomic ice-breaker Sibir; Deputy Chair. USSR State Cttee on Meteorology 1986–92; counsellor, Chair. Russian Supreme Soviet on problems of Arctic and Antarctic 1991–93; Pres. Asscn of Polar Explorers of the Russian Fed. 1991–, mem. Coordinating Council Polus Expeditionary Centre (organizes expeditions for the Asscn) 2002–; mem. State Duma (Parl.) 1993–, Deputy Speaker 1994–; mem. Org. Cttee Otechestvo Movt 1999; joined Yedinstvo and Otechestvo Union (later Yedinaya Rossiya party); Corresp. mem. Russian Acad. of Natural Sciences; Co-Chair. Russian Foundation of int. humanitarian aid and co-operation; Order of Lenin, Labour Red Banner, Sign of Honour; Hero of the Soviet Union, USSR State Prizes. *Leisure interest:* football. *Address:* c/o Coordinating Council, Polus Expeditionary Centre, 119027 Moscow, 2 Reysovaya Street, 2A, PGK airport Vnukovo; State Duma, 103009 Moscow, Okhotny ryad 1, Russia (office). *Telephone:* (495) 436-28-47 (Polus) (office); (495) 292-80-44 (office). *Fax:* (495) 292-76-50 (office). *E-mail:* mail@polus.org (office). *Website:* www.polus.ru (office).

CHILINGIRIAN, Levon, OBE, FRCM, ARCM; British violinist and academic; *Professor, Royal College of Music;* b. 28 May 1948, Nicosia, Cyprus; nephew of Manoug Parikian; m. Susan Paul Pattie 1983; one s.; ed Royal Coll. of Music (RCM), London; f. Chilingirian String Quartet 1971; has performed in N and S America, Africa, Australasia, Europe and Far East; Prof., RCM 1980–; Musical Dir Camerata Nordica of Sweden; BBC Beethoven Competition 1969, Munich Duo Competition (with Clifford Benson) 1971; Hon. DMus (Sussex) 1992; Cobbett Medal 1995, Royal Philharmonic Soc. Chamber Music Award 1995. *Recordings include:* 10 Mozart quartets, last three Schubert quartets, Debussy and Ravel quartets, Schubert octet and quintet, six Bartok quartets and piano quintet, late and middle Dvořák quartets, Tippett Triple Concerto; music by Panufnik, Tavener, Pärt, Chausson, Grieg, Vierne, Hahn, Komitas, McEwan, Michael & Lennox Berkeley, Mozart and Eliasson (with Chilingirian Quartet and Camerata Nordica). *Publications:* Edvard Grieg's F Major Quartet 1999. *Leisure interests:* reading, backgammon, football. *Address:* c/o Grant Rogers Musical Artists' Management, 8 Wren Crescent, Bushey Heath, Hertfordshire, WD23 1AN, England (office); 7 Hollingbourne Road, London, SE24 9NB, England. *Telephone:* (20) 8950-2220 (office); (20) 7978-9104. *Fax:* (20) 8950-3570 (office); (20) 7274-5764. *E-mail:* info@ngrartists.com (office); spplchil@aol.com (home). *Website:* www.ngrartists.com (office).

CHILOSI, Alberto, PhD; Italian economist and academic; *Professor of Economic Policy, University of Pisa;* b. 14 Jan. 1942, Modena; s. of Giuseppe Chilosi and Clara Trabucchi; m. Lucia Ponzini; one s.; ed La Spezia, Univ. of Pisa, Warsaw Cen. School of Planning and Statistics; Asst at Univ. of Pisa 1966–69; Lecturer then Assoc. Prof. of Econs, Univ. Officielle du Congo 1969–72; Lecturer in Theory and Policy of Econ. Devt, Univ. of Pisa 1972–81, Prof. of Econ. Policy 1981–; Pres. Asscn Italiana per lo Studio dei Sistemi Economici Comparati 1988–89. *Publications:* Growth Maximization, Equality and Wage Differentials in the Socialist Economy 1976, Kalecki 1979, Self-Managed Market Socialism with Free Mobility of Labour 1986, L'Economia del Periodo di Transizione 1992; book chapters and articles on the econs and politics of immigration in scholarly journals. *Leisure interests:* cycling, swimming. *Address:* Dipartimento di Scienze Economiche, Sede di Scienze Politiche, Via Serafini, 3, 56126 Pisa (office); Via S. Andrea, 48, 56126 Pisa, Italy (home). *Telephone:* (050) 2212439 (office); (050) 544184 (home). *E-mail:* chilosi@specon.unipi.it (office). *Website:* www-dse.ec.unipi.it/chilosi (office).

CHILUMPHA, Cassim; Malawi politician; *Vice-President and Minister responsible for Statutory Corporations;* Minister of Finance 1998–2000; Vice-Pres. and Minister responsible for Statutory Corpns 2004–. *Address:* Office of the President and Cabinet, Private Bag 301, Capital City, Lilongwe 3, Malawi (office). *Telephone:* 1782655 (office). *Fax:* 1783654 (office).

CHILVER, Baron (Life Peer), cr. 1987, of Cranfield in the County of Bedfordshire; **Henry Chilver,** MA, DSc, FRS, FREng, CCMI; British academic, university administrator and business executive; b. 30 Oct. 1926, Barking, Essex; s. of A. H. Chilver; m. Claudia Grigson 1959; three s. two d.; ed Southend High School and Univ. of Bristol; Structural Engineer, British Railways 1947–48; Lecturer, Univ. of Bristol 1952–54, Univ. of Cambridge 1956–61, Fellow, Corpus Christi Coll., Cambridge 1958–61; Prof. of Civil Eng, Univ. of London 1961–69; Dir Centre for Environmental Studies 1967–69; Vice-Chancellor, Cranfield Inst. of Tech. 1970–89; Dir English China Clays 1973, Chair. 1989–95; Dir ICI 1990–93, Zeneca 1993–95; Chair. RJB Mining 1993–97, Chiroscience Group PLC 1995–98, Univs Computer Bd 1975–78, The Post Office 1980–81, Advisory Council for Applied Research and Devt 1982–85, Milton Keynes Devt Corpn 1983–92, Plymouth Devt Corpn 1996–98; Chair. Univs Funding Council 1988–91; mem. or fmr mem. various cttees of inquiry, review bodies etc.; Hon. Fellow, Corpus Christi Coll., Cambridge; Dr hc (Leeds, Bristol, Salford, Strathclyde, Bath, Buckingham, Cranfield, Compiègne); Telford Gold Medal 1962 and Coopers Hill War Memorial Prize 1977, ICE. *Publications:* Problems in Engineering Structures (with R. J. Ashby) 1958, Strength of Materials and Structures (with J. Case and C. T. F. Ross) 1971; papers on structural eng. and stability. *Telephone:* (20) 7219-8636 (office).

CHIMUTENGWENDE, Chenhamo (Chen), MA; Zimbabwean writer, activist and politician; b. 28 Aug. 1943, Mazowe Dist; m. Edith Matore; three s. two d.; ed Univ. of Bradford, UK; Exec. Dir Europe–Third World Research Centre, London 1969–74; Pres. Kwame Nkrumah Inst. of Writers and Journalists, London 1969–77; Deputy Dir and Sr Lecturer in Mass Communications and Int. Affairs, City Univ., London 1978–79; UNESCO Consultant on Mass Communications (Broadcasting) 1979–80; Corresp. for East and Southern Africa, Inter Press Service, Rome 1980–83; Sr Lecturer and Head, School of Journalism, Univ. of Nairobi 1980–82; MP 1985–2008; fmr Minister of Environment and Tourism, of Information, Posts and Telecommunications, of Public and Interactive Affairs; fmr Zanu PF Prov. Chair. for Mashonaland Central; fmr Pres. United New Africa Global Network; Corresp. UNESCO's Int. Social Science Journal 1980–2003; Chair. Africa Star Holdings Ltd 1986; Pres. UN Convention on Climate Change 1996–98; Chair. UN High Level Cttee of Ministers and Sr Officials 1997–98. *Publication:* South Africa: The Press and the Politics of Liberation 1978. *Leisure interests:* music, travelling, reading, public speaking. *Address:* 6 Duthie Road, Belgravia, Harare, Zimbabwe (home). *Telephone:* (4) 704586 (home). *E-mail:* chenchim@yahoo.com (home).

CHIN, Lt-Col Elias Camsek, AA, BA; Palauan army officer and politician; *Vice-President;* b. 10 Oct. 1949, Peleliu; s. of Taktai Chin and Takeko Kuratomi Chin; m. Miriam Rudimch 1977; one s. one d.; ed Farrington High School, Honolulu, Hawaii, Univ. of Hawaii, Electronic Inst. of Hawaii, Univ. of Hawaii at Manoa, Armor Officer Basic and Advanced Course, US Army Flight School, Air Ground Operations School, US Army Command and Gen. Staff Coll., US Army War Coll., US Army Airborne School, US Army Ranger School,

US Army Motor Officer School, US Army Computer School; served for 23 years in army, achieving rank of Lt-Col in US Army before retiring in 1977, commissioned in Armor Corps of US Army 1975, later transferred to Aviation Corps, spent more than 20 years as US Army combat aviator; Minister of Justice 1997–2000, designed and built three-story BRT Building to house Ministry of Justice Office and Bureau of Public Safety Admin; participated in design, building and fund-raising for construction of Father Felix Yaoch Gymnasium 2000; Senator to Sixth Olbiil Era Kelulau (Palau Nat. Congress) 2000–04; Vice-Pres. of Palau 2004–; Legion of Merit, Meritorious Service Medal with Second Oak Leaf Cluster, Army Commendation Medal with Second Oak Leaf Cluster, Army Achievement Medal with Oak Leaf Cluster, Nat. Defense Service Medal, Army Service Ribbon, Overseas Ribbon, Parachutist Badge, Army Master Aviator Badge, Ranger Tab. *Leisure interests:* baseball, spear fishing. *Address:* Office of the Vice-President, PO Box 10284, Koror 96940, Palau (office). *Telephone:* 767-2702 (office). *Fax:* 767-1310 (office). *E-mail:* vp@vpchin.com (office). *Website:* www.vpchin.com (office).

CHINAMASA, Patrick Anthony, LLB; Zimbabwean politician; *Minister of Justice, Legal and Parliamentary Affairs;* b. 25 Jan. 1947, Nyanga; s. of Anthony Chinamasa and Regina Maunga; m. Monica Chinamasa; two s. two d.; mem. Zimbabwe African Nat. Union–Patriotic Front (ZANU–PF); fmr Attorney Gen.; currently Minister of Justice, Legal and Parl. Affairs, Acting Minister of Finance Feb. 2009. *Leisure interests:* watching sport, jogging, reading. *Address:* Ministry of Justice, Legal and Parliamentary Affairs, cnr. Samora Machel Avenue, and Leopold Takawira St, Private Bag 7751, Causeway, Harare (office); Honeybear Lane, Borrowdale, Harare, Zimbabwe (home). *Telephone:* (4) 774620 (office); (4) 860006 (home). *Fax:* (4) 772999 (office). *Website:* www.justice.gov.zw (office).

CHINCHILLA MIRANDA, Laura, BA, MA; Costa Rican politician; *Vice-President and Minister of Justice;* b. 28 March 1959; m.; one c.; ed Univ. of Costa Rica, Georgetown Univ., USA; adviser, Ministry of Planning and Political Economy 1989–90; consultant on state reform and structural adjustment programmes 1994–96, including with UNDP, IDB, USAID; Vice-Minister for Public Security and Governance 1994–96, Minister of Public Security 1996–98; Deputy, Asamblea Legislativa (Parl.) 2002–06; Interim Minister of Public Security April 2008, Vice-Pres. and Minister for Justice 2008–; mem. Bd Nat. Drugs Council (CONARDO); Pres. Nat. Council on Migration 1996–98; Pres. Bd Centro de Inteligencia Conjunto Antidrogas (CICAD) 2002–06; mem. Comm. on Judicial Affairs, Comm. on Int. Affairs 2006–. *Publications:* various publs on admin. of justice, public security and police reform. *Address:* Ministry of Justice, 50 m norte de la Clínica Bíblica, frente a la Escuela M. García Flamenco, 1000 San José, Costa Rica (office). *Telephone:* 280-9054 (office). *Fax:* 234-7959 (office). *E-mail:* justicia@gobnet.go.cr (office). *Website:* www.mj.go.cr (office).

CHINOFOTIS, Adm. Panagiotis; Greek naval officer and politician; *Deputy Minister of Interior;* b. 12 Aug. 1949, Athens; m. Maria Chinofotis; ed Hellenic Naval Acad., Hellenic Naval War Coll., Naval War Coll., USA, Salve Regina Univ., Newport, RI, USA; commissioned as Ensign, Hellenic Navy 1971; fmr Head, Hellenic Navy Gen. Staff (HNGS), NATO and Nat. Exercises and Operational Training; fmr Dir of Studies, Hellenic Naval War Coll.; Commdr, HS Lemnos (warship) 1991–93; worked for Mil. Rep. to NATO 1993–95; Asst Dir Strategic Plans and Policy Directorate, Hellenic Nat. Defence Gen. Staff (HNDGS) 1995–96; Commdr, First Div. of Destroyers and Frigates 1996–97; Deputy Mil. Rep. to WEU, Brussels 1997–98, concurrently Chair. Mil. Reps Working Group during Greek presidency of WEU; promoted to Commodore 1998; Deputy Chief of Staff, Hellenic Fleet Command 1998–99; Commdr and Flag Officer, Destroyers and Frigates 1999–2001; Dir A Div. HNGS 2001–02; promoted to Rear-Adm. 2002; Dir D Div. HNDGS 2002–04; C-in-C of Hellenic Fleet 2004–05; promoted to Adm. 2005; Chief of Defence 2005–07; Deputy Minister of Interior 2007–; mem. New Democracy Party; Navy Force Formation Command Medal A' and C' Class, Navy Force Meritorious Command Medal A', B' and C' Class, Staff Officer Service Commendation Medal A' and B' Class, Chief of Defence Command Medal. *Address:* 17 Aphrodites Street, Palaio Faliro, Athens 155 61 (home); Ministry of the Interior, 4 P. Kanellopoulou Avenue, Athens 101 77, Greece (office). *Telephone:* (210) 9838797 (home); (210) 6988222 (office). *Fax:* (210) 6911995 (office). *E-mail:* yfypes@mopo.gr (office). *Website:* www.ydt.gr (office); www.ypes.gr (office).

CHIOU, I-Jen, MA; Taiwanese politician; b. 9 May 1950; ed Nat. Taiwan Univ. and Univ. of Chicago, USA; Deputy Chief of Staff, Nat. Security Council 2000–02, Sec.-Gen. 2002–03, 2004–07; Sec.-Gen. Exec. Yuan 2000–02, Vice-Pres. 2007–08 (resgnd); Minister without portfolio 2002; Chief of Staff, Office of the Pres. 2003–04, 2007; Minister responsible for Consumer Protection Comm. 2007–08 (resgnd). *Address:* c/o Executive Yuan, 1 Jhongsiao E. Rd, Sec. 1, Taipei 10058, Taiwan (office).

CHIPMAN, John Miguel Warwick, CMG, BA, MA, DPhil; British administrator and academic; *Director-General and Chief Executive, International Institute for Strategic Studies (IISS);* b. 10 Feb. 1957, Montréal, Canada; s. of Lawrence Carroll Chipman and Maria Isabel Prados; m. Lady Theresa Manners 1997; two s.; ed Westmount High School, Montreal, El Estudio, Madrid, Harvard Univ., USA, London School of Econs and Balliol Coll., Oxford; Research Assoc. IISS, London 1983–84; Asst Dir for Regional Security, IISS 1987–91, Dir of Studies 1991–93, Dir IISS 1993, now Dir-Gen. and Chief Exec., Founder IISS Publ Strategic Comments; Research Assoc. Atlantic Inst. for Int. Affairs, Paris 1985–87; Dir Arundel House Enterprises, US Office IISS, Washington, DC, Asia Office IISS, Singapore; mem. Bd of Dirs Aspen Inst. Italia, Asan Inst. for Policy Studies, South Korea; mem. Int. Advisory Bd Reliance Industries Ltd, Mumbai, Nat. Bank of Kuwait; NATO Fellowship 1983. *Achievements include:* was Capt. of Harvard Fencing Team and earned Full Blue while fencing at Oxford. *Publications:* Cinquième République et Défense de l'Afrique 1986, French Power in Africa 1989; ed. and prin. contrib. to NATO's Southern Allies: Internal and External Challenges 1988; articles in journals and book chapters. *Leisure interests:* tennis, skiing, scuba diving, collecting travel books, music. *Address:* International Institute for Strategic Studies, Arundel House, 13–15 Arundel Street, London, WC2R 3DX, England (office). *Telephone:* (20) 7379-7676 (office). *Fax:* (20) 7836-3108 (office). *E-mail:* iiss@iiss.org (office). *Website:* www.iiss.org (office).

CHIPPERFIELD, David Alan, CBE, DipArch, RA; British architect; *Principal, David Chipperfield Architects;* b. 18 Dec. 1953, London; s. of Alan John Chipperfield and Peggy Chipperfield (née Singleton); m. Dr Evelyn Stern; two s. one d. and one s. from previous m.; ed Architectural Asscn; Prin. David Chipperfield Architects 1984–; Visiting Prof., Harvard Univ., USA 1987–88, Univ. of Naples, Italy 1992, Univ. of Graz, Austria 1992, Ecole Polytechnique Fédérale de Lausanne, Switzerland 1993–94, London Inst. 1997, Università degli Studi Federico II, Naples 2003, Art Inst., Chicago, USA 2003, Università degli Studi di Sassari, Alghero, Italy 2003, Illinois Inst. of Tech., Chicago 2006; Design Tutor, RCA 1988–89; Prof. of Architecture, Staatliche Akad. der Bildenden Künste, Stuttgart, Germany 1995–2001; Mies van der Rohe Chair, Barcelona School of Architecture, Spain 2001; Royal Designer for Industry 2006; Hon. Prof., Univ. of the Arts, London 2004–; Hon. FAIA 2007; Hon. Mem. Bund Deutscher Architekten 2007; Andrea Palladio Prize 1993, RIBA Regional Award 1996, 1998, RIBA Award 1998, 1999, 2002, 2003, 2004, Heinrich Tessenow Gold Medal 1999, Royal Fine Art Comm. Trust/BSkyB Best Building Award 1999, RIBA European and Int. Awards 2007, RIBA Stirling Prize 2007, RIBA Nat. and European Awards 2008. *Completed projects include:* TAK Design Centre, Kyoto 1990, pvt. museum, Japan 1991, Matsumoto Corp. HQ, Okayama 1992, River and Rowing Museum, Henley-on-Thames, Kaistrasse Office Bldg, Düsseldorf, Joseph Store, Sloane Avenue, London 1997, Bryant Park Hotel, New York 1998, Landeszentralbank HQ, Gera, Shore Club Hotel, Miami, Ernsting Service Centre, Coesfeld-Lette 2001, Gormley Studio, London 2003, pvt. house, New York 2004, housing, Villaverde, Madrid, Pantaenius House, Hamburg, Hotel Beaumont, Maastricht, Figge Art Museum, Davenport, Ia, Hotel Puerta America, Madrid 2005, Museum of Modern Literature, Marbach am Neckar, Des Moines Public Library, Ia, America's Cup Bldg 'Veles e Vents', Valencia, BBC Scotland Pacific Quay, Glasgow 2006, Freshfields Bruckhaus Deringer office bldg, Amsterdam, Liangzhu Culture Museum, China, Empire Riverside Hotel, Hamburg, Gallery 'Hinter dem Giesshaus 1', Berlin 2007, Ninetree Village, China, Campus Audiovisual, Barcelona, Kivik Pavilion, Sweden 2008. *Current projects include:* Neues Museum, Berlin, Museum Island Masterplan, Berlin, San Michele Cemetery, Venice, Palace of Justice, Salerno, City of Justice, Barcelona, Turner Contemporary, Margate, The Hepworth, Wakefield, Anchorage Museum at Rasmuson Center, Alaska, Saint Louis Art Museum, Mo. *Publications:* El Croquis (monograph) 1998, 2001, 2004, 2006, David Chipperfield, Idea e Realta 2005, David Chipperfield Architectural Works 1990–2002 2003. *Address:* David Chipperfield Architects, Cobham Mews, Agar Grove, London, NW1 9SB, England (office). *Telephone:* (20) 7267-9422 (office). *Fax:* (20) 7267-9347 (office). *E-mail:* info@davidchipperfield.co.uk (office). *Website:* www.davidchipperfield.co.uk (office).

CHIRAC, Jacques René; French politician and fmr head of state; b. 29 Nov. 1932, Paris; s. of François Chirac and Marie-Louise Valette; m. Bernadette Chodron de Courcel 1956; two d.; ed Lycée Carnot, Lycée Louis-le-Grand, Ecole Nationale d'Admin and Inst. d'Etudes Politiques, Paris; mil. service in Algeria; auditor, Cour des Comptes 1959–62; Special Asst, Secr.-Gen. of Govt 1962; Special Asst, Pvt. Office of M. Pompidou 1962–65; Counsellor, Cour des Comptes 1965–94; Sec. of State for Employment Problems 1967–68; Sec. of State for Economy and Finance 1968–71; Minister for Parl. Relations 1971–72, of Agriculture and Rural Devt 1972–73, 1973–74, of the Interior March–May 1974; Prime Minister of France 1974–1976, 1986–88; Sec.-Gen. UDR 1974–75, Hon. Sec.-Gen. 1975–76; Pres. RPR (fmrly UDR) 1976–94, Hon. Sec.-Gen. 1977–80; mem. European Parl. 1979; Pres. Regional Council, La Corrèze 1970–79; Municipal Counsellor, Sainte-Féréole 1965–77; Mayor of Paris 1977–95; Pres. of France May 1995–2007; Deputy for Corrèze March–May 1967, June–Aug. 1968, March–May 1973, 1976–79, 1981–86, 1988–95; mem. Comm. on Nat. Defence, Nat. Assembly 1980–86; mem. (ex officio) Conseil Constitutionnel 2007–; f. Fondation Jacques Chirac (for sustainable Devt and cultural dialogue) 2008; Grand-Croix, Légion d'honneur; Ordre nat. du Mérite; Croix de la Valeur Militaire; Chevalier du Mérite agricole, des Arts et Lettres, de l'Étoile noire, du Mérite sportif, du Mérite touristique; Grand Cross Merit of the Sovereign Order of Malta; Prix Louise Michel 1986, Médaille de l'Aéronautique, State Prize of the Russian Federation 2008. *Publications:* Discours pour la France à l'heure du choix, La lueur de l'espérance: réflexion du soir pour le matin 1978, Une Nouvelle France, Réflexions 1 1994, La France pour Tous 1995. *Address:* c/o Conseil Constitutionnel, 2 rue de Montpensier, 75001 Paris, France. *Telephone:* 1-40-15-30-00. *Fax:* 1-40-20-93-27. *E-mail:* relations-exterieures@conseil-constitutionnel.fr. *Website:* www.conseil-constitutionnel.fr.

CHIRICĂ, Andrei; Romanian engineer and organization official; *Chairman, Romanian Association of Telecommunications Engineers;* b. 14 June 1939, Ploieşti; ed Electronics and Telecommunications Coll. of Bucharest; engineer in Radio and TV Dept 1961–68; Chief Engineer, Gen. Direction of Post and Telecommunications 1968–84, then Asst Gen. Dir for matters of research and information in telecommunications, Minister of Communications 1990–94; Pres. Romtelecom SA 1994–95; Pres. C. A. Mobil Rom 1996–; Chair. Romanian Asscn of Telecommunications Engineers (AITR) 2003–. *Publications:* numerous specialized works. *Address:* Asociatia Inginerilor de Telecomunicatii din România, Str. Spatiului nr. 3, 051116, Bucharest 5, Romania (office).

Telephone: (21) 4005141 (office). *Fax:* (21) 4005721 (office). *E-mail:* andrei.chirica@orange.ro (office); adminstrator@aitr.ro (office). *Website:* www.aitr.ro (office).

CHISHOLM, Sir John, Kt, KBE, MSc, FREng, CEng, FIEE; British international organization official; *Executive Chairman, QinetiQ;* b. 1946; m. Kitty Chisholm; two c.; ed Cambridge Univ.; began career with General Motors; fmr Man. Scicon Ltd (part of BP); f. CAP Scientific 1979, fmr Dir CAP Group PLC; Man. Dir Sema Group PLC 1988–91; Chief Exec. DERA 1991–2001; Chief Exec. QinetiQ 2001–05, Exec. Chair. 2005–; Dir (non-exec.) Expro International PLC 1994–2003, Bespack PLC 1999–2005; Fellow, IEE (Pres. 2005–06), Royal Acad. of Eng, Royal Aeronautical Soc., Inst. of Physics. *Leisure interests:* historic motor racing. *Address:* QinetiQ, Cody Technology Park, Ively Road, Farnborough GU14 0LX, England (office). *Telephone:* (8700) 100942 (office). *E-mail:* customercontact@qinetiq.com (office). *Website:* www.qinetiq.com (office).

CHISHOLM, Malcolm H., BS, DrSci, PhD, FRS; British chemist and academic; *Distinguished University Professor, Department of Chemistry, Ohio State University;* b. 15 Oct. 1945; ed Queen Mary Coll., London Univ.; Postdoctoral Fellow and Lecturer, Univ. of Western Ontario, Canada 1969–72; Lecturer, Princeton Univ., NJ, USA 1972–78; Lecturer, Indiana Univ., Bloomington 1978–2000; Distinguished Prof. of Math. and Physical Sciences, Ohio State Univ. 2000–, Distinguished Univ. Prof., Dept of Chem. 2006–; mem. Advisory Bd several journals including Organometallics 1987–89, Chemical Communications 1989–96, Inorganic Synthesis 1990–, Dalton Transactions 1998–; Guggenheim Fellow 1985–86; Fellow, AAAS 1987–, Royal Soc. 1990, American Acad. of Arts and Sciences 2004, Deutsche Akademie der Naturforscher Leopoldina 2004; Corresp. Fellow, Royal Soc. of Edinburgh 2005; mem. NAS 2005–. *Publications:* approx. 600 articles in research journals. *Leisure interests:* reading, gardening, squash. *Address:* Department of Chemistry, Ohio State University, 100 West 18th Avenue, Columbus, OH 43210, USA (office). *Telephone:* (614) 292-7216 (office). *Fax:* (614) 292-0368 (office). *E-mail:* chisholm@chemistry.ohio-state.edu (office). *Website:* www.chemistry.ohio-state.edu (office); www.chemistry.ohio-state.edu/~chisholm (office).

CHISHOLM, Sam; New Zealand television executive; b. 8 Oct. 1939; s. of R. and N. Chisholm; m. Susan Chisholm; ed King's Coll. S. Auckland; CEO and Man. Dir Nine Network, Australia 1976–90, Dir 1980–83; CEO and Man. Dir British Sky Broadcasting 1990–97, Dir BSkyB 1990–99; Exec. Dir News Corpn 1993–97; Dir Star TV and Foxtel 1993–97, Telstra 2000–04 Chair. Foxtel 2000–04; Dir Tottenham Hotspur FC 1998–2000; Exec. Dir Publishing and Broadcasting Ltd 2004–06; Dir Prime TV New Zealand 2004–06; Chair., Macquarie Radio Network 2002–04; Dir and Life Gov. Victor Chang Cardiac Research Inst. 2000–08; Dir Sydney Cancer Foundation 2007–; Dr hc (Queensland Univ. of Tech.) 2004. *Leisure interests:* reading, television, fishing. *Address:* Bundarbo Station, Jugiong, NSW 2726, Australia (home).

CHISSANO, Joaquim Alberto; Mozambican politician; *Special Envoy to Northern Uganda, United Nations;* b. 2 Oct. 1939, Chibuto; m. Marcelina Rafael Chissano; four c.; faculty of medicine in Lisbon, Portugal and Poitiers, France; Founding mem. Frente de Libertação de Mozambique (FRELIMO), Asst Sec. to Pres., FRELIMO in charge of Educ. 1963–66, Sec. to Pres., FRELIMO 1966–69; Chief Rep. FRELIMO in Dar es Salaam 1969–74; Prime Minister, Transitional Govt of Mozambique 1974–75, Minister of Foreign Affairs 1975–86, Pres. of Mozambique and C-in-C of Armed Forces 1986–2005; Pres. FRELIMO 1991–2004; Chair. African Union 2002–04; UN Special Envoy to N Uganda 2006–; Order, Augusto César Sandino (Nicaragua) 1988; numerous awards including Chatham House Prize 2006, Mo Ibrahim Prize for Achievement in African Leadership (first recipient) 2007. *Address:* c/o United Nations Peace-Building and Special Missions, Department of Political Affairs, United Nations, New York, NY, 10017 USA.

CHITANAVA, Nodari Amrosievich, PhD; Georgian politician, agricultural specialist and economist; *Director, Economic and Social Problems Research Institute;* b. 10 March 1936, Zugdidi Region, Georgia; s. of Ambrose Chitanava and Tina Chitanava; m. Keto Dimitrovna 1964; two d.; ed Georgian Polytechnic Inst., Moscow High Political School; mem. CPSU 1958–91; Komsomol and party work 1959–; Second Sec. Adzhar obkom 1973–74; Minister of Agric. for Georgian SSR 1974–79; First Deputy Chair., Georgian Council of Ministers 1979–85; Party Sec. for Agric. 1985–89; Chair. Council of Ministers, Georgian SSR 1989–90; Minister of Agric. 1991–93; Dir Econ. and Social Problems Research Inst. 1993–; Chair. Georgian Economists' Soc. *Publications:* 70 scientific works of which there are seven monographs including Social-Economic Pproblems During Transition Perios (three vols). *Leisure interest:* spending time in the country. *Address:* Institute for Macroeconomics, 16 Zandukeli Str., 380008 Tbilisi; Atheni Str. 16, Tbilisi, Georgia (home). *Telephone:* (32) 93-12-55; (32) 99-75-15 (office); (32) 23-37-53 (home).

CHITTISTER, Joan D., MA, PhD; American social psychologist, writer and lecturer; *Executive Director, Benetvision;* b. 26 April 1936, Dubois, Pa; d. of Harold C. Chittister and Loretta Cuneo Chittister; ed St Benedict Acad. Erie, Mercyhurst Coll. Erie, Univ. of Notre Dame and Pa State Univ.; elementary teacher, 1955–59, secondary teacher 1959–74; taught Pa State Univ. 1969–71; Pres. Fed. of St Scholastica 1971–78; Prioress, Benedictine Sisters of Erie 1978–90; Pres. Conf. of American Benedictine Prioresses 1974–90; Invited Visiting Fellow, St Edmund's Coll. Cambridge, UK 1995–96; mem. Exec. Bd Ecumenical and Cultural Inst. St John's Univ. Collegeville 1976–98; Exec. Dir Benetvision 1990–; mem. Bd of Dirs Nat. Catholic Reporter 1983–2000; Co-Chair. Global Initiative of Women Religious and Spiritual Leaders 2002–, Network of Spiritual Progressives/Tikkun Community 2005–; mem. Niwano Peace Foundation, Tokyo 2003–06; 12 hon. degrees; numerous awards, including Notre Dame Alumni Assoc. Women's Award of Achievement 1997, Distinguished Alumni Award (Penn. State Univ.) 2000, Catholic Press Asscn Book Award 1996, 1997, 2001, 2004, 2005, 2006. *Publications include:* Climb Along the Cutting Edge: An Analysis of Change in Religious Life 1977, Women, Church and Ministry 1983, Winds of Change: Women Challenge the Church 1986, Wisdom Distilled from the Daily 1990, The Rule of Benedict: Insights for the Ages 1992, There is a Season 1995, The Fire in these Ashes: A Spirituality of Contemporary Religious Life 1995, The Psalms: Meditations for Every Day of the Year 1996, Beyond Beijing: The Next Step for Women 1996, Passion for Life: Fragments of the Face of God 1996, Songs of Joy: New Meditations on the Psalms 1997, Light in the Darkness: New Reflections on the Psalms 1998, Heart of Flesh: A Feminist Spirituality for Women and Men 1998, In Search of Belief 1999, Gospel Days: Reflections for Every Day of the Year 1999, The Story of Ruth: Twelve Moments in Every Woman's Life 2000, The Illuminated Life: Monastic Wisdom for Seekers of Light 2000, Living Well: Scriptural Reflections for Every Day 2000, The Friendship of Women: A Spiritual Tradition 2000, Seeing With Our Souls 2002, New Designs 2002, Scarred by Struggle, Transformed by Hope (Asscn of Theological Booksellers Award) 2003, Twelve Steps to Inner Freedom 2003, Listening with the Heart 2003, Called to Question: A Spiritual Memoir 2004, In the Heart of the Temple 2004, Becoming Fully Human: The Greatest Glory of God 2005, The Way We Were: A Story of Conversion and Renewal 2005, The Tent of Abraham (co-author) 2006, How Shall We Live? 2006, The Ten Commandments 2006, 25 Windows Into the Soul 2007, Welcome to the Wisdom of the World 2007, The Gift of Years 2008; numerous articles and lectures on religious life, peace and justice issues and women in church and society. *Leisure interests:* computers, music, reading. *Address:* St Scholastica Priory, 355 East 9th Street, Erie, PA 16503, USA. *Telephone:* (814) 454-4052. *Fax:* (814) 459-8066. *E-mail:* office@benetvision.org (office). *Website:* www.benetvision.org (office).

CHITTOLINI, Giorgio; Italian historian and academic; *Professor of Medieval History, University of Milan;* b. 9 Dec. 1940, Parma; s. of Gino Chittolini and Diva Scotti; m. Franca Leverotti 1977; one d.; Assoc. Prof. of History, Univ. of Pisa 1974–76, Univ. of Pavia 1976–79; Fellow at Villa I Tatti, Florence 1980; Prof. of Medieval History, Univ. of Parma 1981–84, Univ. of Milan 1985–; mem. Bd of Eds, Società e Storia 1979–; mem. Scientific Cttee, Istituto Storico Italo-Germanico, Trento 1989–; Pres. Centro Studi Civiltà del tardo Medioevo 1990–; mem. Int. Comm. for the History of Towns 1995. *Publications:* La formazione dello stato regionale e le istituzioni del contado 1979, Gli Sforza, la chiesa lombarda e la corte di Roma (1450–1535) 1990, Comunità, Governi e Feudi nell'Italia Centrosettentrionale 1995, Materiali di storia ecclesiastica lombarda (series ed.) 1995. *Address:* Department of History, Università Degli Studi di Milano, Via Festa del Perdono 7, 20122 Milan (office); Via Madre Cabrini 7, 20122 Milan, Italy. *Telephone:* (02) 58304652 (office). *E-mail:* giorgio.chittolini@unimi.it (office). *Website:* www.lettere.unimi.it/~storia (office).

CHIU, Cheng-hsiung, BA, MA, PhD; Taiwanese banker and politician; *Vice Premier and Minister of the Consumer Protection Commission;* b. 19 Feb. 1942; ed Nat. Taiwan Univ., Ohio State Univ., USA; Deputy Dir-Gen., Dept of Banking, Cen Bank of the Repub. of China, Exec. Yuan 1975–76, Deputy Dir-Gen., Dept of Foreign Exchange 1976–81, Dir-Gen., Dept of Banking 1981–88, Deputy Gov. 1988–96; Pres. Hua Nan Commercial Bank 1988; Minister of Finance 1996–2000; Bd Chair. Grand Cathay Securities Corpn 2000–04, EnTie Commercial Bank 2004–07, Hon. Bd Chair. 2007–08; Vice Premier and Minister of the Consumer Protection Comm. 2008–. *Address:* Consumer Protection Commission, 1 Jihe Road, Taipei 11166, Taiwan (office). *Telephone:* (2) 28863200 (office). *Fax:* (2) 28866646 (office). *E-mail:* tcpc@ms1.hinet.net (office). *Website:* www.cpc.gov.tw (office).

CHIUARIU, Tudor, LLB; Romanian lawyer and politician; b. 1976, Botoşani; ed Al. I. Cuza Univ., Iaşi, Police Acad., Bucharest, Cen. European Univ., Bucharest and Acad. of European Law, Germany; mem. Partidul Naţional Liberal (Nat. Liberal Party) 1997–, Vice-Pres. of Youth Org., Iaşi br. 1997–2002, mem. Political Cttee, Iaşi br. 2001–02, Vice-Pres. Court of Honour and Arbitration 2005–; attorney in Iaşi 2000–; Lecturer in Law, Petre Andrei Univ., Iaşi 2000–07; Sec. of State, Office of the Prime Minister 2005–07; Minister of Justice 2007; Pres. Inter-Ministerial Comm. on Civil Servants' Pay System 2005–06; Vice-Pres. Justice and Human Rights Comm. 2002–05; mem. Implementation of Nat. Anticorruption Strategy Cttee 2005–07; mem. Romanian Bar Asscn. *Publications:* numerous articles on Romanian law in professional journals. *Address:* 1 Victoriei Square, Victoria Palace, Bucharest, Romania (office). *Telephone:* (21) 3181131 (office). *Fax:* (21) 3181151 (office). *E-mail:* tudor.chiuariu@cdep.ro (office). *Website:* www.cdep.ro (office); www.tudorchiuariu.ro (home).

CHIZEN, Bruce R., BS; American business executive; *Strategic Advisor, Adobe Systems Inc.;* b. 5 Sept. 1955; m.; one s. one d.; ed Brooklyn Coll., City Univ. of New York; Retail Merchandising Man. (Eastern Region) Mattel Electronics 1980–83; Sales Dir (Eastern Region) Microsoft Corpn 1983–87; Founding Sr Man. Claris Corpn 1987, later Vice-Pres. Sales, Worldwide Marketing, Vice-Pres. and Gen. Man. Claris Clear Choice; joined Adobe Systems Inc. 1994, Vice-Pres. and Gen. Man. Graphics Professional Div. and Consumer Div., later Exec. Vice-Pres. Worldwide Products and Marketing, Pres. Adobe Systems Inc. 1999–2005, CEO 2000–07, Strategic Advisor 2007–; Dir Synopsys, Inc. 2001–, PBS Foundation 2005–, Children's Discovery Museum of San Jose. *Address:* Adobe Systems Incorporated, 345 Park Avenue, San Jose, CA 95110-2704, USA (office). *Telephone:* (408) 536-6000 (office). *Fax:* (408) 537-6000 (office). *Website:* www.adobe.com (office).

CHIZHOV, Ludvig Aleksandrovich; Russian diplomatist; b. 25 April 1936, Radornishl, Zhitomir Region; m.; one s. one d.; ed Moscow Inst. of Int. Relations; fmr mem. CPSU; attaché, Embassy in Tokyo 1960–65, First Sec.,

Counsellor, 1971–77; Third Sec., Second Sec., Second Far Eastern Dept, Ministry of Foreign Affairs 1966–70, Counsellor, Second Far Eastern Dept 1978–80; Minister Counsellor, Embassy in Tokyo 1980–86; Head of Pacific Ocean Countries Dept, Ministry of Foreign Affairs 1986–89; Russian Amb. to Japan 1990–96; Amb.-at-Large 1996–98; Dir 3rd European Dept, Ministry of Foreign Affairs 1998–2001, on staff of Ministry 2001–2003, Deputy Minister 2003–. *Leisure interests:* fishing, reading. *Address:* c/o Ministry of Foreign Affairs, 119200 Moscow, Smolenskaya-Sennaya pl. 32/34, Russia (office). *Telephone:* (495) 244-16-06 (office). *Fax:* (495) 230-21-30 (office). *E-mail:* ministry@mid.ru (office). *Website:* www.mid.ru (office).

CHKHEIDZE, Peter, PhD; Georgian diplomatist; b. 22 Oct. 1941, Tbilisi; s. of the late Peter Chkheidze and Julia Chkheidze; m. Manana Chkheidze 1963; two s.; ed Tbilisi Nat. Univ., Diplomatic Acad. of USSR Ministry of Foreign Affairs and Inst. of State and Law, USSR Acad. of Sciences; various positions with Attorney Service of Repub. of Georgia 1963–75; First Sec., Dept of Int. Orgs, Ministry of Foreign Affairs of USSR 1978; First Sec., Counsellor, then Chief of Dept Perm. Mission of USSR to UN 1978–84; leading posts in nat. state and public insts 1984–89; Chair. Ind. Trade Unions Confed. of Repub. of Georgia 1989–91; Deputy Prime Minister of Repub. of Georgia and Perm. Rep. of Govt of Georgia to USSR, later Russian Fed. 1991–92; Chargé d'Affaires in Russian Fed. 1992–93; Amb. to USA 1993–94; Perm. Rep. to UN 1993–2002; Amb. to Turkmenistan (also accred to Afghanistan) 2002; Corresp. mem. Int. Informatization Acad. 1994–. *Publications:* various publs in fields of law and int. relations 1975–95. *Leisure interests:* literature, art, horse-riding. *Address:* Inguri St 3, Apt. 52, Tbilisi 380071, Georgia (home). *Telephone:* 33-7056.

CHKHEIDZE, Revaz (Rezo) Davidovich; Georgian film director; *President, Georgian Film;* b. 8 Dec. 1926, Tbilisi; s. of David Chkheidze and Serapime Gogodze; m. Tinatin Gambashidze 1950 (died 2004); one s. two d.; ed Tbilisi State Theatrical Inst., VGIK Moscow (Film School); Pres. Georgian Film 1972–; Deputy USSR Supreme Soviet 1974–84; Chair. of Cinema 1995–; Prof. of Theatre and Cinema, Univ. of Tbilisi 1997–; USSR People's Artist 1980; All-Union Festival Prize 1973; Lenin Prize 1986, Prize for Prominent Contrib. in the World Cinematography 2005–06. *Films include:* Magdana's Donkey (Golden Palm, Int. Cinema Festival Cannes, Diploma, Edinburgh Int. Festival 1956) 1956 (with T. Abuladze), Our Yard (Golden Medal and First Prize, World Festival of Youth Moscow) 1957, Treasure (Jury Prize, Delhi Int. Film Festival 1961) 1961, A Soldier's Father (Cork Int. Film Festival Prize 1965, Best Foreign Film, Salonik Int. Film Festival, Diploma of San Francisco Festival, Capitol of Rome Prize 1965) 1965, Our Youth 1970, The Seedlings (Special Prizes and Diplomas, Moscow Int. Film Festival) 1973, Your Sun, Earth (Prize and Diploma, All-Union Festival of Vilnius 1981) 1981, Life of Don Quixote and Sancho 1989. *Publications:* Cinema and Life. *Leisure interests:* reading, football. *Address:* Larsi Street 5, Apt 3, 010079 Tbilisi, Georgia (home). *Telephone:* (32) 520627 (office); (32) 525674 (home). *E-mail:* tamarchkheidze2000@yahoo.com (home).

CHKHEIDZE, Temur Georgyevich; Georgian theatre director; *Artistic Director, Tovstonogov Bolshoi Drama Theater;* b. 18 Nov. 1943, Tbilisi; ed Tbilisi Rustaveli State Theatre Inst.; Dir Municipal Zugdidi Drama Theatre 1965–67; Dir Georgia Young Spectators Theatre, Tbilisi 1967–70; Dir Tbilisi Academic Rustaveli Theatre 1970–80; Artistic Dir Academic Mardzhanishvili Theatre, Tbilisi 1980–91; Dir Tovstonogov Bolshoi Drama Theatre 1991–2004, Prin. Dir 2004–07, Artistic Dir 2007–; has appeared as producer at St Peterburg Maryinsky Theatre and Milan La Scala;; Peoplés Artist of Russia and Georgia, Lenin Prize 1986. *Address:* Tovstonogov Bolshoi Drama Theater, 190023 St Petersburg, ul. Fontanka 65, Russia (office). *Telephone:* (812) 310-20-05 (office). *E-mail:* bdt@bdt.spb.ru (office). *Website:* www.bdt.spb.ru/theatre.html (office).

CHKHIKVADZE, Ramaz Grigorievich; Georgian actor; b. 28 Feb. 1928; m. Natalia Chkhikvadze; ed Rustaveli Georgian State Drama Inst.; with the Rustaveli State Theatre, Tbilisi 1951–; awards include Best Leading Man at VIIIth Moscow Film Festival for film Saplings, Mardzhanishvili Prize for performance of title role in Kvarkvare, 1975; Georgian State Prize 1974, 1981; USSR State Prize 1979; USSR People's Artist 1981, Hero of Socialist Labour 1988. *Films include:* Chrichina 1954, Eteris simgera 1956, Tsarsuli zapkhuli 1959, Sad aris sheni bedniereba Mzia? 1959, Dge pirveli, dge ukanaskneli 1959, Tkhunela 1962, Londre 1966, Vedreba 1967, Pilatelistis sikvdili 1969, Nutsa 1971, Samkauli satrposatvis 1972, Veris ubnis melodiebi 1973, Nergebi 1973, Mtvaris motatseba 1973, Chiriki da Chikotela 1975, Soplis ashiki 1976, Qalaqi Anara 1976,m Natvris khe 1977, Erti nakhvit shekvareba 1977, Cinema 1978, XIX saukunis qartuli qronika 1979, Tbilisi, Parizi, Tbilisi 1980, Richard III 1980, Ruki vverkh! 1982, Gza shinisaken 1982, Gde-to plachet ivolga 1982, Ya gotov prinyat vyzov 1983, Sizmara (voice) 1983, Tskheli zapkhulis 3 dge 1984, Pobeda 1985, Kak doma, kak dela? 1987, Skorbnoye beschuvstviye 1987, Nazares ukanaskneli lotsva 1988, Ashugi Qaribi 1988, Vozvrashcheniye Khodzhi Nasreddina 1989, Zakat 1990, Kedeli 1991, Amkhanag Stalinis mogzauroba aprikashi 1991, Vostochnyy roman 1992, Shekvarebuli kulinaris ataserti retsepti 1997, Midjachvuli raindebi 2000, V avguste 44-go 2001, Botinki iz America 2001, Der Briefträger 2003, Black Prince 2004, Midioda matarebeli 2005, The Rainbowmaker 2008. *Theatre roles include:* Louis XIV (Bulgakov's Molière), Macheath (Brecht's Threepenny Opera), Adzhak (Caucasian Chalk Circle), Richard (Richard III). *Address:* Rustaveli Theatre, 17 Rustaveli Avenue, 380008 Tbilisi; S. Chikovani Street 20, Apartment 5H, 380015 Tbilisi, Georgia. *Telephone:* (32) 36-45-25.

CHO, Fujio; Japanese motor industry executive; *Chairman and Representative Director, Toyota Motor Corporation;* b. 2 Feb. 1937, Tokyo; ed Tokyo Univ.; joined Toyota Motor Corpn 1960, apprentice 1960–66, Production Control Div. 1966–74 (Man. 1974–1984), Man. Logistics Admin and Project Man., Production Control Div. 1984–86, Admin Man. 1986–87, Man. Toyota N America Project and Exec. Vice Pres., Toyota Motor Manufacturing USA 1987–88, Pres. Toyota Motor Manufacturing USA 1988–94, Man. Dir Toyota Motor Corpn 1994–96, Sr Man. Dir 1996–98, Exec. Vice-Pres. 1998–99, CEO and Pres. 1999–2005, Vice-Chair. then Chair. and Rep. Dir 2006–; included by Time magazine in list of 100 Most Influential People of 2004. *Address:* Toyota Motor Corporation, 1 Toyota-cho, Toyota, Aichi 471-8571, Japan (office). *Telephone:* (565) 28-2121 (office). *Fax:* (565) 23-5800 (office). *Website:* www.toyota.co.jp (office).

CHO, Ramaswamy, BSc, BL; Indian journalist, playwright, actor, lawyer and political commentator; b. 5 Oct. 1934, Madras (now Chennai); s. of R. Srinivasan and Rajammal Srinivasan; m. 1966; one s. one d.; ed P.S. High School, Loyola Coll., Vivekananda Coll., Madras and Madras Law Coll., Madras Univ.; practiced as lawyer, Madras High Court 1957; Legal Adviser to T.T.K. Group of Cos 1961–; film scriptwriter and actor 1966–; theatre dir, actor and playwright 1958–; Ed. Thuglak (Tamil political fortnightly) 1970–; Pres. People's Union of Civil Liberties, Tamilnadu 1980–82; nominated mem. of Rajya Sabha (Parl.); has acted in 180 films, written 14 film scripts, directed four films; written, directed and acted in four TV series and 23 plays in Tamil; Haldi Gati Award, Maharana of Mewar, for nat. service through journalism 1985, Veerakesari Award for investigative journalism 1986, B. D. Goenka Award for Excellence in Journalism, Panchajanya Award for promotion of nationalism 1998. *Publications:* 23 plays and 10 novels in Tamil; numerous articles on politics, in English and Tamil. *Leisure interest:* photography. *Address:* 46 Greenways Road, Chennai, 600028; 35 Meena Bagh, New Delhi, 110011, India. *Telephone:* (44) 4936913 (Chennai); (11) 3792520 (New Delhi). *Fax:* (44) 24936915. *Website:* www.thuglak.com.

CHO, Yung-kil; South Korean politician and army general (retd); b. 9 May 1940, Yongkwangkun, Chollanamdo Prov.; m. Kang Suk; one s. two d.; ed Kwangju Soongil High School, Army Coll., Nat. Defence Coll., Grad. School of Public Admin, Dongkuk Univ.; commissioned Second Lt 1962; Co. Commdr Tiger Unit, Vietnam War 1962–70; Commdr 26th Brigade, Capital Mechanized Div. 1983–84; Chief of Strategic Planning, Policy Planning Office, Army HQ 1984–87, Dir Special Inspection Group 1987–88, Dir of Strategic Planning 1989–91; Dean of Faculty, Nat. Defence Univ. 1988–89; Commdg Gen. 2nd Corps 1995–97, 2nd Repub. of Korea Army 1998–99; Chair. of Jt Chiefs of Staff 1999–2001; Minister of Nat. Defence 2003–04 (resgnd); United States Legion of Merit 2000, 2001 Order of Mil. Merit Hwarang Medal 1970, Vietnam Hero Medal (Silver) and Bronze Star 1970, United States Bronze Star 1970, Order of Nat. Security Medal (Cheonsu) 1987, (Gukson) 1996, (Tongil) 1999. *Address:* c/o Ministry of National Defence, 1, 3-ga, Yonsan-dong, Yeongsan-gu, Seoul, Republic of Korea (office).

CHOE, Jin Su; North Korean diplomatist; *Ambassador to China;* b. 1941, S Hwanghae Prov.; ed Univ. of Int. Affairs, Pyongyang; began career in Ministry of Foreign Affairs, posted to Embassy in Brunei 1969, in Burkina Faso 1974, to Trade Rep. Office, Paris 1978; later Head of W European Affairs, Ministry of Foreign Affairs; Amb. to Switzerland 1986–89, to China 2000–; Deputy Chief, Workers' Party Cen. Cttee Int. Dept 1995–2000. *Address:* Embassy of the Democratic People's Republic of Korea, Ri Tan Bei Lu, Jian Guo Men Wai, Beijing 100600, People's Republic of China (office). *Telephone:* (10) 65321186 (office). *Fax:* (10) 65326056 (office).

CHOEDRA, His Holiness the 70th Je Khenpo Trulku Jigme; Bhutanese ecclesiastic; *Chairman, Council for Ecclesiastical Affairs;* followers believe him to be reincarnation of Maitreya, as well as the Mahasiddha Saraha, Hungchen Kara, Kheuchung Lotsawa, and His Holiness Pema Tsering; elected 70th Je Khenpo of Bhutan 1996, title given to highest religious official of Bhutan, Leader of Cen. Monk Body, also formally the leader of Drukpa sect of Kagyupa School of Tibetan Buddhism; adviser to the King; Chair. Council for Ecclesiastical Affairs (Dratshang Lhentshog). *Address:* Council for Ecclesiastical Affairs (Dratshang Lhentshog), PO Box 254, Thimphu, Bhutan (office). *Telephone:* (2) 322754 (office). *Fax:* 2) 323867 (office). *E-mail:* dratsang@druknet.bt (office).

CHOHAN, Muhammad Anwar; Pakistani diplomatist; *High Commissioner to the Maldives;* ed Asia-Pacific Center for Security Studies; High Commr to the Maldives 2006–. *Address:* High Commission of Pakistan, G. Helengely, Lily Magu, Malé, Maldives (office). *Telephone:* 3323005 (office). *Fax:* 3321832 (office). *E-mail:* pahicmale@hotmail.com (office). *Website:* www.mofa.gov.pk/Green_Book/Maldives_GB.htm.

CHOI, Kil-seon; South Korean business executive; *President and Co-CEO, Hyundai Heavy Industries Company Ltd;* s. of Choi Ma-am and Yu Ok-soon; m. Yang Yang-ja 1971; two c.; ed Seoul Nat. Univ.; Lt in Korean Army 1969–71; Exec. Vice-Pres. Hyundai Heavy Industries Co. Ltd (HHI) 1972–92, Pres. Halla Engineering and Heavy Industries (subsidiary co.) 1993–99, Pres. Hyundai Mipo Dockyard, Ulsan 2004–05, Pres. and Co-CEO HHI 2005–, mem. Bd Dirs 2008–; Chair. Korea Shipbuilders' Asscn 2003–05; Korean Govt Order of Industrial Merit 1977, Korea CEO Forum Grand Prix Award 2006. *Address:* Hyundai Heavy Industries Co. Ltd, 1, 1, Jeonha-dong, Dong-gu, Gyeonsang nam-do, Ulsan, 682-792, Republic of Korea (office). *Telephone:* (52) 202-2114 (office); (52) 230-3899 (office). *Fax:* (52) 230-3450 (office). *E-mail:* ir@hhi.co.kr (office). *Website:* www.hhi.co.kr (office).

CHOI, Man-Duen, PhD, FRSC; Canadian mathematician and academic; *Professor of Mathematics, University of Toronto;* b. 13 June 1945, Nanking, China; m. Pui-Wah Ip 1972; two s. one d.; ed Chinese Univ. of Hong Kong, Univ. of Toronto; Lecturer, Dept of Math., Univ. of California, Berkeley 1973–76; Asst Prof., Dept of Math., Univ. of Toronto 1976–79, Assoc. Prof. 1979–82, Prof. of Math. 1982–; mem. American Math. Soc., Canadian Math. Soc., Math. Asscn of America; Israel Halperin Prize 1980, Coxeter-James

Prize, Canadian Math. Soc. 1983. *Publications:* numerous articles in mathematical journals. *Leisure interests:* yoga, stamps. *Address:* Department of Mathematics, BA6234, University of Toronto, Toronto, ON M5S 2E4, Canada (office). *Telephone:* (416) 978-3318 (office). *Fax:* (416) 978-4107 (office). *E-mail:* choi@math.toronto.edu (office). *Website:* www.math.toronto.edu (office).

CHOI, Seok-young, BA, MBA; South Korean diplomatist and international organization official; *Minister of Economic Affairs, Embassy of South Korea, Washington, DC;* b. 1955, Kangleung; m. Kim Young In; one s. one d.; ed Seoul Nat. Univ., Univ. of Heidelberg, Germany, Korea Devt Inst. School of Public Policy and Man.; joined Ministry of Foreign Affairs (MOF) 1979; Consul in Hamburg, Germany 1986–88; First Sec. in Nairobi, Kenya 1988–91; Asst Dir Environmental Cooperation Div., MOF 1991–94; Counsellor for Econ. and Trade Affairs, Perm. Mission to UN, Geneva 1994–97; Dir for Environment and Science and Chief Negotiator for 1997 UNGA Special Session, MOF 1997–99; Counsellor and Chief of Econ. Section, Perm. Mission to UN, New York 1999–2002; Adviser to Pres. of UN Gen. Ass. 2001; Deputy Dir-Gen. Multilateral Trade Bureau, MOF 2002–03; Deputy Sr Official to APEC 2002–03; Deputy Exec.-Dir, APEC Secr. 2004, Exec.-Dir 2005; Minister of Econ. Affairs, Embassy of South Korea, Washington, DC 2006–, also Deputy Chief of Mission; del. to numerous int. and multilateral forums including UN, WTO and APEC. *Publications:* numerous articles on trade, environmental issues and climate change negotiations. *Address:* Embassy of the Republic of Korea, 2450 Massachusetts Avenue, NW, Washington, DC 20008, USA (office). *Telephone:* (202) 939-5600 (office). *Fax:* (202) 797-0595 (office). *E-mail:* information-usa@mofat.go.kr (office). *Website:* emb.dsdn.net (office).

CHOJNACKA, Elisabeth, MA; French harpsichordist; *Professor of Contemporary Harpsichord, Mozarteum Academy of Music;* b. 10 Sept. 1939, Warsaw, Poland; d. of Tadeusz Chojnacki and Edwarda Chojnacka; m. Georges Lesèvre 1966; ed Warsaw Acad. of Music, Ecole Supérieure de Musique and with Aimée van de Wiele, Paris; first recital of contemporary harpsichord, L'Arc, Paris 1971; a performer of contemporary music, she has inspired many composers (including Xenakis, Ligeti, Halffter, Donatoni, Ferrari, Bussotti, Górecki, Takemitsu, etc.) to write works for and dedicate works to her; has created completely new repertoire for solo modern harpsichord, initiated repertoire combining harpsichord with organ, percussion, bandéon, orchestra; soloist with Orchestre de Paris, Cleveland and Minneapolis Orchestras 1974, Suisse Romande Orchestra 1979, Orchestre National de France 1981; Prof. of Contemporary Harpsichord, Mozarteum Acad. of Music, Salzburg 1995–; numerous tours in Europe, USA, Japan and Mexico; appearances at prin. festivals of contemporary music; master classes; collaborations with choreographer Lucinda Child 1991–; numerous recordings of classical and contemporary music; Chevalier Légion d'honneur, Officier des Arts et des Lettres, Croix d'Officier Ordre de Mérite pour la Pologne; First Prize, Int. Harpsichord Competition, Vercelli, Italy 1968; Orphée Prize 1981, 2000, Grand Prix de la SACEM 1983. *Publications:* articles in La Revue Musicale. *Leisure interests:* cinema, literature, dancing, genetics, astrophysics, theatre, ballet, paintings. *Address:* 17 rue Emile Dubois, 75014 Paris, France. *Telephone:* 1-45-89-52-82 (office); 1-45-65-17-20 (home). *Fax:* 1-45-65-31-90 (office).

CHOMSKY, (Avram) Noam, MA, PhD; American theoretical linguist and writer; *Professor Emeritus, Department of Linguistics, Massachusetts Institute of Technology;* b. 7 Dec. 1928, Philadelphia, PA; s. of William Chomsky and Elsie Simonofsky; m. Carol Schatz 1949 (died 2008); one s. two d.; ed Univ. of Pennsylvania; Asst Prof., MIT 1955–58, Assoc. Prof. 1958–61, Prof. of Modern Languages 1961–66, Ferrari P. Ward Prof. of Modern Languages and Linguistics 1966–76, Institute Prof. 1976–; Visiting Prof., Columbia Univ. 1957–58; NSF Fellow, Princeton Inst. for Advanced Study 1958–59; American Council of Learned Socs Fellow, Center for Cognitive Studies, Harvard Univ. 1964–65; Linguistics Soc. of America Prof., Univ. of California at Los Angeles 1966; Beckman Prof., Univ. of California at Berkeley 1966–67; John Locke Lecturer, Univ. of Oxford 1969; Shearman Lecturer, Univ. Coll. London 1969; Bertrand Russell Memorial Lecturer, Univ. of Cambridge 1971; Nehru Memorial Lecturer, Univ. of New Delhi 1972; Whidden Lecturer, McMaster Univ. 1975; Huizinga Memorial Lecturer, Univ. of Leiden 1977; Woodbridge Lecturer, Columbia Univ. 1978; Kant Lecturer, Stanford Univ. 1979; Jeanette K. Watson Distinguished Visiting Prof., Syracuse Univ. 1982; Pauling Memorial Lecturer, Oregon State Univ. 1995; mem. American Acad. of Arts and Sciences, Linguistic Soc. of America, American Philosophical Asscn, American Acad. of Political and Social Science, NAS, Bertrand Russell Peace Foundation, Deutsche Akademie der Naturforscher Leopoldina, Nat. Acad. of Sciences, Royal Anthropological Inst., Utrecht Soc. of Arts and Sciences; Fellow, American Asscn for the Advancement of Science; Corresp. Fellow, British Acad.; Hon. Fellow, British Psychological Soc. 1985, Royal Anthropological Inst.; Hon. DHL (Chicago) 1967, (Loyola Univ., Swarthmore Coll.) 1970, (Bard Coll.) 1971, (Mass.) 1973, (Maine, Gettysburg Coll.) 1992, (Amherst Coll.) 1995, (Buenos Aires) 1996; Hon. DLitt (London) 1967, (Delhi) 1972, Visva-Bharati (West Bengal) 1980, (Pa) 1984, (Cambridge) 1995; hon. degrees (Tarragona) 1998, (Guelph) 1999, (Columbia) 1999, (Connecticut) 1999, (Pisa) 1999, (Harvard) 2000, (Toronto) 2000, (Western Ontario) 2000, Kolkata (2001); George Orwell Award, Nat. Council of Teachers of English 1987, Kyoto Prize in Basic Sciences 1988, James Killian Award, MIT 1992, Helmholtz Medal, Berlin Brandenburgische Akad. Wissenschaften 1996, Benjamin Franklin Medal, Franklin Inst., Philadelphia 1999, Rabindranath Tagore Centenary Award, Asiatic Soc. 2000, Peace Award, Turkish Publrs Asscn 2002. *Publications include:* Syntactic Structures 1957, Current Issues in Linguistic Theory 1964, Aspects of the Theory of Syntax 1965, Cartesian Linguistics 1966, Topics in the Theory of Generative Grammar 1966, Language and Mind 1968, The Sound Pattern of English (with Morris Halle) 1968, American Power and the New Mandarins 1969, At War with Asia 1970, Problems of Knowledge and Freedom 1971, Studies on Semantics in Genera-tive Grammar 1972, For Reasons of State 1973, The Backroom Boys 1973, Counter-revolutionary Violence (with Edward Herman) 1973, Peace in the Middle East? 1974, Reflections on Language 1975, The Logical Structure of Linguistic Theory 1975, Essays on Form and Interpretation 1977, Human Rights and American Foreign Policy 1978, Language and Responsibility 1979, The Political Economy of Human Rights (two vols, with Edward Herman) 1979, Rules and Representations 1980, Lectures on Government and Binding 1981, Radical Priorities 1981, Towards a New Cold War 1982, Concepts and Consequences of the Theory of Government and Binding 1982, Fateful Triangle: The United States, Israel and the Palestinians 1983, Modular Approaches to the Study of the Mind 1984, Turning the Tide 1985, Knowledge of Language: Its Nature, Origins and Use 1986, Barriers 1986, Pirates and Emperors 1986, Generative Grammar: Its Basis, Development and Prospects 1987, On Power and Ideology 1987, Language and Problems of Knowledge 1987, Language in a Psychological Setting 1987, The Chomsky Reader 1987, The Culture of Terrorism 1988, Manufacturing Consent (with Edward Herman) 1988, Language and Politics 1988, Necessary Illusions 1989, Deterring Democracy 1991, What Uncle Sam Really Wants 1992, Chronicles of Dissent 1992, Year 501: The Conquest Continues 1993, Rethinking Camelot: JFK, the Vietnam War and US Political Culture 1993, Letters from Lexington: Reflections on Propaganda 1993, The Prosperous Few and the Restless Many 1993, Language and Thought 1994, World Orders, Old and New 1994, The Minimalist Program 1995, Powers and Prospects 1996, Class Warfare 1996, The Common Good 1998, Profit over People 1998, The New Military Humanism 1999, New Horizons in the Study of Language and Mind 2000, Rogue States: The Rule of Force in World Affairs 2000, A New Generation Draws the Line 2000, Architecture of Language 2000, Propaganda and the Public Mind 2001, 9-11 2001, Understanding Power 2002, On Nature and Language 2002, Middle East Illusions 2003, Hegemony or Survival: America's Quest for Global Dominance 2003, Failed States: America 2006, Interventions 2007, What We Say Goes 2008, Perilous Power (with Gilbert Achcar) 2008; numerous lectures, contribs. to scholarly journals. *Address:* Department of Linguistics and Philosophy, Massachusetts Institute of Technology, 77 Massachusetts Avenue, Bldg. 32-D808, Cambridge, MA 02139 (office); 15 Suzanne Road, Lexington, MA 02420, USA (home). *Telephone:* (617) 253-7819 (office); (781) 862-6160 (home). *Fax:* (617) 253-9425 (office). *E-mail:* chomsky@mit.edu (office). *Website:* web.mit.edu/linguistics/www (office).

CHONG, Michael; Canadian politician; b. 22 Nov. 1971, Windsor; m. Carrie Davidson 2002; two s.; ed Centre Wellington Dist High School, Fergus, Univ. of Toronto; fmrly with Barclays Bank, Research Capital Corpn; fmr Chief Information Officer Nat. Hockey League Players' Asscn; fmr sr tech. consultant for redevelopment of Pearson Int. Airport, Greater Toronto Airports Authority; co-f. Dominion Inst. 1997, mem. Bd Govs; MP 2004–, mem. House of Commons Standing Cttee on Industry, Natural Resources, Science and Tech. 2004; Pres. Queen's Privy Council for Canada, Minister of Intergovernmental Affairs and of Sport 2006 (resgnd); mem. Corpn Trinity Coll., Univ. of Toronto; mem. Bd Elora Festival. *Address:* House of Commons, Ottawa, ON K1A 0A6, Canada (office). *Telephone:* (613) 992-4179 (office). *E-mail:* Chong.M@parl.gc.ca (office). *Website:* www.michaelchong.ca (home).

CHONG WONG, William, DrLic; Honduran politician; fmr Prof. and Vice-Pres. La Universidad Tecnologica Centroamericana (UNITEC); Deputy Minister of Finance 2002–04, Minister of Finance 2004–06; Gov. for Honduras World Bank, IMF, IDB. *Address:* c/o Ministry of Finance, 5a Avda, 3a Calle, Tegucigalpa, Honduras (office).

CHONGWE, Rodger Masauso Alivas, LLB, SC; Zambian lawyer and politician; *President, Liberal Progressive Front (LPF);* b. 2 Oct. 1940, Chipata; m. Gwenda Fay Eaton 1967; one s. one d.; ed St Mark's Coll., Mapanza, Choma, Munali Secondary School, Lusaka, Univ. of Western Australia School of Law, Perth; Native Courts Asst and Dist Asst, Govt of Northern Rhodesia 1962–63; admitted to practise as barrister, solicitor and Proctor of the Supreme Court of Western Australia and the High Court of the Commonwealth of Australia 1968; admitted as solicitor and barrister before all courts, Zambia 1969; Asst Solicitor, Martin & Co., Lusaka 1969–70, Pnr 1979; Pnr, Mwisiya Chongwe & Co., Lusaka 1970–77; owner, RMA Chongwe & Co., Lusaka 1987; apptd State Counsel 1985; mem. Industrial Relations Court of Zambia 1976–87; Lecturer, Law Practice Inst. 1974–83, Examiner 1975; Dir Tazama Pipelines Ltd 1974–89; Local Dir Jos Hansen & Soehne Zambia Ltd 1983; Dir Standard Chartered Bank of Zambia Ltd 1985; Pres. Liberal Progress Front (LPF) party 1993–, Minister of Local Govt and Housing and Legal Affairs 1997, shot by police 1997, fled Zambia and lived in exile in Australia, returned to Zambia 2003; mem. Int. Bar Asscn 1978, mem. Council 1984–86; Councillor Law Asscn of Zambia 1979, Vice-Chair. 1980, Chair. 1981–86, Councillor 1986, Chair. Human Rights Cttee 1986; Chair. African Bar Asscn 1985; mem. Council of Legal Educ. of Zambia 1982; Commr Law Devt Comm. of Zambia 1981; Exec. mem. Commonwealth Lawyers' Asscn 1983, Sec.-Gen. 1986, Pres. 1990; Gov. Art Centre Foundation 1977; Treasurer Int. Asscn of Artists 1983. *Publications:* numerous papers on legal topics, particularly concerning human rights, the legal profession and legal education. *Address:* Liberal Progressive Front (LPF), POB 31190, Lusaka; Subdivision 36, Farm Number 34A, Great East Road, Lusaka, Zambia (home).

CHOONG, Yong-ahn, MA, PhD; South Korean economist and academic; *Foreign Investment Ombudsman, Korea Trade-Investment Promotion Agency;* ed Kyung-Pook Nat. Univ., Univ. of Hawaii, Ohio State Univ., USA; Prof. of Econs, Chung-Ang Univ. 1974–2006, Chair Prof., Grad. School of Int. Studies 2006–; consultant to World Bank 1978–88, also adviser to Fed. of Korean Industries 1980 and Bank of Korea 1984–87; UNIDO Chief Tech. Adviser to Govt of Malaysia 1990–93; Chair. Chohung Bank 1999–2002; mem. Presidential Econ. Advisory Council 2002–05; Chair. APEC Econ. Cttee 2002–05; Chair. Korean Nat. Cttee for Pacific Econ. Cooperation (KOPEC) 2001; Pres. Korea Inst. for Int. Econ. Policy 2002–05; Foreign Investment Ombudsman, Korea Trade-Investment Promotion Agency (KOTRA) 2006–; mem. Editorial Bd Global Asia (journal); Pres. Korea Econometric Soc. 1991–93, Korea Int. Econs Asscn 1994–95, Devt Econs Asscn 1997–98, Asscn of Trade and Industry Studies 2000–01; mem. Presidential Council on Nat. Competitiveness 2008–; Economist of the Year, Maeil Business Newspaper 1984, Okita Saburo Policy Research Award, Nat. Inst. of Research Investment of Japan 2000, Free Economy Publication Award, Fed. of Korean Industries 2002. Publications: numerous articles and newspapers in journals. Address: Office of the Foreign Investment Ombudsman, 6th Floor, KOTRA Bldg, 13, Heolleungno, Seocho-gu, Seoul 137-749, Republic of Korea (office). Telephone: (2) 3460-7635 (office). Fax: (2) 3460-7949 (office). Website: www.investkorea .org (office).

CHOPLIN, Jean-Luc; French arts management executive; Director, Théâtre du Châtelet; b. 1951; m.; three d.; Gen. Dir Roland Petit Ballet 1980–84; Man. Dir Paris Opéra Ballet 1984–89; Vice Pres. of Entertainment, Disneyland Paris 1989–95, Vice-Pres. Creative Devt, Walt Disney Co., LA 1995–2001; Artistic Consultant 2001–02; Programme and Devt Advisor, Robert Wilson's Watermill Center, New York 2001–02; CEO Sadler's Wells, London 2002–04; Dir Théâtre du Châtelet, Paris 2006–. Address: Théâtre du Châtelet, 1 place du Châtelet, 75001 Paris, France (office). Telephone: 1-40-28-28-40 (office). Website: www.chatelet-theatre.com (office).

CHOPPIN, Gregory R., PhD; American chemist and academic; Senior Scientist and Project Director, Radiochemistry, Institute for International Cooperative Environmental Research, Florida State University; joined Faculty of Florida State Univ. 1956, Chair. Dept of Chem. 1968–76, Robert O. Lawton Distinguished Prof. of Chem., now Prof. Emer., currently Sr Scientist and Project Dir: Radiochemistry, Inst. for Int. Cooperative Environmental Research; consultant, Lawrence Livermore Nat. Lab., Argonne Nat. Lab., Los Alamos Nat. Lab., Sandia Nat. Labs, as well as several pvt. labs; mem. Editorial Bd Chemistry Central Journal; Hon. DSc (Loyola Univ.); Hon. DTC (Chalmers Univ., Sweden); George Hevesy Medal Award 2005. Publications: Introductory Chemistry (co-author) 1972, Nuclear Chemistry (co-author) 1980, Nuclear Chemistry: Theory and Applications 1980, Chemistry (co-author) 1982, Lanthanide Probes in Life, Chemical and Earth Sciences: Theory and Practice (co-author) 1990, Principles and Practices of Solvent Extraction (co-author) 1992, Radio Chemistry and Nuclear Chemistry (co-author) 1995, Separations of F Elements: Proceedings of an ACS Symposium of F Elements Separations Held in San Diego, California, March 13–17, 1994 (co-ed) 1995, Chemical Separation Technologies and Related Methods of Nuclear Waste Management: Applications, Problems, and Research Needs (co-author) 1999, Radiochemistry and Nuclear Chemistry (co-author) 2001, Chemical Separations in Nuclear Waste Management: The State of the Art and a Look to the Future (co-author) 2002; numerous scientific papers in professional journals on inorganic and nuclear chemistry, especially the lanthanide and actinide elements. Address: Institute for International Cooperative Environmental Research, Florida State University, 2035 East Paul Dirac Drive (226 HMB), Tallahassee, FL 32310-3700, USA (office). Telephone: (850) 644-5524 (office); (850) 644-3875 (office). Fax: (850) 574-6704 (office). E-mail: choppin@chem.fsu.edu (home); IICER@mailer.fsu.edu (office). Website: www.chem.fsu.edu/faculty/choppin.htm (office); iicer.fsu.edu (office).

CHOPPIN, Purnell Whittington, MD; American scientist and academic; President Emeritus, Howard Hughes Medical Institute; b. 4 July 1929, Baton Rouge, La.; s. of Arthur Richard Choppin and Eunice Dolores Choppin (née Bolin); m. Joan H. Macdonald 1959; one d.; ed La State Univ.; Intern, Barnes Hosp., St Louis 1953–54, Asst Resident 1956–57; Postdoctoral Fellow, Research Assoc., Rockefeller Univ., New York 1957–60, Asst Prof. 1960–64, Assoc. Prof. 1964–70, Prof., Sr Physician 1970–85, Leon Hess Prof. of Virology 1980–85, Vice-Pres. Acad. Programs 1983–85, Dean of Grad. Studies 1985; Vice-Pres. and Chief Scientific Officer, Howard Hughes Medical Inst. 1985–87, Pres. 1987–99, Pres. Emer. 2000–, Virology 1973–82; Chair. Virology Study Section, NIH 1975–78; mem. Bd of Dirs Royal Soc. of Medicine Foundation Inc., New York 1978–93, Advisory Cttee on Fundamental Research, Nat. Multiple Sclerosis Soc. 1979–84 (Chair. 1983–84), Advisory Council Nat. Inst. of Allergy and Infectious Diseases 1980–83, Sloan-Kettering Cancer Cttee, New York 1983–84, Comm. on Life Sciences, Nat. Research Council 1982–87, Council for Research and Clinical Investigation, American Cancer Soc. 1983–85; Pres. American Soc. of Virology 1985–86; Fellow, AAAS; mem. NAS (Chair. Class IV medical sciences 1983–86, Section 43 microbiology and immunology 1989–93), mem. council 2000–02, mem. Governing Bd NAS Nat. Research Council 1990–92; mem. Council Inst. of Medicine 1986–92, Exec. Cttee 1988–91; mem. American Philosophical Soc. (mem. Council 1999–2001, Vice-Pres. 2000–06); mem. Asscn of American Physicians, American Soc. of Microbiology, American Asscn of Immunologists and other professional orgs; numerous hon. degrees; Howard Taylor Ricketts Award, Univ. of Chicago 1978, Waksman Award for Excellence in Microbiology, NAS 1984. Publications: numerous articles and chapters on virology, cell biology, infectious diseases. Leisure interests: fly fishing, stamp collecting. Address: Howard Hughes Medical Institute, 4000 Jones Bridge Road, Chevy Chase, MD 20815 (office); 2700 Calvert Street, NW, Washington, DC 20008, USA (home). Telephone: (301) 215-8554 (office). Website: www.hhmi.org (office).

CHOPRA, Deepak; writer; founder and Dir of Educational Programs, Chopra Center 1955–; Fellow, American Coll. of Physicians; mem. American Asscn of Clinical Endocrinologists. Publications include: Return of the Rishi 1989, Quantum Healing 1990, Perfect Health 1990, Unconditional Life 1991,

Creating Health 1991, Creating Affluence 1993, Ageless Body, Timeless Mind 1993, Restful Sleep 1994, Perfect Weight 1994, The Seven Spiritual Laws of Success 1995, The Path of Love 1996, How to Create Wealth 1999, Everyday Immortality: A Concise Course in Spiritual Transformation 1999, How to Know God: The Soul's Journey into the Mystery of Mysteries 2000, How to Know God 2001, Grow Younger, Live Longer 2002, Golf for Enlightenment 2003, Book of Secrets 2004, Peace is the Way 2005, Buddha 2007, The Third Jesus: the Christ we cannot ignore 2008. Address: Chopra Centre at La Costa Resort and Spa, 2013 Costa del Mar Road, Carlsbad, CA 92009, USA (office). Telephone: (760) 494-1600 (office). Fax: (760) 494-1608 (office). Website: www .chopra.com (office).

CHOPRA, Yash; Indian film director and film producer; Chairman, Yash Raj Films Pvt. Ltd; b. 27 Sept. 1932, Jalandhar, Punjab, British India (now Pakistan); one s.; began career as Asst Dir to I.S. Johar; directed films for brother B.R. Chopra's co. B.R. Films 1959–69; Founding Chair. Yash Raj Films Pvt. Ltd 1970–; Chair. Entertainment Cttee, Fed. of Indian Chambers of Commerce & Industry (FICCI); Vice-Pres. Film Producers' Guild of India 1994–; mem. Advisory Bd, Information and Broadcasting, Ministry of State; Founding Trustee Film Industry Welfare Trust 1996–; BBC Asia Award 1998, 2001, Dr. Dadabhai Naoroji Millennium Lifetime Achievement Award 2001, Certificate of Recognition, British Tourist Authority and British Film Comm., Vocational Excellence Award, Rotary Club, honoured by Indian Int. Film Awards, Nat. Asscn of Software and Service Cos (NAASCOM), All India Asscn of Industries (AIAI), Priyadarshini Award, Dadasaheb Phalke Award 2001, Padma Bhushan Award 2004. Films include: Dhool ka Phool 1959, Dharmputra (President's Gold Medal) 1961, Wakt (4 Filmfare Awards) 1965, Ittefaq (Best Dir Filmfare Award) 1969, Aaadmi Aur Insaan 1969, Daag (4 Filmfare Awards) 1973, Joshila 1973, Deewar (7 Filmfare Awards) 1975, Kabhi Kabhie 1976, Doosra Aadmi 1977, Trishul 1978, Noorie 1979, Kala Patthar 1979, Nakhuda 1981, Silsila 1981, Sawaal 1982, Mashaal 1984, Faasle 1985, Vijay 1988, Chandni (Nat. Award for Best Film) 1989, Lamhe (5 Filmfare Awards) 1991, Parampara 1992, Darr (Nat. Award for Best Film) 1993, Aaina 1993, Dilwale Dulhania Le Jayenge (10 Filmfare Awards, Nat. Award for Best Film) 1995, Dil To Pagal Hai (7 Filmfare Awards, Nat. Award for Best Film) 1997, Humko Ishq Ne Mara 1997, Mohabbatein 2000, Mere Yaar Ki Shaadi Hai 2002, Mujhse Dosti Karoge! 2002, Saathiya 2002, Hum Tum 2004, Veer-Zaara 2004, Bunty Aur Babli 2005, Dhoom 2 2006, Jhoom Barabar Jhoom 2007, Chak De! India 2007, Tashan 2008, Bachna Ae Haseeno 2008, Roadside Romeo 2008, Rab Ne Bana Di Jodi 2008. Address: Yash Raj Films Private Limited, 5, Shah Industrial Estate, Veera Desai Road, Andheri (West), Mumbai 400 053, India (office). Telephone: (22) 30613500 (office). Fax: (22) 30613599 (office). E-mail: helpdesk@yashrajfilms.com (office). Website: www.yashrajfilms.com (office).

CHOQUEHUANCA CÉSPEDES, David; Bolivian government official; Minister of Foreign Affairs and Worship; b. 7 May 1961, Cota Cota Baja; ed Colegio General José Miguel Lanza, Escuela Nacional de Formación de Cuadros Niceto Pérez, Cuba, Universidad Cordillera; Nat. Co-ordinator NINA 1998; Minister of Foreign Affairs and Worship 2006–. Address: Ministry of Foreign Affairs and Worship, Calle Ingavi, esq. Junín, La Paz, Bolivia (office). Telephone: (2) 237-1150 (office). Fax: (2) 237-1155 (office). E-mail: mreuno@ rree.gov.bo (office). Website: www.rree.gov.bo (office).

CHORLEY, 2nd Baron, cr. 1945, of Kendal; **Roger Richard Edward Chorley,** FCA; British accountant; b. 14 Aug. 1930; s. of 1st Baron Chorley and Katharine Campbell Hopkinson; m. Ann Debenham 1964; two s.; ed Stowe School, Gonville and Caius Coll., Cambridge; joined Cooper Brothers & Co. (later Coopers & Lybrand) 1955, New York office 1959–60, Pakistan (Indus Basin Project) 1961, Partner 1967–89; Accounting Adviser to Nat. Bd.for Prices and Incomes 1965–68; Visiting Prof., Dept of Man. Sciences, Imperial Coll. of Science and Tech., London Univ. 1979–82; mem. Royal Comm. on the Press 1975–77, Finance Act 1960 Tribunal 1974–79, Ordnance Survey Review Cttee 1978–79, British Council Review Cttee 1979–80, Bd British Council 1981–99 (Deputy Chair. 1990–99), Top Salaries Review Body 1981–90, Ordnance Survey Advisory Bd 1983–85, House of Lords Select Cttee on Science and Tech. 1983, 1987, 1990, 2006, Select Cttee on Sustainable Devt 1994–95; elected mem. House of Lords 2001–; Chair. The National Trust 1991–96; fmr Pres. Cambridge Univ. Mountaineering Club, mem. expeditions Himalayas (Rakaposhi) 1954, (Nepal) 1957; Vice-Pres. Council for Nat. Parks 1996–; Hon. Sec. Climbers' Club 1963–67; mem. Man. Cttee Mount Everest Foundation 1968–70; Pres. Alpine Club 1983–85; mem. Council Royal Geographical Soc. 1984–, Vice-Pres. 1986–87, Pres. 1987–90; mem. Finance Cttee Nat. Trust 1972–90, Exec. Cttee 1989–96; mem. Council, Royal Soc. of Arts 1987–89, City and Guilds of London Inst.; mem. Nat. Theatre Bd 1980–91; Patron British Mountaineering Council 1996–; Hon. FRICS; Hon. Fellow Central Lancs. Univ. 1993, Hon. Pres. Asscn for Geographic Information 1995–; Hon. DSc (Reading, Kingston); Hon. LLD (Lancaster). Leisure interest: mountains. Address: House of Lords, Westminster, London, SW1A 0PW, England (office). Telephone: (20) 7219-5353 (office).

CHORY, Joanne, AB, PhD; American biologist and academic; Professor and Director, Plant Molecular and Cellular Biology Laboratory, Salk Institute for Biological Studies; ed Oberlin Coll., Ohio and Univ. of Illinois at Urbana-Champaign; Postdoctoral Research, Harvard Medical School, Boston, Mass 1984–88; Asst Prof., Plant Biology Lab., Salk Inst., La Jolla, Calif. 1988–94, Assoc. Prof. 1994–98, Dir Plant Molecular and Cellular Biology Lab. 1998–, Prof. 1998– (mem. Academic Council Salk Inst. 1992–94, 1995–97, 2000–03); Adjunct Asst Prof., Biology Dept, Univ. of California, San Diego, La Jolla 1992–94, Adjunct Assoc. Prof. 1994–99, Adjunct Prof. 1999–; Assoc. Investigator, Howard Hughes Medical Inst., La Jolla 1997–; mem. Bd of Dirs Int. Soc. for Plant Molecular Biology 1995–98, Boyce Thompson Inst. for Plant

Research 2001–03; mem. Bd on Life Sciences, Nat. Research Council 2001–04, Int. Advisory Cttee 7th Int. Congress of Plant Molecular Biology 2003; mem. NAS 1999–; mem. Editorial Review Bd Plant Journal 1991–99, Plant Physiology 1992–95, 1998–, Genetics 1993–98, Developmental Genetics 1993–99, Cell 1994–97, 2001–, Genes to Cells 1995–, Current Opinion in Plant Biology 1998–, Science 1998–, BioProtocol 2000–01, Faculty of 1000 Section Head 2001–; Fellow, American Acad. of Arts and Sciences 1998–, AAAS; mem. NAS; Trustees' Scholarship, Oberlin Coll. 1975–77, Anna Fuller Fund Jr Research Fellow, Harvard School of Public Health 1977, Award for Initiatives in Research, NAS 1994, Charles Albert Schull Award, American Soc. of Plant Physiologists 1995, Edna Roe Lecturer, Int. Congress of Photobiology 1996, Gatsby Foundation Flying Fellow 1997, L'Oreal-Helena Rubenstein Award for Women in Science 2000, Kumho Award in Plant Molecular Biology. *Publications:* more than 130 publs in scientific journals. *Address:* Plant Biology Laboratory, Salk Institute for Biological Studies, 10010 N Torrey Pines Road, San Diego, CA 92037, USA (office). *Telephone:* (858) 552-1148 (office). *Fax:* (858) 558-6379 (office). *E-mail:* chory@salk.edu (office). *Website:* www.salk.edu/faculty/chory.html (office).

CHOU, Chang-Hung, BS, MS, PhD; Taiwanese researcher and academic; *Chair Professor and Director, Research Center for Biodiversity, China Medical University;* b. 5 Sept. 1942, Tainan, Taiwan; s. of F.K. Chou and C.Y. Shih Chou; m. Ruth L.H. Yang Chou 1970; one s. one d.; ed Nat. Taiwan Univ., Taipei, Univ. of Calif., Santa Barbara, USA, Univ. of Toronto, Canada; Assoc. Research Fellow, Inst. of Botany, Academia Sinica, Taipei 1972–76, Research Fellow 1976–2002, Dir 1989–96; Prof., Dept of Botany, Nat. Taiwan Univ. 1976–99; Vice-Pres. Nat. Sun Yat-sen Univ. 1999–2002; Pres. Nat. Pingtung Univ. of Science and Tech. 2002–06; Nat. Chair Prof., Ministry of Educ. 2001–04; Chair Prof. and Dir Research Center for Biodiversity, China Medical Univ. 2006–; mem. various nat. cttees for Int. Council of Scientific Unions (ICSU) 1974–; Sec. for Int. Affairs, Academia Sinica 1988–, mem. Council Academia Sinica 1989–, Pacific Science Asscn 1989; mem. Cttee for Science Educ., Ministry of Educ. 1986–, Cttee for Environmental Educ. 1991–, Cttee for Cultural and Natural Preservation Council of Agric. 1990; mem. Council Taiwan Livestock Research Inst. 1976–, Taiwan Forestry Research Inst. 1989–, Council Nat. Sustainable Devt 1997–; Dir Life Science Research Promotion Centre Nat. Science Council 1989–; Visiting Scholar, Oklahoma Univ., Univ. of Texas, Washington State Univ. 1979–80; Pres. Botanical Soc. of Repub. of China (Taiwan) 1983–84, Biological Soc. of Repub. of China (Taiwan) 1987–88; Chair. Nat. Cttee Int. Union of Biological Sciences (IUBS) 1990–, Vice-Pres. IUBS 1997, mem. Exec. Cttee 2007–; Chair. SCOPE Nat. Cttee; Exec. Mem. Pacific Science Asscn; Ed. Botanical Bulletin of Academia Sinica 1989–; Fellow, Third World Acad. of Sciences; mem. Academia Sinica, Taipei; Highest Honor, Soka Univ., Japan 2003; awards from Ministry of Educ. and Science Council of Taiwan. *Publications:* over 200 scientific papers, one univ. textbook; 10 monographs. *Leisure interest:* listening to classical music. *Address:* 91, Hseuh-Shih Road, Taichung 404, Taiwan (office). *Telephone:* (4) 2205-3366 (office). *Fax:* (4) 2207-1500 (office). *E-mail:* choumasa@mail.cmu.edu.tw (office). *Website:* www.cmu.edu.tw (office).

CHOUE, Young Seek, LLD; South Korean university chancellor; *Honorary President, Kyung Hee University System;* b. 22 Nov. 1921, Woon San; m. Chung-Myung Oh 1943 (died 2008); two s. two d.; ed Seoul Nat. Univ. and Univ. of Miami; Founder-Pres. Kyung Hee Univ., then Chancellor, Kyung Hee Univ. System, currently Hon. Pres.; Perpetual Pres. Emer. Int. Asscn of Univ. Pres., fmr Chair.; Chair. High Comm. for Peace; Founder and fmr Pres. Global Co-operation Soc. Int., now Hon. Pres.; Pres. Inst. of Brighter Soc., Inst. of Int. Peace Studies, Inst. of Asia-Pacific Studies, Centre for Reconstruction of Human Soc.;; Chair. Korean Ass. for Reunion of Ten Million Separated Families, Oughtopian Peace Foundation; initiated UN Int. Day and Year of Peace; 34 hon. degrees; numerous awards including UN Special Award for Meritorious Services for Peace 1996. *Publications include:* Democratic Freedom 1948, World Peace through Education 1971, Reconstruction of the Human Society 1975, Oughtopia 1979, World Peace Through Pax UN 1984, World Encyclopedia of Peace 1986, White Paper on World Peace 1991, World Citizenship 1995. *Leisure interests:* golf, tennis, table tennis, travel. *Address:* 7-36, 1-Ka, Myungryun-Dong, Jongo-gu, Seoul, Republic of Korea (home). *Telephone:* (2) 762-3278 (home). *Fax:* (2) 741-3195 (home).

CHOUINARD, Yvon; American mountaineer, surfer, sportsman, business executive and writer; *Chairman, Patagonia, Inc.;* b. 9 Nov. 1938, Lewiston, Me; m. Malinda Pennoyer 1970; two c.; served in US Army 1962–64; f. Chouinard Equipment for Alpinists (CEA), Inc. 1960; f. Lost Arrow Corpn 1974; f. Patagonia Inc. 1976–; also a kayaker, falconer and fisherman; writer on climbing issues and ethics and also on mixing environmentalism and sound business practice; mem. American Alpine Club. *Achievements include:* participated in second ascent of The Nose on El Capitan 1960, ascent of North American Wall using no fixed ropes 1964; visited Canadian Rockies with Fred Beckey 1961, made several important first ascents, including North Face of Mount Edith Cavell, Beckey-Chouinard Route on South Howser Tower in the Bugaboos, and North Face of Mount Sir Donald; freeclimbed first pitch of Matinee in the Gunks 1961; climbed Cerro Fitzroy in Patagonia by a new route (The Californian Route) 1968. *Publications:* Climbing Ice 1982, Let My People Go Surfing 2005. *Address:* 259 W Santa Clara Street, Ventura, CA 93001, USA (office). *Telephone:* (805) 643-8616 (office). *Fax:* (800) 543-5522 (office). *E-mail:* info@patagonia.com (office). *Website:* www.patagonia.com (office).

CHOUMMALI, Lt-Gen. Saignason; Laotian army officer, politician and head of state; *President;* b. 6 March 1936, Attapu; mem. Nat. Ass.; Deputy Prime Minister and Minister of Nat. Defence –2001; Vice-Pres. of Laos 2001–06, Pres. 2006–; elected Gen. Sec. Phak Pasason Pativat Lao (Lao People's Revolutionary Party) 2006–. *Address:* Office of the President, Vientiane, Laos (office). *Telephone:* (21) 214200 (office). *Fax:* (21) 214208 (office).

CHOW, Alan Y., BA, MD; American paediatric ophthalmologist and academic; *Paediatric Ophthalmology Specialist, Hauser Ross Eye Institute and Surgicenter;* b. Glen Ellyn, Ill.; ed Univ. of Chicago, Loyola Univ.; completed internships in Paediatrics at Cincinnati Children's/GSH and in Gen. Surgery at Loyola Univ. where he also completed his ophthalmology residency; fmr Knapp Fellow in Ophthalmic Genetics, Wilmer Eye Inst., Johns Hopkins Univ.; fmr Heed Fellow in Paediatric Ophthalmology, Children's Hosp. Nat. Medical Center; Asst Prof., Rush Univ. Medical Center, Chicago; Visiting Assoc. Prof., Univ. of Illinois Eye Center, Chicago; Adjunct Asst Prof., Tulane Univ. Eye Center; Co-founder and COO Optobionics Corpn, led devt of Artificial Silicon Retina 1990; Paediatric Ophthalmology Specialist, Hauser-Ross Eye Inst. and Surgicenter, Sycamore 2007–; frequent nat. and int. lecturer; reviewer for several peer-reviewed journals; spokesperson for American Acad. of Ophthalmology; grants and awards from NASA, Westinghouse Foundation, NSF, NIH and SBA, Chicago Inventor of the Year (together with his brother Vincent) for work in developing Artificial Silicon Retinal Prosthesis 1996, Tibbetts Award, Small Business Innovation Research Program 2000, RP International's Vision Award (with his brother) 2002, Ernst & Young Entrepreneur of the Year Award in the Chicago area 2003, World Tech. Award in Health and Medicine, The World Tech. Network (with his brother) 2004. *Publications:* numerous articles, book chapters and patents. *Address:* Hauser-Ross Eye Institute and Surgicenter, 2240 Gateway Drive, Sycamore, IL 60178, USA (office). *Telephone:* (815) 756-8571 (office); (888) 286-9221 (office). *E-mail:* info@hauserross.org (office). *Website:* www.hauserross.org (office).

CHOW, Sir C. K. (Chung Kong), Kt., CEng, BSc, MSc, DEng, FREng, FCGI, FIChemE, FHKAES; British (b. Hong Kong) business executive; *CEO, MTR Corporation Ltd;* b. 9 Sept. 1950; ed Univs of Wis. and Calif., USA, Chinese Univ. of Hong Kong, Harvard Univ., USA; Research Engineer, Climax Chemical Co., New Mexico 1974–76; Process Engineer, Sybron Asia Ltd, Hong Kong 1976–77; joined BOC Group 1977, with Hong Kong Oxygen, Hong Kong and BOC Australia 1977–84, Man. Dir Hong Kong Oxygen 1984–86, Pres. BOC Japan 1986–89, Group Man. Gases Business Devt, BOC Group PLC, UK and USA 1989–91, Regional Dir N Pacific, Tokyo and Hong Kong 1991–93, CEO Gases 1993–96, apptd to Main Bd 1994, Man. Dir 1994–97; CEO GKN PLC 1997–2001, CEO Brambles Industries Ltd 2001–03, CEO MTR Corpn 2003–; Dir (non-exec.) Standard Chartered PLC 1997–, Pres. 1999–2000, Deputy Pres. 2000–01; Chair. Standard Chartered Bank (Hong Kong) Ltd 2004–; fmr Pres. Soc. of British Aerospace Cos; mem. Governing Body London Business School; Fellow, Inst. of Chemical Engineers, Chartered Inst. of Logistics and Transport; Hon. Fellow, Hong Kong Inst. of Engineers. *Address:* MTR Corporation Ltd, GPO Box 9916, Hong Kong Special Administrative Region, People's Republic of China (office). *Telephone:* 28818888 (office). *Fax:* 27959991 (office). *Website:* www.mtr.com.hk (office).

CHOW, Vincent Y., BS; American electrical engineer and business executive; *President, Vega Technology and Systems, Inc.;* ed Illinois Inst. of Tech.; fmr Dir of Operations, Telco Systems; fmr Man. of Reliability Devt, AT&T Bell Labs/Teletype; Dir of Tech. Operations, Autotech Corpn 1985–89; Dir of Research and Devt, MDA Scientific 1989–94; Co-founder and Vice-Pres., Research and Devt, Optobionics Corpn 1990–94; Pres. Vega Technology and Systems, Inc. (eng consulting firm for optical sensing products and ASIC applications) 1994–; Chicago Inventor of the Year Award (with his brother Alan) for work in developing Artificial Silicon Retina Microchip 1996, Vision Award, RP International (with his brother) 2002, Ernst & Young Entrepreneur of the Year Award in the Chicago area (with his brother) 2003, World Tech. Award in Health and Medicine, The World Tech. Network (with his brother) 2004. *Publications:* more than 220 papers in scientific journals and named inventor on 11 patents. *Address:* Vega Technology and Systems, Inc., 7980 Kingsbury Drive, Bartlett, IL 60133-2348, USA (office). *Telephone:* (630) 855-5068 (office).

CHOW, Yun-Fat; Chinese film actor; b. 18 May 1955, Lamma Island; m. Jasmine Chow 1986; began acting career at TV station TVB, Hong Kong 1973, appearing in over 1,000 TV series; Dr hc (City Univ. of Hong Kong) 2001. *Films include:* The Story of Woo Viet, A Better Tomorrow 1986, God of Gamblers 1989, The Killer 1989, Eighth Happiness, Once a Thief 1991, Full Contact 1992, Hard Boiled 1992, Peace Hotel 1995, Broken Arrow, Anna and the King 1999, Crouching Tiger, Hidden Dragon 2000, King's Ransom 2001, Bulletproof Monk 2003, Yi ma de hou xian dai sheng huo 2006, Man cheng jin dai huang jin jia (Curse of the Golden Flower) 2006, Pirates of the Caribbean: At World's End 2007, The Children of Huang Shi 2008, Shanghai 2008, Dragonball 2009. *Address:* Chow Yun Fat International, PO Box 71288, Kowloon Central, Hong Kong Special Administrative Region, People's Republic of China (office); c/o William Morris Agency, 1 William Morris Place, Beverly Hills, CA 90212, USA.

CHOW MAN YIU, Paul; Chinese business executive; fmr Exec. Dir Sun Hung Kai Securities Ltd; CEO Hong Kong Securities Clearing Corpn 1990–91; CEO Hong Kong Stock Exchange 1991–97; CEO HSBC Asset Management (Hong Kong) Ltd 1997–2003; Chair. Hong Kong Investment Funds Asscn 2000–01; Dir Hong Kong Cyberport Management Co. Ltd 2003–07; mem. Advisory Cttee Securities and Futures Comm. 2001–07; Hon. Fellow, Univ. of Hong Kong; Silver Bauhinia Star 2005. *Address:* c/o The Stock Exchange of Hong Kong Ltd, 1/F One and Two Exchange Square, Central, Hong Kong Special Administrative Region, People's Republic of China.

CHOWDHURY, A. Q. M. Badruddoza, FRCPE, FRCP(CLAS), TDD; Bangladeshi surgeon, politician and fmr head of state; *President, Liberal Democratic Party;* b. 1939; s. of the late Kafil Uddin Chowdhury; m. Hasina Chowdhury; one s. two d.; ed St Gregory High School, Dhaka Coll., Dhaka Medical Coll., Univ. of Wales, UK; practised as physician specializing in treatment of tuberculosis; Founding Sec.-Gen. Bangladesh Nationalist Party 1978, fmr Deputy Leader; fmr Sr Deputy Prime Minister, Minister of Health and Family Planning, of Foreign Affairs; Pres. of Bangladesh 2001–02; Co-founder and Pres. Liberal Democratic Party 2006–; fmr Pres. Nat. Anti-Tuberculosis Asscn of Bangladesh, Int. Union Against Tuberculosis; led Bangladesh del. to World Health Conf., Geneva 1978, 1979 and many dels to int. confs on tuberculosis and chest diseases; Hon. Fellow, Coll. of Physicians and Surgeons (Bangladesh); Nat. TV Award 1976. *Publications:* many research papers in nat. and int. journals; essays and plays. *Address:* Liberal Democratic Party, Dhaka (office); Residence Bari Dhar, near Gulshan, Dhaka, Bangladesh (home).

CHOWDHURY, Anwarul Karim, MA; Bangladeshi diplomatist and international organization official (retd); b. 5 Feb. 1943, Dhaka; m.; three c.; ed Univ. of Dhaka; Dir-Gen. for S and SE Asia, Foreign Ministry 1979–80, for Multilateral Econ. Co-operation 1986–90; Deputy Perm. Rep. to UN 1980–86, Perm. Rep. 1996–2001, Chair. Fifth Cttee (Admin. and Budgetary) of UN 1997–98); UNICEF Dir for Japan, Australia and NZ 1990–93, Sec. Exec. Bd UNICEF, New York 1993–96 (Chair. Bd 1985–86), UN Under-Sec.-Gen. for Least Developed Countries, Landlocked Developing Countries and Small Island Developing States 2002–07 (retd); Dr hc (Soka Univ., Tokyo); U Thant Peace Award, UNESCO Gandhi Gold Medal for Culture and Peace. *Publications:* contribs to journals on devt and human rights issues. *Address:* c/o OHRLLS, United Nations Headquarters, Room S-770, New York, NY 10017. *Telephone:* (212) 963-9078.

CHOWDHURY, M. Nurunnabi; Bangladeshi business executive; fmr Chair. Bangladesh Textile Mills Corpn. *Address:* c/o Bangladesh Textile Mills Corporation, Bastra Bhaban, 7–9 Kawran Bazar, Dhaka 1215, Bangladesh (office).

CHOWDHURY, Shamsher Mobin, BA; Bangladeshi diplomatist; ed Pakistan Mil. Acad.; joined Pakistan army 1969, promoted to rank of Maj. 1973; joined Bangladesh Civil Service 1975; Deputy Chief of Protocol and Dir West Europe, Ministry of Foreign Affairs 1975–77, with Embassy in Rome 1977–81, Counsellor, Embassy in Washington, DC 1981–83, Counsellor and Minister, High Comm. in Ottawa 1983–86, Deputy Chief of Mission, Embassy in Beijing 1986–88, Dir-Gen. SAARC Div., Ministry of Foreign Affairs 1988–91, High Commr to Sri Lanka 1991–95, Amb. to Germany 1995–98, to Viet Nam 1998–2001, Foreign Sec. 2001–05, Amb. to USA 2005–07; Gallantry Award Bir Bikram (BB). *Address:* Ministry of Foreign Affairs, Segunbagicha, Dhaka 1000, Bangladesh (office). *Telephone:* (2) 9562862 (office). *Fax:* (2) 9555283 (office). *E-mail:* info@mofabd.org (office). *Website:* www.mofa.gov.bd (office).

CHRAMOSTOVÁ, Vlasta; Czech actress and human rights activist; b. 17 Nov. 1926, Brno; m. Stanislav Milota 1971; ed Conservatoire of Music and Performing Arts, Brno; with The Free Theatre, Brno 1945, Municipal Theatre, Olomouc 1945–46, State Theatre Brno 1946–49, Theatre in Vinohrady, Prague 1950–69; mem. ensemble, Theatre behind the Gate 1970–72; banned from acting in public; signed Charter 77 Jan. 1977; appealed to artists in the West for support for Charter 77 1977; Charter 77 activist 1977–89; sentenced to imprisonment for 3 months, sentence suspended on one-year-probation April 1989; mem. Nat. Theatre Ensemble Prague 1990–91; joined Drama Co. of Nat. Theatre Prague 1991–; Hon. mem. Masaryk Democratic Movt 1990; Order of T. G. Masaryk 1998; Merited Artist 1965, Czech Theatre Artists' Award 1967, Peace Prize awarded by Paul Lauritzen Foundation 1989, Czech Film Acad. Prize, Czech Lion. *Films include:* Spadla s mesíce 1961, Destivý den 1962, Az prijde kocour (When the Cat Comes) 1963, Letos v zari 1963, Komedie s Klikou (Comedy Around a Door Handle) 1964, Bílá paní (The White Lady) 1965, Spalovac mrtvol (The Cremator) 1968, Lítost (TV) 1970, Becicka (TV) 1971, Sekal Has to Die 1998, Melancholy Chicken 1999, Samota (Solitude) (TV) 2002. *Publications:* Kniha pamětí (memoirs) 1999. *Address:* Národní divadlo, Ostrovní 1, Prague 1, Nové Město; Čelakovského sady 10, 120 00 Prague 2, Czech Republic. *Telephone:* (224) 210892 (office); (224) 225088 (home).

CHRÉTIEN, Rt Hon. Joseph Jacques Jean, PC, QC, BA, LLD; Canadian lawyer and fmr politician; *Of Counsel, Heenan Blaikie LLP;* b. 11 Jan. 1934, Shawinigan; s. of Wellie Chrétien and Marie Boisvert; m. Aline Chaîné 1957; two s. one d.; ed Laval Univ., Québec; Dir Bar of Trois-Rivières 1962; mem. House of Commons (Liberal) 1963–86; Parl. Sec. to Prime Minister 1965, to Minister of Finance 1966; Minister without Portfolio 1967–68, of Nat. Revenue Jan.–July 1968, of Indian Affairs and Northern Devt 1968–74; Pres. Treas. Bd 1974–76; Minister of Industry, Trade and Commerce 1976–77, of Finance 1977–79, of Justice, Attorney-Gen. of Canada and Minister of State for Social Devt 1980–82, of Energy, Mines and Resources 1982–84, Sec. of State for External Affairs, Deputy Prime Minister June–Sept. 1984; MP for Beauséjour 1990–93, for St Maurice 1993–2003, Prime Minister of Canada 1993–2003, Leader Nat. Liberal Party 1990–2003; Legal Counsel, Lang, Michener, Laurence & Shaw, Ottawa, Toronto and Vancouver 1984–90; special adviser on int. energy and power, Bennett Jones LLP 2004; Of Counsel, Heenan Blaikie LLP, Ottawa 2004–; mem. Barreau du Québec, Ont. Bar Asscn; Hon. LLD (Wilfred Laurier Univ.) 1981, (Laurentian Univ.) 1982, (W Ont.) 1982, (York Univ.) 1986, (Alberta) 1987, (Lakehead) 1988, (Ottawa) 1994, (Meiji) 1996, (Queen's Univ.) 2004, (McMaster Univ.) 2005; Dr hc (Ottawa Univ.) 1994, (Meiji Univ., Japan) 1996, (Warsaw School of Econs, Poland) 1999, (Michigan State Univ.) 1999, (Hebrew Univ., Jerusalem) 2000 (Memorial Univ.) 2000, (Université Catholique Pontificate Madre y Maestra in Santiago de los Caballeros, Dominican Repub.) 2003, (Nat. Univ. of Kyiv-Mohyla Acad., Ukraine) 2007, (Univ. of Western Ontario) 2008; Int. Role Model Award, Equality Forum 2005. *Publications:* Straight from the Heart 1985, Finding a Common Ground 1992. *Leisure interests:* skiing, fishing, golf. *Address:* Heenan Blaikie LLP, 55 Metcalfe Street, Suite 300, Ottawa, ON K1P 6L5, Canada (office). *Telephone:* (613) 236-1668 (office). *E-mail:* jchretien@heenan.ca (office). *Website:* www.heenanblaikie.com (office).

CHRÉTIEN, Raymond A. J., BA, LLL; Canadian lawyer, government official and diplomatist (retd); *Partner and Strategic Advisor, Fasken Martineau;* b. 20 May 1942, Shawinigan, Québec; s. of Maurice Chrétien and Cécille Chrétien (née Marcotte); m. Kay Rousseau; one s. one d.; ed Séminaire de Joliette and Laval Univ.; Quebec Bar Exams 1966; mem. Legal Affairs Div., Div. of External Affairs, Govt of Canada 1966–67, Policy Dir Industry, Investments and Competition 1981–82; Asst Under-Sec. for Manufacturing, Tech. and Transportation 1982–83; Insp.-Gen. 1983–85, Assoc. Under-Sec. of State for External Affairs 1988–91; Third Sec., Perm. Mission to UN, New York 1967–68; Asst Sec., Fed. and Provincial Relations Comm., Privy Council Office 1968–70, Exec. Asst to Sec., mem. Treasury Bd 1970–71; Exec. Asst to Pres., Canadian Int. Devt Agency 1971–72; First Sec., Embassy in Beirut 1972–75; First Sec. and Counsellor, Embassy in Paris 1975–78; Amb. to Zaïre 1978–81, to Mexico 1985–88, to Belgium and Luxembourg 1991–94, to USA 1994–2000, to France 2000–03; Pnr and Strategic Advisor, Fasken Martineau (law firm), Montréal 2004–; UN Sec.-Gen.'s Special Envoy to Cen. Africa 1996; Chair. Centre d'études et de recherches internationales de l'Université de Montréal (CÉRIUM); Pres. Comité des gouverneurs des corridors de commerce Québec-Canada-États-Unis of the Fédération des chambres de commerce du Québec; mem. Bd of Dirs Institut de recherches cliniques de Montréal; mem. Trilateral Comm.; Hon. mem. Bar of US Court of Appeal for the Armed Forces 1988; Order of Aztec Eagle, Mexico 1989, Commdr de la Légion d'Honneur 2003; Hon. DLitt (Brock) 1999; Hon. DJur (Laval) 2001, (State Univ. of New York) 2002. *Address:* Fasken Martineau Dumoulin, Stock Exchange Tower, Suite 3400, POB 242, 800 Place Victoria, Montréal, PQ H4Z 1E9, Canada (office). *Telephone:* (514) 397-5230 (office). *Fax:* (514) 397-7600 (office). *E-mail:* rchretien@fasken.com (office). *Website:* www.fasken.com (office).

CHRISOCHOIDHIS, Michalis; Greek politician; *Secretary-General, Panhellenic Socialist Movement (PASOK);* b. 31 Oct. 1955, Imathia; s. of Vasilis Chrisochoidhis and Anna Chrisochoidhis; m. Aggeliu Hondromelidois; one s. one d.; ed Faculty of Law, Aristotle Univ. of Thessaloníki; Founding mem. Panhellenic Socialist Movement (PASOK) 1974–, held numerous elected posts at local level, elected mem. Cen. Cttee 1990, Sec.-Gen. 2003–; elected to Nat. Parl. 1989; Deputy Minister of Commerce 1994–96, of Devt 1996–99; Minister for Public Order 1999–2003. *Address:* Panhellenic Socialist Movement, Panellinion Socialistikon Kinima), Harilaou Trikoupi 50, 10680 Athens, Greece (office). *Telephone:* (210) 3665000 (office). *Fax:* (210) 3606958 (office). *E-mail:* pasok@pasok.gr (office). *Website:* www.pasok.gr (office).

CHRISTENSEN, Helena; Danish model and photographer; b. 25 Dec. 1968, Copenhagen; d. of Flemming Christensen and Elsa Christensen; one s.; grad. in arithmetic and sociology course; fmr child model; began adult modelling career in Paris 1988; has since worked as one of world's leading models in promotions for Versace, Rykiel, Chanel, Lagerfeld, Revlon, Dior, Prada etc.; has appeared on all major magazine covers working for photographers including Herb Ritts, Bruce Weber, Patrick DeMarchelier, Penn, Steven Meisel, Helmut Newton, and others; Co-founder and fmr Creative Dir Nylon Magazine. *Films include:* Inferno (TV) 1992, March of the Anal Sadistic Warrior 1998, Allegro 2005. *Leisure interests:* photography (black and white), oil/watercolour painting. *Address:* One Management, 42 Bond Street, #2, New York, NY 10012, USA (office). *Telephone:* (212) 431-0054 (office). *Website:* www.helena-christensen.com (office).

CHRISTENSEN, Kai; Danish architect; b. 28 Dec. 1916, Copenhagen; s. of late J. C. Christensen and Jenny Christensen; m. Kirsten Vittrup Andersen 1941 (died 1990); two d.; ed Royal Acad. of Fine Arts, Copenhagen; Dir Tech. Dept of Fed. of Danish Architects 1947–52; Man. Dir Danish Bldg Centre 1952–61; Attached to Danish Ministry of Housing 1961–86; Graphic Adviser to Govt Depts 1986–; Chief, Scandinavian Design Cavalcade 1962–69; mem. Fed. of Danish Architects 1943, The Architectural Asscn, London 1955, life mem. 2000, Danish Cttee for Bldg Documentation 1950–79, Danish Soc. of History, Literature and Art 1969, Cttee mem. 1979, Vice-Pres. 1981, Pres. 1985–2001, Hon. Mem. 2001–; Cttee mem. Danish Soc. for Chamber Music 1989; Sec.-Gen. Nordisk Byggedag (Scandinavian Bldg Conf.) VIII 1961, XIII 1977; Pres. Int. Conf. of Building Centres 1960, Danish Ministries Soc. of Art 1982–87; mem. Scandinavian Liaison Cttee concerning Govt Bldg 1963–72; Assoc. Ed. Building Research and Practice/Bâtiment International (CIB magazine) 1968–85; Fellow, Royal Soc. of Arts, London 1977; The Arts Craft Prize 1944, The Cabinetmakers Prize 1945, C. F. Hansens Award 1949, Danish Design Council's Award for Industrial Graphics 1989; awards and prizes in public competition. *Major works:* designs for arts and crafts, graphic design, exhbns, furniture for the Copenhagen Cabinet Makers' exhbns. *Publications:* books about architecture, graphic design, humaniora and music, 90 Years (memoirs) 2007; articles and treatises in technical magazines and daily press. *Leisure interests:* chamber music, chess, fencing. *Address:* 100 Vester Voldgade, 1552 Copenhagen V, Denmark. *Telephone:* (45) 33-12-13-37. *E-mail:* kai.c@mail.tele.dk (home).

CHRISTENSEN, Lars Saabye; Norwegian poet, writer and playwright; b. 21 Sept. 1953, Oslo; Ed., Signaler 1986–90; Commdr, Order of St Olaf 2006; Cappelenprisen 1984, Rivertonprisen 1987, Kritikerpris 1988, Amandaprisen 1991, Doblougprisen 1993, Riksmålprisen 1997, Sargsborgrisen 1999, Aamoudt-statuetten 2001, Brageprisen 2001, Den norske leserprisen 2001, Natt & Dags bokpris 2001, Nordisk Råds Litteratuur Pris 2002. *Plays:*

Columbus' ankomst (Hørespillprisen 1981–82) 1981, Mekka 1994. *Publications:* poetry: Historien om Gly (Tarjei Vesaas' Debutantpris) 1976, Ordbok 1977, Kamelen i mitt hertje 1978, Jaktmarker 1979, Paraply 1982, Åsteder 1986, Stempler 1989, Versterålen: Lyset, livet, landskapet 1989, Hvor er det blitt av alle gutta 1991, Den akustiske skyggen 1993, Nordmarka 1993, Den andre siden av blått 1996, Falleferdig himmel 1998, Pasninger 1998, Under en sort paraply (with Niels Fredriok Dahl) 1998, Pinnsvinsol 2000, Mann for sin katt 2000, Sanger & steiner 2003; novels: Amatøren 1977, Billettene 1980, Jokeren 1981, Beatles 1984, Blodets bånd 1985, Sneglene 1987, Herman (trans. as Herman) 1988, Bly (Bokhandlerprisen) 1990, Gutten som ville være en av gutta 1992, Jubel 1995, Halvbroren (trans. as The Half Brother) (Bokhandlerprisen) 2001, Maskeblomstfamilien 2003, Modellen (trans. as The Model) 2005, Circus 2007; other fiction: Ingens 1992, Den Misunnnelige frisøren 1997, Noen som elsker hverandre 1999, Kongen som ville ha mer enn en krone (with Randall Meyers and Anita Killi) 1999; contrib. to Alexandrias aske 1993. *Address:* J. W. Cappelens Forslag AS, PB 350, 0101, Oslo, Norway (office). *Telephone:* 22-36-50-00 (office). *Fax:* 22-36-50-40 (office). *Website:* www.cappelen.no (office).

CHRISTIE, Sir George William Langham, Kt, CH; British music administrator; b. 31 Dec. 1934; s. of John Christie, CH and Audrey Mildmay Christie; m. Patricia Mary Nicholson 1958; three s. one d.; ed Eton Coll.; Asst to Sec. of Calouste Gulbenkian Foundation 1957–62; Chair. Glyndebourne Productions 1956–99; mem. Arts Council of GB and Chair. Music Panel 1988–92; Founder Chair. of London Sinfonietta; Hon. mem. Guildhall School of Music and Drama 1991; Commdr de l'Ordre des Arts et des Lettres 2006; Hon. DL; Hon. FRCM 1986; Hon. FRNCM 1986; Hon. DMus (Sussex) 1990, (Keele) 1993; Hon. DLitt (Exeter) 1994. *Address:* Old House, Moor Lane, Ringmer, East Sussex, BN8 5UR, England (home).

CHRISTIE, Julie (Frances); British actress; b. 14 April 1940, Assam, India; d. of Frank St John Christie and Rosemary Christie (née Ramsden); ed Brighton Technical Coll. and Central School of Speech and Drama; Dr hc (Warwick) 1994; Motion Picture Laurel Award, Best Dramatic Actress 1967, Motion Picture Herald Award 1967; Fellow BAFTA 1997. *Films include:* Crooks Anonymous 1962, The Fast Lady 1962, Billy Liar 1963, Young Cassidy 1964, Darling 1964 (Acad. Award 1966), Doctor Zhivago (Donatello Award) 1965, Fahrenheit 451 1966, Far From the Madding Crowd 1966, Petulia 1967, In Search of Gregory 1969, The Go-Between 1971, McCabe & Mrs. Miller 1972, Don't Look Now 1973, Shampoo 1974, Demon Seed, Heaven Can Wait 1978, Memoirs of a Survivor 1980, Gold 1980, The Return of the Soldier 1981, Les Quarantièmes rugissants 1981, The Animals Film (voiceover) 1981, Heat and Dust 1982, The Gold Diggers 1984, Miss Mary 1986, The Tattooed Memory 1986, Power 1987, Fathers and Sons 1988, Dadah is Death (TV) 1988, Fools of Fortune 1989, McCabe and Mrs Miller 1990, The Railway Station 1992, Hamlet 1995, Afterglow 1998, The Miracle Maker (voice) 2000, No Such Thing 2001, Snapshots 2001, I'm With Lucy 2002, A Letter to True 2003, Harry Potter and the Prisoner of Azkaban 2004, Finding Neverland 2004, Troy 2004, Away From Her (Best Actress, Nat. Bd of Review 2007, Golden Globe for Best Actress in a Drama 2008, Outstanding Performance by a Female Actor in a Leading Role, Screen Actors Guild 2008) 2007. *Plays:* Old Times 1995, Suzanna Andler 1997, Afterglow 1998. *Address:* c/o ICM Ltd, Oxford House, 76 Oxford Street, London, W1D 1BS, England (office).

CHRISTIE, Linford, OBE; British athletics coach, business executive and fmr athlete; b. 2 April 1960, St Andrew's, Jamaica; s. of James Christie and of the late Mabel Christie; one d.; fmr cashier Wandsworth Co-op; mem. Thames Valley Harriers; winner, UK 100m 1985, 1987, 200m 1985 (tie), 1988; winner Amateur Athletics Asscn 100m 1986, 1988, 200m 1988; winner, European 100m record; silver medallist, 100m, Seoul Olympic Games 1988, Winner 100m gold medal, Commonwealth Games 1990, Olympic Games 1992, World Athletic Championships 1993, Weltklasse Grand Prix Games 1994, European Games 1994; winner 100m Zurich 1995; Capt. of British Athletics Team 1995–97; officially retd 1997; Co-Founder (with Colin Jackson q.v. and Man. Dir Nuff Respect sports man. co. 1992–; successful coach to prominent UK athletes including Katharine Merry and Darren Campbell; Hon. MSc (Portsmouth Univ.) 1993; Male Athlete of the Year 1988, 1992, BBC Sports Personality of the Year 1993. *Publications:* Linford Christie (autobiog.) 1989, To be Honest With You 1995, A Year in the Life of Linford Christie 1996. *Leisure interests:* cooking, gardening. *Address:* c/o Susan Barrett, Nuff Respect, The Coach House, 107 Sherland Road, Twickenham, Middx, TW9 4HB, England. *Telephone:* (20) 8891-4145 (office). *Fax:* (20) 8891-4140 (office). *E-mail:* nuff_respect@msm.com (office). *Website:* www.nuff-respect.co.uk (office).

CHRISTIE, Rt Hon. Perry Gladstone, LLB; Bahamian politician; *Leader, Progressive Liberal Party;* b. 21 Aug. 1943, Nassau; s. of Gladstone L. Christie and Naomi Christie; m. Bernadette Hanna; two s. one d.; ed Eastern Senior School, New Providence, Univ. of London and Univ. of Birmingham, UK; attorney with McKinney Bancroft and Hughes; f. own law practice Christie Ingraham & Co. (now Christie Davis & Co.); mem. Bd of Dirs Broadcasting Corpn of The Bahamas 1973; mem. Progressive Liberal Party (PLP), Co-Deputy Leader 1993–97, Leader 1997–; Senator 1974; mem. House of Ass. (PLP) for Centerville and Farm Road, New Providence 1977–; Minister of Health and Nat. Insurance 1977–82, of Tourism 1977–82, of Agric., Trade and Industry 1990–93; Prime Minister and Minister of Finance 2002–07. *Address:* Progressive Liberal Party, Sir Lynden Pindling Centre, PLP House, Farrington Rd, POB N-547, Nassau, Bahamas (office). *Telephone:* 325-5492 (office). *Fax:* 328-0808 (office). *Website:* www.myplp.com (office).

CHRISTIE, William Lincoln, BA; French (b. American) harpsichordist, conductor and musicologist; b. 19 Dec. 1944, Buffalo, NY; s. of William Christie and Ida Jones; ed Harvard Univ., Yale School of Music; studied harpsichord with Ralph Kirkpatrick, Kenneth Gilbert and David Fuller; moved to France 1971; mem. Five Centuries Ensemble 1971–75, René Jacobs' Concerto vocale 1976–80; f. Les Arts Florissants vocal and instrumental ensemble 1979; Prof., Conservatoire Nat. Supérieur de Musique, Paris 1982–95; conducts his own orchestra as well as many leading int. orchestras (Orchestra of the Age of Enlightenment, Glyndebourne 1996, 2005, Berlin Philharmonic, Zurich Opera, Opéra Nat. de Lyon); career highlights include Handel's Theodora, Glyndebourne 1996, Handel's Semele, Aix-en-Provence Festival 1996, Rameau's Hippolyte et Aricie, Paris 1996–97, Lully's Thésée, Barbican, London 1998, Monteverdi's Il ritorno d'Ulisse in patria, Aix-en-Provence 2002, Hercules, Aix-en-Provence 2004, Rameau's Les Paladins, Théâtre du Chatelet 2004, 2006; Pres. Jury, Concours de Chant Baroque de Chimay, Belgium 2000–; cr. Le Jardin des Voix acad. for young singers in Caen, int. tours 2002, 2005, 2007; Artist-in-Residence (with Les Arts Florissants), Juillard School, New York 2007; mem. Royal Cabinet of Music, Acad. des Beaux-Arts 2008–; Chevalier Légion d'honneur 1993, Officier des Arts et des Lettres; Hon. DMus (New York) 1999; Prix Edison, Netherlands 1981, Grand prix du disque, Prix mondial de Montreux, Switzerland 1982, Gramophone Record of the Year, UK 1984, 1995, 1997, Deutscher Schallplattenpreis 1987, Grand prix de la Critique (best opera performance) 1987, Prix Opus, USA 1987, Prix int. de musique classique 1992, Prix Grand siècle Laurent Perrier 1997, Grammy Award for Handel's Acis and Galatea 2000, Grammy and Cannes Classical Awards for Alcina 2001, Harvard Univ. Arts Medal 2002, Royal Philarmonic Award 2003, Prix George Pompidou 2005. *Recordings:* numerous recordings including all works for harpsichord by Rameau, works by Monteverdi, Purcell, Handel, Couperin, Charpentier, Desmarest, Mozart, etc. *Leisure interests:* gardening, old houses. *Address:* Les Arts Florissants, 46 rue Fortuny, 75017 Paris (office); 81 avenue Victor Hugo, 75116 Paris (home); Le Bâtiment, Thiré, 85210 Sainte-Hermine, France (home). *E-mail:* w.christie@wanadoo.fr (home). *Website:* www.arts-florissants.com (office).

CHRISTO; American (naturalized) artist; b. (Christo Javacheff), 13 June 1935, Gabrovo, Bulgaria; m. Jeanne-Claude Denat de Guillebon (Jeanne-Claude); one s.; ed Acad. of Fine Arts, Sofia and Vienna; went to Paris 1958; solo works include: Wrapped Objects 1958; project for Packaging of Public Building 1960; works with Jeanne-Claude 1961–: Stacked Oil Barrels and Dockside Packages, Cologne 1961–, Iron Curtain Wall of Oil Barrels blocking rue Visconti, Paris, Wrapping a Girl, London 1962, Showcases 1963, Store Front 1964, Air Package and Wrapped Tree, Eindhoven, Netherlands 1966, 42,390 cu. ft. Package, Walker Art Center, Minneapolis School of Art 1966, Wrapped Kunsthalle, Bern 1968, 5,600 cu. m. Package for Kassel Documenta 4 1968, Wrapped Museum of Contemporary Art, Chicago 1969, Wrapped Coast, Little Bay, Sydney, Australia, 1 m. sq. ft. 1969, Valley Curtain, Grand Hogback, Rifle, Colorado, suspended fabric curtain 1970–72, Running Fence, Calif. 1972–76, Wrapped Roman Wall, Rome 1974, Ocean Front, Newport 1974, Wrapped Walk-Ways, Kansas City 1977–78, Surrounded Islands, Biscayne Bay, Miami, Florida 1980–83, The Pont Neuf Wrapped, Paris 1975–85, The Umbrellas, Japan-USA 1984–91, Wrapped Reichstag, Berlin 1971–95, Wrapped Trees, Fondation Beyeler and Berower Park, Riehen, Switzerland 1997–98, The Wall, 13,000 oil barrels, Gasometer, Oberhausen, Germany, indoor installation 1999, The Gates, Central Park, New York City 1979–2005; Praemium Imperiale 1995. *Fax:* (212) 966-2891 (office). *Website:* www.christojeanneclaude.net.

CHRISTODOULAKIS, Nikos M., EngDipl, MPhil, PhD; Greek politician and academic; *Professor of Economic Analysis, Athens University of Economics;* b. 27 Oct. 1952, Chania, Crete; ed Nat. Tech. Univ. of Athens and Univ. of Cambridge, UK; fmr mem. Euro-Communist party, linked with student uprising at Athens polytechnic 1973; Sr Research Officer, Dept of Applied Econs, Univ. of Cambridge 1984–86; Fellow, European Univ. of Florence 1989–90; apptd Prof. of Econ. Analysis, Athens Univ. of Econs 1990, Vice-Rector 1992–94, Prof. of Econ. Analysis 2007–; fmr Visiting Research Fellow, London Business School, Tinbergen Inst.; Prof. of Econs, Grad. School, Charles Univ., Prague 1992–93, Univ. of Cyprus 1996; Sec.-Gen. Research and Tech. 1993–96; Econ. Adviser to Prime Minister 1996; Deputy Minister of Finance 1996–2000; Minister of Devt with portfolios of Energy, Industry, Tech., Tourism and Commerce 2000–01; Minister of Economy and Finance 2001–04; mem. Parl. (Socialist Party) for Chania, Crete 2004–07; First Prize, Greek Math. Soc. 1970, Winbolt Prize 1985. *Publications include:* The New Terrain for Growth (in Greek) 1998, Growth, Employment and the Environment 2002, The Pendulum of Convergence (in Greek) 2006, several books and articles on econ. policy, business cycles, growth, forecasting and econ. models. *Leisure interest:* art, swimming, trekking. *Address:* 9 Kolokotroni Street, 10562 Athens, Greece (office). *Telephone:* (21) 03313488 (office). *Fax:* (21) 03313428 (office). *E-mail:* christodoulakis@parliament.gr (office). *Website:* www.christodoulakis.gr (office).

CHRISTODOULOU, Christodoulos, PhD; Cypriot lawyer, fmr government official and fmr central banker; b. 13 April 1939, Avgorou; m.; one d.; ed Pedagogical Acad. of Cyprus, Nicosia, Pantios High School of Political Sciences, Athens and Aristotelian Univ. of Salonica, Greece, Univ. of Wales, UK; began career as school teacher 1962; joined Publs Section, Press and Information Office 1964, Sr Officer, House of Reps 1968–72, Dir Govt Printing Office 1972–85; Perm. Sec. Ministry of Labour and Social Insurance 1985–89; served in Ministry of Agric. and Natural Resources 1989–94; Minister of Finance 1994–99, of the Interior 1999–2002; Gov. of Cen. Bank of Cyprus 2002–07; mem. Gen. Council of Cyprus Civil Servants Trade Union 1978–94, Exec. Cttee 1980–85; Chair. Bd Dirs of Govt Depts 1982–85; Chair. Bd Dirs Human Resource Devt Authority of Cyprus 1985–89; Rep. of Cyprus to ILO 1985–87; Govt Del. to Int. Labour Conf. 1985–89; del. to numerous other int. orgs including FAO, IBRD, IMF, The Commonwealth; mem. Advisory Bd EP

Global Energy Ltd. 2007–. *Leisure interests:* reading, gardening. *Address:* c/o Advisory Board, EP Global Energy Ltd, 7, Dositheou Street, Parabuilding C, 1071, Nicosia, Cyprus (office).

CHRISTOFIAS, Demetris, PhD; Cypriot politician and head of state; *President;* b. 29 Aug. 1946, Kyrenia; ed Nicosia Commercial Lyceum, Inst. of Social Sciences and Acad. of Social Sciences, Moscow; joined United Democratic Youth Org. (EDON) 1964, elected mem. Central Council 1969, Cen. Organisational Sec. 1974–77, Sec.-Gen. 1977–87; mem. Anorthotiko Komma Ergazomenou Laou (AKEL) 1964–, Sec.-Gen. 1988–; mem. House of Reps representing Kyrenia 1991–, Pres. House of Reps 2001–08; Pres. of Cyprus 2008–; Dr hc (Univ. of Macedonia) 2004. *Address:* Office of the President, Presidential Palace, Dem. Severis Avenue, 1400 Nicosia, Cyprus (office). *Telephone:* 22867400 (office). *Fax:* 22867594 (office). *E-mail:* president@presidency.gov.cy (office). *Website:* www.cyprus.gov.cy (office).

CHRISTOPHER, Ann, BA, RA, FRBS, RWA; British sculptor; b. 4 Dec. 1947, Watford, Herts.; d. of the late William Christopher and Phyllis Christopher; m. Kenneth Cook 1969; ed Watford Girls' Grammar School, Harrow School of Art, West of England Coll. of Art; works include bronze sculpture, Castle Park, Bristol 1993, Corten sculpture, Marsh Mills, Plymouth 1996, Bronze Sculpture for offices of Linklaters and Paines solicitors, London 1997, Bronze Sculpture, Great Barrington, USA 1998, Corten Sculpture, Port Marine, UK 2001; represented by Gallery Pangolin and Pangolin London; RBS Silver Medal for Sculpture of Outstanding Merit 1994, Frampton Award 1996, Otto Beit Medal for Sculpture of Outstanding Merit 1997. *Publications:* Sculpture and Drawings 1969–89, Sculpture 1989–94. *Leisure interests:* cinema, travel, architecture.

CHRISTOPHER, Sir (Duncan) Robin Carmichael, Kt, KBE, CMG; British diplomatist (retd) and international organization executive; *Secretary-General, GLF Global Leadership Foundation;* b. 13 Oct. 1944, Sussex; m. Merril Stevenson 1980; two d.; ed Keble Coll., Oxford and Fletcher School, Tufts Univ., USA; VSO volunteer in Bolivia; philosophy teacher, Univ. of Sussex 1969; joined FCO 1970, New Delhi 1972–76, FCO 1976, Deputy High Commr, Lusaka 1980–83, FCO and Cabinet Office 1983–87, Counsellor, Madrid 1987–91, Head Southern African Dept, FCO 1991–94, Amb. to Ethiopia 1994–97, to Indonesia 1997–2000, to Argentina 2000–04; Sec.-Gen. GLF Global Leadership Foundation 2007–; Dir Rurelec PLC; Trustee, The Brooke, Prospect Burma, St Matthew's Children's Fund (Ethiopia), Redress; Fellow, Univ. of London Inst. for the Study of the Americas. *Publications:* Indonesia in Transition: Democracy or Disintegration? 2000, Justice and Peace 2000 (Czech edn 2007), Remembrance Day 2007. *Leisure interests:* motorcycling, skiing, music. *Address:* GLF Global Leadership Foundation, 14 Curzon Street, London, W1J 5HN, England (office). *Telephone:* (20) 7861-8855 (office). *Fax:* (20) 7861-8856 (office). *E-mail:* Secretariat@g-l-f.org (office); rchristopher2@yahoo.co.uk (home). *Website:* www.g-l-f.org (office).

CHRISTOPHER, Warren M.; American lawyer and fmr government official; *Senior Partner, O'Melveny and Myers LLP;* b. 27 Oct. 1925, Scranton, ND; s. of Ernest Christopher and Catharine Christopher; m. Marie Wyllis 1956; three s. one d.; ed Univ. of Southern California, Stanford Univ. Law School; served in USNR 1943–45; Law Clerk, Justice William O. Douglas, US Supreme Court; mem. O'Melveny and Myers law firm, LA 1950–67, 1969, Pnr 1958–67, 1969–76, 1981–93, Sr Pnr 1997–; special consultant on foreign econ. problems to Under-Sec. of State George Ball 1961–65; a trade negotiator in Kennedy Admin.; Deputy Attorney-Gen. in Johnson Admin.; Deputy Sec. of State in Carter Admin. (chief negotiator for Panama Canal treaties, supervisor human rights policies abroad, negotiated for release of US hostages in Iran 1980) 1977–81; Chair. comm. to review conduct of LA Police Dept in Rodney King case 1991; US Sec. of State 1993–97; Past-Pres. LA Co. Bar Asscn; fmr Chair. Federal Judiciary Cttee, American Bar Asscn; fmr Dir LA World Affairs Council; fmr mem. Trilateral Comm.; several hon. degrees; Medal of Freedom 1981, Los Angeles Chamber of Commerce, First Civic Medal of Honor 2003. *Publications:* In the Stream of History 1998, Chances of a Lifetime 2000. *Address:* O'Melveny and Myers, 1999 Avenue of the Stars, Floor 7, Los Angeles, CA 90067-6035, USA. *Telephone:* (310) 246-6750. *Fax:* (310) 246-6779. *E-mail:* wchristopher@omm.com. *Website:* www.omm.com.

CHRISTOPHERSEN, Henning, MEcon; Danish politician; *Chairman, European Institute of Public Administration;* b. 8 Nov. 1939, Copenhagen; s. of Richard Christophersen and Gretha Christophersen; m. Jytte Risbjerg Nielsen 1961; one s. two d.; ed Univ. of Copenhagen; Head of the Economic Section of the Handicrafts Council 1965–70; mem. Folketing 1971–84, mem. of Parl. Finance Cttee 1972–76, Vice-Chair. 1976–78, Minister of Foreign Affairs 1978–79; Deputy Leader, Danish Liberal Party 1972, Acting Party Leader 1977–78, Party Leader 1978–84; Deputy Prime Minister and Minister of Finance 1982–84; Vice-Pres. Comm. responsible for Budget, Financial Control, Personnel and Admin., Comm. of EC (now European Comm.) 1985–89, Econ. and Financial Affairs 1989–95, Co-ordination of Structural Funds 1989–92; a Vice Pres. of EC (now EU) 1993–95; Swedish Prime Minister's Adviser, Council for Baltic Sea Cooperation 1996–2000; Danish Prime Minister's Personal Rep. to European Convention and mem. Presidium 2002–03; Chair. European Inst. of Public Admin., Netherlands 1996–; Pres. The Energy Charter Treaty Conf., Brussels 1998–2007; Chair. Supervisory Bd of Dirs Örestad Devt Cooperation, Copenhagen 1999–; Vice-Chair. Supervisory Bd of Dirs Scania Danmark A/S, Herlev, Denmark 2000–; Sr Partner, Kreab A/B, Brussels 2002–; mem. Bd of Dirs Den Danske Bank 1996–, Int. Advisory Bd Creditanstalt-Bankverein, Austria, European Advisory Cttee on the Opening-up of Public Procurement, Danish Council for European Policy and the Baltic Sea Council, Sweden; Nat. Order of Merit. *Publications:* En udfordring for de Liberale, Taenker om Danmark i Det Nye Europa 1989 and numerous articles on econs. *Leisure interests:* genealogy, history and languages. *Address:* Kreab A/B, Av. de Tervueren 2, 1040 Brussels, Belgium.

CHROMY, Bronisław; Polish sculptor; b. 3 June 1925, Leńcze nr Lanckorona; m.; two d.; ed Acad. of Fine Arts, Kraków 1956; one-man exhbns in Poland and abroad; int. exhbns and competitions; creator of many monuments commemorating victims of World War II; f. Bronislaw Chromy ART Foundation, Kracόw; mem. Polish Acad. of Arts and Sciences, Kraków; mem. Union of Polish Artists and Designers 1970–; Commdr Cross with Star Order of Polonia Restituta 1999; Meritorious Medal for Nat. Culture 1986. *Achievements:* some works permanently in museums and pvt collections; sculptures include: Pieta Oświęcimska (Monument) 1963, Smok wawelski, Cracow 1970, Pomnik Żołniercy Polskich (Monument to Polish Soldiers), Katowice 1978, Pomnik jana Pawła II (Monument to John Paul II), Tarnów 1981, Zielonki nr Kraków 1998. *Leisure interests:* music, literature, nature. *Address:* Bronislaw Chromy ART Foundation, ul. Cystersow 11, 31-553 Kracόw, Poland. *Telephone:* (12) 4122260. *Fax:* (12) 4122466. *E-mail:* office@chromy.art.pl. *Website:* www.chromy.art.pl.

CHRONOWSKI, Andrzej; Polish politician; b. 9 April 1961, Grybów, Nowy Sącz Dist; m. Barbara Chronowski; two s.; ed Acad. of Mining and Metallurgy, Kraków; helped organize student strikes in univ. cities including Kraków 1980–81; railway repair factory, Nowy Sącz 1987, later Head of Production, Chair. Employees' Council 1991–93; mem. Solidarity Trade Union; Senator 1993–2005; Sec. Solidarity Senate Club Presidium 1993–97; Vice-Marshal of Senate 1997–; Chair. Nowy Sącz Region of Social Movt of Solidarity Electoral Action (RS AWS) 1997, Chair. Małopolski Region, Chair. Senators' Club 2001; Chair. Council of Sądecki Club; Minister of State Treasury 2000–01; Senator to 3rd and 4th term Senate, Deputy Speaker of 4th term Senate 2001–; mem. European Parl. (Group of the European People's Party—Christian Democrats and European Democrats) 2004, mem. Cttee on Budgets; mem. Solidarity Trade Union, Nat. Econ. Cttee, Cttee for Human Rights and Lawfulness, Cttee of Initiatives and Legislative Work. *Leisure interests:* skiing, climbing, time with family. *Address:* ul. Pijarska 17A, 33-300 Nowy Sącz S5C2, Poland (office).

CHRYSANTHOPOULOS, Leonidas T.; Greek diplomatist and international organization executive; *Secretary-General, Organization of the Black Sea Economic Cooperation;* b. 1946, Athens; ed Univ. of Athens; joined Greek Foreign Ministry in 1972, served as Vice-Consul in Toronto, as Second Sec. at Perm. Mission of Greece to EEC, as Dir Diplomatic Cabinet of the Minister in Charge of EEC Affairs, as Consul-Gen. in Istanbul, as Rep. of Greece in Charge of Third Cttee Questions (UN), as Deputy Perm. Rep. of Greece to the UN, as Minister-Counsellor in Beijing, as Amb. of Greece to Armenia 1993, as Alt. Dir-Gen. for EU Affairs, as Amb. to Poland, to Canada 2000–04, as Dir-Gen. for EU Affairs, as Dir-Gen. for Bilateral Econ. Relations and Multilateral Econ. Cooperation; Sec.-Gen. Org. of Black Sea Econ. Cooperation 2006–. *Publication:* Caucasus Chronicles: Nation-Building and Diplomacy in Armenia, 1993–1994 2002. *Address:* Permanent International Secretariat, Black Sea Economic Cooperation, Sakıp Sabancı Caddesi, Müşir Fuad Paşa Yalısı, Eski Tersane, 34460 İstanbul, Turkey (office). *Telephone:* (212) 229-63-30-35 (office). *Fax:* (212) 229-63-36 (office). *E-mail:* info@bsec-organization.org (office). *Website:* www.bsec-organization.org (office).

CHRYSSA; American (b. Greek) artist; b. (Chryssa Mavromichali), 1933, Athens, Greece; ed Acad. Grand Shaumière, Paris and Calif. School of Fine Arts, San Francisco; one-woman shows, Solomon Guggenheim Museum, New York 1961, Museum of Modern Art, New York 1963, Walker Art Centre, Minneapolis 1968, Whitney Museum of Modern Art, New York 1972, Musée d'Art Contemporain, Montreal 1974, Musée d'Art Moderne de la Ville de Paris 1979, Nat. Pinacotheque Museum Alexander Soutsos, Athens 1980, Albright-Knox Gallery, Buffalo 1982, Leo Castelli Gallery 1988 and at galleries in New York, Boston, San Francisco, Paris, Cologne, Düsseldorf, Zurich, Turin and Athens since 1961; work has also appeared in many group exhbns. and belongs to numerous public collections in USA and Europe; Guggenheim Fellowship 1973; CAVS, MIT 1979. *Address:* c/o Leo Castelli Gallery, 59 East 79th Street, New York, NY 10021, USA.

CHRZANOWSKI, Wiesław Marian; Polish politician and lawyer; b. 20 Dec. 1923, Warsaw; s. of Wiesław Chrzanowski and Izabela Chrzanowska; ed Jagiellonian Univ., Kraków, M. Curie-Skłodowska Univ., Lublin; during Nazi occupation active in resistance movt, mem. Nat. Party (Bd bi-weekly Młoda Polska 1942–45), served in Home Army 1942–44, Warsaw Uprising 1944; Pres. clandestine Law Students' Asscn 1942–43; Asst, Sr Asst Civil Law Dept in Warsaw Univ. and Cen. School of Commerce, Warsaw 1945–48; arrested and sentenced to 8 years' imprisonment for attempting to overthrow regime 1948–54, acquitted and rehabilitated 1956; legal counsellor 1955–72; attorney's trainee 1957–60, attorney 1981–90; researcher 1972–79, Asst Prof. 1980–88, Prof. 1988, Cooperative Research Inst.; Asst Prof., Catholic Univ. of Lublin 1982–87, Prof. of Law 1987–, Deputy Dean Canon and Secular Law Faculty 1987–90; mem. informal information group of Primate of Poland 1965–81; mem. Social Council of Primate of Poland 1983–84; mem. Episcopal Comm. for Agric. 1982–86; mem. on behalf of Episcopate of team drawing up convention between Holy See and Poland and Law on State–Church Relations 1987–89; mem. Solidarity Trade Union 1980–89 (adviser to Nat. Comm., plenipotentiary for registration by Voivodship and Supreme Court 1980–81); mem. Labour Party 1945–46, Christian-Nat. Union 1989– (Chair. Main Bd 1989–94); Chair. Supreme Council 1995–98, 2000–01; Minister of Justice and Attorney-Gen. Jan.–Dec. 1991; Deputy to Sejm (Parl.) 1991–93, Marshal (Speaker) of Sejm 1991–93; Senator 1997–2001; Orderem Orła Białego (Order of White Eagle) 2005, Kapitule Orła Białego 2007. *Publications:* over 100 books and articles on civil law and cooperative law, many contribs. in underground journals and Polish journals appearing abroad. *Leisure inter-*

ests: reading, history (19th and 20th century), sociology, theatre, mountain hiking. *Address:* ul. Solec 79a/82, 00-402 Warsaw, Poland. *Telephone:* (22) 629-30-88.

CHSHMARITIAN, Karen, PhD; Armenian economist and politician; b. 12 Sept. 1959, Yerevan; m.; two c.; ed Yerevan Inst. of Nat. Economy; trained as economist, Georgetown Univ. and USAID Tech. Cooperation Program, Int. Law Acad. for Educational Devt, Washington, DC 1995; economist, Armenian Br., Research Inst. of Standards and State Planning, USSR 1980; mil. service in Soviet Army 1981–82; Sr Economist, Chief Specialist and Head of Financial Sub-Div., State Supply, Armenia 1985–90; Vice-Pres. Haielectramekenametzar (state co.), Armenia 1990–91; Head of Dept, State Supply 1991–93; Deputy Minister, Ministry of Material Resources, Repub. of Armenia 1993–96; Head of Foreign Trade Dept, Ministry of Trade, Services and Tourism 1996–97; First Deputy Minister, Ministry of Industry and Trade 1997–98; Minister of Industry and Trade 1999–2000; Minister of Trade and Econ. Devt 2002–07; mem. Azgayin Zhoghov (Nat. Ass.) (Republican Party of Armenia) 2007–. *Address:* Azgayin Zhoghov (National Assembly), 0095 Yerevan, Marshal Baghramian St 19, Armenia (office). *Telephone:* (10) 58-82-25 (office). *Fax:* (10) 52-98-26 (office). *E-mail:* karen.chshmaritian@parliament.am (office). *Website:* www.parliament.am (office).

CHU, Bo; Chinese politician; *Secretary, Committee of Inner Mongolian Autonomous Region, Chinese Communist Party;* b. Oct. 1944, Tongcheng, Anhui Prov.; ed Tianjin Univ.; joined CCP 1969; Deputy Dir and Deputy Sec. CCP Party Cttee, Yueyang Chemical Works 1975–84; fmr Mayor Yueyang City; Del., 13th CCP Nat. Congress 1987–92; mem. Standing Cttee, CCP Hunan Prov. Cttee 1990, Deputy Sec. CCP Hunan Prov. Cttee 1994–99; Exec. Vice-Gov. Hunan Prov. 1993–94, Vice-Gov. (also Acting Gov.) 1998–99, Gov. 1999–2001; Deputy, 9th NPC 1998–2003; Sec. CCP Cttee of Inner Mongolian Autonomous Region 2001–; Alt. mem. 15th CCP Cen. Cttee 1997–2002, mem. 16th CCP Cen. Cttee 2002–07, mem. 17th CCP Cen. Cttee 2007–; Hon. Pres. Hunan Prov. Merchants' Asscn. *Address:* Chinese Communist Party Committee of Inner Mongolian Autonomous Region, Huhot, Inner Mongolia, People's Republic of China (office).

CHU, Lam Yiu; Chinese business executive; *Chairman and President, Huabao International Holdings Ltd;* b. 1971, Sichuan; m. Lam Kwok Man; f. Huabao Food and Flavours and Fragrances Co. Ltd, Shanghai 1996, made public 2006, now called Huabao International Holdings Ltd, Chair. and Pres. 2004–; Deputy Dir China Asscn of Fragrance, Flavour and Cosmetic Industry, China Food Additive Production and Application Industry Asscn; mem. 4th CPPCC Cttee; ranked by Forbes magazine amongst 100 Most Powerful Women (90th) 2007. *Address:* Huabao International Holdings Ltd, Suite 1103, Central Plaza, 18 Harbour Road., Wanchai, Hong Kong Special Administrative Region, People's Republic of China (office). *Telephone:* 28276677 (office). *Fax:* 28278866 (office). *Website:* www.huabao.com.hk (office).

CHU, Paul Ching-Wu, BS, MS, PhD, JP; American (b. Chinese) physicist, academic and university administrator; *President and Professor of Physics, Hong Kong University of Science and Technology;* b. 12 Feb. 1941, Hunan, People's Repub. of China; ed Cheng-Kung Univ., Taiwan, Fordham Univ., Bronx, NY, Univ. of Calif., San Diego; Teaching Asst, Fordham Univ. 1963–65; Research Asst, Univ. of Calif., San Diego 1965–68; mem. Tech. Staff, Bell Labs, Murray Hill, NJ 1968–70; Asst Prof. of Physics, Cleveland State Univ. 1970–73, Assoc. Prof. 1973–75, Prof. 1975–79; Resident Research Assoc., Argonne Nat. Lab., Argonne, Ill. 1972; Visiting Scientist, Stanford Univ., Hansens Physics Lab. 1973; Visiting Staff Mem., Los Alamos Scientific Lab., Los Alamos, NM 1975–80; Prof. of Physics, Univ. of Houston, Tex. 1979–, also Dir Magnetic Information Research Lab. 1984–88, Dir Space Vacuum Epitaxy Center 1986–88, M. D. Anderson Chair. of Physics 1987–89, Exec. Dir Tex. Center for Superconductivity 1987–2001, 2007–, T.L.L. Temple Chair. of Science 1987–; Pres. and Prof. of Physics, Hong Kong Univ. of Science and Tech. 2001–; Visiting Miller Research Prof., Univ. of Calif., Berkeley 1991; Prin. Investigator, Lawrence Berkeley Nat. Lab., Berkeley, Calif. 1999–; mem. Editorial Bd numerous journals including Indian Journal of Pure and Applied Physics 1992–, Brazilian Journal of Physics 1995–, Science in China 1997–, Chinese Science Bulletin 1997–; mem. State of Tex. Science and Tech. Council 1996–; mem. Univ. of Tex. at Dallas Research Advisory Bd 2004–; mem. Academia Sinia Inst. of Physics; Foreign mem., Chinese Acad. of Sciences 1996–; Fellow, Tex. Acad. of Sciences 1992–; Dr hc (Chinese Univ. of Hong Kong) 1988, (NW Univ.) 1988, (Fordham Univ.) 1988, (Florida International Univ.) 1989, (Whittier Coll.) 1991, (Hong Kong Baptist Univ.) 1999; St Martin de Porres Award 1990, Bernd Matthias Award 1994, Univ. of Houston Esther Farfel Award 2000, American Asscn of Eng Socs John Fritz Medal 2001. *Publications:* more than 50 scientific papers in professional journals. *Address:* Office of the President, Hong Kong University of Science and Technology, Clear Water Bay, Kowloon, Hong Kong Special Administrative Region, People's Republic of China (office); Room 262 UHSC, Texas Center for Superconductivity, University of Houston, 202 Houston Science Center, Houston, TX 77204-5002, USA. *Telephone:* 23586113 (office); (713) 743-8222. *Fax:* 23580029 (office). *E-mail:* ophkust@ust.hk (office); cwchu@uh.edu. *Website:* www.ust.hk (home); www.tcsuh.uh.edu.

CHU, Steven, BA, PhD; American physicist, academic and government official; *Secretary of Energy;* b. 28 Feb. 1948, St Louis, Mo.; s. of Ju Chin Chu and Ching Chen Li; m. 1st Lisa Chu-Thielbar; two s.; m. 2nd Jean Fetter 1997; ed Garden City High School, Univ. of Rochester, Univ. of California, Berkeley; Post-doctoral Fellow, Univ. of California, Berkeley 1976–78; with Bell Labs, Murray Hill, NJ 1978–83, Head of Quantum Electronics Research Dept, Bell Labs, Holmdell, NJ 1983–87; Prof. of Physics and Applied Physics, Stanford Univ. 1987–2004, Frances and Theodore Geballe Prof. of Physics and Applied Physics 1990–2004, Chair. Physics Dept 1990–93, 1999–2001; Prof. of Physics and Prof. of Molecular and Cell Biology, Univ. of California, Berkeley 2004–, Dir Lawrence Berkeley Nat. Lab. 2004–08; US Sec. of Energy, Washington, DC 2009–; Visiting Prof., Collège de France 1990; Fellow, American Physics Soc. (Chair. Laser Science Topical Group 1989), Optical Soc. of America, American Acad. of Arts and Sciences; Woodrow Wilson Fellow 1970, NSF Doctoral Fellow 1970–74; mem. NAS, American Philosophical Soc., Academia Sinica; Foreign mem. Chinese Acad. of Sciences, Korean Acad. of Science and Eng; Herbert P. Broida Prize for laser spectroscopy 1987, King Faisal Prize for Science 1993, Schawlow Prize 1994, Meggars Award 1994, Humboldt Sr Scientist Award 1995, Science for Art Prize 1995, shared Nobel Prize for Physics 1997 for developing methods of cooling matter to very low temperatures using lasers. *Publications:* numerous papers on atomic physics and laser spectroscopy. *Leisure interests:* baseball, swimming, cycling, tennis. *Address:* Department of Energy, Forrestal Building, 1000 Independence Avenue, SW, Washington, DC 20585, USA (office). *Telephone:* (202) 586-5000 (office). *Fax:* (202) 586-4403 (office). *E-mail:* the.secretary@hq.doe.gov (office). *Website:* www.energy.gov (office).

CHUA, Nam-Hai, PhD, FRS; Singaporean biologist and academic; *Andrew W. Mellon Professor and Head, Laboratory of Plant Molecular Biology, The Rockefeller University;* b. 8 April 1944; m. Suat-Choo Pearl Chua 1970; two d.; ed Univ. of Singapore and Harvard Univ.; lecturer, Dept of Biochemistry, Univ. of Singapore 1969–71; Research Assoc. Dept of Cell Biology, Rockefeller Univ. 1971–73, Asst Prof. Dept of Cell Biology 1973–77, Prof. and Head, Lab. of Plant Molecular Biology 1988–, Andrew W. Mellon Prof. 1988–; consultant Shanghai Research Centre for Life Sciences, Chinese Acad. of Science 1996–, Global Tech. Centre and Nutrition, Monsanto Co. 1997–; numerous consultancies and bd memberships; Int. Prize for Biology, Japan Soc. for the Promotion of Science 2005. *Publications:* over 260 scientific publs. *Leisure interests:* squash, skiing. *Address:* Laboratory of Plant Molecular Biology, Rockefeller University, 1230 York Avenue, New York, NY 10021, USA (office). *Telephone:* (212) 327-8126 (office). *E-mail:* chua@rockefeller.edu (office). *Website:* www.rockefeller.edu/labheads/chua (office).

CHUA, Sock Koong, CPA; Singaporean accountant and telecommunications industry executive; *Group CEO, Singapore Telecommunications Ltd (SingTel);* m.; two d.; ed Univ. of Singapore; chartered financial analyst; joined Singapore Telecommunications Ltd (SingTel) as Treas. in 1989, Chief Financial Officer 1999–2006, Group Chief Financial Officer 2006–07, CEO International 2006–07, Group CEO 2007–; mem. Bd Dirs JTC Corpn, Bharti Tele-Ventures Ltd; Trustee Singapore Man. Univ.; Best Chief Financial Office, FinanceAsia magazine's 2004 Best Managed Companies poll 2002, 2003, 2004, ranked by Fortune magazine amongst 50 Most Powerful Women in Business outside the US (25th) 2002, (41st) 2003, (43rd) 2004, (50th) 2005, (17th) 2006, (15th) 2007. *Leisure interest:* keeping fit. *Address:* SingTel, 31 Exeter Road, Comcentre, Singapore 239732 (office). *Telephone:* 68383388 (office). *Fax:* 67383769 (office). *E-mail:* contact@singtel.com (office). *Website:* www.singtel.com (office).

CHUAN, Leekpai, LLB; Thai politician; *President of the Advisory Council, Democrat Party;* b. 28 July 1938, Muang Dist, Trang Prov.; ed Trang Wittaya School, Silapakorn Pre-Univ. and Thammasat Univ.; studied for two years with Bar Asscn of Thailand; mem. Parl. for Trang Prov. 1969–; Deputy Minister of Justice 1975; Deputy Minister of Justice and Minister, Prime Minister's Office 1976; Minister of Justice 1980; Minister of Commerce 1981, of Agric. and Co-operatives 1982–83, of Educ. 1983–86; Speaker of House of Reps 1986–88; Minister of Public Health 1988–89, of Agric. and Co-operatives 1990–91; Deputy Prime Minister 1990, Prime Minister of Thailand 1992–95, 1997–2001; Leader Prachatipat (Democrat Party—DP); Leader of Opposition 1995–96, 1996–97, 2001–; Minister of Defence 1997–2001; Vice-Pres. Prince of Songkhla Univ. Council; 6 hon. degrees; Kt Grand Cordon of the Most Noble Order of the Crown of Thailand 1981, Kt Grand Cordon (Special Class) of the Most Exalted Order of the White Elephant 1982, Order of Sukatuna (Special Class), Raja, Philippines 1993, Kt Grand Commdr (2nd Class, Higher Grade) of the Most Illustrious Order of Chula Chom Klao 1998, Order of the Sun (Grand Cross), Peru 1999. *Leisure interest:* drawing. *Address:* Prachatipat (Democrat Party), 67 Thanon Setsiri, Samsen Nai, Phyathai, 10400, Bangkok 10300 (office); 471/2 Rajaprasop Road, Magasasam, Rajatheri District, Metropolitan 10400, Bangkok, Thailand (home). *Telephone:* (2) 278-4042 (office); (2) 245-4415 (home). *Fax:* (2) 279-6086; (2) 278-4218 (office). *E-mail:* admin@democrat.or.th (office). *Website:* www.democrat.or.th (office); www.chuan.org (office).

CHUBACHI, Ryoji, MA, PhD; Japanese business executive; *Vice Chairman, Sony Corporation;* b. 1948; ed Tohoku Univ.; joined Sony Corpn 1977, with Sony Magnetic Products Inc., Ala, USA 1989–92, Gen. Man. Video Tape Div., Recording Media Products Group, Tokyo 1992–94, Gen. Man. Video Tape Dept, Recording Media Div. 1994–98, Pres. Recording Media Co. 1999–2002, Pres. Core Tech. & Network Co. 2002–03, Pres. Micro Systems Network Co. 2003–04, COO in charge of Micro Systems Network Co. June 2004, Pres. Production Strategy Group 2004–05, mem. Bd of Dirs Sony Corpn 2005–, also Rep. Corp. Exec. Officer 2005–, Pres. 2005–09, CEO Global Electronics Business 2005–09, Vice-Chair. 2009–; mem. Asscn of Radio Industries and Businesses (Dir 2005–), Japan Electronics and Information Tech. Industries Asscn (Vice-Chair. Exec. Bd, Trade Affairs). *Address:* Sony Corporation, 1-7-1 Konan, Minato-ku, Tokyo 108-0075, Japan (office). *Telephone:* (3) 6748-2111 (office). *Fax:* (3) 6748-2244 (office). *E-mail:* info@sony.net (office). *Website:* www.sony.net (office).

CHUBAIS, Anatoliy Borisovich, CEconSc, PhD; Russian economist, business executive and politician; *Chief Executive Officer, Russian State Nanotechnology Corporation (Rosnanotech);* b. 16 June 1955, Borisov, Belarusian SSR; m.; one s. one d.; ed Leningrad Inst. of Eng and Econs; engineer and Asst to Chair.

Leningrad (now St Petersburg) Inst. of Econs and Eng 1977–82, Asst Prof. 1982–90; Leader, The Young Economists 1984–87; Deputy, then First Deputy-Chair. of Leningrad Municipal Council Jan.–Nov. 1991; Minister of Russia and Chair. State Cttee for Man. of State Property 1991–98; Deputy Prime Minister and Chair. Co-ordination Council for Privatization 1992–94; First Deputy Prime Minister responsible for economy 1994–96; mem. State Duma (Parl.) 1993–95; Chief of Staff of Presidential Exec. Office 1996–97; First Deputy Prime Minister 1997–98, Minister of Finance March–Nov. 1997; Russian Dir EBRD 1997–98; mem. Russian Security Council 1997–98; Head of Russian Fed. Interdepartmental Comm. on Co-operation with Int. Financial and Econ. Orgs and Group of Seven 1998; CEO Unified Energy Systems of Russia 1998–2001, CEO and Chair. Bd of Man. 2001–08; CEO Russian State Nanotechnology Corpn (Rosnanotech) 2008–; Co-Chair. Round Table of Russian and EU Producers 2000–; Pres. Electric Power Council of CIS 2000–07; mem. Int. Advisory Bd JP Morgan Chase 2008–; mem. Man. Bd Russian Union of Mfrs and Entrepreneurs 2000–; mem. Govt Comm. on Co-operation with EU 2000–; joined Union of Rightist Forces 1999, Co-Chair. 2001–04 (resgnd); Hon. PhD (St Petersburg State Eng, Econ. Univ.); Best Minister of Finance Award (Euromoney magazine) 1997; three commendations from Pres. of Russian Fed. 1995, 1997, 1998; International Union of Economists International Award 2001. *Leisure interests:* music, literature. *Address:* Russian State Nanotechnology Corporation (Rosnanotech), 117420 Moscow, ul. Nametkina 12A, Russia (office). *Telephone:* (495) 542-44-44 (office). *Fax:* (495) 542-44-34 (office). *E-mail:* info@rusnano.com (office). *Website:* www.rusnano.com (office); www.chubais.ru (home).

CHUBB, Ian William, AC, MSc, DPhil; Australian neuroscientist and university administrator; *Vice-Chancellor, Australian National University;* Lecturer in Human Physiology, Flinders Univ. 1977, Vice-Chancellor Flinders Univ. 1995–2000; Deputy Vice-Chancellor Univ. of Wollongong 1986–90; Chair. Higher Educ. Council 1990–93, part-time Chair. 1994–97; Deputy Chair. Nat. Bd of Employment, Educ. and Training 1990–93; Sr Deputy Vice-Chancellor and Foundation Dean Faculty of Business and Econs, Monash Univ. 1993–95; Interim Chair., then Deputy Chair. Nat. Cttee for Quality in Higher Educ. 1993–94; Vice-Chancellor ANU 2001–; mem. Ministerial Task Force 1989, Prime Minister's Science, Eng and Innovation Council 2000–02, Foreign Affairs Council; mem. Bd of Dirs Australia-New Zealand School of Govt, Australian Vice-Chancellors' Cttee (later Deputy Pres., Pres. 2000–01); Chair. Group of Eight Univs; also served in various capacities on Nat. Health and Medical Research Council and Australian Research Cttee; Hon. DSc (Flinders); recipient of several academic awards and named fellowships at Univs of Ghent, Belgium and Oxford, UK, Centenary Medal 2003. *Publications:* numerous articles in scientific journals. *Address:* Office of the Vice-Chancellor, Chancelry Building 10, The Australian National University, Canberra, ACT 0200, Australia (office). *Telephone:* (2) 6125-2510 (office). *Fax:* (2) 6257-3292 (office). *E-mail:* vc@anu.edu.au (office). *Website:* info.anu.edu .au/OVC (office).

CHUBUK, Ion, DrEcon; Moldovan politician; b. 20 May 1943; ed Odessa Inst. of Agric.; First Deputy Chair. Moldovan State Planning Cttee 1984–86; Head of Div. Research Inst. of Agric. 1986–89; Deputy Chair. Moldovan Agricultural-Industrial Council 1989–90; First Deputy Minister of Econs 1990–91; Deputy Prime Minister, Perm. Rep. of Moldovan Govt in USSR Council of Ministers 1991–92; First Deputy Minister of Foreign Affairs 1992–94; First Deputy Minister of Econs April–Dec. 1994; Chair. Moldovan Accountant Chamber 1994–97, Deputy Chair. Accountant Chamber 1999–; Prime Minister of Moldova 1997–99; Deputy Chair. Centrist Union 2000–. *Address:* c/o Centrist Union of Moldova, (Uniunea Centristă din Moldova), Chişinău, str. Tricolorului 35, Moldova (office).

CHUCK D; American rap artist; b. (Carlton Ridenhour), 1 Aug. 1960, Long Island, NY; ed Adelphi Univ.; Super Special Mix Show, radio WBAU 1982; own mobile DJ and concert promotion co., Spectrum City; Founder mem. rap group, Public Enemy 1982–; Man. and Promoter, The Entourage (hip hop venue), Long Island, New York 1986; Founder, Offda Books, Under the Radar Publishing 2003; MOBO Award for Outstanding Contrib. to Black Music 2005. *Recordings include:* albums: with Public Enemy: Yo! Bum Rush The Show 1987, It Takes A Nation of Millions To Hold Us Back 1988, Fear of a Black Planet 1990, Apocalypse 91... The Enemy Strikes Black (Soul Train Music Award for Best Rap Album 1992) 1991, Greatest Misses 1992, Muse Sick-n-Hour Mess Age 1994, He Got Game (film soundtrack) 1998, There's a Poison Goin' On... 1999, Revolverlution 2002, Rebirth of a Nation 2005, New Whirl Odor 2005, How you Sell a Soul to a Soulless People who Sold their Soul??? 2007; solo: No 1996, The Autobiography of Mistachuck 1996. *Publications:* Public Enemy (autobiog.) 1994, Fight the Power: Rap, Race and Reality (non-fiction, with Yusuf Jah) 1997. *E-mail:* Mistachuck@rapstation.com (office). *Website:* www.rapstation.com; www.publicenemy.com.

CHUDAKOVA, Marietta Omarovna, DLit, PhD; Russian academic; *Professor of Literature, Moscow Literary Institute;* b. (Marietta Khan-Magomedova), 2 Jan. 1937, Moscow; m. Alexander Pavlovich Chudakov (died 2005); one d.; ed Moscow State Univ.; school teacher in Moscow 1959–61; Sr Researcher, Div. of Manuscripts, Div. of Rare Books, Div. of Library Research All-Union Lenin's Public Library 1965–84; Ed.-in-Chief Tynyanovski sborniki 1984–; teacher, Moscow Literary Inst. 1986–, Prof. 1992–; main research on history of Russian Literature (Soviet period), archives and literary criticism; Visiting Prof., Stanford 1989, Univ. of Southern Calif. 1990, Ecole Normale Supérieure, Paris 1991, Geneva Univ. and European Inst. in Geneva 1994, Ottawa Univ. 1995, Cologne Univ. 1999; Chair. All-Russian Mikhail Bulgakov Fund; mem. Academia Europaea; Prize of Moscow Komsomol for research on Yuri Olesha 1970. *Publications:* Effendi Kapiev (biog.) 1970, Craftsmanship of Yuri Olesha 1972, Talks about Archives 1975, Poetics of Mikhail Zoshchenko 1979, Life of

Mikhail Bulgakov 1988, Literature of the Soviet Past 2001, Yeltsin and the Cult 2000, Results and Perspectives of the Contemporary Russian Revolution 2002; more than 350 publs in magazines on literary subjects and political essays. *Leisure interests:* rowing, skiing. *Address:* Moscow Literary Institute, Miklukho-Maklaia str. 39, korp. 2, apt. 380, 117485 Moscow, Russia (home). *Telephone:* (495) 202-84-44 (office); (495) 335-92-57 (home). *Fax:* (495) 375-78-03 (office). *E-mail:* marietta@online.ru (home).

CHUDÍK, Ladislav; Slovak actor; b. 27 May 1924, Hronec by Banská Bystrica; m.; one c.; ed Comenius Univ. Bratislava, State Conservatoire, Bratislava; with Slovak Nat. Theatre, Bratislava 1944, 1951–, Nová Scéna 1946–1951; Minister of Culture 1990; tutor Conservatoire and Acad. of Musical Arts, Bratislava—VSMU; Medal of Merit (First Grade) 2003; State Prize 1959, Certificate of Merit 1965, Nat. Artist 1982. *Films include:* Vlcie diery 1948, Muj prítel Fabián (My Friend the Gypsy, UK) 1955, Kapitán Dabac 1959, Piesen o sirom holubovi 1961, Polnocná omsa (Midnight Mass) 1962, Smrt prichádza v dazdi 1965, Vrah zo záhrobia 1966, Volanie démonov 1967, Niet inej cesty 1968, Luk královny Dorotky 1970, Podezrení 1972, Trofej neznámeho strelca 1974, Kean (TV) 1975, Az Idök kezdetén 1975, Do posledneho dychu 1976, Nemocnice na kraji mesta (TV series) 1977, Vojaci slobody 1977, Sol nad zlato (The Salt Prince) 1982, Výlet do mladosti 1983, Výlet do mladosti 1983, Putováni Jana Amose 1983, Velká filmová loupez 1986, Rozruch na onkológii 1991, Vsichni moji blízcí (All My Loved Ones, USA) 1999, Nemocnice na kraji mesta po dvaceti letech (TV series) 2003. *Plays include:* Macbeth, Herodes, Henry IV, Borkman. *Television includes:* Nemocnice na okraji mesta (series). *Leisure interests:* literature, poetry, gardening. *Address:* c/o Slovenské národné divadlo—SND, Gorkého 4, 81586 Bratislava, Slovakia (office).

CHUDINOV, Igor Vitalyevich; Kyrgyzstani politician; *Prime Minister;* b. 21 Aug. 1961; ed Kyrgyz State Univ., Int. Business School, Moscow, Russia; held high-ranking positions in Komsomol; early career as computer programmer; worked in a variety of positions as business exec. 1991–2005; Dir-Gen. Kyrgyzgaz (state co. that procures gas supplies for Kyrgyzstan) 2005–07; Minister of Industry, Energy and Fuel Resources Feb.–Dec. 2007; Prime Minister Dec. 2007–; mem. Ak Zhol party. *Address:* Office of the Prime Minister, 720003 Bishkek, Dom Pravitelstvo, Kyrgyzstan (office). *Telephone:* (312) 66-12-20 (office). *Fax:* (312) 66-66-58 (office). *E-mail:* pmoffice@mail.gov .kg (office). *Website:* www.government.gov.kg (office).

CHUI, Benjamin W., PhD; American electrical engineer; *Consulting Associate, Alissa M. Fitzgerald & Associates;* ed Stanford Univ.; has extensive experience in micro-device design and prototyping; has worked for Lightconnect, Inc. (optical Microelectromechanical systems (MEMS) startup co.); fmr Researcher, IBM Almaden Research Center, San Jose, Calif.; fmr Researcher, Inst. of Microtechnology, Neuchatel, Switzerland; Consulting Assoc., Alissa M. Fitzgerald & Assocs tech. consulting 2005–; World Tech. Award in Materials, The World Tech. Network (co-recipient) 2005. *Achievements include:* part of team that made first demonstrations of magnetic resonance force microscopy (MRFM) 1992, work reached key milestone with manipulation and detection of individual electron spin 2004, designed and fabricated micro-cantilevers used to measure single electron spins. *Publications:* one book and numerous papers on MEMS-related subjects. *Address:* A.M. Fitzgerald & Assocs, LLC, 655 Skyway Road, Suite 118, San Carlos, CA 94070, USA (office). *Telephone:* (650) 592-6100 (office). *Fax:* (650) 592-6111 (office). *E-mail:* info@amfitzgerald.com (office). *Website:* www.amfitzgerald .com (office).

CHUKHRAI, Pavel Grigoryevich; Russian film director and screenwriter; b. 14 Oct. 1946, Bykovo, Moscow; s. of the late Grigoriy Chukhrai; m. Maria Zvereva; two d.; ed All-Union State Inst. of Cinematography; actor, cameraman, scriptwriter; mem. Union of Cinematographers, European Acad. of Cinema and TV; Lenin's Komsomol Prize 1981, All-Union Film Festival Prize 1981, four Kinoshock Festival prizes, six Russian Acad. prizes, four Golden Oven Festival prizes, Grand Prix Prague Film Festival, Jury Prize, Int. Film Festival, Japan. *Films include:* Lyudi v okeane (also writer) 1980, Kto zaplatit za udachu? (writer) 1980, Kletka dlya kanareek (also writer) 1983, Zina-Zinulya 1986, Vor (also writer) 1997, Klassik (writer) 1998, Voditel dlya Very (also writer) 2004. *Address:* Bolshaya Pirogovskaya str. 53/55, apt. 177, Moscow, Russia (home). *Telephone:* (495) 246-98-61 (home). *Fax:* (495) 246-98-61 (home). *E-mail:* pavel@girmet.ru (home).

CHULANONT, Gen. Surayud; Thai army officer and politician; b. 28 Aug. 1943, Phetchaburi province; s. of Lt Col Payom Chulanont; m. Khunying Chitravadee Chulanont; ed Chulachomklao Mil. Acad., Jt Staff Coll., USA, Jt Staff Coll., Thailand; started career as Jr Lt, Royal Thai Army 1965, served in infantry, artillery and counter-insurgency units; Instructor, Special Warfare School 1974–76; Aide to C-in-C 1976; Commdr Gen., Special Warfare Command 1992–94, Second Army Area 1994–97, C-in-C 1998–2002, Supreme Commdr 2002–03; PC 2003–; Interim Prime Minister 2006–08, also Minister of the Interior 2007–08; mem. Exec. Cttee Anandamahidol Foundation 2003–; Kt Order of the Crown of Thailand 1992, Kt Order of the White Elephant 1995, Kt Grand Commdr Order of Chula Chom Kloa 2001; Freeman Safeguarding Medal 1974, Rama Medal of the Hon. Order of Rama 1990. *Address:* c/o Government House, Thanon Nakornpratom Dusit, 10300 Bangkok, Thailand (office).

CHUMA, Kouki; Japanese politician; b. 8 Oct. 1936; ed Univ. of Tokyo; with Sumitomo Heavy Industries Ltd 1961; with Research Bureau, Econ. Planning Agency –1969; mem. House of Reps (Osaka 1st Dist) 1976–, Chair. House of Reps Standing Cttee on Science and Tech. 1991, on Local Admin Div. 1993, Special Cttee on Election Laws 1996, Standing Cttee on Foreign Affairs 1997, Special Cttee on Political Ethics and Election Laws 2001, Dir Special Cttee on

Decentralization of Govt 1993; Chair. Policy Bd, New Liberal Club 1981; State Sec. for Environment 1984; Parl. Vice-Minister for Home Affairs 1990; Dir Local Admin Div., Liberal Democratic Party (LDP) 1991, Acting Head, Nat. Campaign HQ, LDP 1993, Deputy Chair. Policy Research Council, LDP (Local Admin and Transport) 1995, Chief Deputy Sec.-Gen. LDP 2000, Chair. Research Comm. on Local Govt Admin, LDP 2001, 2003, mem. Gen. Council LDP 2002, Deputy Chair. Gen. Council 2004; Chair. Special Cttee to Promote the Devt of Osaka Bay Area 1996; Sr State Sec. for Transport 1999–02; Sr Vice-Minister of Land, Infrastructure and Transport 2002–05; mem. Research Comm. on Local Admin Systems 2004; Minister of State for Admin. Reform, Regulatory Reform, Special Zones for Structural Reform, and Regional Revitalization 2005–06. *Address:* c/o Liberal-Democratic Party—LDP (Jiyu-Minshuto), 1-11-23, Nagata-cho, Chiyoda-ku, Tokyo 100-8910, Japan. *Telephone:* (3) 3581-6211. *E-mail:* koho@ldp.jimin.or.jp. *Website:* www.jimin.jp; www.chuma-koki.jp.

CHUN, Jung-bae, LLM; South Korean lawyer and politician; b. 12 Dec. 1954; ed Seoul Nat. Univ.; founding-mem. Minbyun (Lawyers for a Democratic Soc.) 1988, Co-ordinator, Chair. Int. Human Rights Cttee; elected mem. Nat. Ass. 1996, 2000, 2004, Chair. House Steering Cttee 2004, mem. Commerce, Industry and Energy Cttee 2005; Chief Sec. to Pres. Nat. Congress for New Politics (NCNP) 1998; Vice-Chair. Policy Cttee, Vice Floor Leader, Millennium Democratic Party 2000, Special Advisor on State Affairs to Presidential Cand. 2002, Chief Sec. Advisory Cttee on Political Reform for Presidential Cand. 2002; Chair. Nat. Security and Int. Relations Cttee, Korea-Japan Parliamentarians' Union 2003, Adviser 2005; Chair. Special Cttee on Political Reform, Uri Party 2003, Chair. Gen. Election Planning Cttee, Clean Election Campaign Cttee 2004, Floor Leader 2004; Minister of Justice 2005–06 (resgnd); mem. UNDP (renamed Democratic Party) 2007–; Pres. Korea–UK Parliamentarians' Friendship Asscn 2005; Baek-Bong Memorial Foundation Clean & Gentle Politician Award 1999, Asscn of Korean Journalists Politician of the Year Award 2001. *Address:* c/o Democratic Party, 15–16 Yeouido-dong, Yeongdeungpo-gu, Seoul 150-701, Republic of Korea. *E-mail:* help@undp.kr. *Website:* minjoo.kr.

CHUNG, Dong-soo, BA, MA; South Korean academic and banking executive; b. 24 Sept. 1945; ed Seoul Nat. Univ., Univ. of Wisconsin, USA; fmr Asst Minister, Planning and Man. Office, Ministry of Planning and Budget; Deputy Minister, Ministry of Environment 2001–02; mem. Bd of Dirs Kookmin Bank 2002–, fmr Chair.; Prof., Sangmyung Univ.; Dir Daewoo Shipbuilding and Marine Eng Co. Ltd. *Address:* c/o Board of Directors, Kookmin Bank, 9-1, 2-ga, Namdaemoon-ro, Jung-gu, Seoul 100-703, Republic of Korea (office). *Telephone:* (2) 2073-7114 (office). *Fax:* (2) 2073-8360 (office). *Website:* www.kookmin-bank.com (office).

CHUNG, Dong-young, MA; South Korean politician; b. 17 June 1953, Sunchang Co., N Jeolla Prov.; m.; two s.; ed Jeonju High School, Seoul Nat. Univ. and Cardiff Grad. School, Univ. of Wales, UK; imprisoned for involvement in Mincheong Hakryeon Case 1973; reporter, Moonhwa Broadcasting Corpn (MBC) 1978–88, Anchor, MBC Midnight News 1988–89, MBC Los Angeles Corresp., USA 1989–93, Main Anchor, 9 O'Clock News Desk, MBC 1994–96; mem. 15th Nat. Ass. 1996–2000, Cen. Party Affairs Cttee, Nat. Congress for New Politics (NCNP), 16th Nat. Ass. 2000–04, mem. Science, Tech., Information and Telecommunications Cttee; Special Asst to NCNP Pres. Kim Dae-jung and Campaign Planner; Seoul Mayor Electoral Campaign 1998; Spokesman, NCNP 1998–99; mem. and Spokesman, Millennium Democratic Party 2000; mem. Cen. Cttee Uri Party (subsequently renamed United Nat. Democratic Party—UNDP, now Democratic Party) 2003–, Chair. Uri Party 2004–06 (resgnd), UNDP cand. for Pres. of South Korea 2007; Minister of Unification 2005–06. *Address:* c/o Democratic Party, 15–16 Yeouido-dong, Yeongdeungpo-gu, Seoul 150-701, Republic of Korea. *Telephone:* (2) 784-0114. *E-mail:* help@undp.kr. *Website:* minjoo.kr.

CHUNG, Kyung-wha; South Korean violinist; b. 26 March 1948, Seoul; sister of Myung-whun Chung and Myung-wha Chung; m. Geoffrey Leggett 1984; two s.; ed Juilliard School, New York with Ivan Galamian; started career in USA; European debut 1970; has played with maj. orchestras, including all London orchestras, Chicago, Boston and Pittsburgh Symphony Orchestra, New York, Cleveland, Philadelphia, Berlin, Israel and Vienna Philharmonics, Orchestre de Paris; has toured world; recordings for EMI; played at Salzburg Festival with London Symphony Orchestra 1973, Vienna Festival 1981, 1984, Edinburgh Festival 1981 and at 80th birthday concert of Sir William Walton March 1982; with Hallé Orchestra, BBC Proms, London 1999; winner of Leventritt Competition 1968. *Recordings:* Concertos by Bartók, Beethoven, Bruch, Mendelssohn, Stravinsky, Tchaikovsky, Vieuxtemps, Walton. *Leisure interests:* arts, family. *Address:* Opus 3 Artists, 470 Park Avenue South, 9th Floor North, New York, NY 10016, USA (office). *Telephone:* (212) 584-7500 (office). *Fax:* (646) 300-8200 (office). *E-mail:* info@opus3artists.com (office). *Website:* www.opus3artists.com (office).

CHUNG, Mong-joon, MA, PhD; South Korean politician, sports administrator and business executive; *President, Korea Football Association;* b. 17 Oct. 1951, Pusan; s. of the late Chung Ju-Yung; m.; two s. two d.; ed Joongang High School, Coll. of Commerce, Seoul Nat. Univ., Mass Massachusetts Inst. of Tech. and Johns Hopkins Univ., USA; First Lt Reserve Officers Training Corps; joined Hyundai Heavy Industries 1978, Man. Dir 1980, CEO 1987, Adviser 1991–2002; Pres. Hanjin Heavy Industries & Construction Co. Ltd (HHIC) 1982–87, Chair. 1987; Chief Dir Ulsan Inst. of Tech. Foundation 1983–; elected mem. Nat. Ass. (Ind.) 1988–; f. Nat. Unity 21 party Nov. 2002; Vice-Pres. FIFA 1994–, Chair. Media Cttee 1997–; Pres. Korea Football Asscn 1993–, Co-Chair. Korean Organizing Cttee for 2002 FIFA World Cup, Korea–Japan 2002, Deputy Chair. Bureau Cttee for FIFA Youth Competitions, Organizing Cttees for FIFA U-17 World Championship, Finland 2003, FIFA World Youth Championship, UAE 2003; Chair. Modern Econ. and Social Inst. 1990; Chair Prof., Korea Univ. 1999–; mem. Bd Trustees Ulsan Univ. (Chair. 1983), Johns Hopkins Univ., Korea Univ.; Chair. Bd Asan Foundation 2001–; Hon. PhD (Myongji Univ.) 1998; Hon. LLD (Univ. of Maryland) 1999. *Publications include:* Corporate Management Ideology 1982, Relations Between the Government and the Corporate in Japan 1995. *Leisure interests:* football, tennis, golf, equestrianism, hiking. *Address:* Korea Football Association, 1-131, Shinmunro 2-Ga, Jongro-Gu, Seoul 110-062 (office); 345-1, Pyeongchang-dong, Jongno-gu, Seoul, Republic of Korea. *Telephone:* (2) 733-6764 (office); (2) 735-2755 (office). *Fax:* (2) 735-2755 (office). *Website:* www.mjchung.com (office); www.kfa.or.kr (office).

CHUNG, Mong-koo; South Korean automotive industry executive; *Chairman and Co-CEO, Hyundai Motor Company;* s. of the late Chung Ju-yung; brother of the late Chung Mong-hun; began career in family-owned business Hyundai Automotive Group 1970, various positions include Man. Hyundai Motor Co. 1983, Head of Hyundai Motor Service, Chair. Hyundai Group 1996–99, Chair. and Co-CEO Hyundai Motor Co. and Kia Motor Co. 1999–; received suspended sentence for embezzling co. funds 2007; Automotive Hall of Fame Distinguished Service Citation, Nat. Automobile Dealers Asscn 2001. *Address:* Hyundai Motor Company, 231, Yangjae-dong, Seocho-gu, Seoul 137-1115, Republic of Korea (office). *Telephone:* (82) 2-3464-1114 (office). *E-mail:* dmkim@hyundai-motor.com (office). *Website:* www.hyundai-motor.com (office).

CHUNG, Moon Soul, BA; South Korean business executive; b. 7 March 1938, Chonbuk Imsil; ed Iksan Men's High School, Won Kwang Univ.; Sr Man. Planning and Coordinating Div., Korea Cen. Intelligence Agency 1962–80; Founder, Chair. and CEO Mirae Corpn 1983–2001, Consultant 2001–, Founder and CEO Lycos Korea 1999–2001; apptd Dir (non-exec.) Kookmin Bank 2001, Chair. 2004; Dir (non-exec.) Dongwon Securities; Dr hc (Korea Advanced Inst. of Science and Tech.) 2009. *Address:* Mirae Corporation, 9-2 Cha-Am-dong, Chonan, Chungcheongnam 330-200, Republic of Korea. *Telephone:* (41) 621-5070 (office). *Fax:* (41) 621-5090. *Website:* www.mirae.co.kr.

CHUNG, Myung-whun; South Korean conductor and pianist; *Music Director, Seoul Philharmonic Orchestra;* b. 22 Jan. 1953, Seoul; brother of Kyung-wha Chung and Myung-wha Chung; ed Mannes Coll. of Music and Juilliard School, New York, USA; asst to Carlo Maria Giulini as Assoc. Conductor, Los Angeles Philharmonic 1978–81; moved to Europe 1981, conducting Berlin Philharmonic, Munich Philharmonic, Amsterdam Concertgebouw, Orchestre de Paris, major London orchestras; Music Dir and Prin. Conductor, Radio Orchestra of Saarbrücken 1984–89; in USA has conducted the New York Philharmonic, Nat. Symphony, Washington, DC, Boston Symphony, Cleveland and Chicago Orchestras, Metropolitan Opera, San Francisco Opera 1986–; Guest Conductor, Teatro Comunale, Florence 1987; Musical Dir Opéra de la Bastille, Paris 1989–94; Covent Garden debut, conducting Otello 1997; Music Dir and Prin. Conductor, Orchestra of the Nat. Acad. of Santa Cecilia, Rome 1997–2005; conducted Swedish Radio Symphony Orchestra at London Proms, playing Beethoven's Fourth Piano Concerto and Nielsen's Fifth 1999; Music Dir Asia Philharmonic Orchestra 1997–; Music Dir Radio France Philharmonic Orchestra 2000–; Special Artistic Adviser, Tokyo Philharmonic Orchestra 2001–; Music Dir Seoul Philharmonic Orchestra 2005–; Legion d'Honneur 1992; Second Prize Tchaikovsky Competition, Moscow 1974, Abbiati Prize (Italian critics) 1988, Arturo Toscanini Prize 1989, Victoires de la Musique Best Conductor, Best Lyrical Production, Best French Classical Recording 1995, Record Acad. Prize (Japan), Kumkwan (South Korea). *Address:* Askonas Holt Ltd, Lincoln House, 300 High Holborn, London, WC1V 7JH, England (office). *Telephone:* (20) 7400-1700 (office). *Fax:* (20) 7400-1799 (office). *E-mail:* info@askonasholt.co.uk (office). *Website:* www.askonasholt.co.uk (office); www.seoulphil.co.kr (office).

CHUNG, Shui-ming, BSc, MBA; Hong Kong business executive and fmr government official; *CEO, Shimao Property Holdings Ltd;* b. 23 Nov. 1951, Hong Kong; two c.; ed Univ. of Hong Kong, Chinese Univ. of Hong Kong; fmr Hong Kong Affairs Adviser to Chinese Govt; fmr mem. Exec. Council, Hong Kong Special Admin. Region, Hong Kong Housing Soc. Exec. Cttee, now Chair., fmr mem. Housing Authority Finance Cttee; fmr Chief Exec. Hong Kong Special Admin. Region Land Fund; Exec. Dir and CEO Shimao Property Holdings Ltd 2004–; mem. Bd of Dirs Hantec Investment Holdings Ltd 2004–06, Man. Dir, Exec. Dir and Deputy Chair. 2006–; mem. Nat. Cttee of the Tenth CPPCC; Deputy Chair. Council of City Univ. of Hong Kong; mem. Hong Kong Housing Authority; Court mem. Univ. of Hong Kong; Fellow, Hong Kong Inst. of CPAs, Asscn of Chartered Certified Accountants, Hong Kong Soc. of Accountants; fmr Chinese mem. Sino-British Land Comm. *Address:* Shimao Property Holdings Ltd, 36-28F One Lujiazui, 68 Yin Cheng Road Central, Shanghai 200120, People's Republic of China (office). *Telephone:* (21) 86213861 (office). *Website:* www.shimaogroup.com (office).

CHUNG, Hon. Sir Sze-yuen, Kt, OBE, CBE, GBE, GBM, DEng, PhD, DSc, FREng, FIET, CBIM, JP; Chinese/British business executive; *Chairman, Kowloon Motor Bus 1933 Ltd;* b. 3 Nov. 1917, Hong Kong; m. Nancy Cheung 1942 (died 1977); one s. two d.; ed Hong Kong and Sheffield Univs; consulting engineer 1952–56; Gen. Man. Sonca Industries 1956–50, Man. Dir 1960–77, Chair. 1977–88; mem. Hong Kong Legis. Council 1965–74, Sr Unofficial Mem. 1974–78; mem. Hong Kong Exec. Council 1972–80, Sr Unofficial Mem. 1980–88; Chair. Fed. of Hong Kong Industries 1966–70; Chair. Hong Kong Productivity Council 1974–76; Founding Chair. Hong Kong Polytechnic 1972–86, City Polytechnic of Hong Kong 1984–85, Hong Kong Univ. of Science and Tech. 1987–99, Hong Kong Hosp. Authority 1990–95; Adviser to the Govt of People's Repub. of China on Hong Kong Affairs 1992–97; Founder and Pres. Hong Kong Acad. of Eng Sciences 1994–97; mem. Chinese Govt's Preparatory Cttee for establishment of Hong Kong Special Admin. Region (HKSAR) 1996–97; Convenor

HKSAR Exec. Council 1997–99; Chair. Kowloon Motor Bus 1933 Ltd 1999–; Chair. Transport Int. Holdings Ltd 2006–; Dir CLP Holdings Ltd 1967–; Hon. FIMechE 1983; Order of the Sacred Treasure (Japan) 1984; Hon. DSc (Hong Kong) 1976; Whitworth Prize, IMechE (London) 1952, Silver Jubilee Medal 1977, Gold Medal, Asian Productivity Org. 1980, and other awards and distinctions. *Publications:* Hong Kong's Journey to Reunification – Memoirs of Sze-yuen Chung; articles in professional journals. *Leisure interest:* swimming. *Address:* 128 Argyle Street, 10/F, Kowloon, Hong Kong Special Administrative Region (office); House 25, Bella Vista, Silver Terrace Road, Clear Water Bay, Kowloon, Hong Kong Special Administrative Region, People's Republic of China (home). *Telephone:* 27610281 (office). *Fax:* 27607493 (office). *Website:* www.kmb.com.hk/english.php (office).

CHUNG, Won-shik; South Korean fmr politician; *President, Paradise Welfare Foundation;* fmr Minister of Educ.; Prime Minister of South Korea 1991–92; Pres. Paradise Welfare Foundation (charity associated with Paradise Group); Adviser, Korea Support Cttee for Int. Vaccine Inst.; mem. Democratic Liberal Party. *Address:* Paradise Welfare Foundation, 186-39, Jangchoong Bldg., Jangchoong-dong 2ga, Joong-gu, Seoul 100-855, Republic of Korea (office). *Telephone:* (2) 2277-3296 (office). *Fax:* (2) 2277-3124 (office). *Website:* www.paradise.or.kr (office).

CHURCHILL, Caryl, BA; British playwright; b. 3 Sept. 1938, London; d. of Robert Churchill and Jan Churchill (née Brown); m. David Harter 1961; three s.; ed Trafalgar School, Montréal, Canada, Lady Margaret Hall, Oxford; first play, Downstairs, performed at Nat. Union of Students Drama Festival 1958; writes mainly for theatre but has also written numerous radio plays and several TV plays. *Stage plays include:* Having a Wonderful Time (Oxford Players, 1960), Owners (Royal Court, London) 1972, Objections to Sex and Violence (Royal Court) 1975, Vinegar Tom (Monstrous Regiment toured 1976), Light Shining in Buckinghamshire (performed by Joint Stock Co., Edinburgh Festival 1976, then Royal Court), Traps (Royal Court) 1977, Cloud Nine (Joint Stock Co., Royal Court) 1979, 1980, Lucille Lortel Theater, New York 1981–83, Top Girls (Royal Court) 1982, 1983, Public Theater, New York 1983, Fen (Joint Stock Co., Almeida Theatre, London 1983, Royal Court 1983, Public Theater, New York 1983), Softcops (RSC 1984), A Mouthful of Birds (Joint Stock, Royal Court and tour 1986), Serious Money (Royal Court 1987, Wyndham Theatre 1987, Public Theater New York 1988), Icecream (Royal Court 1989, Public Theater New York 1990), Mad Forest (Cen. School of Drama, Nat. Theatre Bucharest, Royal Court 1990), Lives of the Great Poisoners (Second Stride Co. Riverside Studios, London and tour 1991), The Skriker (Nat. Theatre 1994), Thyestes (by Seneca, translation; Royal Court Theatre Upstairs 1994); Hotel (Second Stride Co., The Place) 1997, This Is A Chair (Royal Court) 1997, Blue Heart (Out of Joint, Royal Court) 1997, Far Away (Royal Court) 2000, (Albery) 2001, A Number (Royal Court) 2002, Drunk Enough to Say I Love You? (Royal Court) 2006, Seven Jewish Children (Royal Court) 2009. *Radio:* The Ants, Not . . Not . . not . . not enough Oxygen, Abortive, Schreiber's Nervous Illness, Identical Twins, Perfect Happiness, Henry's Past. *Television:* The Judge's Wife, The After Dinner Joke, The Legion Hall Bombing, Fugue (jtly). *Publications:* Owners 1973, Light Shining 1976, Traps 1977, Vinegar Tom 1978, Cloud Nine 1979, Top Girls 1982, Fen 1983, Fen and Softcops 1984, A Mouthful of Birds 1986, Serious Money 1987, Plays I 1985, Plays II 1988, Objections to Sex and Violence in Plays by Women Vol. 4 1985, Ice Cream 1989, Mad Forest 1990, Lives of the Great Poisoners 1992, The Striker 1994, Thyestes 1994, Blue Heart 1997, This is a Chair 1999, Far Away 2000, A Number 2002, Drunk Enough to Say I Love You? 2006; anthologies. *Address:* c/o Casarotto Ramsay Ltd, National House, 60–66 Wardour Street, London, W1V 3HP, England. *Telephone:* (20) 7287-4450. *Fax:* (20) 7734-9293.

CHURIKOVA, Inna Mikhailovna; Russian actress and screenwriter; b. 5 Oct. 1945, Belibey, Bashkiria; d. of Mikhail Churikov and Yelizaveta Mantrova; m. Gleb Panfilov 1974; one s.; ed Shchepkin Theatre School; with Moscow Youth Theatre 1965–68; with Lenin Komsomol Theatre (now Lenkom), Moscow 1973–; debut in films 1955; Lenin Komsomol Prize 1976, RSFSR State Prize 1985, USSR People's Artist 1985, Nika Prize 1993, Triumph Prize 1994, Kinotaur Festival Prize 1994, Kamaz Festival First Prize 1994, Russian Fed. State Prize 1997, Cristal Turandot Drama Asscn Award (twice), Treumf Award, several Nika and Golden Eagle (Russian Film Acad.) awards, numerous state awards. *Plays:* The Gambler (Stanislavsky Award) 1996, The Sheep 1997, Old Women 1999, City of Millionaires 2000, Mixed Feelings 2005, Tout Payee 2005. *Roles in:* No Ford Through Fire (Panfilov) 1968, The Beginning 1970, May I Speak? 1976, Valentina 1981, Vassa 1983, War-Novel (Berlin Film Festival Prize) 1984, Three Girls in Blue (theatre) 1985, The Theme 1986, Mother 1991, Adam's Rib (Critics' Prize) 1991, Sorry (theatre) 1992, Casanova's Mantle 1992, The Seagull (theatre) 1994, The Year of the Dog 1994, Father Frost 2001, and many others. *Films include:* Mat 1955, Tuchi nad Borskom 1960, Ya shagayu po Moskve 1963, Morozko 1964, Gde ty teper, Maksim? 1964, Tridtsat tri (Nenauchnaya fantastika) 1965, Stryapukha 1965, Starshaya sestra 1966, Neulovimyye mstiteli 1966, Vogne broda net 1967, Nachalo 1970, Proshu slova 1975, Tema 1979, Valentina 1981, Voenno-polevoy roman 1983, Kurer 1987, Mat 1989, Gamlet 1989, Rebro Adama 1990, Plashch Kazanovy 1993, God sobaki 1993, Kurochka Ryaba 1994, Shirli-Myrli 1995, Blagoslovite zhenshchinu 2003, Casus belli 2003. *Television includes:* Tot samyy Myunkhgauzen 1979, Myortvye dushi (mini series) 1984, Idiot 2003, Moskovskaya saga (series) 2004, Vintovaya lestnitsa 2005, In the First Circle (miniseries) 2006, Carnival Night (part two) 2006. *Recording:* Zemfira featuring Inna Churikova (single). *Address:* Lenkom Theatre, 127006 Moscow, Malaya Dmitrovka 6, Russia (office). *Telephone:* (495) 699-19-92 (office); (495) 130-95-54 (home). *E-mail:* varadero@mail.ru (home); nimfa@lenkom.ru (office). *Website:* www.lenkom.ru (office); www.churikova.com.

CHURKIN, Vitaly Ivanovich, PhD; Russian diplomatist; *Permanent Representative, United Nations;* b. 21 Feb. 1952; m.; one s. one d.; ed Moscow State Inst. of Int. Relations; attaché, Translations Dept, Ministry of Foreign Affairs, interpreter for USSR del. to SALT II negotiations 1974–79; Third Sec., USA Dept of Ministry of Foreign Affairs 1979–82; Second Sec. then First Sec., USSR Embassy in Washington, DC 1982–87; expert, Int. Dept of Cen. Cttee CPSU 1987–89; Counsellor, Ministry of Foreign Affairs 1989–90, Dir Information and Press Dept 1990–92; attained rank of Amb. Extraordinary and Plenipotentiary 1990; Deputy Minister of Foreign Affairs of Russia 1992–94; Amb. to Belgium 1994–97, to Canada 1998–2003; on staff, Ministry of Foreign Affairs 2003–, Chair. Sr Arctic Officials Cttee 2004–06; Perm. Rep. to UN, New York 2006–. *Leisure interest:* tennis. *Address:* Office of the Permanent Representative of the Russian Federation to the United Nations, 136 East 67th Street, New York, NY 10065, USA (office). *Telephone:* (212) 861-4900 (office). *Fax:* (212) 628-0252 (office). *E-mail:* rusun@un.int (office). *Website:* www.un.int/russia (office).

CHUROV, Vladimir Yevgenyevich; Russian politician; *Chairman, Central Electoral Commission;* b. 17 March 1953; ed Physics Dept, Leningrad State Univ.; worked for Cttee of Int. Relations of City of St Petersburg 1992–2003, Vice Chair. 1995–2003; Deputy in State Duma 2003–07, Deputy Chair. of the Cttee on CIS and Russian Diaspora; Chair. Cen. Electoral Comm. 2007–; Prof. of Econs, Humanitarian Univ. of Trade Unions, St Petersburg; mem. Liberal Democratic Party of Russia (Liberalno-demokraticheskaya partiya Rossii); Order of Friendship 2004. *Publications include:* several books on mil., including the history of the imperial army and White Movement, also popular maritime novels for children. *Address:* Central Election Commission, 109012 Moscow, Bolshoi Cherkassky per. 9, Russia (office). *Telephone:* (495) 206-86-51 (office). *Fax:* (495) 956-39-30 (office). *E-mail:* intdiv@A5.kiam.ru (office).

CHUTE, Robert Maurice, ScD; American poet, biologist and academic (retd); *Professor Emeritus of Biology, Bates College;* b. 13 Feb. 1926, Bridgton, Me; s. of James Cleveland and Elizabeth Davis Chute; m. Virginia Hinds 1946; one s. one d.; ed Fryeburg Acad., Univ. of Maine, Johns Hopkins Univ. School of Hygiene and Public Health; Instructor and Asst Prof., Middlebury Coll. 1953–59; Asst Prof. Northridge State Coll. 1959–61; Assoc. Prof. and Chair. of Biology, Lincoln Univ. 1961; Prof. and Chair. of Biology, then Dana Prof. of Biology, Bates Coll. 1962–93, Prof. Emer. 1993–; Fellow, AAAS; Me Arts and Humanities Award 1978, Chad Walsh Award (Beloit Poetry Journal) 1997, Maine Writers and Publrs Alliance Poetry Competition 2001. *Publications:* Environmental Insight 1971, Introduction to Biology 1976, Sweeping the Sky: Soviet Women Flyers in Combat 1999; poetry: Quiet Thunder 1975, Uncle George 1977, Voices Great and Small 1977, Thirteen Moons/Treize Lunes 1982, Samuel Sewell Sails for Home 1986, When Grandmother Decides to Die 1989, Woodshed on the Moon: Thoreau Poems, Barely Time to Study Jesus 1996, Androscoggin Too 1997, Sweeping the Sky 1999, Bent Offerings 2003; trans.: Thirteen Moons into Micmac Maliseet (native American) 2002; contribs to Kansas Quarterly, Beloit Poetry Review, Bitterroot, South Florida Poetry Review, North Dakota Review, Cape Rock, Fiddlehead, Greenfield Review, Literary Review. *Leisure interests:* walking, reading, films, Thoreau studies. *Address:* 85 Echo Cove Lane, Poland Spring, ME 04274, USA. *Telephone:* (207) 998-4338.

CHYLEK, Petr, PhD; American(b. Czech) atmospheric scientist and academic; *Technical Staff Member, Space and Remote Sensing Sciences, Los Alamos National Laboratory;* ed Charles Univ., Prague, Czech Repub., Univ. of California, Riverside; Research Assoc., Dept of Physics, Indiana Univ., Bloomington 1970–72; Post-doctoral Fellow, Advanced Study Program, Nat. Center for Atmospheric Research, Boulder, Colo 1972–73; Asst Prof., Dept of Atmospheric Science, State Univ. of NY, Albany 1973–75, Research Prof. 1978–86; Assoc. Prof., Dept of Geosciences, Purdue Univ., West Lafayette, Ind. 1975–78; Prof., School of Meteorology, Univ. of Oklahoma, Norman 1986–90; Founder and Co-ordinator Atmospheric Science Program, Dalhousie Univ., Halifax, NS, Canada, Prof. of Physics and Atmospheric Science –2001, Sr Chair in Climate Research 1990–2001, Adjunct Prof. of Physics and Atmospheric Science 2001–; Adjunct Prof. of Physics, New Mexico State Univ., Las Cruces 1990–; Tech. Staff Mem. Space and Remote Sensing Sciences, Los Alamos Nat. Lab., Santa Fe, NM 2001–; Visiting Scientist, Instituto di Fisica de la Atmosfera, Frascati, Italy March–May 1966; Visiting Scientist, Air Resources Laboratory, Nat. Oceanic and Atmospheric Admin, Boulder, Colo 2000–01; Chair. Scientific Program Cttee, Second Int. Conf. on Global Warming and the Next Ice Age, Los Alamos Nat. Lab. 2006; mem. American Meteorological Soc., American Geophysical Union 2006; Fellow, Optical Soc. of America 1991, Los Alamos Nat. Lab. 2006; Hon. Fellow, Center for Earth and Planetary Physics, Harvard Univ. 1976–78; Univ. of California Grad. Fellowship 1968–70, Advanced Study Program Post-doctoral Fellowship, Nat. Center for Atmospheric Research 1972–73, Nat. Research Council Sr Fellowship, White Sands Missile Range 1984–85, paper by Chylek, Kiehl & Ko (1978) reprinted in SPIE Milestone Series as one of milestone papers in field of Light Scattering 1988, Sr Research Chair in Climate Research, Natural Sciences and Eng Research Council of Canada 1990–2000, Distinguished Faculty Summer Fellowship, Naval Research Lab. April–June 1992, paper by Chylek and Srivastava (1983) reprinted in SPIE Milestone Series as one of milestone papers in field of linear optical composite materials 1996, paper by Chylek and Borel (2004) selected by American Geophysical Union Eds as a Journal Highlight 2004, Los Alamos Nat. Lab. Award for Scientific and Tech. Leadership 2004. *Publications:* more than 100 scientific papers in professional journals on remote sensing, atmospheric radiation, climate change, cloud and aerosol physics, applied laser physics and ice-core analysis. *Address:* Space and Remote Sensing Sciences (ISR-2), PO Box 1664, MS B241, Los Alamos, NM 87545, USA (office). *Telephone:* (505) 667-2965 (office). *Fax:* (505) 665-

3169 (office). *E-mail:* krodriguez@lanl.gov (office). *Website:* www.lanl.gov/orgs/isr/isr2 (office).

CHYNOWETH, Alan Gerald, BSc, PhD, FIEEE, FInstP; British physicist; b. 18 Nov. 1927, Harrow, Middx; s. of James Charles Chynoweth and Marjorie Fairhurst; m. Betty Freda Edith Boyce 1950; two s.; ed King's College, Univ. of London; Postdoctoral Fellow, Nat. Research Council of Canada, Chem. Div., Ottawa 1950–52; mem. Tech. Staff, Bell Telephone Labs 1953–60, Head of Crystal Electronics Dept 1960–65, Asst Dir Metallurgical Research Lab. 1965–73, Dir Materials Research Lab. 1973–76, Exec. Dir Electronic and Photonic Devices Div. 1976–83, Vice-Pres. Applied Research, Bell Communications Research 1983–92; currently Sr Assoc. Fusfeld Group, Inc.(consulting firm); Survey Dir of NAS Cttee on Survey of Materials Science and Eng 1971–73, Comm. on Mineral Resources and the Environment 1973–75; mem. Nat. Materials Advisory Bd 1975–79, NATO Special Programme Panel on Materials 1977–82, consultant to NATO Advanced Study Inst. Panel 1982–89; mem. Materials Research Soc., Metallurgical Soc.; Alt. Dir Microelectronics and Computer Tech. Corpn 1985–92; Dir Industrial Research Inst. 1990–92; Chair. Tech. Transfer Merit Program, NJ Comm. on Science and Tech. 1992–; consultant to EC Telecommunications Directorate 1995; Lecturer, Electrochemical Soc. 1983; Co.-Ed. Optical Fiber Telecommunications 1979; Assoc. Ed. Solid State Comm. 1975–83; mem. Visiting Cttee, Cornell Univ. Materials Science Centre 1973–76, Natural Sciences Advisory Bd, Univ. of Pennsylvania 1988–92, Advisory Bd Dept of Electrical Eng and Computer Science, Univ. of California, Berkeley 1987–, Advisory Bd, Dept of Electrical Eng, Univ. of Southern California 1988–; mem. Office of Science and Tech. Policy Panel on High Performance Computing and Communications; mem. Frederik Philips Award Cttee 1998–, Corp. Achievement Award Cttee 1999–; Fellow, IEEE, American Physical Soc., Int. Eng Consortium, Inst. of Physics, London; IEEE W. R. G. Baker Prize 1967, IEEE Frederik Philips Award 1992, American Physical Soc. George E. Pake Prize 1992, IEEE Eng Leadership Recognition 1996. *Publications:* Optical Fiber Telecommunications (with Stewart E. Miller) 1979; over 60 papers in professional journals on solid state physics, 11 patents on solid state devices, NAS reports: Materials and Man's Needs, Materials Conservation through Technology, Resource Recovery from Municipal Solid Wastes. *Leisure interests:* travel, boating. *Address:* 6 Londonderry Way, Summit, NJ 07901 (home); The Fusfeld Group, Inc., 15 Laverdure Circle, Framingham, MA 01701, USA. *Telephone:* (908) 273-4581 (home). *E-mail:* algchy@aol.com.

CIAMPI, Carlo Azeglio, LLB; Italian economist, politician, fmr central banker and fmr head of state; *Senator for Life;* b. 9 Dec. 1920, Livorno; s. of Pietro Ciampi and Marie Masino; m. Franca Pilla 1946; one s. one d.; ed Scuola Normale Superiore di Pisa, Pisa Univ.; served in Italian Army 1941–44; with Banca d'Italia 1946, economist, Research Dept 1960–70, Head of Research Dept 1970–73, Sec.-Gen. 1973–76, Deputy Dir-Gen. 1976–78, Dir-Gen. 1978–79, Gov. 1979–93; Chair. Ufficio Italiano dei Cambi, 1979–83 (Hon. Gov. 1994–); Prime Minister 1993–94; Minister of the Treasury and the Budget 1996–98; Pres. of Italy 1999–2006 (retd), Pres. Emer. 2006–; Senator for Life 2006–; Chair. IMF Interim Cttee 1998–99; fmr mem. Bd of Govs for Italy IBRD, IDA, IFC; fmr mem. Cttee of Govs EEC; fmr mem. Bd of Dirs Consiglio Nazionale delle Ricerche, BIS; mem. Istituto Adriano Olivetti di Studi per la Gestione dell'Economia e delle Aziende; Mil. Cross, Grand Officer, Order of Merit of the Italian Repub. Dr hc (École Normale Supérieure) 2005; Charlemagne Award, Aachen 2005. *Publications:* Un metodo per Governare 1996. *Address:* Senate (Senato), Piazza Madama, 00186 Rome, Italy (office). *Telephone:* (06) 67061 (office). *E-mail:* ciampi_ca@posta.senato.it (office). *Website:* www.senato.it (office).

CIAVATTA, Valeria; San Marino government official; *Secretary of State for Internal Affairs, Civil Protection and Implementation of the Government Programme;* b. 1959; m. Giovanni Pacelli; two c.; ed Univ. of Urbino; Co-Capt.-Regent of San Marino 2003–04; currently Secretary of State for Internal Affairs, Civil Protection and Implementation of the Govt Programme; mem. Popular Alliance of Democrats (Alleanza Popolare dei Democratici Sammarinese). *Address:* Secretariat of State for Internal Affairs, Civil Protection and Implementation of the Government Programme, Parva Domus, Piazza della Libertà, 47890 (office); Alleanza Popolare dei Democratici Sammarinese (APDS), Via Luigi Cibrario 25, 47893 Cailungo, San Marino (office). *Telephone:* 0549 882425 (office); 0549 907080 (office). *Fax:* 0549 885080 (office); 0549 907082 (office).

ÇIÇEK, Cemil; Turkish politician; *Deputy Prime Minister;* b. 1946, Yozgat; m.; three c.; ed Faculty of Law, Istanbul Univ.; fmr Mayor of Yozgat; co-f. Motherland Party (now ANAVATAN); fmr State Minister; Minister of Justice –2007; Deputy Prime Minister 2007–. *Address:* Office of the Deputy Prime Minister, Başbakan yard. ve Devlet Bakanı, Bakanlıklar, Ankara, Turkey (office). *Telephone:* (312) 4191621 (office). *Fax:* (312) 4191547 (office).

CICERONE, Ralph J., MS, PhD; American academic, university administrator and chemist; *President, National Academy of Sciences;* b. Pennsylvania; m. Prof. Carol Cicerone; one d.; ed Massachusetts Inst. of Tech. and Univ. of Illinois; Research Scientist and Lecturer, Dept of Electrical Eng, later Asst Prof., Dept of Electrical and Computer Eng, Univ. of Michigan 1971–78; Research Chemist, Scripps Inst. of Oceanography, Univ. of California, San Diego 1978–80; Sr Scientist and Dir Atmospheric Chem. Div., Nat. Center for Atmospheric Research, Boulder, Colo 1980–89; Daniel G. Aldrich, Jr Chair in Earth System Science, Univ. of California, Irvine 1989–2005, Chair. Dept of Earth System Science 1989–94, Prof. of Chem. 1990–2005, Dean of Physical Sciences 1994–98, Chancellor Univ. of California, Irvine 1998–2005; mem. NAS 1990– (served on Council 1996–99 and on Bd on Sustainable Devt), Chair. Climate Change Science: An Analysis of Some Key Questions study 2001, mem. Cttee on Women in Science and Eng, Advisory Bd Koshland Science Museum, Advisory Cttee Div. of Earth and Life Sciences, Pres. NAS 2005–; fmr Pres. American Geophysical Union; mem. ACS 1974, American Acad. of Arts and Sciences, American Philosophical Soc.; expert on chem. of ozone layer and radiative forcing of climate change; James B. Macelwane Award, American Geophysical Union 1979, UNEP Ozone Award 1997, Bower Award and Prize for Achievement in Science, Franklin Inst. 1999, Roger Revelle Medal, American Geophysical Union 2002, Albert Einstein World Award of Science 2004. *Publications:* more than 100 articles in scientific journals and 200 conf. papers. *Address:* Office of the President, National Academy of Sciences, 500 Fifth Street, NW, Washington, DC 20001, USA (office). *Website:* www.nationalacademies.org/president (office).

CICHY, Leszek; Polish bank executive and mountaineer; b. 14 Nov. 1951, Pruszków; m. Maria Gierałtowska; two s.; ed Warsaw Univ. of Tech.; researcher, Geodesic Dept, Warsaw Univ. of Tech. 1977–90; engineer in Syria 1990–92; mem. of staff, Housing Investments, Warsaw 1992–93, Polski Bank Rozwoju 1993–98; Vice-Chair. Dom Inwestycyjny BRE Banku, Warsaw 1998–99, Bank Współpracy Europejskiej, Warsaw 1999–2000; Dir Kredyt Bank, Warsaw 2000–01; Vice-Chair. and Finance Dir, Capital Group ERGIS 2001–; mem. Polish Alpine Club, Pres. 1995–2000; mountaineering expeditions include Tatra, Alps, Andes, Caucasus, Karakoram and Himalayas; first person to climb Mount Everest in the winter (with partner Krzysztof Wielicki q.v.) 1980; first Pole to climb the Crown of the Earth (highest peaks on every continent) 1980–99. *Publication:* Discussing Everest (co-author) 1982. *Leisure interests:* tennis, skiing, astronomy. *Address:* ul. Na Uboczu 16/49, 02-791 Warsaw, Poland (home).

CICO, Carla, MSc (Econs), MBA; Italian telecommunications industry executive; *CEO, Ambrosetti China;* b. 21 Feb. 1961, Verona; d. of Lorenzo Cico and Francesca Provera; ed Normal Superior Univ., Taiwan, Univ. of Venice, Univ. of London and London Business School, UK; Chief Rep. in Beijing office, Italtel 1987–92; Chief Rep. IRI, Beijing 1993–94; Dir Int. Business Operations, STET International SpA, Rome 1995–99; consultant to several telecommunications cos 2000–01; Pres., CEO and Dir of Investor Relations, Brasil Telecom SA 2001–05; CEO Ambrosetti China (consulting firm) 2007–; mem. London Business School Latin America Regional Advisory Bd 2003; mem. Bd Belgacom 2004–05; Hon. Citizen, State of Rio de Janeiro 2003; Sloan Fellowship; elected Exec. of the Year by ANEFAC (Brazil) 2002, ranked by Fortune magazine amongst 50 Most Powerful Women in Business outside the US (37th) 2002, (30th) 2003, (25th) 2004, elected Businesswoman of the Year 2002 by British Chamber of Commerce in Brazil 2003, Comenda da Ordem do Mérito Anhanguera Award, Gov. of Goias 2003, elected Best CEO in Telecommunication Sector in Latin America by Reuters Institutional Investor Research 2003, ranked by Forbes magazine amongst 100 Most Powerful Women (75th) 2004, (32nd) 2005. *Leisure interest:* running in marathons. *Address:* Ambrosetti, Room 3518, Jingguang Center, Hujialou, Chaoyang District, Beijing 100020, People's Republic of China (office). *Telephone:* (10) 65974991 (office). *Fax:* (10) 65974992 (office). *E-mail:* beijing@ambrosetti.it (office). *Website:* www.ambrosetti.com.cn (office).

CICUTTO, Frank J., BCom, MPA, FAIBF, FAICD, FCIOSB; Australian business executive; ed Univ. of New South Wales, Harvard Univ., USA; joined Nat. Bank of Australia (later Nat. Australia Bank) as grad. trainee 1968, served in various man. positions including accountant, Gen. Man., State Man., NSW, Exec. Gen. Man., Products and Services 1994–96, Chief Gen. Man., Australian Financial Services 1996–98, also CEO, Clydesdale Bank, Scotland (subsidiary of Nat. Australia Bank), Man. Dir and CEO Nat. Australia Bank 1999–2004; Chair. ORIX Australia Corpn Ltd 2004–08, also Chair. ORIX New Zealand Ltd; Chair. RUN Corpn Ltd 2005–07; currently Chair. Chord Capital Management Pty Ltd; mem. Bd of Dirs St Vincent's Health 2004–, Melbourne Business School. *Leisure interests:* theatre, rugby, squash, golf. *Address:* c/o Board of Directors, St Vincent's Healthy, PO Box 2900, Fitzroy, VIC 3065, Australia (office).

CIECHANOVER, Aaron, MD, PhD; Israeli physician, molecular biologist and academic; *Professor of Biochemistry, Technion–Israel Institute of Technology;* b. 1 Oct. 1947, Haifa; ed Hebrew Univ. of Jerusalem; mil. service as a doctor in Israeli army; studied protein degradation at biochemical level with Avram Hershko (q.v.) 1976–81; collaborated with Alexander Varshavsky (q.v.) at MIT; currently Dir Rappaport Family Inst. for Research in Medical Sciences and Prof. of Biochemistry, Technion–Israel Inst. of Tech.; Albert Lasker Basic Medical Research Award 2000, Nobel Prize in Chem. (jtly) 2004. *Address:* Faculty of Medicine, Technion–Israel Institute of Technology, 1 Efron Street, PO Box 9697, Bat Galim, Haifa, 31096, Israel (office); 4-8514722 (office). *Fax:* 4-8517008 (office). *E-mail:* c_tzachy@netvision.net.il (office); rafael@biomed.technion.ac.il (office). *Website:* www.technion.ac.il/medicine (office).

CIEMNIEWSKI, Jerzy, JuD; Polish lawyer and politician; b. 2 Aug. 1939, Warsaw; m.; one s.; ed Faculty of Law, Warsaw Univ.; Lecturer, Warsaw Univ. 1962–68; scientific worker, Inst. of Law Studies, Polish Acad. of Sciences, Warsaw 1969–, Lecturer 1972–; mem. Solidarity Independent Self-governing Trade Union 1980–89; Assoc. Understanding Cttee of Creative and Scientific Asscns and Teachers' Solidarity, also scientific worker Social and Labour Study Centre attached to Nat. Comm. of Solidarity 1980–81; mem. Helsinki Cttee in Poland 1983; participant, Round Table debates, mem. group for law and judicature reform, expert group for political reforms Feb.–April 1989; mem. State Election Comm. during election to the Sejm (Parl.) and Senate 1989; Under-Sec. of State in Office of the Council of Ministers, Sec. of Council of Ministers 1989–91; Deputy to Sejm 1991–98; judge, Constitutional Tribunal 1998–2007; mem. Democratic Freedom Union 1990–94, Freedom Union 1994–, Helsinki Foundation for Human Rights, Centre for Human Rights in Eastern Europe; Awards of Gen. Sec. of Polish Acad. of Sciences 1974, 1976. *Publications:* numerous scientific works, mainly on constitutional law, including Ustawa o systemie konstytucyjnym SFR Jugosławii 1976, Sejm Ustawodawczy RP (1947–1952) 1978 (co-author), Studia nad rządem 1985 (co-author), System delegacki na tle ewolucji ustroju politycznego SFR Jugosławii 1988, Draft of the Constitution of the Republic of Poland (co-author) 1990. *Leisure interests:* family life, walking with dog, general history, painting. *Address:* c/o Trybunał Konstytucyjny, al. J. Ch. Szucha 12A, 00-198 Warsaw, Poland.

CIKOTIĆ, Brig.-Gen. Selmo, MA; Bosnia and Herzegovina government official and army officer (retd); *Minister of Defence;* b. 25 Jan. 1964, Berane-Ivangrad, Montenegro; m. Tanja Cikotić; one s. one d.; ed Bratstvo i Jedinstvo Mil. High School, Belgrade, Zadar Mil. Acad., Sarajevo Univ.; PhD cand., Sarajevo Univ.; Duty Officer, Air Defence Educ. Centre, Zadar 1986–92; mem. Bosnia and Herzegovina Army 1992–94; Defence Attaché in Washington, DC 1994–97; Head of Training and Educ. Centre, Joint Command of Fed. of Bosnia and Herzegovina Army 1997–99; Head of Cabinet, Deputy Minister of Defence of Fed. of Bosnia and Herzegovina 1999–2000; Deputy Commdr of 1st Corps, Fed. of Bosnia and Herzegovina Army 2000–01, Commdr 2001–04; retd from active mil. duty 2004; CEO OKI Ltd, Sarajevo 2004–07; Minister of Defence 2007–; mem. Party of Democratic Action (SDA). *Publications:* several articles on defence and security. *Leisure interests:* sharpshooting, skiing, mountain biking, swimming, reading. *Address:* Ministry of Defence, 71000 Sarajevo, Bistrik 5, Bosnia and Herzegovina (office). *Telephone:* (33) 286500 (office). *Fax:* (33) 206094 (office). *E-mail:* mod@mod.gov.ba (office). *Website:* www.mod.gov.ba (office).

ÇİLLER, Tansu, PhD; Turkish politician and academic; b. 1945, Istanbul; m.; two c.; ed Robert Coll., Boğaziçi Univ., Univ. of Connecticut and Yale Univ., USA; Assoc. Prof. 1978, Prof. 1983; served on academic bds of various univs, mainly in Dept of Econs Boğaziçi Univ.; joined True Path Party (DYP) 1990, Leader 1993–96; mem. Parl. 1991–2002; Minister of State for the Economy 1991; Prime Minister 1993–96; Deputy Prime Minister and Minister of Foreign Affairs 1996–97. *Publications:* nine publs on econs. *Address:* c/o True Path Party, Çetýn Emeç Bul. 117, Balgat, Ankara, Turkey. *Website:* www.dyp.org.tr.

CIMINO, Michael, BFA, MFA; American director and screenwriter; b. 1943, New York; ed Yale Univ.; Chevalier des Arts et des Lettres 2001. *Films include:* Silent Running (writer) 1972, Magnum Force (writer) 1973, Thunderbolt and Lightfoot (also writer) 1974, The Deer Hunter (also producer, Academy Award for Best Dir 1979) 1978, Heaven's Gate (also writer) 1980, Year of the Dragon (also writer) 1985, The Sicilian (also producer) 1987, Desperate Hours (also producer) 1990, The Sunchaser (also producer) 1996, To Each His Cinema (segment) 2007. *Publication:* Big Jane (novel) 2001. *Address:* c/o Jeff Berg, ICM, 8942 Wilshire Blvd., Beverly Hills, CA 90211, USA.

CIMOLI, Giancarlo; Italian administrator and airline industry executive; with SNIA Viscosa 1968–74; Chair. and Man. Dir Ferrovie dello Stato (state railways) 1996–2004; Chair. and CEO Alitalia 2004–07; mem. Bd of Dirs Air France-KLM –2007; mem. Aspen Inst. *Address:* c/o Alitalia, Viale A. Marchetti 111, 00148 Rome, Italy (office).

CIMOSZEWICZ, Włodzimierz, MA, PhD, DJur; Polish lawyer, politician and farmer; b. 13 Sept. 1950, Warsaw; m.; one s. one d.; ed Faculty of Law, Warsaw Univ.; Research Assoc. and then Asst Prof., Warsaw Univ. 1972–85; Fullbright Scholar, Columbia Univ., New York, USA 1980–81; farm owner and operator 1985–89; mem. Union of Socialist Youth 1968–73 (Chair. Bd, Warsaw Univ. 1972–73), Union of Polish Students/Socialist Union of Polish Students 1968–75 (Chair. Univ. Council 1973), PZPR 1971–90; Deputy to Sejm (Parl.) 1989–2005, (mem. PZPR caucus 1989–90, Chair. SLD Parl. Group 1990–93, Vice-Chair. Nat. and Ethnic Minorities Comm. 1989–91, mem. Parl. Foreign Affairs Comm. 1989, Special Comm. on Territorial Self-Government 1990, Chair. Constitutional Cttee 1995–96), Deputy Speaker 1995–96; mem. Bd Interparliamentary Union 1989–91; presidential cand. for Democratic Left Alliance (SLD) 1990; mem. Parl. Ass. Council of Europe 1992–96; Deputy Chair. Council of Ministers and Minister of Justice and Attorney-Gen. 1993–95; Prime Minister of Poland 1996–97; Chair. European Integration Cttee 1996–97; mem. Podlaskie Prov. Council 1998–2000; Minister of Foreign Affairs 2001–04; elected Marshal (Speaker) Sejm Jan.–Oct. 2005; teacher, Univ. of Białystok 2006–; mem. Senate for Białystok 2007–; Fullbright Scholar, Columbia Univ., New York, USA 1980–81; Chevalier Ordre nat. du Mérite 1997; Kt Order of the Greek Repub. 1997; Dr hc (Univ. of South Carolina) 1997, (Appalachian Univ.) 1998, (Odessa Univ., Ukraine). *Leisure interests:* family, reading, handiwork, hunting, angling, crafts, ecology. *Address:* Senat (Senate), 00-902 Warsaw, ul. Wiejska 6, Poland (office). *Telephone:* (22) 6949265 (office). *Fax:* (22) 6949428 (office). *Website:* www.senat.gov.pl (office).

CIOCCA, Pierluigi, DIur; Italian economist, central banker and academic; *Professor, Department of Economics, Università degli Studi di Roma 'la Sapienza';* b. 17 Oct. 1941, Pescara; ed Univ. of Rome, Fondazione Einaudi (Univ. of Turin) and Balliol Coll., Oxford, UK; economist, Research Dept Banca d'Italia (Bank of Italy) 1969–82, Cen. Man. for Cen. Bank Operations 1982–88, Cen. Man. for Econ. Research 1988–95, Deputy Dir-Gen. Bank of Italy 1995–2006; mem. Working Party 3 OECD Econ. Policy Cttee 1997; substitute for Gov. Bank of Italy, Governing Council, European Cen. Bank 1998; mem. Financial Stability Forum 1999, EU Econ. and Financial Cttee 2003; currently Prof., Dept of Econs, Università degli Studi di Roma 'la Sapienza'. *Publications:* La nuova finanza in Italia, Una difficile metamorfosi (1980–2000) 2000. *Address:* Via Cesalpino 12, 00161, Rome, Italy. *Telephone:* (06) 4991-7065. *E-mail:* pierluigi.ciocca@uniroma1.it. *Website:* dipartimento.dse.uniroma1.it.

CIOFFI, John M., BS, MS, PhD; American electrical engineer and academic; *Hitachi America Professor of Engineering, Stanford University;* ed Univ. of Illinois, Stanford Univ., Calif.; Hitachi America Prof. of Eng, Stanford Univ. 2002–; Co-founder and Chief Tech. Officer, Amati Communications Inc. 1991–97 (acquired by Texas Instruments 1997); mem. Bd of Dirs ClariPhy Communications, Inc., Teranetics Communications, ASSIA Inc. (Chair.), Vector Silicon Inc., Afond Technologies; mem. Advisory Bd Wavion, Focus Ventures, Quantenna Communications, Inc., Amicus; mem. Nat. Research Council Computer Science and Telecommunications Bd 1998–2003, ASSP Soc. DSP Cttee 1987–93; Assoc. Ed. IEEE Transactions on ASSP (Adaptive Filtering) 1985–87, IEEE JSAC (High-Speed Digital Subscriber Lines) 1991; Chief Ed. IEEE JSAC (Signal Processing and Coding for Recording) 1992; Ed. Dynamic Spectrum Management T1E1.4, American Nat. Standards 2001–; mem. Nat. Acad. of Eng 2001; Fellow, IEEE 1996–; NSF Presidential Investigator 1987–92, Faculty Devt Award, IBM Research 1986–88, Best Paper Award, IEEE Communications Soc. 1990, Outstanding Achievment Award, American Nat. Standards Inst. for contribs to ADSL 1995, Univ. of Illinois Outstanding Alumni Award 1999, IEE J. J. Thomson Medal 2000, IEEE Third Millennium Medal 2000, IEEE Kobayashi Medal 2001, ISSLS Best Paper Prize, IEE 2004, Marconi Prize and Fellowship, Marconi Foundation 2006, Best Paper Award, IEEE ICC (co-recipient) 2006, Best Paper Award, IEEE ICC (co-recipient) 2007, Best Paper Award, IEEE Communications Magazine (co-recipient) 2007, Best Paper Award, IEEE ICC (co-recipient) 2008. *Publications:* more than 90 journal papers and 200 conf. papers and more than 40 licensed patents. *Address:* Room 363, David Packard Electrical Engineering Building, Stanford University, 350 Serra Mall, MC 9515, Stanford, CA 94305-9515, USA (office). *Telephone:* (650) 723-2150 (office). *Fax:* (650) 724-3652 (office). *E-mail:* cioffi@stanford.edu (office). *Website:* www.stanford.edu/group/cioffi (office).

CIORBEA, Victor; Romanian lawyer and fmr politician; b. 26 Oct. 1954, Ponor Village; s. of Vasile Ciorbea and Eugenia Ciorbea; m. 1977; one d.; ed Law School, Cluj-Napoca, Case Western Reserve Univ., Cleveland, Ohio, USA; judge, Court of Bucharest 1979–84; Prosecutor, Dept Civil Cases, Gen. Prosecutor's Office 1984–87; Asst to Lecturer Law School, Bucharest 1987–90; Pres. Free Trade Unions Fed. in Educ. 1990–96, CNSLR 1990–93, CNSLR-FRĂTIA 1993–94, Democratic Union Confed., Romania 1994–96; Mayor of Bucharest 1996; Prime Minister of Romania 1996–98; mem. Exec. Bd ICFTU, ETUC, CES 1993–94, Congress of Local and Regional Powers, Council of Europe, Strasbourg 1996, European Hon. Senate 1999; rep. of Romania at OIM confs; Vice-Pres. PNTCD 1997–99, Pres. 2001; fmr Vice-Pres. and Chair. Christian Democratic Nat. Peasants' Party (now Popular Christian-Democratic Party of Romania); mem. Bd Alianta Civica 1996; Founding mem. Int. Christian Coalition 1999. *Address:* 3 Rosetti Square, sector 1, Bucharest 70 000, Romania (office). *Telephone:* (21) 3153862 (office).

CIOROIANU, Adrian Mihai, PhD; Romanian politician and academic; b. 5 Jan. 1967, Craiova; ed Univ. of Bucharest and Laval Univ., Canada; Lecturer, History Dept, Univ. of Bucharest 2002–; Advisor to Pres. of Nat. Liberal Party (PNL) 2002; elected to Romanian Senate (PNL) 2004–; Observer, European Parl. 2005–07; mem. European Parl. 2007–; Minister of Foreign Affairs 2007–08 (resgnd); mem. editorial team, Dilema Veche 1998–, Gazeta Sporturilor, Interpres, Scrisul Romanesc (newspapers); TV presenter on TVR1, Realitatea TV, Pax TV 2000–04. *Publications include:* The Ashes of a Century: A Hundred and One Superimposed Stories 2001, The Fire Hidden in Stone: On History, Memory and Other Contemporary Vanities 2002, This Ceaușescu Who Is Haunting the Romanians: The Myth, the Images and the Cult of the Leader in Communist Romania 2005, On the Shoulders of Marx: An Incursion into the History of Romanian Communism 2005, Sic Transit Gloria: The Subjective Chronicle of a Five-Year Plan Completed over Three and a Half Years 2006. *Address:* National Liberal Party, 011866, Bucharest, Boulevard Aviatorilor 86, Romania (office). *Telephone:* (21) 2310795 (office). *Fax:* (21) 2310796 (office). *E-mail:* dre@pnl.ro (office). *Website:* www.pnl.ro (office); cioroianu.ro (home).

CIOSEK, Stanisław, MA; Polish politician and diplomatist; b. 2 May 1939, Pawłowice, Radom Prov.; s. of Józef Ciosek and Janina Ciosek; m. Anna Ciosek 1969; two d.; ed Higher School of Econs, Sopot; activist in youth orgs 1957–75; Chair. Regional Council of Polish Students' Asscn (ZSP), Gdańsk, Deputy Chair. and Chair. Chief Council, ZSP 1957–73; Chair. Chief Council of Fed. of Socialist Unions of Polish Youth (FSZMP) 1974–75; mem. Polish United Workers' Party (PZPR) 1959–90, Deputy mem. PZPR Cen. Cttee 1971–80, First Sec., Voivodship Cttee PZPR and Chair. Presidium of Voivodship Nat. Council, Jelenia Góra 1975–80, mem. PZPR Cen. Cttee 1980–81, 1986–90, Sec., PZPR Cen. Cttee 1986–88, Alt. mem. Political Bureau of PZPR Cen. Cttee 1988, mem. Political Bureau 1988–89; Deputy to Sejm 1972–85; Minister for Co-operation with Trade Unions 1980–85, for Labour, for Wages and Social Affairs 1983–84, Vice-Chair. Cttee of Council of Ministers for Co-operation with Trade Unions 1983–85; Sec., Socio-Political Cttee of Council of Ministers 1981–85; Sec.-Gen. Nat. Council of Patriotic Movt for Rebirth (PRON) 1988–89; Co-organizer and participant, Round Table debates 1989; Amb. to USSR 1989–91, to Russia 1991–96; Foreign Policy Adviser to Pres. of Poland 1997–2005; Sec.-Gen. Eastern Club; Commdr's Cross, Order of Polonia Restituta. *Address:* ul. Belgijska 11/11, 02-511 Warsaw, Poland (office). *Telephone:* (22) 542-8240 (office). *Fax:* (22) 542-8244 (office). *E-mail:* ciosek@ipgroup.pl (office).

CIPRIANI THORNE, HE Cardinal Juan Luis; Peruvian ecclesiastic; *Archbishop of Lima;* b. 28 Dec. 1943, Lima; ed St Mary's Catholic High School, Nat. Univ. of Eng, Univ. of Navarra, Spain; mem. Peruvian nat. basketball team in his youth; ordained priest 1977; apptd Coadjutor Bishop of Ayacucho 1988, Bishop of Turuzi 1988–95, Archbishop of Ayacucho 1995–99, Archbishop of Lima 1999–; apptd Cardinal-Priest of S. Camillo de Lellis 2001; Great Chancellor Pontificia Universidad Católica del Perú; mem. Opus Dei; Class of Grand Cross, Order of the Sun 2009. *Address:* Arzobispado, Plaza de Armas s/n, Apdo. 1512, Lima 100 (office); Calle Los Nogales 249, San Isidro, Lima 27, Peru. *Telephone:* (14) 427-5980 (office); (14) 441-1977. *Fax:* (14) 427-1967 (office); (14) 440-9134. *E-mail:* arzolimas@amauta.rcpnet.pe (office).

CIRELLI, Jean-François; French energy industry executive; *Chairman and CEO, Gaz de France Group;* b. 9 July 1958, Chambéry; ed Institut d'Etudes Politiques, Ecole Nationale d'Admin, Paris; with Treasury Dept, Ministry of Economy and Finance 1985–95; Tech. Adviser to Pres. of France 1995–97, Econ. Adviser 1997–2002; Deputy Dir Office of the Prime Minister 2002–04; Chair. and CEO Gaz de France Group 2004–, Chair. Gaz de France Corp. Foundation, Pres. and Vice-Chair. Cie de Suez; mem. Bd Dirs Neuf Cegetel, Atos. *Address:* Gaz de France, 23 rue Philibert Delorme, 75840 Paris Cedex 17, France (office). *Telephone:* 1-47-54-21-16 (office). *Fax:* 1-47-54-24-85 (office). *E-mail:* info@gazdefrance.com (office). *Website:* www.gazdefrance.com (office).

CIRIANI, Henri Edouard; French architect and academic; b. 30 Dec. 1936, Lima, Peru; s. of Enrique Ciriani and Caridad Suito; m. Marcelle Espejo 1962; two d.; ed Santa Maria School, Nat. Univ. of Eng and Town Planning Inst., Lima; Asst Architect, Dept of Architecture, Ministry of Devt and Public Works, Lima, Project Architect 1961–64; pvt. practice with Crousse and Paez 1961–63; Asst Prof. of Design, Nat. Univ. of Eng, Lima 1962–64; emigrated to France 1964; f. pvt. practice 1968; Prof. Ecole des Beaux-Arts de Paris 1969–83; Prof. of Architecture, Ecole d'Architecture de Paris-Belleville 1984–2002; Dist Prof., Univ. Nacional de Ingeniería, Lima 1985–; Visiting Prof., Tulane Univ., New Orleans 1984, Univ. Coll., Dublin 1985, Ecole d'Architecture de Grenoble 1988, Univ. of Pennsylvania 1989 and many others; Sir Banister Fletcher Visiting Lecturer, Univ. Coll., London 1986; Prof., Univ. of Navarra 2006–07; Dir Acad. de France, Rome 1987–91; Fondation Le Corbusier 1989–; mem. Int. Acad. of Architecture; Hon. Fellow, RIBA; Chevalier, Légion d'honneur 1997; Nat. Grand Prix of Architecture 1983, Equerre d'Argent 1983, Palme d'Or de l'Habitat 1988, Brunner Memorial Prize 1997. *Public works include:* public housing at Ventanilla Matute 1963, San Felipe 1964, Rimac Mirones 1965, Marne-la-vallée Noisy II 1980, Noisy III 1981, St Denis 1982, Evry 1985, Lognes 1986, Charcot 1991, Bercy 1994, Colombes 1995, urban landscape at Grenoble 1968–74, public facilities at St Denis Child-care Centre 1983, Cen. kitchen for St Antoine Hosp., Paris 1985, Torcy Child-care Centre 1989, Museum of the First World War, Péronne 1992, extension to Ministry of Finance Bldg, Paris 1993, Arles Archaeological Museum 1995, pvt. bldgs at The Hague Apartment Tower 1995, Stadspoort College 2000, Conf. Centre, French Nat. Inst. for Research in Computer Science and Control 2001, Palais de Justice 2006, retrospective exhbns at Institut Français d'Architecture, Paris 1984, Figueira da Foz, Oporto and Lisbon 1985, New York 1985, Tokyo 1987, Lima 1996, New York 1997, Montreal 1997, Venice 1999, Sao Paulo 2005. *Publications:* Pratique de la pièce urbaine 1996, Paroles d'architecte (ed. by Jean Petit Lugano) 1997. *Leisure interests:* drawing, collecting postcards. *Address:* Atelier Ciriani, 61 rue Pascal, 75013 Paris, France (office). *Telephone:* 1-43-37-41-00 (office).

CIRY, Michel; French composer, painter, etcher and graphic artist; b. 31 Aug. 1919, La Baule; s. of Georges Ciry and Simone Ciry (née Breune); ed Ecole des Arts Appliqués, Paris; studied music with Nadia Boulanger; religious and secular paintings and etchings; apptd Sec. of Peintres Graveurs Français 1941, painter 1951–; Prof., School of Fine Arts Fontainebleau 1957–58, Académie Julian 1960; fmr mem. Conseil Supérieur de l'Enseignement des Beaux-Arts; Vice-Pres. Comité Nat. de la Gravure 1957–; numerous exhbns in Europe and America including Paris, London, New York, Boston, Amsterdam, Rome and Berlin; works in Museums of Europe and America; has illustrated numerous books including books by Montherlant, Green, Claudel and Mauriac; mem. Acad. des Beaux-Arts, Florence 1964–, Belgian Acad. 1988; Officier, Légion d'honneur, Chevalier des Arts et Lettres, Commdr, Ordre Nat. du Mérite; Prix Nat. des Arts 1945, Grande médaille de vermeil de la Ville de Paris 1962, Grand Prix du Conseil Général de la Seine 1962, Prix de l'Ile de France 1964, Prix Eugène Carrière 1964, Grand Prix de Montrouge 1965, Lauréate Acad. des Beaux-Arts 1968, Prix Wildenstein 1968, Biennale Médaille d'Or, Florence 1972, Prix international de la Biennale du Gemmail d'Art Sacré 1973, Lauréat du Grand Prix Georges Baudry 1984. *Major works:* Chemin de croix 1960–64, Stabat Mater 1960, 1961, 1963, 1965, Fièvres 1965, Christ's Passion 1955, 1957, 1960, 1964, Marie-Madeleine 1961, 1963, 1965, Saint François 1950, 1954, 1959, 1960, 1964, 1965, Saint Dominic 1962. *Compositions include:* five sacred symphonies for choir and orchestra 1951–54, Stèle pour un héros 1949, Pietà 1950, Mystère de Jésus 1953, several chamber works. *Publications:* twenty-four vols of autobiog., Brisons nos fers 1992. *Address:* La Bergerie, 76119 Varengeville-sur-Mer, Seine-Maritime, France. *Website:* www.michel-ciry.fr.

CISNEROS, Gustavo A.; Venezuelan media executive; *Chairman and CEO, Cisneros Group;* b. 16 Aug. 1947; s. of Diego Cisneros; m. Patricia Phelps; three c.; ed Babson Coll., Wellesley, Mass., USA; Chair. and CEO Cisneros Group (family-owned co. holding stakes in over 70 cos. in 39 countries including Venevisión, Univisión, Chilevisión, Caracol Televisión de Colombia, Playboy TV Latin America, Caribbean Communications Network, Direct TV Latin America and American Online Latin America (AOLA); Dir Panamco Bottling Co., AOL Latin America, Pueblo Int., Inc., Ibero-American Media Partners 1997–; Owner, Los Leones del Caracas baseball team 2001–; Co-founder (with wife Patricia and brother Ricardo) Fundación Cisneros; mem. Bd of Dirs Barrick Gold Corpn, RRE Ventures LLC; Commr Global Information Infrastructure Comm.; charter mem. UN Information and Communications Technologies Task Force; mem. World Business Council, World Econ. Forum; mem. Int. Advisory Councils, Columbia Univ., Babson Coll.; mem. Int. Advisory Bd Barrick Gold Corpn, Council on Foreign Relations; mem. Advisory Cttee, David Rockefeller Center for Latin American Studies, Harvard Univ.; mem. Bd of Advisers for Panama Canal; mem. Chair.'s Int. Advisory Council, Americas Soc.; mem. Bd of Overseers, Int. Center for Econ. Growth; mem. Bd Govs. Joseph H. Lauder Inst. of Man., Wharton School at Univ. of Pennsylvania; mem. Chair.'s Council, Museum of Modern Art; mem. Bd Trustees, Museum of TV and Radio; Americas Soc. Distinguished Service Award 2003, Woodrow Wilson Award for Public Service 2004. *Address:* Cisneros Group, 36 East 61st Street, New York, NY 10021, USA (office); Edeficio Venevisión, Final Avenida La Salle, Colina de los Caobos, Caracas 1050 (office); Fundación Cisneros, Centro Mozarteum, Final Avenida La Salle, Colina de los Caobos, Caracas 1050, Venezuela (office). *Telephone:* (212) 708-9444 (USA) (office); (582) 708-9697 (Venezuela) (office). *E-mail:* info@cisneros.com (office); info@fundacion.cisneros.org (office). *Website:* www.cisneros.com (office); www.venevision.net (office).

CISNEROS, Henry G., BA, DPA; American real estate industry executive and fmr politician; *Executive Chairman, CityView;* b. 11 June 1947, San Antonio, Tex.; s. of J. George Cisneros and Elvira Munguia; m. Mary-Alice Perez; one s. two d.; ed Tex. A&M, Harvard and George Washington Univs; Asst Dir Dept of Model Cities, San Antonio 1969–70; Asst to Exec. Vice-Pres., Nat. League of Cities, Washington, DC 1970–71; Teaching Asst, Dept of Urban Studies and Planning, MIT 1972–74; Faculty mem. Public Admin. Program, Univ. of Tex. 1974–87; Faculty mem. Dept of Urban Studies, Trinity Univ. 1974–87; mem. City Council, San Antonio 1975–81, Mayor of San Antonio 1981–89; Chair. Cisneros Asset Man. Co., Cisneros Benefit Group, Cisneros Communications 1989–; Sec., US Dept of Housing and Urban Devt, Washington, DC 1993–97; Pres. COO Univision Communications Inc., LA 1997–2000; Exec. Chair. and CEO American CityVista (now CityView), San Antonio 2000–; Co-Chair. Nat. Hispanic Leadership Agenda 1988–92; Vice-Chair. Pres.'s Summit on Volunteerism 1997; Hon. mem. AIA 1986; 23 hon. degrees; numerous honours and awards including Nat. Recognition Award, Mexican Govt 1985, Pres.'s Award, Nat. League of Cities 1989, Hubert Humphrey Award, Leadership Conference for Civil Rights 1994. *Publication:* San Antonio's Place in the Technology Economy 1982. *Leisure interests:* reading, going to the cinema, spending time with his family. *Address:* CityView, 454 Soledad Street, Suite 300, San Antonio, TX 78205 (office); 2002 West Houston Street, San Antonio, TX 78207, USA (home). *Telephone:* (210) 228-9574 (office). *Fax:* (210) 224-7888 (home). *E-mail:* info@cityview.com (office). *Website:* www.cityview.com (office).

CISSÉ, Amadou Boubacar, BA, MEcon, PhD; Niger civil engineer, politician and banker; *Vice-President (Operations), Islamic Development Bank;* b. 29 June 1948; m.; five c.; ed Ecole Nationale des Ponts et Chaussées and Institut des Sciences Politiques, Paris; fmr sr staff mem. in various capacities with World Bank, including Infrastructure Specialist, Prin. Operations Officer, IFC for Privatization and Financial Advisory Advisor to Vice-Pres. Africa Region, Resident Rep. of World Bank in several African countries; fmr Prime Minister of Niger; fmr Minister of Finance and Econ. Reforms; fmr Minister of State in charge of Economy, Finance and Planning; fmr Managing Dir Public Works Dept; fmr Exec. Sec. Railway Authority of Benin-Niger; Vice-Pres. (Operations), Islamic Devt Bank, Jeddah, Saudi Arabia 2002–. *Address:* Islamic Development Bank, PO Box 5925, Jeddah 21432, Saudi Arabia (office). *Telephone:* (2) 6361400 (office). *Fax:* (2) 6366871 (office). *E-mail:* idbarchives@isdb.org (office). *Website:* www.isdb.org (office).

CITERNE, Philippe, BEcons, PhD; French banker; *Co-CEO, Société Générale;* b. 1949; ed Ecole Centrale de Paris; Project Man., Business Dept, INSEE 1972–74; Project Man., Forecasting Dept, Ministry of Finance, becoming Bureau Chief, Energy, Transport and Equipment Div. 1974–79; joined Econ. Research Dept, Société Générale 1979, Dir Econ. Research Dept 1984–86, Dir Financial Man. 1986–90, Dir of Human Resources 1990–95, Deputy CEO in charge of Resources and Services Div. 1995–97, CEO Société Générale 1997–2006, Dir and Co-CEO 2006–. *Address:* Société Générale, 75886 Paris Cedex 18, France (office). *Telephone:* 1-42-14-20-00 (office). *E-mail:* info@socgen.com (office). *Website:* www.socgen.com (office).

CIUHA, Jože; Slovenian artist and painter; b. 26 April 1924, Trbovlje; s. of Jože and Amalija Ciuha; m. Radmila Novak 1962; one s. one d.; ed Acad. of Fine Arts, Ljubljana and Univ. of Rangoon, Burma (Buddhist art and philosophy); work includes painting on plexi-glass, print-making, murals, tapestry, scenography, illustrating and water colours; developed silk-screen technique; his extensive travels in Europe, Asia and S. America inspired deep interest in ancient cultures; over 100 one-man exhbns in Europe and USA; Perm. mem. Russian Acad. of Art 2004; lives in Paris; Chevalier des Art et Letters; more than 20 nat. and int. prizes, including Grand Prix at Int. Graphic Biennale, Seoul, First Prize, Mediterranean Biennale, Alexandria, prizes at Biennale in Kraków and Ljubljana, Golden Medal for Artistic Promotion, Pres. of Austria 2004. *Publications:* Petrified Smile, Conversations with Silence (based on sketchbooks from his S American journey 1964–65), Travels to the Tenth Country (for children), Joze Ciuha. *Leisure interest:* literature. *Address:* 4 place de la Porte de Bagnolet, 75020 Paris, France; Prešernova 12, 61000 Ljubljana, Slovenia. *Telephone:* (61) 218956 (Ljubljana).

CIULEI, Liviu; Romanian actor, scenographer and theatre, film and opera director; b. 7 July 1923, Bucharest; ed Bucharest Inst. of Architecture, Bucharest Conservatory of Music and Theatre; actor 1945–; stage dir and scenographer 1946–; Artistic Dir Lucia Sturdza Bulandra Theatre, Bucharest 1962–72, Hon. Dir 1990–; Artistic Dir Guthrie Theater, Minneapolis, Minn. 1980–86; freelance dir and direction teacher, Columbia Univ., New York 1986–87; Acting Prof. New York Univ. 1988–2003; acted at Bulandra, Odeon and C. Nottara theatres in Bucharest, as Puck in A Midsummer Night's

Dream, Protasov in The Children Of The Sun, Treplev in The Seagull, Dunois in St Joan, Danton in Danton's Death; numerous roles in Romanian films 1951–75; State Prize 1962 for films, Prize for Best Direction, Int. Festival, Cannes 1965. *Plays directed include:* Lower Depths, Bucharest 1960, Munich 1976, Washington, DC, Sydney 1977, Danton's Death, West Berlin 1967, Leonce and Lena, Bucharest 1970, Washington 1974, Vancouver 1976, Macbeth, Bucharest, Berlin 1968, Munich 1973, Richard II, Düsseldorf 1969, Volpone, Berlin 1970, As You Like It, Bucharest 1961, Gottingen 1968, Minneapolis 1982, The Tempest, Bucharest 1979, Minneapolis 1984, Richard II, Düsseldorf 1969, Hamlet, Washington 1978, New York 1987, A Midsummer Night's Dream, New York 1988, The Threepenny Opera, Bucharest 1964, Minneapolis 1986, Volpone, Berlin 1970, Six Characters in Search of an Author, Washington 1988, Long Day's Journey into Night, Bucharest 1976, Bacchantes, Minneapolis 1988, Requiem for a Nun, Minneapolis 1984, Henric 4, Bucharest 2005 etc. *Films directed include:* Eruptia (Eruption) 1957, Valurile Dunarii (The Danube Waves) (Grand Prize, Int. Festival of Karlovy Vary as dir and interpreter 1960, State Prize for Films, Romania 1961) 1959, Padurea spînzuratilor (Forest of the Hanged) (Grand Prize, Int. Festival of Karlovy Vary as dir and interpreter, Prize for Best Direction, Int. Festival Cannes 1965) 1964, O Scrisoare pierduta (A Lost Letter) (TV) 1977. *Operas directed include:* Lady Macbeth of Mtsensk, The Gambler, Così fan tutte, Wozzeck, Falstaff, at Spoleto, Chicago, Washington, Cardiff, Amsterdam etc.; designer Prince Igor, Covent Garden, London 1990; numerous tours abroad with Romanian productions, including Budapest 1960, Leningrad and Moscow 1966, Florence 1969, 1970, Regensburg, Frankfurt Main, Essen 1970, Edin. Festival 1971, The Hague, Amsterdam 1972, etc. *Address:* Teatrul Bulandra, Str. Schitu Măgureanu Nr. 1, Bucharest, Romania; 400 West 119th Street, Apt. 12-0, New York, NY 10027, USA. *Telephone:* 1349696 (Bucharest).

ČIUPAILA, Regimantas, PhD; Lithuanian mathematician, engineer, academic and politician; b. 20 Aug. 1956; m. Dalia Čiupaila; two d.; ed Vilnius Univ.; engineer-programmer, Computation Centre, Vilnius Univ. 1991–92; Dir of Foreign Relations, Vilnius Gediminas Tech. Univ. 1992–96, Docent 1992–; Docent, Mykolas Riomeris Univ. 2001–; mem. Liberal and Centre Union (LCU—Liberalų Centro Sąjunga), mem. LCU Bd 2003–; mem. Council of Vilnius City Municipality 1990–96, Vice-Pres. Vilnius City Council 1990–91; mem. Seimas (Parl.), Vice-Pres. European Affairs Cttee, mem. Foreign Affairs Cttee 1996–2000; mem. Parl. Ass. of Council of Europe 1996–2000; mem. European Parl. Jt Cttee 1997–2000; Vice-Pres. Lithuanian Cen. Union 2001–03; Vice-Minister of the Interior 2006–07, Minister of the Interior 2007–08. *Address:* Ministry of the Interior, Šventaragio 2, 01510 Vilnius, Lithuania (office). *Telephone:* (5) 271-7130 (office). *Fax:* (5) 271-8551 (office). *E-mail:* korespondencija@vrm.lt (office). *Website:* www.vrm.lt (office).

CIVILETTI, Benjamin R., AB, LLB; American lawyer and fmr government official; *Chairman, Venable, Baetjer, Howard & Civiletti LLP;* b. 17 July 1935, Peekskill, NY; s. of Benjamin C. Civiletti and Virginia I. Civiletti; m. Gaile Lundgren 1958; two s. one d.; ed Johns Hopkins Univ., Baltimore, Md, Columbia Univ., New York, Univ. of Maryland School of Law; admitted Md Bar 1961; law clerk to Hon. W. Calvin Chesnut, US District Court for Md 1961–62; Asst US Attorney, Md 1962–64; Pnr Venable, Baetjer & Howard (now Venable, Baetjer, Howard & Civiletti LLP) 1964–77, 1981–, Chair. 1996–; Asst Attorney-Gen., Criminal Div., US Dept of Justice, Washington, DC 1977–79, US Attorney-Gen. 1979–81; Chair. and Dir Healthcorp Inc.; Dir Bethlehem Steel Corpn, Wackenhut Corrections Corpn, MBNA America, MBNA International; Trustee Johns Hopkins Univ. 1980–98; mem. Legal Advisory Bd Martindale-Lexus; mem. Bd of Eds Federal Litigation Guide Reporter; mem. ABA, Federal Bar Asscn, Md State Bar, DC Bar Asscn, Bar Asscn of Baltimore City; Fellow, American Bar Foundation, American Law Inst., American Coll. of Trial Lawyers; Kt-Commdr, Order of Merit of the Italian Repub.; Hon. LLD (Univ. of Baltimore), (New York Law School), (St John's Coll.), (Tulane Univ.) (Univ. of Notre Dame), (Univ. of Maryland); Hon. DHumLitt (Towson State Univ.); Equal Justice Award, Baltimore Urban League 1997, Justice Award, American Judicature Soc. 2005. *Leisure interests:* golf, gardening, antiques. *Address:* Venable, Baetjer, Howard & Civiletti LLP, 1800 Mercantile Bank and Trust Building, 2 Hopkins Plaza, Baltimore, MD 21201, USA (office). *Telephone:* (410) 244-7600 (home). *Fax:* (410) 244-7742 (office). *E-mail:* brciviletti@venable.com (office). *Website:* www.venable.com (office).

CIVITA, Roberto; Brazilian journalist and business executive; *President and CEO, Grupo Abril;* b. 1936, Milan, Italy; s. of Victor Civita; two s.; ed Wharton School, Univ. of Pennsylvania, Columbia Univ., USA; trainee at Time Magazine, USA; Founder and Ed.-in-Chief Veja Magazine 1968–; Pres. Grupo Abril 1990–, CEO 1990–2001, 2006–; Pres. Victor Civita Foundation; mem. Bd Int. Admin of Econ. Devt; Hon. Councillor Superior School of Propaganda and Marketing 2005; Commdr of the Order of the Lion (Finland) 1997; Dr hc (Casper Líbero Univ. of Social Communication) 1997; Personality of the Year for Communications, MegaBrasil Comunicação 2005. *Address:* Grupo Abril, Avenida das Nações Unidas, 7221, Pinheiros, 05425-902 São Paulo, Brazil (office). *Telephone:* (11) 3037-2000 (office). *Website:* www.abril.com.br (office).

CIXOUS, Hélène, DèsSc; French academic and author; b. 5 June 1937, Oran, Algeria; d. of Georges Cixous and Eve Klein; one s. one d.; ed Lycée d'Alger, Lycée de Sceaux, Sorbonne; mem. staff. Univ. of Bordeaux 1962–65; Asst Lecturer, Sorbonne 1965–67; Lecturer, Univ. of Paris X (Nanterre) 1967–68; helped found Univ. of Paris VIII (Vincennes) 1968, Chair. and Prof. of Literature 1968–, Founder and Dir Centre d'Etudes Féminines 1974–; Co-Founder of journal Poétique 1969; Southern Cross of Brazil 1989; Chevalier de la Légion d'honneur 1994; Officier Ordre nat. du Mérite 1998; Dr hc (Queen's Univ., Kingston, Canada) 1991, (Edmonton, Canada) 1992, (York, UK) 1993,

(Georgetown, Washington, DC, USA) 1995, (Northwestern, Chicago, USA) 1996; Prix Médicis 1969, Prix des critiques for best theatrical work of the year 1994, 2000, Amb. of Star Awards, Pakistan 1997. *Theatre:* Portrait de Dora 1976, Le nom d'Oedipe 1978, La prise de l'école de Madhubaï 1984, L'Histoire terrible mais inachevée de Norodom Sihanouk, roi du Cambodge 1985, L'Indiade ou l'Inde de leurs rêves 1987, On ne part pas on ne revient pas 1991, Voile noire voile blanche 1994, L'Histoire qu'on ne connaîtra jamais 1994, La Ville Parjure ou le Réveil des Erinyes 1994, Tambours sur la digue 1999 (Molière Award 2000), Rouen la trentième nuit de mai 31 2001. *Publications include:* Le Prénom de Dieu 1967, Dedans 1969, Le Troisième corps, Les Commencements 1970, Un vrai jardin 1971, Neutre 1972, Tombe, Portrait du Soleil 1973, Révolutions pour plus d'un Faust 1975, Souffles 1975, La 1976, Partie 1976, Angst 1977, Préparatifs de noces au-delà de l'abîme 1978, Vivre l'orange 1979, Anankè 1979, Illa 1980, With ou l'art de l'innocence 1981, Limonade tout était si infini 1982, Le Livre de Promethea 1983, Manne 1988, Jours de l'An 1990, L'Ange au secret 1991, Déluge 1992, Beethoven à jamais 1993, La fiancée juive 1995, Messie 1996, Or, les lettres de mon père 1997, Osnabrück 1999, Les Rêveries de la femme sauvage 2000, Le Jour où je n'étais pas là 2000, Portrait de Jacques Derrida en jeune saint juif 2001, Benjamin à Montaigne, il ne faut pas le dire 2001, Manhattan. Lettres de la Préhistoire 2002; essays: L'exil de James Joyce 1969, Prénoms de personne 1974, La Jeune née 1975, La venue à l'écriture 1977, Entre l'écriture 1986, L'heure de Clarice Lispector 1989, Reading with Clarice Lispector 1990, Readings, the Poetics of Blanchot, Joyce, Kafka, Lispector, Tsvetaeva 1992, Three Steps on the Ladder of Writing 1993, Photos de racines 1994, Stigmata 1998, Escaping Texts 1998. *Address:* Éditions Galilée, 9 rue Linné, 75005 Paris (office); Centre d'études féminines, Université Paris VIII, 2 rue de la Liberté, 93526 Saint-Denis cedex 2, France.

CIZIK, Robert, BS, MBA; American business executive; b. 4 April 1931, Scranton, Pa; s. of John Cizik and Anna Paraska Cizik; m. Jane Morin 1953; three s. two d.; ed Univ. of Connecticut and Harvard Grad. School of Business; accountant, Price, Waterhouse & Co. 1953–54, 1956; financial analyst, Exxon Co. 1958–61; joined Cooper Industries 1961, Dir Cooper Industries 1971–96, Pres. 1973–92, CEO 1975–95, Chair. 1983–96; Prin. Cizik Interests, Houston 1996–; Chair. Easco Inc. 1997–98, Stanadyne Automotive 1998–2000, Koppers Holdings Inc. (fmrly Koppers Industries) 1999–2008; mem. Bd of Dirs Harris Corpn 1988–99, Air Products & Chemicals 1992–2002, Temple-Inland Inc., American Industrial Partners 1996–98; Advisory Dir Wingate Partners 1994–2004; Dir and Co-founder Robert and Jane Cizik Foundation; Hon. LLD (Kenyon Coll.) 1983. *Address:* Cizik Interests, 8839 Harness Creek Lane, Houston, TX 77024 (office); Robert and Jane Cizik Foundation, 8839 Harness Creek Lane, Houston, TX 77024-7044, USA. *Telephone:* (713) 810-0100 (office).

CLAES, Willy; Belgian politician and pianist; b. 24 Nov. 1938, Hasselt; m. Suzanne Meynen 1965; one s. one d.; ed Univ. Libre de Bruxelles; mem. Exec. Cttee Belgian Socialist Party, Jt Pres. 1975–77; mem. Limbourg Council 1964; mem. Chamber of Deputies 1968–94; Minister of Educ. (Flemish) 1972–73, of Econ. Affairs 1973–74, 1977–81, Deputy Prime Minister 1979–81, 1988–94, Minister of Econ. Affairs, Planning and Educ. (Flemish Sector) 1988–91, of Foreign Affairs 1991–94; Sec.-Gen. NATO 1994–95 (resgnd), given suspended three-year prison sentence for corruption Dec. 1998; Pres. European Socialist Party 1992–94; f. Willy Claes Quartet. *Publications include:* Tussen droom en werkelijkheid 1979, La Chine et l'Europe 1980, Livre Blanc de l'Energie 1980, Elementen voor een nieuw energiebeleid 1980, De Derde Weg: beschouwingen over de Wereldcrisis 1987. *Address:* c/o Thienpont: Artiestenbureau, Leernsesteenweg 243A, 9800 Bachte-Maria-Leerne, Deinze; Berkenlaan 62, 3500 Hasselt, Belgium.

CLAIR, Louis Serge; Mauritian politician; *Chief Commissioner, Rodrigues Regional Assembly;* b. 1 April 1940, Rodrigues; s. of Emmanuel Clair and Willida Clair; m. Danielle Limock 1984; two c.; studied philosophy, theology and social sciences in France and TV production in Australia; Dir and Ed. L'Organisation (first local newspaper on island of Rodrigues) 1976–86; Leader Org. du Peuple Rodriguais; mem. Legis. Ass. 1982–2002, Minister for Rodrigues 1982–89, 1989–95, Chief Commr, Rodrigues Regional Ass. 2003–; Grand Commdr of the Star and Key of the Indian Ocean. *Leisure interests:* sight-seeing, gardening. *Address:* Organisation du Peuple Rodriguais, Mont Lubin, Rodrigues, Mauritius (office). *Telephone:* (230) 8310882 (office). *Fax:* (230) 8312404 (office). *E-mail:* chiefcom@mtnet.mn (office).

CLANCY, HE Cardinal Edward Bede, AC; Australian ecclesiastic (retd); *Archbishop Emeritus of Sydney;* b. 13 Dec. 1923, Lithgow, NSW; s. of John Bede Clancy and Ellen Lucy Clancy; ed St Columba's Coll., Springwood, NSW, St Patrick's Coll, Manly, NSW, Pontifical Biblical Inst. and Propaganda Fide Univ., Rome; Auxiliary Bishop, Archdiocese of Sydney 1974–78, Archbishop, Archdiocese of Canberra and Goulburn 1979–83, Archbishop of Sydney 1983–2001 (retd), Archbishop Emer. 2001–; cr. Cardinal 1988, cr. Cardinal-Priest of St Maria in Vallicella 1988; Chancellor Australian Catholic Univ. 1992–2000. *Publications:* The Bible: The Church's Book 1974, Come Back: The Church Loves You 2002, Walk Worthy of Your Vocation 2004. *Leisure interest:* golf. *Address:* 54 Cranbrook Road, Bellevue Hill, NSW 2023, Australia (home).

CLANCY, James, BA; Canadian trade union official; *President, National Union of Public and General Employees;* b. 10 March 1950, Kingston, Ont.; m.; three c.; ed Carleton Univ., Ottawa; social worker in Toronto 1976–84; Pres. Ont. Public Services Employees Union 1984–90; Pres. Nat. Union of Public and Gen. Employees 1990–; Gen. Vice-Pres. Canadian Labour Congress 1990–. *Address:* National Union of Public and General Employees, 15 Auriga Drive, Nepean, ON K2E 1B7, Canada (office). *Telephone:* (613) 228-9800 (office). *Fax:* (613) 228-9801 (office). *E-mail:* national@nupge.ca (office). *Website:* www.nupge.ca (office).

CLANCY, Thomas (Tom) Leo, Jr, BA; American writer; b. 12 March 1947, Baltimore, Md; m. 1st Wanda Thomas 1969 (divorced 1998); one s. three d.; m. 2nd Alexandra Marie Llewellyn 1999; ed Loyola Coll.; Co-founder Red Storm Entertainment (computer game developer) 1996; part-owner of the Baltimore Orioles, a Major League Baseball team. He officially is the Orioles' Vice Chairman of Community Activities and Public Affairs.; Hon. DHumLitt (Rensselaer Polytechnic Inst.) 1992. *Publications:* The Hunt for Red October 1984, Red Storm Rising 1986, Patriot Games 1987, Cardinal of the Kremlin 1988, Clear and Present Danger 1989, The Sum of all Fears 1991, Without Remorse 1992, Submarine 1993, Debt of Honour 1994, Tom Clancy's Op Centre (with Steve Pieczenik) 1994, Reality Check 1995, Games of State: Op Centre 03 (with Steve Pieczenik) 1996, Tom Clancy's Op Centre II (with Steve Pieczenik) 1996, Executive Orders 1996, Into the Storm (with Fred Franks Jr) 1997, Rainbow Six 1998, Carrier 1999, The Bear and the Dragon 2000, Red Rabbit 2002, The Teeth of the Tiger 2003, Battle Ready (with Tony Zinni and Tony Koltz) 2004. *Address:* 111 West 40th Street, New York, NY 10018-2506, USA.

CLAPTON, Eric Patrick, CBE; British musician (guitar), singer and songwriter; b. (Eric Patrick Clapp), 30 March 1945, Ripley, Surrey; m. 1st Patti Harrison (née Boyd) 1979 (divorced 1988); one s. (deceased) by Lori Delsanto; one d.; m. 2nd Melia McEnery 2002; three c.; guitarist with Roosters 1963, Yardbirds 1963–65, John Mayall's Bluesbreakers 1965–66, Cream 1966–68, Blind Faith 1969, Derek and the Dominoes 1970, Delaney and Bonnie 1970–72; solo artist 1972–; six Grammy Awards 1993, Grammy Award for Best Rock Performance by Duo or Group (for The Calling, with Santana) 2000, Grammy Award for Best Male Pop Vocalist 1997. *Film appearances:* Tommy 1974, Blues Brothers 2000 1998. *Recordings include:* albums: Disraeli Gears 1967, Wheels of Fire 1968, Goodbye Cream 1969, Layla 1970, Eric Clapton 1970, Blind Faith 1971, Concert For Bangladesh 1971, Eric Clapton's Rainbow Concert 1973, 461 Ocean Boulevard 1974, There's One In Every Crowd 1975, E. C. Was Here 1975, No Reason To Cry 1976, Slowhand 1977, Backless 1978, Just One Night 1980, Another Ticket 1981, Money and Cigarettes 1983, Too Much Monkey Business 1984, Behind The Sun 1985, August 1986, Homeboy 1989, Journeyman 1989, 24 Nights 1991, Rush 1992, Unplugged 1992, Stages 1993, From The Cradle 1994, Crossroads 2 1996, Live In Montreux 1997, Pilgrim 1998, Rock Report: Deserted Cities Of The Heart 1998, Riding With The King (with B. B. King) (Grammy Award for Best Traditional Blues Album 2001) 2000, Reptile (Grammy Award for Best Pop Instrumental Performance 2002) 2001, One More Car One More Rider 2002, Me And Mr Johnson 2004, She's So Respectable 2004, Sessions For Robert J. 2004, Back Home 2005, The Road to Escondido (with J. J. Cale; Grammy Award for Best Contemporary Blues Album 2008) 2006. *Publication:* Eric Clapton: The Autobiography 2007. *Address:* c/o Michael Eaton, 22 Blades Court, Deodar Road, London, SW15 2NU, England (office). *Website:* www.ericclapton.com.

CLARDY, Jon Christel, BS, PhD; American chemist and academic; *Co-Director, Institute of Chemistry and Cell Biology, Harvard Medical School;* b. 16 May 1943, Washington, DC; m. Andrea Clardy 1966; two s.; ed Yale Univ., Harvard Univ.; Asst Prof., Iowa State Univ. 1969–72, Assoc. Prof. 1972–75, Prof. 1975–77; Prof., Cornell Univ. 1978–90, Chair. Dept of Chem. 1988–93, Horace White Prof. of Chem. and Chemical Biology 1990–2002, Sr Assoc. Dean, Cornell Coll. of Arts and Sciences 2000–02; Prof., Dept of Biological Chem. and Molecular Pharmacology, Harvard Medical School 2003–, Co-Dir Inst. of Chem. and Cell Biology 2003–; mem. Editorial Advisory Bd Chemistry and Biology 1994–; mem. US Nat. Cttee on Crystallography 1994–98, Vice-Chair. 2000–02, Chair. 2003–; mem. Exec. Cttee American Soc. of Pharmacognosy 1999–2002, Pres. 2003–04, mem. Research Achievement Cttee 1997–2000; mem. Review Cttee Novartis Core Technologies 1997, NIH Nat. Cancer Inst. Developmental Therapeutics 1997–98, mem. Bd of Scientific Counselors 1999–2004; Fellow, Camille and Henry Dreyfus Foundation 1972–77, Alfred P. Sloan Foundation 1973–75, John Simon Guggenheim Memorial Foundation 1984–85, AAAS 1985–, American Acad. of Arts and Sciences 1995–; Hon. Fellow, Woodrow Wilson Nat. Fellowship Foundation 1964–; ACS Akron Section Award 1987, Cornell Univ. Clark Distinguished Teaching Award 1990, ACS Arthur C. Cope Scholar Award 1997, Paul J Scheuer Award 1998, American Soc. of Pharmacognosy Research Achievement Award 2004. *Publications:* over 600 papers in scientific journals. *Address:* Department of Biological Chemistry and Molecular Pharmacology, Harvard Medical School, 240 Longwood Avenue, Boston, MA 02115, USA (office). *Telephone:* (617) 432-2845 (office). *Fax:* (617) 432-3702 (office). *E-mail:* jon_clardy@hms.harvard.edu (office). *Website:* www.iccb.med.harvard.edu (office).

CLARK, Rt Hon. (Charles) Joseph (Joe), PC, CC; Canadian politician; b. 5 June 1939, High River, Alberta; s. of Charles A. Clark and Grace R. Welch; m. Maureen Anne (née McTeer) 1973; one d.; ed Univ. of Alberta, Dalhousie Univ.; began career as a journalist; Nat. Pres. Progressive Conservative Party of Canada (PCP) Student Fed. 1963–65; First Vice-Pres. PCP Asscn of Alberta 1966–67; Lecturer, Univ. of Alberta 1965–67; Special Asst to Davie Fulton 1967; Exec. Asst to PCP Leader Robert Stanfield 1967–70; MP for Rocky Mountain 1972–79, for Yellowhead 1979–93; Leader of PCP 1976–83, 2000–03; Prime Minister of Canada 1979–80; Sec. of State for External Affairs 1984–91, Minister responsible for Constitutional Affairs, Pres. of Queen's Privy Council 1991–93; UN Sec.-Gen.'s Special Rep. for Cyprus 1993–96; Founder and Pres. Joe Clark & Assocs (consulting firm), Calgary 1993–; Chair. SMG Canada 1993–98; Chair. CANOP Int. Resource Ventures Inc. 1993–98; Distinguished Statesman-in-Residence, School of Int. Service and Sr Fellow, Center for North American Studies, American Univ., Washington, DC 2004–05; Public Policy Scholar, Woodrow Wilson Int. Center for Scholars 2004; Chair. CANOP Worldwide Corpn, SMG Canada, Canada-

Korea Forum; mem. Bd Bentall Corpn, Hughes Aircraft of Canada, Inuvaluit Energy Inc. and other resource companies, Nat. History Soc. (of Canada), Pacific Council on Int. Policy, North-South Inst.; mem. Advisory Bd Canadian Foundation for Dispute Resolution; mem. Council of Freely Elected Heads of Govt, Int. Council of the Asia Soc.; Hon. LLD (New Brunswick) 1976, (Calgary) 1984, (Alberta) 1985, (Univ. of King's Coll., Concordia Univ.) 1994; Hon. Chief Samson Cree Nation 1992; mem. Alberta Order of Excellence 1983. *Publication:* A Nation Too Good To Lose 1994. *Address:* c/o Joe Clark & Associates, 30th Floor, 237 4th Avenue, SW, Calgary, Alberta T2P 4X7, Canada (office). *Telephone:* (403) 268-6863 (office). *Fax:* (403) 268-3100 (office). *E-mail:* joeclark@cchambers.com (office).

CLARK, Colin Whitcomb, PhD, FRS, FRSC; Canadian mathematician and academic; *Professor Emeritus of Mathematics, University of British Columbia;* b. 18 June 1931, Vancouver; s. of George Savage Clark and Irene Clark (née Stewart); m. Janet Arlene Davidson 1955; one s. two d.; ed Univs of British Columbia and Washington; instructor, Univ. of California, Berkeley 1958–60; Asst Prof., then Assoc. Prof., Prof. of Math., Univ. of British Columbia 1960–94, Prof. Emer. 1994–; Regents' Prof., Univ. of California, Davis 1986; Visiting Prof., Cornell Univ. 1987, Princeton Univ. 1997; Hon. DSc (Univ. of Victoria) 2001. *Publications include:* Dynamic Modelling in Behavioral Ecology (with M. Mangel) 1988, Mathematical Bioeconomics 1990, Dynamic State Variable Models in Ecology (with M. Mangel) 2000, Worldwide Crisis in Fisheries 2006. *Leisure interests:* natural history, hiking, gardening. *Address:* 10995 Springmont Gate, Richmond, BC, V7E 1Y5 (home); Mathematics Department, Math Annex 1217, University of British Columbia, Vancouver, BC V6T 1Z2, Canada (office). *Telephone:* (604) 274-5379 (home). *Fax:* (604) 822-6074 (office). *E-mail:* colin_clark@shaw.ca (home). *Website:* www.math.ubc.ca/people/faculty/keshet/mathbio/clark.html (office).

CLARK, Rt Hon. Helen Elizabeth, PC, MA; New Zealand politician; *Administrator, United Nations Development Programme (UNDP);* b. 26 Feb. 1950, Hamilton; d. of George Clark and Margaret Clark; m. Peter Davis; ed Epsom Girls' Grammar School, Auckland, Auckland Univ.; Jr Lecturer, Dept of Political Studies, Auckland Univ. 1973–75, Lecturer 1977–81; MP for Mount Albert 1981–96, 1999–, for Owairaka 1996–99, mem. Foreign Affairs, Defence and Trade Cttee; Minister of Housing and Minister of Conservation 1987–89, of Health 1989–90, of Labour 1989–90; Deputy Prime Minister 1989–90, Prime Minister of New Zealand Nov. 1999–2008, also Minister for Arts, Culture and Heritage; Deputy Leader of the Opposition 1990–93, Spokesperson on Health and Labour 1990–93, Leader of the Opposition 1993–99; Leader NZ Labour Party 1993–2008; mem. Labour Party 1971–, Spokesperson on Foreign Affairs, on Arts, Culture and Heritage 2008–; Admin. UNDP 2009–; Peace Prize, Danish Peace Foundation 1986, ranked by Forbes magazine amongst 100 Most Powerful Women (43rd) 2004, (24th) 2005, (20th) 2006, (38th) 2007, (56th) 2008. *Leisure interests:* film, theatre, classical music, opera, cross-country skiing, trekking, reading. *Address:* Office of the Administrator, United Nations Development Programme, One United Nations Plaza, New York, NY 10017, USA (office). *Telephone:* (212) 906-5295 (office). *Fax:* (212) 906-5364 (office). *E-mail:* hq@undp.org (office). *Website:* www.undp.org (office).

CLARK, Howard Charles, PhD, FRSC, FCIC; Canadian chemist and academic; b. 4 Sept. 1929, Auckland, NZ; s. of Eric Crago Clark; m. Isabel Joy Dickson-Clark 1954; two d.; ed Takapuna Grammar School, Auckland, Univ. of Auckland, NZ and Univ. of Cambridge, UK; Lecturer, Univ. of Auckland 1954–55; Fellow Univ. of Cambridge 1955–57; Asst Prof. then Prof., Univ. of British Columbia 1957–65; Assoc. Prof., Univ. of Western Ont. 1965–66; Prof. and Head of Chem., Univ. of Guelph 1967–76; Academic Vice-Pres. and Prof. of Chem. 1976–86; Pres., Vice-Chancellor Dalhousie Univ. 1986–95; Ed. Canadian Journal of Chemistry 1974–78; Chair. Int. Relations Cttee, Assoc. of Univs and Colls of Canada 1993; Past Chair. Metro United Way Task Force; Co-Chair. NABST Oceans and Coasts Cttee 1993–94; Dir Corp. Higher Educ. Forum 1990–94; mem. Chem. Inst. of Canada (Pres. 1983–84), Asscn of Atlantic Univs 1986–, Asscn of Univs and Colls of Canada 1986–, Nat. Advisory Bd on Science and Tech. 1991–94, Commonwealth Standing Cttee on Student Mobility and Higher Educ. Co-operation 1992; Hon. DSc (Univ. of Vic.) 1989, (Univ. of Guelph) 1993; Noranda Award of Chem. Inst. of Canada 1968. *Publications:* author or co-author of over 250 articles and chapters in professional journals. *Leisure interests:* tennis, swimming, gardening. *Address:* RR#1, Moffat, ON L0P 1J0, Canada.

CLARK, Ian D., DPhil, MPP; Canadian government official, international civil servant and academic; *Professor, School of Public Policy and Governance, University of Toronto;* b. 15 April 1946, Antrim, UK; s. of Sidney Clark and Zella I. Stade; m. Marjorie Sweet 1968; ed Univs of British Columbia and Oxford and Harvard Univ.; Exec. Asst to Minister of Urban Affairs 1972–74; Dir then Dir-Gen. Analysis and Liaison Br. Dept of Regional Econ. Expansion 1974–79; Dir then Deputy Sec. Ministry of State for Econ. Devt 1979–82; Deputy Sec. Privy Council Office 1982–87; Deputy Minister, Dept of Consumer and Corp. Affairs 1987–89; Sec. Treas. Bd 1989–94, also Comptroller-Gen. of Canada 1993–94; Exec. Dir IMF 1994–96; Pnr, KPMG, Toronto 1996–98; Pres. and CEO Council of Ont. Univs 1998–2007; Prof., School of Public Policy and Governance, Univ. of Toronto 2007–; Harvard Kennedy School Alumni Achievement Award 1997. *Address:* School of Public Policy and Governance, University of Toronto, Canadiana Building, 3rd floor, 14 Queen's Park Cres., West Toronto, ON M5S 3K9 (office); 44 Glenview Avenue, Toronto, ON M4R 1P6 Canada. *Telephone:* (416) 978-2841 (office). *Fax:* (416) 978-5079 (office). *E-mail:* id.clark@utoronto.ca (office). *Website:* www.publicpolicy.utoronto.ca (office).

CLARK, Johnson (John) Pepper, BA; Nigerian poet, dramatist and academic; b. 3 April 1935, Kiagbodo; s. of Fuludu Bekederemo Clark; m.

Ebunoluwa Bolajoko Odutola; one s. three d.; ed Govt Coll. Ughelli, Univ. Coll. Ibadan, Princeton Univ., USA; Ed. The Horn (Ibadan) 1958; Head of Features and editorial writer, Express Group of Newspapers, Lagos 1961–62; Research Fellow, Inst. of African Studies, Univ. of Lagos 1963–64, Lecturer, Dept of English 1965–69, Sr Lecturer 1969–72, Prof. of English 1972–80; consultant to UNESCO 1965–67; Ed. Black Orpheus (journal) 1965–78; Visiting Distinguished Fellow, Center for Humanities, Wesleyan Univ., Conn., USA 1975–76; Visiting Research Prof., Inst. of African Studies, Univ. of Ibadan 1979–80; Distinguished Visiting Prof. of English and Writer in Residence, Lincoln Univ., Pa 1989; Visiting Prof. of English, Yale Univ. 1990; Trustee and mem. Petroleum (Special) Trust Fund and Man. Bd, Abuja 1995–; mem. Nat. Council of Laureates (Nigeria) 1992; Foundation Fellow, Nigerian Acad. of Letters 1996; Nigerian Nat. Order of Merit; Nigerian Nat. Merit Award. *Drama includes:* Song of a Goat 1961, Three Plays 1964, Ozidi 1968, The Bikoroa Plays 1985, The Wives' Revolt. *Poetry published includes:* Poems 1962, A Reed in the Tide 1965, Casualties 1970, A Decade of Tongues 1981, State of the Union 1985, Mandela and Other Poems 1988, A Lot From Paradise 1997. *Other publications:* America, Their America 1964, The Example of Shakespeare 1970, Transcription and Translation from the Oral Tradition of the Izon of the Niger Delta; The Ozidi Saga (trans.) 1977, The Hero as a Villain 1978. *Leisure interests:* walking, swimming, collecting classical European and traditional African music. *Address:* 23 Oduduwa Crescent, GRA, Ikeja, Lagos; Okemeji Place, Funama, Kiagbodo, Burutu Local Government Area, Delta State, Nigeria. *Telephone:* (1) 497-8436 (Lagos). *Fax:* (1) 497-8463 (Lagos).

CLARK, Jonathan Charles Douglas, PhD, FRHistS; British historian and academic; *Joyce and Elizabeth Hall Distinguished Professor of British History, University of Kansas;* b. 28 Feb. 1951, London; s. of Ronald James Clark and Dorothy Margaret Clark; m. Katherine Redwood Penovich 1996; ed Univ. of Cambridge; Research Fellow, Peterhouse, Cambridge 1977–81; Research Fellow, The Leverhulme Trust; Fellow, All Souls Coll., Oxford 1986–95, Sr Research Fellow 1995; Joyce and Elizabeth Hall Distinguished Prof. of British History, Univ. of Kansas, USA 1995–; Visiting Prof., Cttee on Social Thought, Univ. of Chicago 1993; Visiting Prof., Forschungszentrum Europäische Aufklärung, Potsdam 2000, Univ. of Northumbria 2001–03; Visiting Distinguished Lecturer, Univ. of Manitoba 1999; mem. Ecclesiastical History Soc., Church of England Record Soc., N American Conf. on British Studies, British Soc. for Eighteenth Century Studies. *Publications:* The Dynamics of Change 1982, English Society 1688–1832 1985, Revolution and Rebellion 1986; The Memoirs and Speeches of James, 2nd Earl Waldegrave (ed.) 1988, Ideas and Politics in Modern Britain (ed.) 1990, The Language of Liberty 1660–1832 1993, Samuel Johnson 1994, Edmund Burke's Reflections on the Revolution in France (ed.) 2001, English Society 1660–1832 (revised edn) 2000, Samuel Johnson in Historical Context (jt ed.) 2002, Our Shadowed Present 2003; articles on British and American history. *Leisure interest:* history. *Address:* Department of History, University of Kansas, 1445 Jayhawk Boulevard, Lawrence, KS 66045-7590, USA (office). *Telephone:* (785) 864-3569 (office). *Fax:* (785) 864-5046 (office). *E-mail:* jcdclark@ku.edu (office). *Website:* www.history.ku.edu (office).

CLARK, Rt Hon. Joseph (see CLARK, Rt Hon. Charles Joseph).

CLARK, Mary Higgins, BA; American writer and business executive; b. 24 Dec. 1931, New York; d. of Luke Higgins and Nora Durkin; m. Warren Clark 1949 (died 1964); two s. three d.; ed Fordham Univ.; advertising asst Remington Rand 1946; stewardess, Pan Am 1949–50; radio scriptwriter, producer Robert G. Jennings 1965–70; Vice-Pres., Pnr, Creative Dir, Producer Radio Programming, Aerial Communications, New York 1970–80; Chair. and Creative Dir D.J. Clark Enterprises, New York 1980–; mem. American Acad. of Arts and Sciences, Mystery Writers of America, Authors League; several hon. degrees; Grand Prix de Littérature Policière, France 1980. *Publications:* Aspire to the Heavens, A Biography of George Washington 1969, Where Are the Children? 1976, A Stranger is Watching 1978, The Cradle Will Fall 1980, A Cry in the Night 1982, Stillwatch 1984, Weep No More, My Lady 1987, While My Pretty One Sleeps 1989, The Anastasia Syndrome 1989, Loves Music, Loves to Dance 1991, All Around the Town 1992, I'll Be Seeing You 1993, Remember Me 1994, The Lottery Winner 1994, Bad Behavior 1995, Let Me Call You Sweetheart 1995, Silent Night 1996, Moonlight Becomes You 1996, My Gal Sunday 1996, Pretend You Don't See Her 1997, The Plot Thickens 1997, You Belong to Me 1998, All Through the Night 1998, We'll Meet Again 1999, Before I Say Good-Bye 2000, Deck the Halls (with Carol Higgins Clark) 2000, Daddy's Little Girl 2002, On the Street Where You Live 2002, Mount Vernon Love Story: A Novel of George and Martha Washington 2002, The Second Time Around 2003, Nighttime is My Time 2004, No Place Like Home 2005, Little Girls in Blue 2006, Santa Cruise 2006, Ghost Ship: A Cape Cod Story 2007, I Heard that Song Before 2007, Where Are You Now? 2008, Just Take my Heart 2009. *Address:* c/o Simon and Schuster, Inc., 1230 Avenue of the Americas, New York, NY 10020, USA (office). *Website:* www.simonsays .com (office).

CLARK, Maureen Harding, BCL; Irish criminal lawyer and judge; *Judge, International Criminal Court;* b. 3 Jan. 1946; ed Bukit Nanas School, Kuala Lumpur, Malaysia, Muckross Park School, Dublin, Trinity Coll. Dublin, Univ. Coll. Dublin, Univ. of Lyons, France; called to Irish Bar 1975, Irish Inner Bar 1991; criminal defence practice 1976–2001; Regional State Prosecutor 1985–91; Lead Counsel, Court of Criminal Appeal, Dublin 1991–2001; elected Judge Int. Criminal Tribunal for the Fmr Yugoslavia (ICTY) 2001; elected Judge Int. Criminal Court 2003–; governmental adviser on issues relating to victims' rights in sexual offence cases; Sec. and elected mem. Bar Council of Ireland; mem. Int. Asscn of Prosecutors, Irish Women Lawyers Asscn, Irish Human Rights Comm. 2004–; Assoc. mem. American Bar Asscn; Rep. of Irish Bar to numerous int. legal confs. *Address:* International Criminal Court, Maanweg 174, 2516 AB The Hague, The Netherlands (office). *Telephone:* (70) 5158515 (office). *Fax:* (70) 5158555 (office). *E-mail:* pio@icc-cpi.int (office). *Website:* www.icp-cpi.int (office).

CLARK, Petula, CBE; British singer and actress; b. (Sally Olwen), 15 Nov. 1932, Epsom, Surrey; d. of Leslie Norman Clarke and Doris Olwen; m. Claude Wolff 1961; one s. two d.; started career as child singer entertaining troops during Second World War; early appearances in films under contract to Rank Organization; made numerous recordings and television appearances in both England and France; success of single Downtown started career in USA; two Grammy Awards, Medaille de Vermel de Paris 1970, Achievement in Arts Award 1994, Grammy Hall of Fame Award 2003. *Films include:* Medal for the General 1944, Murder in Reverse 1945, London Town 1946, Strawberry Roan 1947, Here Come the Huggets, Vice Versa, Easy Money 1948, Don't Ever Leave Me 1949, Vote for Huggett 1949, The Huggetts Abroad, Dance Hall, The Romantic Age 1950, White Corridors, Madame Louise 1951, Made in Heaven 1952, The Card 1952, The Runaway Bus 1954, My Gay Dog 1954, The Happiness of Three Women 1955, Track the Man Down 1956, That Woman Opposite 1957, Daggers Drawn 1964, Finian's Rainbow 1968, Goodbye Mr Chips 1969, Second Star to the Right 1980. *Stage appearances:* Sound of Music 1981, Someone Like You (also wrote) 1989, Blood Brothers (Broadway) 1993, Sunset Boulevard 1995–96; nat. tour 1994–95, Sunset Boulevard 1995, 1996, New York 1998, US tour 1998–2000, London 2000. *Address:* c/o John Ashby, John Ashby Associates, PO Box 288, Woking, Surrey, GU22 0YN, England (office). *Telephone:* (1483) 799686 (office). *Fax:* (1483) 799687 (office). *Website:* www.petulaclark.net.

CLARK, R. Kerry, BCom; Canadian healthcare industry executive; *Chairman and CEO, Cardinal Health Inc.;* b. 29 April 1952, Ottawa, Ont.; ed Queen's Univ.; joined Procter & Gamble Co. 1974, held various man. positions including Group Vice-Pres. Laundry and Cleaning Products, Pres. Procter & Gamble Asia, Pres. of Global Market Devt and Business Operations, Vice-Chair. and Pres. Global Health, Baby and Family Care 2004–06; Chair. and CEO Cardinal Health Inc. 2006–; mem. Bd of Dirs Textron Inc., CompeteColumbus; mem. The Business Council, Healthcare Leadership Council, Ohio Business Roundtable, The Columbus Partnership, Dean's Advisory Council for Ohio State Univ.'s Fisher Coll. of Business; Hon. Doctor of Commercial Science (St Bonaventure Univ.). *Address:* Cardinal Health Inc., 7000 Cardinal Place, Dublin, OH 43017, USA (office). *Telephone:* (614) 757-5000 (office). *Fax:* (614) 757-8871 (office). *E-mail:* info@cardinal.com (office). *Website:* www .cardinal.com (office).

CLARK, Richard T., BA, MBA; American pharmaceutical industry executive; *Chairman, President and CEO, Merck & Company, Inc.;* ed Washington and Jefferson Coll., American Univ.; Lt in US Army 1970–72; Quality Control Inspector, Industrial Engineer, Quality Control Analyst, Lead Supervisor (Pharmaceutical Production), MSD Pharmaceutical 1972–78, Sr New Products Planner 1978–81, Production Man., Elkton Pharmaceutical Labs 1981–83, Man. Industrial Eng, West Point 1983–84, Sr Man. Industrial Eng, MPMD 1984–85, Dir Operations Improvement, MPMD 1985–86, Sr Dir, Man. Eng, MSD/MPMD 1986–89, Exec. Dir, Man. Eng, Merck Pharmaceutical Mfg Div. 1989–91, Vice-Pres., Materials Man. and Man. Eng, Merck Mfg Div. (MMD) 1991–93, Vice-Pres., Procurement and Materials Man., MMD 1993–94, Vice-Pres., N American Operations, MMD 1994–96, Sr Vice-Pres. 1996–97, Sr Vice-Pres., Quality Commercial Affairs, MMD 1997, Exec. Vice-Pres. and COO, Merck-Medco Managed Care 1997–2000, Pres. Medco Health Solutions Inc. 2000–02, Chair. and CEO 2002–03, Pres. MMD 2003–05, mem. Bd Dirs, Pres. and CEO Merck & Co., Inc. 2005–, Chair. 2007–. *Address:* Merck & Co. Inc., 1 Merck Drive, Whitehouse Station, NJ 08889-0100, USA (office). *Telephone:* (908) 423-1000 (office). *Fax:* (908) 735-1253 (office). *E-mail:* info@merck.com (office). *Website:* www.merck.com (office).

CLARK, Sir Robert Anthony, Kt, DSC; British business executive; *Chairman, RP&C International Ltd;* b. 6 Jan. 1924, London; s. of John Anthony Clark and Gladys Clark (née Dyer); m. Marjorie Lewis 1949; two s. one d.; ed Highgate School, King's Coll., Cambridge; served in RN 1942–46; qualified as lawyer with Messrs. Slaughter and May, became Pnr 1953; Dir Hill Samuel Bank Ltd (fmrly Philip Hill, Higginson, Erlangers Ltd, then Hill Samuel and Co. Ltd) 1962–91, Chair. 1974–87, Chief Exec. 1974–77, also Chief Exec. Hill Samuel Group 1976–80, Chair. 1980–87; Chair. IMI PLC 1980–89, Marley 1984–89, Vodafone Group PLC 1988–98; Co-founder and Chair. RP&C Int. Ltd (fmrly Rauscher Pierce and Clark) 1992–; Dir Mirror Group Newspapers (now called Trinity Mirror Group) 1991, Chair. 1992–98; Dir Rover Group (fmrly BL PLC) 1977–88, Bank of England 1976–85, Shell Transport and Trading Co. 1982–94, Alfred McAlpine PLC 1957–96, SmithKline Beecham PLC 1986–95; Chair. Review Bd on Doctors' and Dentists' Remuneration 1979–86, Charing Cross and Westminster Medical School 1982–96; Dir ENO 1983–87; Hon. DSc (Cranfield) 1982. *Leisure interests:* music, reading, collecting antiquarian books. *Address:* RP&C International Ltd, 31A St James's Square, London, SW1Y 4JR (office); Munstead Wood, Godalming, Surrey, GU7 1UN, England (home). *Telephone:* (20) 7766-7000 (office); (1483) 417867 (home). *Fax:* (20) 7766-7001 (office). *E-mail:* info@rpcint.com (office). *Website:* www.rpcint.com (office).

CLARK, Robin Jon Hawes, CNZM, PhD, FRS, FRSA, FRSC; British chemist and academic; *Sir William Ramsay Professor of Chemistry, University College London;* b. 16 Feb. 1935, Rangiora, NZ; s. of Reginald Hawes Clark, JP and Marjorie Alice Clark (née Thomas); m. Beatrice Rawdin Brown, JP 1964; one s. one d.; ed Marlborough Coll., Blenheim, NZ, Christ's Coll., Christchurch, NZ, Canterbury Univ. Coll., Univ. of NZ, Univ. of Otago, NZ, Univ. Coll. London; Asst Lecturer in Chem., Univ. Coll. London 1962, Lecturer 1963–71, Reader 1972–81, Prof. 1982–88, Head Dept of Chem. 1989–99, Dean, Faculty of

Science 1988–89, Sir William Ramsay Prof. 1989–, mem. Council 1991–94, Fellow, Univ. Coll. London 1992–, mem. Senate and Acad. Council Univ. of London 1988–93; Visiting Prof., Columbia Univ. 1965, Padua 1967, Western Ontario 1968, Texas A&M 1978, Bern and Fribourg 1979, Auckland 1981, Odense 1983, Sydney 1985, Bordeaux 1988, Pretoria 1991, Würzburg 1997, Indiana 1998, Thessaloniki 1999; mem. Dalton Council Royal Soc. of Chem. 1985–88, Vice-Pres. 1988–90; mem. SRC Inorganic Chem. Panel 1977–80, Science and Eng Research Council (SERC) Post-Doctoral Fellowships Panel 1983, SERC Inorganic Chem. Panel 1993–94; Chair. Steering Cttee Int. Conferences on Raman Spectroscopy 1990–92, 11th Int. Conf. on Raman Spectroscopy, London 1988, Advisory Council, Ramsay Memorial Fellowships Trust 1989– (Trustee 1994–); mem. Council, Royal Soc. 1993–94, Royal Institution 1996–, Vice-Pres. 1997–, Sec. 1998–2004; Tilden 1983, Nyholm 1989, Thomas Graham 1991, Harry Hallam 1993, 2000, and Liversidge 2003 Lecturer and Medallist, Royal Soc. of Chem.; Chair. Univ. of Canterbury, NZ Trust 2004–; mem. Academia Europaea 1990; Fellow, Royal Soc. 1990; Foreign Fellow, Nat. Acad. of Sciences (India) 2007; numerous radio and several TV interviews on arts/science subjects in UK, Italy, France and NZ; invited lectures in over 360 insts in 36 countries; Hon. Fellow, Royal Soc. of NZ 1989, Royal Inst. of GB 2004; Companion of the NZ Order of Merit; Hon. DSc (Canterbury, NZ) 2001; Joannes Marcus Marci Medal, Czech Spectroscopy Soc. 1998, UK-Canada Rutherford Lecturer 2000, T.J. Sidey Medal, Royal Soc. of NZ 2001, Ralph Anderson Lecturer Horners' Co. 2003, Lifetime Achievement Award, New Zealand Soc. 2004, Royal Soc. of London Bakerian Lecturer 2008, Inaugural Franklin-Lavoisier Prize, Maison de la Chimie/Chemical Heritage Foundation 2009, Barber-Surgeons Co. Denny Lecturer 2009. *Publications:* The Chemistry of Titanium and Vanadium 1968, The Chemistry of Titanium, Zirconium and Hafnium (jtly) 1973, The Chemistry of Vanadium, Niobium and Tantalum (jtly) 1973, Advances in Spectroscopy (co-ed.) Vols 1–26 1975–98, Raman Spectroscopy (co-ed.) 1988; more than 500 scientific papers in learned journals on topics in transition metal chemistry and spectroscopy and the Arts/Science interface. *Leisure interests:* golf, long distance walking, travel, bridge, music, theatre, wine. *Address:* Christopher Ingold Laboratories, University College London, 20 Gordon Street, London, WC1H 0AJ, England (office). *Telephone:* (1923) 85-7899 (home); (20) 7679-7457 (office). *Fax:* (20) 7679-7463 (office). *E-mail:* r.j.h.clark@ucl.ac.uk (office). *Website:* www.chem.ucl.ac.uk (office).

CLARK, W. Edmund (Ed), MA, DEcon; Canadian banker; *President and CEO, Toronto-Dominion Bank;* b. 1947; m. Frances Clark; four c.; ed Univ. of Toronto, Harvard Univ., USA; various sr positions in Fed. Govt of Canada, Ottawa 1974–84, including heading Nat. Energy Program 1980; Head of Corp. and Govt Finance, Merrill Lynch, Toronto 1985–88, Chair. and CEO Morgan Financial Corpn 1988–91; Vice-Chair. and COO CT Financial Services Inc. 1991–94, Pres. and CEO 1994–2000; Chair. and CEO Toronto-Dominion (TD) Canada Trust (following acquisition of CT Financial Services Inc. by TD Bank 2000) 2000, Pres. and COO TD Bank Financial Group 2000–02, Pres. and CEO 2002–; Co-Chair. Heart and Circulation Campaign, Univ. Health Network (UHN). *Address:* Toronto-Dominion Bank, Toronto-Dominion Centre, King Street West and Bay Street, Toronto, ON M5K 1A2, Canada (office). *Telephone:* (416) 982-8222 (office). *Fax:* (416) 982-5671 (office). *E-mail:* td .capa@td.com (office). *Website:* www.td.com (office).

CLARK, Gen. Wesley Kanne, BA, MA; American politician and fmr army officer; *Chairman and CEO, Wesley Clark & Associates LLC;* b. 23 Dec. 1944, Little Rock, Ark.; m. Gertrude Clark; one s.; ed US Mil. Acad., West Point, Univ. of Oxford (Rhodes Scholar), UK, Nat. War Coll., Command and Gen. Staff Coll., Armor Officer Advanced and Basic Courses, Ranger and Airborne School; served in US Army 1966–2000, held numerous staff and command positions and rose to rank of 4-star Gen., served in Viet Nam; fmr Sr mil. Asst to Gen. Alexander Haig (q.v.); fmr Head Nat. Army Training Center; fmr Dir of Strategy Dept of Defense; Sr mem. American negotiating team at Bosnian peace negotiations, Dayton, OH 1995; fmr Head of US Southern Command, Panama; NATO Supreme Allied Commdr in Europe (SACEUR) 1997–2000; Head of US Forces in Europe (USEUCOM) 1997–2000 (retd); consultant, Stephens Inc., Little Rock, Ark. 2000–01, Man. Dir Stephens Group 2001–03; Distinguished Advisor, Center for Strategic and Int. Studies, Washington, DC 2000; Chair. and CEO Wesley Clark & Assocs LLC (consulting firm), Little Rock, Ark. 2003–; Vice-Chair. and Sr Advisor, James Lee Witt Assocs LLC, Washington, DC 2004–; Chair. Rodman & Renshaw LLC, New York 2006–; unsuccessful cand. for Democratic presidential nomination 2003; mil. analyst for CNN 2001–03; Sr Fellow and Lecturer, Ronald W. Burkle Center for Int. Relations, UCLA 2006–; Hon. OBE; Dr hc Drake Univ. 2002; Hon. DHumLitt, Seton Hall Univ. 2002; Hon. LLD, Univ. of Arkansas 2002, Ripon Coll. 2005, Lyon Coll. 2005; Commdr, Légion d'honneur, Kt Grand Cross, Order of Orange-Nassau, Netherlands; Decorated Defense Distinguished Service Medal (three), Distinguished Service Medal, Silver Star, Legion of Merit (four), Bronze Star Medal (two), Purple Heart, Meritorious Service Medal (two), Army Commendation Medal (two), Presidential Medal of Freedom 2000. *Publication:* Waging Modern War: Bosnia, Kosovo and the Future of Combat 2001, Winning Modern Wars 2003, Time to Lead: For Duty, Honor and Country (co-author) 2007. *Address:* 1 Crestmont Drive, Little Rock, AR 72227; Rodman & Renshaw LLC, Wall Street Plaza, 88 Pine Street, 32nd Floor, New York, NY 10005, USA. *Telephone:* (212) 850-5600 (New York). *E-mail:* rodman@fd.com. *Website:* www.rodmanandrenshaw.com.

CLARK OF CALTON, Baroness (Life Peer), cr. 2005; **Lynda Margaret Clark,** QC, LLB, PhD; British lawyer, former law officer and judge; *Senator of the College of Justice;* b. 26 Feb. 1949, Dundee; ed Univ. of St Andrews and Univ. of Edinburgh; Lecturer Univ. of Dundee 1973–76; admitted as Advocate of the Scots Bar 1977; called to the English Bar, Inner Temple 1988, Bencher 2000; contested constituency of Fife NE (Labour Party) 1992; MP (Labour) for Edinburgh Pentlands 1997–; Advocate Gen. for Scotland 1999–2006; Senator, Coll. of Justice 2006–; mem. Court Univ. of Edinburgh 1995–97; Hon. LLD (Napier) 2007, (Dundee) 2007. *Leisure interests:* reading, arts, swimming. *Address:* Parliament House, Edinburgh, EH7 5BL, Scotland (office).

CLARK OF WINDERMERE, Baron (Life Peer), cr. 2001, of Windermere in the County of Cumbria; **David George Clark,** PC, BA, PhD; British politician; *Chair, Forestry Commission;* b. 19 Oct. 1939, Castle Douglas; s. of George Clark and Janet Clark; m. Christine Kirkby 1970; one d.; ed Univ. of Manchester, Univ. of Sheffield; fmr forester, lab. asst and student teacher; Pres. Univ. of Manchester Union 1963–64; trainee man., USA 1964; univ. lecturer 1965–70; MP for Colne Valley 1970–74, for S. Shields 1979–; Labour spokesman on Agric. and Food 1973–74, on Defence 1980–81, on Environment 1981–86, on Environmental Protection and Devt 1986–87, on Food, Agric. and Rural Affairs 1987–92, on Defence, Disarmament and Arms Control 1992–97; Pres. Open Spaces Soc. 1979–88; mem. Parl. Ass., NATO 1981–; Chancellor of Duchy of Lancaster 1997–98; Chair. Atlantic Council of UK 1998–2001, Forestry Comm. 2001–; Leader UK Del. to NATO-PA 2001–05; mem. House of Lords 2001–; Freeman of South Tyneside 1999. *Publications:* The Industrial Manager 1966, Colne Valley: Radicalisation to Socialism 1981, Victor Grayson: Labour's Lost Leader 1985, We Do Not Want the Earth 1992. *Leisure interests:* walking, gardening, watching football. *Address:* House of Lords, Westminster, London, SW1A 0PW, England. *Telephone:* (20) 7219-2558 (office). *Fax:* (20) 7219-4885 (office). *E-mail:* clarkd@parliament.uk.

CLARKE, Aidan, PhD; Irish historian and academic; *Emeritus Professor, Trinity College, Dublin;* b. 2 May 1933, Watford, England; s. of the late Austin Clarke and of Nora Walker; m. Mary Hughes 1962; two s. two d.; ed The High School, Dublin and Trinity Coll., Dublin; Lecturer in Modern History and Politics, Magee Univ. Coll., Derry 1959–65; Lecturer in Modern History, Trinity Coll., Dublin 1965–78, Assoc. Prof. 1978–86, Erasmus Smith's Prof. 1986–2001, Sr Tutor 1971–73, Registrar 1974–76, Bursar 1980–81, Vice-Provost 1981–87, 1989–91, Fellow 1970–, currently Emer. Prof.; Research Fellow, The 1641 Project 2007–; Chair. Irish Historical Soc. 1978–80; mem. Royal Irish Acad. 1982–, Sr Vice-Pres. 1988–89, Sec. Cttee of Polite Literature and Antiquities 1989–90, Pres. 1990–93; Hon. LittD (Dublin) 1992. *Publications include:* The Old English in Ireland 1625–42 1966, contribs to The New History of Ireland, 111: Early Modern Ireland 1976 Prelude to Restoration in Ireland: the end of the Commonwealth, 1659–1660 1999; numerous articles and essays on early modern Irish history. *Address:* Arts Building, Trinity College, Dublin 2 (office); 160 Rathfarnham Road, Dublin 14, Ireland (home). *Telephone:* (1) 896-2275 (office); (1) 490-3223 (home). *E-mail:* aclarke@tcd.ie (office).

CLARKE, Brian, FRSA; British artist; *Chairman, The Architecture Foundation;* b. 2 July 1953, Oldham, Lancs.; s. of the late Edward Ord Clarke and of Lilian Clarke (née Whitehead); m. Elizabeth Cecilia Finch 1972; one s.; ed Oldham School of Arts and Crafts, Burnley School of Art, The North Devon Coll. of Art and Design; Visiting Prof. of Architectural Art, Univ. Coll. London 1993; mem. Council Winston Churchill Memorial Trust 1985–; Trustee and mem. Cttee Robert Fraser Foundation 1990–; Trustee The Ely Stained Glass Museum; judge, BBC Design Awards 1990, Royal Fine Art Comm. and Sunday Times Architecture Award 1991; stage designs for Paul McCartney World Tour 1989, 1993, The Ruins of Time (Dutch Nat. Ballet) 1993; mem. Cttee, Disability Rights Comm. Comm. for Architecture and the Built Environment 1999–2005; Chair. The Architecture Foundation; Executor, Estate of Francis Bacon; Hon. FRIBA 1993; Churchill Fellowship in architectural art 1974, Art and Work Award special commendation 1989, Europa Nostra award 1990, Leeds Award for Architecture, Special Award for Stained Glass 1990, The European Shopping Centre Award 1995, BDA Auszeichnung guter Bauten, Heidelberg 1996. *Major works:* St Gabriel's Church, Blackburn 1976, All Saints Church, Habergham 1976, Queen's Medical Centre, Nottingham 1978, Laver's & Barraud Bldg, London 1981, Olympus Optical Europa GmbH HQ Bldg, Hamburg 1981, King Khaled Int. Airport, Riyadh, Saudi Arabia 1982, Buxton Thermal Baths, Derbyshire 1987, Lake Sagami Country Club, Yamanishi, Japan (in Asscn with Arata Isozaki) 1988, New Synagogue, Darmstadt, Germany 1988, Victoria Quarter, Leeds 1989, Cibreo Restaurant, Tokyo 1990, Glaxo Pharmaceuticals, Stockley Park, Uxbridge 1990, Stansted Airport, Essex (in Asscn with Sir Norman Foster) 1991, Spindles Shopping Centre, Oldham 1991–93, España Telefónica, Barcelona 1991, Number One America Square, London 1991, 35–38 Chancery Lane, London 1991, The Carmelite, London 1992, 100 New Bridge Street, London 1992, façade of Hôtel de Ville des Bouches-du-Rhône, Marseille (with Will Alsop) 1992–94, Glass Dune, Hamburg (with Future Systems) 1992, EAM Bldg, Kassel, Germany 1992–93, New Synagogue, Heidelberg, Germany 1993, W H Smith & Sons, Abingdon 1994, SMS Lowe The Grace Bldg, New York 1994, Cliveden Hotel 1994, Schadow Arkaden, Düsseldorf 1994, Norte Shopping, Rio de Janeiro 1995, Rye Hosp., Sussex (with Linda McCartney) 1995, Valentino Village, Noci Italy 1996, Kinderhaus Regensburg Germany 1996, Pfizer Pharmaceuticals, New York 1997, 2001, Willis Corroon Bldg, Ipswich 1997, RWE Essen (refurbishment of lobby) 1997, Offenbach Synagogue 1997, New Catholic Church Obersalbach 1997, Praça Norte Clock Tower 1997, Chicago Sinai 1997, Warburg Dillon Read Stamford CT (stained glass cone) 1998, Al Faisaliah Centre, Riyadh (in association with Lord Norman Foster) 2000, Olympus Optical Europa GmbH New HQ Building, Hamburg 2000, Hotel and Thalassotherapy Centre, Nova Yardinia, Italy 2002, Pfizer Security Lobby, New York 2003, Pyramid of Peace, Astana, Kazakhstan (with Norman Foster) 2006. *Design:* Hammersmith Hosp., London 1993, Crossrail, Paddington, London (with Will Alsop) 1994, Q206 Berlin 1994, Frankfurter Allee Plaza, Berlin 1994, New Synagogue, Aachen 1994, Hungerford Bridge, London (with Alsop and Störmer) 1996, Center Villa-Lobos, São Paulo 1997, Future Systems Tower NEC 1997, Heidelberg Cathedral 1997, Chep Lap Kok Airport, Hong

Kong 1997, West Winter Garden, Heron Quays, London 2001, Design for Stained Glass and Rooflight, Ascot Racecourse 2003, Design for Khazakstan Pyramid of Peace, Khazakstan 2004, Apax Partners, London 2007, The Watchtower, Point Village, Dublin, Eire (design) 2008, Mosaic Path "From Life to Life, a Garden for George Harrison", Chelsea Flower Show, London 2008. *Leisure interests:* reading, hoarding. *Address:* Brian Clarke Studio, 6A Trading Estate Road, London, NW10 7LU, England (office). *Telephone:* (20) 8961-9636 (office). *E-mail:* mail@brianclarke.co.uk (office). *Website:* www.brianclarke.co.uk (office).

CLARKE, Bryan Campbell, MA, DPhil, FRS; British geneticist and academic; *Professor Emeritus of Genetics, University of Nottingham;* b. 24 June 1932, Gatley, Cheshire; s. of Robert Campbell Clarke and Gladys Mary Clarke (née Carter); m. Ann Gillian Jewkes 1960; one s. one d.; ed Fay School, Southborough, Mass, USA, Magdalen Coll. School, Oxford and Magdalen Coll., Oxford; Nature Conservancy research student, Univ. of Oxford 1956–59; Asst in Zoology, Univ. of Edin. 1959–63, Lecturer 1963–69, Reader 1969–71; Prof. of Genetics, Univ. of Nottingham 1971–93, Research Prof. 1993–97, Prof. Emer. 1997–, Leverhulme Research Fellow Emer., Inst. of Genetics 1999–2002; Science Research Council Sr Research Fellow 1976–81; Ed. Heredity 1978–85, Proceedings of the Royal Society, series B 1988–93; Vice-Pres. Genetical Soc. 1981–83, Linnean Soc. 1984–86, Soc. for the Study of Evolution 1990–91, Zoological Soc. of London 1998–99; Chair. Biological Sciences Panel, HEFCE 1994–96, Trustee, Charles Darwin Trust 2000–; Co-Founder and Trustee, Frozen Ark Project 2003–; mem. Council of Royal Soc. 1994–96; Foreign mem. American Philosophical Soc. 2003–; Hon. Research Fellow, Natural History Museum 1993–2008; Hon. Foreign mem. American Acad. of Arts and Sciences 2004–; Linnean Medal for Zoology 2003, Darwin-Wallace Medal 2008. *Radio:* about 20 radio broadcasts. *Television:* two programmes based on scientific work: The Open University 1987, Horizon (BBC) 1994. *Publications:* Berber Village 1959; about 130 scientific publications. *Leisure interests:* painting, computing. *Address:* Linden Cottage, School Lane, Colston Bassett, Nottingham, NG12 3FD, England (home). *Telephone:* (1949) 81243 (home). *E-mail:* bryan.clarke@nottingham.ac.uk (office).

CLARKE, Rt Hon. Charles (Rodway), PC, BA; British politician; b. 21 Sept. 1950; s. of Sir Richard Clarke and Brenda Clarke (née Skinner); m. Carol Marika Pearson 1984; two s.; ed Highgate School and King's Coll., Cambridge; Pres. Nat. Union of Students 1975–77; various admin. posts 1977–80; Head, Office of Rt Hon Neil Kinnock, MP 1981–92; Chief Exec. Quality Public Affairs 1992–97; mem. Hackney London Borough Council 1980–86; MP (Labour) for Norwich S 1997–; Parl. Under-Sec. of State, Dept for Educ. and Employment 1998–99; Minister of State, Home Office 1999–2001; Chair. Labour Party and Minister without Portfolio 2001–02; Sec. of State for Educ. and Skills 2002–04, Home Sec. 2004–06; mem. Treasury Select Cttee 1997–98, mem. Parl. Cttee 2001–, Labour Party Nat. Policy Forum 2001–; Chair. Labour Party Donations Cttee 2002–. *Leisure interests:* chess, reading, walking. *Address:* House of Commons, London, SW1A 0AA, U.K (office). *Telephone:* (20) 7219-1194 (office). *Fax:* (20) 7219-0526 (office). *E-mail:* clarkec@parliament.uk (office). *Website:* www.charlesclarke.org.uk (office).

CLARKE, Sir Christopher Simon Courtenay Stephenson, Kt, QC, FRSA; British judge; *High Court Judge, Queen's Bench Division, Commercial Court;* b. 14 March 1947, Plymouth; s. of the late Rev. John Stephenson Clarke and of Enid Courtenay Clarke; m. Caroline Anne Fletcher 1974; one s. two d.; ed Marlborough Coll. and Gonville and Caius Coll., Cambridge; called to the Bar, Middle Temple 1969; apptd QC 1984; Recorder of the Crown Court 1990–, Deputy High Court Judge 1993–2005, High Court Judge, Queen's Bench Div., Commercial Court 2005–; mem. Courts of Appeal of Jersey and Guernsey 1998; Attorney of the Supreme Court of Turks and Caicos Islands 1975–; Bencher of the Middle Temple 1991; Counsel for the Bloody Sunday Inquiry 1998–2004; Councillor Int. Bar Asscn 1988–90; Chair. Commercial Bar Asscn 1993–95; mem. Bar Council 1993–99; Harmsworth Memorial Scholar, Middle Temple 1969; Lloyd Stott Memorial Prizeman (Middle Temple) 1969, J. J. Powell Prizeman (Middle Temple) 1969. *Leisure interest:* opera. *Address:* Royal Courts of Justice, Strand, London, WC2A 2LL, England (office).

CLARKE, David Stuart, AO, BEcons, MBA; Australian business executive; *Non-Executive Chairman, Macquarie Bank Limited ABN;* b. 3 Jan. 1942; s. of Stuart Clarke and Ailsie Clarke; m. 1st Margaret Partridge 1964 (divorced 1994); two s.; m. 2nd Jane Graves 1995; ed Knox Grammar School and Univ. of Sydney and Harvard Univ.; Dir Darling & Co. Ltd (now Schroder Australia Ltd) 1966–71, Babcock Australia Holdings Ltd 1972–81, Hooker Corpn Ltd 1984–86, Reil Corpn Ltd 1986–87; Jt Man. Dir Hill Samuel Australia Ltd 1971–77, Man. Dir 1977–84, Chair. 1984–85, Dir Hill Samuel & Co. Ltd (London) 1978–84; Chair. Accepting Houses Asscn of Australia 1974–76, Sceggs Darlinghurst Ltd 1976–78; Exec. Chair. Macquarie Bank Ltd ABN 1985–2007, Non-Exec. Chair. 2007–; Chair. Australian Vintage Ltd, Goodman Group, Barlile Corpn Ltd 1986–93, NSW Rugby Union 1989–95, Wine Cttee, Royal Agricultural Soc. of NSW 1990–, Brian McGuigan Wines Ltd 1991–, Australian Wool Realization Comm. 1991–93, Menzies Research Centre 1994–97, Goodman Fielder Ltd 1995–2000; Campaign Chair. Salvation Army Educ. Foundation 1996–98; Deputy Chair. Australian Opera 1983–86, Chair. 1986–95, Chair. Opera Australia Capital Fund, Opera Australia 1996–; Pres. Harvard Club of Australia 1977–79; Dir Australian Rugby Union Ltd 1990–97, Deputy Chair. 1997–98, Chair. 1998–; Assoc., ASX Ltd; mem. Exec. Cttee, Cttee for Econ. Devt of Australia 1982–98; mem. Investment Advisory Cttee Australian Olympic Foundation 1996–, Harvard Business School Asia Pacific Advisory Cttee 1997–, Seoul International Business Advisory Council, Bd of the Centre for the Mind, Bloomberg Asia Advisory Bd, Corp. Governance Cttee, Australian Inst. of Co. Dirs, Corp. Citizen's Cttee Children's Cancer Inst. of Australia 1992–; mem. Council Royal Agric. Soc. of New South Wales 1986– (mem. Bd 1991–), Bd of Trustees, Financial Markets Foundation for Children 1989–2000 (Hon. life mem. 2000), Sydney Advisory Bd (Chair. 1999–), The Salvation Army 1990–, Council, Royal Humane Soc. of NSW 1999–2000; Co-convenor Cook Soc. 1988–97; Hon. Fed. Treas. Liberal Party of Australia 1987–89; Hon. DSc (Econ), Univ. of Sydney. *Leisure interests:* opera, skiing, tennis, golf, bridge, philately, personal computers, ballet, wine. *Address:* Macquarie Bank Limited ABN, No 1 Martin Place, Sydney, NSW 2000 (office); 5 Keltie Bay, 15 Sutherland Crescent, Darling Point, NSW 2027, Australia. *Telephone:* (2) 8232-3333 (office). *Fax:* (2) 8232-7780 (office). *Website:* www.macquarie.com.au (office).

CLARKE, Edmund M., BA, MA, PhD; American computer scientist and academic; *FORE Systems University Professor of Computer Science and Professor of Electrical and Computer Engineering, Carnegie-Mellon University;* ed Univ. of Virginia, Charlottesville, Duke Univ., Durham, NC, Cornell Univ., Ithaca, NY; taught in Dept of Computer Science, Duke Univ. –1978; Asst Prof. of Computer Science, Div. of Applied Sciences, Harvard Univ., Cambridge, Mass 1978–82; joined faculty in Computer Science Dept, Carnegie-Mellon Univ., Pittsburgh, Pa 1982, Full Prof. 1989–, first recipient of FORE Systems Professorship, School of Computer Science 1995–, Univ. Prof. 2008–; fmr Ed.-in-Chief Formal Methods in Systems Design; fmr mem. Editorial Bd Distributed Computing, Logic and Computation, IEEE Transactions in Software Engineering; mem. Organizing Cttee Logic in Computer Science, Steering Cttee Computer-Aided Verification; mem. Nat. Acad. of Eng 2005; Fellow, Asscn for Computing Machinery (ACM), IEEE; Tech. Excellence Award, Semiconductor Research Corpn 1995, ACM Kanellakis Award (co-recipient) 1998, Allen Newell Award for Excellence in Research, Carnegie Mellon Computer Science Dept 1999, IEEE Harry H. Goode Memorial Award 2004, ACM A.M. Turing Award (co-recipient) 2007, CADE Herbrand Award for Distinguished Contribs to Automated Reasoning 2008. *Publications:* numerous scientific papers in professional journals on software and hardware verification and automatic theorem proving. *Address:* Wean Hall 7117, School of Computer Science, Carnegie Mellon University, 5000 Forbes Avenue, Pittsburgh, PA 15213-3891, USA (office). *Telephone:* (412) 268-2628 (office). *Fax:* (412) 268-5576 (office). *E-mail:* edmund.clarke@cs.cmu.edu (office). *Website:* www.cs.cmu.edu/~emc (office).

CLARKE, Sir Ellis Emmanuel Innocent, GCMG, LLB; Trinidadian government official, lawyer, diplomatist and fmr head of state; b. 28 Dec. 1917, Belmont, Port of Spain; s. of the late Cecil E. I. Clarke and of Elma Pollard; m. Eyrmyntrude Hagley 1952 (died 2002); two s. one d.; ed St Mary's Coll., Port of Spain, Trinidad, Univ. of London and Gray's Inn, London, UK; pvt. law practice, Trinidad 1941–54; Solicitor-Gen. Trinidad and Tobago 1954–56; Deputy Colonial Sec. 1956–57; Attorney-Gen. 1957–61; Constitutional Adviser to the Cabinet 1961–62; Amb. to USA and Canada 1962–73 (also accred to Mexico 1966–73); Perm. Rep. to UN, New York 1962–66; Rep. on Council of OAS 1967–73; Chair. British West Indian Airways 1968–73; Gov.-Gen. and C-in-C of Trinidad and Tobago 1973–76; Pres. of Trinidad and Tobago 1976–87; Hon. Master of Bench, Gray's Inn 1980; awarded first Trinity Cross (T.C.) 1969, KStJ 1973, El Gran Cordon (Venezuela); Hon. LLD (Univ. of the West Indies). *Leisure interests:* golf, racing, cricket. *Address:* 16 Frederick Street, Port of Spain, Trinidad and Tobago.

CLARKE, Geoffrey, RA, ARCA; British artist and sculptor; b. 28 Nov. 1924; s. of John Moulding Clarke and Janet Petts; m.; two s.; ed RCA; exhbns at Gimpel Fils Gallery 1952, 1955, Redfern Gallery 1965, Taranman Gallery 1975, 1976, 1982, Yorkshire Sculpture Park 1994, Chappel Gallery 1994; touring exhbns at Christchurch Mansions, Ipswich 1994, Herbert Art Gallery, Coventry and Pallant House, Chichester 1995; retrospective Exhbn Fine Art Soc. 2000; commissioned work includes: iron sculpture, Time Life Building, New Bond Street; mosaics, Liverpool Univ. Physics Block; stained glass windows for Treasury, Lincoln Cathedral; bronze sculpture, Thorn Electric Building, Upper St Martin's Lane; three stained glass windows, high altar cross and candle-sticks, the flying cross and crown of thorns, all for Coventry Cathedral, screens in Royal Mil. Chapel, Birdcage Walk; other works at Newcastle Civic Centre, Churchill Coll., Aldershot, Suffolk Police HQ, All Souls, W London, The Majlis, Abu Dhabi, York House, N London, St Paul, Minn. *Address:* Stowe Hill, Hartest, Bury St Edmunds, Suffolk, IP29 4EQ, England. *Telephone:* (1284) 830319.

CLARKE, Graeme Wilber, MA, LittD; Australian professor of classics; *Professor Emeritus, Australian National University;* b. 31 Oct. 1934, Nelson, New Zealand; s. of Wilber P. Clarke and Marjorie E (née Le May) Clarke; m. Nancy J. Jordan 1963; three s. one d.; ed Sacred Heart Coll., Auckland, NZ, Univ. of Auckland, Balliol Coll., Oxford; lecturer, Dept of Classics, Australian Nat. Univ. 1957, 1961–63, Sr Lecturer, Dept of Classics and Ancient History, Univ. of Western Australia 1964–66, Assoc. Prof., Dept of Classical Studies, Monash Univ. 1967–68, Prof. Dept of Classical Studies, Univ. of Melbourne 1969–81, Prof. Emer. 1981–; Deputy Dir Humanities Research Centre, Australian Nat. Univ. 1982–90, Dir 1991–99, Prof. Emer. 2000–; Visting Fellow Dept of History, Australian Nat. Univ. 2000–; Fellow Australian Acad. of the Humanities 1975, Soc. of Antiquaries, London 1989; Dir archaeological excavation in N Syria at Jebel Khalid 1984–. *Publications:* The Octavius of Marcus Minucius Felix 1974, The Letters of St Cyprian (4 Vols) 1984–88, Rediscovering Hellenism (ed.) 1988, Reading the Past in Late Antiquity (ed.) 1990, Identities in the Eastern Mediterranean in Antiquity (ed.) 1998, Jebel Khalid on the Euphrates. Report on Excavations 1986–1996 (Vol. I) 2002. *Leisure interest:* gardening. *Address:* Department of History, Australian National University, Canberra, ACT 0200 (office); 62 Wybalena Grove, Cook, ACT 2614, Australia (home). *Telephone:* (2) 6125-4789 (office); (2) 6251-4576 (home). *Fax:* (2) 6125-4083 (office). *E-mail:* graeme.clarke@anu.edu.au (office).

CLARKE, John, BA, MA, PhD, ScD, FRS; British physicist and academic; *Professor of Physics, University of California, Berkeley;* b. 10 Feb. 1942, Cambridge; s. of Victor P. Clarke and Ethel M. Clarke; m. Grethe Fog Pedersen 1979; one d.; ed Perse School, Cambridge and Univ. of Cambridge; Postdoctoral Scholar, Dept of Physics, Univ. of California, Berkeley 1968–69, Asst Prof. 1969–71, Assoc. Prof. 1971–73, Prof. 1973–, Faculty Research Lecturer 2005; Luis W. Alvarez Memorial Chair in Experimental Physics 1994–99; Faculty Sr Scientist, Lawrence Berkeley Nat. Lab., Berkeley 1969–; Visiting Fellow, Clare Hall, Cambridge 1989; Fellow, AAAS, American Physical Soc., Inst. of Physics; Alfred P. Sloan Foundation Fellowship 1970–72; Adolph C. and Mary Sprague Miller Research Professorship 1975–76, 1994–95; Guggenheim Fellowship 1977–78; Hon. Fellow, Christ's Coll., Cambridge; Calif. Scientist of the Year 1987, Fritz London Memorial Award 1987, Joseph F. Keithley Award, American Physical Soc. 1998, Comstock Prize in Physics, NAS 1999, Hughes Medal, Royal Soc. 2004, Lounasmaa Prize, Finnish Acad. of Arts and Sciences 2004. *Publications:* approx. 400 publs in learned journals. *Address:* Department of Physics, 366 LeConte Hall, University of California, Berkeley, CA 94720-7300, USA (office). *Telephone:* (510) 642-3069 (office). *Fax:* (510) 642-1304 (office). *E-mail:* jclarke@berkeley.edu (office). *Website:* www.physics.berkeley.edu/research/faculty/clarke.html (office); socrates.berkeley.edu/~jclarke2 (office).

CLARKE, (John) Neil, LLB, FCA; British business executive; b. 7 Aug. 1934; s. of the late George P. Clarke and Norah M. Bailey; m. Sonia H. Beckett 1958; three s.; ed Rugby School and King's Coll. London; Pnr, Rowley, Pemberton, Roberts & Co. 1960–69; with Charter Consolidated PLC 1969–88, Deputy Chair. and CEO 1980–88; mem. Bd of Dirs Anglo-American Corpn of South Africa 1976–90, Consolidated Gold Fields 1982–89, Travis Perkins 1990–2002, Porvair 1994–96; Chair. Johnson Matthey 1984–90, Molins 1987–91 (Chair. 1989–91); Chair. Genchem Holdings 1989–2006, British Coal 1991–97; Chevalier, Ordre nat. du Mérite. *Leisure interests:* music, tennis, golf. *Address:* High Willows, 18 Park Avenue, Farnborough Park, Orpington, Kent, BR6 8LL, England. *Telephone:* (1689) 851651 (office). *Fax:* (1689) 862229 (office).

CLARKE, Rt Hon. Kenneth (Ken) Harry, PC, QC, BA, LLB; British politician; *Shadow Secretary of State for Business, Enterprise and Regulatory Reform;* b. 2 July 1940; s. of Kenneth Clarke and Doris Clarke (née Smith); m. Gillian Mary Edwards 1964; one s. one d.; ed Nottingham High School and Gonville and Caius Coll., Cambridge; called to the Bar, Gray's Inn 1963; practising mem. Midland circuit 1963–79; Research Sec. Birmingham Bow Group 1965–66; contested Mansfield, Notts. in General Elections 1964, 1966, MP for Rushcliffe Div. of Notts. 1970–; Parl. Pvt. Sec. to Solicitor Gen. 1971–72; an Asst Govt Whip 1972–74, Govt Whip for Europe 1973–74; Lord Commr, HM Treasury 1974; Opposition Spokesman on Social Services 1974–76, on Industry 1976–79; Parl. Sec., Dept of Transport, later Parl. UnderSec. of State for Transport 1979–82; Minister of State (Minister for Health), Dept of Health and Social Security 1982–85; Paymaster-Gen. and Minister for Employment 1985–87; Chancellor of Duchy of Lancaster and Minister for Trade and Industry 1987–88, Minister for the Inner Cities 1987–88; Sec. of State for Health 1988–90, for Educ. and Science 1990–92, for the Home Dept 1992–93; Chancellor of the Exchequer 1993–97; mem. Parl. Del. to Council of Europe and WEU 1973–74; Dir Alliance UniChem PLC 1997–2001, Deputy Chair. (non-exec.) 2001–; Dir Foreign and Colonial Investment Trust 1997–, Deputy Chair. British American Tobacco 1998–; Dir Ind. News and Media (VIC) 1999–; Chair. Savoy Asset Man. PLC 2000–; Master of Bench, Gray's Inn; Liveryman, Clockmakers' Co. 2001–; Shadow Sec. of State for Business, Enterprise and Regulatory Reform 2009–; Hon. LLD (Nottingham) 1989, (Huddersfield) 1993; Hon. DUniv (Nottingham Trent) 1996. *Publication:* New Hope for the Regions 1969. *Leisure interests:* bird-watching, jazz, cricket, football. *Address:* House of Commons, Westminster, London, SW1A 0AA, England (office). *Telephone:* (20) 7219-3000 (office).

CLARKE, Sir Robert (Cyril), Kt, MA; British business executive (retd); b. 28 March 1929, Eltham; s. of Robert Henry Clarke and Rose Lilian Clarke (née Bratton); m. Evelyn (Lynne) Mary Harper 1952; three s. one d.; ed Dulwich Coll. and Pembroke Coll. Oxford; trainee, Cadbury Bros. Ltd 1952; Gen. Man. John Forrest Ltd 1954; Marketing Dir Cadbury Confectionery 1957; Man. Dir Cadbury Cakes Ltd 1962; Chair. Cadbury Cakes Ltd and Dir Cadbury Schweppes Foods Ltd 1969; Man. Dir McVitie & Cadbury Cakes Ltd 1971–74; mem. Bd United Biscuits (UK) Ltd 1974, Man. Dir UB Biscuits 1977, Chair. and Man. Dir United Biscuits (UK) Ltd and Dir United Biscuits (Holdings) PLC 1984–95, Group Chief Exec. United Biscuits (Holdings) PLC 1986–90, Deputy Chair. 1989, Chair. 1990–95; fmr Dir (non-exec.) Thames Water PLC, Chair. 1994–99; Gov. World Econ. Forum 1990–; Fellow, Dulwich Coll. 2003. *Leisure interests:* reading, walking, renovating old buildings, planting trees.

CLARKSON, Rt Hon. Adrienne, OC, PC, CC, CMM, COM, CD; Canadian broadcaster and fmr government official; *Co-Chair, Institute for Canadian Citizenship;* b. 1939, Hong Kong; d. of William Poy; m. John Ralston Saul; ed Univ. of Toronto, Sorbonne, Paris; broadcaster with CBC TV 1965–82, 1988–98; Ont.'s Agent-Gen. in Paris 1982–87; Pres. McClelland & Stewart Publishing 1987–88; fmr Chair. Bd of Trustees, Canadian Museum of Civilization, Hull, Quebec; fmr Pres. Exec. Bd IMZ, Vienna (int. audio-visual assen of music, dance and cultural programmers); Gov.-Gen. of Canada 1999–2005; Co-founder and Co-Chair. Inst. for Canadian Citizenship; Chair. of jury, Man Asian Literary Prize 2007; fmr Bencher of Law Soc. of Upper Canada; Colonel-in-Chief of Princess Patricia's Canadian Light Infantry on February 7, 2007,; Order of Friendship of the Russian Fed. Federation 2003; numerous Canadian decorations 21 hon. doctorates. *TV includes:* Take Thirty, Adrienne at Large, The Fifth Estate, Adrienne Clarkson's Summer Festival, Adrienne Clarkson Presents, Something Special. *Publications include:* Heart Matters (memoirs) 2006; three other books and numerous magazine and newspaper articles. *Address:* Institute for Canadian Citizenship, 260 Spadina Avenue, Suite 500, Toronto, ON M5T 2E4, Canada (office). *Telephone:* (416) 593-6998 (office). *Fax:* (416) 593-9028 (office). *E-mail:* icc@icc-icc.ca (office). *Website:* www.icc-icc.ca (office).

CLARKSON, Thomas William, BS, PhD; British toxicologist and academic; *J. Lowell Orbison Distinguished Alumni Professor Emeritus, Department of Environmental Medicine and Professor of Biochemistry and Biophysics, and Pharmacology and Physiology, University of Rochester;* b. 1 Aug. 1932, Blackburn, Lancs.; s. of William Clarkson and Olive Jackson; m. Winifred Browne 1957; one s. two d.; ed Univ. of Manchester; Instructor, Univ. of Rochester School of Medicine, USA 1958–61, Asst Prof. 1961–62, Assoc. Prof. 1965–71, Prof. of Biochemistry and Biophysics, and Pharmacology and Physiology 1971–, Head of Div. of Toxicology 1980–86, J. Lowell Orbison Distinguished Alumni Prof. 1983–2008, now Emer., Dir Environmental Health Sciences Center 1986–98, Chair. Dept of Environmental Medicine 1992–98; Scientific Officer, MRC, UK 1962–64; Sterling Drug Visiting Prof., Albany Medical Coll. 1989; Sr Fellowship, Weizmann Inst. of Science, Israel 1964–65; Post-Doctoral Fellow, Nuffield Foundation 1956–57 and US Atomic Energy Comm., Univ. of Rochester, NY 1957–58; mem. Inst. of Medicine of NAS; Dir NASA Center in Space Environmental Health 1991–95; mem. La Academia Nacional de Medicina de Buenos Aires 1984; mem. Collegium Ramazzini 1983; Hon. Dr Med. (Umeå Univ., Sweden) 1986; Merit Award, SOT 1999, Arthur Kornberg Award, Univ. of Rochester 1999. *Publications:* Reproductive and Developmental Toxicology (co-ed.), The Cytoskeleton as a Target for Toxic Agents (co-ed.), Biological Monitoring of Toxic Metals (co-ed.), Advances in Mercury Toxicology (co-ed.); more than 200 published papers. *Address:* Department of Environmental Medicine, University of Rochester School of Medicine, Box EHSC, Rochester, NY 14642, USA (office). *Telephone:* (716) 275-3911 (office). *Fax:* (716) 256-2591 (office). *E-mail:* tom_clarkson@urmc.rochester.edu (office). *Website:* www2.envmed.rochester.edu/envmed (office).

CLARY, David Charles, PhD, ScD, FRS, FRSC, FInstP, FRSA; British chemist and academic; *President, Magdalen College, Oxford;* b. 14 Jan. 1953, Halesworth, Suffolk; s. of Cecil Raymond Clary and Mary Mildred Clary (née Hill); m. Heather Ann Vinson 1975; three s.; ed Colchester Royal Grammar School, Univ. of Sussex, Corpus Christi Coll., Cambridge; researcher, IBM Research Lab., San Jose, Calif. 1977–78; post-doctoral research at Univ. of Manchester 1978–80; Research Lecturer in Chem., UMIST 1980–83; Lecturer, then Reader in Theoretical Chem., Dept of Chem., Univ. of Cambridge 1983–96; Fellow, Magdalene Coll., Cambridge 1983–96, Sr Tutor 1989–93, Fellow Commoner 1996–2002, Hon. Fellow 2002; Prof. of Chem., Dir of Centre for Theoretical and Computational Chem., Univ. Coll. London 1996–2002; Head of Math. and Physical Sciences, Univ. of Oxford 2002–05, Professorial Fellow, St John's Coll., Oxford 2002–05; Pres. Magdalen Coll., Oxford 2005–; Miller Fellow, Univ. of California, Berkeley 2001; Pres. Faraday Div. Royal Soc. of Chem. 2006; mem. Int. Acad. of Quantum Molecular Science 1998; Ed. Chemical Physics Letters 2000–; Fellow, AAAS 2003, American Physical Soc. 2003; mem. Council Royal Soc. 2004–05; Foreign Hon. Mem. American Acad. of Arts and Sciences 2003; Kistiakowsky Lecture, Harvard 2002, Pitzer Lecture, Berkeley 2003, Polanyi Lecture 2004; Annual Medal of Int. Acad. of Quantum Molecular Science 1989; medals of the Royal Soc. of Chem.: Meldola 1981, Marlow 1986 Corday-Morgan 1989, Tilden 1998, Chemical Dynamics 1998. *Achievements:* developed quantum theory for chemical reactions of polyatomic molecules. *Publications:* more than 300 research papers on chemical physics and theoretical chem. in learned journals. *Leisure interests:* family, football. *Address:* Magdalen College, Oxford, OX1 4AU, England (office). *Telephone:* (1865) 276100 (office). *Fax:* (1865) 286730 (office). *Website:* www.chem.ox.ac.uk (office); www.mag.ox.ac.uk (office).

CLASPER, Michael (Mike), CBE, BEng; British airport executive and music industry executive; *Chairman, HM Revenue and Customs;* b. 21 April 1953, Sunderland; s. of Douglas Clasper and Hilda Clasper; m. Susan Rosemary Shore 1975; two s. one d.; ed Bede School, Sunderland, St John's Coll., Cambridge; with British Rail 1974–78; joined Proctor & Gamble 1978, Advertising Dir 1985–88, Gen. Man. Proctor & Gamble Holland 1988–91, Man. Dir and Vice-Pres. Proctor & Gamble UK 1991–95, Regional Vice-Pres. Laundry Products, Proctor & Gamble Europe 1995–99, Pres. Global Home Care and New Business Devt, Proctor & Gamble, Brussels 1999–2001; Deputy CEO and Chair. Airports Bd BAA PLC 2001–03, CEO 2003–06; Head of EVP Marketing Sales and Operations, EMI Group 2008; Chair., HM Revenue and Customs 2008–; Dir (non-exec.) ITV plc 2006–; mem. Advisory Council on Business and the Environment 1993–99; mem. Man. Cttee Business and Environment Programme, Univ. of Cambridge Programme for Industry 2000–, Prince of Wales Business and Environment Programme; mem. Investor Bd EMI Group 2007; Fellow, Inst. of Grocery Distribution; Hon. PhD (Sunderland). *Leisure interests:* swimming, cycling, skiing, tennis, golf. *Address:* c/o EMI Group Ltd, 27 Wrights Lane, London, W8 5SW, England (office).

CLATWORTHY, Robert, RA; British sculptor; b. 31 Jan. 1928; s. of E. W. and G. Clatworthy; m. 1st Pamela Gordon 1954 (divorced); two s. one d.; m. 2nd Jane Clatworthy (née Illingworth Stubbs) 1989; ed Dr Morgan's Grammar School, Bridgwater, West of England Coll. of Art, Chelsea School of Art, The Slade; teacher, West of England Coll. of Art 1967–71; Visiting Tutor, RCA 1960–72; mem. Fine Art Panel of Nat. Council for Diplomas in Art and Design 1961–72; Governor, St Martin's School of Art 1970–71; Head of Dept of Fine Art, Central School of Art and Design 1971–75; work in collections of Arts Council, Contemporary Art Soc., Tate Gallery, Victoria and Albert Museum,

GLC, Nat. Portrait Gallery (portrait of Dame Elisabeth Frink 1985). *Works include:* public sculptures: Large Bull, Alton Housing Estate, London SW15; Monumental Horse and Rider in grounds of Charing Cross Hosp., London W6. *Address:* Moelfre, Cynghordy, Llandovery, Carmarthenshire, SA20 0UW, Wales (home). *Telephone:* (1550) 720201. *E-mail:* robertclatworthy@hotmail.com (office). *Website:* www.robertclatworthy.homestead.com (office).

CLAUSEN, Christian, MEconSc; Danish banking executive; *President and Group CEO, Nordea Bank AB;* b. 6 March 1955, Copenhagen; Man. Dir Privatbørsen, Privatbanken 1988–90, Man. Dir and CEO Unibørs Securities (later Nordea) 1990–96, Man. Dir and CEO Unibank Markets 1996–98, mem. Exec. Bd Unibank 1998–2000, mem. Group Exec. Man. Nordea Bank AB (parent co.) 2001–, also Exec. Vice-Pres., Head of Asset Man. & Life 2000–07, Pres. and Group CEO Nordea Bank AB 2007–; Dir OMX Nordic Exchange Group Oy 2005–. *Address:* Nordea Bank AB, Hamngatan 10, 10571 Stockholm, Sweden (office). *Telephone:* (8) 61-47-800 (office). *Fax:* (8) 10-50-69 (office). *E-mail:* info@nordea.com (office). *Website:* www.nordea.com (office).

CLAVEL, Bernard; French writer; b. 29 May 1923, Lons-le-Saunier; s. of Henri Clavel and Héloïse Dubois; m. 2nd Josette Pratte 1982; three s. (from first marriage); ed primary school; left school aged 14 and apprenticed as pâtissier 1937; subsequently held various jobs on the land and in offices; painter and writer since age 15; has written numerous plays for radio and television and contributed to reviews on the arts and pacifist journals; Prix Eugène Leroy, Prix populiste, Prix Jean Macé, Prix Goncourt (for Les fruits de l'hiver) 1968, Grand Prix littéraire de la Ville de Paris 1968, Prix Ardua de l'Université 1997, Prix des maisons de la presse 1998. *Publications include:* L'Ouvrier de la nuit 1956, Qui m'emporte 1958, L'espagnol 1959, Malataverne 1960, La maison des autres 1962, Celui qui voulait voir la mer 1963, Le coeur des vivants 1964, Le voyage du père 1965, L'Hercule sur la place 1966, Les fruits de l'hiver 1968, Victoire au Mans 1968, L'espion aux yeux verts 1969, Le tambour du bief 1970, Le massacre des innocents 1970, Le seigneur du fleuve 1972, Le silence des armes 1974, Lettre à un képi blanc 1975, La boule de neige 1975, La saison des loups 1976, La lumière du lac 1977, Ecrit sur la neige 1977, La fleur de sel 1977, La femme de guerre 1978, Le Rhône ou la métamorphose d'un dieu 1979, Le chien des Laurentides 1979, L'Iroquoise 1979, Marie Bon Pain 1980, La bourrelle 1980, Felicien le fantôme (with Josette Pratte) 1980, Terres de Mémoire 1980, Compagnons du Nouveau-Monde 1981, Arbres 1981, Odile et le vent du large 1981, Le Hibou qui avait avalé la lune 1981, L'Homme du Labrador 1982, Harricana 1983, L'Or de la terre 1984, Le mouton noir et le loup blanc 1984, Le roi des poissons 1984, L'oie qui avait perdu le nord 1985, Miserere 1985, Bernard Clavel qui êtes-vous? 1985, Amarok 1986, Au cochon qui danse 1986, L'Angélus du soir 1988, Le grand voyage de Quick Beaver 1988, Quand j'étais capitaine 1990, Retour au pays 1990, Meurtre sur le Grandvaux 1991, La révolte à deux sous 1992, Cargo pour l'enfer 1993, Les roses de Verdun 1994, Le Carcajou 1995, Jésus le fils du charpentier 1996, Contes et légendes du Bordelais 1997, La Guinguette 1997, Le Soleil des morts 1998, Achille le singe 1998, Les Petits bonheurs 1999, Le Commencement du monde 1999, La Louve du Noirmont 2000, Le Cavalier du Baïkal 2000, Histoires de chiens 2000, Brutus 2001, La Retraîte aux flambeaux 2002, La Table du roi 2003, Les Grands malheurs 2004, numerous essays, short stories and children's books. *Leisure interests:* sport, painting, handicraft. *Address:* 8 rue Crébillon, 75006 Paris, France (office). *E-mail:* iroquoise.jp@wanadoo.fr (office). *Website:* www.bernard-clavel.com.

CLAVIER, Christian Jean-Marie; French actor and film producer; b. 6 May 1952, Paris; s. of Jean-Claude Clavier and Phanette Rousset-Rouard; one d. by Marie-Anne Chazel; f. Ouille Productions; Chevalier Ordre nat. du Mérite, Officier Ordre nat. des Arts et des lettres. *Stage appearances include:* Ginette Lacaze, La Dame de chez Maxim's, Non Georges pas ici 1972, Ma tête est malade 1976, Le Pot de terre contre le pot de vin 1977, Amours, coquillages et crustacés 1978, Le Père Noël est une ordure 1979–80, Papy fait de la résistance 1981, Double Mixte 1986–88, Un fil à la patte 1989, Panique au plaza 1995. *Films include:* Que la fête commence 1974, F. comme Fairbanks 1976, Le Diable dans la boîte 1976, L'Amour en herbe 1977, Des enfants gâtés 1977, Dîtes-lui que je l'aime 1977, Les Bronzés font du ski (also co-writer) 1979, Cocktail Molotov 1980, Je vais craquer 1980, Clara et les chics types 1980, Quand tu seras débloqué, fais-moi signe 1981, Elle voit des nains partout 1981, le Père Noël est une ordure (also co-writer) 1982, Rock and Torah 1982, la Vengeance d'une blonde 1993, les Anges gardiens (also co-writer) 1994, Les Couloirs du temps (also co-writer) 1998, Astérix et Obélix contre César 1999, The Visitors 2000, Astérix et Obélix: Mission Cleopatra 2002, Lovely Rita, sainte patronne des cas désespérés 2003, Albert est méchant 2004, L'Enquête corse 2004, L'Antidote 2005, Les Bronzés 3: amis pour la vie 2006, L'Entente cordiale 2006, Le Prix à payer 2006, L'Auberge rouge 2007. *Television includes:* l'Été 1985, Sueurs froides 1988, Palace 1988, Si Guitry m'était conté 1989, Bougez pas j'arrive 1989, Mieux vaut courir 1989, Fantôme sur l'oreiller (co-writer 1989), Charmante soirée (co-writer 1990), Les Misérables (miniseries) 2000, Napoléon 2002, Kronprinz Rudolf 2006, Kaamelott 2007. *Leisure interests:* skiing, cycling, swimming. *Address:* Ouille Productions, 7 rue des Dames Augustines, 92200 Neuilly, France (office). *Telephone:* 1-41-34-13-34 (office). *Fax:* 1-41-34-13-10 (office). *E-mail:* ouille2@wanadoo.fr (office).

CLAYBURGH, Jill, BA; American actress; b. 30 April 1944, New York; d. of Albert H. Clayburgh and Julia (née Door) Clayburgh; m. David Rabe 1979; ed Sarah Lawrence Coll., Bronxville, New York; Broadway debut in The Rothschilds 1979; James Turner Butler Creative Lecture (jtly), Stetson Univ. 2007. *Stage appearances include:* In the Boom Boom Room, Design for Living. *Television includes:* The Snoop Sisters 1972, Going Places 1973, Hustling 1975, The Art of Crime 1975, Griffin and Phoenix: A Love Story 1976, Miles to Go 1986, Who Gets the Friends? 1988, Fear Stalk 1989, Unspeakable Acts 1990, Reason for Living: The Jill Ireland Story 1991, Trial: The Price of Passion 1992, Firestorm: 72 Hours in Oakland 1993, Honor Thy Father and Mother: The True Story of the Menendez Murders 1994, For the Love of Nancy 1994, The Face on the Milk Carton 1995, When Innocence Is Lost 1997, Sins of the Mind 1997, Crowned and Dangerous 1998, Trinity (series) 1998, My Little Assassin 1999, Everything's Relative (series) 1999, Leap of Faith (series) 2002, Phenomenon 2002, Phenomenon II 2003, Dirty Sexy Money (series) 2007–08. *Films include:* Portnoy's Complaint 1972, The Thief Who Came to Dinner 1973, The Terminal Man 1974, Gable and Lombard 1976, Silver Streak 1976, Semi-Tough 1977, An Unmarried Woman (Best Actress Award, Cannes Film Festival, Golden Apple Award for Best Film Actress) 1978, La Luna 1979, Starting Over 1979, It's My Turn 1980, I'm Dancing as Fast as I Can 1982, Hannah K 1983, Shy People 1987, Beyond the Ocean, Between the Lines 1990, Naked in New York 1994, Fools Rush In 1997, Going All the Way 1997, Never Again 2001, Vallen 2001, Running with Scissors 2006. *Address:* PO Box 432, Lakeville, CT 06039, USA.

CLAYTON, Adam; British musician (bass guitar); b. 13 March 1960, Chinnor, Oxon.; founder mem. the Feedback 1976, renamed the Hype, finally renamed U2 1978–; numerous concerts, including Live Aid Wembley 1985, Self Aid Dublin, A Conspiracy of Hope (Amnesty Int. Tour) 1986, Smile Jamaica (hurricane relief fundraiser) 1988, Very Special Arts Festival, White House, Washington, DC 1988; numerous tours worldwide; Grammy awards for Album of the Year and Best Rock Performance by a Duo or Group with Vocal (for The Joshua Tree) 1987, Grammy awards for Best Rock Performance by a Duo or Group with Vocal (for Desire) and Best Performance Video, short form (for Where the Streets Have No Name) 1988, BRIT Awards for Best Int. Act 1988–90, 1992, 1998, 2001, Best Live Act 1993, Outstanding Contribution to the British Music Industry 2001, JUNO Award 1992, World Music Award 1992, Grammy Award for Best Rock Vocal by a Duo or Group (for Achtung Baby) 1992, Grammy Award for Best Alternative Music Album (for Zooropa) 1993, Grammy Award for Best Music Video, long form (for Zoo TV Live from Sydney) 1994, Grammy Award for Song of the Year, Record of the Year, Best Rock Performance by a Duo or Group with Vocal (all for Beautiful Day) 2000, Grammy Awards for Best Pop Performance by a Duo or Group with Vocal (for Stuck In A Moment You Can't Get Out Of), for Record of the Year (for Walk On), for Best Rock Performance by a Duo or Group with Vocal (for Elevation), for Rock Album of the Year (All That You Can't Leave Behind) 2001, American Music Award for Favorite Internet Artist of the Year 2002, Ivor Novello Award for Best Song Musically and Lyrically (for Walk On) 2002, Golden Globe for Best Original Song (for The Hands That Built America, from film Gangs of New York) 2003, Grammy Awards for Best Rock Performance by a Duo or Group with Vocal, Best Rock Song, Best Short Form Music Video (all for Vertigo) 2004, TED Prize 2004, Nordoff-Robbins Silver Clef Award for lifetime achievement 2005, Q Award for Best Live Act 2005, Digital Music Award for Favourite Download Single (for Vertigo) 2005, Meteor Ireland Music Award for Best Irish Band, Best Live Performance 2006, Grammy Awards for Song of the Year, for Best Rock Performance by a Duo or Group with Vocal (both for Sometimes You Can't Make it on Your Own), for Best Rock Song (for City of Blinding Lights), for Album of the Year and Best Rock Album of the Year (both for How to Dismantle an Atomic Bomb) 2006; Portuguese Order of Liberty 2005; Amnesty Int. Ambs of Conscience Award 2006. *Films:* Rattle and Hum 1988. *Recordings include:* albums: Boy 1980, October 1981, War 1983, Under a Blood Red Sky 1983, The Unforgettable Fire 1984, Wide Awake In America 1985, The Joshua Tree (Grammy Award for Album of the Year, Best Rock Performance by a Duo or Group with Vocal) 1987, Rattle and Hum 1988, Achtung Baby (Grammy Award for Best Rock Performance by a Duo or Group with Vocal 1992) 1991, Zooropa (Grammy Award for Best Alternative Music Album) 1993, Passengers (film soundtrack with Brian Eno) 1995, Pop 1997, The Best Of 1980–90 1998, All That You Can't Leave Behind (Grammy Award for Best Rock Album 2001) 2000, The Best Of 1990–2000 2002, How To Dismantle An Atomic Bomb (Meteor Ireland Music Award for Best Irish Album 2006, Grammy Awards for Album of the Year, for Best Rock Album 2006) 2004, No Line on the Horizon 2009. *Address:* Principle Management, 30–32 Sir John Rogersons Quay, Dublin 2, Ireland (office). *E-mail:* candida@numb.ie (office). *Website:* www.u2.com (office).

CLAYTON, Dame Barbara, DBE, PhD, MD, CBiol, FRCP, FRCPE, FRCPI, FRCPath, FMedSci; British professor of chemical pathology; *Honorary Research Professor in Metabolism, University of Southampton;* b. 2 Sept. 1922, Liverpool; d. of William Clayton and Constance Clayton; m. William Klyne 1949 (died 1977); one s. one d.; ed Bromley County School for Girls, Edinburgh Univ.; consultant, Hosp. for Sick Children 1959–78 (mem. Bd of Govs 1968–78); Prof. Inst. of Child Health, Univ. of London 1970–78, Univ. of Southampton 1979–87 (Hon. Research Prof. in Metabolism 1989–); Pres. Asscn of Clinical Biochemists 1977–78, Soc. for the Study of Inborn Errors of Metabolism 1981–82 (Hon. mem. 1988), Royal Coll. of Pathologists 1984–87, Nat. Soc. for Clean Air and Environmental Protection 1995–97; Chair. Standing Cttee on Postgrad. Medical and Dental Educ. 1988–99, Health of the Nation Task Force on Nutrition 1992–95, Medical and Scientific Panel, Leukaemia Research Fund 1988–2003; Dean Faculty of Medicine Univ. of Southampton 1983–86; Hon. Pres. British Dietetic Asscn 1989–; mem. Royal Comm. on Environmental Pollution 1981–96, Gen. Medical Council 1983–87; Leverhulme Emerita Fellowship 1988–90; Gov. British Nutrition Foundation, Hon. Pres. 1999–; Corresp. mem. Soc. Française Pédiatric 1975; Gesellschaft für Laboritoriumsmedizin 1990; Hon. Fellow, Royal Coll. of Paediatrics and Child Health 1968, American Soc. of Clinical Pathologists 1987; Hon. FRCPI 1987; Hon. FIBiol 2000; Hon. DSc (Edin.) 1987, (Southampton) 1992, (London) 2000; RCPE Jessie MacGregor Prize for Medical Science 1955, 1985, Wellcome Prize, Asscn of Clinical Biochemists 1988, BMA Gold Medal for Distinguished Merit 1999; numerous named lectures including Stanley Davidson, Royal

Coll. of Physicians, Edinburgh (RCPE) 1973; Hartley Lecture, Southampton Univ. 1990, Wilfrid Fish GDC 1995, British Nutrition Foundation Lecture 1997. *Publications:* Clinical Biochemistry and the Sick Child (jtly) 1994, numerous publs on nutrition, pediatrics and the environment. *Leisure interests:* natural history, visiting the Arctic. *Address:* Level B (801), South Academic Block, Southampton General Hospital, Tremona Toad, Southampton, SO16 6YD (office); 16 Chetwynd Drive, Bassett, Southampton, SO16 3HZ, England (home). *Telephone:* (23) 8079-6800 (office); (23) 8076-9937 (home). *Fax:* (23) 8079-4760 (office).

CLAYTON, Robert Norman, MSc, PhD, FRS; Canadian geochemist and academic; *Enrico Fermi Distinguished Service Professor Emeritus, Department of Chemistry, University of Chicago;* b. 20 March 1930; s. of Norman Clayton and Gwenda Clayton; m. Cathleen Shelbourne Clayton 1971; one d.; ed Queen's Univ. Canada and Calif. Inst. of Tech.; Research Fellow, California Inst. of Tech. 1955–56; Asst Prof., Pennsylvania State Univ. 1956–58; Asst Prof., Univ. of Chicago 1958–62, Assoc. Prof. 1962–66, Prof., Depts of Chem. and of Geophysical Sciences 1966–80, Enrico Fermi Distinguished Service Prof. 1980–, now Prof. Emer.; mem. NAS; Fellow, AAAS, RSC, Royal Soc., London, American Acad. of Arts and Sciences, Meteoritical Soc., American Geophysical Union; NASA Exceptional Scientific Achievement Medal 1976, George P. Merrill Award, NAS 1980, Goldschmidt Medal, Geochemical Soc. 1981, Leonard Medal, Meteoritical Society 1982, Elliot Cresson Medal, Franklin Inst. 1985, William Bowie Medal, American Geophysical Union 1987, Award in Nuclear Chemistry, ACS 1992, Urey Medal, European Asscn of Geochemistry 1995, US Nat. Medal of Science 2004. *Publications:* over 200 papers in geochemical journals. *Address:* Department of Chemistry, University of Chicago, RI 440, 5640 South Ellis Avenue, Chicago, IL 60637 (office); 5201 South Cornell, Chicago, IL 60615, USA (home). *Telephone:* (773) 702-7777 (office). *Fax:* (773) 702-5863 (office). *E-mail:* rclayton@uchicago.edu (office). *Website:* chemistry.uchicago.edu/fac/clayton.shtml (office).

CLEARY, Jon Stephen; Australian author; b. 22 Nov. 1917, Sydney, NSW; s. of Mathew Cleary and Ida F. Brown; m. Constantine E. Lucas 1946 (deceased); two d. (one deceased); ed Marist Brothers School, NSW; various jobs, including bush-working and commercial art 1932–40; served in Australian Imperial Forces, Middle East, New Britain, New Guinea 1940–45; full-time writer since 1945, except for three years as journalist, Australian News and Information Bureau, London and New York 1948–51; winner, ABC Nat. Play Competition 1945, Crouch Literary Prize 1951, Edgar Award for Best Crime Novel 1974, First Lifetime Award, Australian Crime Writers Soc. 1998, Ned Kelly Award for Best Crime Novel 2003. *Cinema:* The Siege of Pinchgut 1958, The Sundowners 1960, The Green Helmet 1960. *Television includes:* No Friend like an Old Friend (CBS) 1951, Just Let Me Be (ATV) 1958, Bus Stop (Fox) 1967. *Publications include:* two books of short stories 1983; novels: These Small Glories 1945, You Can't See Round Corners 1948, The Long Shadow 1949, Just Let Me Be 1950, The Sundowners 1952, The Climate of Courage 1954, Justin Bayard 1955, The Green Helmet 1957, Back of Sunset 1959, The Siege of Pinchgut 1959, North from Thursday 1960, The Country of Marriage 1961, Forests of the Night 1962, Pillar of Salt 1963, A Flight of Chariots 1964, The Fall of An Eagle 1965, The Pulse of Danger 1966, The High Commissioner 1966, The Long Pursuit 1968, Season of Doubt 1969, Remember Jack Hoxie 1970, Helga's Webb 1971, The Liberators 1971, The Ninth Marquess 1972, Ransom 1973, Peter's Pence 1974, The Safe House 1975, A Sound of Lightning 1976, High Road to China 1977, Vortex 1977, The Beaufort Sisters 1979, A Very Private War 1980, The Golden Sabre 1981, The Faraway Drums 1981, Spearfield's Daughter 1982, The Phoenix Tree 1984, The City of Fading Light 1985, Dragons at the Party 1987, Now and Then, Amen 1988, Babylon South 1989, Murder Song 1990, Pride's Harvest 1991, Dark Summer 1992, Bleak Spring 1993, Autumn Maze 1994, Winter Chill 1995, Endpeace 1996, A Different Turf 1997, Five-Ring Circus 1998, Dilemma 1999, Bear Pit 2000, Yesterday's Shadow 2001, The Easy Sin 2002, Degrees of Connection 2003, Miss Ambar Regrets 2004, Morning's Gone 2006, Four-Cornered Circle 2007. *Leisure interests:* watching cricket, filmgoing, reading. *Address:* c/o HarperCollins, 23 Ryde Road, Pymble, NSW 2073, Australia.

CLEAVER, Sir Anthony Brian, Kt, MA; British business executive; *Chairman of the Executive Board, Caithness and North Sutherland Regeneration Partnership;* b. 10 April 1938, London; s. of the late William Brian Cleaver and Dorothea Early Cleaver (née Peeks); m. Mary Teresa Cotter 1962 (died 1999); one s. one d.; m. 2nd Jennifer Lloyd Graham 2000; ed Berkhamsted School and Trinity Coll. Oxford; nat. service in Intelligence Corps 1956–58; joined IBM 1962, UK Sales Dir 1976–77, DP Dir, mem. Bd, IBM UK (Holdings) 1977–80, Vice-Pres. of Marketing IBM Europe 1981–82, Asst Gen. Man. IBM UK 1982–84, Gen. Man. 1984–85, Chief Exec. 1986–91, Chair. 1990–94 (retd); Chair. UK Atomic Energy Authority (UKAEA) 1993–96, Chair. AEA Tech. PLC (after privatisation and flotation of UKAEA) 1996–2001; Chair. Industrial Devt Advisory Bd Dept of Trade and Industry 1993–99, UKAEA 1993–96, The Strategic Partnership 1996–2000, Medical Research Council 1998, IX Holdings Ltd 1999, Baxi Partnership 1999–2000, SThree 2000, UK eUniversities Worldwide Ltd 2000, Working Links (Employment) Ltd 2002, Royal Coll. of Music; Deputy Chair. ENO –2000; Pres. Involvement and Participation Asscn 1997–2002, Inst. of Man. 1998–2000; mem. Bd of Dirs Nat. Computing Centre 1977–80, Gen. Accident PLC (fmrly Gen. Accident) Fire and Life Assurance Corpn 1988–98, Gen. Cable PLC 1994–98 (Chair. 1995–98), Smith and Nephew PLC 1993; mem. Council, Templeton Coll. Oxford 1982–93, Asscn for Business Sponsorship of the Arts 1985–97; mem. Bd CEED 1985–98 (Deputy Chair. 1992–98); mem. Cttee on Standards in Public Life 1997–, British Govt Panel on Sustainable Devt 1998–2000; Chair. Nuclear Decommissioning Authority (NDA) 2004–07; Chair. Exec. Bd Caithness and North Sutherland Regeneration Partnership 2008–; Chair. Bd of Govs, Birkbeck Coll. 1989–98; Fellow, British Computer Soc.; Hon. Fellow, Birkbeck Coll. 1999; Hon. LLD (Nottingham) 1991, (Portsmouth) 1996; Hon. DSc (Cranfield) 1995, (City) 2001, (Hull) 2001; Global 500 Roll of Honour (UN Environment Program) 1989. *Leisure interests:* sport, especially cricket, music, especially opera and reading. *Address:* Caithness Regeneration Partnership, T3UK, Janetstown Industrial Estate, Janetstown, KW14 7XF, Scotland (office). *Telephone:* (1847) 890017 (office). *Website:* www.caithness.org/regeneration (office).

CLEESE, John Marwood, MA; British actor and writer; b. 27 Oct. 1939; s. of Reginald Cleese and Muriel Cleese; m. 1st Connie Booth 1968 (divorced 1978); one d.; m. 2nd Barbara Trentham 1981 (divorced 1990); one d.; m. 3rd Alyce Faye Eichelberger 1992; ed Clifton Sports Acad. and Downing Coll., Cambridge; started writing and making jokes professionally 1963; first appearance on British TV 1966; appeared in and co-wrote TV series: The Frost Report, At Last the 1948 Show, Monty Python's Flying Circus, Fawlty Towers, The Human Face; Founder and Dir Video Arts Ltd 1972–89; appeared as Petruchio in The Taming of the Shrew, BBC TV Shakespeare cycle 1981; appeared in Cheers, for which he received an Emmy Award; guest appearances in Third Rock From the Sun, Will and Grace; Hon. A.D. White Prof.-at-Large, Cornell Univ. 1999–; Hon. LLD (St Andrews). *Films include:* Interlude, The Magic Christian, And Now For Something Completely Different, Monty Python and the Holy Grail, Romance with a Double Bass, Life of Brian, Time Bandits, Privates on Parade, Yellowbeard 1982, The Meaning of Life 1983, Silverado 1985, Clockwise 1986, A Fish Called Wanda (BAFTA Award for Best Film Actor) 1988, Erik the Viking 1988, Splitting Heirs 1992, Mary Shelley's Frankenstein 1993, The Jungle Book 1994, Fierce Creatures 1996, The Out of Towners 1998, Isn't She Great 1998, The World Is Not Enough 1999, The Quantum Project 2000, Rat Race 2000, Pluto Nash 2000, Harry Potter and the Philosopher's Stone 2001, Scorched 2002, Die Another Day 2002, Harry Potter and the Chamber of Secrets 2002, Charlie's Angels: Full Throttle 2003, George of the Jungle 2 (voice) 2003, Shrek 2 (voice) 2004, Around the World in 80 Days 2004, Valiant (voice) 2005, Man About Town 2006, Complete Guide to Guys 2006, L'Entente cordiale 2006, Charlotte's Web (voice) 2006, Shrek the Third (voice) 2007, Igor (voice) 2008. *Publications:* Families and How to Survive Them, Life and How to Survive It (both with Robin Skynner), The Human Face (with Brian Bates), The Pythons Autobiography (co-author) 2003. *Leisure interests:* gluttony, sloth. *Address:* c/o David Wilkinson, 115 Hazlebury Road, London, SW6 2LX, England. *Telephone:* (20) 7371-5188. *Fax:* (20) 7371-5161.

CLEGG, Nick, MA; British politician; *Leader, Liberal Democratic Party;* b. 7 Jan. 1967, Chalfont St Giles, Bucks.; s. of Nick Clegg and Hermance van den Wall Bake; m. Miriam Gonzalez Durantez; two s.; ed Westminster School, Cambridge Univ., Univ. of Minn., USA, Coll. d'Europe, Belgium; began career as trainee journalist at The Nation magazine, Washington, DC; Aid and Trade Adviser, European Comm., Brussels 1994–96; Adviser to Sir Leon Brittan 1996–99; Liberal Democrat MEP for E Midlands 1996–2004; Lecturer, Sheffield and Cambridge Univs 2004; MP (Liberal Democrats) for Sheffield Hallam 2005–, Shadow Spokesperson on Foreign Affairs 2005–06, Shadow Home Sec. 2006–07, Leader Liberal Democratic Party 2007–; Founder mem. Campaign for Parl. Reform; columnist Guardian Politics Unlimited. *Leisure interests:* skiing, mountaineering. *Address:* Liberal Democratic Party, 4 Cowley Street, London, SW1P 3NB (office); 85 Nethergreen Road, Sheffield, S11 7EH, England (office). *Telephone:* (20) 7222-7999 (office); (114) 230-9002 (Sheffield) (office). *Fax:* (20) 7799-2170 (office); (114) 230-9614 (Sheffield) (office). *E-mail:* info@libdems.org.uk (office); nickclegg@sheffieldhallam.org.uk (office). *Website:* www.libdems.org.uk (office); www.nickclegg.org.uk (office).

CLEGHORN, John E., OC, FCA, BComm, CA; Canadian banker and business executive; *Chairman, Canadian Pacific Railway Ltd;* b. 7 July 1941, Montreal, PQ; s. of H. W. Edward Cleghorn and Hazel Miriam Dunham; m. Pattie E. Hart 1963; two s. one d.; ed McGill Univ.; Clarkson Gordon & Co. (chartered accountants) 1962–64; sugar buyer and futures trader, St Lawrence Sugar Ltd, Montréal 1964–66; Mercantile Bank of Canada 1966–74; joined Royal Bank of Canada 1974, various sr exec. positions 1975–83, including Pres. 1983, Pres., COO 1986, Pres. CEO 1994–95, Chair. CEO 1995–2001; Chair. SNC-Lavalin Group 2002–07 (retd); mem. Bd of Dirs Canadian Pacific Railway Ltd 2001–, Chair. 2006–; mem. Bd of Dirs Molson Coors Brewing Co.) 2003–; fmr mem. McGill Univ. Bd of Govs, now Govs Emer. and mem. McGill Desautels Faculty of Man.'s Int. Advisory Bd; Chancellor Wilfrid Laurier Univ. 1996–2003; mem. Canadian and BC Insts. of Chartered Accountants; Fellow, Ordre des Comptables Agréés du Québec, Inst. of Chartered Accountants of Ont.; Hon. DCL (Bishop's Univ.) 1989, (Acadia Univ.) 1996; Hon. LLD (Wilfrid Laurier Univ.) 1991. *Leisure interests:* skiing, jogging, tennis, fishing. *Address:* Canadian Pacific Railway Ltd, Gulf Canada Square, 401 9th Ave. SW, Calgary, Alberta T2P 4Z4, Canada (office). *Telephone:* (403) 319-7000 (office). *Website:* www8.cpr.ca (office).

CLELAND, Joseph Maxwell (Max), MA; American fmr politician; b. 24 Aug. 1942, Atlanta, Ga; s. of Joseph Cleland and Juanita Kesler; ed Stetson Univ. Deland, Fla, Emory Univ.; served in US Army during Vietnam War, lost both legs and part of one arm 1968; mem. Ga Senate, Atlanta 1971–75; consultant, Comm. on Veterans Affairs, US Senate 1975–77; Admin. Veterans Affairs, Washington, DC 1977–81; Sec. of State, State of Ga 1982–95; Senator from Georgia 1997–2003; mem. Senate Armed Services Cttee 1997–2002, Cttee on Governmental Affairs 1997–2002, Cttee on Small Businesses 1997–2002, Commerce Cttee 1999–2002; mem. Nat. Comm. on Terrorist Attacks Upon the US 2002–03 (resgnd); Distinguished Adjunct Prof., American Univ. Washington Semester Program and Fellow, Center for Congressional and Presidential Studies 2003; mem. Bd of Dirs Export-Import Bank of the United States 2003–07; worked for presidential campaign of John Kerry

2004; Democrat; Silver Star and Bronze Star for valorous action in combat. *Publications:* Strong at the Broken Places 2000, Going for the Max!: 12 Principles for Living Life to the Fullest 2000. *Address:* 340 Mockingbird Lane, SE, Smyrna, GA 30082, USA (office).

CLÉMENT, Jérôme, LenD; French government official and broadcasting executive; *President, d'Arte France;* b. 18 May 1945, Paris; s. of Yves-André Clément and Raymonde Gornik; m. Marie-Christine Sterin 1974; one s. three d.; ed Lycées Montaigne and Louis-le-Grand, Paris, Facultés de Droit et des Lettres, Paris and Ecole Nat. d'Admin; Ministry of Culture 1974–76, 1978–80; Cour des Comptes 1976–78; Cultural Counsellor, French Embassy, Cairo 1980–81; Counsellor, Office of Prime Minister Mauroy 1981–84; Dir-Gen. Centre nat. de la cinématographie 1984–89; mem. Supervisory Bd Soc. Européenne de Programmes de Télévision (La Sept) 1986–89, Pres. 1989–; Pres. Asscn Int. des Télévisions de l'Educ. et de la Découverte 1999–2001; Pres. d'Arte France 1991–99, Vice-Pres. 1999–2003, Pres. 2003–; Pres. la Cinquième (TV channel) 1997–2000; Dir Réunion des musées nationaux, Orchestre de Paris; municipal councillor Clamart 2001–; Chevalier, Ordre nat. du Mérite, Commdr des Arts et des Lettres, Commdr Ordre du Mérite (FRG). *Publications:* Socialisme et multinationales 1976, Cahiers de l'Atelier, Un Homme en quête de Vertu 1992, Lettres à Pierre Bérégovoy 1993, La Culture expliquée à ma fille 2000. *Leisure interests:* piano, music, painting, tennis, running. *Address:* d'Arte France, 8, Rue Marceau, 92785 Issy-les-Moulineaux Cedex 9 (office); 205 avenue Jean-Jaurès, 92140 Clamart, France (home); Le Vieux Castel, 49350 Gennes. *Telephone:* 1-55-00-77-77 (office). *Fax:* 1-55-00-77-00 (office). *Website:* www.arte-tv.com/fr (office).

CLEMENT, John, CBIM; British business executive; *Chairman, Allianz Dresdner Second Endowment Policy Trust;* b. 18 May 1932; s. of Frederick and Alice Eleanor Clement; m. Elisabeth Anne Emery 1956; two s. one d.; ed Bishop's Stortford Coll.; Howards Dairies, Westcliff on Sea 1949–64; United Dairies London Ltd 1964–69; Asst Man. Dir Rank Leisure Services Ltd 1969–73; Chair. Unigate Foods Div. 1973; Chief Exec. Unigate PLC 1976–90, Chair. 1977–91; Dir Eagle Star Holdings 1981–86; Chair. (non-exec.) The Littlewoods Org. 1982–90; Chair. Culpho Consultants 1991–, Chair. Tuddenham Hall Foods 1979–; Chair. Kleinwort 2nd Endowment Trust PLC (now Allianz Dresdner Second Endowment Policy Trust PLC); Dir (non-exec.) Ransomes PLC 1991–, Chair. 1993–98; Dir Anglo American Insurance Co. Ltd 1991–94, Chair. 1993–94; Dir Jarvis Hotels Ltd 1994–2004; Chair. Nat. Car Auctions Ltd 1995–; mem. Supervisory Bd Nutricia N.V.; mem. Securities and Investment Bd 1986–89; High Sheriff, Suffolk 2000–01; Fellow, Inst. of Grocery Distribution. *Leisure interests:* tennis, shooting, sailing, bridge, rugby. *Address:* Allianz Dresdner Second Endowment Policy Trust Plc, 55 Bishopsgate, London, EC M 3AD, England (office). *Telephone:* (20) 7859-9000 (office).

CLEMENT, Pascal; French government official and barrister; b. 12 May 1945, Boulogne-Billancourt (Hauts-de-Seine); fmr Marketing Dir Rank-Xerox; Mayor of Saint-Marcel-de-Félines (Loire) 1977–2001, mem. Municipal Council; Deputy Nat. Ass. 1978–93, 1995–2005, fmr Chair. Cttee on Constitutional Laws and Legislation; Vice-Chair. Loire Gen. Council 1982–94, Chair. 1994–2008; Minister Del. attached to the Prime Minister, responsible for relations with the Nat. Ass. 1993–95; Keeper of the Seals and Minister of Justice 2005–07. *Address:* c/o Ministry of Justice, 13 place Vendôme, 75042 Paris Cédex 01, France (office).

CLEMENT, Tony, BA, LLB; Canadian politician; *Minister of Industry;* b. 1961, Manchester, UK; m. Lynne Golding; three c.; ed Univ. of Toronto; fmr Pres. Progressive Conservative Party of Ont.; prov. Minister of Transportation 1997–99, of the Environment 1999–2000, of Municipal Affairs and Housing 1999–2001, of Health and Long-Term Care 2001–03; defeated in 2003 election; Counsel, Bennett Jones LLP 2003–06; MP 2006–; Minister of Health and Minister for the Fed. Econ. Devt Initiative for Northern Ont. 2006–08, of Industry 2008–; Founding Pres. Canadian Alliance 2000;. *Address:* Industry Canada, C. D. Howe Building, 11th Floor, East Tower, 235 Queen Street, Ottawa, ON K1A 0H5, Canada (office). *Telephone:* (613) 954-5031 (office). *Fax:* (613) 954-2340 (office). *E-mail:* info@ic.gc.ca (office). *Website:* www.ic.gc.ca (office).

CLEMENT, Wolfgang; German politician; b. 7 July 1940, Bochum; five d.; ed Univ. of Münster; journalist, Westfälische Rundschau newspaper –1967, various positions including Deputy Ed.-in-Chief 1968–81; Research Asst, Inst. for Procedural Law, Univ. of Marburg 1967–68; Press Spokesman, SPD Nat. Exec., Bonn 1981–86, resgnd over campaign controversy 1986; Ed.-in-Chief Hamburger Morgenpost newspaper 1986–88; Chief-of-Staff N Rhine-Westphalia State Chancellery 1989–90, Minister without Portfolio 1990–95, Head of Ministry of Industry, Small Business, Tech. and Transport 1995–96; mem. N Rhine-Westphalia State Ass. 1993–2001; elected Deputy Chair. SPD Exec. for State of N Rhine-Westphalia 1996; Premier of State of N Rhine-Westphalia 1998–2002; Deputy Chair. SPD Nat. Exec. 1999–2008 (resgnd); Fed. Minister of Econs and Labour 2002–05. *Address:* c/o Federal Ministry of Economics and Labour, Scharnhorststrasse 34–37, 10115 Berlin, Germany (office).

CLEMENTE, Carmine Domenic, AB, MA, PhD; American professor of anatomy and neurobiology; *Professor Emeritus, UCLA;* b. 29 April 1928, Penns Grove, NJ; s. of Ermanno Clemente and Caroline Clemente (née Friozzi); m. Juliette G. Clemente 1968; ed Univ. of Pennsylvania and Univ. Coll. London; US Public Health Service Fellow and Asst Instructor in Anatomy, Univ. of Pennsylvania 1950–52; Instructor in Anatomy, UCLA 1952–53, Asst Prof. 1954–59, Assoc. Prof. 1959–63, Prof. and Chair. Dept of Anatomy 1963–73, Prof. of Anatomy 1973–94, Prof. Emer. 1994–; Prof. of Surgery (Anatomy), Charles R. Drew Postgrad. Medical School 1974– (mem.

Bd 1985–), Dir Brain Research Inst. 1976–87; John Simon Guggenheim Memorial Scholar, Nat. Inst. for Medical Research, Mill Hill, London 1988–89, 1991; Consultant in Surgical Anatomy, Martin Luther King Hosp., Los Angeles 1971; Consultant in Research Neurophysiology, Sepulveda Veterans Admin. Hosp.; mem. Inst. of Medicine of NAS; consultant, Robert Wood Johnson Foundation, Princeton, NJ 1990–; numerous awards and distinctions. *Publications:* ed. Gray's Anatomy 1973–; numerous books, films and some 200 scientific publs, including: Anatomy, An Atlas of the Human Body 1975 (5th edition 2007). *Leisure interest:* philately. *Address:* Dept of Neurobiology, UCLA School of Medicine, Los Angeles, CA 90095 (office); 11737 Bellagio Road, Los Angeles, CA 90049, USA (home). *Telephone:* (310) 825-9566 (office); (310) 472-1149 (home). *E-mail:* cdclem@ucla.edu.

CLEMENTE, Francesco; Italian painter; b. 23 March 1952, Naples; s. of Marquess Lorenzo Clemente; m. Alba Primiceri 1974; four c.; ed Univ. degli Studi di Roma, La Sapienza; collaborated with Andy Warhol and Jean-Michel Basquiat 1984; mem. American Acad. of Arts and Letters. *Address:* c/o Gagosian Gallery, 980 Madison Avenue, New York, NY 10021, USA.

CLEMENTI, Sir David Cecil, Kt, CA, FCA; British financial executive; *Chairman, Prudential plc;* b. 25 Feb. 1949, Hunts.; s. of Air Vice-Marshal Creswell Montagu Clementi and Susan Clementi (née Pelham); m. Sarah Louise (Sally) Cowley 1972; one s. one d.; ed Winchester Coll., Lincoln Coll., Oxford, Harvard Business School, USA; with Corp. Finance Div. Kleinwort Benson Ltd 1975–87, Head 1989–94; Head Kleinwort Benson Securities 1987–89; Chief Exec. Kleinwort Benson Ltd 1994–97; Vice-Chair. Kleinwort Benson Group PLC 1997; Deputy Gov. Bank of England 1997–2002; Chair. Prudential PLC 2002–; mem. Monetary Policy Cttee; Dir (non-exec.) Financial Services Authority, mem. Financial Capability Steering Group 2003–, apptd by Sec. of State for Constitutional Affairs to carry out review of regulation of legal services in England and Wales (completed 2004); Dir (non-exec.) Rio Tinto plc 2003–, Foreign & Colonial Investment Trust PLC 2008–; Pres. Investment Property Forum 2005–; Trustee, Royal Opera House. *Leisure interests:* sailing. *Address:* Prudential plc, Laurence Pountney Hill, London, EC4R 0HH, England (office). *Telephone:* (20) 7548-3901 (office). *Fax:* (20) 7548-3631 (office). *E-mail:* info@prudential.co.uk (office). *Website:* www.prudential.co.uk (office).

CLEMENTS, John Allen, MD, FRCP, FAAS; American paediatrician, physiologist and academic; *Professor of Pulmonary Biology and Professor of Pediatrics Emeritus, University of California, San Francisco;* Research Asst, Cornell Univ. Medical Coll. 1947–49; with US Army studying defences against war gasses 1949–61; with Cardiovascular Research Inst., Univ. of California 1961–; Julius H. Comroe, Jr Prof. of Pulmonary Biology, Univ. of California, San Francisco 1987, currently Prof. of Pulmonary Biology and Prof. of Pediatrics Emer.; Fellow, American Acad. of Arts and Sciences 2002–; Bowditch Lecturer, American Physiological Soc. 1961; Harold and Marilyn Menkes Memorial Lecture, Johns Hopkins Univ. 1991; Distinguished Lecturer in Medical Science, Mayo Clinic 1993; Ulf von Euler Memorial Lecture of the Karolinska Inst., Nobel Foundation 1996; mem. WHO immunisation programme, Nat. Heart, Lung and Blood Inst. Advisory Council 1990–93; Hon. Fellow, American Coll. of Chest Physicians 1978, Hon. Dir La Sociedad Chilena de Enfermedades del Thorax y Tuberculosis 1982, Hon. Life Mem. American Lung Asscn 1983; Hon. MD (Universität Bern) 1990, (Philipps Universität Marburg) 1992, Hon. DSc (Univ. of Manitoba) 1993; Modern Medicine Distinguished Achievement Award 1973, Howard Taylor Ricketts Medal and Award, Univ. of Chicago 1975, 57th Mellon Award, Univ. of Pittsburgh 1976, Edward Livingston Trudeau Medal, American Lung Asscn 1982, Gairdner Foundation Int. Award 1983, Research Achievement Award, American Heart Asscn 1991, Christopher Columbus Discovery Award in Biomedical Research, NIH Christopher Columbus Quincentenary Jubilee Comm. of US Congress 1992, Nat. Medical Research Award, Nat. Health Council 1992, American Acad. of Pediatrics Virginia Apgar Award for Distinguished Contribs to Neonatology 1994, Albert Lasker Award for Clinical Research 1994, Warren Alpert Foundation Prize, Harvard Medical School 1996, Discoverers Award, Pharmaceutical Manufacturers Asscn 1997. *Achievements include:* Co-discoverer of lung surfactant and elucidator of its composition and functions 1955–; inventor of synthetic surfactant replacements 1980. *Publications:* numerous scholarly articles in journals and books. *Leisure interests:* piano, musical concerts, tennis, swimming, biography, history of science. *Address:* Box 1245, University of California, San Francisco, 3333 California Street, Laurel Heights 150, San Francisco, CA 94143-1245, USA (office). *Telephone:* (415) 476-1509 (office). *Fax:* (415) 476-3586 (office). *E-mail:* clement@itsa.ucsf.edu (office).

CLEMENTS, William Perry, Jr; American fmr politician; b. 13 April 1917, Dallas, Tex.; s. of William P. Clements and Evelyn Cammack Clements; m. Rita Crocker Clements 1975; one s. one d. (by previous marriage); ed Highland Park High School, Dallas and Southern Methodist Univ., Dallas; founder, Chair., CEO SEDCO Inc., Dallas 1947–73, 1977, 1983–; mem. Nat. Exec. Bd, Boy Scouts of America; mem. Bd of Trustees and Bd of Govs, Southern Methodist Univ.; Deputy Sec. for Defense 1974–77; Gov. of Texas 1979–83, 1987–91; mem. Nat. Bipartisan Comm. of Cen. America 1983–84. *Address:* 1901 North Akard, Dallas, TX 75201, USA. *Telephone:* (214) 720-0336 (office). *Fax:* (214) 720-0378 (office).

CLEMINSON, Sir James Arnold Stacey, KBE, MC; British fmr company director; b. 31 Aug. 1921, Hull, Yorkshire; s. of Arnold Russell Cleminson and Florence Stacey Cleminson; m. Helen Juliet Measor; one s. two d.; ed Bramcote and Rugby Schools; served British Army, Parachute Regt 1940–46; joined Reckitt Colman Overseas 1946; Dir and later Vice-Chair. J. J. Colman Norwich 1960–69; Dir Reckitt and Colman 1969, Chair. Food Div. 1970, CEO 1973–80, Chair. 1977–86; Vice-Chair. Norwich Union 1981–92 (Dir 1979–92);

Dir United Biscuits Holdings 1982–89; Pres. CBI 1984–86; Pres. Endeavour Training 1984–97; Chair. British Overseas Trade Bd 1986–90, Jeyes Hygiene PLC 1986–89, Riggs A. P. Bank 1987–91 (Dir 1985–2002); Dir Eastern Counties Newspaper Group 1986–92, J. H. Fenner PLC 1985–97 (Vice-Chair. 1993–97), Riggs Nat. Bank of Washington DC 1991–93; Pro-Chancellor Hull Univ. 1986–94; fmr Trustee, Army Benevolent Fund; Trustee Airborne Forces Security Fund, Norwich Cathedral Trust; Pres. Norfolk SSAFA 1994–2000; fmr DL (retd); Pres. Arnhem Veterans' Club; Hon. LLD (Hull) 1985. *Leisure interests:* fishing, golf. *Address:* 18 Earsman Street, Bungay, Norfolk, NR35 1AG, England (office). *Telephone:* (1986) 894945 (home). *Fax:* (1986) 895664 (office).

CLEOBURY, Nicholas Randall, MA, FRCO; British conductor; *Associate Director, Orchestra of the Swan;* b. 23 June 1950, Bromley, Kent; s. of John Cleobury and Brenda Cleobury; m. Heather Kay 1978; one s. one d.; ed King's School, Worcester and Worcester Coll., Oxford; Asst Organist, Chichester Cathedral 1971–72, Christ Church, Oxford 1972–76; Conductor, Schola Cantorum of Oxford 1973–76; Chorus Master, Glyndebourne Festival Opera 1977–79; Asst Dir BBC Singers 1977–79; Prin. Opera Conductor, RAM 1980–87; Guest Conductor, Zurich Opera House 1992–; Music Dir Oxford Bach Choir 1997–; Artistic Dir Aquarius 1983–92, Cambridge Symphony Soloists 1990–92, Britten Sinfonia 1992–2005, Sounds New 1996–; Music Dir Broomhill 1990–94, Artistic Dir Cambridge Festival 1992, Mozart Ways Canterbury 2003–; Artistic Advisor, Berkshire Choral Festival 2002–; Assoc. Dir Orchestra of the Swan 2004–; has conducted world-wide from Australia to USA 1979–; Fellow, Christ Church Univ. Coll., Canterbury 2005; numerous recordings; Hon. RAM 1985. *Leisure interests:* cricket, food, wine, reading, theatre. *Address:* Robert Gilder and Co., 91 Great Russell Street, London WC1B 3PS, England (office); 20 Denbigh Street, London, SW1V 2ER (office); Barcheston House, Northside Steeple, Aston, Oxfordshire, OX25 4SE, England (home). *Telephone:* (20) 7580-7758 (office); (7831) 148637 (office); (1869) 340363 (home). *E-mail:* cathy@robert-gilder.com (office); nicholascleobury@btinternet.com (home). *Website:* www.robert-gilder.com (office); www.nicholascleobury.net.

CLEOBURY, Stephen John, MusB, MA, FRCM, FRCO; British conductor and academic; *Director of Music, King's College, Cambridge;* b. 31 Dec. 1948, Bromley; s. of John Frank Cleobury and Brenda Julie Cleobury (née Randall); m. 2nd Emma Sian Disley; three d. (two from previous m.); ed King's School, Worcester and St John's Coll., Cambridge; organist, St Matthew's, Northampton 1971–74; sub-organist, Westminster Abbey 1974–78; Master of Music, Westminster Cathedral 1979–82; Dir of Music, King's Coll. Cambridge 1982–; mem. Council, Royal School of Church Music 1982–; Pres. Inc. Asscn of Organists 1985–87, Cathedral Organists' Asscn 1988–90, Royal Coll. of Organists 1990–92 (Hon. Sec. 1981–90); Chief Conductor BBC Singers 1995–2007, Conductor Laureate 2007–; Hon. DMus (Anglia Polytechnic) 2001. *Recordings:* solo organ works and directing choir of King's Coll. and BBC Singers. *Leisure interest:* reading, opera. *Address:* c/o Lundstrom Arts Management, 86 Ard na Mara, Malahide, Co. Dublin, Ireland (office); King's College, Cambridge, CB2 1ST, England (office). *Telephone:* (1) 8450444 (office); (1223) 331224 (office). *E-mail:* info@lundstrom-am.com (office); choir@kings.cam.ac.uk (office). *Website:* www.lundstrom-am.com (office). *Fax:* (1223) 331890 (office).

CLERCQ, Willy De, MA, LLD; Belgian politician and barrister; b. 8 July 1927, Ghent; s. of Frans De Clercq and Yvonne Catry; m. Fernande Fazzi 1953; two s. one d.; Barrister, Court of Appeal, Ghent 1951; with Gen. Secretariat of UN, New York 1952; mem. Chamber of Reps. for Ghent-Eekloo 1958–85; Deputy Prime Minister, in charge of Budget 1966–68; Deputy Prime Minister and Minister of Finance 1973–74, Minister of Finance 1973–77, Deputy Prime Minister and Minister of Finance and Foreign Trade Dec. 1981–85; Vice-Pres. Partij voor Vrijheid en Vooruitgang (PVV) 1961; Pres. PVV 1971–73, 1977–81; mem. European Parl. 1979–81, 1989–; Pres. Cttee for External Econ. Relations and Legal Affairs Cttee 1989–99; Minister of State 1985; Hon. Pres. European Liberal and Democratic Party (ELD) 1980–85; part-time Prof. Univs of Ghent and Brussels; Chair. of Interim Cttee of the IMF 1976–77, 1983–85; Commr for External Relations and Trade Policy, Comm. of European Communities 1985–89; mem. Bd Care Int., China Europe Int. Business School, Shanghai; Hon. Pres. European Movt, Belgium, Union of European Federalists; Grand Cross Order of Leopold II, Officier Légion d'honneur, Grand Cross First Class, Order of Merit (Germany) and several other honours. *Publications:* Europe, Back to the Top; numerous contribs to Belgian newspapers. *Leisure interests:* sport, travel. *Address:* Cyriel Buyssestraat 12, 9000 Ghent, Belgium (home). *Telephone:* (2) 284-26-60 (office); (9) 221-18-13 (home). *Fax:* (2) 284-91-49 (office); (9) 220-07-77 (home). *E-mail:* wdeclercq@europarl.eu.int (office); info@fazzi.be (home). *Website:* www.wdeclercq.be (office).

CLERIDES, Glafcos, BA, LLB; Cypriot lawyer, politician and fmr head of state; *Honourary President, Dimokratikos Synagermos (Democratic Rally);* b. 24 April 1919, Nicosia; s. of the late Yiannis Clerides and Elli Clerides; m. Lilla-Irene Erulkar 1946 (died 2007); one d.; ed Pancyprian Gymnasium, Nicosia, King's Coll., London, UK; served with RAF 1939–45, POW 1942–45; called to Bar, Gray's Inn 1951; practised law in Cyprus 1951–60; Minister of Justice 1959–60; Head of Greek Cypriot Del. to Jt Constitutional Comm. 1959–60, Greek Cypriot Del., London Conf. 1964, Rep. Negotiator Greek Cypriot Community Intercommunal Talks 1968; mem. House of Reps 1960–76, 1981–93, Pres. 1960–76; Acting Pres. of Cyprus July–Dec. 1974, Pres. 1993–2003; Pres. Cyprus Red Cross 1961–63 (Hon. Certificate and Hon. Life mem., Recognition of Distinguished Service); f. Unified Party 1969, Democratic Rally 1976; leading mem. Unified Party, Progressive Front; FounderDimokratikos Synagermos (Democratic Rally) 1976, currently Hon. Pres.; Hon. Mem. Int. Raoul Wallenberg Foundation; Grand Cross of the Saviour (Greece); Gold Medal (Order of Holy Sepulchre), Recognized Services and Understanding of Roman Catholic Religious Group (by approval of His Holiness Pope John XXIII). *Publications:* My Deposition (four vols). *Leisure interests:* sailing. *Address:* c/o Dimokratikos Synagermos (Democratic Rally), POB 25305, 25 Pindarou St, 1308 Nicosia (office); 5 Ioannis Clerides Street, Nicosia, Cyprus (home). *Telephone:* 22883000 (office). *Fax:* 22752751 (office). *E-mail:* disy@disy.org.cy (office). *Website:* www.disy.org.cy (office).

CLERISME, Jean Renald, BA, MA, MPhil, PhD; Haitian anthropologist, politician and diplomatist; b. 7 Nov. 1937, Arniquet; m. Dr Linda Geralde; three s.; ed Université d'Haiti, New York Univ. and Yale Univ., USA; Amb. of Haiti to WTO, Int. Trade Center, UNCTAD, ITU, Geneva, Switzerland 2001–03; Del. Plenipotentiary to IAEA, Vienna 2001–03; Del. to Gen. Ass., Complete Test Ban Treaty Org. (CTBTO), Vienna 2003; Minister of Foreign Affairs 2006–08; past positions include Pres. and Co-Pres. of Task Forces, WTO on Budget, Finances and Admin Cttee, Minister Counsellor to Perm. Mission to UN Office, Geneva, Rep. to UNIDO, Vienna; fmr Del. to WTO Confs, Singapore, Geneva, Seattle, Cancun, to UNCTAD Confs in Geneva, Bangkok, Brussels, to WIPO, Lisbon; Fulbright/LASPAU Scholarship, Mellon Fondation Grant. *Publication:* Main-d'oeuvre haïtienne and capital dominicain (Haitian Labor and Dominican Capital) 2003. *Address:* c/o Ministry of Foreign Affairs, Blvd Harry S. Truman, Cité de l'Exposition, Port-au-Prince, Haiti (office).

CLERMONT, Yves Wilfrid, PhD, FRSC; Canadian anatomist and academic; *Professor Emeritus of Anatomy and Cell Biology, McGill University;* b. 14 Aug. 1926, Montréal; s. of Rodolphe Clermont and Fernande Primeau; m. Madeleine Bonneau 1950; two s. one d.; ed Univ. of Montréal, McGill Univ., Collège de France, Paris; Teaching Fellow, Dept of Anatomy, Faculty of Medicine, McGill Univ., Montréal 1952–53, Lecturer 1953–56, Asst Prof. 1956–60, Assoc. Prof. 1960–63, Prof. 1963–97, Chair. of Dept 1975–85, Prof. Emer. 1997–; Vice-Pres. American Asscn of Anatomists 1979–83; mem. Review Group and Advisory Group of Expanded Programme of Research in Human Reproduction, WHO, Geneva 1971–76, RSC 1972–; Ortho Prize, Canadian Soc. of Fertility 1958, Prix Scientifique de la Province de Québec 1963, Siegler Award, American Fertility Soc. 1966, Van Campenhout Award, Canadian Fertility Soc. 1986, J.C.B. Brant Award, Canadian Asscn of Anatomists 1986, Distinguished Andrologist Award, American Asscn of Andrology 1988, Osler Teaching Award, Faculty of Medicine, McGill Univ. 1990, Serono Award American Asscn of Andrology. *Publications:* more than 140 scientific articles in journals and books in the field of biology of reproduction and cell biology. *Leisure interests:* reading history and biography, gardening, listening to classical music. *Address:* 567 Townshend, St Lambert, PQ J4R 1M4 (home); Department of Anatomy, McGill University, 3640 University Street, Montréal, PQ H3A 2B2, Canada (office). *Telephone:* (450) 671-5606 (home); (514) 398-6349 (office). *Fax:* (514) 398-5047 (office). *E-mail:* yves.clermont@mcgill.ca (office).

CLEWLOW, Warren (Alexander Morten); South African business executive and chartered accountant; b. 13 July 1936, Durban; s. of Percy Edward Clewlow; m. Margaret Brokensha 1964; two s. three d.; ed Glenwood High School, Univ. of Natal; joined Barlow Group as Co. Sec. Barlow's (OFS) Ltd 1963; Alt. Dir Barlow Rand Ltd 1974, Dir 1975; mem. Exec. Cttee with various responsibilities Barlow Group 1978–83; CEO Barlow Rand Ltd (now Barloworld) 1983–86, Deputy Chair. and Chief Exec. 1985, Chair. 1991–2007 (resgnd); Chair. Nedbank Ltd and Nedcor Ltd 2004–06; Chair. Pretoria Portland Cement 1993–2004; fmr Dir SA Mutual Life Assurance Soc., Sasol Ltd; Regional Gov. Univ. of Cape Town Foundation; Council mem. South Africa Foundation; Chair. State Pres. Econ. Advisory Council 1985; mem. Bd Asscn of Marketers; Trustee Project South African Trust, Nelson Mandela Children's Fund; Chair. Duke of Edinburgh's South African Foundation; Chair. The President's Award for Youth Empowerment Trust; Hon. Treas. African Children's Feeding Scheme; Hon. Prof. Univ. of Stellenbosch 1986; Order for Meritorious Service (Gold Class) 1988; Hon. DEcon (Natal) 1988; Businessman of the Year, Sunday Times 1984, Marketing Man of the Year, SA Inst. of Marketing 1984, Dr G. Malherbe Award, Univ. of Natal 1986. *Leisure interests:* tennis, horticulture, historical reading, sugar plantation farmering. *Address:* c/o Barloworld Ltd, P.O. Box 782248, Sandton, 2146, South Africa (office).

CLIBURN, Harvey Lavan (Van), Jr; American pianist; b. 12 July 1934, Shreveport; s. of Harvey Lavan and Rildia Bee Cliburn (née O'Bryan); studied with mother and at Juilliard School; public appearances, Shreveport 1940; début, Houston Symphony Orchestra 1952, New York Philharmonic Orchestra 1954, 1958; concert pianist on tour in USA 1955–56, USSR 1958; appearances in Brussels, London, Amsterdam, Paris, etc.; Hon. HHD (Baylor), MFA (Moscow Conservatory) 1989; Leventritt Award 1954, Winner first Int. Tchaikovsky Piano Competition, Moscow 1958, Arturo Toscanini Award, Classical Music Broadcaster's Asscn 1998, Kennedy Center Honor 2001. *Address:* PO Box 470219, Fort Worth, TX 76147-0219 (office); Van Cliburn Foundation, 2525 Ridgmar Boulevard, Suite 307, Fort Worth, TX 76116-4583, USA (office). *Telephone:* (817) 738-6536 (office). *Fax:* (817) 738-6534 (office). *Website:* www.cliburn.org (office).

CLIFF, Ian Cameron, OBE, MA; British diplomatist; *Ambassador and Head of Delegation to the Organization for Security and Co-operation in Europe (OSCE);* b. 11 Sept. 1952, Twickenham; s. of Gerald Shaw Cliff and Dorothy Cliff; m. Caroline Redman 1988; one s. two d.; ed Hampton Grammar School and Univ. of Oxford; history teacher, Dr Challoner's Grammar School, Amersham 1975–79; joined FCO 1979; First Sec., Khartoum 1982–85, FCO 1985–89, UK Mission to UN, New York 1989–93; Dir Exports to Middle East, Near East and N Africa, Dept of Trade and Industry 1993–96; Deputy Head of

Mission, Embassy in Vienna 1995–2001; Amb. to Bosnia and Herzegovina 2001–05, to Sudan 2005–07, Amb. and Head of Del. to OSCE, Vienna 2007–. *Leisure interests:* music, railways, philately. *Address:* UK Delegation to the OSCE, Jauresgasse 12, 1030 Vienna, Austria (office). *Telephone:* (1) 716133304 (office). *Fax:* (1) 716133900 (office). *E-mail:* ian.cliff@fco.gov.uk (office). *Website:* www.britishembassy.gov.uk/austria (office).

CLIFF, Jimmy; Jamaican reggae singer and composer; b. (James Chambers), 1 April 1948, St Catherine; one s.; ed Kingston Tech. School; singer, songwriter 1960s–; backing vocalist, London 1963; tours world-wide, especially USA, Europe, South America, Africa; concerts include Montreux Jazz Festival 1980, World Music Festival, Jamaica 1982, Rock In Rio II, Brazil 1991, Worlds Beat Reggae Festival, Portand, USA 1992; formed own record label, Cliff Records 1989, own production company, Cliff Sounds and Films 1990; Grammy Award, Best Reggae Recording 1985, MOBO Award, Contribution to Urban Music 2002. *Films:* The Harder They Come 1972, Bongo Man 1980, Club Paradise 1986. *Compositions include:* You Can Get It If You Really Want (recorded by Desmond Dekker), Let Your Yeah Be Yeah (recorded by The Pioneers), Trapped (recorded by Bruce Springsteen). *Recordings include:* albums: Hard Road 1967, Jimmy Cliff 1969, Can't Get Enough 1969, Wonderful World 1970, Another Cycle 1971, The Harder They Come 1972, Struggling Man 1974, Follow My Mind 1975, Give Thanx 1978, I Am The Living 1980, Give The People What They Want 1981, Special 1982, The Power and The Glory 1983, Cliff Hanger 1985, Hanging Fire 1988, Images 1990, Breakout 1992, 100% Pure Reggae 1997, Shout for Freedom 1999, Humanitarian 1999, Live And In The Studio 2000, Wanted (compilation) 2000, Best of Jimmy Cliff 2001, Fantastic Plastic People 2002, Sunshine in the Music 2003, Black Magic 2005. *E-mail:* sunpowerproductions3@yahoo.fr (office). *Website:* www.jimmycliff.com.

CLIFFORD, Maxwell (Max); British public relations executive; b. April 1943, Kingston-upon-Thames; s. of Frank Clifford and Lilian Clifford; m. Elizabeth Clifford; one d.; ed secondary modern school, South Wimbledon; worked in dept store (sacked); fmr jr reporter, Merton and Morden News; fmr jr press officer, EMI Records (promoted the Beatles); worked in public relations; Founder Max Clifford Assocs (press and public relations consultancy) 1968–, clients have included Muhammad Ali, Geoffrey Boycott, Marlon Brando, David Copperfield, Diana Ross, O. J. Simpson, Frank Sinatra, SEAT, Laing Homes, Simon Cowell, Kerry Katona. *Publication:* Max Clifford, Read All About It (autobiog. with Angela Levin) 2005. *Address:* Max Clifford Associates Ltd, Moss House, 15-16 Brooks Mews, Mayfair, London, W1K 4DS, England (office). *Telephone:* (20) 7408-2350 (office). *Fax:* (20) 7409-2294 (office). *E-mail:* max@maxclifford.com (office). *Website:* www.maxclifford.com (office).

CLIFFORD, R. Leigh, BEng, MEng Sci; Australian business executive; *Chairman, Qantas Airways Ltd;* ed Univ. of Melbourne; joined Rio Tinto Group 1970, has held posts including Man. Dir Rio Tinto Ltd, Chief Exec. Energy Div., CEO Rio Tinto Group 2000–07 (retd), mem. Bd of Dirs 1994–2007; mem. Bd of Dirs Qantas Airways 2007–, Chair. 2007–; mem. Bd of Dirs Barclays PLC 2004–; mem. Bechtel Bd of Counsellors 2007–; Chair. IEA's Coal Industry Advisory Bd 1998–2000. *Address:* Qantas Airways Ltd, Level 12, Exhibition Street, Melbourne, Vic. 3000, Australia (office). *Telephone:* (3) 8656-6006 (office). *Fax:* (3) 8656-6011 (office). *Website:* www.qantas.com.au (office).

CLIFFORD, Sir Timothy Peter Plint, Kt, BA, FRSA, FRSE, FSA; British art historian and museum administrator; b. 26 Jan. 1946; s. of the late Derek Plint Clifford and Anne Clifford (née Pierson); m. Jane Olivia Paterson 1968; one d.; ed Sherborne, Dorset, Perugia Univ., Courtauld Inst., Univ. of London; Asst Keeper, Dept of Paintings, Manchester City Art Galleries 1968–72, Acting Keeper 1972; Asst Keeper, Dept of Ceramics, Victoria and Albert Museum, London 1972–76; Dir Manchester City Art Galleries 1978–84; Dir Nat. Galleries of Scotland 1984–2001, Dir Gen. 2001–05; mem. Cttee ICOM (UK) 1980–82, Chair. Int. Cttee for Museums of Fine Art 1980–83, mem. Exec. Cttee 1983–88; mem. Bd Museums and Galleries Comm. 1983–88, British Council 1987–92; mem. Exec. Cttee Scottish Museums Council 1984; Vice-Pres. Turner Soc. 1984–86, 1989–; mem. Advisory Council, Friends of the Courtauld Inst.; Trustee Wallace Collection 2003–, Attingham Summer School, The American Friends of the Nat. Galleries of Scotland, Hermitage Devt Trust 1999–2003; Pres. Nat. Asscn of Decorative and Fine Arts Socs 1996–2006; Patron, Friends of Sherborne House 1997–; Freeman, Goldsmiths Co. 1989, City of London 1989; Cavaliere al Ordine della Repubblica Italiana 1988, Commendatore 1999; Hon. LLD (St Andrews) 1996; Hon. DLitt (Glasgow) 2001; Special Award, BIM 1991, Ateneo Veneto, Italy 1997, Gulbenkian Prize for Charles Jenck's Landform 2004, Garrett Lifetime Award for Business Sponsorship for the Arts 2005. *Publications include:* John Crome (with Derek Clifford) 1968, The Man at Hyde Park Corner: Sculpture by John Cheere (with T. Friedmann) 1974, Vues pittoresques de Luxembourg . . . par J.M.W. Turner 1977, Ceramics of Derbyshire 1750–1975 1978, J.M.W. Turner, Acquerelli e incisioni 1980, The Nat. Gallery of Scotland: an Architectural and Decorative History (with Ian Gow) 1988, Raphael: the Pursuit of Perfection (co-author) 1994, Effigies and Ecstasies: Roman Baroque Sculpture and Design in the Age of Bernini (with A. Weston-Lewis) 1998, Designs of Desire: Architectural and Ornament Prints and Drawings 1500–1850 2000, (co-author) A Poet in Paradise: Lord Lindsay and Christian Art 2000. *Leisure interests:* bird watching, entomology. *Address:* c/o Board of Trustees, Wallace Collection, Hertford House, Manchester Square, London, W1U 3BN, England. *Telephone:* (20) 7563-9500. *Fax:* (20) 7224-2155. *Website:* www.wallacecollection.org.

CLIFTON, James Albert, BA, MD; American gastroenterologist, academic and university administrator; *Roy J. Carver Professor Emeritus, College of Medicine, University of Iowa;* b. 18 Sept. 1923, Fayetteville, NC; s. of the late James A. Clifton, Sr and Flora McNair Clifton; m. Katherine Rathe 1949; two d. (and one d. deceased); ed Vanderbilt Univ.; Asst Prof. of Medicine, Univ. of Ia Coll. of Medicine 1954–58, Assoc. Prof. 1958–63, Prof. 1963–76, Roy J. Carver Prof. of Medicine 1976–90, Dir Center for Digestive Diseases 1985–90, Prof. Emer. 1991–, Interim Dean 1991–93; Chief, Div. of Gastroenterology, Univ. of Ia, Dept of Medicine 1953–71, Prof. Emer. 1991–; Chair. Dept of Medicine, Univ. of Ia Coll. of Medicine 1970–76; Pres. American Coll. of Physicians 1977–78, American Gastroenterological Asscn 1970–71; Chair. Subspecialty Bd in Gastroenterology, American Bd of Internal Medicine 1972–75, American Bd of Internal Medicine 1980–81; Pres. Univ. of Iowa Retirees Asscn 1999–2000, Emer. Faculty Asscn 2000; mem. Ludwig Inst. for Cancer Research, Zürich, Switzerland 1984–95, Central Soc. for Clinical Research, American Physiological Soc., Asscn of American Physicians, Inst. of Medicine (NAS), Royal Soc. of Medicine, London, Scientific Advisory Cttee, Health Task Force Cttee (Nat. Insts of Health), Nat. Advisory Council, Nat. Insts of Arthritis, Metabolism and Digestive Diseases (Nat. Insts of Health); consultant to numerous US medical schools; Visiting Scientist, Mount Desert Island Biological Research Lab., Bar Harbor, Maine 1964; Visiting Prof. of Medicine, St Mark's Hosp. (Univ. of London), England 1984–85; Distinguished Medical Alumnus Award, Vanderbilt Univ., Alfred Stengel Award, American Coll. of Physicians, Distinguished Medical Alumnus Award, Univ. of Iowa 2000, Distinguished Mentoring Award 2002. *Publications:* numerous scientific papers on intestinal absorption of nutrients, gastrointestinal motility and numerous publs regarding philosophy and current affairs in internal medicine. *Leisure interests:* music, photography and travel. *Address:* University of Iowa Hospital and Clinics, 4 J.C.P., Hawkins Drive, Iowa City, IA 52242 (office); 39 Audubon Place, Iowa City, IA 52245, USA (home). *Telephone:* (319) 356-1771 (office); (319) 351-1561 (home). *Fax:* (319) 353-6399 (office); (319) 351-1561 (home). *E-mail:* james-clifton@uiowa.edu (office); zybumjim@home.com (home).

CLINTON, Hillary Rodham, MA, DJur; American lawyer, politician and governmment official; *Secretary of State;* b. 26 Oct. 1947, Chicago, Ill.; d. of the late Hugh Ellsworth and Dorothy Howell Rodham; m. William (Bill) Jefferson Clinton (q.v.) (fmr Pres. of USA), 1975; one d.; ed Wellesley Coll. and Yale Univ.; joined Rose Law Firm 1977, fmr Sr Pnr; Legal Counsel, Nixon impeachment staff, US House Judiciary Cttee 1974; Asst Prof. of Law, Univ. of Ark., Fayetteville and Dir Legal Aid Clinic 1974–77; Lecturer in Law, Univ. of Ark., Little Rock 1979–80; Chair. Comm. on Women in the Profession, ABA 1987–91; First Lady of USA 1993–2001; Head of Pres.'s Task Force on Nat. Health Reform 1993–94; newspaper columnist 1995; Senator from New York 2001–09, mem. Armed Services Cttee, Environment and Public Works Cttee, Health, Educ., Labor and Pensions Cttee, Special Cttee on Aging; Co-Chair. Children's Defense Fund 1973–74; unsuccessful cand. for Democratic party nomination for US Pres. 2008; US Sec. of State, Washington, DC 2009–; mem. Bd of Dirs Southern Devt Bancorpn 1986, Nat. Center on Educ. and the Economy 1987, Franklin and Eleanor Roosevelt Inst. 1988, Children's TV Workshop 1989, Public/Pvt. Ventures 1990, Arkansas Single Parent Scholarship Fund Program 1990; Hon. LLD (Arkansas, Little Rock) 1985, (Arkansas Coll.) 1988, (Hendrix Coll.) 1992; Hon. DHL (Drew) 1996; numerous awards and distinctions including One of Most Influential Lawyers in America (Nat. Law Journal) 1988, 1991, Outstanding Lawyer-Citizen Award (Ark. Bar Asscn) 1992, Lewis Hine Award, Nat. Child Labor Law Comm. 1993, Friend of Family Award, American Home Econs Foundation 1993, Humanitarian Award, Alzheimer's Asscn 1994, Elie Wiesel Foundation 1994, AIDS Awareness Award 1994, Grammy Award 1996, ranked by Forbes magazine amongst 100 Most Powerful Women (fifth) 2004, (26th) 2005, (18th) 2006, (25th) 2007, (28th) 2008. *Publications:* It Takes a Village 1996, Dear Socks, Dear Buddy 1998, An Invitation to the White House 2000, Living History (memoirs) 2003; numerous contribs to professional journals. *Leisure interests:* reading, walking, tennis. *Address:* Department of State, 2201 C Street, NW, Washington, DC 20520, USA (office). *Telephone:* (202) 647-4000 (office). *Fax:* (202) 647-6738 (office). *Website:* www.state.gov (office).

CLINTON, William (Bill) Jefferson, JD; American lawyer, fmr politician and fmr head of state; b. 19 Aug. 1946, Hope, Ark.; s. of the late William Jefferson Blythe III and the late Virginia Dwire Kelley; stepfather the late Roger Clinton; m. Hillary Rodham Clinton (q.v.) 1975; one d.; ed Hot Springs High School, Ark., Georgetown Univ., Univ. Coll., Oxford UK, Yale Law School; Professor, Univ. of Ark. Law School 1974–76; Democratic Nominee, US House Third Dist., Ark. 1974; Attorney-Gen., Ark. 1977–79, Gov. of Ark. 1979–81, 1983–93; Pres. of USA 1993–2001; impeached by US House of Reps for perjury and obstruction of justice Dec. 1998, acquitted in Senate on both counts Jan. 1999; suspended from practising law in Supreme Court 2001–06; mem. counsel firm Wright, Lindsey & Jennings 1981–83; UN Special Envoy for Tsunami Recovery 2005–; Chair. Southern Growth Policies Bd 1985–86; Chair. Nat. Govs.' Asscn 1987, Co-Chair. Task Force on Educ. 1990–91; Vice-Chair. Democratic Govs' Asscn 1987–88, Chair. (elect) 1988–89, Chair. 1989–90; Chair. Educ. Comm. of the States 1987; Chair. Democratic Party Affirmative Action 1975, Southern Growth Policies Bd 1980; Chair. Democratic Leadership Council 1990–91; mem. US Supreme Court Bar, Bd of Trustees, Southern Center for Int. Studies of Atlanta, Ga; Chair. Bd of Dirs Global Fairness Initiative; Founder William J. Clinton Foundation, NY and Clinton Presidential Center, Ark.; Hon. Co-Chair. Club of Madrid; Hon. Fellow, Univ. Coll. Oxford 1992; Hon. DCL (Oxford) 1994; Hon. DLitt (Ulster) 1995; TED (Tech. Entertainment Design) Prize (co-recipient) 2007. *Recordings include:* Peter and the Wolf: Wolf Tracks (Grammy Award, Best Spoken Word Album for Children (jtly) 2004) 2003, My Life (Grammy Award, Best Spoken Word Album) 2005. *Publication:* Between Hope and History 1996, My Life (memoir) (British Book Award for Biography of the Year 2005) 2004,

Giving: How Each of Us Can Change the World 2008. *Leisure interests:* jogging, swimming, golf, reading. *Address:* William J. Clinton Foundation, 55 West 125th Street, New York, NY 10027; Clinton Presidential Center, 1200 President Clinton Avenue, Little Rock, AR 72201, USA. *Website:* www.clintonpresidentialcenter.org; www.clintonfoundation.org.

CLINTON-DAVIS, Baron (Life Peer), cr. 1990, of Hackney in the London Borough of Hackney; **Stanley Clinton-Davis,** PC, LLB; British politician, solicitor and international organization official; b. 6 Dec. 1928, London; s. of the late Sidney Davis and of Lily Davis; m. Frances Jane Lucas 1954; one s. three d.; ed Hackney Downs School, Bournemouth School, Mercers' School and King's Coll., London; fmr Councillor and Mayor, London Borough of Hackney; MP for Hackney Cen. 1970–83; Parl. Under-Sec. of State for Trade 1974–79; Opposition Spokesman for Trade 1979–81, for Transport, House of Lords 1990–97; Minister of State, Dept of Trade and Industry 1997–98; Deputy Opposition Spokesman for Foreign Affairs 1981–83; Commr EC for the Environment, Consumer Protection, Nuclear Safety, Forests and Transport 1985–86, for Environment, Transport and Nuclear Safety 1986–88; Chair. Refugee Council 1989–97, Advisory Cttee on Protection of the Sea 1989–97, 1998–2001 (Pres. 2001–03); consultant on European affairs and law, S. J. Berwin & Co. 1989–97, 1998–2003, European Cockpit Asscn 1995–97; Pres. Asscn of Metropolitan Authorities 1992–97, 1998–2003, Airfields Environment Fed. 1994–97, British Airline Pilots Asscn 1994–; Deputy Chair. Labour Finance and Industry Group 1993–; Fellow, King's Coll. and Queen Mary and Westfield Coll., London Metropolitan Univ.; Labour; Grand Cross, Order of Leopold II, for services to EC (Belgium) 1990; Dr hc (Polytechnical Inst., Bucharest) 1993; First Medal for Outstanding Services to Animal Welfare in Europe (Eurogroup for Animal Welfare) 1988. *Publication:* Good Neighbours? Nicaragua, Central America and the United States (co-author) 1982. *Leisure interests:* reading political biographies, golf. *Address:* House of Lords, Westminster, London, SW1A 0PW (office); 22 Bracknell Gate, Frognal Lane, Hampstead, London, NW3 7EP, England (home). *Telephone:* (20) 7435-0541 (home).

CLODUMAR, Kinza (Godfrey); Nauruan politician; b. 1944; entered parl. 1977; prin. financial adviser to Pres. 1992–95; Pres. of Nauru 1997–98, Jan.–May 2003; Minister of Finance several times between 1977–92, also 2003–04; Minister of the Environment 2004; fmr Chair. Nauru Insurance Corpn.

CLONINGER, Kriss, III, BBA, MBA; American insurance industry executive; *President and Chief Financial Officer, Aflac Incorporated;* b. 21 Oct. 1947, Houston; m. Lisa Cloninger (neé Welch); two c. two step-c.; ed Univ. of Tex.; served as First Lt, USAF 1971–73; Consulting Actuary and Pnr, Rudd and Wisdom, Austin, Tex. 1974–77; Prin. KPMG, Atlanta 1977–92; joined Aflac Inc. as Sr Vice-Pres. and Chief Financial Officer 1992, Sr Vice-Pres. 1992–93, Exec. Vice-Pres. 1993–2001, Pres. and Chief Financial Officer 2001–; mem. Bd of Dirs Total System Services Inc., Tupperware Brands Corpn, RiverCenter for the Performing Arts, Historic Columbus Foundation, Little Blessings Nurturing Center, Columbus, Ga; Fellow, Soc. of Actuaries; Institutional Investor Best Insurance CFO 2003–06. *Address:* Aflac Incorporated, 1932 Wynnton Road, Columbus, GA 31999, USA (office). *Telephone:* (706) 323-3431 (office). *Fax:* (706) 324-6330 (office). *Website:* www.aflac.com (office).

CLOONEY, George; American actor and film director; b. 6 May 1961, Lexington, Ky; s. of Nick Clooney; m. Talia Blasam (divorced); ed Northern Ky Univ.; founder Section Eight (production co.) –2006; Co-founder Smoke House (production co.) 2006–; Chevalier des Arts et des Lettres 2007; Spirit of Independence Award 2005, Modern Master Award, Santa Barbara Film Festival 2006, American Cinemathèque Award 2006. *Films:* Grizzly II: The Predator 1987, Return to Horror High 1987, Return of the Killer Tomatoes 1988, Red Surf 1990, Unbecoming Age 1992, The Harvest 1993, From Dusk Till Dawn 1996, Curdled 1996, One Fine Day 1996, Batman & Robin 1997, The Peacemaker 1997, Out of Sight 1998, The Thin Red Line 1998, South Park: Bigger Longer & Uncut (voice) 1999, Three Kings 1999, O Brother, Where Art Thou? 2000, The Perfect Storm 2000, Rock Star (exec. producer) 2001, Spy Kids 2001, Ocean's Eleven 2001, Insomnia (exec. producer) 2002, Far From Heaven (exec. producer) 2002, Welcome to Collinwood (also producer) 2002, Solaris 2002, Confessions of a Dangerous Mind (also dir) 2002, Spy Kids 3-D: Game Over 2003, Intolerable Cruelty 2003, Criminal (producer) 2004, Ocean's Twelve (also exec. producer) 2004, The Big Empty (exec. producer) 2005, The Jacket (producer) 2005, Goodnight And Good Luck (also dir, co-writer, Freedom Award 2006 from Critics' Choice Awards) 2005, Syriana (also producer, Golden Globe Award for Best Supporting Actor 2006, Acad. Award for Best Supporting Actor 2006) 2006, The Good German 2006, Ocean's Thirteen 2007, Michael Clayton (Best Actor, Nat. Bd of Review 2007) 2007, Leatherheads 2008, Burn After Reading 2008. *Television:* E/R (series) 1984–85, The Facts of Life (series) 1985–86, Combat High (film) 1986, Roseanne (series) 1988–89, Knights of the Kitchen Table (film) 1990, Sunset Beat (series) 1990, Rewrite for Murder (film) 1991, Baby Talk (series) 1991, Bodies of Evidence (series) 1992–93, Sisters (series) 1993–94, ER (series) 1994–99, Kilroy (film, writer and producer) 1999, Fail Safe (film, also exec. producer) 2000, K Street (series, exec. producer) 2003, Unscripted (series, dir and exec. producer) 2005. *Address:* Smoke House, c/o Warner Bros., 4000 Warner Blvd., Bldg. 15, Burbank, CA 91522; c/o Bryan Lourd, Creative Artists Agency, 9830 Wilshire Boulevard, Beverly Hills, CA 90212 (office); Stan Rosenfeld & Associates Ltd., 2029 Century Park East, Suite 1190, Los Angeles, CA 90067, USA. *Telephone:* (818) 954-4840 (Smoke House); (310) 286-7474 (Rosenfeld). *Fax:* (818) 954-4860 (Smoke House); (310) 286-2255 (Rosenfeld).

CLOSE, Chuck, BA, MFA; American artist; b. (Charles Thomas Close), 1940, Monroe, Wash.; ed Univ. of Washington, Seattle, Yale Univ., Akad. der Bildenen Kunste, Vienna, Austria; works in perm. collections of Museum of Modern Art, New York, Louisiana Museum of Modern Art, Denmark, Centres George Pompidou, Paris, France, Tate Modern, London, UK; works include Big Self-Portrait 1967–68, Self-Portrait/White Ink 1977, Phil/Fingerprint 1978, John/Color Fingerprint 1983, Georgia/Fingerpainting 1984, Leslie 1986, Self-Portrait (spitbite aquatint) 1988, Lucas (seven-step reduction block/linoleum cut print) 1988, Alex/Reduction Block (silk screen print) 1993, Lucas/Rug 1993, Self-Portrait I 1999, Self-Portrait II 1999, Lyle (etching) 2000, Self-Portrait/Scribble/Etching Portfolio (etching) 2000, Emma (woodblock print) 2002; mem. American Acad. and Inst. of Arts and Letters 1992; Hon. DFA (Colby Coll., Me) 1994, (Univ. of Massachusetts) 1995, (Yale Univ.) 1996; Dr hc (Rhode Island School of Design) 1997; Acad.-Inst. Award in Art, American Acad. and Inst. of Arts and Letters 1991, Univ. of Washington Alumnus Summa Laude Dignatus 1997, Dieu Donné Art Award (jtly) 2000. *Address:* c/o PaceWildenstein, 32 East 57th Street, New York, NY 10022, USA (office). *Telephone:* (212) 421-3292. *Fax:* (212) 421-0835.

CLOSE, Glenn; American actress; b. 19 March 1947, Greenwich, Conn.; d. of William Close and Bettine Close; m. 1st Cabot Wade (divorced); m. 2nd James Marlas 1984 (divorced); one d. by John Starke; m. 3rd David Shaw 2006; ed William and Mary Coll.; joined New Phoenix Repertory Co. 1974; Co-owner The Leaf and Bean Coffee House, Bozeman, Mont. 1991–. *Stage appearances include:* Love for Love, The Rules of the Game, The Singular Life of Albert Nobbs, Childhood, Real Thing (Tony Award), King Lear, The Rose Tattoo, Benefactors, Death and the Maiden, Sunset Boulevard, A Streetcar Named Desire (Royal Nat. Theatre) 2002. *Films include:* The World According to Garp 1982, The Big Chill 1983, The Natural 1984, The Stone Boy 1984, Maxie 1985, Jagged Edge 1985, Fatal Attraction 1987, Dangerous Liaisons 1989, Hamlet 1989, Reversal of Fortune 1989, The House of Spirits 1990, Meeting Venus 1990, Immediate Family 1991, The Paper 1994, Mary Reilly 1994, Serving in Silence: The Margaret Cammermeyer Story 1995, 101 Dalmatians 1996, Mars Attacks! 1996, Air Force One 1997, Paradise Road 1997, Tarzan 1999, Cookie's Fortune 1999, 102 Dalmatians 2000, The Safety of Objects 2001, Pinocchio (voice) 2002, Le Divorce 2003, The Stepford Wives 2004, Heights 2004, Nine Lives 2005, The Chumscrubber 2005, Tarzan II (voice) 2005, Hoodwinked (voice) 2006, Evening 2007. *Television includes:* The Lion in Winter (Best Actress in a Miniseries or TV Movie, Golden Globe Awards 2005, Screen Actors Guild Awards 2005) 2004, The Shield (series) 2005, Damages (series) (Golden Globe for Best Actress in a TV series 2008) 2007–. *Address:* c/o Creative Artists Agency, 9830 Wilshire Boulevard, Beverly Hills, CA 90212, USA.

CLOSETS, François de; French writer, journalist and producer; b. 25 Dec. 1933, Enghien-les-Bains; s. of Louis-Xavier de Closets and Marie-Antoinette Masson; m. 1st Danièle Lebrun; one s.; m. 2nd Janick Jossin 1970; one s. one d.; ed Lycée d'Enghien, Faculté de Droit de Paris and Inst. d'Etudes Politiques, Paris; Ed. then special envoy of Agence France-Presse in Algeria 1961–65; scientific journalist, Sciences et Avenir 1964–, Acualités Télévisées 1965–68; contrib. L'Express 1968–69; Head of Scientific Service, TV Channel 1 1969–72; Head of Scientific and Tech. Service of TV Channel 2 1972; contrib. to Channel 1 1974; Asst Ed.-in-Chief TF1; Co-producer l'Enjeu (econ. magazine) 1978–88; Dir of Econ. Affairs, TFI 1987; Co-producer, Médiations magazine 1987–93; Producer, illustrator "Savoir Plus" for France 2 1992–2000, "Les Grandes Enigmes de la Science" for France 2 1992–2003; Grand Prix du reportage du Syndicat des journalistes et écrivains 1966, Prix Cazes 1974, 7 d'or du meilleur journaliste 1985, Prix Aujourd'hui 1985, Roland Dorgelès Prize 1997. *Publications:* L'Espace, terre des hommes, La lune est à vendre 1969, En danger de progrès 1970, Le Bonheur en plus 1974, La France et ses mensonges 1977, Scénarios du futur (Vol. I) 1978, Le monde de l'an 2000 (Vol. II) 1979, Le Système EPM 1980, Toujours plus 1982, Tous ensemble pour en finir avec la syndicatrie 1985, La Grande Manip 1990, Tant et Plus 1992, Le Bonheur d'apprendre, et comment on l'assassine 1996, Le compte à Rebours 1998, L'Imposture informatique 2000, La dernière liberté 2001, Ne dites pas à Dieu ce qu'il doit faire 2004, Plus encore 2006, Le divorce français 2008. *Address:* France 2, 7 esplanade Henri de France, 75907 Paris Cedex 15 (office); VM Group, 99 rue Leblanc, Paris 75015 (office); 1 Villa George Sand, Paris 75016, France (home). *Telephone:* 1-53-90-16-71, ext. 75 (office). *Fax:* 1-45-45-45-33 (office). *E-mail:* f.declosets@france2.fr (office).

CLOTET, Lluis; Spanish architect and designer; *Principal, Clotet, Paricio i Associats sl;* b. 31 July 1941, Barcelona; s. of Jaime Clotet and Concepción Clotet; ed Barcelona Escuela Técnica Superior de Arquitectura; worked for Federico Correa and Alfonso Milás's Studio 1961–64; co-f. (with Pep Bonet, Cristian Cirici and Oscar Tusquets) Studio PER 1964; co-f. B.D. Ediciones de Diseño; collaborator, XV Triennale de Milano 1973, Festival of Fine Architecture, Paris 1978, Transformations in Modern Architecture, Museum of Modern Art, New York 1979, Forum Design, Linz 1980, Biennale de Venezia 1980, The House as Image, Louisiana Museum of Modern Art 1981, The Presence of the Past, San Francisco 1982, Ten New Buildings, Inst. of Contemporary Art, London 1983, Contemporary Spanish Architecture, New York 1986; associated with with Ignacio Paricio 1983–; Prof. in Drawing, Barcelona Higher Tech. School in Architecture 1977–84; numerous prizes. *Major works include:* Banco España 1981–89, Water Cistern Ciutadella Park, Barcelona 1985–88, SIMON SA Bldg, Canovelles 1987–88, Museum of Art, Convent dels Angels, Barcelona (Restoration and extension plan) 1984–89, Teleport, Castellbisbal, Barcelona (plan) 1988, Sport Pavilion in Granada, 100 dwellings at the Olympic Village. *Address:* Clotet, Paricio i Associats sl, Pujades 63, 3.pl, 08005 Barcelona, Spain (office). *Telephone:* (93) 4853625 (office). *Fax:* (93) 3090567 (office). *E-mail:* cpa@coac.es (office).

CLOUDSLEY-THOMPSON, John Leonard, MA, PhD, DSc, CBiol, FIBiol, FRES, FZS, FWAAS, FLS; British zoologist, academic and writer; *Professor Emeritus of Zoology, Birkbeck College, University of London;* b. (John Leonard

Thompson), 23 May 1921, Murree, India; s. of Dr A. G. G. Thompson and Muriel Elaine (née Griffiths) Thompson; m. J. Anne Cloudsley 1944; three s.; ed Marlborough Coll., Pembroke Coll., Cambridge; war service 1940–44, commissioned, 4th Queen's Own Hussars 1941, transferred to 4th Co. of London Yeomanry (Sharpshooters), Hon. Capt. 1944; Lecturer in Zoology, King's Coll., London 1950–60; Prof. of Zoology, Univ. of Khartoum and Keeper, Sudan Natural History Museum 1960–71; Prof. of Zoology, Birkbeck Coll., London 1972–86, Prof. Emer. 1986–; Nat. Science Senior Research Fellow, Univ. of New Mexico, Albuquerque 1969; Leverhulme Emer. Fellowship, Univ. Coll. London 1987–89; Visiting Prof., Univ. of Kuwait 1978, 1983, Univ. of Nigeria, Nsukka 1981, Univ. of Qatar 1986; Visiting Research Fellow, ANU 1987, Desert Ecological Research Unit of Namibia 1989; Chair. British Naturalists' Asscn 1974–83, Vice-Pres. 1985–; Chair. Biological Council 1977–82 (Medal 1985); Pres. British Arachnological Soc. 1982–85, British Soc. for Chronobiology 1985–87; Vice-Pres. Linnean Soc. 1975–76, 1977–78; Ed.-in-Chief Journal of Arid Environments Vols 1–37 1978–97; Liveryman, Worshipful Co. of Skinners 1952; Hon. FLS 1997; Hon. mem. Royal African Soc. 1969 (Medal 1969), British Herpetological Soc. 1983 (Pres. 1991–96), Centre Int. de Documentation Arachnologique, Paris 1995, Hon. Fellow, British Naturalists' Asscn 2007; Hon. DSc (Khartoum Univ.); Silver Jubilee Gold Medal 1981, Inst. of Biology KSS Charter Award 1981, J. H. Grundy Memorial Medal, Royal Army Medical Coll. 1987, Peter Scott Memorial Award, BNA 1993. *Publications:* Spiders, Scorpions, Centipedes and Mites 1958, Animal Behaviour 1960, Rhythmic Activity in Animal Physiology and Behaviour 1961, Animal Conflict and Adaptation 1965, Animal Twilight 1967, Zoology of Tropical Africa 1969, The Temperature and Water Relations of Reptiles 1971, Desert Life 1974, Terrestrial Environments 1975, Insects and History 1976, Man and the Biology of Arid Zones 1977, The Desert 1977, Animal Migration 1978, Biological Clocks 1980, Tooth and Claw 1980, Evolution and Adaptation of Terrestrial Arthropods 1988, Adaptations of Desert Organisms (book series ed., 25 vols) 1989–2000, Ecophysiology of Desert Arthropods and Reptiles 1991, The Nile Quest (novel) 1994, Predation and Defence Amongst Reptiles 1994, Biotic Interactions in Arid Lands 1996, Teach Yourself Ecology 1998, The Diversity of Amphibians and Reptiles 1999, Ecology and Behaviour of Mesozoic Reptiles 2005, Sharpshooter: Memories of Armoured Warfare 1939–45 2006. *Leisure interests:* music, photography, travel. *Address:* 10 Battishill Street, London, N1 1TE, England (home). *Telephone:* (20) 7359-7197 (home).

CLOUGH, Ray William, Jr, ScD; American structural engineer and academic; *Byron and Elvira Nishkian Professor of Structural Engineering Emeritus, University of California, Berkeley;* b. 23 July 1920, Seattle; s. of Ray W Clough, Sr and Mildred Eva Nelson; m. Shirley Claire Potter 1942; one s. two d.; ed Univ. of Washington, Seattle, California Inst. of Tech., Pasadena, Calif. and Massachusetts Inst. of Tech., Cambridge, Mass.; served in USAF 1942–46; joined Civil Eng Faculty, Univ. of California, Berkeley as Asst Prof. of Civil Eng 1949, Assoc. Prof. 1954–59, Prof. 1959–83, Chair. Div. of Structural Eng and Structural Mechanics 1967–70, Byron and Elvira Nishkian Prof. of Structural Eng 1983–87, Prof. Emer. 1987–; consultant in structural eng specializing in structural dynamics, computer methods of structural analysis and earthquake eng 1953–; mem. US Army Corps of Engineers Structural Design Advisory Bd 1967–; mem. NAS, Nat. Acad. of Eng; Hon. mem. American Soc. of Civil Eng 1988; Research Prize, Howard Medal, Newmark Medal, Moisieff Medal, Th. von Karman Medal (American Soc. of Civil Engineers), George W. Housner Medal 1996, Prince Philip Medal, Royal Acad. of Eng 1997, Benjamin Franklin Medal in Civil Eng 2006. *Publication:* Dynamics of Structures (with J. Penzien) 1975, 1993. *Leisure interests:* skiing (cross-country) and hiking. *Address:* PO Box 4625, Sunriver, OR 97707-1625, USA (home). *Telephone:* (541) 593-5064 (home). *Fax:* (541) 593-2823 (home). *Website:* semm.berkeley.edu/index.htm (office).

CLOUTIER, Gilles G., CC, PhD, FRSC; Canadian engineer, physicist and university administrator; b. 27 June 1928, Québec City; s. of the late Philéas Cloutier and Valéda Nadeau; m. Colette Michaud 1954; two s. three d.; ed Univ. Laval, Québec and McGill Univ.; Prof. of Physics, Univ. of Montréal 1963–68; Man. of Basic Research Lab., Dir of Research and Asst Dir of Inst., Research Inst. of Hydro-Québec 1968–78; Pres. Alberta Research Council 1978–83; Exec. Vice-Pres. Tech. and Int. Affairs, Hydro-Québec 1983–85; Rector Univ. of Montréal 1985–93; Pres. Conf. of Rectors and Prins of Québec Univs 1987–89; Chair. of Corp. Higher Educ. Forum 1992–93; Deputy Chair. Advisory Council on Science and Tech. 1998–; currently consultant in high tech. commercialization; mem. Bd Centre d'initiative technologique de Montréal 1985–93, Chamber of Commerce of Greater Montréal 1989–93; Fellow, Royal Soc. of Canada; mem. Bd of Trustees of Manning Awards; Officier Order of Québec, Chevalier Légion d'honneur 1991; Dr hc (Montreal, Alberta, McGill, Lyon II, Toronto). *Address:* 4500 Promenade Paton, Apt 1208, Laval, PQ H7W 4Y6 (home); 2910 boulevard Edouard-Montpetit, Bureau 6, Montréal, PQ H3C 3J7, Canada (office). *Telephone:* (450) 687-3520 (home); (514) 343-5775 (office). *Fax:* (450) 687-7477 (office).

CLUFF, John Gordon (Algy); British business executive; *Chairman and CEO, Cluff Gold plc;* b. 19 April 1940, Bucklow, Cheshire; s. of the late Harold Cluff and of Freda Cluff; m. Blondel Hodge 1993; three s.; ed Stowe School; army officer, served W Africa, Cyprus, Malaysia 1959–64; Chief Exec. Cluff Resources (fmrly Cluff Oil) 1971, Chair. (and Chair. Zimbabwe) 1979, Chair. and CEO Cluff Mining 1996–2003 (acquired by Ashanti Goldfields), Chair. and CEO Cluff Gold plc 2003–; Proprietor, The Spectator 1981–85, Chair. 1985–2004; Chair. Apollo Magazine Ltd 1985; Trustee Anglo-Hong Kong Trust 1989–, Stowe House Preservation Trust 1999–; Dir Centre for Policy Studies 1998–; Gov. Commonwealth Inst. 1995–, Chair. Conservative Comm. on the Commonwealth 2001; mem. Bd of Govs Stowe School 1998–; Chair. Trustees, War Memorial Trust 2003–. *Leisure interests:* collecting books and paintings, golf, shooting. *Address:* Cluff Gold plc, 24 Queen Anne's Gate, London, SW1H 9AA, England (office). *Telephone:* (20) 7340-9790 (office). *Fax:* (20) 7233-4780 (office). *E-mail:* admin@cluffgold.com (office). *Website:* www.cluffgold.com (office).

CLUZEL, Jean, LenD; French politician and business executive; *President, Canal Académie;* b. 18 Nov. 1923, Moulins; s. of Pierre Cluzel and Jeanne Cluzel (née Dumont); m. Madeleine Bonnaud 1947; three s. one d.; ed Lycée de Vichy and Univ. of Paris; Pres. and Dir-Gen. Cluzel-Dumont 1947–71; Municipal Councillor St Pourcain/Sioule 1959–65; Admin., later Senator, Allier 1971, 1980, 1989; Conseiller Général, Moulins-Ouest 1967, 1973, 1979, 1985; Pres. Conseil Général, Allier 1970–76, 1985–92; Senator, Allier 1971, 1980, 1989; mem. l'Union Centriste, Spokesman and Vice-Pres. Comm. des Finances du Senat; Pres. Cttee for Econ. Expansion of Allier 1959–67; Pres. 'Positions' and 'L'Allier Demain', Fed. des Elus Bourbonnais 1972, Univ. Populaire de Bransat 1981, Comité Français pour l'Audiovisuel 1993; Dir Cahiers de l'audiovisuel 1994; Admin. France 2 1998, Singer Polignac Foundation 1999; Perm. Sec. Académie des Sciences Morales et Politiques 1999–2004, now mem. Morale et sociologie, Section II; Founder and Pres. Canal Académie, Institut de France (internet radio service) 2004–; Council mem. Admin. du conseil mondial pour la Radio et la Télévision; mem. Supervisory Cttee European Business School; Officier Légion d'honneur. *Publications:* Horizons Bourbonnais 1973, Les boutiques en colère 1975, Elu de peuple 1977, Télé Violence 1978, L'argent de la télévision 1979, Finances publiques et pouvoir local 1980, Les pouvoirs publics et la transmission de la culture 1983, Les pouvoirs publics et les caisses d'épargne 1984, Les anti-monarque de la Vème 1985, Un projet pour la presse 1986, La loi de 1987 sur l'épargne 1987, La télévision après six réformes 1988, Les finances locales decentralisées 1989, Le Sénat dans la société française 1990, Une ambition pour l'Allier 1992, Une autre bataille de France 1993, Mots pour Mots 1993, Pour qui sont ces tuyaux qui sifflent sur nos têtes? 1993, Feu d'artifices pour fin de législature 1993, L'age de la télévision 1993, Lettre à mes collègues représentants du peuple 1993, Education, culture et télévision 1994, Du modèle canadien à l'appel sud-africain 1996, L'audiovisuel en Europe centrale et orientale 1996, La télévision 1996, Presse et démocratie 1997, L'indispensable Sénat 1998, A propos du Sénat et de ceux qui voudraient en finir avec lui 1999, Anne de France 2002, Propos impertinents sur le cinéma français 2003. *Address:* Canal Académie, 23, quai Conti, 75006 Paris; 12 villa Dupont, 75116 Paris (home); c/o L'Académie des Sciences Morales et Politiques, 23, quai Conti, 75006 Paris, France. *Website:* www.canalacademie.com.

CLUZET, François; French actor; b. 21 Sept. 1955, Paris; four c. and one s. with actress Marie Trintignant; ed acting lessons at Cours Simon and Cours de Périmony et Cochet; Prix Jean Gabin 1984. *Films:* Un enfant sans histoire 1979, Cocktail Molotov 1980, Le cheval d'orgueil (The Horse of Pride) 1980, Une histoire de trains 1982, Les fantômes du chapelier (The Hatter's Ghost) 1982, Coup de foudre (Between Us) 1983, L'Été meurtrier (One Deadly Summer) 1983, Vive la sociale! 1983, Les enragés 1985, Elsa, Elsa 1985, États d'âme 1986, 'Round Midnight (Autour de minuit) 1986, Rue du Départ 1986, Association de malfaiteurs 1987, Jaune revolver 1988, Chocolat 1988, Une affaire de femmes (Story of Women) 1988, Deux (Two) 1989, Un tour de manège (Roundabout) 1989, Force majeure (Uncontrollable Circumstances) 1989, Trop belle pour toi (Too Beautiful for You) 1989, La Révolution française (The French Revolution) 1989, Olivier, Olivier 1992, Sexes faibles! (The Weaker Sexes!) 1992, À demain (See You Tomorrow) 1992, L'Instinct de l'ange 1993, L'Enfer (Hell) 1994, Le vent du Wyoming (Wind from Wyoming) 1994, Prêt-à-Porter (Ready to Wear) 1994, French Kiss (Paris Match) 1995, Le hussard sur le toit (The Horseman on the Roof) 1995, Les apprentis 1995, Dialogue au sommet 1996, Enfants de salaud (Bastard Brood) 1996, Le déménagement 1997, Le silence de Rak (Best Actor Award, Paris Film Festival 1996) 1997, Rien ne va plus (The Swindle) 1997, La Voie est libre 1998, Fin août, début septembre (Late August, Early September) 1998, Dolce far niente (Sweet Idleness) 1998, L'Examen de minuit (Midnight Exam) 1998, L'Adversaire (The Adversary) 2002, Quand je vois le soleil 2003, Mais qui a tué Pamela Rose? 2003, Janis et John (Janis and John) 2003, France Boutique 2003, Je suis un assassin (The Hook) 2004, Le domaine perdu (The Lost Domain) 2005, La cloche a sonné 2005, Ne le dis à personne (Tell No One) (César Award for Best Actor 2007, Étoile d'Or for Best Actor 2007) 2006, Ma place au soleil (My Place in the Sun) 2007, La vérité ou presque 2007, Détrompez-vous 2007, Les liens du sang (Rivals) 2008, Paris 2008. *Television:* Au théâtre ce soir (episode Madame Jonas dans la baleine)1977, Histoires de voyous: L'élégant 1979, journal (mini-series) 1979, Chère Olga 1980, Le gros oiseau 1981, Le boulanger de Suresnes 1981, Paris-Saint-Lazare (mini-series) 1982, Julien Fontanes, magistrat (episode Perpète) 1983, Un manteau de chinchilla 1983, Pablo est mort 1983, Le bout du lac 1984, Série noire (episode Aveugle, que veux-tu?) 1984, La mèche en bataille 1984, Manipulations 1984, Sueurs froides (episode À la mémoire d'un ange) 1988, Lucas 1993, 3000 scénarios contre un virus (3,000 Scenarios to Combat a Virus; segment L'Appel d'un ami) 1994, Sweet home 1995, L'huile sur le feu 1996, Le goût des fraises 1998, La cape et l'épée (episode La mise à mort) 1999, Les enfants du printemps (mini-series) 2000, L'Algérie des chimères (mini-series) 2001, Un mois à nous 2002, La famille Guérin (series) 2002, Vénus & Apollon (Venus and Apollo (episode Soin ultime) 2005, Quatre étoiles (Four Stars) 2006. *Address:* c/o Isabelle de la Patellière, VMA, 20 avenue Rapp, 75007 Paris, France. *Telephone:* 1-43-17-37-00. *Fax:* 1-47-20-15-86. *E-mail:* d.leprestre@vma.fr. *Website:* www.vma.fr.

CLWYD, Rt Hon. Ann, PC; British politician, journalist and broadcaster; *Prime Minister's Special Envoy on Human Rights in Iraq;* b. 21 March 1937; d. of Gwilym Henri Lewis and Elizabeth Ann Lewis; m. Owen Dryhurst Roberts 1963; ed Holywell Grammar School, The Queen's School, Chester and Univ. Coll., Bangor; fmr BBC studio man., freelance reporter and producer; Welsh corresp. The Guardian and The Observer 1964–79; Vice-Chair. Welsh Arts Council 1975–79; mem. Royal Comm. on NHS 1976–79, Arts Council of GB 1975–80; various public and political appointments; MEP for Mid- and West Wales 1979–84; MP (Labour) for Cynon Valley 1984–; Opposition Front Bench Spokesperson on Women 1987–88, on Educ. 1987–88; Shadow Sec. of State on Overseas Devt and Co-operation 1989–92, on Wales 1992, for Nat. Heritage 1992–93; Opposition Front Bench Spokesperson on Employment 1993–94, on Foreign Affairs 1994–95; mem. Select Cttee on Int. Devt 1997–; Chair. All-Party Group on Human Rights 1997–; Chair. INDICT 1997–; Prime Minister's Special Envoy on Human Rights in Iraq 2003–; Hon. Fellow, North East Wales Inst. of Educ. 1996, Univ. of Wales, Bangor 2004; White Robed Bard of the Nat. Eisteddfod 1991; Hon. LLD (Univ. of Wales) 2007. *Address:* House of Commons, Westminster, London, SW1A 0AA, England; 6 Deans Court, Dean Street, Aberdare, Mid Glamorgan, CF44 7BN, Wales (office). *Telephone:* (1685) 871394 (office); (20) 7219-3000. *Fax:* (20) 7219-5943. *E-mail:* clwyda@parliament.uk (office).

CLYNE, Cameron; Australian banking executive; *Group CEO, National Australia Bank;* Man. Pnr, PricewaterhouseCoopers financial services consulting practice across Asia-Pacific –2005, also worked in their financial services practices in New York; Exec. Gen., Group Devt, National Australia Bank Group 2005–07, Man. Dir and CEO Bank of New Zealand 2007–09, Group CEO National Australia Bank 2009–. *Address:* National Australia Bank Ltd, 500 Bourke Street, Melbourne, Victoria 3000, Australia (office). *Telephone:* (3) 8641-3500 (office). *Fax:* (3) 9208-5695 (office). *E-mail:* info@nabgroup.com (office). *Website:* www.nabgroup.com (office).

CLYNE, Michael George, AM, MA, PhD; Australian professor of linguistics; *Emeritus Professor, Monash University; Honorary Professorial Fellow, University of Melbourne;* b. 12 Oct. 1939, Melbourne; s. of Dr John Clyne and Edith Clyne; m. Irene Donohoue 1977; one d.; ed Caulfield Grammar School, Univs of Melbourne, Bonn and Utrecht and Monash Univ.; Tutor then Sr Tutor, Monash Univ. 1962–64, Lecturer then Sr Lecturer 1965–71, Assoc. Prof. of German 1972–88, Prof. of Linguistics 1988–2000, Prof. Emer. 2005–, Research Dir, Language and Soc. Centre 1990–2000; Professorial Fellow in Linguistics, Univ. of Melbourne 2001–04, Hon. Professorial Fellow 2005–, Dir, Research Unit for Multilingualism and Cross-Cultural Communication 2001–04; Adjunct Prof., Univ. of Queensland 2005–; Pres. Australian Linguistic Soc. 1986–88, Vice-Pres. 1989–90; Fellow, Acad. of Social Sciences in Australia 1982, Australian Acad. of Social Sciences 1983; Foreign mem., Royal Netherlands Acad. of Sciences 2005; Patron, Victorian School of Languages 2005–; mem. Ministerial Advisory Council on Languages, ESL and Multicultural Educ. (Vic.) 2008–; Hon. life mem. Applied Linguistics Asscn of Australia 1989–, Australian Linguistic Soc. 2005–, Modern Language Teachers Asscn of Vic. 2007–; Austrian Cross of Honour for Science and the Arts (1st class) 1996, German Cross of Merit (1st class) 2003; Hon. DPhil (Munich); Jakob- and Wilhelm-Grimm Prize 1999, Humboldt Research Prize 2003. *Publications include:* Transference and Triggering 1967, Perspectives on Language Contact 1972, Deutsch als Muttersprache in Australien 1981, Multilingual Australia 1982, Language and Society in the German-Speaking Countries 1984, Australia: Meeting Place of Languages 1985, An Early Start: Second Language at the Primary School 1986, Community Languages, the Australian Experience 1991, Pluricentric Languages 1992, Inter-cultural Communication at Work 1994, Developing Second Language From Primary School 1995, The German Language in a Changing Europe 1995, Background Speakers 1997, Undoing and Redoing Corpus Planning 1997, Pluricentric Languages in an Immigrant Context 1999, Dynamics of Language Contact 2003, Australia's Language Potential 2005, Tiles in a Multilingual Mosiac 2006, Language and Human Relations 2008. *Leisure interests:* music, reading. *Address:* School of Languages and Linguistics, University of Melbourne, Melbourne, Vic. 3010 (office); School of Languages Cultures and Linguistics, Monash University, Vic. 3800 (office); 1/58 St Albans Street, Mount Waverley, Vic. 3149, Australia (home). *Telephone:* (3) 8344-8991 (office); (3) 9902-0781 (office); (3) 9807-7180 (home). *E-mail:* mgclyne@gmail.com (office).

COAKLEY, Rev. Sarah Anne, MA, ThM, PhD; British academic; *Norris-Hulse Professor of Divinity, University of Cambridge;* b. 10 Sept. 1951, London; d. of F. Robert Furber and Anne McArthur; m. James F. Coakley 1975; two d.; ed Blackheath High School for Girls, New Hall, Cambridge and Harvard Divinity School, USA; Lecturer in Religious Studies, Univ. of Lancaster 1976–90, Sr Lecturer 1990–91; Tutorial Fellow in Theology and Univ. Lecturer, Oriel Coll., Oxford 1991–93; Prof. of Christian Theology, The Divinity School, Harvard Univ., USA 1993–95, Edward Mallinckrodt, Jr, Prof. of Divinity 1995–2007; Norris-Hulse Professor of Divinity, Univ. of Cambridge 2007–; Harkness Fellowship 1973–75; Select Preacher, Univ. of Oxford 1991; Visiting Professorial Fellow, Princeton Univ., USA 2003–04; Hon. DTheol (Lund); Hulsean Prize, Univ. of Cambridge 1977, Hulsean Lecturer, Univ. of Cambridge 1991–92, Hulsean Preacher 1996, Samuel Ferguson Lecturer, Univ. of Manchester 1997, Riddell Lecturer, Univ. of Newcastle 1999, Tate-Wilson Lecturer, Southern Methodist Univ. 1999, Prideaux Lecturer, Univ. of Exeter 2000, Jellema Lecturer, Calvin Coll. 2001, Stone Lecturer, Princeton Theological Seminary 2002, Cheney Lecturer, Berkeley Divinity School at Yale 2002, Reynolds Lecturer, Princeton Univ. 2005, Hensley Henson Lecturer, Univ. of Oxford 2005. *Publications:* Christ Without Absolutes: A Study of the Christology of Ernst Troeltsch 1988, The Making and Remaking of Christian Doctrine (co-ed. with David Pailin) 1993, Religion and the Body (ed.) 1997, Powers and Submissions: Spirituality, Philosophy and Gender 2002, Rethinking Gregory of Nyssa (ed) 2003, Pain and its Transformations: The Interface of Biology and Culture (co-ed.) 2007; contribs to Church of England Doctrine Comm. Reports 1987, 1991; articles in theological journals. *Leisure interests:* musical activities, thinking about the garden. *Address:* Faculty of Divinity, West Road, Cambridge, CB3 9BS, England (office); c/o The Divinity School, Harvard University, 45 Francis Avenue, Cambridge, MA 02138, USA (office). *Telephone:* (1223) 763002 (UK) (office); (617) 496-2446 (office). *Fax:* (1223) 763003 (UK) (office); (617) 496-0585 (office). *E-mail:* faculty-office@divinity.cam.ac.uk (office). *Website:* www.divinity.cam.ac.uk (office); www.hds.harvard.edu (office).

COASE, Ronald Harry, BCom, DScEcon; British economist and academic; *Clifton R. Musser Professor Emeritus of Economics, The Law School, University of Chicago;* b. 29 Dec. 1910, London; s. of Henry Coase and Rosalie Coase; m. Marian Hartung 1937; ed London School of Econs; Asst Lecturer, Dundee School of Econs 1932–34; Asst Lecturer, Univ. of Liverpool 1934–35; Asst Lecturer to Reader, LSE, 1935–40, 1946–51; Head, Statistical Division, Forestry Comm. 1940–41; Statistician, later Chief Statistician, Cen. Statistical Office, Offices of War Cabinet, 1941–46; Prof., Univ. of Buffalo 1951–58; Prof., Univ. of Virginia 1958–64; Ed. Journal of Law and Economics 1964–92; Clifford R. Musser Prof. of Econs, Univ. of Chicago 1964–82, Prof. Emer. and Sr Fellow in Law and Econs 1982–; Fellow, American Acad. of Arts and Sciences; Distinguished Fellow, American Econ Asscn; Rockefeller Fellow 1948; Sr Research Fellow, Hoover Inst., Stanford Univ. 1977; Corresponding Fellow, British Acad., European Acad.; Hon. Fellow, LSE, Royal Econ. Soc.; numerous hon. degrees; Nobel Prize for Economic Science 1991. *Publications:* British Broadcasting: a study in Monopoly 1950, The Firm, the Market and the Law 1988, Essays on Economics and Economists 1994. *Address:* University of Chicago Law School, 1111 East 60th Street, Chicago, IL 60637 (office); The Hallmark, Apt 1100, 2960 North Lake Shore Drive, Chicago, IL 60657, USA (home). *Telephone:* (773) 702-7342 (office). *Website:* www.law.uchicago.edu (office).

COATES, Anne Voase, OBE; British film editor and producer; b. 12 Dec. 1925, Reigate, Surrey; m. Douglas Hickox (deceased); two s. one d.; ed Bartrum Gables Coll.; worked as nurse, East Grinstead Plastic Surgery Hosp.; Woman in Film Crystal Awards Int. Award 1997, Lifetime Achievement Award, American Cinema Eds 1998, Woman in Film and TV Awards Channel Four Lifetime Achievement Award 2000, BAFTA Fellowship 2007. *Films edited include:* Pickwick Papers 1952, Grand National Night 1953, Forbidden Cargo 1954, To Paris With Love 1955, The Truth About Women 1957, The Horse's Mouth 1958, Tunes of Glory 1960, Don't Bother to Knock 1961, Lawrence of Arabia (Academy Award 1962) 1962, Becket 1964, Young Cassidy 1965, Those Magnificent Men in their Flying Machines (co-ed.) 1965, Hotel Paradiso 1966, Great Catherine 1968, The Adventurers 1970, Friends 1971, The Public Eye 1972, The Nelson Affair 1973, 11 Harrowhouse 1974, Murder on the Orient Express 1974, Man Friday 1975, Aces High 1976, The Eagle Has Landed 1976, The Legacy 1978, The Elephant Man 1980, The Pirates of Penzance 1983, Greystoke: The Legend of Tarzan, Lord of the Apes 1984, Lady Jane 1986, Raw Deal 1986, Masters of the Universe 1987, Farewell to the King (co-ed.) 1989, Listen to Me 1989, I Love You to Death 1990, What About Bob? 1991, Chaplin 1992, In the Line of Fire (Guild of British Film Eds Award) 1993, Pontiac Moon 1994, Congo 1995, Striptease 1996, Out to Sea 1997, Out of Sight 1998, Passion of Mind 2000, Erin Brockovich 2000, Sweet November 2001, Unfaithful 2002, Taking Lives 2004, Catch and Release 2006, The Golden Compass 2007; producer The Medusa Touch 1978; The Aviator (cameo role) 2005. *Leisure interests:* cinema, theatre, travelling, horseback riding, swimming, skiing. *Address:* 8455 Fountain Avenue, Apartment 621, Los Angeles, CA 90069 (office); c/o United Talent Agency, 9560 Wilshire Blvd, Beverly Hills, CA 90210, USA (office). *Telephone:* (323) 654-7282 (home). *Fax:* (323) 654-4574 (home).

COATES, John Henry, BA, PhD, FRS; Australian mathematician and academic; *Sadleirian Professor of Pure Mathematics, University of Cambridge;* b. 26 Jan. 1945, New South Wales; s. of J. H. Coates and B. L. Lee; m. Julie Turner 1966; three s.; ed Australian Nat. Univ., Ecole Normale Supérieure, Paris, France, Univ. of Cambridge UK; Asst Prof., Harvard Univ., USA 1969–72; Assoc. Prof. (with tenure), Stanford Univ., USA 1972–75; Lecturer, Univ. of Cambridge, UK 1975–77, Sadleirian Prof. of Pure Math. 1986–, Head of Dept of Pure Math. and Math. Statistics 1991–97; Prof., ANU 1977–78; Prof., Université de Paris XI (Orsay) 1978–85; Prof. and Dir of Math., Ecole Normale Supérieure, Paris 1985–86; Professorial Fellow, Emmanuel Coll., Cambridge 1975–77, 1986–; Vice-Pres. Int. Mathematical Union 1991–95; Fellow, Academia Europa; Dr hc (Ecole Normale Supérieure) 1997. *Leisure interest:* reading, early Japanese porcelain. *Address:* Emmanuel College, Department of Pure Mathematics and Mathematical Statistics, Room C1.08, Cambridge, CB1 2EA (office); 104 Mawson Road, Cambridge, CB1 2EA, England (office). *Telephone:* (1223) 337989 (office). *E-mail:* J.H.Coates@dpmms.cam.ac.uk (office). *Website:* www.dpmms.cam.ac.uk (office).

COATS, Daniel Ray, BA, JD; American lawyer, politician and diplomatist; *Senior Policy Advisor, Government Advocacy and Public Policy Practice Group, King & Spalding LLP;* b. 16 May 1943, Jackson, Mich.; s. of Edward R. Coats and Vera E. Coats; m. Marcia Crawford 1965; one s. two d.; ed Wheaton Coll., Ill., Univ. of Indiana; served in US Army 1966–68; called to Bar of Ind. 1972; mem. US House of Reps from 4th Dist of Ind. 1981–89; Dist Rep. for Congressman Dan Quayle (q.v.) 1976–80; Senator from Indiana 1989–99; Amb. to Germany 2001–05; Sr Policy Advisor, Govt Advocacy and Public Policy Practice Group, King & Spalding LLP, Washington, DC 2005–; fmr lobbyist, Pharmaceutical Research and Mfrs of America; mem. Bd of Trustees American Inst. For Contemporary German Studies 2005–; mem. Bd of Dirs IPALCO, Lear Siegler Services Inc., Int. Republic Inst., The Empowerment Network. *Publication:* Mending Fences: Renewing Justice Between Government and Civil Society 1998. *Address:* King & Spalding LLP, 1700 Pennsylvania Avenue, NW, Suite 200, Washington, DC 20006-4706, USA (office). *Telephone:* (202) 626-3733 (office). *Fax:* (202) 626-3737 (office). *E-mail:* dcoats@kslaw.com (office). *Website:* www.kslaw.com (office).

COBBOLD, Rear Adm. Richard, CB, FRAeS; British research institute director and military analyst; *Director, Royal United Services Institute;* served in RN 1961–94, first as seaman officer and helicopter observer, commanded frigates HMS Mohawk and HMS Brazen, then Capt. of 2nd Frigate Squadron in HMS Brilliant; promoted Rear Adm. 1991; Asst Chief Defence Staff Operational Requirements for Sea Systems –1994, ACDS (Jt Systems) 1992–94; mem. Royal Coll. of Defence Studies 1984; Dir of Defence Concepts, Ministry of Defence 1987; Dir Royal United Services Inst. for Defence Studies 1994–; specialist adviser to House of Commons Defence Cttee 1997–; Gov., London Nautical School. *Publications:* numerous articles on defence and security issues. *Address:* Royal United Services Institute for Defence Studies, Whitehall, London, SW1 2ET, England (office). *Telephone:* (20) 7747-2602 (office). *Fax:* (20) 7321-0943 (office). *E-mail:* director@rusi.org (office). *Website:* www.rusi.org (office).

COBEN, Harlan, BA; American writer; b. 4 Jan. 1962, Newark, NJ; m. Anne Armstrong 1988; two s. two d.; ed Amherst Coll.; mem. MWA, Sisters in Crime. *Publications:* novels: Play Dead 1990, Miracle Cure 1991, Deal Breaker (World Mystery Conference Anthony Award for Best Paperback Original Novel 1996) 1995, Drop Shot 1996, Fade Away (MWA Edgar Award for Best Paperback Original Mystery Novel, Shamus Award for Best Paperback Original Novel, Private Eye Writers of America 1997) 1996, Back Spin 1997, One False Move (WH Smith Fresh Talent Award) 1997, The Final Detail 1999, Darkest Fear 2000, Tell No One 2001, Gone For Good (WH Smith Thumping Good Read Award) 2002, No Second Chance 2003, Just One Look 2004, The Innocent 2005, Promise Me 2006, The Woods 2007, Hold Tight 2008, Long Lost 2009; short stories: A Simple Philosophy 1999, The Key to My Father 2003. *Address:* Aaron Priest Literary Agency, 708 Third Avenue, New York, NY 10017, USA (office). *E-mail:* me@harlancoben.com. *Website:* www .harlancoben.com.

COBOS, Julio César Cleto; Argentine engineer and politician; *Vice-President;* b. 30 April 1955, Mendoza; m María Cristina Cerutti; one s two d; ed Universidad Tecnológica Nacional; taught at Universidad Tecnológica Nacional and at Universidad Nacional de Cuyo, Universidad de Mendoza, Dean of Prov. Faculty of Universidad Tecnológica Nacional 1997–2003; joined Unión Cívica Radical 1991, has been involved in Mendoza local politics since early 1990s; Minister of Environment and Public Works, Mendoza Prov. 1999–2000; Gov. of Mendoza Prov. (in a coalition with Recrear Liberals and Federalists) 2003–07; Vice-Pres. of Argentina 2007–. *Publications include:* Principios fundamentales de la hidráulica, Materias integradoras en ingeniería civil. *Address:* c/o Office of the President, Balcarce 50, C1064AAB, Buenos Aires, Argentina (office). *E-mail:* dgi@presidencia.gov.ar (office). *Website:* www.presidencia.gov.ar (office).

COBURN, Thomas (Tom) Allen, BS, MD; American physician and politician; *Senator from Oklahoma;* b. 14 March 1948, Muskogee; m. Carolyn Coburn; three c.; ed Oklahoma State Univ.; fmr Pres. Coll. of Business Student Council, Oklahoma State Univ.; Mfg Man., Ophthalmic Div., Coburn Optical Industries (family-owned co.), Colonial Heights, Va 1970–78; trained as physician 1978–83; internship in gen. surgery, St Anthony's Hosp., Oklahoma City 1983–84; family practice residency, Univ. of Arkansas, Fort Smith 1984–86; family practice physician, specialising in obstetrics and allergy, Muskogee 1986–94; mem. US House of Reps from Okla 2nd Dist, Washington, DC 1995–2001, mem. House Commerce Cttee; Co-Chair. Pres.'s Advisory Council on HIV/AIDS 2001–;, f. Family Caucus; Senator from Okla 2005–; mem. Ark. Medical Soc., Okla Medical Asscn, American Medical Asscn, American Acad. of Otolaryngic Allergy, American Acad. of Family Practice; Republican. *Publication:* Breach of Trust: How Washington Turns Outsiders Into Insiders (with John Hart) 2003. *Address:* 172 Russell Senate Office Building, Washington, DC 20510, USA (office). *Telephone:* (202) 224-5754 (office). *Fax:* (202) 224-6008 (office). *Website:* coburn.senate.gov (office).

COCHRAN, (William) Thad, BA, JD; American politician; *Senator from Mississippi;* b. 7 Dec. 1937, Pontotoc, Miss.; s. of William Holmes Cochran and Emma Grace Cochran (née Berry); m. Rose Clayton 1964; two c.; ed Univ. of Mississippi and School of Law, Univ. of Dublin, Ireland; served as Lt in USNR 1959–61; called to the Bar 1995, pvt. law practice in Jackson, Miss. 1965–72; mem. US House of Reps, Washington, DC 1973–78; Senator from Mississippi 1979–; Sec. Republican Conf. in US Senate 1985–90, Chair. Republican Conf., US Senate 1990–96; mem. Agric. Nutrition and Forestry Cttee, Appropriations Cttee, Govt Affairs Cttee, Rules and Admin. Cttee and Select Cttee on Indian Affairs; mem. Bd of Dirs US Naval Acad.; mem. Bd of Regents Smithsonian Inst.; Trustee Kennedy Center, Washington, DC; fmr Pres. Young Lawyers' section of Miss. State Bar; fmr Chair. Miss. Law Inst.; mem. ABA; Republican; Dr hc (Kentucky Wesleyan Coll., Mississippi Coll., Blue Mountain Coll., Univ. of Richmond, Tougaloo Coll.). *Address:* 113 Dirksen Senate Office Building Washington, DC 20510-2402, USA. *Telephone:* (202) 224-5054 (office). *Website:* cochran.senate.gov (office).

COCKBURN, William, CBE, TD, FRSA; British business executive; b. 28 Feb. 1943; joined Post Office 1961, Personal Asst to Chair. 1971–73, Asst Dir of Planning and Finance 1973–77, Dir Cen. Finance Planning 1977–78, Dir Postal Finance 1978–79, Dir London Postal Region 1979–82, mem. Bd 1981–95, Man. Dir Royal Mail 1986–92, Chief Exec. The Post Office 1992–95; Chair. Int. Post Corpn 1994–95; Group Chief Exec., WH Smith Group PLC 1995–97; Group Man. Dir British Telecommunications PLC 1997–2001; Chair. Parity Group PLC 2001–04; Deputy Chair. Business Post PLC 2002–; Deputy Chair. AWG PLC 2003–06, now Dir (non-exec.); Dir (non-exec.) Watkins Holdings Ltd 1985–93, Lex Service PLC 1993–2002, Centrica PLC 1997–99; Dir Business in the Community 1990–; Chair. Schoolteachers' Review Body 2002–; Pres. Inst. of Direct Marketing 2001–; Fellow, Chartered Inst. of Transport; Freeman City of London. *Address:* c/o Board of Directors,

Business Post Group plc, Express House, Wolseley Drive, Heartlands, Birmingham, B8 2SQ; 9 Avenue Road, Farnborough, Hants., GU14 7BW, England (home).

COCKER, James Cecil; Tongan economist, politician and diplomatist; *Consul-General in San Francisco;* m. Malia Cocker; eight c.; fmr Minister of Finance, of Works and Disasters Relief Activities, of Marines, of Police, of Labour and Commerce, fmr Deputy Prime Minister and Minister of Internal Affairs; Consul-Gen. in San Francisco 2006–. *Address:* Consulate-General of Tonga, 360 Post St, Suite 604, San Francisco, CA 94108, USA (office). *Telephone:* (415) 781-0365 (office). *Fax:* (415) 781-3964 (office). *E-mail:* consulategeneraloftonga@gmail.com (office). *Website:* tongaconsul.com (office).

CODRON, Michael Victor, CBE, MA; British theatre producer; b. 8 June 1930, London; s. of Isaac A. Codron and Lily Codron (née Morgenstern); ed St Paul's School, Worcester Coll., Oxford; Dir Aldwych Theatre, Hampstead Theatre, Royal Nat. Theatre; Cameron Mackintosh Prof. Oxford Univ. 1993; mem. Bd of Trustees Oxford School of Drama. *Plays:* has produced over 300 shows in West End, London including: The Birthday Party 1958, The Caretaker 1960, The Killing of Sister George, Little Malcolm and his Struggle against the Eunuchs, Big Bad Mouse 1966, The Boyfriend (revival) 1967, A Voyage Round My Father, The Homecoming (revival), Dr. Faustus, The Dresser, Three Sisters, Uncle Vanya, The Cherry Orchard 1989, Man of the Moment, Private Lives 1990, The Rise and Fall of Little Voice 1992, Time of My Life, Jamais Vu 1993, Kit and the Widow, Dead Funny, Arcadia, The Sisters Rosensweig 1994, Indian Ink, Dealer's Choice 1995, The Shakespeare Revue 1996, A Talent to Amuse 1996, Tom and Clem 1997, Silhouette 1997, Heritage 1997, Things We Do For Love, The Invention of Love, Alarms and Excursions 1998, Copenhagen 1999, Quartet, Comic Potential 1999, Peggy for You 2000, Blue/Orange 2001, Life After George 2002, Bedroom Farce 2002. *Film:* Clockwise 1986. *Leisure interest:* collecting Caroline of Brunswick memorabilia. *Address:* Aldwych Theatre Offices, Aldwych, London, WC2B 4DF (office); 12 Tower Bridge Wharf, London, E1 9UR, England (home). *Telephone:* (20) 7240-8291 (office); (20) 7925-6243. *Fax:* (20) 7240-8467 (office); (20) 7240-8467.

COE, Jonathan, BA, MA, PhD; British writer; b. 19 Aug. 1961, Birmingham, England; m. Janine McKeown 1989; ed Trinity Coll., Cambridge, Warwick Univ.; fmr legal proofreader; John Llewellyn Rhys Prize 1995, Prix du Meilleur Livre Étranger 1996, Writers' Guild Award 1997, Prix Médicis Étranger 1998, Bollinger Everyman Wodehouse Prize 2001. *Publications:* The Accidental Woman 1987, A Touch of Love 1989, The Dwarves of Death 1990, Humphrey Bogart: Take It and Like It 1991, James Stewart: Leading Man 1994, What A Carve Up! 1994, The House of Sleep 1997, The Rotters' Club 2001, The Closed Circle 2004, Like a Fiery Elephant: the Story of B. S. Johnson (BBC Four Samuel Johnson Prize for non-fiction 2005) 2004, The Rain Before It Falls 2007; contrib. to periodicals. *Address:* c/o Peake Associates, 14 Grafton Crescent, London, NW1 8SL, England (office).

COE, Baron (Life Peer), cr. 2000, of Ranmore in the County of Surrey; **Sebastian Newbold Coe,** OBE, KBE, BSc; British fmr politician and fmr athlete; *Chairman, London Organizing Committee of the Olympic Games and Paralympic Games;* b. 29 Sept. 1956, London; s. of Peter Coe and Angela Coe; m. Nicola Susan Elliott 1990; two s. two d.; ed Univ. of Loughborough; competed in Olympic Games, Moscow 1980, won Gold Medal at 1500m and Silver Medal at 800m and repeated this in Los Angeles 1984; European Jr Bronze Medallist at 1500m 1975; European Bronze Medallist at 800m 1978; European Silver Medallist at 800m 1982; European 800m Champion 1986; held world records at 800m, 1000m, 1500m and mile; est. new records at 800m, 1000m and mile 1981; mem. 4×400m world record relay squad 1982; only athlete to hold world records at 800m, 1000m, 1500m and mile simultaneously; Pres. first athletes' del. to IOC, Baden-Baden 1981 and mem. first athletes' comm. set up after Congress by IOC 1981–; Conservative MP for Falmouth and Camborne 1992–97; mem. Employment Select Cttee 1992–94, Nat. Heritage Select Cttee 1995–97; Parl. Pvt. Sec. to Chancellor of Duchy of Lancaster 1994–95, to Michael Heseltine 1995–96; Jr Govt Whip 1996–97; Deputy Chief of Staff then Pvt. Sec. to William Hague, Leader of the Opposition 1997–2001; Chair. Diadora UK 1987–94, ADT Health Quest Charitable Trust 1991–; Vice-Chair. Sports Council 1986–89, Sports Aid Trust 1987; Vice-Chair. London 2012 Olympic Games Bid 2003–04, Chair. and Pres. London 2012 Olympic and Paralympic Bid 2004–05, London Organizing Cttee of the Olympic Games and Paralympic Games (in 2012) 2005–; Chair. FIFA Ethics Cttee 2006–; Vice-Pres. Int. Asscn of Athletics Feds mem. Health Educ. Authority 1987–92, Health Educ. Council (now Authority) 1986–, Council IAAF 2003–; Vice-Patron Sharon Allen Leukemia Trust 1987–, Olympic Cttee Medical Comm. 1987–95, Sport for All Comm. 1997–; Admin. Steward, British Boxing Bd of Control 1995–; Global Adviser NIKE 2000–; Founding mem. World Sports Acad. 2000–; sports columnist, Daily Telegraph 2000–; Hon. D. Tech. (Loughborough) 1985; Hon. DSc (Hull) 1988; Hon. LLB (Sheffield) 1991; BBC Sports Personality of 1979, Sir John Cohen Memorial Award 1981, Príncipe de Asturias Award (Spain) 1987, BBC Sports Personality of the Year Special Award 2005. *Publications:* Running Free (with David Miller) 1981, Running for Fitness 1983, The Olympians 1984, More Than a Game 1992, Born to Run (autobiog.) 1992. *Leisure interests:* jazz, theatre, reading, some writing. *Address:* House of Lords, Westminster, London, SW1A 0PW, England. *Telephone:* (20) 3201-2000. *Website:* www.london2012.com.

COELHO, Paulo; Brazilian writer; b. Aug. 1947, Rio de Janeiro; ed law school; fmr playwright, theatre director and popular songwriter; imprisoned for alleged subversive activities against Brazilian Govt 1974; regular columnist for O Globo (newspaper) 2007–; elected mem. Brazilian Acad. of Arts 2002–; Chevalier, Ordre des Arts et des Lettres 1996, Comendador de Ordem do Rio Branco, Brazil 1998, Chevalier, Légion d'honneur 2000, Order of St Sophia, Ukraine 2004, Cruz do Mérito do Empreendedor Juscelino Kubitschek 2006; Prix Lectrices d'Elle, France 1995, Golden Book Awards, Yugoslavia 1995, 1996, 1997, 1998, 1999, 2000, Flaiano Int. Award, Italy 1996, Super Grinzane Cavour Book Award, Italy 1996, Golden Medal of Galicia, Spain 1999, Crystal Mirror Award, Poland 2000, XXIII Premio Internazionale Fregene, Italy 2001, Bambi Award, Germany 2001; Budapest Prize, Hungary 2005. *Publications:* Arquivos do inferno 1982, O Diário de um mago (trans. as The Pilgrimage, aka The Diary of a Magus: The Road to Santiago) 1987, O Alquimista (trans. as The Alchemist) 1988, Brida 1990, O Dom Supremo (trans. as The Gift) 1991, As Valkírias (trans. as The Valkyries) 1992, Maktub 1994, Na margem do rio Piedra eu sentei e chorei (trans. as By the River Piedra I Sat Down and Wept) 1994, Frases 1995, O Monte Cinco (trans. as The Fifth Mountain) 1996, Cartas de Amor do Profeta (trans. as Love Letters from a Prophet) 1997, Manual do guerreiro da luz (trans. as Manual of the Warrior of Light) 1997, Veronika decide morrer (trans. as Veronika Decides to Die) 1998, Palavras essenciais (trans. as The Confessions of a Pilgrim) 1999, O demônio e a Srta Prym (trans. as The Devil and Miss Prym) 2000, Histórias para pais, filhos e netos (trans. as Fathers, Sons and Grandsons) 2001, Onze minutos (trans. as Eleven Minutes) 2003, O Gênio e as Rosas (trans. as The Genie and the Roses, juvenile) 2004, O Zahir (trans. as The Zahir) 2005, Like the Flowing River (thoughts and short stories) 2006, A Bruxa do Portobello (trans. as The Witch of Portobello) 2006, O Vencedor está Só (trans. as The Winner Stands Alone) 2008. *Address:* Sant Jordi Asociados Agencia Literaria SL, Paseo García Faria, 73–75, 08019 Barcelona, Spain (office). *Telephone:* (93) 2240107 (office). *Fax:* (93) 3562696 (office). *Website:* www.santjordi-asociados.com (office); www.paulocoelho.com. *E-mail:* paulo@paulocoelho.com (office).

COËME, Guy; Belgian politician; *Mayor of Waremme;* b. 21 Aug. 1946, Waremme; m.; two c.; ed Univ. of Liège; mem. Nat. Office, Parti Socialiste (PS) 1970–74, Vice-Pres. PS 1983–; Deputy Mayor, Waremme 1971–74, 1982–87; Prov. Councillor, Liège 1971–74; Deputy, Liège 1974–81, Huy-Waremme 1982–; Burgomaster, Waremme 1987–; Sec. of State for the Wallonne Region, with responsibility for the Environment and Planning 1981–82; Minister-Pres. Wallonne Regional Exec., with responsibility for Water, Rural Devt, Conservation and Admin. Feb.–May 1988; Minister of Nat. Defence 1988–92; Deputy Prime Minister and Minister of Communications and Public Services 1992–94 (resgnd); convicted in government bribery case and received suspended sentenced 1998; cand. in regional elections Huy-Waremme 2004; Pres. Soc. for the Regional Devt of Wallonne 1978; Vice-Pres. Socialist Party 1983; Admin. Soc. for Regional Investment in Wallonne 1979. *Address:* Office of the Mayor, Rue Joseph Wauters, 2, Waremme, Belgium (office). *E-mail:* guy.coeme@waremme.be (office). *Website:* www.waremme.be (office).

COEN, Enrico Sandro, CBE, PhD, FRS, FLS; British geneticist; *Group Leader, Department of Cell and Developmental Biology, John Innes Institute;* b. 29 Sept. 1957, Southport, Lancs.; s. of Ernesto Coen and Dorothea Coen (née Cattani); m. Lucinda Poliakoff 1984; two s. one d.; ed King's Coll., Cambridge; joined John Innes Inst., Norwich 1984, Project Leader 1995–98, Deputy Head Dept of Genetics 1998–2000, Group Leader Dept of Cell and Developmental Biology 2000–; Foreign Assoc. mem. NAS 2001; Corresp. mem. Botanical Soc. of America 2003; Hon. Lecturer Univ. of E Anglia 1989, Hon. Reader 1994, Hon. Prof. 1998; EMBO Medal, Rome 1996, Science for Art Prize, Paris 1996, Linnean Gold Medal, London 1997, Royal Soc. Darwin Medal (jtly) 2004. *Publications:* The Art of Genes 1999; 80 articles in int. scientific research journals. *Leisure interests:* painting, children. *Address:* John Innes Centre, Colney Lane, Norwich, NR4 7UH, England (office). *Telephone:* (1603) 450274 (office). *Fax:* (1603) 450022 (office). *E-mail:* enrico.coen@bbsrc.ac.uk (office). *Website:* www.jic.bbsrc.ac.uk (office).

COEN, Ethan; American film producer and screenwriter; b. 1958, St Louis Park, Minn.; s. of Ed Coen and Rena Coen; brother of Joel Coen (q.v.); m.; ed Princeton Univ.; screenwriter (with Joel Coen) Crime Wave (fmrly XYZ Murders); producer, screenplay; ed. Blood Simple 1984. *Films include:* Raising Arizona 1987, Miller's Crossing 1990, Barton Fink 1991 (Palme d'Or, Cannes Festival), The Hudsucker Proxy 1994, Fargo 1996, The Naked Man, The Big Lebowski 1998, O Brother, Where Art Thou? 2000, The Man Who Wasn't There 2001, A Fever in the Blood 2002, Intolerable Cruelty 2003, The Ladykillers 2004, Paris, je t'aime (segment) 2006, No Country for Old Men (Best Film, Nat. Bd of Review 2007, Academy Awards for Best Film, Best Direction, Best Adapted Screenplay 2008) 2007, Burn After Reading 2008. *Publication:* Gates of Eden 1998. *Address:* c/o UTA, 9560 Wilshire Boulevard, Beverly Hills, CA 90212, USA.

COEN, Joel; American film director and screenwriter; b. 1955, St Louis Park, Minn.; s. of Ed Coen and Rena Coen; brother of Ethan Coen (q.v.); m. (divorced); ed Simon's Rock Coll. and New York Univ.; Asst Ed. Fear No Evil, Evil Dead; worked with rock video crews; screenwriter (with Ethan Coen) Crime Wave (fmrly XYZ Murders). *Films include:* (with Ethan Coen): Blood Simple 1984, Raising Arizona 1987, Miller's Crossing 1990, Barton Fink (Palme d'Or, Cannes Festival) 1991, The Hudsucker Proxy 1994, Fargo 1996 (Best Dir Award, Cannes Int. Film Festival 1996), The Big Lebowski 1998, O Brother, Where Art Thou? 2000, The Man Who Wasn't There 2001, Intolerable Cruelty 2003, The Ladykillers 2004, Paris, je t'aime (segment) 2006, No Country for Old Men (Best Film, Nat. Bd of Review 2007, Academy Awards for Best Film, Best Direction, Best Adapted Screenplay 2008) 2007, Burn After Reading 2008. *Address:* c/o UTA, 9560 Wilshire Boulevard, Beverly Hills, CA 90212, USA.

COETZEE, John Maxwell (J. M.), MA, PhD; South African/Australian writer and academic; b. 9 Feb. 1940, Cape Town; one s. one d.; ed Univ. of Cape Town, Univ. of Texas; Asst Prof. of English, State Univ. of NY Buffalo 1968–71;

Lecturer, Univ. of Cape Town 1972–76, Sr Lecturer 1977–80, Assoc. Prof. 1981–83, Prof. of Gen. Literature 1984–2001; Research Fellow, Univ. of Adelaide, Australia 2002–; Prof. of Social Thought, Univ. of Chicago, USA 2001–, Distinguished Service Prof.; Dr hc (Strathclyde) 1985, (State Univ. of New York) 1989, (Cape Town) 1995, (Oxford) 2002; CNA Literary Award 1977, 1980, 1983, Geoffrey Faber Prize 1980, James Tait Black Memorial Prize 1980, Jerusalem Prize 1987, Prix Meilleur Livre 2002, Premio Grinzane 2003, Nobel Prize for Literature 2003. *Publications:* Dusklands 1974, In the Heart of the Country 1977, Waiting for the Barbarians 1980, Life and Times of Michael K (Booker-McConnell Prize 1983, Prix Femina Etranger 1985) 1983, Foe 1986, White Writing 1988, Age of Iron (Sunday Express Book of the Year Prize 1990) 1990, Doubling the Point: Essays and Interviews (ed. by David Atwell) 1992, The Master of Petersburg (Premio Mondello 1994, Irish Times Int. Fiction Prize 1995) 1994, Giving Offence: Essays on Censorship 1996, Boyhood 1997, The Lives of Animals (lecture) 1999, Disgrace (Booker Prize 1999, Commonwealth Writers Prize 2000) 1999, The Humanities in Africa 2001, Stranger Shores: Essays 1986–1999 2001, Youth 2002, Elizabeth Costello: Eight Lessons 2003, Slow Man (novel) 2005, Inner Workings (essays) 2007, Diary of a Bad Year (novel) 2007. *Address:* POB 3045, Newton, SA 5074, Australia. *E-mail:* john.coetzee@adelaide.edu.au (home).

COEY, John Michael David, DSc, FRS; Irish physicist and academic; *Erasmus Smith's Professor of Natural and Experimental Philosophy, Trinity College Dublin;* b. 24 Feb. 1945, Belfast; s. of David S. Coey and Joan E. Newsam; m. Wong May 1973; two s.; ed Tonbridge School, Jesus Coll. Cambridge, UK and Univ. of Manitoba, Canada; Chargé de Recherches, CNRS, Grenoble 1974–78; Lecturer/Prof., Trinity Coll. Dublin 1978–, Prof. of Experimental Physics 1987–2007, Erasmus Smith's Prof. of Natural and Experimental Philosophy 2007–, Head, Dept of Physics 1989–92; Visiting Scientist, IBM Research Center, Yorktown Heights, NY 1976–77, 1988, Univ. of Bordeaux 1984, Centre d'Etudes Nucléaires de Grenoble 1985–86, Johns Hopkins Univ. Applied Physics Lab. 1986, Univ. de Paris 7 1992, Univ. of Calif., San Diego 1997, Florida State Univ. 1998; Co-inventor, thermopiezic analyser 1986, nitromag 1990; Chief Coordinator, Concerted European Action on Magnets 1987–94; Dir Magnetic Solutions Ltd 1994–; mem. Academic Cttee Magnetism Lab. Inst. of Physics, Beijing 1988–; mem. Royal Irish Acad., Vice-Pres. 1989; Fulbright Fellow 1997–98; Fellow, American Physical Soc. 2000; Hon. DSc (Inst. Nat. Polytechnique de Grenoble) 1994; Charles Chree Prize and Medal, Inst. of Physics London, Gold Medal, Royal Irish Acad. 2005. *Publications:* Magnetic Glasses (with K. Moorjani) 1984, Structural and Magnetic Phase Transitions in Minerals (with S. Ghose and E. Salje) 1988, Rare-Earth Iron Permanent Magnets 1996, Permanent Magnetism (with R. Skomski) 1999; numerous papers on magnetic and electronic properties of solids. *Leisure interest:* gardening. *Address:* Department of Physics, University of Dublin Trinity College, Dublin 2 (office); Hillbrook House, Castleknock, Dublin 15, Ireland (home). *Telephone:* (1) 6081470 (office). *Fax:* (1) 6711759 (office). *E-mail:* jcoey@tcd.ie (office). *Website:* www.tcd.ie/Physics (office).

COFFEY, Rev. David Roy, OBE, BA; British Baptist leader and minister of religion; *President, Baptist World Alliance;* b. 13 Nov. 1941, Purley, Surrey; s. of Arthur Coffey and Elsie Maud Willis; m. Janet Anne Dunbar 1966; one s. one d.; ed Spurgeon's Coll., London; ordained to Baptist ministry 1967; Minister Whetstone Baptist Church, Leicester 1967–72, N Cheam Baptist Church, London 1972–80; Sr Minister Upton Vale Baptist Church, Torquay 1980–88; Sec. for Evangelism, Baptist Union of GB 1988–91, Gen. Sec. 1991–; Pres. Baptist Union 1986–87; Vice-Pres. European Baptist Fed. 1995–, Pres. 1997–99; Vice-Pres. Baptist World Alliance 2000–05, Pres. 2005–; Free Churches Moderator and Co-Pres. Churches Together in England 2003–07; Hon. DD (Dallas Baptist Univ.) 2008, (Palmer Seminary) 2009. *Publications:* Build that Bridge: a Study in Conflict and Reconciliation 1986, Discovering Romans: a Crossway Bible Guide 2000, Joy to the World 2008, Unity 2009. *Leisure interests:* grandchildren, music, soccer, bookshops, Elgar Soc. *Address:* Baptist House, 129 Broadway, Didcot, Oxon., OX11 8RT, England (office). *Telephone:* (1235) 517699 (office). *Fax:* (1235) 517601 (office). *E-mail:* bwapresident@tiscali.co.uk (office). *Website:* www.bwanet.org (office).

COFFEY, Shelby, III; American journalist; *Senior Fellow, Freedom Forum;* m. Mary Lee Coffey; ed Univ. of Virginia; with Washington Post 1968–85, latterly Asst Man. Ed. for nat. news and Deputy Man. Ed. for features; Ed. US News and World Report 1985–86; Ed. Dallas Times Herald 1986; Deputy Assoc. Ed. Los Angeles Times, subsequently Exec. Ed. 1986–89, Ed. and Exec. Vice-Pres. 1989; currently Sr Fellow, Freedom Forum 2001–; Nat. Press Foundation Ed. of the Year 1994. *Address:* Freedom Forum Headquarters, 555 Pennsylvania Avenue, N.W, Washington, DC 20001, USA (office). *Telephone:* (202) 292-6100 (office). *E-mail:* news@freedomforum.org (office). *Website:* www.freedomforum.org (office).

COFFIN, Frank Morey, AB, LLD; American fmr government official and judge (retd); b. 11 July 1919, Lewiston, Androscoggin Co., Me; s. of Herbert Coffin and Ruth Coffin; m. Ruth Ulrich 1942; one s. three d.; ed Bates Coll. and Harvard Univ.; served as Lt in USNR 1943–46; admitted to Maine Bar 1947, legal practice 1947–56; mem. US House of Reps, Washington, DC 1957–61; Man. Dir Devt Loan Fund, US Dept of State, Washington, DC 1961; Deputy Admin., Agency for Int. Devt 1961–62; Deputy Admin. for Operations 1962–64; US Rep. to Devt Assistance Cttee, OECD, Paris 1964–65; US Circuit Judge, Court of Appeals for First Circuit 1965–89, Chief Judge 1972–83, Sr Judge 1989–2006; Chair. Judicial Br. Cttee US Judicial Conf. 1984–90; Adjunct Prof., Univ. of Maine School of Law 1986–89; Co-founder and Dir Governance Inst., Washington, DC (now affiliated with Brookings Inst.) 1987–; Chair. Maine Justice Action Group 1996–2001; mem. ABA, American Acad. of Arts and Sciences; Trustee Emer. Bates Coll. 2005. *Publications:* Witness for Aid 1964, The Ways of a Judge 1980, A Lexicon of Oral Advocacy

1984, On Appeal 1994. *Leisure interests:* sculpture, painting, boating. *Address:* c/o United States Court of Appeals, 156 Federal Street, Portland, ME 04101-4152, USA (office).

COFFMAN, Vance D., BS, MS, PhD; American aerospace company executive (retd); b. 3 April 1944; m. Arlene Coffman; two d.; ed Iowa State Univ., Stanford Univ.; joined Lockheed Corpn as guidance and control systems analyst, Space Systems Div. (led devt of several major space programmes) 1967, apptd Div. Vice-Pres. 1985, Div. Vice-Pres. and Asst Gen. Man. 1987, Div. Pres. (responsible for Hubble Space Telescope and MILSTAR satellite communications programme) 1988, Pres. Space Systems Div. Lockheed Missiles & Space Co. and Vice-Pres. Corpn, Exec. Vice-Pres. Corpn –1995; Pres. and COO Space & Strategic Missiles Sector, Lockheed Martin Corpn (following merger of Lockheed and Martin Marietta Corpns) 1995, Pres., COO and Exec. Vice-Pres. –1997, Vice-Chair. 1997–98, CEO 1997–2004, Chair. 1998–2005 (retd); mem. Bd of Dirs Bristol-Myers Squibb 1998, United Negro Coll. Fund 2001, 3M Co. 2002; mem. Nat. Acad. of Eng, Security Affairs Support Asscn; Fellow, American Astronomical Soc. 1991, AIAA 1996; Hon. Dr Aerospace Eng (Embry-Riddle Univ.) 1998; Hon. DEng (Stevens Inst. of Tech.) 1998; Hon. LLD (Pepperdine Univ.) 2000; Professional Progress in Engineering Award, Iowa State Univ. 1989, Distinguished Achievement Citation, Iowa State 1999, Rear Admiral John J. Bergen Industry Award, New York Council of the Navy League 2000, Fleet Admiral Chester W. Nimitz Award, Navy League of USA 2001, Executive of the Year, Washington Techway 2001, Bob Hope Distinguished Citizen Award, Nat. Defense Industrial Asscn (Los Angeles Chapter) 2002. *Address:* POB 1785, Pebble Beach, CA 93953, USA.

COHAN, Robert Paul, CBE; British choreographer; b. 27 March 1925; s. of Walter Cohan and Billie Cohan; ed Martha Graham School, New York; Pnr, Martha Graham School 1950, Co-Dir Martha Graham Co. 1966; Artistic Dir Contemporary Dance Trust Ltd, London 1967–; Artistic Dir and Prin. Choreographer, London Contemporary Dance Theatre 1969–87, Founder-Artistic Dir 1987–89; Artistic Adviser, Batsheva Co., Israel 1980–89; Dir York Univ., Toronto Choreographic Summer School 1977, Gulbenkian Choreographic Summer School, Univ. of Surrey 1978, 1979, 1982 and other int. courses; Gov. Contemporary Dance Trust; Ed., Choreography and Dance (journal) 1988–; Chair. Robin Howard Foundation; with London Contemporary Dance Theatre has toured Europe, S. America, N Africa, USA; maj. works created: Cell 1969, Stages 1971, Waterless Method of Swimming Instruction 1974, Class 1975, Stabat Mater 1975, Masque of Separation 1975, Khamsin 1976, Nympheas 1976, Forest 1977, Eos 1978, Songs, Lamentations and Praises 1979, Dances of Love and Death 1981, Agora 1984, A Mass for Man 1985, Ceremony 1986, Interrogations 1986, Video Life 1986, Phantasmagoria 1987, A Midsummer Night's Dream 1993, The Four Seasons 1996, Aladdin 2000; Hon. Fellow York Univ., Toronto; Hon. DLitt (Exeter Univ.) 1993, (Univ. of Kent) 1996; Dr. hc (Middx) 1994, (Winchester) 2006; Evening Standard Award for outstanding achievement in ballet 1975, Soc. of West End Theatres Award for outstanding achievement in ballet 1978, UK Dance Critics Circle Award for Lifetime Achievement 2005. *Publication:* The Dance Workshop 1986. *Leisure interest:* dancing. *Address:* The Place, 17 Dukes Road, London, WC1H 9AB, England. *Telephone:* (20) 7387-0161.

COHEN, Abby Joseph, BA, MS, CFA; American economist and investment bank executive; *Partner and Chief US Portfolio Strategist, Goldman Sachs Group, Inc.;* b. 29 Feb. 1952, Queens, New York; d. of Raymond Joseph Cohen and the late Shirley Joseph (née Silverstein); m. David M. Cohen 1973; two d.; ed Martin Van Buren High School, Cornell Univ., George Washington Univ.; Jr Economist, Fed. Reserve Bd, Washington, DC 1973–76; Economist/Analyst, T. Rowe Price Assocs, Baltimore, Md 1976–83; Investment Strategist, Drexel Burnham Lambert, New York 1983–90; BZW, New York 1990; Investment Strategist, Goldman, Sachs & Co. 1990–, Man. Dir 1996–, Man. Pnr 1998–, Chair. Investment Policy Cttee, also Chief US Portfolio Strategist; Chair. Inst. of Chartered Financial Analysts; mem. Bd Govs Nat. Economists Club, New York Soc. of Security Analysts; Vice-Chair. Asscn for Investment Man. Research; mem. Nat. Asscn of Business Economists; Trustee/Fellow, Cornell Univ.; Trustee Jewish Theological Seminary of America; Woman Achiever (Woman of the Year) Award, YWCA, New York 1989, ranked 19th by Forbes magazine amongst 100 Most Powerful Women 2005. *Address:* Goldman Sachs Group, Inc., 85 Broad Street, New York, NY 10004, USA (office). *Telephone:* (212) 902-1000 (office). *Fax:* (212) 902-3000 (office). *Website:* www.goldmansachs.com (office).

COHEN, Ben; American business executive; *President, TrueMajority.org;* b. 1951, Brooklyn, NY; ed Calhoun High School, Merrick, LI, Colgate Univ., Skidmore Coll., New School, NY, NY Univ.; various jobs whilst studying pottery and jewellery, including pottery wheel delivery person, paediatric emergency room clerk, taxi cab driver; fmr craft therapist intern, Jacobi Hosp., Bronx, New York and Grand Street Settlement House, Manhattan; craft teacher, Highland Community School, Paradox, NY 1974–77; Co-founder Ben & Jerry's Homemade Inc. (with Jerry Greenfield) 1977, opened first Ice Cream Parlour in Burlington, Vt 1978, held various positions including Marketing Dir, Salesperson, Pres., CEO and Chair., est. Ben & Jerry's Foundation (to oversee donation of 7.5% of profits to non-profit orgs), co. sold to Unilever; f. TrueMajority.org (non-profit educ. and advocacy group); Founding mem. Businesses for Social Responsibility (org. that promotes socially responsible business practices); mem. numerous non-profit orgs; Corp. Giving Award, Council on Econ. Priorities 1988, US Small Business Persons of the Year, US Small Business Admin 1988. *Publications include:* Ben & Jerry's Homemade Ice Cream and Dessert Book (co-author with Jerry Greenfield) 1987. *Address:* TrueMajority.org, 1825 K St., NW, Suite 210, Washington, DC 20006, USA (office). *Telephone:* (802) 735-9110 (office). *Website:* www.truemajority.org (office).

COHEN, Bernard Woolf, DFA; British artist and academic; *Slade Professor Emeritus, University College London;* b. 28 July 1933, London; m. Jean Britton 1959; one s. one d.; ed South West Essex School of Art, St Martin's School of Art, London and Slade School of Fine Art, London; held teaching appointments at several art schools 1957–67; teacher of painting and drawing, Slade School of Fine Art 1967–73, 1977; Visiting Prof., Univ. of New Mexico 1969–70, faculty alumni 1974; Guest Lecturer, Royal Coll. of Art 1974–75; Visiting Artist, Minneapolis School of Art 1964, 1969, 1971, 1975, Ont. Coll. of Art 1971, San Francisco Art Inst., Univ. of Victoria, BC 1975; has lectured at several Canadian univs since 1969; fmrly Principal Lecturer (Painting), Wimbledon School of Art 1980–84; Slade Prof., Chair. of Fine Art, Univ. Coll. London 1988–2000, Prof. Emer. 2000–, Fellow, Univ. Coll. London 1992; Hon. DFA (Univ. of London, Slade School). *Publications:* articles and statements in journals and catalogues. *Leisure interests:* music, cinema, travel, museums. *Address:* 80 Camberwell Grove, London, SE5 8RF, England (home). *Telephone:* (20) 7708-4480 (home). *Fax:* (20) 7708-4480 (home). *E-mail:* bwc44@hotmail.com (home). *Website:* wwwflowerseast.com (office).

COHEN, Gerald Allan, MA, BPhil, FBA; Canadian academic; *Quain Professor of Jurisprudence, University College London;* b. 14 April 1941, Montreal; s. of Morrie Cohen and Bella Lipkin; m. 1st Margaret Florence Pearce 1965 (divorced 1996); one s. two d.; m. 2nd Michèle Jacottet 1999; ed Morris Winchewsky Jewish School, Strathcona Acad. and McGill Univ., Montreal and New Coll. Oxford, England; Lecturer in Philosophy, Univ. Coll. London 1963–78, Reader 1978–84, Quain Prof. of Jurisprudence 2008–09; Chichele Prof. of Social and Political Theory and Fellow of All Souls, Oxford 1985–2008; Isaac Deutscher Memorial Prize 1980. *Publications:* Karl Marx's Theory of History: A Defence 1978, History, Labour and Freedom: Themes from Marx 1988, Self-Ownership, Freedom and Equality 1995, If You're an Egalitarian, How Come You're so Rich? 2000, Rescuing Justice and Equality 2008. *Leisure interests:* Guardian crossword puzzles, American popular music 1920–60, painting, architecture, travel, patience. *Address:* Faculty of Laws, University College London, Endsleigh Gardens, London, WC1H 0EG, England (office). *Telephone:* (207) 679-2000 (office). *Website:* www.ucl.ac.uk/laws/jurisprudence.

COHEN, Joel E., BA, PhD, DrPH; American mathematical biologist and academic; *Abby Rockefeller Mauzé Professor of Populations, The Rockefeller University;* b. 10 Feb. 1944; ed Harvard Univ.; taught at Harvard Univ. 1971–75; Prof., The Rockefeller Univ. 1975–, currently Abby Rockefeller Mauzé Prof. of Populations; also Prof. of Populations, Earth Inst., Columbia Univ., New York; mem. Bd of Dirs The Nature Conservancy; mem. Bd of Trustees Population Reference Bureau; mem. NAS; MacArthur Foundation Fellow; Fred L. Soper Prize, Pan American Health Org., Washington, DC 1998 for work on Chagas disease, Tyler Prize for Environmental Achievement 1999. *Publications:* numerous scientific papers in professional journals on demography, epidemiology and ecology. *Address:* Cohen Joel Laboratory, The Rockefeller University, 1230 York Avenue, New York, NY 10065, USA (office). *Telephone:* (212) 327-8000 (office). *E-mail:* cohen@rockefeller.edu (office); joel.cohen@mail.rockefeller.edu (office). *Website:* www.rockefeller.edu/research/abstract.php?id=23 (office).

COHEN, Leonard, BA, CC; Canadian singer and songwriter; b. 21 Sept. 1934, Montreal; s. of Nathan B. Cohen and Masha Klinitsky; two c.; ed McGill Univ.; f. country-and-western band, The Buckskin Boys 1951; initially wrote poetry, winning McGill Literary Award for first collection; moved to New York in early 1960s; hon. degree (Dalhousie Univ.) 1970, (McGill Univ.) 1992; numerous awards including William Harold Moon Award (Recording Rights Org. of Canada) 1984, Juno Hall of Fame 1991, Gov. Gen.'s Performing Arts Award 1993. *Recordings include:* albums: The Songs of Leonard Cohen 1968, Songs From A Room 1969, Songs of Love and Hate 1971, Live Songs 1973, New Skin For the Old Ceremony 1974, Greatest Hits 1975, The Best of Leonard Cohen 1976, Death of a Ladies' Man 1977, Recent Songs 1979, Various Positions 1985, I'm Your Man 1988, The Future 1992, Cohen Live 1994, More Best Of 1997, Live Songs 1998, Ten New Songs 2001, Field Commander Cohen 2001, The Essential Leonard Cohen 2002, Dear Heather 2004. *Film:* Leonard Cohen I'm Your Man 2006. *Publications:* Let Us Compare Mythologies (McGill Literary Award) 1956, The Spice-Box of Earth 1961, The Favourite Game (Quebec Literary Prize) 1963, Flowers for Hitler 1964, Beautiful Losers 1966, Parasites of Heaven 1966, Selected Poems 1956–1968 1968, The Energy of Slaves 1972, Death of a Ladies' Man 1978, Book of Mercy (Canadian Authors' Asscn Literary Award) 1984, Stranger Music: Selected Poems and Songs 1993, Book of Longing (poems) 2006. *Address:* 5042 Wilshire Boulevard, Suite 845, Los Angeles, CA 90036, USA (office).

COHEN, Lyor; American music company executive; *Vice-Chairman and CEO of US and UK Recorded Music, Warner Music Group;* b. New York, NY; ed Univ. of Miami; financial officer, Bank Leumi; Hip-Hop Performance Promoter, Mix Club, Los Angeles; joined Rush Entertainment 1985, later Partner; Pres. and CEO Island Def Jam Records 1988–2004; Vice-Chair. and CEO US and UK Recorded Music, Warner Music Group 2004–. *Address:* Warner Music Group, 75 Rockefeller Plaza, New York, NY 10019, USA (office). *Website:* www.wmg.com.

COHEN, Marius (Job), PhD; Dutch politician and academic; *Mayor of Amsterdam;* b. 18 Oct. 1947, Haarlem; s. of Adolf Emiel Cohen and Hetty Koster; m. 1972; one s. one d.; ed Stedelijk Gymnasium Haarlem and Univ. of Groningen; joined PvdA (Netherlands Labour Party) 1967; held a scientific position at Bureau Research of Educ., Leiden Univ. 1971–81; Lecturer, Maastricht Univ. 1981–83, Chair. Comm. that prepared establishment of faculty of law, Prof. of Methods and Techniques, Faculty of Law 1983, Rector Magnificus 1991–93; State Sec. (Deputy Minister) of Educ. 1993–94; mem. Eerste Kamer (Upper House) 1995–98; Interim Dir VRPO TV station

Feb.–Aug. 1998; State Sec., Ministry of Justice, with responsibility for Immigration 1998–2000; Mayor of Amsterdam 2001–; Labour Party cand. for Prime Minister in gen. elections 2003; Dr hc (Univ. of Windsor) 2007, (Radboud Univ. Nijmegen) 2008; Cleveringa Lecturer, Univ. of Leiden 2002, named a Time magazine 'European Hero' 2005. *Address:* Office of the Mayor, Postbus 202, 1000 AE Amsterdam, Netherlands (office). *Telephone:* (20) 5522000. *E-mail:* jcohen@amsterdam.nl (office). *Website:* www.amsterdam.nl (office).

COHEN, Marvin Lou, PhD; American (b. Canadian) physicist and academic; *University Professor of Physics, University of California, Berkeley;* b. 3 March 1935, Montreal, Canada; s. of Elmo Cohen and Molly Zaritsky; m. 1st Merrill Leigh Gardner 1958 (died 1994); one s. one d.; m. 2nd Suzy R. Locke 1996; ed Univs of California, Berkeley and Chicago; mem. Tech. Staff, Bell Labs, Murray Hill, NJ 1963–64; Asst Prof. of Physics, Univ. of Calif., Berkeley 1964–66, Assoc. Prof. 1966–68, Prof. 1969–95, Univ. Prof. 1995–; Prof., Miller Inst. Basic Research in Science, Univ. of Calif. 1969–70, 1976–77, 1988, Chair. 1977–81, Univ. Prof. 1995–, Faculty Research Lecturer 1996–97, Faculty Research Prof., Lecturer 1997–; Distinguished Lecturer in Physics and Electrical Eng, Columbia Univ. 1996; Chair. Gordon Research Conf. on Chem. and Physics of Solids 1972; US Rep., Semiconductor Comm., IUPAP 1975–81; Visiting Prof., Univ. of Cambridge, UK 1966, Univ. of Paris 1972–73, Univ. of Hawaii 1978–79, Technion, Haifa, Israel 1987–88; Alfred P. Sloan Fellow, Univ. of Cambridge 1965–67; Guggenheim Fellow 1978–79, 1990–91; Fellow, American Physics Soc. Exec. Council 1975–79, Chair. 1977–78; mem. NAS 1980, American Acad. of Arts and Sciences, Oliver E. Buckley Prize Comm. 1980–81, Chair. 1981; mem. Selection Cttee for Presidential Young Investigator Awards 1983; mem. Cttee on Nat. Synchotron Radiation Facilities 1983–84; Chair. 17th Int. Conf. on the Physics of Semiconductors 1984; Chair. Screening/Search Cttee, NAS 1997–99; mem. Govt-Univ.-Industry Research Round Table 1984–, Vice-Chair. Working Group on Science and Eng Talent 1984–, Advisory Bd Tex. Center for Superconductivity 1991– (mem. 1988–90), mem. Search Cttee for Dir 2000–01; mem. Research Briefing Panels NAS on Funding and on High Temperature Superconductivity 1987, US–Japan Workshop on Univ. Research 1988–89, Science Policy Bd Stanford Synchrotron Radiation Lab. 1990–92, Visiting Cttee, The Ginzton Lab., Stanford Univ. 1991, American Acad. of Arts and Sciences 1993, Scientific Policy Cttee, Stanford Linear Accelerator Center 1993–95, Chair. Comstock Prize Cttee NAS; Assoc. Ed. Materials Science and Eng 1987, Chair. Exec. Bd Council, Panel on Public Affairs, Investment Cttee, American Physical Soc. Fellowship Cttee, Congressional Fellowship Cttee, 2003; mem. Advisory Bd Int. Journal of Modern Physics B 1987–, Editorial Bd Perspectives in Condensed Matter Physics 1987–, AAAS 1993–, American Physical Society Lilienfeld Prize Cttee 1994–95, mem. Bd of Advisors, Discover Magazine 1998–2000, Prize Cttee for Nanoscience Prize ACSIN 1999, 2001, Cttee on Faculty Research Lectureship, Univ. of Calif. 1999–2002, Visiting Advisory Cttee on Computational Science and Eng, Univ. of Calif., Davis 2000, Int. Advisory Bd, Nanonetwork Materials, Kamakura, Japan 2000, Advisory Cttee, Inst. of Nano Science and Tech., Hong Kong Univ. of Science and Tech. 2001–; mem. Bd of Govs Weizmann Inst. of Science 2002–, Scientific and Academic Advisory Cttee, Weizmann Inst. of Science 2002–; Invited Speaker, Nobel Symposium 1996; Inauguration Speaker, Korea Inst. for Advanced Study 1996; Gerhard Schmidt Memorial Lecture, Weizmann Inst. of Science 1997; Fellow AAAS 1997; Hubert M. James Lecturer, Purdue Univ. 1999; Distinguished Lecturer, Hong Kong Univ. of Science and Tech. 2001; elected to American Physical Soc. 2002, Vice-Pres. 2003, Pres. Elect 2004, Pres. 2005, Past Pres. 2006; mem. American Philosophical Soc. 2003; mem. Regional Bd, American Cttee for Weizmann Inst. of Science; mem. Governing Bd, American Inst. of Physics 2003–07; mem. Nominating Cttee, American Inst. of Physics 2003–06; Loeb Lecturer, Harvard Univ. 2004; Chief Scientific Officer, Nanomix Inc. 2006–; Oliver E. Buckley Prize for Solid State Physics 1979; Dept of Energy Award 1981, 1990, Lawrence Berkeley Lab. Certificate of Merit 1991, Julius Edgar Lilienfeld Prize (American Physical Soc.) 1994 Dr hc (Montreal) 2005; Outstanding Performance Award, Lawrence Berkeley Nat. Lab. 1995, Nat. Medal of Science 2001, Presidential Award 2002, Foresight Inst. Richard P. Feynman Prize in Nanotechnology (with Steven G. Louie) 2003, Technology Pioneer Award, World Econ. Forum 2007. *Publications:* over 700 articles on research topics. *Leisure interests:* music (clarinet), running. *Address:* Department of Physics, 366 Le Conte Hall, # 7300, Berkeley, CA 94720-7300 (office); 201 Estates Drive, Piedmont, CA 94611, USA (home). *Telephone:* (510) 642-4753 (office). *Fax:* (510) 643-9473 (office). *E-mail:* mlcohen@berkeley.edu (office). *Website:* civet.berkeley.edu/cohen/index.html.

COHEN, Sir Philip, Kt, PhD, FRS, FRSE; British research biochemist and academic; *Royal Society Research Professor, School of Life Sciences Research, University of Dundee;* b. 22 July 1945, Edgware, Middx; s. of Jacob Davis Cohen and Fanny Bragman; m. Patricia T. Wade 1969; one s. one d.; ed Hendon County Grammar School and Univ. Coll. London; SRC/NATO Postdoctoral Fellow, Univ. of Washington, Seattle 1969–71; Lecturer in Biochemistry, Univ. of Dundee 1971–77, Reader 1977–81, Prof. of Enzymology 1981–84, Royal Soc. Research Prof. 1984–; Dir MRC Protein Phosphorylation Unit 1990–; Dir Wellcome Trust Biocentre 1997–; Fellow, Univ. Coll. London 1993, Acad. of Medical Sciences 1998; mem. Discovery Advisory Bd SmithKline Beecham Pharmaceutical Co. 1993–97; mem. European Molecular Biology Org. 1982, Academia Europaea 1990; Croonian Lecturer, Royal Soc. 1998; hon. mem. British Biochemical Soc. 2003, Pres. 2006–; Hon. Fellow, Royal Coll. of Pathologists 1998; Hon. DSc (Abertay) 1998, (Strathclyde) 1999, (Debrecen, Hungary) 2004, Hon. MD (Linkoping, Sweden) 2004, (St Andrews) 2005; Anniversary Prize, Fed. of European Biochemical Socs 1977, Colworth Medal 1977, CIBA Medal and Prize 1991, British Biochemical Soc.; Prix Van Gysel, Belgian Royal Acads of Medicine 1992; Bruce Preller Prize, Royal Soc. of Edin. 1993, Louis Jeantet Prize for Medicine 1997, Pfizer Award for Innovative Science in Europe 1999, Sir Hans Krebs Medal, Fed. of European Biological Socs 2001; Bristol-Myers Squibb Distinguished Achievement Award for Metabolic Research 2002, Royal Medal, Royal Soc. of Edin. 2004, Debrecen Award for Molecular Medicine 2004. *Publications:* Control of Enzyme Activity 1976; over 470 articles in scientific journals. *Leisure interests:* bridge, golf, ornithology, picking wild mushrooms, cooking. *Address:* MRC Protein Phosphorylation Unit, School of Life Sciences, MSI/WTB Complex, University of Dundee, Dow Street, Dundee, DD1 5EH (office); Inverbay II, Invergowrie, Dundee, DD2 5DQ, Scotland (home). *Telephone:* (1382) 344238 (office); (1382) 562328 (home). *Fax:* (1382) 223778 (office). *E-mail:* p.cohen@dundee.ac.uk (office). *Website:* www.dundee.ac.uk/biocentre/SLSBDIV5pc.htm (office); www.dundee.ac.uk/lifesciences/mrcppu (office).

COHEN, Preston Scott, MArch; American architect and academic; *Gerald M. McCue Prof. of Architecture and Chair, Department of Architecture, Graduate School of Design, Harvard University;* b. 1961, Asheville, North Carolina; ed Rhode Island School of Design, Harvard Univ. Grad. School of Design; Adjunct Asst Prof. of Architecture, Ohio State Univ. 1989; f. Preston Scott Cohen (architectural firm), Cambridge, Mass 1989; Design Critic in Architecture, Harvard Univ. Grad. School of Design 1989–92, Asst Prof. of Architecture 1992–95, Assoc. Prof. of Architecture 1995–2001, Prof. of Architecture 2002–03, Dir Master of Architecture Degree Programs 2003–08, Gerald M. McCue Prof. of Architecture 2003–, Chair Dept of Architecture 2008–; Visiting Faculty Mem., Rhode Island School of Design 1993–98; Visiting Assoc. Prof. of Architecture, Princeton Univ. 1997; Perloff Visiting Prof., UCLA 2002; Frank Gehry Int. Visiting Chair, Univ. of Toronto 2004; Young Architects Award, Architectural League of New York 1992, Progressive Architecture Award 1998, 2000, First Prize, Herta and Paul Amir Int. Competition 2003, PA Award, Architecture, Tel Aviv Museum of Art 2004, Acad. Award in Architecture, American Acad. of Arts and Letters 2004. *Publications:* Contested Symmetries and Other Predicaments in Architecture 2001, Permutations of Descriptive Geometry 2002. *Address:* Preston Scott Cohen Inc., 675 Massachusetts Avenue, Cambridge, MA 02139 (office); Harvard University Graduate School of Design, 48 Quincy Street, Gund Hall, Cambridge, MA 02138, USA (office). *Telephone:* (617) 441-2110 (office); (617) 495-2591 (office). *Fax:* (617) 441-2113 (office); (617) 495-8916 (office). *E-mail:* scott@pscohen.com (office). *Website:* www.pscohen.com (office); www.gsd.harvard.edu (office).

COHEN, Ra'anan, PhD; Israeli politician; b. 1941, Iraq; m.; four c.; ed Tel-Aviv Univ.; moved to Israel 1951; army service; mem. Knesset 1988–; served on Immigration and Absorption, Labour and Welfare, State Control, Finance, Anti-Drug Abuse, Knesset, Foreign Affairs and Defence Cttees; Chair. Meretz Parl. Group 1992–99; Chair. of House of Reps of Histadrut 1994–98; Sec.-Gen. Labor Party 1998–; mem. Meretz leadership; Sec. Israel Ahat; Chair. Beit Or Aviva (org. for the rehabilitation of drug addicts); Minister of Labor and Social Welfare 2000–2001, Minister without Portfolio 2001–; Chair. Industrial Devt Bank of Israel Ltd. *Address:* The Knesset, Jerusalem, Israel (office); Israel Ahat, Ramat-Gan, Tel-Aviv. *E-mail:* amuta@ehudbarak.co.il (office).

COHEN, Robert; British cellist, conductor and academic; *Professor of Advanced Cello Studies, Conservatorio della Svizzera Italiana di Lugano;* b. 15 June 1959, London; s. of Raymond Cohen and Anthya Rael; m. Rachel Smith 1987; four s.; ed Purcell School and Guildhall School of Music, cello studies with William Pleeth, André Navarra, Jacqueline du Pré and Mstislav Rostropovich; started playing cello aged five; Royal Festival Hall debut (Boccherini Concerto), aged 12; London recital debut, Wigmore Hall, aged 17; Tanglewood Festival, USA 1978; recording debut (Elgar concerto) 1979; concerts USA, Europe and Eastern Europe 1979; since 1980, concerts worldwide with major orchestras and with conductors including Muti, Abbado, Dorati, Sinopoli, Otaka, Mazur, Davis, Marriner and Rattle; Dir Charleston Manor Festival, E Sussex 1989–; regular int. radio broadcasts and many int. TV appearances; plays on the 'Ex-Roser' David Tecchler of Rome cello dated 1723; conductor, various chamber orchestras 1990–, symphony orchestras 1997–; Visiting Prof., RAM 1998–; Prof. of Advanced Cello Studies, Conservatorio della Svizzera Italiana di Lugano 2000–; Fellow, Purcell School for Young Musicians 1992–; Hon. RAM 2009; Winner, Young Concert Artists Int. Competition, New York 1978, Piatigorsky Prize, Tanglewood Festival 1978, Winner, UNESCO Int. Competition, Czechoslovakia 1981. *Recordings include:* Elgar concerto (new Elgar concerto 1993), Dvořák concerto, Tchaikovsky Rococo Variations, Rodrigo Concierto en modo Galante, Beethoven Triple concerto, Grieg sonata, Franck sonata, Virtuoso Cello Music record, Dvořák Complete Piano trios with Cohen Trio, Schubert String Quintet with Amadeus Quartet, Complete Bach solo cello Suites, Howard Blake Diversions, Bliss Concerto 1992, Walton Concerto 1995, Britten Cello Suites 1997, Morton Feldman Concerto 1998, Britten Cello Symphony 1998, Sally Beamish Cello Concerto River 1999, HK Gruber Cello Concerto 2003. *Television:* Bach Sarabandes (BBC), Elgar Cello Concerto (BBC), Beamish Cello Concerto (BBC). *Leisure interests:* photography, computers, playing sports with my children. *Address:* 10C Gateley Road, London SW9 9SZ, England (office); 15 Birchwood Avenue, London, N10 3BE, England (office). *Telephone:* (20) 7737-5994 (office); (20) 8444-1065 (office). *E-mail:* jo@jocarpenter.com (office); office@robertcohen.info (office). *Website:* www.robertcohen.info (office).

COHEN, Sir Ronald, Kt, MBA; British venture capital executive; *Founder and Chairman, The Portland Trust;* b. 1945, Egypt; m. 1st Carol Belmont 1972 (divorced 1975); m. 2nd Claire Enders 1983 (divorced 1986); m. 3rd Sharon Harel-Cohen; two c.; ed Exeter Coll., Univ. of Oxford, Harvard Business School; emigrated to England 1957; worked as man. consultant for McKinsey & Co. in UK and Italy; f. Britain's first venture capital firm Apax Pnrs 1971,

Chair. –2005; helped establish EASDAQ (European tech. stock exchange) 1996; stood as parl. cand. for Liberal Party, Kensington North 1974, European Parl. cand., London West 1979, later served as financial supporter of Labour Party; Chair. HM Treasury's Social Investment Task Force 2000–; Founder and Chair. The Portland Trust (non-profit investment foundation) 2003–; Founder and Chair. Bridges Community Ventures Ltd, Portland Capital LLP; Chair. Comm. on Unclaimed Assets 2005–; Vice-Chair. Ben Gurion Univ. of the Negev; mem. Exec. Cttee IISS; Founder Dir and past Chair. British Venture Capital Asscn; Founder Dir European Venture Capital Asscn, Quoted Companies Alliance; Trustee, British Museum; Hon. Fellow, Exeter Coll.; Jubilee Award for services to Israeli business. *Address:* The Portland Trust, 42 Portland Place, London, W1B 1NB, England (office). *Telephone:* (20) 7182-7780 (office). *Fax:* (20) 7182-7895 (office). *Website:* www.portlandtrust.org (office).

COHEN, Sacha Baron; British actor and screenwriter; b. 13 Oct. 1971, London; pnr Isla Fisher; one d.; ed Christ's Coll., Univ. of Cambridge. *Films include:* Punch 1996, The Jolly Boys' Last Stand 2000, Ali G Indahouse 2002, Spyz 2003, Madagascar (voice) 2005, Borat: Cultural Learnings of America for Make Benefit Glorious Nation of Kazakhstan (Best Actor, Los Angeles Film Critics Asscn, Toronto Film Critics Asscn 2006, London Evening Standard Peter Sellers Award for Best Comedy 2007) 2006, Talladega Nights: The Ballad of Ricky Bobby 2006, Sweeney Todd 2007. *Television includes:* The 11 O'Clock Show 1998–99, Da Ali G Show (series) 2000–04. *Publication:* Borat: Touristic Guidings to Glorious Nation of Kazakhstan (as Borat Sagdiyev) 2007. *Address:* c/o Jimmy Miller, 10th Floor, 9200 Sunset Blvd, Los Angeles, CA 90069; Endeavor Agency, 9601 Wilshire Blvd, 10th Floor, Beverly Hills, CA 90212, USA. *Telephone:* (310) 248-2000 (Endeavor). *Fax:* (310) 248-2020 (Endeavor).

COHEN, Stanley, BA, PhD; American biochemist and academic; *Distinguished Professor Emeritus, School of Medicine, Vanderbilt University;* b. 17 Nov. 1922, Brooklyn, New York; s. of Louis Cohen and Fruma Feitel; m. 1st Olivia Larson 1951; m. 2nd Jan Elizabeth Jordan 1981; three s.; ed Brooklyn and Oberlin Colls., Univ. of Michigan; Teaching Fellow, Dept of Biochemistry, Univ. of Michigan 1946–48; Instructor, Depts of Biochemistry and Pediatrics, Univ. of Colorado School of Medicine, Denver 1948–52; Postdoctoral Fellow, American Cancer Soc., Dept of Radiology, Washington Univ., St Louis 1952–53; Research Prof. of Biochemistry, American Cancer Soc., Nashville 1976–; Asst Prof. of Biochemistry, Vanderbilt Univ. School of Medicine, Nashville 1959–62, Assoc. Prof. 1962–67, Prof. 1967–86, Distinguished Prof. 1986–2000, Distinguished Prof. Emer. 2000–; mem. Editorial Bds Excerpta Medica, Abstracts of Human Developmental Biology, Journal of Cellular Physiology; mem. NAS, American Soc. of Biological Chemists, Int. Inst. of Embryology, American Acad. of Arts and Sciences; Hon. DSc (Chicago) 1985; Nobel Prize for Physiology and Medicine 1986, and many other prizes and awards. *Leisure interests:* camping, tennis. *Address:* 11306 East Limberlost Road, Tucson, AZ 85749 (home); Department of Biochemistry, Vanderbilt University School of Medicine, 607 Light Hall, Nashville, TN 37232, USA (office). *Telephone:* (615) 322-3318 (office). *Fax:* (615) 322-4349 (office). *Website:* medschool.mc.vanderbilt.edu/biochemistry (office).

COHEN, Stanley, MD; American pathologist; b. 4 June 1937, New York; s. of Herman Joseph Cohen and Eva Lapidus; m. Marion Doris Cantor 1959; two s. one d.; ed Stuyvesant High School, Columbia Coll. and Columbia Univ. Coll. of Physicians and Surgeons; Internship and Residency, Albert Einstein Medical Center and Harvard-Mass. Gen. 1962–64; Instructor, Dept of Pathology, New York Univ. Medical Center 1965–66; Captain, MC, USA, Walter Reed Inst. of Research 1966–68; Assoc. Prof., State Univ. of New York at Buffalo 1968–72, Assoc. Dir, Center for Immunology 1972–74, Prof. of Pathology 1972–74; Assoc. Chair. Dept of Pathology, Univ. of Conn. Health Center 1976–80, Prof. of Pathology 1974–87; Prof., Chair. Bd Hahnemann Univ., Philadelphia 1987–94; Chair. Dept of Pathology, Hahnemann Medical Center 1986–94; Prof., Chair. Univ. Medicine and Dentistry, NJ Medical School 1994; Vice-Pres. American Soc. for Investigative Pathology; Treasurer, Fed. of Socs of Experimental Biology; Kinne Award 1954; Borden Award 1961; Parke-Davis Award in Experimental Pathology 1977; Outstanding Investigator Award, Nat. Cancer Inst. 1986; Co-Chair. Int. Lymphokine Workshop 1979, 1982 and 1984. *Publications:* 200 scientific articles on cellular immunity; ed. 7 books including Mechanisms of Cell-Medicated Immunity 1977, Mechanisms of Immunopathology 1979, The Biology of the Lymphokines 1979, Interleukins, Lymphokines and Cytokines 1983, Molecular Basis of Lymphatic Action 1986, The Role of Lymphatics in the Immune Response 1989. *Leisure interests:* music, photography, karate. *Address:* c/o Department of Pathology and Laborator Medicine, UMDNJ-New Jersey Medical School, 185 South Orange Avenue, Newark, NJ 07103 (office); 79 Ettl Circle, Princeton, NJ 08540-2334, USA (home). *Telephone:* (973) 972-4520 (office). *Fax:* (973) 972-5909 (office). *E-mail:* cohenst@umdnj.com (office).

COHEN, Stanley Norman, BS, MD; American physician, geneticist and academic; *Professor and Principal Investigator, Stanley N. Cohen Laboratory, Stanford University;* b. 17 Feb. 1935, Perth Amboy, NJ; s. of Bernard Cohen and Ida Cohen (née Stolz); m. Joanna Lucy Wolter 1961; one s. one d.; ed Rutgers Univ. and Univ. of Pennsylvania School of Medicine; intern, Mount Sinai Hosp., New York 1960–61; Asst Resident in Medicine, Univ. Hosp., Ann Arbor, Mich. 1961–62; Clinical Assoc., Arthritis and Rheumatism Branch, Nat. Inst. of Arthritis and Metabolic Diseases 1962–64; Sr Resident in Medicine, Duke Univ. Hosp., Durham, NC 1964–65; American Cancer Soc. Postdoctoral Research Fellow, Dept of Molecular Biology and Dept of Developmental Biology and Cancer, Albert Einstein Coll. of Medicine, Bronx, New York 1965–67, Asst Prof. 1967–68; Asst Prof. of Medicine, Stanford Univ. School of Medicine 1968–71, Head, Div. of Clinical Pharmacology 1969–78, Assoc. Prof. of Medicine 1971–75, Prof. of Genetics 1977 and Prof. of Medicine 1975–, Chair. Dept of Genetics 1978–86, K.-T. Li Prof. of Genetics 1993–; mem. of various scientific orgs including NAS; Fellow, American Acad. of Arts and Sciences (Chair. Genetics Section 1988–91), American Acad. of Microbiology, AAAS; Trustee Univ. of Pennsylvania 1997–2002; Hon. ScD (Rutgers Univ.) 1994, (Univ. of Pennsylvania) 1995; Baldouin Lucke Research Award, Univ. of Pa School of Medicine 1960, Research Career Devt Award, US Public Health Service 1969, Burroughs Wellcome Scholar Award 1970, Mattia Award, Roche Inst. for Molecular Biology 1977, Harvey Soc. Lecturer 1979, Calif. Inventor of the Year Award 1980, Wolf Prize in Medicine 1981, Kinyoun Lecturer 1981, Marvin J. Johnson Award, ACS 1981, Albert Lasker Basic Medical Research Award 1980, Distinguished Grad. Award Univ. of Pa School of Medicine 1986, Distinguished Service Award, Miami Winter Symposium 1986, Nat. Medal of Science 1988, Cetus Award 1988, LVMH Institut de la Vie Prize 1988, City of Medicine Award 1988, Nat. Biotechnology Award 1989, Nat. Medal of Tech. 1989, ACS Special Award 1992, Helmut Horten Research Award 1993; Distinguished Grad. Award, Rutgers Univ. 1994, Lemelson-MIT Prize 1996, Albany Medical Center Prize in Medicine and Biomedical Research (jtly) 2004, Shaw Prize in Life Science and Medicine 2004; Guggenheim Fellow 1975, Josiah Macy Jr Foundation Faculty Scholar 1975–76; Nat. Inventors Hall of Fame 2001, Economist Innovation Award 2005. *Address:* Stanley N. Cohen Laboratory, Stanford University Medical Center, Lane Medical Building, L-312, Stanford, CA 94305 (office); Department of Genetics, School of Medicine, Stanford University, Stanford, CA 94305-5120, USA (office). *Telephone:* (650) 723-5315 (office). *Fax:* (650) 725-1536 (office). *E-mail:* sncohen@stanford.edu (office). *Website:* sncohenlab.stanford.edu (office).

COHEN, Sydney, CBE, MD, PhD, FRS, FRCPath; British professor of medicine; *Professor Emeritus of Chemical Pathology, Guy's Hospital Medical School;* b. 18 Sept. 1921, Johannesburg, S. Africa; s. of Morris Cohen and Pauline Cohen; m. 1st June Bernice Adler 1950 (died 1999); one s. one d.; m. 2nd Deirdre Maureen Ann Boyd 1999; ed King Edward VII School, Witwatersrand Univ., Johannesburg, Univ. of London; with Emergency Medical Service, UK 1944–46; Lecturer, Dept of Physiology, Univ. of Witwatersrand 1947–53; mem. Scientific Staff, Nat. Inst. for Medical Research, London 1954–60; Reader, Dept of Immunology, St Mary's Hosp., London 1960–65; Prof. of Chemical Pathology, Guy's Hosp. Medical School, London 1965–86, now Prof. Emer.; mem. MRC 1974–76, Chair. Tropical Medicine Research Bd 1974–76, Royal Soc. Assessor 1983–85; Chair. WHO Scientific group on Immunity to Malaria 1976–81; mem. Council, Royal Soc. 1981–83; Nuffield Dominion Fellow in Medicine 1954; Founding Fellow, Royal Coll. of Pathologists 1964; Hon. DSc (Witwatersrand) 1987. *Publications:* papers and books on immunology and parasitic infections. *Leisure interests:* golf, gardening, forestry. *Address:* 8 Gibson Place, St Andrews, KY16 9JE, Scotland (home); Hafodfraith, Llangurig, SY18 6QG, Wales (home). *Telephone:* (1334) 476568 (home).

COHEN, William Sebastian, BA, LLB; American consultant, fmr politician and fmr government official; *Chairman and CEO, Cohen Group;* b. 28 Aug. 1940, Bangor, Me; s. of Reuben Cohen and Clara Cohen (née Hartley); two s.; ed Bangor High School, Bowdoin Coll., Boston Univ. Law School; admitted to Maine Bar, Mass. Bar, DC Bar; Pnr, Prairie, Cohen, Lynch, Weatherbee and Kobritz, Bangor 1966–72; Asst Co. Attorney, Penobscot Co., Me 1968–70, instructor, Univ. of Maine at Orono 1968–72; mem. Bd of Overseers, Bowdoin Coll. 1973–85; City Councillor, Bangor 1969–72, Mayor of Bangor 1971–72; mem. US House of Reps, Washington, DC 1972–78; Senator from Maine 1979–96; US Sec. of Defense 1997–2001; Founder and CEO The Cohen Group (consulting firm), Washington, DC 2001–; Trustee and Counselor, Center Strategic and Int. Studies 2001–; Fellow of John F. Kennedy Inst. of Politics, Harvard Univ. 1972; mem. Bd of Dirs AIG –2006; Distinguished Public Service, Boston Univ. Alumni Asscn 1976, L. Mendel Rivers Award, Non-Commissioned Officers' Asscn 1983, Pres.'s Award, New England Asscn of School Superintendents 1984, Silver Anniversary Award, Nat. Collegiate Athletic Asscn 1987, Nat. Asscn Basketball Coaches, US 1987, numerous other awards. *Publications:* Of Sons and Seasons 1978, Roll Call 1981, Getting the Most Out of Washington 1982 (with Prof. Kenneth Lasson), The Double Man 1985 (with Senator Gary Hart), A Baker's Nickel 1986, Men of Zeal (with Senator George Mitchell) 1988, One-Eyed Kings 1991, Murder in the Senate (with Thomas B. Allen) 1993. *Leisure interests:* poetry, sport. *Address:* The Cohen Group, 1200 19th Street, NW, Suite 400, Washington, DC 20036, USA (office). *Telephone:* (202) 689-7900 (office). *Fax:* (202) 689-7910 (office). *E-mail:* wsc@cohengroup.net (office). *Website:* www.cohengroup.net (office).

COHEN, Yitzhak; Israeli politician; b. 2 Dec. 1951; m.; ten c.; army service; fmr Deputy Mayor of Ashkelon and Sec.-Gen. of El Hama'ayan (Shas-affiliated educational inst.); mem. Knesset (Parl.) 1996–; mem. of Labour and Social Affairs and Finance Cttees; Minister of Religious Affairs 1999–2000; Deputy Minister of Finance 2001–03; Minister without Portfolio (responsible for religious councils) 2006–. *Address:* The Knesset, HaKiryah, Jerusalem, 91950, Israel (office). *Telephone:* (2) 5311170 (office). *Fax:* (2) 6535469 (office).

COHEN-TANNOUDJI, Claude Nessim, PhD; French academic; b. 1 April 1933, Constantine; s. of Abraham Cohen-Tannoudji and Sarah Sebbah; m. Jacqueline Veyrat 1958; two s. one d.; ed Ecole Normale Supérieure; Research Assoc., CNRS 1962–64; Maître de Conférences, then Prof., Faculté des Sciences, Paris 1964–73; Prof., Collège de France 1973–2004; mem. Acad. des Sciences; Foreign Assoc. NAS; Fellow, American Physical Soc.; Foreign Hon. mem. American Acad. of Arts and Sciences, Accademia dei Lincei, Russian Acad. of Sciences, Nat. Acad. of Sciences, Pontifical Acad. of Sciences of USA, Indian Nat. Acad. of Sciences, Brazilian Acad. of Sciences; Commdr Ordre nat. du Mérite, Commdr Officier Légion d'honneur; Dr hc (Uppsala,

Jerusalem, Brussels, Liege, Tel Aviv, Sussex); Ampère Prize, Acad. des Sciences 1980, Lilienfeld Prize, American Physical Soc., Charles Townes Award, Optical Soc. of America 1993; Harvey Prize, Technion, Haifa, CNRS Gold Medal 1996, Nobel Prize for Physics 1997;. *Publications:* in collaboration: Optique et Electronique Quantiques 1965, Mécanique Quantique (two vols) 1973, Photons et Atomes, Introduction à l'Electrodynamique Quantique 1987, Processus d'Interaction entre Photons et Atomes 1988, Atoms in Electromagnetic Fields 1994, Lévy Statistics and Laser Cooling. How Rare Events Bring Atoms to Rest 2001. *Leisure interest:* music. *Address:* Laboratoire Kastler Brossel, 24 rue Lhomond, 75231 Paris Cedex 05 (office); 38 rue des Cordelières, 75013 Paris, France (home). *Telephone:* 1-47-07-77-83 (office); 1-45-35-02-18 (home). *Fax:* 1-44-32-34-34 (office). *E-mail:* cct@lkb.ens.fr (office).

COHN, Gary D.; American financial services industry executive; *President and COO, Goldman Sachs Group;* b. 27 Aug. 1960, Cleveland; m. Lisa Pevaroff Cohn; ed American Univ.; has served in various sr man. positions with Goldman Sachs Group including Head of Commodities Div. 1996–99, managed Fixed Income, Currency and Commodities (FICC) macro businesses 1999–2002, Co-COO FICC 2002, Co-Head FICC 2002–, Co-Head Equities 2003–, Co-Head Global Securities 2004–06, Pres. and COO 2006–, mem. Bd of Dirs; mem. Bd of Dirs New York Mercantile Exchange 1998–2000; mem. Treasury Borrowing Advisory Cttee, Bond Market Asscn; Trustee Gilmour Acad., Cleveland, New York Univ. (NYU) Child Study Center, NYU Hospital, NYU Medical School, Harlem Children's Zone, Columbia Grammar and Preparatory School, American Univ.; est. Gary D. Cohn Endowed Research Professorship in Finance, American Univ.; Effecting Change Award, 100 Women in Hedge Funds 2005. *Address:* Goldman Sachs Group, 85 Broad Street, New York, NY 10004, USA (office). *Telephone:* (212) 902-1000 (office). *Fax:* (212) 902-3000 (office). *Website:* www.goldmansachs.com (office).

COHN, Mildred, MA, PhD; American professor of biochemistry and biophysics; *Benjamin Rush Professor Emerita, University of Pennsylvania;* b. 12 July 1913, New York City; d. of Isidore M. Cohn and Bertha Klein; m. Henry Primakoff 1938 (deceased); one s. two d.; ed Hunter Coll. and Columbia Univ., New York; Cornell Univ. Medical Coll., New York 1938–46; Washington Univ. Medical School, St Louis, Mo. 1946–60; Prof. of Biophysics and Biophysical Chem., Univ. of Pa School of Medicine 1961–75, Prof. of Biochemistry and Biophysics 1975–82; Pres. American Soc. of Biology and Chem. 1978; Benjamin Rush Prof. of Physiological Chem. 1978–82, Benjamin Rush Prof. Emer. 1982–; Visiting Prof., Univ. of California, Berkeley 1981, Johns Hopkins Univ. Medical School 1982–91; Career Investigator, American Heart Asscn 1964–78; Sr mem. Inst. for Cancer Research 1982–85; mem. Bd Journal of Biological Chem. (first woman), Ed. 1958–63, 1968–73; mem. American Acad. of Arts and Sciences, NAS, American Philosophical Soc., Vice-Pres. 1944–2000; Hon. ScD (Women's Medical Coll. of Pennsylvania) 1966, (Radcliffe Coll.) 1978, (Washington Univ.) 1981, (Brandeis, Hunter Coll., Univ. of Pennsylvania) 1984, (N Carolina) 1985, (Miami) 1990, Hon. PhD (Weizmann Inst. of Science) 1988; Cresson Medal, Franklin Inst. 1975, ACS Garvan Medal 1963, Nat. Medal for Science 1982, Mack Award, Ohio State Univ. 1985, Chandler Medal, Columbia Univ. 1986, Distinguished Service Award, Coll. of Physicians, Phila 1987, ACS (Maryland Section) Remsen Award 1988, Pennsylvania Gov.'s Award for Excellence in Science 1993, Stein-Moore Award, Protein Soc. 1997, Oesper Award, Univ. of Cincinnati 2000, and several other awards. *Achievements include:* performed with the Denishawn Dancers 1929–31. *Publications:* more than 160 articles in professional journals. *Leisure interests:* hiking, writing, history of science. *Address:* Department of Biochemistry and Biophysics, University of Pennsylvania School of Medicine, 242 Anat-Chem Philadelphia, PA 19104-6059 (office); 226 W Rittenhouse Square #1806, Philadelphia, PA 19103, USA (home). *Telephone:* (215) 898-8404 (office). *Fax:* (215) 898-4217 (office).

COHN-BENDIT, (Marc) Daniel; French/German politician; *Co-President, European Greens–European Free Alliance, European Parliament;* b. 4 April 1945, Montauban, Tarn-et-Garonne, France; s. of Erich Cohn-Bendit and Herta Cohn-Bendit (née David); m. Ingrid Voigt 1997; one c.; ed Odenwaldschule, Heppenheim, Germany, Univ. de Paris X-Nanterre; moved to Germany 1958; student movt's spokesman, Paris 1968; deported from France May 1968; nursery school teacher, Frankfurt 1968–73; co-f. German students' group Revolutionärer Kampf, Bockenheim 1970; co-f. cultural magazine Pflasterstrand 1970, Ed.-in-Chief 1978–84; Deputy Mayor of Frankfurt 1989–97; mem. European Parl. (Greens) 1994–99, (Ecology Greens) 1999–2004, (Alliance 90/Greens) 2004–, Vice-Pres. Parl. Comm. on Culture, Youth, Media and Sport 1994–95, mem. Foreign Affairs Comm, Public Freedoms Comm., N Africa Comm., Deputy mem. Budget Comm., Rapporteur on regional co-operation between states of Fmr Yugoslavia 1996, Rapporteur for Foreign Affairs Parl. Comm. on Jt EU-Mediterranean Accord, mem. Steering Cttee SOS Europe 1997, Chair. Del. to Jt EU-Turkey Parl. Comm. 1999–2002, Pres. Green Parl. Group 2001–04, Co-Pres. European Greens–European Free Alliance 2004–; Adviser to Joschka Fischer, Vice-Chancellor and Minister of Foreign Affairs 1998; mem. German Green Party 1984, French Green Party 1998–; co-f. Forum Européen de Prévention Active des Conflicts (Fepac) 1994; presenter monthly literary programme Literaturclub, Swiss German TV 1995; f. monthly Eurospeed 1997; Dr hc (Catholic Univ. of Tilburg, Netherlands) 1997; Trombinoscope 'Political Discovery' Award 1998. *Documentary films:* (writer) A chacun son allemagne 1976, Nous l'avons tant aimée, la révolution (four films) 1983, C'est la vie (full-length film) 1990, Angst im Rüchen hat jeder von uns 1992. *Publications include:* Obsolete Communism: The Left-Wing Alternative (co-author) 1968, La Révolte étudiante 1968, Le Grand bazar 1976, Nous l'avons tant aimée, la révolution 1987; co-author numerous other books. *Leisure interest:* football. *Address:* European Parliament, Bâtiment Altiero Spinelli 08G201, 60 rue Wiertz/Wiertzstraat 60, 1047 Brussels, Belgium (office). *Telephone:* (2) 284-54-98 (office). *Fax:* (2) 284-94-98 (office). *Website:* www.europarl.europa.eu (office); www.cohn-bendit.de.

COHN-SHERBOK, Dan, MLitt, PhD, DD, MAHL; American rabbi and academic; *Professor of Judaism and Director, Centre for the Study of the World's Religions, University of Wales at Lampeter;* b. 1 Feb. 1945, Denver, Colo; s. of Bernard Sherbok and Ruth Sherbok; m. Lavinia C. Heath 1976; ed Williams Coll., Hebrew Union Coll. and Univ. of Cambridge, UK; rabbi in USA, UK, Australia and South Africa 1968–74; Chaplain, Colorado State House of Reps 1971; Univ. Lecturer in Theology, Univ. of Kent, UK 1975–97, Dir Centre for Study of Religion and Society 1982–90; Visiting Prof. of Judaism, Univ. of Wales at Lampeter 1995–97, Prof. 1997–, Dir Centre for the Study of the World's Religions 2003–; Visiting Prof., Univ. of Essex, UK 1993–94, Middx Univ. 1994–, UK, Univ. of St Andrews, UK 1995–96, St Andrew's Biblical Theological Coll., Moscow, Russia 1996, Univ. of Wales, Bangor, Univ. of Vilnius, Lithuania 1999, Univ. of Durham, UK 2002; Visiting Scholar, Sarum Coll. 2006–; Fellow, Hebrew Union Coll., Acad. of Jewish Philosophy; Hon. DD (Hebrew Union Coll., Jewish Inst. of Religion) 1995. *Publications:* The Jewish Heritage 1988, The Crucified Jew 1992, The Jewish Faith 1993, Not a Nice Job for a Nice Jewish Boy 1993, Judaism and Other Faiths 1994, The Future of Judaism 1994, The American Jew 1994, Jewish and Christian Mysticism 1994, Modern Judaism 1995, Jewish Mysticism 1995, The Hebrew Bible 1996, Biblical Hebrew for Beginners 1996, The Liberation Debate 1996, Atlas of Jewish History 1996, Medieval Jewish Philosophy 1996, Fifty Key Jewish Thinkers 1996, The Jewish Messiah 1997, After Noah: Animals and the Liberation of Theology 1997, Understanding the Holocaust 1999, Jews, Christians and Religious Pluralism 1999, Messianic Judaism 2000, Interfaith Theology 2001, Holocaust Theology: A Reader 2001, Anti-Semitism 2002, Judaism: History, Belief, Practice 2003, The Vision of Judaism 2004, The Dictionary of Jewish Biography 2005, Pursuing the Dream: Jewish Christian Dialogue 2005, The Paradox of Antisemitism 2006, Politics of Apocalypse 2006. *Leisure interests:* keeping cats, walking, drawing cartoons. *Address:* Department of Theology and Religious Studies, University of Wales, Lampeter, Ceredigion, SA48 7ED, Wales (office); The Old Coach House, Bwlchllan, SA48 7ED, Wales (home). *Telephone:* (1570) 424968 (office); (1570) 424968 (home). *Fax:* (1570) 423641 (office). *E-mail:* d.cohn-sherbok@lamp.ac.uk (office); cohn-sherbok@lamp.ac.uk (home). *Website:* www.lamp.ac.uk/trs/Index.htm (office); www.lamp.ac.uk/trs/Staff_Home_Pages/Dan.htm (office); www.cohn-sherbok.co.uk (home).

COHON, Jared L., BS, PhD; American university administrator and academic; *President, Carnegie Mellon University;* ed Univ. of Pennsylvania, Massachusetts Inst. of Tech.; Faculty mem. in Dept of Geography and Environmental Eng, Johns Hopkins Univ. 1973–92, later Asst and Assoc. Dean of Eng and Vice-Provost for Research; Prof. of Environmental Systems Analysis and Dean of School of Forestry and Environmental Studies, Yale Univ. 1992–97; Pres. Carnegie Mellon Univ. 1997–; Legis. Asst for Energy and the Environment to the late Daniel Patrick Moynihan, US Senator from NY 1977–78; mem. Nuclear Waste Tech. Review Bd 1995– (Chair. 1997–2002), Homeland Security Advisory Council 2002– (Chair. Sr Advisory Cttee on Academia and Policy Research); mem. Bd of Dirs Mellon Financial Corpn, American Standard, Inc.; serves on bds of several nat. and local non-profit orgs, including Health Effects Inst., Heinz Center for Science, Econs and the Environment, Council on Competitiveness, Carnegie Museums of Pittsburgh, Pittsburgh Cultural Trust, Urban League of Pittsburgh, Allegheny Conf. on Community Devt; shared Pittsburgh Magazine's 'Pittsburgher of the Year'. *Publications:* Multiobjective Programming and Planning 1978 (re-issued as a Classic of Operations Research 2004); author, co-author or editor of more than 80 professional publs on environmental and water resource systems analysis. *Address:* Office of the President, Carnegie Mellon University, 5000 Forbes Avenue, Pittsburgh, PA 15213, USA (office). *Telephone:* (412) 268-2201 (office). *E-mail:* jaredcohon@cmu.edu (office). *Website:* www.cmu.edu (office).

COINTAT, Michel; French politician and agronomist; b. 13 April 1921, Paris; s. of Lucien Cointat and Marie-Louise Adam; m. Simone Dubois 1942; two s.; ed Ecole Nat. des Eaux et Forêts; insp. of water and forests, Uzès, Gard 1943–49; insp. of forests, Haute-Marne 1950–58; Dir Gen. Soc. for Devt of Waste Ground and Scrub Lands of the East 1948–61, Pres. 1961–71; Dir du Cabinet, Ministry of Agriculture 1961–62, Dir Gen. of Production and Supply 1962–67; Pres. Special Agricultural Cttee to EEC 1965; Minister of Agric. 1971–72, of External Trade 1980–81; Deputy RPR (fmrly Union Démocratique pour la République) for Ille-et-Vilaine 1967–71, 1981–93; mem. European Parl. 1968–71, 1974–79; Mayor of Fougères 1971–83; Pres. Financial Comm. in Regional Council of Brittany; Pres. Special Comm. to examine proposed land law; Dir Editions Ufap 1975–83; Questeur (Admin. Official), Assemblée Nat. 1988–90; Pres. Paneurope France 1990–92; Pres. Echanges et consultations techniques internationaux 1997–; mem. Acad. d'Agric. de France 1987–, Pres. 1996–; mem. Acad. de l'art de vivre 1994–, Pres. 2000–; Commdr, Légion d'honneur, Officier, Ordre nat. du Mérite, Commdr du Mérite agricole, Officier des Palmes académiques, Chevalier, Economie nationale, Grand Officier du Mérite (FRG), Grand Officier, Ordre de Victoria, Commdr du Mérite Italien, Grand Officier, Ordre de la Haute-Volta, Grand Officier du Rio Branco, Mérite Européen. *Publications:* about 500 articles on agric., forestry, fishing and related subjects; collections of poems: Souvenirs du temps perdu 1957, Poèmes à Clio 1965, Les heures orangées 1974, les moments inutiles 1983, le neveu de Jules Ferry: Abel 1987, 1789: Sept députés bretons à Versailles 1988, Souvenirs de l'Uzège 1992, Poèmes en fleurs 1996, Fleurs en fêtes 1997, Rivarol 2001, Les couloirs de l'Europe 2001, Histoires de fleurs 2003, La Moyen Age moderne 2004. *Address:* 89 rue du Faubourg Saint-Denis, 75010 Paris, France (home).

ČOLAK, Bariša; Bosnia and Herzegovina politician; *Minister of Justice;* b. 1 Jan. 1956, Široki Brijeg; ed Univ. of Mostar; Judge, Magistrates Court, Široki Brijeg 1988–93; Deputy Minister of Justice 1993–96; Chair. local govt 1996–99; mem. Parl., Fed. of Bosnia and Herzegovina 2001–02, Minister of Justice 1999–2001, 2007–; Vice-Pres. and Minister of Security, Bosnia and Herzegovina 2003–07; mem. Croatian Democratic Union of Bosnia and Herzegovina (Hrvatska Demokratska Zajednica Bosne i Hercegovine). *Address:* Ministry of Justice, 71000 Sarajevo, trg Bosne i Hercegovine 1, Bosnia and Herzegovina (office). *Telephone:* (33) 223501 (office). *Fax:* (33) 223504 (office). *E-mail:* kontakt@mpr.gov.ba (office). *Website:* www.mpr.gov.ba (office).

COLANINNO, Roberto; Italian business executive; *Chairman and CEO, Piaggio & Co SpA;* b. 16 Aug. 1943, Mantua; began career with Fiamm SpA, fmr Chief Exec.; f. jtly Sogefi SpA (finance co.) 1981; mem. Bd several regional and nat. banks in Italy including Mediobanco, Efibanca SpA, Gruppo Bancario Capitalia; CEO Olivetti & Co. 1996–2001; Chair. and CEO Telecom Italia 1999–2001, also Chair. Telecom Italia Mobile SpA 1999–2001; f. Omniaholding SpA 1998; Chair. IMMSI 2002–; Chair. and CEO Piaggio & Co. SpA 2006–; mem. Man. Cttee and Nat. Advisory Cttee Confindustria 1997–2002; Hon. DEcon (Lecce) 2001; Cavaliere del Lavoro. *Address:* Piaggio Group, Via Vivaio 6, 20122 Milan, Italy (office). *Website:* www.piaggiogroup.com (office).

COLARIČ, Jože, BEcons; Slovenian business executive; *President of the Management Board and CEO, KrKa d.d.;* b. 27 Aug. 1955, Brežice; ed Faculty of Econs, Univ. of Ljubljana; joined KrKa d.d. 1982, Head of Foreign Exchange Trade Dept and later Asst Dir 1982–89, Head of Export Service, Export-Import Div. 1989–91, Deputy Dir 1991–93, Deputy to CEO for Marketing and Finance 1993–97, mem. Man. Bd 1997–, Deputy Pres. 1998–2004, Pres. of Man. Bd and CEO 2005–. *Address:* KrKa d.d., Šmarješka cesto 6, 8501 Novo Mesto, Slovenia (office). *Telephone:* (7) 3312111 (office). *Fax:* (7) 3321537 (office). *E-mail:* info@krka.biz (office). *Website:* www.krka.si (office).

COLBORN, Theodora Emily Decker (Theo), BS, MA, PhD; American zoologist and academic; *Professor Emeritus of Zoology, University of Florida;* ed Western State Coll. of Colorado, Rutgers Univ., Univ. of Wisconsin; Congressional Fellow 1985–86, Science Analyst, Office of Tech. Assessment, US Congress, Washington, DC 1986–87; Assoc., Conservation Foundation, Washington, DC 1987–88, Consultant, Environmental Health Analysis 1987–90; Sr Fellow, World Wildlife Fund 1988–93 (on sabbatical 1990–93); Sr Fellow, W. Alton Jones Foundation 1990–93; Sr Scientist and Dir Wildlife and Contaminants Program, World Wildlife Fund 1993–2003; Prof. of Zoology, Univ. of Florida, Gainesville 2004–07, Prof. Emer. 2008–; Founder and Pres. The Endocrine Disruption Exchange, Paonia, Colo 2003–08; has served on numerous advisory panels, including US Environmental Protection Agency (EPA) Science Advisory Bd, Ecosystem Health Cttee of Int. Jt Comm. of US and Canada, Science Man. Cttee of Toxic Substances Research Initiative of Canada, EPA Endocrine Disruptor Screening and Testing Advisory Cttee, EPA Endocrine Disruption Methods and Validation Sub-cttee; mem. Bd of Dirs Rachel Carson Council 2006–; mem. Bd of Scientific Advisors, Children's Health Environmental Coalition 2006–; est. and directed Wildlife and Contaminants Program at World Wildlife Fund US; Nat. Water Alliance Award for Excellence in Protecting the Nation's Aquatic Resources 1991, Pew Fellows Award 1993–96, Nat. Conservation Achievement Award in Science, Nat. Wildlife Fed. 1994, Rachel Carson Award, Chatham Coll. 1997, Norwegian Int. Rachel Carson Prize 1999, UNEP Women Leadership for the Environment Award 1997, State of the World Forum, Mikhail Gorbachev, Change Makers Award 1997, Audubon Magazine: A Century of Conservation, 100 Champions of Conservation 1998, Int. Blue Planet Prize, Asahi Glass Foundation, Japan 2000, Rachel Carson Award, Soc. of Toxicology and Environmental Chem. 2003, Rachel Carson Award, Center for Science in the Public Interest 2004, Beyond Pesticides Dragonfly Award 2006, Woman on the Forefront: Leadership and Integrity in Science 2007, Lifetime Achievement Award, Nat. Council for Science and the Environment 2007, Time magazine Global Environmental Heroes Award 2007. *Achievements include:* provided scientific guidance for book, *Great Lakes, Great Legacy?* in collaboration with Inst. for Research and Public Policy, Ottawa, Canada at request of Canada/US Int. Jt Comm. 1990. *Publications:* Chemically Induced Alterations in Sexual and Functional Development: The Wildlife/Human Connection (ed.) 1992, Our Stolen Future: How We Are Threatening Our Fertility, Intelligence and Survival (co-author) 1996; numerous scientific papers in professional journals on the consequences of prenatal exposure to synthetic chemicals by the developing embryo and foetus in wildlife, lab. animals and humans. *Address:* PO Box 1253, 121 Main Avenue Paonia, CO 81428, USA; University of Florida, PO Box 118525, Gainesville, FL 32611-8525 (office); The Endocrine Disruption Exchange, PO Box 1407, Paonia, CO 81428 (office). *Telephone:* (352) 392-1107 (Gainesville) (office); (970) 527-4082 (TEDX) (office); (970) 527-6548. *Fax:* (970) 527-6548. *E-mail:* colborn@tds.net (office). *Website:* www.endocrinedisruption.org (office); www.ourstolenfuture.org (office).

COLCLEUGH, D. W. (Dave), PhD; Canadian business executive (retd) and academic; *Leadership Development Professor, Faculty of Applied Science and Engineering, University of Toronto;* b. Fort Erie, Ont.; m.; two c.; ed Univ. of Toronto and Univ. of Cambridge, UK; research engineer, DuPont Canada, Kingston 1963–68, polymer tech. supervisor, Fibres Div. 1968–73, tech. supt. Explosives Div., North Bay 1973–75, Tech. and Planning Man., Explosives Div., Montréal 1975–79, Rubber Industry Man., Tyre and Industrial Div. 1979–82, Man. of Gen. Products, Mississauga 1982–85, Prin. Consultant, Corp. Planning Div., Wilmington April–Dec. 1985, Gen. Man. of Finishes, Toronto 1985–89, Dir of Corp. Planning and Devt April–Nov. 1989, Vice-Pres. of Mfg and Eng 1989–92, Sr Vice-Pres. with responsibility for Fibres and Intermediates, Eng Polymers Units and Mfg and Eng 1992–94; Vice-Pres.,

Gen. Man. of Nylon, DuPont Asia-Pacific 1994–95, Pres. 1995–97; Pres. and CEO DuPont Canada Inc. 1997–2003, Chair of Bd 1998–2003 (retd); Leadership Development Professor, Faculty of Applied Science and Eng, Univ. of Toronto 2006–; mem. Bd of Dirs Let's Talk Science (LTS) 2003–, Chair. 2005–; mem. Bd of Dirs ZENON Environmental Inc. 2000–, Hudson's Bay Co., Canadian Chemicals Producers Asscn, Textiles Human Resources Council, Art Gallery of Mississauga; mem. Dean's Advisory Bd Univ. of Toronto; . *Address:* Faculty of Applied Science and Engineering, University of Toronto, 35 St. George Street, Toronto, ON M5S 1A4, Canada (office). *Telephone:* (416) 978-8605 (office). *E-mail:* colcleugh333@rogers.com (office). *Website:* www.undergrad.engineering.utoronto.ca/home.htm (office).

COLDITZ, Graham A., BSc (Med.), MBBS, MPH, DrPH, MD; Australian epidemiologist and academic; *Niess-Gain Professor in Medicine, Department of Surgery, School of Medicine, Washington University;* b. 1 Nov. 1954, Sydney; ed Univ. of Queensland and Harvard School of Public Health, Boston, Mass, USA; Instructor in Medicine, Harvard Medical School 1986–88, Asst Prof. of Medicine 1988–91, Assoc. Prof. 1991–98, Prof. 1998–2006, Prof. of Epidemiology, Grad. School of Public Health 1998–2006, Program Leader, Cancer Epidemiology, Dana-Farber/Harvard Cancer Center, Dir of Educ., Harvard Center for Cancer Prevention; Niess-Gain Prof. in Medicine, Dept of Surgery, Washington Univ. School of Medicine, St Louis 2006–, also Assoc. Dir for Prevention and Control, Alvin J. Siteman Cancer Center; Raine Visiting Prof., Univ. of Western Australia 1997; Adjunct Prof., Univ. of Queensland School of Population Health 2001–; fmr Dir American Cancer Soc. New England Div., Inc.; mem. Inst. of Medicine 2006–; mem. Advisory Cttee on Research, Alberta Cancer Bd 2000–; Fellow, Australian Faculty of Public Health Medicine, Royal Australian Coll. of Physicians 1990; Frank Knox Memorial Fellowship, Harvard Univ. 1981–83, Faculty Research Award, American Cancer Soc. 1991–96, ACS Clinical Research Professorship Award 2003, DeWitt S. Goodman Lectureship, American Asscn for Cancer Research 2003. *Publications:* more than 580 publs in medical journals. *Address:* Washington University School of Medicine, 660 South Euclid Ave., Campus Box 8100, St Louis, MO 63108, USA (office). *Telephone:* (314) 454-7940 (office). *E-mail:* colditzg@wustl.edu (office). *Website:* medschool.wustl.edu (office).

COLE, Natalie Maria, BA; American singer; b. 6 Feb. 1950, Los Angeles; d. of Nathaniel Adam Cole (Nat 'King' Cole) and Maria Hawkins; m. 1st Marvin J. Yancy 1976 (divorced); m. 2nd Andre Fisher (divorced); ed Univ. of Massachusetts; recordings of albums and singles 1975–; recipient of eight Grammys and other music awards. *Albums include:* Inseparable 1975, Natalie 1976, Unpredictable 1977, Thankful 1977, Live 1978, I Love You So 1979, We're The Best Of Friends 1979, Don't Look Back 1980, Happy Love 1981, I'm Ready 1983, Unforgettable – A Tribute to Nat 'King' Cole (with Johnny Mathis) 1983, Dangerous 1985, Everlasting 1987, Good To Be Back 1989, Unforgettable 1991, Too Much Weekend 1992, Take A Look 1993, Holly and Ivy 1994, Stardust (two Grammy Awards) 1996, This Will Be 1997, Magic of Christmas 1999, Snowfall on the Sahara 1999, Love Songs (compilation) 2000, Ask a Woman Who Knows 2002, Leavin' 2006, Still Unforgettable (Grammy Award for Best Traditional Pop Vocal Album 2009) 2008. *E-mail:* babswest@aol.com (office). *Website:* www.nataliecole.com (home).

COLE-HAMILTON, David John, PhD, CChem, FRSC, FRSE; British chemist and academic; *Professor of Chemistry, University of St Andrews;* b. 22 May 1948, Bovey Tracey; s. of A.M. Cole-Hamilton and the late M.M Cartwright; m. 1st Elizabeth A. Brown 1973 (divorced); two s. two d.; m. 2nd Rosemary E. Macrae (née Semple) 2008; ed Haileybury & Imperial Service Coll. and Univ. of Edinburgh; Research Asst and temporary Lecturer, Imperial Coll. London 1974–78; Lecturer, Univ. of Liverpool 1978–83, Sr Lecturer 1983–85; Irvine Prof. of Chem., St Andrews Univ. 1985–, Chair. of Chem. 1985–90; Sir Edward Frankland Fellowship 1985, Corday Morgan Medal and Prize 1983, Industrial Award for Organo-metallic Chem. 1998, Sir Geoffrey Wilkinson Prize, Tilden Lecturer, Royal Soc. of Chem. 2000–01, Eminent Visitor, Catalysis Soc. of S Africa 2004, Sir Geoffrey Wilkinson Prize Lecturer, Royal Soc. of Chem. 2005–06. *Publications:* more than 300 articles on homogeneous catalysis and organometallic chem. *Address:* School of Chemistry, Purdie 340, University of St Andrews, St Andrews, Fife, KY16 9ST (office); 22, Buchanan Gardens, St Andrews, Fife, KY16 9LU, Scotland (home). *Telephone:* (1334) 463805 (office). *Fax:* (1334) 463808 (office). *E-mail:* djc@st-and.ac.uk (office). *Website:* ch-www.st-andrews.ac.uk (office).

COLEGATE, Isabel, FRSL; British writer; b. 10 Sept. 1931, London; d. of Arthur Colegate and Winifred Colegate; m. Michael Briggs 1953; two s. one d.; ed Runton Hill School, Norfolk; literary agent, Anthony Blond Ltd, London 1952–57; Dr hc (Bath) 1988. *Publications include:* The Blackmailer 1958, A Man of Power 1960, The Great Occasion 1962, Statues in a Garden 1964, The Orlando Trilogy 1968–72, News From the City of the Sun 1979, The Shooting Party 1980 (WH Smith Literary Award; filmed 1985), A Glimpse of Sion's Glory 1985, Deceits of Time 1988, The Summer of the Royal Visit 1991, Winter Journey 1995, A Pelican in the Wilderness – Hermits Solitaries and Recluses 2002. *Address:* c/o Penguin Publicity, 80 Strand, London, WC2R 0RL, England (office). *Website:* www.penguin.co.uk (office).

COLEMAN, Mary Sue, BA, PhD; American university administrator and academic; *President, University of Michigan;* b. Ky; m. Kenneth Coleman; one s.; ed Grinnell Coll., Univ. of North Carolina, Univ. of Texas; mem. Biochemistry Faculty, Univ. of Kentucky, Lexington 1971–90, Cancer Care Admin 1982–90; Assoc. Provost and Dean of Research, Univ. of North Carolina 1990–92, Vice-Chancellor Grad. Studies and Research 1992–93; Provost and Vice-Pres. of Academic Affairs Univ. of New Mexico 1993–95; Pres. Univ. of Iowa 1995–2002; Pres. Univ. of Michigan 2002–, also Prof. of Biological Chem. and Medical School Prof.; elected to NAS Inst. of Medicine 1997, Co-Chair. Cttee on Consequences of Uninsurance; Chair. Hitchings-Elion Postdoctoral

Fellowship Program, Burroughs-Wellcome Fund 1997; mem. Bd of Dirs Johnson & Johnson 2003–, Meredith Corpn; Trustee, Knight Foundation 2005–; fmr mem. Exec. Cttee Asscn of American Univs (AAU); mem. Bd of Dirs American Council of Educ. (ACE), Nat. Collegiate Athletic Asscn (NCAA); mem. Knight Comm. on Intercollegiate Athletics 2000–01; mem. Bd of Trustees Univs Research Asscn, ACE Task Force on Teacher Educ. and Comm. Minorities in Higher Educ., Business-Higher Educ. Forum, Imagining America Pres.'s Council, AAU Task Force Research Accountability, NCAA Standards for Success Advisory Bd, Pres.'s Leadership Group for Higher Educ., Center for Alcohol and Other Drug Prevention; Fellow, American Acad. Arts and Sciences, AAAS. *Address:* Office of the President, University of Michigan, 2074 Fleming Administration Building, Ann Arbor, MI 41809-1340, USA (office). *Telephone:* (734) 764-6270 (office). *Fax:* (734) 936-3529 (office). *E-mail:* presoff@umich.edu (office). *Website:* www.umich.edu (office).

COLEMAN, Norm, BA, JD; American lawyer and politician; b. Brooklyn; m. Laurie Coleman; one s. one d.; ed Hofstra Univ., Univ. of Iowa; served in Office of Attorney-Gen. of Minn. in various positions including Chief Prosecutor and Solicitor-Gen. of State of Minn. 1976–93; elected Mayor of St Paul (Conservative Democrat) 1993, re-elected 1997 (Republican); unsuccessful Republican cand. for Gov. of Minn. 1998; Senator from Minn. 2003–09, mem. Foreign Relations Cttee, Chair. Sub-Cttee on Western Hemisphere, Peace Corps and Narcotics Affairs; advisor, Republican Jewish Coalition, Washington, DC 2009–. *Leisure interests:* playing basketball with his daughter, juggling, Bob Dylan's music. *Address:* Republican Jewish Coalition, 50 F Street, NW, Suite 100, Washington, DC 20001, USA. *Telephone:* (202) 638-6688. *Fax:* (202) 638-6694. *Website:* www.rjchq.org.

COLEMAN, Ornette; American jazz musician; b. 9 March 1930, Fort Worth, Tex.; s. of Randolph Coleman and Rosa Coleman; m. Jayne Cortez (divorced 1964); one s.; ed Lennox School of Jazz; player of alto and tenor saxophone, trumpet, violin, bassoon; developed Harmoldic music theory; mem. various bands including own Coleman Quartet and Prime Time mid-1970s–, currently with Sound Grammer quartet; has appeared in numerous major festivals worldwide; has toured in Japan, Europe, Africa; Guggenheim Foundation Fellow 1967, 1974; mem. American Acad. of Arts and Letters; Dr hc (Univ. of Pennsylvania), (Bard Coll.), (New School for Social Research), (Berklee School of Music); Praemium Imperiale, Japan Art Asscn 2001, MacArthur "Genius"Award, American Music Center Letter of Distinction, Lillian Gisch Prize, NY State Gov. Arts Award, Grammy Lifetime Achievement Award 2007. *Film:* Ornette: Made in America 1986. *Compositions include:* Music of Ornette Coleman (works for string quartet and woodwind quintet), Skies of America and over 100 compositions for small jazz group and larger ensembles. *Recordings include:* albums: Something Else 1958, Tomorrow is the Question 1959, The Shape of Jazz to Come 1959, Change of the Century 1960, This is Our Music 1960, Free Jazz 1961, Ornette! 1961, Ornette on Tenor 1961, The Town Hall Concert 1962, 1963, Chappaqua Suite 1965, Live at the Tivoli 1965, The Great London Concert 1966, The Empty Foxhole 1966, Music of Ornette Coleman 1967, Live in Milano 1968, New York is Now 1968, Love Call 1968, Ornette At 12 1969, Crisis 1969, Friends and Neighbours 1970, The Art of Improvisation 1970, Science Fiction 1972, Skies of America 1972, Twins 1972, Dancing in Your Head 1976, Body Meta 1976, Soapsuds (with Charlie Haden) 1977, Broken Shadows 1982, Opening the Caravan of Dreams 1985, Prime Time/Time Design 1985, Song X 1986, In All Languages 1987, Virgin Beauty 1988, At the Golden Circle, Stockholm 1987, Naked Lunch 1992, Tone Dialling 1995, Colours: Live from Leipzig 1996, Complete Science Fiction Sessions 2000, Song X (with Pat Metheny) 2005, Sound Grammar (Pulitzer Prize for Music 2007) 2006. *Address:* Sound Grammar, c/o Phrase Text, Inc., POB 20071, London Terrace Station, New York, NY 10011, USA. *Telephone:* 9646) 238-9942. *Fax:* (212) 431-1753. *E-mail:* phrasetext@gmail.com. *Website:* www .ornettecoleman.com.

COLEMAN, Sir Robert John, MA, JD, KCMG; British lawyer, academic and international organization official; *Visiting Professor, School of Law and Social Science, University of Plymouth;* b. 8 Sept. 1943; m. Malinda Tigay Cutler 1966; two d.; ed Devonport High School for Boys, Plymouth, Jesus Coll. Oxford and Univ. of Chicago Law School, USA; Lecturer in Law, Univ. of Birmingham 1967–70; called to the Bar 1969; in practice as barrister-at-law, London 1970–73; Admin., subsequently Prin. Admin., EC 1974–82, Deputy Head of Div. 1983, Head of Div. 1984–87, Dir Public Procurement 1987–90, Dir Approximation of Laws, Freedom of Establishment and Freedom to Provide Services, the Professions 1990–91, Dir-Gen. Transport, EC 1991–99; Dir-Gen. Health and Consumer Protection 1999–2003; Sr Practitioner Fellow, Inst. of Governance, Queen's Univ., Belfast 2003–04, Visiting Research Fellow 2004–07; Visiting Prof., School of Law and Social Science, Univ. of Plymouth 2005–; also teaches at World Maritime Univ., Malmo, Sweden and Inst. of Maritime Law, Malta; EU Liaison Officer, Baltic and Int. Maritime Council 2005–; mem. Admin. Bd European Maritime Safety Agency, Lisbon 2008–. *Publications:* numerous articles in professional journals. *Leisure interest:* singing. *Address:* School of Social Science and Law, University of Plymouth, 20 Portland Villas, Drake Circus, Plymouth, Devon, PL4 8AA, England (office). *Telephone:* (1752) 585500 (office). *Fax:* (1752) 585501 (office). *E-mail:* robert.coleman18@btinternet.com (office). *Website:* www.plymouth.ac.uk (office).

COLEMAN, Terence (Terry) Francis Frank, LLB, FRSA; British journalist and writer; b. 13 Feb. 1931; s. of Jack Coleman and D. I. B. Coleman; m. 1st Lesley Fox-Strangeways Vane 1954 (divorced); two d.; m. 2nd Vivien Rosemary Lumsdaine Wallace 1981; one s. one d.; ed 14 schools and Univ. of London; fmr reporter, Poole Herald; fmr Ed. Savoir Faire; fmr Sub-Ed. Sunday Mercury, Birmingham Post; Reporter then Arts Corresp. The Guardian 1961–70, Chief Feature Writer 1970–74, 1976–79, New York Corresp. 1981, Special Corresp. 1982–89; Special Writer with Daily Mail 1974–76; Assoc. Ed. The Independent 1989–91; columnist, The Guardian 1992–; Feature Writer of the Year, British Press Awards 1982, Journalist of the Year (What the Papers Say Award) 1988. *Publications:* The Railway Navvies 1965 (Yorkshire Post Prize for Best First Book of the Year), A Girl for the Afternoons 1965, Providence and Mr Hardy (with Lois Deacon) 1966, The Only True History: collected journalism 1969, Passage to America 1972, An Indiscretion in the Life of an Heiress (Hardy's first novel) (ed.) 1976, The Liners 1976, The Scented Brawl: Collected Journalism 1978, Southern Cross 1979, Thanksgiving 1981, Movers and Shakers: Collected Interviews 1987, Thatcher's Britain 1987, Empire 1994, W. G. Grace: A Biography 1997, Nelson: The Man and the Legend (biog.) 2001, Olivier: The Authorised Biography 2005. *Leisure interests:* cricket, opera and circumnavigation. *Address:* PFD, Drury House, 34–43 Russell Street, London, WC2B 5HA, England (office). *Telephone:* (20) 7344-1000 (office); (20) 7720-2651 (home). *Fax:* (20) 7836-9543 (office). *Website:* www.pfd.co.uk (office).

COLERIDGE, David Ean; British insurance executive; b. 7 June 1932; s. of Guy Cecil Richard Coleridge and Katherine Cicely Stewart Smith; m. Susan Senior 1955; three s.; ed Eton Coll.; with Glanvill Enthoven 1950–57; joined R. W. Sturge & Co. 1957, Dir 1966–95; Chair. A. L. Sturge (Holdings) Ltd (now Sturge Holdings PLC) 1978–95; mem. Cttee of Lloyd's Underwriting Agents Asscn 1974–82, Chair. 1981–82; mem. Council and Cttee of Lloyd's 1983–86, 1988–92; Deputy Chair. Lloyd's 1985, 1988, 1989, Chair. 1991–92; Dir Wise Speke Holdings Ltd 1987–94, Ockham Holdings PLC (now Highway Insurance PLC) 1996– (Chair. 1995). *Leisure interests:* golf, racing, gardening, family. *Address:* Spring Pond House, Wispers, nr Midhurst, West Sussex, GU29 0QH; 37 Egerton Terrace, London, SW3 2BU, England. *Telephone:* (1730) 813277. *Fax:* (20) 7591-0637 (London) (home).

COLERIDGE, Nicholas David; British publisher, journalist and author; *Vice-President, Condé Nast International;* b. 4 March 1957; s. of David Ean Coleridge (q.v.) and Susan Coleridge (née Senior); m. Georgia Metcalfe 1989; three s. one d.; ed Eton, Trinity Coll., Cambridge; Assoc. Ed. Tatler 1979–81; columnist Evening Standard 1981–84; Features Ed. Harpers and Queen 1985–86, Ed. 1986–89; Editorial Dir Condé Nast Publs 1989–91, Man. Dir Condé Nast UK 1992–, Vice-Pres. Condé Nast Int. 1999–, Dir Condé Nast France, Condé Nast India; Chair. British Fashion Council 2000–03, Fashion Rocks for The Prince's Trust 2003, Periodical Publrs Asscn 2004–07; mem. Council RCA 1995–2000; Young Journalist of the Year, British Press Awards 1983, Mark Boxer Award for Editorial Excellence 2001. *Publications:* Tunnel Vision 1982, Around the World in 78 Days 1984, Shooting Stars 1984, The Fashion Conspiracy 1988, How I Met My Wife and Other Stories 1991, Paper Tigers 1993, With Friends Like These 1997, Streetsmart 1999, Godchildren 2002, A Much Married Man 2006, Deadly Sins 2009. *Address:* Condé Nast, Vogue House, Hanover Square, London, W1S 1JU (office); 29 Royal Avenue, London, SW3 4QE; Wolverton Hall, Nr. Pershore, Worcs., WR10 2AU, England. *Telephone:* (20) 7330-5998 (office). *Website:* www.condenast.co.uk (office).

COLES, Anna L. Bailey, PhD; American professor of nursing; *Dean Emerita of Nursing, Howard University;* b. 16 Jan. 1925, Kansas City; d. of Lillie Mai Buchanan and Gordon A. Bailey; m. 1953 (divorced 1980); three d.; ed Freedmen's Hosp. School of Nursing, Washington, DC, Avila Coll., Kansas City, Mo. and Catholic Univ. of America; Instructor, Veterans Admin. Hosp., Topeka, Kan. 1950–52; Supervisor, Veterans Admin. Hosp., Kansas City 1952–58; Asst Dir In-Service Educ., Freedmen's Hosp. 1960–61, Admin. Asst to Dir 1961–66, Assoc. Dir Nursing Service 1966–67, Dir of Nursing 1967–69; Prof. and Dean, Howard Univ. Coll. of Nursing 1968–86, Dean Emer. 1986–, retd 1986; Dir Minority Devt, Univ. of Kansas School of Nursing 1991–95; Pres. Societas Docta, Inc. 1996–99; mem. Inst. of Medicine; Meritorious Public Service Award, DC 1968; Distinguished Alumni Award, Howard Univ.; Lifetime Achievement Award Asscn of Black Nursing Faculty in Higher Educ. 1993; numerous other awards. *Publications:* articles in professional journals; contrib. to Fundamentals of Stroke Care 1976; Nurses, an Encyclopedia of Black America 1981. *Leisure interests:* reading, outdoor cooking and travelling. *Address:* 15107 Interlachen Drive, #315, Silver Spring, MD 20906, USA (home). *Telephone:* (301) 598-3680 (home). *Fax:* (301) 598-3680 (home).

COLES, Sir (Arthur) John, MA, GCMG; British diplomatist (retd); b. 13 Nov. 1937; s. of Arthur S. Coles and Doris G. Coles; m. Anne M. S. Graham 1965; two s. one d.; ed Magdalen Coll. School, Brackley and Magdalen Coll., Oxford; joined HM Diplomatic Service 1960; Middle Eastern Centre for Arabic Studies, Lebanon 1960–62; Third Sec. Khartoum 1962–64; Asst Political Agent, Trucial States (Dubai) 1968–71; Head of Chancery, Cairo 1975–77; Counsellor, UK Perm. Mission to EEC 1977–80; Head of S Asian Dept FCO 1980–81; Pvt. Sec. to Prime Minister 1981–84; Amb. to Jordan 1984–88; High Commr in Australia 1988–91; Deputy Under-Sec. of State, FCO 1991–94; Perm. Under-Sec. of State and Head of HM Diplomatic Service 1994–97; Dir B.G. PLC 1998–; Visiting Fellow, All Souls Coll. Oxford 1998–99; Trustee Imperial War Museum 1999–2004; Chair. Sight Savers Int. 2001–07. *Publications:* British Influence and the Euro 1999, Making Foreign Policy: A Certain Idea of Britain 2000, Blindness and the Visionary: The Life and Work of John Wilson 2006. *Leisure interests:* walking, cricket, bird-watching, reading, music. *Address:* Kelham, Dock Lane, Beaulieu, Hants., SO42 7YH, England (home).

COLES, John Morton, MA, PhD, ScD, FBA, FSA, FRSA; British/Canadian archaeologist and academic; b. 25 March 1930, Canada; s. of John L. Coles and Alice M. Brown; m. 1st Mona Shiach 1958 (divorced 1985); two s. two d.; m. 2nd Bryony Orme 1985; ed Univs of Toronto, Edinburgh and Cambridge; Carnegie Scholar 1959–60; Research Fellow, Univ. of Edinburgh 1959–60; Univ. Lecturer and Reader, Univ. of Cambridge 1960–80, Prof. of European

Prehistory 1980–86; Visiting Prof., Centre for Maritime Archaeology, Nat. Museum of Denmark 1994; Pres. The Prehistoric Soc. 1978–82; mem. Academia Europaea 1989–, Royal Comm. on Ancient and Historical Monuments of Scotland 1992–2002, Discovery Programme Ireland 2001–05; Corresp. mem. Deutsches Archaeologisches Institut 1979; Fellow, Fitzwilliam Coll. Cambridge 1963–; British Acad. Fellow, Royal Swedish Acad. of Letters, History and Antiquities 1990, 1998, 2002; Visiting Fellow, Japan Asscn for the Promotion of Science 1994–95; Hon. Prof., Univ. of Exeter 1993–2003, Univ. of Hull 1996–99; Hon. FSA (Scotland) 2000; Hon. mem. Inst. of Field Archaeologists 1991; Dr hc (Uppsala) 1997; Chalmers-Jervise Prize 1960, Rhind Lecturer (with B. Coles), Soc. of Antiquaries of Scotland 1994–95, Grahame Clark Medal, British Acad. 1995, ICI Medal (jtly), British Archaeological Awards 1998, Europa Prize for Prehistory 2000, Gold Medal, Soc. of Antiquaries of London 2002, European Archaeological Heritage Prize 2006. *Publications:* The Archaeology of Early Man (with E. Higgs) 1969, Field Archaeology in Britain 1972, Archaeology by Experiment 1973, The Bronze Age in Europe (with A. Harding) 1979, Experimental Archaeology 1979, Prehistory of the Somerset Levels (with B. Orme) 1980, The Archaeology of Wetlands 1984, Sweet Track to Glastonbury (with B. Coles) 1986, Meare Village East: The Excavations of A. Bulleid and H. St George Gray 1932–1956 1987, People of the Wetlands (with B. Coles) 1989, Images of the Past 1990, From The Waters of Oblivion 1991, Arthur Bulleid and the Glastonbury Lake Village 1892–1992 (with A. Goodall and S. Minnitt) 1992, Fenland Survey (with D. Hall) 1994, Rock Carvings of Uppland 1995, Industrious and Fairly Civilised: the Glastonbury Lake Village (with S. Minnitt) 1995, Enlarging the Past (with B. Coles) 1996, Lake Villages of Somerset (with S. Minnitt) 1996, Changing Landscapes: The Ancient Fenland (with D. Hall) 1998, Patterns in a Rocky Land: Rock Carvings in South-West Uppland, Sweden 2000, Shadows of a Northern Past: Rock Carvings of Bohuslän and Østfold 2005; numerous papers on European prehistory, field archaeology, experimental archaeology, wetland archaeology. *Leisure interests:* music, travel, wetlands. *Address:* Fursdon Mill Cottage, Thorverton, Devon, EX5 5JS, England (home). *Telephone:* (1392) 860125 (home). *E-mail:* jmcoles@btinternet.com (office).

COLES, Robert Martin, AB, MD; American child psychiatrist; b. 12 Oct. 1929, Boston, Mass.; s. of Philip W. Coles and Sandra Coles (née Young); m. Jane Hallowell 1960; three s.; ed Harvard Coll. and Columbia Univ.; Intern, Univ. of Chicago clinics 1954–55; Resident in Psychiatry, Mass. Gen. Hosp., Boston 1955–56, McLean Hosp., Belmont 1956–57; Resident in Child Psychiatry, Judge Baker Guidance Center, Children's Hosp., Roxbury, Mass. 1957–58, Fellow 1960–61; mem. psychiatric staff, Mass. Gen. Hosp. 1960–62; Clinical Asst in Psychiatry, Harvard Univ. Medical School 1960–62; Research Psychiatrist in Health Services, Harvard Univ. 1963–, Lecturer in Gen. Educ. 1966–, Prof. of Psychiatry and Medical Humanities, Harvard Univ. Medical School 1977–; mem. American Psychiatric Asscn; Fellow, American Acad. of Arts and Sciences; awards include Pulitzer Prize for vols II and III of Children of Crisis 1973, Sara Josepha Hale Award 1986. *Publications:* Harvard Diary 1988, Times of Surrender: Selected Essays 1989, The Spiritual Life of Children; numerous books and articles in professional journals. *Leisure interests:* tennis, bicycle riding, skiing. *Address:* POB 674, Concord, MA 01742-0674; 81 Carr Road, Concord, 01742, USA (home). *Telephone:* (617) 495-3736 (office); (617) 369-6498 (home).

COLFER, Eoin; Irish children's writer; b. 14 May 1965, Wexford; m. Jackie; two s.; fmr teacher; invited to write new novel in Hitchhiker's Guide to the Galaxy series 2008; British Book Awards WH Smith Children's Book of the Year 2001, WH Smith Book Award 2002, German Children's Book Award 2004. *Publications:* juvenile: Benny and Omar 1998, Benny and Babe 1999, The Wish List 2000, Artemis Fowl 2001, Artemis Fowl: The Arctic Incident 2002, Artemis Fowl: The Eternity Code 2003, The Seventh Dwarf (novella) 2004, The Legend of Spud Murphy 2004, The Supernaturalist 2004, The Artemis Fowl Files 2004, Artemis Fowl: The Opal Deception 2005, Artemis Fowl and the Lost Colony 2006, Half Moon Investigations 2006, Airman 2008; for younger children: Going Potty 1999, Ed's Funny Feet 2000, Ed's Bed 2001; has also written plays. *Address:* 1 Priory Hall, Spawell Road, Wexford, Ireland (office); Brookes Batchellor LLP, 102–108 Clerkenwell Road, London, EC1M 5SA, England. *Website:* www.eoincolfer.com.

COLGAN, Michael Anthony, BA; Irish theatre, film and television producer; *Artistic Director, The Gate Theatre, Dublin;* b. 17 July 1950, Dublin; s. of James Joseph Colgan and Josephine Patricia Colgan (née Geoghegan); m. Susan Mary FitzGerald 1975; one s. two d.; ed Trinity Coll. Dublin; Theatre Dir Abbey Theatre, Dublin 1974–78; Co. Man. Irish Theatre Co., Dublin 1977–78; Man. Dublin Theatre Festival 1978–81, Artistic Dir 1981–83, mem. Bd of Dirs 1983–; Artistic Dir Gate Theatre, Dublin 1983– (also mem. Bd of Dirs); Exec. Dir Little Bird Films, Dublin and London 1986–; Co-Founder Belacqua Film Co. 1998, Blue Angel Film Co. 1999; Artistic Dir Parma Festival, Italy 1982; mem. Irish Arts Council 1989–94; Gov. Dublin City Univ. 1998–2001; Chair. St Patrick's Festival 1996–99; mem. Bd Millennium Festivals Ltd, Laura Pels Foundation, New York 2000–04; mem. Irish Arts Council 1989–94, Governing Authority, Dublin City Univ.; Chevalier dans l'Ordre des Arts et des Lettres 2007; Hon. LLD (Trinity Coll. Dublin) 2000; Arts Award, Irish Independent 1985, 1987, Nat. Entertainment Award 1996, People of the Year Award 1999, Irish Times Lifetime Achievement Award 2006. *Plays produced:* I'll Go On (Samuel Beckett), Dublin, Paris, London, New York; Juno and the Paycock (Sean O'Casey), Dublin, New York; Salomé (Oscar Wilde), Dublin, Edin., Charleston, SC; Three Sisters (Anton Chekhov), Dublin and Royal Court Theatre, London, four Beckett Festivals, Dublin, London, New York (all 19 Samuel Beckett stage plays), four Pinter Festivals, Dublin and New York. *World premieres include:* Molly Sweeney (Brian Friel), Dublin, London and New York, Port Authority (Conor McPherson), Afterplay (Brian Friel), See You Next Tuesday (Francis Veber), Shining City (Conor McPherson), The Home Place (Brian Friel). *Television:* Two Lives (exec. producer) for RTÉ 1986, Troubles (two two-hour films) for LWT 1996. *Film:* Beckett on Film (co-producer) 2000: all 19 of Beckett's plays filmed using internationally known dirs and actors (Best Drama Award 2002, South Bank Show, Peabody Award 2002). *Leisure interests:* Schubert, Beckett, New York City, middle distance running, chamber music. *Address:* The Gate Theatre, 1 Cavendish Row, Dublin 1, Ireland (office). *Telephone:* (1) 874-4369 (office). *Fax:* (1) 874-5373 (office). *E-mail:* info@gate-theatre.ie (office). *Website:* www.gate-theatre.ie (office).

COLLARD, Jean Philippe; French pianist; b. 27 Jan. 1948, Mareuil-sur-Aÿ (Marne); s. of Michel Collard and Monique (Philipponnat) Collard; m. 2nd Ariane de Brion; three s. (two from previous m.) one d.; ed Conservatoire Nat. de Musique de Paris; Chevalier, Ordre des Arts et des Lettres, Chevalier, Ordre nat. du Mérite, Chevalier Légion d'honneur 2003. *Recordings include:* music by Bach, Brahms, Debussy, Fauré, Franck, Rachmaninov, Ravel, Saint-Saëns, Schubert, Chopin, Mozart. *Leisure interests:* windsurfing, tennis. *Address:* Angela Sulivan, Sulivan Sweetland, 1 Hillgate Place, Balham Hill, London SW12 9ER, England (office). *Telephone:* (20) 8772-3470 (office). *E-mail:* info@sulivansweetland.co.uk (office); pianojpc@aol.com (home). *Website:* www.sulivansweetland.co.uk (office).

COLLENETTE, David Michael, PC, BA (Hons), MA; Canadian academic and fmr politician; *Distinguished Fellow, Glendon School of Public and International Affairs, York University;* b. 24 June 1946, London, UK; s. of David H. Collenette and Sarah M. Collenette; m. Penny Collenette 1975; one s.; ed Glendon Coll., York Univ.; fmrly worked in life insurance, plastics and exec. recruitment; fmr Exec. Vice-Pres. Mandrake Man. Consultants; elected to House of Commons 1974, 1980, 1993, 1997, 2000, retd 2004; fmr Minister of State (Multiculturalism), Parl. Sec. to Postmaster-Gen. and to Pres. of Privy Council; Minister of Nat. Defence and Minister of Veterans Affairs 1993–96, of Transport 1997–2003; mem. Liberal Party, Minister responsible for Crown Corpns 2002–03; Chancellor Royal Mil. Coll. of Canada 1993–96; mem. Int. Advisory Council, Inst. of Int. Studies, Stanford Univ. 1999–; Distinguished Fellow, Dept of Political Science, Glendon Coll., York Univ. 2004–; Head of Ottawa Transportation Task Force Cttee 2007; Fellow, Chartered Inst. of Logistics and Transport. *Leisure interests:* squash, soccer, swimming, classical music and theatre. *Address:* Glendon School of Public and International Affairs, 220 Glendon Hall, Glendon Campus, York University, 2275 Bayview Avenue, Toronto, ON M4N 3M6, Canada (office). *Telephone:* (416) 736-2100 (office). *E-mail:* dcollenette@glendon.yorku.ca (office). *Website:* www.glendon.yorku.ca/publicaffairs (office); www.davidcollenette.ca.

COLLETTE, Toni; Australian actress; b. 1 Dec. 1972, Sydney; m. Dave Galafassi 2003; one d.; ed Nat. Inst. for Dramatic Art, Sydney; jury mem. Cannes Film Festival 2007. *Films include:* Spotswood 1991, Muriel's Wedding 1994, This Marching Girl Thing 1994, Arabian Knight (voice) 1995, Lilian's Story 1995, Cosí 1996, The Pallbearer 1996, Emma 1996, Clockwatchers 1997, The James Gang 1997, Diana & Me 1997, The Boys 1997, Velvet Goldmine 1998, 8½ Women 1999, The Sixth Sense 1999, Shaft 2000, Hotel Splendide 2000, Changing Lanes 2002, Dirty Deeds 2002, About a Boy 2002, The Hours 2003, Japanese Story 2003, Connie and Carla 2004, The Last Shot 2004, In Her Shoes 2005, The Night Listener 2006, Little Miss Sunshine (Screen Actors' Guild Award for Outstanding Performance by a Cast 2007) 2006, Like Minds 2006, The Dead Girl 2006, Evening 2007. *Television includes:* Tsunami: The Aftermath 2006. *Leisure interests:* yoga, mental and spiritual retreats in India, climbing Tibetan Himalayas. *Address:* c/o Shanahan Management, Level 3, Berman House, 91 Campbell Street, Surry Hills, NSW 2010, Australia; United Talent Agency Inc.(UTA), 9560 Wilshire Blvd., Suite 500, Beverly Hills, CA 90212, USA. *Telephone:* (2) 8202-1800; (310) 273-6700 (UTA). *Fax:* (2) 8202-1801; (310) 247-1111 (UTA).

COLLEY, Linda Jane, PhD, FRSL, FBA, CBE; British academic and writer; *Shelby M.C. Davis 1958 Professor of History, Princeton University;* b. 13 Sept. 1949, Chester; d. of Roy Colley and the late Marjorie Colley (née Hughes); m. David Nicholas Cannadine (q.v.) 1982; one d. (deceased); ed Univs of Bristol and Cambridge; Eugenie Strong Research Fellow, Girton Coll., Cambridge 1975–78; Fellow, Newnham Coll., Cambridge 1978–79, Christ's Coll., Cambridge 1979–81; Asst Prof. of History, Yale Univ. 1982–85, Assoc. Prof. 1985–90, Prof. of History 1990–92, Richard M. Colgate Prof. of History 1992–98, Dir Lewis Walpole Library 1982–96; Prof., School of History, LSE 1998–2003, Leverhulme Personal Research Prof., European Inst. 1998–2003; Shelby M.C. Davis 1958 Prof. of History, Princeton Univ. 2003–; mem. Bd British Library 1999–2003, Princeton Univ. Press 2007–; mem. Advisory Bd Tate Britain 1999–2003, Paul Mellon Centre for British Art 1999–2003; Visiting Fellowship, Humanities Research Centre, ANU, Canberra 2005; Glaxo-Smith-Kline Sr Fellowship Nat. Humanities Center, NC 2006; Hon. Fellow, Christ's Coll., Cambridge 2005; Dr hc (South Bank, London) 1999, (Essex) 2004, (East Anglia) 2005, (Bristol) 2006; Wolfson Prize 1993, Anstey Lecturer Univ. of Kent 1994; William Church Memorial Lecturer, Brown Univ. 1994, Distinguished Lecturer in British History, Univ. of Texas 1995, Trevelyan Lecturer, Univ. of Cambridge 1997, Wiles Lecturer, Queen's Univ. Belfast 1997, Prime Minister's Millennium Lecture 2000, Raleigh Lecturer, British Acad. 2002, Nehru Lecturer 2002, Bateson Lecturer, Oxford 2003, Chancellor Dunning Trust Lecturer, Queen's Univ., Ont. 2004, Byrn Lecturer, Vanderbilt Univ. 2005, Annual Lecture in Int. History, LSE 2006, C.P.Snow Lecture, Cambridge 2007, Pres's Lecture, Princeton Univ. 2007, Political Science Quarterly Lecture 2007. *Publications:* In Defiance of Oligarchy: The Tory Party 1714–60 1982, Namier 1989, Crown Pictorial: Art and the British Monarchy 1990, Britons: Forging the Nation 1707–1837 (Wolfson Prize 1993) 1992, Captives: Britain, Empire and the World 1600–1850 2002, The Ordeal of Elizabeth Marsh: A Woman in World History 2007 (rated one of the ten best books of the year by The New York Times 2007), Taking Stock of Taking Liberties (catalogue of British Library exhbn) 2008; numerous articles and reviews in UK and American learned journals. *Leisure interests:* travel, looking at art, politics. *Address:* c/o Gill Coleridge, RCW Ltd, 20 Powis Mews, London, W11 1JN, England (office); Department of History, Princeton University, 129 Dickinson Hall, Princeton, NJ 08544-1017, USA (office). *Telephone:* (609) 258-8076 (office). *E-mail:* lcolley@princeton.edu (office). *Website:* his.princeton.edu (office).

COLLIGNON, Stefan Colin, PhD; German economist and academic; *Professor of Political Economy, Sant'Anna School of Advanced Studies;* b. 11 Dec. 1951, Munich; s. of Klaus Collignon and Rosemarie Collignon; m. Judith Zahler 1984; ed Institut d'Etudes Politiques, Paris, Free Univ. of Berlin, Univ. of Dar es Salaam, Tanzania, Queen Elizabeth House, Oxford, UK, London School of Econs; financial analyst, First Nat. Bank in Dallas, Paris 1975–76; teacher, Lindi Secondary School, Deutscher Entwicklungsdienst (German Volunteer Service), Tanzania 1977–79; Man. Dir and Chair. Dorcas Ltd, London 1981–88; Dir Research and Communication, Asscn for the Monetary Union of Europe, Paris 1989–98; Lecturer, Institut d'Etudes Politiques, Paris 1990–95, Free Univ. of Berlin 1997–2000; Prof., Collège d'Europe, Bruge 1998–2005; Centennial Prof. of European Political Economy, LSE 2001–08; Visiting Prof., Harvard Univ. 2005–07, also Assoc., Minda de Gunzburg Centre for European Studies; Prof. of Political Economy, Sant'Anna School of Advanced Studies, Pisa 2007–; Chair. Scientific Cttee Centro Europa Ricerche, Rome 2007–; Visiting Prof., Institut d'Etudes Politiques, Lille 2005–, Univ. of Hamburg 2007–08; Pres. Asscn France-Birmanie 1990–; mem. Bd of Dirs Glunz AG 1998–, Sonae Industria SGPS, Portugal 2003–05. *Publications:* Europe's Monetary Future (Vol. I) 1994, The Monetary Economics of Europe: Causes of the EMS Crisis (Vol. II) 1994, European Monetary Policy (ed.) 1997, Exchange Rate Policies in Emerging Asian Countries 1999, Monetary Stability in Europe 2002, Private Sector Involvement in the Euro 2003, The European Republic (Prix du meilleur livre politique 2004) 2003; numerous articles and book chapters on monetary union. *Address:* 11, rue d'Ormesson, 75004 Paris, France (home); Scuola Superiore Sant'Anna, Piazza Martiri della Libertà, 33, 56127 Pisa, Italy. *Telephone:* 1-40-27-95-63 (home); (050) 883111 (office). *Fax:* 1-40-27-90-45 (home); (050) 883225 (office). *E-mail:* stefan.collignon@sssup.it (office). *Website:* www.stefancollignon.de.

COLLIN, Jean-Philippe, MEng; French business executive; *Executive Vice-President, Automobiles Peugeot;* b. 28 May 1956; ed Ecole Supérieure d'Electricité (Supelec); began career with IBM in 1982, served as man. of components procurement centre in USA and Chair. of one of co.'s Global Purchasing Councils, was also in charge of Tech. and Quality Lab.; joined Valeo 1995, Vice-Pres., Purchasing, for Electronics Div., later promoted to Vice-Pres. Purchasing Valeo Group; Sr Vice-Pres., Sourcing, Thomson 1999–2002, put in charge of spring cost reduction programme 2002, later served as Sr Vice-Pres., Integrated Circuits, Thomson Optical Systems, mem. Thomson Exec. Cttee; Vice-Pres., Purchasing, for PSA Peugeot Citroën, as part of Group's Platforms, Eng and Purchasing Dept 2004–07, reported directly to Chair. and Pres. PSA Peugeot Citroën Group as mem. Extended Exec. Cttee 2007, mem. PSA Peugeot Citroën Man. Bd and Exec. Vice-Pres. Automobiles Peugeot 2008–. *Address:* PSA Peugeot Citroën SA, 75 avenue de la Grande-Armée, 75116 Paris, France (office). *Telephone:* 1-40-66-55-11 (office). *Fax:* 1-40-66-54-14 (office). *E-mail:* info@psa-peugeot-citroen.com (office). *Website:* www.psa-peugeot-citroen.com (office); www.peugeot.com (office).

COLLINS, Billy, PhD; American poet and academic; *Distinguished Professor, Lehman College, City University of New York;* b. 22 March 1941, New York; m. Diane Collins 1979; ed Holy Cross Coll., Univ. of California at Riverside; Prof. of English Lehman Coll., City Univ. of New York 1969–2001, Distinguished Prof. 2001–; Visiting Writer Poets House, N Ireland 1993–96, Lenoir-Rhyne Coll. 1994, Ohio State Univ. 1998; Resident Poet Burren Coll. of Art, Ireland 1996, Sarah Lawrence Coll. 1998–2000; Adjunct Prof. Columbia Univ. 2000–01; conducts summer poetry workshops at Univ. Coll. Galway, Ireland; Library of Congress's Poet Laureate Consultant in Poetry 2001, US Poet Laureate 2001–03; Fellow, New York Foundation for the Arts, Nat. Endowment for the Arts, Guggenheim Foundation; NEA Fellowship 1993; Guggenheim Fellowship 1995; New York Foundation for the Arts Poetry Fellowship 1986, Nat. Endowment for the Arts Creative Writing Fellowship 1988, Nat. Poetry Series Competition Winner 1990, Bess Hokin Prize 1991, Literary Lion, New York Public Library 1992, Frederick Bock Prize 1992, Guggenheim Fellowship 1993, Levinson Prize 1995, Paterson Poetry Prize 1999, J. Howard and Barbara M. J. Wood Prize 1999, Pushcart Prize 2002, Poet Laureate of New York State 2004–06. *Publications include:* Pokerface 1977, Video Poems 1980, The Apple that Astonished Paris 1988, Questions About Angels 1991, The Art of Drowning 1995, Picnic, Lightning 1998, Taking Off Emily Dickinson's Clothes 2000, Sailing Alone Around the Room: New and Selected Poems 2001, Nine Horses 2002, The Trouble with Poetry 2005, She Was Just Seventeen 2006, Ballistics 2008; editor: Poetry 180: A Turning Back to Poetry, 180 More: Extraordinary Poems for Everyday Life; poems in many anthologies, including The Best American Poetry 1992, 1993, 1997 and periodicals, including Poetry, American Poetry, Review, American Scholar, Harper's, Paris Review and The New Yorker. *Address:* Steven Barclay Agency, 12 Western Avenue, Petaluma, CA 94952, USA (office); c/o Lehman College, 250 Bedford Park Boulevard West, Business Office, Shuster Hall Building, Bronx, New York, NY 10468, USA (office); 185 Route 202, Somers, NY 10589 (home). *Telephone:* (718) 960-8550 (office). *Website:* www.barclayagency.com (office); www.lehman.cuny.edu (office); www.bigsnap.com (home).

COLLINS, Christopher Douglas, FCA; British business executive; *Chairman, Old Mutual PLC;* b. 19 Jan. 1940, Welwyn; s. of Douglas Collins and Patricia Collins; m. Susan Lumb 1976; one s. one d.; ed Eton Coll.; articled clerk, Peat Marwick Mitchell 1958–64; Man. Dir Goya Ltd 1968–75, Dir 1975–80; amateur steeplechase jockey 1965–75; rep. of GB in three-day equestrian events 1974–80; Steward, Jockey Club 1980–81; mem. Horse Race Betting Levy Board 1982–84; Chair. Aintree Racecourse Ltd 1983–88, Nat. Stud 1986–88; joined Hanson PLC 1989, Dir 1991, Vice-Chair. 1995, Deputy Chair. 1997, Chair. 1998–2005; Chair. Forth Ports PLC 2000–, Racecourse Holdings Trust 2005–; Dir Old Mutual PLC 1999–2005, Chair. 2005–; Dir The Go-Ahead Group PLC 1999–, Alfred McAlpine PLC 2000–. *Leisure interests:* riding, skiing. *Address:* Old Mutual Place plc, 5th Floor, Old Mutual Place, 2 Lambeth Hill, London, EC4V 4GG, England (office). *Telephone:* (20) 7002-7204 (office). *Fax:* (20) 7002-7299 (office). *E-mail:* matthew.gregorowski@omg.co.uk (office). *Website:* www.oldmutual.com (office).

COLLINS, Col (retd) Eileen Marie; American pilot and astronaut (retd) and air force officer (retd); b. 19 Nov. 1956, Elmira, NY; m. Pat Youngs 1987; one s. one d.; ed Elmira Free Acad., Corning Community Coll., Syracuse Univ., Stanford Univ., Webster Univ., Air Force Inst. of Tech.; trained as USAF pilot, Vance Air Force Base, Okla 1979–82; C-141 Aircraft Commdr and Instructor Pilot, Travis Air Force Base, Calif. 1983–85; Asst Prof. of Math. and T-41 Instructor Pilot, USAF Acad., Colo 1986–89; attended Air Force Test Pilot School, Edwards Air Force Base, Calif. 1990; selected by NASA to become astronaut 1991, served in various roles including assignment to Orbiter eng support, mem. support team responsible for Orbiter prelaunch checkout, final launch configuration, crew ingress/egress, landing/recovery, worked in NASA Mission Control as spacecraft communicator (CAPCOM), Astronaut Office Spacecraft Systems Br. Chief, Chief Information Officer, Shuttle Br. Chief, Astronaut Safety Br. Chief, pilot on STS-63 mission 1995 (first woman to pilot space shuttle), STS-84 mission 1997, Commdr STS-93 mission 1999 (first woman to command space shuttle mission), Commdr STS-114 2005; retd from USAF 2005; mem. NASA Advisory Council 2006–; mem. Air Force Asscn, Order of Dedalians, Women Mil. Aviators, US Space Foundation, American Inst. of Aeronautics and Astronautics, Ninety-Nines; Hon. DSc (Univ. Coll. Dublin) 2006; Jackie Robinson Empire State Freedom Medal 1999, Soc. of Women Engineers (SWE) Resnik Challenger Medal 2003; Defense Superior Service Medal, Distinguished Flying Cross, Defense Meritorious Service Medal, Air Force Meritorious Service Medal with one oak leaf cluster, Air Force Commendation Medal with one oak leaf cluster, Armed Forces Expeditionary Medal for Service in Grenada (Operation Urgent Fury) 1983, NASA Outstanding Leadership Medal, NASA Space Flight Medals, Women in Space Science Award, Adler Planetarium 2006; Howard Hughes Memorial Award 2006; elected mem. Aviation Hall of Fame 2009; French Legion of Honor. *Address:* c/o NASA Advisory Council, Washington, DC 20546, USA. *Website:* www.hq.nasa.gov/office/oer/nac/index.html.

COLLINS, Francis S., MD, PhD; American research scientist; ed Univ. of Virginia, Yale Univ., Univ. of N Carolina at Chapel Hill; Fellowship in Human Genetics, Yale Univ.; fmr staff mem. Howard Hughes Medical Inst., Univ. of Mich. Medical Center, Ann Arbor 1984; with research team identified gene for cystic fibrosis 1989, for neurofibromatosis 1990, for Huntington disease 1993; Dir Nat. Human Genome Research Inst. —2008, also Sr Investigator, Genome Tech. Br.; mem. Inst. of Medicine, NAS; co-recipient Gairdner Foundation Int. Award for work on Cystic Fibrosis 1990. *Publication:* The Language of God: A Scientist Presents Evidence for Belief 2006. *Address:* c/o National Human Genome Research Institute, Building 31, Room 4B09, 31 Center Drive, MSC 2152, Bethesda, MD 20892-2152, USA (office).

COLLINS, Gerard; Irish politician; b. 16 Oct. 1938, Abbeyfeale, Co. Limerick; s. of the late James J. Collins and Margaret Collins; m. Hilary Tattan; ed Univ. Coll. Dublin; fmr vocational teacher; mem. Dáil 1967–; Acting Gen. Sec. Fianna Fáil Party 1964–67; Parl. Sec. to Minister for Industry and Commerce and to Minister for the Gaeltacht 1969–70; Minister for Posts and Telegraphs 1970–73; mem. Consultative Ass. of Council of Europe 1973–75; Limerick Co. Council 1974–77; Minister for Justice 1977–81, 1987–89, for Foreign Affairs March–Dec. 1982, 1989–93; Chair. Parl. Cttee on EEC Affairs 1983–87; mem. European Parl. 1994–, Leader Fianna Fáil Group, Vice-Pres. Union for Europe Group, Pres. European Parl. Del. to S. Asia and South Asian Asscn for Regional Co-operation (SAARC); Chair. of the EU-South Africa Interparliamentary Del. *Address:* The Hill, Abbeyfeale, Co. Limerick, Ireland (home); 6F 365, European Parliament, 97–113 rue Wiertz, 1047 Brussels, Belgium (office). *Telephone:* (2) 284-56-22 (office); (68) 32441. *Fax:* (2) 284-96-22 (office). *E-mail:* gcollins@europarl.eu.int (office). *Website:* www.europarl.ep.ec (office).

COLLINS, Jackie; British novelist; sister of Joan Collins (q.v.). *Mini-series:* Hollywood Wives (ABC TV), Lucky Chances (NBC TV), Lady Boss (NBC TV). *Screenplays:* Yesterday's Hero, The World is Full of Married Men, The Stud. *Publications:* The World is Full of Married Men 1968, The Stud 1969, Sunday Simmons and Charlie Brick 1971, Lovehead 1974, The World is Full of Divorced Women 1975, Lovers and Gamblers 1977, The Bitch 1979, Chances 1981, Hollywood Wives 1983, Lucky 1985, Hollywood Husbands 1986, Rock Star 1988, Lady Boss 1990, American Star 1993, Hollywood Kids 1994, Vendetta – Lucky's Revenge 1996, Thrill 1998, LA Connections (four-part serial novel) 1998, Dangerous Kiss 1999, Hollywood Wives: The New Generation 2001, Lethal Seduction 2001, Deadly Embrace 2002, Hollywood Divorces 2003, Lovers and Players 2006, Drop Dead Beautiful 2007, Married Lovers 2008. *Address:* c/o Steve Troha, St Martin's Press, 175 Fifth Avenue, New York, NY 10010, USA (office). *Telephone:* (646) 307-5569 (office). *E-mail:* steve.troha@stmartins.com (office). *Website:* www.jackiecollins.com.

COLLINS, James Franklin; American diplomatist (retd); *Senior International Adviser, Akin Gump Strauss Hauer & Feld LLP;* b. 4 June 1939, Aurora, Illinois; ed Harvard Univ., Indiana Univ.; Dir for Intelligence Policy, Nat. Security Council, Washington; Deputy Exec. Sec. Europe and Latin America, US Dept of State, Washington; Vice-Counsel Izmir, Turkey; Political Counsellor Amman, Jordan; Deputy Chief of Mission, American Embassy Moscow 1990–93, Co-ordinator for Regional Affairs for New Ind. States, US Dept of State 1993–94, Sr Co-ordinator Office of Amb.-at-Large for New Ind. States 1994–97; Amb. to Russia 1997–2001; retd 2001; sr int. adviser Akin, Gump, Strauss, Hauer & Feld 2001–;*Telephone:* (202) 887-4066 (office). *E-mail:* jcollins@akingump.com (office); jfcollins@aol.com (home). *Website:* www.akingump.com (office).

COLLINS, Joan Henrietta, OBE; British actress and author; b. 23 May 1933, London; d. of Joseph William Collins and Elsa Collins (née Bessant); sister of Jackie Collins (q.v.); m. 1st Maxwell Reed 1954 (divorced 1957); m. 2nd George Anthony Newley 1963 (divorced 1970); one s. one d.; m. 3rd Ronald S. Kass 1972 (divorced 1983); one d.; m. 4th Peter Holm 1985 (divorced 1987); m. 5th Percy Gibson 2002; ed RADA; actress in numerous stage, film, and TV productions, producer and author; Best TV Actress, Golden Globe, 1982; Favourite TV Performer, People's Choice 1985. *Plays include:* The Last of Mrs Cheyne, London 1979–80, Private Lives London 1990, Broadway 1991, Love Letters, USA tour 2000, Over the Moon, London 2001, Full Circle (UK tour) 2004. *Films include:* I Believe in You 1952, Our Girl Friday 1953, The Good Die Young 1954, Land of the Pharaohs 1955, The Virgin Queen 1955, The Girl in the Red Velvet Swing 1955, The Opposite Sex 1956, Island in the Sun 1957, Sea Wife 1957, The Bravados 1958, Seven Thieves 1960, Road to Hong Kong 1962, Warning Shot 1966, The Executioner 1969, Quest for Love 1971, Revenge 1971, Alfie Darling 1974, The Stud 1979, The Bitch 1980, The Big Sleep, Tales of the Unexpected, Neck 1983, Georgy Porgy 1983, Nutcracker 1984, Decadence 1994, In the Bleak Midwinter 1995, Hart to Hart 1995, Annie: A Royal Adventure 1995, The Clandestine Marriage 1998, Joseph and the Amazing Technicolor Dreamcoat 1999, The Flintstones – Viva Rock Vegas 2000, These Old Broads 2000, Clandestine Marriage 2001, Ozzie 2001. *Television appearances include:* Dynasty (series) 1981–89, Cartier Affair 1985, Sins 1986, Monte Carlo 1986, Tonight at 8.30 1991, Pacific Palisades (series) 1997, Will and Grace 2000, Guiding Light 2002, Hotel Babylon 2006, Footballers Wives 2006. *Publications include:* Past Imperfect 1978, The Joan Collins Beauty Book 1980, Katy, A Fight for Life 1982, Prime Time 1988, Love and Desire and Hate 1990, My Secrets 1994, Too Damn Famous 1995, Second Act 1996, My Friends' Secrets 1999, Star Quality 2002, Joan's Way 2002, Misfortune's Daughters 2004. *Address:* c/o Paul Keylock, 16 Bulbecks Walk, South Woodham Ferrers, Essex, CM3 5ZN, England (office). *Telephone:* (1245) 328367 (office). *Fax:* (1245) 328625 (office). *E-mail:* pkeylock@aol.com (office). *Website:* www.joancollins.net (office).

COLLINS, Sir John (Alexander), Kt., BSc; British business executive; *Chairman, DSG International PLC;* b. 10 Dec. 1941; s. of John Constantine Collins and Nancy Isobel Mitchell; m. Susan Mary Hooper 1965; ed Campbell Coll., Belfast, Reading Univ.; with Shell Int. Chemicals 1964, seconded to Kenya, Nigeria, Colombia, UK 1964–89, Supply and Marketing Co-ordinator and Dir Shell Int. Petroleum Co. Ltd 1989–90, Chair. and CEO Shell UK 1990–93; CEO Vestey Group 1993–2001; Deputy Chair. (non-exec.) and Dir (non-exec.) Dixons Group PLC (now DSG International PLC) 2001–02, Chair. 2002–; Chair. Cantab Pharmaceuticals 1996–99, Nat. Power 1997–2000; Dir BSkyB 1994–97, N.M. Rothschild & Sons (now Rothschild Continuation Holdings) 1995–, London Symphony Orchestra 1997–, Peninsular & Oriental Steam Navigation Co. Ltd 1998–, Stoll Moss Theatres Ltd 1999–2000; Chair. Advisory Cttee on Business and the Environment 1991–93, Dept of Trade & Industry Energy Advisory Panel; mem. Prime Minister's Advisory Cttee for Queen's Awards for Export, Tech. and Environmental Achievement 1992–99; Gov. Wellington Coll. 1995–99. *Leisure interests:* opera, theatre, sailing, riding, golf, tennis, the New Forest. *Address:* DSG International PLC, Maylands Ave., Hemel Hempstead, HP2 7TG, England (office). *Telephone:* (20) 7499-3494 (office). *Fax:* (20) 7499-2071 (office). *Website:* www.dixons-group-plc.co.uk (office).

COLLINS, Joseph Jameson, AB, MBA; American communications industry executive; b. 27 July 1944, Troy, New York; s. of Mark Francis Collins and Olive Elizabeth Collins (née Jameson); m. Maura McManmon 1972; one s. three d.; ed Brown Univ., Harvard Business School; several exec. positions with American TV and Communications Corpn (ATC) 1964–84, Chair. and CEO 1988–90; Pres. Home Box Office, Time Inc. 1984–88; Chair. and CEO Time Warner Cable (after merger with ATC) 1990–2001, CEO Time Warner Interactive Video div. 2001–03 (retd); currently Chair. Aegis LLC; mem. Bd of Dirs Comcast Corpn 2004–; Dir Emer. Cable TV Labs Inc.; Distinguished Vanguard Award for Leadership, Nat. Cable and Telecommunications Asscn, President's Award and Grand TAM Award, Cable and Telecommunications Asscn for Marketing. *Address:* c/o Board of Directors, Comcast Corporation, 1500 Market Street, Philadelphia, PA 19102-2148, USA.

COLLINS, Kim; Saint Christopher and Nevis professional athlete; b. 5 April 1976, Saint Kitts; ed Texas Christian Univ.; sprinter; 60m personal best 6.53 seconds (Fayetteville, AR, USA, March 2000); 100m personal best 9.98 seconds (Paris, France, Sept. 2002); 200m 20.20 seconds (Edmonton, Alberta, Canada, Aug. 2001); winner: World Championships 100m 2003, Commonwealth Games 100m 2002; runner-up: World Cup 100m 2002, Indoor World Championships 60m 2003; 3rd: World Championships 200m 2001, 4th: International Amateur Athletics Federation Grand Final 100m 2002; finalist: Olympic Games 100m 2000, World Championships 100m 2001; ranked 1st in 2003; coach Monte Stratton. *Address:* c/o Saint Kitts and Nevis Olympic Association, Olympic House, 18 Taylor's Range, Bosseterre, Saint Kitts. *Telephone:* 465-6601. *Fax:* 465-8321. *Website:* sknoc@caribsurf.com.

COLLINS, Michael; American fmr astronaut and fmr museum director; b. 31 Oct. 1930, Rome, Italy; m. Patricia M. Finnegan 1957; one s. two d.; ed US Mil. Acad., West Point and Harvard Univ.; commissioned by USAF, served as experimental flight test officer, AF Flight Test Center, Edwards AF Base, Calif.; selected by NASA as astronaut Oct. 1963; backup pilot for Gemini VII mission 1965; pilot of Gemini X 1966; command pilot, Apollo XI mission for first moon landing July 1969; Asst Sec. for Public Affairs, Dept of State 1970–71; Dir Nat. Air and Space Museum 1971–78, Under-Sec. Smithsonian Inst. 1978–80; Maj.-Gen. USAF Reserve; Vice-Pres. LTV Aerospace and Defense Co. 1980–85; Pres. Michael Collins Assocs (aerospace consulting firm), Washington, DC 1985–; Fellow, Royal Aeronautical Soc., American Inst. of Aeronautics and Astronautics; mem. Int. Acad. of Astronautics, Int. Astronautical Fed.; Exceptional Service Medal (NASA), DSM (NASA), Presidential Medal of Freedom, DCM (USAF), DFC, F.A.I. Gold Space Medal. *Publications:* Carrying the Fire 1974, Flying to the Moon and Other Strange Places 1976, Liftoff 1988, Mission to Mars 1990.

COLLINS, Pauline, OBE; British actress; b. 3 Sept. 1940, Exmouth, Devon; d. of William Henry Collins and Mary Honora Callanan; m. John Alderton; two s. one d.; ed Convent of the Sacred Heart, Hammersmith, Cen. School of Speech and Drama; Dr hc (Liverpool Polytechnic) 1991. *Stage appearances include:* A Gazelle in Park Lane (stage debut, Windsor 1962), Passion Flower Hotel 1965, The Erpingham Camp 1967, The Happy Apple 1967, 1970, The Importance of Being Earnest 1968, The Night I Chased the Women with an Eel 1969, Come as You Are 1970, Judies 1974, Engaged 1975, Confusions 1976, Rattle of a Simple Man 1980, Romantic Comedy 1983, Woman in Mind, Shirley Valentine (Olivier Award for best actress, London, Tony, Drama Desk and Outer Critics' Circle awards, New York) 1988, 1989, Shades 1992. *Films include:* Shirley Valentine (Evening Standard Film Actress of the Year 1989, BAFTA Best Actress Award 1990) 1989, City of Joy 1992, My Mother's Courage 1997, Paradise Road 1997, One Life Stand 2000, Mrs Caldicott's Cabbage War 2002. *Television includes:* Emergency-Ward 10 (series) 1957, Amerika 1966, The Making of Jericho 1966, Happy 1969, The Liver Birds (series), 1969, Upstairs Downstairs (series) 1974, Kings Cross 1972, No, Honestly (series) 1974, Wodehouse Playhouse (series) 1975, Thomas and Sarah (series) 1979, Long Distance Information 1979, Little Miss Trouble and Friends (series, voice) 1983, Knockback 1984, Tropical Moon Over Dorking 1985, The Black Tower (miniseries) 1985, Forever Green (series) 1989, The Ambassador (series) 1998, Little Grey Rabbit (series) 2000, Man and Boy 2002, Sparkling Cyanide 2003, Bleak House (series) 2005, Doctor Who (series) 2006. *Publication:* Letter to Louise 1992. *Address:* c/o ICM, Oxford House, 76 Oxford Street, London W1D 1BS, England.

COLLINS, Philip (Phil), LVO; British singer, songwriter, musician (drums) and producer; b. 30 Jan. 1951, Chiswick, London; s. of Greville Collins and June Collins; m. 1st 1976 (divorced); one s. one d.; m. 2nd Jill Tavelman 1984 (divorced 1995); one d.; m. 3rd Orianne Cevey 1999; one s.; ed Barbara Speake Stage School; fmr child actor, appearing as Artful Dodger in London production of Oliver Twist; fmr mem. various music groups, including The Real Thing, The Freehold, Hickory, Flaming Youth 1967–70; mem. rock group, Genesis, as drummer 1970–96, as lead singer 1975–96, 2006–; mem. Brand X 1975–; solo artist 1981–; record producer for various artists; Trustee Prince of Wales Trust 1983–; Grammy Awards (seven), Ivor Novello Awards (six), BRIT Awards (four), Variety Club of Great Britain Awards (two), Silver Clef Awards (two), Elvis Awards, Acad. Award (for You'll be in my Heart, from film Tarzan) 1999, American Music Award for Favorite Adult Contemporary Artist 2000. *Films:* Buster 1988, Frauds 1993. *Recordings include:* albums: with Genesis: From Genesis To Revelation 1969, Trespass 1970, Nursery Cryme 1971, Foxtrot 1972, Genesis Live 1973, Selling England By The Pound 1973, The Lamb Lies Down On Broadway 1974, A Trick Of The Tail 1976, Seconds Out 1977, Wind And Wuthering 1977, And Then There Were Three 1978, Duke 1980, Abacab 1981, Three Sides Live 1982, Genesis 1983, Invisible Touch 1986, We Can't Dance 1991, The Way We Walk: The Shorts 1992, The Way We Walk: The Longs 1993, Calling All Stations 1997, Turn It On Again 1999, Archive 1967–75 1999, Archive 1976–92 2001; with Brand X: Unorthodox Behaviour, Moroccan Roll 1977, Livestock 1977, Product 1979, Do They Hurt? 1980, Is There Anything About? 1982, Xtrax 1986, The Plot Thins 1992, Brand X Featuring Phil Collins 1996, Live At The Roxy 1996, Missing Period 1997, A History 1976–80 1997, The X-Files 1999; solo: Face Value 1981, Hello, I Must Be Going! 1982, No Jacket Required 1985, 12"ers 1987, ...But Seriously 1989, Serious Hits... Live! 1990, Both Sides 1993, Dance Into The Light 1996, ...Hits! 1998, A Hot Night In Paris 1999, Tarzan 1999, Testify 2002, Love Songs: A Complication Old And New 2004, The Platinum Collection 2004. *Publication:* Genesis: Chapter and Verse (with other band mems) 2007. *Address:* Hit and Run Music, 30 Ives Street, London, SW3 2ND, England (office). *E-mail:* info@genesis-music.com. *Website:* www.philcollins.co.uk; www.genesis-music.com.

COLLINS, Rory E., PhD, FRCP, FMedSci, FFPM; British epidemiologist and academic; *BHF Professor of Medicine and Epidemiologist and Co-Director, Clinical Trial Service Unit, University of Oxford;* Co-Dir Clinical Trial Service Unit (CTSU), Nuffield Dept of Clinical Medicine, Univ. of Oxford 1985–, BHF Prof. of Medicine and Epidemiology 1996–; Prin. Investigator and Chief Exec. UK Biobank prospective study of 0.5M British men and women aged 40–69 2005–; CTSU awarded a Queen's Anniversary Prize for Higher and Further Educ. 2006, J. Allyn Taylor Int. Prize in Medicine, Robarts Research Inst. 2007. *Publications:* numerous scientific papers in professional journals on the establishment of large-scale epidemiological studies of the causes, prevention and treatment of heart attacks, other vascular disease, and cancer. *Address:*

Clinical Trial Service Unit, Richard Doll Building, Old Road Campus, Roosevelt Drive, Oxford, OX3 7LF, England (office). *Telephone:* (1865) 743834 (office). *Fax:* (1865) 743985 (office). *E-mail:* secretary@ctsu.ox.ac.uk (office). *Website:* www.ctsu.ox.ac.uk (office).

COLLINS, Susan Margaret, BA; American politician; *Senator from Maine;* b. 7 Dec. 1952, Caribou, Me; ed St Lawrence Univ.; Prin. Adviser on Business Affairs to Senator Bill Cohen 1975–78; Staff Dir Senate Sub-Cttee on Oversight Govt Man. 1981–87; Commr Maine Dept of Professional and Financial Regulation 1987–92; Dir New England Operations, US Small Business Admin 1992–93; Exec. Dir Center Family Business, Husson Coll., Bangor 1993–96; Senator from Maine 1997–, mem. Cttee on Health, Educ., Labor and Pensions 1997–, Sub-Cttee on Children and Families 1997–, Sub-Cttee on Public Health and Safety 1997–, Cttee on Govt Affairs 1997–, Chair. Perm. Sub-Cttee on Investigation 1997–, mem. Special Cttee on Ageing; Chair. Maine Cabinet Council on Health Care Policy; Republican cand. for Gov. of Maine 1994; Outstanding Alumni Award, St Lawrence Univ. 1992. *Address:* 461 Dirksen Senate Office Building, US Senate, Washington, DC 20510, USA (office). *Telephone:* (202) 224-2523 (office). *Fax:* (202) 224-2693 (office). *Website:* collins.senate.gov (office).

COLLINSON, Patrick, CBE, PhD, FBA, FRHistS, FAHA; British historian and academic; *Professor Emeritus of Modern History, University of Cambridge;* b. 10 Aug. 1929, Ipswich; s. of William Cecil Collinson and Belle Hay Collinson (née Patrick); m. Elizabeth Albinia Susan Selwyn 1960; two s. two d.; ed King's School, Ely, Pembroke Coll., Cambridge and Univ. of London; Research Asst, Univ. Coll. London 1955–56; Lecturer in History, Univ. of Khartoum, Sudan 1956–61; Lecturer in Ecclesiastical History, King's Coll. London 1961–69; Prof. of History, Univ. of Sydney, Australia 1969–75; Prof. of History, Univ. of Kent at Canterbury 1976–84; Prof. of Modern History, Univ. of Sheffield 1984–88; Regius Prof. of Modern History, Univ. of Cambridge 1988–96, now Emer.; Ford's Lecturer in English History, Univ. of Oxford 1979; Visiting Prof. Univ. of Richmond, VA 1999; Assoc. Visiting Prof., Univ. of Warwick 2000–03; Fellow, Trinity Coll., Cambridge 1988–; Chair. Advisory Ed. Bd Journal of Ecclesiastical History 1982–93; Pres. Ecclesiastical History Soc. 1985–86, Church of England Record Soc. 1991–92; mem. Council British Acad. 1986–89; Hon. DUniv (York) 1988; Hon. DLitt (Kent) 1989, (Trinity Coll. Dublin) 1992, (Sheffield) 1994, (Oxford) 1997, (Essex) 2000, (Warwick) 2003; Medlicott Medal, Historical Asscn 1998. *Publications:* The Elizabethan Puritan Movement 1967, Archbishop Grindal 1519–1583: The Struggle for a Reformed Church 1979, The Religion of Protestants: the Church in English Society 1559–1625 (The Ford Lectures 1979) 1982, Godly People: Essays on English Protestantism and Puritanism 1984, English Puritanism 1984, The Birthpangs of Protestant England: Religious and Cultural Change in the 16th and 17th Centuries 1988, Elizabethan Essays 1993, A History of Canterbury Cathedral (jtly) 1995, The Reformation in English Towns (jtly) 1998, A History of Emmanuel College, Cambridge (jtly) 1999, Short Oxford History of the British Isles: The Sixteenth Century (ed) 2002, Reformation 2003, Elizabethans 2003, Conferences and Combination Lectures in the Elizabethan Church (jtly) 2003, Oxford Dictionary of National Biography 2004, From Cranmer to Sancroft 2006. *Leisure interests:* grandchildren, music. *Address:* New House, Crown Square, Shaldon, Devon TQ14 0DS (home); Trinity College, Cambridge, CB2 1TQ, England (office). *Telephone:* (1626) 871245 (home); (1223) 338400 (office). *Fax:* (1626) 871245 (home); (1433) 650918. *E-mail:* patrickcollinson@btinternet.com (home).

COLLMAN, James Paddock, PhD; American chemist and academic; *George A. and Hilda M. Daubert Professor of Chemistry, Stanford University;* b. 31 Oct. 1932, Beatrice, Neb.; s. of Perry G. Collman and Frances Dorothy Palmer; m. Patricia Tincher 1955; four d.; ed Univs. of Nebraska and Illinois; Instructor, Univ. of NC 1958–59, Asst Prof. 1959–62, Assoc. Prof. 1962–66, Prof. of Organic and Inorganic Chem. 1966–67; Prof., Stanford Univ. 1967–, George A. and Hilda M. Daubert Prof. of Chem. 1980–; mem. NAS, American Acad. of Arts and Sciences; Alfred P. Sloan Foundation Fellow 1963–66; Nat. Science Foundation Sr Postdoctoral Fellow 1965–66; Guggenheim Fellow 1977–78, 1985–86; Churchill Fellow (Cambridge) 1977–; Dr. hc (Univ. of Nebraska) 1988, (Univ. de Bourgogne) 1988; American Chemical Soc. (ACS) Award in Inorganic Chem. 1975, Calif. Scientist of the Year Award 1983, Arthur C. Cope Scholar Award (ACS) 1986, Pauling Award 1990, ACS Award for Distinguished Service in the Advancement of Inorganic Chem. 1991, LAS Alumni Achievement Award, Coll. of Liberal Arts and Sciences Univ. of Ill. 1994, Marker Lecturer Medal 1999, Japanese Coordination Chemistry Award 2008, Ronald Breslow Award for Biomimetic Chemistry 2009. *Publications:* Principles and Applications of Organo-transition Metal Chemistry (with Louis S. Hegedus) 1980, 1987, Naturally Dangerous 2001; and 300 scientific papers. *Leisure interest:* fishing. *Address:* Department of Chemistry, Stauffer II, Room 201, Stanford University, Stanford, CA 94305-5080, USA; 794 Tolman Drive, Stanford, CA 94305-5080, USA (home). *Telephone:* (650) 725-0283 (office); (650) 493-0934 (home). *Fax:* (650) 725-0259 (office). *E-mail:* jpc@stanford.edu (office). *Website:* stanford.edu/group/collman (office).

COLLOMB, Bertrand Pierre Charles, PhD; French business executive; *Honorary Chairman, Lafarge;* b. 14 Aug. 1942, Lyon; s. of Charles Collomb and Hélène Traon; m. Marie-Caroline Collomb 1967; two s. one d.; ed Ecole Polytechnique, Paris, Ecole des Mines, Paris and Univ. of Texas, Austin, USA; worked with French Govt, Founder and Man. Centre for Man. Research, Ecole Polytechnique 1972–75; joined Lafarge as Regional Man. 1975, later Pres. and CEO Ciments Lafarge France; CEO Orsan (Biotechnology Co. of the Lafarge Group) 1983; CEO Lafarge Corp. 1987–88; Vice-Chair. and CEO Lafarge 1989, Chair. and CEO 1989–2003, Chair. 2003–07, currently Hon. Chair.; Chair. IFRI (French Inst. of Int. Relations); Chair. IHEST (Inst. for Science and Tech.); mem. Governing Body EIT (European Inst. of Tech.); mem. European Corporate Governance Forum; mem. Institut de France (Acad. des Sciences, Morales et Politiques); Officier, Légion d'honneur, Commdr, Ordre nat. du Mérite. *Leisure interests:* horse riding, hunting. *Address:* Lafarge, 61 rue des Belles Feuilles, BP 40, 75782 Paris Cedex 16 (office); 4 rue de Lota, 75116 Paris, France (home). *Telephone:* 1-44-34-12-02 (office); 1-45-53-02-86 (home). *Fax:* 1-44-34-12-07 (office); 1-47-27-46-99 (home). *E-mail:* bertrand.collomb@lafarge.com (office). *Website:* www.lafarge.com (office).

COLMAN, Sir Michael Jeremiah, 3rd Bt, cr. 1907; British business executive; b. 7 July 1928, London; s. of Sir Jeremiah Colman, 2nd Bt and Edith Gwendolyn Tritton; m. Judith Jean Wallop (née William-Powlett) 1955; two s. three d.; ed Eton Coll.; Capt. Yorks Yeomanry 1967; Dir Reckitt and Colman PLC 1970–95, Chair. 1986–95; First Church Estates Commr 1993–99; Dir Foreign and Colonial Ventures Advisors Ltd 1988–99; Trade Affairs Bd Chemical Industries Asscn 1978–84, Council 1983–84; Council Mem. Royal Warrant Holders Asscn 1977–, Pres. 1984; mem. Gen. Council and Investment Cttee, King Edward's Hosp. Fund for London 1978–2004; Assoc. of Trinity House, mem. Lighthouse Bd 1985–94, Younger Brother 1994; mem. Bd UK Centre for Econ. and Environmental Devt 1985–99, Chair. 1996–99; mem. of the Court of Skinners' Co. 1985– (Master 1991–92); mem. Council of Scouts Asscn 1985–2000; Assoc. Trustee St Mary's Hosp., London 1988–2000; Archbishop's Cross of St Augustine 1999; Hon. LLD (Hull) 1993. *Leisure interests:* farming, shooting, forestry, golf. *Address:* Malshanger, Basingstoke, Hants., RG23 7EY (home); 40 Chester Square, London, SW1W 9HT, England. *Telephone:* (1256) 780241 (home).

COLMAN, Peter Malcolm, PhD, FAA, FTSE; Australian medical research scientist; *Division Head, Walter and Eliza Hall Institute of Medical Research;* b. 3 April 1944, Adelaide; s. of Clement Colman and Kathleen Colman; m. Anne Elizabeth Smith 1967; two s.; ed Univ. of Adelaide; Post-Doctoral Fellow, Univ. of Oregon 1969–72, Deutsche Forschungsgemeinschaft, Max Planck Inst., Munich 1972–75; Queen Elizabeth II Fellow, Univ. of Sydney 1975–77; consultant, Univ. of Utah 1977; Prin. Investigator, Nat. Health and Medical Research Council, Univ. of Sydney 1977–78, Officer, CSIRO 1978–89, Chief Div. of Biomolecular Eng 1989–97, Dir Biomolecular Research Inst. 1991–2000; Professorial Assoc., Univ. of Melbourne 1988–98, Professorial Fellow 1998–2003; Adjunct Prof., La Trobe Univ. 1998–2001; Sr Prin. Research Fellow (NHMRC), Walter and Eliza Hall Inst. of Medical Research, Div. Head 2001–; Dir Biota Holdings Ltd 1985–91; Royal Soc. Victorian Medal 1986, Lemberg Medallist and lecturer, Australian Biochemical Soc. 1988, Burnet Medal, Australian Acad. of Sciences 1995, Australia Prize 1996, Mayne-Florey Medal 2004, Victoria Prize 2008. *Achievements:* co-discoverer of neuraminidase inhibitors as medicines for influenza virus infection. *Leisure interest:* music. *Address:* 74 Hotham Street, East Melbourne, Vic. 3002 (home); Walter and Eliza Hall Institute of Medical Research, 1G Royal Parade, Parkville, Vic. 3050, Australia (office). *Website:* www.wehi.edu.au (office).

COLOM CABALLEROS, Álvaro, BEng; Guatemalan industrial engineer, business executive, politician and head of state; *President;* b. 15 June 1951, Guatemala City; m.; ed Univ. de San Carlos; Deputy Minister for the Economy 1991; Founder and Pres., Unidad Nacional de la Esperanza (UNE) 2001–, runner up in primary elections for Pres. 2003, Pres. 2008–; Founder and Pres. Grupo Mega; Exec. Dir Dependencia Presidencial de Asistencia Legal y Resolución de Conflictors sobre la Tierra (CONTIERRA); Founder, Pnr and Production Man. Roprisma, Intraexsa; Man. Dept Industrial de DINAH SA; Dir Clothing Comm., Chamber of Industry and Commerce 1977–82; Vice Pres. Asscn of Guatemalan Exporters 1990–; Dir Fundación para el Análisis y Desarollo de Centroamérica (FADES) 1999–; Adviser, Consejo Nacional de Ancianos Mayas (Mayan Council) 1996–; mem. Consultative Bd, AGEXPRONT 1977–82, Dir 1982–90; Founder and Pres. Nat. Comm. for the Clothing Industry 1984; Adviser, Secretaría de la Paz (SEPAZ) 1997; serves as an ordained Mayan minister. *Address:* Office of the President, Guatemala City; Unidad Nacional de la Esperanza (UNE), 2a Avenida 5-11, Zona 9, Guatemala City, Guatemala (office). *Telephone:* 232-4685 (office). *E-mail:* ideas@une.org.gt (office). *Website:* www.une.org.gt (office).

COLOMBANI, Jean-Marie; French journalist; b. 7 July 1948, Dakar, Senegal; m. Catherine Sénès 1976; five c.; ed Lycée Hoche, Versailles, Lycée La Pérouse, Nouméa, New Caledonia, Univ. of Paris II-Assas, Univ. of Paris I Panthéon-Sorbonne, Inst. d'Etudes Politiques, Paris and Inst. d'Etudes Supérieures de Droit Public; journalist, ORTF, later Office of FR3, Nouméa 1973; Ed. Political Service, Le Monde 1977, Head of Political Service 1983, Ed.-in-Chief 1990, Deputy Editorial Dir 1991; Man. Dir S.A.–Le Monde March–Dec. 1994, Chair. of Bd and Dir of Publs 1994–2007, mem. Bd of Dirs 2007–08; Co-founder online magazine in France based on Slate.com 2009; Chair. Advisory Council, Midi-Libre Group 2000–. *Publications:* Contradictions: entretiens avec Anicet Le Poro 1984, L'utopie calédonienne 1985, Portrait du président ou le monarque imaginaire 1985, Le mariage blanc (co-author) 1986, Questions de confiance: entretiens avec Raymond Barre 1987, Les héritiers (co-author), La France sans Mitterrand 1992, La gauche survivra-t-elle aux socialistes? 1994, Le Double Septennat de François Mitterrand, Dernier Inventaire (jtly) 1995, De la France en général et de ses dirigeants en particulier 1996, Le Résident de la République 1998, La Cinquième ou la République des phratries (co-author) 1999, Les infortunes de la Republique 2000, Tous Américains? 2002. *Leisure interest:* cinema. *Address:* 5 rue Joseph Bara, 75006 Paris, France (home). *Website:* www .slate.fr.

COLOMBO, Emilio; Italian politician; *President, Italian Atlantic Committee;* b. 11 April 1920; ed Rome Univ.; took active part in Catholic youth orgs; fmr Vice-Pres. Italian Catholic Youth Asscn; Deputy, Constituent Ass. 1946–48, Parl. 1948–; Under-Sec. of Agric. 1948–51, of Public Works 1953–55; Minister of Agric. 1955–58, of Foreign Trade 1958–59, of Industry and Commerce 1959–60, March–April 1960, 1960–63, of the Treasury 1963–70, Feb.–May 1972; Prime Minister 1970–72; Minister without Portfolio in charge of Italian representation of UN 1972–73; Minister of Finance 1973–74, of the Treasury 1974–76, of Foreign Affairs 1980–83, 1992–93, of Budget and Econ. Planning 1987–88, of Finance 1988–89; 1976–80 (Pres. 1977–79); currently Pres. Italian Atlantic Cttee; Pres. Nat. Cttee for Nuclear Research 1961; mem. Cen. Cttee Christian Democratic Party 1952, 1953; named Senator for Life 2003. *Address:* Italian Atlantic Committee, Piazza Firenze 27, 00186 Rome, Italy (office). *Telephone:* (06) 6873786 (office). *Fax:* (06) 6873376 (office). *E-mail:* italata@iol.it (office); info@emiliocolombo.it. *Website:* www.emiliocolombo.it; www.comitatoatlantico.it (office).

COLOMBO, John Robert, CM, OC, BA, DLitt; Canadian editor, author and consultant; b. 24 March 1936, Kitchener, Ont.; m. Ruth F. Brown 1959; two s. one d.; ed Kitchener-Waterloo Collegiate Inst., Waterloo Coll. and Univ. Coll., Univ. of Toronto; editorial asst, Univ. of Toronto Press 1957–59; Asst Ed. The Ryerson Press 1960–63; Instructor, York Univ., Downsview, Ont. 1963–65; Consulting Ed. McClelland & Stewart 1963–70, Ed.-at-Large 1963–; Gen. Ed. The Canadian Global Almanac 1992–2000; Writer-in-residence, Mohawk Coll., Hamilton, Ont. 1979–80; Consultant, American Man. Asscn/Canadian Man. Centre; Assoc. Northrop Frye Centre, Victoria Coll., Univ. of Toronto; Order of Cyril and Methodius 1979; Esteemed Kt of Mark Twain 1979; Hon. DLitt (York Univ., Toronto) 1998; Centennial Medal 1967, Harbour Front Literary Prize 1985. *Television:* Presenter: Colombo Quotes (series), CBC-TV 1978, Unexplained Canada (series), Space Network 2006. *Publications include:* over 200 books of poetry, prose, reference, science fiction anthologies and translations including Colombo's Canadian Quotations 1974, Colombo's Canadian References 1976, Colombo's Book of Canada 1978, Canadian Literary Landmarks 1984, 1,001 Questions about Canada 1986, Colombo's New Canadian Quotations 1987, Mysterious Canada 1988, Songs of the Great Land 1989, Mysterious Encounters 1990, The Dictionary of Canadian Quotations 1991, UFOs over Canada 1991, Dark Visions 1992, Worlds in Small 1992, The Mystery of the Shaking Tent 1993, Walt Whitman's Canada 1993, Voices of Rama 1994, 1995, Close Encounters of the Canadian Kind 1995, Ghost Stories of Ontario 1995, Haunted Toronto 1996, Iron Curtains 1996, The New Consciousness 1997, Weird Stories 1999, Ghosts in our Past 2000, The UFO Quote Book 2000, 1000 Questions about Canada 2001, Famous Lasting Words 2001, The Penguin Book of Canadian Jokes 2002, The Penguin Treasury of Popular Canadian Poems and Songs 2002, The Penguin Book of More Canadian Jokes 2003, O Rare Denis Saurat 2003, True Canadian Ghost Stories 2003, The Midnight Hour 2004, The Denis Saurat Reader 2004, The Monster Book of Canadian Monsters 2004, The Native Series 2005, Early Earth 2006, All the Poems 2006, All the Aphorisms 2006, Autumn in August 2006, Miniatures 2006, The Penguin Dictionary of Popular Canadian Quotations 2006, Terrors of the Night 2007, The Big Book of Canadian Ghost Stories 2008, Whistle While You Work 2008, A Far Cry 2009. *Leisure interest:* reading. *Address:* 42 Dell Park Avenue, Toronto, ON M6B 2T6, Canada (home). *Telephone:* (416) 782-6853 (home). *Fax:* (416) 782-0285 (home). *E-mail:* jrc@ca.inter.net (office). *Website:* www.colombo-plus.ca (home).

COLOMBO, Umberto, ScD; Italian chemical engineer and government official; b. 20 Dec. 1927, Livorno; s. of Eugenio Colombo and Maria Eminente Colombo; m. Milena Piperno 1951; two d.; ed Univ. of Pavia, MIT, USA; Dir Montedison's G. Donegani Research Centre 1967–70, Dir-Gen. for Research and Corp. Strategies, Montedison 1971–78; Chair. Italian Atomic Energy Comm. 1979–82; Chair. ENEA (Italian Nat. Agency for New Tech., Energy and the Environment) 1982–93; Pres. European Science Foundation 1991; Minister for Univs and Scientific Research 1993–94; fmr mem. Council, UN Univ.; fmr Chair. EC's Cttee on Science and Tech. (CODEST), UN Advisory Cttee on Science and Tech. for Devt, OECD Cttee on Scientific and Tech. Policy, European Industrial Research Man. Asscn; Chair. Novamont SpA, Dike Aedifica SpA; mem. Bd of Dirs SAES Getters SpA, Impregilo SpA, Telecom Italia Media SpA; mem. Accademia Nazionale dei Lincei, Academia Europaea, Italian Nat. Council of Economy and Labour, China Council for Int. Cooperation on Environment and Devt; Foreign mem. Swiss, Swedish, Japanese and US Acads of Eng Sciences, American Acad. of Arts and Sciences, Fellowship of Eng, UK; Assoc. Fellow, Third World Acad. of Sciences, New York Acad. of Sciences; Hon. mem., Club of Rome; Hon. Trustee Aspen Inst. of Humanistic Studies; Hon. Degree in Science (Anna Univ., Madras) 1991;, Hon. Degree in Engineering (Mendelejev Univ., Moscow) 1994; Conrad Schlumberger Prize 1958, Roncaglia Mari Prize 1977, Honda Prize for Ecotechnology 1984, Giulio Natta Medal, Italian Chemistry Asscn 1991. *Publications:* (co-author): Beyond the Age of Waste 1976, WAES Report Italy 1978, La Speranza Tecnologica 1979, Il Secondo Pianeta 1982, Scienza e Tecnologia verso il XXI Secolo 1988, La Frontiere della Tecnologica 1990; over 200 essays and articles on energy, scientific and technology policy. *Leisure interests:* music, farming. *Address:* Via del Viminale, 43, 00184 Rome; Novamont S.p.A. Via Fauser 8, 28100 Novara; Via San Martino ai Monti 26 bis, 00184 Rome, Italy.

COLOMINA, Beatriz, PhD; Spanish architect and academic; *Professor of History and Architecture, Princeton University;* ed Escuela Tecnica Superior de Arquitectura Universidad de Barcelona; trained as architect, Valencia and Barcelona –1976; Asst Prof. Columbia Univ., New York, USA 1984–88; Asst Prof. Princeton Univ. 1988, later Assoc. Prof. of the History and Theory of Architecture, currently Prof. of History and Architecture; has lectured extensively throughout world including Museum of Modern Art, New York, Architectural Inst. of Japan, Tokyo, Centre for Contemporary Art and Architecture, Stockholm, DIA Art Foundation, New York, Museum of Contemporary Art, Barcelona, Museo de Bellas Artes, Buenos Aires, Harvard and Yale Univs, Architectural Asscn, London, Helsinki Univ., Auckland Univ., Wissenschaftskolleg, Berlin; Titulo de Architecto; recipient of grants

and fellowships from Chicago Inst. for Architecture, SOM Foundation, Graham Foundation, Fondation Le Corbusier, Center for Advanced Studies in the Visual Arts, Washington, DC, Canadian Centre for Architecture, Montréal. *Publications include:* Architectureproduction (ed.) 1988, Sexuality and Space (ed., AIA Int. Book Award 1993) 1992, Privacy and Publicity: Modern Architecture as Mass Media (AIA Int. Book Award 1995) 1994, The Work of Charles and Ray Eames (co-author) 1997, Frank Gehry Architect (co-author) 2001, Cold War Hothouses (co-ed.) 2004, Doble Exposicion: La Arquitectura a través del Arte 2006, Domesticity at War 2006; numerous articles. *Address:* School of Architecture, Princeton University, Princeton, NJ 08544-5264, USA (office). *Telephone:* (609) 258-3741 (office). *Fax:* (609) 258-4740 (office). *E-mail:* colomina@princeton.edu (office). *Website:* www .princeton.edu/~soa (office).

COLSON, Charles (Chuck) Wendell, BA, JD; American writer and fmr government official; *Chairman, Prison Fellowship;* b. 16 Oct. 1931, Boston; s. of Wendell Colson and Inez Ducrow; m. 1st Nancy Billings 1953; two s. one d.; m. 2nd Patricia Hughes 1964; ed Brown Univ. and George Washington Univ.; Capt. in US Marine Corps 1953–55; Asst to Asst Sec. of US Navy 1955–56; admin. asst to US Senator L. Saltonstall 1956–61; Sr Pnr, Gadsby & Hannah (law firm) 1961–69; Special Counsel to Pres. Richard Nixon 1969–73; Pnr Colson & Shapiro, Washington, DC 1973–74; received seven-month jail sentence for role in Watergate scandal 1974; Founder and Chair. Prison Fellowship and Prison Fellowship Int. 1976–; Distinguished Sr Fellow, Coalition for Christian Colls and Univs 1997; Trustee Gordon Conwell Theological Seminary; recipient of several hon. degrees; The Others Award, Salvation Army 1990, Templeton Prize 1993 and other awards. *Radio:* "Breakpoint" (daily radio commentary). *Publications:* Born Again 1975, Life Sentence 1979, Crime and The Responsible Community 1980, Loving God 1983, Who Speaks for God? 1985, Kingdoms in Conflict 1987, Against the Night 1989, The God of Stones and Spiders 1990, Why America Doesn't Work (with J. Eckerd) 1991, The Body 1992, A Dance with Deception 1993, A Dangerous Grace 1994, Gideon's Torch 1995, Burden of Truth 1997, Evangelicals and Catholics Together (with R. Neuhaus) 1995, How Now Shall We Live (with N. Pearcey) 1999, Chuck Colson Speaks 2000, Answers to Your Kids' Questions 2000, Justice that Restores 2001, Being The Body 2003. *Leisure interests:* writing, fishing. *Address:* Prison Fellowship, 44180 Riverside Parkway, Lansdowne, VA 20176, USA (office). *Telephone:* (703) 478-0100 (office). *Fax:* (703) 834-3658 (office). *Website:* www.pfm.org (office).

COLSON, Elizabeth Florence, PhD; American anthropologist and academic; *Professor Emerita of Anthropology, University of California, Berkeley;* b. 15 June 1917, Hewitt, Minn.; d. of Louis Henry Colson and Metta Damon Colson; ed Wadena Public High School, Univ. of Minnesota, Radcliffe Coll.; Sr Research Officer, Rhodes-Livingstone Inst. 1946–47, Dir 1948–51; Sr Lecturer, Manchester Univ., UK 1951–53; Assoc. Prof., Goucher Coll. 1954–55; Assoc. Prof. and Research Assoc., Boston Univ. 1955–59; Prof., Brandeis Univ. 1959–63; Prof., Univ. of California, Berkeley 1964–84, Prof. Emer. 1984–; Lewis Henry Morgan Lecturer, Univ. of Rochester 1973; Visiting Prof., Univ. of Zambia 1987; mem. NAS, American Acad. of Arts and Science; Fellow, Center for Advanced Study in the Behavioral Sciences, Stanford Univ.; Fairchild Fellow, California Inst. of Tech.; Hon. Fellow, Royal Anthropological Soc., UK; Dr hc (Brown, Rochester, Univ. of Zambia); Rivers Memorial Medal, Distinguished Lecture, American Anthropological Asscn 1975, Faculty Research Lecture, Univ. of California, Berkeley 1983, Malinowski Distinguished Lecture, Soc. for Applied Anthropology 1984, Distinguished Africanist Award, AAAS 1988. *Publications:* Seven Tribes of British Central Africa, 1951, The Makah 1953, Marriage and the Family among the Plateau Tonga 1958, Social Organization of the Gwembe Tonga 1962, Social Consequences of Resettlement 1971, Tradition and Contract 1974, Autobiographies of three Pomo Women 1974; (with Thayer Scudder) Secondary Education and the Formation of an Elite 1980, People in Upheaval 1987 (with Thayer Scuddes), For Prayer and Profit 1988; (with Lenore Ralstrom and James Anderson) Voluntary Efforts in Decentralized Management 1983, The History of Nampeyo 1991. *Address:* c/o Department of Anthropology, University of California, Berkeley, CA 94720, USA. *Telephone:* (510) 526-3743. *E-mail:* gwembe@uclink.berkeley.

COLTRANE, Robbie, OBE; British actor; b. 31 March 1950, Glasgow; m. Rhona Irene Gemmel 2000; one s. one d.; ed Glasgow School of Art; Co-Producer, Young Mental Health (documentary) 1973; Co-Writer and Dir Jealousy (BBC) 1992, Brothers Bloom 2007; Peter Sellers Comedy Award, Evening Standard 1990, Best Actor, Royal Television Soc. 1993, Best Actor, Broadcasting Press Guild 1993, Best Actor TV Series, British Acad. of Film and TV Arts 1993, 1994, 1995, Best Actor, Monte Carlo TV Festival 1994, Fipa d'Or for Best Actor, Nice Film and Television Festival 1995, Best Actor in Film or Mini-series, Nat. Cable Ace Awards (USA) 1996, Best Actor in TV Series, Royal Television Soc. 1996, Goldener Gong for Best Actor, German TV 1996. *Films include:* Mona Lisa, Subway Riders, Britannia Hospital, Defence of the Realm, Caravaggio, Eat The Rich, Absolute Beginners, The Fruit Machine, Slipstream, Nuns On The Run, Huckleberry Finn, Bert Rigby, You're A Fool, Danny, Champion of the World, Henry V, Let It Ride, The Adventures of Huckleberry Finn, Goldeneye, Buddy, Montana, Frogs for Snakes, Message in a Bottle, The World is Not Enough 1999, On the Nose 2000, From Hell 2000, Harry Potter and the Philosopher's Stone 2001, Harry Potter and the Chamber of Secrets 2002, Harry Potter and the Prisoner of Azkaban 2004, Ocean's 12 2004, Harry Potter and the Goblet of Fire 2005, Stormbreaker 2006, Provoked 2006, Harry Potter and the Order of the Phoenix 2007, The Brothers Bloom 2008, Tales of Despereaux 2008. *Stage appearances include:* Waiting for Godot, Endgame, The Bug, Mr Joyce is Leaving, The Slab Boys, The Transfiguration of Benno Blimpie, The Loveliest Night of the Year, Snobs and Yobs, Your Obedient Servant (one-man show) 1987, Mistero Buffo 1990,

The Brother's Suit 2005. *Television appearances include:* The Comic Strip Presents…, Five Go Mad In Dorset, The Beat Generation, War, Summer School, Five Go Mad on Mescalin, Susie, Gino, Dirty Movie, The Miner's Strike, The Supergrass (feature film), The Ebb-tide, Alice in Wonderland, The Young Ones, Kick Up the Eighties, The Tube, Saturday Night Live, Lenny Henry Show, Blackadder, Tutti Frutti, Coltrane in a Cadillac, Cracker, Boswell and Johnson's Tour of the Western Isles 1990, The Plan Man 2003, Cracker 9/11 2005, Coltrane's B-Road Britain 2007. *Publications:* Coltrane in a Cadillac 1992, Coltrane's Planes and Automobiles 1999. *Leisure interests:* sailing, film, vintage cars, music, art. *Address:* 125 Gloucester Road, London, SW7 4TE, England. *Telephone:* (20) 7373-3323.

COLUMBUS, Chris; American film director and screenwriter; b. 10 Sept. 1958, Spangler, Pa; s. of Alex Michael Columbus and Mary Irene Puskar; m. Monica Devereux 1983; two d.; ed New York Univ. Film School; wrote and developed TV cartoon series Galaxy High School; f. 1942 Productions (production co.). *Screenplays include:* Reckless 1983, Gremlins 1984, The Goonies 1985, The Young Sherlock Holmes 1985, Only the Lonely 1991, Little Nemo: Adventures in Slumberland (jtly) 1992, Nine Months 1995, Christmas with the Kranks 2004. *Films include:* Adventures in Babysitting 1987, Heartbreak Hotel 1988, Home Alone 1990, Only the Lonely 1991, Home Alone 2: Lost in New York 1992, Mrs Doubtfire 1993, Nine Months (also producer) 1995, Jingle All the Way (also producer) 1996, Stepmom (also producer) 1998, Monkey Bone 1999, Bicentennial Man (also producer) 1999, Harry Potter and the Philosopher's Stone (also producer) 2001, Harry Potter and the Chamber of Secrets (also producer) 2002, Rent (also producer) 2005, Night at the Museum (producer) 2006, 4: Rise of the Silver Surfer (producer) 2007, . *TV directed includes:* Amazing Stories, Twilight Zone, Alfred Hitchcock Presents (series). *Address:* c/o Beth Swofford, CAA, 9830 Wilshire Boulevard, Beverly Hills, CA 90212, USA.

COLVILLE OF CULROSS, 4th Viscount, cr. 1902; 14th Baron (Scotland), cr. 1604; 4th Baron (UK), cr. 1885; **John Mark Alexander Colville,** QC, MA; British judge; *Assistant Surveillance Commissioner;* b. 19 July 1933; s. of the late Viscount Colville of Culross and Kathleen Myrtle Gale; m. 1st Mary Elizabeth Webb-Bowen 1958 (divorced 1973); four s.; m. 2nd Margaret Birgitta, Viscountess Davidson (née Norton) 1974; one s.; ed Rugby School, New Coll. Oxford; called to Bar, Lincoln's Inn 1960, QC 1978, Bencher 1986, a Recorder 1990–93, Judge, South Eastern Circuit 1993–99; Minister of State, Home Office 1972–74; UK Rep., UN Human Rights Comm. 1980–83, mem. UN Working Group on Disappeared Persons 1980–84 (Chair. 1981–84), Special Rapporteur on Human Rights in Guatemala 1983–87, mem. UN Human Rights Cttee 1996–2000; Asst Surveillance Commr 2001–; Dir Securities and Futures Authority (fmrly Securities Asscn) 1987–93; Chair. Mental Health Act Comm. 1983–88, Alcohol Educ. and Research Council 1984–90, Parole Bd for England and Wales 1988–92; author of reports for Govt on Prevention of Terrorism Act and Northern Ireland Emergency Powers Act 1986–93; Chair. Norwich Information and Tech. Centre 1983–85; Dir Rediffusion TV Ltd 1961–68, British Electric Traction Co. Ltd 1968–72, 1974–84 (Deputy Chair. 1980–81); mem. CBI Council 1982–84; Gov. BUPA 1990–93; mem. Royal Co. of Archers (Queen's Body Guard for Scotland); Hon. Fellow New Coll. Oxford; Hon. DCL (East Anglia). *Address:* House of Lords, Westminster, London, SW1A 0PW (office); West Lexham Manor, King's Lynn, Norfolk, PE32 2QN, England (home).

COLVIN, Marie Catherine, BA; American journalist; *Foreign Affairs Correspondent, The Sunday Times (UK);* b. 12 Jan. 1956, New York; d. of William Joseph Colvin and Rosemarie Marron; m. Patrick Bishop 1989 (divorced); ed Yale Univ.; with United Press Int. (UPI), New York and Washington, DC 1982–84, Paris Bureau Chief 1984–86; Middle East Corresp., The Sunday Times, London 1986–96, Foreign Affairs Corresp. 1996–; Woman of the Year (for work in Timor-Leste), Women of the Year Foundation, London 2000, Courage in Journalism Award, Int. Women's Media Foundation, USA 2000, Journalist of the Year, USA Foreign Corresps' Asscn 2001, Foreign Reporter of the Year, UK Press Awards 2001. *Television:* Behind the Myth: Yasser Arafat (BBC documentary), Martha Gelhorn (BBC documentary). *Leisure interests:* sailing, reading. *Address:* c/o Sunday Times Foreign Desk, 1 Pennington Street, London, E1 9XW, England (office). *Telephone:* (20) 7782-5701 (office). *Fax:* (20) 7782-5050 (office). *E-mail:* mariecolvin@hotmail.com (home).

COLWELL, Rita Rossi, BS, MS, PhD; American marine microbiologist, epidemiologist and academic; *Senior Advisor and Honorary Chairperson, Canon US Life Sciences Inc.;* b. 23 Nov. 1934, Mass.; d. of Louis Rossi and Louise DiPalma; m. Jack H. Colwell 1956; two d.; ed Purdue Univ. and Univ. of Wash.; Research Asst, Drosophila Genetics Lab. Purdue Univ. 1956–57; Research Asst, Dept of Microbiology, Univ. of Washington 1957–58, Predoctoral Assoc. 1959–60, Asst Research Prof. 1961–64; Asst Prof. of Biology, Georgetown Univ. 1964–66, Assoc. Prof. 1966–72; Prof. of Microbiology, Univ. of Maryland 1972–98, Vice-Pres. for Academic Affairs 1983–87, Founding Dir Center of Marine Biotechnology 1987–91, Founder and Pres. Biotechnology Inst. 1991–98, Distinguished Univ. Prof. 2004–; Distinguished Univ. Prof., Bloomberg School of Public Health, Johns Hopkins Univ. 2004–; Dir NSF 1998–2004; Chair., Canon US Life Sciences, Inc. 2004–06, Sr Advisor and Hon. Chair. 2006–; fmr Chair. Bd of Govs American Acad. of Microbiology; fmr Pres. AAAS, American Society for Microbiology, Int Union of Microbiological Societies, Sigma Xi Nat Science Hon. Society; mem. NAS, Royal Swedish Acad. of Sciences, Stockholm, American Acad. of Arts and Sciences, American Philosophical Society; 22 hon. doctorates; Gold Medal, Canterbury, UK 1990, Purkinje Gold Award, Prague 1991, Maryland Pate Civic Award 1991, Barnard Medal, Colorado Univ. 1996, Gold Medal, UCLA 2000, Achievement Award, American Asscn of Univ. Women 2001, Carey Award, AAAS 2001, Nat. Medal of Science 2007. *Publications:* 16 books, over 600 articles in journals, book chapters, abstracts. *Leisure interests:* gardening, sailing, jogging. *Address:* Canon US Life Sciences, Inc., 9800 Medical Center Drive, Suite A-100, Rockville, MD 20850 (office); 5010 River Hill Road, Bethesda, MD 20816, USA (home). *Telephone:* (301) 762-7070 (office); (301) 229-5129 (home). *Fax:* (301) 762-0406 (office); (301) 320-2795 (home). *E-mail:* culs@canon.uslifesciences.com (office). *Website:* www.uslifesciences.com (office).

COMANECI, Nadia; American (b. Romanian) fmr gymnast; b. 12 Nov. 1961, Oneşti, Bacău Co.; d. of Gheorghe Comaneci and Stefania-Alexandria Comaneci; m. Bart Connor 1996; one s.; ed Coll. of Physical Educ. and Sports, Bucharest; overall European champion Skien 1975, Prague 1977, Copenhagen 1979; overall Olympic champion, Montreal 1976, first gymnast to be awarded a 10; overall World Univ. Games Champion, Bucharest 1981; gold medals European Championships, Skien 1975 (vault, asymmetric bars, beam), Prague 1977 (bars), Copenhagen 1979 (vault, floor exercises), World Championships, Strasbourg 1978 (beam), Fort Worth 1979 (team title), Olympic Games, Montreal 1976 (bars, beam), Moscow (beam, floor), World Cup, Tokyo 1979 (vault, floor); World Univ. Games, Bucharest 1981 (vault, bars, floor and team title); silver medals European Championships, Skien 1975 (floor), Prague 1977 (vault), World Championships, Strasbourg 1978 (vault), Olympic Games, Montreal 1976 (team title), Moscow 1980 (individual all-round, team title), World Cup, Tokyo 1979 (beam); bronze medal Olympic Games, Montreal 1976 (floor); retd May 1984, jr team coach 1984–89; granted refugee status in USA 1989; currently with Bart Connor Gymnastics Acad., Okla, USA; performs as dancer, gymnastics entertainer and promotes commercial products; Contributing Ed. International Gymnast magazine; Prin. (with husband) Perfect 10 Productions, Inc. (TV production co.), Grips, Etc.(gymnastics supply co.); UN Spokesperson for Int. Year of Volunteers 2001; f. Nadia Comaneci Children's Clinic, Bucharest 2004; Vice-Chair. Special Olympics Int.; Vice-Pres. Muscular Dystrophy Asscn; mem. Bd of Dirs Laureus Sports For Good Foundation; Sportswomen of the Century Prize, Athletic Sports Category 1999, Govt Excellence Diploma 2001. *Publication:* Letters to a Young Gymnast 2004. *Address:* c/o Bart Conner Gymnastics Academy, 3206 Bart Conner Drive, POB 720217, Norman, OK 73070-4166, USA (office). *Telephone:* (405) 447-7500 (office). *Fax:* (405) 447-7600 (office). *Website:* www.bartconnergymnastics.com (office); www.bartandnadia.com.

COMĂNESCU, Lazăr, PhD; Romanian diplomatist and politician; b. 4 June 1949, Horezu (Ursani), Vâlcea; m. Mihaela Comănescu; one d.; ed Acad. of Econ. Studies, Bucharest, Sorbonne, Paris; Jr Diplomat, Ministry of Foreign Affairs 1972–82, Counsellor, later Minister-Counsellor, Mission to EU, Brussels 1990–94, Dir EU Directorate, Ministry of Foreign Affairs 1994–95, Dir-Gen. and Adviser to Minister of Foreign Affairs, also Head of Minister's office 1995, State Sec., Ministry of Foreign Affairs 1995–98, Amb. and Head, Mission to NATO and WEU 1998–2001, Amb. and Head of Mission to EU 2001–07, Perm. Rep., EU, Brussels 2007–08; Minister of Foreign Affairs 2008; Prof. of Int. Econs, Acad. of Econ. Studies, Bucharest 1982–90; mem. Scientific Consultative Bd European Inst. in Romania; mem. Scientific Bd Romanian Inst. for Int. Studies; Founding mem. Warsaw Cen. European Forum; Grand Officer, Romanian Nat. Order of Loyal Service 2000, Romanian Nat. Order of Loyal Service with Great Cross 2007. *Publications:* author of several univ. courses and books; numerous articles in journals. *Address:* c/o Ministry of Foreign Affairs, Al. Alexandru 31, 011822 Bucharest, Romania (office).

COMASTRI, HE Cardinal Angelo; Italian ecclesiastic; *President of the Fabric of St Peter;* b. 17 Sept. 1943, Sorano; ordained priest 1967; Bishop of Massa Marittima-Piombino 1990–94; Archbishop (Personal Title) of Loreto 1996–2005 (retd); Pres. Fabric of St Peter 2005–; Coadjutor Archpriest of the Basilica di San Pietro in Vaticano and Coadjutor Papal Vicar for the Vatican City 2005–06, Archpriest of the Basilica di San Pietro in Vaticano and Papal Vicar for the Vatican City 2006–; Dir Italian Bishops' Nat. Vocations Centre 1994; Pres. Nat. Cttee for the Great Jubilee of the Year 2000 1994; cr. Cardinal 2007–, cr. *Address:* Fabbrica di San Pietro, 00120 Vatican City, Rome, Italy (office). *Telephone:* (06) 6988-5318 (office). *Fax:* (06) 6988-5518 (office). *E-mail:* info@fsp.va (office). *Website:* www.vatican.va/roman_curia/institutions_connected/uffscavi/index.htm (office).

COMBS, Sean John, (Diddy); American rap artist, record producer, fashion designer and business executive; *Chairman and CEO, Bad Boy Worldwide Entertainment Group;* b. 4 Nov. 1969, Harlem, NY; s. of Melvin Combs and Janice Combs; fmr pnr Misa Hylton-Brim; one s.; fmr pnr Kim Porter; two s. twin d.; ed Howard Univ.; early positions at Uptown Records (R&B label) 1990–93; talent spotter for artists such as Jodeci and Mary J. Blige; producer for Ma$e, Sting, MC Lyte, Faith Evans, The Lox, Mariah Carey, Aretha Franklin, 112, Notorious BIG; f. Bad Boy Entertainment record label 1994 (now a part of Bad Boy Worldwide Entertainment Group); remixed and reworked songs by artists including Jackson 5, Sting, Goldie, Trent Reznor and The Police; co-producer (with Jimmy Page) of soundtrack to film Godzilla; launched fashion collection under name Sean John 1998, opened flagship store in Manhattan 2002; known as 'Puff Daddy' until 2001, when he changed his pseudonym to 'P Diddy', then 'Diddy' 2005–; launched fragrances Unforgiveable 2006, I Am King 2009; Grammy Award for Best Rap Performance by a Duo or Group for I'll Be Missing You, with Faith Evans 1998, for Shake Ya Tailfeather 2004, Council of Fashion Designers of America menswear designer of the year award 2004. *Play:* A Raisin in the Sun (actor) 2004. *Recordings include:* albums: No Way Out (Grammy Award for Best Rap Album 1998) 1997, Shake Ya TailfeatherForever 1999, The Saga Continues 2001, Maximum Puff Daddy 2003, Press Play 2006. *Address:* Bad Boy Worldwide Entertainment Group, 1710 Broadway, New York, NY 10019, USA (office). *Telephone:* (212) 381-1540 (office). *Fax:* (212) 381-1599 (office). *Website:* www.diddy.com; www.seanjohn.com; www.badboyonline.com.

COMOLLI, Jean-Dominique, MEconSc; French business executive and fmr public servant; *Chairman, Altadis SA;* b. 25 April 1948, Bougie, Algeria; s. of Ivan Comolli and Jacqueline Courtin; m. Catherine Delmas 1968; two s. one d.; ed Institut d'Etudes Politiques, Paris, Ecole Nat. d'Admin; civil servant, Budget Dept, Ministry of Economy, Finance and Budget 1977–81, Minister of the Budget's Tech. Adviser to Cabinet, then Prime Minister's Tech. Adviser to Cabinet 1981–86, Asst Dir Budget Dept 1986–88, Prin. Pvt. Sec. to Minister of the Budget 1988–89, Dir-Gen. Customs and Indirect Duties, Ministry of the Budget 1989–95; Chair. and CEO Soc. Nat. d'Exploitation Industrielle des Tabacs et Allumettes (Seita) 1993–99; Co-Chair. Bd of Dirs Altadis SA (tobacco co. cr. out of merger of Seita and Tabacalera) 1999–2005, Chair. 2005–; Chevalier, Légion d'honneur, Ordre nat. du Mérite. *Address:* Altadis, 182–188 avenue de France, 75639 Paris Cedex 13 (office); 23 avenue de l'Observatoire, 75006 Paris, France (home). *Telephone:* 1-44-97-65-65 (office). *Fax:* 1-44-97-62-43 (office). *E-mail:* jean-dominique.comolli@altadis.com (office). *Website:* www.altadis.com (office).

COMPAGNON, Antoine Marcel Thomas; French academic and writer; *Blanche W. Knopf Professor of French and Comparative Literature, Columbia University;* b. 20 July 1950, Brussels, Belgium; s. of Gen. Jean Compagnon and Jacqueline Terlinden; ed Lycée Condorcet, The Maret School, Washington, DC, USA, Prytanée Militaire, La Flèche, Ecole Polytechnique, Paris, Ecole Nat. des Ponts et Chaussées, Paris, Univ. of Paris VII; with Fondation Thiers and Research Attaché, CNRS 1975–78; Asst Lecturer, Univ. of Paris VII 1975–80; Asst Lecturer, Ecole des Hautes Etudes en Sciences Sociales, Paris 1977–79; Lecturer, Ecole Polytechnique, Paris 1978–85; teacher at French Inst., London 1980–81; Lecturer, Univ. of Rouen 1981–85; Prof. of French, Columbia Univ., New York 1985–91; Visiting Prof., Univ. of Pennsylvania 1986, 1990; Prof., Univ. of Le Mans 1989–90; Blanche W. Knopf Prof. of French and Comparative Literature, Columbia Univ., New York 1991–; Prof., Univ. of Paris IV-Sorbonne 1994–2006, Collège de France 2006–; Sec. Gen. Int. Asscn of French Studies 1998–2008; Guggenheim Fellow 1988; Visiting Fellow, All Souls Coll., Oxford 1994; Fellow, American Acad. of Arts and Sciences 1997, Academia Europaea 2006; Commdr des Palmes académiques, Chevalier de la Légion d'honneur. *Publications:* La Seconde Main ou le travail de la citation 1979, Le Deuil antérieur 1979, Nous, Michel de Montaigne 1980, La Troisième République des lettres, de Flaubert à Proust 1983, Ferragosto 1985, critical edn of Marcel Proust, Sodome et Gomorrhe 1988, Proust entre deux siècles 1989, Les Cinq Paradoxes de la modernité 1990, Chat en poche: Montaigne et l'allégorie 1993, Connaissez-vous Brunetière? 1997, Le Démon de la théorie 1998, Baudelaire devant l'innombrable 2003, Les Antimodernes 2005; numerous articles on French literature and culture. *Address:* Columbia University, Department of French and Romance Philology, 513 Philosophy Hall, 1150 Amsterdam Avenue, New York, NY 10027, USA (office); Collège de France, 11 place Marcelin-Berthelot, 75005 Paris, France (office). *Telephone:* (212) 854-2500 (NY) (office); 1-44-27-10-79 (Paris) (office). *Fax:* (212) 854-5863 (NY) (office). *E-mail:* amc6@columbia.edu (office); antoine.compagnon@college-de-france.fr (office). *Website:* www.columbia.edu/cu/french (office).

COMPAORÉ, Blaise; Burkinabè head of state and fmr army officer; *President;* b. 3 Feb. 1951, Ouagadougou; m. Chantal K. Terrasson; one d.; trained as soldier in Cameroon and Morocco; fmr second in command to Capt. Thomas Sankara whom he overthrew in a coup in Oct. 1987; Minister of State to the Pres., then Minister for Justice 1983–87; Chair. Popular Front of Burkina Faso and Head of Govt Oct. 1987–, Interim Head of State June–Dec. 1991, Pres. of Burkina Faso Dec. 1991–; Assoc. mem. Overseas Acad. of Sciences, France 1995–; Commdr, Ordre Int. des Palmes académiques 2005; Dr hc (Ecole des Hautes Etudes Ints de Paris) 1992, (Soka Univ., Japan) 1995, (Jean-Moulin de Lyon 3 Univ., France) 2004, (Ramkhamaeng Univ., Thailand) 2005. *Address:* Office of the President, 03 BP 7030, Ouagadougou 03, Burkina Faso (office). *Telephone:* 30-66-30 (office). *Fax:* 31-49-26 (office). *Website:* www.primature.gov.bf (office).

COMPAORE, Jean-Baptiste Marie Pascal, MEconSc, DES; Burkinabè politician, banker and economist; *Vice-Governor, Banque Centrale des États de l'Afrique de l'ouest (BCEAO);* b. 12 April 1954, Ouagadougou; m.; four c.; ed Phillipe Zinda Kabore Coll., Ouagadougou, Univ. of Benin, Lome, Togo, Centre Ouest Africain de Formation aux Études Bancaires (COFEB); joined Banque Centrale des États de l'Afrique de l'ouest (BCEAO), Dakar 1981, served in Credit and Inspection Divs; Inspector of Banks, Banking Comm. of W Africa Monetary Union 1990–95, currently Vice-Gov.; Counsellor, Dir of Econ. and Social Affairs, Office of the Pres. 1995–96, Sec.-Gen. of Ministry 1996–2000; Minister to the Prime Minister, responsible for Finance and the Budget 2000–02; Minister of Finance and the Budget 2002–07; Minister of the Economy and Finances 2007–08; Gov. IMF, World Bank Group, African Devt Bank, Econ. Community of West African States; fmr Lecturer (part-time) Lome Tech. School, Togo; Coordinator Program of Admin. Support 1997–; fmr Chair. Inter-Departmental Cttee to Follow-up Recommendations of Arbitrator of Faso; Officier, Ordre Nat. *Address:* BCEAO, siège BP 3108, Dakar, Senegal (office). *Telephone:* 33-839-0500 (office). *Website:* www.bceao.int (office).

COMPER, Francis Anthony (Tony), BA; Canadian banker; b. 24 April 1945, Toronto, Ont.; m. Elizabeth Comper 1971; ed Univ. of Toronto; began career with BMO Financial Group 1967, Sr Vice-Pres., Personal Banking 1982, Sr Vice-Pres. and Sr Operations Officer, Treasury Group 1982–84, Man., London, UK Br. 1984–86, Sr Marketing Officer, Corp. and Govt Banking 1986–87, Exec. Vice-Pres., Operation 1987–89, Chief Gen. Man. and COO 1989–90, Pres., COO and Dir 1990–99, Pres. CEO and Dir 1999, Chair., CEO and Dir 1999–2007; Chair. Capital Campaign for the Univ. of Toronto 1997–2002; mem. Bd of Dirs Spectra Energy Corpn, Canadian Inst. of Advanced Research, Harris Bancorp, Inc., Harris Trust and Savings Bank, Toronto, C. D. Howe Inst., C. D. Howe Memorial Foundation, Canadian Club, BMO Nesbitt Burns Inc., Catalyst, NY; Trustee Canadian Centre for Architecture; mem. Int. Advisory Cttee, Li Ka Shing Knowledge Inst. of St Michael's Hosp.; Hon. Chair. Bd of Govs The Yee Hong Centre for Geriatric Care; Hon. DHumLitt (Mount Saint Vincent), Hon. LLD (Univ. of Toronto), Hon. DLitt (Univ. of New Brunswick); Human Relations Award, Canadian Council of Christians and Jews 1998, B'nai Brith Order of Merit 2003, Scopus Award (with his wife), Hebrew Univ. of Jerusalem. *Leisure interests:* golf, tennis, theatre, arts, reading. *Address:* c/o BMO Financial Group, First Bank Tower, First Canadian Place, Toronto, ON M5X 1A1, Canada (office).

COMSTOCK, Beth; American broadcasting executive; *President, Integrated Media, NBC Universal;* b. Va; m.; two d.; ed Coll. of William and Mary, Williamsburg, Va; began career working for a TV news service and in local cable programming in Va; held a succession of communications and publicity positions at NBC, Turner Broadcasting and CBS Entertainment from 1986; Vice-Pres. NBC News Communications 1993–96, Sr Vice-Pres. Communications, NBC 1996–98, Vice-Pres. Corp. Communications, General Electric (GE) 1998–2003, Corp. Vice-Pres. and Chief Marketing Officer, GE 2003–05, Pres. NBC Universal Digital Media and Market Devt (now Integrated Media) 2005–; named by Business Week an innovation "transformer" 2005, named by BtoB Magazine Marketing Exec. of the Year, named by PR Week PR Professional of the Year, Matrix Award, New York Women in Communications 2006. *Address:* NBC Universal, Inc., 30 Rockefeller Plaza, New York, NY 10112, USA (office). *Telephone:* (212) 664-4444 (office). *Fax:* (212) 664-4085 (office). *Website:* www.nbcuni.com (office).

CONANT, Douglas R.; American food industry executive; *President and CEO, Campbell Soup Company;* began career in marketing dept, General Mills Inc. 1976; joined Kraft Foods 1986; Pres. Nabisco Foods Co. 1995–2000; Pres. and CEO Campbell Soup Co. 2001–; mem. Bd of Dirs Applebee's Int. Inc.; Chair. Bd of Dirs Students In Free Enterprise; Chair. and Trustee The Conference Bd; Chair. Grocery Mfrs Asscn/Food Processors of America; Trustee Int. Tennis Hall of Fame. *Address:* Campbell Soup Company, 1 Campbell Place, Camden, NJ 08103-1701, USA (office). *Telephone:* (856) 342-4800 (office). *Fax:* (856) 342-3878 (office). *Website:* www.campbellsoup.com (office).

CONDÉ, Mamadi; Guinean fmr government official; fmr Minister of Information; Minister of Foreign Affairs and Co-operation 2004–05, 2006–07. *Address:* c/o Ministry of Foreign Affairs, face au Port, ex-Primature, BP 2519, Conakry, Guinea (office).

CONDE de SARO, Francisco Javier, M.L.; Spanish business executive and fmr diplomatist; *President, Sociedad Estatal para Exposiciones Internacionales;* b. 13 March 1946, Madrid; s. of Francisco Javier Conde and María Jesús de Saro; m. Ana Martínez de Irujo; one s. two d.; ed Univ. of Madrid, Diplomatic School, Madrid; Dir-Gen. for Int. Econ. Relations, Ministry of Foreign Affairs 1971; Asst Dir-Gen. for Int. Relations, Directorate of Maritime Fisheries 1976; Dir of Political Affairs for Africa and Asia, Ministry of Foreign Affairs 1978; counsellor Ministry of Transport, Tourism and Communications 1978; Econ. and Commercial Counsellor, Embassy in Rabat 1979–83, in Buenos Aires 1983–86; Dir-Gen. Juridical and Institutional Co-ordination, Sec. of State for EU, Ministry of Foreign Affairs 1986–90, Sec.-Gen. 1994; Amb. to Algeria 1990–94; Perm. Rep. to NATO,Brussels 1996–2000; Perm. Rep. to EU, Brussels 2000–04; Amb. to Japan 2004–06; currently Pres. Sociedad Estatal para Exposiciones Internacionales (State Co. for Int. Exhibitions); Kt Commdr of Civil Merit (Spain), of Isabel la Católica (Spain), of Mayo Order (Argentina), of Order of the Lion (Senegal); Kt of Order of El Ouissam El Mohammadi (Morocco); Grand Cross for Naval Merit (Spain), Grand Cross of Merit (Austria). *Address:* Sociedad Estatal para Exposiciones Internacionales, C/José Abascal, 4–4° B, 28003 Madrid, Spain (office). *Telephone:* (91) 7004000 (office). *E-mail:* info@expo-int.com (office). *Website:* www.expo-int.com (office).

CONDON, Baron (Life Peer), cr. 2001, of Langton Green in the County of Kent; **Paul Leslie Condon,** QPM, DL, CCMI (CIMgt), FRSA; British international organization official and fmr police commissioner; b. 1 Jan. 1946, Dorset; m.; two s. one d.; ed St Peter's Coll. Oxford; joined Metropolitan Police 1967, Insp. 1975–78, Chief Insp. 1978–81; Superintendent, Bethnal Green 1981–82; Staff Officer to Commr as Superintendent, then as Chief Superintendent 1982–84; Asst Chief Constable of Kent 1984–87; Deputy Asst Commr Metropolitan Police 1987–88, Asst Commr 1988–89; Chief Constable of Kent 1989–92; Commr, Metropolitan Police 1993–2000; Dir Anti-Corruption Unit, Int. Cricket Council 2001–; mem. Bd of Dirs (non-exec.) Securicor PLC 2000–, G4S 2004– (Deputy Chair. 2006–), Tenix (Holdings) UK Ltd, Vidient Systems Inc; Vice-Chair. Private Security Group, House of Lords 2006–; Pres. British Security Industry Asscn. *Address:* House of Lords, London, SW1A 0PW, England. *Telephone:* (20) 7219-3617.

CONDOR, Sam Terence, BA; Saint Christopher and Nevis politician and business executive; *Deputy Prime Minister and Minister of Education, Youth, Social and Community Development and Gender Affairs;* b. 4 Nov. 1949; m.; one s. two d.; ed Ruskin Coll., Oxford, Univ. of Sussex, UK; printer, Saint Christopher and Nevis Govt Printery 1967–82; Sr Clerk, Inland Revenue Dept 1980–82; Man. Dir Quality Foods Ltd 1986–95; MP 1989–; Deputy Prime Minister, Minister of Trade, Industry, Caricom Affairs, Youth, Sports and Community Devt 1995–99, Deputy Prime Minister, Minister of Foreign Affairs, Int. Trade and Caricom Affairs, Community and Social Devt and Gender Affairs 2000–01; apptd Deputy Prime Minister and Minister of CARICOM Affairs, Int. Trade, Labour, Social Security, Telecommunications

www.worldwhoswho.com

and Tech. 2001; currently Deputy Prime Minister and Minister of Educ., Youth, Social and Community Devt and Gender Affairs; Vice-Chair. Young Labour 1980–82, Deputy Leader Saint Christopher and Nevis Labour Party 1990–; mem. Saint Christopher and Nevis Tourist Bd 1975–78; Nat. Football Player 1969–72, Man. and Coach Nat. Football Team 1986–88; Margaret Marsh Prize for Most Outstanding Overseas Student, Ruskin Coll. 1979–80. *Leisure interests:* playing football, jogging, fast walking, drama. *Address:* Ministry of Education, Youth, Social and Community Development and Gender, Church Street, PO Box 186, Basseterre (office); North Pelican Drive, Bird Rock, Saint Christopher, Saint Christopher and Nevis, West Indies (home). *Telephone:* 465-2521 (office); 465-1545 (home). *Fax:* 465-2556 (office). *E-mail:* dpmin@caribsurf.com (office).

CONFALONIERI-RICCA, Fedele; Italian media executive; *Chairman, Mediaset SpA;* b. 6 Aug. 1937, Milan; ed State Univ. of Milan; Chair. Mediaset SpA (commercial TV broadcaster); mem. Bd of Dirs Il Giornale (nat. daily newspaper); mem. Bd of Dirs and Vice-Pres. Gestevision Telecinco SA 2000–; mem. Bd Italian Confed. of Industry (Confindustria); mem. Exec. Cttee and Bd Lombardy Industrialists Confed. (Assolombarda); Chair. Nat. Television Broadcasters Asscn (part of Nat. Broadcasting Fed.); mem. Man. Council of Assonime (Asscn for Italian limited liability cos); Founding mem. ACT (European Asscn of Commercial Television Broadcasters). *Address:* Mediaset SpA, Viale Europa 46, 6th Floor, 20093 Cologno Monzese, Milan, Italy (office). *Telephone:* (02) 25141 (office). *E-mail:* simone.sole@mediaset.it (office). *Website:* www.mediaset.it (office).

CONLON, James Joseph, BMus; American conductor; *Music Director, Los Angeles Opera;* b. 18 March 1950, New York; s. of Joseph Conlon and Angeline Conlon; m. Jennifer Ringo; two d.; ed High School of Music and Art, New York and Juilliard School; fmr faculty mem. Juilliard School of Music; since making debut with New York Philharmonic has conducted every major US orchestra and many leading European orchestras; Conductor, New York Philharmonic Orchestra 1974–, Metropolitan Opera, New York 1976–; debut at Metropolitan Opera 1976, Covent Garden 1979, Paris Opera 1982, Lyric Opera of Chicago 1988, La Scala, Milan 1993, Kirov Opera 1994; Music Dir Cincinnati May Festival 1979–, Berlin Philharmonic Orchestra 1979, Rotterdam Philharmonic Orchestra 1983–91, Ravinia Festival 2005–; Musical Adviser to Dir, Paris Opera 1995– (Prin. Conductor 1996–2004); conducted opening of Maggio Musicale, Florence 1985; Gen. Music Dir and Chief Conductor, Cologne Opera 1989–2002; Music Dir Los Angeles Opera 2006–; residency at Juilliard School, New York 2007–; has conducted at major int. music festivals and with numerous leading orchestras; Officier, Ordre des Arts et Lettres 1996; Grand Prix du Disque for recording of Poulenc Piano Concertos, Opera News Award 2005, Galileo 2000 Music Prize, Florence 2008. *Recordings:* numerous works by Mozart, Liszt, Poulenc etc. *Address:* Opus 3 Artists, 470 Park Avenue South, 9th Floor North, New York, NY 10016, USA (office). *Telephone:* (212) 584-7500 (office). *Fax:* (646) 300-8200 (office). *E-mail:* info@opus3artists.com (office). *Website:* www.opus3artists.com (office).

CONNEH, Sekou Damate, Jr; Liberian politician; *Leader, Progressive Democratic Party;* b. 1960, Gbarnga; s. of Sekou Damate Conneh Sr and Margaret Makay; m. Aisha Keita Conneh; ed William V. C. Tubman Methodist High School; joined Progressive People's Party 1980, served as Sr Coordinator Kokoyah Dist; exiled in Uganda 1980–1985; apptd revenue agent Ministry of Finance 1986; f. and served as Man. Dir Damate Corpn (import/export co.); Pres. of Nat. Exec. Cttee Liberians United for Reconciliation and Democracy (now Progressive Democratic Party) 2003–, currently Leader; f. Damate Peace Foundation. *Address:* Progressive Democratic Party, McDonald St, Monrovia, Liberia. *Telephone:* (6) 521091.

CONNELL, HE Cardinal Desmond, BA, MA, BD, PhDr; Irish ecclesiastic; *Archbishop Emeritus of Dublin;* b. 24 March 1926, Dublin; ed Univ. Coll. Dublin, Maynooth, Univ. of Louvain, Belgium; ordained priest 1951; worked in Dept of Metaphysics, Univ. Coll. Dublin 1953–72, apptd Prof. of Gen. Metaphysics 1972, elected Dean Faculty of Philosophy and Sociology 1983; Archbishop of Dublin 1988–2004, now Archbishop Emer.; cr. Cardinal 2001, apptd Cardinal-Priest of S. Silvestro in Capite; fmr mem. Pontifical Council for the Pastoral Care of Migrants and Itinerant People, Irish Hierarchy's Theological Comm., Diocesan Cttee on Ecumenism. *Address:* c/o Archbishop's House, Drumcondra, Dublin 9, Ireland. *Telephone:* (1) 8373732. *Fax:* (1) 8369796. *E-mail:* communications@dublindiocese.ie. *Website:* www.dublindiocese.ie.

CONNELL, Elizabeth, BMus; Irish singer (soprano); b. 22 Oct. 1946, Port Elizabeth, SA; d. of the late (Gordon) Raymond Connell and (Maud) Elizabeth Connell (née Scott); ed Univ. of the Witwatersrand and Johannesburg Coll. of Educ., SA and London Opera Centre; debut at Wexford Festival, Ireland as Varvara in Katya Kabanova 1972; Australian Opera 1973–75; ENO 1975–80; debut Royal Opera House, Covent Garden, London as Viclinda in I Lombardi 1976; Ortrud in Lohengrin, Bayreuth Festival 1980; Electra in Idomeneo, Salzburg Festival 1984; debut Metropolitan Opera, New York as Vitellia in La Clemenza di Tito 1985; debut Vienna State Opera as Elisabeth in Tannhäuser 1985; debut Glyndebourne, England as Electra in Idomeneo 1985; debut La Scala, Milan as Ortrud in Lohengrin 1981; sang full range of dramatic mezzo repertoire until 1983 when moved into dramatic soprano field; sings worldwide, freelance in opera, oratorio, concert and recital work; Maggie Teyte Prize 1972. *Leisure interests:* reading, theatre, concerts, cooking, embroidery, writing, composing. *Address:* Askonas Holt Ltd, Lincoln House, 300 High Holborn, London, WC1V 7JH, England (office). *Telephone:* (20) 7400-1700 (office). *Fax:* (20) 7400-1799 (office). *E-mail:* info@askonasholt.co.uk (office). *Website:* www.askonasholt.co.uk (office).

CONNELLY, Deirdre P., BA; American business executive; *President, North America Pharmaceuticals, GlaxoSmithKline PLC;* b. San Juan, Puerto Rico; ed Lycoming Coll., Pa, Harvard Univ.'s Advanced Man. Program; joined Lilly as Sales Rep. 1983, Marketing Assoc. in San Juan 1984–89, joined Int. Man. Devt Program at Lilly Corp. Center 1989, Sales Supervisor in Phila, Pa 1989–90, Diabetes Product Man., San Juan 1990–91, Nat. Sales Man. for Puerto Rico affiliate 1991–92, Marketing and Sales Dir for Puerto Rico 1992–93, Dir of Sales and Marketing for Caribbean Basin Region, including Cen. America, Puerto Rico and Caribbean Island countries 1993–95, Gen. Man. Eli Lilly Puerto Rico, SA 1995–97, returned to Indianapolis 1997, held positions of Regional Sales Dir, Exec. Dir Global Marketing for Evista, and Team Leader for Evista Product Team 1997–2001, Leader, Woman's Health Business Unit in US affiliate 2001–03, Exec. Dir Human Resources for US affiliate 2003–04, Vice-Pres. Human Resources for Pharmaceutical Operations 2004–05, Sr Vice-Pres. Human Resources for Lilly and mem. Operations Cttee and Sr Man. Council 2005, Pres. Lilly USA, Eli Lilly & Co. 2005–09 (resgnd); Pres. North American Pharmaceuticals, GlaxoSmithKline PLC 2009–; mem. Bd of Dirs Macy's Inc. 2007–; ranked by Fortune magazine amongst 50 Most Powerful Women in Business in US (43rd) 2006, (47th) 2007, 2008; Outstanding Achievement Award, Lycoming Coll. Alumni Asscn 2007. *Address:* GlaxoSmithKline, 5 Moore Drive, POB 13398, Research Triangle Park, NC 27709, USA (office). *Website:* us.gsk.com (office).

CONNELLY, Jennifer; American actress; b. 12 Dec. 1970; d. of Gerard Connelly and Eileen Connelly; one s. with David Dugan; m. Paul Bettany 2002; one s.; ed Saint Ann's School, Brooklyn, Yale Univ. and Stanford Univ.; fmr model. *Films include:* Once Upon A Time in America 1984, Il mondo dell'orrore di Dario Argento 1985, Seven Minutes in Heaven 1985, The Valley 1985, Phenomena 1985, Labyrinth 1986, Inside the Labyrinth 1986, Some Girls 1988, Etoile 1988, The Hot Spot 1990, Career Opportunities 1991, The Rocketeer 1991, Of Love and Shadows 1994, Higher Learning 1995, Far Harbor 1996, Mulholland Falls 1996, Inventing the Abbotts 1997, Dark City 1998, Requiem for a Dream 2000, Waking the Dead 2000, A Beautiful Mind (Acad. Award, BAFTA Award and Golden Globe Award for Best Supporting Actress 2002) 2001, Pollock 2001, House of Sand and Fog 2003, Hulk 2003, Dark Water 2005, Little Children 2006, Blood Diamond 2006, Reservation Road 2007. *TV appearances include:* Tales of the Unexpected 1984, The $treet 2001. *Recording:* Monologue of Love (single, in Japanese). *Leisure interests:* hiking, camping, swimming, bike riding, quantum physics, philosophy. *Address:* c/o CAA, 2000 Avenue of the Stars, Los Angeles, CA 90067211, USA (office).

CONNERY, Sir Sean, Kt; British actor; b. 25 Aug. 1930, Edinburgh, Scotland; s. of Joseph and Euphamia Connery; m. 1st Diane Cilento 1962 (divorced 1974); one s. one step-d.; m. 2nd Micheline Boglio Roquebrun 1975; served in RN; Dir Tantallon Films Ltd 1972–; Fellow, Royal Scottish Acad. of Music and Drama 1984; mem. Scottish Nat. Party 1992–; Dir Fountainbridge Films (production co.) –2002; Freeman City of Edinburgh 1991; Commdr des Arts et Lettres 1987, Chevalier, Légion d'honneur; Hon. DLitt (Heriot-Watt) 1981, (St Andrew's) 1988; American Cinematique Award 1991, Rudolph Valentino Award 1992, Nat. Board of Review Award, BAFTA Lifetime Achievement Award 1990, BAFTA Fellowship 1998. *Films include:* No Road Back 1955, Time Lock 1956, Action of the Tiger 1957, Another Time, Another Place, Hell Drivers, 1958, Darby O'Gill and the Little People 1959, Tarzan's Greatest Adventure 1959, On the Fiddle 1961, The Longest Day 1962, The Frightened City 1962, Woman of Straw 1964, Marnie 1964, The Hill 1965, A Fine Madness 1966, Shalako 1968, The Molly Maguires 1968, The Red Tent 1969, The Anderson Tapes 1970, The Offence 1973, Zardoz 1974, Murder on the Orient Express 1974, Ransom 1974, The Wind and the Lion 1975, The Man Who Would Be King 1975, Robin and Marian 1976, A Bridge Too Far 1977, The Great Train Robbery 1978, Meteor 1978, Cuba 1979, Outland 1981, The Man with the Deadly Lens 1982, The Untouchables (Acad. Award, Best Supporting Actor 1987) 1986, The Name of the Rose 1987, The Presidio 1988, Rosencrantz and Guildenstern are Dead, A Small Family Business, Indiana Jones and the Last Crusade 1989, Hunt for Red October 1989, The Russia House 1989 (BAFTA Award 1990), Mutant Ninja Turtles 1990, Highlander 2 1990, Medicine Man 1992, Rising Sun 1993, A Good Man in Africa 1994, First Knight 1994, Just Cause 1994, The Rock 1996, Dragonheart 1996, The Avengers 1998, Entrapment 1999, Playing By Heart 1999, Finding Forrester 2000, The League of Extraordinary Gentlemen 2003, Sir Billi the Vet (voice) 2006; as James Bond in Dr. No 1963, From Russia with Love 1964, Goldfinger 1965, Thunderball 1965, You Only Live Twice 1967, Diamonds are Forever 1971, Never Say Never Again 1983. *Publication:* Neither Shaken Nor Stirred 1994, Being a Scot (memoirs) (with Murray Grigor) 2008. *Leisure interests:* golf, tennis, reading. *Address:* c/o Creative Artists Agency Inc., 9830 Wilshire Boulevard, Beverly Hills, CA 90212, USA (office); Fountainbridge Films 8428 Melrose Place, Unit C Los Angeles, CA 90069 323-782-1177. *Website:* www.seanconnery.com.

CONNES, Alain, PhD; French mathematician and academic; *Professor, Collège de France;* b. 1 April 1947, Draguignan (Var); ed Ecole Normale Supérieur, Paris; Research Fellow, CNRS 1970–74, Dir of Research 1981–84; Visiting Research Fellow, Queen's Univ., Kingston, Canada 1975; Assoc. Prof. and Prof., Univ. of Paris VI 1976–80; Long Term Prof. and Léon Motchane Prof., Institut des Hautes Etudes Scientifiques 1979–; Prof., Collège de France (chaire d'Analyse et Géométrie) 1984–; Distinguished Prof., Vanderbilt Univ., Nashville, Tenn., USA 2003–; Ed. Journal of Functional Analysis, Inventiones Mathematicae 1978–98, Communications in Mathematical Physic, Journal of Operator Theor, Ergodic Theory and Dynamical Systems 1981–93, Comptes rendus de l'Académie des sciences, Letters in Mathematical Physics, K-theory, Selecta Mathematica, Publications Mathématiques de l'I.H.E.S., Advances in Mathematics; Corresp. mem. Acad. des Sciences 1980, mem. 1983–; Foreign

Assoc. mem. Royal Danish Acad. of Sciences 1980, Norwegian Acad. of Science 1993, NAS 1997, Russian Acad. of Sciences 2003; Foreign Fellow, Royal Soc. of Canada 1996; Hon. Foreign mem. American Acad. of Arts and Sciences 1990; Dr hc (Queen's Univ., Kingston) 1979, (Univ. of Rome Tor Vergata) 1997, (Univ. of Oslo) 1999; Prix Aimé Berthé, Acad. des Sciences 1975, Prix Peccot-Vimont, Collège de France 1976, Médaille d'argent, CNRS 1977, Prix Ampère, Acad. des Sciences 1980, Fields Medal 1982, Clay Research Award 2000, Crafoord Prize 2001, CNRS Gold Medal 2004. *Publications:* Matière à pensée (co-author) 1989, Géométrie non commutative 1990, Noncommutative geometry 1994, Conversations on Mind, Matter, and Mathematics (co-author) 1995, Triangle de pensées (co-author) 2000, Triangle of Thought (co-author) 2001; more than 150 publs in scientific journals. *Address:* Collège de France, 3 rue d'Ulm, 75231 Paris Cedex 05, France (office). *Telephone:* 1-44-27-17-05 (office). *Fax:* 1-44-27-17-04 (office). *E-mail:* alain@connes.org (office). *Website:* www.college-de-france.fr (office); www.ihes.fr (office); www.alainconnes.org; www.vanderbilt.edu (office).

CONNICK, Harry, Jr; American jazz musician (piano), singer and actor; b. 11 Sept. 1967, New Orleans, LA; m. Jill Goodacre 1994; ed New Orleans Center for the Creative Arts, Hunter Coll. and Manhattan School of Music; studied with Ellis Marsalis. *Films:* Memphis Belle 1990, Little Man Tate 1991, Copycat 1995, Independence Day 1996, Excess Baggage 1997, Action League Now!! (voice) 1997, Hope Floats 1998, The Iron Giant (voice) 1999, Wayward Son 1999, My Dog Skip (voice) 2000, The Simian Line 2000, Life Without Dick 2001, Basic 2003, Mickey 2004, The Happy Elf (voice) 2005, Bug 2006, P.S. I Love You 2007. *Television includes:* South Pacific 2001, Will & Grace (series) 2002–06. *Theatre:* Thou Shalt Not (composer, Broadway) 2001, The Pajama Game (actor, Broadway) 2005. *Recordings include:* albums: 11 1978, Harry Connick Jr 1987, 20 1988, When Harry Met Sally (Grammy Award for Male Jazz Vocal Performance 1990) 1989, Lofty's Roach Soufflé 1990, We Are In Love 1990, Blue Light, Red Light 1991, 25 1992, When My Heart Finds Christmas 1993, Imagination 1994, She 1994, Whisper Your Name 1995, Star Turtle 1995, All Of Me 1996, To See You 1997, Come By Me 1999, 30 2001, Songs I Heard 2001, Other Hours: Connick On Piano, Vol. I 2003, Harry For The Holidays 2003, Only You 2004, My New Orleans 2007; contrib. music for films Memphis Belle 1990, Little Man Tate 1991. *Address:* Wilkins Management Inc., 323 Broadway, Cambridge, MA 02139, USA (office); c/o Columbia Records, 51/12, 550 Madison Avenue, PO Box 4450, New York, NY 10101, USA. *Website:* www.hconnickjr.com.

CONNOLLY, Billy, CBE; British actor, comedian, playwright and presenter; b. 24 Nov. 1942, Anderston, Glasgow, Scotland; m. 1st Iris Connolly (divorced 1985); one s. one d.; m. 2nd Pamela Stephenson 1990; three d.; worked as apprentice welder; performed originally with Gerry Rafferty and The Humblebums; first play, The Red Runner, staged at Edinburgh Fringe 1979; Hon. DLitt (Glasgow) 2001, Dr hc (Royal Scottish Acad. of Music and Drama, Glasgow) 2006. *Theatre:* The Great Northern Welly Boot Show, The Beastly Beatitudes of Balthazar B 1982. *Films include:* Absolution 1978, Worzel Gummidge: A Cup o' Tea an' a Slice o' Cake 1980, Bullshot 1983, Water 1985, To the North of Katmandu 1986, The Hunting of the Snark 1987, The Return of the Musketeers 1989, The Big Man 1990, Indecent Proposal 1993, Pocahontas (voice) 1995, Treasure Island (Muppet Movie) 1996, Deacon Brodie (BBC Film) 1996, Beverly Hills Ninja 1997, Mrs Brown 1997, Ship of Fools 1997, Paws (voice) 1997, Middleton's Changeling 1998, The Impostors 1998, Still Crazy 1998, The Debt Collector 1999, The Boondock Saints 1999, Beautiful Joe 2000, An Everlasting Piece 2000, The Man Who Sued God 2001, White Oleander, Gabriel and Me 2002, The Last Samurai 2003, Timeline 2003, Lemony Snicket's A Series of Unfortunate Events 2004, Garfield 2 2006, Open Season (voice) 2006, Fido 2006; numerous video releases of live performances including Bite Your Bum 1981 (Music Week and Record Business Award 1982), An Audience with Billy Connolly 1985, Billy Connolly – Live in New York 2005, Billy Connolly Live – Was It Something I Said?, The X Files: I Want to Believe 2008. *Television includes:* Just Another Saturday (play) 1975, The Elephants' Graveyard (play) 1976, Blue Money 1982, Androcles and the Lion 1984, Return to Nose and Beak (Comic Relief), Head of the Class (series) 1990–91, South Bank Show Special (25th Anniversary Commemoration) 1992, Billy (series) 1992, Down Among the Big Boys 1993, Billy Connolly's World Tour of Scotland (six-part documentary) 1994, The Big Picture 1995, Billy Connolly's World Tour of Australia 1996, Deacon Brodie 1997, Erect for 30 Years 1998, Columbo: Murder with Too Many Notes 2000, Gentlemen's Relish 2001, Prince Charming 2001, Billy Connolly's World Tour of England, Ireland and Wales 2002, Gentleman's Relish, Billy Connolly's World Tour of New Zealand. *Albums include:* The Great Northern Welly Boot Show (contains No. 1 hit DIVORCE), Pick of Billy Connolly (Gold Disc) 1982. *Publications include:* Gullible's Travels 1982. *Address:* c/o Tickety-boo Limited, 2 Triq il-Barriera, Balzan, BZN 06, Malta (office). *Telephone:* 21556166 (office). *Fax:* 21557316 (office). *E-mail:* tickety-boo@tickety-boo.com (office). *Website:* www.tickety-boo.com (office); www.billyconnolly.com.

CONNORS, James Scott (Jimmy); American tennis player; b. 2 Sept. 1952, East St. Louis, Ill.; s. of James Scott Connors I and the late Gloria Thompson Connors; m. Patti McGuire 1978; one s. one d.; ed Univ. of California, Los Angeles; amateur player 1970–72, professional since 1972; Australian Open Champion 1974; Wimbledon Champion 1974, 1982; US Open Champion 1974, 1976, 1978, 1982, 1983; SA Champion 1973, 1974; WCT Champion 1977, 1980; Grand Prix Champion 1978; commentator for NBC; played Davis Cup for USA 1976, 1981; ranked World Number 1 for a record 157 weeks; won 109 tournament titles; joined BBC tennis commentary team for 2005 Wimbledon championships; coached Andy Roddick 2006–08; BBC Overseas Sports Personality 1982; inducted into International Tennis Hall of Fame 1998. *Leisure interest:* golf. *Address:* Tennis Management Inc., 109 Red Fox Road, Belleville, IL 62223; RHB Ventures, 1320 18th Street, NW, Suite 100, Washington DC 20036, USA.

CONQUEST, (George) Robert (Acworth), CMG, OBE, MA, DLitt, FBA, FRSL; British writer, academic and fmr diplomatist; *Senior Research Fellow, Hoover Institution, Stanford University;* b. 15 July 1917, Malvern, England; s. of Robert F. W. Conquest and Rosamund A. Acworth; m. 1st Joan Watkins 1942 (divorced 1948); two s.; m. 2nd Tatiana Milhailova 1948 (divorced 1962); m. 3rd Caroleen Macfarlane 1964 (divorced 1978); m. 4th Elizabeth Neece 1979; ed Winchester Coll., Univ. of Grenoble and Magdalen Coll., Oxford; mil. service 1939–46; HM Foreign Service 1946–56; Sydney and Beatrice Webb Research Fellow, LSE 1956–58; Visiting Poet, Univ. of Buffalo 1959–60; Literary Ed. The Spectator 1962–63; Sr Fellow, Columbia Univ. Russian Inst. 1964–65; Fellow, Woodrow Wilson Int. Center, Washington, DC 1976–77; Sr Research Fellow, Hoover Inst., Stanford Univ. 1977–79, 1981–; Distinguished Visiting Fellow, Heritage Foundation 1980–81; Fellow, Royal Soc. of Literature, British Acad., British Interplanetary Soc., American Acad. of Arts and Sciences; mem. Soc. for the Promotion of Roman Studies, The Literary Soc.; Adjunct Fellow, Center for Strategic and Int. Studies 1983–; Alexis de Tocqueville Award 1992, Jefferson Lectureship 1993, Michael Braude Award for Light Verse, American Acad. of Arts and Letters 1997, Richard Weaver Award for Scholary Letters 1999, Fondazione Liberal Career Award 2004, Presidential Medal of Freedom 2005, Ukranian Medal of Honor 2006. *Publications:* Common Sense About Russia 1960, Power and Policy in the USSR 1960, Soviet Deportation of Nationalities 1960, Courage of Genius: The Pasternak Affair 1961, Industrial Workers in the USSR 1967, Soviet Nationalities Policy in Practice 1967, Agricultural Workers in the USSR 1968, The Soviet Police System 1968, Religion in the USSR 1968, The Soviet Political System 1968, Justice and the Legal System in the USSR 1968, The Great Terror: Stalin's Purge of the Thirties 1968, The Nation Killers: The Soviet Deportation of Nationalities 1970, Where Marx Went Wrong 1970, Lenin 1972, Kolyma: The Arctic Death Camps 1978, Inside Stalin's Secret Police: NKVD Politics, 1936–1939 1985, The Harvest of Sorrow: Soviet Collectivization and the Terror-Famine 1986, New and Collected Poems 1988, Tyrants and Typewriters: Communiques in the Struggle for Truth 1989, Stalin and the Kirov Murder 1989, The Great Terror: A Reassessment 1990, Stalin: Breaker of Nations 1991, History, Humanity, and Truth 1993, Demons Don't 1999, Reflections on a Ravaged Century 1999, Dragons of Expectation: Reality and Delusion in the Course of History 2005. *Address:* Hoover Institution, Stanford University, Stanford, CA 94305-6010; 52 Peter Coutts Circle, Stanford, CA 94305, USA (home). *Telephone:* (650) 723-1647. *Fax:* (650) 723-1687. *Website:* www.hoover.org/bios/conquest.html.

CONRAD, Donald Glover, BS, MBA; American insurance industry executive; b. 23 April 1930, St Louis; s. of Harold Armin and Velma Glover Conrad (née Morris); m. M. Stephania Shimkus 1980; one d. one step-d.; one s. two d. by previous marriage; ed Wesleyan and Northwestern Univs and Univ. of Michigan; with Exxon Co. 1957–70; Financial Adviser, Esso Natural Gas, The Hague, Netherlands 1965–66, Treasurer Esso Europe, London 1966–70; CFO and Sr Vice-Pres. Aetna Life & Casualty Co., Hartford, Conn. 1970–72, Exec. Vice-Pres. and Dir; Dir Terra Nova Insurance Co., Federated Investors Inc. –1988; Co-owner and CEO Hartford Whalers Hockey Club 1988–92; Sr Adviser to Pres. of World Bank 1995–2002; mem. Bd of Dirs Chevy Chase Bank, Washington, DC, Palm Beach (Fla) Civic Asscn; Vice-Chair. Ind. Energy Corpn 1989; Chair. Emer., American Council for the Arts; Founder Greater Hartford Arts Council. *Address:* 105 Banyan Road, Palm Beach, FL 33480, USA.

CONRAD, (Gaylord) Kent, MBA; American politician; *Senator from North Dakota;* b. 12 March 1948, Bismarck, ND; m. Lucy Calautti 1987; one d.; ed Univ. of Missouri, Stanford Univ. and George Washington Univ.; Asst to Tax Commr, State of ND Tax Dept, Bismarck 1974–80, Tax Commr 1981–86; Senator from North Dakota 1987–, Chair. Budget Cttee 2001–; Democrat. *Address:* 530 Hart Senate Office Bldg, Washington, DC 20510-3403, USA (office). *Telephone:* (202) 224-2043 (office). *Fax:* (202) 224-7776 (office). *Website:* conrad.senate.gov (office).

CONRAD, Kevin M., BS; Papua New Guinea/American diplomatist and international organization official; *Executive Director, Coalition of Rainforest Nations;* m.; ed Ukarumpa High School, Eastern Highlands Prov., Univ. of Southern California, USA, London Business School, UK, Columbia Business School, New York, USA; grew up in Arapesh tribe nr Wewak, East Sepik Prov., New Guinea; worked in investment banking; serves as Special Envoy and Amb. for Environment and Climate Change for Papua New Guinea; on faculty, School for Int. and Public Affairs, Columbia Univ., Exec. Dir Coalition for Rainforest Nations, has been instrumental in establishment of World Bank's Forest Carbon Partnership Facility and UN's UN-REDD (Reducing Emissions from Deforestation and Forest Degradation in developing countries) programme; has advised govts in Africa, Asia, Latin America and the Pacific on sustainable devt, econ. reform and investment incentive programmes; named by Time magazine No. 1 in 'Leaders & Visionaries' category of Heroes of the Environment 2008. *Address:* Coalition for Rainforest Nations, 2852 Broadway, New York, NY 10025, USA (office). *Telephone:* (212) 854-8181 (office). *Fax:* (212) 504-2622 (office). *E-mail:* kconrad@rainforestcoalition.org (office). *Website:* www.rainforestcoalition.org (office).

CONRAN, Jasper Alexander Thirlby, OBE; British fashion designer; b. 12 Dec. 1959, London; s. of Sir Terence Conran (q.v.) and Shirley Conran; ed Bryanston School, Dorset, Parsons School of Art and Design, New York; Fashion Designer, Man. Dir Jasper Conran Ltd 1978–; designer of lines for Debenhams 1997–; theatre costumes, Jean Anouilh's The Rehearsal, Almeida Theatre 1990, My Fair Lady 1992; Sleeping Beauty, Scottish Ballet 1994, The Nutcracker Sweeties, Birmingham Royal Ballet 1996, Edward II 1997, Arthur

2000; Fil d'Or (Int. Linen Award) 1982, 1983, British Fashion Council Designer of the Year Award 1986–87, Fashion Group of America Award 1987, Laurence Olivier Award for Costume Designer of the Year 1991, British Collections Award (in British Fashion Awards) 1991. *Address:* Jasper Conran Ltd, 1-7 Rostrevor Mews, Fulham, London, SW6 5AZ, England. *Telephone:* (20) 7384-0800. *Fax:* (20) 7384-0801. *E-mail:* info@jasperconran.com. *Website:* www.jasperconran.com.

CONRAN, Sir Terence Orby, Kt; British designer and retail executive; b. 4 Oct. 1931, Esher, Surrey; s. of Rupert Conran and Christina Halstead; m. 1st Brenda Davison (divorced); m. 2nd Shirley Conran (divorced 1962); two s.; m. 3rd Caroline Herbert 1963 (divorced 1996); two s. one d.; m. 4th Vicki Davis 2000; ed Bryanston School and Cen. School of Art and Design, London; Chair. Conran Holdings Ltd 1965–68; Jt Chair. Ryman Conran Ltd 1968–71; Chair. Habitat Group Ltd 1971–88, Habitat/Mothercare PLC 1982–88; Chair. Habitat France SA 1973–88, Conran Stores Inc. 1977–88, J. Hepworth & Son Ltd 1981–83 (Dir 1979–83), Richard Shops 1983; Chair. Storehouse PLC 1986–90, CEO 1986–88, non-exec. Dir 1990; Chair. The Conran Shop Ltd 1976–, Conran Roche 1980–, Jasper Conran 1982–, Butlers Wharf 1984–90, Bibendum Restaurant 1986–, Benchmark Ltd 1989–, Blueprint Café 1989–, Terence Conran Ltd 1990–, Conran Holdings 1990–, The Conran Shop SNC 1990–, Le Pont de la Tour 1991–, Quaglino's Restaurant Ltd 1991–, The Butler's Wharf Chop House Ltd 1992–; CD Partnership 1993–, Conran Restaurants Ltd 1994–, Bluebird Store Ltd 1994–, Mezzo Ltd 1995–, Conran Shop Marylebone 1995–, Conran Shop Germany 1996–, Coq d'Argent Ltd 1997–, Orrery Ltd 1997–; Vice-Pres. FNAC 1985–89; Dir Conran Ink Ltd 1969–, The Neal Street Restaurant 1972–89, Electra Risk Capital 1981–84, Conran Octopus Ltd 1983–, Heal & Son Ltd 1983–87, Savacentre 1986–88, British Home Stores 1986–88, Michelin House Investment Co. Ltd 1989–; f. Conran Foundation, Butler's Wharf; launched Content by Conran range of furniture for Christie Tyler 2003; mem. Royal Comm. on Environmental Pollution 1973–76; mem. Council, Royal Coll. of Art 1978–81, 1986–; mem. Advisory Council, Victoria & Albert Museum 1979–83, Trustee 1984–90; Trustee Design Museum 1989–, Chair. 1992–; mem. Creative Leaders' Network; Dr hc (RCA) 1996, Hon. DLitt (Portsmouth) 1996; RSA Bicentenary Medal 1982, Commdr Ordre des Arts et des Lettres 1991 and other awards for design. *Publications:* The House Book 1974, The Kitchen Book 1977, The Bedroom & Bathroom Book 1978, The Cook Book (with Caroline Conran) 1980, The New House Book 1985, The Conran Directory of Design 1985, The Soft Furnishings Book 1986, Plants at Home 1986, Terence Conran's France 1987, Terence Conran's D.I.Y. by Design 1989, D.I.Y. in the Garden 1991, Terence Conran's Toys and Children's Furniture 1992, Terence Conran's Kitchen Book 1993, The Essential House Book 1994, Terence Conran on Design 1996, The Essential Garden Book 1998, Easy Living 1999, Chef's Garden 1999, Terence Conran on Restaurants 1999, Terence Conran on London 2000; Q and A: A Sort of Autobiography 2001, Terence Conran on Small Spaces 2001, How to Live in Small Spaces 2006, Eat London (with Peter Prescott) 2007, Outdoors: The Garden Design Book for the Twenty-First Century (with Diarmuid Gavin) 2007. *Leisure interests:* gardening, cooking. *Address:* 22 Shad Thames, London, SE1 2YU, England. *Telephone:* (20) 7378-1161. *Fax:* (20) 7403-4309. *Website:* www.conran.com.

CONROY, (Donald) Patrick (Pat), BA; American writer; b. 26 Oct. 1945, Atlanta, GA; s. of Col Donald Conroy and Frances (Peg) Dorothy Conroy; m. 1st Barbara Bolling 1969 (divorced 1977); m. 2nd Lenore Gurewitz 1981 (divorced 1995); one s. five d.; ed The Citadel; mem. Authors' Guild of America, PEN, Writers Guild; Ford Foundation Leadership Devt Grant 1971, Nat. Endowment for the Arts Award for Achievement in Educ. 1974, SC Hall of Fame, Acad. of Authors 1988, Golden Plate Award, American Acad. of Achievement 1992, Ga Comm. on the Holocaust Humanitarian Award 1996, Lotos Medal of Merit for Outstanding Literary Achievement 1996 and many others. *Film screenplays:* Invictus 1988, The Prince of Tides (with Becky Johnson) 1991, Beach Music 1997. *Publications:* non-fiction: The Boo 1970, The Water is Wide 1972; novels: The Great Santini 1976, The Lords of Discipline 1980, The Prince of Tides 1986, Beach Music 1995, My Losing Season 2002. *Address:* Marly Rusoff and Associates, PO Box 524, Bronxville, NY 10708, USA (office). *Telephone:* (914) 961-7939 (office). *E-mail:* mra_queries@rusoffagency.com (office). *Website:* www.rusoffagency.com (office).

CONSALVI, Simón Alberto; Venezuelan historian and diplomatist; b. 7 July 1929; m.; two c.; ed Univ. Cen. de Venezuela; mem. Nat. Congress 1959–64, 1974–; Amb. to Yugoslavia 1961–64; Dir Cen. Office of Information for the Presidency 1964–67; Pres. Nat. Inst. of Culture and Art 1967–69; Dir Nat. Magazine of Culture; Int. Ed. El Nacional newspaper 1971–74, now mem. Editorial Bd; Minister of State for Information 1974; Perm. Rep. to UN, New York 1974–77; Pres. UN Security Council 1977; Minister of Foreign Affairs 1977–79, 1985–88; Amb. to USA 1990–94; Founder and Dir Biblioteca Biográfica Venezolana; fmr Sec.-Gen. of Presidency; mem. Nat. Congress Foreign Relations Comm. *Publications:* El Perfil y la sombra 1997; numerous articles and assays. *Address:* c/o El Nacional, Edif. El Nacional, Puente Nuevo a Puerto Escondido, El Silencio, Apdo 209, Caracas, Venezuela. *Telephone:* (212) 408-3111. *Fax:* (212) 408-3169. *E-mail:* contactenos@el-nacional.com. *Website:* www.el-nacional.com.

CONSIDINE, Frank William; American business executive; b. 15 Aug. 1921, Chicago; s. of Frank J. Considine and Minnie Regan; m. Nancy Scott 1948; ed Loyola Univ., Chicago; Pnr, F. J. Hogan Agency, Chicago 1945–47; Asst to Pres. Graham Glass Co. Chicago 1947–51; Prin., F. W. Considine Co., Chicago 1951–55; Vice-Pres. Metro Glass Div. Kraftco, Chicago 1955–60; Vice-Pres. and Dir Nat. Can Corpn (now American Nat. Can Co.), Chicago 1961–67, Exec. Vice-Pres. 1967–69, Pres. 1969–88, CEO 1973–88, Chair. 1983–90, Hon.

Chair. and Chair. Exec. Cttee 1990–; Vice-Chair. Triangle Industries Inc. (parent corpn) 1985–88; Vice-Pres. Lyric Opera of Chicago; mem. Bd of Dirs Encyclopaedia Britannica, First Chicago Corpn, First Nat. Bank of Chicago, Helene Curtis Industries Inc., Ill. Power Co., Schwitzer Inc., Scotsman Industries, Maytag Co., Tribune Co., IMC Fertilizer Group Inc.; Chair. Bd of Trustees Loyola Univ., Chicago –1999, Loyola Univ. Health System; Hon. LLD (Loyola) 1986; Hon. LHD (Northwestern) 1987. *Address:* 140 Thorn Tree Land, Winnetka, IL 60093, USA.

CONSTÂNCIO, Vitor Manuel Ribeiro; Portuguese central banker and fmr politician; *Governor, Banco de Portugal;* b. 12 Oct. 1943, Lisbon; s. of António Francisco Constâncio and Ester Ribeiro Vieira Constâncio; m. Maria José Constâncio 1968; one s. one d.; ed Instituto Superior de Ciências Económicas e Financeiras, Lisbon and Univ. of Bristol; Asst Prof., Faculty of Econs 1965–73, 1989–; Dir of Global Planning Studies, Planning Research Centre 1973; Sec. of State for Planning and Budget 1974–75; Head of Econ. Research Dept, Banco de Portugal 1975, Vice-Gov. 1977, 1979–85, Gov. 1985–86, 2000–, Adviser 1989–95; mem. Parl. 1976, 1980-81, 1987–88, Chair. Parl. Comm. of Econ. and Finance 1976; Pres. of Comm. formed to negotiate with EEC 1977; Minister of Finance and Planning 1978; Sec.-Gen. Socialist Party 1986–89; mem. Council of State 1996–; Prof. of Econs Tech. Univ. of Lisbon 1989–; mem. Bd Banco BPI 1995–2000. *Address:* Office of the Governor, Banco de Portugal, Rua do Ouro 27, 1100-150 Lisbon, Portugal (office). *Telephone:* (21) 3213200 (office). *Fax:* (21) 3464843 (office). *E-mail:* info@bportugal.pt (office). *Website:* www.bportugal.pt (office).

CONSTANT, Paule, DèsSc; French author; b. 25 Jan. 1944, Gan; d. of Yves Constant and Jeanne Tauzin; m. Auguste Bourgeade 1968; one s. one d.; ed Univ. of Bordeaux and Univ. of Paris (Sorbonne); Asst Lecturer in French Literature, Univ. of Abidjan 1968–75; Maître-assistant, then Maître de Conférences in French Literature and Civilization, Univ. of Aix-Marseille III 1975–90, Inst. of French Studies for Foreign Students 1986–95; Prof. Université Aix–Marseille III 1995–; diarist, Revue des Deux Mondes, Paris 1990–92; Founder and Pres. Centre des Ecrivains du Sud - Jean Giono; Chevalier, Légion d'honneur, Ordre de l'Educ. Nat. de Côte d'Ivoire. *Television includes:* L'Education des Jeunes Filles de la Légion d'Honneur 1992, Mon héros préféré: La Princesse de Clèves 1996, Les grands fleuves racontés par des écrivains: L'Amazone 1997, Galilée: Paule Constant sur les traces de Jean Giono 2001. *Publications:* novels: Ouregano 1980 (Prix Valery Larbaud), Propriété privée 1981, Balta 1983, White Spirit 1989 (Prix François Mauriac, Prix Lutèce, Prix du Sud Jean-Baumel, Grand Prix du Roman, Acad. Française), Le Grand Ghâpal 1991, La Fille du Gobernator 1994, Confidence pour confidence 1998 (Prix du roman France-Télévision, Prix Goncourt Un monde à l'usage des demoiselles (essay) 1987 (Grand Prix de l'Essai, Acad. Française 1987), Sucre et Secret 2003 (Prix du roman, Amnesty inter-national), La Bête à Chagrin 2007. *Leisure interest:* bibliophile (18th and 19th century works on educ.). *Address:* Institut d'études françaises pour étudiants étrangers, 23 rue Gaston de Saporta, 13100 Aix-en-Provence; 29 rue Cardinale, 13100 Aix-en-Provence, France. *Telephone:* 4-42-38-45-08 (office). *Fax:* 4-42-23-02-64 (office). *Website:* www.pauleconstant.com.

CONSTANTINE II, King of the Hellenes; b. 2 June 1940; m. Princess Anne-Marie of Denmark 1964; three s. two d.; ed Anavryta School and Law School, Athens Univ.; military training 1956–58; visited USA 1958, 1959; succeeded to throne March 1964; left Greece Dec. 1967; deposed June 1973; monarchy abolished by Nat. Referendum Dec. 1974; deprived of Greek citizenship, remaining property in Greece nationalized April 1994; won ruling in European Court of Human Rights for compensation; Gold Medal, Yachting, Olympic Games, Rome 1960. *Address:* 15 Grosvenor Square, London, W1K 6LD, England (office). *Website:* www.greekroyalfamily.org.

CONSTANTINE, David John, BA, PhD; British poet, writer and translator; *Co-Editor, Modern Poetry in Translation;* b. 4 March 1944, Salford, Lancs., England; m. Helen Frances Best 1966; one s. one d.; ed Wadham Coll., Oxford; Lecturer to Sr Lecturer in German, Univ. of Durham 1969–81; Fellow in German, Queens' Coll. Oxford 1981–2000; Co-Ed. (with Bernard O'Donoghue) Oxford Poets anthologies 2000–, (with Helen Constantine), Modern Poetry in Translation magazine 2004–; mem. Poetry Soc., Soc. of Authors; Alice Hunt Bartlett Prize 1984, Runciman Prize 1985, Southern Arts Literature Prize 1987, European Poetry Translation Prize 1998. *Publications:* poetry: A Brightness to Cast Shadows 1980, Watching for Dolphins 1983, Mappi Mundi 1984, Madder 1987, Selected Poems 1991, Caspar Hauser 1994, Sleeper 1995, The Pelt of Wasps 1998, Something for the Ghosts 2002, Collected Poems 2004, A Poetry Primer 2004; fiction: Davies 1985, Back at the Spike 1994, Under the Dam (short stories) 2005; non-fiction: The Significance of Locality in the Poetry of Friedrich Hölderlin 1979, Early Greek Travellers and the Hellenic Ideal 1984, Hölderlin 1988, Friedrich Hölderlin 1992, Fields of Fire: A Life of Sir William Hamilton 2001, A Living Language 2004; translator: Hölderlin: Selected Poems 1996, Henri Michaux: Spaced, Displaced (with Helen Constantine) 1992, Philippe Jaccottet: Under Clouded Skies/Beaure-gard (with Mark Treharne) 1994, Goethe: Elective Affinities 1994, Kleist: Selected Writings 1998, Hölderlin's Sophocles 2001, Hans Magnus Enzens-berger: Lighter Than Air 2002; editor: German Short Stories 2 1972. *Leisure interest:* walking. *Address:* Modern Poetry in Translation, The Queens' College, Oxford, OX1 4AW (office); 1 Hill Top Road, Oxford, OX4 1PB, England (home). *Telephone:* (1865) 244701 (office). *E-mail:* david.constantine@queens.ox.ac.uk (office). *Website:* www.mptmagazine.com.

CONSTANTINESCU, Emil, PhD, DSc; Romanian politician, jurist, geologist and fmr head of state; *Chairman, Actiunea Populara;* b. 19 Nov. 1939, Tighina (now Repub. of Moldova); s. of Ion Constantinescu and Maria Constantinescu; m. Nadia Ileana Bogorin; one s. one d.; ed Bucharest Univ.; practising lawyer 1960–61; Lecturer and Sr Lecturer, Bucharest Univ. 1966–90, Prof. of

Mineralogy 1990–, Vice-Rector 1990–92, Rector 1992–96, Hon. Pres. of Senate 1996–, Prof. of Mineralogy-Crystallography 2001–; Visiting Prof., Duke Univ., NC, USA 1991–92; Chair Nat. Romanian Council of Univ. Rectors 1992–96; mem. Steering Cttee of European Univs Assoc. (CRE) 1992–98, Int. Assoc. of Univ. Presidents 1994–96, Founder-mem. Univ. Solidarity 1990; Pres. Civic Acad. 1990–92; Acting Chair. Romanian Anti-Totalitarian Forum 1991; Pres. Democratic Convention 1992–96; Pres. of Romania 1996–2000; Gen. Sec. Romanian Geological Soc. 1987–93, 1990–93; Chair. Actiunea Populara (Popular Action) 2003–; Co-Chair. World Justice Project (sponsored by ABA, European Bar Asscn, World Bar Asscn) 2007–; mem. A Global Forum on New Democracies, Taipei 2008; Hon. Citizen of Athens, Prague, Budapest, San Francisco and Helsinki; Hon. mem. Geological and Mineralogical Socs of America, UK, Germany, SA, Japan, Greece; Hon. mem. Nat. Geographical Soc. of USA and Geographical Soc. of France; Grand Croix, Légion d'honneur, Order of Merit (Austria), Stara Planina with Ribbon (Romania), White Rose of Finland with Collar, Great Cross of The Saviour (Greece), Great Cross of St Olaf (Norway), Great Cross with Brilliants (The Sun of Peru), The Independence Order with Collar (Qatar), State Decoration (Turkey), St Andrew Order, Patriarchy of Constantinople, Skanderberg Order (Albania), Orthodox Order of the Holy Grave with Collar, Orthodox Patriarchy in Jerusalem, Collar of Don Infante Henrique (Portugal), Great Cross of High Order of St Michael and St George (UK), Kt, Order of the Elephant (Denmark); Hon. DSc (Univs of Athens, Liège, Montréal, Delhi, Beijing, Ankara, Chişinău, Astana, Maribor, Bangkok, Sofia, Ecole Nationale Supérieur, Paris); Romanian Acad. Award in Geology 1980, Aristide Calvany Award for Peace, Democracy and Human Devt Paris 1997, Award for Democracy of Democratic Center Washington, DC 1998, European Statesman of the Year Award New York 1998, European Coudenhove-Kalergi Award for Contrib. to Devt of Europe and Free Movt of Ideas, Bern 1998, American Bar Asscn Award 1999, Palmas Académicas from Acad. of Brazil 2000, Bethleem 2000 Medal, Nat. Palestinian Authority 2000; awards and medals from Acad. des Sciences Inst. de France, Univs of Paris-Sorbonne, Prague, Amsterdam, Bratislava, Szeged, São Paulo. *Publications:* 12 books and more than 60 articles in scientific journals and more than 100 articles, speeches and essays on political, econ., social, educational, cultural and environmental issues. *Address:* 050093 Bucharest 5, Splaiul Independenţei 17/101, Romania. *Telephone:* (21) 3160293 (office); (21) 2229100 (home). *Fax:* (21) 3160399 (office); (21) 2229038 (home). *E-mail:* emil@constantinescu.ro; office@actiunea.ro (office). *Website:* www.actiunea.ro (office); www.constantinescu.ro.

CONSTAS, Dimitri, LLB, PhD; Greek academic, research institute director and fmr government official; ed Panteion Univ., Univ. of Thessaloniki, Carleton Univ., Canada, Tufts Univ., USA; Rector, Panteion Univ. 1990–95; Interim Minister for Press and Mass Media 1996; Perm. Rep. to Council of Europe, Strasbourg 1997–99; Head of Task Forces on Euro-Mediterranean Co-operation, Middle East Peace Process, Greek role in Int. Conflict Resolution 2000; Founder Inst. of Int. Relations, Panteion Univ., Athens 1989; Pres. Hellenic Soc. of Int. Law and Int. Relations 1989–91; Vice-Pres. Foundation for Hellenic Culture 1994–95; Fellow, Woodrow Wilson Int. Center for Scholars 1998; Fulbright Scholar 1976–79, MacJannet Fellow, Institut des Hautes Etudes Internationaux 1978, Robert Schumann Fellow in European Integration 1979, Noted Scholar, Univ. of British Columbia 1996, Sr Fulbright Scholar, Princeton Univ. 1996. *Publications include:* The Greek–Turkish Conflict in the 1990s (ed.) 1991, Modern Diasporas in World Politics: the Greeks in Comparative Perspective (co-ed.) 1993, Greece Prepares for the Twenty-First Century (co-ed.) 1995, Greek and European Foreign Policy (1991–99), Diplomacy and Politics 2003. *Address:* Institute of International Relations, 3–5 Hill Street, Athens 10558, Greece (office). *Telephone:* (21) 13312325 (office). *Fax:* (21) 13313575 (office). *E-mail:* constas@idis.gr (office). *Website:* www.idis.gr (office).

CONTAMINE, Claude Maurice; French television executive; b. 29 Aug. 1929, Metz, Moselle; s. of the late Henry Contamine and Marie-Thérèse Dufays; m. Renée Jaugeon (deceased); one s.; ed Lycée Malherbe, Caen, Facultés de Droit, Caen and Paris and Ecole Nat. d'Admin; public servant until 1964; Asst Dir-Gen. ORTF and Dir of TV 1964–67; Pres. Dir-Gen. Union générale cinématographique (UGC) 1967–71; Consul-Gen. Milan 1971–72; Asst Dir-Gen. in charge of external affairs and co-operation, ORTF 1973–74; Minister plenipotentiary 1974; mem. Haut Conseil de l'Audiovisuel 1973–80; Pres. France-Régions (FR3) 1975–81; Conseiller Maître, Cour des Comptes 1981; Pres. Télédiffusion de France (TDF) 1986; Pres. Dir-Gen. Soc. nat. de programme Antenne 2 1986–89; Rapporteur général European TV and Film Forum 1990–; Pres. Conservatoire Européen d'Ecriture Audiovisuelle 1996–2002; mem. Conseil Supérieur de la Magistrature 1998–2002, Comm. nationale consultative des droits de l'homme 2002; Commdr, Légion d'honneur 2003, Commdr, Ordre nat. du Mérite, Officier des Arts et des Lettres. *Address:* 12 rue de Bassano, 75116 Paris, France (home).

CONTAMINE, Philippe, DèsSc; French historian and academic; *Professor Emeritus of Medieval History, Université Paris-Sorbonne;* b. 7 May 1932, Metz; s. of Henry Contamine and Marie-Thérèse Dufays; m. Geneviève Bernard 1956; two s. one d.; ed Lycée Malherbe, Caen, Lycée Louis-le-Grand, Paris, Sorbonne; history and geography teacher, Lycée, Sens 1957–60, Lycée Carnot, Paris 1960–61; Asst Prof. of Medieval History, Sorbonne 1962–65; Asst Lecturer, Lecturer then Prof. of Medieval History, Univ. of Nancy 1965–73; Prof. of Medieval History, Univ. of Paris (Nanterre) 1973–89; Prof. of Medieval History, Univ. of Paris (Sorbonne) 1989–2000, Prof. Emer. 2000–; Dir Dept of History 1976–79; Sec. to Soc. de l'histoire de France 1984–; Pres. Nat. Soc. of Antique Dealers 1999; mem. Institut de France (Acad. des Inscriptions et Belles-Lettres, Pres. 2000) 1990, Academia Europaea 1993; Corresp. Fellow Royal Historical Soc. 1993; Pres. Soc. Nat. des Antiquaires de France 1999; Chevalier Légion d'honneur, Commdr des Palmes académiques, Officier des Arts et Lettres. *Publications:* La Guerre de cent ans 1968, Guerre, Etat et Société à la fin du Moyen Age 1972, La Vie quotidienne en France et en Angleterre pendant la guerre de cent ans 1976, La guerre au Moyen Age 1980, La France aux XIVe et XVe siècles 1981, La France de la fin du XVe siècle (co-ed.) 1985, L'Etat et Les Aristocraties (ed.) 1989, L'histoire militaire de la France 1992, Des pouvoirs en France 1300–1500 1992, L'Economie Mediévale 1993, De Jeanne d'Arc aux guerres d'Italie 1994, La Noblesse au royaume de France de Philippe Le Bel à Louis XII 1997, Guerre et concurrence entre les Etats européens du XIVe au XVIIIe siècle (ed.) 1998, Autour de Marguerite d'Ecosse: reines, princesses et dames du XVe siècle (ed.) 1999, Les enceintes urbaines XIIIe-XVIe (jtly) 2002, Histoire de la France politique 2002. *Address:* 11–15 rue de l'Amiral Roussin, 75015 Paris, France.

CONTE, Arthur; French politician, journalist and broadcasting executive; b. 31 March 1920, Salses, Pyrénées-Orientales; s. of Pierre Conte and Marie-Thérèse Parazols; m. Colette Lacassagne 1951 (died 2001); one s. one d.; ed Montpellier Univ.; foreign leader writer, Indépendant de Perpignan 1945; later worked for Paris Match; subsequently leader-writer for Les Informations and contrib. to Le Figaro, Historia, Les Nouvelles Littéraires; Sec. Socialist Party Fed. for Pyrénées-Orientales; Deputy to Nat. Assembly 1951–62, 1968–72; Sec. of State for Industry and Commerce 1957; Mayor of Salses 1947–72; Del. to Assembly of Council of Europe 1956–62; Pres. WEU Assembly 1961–62; Chair. and Dir-Gen. ORTF 1972–73; Chevalier, Légion d'honneur. *Publications:* La légende de Pablo Casals, Les étonnements de Mister Newborn, Les promenades de M. Tripoire, Les hommes ne sont pas des héros, La vigne sous le rempart, Yalta ou le partage du monde, Bandoung, tournant de l'histoire, sans de Gaulle, Lénine et Staline, Les frères Burns, Hommes libres, L'épopée mondiale d'un siècle (5 Vols), Le premier janvier 1900, Le premier janvier 1920, Le premier janvier 1940, Le premier janvier 1960, Le premier janvier 1983, L'aventure européenne (2 Vols), L'homme Giscard, L'Après-Yalta, Karl Marx face à son temps, Les dictateurs du vingtième siècle, Les présidents de la cinquième république, Les premiers ministres de la Verépublique, Verdun, Le 1er janvier 1789 1988, Billaud Varenne, géant de la Révolution 1989, Joffre 1991, L'epopée coloniale de la France 1992, Nostalgies françaises 1993, Au village de mon enfance 1994, L'epopée des chemins de fer français 1996, C'était la IVeRépublique 1998, La drôle de guerre 1999, Les paysans de France 2000, Soldats de France 2001, Ma terre de toujours 2002. *Leisure interest:* golf. *Address:* 94 avenue de Suffren, 75015 Paris, France. *Telephone:* 1-47-83-23-45.

CONTE, Fernando, BSc, MBA; Spanish airline executive; *Chairman and CEO, Iberia Group;* b. 28 Feb. 1950, Mérida, Mexico; m.; two d.; ed Instituto Catolico de Artes e Industrias, Instituto de Empresa (pvt. business school); worked for Asea Brown Boveri 1974–2003, positions included Sales Engineer/ Product Man., Madrid, Regional Man. for Cen. America/Caribbean, Asea AB, Guatemala City, Industrial Div. Man. for Asea in Venezuela, Cen. Region Man., Asea Eléctrica, Madrid, Man. Power Transmission and Distribution Div., ASEA/ABB Energía, Madrid, Gen. Man. ABB Subestaciones, Madrid, Gen. Man. ABB Trafo, Madrid, Segment Vice-Pres. Asea Brown Boveri, SA, Madrid, Exec. Vice-Pres. and CEO Asea Brown Boveri, SA, Madrid, mem. Bd ABB Portugal, mem. ABB Ltd Group Exec. Team, Zürich; ind. Bd mem. Iberia 2001–03, Chair. and CEO Iberia Group 2003–; ind. Bd mem. Amadeus 2000–03; Chair. oneworld (airline alliance) 2005–06, Audit Cttee IATA 2005–, Asscn of European Airlines 2007–; Javier Benjumea Prize, Coll. Asscn of Engineers–ICAI 2005. *Address:* Iberia Aéreas de España, Velázquez 130, 28006 Madrid, Spain (office). *Telephone:* (91) 587-87-87 (office). *E-mail:* presidencia@iberia.es (office). *Website:* www.iberia.es (office).

CONTEH, Maj. (Alfred) Paolo, LLB (Hons), LLM; Sierra Leone army officer (retd) and government official; *Minister of Defence;* ed Univs of London and East London, UK; served in Sierra Leone army 1976–92, rose to rank of Maj. and CO of the Mil. Police; went to UK on leave to pursue legal studies 1986; Court Liaison Officer and Prosecution Sec., Dept for Work and Pensions for the investigation service in London –2007; Minister of Defence 2007–. *Address:* Ministry of Defence, State Avenue, Freetown, Sierra Leone (office). *Telephone:* (22) 227369 (office). *Fax:* (22) 229380 (office).

CONTI, Fulvio; Italian business executive; *CEO and General Manager, Enel SpA;* b. 28 Oct. 1947, Rome; m.; one s.; ed Univ. of Rome 'La Sapienza'; joined Mobil Group 1969, Chief of Finance for Europe 1989–90; Head, Accounting, Finance and Control Dept Montecatini 1991–93; Head of Finance Montedison-Compart 1993–96; Gen. Man. and Chief Financial Officer Italian Nat. Railways 1996–98; also held important positions in other cos, including Metropolis and Grandi Stazioni; Vice-Chair. Eurofima 1997; Gen. Man. and Chief Financial Officer Telecom Italia 1998–99, also held important positions in other cos of the group, including Finsiel, TIM, Sirti, Italtel, Meie and STET International; Chief Financial Officer Enel SpA 1999–2005, CEO and Gen. Man. 2005–; Deputy Chair. Eurelectric; mem. Bd Dirs Barclays plc, AON Corpn, Nat. Acad. of Santa Cecilia. *Address:* Enel SpA, Viale Regina Margherita 137, 00198 Rome, Italy (office). *Telephone:* (06) 83057866 (office). *Fax:* (06) 83053472 (office). *E-mail:* secireteriaad@enel.it (office). *Website:* www.enel.it (office).

CONTI, Most Rev. Mario Joseph, PhL, STL, FRSE; British ecclesiastic; *Archbishop of Glasgow;* b. 20 March 1934, Elgin; s. of Louis Joseph Conti and Josephine Quintilia Panicali; ed Blairs Coll., Aberdeen, Pontifical Scots Coll. and Gregorian Univ., Rome; ordained priest 1958; apptd Curate, St Mary's Cathedral, Aberdeen 1959, apptd Parish Priest, St Joachim's Wick 1962; Bishop of Aberdeen 1977–2002; Archbishop of Glasgow 2002–; Apostolic Admin. Diocese of Paisley 2004–05; Pres.-Treas. Scottish Catholic Int. Aid Fund 1978–84; Pres. Nat. Liturgy Comm. 1981–85, Nat. Comm. for Christian Doctrine and Unity 1985–; Vice-Pres. Comm. for Migrant Workers and Tourism 1978–84, Scottish Catholic Heritage Comm. 1980–; mem. Council for

Promotion of Christian Unity (Rome) 1984–, Int. Comm. for English in the Liturgy 1978–87, Pontificial Comm. for Cultural Heritage of the Church, Rome 1994–2004; Convener, Action of Churches Together in Scotland 1990–93; Co-Moderator of Jt Working Group, RC Church and WCC 1995–2008; Prin. Chaplain to British Asscn of the Order of Malta 1995–2000, 2005–, Conventual Chaplain Grand Cross 2001–; mem. Historic Buildings Council of Scotland 1995–2000; Order of Merit of the Italian Repub. 1982; Kt Commdr of Holy Sepulchre 1989; Hon. DD (Aberdeen) 1989. *Publications:* Oh Help! The Making of an Archbishop 2003; occasional articles and letters in nat. and local press. *Leisure interests:* walking, travel, swimming, music and the arts. *Address:* Curial Offices, 196 Clyde Street, Glasgow, G1 4JY (office); 40 Newlands Road, Glasgow G43 2JD, Scotland (home). *Telephone:* (141) 226-5898 (office). *Fax:* (141) 225-2600 (office). *E-mail:* curia@rcag.org.uk (office). *Website:* www.rcag.org.uk (office).

CONTI, Tom; British actor and director; s. of Alfonso Conti and Mary McGoldrick; m. Kara Wilson 1967; one d.; ed Royal Scottish Acad. of Music; West End Theatre Mans' Award, Royal Television Soc. Award, Variety Club of Great Britain Award 1978, Tony Award of New York 1979. *London theatre includes:* Savages (Christopher Hampton) 1973, The Devil's Disciple (Shaw) 1976, Whose Life is it Anyway? (Brian Clarke) 1978, They're Playing Our Song (Neil Simon/Marvin Hamlisch) 1980, Romantic Comedy (Bernard Salde), An Italian Straw Hat 1986, Two Into One, Treats 1989, Jeffrey Bernard is Unwell 1990, The Ride Down Mt. Morgan 1991, Present Laughter (also dir) 1993, Chapter Two 1996, Jesus My Boy 1998. *Films include:* Flame, Full Circle, Merry Christmas Mr. Lawrence, Reuben, American Dreamer, Saving Grace, Miracles, Heavenly Pursuits, Beyond Therapy, Roman Holiday, Two Brothers Running, White Roses, Shirley Valentine, Someone Else's America, Crush Depth, Something to Believe In 1996, Out of Control 1997, The Enemy 2000, Derailed 2005, Rabbit Fever 2006, Paid 2006, Almost Heaven 2006, O Jerusalem 2006, Dangerous Parking 2007. *Television work includes:* Madame Bovary, Treats, The Glittering Prizes, The Norman Conquests, The Beate Klarsfield Story, Fatal Dosage, The Quick and the Dead, Blade on the Feather, The Wright Verdicts, Deadline, Friends 1998, Deadline 2000–01, I Was a Rat 2001, Donovan 2004, Deeply Irresponsible 2007. *Directed:* Last Licks, Broadway 1979, Before the Party 1980, The Housekeeper 1982, Treats 1989, Present Laughter 1993, Last of the Red Hot Lovers 1999. *Publication:* The Doctor (novel) 2004. *Leisure interest:* music. *Address:* Artists Independent Network, 32 Tavistock Street, London, WC2E 7PB, England. *Telephone:* (20) 7352-7722.

CONTOGEORGIS, George, MA, PhD; Greek academic; *Professor of Political Science, Panteion University of Athens;* b. 14 Feb. 1947, Letkas; s. of Dimitri Contogeorgis and Elia Contogeorgis; m. Catherine Kampourgiannidou 1972; two d.; ed Univ. of Athens, Univ. of Paris II, Ecole Pratique des Hautes Etudes, Ecole des Hautes Etudes en Sciences Sociales; Prof. of Political Science, Panteion Univ. Athens 1983–, Rector 1984–90; Gen. Dir ERT SA (Hellenic Broadcasting Corpn) 1985, Pres.-Gen. Dir 1989; Minister, Ministry of the Presidency (State Admin., Communication, Media), Govt Spokesman 1993; Founding mem. European Political Science Network (EPSNET); Dir European Masters Programme in Political Science; Founder-mem. and Sec.-Gen. Greek Political Sciences Asscn 1975–80; leader writer in Athenian daily newspapers; mem. High Council and Research Council, European Univ. Florence 1986–94; mem. High Council, Univ. of Europe, Paris and Centre of Regional Studies, Montpellier; Visiting Prof., Inst. d'Etudes Politiques, Paris, Univ. Libre de Bruxelles, Univ. Catholique de Louvain, Univs of Montpellier, Tokyo, IEP Bordeaux, Lille etc.; Prof., Franqui Chair., Univ. of Brussels; Prof. of European Studies, Univ. of Siena; mem. Council Pôle Sud, Political Science Review, Revue Internationale de Politique Comparée; corresponding mem. Acad. of Culture, Portugal; mem. French Political Science Asscn, IPSA and other int. asscns; Chevalier, des Palmes Academiques. *Publications:* The Theory of Revolution in Aristotle 1975, The Popular Ideology: Socio-political Study of the Greek Folk Song 1979, Political System and Politics 1985, Social Process and Political Self-government: The Greek City-State Under the Ottoman Empire 1982, The Local Government in the State 1985, Nuclear Energy and Public Opinion in Europe 1991, History of Greece 1992, Système de communication et système d'échange: La télévision 1993, After Communism (in collaboration) 1993, Greek Society in the 20th Century 1995, Democracy in the Technological Society 1995, Society and Politics 1996, New World Order 1998, Identité cosmosystémique ou identité nationale? Le Paradigme hellénique 1999, Le Citoyen dans la cité (Typology of Citizenship) 2000, Religion and Politics 2000, Modernity and Progress 2001, State and Globalization 2003, Work and Freedom 2003, Citizenship and State, Concept and Typology of Citizenship 2004, The Authoritarian Phenomenon 2004, Nation and Modernity 2006, The Hellenic Cosmosystem: Vol. 1, The Statocentric Period 2006, Democracy as Freedom 2007, Democracy and Representation 2007, The 'Greek Cosmopolitean Democracy' of Rhigas Feraios 2008. *Leisure interest:* water sports. *Address:* Panteion University of Athens, 136 Sygrou Avenue, Athens 176 71 (office); 7 Tassopoulou Street, Athens 153 42, Greece (home). *Telephone:* (210) 9201743 (office); (210) 6399662 (home); (210) 6081780 (home). *Fax:* (210) 9201743 (office); (210) 6081780 (home). *E-mail:* gdc14247@gmail.com (office). *Website:* www .panteion.gr (office).

CONWAY, Craig A., BSc; American business executive (retd); b. 17 Oct. 1954, Fort Wayne, Ind.; m. Tina Conway; two c.; ed State Univ. of NY, Brockport; began career as Exec. Vice Pres. of Marketing, Sales and Operations, Oracle Corpn; fmr Pres. and CEO TGV Software; Pres. and CEO One Touch Systems –1999; joined PeopleSoft Inc. May 1999, Pres. and CEO 1999– 2004; mem. Bd of Dirs Salesforce.com 2005–, Kazeon Systems, Inc. 2006–, Unisys Corpn 2007–. *Address:* 170 Olive Hill Lane, Woodside, CA 94062, USA.

CONWAY, John Horton, MA, PhD, FRS; British mathematician and academic; *John von Neumann Distinguished Professor of Mathematics, Princeton University;* b. 26 Dec. 1937, Liverpool; m. Diana Conway; three s. four d.; ed Gonville and Caius Coll., Cambridge; Lecturer in Pure Math., Cambridge Univ. –1973, Reader in Pure Math. and Math. Statistics 1973–83, Prof. of Math. 1983–87; John von Neumann Distinguished Prof. of Math., Princeton Univ. 1986–; Fellow Sidney Sussex Coll., Cambridge 1964–70, Gonville and Caius Coll., Cambridge 1970–87; Hon. Fellow Gonville and Caius Coll. 1999; Hon. DSc (Liverpool) 2001; Polya Prize London Math. Soc. 1987, Frederic Esser Nemmers Prize, Northwestern Univ. 1999, Steele Prize, American Math. Soc. 1999, Joseph Priestley Award, Dickinson Coll. 2001. *Publications:* Regular Algebra and Finite Machines 1971, On Numbers and Games 1976, Winning Ways for Your Mathematical Plays (vol 2) 1982, 2003, Atlas of Finite Groups 1985, Sphere Packings, Lattices and Groups 1987, The Book of Numbers 1996, The Sensual Quadratic Form 1997, On Numbers and Games 2000, Winning Ways for You Mathematical Plays (vol 1) 2001, On Quaternions and Octonions, Winning Ways for Your Mathematical Plays (vol 3) 2003, Winning Ways for Your Mathematical Plays (vol 4) 2004. *Leisure interests:* puzzles, games, knots, knowlege. *Address:* Department of Mathematics, Fine Hall, Princeton University, Washington Road, Princeton, NJ 08544 (office); 71 Patton Avenue, Princeton, NJ 08540, USA (home). *Telephone:* (609) 258-6468 (office); (609) 683-0206 (home). *Fax:* (609) 921-0353 (home). *Website:* www.math.princeton.edu/menusa/index0.html (office).

COOK, Christopher Paul, BA, MA; British artist, poet and academic; *Reader in Painting, University of Plymouth;* b. 24 Jan. 1959, Great Ayton, N Yorks.; s. of E. P. Cook and J. Leyland; m. Jennifer Jane Mellings 1982; two s.; ed Univ. of Exeter, Royal Coll. of Art; Italian Govt Scholar, Accad. di Belle Arti, Bologna 1986–89; Fellow in Painting, Exeter Coll. of Art 1989–90; guest artist, Stadelschule, Frankfurt 1991; Visiting Fellow, Ruskin School, Univ. of Oxford 1992–93; Distinguished Visiting Artist, Calif. State Univ., Long Beach 1994; Visiting Artist to Banaras Hindu Univ., Varanasi, India 1994, 1996; Reader in Painting, Univ. of Plymouth 1997–; Artist in Residence, Eden Project, Cornwall 2001–03; Resident Artist, Univ. of Memphis 2004; Yokohama Museum residency, Japan 2005; Phillips Award, British School at Rome, Italy 2008; Prizewinner John Moores Liverpool XXI 1999, Arts Council of England Award 2000, British Council Award to Artists 2003, Daiwa Award 2005, AHRC Award 2005, British Council Award 2006. *Publications:* Dust on the Mirror 1997, For and Against Nature 2000, A Thoroughbred Golden Calf 2003. *Leisure interest:* the outdoors. *Address:* c/o Mary Ryan Gallery, Inc., 24 West 57th Street, 2nd Floor, New York, NY 10019, USA (office). *Telephone:* (212) 397-0669 (home). *Fax:* (212) 397-0766 (office). *E-mail:* c1cook@plymouth.ac.uk (home). *Website:* www.cookgraphites.com (office).

COOK, Gordon Charles, MD, DSc, MRCS, FRCP, FRCPE, FRACP, FLS; British physician in tropical medicine and infectious diseases; *Visiting Professor, University College London;* b. 17 Feb. 1932, Wimbledon; s. of Charles F. Cook and Kate Cook (née Kraninger, then Grainger); m. Elizabeth J. Agg-Large 1963; one s. three d.; ed Wellingborough Grammar School, Kingston-upon-Thames, Raynes Park Grammar Schools and Royal Free Hosp. School of Medicine, Univ. of London; jr appointments, Royal Free Hosp., Brompton Hosp. and Royal Northern Hosp. 1958–60; medical specialist, captain, RAMC and Royal Nigerian Army 1960–62; Lecturer in Medicine, Royal Free Hosp. School of Medicine 1963–65, 1967–69, Makerere Univ. Coll., Uganda 1965–67; Prof. of Medicine, Univ. of Zambia 1969–74, Univ. of Riyadh, Saudi Arabia 1974–75; Visiting Prof. of Medicine, Univs of Basrah and Mosul, Iraq 1976; Sr Lecturer in Clinical Tropical Medicine, London School of Hygiene and Tropical Medicine 1976–97; Consultant Physician, Univ. Coll. London Hosps. and Hosp. for Tropical Diseases, London 1976–97; Prof. of Medicine and Chair. Clinical Sciences Dept, Univ. of Papua New Guinea 1978–81; Hon. Sr Lecturer in Medicine, Univ. Coll. London 1981–2002, Visiting Prof. 2002–; Hon. Consultant Physician, St Luke's Hosp. for the Clergy 1988–; Visiting Prof. of Medicine, Doha, Qatar 1989; Hon. Lecturer in Clinical Parasitology, Medical Coll. of St Bartholomew's Hosp., London 1992–; Sr Research Fellow, Wellcome Centre for the History of Medicine 1997–2002; Chair. Erasmus Darwin Foundation, Lichfield 1994–; Chair. Medical Writers Group, Soc. of Authors 1997–99; Vice-Pres. Royal Soc. of Tropical Medicine and Hygiene 1991–93, Pres. 1993–95; Vice-Pres. History of Medicine Section, Royal Soc. of Medicine 1994–96, Pres. 2003–04; Vice-Pres. Fellowship of Postgraduate Medicine 1996–2000, Pres. 2000–; mem. Council, Galton Inst. 2005–; mem. Cttee, Friends of the Florence Nightingale Museum 2005– (Vice-Chair. 2006–); Examiner, Royal Coll. of Physicians, Univs of London and Makerere, Uganda; Ed. Journal of Infection 1995–97; mem. Editorial Bd, The Postgraduate Medical Journal; mem. Jt Cttee on Higher Medical Training, Exec. Cttee and Examiner Faculty of History and Philosophy of Medicine and Pharmacy, The Worshipful Soc. of Apothecaries 1997–; mem. of Council, History of Medicine Section, Royal Soc. of Medicine 1999–; mem. Code of Practice Cttee, Asscn of British Pharmaceutical Industry; mem. Asscn of Physicians of GB and Ireland 1973–; mem. numerous other medical and scientific socs; Trustee Overseas Devt Admin., Bookpower (fmrly Educational Low-Priced Sponsored Texts—ELST) 1996–; Hon. Research Assoc., Greenwich Maritime Inst. 2003–; Hon. Archivist, Seamen's Hosp. Soc. 2002–; Charlotte Brown Prize, Cunning and Legg Awards, Royal Free Hosp. School of Medicine, Frederick Murgatroyd Memorial Prize, Royal Coll. of Physicians, London 1973, Hugh L'Etang Prize, Royal Soc. of Medicine 1999, Monckton Copeman Lecturer, Soc. of Apothecaries 2000, Denny Lecturer, Barbers Co. 2003. *Publications:* Acute Renal Failure (jtly) 1964, Tropical Gastroenterology 1980, Communicable and Tropical Diseases 1988, Parasitic Disease in Clinical Practice 1990, From the Greenwich Hulks to Old St Pancras: a history of tropical disease in London 1992; 100 Clinical Problems in Tropical Medicine (co-ed.) 1987, Travel-associated Disease (ed.) 1995, Gastroenterological Problems from the Tropics (ed.) 1995, Manson's Tropical Diseases (ed.) (21st edn) 2003, Victorian Incurables: A History of the Royal Hospital for Neuro-Disability, Putney 2004, John MacAllister's Other Vision: A History of the Fellowship of Postgraduate Medicine 2005, The Incurables Movement: An Illustrated History of the British Home 2006, Tropical Medicine: an Illustrated History of the Pioneers 2007; more than 500 papers on physiology, gastroenterology, tropical medicine, nutrition and medical history. *Leisure interests:* cricket, walking, medical and scientific history, African and Pacific artefacts. *Address:* Infectious Diseases Unit, Windeyer Building, 46 Cleveland Street, London, W1P 6DB (office); 11 Old London Road, St Albans, Herts., AL1 1QE, England (home). *Telephone:* (20) 7636-6334 (office); (1727) 869000 (home). *Fax:* (20) 7436-2535 (office). *E-mail:* admin@fpm.uk.org (office).

COOK, Linda Zarda, BEng; American energy industry executive; *Executive Director, Gas and Power, Royal Dutch/Shell Group;* b. June 1958, Kansas City; m. Steve Cook; three c.; ed Univ. of Kansas; a Shawnee native; joined Royal Dutch/Shell Group, Houston, TX 1980, worked for Shell Oil Co. in Houston and Calif. in a variety of tech. and managerial positions until 1998 when moved to The Hague, Netherlands, Exec. Dir Global Gas and Power Unit 2000–03, 2004–, Pres. and CEO Shell Canada Ltd 2003–04, mem. Bd of Man. Royal Dutch Petroleum Co., mem. Cttee of Man. Dirs Royal Dutch/Shell Group 2004–; mem. Bd of Dirs Boeing Co. 2003–; mem. Soc. of Petroleum Engineers, Harvard School of Govt Dean's Council, Canadian Council of Chief Execs; ranked by Fortune magazine amongst 50 Most Powerful Women in Business outside the US 2001, (11th) 2002, (17th) 2003, (seventh) 2004, (fourth) 2005, (fourth) 2006, (fifth) 2007, Balmoral Hall School 'Yes She Can' Award 2004, ranked by Forbes magazine amongst 100 Most Powerful Women (83rd) 2005, (56th) 2006, (44th) 2007, (43rd) 2008, ranked by the Financial Times amongst Top 25 Businesswomen in Europe (14th) 2005, (12th) 2006, (16th) 2007. *Address:* Royal Dutch Petroleum Company, Carel van Bylandtlaan 30, 2596 HR, The Hague, The Netherlands (office). *Telephone:* (70) 377-9111 (office). *Fax:* (70) 377-3115 (office). *Website:* www.shell.com (office).

COOK, Michael John, AO, LLB; Australian diplomatist; b. 28 Oct. 1931, Burma; s. of H. J. M. Cook and Maureen H. Taylor; m. 1st Helen Ibbitson 1957 (divorced 1970); one s. three d.; m. 2nd Catriona Matheson 1970; one s. one d.; ed Geelong Grammar School, Univ. of Melbourne, Canberra Univ. Coll. and Imperial Defence Coll.; joined Australian Dept of Foreign Affairs 1954; Amb. to Vietnam 1973–74; CEO Pvt. Office of Prime Minister 1979–81; Dir-Gen. Office of Nat. Assessments 1981–89; Amb. to USA 1989–93; Distinguished Visiting Fellow, Menzies Centre, Univ. of London 1993–94. *Leisure interests:* tennis, history, Bach. *Address:* 126 Loudoun Road, London, NW8 0ND, England.

COOK, Peter, CBE, PhD; Australian scientist, academic and environmental organization administrator; *Chief Executive, Cooperative Research Centre for Greenhouse Gas Technologies (CO2CRC);* fmr Exec. Dir Petroleum CRC; fmr Dir British Geological Survey; fmr Pres. EuroGeoSurveys; fmr Assoc. Dir, Bureau of Mineral Resources; fmr Sr Research Fellow, ANU; est. GEODISC programme, and subsequently Cooperative Research Centre for Greenhouse Gas Technologies (CO2CRC), now Chief Exec.; coordinating lead author of Special IPCC Vol. on CO_2 Capture and Storage; Fellow, Australian Acad. of Technological Sciences; John Coke Medal, Public Service Medal, Centennial Medal, Lewis G. Weeks Medal, Leopold von Buch Medal. *Publications:* numerous scientific papers in professional journals. *Address:* CO2CRC, GPO Box 463, Canberra, ACT 2601, Australia (office). *Telephone:* (2) 6200-3366 (office); (419) 490044 (mobile). *Fax:* (2) 6273-7181 (office). *E-mail:* pjcook@co2crc.com.au (office). *Website:* www.co2crc.com.au (office).

COOK, Sir Peter Frederick Chester, Kt, AADip, RIBA, BDA, FRSA, MEASA; British architect and academic; b. 22 Oct. 1936, Southend-on-Sea; s. of late Maj. Frederick William Cook and Ada Alice Cook (née Shaw); m. 1st Hazel Aimée Fennell 1960 (divorced 1990); m. 2nd Yael Reisner 1990; one s.; ed Bournemouth Coll. of Art, Architectural Asscn (A.A.), London; Architectural Asst, James Cubitt & Partners, London 1960–62; Asst Architect, Taylor Woodrow Design Group, London 1962–64; taught at A.A. 1964–89; Partner, Archigram Architects 1964–75, Cook and Hawley Architects, London 1976–; Bartlett Prof. of Architecture, Bartlett School of Architecture and Planning, Univ. Coll. London 1990–2005, also Chair. Bartlett School of Architecture; Prof. of Architecture, HBK Frankfurt, Germany 1984–; visiting critic many schools of architecture USA and abroad; Visiting Prof. Oslo Architecture School 1982–83, RI School of Design 1981, 1984; Architect of 'Plug-in-City', 'Instant City', etc., of the Lutlowplatz Housing, Berlin 1990 (with Christine Hawley) and the Kunsthaus, Graz (with Colin Fournier), under construction; works featured in several books; Graham Foundation Award 1970, Monte Carlo Competition 1st Prize 1970, Landstuhl Housing Competition 1st Prize 1980, LA Prize (AIA) 1988, Int. Competition for Historic Museum 1st Prize, Austria 1995, Jean Tschumi Prize (U.I.A.) 1996, Int. Competition for Kunsthaus, Graz 1st Prize, Austria 2000, Grand Prize of the Buenos Aires Biennale 2001, Royal Gold Medal of the Royal Inst. of British Architects (RIBA) 2000 (as mem. of Archigram). *Publications:* Primer 1996, The Power of Contemporary Architecture 1999, The Paradox of Contemporary Architecture 2001, The City as Inspiration 2001. *Leisure interests:* listening to music, talking to young architects, restaurants. *Address:* 54 Compayne Gardens, London, NW6 3RY, England (home). *Telephone:* (20) 7372-3784 (home).

COOK, Stephen Arthur, PhD, FRSC, OM, FRS; American/Canadian computer scientist and academic; *University Professor, Department of Computer Science, University of Toronto;* b. 1939, Buffalo, NY; s. of Gerhard A. Cook and Lura Cook; m. Linda Cook 1968; two s.; ed Univ. of Michigan and Harvard Univ.; Asst Prof. of Math., Univ. of Calif., Berkeley 1966–70; Assoc. Prof. of Computer Science, Univ. of Toronto, Canada 1970–75, Prof. 1975–85, Univ. Prof. 1985–; E.W.R. Staecie Memorial Fellowship 1977–78; Killam Research

Fellow, Canada Council 1982–83; mem. NAS, American Acad. of Arts and Science; Turing Award, Assoc. Computing Machinery 1982, Killam Prize 1997, CRM/Fields Inst. Prize 1999. *Publications:* numerous articles in professional journals on theory of computation. *Leisure interest:* sailing. *Address:* Department of Computer Science, 10 King's College Road, Sandford Fleming Building, Room SF2303C, University of Toronto, Toronto, ON M5S 3G4, Canada (office). *Telephone:* (416) 978-5183 (office). *Fax:* (416) 978-1931 (office). *E-mail:* sacook@cs.toronto.edu (office). *Website:* www.cs.toronto.edu/dcs/people/faculty/sacook.html (office); www.cs.toronto.edu/~sacook (office).

COOK, William Alfred, BSc; American medical device industry executive; *Chairman, Cook Group Incorporated;* b. 1931; m. Gayle Cook; one s.; ed Northwestern Univ.; Founder and Chair. Cook Inc., Bloomington, Ind. (manufacturer of medical devices and supplies) 1963, now Cook Group Inc. *Address:* Cook Group Inc., PO Box 489, Bloomington, IN 47402-0489, USA (office). *Telephone:* (812) 339-2235 (office). *Website:* www.cookgroup.com (office).

COOK-BENNETT, Gail C. A., BA, PhD; Canadian business executive and academic; *Chairwoman, Manulife Financial Corporation;* ed Carleton Univ., Univ. of Michigan; fmr Exec. Vice-Pres. C.D. Howe Inst., Montreal; fmr Prof., Dept of Political Economy, Univ. of Toronto; mem. Bd of Dirs Manulife Financial Corpn 1978–, mem. Man. Resources and Compensation Cttee, Vice-Chair. 2007–08, Chair. (first woman) 2008–; Chair. Canada Pension Plan Investment Bd 1998–2008, Chair. and mem. Investment Cttee, mem. Governance Cttee; Vice-Chair. Bennecon Ltd –1998; mem. Bd of Dirs Petro-Canada 1991– (Chair. Pension Cttee, mem. Audit, Finance and Risk Cttee), Transcontinental Inc. (also known as Groupe Transcontinental GTC Ltée; fmr mem. Audit Cttee), Cadillac Fairview Inc., Enbridge Consumers Gas Co., Mackenzie Financial Corpn, Emera Inc. (mem. Audit Cttee, Nominating and Corp. Governance Cttee), Nova Scotia Power Inc. (mem. Nominating and Corp. Governance Cttee); Fellow, Inst. of Corp. Dirs; Hon. LLD (Carleton Univ.). *Address:* Manulife Financial Corpn, 200 Bloor Street East, NT 11, Toronto, ON M4W 1E5, Canada (office). *Telephone:* (416) 926-3000 (office). *Fax:* (416) 926-5410 (office). *E-mail:* info@manulife.com (office). *Website:* www.manulife.com (office).

COOKE, Dominic; British theatre director and playwright; *Artistic Director, Royal Court Theatre;* b. 1966; Assoc. Dir Royal Court Theatre 1998–2002, Artistic Dir 2007–; Assoc. Dir RSC 2002–07. *Productions include:* Royal Court Theatre: Other People 2000, Fireplace 2000, Spinning into Butter 2001, Redundant 2001, Fucking Games 2001, Plasticine, The People are Friendly, This is a Chair (co-dir) 2002, Identical Twins 2002, The Pain and the Itch 2007, Rhinoceros 2007; RSC: The Malcontent 2002, Cymbeline 2003, Macbeth 2004, As You Like It 2005, Postcards From America 2005, The Winter's Tale, Pericles, The Crucible (Gielgud; Best Dir and Best Revival, Laurence Olivier Awards 2007) 2006; other: Arabian Nights (Old Vic and on tour) (TMA/Equity Award for Best Show for Young People) 1998, Noughts and Crosses 2007. *Radio:* directed a version of Plasticine; currently adapting his version of Arabian Nights for BBC Radio 4. *Publication:* Arabian Nights (adaptation) 1998, Noughts and Crosses (adaption) 2007. *Address:* Royal Court Theatre, Sloane Square, London, SW1W 8AS, England (office). *Telephone:* (20) 7565-5050 (office). *Fax:* (20) 7565-5001 (office). *E-mail:* info@royalcourttheatre.com (office). *Website:* www.royalcourttheatre.com (office).

COOKE, Sir Howard (Felix Hanlan), ON, GCMG, GCVO, CD; Jamaican politician, schoolteacher and insurance company executive; b. 13 Nov. 1915, Goodwill; s. of David Brown Cooke and Mary Jane Minto; m. Ivy Sylvia Lucille Tai 1939; two s. one d.; teacher, Mico Training Coll. 1936–38; Headmaster, Belle-Castle All-Age School 1939–50; teacher, Port Antonio Upper School 1951, Montego Bay Boys' School 1952–58; Br. Man. Standard Life Insurance Co. Ltd 1960–71; Unit Man. Jamaica Mutual Life Assurance Co. Ltd 1971–81; Br. Man. Alico Jamaica 1982–91; mem. West Indies Fed. Parl. 1958–62, Senate 1962–67, House of Reps 1967–80; Govt Minister 1972–80; Gov.-Gen. of Jamaica 1991–2006; Sr Elder United Church of Jamaica and Grand Cayman; lay pastor and fmr Chair. Cornwall Council of Churches; mem. Ancient and Accepted Order of Masons; Kt of St John (St John's Council) 1993; Jamaica Independence Medal 1962, Special Plaque for Distinguished Services (CPA) 1980. *Leisure interests:* gardening, cricket, football, reading. *Address:* c/o Office of the Governor-General, King's House, Hope Road, Kingston 10, Jamaica (office).

COOLEY, Denton Arthur, BA, MD; American surgeon; *Surgeon-in-Chief, Texas Heart Institute;* b. 22 Aug. 1920, Houston, Tex.; s. of Ralph C. Cooley and Mary Fraley Cooley; m. Louise Goldsborough Thomas 1949; five d.; ed Univ. of Texas and Johns Hopkins Univ. School of Medicine; Intern, Johns Hopkins School of Medicine, Baltimore 1944–45, Instructor in surgery 1945–50; Sr Surgical Registrar in Thoracic Surgery, Brompton Hospital for Chest Diseases, London 1950–51; Assoc. Prof. of Surgery, Baylor Univ. Coll. of Medicine, Houston 1954–62, Prof. 1962–69; Founder and Surgeon-in-Chief, Texas Heart Inst., Houston 1962–; Clinical Prof. of Surgery, Univ. of Texas Medical School, Houston 1975–; served as Capt., Chief Surgical Service, US Army Medical Corps, Linz, Austria 1946–48; has performed numerous heart transplants; mem. numerous socs and asscns; Hon. Doctorem Medicinae (Turin) 1969; Hon. Fellow, Royal Coll. of Physicians and Surgeons 1980, Royal Coll. of Surgeons 1984, Royal Australasian Coll. of Surgeons 1986; Kt Commdr, Order of Merit of Italian Repub., Order of the Sun, Peru and others; Hoktoen Gold Medal 1954, Grande Médaille, Univ. of Ghent, Belgium 1963, René Leriche Prize, Int. Surgical Soc. 1965–67, Billings Gold Medal, American Medical Asscn 1967, Semmelweis Medal 1973, St Francis Cabrini Gold Medal (first recipient) 1980, Theodore Roosevelt Award, Nat. Collegiate Athletic Asscn 1980, Presidential Medal of Freedom 1984, Nat. Medal of Tech., US Dept of Commerce 1999, Grand Hamdan Int. Award for Medical Science 2000.

Achievements include: implanted first artificial heart 1969. *Publications:* Surgical Treatment of Congenital Heart Disease 1966, Techniques in Cardiac Surgery 1975, 1984, Techniques in Vascular Surgery 1979, Essays of Denton A. Cooley—Reflections and Observations 1984; over 1,000 scientific articles. *Leisure interests:* golf, ranching. *Address:* Texas Heart Institute, PO Box 20345, 1101 Bates Street, Houston, TX 77225-0345, USA (office). *Telephone:* (832) 355-4900 (office). *Fax:* (832) 355-3424 (office). *E-mail:* dcooley@heart.thi .tmc.edu (office). *Website:* www.texasheartinstitute.org (office).

COOLIDGE, Martha; American film director and producer; b. 17 Aug. 1946, New Haven, Conn.; d. of Robert Tilton Coolidge and Jean McMullen; one s.; ed Rhode Island School of Design, Columbia Univ. and New York Univ. Inst. of Film and TV Grad. School; producer, dir and writer of documentaries including Passing Quietly Through, David: Off and On, Old Fashioned Woman; wrote and produced daily children's TV show Magic Tom, Canada; Pres. Dirs Guild Asscn 2002–03; Blue Ribbon Award, American Film Festival (Not a Pretty Picture), Independent Spirit Award, Best Dir (Rambling Rose), Crystal Award, Women in Film, Breakthrough Award, Method Fest, Robert Aldrich Award, Dirs Guild Award. *Films include:* Valley Girl 1983, City Girl 1984, Joy of Sex 1984, Real Genius 1985, Plain Clothes 1988, Rambling Rose 1991, Lost in Yonkers 1993, Angie 1994, Three Wishes 1995, Out to Sea 1997, The Prince and Me 2004, Material Girls 2006. *Television includes:* The Twilight Zone, Sledge Hammer (pilot), House and Home (pilot), Trenchcoat in Paradise (film), Bare Essentials, Crazy in Love, Introducing Dorothy Dandridge 1999, If These Walls Could Talk II 2000, The Ponder Heart 2000, The Flamingo Rising 2001, Leap Years 2001, Sex and the City (2 Episodes). *Leisure interest:* breeding Paso-Fino horses. *Address:* c/o Beverly Magid Guttman Associates, 118 South Beverly Drive, Suite 201, Beverly Hills, CA 90212, USA. *Telephone:* (310) 246-4600 (office). *Website:* www.marthacoolidge .com (office).

COOMARASWAMY, Radhika, BA, LLM, JD; Sri Lankan lawyer and international organization executive; *Special Representative of the Secretary-General, Office of the Special Representative of the Secretary-General for Children and Armed Conflict, United Nations;* ed Yale, Columbia and Harvard Univs and UN Int. School, New York, USA; Special Rapporteur on Violence Against Women 1994–2003; Chair. Sri Lanka Human Rights Comm. 2003–; Dir Int. Centre for Ethnic Studies, Colombo; Special Rep. of the Sec.-Gen., UN Office of the Special Rep. of the Sec.-Gen. for Children and Armed Conflict 2006–; mem. Global Faculty, New York Univ. School of Law; teaches a summer course at New Coll., Oxford, UK every July; title of 'Deshamanya' conferred on her by Pres. of Sri Lanka 2005 (only female recipient); Hon. PhD (Amherst Coll., Univ. of Edinburgh, Univ. of Essex); ABA Int. Law Award, Human Rights Award, Int. Human Rights Law Group, Bruno Kreisky Award 2000, Leo Ettinger Human Rights Prize, Univ. of Oslo, Cesar Romero Award, Univ. of Dayton, William J. Butler Award, Univ. of Cincinnati, Robert S. Litvack Award, McGill Univ. *Publications:* two books on constitutional law and numerous articles on ethnic studies and the status of women. *Address:* Office of the Special Representative of the Secretary-General for Children and Armed Conflict, United Nations, Room S-3161, New York, NY 10017, USA (office). *Telephone:* (212) 963-3178 (office). *Fax:* (212) 963-0807 (office). *Website:* www.un.org/special-rep/children-armed-conflict (office).

COOMBER, John R., BSc; British insurance executive; *Executive Vice-Chairman, Pension Corporation;* b. 7 Feb. 1949; m.; ed Nottingham Univ.; began career with Phoenix Insurance Co.; joined Swiss Re 1973, specialized in life reinsurance, Company Actuary 1983–90, Head of Life Div. 1987, Head of UK Operations 1993, apptd mem. Exec. Bd 1995, Head of Life and Health Div. 1995–2000, mem. Exec. Bd Cttee 2000–03, CEO Swiss Reinsurance Co. (first non-Swiss person in position) 2003–05 (retd), mem. Bd of Dirs (non-exec.) 2005; Chair. telent plc 2007–; Exec. Vice-Chair. Pension Corpn 2008–; mem. Supervisory Bd Euler Hermes; Trustee Climate Group. *Address:* Pension Corporation, 14 Cornhill, London, EC3V 3ND (office); telent, Point 3, Haywood Road, Warwick, CV34 5AH, England. *Telephone:* (20) 7105-2000 (office); (1926) 693-000 (telent) (office). *Fax:* (20) 7105-2001 (office). *Website:* www.pensioncorporation.com (office); www.telent.com (office).

COOMBS, Douglas Saxon, CNZM, PhD, MSc, FRSNZ; New Zealand geologist and academic; *Emeritus Professor of Geology, University of Otago;* b. 23 Nov. 1924, Dunedin; s. of Leslie D. Coombs and Nellie Véra Coombs; m. Anne G. Tarrant 1956; two s. one d.; ed King's High School, Dunedin, Univ. of Otago, Emmanuel Coll., Cambridge; Asst Lecturer in Geology, Univ. of Otago 1947–48, Lecturer 1949, 1952–55, Prof. 1956–90, Prof. Emer. 1990–; 1851 Exhbn Scholar, Emmanuel Coll., Cambridge 1949–52; Visiting Prof. Pa State Univ. 1960, Yale Univ. 1967–68, Geneva Univ. 1968, 1975, Univ. of Calif. at Santa Barbara 1982; Vice-Pres. Int. Mineralogical Asscn 1974–86; Chair. Bd of Govs, King's High School 1979–88; Life Fellow Mineralogical Soc. of America 1961; Foreign Assoc. NAS 1977; Fellow Japan Soc. for Promotion of Science 1988; Hon. Fellow Geological Soc. of London 1968, Geological Soc. of America 1983; Hon. mem. Mineralogical Soc. of Great Britain and Ireland 1986; Hon. DSc (Geneva); McKay Hammer Award, Geological Soc. of NZ 1961, Hector Medal, Royal Soc. of NZ 1969. *Publications:* numerous scientific papers, especially on very low-grade metamorphism. *Leisure interests:* genealogy, cricket, tramping. *Address:* Geology Department, University of Otago, P.O. Box 56, Dunedin (office); 6 Tolcarne Avenue, Dunedin, New Zealand (home). *Telephone:* (3) 479-7505 (office); (3) 467-5699 (home). *Fax:* (3) 479-7527 (office). *E-mail:* doug.coombs@stonebow.otago.ac.nz (office).

COOMBS, Stephen; British pianist; *Director of Instrumental Studies, Blackheath Conservatoire of Music and the Arts;* b. 11 July 1960; s. of Geoffrey Samuel Coombs and Joan Margaret Jones; ed Royal Northern Coll. of Music, RAM; debut at Wigmore Hall 1975; has given concerts and masterclasses in UK, France, Germany, Italy, Hungary, Portugal, Switzerland, Scandinavia, Korea, Thailand, the Philippines, Hong Kong, USA; has appeared in festivals at Cheltenham, Salisbury, Snape Maltings Proms, Henley, the Three Choirs, Radley, Bath, Lichfield, Cardiff, Spoleto, Italy, St Nazaire, France, Sintra, Portugal; Visiting Lecturer, Univ. of Cen. England 1994–96; Founder and Artistic Dir 'Pianoworks' Int. Piano Festival, London 1998–99; Dir of Instrumental Studies, Blackheath Conservatoire of Music and the Arts 2001–; Gold Medal, First Int. Liszt Concourse, Hungary 1977, Worshipful Co. of Musicians/Maisie Lewis Award 1986 and numerous other awards and prizes. *Recordings include:* Two Piano Works of Debussy 1989, Ravel Works for Two Pianos 1990, Mendelssohn Two Double Piano Concertos 1992, Arensky Piano Concerto in F Minor and Fantasy on Russian Folk Songs 1992, Bortkiewicz Piano Concerto No. 1 1992, Arensky Suites for Two Pianos 1994, Glazunov Complete Piano Works (four vols) 1995, Glazunov Piano Concertos Nos 1 & 2 1996, Goedicke Concertstück 1996, Reynaldo Hahn Piano Concerto 1997, Massenet Piano Concerto 1997, Bortkiewicz Piano Works 1997, Liadov Piano Works 1998, Milhaud Works for Two Pianos 1998, Arensky Piano Works 1998, Scriabin Early Piano Works 2001, Hahn Piano Quintet 2001, Verne Piano Quintet 2001. *Leisure interests:* genealogy, pubs, reading. *Address:* The Conservatoire, 19–21 Lee Road, Blackheath, London, SE3 9RQ; c/o Hyperion Records Ltd, 19–20 Chiltonian Industrial Estate, Manor Lane, London, SE12 0TX, England. *Website:* www.conservatoire.org .uk.

COOPER, Alice; American singer; b. (Vincent Damon Furnier), 4 Feb. 1948, Detroit; s. of the late Mick Furnier and of Ella Furnier; m. Sheryl Goddard; one s. two d.; ed Cortez High School, Phoenix, Ariz.; mem. of band Alice Cooper, adopted this name after band split; first to stage theatrical rock concert tours; among first to film conceptual rock promotional videos (pre-MTV); considered among originators and greatest hard rock artists; host on Virgin Radio Classic Rock 2005–; mem. BMI, NARAS, SAG, AFTRA, AFofM; Foundations Forum Lifetime Achievement Award 1994. *Film appearances:* Sextette 1978, Sgt. Pepper's Lonely Hearts Club Band 1978, Leviatán 1984, Prince of Darkness 1987, Freddy's Dead: The Final Nightmare 1991, The Attic Expeditions 2001. *Recordings include:* with band Alice Cooper: Pretties For You 1969, Live At The Whisky 1969, Easy Action 1970, Love It To Death 1971, Killer 1971, School's Out 1972, Billion Dollar Babies 1973, Muscle of Love 1973, Alice Cooper's Greatest Hits 1974; solo: Welcome To My Nightmare 1975, Alice Cooper Goes To Hell 1976, Lace And Whiskey 1977, Alice Cooper Show (live) 1977, From The Inside 1978, Flush The Fashion 1980, Special Forces 1981, Zipper Catches The Skin 1982, Dada 1982, Constrictor 1986, Raise Your Fist And Yell 1987, Trash 1989, Prince Of Darkness 1989, Hey Stoopid 1991, The Last Temptation 1994, Fistful Of Alice (live) 1997, He's Back 1997, Science Fiction 2000, Brutal Planet 2000, Alice Cooper Live 2001, Take 2 2001, Dragontown 2001, Eyes Of Alice Cooper 2003, Hell Is 2003, Dirty Diamonds 2005, Along Came a Spider 2008. *Address:* Alive Enterprises, PO Box 5542, Beverly Hills, CA 90211, USA (office). *Website:* www.alicecooper .com.

COOPER, Chris; American actor; b. 9 July 1951, Kansas City, Mo.; s. of Charles Cooper and Mary Ann Cooper; m. Marianne Leone 1983; one s.; ed Univ. of Missouri; studied ballet at Stephens Coll., Mo.; entered US Coast Guard Reserves following high school graduation; studied theatre acting under Stella Adler and Wynn Handman, NY 1976; first Broadway appearance in Of the Fields Lately 1980; Best Actor Award, Cowboy Hall of Fame 1991, Peter J. Owens Award, San Francisco International Film Festival 2004. *Films include:* Bad Timing 1980, Matewan 1987, Non date da mangiare agli animali 1987, Guilty by Suspicion 1991, Thousand Pieces of Gold 1991, City of Hope 1991, This Boy's Life 1993, Money Train 1995, Pharaoh's Army 1995, Boys 1996, Lone Star 1996, A Time to Kill 1996, Great Expectations 1998, The Horse Whisperer 1998, The 24 Hour Woman 1999, October Sky 1999, American Beauty (Screen Actors Guild Award 2000) 1999, Me, Myself & Irene 2000, The Patriot 2000, Interstate 60 2002, The Bourne Identity 2002, Adaptation (Best Supporting Actor, Acad. Awards 2004, Golden Globe Awards, Nat. Bd of Review, San Francisco Film Critics, Toronto Film Critics, San Diego Film Critics, Broadcast Film Asscn, LA Critics Asscn) 2002, Seabiscuit 2003, Silver City 2004, Syriana 2005, Capote 2005, Jarhead 2005, Breach 2007, The Kingdom 2007, Married Life 2007. *Television includes:* Lonesome Dove (miniseries) 1989, Return to Lonesome Dove (miniseries) 1993, My House in Umbria 2003. *Stage appearances include:* Of the Fields Lately 1980, The Ballad of Soapy Smith 1983, A Different Moon 1983, Cobb, The Grapes of Wrath, Sweet Bird of Youth, Love Letters. *Address:* Paradigm Talent Agency, 10100 Santa Monica Boulevard, Suite 2500, Los Angeles, CA 90067 (office); c/o PMK, 8500 Wiltshire Boulevard, Suite 700, Beverly Hills, CA 90211-3105, USA (office).

COOPER, Emmanuel, OBE, PhD; British ceramic potter, writer and critic; *Editor, Ceramic Review;* b. 12 Dec. 1938, Chesterfield; s. of Fred Cooper and Kate Elizabeth Cooper (née Cook); partner, David Horbury; ed Clay Cross Tupton Hall Grammar School, Dudley Training Coll., Bournemouth and Hornsey Schools of Art; est. own studio in London 1965; part-time lecturer, Middx Polytechnic (now Univ.) –1998; Ed. Ceramic Review 1997–; Visiting Prof. of Ceramics and Glass RCA 2000–; mem. Crafts Council Index, Visual Art and Architecture Panel, Arts Council 1998–2000; mem. Council Craft Potters Asscn, Arts Council of England 2000–02, Arts Council, London 2002–. *Publications:* People's Art: Visual Art and Working Class Culture 1992, Fully Exposed – The Male Nude in Photography 1996, Ten Thousand Years of Studio Pottery 2000, Lucie Rie (ed) 2002, Bernard Leach – Life and Work 2003, David Leach 2003, Male Bodies: Male Nude in Photography 2004, Janet Leach: A Potter's Life 2006. *Leisure interests:* theatre, film, art, craft. *Address:* 38 Chalcot Road, London, NW1 8LP, England (home). *Telephone:* (20) 7722-9090 (home). *E-mail:* emmanuelcooper@lineone.net (home).

COOPER, Imogen, CBE; British pianist; b. 28 Aug. 1949, London; d. of the late Martin Du Pré Cooper and of Mary Stewart; ed Paris Conservatoire and in Vienna with Alfred Brendel; TV début at Promenade Concerts, London 1975, has appeared regularly since then; first British pianist and first woman pianist in South Bank Piano series, Queen Elizabeth Hall, London; broadcasts regularly for BBC; performs with New York, Berlin, Vienna and LA Philharmonic orchestras and with Boston, London, Sydney, Melbourne and Concertgebouw Symphony orchestras; gives solo recitals worldwide; Hon. MusD (Exon) 1999; Paris Conservatoire Premier Prix 1967, Mozart Memorial Prize 1969, Royal Philharmonic Soc. Award for Best Instrumentalist 2008. *Recordings include:* Schubert's Schwannengesang, Winterreise, Die Schöne Mullerin and Schumann's Heine Lieder and Kerner Lieder (with Wolfgang Holzmair), Mozart's Concerto for two pianos K.365 (with Alfred Brendel), Schubert four-hand piano music (with Anne Queffélec), 'The Last Six Years' of Schubert's piano music, Imogen Cooper and Friends (solo, chamber and lieder), Mozart Concertos (with the Northern Sinfonia). *Leisure interests:* visual arts, reading, walking, architecture. *Address:* Askonas Holt Ltd, Lincoln House, 300 High Holborn, London, WC1V 7JH, England (office). *Telephone:* (20) 7400-1743 (office). *Fax:* (20) 7400-1799 (office). *E-mail:* info@askonasholt.co.uk (office). *Website:* www.askonasholt.co.uk (office).

COOPER, Jilly, OBE; British writer; b. 21 Feb. 1937, Hornchurch, Essex; d. of Brig. W. B. Sallitt, OBE and Mary Elaine Whincup; m. Leo Cooper 1961; one s. one d.; ed Godolphin School, Salisbury; reporter, Middx Ind. 1957–59; account exec.; copy writer; publr's reader; various temporary roles 1959–69; columnist The Sunday Times 1969–82, Mail on Sunday 1982–87; British Book Awards Lifetime Achievement Award 1998. *Publications:* How to Stay Married 1969, How to Survive from Nine to Five 1970, Jolly Super 1971, Men and Super Men 1972, Jolly Super Too 1973, Women and Super Women 1974, Jolly Superlative 1975, Emily 1975, Super Men and Super Women 1976, Bella 1976, Harriet 1976, Octavia 1977, Work and Wedlock 1977, Superjilly 1977, Imogen 1978, Prudence 1978, Class 1979, Intelligent and Loyal 1980, Supercooper 1980, Violets and Vinegar (ed with Tom Hartman) 1980, The British in Love (ed) 1980, Love and Other Heartaches 1981, Jolly Marsupial 1982, Animals in War 1983, Leo and Jilly Cooper on Rugby 1984, The Common Years 1984, Riders 1985, Hotfoot to Zabriskie Point 1985, How to Survive Christmas 1986, 1996, Turn Right at the Spotted Dog 1987, Rivals 1988, Angels Rush In 1990, Polo 1991, The Man Who Made Husbands Jealous 1993, Araminta's Wedding 1993, Apassionata 1996, Score! 1999, Pandora 2002, Wicked! 2006. *Leisure interests:* merry-making, mongrels, music, wild flowers, greyhounds. *Address:* c/o Vivienne Schuster, Curtis Brown Ltd, Fourth Floor, Haymarket House, 28–29 Haymarket, London, SW1Y 4SP, England (office). *Telephone:* (20) 7393-4400 (office). *Fax:* (20) 7393-4401 (office). *E-mail:* cb@curtisbrown.co.uk (office). *Website:* www.curtisbrown.co.uk (office).

COOPER, Leon, DSc, PhD; American scientist and academic; *Thomas J. Watson, Sr Professor of Physics, Brain Science Program, Brown University;* b. 28 Feb. 1930, New York; s. of Irving Cooper and Anna Zola; m. Kay Anne Allard 1969; two d.; ed Columbia Univ.; mem. Inst. for Advanced Study 1954–55; Research Assoc., Univ. of Ill. 1955–57; Asst Prof., Ohio State Univ. 1957–58; Assoc. Prof., Brown Univ. 1958–62, Prof. 1974–, Thomas J. Watson, Sr Prof. of Science 1974–, Dir Center for Neural Science 1978–90, Inst. for Brain and Neural Systems 1991–, Brain Science Program 2000–; Visiting Lecturer, Varenna, Italy 1955; Visiting Prof., Brandeis Summer Inst. 1959, Bergen Int. School of Physics, Norway 1961, Scuola Internazionale Di Fisica, Erice, Italy 1965, L'Ecole Normale Supérieure, Centre Universitaire Int., Paris 1966, Cargèse Summer School 1966, Radiation Lab., Univ. of Calif., Berkeley 1969, Faculty of Sciences, Quai St Bernard, Paris 1970, 1971, Brookhaven Nat. Lab. 1972; consultant for various industrial and educational orgs; Chair. of Math. Models of Nervous System Fondation de France 1977–83; mem. Conseil supérieur de la Recherche Univ. René Descartes, Paris 1981–88; mem. Defence Science Bd 1989–93; NSF Post-doctoral Fellow 1954–55; Alfred P. Sloan Foundation Research Fellow 1959–66; John Simon Guggenheim Memorial Foundation Fellow 1965–66; Fellow, American Physical Soc., American Acad. of Arts and Sciences; Sponsor, American Fed. of Scientists; mem. NAS, American Philosophical Soc.; Hon. DSc (Columbia, Sussex), 1973, (Illinois, Brown) 1974, (Gustavus Adolphus Coll.) 1975, (Ohio State Univ.) 1976, (Univ. Pierre et Marie Curie, Paris) 1977; Comstock Prize, NAS 1968, Nobel Prize 1972, Award in Excellence, Columbia Univ. 1974; Descartes Medal, Acad. de Paris, Univ. René Descartes 1977, John Jay Award, Columbia Coll. 1985. *Publications:* An Introduction to the Meaning and Structure of Physics 1968, Structure and Meaning 1992, How We Learn, How We Remember 1995; numerous scientific papers. *Leisure interests:* skiing, music, theatre. *Address:* Department of Physics and Neuroscience, Box 1843, Barus & Holley, Room 718, Brown University, Providence, RI 02912-1843, USA (office). *Telephone:* (401) 863-2585 (office). *E-mail:* Leon_Cooper@brown.edu (office). *Website:* physics/userpages/faculty/Leon_Cooper/cooper.htm (office); www.physics.brown.edu/people/detail.asp?id=5 (office); www.brainscience.brown.edu (office).

COOPER, Richard Newell, PhD; American economist, academic and fmr public official; *Maurits C. Boas Professor of International Economics, Harvard University;* b. 14 June 1934, Seattle, Wash.; s. of Richard W. Cooper and Lucile Newell; m. 1st Carolyn Cahalan 1956 (divorced 1980); m. 2nd Ann Lorraine Hollick 1982 (divorced 1994); m. 3rd Jin Chen 2000; two s. two d.; ed Oberlin Coll., London School of Econs, UK, Harvard Univ.; Sr Staff Economist, Council of Econ. Advisers, The White House 1961–63; Deputy Asst Sec. of State for Monetary Affairs, US State Dept, Washington, DC 1965–66; Prof. of Econs, Yale Univ. 1966–77, Provost 1972–74; Under-Sec. of State for Econ. Affairs, 1977–81; Maurits C. Boas Prof. of Int. Econs, Harvard Univ. 1981–; Chair. Nat. Intelligence Council 1995–97; mem. Bd of Dirs Fed. Reserve Bank of Boston 1987–92, Chair. 1990–92; mem. Bd of Dirs Rockefeller Brothers Fund 1975–77, Schroders Bank and Trust Co. 1975–77, Warburg-Pincus Funds 1986–98, Center for Naval Analysis 1992–95, Phoenix Cos 1983–2005, Circuit City Stores 1983–2004, CNA Corpn 1997–, Inst. for Int. Econs 1983–; consultant to US Treasury, Nat. Security Council, World Bank, IMF, USN; Marshall Scholarship (UK) 1956–58; Fellow, American Acad. of Sciences 1974; Hon. LLD (Oberlin Coll.) 1958; Dr hc (Paris II) 2000; Nat. Intelligence Distinguished Service Medal 1996. *Publications:* The Economics of Interdependence 1968, Economic Policy in an Interdependent World 1986, The International Monetary System 1987, Stabilization and Debt in Developing Countries 1992, Boom, Crisis and Adjustment (co-author) 1993, Environment and Resource Policies for the World Economy 1994, Trade Growth in Transition Economies (ed.) 1997, What The Future Holds (ed.) 2002; more than 300 articles. *Address:* Center for International Affairs, Harvard University, 1737 Cambridge Street, Cambridge, MA 02138 (office); 33 Washington Avenue, Cambridge, MA 02140, USA (home). *Telephone:* (617) 495-5076 (office). *Fax:* (617) 495-7730 (office). *E-mail:* rcooper@harvard.edu (office). *Website:* www.economics.harvard.edu (office).

COOPER, Robert, BA, MA, MVO, CMG; British diplomatist; *Director General, External and Politico-Military Affairs, Council of the European Union;* b. 28 Aug. 1947, Brentwood, Essex; ed Delamere School, Nairobi, Worcester Coll. Univ. of Oxford, Univ. of Pennsylvania, USA; fmr Adviser to UK Prime Minister Tony Blair; currently Dir-Gen. External and Politico-Mil. Affairs, Council of the EU; Orwell Prize for Political Writing 2003. *Publication:* Breaking of Nations 2003. *Address:* Council of the EU, Directorate-General E, 175 rue de la Loi, 1048 Brussels, Belgium (office). *Telephone:* (2) 281-85-52 (office). *Fax:* (2) 281-62-18 (office). *E-mail:* robert.cooper@consilium.europa.eu (office).

COOPER, Yvette; British politician; *Chief Secretary to the Treasury;* b. 1969, Inverness; d. of Tony Cooper and June Cooper; m. Ed Balls; one s. two d.; ed Oxford Univ., Harvard Univ., USA and London School of Econs; fmr Econ. Researcher for John Smith; fmr Policy Adviser, Bill Clinton Presidential Campaign, USA; fmr Policy Adviser to Labour Treasury Team on public spending; econs columnist and leader writer, The Independent (daily newspaper); MP (Labour) for Pontefract and Castleford 1997–; Parl. Under-Sec. of State for Public Health 1999–2002, Parl. Sec. at Lord Chancellor's Dept 2002–03, in Office of Deputy Prime Minister 2003–05, Minister of State (Minister for Housing and Planning), Dept for Communities and Local Govt 2005–07, Minister for Housing 2007–08, Chief Sec. to Treasury 2008–. *Address:* House of Commons, London SW1A 0AA (office); 1 York Street, Castleford, WF10 1JS, England (office). *Telephone:* (20) 7219-5080 (office). *E-mail:* coopery@parliament.uk (office). *Website:* www.yvettecooper.com (office).

COOR, Lattie Finch, PhD; American academic; *President Emeritus, Arizona State University;* b. 26 Sept. 1936, Phoenix, Ariz.; s. of Lattie F. Coor and Elnora Coor (née Witten); m. Elva Wingfield 1994; three c. from a previous marriage; ed Northern Arizona Univ., Washington Univ., St Louis, American Coll., Greece; Admin. Asst to Gov. of Mich. 1961–62; Asst to Chancellor, Washington Univ., St Louis 1963–67, Asst Dean, Grad. School of Arts and Sciences 1967–69, Dir Int. Studies 1967–69, Asst Prof. of Political Science 1967–76, Vice-Chancellor 1969–74, Univ. Vice-Chancellor 1974–76; Pres., Univ. of Vt, Burlington 1976–89; Pres. Ariz. State Univ. 1990–2002, Pres. Emer. 2002–, Prof. and Ernest W. McFarland Chair in Leadership and Public Policy, School of Public Affairs 2002–; Chair. and CEO Center for the Future of Arizona 2002–; consultant for Dept of Health, Educ. and Welfare; special consultant to US Commr for Educ. 1971–74; Chair., Cttee on governmental relations, American Council on Educ. 1976–80; Dir New England Bd of Higher Educ. 1976–; mem. Pres.'s Comm., Nat. Coll. Athletic Asscn, Nat. Asscn State Univs and Land Grant Colls (Chair. Bd 1991–92). *Address:* Downtown Center B5, Arizona State University, 541 E Van Buren, Phoenix, AZ 85004, USA (office). *Telephone:* (480) 727-5005 (office). *E-mail:* lattie.coor@asu.edu (office).

COORE, David Hilton, OJ, BA, BCL, QC; Jamaican politician, business executive and lawyer; b. 22 Aug. 1925, St Andrew; s. of Clarence Reuben Coore and Ethlyn Maud Hilton; m. Rita Innis 1949; three s.; ed Jamaica Coll., McGill Univ., Canada and Exeter Coll., Oxford, UK; practised as barrister-at-law in Jamaica 1950–72; mem. Legis. Council 1960–62; Opposition Spokesman on Finance 1967–72; Chair. People's Nat. Party 1969–78; elected MP 1972; Deputy Prime Minister 1972–78, also Minister of Finance 1972–78, of Planning 1977–78, of Foreign Affairs and Foreign Trade 1989, of Legal Affairs and Attorney Gen. 1993–95; Leader Govt Business 1989; Chair. Bd of Govs Caribbean Devt Bank 1972–73, IDB 1973–74; consultant to Myers Fletcher & Gordon (law firm); fmr Chair. Nat. Investment Bank of Jamaica (NIBJ); fmr mem. Bd of Dirs FINSAC Ltd. *Leisure interests:* reading, swimming, golf. *Address:* 21 East Street, Kingston, Jamaica (office). *Telephone:* 922-5860 (office).

COORS, Peter H., BEng, MBA; American business executive; *Chairman, Coors Brewing Company; Vice-Chairman, Molson Coors Brewing Company;* b. 20 Sept. 1946, Golden, Colo; great-grand s. of Adolph Coors, founder of the Golden brewery in 1873; ed Phillips Exeter Acad., NH, Cornell Univ., NY, Univ. of Denver; has served in several exec. positions at Coors, including Dir Coors and Coors Brewing Co. 1973–2005, Exec. Vice-Pres. and Chair. brewing div. of Coors (before being organized as Coors Brewing Co.) –1993, interim Treasurer and Chief Financial Officer, Coors 1993–95, Vice-Chair. and CEO Coors Brewing Co. 1993, Chair. Coors Brewing Co. and Pres. and CEO Adolph Coors Co. 2000–02, Chair. Adolph Coors Co. and Coors Brewing Co. 2002–05, Chair. Coors Brewing Co. and Vice-Chair. Molson Coors Brewing Co. 2005–; Chair. Univ. of Colorado Hosp. Foundation 2006–; mem. Bd of Dirs U.S. Bancorp 1996–, Inc., Energy Corporation of America 1996–, H.J. Heinz Co. 2001–; mem. Int. Chapter of Young Presidents Org., Denver Univ.'s Daniels

www.worldwhoswho.com

School of Business Advisory Bd; mem. Exec. Cttee Nat. Western Stock Show Asscn; fmr Nat. Pres. and Chair. Ducks Unlimited; Trustee and mem. Exec. Bd Denver Area Council of the Boy Scouts of America; Trustee Seeds of Hope Foundation, Univ. of Northern Colorado; serves on bds of several conservation groups; Dr hc (Regis Univ.) 1991, (Wilberforce Univ.) 1992, (Johnson & Wales Univ.) 1997. *Leisure interests:* outdoor pursuits, wildlife conservation. *Address:* Coors Brewing Co., 17735 West 32nd Avenue, Golden CO 80401-1217 (office); Molson Coors Brewing Co., 1225 17th Street, Denver, CO 80202, USA. *Telephone:* (303) 279-6565 (office). *Fax:* (303) 277-5415 (office). *E-mail:* webmaster@coors.com (office). *Website:* www.molsoncoors.com (office).

COOTE, Alice; British singer (mezzo-soprano); b. 10 May 1968, Frodsham, Cheshire; ed Guildhall School of Music and Drama, London, Royal Northern Coll. of Music and Nat. Opera Studio; concerts include oratorio with London and Liverpool Philharmonic Orchestras, Bergen Philharmonic, London Mozart Players, appearances at the BBC Proms 1997, 2002, 2003, recitals at Cheltenham and Edinburgh Festivals, on BBC Radio 3, and at the Wigmore Hall, London; roles include Cherubino in Figaro, Dorabella in Così fan tutte, Penelope in The Return of Ulysses, Kate Pinkerton in Madama Butterfly, Suzy in La Rondine, the Page in Salome, Glycère in Cherubini's Anacréon ou l'amour fugitif, Fortuna and Valletto in Poppea, Hanna Kennedy in Mary Stuart; season 1998–99 included her debut at Opéra Bastille in Parsifal, the title role in Rape of Lucretia at Nantes, Tamyris in Il Re Pastore for Opera North, Ruggiero in Alcina at Stuttgart; season 2002–03 included Covent Garden debut as Dryade in Ariadne auf Naxos, Ruggiero in Alcina at San Francisco, Octavian in Der Rosenkavalier for ENO, Strauss' Composer in Chicago, Dido in Les Troyens for San Francisco Opera, Turnspit in Rusalka and Orlando at Covent Garden; Rinaldo at Göttingen, Der Komponist in Ariadne auf Naxos for WNO 2004; numerous performances with Julius Drake; Brigitte Fassbaender Award for Lieder Interpretation, Decca-Kathleen Ferrier Prize 1992. *Recordings include:* Vaughan Williams' Hugh the Drover 1994, Rossini's Ricciardo e Zoraide 1997, Great Operatic Arias 2002, Verdi's Falstaff 2002, Handel: The Choice of Hercules 2002, Songs 2003, Walton's Gloria, The Choice of Hercules, Orfeo. *Address:* c/o Stefania Almansi, IMG Artists, The Light Box, 111 Power Road, London, W4 5PY, England (office). *Telephone:* (20) 7957-5800 (office). *Fax:* (20) 7957-5801 (office). *E-mail:* salmansi@imgartists.com (office). *Website:* www.imgartists.com (office).

COPE, George A., BBA; Canadian telecommunications executive; *CEO, Bell Canada Enterprises (BCE) Inc;* b. 1961, Scarborough, Ont.; ed Univ. of Western Ont.; Pres. and CEO Clearnet Communications Inc. 1987–2000 (acquired by TELUS Mobility 2000), Pres. and CEO TELUS Mobility 2000–05; Pres. and CEO Bell Canada 2005–08, CEO Bell Canada Enterprises (BCE) Inc. 2008–; Dir BMO Financial Group, NII Holdings Inc.; mem. Advisory Bd Richard Ivey School of Business, Univ. of Western Ont.; Canada's Top 40 Under 40 Award 1996. *Address:* Bell Canada Enterprises Inc., 1000 rue de la Gauchetière Ouest, Suite 3700, Montreal, PQ H3B 4Y7, Canada (office). *Telephone:* (514) 870-8777 (office). *Fax:* (514) 870-4385 (office). *Website:* www.bce.ca (office).

COPE, Jonathan, CBE; British ballet dancer (retd) and répétiteur; b. 1963, Crediton, Devon; m. Maria Almeida, one s. one d.; ed Royal Ballet School; joined Royal Ballet 1982, Soloist 1985–86, Prin. 1987–90, 1992–2005 (retd), Répétiteur 2005–; est. property devt business 1990–92; South Bank Show Dance Award 2003, Critics' Circle/Nat. Dance Awards, Best Male Dancer 2004. *Leading roles (with Royal Ballet) include:* Prince in Swan Lake, The Sleeping Beauty and The Nutcracker, Romeo and Juliet (partnering Sylvie Guillem and Darcey Bussell), Solor in La Bayadère, Albrecht in Giselle, Le Baiser de la Fée, The Prince of the Pagodas, Cinderella, Palemon in Ondine, Serenade, Agon, Apollo, Opus 19/The Dreamer, The Sons of Horus, Young Apollo, Galanteries, The Planets, Still Life at the Penguin Café, The Spirit of Fugue, Concerto, Gloria, Requiem, A Broken Set of Rules, Pursuit, Piano, Grand Pas Classique, Monotones, Crown Prince Rudolph in Mayerling, Woyzeck in Different Drummer, Second Friend in The Judas Tree, Beliaev in A Month in the Country, Birthday Offering, La Valise, Air Monotones II, Fox in Renard, Fearful Symmetries, Symphony in C (partnering Sylvie Guillem), Duo Concertant, If This Is Still a Problem, Des Grieux in Manon, Illuminations. *Address:* The Royal Ballet, Royal Opera House, Bow Street, Covent Garden, London, WC2E 9DD, England. *Telephone:* (20) 7240-1200. *Fax:* (20) 7212-9121. *Website:* info.royaloperahouse.org/ballet.

COPE, Wendy Mary, MA, FRSL; British writer; b. 21 July 1945, Erith, Kent; d. of Fred Stanley Cope and Alice Mary Cope (née Hand); m. Lachlan Mackinnon; ed Farringtons School, St Hilda's Coll., Oxford, Westminster Coll. of Educ., Oxford; primary school teacher, London 1967–86; freelance writer 1986–; mem. Soc. of Authors (man. cttee 1992–95); Hon. DLitt (Winchester) 2000, (Oxford Brookes) 2003; Cholmondeley Award for Poetry 1987, Michael Braude Award for Light Verse, American Acad. of Arts and Letters 1995. *Publications include:* Across the City 1980, Hope and the 42 1984, Making Cocoa for Kingsley Amis 1986, Poem from a Colour Chart of House Paints 1986, Men and Their Boring Arguments 1988, Does She Like Wordgames? 1988, Twiddling Your Thumbs 1988, The River Girl 1990, Serious Concerns 1992, If I Don't Know 2001; editor: Is That the New Moon? – Poems by Women Poets 1989, The Orchard Book of Funny Poems 1993, The Funny Side 1998, The Faber Book of Bedtime Stories 2000, Heaven on Earth – 101 Happy Poems 2001, George Herbert: Verse and Prose (a selection) 2002, Two Cures for Love: Selected Poems 2008; contribs to newspapers and reviews. *Leisure interest:* playing the piano. *Address:* c/o Faber and Faber, Bloomsbury House, 74–77 Great Russell Street, London WC1B 3DA, England (office). *Telephone:* (20) 7927-3800 (office). *Website:* www.faber.co.uk (office).

COPPA, HE Cardinal Giovanni; Italian ecclesiastic; b. 9 Nov. 1925, Alba; ed Catholic Univ. of Milan; ordained priest 1949; began working at the

Vatican in what was known as the Apostolic Chancery; served as Latinist at Second Vatican Council and later worked in Vatican Secr. of State, which had taken over duties of Apostolic Chancery; apptd Titular Archbishop of Serta and Official of Secr. of State 1979; Apostolic Nuncio to Czechoslovakia 1990–93, to Czech Repub. 1993–2001 (also accred to Slovakia 1993–94 (resgnd)); cr. Cardinal 2007–, apptd Cardinal-Deacon of S. Lino 2006–. *Address:* c/o Apostolic Nunciature to Czech Republic, Vorsilska ul. 12, 11000 Prague 1, Czech Republic. *Telephone:* (2) 2499-9811. *Fax:* (2) 2499-9833.

COPPENS, Yves; French professor of palaeoanthropology and prehistory; *Professor Emeritus, Collège de France;* b. 9 Aug. 1934, Vannes; s. of René Coppens and Andrée Coppens; m. Françoise Le Guennec 1959; ed Univ. of Rennes, Univ. of Paris (Sorbonne); Research Asst, CNRS, Paris 1956–69; Assoc. Prof., then Prof., Nat. Museum of Natural History 1969–83; Prof. of Palaeoanthropology and Prehistory, Collège de France 1983, now Prof. Emer.; mem. Acad. of Sciences 1985–, Nat. Acad. of Medicine 1991–, Royal Acad. of Sciences (Belgium) 1992–; Chevalier, Légion d'honneur, Officier, Ordre Nat. du Mérite, Officier des Palmes Académiques, Officier, des Arts et Lettres, Officier, Ordre Nat. Tchadien; Dr. hc (Bologna) 1988, (Liège) 1992; Le prix Edmond Hébert 1963, Le prix André C. Bonnet 1969, La médaille d'or de l'Empereur d'Éthiopie 1973, Le grand prix Jaffé de l'Académie des Sciences 1974, Le grand prix scientifique de la Fondation de France 1975, La médaille Fourmarier de la Société Géologique de Belgique 1975, Le prix Glaxo 1978, La médaille d'argent du CNRS 1982, Le prix Kalinga de l'UNESCO 1984, La médaille Vandenbroeck de la Société belge de géologie, de paléontologie et d'hydrologie 1987, La médaille André Duveyrier de la Société de Géographie 1989, La médaille d'or de l'encouragement au progrèscience 1991. *Documentary film:* Homo sapiens 2005. *Publications:* Le Singe, l'Afrique et l'homme 1983, Préhistoire de l'art occidental (with Brigitte Delluc, André Leroi-gourhan) 1990, Origines de la bipédie (with Brigitte Senut) 1992, La plus belle histoire du monde 1996, Le genou de Lucy 1999, Pré-ambules : les premiers pas de l'homme 1999, Grand entretien 2001, Aux origines de l'humanité 2001, Les origines de l'homme T 1 et T 2 (with Pascal Picq) 2002, L'Odyssée de l'espèce 2003, Homo sapiens 2004; over 400 scientific papers. *Address:* Collège de France, 3, rue d'Ulm, 75231 Paris, Cedex 5; Musée de l'Homme, Palais de Chaillot, place du Trocadéro, 75116 Paris (office); 4 rue du Pont-aux-Choux, 75003 Paris, France (home). *Telephone:* 1-44-27-10-23. *E-mail:* yves.coppens@ college-of-france.fr. *Website:* www.college-de-france.fr/site/pal_pre/ p998923969623.htm.

COPPERFIELD, David; American magician; b. (David Kotkin), 1956, Metuchen, NJ; ed Fordham Univ.; Prof. of Magic, New York Univ. 1974; appeared in musical Magic Man 1974; presenter, The Magic of ABC; performer, dir, producer, writer, The Magic of David Copperfield 1978–; Founder and Chair. Project Magic 1982–; Founder Int. Museum and Library of Conjuring Arts, Nev. 1991; owner, Musha Cay resort, Bahamas; performs more than 550 shows per year worldwide; Dr hc (Fordham Univ.); Chevalier de l'Ordre des Arts et Letters; Golden Rose Award, Montreux Film Festival 1987; Bambi Award 1993; 19 Emmy Awards. *Film:* Terror Train 1980. *Achievements include:* illusions include levitating across Grand Canyon 1984, walking through Great Wall of China 1986, escaping from Alcatraz prison 1987, making Statue of Liberty disappear 1989, going over Niagara Falls 1990, making Orient Express disappear 1991; introduced flying illusion 1992; escaped from burning ropes 13 storeys above ground, Caesar's Palace 1993. *Website:* www.davidcopperfield.com.

COPPERWHEAT, Lee; British fashion designer; s. of Terence Copperwheat and Diana Frances Brooks; ed Tresham Coll., Northampton, London Coll. of Fashion; fmrly tailor with Aquascutum; est. design room and fmr man. of sampling and production Passenger sportswear; freelance design projects for numerous clients; fmr teacher menswear tailoring Brighton Univ.; fmr Lecturer, St Martin's School of Art, London; est. Copperwheat Blundell with Pamela Blundell (q.v.); Young Designer of the Year 1994 (with Pamela Blundell).

COPPOLA, Francis Ford; American film director, film producer and screenwriter; b. 7 April 1939, Detroit, Michigan; s. of the late Carmine Coppola and Italia Coppola; m. Eleanor Neil; two s. (one deceased) one d. Sophia Coppola (q.v.); ed Hofstra Univ., Univ. of California; theatre direction includes Private Lives, The Visit of the Old Lady, San Francisco Opera Co. 1972; founder and Artistic Dir Zoetrope Studios 1969–; owner Niebaum-Coppola Estate (winery), Napa Valley; f. Zoetrope Argentina, Buenos Aires; Commdr Ordre des Arts et des Lettres; Cannes Film Award for The Conversation 1974; Dir's Guild Award for The Godfather; Acad. Award for Best Screenplay for Patton, Golden Palm (Cannes) 1979 for Apocalypse Now, also awarded Best Screenplay, Best Dir and Best Picture Oscars for The Godfather Part II; US Army Civilian Service Award. *Films directed include:* The Playgirls and the Bellboy 1962, Tonight for Sure 1962, Dementia 13 1963, You're a Big Boy Now 1966, Finian's Rainbow 1968, The Rain People 1969, The Godfather 1972, The Conversation 1974, The Godfather: Part II 1974, Apocalypse Now 1979, One from the Heart 1982, The Outsiders 1983, Rumble Fish 1983, The Cotton Club 1984, Captain EO 1986, Peggy Sue Got Married 1986, Gardens of Stone 1987, Tucker: The Man and His Dream 1988, New York Stories 1989, The Godfather: Part III 1990, Dracula 1992, Jack 1996, The Rainmaker 1997, Youth Without Youth 2007; also numerous screenplays and films produced including American Graffiti. *Address:* Zoetrope Studios, 916 Kearny Street, San Francisco, CA 94133; Niebaum Coppola, POB 208, Rutherford, CA 94573; c/o CAA, 9830 Wilshire Boulevard, Beverly Hills, CA 90212, USA. *Website:* www.zoetrope.com; www.niebaum-coppola.com.

COPPOLA, Sofia; American actress, film director, screenwriter, film producer and photographer; b. 14 May 1971, New York; d. of Francis Ford Coppola and Italia Coppola; m. Spike Jonze 1999 (divorced 2003); Pnr Thomas Mars;

one d.; cr. pop-culture magazine show Hi-Octane 1994; fmr designer Milkfed fashion label; photography has appeared in Interview, Paris Vogue and Allure; mem. Writers Guild of America. *Films include:* Frankenweenie 1984, Peggy Sue Got Married 1986, Anna 1987, The Godfather: Part III 1990, Inside Monkey Zetterland 1992, Ciao L.A. 1994, Lick the Star (dir, producer and writer) 1998, The Virgin Suicides (dir and writer) 1999, Star Wars: Episode I: The Phantom Menace 1999, CQ 2001, Lost in Translation (dir, producer and writer) (Acad. Award for Best Original Screenplay 2004, Golden Globe Awards for Best Picture, Best Screenplay 2004, Independent Spirit Awards for Best Screenplay, Best Dir, Best Picture 2004, Cesar Award for Best Foreign Feature 2005) 2003, Marie-Antoinette (dir, producer and writer) 2006. *Address:* c/o Bart Walker, Creative Artists Agency LLC, 162 5th Avenue, 6th Floor, New York, NY 10010, USA. *Telephone:* (212) 277-9000.

COPPS, Sheila Maureen, PC, BA; Canadian consultant and fmr politician; *President, Sheila Copps and Associates;* b. 27 Nov. 1952, Hamilton, Ont.; d. of Victor Kennedy Copps and Geraldine Florence Copps (née Guthro); m. Austin Thorne; one d.; ed Univ. of Western Ontario, Univ. of Rouen, France, McMaster Univ.; journalist, Ottawa Citizen 1974–76, Hamilton Spectator 1977; Constituency Asst to Leader Liberal Party, Ont. 1977–81; mem. Ont. Legis. Ass. for Hamilton Centre 1981–84; mem. House of Commons Parl.) 1984–2004, Deputy Leader of Opposition, Fed. Liberal Party 1991; Deputy Prime Minister 1993–97, Minister of the Environment 1993–96, Minister of Canadian Heritage 1996–2004; currently Pres. Sheila Copps and Assocs, Hamilton; Achievement Award, Canadian Council for the Arts 2003. *Publication:* Nobody's Baby 1986, Worth Fighting For 2004. *Address:* Sheila Copps and Associates, 370 Main East, Suite 301, Hamilton Ont., L8N 1J6, Canada (office). *Telephone:* (905) 522-7712 (office). *Fax:* (905) 522-7715 (office). *E-mail:* info@sheilacopps.ca (office).

CORBETT, Gerald Michael Nolan, MA, MSc; British business executive; *Chairman, Britvic PLC;* b. 7 Sept. 1951, Hastings, Sussex; s. of the late John Michael Nolan Corbett and of Pamela Muriel Corbett (née Gay); m. Virginia Moore Newsum; one s. three d.; ed Tonbridge School, Pembroke Coll. Cambridge, London Business School, Harvard Business School; with Boston Consulting Group 1975–82; Group Financial Controller Dixons Group PLC 1982–86, Corp. Finance Dir 1986–87; Group Finance Dir Redland PLC 1987–94, Grand Metropolitan PLC 1994–97; Dir (non-exec.) MEPC PLC 1995–98, Burmah Castrol PLC 1998–2000; CEO Railtrack PLC 1997–2000; Chair. Woolworths Group PLC 2001–07, Health Club Holdings, Holmes Place 2003–, SSL Int. 2005–, Britvic PLC 2005–, Moneysupermarket.com Group Ltd; Chair. Bd of Govs Abbots Hill School 1997–2002, Royal Nat. Inst. for the Deaf (RNID) 2007–; Foundation Scholar, Pembroke Coll., Cambridge 1972–75, William Pitt Prize 1974, London Business School Prize 1979. *Leisure interests:* golf, country pursuits. *Address:* Britvic PLC, Britvic House, Bloomfield Road, CM1 1TU, Chelmsford, Essex, UK (office). *Telephone:* (1245) 261871 (office). *Fax:* (1245) 267147 (office). *Website:* www.britvic.co.uk (office).

CORBETT, Roger Campbell, AM, BComm; Australian business executive; b. 1944; m.; ed Univ. of NSW; began career working on dock, Woolworths Store, Chatswood; fmr Dir of Operations and mem. Bd Dirs, David Jones (Australia) Pty Ltd; fmr Merchandising and Stores Dir and mem. Bd Dirs Grace Brothers; Man.-Dir Big W (gen. merchandise discount stores), Woolworths Ltd (Australia) 1990–97, apptd Exec. Dir Woolworths Ltd (Australia) 1990, Man.-Dir of Retail 1997–98, COO 1998–99, CEO, Group Man.-Dir and mem. Bd Dirs 1999–2006 (retd); mem. Bd Dirs Wal-Mart Stores Inc. 2006–, Reserve Bank of Australia, Fairfax Media Ltd, Outback Stores; Chair. ALH Group Pty Ltd; fmr Chair. CIES Food Business Forum, France; Deputy Chair. PrimeAg Australia; mem. Advisory Council, Australian Grad. School of Man., Univ. of New South Wales; B'nai B'rith (Australia-NZ) Gold Medal. *Address:* ALH Group Pty Ltd., Ground Floor, 16-20 Claremont Street, South Yarra, Vic. 3141, Australia (office). *Telephone:* (3) 9829-1000 (office). *Website:* www .alhgroup.com.au (office).

CORBO, Vittorio, PhD; Chilean economist, academic, business executive and fmr central banker; *President, ING Seguros de Vida SA;* b. 22 March 1943, Iquique; s. of Gerardo Corbo and Maria Lioi; m. Veronica Urzua 1967; one s. one d.; ed Universidad de Chile and Mass Inst. of Tech.; Asst Prof., Concordia Univ. 1972–81, Prof., Inst. of Econs, Pontificia Univ. Católica de Chile 1981–84, 1991–; Sr Adviser, IBRD 1984–87, Div. Chief. 1987–91; Chief, Macroeconomic Devt and Growth Div., World Bank 1984–91, mem. Chief Economist Advisory Council 2004–; Economic Adviser to Santander Group in Chile 1991–2003, 2008–, mem. Bd of Dirs Banco Santander-Chile 1995–2003; Chair. Cen. Bank of Chile 2003–07; Pres. ING Seguros de Vida SA (insurance co.), Santiago 2008–; Vice-Chair. Inmobiliaria Simonetti 2008–; mem. Bd of Dirs Global Devt Network 1999–2003, Universia-Chile 2000–03, Chilean Pacific Foundation 2000–, Cruz Verde Pharmacies 2008–; Prof. of Econs, Concordia Univ., Canada 1972–81; Visiting Prof., Georgetown Univ., Washington, DC 1984–91; Vice-Pres. Int. Econ. Asscn 1998–2002; mem. Man. Council, Global Devt Network 1993–2003, Int. Advisory Council, Center for Social and Econ. Research (CASE), Warsaw, Poland, Advisory Bd, Stanford Center for Int. Devt 1999–; Sr Research Fellow, Research Center for Econ. Devt and Policy Reform, Stanford Univ. 1999; Visiting Sr Scholar, Research Dept, IMF 2000, 2003; mem. editorial cttee Journal of Development Economics, Journal of Applied Economics; Economist of the Year, El Mercurio newspaper 2003. *Publications include:* Inflation in Developing Countries 1974, Monetary Policy in Latin America in the 1990s 2000. *Leisure interest:* skiing. *Address:* ING Seguros de Vida SA, Ave Sucecia #211 Santiago, Piso 7, Santiago, Chile (office). *Telephone:* (2) 252-1464 (office). *Website:* www.ingvida .cl (office).

CORBY, Sir (Frederick) Brian, Kt, MA, FIA; British business executive and actuary; b. 10 May 1929, Raunds, Northants.; s. of Charles Walter Corby and

Millicent Corby; m. Elizabeth Mairi McInnes 1952; one s. two d.; ed Kimbolton School and St John's Coll., Cambridge; joined Prudential Assurance Co. Ltd 1952, Asst Gen. Man. (Overseas) 1968–73, Deputy Gen. Man. 1974–75, Gen. Man. 1976–79, Chief Actuary 1980–81, Group Gen. Man., Prudential Corpn PLC 1979–82, CEO 1982–90, Chair. 1990–95; Chief Gen. Man. Prudential Assurance Co. Ltd 1982–85, Chair. 1985–90; Deputy Pres. CBI 1989–90, Pres. 1990–92; Pres. Nat. Inst. for Econ. and Social Research 1994–2003; Vice-Pres. Inst. of Actuaries 1979–83; Chair. South Bank Bd 1990–98; Deputy Chair. British Insurance Asscn 1984–85; Chair. Asscn of British Insurers 1985–87; Dir Bank of England 1985–93, Pan-Holding 1993–, Montanaro Small Cos Investment Trust PLC (Chair.) 1995–99, Mid-Ocean Reinsurance 1995–98, Brockbank Holdings Ltd (Chair.) 1995–99, Moorfield Estates PLC (Chair.) 1996–2000, XL Capital 1998–2003, Nat. Asscn of Security Dealers, Inc. 2000–; Chancellor Univ. of Herts. 1992–96; Hon. DSc (City Univ., London) 1989, (Hertfordshire) 1996, Hon. DLitt (CNAA) 1991. *Publications:* articles in Journal of Inst. of Actuaries. *Leisure interests:* reading, golf, gardening. *Address:* Fairings, Church End, Albury, Ware, Herts., SG11 2JG, England (home). *Telephone:* (1279) 771422 (home). *Fax:* (1279) 771488 (home).

CORDEN, Warner Max, AC, MComm, MA, PhD, FBA, FASSA; Australian economist and academic; *Professorial Fellow, Department of Economics, University of Melbourne;* b. 13 Aug. 1927, Breslau, Germany (now Wrocław, Poland); s. of the late Ralph S. Corden; m. Dorothy Martin 1957; one d.; ed Melbourne Boys High School, Univ. of Melbourne and London School of Econs; Lecturer, Univ. of Melbourne 1958–61, Professorial Fellow 2002–; Nuffield Reader in Int. Econs and Fellow of Nuffield Coll., Oxford 1967–76; Professorial Fellow, ANU 1962–67, Prof. of Econs 1976–88; Chung Ju Yung Prof. of Int. Econs, Paul H. Nitze School of Advanced Int. Studies, Johns Hopkins Univ., Washington, DC, USA 1989–2002, Prof. Emer. of Int. Econs 2002–; Visiting Prof., Univ. of California, Berkeley 1965, Univ. of Minnesota 1971, Princeton Univ. 1973, Harvard Univ. 1986; Sr Adviser, IMF 1986–88; Pres. Econ. Soc. of Australia and New Zealand 1977–80; mem. Group of Thirty 1982–90; Foreign Hon. mem. American Econ. Asscn 1986; Distinguished Fellow, Econ. Soc. of Australia 1995; Dr hc (Melbourne) 1995; Bernard Harms Prize 1986. *Publications:* The Theory of Protection 1971, Trade Policy and Economic Welfare 1974, 1997, Inflation, Exchange Rates and the World Economy 1977, 1985, Protection, Growth and Trade 1985, International Trade Theory and Policy 1992, Economic Policy, Exchange Rates and the International System 1994, The Road to Reform 1997, Too Sensational: On the Choice of Exchange Rate Regimes 2002. *Address:* Department of Economics, University of Melbourne, Melbourne, Victoria 3010, Australia (office). *Telephone:* (3) 8344-5296 (office). *Fax:* (3) 8344-6899 (office). *E-mail:* m.corden@unimelb.edu.au (office). *Website:* www.economics.unimelb.edu.au/SITE/mcorden/mcorden .shtml (office).

CORDES, Eckhard, MBA, PhD; German business executive; *Chairman of the Management Board and CEO, METRO AG;* b. 25 Nov. 1950, Neumünster; ed Hamburg Univ.; joined DaimlerChrysler Group 1976, Asst Plant Man. Sindelfingen Plant 1977–81, Sr Man. Investment Planning, Sindelfingen Plant 1981–83, Head, Product Control, New Commercial Vehicle P 1983–86, Dir Accounting and Control, Mercedes-Benz, Sao Paulo, Brazil 1986–89, Dir Control AEG, Frankfurt 1989–91, Sr Vice Pres. Control, Corp. Planning and Mergers and Acquisitions 1991–94, Sr Vice Pres. Corp. Planning and Control, Daimler-Benz AG 1994–95, Sr Vice Pres. Corp. Devt 1995–96, mem. Man. Bd, Corp. Devt and Directly-Managed Businesses 1997, Corp. Devt and IT Man. and MTU/Diesel Engines and TEMIC DaimlerChrysler AG 1998–2000 (after Daimler-Benz merged with Chrysler Corpn 1998), mem. Man. Bd, Corp. Devt and IT Man. DaimlerChrysler AG 2000–04, Commercial Vehicles Div. 2000–04, Head, Mercedes Car Group 2004–05; Chair. Man. Bd Franz Haniel & Cie. GmbH 2006–; Chair. Supervisory Bd METRO AG 2006–07, Chair. Man. Bd and CEO 2007–. *Address:* METRO AG, Schlüterstrasse 1, 40235 Düsseldorf, Germany (office). *Telephone:* (211) 6886-0 (office). *E-mail:* kontakt@metro.de (office). *Website:* www.metrogroup.de (office).

CORDES, HE Cardinal Paul Josef; German ecclesiastic; *President of the Pontifical Council 'Cor Unum';* b. 5 Sept. 1934, Kirchhundem; ed briefly studied medicine before entering the seminary, doctoral studies at Univ. of Mainz; ordained priest of Paderborn 1961; apptd Titular Bishop of Naissus and Auxiliary Bishop of Paderborn 1975, Titular Archbishop of Naissus 1995; Vice-Pres. Pontifical Council for the Laity 1980; Pres. Pontifical Council 'Cor Unum' 1995–2 April 2005, 21 April 2005–; cr. Cardinal 2007–, apptd Cardinal-Deacon of S. Lorenzo in Piscibus 2007–. *Address:* Pontifical Council 'Cor Unum', Piazza S. Calisto 16, 00153 Rome, Italy (office). *Telephone:* (06) 6988-9411 (office). *Fax:* (06) 6988-7301 (office).

CÓRDOBA RUIZ, Piedad Esneda; Colombian lawyer and politician; *Senator;* b. 25 Jan. 1955, Medellín, Antioquia; d. of Zabulón Córdoba and Lía Ruiz; ed Universidad Pontificia Bolivariana, Medellín; began her political career working as community leader in several neighbourhoods in Medellín; Municipal Sub-controller 1984–86; Pvt. Sec. to Mayor William Jaramillo 1986; elected Councilwoman, Medellín 1988–90; cand. for Chamber of Reps of Colombia 1990; elected Deputy of Antioquia Dept Ass. 1990; Deputy, Chamber of Reps 1992–94; Mayor of Medellín 1994; elected to Senate 1994–98, re-elected 1998, 2002 (lost her seat in Congress following modification of electoral results in Valle del Cauca and Atlántico by Council of State 2005); Senator and mem. Seventh Comm. of Congress 2006–, in charge of debating labour topics, previously worked on Third Comm. (Financial affairs), Fifth Comm. (Mining and Energy) and Second Comm. (Foreign Affairs), Pres. Senate's Human Rights Comm. and the Peace Comm.; leading figure of Latin American feminist movt in Colombia, represents minority groups as part of Poder Ciudadano Siglo XXI Movt; participated in Fourth World Conf. on Women, Beijing 1995; kidnapped by leader of paramilitary group United Self-Defense

Forces of Colombia (AUC) 1999, eventually freed and exiled with her family in Canada, returned to Colombia in 2000; subject of two assassination attempts; Pres. Liberal Nat. Directorate (Head of Partido Liberal Colombiano—Colombian Liberal Party) 2003–; judicially denounced for treason under Colombian law after making controversial declarations against Colombian Govt and Columbian Pres. during political event in Mexico March 2007, charge currently under investigation by Supreme Court; participated as official Govt mediator, along with Pres. Hugo Chávez of Venezuela, in humanitarian exchange discussions between Colombia Govt and Fuerzas Armadas Revolucionarias de Colombia (FARC) guerrilla group Aug.–Nov. 2007. *Address:* Senado de la República de Colombia, Bogotá, Colombia (office). *E-mail:* piedad.cordoba.ruiz@senado.gov.co (office); info@piedadcordoba.net. *Website:* www.senado.gov.co (office); www.piedadcordoba.net.

CÓRDOVA, France Anne, PhD; American astrophysicist, academic and university administrator; *President, Purdue University;* b. Paris, France; m. Christian J. Foster; two c.; ed Stanford Univ., Calif. Inst. of Tech.; early career at LA Times News Service 1971; Staff Scientist, Earth and Space Science Div., Los Alamos Nat. Lab. (LANL) 1979–89, Deputy Group Leader, Space Astronomy and Astrophysics Group 1989; Prof. of Astronomy and Astrophysics, Pa State Univ. 1989–96, Dept Head 1989-93; Chief Scientist, NASA 1993–96; Prof. of Physics, Univ. of Calif., Santa Barbara 1996–2002, Vice-Chancellor Research 1996–2002; Chancellor Univ. of Calif., Riverside 2002–07; Pres. Purdue Univ. 2007–; fmr Chair. numerous NASA bds including Exceptional Scientific Achievement Medal Panel 1993–96, Science Council 1994–96, Search Cttee for Dir Astrobiology Inst. 1998, Science Working Group, Constellation X Mission 1998–2000, Hubble Space Telescope Time Allocation Cttee 2001, Strategic Roadmap Cttee on Educ. (Co-Chair.) 2004; Chair. Research Advisory Council, Earth and Environmental Sciences Div. (LANL) 1985–86, Geosciences Space Science and Astrophysics (GSSA) Category Team (LANL) 1986–88, Science and Eng Advisory Council (SEAC) 1988–89; co-founder Int. Astronomical Union Working Group on Multi-Frequency and Multi-Facility Astrophysics 1988; Vice-Chair. High Energy Astrophysics Div., American Astronomical Soc. 1989, Chair. 1990, Vice-Pres. American Astronomical Soc. 1993–96; Chair.-Elect Comm. on Human Resources and Social Change, Nat. Asscn State Univs. and Land-Grant Colls. (NASULGC) 2005–07; mem. of numerous panels and bds including Scientific Program Cttee, AAAS 2000–, NRC Policy and Global Affairs Advisory Cttee 2001–, Univ. of Calif. Mexico Comm. on Educ. Science Tech. 2002–, Univ. of Calif. Pres.'s Council on Nat. Labs 2002–, Calif. Council on Science and Tech. 2003–, Belo 2003–, NAS Roundtable on Scientific Communication and Security 2003–, Edison Int. 2004–, Nat. Panel of Pres and Chancellors, Models for Flexible Tenure-track Faculty Career Pathways, American Council on Educ. (ACE) 2004–, Univ. Calif. Long-Range Guidance Team 2005–; Fellow, Asscn for Women in Science 1999; Dr hc (Loyola-Marymount Univ.) 1997; NASA Group Achievement Award for Outstanding Teamwork, Swift Midsize Explorer Team 2000, Kilby Prize Laureate, Jack Kilby Int. Awards Foundation 2000, Nat. Assoc. of Nat. Acads 2002. *Publications:* approx. 140 scientific reports and papers, as ed.: Multiwavelength Astrophysics 1988, The Spectroscopic Survey Telescope 1990; contribs. to Mademoiselle magazine; fiction: The Women of Santo Domingo. *Address:* Office of the President, Purdue University, Hovde Hall, Room 200, 610 Purdue Mall, West Lafayette, IN 47907-2040, USA (office). *Telephone:* (765) 494-4600 (office). *Website:* www.purdue.edu/president (office).

CORDOVEZ, Diego; Ecuadorean diplomatist and lawyer; b. 3 Nov. 1935, Quito; s. of Luis Cordovez-Borja and Isidora Zegers de Cordovez; m. Maria Teresa Somavia 1960; one s.; ed Univ. of Chile; admitted to Bar 1962; served in Foreign Service of Ecuador until 1963; joined UN as Econ. Affairs Officer 1963; Political Officer on special missions to Dominican Repub. 1965, Pakistan 1971; Dir UN Econ. and Social Council Secr. 1973–78, Asst Sec.-Gen. for Econ. and Social Matters, UN 1978–81; Special Rep. of UN Sec.-Gen. on Libya–Malta dispute 1980–82; Sec.-Gen.'s rep. on UN Comm. of Inquiry on hostage crisis in Tehran 1980; Sr officer responsible for efforts to resolve Iran/Iraq war 1980–88; Under-Sec.-Gen. for Special Political Affairs 1981–1988; Special Envoy to Grenada 1983; UN Mediator, Afghanistan 1982–88, Rep. for implementation of Geneva Accords 1988–89; Minister for Foreign Affairs 1988–92; Pres. World Trade Center (Ecuador) 1993–98; Special Counsel LeBoeuf, Lamb, Greene and Macrae 1993–98; Special Adviser to UN Sec.-Gen. for Cyprus 1997–99, for Latin American Affairs 1999–2005; Perm. Rep. to UN, New York 2005–08; Pres. Andean Centre for Int. Studies 2000; mem. American Soc. of Int. Law; Order of Merit (Ecuador), Légion d'honneur, Grand Cross (Spain, Portugal, Brazil, Argentina, Chile, Peru, Colombia, Venezuela). *Publications:* UNCTAD and Development Diplomacy 1971, Out of Afghanistan: The Inside Story of the Soviet Withdrawal (with Selig S. Harrison) 1995, Nuestra Propuesta Inconclusa (Ecuador–Perú: Del Inmovilismo al Acuerdo de Brasilia) 2000. *Leisure interests:* reading, carpentry. *Address:* c/o Ministry of External Relations, Trade and Integration, Avda 10 de Agosto y Carrión, Quito (office); Calle Afganistán N41–90, El Bosque, Quito, Ecuador (office).

CORELL, Hans Axel Valdemar, LLB; Swedish lawyer, judge and diplomatist; *Senior Counsel, Mannheimer Swartling Advokatbyrå AB;* b. 7 July 1939, Västermo; s. of Alf Corell and Margit Norrman; m. Inger Peijfors 1964; one s. one d.; ed Univ. of Uppsala; court clerk, Eksjö Dist Court and Göta Court of Appeal 1962–67; Asst Judge, Västervik Dist Court 1968–72; Legal Adviser, Ministry of Justice 1972, 1974–79; Additional mem. and Assoc. Judge of Appeal, Svea Court of Appeal 1973; Asst Under-Sec. Div. for Constitutional and Admin. Law, Ministry of Justice 1979–81; Judge of Appeal 1980; Under-Sec. for Legal Affairs, Ministry of Justice 1981–84; Amb. and Under-Sec. for Legal and Consular Affairs, Ministry of Foreign Affairs 1984–94; mem. Perm. Court of Arbitration, The Hague 1990–; Under-Sec.-Gen. for Legal Affairs, The Legal Counsel of the UN 1994–2004; Sr Counsel, Mannheimer Swartling Advokatbyrå AB (law firm), Stockholm 2005–; Chair. Bd of Trustees Raoul Wallenberg Inst. of Human Rights and Humanitarian Law 2006–; mem. Advisory Bd Int. Center for Ethics, Justice and Public Life, Brandeis Univ. 2005–; mem. Council Human Rights Inst., Int. Bar Asscn 2005–; Counsellor, American Soc. of Int. Law 2006–; mem. Int. Law Asscn; Hon. LLD (Stockholm) 1997, (Lund) 2007; William J. Butler Human Rights Medal, Univ. of Cincinnati Coll. of Law 2001, Cox Int. Humanitarian Award for Advancing Global Justice, Case Western Reserve Univ. 2005. *Publications:* Sekretesslagen (co-author) 1992, Proposal for an International War Crimes Tribunal for the Former Yugoslavia (CSCE Report) (co-author) 1993; various legal publs. *Leisure interests:* art, music (Piper of the Caledonian Pipes and Drums of Stockholm 1975–84), ornithology. *Address:* Mannheimer Swartling Advokatbyrå AB, Norrlandsgatan 21, Box 1711, 111 87 Stockholm (office); Norr Mälarstrand 70, 112 35 Stockholm, Sweden. *Telephone:* (8) 595-06303 (office). *Fax:* (8) 595-06001 (office). *E-mail:* hac@msa.se (office); hans.corell@tele2.se. *Website:* www.mannheimerswartling.se (office); www.havc.se.

COREY, Elias James, PhD; American chemist and academic; *Professor Emeritus of Chemistry, Harvard University;* b. 12 July 1928, Methuen, Mass.; s. of Elias J. Corey and Tina Hasham; m. Claire Higham 1961; two s. one d.; ed Mass. Inst. of Tech.; Instructor in Chem., Univ. of Ill. 1951–53, Asst Prof. of Chem. 1953–55, Prof. 1956–59; Prof. of Chem., Harvard Univ. 1959–68, Chair. Dept of Chem. 1965–68, Sheldon Emery Prof. 1968, currently Prof. Emer.; Alfred P. Sloan Foundation Fellow 1955–57, Guggenheim Fellow 1957, 1968–69; mem. American Acad. of Arts and Sciences 1960–68, NAS 1966; Hon. AM, Hon. DSc; Pure Chem. Award of ACS 1960, Fritzsche Award of ACS 1967, Intra-Science Foundation Award 1967, Harrison Howe Award, ACS 1970, Award for Synthetic Organic Chem. 1971, CIBA Foundation Award 1972, Evans Award, Ohio State Univ. 1972, Linus Pauling Award 1973, Dickson Prize in Science, Carnegie Mellon Univ. 1973, George Ledlie Prize, (Harvard) 1973, Remsen Award, Arthur C. Cope Award 1976, Nichols Medal 1977, Buchman Memorial Award (Calif. Inst. of Tech.) 1978, Franklin Medal 1978, Scientific Achievement Award Medal 1979, J. G. Kirkwood Award (Yale) 1980, C. S. Hamilton Award (Univ. of Nebraska) 1980, Chemical Pioneer Award (American Inst. of Chemists) 1981, Rosenstiel Award (Brandeis Univ.) 1982, Paul Karrer Award (Zurich Univ.) 1982, Medal of Excellence (Helsinki Univ.) 1982, Tetrahedron Prize 1983, Gibbs Award (ACS) 1984, Paracelsus Award (Swiss Chem. Soc.) 1984, V. D. Mattia Award (Roche Inst. of Molecular Biology) 1985, Wolf Prize in Chemistry (Wolf Foundation) 1986, Silliman Award (Yale Univ.) 1986, Nat. Medal of Science 1988, Japan Prize 1989, Nobel Prize for Chem. 1990, Priestley Medal of ACS 2004 and numerous other awards and honours. *Publications:* nearly 1,000 scientific publs. *Leisure interests:* outdoor activities and music. *Address:* Department of Chemistry, Harvard University, 12 Oxford Street, Cambridge, MA 02138-2902 (office); 20 Avon Hill Street, Cambridge, MA 02140, USA (home). *Telephone:* (617) 495-4033 (office); (617) 864-0627 (home). *Fax:* (617) 495-0376 (office). *E-mail:* corey@chemistry.harvard.edu (office). *Website:* www.chem.harvard.edu (office).

CORFIELD, Sir Kenneth (George), Kt, CE, FREng, FIEE, FIMechE; British business executive and engineer; *Chairman, Tanks Consolidated Investments Ltd;* b. 27 Jan. 1924, Rushall; s. of Stanley Corfield and Dorothy Elizabeth Corfield (née Mason); m. Patricia Jean Williams 1960; one d.; ed Elmore Green High School, South Staffs. Coll. of Advanced Tech.; Tech. Officer, ICI Ltd 1947–50; Chief Exec., KG Corfield Ltd, camera Mfrs 1950–61; Exec. Dir Parkinson Cowan Ltd 1962–67; Vice-Pres., Dir ITT Europe Inc. 1967–70; Man. Dir Standard Telephones and Cables Ltd 1970–85, Deputy Chair. 1974–79, Chair. and CEO 1979–85; Chair. Standard Telephones and Cables (NI) 1974–85; Vice-Pres. Int. Standard Electric Corpn, ITT Sr Officer in UK 1974–84; Chair. Nat. Econ. Devt Cttee for Ferrous Foundries Industry 1975–78; Vice-Chair. British Inst. of Man. 1978–84; Vice-Pres. Inst. of Marketing 1980–; Chair. Eng Council 1981–85, Distributed Information Processing Ltd 1987–, Octagon Investment Man. 1987–96, Gandolfi Ltd 1987–, Tanks Consolidated Investments 1990–, Linhof & Studio Ltd 1993–; Dir Midland Bank Group 1979–91, Britoil 1982–88, Vice-Pres. Eng Employers Fed. –1985; mem. Pres.'s Cttee and Council, CBI –1985; mem. Council, Inst. of Dirs. 1981–85 (Pres. 1984–85); mem. Advisory Council, Science Museum 1975–83, Trustee 1984–92; mem. Advisory Council for Applied Research and Devt 1981, Nat. Econ. Devt Cttee for Electronics 1981; Hon. FIEE; Hon. Fellow, Sheffield City Polytechnic 1983, Wolverhampton Polytechnic 1986; Dr hc (Surrey), (Open Univ.) 1985; Hon. DSc (City Univ.) 1981, (Bath) 1982, (Queen's, Belfast) 1982, (Loughborough) 1982, (Aston) 1985; Hon. LLD (Strathclyde) 1982; Hon. DSc (Eng) Univ. of London 1982; Hon. DEng (Bradford) 1983. *Publications:* Report on Product Design for NEDC 1979, No Man an Island 1982, Patterns of Change: Collected Essays 1983. *Leisure interests:* photography, cinema, music. *Address:* 10 Chapel Place, Rivington Street, London, EC2A 3DQ, England. *Telephone:* (20) 7729-5765. *Fax:* (20) 7729-5791.

CORISH, Patrick Joseph, MA, DD, MRIA; Irish historian (retd); b. 20 March 1921, Co. Wexford; s. of Peter William Corish and Brigid Mary O'Shaughnessy; ed St Peter's Coll., Wexford and Nat. Univ. of Ireland, St Patrick's Coll., Maynooth and Univ. Coll., Dublin; ordained priest 1945; Prof. of Ecclesiastical History, Pontifical Univ., Maynooth 1947–75; Prof. of Modern History, Maynooth, Nat. Univ. of Ireland 1975–88; Sec. Catholic Record Soc. of Ireland 1948; ed. Soc.'s journal Archivium Hibernicum 1948–77; mem. Irish Manuscripts Comm. 1949, Royal Irish Acad. 1956; Domestic Prelate 1967. *Publications:* A History of Irish Catholicism (ed. and contrib.) 1967–71, The Catholic Community in the Seventeenth and Eighteenth Centuries 1981, The Irish Catholic Experience 1985, Maynooth College: A Bicentenary History 1995, Records of the Irish Catholic Church (with David C. Sheehy) 2001, The

Beatified Irish Martyrs (co-ed. with B. Millett) 2004). *Leisure interest:* gardening. *Address:* St Patrick's College, Maynooth, Co. Kildare, Ireland. *Telephone:* (1) 6285222. *Fax:* (1) 6289063.

CORKER, Robert Phillips (Bob), Jr, BS; American business executive and politician; *Senator from Tennessee;* b. 24 Aug. 1952, Orangeburg, SC; m. Elizabeth Corker 1987; two d.; ed Univ. of Tennessee, Knoxville; moved to Tenn. aged 11; worked for four years as construction supt then f. own construction co., Bencor, sold in 1990; purchased two largest real estate cos in Chattanooga 1999, sold most of these holdings 2006; cand. for US Senate 1994; Commr of Finance and Admin for State of Tennessee 1995–2001; Mayor of Chattanooga 2001–05; Senator from Tennessee 2007–; Republican; Entrepreneurial Hall of Fame, Univ. of Tennessee at Chattanooga. *Address:* Dirksen Senate Building, SD-B40A, Washington, DC 20510, USA (office). *Telephone:* (202) 224-3344 (office). *Fax:* (202) 228-0566 (office). *Website:* corker.senate.gov (office).

CORKUM, Paul Bruce, OC, BSc, MS, PhD, FRS, FRSC; Canadian physicist; *Project Leader, Attosecond Science, Steacie Institute for Molecular Sciences, National Research Council of Canada;* b. 30 Oct. 1943; ed Acadia Univ., Wolfville, NS, Lehigh Univ., Bethlehem, Pa; Post-doctoral Fellow, Nat. Research Council of Canada 1973–, Project Leader, Attosecond Science, Steacie Inst. for Molecular Sciences; Adjunct Prof. of Chem., Univ. of Toronto; Adjunct Prof. of Physics, McMaster Univ., Univ. of British Columbia, Ottawa Univ.; mem. Int. Advisory Bd Max Planck Inst. for Quantenoptik, Garching, Germany 1996–, Advisory Bd for Advanced Synchronton Sources, Brookhaven Nat. Labs 2001, Networks of Centres of Excellence: Canadian Inst. for Photonics Innovation and Team Leader for Ultrafast Dynamic Imaging Thrust; Program Chair. Conf. on Lasers and Electro-Optics/Int. Quantum Electronics Conf. 1996, Gen. Chair. 1998; Co-Chair. two Canadian workshops on femtosecond X-rays 2001–02; Program Chair. Int. Conf. on Ultrafast Optics 2001, Gen. Chair. 2003; Co-Chair. Gordon Conf. on Control of Light with Matter and Matter with Light 2003 (Chair. 2005), Dynamic Imaging Workshop, Sherbrooke, PQ 2003, Harvard-ITAMP Workshop on Attosecond Science 2003, 10th Int. Conf. on Multiphoton Processes 2005, Ultrafast Phenomena Conf. 2006; mem. Editorial Advisory Bd International Journal of Nonlinear Optics, Editorial Bd Journal of Physics B; Hon. PhD (Acadia) 2006; Canadian Asscn of Physicists' Gold Medal for Lifetime Achievement in Physics 1996, Einstein Award, Soc. for Optical and Quantum Electronics 1999, LEOS Distinguished Lecturer 2001–03, Queen's Golden Jubilee Medal 2003, RSC Tory Medal 2003, Charles Townes Award, Optical Soc. of America 2005, IEEE Quantum Electronics Award 2005, Killam Prize for Physical Sciences 2006, Arthur Schawlow Award for Quantum Electronics, American Physical Soc. 2006. *Publications:* more than 170 scientific papers in professional journals. *Address:* Steacie Institute for Molecular Sciences, National Research Council of Canada, 100 Sussex Drive, Room 2063, Ottawa, ON K1A OR6, Canada (office). *Telephone:* (613) 993-7390 (office). *Fax:* (613) 991-3437 (office). *E-mail:* paul.corkum@nrc-cnrc.gc.ca (office). *Website:* steacie.nrc-cnrc.gc.ca (office).

CORMAN, Roger William, AB, AFM; American film director and film producer; *President, Concorde New Horizons Corporation;* b. 5 April 1926, Detroit; m. Julie Ann Halloran; two s. two d.; ed Stanford Univ., Calif., Univ. of Oxford, UK; founder and Pres. New World Pictures 1970–83, Concorde-New Horizons Corpn 1983–; distributed films including: Cries and Whispers, Amarcord, Fantastic Planet, The Story of Adele H, Small Change, The Tin Drum; mem. Producers' Guild of America, Directors' Guild of America; Dr hc (American Film Inst.); Lifetime Achievement Award, LA Film Critics 1997, 1st Producers of Century Award, Cannes Film Festival 1998, Award of Venice Film Festival, PGA Lifetime Achievement Award. *Films directed include:* Swamp Women 1955, Apache Woman 1955, Five Guns West 1955, Day the World Ended 1956, The Oklahoma Woman 1956, It Conquered the World 1956, Naked Paradise 1957, Carnival Rock 1957, Not of This Earth 1957, Attack of the Crab Monsters 1957, The Undead 1957, Rock All Night 1957, Teenage Doll 1957, Sorority Girl 1957, The Saga of the Viking Women 1957, I Mobster 1958, War of the Satellites 1958, Machine-Gun Kelly 1958, Prehistoric World 1958, She Gods of Shark Reef 1958, A Bucket of Blood 1959, Ski Troop Attack 1960, The Wasp Woman 1960, House of Usher 1960, The Little Shop of Horrors 1960, Last Woman on Earth 1960, Atlas 1961, Creature from the Haunted Sea 1961, Pit and the Pendulum 1961, The Premature Burial 1962, The Intruder 1962, Tales of Terror 1962, Tower of London 1962, The Young Racers 1963, The Raven 1963, The Terror 1963, The Haunted Palace 1963, Man with the X-Ray Eyes 1963, The Masque of the Red Death 1964, The Secret Invasion 1964, The Tomb of Ligeia 1965, The Wild Angels 1966, The St. Valentine's Day Massacre 1967, The Trip 1967, Target: Harry 1969, Bloody Mama 1970, Gas-s-s-s 1971, The Red Baron 1971, Frankenstein Unbound 1990. *Films produced include:* more than 300 films including The Fast and the Furious 1954, Attack of the Crab Monsters 1957, Teenage Cave Man 1958, Attack of the Giant Leeches 1959, The Premature Burial 1962, Queen of Blood 1966, Big Bad Mama 1974, Death Race 2000 1975, I Never Promised You a Rose Garden 1977, Saint Jack 1979, Rage and Discipline 2004, DinoCroc 2004, Scorpius Gigantus 2005. *Film appearances include:* The Silence of the Lambs, The Godfather Part II, Philadelphia, Apollo 13, Scream 3, The Independent, A Galaxy Far Far Away. *Publication:* How I Made 100 Films in Hollywood and Never Lost a Dime (autobiog.) 1990. *Address:* c/o Concorde-New Horizons Corporation, 11600 San Vicente Blvd., Los Angeles, CA 90049, USA.

CORNEA, Doina; Romanian philologist; b. 30 May 1929, Braşov; m.; one d.; ed Faculty of Philology, Univ. of Cluj; Asst Lecturer in French Literature, Univ. of Cluj; dismissed for writing an open letter to Those Who Haven't Ceased to Think 1982; 30 other open letters followed 1983–89; held for interrogation for five weeks Nov. 1987; under house arrest 1988–89; mem. Romanian Nat. Salvation Front 1989–90, Memory Foundation; Founder-mem. Social Dialogue Group (GDS) 1989, Civil Alliance; Co-founder Antitotalitarian Forum of Romania 1990; Officier, Légion d'honneur 1999, Steaua României, Mare Cruce 2000, Magyar Köztársasági Érdemrend Tisztikeresztje 2002, Domina Ordinis Sancti Silvestri Papae (Vatican) 2003; Dr hc (Brussels) 1989; int. awards for activities in furtherance of human rights, including Thorolf Rafto Human Rights Award, Norway 1989. *Publications:* Liberté? 1990, Opened Letters and Other Texts 1991, translations from French, Fata Nevazuta a Lucrurilor 1990–99 1999, La face cachée des choses 2000, Puterea fragilitătii 2005. *Address:* Str. Alba Iulia Nr. 16, Ro-Cluj 400197, Romania. *Telephone:* (264) 598460. *Fax:* (64) 433623.

CORNELIS, François; Belgian business executive; *Executive Vice-President and President of Chemicals, Total SA;* b. 25 Oct. 1949, Uccle, Brussels; m. Colette Durant 1973; two s. two d.; ed Universite Catholique de Louvain; joined Petrofina SA as systems engineer, subsequently Co-ordinator of Supply and Refining Operations, Brussels, Supply and Shipping Man., Petrofina UK, London, Vice-Pres., Special Asst to Pres., American Petrofina, Dallas, Tex., USA 1983–84, Gen. Man. and Asst to Pres., Petrofina 1984–86, Exec. Dir, Office of the Chair. 1986–90, CEO and Vice-Chair. 1991–99, after merger with Total Vice-Chair. of Exec. Cttee, Totalfina and Sr Vice-Pres., Petrochemicals, Paints and US Operations (after merger with Total) 1999–2000, Exec. Vice-Pres. Chemicals Div., TotalFinaElf 2000, Chair. Atofina 2000–03, Vice-Chair. Exec. Cttee and Pres. of Chemicals, Total SA 2003–; Chair. European Chemical Industry Council, Royal Automobile Club of Belgium; mem. Bd of Dirs Delhaize Freres et Cie Le Lion SA ADS, Sofina; mem. Global Advisory Council of The Conference Board and Chair. European Steering Cttee. *Address:* Total, SA, 2 place de la Coupole, La Défense 6, 92400 Courbevoie, France (office). *Telephone:* 1-47-44-58-53 (office). *Fax:* 1-47-44-58-24 (office). *Website:* www.total.com (office).

CORNELIUS, James M., BA, MBA; American pharmaceutical industry executive; *Chairman and CEO, Bristol-Myers Squibb;* b. Kalamazoo, Mich.; m.; two c.; ed Michigan State Univ.; Pres. and CEO IVAC Corpn 1980–82; Chief Financial Officer, mem. Bd of Dirs and Exec. Bd Lilly 1983–95; Chair. Guidant 1994–2006, Chair. Emer. 2006–; mem. Bd of Dirs Bristol-Myers Squibb 2005–, Interim Chief Exec. 2006, CEO 2006–, Chair. 2008–; Pres. Cornelius Family Charitable Foundation. *Leisure interest:* American football. *Address:* Bristol-Myers Squibb, 345 Park Avenue, New York, NY 10154-0037, USA (office). *Telephone:* (212) 546-4000 (office). *Fax:* (212) 546-4020 (office). *E-mail:* info@bms.com (office). *Website:* www.bms.com (office).

CORNELL, Eric Allin, BS, PhD; American physicist and academic; *Professor Adjoint, Department of Physics, University of Colorado;* b. 1961, Palo Alto, Calif.; s. of Allin Cornell and Elizabeth Cornell (née Greenberg); m. Celeste Landry; two d.; ed Stanford Univ., Massachusetts Inst. of Tech.; Research Asst, Stanford Univ. 1982–85, MIT 1985–90; Teaching Fellow, Harvard Extension School 1989; Post-doctoral research, Jt Inst. for Lab. Astrophysics, Boulder 1990–92, Fellow 1994–; Asst Prof. Adjoint, Dept of Physics, Univ. of Colorado at Boulder 1992–95, Prof. Adjoint 1995–; Sr Scientist, Nat. Inst. of Standards and Tech., Boulder 1992–, Fellow 1994–; Fellow, American Physical Soc. 1997–, Optical Soc. of America 2000–; mem. NAS 2000–; numerous awards including Dept of Commerce Gold Medal 1996, Fritz London Prize in Low Temperature Physics 1996, King Faisal Int. Prize in Science 1997, I. I. Rabi Prize 1997, Lorentz Medal, Royal Netherlands Acad. of Arts and Sciences 1998, Benjamin Franklin Medal in Physics 1999, Nobel Prize in Physics (jt recipient) 2001. *Address:* Joint Institute for Laboratory Astrophysics, University of Colorado, Campus Box 440, Boulder, CO 80309-0440, USA (office). *Telephone:* (303) 492-6281 (office). *Fax:* (303) 492-5235 (office). *E-mail:* cornell@jila.colorado.edu (office). *Website:* jilawww.colorado.edu/bec/CornellGroup/index.html (office); jilawww.colorado.edu (office).

CORNESS, Sir Colin (Ross), Kt, MA; British business executive; b. 9 Oct. 1931, Chorlton; s. of the late Thomas Corness and Mary Evlyne Corness; ed Uppingham School, Magdalene Coll., Cambridge, Harvard Grad. School of Business, USA; Dir Taylor Woodrow Construction Ltd 1961–1964; Man. Dir Redland Tiles Ltd 1965–70, Group Man. Dir Redland PLC 1967–82, Deputy Chair. and Man. Dir 1974–77, Chair. 1977–95; CEO 1977–91; Chair. Nationwide Bldg Soc. 1991–96; Dir Chubb and Son PLC 1974–84, W.H. Smith and Son Holdings PLC 1980–87, SE Region, Nat. Westminster Bank PLC 1982–86, Courtaulds PLC 1986–91, Gordon Russell PLC 1985–89, Bank of England 1987–95, S. G. Warburg Group PLC 1987–95, Unitech PLC 1987–95, Union Camp Corpn 1991–99, Chubb Security PLC 1992–97, Glaxo Wellcome PLC 1994–97 (Chair. 1995–97), Taylor Woodrow PLC 1997–2001; Chair. Bldg Centre 1974–77; mem. Econ. Devt Cttee for Bldg 1980–84, Industrial Devt Advisory Bd 1982–84, UK Advisory Bd of the British-American Chamber of Commerce 1987–; Trustee, Uppingham School 1996–99; Hon. Fellow, Magdalene Coll. 2001; Hon. DBA (Kingston) 1994. *Leisure interests:* travel, music, tennis.

CORNILLAC, Clovis; French actor; b. 16 Aug. 1967, Lyon (Rhône); s. of Roger Cornillac and Myriam Boyer; two twin d.; acted in Peter Brooke's Mahabharata 1984–86; Commdr, Ordre des Arts et des Lettres 2005; César Award for Best Supporting Actor 2005. *Films include:* Hors-la-loi (aka Outlaws) 1985, Il y a maldonne 1988, The Unbearable Lightness of Being 1988, Les années sandwiches 1988, Suivez cet avion 1989, Le trésor des îles chiennes 1990, Trois nuits 1991, Traverser le jardin 1993, Pétain 1993, Les Mickeys 1994, Les amoureux 1994, Bons baisers de Suzanne 1995, Marie-Louise ou la permission 1995, Ouvrez le chien 1997, La mère Christain 1998, Karnaval 1999, Tea Time 2001, Grégoire Moulin contre l'humanité 2001, Bois ta Suze 2002, Une affaire privée 2002, Carnages 2002, Maléfique 2002, Une affaire qui roule (aka A Great Little Business) 2003, À la petite semaine (aka Nickel and Dime) 2003, Après la pluie, le beau temps 2003, Mariées mais pas

www.worldwhoswho.com

trop (aka The Very Merry Widows) 2003, Vert paradis (aka Les cadets de Gascogne, TV title) 2003, Je t'aime, je t'adore 2003, Malabar Princess 2004, Doo Wop 2004, Grossesse nerveuse 2004, La femme de Gilles 2004, Mensonges et trahisons et plus si affinités... 2004, Un long dimanche de fiançailles (A Very Long Engagement) 2004, Close-Up 2005, Brice de Nice 2005, Au suivant! 2005, Les chevaliers du ciel (Sky Fighters) 2005, Le cactus 2005, Les brigades du Tigre 2006, Poltergay 2006, Le serpent 2007, Scorpion 2007, Astérix at the Olympic Games 2008. *Television includes:* Le village sur la colline (mini-series) 1982, Tu peux toujours faire tes bagages 1984, Les cadavres exquis de Patricia Highsmith: Légitime défense (episode) 1990, Les dessous de la passion 1991, Bonne chance Frenchie (mini-series) 1992, Van Loc: un grand flic de Marseille – La Grenade (episode) 1993, Le juge est une femme: Aux marches du palais (episode) 1993, Le JAP, juge d'application des peines: Chacun sa gueule (episode) 1993, Navarro: En suivant la caillera (episode) 1994, Un été à l'envers 1994, La bavure 1994, Les cordier, juge et flic: Un si joli témoin (episode) 1995, Billard à l'étage 1996, L'échappée 1998, Les vilains 1999, Sam 1999, L'amour prisonnier 2000, L'île bleue 2001, Orages 2003, Central nuit (aka Night Squad) episodes: Nuit de chien 2001, La petite fille dans le placard 2001, Vol à la poussette 2004; Gris blanc 2005.

CORNILLET, Thierry Pierre Fernand, DèsScPol; French politician and international organization official; *President, Association Internationnale des Régions Francophones;* b. 23 July 1951, Montélimar, Drôme; s. of Col Jean-Baptiste Cornillet and Inès Genoud; m. Marie-France Rossi 1983; one s. one d.; ed Lycée Alain Borne, Montélimar, Univs of Lyon II, Lyon III and Paris I–Panthéon Sorbonne; Head of Dept, Office of Dir of Civil Security at Ministry of Interior 1977–81; Head of Dept, Office of Minister of External Trade, then of Admin. Reform 1980–81; Export Man., Lagarde SA, Montélimar 1981–83; Dir Office of Deputy Mayor of Nancy 1983–85; Legal Adviser to Jr Minister, Ministry of Interior 1985–86, Chef de Cabinet 1986–88; Head of Dept, Cie nationale du Rhône 1988–93; Municipal Councillor, Montélimar 1983, Mayor 1989–99; mem. Gen. Council of Drôme 1985–93, Vice-Chair. 1992–93; mem. and Sec. Regional Council of Rhône-Alpes 1986, Vice-Pres. 1999–; mem. Assemblée nationale (UDF) from Drôme 1993–97; Vice-Chair. Parti Radical 1988–97, Chair. 1997–, mem. European Parl. 1999–, Vice-Chair. EU Jt Parl. Ass. on Africa, Caribbean, Pacific; Pres. Association Internationale des Régions Francophones; Chevalier Ordre nat. du Mérite. *Address:* European Parliament, Bât. Altiero Spinelli, 09G103, 60, rue Wiertz, 1047 Brussels, Belgium; Rhône-Alpes Regional Council, Groupe UDF, 78 route de Paris, BP 19, 69751 Charbonnières-les-Bains, France. *E-mail:* thierry.cornillet@europarl.europa.eu. *Website:* www.rhonealpes.fr; www.regions-francophones.com; www.cornillet.net.

CORNISH, (Robert) Francis, CMG, LVO, FRSA; British business executive and diplomatist (retd); *Chairman, South West Tourism Ltd;* b. 18 May 1942, Bolton; m. Alison Jane Dundas 1964; three d.; ed Charterhouse, Royal Mil. Acad., Sandhurst; commissioned 14th/20th King's Hussars and served in Libya, UK and Germany, becoming Adjutant 1966; joined HM Diplomatic Service 1968, served in Kuala Lumpur and Jakarta before becoming Head of Greek Desk, London; First Sec. (EEC), Bonn 1976–80; apptd Asst Pvt. Sec. to Prince of Wales 1980, also worked for Princess of Wales 1980–83; High Commr to Brunei 1983–86; Dir of Public Diplomacy, Washington, DC and Head of British Information Services, New York 1986–90; Head of News Dept, FCO and Spokesman for Foreign Sec. 1990–93, Sr British Trade Commr, Hong Kong 1993, first Consul-Gen. Hong Kong 1997; Sr Directing Staff, Royal Coll. of Defence Studies 1998; Amb. to Israel 1998–2001; Chair. South West Tourism Ltd 2003–, Taunton Town Centre Co.; Dir Grosshill Properties 2002–, Sydney & London Properties 2003–. *Leisure interests:* farming, theatre, riding, hill walking. *Address:* South West Tourism Ltd, Woodwater Park, Exeter, EX2 5WT (office); Coombe Farm, West Monkton, Somerset, TA2 8RB, England (home). *Telephone:* (1392) 353201 (office). *Fax:* (1392) 445112 (office). *E-mail:* sthompson@swtourism.co.uk (office). *Website:* www.swtourism.co.uk (office).

CORNISH, William Rodolph, LLD, BCL, FBA; British/Australian barrister; b. 9 Aug. 1937, S Australia; s. of Jack R. Cornish and Elizabeth E. Cornish; m. Lovedy E. Moule 1964; one s. two d.; ed St Peter's Coll., Adelaide, Adelaide Univ. and Univ. of Oxford, England; Lecturer in Law, LSE 1962–68; Reader in Law, Queen Mary Coll., London 1969–70; Prof. of English Law, LSE 1970–90; Prof. of Law, Univ. of Cambridge 1990–95, Dir Centre for Euro Legal Studies 1991–94, Herchel Smith Prof. of Intellectual Property Law, Univ. of Cambridge 1995–2004; Fellow, Magdalene Coll., Cambridge 1990–, Pres. 1998–2001; Academic Dir British Law Centre, Warsaw Univ., Poland 1992–2005; External Academic Mem. Max-Planck-Institute, Intellectual Property 1990–; Hon. QC 1997, Bencher Gray's Inn 1998; Hon. LLD (Edinburgh) 2005. *Publications:* The Jury 1968, Intellectual Property 1981–2003, Encyclopaedia of UK and European Patent Law (with others) 1978, Law and Society in England 1750–1950 1989; numerous articles in legal periodicals. *Address:* Magdalene College, Cambridge, CB3 0AG, England. *Telephone:* (1223) 330062. *Fax:* (1223) 330055. *E-mail:* wrc1000@cam.ac.uk (office). *Website:* www.law.cam.ac.uk.

CORNWALL, HRH The Duchess of; British b. (Camilla Rosemary Shand), 17 July 1947, London; d. of the late Major Bruce Shand and Hon. Rosalind Cubitt; m. 1st Andrew Parker Bowles 1973 (divorced); one s. one d.; m. 2nd HRH The Prince of Wales 2005; ed Dumbrells School, Sussex, Queen's Gate School, South Kensington, Mon Fertile, Switzerland, Institut Britannique, Paris; made debut in London 1965; Patron, Animal Care Trust, Cornwall Community Foundation, Friends of Westonbirt Arboretum, London Chamber Orchestra, New Queen's Hall Orchestra, Public Catalogue Foundation's Cornish Catalogue, Soc. of Chiropodists and Podiatrists, St John's Smith Square Charitable Trust, Unicorn Theatre for Children, Wiltshire Bobby Van Trust, Youth Action Wiltshire; Pres. Nat. Osteoporosis Soc., Scotland's Gardens Scheme. *Address:* Clarence House, St James's Palace, London, SW1A 1BA, England. *Website:* www.princeofwales.gov.uk.

CORNWELL, Andrew, BSc, MSc; British politician and journalist; *Councillor and Executive Member for Finance, London Borough of Islington;* b. 30 Sept. 1966, London; ed London School of Econs; financial journalist 1988–98; mem. Bd London Pensions Fund Authority 2001–06; European Media Officer BOND (British Overseas NGOs for Devt) 2001; Green Party cand in Gen. Election 2001; Chair. Green Party of England and Wales 2002–03; Vice-Chair. Green Liberal Democrats 2004–; Councillor and Exec. Mem. for Finance, London Borough of Islington 2006–. *Address:* London Borough of Islington, Town Hall, Upper Street, London, N1 2UD, England (office). *Telephone:* (20) 7527-2986 (office). *E-mail:* andrew.cornwell@islington.gov.uk (office). *Website:* www.islington.gov.uk (office).

CORNWELL, Bernard, (Susannah Kells), BA; British writer; b. 23 Feb. 1944, London, England; m. Judy Acker 1980; ed Univ. of London. *Publications:* Redcoat 1987, Wildtrack 1988, Sea Lord (aka Killer's Wake) 1989, Crackdown (aka Murder Cay) 1990, Stormchild 1991, Scoundrel 1992, Stonehenge 2000 BC 1999, The Archer's Tale 2001, Gallows Thief 2001, The Last Kingdom 2004, The Pale Horseman 2005, Lords of the North Country 2006, Sword Song 2007, Agincourt 2008; Starbuck Chronicles series: Rebel 1993, Copperhead 1994, Battle Flag 1995, The Bloody Ground 1996; Arthur series: The Winter King 1995, Enemy of God 1996, Excalibur 1997; Sharpe series: Sharpe's Eagle 1981, Sharpe's Gold 1981, Sharpe's Company 1982, Sharpe's Sword 1983, Sharpe's Enemy 1984, Sharpe's Honour 1985, Sharpe's Regiment 1986, Sharpe's Siege 1987, Sharpe's Rifles 1988, Sharpe's Revenge 1989, Sharpe's Waterloo 1990, Sharpe's Devil 1992, Sharpe's Battle 1995, Sharpe's Tiger 1997, Sharpe's Triumph 1998, Sharpe's Fortress 1999, Sharpe's Trafalgar 2000, Sharpe's Prey 2001, Sharpe's Skirmish (short story) 2002, Sharpe's Havoc 2003, Sharpe's Escape 2004, Sharpe's Fury 2006; Grail Quest series: Harlequin 2000, Vagabond 2002, Heretic 2003; as Susannah Kells: A Crowning Mercy 1983, The Fallen Angels 1984, Coat of Arms 1986, The Aristocrats 1987. *Address:* Toby Eady Associates Ltd, Third Floor, 9 Orme Court, London, W2 4RL, England (office). *Telephone:* (20) 7792-0092 (office). *Fax:* (20) 7792-0879 (office). *E-mail:* toby@tobyeady.demon.co.uk (office). *Website:* www.tobyeadyassociates.co.uk (office); www.bernardcornwell.net (office).

CORNWELL, David John Moore, (John le Carré), BA; British writer; b. 19 Oct. 1931, Poole, Dorset; s. of Ronald Thomas Archibald Cornwell and Olive Glassy; m. 1st Alison Ann Veronica Sharp 1954 (divorced 1971); three s.; m. 2nd Valerie Jane Eustace 1972; one s.; ed St Andrew's Preparatory School, Pangbourne, Sherborne School, Berne Univ., Switzerland and Lincoln Coll., Oxford; teacher, Eton Coll. 1956–58; in Foreign Service (Second Sec., Bonn, then Political Consul Hamburg) 1959–64; Hon. Fellow Lincoln Coll. Oxford 1984–; Commdr de l'Ordre des Arts et des Lettres 2005; Hon. DLitt (Exeter) 1990, (St Andrews) 1996, (Southampton) 1997, (Bath) 1998, (Berne Univ., Switzerland) 2008; Somerset Maugham Award 1963, MWA Edgar Allan Poe Award 1965, James Tait Black Award 1977, CWA Gold Dagger 1978, MWA 'Grand Master Award' 1986, Premio Malaparte 1987, CWA Diamond Dagger 1988, Nikos Kazantzakis Prize 1991, CWA 'Dagger of Daggers' 2005. *Publications:* Call for the Dead 1961, Murder of Quality 1962, The Spy Who Came in From the Cold 1963, The Looking Glass War 1965, A Small Town in Germany 1968, The Naive and Sentimental Lover 1971, Tinker, Tailor, Soldier, Spy 1974, The Honourable Schoolboy 1977, Smiley's People 1979, The Quest for Carla (collected edn of previous three titles) 1982, The Little Drummer Girl 1983, A Perfect Spy 1986, The Russia House 1989, The Secret Pilgrim 1991, The Night Manager 1993, Our Game 1995, The Tailor of Panama 1996, Single and Single 1999, The Constant Gardener (British Book Awards Play.com TV & Film Book of the Year 2006) 2000, Absolute Friends 2004, The Mission Song 2006, A Most Wanted Man 2008. *Address:* Curtis Brown, 28–29 Haymarket, London, SW1Y 4SP, England (office). *Telephone:* (20) 7393-4400 (office). *Fax:* (20) 7393-4401 (office).

CORNWELL, Patricia Daniels, BA; American writer; b. 9 June 1957, Miami, FL; ed Davidson Coll. (NC); police reporter, Charlotte Observer, NC 1979–81; computer analyst, Office of the Chief Medical Examiner, Richmond, Va 1985–91; mem. Authors' Guild, Int. Asscn of Identification, Int. Crime Writers Asscn, Nat. Asscn of Medical Examiners; Investigative Reporting Award, N Carolina Press Asscn 1980, Gold Medallion Book Award, Evangelical Christian Publishers Asscn 1985, Edgar Award 1990, Prix du Roman d'Aventure 1991, Gold Dagger Award 1993, Sherlock Holmes Award 1999. *Publications include:* non-fiction: A Time of Remembering: The Story of Ruth Bell Graham 1983 (re-issued as Ruth: a Portrait 1997); fiction: Postmortem (John Creasey Award, British Crime Writers' Asscn 1991, Anthony Award, Boucheron Award, World Mystery Convention, MacAvity Award, Mystery Readers Int) 1990, Body of Evidence 1991, All That Remains 1992, Cruel and Unusual 1993, The Body Farm 1994, From Potter's Field 1995, Cause of Death 1996, Hornet's Nest 1996, Unnatural Exposure 1997, Point of Origin 1998, Southern Cross 1999, Black Notice 1999, The Last Precinct 2001, Isle of Dogs 2001, Portrait of a Killer: Jack the Ripper 2002, Blow Fly 2003, Trace 2004, Predator 2005, At Risk 2006, Book of the Dead (British Book Award for Best Crime Thriller 2008) 2007, Scarpetta 2008, The Front 2008. *Address:* c/o Don Congdon Associates Inc., 156 5th Avenue, Suite 625, New York, NY 10010-7002, USA; c/o Little, Brown & Co., Brettenham House, Lancaster Place, London, WC2E 7EN, England. *Website:* www.patriciacornwell.com.

CORNYN, John, LLM; American politician; *Senator from Texas;* b. 2 Feb. 1952, Houston, Tex.; s. of John Cornyn and Gale Cornyn; ed Trinity Univ. and St Mary's School of Law, San Antonio, Univ. of Virginia Law School; Dist Court Judge, San Antonio 1984–90; elected to Tex. Supreme Court 1990, re-

www.worldwhoswho.com

elected 1996; Attorney-Gen. of Tex. 1997–2003; Senator from Tex. 2003–; mem. Bush–Cheney Transition Advisory Cttee 2000; St Mary's Distinguished Law School Grad. 1994; Trinity Univ. Distinguished Alumnus 2001; Outstanding Texas Leader Award, John Ben Shepperd Foundation of Texas 2000, James Madison Award, Freedom of Information Foundation of Texas 2001. *Address:* 517 Hart Senate Office Bldg, Washington, DC 20510, USA (office). *Telephone:* (202) 224-2934 (office). *Fax:* (202) 228-2856 (office). *Website:* cornyn.senate.gov (office).

CORONEL, Sheila S., BA, MA; Philippine journalist; *Executive Director, Toni Stabile Center for Investigative Journalism, Columbia University;* b. 1958, Manila; ed Univ. of the Philippines, London School of Econs; began as cub reporter for Philippine Panorama 1983; reporter for The Manila Times, Manila Chronicle; Co-founder Philippine Center for Investigative Journalism 1989, later Exec. Dir; Exec. Dir, Toni Stabile Center for Investigative Journalism and Prof. of Professional Practice, Columbia Univ. 2006–; Ramón Magsaysay Award for Journalism 2003. *Publications:* more than 12 books including Coups, Cults and Cannibals, The Rulemakers, Pork and other Perks. *Address:* Toni Stabile Center for Investigative Journalism, School of Journalism Columbia University, 2950 Broadway, New York, NY 10027, USA (office). *Telephone:* (212) 854-5748 (office). *E-mail:* ssc2136@columbia.edu (office). *Website:* www.journalism.columbia.edu (office).

COROPCEAN, Div. Gen. Ion; Moldovan army officer; *Chief of General Staff, Commander of the National Army of the Republic;* b. 11 March 1960, Liveden' vill; s. of Ştefan Coropcean; m. Valentina Coropcean; one s. one d.; ed Poltava Mil. Air Defence High School, Mil. Air Defence Acad.; cadet 1977–81, Air Defence Platoon Commdr 1981–84, Air Defence Battery Commdr 1984–87, Air Defence Bn Commdr 1987–88, Air Defence Acad. 1988–91, Chief of Staff and Deputy Commdr Air Defence Regt 1991–92, Deputy Commdr Air Defence Brigade 1992–97, Commdr Mil. Coll. 1997–98, Chief of Gen. Staff Nat. Army and Deputy Minister of Defence 1998–2006, Chief of Gen. Staff, Commdr Nat. Army 2006–; Medal of Courage, Medal of Mil. Merit, Award for Allegiance to the Motherland. *Publications:* The Foreign Policy of the Republic of Moldova in the Context of Integration Processes: Interests and Priorities. *Leisure interests:* books, football, literature. *Address:* ŞOS. Hînceşti 84, 2021 Chişinău (office); str. Alba Julia 200/1, Ap. 100, 2071 Chişinău, Republic of Moldova (home). *Telephone:* (2) 252444 (office); (2) 514874 (home). *Fax:* (2) 234434 (office). *E-mail:* coropcei@md.pims.org (office); ion.coropcean@army.md (office). *Website:* www.army.md (office).

CORR, Edwin Gharst, MA; American diplomatist and academic; b. 6 Aug. 1934, Edmond, Okla; s. of E. L. Corr and Rowena Gharst; m. Susanne Springer 1957; three d.; ed Univs of Oklahoma and Texas; officer, Dept of State, Foreign Office 1961–62; sent to Mexico 1962–66; Dir Peace Corps, Cali, Colombia 1966–68; Panama Desk Officer, Dept of State 1969–71; Program Officer InterAmerican Foundation 1971; Exec. Asst to Amb., American Embassy, Bangkok 1972–75; Counsellor Political Affairs, American Embassy, Ecuador 1976; Deputy Chief of Mission 1977–78; Deputy Asst Sec. Int. Narcotics Matters, State Dept 1978–80; Amb. to Peru 1980–81, Bolivia 1981–85, El Salvador 1985–88; State Dept Diplomat-in-Residence, Univ. of Okla 1988–90, Prof. of Political Science 1990–96, Dir Energy Inst. of the Americas 1996–2001, Assoc. Dir Int. Programs Center 1996–2006, Sr Research Fellow 2006–07 (retd); ind. consultant to US Govt 2007–09; Nat. Order of Merit (Ecuador) 1978; Condor of the Andes (Bolivia) 1985; Jose Matias Delgado Decoration (El Salvador) 1988; US Pres.'s Meritorious Service Award 1985, US State Dept Distinguished Honor Award 1988. *Publications:* The Political Process in Colombia 1971, Low-Intensity Conflict: Old Threats in a New World (co-ed.) 1992, The Middle East Peace Process: Vision vs Reality (co-ed.) 2002, The Search for Security: The US Grand Strategy in the 21st Century (co-ed.) 2003, The Search for Israel Peace (co-ed.) 2007; numerous articles in English and Spanish. *Leisure interests:* ranching, reading, public speaking, writing, exercise. *Address:* c/o International Programs Center, University of Oklahoma, Norman, OK 73019 (office); 1617 Jenkins Street, Norman, OK 73072, USA (home). *Telephone:* (405) 321-7036 (home).

CORREA, Charles M., BArch, MArch; Indian architect and planner; b. 1 Sept. 1930, Secunderabad; s. of Carlos Marcos Correa and Ana Florinda de Heredia; m. Monika Sequeira 1961; one s. one d.; ed Univ. of Michigan and Massachusetts Inst. of Tech., USA; Prin., Charles Correa Assocs, Mumbia (pvt. practice) 1958–; Chief Architect Navi Mumbai 1971–74, mem. Bd of Dirs CIDCO (Navi Mumbai) 1975–89; Consulting Architect, Govt of Kamataka 1975–78; Chair. Housing Urban Renewal and Ecology Bd, Mumbai 1975–83; Chair. Nat. Comm. on Urbanization 1985–88; Pres. World Soc. of EKISTICS, Athens 1996–98; Consulting Architect, Govt of Goa 1999–; Farwell Bernis Prof., MIT 2001–; Chair. Delhi Urban Arts Comm. 2005–; Founder Mem. Indian Nat. Trust for Art and Cultural Heritage 1983, Trust for Urban Design Research Inst. 1984; Fellow, Indian Inst. of Architects 1964–; mem. Council of Architecture 1974–; Hon. FAIA 1979; Hon. FRIBA 1993; Hon. Fellow, Academie d' Architecture Francais 1985, Int. Acad. of Architecture, Sofia, Bulgaria 1987, United Architects of the Philippines 1990, Finnish Asscn of Architects 1992, American Acad. of Arts and Sciences 1993, Royal Inst. of Architects of Ireland 1997, American Acad. of Arts and Letters 1998, Trinidad Inst. of Architects 1999, Royal Architectural Inst. of Canada 2002; Dr hc (Univ. of Michigan) 1980; Padma Shri, Pres. of India 1972; RIBA Gold Medal 1984, Gold Medal, Indian Inst. of Architects 1987, Gold Medal, Int. Union of Architects 1990, Praemium Imperiale for Architecture, Japan Art Asscn 1994, Aga Khan Award for Architecture 1998. *Major works include:* Mahatma Gandhi Memorial Museum, Sabarmati Ashram, Ahmedabad, Kovalam Beach Devt, Kerala, Kanchanjunga apartments, Mumbai, Cidade de Goa, Dona Paula, New India Centre, Delhi, Performing Arts Centre, Kala Acad., Goa, Previ low-income housing, Peru, Bharat Bhavan, Bhopal, Jawahar Kala Kendra, Jaipur, Nat. Crafts Museum, Delhi, British Council, Delhi, IUCCA, Pune Univ. *Publication:* The New Landscape 1985, Housing and Urbanisation 1999. *Leisure interests:* model railways, old films, swimming. *Address:* Charles Correa Associates, 9 Mathew Road, Mumbai 400004 (office); Sonmarg, Nepean Sea Road, Mumbai 400 006, India (home). *Telephone:* (22) 23633307 (office); (22) 23633306 (home). *Fax:* (22) 23631138 (office). *E-mail:* cmc@charlescorrea.net (office). *Website:* www.charlescorrea.net (office).

CORREA DELGADO, Rafael, MSc, PhD; Ecuadorean economist, politician and head of state; *President;* b. 6 April 1963, Guayaquil; ed Universidad Católica de Santiago de Guayaquil, Catholic Univ. of Louvain, Belgium, Univ. of Illinois, USA; teaching asst, Econs Faculty, Universidad Católica de Santiago de Guayaquil 1983–85, Assoc. Prof. 1988–1989; Industrial Specialist, Centre of Industrial Devt 1984–87; volunteer in Mission of the Salesian Fathers, Zumbahua, Cotopaxi 1987–88; Admin. Dir in charge of educational projects financed by IDB 1992–93; Head Prof., Dept of Econs, Universidad San Francisco de Quito 1993–2005; Minister of the Economy following overthrow of Lucio Gutierrez April–Aug. 2005 (resgnd); Founder,Alianza PAIS (Patria Altiva i Soberana); Pres. of Ecuador 2007–. *Publications:* El Reto del Desarrollo: ¿Estamos Preparados para el Futuro? 1996, La Vulnerabilidad de la Economía Ecuatoriana 2004; numerous journal Contribs. *Address:* Office of the President, Palacio Nacional, García Moreno 1043, Quito (office); Diego de Almagro N32-27 y Whimper, Edif. Torres Whimper, Of. 501, Quito, Ecuador. *Telephone:* (2) 221-6300 (office); (2) 600-0630; (2) 600-1029. *E-mail:* info@rafaelcorrea.com. *Website:* www.presidencia.gov.ec (office); www.rafaelcorrea.com.

CORREIA, Carlos; Guinea-Bissau politician; b. 6 Nov. 1933; mem. Partido Africano da Independência da Guiné e Cabo Verde (PAIGC)–1999; fmr Minister of State for Rural Devt and Agric.; Prime Minister of Guinea-Bissau 1991–94, 1997–98, Aug.–Dec. 2008; fmr Perm. Sec. Council of State; fmr Gov. for Guinea Bissau, African Devt Bank. *Address:* c/o Office of the Prime Minister, Av. Unidade Africana, CP 137, Bissau, Guinea-Bissau.

CORRELL, A(lston) D(ayton) (Pete), MS; American paper industry executive; *Chairman Emeritus, Georgia–Pacific Corporation;* b. 28 April 1941, Brunswick, Ga; s. of Alston Dayton Correll and Elizabeth Correll (née Flippo); m. Ada Lee Fulford 1963; one s. one d.; ed Univs of Georgia and Maine; tech. service engineer, Westvaco 1963–64; instructor, Univ. of Maine (Orono) 1964–67; various positions in pulp and paper man., Weyerhaeuser Co. 1967–77; Div. Pres., Paperboard, Mead Corpn 1977–80, Group Vice-Pres. 1980–83, Sr Vice-Pres., Forest Products 1983–88; Sr Vice-Pres., Pulp and Printing Paper, Georgia–Pacific Corpn 1988–89, Exec. Vice-Pres., Pulp and Paper 1989–91, Pres., COO 1991–93, CEO 1993–2005, Chair. 1993–2006, Chair. Emer. 2006–; mem. Bd of Dirs Univ. of Maine Pulp and Paper Foundation (Vice-Pres.), Engraph Inc., Trust Co. Bank of Atlanta, Trust Co. of Ga, Atlanta Chamber of Commerce, Atlanta Symphony Orchestra, Robert W. Woodruff Arts Center; Nat. Brotherhood Award 1991, Distinguished Alumnus Award, Univ. Georgia Terry Coll. of Business 1994, Salute to Greatness Award, The King Center 1999, Atlanta Urban League Distinguished Community Service Award 2001, Oglethorpe Sword, British American Business Group 2002, Silver Hope Award, Nat. Multiple Sclerosis Soc. 2003, CEO of the Year, Business to Business Magazine 2004, Paperloop CEO of the Year 2005; elected Business Hall of Fame, Georgia State Univ. 2005. *Address:* Georgia-Pacific Corporation, PO Box 105605, 133 Peachtree Street, NE, Atlanta, GA 30303-1808, USA (office). *Telephone:* (404) 652-4000 (office). *Fax:* (404) 230-1674 (office). *Website:* www.gp.com (office).

CORRIGAN, E(dward) Gerald, BS, MA, PhD; American banker and economist; b. 3 June 1941, Waterbury, Conn.; ed Fairfield and Fordham Univs; Group Vice-Pres. (Man. and Planning) Fed. Reserve Bank of New York 1976–80, Pres. 1985–93; Special Asst to Chair., Bd of Govs Fed. Reserve System, Washington, DC 1979–80; Pres. Fed. Reserve Bank of Minneapolis 1981–84; Chair. Basel Cttee on Banking Supervision 1991–93; Chair. Int. Advisers, Goldman Sachs & Co. 1994–96, Man. Dir 1996–, now Pnr and Man. Dir, Chair. GS USA (bank holding co.) 2008–; Chair. Russian-American Enterprise Fund 1993; Chair. Counterparty Risk Man. Policy Group 1999–; Trustee, Macalester Coll. 1981–, Jt Council for Econ. Educ. 1981–, Fairfield Univ. 1985–; mem. Trilateral Comm. 1986–; Pres. BRI 1991–; Fellow, American Acad. of Arts and Sciences 2005; Risk Man. of the Year, Global Asscn of Risk Professionals 2006. *Address:* Goldman Sachs & Co., 85 Broad Street, New York, NY 10004, USA. *Website:* www.gs.com (office).

CORRIGAN, (Francis) Edward, PhD, FRS; British mathematician and academic; *Professor of Mathematics, University of York;* b. 10 Aug. 1946, Birkenhead; s. of the late Anthony Corrigan and of Eileen Corrigan (née Ryan); m. Jane Mary Halton 1970; two s. two d.; ed St Bede's Coll., Manchester, Christ's Coll., Cambridge; Addison Wheeler Fellow, Univ. of Durham 1972–74; CERN Fellow, CERN, Geneva 1974–76; Lecturer, Univ. of Durham 1976, Reader 1987, Prof. of Math. 1992–99; Prof. of Math., Univ. of York 1999–, Head of Dept 1999–2004, 2005–07; Visiting Prof., Centre for Partide Theory, Univ. of Durham 1999–, Kyoto Univ. 2005; Visiting Research Assoc., ENS-Lyon 2005, Bologna Univ. 2005; Life mem. Clare Hall, Cambridge; Ed.-in-Chief, Journal of Physics A 1999–2003; Adrian-Daiwa Prize 1998. *Publications:* over 90 articles in learned journals and conf. proceedings. *Leisure interests:* music, squash, walking. *Address:* University of York, Department of Mathematics, Heslington, Yorks., YO10 5DD (office); Acorn Cottage, Youlthorpe, YO41 5QW, England (home). *Telephone:* (1904) 433774 (office). *Fax:* (1904) 433071 (office). *E-mail:* ec9@york.ac.uk (office). *Website:* maths.york.ac.uk (office).

CORSARO, Frank Andrew; American theatre and opera director; b. 22 Dec. 1924, New York; s. of Joseph Corsaro and Marie Corsaro (née Quarino); m.

www.worldwhoswho.com

Mary Cross Bonnie Lueders 1971; one s.; ed Yale Univ.; began career as actor 1948, appearing since in productions including Mrs. McThing, Broadway 1951; first film appearance in Rachel 1967; Dir of numerous plays including A Hatful of Rain, Broadway 1955–56, The Night of the Iguana 1961–62, Tremonisha 1975, 1600 Pennsylvania Avenue 1976, Cold Storage, Lyceum 1977–, Whoopee! 1979, Knockout 1979; directed and acted in numerous TV productions; one-man art show 1976; Dir numerous operas with New York City Opera 1958–, Washington Opera Soc. 1970–74, St Paul Opera 1971, Houston Grand Opera 1973–77, Assoc. Artistic Dir 1977–; Artistic Dir The Actors Studio 1977–85; Drama Dir Juilliard Opera Centre 1989, Artistic Dir, Vocal Arts Dept, Juilliard School 1988–2008, Faculty Emer. 2008–; Nat. Endowment for the Arts Opera Award 2009. *Theatre productions include:* La Traviata, Madame Butterfly, Faust, Manon Lescaut, A Village Romeo and Juliet, L'Incoronazione di Poppea, The Angel of Fire, Hugh the Drover, Rinaldo, Love for Three Oranges (Glyndebourne 1983), La Fanciulla del West (Deutsches Oper Berlin 1983), Rinaldo (Metropolitan Opera 1983), Fennimore and Gerda (Edinburgh Festival 1983), Where the Wild Things Are, Higgeldy, Piggeldy, Pop (Glyndebourne 1985), Alcina (Spitalfields 1985), (LA Opera Centre 1986), L'Enfant et les Sortilèges, L'Heure espagnole, Glyndebourne Festival 1987, Hansel and Gretel (Houston, Toronto, Zurich 1997–98), Kuhlhandel (Juilliard 1998). *Publications include:* L'histoire du soldat (adaptation), La Bohème (adaptation), A Piece of Blue Sky (play), Maverik 1978, Libretto: Before Breakfast (music by Thomas Pasatieri), Libretto: Heloise and Abelard (music by Steven Paulus), Kunma (novel). *Leisure interests:* painting, piano playing, writing. *Address:* c/o Columbia Artists Management Inc., 1790 Broadway, New York, NY 10019-1412, USA (office).

CORSTENS, Geert J.M., PhD; Dutch judge; *President, Supreme Court of the Netherlands;* b. 1 Feb. 1946, Helvoirt; m. Madeleine Mignot; three d.; ed Radboud Univ., Nijmegen, Univ. of Amsterdam; Asst Public Prosecutor, Amsterdam 1973–1975; Law Clerk, Dist Court of Amsterdam 1975–1976; lawyer, Goudsmit & Branbergen (law firm), Amsterdam 1976–1977; Public Prosecutor, Arnhem 1977–1981; Prof. of Criminal law, Catholic Univ. Nijmegen, 1982–1995; Visiting Prof., Univ. of Poitiers 1986; Justice, Supreme Court of the Netherlands 1995–2006, Vice-Pres. 2006–2008, Pres. 2008–; Pres. Advisory Bd Nat. Research Project on Criminal Procedure 1998–2003, on the Quality of Criminal Judgements 2005–; mem. Dutch Law Asscn 1983–86, Nat. Cttee for the Reform of Criminal Procedure 1989–93; mem. Bd of Int. Advisors, Int. Judicial Acad., Washington, DC 2001–; mem. Editorial Bd Nederlands Juristenblad 2004–06; Officier, l'Ordre des Palmes académiques, Chevalier, Légion d'honneur. *Publications:* European Criminal Law (with Jean Pradel) 2002, Het Nederlands strafprocesrecht 2005; 300 contribs to books and legal journals. *Address:* Hoge Raad der Nederlanden, PO Box 20303, 2500 EH The Hague, Netherlands (office). *Telephone:* (70) 3611237 (office). *Fax:* (70) 3658700 (office). *E-mail:* g.corstens@hogeraad.nl (office). *Website:* www.hogeraad.nl (office).

CORT, Errol; Antigua and Barbuda politician, economist and lawyer; *Minister of National Security and Labour;* m.; c.; ed trained as economist and attorney; Attorney-Gen. of Antigua and Barbuda 1999–2001; elected mem. Parl. for St John's E; Minister of Finance, Econ. Devt and Planning 2004–09, of Nat. Security and Labour 2009–. *Address:* Ministry of National Security and Labour, Government Office Complex, Parliament Drive, St John's, Antigua (office).

CORTAZZI, Sir (Henry Arthur) Hugh, Kt, GCMG, MA; British diplomatist (retd); b. 2 May 1924, Sedbergh, Yorks. (now Cumbria); s. of F. E. M. Cortazzi and M. Cortazzi; m. Elizabeth Esther Montagu 1956; one s. two d.; ed Sedbergh School, Univs of St Andrews and London; served in RAF 1943–48; joined Foreign Office 1949; Third Sec., Singapore 1950–51; Second Sec., Tokyo 1951–54; Foreign Office, London 1954–58; First Sec., Bonn 1958–60, Tokyo 1961–65 (Head of Chancery 1963); Foreign Office 1965–66; Counsellor (Commercial), Tokyo 1966–70; Royal Coll. of Defence Studies 1971; Minister (Commercial), Washington, DC 1972–75; Deputy Under-Sec. of State FCO 1975–80; Amb. to Japan 1980–84 (retd); apptd Dir Hill Samuel and Co. Ltd (later Hill Samuel Bank Ltd) 1984–91, Foreign and Colonial Pacific Investment Trust 1984–98, G. T. Japan Investment Trust 1984–99, Thornton Pacific Investment Trust SA 1986–2002; Adviser to Mitsukoshi Dept Store, Tokyo, Japan 1984–2004; Sr Adviser, NEC Corpn, Japan 1992–98, Dai-Ichi Kangyo Bank, Japan 1992–99, Bank of Kyoto 1992–99, Wilde Sapte, solicitors 1992–99; mem. Econ. and Social Research Council 1984–90; Hon. Fellow, Robinson Coll., Cambridge 1988; Grand Cordon, Order of the Sacred Treasure (Japan) 1995; Hon. DUniv (Stirling) 1988, Hon. DLitt (East Anglia) 2006; Yamagata Banto Prize, Osaka 1990. *Publications:* trans. of Japanese short stories by Keita Genji 1972, A Diplomat's Wife in Japan: Sketches at the Turn of the Century (ed.) 1982, Isles of Gold: Antique Maps of Japan 1983, Higashi No Shimaguni, Nishi No Shimaguni 1984, Dr. Willis in Japan (1862–1877) 1985, Mitford's Japan (ed.) 1985, Zoku Higashi No Shimaguni, Nishi No Shimaguni (ed.) 1987, Victorians in Japan: In and Around the Treaty Ports 1987, Kipling's Japan (ed.) 1988, The Japanese Achievement, A Short History of Japan and Japanese Culture 1990, Britain and Japan 1859–1991: Themes and Personalities 1991, A British Artist in Meiji Japan (ed.) 1991, Building Japan 1868–1876 1991, Modern Japan: A Concise Survey 1993, Caught In Time: Japan (ed.) 1995, Japan and Back and Places Elsewhere: A Memoir 1998, Japan Experiences (ed.) 2001, Britain and Japan: Biographical Portraits Vol. IV (ed.) 2002, Vol. V (ed.) 2004, Vol. VI (ed.) 2007, British Envoys in Japan 1859–1972 (ed.) 2004, The Thames and I : A Memoir by the Crown Prince of Japan (trans.) 2007. *Leisure interests:* the arts, literature, Japanese studies. *Address:* Ballsocks, Vines Cross, Heathfield, East Sussex, TN21 9ET, England (home).

CORTES, Joaquín; Spanish dancer and actor; b. 22 Feb. 1969, Córdoba; joined Spanish Nat. Ballet 1985, Prin. Dancer 1987–90; f. Joaquín Cortés Flamenco Ballet 1992; now appears in own shows, blending gypsy dancing, jazz blues and classical ballet; appeared in Pedro Almodóvar's film The Flower Of My Secret and Carlos Saura's film Flamenco; launched Stop Anti-Gypsyism campaign 2000; apptd Amb. for the Roma people to EU 2007. *Films include:* Flamenco (de Carlos Saura) 1995, Flor de mi secreto, La 1995, Gitano 2000, Vaniglia e cioccolato 2004. *Television includes:* Sabadabada (series) 1981, Hola Raffaella! (series) 1992. *Address:* C/ Alcalá, 155. E.Izda. 2ºC, Madrid, Spain. *Telephone:* (91) 7580350. *Fax:* (91) 5595245.

CORTINA DE ALCOCER, Alfonso, BEng; Spanish business executive; *President, Fundación Repsol;* b. 13 March 1944, Madrid; ed Univ. of Madrid; Vice-Pres. Sociedad Hispano Hipotecario 1981–84; Vice-Pres. Cementera Portland Valderrivas 1984–93, Pres. 1993–96; CEO Repsol YPF 1996–2004, Pres. Fundación Repsol 2004–; Chair. Inmobiliaria Colonial 2005–06; Vice Chair. Rothschild Europe and Sr Adviser for Spain and Latin America and mem. European Advisory Council, Rothschild; Sr Adviser Texas Pacific Group, Madrid 2007–; mem. Exec. Cttee Foundation for Technological Innovation; mem. Bd of Dirs Mutua Madrileña Automovilística Sociedad de Seguros a Prima Fija, Recoletos Grupo de Comunicación SA; mem. Int. Advisory Bd and Jt Advisory Council, Allianz Companies; mem. Advisory Cttee Altamar Private Equity; mem. Trilateral Comm. *Address:* Fundación Repsol, Velázquez, 166, 28002 Madrid, Spain. *Telephone:* (91) 3489079. *Fax:* (91) 3489370. *E-mail:* fundacion@fundacion.repsolypf.org.

CORWIN, Norman; American writer, producer, director and academic; *Professor, School of Journalism, University of Southern California;* b. 3 May 1910, Boston, Mass.; s. of Samuel H. Corwin and Rose Ober; m. Katherine Locke 1947; one s. one d.; Newspaperman 1929–38; writer, dir, producer for CBS 1938–48; Chief, Special Projects, UN Radio 1949–53; mem. Faculty of Theatre Arts, UCLA; Regents Lecturer, Univ. of Calif., Santa Barbara; Visiting Prof., School of Journalism, Univ. of Southern Calif. 1981, Prof. 1989–; Writer-in-Residence, Univ. of N Carolina; Patten Memorial Lecturer, Indiana Univ. 1981; Co-Chair. Scholarship Cttee of Acad. of Motion Picture Arts and Sciences, Chair. Writers Exec. Cttee, mem. Bd of Govs 1979–88, Chair. Documentary Awards Comm. 1967–82, 1985–94, Sec. Acad. Foundation 1983–88; mem. Bd of Dirs Writers Guild of America, Selden Ring Journalism Award 1994–, Bette Davis Foundation 1997–; Trustee Filmex; writer, dir and host Norman Corwin Presents (TV series), Westinghouse Broadcasting Co.; host, More by Corwin (radio series), Nat. Public Radio 1996–97; Sec. Acad. of Arts and Sciences Foundation 1983; First Vice-Pres. Acad. of Motion Picture Arts and Sciences 1988; Stasheff Lecturer, Univ. of Mich. 1984; papers acquired by Thousand Oaks Library Foundation 1993; subject of 90-minute TV documentary 1995; three hon. degrees; Peabody Medal, Edward Bok Medal, Award of American Acad. of Arts and Sciences 1942, American Newspaper Guild Page One Award 1944, 1945, Wendell Wilkie One-World Award 1946, PEN Award 1986, inducted Radio Hall of Fame 1993, Dupont Award, Columbia Univ. 1996, ICON Award, Bradbury Creativity Award 2001 and other awards. *Films:* The Blue Veil, The Grand Design, Lust for Life, The Story of Ruth, Yamashita, The Tiger of Malaya, Scandal at Scourie. *Cantatas:* The Golden Door, Yes Speak Out Yes (commissioned by UN 1968). *Stage plays:* The Rivalry, The World of Carl Sandburg, The Hyphen, Cervantes, Together Tonight 1975, The Strange Affliction 1995, Fifty Years After 14 August (on surrender of Japan) 1995. *Radio:* No Love Lost, The Curse of 589, The Secretariat 1998, Our Lady of the Freedoms and Some of Her Friends, The Writer with the Lame Left Hand (Cervantes) 1999, Memos to a New Millennium 2000, College Collage 2002. *Publications:* They Fly through the Air 1939, Thirteen by Corwin 1942, More by Corwin 1944, On a Note of Triumph (both as a book and album of recordings) 1945, Untitled and Other Dramas 1947, Dog in the Sky 1952, Overkill and Megalove 1962, Prayer for the 70's 1969, Holes in a Stained Glass Window 1978, Jerusalem Printout 1978, Greater than the Bomb 1981, A Date with Sandburg 1981, Trivializing America 1984, Network at Fifty 1984, CONartist 1993, Norman Corwin's Letters 1994, Years of the Electric Ear 1994, Limericks, Freebies and Never Once Drunk 1999, Message for the Millennium 2000, The Huntington 2002. *Leisure interests:* mineralogy, music, painting, chess. *Address:* School of Journalism, ASC 325, University of Southern California, University Park, Los Angeles, CA 90089-1695 (office); Suite 302, 1840 Fairburn Avenue, Los Angeles, CA 90025-4958, USA (home). *Telephone:* (213) 740-3914; (310) 475-3179 (office). *Fax:* (310) 475-3179 (office). *E-mail:* corwin@usc.edu (office). *Website:* annenberg.usc.edu (office).

CORY, Hon. Peter deCarteret, CC, CD, BA; Canadian judge; b. 25 Oct. 1925, Windsor, Ont.; s. of Andrew Cory and Mildred Cory (née Beresford Howe); m. 1st Edith Nash 1947 (died); three s.; m. Mary Elizabeth Dayton 2007; three step-c.; ed Univ. of Western Ontario, Osgoode Hall Law School; pilot, 6th Bomber Group, RCAF 1943–46; called to Bar of Ont. 1950; apptd QC 1963; Bencher, Law Soc. of Upper Canada 1971–74; Trial Div., Supreme Court of Canada 1974; apptd to Court of Appeal, Ont. 1981; apptd to Supreme Court of Canada 1989, Judge 1989–99 (retd); apptd by British and Irish Govts to lead investigations into suspected collusion of intelligence services and IRA in six cross-border Irish killings 2002; fmr Pres. Advocates Soc., York Co. Law Asscn; fmr Chair. Ont. Civil Liberties Section, Canadian Bar Asscn, fmr mem. Council. *Leisure interests:* tennis, squash, sailing, canoeing. *Address:* POB 50, First Canadian Place, Toronto, ON M5X 1B8, Canada (office). *Telephone:* (416) 862-6732 (office). (416) 973-8324. *E-mail:* pcory@osier.com (office).

CORY, Suzanne, AC, PhD, FAA, FRS; Australian biochemist, geneticist and academic; *Director, Walter and Eliza Hall Institute of Medical Research, Joint Head, Molecular Genetics of Cancer Division, and Professor of Medical Biology, University of Melbourne;* b. 11 March 1942, Melbourne; m. Dr Jerry

McKee Adams; two d.; ed Canterbury Girls' Secondary School, Univ. High School, Univ. of Melbourne, MRC Laboratory of Molecular Biology, Cambridge, UK; Post-doctoral Fellow, Univ. of Geneva, Switzerland 1969–71; Queen Elizabeth II Fellow, The Walter and Eliza Hall Inst. of Medical Research, Melbourne 1971–74, Roche Fellow 1974–76, Research Fellow 1977, Sr Research Fellow 1978–83, Principal Research Fellow 1984–88, NHMRC Sr Principal Research Fellow and Jt Head, Molecular Genetics of Cancer Div. 1988–96, Dir Walter and Eliza Hall Inst. 1996–; Int. Research Scholar, Howard Hughes Medical Inst. 1992–97; Research Prof. of Molecular Oncology, Univ. of Melbourne 1993–96, Prof. of Medical Biology 1996–; Dir Bio21 Australia Ltd; mem. Bd CSIRO 2002–; mem. Knowledge, Innovation, Science and Eng Council of Victorian Govt, Council of The Cancer Council Victoria, Cttee for Melbourne Bd, Bd of Man. of CRC for Cellular Growth Factors, Council of Australian Acad. of Science; Foreign mem. NAS; Assoc. Foreign mem. Acad. des Sciences; Fellow, Royal Soc. of Victoria 1997; hon. mem. American Asscn for Immunology; Foreign Hon. mem. American Acad. of Arts and Sciences; David Syme Prize, Univ. of Melbourne 1982, Charles S. Mott Prize, General Motors Cancer Research Foundation (jtly) 1988, Avon Australia Spirit of Achievement Award 1992, Lemberg Medal, Australian Soc. for Biochemistry and Molecular Biology 1995, Burnet Lecturer, Australian Acad. of Science 1997, Australia Prize 1998, L'Oreal-UNESCO Women in Science Award 2001. *Publications:* numerous articles in scientific journals. *Address:* The Walter and Eliza Hall Institute of Medical Research, 1G Royal Parade, Parkville Vic. 3050, Australia (office). *Telephone:* (3) 9345-2551 (office). *Fax:* (3) 9345-2508 (office). *E-mail:* cory@wehi.edu.au (office). *Website:* www.wehi.edu.au (office).

CORZINE, Jon Stevens, MBA; American politician, business executive and state official; *Governor of New Jersey;* b. 1 Jan. 1947, Taylorville, Ill.; s. of Roy Allen Corzine and Nancy June Corzine (née Hedrick); m. Joanne Dougherty 1968 (divorced 2003); two s. one d.; ed Univs of Chicago and Ill.; bond officer, Continental Ill. Nat. Bank 1970; Asst Vice-Pres. BancOhio Corpn 1974–75; joined Goldman, Sachs & Co. 1975, Vice-Pres. 1977, Pnr 1980–98, man. consultant 1985–94, Co-Head, Fixed Income Div. 1988–94, Sr Pnr and Chair. Man. Cttee, CEO 1994–99; Senator from NJ 2001–05, mem. Foreign Relations Cttee; Gov. of NJ 2005–; mem. Bd of Dirs NY Philharmonic 1996–, Public Securities Asscn (Vice-Chair. 1985, Chair. 1986). *Address:* Office of the Governor, POB 001, Trenton, NJ 08625, USA (office). *Telephone:* (609) 292-6000 (office). *Website:* www.state.nj.us/governor (office).

COSBY, William (Bill) H., Jr, MA, EdD; American actor; b. 12 July 1937, Philadelphia; s. of William Cosby and Anna Cosby; m. Camille Hanks 1964; five c. (one s. deceased); ed Temple Univ. and Univ. of Mass.; served USNR 1956–60; Pres. Rhythm and Blues Hall of Fame 1968–; mem. Bd of Dirs Sickle Cell Anemia Foundation, United Negro Coll. Fund, Operation PUSH; Hon. MusD, Berklee Coll. of Music 2004; recipient of four Emmy Awards and eight Grammy Awards, Bob Hope Humanitarian Award, Acad. of TV Arts and Sciences 2003; named to Hall of Fame, Acad. of TV Arts and Sciences 1994, to Nat. Asscn for the Advancement of Colored People Image Awards Hall of Fame 2007, Mark Twain Prize for American Humor 2009. *Films include:* Hickey and Boggs 1972, Man and Boy 1972, Uptown Saturday Night 1974, Let's Do It Again 1975, Mother, Jugs and Speed 1976, Aesop's Fables, A Piece of Action 1977, California Suite 1978, Devil and Max Devlin 1979, Leonard: Part VI 1987, Ghost Dad 1990, The Meteor Man 1993, Jack 1996. *Television:* The Bill Cosby Show 1969, 1972–73, I Spy, The Cosby Show 1984–92, Cosby Mystery Series 1994–; recitals include: Revenge, To Russell, My Brother, With Whom I Slept, Top Secret, 200 M.P.H., Why Is There Air, Wonderfulness, It's True, It's True, Bill Cosby is a Very Funny Fellow: Right, I Started Out as a Child, 8:15, 12:15, Hungry, Reunion 1982, Bill Cosby . . . Himself 1983, Those of You With or Without Children, You'll Understand; Exec. Producer A Different Kind of World (TV series) 1987–93; Presenter Kids Say the Darndest Things 1998–, As I Was Saying 1997. *Publications:* The Wit and Wisdom of Fat Albert 1973, Bill Cosby's Personal Guide to Power Tennis, Fatherhood 1986, Time Flies 1988, Love and Marriage 1989, Childhood 1991, Little Bill Series 1999, Congratulations! Now What? 1999, Friends of a Feather (juvenile). *Address:* c/o William Morris Agency, 1 William Morris Place, Beverly Hills, CA 90212; c/o The Brokaw Co., 9255 Sunset Boulevard, Los Angeles, CA 90069, USA.

COSENZA JIMENEZ, Luis, BS, PhD; Honduran engineer, development banker, politician and academic; *Hewlett Visiting Fellow for Public Policy, Kellogg Institute for International Studies, University of Notre Dame;* ed Univ. of Notre Dame, USA; worked for Empresa Nacional De Energía Eléctrica (state-owned power utility) becoming CEO 1976; Energy Specialist, IDB 1981–89; Prin. Power Engineer responsible for east Africa and much of central American region, World Bank 1989; campaign man. for Ricardo Maduro (Arriba Honduras cand.) during presidential election in 2000; Minister of the Presidency 2002–05; Exec. Dir for Belize, Costa Rica, El Salvador, Guatemala, Honduras and Nicaragua, IDB 2005–06; Visiting Fellow, Kellogg Inst. for Int. Studies, Univ. of Notre Dame 2006–07, Hewlett Visiting Fellow for Public Policy 2008–; mem. Bd of Advisors Concern Yourself, Inc.; fmr Exec. Pres. Honduran Foundation for Investment and Promotion of Exports (FIDES). *Address:* Kellogg Institute for International Studies, 130 Hesburgh Center, Notre Dame, IN 46556, USA (office). *Telephone:* (574) 631-6580 (office). *Fax:* (574) 631-6717 (office). *Website:* kellogg.nd.edu (office).

COSGRAVE, Liam; Irish politician; b. 13 April 1920, Templeogue, Co. Dublin; s. of the late William T. Cosgrave (Pres. of the Exec. Council of the Irish Free State 1922–32) and Louise Flanagan; m. Vera Osborne 1952; two s. one d.; ed Synge Street Christian Brothers' Schools, Dublin, St Vincent's Coll., Castleknock, Co. Dublin and Kings Inns; called to the Bar 1943; SC 1958; served in army; TD, Dublin Co. 1943–48, Dún Laoghaire and Rathdown 1948–81; Leader, Fine Gael Party 1965–77; Parl. Sec. to the Prime Minister and to Minister for Industry and Commerce 1948–51; Minister for External Affairs 1954–57; Prime Minister 1973–77; Minister for Defence 1976; Chair. and Leader of first Irish Del. to UN Gen. Ass. 1956; Kt Grand Cross of Pius IX (Ordine Piano); Hon. LLD (Duquesne Univ., St John's Univ.) 1956, (De Paul Univ.) 1958, (Nat. Univ. of Ireland and Univ. of Dublin) 1974. *Address:* Beechpark, Templeogue, Co. Dublin, Ireland.

COSGROVE, Art, BA, PhD; Irish historian, academic, barrister and fmr university president; b. 1 June 1940, Newry, Co. Down, NI; m. Emer Sweeney 1968; nine c.; ed Abbey Christian Brothers School, Newry, Co. Down, NI and Queen's Univ., Belfast, NI; mem. academic staff, Univ. Coll. Dublin 1963–94, Sr Lecturer, Dept of Medieval History 1976, Assoc. Prof. and Acting Head of Dept 1990, apptd Chair. Combined Depts of History 1991, Pres. Univ. Coll. Dublin 1994–2003; mem. Bd of Dirs racecaller.com; Visiting Prof., History Dept, Univ. of Kansas 1974; Hon. LLD (Queen's Univ., Belfast) 1995. *Publications:* Studies in Irish History presented to R. D. Edwards (jtly) 1979, Late Medieval Ireland 1370–1541 1981, Parliament and Community (jtly) 1981, Marriage in Ireland 1985, A New History of Ireland II: Medieval Ireland 1169–1534 1987, Dublin Through the Ages 1988. *Website:* www.racecaller.com.

ĆOSIĆ, Dobrica; Serbian writer and politician; b. 29 Dec. 1921, Velika Drenova; m. Božica Ćosić; one d.; ed Belgrade Univ., Higher Party School; war service 1941–45; worked as journalist, then as freelance writer; corresp. mem. Serbian Acad. of Arts and Sciences 1970, mem. 1976; left League of Communists of Yugoslavia (LCY), prosecuted; resumed active political activity 1980s; Pres. of Repub. of Yugoslavia 1992–93. *Publications:* The Sun is Far 1951, Roots 1954, Sections 1961, Fairy Tale 1965, The Time of Death (Vols 1–4) 1972–79, The Time of Evil: Sinner (Vols 1–4) 1985, Apostate 1986, Believer 1990, The Time of Power 1995, Kosovo; studies and essays: Hope and Fear 2001, Real and Possible 2001, Serbian Question (Vols 1–4) 2002, Writer's Notes (Vols 1–4) 2002. *Address:* Serbian Academy of Sciences and Arts, Knez Mikhailova Str. 35, Belgrade (office); Branka Djonovića 6, Belgrade, Serbia (home). *Telephone:* (11) 3342400 (office); (11) 663437 (home). (11) 182825*E-mail:* sasapres@bib.sanu.ac.yu (office).

COŞKUN, Ali, MSc; Turkish politician and business executive; b. 1939, Kemaliye, Erzincan; m.; two c.; ed Faculty of Electrical Eng, Yildiz Tech. Univ., Wirtschaft Academie, Hamburg, Germany; fmr Pres. Admin. Bd, Ihlas Finance Inst. and Bisan Bicycle Industry and Commerce; fmr Deputy Pres. Istanbul Chamber of Commerce; fmr Pres. Turkish Union of Chambers and Commodities Exchanges (TOBB); fmr Deputy Pres. Islamic Countries Union of Chambers; mem. Parl. (ANAP) for Istanbul Constituency 1995–2005, Chair. Nat. Defense Comm., mem. Plan and Budget Comm., Industry, Trade, Energy and Technology Comm.; Minister of Industry and Commerce 2005–07; Hon. Pres. TOBB; Hon. mem. Ass. of İstanbul Chamber Industry, Ass. of Ankara Chamber of Trade, Ass. of Turkish Exporters. *Publication:* Energy Problems of Turkey and Solutions 1986. *Address:* Öğretmenler Cad. Usta Apt. A Blok 1/1, 06140Çukurambar Ankara, Turkey. *Telephone:* (312) 2857037. *Fax:* (312) 2857034. *E-mail:* bilgi@alicoskun.com.tr. *Website:* www.alicoskun.com.tr.

COSMOS, Jean; French playwright; b. (Jean Louis Gaudrat), 14 June 1923, Paris; s. of Albert Gaudrat and Maria Maillebuau; m. Alice Jarrousse 1948; one s. two d.; ed Inst. St Nicholas, Igny, Coll. Jean-Baptiste Say, Paris; songwriter 1945–50, writer for radio 1952–60, for TV 1964–; mem. Comm. Soc. des auteurs dramatiques 1971–; co-librettist Goya 1996 (opera); Chevalier Légion d'honneur, Officier des Arts et des Lettres; Soc. des auteurs et compositeurs prizes 1970. *Plays:* author or adapter of numerous plays for the theatre including la Fille du roi 1952, Au jour le jour 1952, les Grenadiers de la reine 1957, Macbeth 1959, 1965, le Manteau 1963, la Vie et la Mort du roi Jean 1964, Arden de Faversham 1964, Monsieur Alexandre 1965, la Bataille de Lobositz 1969, Major Barbara 1970, le Marchand de Venise 1971, Sainte Jeanne des Abattoirs 1972, Ce sacré Bonheur 1987; author of numerous TV plays including les Oranges (Albert Ollivier prize) 1964, le Pacte 1966, Un homme, un cheval 1968, la Pomme oubliée (after Jean Anglade), l'Ingénu (after Voltaire), Bonsoir Léon, la Tête à l'envers, le Trêve, le Coup Monté, Aide-toi, Julien Fontanes, magistrat (TV Series 1980–89), La Dictée 1984; with Jean Chatenêt: 16 à Kerbriant, Ardéchois coeur fidèle (Critics' choice) 1975, Les Yeux Bleus, la Lumière des Justes (after Henri Troyat); with Gilles Perrault: le Secret des dieux, la Filière, Fabien de la Drôme, seven-part serial of Julien Fontanes, Magistrat, regular contrib. to les Cinq dernières minutes. *Films include:* Bonjour toubib 1959 La vie et rien d'autre 1989, Le Colonel Chabert 1994, La fille de d'Artagnan 1994, Capitaine Conan 1996, Le bossu 1997, Laissez-passer 2002, Effroyables jardins 2003, Fanfan la tulipe 2003, Agents secrets 2004, Aurore 2006, Le Grand Meaulnes 2006, Michou d'Auber 2007, Dialogue avec mon jardinier 2007. *Address:* c/o Artmédia, 20 avenue Rapp, 75007 Paris (office); 57 rue de Versailles, 92410 Ville d'Avray, France (home). *Telephone:* 1-43-17-33-00 (office). *E-mail:* info@artmedia.fr (office).

COSSART, Pascale, MSc, PhD; French bacteriologist and academic; *Director of Cell Biology and Infection Department, Institut Pasteur;* ed Lille Univ., Georgetown Univ., Washington, DC, USA, Univ. of Paris VII; Asst, Univ. Inst. Tech., Lille; Fellow, Georgetown Univ. 1970–71; Prof., Royal School of Medicine, Laos 1974–75; joined Institut Pasteur, Paris 1972, Head of Listeria Molecular Genetics Lab. 1991–94, Prof. and Head of Bacterial-Cellular Interactions Unit 1994, Dir Cell Biology and Infection Dept 2006–; Int. Research Scholar, Howard Hughes Medical Inst. 2000–; mem. Scientific Advisory Bd at Research Centre for Infectious Diseases, Würzburg Univ., Germany 2000–, at Biozentrum, Univ., Basel, Switzerland 2002–; mem. Scientific Council, Ville de Paris 2003–, Nat. Ethics Consultative Cttee 2003, EMBO Course and Workshop Cttee 1999–2004, Chair. 2001–04; mem. Scientific Council, Institut Pasteur 2002–06, Pres. 2003–05; mem. Scientific

Council, CNRS 2005–06, Soc. Francaise de Microbiologie 1977–, American Soc. for Microbiology 1987, American Soc. for Cell Biology 1993–, Soc. Francaise de Biologie Cellulaire 2007–, Soc. Francaise de Biochimie et de Biologie Moléculaire 2007–; mem. Cttee de Pilotage, Agence Nat. pour la Recherche 2006–; mem. editorial bds of several journals; mem. Deutsche Akad. der Naturforscher Leopoldina, Acad. des Sciences 2002–, American Acad. of Microbiology 2004; Chevalier, Légion d'honneur 1998, Officier 2007, Officier de l'Ordre National du Mérite 2002; UNESCO Carlos Finlay Prize 1995, Louis Rapkin Award 1997, Richard Lounsbery Prize, L'Oreal-UNESCO Women in Science Award 1998, Louis Pasteur Gold Medal, Swedish Soc. of Medicine 2000, Nestle Prize 2000, Valade Senior Price, Fondation de France 2003, INSERM Prize of Fundamental Research 2005, Glaxo Smith Kline Int. Mem. of the Year Award 2007, Robert Koch Prize 2007. *Publications:* numerous publs in scientific journals. *Address:* Institut Pasteur, 25–28 rue du Dr Roux, 75015 Paris, France (office). *Telephone:* 1-45-68-80-00 (office). *E-mail:* pcossart@pasteur.fr (office). *Website:* www.pasteur.fr (office).

COSSIGA, Francesco, LLD; Italian politician; *Life Senator;* b. 26 July 1928, Sassari; two s.; joined Democrazia Cristiana 1945, Provincial Sec. 1956–58, mem. Nat. Council 1956–85; mem. Parl. for Sassari 1958–85; Under-Sec. of State for Defence 1966–70; Minister for Public Admin. 1974–76, of the Interior 1976–78; Prime Minister 1979–80; Pres. of Senate 1983–85; Pres. of Italy 1985–92; Life-term Senator (Ind. Group) 1992–; Dr hc (Oxford) 1987. *Publications:* Italiani sono Sempre gli Altri, Per Carita di Patria. *Address:* c/o Senato, Piazza Madama, 00186 Rome, Italy. *Telephone:* (6) 6706-20-12 (office). *Fax:* (6) 6706-36-58 (office). *E-mail:* f.cossiga@senato.it (office).

COSSONS, Sir Neil, Kt, OBE, MA, FSA; British foundation executive; b. 15 Jan. 1939, Nottingham; s. of Arthur Cossons and Evelyn Cossons (née Bettle); m. Veronica Edwards 1965; two s. one d.; ed Henry Mellish Grammar School, Nottingham, Univ. of Liverpool; Curator of Tech., Bristol City Museum 1964; Deputy Dir, City of Liverpool Museums 1969; Dir Ironbridge Gorge Museum 1971; Dir Nat. Maritime Museum, Greenwich 1983; Dir Science Museum, London 1986–2000; Commr Historic Buildings and Monuments Comm. for England (English Heritage) 1989–95, 1999–2000, Chair. 2000–07; Pres. Royal Geographical Soc. 2003–; mem. Royal Coll. of Art Council 1989–, Design Council 1990–94, British Waterways Bd 1995–2001; Pres. European Museum Forum 2001–; mem. Council Foundation for Mfg and Industry 1993–98; Fellow and Past Pres. of the Museums Asscn; Comité Scientifique, Conservatoire Nat. des Arts et Métiers 1991–2000; mem. of bd Liverpool Culture Co.; Hon. Fellow, RCA; Hon. Companion Royal Aeronautical Soc. 1996; Hon. mem. Soc. of Chemical Industry 2002; Hon. FRIBA 2002; Hon. DSocSc (Birmingham) 1979; Hon. DUniv (Open Univ.) 1984, (Sheffield Hallam) 1995, (York) 1998; Hon. DLitt (Liverpool) 1989, (Bradford) 1991, (Nottingham Trent) 1994, (Univ. of West of England) 1995, (Bath) 1997, (Greenwich) 2004; Hon. DSc (Leicester) 1995, (Nottingham) 2000; Hon. DArts (De Montfort) 1997; Norton Medlicott Medal, Historical Asscn 1991, Pres.'s Medal, Royal Acad. of Eng 1993. *Publications:* Industrial Archaeology of the Bristol Region (with R. A. Buchanan) 1968, Industrial Archaeology 1975, Transactions of the First International Congress on the Conservation of Industrial Monuments (ed.) 1975, Rees's Manufacturing Industry (ed.) 1975, Ironbridge—Landscape of Industry (with H. Sowden) 1977, The Iron Bridge – Symbol of the Industrial Revolution (with B.S. Trinder) 1979, The Management of Change in Museums (ed.) 1985, Making of the Modern World (ed.) 1992, Perspectives on Industrial Archaeology (ed.) 2000. *Leisure interests:* travel, industrial archaeology. *Address:* c/o English Heritage, 23 Savile Row, London, W1S 2ET (office); The Old Rectory, Rushbury, Shropshire, SY6 7EB, England (home). *E-mail:* nc@cossons.org.uk (office).

COSTA, Antonio; Portuguese lawyer and politician; *Mayor of Lisbon;* b. 17 July 1961; s. of Orlando da Costa and Maria Antónia Palla; m.; two c.; ed Univ. of Lisbon; mem. Municipal Ass. of Lisbon 1982–93; Deputy Ass. of Repub. 1991–2007, mem. Partido Socialista, Pres. Parl. Group 2002–04; Sec. of State for Parl. Affairs 1995–97; Govt Rep. Expo '98 1997–98; Minister of Justice 1999–2002; MEP 2004–05, Vice-Pres. European Parl.; Minister of State and Internal Admin 2005–07; Mayor of Lisbon 2007–. *Address:* Câmara Municipal de Lisboa, Paços do Concelho -Praça do Município, 1100-365 Lisbon, Portugal (office). *Telephone:* (21) 3227000 (office). *Fax:* (21) 3227008 (office). *E-mail:* geral@cm-lisboa.pt (office). *Website:* www.cm-lisboa.pt (office).

COSTA, Antonio Maria, PhD; Italian UN official and economist; *Executive Director, Office on Drugs and Crime and Director-General, United Nations, Vienna;* b. 16 June 1941, Mondovi; s. of Francesco Costa and Maria Costa; m. Patricia Agnes Wallace 1971; two s. one d.; ed Univ. of California, Berkeley, Acad. of Sciences of the USSR and Univ. of Turin; Visiting Prof. of Econs, Moscow Univ. and Acad. of Sciences of the USSR 1965–67; Instructor of Econs, Univ. of Calif., Berkeley 1968–70; Prof. of Econs, New York Univ., 1976–83; Sr Econ. Adviser to the UN 1970–83; Special Counsellor in Econs to the Sec.-Gen. of OECD 1983–87; Dir Gen. Econ. and Financial Affairs, EC 1987–92; Sec.-Gen. EBRD, London, UK 1992–2001; Dir-Gen. UN Office on Drugs and Crime (fmrly UN Office for Drug Control and Crime Prevention), Vienna, Austria 2002–. *Publications:* articles on econs and politics. *Leisure interest:* work. *Address:* United Nations Office on Drugs and Crime, Vienna International Centre, PO Box 500, 1400 Vienna, Austria. *Telephone:* (1) 26060-0 (office). *Fax:* (1) 26060-5819 (office). *E-mail:* unodc@unodc.org (office). *Website:* www.unodc.org (office).

COSTA, Francisco; Brazilian fashion designer; *Creative Director, Calvin Klein Collection for Women, Calvin Klein Inc.;* b. 1969; fmr designer for Gucci, Balmain and Oscar de la Renta; joined Calvin Klein 2002, Design Dir for Womenswear (following sale of co. to Phillips-Van Heusen and retirement of Calvin Klein as Design Dir) 2003–, debut collection at NY Fashion Week 2003.

Address: Calvin Klein Inc., 205 West 39th Street, New York, NY 10018, USA (office).

COSTA, Gabriel Arcanjo Ferreira da, BLL; São Tomé and Príncipe politician, lawyer and diplomatist; b. 11 Dec. 1954; lawyer and magistrate; mem. Parl. (Juventude Movimento Libertação de São Tomé e Príncipe) in first Ass. following nat. independence 1975–98; Counsellor for Legal and Political Affairs to Pres. Trovoada 1991–95, Head of Cabinet of Pres. 1996–98; State Minister of Justice, Admin. Reform and Local Admin –1998; Special Rep. of Exec. of CPLP for Guinea-Bissau 1998–2000; Amb. to Portugal, Morocco and Spain 2000–02; Prime Minister of São Tomé e Príncipe March–Oct. 2002; mem. Movimento de Libertação de São Tomé e Príncipe—Partido Social Democrata. *Address:* c/o Movimento de Libertação de São Tomé e Príncipe—Partido Social Democrata, Estrada Riboque, Edif. Sede do MLSTP, São Tomé, São Tomé e Príncipe (office).

COSTA, Jean-Paul, LLM, PhD; French judge; *President, European Court of Human Rights;* b. 3 Nov. 1941, Tunis, Tunisia; ed Inst. of Political Studies, Nat. School of Man., Paris; clerk, Council of State 1966, Advisor, Judicial Section 1966–71, 1977–80, 1987–89, Assessor of Sub-section of Judicial Section 1989–93, Pres. of Sub-section of Judicial Section 1993–98; Political Sec. to Minister of Educ. 1981–84; Assoc. Prof., Orléans Univ. 1989–98, Panthéon-Sorbonne Univ. 1992–98; Judge, European Court of Human Rights 1998–, Vice-Pres. 2001–07, Pres. 2007–. *Address:* Office of the President, European Court of Human Rights, Council of Europe, 67075 Strasbourg, France (office). *Telephone:* 3-88-41-38-24 (office). *Fax:* 3-88-41-27-91 (office). *Website:* www.echr.coe.int (office).

COSTA, Manuel Pinto da; São Tomé and Príncipe politician; b. 5 Aug. 1937, Água Grande; f. Movt for the Liberation of São Tomé e Príncipe (MLSTP) 1972; Sec.-Gen. MLSTP, based in Gabon 1972–75, Pres. 1978; Pres. of São Tomé e Príncipe 1975–91; Minister of Agric., Land Reform and Defence 1975–78, of Labour and Social Security 1977–78, of Territorial Admin. 1978–82, of Defence and Nat. Security 1982–86, fmr Minister of Planning and Econs; Prime Minister 1978–88; visited China and N Korea Dec. 1975; Dr hc (Berlin); José Marti Medal, Cuba. *Address:* c/o Office of the President, CP 38, São Tomé, São Tomé e Príncipe.

COSTA, Pedro; Portuguese film director and writer; b. 3 March 1959, Lisbon; s. of dir and writer Luís Filipe Costa; ed Univ. of Lisbon, Escola Superior de Teatro e Cinema. *Films:* É Tudo Invenção Nossa (also producer) 1984, Um Adeus Português (asst dir) 1986, Uma Rapariga no Verão (asst dir) 1986, Agosto (August) (asst dir) 1987, O Sangue (The Blood) (also writer) 1989, Casa de Lava (Down to Earth) (also writer) (Special Artistic Achievement, Thessaloniki Film Festival 1994, Grand Prix for Best Foreign Film, Entrevues Film Festival 1994) 1994, Ossos (Bones) (also writer) (Grand Prix for Best Foreign Film, Entrevues Film Festival 1997) 1997, No Quarto da Vanda (In Vanda's Room) (also cinematographer) (Don Quixote Award (Special Mention), Special Mention, and Youth Jury Award, Locarno Int. Film Festival 2000, FIPRESCI Prize (Int. Competition), Yamagata Int. Documentary Festival 2001, France Culture Award for Cineaste of the Year, Cannes Film Festival 2002) 2000, 6 Bagatelas (video) 2001, Ne change rien 2005, Juventude Em Marcha (Colossal Youth) (also writer and cinematographer) (Independent/ Experimental Film and Video Award, Los Angeles Film Critics Association Awards 2007) 2006, O Estado do Mundo (State of the World; segment Tarrafal) (also cinematographer) 2007. *Television:* Cinéma, de notre temps (episode Danièle Huillet/Jean-Marie Straub: Où gît votre sourire enfoui?) (also cinematographer) 2001.

COSTA-GAVRAS, Constantin; French (b. Greek) film director and screenwriter; b. (Constantin Gavras), 13 Feb. 1933, Arcadia; s. of Panayotis Gavras and Panayota Gavras; m. Michele Ray 1968; three c.; ed Sorbonne and Institut de Hautes Etudes Cinématographiques, Paris; worked as asst to film dirs Yves Allegret, Jacques Demy, René Clair, René Clément; Pres. Soc. des Réalisateurs Français 1973–75, Cinémathèque Française 1982–87, Festival Paris-Cinéma 2003–; Chevalier, Légion d'honneur; Commdr Arts et Lettres; Officier Ordre nat. du Mérite; Prix Académie Française for Life Achievement 1998. *Films directed include:* The Sleeping Car Murder (also writer) 1965 (MWA Award), Un Homme de Trop 1966 (Moscow Film Festival Prize), Z (co-writer) 1969 (Jury Award, Cannes, Award for Best Foreign-Language Film), L'Aveu (co-writer) 1970, State of Siege (co-writer) 1973 (Louis Delluc Prize), Section Spéciale (co-writer) 1975 (Best Dir, Cannes), Clair de Femme (writer) 1979, Missing (co-writer) 1982 (Gold Palm, Cannes, Academy Award, best screenplay, British Acad. best screenplay), Hanna K (co-writer) 1983, Family Business (writer) 1985, Betrayed 1988 (ACLUF Award), Music Box 1989 (Golden Bear, Berlin), The Little Apocalypse (dir and co-writer) 1993, Mad City 1996; directed opera Il Mondo della Luna (Joseph Haydn), Teatro San Carlo, Naples 1994, Amen 2001, Parthenon (short) 2003. *Publication:* Etat de Siège: The making of the film. *Leisure interests:* theatre, opera, books, films. *Address:* 244 rue Saint-Jacques, 75005 Paris (office); c/o Artmédia, 20 avenue Rapp, 75007, Paris, France. *Telephone:* 1-44-41-13-73 (office). *Fax:* 1-44-41-13-74 (office). *E-mail:* kgprod@wanadoo.fr (office).

COSTA PEREIRA, Renato Claudio; Brazilian aviation official and international organization official; b. 30 Nov. 1936; m.; ed Brazilian Air Force Academy; Personnel Commdr, Belo Horizonte Air Force Base 1961–67; Officer, Brazilian Air Force Gen. Personnel Command 1967–70, Instructor Officer, Brazilian Air Force Improvement Officer School 1970–74; Pilot Instructor, Brazilian Air Force Acad. 1974–77; Man. and Co-ordinator of Research and Devt project 1978–84; Dir Flight Protection Inst. 1984–85; Logistics Adviser to Minister of Aeronautics 1985–87; Chief, Brazilian Air Comm., London, England 1987–89; Sec. of Planning and Contracting, Secr. of Econ. and Finance, Ministry of Aeronautics 1989–90; Dir Operations Sub-

Dept, Civil Aviation Dept 1990–92, Dir Planning Sub-Dept 1990–94; Pres. Latin American Comm. of Civil Aviation 1990–97, responsible for establishing the basis for the enlargement of the Comm. to a Pan-American body in 1997; Pres. Brazilian Govt agency for int. air navigation affairs 1990–97; Sec.-Gen. ICAO 1997–2003. *Address:* c/o International Civil Aviation Organization, 999 University Street, Montreal, PQ H3A 5H7, Canada (office).

COSTEDOAT, Lt-Gen. Pierre-Jacques; French army officer and consultant; b. 27 Jan. 1942, Casablanca, Morocco; s. of René Costedoat and Marguerite Bosc; m. Anne-Marie Delamare 1965; four d.; ed Saint-Cyr-Coëtquidan Mil. Acad.; Second Lt, 74th Artillery Regt 1964, Lt 1966; Capt., 1st Artillery Regt 1972, then Battery CO; Maj., 11th Artillery Regt 1977, Lt-Col 1981, Col 1984; attended as auditeur Centre des hautes études militaires and Institut des hautes études de défense nationale 1987–88; CO 93rd Mountain Artillery Regt, then Staff 1988–89, at Direction Générale de la Sécurité extérieure 1989–95; Brig. 1992; CO Saint-Cyr Coëtquidan Mil. Acad. 1995–98; rank of Maj.-Gen. 1995, later Lt-Gen.; Asst Gen. Sec. of Nat. Defence 1998–2000; Gen. de corps 1998–; Mil. Gov. of Paris, Commdr of Ile-de-France, Officer Gen. Paris Zone of Defence 2000–02; Advisor to Pres. of Sécurité Sans Frontières (risk prevention and man. consultancy) 2003–; Officier Légion d'honneur, Commdr Ordre nat. du Mérite. *Leisure interests:* skiing, tennis, golf, hiking. *Address:* c/o Office of the President, Sécurité Sans Frontières, Sofema Groupe, 58 avenue Marceau, 75008 Paris France. *Website:* www.securite-sf.com.

COSTELLO, Elvis; British singer and songwriter; b. (Declan Patrick Aloysius McManus), 25 Aug. 1954, London, England; s. of Ross McManus and Lillian McManus (née Costello); m. 1st Mary Costello 1974; one s.; m. 2nd Cait O'Riordan 1986 (divorced 2003); m. 3rd Diana Krall 2003; twin s.; fmr mem. Flip City; formed Elvis Costello and the Attractions 1977–; concert appearances, UK and USA 1978–; Dir South Bank Meltdown 1995; BAFTA Award for Best Original Television Music (for G.B.H.) 1992, MTV Video Award for Best Male Video 1989, Rolling Stone Award for Best Songwriter 1990, two Ivor Novello Awards, Nordoff-Robbins Silver Clef Award, ASCAP Founders Award 2003. *Film:* Americathon 1979, No Surrender 1985, Straight to Hell 1987, Prison Song 2001, De-Lovely 2004. *Television:* Scully (Granada TV for Channel 4) 1984, The Juliet Letters 1993, presenter, Spectacle: Elvis Costello With... (Sundance Channel) 2008–. *Recordings include:* albums: My Aim Is True 1977, This Year's Model 1978, Armed Forces 1979, Get Happy 1980, Trust 1980, Almost Blue 1981, Taking Liberties 1982, Imperial Bedroom 1982, Goodbye Cruel World 1984, Punch The Clock 1983, The Best Of 1985, Blood and Chocolate 1986, King of America 1986, Spike 1989, Mighty Like A Rose 1991, The Juliet Letters (with the Brodsky Quartet) 1993, Brutal Youth (with Steve Nieve, Pete Thomas, Bruce Thomas and Nick Lowe) 1994, The Very Best of Elvis Costello and The Attractions 1995, Kojak Variety 1995, Deep Dead Blue, Live At Meltdown (with Bill Frisell) 1995, All This Useless Beauty 1996, Extreme Honey 1997, Terror and Magnificence 1997, Painted From Memory (Grammy Award 1999) 1998, The Sweetest Punch: The Songs of Costello 1999, Best of Elvis Costello 1999, For The Stars (with Anne-Sofie von Otter) 2001, When I Was Cruel 2002, North 2003, My Flame Burns Blue 2006, The River in Reverse (with Allen Toussaint) 2006, Momofuku 2008. *Address:* By Eleven Management, 12 Tideway Yard, 125 Mortlake High Street, London, SW14 8SN, England (office). *Website:* www.elviscostello.com.

COSTELLO, Peter Howard, BA, LLB; Australian politician; b. 14 Aug. 1957; s. of R. J. Costello and M. A. Costello; m. Tanya Costello 1982; one s. two d.; ed Carey Grammar School, Monash Univ.; solicitor, Mallesons, Melbourne 1981–84; tutor (part-time) Monash Univ. 1984–86; mem. Victorian Bar 1984–90; MP for Higgins, Victoria, 1990–2007; Shadow Minister for Corp. Law Reform and Consumer Affairs 1990–92; Shadow Attorney-Gen. and Shadow Minister for Justice 1992–93, for Finance 1993–94; Deputy Leader of the Opposition and Shadow Treas. 1994–96; Deputy Leader Liberal Party 1996–2007, Commonwealth of Australia Treas. 1996–2007; mem. Liberal Party. *Publication:* Arbitration in Contempt (jtly) 1986; articles for periodicals and journals. *Leisure interests:* swimming, football, reading. *Address:* c/o Liberal Party of Australia, Federal Secretariat, cnr Blackall and Macquarie Streets, Barton, ACT 2600, Australia.

COSTELLOE, Paul; Irish fashion designer and artist; b. 23 June 1945, Dublin; m. 1982; six s. one d.; ed Blackrock Coll., Dublin, design coll. in Dublin and Chambre Syndical Paris; Design Asst Jacques Esterel, Paris 1969–71; Designer, Marks & Spencer 1972; Chief House Designer, A. Rinascente, Milan 1972–74; Designer, Anne Fogerty, New York, Pennaco, New York and Trimfit, Philadelphia 1974–79; established own design house, Paul Costelloe Int. Ltd in conjunction with business pnr Robert Eitel 1979; merchandise sold in UK, Ireland, Europe, Scandinavia and N America under Paul Costelloe Collection and Dressage labels; opened flagship store, Knightsbridge 1994; designer of British Airways uniform 1994; Hon. DLitt (Ulster) 1996; Fil d'Or award, Int. Linen Council, 1987, 1988, 1989; British Designer of the Year 1989 and other awards. *Leisure interests:* rugby, tennis, golf. *Address:* Main Road, Moygashel, Dungannon, County Tyrone, BT71 7QR, Ireland; c/o Signature Brands Group plc, 4 Fitzhardinge Street, London, W1H 6EG, England. *Website:* www.paulcostelloe.com.

COSTNER, Kevin; American actor and film director; b. 18 Jan. 1955; m. 1st Cindy Silva (divorced); one s. two d.; one s. by Bridget Rooney; m. 2nd Christine Baumgartner 2004; one s.; ed California State Univ., Fullerton; directing debut in Dances with Wolves 1990 (Acad. Award for Best Picture 1991); mem. band, Modern West. *Films include:* Frances 1982, Testament 1983, Silverado 1985, The Untouchables 1987, No Way Out 1987, Bull Durham 1988, Field of Dreams 1989, Revenge 1989, Robin Hood: Prince of Thieves 1990, JFK 1991, The Bodyguard 1992, A Perfect World 1993, Wyatt Earp 1994, The War 1994, Waterworld 1995, Tin Cup 1996, The Postman 1997, Message in a Bottle 1998, For Love of the Game 1999, Thirteen Days 2000, 3000 Miles to Graceland 2001, Dragonfly 2002, Open Range 2003, The Upside of Anger 2005, Rumor Has It 2005, The Guardian 2006, Mr. Brooks 2007, Swing Vote 2008; co-producer Rapa Nui, China Moon 1993, exec. producer Rapa Nui 1994. *Recording:* album: with Modern West: Untold Truths 2008. *Leisure interest:* golf. *Address:* c/o J.J. Harris, One Entertainment, 9220 Sunset Blvd, Suite 306, Los Angeles, CA 90069; TIG Productions, Producers' Building 5, 4000 Warner Boulevard, Burbank, CA 91523, USA. *Website:* www.kevincostner.com; www.kevincostnermodernwest.com.

COT, Jean-Pierre; French politician, international organization official and academic; *Judge, International Tribunal for the Law of the Sea;* b. 23 Oct. 1937, Geneva, Switzerland; s. of Pierre Cot and Luisa Phelps; m.; three c.; Prof., then Dean, Faculty of Law, Amiens 1968; Prof. of Int. Law and Political Sociology, Univ. of Paris I (Panthéon-Sorbonne) 1969, Dir Disarmament Research and Study Centre (CEREDE); mem. Steering Cttee, Parti Socialiste (PS) 1970, 1973, mem. Exec. Bureau 1976; Mayor of Coise-Saint-Jean-Pied-Gauthier 1971–95; Deputy (Savoie) to Nat. Ass. 1973–81; Gen. Councillor, Savoie 1973–81; PS Nat. Del. for matters relating to the EC 1976–79; mem. European Parl. 1978–79, 1984–99, Pres. Budget Cttee 1984–87, Chair. Socialist Group 1989–94, Vice-Pres. 1997–99; Judge, Int. Tribunal for the Law of the Sea 2002–; Minister-Del. for Co-operation, attached to Minister for External Relations 1981–82; mem. Exec. Council UNESCO 1983–84. *Publication:* A l'épreuve du pouvoir: le tiers-mondisme, pour quoi faire? 1984 and numerous works on int. law and political science. *Address:* Coise-Saint-Jean-Pied-Gauthier, 73800 Montmélian, France (home).

COTE, David M., BBA; American business executive; *Chairman and CEO, Honeywell International Inc.;* ed Univ. of New Hampshire; various man. positions General Electric –1996, Corp. Sr Vice-Pres., Pres. and CEO General Electric Appliances 1996–99; Pres., CEO and Chair. TRW, Cleveland 1999–2002; Pres. and CEO Honeywell International Inc. Feb.–July 2002, Chair. and CEO July 2002–; mem. Nat. Security Telecommunications Advisory Cttee; one of 10 US CEOs invited to serve on US-India CEO Forum est. by Pres. George W. Bush and Indian Prime Minister Manmohan Singh 2005; Hon. LLD (Pepperdine Univ.) 2001; Corporate Social Responsibility Award, Foreign Policy Asscn 2007. *Address:* Honeywell International Inc., 101 Columbia Road, Morristown, NJ 07962-1219, USA (office). *Telephone:* (973) 455-2000 (office). *Fax:* (973) 455-4807 (office). *E-mail:* ecccustomercare@honeywell.com (office). *Website:* www.honeywell.com (office).

COTILLARD, Marion; French actress; b. 30 Sept. 1975, Paris; d. of Jean-Claude Cotillard (actor, playwright and dir) and Niseema Theillaud (actress and drama teacher); ed Conservatoire d'Art Dramatique, Orléans; raised in Orléans; made acting debut as child with role in one of her father's plays; cinema debut with film L'Histoire du garçon qui voulait qu'on l'embrasse 1994; first prominent screen role was in Taxi 1998, reprised role as Lili Bertineau in two sequels; only second actress to win Best Actress Academy Award performing in a language other than English (along with Sophia Lauren in La Ciociara 1960). *Films:* L'Histoire du garçon qui voulait qu'on l'embrasse 1994, Snuff Movie 1995, Comment je me suis disputé... (ma vie sexuelle) (aka My Sex Life... or How I Got Into an Argument, USA) 1996, La belle verte 1996, Taxi 1998, La guerre dans le Haut Pays (aka War in the Highlands) 1999, Furia 1999, L'Appel de la cave 1999, Du bleu jusqu'en Amérique (aka Blue Away to America) 1999, Quelques jours de trop 2000, Le Marquis 2000, Taxi 2 2000, Heureuse 2001, Boomer 2001, Lisa 2001, Les jolies choses (aka Pretty Things) 2001, Une affaire privée (aka A Private Affair) 2002, Taxi 3 2003, Jeux d'enfants (aka Love Me If You Dare) 2003, Big Fish 2003, Innocence 2004, Un long dimanche de fiançaille (aka A Very Long Engagement) (César Award for Best Supporting Actress) 2004, Edy 2005, Cavalcade 2005, Ma vie en l'air 2005, Mary 2005, Sauf le respect que je vous dois 2005, La boîte noire 2005, Toi et moi 2006, Dikkenek 2006, Fair Play 2006, A Good Year 2006, played and sang role of Édith Piaf in La Môme (retitled 'La Vie en Rose' in USA) (Academy Award for Best Actress 2008, César Award for Best Actress 2008, BAFTA Award for Best Actress in a Leading Role 2008, Golden Globe Award 2008, Czech Lion Award for Best Actress 2008, Los Angeles Film Critics' Asscn Award 2008, London Critics' Circle Film Award 2008, Boston Soc. of Film Critics Award 2008, Palm Springs Int. Film Festival Award 2008, Cabourg Romantic Film Festival Award 2008) 2007. *Television:* Extrême limite (series) 1994, Chloé 1996, Interdit de vieillir 1998, Les redoutables (series) 2001, Une femme piégée 2001. *Address:* c/o Creative Artists Agency, 4th Floor, Space One, 1 Beadon Road, London, W6 0EA, England. *E-mail:* info@cotillard.net. *Website:* www.cotillard.net.

COTLER, Irwin, OC; Canadian lawyer, politician and professor of law; b. 8 May 1940, Montreal; Prof. of Law, McGill Univ., Dir Human Rights Programme, Chair. InterAmicus Int. Human Rights Advocacy Centre (on leave); fmr Visiting Prof., Harvard Law School; fmr Woodrow Wilson Fellow, Yale Law School; MP 1999–, mem. Standing Cttee on Foreign Affairs, sub-Cttee on Human Rights and Int. Devt, Cttee on Justice and Human Rights; Special Advisor to Minister of Foreign Affairs on Int. Criminal Court 2000–03; Minister of Justice and Attorney-Gen. 2003–06; Chair. Int. Comm. of Inquiry into the Fate and Whereabouts of Raoul Wallenberg, Comm. on Econ. Coercion and Discrimination. *Address:* House of Commons, 491 West Block, Ottawa, ON K1A 0A6, Canada (office). *Telephone:* (613) 995-0121 (office). *Fax:* (613) 992-6762 (office). *E-mail:* cotlei@parl.gc.ca (office). *Website:* www.irwincotler.parl.gc.ca (office).

COTTA, Michèle, LèsL, DrèsScPol; French journalist; *Director General, JLA Groupe;* b. 15 June 1937, Nice; d. of Jacques Cotta and Helène Scoffier; m. 1st Claude Tchou (divorced); one s. (deceased) one d.; m. 2nd Phillipe Barret 1992; ed Lycée de Nice, Faculté de Lettres de Nice and Inst. d'études politiques de Paris; journalist with L'Express 1963–69, 1971–76; Europ I 1970–71, 1986;

political diarist, France-Inter 1976–80; Head of political service, Le Point 1977–80, Reporter 1986; Chief Political Ed. RTL 1980–81; Pres. Dir-Gen. Radio France 1981–82; Pres. Haute Autorité de la Communication Audiovisuelle 1982–86; Producer Faits de Soc. on TF1 1987, Dir of Information 1987–92, Pres. Sofica Images Investissements 1987; producer and presenter La Revue de presse, France 2 1993–95; political ed. Nouvel Economiste 1993–96; producer and presenter Polémiques, France 2 1995–99, Dir-Gen. France 2 1999–2002 (retd); Dir-Gen. JLA Groupe 2002–; editorial writer, RTL 1996–99; mem. Conseil économique et social; Chevalier, Légion d'honneur, Officier, Ordre nat. du mérite. *Publications:* La collaboration 1940–1944, 1964, Les elections présidentielles 1966, Prague, l'été des Tanks 1968, La Vième République 1974, Les miroirs de Jupiter 1986, Les Secrets d'une Victoire 1995. *Address:* JLA Groupe, 7 rue des Bretons, 93210 Paris (office); 70 boulevard Port Royal, 75005 Paris, France (home). *Telephone:* 1-49-17-27-27 (office); 6-09-48-10-00. *Fax:* 1-49-17-27-67 (office). *E-mail:* contact@groupe-jla.com (office); mcotta@noos.fr (home). *Website:* www.groupe-jla.com (office).

COTTE, Bruno; French judge; *Judge, International Criminal Court;* b. 10 June 1945, Lyons; m.; three c.; ed Univ. of Lyons, Ecole Nationale de la Magistrature, Bordeaux; studies in Paris; Teaching Asst in Criminology, Faculty of Law, Univ. of Paris II 1970; Magistrate in Ministry of Justice and Head, Office of Dir of Criminal Affairs and Pardons 1970–73; Deputy Public Prosecutor, Tribunal de Grande Instance de Lyon (Lyons Dist Court) 1973–75; Head of Prosecution Bureau, Directorate of Criminal Affairs and Pardons, Ministry of Justice with competence in econ., financial and social criminal matters 1975–80; Lecturer, French Nat. School for Judiciary, Bordeaux 1975–80; Special Asst to First Pres. of Supreme Court of Appeal (judicial competence of First Pres.) 1980–81; Special Asst to Attorney Gen., Paris Court of Appeal, serving as Sec.-Gen. of Public Prosecutor's Dept 1981–84; Deputy Dir of Criminal Justice, Directorate of Criminal Affairs and Pardons, Ministry of Justice 1983–84, Dir for Criminal Affairs and Pardons 1984–90; Attorney Gen. to Versailles Court of Appeal May–Sept. 1990; Public Prosecutor in Tribunal de Grande Instance de Paris (Paris Dist Court) 1990–95; Counsel for Prosecution to Supreme Court of Appeal (Criminal Chamber) 1995–2000; Lecturer in Criminal Procedure to mems of Prefectural Police, Ministry of the Interior 1995–2000; Pres. of jury that confers rank of judicial police officers to student inspectors of Nat. Police Force, Ministry of the Interior 1996–2000; Pres. Criminal Chamber of Supreme Court of Appeal 2000–08; Lecturer in Criminal Procedure, Nat. School for the Judiciary, Paris 2000–07; Acting First Pres. Cour de Cassation (Supreme Court of Appeal) March–May 2007; Judge, Int. Criminal Court, The Hague 2008–; mem. Paris Aide aux Victimes, amongst others; Chevalier du Mérite agricole 1979, Commdr Ordre nat. du Mérite 2001, Commdr Légion d'honneur 2005; Penitentiary Medal. *Address:* International Criminal Court, PO Box 19519, 2500 CM The Hague, The Netherlands (office). *Telephone:* (70) 515-8515 (office). *Fax:* (70) 515-8555 (office). *E-mail:* info@icc-cpi.int (office). *Website:* www.icc-cpi.int (office).

COTTERILL, Rodney Michael John, PhD, DSc; British/Danish biophysicist and academic; *Professor of Biophysics, Danish Technical University;* b. 27 Sept. 1933, Bodmin, UK; s. of Herbert Cotterill and Aline Le Cerf; m. Vibeke Nielsen 1959; two d.; ed Cowes and Newport High Schools, Isle of Wight, Univ. Coll. London, Yale Univ. and Emmanuel Coll. Cambridge; served with RAF 1952–54; Assoc. Scientist, Argonne Nat. Lab. 1962–67; Prof., Tech. Univ. of Denmark (now Danish Tech. Univ.) 1967–; Visiting Prof., Tokyo Univ. 1978, 1985; Fellow, Royal Danish Acad. of Sciences and Letters, Danish Acad. of Tech. Sciences, Inst. of Physics (UK); Kt, Order of the Dannebrog 1979 (First Class 1994); Ellen and Hans Hermer Memorial Prize 1978, James Arthur Lecturer (American Museum of Natural History, New York) 2003. *Publications:* The Cambridge Guide to the Material World 1985, Computer Simulation in Brain Science (ed.) 1988, No Ghost in the Machine 1989, Models of Brain Function (ed.) 1989, Neural Network Dynamics (co-ed.) 1992, Brain and Mind (ed.) 1994, Autism, Intelligence and Consciousness 1994, Enchanted Looms 1998, Biophysics 2002; articles on topics in physics, biology and medicine. *Leisure interests:* sailing, choral singing, writing. *Address:* Biophysics, Danish Technical University, Building 309, 2800 Lyngby, Denmark (office). *Telephone:* 45-25-32-03 (office). *Fax:* 45-93-16-69 (office). *E-mail:* rodney.cotterill@fysik.dtu.dk (office). *Website:* www.fys.dtu.dk/~rodney/people/rodney.html (office).

COTTI, Flavio; Swiss politician; b. 18 Oct. 1939, Muralto; m. Renata Naretto; one d.; ed Univ. of Freiburg; barrister and public notary in Locarno 1965–75; mem. Locarno Communal Council 1964–75; mem. of cantonal Parl. of Ticino 1967–75; mem. of Govt, canton of Ticino, Head of Dept of Home Affairs, Econ. Affairs, Justice and Mil. Matters 1975–83; mem. Nat. Council 1983–86; mem. Fed. Council 1987–99; Head of Fed. Dept of Home Affairs 1987–93, Dept of Foreign Affairs 1994–99, Pres. of Swiss Confed. 1991 and 1998, Vice-Pres. 1990, 1997; Pres. Bd of Dirs Ticino Cantonal Tourist Office 1976–84; Pres. Christian Democratic People's Party (CDPP) of Ticino 1981, CDPP of Switzerland 1984; Chair. OSCE 1996; Chair. Int. Advisory Bd Credit Suisse Group –2007; mem. Bd of Dirs Fiat SpA 2000–05, Jakobs Foundation 1999–, Georg Fischer Ltd 2000–, Intier Automotive Inc.2002–; Trustee Jacobs Foundation; mem. Foundation Bd World Econ. Forum. *Address:* c/o Christlichdemokratische Volkspartei der Schweiz—Parti démocrate-chrétien suisse (Christian Democratic People's Party), Klaraweg 6, Postfach 5835, 3001 Bern, Switzerland.

COTTINGHAM, Robert; American artist; b. 26 Sept. 1935, Brooklyn, New York; s. of James and Aurelia Cottingham; m. Jane Weismann 1967; three d.; ed Brooklyn Tech. High School, Pratt Inst.; served in US army 1955–58; Art Dir with Young and Rubicam Advertising Inc., New York 1959–64, Los Angeles 1964–68; left advertising to paint 1968–; taught at Art Centre Coll. of Design, Los Angeles 1969–70; moved to London 1972–76; returned to USA 1976; Nat. Endowment for the Arts 1974–75; numerous solo exhbns; works in many public galleries in USA and also in Hamburg Museum, Tate Gallery, London and Utrecht Museum; MacDowell Colony Residency 1993, 1994; Walter Gropius Fellowship, Huntington Museum of Art 1992; mem. Nat. Acad. of Design. *Publications:* numerous print publs (lithographs, etchings). *Leisure interests:* travel, music, history. *Address:* PO Box 604, Blackman Road, Newtown, CT 06470; c/o Forum Gallery, 8069 Beverly Blvd, Los Angeles, CA 90048, USA.

COTTRELL, Sir Alan (Howard), Kt, PhD, ScD, FRS, FREng; British fmr scientist and fmr professor of physical metallurgy; b. 17 July 1919, Birmingham; s. of Albert Cottrell and Elizabeth Cottrell; m. Jean Elizabeth Harber 1944 (died 1999); one s.; ed Moseley Grammar School, Univs of Birmingham and Cambridge; Lecturer in Metallurgy, Univ. of Birmingham 1943–49, Prof. of Physical Metallurgy 1949–55; Deputy Head, Metallurgy Div., AERE, Harwell, Berks. 1955–58; Goldsmiths' Prof. of Metallurgy, Cambridge Univ. 1958–65; Deputy Chief Scientific Adviser (Studies), Ministry of Defence 1965–67; Chief Adviser 1967; Deputy Chief Scientific Adviser to HM Govt 1968–71; Chief Scientific Adviser 1971–74; Master, Jesus Coll., Cambridge 1974–86, Vice-Chancellor, Cambridge Univ. 1977–79; Part-time mem. UKAEA 1962–65, 1983–87; Dir Fisons PLC 1979–90; mem. Advisory Council on Scientific Policy 1963–64, Cen. Advisory Council for Science and Technology 1967–, Exec. Cttee British Council 1974–87, Advisory Council, Science Policy Foundation 1976–, UK Perm. Security Comm. 1981–92; Foreign Assoc. NAS 1972, Nat. Acad. of Eng, USA 1976; Foreign Hon. mem. American Acad. of Arts and Sciences 1960; Fellow, Royal Soc. (Vice-Pres. 1964, 1976, 1977), Royal Swedish Acad. of Sciences 1970; mem. Academia Europaea 1991; Hon. Fellow, Christ's Coll., Cambridge 1970 (Fellow 1958–70), Jesus Coll., Cambridge 1986, Imperial Coll., London 1991, Inst. of Metals 1989; Hon. mem. American Soc. for Metals 1972, Fellow 1974; Hon. mem. The Metals Soc. 1977, Japan Inst. of Metals 1981; Hon. DSc (Columbia) 1965, (Newcastle) 1967, (Liverpool) 1969, (Manchester) 1970, (Warwick) 1971, (Sussex) 1972, (Bath) 1973, (Strathclyde and Aston in Birmingham) 1975, (Cranfield Inst. of Tech.) 1975, (Oxford) 1979, (Essex) 1982, (Birmingham) 1983; Hon. DEng (Tech. Univ. of Nova Scotia) 1984; Hon. ScD (Cambridge) 1976; Hon. LLD (Cambridge) 1996; Rosenhain Medal, Inst. of Metals, Hughes Medal, Royal Soc. 1961, Réaumur Medal, Soc. Française de Métallurgie 1964; Inst. of Metals (Platinum) Medal 1965, James Alfred Ewing Medal, ICE 1967, Holweck Medal, Soc. Française de Physique 1969, Albert Sauveur Achievement Award, American Soc. for Metals 1969, James Douglas Gold Medal, American Inst. of Mining, Metallurgy and Petroleum Engineers 1974, Rumford Medal, Royal Soc. 1974, Harvey Prize (Technion, Israel) 1974, Acta Metallurgica Gold Medal 1976, Guthrie Medal and Prize, Inst. of Physics 1977, Gold Medal, American Soc. for Metals 1980, Brinell Medal, Royal Swedish Acad. of Eng Sciences 1980, Kelvin Medal, ICE 1986, Hollomon Award, Acta Metallurgica 1990, Copley Medal, Royal Soc. 1996, Von Hippel Award, Materials Research Soc. 1996. *Publications:* Theoretical Structural Metallurgy 1948, Dislocations and Plastic Flow in Crystals 1953, The Mechanical Properties of Matter 1964, Theory of Crystal Dislocations 1964, An Introduction to Metallurgy 1967, Portrait of Nature 1975, Environmental Economics 1978, How Safe is Nuclear Energy? 1981, Introduction to the Modern Theory of Metals 1988, Chemical Bonding in Transition Metal Carbides 1995, Concepts in the Electron Theory of Alloys 1998 and scientific papers in various learned journals. *Leisure interests:* music. *Address:* 40 Maids Causeway, Cambridge, CB5 8DD, England. *Telephone:* (1223) 363806 (home). *E-mail:* ah.cottrell@virgin.net (home).

COTTRILL, Ross, FAIM; Australian diplomatist, research institute director and academic; *Visiting Fellow, Asia-Pacific College of Diplomacy, Australian National University;* served as diplomat in several Asian posts 1964–79; Head of Dept of Foreign Affairs Policy Planning Unit 1975–76; Special Advisor and Div. Head of Defence and Foreign Affairs at depts of Prime Minister, Cabinet and Defence; Foundation Dir of Studies, Australian Coll. of Defence and Strategic Studies 1994–96; Exec. Dir Australian Inst. of Int. Affairs 1998–2004; currently Visiting Fellow, Asia-Pacific Coll. of Diplomacy, ANU Fellow, Australian Insts of Company Dirs and Mans. *Address:* Asia-Pacific College of Diplomacy, Hedley Bull Centre Building 130, Canberra ACT 0200, Australia (office). *Website:* apcd.anu.edu.au.

COUCHEPIN, François; Swiss lawyer; b. 19 Jan. 1935, Martigny; s. of Louis Couchepin and Andrée Couchepin; m. Anne Marie Cottier 1957; six c.; ed Univ. of Lausanne; legal practitioner at Rodolphe Tissières 1959–64; own legal practice in Martigny 1964–; elected to Cantonal Council of Canton Valais 1965, re-elected 1969, 1973, 1977; Sec. Radical Group 1965–77, Pres. 1977–79; Head of French Section, Cen. Language Service, Fed. Chancellery 1980; Vice-Chancellor responsible for gen. admin. of Fed. Chancellery 1981; Chancellor of the Swiss Fed. 1991–99; mem. Defence Staff. *Address:* c/o Federal Chancellery, Bundeshaus-West, 3003 Berne, Switzerland.

COUCHEPIN, Pascal; Swiss politician and fmr head of state; *President of the Swiss Confederation and Head, Federal Department of Home Affairs;* b. 5 April 1942, Martigny; m.; three c.; ed Lausanne Univ.; elected mem. local council Martigny 1968; Deputy Mayor of Martigny 1976, Mayor 1984–98; elected to the Nat. Council 1979; Chair. Parl. Group, Liberal Democrat Party (LDP) 1989–96; fmr Chair. Nat. Council's Cttee for Science and Research; fmr Chair. Fed. Dept of Justice and Police section of the Control Cttee; elected to Federal Council 1998; Vice-Pres. of the Swiss Confederation 2002, 2007, Pres. of the Swiss Confederation 2003, 2008; Head of Fed. Dept of Econ. Affairs 1998–2002, of Home Affairs 2003–; fmr Gov. IBRD, EBRD. *Address:* Federal Department of Home Affairs, Bundeshaus, Inselgasse, 3003 Bern, Switzerland (office). *Telephone:* (31) 3228001 (office). *Fax:* (31) 3227901 (office). *E-mail:* info@gs-edi.admin.ch. *Website:* www.edi.admin.ch (office).

COUCHER, Iain, MBA; British transport industry executive; *CEO, Network Rail;* m.; two c.; ed Imperial Coll., London and Open Univ.; worked for EDS 1983–99, positions included Head of Mergers and Acquisitions; CEO TubeLines 1999–2002, seconded as CEO to TranSys consortium 1996–98; Man. Dir Network Rail 2002, Deputy CEO 2002–07, CEO 2007–. *Address:* Network Rail, 40 Melton Street, London, NW1 2EE England (office). *Telephone:* (20) 7557-8000 (office). *Fax:* (20) 7557-9000 (office). *Website:* www.networkrail.co.uk (office).

COUGHLAN, Mary, B.Soc.Sc; Irish politician; *Tánaiste and Minister for Enterprise, Trade and Employment;* b. 1965, Co. Donegal; d. of the late Cathal Coughlan; m. David Charlton; one s. one d.; ed Ursuline Convent, Sligo, Univ. Coll., Dublin; early career in social work; mem. Co. Donegal Co. Council 1986–2001; mem. North Western Health Bd 1987–2001; mem. Fianna Fáil; TD for Donegal SW 1987–; Chair. Oireachtas Jt Cttee on Irish Language 1993–95; Minister of State Dept of Arts, Heritage, Gaeltacht and the Islands 2000–02, Minister for Social, Community and Family Affairs 2002–04, Minister for Agriculture and Food (now Agriculture, Fisheries and Food) 2004–08, Tánaiste (Deputy Prime Minister) and Minister for Enterprise, Trade and Employment 2008–; mem. Co. Donegal Vocational Educ. Cttee 1986–99 (Chair. 1991–92); Chair. Bd of Man. Abbey Vocational School, Donegal Town; mem. Bd of Man. Tourism Coll., Killybegs; fmr mem. Comhchoiste na Gaeilge (Chair. 1993–94); Pres. Killybegs Coast and Cliff Rescue Service; Hon. Sec. Fianna Fáil Party 1995. *Address:* Department of Enterprise, Trade and Employment, 23 Kildare Street, Dublin 2, Ireland (office). *Telephone:* (1) 6312121 (office). *Fax:* (1) 6312827 (office). *Website:* www.entemp.ie (home).

COULOMBE, Pierre, BA, BSc, PhD; Canadian medical researcher and administrator; *President, National Research Council;* ed Yeshiva Univ. of New York and Univ. of Minnesota; fmr Medical Research Council Scholar and Asst Prof. of Medicine, Université Laval, Québec; fmr Dir for Technological Innovation, Ministère de l'Enseignement supérieur et de la Science; fmr Sr Exec., Ministère de la Science et de la Technologie; various public service positions with Québec prov. govt, including Asst Deputy Minister for Tech., Ministère de l'Industrie et du Commerce and Asst Deputy Minister for Operations, Ministère du Commerce extérieur et de la Technologie; worked as pvt. industry exec., a consultant; fmr Chair. and CEO Centre de recherche industrielle du Québec; fmr Pres. and CEO Centre de recherche informatique de Montréal, Infectio Diagnostic Inc.; Pres. Nat. Research Council 2005–; has served on numerous bds of dirs and cttees; mem. Ordre des Ingénieurs du Québec, Ordre des Administrateurs Agrées du Québec; Assoc. mem. CFA Inst. *Publications:* numerous publs and communications on endocrinology. *Address:* Executive Offices, National Research Council – EXEC, Room W-307 Build M-58, 1200 Montreal Road, Ottawa, ON K1A 0R6, Canada (office). *Telephone:* (613) 993-2024 (office). *Fax:* (613) 957-8850 (office). *E-mail:* pierre.coulombe@nrc-cnrc.gc.ca (office). *Website:* www.nrc-cnrc.gc.ca (office).

COUMAKOYE, Kassiré Delwa, DenD; Chadian politician; b. 31 Dec. 1949, Bongor; ed Ecole Nat. d'Admin, Chad, Inst. Int. d'Admin Publique, Paris, Univ. de Paris I and II; Minister of Justice 1981–82, of Public Works, Housing and Town Planning 1987–88, of Justice 1988–89, of Posts and Telecommunications 1989–90, of Higher Educ. and Scientific Research 1989–90, of Communications and Liberties, of Justice June–Nov. 1993; Govt Spokesperson April–June 1993; Gen. Inspector of Admin 1987–; Prime Minister of Chad 1993–95, 2007–08; mem. and Pres. Rassemblement nat. pour la démocratie et le progrès 1992–; also Leader, Convention de l'opposition démocratique (alliance of opposition parties); sentenced to three months' imprisonment for possessing illegal weapons 1996; Chevalier Ordre de Mérite Centrafricain 1976, Commdr Ordre nat. du Tchad 1994. *Achievements include:* Cen. African champion in 3,000m. steeple chase 1965 (record unbroken). *Address:* Rassemblement Pour La Démocratie et Le Progrès, N'Djamena, Chad (office).

COUPLES, Frederick Stephen (Fred); American golfer; b. 3 Oct. 1959, Seattle, Wash.; m. Thais Couples; one s. one d.; ed Univ. of Houston; turned professional 1980; mem. US Ryder Cup Team 1989, 1991, 1993, 1995, 1997; mem. Pres.'s Cup 1994, 1996, 1998; won Kemper Open 1984, Tournament Players Championship 1984, Byron Nelson Golf Classic 1987, Nissan Los Angeles Open 1990, Federal Express St Jude Classic BC Open, Johnnie Walker World Championship 1991, Nissan Los Angeles Open, Nestlé Int., Masters 1992, Honda Classic 1993, Buick Open 1994, World Cup 1994, Dubai Desert Classic, Johnnie Walker Classic 1995, The Players' Championship 1996, Bob Hope Chrysler Classic 1998, Memorial Tournament 1998, Houston Open 2004; Capt. US Pres.'s Cup team 2009; PGA Tour Player of the Year 1991, 1992, Arnold Palmer Award 1992. *Leisure interests:* tennis, all sports, antiques, bicycling, vintage cars. *Address:* c/o PGA Tour, 100 Avenue of the Champions, P.O. Box 109601, Palm Beach Gardens, FL 33410, USA.

COURANT, Ernest David, PhD; American (naturalized) physicist and academic; *Distinguished Scientist Emeritus, Brookhaven National Laboratory;* b. 26 March 1920, Göttingen, Germany; s. of Richard Courant and Nina Runge; m. Sara Paul 1944; two s.; ed Swarthmore Coll. and Univ. of Rochester, USA; Scientist, Nat. Research Council (Canada), Montreal 1943–46; Research Assoc. in Physics, Cornell Univ. 1946–48; Physicist, Brookhaven Nat. Lab., Upton, NY 1948–60, Sr Physicist 1960–89, Distinguished Scientist Emer. 1990–; Prof. (part-time), Yale Univ. 1961–67, State Univ. of NY, Stony Brook 1967–85; Visiting Prof., Univ. of Mich. 1989–; Hon. Prof., Univ. of Science and Tech. of China, Hefei 1994; co-discoverer of Strong-focusing principle, particle accelerators; mem. NAS 1976; Fellow, AAAS 1981; Hon. DSc (Swarthmore Coll.) 1988; Pregel Prize, New York Acad. of Sciences 1979, Fermi Award 1986, R. R. Wilson Prize 1987. *Publications:* various articles; contrib. to Handbuch der Physik 1959, Annual Review of Nuclear Science 1968. *Address:* 40 West 72nd Street, New York, NY 10023, USA (home). *Telephone:* (212) 580-1006 (home). *E-mail:* ecourant@msn.com (home).

COURIC, Katherine (Katie); American broadcast journalist; *Anchor and Managing Editor, CBS Evening News;* b. 7 Jan. 1957, Arlington, Va; m. Jay Monahan (deceased); two d.; ed Univ. of Virgina; began career as desk asst for ABC news bureau, Washington, DC 1979; Assignment Ed., CNN 1980, later Assoc. Producer, Atlanta, later Producer of Take Two; worked at WTVJ, Miami for three years; joined NBC Network News 1989, later Nat. Corresp., The Today Show, Washington, DC, Co-Anchor 1991–2006; Anchor and Man. Ed. CBS Evening News 2006–, also contrib. to 60 Minutes and other CBS News specials; Co-host, NBC's morning coverage of Summer Olympics, Barcelona 1992, Co-host, Now with Tom Brokaw and Katie Couric 1993–94, Contributing Anchor, Dateline NBC 2005; six Emmy Awards, named Best in the Business by Washington Journalism Review 1993, ranked by Forbes magazine amongst 100 Most Powerful Women (57th) 2004, (47th) 2005, (54th) 2006, (63rd) 2007, (62nd) 2008. *Address:* CBS Evening News, 524 West 57th Street, New York, NY 10019, USA (office). *Telephone:* (212) 975-3247 (office). *Fax:* (212) 975-1893 (office). *E-mail:* evening@cbsnews.com (office). *Website:* www.cbsnews.com/sections/eveningnews/main3420.shtml (office).

COURIER, Jim; American business executive and fmr professional tennis player; b. 17 Aug. 1970, Sanford Fla; ed Nick Bollettieri Tennis Acad.; coached by José Higueras; winner, French Open 1991, 1992, Indian Wells (doubles) 1991; runner-up, US Open 1991, ATP World Championship 1991; winner, Australian Open 1992–93, Italian Open 1993; runner-up, French Open 1993, Wimbledon 1993; winner of 23 singles titles and six doubles titles and over $16 million in prize money at retirement in May 2000; now plays Delta Tour of Champions 2004–; Founding Pnr, InsideOut Sports & Entertainment, LLC 2004–; f. Raymond James Courier's Kids (inner-city youth tennis program); mem. Bd of Dirs First Serve, Gullikson Foundation; mem. Advisory Bd Falconhead Capital; elected to Int. Tennis Hall of Fame 2005. *Address:* InsideOut Sports & Entertainment LLC, 401 Lafayette, Suite 600, New York, NY 10003, USA (office). *Telephone:* (646) 367-2770 (office). *Fax:* (646) 367-2780 (office). *E-mail:* info@insideoutse.com (office). *Website:* www.insideoutse.com (office).

COURRÈGES, André; French couturier; b. 9 March 1923, Pau (Pyrénées-Atlantiques); s. of Lucien Courrèges and Céline Coupe; m. Jacqueline Barrière 1966; one d.; ed Ecole Supérieure Technique; studied eng; moved to Paris and spent year as fashion designer 1945; went to Balenciaga's workrooms 1948 and served 11 years apprenticeship; f. Société André Courrèges 1961, founder and Dir, then Chair. and Man. Dir 1966; founder and Dir and Admin, Sport et Couture Amy Linker 1969; founder and Dir Société Courrèges Design 1981; launched 'Couture-Future' 1967; credited with inventing miniskirt. *Leisure interests:* Basque pelota, physical fitness, rugby. *Address:* 40 rue François 1er, 75008 Paris (office); 27 rue Delabordère, 92200 Neuilly-sur-Seine, France (home).

COURT, Rev. Margaret, AO, MBE LLD; Australian fmr tennis player and ecclesiastic; b. 16 July 1942, Albury, NSW; d. of Lawrence Smith and Maud Smith; m. Barry Court 1967; one s. three d.; ed St Augustines, Wodonga, Victoria; amateur player 1960–67; professional 1968–77; Australian champion 1960, 1961, 1962, 1963, 1964, 1965, 1966, 1969, 1970, 1971, 1973; French champion 1962, 1964, 1969, 1970, 1973; Wimbledon champion 1963, 1965, 1970; US champion 1962, 1965, 1969, 1970, 1973; held more major titles in singles, doubles and mixed doubles than any other player in history; won two Grand Slams, in mixed doubles 1963 and singles 1970; played Federation Cup for Australia 1963, 1964, 1965, 1966, 1968, 1969, 1971; ordained a Pentecostal minister in 1991, f. the Victory Life Centre, Perth 1996; elected to Int. Tennis Hall of Fame 1979, Australian Tennis Hall of Fame 1993; Australian Sports Medal 2000, Centenary Medal 2001; Show Court One at Melbourne Park renamed Margaret Court Arena on eve of Australian Open Jan. 2003. *Publications:* The Margaret Smith Story 1964, Court on Court 1974, Winning Faith (with Barbara Oldfield) 1993, Winning Words 1999, Our Winning Position 2003. *Address:* Victory Life Center PO Box 20, Osborne Park, WA 6917, Australia. *Telephone:* (08) 92011266 (office). *Fax:* (08) 92011299 (office). *E-mail:* mcourt@victorylifecentral.com.au (office). *Website:* dev.victorylifecentre.com.au (office).

COURTENAY, Sir Thomas (Tom) Daniel, Kt, KBE; British actor; b. 25 Feb. 1937; s. of the late Thomas Henry Courtenay and Annie Eliza Quest; m. 1st Cheryl Kennedy 1973 (divorced 1982); m. 2nd Isabel Crossley 1988; ed Kingston High School, Hull, Univ. Coll. London, Royal Acad. of Dramatic Art; started acting professionally 1960; Fellow, Univ. Coll. London; Hon. DLitt (Hull); Best Actor Award, Prague Festival 1968, TV Drama Award (for Oswald in Ghosts) 1968, Golden Globe Award for Best Actor 1983, Drama Critics' Award and Evening Standard Award 1980, 1983, BAFTA Award for Best Actor 1999. *Films include:* The Loneliness of the Long Distance Runner 1962, Private Potter 1962, Billy Liar 1963, King and Country 1964, Operation Crossbow 1965, King Rat 1965, Doctor Zhivago 1965, The Night of the Generals 1967, The Day the Fish Came Out 1967, A Dandy in Aspic 1968, Otley 1969, One Day in the Life of Ivan Denisovich 1970, Catch Me a Spy 1971, The Dresser 1983, The Last Butterfly 1990, Redemption (TV) 1991, Let Him Have It 1991, Old Curiosity Shop (TV) 1995, The Boy from Mercury 1996, A Rather English Marriage (TV) 1998, Whatever Happened to Harold Smith 1999, Last Orders 2002, Nicholas Nickleby 2002, Ready When You Are Mr. McGill (TV) 2003, Flood 2006, The Golden Compass 2007. *Plays include:* Billy Liar 1961–62, The Cherry Orchard 1966, Macbeth 1966, Hamlet 1968, She Stoops to Conquer 1969, Charley's Aunt 1971, Time and Time Again (Variety Club of GB Stage Actor Award) 1972, Table Manners 1974, The Norman Conquests 1974–75, The Fool 1975, The Rivals 1976, Clouds 1978, Crime and Punishment 1978, The Dresser (Drama Critics Award and Evening Standard

Award for Best Actor) 1980, 1983, The Misanthrope 1981, Andy Capp 1982, Jumpers 1984, Rookery Nook 1986, The Hypochondriac 1987, Dealing with Clair 1988, The Miser 1992, Moscow Stations, Edinburgh 1993, London 1994, New York 1995, Poison Pen, Manchester 1993, Uncle Vanya, New York 1995, Art, London 1996, King Lear, Manchester 1999. *Television includes:* She Stoops to Conquer 1971, I Heard the Owl Call My Name 1973, Me and the Girls 1985, Absent Friends 1985, Redemption 1991, The Adventures of Young Indiana Jones: Treasure of the Peacock's Eye 1995, The Old Curiosity Shop 1995, A Rather English Marriage 1998, Ready When You Are Mr. McGill 2003, Little Dorrit (series) 2008. *Publication:* Dear Tom: Letters from Home (memoirs) 2000. *Leisure interests:* playing the flute, watching sport. *Address:* c/o Jonathan Altaras Associates, 11 Garrick Street, London, WC2E 9AR, England (office). *Telephone:* (20) 7836-8722 (office).

COUSINS, Richard J., BSc, MSc; British food services industry executive; *Group Chief Executive, Compass Group PLC;* ed Univs of Sheffield and Lancaster; began career with Cadbury Schweppes PLC; joined BTR PLC 1984, becoming Corp. Planning Man., Newey & Eyre (subsidiary co.); joined BPB Group (plasterboard mfr) 1990, apptd Group Financial Controller 1992, served as Gen. Man. then Man. Dir for Packaging, Pres. (Canada) 1998–2000, Group CEO 2000–05; mem. Bd Dirs and Group Chief Exec. Compass Group PLC 2006–, mem. Corp. Responsibility and Exec. Cttees; Dir (non-exec.) HBOS plc; fmr Dir (non-exec.) P&O. *Address:* Compass Group PLC, Compass House, Guildford Street, Chertsey, Surrey, KT16 9BQ, England (office). *Telephone:* (1932) 573000 (office). *Fax:* (1932) 569956 (office). *E-mail:* info@ compass-group.com (office). *Website:* www.compass-group.com (office).

COUSTEAU, Jean-Michel; French explorer, oceanographer, environmentalist activist, educator and film producer; *President, Ocean Futures Society;* b. 8 May 1938; first s. of ocean explorer Jacques-Yves Cousteau and Simone Melchior; one s. one d.; pnr, Nancy Marr; Exec. Vice-Pres. The Cousteau Soc. for nearly 20 years; est. Ocean Futures Soc., Santa Barbara, Calif. (non-profit marine conservation and educ. org.) 1999, now offices in France, Brazil and Italy; has served as spokesman on water issues at UN World Summit on Sustainable Devt in Johannesburg, at 3rd World Water Forum in Kyoto, at Dialogues on Water for Life and Security in Barcelona; spokesperson for US Pavilion at Expo '98, Lisbon, Portugal 1998; merged Jean-Michel Cousteau Inst. with Free Willy Keiko Foundation to continue research and care for Keiko (captive killer whale) 1999; mem. Bd of Dirs Athens Environmental Foundation for Athens 2004 Olympic Games; launched Sustainable Reefs Program (package of materials including CD-ROM, cartoon book and video on sustainable man. of coral reef systems) 2004; Hon. DHumLitt (Pepperdine Univ.) 1976; DEMA Reaching Out Award 1994, NOGI Award, Acad. of Underwater Arts and Sciences 1995, SeaKeepers Award, Showboats International 1996, John M. Olguin Marine Environment Award, Cabrillo Marine Aquarium 1996, Environmental Hero Award, White House Nat. Oceans Conf. 1998, first Oceana Ocean Hero Award 2003, inducted into Int. Scuba Diving Hall of Fame 2003, Poseidon/Lifetime Achievement Award, Reef Check 2006, Emmy Award, Peabody Award, 7 d'Or, Cable Ace Award. *Achievements include:* first person to represent the Environment in Opening Ceremony of Olympic Games, Salt Lake City 2002. *Films:* has produced more than 75 films, including Jean-Michel Cousteau's Ocean Adventures (three-year series of HD TV specials on PBS and internationally) (exec. producer), Sharks 3D, Return to the Amazon 2008, Dolphins and Whales 3D: Tribes of the Ocean 2008; appears in IMAX documentary film Coral Reef Adventure; also appeared in documentary-type special feature on DVD version of Spongebob Squarepants Movie; did similar feature for DVD of Disney/Pixar movie Finding Nemo. *Publications include:* Water Culture (ed. and contributing author), My Father, the Captain 2004, America's Underwater Treasures (co-author) 2006. *Address:* Ocean Futures Society, 325 Chapala Street, Santa Barbara, CA 93101, USA (office). *Telephone:* (805) 899-8899 (office). *E-mail:* contact@ oceanfutures.org (office). *Website:* www.oceanfutures.org (office).

COUTARD, Raoul; French cinematographer and film director; b. 16 Sept. 1924, Paris; with French mil. Information Service, Vietnam, subsequently civilian photographer for Time and Paris-Match; worked in photographic labs during World War II; f. production co. making documentary films; head of photography for French New Wave directors including Godard and Truffaut; later with Costa-Gavras. *Films include:* La Passe du diable 1958, Ramuntcho 1959, Pêcheur d'Islande 1959, Petit jour 1960, Au bout de souffle 1960, Shoot the Pianist 1960, Les Grandes personnes 1961, Lola 1961, Une femme est une femme 1961, Chronique d'un été 1961, Et satan conduit le bal 1962, Jules et Jim 1962, L'Amour à vingt ans 1962, La Poupée 1962, Vivre sa vie 1962, Le Petit soldat 1963, Als twee druppels water 1963, Baie des Anges, Les Carabiniers 1963, Vacances portugaises 1963, Le Mépris 1963, La Peau Douce 1964, Baisers 1964, La Difficulté d'être infidèle 1964, Bande à part 1964, Les Plus belles escroqueries du monde 1964, Une femme mariée 1964, Un monsieur de compagnie 1964, Scruggs 1965, L'Avatar botanique de Mlle Flora 1965, Alphaville 1965, Je vous salue mafia 1965, Pierrot Le Fou 1965, La 317ème Section 1965, The Defector 1966, Made in USA 1966, Horizon 1967, Two or Three Things I Know About Her 1967, Weekend 1967, Sailor from Gibraltar 1967, Rocky Road to Dublin 1968, The Bride Wore Black 1968, Z 1969, The Southern Star 1969, L'Aveu 1970, La Liberté en croupe 1970, L'Explosion 1970, Êtes-vous fiancée à un marin grec ou à un pilote de ligne? 1971, Les Aveux les plus doux 1971, Embassy 1972, The Jerusalem File 1972, Le Trèfle à cinq feuilles 1972, Le Gang des otages 1973, L'Emmerdeur 1973, Comme un pot de fraises 1974, Le Crabe-Tambour 1977, Passion 1982Carmen 1983, Dangerous Moves 1984, La Garce 1984, Parachute 1985, Max mon amour 1986, Blanc de Chine 1988, Brennende Betten 1988, Let Sleeping Cops Lie 1988, Nachbarschaft 1990, Kaffeeklatsch 1990, Bethune: The Making of a Hero 1989, Les Enfants Volants 1990, La Femme Fardée 1990, Maigret et les Plaisirs de la Nuit 1991, La Vie Crevee 1992, The Birth of Love 1994, À

Naissance De L'Amour 1994, Faut pas rire du bonheur 1994, Le Coeur Fantome 1996, Sauvage innocence 2001. *Publication:* L'Impériale de Van Su - Ou comment je suis entré dans le cinéma en dégustant une soupe chinoise (autobiography) 2007. *Address:* c/o Editions Ramsay, 91 bis rue de Cherche-Midi, 75006 Paris, France (office).

COUTAZ, Bernard Edouard; French music industry executive; *Chairman and CEO, Harmonia Mundi SA;* b. 30 Dec. 1922, Saint-Auban-sur-l'Ouvèze (Drôme); s. of Edouard Coutaz and Louise Barlatier; m. Eva Coutaz; ed Faculté catholique de Lyon; journalist, Bayard Presse 1954–60; Founder and Pres. Harmonia Mundi SA (recording co.) 1958, Editions Bernard Coutaz (books on music) 1987, Diffusion livres d'Harmonia Mundi 1987, Chair. and CEO Harmonia Mundi holding co., Mas de vert 1960–; Chevalier Légion d'honneur, Officier des Arts et des Lettres. *Address:* Harmonia Mundi, Mas de vert, BP 20150, 13631 Arles cedex (office); 23 rue Baudanoni, 13200 Arles, France (home). *Telephone:* 4-90-49-90-49 (office). *E-mail:* bcoutaz@ harmoniamundi.com. *Website:* www.harmoniamundi.com (office).

COUTO, Mia; Mozambican biologist, writer and journalist; b. (António Emílio Leite Couto), 5 July 1955, Beira; fmr Dir Mozambique Information Agency; columnist, Notícias daily newspaper, Tempo magazine; currently works as environmental biologist at Limpopo Transfrontier Park; Nat. Award for Literature, Mozambican Nat. Journalistic Asscn 1991, "Best of 1995" Award, Sao Paulo Art Critics Asscn 1996, Prémio Vergílio Ferreira 1999, Latin Union Prize for Literature 2007,. *Publications include:* Raiz d'orvalho (poems) 1983, Vozes Anoitecidas (trans. as Voices Made Night) 1986, Cada homem e uma raca 1991 (trans. as Every Man is a Race 1994), Terra Sonambula 1992, Under the Frangipani 2001, Um Rio Chamado Tempo, Uma Casa Chamada Terra 2002, Vozes Anoitecidas 2002, Contos do Nascer da Terra 2002, The Last Flight of the Flamingo 2004, O fio das missangas 2002, A chuva pasmada 2004, Pensatempos 2005, O outro pé da Sereia 2006, Sleepwalking Land 2006, A River Called Time 2008 and collections of short stories. *Address:* c/o Serpent's Tail, 3A Exmouth House, Pine Street, London, EC1R 0JH, England (office).

COUTTS, Ronald Thomson, PhD, DSc, FRSC; Canadian professor of medicinal chemistry; *Professor Emeritus of Psychiatry, University of Alberta;* b. 19 June 1931, Glasgow, Scotland; s. of Ronald Miller Coutts and Helen Alexanderina Crombie; m. Sheenah Kirk Black 1957; two s. one d.; ed Woodside Secondary School, Glasgow, Univ. of Strathclyde, Glasgow Univ. and Chelsea Coll., London; Lecturer in Medicinal Chem., Sunderland Tech. Coll., England 1959–63; Asst then Assoc. Prof., Univ. of Saskatchewan, Canada 1963–66; Prof., Univ. of Alberta 1966–97, Distinguished Univ. Prof. 1984–, Pres. Faculty Asscn 1978–79, mem. Bd of Govs 1982–85, Hon. Prof. of Psychiatry 1979–, Prof. Emer. 1997–; McCalla Prof., Univ. of Alberta 1985–86; Pres. Xenotox Services Ltd 1978–; Scientific Ed. Canadian Journal of Pharmaceutical Sciences 1967–72; mem. Ed. Bd Asian Journal of Pharmaceutical Sciences 1978–85; Ed. Journal of Pharmacological Methods 1984–98; Ed. Bd Chirality 1989–95; Pres. Asscn of Faculties of Pharmacy of Canada 1994–96; Fellow, Pharmaceutical Soc. of GB, Canadian Inst. of Chemistry, American Asscn of Pharmaceutical Scientists; McNeil Research Award 1982, Canadian Coll. of Neuropsychopharmacology Medal 1992, Innovation in Neuropsychopharmacology Research Award 1999. *Publications:* over 350 research manuscripts and reviews; several textbooks and chapters in textbooks. *Leisure interests:* golf, cross-country skiing, squash and music (playing and listening). *Address:* 4724 139 Street, NW, Edmonton, AB, Canada (home). *Telephone:* (780) 436-4313 (home).

COUTU, Jean, OC, OQ; Canadian pharmacist and business executive; *Chairman of the Board, Jean Coutu Group;* b. 29 May 1927, Montréal; s. of Lucien Coutu; m. Marcelle Coutu; ed Université de Montréal; f. Jean Coutu Group (pharmacy business) 1969, currently Chair. of Bd; f. l'Association Québécoise des pharmaciens propriétaires 1966, Fondation Marcelle et Jean Coutu 1990. *Address:* Jean Coutu Group, 530 Bériault Street, Longueuil, PQ J4G 1S8, Canada (office). *Telephone:* (450) 646-9760 (office). *Website:* www .jeancoutu.com (office).

COUTURE, Lise Anne, MArch; Canadian architect and academic; *Partner, Asymptote Architecture;* b. 1959; ed Carleton Coll., Yale Univ., USA; Pnr (with Hani Rashid) Asymptote Architecture, New York 1989–; Prof. of Architecture, Parsons School of Design 1990–; currently Adjunct Asst Prof. of Architecture, Grad. School of Architecture, Columbia Univ.; fmr Bishop Chair and Saarinen Chair, Yale Univ.; Mushenheim Fellow, New York Foundation for the Arts 1992; fmr Visiting Prof., Princeton Univ., Harvard Univ., Sciarc, Univ. of Virginia, Univ. of Montréal, Berlage Inst., Univ. of Michigan, MIT; comms include Guggenheim Virtual Museums, New York Stock Exchange Virtual Environment and Advanced Command Area; exhbn Stratascope Asymptote, Pa 2001–02; Frederick Kiesler Award (jtly) 2004. *Architectural works include:* Moscow State Theatre, Russia; Library, Alexandria, Egypt; Nat. Courthouse, Groningen, The Netherlands; LA W Coast Highway; Univers Theater, Århus, Denmark. *Publications include:* numerous articles in professional journals. *Address:* Asymptote Architecture, 11–45 46th Avenue, LIC, New York, NY 11101 (office); Graduate School of Architecture, Planning and Preservation, Columbia University, 2960 Broadway, New York, NY 10027-6902, USA. *Telephone:* (212) 343-7333 (office). *Fax:* (718) 937-3320 (office). *E-mail:* info@ asymptote.net (office). *Website:* www.asymptote.net (office).

COUTURE, Pierre-François; French business executive and civil servant; *Special Delegate for Economic Development in Ardennes;* b. 15 May 1946, Grenoble; s. of André Couture and Françoise Couture (née Dubourguez); brother of Xavier Couture (q.v.); m. 2nd Jocelyne Kerjouan; one s.; three c. from previous m.; ed Ecole Nat. d'Admin., Inst. d'Etudes Politiques, Paris, Univ. of Paris II; Dir Industry and Energy Dept, Ministry of the Econ. and

Finance 1974–78, mem. Oil Co. Audit Programme 1979; Dir of Budgets Ministries of Finance and Justice and Office of the Prime Minister 1978–79; Gen. Sec. Exploration and Production Div., Cie Française des Pétroles 1979–81; Tech. Adviser Ministry of the Budget 1981–83; Tech. Adviser Ministry of Industry 1983–84, Dir of Gas, Electricity and Coal 1983–1990; Adviser to Chair. of La Poste 1996; Special Adviser to Industry Sec. in charge of Postal Services and Telecommunications, Ministry of the Economy, Finance and Industry 1997–99; Chair. Enterprise Minière et Chimique (EMC) 1999–2004; Head of Econ. and Financial Audit Programme, Ministry of Economy, Finance and Industry 2005–; Special Del. for Econ. Devt in Ardennes 2006–; mem. Bd of Dirs Charbonnages de France; Chair. Viet Nam Cttee, Medef Int; Chevalier, Ordre Nat. du Mérite, Légion d'honneur. *Leisure interests:* travel, mountain sports, golf. *Address:* Conseil Général des Ardennes, Hôtel du Département, 08011 Charleville-Mézières Cedex, France (office). *Telephone:* 3-24-59-60-60 (office). *Fax:* 3-24-37-76-76 (office). *E-mail:* conseil-general-ardennes@cg08.fr (office). *Website:* www.cg08.fr (office).

COUVREUR, Philippe; Belgian lawyer and international organization official; *Registrar, International Court of Justice;* b. 29 Nov. 1951, Schaerbeek; ed Collège Jean XXIII, Brussels, Facultés Notre-Dame de la Paix, Namur, Université Catholique de Louvain, King's Coll., London, UK, Universidad Complutense de Madrid, Spain; Intern, Legal Service, Comm. of EC 1978–79 (worked on accessions of Spain and Portugal to join EC); Special Asst in offices Registrar and Deputy-Registrar, Int. Court of Justice 1982–86, Sec. 1986–94, First Sec. 1994–95, Prin. Legal Sec. 1995–2000; Registrar Int. Court of Justice 2000– (re-elected 2007); Asst Prof., Centre d'études européennes and in Law Faculty of Université Catholique de Louvain 1976–82; Visiting Prof. in the Law of Int. Orgs, Univ. of Ouagadougou, Burkina Faso 1980–82; Professeur extraordinaire in Law of Nations and Comparative Constitutional Law, Ecole des Hautes études commerciales Saint-Louis, Brussels 1986–96; Guest Lecturer in Public Int. Law, Université Catholique de Louvain 1997–; Corresp. mem. Spanish Royal Acad. of Moral and Political Sciences; mem. various other learned socs; Netherlands Embassy Prize 1969. *Publications:* numerous publs and articles. *Address:* International Court of Justice, Peace Palace, Carnegieplein 2, 2517 KJ The Hague, The Netherlands (office). *Telephone:* (70) 302-23-23 (office). *Fax:* (70) 364-99-28 (office). *E-mail:* info@icj-cij.org (office). *Website:* www.icj-cij.org (office).

COVENEY, James, BA, DUniv; British academic; *Professor Emeritus of French, University of Bath;* b. 4 April 1920, London; s. of James Coveney and Mary Coveney; m. Patricia Yvonne Townsend 1955; two s.; ed St Ignatius Coll. and Univs of Reading and Strasbourg; served in Welch Regt, Royal West Kent Regt, and RAF as Pilot (Flight-Lt), World War II; Lecturer, Univ. of Strasbourg 1951–53; Lecturer in Medieval French, Univ. of Hull 1953–58; Asst Dir, Civil Service Comm. 1958–59; UN Secr., New York 1959–61; NATO Secr. 1961–64; Sr Lecturer, Head of Modern Languages, Univ. of Bath 1964–68, Prof. of French 1969–85, Prof. Emer. 1985–; Visiting Prof., Ecole Nat. d'Admin, Paris 1974–85, Univ. of Buckingham 1974–86, Bethlehem Univ. 1985; Consultant, Univ. of Macau 1988, Int. Communications, Inc., Tokyo 1991–94; Corresp. mem. Acad. des Sciences, Agric., Arts et Belles-lettres, Aix-en-Provence 1975; Officier, Ordre nat. du Mérite 1986, Officier, Ordre des Palmes Académiques 2007. *Publications:* La légende de l'Empereur Constant 1955; co-author: Glossary of French and English Management Terms 1972, Le français pour l'ingénieur 1974, Guide to French Institutions 1978, French Business Management Dictionary 1993. *Address:* 2 Campions court, Graemesdyke Road, Berkhamsted, Herts., HP4 3PD, England. *Telephone:* (1442) 865657.

COVENTRY, Kirsty Leigh; swimmer; b. 16 Sept. 1983, Harare; ed Dominican Convent High School; Gold Medal 200m Individual Medley, Commonwealth Games, Manchester 2002; swam competitively for Auburn Univ., Ala, USA, winner 100m Freestyle, 200m Freestyle, 200m Backstroke, Nat. Collegiate Athletic Asscn (NCAA) Championships 2005; Gold Medal 200m Backstroke, Athens Olympics 2004, Silver Medal 100m Backstroke, Bronze Medal 200m. Individual Medley; Gold Medal 100m Backstroke, 200m Backstroke, World Championships, Montreal 2005, Silver Medal 200m Individual Medley, 400m Individual Medley; Gold Medal 200m Individual Medley, 400m Individual Medley, 50m freestyle, 800m freestyle, 50m backstroke, 100m backstroke, 200m backstroke, All-Africa Games, Algiers 2007, Silver Medal 100m breaststroke, 4×100m medley relay, 4×200m freestyle relay; Silver Medal 200m Backstroke, 200m Individual Medley, World Championships, Melbourne 2007; Gold Medal 200m Backstroke, Olympic Games, Beijing 2008, Silver Medal 100m Backstroke, 200m Individual Medley, 400m Individual Medley; Zimbabwe Sports Woman of the Year 2000, SEC Female Athlete of the Year 2004–05, College Swimming Coaches Asscn Swimmer of the Meet 2005, SEC Swimmer of the Year 2005, Honda Award for Swimming 2005, World African Swimmer of the Year 2005, 2007. *Address:* c/o Zimbabwe Olympic Committee, PO Box 4718, City Sport Centre Complex, off Rekai Tangwena Street, Harare, Zimbabwe. *Telephone:* (4) 751107. *Fax:* (4) 751107. *E-mail:* olympic@ecoweb.co.zw.

ČOVIĆ, Dragan, PhD; Bosnia and Herzegovina politician; *President, Croatian Democratic Union of Bosnia and Herzegovina;* b. 20 Aug. 1956, Mostar; m.; two d.; ed Univ. of Mostar, Sarajevo Univ.; with SOKO co., Mostar, holding sr managerial positions 1977–98; Assoc. Prof., then Prof., Univ. of Mostar 1996–; mem. Croat Democratic Union; Deputy Prime Minister and Minister of Finance, Fed. of Bosnia and Herzegovina 1998–2001; elected to Tripartite Presidency 2002, Leader of Presidency 2003–04, dismissed by High Rep. of the Int. Community in Bosnia and Herzegovina Paddy Ashdown following indictment for financial corruption, before trial took place 29 March 2005; Vice-Pres., Croatian Democratic Union of Bosnia and Herzegovina 1998–2005, Pres. 2005–. *Address:* Croatian Democratic Union of Bosnia and

Herzegovina, 88000 Mostar, Mostar-Zapad, Kneza Domagoja b.b, Bosnia and Herzegovina. *Telephone:* (36) 310701. *Fax:* (36) 315024. *E-mail:* hdzbih@hdzbih.org. *Website:* www.hdzbih.org.

ČOVIĆ, Željko, MSc; Croatian business executive; *President of the Management Board and CEO, PLIVA Pharmaceuticals Inc.;* b. 9 Jan. 1953, Zagreb; ed Zagreb Univ., Int. Inst. of Man. Devt; joined PLIVA, Zagreb 1980, Dir Foodstuffs Div. 1985–86, Head of Sales, Foodstuffs Div. 1986–88, Head of Marketing and Sales 1988–91, Chair. Bd of Dirs and CEO PLIVA d.d. 1993–95, Pres. Man. Bd and CEO 1995–; mem. Exec. City Council and Sec. for Econ. Affairs, City of Zagreb 1991–93, Advisor to Vice-Pres. of the Economy, Croatian Govt 1993; mem. American Chamber of Commerce, Croatian Nat. Council on Competitiveness (Pres. 2002–05), Croatian Employers' Asscn (Pres. 2001–02); Order of the Croatian Star 1995, Order of the Croatian Pleter 1995; Croatian Chamber of Commerce Golden Award 1994, Managers and Entrepreneurs Asscn Manager of the Year 1995, ING Barings and Emerging Markets CEO of the Year Award 1999. *Address:* PLIVA Pharmaceuticals Inc., Ulica grada Vukovara 49, 10000 Zagreb, Croatia (office). *Telephone:* (1) 6160355 (office). *Fax:* (1) 6114413 (office). *Website:* www.pliva.com (office).

COWELL, Simon; British broadcaster, television executive, record company executive and A & R consultant; b. 7 Oct. 1959, England; ed Dover Coll., St Columba's Coll., St Albans; worked for EMI Music Publishing 1977–82; founder, Fanfare Records (with Iain Burton) 1982–89; A & R Consultant BMG Records 1989–; founder and co-owner S Records 2001; f. Syco record label (subsidiary of Sony BMG) 2002, artists include Westlife, Five, Robson & Jerome, Zig & Zag, Girl Thing, Will Young, Gareth Gates, Six, Il Divo, Steve Brookstein, Shayne Ward, Journey South, Paul Potts, Ray Quinn, Leona Lewis; Record Exec. of the Year 1998, 1999, A & R Man. of the Year 1999, Variety Club Showbusiness Personality of the Year 2005. *Television:* producer and judge Pop Idol (ITV 1) 2001–02, American Idol: The Search for a Superstar (Fox TV) 2002–, The X Factor (ITV) 2004–, America's Got Talent 2006–, Britain's Got Talent 2007–. *Address:* Syco Music, Bedford House, 69–79 Fulham High Street, London, SW6 3JW, England. *E-mail:* simon.cowell@bmg.com.

COWEN, Brian, BCL; Irish solicitor and politician; *Taoiseach (Prime Minister);* b. 10 Jan. 1960, Tullamore; s. of the late Bernard Cowen and of Mary Cowen; m. Mary Molloy 1990; two d.; ed Univ. Coll. Dublin and Inc. Law Soc. of Ireland; mem. Offaly Co. Council 1984–93; mem. Dáil for for Laois-Offaly 1984–; Minister for Labour 1991–92, for Transport, Energy and Communications 1992–94, for Health and Children 1997–2000, for Foreign Affairs 2000–04, for Finance 2004–08 (also Deputy Prime Minister), Taoiseach (Prime Minister) 2008–, Leader, Fianna Fáil 2008, Leader Parl. Party 2008–; fmr Opposition Spokesperson on Agric. and Food. *Leisure interests:* sport, reading, music. *Address:* Department of the Taoiseach, Government Bldgs, Upper Merrion Street, Dublin 2; Ballard, Tullamore, Co. Offaly, Ireland. *Telephone:* (1) 6194000. *Fax:* (1) 6194297. *E-mail:* webmaster@taoiseach.gov.ie. *Website:* www.taoiseach.gov.ie.

COWEN, Rt Hon. Sir Zelman, Kt, PC, AK, GCMG, GCVO, QC; Australian academic; b. 7 Oct. 1919, Melbourne; s. of the late Bernard Cowen and of Sara Granat; m. Anna Wittner 1945; three s. one d.; ed Scotch Coll., Melbourne, Univ. of Melbourne, Univ. of Oxford; served in Royal Australian Naval Volunteer Reserve 1940–45; consultant to Mil. Govt in Germany 1947; Australian Dominion Liaison Officer to Colonial Office 1951–66; Dean of Faculty of Law, Prof. of Public Law, Univ. of Melbourne 1951–66; Vice-Chancellor, Univ. of New England, NSW 1967–70, Univ. of Queensland 1970–77; Gov.-Gen. of Australia 1977–82; Provost of Oriel Coll., Oxford 1982–90; Pro-Vice Chancellor of Oxford Univ. 1988–90; Chair. John Fairfax Holdings Ltd 1992–94 (Dir 1994–96); Visiting Prof., Univ. of Chicago 1949, Harvard Law School and Fletcher School of Law and Diplomacy 1953–54, 1963–64, Univ. of Utah 1954, Ill. 1957–58, Wash. 1959, Univ. of Calcutta, India 1975; Menzies Scholar in Residence, Univ. of Va, 1983; Pres. Adult Educ. Asscn of Australia 1968–70; mem. and (at various times) Chair. Victorian State Advisory Cttee to Australian Broadcasting Comm.; mem. Devt Corpn of NSW 1969–70, Bd of Int. Asscn for Cultural Freedom 1970–75; Academic Gov. of Bd of Govs, Hebrew Univ. of Jerusalem 1969–77, 1982–; mem. Club of Rome 1974–77; Pres. Australian Inst. of Urban Studies 1973–77; Chair. Bd of Govs, Utah Foundation 1975–77; Law Reform Commr, Commonwealth of Australia 1976–77; Chair. Australian Vice-Chancellor's Cttee 1977, Australian Studies Centre Cttee (London) 1982–90, Press Council (UK) 1983–88, Victoria League for Commonwealth Friendship 1986–89, of Trustees, Visnews Ltd 1986–91, Bd of Dirs Sir Robert Menzies Memorial Foundation 1990–97, Australian Nat. Acad. of Music 1995–2000, Australian Mutual Provident Soc. 1982–90; mem. Nat. Council of Australian Opera (Chair. 1983–95); Trustee Sydney Opera House 1969–70, Queensland Overseas Foundation 1976–77, Sir Robert Menzies Memorial Trust (UK), Winston Churchill Memorial Trust (UK), Van Leer Inst. of Jerusalem (Chair. 1988–95, Hon. Chair. 1995–); Pres. Order of Australia Asscn 1992–95; Nat. Pres. Australia-Britain Soc. 1993–95; Foreign Hon. Mem. American Acad. of Arts and Sciences; Fellow, Acad. of Social Sciences in Australia, Australian Coll. of Educ., Australian and NZ Asscn for the Advancement of Science (now Hon. Fellow), Australian Nat. Acad. of Music 2000; Hon. Fellow, New Coll., Oxford, Univ. House, Australian Inst. of Architects, Australian Acad. of Social Sciences, Australian Coll. of Educ., Univ. House of Australia, Nat. Univ., Australian Acad. of Technological Sciences, Royal Australasian Coll. of Physicians, Royal Australian Coll. of Medical Administrators, Royal Australian Coll. of Obstetricians and Gynae-cologists, Australian Acad. of the Humanities, Australian Soc. of Accountants, Australian Inst. of Chartered Accountants, Australian Coll. of Rehabilitation Medicine, Trinity Coll., Dublin, Oriel Coll., Oxford; Hon. Master, Gray's Inn Bench 1976, QC of the Queensland Bar, mem. Victorian Bar and Hon. Life mem. NSW Bar Asscn; Hon. LLD (Univs. of Hong Kong, Queensland, Melbourne, WA, Turin, Australian Nat. Univ., Tasmania, Victoria Univ. of Tech., Deakin Univ., Monash Univ.), Hon. DLitt (Univs. of New England, Sydney, Oxford, James Cook Univ. of N Queensland), Hon. DHL (Hebrew Union Coll., Cincinnati), (Univ. of Redlands, Calif.), Hon. DUniv (Newcastle, Griffith, Sunshine Coast Univ. Queensland), Hon. DPhil (Hebrew Univ. of Jerusalem, Univ. of Tel Aviv); Kt, Order of Australia, Kt Grand Cross, Order of St Michael and St George, Royal Victorian Order, KStJ, Kt Grand Cross, Order of Merit, Italy. *Publications:* Specialist Editor, Dicey: Conflict of Laws 1949, Australia and the United States: Some Legal Comparisons 1954, (with P. B. Carter) Essays on the Law of Evidence 1956, American-Australian Private International Law 1957, Federal Jurisdiction in Australia 1959 (with Leslie Zines), Matrimonial Causes Jurisdiction 1961, The British Commonwealth of Nations in a Changing World 1964, Sir John Latham and Other Papers 1965, Sir Isaac Isaacs 1967, 1993, The Private Man (A.B.C. Boyer Lectures 1969), Individual Liberty and the Law (Tagore Law Lectures 1975), The Virginia Lectures 1984, Reflections on Medicine, Biotechnology and the Law (Pound Lectures, Neb. Univ.) 1986, A Touch of Healing (3 Vols) 1986, Memoirs of Zelman Cowen: A Public Life 2006. *Leisure interests:* music, performing and visual arts. *Address:* 4 Treasury Place, East Melbourne, Vic. 3002, Australia (office). *Telephone:* (3) 96500299 (office). *Fax:* (3) 96500301 (office). *E-mail:* zelman.cowen@dpmc.gov.au (office).

COWLEY, Alan Herbert, BS, MS, PhD, FRS; British chemist and academic; *Robert A. Welch Professor of Chemistry, University of Texas;* b. 29 Jan. 1934, Manchester; s. of the late Herbert Cowley and Dora Cowley; m. Deborah Elaine Cole 1975; two s. three d.; ed Univ. of Manchester; Postdoctoral Fellow, then Instructor, Univ. of Florida, USA 1958–60; Tech. Officer, Exploratory Group, ICI (Billingham Div.), UK 1960–61; Asst Prof. of Chem., Univ. of Texas at Austin 1962–67, Assoc. Prof. 1967–70, Prof. 1970–84, George W. Watt Centennial Prof. of Chem. 1984–88, Richard J.V. Johnson Regent's Prof. of Chem. 1989–91, Robert A. Welch Prof. of Chem. 1991–; Sir Edward Frankland Prof. of Inorganic Chem., Imperial Coll., London 1988–89; Vice-Chair. Bd of Trustees, Gordon Research Confs. 1993–94 (Chair. 1994–95) mem. Editorial Bd Inorganic Chemistry 1979–83, Chemical Reviews 1984–88, Polyhedron 1984–2000, Journal of American Chem. Soc. 1986–91, Journal of Organometallic Chemistry 1987–, Organometallics 1988–91, Dalton Trans 1997–2000, Inorganic Syntheses 1983–; Corresp. Mem. Mexican Acad. of Sciences 2004; Guggenheim Fellowship 1976–77; Chevalier, Ordre des Palmes Académiques 1997; Dr hc (Univ. of Bordeaux) 2003; Royal Soc. of Chem. Award for Main-Group Element Chem. 1980, Centenary Medal and Lectureship, Royal Soc. of Chem. 1986, ACS Southwest Regional Award 1986, Stiefvater Memorial Award and Lectureship, Univ. of Nebraska 1987, Chemical Pioneer Award, American Inst. of Chemists 1994, Von Humboldt Prize 1996. *Publications:* more than 450 articles in learned journals. *Leisure interests:* squash, sailing, classical music, literature. *Address:* Department of Chemistry and Biochemistry, WEL 4.330, University of Texas, Austin, TX 78712, USA. *Telephone:* (512) 471-7484 (office). *Fax:* (512) 471-6822 (office). *E-mail:* cowley@mail.utexas.edu (office). *Website:* www.cm.utexas.edu/alan_cowley (office); cowley.cm.utexas.edu/acowley (office).

COWLEY, Roger Arthur, FRS, FRSE, FRSC; British physicist and academic; *Emeritus Professor of Experimental Philosophy and Fellow, Wadham College, University of Oxford;* b. 24 Feb. 1939, Essex; s. of C. A. Cowley; m. Sheila Joyce Wells 1964; one s. one d.; ed Brentwood School and Univ. of Cambridge; Fellow of Trinity Hall, Cambridge 1962–64; Research Officer, Atomic Energy of Canada Ltd 1964–70; Prof. of Physics, Univ. of Edinburgh 1970–88; Dr Lee's Prof. of Experimental Philosophy and Fellow of Wadham Coll., Oxford 1988–2007, Emer. Prof. 2007–, Chair. of Physics Dept 1993–96, 1999–2002; Max Born Medal and Prize 1973, Holweck Medal and Prize 1990, Walter Hälg Prize and Medal 2003, Faraday Medal and Prize 2008. *Publications:* over 350 scientific publs. *Leisure interests:* gardening, tennis, walking. *Address:* Oxford Physics, Clarendon Laboratory, Parks Road, Oxford, OX1 3PU (office); Tredinnock, Harcourt Hill, Oxford, OX2 9AS, England (home). *Telephone:* (1865) 272224 (office); (1865) 247570 (home). *Fax:* (1865) 272400 (office). *E-mail:* r.cowley@physics.ox.ac.uk (office). *Website:* www.physics.ox.ac.uk (office).

COWPER-COLES, Sir Sherard Louis, Kt, KCMG, LVO; British diplomatist; *Ambassador to Afghanistan;* b. 8 Jan. 1955, London; s. of Sherard Hamilton Cowper-Coles and Dorothy Short; m. Bridget Cowper-Coles; four s. one d.; ed Tonbridge School, Hertford Coll., Oxford; joined FCO 1977; Third, then Second Sec., Cairo 1980–83; First Sec. Planning Office, FCO 1983–85, Pvt. Sec. to Perm. Under-Sec. of State 1985–87; First Sec., Washington, DC 1987–91; Asst Security Policy Dept, FCO 1991–93, Head Hong Kong Dept 1994–97; Counsellor, Paris 1997–99; Prin. Pvt. Sec. to Sec. of State for Foreign and Commonwealth Affairs 1999–2001; Amb. to Israel 2001–03, to Saudi Arabia 2003–07, to Afghanistan 2007–; Hon. Fellow, Hertford Coll. Oxford 2002. *Publication:* From Defence to Security 2004. *Address:* BFPO 5426, HA4 6EP, England (office). *Telephone:* 70-102201 (Afghanistan, mobile) (office). *E-mail:* sherard.cowper-coles@fco.gov.uk (office). *Website:* www.britishembassy.gov.uk/afghanistan (office).

COX, Barry Geoffrey, BA, FRTS; British journalist and television industry executive; b. 25 May 1942, Guildford; m. 1st Pamela Doran 1967 (divorced 1977); m. 2nd Kathryn Kay 1984 (divorced 1992); two s. two d.; ed Tiffin School, Kingston, Surrey and Magdalen Coll., Oxford; reporter, The Scotsman 1965–67; feature writer, Sunday Telegraph 1967–70; Producer/Dir World in Action, Granada TV 1970–74; The London Programme, London Weekend TV 1974–77, Head of Current Affairs 1977–81, Controller of Features and Current Affairs 1981–87, Dir of Corp. Affairs 1987–94, Special Adviser to Chief Exec. 1994–95; Dir Ind. TV Asscn 1995–98; Deputy Chair. Channel 4 1999–2006; consultant to United Broadcasting and Entertainment 1998–2001, to Ind. TV News 1998–; Chair. Digital TV Stakeholders Group 2002–04; Chair. SwitchCo Ltd 2005–; Chair. of Bd Oval House Theatre 2001–; News Int. Visiting Prof. of Broadcast Media, Oxford Univ. 2003; mem. Council Inst. of Educ. 2000; Owner, Mapledene TV Productions Ltd. *Publications:* Civil Liberties in Britain 1975, The Fall of Scotland Yard 1977, Free For All: Public Service Television in the Digital Age 2004. *Leisure interests:* tennis, walking, theatre. *Address:* Mapledene TV Productions Ltd, 72 Wilton Road, Victoria, London, SW1V 1DE, England. *E-mail:* barry.cox3@btopenworld.com. *Website:* www.digitaluk.co.uk.

COX, Brian Denis, CBE; British actor, director and writer; b. 1 June 1946; s. of Charles Mcardle Campbell Cox and Mary Ann Gillerine (née Mccann); m. 1st Caroline Burt 1968 (divorced 1987); one s. one d.; m. 2nd Nicole Ansari 2001; two s.; ed London Acad. of Music and Dramatic Art; Hon. LLD (Dundee) 2006; Hon. Dr of Drama (Royal Scottish Acad. of Music and Drama) 2006; Scottish BAFTA Award for Contrib. to Scottish Broadcasting 2004. *Stage appearances include:* debut at Dundee Repertory 1961; Royal Lyceum, Edinburgh 1965–66, Birmingham Repertory 1966–68, As You Like It, Birmingham and Vaudeville (London debut) 1967, Peer Gynt, Birmingham 1967, When We Dead Awaken, Edinburgh Festival 1968, In Celebration, Royal Court 1969, The Wild Duck, Edinburgh Festival 1969, The Big Romance, Royal Court 1970, Don't Start Without Me, Garrick 1971, Mirandolina, Brighton 1971, Getting On, Queen's 1971, The Creditors, Open Space 1972, Hedda Gabler, Royal Court 1972; Playhouse, Nottingham: Love's Labour's Lost, Brand, What The Butler Saw, The Three Musketeers 1972; Cromwell, Royal Court 1973; Royal Exchange, Manchester: Arms and the Man 1974, The Cocktail Party 1975; Pilgrims Progress, Prospect Theatre 1975, Emigres, Nat. Theatre Co., Young Vic 1976; Olivier Theatre: Tamburlaine the Great 1976, Julius Caesar 1977; The Changeling, Riverside Studios 1978; Nat. Theatre: Herod, The Putney Debates 1978; On Top, Royal Court 1979, Macbeth, Cambridge Theatre and tour of India 1980, Summer Party, Crucible 1980, Have You Anything to Declare?, Manchester then Round House 1981, Danton's Death, Nat. Theatre Co., Olivier 1982, Strange Interlude, Duke of York (Drama Magazine Best Actor Award 1985) 1984 and Nederlander, New York 1985, Rat in the Skull, Royal Court (Drama Magazine and Olivier Best Actor Awards 1985) 1984 and New York 1985, Fashion, The Danton Affair, Misalliance, Penny for a Song 1986, The Taming of the Shrew, Titus Andronicus 1987, The Three Sisters 1989, RSC and Titus Andronicus on tour, Madrid, Paris, Copenhagen (Olivier Award for Best Actor in a Revival and Drama Magazine Best Actor Award for RSC 1988) 1988, Frankie and Johnny in the Claire-de-Lune, Comedy 1989, Richard III, King Lear, nat. and world tour 1990–91, The Master Builder, Edinburgh 1993, Riverside 1994, St Nicholas, The Bush Theatre 1997, New York (Lucille Lortel Award 1998) 1998, Skylight, Los Angeles 1997, Dublin Carol, Old Vic and Royal Court 2000, Uncle Varrick, Royal Lyceum, Edinburgh 2004, Rock 'n' Roll, Royal Court Theatre. *Plays directed:* Edinburgh Festival: The Man with a Flower in his Mouth 1973, The Stronger 1973; Orange Tree, Richmond: I Love My Love 1982, Mrs Warren's Profession 1989; The Crucible, Moscow Art Theatre, London and Edinburgh 1989, The Philanderer, Hampstead Theatre Club (world premier of complete version) (Int. Theatre Inst. Award 1990) 1991. *Radio:* McLevy (BBC series). *Films include:* Nicholas and Alexandra 1971, In Celebration 1975, Manhunter 1986, Shoot for the Sun 1986, Hidden Agenda 1990, The Cutter 1994, Braveheart 1995, Rob Roy 1995, Chain Reaction 1996, The Glimmer Man 1996, The Long Kiss Goodnight 1996, Desperate Measures 1997, Food for Ravens 1997, Poodle Spring 1997, The Boxer 1998, The Corruptor 1998, Mad About Mamba 1998, The Minus Man 198, Rushmore 1998, The Biographer 2000, Saltwater 2001, LIE 2001, Morality Play, Affair of the Necklace, The Bourne Identity 2002, Adaptation 2002, The Ring 2002, X-Men 2 2003, Troy 2004, The Bourne Supremacy 2004, Get the Picture 2004, Match Point 2005, A Woman in Winter 2005, Red Eye 2005, The Ringer 2005, The Flying Scotsman 2006, Burns 2006, Running with Scissors 2006, The Escapist 2007, Zodiac 2007. *TV appearances include:* Churchill's People: The Wallace 1972, The Master of Ballantrae 1975, Henry II in The Devil's Crown 1978, Thérèse Raquin 1979, Dalhousie's Luck 1980, Bothwell 1980, Bach 1981, Pope John Paul II 1984, Florence Nightingale 1985, Beryl Markham: A Shadow in the Sun 1988, Secret Weapon 1990, Acting in Tragedy (BBC Masterclass) 1990, The Lost Language of Cranes 1992, The Cloning of Joanna May 1992, The Big Battalions 1992, The Negotiator 1994, Witness for Hitler 1995, Blow Your Mind See A Play 1995, Nuremberg (Emmy Award for Best Actor) 2001, Frasier 2002, The Court 2002, Blue/Orange 2005, Deadwood 2006, The Outsiders 2006. *Publications include:* Salem to Moscow: An Actor's Odyssey 1991, The Lear Diaries 1992. *Leisure interests:* keeping fit, tango. *Address:* c/o Conway van Gelder, 18–21 Jermyn Street, London, SW1Y 6HP, England (office). *Telephone:* (20) 7287-0077 (office).

COX, Carrie S., BS; American pharmacist and business executive; *Executive Vice-President and President of Global Pharmaceuticals, Schering-Plough Corporation;* ed Mass Coll. of Pharmacy and Health Sciences; held a variety of positions in market research, sales and product man. during a 10-year career with Sandoz Pharmaceuticals; Vice-Pres. Women's Health Care, Wyeth-Ayerst for seven years; Exec. Vice-Pres. and Pres. Global Prescription Business, Pharmacia Corpn (fmrly Pharmacia & Upjohn) 1997–2003; Exec. Vice-Pres. and Pres. Global Pharmaceuticals, Schering-Plough Corpn 2003–; mem. Bd of Dirs Texas Instruments Inc. 2004–; ranked by Fortune magazine amongst 50 Most Powerful Women in Business in the US 2001, (37th) 2005, (39th) 2006, (32nd) 2007. *Address:* Global Headquarters, Schering-Plough Corporation, 2000 Galloping Hill Road, Kenilworth, NJ 07033-0530, USA (office). *Telephone:* (908) 298-4000 (office). *Website:* www.schering-plough.com (office).

COX, Christopher, BA, MBA, JD; American lawyer, politician and fmr government official; b. 16 Oct. 1952; m. Rebecca Gernhardt; three c.; ed Univ. of Southern California, Harvard Business School, Harvard Law School; fmr Ed. Harvard Law Review; Clerk US Court of Appeals 1977–78; Assoc. Latham & Watkins 1978–82, Pnr 1984–86; Lecturer in Business Admin, Harvard Business School 1982–83; Sr Assoc. Counsel to Pres., White House 1986–88; mem. US House of Reps from Calif. 1988–2005, Chair. House Cttee on Homeland Security, House Policy Cttee 1994–2005; Chair. SEC 2005–09. *Address:* c/o SEC Headquarters, 100 F Street, NE, Washington, DC 20549, USA (office).

COX, Sir David Roxbee, Kt, PhD, FRS; British statistician; b. 15 July 1924, Birmingham; s. of Sam R. Cox and Lilian Cox (née Braines); m. Joyce Drummond 1948; one d. three s.; ed Handsworth Grammar School, Birmingham and St John's Coll. Cambridge; with Royal Aircraft Establishment 1944–46; Wool Industries Research Asscn 1946–50; Statistical Lab., Univ. of Cambridge 1950–55; with Dept of Biostatistics, Univ. of North Carolina 1955–56, Birkbeck Coll., London 1956–66; Bell Telephone Labs 1965; Prof. of Statistics, Imperial Coll. of Science and Tech., London 1966–88; Warden, Nuffield Coll., Oxford 1988–94; Science and Eng Research Council Sr Research Fellow 1983–88; Ed. Biometrika 1966–91; Pres. Int. Statistics Inst. 1995–97; Fellow, Imperial Coll., Birkbeck Coll. London; Hon. Fellow, St John's Coll. Cambridge, Inst. of Actuaries, Nuffield Coll. Oxford, British Acad.; Hon. Foreign mem.: US Acad. of Arts and Sciences, Royal Danish Acad., NAS, American Philosophical Soc., Indian Acad. of Sciences; Hon. DSc (Reading, Bradford, Heriot Watt, Helsinki, Limburg, Queen's, Kingston, Ont., Waterloo, Neuchâtel, Padua, Minn., Toronto, Abertay Dundee, Crete, Bordeaux 2, Athens Univ. of Econs, Harvard, Elche, Rio de Janeiro, Leeds); Guy Medals in silver and gold, Royal Statistical Soc., Weldon Medal, Univ. of Oxford, Deming Medal, ASQC, Kettering Medal and Prize, Gen. Motors Cancer Research Foundation, Max Planck Prize. *Publications:* several books on statistics, articles in Journal of the Royal Statistical Soc., Biometrika etc. *Address:* c/o Nuffield Coll., Oxford, OX1 1NF, England. *Telephone:* (1865) 278690 (office). *Fax:* (1865) 278621 (office). *E-mail:* david.cox@nuf.ox.ac.uk (office). *Website:* www.stats.ox.ac.uk/people/cox (office).

COX, Sir George Edwin, Kt, BSc; British business executive; b. 28 May 1940; s. of George Herbert Cox and Beatrice Mary Cox; m. 1st Gillian Mary Mannings (divorced 1996); two s.; m. 2nd Lorna Janet Peach 1996; two d.; ed Quintin School, Queen Mary Coll., Univ. of London; began career in aircraft industry, in factory man. and in precision eng; Man. Dir Butler Cox (IT consultancy and research group) 1977; Chief Exec. then Chair. PE Int.; fmr UK Chief Exec. Unisys UK, Head of Unisys Services Businesses across Europe; Dir-Gen. Inst. of Dirs 1999–2004; Chair. The Design Council 2004–07; fmr Chair. Merlin (Medical Emergency Relief Int.); mem. Bd of Dirs Shorts 2000–; fmr Dir Inland Revenue 1996–99, London Int. Financial Futures and Options Exchange (LIFFE) 1995–2002, Bradford & Bingley PLC; Visiting Prof., Man. School, Royal Holloway, Univ. of London 1995–; Pres. Royal Coll. of Speech Therapists 2004–; mem. Supervisory Bd Euronext 2003–; mem. Advisory Bd Warwick Business School 2003–, Chair. 2005–; mem. Council Warwick Univ. 2004–; Trustee VSO 2005–; Past Pres. Man. Consultancies Asscn; Past Master of Worshipful Co. of Man. Consultants; carried out Cox Review of Creativity in Business, commissioned by HM Govt 2005; Hon. Fellow, Queen Mary, London; Companion of Chartered Inst. of Man., Royal Aeronautical Soc.; Dr hc (Univ. of Middlesex) 2002, (Univ. of Wolverhampton) 2004, (Northumbria Univ.) 2007, (Univ. of Huddersfield) 2008. *Leisure interest:* rowing, history of aviation, theatre. *Address:* c/o Warwick Business School, Scarman Road, University of Warwick, Coventry, CV4 7AL, England (office). *Telephone:* (24) 7652-4306 (office). *Website:* www.wbs.ac.uk (office).

COX, Pat; Irish EU official and politician; b. 28 Nov. 1952; m.; six c.; ed Trinity Coll., Dublin; Lecturer, Dept of Econs, Inst. of Public Admin, Dublin and Univ. of Limerick (fmrly Nat. Inst. of Higher Educ. —NIHE) 1974–82; TV Current Affairs Reporter for 'Today Tonight' 1982–86; Gen. Sec. Progressive Democrats 1985–94, Deputy Leader 1990–94, MEP for Munster 1989–2004, served on Econ. and Monetary Affairs, Institutional Affairs, and Legal Affairs Cttees, Deputy Leader European Liberal Democrats (ELDR) 1994–98, Pres. 1998–2002; Pres. European Parl. 2002–04; TD (Irish Parl.) for Cork S Cen. and Progressive Democrats Spokesperson on Finance 1992–94; fmr mem. Jt Parl. Cttees to Sweden, Austria and Hungary, Parl. Del. to S Africa; mem. Bd Trustees Int. Crisis Group, Friends of Europe; Freeman of City of Limerick; honoured with highest nat. honours by Pres of Italy, Lithuania, Bulgaria and Romania; Dr hc (Nat. Univ. of Ireland, Trinity Coll. Dublin, American Coll. Dublin); Pres.'s Medal, Univ. of Limerick, MEP of the Year 2001, Campaigner of the Year, Brussels 2003, Special Diploma of Minister of Foreign Affairs (Poland) 2003, Polish Business Oscar 2003, Transatlantic Business Award of the Year, American Chamber of Commerce to the EU 2004, Int. Charlemagne Prize 2004. *Address:* Crawford Hall, Western Road, Cork, Ireland. *Telephone:* (21) 4975833. *Fax:* (21) 4975834. *E-mail:* pcoxmep@eircom.net (office). *Website:* www.patcox.ie (office).

COX, Paul; Dutch film director, screenwriter and author; b. 16 April 1940, Venlo, The Netherlands; s. of W Cox; two s. one d.; ed Melbourne Univ.; settled in Australia 1965; photographic exhbns in Australia, The Netherlands, Germany, Japan, India and USA; taught photography and cinematography for several years; f. Illumination Films (production co.) with Tony Llewellyn-Jones and Bernard Eddy 1977; numerous awards and prizes. *Films include:* directed: (shorts) Mantuta 1965, Time Past 1966, Skindeep 1968, Marcel 1969, Symphony 1969, Mirka 1970, Phyllis 1971, Island 1975, We are All Alone My Dear 1975, Ways of Seeing 1977, Ritual 1978; (feature length) The Journey 1972, Illuminations 1976, Inside Looking Out 1977, Kostas 1978, Lonely Hearts 1981, Man of Flowers 1983, Death and Destiny (A Journey into Ancient Egypt) 1984, My First Wife 1984, Cactus 1986, Vincent 1988, Island 1989, Golden Braid 1990, A Woman's Tale 1991, The Nun and the Bandit 1992, Exile 1993, Lust and Revenge 1996, The Hidden Dimension 1997, Molokai 1998, Innocence 1998, The Diaries of Vaslav Nijinsky 2001, Human Touch 2004, Salvation 2008; (documentaries) Calcutta 1970, All Set Backstage 1974, For A Child Called Michael 1979, The Kingdom of Nek Chand 1980, Underdog 1980, Death and Destiny 1984, Handle with Care 1985; (for Children's TV) The Paper Boy 1985, The Secret Life of Trees 1986, The Gift 1988, Exile 1993. *Publications:* Home of Man (jtly), Human Still Lives of Nepal, I Am 1997, Reflections 1998. *Address:* Illumination Films, 1 Victoria Avenue, Albert Park, Vic. 3206, Australia. *Telephone:* (3) 9690-5266 (office). *Fax:* (3) 9696-5625.

COX, Hon. Paula Ann, JP, BA; Bermudian politician and lawyer; *Deputy Premier and Minister of Finance;* d. of the late C. Eugene Cox MP, CBE, JP and Alinda Cox; m. Germain Nkeuleu; ed McGill Univ., Canada, Univ. of Manchester, UK; fmr Vice Pres. and Sr Legal Counsel, Global Funds Bank of Bermuda Ltd; Corp. Counsel, ACE Ltd 1996; mem. of Parl. 1996–, Minister of Labour, Home Affairs and Public Safety 1998–2001, Minister of Educ. and Devt 2001–02, Attorney-Gen. and Minister of Educ. 2003–04, Minister of Finance 2004–, also Deputy Premier; Deputy Leader Progressive Labour Party; Dr hc (Wheelock Coll.) 2004; Most Effective Politician 2001, 2003. *Address:* Ministry of Finance, Government Administration Building, 30 Parliament Street, Hamilton, HM 12, Bermuda (office). *Telephone:* 295-5151 (office). *Fax:* 296-5727 (office). *E-mail:* pcox@gov.bm (office).

COX, Philip Sutton, AO, BArch, PhD, RIBA; Australian architect; *Director, Cox Richardson Architects & Planners;* b. 1 Oct. 1939, Killara, Sydney; s. of Ronald Albert Cox and Lilian May Cox; m. Virginia Louise Gowing 1972; two d.; ed Sydney Church of England Grammar School, Sydney Univ.; worked in New Guinea 1962; apptd Tutor in Architecture, Univ. of Sydney 1963; est. Ian McKay & Philip Cox pvt. practice with Ian McKay 1963; est. Philip Cox and Assocs (now Cox Richardson Architects & Planners) 1967; Architect Sydney Olympics, Stage I; Tutor in Architecture, Univ. of NSW 1971, 1973, 1978, Prof. 1989–; Founding mem. The Australian Acad. of Design 1990–; Life Fellow, Royal Australian Inst. of Architects, Chair. Educ. Bd, Fed. Chapter; Vice-Chair. Architecture and Design Panel, Visual Arts Bd, Australia Council; Patron Cancer Patients Assistance Soc. of NSW; Fellow, Australian Acad. of Humanities; Hon. FAIA Commonwealth Scholarship 1956; numerous awards and prizes including Royal Australian Inst. of Architects Gold Medal and Merit Awards, Commonwealth Asscn of Architects Sir Robert Matthew Award, Blacket Award, Sir John Sulman Medal. *Major Artistic Works:* Darling Harbour, Freemantle Harbour, Emirates Univ. Uluru, Doya Stadium, Sydney Football Stadium, Sydney, Brisbane, Perth Exhbn Centres. *Publications:* several books including The Australian Homestead (with Wesley Stacey) 1972, Historic Towns of Australia (with Wesley Stacey) 1973, Restoring Old Australian Houses and Buildings, an Architectural Guide (with others) 1975, Australian Colonial Architecture (with Clive Lucas), The Functional Tradition (with David Moore) 1987. *Leisure interests:* gardening, swimming, walking, painting. *Address:* Cox Richardson Architects and Planners, Level 2, 204 Clarence Street, Sydney, NSW 2000, Australia (office). *Telephone:* (2) 9267-9599 (office). *Fax:* (2) 9264-5844 (office). *E-mail:* sydney@cox.com.au (office); www.cox.com.au (office).

COX, Robert W., MA, FRSC; Canadian academic, political scientist and international civil servant; *Professor Emeritus, Department of Political Science, York University;* b. 18 Sept. 1926, Montreal; ed McGill Univ.; fmr Asst Dir-Gen. ILO; fmr Dir Int. Inst. for Labour Studies, Geneva, Switzerland; fmr Prof. of Political Science, Grad. Inst. of Int. Studies, Geneva; Prof. of Int. Org., Columbia Univ., New York 1972–77; Visiting Prof., Yale Univ., Univ. de Laval, Québec, Univ. of Toronto, Univ. of Denver; Programme Co-ordinator on Multilateralism and the UN System, UN Univ., Tokyo; currently Prof. Emer., Dept of Political Science, York Univ., Toronto. *Publications include:* The Anatomy of Influence 1975, Production, Power and World Order 1987, International Political Economy: Understanding Global Disorder 1995, Approaches to World Order 1996, The New Realism (ed.) 1997, Political Economy of a Plural World: Critical Reflections on Power, Morals and Civilizations 2002. *Address:* Department of Political Science, Faculty of Arts, S652 Ross Building, York University, 4700 Keele Street, Toronto, ON M3J 1P3 (office); 5 Metcalfe Street, Toronto, ON M4X 1R5, Canada (home). *Telephone:* (416) 736-5265 (office); (416) 925-7307 (home). *Fax:* (416) 736-5700 (office); (416) 925-8892 (home). *E-mail:* rwcox@yorku.ca (office). *Website:* www.yorku.ca/polisci (office).

COX, Stephen Joseph; British artist; b. 16 Sept. 1946, Bristol; s. of Leonard John Cox and Ethel Minnie May McGill; m. Judith Atkins 1970; two d.; ed St Mary Redcliffe, Bristol, West of England Coll. of Art, Bristol and Cen. School of Art and Design, London; lives and practices near Ludlow, England as well as, Italy, India and Egypt; works in collections of Tate Gallery, Victoria and Albert Museum, British Museum, South Bank Centre, Arts Council of GB, British Council, Walker Art Gallery, Liverpool, Henry Moore Centre for Sculpture, Leeds City Gallery, Southampton Museum, Fogg Museum, USA, Groningen Museum, Netherlands, Peter Ludwig Collection, FRG, Uffizi Gallery, Florence, Fattoria di Celle, Pistoia, Palazzo del Commune, Spoleto, Santa Maria della Scala, Siena, Regione di Aosta and pvt. collections in India, Egypt, USA and Europe; numerous public sculptures in England including Broadgate, Ludgate and Finsbury Square, London, St Paul's Church, Harringay, St Luke's, Chelsea, St Nicholas, Newcastle upon Tyne, Altar for St Anselm's Chapel, Canterbury Cathedral and British govt comms in Delhi, Cairo and Canberra; consultant sculptor, Rajiv Gandhi Samadhi, Delhi; Sr Research Fellow, Wimbledon School of Art 1995–96; Brian Montgomery Visiting Fellow in Sculpture, Lincoln Coll., Oxford 2009; subject of book The

Sculpture of Stephen Cox by Stephen Bann 1995; Gold Medal Indian Triennale, Arts Council Major Awards 1978, 1980, British Council Bursaries 1978, 1979, Hakone Open Air Museum Prize, Japan 1985, Goldhill Sculpture Prize, Royal Acad. 1988, Arts & Business Award 1988, ACE (Art and Christianity Enquiry) Award 2007. *Television:* contributor The Divine Michelangelo (BBC) 2004. *Address:* Lower House Farm, Coreley, nr Ludlow, Salop., SY8 3AS, England (home). *Telephone:* (1584) 891532 (home). *E-mail:* coxstepstone@aol.com (home). *Website:* www.stephencox.info.

COX, Vivienne, BSc, MSc, MBA; British energy industry executive; *Executive Vice-President and CEO, Alternative Energy, BP PLC;* b. 29 May 1959; m.; two d.; ed Univ. of Oxford and Institut européenne d'admin des affaires (INSEAD), Paris, France; joined BP Chemicals 1981, various sales and marketing posts 1981–85, moved to BP Exploration 1985, moved to BP Finance 1987, set up commodity derivatives group within oil trading 1990–93, took over responsibility for BP's share holding in Rotterdam refinery 1993–96, Man. New Business in Cen. and Eastern Europe, Vienna 1996–98, CEO Air BP 1998, mem. BP Group Chief Execs, Exec. Vice-Pres. for Gas, Power and Renewables 1999–, Integrated Supply and Trading 2001, Group Vice-Pres. 2004, currently Exec. Vice-Pres. and CEO, Alternative Energy; mem. Bd of Dirs (non-exec.) Eurotunnel PLC 2002–04, Rio Tinto plc 2005–, Climate Change Capital Ltd 2008–, St Francis Hospice; mem. Int. Council of INSEAD; ranked by Fortune magazine amongst 50 Most Powerful Women in Business outside the US (19th) 2002, (19th) 2003, (15th) 2004, (12th) 2005, (15th) 2006, (16th) 2007, Harpers and Queen Businesswoman of the Year 2004, Veuve Clicquot Businesswoman of the Year 2006, ranked by the Financial Times amongst Top 25 Businesswomen in Europe (21st) 2005, (20th) 2006, (21st) 2007. *Address:* BP PLC, International Headquarters, 1 St James's Square, London, SW1Y 4PD, England (office). *Telephone:* (20) 7496-4000 (office). *Fax:* (20) 7496-4630 (office). *Website:* www.bp.com (office).

COX, Warren Jacob, BA, MArch, FAIA; American architect; *Partner, Hartman-Cox Architects;* b. 28 Aug. 1935, New York; s. of Oscar Sydney Cox and Louise Bryson Cox (née Black); m. Claire Christie-Miller 1975; one s. one d.; ed The Hill School, Yale Univ., Yale Univ. School of Architecture; Pnr Hartman-Cox Architects, Washington DC 1965–; Visiting Architectural Critic, Yale Univ. 1966, Catholic Univ. of America 1967, Univ. of Va 1976; Dir Center for Palladian Studies in America 1982–; lecturer numerous architectural schools and insts; juror for design awards programs; mem. Editorial Bd Guide to the Architecture of Washington, DC 1965, 1974; AIA Architectural Firm Award 1988, AIA Nat. Honor Awards 1970, 1971, 1981, 1983, 1989, 1994, Louis Sullivan Prize 1972, Arthur Ross Award, Centennial Award DC AIA, History of Art Prize, Henry Adams Prize, and over 100 other awards. *Work includes:* Euram Bldg, Nat. Perm. Bldg, Sumner Square, Market Square, Mount Vernon Coll. Chapel, Folger Shakespeare Library Additions, Immanuel Presbyterian Church, Concert Hall Redesign, Kennedy Center, Renovation of the Nat. Archives, Patent Office Bldg and Lincoln and Jefferson Memorials, Washington, DC; Winterthur Museum New Exhbn Bldg, Wilmington, Del.; Chrysler Museum, Norfolk, Va; John Carter Brown Library Addition, Providence, RI; H.E.B. Corp. HQ, San Antonio, Tex.; Nat. Humanities Center, Raleigh, NC; US Embassy, Malaysia; Law School, Washington Univ.; Law School, Tulane Univ.; Library, Addition and Residence Hall, Georgetown Univ. Law Center, Washington; Library, Case Western Reserve Univ., Cleveland, Ohio; Law Library, Univ. of Conn., Hartford, Conn., Fed. Courthouse, Corpus Christi, Tex., Divinity School Addition, Duke Univ., Durham, NC, City and County Courthouses, Lexington, Ky, McIntire School of Commerce, Monroe Hall Addition and Special Collections Library, Univ. of VA, Charlottesville, VA, Jefferson Library, Charlottesville, VA. *Publication:* Hartman-Cox Architects/Master Architects Series 1994, various books and periodicals. *Leisure interests:* architectural history, automobile racing, shooting, golden retriever dogs, farming, book collecting. *Address:* Hartman-Cox Architects, 1074 Jefferson Street, NW, Washington, DC 20007 (office); 3111 N Street, NW, Washington, DC 20007 (home); Kennersley, P.O. Box 1, Church Hill, MD 21623, USA (home). *Telephone:* (202) 333-6446 (office); (202) 965-0615 (home). *Fax:* (202) 333-3802 (office). *E-mail:* wcox@hartmancox.com (office).

COX, Winston A., MSc (Econs); Barbadian banker and international organization official; *Executive Director for the Bahamas, Barbados, Guyana, Jamaica, and Trinidad and Tobago, Inter-American Development Bank;* m. Sylvia Potvin; five c.; ed Univ. of the West Indies, Inst. of Social Studies, Netherlands; joined Cen. Bank of Barbados 1974, Adviser to Gov. 1982–87, Gov. 1997; Dir of Finance, Ministry of Finance 1987–91; mem. Exec. Bd IBRD 1994–97; Gov. Cen. Bank of Barbados 1997–99; Deputy Sec.-Gen. (for Devt Co-operation) of the Commonwealth 2000–06; Alt. Exec. Dir for the Bahamas, Barbados, Guyana, Jamaica, and Trinidad and Tobago, IDB 2006–08, Exec. Dir 2008–. *Address:* Inter-American Development Bank, 1300 New York Avenue, NW, Washington, DC 20577, USA (office). *Telephone:* (202) 623-1039 (office). *Fax:* (202) 942-8100 (office). *E-mail:* winstonc@iadb.org (office). *Website:* www.iadb.org (office).

COX ARQUETTE, Courteney; American actress and film producer; b. 15 June 1964, Birmingham, Ala; d. of Richard Lewis and Courteney Cox (née Bass-Copland); m. David Arquette 1999; one d.; modelling career in New York; appeared in Bruce Springsteen music video Dancing in the Dark 1984; Co-founder (with husband) Coquette Productions 2004. *Films include:* Down Twisted 1986, Masters of the Universe 1987, Cocoon: The Return 1988, Mr. Destiny 1990, Blue Desert 1990, Shaking the Tree 1992, The Opposite Sex 1993, Ace Ventura, Pet Detective 1994, Scream 1996, Commandments 1996, Scream 2 1997, The Runner 1999, Alien Love Triangle 1999, Scream 3 2000, The Shrink Is In 2000, 3000 Miles to Graceland 2001, Get Well Soon 2001, Alien Love Triangle 2002, November 2004, Alpha Dog 2006, Barnyard (voice)

2006, Zoom 2006, The Tripper (also producer) 2006, The Monday Before Thanksgiving 2008, Bedtime Stories 2008. *Television series:* Misfits of Science 1985–86, Family Ties 1987–88, The Trouble with Larry 1993, Friends 1994–2004, Dirt (also exec. producer) 2007–08. *Television films include:* Roxanne: The Prize Pulitzer 1989, Till We Meet Again 1989, Curiosity Kills 1990, Morton and Hays 1991, Topper 1992, Sketch Artist II: Hands That See 1995. *Address:* Coquette Productions, 8015 West 3rd Street, Los Angeles, CA 90048; c/o William Morris Agency, One William Morris Place, Beverly Hills, CA 90212,; c/o Brillstein-Grey Entertainment, 9150 Wilshire Blvd., Suite 350, Beverly Hills, CA 90212, USA. *Telephone:* (323) 801-1000 (Coquette).

COZ, Steve; American editor and publishing executive; b. 26 March 1957, Grafton, Mass.; s. of Henry Coz and Mary Coz; m. Valerie Virga 1987; ed Harvard Univ.; freelance writer for various US publs 1979–82; reporter, Nat. Enquirer, Fla 1982–95, Ed.-in-Chief 1995, then Editorial Dir and Exec. Vice-Pres. American Media Inc.; Founder and Pres. Coz Media Group LLC; Co-founder and Man. Pnr, MyReforma 2007–; American celebrity analyst BBC Radio 1995–96; Edgar Hoover Memorial Award for Distinguished Public Service 1996; Haven House Award of Excellence for Outstanding Reporting on Domestic Violence Issues 1996. *Address:* Coz Media Group LLC, 2 Osprey Court, Boynton Beach, FL 33435-7033 (office); MyReforma, 1122 East Atlantic Ave, #4, Delray Beach, FL 33483, USA. *Telephone:* (561) 736-9159 (office). *Website:* www.myreforma.com.

CRABTREE, Robert H., MA, DSc, DPhil; British/American chemist and academic; *Professor of Chemistry, Yale University;* b. 17 April 1948, London; s. of Arthur Crabtree; ed Brighton Coll. and Univs of Oxford and Sussex; Attaché de Recherche, CNRS, France 1975–77; Asst Prof. of Chem., Yale Univ. 1977–82, Assoc. Prof. 1982–85, Prof. 1985–; Mond Lecturer 2009; Ed.-in-Chief Encyclopedia of Inorganic Chemistry, Comprehensive Organometallic Chemistry; Dreyfus Teacher-Scholar 1982, Corday-Morgan Medal 1984, Organometallic Chem. Award, Royal Soc. of Chem. 1991, ACS Organometallic Chem. Award 1993, Dow Lecturer, Berkeley 2004, Williams Lecturer, Oxford 2004, Sabatier Lecturer, Toulouse 2006, Osborn Lecturer, Strasbourg 2009. *Publication:* The Organometallic Chemistry of the Transition Metals 2005. *Leisure interest:* travel. *Address:* Yale Chemistry Department, PO Box 208107, 225 Prospect Street, New Haven, CT 06520-8107 (office); 97 Fairwood Road, Bethany, CT 06524, USA (home). *Telephone:* (203) 432-3925 (office). *Fax:* (203) 432-6144 (office). *E-mail:* robert.crabtree@yale.edu (office). *Website:* www.chem.yale.edu/faculty/crabtree.html (office).

CRACE, Jim, BA; British writer and dramatist; b. 1 March 1946, Brocket Hall, Lemsford, Hertfordshire; m. Pamela Ann Turton 1975; one s. one d.; ed Birmingham Coll. of Commerce, Univ. of London; freelance writer and journalist 1976–87; Distinguished Writer in Residence, James Michener Center, Univ. of Texas, Austin 2008; Dr hc (Univ. of Central England) 2000; David Higham Award 1986, Guardian Prize for Fiction 1986, Whitbread Awards 1986, 1997, Antico Fattore Prize, Italy 1988, GAP Int. Prize for Literature 1989, Soc. of Authors Travel Award 1992, RSL Winifred Holtby Memorial Prize 1995, E. M. Forster Award 1996, Nat. Critics' Circle Award, USA 2001. *Publications:* Continent 1986, The Gift of Stones 1988, Arcadia 1992, Signals of Distress 1994, The Slow Digestions of the Night 1995, Quarantine 1997, Being Dead 1999, The Devil's Larder 2001, Genes 2001, Six 2003, Genesis 2003, The Pesthouse 2007; short stories: Refugees 1977, Annie, California Plates 1977, Helter Skelter, Hang Sorrow, Care'll Kill a Cat 1977, Seven Ages 1980; other: radio plays. *Address:* c/o David Godwin Associates, 55 Monmouth Street, London, WC2H 9DG, England (office).

CRACKNELL, James, MBE; British oarsman; b. 5 May 1972, Sutton, Surrey; m. Beverley Turner 2002; two c.; ed Kingston Grammar School; int. debut in 1989 in coxed pair (finished tenth at Jr World Championships); won gold medal in coxless four Jr World Championships 1990; sr int. debut in 1991 in coxless four (finished seventh in World Championships); won silver medal in the Eight at World Student Games 1993; part of British coxless four team 1997: gold medals at World Championships 1997–99, gold medals, FISA (Fédération Internationale des Sociétés d'Aviron) World Cup 1997, 1999, 2000, gold medals at Olympic Games, Sydney 2000, Athens 2004; with Matthew Pinsent won gold medals in the pair at World Championships 2001 and 2002 (also gold medal in coxed pair); qualified geography teacher; took a 12-month break from rowing 2004; currently presenter for Channel 4 and ITV, also columnist for Daily Telegraph. *Publication:* The Crossing (with Ben Fogle) 2006. *Address:* c/o MTC (UK) Ltd, 20 York Street, London, W1U 6PU, England (office).

CRADDOCK, Gen. (Bantz) John, BA, MA; American army officer; *Supreme Allied Commander Europe and Commander of US European Command, NATO;* b. 1950, West Union, Doddridge Co., W Va; m. Linda Craddock; one s. one d.; ed West Virginia Univ., Command and Gen. Staff Coll., US Army War Coll.; commissioned as Armour Officer; Tank Co. Commdr, 3rd Armoured Div.; Systems Analyst then Exec. Officer, Office of Program Man., Abrams Tank System, Warren, Mich. 1981; assumed command of 4th Bn 64th Armour 24th Infantry Div. (Mechanised), Fort Stewart, Ga 1989; Asst Chief of Staff, (Operations) for 24th Div.; assumed command of 194th Separate Armoured Brigade 1993–95, then Asst Chief of Staff (Operations) for III Corps, Fort Hood, Tex.; Asst Deputy Dir (Plans and Policy), Jt Staff at Pentagon 1996–98; Asst Divisional Commdr for Manoeuvre of 1st Infantry Div. (Mechanised), Germany 1998; Commanding Gen. 7th Army Training Command, US Army Europe, then assumed command of 1st Infantry Div. (Mechanised); Sr Mil. Asst to Sec. of Defense; Combatant Commdr US Southern Command –2004, led US Southern Command 2004–06; Supreme Allied Commdr Europe and Commdr US European Command, NATO 2006–; served in Operation Desert Storm and Kosovo War; Valorous Unit Award, Defense Distinguished Service Medal, Distinguished Service Medal, Silver Star, Defense Superior Service

Medal with 1 Oak Leaf Cluster, Legion of Merit with 2 Oak Leaf Clusters, Bronze Star. *Address:* NATO Allied Commander Europe, NATO Headquarters, boulevard Léopold III, 1110 Brussels, Belgium (office). *E-mail:* natodoc@ hq.nato.int (office). *Website:* www.nato.int/shape (office); www.eucom.mil/ english/index.asp (office).

CRADOCK, Rt Hon. Sir Percy, PC, GCMG; British diplomatist; b. 26 Oct. 1923; m. Birthe Marie Dyrlund 1953; joined FCO 1954; First Sec. Kuala Lumpur, Malaya 1957–61, Hong Kong 1961–62, Beijing 1962–63; Foreign Office 1963–66; Counsellor and Head of Chancery, Beijing 1966–68, Chargé d'affaires 1968–69; Head of FCO Planning Staff 1969–71; Asst Under-Sec. of State and Head of Cabinet Office Assessments Staff 1971–76; Amb. to GDR 1976–78, concurrently Leader UK Mission to Comprehensive Test Ban Negotiations, Geneva 1977–78; Amb. to People's Repub. of China 1978–83; Leader of Negotiating Team with China over Hong Kong 1982–83; Deputy Under-Sec. with special responsibility for negotiations with China over Hong Kong 1983–85; Foreign Policy Adviser to the Prime Minister 1984–92; Chair. Jt Intelligence Cttee 1985–92; Dir South China Morning Post 1996–2000; Hon. Fellow, St John's, Cambridge 1982. *Publications:* Experiences of China 1993, In Pursuit of British Interests 1997, Know Your Enemy: How the Joint Intelligence Committee Saw the World 2002. *Address:* c/o The Reform Club, 104 Pall Mall, London, SW1Y 5EW, England.

CRAGG, Anthony (Tony) Douglas, CBE, MA; British sculptor; b. 9 April 1949, Liverpool; s. of Douglas R. Cragg and Audrey M. Rutter; m. 1st Ute Oberste-Lehn 1977; two s.; m. 2nd Tatjana Verhasselt 1990; one s. one d.; ed Cheltenham and Wimbledon Schools of Art and RCA; Lab. Technician, Nat. Rubber Producers Research Asscn 1966–68; moved to Wuppertal 1977, first exhbn 1977; teacher, Düsseldorf Kunstakademie 1978–2001, Prof. and Co-Dir 1988–2001; Prof. Hochschule der Künste (HdK), Berlin 2001–; Visiting Prof., Univ. of the Arts, London 2005; elected to Akademie der Künste, Berlin 2001; Hon. Fellowship John Moores Univ. 2001; Chevalier des Arts et des Lettres 1992; Dr hc (Univ. of Surrey) 2001; Von-der-Heydt Prize 1989, Turner Prize 1988, Shakespeare Prize 2001, Peipenbrock Prize for Sculpture 2002, First Prize for Best Sculpture, Beijing Biennale 2005. *Leisure interests:* walking, geology. *Address:* Lise-Meitner-Str. 33, 42119 Wuppertal Germany. *Telephone:* (202) 55-13-50. *Fax:* (202) 55-13-512. *E-mail:* jm@tony-cragg.com. *Website:* www.tony-cragg.com.

CRAIG, Daniel; British actor; b. 2 March 1968, Chester; s. of Timothy Craig and Carol Olivia Craig; m. Fiona Loudon 1992 (divorced); one d.; ed Guildhall School of Music and Drama. *Films include:* The Power of One 1992, A Kid in King Arthur's Court 1995, Obsession 1997, Love and Rage 1998, Elizabeth 1998, Love Is the Devil: Study for a Portrait of Francis Bacon 1998, The Trench 1999, I Dreamed of Africa 2000, Some Voices 2000, Hotel Splendide 2000, Lara Croft: Tomb Raider 2001, Road to Perdition 2002, Ten Minutes Older: The Cello 2002, Occasional, Strong 2002, The Mother 2003, Sylvia 2003, Enduring Love 2004, Layer Cake 2004, The Jacket 2005, Sorstalanság 2005, Munich 2005, Renaissance (voice) 2006, Infamous 2006, Casino Royale (Evening Standard British Film Award for Best Actor 2007) 2006, The Invasion 2007, The Golden Compass 2007, Flashbacks of a Fool 2008, Quantum of Solace 2008, Defiance 2008. *Television includes:* Our Friends in the North 1996, Shockers: The Visitor 1999, Sword of Honour 2001, Copenhagen 2002, Archangel 2005. *Address:* c/o Creative Artists Agency, Inc., 9830 Wilshire Blvd., Beverly Hills, CA 90212-1825, USA. *Telephone:* (310) 288-4545. *Fax:* (310) 288-4800. *Website:* www.caa.com.

CRAIG, David Parker, AO, DSc, FRS, FRSA, FAA; Australian chemist and academic; *Professor Emeritus of Chemistry, Australian National University;* b. 23 Nov. 1919, Sydney; s. of Andrew Hunter Craig and Mary Jane Parker; m. Veronica Bryden-Brown 1948; three s. one d.; ed Univ. of Sydney and Univ. Coll. London; Capt., Australian Imperial Force 1941–44; Lecturer in Chem., Univ. of Sydney 1944–46, Prof. of Physical Chem. 1952–56; Turner and Newall Research Fellow 1946–49; Lecturer in Chem., Univ. Coll. London, UK 1949–52, Prof. 1956–67, Visiting Prof. 1968; Prof. of Chem., ANU 1967–85, Prof. Emer. 1985–, Dean, Research School of Chem. 1970–73, 1977–81; Firth Visiting Prof., Univ. of Sheffield, UK 1973; Visiting Prof., Univ. Coll. Cardiff UK 1975–89; Visiting Foreign Prof., Univ. of Bologna, Italy 1984; part-time mem. Exec. CSIRO 1980–85; Pres. Australian Acad. of Science 1990–94; Fellow, Univ. Coll. London; Hon. FRSC; Hon. DSc (Sydney), (Bologna); H. G. Smith Memorial Medal, Leighton Medal, David Craig Medal named in honour of him by Australian Acad. of Science 2005. *Publications:* Excitons in Molecular Crystals – Theory and Applications (co-author) 1968, Molecular Quantum Electrodynamics: An Introduction to Radiation-Molecule Interactions (co-author) 1984; original papers on chemistry in scientific journals. *Leisure interest:* tennis. *Address:* 216 Dryandra Street, O'Connor, ACT 2602, Australia (home). *Telephone:* (2) 6125-2839 (office); (2) 6249-1976 (home). *Fax:* (2) 6125-3216 (office). *E-mail:* david.craig@anu.edu.au (office).

CRAIG, George; American publishing executive; Dir Production, Honeywell Computers Scotland 1965–74; Vice-Chair. and Group Man. Dir William Collins, UK 1974–87; Pres. and CEO Harper & Row Publrs Inc. (now HarperCollins Publrs), New York 1987–96; mem. Bd of Dirs The News Corpn Ltd; mem. Editorial Advisory Bd Publrs Weekly Int.

CRAIG, Ian Jonathan David, BSc, PhD; British astrophysicist and academic; *Professor, Department of Mathematics, University of Waikato;* b. 30 Aug. 1950, Sheffield; s. of Ronald W. Craig and Beatrice I. Craig; m. Fiona M. Jardine 1979; one s. one d.; ed Chesterfield Coll. of Tech. and Westfield Coll. and Univ. Coll., London; Research Fellow, Dept of Astronomy, Univ. of Glasgow 1974–76, 1977–79; Research Assoc. Inst. for Plasma Research, Stanford Univ. 1976–77; Lecturer in Math., Univ. of Waikato, NZ 1979–85, Sr Lecturer 1985–93, Assoc. Prof. 1993–2002; Prof. 2002–, fmr Chair. of Dept 2002;

Research Astronomer, Inst. for Astronomy, Univ. of Hawaii 1990–91; guest investigator on Skylab 1977; mem. Int. Astronomical Union. *Publications include:* Inverse Problems in Astronomy—A Guide to Inversion Strategies For Remotely Sensed Data (with J. C. Brown) 1986. *Leisure interests:* cycling, swimming, skiing, windsurfing; wood: growing it, working it and burning it. *Address:* Department of Mathematics, Room G3.21, University of Waikato, Private Bag, Hamilton (office); 25 Cranwell Place, Hamilton, New Zealand (home). *Telephone:* (7) 838-4466 (office). *Fax:* (7) 838-4666 (office). *E-mail:* i.craig@waikato.ac.nz (office). *Website:* www.math.waikato.ac.nz (office).

CRAIG, Larry Edwin, BA; American politician; b. 20 July 1945, Council, Ida; s. of Elvin Craig and Dorothy Craig; m. Suzanne Thompson 1983; two s. one d.; ed Univ. of Idaho and George Washington Univ.; farmer and rancher in Midvale, Ida area; mem. Ida Farm Bureau 1965–79; mem. Nat. Rifle Asscn, Future Farmers of America; Pres. Ida Young Republican League 1976–77; mem. Ida Republican Exec. Cttee 1976–78; mem. Ida Senate 1974–80; mem. US House of Reps from 1st Dist of Ida 1981–91; Senator from Idaho 1991–2009 (retd); Republican. *Leisure interest:* gardening.

CRAIG, Mary, MA; British author and broadcaster; b. 2 July 1928, St Helens, Lancs.; d. of William Joseph Clarkson and Anne Mary Clarkson; m. Francis John Craig 1952 (died 1995); four s. (one deceased); ed Notre Dame Convent, St Helens, Liverpool Univ., St Anne's Coll., Oxford Univ.; NW Organizer, Sue Ryder Trust 1962–68; TV Critic, Catholic Herald 1971–76; presenter and features writer (freelance) with BBC Radio 1969–77; interviewer, Thames TV, Southern TV (freelance); freelance journalist and book reviewer; Officer's Cross, Order of Polonia Restituta 1987; John Harriott Award 1993 and other awards. *Publications:* Longford 1978, Woodruff at Random 1978, Blessings (The Christopher Book Award, USA 1979) 1979, Man from a Far Country 1979, Candles in the Dark 1983, The Crystal Spirit 1986, Spark from Heaven 1988, Tears of Blood: A Cry for Tibet 1992, Kundun: The Dalai Lama, His Family and His Times 1997, The Last Freedom: A Journal 1997, Waiting for the Sun: A Peasant Boy in Occupied Tibet 1999, His Holiness the Dalai Lama (anthology, ed.) 2001; for children: Pope John Paul II 1982, Mother Teresa 1984, Lech Wałęsa 1989. *Leisure interests:* reading modern history and biography, logic puzzles, listening to music, playing the piano, travel. *Address:* PFD, Drury House, 34–43 Russell Street, London, WC2B 5HA (office); 1 Lodge Gardens, Penwood, Burghclere, nr Newbury, Berks., RG20 9EF, England (home). *Telephone:* (20) 7344-1000 (office). *Fax:* (20) 7836-9543 (office). *Website:* www.pfd.co.uk (office).

CRAIG, Michael; British actor; b. 27 Jan. 1929, Pune, India; appeared in The Homecoming, New York 1967–68; frequent appearances on stage in Australia; actor and scriptwriter for TV plays and films in Australia; TV appearances in UK. *Films include:* The Love Lottery, Passage Home, The Black Tents, To the Night, Eyewitness, House of Secrets, High Tide at Noon, Campbell's Kingdom, The Silent Enemy, Nor the Moon by Night, The Angry Silence, Doctor in Love, The Mysterious Island, Payroll, No My Darling Daughter, A Life for Ruth, The Iron Maiden, Captive City, Summer Flight, Of a Thousand Delights, Life at the Top, Modesty Blaise, Funny Girl, Royal Hunt of the Sun, Twinky, Country Dance, Royal Hunt of the Sun, The Second Mrs Anderson, Inn of the Damned, A Sporting Proposition, The Irishman, Turkey Shoot, Stanley, The Timeless Land, Appointment with Death. *Television includes:* The Emigrants 1976, The Timeless Land (miniseries) 1980, Triangle (series) 1981, G.P. (series) 1989, Brides of Christ (miniseries) 1991, Grass Roots (series) 2000, Mary Bryant (miniseries) 2005. *Address:* c/o Shanahans, PO Box 478, King's Cross, Sydney, NSW 2033, Australia.

CRAIG-MARTIN, Michael, CBE, MFA, RA; Irish artist; *Professor Emeritus of Fine Art, Goldsmith's College;* b. 28 Aug. 1941, Dublin; s. of Paul F. Craig-Martin and Rhona Gargan Craig-Martin; m. Janice Hashey 1963 (divorced); one d.; ed Yale Univ.; family moved to USA 1946, returned to UK 1966; Lecturer, Bath Acad. of Art 1966–69; Artist in Residence, King's Coll., Cambridge 1970–72; Sr Lecturer, Goldsmith's Coll., Univ. of London 1974–88, Millard Prof. of Fine Art 1994–2000, now Prof. Emer.; Trustee, Tate Gallery 1989–99; Hon. Fellow, Goldsmith's Coll.; Dr hc (San Francisco Art Inst.) 2001. *Address:* c/o Gagosian Gallery, 4–24 Britannia Street, London, WC1X 9JD, England. *Telephone:* (20) 7841-9960. *E-mail:* mcraigm@dircon.co.uk (office). *Website:* www.michaelcraig-martin.com (office).

CRAIG OF RADLEY, Baron (Life Peer), cr. 1991, of Helhoughton in the County of Norfolk; *Marshal of the RAF David Brownrigg Craig,* GCB, OBE, MA, DSc, FRAeS; British fmr air force officer; b. 17 Sept. 1929, Dublin, Ireland; s. of Maj. Francis Brownrigg Craig and Olive Craig; m. Elizabeth June Derenburg 1955; one s. one d.; ed Radley Coll. and Lincoln Coll., Oxford; commissioned in RAF 1951, Commanding Officer RAF Cranwell 1968–70; ADC to The Queen 1969–71; Dir Plans and Operations, HQ Far East Command 1970–71, Commanding Officer RAF Akrotiri 1972–73, ACAS (Ops) Ministry of Defence 1975–78, Air Officer Commanding No. 1 Group RAF Strike Command 1978–80, Vice-Chief of the Air Staff 1980–82, Air Officer, C-in-C, RAF Strike Command and C-in-C UK Air Forces 1982–85, Chief of Air Staff 1985–88, Chief of Defence Staff 1988–91; Air ADC to The Queen 1985–88; Chair. Council of King Edward VII Hosp. (Sister Agnes) 1998–2004; Deputy Chair. RAF Benevolent Fund 1996–; mem. House of Lords Select Cttee on Science and Tech. 1993–99; Convenor Cross-bench Peers 1999–2004; Pres. RAF Club 2002–; Hon. Fellow Lincoln Coll. Oxford 1984; Hon. DSc (Cranfield). *Leisure interests:* fishing, shooting. *Address:* House of Lords, Westminster, London, SW1A 0PW, England. *Fax:* (20) 7219-0147 (office). *E-mail:* craigd@ parliament.uk (office).

CRAIK, Fergus Ian Muirden, PhD, FRSC, FRS; British/Canadian psychologist and academic; *Senior Scientist, Rotman Research Institute;* b. 17 April 1935, Edinburgh; s. of George Craik and Frances Crabbe; m. Anne Catherall

1961; one s. one d.; ed George Watson's Boys' Coll., Edinburgh and Univs. of Edinburgh and Liverpool; mem. scientific staff, MRC Unit for Research on Occupational Aspects of Ageing, Univ. of Liverpool 1960–65; lecturer in Psychology, Birkbeck Coll. London 1965–71; Assoc. Prof. then Prof. of Psychology, Univ. of Toronto 1971–, now Prof. Emer., Chair. Dept of Psychology 1985–90; Sr Scientist, Rotman Research Inst., Baycrest Centre for Geriatric Care 2000–; Fellow, Killam Research Fellowship 1982–84; Guggenheim Fellowship 1982–83; Fellow, Center for Advanced Study in Behavioral Sciences, Stanford Univ. 1982–83, Soc. of Experimental Psychologists, Canadian Psychological Asscn, American Psychological Asscn; Dr hc (Bordeaux) 2006; William James Fellow Award 1993, D. O. Hebb Award 1998, Killam Prize for Science 2000. *Publications:* Levels of Processing in Human Memory (ed. with L. S. Cermak) 1979, Aging and Cognitive Processes (ed. with S. Trehub) 1982, Varieties of Memory and Consciousness (ed. with H. L. Roediger III) 1989, The Handbook of Aging and Cognition (ed. with T. A. Salthouse) 1992, 2000, The Oxford Handbook of Memory (ed. with E. Tulving) 2000. *Leisure interests:* reading, walking, tennis, music. *Address:* Rotman Research Institute, Baycrest Centre for Geriatric Care, 3560 Bathurst Street, Toronto, ON M6A 2E1, Canada (office). *Telephone:* (416) 785-2500 ext. 2526 (office). *Fax:* (416) 785-2862 (office). *E-mail:* craik@psych.utoronto.ca (office). *Website:* www.rotman-baycrest.on.ca/content/people/profiles/craik.html (office).

CRAINZ, Franco, MD, FRCOG; Italian physician and academic; *Professor Emeritus of Obstetrics and Gynaecology, University of Rome;* b. 18 May 1913, Rome; s. of the late Silvio Crainz and Ada Fanelli Crainz; ed Rome Univ.; Prof. and Head of Dept, School for Midwives, Novara 1956–64; Prof. and Head, Dept of Obstetrics and Gynaecology, Univ. of Cagliari 1964–66, of Messina 1966–67, of Bari 1967–72; Prof. of Obstetrics and Gynaecology, Rome Univ. 1972–88, Prof. Emer. 1988–; Vice-Pres. Italian Soc. of the History of Medicine; Hon. Pres. Italian Soc. of Obstetrics and Gynaecology (Pres. 1977–80); Corresp. mem. German Soc.; Hon. mem. European Soc. of Gynaecology and of the Austrian, Portuguese, Romanian, Spanish and Swiss Socs. *Publications:* An Obstetric Tragedy – The Case of HRH the Princess Charlotte Augusta 1977, The Birth of an Heir to the 5th Duke of Devonshire 1989, Dr. Matthew Baillie 1995, The Pregnant Madonna in Christian Art (with J. Dewhurst) 2001, Saints and Sickness (jtly) 2003, Saints and Sickness (with J. Dewhurst) 2003; over 100 medical papers. *Leisure interests:* history of medicine, music, archaeology, history, gardening. *Address:* Via P. Mascagni 124, 00199 Rome, Italy. *Telephone:* (06) 8610433.

CRANBROOK, 5th Earl of (cr. 1892), 5th Viscount (cr. 1878); **Gathorne Gathorne-Hardy,** MA, PhD, CBiol, DL; British biologist; b. 20 June 1933, London; m. Caroline Jarvis 1967; two s. one d.; ed Eton Coll., Corpus Christi Coll., Cambridge and Univ. of Birmingham; Lecturer, Sr Lecturer in Zoology, Univ. of Malaya 1961–70; Ed. Ibis (journal of British Ornithologists' Union) 1973–80; mem. Royal Comm. on Environmental Pollution 1981–92; Trustee, Natural History Museum 1982–86; mem. Natural Environment Research Council 1982–88; mem. Nature Conservancy Council 1990–91; Chair. English Nature 1991–98, ENTRUST 1996–2002; Dir (non-exec.) Anglian Water 1989–98; mem. Broads Authority, Harwich Haven Authority 1988–98; mem. Bd Foundation for European Environmental Policy 1987–98, Chair. 1990–98; Vice-Pres. Nat. Soc. for Clean Air and Environmental Protection; also partner in family farming business in Suffolk; Chair. Inst. for European Environmental Policy 1990–; Chair. Int. Trust for Zoological Nomenclature 2001–; Hon. Johan Bintang Sarawak (JBS) 1997, Hon. Panglima Negara Bintang Sarawak (PNBS) 2005; Hon. DSc (Aberdeen) 1989, (Cranfield) 1996. *Publications:* Mammals of Borneo 1965, Birds of the Malay Peninsula (jtly) 1974, Riches of the Wild: Mammals of South East Asia 1987, Belalong: a tropical rain forest (jtly) 1994, Wonders of Nature in South East Asia 1997, Ballad of Jerjezang (jtly) 2001, Swiftlets of Borneo (jtly) 2002. *Leisure interest:* walking. *Address:* Glemham House, Great Glemham, Saxmundham, IP17 1LP, England (home). *Telephone:* (7775) 755825 (home). *Fax:* (1728) 663339 (home). *E-mail:* lordcranbook@greatglemhamfarms.co.uk (office).

CRANDALL, Robert Lloyd, BA; American business executive; *Chairman, Celestica Inc.;* b. 6 Dec. 1935, Westerly, RI; s. of Lloyd Evans Crandall and Virginia Crandall (née Beard); m. Margaret Jan Schmults 1957; two s. one d.; ed William and Mary Coll., Univ. of Rhode Island, Wharton School, Univ. of Pennsylvania; Dir of Credit and Collections, then Vice-Pres. Data Services TWA 1967–73; COO American Airlines 1973–85, Sr Vice-Pres. (Finance) 1973–74, Sr Vice-Pres. Marketing 1974–80, Dir 1976–, Pres. 1980–95, Chair. and CEO 1985–98 (retd), Pres., Chair. and CEO AMR Corpn 1985–98, now Chair. Emer.; Chair. Celestica Inc. 2004–; also currently Chair. Pogo Jet Inc.; mem. Bd of Dirs Anixter International Inc., Halliburton Co.; mem. US Fed. Aviation Admin Man. Advisory Cttee; Horatio Alger Award 1997, Wright Brothers Memorial Trophy, Nat. Aeronautic Asscn 2004, Eagle of Aviation Award, Embry-Riddle Aeronautical Univ. 2004. *Leisure interests:* skiing, tennis, running, reading. *Address:* Celestica Inc., 12 Concorde Place, 5th Floor, Toronto, ON M3C 3R8, Canada (office); Pogo Jet, Inc., 611 Access Road, Suite 105, Stratford, CT 06615, USA (office). *Telephone:* (416) 448-5800 (Celestica) (office). *E-mail:* contactus@celestica.com (office); contact@flypogo.com (office). *Website:* www.celestica.com (office); www.flypogo.com (office).

CRANE, Sir Peter Robert, Kt, PhD, FRS; British environmentalist and academic; *Dean, School of Forestry and Environmental Studies, Yale University;* b. 18 July 1954, Kettering; s. of Walter Robert Crane and Dorothy Mary Crane (née Mills); m. Elinor Margaret Hamer 1986; one s. one d.; ed Univ. of Reading; Lecturer, Dept of Botany, Univ. of Reading 1978–82; Post-doctoral Research Scholar, Dept of Biology, Indiana Univ. 1981–82; Curator Dept of Geology, The Field Museum, Chicago 1982–92, Vice-Pres. Center for Evolutionary and Environmental Biology 1992–93, Vice-Pres. Academic Affairs and Dir The Field Museum 1994–99; mem. Paleontological Soc. (Pres. 1998–2000); Dir Royal Botanic Gardens, Kew 1999–2005; Prof., Department of Geophysical Sciences, Univ. of Chicago 2006–09; Dean, School of Forestry and Environmental Studies, Yale Univ. 2009–; Foreign Assoc. NAS 2001; Foreign mem. Royal Swedish Acad. of Sciences 2002; Bicentenary Medal, Linnean Soc. 1984, Schuchert Award, Paleontological Soc. 1993. *Publication:* (co-ed) The Origins of Angiosperms and their Biological Consequences 1987, (co-ed) The Evolution, Systematics and Fossil History of the Hamamelidae Vols 1 and 2 1989; (jtly) The Origin and Diversification of Land Plants 1997. *Address:* Yale School of Forestry and Environmental Studies, 205 Prospect Street, New Haven, CT 06511, USA (office). *Telephone:* (203) 432-5100 (office). *Fax:* (203) 432-5942 (office). *Website:* environment.yale.edu (office).

CRANFIELD, Rev. Charles Ernest Burland, MA, FBA; British academic; *Professor Emeritus of Theology, University of Durham;* b. 13 Sept. 1915, London; s. of Charles Ernest Cranfield and Beatrice Mary Cranfield (née Tubbs); m. Ruth Elizabeth Gertrude Bole 1953; two d.; ed Mill Hill School, Jesus Coll., Cambridge and Wesley House, Cambridge; research in Basle until outbreak of World War II; Probationer in Methodist Church 1939; ordained 1941; Minister in Shoeburyness 1940–42; Chaplain to the Forces (from end of hostilities worked with German Prisoners of War, was first staff chaplain to POW Directorate in War Office) 1942–46; Minister in Cleethorpes 1946–50; admitted to Presbyterian Church of England (now part of United Reformed Church) 1954; Lecturer in Theology, Univ. of Durham 1950–62, Sr Lecturer 1962–66, Reader 1966–78, Prof. of Theology (personal) 1978–80, Prof. Emer. 1980–; Jt Gen. Ed. new series of International Critical Commentary 1966–2005; Hon. DD (Aberdeen) 1980; Burkitt Medal for Biblical Studies 1989. *Publications:* The First Epistle of Peter 1950, The Gospel according to Saint Mark 1959, I and II Peter and Jude 1960, A Critical and Exegetical Commentary on the Epistle to the Romans, Vol. 1 1975, Vol. 2 1979, Romans: A Shorter Commentary 1985, The Bible and Christian Life: A Collection of Essays 1985, If God Be For Us: a Collection of Sermons 1985, The Apostles' Creed: a Faith to Live By 1993, On Romans and Other New Testament Essays 1998. *Address:* 30 Albert Street, Western Hill, Durham City, Durham, DH1 4RL, England (home). *Telephone:* (191) 384-3096 (home).

CRANFIELD, Thomas L., BA; Irish banker and civil servant; *Director-General, Office for Official Publications, European Union;* b. 3 Feb. 1945, Dublin; m.; three d.; ed Univ. Coll. Dublin; personal admin. in American biomedical eng co., Dublin 1970–73; Head of Div. EIB (Luxembourg) 1973–90; Deputy Registrar European Court of Justice (Luxembourg) 1990–2000; Dir-Gen. Office for Official Publs of the EU 2000–. *Address:* Office for Official Publications of the European Union, 2 rue Mercier, 2985 Luxembourg (office). *Telephone:* 2929-1 (office). *Fax:* 2929-44691 (office). *E-mail:* ThomasL.Cranfield@publications.europa.eu (office). *Website:* www.publications.europa.eu (office).

CRANHAM, Kenneth Raymond; British actor; b. 12 Dec. 1944, Dunfermline, Scotland; s. of Ronald Cranham and Margaret McKay Ferguson; m. Fiona Victory; two d.; ed Tulse Hill School, London, Royal Acad. of Dramatic Art (RADA), Nat. Youth Theatre; Bancroft Gold Medal, RADA 1966. *Films include:* Two Men Went to War, Born Romantic, Shiner, Gangster No. 1, Women Talking Dirty, The Last Yellow, Under Suspicion, Chocolat, The Clot, Oliver, Brother Sun Sister Moon, Joseph Andrews, The Rising, Layer Cake, Trauma, Mandancin, A Good Year, Hot Fuzz, Valkyrie. *Plays include:* RSC: School for Scandal, Ivanov, The Iceman Cometh; Nat. Theatre: Flight, An Inspector Calls, Kick for Touch, Cardiff East, From Kipling to Vietnam, The Caretaker, Strawberry Fields, Love Letters on Blue Paper, The Passion, The Country Wife, Old Movies, Madras House, The UN Inspector; Royal Court: Saved, Ruffian on the Stair, Samuel Beckett's Play, Cascando, The London Cuckolds, Tibetan in Roads, Magnificence, Cheek, Owners, Geography of a Horse Dreamer; West End: Loot, Comedians, Entertaining Mr Sloane, The Novice, Doctor's Dilemma, Paul Bunyan (Royal Opera House), Endgame; Broadway: Loot, An Inspector Calls, Gaslight (Old Vic), The Homecoming. *Radio:* The Barchester Chronicles, New Grub Street, Sons and Lovers, Hard Times, Answered Prayers, Earthly Powers, Barrack Room Ballads, Gilgamesh. *Television includes:* Night Flight, Without Motive, The Murder of Stephen Lawrence, Our Mutual Friend, Oranges are Not the Only Fruit, Rules of Engagement, The Contractor, The Birthday Party, Lady Windermere's Fan, Thérèse Raquin, 'Tis a Pity She's a Whore, Merchant of Venice, The Caretaker, The Dumb Waiter, La Ronde, The Sound of Guns, Sling Your Hook, Shine On Harvey Moon (Harvey Moon), The Genius of Mozart (Leopold Mozart), Rome (Pompey), The Party, Polyanna, The Lavender List (Harold Wilson), The Addiction of Sin (W.H. Auden), Black and Blue Lamp, A Little Bit of Lippy, El C.I.D, Reilly Ace of Spies (Lenin), Lillies, Afterlife, Dickens, Requiem Apache, Chimera, The Chatterley Affair, Justice in Wonderland (George Carmen QC), The Tenant of Wildfell Hall, The Line of Beauty, Tess of the D'Urbervilles, Merlin. *Leisure interests:* vernacular music, art, food, travel, some people, thinking on trains. *Address:* c/o Markham & Froggatt Ltd, 4 Windmill Street, London, W1P 1HF, England (office). *Telephone:* (20) 7636-4412 (office).

CRANSTON, David Alan, CBE; British business executive and fmr army officer; b. 20 Oct. 1945, Windermere, Cumbria; s. of Stanley Cranston and Mary Cranston (née Fitzherbert); m. Pippa Ann Reynolds 1968; three d.; ed Strathallan School, Perthshire, Royal Mil. Acad., Sandhurst; served in army first in artillery and then as aviator 1966–95, retd with rank of Brig.; with Personal Investment Authority 1995–97, Royal Bank of Scotland Group 1997–2000; Dir-Gen. Nat. Asscn of Pension Funds 2000–02; Dir (non-exec.) Voller Energy Group PLC, Scandia UK, Austin Reed Group Pension Fund Ltd, WBB Minerals Pension Fund Ltd; Chair. British Biathlon Union 1996–. *Leisure interests:* gardening, reading, sport, qualified helicopter pilot.

Address: West End Manor, Durrington, Wilts., SP4 8AQ, England (office). *Telephone:* (7887) 600658 (office).

CRAPO, Michael Dean, BA, JD; American lawyer and politician; *Senator from Idaho;* b. 20 May 1951, Idaho Falls; s. of George Lavelle Crapo and Melba Crapo (née Olsen); m. Susan Diane Hasleton 1974; two s. three d.; ed Brigham Young Univ., Univ. of Utah, Harvard Univ.; called to Bar in Calif. 1977, in Idaho 1979; law clerk, US Ninth Circuit Court of Appeals, San Diego 1977–78; Assoc., Gibson, Dunn & Crutcher (law firm) 1978–79; attorney, Holden, Kidwell, Hahn & Crapo 1979–92, Pnr 1983–92; mem. Idaho State Senate 1984–93, Asst Majority Leader 1987–88, Pres. Pro Tempore 1989–92; mem. US House of Reps from 2nd Idaho Dist 1992–99; Senator from Idaho 1999–, mem. Banking, Housing, and Urban Affairs Cttee, Budget Cttee, Environment and Public Works Cttee, Finance Cttee, Indian Affairs Cttee, # Co-Chair. Canada-US Interparliamentary Group, Chair. Republican Capital Markets Task Force; Republican. *Leisure interests:* backpacking, skiing. *Address:* 239 Dirksen Senate Building, Washington, DC 20510, USA. *Telephone:* (202) 224-6142 (office). *Fax:* (202) 228-1375 (office). *Website:* crapo.senate.gov (office).

CRAVEN, Sir John Anthony, Kt, BA; Canadian/British merchant banker; *Chairman, Lonmin Plc;* b. 23 Oct. 1940; m. 3rd Ning Ning Chang 2005; three s. from 3rd m.; one s. one d. from 1st m.; ed Michaelhouse, S Africa, Jesus Coll., Cambridge, Queen's Univ., Kingston, Ont.; with Clarkson & Co., Toronto 1961–64, Wood Gundy Bankers 1964–67; Dir S. G. Warburg & Co. 1967–73, Vice-Chair. 1979; Chief Exec. White Weld & Co. Ltd 1973–78; Founder and Chair. Phoenix Securities Ltd 1981–89; CEO Morgan Grenfell Group 1987–89, Chair. 1989–97; mem. Bd Man. Dirs Deutsche Bank AG, Frankfurt 1990–96, Supervisory Bd Société Générale de Surveillance Holding, Geneva 1989–98; Chair. (non-exec.) Tootal Group 1985–91, Lonmin PLC 1997–; Dir Securities and Investment Bd 1990–93; Dir Rothmans Int. PLC 1991–99; Dir (non-exec.) Reuters 1997–2004, Robert Fleming Holdings Ltd 1999–2000; Dir Gleacher & Co. Ltd 2000–2003, Fleming Family & Pnrs Ltd 2000–2003, Chair. 2003–07; Ducati Motor Holdings SpA 1999–2000; mem. Ont. Inst. of Chartered Accountants, Canadian Inst. of Chartered Accountants. *Leisure interests:* hunting, shooting, skiing. *Address:* Lonmin Plc, 4 Grosvenor Place, London, SW1X 7YL, England (office). *Telephone:* (20) 7201-6000 (office). *Fax:* (20) 7201-6100 (office). *E-mail:* contact@lonmin.com (office). *Website:* www .lonmin.com (office).

CRAVEN, Wes, MA; American director, screenwriter and actor; b. 2 Aug. 1939, Cleveland, Ohio; ed Wheaton Coll., Johns Hopkins Univ.; fmr Prof. of Humanities; began film career at film production house, became Asst to Co. Pres. working on post-production; Asst Ed. to Sena Cunningham; mem. Dirs Guild of America. *Films include:* The Last House on the Left (also screenplay and ed.) 1972, The Hills Have Eyes (also screenplay and ed.) 1976, You've Got to Walk It Like You Talk It or You'll Lose That Beat, Deadly Blessing (also co-writer) 1979, Swamp Thing (also screenplay) 1980, The Hills Have Eyes II (also screenplay) 1983, Invitation To Hell 1984, A Nightmare on Elm Street (also screenplay) 1984, Deadly Friend (co-writer) 1986, The Serpent and the Rainbow 1988, A Nightmare on Elm Street III (co-writer, co-exec. producer) 1986, Shocker (also screenplay and co-exec. producer) 1989, The People Under the Stars (also screenplay and co -exec. producer) 1991, Wes Craven's New Nightmare (also screenplay and actor) 1994, Vampire in Brooklyn 1995, The Fear (actor), Scream 1998, Scream 2 1999, Music of the Heart 1999 (dir), Scream 3, Carnival of Souls (exec. producer), Alice (producer), Red Eye (dir) 2005, Paris je t'aime (segment) 2006. *TV includes:* (films) A Stranger in our House (co-writer) 1978, Invitation to Hell 1982, Chiller 1983, Casebusters 1985, A Little Peace and Quiet 1987, Wordplay 1987, Chameleon 1987, Her Pilgrim Soul 1987, Shatterday 1987, Dealer's Choice 1987, The Road Not Taken 1988, Night Visions (also co-writer and exec. producer) 1990, Nightmare Café (exec. producer) 1991, Laurel Canyon (exec. producer), Body Bags (actor); (series) Twilight Zone, Crimebusters. *Address:* c/o William Morris Agency, 1 William Morris Place, Beverly Hills, CA 90212; c/o Joe Quenqua, PMK, 1775 Broadway, Suite 701, New York, NY 10019, USA.

CRAVID, Raul; São Tomé and Príncipe politician; *Minister of Public Administration, State Reform and Territorial Administration;* fmr Dir Empresa de Agua e Electricidade (EMAE—electricity and water utility co.); Minister of Planning and Finance 2008, of Public Admin, State Reform and Territorial Admin 2008–. *Address:* Ministry of Public Administration, State Reform and Territorial Administration, Av. Kwame Nkrumah, CP 136, São Tomé, São Tomé and Príncipe (office). *Telephone:* 224750 (office). *Fax:* 222824 (office).

CRAWFORD, Bryce, Jr, PhD; American chemist and academic; *Regents Professor Emeritus, Department of Chemistry, University of Minnesota;* b. 27 Nov. 1914, New Orleans, La.; s. of Bryce Low Crawford and Clara Hall Crawford; m. Ruth Raney 1940; two s. one d.; ed Stanford Univ.; Nat. Research Council Fellow, Harvard Univ. 1937–39; Instructor, Yale Univ. 1939–40; Asst Prof., Univ. of Minn. 1940–43, Assoc. Prof. 1943–46, Prof. 1946–82, Regents' Prof. 1982–85, Prof. Emer. 1985–, Chair. Dept of Chem. 1955–60, Dean, Grad. School 1960–72; Fulbright Prof., Oxford Univ. 1951, Tokyo Univ. 1966; Ed. Journal of Physical Chem. 1970–80; Chair. Council of Grad. Schools 1962–63; Pres. Asscn of Grad. Schools 1970, Grad. Record Examinations Bd 1968–72; mem. NAS (Council 1975–78), Home Sec. 1979–87; mem. American Acad. of Arts and Sciences 1977; American Chem. Soc. (Bd of Dirs 1969–77), Coblentz Soc., American Philosophical Soc.; Fellow, American Physical Soc.; Presidential Certificate of Merit 1946; Guggenheim Fellowships 1950, 1972; Fulbright Professorship 1951, 1966; Minn. Award, American Chem. Soc. 1969, Pittsburgh Spectroscopy Award 1977, Ellis Lippincott Award 1978, Priestley Medal 1982. *Publications:* articles in scientific journals.

CRAWFORD, Cynthia (Cindy) Ann; American model; b. 20 Feb. 1966, DeKalb, Ill.; m. 1st Richard Gere (q.v.) 1991 (divorced); m. 2nd Rande Gerber 1998; one s. one d.; promoted Revlon (cosmetics) and Pepsi Cola; presented own fashion show on MTV (cable and satellite); has appeared on numerous covers for magazines; model for numerous fashion designers; has released several exercise videos; face of Kelloggs Special K 2000; spokesperson for eStyle.com, Omega watches, 24 Hr. Fitness (also Dir), EAS Health and Sports Products; signature fragrance collection launched 2002, Cindy Crawford Feminine launched 2003. *Films include:* Fair Game 1995, 54 1998, The Simian Line 2000. *Publications:* Cindy Crawford's Basic Face 1996, About Face (for children) 2001. *Address:* 21650 Oxnard Street, Suite 1925, Woodland Hills, CA 91367-7888; c/o Wolf-Kasteler Inc., 335 North Maple Drive, Suite 351, Beverly Hills, CA 90210, USA. *Website:* www.cindy.com.

CRAWFORD, Edwin M. (Mac), BS; American business executive; *Chairman and CEO, CrawfordSpalding Group;* b. 1949; m. Linda Crawford; one s. one d.; ed Auburn Univ.; positions with Arthur Young & Co. 1971–77, 1978–81, Salem Nat. Corpn 1977–78, GTI Ltd 1981–85, 1986, Oxylance Corpn 1985–86, Mulberry Street Investment Co. 1986–90; Exec. Vice-Pres. Hosp. Operations Charter Medical Corpn 1990–92, Pres. and COO Magellan (previously Charter Medical Corpn) 1992–93, Chair., CEO and Pres. 1993–97; CEO and Pres. MedPartners Inc. 1997–98, Chair. and CEO Caremark Rx Inc. (previously MedPartners Inc.) 1998–2007, Pres. 1998–2000, 2004–07, Chair. CVS Caremark Corpn (following merger between Caremark Rx Inc. and CVS Corpn 2007) 2007 (retd); Co-founder, Chair. and CEO CrawfordSpalding Group (consultancy) 2008–; mem. Bd of Dirs Pharmaceutical Care Man. Asscn. *Address:* CrawfordSpalding Group, 12 Cadillac Drive, Suite 200, Brentwood, TN 37027, USA (office). *Telephone:* 615 309 9200 (office). *Fax:* 615 373 0104 (office). *E-mail:* info@crawfordspalding.com (office). *Website:* www .crawfordspalding.com (office).

CRAWFORD, Sir Frederick William, Kt, DL, DEng, DSc, CCIM, FREng, FIEEE, FIET, FInstP, FIMA; British scientist; b. 28 July 1931, Birmingham; s. of William Crawford and Victoria Maud Crawford; m. Béatrice Madeleine Jacqueline Hutter 1963; one s. (deceased) one d.; ed George Dixon Grammar School, Birmingham, Univs of London and Liverpool; Research Trainee, J. Lucas Ltd 1948–52; scientist, Nat. Coal Bd Mining Research Establishment 1956–57; Sr Lecturer in Electrical Eng, Birmingham Coll. of Advanced Tech. 1958–59; Stanford Univ., Calif., USA 1959–82; Prof. (Research), Inst. for Plasma Research 1964–67, Assoc. Prof. 1967–69, Prof. 1969–82, Consulting Prof. 1982–84, Chair. 1974–80; Dir Centre for Interdisciplinary Research 1973–77; Visiting Prof., Math. Inst. 1977–78, Visiting Fellow, St Catherine's Coll., Oxford 1977–78, 1996–97; Vice-Chancellor of Aston Univ. 1980–96; Criminal Cases Review Comm. 1996–2003; Chair. US Nat. Cttee, Union Radio-Scientifique Internationale 1975–81, Int. Comm. 1978–81, UK Rep. 1982–84, Int. Scientific Cttee, Int. Conf. on Phenomena in Ionised Gases 1979–81; mem. US –UK Educ. Comm. 1981–84, British North-American Cttee 1987–, Franco-British Council 1987–98; Chair. Birmingham Civic Soc. 1983–88; High Sheriff, W Midlands Co. 1995; Fellow, Inst. of Math. and its Applications; Freeman, City of London 1986; Hon. Fellow, Inst. of Linguists 1987; Master, Worshipful Co. of Engineers 1996, Co. of Information Technologists 2000; Hon. Bencher, Inner Temple 1996; Hon. DSc (Buckingham) 1996. *Publications:* numerous publs on higher educ. and plasma physics. *Address:* 47 Charlbury Road, Oxford, OX2 6UX, England (home). *E-mail:* f.w .crawford@btinternet.com (home).

CRAWFORD, James Richard, BA, DPhil, LLD, SC, FBA; Australian academic; *Whewell Professor of International Law, University of Cambridge;* b. 14 Nov. 1948, Adelaide; s. of James Crawford and Josephine Bond; m. 1st Marisa Luigina Ballini 1971 (divorced 1990); four d.; m. 2nd Patricia Hyndman 1992 (divorced 1998); m. 3rd Joanna Gomula 1998; one s.; ed Brighton High School and Univs of Adelaide and Oxford; Lecturer, then Sr Lecturer, Reader, Prof. of Law, Univ. of Adelaide 1974–86; mem. Australian Law Reform Comm. 1982–84, part-time 1984–90; Challis Prof. of Int. Law, Univ. of Sydney 1986–92, Dean, Faculty of Law 1990–92; Whewell Prof. of Int. Law, Univ. of Cambridge 1992–; Dir Lauterpacht Research Centre for Int. Law 1997–2003, Chair. Faculty Bd of Law 2003–06; barrister, SC (NSW, Australia) 1997; mem. UN Int. Law Comm. 1992–2001; mem. Matrix Chambers; Wolfgang Friedmann Memorial Award 2009. *Publications:* The Creation of States in International Law 1979, The Rights of Peoples (ed.) 1988, Australian Courts of Law (third edn) 1993, The International Law Commission Articles on State Responsibility 2002, International Law as an Open System 2002. *Leisure interests:* reading, cricket, walking. *Address:* Lauterpacht Research Centre for International Law, 5 Cranmer Road, Cambridge, CB3 9BL (office); 7 Archway Court, Barton Road, Cambridge, CB3 9LW, England (home). *Telephone:* (1223) 335358 (office). *Fax:* (1223) 311668 (office). *E-mail:* jrc1000@cam.ac.uk (office). *Website:* www.law.cam.ac.uk (office).

CRAWFORD, Lionel, BA, PhD, FRS, FRSE; British virologist and academic; ed Rendcomb Coll., Glos., Emmanuel Coll., Cambridge (State Scholarship and an Emmanuel Coll. Sr Scholarship), Dept of Chemical Microbiology, Univ. of Cambridge; Nat. Service 1950–52; mem. scientific staff, MRC Inst. of Virology, Glasgow 1960–68; Head of Dept of Molecular Virology, Imperial Cancer Research Fund (ICRF, now Cancer UK), London 1968–88 (Chair. Cellular and Molecular Biology Groups 1968–70), Head of ICRF Tumour Virus Group, Pathology Dept, Univ. of Cambridge 1988–95; Visiting Research Fellow (Rockefeller Foundation Travel Fellowship), Virus Lab., Univ. of California, Berkeley 1958, Div. of Biology, California Inst. of Tech., Pasadena 1959; Co-organizer first Tumour Virus Workshops, Cold Spring Harbor 1969, European Molecular Biology Org. 1972; Ed. Journal of General Virology 1975–80, Oncogene Research 1986; expert in the field of DNA tumour viruses; Hon. mem. Biochemical Soc. 2004; Royal Soc. Gabor Medal 2005. *Publications:*

numerous scientific papers in professional journals on small DNA tumour viruses. *Address:* 18 Salters Road, Gosforth, NE3 1DJ, England (home).

CRAWFORD, Michael, OBE; British actor and singer; b. (Michael Dumbell-Smith), 19 Jan. 1942; ed St Michael's Coll., Bexley, Oakfield School, Dulwich; actor 1955–; films for Children's Film Foundation; hundreds of radio broadcasts; appeared in original productions of Noyes Fludde and Let's Make an Opera by Benjamin Britten; has toured in UK, USA and Australia. *Stage roles include:* Travelling Light 1965, the Anniversary 1966, No Sex Please, We're British 1971, Billy 1974, Same Time, Next Year 1976, Flowers for Algernon 1979, Barnum 1981–83, 1984–86, Phantom of the Opera, London (Olivier Award for Best Actor in a Musical) 1986–87, Broadway (Tony Award for Best Actor in a Musical) 1988, Los Angeles 1989, The Music of Andrew Lloyd Webber (concert tour), USA, Australia, UK 1991–92, EFX, Las Vegas 1995–96, Dance of the Vampires, Broadway 2002–03, The Woman in White 2004–05. *Films include:* Soap Box Derby 1950, Blow Your Own Trumpet 1954, Two Living One Dead 1962, The War Lover 1963, Two Left Feet 1963, The Knack 1965, A Funny Thing Happened on the Way to the Forum 1966, The Jokers 1966, How I Won the War 1967, Hello Dolly 1969, The Games 1969, Hello Goodbye 1970, Alice's Adventures in Wonderland 1972, The Condorman 1980. *TV appearances include:* Sir Francis Drake (series) 1962, Some Mothers Do 'Ave 'Em (several series), Chalk and Cheese (series), Sorry (play) 1979. *Publication:* Parcel Arrived Safely: Tied with String (autobiog.) 2000. *Address:* Knight Ayton Management, 114 St Martins Lane, London, WC2N 4BE, England (office). *Telephone:* (20) 7836-5333 (office). *Fax:* (20) 7836-8333 (office). *E-mail:* info@knightayton.co.uk (office). *Website:* www.knightayton.co.uk (office).

CRAWFORD, Michael Hewson, MA, FBA; British historian and academic; *Professor Emeritus of Ancient History, University College, London;* b. 7 Dec. 1939, Twickenham, Middx; s. of Brian Hewson Crawford and Margarethe Bettina Crawford (née Nagel); ed St Paul's School, London and Oriel Coll. Oxford; Research Fellow, Christ's Coll. Cambridge 1964–69; Univ. Lecturer, Cambridge 1969–86; Jt Dir Excavations of Fregellae 1980–86, Valpolcevera Project 1987–94, Velleia Project 1994–95, S. Martino Project 1996–; Chair. British Epigraphy Soc. 1996–99; Visiting Prof. Pavia Univ. 1983, 1992, Ecole Normale Supérieure, Paris 1984, Padua Univ. 1986, Sorbonne, Paris 1989, San Marino Univ. 1989, Milan Univ. 1990, L'Aquila Univ. 1990, Ecole des Hautes Etudes, Paris 1997, Ecole des Hautes Etudes en Sciences Sociales, Paris 1999; Prof. of Ancient History, Univ. Coll. London 1986, now Prof. Emer.; Foreign mem. Istituto Lombardo, Reial Academia de Bones Lletres; mem. Academia Europaea; Joseph Crabtree Orator 2000; Trustee, Entente Cordiale Scholarships 2000; Officier des Palmes Académiques 2001; Archer Huntington Medal of the American Numismatic Society 2002. *Publications:* Roman Republican Coinage 1974, The Roman Republic 1978, La Moneta in Grecia e a Roma 1981, Sources for Ancient History 1983, Coinage and Money under the Roman Republic 1985, L'Impero romano e la struttura economica e sociale delle province 1986, Medals and Coins from Budé to Mommsen (with C. Ligota and J. B. Trapp) 1990, Antonio Agustín between Renaissance and Counter-reform 1993, Roman Statutes (Ed.) 1995, Historia Numorum (with N.K. Rutter et al.) 2001. *Address:* 24 Gordon Square, Office B21, London, WC1H, England. *Telephone:* (20) 7679-7363. *E-mail:* imagines.italicae@sas.ac.uk.

CRAWFORD, Shawn; American sprinter; b. 14 Jan. 1978, Van Wyck, SC; ed Indian Land High School, Clemson Univ.; fmr 100m and 200m SC State Champion; Goodwill Games Champion 2001; Bronze Medal 200m, World Outdoor Championships 2001; Gold Medal 200m, World Indoor Championships 2001, US Outdoor Championships 2001, 2002, Athens Olympics 2004; Silver Medal 60m, World Indoor Championships 2004; Silver Medal 4×100m, Athens Olympics 2004; Gold Medal 60m, US Indoor Championships 2004; Silver Medal 200m, Beijing Olympics 2008; coach Bob Kersee. *Address:* c/o USA Track and Field, One RCA Dome, Suite 140, Indianapolis, IN 46225, USA (office). *Telephone:* (317) 261-0500 (office). *Website:* www.usatf.org (office).

CRAWLEY, Frederick William, CBE, FCIB, FRAeS; British banker; *Chairman, Royal Air Force Charitable Trust Enterprises;* b. 10 June 1926, London; s. of William Crawley and Elsie Crawley; m. Ruth E. Jungman 1951 (deceased); two d.; entered Lloyds Bank 1942, Chief Accountant 1969, Asst Gen. Man. 1973, Exec. Dir Lloyds Bank Int. 1975, Asst Chief Gen. Man. 1977, Deputy Chief Gen. Man. 1978–82, 1983–84, Vice-Chair. and CEO Lloyds Bank Calif. 1982–83, Chief Gen. Man. Lloyds Bank PLC 1984–85, Deputy Group Chief Exec. 1985–87; Chair. Black Horse Agencies Ltd 1985–88; Deputy Chair. Girobank PLC 1991, Chair. 1991–94; Chair. Betta Stores PLC 1990–92, Alliance & Leicester Bldg Soc. 1991–94, Legal and Gen. Recovery Investment Trust PLC 1994–98; Dir Lloyds Bank 1984–88, Lloyds Devt Capital Ltd 1987–92, FS Assurance Ltd 1988–89, FS Investment Mans. Ltd 1988–89, FS Investment Services Ltd 1988–89, Barratt Devts Ltd 1988–96, Alliance & Leicester Estate Agents Ltd 1988–92, Legal and Gen. Bank Ltd 1997–2001; Consultant Anglo-Airlines Ltd 1988–92; Hon. Treas. RAF Benevolent Fund 1988–2004, Deputy Chair. RAF Benevolent Fund Enterprises Ltd 1988–2004; Chair. RAF Charitable Trust Enterprises 2005–, Trustee RAF Charitable Trust 2005–; Fellow, St Andrew's Man. Inst. 1996–97; Assoc. Royal Aeronautical Soc. 1984, Fellow 2006; Freeman, Gapan 1992–, Liveryman, Gapan 2006, Freeman of the City of London 2006. *Leisure interests:* aviation, shooting, photography. *Address:* 4 The Hexagon, Fitzroy Park, London, N6 6HR, England (home). *Telephone:* (20) 8341-2279 (home). *Fax:* (20) 8341-2279 (home). *E-mail:* fredcrawleyis@yahoo.com (home).

CRAWLEY, Phillip; British/Canadian newspaper executive; *Publisher and CEO, The Globe and Mail;* b. 1944, Northumberland, England; m. Stephanie Crawley; three c., two step-c.; ed Univ. of Manchester; worked in various editorial roles for Thomson Regional Newspapers, UK –1979; Ed. The Journal, Newcastle upon Tyne 1979–87; Northern Ed. The Daily Telegraph, London 1987–88; Ed., then Ed.-in-Chief South China Morning Post, Hong Kong and Editorial Dir Asia Magazine 1988–93; Man. Dir The Times Supplements, London (subsidiary of News International, publr of The Times Educational Supplement, The Times Higher Educational Supplement and The Times Literary Supplement) 1993–97; Man. Dir The New Zealand Herald 1997–98, later CEO Designate Wilson & Horton, owner of NZ's largest media group, including newspapers, radio, magazines and print (wholly-owned subsidiary of Independent Newspapers of Dublin); Pres. and COO The Globe and Mail, Toronto 1998–99, Publr and CEO 1999–; Chair. The Canadian Press (nat. news agency); mem. Bd and fmr Chair. Canadian Newspaper Asscn; Chair. Charter for Business; mem. Bd Sunnybrook Health Sciences Centre, Toronto; cabinet mem. United Way of Toronto; mem. campaign cabinet, Royal Conservatory of Music. *Address:* The Globe and Mail, 444 Front Street West, Toronto, ON M5V 2S9, Canada (office). *Telephone:* (416) 585-5000 (office). *Fax:* (416) 585-5150 (office). *E-mail:* pcrawley@globeandmail.com (office). *Website:* www.globeandmail.com (office).

CRAXTON, John Leith, RA; British artist; b. 3 Oct. 1922; s. of the late Harold Craxton and Essie Craxton; ed Betteshanger, Kent, Westminster School of Art, London, Cen. School of Art, London, Goldsmiths' Coll., London; has designed sets for Royal Ballet, London; works exhibited in Tate Gallery, London, Victoria and Albert Museum, London, British Museum, London, Gallery of Modern Art, Edin., Nat. Museum of Wales, Arts Council, British Council, British Govt Picture Collection, Nat. Gallery, Melbourne, Metropolitan Museum, NY; HM Consular Corresp., Hania, Crete 1992–. *Leisure interests:* music, museums, motorbikes, seafood. *Address:* Moshon 1, Hania, Crete, Greece (office); c/o Royal Academy of Arts, Burlington House, Piccadilly, London, W1V 0DS, England.

CREAN, Hon. Simon Findlay, BEcons, LLB; Australian politician and trade union official; *Federal Minister for Trade;* b. 26 Feb. 1949, Melbourne; s. of Frank Crean and Mary Crean; m. Carole Lamb 1973; two d.; ed Middle Park Cen. School, Melbourne High School and Monash Univ.; Research Officer, Federated Storemen and Packers' Union of Australia 1970–74, Asst Gen. Sec. 1976–79, Gen. Sec. 1979–85; Jr Vice-Pres. Australian Council of Trade Unions 1981–83, Sr Vice-Pres. 1983–85, Pres. 1985–90; mem. House of Reps (for Hotham, Vic.) 1990–, Minister of Science and Tech. and Treas. 1990–91, of Primary Industries and Energy 1991–93, of Employment, Educ. and Training 1993–96; Man. Opposition Business, Shadow Minister for Industry and Regional Devt 1996–98, Shadow Treas. and Deputy Leader of the Opposition 1998–2001, Leader of the Opposition 2001–02, Shadow Treas. 2003–04, Shadow Minister for Regional Devt 2005–06, Shadow Minister for Trade and Regional Devt 2006–07, Fed. Minister for Trade 2007–; Deputy Leader of the Australian Labor Party 1998–2001, Leader 2001–02; Pres. Australian Council of Trades Unions 1985–90; mem. Econ. Planning Advisory Council, Nat. Labor Consultative Council, ILO Governing Body, Qantas Bd, Transport Industry Advisory Council, Business Educ. Council. *Leisure interest:* tennis, swimming, cycling, bushwalking. *Address:* Department of Foreign Affairs and Trade, R.G. Casey Building, John McEwen Crescent, Barton ACT 0221 (office); PO Box 6022, House of Representatives, Parliament House, Canberra, ACT 2600 (office); 401 Clayton Road, Clayton, Vic. 3168, Australia (office). *Telephone:* (2) 6261-1111 (office); (2) 6277-7420 (office); (2) 6277-4911 (office). *Fax:* (2) 6261-3111 (office); (2) 6273-4128 (office); (2) 6277-8547 (office). *E-mail:* simon.crean@dfat.gov.au (office). *Website:* www.dfat.gov.au (office); www.simoncrean.net.

CREECH, Rt Hon. Wyatt (W. B.), BA; New Zealand accountant, vintner and fmr politician; b. Oct. 1946, Oceanside, Calif., USA; m. Danny (Diana) Creech; three s.; ed Massey and Victoria Univs; mem. Martinborough Council 1980–86; MP for Wairarapa 1988–99; Minister of Revenue, Customs, in Charge of the Public Trust Office and responsible for Govt Superannuation Fund 1990–91, Minister of Revenue, in Charge of the Public Trust Office and responsible for Govt Superannuation Fund and Sr Citizens, Assoc. Minister of Finance and Social Welfare 1991–93, Minister of Revenue and Employment, Deputy Minister of Finance 1993–96, Minister of Educ., for Courts, for Ministerial Services and Leader of the House 1996–98, Deputy Prime Minister 1998–99; Assoc. Spokesperson for Foreign Affairs and Trade; Deputy Leader Nat. Party 1997–2001; Chair. Cabinet Social Policy Cttee, Cabinet Legislation Cttee; mem. Nat. Party. *Leisure interests:* gardening, outdoor pursuits, wine tasting.

CREED, Martin; British artist; b. 21 Oct. 1968, Wakefield; s. of John Creed and Gisela Grosscurth; pnr Paola Pivi; ed Slade School of Fine Art, London. *Music:* sings with punk band owada. *Address:* c/o Hauser & Wirth London, 196a Piccadilly, London, W1J 9DY, England. *E-mail:* mail@martincreed.com. *Website:* www.martincreed.com.

CREEL MIRANDA, Santiago; Mexican lawyer and politician; b. 11 Dec. 1954, Mexico City; ed Univ. Nacional Autónoma de México, Univ. of Michigan, USA; lawyer, pvt. law firm; fmr Sec. Vuelta periodical; f. Este País magazine; fmr Prof. Autonomous Tech. Inst. of Mexico, Head Acad. Dept; Citizen Adviser to Gen. Council, Fed. Electoral Inst. 1994–96, Fed. Deputy 1997–; joined Partido Acción Nacional (PAN), cand. for Head of Govt of Fed. Dist 1999; Sec. of the Interior 2000–05; mem. Senado (Senate) 2006–; mem. Mexican Bar, Coll. of Lawyers, Mexican Acad. of Human Rights, Lawyers' Cttee for Human Rights. *Address:* Torre Azul Piso 20, Oficina A 20th floor, Reforma 136, Col. Juarez Del. Cuauhtémoc, 06600 México, DF, Mexico (office). *Telephone:* (55) 5345-3000, ext. 3493 (office). *E-mail:* santiago.creel@pan.senado.gob.mx (office). *Website:* www.senado.gob.mx (office).

CREMONA, Hon. John Joseph, KM, LLD, DLitt, PhD, DJur; Maltese jurist, historian and writer; b. 6 Jan. 1918, Gozo; s. of Dr Antonio Cremona and Anne

Camilleri; m. Beatrice Barbaro Marchioness of St George 1949; one s. two d.; ed Malta, Rome, London, Cambridge and Trieste Univs; Crown Counsel 1947; Lecturer in Constitutional Law, Royal Univ. of Malta 1947–65; Attorney Gen. 1957–64; Prof. of Criminal Law, Univ. of Malta 1959–65; Prof. Emer. 1965–; Pres. of Council 1972–75; Crown Advocate-Gen. 1964–65; Vice Pres. Constitutional Court and Court of Appeal 1965–71; Judge, European Court of Human Rights 1965–92, Vice-Pres. 1986–92; Pro-Chancellor, Univ. of Malta 1971–74; Chief Justice of Malta, Pres. of the Constitutional Court, the Court of Appeal and the Court of Criminal Appeal 1971–81; mem. UN Cttee on Elimination of Racial Discrimination 1984–88, Chair. 1986–88; Judge, European Tribunal in Matters of State Immunity 1986–92, Vice-Pres. 1986–92; fmr Acting Gov.-Gen., Acting Pres. of Malta; Chair. Human Rights Section, World Asscn of Lawyers; Chair. Public Broadcasting Services Ltd 1996–98; Pres. Malta Human Rights Asscn; Vice-Pres. Int. Inst. of Studies Documentation and Information for the Protection of the Environment 1980–; mem. Int. Inst. of Human Rights 1992; mem. Editorial Bd several human rights journals in Europe and America; Fellow, Royal Historical Soc.; Hon. Fellow LSE; Hon. mem. Real Academia de Jurisprudencia y Legislación, Madrid; Kt of Magisterial Grace, Sovereign Mil. Order of Malta; Kt Grand Cross Order of Merit (Italy); Kt Grand Cross, Constantine St George; Kt Order of St Gregory the Great; Kt Most Venerable Order of St John of Jerusalem; Companion of the Nat. Order of Merit (Malta); Chevalier, Légion d'honneur. *Publications include:* The Treatment of Young Offenders in Malta 1956, The Malta Constitution of 1835 1959, The Legal Consequences of a Conviction in the Criminal Law of Malta 1962, The Constitutional Development of Malta 1963, From the Declaration of Rights to Independence 1965, Human Rights Documentation in Malta 1966, Selected Papers (1946–89) 1990, The Maltese Constitution and Constitutional History 1994, Malta and Britain: The Early Constitutions 1996; three volumes of poetry; articles in French, Italian, German, Portuguese and American law reviews. *Address:* Villa Barbaro, Main Street, Attard, Malta. *Telephone:* 440818.

CRENSHAW, William Edwin (Ed), BBA; American retail executive; *CEO, Publix Supermarkets Inc.;* b. 1951, grandson of George Jenkins (founder of Publix); m. Denise Crenshaw; ed Baylor Univ.; joined Publix Supermarkets Inc. 1974, becoming Dir of Retail Operations, Lakeland, Fla Div. 1984–90, Vice-Pres. Lakeland Div. 1990–91, Dir Publix Supermarkets Inc. 1990–, Vice-Pres. Publix Atlanta Div. 1991–94, Exec. Vice-Pres. of Retailing 1994–96, Pres. 1996–2008, CEO 2008–; mem. Advisory Bd Hankamer School of Business. *Address:* Publix Super Markets Corporate Office, PO Box 407, Lakeland, FL 33802-0407, USA (office). *Telephone:* (863) 688-1188 (office). *Fax:* (863) 284-5532 (office). *E-mail:* info@publix.com (office). *Website:* www.publix.com (office).

CRÉPEAU, Paul-André, CC, OQ, QC, LPh, LLL, BCL, DenD; Canadian legal scholar; *Professor Emeritus and Director, Quebec Research Centre of Private and Comparative Law, McGill University;* b. 20 May 1926, Gravelbourg, Sask.; s. of J. B. Crépeau and Blanche Provencher; m. Nicole Thomas 1959; two s. one d.; ed Univs of Ottawa, Montreal, Oxford and Paris; Pres. Civil Code Revision Office 1965–77; Prof. of Civil Law, McGill Univ. 1966–94, Wainwright Chair. of Civil Law 1976–94, Dir Inst. of Comparative Law 1975–84, now Prof. Emer.; Dir Québec Research Centre of Pvt. and Comparative Law 1975–; Pres. Int. Acad. of Comparative Law 1990–98; KStJ (Malta), Chevalier Ordre nat. du Mérite 2002, Commdr Ordre Nat. des Arts et Lettres 2004; Hon. LLD (Ottawa) 1971, (York) 1984, (Dalhousie) 1989, (Strasbourg) 1990, (Montréal) 1994, (Paris II, Panthéon-Arras) 2001, (Laval) 2004; Killam Award 1984–85, 1985–86, Gov. Gen. Prize for Law 1993. *Publications:* La responsabilité civile du médecin et de l'établissement hospitalier 1956, Rapport sur le Code civil 1978, Code civil, Edition historique et critique 1966–1980 1981, L'intensité de l'obligation juridique 1989, L'Affaire Daigle et la Cour Suprême du Canada ou la Méconnaissance de la tradition civiliste en Mélanges Brière 1993, Lecture du message législatif in Mélanges Beetz 1995, Abuse of Rights in the Civil Law of Quebec in Aequitas and Equity 1997, Les Principes d'Unidroit et le Code civil du Québec: Valeurs partagées? 1998, La Réforme du Droit civil canadien: une certaine conception de la Recodification 2001. *Leisure interests:* reading, gardening. *Address:* Institute of Comparative Law/Institut de droit comparé, McGill University, 3661 Peel Street, Montréal, PQ H3A 1X1 (office); 5 Place du Vésinet, Montréal, PQ H2V 2L6, Canada (home). *Telephone:* (514) 398-2770 (office); (514) 272-5941 (home). *Fax:* (514) 398-7145 (office). *Website:* people.mcgill.ca/paul.crepeau (office).

CRESSON, Edith; French politician; *President, Fondation des écoles de la deuxième chance;* b. (Edith Campion), 27 Jan. 1934, Boulogne-sur-Seine; d. of Gabriel and Jacqueline Campion; m. Jacques Cresson 1959 (died 2001); two d.; ed l'Ecole de Haut Enseignement Commercial pour les Jeunes Filles (HECJF); Nat. Sec. Parti Socialiste; Youth Organizer, Parti Socialiste 1975; Mayor, Châtellerault 1983–97; Gen. Counsellor Châtellerault-Ouest 1982–97; mem. European Parl. 1979–81; Minister of Agric. 1981–83, of Foreign Trade and Tourism 1983–84, of Industrial Redeployment and Foreign Trade 1984–86, of European Affairs 1988–90; Prime Minister of France 1991–92; Pres. L'Association démocratique des français de l'étranger 1986; Pres. SISIE 1992–94; European Commr for Educ., Research, Science and Devt 1994–99; mem. Nat. Ass. for Vienne 1981, 1986–88; mem. Nat. Secr. Parti Socialiste 1974–90; Pres. Fondation des écoles de la deuxième chance 2002–; Pres. Inst. d'Etudes Européennes Univ. de Seine St Denis 1992; Chevalier de la Légion d'honneur, Grand-Croix de l'Ordre Nat. du Mérite; Dr hc (Weizmann Inst., Open Univ., UK). *Publications:* Avec le soleil 1976, Innover ou subir 1998, Histoires Françaises 2006. *Address:* 21, Boulevard de Grenelle, 75015 Paris, France (office). *Telephone:* 1-45-78-34-15 (office). *E-mail:* edith.cresson@wanadoo.fr (office).

CRESSWELL, Peter, MSc, PhD, FRS; British immunobiologist and academic; *Professor of Immunobiology, Cell Biology and Dermatology, School of Medicine, Yale University;* b. 6 March 1945; s. of Maurice Cresswell and Mary Cresswell; m. Ann K. Cooney 1969; two s.; ed Univ. of Newcastle Upon Tyne, London Univ., Harvard Univ.; fmrly Chief Div. of Immunology, Duke Univ. Medical Center; Prof. of Immunobiology and Biology (now Prof. of Immunobiology, Cell Biology and Dermatology), Yale Univ. School of Medicine 1991–; also currently Investigator, Howard Hughes Medical Inst., Chevy Chase, MD; research into mechanisms regulating generation of complexes of peptides with Major Histocompatability Complex (MHC) molecules, essential in the immune response; Fellow, Royal Soc., UK; mem. NAS. *Address:* Yale University School of Medicine, PO Box 208011, New Haven, CT 06520 (office); Howard Hughes Medical Institute, 4000 Jones Bridge Road, Chevy Chase, MD 20815-6789, USA (office). *Telephone:* (203) 7855-176 (Yale) (office); (301) 215-8500 (office). *Fax:* (203) 785-4461 (Yale) (office). *E-mail:* peter.cresswell@yale.edu (office). *Website:* info.med.yale.edu/ysm (office); www.hhmi.org (office).

CRETNEY, Stephen Michael, MA, DCL, FBA; British professor of law; *Fellow Emeritus, All Souls College, University of Oxford;* b. 25 Feb. 1936, Witney, Oxon.; s. of Fred Cretney and Winifred Cretney; m. Rev. Antonia L. Vanrenen 1973; two s.; ed Cheadle Hulme School, Magdalen Coll., Oxford; Pnr, Macfarlanes (Solicitors), London 1964–65; Lecturer, Kenya School of Law, Nairobi 1966–67, Univ. of Southampton 1968–69; Fellow and Tutor in Law, Exeter Coll., Oxford 1969–78; mem. Law Comm. for England and Wales 1978–83; Prof. of Law (Dean of Faculty 1984–88), Univ. of Bristol 1984–93; Fellow, All Souls Coll. Oxford 1993–2001, Fellow Emer. 2001–; Hon. QC; Hon. LLD (Bristol). *Publications:* Enduring Powers of Attorney (4th edn) 1996, Principles of Family Law (7th edn) 2002, Law, Law Reform and the Family 1998, Family Law (4th edn) 2000, Family Law in the 20th Century: A History 2003, Same Sex Relationships, from 'Odious Crime' to 'Gay Marriage' 2006. *Address:* 8 Elm Farm Close, Wantage, Berks., OX12 9FD, England (home). *E-mail:* Smcretney@aol.com (home).

CREWE, Albert Victor, PhD; American physicist and academic; *Professor Emeritus, University of Chicago;* b. 18 Feb. 1927, Bradford, England; s. of Wilfred Crewe and Edith Fish Crewe (née Lawrence); m. Doreen Crewe; one s. three d.; ed Liverpool Univ.; Asst Lecturer, Liverpool Univ. 1950–52, lecturer 1952–53; Research Assoc. Chicago Univ. 1955–56, Asst Prof. of Physics 1956–59, Assoc. Prof. 1959–63; Dir Particle Accelerator Div., Argonne Nat. Lab. 1958–61, Dir 1961–67; Prof. Dept of Physics and Biophysics Enrico Fermi Inst. 1963–71, Univ. of Chicago 1963–71, Dean, Physical Sciences Div. 1971–81, William E. Wrather Distinguished Service Prof. 1977–96, Prof. Emer. 1996–; Pres. Orchid One Corpn 1987–90; as Dir Argonne Nat. Lab., developed relationships with U.S. Atomic Energy Comm., Argonne Univ. and Chicago Univ., expressed in Tripartite Agreement; Fellow, American Physical Soc., American Nuclear Soc.; mem. NAS, American Acad. of Arts and Sciences, Scientific Research Soc. for America, Electron Microscopy Soc. of America, Chicago Area Research and Devt Council (Chair. 1964), Gov.'s Science Advisory Cttee for State of Ill.; artist mem. Palette and Chisel Acad. of Fine Arts, Chicago;; Hon. Fellow, Royal Microscopical Soc. 1984; Dr hc (Univ. of Missouri) 1972, (Lakeforest Coll.) 1972, (Elmhurst Coll.) 1973, (Univ. of Liverpool) 2001; Immigrant's Service League's Annual Award for Outstanding Achievement in the Field of Science 1962; "Industrial Research Man of the Year 1970"; Michelson Medal (Franklin Inst.) 1978; Ernst Abbe Award, New York Microscope Soc. 1979; Duddell Medal, Inst. of Physics, UK 1980;. *Achievements include:* constructed England's first diffusion cloud chamber with Dr W. H. Evans at Liverpool Univ.; directed construction of large magnetic spectrometer for Chicago Univ.'s synchrocyclotron; consultant Sweden, Argentina; directed much of design and construction of Argonne's Zero Gradient Synchrotron; invented the scanning transmission electron microscope; obtained first atom images 1971. *Leisure interests:* sculpture, painting. *Address:* 8 Summit Drive, Dune Acres, Chesterton, IN 46304 (home); Enrico Fermi Institute, University of Chicago, 5640 South Ellis Avenue, Chicago, IL 60637, USA (office). *Telephone:* (773) 702-7821 (office); (219) 787-5018 (home). *E-mail:* crewe@midway.uchicago.edu (office); avdbc@comcast.net (home).

CRIADO-PEREZ TREFAULT, Carlos; Argentine retail executive; *Executive Chairman, Dinosol Supermercados;* b. 1954, Buenos Aires; m.; three c.; with SHV Makro 1976–90, worked in Portugal, Brazil, and Taiwan 1990–97, also Exec. Dir; COO Int. Div. Wal-Mart Inc. 1997–99; COO Safeway PLC 1999, CEO 1999–2004; Exec. Chair. Dinosol Supermercados, Madrid 2004–; mem. Bd of Dirs X5 Retail Group N.V; Sr Advisor, UBS Bank 2007–; mem. Permira UK Advisory Bd; serves as adviser to Marks and Spencer's on int. expansion; Retail Personality of the Year, Retek 2001. *Leisure interests:* opera (Mozart), running marathons. *Address:* Dinosol Supermercados, Camino de la Zarzuela, 11, 28023 Madrid, Spain (office). *Website:* dinosol.es (office).

CRICHTON-BROWN, Sir Robert, KCMG, CBE, TD; Australian business executive; b. 23 Aug. 1919, Melbourne; s. of the late L. Crichton-Brown; m. Norah I. Turnbull 1941; one s. one d.; ed Sydney Grammar School; Man. Dir Security and Gen. Insurance Co. Ltd 1952; Chair. Security Life Assurances Ltd 1961–85, NEI Pacific Ltd 1961–85, Edward Lumley Ltd (Group), Australia 1974–89 (Man. Dir 1952–82, Dir 1989–), The Commercial Banking Co. of Sydney Ltd 1976–82, Commercial and General Acceptance Ltd 1977–82, Westham Dredging Co. Pty Ltd 1975–85, Rothmans of Pall Mall (Australia) Ltd 1981–85 (Exec. Chair. 1985–88); Vice-Chair. Nat. Australia Bank Ltd 1982–85, Custom Credit Corpn Ltd 1982–85; Dir Daily Mail & General Trust Ltd, UK 1979–95, The Maritime Trust; Exec. Chair. Rothmans Int. PLC 1985–88; Underwriting mem. Lloyd's 1946–97; Dir Royal Prince Alfred Hosp. 1970–84; Fed. Pres. Inst. of Dirs in Australia 1967–80; Fed. Hon. Treas. Liberal Party of Australia 1973–85; mem. Council, Medical Foundation, Univ.

www.worldwhoswho.com

of Sydney 2005–, Pres. 1962–87; Nat. Co-ordinator, Duke of Edinburgh's Award Scheme in Australia 1980–85; mem. numerous professional and charitable orgs in Australia; Hon. Fellow, Univ. of Sydney 1987, Hon. Life Gov., Australian Postgraduate Fed. in Medicine. *Achievements include:* mem. Australia's winning Admiral's Cup Team (Balandra) 1967; winner, Sydney-Hobart Yacht Race (Pacha) 1970. *Leisure interest:* sailing. *Address:* c/o Medical Foundation, Edward Ford Building A27, The University of Sydney, Sydney NSW 2006, Australia.

CRICK, Ronald Pitts, FRCS, FRCOphth; British ophthalmic surgeon; b. 5 Feb. 1917, Toronto, Canada; s. of Owen John Pitts Crick and Margaret Daw; m. Jocelyn Mary Grenfell Robins 1941; four s. one d.; ed Latymer Upper School, London, King's Coll. Hosp. Medical School, London; surgeon, Merchant Navy 1939–40; Surgeon-Lt, RNVR 1940–46; Ophthalmic Registrar, King's Coll. Hosp. 1946–48; Surgical First Asst, Royal Eye Hosp., London 1947–50, Surgeon 1950–69; Ophthalmic Surgeon, Belgrave Hosp. for Children 1950–66; Ophthalmic Surgeon, King's Coll. Hosp. 1950–82, Hon. Ophthalmic Surgeon 1982–; Recognized Teacher in Ophthalmology, Univ. of London 1960–82, Lecturer Emer., School of Medicine and Dentistry, King's Coll. 1982–; Chair. Ophthalmic Training Cttee, SE Thames Regional Health Authority 1973–82; Fellow and Vice-Pres. Ophthalmology Section, Royal Soc. of Medicine 1964; Charter mem. Int. Glaucoma Congress of American Soc. of Contemporary Ophthalmology 1977–; f. Int. Glaucoma Asscn 1974, Chair. 1974–2000, Pres. 2000–05; Co-Ed. Glaucoma Forum (quarterly journal); Hon. FRCOphth 2008; Open Science Scholarship, King's Coll. Hosp. Medical School 1934, Sir Stewart Duke-Elder Glaucoma Award (Int. Glaucoma Congress) 1985, Alim Memorial Lecturer, Ophthalmological Soc. of Bangladesh 1991. *Publications:* All About Glaucoma (with W. Leydhecker) 1981, A Text Book of Clinical Ophthalmology (with P. T. Khaw) 2003; numerous articles in ophthalmic books and journals. *Leisure interests:* natural history, motoring, sailing, designing ophthalmic instruments. *Address:* International Glaucoma Association, Woodcote House, 15A, Highpoint Business Village, Henwood, Ashford, Kent, TN24 8DH (office); 10 Golden Gates, Sandbanks, Poole, Dorset, BH13 7QN, England. *Telephone:* (1233) 648164 (office); (1202) 707560 (home). *Fax:* (1233) 648179 (office); (1202) 701560 (home). *E-mail:* info@iga.org.uk (office). *Website:* www.glaucoma-association.com (office).

CRICKHOWELL, Baron (Life Peer), cr. 1987, of Pont Esgob in the Black Mountains and County of Powys; **(Roger) Nicholas Edwards,** PC, MA; British politician; b. 25 Feb. 1934; s. of the late Ralph Edwards and Marjorie Ingham Brooke; m. Ankaret Healing 1963; one s. two d.; ed Westminster School, Trinity Coll., Cambridge; mem. Lloyd's 1965–2002; MP for Pembroke 1970–87; Opposition Spokesman on Welsh Affairs 1975–79; Sec. of State for Wales 1979–87; Chair. Nat. Rivers Authority 1989–96, ITNET PLC 1997–2004; Pres. Univ. of Wales, Cardiff 1988–98, Contemporary Art Soc. for Wales 1988–93; Dir HTV Ltd 1987–2002 (Chair. 1997–2002), Associated British Port Holdings PLC 1988–99; mem. Cttee Automobile Asscn 1997–98; mem. Conservative Party; Hon. LLD. *Publications:* Opera House Lottery 1997, Westminster, Wales and Water 1999. *Leisure interests:* gardening, fishing. *Address:* 4 Henning Street, London, SW11 3DR, England; Pont Esgob Mill, Fforest Coal Pit, nr Abergavenny, Mon., NP7 7LS, Wales.

CRISP, Baron (Life Peer), cr. 2006, of Eaglescliffe in the County of Durham; **(Edmund) Nigel (Ramsay) Crisp,** KCB, MA; British civil servant; b. 14 Jan. 1952; s. of Edmund Theodore Crisp and Dorothy Shephard Crisp (née Ramsay); m. Siân Elaine Jenkins 1976; one s. one d.; ed Uppingham School and St John's Coll., Cambridge; Deputy Dir Halewood Community Council 1973; Production Man. Trebor 1978; Dir Cambs. Community Council 1981; Unit Gen. Man. E Berks. Health Authority 1986; Chief Exec. Heatherwood and Wexham Park Hosps 1988; Chief Exec. Oxford Radcliffe Hosps NHS Trust 1993–96; Regional Dir S Thames 1977–98, London 1999–2000; Perm. Sec. Dept of Health and Chief Exec. Nat. Health Service 2000–06 (retd). *Leisure interest:* the countryside. *Address:* House of Lords, London, SW1A 0PW, England. *Telephone:* (20) 7219-3873. *Website:* www.nigelcrisp.com.

CRIST, Charles Joseph (Charlie), Jr, BA, JD; American lawyer, politician and state official; *Governor of Florida;* b. 24 July 1956, Altoona, Pa; s. of Charles Crist, Sr and Nancy Crist (née Lee); m. 1st Amanda Morrow 1979 (divorced); m. 2nd Carole Rome 2008; ed St Petersburg High School, Wake Forest Univ., Florida State Univ., Cumberland School of Law, Birmingham, Ala; worked as intern in Fla State Attorney's Office before accepting position as Gen. Counsel for Nat. Asscn of Professional Baseball Leagues 1982–87; cand. for Fla State Senate 1986; began his govt service as State Dir for US Senator Connie Mack, Chair. Baseball Anti-Trust Advisory Cttee, mem. Fed. Judicial Advisory Comm. 1989–92; attorney, Wood & Crist law firm, Tampa 1987–; Fla State Senator 1993–99, Chair. Senate Ethics and Elections Cttee, Appropriations Criminal Justice Sub-cttee; cand. for US Senate 1998; Deputy Sec. Fla Dept of Business and Professional Regulation 1999–2000; Commr of Educ. 2001–03; State Attorney Gen. 2003–06; Gov. of Fla 2007–; mem. Domestic Security Oversight Bd, ABA Pres.'s Council, American Lung Asscn, Admin. Bd American Swiss Asscn Center Against Spouse Abuse, First United Methodist Church Ethics Cttee, Fla Bar Asscn, Bd Fla Conservation Asscn, Foundation for Fla's Future, Hillsborough Bar Asscn, Pinellas Park Chamber of Commerce, Rotary, Saint Petersburg Bar Asscn, Saint Petersburg Chamber of Commerce, Bd of Dirs Suncoasters Civic Club; Pinellas Co. Fellow; Republican; Hon. Sheriff, Fla Sheriffs' Asscn. *Address:* Office of the Governor, The Capitol, 400 South Monroe Street, Tallahassee, FL 32399, USA (office). *Telephone:* (850) 488-7146 (office). *Fax:* (850) 487-0801 (office). *Website:* www.flgov.com (office); www.charliecrist.com.

CRISTEA, Valerian; Moldovan politician and diplomatist; b. 1 Aug. 1950, Viprova, Orhei Co.; ed Polytechnic Inst., Chişinău; party instructor, Chisinau 1979–82; Chair. union of the State Enterprise 'Energoreparaţia' 1982–86; Chair. Republican Cttee of Trades Unions 'Sindenergo' 1986–94, Deputy Chairmanship of the Gen. Fed. of Trades Unions of Moldova 1994–98; mem. Parl. (CP of Moldova) 1998–2006, Chair. Perm. Comm. for Social Protection, Health and Family 1998–2001, Deputy Prime Minister 2001–06; Amb. to Czech Repub. 2007–; Merit Prize of the alliance War Against Trafficking (USA). *Address:* Embassy of Moldova, Na Zátorce 12, 160 00 Prague 6, Czech Repub. (office). *Telephone:* 233323762 (office). *Fax:* 233323765 (office). *E-mail:* secretariat@ambasadamoldova.cz (office). *Website:* www.ambasadamoldova.cz (office).

CROCKER, Chester Arthur, PhD; American academic and fmr government official; *James R. Schlesinger Professor of Strategic Studies, Edmund A. Walsh School of Foreign Service, Georgetown University;* b. 29 Oct. 1941, New York; s. of Arthur Crocker and Clare Crocker; m. Saone Baron 1965; three d.; ed Ohio State Univ., Johns Hopkins Univ.; editorial asst, Africa Report 1965–66, News Ed. 1968–69; Lecturer, American Univ. 1969–70; staff officer, Nat. Security Council 1970–72; Dir Master of Science, Foreign Service Program, Georgetown Univ. 1972–78, James R. Schlesinger Prof. of Strategic Studies 1989–; Dir African Studies, Center for Strategic and Inst. Studies 1976–81; Asst Sec. of State for African Affairs 1981–89; Chair. African Working Group, Reagan Campaign 1980; Chair. US Inst. of Peace 1992–2004; work as int. consultant; mem. Bd of Dirs ASA Ltd, Nat. Defense Univ., US Inst. of Peace, Universal Corpn, Bell Pottinger Communications USA LLC, First Africa Holdings Ltd, G3 Good Governance Group Holdings Ltd; Presidential Citizen's Medal, Sec. of State's Distinguished Service Award, Vicennial Award for Service and John Carroll Medal, Georgetown Univ., Woodrow Wilson Award for Distinguished Public Service, Johns Hopkins Univ. *Publications:* South Africa's Defense Posture 1982, South Africa into the 1980s 1979, High Noon in Southern Africa 1992, African Conflict Resolution 1995, Managing Global Chaos 1996, Herding Cats: Multiparty Mediation in a Complex World 1999, Turbulent Peace: The Challenges of Managing International Conflict 2001, Taming Intractable Conflicts 2004, Grasping the Nettle: Analysing Cases of Intractable Conflict 2005, Leashing the Dogs of War: Conflict Management in a Divided World 2007; numerous articles. *Address:* Room 801, Intercultural Center, School of Foreign Service, Georgetown University, Washington, DC 20057, USA (office). *Telephone:* (202) 687-5074 (office). *Fax:* (202) 687-2315 (office). *E-mail:* crockerc@georgetown.edu (office). *Website:* www.georgetown.edu/sfs (office).

CROCKER, Ryan C., BA; American diplomatist; b. 19 June 1949, Spokane, Wash.; s. of Carol Crocker; m. Christine Barnes; ed schools in Morocco, Canada, Turkey and USA, Univ. Coll. Dublin, Ireland, Whitman Coll., Walla Walla, Wash., Princeton Univ.; joined Foreign Service in 1971, diplomatic positions in Iran 1972–74, Qatar 1974–76, Iraq 1978–80, Lebanon 1981–84; Deputy Dir Office of Arab-Israeli Affairs 1985–87; Political Counselor, Embassy in Cairo 1987–90; Dir State Dept's Iraq-Kuwait Task Force Aug. 1990; Amb. to Lebanon 1990–93, to Kuwait 1994–97, to Syria 1998–2001; Deputy Asst Sec. of State for Near Eastern Affairs 2001–03; Interim Envoy to new Govt of Afghanistan 2002–04; Int. Affairs Advisor, Nat. War Coll., Washington, DC 2003–04; Amb. to Pakistan 2004–07, to Iraq 2007–09, rank of Career Amb. 2004; Hon. LLD (Whitman Coll.) 2001; Presidential Distinguished Service Award 1994, Dept of Defense Medal for Distinguished Civilian Service 1997, Presidential Meritorious Service Award 1999, 2003, State Dept Award for Valor, Three Superior Honor Awards, American Foreign Service Asscn Rivkin Award, State Dept Distinguished Honor Award 2004. *Address:* c/o Department of State, 2201 C St, NW, Washington, DC 20520, USA (office).

CROCKETT, Sir Andrew Duncan, Kt, MA; British banker; *President of International Operations, J.P. Morgan Chase & Company;* b. 23 March 1943, Glasgow; s. of Andrew Crockett and Sheilah Stewart; m. Marjorie Hlavacek 1966; two s. one d.; ed Queens' Coll. Cambridge and Yale Univ.; with Bank of England 1966–72, Exec. Dir 1989–93; with IMF 1972–89; Gen. Man. BIS 1994–2003; Chair. Financial Stability Forum 1999–; Monetary Policy Adviser to IMF 2002–; Pres. Int. Operations, J.P. Morgan & Chase 2003–. *Publications:* Money: Theory, Policy, Institutions 1973, International Money: Issues and Analysis 1977; contribs to professional journals. *Leisure interests:* reading, golf, tennis. *Address:* J.P. Morgan Chase & Co., 270 Park Avenue, New York, NY 10017, USA (office). *Telephone:* (212) 270-6000 (office). *Fax:* (212) 270-2613 (office). *Website:* www.jpmorganchase.com (office).

CROFF, Davide; Italian business executive; *Chairman, Permasteelisa SpA;* b. 1 Oct. 1947; ed in Venice, Pembroke Coll. Oxford; Asst Prof. of Political Econ., Univ. of Padua 1971–72; Research Dept Officer, Banca d'Italia, Rome 1974–79; Foreign and Financial Affairs Dept, Fiat SpA, Turin 1979–83, in charge of Int. Treasury Dept 1982, Finance Man. 1983–86, Sr Vice-Pres. 1986–89; CEO Finance and Int., Banca Nazionale del Lavoro, Rome 1989–90, Man. Dir 1990–2003; Chair. Permasteelisa SpA 2006–; Pres. la Biennale di Venezia 2004–; Chair. BPM 360 Gradi; Sr Adviser to Texas Pacific Group in Italy. *Address:* Permasteelisa SpA, Viale E. Mattei, 21/23, 31029 Vittorio Veneto (office); la Biennale di Venezia, Ca' Giustinian, 1364 San Marco, 30124 Venice, Italy. *Telephone:* (04) 38 505000 (office). *Fax:* (04) 38505125 (office). *E-mail:* info@permasteelisa.com (office). *Website:* www.permasteelisa.com (office); www.labiennale.org.

CROHAM, Baron (Life Peer), cr. 1978, of the London Borough of Croydon; **Douglas Albert Vivian Allen,** BSc, CB, GCB, KCB; British civil servant (retd); b. 15 Dec. 1917, Surrey; s. of Albert Allen and Elsie Maria Allen (née Davies); m. Sybil Eileen Allegro 1941 (died 1994); two s. one d.; ed Wallington County Grammar School and London School of Econs; Asst Prin., Bd of Trade 1939; served in Royal Artillery 1940–45; Prin., Bd of Trade 1945, Cabinet Office 1947, Treasury 1948; Asst Sec., Treasury 1949–58; Under-Sec., Ministry of Health 1958–60, Treasury 1960–62; Third Sec., Treasury 1962–64; Deputy

Under-Sec. of State, Dept of Econ. Affairs 1964–66, Second Perm. Under-Sec. of State 1966, Perm. Under-Sec. of State 1966–68; Perm. Sec., Treasury 1968–74; Head, Home Civil Service, Perm. Sec., Civil Service Dept 1974–77; Chair. Econ. Policy Cttee, OECD 1972–77, Deputy Chair. BNOC 1978–82, Chair. 1982–86; Adviser to Gov., Bank of England 1978–83; Trustee, Anglo-German Foundation 1977–, Chair. 1982–98; Pres. Inst. of Fiscal Studies 1978–92; Chair. Inst. of Man. Econ. and Social Affairs Cttee 1982–85, Trinity Insurance 1988–92; Dir (non-exec.) Pilkington PLC 1978–92, Guinness Peat Group 1983–87 (Chair. 1983–86), Guinness Mahon and Co. Ltd 1989–92. *Leisure interest:* bridge. *Address:* 9 Manor Way, South Croydon, Surrey, CR2, England (home). *Telephone:* (20) 8688-0496 (home).

CROLL, Peter; German economist and research institute director; *Director, Bonn International Centre for Conversion;* early position at ECLA; held several positions with German Tech. Cooperation (GTZ), including Country Dir Kenya; facilitator, UNDP/FAO cross-border ecological program in S Africa and other programs in Africa and India; currently Dir Bonn Int. Centre for Conversion. *Address:* Bonn International Centre for Conversion, An der Elisabethkirche 25, Bonn, 53113, Germany (office). *Telephone:* (228) 911960 (office). *Fax:* (228) 241215 (office). *E-mail:* bicc@bicc.de (office). *Website:* www .bicc.de (office).

CROMBIE, Sir Sandy, Kt; British insurance executive; *Group Chief Executive, Standard Life PLC;* b. 1949; joined Standard Life Insurance Co. 1966, various sr and man. positions including CEO Standard Life Investments (SLI) 1998–2004, Dir 2000–06, CEO Standard Life Assurance Co. 2004–06, Group Chief Exec. Standard Life PLC 2006–; mem. Chancellor of the Exchequer's high-level business group; mem. Bd Dirs Asscn of British Insurers; The Prince's Amb. for Corp. Social Responsibility in Scotland 2007; Fellow, Faculty of Actuaries. *Address:* Standard Life House, 30 Lothian Road, Edinburgh, EH1 2DH, Scotland (office). *Telephone:* (131) 225-2552 (office). *Fax:* (131) 245-7990 (office). *E-mail:* info@standardlife.com (office). *Website:* www.standardlife.com (office).

CROMME, Gerhard, DJur; German business executive; *Chairman of the Supervisory Board, ThyssenKrupp AG;* b. 25 Feb. 1943, Vechta/Oldenburg; m.; four d.; ed Münster, Lausanne, Switzerland, Univ. of Paris, France and Harvard Univ., USA; joined Compagnie de Saint-Gobain 1971, latterly Deputy Del.-Gen. for FRG and Chair. Man. Bd VEGLA/Vereinigte Glaswerke GmbH, Aachen; Chair. Man. Bd Krupp Stahl AG, Bochum 1986; mem. Exec. Bd Fried. Krupp GmbH, Essen 1988 (now Fried. Krupp AG Hoesch-Krupp), CEO 1989–99; CEO ThyssenKrupp AG 1999–2001, Chair. Supervisory Bd 2001–; Chair. Supervisory Bd Siemens AG 2007–; Chair. and mem. several supervisory bds and advisory councils; Chair. German Corp. Governance Code Comm., European Round Table of Industrialists. *Address:* ThyssenKrupp AG, August-Thyssen-Strasse 1, 40211 Düsseldorf (office); Siemens AG, Wittelsbacherplatz 2, 80333 Munich, Germany (office). *Telephone:* (211) 824-36001 (Düsseldorf) (office); (69) 797-6660 (Munich) (office). *Fax:* (211) 824-36005 (Düsseldorf) (office). *Website:* www.thyssenkrupp.com (office); www.siemens .com (office).

CRONENBERG, David; Canadian film director and screenwriter; b. 15 March 1943, Toronto; ed Univ. of Toronto; fmr cinematographer and film editor; has directed fillers and short dramas for TV; Chevalier, Légion d'Honneur 2009. *Plays:* Opera version of The Fly, Théâtre du Châtelet, Paris 2008. *Films:* Transfer (writer, dir, prod.) 1966, From the Drain (writer, dir) 1967, Stereo (writer, dir, prod.) 1969, Crimes of the Future (writer, dir, prod.) 1970, The Victim (dir) 1974, Shivers (writer, dir) 1974, Rabid (writer, dir) 1976, Fast Company (writer, dir) 1979, The Brood (writer, dir) 1979, Scanners (writer, dir) 1980, Videodrome (writer, dir) 1982, The Dead Zone (dir) 1983, Into the Night (actor) 1985, The Fly (writer, dir, actor) 1986, Dead Ringers (writer, dir, prod.) 1988, Nightbreed (actor) 1990, Naked Lunch (writer, dir) 1991, Blue (actor) 1992, M. Butterfly (dir) 1993, Henry & Verlin (actor) 1994, Boozecan (actor) 1994, Trial by Jury (actor) 1994, To Die For (actor) 1995, Blood & Donuts (actor) 1995, Crash (writer, dir, prod.) (Cannes Jury Special Prize 1997) 1996, The Stupids (actor) 1996, Extreme Measures (actor) 1996, I'm Losing You (exec. prod.) 1998, Last Night (actor) 1998, Resurrection (actor) 1999, eXistenZ (writer, dir, prod.) (Silver Berlin Bear 1999) 1998, Camera (writer, dir) 2000, Jason X (actor) 2001, Spider (dir, prod.) 2002, A History of Violence (dir, prod.) 2005, Chacun son cinéma (dir, segment) 2007, Eastern Promises (People's Choice Award, Toronto Int. Film Festival 2007) 2007. *Television:* Programme X (dir episode: Secret Weapons) 1970, Tourettes (film dir, writer) 1971, Letter from Michelangelo (film dir, writer) 1971, Jim Ritchie Sculptor (film dir, writer, prod.) 1971, Winter Garden (film dir, writer) 1972, Scarborough Bluffs (film dir, writer) 1972, Lakeshore (film dir, writer) 1972, In the Dirt (film dir, writer) 1972, Fort York (film dir, writer) 1972, Don Valley (film dir, writer) 1972, Peep Show (dir episodes: The Lie Chair, The Victim) 1975, Teleplay (writer, dir episode: The Italian Machine) 1976, Friday the 13th (dir episode: Faith Healer) 1987, Scales of Justice (dir episode: Regina vs Horvath) 1990, Moonshine Highway (actor) 1996, The Judge (actor) 2001. *Publications:* Crash 1996, Cronenberg on Cronenberg 1996. *Address:* David Cronenberg Productions Ltd, 217 Avenue Road, Toronto, ON M5R 2J3, Canada (office); c/o John Burnham, William Morris Agency, 151 South El Camino Drive, Beverly Hills, CA 90212, USA (office).

CRONIN, Anthony; Irish author; b. 23 Dec. 1928, Co. Wexford; s. of John Cronin and Hannah Barron; m. 1st Thérèse Campbell 1955; two d.; m. 2nd Anne Haverty 2003; ed Blackrock Coll., Univ. Coll., Dublin and Kings Inns, Dublin; Assoc. Ed. The Bell 1952–54; Literary Ed. Time and Tide 1956–58; Visiting Lecturer in English, Univ. of Montana, USA 1966–68; Writer-in-Residence, Drake Univ., Ia 1968–70; columnist, Irish Times 1973–80; cultural and artistic adviser to the Prime Minister of Ireland 1980–83, 1987–92; Founding mem. Aosdána (arts asscn), elected Saoi 2003; Hon. DLitt (Trinity Coll., Dublin, Univ. of Ulster); Martin Toonder Award for contrib. to Irish literature 1983. *Publications:* Poems 1958, The Life of Riley 1964, A Question of Modernity 1966, Dead as Doornails 1976, Identity Papers 1980, New and Selected Poems 1982, Heritage Now 1982, An Irish Eye 1985, No Laughing Matter, The Life and Times of Flann O'Brien 1989, The End of the Modern World 1989, Relationships 1994, Samuel Beckett: The Last Modernist 1996, The Minotaur and Other Poems 1999, Anthony Cronin's Personal Authology 2000, Collected Poems 2004. *Leisure interests:* reading, walking, travelling, watching horse-racing. *Address:* 30 Oakley Road, Dublin 6, Ireland. *Telephone:* (1) 4970490. *Fax:* (1) 4970490.

CRONIN, James Watson, PhD; American physicist and academic; *University Professor Emeritus of Astronomy and Astrophysics and Physics, Enrico Fermi Insitute, University of Chicago;* b. 29 Sept. 1931, Chicago, Ill.; s. of James Farley Cronin and Dorothy Watson Cronin; m. Annette Martin 1954; one s. two d.; ed Southern Methodist Univ., Univ. of Chicago; Nat. Science Foundation Fellow 1952–55; Assoc. Brookhaven Nat. Lab. 1955–58; Asst Prof. of Physics, Princeton Univ. 1958–62, Assoc. Prof. 1962–64, Prof. of Physics 1965–71; Prof. of Physics, Univ. of Chicago 1971, now Univ. Prof. Emer. of Astronomy and Astrophysics and Physics; Loeb Lecturer in Physics, Harvard Univ. 1976, lecturer Nashima Foundation 1993; mem. NAS, American Acad. of Arts and Sciences, American Physical Soc.; Hon. DSc (Leeds) 1996; Research Corpn Award 1968, Ernest O Lawrence Award 1977, John Price Wetherill Medal, Franklin Inst. 1975, shared Nobel Prize for Physics 1980 with Prof. Val Fitch (q.v.) for work on elementary particles, Nat. Medal of Science 1999. *Publications:* Fermi Remembered (ed.) 2004; numerous articles on physics. *Address:* Enrico Fermi Institute, University of Chicago, 5630 South Ellis Avenue, Chicago, IL 60637 (office); 5825 South Dorchester Avenue, Chicago, IL 60637, USA. *Telephone:* (773) 962-7102 (office). *Fax:* (773) 702-6645 (office). *E-mail:* jwc@hep.uchicago.edu (office). *Website:* efi.uchicago .edu (office).

CRONKITE, Walter Leland, Jr; American broadcast journalist (retd); b. 4 Nov. 1916, St Joseph, Mo.; s. of the late W. L. Cronkite and of Helene Fritsche; m. Mary Elizabeth Maxwell 1940; one s. two d.; ed Univ. of Texas; news writer and Editor, Scripps-Howard & United Press, Houston, Kansas City, Dallas, Austin, El Paso and New York; United Press War Corresp. 1942–45, later Foreign Corresp., Chief Corresp. Nuremberg War Crimes Trials, Bureau Man., Moscow 1946–48; Lecturer 1948–49; news corresp., CBS 1950–81; anchor and Man. Ed., CBS Evening News with Walter Cronkite 1962–81, CBS News Special Corresp. 1981–; fmr mem. Bd of Dirs CBS Inc., Pan American World Airways; co-founder and Chair. The Cronkite Ward Co. (production co. 1993–; mem. Advisory Cttee The Smile Train; provides commentary on Nat. Public Radio (NPR); Hon. Chair. Interfaith Alliance USA; Hon. Chair. Cttee to Protect Journalists, Hon. Commodore US Coast Guard Auxiliary; several hon. degrees; Emmy Award (several times), Acad. TV Arts and Sciences 1970, George Polk Journalism Award 1971, Jefferson Award 1981, Presidential Medal of Freedom 1981, George Foster Peabody Award 1981, Distinguished Service Award from the Nat. Asscn of Broadcasters 1982, Trustees' Award from the Nat. Acad. of Television Arts and Sciences 1982, Amb. of Exploration Award, NASA 2006. *Television:* The Cronkite Reports (mini-series, Discovery Channel) 1994–96, Cronkite Remembers (mini-series, CBS and Discovery Channel) 1996. *Publications:* Eye on the World 1971, Challenges of Change 1971; co-author South by Southeast 1983, North by Northeast 1986, Westwind 1990, A Reporter's Life 1996, Around America 2001. *Leisure interest:* yachting. *Address:* Cronkite Unit, CBS Inc., 51 West 52nd Street, New York, NY 10019, USA.

CROSBIE, John Carnell, PC, OC, QC, BA, LLB; Canadian politician; *Lieutenant Governor, Newfoundland and Labrador;* b. 30 Jan. 1931, St John's, Newfoundland; s. of Chesley A. Crosbie and Jessie Crosbie (née Carnell); m. Jane Furneaux; two s. one d.; ed St Andrew's Coll., Aurora, Ont., Queen's Univ., Ont., Dalhousie Law School, Univ. of London, LSE; called to Newfoundland Bar 1957; Prov. Minister of Municipal Affairs and Housing 1966, mem. Newfoundland House of Ass. 1966, 1971–76; Minister of Finance, Econ. Devt, Fisheries, Inter-Govt Affairs, Mines and Energy and Pres. of the Treasury Bd, Leader of House of Ass. 1975; mem. House of Commons 1976–93; Minister of Finance 1979, of Justice and Attorney-Gen. of Canada 1984–86, of Transport 1986–89, of Int. Trade 1989–91, of Fisheries and Oceans and the Atlantic Canada Opportunities Agency 1991–93; Counsel to Patterson Palmer Law (now Cox and Palmer) 1994–; Chancellor Memorial Univ. of Newfoundland 1994–; Dir Atlantic Inst. of Market Studies and other Canadian corpns.; Trustee, Oceanex Income Fund; Lt Gov. Newfoundland and Labrador 2008–; mem. Progressive Conservative Party; Hon. Consul of Mexico to Newfoundland and Labrador 1996–. *Publication:* No Holds Barred 1997. *Leisure interests:* reading, tennis, salmon and trout fishing. *Address:* Government House, Military Road, PO Box 5517, St. John's, Newfoundland, A1C 5W4 (office); Cox and Partner, Scotia Centre, 235 Water Street, PO Box 610, St John's, Newfoundland, A1C 5L3 (office); PO Box 23119, St John's, Newfoundland, A1B 4J9, Canada (home). *Telephone:* (709) 729-4494 (office); (709) 726-6124 (office); (709) 895-3308 (home). *Fax:* (709) 729-2234 (office); (709) 722-0483 (office); (709) 895-3343 (home). *E-mail:* info@gov.nl.ca (office); jcrosbie@pattersonpalmer.ca (office); jane.crosbie@hf.sympatico.ca (home). *Website:* www.gov.nl.ca (office); www.pattersonpalmer.ca (office).

CROSBY, Sir James Robert, Kt; British business executive; b. 14 March 1956; m.; four c.; ed Lancaster Royal Grammar School and Brasenose Coll., Oxford; joined Scottish Amicable 1977, Investment Dir, Fund Man. 1983–, later Gen. Man. –1994; Man. Dir Halifax Life 1994–96, Financial Services and Insurance Dir Halifax PLC 1996–99, CEO Halifax Group PLC 1999–2001, Group CEO HBOS PLC (after merger of Halifax PLC and Bank of Scotland) 2001–06; Chair. Public Pvt. Forum on Identity Man., HM Treasury 2006–;

mem. Bd of Dirs ITV plc 2002–, Financial Services Authority 2003–09 (Deputy Chair. 2004–09); Compass Group plc 2007–; Fellow, Faculty of Actuaries 1980. *Address:* Public-Private Forum on Identity Management, HM Treasury, 1 Horse Guards Road, London, SW1A 2HQ, Scotland (office). *Telephone:* (20) 7270-4558 (office). *Fax:* (20) 7270-4861 (office). *E-mail:* ministers@hm-treasury.gsi.gov.uk (office). *Website:* www.hm-treasury.gov.uk (office).

CROSBY, Sidney Patrick; Canadian professional ice hockey player; b. 7 Aug. 1987, Cole Harbour, Nova Scotia; s. of Troy and Trina Crosby; ed Shattuck-Saint Mary's Boarding School, Minn., USA; played amateur ice hockey with Dartmouth Subways and Shattuck-Saint Mary's Sabres; leading scorer in Quebec Major Junior Hockey League 2004, 2005; first pick overall in Nat. Hockey League (NHL) Entry Draft 2005 by Pittsburgh Penguins; youngest player in NHL history to be named team capt., to record 100 points in a season, to record 200 career points, to have two consecutive 100 point seasons, to be named to All-Star Team; Quebec Major Junior Hockey League: Michel Briere Trophy (most valuable player) 2004, 2005, Jean Béliveau Trophy (league leading scorer) 2004, 2005, Mike Bossy Trophy (best professional prospect) 2005, Paul Dumont Trophy (personality of the year) 2004, 2005, Guy Lafleur Trophy (playoff MVP) 2005, Michel Bergeron Trophy (offensive rookie of the year) 2004; Canadian Hockey League: Rookie of the Year 2004, Player of the Year 2004, 2005; NHL: Art Ross Trophy 2007, Lester B. Pearson Award 2007, Hart Memorial Trophy 2007, First Team All-Star 2007, Mark Messier Leadership Award 2007. *Address:* c/o Pittsburgh Penguins, 1 Chatham Center, Suite 400, Pittsburgh, PA 15219-3447, USA. *Telephone:* (412) 642-1300. *Fax:* (412) 642-1859. *Website:* www.pittsburghpenguins.com; www.crosby87.com (office).

CROSS, George Alan Martin, PhD, FRS; British scientist and academic; *Professor and Head, Laboratory of Molecular Parasitology, Rockefeller University;* b. 27 Sept. 1942, Cheshire; s. of George Bernard Cross and Beatrice Mary Cross (née Horton); one d.; ed Cheadle Hulme School, Downing Coll. Cambridge; Scientist, Biochemical Parasitology, MRC 1969–77; Head, Dept of Immunochemistry and Molecular Biology, Wellcome Foundation Research Labs 1977–82; André and Bella Meyer Prof. of Molecular Parasitology, Rockefeller Univ. 1982–, Dean Grad. and Postgraduate Studies 1995–99; Leeuwenhock Lecturer, The Royal Soc. 1998; Fleming Prize, Soc. for Gen. Microbiology 1978, Chalmers Medal, Royal Soc. of Tropical Medicine and Hygiene 1983, Paul Ehrlich and Ludwig Darmstaedter Prize 1984. *Leisure interests:* sailing, tennis. *Address:* The Rockefeller University, 1230 York Avenue, New York, NY 10021, USA (office). *Telephone:* (212) 327-7571 (office). *Fax:* (212) 327-7845 (office). *E-mail:* gamc@rockefeller.edu (office). *Website:* tryps.rockefeller.edu (office).

CROSSLAND, Sir Bernard, Kt, CBE, DSc, FRS, FREng, FIAE, MRIA; British mechanical engineer and academic; *Professor Emeritus, Queen's University, Belfast;* b. 20 Oct. 1923, Sydenham; s. of Reginald F. Crossland and Kathleen M. Crossland (née Rudduck); m. Audrey Elliot Birks 1946; two d.; ed Simon Langton's Grammar School, Derby Tech. Coll. and Nottingham Univ. Coll.; eng apprentice and later Tech. Asst, Rolls-Royce, Derby 1940–44, Tech. Asst 1943–45; Asst Lecturer, Lecturer, Sr Lecturer in Mechanical Eng, Univ. of Bristol 1946–59; Prof. and Head, Dept of Mechanical and Industrial Eng, Queen's Univ., Belfast 1959–82, Dean, Faculty of Eng 1964–67, Pro-Vice-Chancellor 1978–82, Special Research Prof. 1982–84, Prof. Emer. 1984–; Consulting Engineer 1984–; Chair. NI Manpower Council 1981–86; Pres. IMechE 1986–87, Past Pres. 1987–91; Pres. The Welding Inst. 1995–98; mem. Industrial Devt Bd for NI 1982–87, NI Econ. Council 1981–85; mem. Agricultural and Food Research Council 1981–87, Eng Council 1983–88; Chair. Postgraduate Advisory Bd to Dept of Educ. for NI 1982–95, Bd for Engineers Registration 1983–86, Hazards Forum 1991–93, Bilsthorpe Colliery Accident Public Hearing 1994; non-exec. Dir Gilbert Assocs (Europe) Ltd 1991–94; Assessor of King's Cross Underground Fire Investigation; Founder-Fellow, Irish Acad. of Eng 1998; Hon. mem. ASME; Hon. Fellow, Welding Inst., Inst. of Engineers of Ireland, IMechE, Inst. of Structural Engineers; Hon. Fellow, Univ. of Luton 1994; Hon. DSc (Ireland) 1984, (Dublin) 1985, (Edin.) 1987, (Aston) 1988, (Queen's Univ., Belfast) 1988, (Cranfield Inst. of Tech.) 1989; Hon. D. Eng (Bristol) 1992, (Limerick) 1993, (Liverpool) 1993; George Stephenson Research Prize, Inst. of Mechanical Eng (IMechE) 1956, Thomas Hawksley Gold Medal, IMechE 1968, George Stephenson Lecture, IMechE 1989, Kelvin Medal, Inst. of Civil Eng 1992, James Watt Int. Medal, IMechE 1999, Thomas Lowe Gray Lecture, IMechE 1999, Cunningham Medal, Royal Irish Acad. 2001. *Publications:* An Introduction to Mechanics of Machines 1964, Explosive Welding of Metals 1982, The Lives of Great Engineers of Ulster Vol. 1 2003, Industry's Needs in the Education and Training of Engineers (report); numerous papers on high-pressure eng and explosive welding in int. journals. *Leisure interests:* hobbling, reading, travel. *Address:* The Queen's University, Belfast, BT7 1NN (office); 16 Malone Court, Belfast, BT9 6PA, Northern Ireland (home). *Telephone:* (28) 9097-4238 (office); (28) 9066-7495 (home). *Fax:* (28) 90974627 (office). *E-mail:* b.crossland@qub.ac.uk (office).

CROSSLEY, Paul Christopher Richard, CBE, MA; British concert pianist and music director; b. 17 May 1944, Dewsbury; s. of the late Frank Crossley and Myra Crossley (née Barrowcliffe); ed Silcoates School, Wakefield, Mansfield Coll., Oxford; has performed world-wide as concert pianist; dedicatee and first performer of works by Tippett, Henze, Berio, Takemitsu, Adams, Lindberg, Salonen, Knussen, Benjamin; Artistic Dir London Sinfonietta 1988–94; 15 major films on twentieth-century composers; Hon. Fellow, Mansfield Coll., Oxford 1991. *Recordings include:* complete piano music of Franck, Fauré, Debussy, Ravel, Poulenc, Janacek, Tippett, Takemitsu; works for piano and orchestra by Franck, Messiaen, Takemitsu, Lutoslawski, Stravinksi, Adams. *Leisure interests:* reading and mah-jong. *Address:* Connaught Artists Management, 2 Molasses Row, Plantation Wharf, London, SW11 3UX, England (office). *Telephone:* (20) 7738-0017 (office). *Fax:* (20) 7738-0909 (office). *E-mail:* classicalmusic@connaughtartists.com (office).

CROW, Michael M., BA, PhD; American university administrator; *President, Arizona State University;* b. 11 Oct. 1955, San Diego; m. Sybil Francis; one s. two d.; ed Iowa State Univ.; Research Asst, Energy and Mineral Resources, Iowa State Univ. 1974–77, Assoc. Prof. of Man. 1988–91; Research Assoc., Inst. for Energy Research, Syracuse Univ. 1982–83, Sr Research Assoc., Maxwell School of Citizenship and Public Affairs, Syracuse Univ. 1983–87, Research Fellow 1987–89; Asst Prof. of Public Admin, Univ. of Kentucky 1984–85; Prof. of Science and Tech. Policy, School of Int. and Public Affairs, Columbia Univ. 1992–2002, Assoc. Vice Provost 1991–92, Vice Provost 1992–98, Exec. Vice Provost 1998–2002; Prof., School of Public Affairs, Arizona State Univ. 2002–, Pres. Arizona State Univ. 2002–; f. Center for Science, Policy and Outcomes, Washington, DC 1998; Fellow, Nat. Acad. of Public Admin 2006–. *Address:* Office of the President, Arizona State University, PO Box 877705, Tempe, AZ 85287-7705, USA (office). *Telephone:* (480) 965-8972 (office). *Fax:* (480) 965-0865 (office). *E-mail:* Michael.Crow@asu.edu (office). *Website:* president.asu.edu (office).

CROW, Sheryl; American singer, songwriter and musician (guitar); b. 11 Feb. 1962, Kennett, MO; one adopted s.; ed Univ. of Missouri; trained as classical pianist; worked as music teacher and part-time bar singer; fmr backing singer to Rod Stewart, Eric Clapton, Don Henley, Michael Jackson, Joe Cocker; solo artist mid-1980s–; int. concerts and tours; BRIT Award for Best Int. Female Artist 1997, American Music Awards for Best Female Pop/Rock Artist 2003, 2004. *Film appearance:* De-Lovely 2004. *Recordings include:* albums: Tuesday Night Club Music (three Grammy Awards 1995) 1993, Sheryl Crow 1996, The Globe Sessions 1999, Sheryl Crow and Friends: Live in Central Park 1999, C'mon C'mon 2002, Sheryl Crow: Live At Budokan 2003, Wildflower 2005, Hits and Rarities 2007, Detours 2008. *Address:* Helter Skelter, The Plaza, 535 Kings Road, London, SW10 0SZ, England (office); c/o A&M Records, 2220 Colorado Avenue, Santa Monica, CA 90404, USA. *Telephone:* (20) 7376-8501 (office). *Fax:* (20) 7376-8336 (office). *E-mail:* info@helterskelter.co.uk (office); sheryl@sherylcrow.com. *Website:* www.sherylcrow.com.

CROWE, Cameron; American film director and screenwriter; b. 13 July 1957, Palm Springs, Calif.; ed California State Univ., San Diego; writer Rolling Stone magazine. *Films:* American Hot Wax (actor) 1978, Fast Times at Ridgemont High (writer) 1982, The Wild Life (writer, prod., actor) 1984, Say Anything... (writer, dir) 1989, Singles (writer, dir, prod., actor) 1992, Jerry Maguire (writer, dir, prod.) 1996, Almost Famous (writer, dir, prod.) 2000, Minority Report (actor) 2002, Vanilla Sky (screenplay, dir, prod.) 2001, Hitting It Hard (prod.) 2002, Elizabethtown (writer, dir, prod.) 2005. *Television:* creative consultant on series, Fast Times 1986. *Address:* c/o Columbia Tristar, 10202 Washington Boulevard, Culver City, CA 90232, USA (office).

CROWE, Martin David, MBE; New Zealand fmr professional cricketer; b. 22 Sept. 1962, Auckland; s. of David Crowe and Audrey Crowe; m. Simone Curtice 1991 (separated 1996); ed Auckland Grammar School; right-hand batsman, slip fielder; played for Auckland 1979–80 to 1982–83, Cen. Dists. 1983–84 to 1989–90 (Capt. 1984–85 to 1989–90), Somerset 1984–88, Wellington 1990–91 to 1994–95 (Capt. 1993–94); played in 77 Tests for NZ 1981–82 to 1995–96, 16 as Capt., scored 5,444 runs (average 45.36) with 17 hundreds, including NZ record 299 v. Sri Lanka, Wellington, Feb. 1991); scored 19,608 first-class runs (71 hundreds); toured England 1983, 1986, 1990 and 1994; 143 limited-overs internationals; Exec. Producer Sky TV cricket broadcasts; Wisden Cricketer of the Year 1985, NZ Sportsman of the Year 1991; selected World Cup Champion Cricketer 1992. *Publication:* Out on a Limb 1996. *Leisure interests:* tennis, golf, wine. *Address:* P.O. Box 109302, Newmarket, Auckland, New Zealand.

CROWE, Russell; New Zealand actor; b. 7 April 1964; m. Danielle Spencer 2003; two s.; singer, 30 Odd Foot of Grunts –2005, The Ordinary Fear of God 2006–; Variety Club Award (Australia) 1993, Film Critics Circle Award 1993, Best Actor Seattle Int. Film Festival 1993, Man. Film and TV Awards, Motion Pictures Exhibitors Asscn 1993, LA Film Critics Asscn 1999, Nat. Bd of Review 1999, Nat. Soc. of Film Critics 1999, Acad. Award for Best Actor 2000. *Films include:* Romper Stomper 1992, The Crossing 1993, The Quick and the Dead 1995, Rough Magic 1995, Virtuosity 1995, Under the Gun 1995, Heaven's Burning 1997, Breaking Up 1997, LA Confidential 1997, Mystery Alaska 1999, The Insider 1999, Gladiator 2000, Proof of Life 2000, A Beautiful Mind (Golden Globe, BAFTA Award and Screen Actors' Guild Award for Best Actor) 2001, Master and Commander 2003, Cinderella Man 2005, A Good Year 2006, 3:10 to Yuma 2007, American Gangster 2007, Body of Lies 2008. *Address:* William Morris Agency, One William Morris Place, Beverly Hills, CA 90212, USA (office); Bedford & Pearke Management Ltd, PO Box 171, Cameray, NSW 2062, Australia (office).

CROZIER, Adam Alexander, BA; British business executive; *Chairman of the Group Executive Team and Chief Executive, Royal Mail Group;* b. 26 Jan. 1964, Bute; s. of Robert Crozier and Elinor Crozier; m. Annette Edwards 1994; two d.; ed Heriot-Watt Univ., Edinburgh; with Pedigree Petfoods, Mars (UK) Ltd 1984–86; with Daily Telegraph 1986–88; joined Saatchi & Saatchi 1988, Dir 1990, Media Dir 1992, Vice-Chair. 1994, Jt Chief Exec. 1995–99; Chief Exec. Football Asscn 2000–02; Chair. Group Exec. Team and Chief Exec. Royal Mail Group, Royal Mail Holdings PLC 2003–; mem. Bd of Dirs Camelot PLC 2006–, Debenhams PLC 2006–; mem. Pres.'s Cttee of CBI. *Leisure interests:* football, golf, music. *Address:* Royal Mail Group PLC, 148 Old Street, London, EC1V 9HQ, England (office). *Telephone:* (20) 7250-2888 (office). *Fax:* (20) 7250-2244 (office). *E-mail:* info@royalmailgroup.com (office). *Website:* www.royalmailgroup.com (office).

CROZIER, Brian Rossiter, (John Rossiter); British writer and journalist; b. 4 Aug. 1918, Kuridala, Queensland, Australia; s. of R.H. Crozier and Elsa Crozier (née McGillivray); m. 1st Mary Lillian Samuel 1940 (died 1993); one s. three d.; m. 2nd Jacqueline Marie Mitchell 1999; ed Lycée, Montpellier, Peterborough Coll., Harrow, Trinity Coll. of Music, London; music and art critic, London 1936–39; reporter and sub-ed., Stoke-on-Trent, Stockport, London 1940–41; aeronautical inspection 1941–43; sub-ed., Reuters 1943–44, News Chronicle 1944–48, sub-ed. and writer Sydney Morning Herald, Australia 1948–51; corresp., Reuters-AAP 1951–52; Features Ed., Straits Times, Singapore 1952–53; leader writer and corresp., The Economist 1954–64; BBC commentator, English, French and Spanish overseas services 1954–66, Chair. Forum World Features 1965–74; Ed., Conflict Studies 1970–75; Co-founder and Dir Inst. for the Study of Conflict 1970–79, Consultant 1979–; Columnist, Now!, London 1980–81, Nat. Review, New York 1978–90 (contributing ed. 1982–), The Times 1982–84, The Free Nation, London 1982–89; Adjunct Scholar, The Heritage Foundation 1983–95; Distinguished Visiting Fellow, Hoover Inst., Stanford, Calif., USA 1996–2001. *Publications:* The Rebels 1960, The Morning After 1963, Neo-Colonialism 1964, South-East Asia in Turmoil 1965, The Struggle for the Third World 1966, Franco 1967, The Masters of Power 1969, The Future of Communist Power (in USA: Since Stalin) 1970, De Gaulle (vol. I) 1973, (vol. II) 1974, A Theory of Conflict 1974, The Man Who Lost China (Chiang Kai-shek) 1977, Strategy of Survival 1978, The Minimum State 1979, Franco: Crepúsculo de un hombre 1980, The Price of Peace 1980, Socialism Explained (co-author) 1984, This War Called Peace (co-author) 1984, The Andropov Deception (novel) (under pseudonym John Rossiter) 1984, The Grenada Documents (ed.) 1987, Socialism: Dream and Reality 1987, The Gorbachev Phenomenon 1990, Communism: Why Prolong its Death Throes? 1990, Free Agent: The Unseen War 1993, The KGB Lawsuits 1995, Le Phénix rouge (co-author) 1995, The Rise and Fall of the Soviet Empire 1999 and contribs to journals in numerous countries. *Leisure interests:* taping stereo, piano. *Address:* 18 Wickliffe Avenue, Finchley, London, N3 3EJ, England (home). *Telephone:* (20) 8346-8124 (home). *Fax:* (20) 8346-4599 (home). *E-mail:* b-crozier@ntlworld.com (home).

CRUICKSHANK, Sir Donald Gordon, Kt, MA, MBA, LLD, CA; British government official, financial administrator and business executive; b. 17 Sept. 1942; s. of Donald C. Cruickshank and Margaret Morrison; m. Elizabeth B. Taylor 1964; one s. one d.; ed Univ. of Aberdeen and Manchester Business School; consultant, McKinsey & Co. 1972–77; Gen. Man. Sunday Times, Times Newspapers 1977–80; Pearson PLC 1980–84; Man. Dir Virgin Group 1984–89; Chair. Wandsworth Health Authority 1986–89; CEO Nat. Health Service in Scotland 1989–93; Dir-Gen. UK Office of Telecommunications 1993–98; Chair. Action 2000 1997–2000; Chair. UK Banking Review 1998–2000; Chair. SMG PLC 1999–2004, London Stock Exchange 2000–03; mem. Financial Reporting Council 2002–; mem. Bd of Dirs (non-exec.) and Chair. Taylor & Francis PLC 2004, mem. Bd of Dirs T&F Informa plc (formed by merger of Taylor & Francis and Informa) 2004–05; Chair. (non-exec.) Formscape Group Ltd 2003–06, Clinovia 2004–06; mem. Bd of Dirs Qualcomm, Inc. 2005–; mem. Inst. of Chartered Accountants of Scotland. *Leisure interests:* sport, golf, opera. *Address:* c/o Financial Reporting Council, Aldwych House 71-91 Aldwych, London, WC2B 4HN, England.

CRUICKSHANK, John; Canadian journalist and publisher; *Publisher, CBC News;* began career at Montreal Gazette and the Kingston Whig-Standard newspapers before holding several positions at The Globe and Mail 1981–95, beats included educ. and Queen's Park, then Vancouver bureau chief, editorial writer, Assoc. Ed., Man. Ed. 1992–95; Ed. The Vancouver Sun 1995–2000; Vice-Pres. Editorial and Co-Ed. Chicago Sun-Times 2000–03, Publr 2003–07, also COO Sun-Times Media Group; Publr CBC News, Toronto 2007–. *Address:* CBC News, 181 Queen Street, Station C, Ottawa, ON K1Y 1E4, Canada (office). *Telephone:* (613) 288-6000 (office). *E-mail:* webmaster@cbc.ca (office). *Website:* www.cbc.ca/news (office).

CRUISE, Tom; American actor and film producer; b. (Thomas Cruise Mapother IV), 3 July 1962, Syracuse, NY; m. 1st Mimi Rogers 1987 (divorced 1990); m. 2nd Nicole Kidman 1990 (divorced 2001); one adopted s. one adopted d.; m. 3rd Katie Noelle Holmes 2006; one d.; Exec. Producer, United Artists Corpn 2006–; David di Donatello Lifetime Achievement Award 2005. *Films include:* Endless Love 1981, Taps 1981, All the Right Moves 1983, Losin' It 1983, The Outsiders 1983, Risky Business 1983, Legend 1985, Top Gun 1986, The Color of Money 1986, Rain Man 1988, Young Guns (uncredited) 1988, Cocktail 1989, Born on the Fourth of July 1989, Days of Thunder (also writer) 1990, Sure as the Moon 1991, Far and Away 1992, A Few Good Men 1992, The Firm 1993, Interview with the Vampire 1994, Mission: Impossible (also producer) 1996, Jerry Maguire 1996, Without Limits (producer) 1998, Eyes Wide Shut 1999, Magnolia 1999 (Golden Globe 2000), Mission: Impossible II (also producer) 2000, Vanilla Sky (also producer) 2001, Minority Report 2002, Narc (exec. producer) 2002, Space Station 3D (voice) 2002, Hitting It Hard (video) (producer) 2002, Shattered Glass (exec. producer) 2003, The Last Samurai (also producer) 2003, Collateral 2004, Ask the Dust (producer), Elizabethtown (producer) 2005, War of the Worlds 2005, Mission: Impossible III (also producer), Ask the Dust (producer) 2006, Lions for Lambs 2007, Tropic Thunder 2008. *Television includes:* Fallen Angels (dir series episode The Frightning Frammis) 1993, hosted Nobel Peace Prize Concert 2004. *Address:* Creative Artists Agency, 9830 Wilshire Boulevard, Beverly Hills, CA 90212-1825 (office); United Artists Corporation, 10250 Constellation Blvd., Los Angeles, CA 90067, USA (office). *Telephone:* (310) 288-4545 (CAA) (office); (310) 449-3000 (UA) (office). *Fax:* (310) 288-4800 (CAA) (office); (310) 449-8857 (UA) (office). *Website:* www.caa.com (office); www.unitedartists.com (office).

CRUMB, George, BM, MM, DMA; American composer; b. 24 Oct. 1929, Charleston, WV; s. of George Henry and Vivian Reed; m. Elizabeth Brown 1949; two s. one d.; ed Mason Coll. of Music, Charleston, Univ. of Illinois, Univ. of Michigan at Ann Arbor, Hochschule für Musik, Berlin; Prof., Univ. of Colorado 1959–63; Creative Assoc., State Univ. of New York at Buffalo 1963–64; Prof. of Composition, Univ. of Pa 1971–83, Annenberg Prof. of the Humanities 1983–97, Emer. 1997–; mem. Nat. Inst. of Arts and Letters 1975–; Fulbright Scholarship 1955, Rockefeller Grant 1964, Guggenheim Grant 1967, 1973, Koussevitsky Int. Recording Award 1971, UNESCO Int. Rostrum of Composers Award 1971, Fromm Grant 1973, Ford Grant 1976, Prince Pierre de Monaco Prize 1989, Edward MacDowell Colony Medal, Peterborough 1995, Grammy Award (for Star Child) 2000. *Compositions include:* Two Duos for flute and clarinet 1944, Four Songs for voice, clarinet and piano 1945, Sonata for piano 1945, Four Pieces for violin and piano 1945, Poem 1946, Three Early Songs for voice and piano 1947, Gethsemane for orchestra 1947, Alleluja for chorus 1948, Sonata for violin and piano 1949, A Cycle of Greek Lyrics 1950, Prelude and Toccata 1951, Three Pastoral Pieces for oboe and piano 1952, String Trio 1952, Sonata for viola and piano 1953, String Quartet 1954, Sonata for cello 1955, Diptych for orchestra 1955, Variazioni for orchestra 1959, Five Pieces for piano 1962, Night Music I for soprano, piano and two percussionists 1963, Four Nocturnes for violin and piano 1964, Eleven Echoes of Autumn 1966, Madrigals, Books 1–4 1965–69, Songs, Drones and Refrains of Death 1968, Echoes of Time and the River (Pulitzer Prize for Music) 1968, Night of the Four Moons 1969, Ancient Voices of Children 1970, Black Angels for electric string quartet 1970, Vox Balaenae for three masked musicians 1971, Lux Aeterna 1971, Makrokosmos vols I–V 1972–79, Dream Sequence for violin, cello, piano and percussion 1976, Star-Child for soprano, children's chorus and orchestra (Grammy Award for Best Contemporary Composition 2001) 1977, Apparition 1979, A Little Suite for Christmas 1979, Gnomic Variations for piano 1981, Pastoral Drone for organ 1982, Processional for piano 1983, A Haunted Landscape for orchestra 1984, The Sleeper 1984, An Idyll for the Misbegotten 1986, Federico's Little Songs for Children for soprano, flute and percussion 1986, Zeitgeist for two amplified pianos 1988, Easter Dawning for carillon 1991, Quest for guitar and ensemble 1994, Mundus Canis for guitar and percussion 1998, American Songbook 2001–04, Unto the Hills 2001, A Journey Beyond Time 2002, Eine Kleine Mitternachtmusik 2002, Otherworldly Resonances 2002, River of Life 2003, Winds of Destiny 2004, Voices from a Forgotten World 2006, Voices from the Morning of the Earth 2007. *Leisure interest:* reading. *Address:* c/o Becky Starobin, Bridge Records, Inc., 200 Clinton Avenue, New Rochelle, NY 10801, USA (office). *Telephone:* (914) 654-9270 (office). *Fax:* (914) 636-1383 (office). *E-mail:* bridgerec@aol.com (office). *Website:* www.bridgerecords.com (office); www.georgecrumb.net.

CRUMPTON, Michael Joseph, CBE, PhD, FRS, FMedSci; British biochemist and immunologist; b. 7 June 1929; s. of Charles E. Crumpton and Edith Crumpton; m. Janet Elizabeth Dean 1960; one s. two d.; ed Poole Grammar School, Univ. Coll., Southampton and Lister Inst. of Preventive Medicine, London; joined scientific staff Microbiological Research Establishment, Porton, Wilts. 1955–60; Deputy Dir Research Labs., Imperial Cancer Research Fund Labs., London 1979–91, Dir 1991–93; Dir Imperial Cancer Research Tech. Ltd 1989–99 (COO 1993–94); Visiting Scientist Fellowship, NIH, Bethesda, Md, USA 1959–60; Research Fellow, Dept of Immunology, St Mary's Hosp. Medical School, London 1960–66; mem. scientific staff, Nat. Inst. for Medical Research, Mill Hill 1966–79, Head of Biochemistry Div. 1976–79; Visiting Fellow, John Curtin School for Medical Research, Australian Nat. Univ., Canberra 1973–74; mem. Cell Bd MRC 1979–83, Science Council, Celltech Ltd 1980–90, EMBO 1982–, WHO Steering Cttee for Encapsulated Bacteria 1984–91 (Chair. 1988–91), Sloan Cttee Gen. Motors Research Foundation 1986–88 (Chair. 1988), Council Royal Inst. 1986–90 (mem. Davy Faraday Lab. Comm. 1985–90, Chair. 1988–90), MRC 1986–90, Royal Soc. 1990–92, Scientific Advisory Comm., Lister Inst. 1986–91, MRC AIDS Directed Prog. Steering Cttee 1987–91, Scientific Cttee Swiss Inst. for Experimental Cancer Research 1989–96; Chair. Scientific Advisory Bd Biomedical Research Centre, Univ. of British Columbia 1987–91, Health and Safety Exec., Dept of Health Advisory Comm. on Dangerous Pathogens 1991–99; Dir (non-exec.) Amersham Int. PLC 1990–97, Amersham Pharmacia Biotech Ltd 1997–2001, Amersham Pharmacia Biotech Inc. 2001–02; mem. Governing Body British Postgraduate Medical Foundation 1987–95, Academia Europea 1996–, Governing Body Imperial Coll. 1994–98; mem. numerous Editorial Bds; Biochemistry Soc. Visiting Lecturer, Australia 1983; Trustee EMF Biological Research Trust 1995–, Breakthrough Breast Cancer 1997–; Hon. FRCPath; Hon. mem. American Assen of Immunology 1995. *Publications:* numerous scientific papers. *Leisure interests:* gardening, reading. *Address:* 33 Homefield Road, Radlett, Herts., WD7 8PX, England. *Telephone:* (1923) 854675. *Fax:* (1923) 853866.

CRUTZEN, Paul Josef; Dutch professor of atmospheric chemistry; *Professor Emeritus, Institute for Marine and Atmospheric Sciences, Utrecht University;* b. 3 Dec. 1933, Amsterdam; s. of the late Josef Crutzen and Anna Crutzen; m.; two c.; ed Stockholm Univ., Sweden; various computer consulting, teaching and research positions at Dept of Meteorology, Stockholm Univ. 1959–74; Post-doctoral Fellow, European Space Research Org., Clarendon Lab., Univ. of Oxford, UK 1969–71; Research Scientist, Upper Atmosphere Project, Nat. Center for Atmospheric Research (NCAR), Boulder, Colo, USA and Consultant at Aeronomy Lab., Environmental Research Labs, Nat. Oceanic and Atmospheric Admin, Boulder 1974–77; Sr Scientist and Dir Air Quality Div., NCAR 1977–80; Adjunct Prof., Atmospheric Sciences Dept, Colorado State Univ. 1976–81; Dir Atmospheric Chem. Div., Max Planck Inst. for Chem.,

Mainz, Germany 1980–2000; Exec. Dir Max Planck Inst. for Chem. 1983–85; Prof., Dept of Geophysical Sciences, Univ. of Chicago, USA 1987–91; Prof., Scripps Inst. of Oceanography, Univ. of California, San Diego 1992–2000; Prof., Inst. for Marine and Atmospheric Sciences (IMAU), Utrecht Univ., Netherlands 1997–2000, Prof. Emer. 2000–; mem. Royal Swedish Acad. of Sciences 1991, Royal Swedish Acad. of Eng 1991, Leopoldina, halle 1991, Accad. Nazionale dei Lincei 1997; mem. Council of Pontifical Acad. of Sciences 2001; Founding mem. Academia Europaea 1988; Foreign Assoc. NAS 1994; Corresp. mem. Royal Netherlands Acad. of Science 1990; Foreign mem. Russian Acad. of Sciences 1999; Fellow, American Geophysical Union 1986; Foreign Hon. mem. American Acad. of Arts and Sciences 1986; Hon. mem. American Meteorological Soc. 1997, European Geophysical Soc. 1997, Comm. on Atmospheric Chem. and Global Pollution 1998, Swedish Meteorological Soc. 2000, World Innovation Foundation 2002; Hon. Prof., Johannes Gutenberg Univ. of Mainz 1993; Hon. Chair. Climate Conference 2001, Utrecht 2001; Dr hc (York Univ., Canada) 1986, (Université Catholique de Louvain) 1992, (Univ. of East Anglia, UK) 1994, (Aristotle Univ., Thessaloniki, Greece) 1996, (Univ. of Liège, Belgium) 1997, (Univ. of San José, Costa Rica) 1997, (Tel-Aviv Univ.) 1997, (Oregon State Univ.) 1997, (Univ. of Chile) 1997, (Université de Bourgogne, Dijon, France) 1997, (Univ. of Athens, Greece) 1998, (Democritus Univ. of Thrace, Greece) 2001, (Nova Gorica Polytechnic, Slovenia) 2002, (Univ. of Hull, UK) 2002; Tyler Environment Prize 1989, Volvo Environmental Prize 1991, German Environmental Prize 1994, Max-Planck Research Prize 1994, shared Nobel Prize in Chem. 1995, most cited author in the geosciences world-wide 2002. *Publications include:* Atmospheric Change; An Earth System Perspective (with T. E. Graedel) 1993. *Address:* IMAU, Utrecht University, Buys Ballotlaboratorium, Princetonplein 5, 3584 Utrecht, Netherlands (office). *E-mail:* air@mpch-mainz.mpgde (office). *Website:* www.mpch-mainz.mpg.de/~air/crutzen (office); www.universiteitutrecht.nl (office).

CRUYFF, Johan; Dutch professional football manager and fmr professional football player; b. 25 April 1947, Amsterdam; one s.; played for Ajax 1964–73, top scorer in Dutch League, with 33 goals 1967; with FC Barcelona 1973–78; played for Los Angeles Aztecs 1979–80, for Washington Diplomats 1980–81, for Levante, Spain 1981, for Ajax 1981–83, for Feyenoord 1983–84; capped 48 times, scored 33 int. goals and captained Netherlands 1974 World Cup final; Man. Ajax 1985–87, winning European Cup Winners' Cup 1987; Man. FC Barcelona 1988–96, winning Cup Winners' Cup 1989, European Cup 1992, Spanish League title 1991, 1992, 1993, Spanish Super Cup 1992; f. Cruyff Foundation 1997, Johan Cruyff Univ. (to assist retd sportspeople) 1998; European Footballer of the Year 1971, 1973–74, Golden Player of the Netherlands (best player of past 50 years) 2003, Laureus Lifetime Achievement Award 2006, Lifetime Achievement Award, Royal Netherlands Football Asscn 2006. *Address:* c/o Johan Cruyff Foundation, Olympisch Stadion 5, 1076 DE Amsterdam, Netherlands (office). *Telephone:* (20) 3057766 (office). *Fax:* (20) 3057760 (office). *Website:* www.cruyff-foundation.org (office).

CRUZ, Avelino, Jr; Philippine lawyer and government official; ed Univ. of the Philippines Coll. of Law; Presidential Legal Counsel 2001–04; fmr mem. Cabinet Oversight Cttee on Internal Security; Sec. of Nat. Defense 2004–06 (resgnd), fmr mem. Nat. Security Council; currently adviser to Liberal Party Pres. Manuel Roxas II;. *Address:* c/o Liberal Party, 2nd Floor, Matrinco Bldg, Chino Roces Ave, Makati City, 1231 Metro Manila, Philippines.

CRUZ, Penélope; Spanish actress; b. 28 April 1974, Madrid; d. of Eduardo and Encarna Cruz Sánchez; ed Nat. Conservatory, Madrid; Chevalier, Ordre des Arts et des Lettres 2006. *Films:* Live Flesh, Belle Epoque 1992, Jamón, Jamón 1992, La Celestina 1996, Open Your Eyes 1997, The Hi-Lo Country 1998, Talk of Angels 1998, The Girl of Your Dreams (Goya Award) 1998, All About My Mother 1999, Woman on Top 1999, All the Pretty Horses 2000, Captain Corelli's Mandolin 2001, Blow 2001, Vanilla Sky 2001, Fanfan La Tulipe 2003, Gothika 2003, Noel 2004, Head in the Clouds 2004, Non ti muovere (Don't Move) 2004, Bandidas 2006, Volver (Goya Award for Best Actress 2007) 2006, The Good Night 2007, Elegy 2007, Vicky Cristina Barcelona (BAFTA Award for Best Supporting Actress 2009, Acad. Award for Best Supporting Actress 2009) 2008. *Address:* c/o Kuranda Management International, 8626 Skyline Drive, Los Angeles, CA 90046, USA (office).

CRUZ-DIEZ, Carlos; Venezuelan painter; b. 17 Aug. 1923; ed School of Plastic and Applied Arts, Caracas; Graphic Designer, Creole Petroleum Corpn, Venezuela 1940–45; Creative Dir, Venezuelan subsidiary of McCann-Erickson Advertising Agency 1946–51; Prof., History of Applied Arts, School of Arts, Caracas 1953–55; in Barcelona and Paris working on physical qualities of colour now named Physichromies 1955–56; opened studio of visual arts and industrial design, Caracas 1957; Prof. and Asst Dir School of Arts, Caracas 1959–60; moved to Paris 1960; Pres. for Life Carlos Cruz-Diez Museum of Print and Design Foundation, Caracas; 1986-1993 Titular Prof. and Dir, Art Unit of Inst. of Advanced Studies (IDEA), Caracas 1986–93; first one-man exhbn, Caracas 1947, later including Madrid, Genoa, Turin, London, Paris, Cologne, Munich, Oslo, Brussels, Ostwald Museum, Dortmund, Bottrop (Germany), New York, Bogotá, Rome, Venice and Essen; retrospective exhbns at Signals, London and Galerie Kerchache, Paris 1965, Galerie Denise René, Paris 1994, Städtisches Museum, Gelsenkirchen, Museo de Arte Moderno, Bogotá and Museo de Arte Moderno J. Soto, Ciudad Bolívar 1998, Galerie Schoeller, Düsseldorf 2001, Centro Cultural Corp Group, Caracas 2001, Galerie d'art de Créteil, France 2002, Galería Marci Gaymu, Madrid 2004, Sicardi Gallery, Houston 2005; represented at numerous group exhbns including L'oeil Moteur : Art Optique et Cinétique /1950-1975, Musée d'Art Moderne et Contemporain, Strasbourg. France 2005; works exhibited in Museo de Bellas Artes, Caracas, Victoria and Albert Museum, Tate Gallery, London, Casa de las Américas, Havana, Städtisches Museum, Leverkusen, Germany, Museum of Modern Art, New York, Museum of Contemporary Art, Montréal, Museum des 20. Jahrhunderts, Vienna, Univ. of Dublin, Museo Civico di Torino, Wallraf-Richartz Museum, Cologne, Musée de Grenoble, Centre Georges Pompidou, Musée d'Art Moderne, Paris, Neue Pinakothek, Munich; mem. l'Académie des Sciences Arts et Lettres de Mérida. Vénézuéla; Hon. Mem. de Ciencias, Arte y Letras, Merida, Venezuela; Orden Andres Bello (Venezuela) 1981, Officier des Arts et Lettres (France) 1985, Orden Ciudad de Barquisimeto en Primera Clase (Venezuela) 2000, Commandeur des Arts et des Lettres 2002, Orden Universidad Católica Andrés Bello (Venezuela) 2006, Ordre Ciudad de Tovar y Ciudad de Bailadores (Venezuela) 2007; Dr hc (Universidad Simón Bolívar) 2006, (Universidad de Los Andes) 2007; Second Prize, Festival Int. de Peinture, Cagnes-sur-Mer, France 1969, First Prize III American Art Biennial, Cordoba, Argentina 1970, Int. Painting Prize IXth Biennial of Sao Paulo, Brazil 1971, Nat. Prize of Fine Arts, Venezuela 1971, Prize Intervencion del Arte en la Arquitectura, VI Biennial of Architecture, Venezuela 1976, Prize Carlos Raul Villanueva, XXXVI Salon de Arte Arturo Michelena, Valencia, Venezuela 1978, Gold Medal, Norwegian Int. Print Triennale, Fredrikstad, Norway 1992. *Publications:* My Reflection on Colour 1989, Interactive Random Chromatic Experience (software) 1995. *Address:* 23 rue Pierre Semard, 75009 Paris, France. *E-mail:* carlos@cruz-diez.com (office). *Website:* www.cruz-diez.com (office).

CRVENKOVSKI, Branko; Macedonian politician, engineer and fmr head of state; b. 12 Oct. 1962, Sarajevo, Bosnia and Herzegovina; m. Jasmina Crvenkovska; one s. one d.; ed Sts Cyril and Methodius Univ., Skopje; computer engineer, SEMOS Co. 1987–90; mem. Nat. Ass. 1990–2004; Chair. Social-Democratic Union of Macedonia (SDUM) 1990–92, Pres. 1991–2004; Chair. Cabinet of Ministers (Prime Minister) 1992–98, 2002–04; Pres. 2004–09; Hon. mem. Int. Raoul Wallenberg Foundation. *Address:* c/o Office of the President, 1000 Skopje, 11 Oktomvri bb, Former Yugoslav Republic of Macedonia. *Telephone:* (2) 3113318.

CRYSTAL, Billy; American actor and comedian; b. 14 March 1947, Long Beach, NY; s. of Jack Crystal and Helen Crystal; m. Janice Crystal (née Goldfinger); two d.; ed Marshall Univ., Nassau Community Coll., New York Univ.; mem. of the group 3's Company; solo appearances as a stand-up comedian; Emmy Award for Outstanding Writing 1991, Mark Twain Prize for American Humor 2007. *Television:* Soap (series) 1977–81, The Billy Crystal Hour 1982, Saturday Night Live 1984–85, The Love Boat, The Tonight Show; TV films include: Breaking up is Hard to do 1979, Enola Gay, The Men, The Mission, The Atomic Bomb 1980, Death Flight. *Stage appearances include:* 700 Sundays (one-man show) (Tony Award for special theatrical event 2005). *Films include:* The Rabbit Test 1978, This is Spinal Tap 1984, Running Scared 1986, The Princess Bride 1987, Throw Momma from the Train 1987, When Harry Met Sally 1989, City Slickers 1991, Mr Saturday Night (also dir producer, co-screen-play writer) 1993, Forget Paris 1995, Hamlet, Father's Day, Deconstructing Harry, My Giant 1998, Analyze This 1998, The Adventures of Rocky & Bullwinkle 2000, Monsters Inc. (voice) 2001, Mike's New Car (voice) 2002, Analyze That 2002, Howl's Moving Castle (voice) 2004, Cars (voice) 2006. *Publications:* Absolutley Mahvelous 1986, I Already Know I Love You (juvenile) 2004, 700 Sundays (autobiog.) 2005. *Address:* c/o CAA, 2000 Avenue of the Stars, Los Angeles, CA 90067, USA.

CSABA, László, PhD, DrSci, DrHab; Hungarian economist and academic; *Professor of Economics and European Studies, Central European University;* b. 27 March 1954, Budapest; s. of Ede Csaba and Márta Biró; m. Gabriella Ónody 1980; one s. one d.; ed Univ. of Budapest, Hungarian Acad. of Sciences; Fellow, Inst. for World Econs, Budapest 1976–87; economist/researcher, then Sr Economist, Kopint-Datorg Econ. Research 1988–2000; Hon. Prof. of Int. Econs, Coll. of Foreign Trade, Budapest Univ. of Econs 1991–97, Prof. 1997–; Prof. of Econs and European Studies, Cen. European Univ. 2000–; Head of Doctoral Programme, Univ. of Debrecen 1999–2004; Vice-Pres. European Asscn for Comparative Econs 1990–94, 1996–98, Pres. 1999–2000; mem. Econs Cttee Hungarian Acad. of Sciences 1986–, Co-Chair. 1996–99, 2000–02, Chair. 2003–05; Visiting Prof., Bocconi Univ., Milan 1991, Helsinki Univ. 1993, Europa Univ., Viadrina, Frankfurt 1997, Freie Univ., Berlin 1998–2000, Cen. European Univ. 1998; mem. Bd TIGER Inst., Poland, NORDI Inst., Finland; mem. editorial bd of various journals; Ministry of External Econ. Affairs Prize 1994, Bezeredi Prize for European Integration 2003, Nat. Bank of Hungary Prize 2004, Akademia Publishing House Best Economics Book Award 2005. *Publications:* Eastern Europe in the World Economy 1990, The Capitalist Revolution in Eastern Europe 1995, The New Political Economy of Emerging Europe 2005; ed. six books; over 190 articles and chapters in books published in 18 countries. *Leisure interests:* classical music, travel, soccer. *Address:* Department of International Relations and European Studies, Central European University, 1051 Budapest, Nador u.9 (office); 1074 Budapest, Dohány u. 94, Hungary (home). *Telephone:* (1) 327-30-17 (office); (1) 322-05-19 (home). *Fax:* (1) 327-32-43 (office). *E-mail:* csabal@ceu.hu (office). *Website:* www.ceu.hu (office); www.csabal.com.

CSÁKY, Pál, MSc; Slovak politician; *Chairman, Party of the Hungarian Coalition (Strana maďarskej koalície);* b. 21 March 1956, Sahy; m.; four d.; ed Univ. of Pardubice, Czech Repub.; Chief Technologist, Levitex textile factory, Levice 1981–90; mem. Nat. Council of Slovak Repub. 1990–, mem. Jt Parl. Cttee Nat. Council of Slovak Repub. and European Parl. 1994–98; Deputy Chair. for Foreign Affairs, Hungarian Christian-Democratic Movt (HCDM) 1991–98, Chair. HCDM Parl. Group 1992–98; mem. Parl. Ass. of Council of Europe 1993–94; Deputy Chair. Hungarian Coalition Party 1998–; Deputy Prime Minister for Human Rights, Minorities, and Regional Devt 1998–2002, for European Affairs, Human Rights and Minorities 2002–06; Chair. Party of the Hungarian Coalition (Strana maďarskej koalície/Magyar Koalíció Pártja) 2007–; Chair. Govt Council for Minorities and Ethnic Groups, Cttee of

Ministers for European Affairs, Govt Council for Regional Policy and Control over Structural Operations, Govt Council for Third Sector, Govt Council for Sustainable Devt, Cttee of Ministers Against Drug Abuse and Drug Dependencies. *Publications include:* in Hungarian: Emlékek könyve (Book of Memoirs) 1992, Csillagok a falu felett (Stars Above the Village) 1993, Úton (On the Way) 1994, Magyarként Szlovákiában (Being a Hungarian in Slovakia) 1994, Két világ között (Between Two Worlds) 1998; more than 1000 articles, political literature and fiction, mainly in Hungarian. *Leisure interests:* music, piano, literature, theatre, fitness, swimming. *Address:* Party of the Hungarian Coalition (Strana maďarskej koalície), 811 05 Bratislava, Čajakova 8, Slovakia (office). *Telephone:* (2) 5249-5164 (office). *Fax:* (2) 5249-5264 (office). *Website:* www.mkp.sk (office).

CSÁNYI, Sándor, MSc, PhD; Hungarian banker; *Chairman and CEO, OTP Bank plc;* b. 20 March 1953, Jászárokszállás; m.; five c.; ed Inst. of Finance and Accounting, Budapest Univ. of Econ. Sciences; with Fiscal Dept, Ministry of Finance 1974–83; Dept Head of Ministry of Agric. and Food 1983–86, of Hungarian Credit Bank Co. 1986–89; Deputy CEO Commercial and Credit Bank Co. 1989–92, Pres. 1992–; Chair. and CEO OTP Bank-Nat. Savings and Commercial Bank plc, Budapest; Vice-Pres. Bd Hungarian Bankers Asscn; Co-Chair. Nat. Asscn of Entrepreneurs and Employers; mem. Bd MasterCard, Mol; Hon. Citizen Budapest Corvinus Univ. 2005; Global Leader of Tomorrow World Econ. Forum, Davos 1996, One of Top Executives in Central Europe, Wall Street Journal 1999, Entrepreneur of Hungary 2000, Hungarian Banker of the Year 2001, Ernst & Young Businessman of the Year 2004, Mercur Award for Outstanding Performance in Business, Hungarian Chamber of Industry and Trade 2005. *Leisure interests:* hunting, sports, reading. *Address:* Nádor u. 16, 1051 Budapest, Hungary (office). *Telephone:* (1) 311-5093 (office). *Fax:* (1) 311-0072 (office). *E-mail:* csanyis@otpbank.hu (office). *Website:* www.otpbank.hu (office).

CSÁSZÁR, Ákos, PhD; Hungarian mathematician and academic; *Professor Emeritus, Eötvös Loránd University;* b. 26 Feb. 1924, Budapest; s. of Károly Császár and Gizella Szücs; m. Klára Cseley; ed Budapest Univ.; Prof., Eötvös Loránd Univ., Budapest 1957–94, Prof. Emer. 1994–, Dir Inst. of Math. 1983–86; Visiting Prof., Technische Universität, Stuttgart 1975, Università di Torino 1979, Technische Universität, Graz 1983; fmr mem. Editorial Bd Periodica Mathematica Hungarica, Studia Mathematica Hungarica; Chief Ed. Acta Mathematica Hungarica 1996, Annales Univ. Scientiarum Budapestinensis Sectio Mathematica; Gen. Sec. János Bolyai Mathematical Soc. 1966–80, Pres. 1980–90, Hon. Pres. 1990–; Corresp. mem. Hungarian Acad. of Sciences 1970, Full mem. 1979–, mem. St Stephen's Acad. 1999–; Hon. Dr and Prof. (Budapest) 2004; Kossuth Prize 1963, Bolzano Medal (Prague) 1981, Arany János Prize 1999. *Publications:* Foundations of General Topology 1960, General Topology 1974, Valós analízis (Real Analysis) (two vols) 1983; articles in int. math. periodicals. *Leisure interests:* music, botany, bridge. *Address:* Párizsi utca 6/a, 1052 Budapest, Hungary (home). *Telephone:* (1) 318-5172 (home).

CSIKÓS-NAGY, Béla, DrEconSc; Hungarian economist; b. 9 Sept. 1915, Szeged; s. of Dr József Csikós-Nagy and Jolán Jedlicska; m. Dr Livia Kneppó 1944; two d.; ed Szeged Univ. and Univ. of Pécs; joined Hungarian CP 1945; Chair. Hungarian Bd of Prices and Materials 1957–84; Exec. Co-Chair. Council of Industrial Policy 1984–90; Lecturer in Price Theory, Karl Marx Univ. of Econ. Sciences, Budapest 1959–90, title of Univ. Prof. 1964; Under-Sec. of State 1968–84; Pres. Hungarian Econ. Asscn 1970–90, Hon. Chair. 1994–; mem. Exec. Cttee Int. Econ. Asscn 1971–77, 1983–86; mem. Oxford Energy Club 1977, Hungarian Acad. of Sciences 1982–; Corresp. mem. Austrian Acad. of Sciences; Pres. Hungarian Bridge Fed. 1983–90; Hon. Chair. Int. Soc. of Econs; Hon. Prof., Univ. of Vienna; Banner Order of Hungarian People's Repub.; Hungarian State Prize 1970. *Publications:* Pricing in Hungary 1968, General and Socialist Price Theory 1968, Hungarian Economic Policy 1971, Socialist Economic Policy 1973, Socialist Price Theory and Price Policy 1975, Towards a New Price Revolution 1978, On Hungarian Price Policy 1980, Economic Policy 1982, The Price Law in Socialist Planned Economy 1983, Topical Issues of Hungarian Price Policy 1985, Socialist Market Economy 1987, Price and Power (with Peter S. Elek) 1995, Hungarian Economic Policy in the 20th Century 1996, Economics in the World of Globalization 2002 (English edn 2005), East-West Economic Relations in the Changing Global Environment: Proceedings of a Conference Held by the International Economic Association in Budapest, Hungary, and Vienna, Austria (co-ed.). *Leisure interest:* patience (card game). *Address:* Bp. V. Sas-u.25.VI.em., Budapest 1245, Pf. 1044 (office); Budapest XII, Varosmajor u. 26/c, Hungary (home). *Telephone:* 331-6906 (office); 3554-081 (home). *Fax:* 331-6906 (office).

CSIKSZENTMIHALYI, Mihaly, BA, PhD; American psychologist and academic; *Distinguished Professor of Psychology, Claremont Graduate University;* b. 29 Sept. 1934, Fiume, Italy; s. of Alfred Csikszentmihályi and Edith (Jankovich de Jessenice) Csikszentmihályi; m. Isabella Selega 1961; two s.; ed Univ. of Chicago; emigrated to USA in 1956; Assoc. Prof. and Chair., Dept of Sociology and Anthropology, Lake Forest Coll. 1965–71; Prof. of Human Devt, Univ. of Chicago 1971, Chair. Dept of Behavioral Sciences 1985–87; Davidson Prof. of Man., Drucker School of Man., Claremont Grad. Univ. 1999, now Distinguished Prof. of Psychology, also Dir Quality of Life Research Center; mem. Bd of Advisers, Encyclopaedia Britannica 1985–; Consultant, The JP Getty Museum, Malibu 1985–; Sr Fulbright Scholar, Brazil 1984, New Zealand 1990; Fellow, American Acad. of Arts and Sciences, American Acad. of Political and Social Sciences, Hungarian Acad. of Sciences, Nat. Acad. of Educ., Nat. Acad. of Leisure Sciences, World Economic Forum, Center for Advanced Study in the Behavioral Sciences; Hon. DSc (Lake Forest Coll.) 1999, (Colorado Coll.) 2002, (Rhode Island School of Design) 2003. *Publications:* Beyond Boredom and Anxiety 1975, The Creative Vision 1976, The Meaning of Things 1981, Being Adolescent 1984, Optimal Experience 1988, Flow—The Psychology of Optimal Experience 1990, Television and the Quality of Life 1990, The Art of Seeing 1990, Talented Teenagers 1993, The Evolving Self 1993, Creativity 1996, Finding Flow in Everyday Life 1997, Flow in Sport 1999, Becoming Adult 2000, Good Work 2001, Good Business 2003; contrib. to several other books. *Leisure interests:* mountain climbing, chess and history. *Address:* School of Behavioral and Organizational Sciences, Claremont Graduate University, 150 East 10th St, Claremont, CA 91711; 700 East Alamosa Drive, Claremont, CA 91711, USA (home). *Telephone:* (909) 607-3307 (office); (909) 621-7345 (home). *Fax:* (909) 621-8543 (office). *E-mail:* miska@cgu.edu (office). *Website:* www.cgu.edu/pages/154.asp (office).

CSOÓRI, Sándor; Hungarian poet and writer; b. 3 Feb. 1930, Zámoly, Co. Fejér; ed Lenin Inst., Budapest; contrib. to Irodalmi Újság (monthly) 1954–55, Új hang (monthly) 1955–56; drama critic Mafilm Studio 1968; joined opposition movt 1980; participated in political discussions of Monor 1985 and Lakitelek 1987; Founding mem. Hungarian Democratic Forum 1987, presidium mem. 1988–92; Chair. Illyés Gyula Foundation 1990–94; Pres. World Fed. of Hungarians 1991–2000; Attila József Prize 1954, Cannes Film Festival Prize 1964, 1968, Herder Prize 1981, Kossuth Prize 1990, Eeva Joenpelto Prize 1995, The Hungarian Book of the Year Award 1995, Karoli Gaspar Award, Hungarian Heritage Award. *Publications:* selected poems: Fölröppen a madár (The Bird Takes Wing) 1954, Ördögpille (Demon Butterfly) 1957, Menekülés a magányból (Escape from Loneliness) 1962, Elmaradt lázálom (Postponed Nightmare) 1980, Knives and Nails 1981, Hóemléke (Memory of Snow) 1983, Várakozás a tavaszban (Waiting in the Spring) 1983, Hattyúkkal ágyútűzben (In Cannon Fire with Swans) 1995, Ha volna életem (If I Had a Life) 1996, Quiet Vertigo 2001, Before and After the Fall 2004; sociographies: Tudósítás a toronyból (Report From the Tower) 1963, Kubai utinapló (Cuban Travel Diary) 1965; essay volumes: Faltól falig (From Wall to Wall) 1968, Nomád napló (Nomadic Diary) 1979, Félig bevallott élet (Half Confessed Life) 1984, Készülődés a számadásra (Preparation for Final Reckoning) 1987, Nappali hold (Daytime Moon) 1991, Tenger és diólevél I. II. (The Sea and Nut Leaves) 1994, Száll a alá poklokra (Descent into Hell) 1997; film scripts: Tízezer nap (Ten thousand days), Földobott kő (The thrown-up stone), 80 huszár (Eighty Hussars), Tüske a köröm alatt (A Thorn under the Fingernail), Hószakadás (Snow-Storm), Nincs idö (No Time Left). *Address:* Benczúr u. 15, 1068 Budapest, Hungary.

CUARÓN, Alfonso; Mexican film director and producer; b. 28 Nov. 1961, Mexico City; m. 1st Mariana Elizondo 1980 (divorced 1993); one c.; m. 2nd Annalisa Bugliani 2001; two c.; ed Centro Universitario de Estudios Cinematográficos. *Films include:* Quartet for the End of Time (also writer) 1983, Who's He Anyway (also screenplay) 1983, Cita con la muerte 1989, Sólo con tu pareja (also screenplay and producer) 1991, Camino largo a Tijuana (co-producer) 1991, A Little Princess 1995, Sistole Diastole (screenplay) 1997, Great Expectations 1998, Y tu mamá también (also screenplay and producer) 2001, Me la debes (exec. producer) 2001, Harry Potter and the Prisoner of Azkaban 2004, Temporada de patos (exec. producer) 2004, Crónicas (producer) 2004, The Assassination of Richard Nixon (producer) 2004, Black Sun (exec. producer) 2005, Paris, je t'aime (writer segment "Parc Monceau") 2006, Pan's Labyrinth (producer) (BAFTA Award for Best Film Not in the English Language 2007) 2006, Children of Men (also screenplay) 2006, The Shock Doctrine (short-film made with Naomi Klein) 2007. *Television includes:* Hora Marcada 1988–90. *Address:* c/o Endeavor Agency, 9701 Wilshire Blvd, 10th Floor, Beverly Hills, CA 90212, USA (office).

CUBAS GRAU, Raúl; Paraguayan politician and business executive; b. 23 Aug. 1943, Asunción; m. Mirta Gusinsky de Cubas; two d. (one deceased); ed Universidade Católica do Rio de Janeiro; worked as engineer for ANDE 1967–73; Commercial Dir CIE SRL 1977–79; Dir CONCRET-MIX SA 1970–88; Legal Rep. 14 de Julio SA 1980–1993; Dir COPAC VIAL SA 1987–91; Legal Rep. of consortium OCHO A SACI–14 Julio SA–CONPASA 1992; Exec. Minister of State for Ministry of Econ. and Social Planning and Devt 1994–96; Minister of Finance 1996; Pres. of Paraguay 1998–99.

CUBITT, Sir Hugh (Guy), Kt, CBE, JP, DL, FRICS, FRSA; British fmr business executive; b. 2 July 1928, London; s. of the late Col the Hon. Guy Cubitt and Rosamond M. E. Cholmeley; m. Linda I. Campbell 1958; one s. two d.; ed Royal Naval Coll., Dartmouth and Greenwich; served in RN 1949–53; Pnr, Rogers, Chapman & Thomas 1958–67, Cubitt & West 1962–79; Chair. The Housing Corpn 1980–90, Lombard North Cen. PLC 1980–91; Commr English Heritage 1988–94; Chair. Anchor Group of Housing Assocs 1991–98; Chair. Rea Brothers Group PLC 1996–98; Dir PSIT PLC 1962–97; Dir Nat. Westminster Bank 1977–90, mem. UK Advisory Bd 1990–91; Gov. Peabody Trust 1991–2003 (Chair. 1998–2003); mem. Westminster City Council 1963–78; Lord Mayor of Westminster 1977–78; Hon. Steward Westminster Abbey 1978–2002 (Chief Steward 1997–2002); Pres. London Chamber of Commerce 1988–91; High Sheriff of Surrey 1983–84; Hon. FRAM. *Leisure interests:* country sports, travel, photography, painting. *Address:* Chapel House, West Humble, Dorking, Surrey, RH5 6AY, England (home). *Telephone:* (1306) 882994 (home). *Fax:* (1306) 886825 (home). *E-mail:* hughcubitt@uk2.net (home).

CUEVAS, José Luis; Mexican painter; b. 26 Feb. 1934, México, DF; s. of Alberto Cuevas and María Regla; m. Bertha Riestra 1961; three d.; ed Univ. de México, School of Painting and Sculpture 'La Esmeralda', Mexico; over forty solo exhbns; group exhbns in N and S America, Europe, India and Japan; works are in Museum of Modern Art, Solomon R. Guggenheim Museum, Brooklyn Museum, Art Inst. Chicago, Phillips Collection, Washington, DC, Museums of Albi and Lyons, France, and others; First Int. Award for Drawing, São Paulo Bienal 1959, First Int. Award, Mostra Internazionale di Bianco e

Nero de Lugano, Zürich 1962, First Prize, Bienal de Grabado, Santiago, Chile 1964, First Int. Prize for engraving, first Biennial of New Delhi, India 1968, Nat. Fine Arts Award Mexico 1981. *Publications:* Cuevas por Cuevas 1964, Cuevario 1973, Confesiones de José Luis Cuevas 1975, Cuevas por Daisy Ascher 1979; has illustrated following books: The Worlds of Kafka and Cuevas 1959, The Ends of Legends String, Recollections of Childhood 1962, Cuevas por Cuevas 1964, Cuevas Charenton 1965, Crime by Cuevas 1968, Homage to Quevedo 1969, El Mundo de José Luis Cuevas 1970, Cuaderno de Paris 1977, Zarathustra 1979, Les Obsessions Noirs 1982, Letters to Tasenda 1982. *Address:* c/o Adani Gallery, 16118 Shadybank Drive, Dallas, TX 75248, USA. *Telephone:* (972) 503-5662. *Fax:* (972) 503-7411.

CUEVAS ARGOTE, Javier Gonzalo, MBS; Bolivian government official; b. 1955, La Paz; ed Universidad Mayor de san Andrés, Universidad de Chile, Universidad Privada Boliviana, Florida Int. Univ., USA; director of numerous public and private finance insts; adviser to Pres. of Central Bank; Vice-Minister, Ministry of Finance, Minister of Finance 2003–06. *Address:* c/o Ministry of Finance, Edif. Palacio de Communicaciones, Avda. Mariscal Santa Cruz, La Paz, Bolivia (office).

CUI, Naifu; Chinese politician (retired); b. 8 Oct. 1928, Beijing; s. of Cui Yu Lian and Chang Wei Fung Cui; m. 1955; one s. one d.; joined CCP 1948; Dir Propaganda Dept and Dean of Studies, Lanzhou Univ.; Vice-Chair. Lanzhou Univ. Revolutionary Cttee; Vice-Minister of Civil Affairs 1981, Minister 1982–93; mem. 12th Cen. Cttee CCP 1982–87, 13th Cen. Cttee CCP 1987–92, 14th Cen. Cttee 1992–97; mem. 8th NPC 1993–98, NPC Deputy Jiangxi Prov.; Deputy Head, Group for Resettlement of Ex-Servicemen and Retired Officers 1983–88, Head 1988–; Research Soc. for Theory of Civil Admin. and Social Welfare 1985; Chair. China Org. Comm. of UN Decade of Disabled Persons 1986; Hon. Pres. China Asscn of Social Workers 1991–; Deputy Dir China Org. Comm. of Int. Decade of Natural Disaster Reduction 1991–; Pres. China Charity Fed. 1994–; Hon. Dir China Welfare Fund for the Handicapped 1985–; Hon. Pres. China Asscn for the Blind and Deaf Mutes 1984. *Leisure interest:* calligraphy. *Address:* No. 9, Xi Huang Cheng Gen Street, Beijing 100032, People's Republic of China. *Telephone:* 66017240. *Fax:* 66017240.

CUKJATI, France, MD; Slovenian physician and politician; b. 15 Feb. 1943; m.; four c.; ed Jesuit Inst. of Philosophy, Zagreb, Croatia and Univ. of Ljubljana; practised medicine at Health Centre of Ljubljana-Šiška; fmr Dir Vrhnika Health Centre, entered pvt. practice 1994; mem. Državni zbor (Nat. Ass.) 2000–, Chair. (Speaker) 2004–08; Founding mem. and fmr Sec.-Gen. Slovenian Chamber of Medicine. *Address:* Office of the Speaker, Državni zbor, 1000 Ljubljana, Šubičeva 4, Slovenia (office). *Telephone:* (1) 4789400 (office). *Fax:* (1) 4789845 (office). *E-mail:* info@dz-rs.si (office). *Website:* www.dz-rs.si (office).

CULHANE, John Leonard, PhD, CPhys, FInstP, FRS; Irish physicist and academic; *Professor of Physics, University College London;* b. 14 Oct. 1937, Dublin; s. of the late John Thomas Culhane and Mary Agnes Culhane (née Durkin); m. Mary Brigid Smith 1961; two s.; ed Univ. Coll., Dublin, Univ. Coll., London; Lecturer in Physics, Univ. Coll. London 1967–69, 1970–76, Reader 1976–81, Prof. 1981–; research scientist, Lockheed Palo Alto Lab. 1969–70; Dir Mullard Space Science Lab., Univ. Coll. London 1983–2003, Head Dept of Space and Climate Physics 1993–2003; UK Del. and Vice-Pres. European Space Agency Science Programme Cttee 1989–94; Chair. British Nat. Space Centre Space Science Programme Bd 1989–92, COSPAR Comm. 1994–2002, European Space Science Cttee, European Science Foundation 1997–2002; mem. Advisory Panel European Space Agency Space Science Dept 1995–2000, UK Particle Physics and Astronomy Research 1996–2000; Foreign mem. Norwegian Acad. of Sciences and Letters 1996; Hon. DSc (Wrocław) 1996; Gold Medal, Royal Astronomical Soc. 2007. *Publications:* X-Ray Astronomy, over 350 papers on Solar and Cosmic X-Ray Astronomy, X-Ray Instrumentation and Plasma Spectroscopy. *Leisure interests:* music, motor racing. *Telephone:* (1483) 274111 (office). *Fax:* (1483) 278312. *E-mail:* jlc@mssl.ucl.ac.uk (office).

CULKIN, Macaulay; American actor; b. 26 Aug. 1980, New York; s. of Christopher "Kit" Culkin and Pat Culkin; m. Rachel Milner 1998; ed St Joseph's School of Yorkville, New York and George Balanchine's School of Ballet, New York. *Films include:* Rocket Gibraltar 1988, Uncle Buck 1989, See You In The Morning 1989, Jacob's Ladder 1990, Home Alone 1990, My Girl 1991, Only the Lonely 1991, Home Alone 2: Lost in New York 1992, The Nutcracker, The Good Son 1993, The Pagemaster 1994, Getting Even With Dad 1994, Richie Rich 1995, Body Piercer 1998, Saved! 2004, Jerusalemski sindrom 2004, Sex and Breakfast 2007. *Play:* Madame Melville, Vaudeville Theatre, London 2000. *Television includes:* Foster Hall 2004, Kings (series) 2009. *Publication:* Junior 2006. *Address:* c/o William Morris Agency, One William Morris Place, Beverly Hills, CA 90212, USA.

CULLEN, Michael John, MA, PhD; New Zealand politician; *Shadow Leader of the House and Shadow Minister for Treaty of Waitingi Negotiations;* b. 1945, London, England; m. 1st Rowena Joy Knight; two d.; m. 2nd Anne Lowson Collins; ed Christ's Coll. Christchurch, Univ. of Canterbury and Univ. of Edinburgh, UK; Asst Lecturer, Univ. of Canterbury, Tutor Univ. of Stirling, Sr Lecturer in History, Univ. of Otago, Dunedin and Visiting Fellow, ANU 1968–81; MP for St Kilda 1981–86, for Dunedin South 1986–89; Sr Govt Whip 1984–87; Minister of Social Welfare 1987–90; Assoc. Minister of Finance 1987–89, of Health 1989–90, of Labour 1989–90; Opposition Spokesperson on Finance 1991, apptd Deputy Leader of Opposition 1996; Acting Minister for Accident Insurance 1999–2001; Minister of Revenue 1999–2005, of Finance 1999–2008; Leader of the House 1999–2008; Deputy Prime Minister 2002–08, Minister of Tertiary Educ. 2005–07, Minister in charge of Treaty of Waitingi Negotiations 2007–08, Attorney-Gen 2005, 2006–08; Shadow Leader of the House and Shadow Minister for Treaty of Waitingi Negotiations 2008–; mem. Labour Party 1974–, mem. Party Exec. 1976–81, Party Council 1976–. *Leisure interests:* music, reading, house renovation, golf. *Address:* Executive Wing, Parliament Buildings, Wellington, New Zealand (office). *Telephone:* 470-6551 (office). *Fax:* 495-8442 (office). *E-mail:* michael.cullen@parliament.govt.nz (office). *Website:* www.beehive.govt.nz (office).

CULLINAN, Brendan Peter; Irish judge; b. 24 July 1927, Dublin; s. of Patrick J. Cullinan and Elizabeth Kitchen; one s. (one deceased) two d.; ed Christian Brothers School, Dublin, Univ. Coll. Dublin, Nat. Univ. of Ireland, King's Inns, Dublin and Irish Mil. Coll.; mil. service 1946–65; mem. Irish contingent, Equestrian Games of XVIth Olympiad, Stockholm 1956; called to Irish Bar 1963; legal officer, army Legal Service, Dublin 1963–65; seconded to Inst. of Public Admin. Dublin for service in Zambia and designated under Overseas Service Aid Scheme of Ministry of Overseas Devt (now Overseas Devt Admin.), London 1965–68; Lecturer, Sr Lecturer and Acting Head of Law School, Lusaka, Zambia 1965–68; legal officer, Army Legal Service, Dublin 1968–69; Resident Magistrate and Deputy Registrar, High Court, Lusaka 1969–70, Sr Resident Magistrate and Registrar 1970–73; admitted to practice as legal practitioner in Zambia 1971; Puisne Judge 1973; called to Bar, Lincoln's Inn, London 1977; frequently Acting Judge of Supreme Court, Lusaka 1976–80, Judge of Supreme Court 1980; Dir of Legal Services Corpn Lusaka 1982–83; Puisne Judge of Supreme Court of Fiji, Lautoka and Suva 1984–87; Chief Justice of Lesotho 1987–95 (retd), Judge of Court of Appeal (ex officio) and Chair. Judicial Services Comm., recalled several times to preside over high profile trials; mem. Bd of Trustees Protimos (charity). *Leisure interests:* golf, swimming, gardening.

CULLINAN, Edward Horder, CBE, RA; British architect; b. 17 July 1931, London; s. of Edward Revil Cullinan and Dorothea Joy Horder; m. Rosalind Sylvia Yeates 1961; one s. two d.; ed Ampleforth Coll., Univ. ofCambridge, Architectural Asscn, Univ. of Calif., Berkeley, USA; with Denys Lasdun 1958–65; est. Edward Cullinan Architects 1965; numerous professorships include Bannister Fletcher Prof., Univ. of London 1978–79; Graham Willis Prof., Univ. of Sheffield 1985–87; George Simpson Prof., Univ. of Edinburgh 1987–; currently Visiting Prof., Univ. of Nottingham; designed and built Horder House, Hants. 1959–60, Minster Lovell Mill, Oxon. 1969–72, Parish Church of St Mary, Barnes 1978–84, Lambeth Community Care Centre 1979–84, R.M.C. Int. H.Q. 1985–90, Visitor Centre and Landscape at Fountains Abbey and Studley Royal 1988–92, Media Bldg Cheltenham Art Coll. 1990–93, Library St John's Coll. Cambridge 1991–94, Faculty of Divinity, Cambridge Univ. 1995–2000, Archaeolink Visitor Centre, Aberdeenshire 1996–97, Faculty of Math., Cambridge Univ. 1996–, Docklands Campus, Univ. of E London 1996–99, Downland Gridshell, Weald & Downland Open Air Museum 1997–2002, Greenwich Millennium School and Health Centre 1998–2001, Bristol Harbourside Masterplan 2000–, Singapore Man. Univ. 2000–06, New Gateway Bldg, Royal Botanic Garden, Edinburgh 2003–, New Gateway to Petra, Jordan 2003–; represented at Royal Acad. Summer Exhbn and many others; Financial Times Architecture at Work Award 1991, Special Commendation at Prince Philip Designers Prize 2005, many other awards and prizes. *Publications:* Edward Cullinan Architects 1984, Edward Cullinan Architects 1995, Master Plan for the University of North Carolina at Charlotte 1995, Ends Middles Beginnings 2005; contribs to journals. *Leisure interests:* horticulture, cycling, surfing, Arctic and Sahara travel, history, building, geography. *Address:* 1 Baldwin Terrace, London, N1 7RU, England. *Telephone:* (20) 7704-1975. *Fax:* (20) 7354-2739. *E-mail:* eca@ecarch.co.uk. *Website:* www.edwardcullinanarchitects.com.

CULVER, Chester John (Chet), BA, MA; American teacher, politician and state official; *Governor of Iowa;* b. 25 Jan. 1966, Washington, DC; s. of fmr US Senator John Culver and Ann Cooper Culver; m. Mariclare Thinnes Culver; one s. one d.; ed Bethesda-Chevy Chase High School, Md, Virginia Polytechnic Inst. and State Univ., Drake Univ.; worked as lobbyist 1989–90, clients included Ia Trial Lawyers' Asscn, Ia Beef Processors, Des Moines Univ.; began public service career as environmental and consumer advocate in Ia Attorney Gen.'s Office; taught govt and history at Roosevelt High School and Hoover High School, Des Moines, also coached both football and basketball; Sec. of State for Ia (youngest Sec. of State in USA) 1999–2006, mem. Exec. Council, Chair. Exec. Council Insurance Advisory Cttee, Chair. State Voter Registration Comm., mem. State Records Man. Cttee; mem. Nat. Asscn of Secs of State (mem. Elections and Voter Participation Cttee, Presidential Caucuses and Primaries Cttee, New Millennium Youth Initiative), Elections Task Force, Council of State Govts; Gov. of Ia 2007–; Democrat; Fulbright Memorial Fund Teacher's Scholarship to Japan, Ia State Educ. Asscn 1997. *Address:* Office of the Governor, State Capitol, Des Moines, IA 50319, USA (office). *Telephone:* (515) 281-5211 (office). *Fax:* (515) 281-6611 (office). *Website:* www.governor.state.ia.us (office); www.chetculver.com.

CUMING, Frederick George Rees, RA, ARCA; British painter; b. 16 Feb. 1930; s. of Harold Cuming and Grace Cuming; m. Audrey Lee Cuming 1962; one s. one d.; ed Univ. School, Bexleyheath, Sidcup Art School, Royal Coll. of Art; travelling scholarship to Italy; exhbns in Redfern, Walker, New Grafton, Thackeray and Fieldborne Galleries; works in collections including Dept of the Environment, Treasury, Chantrey Bequest, RA, Kendal Museum, Scunthorpe Museum, Bradford, Carlisle, Nat. Museum of Wales, Brighton and Hove Museum, Maidstone Museum, Towner Gallery, Eastbourne, Monte Carlo Museum, Farringdon Trust, Worcester Coll. Oxford, St John's Coll. Oxford, W. H. Smith, Thames TV, Nat. Trust Foundation for Art; Assoc. RCA; mem. New English Art Club; Hon. DLitt (Univ. of Kent) 2004; Grand Prix, Art Contemporaine, Monte Carlo. *Publication:* A Figure in the Landscape, A Painter's Progress, Practical Art School. *Leisure interests:* tennis, golf, snooker, reading, music, travelling. *Address:* The Gables, Wittersham Road,

Iden, Nr. Rye, East Sussex, TN31 7WY, England. *Telephone:* (1797) 280322. *Website:* www.fredcumingra.com (office).

CUNLIFFE, Jonathan Stephen, CB, MA; British civil servant; *Head of the European and Global Issues Secretariat and International Economic and EU Advisor to the Prime Minister;* b. 2 June 1953; s. of Ralph Cunliffe and Cynthia Cunliffe; m. Naomi Brandler 1984; two d.; ed St Marylebone Grammar School, London and Manchester Univs.; joined Civil Service 1980, various posts in Depts of Environment and Transport 1980–90; Head Public Sector Pay Div., HM Treasury 1990–92, Head Int. Financial Insts Div. 1992–94, Treasury Debt and Reserves Man. Div. 1994–96, Deputy Dir Macroeconomic Policy and Prospects and Head of Treasury European Monetary Union team 1996–98, Deputy Dir Macroeconomic Policy and Int. Finance 1998–2001, Man. Dir Finance Regulation and Industry, HM Treasury 2001–02, Man. Dir Macroeconomic Policy and Int. Finance 2002–05, Second Perm. Sec. 2005–07; Head of the European and Global Issues Secr. and Int. Econ. and EU Advisor to the Prime Minister, Cabinet Office 2007–; Alt. Dir EBRD 1992–94; Alt. mem. EU Monetary Cttee responsible for Debt and Reserves Man. 1996–98. *Leisure interests:* tennis, cooking, walking. *Address:* European and Global Issues Secretariat, Cabinet Office, 70 Whitehall, London, SW1A 2WH, England (office). *Telephone:* (20) 7276-0185 (office). *Fax:* (20) 7276-0074 (office). *Website:* www.cabinetoffice.gov.uk/secretariats/european_secretariat.aspx (office).

CUNNINGHAM, Edward Patrick, MAgrSc, PhD, MRIA; Irish academic and international public servant; *Professor of Animal Genetics, Trinity College Dublin;* b. 4 Aug. 1934, Dublin; s. of Eugene Cunningham and Kathleen Moran; m. Catherine Dee 1965, died 1998; four s. two d.; ed Clongowes Wood Coll., Univ. Coll. Dublin and Cornell Univ., Ithaca, NY, USA; Housemaster, Albert Agricultural Coll. Dublin 1956–57; Research and Teaching Asst, Univ. Coll. Dublin 1957–58, Cornell Univ. 1960–62; Research Officer, The Agricultural Inst., Dublin 1962, Head Dept of Animal Breeding and Genetics 1970, Deputy Dir Agricultural Inst. 1980–88; Prof. of Animal Genetics, Trinity Coll., Dublin 1974–; Dir Animal Production and Health Div., FAO, Rome 1990–93, Dir Screwworm Emergency Centre for N Africa 1990–92; Jt Founder and Chair. Identigen Ltd 1997–; Visiting Prof., Agricultural Univ. of Norway 1968–69, Econ. Devt Inst., IBRD 1988; mem. Royal Swedish Acad. of Agriculture and Forestry, Royal Norwegian Acad. of Science and Letters, Russian Acad. of Agricultural Sciences, Acad. d'Agriculture de France; A. M. Leroy Fellowship 1991; Ordre du Mérite Agricole; Hon. DAgric (Agric. Univ., Norway) 1997; Hon. ScD (Dublin Univ.) 1997; Golden Egg Int. Award, Verona 1983; Boyle Medal, Royal Dublin Soc. 1996. *Publications:* Animal Breeding Theory 1969, Development Issues in the Livestock Sector 1992. *Leisure interests:* farming, history. *Address:* Department of Genetics, Trinity College, Dublin 2 (office); Vesington House, Dunboyne, Co. Meath, Ireland (home). *Telephone:* (1) 608 1064 (office); (1) 825 5350 (home). *Fax:* (1) 679 8558 (office); (1) 825 5350 (home). *E-mail:* epcnnghm@tcd.ie (office). *Website:* www.tcd.ie (office).

CUNNINGHAM, Merce; American choreographer and dancer; *Artistic Director, Merce Cunningham Dance Company;* b. 16 April 1919, Centralia, Wash.; s. of Mr and Mrs C. D. Cunningham; ed Cornish School, Seattle and Bennington Coll. School of Dance; soloist with Martha Graham Dance Co. 1939–45; began solo concerts 1942; mem. Faculty, School of American Ballet, New York 1948, 1950–51; Founder and Artistic Dir Merce Cunningham Dance Co. 1953–; opened own dance school in New York 1959; Hon. Mem. American Acad. and Inst. of Arts and Letters 1984; Ordre des Arts et Lettres 1982, Légion d'honneur 1989; Hon. DLitt (Univ. of Ill.) 1972; Hon. DFA (Wesleyan Univ., Conn.) 1995; Dr hc (Western Australian Acad. of Performing Arts) 2001; Guggenheim Fellowships 1954, 1959, Dance Magazine Award 1960, Soc. for Advancement of The Dance in Sweden Gold Medal 1964, Gold Star for Choreographic Invention Paris 1966, New York State Award 1975, Capezio Award 1977, Wash. State Award 1977, Samuel H. Scripps American Dance Festival Award 1982, Mayor of New York's Award of Honor for Arts and Culture 1983, MacArthur Fellowship 1985, Kennedy Center Honors 1985, Laurence Olivier Award 1985, Algur H. Meadows Award (Southern Methodist Univ., Dallas) 1987, Digital Dance Premier Award 1990, Nat. Medal of Arts 1990, Medal of Honor, Universidad Complutense of Madrid 1993, Dance and Performance Award, London 1993, Golden Lion of Venice Biennale 1995, Nellie Cornish Arts Archievement Award, Seattle 1996; Wexner Prize, Ohio State Univ. 1993, Premio Internazionale 'Gino Tani' 1999, Nijinsky Special Prize, Monaco 2000, Dorothy and Lillian Gish Prize 2000, Edward MacDowell Medal 2003, Praemium Imperiale, Tokyo 2005. *Dance:* The Seasons 1947, 16 Dances for Soloist and Company of Three 1951, Septet 1953, Minutiae 1954, Springweather and People 1955, Suite for Five 1956, Nocturnes 1956, Antic Meet 1958, Summerspace 1958, Rune 1959, Crises 1960, Aeon 1961, Story 1963, Winterbranch 1964, Variations V 1965, How to Pass, Kick, Fall and Run 1965, Place 1966, Scramble 1967, RainForest 1968, Walkaround Time 1968, Canfield 1969, Second Hand 1970, Tread 1970, Signals 1970, Un Jour ou Deux 1973, Sounddance 1975, Rebus 1975, Torse 1976, Squaregame 1976, Travelogue 1977, Inlets 1977, Exchange 1978, Locale 1979, Duets 1980, Gallopade 1981, Trails 1982, Quartet 1982, Roaratorio 1983, Pictures 1984, Doubles 1984, Phrases 1984, Native Green 1985, Arcade 1985, Grange Eve 1986, Carousal 1987, Five Stone Wind 1988, Cargo X 1989, Field and Figures 1989, Inventions 1989, August Pace 1989, Polarity 1990, Neighbors 1991, Trackers 1991, Beach Birds 1991, Loosestrife 1991, Change of Address 1992, Enter 1992, Doubletoss 1993, CRWDSPCR 1993, Breakers 1994, Ocean 1994, Ground Level Overlay 1995, Windows 1995, Rondo 1996, Installations 1996, Scenario 1997, Pond Way 1998, Biped 1999, Interscape 2000, Way Station 2001, Loose Time 2002, Fluid Canvas 2002, Split Sides 2003, Views on Stage 2004, eyeSpace 2006, Xover 2007. *Plays:* An Alphabet (Edinburgh Festival 2001, Western Australia Int. Festival, Perth 2002). *Films:* Fractions 1978, Channels/Inserts 1981, Coast Zone 1985, Points in Space 1986. *TV productions include:* 'Dance in America' Event for TV 1977. *Publications:* Changes: Notes on Choreography 1969, The Dancer and the Dance, Conversations with Jacqueline Lesschaeve 1985, Other Animals (drawings and journals) 2002. *Leisure interest:* drawing. *Address:* Cunningham Dance Foundation, 55 Bethune Street, New York, NY 10014, USA (office). *Telephone:* (212) 255-8240 (office). *Fax:* (212) 633-2453 (office). *E-mail:* info@merce.org (office). *Website:* www.merce.org (office).

CUNNINGHAM, Michael, MA, MFA; American novelist and screenwriter; b. 6 Nov. 1952, Cincinnati; ed Stanford Univ., Univ. of Iowa; fmr bartender; joined Univ. of Iowa Writers' Workshop 1978; writer for Carnegie Corpn; fmr Adjunct Asst Prof., Columbia Univ.; Donald I. Fine Prof. in Creative Writing, Brooklyn Coll. 2001, Distinguished Prof. of English 2001, also head of MFA Writing Program, now Visiting Prof.; Guggenheim Fellowship 1993; Lambda Literary Award for Gay Men's Fiction 1995. *Screenplays include:* A Home at the End of the World 2004, Evening 2007. *Publications:* Golden States 1984, A Home at the End of the World 1990, Flesh and Blood 1995, The Hours (Pulitzer Prize, PEN/Faulkner Award for Fiction 1999) 1998, Specimen Days 2005. *Address:* Steven Barclay Agency, 12 Western Avenue, Petaluma, CA 94952, USA (office); English Department, 2308 Boylan Hall, Brooklyn College, 2900 Bedford Avenue, Brooklyn, NY 11210, USA (office). *Website:* www.barclayagency.com/cunningham.html (office); academic.brooklyn.cuny.edu/english (office). *Telephone:* (718) 951-5195 (office).

CUNNINGHAM, William Hughes, BA, MBA, PhD; American marketer, academic and fmr university administrator; *James L. Bayless Chair for Free Enterprise, McCombs School of Business, Department of Marketing, University of Texas;* b. 5 Jan. 1944, Detroit, Mich.; m.; one s.; ed Michigan State Univ.; Asst Prof. of Marketing, Univ. of Texas at Austin 1971–73, Assoc. Prof. 1973–79, Prof. 1979–, Foley's/Sanger Harris Prof. of Retail Merchandising 1982–83, Dean, Coll. of Business Admin/Grad. School of Business 1983–85, Regents Chair in Higher Educ. Leadership 1985–92, James L. Bayless Chair. for Free Enterprise, McCombs School of Business, Dept of Marketing 1988–, Pres. Univ. of Texas at Austin 1985–92, Chancellor Univ. of Texas System 1992–2000, Lee Hage and Joseph D. Jamail Regents Chair in Higher Educ. Leadership 1992–2000, Fellow, IC^2 Institute; mem. Bd of Dirs Lincoln National Corpn, Southwest Airlines 2000–, Introgen Therapeutics 2000–, Pinnacle Foods Corpn 2000–, Hicks Acquisition Co. I, Inc, John Hancock Mutual Funds 1986–, Jefferson-Pilot Corpn 1985–; mem. Bd of Dirs College Football Assn 1988–89; mem. Econ. Advisory Cttee of US Dept of Commerce 1983–85; Hon. LLD (Michigan State Univ.) 1993; Outstanding Tex. Leader, John Ben Shepperd Leadership Forum 1987, Jewish Nat. Fund Tree of Life Award 1992, Distinguished Alumnus Award, Michigan State Univ. 1993. *Publications:* with others: The Personal Force in Marketing 1977, Consumer Energy Attitudes and Behavior in the Southwest 1977, Effective Selling 1977, Métodos Efectivos de Ventas 1980, Marketing: A Managerial Approach 1987, Grondslagen van het Marketing Management 1984, Introduction to Business 1988, Business in a Changing World 1992. *Leisure interests:* golf, tennis, racquetball, horseback riding. *Address:* HRHRC-Ransom Center, F1900, 1 University Station, Austin, TX 78712 (office); 1909 Hills Oak Court, Austin, TX 78703, USA (home). *Telephone:* (512) 232-7540 (office). *Fax:* (512) 232-7541 (office). *E-mail:* whc@po.utexas.edu (office). *Website:* acsprod.mccombs.utexas.edu (office).

CUNNINGHAM OF FELLING, Baron (Life Peer), cr. 2005, of Felling in the County of Tyne and Wear; **John A. (Jack) Cunningham,** PC, DL, PhD; British politician; b. 4 Aug. 1939, Newcastle upon Tyne; s. of Andrew Cunningham; m. Maureen Cunningham 1964; one s. two d.; ed Jarrow Grammar School and Bede Coll., Univ. of Durham; fmr Research Fellow in Chem., Univ. of Durham; fmr school teacher, trades union officer; MP for Whitehaven, Cumbria 1970–83, for Copeland 1983–2005; Parl. Pvt. Sec. to Rt Hon. James Callaghan 1972–76; Parl. Under-Sec. of State, Dept of Energy 1976–79; Opposition Spokesman on Industry 1979–83, on Environment 1983–89, Shadow Leader of the House and Campaigns Co-ordinator 1989–92, Opposition Spokesman on Foreign and Commonwealth Affairs 1992–94, on Trade and Industry 1994–95, on Nat. Heritage 1995–97; Minister of Agric., Fisheries and Food 1997–98, for the Cabinet Office and Chancellor of the Duchy of Lancaster 1998–99; DL (Cumbria) 1991; mem. Labour Party. *Leisure interests:* fell walking, fly fishing, gardening, theatre, classical and folk music, reading, Newcastle United Football Club, listening to other people's opinions. *Address:* House of Lords, London, SW1A 0PW, England (office).

CUNY, Jean-Pierre, MSc; French business executive; *Chairman and CEO, Bigot Mécanique;* b. 8 April 1940, Menton; s. of Robert Cuny and Marie-Louise Marchal; m. Anne-Marie Fousse 1968; two d.; ed Ecole Centrale, Paris and Massachusetts Inst. of Tech., USA; engineer, Serete 1968–70; Information Man. Firmin Didot 1970–73; Gen. Man. Dafsa Documentation 1973-76; Project Man. CGA 1976–77; Cost Controller Placoplatre 1977–78, Production Dir 1978–82, Marketing Dir 1982–85, Gen. Man. 1985–86, Chair. and CEO 1986–89, Dir BPB PLC (parent co. of Placoplatre) 1988–89, Deputy Chair. Gypsum Div. 1988–94, CEO 1994–99; Pres. Eurogypsum 1996–99; Chair. and CEO Bigot Mécanique 2002–, Sopram 2003–; Chevalier, Légion d'honneur. *Leisure interests:* skiing, theatre, reading, music, film. *Address:* 50 Avenue de Saxe, 75015 Paris, France (home). *Telephone:* 1-39-95-60-45 (office). *E-mail:* jean-pierre.cuny@wanadoo.fr (office).

CUOMO, Andrew M., BA, JD; American lawyer and state government official; *Attorney General of New York;* s. of Mario Cuomo (q.v.); m. Kerry Cuomo; three d.; ed Fordham Univ., Albany Law School; fmr Asst Dist Attorney, Manhattan; fmr Pnr, Blutrich, Falcone and Miller, NY; Chair. NY Comm. on the Homeless 1991–93; Asst Sec. Community Planning and Devt, Dept of

Housing and Urban Devt 1993–97, Sec. of Housing and Urban Devt 1997–2001; Attorney Gen. of New York 2006–; f. H.E.L.P. - Housing Enterprise for the Less Privileged (now HELP USA) 1986, Co-Chair. 2001. *Publications:* Crossroads 2004;. *Address:* Office of the Attorney General, The Capitol, Albany, NY 12224-0341, USA (office). *Telephone:* (518) 474-7330 (office). *Website:* www.oag.state.ny.us (office).

CUOMO, Mario Matthew, LLB; American fmr state governor and lawyer; *Of Counsel, Wilkie Farr & Gallagher LLP;* b. 15 June 1932, Queen's County NY; s. of Andrea and Immaculata Cuomo; m. Matilda Raffa; two s. (including Andrew Cuomo q.v.) three d.; ed St John's Coll. and St John's Univ.; admitted to NY Bar 1956, Supreme Court Bar 1960; Confidential Legal Asst to Hon. Adrian P. Burke, NY State Court of Appeals 1956–58; Assoc., Corner, Weisbrod, Froeb and Charles, Brooklyn 1958–63, partner 1963–75; Sec. of State, NY 1975–79; Lt-Gov. of New York State 1979–82, Gov. 1983–95; partner Wilkie Farr and Gallagher LLP 1995–; mem. faculty St John's Univ. Law School 1963–75; counsel to community groups 1966–72; fmr Co-Chairman and mem. Bd of Dirs Partnership for a Drug-Free America; Democrat; NY Rapallo Award, Columbia Lawyers' Asscn 1976, Dante Medal, Italian Govt./American Asscn of Italian Teachers 1976, Silver Medallion, Columbia Coalition 1976, Public Admin. Award, C.W. Post Coll. 1977. *Publications:* Forest Hills Diary: The Crisis of Low-Income Housing 1974, Maya 1984, Lincoln on Democracy (jtly) 1990, The New York Idea 1994, Common Sense 1995, Reason to Believe 1995, The Blue Spruce 1999, Why Lincoln Matters Today More Than Ever 2004; articles in legal journals. *Address:* Wilkie, Farr and Gallagher LLP, 787 7th Avenue, New York, NY 10019-6099 (office); 50 Sutton Place South, New York, NY 10022, USA. *Telephone:* (212) 728-8260 (office). *Fax:* (212) 728-9260 (office). *E-mail:* mcuomo@willkie.com (office). *Website:* www.willkie.com (office).

CUPITT, Rev. Don, MA; British ecclesiastic and university lecturer; b. 22 May 1934, Oldham; s. of Robert Cupitt and Norah Cupitt; m. Susan Marianne Day 1963; one s. two d.; ed Charterhouse, Trinity Hall, Cambridge, Westcott House, Cambridge; ordained 1959; Curate, St Philip's Church, Salford 1959–62; Vice-Prin. Westcott House, Cambridge 1962–65; Fellow, Emmanuel Coll., Cambridge 1965–96, Dean 1966–91, Life Fellow 1996–; Asst Lecturer, Univ. of Cambridge 1968–73, Lecturer in Divinity 1973–96; Fellow of the Jesus Seminar, Westar Inst., Calif., USA 2001; Hon. DLitt (Bristol) 1985. *Television documentaries:* Who Was Jesus? 1977, The Sea of Faith (series) 1984. *Publications:* Christ and the Hiddenness of God 1971, Crisis of Moral Authority 1972, The Leap of Reason 1976, The Worlds of Science and Religion 1976, Who Was Jesus? (with Peter Armstrong) 1977, The Nature of Man 1979, Explorations in Theology 1979, The Debate about Christ 1979, Jesus and the Gospel of God 1979, Taking Leave of God 1980, The World to Come 1982, The Sea of Faith 1984, Only Human 1985, Life Lines 1986, The Long-Legged Fly 1987, The New Christian Ethics 1988, Radicals and the Future of the Church 1989, Creation out of Nothing 1990, What is a Story? 1991, The Time Being 1992, After All 1994, The Last Philosophy 1995, Solar Ethics 1995, After God: The Future of Religion 1997, Mysticism after Modernity 1997, The Religion of Being 1998, The Revelation of Being 1998, The New Religion of Life in Everyday Speech 1999, The Meaning of It All in Everyday Speech 1999, Kingdom Come in Everyday Speech 2000, Philosophy's Own Religion 2000, Reforming Christianity 2001, Emptiness and Brightness 2001, Is Nothing Sacred? 2002, Life, Life 2003, The Way to Happiness: A Theory of Religion 2005, The Great Questions of Life 2006, The Old Creed and the New 2006, Radical Theology 2006. *Leisure interests:* hill-walking, the arts. *Address:* Emmanuel College, Cambridge, CB2 3AP, England. *Telephone:* (1223) 334200. *Fax:* (1223) 334426. *E-mail:* susancupitt@waitrose.com (home). *Website:* www.doncupitt.com.

CURA, José; Argentine singer (tenor) and conductor; *President, Cuibar Productions S. L.;* b. 1962, Rosario, Santa Fe; m. Silvia Ibarra 1985; two s. one d.; ed Univ. of Rosario, School of Arts, Teatro Colon, Buenos Aires, vocal studies with Horacio Amauri in Argentina and Vittorio Terranova in Italy; appearances at leading int. opera houses 1992–; Pres., Cuibar Productions SL; Chevalier, Lebanese Govt; Premio Abbiatti, Italian Critics' Award, Premio Carrara, Cultura Millenaria 1997, XII Premio Internazionale di Arte e Cultura Cilea 1997. *Opera includes:* Makropoulos Affair, Le Villi, Fedora, Stiffelio, Iris, Samson et Dalila, Carmen, Cavalleria Rusticana, Norma, Tosca, La Gioconda, I Pagliacci, Otello, Aida; *Recordings include:* Le Villi, Iris, Argentine Songs, Puccini Arias, Samson et Dalila, Otello, I Pagliacci, Manon Lescaut. *Address:* Cuibar Productions S.L., Ronda de la Abubilla, 30b, 28043 Madrid, Spain (office). *Telephone:* (91) 3000134 (office). *Fax:* (91) 3002343 (office). *E-mail:* git-w-s-c@cv.bar.com (office). *Website:* www.cuibar.com (office); www.josecura.com (home).

CURRAN, Charles E., STD; American academic and ecclesiastic; *Elizabeth Scurlock University Professor of Human Values, Southern Methodist University;* b. 30 March 1934, Rochester, NY; s. of John F. Curran and Gertrude L. Beisner; ed St Bernard's Coll. Rochester, Gregorian Univ. Rome and Accad. Alfonsiana, Rome; ordained RC priest 1958; Prof. of Moral Theology, St Bernard's Seminary, Rochester, NY 1961–65; Asst Prof., then Assoc. Prof., then Prof. of Moral Theology, Catholic Univ. of America, Washington, DC 1965–89; Sr Research Scholar, Kennedy Center for Bio-Ethics, Georgetown Univ. 1972; External Examiner in Christian Ethics, Univ. of West Indies 1982–86; Visiting Prof. of Catholic Studies, Cornell Univ. 1987–88; Visiting Brooks and Firestone Prof. of Religion, Univ. of Southern California 1988–90; Visiting Eminent Scholar in Religion, Auburn Univ. 1990–91; Elizabeth Scurlock Univ. Prof. of Human Values, Southern Methodist Univ. 1991–; Pres. Catholic Theological Soc. of America 1969–70, Soc. of Christian Ethics 1971–72; American Theological Soc. 1989–90; Dr hc (Charleston, W Va) 1987, (Concordia Coll., Portland, Ore.) 1992; J. C. Murray Award (Catholic Theol.

Soc.) 1972, Building Bridges Award, New Ways Ministry 1992, Presidential Award, Coll. Theology Soc. 2003. *Publications:* Catholic Social Teaching 1891–Present: A Historical, Theological and Ethical Analysis, The Origins of Moral Theology in the United States: Three Different Approaches, The Catholic Moral Tradition Today: A Synthesis, The Moral Theology of Pope John Paul II; numerous books, articles, lectures and addresses. *Leisure interests:* reading, golf, swimming. *Address:* Southern Methodist University, 317 Dallas Hall, POB 750317, Dallas, TX 75275-0317 (office); 4125 Woodcreek, Dallas, TX 75220, USA (home). *Telephone:* (214) 768-4073 (office); (214) 352–8974 (home). *Fax:* (214) 768-4129 (office). *E-mail:* ccurran@mail.smu.edu (office). *Website:* www.smu.edu/theology (office).

CURRAN, Kevin; British trade union official; b. 1954, Stepney, London; s. of John Curran; m. June Curran; two c.; ed LSE; trained as welder in eng construction industry, Tipton, E Midlands; joined GMB (fmrly Boilermakers Union) as shop steward 1975, led disputes at Ford Motor Co., Dagenham and W Thurrock Power Station, Essex 1976, elected Br. Sec. Penge Boilermakers Br. 1978, GMB Safety Rep. 1978, elected Chair. London Dist Cttee of Boilermakers Soc. 1982, mem. GMB London Regional Council 1982, Regional Health and Safety Officer, London Region 1988–90, Regional Organiser, Southern Region 1990–96, Sr Organiser, Southern Region 1996–97, Regional Sec., Northern Region 1997–2003, est. North East Maritime Group (NEMG) to revitalise shipbuilding industry in NE 1997, Gen. Sec. GMB 2003–05; welding instructor in voluntary sector, London 1980–; apptd to Bd of Regional Devt Agency by Sec. of State 1998; mem. Working Group on productivity and industrial clusters devt policy, Dept of Trade and Industry 2001; mem. Treasury Cttee, TU(C)/CBI. *Leisure interests:* running (marathons), football, history.

CURRAN, Patricia (Pat) A.; American business executive; *Executive Vice-President, People, Wal-Mart Stores Division, Wal-Mart Inc.;* began career with Wal-Mart as hourly assoc. in Pets Dept 1983, promoted to Dept Man., then Asst Man., then Co-Man., then Store Man., also worked as Regional Personnel Man., Dist Man., Operations Coordinator, Regional Vice-Pres. and Div. Merchandise Man., promoted to Sr Vice-Pres. Wal-Mart Store Operations for div. that included Ga, NC, SC, Md, Va, Pa, W Va, Ky, Tenn., Del. and OH 2003–05, Exec. Vice-Pres. Store Operations, Wal-Mart Stores Div. 2005–07, Exec. Vice-Pres., People 2007–; mem. Center for Retailing Excellence, Sam M. Walton Coll. of Business at Univ. of Ark., Network of Exec. Women, Coca-Cola Retailing Research Council, Single Parent Scholarship Fund of Washington Co.; Exec. Sponsor PRIDE (Wal-Mart's gay, lesbian, bi-sexual and transgender assoc. resource group), Speaking of Women's Health (Wal-Mart's educational initiative for women's health); ranked 32nd by Fortune magazine amongst 50 Most Powerful Women in Business in the US 2006. *Address:* Wal-Mart Stores, Inc., Bentonville, AR 72716-8611, USA (office). *Telephone:* (479) 273-4314 (office). *Website:* walmartstores.com (office).

CURRIE, James McGill, MA; British company director, civil servant and EU official; b. 17 Nov. 1941, Kilmarnock; s. of the late David Currie and of Mary Currie (née Smith); m. Evelyn Barbara MacIntyre 1968; one s. one d.; ed St Joseph's High School, Kilmarnock, Blairs Coll., Aberdeen, Royal Scots Coll., Valladolid, Univ. of Glasgow; admin. trainee, Scottish Office, Edinburgh 1968–72; Prin. Scottish Educ. and Devt Depts 1972–77; Asst Sec. Scottish Industry Dept 1977–82; Transport and Environment Counsellor, UK Perm. Representation to EC 1982–86; Dir of Programmes Directorate-Gen. XVI Regional Policy 1987–88; Chief of Staff to Competition Policy Commr Sir Leon Brittan 1989–93; Deputy Head of Del., Washington, DC 1993–96; Dir-Gen. (Customs and Indirect Taxation), EC 1996–97, (Environment, Nuclear Safety and Civil Protection) 1997–2001; Visiting Prof. of Law, Georgetown Law Center, Washington, DC USA 1997–; Dir (non-exec.) Royal Bank of Scotland Group 2001–, British Nuclear Fuels plc 2002–05, Total UK Holdings; Int. Adviser, Eversheds LLP; Hon. DLitt (Glasgow) 2001. *Leisure interests:* golf, guitar, good food, tennis. *Address:* Flat 7, 54 Queens Gate Terrace, London, SW7 5PJ, UK (home). *E-mail:* jamesmcurrie@hotmail.com.

CURRIE, Lt-Col Nancy Jane, BA, MS, DEng; American astronaut; b. 29 Dec. 1958, Wilmington, Del.; d. of Warren Decker and Shirley Decker; m. David W. Currie (divorced); one d.; ed Ohio State Univ., Univ. of Southern California, Univ. of Houston; Neuropathology Research Asst, Coll. of Medicine, Ohio State Univ.; command 2nd Lt US Army 1981, helicopter instructor pilot, section leader, platoon leader, brigade flight standardization officer, master and aviator; flight simulation engineer, shuttle training aircraft, NASA Johnson Space Center, Houston 1987, astronaut 1991–, flight crew rep. for crew equipment, lead for remote manipulator system, spacecraft communicator; flight engineer mission specialist on STS-57 (Endeavour space shuttle) 1993, STS-70 (Discovery space shuttle) 1995, STS-88 (Endeavour space shuttle)1998, STS-109 (Columbia space shuttle) 2002; chief astronaut robotics br.; currently Chief Engineer for NASA Eng and Safety Center, Johnson Space Center; mem. Army Aviation Asscn, Ohio State Univ. and ROTC Alumni Asscns, Inst. of Industrial Engineers, Human Factors and Ergonomics Soc.; Phi Beta Kappa NASA Flight Simulation Eng Award 1988, Defence Superior Service Medal 1993, Silver Order of St Michael, Army Aviation Award 1997, NASA Space Flight Medal 1993, 1995, 1998, 2002; inducted into Ohio Veterans Hall of Fame 1994, Troy Hall of Fame 1996, Ohio State Univ. Army ROTC Hall of Fame 1996. *Leisure interests:* weightlifting, running, swimming, scuba-diving, skiing. *Address:* NASA Lyndon B. Johnson Space Center, Houston, TX 77058, USA (office). *Website:* www.nasa.gov/centers/johnson/home/index.html.

CURRIE, Richard (Dick) J., OC, BS, MBA; Canadian business executive; b. St John, New Brunswick; ed Univ. of New Brunswick, Tech. Univ. of Nova Scotia (TUNS), Harvard Business School, USA; began career with Atlantic Sugar Refineries; staff mem. McKinsey & Co., NY –1972; joined Loblaw Cos

Ltd, Toronto 1972, Pres. 1976–96; Pres. and Dir George Weston Ltd 1996–2002; Dir Bell Canada Enterprises (BCE) Inc. 1995–2008, Chair. 2002–08; Chancellor Univ. of New Brunswick 2003–; mem. Bd of Dirs CAE Inc., Staples Inc., Petro-Canada; mem. Int. Advisory Bd RJR Nabisco, Atlanta, USA, Jacobs Suchard, Zürich, Switzerland; fmr Chair. Food Marketing Inst., Washington DC; fmr Chair. Advisory Bd, Richard Ivey Business School, Univ. of Western Ontario; fmr mem. Visiting Cttee, Harvard Business School; Fellow, Inst. of Corp. Dirs 2004; Hon. PhD (Univ. of New Brunswick, TUNS); The Golden Pencil Award, The Rabb Award, Distinguished Retailer of the Year 1997, Canada's Outstanding CEO of the Year(TM) 2001, elected to Canadian Business Hall of Fame 2003, McGill Man. Achievement Award 2004, Retail Council of Canada Lifetime Achievement Award 2005, Business Leader of the Year, Richard Ivey School of Business, Univ. of Western Ontario 2009. *Address:* c/o Office of the Chancellor, University of New Brunswick, Fredericton, P.O. Box 4400, Fredericton, NB E3B 5A3, Canada.

CURRIE OF MARYLEBONE, Baron (Life Peer), cr. 1996, of Marylebone, in the City of Westminster; **David Anthony Currie,** MSocSc, DLitt, PhD, DSc; British communications industry regulator and university professor; *Chairman, Office of Communications (Ofcom);* b. 9 Dec. 1946, London; s. of Kennedy Moir Currie and Marjorie (née Thompson); m. 1st Shaziye Gazioglu 1965 (divorced); two s.; m. 2nd Angela Mary Piers Dumas 1995; ed Battersea Grammar School, Univs of Manchester, Birmingham, London; economist, Hoare Govett 1971–72, Sr Economist Econ. Models 1972; Lecturer in Econs, Queen Mary Coll., Univ. of London 1972–79, Reader 1979–81, Prof. 1981–88; Prof. of Econs, London Business School 1988–, Dir Centre for Econ. Forecasting 1988–95, Research Dean 1989–92, Deputy Prin. 1992–95; Deputy Dean External Relations 1999–2000; Dean City Univ.'s Cass Business School 2001–; Houblon-Norman Research Fellow Bank of England 1985–86, Visiting Scholar IMF 1987; mem. Advisory Bd to Research Councils 1992–93, Retail Price Index Advisory Cttee 1992–93, Treasury's Panel of Ind. Forecasters 1992–95; Trustee Joseph Rowntree Reform Trust 1991–2002; Dir Int. Schools of Business Man.; Gov. London Business School 1989–95, 1997–2000; OFGEM Man. Bd 1999–2001; Dir Abbey Nat. PLC 2001–02; Chair. Ofcom (communications regulator) 2002–; Chair. Coredeal MTS 2002, Ind. Audit Ltd 2003–. *Publications:* Advances in Monetary Economics 1985, The Operation and Regulation of Financial Markets (jtly) 1986, Macroeconomic Interactions Between North and South (jtly) 1988, Macroeconomic Policies in an Interdependent World (jtly) 1989, Rules, Reputation and Macroeconomic Policy Coordination (jtly) 1993, European Monetary Union: Problems in the Transition to a Single European Currency (jtly) 1995, North-South Linkages and International Macroeconomic Policy (jtly) 1995, The Pros and Cons of EMU 1997, Will the Euro Work? 1998. *Leisure interests:* music (playing the cello), literature, swimming. *Address:* City University's Cass Business School, Barbican Centre, London, EC2Y 8HB (office); 106 Bunhill Row, London, EC1Y 8TZ, England. *Telephone:* (20) 7040-8601 (office). *Fax:* (20) 7040-8899 (office). *E-mail:* dcurrie@city.ac.uk (office). *Website:* www.ofcom.org.uk (office); www.cass.city.ac.uk (office).

CURTEIS, Ian Bayley; British dramatist; b. 1 May 1935, London; m. 1st Dorothy Joan Armstrong 1964; two s.; m. 2nd Joanna Trollope (q.v.) 1985; two step-d.; m. 3rd Lady Deirdre Grantley; two step-s.; ed Univ. of London; dir and actor in theatres throughout UK and BBC TV script reader 1956–63; BBC and ATV staff dir (drama) 1963–67; Chair. Cttee on Censorship, Writers' Guild of Great Britain 1981–85, Pres. of Guild 1998–2001. *Plays for TV:* Beethoven, Sir Alexander Fleming (BBC entry, Prague Festival 1973), Mr. Rolls and Mr. Royce, Long Voyage Out of War (trilogy), The Folly, The Haunting, Second Time Round, A Distinct Chill, The Portland Millions, Philby, Burgess and Maclean (British entry, Monte Carlo Festival 1978), Hess, The Atom Spies, Churchill and the Generals (Grand Prize for Best Programme of 1981, New York Int. Film and TV Festival), Suez 1956, Miss Morrison's Ghosts (British entry Monte Carlo Festival), BB and Lord D.; writer of numerous TV series; screenplays: La Condition humaine (André Malraux), Lost Empires (adapted from J. B. Priestley), Eureka, Graham Greene's The Man Within (TV) 1983, The Nightmare Years (TV) 1989, The Zimmerman Telegram 1990, Yalta 1991, The Choir (BBC 1), The Falklands Play 2002, More Love 2003, Yet More Love 2004, Miss Morrison's Ghosts 2004, The Bargain 2007; numerous articles and speeches on the ethics and politics of broadcasting. *Plays for radio:* Eroica 2000, Love 2001, After the Break, The Falklands Play 2002. *Publications:* Long Voyage Out of War (trilogy) 1971, Churchill and the Generals 1980, Suez 1956, 1980, The Falklands Play 1987. *Leisure interest:* avoiding television. *Address:* Markenfield Hall, North Yorks., HG4 3AD; 2 Warwick Square, London, SW1V 2AA, England. *Telephone:* (1765) 603411 (office); (20) 7821-8606 (home). *Fax:* (1765) 607195 (office).

CURTIS, David Roderick, AC, MB, BS, PhD, FRS, FRACP, FAA; Australian pharmacologist and academic; *Professor Emeritus, Australian National University;* b. 3 June 1927, Melbourne; s. of E. D. Curtis and E. V. Curtis; m. Lauris Sewell 1951; one s. one d.; ed Melbourne High School, Univ. of Melbourne and Australian Nat. Univ., Canberra; resident medical positions 1950–53; Research Scholar, ANU 1954–56, Research Fellow 1956–57, Fellow 1957–59, Sr Fellow 1959–62, Professorial Fellow 1962–65, Prof. of Pharmacology 1966–68, Prof. of Neuropharmacology 1968–73; Prof. and Head, Dept of Pharmacology, John Curtin School of Medical Research, ANU 1973–89, Dir and Howard Florey Prof. of Medical Research 1989–92, Univ. Fellow 1993–95, Prof. Emer. 1993–, Visiting Fellow 1995–2000; Burnet Lecturer 1983; Pres. Australian Acad. of Science 1986–90; Chair. Inaugural Australia Prize Cttee 1989–90. *Publications:* scientific papers on various topics concerned with neurophysiology and neuropharmacology. *Leisure interests:* gardening, turning wood, wombling. *Address:* 7 Patey Street, Campbell, ACT 2612, Australia. *Telephone:* (2) 6248-5664 (home). *Fax:* (2) 6248-5664 (home).

CURTIS, Jamie Lee, Lady Haden-Guest; American actress and author; b. 22 Nov. 1958, Los Angeles, Calif.; d. of Tony Curtis (q.v.) and Janet Leigh; m. Christopher Guest; one s. one d.; ed Choate School, Conn., Univ. of the Pacific, Calif. *Films include:* Halloween, The Fog, Terror Train, Halloween II, Road Games, Prom Night, Love Letters, Trading Places, The Adventures of Buckaroo Banzai: Across the 8th Dimension, Grandview, USA, Perfect, 8 Million Ways to Die, Mother's Boys, Drowning Mona, Amazing Grace and Chuck, A Man in Love, Dominick and Eugene, A Fish Called Wanda, Blue Steel, My Girl, Forever Young, My Girl 2, True Lies 1994 (Golden Globe Award for Best Actress in a musical or comedy), House Arrest 1996, Fierce Creatures 1996, Halloween H20 1998, Virus 1999, The Tailor of Panama 2000, Daddy and Them 2001, Halloween: Resurrection 2002, True Lies 2 2003, Freaky Friday 2003, Christmas with the Cranks 2004, The Kid and I 2005. *Television includes:* She's In The Army Now, Dorothy Stratten: Death of a Centrefold, Operation Petticoat, The Love Boat, Columbo, Quincy, Charlie's Angels, Anything but Love (dir), Money on the Side, As Summers Die, Anything but Love, Actor, The Heidi Chronicles, Nichoas' Gift. *Publications:* When I Was Little, A Four-Year-Old's Memoir of her Youth 1993, Tell Me Again About the Night I Was Born 1996, Today I Feel Silly and Other Moods That Make My Day 1999, Where Do Balloons Go? An Uplifting Mystery 2000, I'm Gonna Like Me Letting Off a Little Self-Esteem 2002, It's Hard To Be Five, Learning How To Work My Control Panel 2004, Is There Really a Human Race? 2006. *Leisure interests:* photography. *Address:* c/o Rick Kurtzman, CAA, 9830 Wilshire Blvd, Beverly Hills, CA 90212, USA (office). *Telephone:* (310) 288-4545 (office).

CURTIS, Richard Whalley Anthony, CBE, BA; British screenwriter, film director and film producer; b. 8 Nov. 1956, New Zealand; s. of Anthony J. Curtis and Glynness S. Curtis; two s. one d. by Emma Vallencey Freud; ed Harrow School, Christ Church, Oxford; Co-founder and Producer Comic Relief 1985–2000; BAFTA Fellowship 2007. *Films:* Dead On Time 1983, The Tall Guy (writer) 1988, Four Weddings and a Funeral (writer, exec. producer) 1994, Bean (writer, exec. producer) 1997, Notting Hill (writer, exec. producer) 1999, Bridget Jones's Diary (screenplay) 2001, Love Actually (writer, dir) 2003, Bridget Jones: The Edge of Reason (screenplay) 2004. *Television:* Not the Nine O'Clock News (series writer) 1979–82, The Black Adder (series writer) 1983, Spitting Image (series writer) 1984, Blackadder II (series writer) 1986, Blackadder the Third (series writer) 1987, Blackadder's Christmas Carol (writer) 1988, Blackadder: The Cavalier Years (writer) 1988, Blackadder Goes Forth (series writer) 1989, The Robbie Coltrane Special (contrib.) 1989, Mr Bean (series writer) 1989–95, Bernard and the Genie (writer) 1991, Merry Christmas Mr Bean (writer) 1992, Rowan Atkinson Live (contrib.) 1992, The Vicar of Dibley (series writer, exec. producer) 1994–, Hooves of Fire (writer) 1999, French & Saunders Live (contrib.) 2000, Legend of the Lost Tribe (exec. producer) 2002, The Girl in the Café (writer and exec. producer) (Humanitas Prize 2006) 2005. *Leisure interests:* TV, films, pop music. *Address:* United Agents, 12–26 Lexington Street, London, W1F 0LE, England (office); Portobello Studios, 138 Portobello Road, London W11 2DZ, England (office). *Telephone:* (20) 3214-0800 (office). *Fax:* (20) 3214-0801 (office). *E-mail:* info@unitedagents.co.uk (office). *Website:* unitedagents.co.uk (office).

CURTIS, Tony; American actor; b. (Bernard Schwarz), 3 June 1925, New York; s. of Manuel Schwarz and Helen Schwarz (née Klein); m. 1st Janet Leigh 1951 (divorced 1962); two d. (including Jamie Lee Curtis q.v.); m. 2nd Christine Kaufmann 1963 (divorced 1967); two d.; m. 3rd Leslie Allen 1968; two s.; m. 4th Lisa Deutsch 1993; ed New School of Social Research; served in USN; Kt Order of the Repub. of Hungary 1996. *Films include:* Houdini 1953, Black Shield of Falworth 1954, So This is Paris? 1954, Six Bridges to Cross 1955, Trapeze 1956, Mister Cory 1957, Sweet Smell of Success 1957, Midnight Story 1957, The Vikings 1958, Defiant Ones 1958, Perfect Furlough 1958, Some Like It Hot 1959, Spartacus 1960, The Great Imposter 1960, Pepe 1960, The Outsider 1961, Taras Bulba 1962, Forty Pounds of Trouble 1962, The List of Adrian Messenger 1963, Captain Newman 1963, Paris When It Sizzles 1964, Wild and Wonderful 1964, Sex and the Single Girl 1964, Goodbye Charlie 1964, The Great Race 1965, Boeing, Boeing 1965, Arriverderci, Baby 1966, Not with My Wife You Don't 1966, Don't Make Waves 1967, Boston Strangler 1968, Lepke 1975, Casanova 1976, The Last Tycoon 1976, The Manitou 1978, Sextette 1978, The Mirror Crack'd 1980, Venom 1982, Insignificance 1985, Club Life 1986, The Last of Phillip Banter 1988, Balboa, Midnight, Lobster Man from Mars, The High-Flying Mermaid, Prime Target, Center of the Web, Naked in New York, The Reptile Man, The Immortals 1995, The Celluloid Closet 1995, Brittle Glory 1997, Hardball 1997, Alien X Factor 1997, Stargames 1998, Louis & Frank 1998, Reflections of Evil 2002, The Blacksmith and the Carpenter (voice) 2007, David & Fatima 2008. *Television includes:* Third Girl from the Left 1973, The Persuaders 1971–72, The Count of Monte Cristo 1976, Vegas 1978, Mafia Princess 1986, Christmas in Conneticut 1992, A Perry Mason Mystery: The Case of the Grimacing Governor, Elvis Meets Nixon. *Publications:* Kid Andrew Cody and Julie Sparrow 1977, Tony Curtis: An Autobiography 1993. *Leisure interest:* painting. *Address:* 2598 Forest City Drive, Henderson, NV 89052; c/o William Morris Agency, 1 William Morris Place, Beverly Hills, CA 90212, USA (office).

CUSACK, John; American actor; b. 28 June 1966, Evanston, Ill.; s. of Richard Cusack and Nancy Cusack; brother of Joan Cusack; mem. Piven Theatre Workshop, Evanston from age 9–19; f. New Criminals Theatrical Co., Chicago 1988; f. New Crime Productions 1992. *Films include:* Class 1983, Sixteen Candles 1984, Grandview USA 1984, The Sure Thing 1985, Journey of Natty Gann 1985, Better Off Dead 1985, Stand By Me 1985, One Crazy Summer 1986, Broadcast News 1987, Hot Pursuit 1987, Eight Men Out 1988, Tapeheads 1988, Say Anything 1989, Fatman and Little Boy 1989, The Grifters 1990, True Colors 1991, Shadows and Fog 1992, Roadside Prophets 1992, The Player 1992, Map of the Human Heart 1992, Bob Roberts 1992,

Money for Nothing 1993, Bullets Over Broadway 1994, The Road to Wellville 1994, City Hall 1995, Anastasia 1997, Con Air 1997, Hellcab 1997, Midnight in the Garden of Good and Evil 1997, Grosse Pointe Blank (also dir, writer) 1997, High Fidelity (also screenwriter) 1997, This is My Father 1998, The Thin Red Line 1999, Pushing Tin 1998, Being John Malkovich 1999, The Cradle Will Rock (also screenwriter) 1999, America's Sweethearts 2001, Life of the Party 2000, Arigo (also prod.) 2000, Serendipity 2001, Max 2002, Adaptation 2002, Identity 2003, Runaway Jury 2003, The Ice Harvest 2005, Must Love Dogs 2005, The Contract 2006, Grace Is Gone 2007, 1408 2007, War, Inc. 2007, Martian Child 2007, Igor (voice) 2008. *Address:* New Crime Productions, 555 Rose Avenue, Venice, CA 90291 (office); c/o William Morris Agency, 1 William Morris Place, Beverly Hills, CA 90212, USA. *Telephone:* (310) 396-2199 (office). *Fax:* (310) 396-4249 (office).

CUSACK, Sinead Mary; Irish actress; b. 1948; d. of late Cyril Cusack and Maureen Kiely; m. Jeremy Irons (q.v.) 1977; two s.; numerous appearances in TV drama. *Films include:* Alfred the Great, Tamlyn, Hoffman 1969, David Copperfield 1970, Revenge 1971, The Devil's Widow 1971, Horowitz in Dublin Castle, The Last Remake of Beau Geste 1977, Rocket Gibraltar, Venus Peter, Waterland, God on the Rocks 1992, Bad Behaviour 1993, The Cement Garden 1993, The Sparrow, Flemish Board, Stealing Beauty 1996, Passion of Mind 2000, I Capture the Castle 2003, V for Vendetta 2006, The Tiger's Tail 2006, Eastern Promises 2007. *Theatre includes:* Lady Amaranth in Wild Oats, Lisa in Children of the Sun, Isabella in Measure for Measure, Celia in As You Like It, Evadne in The Maid's Tragedy, Lady Anne in Richard III, Portia in The Merchant of Venice, Ingrid in Peer Gynt, Kate in The Taming of the Shrew, Beatrice in Much Ado About Nothing, Lady Macbeth in Macbeth, Roxanne in Cyrano de Bergerac (all for RSC), Virago in A Lie of the Mind 2001, The Mercy Seat 2003, Oxford Festival, Gate Theatre, Dublin, Royal Court etc. *Address:* c/o Curtis Brown Group, 4th Floor, Haymarket House, 28–29 Haymarket, London, SW1Y 4SP, England.

CUSHING, Sir Selwyn (John), KNZM, CMG, FCA; New Zealand business executive; b. 1 Sept. 1936; s. of Cyril John Cushing and Henrietta Marjory Belle Cushing; m. Kaye Dorothy Anderson 1964; two s.; ed Hastings High School, Univ. of New Zealand; pnr Esam Cushing and Co., Hastings 1960–86; Dir Brierly Investments Ltd 1986–93, Chair., CEO 1999–2001; Deputy Chair. Air New Zealand 1988, Chair. –2001; Chair. Carter Holt Harvey Ltd 1991–93, Electricity Corpn of NZ 1993–97, New Zealand Symphony Orchestra 1996–2005. *Leisure interests:* cricket, music. *Address:* c/o New Zealand Symphony Orchestra, POB 6640, Wellington 6001, (office); 1 Beaston Road, Hastings, New Zealand.

CUSHMAN, David W., PhD; American biochemist; ed Univ. of Illinois; began career as researcher at Squibb Inst. for Medical Research (later the Bristol-Myers Squibb Pharmaceutical Research Inst.) 1969, Distinguished Research Fellow, Dept of Biochemistry –1994 (retd); Ciba Award For Hypertension Research 1983, Warren Alpert Foundation Prize 1991, Albert Lasker Award for Clinical Medical Research 1999, named by ACS one of 12 Heroes of Chemistry 2000. *Publications:* numerous publs in scientific journals. *Address:* c/o Bristol-Myers Squibb Pharmaceutical Research Institute, PO Box 4000, Princeton, NJ 08545-4000, USA (office). *Telephone:* (607) 252-4716 (office).

CUSSLER, Clive Eric, PhD; American novelist; b. 15 July 1931, Aurora, IL; s. of Eric Cussler and Amy Hunnewell; m. Barbara Knight 1955; three c.; ed Pasadena City Coll., Orange Coast Coll., California State Univ.; Owner Bestgen & Cussler Advertising, Newport Beach, Calif. 1961–65; Copy Dir Darcy Advertising, Hollywood, Calif. and Instr. in Advertising Communications, Orange Coast Coll. 1965–67; Advertising Dir Aquatic Marine Corpn, Newport Beach, Calif. 1967–79; Vice-Pres. and Creative Dir of Broadcast, Meffon, Wolff and Weir Advertising, Denver, Colo 1970–73; Chair. Nat. Underwater and Marine Agency; Fellow, New York Explorers Club, Royal Geographical Soc.; Lowel Thomas Award, New York Explorers Club. *Publications include:* The Mediterranean Caper 1973, Iceberg 1975, Raise the Titanic 1976, Vixen O-Three 1978, Night Probe 1981, Pacific Vortex 1982, Deep Six 1984, Cyclops 1986, Treasure 1988, Dragon 1990, Sahara 1992, Inca Gold 1994, Shock Wave 1995, Sea Hunters 1996, Flood Tide 1997, Clive Cussler and Dirk Pitt Revealed 1997, Serpent 1998, Atlantis Found 1999, Blue Gold 2000, Valhalla Rising 2001, Fire Ice (with Paul Kemprecos) 2002, Sea Hunters II 2002, The Golden Buddha (with Craig Dirgo) 2003, White Death 2003, Trojan Odyssey 2003, Black Wind (with Dirk Cussler) 2004, Sacred Stone 2005, Lost City (with Paul Kemprecos) 2006, Skeleton Coast 2006, Treasure of Khan (with Dirk Cussler) 2006, Dark Watch (with Jack Du Brul) 2007, The Chase 2007, Polar Shift 2007, Plague Ship 2008, Arctic Drift 2008, Corsair 2009, Medusa (with Paul Kemprecos) 2009. *Leisure interest:* discovering shipwrecks, collecting classic cars. *Address:* c/o Penguin Group (USA) Inc., Putnam Publicity, 375 Hudson Street, New York, NY 10014, USA (office). *Website:* www.penguin.com (office).

CUTHBERT, Alan William, BPharm, BSc, MA, PhD, ScD, FRS, FMedSci; British academic; *Shield Professor Emeritus of Pharmacology, Department of Medicine, University of Cambridge;* b. 7 May 1932, Peterborough; s. of the late Thomas William Cuthbert and Florence Mary Cuthbert (née Griffin); m. Harriet Jane Webster 1957; two s.; ed Deacons Grammar School, Peterborough, Leicester Coll. of Tech., Univs of St Andrews and London; Reader in Pharmacology, Univ. of Cambridge 1973–79, Shield Prof. of Pharmacology 1979–99, Prof. Emer. 1999–; Master, Fitzwilliam Coll. Cambridge 1991–99, Hon. Fellow 1999; Deputy Vice-Chancellor Univ. of Cambridge 1995–99; Gov. De Montfort Univ. 1998–2005; Chair. Editorial Bd British Journal of Pharmacology 1974–82; Vice-Pres. Ephar 1997–2002, Pres. 2002–04; Foreign Sec. British Pharmacological Soc. 1997–2000, Hon. mem. 2000; mem. Academia Europaea 2000, Acad. Royale de Médecine de Belgique; Fellow, Jesus Coll. Cambridge 1968–91, Hon. Fellow 1991–; Hon. Fellow, Academia

Europaea 2004; Hon. DSc (De Montfort Univ., Aston Univ.), Hon. LLD (Dundee Univ.); Wellcome Gold Medal 2005. *Publications:* numerous articles on physiology, pharmacology and biology. *Leisure interests:* painting, sculpture, photography, gardening, travel. *Address:* Department of Medicine, University of Cambridge, Addenbrooke's Hospital, Hills Road, Cambridge, CB2 3QQ (office); 7 Longstanton Road, Oakington, Cambridge CB4 5BB, England (home). *Telephone:* (1223) 336853 (office); (1223) 233676 (home). *Fax:* (1223) 336846 (office). *E-mail:* awc1000@cam.ac.uk (office). *Website:* www.med .cam.ac.uk (office).

CUTLER, Walter Leon, MA; American diplomatist; b. 25 Nov. 1931, Boston, Mass.; s. of Walter Leon Cutler and Esther Dewey; m. 1st Sarah Gerard Beeson 1957 (divorced 1981); two s.; m. 2nd Isabel Kugel Brookfield 1981; ed Wesleyan Univ. and Fletcher School of Int. Law and Diplomacy, Tufts Univ.; Vice-Consul, Yaoundé, Cameroon 1957–59; Staff Asst to Sec. of State 1960–62; Political-Econ. Officer, Algiers 1962–65; Consul, Tabriz, Iran 1965–67; Political-Mil. Officer, Seoul, Repub. of Korea 1967–69; Political Officer, Saigon, Repub. of Viet Nam 1969–71; Special Asst, Bureau of Far Eastern Affairs, Dept of State 1971–73, mem. Sr Seminar on Foreign Policy 1973–74; Dir Office of Cen. Africa 1974–75; Amb. to Zaïre 1975–79, to Iran 1979; Deputy Asst Sec. of State for Congressional Relations 1979–81; Amb. to Tunisia 1981–83, to Saudi Arabia 1983–87, 1988–89; Pres. Meridian Int. Center, Washington, DC 1989–2006; Sr Advisor Trust Co. of the West, LA 1990; Research Prof. of Diplomacy, Georgetown Univ. 1987–88; Special Emissary for Sec.-Gen. of UN, New York 1994; mem. Council on Foreign Relations, New York, American Acad. of Diplomacy, Washington Inst. of Foreign Affairs; Wilbur J. Carr Award 1989, Dir-Gen.'s Cup, Dept of State 1993; Order of the Leopard (Repub. of Zaïre) 1979; King Abdulaziz Decoration (Saudi Arabia) 1985. *Leisure interests:* sports, ornithology. *Address:* c/o Meridian International Center, 1630 Crescent Place, NW, Washington, DC 20009; 1705 34th Street, NW, Washington, DC 20007, USA.

CUTTAREE, Hon. Jayakrishna, BSc, MSc, PhD; Mauritian lawyer and politician; ed Univ. of Edinburgh, UK, Uppsala Univ., Sweden, Univ. of Cambridge, UK; called to the Bar, Lincoln's Inn, London, UK; fmr Asst Conservator of Forests, Ministry of Agric. and Natural Resources; fmr Gen. Man. Sugar Planters' Mechanical Pool Corpn; fmr Chief of Natural Resources Div., OAU, Addis Ababa, Ethiopia; fmr Programme Specialist (Research and Devt in Natural Resources), UNESCO, Paris, France; mem. Legis. Ass. 1982–; Minister of Labour and Industrial Relations 1982–83, Attorney-Gen. and Minister of Housing, Lands, Town and Country Planning 1991, of Industry, Industrial Tech., Scientific Research and Handicraft 1996, of Industry and Commerce 1996–97, of Industry, Commerce and Int. Trade 2000–03, of Foreign Affairs, Int. Trade and Regional Co-operation 2003–05; Deputy Leader, Mouvement Militant Mauricien; Spokesman, Pacific Common Market, Indian Ocean Comm. and Pacific Forum at WTO meeting, Doha, Qatar 2001; led negotiations between EU and African Pacific Caribbean countries under Cotonou Agreement 2002; Spokesman of African Union at WTO meeting, Cancun, Mexico 2003; Head of Mauritian Del. and Spokesman of the African Union at Africa Growth and Opportunity Act (AGOA) Conf., Washington, DC, 2003. *Address:* c/o Mouvement Militant Mauricien, 21 Poudrière St, Port Louis, Mauritius. *Telephone:* 212-6553. *Fax:* 208-9939. *Website:* mmm.mmmonline.org.

CUTTS, Simon; British artist, poet and publisher; *Director, Coracle Press;* b. 30 Dec. 1944, Derby; s. of George Tom Cutts and Elizabeth Purdy; m. 1st Annira Uusi-Illikainen (divorced 1973); one s.; m. 2nd Margot Hapgood (died 1985); ed Herbert Strutt Grammar School, Belper, Derbyshire, Nottingham Coll. of Art, Trent Polytechnic; travel and miscellaneous employment including The Trent Bookshop, Nottingham 1962–69; Jt Ed. Tarasque Press 1964–72; publishing, lecturing and writing 1972–74; Dir and Co-Partner Coracle Press Books (now Coracle Production and Distribution) 1975–87, 1996–; Dir, Coracle Press Gallery 1983–86; Dir Victoria Miro Gallery 1985–; org. of exhbns in Europe and New York. *Publications:* numerous publs, including Quelques Pianos 1976, Pianostool Footnotes 1983, Petits-Airs for Margot 1986, Seepages 1988, The Rubber Stamp Mini Printer 1993, 1995, After Frank O'Hara and Morton Feldman (with Erica van Horn) 1996, The A. Goldsworthy Questionnaires 1997, A Smell of Printing 2000, Eclogues 2004, A English Dictionary of French Place Names 2004, Ceillets des Poètes 2005, Some Forms of Availability 2006, as if it is at all 2007. *Leisure interests:* walking, running, cooking, eating, drinking and the nostalgia of innocence. *E-mail:* books@coracle.ie (office). *Website:* www.coracle.ie (office).

CVETKOVIĆ, Mirko, MA, PhD; Serbian economist and politician; *Prime Minister;* b. 1950, Zaječar; m.; two c.; ed Faculty of Econs, Univ. of Belgrade; began career as economist at Inst. of Mining and Inst. of Econs; consultant, CES MECON (advisory and research firm.); fmr foreign consultant on World Bank projects in Pakistan, India and Turkey; Econ. Adviser, Inst. of Mining 1998–2001; Deputy Minister of Economy and Privatization 2001–04; Dir Privatization Agency 2003–04; Special Adviser to CEO Intercom Consulting/ CES MECON 2005–; Minister of Finance 2007–08; Prime Minister 2008–. *Address:* Office of the Prime Minister, 11000 Belgrade, Nemanjina 11, Serbia (office). *Telephone:* (11) 3617719 (office). *Fax:* (11) 3617609 (office). *E-mail:* predsednikvladesrbije@srbija.sr.gov.yu (office).

CYPRIANO, Márcio Artur Laurelli; Brazilian banker; *President, Executive Director and CEO, Banco Bradesco SA;* b. 20 Nov. 1943; ed Mackenzie Presbyterian Univ.; began career with Banco da Bahia SA 1967; joined Banco Bradesco SA 1973, Dept Dir 1984, Asst Dir 1986, Man. Dir 1988, Dir and Vice-Pres. 1995, Pres. and CEO 1999–, mem. Exec. Cttee 2002–; Dir Fed. of Brazilian Banking Asscn (FEBRABAN) 2001–, Pres. of the Bd 2002–; Dir Bradespar SA 2002–; Dir Serasa SA 1984–86, Empresas BCN 1998–99. *Address:* Cidade de Deus, Predio Novo 4 andar, Sao Paulo 06029-900, Brazil (office). *Telephone:* (11) 3684-9229 (office). *Fax:* (11) 3684-4570 (office). *E-mail:* info@bradesco.com.br (office). *Website:* www.bradesco.com.br (office).

CYWIŃSKA, Izabella, MA; Polish theatre producer and director; b. 22 March 1935, Kamień; d. of Andrzej Cywiński and Elżbieta Łuszczewska; m. Janusz Michałowski 1968; ed Warsaw Univ., State Acad. of Drama, Warsaw; Asst, Rural Architecture Faculty, Warsaw Univ. of Tech. 1956–58; Stage Dir, Theatre in Cracow-Nowa Huta 1966–68, Polski Theatre, Poznań 1966–68; Dir and Artistic Man. Wojciech Bogusławski Theatre, Kalisz 1969–73, Nowy Theatre, Poznań 1973–88; Vice-Pres. Understanding Cttee of Creative Circles, Poznań 1980–81; Minister of Culture and Art 1989–91; Founder and Vice-Pres. Culture Foundation 1991–93; Artistic Dir 50th Anniversary of the Revolt in the Warsaw Ghetto; mem. Polish Stage Artists' Asscn, Presidential Council for Culture 1992–95, Gen. Ass. European Cooperation Foundation, Brussels; Minister of Culture and Art Award (2nd class) 1977; Kt.'s Cross of Polonia Restituta Order; ; All-Poland Drama Festivals, Kalisz 1970, 1973, 1980, Opole 1976, Wrocław 1976, Medal Kalos Kagathos, Gold Cross of Merit, Nat. Educ. Comm. Medal, Nat. Broadcasting Council of Poland Award 1999, Special Prix Europa Award 2000, Willy Brandt Award, Prix Europa Int. TV Festival, Berlin 2000. *Plays directed include:* Iphigenie auf Tauris 1968, The Morals of Mrs Dulska 1970, The Death of Tarelkin 1973, I giganti della montagna 1973, Lower Depths 1974, They 1975, Wijuny 1976, Bath-house 1978, Judas from Karioth 1980, The Accused: June '56 1981, Enemy of the People 1982, Dawn 1986, Virginity 1986, Cemeteries 1988, Tartuffe 1989, Antygona in New York 1993, Hanemann 2002, Your Excellency 2006; also Dir in USA and USSR, I Leave You 2003. *TV films:* Frédéric's Enchantment (about Chopin) 1998, Purym's Miracle 1999. *Television productions include:* God's Lining (series) 1997, Beauty (TV theatre) 1998 (First Prize', Int. TV Festival, Plovdiv, Bulgaria 1997), Second Mother 1999, Touch (TV theatre) 2001, Marilyn Mongol (TV theatre) 2002, Bar World (TV theatre) 2003, God's Lining II (series) 2004, Lovers from Marona (feature film) 2004. *Publication:* Nagłe zastępstwo 1992. *Leisure interests:* foreign travel, politics. *Address:* ul. Piwna 7A m. 5, 00-265 Warsaw, Poland (home). *Telephone:* (22)

635-32-33. *Fax:* (22) 635-32-33; (22) 635-32-33 (home). *E-mail:* cywinska@hoga .pl (home).

CZERWIŃSKA, Anna, PharmD; Polish mountaineer; b. 10 July 1949, Warsaw; ed Acad. of Medicine, Warsaw; mem. of staff, CEFARM, Warsaw 1977–79, Centre of Rehabilitation STOCER 1980–83, Children's Hosp., Dziekanów Leśny 1984–87; Dir own firm Anamax–Import-Export, Warsaw 1989–; mountaineering expeditions include Tatra, Alps, Karakoram, Himalayas (female teams), Mount Everest (solo) 2000 (oldest woman to reach summit); solo climbing the length of the Tatra ridge 1991; first Polish woman to climb the Crown of the Earth (highest peaks on every continent) 1995–2000; has reached the summit of six of the world's 8000m peaks. *Publications:* Twice Matterhorn (with Krystyna Palmowska) 1980, Difficult Mountain Rakaposhi 1982, Broad Peak – Only Two 1988, Nanga Parbat – Ill-Fated Mountain 1989, Threat Around K2 1990, Crown of the Earth 2000. *Leisure interests:* do-it-yourself, gardening; mountain biking, white-water rafting. *E-mail:* anka@ szkolagorska.com. *Website:* www.czerwinska.szkolagorska.com.

CZIBERE, Tibor; Hungarian engineer, politician and academic; *Professor Emeritus of Mechanical Engineering, University of Miskolc;* b. 16 Oct. 1930, Tapolca; s. of Jozsef Czibere and Maria Loppert; m. Gabriella Nagy 1956; two d.; ed Tech. Univ. of Heavy Industry, Miskolc; engineer with Ganz-MÁVAG Machine Works 1956; rejoined Miskolc Univ. and active as lecturer 1963, Prof. and fmr Dean of Mechanical Eng Faculty 1968, Rector 1978–86, Prof. 1986–88, 1989, now Prof. Emer.; Minister of Culture 1988–89; Corresp. mem. Hungarian Acad. of Sciences 1976, mem. 1985–, mem. Parl. 1983–85, 1988–90; Vice-Pres. Nat. Council of Patriotic People's Front 1985–89; mem. Local Editoral Council, Journal of Computational and Applied Mechanics; Labour Order of Merit 1971, Star Order of the People's Repub. 1986; Kossuth Prize 1962, Szetgyörgyi Albert Prize 1996. *Address:* Department of Fluid and Heat Engineering, University of Miskolc, 3515 Miskolc-Egyetemváros, Hungary (office). *Telephone:* (46) 365-111 (office). *E-mail:* aramczt@gold.uni -miskolc.hu (office). *Website:* www.uni-miskolc.hu (office).

D

DA COSTA, Zacarias; Timor-Leste politician; *Minister of Foreign Affairs;* m. Milena Pires; served as Conselho Nacional da Resistência Timorense (CNRT) rep. to EU in Brussels, UN in Geneva –1999; fmr Vice-Pres. União Democrática Timorense; Co-founder Partido Social Democrata (PSD) 2000, held several posts including Gen.-Sec., Pres. Nat. Congress and Nat. Chair.; consultant for Asian Bank of Devt; Minister of Foreign Affairs 2007–. *Address:* Ministry of Foreign Affairs and Cooperation, GPA Building 1, Ground Floor, Rua Avenida Presidente Nicolau Lobato, PO BOX 6, Dili, Timor-Leste (office). *Telephone:* 3339600 (office). *Fax:* 3339025 (office). *E-mail:* administration@mnec.gov-tl.net (office). *Website:* www.mfac.gov.tp (office).

DA CRUZ POLICARPO, HE Cardinal José, DTheol; Portuguese ecclesiastic; *Patriarch of Lisbon;* b. 26 Feb. 1936, Alvorninha; ed Seminary of Santarem, Seminary of Almada, Major Seminary Cristo-Rei of the Olivais, Pontifical Gregorian Univ., Rome, Italy; ordained priest 1961; Rector Seminary of the Olivais 1970–97; mem. Faculty of Theology, Catholic Univ. of Portugal 1970–86, Dir Faculty of Theology 1974–80, 1985–88, mem. Superior Council, Pres. Organizing Comm. of the Regional Centre of Porto 1985–87, Rector Catholic Univ. of Portugal 1988–92, 1992–96, Grand Chancellor 1998–; Titular Bishop of Caliabria and Auxiliary Bishop of Lisbon 1978–97; Coadjutor Archbishop of Lisbon 1997–98; Patriarch of Lisbon 1998–; Pres. Portuguese Episcopal Conf. 1999–; cr. Cardinal (Cardinal Priest of Sant'Antonio in Campo Marzio) 2001; attended Seventh Ordinary Ass. of World Synod of Bishops, Vatican City 1987, Second Special Ass. for Europe 1999, Tenth Ordinary Ass. 2001; Chancellor Catholic Univ. of Portugal 1998; Hon. mem. Portuguese Acad. of History 2000, Portuguese Acad. of Sciences 2006; Academic of Merit, Portuguese Acad. of History 2006. *Publications:* numerous papers on theology. *Address:* Archdiocese of Lisbon, Mosteiro de Sao Vicente de Fora, Campo de Santa Clara, 1149-085 Lisbon (office); Casa Patriarcal, Seminário dos Olivais, Quinta do Cabeço, 1800 Lisbon, Portugal. *Telephone:* (218) 81-0500 (office); (219) 45-7310. *Fax:* (218) 81-0555 (office); (219) 45-7329. *E-mail:* infodoc@patriarcado-lisboa.pt. *Website:* www.patriarcado-lisboa.pt (office).

DA CRUZ VILAÇA, José Luís, DEcon; Portuguese judge, lawyer and professor of law; *Partner, PLMJ – A.M. Pereira, Sáragga Leal, Oliveira Martins, Júdice e Associados;* b. 20 Sept. 1944, Braga; s. of Fernando da Costa Vilaça and Maria das Dores G. Cruz Vilaça; m. Marie-Charlotte Opitz 1995; two s. two d. (three c. from previous m.); ed Univs. of Coimbra, Paris and Oxford; Asst Faculty of Law, Univ. of Coimbra 1966, Prof. of Fiscal Law and Community Law 1979; mil. service, Naval Legal Dept 1969–72; mem. Parl. 1980–86; Sec. of State for Home Affairs 1980, for Presidency of Council of Ministers 1981, for European Affairs 1982; Advocate-Gen. Court of Justice of EC 1986–89; Full Prof. and Dir Inst. for European Studies, Lusiada Univ. Lisbon 1988–2000; Pres. Court of First Instance of EC 1989–95; Pnr, PLMJ – A.M. Pereira, Sáragga Leal, Oliveira Martins, Júdice e Associados (law firm), Lisbon 1998–; Sec.-Gen. Portuguese Asscn of European Law (APDE) 1998; Visiting Prof. Univ. Nova de Lisboa 2001–; Visiting Researcher, Fordham Univ. School of Law 2002, 2004; Chair. Disciplinary Bd of EC 2003–; Visiting Prof., Portuguese Catholic Univ., Lisbon 2004–; Gran Croce, Ordine di Merito (Italy), Grand-Croix, Couronne de Chêne (Luxembourg), Officier, Légion d'Honneur (France), Grã-Cruz, Ordem do Infante (Portugal). *Publications:* A empresa cooperativa 1969, L'économie portugaise face à l'intégration économique européenne 1978, Introdução ao estudo da Economia 1979, Modelo económico da CEE e modelo económico português 1984, The Court of First Instance of the European Communities: A Significant Step Towards the Consolidation of the European Community as a Community Governed by the Rule of Law 1993, Yatil des limites matérielles à la révision des traités instituant les communautés européennes? 1993, The Development of the Community Judicial System Before and After Maastricht 1994, La procédure en référé comme instrument de protection juridictionnelle des particuliers en droit communautaire 1998, An Exercise on the Application of Keck & Mithouard in the Field of Free Provision of Services 1999, Código da União Europeia 2001, Código da Concorrência 2004. *Leisure interests:* tennis, gardening, literature. *Address:* PLMJ – A.M. Pereira, Sáragga Leal, Oliveira Martins, Júdice e Associados, Avenida da Liberdade 224, 1250-148 Lisbon, Portugal (office). *Telephone:* (213) 197321 (office). *Fax:* (213) 197319 (office). *E-mail:* jcv@plmj.pt (office). *Website:* www.plmj.com (office).

DA GRAÇA VERÍSSIMO DA COSTA, Desidério; Angolan politician; *Minister of Petroleum;* b. 4 April 1934, Luanda; s. of Fernando Pascoal da Costa; m.; five c.; ed Montanuniversität Leoben, Austria, studies in Petroleum Man. in Cambridge, Mass, USA; went to school in Portugal and later sought refuge in FRG from prosecution by Polícia Internacional e de Defesa do Estado secret police, prepared to study medicine, then served for several years as pres. of asscn of students from Portuguese colonies with seat in Morocco, before turning to study of petroleum eng; mem. Angolan Nat. Comm. for Restructuring the Petroleum Industry 1976–77; Gen. Deputy Dir Sonangol 1977–79; Nat. Dir of Petroleum 1982–84; Vice-Minister of Petroleum 1984–2002, Minister of Petroleum 2002–; Chair. African Petroleum Producers Asscn 2005–06. *Address:* Ministry of Petroleum, Av. 4 de Fevereiro, Luanda, Angola (office). *Telephone:* (222) 385847 (office). *Fax:* (222) 385847 (office).

DA GRAÇA VIEGAS SANTIAGO, Ângela Maria, MSc; São Tomé and Príncipe politician; *Minister of Planning and Finance;* b. 14 Oct. 1961; ed Donetsk Univ., Ukraine, Bricham Int. Univ.; economist, Ministry of Econ. and Financial Affairs 1988–93; Dir Dept of Statistics and Econ. Studies, Banco Central de São Tomé e Príncipe 1997–98; prin. adviser to Minister of Planning and Finance 1999–2001; mem. Nat. Ass. 2002–, adviser to Prime Minister 2002–04; Minister of Finance and Planning 2008–; mem. Movimento de Libertação de São Tomé e Príncipe–Partido Social Democrata (MLSTP–PSD). *Address:* Ministry of Planning and Finance, Largo Alfândega, CP 168, São Tomé, São Tomé and Príncipe (office). *Telephone:* 224173 (office). *Fax:* 222683 (office). *E-mail:* mpfc@cstome.net (office). *Website:* www.minfinancas.gov.st (office).

DA SILVA, Luis Inácio (Lula) (see LULA DA SILVA, Inácio).

DA SILVA, Marta Vieira; Brazilian professional footballer; b. 19 Feb. 1986, Dois Riachos, Alagoas; d. of Aldário da Silva and Tereza da Silva; player with Vasco da Gama club, Rio 1999–2001, Brazilian Nat. Women's Team, played in Olympic Games 2004, 2008; with Umeå IK, Sweden 2004–08, Los Angeles Sol, USA 2009–; top scorer in Damallsvenskan league (Sweden) 2004, 2005, 2006; U-20 World Cup Golden Ball 2004, Golden Ball (MVP) FIFA Under-19s Women's World Championship 2004, FIFA Women's World Player of the Year 2006, 2007, 2008, Golden Ball Award, Women's World Cup 2007, Golden Boot Award, Women's World Cup 2007. *Address:* c/o Los Angeles Sol, 714 West Olympic Boulevard, Suite 200, Los Angeles, CA 90015, USA (office). *Website:* www.womensprosoccer.com/la (office).

DA VEIGA, Marias de Fátima Lima; Cape Verde politician and diplomatist; *Ambassador to USA;* b. 22 June 1957, São Vicente; m.; two c.; ed Univ. of Aix-ex-Provence, France; Amb. to Cuba 1999–2001; fmr adviser, Ministry of Foreign Affairs, Chief of Staff, Office of the Minister for Foreign Affairs 1995–99, Sec. of State for Foreign Affairs 2001–02, Minister of Foreign Affairs, Co-operation and Communities 2002–04, Perm. Rep. to UN, New York 2004–07, Amb. to USA 2007–; mem. Nat. Comm. CILSS. *Address:* Embassy of Cape Verde, 3415 Massachusetts Avenue, NW, Washington DC, 20007, USA (office). *Telephone:* (202) 965-6820 (office). *Fax:* (202) 965-1207 (office). *E-mail:* ambacvus@sysnet.net (office). *Website:* www.virtualcapeverde.net (office).

DAAN, Serge, PhD, FRSC; Dutch biologist and academic; *Niko Tinbergen Professor of Behavioural Biology and Dean, Faculty of Mathematical and Natural Sciences, University of Groningen;* b. 11 June 1940, Mook; m. Ruth Hohe-Daan 1982; three c.; ed Gymnasium β, Deventer, Univ. of Amsterdam; Postdoctoral Fellow, Max Planck Inst. for Behavioural Physiology, Andechs, Germany; Postdoctoral Fellow, Stanford Univ., Calif., USA 1973–75; Sr Scientist, Zoological Lab., Univ. of Groningen 1975–85, Assoc. Prof. of Animal Ecology and Ethology 1985–90, Assoc. Prof. of Chronobiology 1994–96, Prof. of Ethology 1996–2004, Niko Tinbergen Prof. of Behavioural Biology 2003–, Vice-Dean for Research, Faculty of Math. and Natural Sciences 2001–04, Dean 2004–, Coordinator Topmaster programme in Behavioural and Cognitive Neurosciences; mem. Bd Earth and Life Sciences, Netherlands Org. for Scientific Research (NWO) 1997–2002, Chair. NWO program, Evolution and Behaviour 2002–; Pres. Dutch Soc. for Behavioural Biology 1996–2001; has served on numerous nat. and int. cttees and editorial bds; mem. Dutch Soc. of Sciences 1999; mem. Bd Dobberke Foundation for Biological Psychology, Amsterdam Advisory Bd, Institut für Vogelforschung, Wilhelmshaven Advisory Bd, Otto Creutzfeld Centre for Cognitive and Behavioural Neuroscience, Münster Editorial Bd, Journal of Biological Rhythms Editorial Bd, International Journal of Zoology; Chair. Leonardo da Vinci Foundation; Kt, Order of the Dutch Lion 2004; Victor and Erna Hasselblad Award 1982, Eighth Laurence Irving-Per Scholander Memorial Lecturer, Univ. of Alaska 1990, Prize of Dutch Soc. for Light Therapy 1992, Alexander von Humboldt Research Prize 1992, Niko Tinbergen Lecturer, London 1996, First Colin S. Pittendrigh Lecturer, Florida 1998, Int. Prize for Biology, Japan Soc. for the Promotion of Science 2006, Award for Eminent Scientists, Japan Soc. for the Promotion of Science 2008. *Achievements include:* contributed several key concepts and models, including 'circadian' (*c.* 24-h) rhythms of rest and activity, the regulation of human sleep, and the annual timing of reproduction. *Publications:* The Prudent Parent (with R. H. Drent) 1980; more than 250 scientific papers in professional journals on the temporal organization of behaviour in animals and humans. *Address:* Room 5161.0504, Faculty of Mathematics and Natural Sciences, University of Groningen, Nijenborgh 9, 9747 AG Groningen, The Netherlands (office). *Telephone:* (50) 363-46-15 (Sec.) (office). *E-mail:* s.daan@rug.nl (office). *Website:* www.rug.nl (office); www.rug.nl/biologie/onderzoek/onderzoekgroepen/gedragsbiologie/index (office).

DAANE, J(ames) Dewey; American banker, academic and fmr government official; *Frank K. Houston Professor Emeritus of Finance and Senior Advisor, Financial Markets Research Center, Owen Graduate School of Management, Vanderbilt University;* b. 6 July 1918, Grand Rapids, Mich.; s. of Gilbert L. Daane and Mamie Daane (née Blocksma); m. 1st Blanche M. Tichenor 1941 (divorced); one d.; m. 2nd Onnie B. Selby 1953 (deceased); m. 3rd Barbara W. McMann 1963; two d.; ed Duke Univ. and Harvard Univ.; with Fed. Reserve Bank of Richmond 1939–60, Monetary Economist 1947, Asst Vice-Pres. 1953, Vice-Pres., Dir, Research Dept, 1957; Chief, IMF Mission to Paraguay 1950–51; Vice-Pres. and Econ. Adviser, Fed. Reserve Bank of Minneapolis May-July 1960; Asst to Sec. of US Treasury, Prin. Adviser to Under-Sec. for Monetary Affairs 1960–61, Deputy Under-Sec. of Treasury for Monetary Affairs and Gen. Deputy to Under-Sec. for Monetary Affairs 1961–63; mem. Bd of Govs US Fed. Reserve System, Washington, DC 1963–74; Vice-Chair. Commerce Union Bank 1974–78; Vice-Chair. Tennessee Valley Bancorp 1975–78; Chair. Int. Policy Cttee, Sovran Financial Corpn/Cen. South 1978–87; Dir Nat. Futures Asscn, Ill. 1983–2003; Chair. Money Market Cttee South Sovran Bank 1988–90; Frank K. Houston Prof. of Banking and Finance, Grad. School of Man., Vanderbilt Univ. 1974–85, Valere Blair Potter Prof. of

Banking and Finance 1985–89, Prof. Emer. 1989–, also Sr Advisor Financial Markets Research Center; Alan R. Holmes Prof. of Econs, Middlebury Coll. 1991–93; Dir Whittaker Corpn 1974–89, Chicago Bd of Trade 1979–82; mem. American Finance Asscn, American Econ. Asscn. *Address:* Vanderbilt University, Owen Graduate School of Management, 401 21st Avenue, South Nashville, TN 37203 (office); 102 Westhampton Place, Nashville, TN 37205, USA (home). *Telephone:* (615) 322-3632 (office). *Fax:* (615) 343-7177 (office). *E-mail:* dewey.daane@owen.vanderbilt.edu (office). *Website:* www.owen .vanderbilt.edu/vanderbilt (office).

DABOUB, Juan José; Salvadorean politician and international organization official; *Managing Director, World Bank Group;* led family-owned businesses for nearly a decade before joining Bd of CEL (electricity utility); fmr Pres. ANTEL (state-owned telecommunications co. which he privatized); served three different govts for 12 years and then returned to pvt. sector; fmr Chief of Staff to Pres. of El Salvador, co-ordinated donors and oversaw reconstruction of El Salvador after two earthquakes of 2001; Minister of Finance –2006; Man. Dir World Bank Group 2006–. *Address:* The World Bank Group, 1818 H Street, NW, Washington, DC 20433, USA (office). *Telephone:* (202) 473-1000 (office). *Fax:* (202) 477-6391 (office). *E-mail:* webmaster@worldbank.org (office). *Website:* www.worldbank.org (office).

DĄBROWSKI, Waldemar; Polish arts administrator and fmr government official; *CEO, Teatr Wielki—Opera Narodowa;* ed Electronics Faculty, Warsaw Polytechnic, Exec. Programme for Leaders in Devt, Harvard Univ., USA; Founder and Dir Riwiera-Remont student club 1973–78; Deputy Dir Cultural Dept, City of Warsaw 1979–81; Co-Man. Warsaw Studio Art Centre 1982, produced more than 70 plays, co-f. Sinfonia Varsovia with Jerzy Maksymiuk and Yehudi Menuhin; Deputy Minister of Culture and Art and Head, Cttee of Cinematography 1990–94; Pres. State Foreign Investment Agency 1994–98, conceived and created Vacation Festival of Stars in Miedzyzdroje (West Pomerania voivodship); Gen. Dir Wielki Theatre Nat. Opera 1998–2002, currently CEO; Minister of Culture 2002–05; fmr Pres. Soc. for the Encouragement of the Fine Arts; fmr Vice-Pres. American-Polish-Israeli Foundation 'Shalom'; fmr Hon. Pres. Polish Golfing Asscn; Chevalier, Ordre des Arts et Lettres, Orderem Świętego Stanisława Pierwszej Klasy 2005; scholarships from British Council, Goethe Inst., US Dept of State; Merited for Warsaw Distinction, Warsaw City Council 2001. *Address:* Teatr Wielki—Opera Narodowa, Plac Teatralny 1, 00-950 Warsaw, skrytka pocztowa 59, Poland (office). *Telephone:* (22) 6920200 (office). *Fax:* (22) 8260423 (office). *E-mail:* office@teatrwielki.pl (office). *Website:* www.teatrwielki.pl (office).

DACHEVILLE, Colette, (pseudonym Stéphane Audran); French actress; b. 8 Nov. 1932, Versailles; d. of Corneille Dacheville and Jeanne Rossi; m. 1st Jean-Louis Trintignant; m. 2nd Claude Chabrol 1964; one s.; ed Lycée Lamartine, Paris, Cours Charles Dullin; studied drama under Tania Balachova and Michel Vitold; Commdr Légion d'honneur. *Films include:* Les bonnes femmes 1959, L'oeil du malin 1961, Landru 1962, Ligne de démarcation 1966, Champagne Murders 1966, Les biches 1968 (Best Actress, Berlin), La femme infidèle 1968, La peau de torpédo 1969, La dame dans l'auto avec les lunettes et un fusil 1969, Le boucher 1970 (Best Actress, San Sebastián), La rupture 1970, Aussi loin que l'amour 1970, Juste avant la nuit 1971, Without Apparent Motive 1971, Un meurtre est un meurtre 1972, Dead Pigeon on Beethoven Street 1972, Discreet Charm of the Bourgeoisie 1972 (Best Actress, Soc. of Film and TV Arts), Les noces rouges 1973, Comment réussir dans la vie quand on est con et pleurnichard 1973, Le cri du coeur 1974, Ten Little Indians 1974, B Must Die 1974, The Black Bird 1975, Vincent, François, Paul and Others 1975, Folies bourgeoises 1976, Silver Bears 1976, Devil's Advocate 1976, Violette Nozière 1978, Le Soleil en face 1979, The Big Red One 1980, Coup de Torchon 1981, Boulevard des assassins 1982, Le choc 1982, On ira tous au paradis, Le sang des autres 1983, Poulet au vinaigre 1984, Babette's Feast 1988 (Best Actress, Taormina), La Cage aux Folles III: The Wedding, Manika: The Girl Who Lived Twice 1989, Quiet Days in Clichy 1989, Betty 1991, The Turn of the Screw 1994, Au petit Marguery 1995, Maximum Risk 1996, Arlette 1997, Madeline 1998, Belle maman 1999, Le Pique-nique de Lulu Kreutz 2000, J'ai faim!!! 2001, Ma femme... s'appelle Maurice 2002. *TV appearances in:* Brideshead Revisited 1981, Mistral's Daughter 1984, The Sun Also Rises 1984, Poor Little Rich Girl 1986, Tecx 1989, Cry No More My Lady 1992, Le Droit à l'oubli 1992, L'Évanouie 1994, Petit 1996, Un printemps de chien 1997, La Bicyclette bleue 2000, Sissi, l'impératrice rebelle 2004, La Battante 2005, Trois Femmes: un soir d'été 2005. *Address:* c/o 2F De Marthod, 11 rue Chanez, 75016 Paris, France. *Telephone:* 1-47-43-13-14.

DACI, Nexhat, MA, PhD; Kosovo politician and academic; *University Professor, University of Priština;* b. 26 July 1944, Tërnoc, Serbia and Montenegro (now in Kosovo); m. Zineta Daci; two s. one d.; ed Univ. of Priština, also educated in UK and Belgium; Univ. Prof., Univ. of Priština 1983–; Pres. and Sec., Kosovo Acad. of Sciences and Arts 1995–2002; Pres. of Kosovo Ass. 2001–06; Acting Pres. of Kosovo Jan.-Feb. 2006; mem. Democratic League of Kosovo, European Acad. for the Environment, American Chem. Asscn. *Publications:* author of four text books. *Address:* Velania 18/IV, Priština, Kosovo (home). *E-mail:* nexhat.daci@assembly-kosova.org (office). *Website:* www.kuvendikosoves.org (office).

DAČIĆ, Ivica; Serbian politician; *First Deputy Prime Minister and Minister of Internal Affairs;* b. 1 Jan. 1966, Prizren; m. Sonja Dačić; one s. one d.; ed Faculty of Political Science, Univ. of Belgrade; Pres. Socialist Youth Brigade, Belgrade 1990; Deputy, Fed. Ass. of Yugoslavia 1992–2004; mem. Socialist Party of Serbia (Socijalistička partija Srbije), Party Spokesman 1992–2000, Vice-Chair. 2000–03, Pres. 2006–; mem. Nat. Ass. of Serbia 2007–; mem. Parl. Ass., Council of Europe, Brussels 2003–04, 2006–, mem. Cttee on Culture, Science and Educ., on Equal Opportunities for Women, on Migration, Refugees and Population; unsuccessful cand. for Pres. of Serbia 2004; Minister of Finance 2007–08; First Deputy Prime Minister and Minister of Internal Affairs 2008–. *Address:* Ministry of Internal Affairs, 11000 Belgrade, Kneza Miloša 101 (office); Socialist Party of Serbia (Socijalistička partija Srbije), 11000 Belgrade, Studentski trg 15, Serbia (office). *Telephone:* (11) 3612410 (office). *Fax:* (11) 3617814 (office). *E-mail:* mupr s@mup.sr.gov.yu (office). *Website:* www.mup.sr.gov.yu (office); www.sps.org.yu (office).

DACRE, Paul Michael, BA; British newspaper editor; *Editor-in-Chief, Associated Newspapers;* b. 14 Nov. 1948, London; s. of Peter Dacre and Joan Dacre (née Hill); m. Kathleen Thomson 1973; two s.; ed Univ. Coll. School, London, Leeds Univ.; reporter, feature writer, Assoc. Features Ed., Daily Express 1970–76, Washington and New York Corresp. 1976–79; New York Bureau Chief, Daily Mail 1980, News Ed., London 1981–85, Asst Ed. (News and Foreign) 1986, Asst Ed. (Features) 1987, Exec. Ed. 1988, Assoc. Ed. 1989–91, Ed. 1992–, Ed.-in-Chief Assoc. Newspapers 1998–; Ed. Evening Standard 1991–92; Dir Associated Newspaper Holdings 1991–, Daily Mail & General Trust PLC 1998–, Teletext Holdings Ltd 2000–; Chair. Editors' Code of Practice Cttee 2008–; mem. Press Complaints Comm. 1998–2008. *Address:* Daily Mail, Northcliffe House, 2 Derry Street, London, W8 5TT, England (office). *Telephone:* (20) 7938-6000 (office). *Fax:* (20) 7937-7977 (office). *E-mail:* news@dailymail.co.uk (office). *Website:* www.dailymail.co.uk (office).

DADAE, Bob; Papua New Guinea politician; *Minister of Defence;* fmr Deputy Speaker of Parl.; Minister of Defence 2007–; MP for Kabwum; Leader, United Party 2007–. *Address:* Department of Defence, Murray Barracks, Free Mail Bag, Boroko 111, National Capital District, Papua New Guinea (office). *Telephone:* 3242480 (office). *Fax:* 3256117 (office). *Website:* www.defence.gov .pg (office).

DAFA, Bader Omar ad-, MA; Qatari UN official and diplomatist; *Executive Secretary, United Nations Economic and Social Commission for Western Asia (ESCWA);* b. 2 Oct. 1950; m. Awatef Mohamed Al-Dafa; one s. two d.; ed Kalamazoo Community Coll., Western Michigan Univ., School of Advanced Int. Studies, Johns Hopkins Univ., USA; diplomatic attaché, Ministry of Foreign Affairs 1976–77, 1981–82; First Sec., Qatar Embassy, Washington, DC 1977–81; Amb. to Spain 1982–88, to Egypt (also Perm. Rep. to Arab League) 1988–93, to France (also accred to Greece and Switzerland) 1993–95, to Russia (also accred to Finland, Latvia, Lithuania and Estonia) 1995–98; Dir of European and American Affairs, Ministry of Foreign Affairs 1998–2000; Amb. to USA and Perm. Observer to OAS 2000–05, non-resident Amb. . to Mexico 2002–07; Exec. Sec. UN Econ. and Social Comm. for Western Asia (ESCWA) 2007–; Ordre nat. du Mérite. *Leisure interests:* reading, painting, music. *Address:* Economic and Social Commission for Western Asia, Riad es-Solh Square, PO Box 11-8575, Beirut, Lebanon (office). *Telephone:* (1) 981301 (office). *Fax:* (1) 981510 (office). *E-mail:* webmaster-escwa@un.org (office). *Website:* www.escwa.org.lb (office); al-dafa.com/bader (office).

DAFFA, Ali Abdullah ad-, BS, MS, PhD; Saudi Arabian mathematician and academic; *Professor, King Fahd University;* b. 1940, Unaizah; m.; four c.; ed Stephen F. Austin State Univ., East Texas State Univ., Vanderbilt Univ.; Asst Prof. of Math., King Fahd Univ. of Petroleum and Minerals, Dhahran 1973–74, Chair. Dept of Math. 1974–77, Dean Coll. of Sciences 1977–84, Prof. of Math. and History of Pure Science 1980–; Visiting Prof., King Saud Univ., Riyadh 1979–82, Harvard Univ. 1981, Princeton Univ.; Pres. Union of Arab Mathematicians and Physicists 1974–81, 1986–88, Supreme Council of Union of Arab Physicists and Mathematicians; mem. editorial Bd Encyclopedia of Islamic Civilization; mem. Int. Comm. on the History Science, Nat. Library Bd, Islamic Foundation for Science, Tech. and Devt, Bd of King Faisal for Islamic Research, Asscn of Muslim Scientist and Engineers, Asscn of Arab Scientists, The Arabic Acad. (Jordan), Islamic World Acad. of Science, Arabic Scientific Soc., American Math. Soc., British Soc. for History of Science; Hon. mem. Acad. of Arabic Language. *Publications:* 36 books and more than 250 articles on math. and history of science. *Address:* King Fahd University of Petroleum and Minerals, Dhahran 31261, Saudi Arabia (office). *Telephone:* (3) 860-0000 (office). *Fax:* (3) 860-3306 (office). *E-mail:* rector@kfupm.edu.sa (office). *Website:* www.kfupm.edu.sa (office).

DAFOE, Willem; American actor; b. 22 July 1955, Appleton, Wis.; s. of William Dafoe; ed Univ. of Wisconsin; Lifetime Achievement Award, San Sebastian Film Festival 2005. *Films include:* The Loveless 1981, New York Nights 1981, The Hunger 1982, Communists are Comfortable (and three other stories) 1984, Roadhouse 66 1984, Streets of Fire 1984, To Live and Die in LA 1985, Platoon 1986, The Last Temptation of Christ 1988, Saigon 1988, Mississippi Burning 1989, Triumph of the Spirit 1989, Born on the 4th of July 1990, Flight of the Intruder 1990, Wild at Heart 1990, The Light Sleeper 1991, Body of Evidence 1992, Far Away, So Close 1994, Tom and Viv 1994, The Night and the Moment 1994, Clear and Present Danger 1994, The English Patient 1996, Basquiat 1996, Speed 2: Cruise Control 1997, Affliction 1997, Lulu on the Bridge 1998, eXistenZ 1998, American Psycho 1999, Shadow of the Vampire 2000, Bullfighter 2000, The Animal Factory 2000, Edges of the Lord 2001, Spider-Man 2002, Auto Focus 2002, Once Upon a Time in Mexico 2003, The Clearing 2004, The Reckoning 2004, The Life Aquatic with Steve Zissou 2004, The Aviator 2004, xXx: State of the Union 2005, Ripley Under Ground 2005, Manderlay 2005, Inside Man 2006, American Dreamz 2006, Paris, je t'aime 2006, The Walker 2007, Mr. Bean's Holiday 2007, Spider-Man 3 2007, Go Go Tales 2007, Anamorph 2007, Fireflies in the Garden 2008, Adam Resurrected 2008, I skoni tou hronou 2008, Farewell 2009. *Address:* c/o Widescreen Management, 270 Lafayette Street, Suite 402, New York, NY 10012; c/o Endeavor Agency, LLC, 9601 Wilshire Blvd., 3rd Floor, Beverly Hills, CA 90210, USA.

DAFT, Douglas (Doug) N.; Australian business executive; b. 1944; joined Coca-Cola Co., Australia 1969, Pres. Cen. Pacific Div. 1984, N Pacific Div. 1988, Pres. Coca-Cola (Japan) Co. 1988, Pres. Pacific Group, Atlanta 1991, Head of Middle and Far East and Africa Groups, Head of Schweppes Div. 1999, Chair. and CEO 2000–04 (retd); mem. Bd of Dirs McGraw-Hill Ryerson Ltd 2003–, Wal-Mart Stores Inc. 2005–, Sistema-Hals; Chair. Advisory Bd Churchill Archives Center, Churchill Coll., Cambridge; mem. Advisory Bd Longreach, Inc., Tisbury Capital, Thomas H. Lee Partners; mem. European Advisory Council N.M. Rothschild & Sons Ltd; mem. Bd of Overseers Int. Business School, Brandeis Univ.; Patron American Australian Asscn; Trustee, Thunderbird School of Global Man., Cambridge Foundation. *Address:* c/o Board of Directors, Wal-Mart Stores Inc.,702 Southwest 8th Street, Bentonville, AR 72716, USA (office).

DAGAN, Maj.-Gen. (retd) Meir; Israeli army officer (retd) and government official; *Director, Mossad (Institute for Intelligence and Special Operations);* b. (Meir Huberman), 1945, USSR; m.; three c.; family emigrated to Israel 1950; army officer, Head of Rimon undercover unit, Gaza Strip, early 1970s, mem. 143 Div., Yom Kippur War 1973, Commdr in S Lebanon 1982, Special Asst to Army Chief of Staff 1987–93, retd from army 1995; joined Mossad (Inst. for Intelligence and Special Operations) 1995, Deputy Dir 1995–97, Counter-Terrorism Adviser to Prime Minister 1997–2000, Head of Israeli negotiating team Nov. 2001, Dir Mossad 2002–; several citations for bravery during army service. *Address:* Mossad, c/o Ministry of Defence, Kaplan Street, Hakirya, Tel-Aviv 67659, Israel. *Website:* www.mossad.gov.il.

DAGHESTANI, Fakhruddin, PhD; Jordanian civil servant and engineer; b. 1936; m.; six c.; ed Univ. of Missouri, USA; Lecturer, Coll. of Eng, Univ. of Missouri 1961–67; Lecturer, IBM Rochester, Minn. 1968–71; Dir Mechanical Eng Dept, Royal Scientific Soc. 1971–76, Vice-Pres. 1976–83, Acting Pres. 1983–84, Pres. 1984–86, Adviser and Prin. Researcher 1986–91, Dir Centre for Int. Studies 1991–93, currently mem. Bd of Govs; Dir Gen. Natural Resources Authority 1993–96, Mineral Investment Co. 1996–; mem. Scientific Council Islamic Foundation for Science, Tech. and Devt 1984–86; mem. Exec. Cttee Org. of the Islamic Conf. Standing Cttee on Scientific and Technological Co-operation (COMSTECH) 1986–94; mem. Arab Fed. of Scientific Research 1983–86; Founding Fellow, Islamic Acad. of Sciences, mem. Council 1986–99; mem. Bd of Govs Telecommunications Corpn, Natural Resources Authority, Jordan Electricity Authority, Arab Potash Co., Nat. Petroleum Co., Jordan Phosphate Mining Co.; mem. Bd Faculties of Grad. Studies and Scientific Research, Jordan Univ.; mem. Editorial Bd Journal of the Islamic Academy of Sciences; fmr mem. Editorial Bd Islamic Thought and Scientific Creativity (journal) 1990–95. *Publications:* ed. and co-ed. of 11 books, author of over 40 technical papers on applied mechanics. *Address:* c/o Royal Scientific Society, PO Box 1438, Al-Jubaiha 11941; PO Box 419, Al-Jubaiha 11941, Jordan (office).

DAGWORTHY PREW, Wendy Ann, BA; British fashion designer and academic; *Head, School of Fashion and Textiles, Royal College of Art;* b. (Wendy Ann Dagworthy), 4 March 1950, Gravesend; d. of Arthur S. Dagworthy and Jean A. Stubbs; m. Jonathan W. Prew 1973; two s.; ed Medway Coll. of Design and Hornsey Coll. of Art; founder, designer and Dir Wendy Dagworthy Ltd (design co.) 1972–; Dir London Designer Collections 1982; consultant to CNAA Fashion/Textiles Bd 1982–; Course Dir Fashion BA Hons Degree, Cen. St Martin's Coll. of Art and Design 1989–, Prof. of Fashion 1998–; Prof. of Fashion and Head of School of Fashion and Textiles, Royal Coll. of Art 1998–; Judge, Royal Soc. of Arts Bd; judge of art and design projects for various mfrs; participating designer in Fashion Aid and many charity shows; exhibited seasonally in London, Milan, New York and Paris; Lecturer and External Assessor at numerous polytechnics and colls of art and design; frequent TV appearances; Hon. Fellow, Kent Inst. of Design, Univ. of the Creative Arts 2005; Fil d'Or Int. Linen Award 1986. *Leisure interests:* dining out, cooking, reading, painting, drawing. *Address:* Royal College of Art, Kensington Gore, London SW7 3EU (office); 18 Melrose Terrace, London, W6, England (home). *Telephone:* (20) 7590-4444 (office); (20) 7602-6676 (home). *Fax:* (20) 7590-4360 (office). *E-mail:* w.dagworthy@rca.ac.uk (office). *Website:* www.rca.ac.uk (office).

DAHABI, Nader al-, MSc, MPA; Jordanian politician; *Prime Minister and Minister of Defence;* b. 1946, Amman; m.; two s. one d.; ed Al Hussein Coll., Amman, Hellenic Air Force Acad., Tatoi, Greece, Cranfield Inst. of Tech., UK, Auburn Univ., USA; cadet in Royal Jordanian Air Force 1964, served 30 years becoming Asst Commdr for Logistics 1992–94; CEO Royal Jordanian Airlines 1994–2001; Minister of Transport 2001–03; Chief Commr Aqaba Special Econ. Zone Authority 2004–07; Prime Minister and Minister of Defence 2007–; mem. Exec. Cttee Arab Air Carriers Org. (AACO), Chair. 1994–95; Chair. Royal Jordanian Air Falcons 1994–; Dir Royal Jordanian Acad.; mem. Higher Cttee Jerash Festival for Culture and Arts; mem. Higher Council of Tourism; Pres. IATA 1996–97, mem. Bd of Govs 1995–98. *Address:* Office of the Prime Minister, POB 80, Amman 11180, Jordan (office). *Telephone:* (6) 4641211 (office). *Fax:* (6) 5695541 (office). *E-mail:* info@pm.gov.jo (office). *Website:* www.pm.gov.jo (office).

DAHAL, Pushpa Kamal, (Prachanda); Nepalese politician and fmr guerrilla leader; Gen. Sec. Communist Party of Nepal (Maoist) 1989–2001, Chair. 2001–, leader of Maoist insurgency –2006, negotiated with seven-party alliance, signed comprehensive peace agreement with Govt Nov. 2006, Communist Party of Nepal (Maoist) entered Parl. and Govt 2007; Prime Minister 2008–09 (resgnd). *Address:* c/o Prime Minister's Office, Singha Durbar, POB 43312, Kathmandu, Nepal (office).

DAHAN, René; Dutch business executive; *Chairman of the Supervisory Board, Royal Ahold NV;* b. 26 Aug. 1941; began career as process technician in refinery, Exxon Corpn, Rotterdam 1963, Man. Supply and Planning Dept, Esso Nederland 1973–74, Man. Refining Dept 1974–77, Head Corp. Planning Div., Esso Europe, London 1977–79, Man. Natural Gas Dept 1979-81, Deputy Man. Petroleum Products Dept, Exxon Corpn HQ, USA 1981–83, Exec. Vice-Pres. Esso BV, Breda 1983–85, Pres. and CEO Esso BV 1985–91, Exec. Vice-Pres. ECI 1991–92, Vice-Pres. Exxon Corpn 1992–95, Sr Vice-Pres. 1995–2001, Dir 1998–2001, Exec. Vice-Pres. Exxon Mobil Corpn 2001–04; Chair. Supervisory Bd Royal Ahold NV 2004–, Chair. Selection and Appointment Cttees; mem. Supervisory Bd VNU NV, TPG NV 2003–, Aegon NV; mem. Int. Advisory Bd, CVC Capital Partners, Inst. de Empresa; mem. Bd Dirs, Jr Achievement Int.; mem. Bd Trustees, US Council for Int. Business. *Address:* Royal Ahold NV, Albert Hijnweg 1, 1507 EH Zaandam, The Netherlands (office). *Telephone:* (75) 659-9111 (office). *Fax:* (75) 659-8350 (office). *E-mail:* info@ahold.com (office). *Website:* www.ahold.com (office).

DAHL, Birgitta, BA; Swedish politician; b. 20 Sept. 1937, Råda; d. of Sven Dahl and Anna-Brita Axelsson; m. Enn Kokk; one s. two d.; ed Univ. of Uppsala; teacher, clerical officer, Scandinavian Inst. of African Studies, Uppsala 1960–65; Sr Admin. Officer, Dag Hammarskjöld Foundation 1965–68, Swedish Int. Devt Authority 1965–82; mem. Parl. 1968–2002; mem. Advisory Council of Foreign Affairs; del. to UN Gen. Ass.; mem. Exec. Cttee Social Democratic Party 1975–96; Minister with special responsibility for Energy Issues, Ministry of Energy 1982–86, for the Environment and Energy 1987–90, for the Environment 1990–91; Spokesperson on Social Welfare; Chair. Environment Cttee of Socialist Int. 1986–93, Confed. of Socialist Parties of EC 1990–94, Chair. High Level Advisory Bd on Sustainable Devt to Sec.-Gen. 1996–97; Speaker of Riksdag (Swedish Parl.) 1994–2002; Chair. Bd Swedish Coral Asscn 2002–05, Nat. Museum of Cultural History, Centre for Gender Research, Uppsala Univ.; Pres. UNICEF Sweden World Infections Foundation; Sr Adviser Global Environment Facility 1998–; mem. Panel of Eminent Persons on United Nations-Civil Society; mem. Bd Stockholm Environment Inst., Int. Inst. for Industrial Environment Econs, Lund Univ.; fmr mem. Bd of Dirs Nat. Housing Bd; Gran Condecoración de Honor del Senado (Chile) 2000, Grand Cross Order of the White Rose (Finland) 2002; Cross of Terra Mariana (Estonia) 2002, Das Grosse Goldene Ehrenzeichens am Bande für Verdienste (Austria) 2002, Illis Quorum Meruere Labores (Sweden) 2003, Medal of Merit (Algeria) 2006. *Publications:* contrib. numerous articles and chapters to magazines and books on democracy and human rights, peace and int. cooperation, sexual equality, children's rights, education and science, the environment and sustainable devt. *Address:* Idrottsgatan 12, 753 35 Uppsala, Sweden (home). *Telephone:* (18) 211793 (home). *Fax:* (18) 211793 (home). *E-mail:* 34dahl@telia.com (home).

DAHL, Lawrence F., BS, PhD; American chemist and academic; *Professor Emeritus, Department of Chemistry, University of Wisconsin;* b. 1929; ed Univ. of Louisville, Iowa State Univ.; R.E. Rundle Prof. of Chemistry, Univ. of Wisconsin 1978–, Hilldale Chair Prof. 1991, now Prof.; Emer. fmr Visiting Lecturer, Technische Universität, Munich, Germany 1965, Univ. of Louisville 1969, Univ. of Notre Dame 1987, Univ. of Illinois 1990, Texas A & M Univ. 1996, Bristol Univ., England 1997, Tulane Univ. 1998; mem. NAS 1988–; Guggenheim Fellow 1969-70; Fellow, NY Acad. of Sciences, 1975–, AAAS 1980–, American Acad. of Arts and Sciences 1992–; Hon. DSc (Univ. of Louisville) 1991; ACS Award in Inorganic Chemistry 1974, Alexander von-Humboldt-Stiftung Sr US Scientist Humboldt Award 1985, Hilldale Award in the Physical Sciences, Univ. of Wisconsin 1994, Amoco Distinguished Lecturer, Ind. Univ. 1996, ACS Willard Gibbs Medal 1999, American Inst. of Chemists Pioneer Award 2000. *Address:* University of Wisconsin, Department of Chemistry, Room 6375a, Chemistry Building, 1101 University Avenue, Madison, WI 53706, USA (office). *Telephone:* (608) 262-5859 (office). *Fax:* (608) 262-6143 (office). *E-mail:* dahl@chem.wisc.edu (office). *Website:* www.chem.wisc.edu (office).

DAHL, Robert Alan, PhD; American academic and political scientist; *Sterling Professor Emeritus of Political Science, Yale University;* b. 17 Dec. 1915, Inwood, Ia; s. of Peter I. Dahl and Vera Lewis Dahl; m. 1st Mary Louise Barlett 1940 (died 1970); three s. one d.; m. 2nd Ann Goodrich Sale 1973; ed Univ. of Washington, Div. of Econ. Research, Nat. Labor Relations Bd and Yale Univ.; Man. Analyst, US Dept of Agric. 1940; Economist, Office of Production Man., OPACS and War Production Bd 1940–42; US Army 1943–45; with Yale Univ., successively Instructor, Asst Prof., Assoc. Prof. and Sterling Prof. of Political Science 1964–86, Sterling Prof. Emer. of Political Science 1986–, fmr Sr Research Scientist in Sociology; Chair. Dept of Political Science 1957–62; Ford Research Prof. 1957; Lecturer in Political Science, Flacso, Santiago, Chile 1967; Guggenheim Fellow 1950 and 1978; Fellow, Center for Advanced Study in the Behavioral Sciences 1955–56, 1967; Pres. American Political Science Asscn 1967; mem. American Acad. of Arts and Sciences, American Philosophical Soc., NAS; Corresp. mem. British Acad.; fmr Trustee, Center for Advanced Study in the Behavioral Sciences; fmr mem. Educ. Advisory Bd, Guggenheim Foundation; Bronze Star Medal with Cluster, Cavaliere of Repub. of Italy; Hon. LLD (Mich.) 1983, (Alaska) 1987, (Harvard) 1996; Hon. DHumLitt (Georgetown) 1993; Woodrow Wilson Prize 1963, Talcott Parsons Prize 1977 and other prizes. *Publications:* Congress and Foreign Policy 1950, Domestic Control of Atomic Energy (with R. Brown) 1951, Politics, Economics and Welfare (with C. E. Lindblom) 1953, A Preface to Democratic Theory 1956, Social Science Research on Business (with Haire and Lazarsfeld) 1959, Who Governs? 1961, Modern Political Analysis 1963, Political Oppositions in Western Democracies 1966, Pluralist Democracy in the United States 1967, After the Revolution 1970, Polyarchy: Participation and Opposition 1971, Regimes and Opposition 1972, Democracy in the United States 1972, Size and Democracy (with E. R. Tufte) 1973, Dilemmas of Pluralist Democracy 1982, A Preface to Economic Democracy 1985, The Control of Nuclear Weapons: Democracy v. Guardianship 1985,

Democracy, Liberty and Equality 1986, Democracy and the Critics 1989, Towards Democracy: A Journey 1997, Reflections (1940–1997) 1997, On Democracy 1999, Politica e Virtú 2001: La teoria democratica de nuovo secolo, How Democratic is the American Constitution? 2002, Intervista sul Pluralismo 2002. *Leisure interests:* tennis, sailing, fly-fishing. *Address:* 124 Prospect Street, Room 209, Yale University, North Haven, CT 06520 (office); 17 Cooper Road, North Haven, CT 06473, USA (home). *Telephone:* (203) 432-5283 (office); (203) 288-3126 (home). *Fax:* (203) 432-6196 (home). *E-mail:* robert.dahl@yale.edu (office). *Website:* www.yale.edu/polisci/dahl/index.htm (office).

DAHL, Sophie; British writer and model; b. 1978, granddaughter of Patricia Neal (q.v.) and the late Roald Dahl; discovered as a model by Isabella Blow who saw her crying in the street; has worked with fashion photographers Nick Knight, David La Chapelle, Karl Lagerfeld, David Bailey, Enrique Badulescu, Herb Ritts and Ellen Von Unwerth; has appeared in ID, The Face, Arena, Elle, Esquire, Scene magazines and advertising campaigns for Lainey Keogh, Bella Freud, Printemps, Nina Ricci, Karl Lagerfeld, Oil of Ulay, Hennes; music videos for U2, Elton John and Duran Duran; contribs to The Daily Telegraph, The Sunday Times, Tatler, Men's Vogue, American Vogue, The Spectator, and Elle magazine; cameo appearance in films Mad Cows and Best 1999; stage appearance in The Vagina Monologues, The Old Vic 1999; judge Orange Prize for Fiction 2003. *Publications:* The Man with the Dancing Eyes (novella) 2003, Playing with the Grown Ups 2007. *Address:* Ed Victor Ltd., 6 Bayley Street, Bedford Square, London, WC1B 3HE, England (office). *Telephone:* (20) 7304-4100 (office). *Fax:* (20) 7304-4111 (office). *E-mail:* sophie@edvictor.com (office).

DAHLAN, Mohammed, BA; Palestinian politician; b. 1961, Gaza; m.; three c.; ed Islamic Univ. of Gaza; brought up in refugee camp in Gaza after fleeing 1948 war; grassroots organizer of Youth Br. of Fatah; arrested for subversive pro-Palestinian activities (ten times) 1981–86, deported to Jordan during intifada 1987; mem. Palestinian Liberation Org. (PLO) 1988–; involved in secret negotiations with Israel, leading to Oslo Peace Accords and creation of Palestinian Authority (PA) 1993–94; apptd Head of PA Preventative Security Force by Yasser Arafat 1994, resgnd June 2002; Minister of State for Security Affairs, PA April–Oct. 2003; visited UK to study English, returned to Gaza June 2004; Minister for Civil Affairs 2005–06; Nat. Security Adviser to Pres. Abbas 2006–07; mem. Fatah Party. *Address:* c/o Fatah, Ramallah, Palestinian Autonomous Areas. *E-mail:* fateh@fateh.org. *Website:* www.fateh.net.

DAHLBÄCK, Claes, MSc (Econs); Swedish business executive; *Chairman, Stora Enso Oyj;* b. 1947; Pres. and CEO Investor AB 1978–99, Exec. Vice-Chair. 1999–2001, Chair. 2002–05; Dir Stora 1990–98, Chair. 1997–98, Chair. Stora Enso Oyj (following merger of Stora and Enso 1998) 1998–; Vice-Chair. Skandinaviska Enskilda Banken 1997–2002; also Chair. Vin & Spirit AB, Gambro AB, EQT Funds; Dir (non-exec.) Goldman Sachs, USA; mem. Bd Dirs ABB, Zürich, Switzerland 1991–96, Ericsson 1993–96; Hon. PhD. *Address:* Stora Enso Oyj, Kanavaranta 1, PO Box 309, 00101 Helsinki, Finland (office). *Telephone:* 2046-131 (home). *Fax:* 2046-21471 (office). *E-mail:* info@storaenso .com (office). *Website:* www.storaenso.com (office).

DAHLFORS, John Ragnar, MCE; Swedish civil engineer; *Management Consultant, JD Management AB;* b. 31 Dec. 1934, Stockholm; s. of Mats Dahlfors and Astrid Dahlfors; m. 1st Anita Roger 1962 (divorced); one s. two d.; m. 2nd Ing-Britt Schlyter 1998; ed Royal Inst. of Tech., Stockholm; engineer with Gränges AB Liberia project 1962–66, Sales Man. Gränges Hedlund AB 1967–68, Pres. 1970–74, Tech. Man. Gränges Construction AB 1969, Pres. Gränges Aluminium AB 1974–78; Pres. Boliden AB 1978–86; fmr man. consultant Sevenco, currently consultant JD Management AB; mem. Bd, ABA of Sweden, Perten Instruments, Vemdalsfjäll; mem. Swedish Acad. of Eng Sciences. *Leisure interests:* sailing, golf, tennis, hunting. *Address:* Karlaplan 12, 115 20 Stockholm, Sweden (home). *Telephone:* (8) 66-02-404 (office); (8) 66-02-404 (home). *Fax:* (8) 66-02-404 (home). *E-mail:* john .dahlfors@telia.com (home).

DAHLIE, Bjorn; Norwegian fmr Olympic skier; b. 19 June 1967; pnr Vilde; two s.; winner of a record total of 29 medals (gold, silver and bronze) 1991–99, including eight Gold Olympic medals; Hon. Pres. Cross Country World Championships 2005; retd 2001; introduced Nordic skiwear collection 1996; majority stockholder Bj Sport AS. *Publication:* Gulljakten (autobiog.). *Leisure interest:* hunting. *Address:* Bj Sport AS, Adminbygget Hellerudsletta, 2013 Skjetten, Norway (office). *Telephone:* 45-28-03-33 (office). *Fax:* 63-84-16-70 (office). *E-mail:* info@bjsport.no (office). *Website:* www.bjorn-daehlie.com (office).

DAHLLÖF, Urban Sigurd, FilD; Swedish academic; *Professor Emeritus of Education, University of Uppsala;* b. 11 Nov. 1928, Göteborg; s. of Sigurd Dahllöf and Karin Hansson; m. Tordis Larsson 1950; two s. one d.; ed Uppsala Univ. and Univ. of Stockholm; Research Asst, Stockholm School of Educ. 1956–60, Asst Prof. 1963–66; Asst Prof., Univ. of Göteborg 1960–62, Assoc. Prof. 1966–72, Prof. of Educ. 1972–76; Prof. of Educ., Uppsala Univ. 1976–93; Project Leader (part-time) Mid-Sweden Univ. Coll. 1991–96; Research Dir (part-time) Univ. of Trondheim 1991–96; Adjunct Prof., Møre Research/Volda Coll., Volda, Norway 1994–99; Head of Bureau, Nat. Bd of Educ., Stockholm 1962–63, Office of the Swedish Chancellor of the Univs, Stockholm 1973–75; Visiting Prof., Univ. of Melbourne, Australia 1984; Sr Consultant, Interior Univ. Soc., Prince George, BC 1988; Chair. Study Group on Evaluation in Higher Educ., OECD, Paris 1988–90; Chair. Swedish School Research Cttee 1978–80, Swedish Secondary School Planning Cttee 1979–81; Pres. Swedish Psychological Asscn 1966–68; mem. Swedish Royal Acad. of Sciences, Swedish Acad. of Letters, History and Antiquities; Hon. Rector Mid-Sweden Univ. Coll. 1997; Hon. mem. Swedish Psychological Asscn; Sidney Suslow Award for Outstanding Research, Asscn for Int. Research 1989. *Publications include:* Demands on the Secondary School 1963, Ability Grouping, Content Validity and Curriculum Process Analysis 1971, Reforming Higher Education and External Studies in Sweden and Australia 1977, Regional Universities in a Comparative Western Perspective 1988, Dimensions of Evaluation in Higher Education (jtly) 1991, New Universities and Regional Context (jtly) 1994, Expanding Colleges and New Universities (jtly) 1996, Towards the Responsive University (jtly) 1998, Tertiary Education and Regional Development in Cross-National Perspective 1999, Municipal Study Centres for Higher Education in Sweden (jtly) 2000. *Leisure interest:* train timetables. *Address:* Department of Education, Box 2109, 750 02 Uppsala (office); Östra Ågatan 17, 753 22 Uppsala, Sweden (home). *Telephone:* (18) 471-16-68 (office); (18) 14-16-94 (home). *Fax:* (18) 471-16-51 (office). *E-mail:* urban.dahllof@ped.uu.se (office).

DAHRENDORF, Baron (Life Peer), cr. 1993, of Clare Market in the City of Westminster; **Ralf (Gustav) Dahrendorf,** KBE, FBA, DPhil, PhD; British (b. German) sociologist, politician, university administrator and writer; *Chairman, Delegated Powers Select Committee, House of Lords;* b. 1 May 1929, Hamburg; s. of Gustav Dahrendorf and Lina Witt; ed Hamburg Univ. and London School of Econs; active in anti-Nazi resistance during Second World War; Asst, Univ. of Saar, Saarbrücken 1954, Privatdozent in sociology 1957; Fellow, Center for Advanced Study in the Behavioral Sciences, Palo Alto, USA 1957–58; Prof. of Sociology, Hamburg 1958, Tübingen 1960, Konstanz 1966 (on leave since 1969); Visiting Prof. at several European and US Univs; Vice-Chair. Founding Cttee Univ. of Konstanz 1964–66, First Dean Faculty of Social Science 1966–67; Adviser on educational questions to the Land Govt of Baden-Württemberg 1964–68; mem. German Council of Educ. 1966–68; Chair. Comm. on Comprehensive Univ. Planning 1967–68; mem. Free Democratic Party (FDP) 1967, Fed. Exec. 1968–74; mem. Land Diet of Baden-Württemberg and Vice-Chair. FDP Parl. Party 1968–70; mem. Fed. Parl. (Bundestag) and Parl. Sec. of State in Foreign Office 1969–70; mem. Comm. of the European Communities 1970–74; Chair. Royal Univ. of Malta Comm. 1972–74; mem. Hansard Soc. Comm. for Electoral Reform 1975–76, Royal Comm. on Legal Services 1976–78, Cttee to Review the Functioning of Financial Insts 1977–80; Dir European Centre for Research and Documentation in Social Sciences 1966–82, LSE 1974–84; BBC Reith Lecturer 1974; Chair. OECD High-Level Group on Labour Market Flexibility 1985–86; Visiting Scholar, Russell Sage Foundation, New York 1986–87; Warden, St Antony's Coll. Oxford 1987–97; Pro-Vice-Chancellor Univ. of Oxford 1991–97; Chair. OECD Comm. on Wealth Creation and Social Cohesion 1994–95; Chair. Delegated Powers Select Cttee 2002–; Pres. German Sociological Soc. 1967–70; Hon. Presidium Anglo-German Soc. 1973–; Chair. Social Science Council of the European Science Foundation 1976–77, Newspaper Publishing 1992–93; Trustee Ford Foundation 1976–88; Chair. Bd Friedrich-Naumann-Stiftung 1982–87; Dir (non-exec.) Bankges. Berlin (UK) PLC 1996–2001; fmr mem. of advisory boards of Volvo, Honeywell, St. Gobain; mem. Council, British Acad. 1980–81, Vice-Pres. 1983–85; mem. German PEN Centre 1971–; Foreign Assoc., NAS 1977; Foreign mem. American Philosophical Soc., Phila 1977; Fellow, Imperial Coll., London 1974, Royal Soc. of Arts 1977, British Acad. 1977; mem. Académie des Sciences Morales, Polish Acad. of Sciences, Russian Acad. of Sciences; Hon. mem. Royal Irish Acad. 1974; Foreign Hon. mem. American Acad. of Arts and Sciences 1975, Hon. mem. Royal Coll. of Surgeons 1982; Hon. Fellow, LSE 1973; Hon. DLitt (Reading) 1973, (Malta) 1992, Hon. DSc (Ulster) 1973, (Bath) 1977, Hon. DUniv (Open Univ.) 1974, (Surrey) 1978, Hon. DHL (Kalamazoo Coll.) 1974, (Maryland) 1978, (Johns Hopkins Univ.) 1982, Hon. LittD (Trinity Coll., Dublin) 1975, Hon. Dr (Univ. Catholique de Louvain) 1977, (Univ. of Buenos Aires) 1993, Hon. LLD (Wagner Coll., Staten Island, New York, Columbia Univ., NY, York, Ontario Univs, Westminster, UK, Manchester, UK) Dr Social Sc. (Queen's Belfast), (Birmingham); Hon. DPolSci (Bologna) 1991; Dr hc (Urbino) 1993, (Univ. René Descartes) 1994; Hon. PhD (Univ. of Haifa) 1994; mem. German Order Pour le Mérite, Grand-Croix de l'Ordre du Mérite du Sénégal 1971, Grand-Croix de l'Ordre du Mérite du Luxembourg 1974, Grosses Bundesverdienstkreuz mit Stern und Schulterband (FRG) 1974, Grosses goldenes Ehrenzeichen am Bande (Austria) 1975, Grand-Croix de l'Ordre de Léopold II (Belgium) 1975, Knight Grand Cross Order of the Italian Repub.; Agnelli Prize 1992, Toynbee Prize 1990, Journal Fund Award for Learned Publications 1966, Theodor Heuss Prize 1997, Garrigues Walker Prize 1998, Goethe Medal 1998, Prince of Asturias Award 2007. *Publications include:* Marx in Perspective 1953, Industrie- und Betriebssoziologie 1956, Homo Sociologicus 1958, Soziale Klassen und Klassenkonflikt 1957 and 1959, Die angewandte Aufklärung 1963, Gesellschaft und Demokratie in Deutschland 1967, Pfade aus Utopia 1967, Essays in the Theory of Society 1968, Konflikt und Freiheit 1972, Plädoyer für die Europäische Union 1973, The New Liberty: Survival and Justice in a Changing World (Reith Lectures) 1975, A New World Order? (Ghana Lectures 1978) 1979, Life Chances (also in German) 1978, On Britain (BBC TV Lectures) 1982/83, Reisen nach innen und aussen 1984, Law and Order 1985, The Modern Social Conflict 1988 (revised edn 2008), Reflections on the Revolution in Europe 1990, History of the London School of Economics and Political Science 1895–1995 1995, Liberale und Andere: Portraits 1995, After 1989: Morals, Revolution and Civil Society 1997, Liberal und Unabhängig, Gerd Bucerius und Seine Zeit 2000, Universities After Communism 2000, Über Grenzen 2002, Auf der Suche nach einer neuen Ordnung 2003, Der Wiederbeginn der Geschichte 2004, Versuchungen der Unfreiheit 2006. *Address:* House of Lords, London, SW1A 0PW, England (office). *Telephone:* (20) 8930-8982 (office). *Fax:* (20) 857-5080 (office). *E-mail:* edith .emmenegger@arcor.de (office).

DAI, Bingguo; Chinese politician and diplomatist; *Member, State Council;* b. 1941, Yinjiang Co., Guizhou Prov.; ed Foreign Affairs Coll., Sichuan Univ.; joined CCP 1973; Deputy Div. Chief, later Div. Chief, Dept of USSR and

Eastern European Affairs, Ministry of Foreign Affairs 1973–85, Deputy Dir 1985–86, Dir 1986–89, Amb. to Hungary 1989–91, Asst Minister of Foreign Affairs 1991–93, Deputy Minister of Foreign Affairs 1993–95, 2003–07; Deputy Head Int. Liaison Dept of CCP Cen. Cttee 1995–97, Head 1997–2003; mem. 15th CCP Cen. Cttee 1997–2002, 16th CCP Cen. Cttee 2002–07, 17th CCP Cen. Cttee 2007–; mem. State Council 2008–. *Address:* State Council, Beijing, People's Republic of China (home).

DAI, Hongjie, MS, PhD; American (b. Chinese) chemist and academic; *J.G. Jackson and C.J. Wood Professor in Chemistry, Stanford University;* b. 1966; ed Tsing Hua Univ., People's Repub. of China, Columbia Univ., Harvard Univ.; Postdoctoral Fellow, Harvard Univ. 1995–97; Postdoctoral Fellow, Rice Univ. 1997; Terman Fellow, Stanford Univ. 1998, Packard Fellow for Science and Eng 1999, Alfred P. Sloan Research Fellow 2001, Asst Prof. of Chem. 1997–2002, Assoc. Prof. 2002–05, Prof. of Chem. 2005–07, J.G. Jackson and C.J. Wood Prof. in Chem. 2007–; Founder, Molecular Nanosystems Inc. 2001; Changjian Visiting Professorship, Tsinghua Univ. 2005–08; Fellow, American Acad. of Arts and Sciences 2009–; mem. Editorial Bd several journals including Nano Letters, Chemical Physics Letters, International Journal of Nanoscience; Camille Dreyfus Teacher-Scholar Award 2002, ACS Pure Chem. Award 2002, Julius Springer Prize for Applied Physics 2004, American Physical Soc. James McGroddy Prize for New Materials 2006, Ramabrahmam and Balamani Guthikonda Award, Columbia Univ. 2009. *Publications:* more than 150 articles in profesional journals. *Address:* Stanford University, Department of Chemistry, Keck Chemistry Building, Room 125A, Stanford, CA 94305-5080, USA (office). *Telephone:* (650) 725-9156 (office). *Fax:* (650) 725-0259 (office). *E-mail:* hdai1@stanford.edu (office). *Website:* www.stanford .edu/dept/chemistry/faculty/dai/group (office).

DAI, Gen. (retd) Tobias Joaquim; Mozambican politician and fmr army officer; b. 25 Nov. 1950, Manica City; s. of Joaquin Dai and Beatriz Mucudo Dai; m.; two c.; ed João XXII and Pêro de Anaia Secondary Schools; joined Mozambique Armed Forces 1971; instructor and Commdr, Nachingweia 1971–76; Weapons Commdr, Vestrel de Moscovo Mil. Acad., USSR 1976–78; Commdr Mil. Garrison, City of Maputo 1978–80; several sr mil. positions including Vice-Commdt and Head of Mil. House of Pres. of the Repub., Prov. Mil. Commdr in Manica, Head of Directorate of Operations, and Commdr-in-Chief of Armed Forces 1980–95; Sec.-Gen. Ministry of Nat. Defence 1995–2000; Minister of Nat. Defence 2000–08; participated in Peace Negotiations 1993–94; elected to House of Reps 1987–94; mem. Frelimo Party; Veteran of the Struggle for Nat. Independence of Mozambique Medal. *Leisure interests:* sports, reading. *Address:* c/o Ministry of National Defence, Avda Mártires de Mueda 280, CP 3216, Maputo, Mozambique (office).

DAI, Xianglong; Chinese politician, banker and economist; *Chairman, National Council for Social Security Fund;* b. Oct. 1944, Yizheng City, Jiangsu Prov.; ed Cen. Inst. of Finance and Banking; mem. CCP 1973–; Deputy Section Chief, People's Bank of China (PBC), Jiangsu Prov. Br. 1978; Deputy Section Chief and Deputy Head of Dept Agricultural Bank of China (ABC), Jiangsu Br., Vice-Gov. 1983; Sec. CCP Group, Communications Bank of China (CBC), also Gen. Man. and Vice-Chair. Bd CBC 1989; Chair. Bd China Pacific Insurance Co. Ltd 1990–93; Vice-Gov. People's Bank of China 1993–95, Gov. 1995–2003; Alt. mem. 14th CCP Cen. Cttee 1992–97, 15th CCP Cen. Cttee 1997–2002, 16th CCP Cen. Cttee 2002–07, 17th CCP Cen. Cttee 2007–; Acting Mayor Tianjin Municipality 2002–03, Vice-Mayor 2002–03, Mayor 2003–07, Deputy Sec. CCP Municipal Cttee 2003–07; Chair. Nat. Council for Social Security Fund 2007–. *Address:* National Council for Social Security Fund, Mailbox No.2, South Tower, Fortune Time, Building 11, Fenghuiyuan, Xicheng District, Beijing 100032, People's Republic of China (office). *Website:* www.ssf.gov.cn (office).

DAIANU, Daniel, PhD; Romanian economist, academic and politician; b. 30 Aug. 1952, Bucharest; ed Acad. of Econ. Studies, Bucharest, Acad. of Sciences, Bucharest and Harvard Business School, USA; Visiting Scholar, Russian Research Center, Harvard Univ. 1990–92; Deputy Minister of Finance Feb.–Aug. 1992; Chief Economist, Nat. Bank of Romania 1992–97; Minister of Finance 1997–98; currently Prof. of Econs, Acad. of Econ. Studies, Bucharest; Pres. Supervisory Bd Banca Comercială Română 2005–07; mem. European Parl. (Nat. Liberal Party) 2007–; Visiting Scholar, Woodrow Wilson Center, Washington, DC 1992, IMF, Washington, DC 1993, UN/ECE; Visiting Sr Fellow, NATO Defense Coll., Rome 1995; Visiting Prof., Univ. of California, Berkeley 1999, Anderson School of Man., UCLA 2000–02, Univ. of Bologna 2000–02; Fellow, William Davidson Inst., Univ. of Michigan Business School; Chair. Romanian Econ. Soc.; Pres. European Asscn for Comparative Econ. Studies 2002–04, OSCE Econ. Forum 2001; Corresp. mem. Romanian Acad.; Pres. Junior Achievement Romania; mem. Aspen Inst. Romania; Hon. Pres. Romanian Acad. of European Studies; Acad. of Sciences Highest Award for Econs 1994. *Publications:* Transformation of Economies as a Real Process – An Insider's Perspective 1998, Economic Vitality and Viability – A Dual Challenge for European Security 1996, Romania—Winners and Losers: The Impact of Reform of Intergovernmental Transfers (research report, co-author) 1999, Balkan Reconstruction (co-ed.) 2001. *Leisure interests:* reading, football, basketball. *Address:* European Parliament, Bât. Altiero Spinelli, 02F158, 60, rue Wiertz, 1047 Brussels, Belgium (office). *Telephone:* (2) 284-58-91 (office). *Fax:* (2) 284-98-91 (office). *E-mail:* daniel.daianu@europarl.europa.eu (office). *Website:* www.daniel-daianu.eu (office).

DAIBER, Hans Joachim, DPhil, DPhil.habil; German academic; *Professor of Oriental Philology and Islam, University of Frankfurt am Main;* b. 1 April 1942, Stuttgart; s. of Otto Daiber and Martha Daiber; m. Helga Brosamler 1971; one s. one d.; ed Theological Seminaries of Maulbronn and Blaubeuren, Univs of Tübingen and Saarbrücken; Lecturer in Arabic, Univ. of Heidelberg 1975–77; Prof. of Arabic, Free Univ., Amsterdam 1977–95; Prof. of Oriental

Philology and Islam, Univ. of Frankfurt am Main 1995–; Special Visiting Prof., Univ. of Tokyo 1992; Visiting Prof., Int. Inst. of Islamic Thought and Civilization, Kuala Lumpur 2001; mem. Royal Netherlands Acad. of Arts and Sciences, German Oriental Inst., Beirut 1973–75; ed. Aristoteles Semitico-Latinus, Islamic Philosophy, Theology and Science. *Publications:* Die arabische Übersetzung der Placita philosophorum 1968, Ein Kompendium der aristotelischen Meteorologie in der Fassung des Hunain Ibn Ishaq 1975, Das theologisch-philosophische System des Muammar Ibn Abbad as-Sulami 1975, Gott, Natur und menschlicher Wille im frühen islamischen Denken 1978, Aetius Arabus 1980, The Ruler as Philosopher: A New interpretation of al-Farabi's View 1986, Wasil Ibn Ata' als Prediger und Theologe 1988, Catalogue of Arabic Manuscripts in the Daiber Collection (Vol. I) 1988, (Vol. II) 1996, Naturwissenschaft bei den Arabern im 10 Jahrhundert nach Christus 1993, Neuplatonische Pythagorica in arabischem Gewande 1995, The Islamic Concept of Belief in the 4th/10th Century 1995, Bibliography of Islamic Philosophy (two vols) 1999, (Supplement) 2006, The Struggle for Knowledge in Islam: Some Historical Aspects 2004, Islamic Thought in the Dialogue of Cultures. Innovation and mediation between antiquity and Middle Ages 2008; numerous articles in journals on Islamic philosophy, theology, history of sciences, Greek heritage in Islam. *Address:* University of Frankfurt am Main, Department of Oriental Studies, PB 111932, 60054 Frankfurt am Main (office); Am Hüttenhof 10, 40489 Düsseldorf, Germany (home). *Telephone:* (211) 403714 (home); (69) 798-22131 (office). *Fax:* (69) 798-24964 (office); (211) 403725 (home). *E-mail:* daiber@em.uni-frankfurt.de (office). *Website:* www.rz.uni-frankfurt.de/fb9/orientalistik (office).

DAILY, Gretchen C., BS, MS, PhD; American ecologist and academic; *Associate Professor (Research), Department of Biological Sciences, Stanford University;* b. 1964; ed Stanford Univ.; fmrly Bing Interdisciplinary Research Scientist, Dept of Biological Sciences, Stanford Univ., currently Assoc. Prof. (Research), also Sr Fellow, Freeman Spogli Inst. for Int. Studies, Dir Center for Conservation Biology, Dir Interdisciplinary Program in Environment and Resources; Sr Fellow, Woods Inst. for the Environment; Chair. The Natural Capital Project; mem. or fmr mem. Bd of Eds Ecological Applications, Ecological Economics, Ecosystems, Encyclopedia of Biodiversity; Fellow, American Acad. of Arts and Sciences 2003, NAS 2005; Frances Lou Kallman Award for Excellence in Science and Grad. Study 1992, Pew Fellow in Conservation and the Environment 1994, Fellow, Aldo Leopold Leadership Program 1999, 21st Century Scientist Award 2000, Smith Sr Scholar of The Nature Conservancy 2003, Sophie Prize 2008. *Achievements include:* has developed concepts of countryside biogeography, ecosystem services and conservation finance; works extensively with economists, lawyers, business people and govt agencies to incorporate environmental issues into business practice and govt policy. *Publications:* Nature's Services: Societal Dependence on Natural Ecosystems (ed.) 1997, The Stork and the Plow: The Equity Solution to the Human Dilemma (co-author) 1995, The Encyclopedia of Biodiversity (co-ed.) 2001, The New Economy of Nature: The Quest to Make Conservation Profitable (with Katherine Ellison) 2002; more than 150 scientific papers and popular articles. *Address:* Department of Biological Sciences, Stanford University, 371 Serra Mall, Stanford, CA 94305, USA (office). *Telephone:* (650) 723-9452 (office). *Fax:* (650) 725-1992 (office). *E-mail:* gdaily@stanford.edu (office). *Website:* www.stanford.edu/group/CCB/Staff/gretchen.htm (office).

DAINBA, Gyaincan; Chinese government official; b. 1940, Lhasa, Tibet; joined CCP 1964; Mayor of Lhasa Municipality 1980–87. *Address:* Government of Xizang Autonomous Region, Lhasa City, People's Republic of China.

DAINTITH, Terence Charles, MA; British legal scholar; *Professor Emeritus of Law, University of London;* b. 8 May 1942, Coulsdon; s. of Edward Daintith and Irene M. Parsons; m. Christine Bulport 1965; one s. one d.; ed Wimbledon Coll. and St Edmund Hall, Oxford; called to Bar, Lincoln's Inn 1966; Assoc. in Law, Univ. of California Berkeley 1963–64; Lecturer in Constitutional and Admin. Law, Univ. of Edin. 1964–72; Prof. of Public Law, Univ. of Dundee 1972–83, Dir Centre for Petroleum and Mineral Law Studies 1977–83; Prof. of Law, European Univ. Inst., Florence 1981–87; Prof. of Law, Univ. of London 1988–2002, Prof. Emer. 2002–, Dir Inst. of Advanced Legal Studies 1988–95, Dean School of Advanced Study 1994–2001; Prof. of Law, Univ. of Western Australia 2002–; Visiting Prof. of Law, Univ. of Melbourne 2004; Bencher, Lincoln's Inn 2000; Ed. Journal of Energy and Natural Resources Law 1983–92; mem. Academia Europaea (Chair. Law Cttee 1993–96, Social Sciences Section 1996–98); Hon. LLD (De Montfort) 2001. *Publications:* The Economic Law of the United Kingdom 1974, United Kingdom Oil and Gas Law (with G. D. M. Willoughby) 1977, Energy Strategy in Europe (with L. Hancher) 1986, The Legal Integration of Energy Markets (with S. Williams) 1987, Law as an Instrument of Economic Policy 1988, Harmonization and Hazard (with G. R. Baldwin) 1992, Implementation of EC Law in the United Kingdom 1995, The Executive in the Constitution (with A. C. Page) 1999, Discretion in the Administration of Offshore Oil and Gas: A Comparative Study 2006. *Address:* Institute of Advanced Legal Studies, 17 Russell Square, London, WC1B 5DR, England (office); Law School, University of Western Australia, Crawley, WA 6009, Australia (office); 79 rue d'Amsterdam, 75008 Paris, France (home). *Telephone:* (20) 7862-5839 (London) (office). *Fax:* (20) 7862-5850 (London) (office).

DALAI LAMA, The, temporal and spiritual head of Tibet; Fourteenth Incarnation (Tenzin Gyatso); Tibetan; b. 6 July 1935, Taktser, Amdo Prov., NE Tibet; s. of Chujon Tsering and Tsering Dekyi; born of Tibetan peasant family in Amdo Prov.; enthroned at Lhasa 1940; rights exercised by regency 1934–50; assumed political power 1950; fled to Chumbi in S Tibet after abortive resistance to Chinese State 1950; negotiated agreement with China 1951; Vice-Chair. Standing Cttee CPPCC, mem. Nat. Cttee 1951–59; Hon.

Chair. Chinese Buddhist Asscn 1953–59; Del. to Nat. People's Congress 1954–59; Chair. Preparatory Cttee for the 'Autonomous Region of Tibet' 1955–59; fled Tibet to India after suppression of Tibetan national uprising 1959; Dr of Buddhist Philosophy (Monasteries of Sera, Drepung and Gaden, Lhasa) 1959; Supreme Head of all Buddhist sects in Tibet (Xizang); Presidential Distinguished Prof., Emory Univ., USA 2007–; Hon. Citizen of Paris 2008; Memory Prize 1989, Congressional Human Rights Award 1989, Nobel Peace Prize 1989, Freedom Award (USA) 1991, Presidential Congressional Gold Medal (USA) 2007. *Publications:* My Land and People 1962, The Opening of the Wisdom Eye 1963, The Buddhism of Tibet and the Key to the Middle Way 1975, Kindness, Clarity and Insight 1984, A Human Approach to World Peace 1984, Freedom in Exile (autobiog.) 1990, My Tibet 1990, The Way to Freedom 1995, The Good Heart 1996, Beyond Dogma 1996, Ethics for the New Millennium 1998, Violence and Compassion 1998, Art of Happiness (co-author) 1999, Ancient Wisdom, Modern World 1999, The Path to Tranquility: Daily Wisdom 1999, Transforming the Mind: Eight Verses on Generating Compassion and Transforming Your Life 2000, A Simple Path: Basic Buddhist Teachings by His Holiness the Dalai Lama 2000, The Art of Living: A Guide to Contentment, Joy and Fulfillment 2001, Stages of Meditation: Training the Mind for Wisdom 2001, Compassionate Life 2001, His Holiness the Dalai Lama: In My Own Words 2001, Essence of the Heart Sutra 2002, How to Practice 2002, The Spirit of Peace 2002, How to See Yourself As You Really Are 2007, Comfort, Ease and Enlightenment: Living the Great Perfection 2007. *Leisure interests:* gardening, mechanics. *Address:* Thekchen Choeling, McLeod Ganj 176219, Dharamsala, Himachal Pradesh, India.

DALBERTO, Michel; French pianist; b. 2 June 1955, Paris; s. of Jean Dalberto and Paulette Girard-Dalberto; ed Lycée Claude Bernard, Lycée Racine, Conservatoire Nat. Supérieur de Musique, Paris; prin. teachers at Conservatoire: Vlado Perlemuter, Jean Hubeau; started professional career 1975; concerts in major musical centres and at int. festivals; Artistic Dir Festival des Arcs 1991–; Pres. Jury, Clara Haskil Competition 1991–; Chevalier Ordre nat. du Mérite; Clara Haskil Prize 1975; First Prize Leeds Int. Pianoforte Competition 1978; Acad. Charles Cros Award 1980 and Acad. Disque Français Award 1984 for recordings; Diapason d'Or Award for Best Concerto Recording 1991. *Recordings include:* albums: Schubert Piano Music (complete recordings), French Mélodies (with Barbara Hendricks), Debussy Preludes, Mozart Concerti. *Leisure interests:* skiing, scuba diving, vintage cars. *Address:* c/o IMG Artists, The Light Box, 111 Power Road, London, W4 5PY, England (office). *Telephone:* (20) 7957-5800 (office). *Fax:* (20) 7957-5801 (office). *E-mail:* knaish@imgworld.com (office). *Website:* www.imgartists.com (office).

DALBORG, Hans Folkeson, MBA, PhD; Swedish banker; *Chairman, Nordea Bank AB;* b. 21 May 1941, Säter; m. Anna Ljungqvist 1965; one s. two d.; ed Univ. of Uppsala and Stockholm School of Econs; teacher and admin., Stockholm School of Econs 1967–72; joined Skandia 1972, Deputy Man. Dir responsible for int. business 1981–83, Pres. and COO Skandia Int. Insurance Corpn 1983–89, Sr Exec., Vice-Pres., COO Skandia Group and CEO Skandia Int. Insurance Corpn 1989–91; Pres. and CEO Nordbanken AB 1991–97, Pres., Group CEO MeritaNordbanken PLC 1998–99; Pres. and CEO Nordea Bank AB 2000–04, Chair. 2004–; Chair. Swedish Code of Corp. Governance, Uppsala Univ.; mem. Bd of Dirs Axel Johnson AB, Stockholm Inst. of Transition Econs and East European Economies (SITE), Stockholm Inst. for Financial Research; mem. European Round Table of Financial Services (EFR). *Address:* Nordea Bank AB, Smålandsgatan 17, 105 71 Stockholm, Sweden (office). *Telephone:* (8) 614-78-00 (office). *Fax:* (8) 614-78-10 (office). *E-mail:* hans.dalborg@nordea.com (office). *Website:* www.nordea.com (office).

DALDRY, Stephen, CBE BA; British theatre and film director; b. 2 May 1960, Dorset; s. of the late Patrick Daldry and of Cherry Daldry (née Thompson); m. Lucy Daldry 2001; ed Huish Grammar School, Taunton, Univ. of Sheffield; trained with Il Circo di Nando Orfei, Italy; f. Metro Theatre Co., Artistic Dir 1984–86; Assoc. Artist, Crucible Theatre, Sheffield 1986–88; Artistic Dir Gate Theatre, London 1989–92; Artistic Dir English Stage Co., Royal Court Theatre, London 1992–99, Assoc. Dir 1999–; Dir Stephen Daldry Pictures 1998–; Cameron Mackintosh Visiting Prof. of Contemporary Theatre, Oxford Univ. 2002. *Films include:* Eight 1998, Via Dolorosa 1999, Dancer (Dir) 2000, Billy Elliot (Dir) (BAFTA Award) 2000, The Hours 2002, The Reader 2008. *Theatre includes:* Billy Elliot (Dir, musical) 2004. *Producer:* Six Degrees of Separation, Oleanna, Damned for Despair (Gate) 1991, An Inspector Calls (Royal Nat. Theatre) 1992, (Aldwych) 1994, (Garrick) 1995, (NY) 1995, (Playhouse) 2001, Machinal (Royal Nat. Theatre) 1993, The Kitchen (Royal Court) 1995, Via Dolorosa (Royal Court) 1998, (NY) 1999, Far Away (Royal Court) 2000, (Albery) 2001, Judgement Day, Ingoldstadt, Figaro Gets Divorced, Rat in the Skull. *Address:* c/o Creative Artists Agency, 2000 Avenue Of The Stars, Los Angeles, CA 90067, USA.

DALE, Jim; British actor; b. (James Smith), 15 Aug. 1935; m.; three s. one d.; ed Kettering Grammar School; music hall comedian 1951; singing, compering, directing 1951–61; first film appearance 1965; appeared in nine Carry On films; later appeared with Nat. Theatre and Young Vic; appeared in London's West End in The Card 1973; host, Sunday Night at the London Palladium (TV show) 1994; with Young Vic appeared on Broadway in The Taming of the Shrew and Scapino 1974; Broadway appearances: Barnum (Tony Award) 1980, Joe Egg 1985, Me and My Girl 1987–88, Candide 1997; other stage appearances include: Privates on Parade (New York), Travels With My Aunt (off-Broadway) 1995, Fagin in Oliver! (London Palladium) 1995–97; lyricist for film Georgy Girl; Grammy Award for Best Spoken Word Album for Children (for Harry Potter and the Deathly Hallows) 2008. *Films include:* Lock Up Your Daughters, The Winter's Tale, The Biggest Dog in the World, National Health, Adolf Hitler—My Part in his Downfall, Joseph Andrews, Pete's Dragon, Hot Lead Cold Feet, Bloodshy, The Spaceman and King Arthur, Scandalous, Carry On Cabby, Carry On Cleo, Carry On Jack, Carry On Cowboy, Carry On Screaming, Carry On Spying, Carry On Constable, Carry On Doctor, Carry On Don't Lose Your Head, Carry On Follow That Camel, Carry On Columbus 1992, Hunchback of Notre Dame 1997. *Address:* c/o Sharon Bierut, CED, 257 Park Avenue South, New York, NY 10010, USA; c/o Janet Glass, 28 Berkeley Square, London, W1X 6HD, England.

D'ALEMA, Massimo; Italian politician and journalist; b. 20 April 1949, Rome; m. Linda Giuva; two c.; ed Univ. of Pisa; Dir L'Unità 1988–90; Sec. Partito Democratico della Sinistra, renamed Democratici di Sinistra (DS) 1998, Pres. 2000–07, mem. Partito Democratico (formed by merger of Democratici di Sinistra and Democrazia è Libertà) 2007–; mem. Camera dei Deputati for Apulia 2006–; fmr mem. Progressisti Federativo; Chair. Parl. Cttee on Institutional Reform 1997; fmr mem. Budget Comm.; Prime Minister of Italy 1998–2000; Pres. Fondazione Italianieuropei 2000–, founder and Pres. Associazione dei Riformisti e Democratici (affiliated to Fondazione Italianieuropei) 2008–; Deputy Prime Minister and Minister of Foreign Affairs 2006–08. *Publications:* Dialogo su Berlinguer (jtly) 1994, Un paese Normale: La Sinistra e il Futuro dell'Italia 1995, Progettare il Futuro 1996, La Sinistra nell'Italia che Cambia 1997, La Grande Occasione. L'Italia verso le Riforme 1997, Parole a Vista (jtly) 1998, Kosovo: Gli italiani e la Guerra (jtly) 1999, Oltre la Paura 2002, La Politica ai Tempi della Globalizzazione 2003, A Mosca l'Ultima Volta 2004. *Address:* Partito Democratico, Piazza Saint'Anastasia 7, 00186 Rome, Italy (office). *Telephone:* (06) 675471 (office). *Fax:* (06) 67547319 (office). *E-mail:* info@partitodemocratico.it (office). *Website:* www.partitodemocratico.it (office).

DALES, Sir Richard Nigel, Kt, KCVO, CMG, MA; British diplomatist; b. 26 Aug. 1942, Woodford, Essex; s. of the late Maj. K. Dales and of O. M. Dales; m. Elizabeth M. Martin 1966; one s. one d.; ed Chigwell School, Essex and St Catharine's Coll. Cambridge; joined Foreign Office 1964; Third Sec. Yaoundé, Cameroon 1965–67; with FCO, London 1968–70; Second Sec., later First Sec., Copenhagen 1970–73; Asst Pvt. Sec. to Sec. of State for Foreign and Commonwealth Affairs 1974–77; Head of Chancery, Sofia 1977–81; FCO 1981–82; Head of Chancery, Copenhagen 1982–86; Deputy High Commr in Zimbabwe 1986–89; Head of Southern Africa Dept FCO 1989–91; seconded to Civil Service Comm. 1991–92; High Commr in Zimbabwe 1992–95; Dir (Africa and Commonwealth), FCO 1995–98; Amb. to Norway 1998–2002; Chair. Anglo-Norse Soc. 2003–; mem. Bd Norfolk and Norwich Festival 2003–; mem. Council of Univ. of East Anglia 2004–; Vice Chair. International Alert 2005–. *Leisure interests:* music and the arts, walking, reading. *Address:* 521 Bunyan Court, Barbican, London, EC2Y 8DH, England.

D'ALESSANDRO, Dominic, OC, BSc; Italian chartered accountant and financial services executive; *President and CEO, Manulife Financial Corporation;* b. Molise; m. Pearl D'Alessandro; two s. one d.; ed Loyola Coll., Montreal, Canada; accountant, Coopers & Lybrand 1968–75; with Genstar Ltd 1975–81, Dir of Finance, Dhahran, Saudi Arabia, subsequently Gen. Man., Dhahran, later Vice-Pres. Materials and Construction Group, San Francisco; with Royal Bank of Canada 1981–88, Vice-Pres. and Controller, then Exec. Vice-Pres. for Finance –1988; Pres. and CEO Laurentian Bank of Canada 1988–94; mem. Bd Dirs, Pres. and CEO Manulife Financial Corpn 1994–; Dir American Council of Life Insurance; mem. Bd The Hudson's Bay Co., TransCanada PipeLines; mem. Business Council on Nat. Issues; fmr Chair. Bd Canadian Life and Health Insurance Asscn; mem. Advisory Cttee on the Public Service of Canada 2006–, North American Competitiveness Council of North American Free Trade Agreement (NAFTA) 2006–; Fellow Inst. Chartered Accountants 1993; Co-Chair. Corp. Fund for Breast Cancer Research Campaign 1996; Campaign Chair. for the Salvation Army, Ont. Cen. Div., for Greater Toronto United Way Campaign 1998; Dr hc (Concordia Univ.) 1998; Bronze Medal, Inst. of Chartered Accountants 1971, Man. Achievement Award, McGill Univ. 1999, Arbour Award, Univ. of Toronto 1999, CEO Award of Excellence in Public Relations, Canadian Public Relations Soc. 2001, named Canada's Outstanding CEO for 2002, voted Canada's Most Respected CEO 2004. *Address:* Manulife Financial, 200 Bloor Street East, Toronto, ON M4W 1E5, Canada (office). *Telephone:* (416) 926-3000 (office). *Fax:* (416) 926-5454 (office). *E-mail:* info@manulife.com (office). *Website:* www.manulife.com (office).

DALEY, Richard Michael, BA, JD; American lawyer and politician; *Mayor of Chicago;* b. 24 April 1942, Chicago, Ill.; s. of the late Richard J. Daley and of Eleanor Guilfoyle; m. Margaret Corbett 1972; one s. (and one s. deceased) two d.; ed De La Salle High School, Providence Coll. and DePaul Univ.; Asst Corpn Counsel, City of Chicago 1969; Del. Ill. Constitutional Convention 1970; Pnr, Simon and Daley (law firm) 1970–72, Daley, Riley & Daley 1972–80; mem. Ill. State Senate 1973–80; State's Attorney, Cook Co., Ill. 1980–89; Mayor of Chicago 1989–; mem. Chicago Bar Asscn, Illinois State Bar Asscn, ABA, Catholic Lawyers Guild; Democrat; numerous awards including Outstanding Leader, Ill. Asscn of Social Workers 1978, Public Official of Year, Governing magazine 1997, Politician of Year, Library Journal 1997, J. Sterling Morton Award, Nat. Arbor Day Foundation 1999, Nat. Trust for Historic Preservation Nat. Preservation Award, 2000, 2002, Lifetime Achievement Award, US Conference Mayors 2005, Kevin Lynch Award, MIT 2005. *Leisure interests:* cinema, reading. *Address:* Office of the Mayor, City Hall, Room 507, 121 North LaSalle Street, Chicago, IL 60602–1202, USA (office). *Telephone:* (312) 744–3300 (office). *E-mail:* MayorDaley@ci.chi.il.us (office). *Website:* www.ci.chi.il.us (office).

DALEY, William M., BA, LLD; American lawyer, business executive and fmr government official; *Chairman, Midwest Region, J.P. Morgan Chase & Company;* b. 1948; s. of the late Richard J. Daley and of Eleanor Guilfoyle, brother of Richard Michael Daley (q.v.); m. Loretta Daley; three c.; ed Loyola

Univ., John Marshall Law School; called to Ill. Bar 1975; fmrly with Daley and George, Chicago; Pnr, Mayer, Brown and Platt; Vice-Chair. Amalgamated Bank, Chicago 1989, Pres., COO 1990–93; Sec. US Dept of Commerce, Washington 1997–2000; Chair. Vice Pres. Albert Gore's presidential election campaign 2000; Vice Chair. Evercore Capital Pnrs LP Jan.–Nov. 2001; Pres. SBC Communications 2001–04; Chair. Midwest Operations J. P. Morgan Chase, Chicago 2004–, also mem. Exec. Cttee, Operating Cttee and Int. Advisory Council; mem. Bd of Dirs Boeing Co., Abbott Laboratories 2004–, Boston Properties Inc.2003–, Art Inst. of Chicago, Joffrey Ballet of Chicago, Loyola Univ. of Chicago, Northwestern Memorial Hosp., Northwestern Univ.; fmr Special Counsel to Pres. for NAFTA; mem. Council on Foreign Relations; St Ignatius Award for Excellence in the Practice of Law, World Trade Award, World Trade Center, Chicago 1994. *Address:* c/o J.P. Morgan Chase & Co., 270 Park Avenue, New York, NY 10017, USA (office). *Website:* www .jpmorganchase.com (office).

DALGARNO, Alexander, PhD, FRS, MRIA, FInstP; American (b. British) astronomer and academic; *Phillips Professor of Astronomy, Harvard University;* b. 5 Jan. 1928, London; s. of William Dalgarno and Margaret Dalgarno; m. 1st Barbara Kane 1957 (divorced 1972); two s. two d.; m. 2nd Emily Izsák 1972 (divorced 1987); ed Univ. Coll. London; mem. Faculty, Applied Math., Queen's Univ., Belfast 1951–67; Prof. of Astronomy, Harvard Univ. 1967–77, Chair. Dept of Astronomy 1971–76, Dir Harvard Coll. Observatory 1971–72, Phillips Prof. of Astronomy 1977–; mem. Smithsonian Astrophysical Observatory 1967–, US Nat. Acad. of Science; Ed. Astrophysical Journal Letters 1973–2002; Fellow, American Geophysical Union, American Physical Soc., Univ. College London, Univ. of Manchester Inst. of Science and Technology, Royal Soc.; mem. American Acad. of Arts and Science, Royal Irish Acad.; Hon. DSc (Queen's, Belfast) 1972, (York, Canada) 2000; Medal of Int. Acad. of Quantum Molecular Science 1969, Hodgkins Medal, Smithsonian Inst. 1977, Davisson-Germer Prize, American Physical Soc. 1980, Meggers Award, Optical Soc. of America 1986, Gold Medal, Royal Astronomical Soc. 1986, Spiers Medal, Royal Soc. of Chem., Fleming Medal, American Geophysical Union 1995, Hughes Medal, Royal Soc. 2002. *Publications:* numerous scientific papers in journals. *Address:* Harvard-Smithsonian Center for Astrophysics, 60 Garden Street, Cambridge, MA 02138 (office); 27 Robinson Street, Cambridge, MA 02138, USA (home). *Telephone:* (617) 495-4403 (office); (617) 354-8660 (home). *Fax:* (617) 495-5970 (office). *E-mail:* adalgarno@cfa .harvard.edu (office). *Website:* cfa-www.harvard.edu/ast (office).

DALGLISH, Kenneth (Kenny) Mathieson, MBE; British professional football manager and fmr professional football player; b. 4 March 1951, Glasgow; m. Marina Dalglish; four c.; played for Celtic, Scottish League champions 1972–74, 1977, Scottish Cup Winners 1972, 1974, 1975, 1977, Scottish League Cup winners 1975; played for Liverpool, European Cup winners 1978, 1981, 1984, FA Cup winners 1986, 1989, League Cup winners 1981–84, Man. 1986–91; Man. Blackburn Rovers 1991–97, Newcastle United 1997–98; Dir of Football Operations, Celtic 1999–2000; 102 full caps for Scotland scoring 30 goals; Co-founder (with wife) Marina Dalglish Appeal; Freeman of Glasgow; Footballer of the Year 1979, 1983, Manager of the Year (three times), elected to Scottish Sports Hall of Fame 2001, Scottish Football Hall of Fame 2004. *Address:* c/o Marina Dalglish Appeal, 78 Seel Street, Liverpool, L1 4BH, England.

DALIBARD, Barbara, MA; French telecommunications executive; *Executive Vice-President, Enterprise Communications Services, France Télécom SA; President and CEO, Orange Business Services;* b. 1958; ed Ecole Normale Supérieure; math. teacher; began career with France Télécom SA in 1982, various man. positions in sales, Corp. Services Dir Orange France and Vice-Pres. Orange Business 2001–02, Exec. Vice-Pres. Corp. Solutions 2003–04, Exec. Vice-Pres. Enterprise Communications Services 2004–, Chair. Supervisory Bd Equant (now Orange Business Services—subsidiary of France Télécom) 2003–05 (mem. Strategy and Compensation Cttees), Pres. and CEO Equant 2005–; Pres. Alcanet International SAS 1998, Sales Man. for New Operators, Alcatel CIT 1999, later Sales Man. for France; ranked by Fortune magazine amongst 50 Most Powerful Women in Business outside the US (27th) 2004, (26th) 2005, (35th) 2006, (40th) 2007. *Address:* France Télécom SA, 6 place d'Alleray, 75505 Paris Cedex 15, France (office). *Telephone:* 1-44-44-22-22 (office). *Fax:* 1-44-44-95-95 (office). *Website:* www.francetelecom.com (office); www.mnc.orange-business.com (office).

DALLARA, Charles H., MA, PhD, MALD; American fmr government official and international organization official; *Managing Director, Institute of International Finance;* b. 1948, Spartanburg, NC; m. 1st Carolyn Gault; one s. one d.; m. 2nd Peixin Li; ed Univ. of S Carolina and Fletcher School of Law and Diplomacy; int. economist, US Treasury Dept 1976–79; Special Asst to Under-Sec. for Monetary Affairs 1979–80; Guest Scholar Brookings Inst. 1980–81; Special Asst to Asst Sec. for Int. Affairs 1981–82; Alt. Exec. Dir IMF 1982–83; Deputy Asst Sec. for Int. Monetary Affairs, US Treasury Dept 1983–85; Exec. Dir IMF 1984–89; Asst Sec. for Policy Devt and Sr Adviser for Policy 1988–89; Asst Sec. for Internal Affairs 1989–93; Man. Dir JP Morgan 1991–93; Man. Dir Inst. of Int. Finance 1993–. *Address:* Institute of International Finance, Inc., 1333 H Street, NW, Suite 800E, Washington, DC 20005-4770 (office); 12196 Goldenchair Court, Oak Hill, VA 20171, USA (home). *Telephone:* (202) 857-3604 (office). *Fax:* (202) 833-1194 (office). *E-mail:* cdallara@iif.com (office). *Website:* www.iif.com (office).

D'ALLEST, Frédéric Jean Pierre; French engineer; b. 1 Sept. 1940, Marseilles; s. of Pierre d'Allest and Luce d'Allest; m. Anne-Marie Morel 1963; three s.; ed Ecole St Joseph and Lycée Thiers, Marseilles, Ecole Polytechnique and Ecole Nat. Supérieure d'Aéronautique; with Centre Nat. d'Etudes Spatiales (CNES) 1966–70, Head of Ariane Project 1973–76, Dir Ariane Programme 1976–82, Dir-Gen. CNES 1982–89; with Europa III project,

European Launcher Devt Org. 1970–72; Pres. Soc. Arianespace 1980–90 (Hon. Pres. 1990–), Matra Transport 1992–, Matra Hachette 1993–; Dir-Gen. Groupe Matra 1990–93, Groupe Lagardère 1996–2000; f. Marseille Provence 1988; Officier, Légion d'honneur, Officier Ordre Nat. du Mérite; Prix de l'Aéronautique, IMechE James Watt Prize 1993. *Leisure interests:* sport, alpinism. *Address:* 6 rue Marcel Allegot, 92190 Meudon, France (home). *E-mail:* fjpdallest@wanadoo.fr.

DALLI, Hon. John, FCCA, CPA, CIM; Maltese politician and accountant; *Executive Chairman, John Dalli and Associates;* b. 5 Oct. 1948, Qormi; s. of Carmelo Dalli and Emma Bonnici; m. Josette Callus; two d.; ed Malta Coll. of Arts, Science and Tech.; posts in financial admin and gen. man., Malta and Brussels; Man. Consultant; MP, Nationalist Party 1987–; Parl. Sec. for Industry 1987–90; Minister for Econ. Affairs 1990–92, of Finance 1992–96, 1998–2003, of Finance and Econ. Affairs 2003–04, of Foreign Affairs and Investment Promotion 2004 (resgnd); Shadow Minister and Opposition Spokesman for Finance 1996–98; currently Exec. Chair. John Dalli and Assocs; mem. Inst. of Man., Malta, Nat. Asscn of Accountants, USA. *Address:* 1400 Blk 14, Portohaso, St Julians PTH01 (office); 2461 Blk 24, Portohaso, St Julians PTH01, Malta (home). *Telephone:* 377948 (office). *Fax:* 377187 (office). *E-mail:* jd@dbms.com.mt (office). *Website:* www.dbms.com.mt (office); www .johndalli.com (home).

D'ALMEIDA, Armindo Vaz; São Tomé and Príncipe politician; Prime Minister 1995–96. *Address:* c/o Office of the Prime Minister, Praça Yon Gato, CP 302, São Tomé, São Tomé e Príncipe.

D'ALOISIO, Tony, BA, LLB (Hons); Australian barrister and business executive; *Chairman, Australian Securities and Investments Commission;* b. 6 Nov. 1946; ed Monash Univ.; admitted to practice as a barrister and solicitor in Vic., WA, Queensland and the ACT, and as a solicitor in NSW; Prin. legal officer with Commonwealth Attorney-Gen.'s Dept in Business and Consumer Affairs Div., Canberra –1977; joined Mallesons Stephen Jaques in 1977, practised as commercial lawyer 1977–92, Chief Exec. 1992, Chief Exec. Pnr, Mallesons 1992–2004; Man. Dir and CEO Australian Securities Exchange (ASX) 2004–06; Commr Australian Securities and Investments Comm. (ASIC) 2006–07, Chair. ASIC 2007–; mem. Business Council of Australia 1994–2006 (mem. Bd of Dirs 2003–06), Int. Legal Services Advisory Council 1998–2004 (Chair. Globalisation of Legal Services Cttee), Bd of Taxation 2002–04; mem. Bd of Dirs Australian Charities Fund 2001–, World Fed. of Stock Exchanges 2002–04, Boral Ltd 2003–04; Australian Law Awards Man. Pnr of the Year 2001, 2002, Australian Govt Centenary Medal for services to law and taxation 2000. *Address:* Australian Securities and Investments Commission, GPO Box 9827, Sydney, NSW 2001, Australia (office). *Telephone:* (2) 9911-2200 (office). *Fax:* (2) 9911-2333 (office). *E-mail:* infoline@asic.gov.au (office). *Website:* www .asic.gov.au (office).

DALRYMPLE, Frederick Rawdon, AO; Australian diplomatist; b. 6 Nov. 1930, Sydney; s. of Frederick Dalrymple and Evelyn Dalrymple; m. Ross E. Williams 1957; one s. one d.; ed Sydney Church of England Grammar School and Univs of Sydney and Oxford; Lecturer in Philosophy, Univ. of Sydney 1955–57; joined Dept of External Affairs 1957, served in Bonn, London 1959–64; Alt. Dir Asian Devt Bank, Manila 1967–69; Minister, Djakarta 1969–71; Amb. to Israel 1972–75, to Indonesia 1981–85, to USA 1985–89, to Japan 1989–93; Chair. ASEAN Focus Group Pty Ltd 1994–2001; Visiting Prof., Univ. of Sydney 1994–2002; Hon. Fellow, Univ. of Sydney 2003. *Publications:* Looking East and West from Down Under 1992; Continental Drift: Australia's Search for a Regional Identity 2003. *Leisure interests:* reading, golf. *Address:* 34 Glenmore Road, Paddington, NSW 2021, Australia (home). *E-mail:* rdalrymp@ozemail.com.au (home).

DALTON, Grant; New Zealand yachtsman; *Managing Director, Emirates Team New Zealand;* b. 1957; m. Nicki Dalton; one s. one d.; fmr accountant; trainee sailmaker 1977; first participation in Whitbread round the world race (now the Volvo Ocean Race) on board Dutch Flyer II 1981–82, Lion New Zealand 1985–86; skipper, Fischer & Peykel 1989–90, New Zealand Endeavour 1993–94 (race winner), Wor 60 1997–98 (Merit Cup), Club Med Catamaran, The Race (winner) March 2001, Nautor Challenge Team, Volvo Ocean Race 2001; other races include Sydney-Hobart race (four times), Fastnet Race (five times), Admirals' Cup 1985, Americas Cup, Fremantle, Australia 1987; Man. Dir Emirates Team New Zealand 2003–, won Louis Vuitton ACC Championship 2004, 2006; New Zealand Yachtsman of the Year 2001. *Address:* Emirates Team New Zealand, 141 Halsey Street, Freemans Bay, Auckland, New Zealand (office). *Telephone:* (9) 355-0900 (office). *Fax:* (9) 355-0901 (office). *E-mail:* info@emiratesteamnz.com (office). *Website:* www .emiratesteamnz.com (office).

DALTON, Timothy; British actor; b. 21 March 1946; ed Royal Acad. of Dramatic Art; joined Nat. Youth Theatre; first London appearance at Royal Court Theatre; toured with Prospect Theatre Co.; guest artist with RSC. *Film appearances include:* The Lion in Winter, Le Voyeur (France), Cromwell, Wuthering Heights, Mary Queen of Scots, Permission to Kill, The Man Who Knew Love (Spain), Sextette, Agatha 1978, Flash Gordon 1979, Chanel Solitaire 1980, The Doctor and the Devils 1985, Brenda Starr, role of Ian Fleming's James Bond in The Living Daylights 1987 and Licence to Kill 1989, Hawks 1987, The King's Whore 1989, The Rocketeer 1990, The Informant 1996, The Reef 1996, The Beautician and the Beast 1996, Made Men 1998, Cleopatra 1998, Possessed 1999, Timeshare 2000, American Outlaws 2001, Looney Tunes – Back in Action 2002, Hercules 2004, Hot Fuzz 2007. *Stage appearances include:* King Lear, Love's Labour's Lost, Henry IV, Henry V (all with Prospect Theatre Co.), Romeo and Juliet (RSC), The Samaritan, Black Comedy and White Liars, The Vortex, The Lunatic, The Lover and the Poet 1980, The Romans 1980, Henry IV, Part I (RSC) 1981, Antony and Cleopatra

1986, The Taming of the Shrew 1986, A Touch of the Poet 1988, His Dark Materials (Royal Nat. Theatre) 2003–04. *Television appearances include:* Centennial 1979, Jane Eyre, The Master of Ballantrae, Mistral's Daughter 1984, Florence Nightingale 1984, Sins 1985, Framed 1992, Scarlett 1994, Salt Water Moose 1995, Cleopatra 1998, Possessed 1999, Time Share 2000. *Address:* c/o ICM, Oxford House, 76 Oxford Street, London, W1D 1BS, England. *Telephone:* (20) 7636-6565. *Fax:* (20) 7323-0101 (office).

DALTREY, Roger Harry, CBE; British singer and actor; b. 1 March 1944, Hammersmith, London, England; m. Heather Daltrey; two d. two s. (one by previous m.); mem. rock group, The Detours, renamed The Who 1964–84 (various reunion tours and recordings); numerous festival appearances and tours; solo artist 1984–; Gold Ticket Madison Square Garden 1979, Ivor Novello Award for Outstanding Contribution to British Music 1982, BRIT Award for Outstanding Contribution to British Music 1988, Q Legend Award 2006, South Bank Show Award for Lifetime Achievement 2007, Kennedy Center Honor 2008. *Films include:* Tommy 1974, Lisztomania 1975, The Legacy 1979, McVicar 1980, Threepenny Opera 1989. *Recordings include:* albums: with The Who: My Generation 1965, A Quick One 1966, Happy Jack 1967, The Who Sell Out 1967, Magic Bus 1968, Tommy 1969, Live At Leeds 1970, Who's Next 1971, Meaty Beefy Big And Bouncy 1971, Quadrophenia 1973, The Who By Numbers 1975, The Story Of The Who 1976, Who Are You 1978, The Kids Are Alright (live) 1979, Face Dances 1981, Hooligans 1982, It's Hard 1982, Once Upon A Time 1983, Who's Last (live) 1984, Two's Missing 1987, Joined Together (live) 1990, Live At The Isle Of Wight Festival 1970 1996, The BBC Sessions 2000, Moonlighting 2005, Endless Wire 2006; solo: Daltrey 1973, Ride A Rock Horse 1975, One Of The Boys 1977, If Parting Should Be Painless 1984, Under A Raging Moon 1985, I Can't Wait To See The Movie 1987, Rocks In The Head 1992, McVicar 1996, Martyrs And Madmen 1997, Anthology 2002. *Address:* Trinifold Management Ltd, 12 Oval Road, London, NW1 7DH, England (office). *Telephone:* (20) 7419-4300 (office). *Fax:* (20) 7419-4325 (office). *E-mail:* trinuk@globalnet.co.uk (office). *Website:* www .trinifold.co.uk (office).

DALY, Brendan; Irish fmr politician; b. 2 Feb. 1940, Cooraclare, Co. Clare; m. Patricia Carmody; two s. one d.; ed Kilrush Co. Boys' School; mem. Dáil 1973–89, 1997–2002; Minister of State, Dept of Labour 1980–81; Minister for Fisheries and Forestry March–Dec. 1982, for the Marine 1987–89, for Defence Feb.–Nov. 1991, for Social Welfare 1991–92; Minister of State, Dept of Foreign Affairs 1992–93; mem. Seanad Éireann 1993–97, 2002–07; mem. NI Peace Forum 1994; mem. Irish Parl. Foreign Affairs Cttee 1993–; mem. Fianna Fáil. *Address:* Cooraclare, Kilrush, Co. Clare, Ireland (home). *Telephone:* (65) 9059040 (home). *Fax:* (65) 9059218 (home).

DALY, HE Cardinal Cahal Brendan, MA, DD, DHumLitt, DTheol; Irish ecclesiastic; *Archbishop Emeritus of Armagh;* b. 1 Oct. 1917, Loughguile, Co. Antrim; s. of Charles Daly and Susan Connolly; ed St Malachy's Coll., Belfast, Queen's Univ., Belfast, St Patrick's Coll., Maynooth, Institut Catholique, Paris; ordained priest 1941; Classics Master, St Malachy's Coll. 1945–46; Lecturer in Scholastic Philosophy, Queen's Univ., Belfast 1946–63, Reader 1963–67; Bishop of Ardagh and Clonmacnois 1967–82; Bishop of Down and Connor 1982–90; Archbishop of Armagh and Primate of All Ireland 1990–96, Archbishop Emer. 1996–; cr. Cardinal-Priest of S. Patrizio 1991; Chancellor St Patrick's Pontificial Univ., Maynooth 1990–96; mem. Congregation for Clergy, for Evangelization of the Peoples, Pontifical Council for the Union of Christians; Hon. DD (Queen's Univ. of Belfast) 1990, (St John's, New York); Hon. Dr of Law (Sacred Heart Univ., Conn.), (Notre Dame Univ., Ind.), (Exeter); Hon. DLitt (Trinity Coll., Dublin); Hon. LLD (Nat. Univ. of Ireland). *Publications:* Morals, Law and Life 1962, Natural Law Morality Today 1965, Violence in Ireland and Christian Conscience 1973, Theologians and the Magisterium 1977, Peace and the Work of Justice 1979, Communities Without Consensus: The Northern Irish Tragedy 1984, Renewed Heart for Peace 1984, Cry of the Poor 1986, The Price of Peace 1991, Tertullian: the Puritan and his Influence 1993, Moral Philosophy in Britain from Bradley to Wittgenstein 1996, Steps on my Pilgrim Journey 1998, The Minding of Planet Earth 2000, Philosophical Papers 2007, The Breaking of Bread: Biblical Reflections on the Eucharist 2008, contrib. to various philosophical works. *Address:* 23 Rosetta Avenue, Ormeau Road, Belfast, BT7 3HG, Northern Ireland. *Telephone:* (28) 9064-2431. *Fax:* (28) 9049-2684.

DALY, John Patrick; American golfer; b. 28 April 1966, Carmichael, Calif.; m. Cherie Daly; two c.; ed Univ. of Arkansas; turned professional 1987; won Missouri Open 1987, Ben Hogan Utah Classic 1990, PGA Championship, Crooked Stick 1991, BC Open 1992, BellSouth Classic 1994, British Open 1995, Dunhill Cup 1993, 1998, BMW Int. Open 2001; f. John Daly Enterprises LLC 2000. *Recording:* My Life (album). *Leisure interests:* sports, writing lyrics, playing the guitar. *Address:* John Daly Enterprises, LLC, 432 South Military Trail, Deerfield Beach, FL 33442, USA (office). *Telephone:* (954) 596-1591 (office). *Fax:* (954) 425-0615 (office). *Website:* www.johndaly.com (office).

DALY, Robert Anthony; American business executive; *President, Rulemaker Inc.;* b. 8 Dec. 1936, Brooklyn,New York; s. of James Daly and Eleanor Daly; m. Carole Bayer Sager; two s. one d.; one step-s.; ed Brooklyn Coll.; Dir Business Affairs, then Vice-Pres. Business Affairs, then Exec. Vice-Pres. CBS TV Network 1955–80; Pres. CBS Entertainment Co. 1977–80; Chair. and Co-CEO Warner Bros, Burbank, Calif. 1980, Chair., CEO 1982–99, Chair. and Co-CEO 1994; Chair. and Co-CEO Warner Music Group 1995–99 (resgnd); Man. Gen. Pnr, Chair. and CEO LA Dodgers professional baseball team 1999–2004; currently Pres. Rulemaker Inc., LA; mem. Bd of Dirs American Film Inst., Museum of TV and Radio; mem. Acad. of Motion Picture Arts and Sciences, Nat. Acad. of TV Arts and Sciences; Chair. Save the Children Bd of Trustees 2005–; Hon. DFA (American Film Inst.) 1999, Hon. DHumLitt (Trinity Coll.) 2001; Steven J. Ross/Time Warner Award from Univ. of Southern Calif. School of Cinema-TV 2004. *Address:* Rulemaker Inc., 10877 Wilshire Boulevard, Suite 610, Los Angeles, CA 90024, USA (office). *Telephone:* (310) 208-1555 (office). *E-mail:* bdaly@rulemakerinc.com (office).

DAM, Kenneth W., JD; American lawyer, academic and fmr government official; *Max Pam Professor Emeritus and Senior Lecturer, Law School, University of Chicago;* b. 10 Aug. 1932, Marysville, Kan.; s. of Oliver W. Dam and Ida L. Dam; m. Marcia Wachs 1962; one s. one d.; ed Univs of Kansas and Chicago; law clerk, Mr Justice Whittaker, US Supreme Court 1957–58; Assoc., Cravath, Swaine & Moore, New York 1958–60; Asst Prof., Univ. of Chicago Law School 1960–61, Assoc. Prof. 1961–64, Prof. 1964–71, 1974–76, Harold J. & Marion F. Green Prof. of Int. Legal Studies 1976–85; Max Pam Prof. of American and Foreign Law 1992–2001, Sr Lecturer 2003–; Provost, Univ. of Chicago 1980–82; Consultant, Kirkland & Ellis, Chicago 1961–71, 1974–80, 1993–; Exec. Dir Council on Econ. Policy 1973; Asst Dir for Nat. Security and Int. Affairs, Office of Man. and Budget 1971–73; Deputy Sec. of State 1982–85; Deputy Sec. US Treasury 2001–03; Vice-Pres., Law and External Relations, IBM Corpn 1985–92; Pres., CEO United Way America 1992; mem. Bd of Dirs Alcoa 1987–2001; Trustee Brookings Inst. 1989–2001, 2003–, Council on Foreign Relations 1992–2001, Chicago Council on Foreign Relations 1992–2001; mem. American Acad. of Arts and Sciences, American Acad. of Diplomacy, American Bar Asscn, American Law Inst.; Chair. German-American Academic Council 1999–2001. *Publications:* Federal Tax Treatment of Foreign Income (with L. Krause) 1964, The GATT: Law and International Economic Organization 1970, Oil Resources: Who Gets What How? 1976, Economic Policy Beyond the Headlines (with George P. Shultz) 1978, The Rules of the Game: Reform and Evolution in the International Monetary System 1982, Cryptography's Role in Securing the Information Society 1996 (co-ed.), The Rules of the Global Game: A New Look at US International Economic Policy 2001, The Law–Growth Nexus: The Rule of Law and Economic Development 2006; numerous articles on legal and economic issues. *Address:* University of Chicago Law School, 1111 East 60th Street, Chicago, IL 60637, USA (office). *Telephone:* (773) 255-2428 (office). *E-mail:* kenneth_dam@law.uchicago.edu (office). *Website:* www.law.uchicago.edu (office).

DAM-JENSEN, Inger; Danish singer (soprano); b. 13 March 1964, Copenhagen; m. Morten Ernst Lassen; ed Royal Danish Acad. of Music, Danish Opera School, studied with Kirsten Buhl Møller; started career 1992, winner Cardiff Singer of the World Competition 1993; roles include Zdenka (Arabella), Ophelia (Hamlet), Norina (Don Pasquale), Sophie (Der Rosenkavalier), Adina (L'elisir d'amore), Susanna (Le Nozze di Figaro), Musetta (La Bohème), Gilda (Rigoletto), Cleopatra (Giulio Cesare), Despina (Così fan Tutte), Lisa (La Sonnambula), Blöndchen (Die Entführung aus dem Serail), Sifare (Mitridate), Pamina (Die Zauberflöte); concert appearances with numerous orchestras, including Danish Radio Symphony, New York Philharmonic, Berlin Philharmonic, Czech Philharmonic, Philharmonia Orchestra, Bastille Orchestra, Sydney Symphony Orchestra, Toronto Symphony Orchestra, Czech Philarmonic Orchestra and Gabrieli Consort; performed closing scene from Strauss' Daphne, London Proms 1999; has performed at Edin. Festival; winner, Cardiff Int. Singing Competition 1993. *Recordings:* Mahler's Fourth Symphony, Grieg's Peer Gynt, Brahms' Ein Deutsches Requiem. *Address:* Internusica Artists' Management Ltd, 16 Duncan Terrace, London, N1 8BZ, England (office). *Telephone:* (20) 7278-5455 (office). *Fax:* (20) 7278-8434 (office). *E-mail:* mail@intermusica.co.uk (office); inger@danlassen.dk. *Website:* www.intermusica.co.uk (office).

DAMADIAN, Raymond V., BS, MD; American scientist and business executive; *CEO, Fonar Corporation;* b. 1936, Forest Hills, NY; ed Juilliard School of Music, New York, Univ. of WI, Albert Einstein School of Medicine, Yeshiva Univ., Israel; developed first Magnetic Resonance scanning machine named Indomitable 1977; est. Fonar Corpn 1978, now CEO; introduced first commercial MRI (Magnetic Resonance Imaging) scanner 1980; Prof., State Univ. of NY Health Science Center, Brooklyn, NY; Nat. Medal of Tech. 1988, inducted into Nat. Inventors Hall of Fame 1989, Lemelson-MIT Lifetime Achievement Award 2001. *Address:* Fonar Corporation, 110 Marcus Drive, Melville, NY 11747, USA (office). *Telephone:* (631) 694-2929 (office). *Fax:* (631) 753-5150 (office). *E-mail:* info@fonar.com (office). *Website:* www.fonar.com (office).

D'AMATO, Alfonse M., BA, LLB; American lawyer, business executive and fmr politician; *Founder, Park Strategies LLC;* b. 1 Aug. 1937, Brooklyn, New York; m. Penelope Ann Collenburg 1960 (divorced); two s. two d.; ed Syracuse Univ.; Receiver of Taxes, Town of Hempstead 1971–72, Supervisor, Hempstead 1972–78, Presiding Supervisor 1978–81; Senator from NY 1981–98, mem. Banking, Housing and Urban Affairs Cttee (Chair. 1995), Finance Cttee, Appropriations Cttee; Founder, Park Strategies LLC 1999–; mem. Bd of Dirs Computer Associates Int. Inc. 1999–. *Publications:* Power, Pasta and Politics (autobiog.) 1995. *Address:* Park Strategies LLC, 101 Park Avenue, Suite 2506, New York, NY 10178, USA (office). *Telephone:* (212) 883-5608 (office). *Website:* www.parkstrategies.com (office).

DAMAZER, Mark David, BA; British broadcasting executive; *Controller, BBC Radio 4, BBC Radio 7;* b. 15 April 1955; s. of Stanislaw Damazer and Suzanne Damazer; m. Rosemary Jane Morgan 1981; one s. one d.; ed Gonville and Caius Coll., Cambridge, Harvard Univ., USA; trainee with ITN 1979–81; Producer BBC World Service 1981–83, TV-AM 1983–84, BBC Six O'Clock News 1984–86, Output Ed. Newsnight 1986–88, Deputy Ed., Nine O'Clock Main Evening News 1988–89, Ed. 1989–94, Ed. TV News 1994–96, Head of Current Affairs 1996–98, Head of Political Programmes 1998–2000, Asst Dir BBC News 1999–2001, Deputy Dir 2001–04, Controller BBC Radio 4 and BBC Radio 7 2004–; mem. Bd Inst. of Contemporary British History; Fellow American Political Soc. 1978–79; Vice-Chair. and mem., Int. Press Inst.;

Fellow, Royal Acad. 2008; Harkness Fellowship. *Publications:* articles in various newspapers and magazines. *Leisure interests:* opera, Tottenham Hotspur, Boston Red Sox, gardening, coarse tennis, Italian painting. *Address:* BBC Radio 4, Broadcasting House, 10–22 Portland Place, London, W1A 1AA, England (office). *Telephone:* (20) 7580-4468 (office). *Website:* www.bbc.co.uk (office).

D'AMICO DE CARVALHO, Caterina; Italian film industry executive, screenwriter and academic; *CEO, RAI Cinema SpA;* d. of Suso Cecchi D'Amico; Dean of Centro Sperimentale di Cinematografia (nat. film school) –2007; CEO RAI Cinema SpA (film production and distribution arm of Govt-run Italian broadcaster RAI) 2007–. *Films:* Luchino Visconti (consultant) 1999, My Voyage to Italy (assoc. producer) 2001. *Address:* RAI Cinema SpA, Piazza Adriana 12, 00193 Rome, Italy (office). *Telephone:* (06) 684701 (office). *E-mail:* info@raicinema.it (office). *Website:* www.raicinema.it (office).

DAMON, Matt; American actor; b. 8 Oct. 1970, Cambridge, Mass.; m. Luciana Barroso 2005; two d.; numerous awards for Good Will Hunting including Acad. Award for Best Writing, Screenplay written directly for Screen, Silver Berlin Bear Award for Outstanding Single Achievement 1997. *Films include:* Mystic Pizza 1988, Rising Son (TV) 1990, School Ties 1992, Geronimo: An American Legend 1993, The Good Old Boys (TV) 1995, Courage Under Fire 1996, Glory Daze 1996, Chasing Amy 1997, The Rainmaker 1997, Good Will Hunting (also co-writer) 1997, Saving Private Ryan 1998, Rounders 1998, Dogma 1999, The Talented Mr Ripley 1999, Titan A.E. (voice) 1999, All the Pretty Horses 1999, The Legend of Baggar Vance 2000, Finding Forrester 2000, Ocean's Eleven 2001, The Majestic (voice) 2001, Gerry (also writer) 2002, Spirit: Stallion of the Cimarron (voice) 2002, The Third Wheel 2002, The Bourne Identity 2002, Confessions of a Dangerous Mind 2003, Stuck on You 2003, Eurotrip 2004, Jersey Girl 2004, The Bourne Supremacy (Empire Film Award for Best Actor 2005) 2004, Ocean's Twelve 2004, The Brothers Grimm 2005, Syriana 2005, The Departed 2006, The Good Shepherd 2006, Ocean's Thirteen 2007, The Bourne Ultimatum 2007. *Address:* Endeavor Agency, 9601 Wilshire Blvd., 10th Floor, Beverly Hills, CA 90212, USA (office). *Telephone:* (310) 248-2000. *Fax:* (310) 248-2020.

DAN, Hiroaki; Japanese business executive; *President and COO, Japan Post Service Co., Ltd;* various roles at Japan Post including Dir-Gen. of Telecommunications Business Dept, Dir-Gen. of Postal Savings Bureau 1999, Dir Secr. 2001, Dir-Gen. of Postal Services Policy 2002, Sr Exec. Vice-Pres. –2007, Pres. and COO Japan Post Service Co. Ltd (following privatization Oct. 2007) 2007–. *Address:* Japan Post Service Co. Ltd, 1-3-2 Kasumigaseki, Chiyoda-ku, Tokyo 100-8798, Japan (office). *Telephone:* (03) 3504-4411 (office). *Website:* www.post.japanpost.jp (office).

DANAILOV, Stefan, MA; Bulgarian actor and politician; *Minister of Culture;* b. Sept. 1942, Sofia; ed Krastyo Sarafov Nat. Acad. for Theatre and Film Arts; currently Prof., Nat. Acad. of Theatre and Film Arts; mem. Nat. Ass. 2001–, Chair. Parl. Cttee on Culture 2001–05; Minister of Culture 2005–; Order of Stara Planina, Commdr, l'Ordre des Arts et des Lettres 2006; Paisiy Hilendarsky (Ministry of Culture) 2002. *Plays:* prominent roles include Camille Demolen, The Danton Case (Psibishevska), Stylo, Banzy is Dead (Ethole Fewgard), Edmond, Long Day's Journey into the Night (Eugene O'Neil), Chadski, Blame His Misfortunes on His Wits (Griboedov), Hamlet (Shakespeare), Stavrogin, The Possessed (Dostoyevsky), Peer Gynt (Ibsen), Shylock, The Price (Arthur Miller), Alessandro Medici, Lorenzaccio (Alfred de Musset), Danton, Danton's Death (Buchner), Trigorin, The Seagull (Chekov). *Films:* The Traces Remain 1956, The Inspector and the Night 1963, Quiet Paths 1967, The Sea 1967, Taste of Almonds 1967, The First Courier 1968, At Each Kilometer 1969, The Prince 1970, The Black Angels 1970, There Is Nothing Finer Than Bad Weather 1971, At Each Kilometer 1971, Affection 1972, Ivan Kondarev 1974, Houses Without Fences 1974, Glow Over the Drava River 1974, Life or Death 1974, The Weddings of King Ioan Assen 1975, A Real Man 1975, Beginning of the Day 1975, The Soldier of the Supply Column 1976, Guilt 1976, Amendment to the Defense-of-State Act 1976, RMS Five 1977, A Year of Mondays 1977, Warmth 1978, Moments in a Matchbox 1979, Something Out of Nothing 1979, The Porcupines' War 1979, The Blood Remains 1980, Ladies Choice 1980, The Queen of Turnovo 1981, Autumn Sun 1982, Crystals 1982, Twenty-Four Hours Raining 1982, The Odyssey in the Deliorman 1983, Balance 1983, Blood That Had to Be Shed 1985, The Conversion to Christianity & Discourse of Letters 1985, Manoeuvres on the Fifth Floor 1985, Misty Shores 1986, Transports of Death 1986, Three Marias and Ivan 1986, Ballad 1986, Dreamers 1987, A Sky for All 1987, The Mooncalf 1987, Protect the Small Animals 1988, Monday Morning 1988, The Carnival 1990, I Want Amerika 1991, The Berlin Conspiracy 1992, Crisis in the Kremlin 1992, Don Quixote Returns 1996, A Spanish Fly 1998, After the End of the World 1998, Vercingétorix 2001, The Lark Farm 2007, St. George Shoots the Dragon 2008. *Television:* Dying in the Worst 1978, Oncoming Traffic 1978, Time for Travelling 1987, Home for Our Children 1987, Big Game 1988, People Who Never Disappear 1988, The Black Frames 1989, Live Dangerously 1990, Fathers and Sons 1990, In fondo al cuore 1997, Racket 1997, Fine secolo 1999, Aleph 2000, Forgive Us 2003. *Address:* Ministry of Culture, 1040 Sofia, bul. A. Stamboliyski 17, Bulgaria (office). *Telephone:* (2) 940-08-63 (office). *Fax:* (2) 981-81-45 (office). *E-mail:* press@mc.government.bg (office). *Website:* www.mc.government.bg (office).

DANCE, Charles, OBE; British actor, writer and film director; b. 10 Oct. 1946, Rednal, Worcs.; s. of the late Walter Dance and Eleanor Perks; m. Joanna Haythorn 1970; one s. one d.; worked in industry; with RSC 1975–80, 1981–92; Best Actor, Paris Film Festival 1996. *Television appearances include:* The Fatal Spring, Nancy Astor, Frost in May, Saigon–The Last Day, Thunder Rock (drama), Rainy Day Women, The Jewel in the Crown, The Secret Servant, The McGuffin, The Phantom of the Opera 1989, Rebecca 1996,

In the Presence of Mine Enemies 1997, Murder Rooms 1999, Justice in Wonderland 2000, Nicholas Nickleby 2001, Trial and Retribution 2003, To the Ends of the Earth (miniseries) 2005, Fingersmith 2005, Last Rights 2005, Bleak House (BBC) 2005 (British Press Guild Best Actor Award 2006), Fallen Angel 2007. *Films include:* For Your Eyes Only, Plenty, The Golden Child, White Mischief, Good Morning Babylon, Hidden City, Pascali's Island 1988, China Moon 1990, Alien III 1991, Limestone 1991, Kabloonak (Best Actor, Paris Film Festival 1991), Century, Last Action Hero, Exquisite Tenderness 1993, Short Cut to Paradise 1993, Undertow 1994, Michael Collins, Space Truckers 1996, Goldeneye, The Blood Oranges, What Rats Won't Do, Hilary and Jackie 1998, Don't go Breaking my Heart 1999, Jurij 1999, Dark Blue World 2000, Gosford Park 2001, Ali G in da House 2001, Black and White 2002, Swimming Pool 2003, City and Crimes 2003, Ladies in Lavender (writer and dir) 2004, Remake 2005, Starter for Ten 2006, Scoop 2006, Désaccord parfait 2006, The Contractor 2006. *Theatre:* Coriolanus (title role) (RSC) 1989, Irma La Douce, Turning Over, Henry V, Three Sisters 1998, Good 1999, Long Day's Journey Into Night 2001, The Play What I Wrote 2002, Eh Joe (Sydney Theatre Festival), Shadowlands 2007–08 (London Theatre Critics Circle Best Actor Award 2008). *Radio:* The Heart of the Matter 2001, The Charge of the Light Brigade 2001. *Address:* c/o Independent Talent Group, Oxford House, 76 Oxford Street, London, W1D 1BS, England. *Telephone:* (20) 7636-6565.

D'ANCONA, Hedy, PhD, DSc; Dutch politician and journalist; b. 1 Oct. 1937; ed HBS-b, Leiden, Univ. of Amsterdam; Producer, Host and Ed. VARA-NOS TV 1962–65; Lecturer in Social Geography, Univ. of Amsterdam 1965–75; Dir Govt Centre for Policy Research 1975–82; mem. Senate (PvdA—Partij van de Arbeid) 1974–81, Spokesperson for Public Housing, and Town and Country Planning; State Sec. for Social Affairs and Employment, responsible for Emancipation Issues, Working Conditions and Adult Educ. 1981–82; mem. European Parl. 1984–89 (Chair. Comm. on Equal Rights for Women, Comm. on Social Affairs and Employment), 1994–99 (Vice-Chair. European Cttee of the Social Democrats, Chair. Comm. of Urgent Resolutions –1996, Chair. Comm. of Justice and Home Affairs 1996–99); Minister of Welfare, Public Health and Culture 1989–94; Chair. Bd of Novib (Dutch Oxfam) 1995–; Vice-Chair. Oxfam Int. 1999–; Chair. various cultural insts 1999–; adviser to Govt on Welfare Policies 1999–; freelance journalist 1999–. *Address:* PO Box 1310, 1000 BH Amsterdam, Netherlands.

D'ANCONA, Matthew; British journalist and writer; *Editor, The Spectator;* b. 1968, London; m. Sarah Schaefer; two s.; ed St Dunstan's Coll., Magdalen Coll., Oxford; fmrly worked for human rights magazine, Index on Censorship; trainee, news reporter, education correspondent The Times 1991–94, Asst Ed. 1994–95; Deputy Ed. comment section and political columnist The Sunday Telegraph 1996–98, Deputy Ed. 1998–2006; Ed. The Spectator 2006–; political columnist GQ magazine 2006–; mem. Millennium Commission 2001–; Fellow All Souls, Oxford 1989–96; British Press Award for Political Journalist of the Year 2004. *Publications:* The Jesus Papyrus (non-fiction, with Carsten Peter Thiede) 1997, The Quest for the True Cross (non-fiction, with Carsten Peter Thiede) 2002, Going East (novel) 2004, Tabatha's Code (novel) 2006, Nothing to Fear 2008. *Address:* The Spectator, 22 Old Queen Street, London, SW1H 9HP, England (office). *Telephone:* (20) 7961-0200 (office). *Website:* www .spectator.co.uk (office).

DANCZOWSKA, Kaja; Polish violinist; b. 25 March 1949, Kraków; one d.; ed State Higher Music School in Kraków, Moscow Conservatory; studied violin under teachers Eugenia Uminska and David Oistrakh; Head of Violin Class, Acad. of Music, Kraków 1972–, Prof. 1989–; formed trio with Maja Nosowska and Tadeusz Wojciechowski 1974; Prof. at courses of interpretation in Poland and abroad 1984–; Ordinary Prof. 1997; mem. of jury int. violin competitions in Poznań, Munich, New York and Tokyo 1986–; tours to most European countries, USA, Canada, Australia, NZ, Japan, Mexico and Venezuela; participated in major festivals, including Salzburg, Bordeaux, Sofia and Istanbul; co-operation with the greatest conductors and orchestras; mem. juries of int. competitions in Tokyo, Munich, New York, Poznań and Odense; more than 300 recordings for Wifon, Polskie Nagrania, Deutsche Grammophon, Philips; Officer's Cross, Order of Polonia Restituta 2001; numerous awards including Wieniawski Competition, Poznań (Third Prize) 1967, Curci Competition, Naples (Second Prize) 1969, in Geneva (Second Prize) 1970, in Munich (Third Prize) 1975, Queen Elizabeth Prize, Brussels 1976 (Silver Medal), Individual Prize of Minister of Culture and Art 1991, Prize of Minister of Culture and Art 1998; Excellence in Teaching Award, USA 1998, Polish Culture Foundation Award 1998. *Leisure interests:* film, literature. *Address:* Academy of Music, ul. św. Tomasza 43, 31-027 Kraków, Poland (office). *Fax:* (12) 4222343 (office).

DANELIUS, Hans Carl Yngve; Swedish judge and diplomatist; b. 2 April 1934, Stockholm; s. of Sven Danelius and Inga Danelius (née Svensson); m. Hannah Schadee 1961; three s. one d.; ed Dept of Legal Studies, Stockholm Univ.; law practice in Swedish courts 1957–64; mem. Secr., European Comm. of Human Rights, Strasbourg 1964–67, mem. European Comm. of Human Rights 1983–99; Asst Judge, Svea Court of Appeal 1967–68; Adviser, Ministry of Justice 1968–71; Deputy Head, Legal Dept, Ministry for Foreign Affairs 1971–75, Head 1975–84, rank of Amb. 1977–84; Amb. to Netherlands 1984–88; Judge, Supreme Court of Sweden 1988–2001; Pres. Council on Legislation 2001–03; Arbitrator, ICSID 1999–; mem. Perm. Court of Arbitration at The Hague 1982–; mem. Court of Conciliation and Arbitration, OSCE 1995–2007; mem. Constitutional Court of Bosnia and Herzegovina 1996–2002; Chief Ed. Svensk Juristtidning (Swedish Law Journal) 1973–84; Swedish and foreign decorations; Dr hc (Stockholm) 1988. *Publications:* The United Nations Convention Against Torture 1988, Mänskliga Rättigheter (Human Rights) (5th edn) 1993, Mänskliga Rättigheter i Europeisk Praxis (Human Rights in European Practice) (3rd edn) 2007; numerous articles in

Swedish and foreign journals. *Address:* Roslinvägen 33, 16851 Bromma, Sweden (home). *Telephone:* (8) 37-34-91 (home). *Fax:* (8) 37-34-91 (home). *E-mail:* hans.danelius@telia.com (home).

DANELIYA, Georgy Nikolayevich; Georgian film director; b. 25 Aug. 1930, Tbilisi; m. Galina Daneliya; one s. one d.; ed Moscow Inst. of Architecture, Higher Courses of Film Direction; worked at Inst. for City Designing; Prof. All-Russian Inst. of Cinematography 1975–85; film Dir studio Mosfilm; State Prizes of USSR and Russia; USSR People's Artist; more than 70 prizes in int. film festivals. *Films include:* Serezha 1960, I am Wailing About Moscow 1963, Thirty Three 1965, Don't Grieve 1969, Aphonya 1975, Mimino 1978 (Gold Prize Avelino Festival, Italy), Autumn Marathon 1979 (Grand Prix San Sebastián Festival, Spain, Grand Prix Chambourci Festival, France), Gentlemen of Luck 1981, Tears were Dropping 1982, Kin-Dza-Dza 1987, Passport 1989, White Dance 1992, Nastya 1993, Heads and Tails? 1995, Fortuna 2000. *Address:* 103062 Moscow, Makarenko 1/19 apt. 15, Russia. *Telephone:* (495) 921-43-74.

DANES, Claire; American actress; b. 12 April 1979, New York; d. of Chris Danes and Carla Danes; ed performing arts school, NY and Lee Strasberg Studio; first acting roles in off-Broadway theatre productions: Happiness, Punk Ballet and Kids on Stage. *Films:* Dreams of Love (debut) 1992, Thirty (short) 1993, The Pesky Suitor (short), Little Women 1994, Romeo and Juliet 1996, To Gillian on Her 37th Birthday 1996, Polish Wedding, U-Turn 1997, The Rainmaker 1997, Les Misérables 1998, The Mod Squad 1999, Brokedown Place 1999, Monterey Pop 2000, Dr T and the Women 2000, Flora Plum 2000, The Cherry Orchard 2002, Igby Goes Down 2002, The Hours 2002, Terminator 3: Rise of the Machines 2003, Stage Beauty 2004, Shopgirl 2005, Family Stone 2005, Evening 2007, The Flock 2007, Stardust 2007, Me and Orson Welles 2008. *Plays include:* Pygmalion (Broadway) 2007. *Television includes:* My So-Called Life (series), No Room for Opal (film), The Coming Out of Heidi Leiter. *Address:* c/o ICM, 8942 Wilshire Boulevard, Beverly Hills, CA 90211-1934, USA. *Telephone:* (310) 550-4000. *Website:* www.icmtalent.com.

DANESH JAFARI, Davoud, PhD; Iranian government official; b. 1954; ed Indian Univ. of Kashmir, Allameh Tabatabaei Univ., Tehran; expert Construction Jihad, Tehran Prov. 1979, later Commdr Eng Section, with Cen. HQ for Reconstruction 1983, Head, Logistics and Eng HQ, Construction Jihad 1984, mem. Cen. Council 1988; Man. Dir Inst. for Devt Jihad 1988; Deputy Minister of Construction Jihad for Reconstruction of Gilan and Zanjan Provs 1989, for Reconstruction of Palm Groves 1990, for Planning 1992; mem. Parl.; Minister of Econ. Affairs and Finance 2005–08; mem. High Monetary and Credit Council, High Council on Banks; Medal of Honour. *Address:* c/o Ministry of Economic Affairs and Finance, Sour Esrafil Avenue, Nasser Khosrou Street, Tehran 11149-43661, Iran (office).

DANEV, Bojidar, MSc, PhD; Bulgarian economist and business executive; *Chairman and Executive President, Bulgarian Industrial Association;* b. 5 Nov. 1939, Sofia; ed Tech. Univ., Sofia; began career at Inst. of Cybernetics, Bulgarian Acad. of Sciences, attained rank of Sr Research Assoc.; worked for two years at Univ. of Hanover, Germany; returned to Bulgaria 1980 to work as expert in Econ. Analysis Dept, Bulgarian Industrial Econ. Asscn (now Bulgarian Industrial Asscn) 1980–87, Vice-Pres. 1989–91, Chair. and Exec. Pres. 1993–; Vice-Chair. on financial issues, Cen. Cooperative Union 1987–89; Man. Sofia Stock Exchange 1991–97; Co-Chair. EU-Bulgaria Jt Consultative Cttee 1999–2004; Vice-Pres. Econ. and Social Council of Repub. of Bulgaria and of Nat. Council of Tripartite Cooperation 2006–, mem. European and Social Cttee and Head of working group on Lisbon Strategy; mem. Man. Cttee Bulgarian Acad. of Sciences; Vice-Pres. New Bulgarian Univ. Bd; Exec. Dir and mem. Man. Bd Interlease AD 1995–; mem. Man. Bd Solvay-Sodi AD, Industrial Holding Bulgaria, Doverie Insurance Company; and Chair., Industrial Holding Bulgaria AD; Chair. Man. Bd and Exec. Chair., Bulgarian Industrial Asscn. *Publications:* three books and more than 150 articles in scientific publications. *Address:* Bulgarian Industrial Association, 1000 Sofia, 16-20 Alabin Str., Bulgaria (office). *Telephone:* (2) 9800303 (office). *E-mail:* danev@bia-bg.com (office). *Website:* www.bia-bg.com (office).

DANFORTH, John Claggett, AB, BD, LLB; American politician, lawyer and diplomatist; *Partner, Bryan Cave LLP;* b. 5 Sept. 1936, St Louis, Mo.; s. of Donald and Dorothy Danforth; m. Sally B. Dobson 1957; one s. four d.; ed St Louis County Day (High) School, Princeton Univ., Yale Univ. Law School and Yale Divinity School; admitted to NY Bar 1963, Mo. Bar 1966; Davis Polk (law firm) 1963–66; Pnr Bryan Cave LLP (law firm) 1966–68, 1995–2004, 2005–; Attorney-Gen. of Mo. 1969–76; Senator from Missouri 1976–95; mem. Senate Cttees on Finance, Commerce, Science and Transportation, Select Cttee on Intelligence; Head of Special Envoy to Sudan 2001–04; US Perm. Rep. to UN, New York 2004 (resgnd); ordained priest, Episcopal Church 1964; asst or assoc. rector of churches in New York City, St Louis, Jefferson City; Assoc. Rector Church of the Holy Communion, Univ. City, Mo. 1995–; Hon. Assoc. St Alban's Church, Washington; awards include Presidential World Without Hunger Award, Legislative Leadership Award of Nat. Comm. against Drunk Driving, Brotherhood and Distinguished Missourian awards of Nat. Conf. of Christians and Jews. *Film appearance:* The Devil Came on Horseback 2006. *Publication:* Resurrection: The Confirmation of Clarence Thomas 1994. *Address:* Bryan Cave LLP, One Metropolitan Square, 211 North Broadway, Suite 3600, St. Louis, MO 63102-2750, USA. *Telephone:* (314) 259-2980 (office). *Fax:* (314) 552-8980 (office). *E-mail:* jcdanforth@bryancave.com (office). *Website:* www.bryancave.com (office).

DANIEL, Bernard; French retail executive; *Chairman, Provestis;* Dir Mammouth and Delta hypermarket chains 1975–81; Man. Dir Metro France 1981–89, mem. Bd of Dirs Metro Int., Switzerland 1989–92; CEO Carrefour SA 1992–2005, also Chair. 1998–2005, fmr Dir Carrefour Commercio e Industria, Brazil; Exec. Deputy Chair. Kingfisher PLC 2006–; Founder and Chair. Provestis; mem. Bd of Dirs Alcatel Lucent, Saint-Gobain, Gémini; fmr Vice-Chair. DIA SA, Finiper, GS, Presicarre. *Address:* Kingfisher plc, 3 Sheldon Square, Paddington, London W2 6PX, England (office); Provestis, 22 rue de la Trémoille, 75008 Paris, France (office). *Telephone:* (20) 7372-8008 (office). *Fax:* (20) 7644-1001 (office). *Website:* www.kingfisher.co.uk (office).

DANIEL, Jean, LèsL; French (b. Algerian) journalist and writer; *Editor-in-Chief, Editorial Director and Director, Le Nouvel Observateur;* b. 21 July 1920, Blida, Algeria; s. of Jules Bensaïd and Rachel Bensimon; m. Michèle Bancilhon 1965; one d.; ed Sorbonne, Paris; Cabinet of Félix Gouin, Pres. Council of Ministers 1946; Founder and Dir Caliban (cultural review) 1947–51; Prof. of Philosophy, Oran 1953; Asst Ed.-in-Chief, subsequently Ed.-in-Chief, L'Express 1955–64; Corresp., New Repub., Washington 1956–65; Assoc., Le Monde 1964; Ed.-in-Chief Le Nouvel Observateur 1964–, Ed. Dir 1965–, Dir 1978–; Admin. Louvre Museum 1992–99; Dir Monde des débats 2001; mem. Comité Nat. d'Ethique; Officier, Légion d'honneur, Croix de Guerre, Commdr Arts et Lettres, Commdr Ordre Nat. du Mérite; Prince of Asturias Award for Communication and the Humanities 2004. *Publications:* L'Erreur 1953, Journal d'un journaliste, Le Temps qui reste 1973, Le Refuge et la source 1977, L'Ere des ruptures 1979, De Gaulle et l'Algérie 1985, Les religions d'un président 1988, Cette grande lueur à l'Est 1989, La Blessure 1992, Le Temps qui vient 1992, L'ami anglais 1994, Voyage au bout de la Nation (essay) 1995, Dieu, est-il fanatique? 1996, Avec le temps. Carnets 1970–1998 1998 (Prix Méditerranée 1999), Soleils d'Hiver 2001, Lettres de France 2002, Oeuvres autobiographiques 2002, La Guerre et la Paix 2003, La Prison Juive 2003, Cet étranger qui me ressemble 2004, Avec Camus 2006. *Leisure interest:* tennis. *Address:* Le Nouvel Observateur, 12 place de la Bourse, 75002 Paris, France (office). *Telephone:* 1-44-88-34-34 (office). *E-mail:* jdaniel@nouvelobs.com (office). *Website:* www.nouvelobs.com (office); jean-daniel.blogs.nouvelobs.com.

DANIEL, Sir John Sagar, Kt, MA, MAEd.Tech, ATh, DèsSc; British/Canadian academic, university administrator and international official; *President and CEO, Commonwealth of Learning;* b. 31 May 1942, Banstead, Surrey, UK; s. of John Edward Daniel Sagar and Winifred Sagar; m. Kristin Anne Swanson 1966; one s. two d.; ed Christ's Hosp., Sussex, St Edmund Hall, Oxford, Univ. of Paris, Concordia Univ., Montréal; Assoc. Prof. Ecole Polytechnique, Univ. de Montréal 1969–73; Dir des Etudes, Télé-Univ., Univ. de Québec 1973–77; Vice-Pres. Athabasca Univ., Alberta 1977–80; Academic Vice-Rector Concordia Univ. 1980–84; Pres. Laurentian Univ., Sudbury 1984–90; Vice-Chancellor Open Univ., UK 1990–2001; Pres. Open Univ., USA 1999–2001; Asst Dir-Gen. for Educ., UNESCO 2001–04; Pres. and CEO Commonwealth of Learning 2004–; mem. Council of Foundation, Int. Baccalaureate 1992– (Vice-Pres. 1996–99), British North American Cttee 1995–; mem. Council Open Univ., Hong Kong 1996–, CBI 1996–; mem. Bd Canadian Council on Learning 2005–; Trustee Carnegie Foundation for the Advancement of Teaching 1993–; Forum Fellow, World Econ. Forum, Switzerland 1998; Fellow, Open Univ. (UK); Senior Fellow, European Distance Educ. Network 2007; Hon. Fellow, St Edmund Hall, Oxford; Officier, Ordre des Palmes Académiques; Hon. DLitt (Deakin Univ., Australia), (Univ. of Lincs. and Humberside) 1996, (Indira Gandhi Nat. Open, India) 2003, (Thompson Rivers, Canada) 2005, (Netaji Subhas Open, India) 2005, (Kota Open, India), (McGill Univ., Canada), Hon. DSc (Coll. Mil. Royal, Saint-Jean) 1988, (Open Univ. of Sri Lanka) 1994, (Univ. de Paris VI) 2001 (Univ. of Winneba, Ghana) 2006, Hon. D.Ed. (CNAA) 1992, Hon. LLD (Waterloo, Canada) 1993, (Univ. of Wales) 2002, (Laurentian Univ. Canada) 2006, (Univ. Canada West) 2008, Hon. DUniv (Univs of Athabasca, Portugal, Humberside, Anadolu Univ., Turkey, Sukhothai Thammathirat Open Univ., Thailand, Télé-université, Université du Québec, Canada, Univ. of Derby, Open Univ., Hong Kong, New Bulgarian Univ., Univ. de Montreal); Hon. D.Hum.Lit. (Thomas Edison State Coll., USA, Richmond, American Int. Univ. in London); Individual Award of Excellence, Commonwealth of Learning 1995, Morris T. Keeton Award, Council for Adult and Experiential Learning (USA) 1999; Queen's Jubilee Medal (Canada), Symons Medal, Asscn of Commonwealth Univs 2008. *Publications:* over 280 articles and books including Learning at a Distance: A World Perspective 1982, Developing Distance Education (jtly) 1988, Mega-universities and Knowledge Media: Technology Strategies for Higher Education 1996. *Leisure interests:* walking, boating, reading. *Address:* Commonwealth of Learning, 1055 West Hastings #1200, Vancouver, BC V6E 3E9, Canada (office). *Telephone:* (604) 775-8200 (office). *Fax:* (604) 775-8210 (office). *E-mail:* jdaniel@col.org (office). *Website:* www.col.org (office).

DANIEL, Patrick, BA (Hons), MPA; Singaporean journalist and newspaper executive; *Editor-in-Chief, English and Malay Newspapers Division, Singapore Press Holdings Ltd;* ed Univ. Coll., Oxford, UK, Kennedy School of Govt, Harvard Univ., USA; with Singapore Govt's Admin. Service, including post of Dir in Ministry of Trade and Industry –1986; Sr Leader/Feature Writer, The Straits Times Press Ltd 1975, Econs Ed., The Straits Times 1989, Man. Ed. 1990–92, Ed. The Business Times 1992–2002, Man. Ed. English and Malay Newspapers Div., Singapore Press Holdings Ltd 2002–06, Ed.-in-Chief 2006–. *Address:* Singapore Press Holdings Ltd, SPH News Centre, P2M, 1000 Toa Payoh North, Singapore City, 318994, Singapore (office). *Telephone:* 6319-5111 (office). *Fax:* 6319-8282 (office). *E-mail:* pdaniel@sph.com.sg (office). *Website:* www.sph.com.sg (office); www.straitstimes.com (office).

DANIEL, Paul Wilson, CBE; British conductor; b. 5 July 1958, Birmingham; m. Joan Rodgers (q.v.) 1988; two d.; ed sang in choir of Coventry Cathedral, King's Coll., Cambridge, Guildhall School of Music and Drama, London, studied with Franco Ferrara in Italy and with Adrian Boult and Edward Downes; mem. music staff ENO, London 1982–87, Music Dir 1997–2005; Music Dir Opera Factory 1987–90, Opera North, Leeds 1990–97; Prin.

Conductor English Northern Philharmonia 1990–97; Music Dir ENO 1997–2005; Prin. Conductor and Artistic Adviser, West Australian Symphony Orchestra (2009–); has conducted all the maj. London orchestras and most of the regional UK orchestras and orchestras in USA, Germany, Netherlands, France and Australia; Olivier Award for Outstanding Achievement in Opera 1997, Gramophone Award for English Music Series 1999. *Operas conducted include:* (ENO) The Mask of Orpheus, Akhnaten, Tosca, Rigoletto, Carmen, Figaro's Wedding, King Priam, Flying Dutchman, From the House of the Dead, Tales of Hoffman, Falstaff, Manon, Othello, Boris Godunov, La Traviata, The Carmelites, Nixon in China, The Silver Tassie, War and Peace, Lulu, The Trojans, Twilight of the Gods; (Opera North) Ariane et Barbe-Bleue, Attila, King Priam, Don Giovanni, Der Ferne Klang, Boris Godunov (also at BBC Proms 1992), Rigoletto, Don Carlos, Wozzeck, Gloriana, Baa Baa Black Sheep (world premiere), Playing Away, Il Trovatore, Pelléas et Mélisande, Jenůfa, Luisa Miller; (Royal Opera Covent Garden) Mitridate; has also conducted opera productions in Nancy, Munich, Brussels, Geneva. *Address:* West Australian Symphony Orchestra, 445 Hay Street, Perth, WA 6832, Australia. *Website:* www.waso.com.au.

DANIEL, Hon. Wilmoth; Antigua and Barbuda politician and auctioneer; *Deputy Prime Minister and Minister of Works, Transportation and The Environment;* b. 18 Aug. 1948, Bolans; m.; one s. one d.; ed Hill Secondary School; fmr Man. Brysons Wholesale Dept, Bottling Plant and Building Supplies Dept; United Nat. Democratic Party cand. in St Phillip's South Constituency 1984; Senator in Upper House 1989–94; mem. Parl. for St Phillip's South 1994–99, 2004–; Deputy Prime Minister and Minister of Works, Transportation and The Environment 2004–; Co-founding mem. and currently Deputy Leader of United Progressive Party. *Address:* Ministry Public Works, Telecommunications and The Environment, New Administration Building, Queen Elizabeth Highway, St John's, Antigua (office). *Telephone:* 462-4625 (office); 462-0651 (office). *Fax:* 462-6398 (office); 462-2836 (office). *E-mail:* environment@antiguabarbuda.net (office). *Website:* www.ab.gov.ag/gov_v2/government/shared/bio_wilmothdaniel.html (office); www.uppantigua.com/leadership/daniel (office).

DANIELEWSKI, Michał, BEng; Polish business executive; *Chairman, Sygnity SA;* ed Warsaw Univ. of Tech.; joined ComputerLand SA (now Sygnity SA after merger with Emax) 1992, Dir, Warsaw Br. 1994, mem. Man. Bd 1997, Gen. Dir 2002–05, Pres. 2005–07, currently Chair. *Address:* Sygnity SA, Al. Jerozolimskie 180, 02–486 Warsaw, Poland (office). *Telephone:* (22) 5711000 (office). *Fax:* (22) 5711001 (office). *E-mail:* info@computerland.pl (office). *Website:* www.computerland.pl (office).

DANIELL, Robert F.; American business executive; b. 1933, Milton, Mass; m.; ed Boston Univ. Coll. of Industrial Tech.; joined Sikorsky as design engineer 1956, programme man. for S-61, S-62 and S-58 commercial helicopter programmes 1968, Commercial Marketing Man. 1971, Vice-Pres. (Commercial Marketing) 1974, Vice-Pres. (Marketing) 1976, Exec. Vice-Pres. 1977, later Pres. and CEO until 1982; Vice-Pres. United Technologies Corpn 1982, Sr Vice-Pres. (Defense Systems) 1983, Pres., COO and Dir 1984–92, CEO 1986–94, Chair. 1987–97 (retd); mem. Bd of Dirs Travelers Corpn, Hartford Insurance Co., Shell Oil Co., Houston; Fellow, Univ. of Bridgeport; Hon. DSc (Bridgeport); Hon. LLD (Trinity Coll. and Boston Univ.);. *Address:* c/o United Technologies Corporation, United Technologies Building, One Financial Plaza, Hartford, CT 06101, USA.

DANIELS, J(ohn) Eric, BA, MSc; American banker; *Group Chief Executive, Lloyds TSB Group;* b. 14 Aug. 1951, Montana; ed Cornell Univ., Massachusetts Inst. of Tech.; joined Citibank 1975, Corp. Banking 1975–80 Panama City, Chief Financial Officer and Br. Man. of 15 brs in Argentina 1980–82, Business Man. Citibank, Chile 1982–85, Country Head, Citibank, Argentina 1985–88, Divisional Exec. Citibank Private Bank, London 1988–91, Head, Citibank Corp. Taskforce (charged with restoring bank's profitability) NY 1992, Pres. FSB Calif. (Citibank consumer franchise) San Francisco 1992–96, Regional Head, Citibank Consumer Bank Europe, Brussels 1996–97, COO Citigroup Consumer Bank NY 1998, Chair. and CEO Travelers Life & Annuity, Hartford, Conn. 1998–2000; Founder, Chair. and CEO Zona Financiera 2000–01; Group Exec. Dir UK Retail Banking Lloyds TSB 2001–03, Group Chief Exec. Lloyds TSB Group 2003–; Dir (non-exec.) BT Group. *Address:* Lloyds TSB Group PLC, 25 Gresham Street, London, EC2V 7HN, England (office). *Telephone:* (20) 7626-1500 (office). *Fax:* (20) 7356–2049 (office). *E-mail:* info@lloydstsb.com (office). *Website:* www.lloydstsb.com (office).

DANIELS, Jeff; American actor; *Executive Director, Purple Rose Theatre;* b. 19 Feb. 1955, Athens, Ga; m. Kathleen Treado; 3 c.; ed Cen. Mich. Univ.; apprentice Circle Repertory Theatre, New York; f. Purple Rose Theatre Co., Chelsea, Mich. *Theatre:* The Farm 1976, Brontosaurus 1977, My Life 1977, Feedlot 1977, Lulu 1978, Slugger 1978, The Fifth of July 1978, Johnny Got His Gun 1982 (Obie Award), The Three Sisters 1982–83, The Golden Age 1984, Redwood Curtain 1993, Short-Changed Review 1993, Lemon Sky. *Films include:* Ragtime 1981, Terms of Endearment 1983, The Purple Rose of Cairo 1985, Marie 1985, Heartburn 1986, Something Wild 1986, Radio Days 1987, The House on Carroll Street 1988, Sweet Hearts Dance 1988, Grand Tour 1989, Checking Out 1989, Arachnophobia 1990, Welcome Home, Roxy Carmichael 1990, Love Hurts 1990, The Butcher's Wife 1992, Gettysburg 1993, Speed 1994, Dumb and Dumber 1994, Fly Away Home 1996, Two Days in the Valley 1996, 101 Dalmatians 1996, Trial and Error 1997, Pleasantville 1998, All the Rage 1999, My Favorite Martian 1999, Chasing Sleep 2000, Escanaba in da Moonlight 2000, Super Sucker 2002, Blood Work 2002, The Hours 2002, Gods and Generals 2002, I Witness 2003, Imaginary Heroes 2004, Because of Winn-Dixie 2005, The Squid and the Whale 2005, Good Night and Good Luck 2005, RV 2006, Infamous 2006, The Lookout 2007, Space Chimp (voice) 2008. *Television includes:* A Rumor of War 1980, Fifth of July 1982, Invasion of Privacy 1983, The Caine Mutiny Court Martial 1988, No Place Like Home 1989, Disaster in Time 1992, Redwood Curtain 1995, Teamster Boss: The Jackie Presser Story, The Goodbye Girl 2004, The Five People You Meet in Heaven 2004. *Plays (author):* Shoeman 1991, The Tropical Pickle 1992, The Vast Difference 1993, Thy Kingdom's Coming 1994, Escanaba in da Moonlight 1995, Guest Artists 2005. *Address:* Purple Rose Theatre, 137 Park Street, Chelsea, MI 48118, USA (office). *Telephone:* (734) 433-7782 (office). *Fax:* (734) 475-0802 (office). *E-mail:* purplerose@purplerosetheatre.org (office). *Website:* www.purplerosetheatre.org (office).

DANIELS, Mitchell E.; American business executive and state official; *Governor of Indiana;* m. Cheri Lynn Herman Daniels; four d.; ed North Central High School, Indianapolis, Princeton Univ., Ind. Univ. School of Law, Georgetown Univ. Law Center; Chief of Staff to Richard Luger, Mayor of Indianapolis 1971–82; Exec. Dir Nat. Republican Senatorial Cttee 1983–84; political advisor and asst to Pres. Ronald Reagan and liaison with state and local officials, Washington, DC 1985–87; Exec. Vice-Pres. and COO Hudson Inst. 1987–90; also Pnr, Baker & Daniels (law firm); Vice-Pres. Corp. Affairs Eli Lilly and Co. 1990–93, Pres. N American Pharmaceutical Operations 1993-97, Sr Vice-Pres. of Corp. Strategy and Policy 1997–2001; Dir Office of Man. and Budget, Washington, DC 2001–03; Gov. of Indiana 2005–. *Address:* Governor's Residence, 4750 North Meridian Street, Indianapolis, IN 46208; Office of the Governor, Statehouse Room 206, 200 West Washington Street, Indianapolis, IN 46204, USA (office). *Telephone:* (317) 931-3076. *Fax:* (317) 283-1201. *Website:* www.in.gov/gov (office).

DANIELS, Ronald J., BA, JD, LLM; Canadian professor of law and university administrator; *President, Johns Hopkins University;* b. 16 Aug. 1959; m. Joanne Rosen; four c.; ed Univ. of Toronto, Yale Univ. Law School; Asst Prof., Faculty of Law, Univ. of Toronto 1988–93, Assoc. Prof. 1993–99, Dean and James M. Tory Prof. of Law 1995–2002; John M. Olin Visiting Fellow, Cornell Univ. Law School 1993; Visiting Prof. and Coca-Cola World Fellow, Yale Univ. Law School 2003–04; Prof., Univ. of Pennsylvania Law School 2005–08, Provost 2005–08; Pres. Johns Hopkins Univ. 2009–. *Address:* Office of the President, Johns Hopkins University, 242 Garland Hall, 3400 N. Charles Street, Baltimore, MD 21218, USA (office). *Telephone:* (410) 516-8068 (office). *Fax:* (410) 516-6097 (office). *E-mail:* rjdaniels@jhu.edu (office). *Website:* web.jhu.edu/president (office).

DANIELS, William Burton, MS, PhD; American physicist and academic; *Unidel Professor Emeritus of Physics, University of Delaware;* b. 21 Dec. 1930, Buffalo, NY; s. of William C. Daniels and Sophia P. Daniels; m. Adriana A. Braakman 1958; two s. one d.; ed Univ. of Buffalo and Case Inst. (now Case-Western Reserve Univ.); Asst Prof. of Physics, Case Tech. 1957–59; Research Scientist, Union Carbide Corpn 1959–61; Asst Prof. Princeton Univ. 1961–63, Assoc. Prof. 1963–66, Prof. of Mechanical Eng 1966–72; Unidel Prof. of Physics, also of Astronomy, Univ. of Del. 1972–2000, Unidel Prof. Emer. 2001–, Chair. Physics Dept 1977–80; Fellow, American Physical Soc.; John Simon Guggenheim Memorial Fellow 1976–77; Humboldt Sr Award 1982, 1992. *Publications:* more than 100 articles on the physics of solids at high pressures. *Leisure interests:* sailing, mountaineering. *Address:* Physics Department, University of Delaware, Newark, DE 19716 (office); 283 Dallam Road, Newark, DE 19711, USA (home). *Telephone:* (302) 451-2667 (office). *Fax:* (302) 831-1637 (home). *E-mail:* Family.Daniels@yahoo.com (home).

DANILOV, Yuri Mikhailovich; Russian judge; *Constitutional Court Judge;* b. 1 Aug. 1950, Mukachevo, Ukraine; m.; two s. one d.; ed Voronezh State Univ.; fmr metalworker in Lugansk; People's Judge, Povorinsk Dist Court, Voronezh Region 1971–80; mem. Voronezh Regional Court 1980–83, Chair. 1985–89; instructor, Voronezh Regional CP Cttee 1983–85; First Deputy Head of Dept of Gen. Courts, USSR Ministry of Justice 1989–91, Deputy Minister of Justice 1991–92; Chief Jurist, Vice-Pres. Int. Food Exchange 1992–93; Deputy Chair. State Cttee on Anti-Monopoly Policy and Support of New Econ. Structures; Chair. Comm. on Stock Exchanges 1993–94; Judge Sec. Constitutional Court of Russian Fed. 1994–, mem. Second Chamber 1995–; Merited Jurist of Russian Fed.; Distinguished Jurist of the Russian Fed. *Address:* Constitutional Court of Justice of the Russian Federation, 103132 Moscow,, Ilyinka str. 21, Russia (office). *Telephone:* (495) 206-16-29 (office). *Website:* www.ksrf.ru (office).

DANILOV-DANILYAN, Victor Ivanovich, DEcon; Russian politician; *Director, Institute of Aquatic Studies, Russian Academy of Sciences;* b. 9 May 1938, Moscow; m.; three s.; ed Moscow State Univ.; jr researcher, engineer, sr engineer, Computation Cen., Moscow State Univ. 1960–64; researcher, leading engineer, Head of lab., Cen. Inst. of Math. and Econs, USSR Acad. of Sciences 1964–76; Head of Lab., Prof., All-Union Research Inst. of System Studies, USSR Acad. of Sciences 1976–80; Head of lab., Chair. Acad. of Nat. Econ., USSR Council of Ministers 1980–91; Deputy Minister of Nature Man. and Environmental Control of USSR Aug.–Nov. 1991, Minister of Ecology and Natural Resources, Russian Fed. 1991–92, of Environmental Control and Natural Resources 1992–96; Chair. State Cttee for Environmental Control 1996–; Pres.-Rector Int. Industrial Ecology and Political Univ. (MNEPU) 1991–; mem. State Duma (parl.) 1993–96; founder and author, ecological programme of Kedr (Cedar) Movt 1994; Dir and corresponding mem., Inst. of Aquatic Studies, Russian Acad. of Sciences 2003–; mem. Russian Acad. of Natural Sciences. *Address:* Institute of Aquatic Studies, Russian Academy of Sciences, 119333 Moscow, 3 Gubkina Street (office); MNEPU, 111250 Moscow, Krasnokazarmennaya str. 14, Russia (office). *Telephone:* (499) 135-54-56 (office); (495) 273-55-48 (office). *Fax:* (499) 135-54-15 (office). *E-mail:* vidd@aqua.laser.ru (office). *Website:* www.iwp.ru (office).

DANIÑO ZAPATA, Roberto Enrique; Peruvian lawyer; *Deputy Chairman, Hochschild Mining plc;* b. 1951; ed Catholic Univ. of Peru, Harvard Univ., USA; fmr Sec.-Gen. Ministry of Economy, Finance and Trade; fmr Pres. Foreign Investment and Tech. Agency, Chair. Foreign Public Debt Comm.; Founding Gen. Counsel Inter-American Investment Corpn, Washington, DC, Chair. Inter-American Devt Bank's External Review Group for Pvt. Sector Operations; Pnr, Wilmer, Cutler & Pickering, Head of Latin American Practice Group 1996–2001; Pres. Council of Ministers (Prime Minister) of Peru 2001–02; Sec.-Gen. Int. Centre for Settlement of Investment Disputes (ICSID) 2003–06 (resgnd); fmr mem. Bd Newbridge Andean Pnrs, Royal & SunAlliance/Fenix, Cementos Pacasmayo, Sindicato Pesquero, Violy, Byorum & Pnrs, The Mountain Inst., The Infant Nutrition Fund; fmr mem. The Coca-Cola Co. Latin American Advisory Bd, Americas Soc. Chair.'s Council, Carnegie Endowment's G-50 Bd; currently Deputy Chair. Hochschild Mining plc. *Address:* Hochschild Mining plc, Calle La Colonia No. 180, Urb. El Vivero Santiago de Surco, Lima 33, Peru (office).

DANISHEFSKY, Samuel J., BS, PhD; American chemist and academic; *Professor, Department of Chemistry, Columbia University;* b. 10 March 1936, Bayonne, NJ; ed Yeshiva and Columbia Univs, New York, Harvard Univ., Cambridge, Mass; Asst Prof., Univ. of Pittsburgh 1964–68, Assoc. Prof. 1968–71, Prof. 1971–79, Univ. Prof. 1978–79; Prof., Yale Univ. 1979–93, Chair. 1981–87, Eugene Higgins Prof. 1983–89, Sterling Prof. 1989–93; Dir Sloan-Kettering Inst. for Cancer Research, Lab. for Bioorganic Chem. 1991–, Kettering Chair 1993–; Prof., Dept of Chem., Columbia Univ. 1993–; mem. NAS 1986, Connecticut Acad. of Sciences 1987; Fellow, Japanese Soc. for the Promotion of Science 1980, AAAS 1985; Hon. DSc (Yeshiva Univ.) 1987; ACS Guenther Award 1980, Arthur C. Cope Scholar 1986, ACS Aldrich Award for Creative Work in Synthetic Organic Chem. 1986, Edgar Fahs Smith Award, Philadelphia Section, ACS 1988, Pfizer Grad. Training Award 1991, Cliff Hamilton Award Univ. of Nebraska 1994, Max Tishler Prize Lecturer, Harvard Univ. 1995, Wolf Prize in Chem. 1996, Tetrahedron Prize 1996, ACS Claude S. Hudson Award in Carbohydrate Chem. 1996, Allan Day Medal, Univ. of Pennsylvania 1997, ACS Cope Medal 1998, Paul Ehrlich Lecture Prize 1998, ACS Nichols Medal 1999, Nagoya Gold Medal 1999, ACS H.C. Brown Medal 2000, F.A. Cotton Medal 2001, New York City (Mayor's) Award for Science and Tech. 2003, Remsen Prize for Maryland Section, Johns Hopkins Univ. 2004, Benjamin Franklin Award in Chem. 2006, Bristol Myers Squibb Lifetime Achievement Award 2006, NAS Award in the Chemical Sciences 2006, ACS North Jersey Section Award for Creativity in Molecular Design and Synthesis 2006, ACS Roger Adams Award in Organic Chem. 2007, Inaugural Award for Chem. in Cancer Research, American Asscn for Cancer Research 2007. *Address:* Department of Chemistry, Columbia University, 3000 Broadway, MC 3106, New York, NY 10027; Department of Bioorganic Chemistry, Sloan-Kettering Institute, 1275 York Avenue, New York, NY 10021, USA (office). *Telephone:* (212) 854-6195 (Columbia); (212) 639-5502 (office). *Fax:* (212) 854-7142 (Columbia) (office); (212) 772-8691 (home). *E-mail:* sjd15@columbia.edu (office); s-danishefsky@ski.mskcc.org (office). *Website:* www.columbia.edu/cu/chemistry (office); www.ski.edu/lab (office).

DANKWORTH, Sir John Philip William, Kt, FRAM; British musician; b. 20 Sept. 1927, London; m. Cleo Laine (q.v.) 1958; one s. one d.; ed Monoux Grammar School, Royal Acad. of Music; f. large jazz orchestra 1953; with Cleo Laine f. Wavendon Stables (performing arts centre) 1970; Pops Music Dir London Symphony Orchestra 1985–90; Hon. Fellow Leeds Coll. of Music; numerous record albums, most recent include Echoes of Harlem, Misty, Symphonic Fusions, Moon Valley; Hon. MA (Open Univ.) 1975; Hon. DMus (Berklee School of Music) 1982, (York Univ.) 1993, (Cambridge Univ.) 2004; Variety Club of GB Show Business Personality Award (with Cleo Laine) 1977, ISPA Distinguished Artists Award 1999, Bob Harrington Lifetime Achievement Award (with Cleo Laine) 2001, BBC British Jazz Awards Lifetime Achievement Award (with Cleo Laine) 2002. *Compositions include:* Improvisations (with Matyas Seiber) 1959, Escapade (commissioned by Northern Sinfonia Orchestra) 1967, Tom Sawyer's Saturday, for narrator and orchestra (commissioned by Farnham Festival) 1967, String Quartet 1971, Piano Concerto (commissioned by Westminster Festival) 1972, Grace Abounding (for Royal Philharmonic Orchestra) 1980, The Diamond and the Goose (for City of Birmingham Choir and Orchestra) 1981, Reconciliation (for Silver Jubilee of Coventry Cathedral) 1987, Woolwich Concerto (clarinet concerto for Emma Johnson) 1995, Double Vision 1997, Dreams '42 (string quartet for Kidderminster Festival) 1997, Objective 2000 (for combined orchestras of the Harpur Trust Schools) 2000, Mariposas (piano and violin concerto, written for Peter Fisher) 2001 (orchestrated for London Chamber Ensemble 2002). *Film scores include:* Saturday Night and Sunday Morning, Darling, The Servant, Morgan, Accident, Gangster No. 1. *Recordings include:* album: I Hear Music 2007. *Publications:* Sax from the Start 1996, Jazz in Revolution 1998. *Leisure interests:* driving, household maintenance. *Address:* The Old Rectory, Wavendon, Milton Keynes, MK17 8LT, England. *Fax:* (1908) 584414. *Website:* www.quarternotes.com.

DANNATT, Gen. Sir Richard, Kt, KCB, CBE, MC; British army officer; b. 23 Dec. 1950; ed Felsted School, St Lawrence Coll.; commissioned into The Green Howards 1971; has served with 1st Battalioin in NI, Cyprus and Germany, Commdr in Airmobile role 1989–91; Commdr 4th Armoured Brigade in Germany and Bosnia 1994–96; Commdr 3rd (UK) Div. and Commdr British Forces in Kosovo 1999, Deputy Commdr, Operations of the Stabilisation Force (SFOR) 2000; Asst Chief of Gen. Staff, Ministry of Defence 2001–02; Commdr NATO Allied Rapid Reaction Corps 2002–05; C-in-C Land Command 2005–06; Chief of the Gen. Staff 2006–08; Pres. Army Rifle Asscn, Army Rugby Union, Army Winter Sports Asscn, Soldiers' and Airmen's Scripture Readers Asscn; Vice-Pres. Armed Forces Christian Union. *Leisure interests:* cricket, rugby, tennis, skiing, shooting and fishing. *Address:* Ministry of Defence, Main

Building, Whitehall, London, SW1A 2HB, England (office). *Telephone:* (20) 7218-9000 (office). *Fax:* (20) 7218-2340 (office). *E-mail:* webmaster@dgics.mod.uk (office). *Website:* www.mod.uk (office).

DANNEELS, HE Cardinal Godfried; Belgian ecclesiastic; *Archbishop of Mechelen-Brussels;* b. 4 June 1933, Kanegem, Bruges; ordained priest 1957; Bishop of Antwerp 1977; Archbishop of Mechelen-Brussels 1979–; Castrene Bishop of Belgium 1980–; Pres. Episcopal Conf. of Belgium, Pax Christi Int.; mem. Synod of Bishops, Sacred Congregation for Evangelization, Council for the Public Affairs of the Church, Congregation of Catholic Educ., Congregation of Divine Worship, Secr. for Non-believers, Congregation for the Oriental Churches; cr. Cardinal (Cardinal-Priest of S Anastasia) 1983. *Address:* Aartsbisdom, Wollemarkt 15, 2800 Mechelen, Belgium. *Telephone:* (15) 216-501. *Fax:* (15) 209-485. *E-mail:* aartsbisdom@kerknet.be (office).

DANON, Laurence; French business executive; *Member of the Executive Board, Edmond de Rothschild Corporate Finance;* m.; two c.; ed Ecole Normale Superieur and Ecoles des Mines, Paris; joined civil service, later head, public office for investment assistance, Picardie; worked in chemical industry; joined Printemps in 2001, Chair. Man. Bd and CEO France Printemps 2002–07 (led buyout of Printemps from PPR); mem. Bd of Dirs Diageo plc 2006–, Experian Group Ltd, Plastic Omnium, Rhodia SA; mem. Exec. Bd Edmond de Rothschild Corp. Finance 2007–; ranked by the Financial Times amongst Top 25 Businesswomen in Europe (19th) 2005, (19th) 2006. *Address:* Edmond de Rothschild Corporate Finance, 47 rue du Faubourg Saint Honoré, 75401 Paris Cedex 08, France (office). *Telephone:* 1-40-17-21-17 (office). *Website:* www.lcf-rothschild.fr (office).

DANSEREAU, Pierre, CC, DSc, FRSC; Canadian ecologist and academic; *Professor Emeritus of Ecology, University of Québec;* b. 5 Oct. 1911, Outremont, Quebec (now part of Montreal); s. of J.-Lucien Dansereau and Marie Archambault; m. Françoise Masson 1935; ed Collège Sainte-Marie, Montréal, Institut Agricole d'Oka, Univ. of Geneva, Switzerland; Asst Dir of Tech. Services, Montréal Botanical Garden 1939–42; Dir Service de Biogéographie, Montréal 1943–50; Assoc. Prof. of Botany, Univ. of Mich., Ann Arbor, USA 1950–55; Dean of Faculty of Science and Dir of Botanical Inst., Univ. of Montréal 1955–61; Asst Dir and Head, Dept of Ecology, The New York Botanical Garden, Bronx, 1961–68; Prof., Inst. of Urban Studies, Univ. of Montréal 1968–71; Prof. and Scientific Dir, Centre de Recherches Ecologiques de Montréal, Univ. of Québec 1971–72, Prof. of Ecology attached to Centre de Recherches en Sciences de l'Environnement 1972–76, Hon. Prof. and Prof. of Ecology in Master's Programme in Environmental Sciences 1976–, doctoral programme 1987–, Prof. Emer. 1989–; many visiting professorships; Commonwealth Prestige Fellowship, Univ. of NZ 1961; Grand Officier, Ordre nat. du Québec 1992; numerous hon. degrees; First Prize (Prix David) Québec, science section 1959, Massey Medal, Royal Canadian Geographical Soc. 1974, Molson Prize 1974, Canada Council 1975, Izaak Walton Killam Prize, Canada Council 1985, Lawson Medal, Canadian Botanical Asscn 1986, Dawson Medal, Royal Soc. of Canada 1995, Canadian Science and Engineering Hall of Fame 2001. *Films:* An Ecologist's Notebook (six half-hour films in English and French), Ecology Close-up (6 15-minute films in English and French) 1979–83, 3 films about his life, work and ideas have been made by the Nat. Film Bd of Canada and Univ. of Québec 2000–01. *Publications:* Biogeography: an ecological perspective 1957, Contradictions & Biculture 1964, Dimensions of Environmental Quality 1971, Inscape and Landscape 1973, La terre des hommes et le paysage intérieur 1973, Harmony and Disorder in the Canadian Environment 1975, EZAIM: Écologie de la Zone de l'Aéroport International de Montréal – Le cadre d'une recherche écologique interdisciplinaire 1976, Essai de classification et de cartographie écologique des espaces 1985, Les dimensions écologiques de l'espace urbain 1987, Interdisciplinary perspective on production-investment-control processes in the environment 1990, L'envers et l'endroit: le désir, le besoin et la capacité 1994, Postface: la voie forestière, la vérité biologique, la vie durable 1994, Biodiversity, ecodiversity, sociodiversity 1997, A ética ecologica e a educação para o desenvolvimento sustentável: a mensagem de Pierre Dansereau 1999. *Leisure interests:* swimming, travel, theatre. *Address:* Université du Québec à Montréal, B.P. 8888, Succ. Centre-Ville, Montréal, PQ H3C 3P8 (office); 205 chemin Côte-Sainte-Catherine, Apt 104, Outremont, Montréal, PQ H2V 2A9, Canada (home). *Telephone:* (514) 987-3000 (office). *Fax:* (514) 987-4054 (office). *E-mail:* dansereau.pierre@uqam.ca (office).

DANSGAARD, Willi, PhD; Danish paleoclimatologist and academic; *Professor Emeritus of Geophysics, University of Copenhagen;* b. 1922, Copenhagen; ed Univ. of Copenhagen; Prof. of Geophysics, Univ. of Copenhagen –1992, Prof. Emer. 1992–; mem. Royal Danish Acad. of Science and Letters, Royal Swedish Acad. of Sciences, Icelandic Acad. of Sciences, Danish Geophysical Soc.; Hans Egede Award 1971, Tyler Prize for Environmental Achievement 1996, Crafoord Prize, Royal Swedish Acad. of Sciences 1995, Seligman Crystal, Int. Glaciological Soc., Vega Medal, Swedish Soc. of Geography and Anthropology. *Achievements:* first paleoclimatologist to demonstrate that measurements of trace isotopes oxygen-18 and deuterium in accumulated glacier ice could be used as indicator of past climate; first to note deuterium excess, or a water sample's deviation from global meteoric water line (GMWL) in ice cores; first scientist to extract palaeoclimatic information from American Camp Century ice core from Greenland drilled by US Army Cold Regions Research and Eng Lab.; repeated events of abrupt climate change during last glacial period named after him and Swiss colleague, Hans Oeschger, and are known as Dansgaard-Oeschger events. *Publications:* Isen fortæller verdenshistorie (with Steen Dansgaard) 1983, Drivhuseffekt og forsuring (with Henning Sørensen) 1984, Greenland Ice Core: Geophysics Geochemistry 1985, Klima vejr og menneske 1987, Les glaces racontent 1993, Grønland i Istid og Nutid 2000 (published in English as Frozen Annals, Greenland Ice Sheet

Research 2005; numerous scientific papers in professional journals. *Address:* Centre for Ice and Climate, Niels Bohr Institute, University of Copenhagen, Juliane Maries Vej 30, 2100 Copenhagen, Denmark (office). *Fax:* 35-32-06-21 (office). *E-mail:* ice_and_climate@gfy.ku.dk (office). *Website:* www.icecores.dk (office).

DANSON, Ted; American actor; b. 29 Dec. 1947, San Diego, Calif.; s. of Edward Danson and Jessica McMaster; m. 1st Randall L. Gosch 1970 (divorced 1977); m. 2nd Cassandra Coates 1977 (divorced); two d.; m. 3rd Mary Steenburgen (1995); ed The Kent School, Connecticut and Stanford and Carnegie-Mellon Univs; teacher, The Actor's Inst. Los Angeles 1978; CEO Anasazi Productions (fmrly Danson/Fauci Productions). *Films include:* The Onion Field 1979, Body Heat 1981, Creepshow 1983, A Little Treasure 1985, A Fine Mess 1986, Just Between Friends 1986, Three Men and a Baby 1987, Cousins 1989, Dad 1989, Three Men and a Little Lady 1990, Made in America 1992, Getting Even With Dad 1993, Pontiac Moon 1993, Gulliver's Travels (TV) 1995, Loch Ness 1996, Homegrown 1998, Thanks of a Grateful Nation 1998, Saving Private Ryan 1998, Mumford 1999, Fronterz 2004, Our Fathers 2005, The Moguls 2005, Bye Bye Benjamin (also producer) 2006, Nobel Son 2007, Mad Money 2008, The Human Contract 2008. *Theatre includes:* The Real Inspector Hound 1972, Comedy of Errors. *Television:* series include Cheers (American Comedy Award 1991) 1982–93, Ink (also producer) 1996–97, Becker 1998–2004, Help Me Help You 2006; TV films include When the Bough Breaks 1986, We Are The Children 1987, Walk Me to the Distance 1989, Down Home 1989, Mercy Mission: The Rescue of Flight 771 1993, On Promised Land 1994, Thanks of a Grateful Nation 1998, Living with the Dead 2002, It Must Be Love 2004, Knights of the South Bronx 2005, Guy Walks Into a Bar 2006, Help Me Help You (series) 2006–09, Damages (series) 2007–09. *Address:* 10345 North Olympic Blvd, Suite 200, Los Angeles, CA 90054-2524; c/o Josh Liberman, Creative Artists Agency, 9830 Wilshire Boulevard, Beverly Hills, CA 90212, USA.

DANTICAT, Edwidge, BA, MFA; American writer; b. 19 Jan. 1969, Port-au-Prince, Haiti; m. Faidherbe Boyer 2002; ed Clara Barton High School, New York, Barnard Coll., New York and Brown Univ., Rhode Island; documentary film work with Jonathan Demme 1993–95; teacher at univs in Miami, New York and Texas; Pushcart Short Story Prize 1995, Granta's Best of American Novelists Citation 1996, American Book Award 1998. *Films as associate producer:* Courage and Pain 1996, The Agronomist 2003. *Publications:* fiction: Breath, Eyes, Memory 1994, Krik? Krak! (short stories) 1995, The Farming of Bones 1998, Behind the Mountains 2002, The Dew Breaker 2004; non-fiction: Odillon Pierre, Artist of Haiti (with Jonathan Demme) 1999, The Beacon Best of 2000: Great Writing by Women and Men of All Colors and Cultures (ed.) 2000, The Butterfly's Way: Voices from the Haitian Dyaspora in the United States (ed.) 2001, After the Dance 2002, Brother, I'm Dying (Nat. Book Critics' Circle Award for Autobiography 2007) 2007. *Address:* c/o Soho Press, 853 Broadway, No. 1903, New York, NY 10003, USA.

DANYLYSHYN, Bohdan Myhaylovich, DEcon; Ukrainian economist, academic and government official; *Minister of the Economy;* b. 6 June 1965, Tserkivna, Dolyn dist, Ivano-Frankivsk Oblast; ed Ternopol State Pedagogical Inst.; Prof. of Econs 2003–; fmr Head of Council on Productive Forces Research, Nat. Acad. of Sciences of Ukraine; Minister of the Economy 2007–; Corresp. mem. Nat. Acad. of Sciences of Ukraine 2004–; State Prize of Ukraine in Science and Tech. *Publications include:* more than 150 scientific papers on regional policy, econs and exploration of nature resources. *Address:* Ministry of the Economy, 01008 Kyiv, vul. M. Hrushevskoho 12/2, Ukraine (office). *Telephone:* (44) 253-93-94 (office). *Fax:* (44) 226-31-81 (office). *E-mail:* meconomy@me.gov.ua (office). *Website:* www.me.gov.ua (office).

DAOUD, HE Cardinal Ignace Moussa I; Syrian ecclesiastic; *Prefect Emeritus, Congregation for the Oriental Churches;* b. 18 Sept. 1930, Meskané, Homs; ed Pontifical Lateran Univ., Rome; ordained priest 1954; Bishop of Le Caire dei Siri 1977–94; Archbishop of Homs dei Siri 1994–98; Patriarch of Antioch 1998–2001 (resgnd), Patriarch Emer. 2001–; cr. Cardinal 2001; Prefect Congregation for the Oriental Churches 2000–07, Prefect Emer. 2007–. *Address:* c/o Congregation for the Oriental Churches, Palazzo del Bramante, Via della Conciliazione 34, 00193, Rome, Italy (office).

DAOUDI, Riad Rashad ad-, PhD; Syrian lawyer, professor of law, international arbitrator and university administrator; *President, Syrian Virtual University;* b. 22 July 1942, Damascus; s. of Rashad Daoudi and Adallat Daoudi; m. Viviane Collin 1978; two s. one d.; ed Institut des Hautes Etudes Internationales, Paris; Prof. of Int. Law, Damascus Law School 1978–91; Asst Dean for Academic Affairs, Faculty of Law, Univ. of Damascus 1980–82; lawyer, mem. Syrian Bar 1982–; Registrar, Judicial Tribunal OAPEC 1983, now lawyer and legal adviser, Registrar Judicial Tribunal OAPEC; Legal Adviser to Ministry of Foreign Affairs 1991–; mem. UN Int. Law Comm. 2001–06; currently Pres. Syrian Virtual Univ., Damascus; Lauréat, best doctoral thesis, Univ. of Paris 1977–78. *Publications:* Parliamentary Immunities: Comparative Study in Arab Constitutions (in Arabic) 1982, Peace Negotiations – Treaty of Versailles (textbook for law students, in Arabic) 1983, Arab Commission for Human Rights, An Encyclopedia of Public International Law (in English) 1985; articles and contribs to books on int. affairs and int. law. *Leisure interests:* tennis, reading. *Address:* c/o Syrian Virtual University, Ministry of Higher Education, BP 9251, place Mezzeh Gamarik, Damascus; Dam Zoukak Al Sakhar Salim Al Sharah Street, Hadjar Building, 3rd Floor, Damascus, Syria (home). *Telephone:* +963-11-2149 9531. *E-mail:* rdaoudi@svuonline.org. *Website:* www.svuonline.org.

DAR, Muhammad Ishaq, BCom; Pakistani economist and politician; *Minister of Finance and Minister for Economic Affairs and Statistics;* ed Hailey Coll. of Commerce, Univ. of Punjab, Lahore; Minister of Commerce 1997–99, of Finance 1998–99; Chair. Bd of Govs Islamic Devt Bank 1998–99; Senator (Pakistan Muslim League—Nawaz (PML—N)) 2006–, also PML—N Parl. Leader; Minister of Finance and Minister for Econ. Affairs and Statistics 2008–; President, Int. Affairs, PML—N; fmr Pres. Lahore Chamber of Commerce and Industry; fmr Dir IMF, Asian Devt Bank, Islamic Devt Bank.; Fellow, Inst. of Chartered Accountants in England and Wales, Inst. of Chartered Accountants of Pakistan, Inst. of Public Finance Accountants of Pakistan. *Address:* Ministry of Finance, Block Q, Pakistan Secretariat, Islamabad (office); 7-H, Gulberg-III, Lahore, Pakistan. *Telephone:* (51) 9201941 (office); (42) 5881594 (home). *Fax:* (51) 9202640 (office). *E-mail:* webmaster@finance.gov.pk (office); midar50@hotmail.com. *Website:* www.finance.gov.pk (office).

DARABOS, Norbert, MA; Austrian politician; *Minister of Defence;* b. 31 May 1964, Vienna; m.; one s. one d.; ed Univ. of Vienna; Chief Exec. Dr.-Karl-Renner-Inst., Burgenland 1988–91; mem. Municipal Council of Nikitsch/Burgenland 1987–2003; Press Speaker for Gov. of Prov. of Burgenland Karl Stix 1991–98; mem. Diet of Burgenland 1999–2004, Pres. SPÖ Club 2000–03; Leader of Burgenland Prov. Social-Democratic Party of Austria—SPÖ 1998–2003, Sec.-Gen. Social Democratic Party of Austria 2003–; mem. Austrian Parl. 2004–; Minister of Defence 2007–; Supreme Commdr, Austrian Armed Forces 2007–. *Address:* Ministry of Defence, Roßauer Lände 1, Vienna 1090, Austria (office). *Telephone:* (1) 5200-21160 (office). *Fax:* (1) 520-17111 (office). *E-mail:* norbert.darabos@bmlv.gv.at (office); buergerservice@bmlv.gv.at (office). *Website:* www.bmlv.gv.at (office).

DARBINYAN, Armen Razmikovich, CandEcon; Armenian politician and university rector; *Rector and President, Russian-Armenian State University;* b. 23 Jan. 1965, Gyumri, Armenia; m.; one d.; ed Moscow State Univ.; Lecturer, Moscow State Univ. 1986–89; Sr Expert, Head of Dept, Perm. Mission of Armenia to Russian Fed., Plenipotentiary Rep., Intergovt Comm. on Debts of Vnesheconombank 1989–92; Dir-Gen. Armenian Foreign Trade Co. Armenintorg 1992–94; First Deputy Chair. Cen. Bank of Armenia 1994–97; Minister of Finance 1997, of Finance and Econs 1997–98; Prime Minister of Armenia 1998–99; Minister of Nat. Economy 1999–2000; Chair. Fund for Devt, Yerevan 2000–; Chair. Bd Trustees, Int. Center for Human Devt 2000–; Rector and Pres., Russian-Armenian State Univ. 2001–; mem. Russian Acad. of Natural Sciences; Commdr World Order of Science, Education and Culture 2002; Int. Socrates Award 2006. *Publications:* over 40 publs including Role of the State in Countries with Transition Economies, Economic Development: Prospects and Role of the Diaspora, From Stability to Economic Growth. *Leisure interests:* music and composing songs. *Address:* 19 str. Sayat Nova, 375001 Yerevan, Armenia. *Telephone:* (10) 28-97-00 (office). *Fax:* (10) 22-14-63 (office). *E-mail:* adarbinian@ichd.org (office). *Website:* www.ichd.org (office).

DARBOE, Ousainou N., LLB, BL, LLM; Gambian lawyer and politician; *Leader, United Democratic Party;* b. 8 Aug. 1948; ed Univ. of Ottawa, Canada, Fed. Law School, Lagos, Univ. of Lagos; State Counsel, Attorney Gen.'s Chambers, Banjul, Chief Prosecutor and Legal Advisor to Govt 1973–76, Acting Registrar-Gen. 1976–77; legal draftsman 1979–80; represented two-thirds of people detained under Govt's Emergency Powers regulations after 1981 abortive coup 1981–82, successfully defended leader of opposition Nat. Convention Party against charges of treason, also defended 16 other people charged with treason, of whom 13 were acquitted 1982; pvt. legal practice, Banjul, legal adviser to Gambia Public Transport Corpn, Continent Bank Ltd, Social Security and Housing Finance Corpn, Gambia Airways, Gambia Telecommunications Co. Ltd, Cen. Bank of The Gambia 1991–; mem. Bd of Dirs Gambia Public Transport Corpn 1987–92; mem. Nat. Advisory Cttee for nomination of judges to Int. Court of Justice 1992–, OAU Observer team in Eritrean referendum 1993–; Vice-Pres. Gambian Bar Assn 1991–; Deputy Chair. Gambia Law Reform Comm. 1992–; Sec. Gambia Nat. Br. African Soc. of Int. and Comparative Law 1993–; Chair. Gambian Wrestling Fed. 1985–95, Bansang Yeriwa Kafo (charity) 1990–; First Vice-Pres. The Gambia Nat. Olympic and Sports Cttee 1989–. *Publications:* numerous articles in professional journals. *Address:* United Democratic Party, 1 ECOWAS Avenue, Banjul (office); Bansang Chambers, 18/19 Liberation Avenue, PO Box 688, Banjul, The Gambia (office). *Telephone:* 4227442 (office); 4228203 (office); 4222000 (office). *Fax:* 4224601 (office). *E-mail:* info@udpgambia.org (office).

DARBOVEN, Hanne; German artist, writer and musician; b. 29 April 1941, Munich; ed Hochschule für Bildende Künste, Hamburg; has participated in numerous group exhbns of contemporary art in galleries in Europe, USA, Canada and also São Paulo Biennale 1973 and Venice Biennale 1982. *Compositions:* series of pieces for solo instruments, chamber and full orchestra. *Publications:* books including: El Lissitzky, Hosmann, Hamburg und Yves Gevaert 1974, Atta Troll Kunstmuseum 1975, Baudelaire, Heine, Disecpolo, Maizi, Flores, Kraus: Pour écrire la liberté 1975, New York Diary 1976, Ein Jahrhundert, Vol. 1 1971–77, Schreibzeit 1999. *Leisure interest:* keeping goats. *Address:* Am Burgberg 26, 21 Hamburg 90, Germany. *Telephone:* (40) 7633033.

D'ARCEVIA, Bruno; Italian painter and sculptor; b. 21 Oct. 1946, Arcevia, Ancona; s. of Benedetto Bruni and Amelia Filippini; m. Maria Falconetti 1972; one s. one d.; worked in France and Venezuela 1975–78; co-f. Nuova Maniera Italiana Movt 1982–83; one of 20 Italian artists included in ArToday review, London 1996; Commendatore Ordine della Repubblica Italiana; Gold San Valentino Award, named Marchigiano dell'Anno 1998. *Leisure interests:* underwater fishing. *Address:* Via dei Campi Sportivi 2A, 00197 Rome (office); Via Luigi Angeloni 29, 00149 Rome, Italy (home). *Telephone:* (06) 8070185 (office); (06) 5503637 (home). *Fax:* (06) 8070185. *E-mail:* info@brunodarcevia.net. *Website:* www.brunodarcevia.net.

DARCOS, Xavier, DèsL; French politician; *Minister of National Education;* b. 14 Aug. 1947, Limoges; s. of Jean-Gabriel Darcos and Anne-Marie Banvillet; m. 1st Marie-Lys Beaudry (deceased); one s. one d.; m. 2nd Laure Driant 1999; one s.; began careeer as teacher, Périgueux, at Lycée Montaigne, Bordeaux 1982–87, at Lycée Louis-le-Grand, Paris 1987–92; Insp.-Gen. of Educ. 1992–98; Assoc. Prof., Univ. de Paris-Sorbonne 1996; Counsellor, Ministry of Educ. 1993–94, 1995–97, Vice-Minister for School Educ. 2002–04, for Coopération, Devt and Francophony 2004–05, Minister of Nat. Educ. 2007–; Mayor of Périgueux 1997–2008; Senator for Dordogne 1998–2002, Vice-Pres. Senate Cultural Comm. 2001; Perm. Rep. to OECD 2005; mem. Académie des sciences morales et politiques 2006–. *Publications:* Prosper Mérimée 1998, Deux voix pour une école 2003, L'école de Jules Ferry 2005, L'État et les églises 2006, Tacite, ses vérités sont les nôtres 2006. *Address:* Ministry of National Education, 110 rue de Grenelle, 75357 Paris Cedex 07, France (office). *Telephone:* 1-55-55-10-10 (office). *Fax:* 1-45-51-53-63 (office). *Website:* www.education.gouv.fr (office).

D'ARCY, Margaretta Ruth; Irish playwright, writer, broadcaster and film maker; b. 14 June 1934, London, England; m. John Arden (q.v.) 1957; five s. (one deceased); Artistic Dir Corrandulla Arts and Entertainment Club 1973, Galway Women's Entertainment 1982, Galway Women's Sceal Radio, Radio Pirate-Woman 1986, Women in Media and Entertainment 1987; mem. Aosdána 1982; Arts Council Playwriting Award (with John Arden) 1972, Women's Int. Newsgathering Service, Katherine Davenport Journalist of the Year Award 1998, Documentary Award Galway Film Fleadh 2005. *Plays produced:* The Happy Haven 1961, Business of Good Government 1962, Ars Longa Vita Brevis 1964, The Royal Pardon 1966, Friday's Hiding 1967, The Hero Rises Up 1969, The Island of the Mighty 1974, The Non-Stop Connolly Show 1975, Vandaleur's Folly 1978, The Little Gray Home in the West 1978, The Making of Muswell Hill 1979 (all with John Arden), A Pinprick of History 1977. *Radio includes:* Keep Those People Moving 1972, The Manchester Enthusiasts 1984, Whose Is the Kingdom? 1988, A Suburban Suicide 1994 (all with John Arden). *Television documentary:* Profile of Sean O'Casey (with John Arden) 1973. *Films:* Circus Exposé 1987, Big Plane Small Axe (the Mis-Trials of Mary Kelly) 2005, Shell Hell 2005, Yellow Gate Women. *Publications:* Tell Them Everything (Prison Memoirs) 1981, Awkward Corners (with John Arden) 1988, Galway's Pirate Women, a Global Trawl 1996, Loose Theatre (Memoirs of a Guerrilla Theatre Activist) 2005. *Address:* c/o Casarotto Ramsay, 60–66 Wardour Street, London, W1V 3HP, England. *Telephone:* (91) 565430 (home).

DARCY LILO, Gordon; Solomon Islands politician; *Minister of Environment and Conservation;* b. 28 Aug. 1965; ed Univ. of Papua New Guinea, Australian Nat. Univ.; fmr Perm. Sec. for Ministry of Finance, for Ministry of Forestry, Environment and Conservation; mem. Parl. (Peoples Alliance Party) for Gizo, Kolombangara 2001–, Leader Ind. Group in Parl. 2001–06; Minister for Nat. Planning and Aid Co-ordination –2006, of Finance and Treasury 2006–07 (also Gov. World Bank for Solomon Islands), for Justice and Legal Affairs Nov. 2007, for Environment and Conservation Dec. 2007–; Chair. Forum Econ. Ministers Meeting 2006. *Address:* Ministry of Environment and Conservation, PO Box G13, Honiara, Solomon Islands (office). *Telephone:* 28611 (office). *Fax:* 28735 (office). *E-mail:* psforestry@pmc.gov.sb (office).

DARDARI, Abdullah ad-, DEcon; Syrian politician and fmr journalist; *Deputy Prime Minister, responsible for Economic Affairs;* b. Damascus; fmr journalist; fmr Chair. State Planning Comm.; Deputy Prime Minister, responsible for Econ. Affairs 2005–. *Address:* State Planning Commission, Ibn Alnafees, Rukin Al Deen, Damascus, Syria (office). *Telephone:* (11) 5161015 (office). *Fax:* (11) 5161011 (office). *E-mail:* info@planning.gov.sy (office). *Website:* www.planning.gov.sy (office).

DARDENNE, Jean-Pierre; Belgian film producer, director and screenwriter; b. (Carl Higgans), 21 April 1951, Liège; brother of Luc Dardenne; ed Arts Inst.; made several videos with his brother Luc about rough life in blue-collar small towns in the Wallonie 1970s; Pres. Jury Cannes Film Festival, Short Films 2000, Caméra d'Or 2006. *Films produced include:* Je pense à vous 1992, L'héritier (exec. producer) 1999, Rosetta 1999, La devinière (line producer) 2000, Premier amour (First Love) 2001, Le lait de la tendresse humaine (The Milk of Human Kindness) (co-producer) 2001, Le fils (The Son) 2002, Romances de terre et d'eau 2002, Stormy Weather 2003, Le monde vivant (The Living World) (co-producer) 2003, Le soleil assassiné (The Assassinated Sun) 2003, Le couperet (The Ax) (co-producer) 2005, L'enfant (The Child) 2005, Mon colonel (The Colonel) 2006. *Films directed include:* Le chant du rossignol 1978, Lorsque le bateau de Léon M. descendit la Meuse pour la première fois 1979, Pour que la guerre s'achève, les murs devaient s'écrouter 1980, R... ne répond plus 1982, Leçons d'une université volante 1982, Regard Jonathan/Jean Louvet, son oeuvre 1983, Il court... il court le monde 1987, Falsch 1987, Je pense à vous (I Think of You) 1992, La promesse (The Promise) (numerous awards in many festivals) 1996, Gigi, Monica... et Bianca 1997, Rosetta (Palme d'Or, Cannes Festival 1999) 1999, Le fils (The Son) (Ecumenical Jury Prize, Cannes Festival 2002) 2002, L'enfant (The Child) (Palme d'Or, Cannes Festival 2005, Best Foreign Film and co-winner Best Dir, Toronto Film Critics Asscn 2006) 2005, Le Silence de Lorna (Best Screenplay, Cannes Festival) 2008. *Television includes:* Brook by Brook (co-producer) 2002.

DARDENNE, Luc; Belgian film producer, director and screenwriter; b. (Eric Higgans), 10 March 1954, Awirs; brother of Jean-Pierre Dardenne; ed Arts Inst.; made several videos with brother Jean-Pierre about rough life in blue-collar small towns in Wallonie 1970s. *Films produced include:* Nous étions tous des noms d'arbres 1982, Je pense à vous 1992, Rosetta 1999, Les siestes Grenadine 1999, Premier amour (First Love) 2001, Le lait de la tendresse humaine (The Milk of Human Kindness) (co-producer) 2001, Le fils (The Son) 2002, Romances de terre et d'eau 2002, Stormy Weather 2003, Le monde vivant (The Living World) (co-producer) 2003, Le soleil assassiné (The Assassinated Sun) 2003, Le couperet (The Ax) (co-producer) 2005, L'enfant (The Child) 2005, Mon colonel (The Colonel) 2006. *Films directed include:* Le chant du rossignol 1978, Lorsque le bateau de Léon M. descendit la Meuse pour la première fois 1979, Pour que la guerre s'achève, les murs devaient s'écrouter 1980, R... ne répond plus 1982, Leçons d'une université volante 1982, Regard Jonathan/Jean Louvet, son oeuvre 1983, Il court... il court le monde 1987, Falsch 1987, Je pense à vous (I Think of You) 1992, La promesse (The Promise) (numerous awards in many festivals) 1996, Rosetta (Palme d'Or, Cannes Festival 1999) 1999, Le fils (The Son) (Ecumenical Jury Prize, Cannes Festival 2002) 2002, L'enfant (The Child) (Palme d'Or, Cannes Festival 2005, Best Foreign Film and co-winner Best Dir Toronto Film Critics Asscn 2006) 2005, Le Silence de Lorna (Best Screenplay, Cannes Festival) 2008. *Television includes:* Brook by Brook (co-producer) 2002.

DARLING, Rt Hon. Alistair (Maclean), PC; British politician and lawyer; *Chancellor of the Exchequer;* b. 28 Nov. 1953; m. Margaret McQueen Vaughan 1986; one s. one d; ed Loretto School, Musselburgh, Univ. of Aberdeen; advocate 1978–82; admitted to Faculty of Advocates 1984; mem. Lothian Regional Council 1982–87 (Chair. Transport Cttee 1986–87), Lothian and Borders Police Bd 1982–86; Gov. Napier Coll., Edinburgh 1982–87; MP (Labour) for Edin. Cen. 1987–; Shadow Chief Sec. to HM Treasury 1996–97; Chief Sec. to HM Treasury 1997–98; Sec. of State for Social Security 1998–2001, for Work and Pensions 2001–02, for Transport 2002–06, and for Scotland 2005–06, for Trade and Industry 2006–07; Chancellor of the Exchequer 2007–. *Address:* HM Treasury, 1 Horse Guards Road, London, SW1A 2HQ; House of Commons, London, SW1A 0AA (office); 22A Rutland Square, Edinburgh, EH1 2BB, U.K (office). *Telephone:* (20) 7270-4558 (office); (131) 476-2552 (office). *Fax:* (20) 7270-4861 (office); (131) 656-0368 (office). *E-mail:* darlinga@parliament.uk (office). *Website:* www.hm-treasury.gov.uk (office); www.alistairdarlingmp.org.uk (home).

DARMAATMADJA, HE Cardinal Julius Riyadi, BPhil; Indonesian ecclesiastic; *Archbishop of Jakarta;* b. 20 Dec. 1934, Muntilan, Magelang, Cen. Java; s. of Joachim Djasman Darmaatmadja (died 1973) and Maria Soepartimah (died 1966); ed Canisius Secondary School, Muntilan, St Peter Canisius Minor Seminary Nertoyudan, Magelang, St Stanislaus Coll., De Nobili Coll., Pontifical Athenaeum, Poona, India, St Ignatius Coll., Yogyakarta; entered St Stanislaus Novitiate of Soc. of Jesus, Giri Sonta-Klepu, Semarang 1957, took first vows 1959; teacher, St Peter Canisius Minor Seminary 1964–66, Vice-Prefect 1971–83, Rector 1977–81; ordained priest by Cardinal Justinus Darmojuwono, Archbishop of Semerang 1969; parish priest, Kalasan Parish, Yogyakarta 1971, Giri Sonta-Klepu 1971–73; Socius Magistri and House Minister, St Stanislaus Novitiate 1971–73; Socius Provincialis in Karangpanas 1973–77; Provincial of Indonesian Prov. of Soc. of Jesus 1981–83; Archbishop of Semarang 1983–96; Mil. Ordinary for Catholic Mems of Indonesian Armed Forces 1984–2006; Pres. Nat. Bishops' Conf. of Indonesia 1988–97, 2001; Cardinal Priest of S. Cuore di Maria 1994–; Archbishop of Jakarta 1996–; Pres.-Del. Special Ass. for Asia, World Synod of Bishops 1998; del. to Ordinary Ass., World Synod of Bishops, Vatican 2001. *Address:* Archdiocese of Jakarta, Keuskupan Agung, Jl. Katedral 7, Jakarta 10710, Indonesia (office). *Telephone:* (21) 3813345 (office). *Fax:* (21) 3855681 (office).

DARNTON, Robert Choate, DPhil; American historian and academic; *Carl H. Pforzheimer Professor and Director of the University Library, Harvard University;* b. 10 May 1939, New York; s. of the late Byron Darnton and Eleanor Darnton; m. Susan Lee Glover 1963; one s. two d.; ed Harvard Univ., Oxford Univ., UK; reporter, The New York Times 1964–65; Jr Fellow, Harvard Univ., 1965–68; Asst Prof., subsequently Assoc. Prof., Prof., Princeton Univ. 1968–, Shelby Cullom Davis Prof. of European History 1984–2007, Dir Program in European Cultural Studies 1987–95; Carl H. Pforzheimer Prof. and Dir of Univ. Library, Harvard Univ. 2007–; fellowships and visiting professorships include Ecole des Hautes Etudes en Sciences Sociales, Paris 1971, 1981, 1985, Netherlands Inst. for Advanced Study 1976–77, Inst. for Advanced Study, Princeton 1977–81, Oxford Univ. (George Eastman Visiting Prof.) 1986–87, Collège de France, Wissenschafts-Kolleg zu Berlin 1989–90, 1993–94; Pres. Int. Soc. for Eighteenth-Century Studies 1987–91, American Historical Asscn 1999–2000; mem. Bd of Dirs, Voltaire Foundation, Oxford, Social Science Research Council 1988–91; mem. Bd of Trustees Center for Advanced Study in the Behavioral Sciences 1992–96, Oxford Univ. Press, USA 1993–, The New York Public Library 1994–; mem. various editorial bds; Fellow, American Acad. of Arts and Sciences, American Philosophical Soc., American Antiquarian Soc.; Adviser, Wissenschafts-Kolleg zu Berlin 1994–; Foreign mem. Academia Europaea, Acad. Royale de Langue et de Littérature Françaises de Belgique; Guggenheim Fellow 1970; Corresp. Fellow, British Acad. 2001; Officier Ordre des Arts et des Lettres 1995, Chevalier Légion d'Honneur 2000; Dr hc (Neuchâtel) 1986, (Lafayette Coll.) 1989, (Univ. of Bristol) 1991, (Univ. of Warwick) 2001, (Univ. of Bordeaux) 2005; Leo Gershoy Prize, American Historical Asscn 1979, MacArthur Prize 1982, Los Angeles Times Book Prize 1984, Prix Médicis 1991, Prix Chateaubriand 1991, Nat. Book Critics Circle Award 1996, Gutenberg Prize 2004. *Television series:* Démocratie (co-ed.), France 1999. *Publications:* Mesmerism and the End of the Enlightenment in France 1968, The Business of Enlightenment 1979, The Literary Underground of the Old Regime 1982, The Great Cat Massacre 1984, The Kiss of Lamourette 1989, Revolution in Print (co-ed.) 1989, Edition et sédition 1991, Berlin Journal, 1989–1900 1991, Gens de lettres, gens du livre 1992, The Forbidden Best-Sellers of Pre-Revolutionary France 1995, The Corpus of Clandestine Literature 1769–1789 1995, Démocratie (co-ed.) 1998, J.-P. Brissot: His Career and Correspondence 1779–1787 2001, Poesie und Polizei 2002, Pour les Lumières 2002, George

Washington's False Teeth: An Unconventional Guide to the 18th Century 2003. *Leisure interests:* squash, travel. *Address:* Office of the Director, Harvard University Library, Wadsworth House, 1341 Massachusetts Avenue, Cambridge, MA 02138, USA (office). *Telephone:* (617) 495-3650 (office); (609) 924-6905 (home). *Fax:* (617) 495-0370 (office). *E-mail:* administration@ hulmail.harvard.edu (office). *Website:* hul.harvard.edu (office).

DARRIEUX, Danielle; French actress; b. 1 May 1917, Bordeaux; d. of Jean and Marie-Louise (née Witkowski) Darrieux; m. 3rd Georges Mitsinkides 1948; one s.; ed Paris Univ.; first appeared in films 1931, in theatre 1937; numerous TV film appearances; Chevalier, Légion d'honneur, Commdr, Ordre des Arts et Lettres, César d'honneur 1985; Prix de l'Amicale des Cadres de l'Industrie Cinématographique 1987. *Plays:* La robe mauve de Valentine 1963, Gillian 1965, Comme un oiseau 1965, Secretissimo 1965, Laurette 1966, CoCo 1970, Ambassador (musical) 1971, Folie douce 1972, Les amants terribles 1973, Boulevard Feydau 1978, L'intoxe 1981, Gigi 1985, Adorable Julia 1987, Adelaïde 90 1990, George et Margaret 1992, Les Mamies 1992, Harold et Maude 1995, Ma petite fille, mon amour 1998, Une Douche écossaise 1998, Oscar et la dame en rose 2003. *Films include:* Le bal, Mayerling, Un mauvais garçon, Battement de coeur, Premier rendez-vous, Ruy Blas, Le plaisir, Madame de . . ., Le rouge et le noir, Bonnes à tuer, Le salaire du péché, L'amant de Lady Chatterley, Typhon sur Nagasaki, La ronde, Alexander the Great, Marie Octobre, L'homme à femmes, Les lions sont lâchés, Le crime ne paie pas, Le diable et les dix commandements, Le coup de grâce, Patate, Greengage Summer, Les demoiselles de Rochefort, 24 heures de la vie d'une femme, Divine, L'année sainte, En haut des marches, Le lieu du crime, Corps et biens, Quelques jours avec moi, Bille en tête, Le jour des rois, Les Mamies, Ça ira mieux demain 2000, 8 Femmes 2002 (Silver Bear Award, Berlin Film Festival, European Film Award), Les liaisons dangereuses (TV) 2003, Une vie à t'attendre 2004, Nouvelle chance 2006, L'Heure zéro 2007, Persepolis (voice) 2007. *Address:* Agence Nicole Cann, 1 rue Alfred de Vigny, 75008 Paris, France. *Telephone:* 1-44-15-14-20 (office). *Fax:* 1-44-15-14-21 (office). *E-mail:* nicolecann@wanadoo.fr (office).

DAS, Maarten; Dutch lawyer and business executive; *Chairman, Heineken Holding NV;* b. 19 June 1948, Amsterdam; m.; three c.; ed Free Univ., Amsterdam; attorney, Loyens & Loeff 1975–, Pnr 1980–; mem. Supervisory Bd Heineken NV 1994–95, Del. mem. Supervisory Bd 1995–, mem. Bd of Dirs Heineken Holding NV 1994–2002, Chair. 2002–. *Address:* Heineken NV, PO Box 28, 1000 AA Amsterdam (office); Heineken NV, Tweede Weteringplantsoen 21, 1017 ZD Amsterdam, The Netherlands (office). *Telephone:* (20) 523-92-39 (office). *Fax:* (20) 626-35-03 (office). *E-mail:* info@heinekeninternational.com (office). *Website:* www.heinekeninternational.com (office).

DAS NEVES CEITA BAPTISTA DE SOUSA, Maria; São Tomé and Príncipe economist and politician; b. 1958; two c.; ed Univ. of the East, Santiago de Cuba, Cuba; fmr economist at World Bank and UNICEF; mem. Movimento de Libertação de São Tomé e Príncipe—Partido Social Democrata; Minister of Trade, Industry and Tourism and Minister of the Economy –2002; Prime Minister of São Tomé e Príncipe (first woman premier in W Africa) 2002–04. *Address:* c/o Movimento de Libertação de São Tomé e Príncipe—Partido Social Democrata, Estrada Riboque, Edif. Sede do MLSTP, São Tomé, São Tomé e Príncipe (office). *Telephone:* 222253.

DASCHLE, Thomas (Tom) Andrew, BA; American lawyer, government official and fmr politician; b. 9 Dec. 1947, Aberdeen, S Dakota; m. Linda Hall Daschle; one s. two d.; ed S Dakota State Univ.; served as 1st Lt, USAF 1969–72; Chief Legis. Aide and then Field Co-ordinator to US Senator 1973–77; mem. 96th–97th Congresses from 1st S Dakota Dist, 98th Congress 1977–87; Senator from S Dakota 1987–2005, Senate Minority Leader Congress 1995–2001, 2002–05, Majority Leader 2001–02; Special Policy Advisor, Alston & Bird LLP, Washington, DC 2005–08; Distinguished Sr Fellow, Center for American Progress 2005–08; Visiting Prof., Public Policy Inst., Georgetown Univ. 2005–08; Co-founder Bipartisan Policy Center, Washington, DC 2007; Richard von Weizsäcker Distinguished Visitor, American Acad. in Berlin, Germany 2008; Democrat; numerous awards including Distinguished Service Award, Nat. Rural Electric Cooperation Asscn 2000. *Publication:* Critical: What We Can Do About the Health Care Crisis 2008. *Address:* c/o Bipartisan Policy Center, 1225 I Street, NW, Suite 1000, Washington, DC 20005, USA.

D'ASCOLI, Bernard Jacques-Henri Marc; French concert pianist; b. 18 Nov. 1958, Aubagne; one s.; ed Marseille Conservatoire; became blind 1962; took up music 1970; youngest Baccalauréat matriculate of France 1974; first public appearances on both piano and organ 1974; elected as most talented French artist of the year (Megève) 1976; began int. professional career 1982, following débuts at maj. London concert halls with Royal Philharmonic Orchestra and first recording; toured Australia with Chamber Orchestra of Europe 1983; début Amsterdam Concertgebouw 1984, USA, with Houston Symphony Orchestra 1985, Musikverein, Vienna 1986, Henry Wood Promenade Concerts, London 1986, Tokyo Casals Hall and Bunka Kaikan Hall 1988, with Boston Symphony Orchestra 1992; recordings of Chopin and Schumann (with Schidlof Quartet); first prize Int. Maria Casals competition, Barcelona 1979; prizewinner, Leipzig Bach competition and Warsaw Chopin competition 1980; 3rd prize, Leeds Int. piano competition 1981. *Leisure interests:* reading, swimming, humane sciences. *Address:* c/o CLB Management, 28 Earlsmead Road, London, NW10 5QB, England (office). *Telephone:* (20) 8964-4513 (office). *Fax:* (20) 8964-4514 (office). *E-mail:* clb@clbmanagement.co.uk (office). *Website:* www.clbmanagement.co.uk/Bernard-d-Ascoli (office).

DASGUPTA, Sir Partha Sarathi, Kt, PhD, FBA; Indian/British professor of economics and philosophy; *Frank Ramsey Professor of Economics, University of Cambridge;* b. 17 Nov. 1942, Dacca; s. of the late Prof. Amiya Dasgupta and Shanti Dasgupta; m. Carol M. Meade 1968; one s. two d.; ed Univs of Delhi and Cambridge; Lecturer in Econs, LSE 1971–75, Reader 1975–78, Prof. of Econs 1978–85; Prof. of Econs, Univ. of Cambridge and Fellow, St John's Coll. Cambridge 1985–, Frank Ramsey Prof. of Econs 1994–; Prof. of Econs and Prof. of Philosophy and Dir of Program on Ethics in Society, Stanford Univ., Calif., USA 1989–92; Chair. Beijer Int. Inst. of Ecological Econs, Stockholm; Pres. European Econ. Asscn 1999, Royal Econ. Soc. 1998–2001; mem. Pontifical Acad. of Social Science; Foreign mem. Royal Swedish Acad. of Sciences, American Philosophical Soc. 2005; Foreign Assoc. NAS; Fellow, Third World Acad. of Sciences, Econometric Soc.; Hon. mem. American Econ. Asscn; Foreign Hon. mem. American Acad. of Arts and Sciences; Hon. Fellow, LSE; Dr hc (Wageningen Univ.) 2000, (Catholic Univ. of Louvain) 2007; Volvo Environment Prize 2002, John Kenneth Galbraith Award, American Agricultural Econs Asscn 2007. *Publications:* An Inquiry into Well-Being and Destitution 1993, Human Well-Being and the Natural Environment 2001, Economics: A Very Short Introduction 2007; books and articles on econs of environmental and natural resources, technological change, normative population theory, political philosophy, devt planning and the political economy of destitution. *Leisure interests:* cinema, theatre, reading. *Address:* Faculty of Economics and Politics, Sidgwick Avenue, Cambridge, CB3 9DD (office); 1 Dean Drive, Holbrook Road, Cambridge, England. *Telephone:* (1223) 212179 (office). *Website:* www.econ.cam.ac.uk/faculty/dasgupta (office).

DASH-YONDON, Budragchaagiin, PhD; Mongolian politician and diplomatist; b. 17 Feb. 1946, Huvsgul; s. of Jugnaa Budragchaa and Sengee Chogjmoo; m. Choijamts Batjargal; one s. two d.; ed Mongolian State Univ., State Univ. of Kiev, USSR; Prof., Mongolian State Univ. 1968–74; officer at Scientific and Educational Dept, Mongolian People's Revolutionary Party (MPRP) Cen. Cttee 1978–79; Vice-Chancellor, Higher Party School, MPRP Cen. Cttee 1979–85; Deputy Head and Head of Dept, MPRP Cen. Cttee 1985–90; First Sec.-Gen., MPRP Ulan Bator City Party Cttee 1990–91; MPRP Sec.-Gen. 1991–96; apptd Political Adviser to Pres. 1997; fmr Amb. to Bulgaria. *Leisure interests:* reading, chess. *Address:* c/o Mongolian People's Revolutionary Party, Baga Toiruu 37/1, Ulan Bator, Mongolia. *Telephone:* (6) 50067805. *E-mail:* contact@mprp.mn. *Website:* www.mprp.mn.

DASSAULT, Serge; French engineer, business executive and politician; *Chairman and CEO, Groupe Industriel Marcel Dassault SA;* b. 4 April 1925, Paris; s. of the late Marcel Dassault and Madeleine Minckès; m. Nicole Raffel 1950; three s. one d.; ed Lycée Janson-de-Sailly, Ecole Polytechnique, Ecole Nat. Supérieure de l'Aéronautique, Centre de Perfectionnement dans l'Administration des Affaires, Inst. des Hautes Etudes de la Défense Nationale; Dir of Flight Testing, Avions Marcel Dassault 1955–61, Export Dir 1961–63; Dir-Gen. Société Electronique Marcel Dassault 1963–67, Pres. Dir-Gen. 1967–86; Admin. Avions Marcel Dassault-Bréguet Aviation 1967, Pres. Dir-Gen. 1986–2000, Adviser, Hon. Pres. 2000–; currently Chair. and CEO Groupe Industriel Marcel Dassault SA, subsidiary cos include Dassault Aviation, Dassault Systemes, Socpresse; Vice-Pres. Société de Gestion de Participations Aéronautiques (SOGEPA); Admin. Dassault Belgique Aviation 1968; Town Councillor, Corbeil-Essonnes 1983–95, Mayor 1995–; Regional Councillor, Ile de France 1986–95; Gen. Councillor Essonne 1988–; Pres. Departmental Cttee RPR de l'Essonne 1998–; mem. Comité de direction du Groupement des industries électroniques 1968, Groupement des Industries Françaises Aéronautiques et Spatiales 1968; Hon. Pres. Fondation des Œuvres Sociales de l'Air 1968; Commissaire Général des Salons Internationaux de l'Aéronautique et de l'Espace 1974–93; Chief Engineer Armaments 1974; Pres. Asscn Française pour la Participation dans les Entreprises 1972; Chair. working group, Participation active dans l'entreprise, Nat. Council, Patronat Français 1985; Pres. of Section Asscn européenne des constructeurs de matériel spatial (AECMA) 1987–, Groupement des Industries Françaises Aéronautiques et Spatiales (Gifas) 1993–97, Council of French Defence Industry 1994–96; mem. Sénat 2004–; mem. Union pour un Mouvement Populaire (UMP); Chevalier, Légion d'honneur, Médaille de l'Aéronautique, Officier de l'Ordre national du Mérite ivoirien. *Publications:* La Gestion participative, J'ai choisi la vérité 1983. *Leisure interests:* golf, hunting, fishing. *Address:* Groupe Dassault, 9 rond-point des Champs-Elysées-Marcel Dassault, 75008 Paris (office); Mairie, place Galignani, 91100 Corbeil-Essonnes, France (office). *Telephone:* 1-53-76-93-00 (office). *Website:* www.dassault.fr (office); www.senat.fr/senfic/dassault_serge04055h.html.

DASSONVILLE, Yves, MEcon; French civil servant and government official; *High Commissioner of New Caledonia;* b. 1948; ed Ecole Nat. d'Admin, Paris; apptd Civil Admin. (2nd Class), Ministry of the Interior and Decentralization 1983; apptd Chief of Staff to Commr of Eure-et-Loire 1983; Deputy Sec.-Gen. of French Polynesia, Overseas Secr. 1984–86; Chief of Staff to Sec. of State to Minister in charge of South Pacific issues 1986; Sec.-Gen. Landes Pref. 1986–88; Civil Admin. (1st Class) and Deputy Prefect of Saint-Dizier 1988–92; Civil Admin. (unclassified), Sec.-Gen. for Regional Affairs of Languedoc and Sr Deputy Prefect 1992–95; Sec.-Gen. Pref. of Réunion 1995–98; Deputy Prefect of Lorient 1998–2001; Prefect Del. for Security and Defence to Prefect of the Southern Defence Zone 2001–02; Prefect of Jura 2002–04; Prefect (Commr) of Martinique 2004; Chief of Staff to Sec. of State for Overseas 2004–07; High Commr of New Caledonia 2007–; Chevalier de la Légion d'honneur, Chevalier de l'Ordre nat. du mérite. *Address:* Office of the High Commissioner, Nouméa, New Caledonia (office). *Telephone:* 24-65-72 (office). *E-mail:* cellule .communication@gouv.nc (office). *Website:* www.gouv.nc (office).

DÄUBLER-GMELIN, Herta, DJur; German lawyer and politician; b. 12 Aug. 1943, Bratislava, Slovakia; m. Wolfgang Däubler 1969; one s. one d.; ed Univs of Tübingen and Berlin; mem. Social Democratic Party of Germany (SPD) 1965–, Chair. Tübingen Dist br. 1971–72; State Chair. Asscn of Social

Democrat Women Baden-Württemberg 1971–76; mem. Bundestag 1972–; mem. State Exec. Baden-Württemburg, elected to Fed. Exec. Cttee 1979, Deputy Chair. Bundestag Parl. Group 1983, 1991–93, elected mem. Party Presidium 1984, 1997, Deputy Chair. 1988–, legal adviser to Parl. Group 1994, elected to Party Exec. Cttee 1997; Fed. Minister of Justice 1998–2002 (resgnd); Chair. working group on Equality for Women 1983, Bundestag Legal Affairs Cttee 1980–83, Legal Policy Working Group 1994; Dr hc (Freie Univ. Berlin). *Publications:* numerous books, articles in political journals and newspapers. *Address:* Bundestag, Platz der Republik 1, 11011 Berlin (office); Karlstrasse 3, 72072 Tübingen, Germany. *Telephone:* (30) 22773335 (office). *Fax:* (30) 22776147 (office). *E-mail:* herta.daeubler-gmelin@bundestag.de (office). *Website:* www.bundestag.de (office); www.daeubler-gmelin.de.

DAUD, Datuk Sulaiman bin Haji, BDS; Malaysian politician; b. 4 March 1933, Kuching, Sarawak; m.; four c.; ed Univ. of Otago, New Zealand and Univ. of Toronto; teacher 1954–56; Dental Officer, State Govt of Sarawak 1963–68; State Dental Officer, Brunei 1971; Political Sec. Ministry of Primary Industries 1972; Minister for Land and Mineral Resources, Sarawak 1973–74; mem. Parl. 1974–; Deputy Minister of Land Devt 1974–75, of Land and Mines 1975–76, of Land and Regional Devt 1976–77, of Health 1978–81; Minister of Fed. Territory March 1981; Minister of Educ. July 1981, of Sport, Youth and Culture 1984–86, of Land and Regional Devt 1986–89; Minister in the Prime Minister's Dept 1989–90; Vice-Pres. Party Pesaka Bumiputra Bersatu, Sarawak; other public appts and leader of Malaysian dels to int. confs; Hon. LLD (Univ. of Otago) 1993; DUniv (Flinders Univ.) 1993; Johan Bintang Sarawak, Panglima Negara Nintang Sarawak. *Address:* c/o Parti Pesaka Bumiputra Bersatu, Lot 401, Jalan Bako, POB 1953, 93400 Kuching, Sarawak, Malaysia.

DAUDA, Joseph B., LLB; Sierra Leonean lawyer and politician; b. 24 Dec. 1942, Bambawo; m.; two c.; ed Fourah Bay Coll., King's Coll., Univ. of London; teacher, St Edwards Secondary School, Freetown 1967–68; with Council of Legal Educ. 1969–72; called to the Bar, Middle Temple 1972; pvt. legal practice 1972–86, 1992–99; mem. and Legal Adviser to Man. Cttee Kenema Town Council 1980–86; mem. Parl. 1986–92; Minister of State in Office of Attorney-Gen. and Minister of Justice 1987–88, Minister of Trade and Industry 1988–91, Second Vice-Pres., Attorney-Gen. and Minister of Justice 1991–92, Minister of Rural Devt and Local Govt 1999–2002, Minister of Finance 2002–05; Gov. for Sierra Leone, IBRD, IDA, IFC; mem. Sierra Leone People's Party (SLPP). *Address:* c/o Sierra Leone People's Party, 15 Wallace Johnson St, Freetown, Sierra Leone. *Telephone:* (22) 2256341. *E-mail:* info@slpp.ws. *Website:* www.slpp.ws.

DAUDZAI, Mohammad Omar; Afghan diplomatist and government official; *Chief of Staff, Office of the President;* fmr Asst Resident Rep., UNDP, Afghanistan, fmr Afghanistan Focal Point, Bureau for Crisis Prevention and Recovery, UNDP, Geneva, Switzerland; Chief of Staff for Pres. Hamid Karzai –2005; Amb. to Iran and Perm. Rep. to Secr. of ECO 2005–07; Chief of Staff, Office of the Pres. 2007–. *Address:* Office of the President, Gul Khana Palace, Presidential Palace, Kabul, Afghanistan (office). *E-mail:* president@afghanistangov.org (office). *Website:* www.president.gov.af (office).

DAUDZE, Gundars; Latvian physician and politician; *Chairman, Saeima (Parliament);* b. 1965, Ventspils; mem. Saeima (Parl.) (Union of Greens and Farmers—ZZS list) for Kurzeme constituency, Chair. (Speaker) Saeima 2007–, Sec. Nat. Security Cttee, mem. Foreign Affairs Cttee, Employment Sub-cttee, Public Health Sub-cttee and Social Security Sub-cttee of Social and Employment Matters Cttee, Latvian Nat. Group at Inter-Parl. Union. *Address:* Saeima, Jekaba iela 11, Rīga 1811, Latvia (office). *Telephone:* 6708-7111 (office). *Fax:* 6708-7100 (office). *E-mail:* Gundars.Daudze@saeima.lv (office). *Website:* www.saeima.lv (office).

DAUGHTRY, Chris(topher Adam); American singer, songwriter and musician (guitar); b. 26 Dec. 1979, Roanoke Rapids, NC; s. of Pete Daughtry and Sandra Daughtry; m. Deanna Robertson 2000; one step-d. one adopted s.; competitor on American Idol 2006; founder mem. and lead singer Daughtry 2006–; American Music Awards for Breakthrough Artist, Best Adult Contemporary Artist 2007, People Choice Award for Best Rock Song (for Home) 2007, Billboard Music Awards for Top Artists (Pop Duo or Group), Top New Artist, Top Comprehensive Artist, Hot 100 Artists (Duo or Group), and Hot Adult Top 40 Artist 2007, World Music Awards for World's Best-Selling Rock Group of 2007, for World's Best-Selling New Artist of 2007. *Recordings include:* album: Daughtry (American Music Award for Best Pop/Rock Album 2007, Top Billboard 200 Album 2007) 2006. *Address:* 19 Entertainment Limited, 32/33 Ransomes Dock, 35–37 Parkgate Road, London, SW11 4NP, England (office). *Website:* www.19.co.uk (office); www.daughtryofficial.com.

DAUGNY, Bertrand, L.ÈS SC.; French business executive and engineer; b. 5 Jan. 1925, Paris; s. of Pierre-Marie Daugny and Suzanne Hauser; m. 1st Nicole Wolff (deceased); one s. one d.; m. 2nd Elisabeth Joussellin 1958; two d.; ed Faculté des Sciences, Paris and Ecole Supérieure d'Electricité; engineer, later Head of Dept Cie Française Thomson-Houston 1948–54; Founder, Electronic Dept, Avions Marcel Dassault 1954, Admin. Deputy and Man. Dir Electronique Marcel Dassault (now Dassault Electronique) 1963, Admin. and Man. Dir 1967, Vice-Chair. and Man. Dir Electronique Serge Dassault 1983–86, Chair. and CEO Dassault Electronique 1986–99; mem. Bd of Dirs Dassault Industries 1990–99, Dassault Aviation 1991–99, Dassault Automatismes et Télécommunications 1991–99; Commdr Légion d'honneur, Médaille Militaire, Chevalier Ordre nat. du Mérite, Croix de Guerre; Médaille Aéronautique. *Address:* 38 boulevard de la Saussaye, 92200 Neuilly-sur-Seine, France.

DAUKORU, Edmund Maduabebe, CON, PhD; Nigerian geologist, politician and international organization official; ed Imperial Coll. of Science and Tech., London, UK; Special Studies Geologist, Shell Int. Petroleum Co. 1978, held various positions in co. both in Nigeria and internationally, including Chief Geologist, apptd Div. Man. SPDC 1984; Group Man. Dir and CEO Nigerian Nat. Petroleum Corpn 1992–2003, Alt. Chair. 2003–; Special Adviser on Petroleum and Energy to Pres. of Nigeria 2003–05; Minister of State for Petroleum Resources 2005–06; Minister of Energy 2006–07; Sec.-Gen. OPEC and Pres. OPEC Conf. 2006–07; Chair. Solid Mineral Cttee for Bayelsa State; mem. Niger Delta Peace Forum, Ijaw Elder's Forum (Bayelsa State); Trustee Bayelsa State Devt Fund; apptd King Mingi XII Amanyanabo of Nembe Kingdom 2008. *Address:* c/o Ministry of Energy, Annex 3, Federal Secretariat Complex, Shehu Shagari Way, Central Area, PMB 278, Garki, Abuja, Nigeria (office).

DAUKŠYS, Kęstutis; Lithuanian politician; b. 31 Jan. 1960, Alytus; m.; two s.; ed Univ. of Vilnius and G. Plechanov Russian Acad. of Econs, Moscow; Asst, Political Economy Dept, Univ. of Vilnius 1983–85; Deputy Head of Planning Div., Furniture Design Construction Bureau 1985–87, Specialist of Foreign Trade Div. 1989–90; mil. service 1987–89; Dir UAB Balticum 1990–95, UAB Balticum grupė 1995–98, 2004; Dir Gen. AB Kilimai 1998–2003, Chair. 1999–2004;; mem. Seimas (Parl.) 2004–, mem. Cttee on Foreign Affairs 2008–, Nuclear Energy Comm. 2008–; Minister of the Economy 2005–06; mem. Darbo Partija (Labour Party). *Leisure interests:* music, fishing. *Address:* Seimas, Room I-438, Gedimino pr. 53, Vilnius 01109, Lithuania (office). *Telephone:* (5) 239-6958 (office). *E-mail:* Kestutis.Dauksys@lrs.lt (office). *Website:* www.lrs.lt (office).

DAUMAN, Philippe P., BA, JD; American lawyer and media executive; *President and CEO, Viacom;* b. 1 March 1954; m. Deborah Dauman; two c.; ed Yale Univ., Columbia Univ. Law School; Pnr, Shearman & Sterling (law firm), New York 1978–93, prin. outside counsel to Viacom, Sr mem. Mergers and Acquisitions Practice Group; mem. Bd of Dirs Viacom Inc. (predecessor of Viacom) 1987–, Gen. Counsel and Sec. 1993–98, Deputy Chair. 1996–2000, mem. Exec. Cttee and Exec. Vice-Pres. in charge of strategic transactions, legal and govt affairs, human resources and admin, supervising Paramount Entertainment, Showtime Networks and Simon & Schuster 1994–2000, mem. Bd of Dirs Viacom Jan. 2006–, Pres. and CEO Viacom Sept. 2006–; Co-founder, Co-Chair. and CEO DND Capital Pnrs LLC (pvt. equity firm) 2000–; mem. Bd of Dirs National Amusements, Inc., Lafarge North America Inc., CBS Corpn; mem. Bd Trustees, Museum of the City of New York; mem. Bd Visitors, Columbia Law School. *Address:* Viacom, 1515 Broadway, New York, NY 10036, USA (office). *Telephone:* (212) 258-6000 (office). *E-mail:* press@viacom.com (office). *Website:* www.viacom.com (office).

DAUNT, Sir Timothy Lewis Achilles, KCMG; British diplomatist; b. 11 Oct. 1935; s. of L. H. G. Daunt and Margery Daunt (née Lewis Jones); m. Patricia Susan Knight 1962; one s. two d.; ed Sherborne School, St Catharine's Coll., Cambridge; mil. service with King's Royal Irish Hussars 1954–56; entered diplomatic service 1959; Ankara 1960; Foreign Office 1964; Nicosia 1967; Pvt. Sec. to Perm. Under-Sec. of State, FCO 1970; with Bank of England 1972; mem. UK Mission, New York 1973; Counsellor OECD, Paris 1975; Head of S European Dept, FCO 1978–81; Assoc. Centre d'études et de recherches internationales, Paris 1982; Minister and Deputy Perm. Rep. to NATO, Brussels 1982–85; Asst Under-Sec. of State (Defence), FCO 1985–86; Amb. to Turkey 1986–92; Deputy Under-Sec. of State (Defence), FCO 1992–95; Lt-Gov. Isle of Man 1995–2000; Chair. British Inst. of Archaeology, Ankara 1995–2006, Anglo-Turkish Soc. 2001–09, The Ottoman Fund Ltd 2005–. *Address:* 20 Ripplevale Grove, London, N1 1HU, England (home). *Telephone:* (20) 7697-8177. *E-mail:* daunt@ripplevale.fsnet.co.uk.

DAUTRY-VARSAT, Alice, DSci; French cell biologist and academic; *President, Institut Pasteur;* b. 1950, Paris; ed Paris-Sud Univ., State Univ. of New York at Stony Brook; training in solid-state physics and molecular biology, France and USA; joined Institut Pasteur, Paris 1977, currently Prof. and Dir Biology of Cell Interaction Unit, Pres. 2005–; mem. Scientific Council, Life Sciences Dept, CNRS; Prof. École Polytechnique; fmr Visiting Scientist, MIT; mem. External Reference Group for Health Research Strategy, WHO; Trustee Ecole Polytechnique, ISTA (Austria), DNDi (Switzerland); Chevalier Légion d'honneur. *Publications:* over 130 publs on receptors and infections by intracellular bacteria. *Address:* Institut Pasteur, 25–28, rue du Dr Roux, 75724 Paris, Cedex 15, France (office). *Telephone:* 1-45-68-85-74 (office). *Fax:* 1-40-61-32-28 (office). *E-mail:* adautry@pasteur.fr (office). *Website:* www.pasteur.fr (office).

DAVENPORT, (Arthur) Nigel, MA; British actor; b. 23 May 1928, Shelford, Cambridge; s. of Arthur Henry Davenport and Katherine Lucy Davenport (née Meiklejohn); m. 1st Helena White 1951 (died 1978); one s. one d.; m. 2nd Maria Aitken 1972 (divorced); one s.; ed Cheltenham Coll. and Trinity Coll. Oxford; entered theatrical profession 1951; worked mainly in theatre 1951–61; Vice-Pres. British Actors' Equity Assen 1978–82, 1985–86, Pres. 1986–92. *Plays include:* A Taste of Honey (Broadway) 1960, Murder is Easy (Duke of York's) 1993, Our Betters (Chichester) 1997; Nat. tours: King Lear 1986, The Old Country 1989, Sleuth 1990, The Constant Wife 1994–95, Brideshead Revisited 1995, On That Day 1996. *Films include:* Look Back in Anger 1958, Peeping Tom 1960, In the Cool of the Day 1963, The Third Secret 1964, A High Wind in Jamaica 1965, Life at the Top 1965, Sands of the Kalahari 1965, Where the Spies Are 1965, A Man for All Seasons 1966, Play Dirty 1968, Sebastian/Mr Sebastian 1968, The Strange Affair 1968, Royal Hunt of the Sun 1969, Sinful Davey 1969, Virgin Soldiers 1969, The Last Valley 1970, The Mind of Mr Soames 1970, No Blade of Grass 1970, Mary Queen of Scots 1971, Villain 1971, Living Free 1972, Charlie One-Eye 1973, La Regenta, Phase IV 1974, The Island of Dr Moreau 1977, Stand Up Virgin Soldiers 1977, The Omega Connection 1979, Zulu Dawn 1979, Nighthawks 1981, Chariots of Fire 1981, Strata 1982, Greystoke 1984, Caravaggio 1986,

Without a Clue 1988, The Cutter 1992, Hotel Shanghai 1995, La Revuelta de El Coyote 1997, David Copperfield 1999, Mumbo Jumbo 2000. *Television includes:* South Riding, The Prince Regent, Howard's Way 1987–88, 1990, Trainer 1991, The Treasure Seekers 1996, The Opium Wars 1996, Longitude 1999, David Copperfield 2000. *Leisure interests:* gardening, travel.

DAVENPORT, Lindsay; American professional tennis player; b. 8 June 1976, Palos Verdes, Calif.; d. of Wink Davenport and Ann Davenport; m. Jon Leach 2003; one s.; ed Murriela Valley High School; turned professional 1993; has won 51 singles titles including Lucerne 1993, 1994, Brisbane 1994, singles and doubles (with Jana Novotna), Bausch & Lomb Championships 1997, Bank of the West 1998, Toshiba Classic 1998, Acura Invitational 1998, US Open 1998, European Championships 1998, Tokyo Pan Pacific 1998, 2001, 2003, Sydney Int. 1999, Wimbledon 1999 (singles and doubles), Advanta Championships, Philadelphia 1999, Chase Championships, New York 1999, Australian Open 2000, Indian Wells 2000; mem. Olympic Team 1996, gold medallist singles 2000; mem. US Fed. Cup Team 1993–2000, 2002; 86 career professional titles in total (35 doubles titles). *Leisure interests:* watching hockey, sports in general, music, crosswords, going to the beach. *Address:* c/o IMG Tennis, IMG Center, 1360 East 9th Street, Suite 100, Cleveland, OH 44114, USA. *Telephone:* (216) 522-1200. *Fax:* (216) 436-3477.

DAVENPORT, Paul Theodore, OC, BA, MA, PhD; Canadian economist, academic and university administrator; *President and Vice Chancellor, University of Western Ontario;* b. 24 Dec. 1946, Summit, NJ; s. of Theodore Davenport and Charlotte Lomax Paul; m. Josette Brotons 1969; one s. two d.; ed Stanford Univ. and Univ. of Toronto; Prof., Dept of Econs McGill Univ. 1973–89, Assoc. Dean, Faculty of Grad. Studies and Research, 1982–86, Vice-Prin. (Planning and Computer Services) 1986–89; Pres. and Vice-Chancellor Univ. of Alberta 1989–94, Univ. of Western Ontario 1994–; Chair. Asscn of Univs and Colls of Canada 1997–99, Council of Ont. Univs 1999–2001; Chevalier Légion d'Honneur 2001; Hon. LLD (Alta) 1994, (Toronto) 2000, (Int. Univ. of Moscow) 2002. *Publications:* Reshaping Confederation: The 1982 Reform of the Canadian Constitution (ed. with R. Leach) 1984, Universities and the Knowledge Economy in Renovating the Ivory Tower (ed. David Laidler) 2002. *Leisure interests:* biking, Impressionist painting, modern jazz, photography. *Address:* Office of the President, University of Western Ontario, Natural Sciences Centre, Room 120A, London, Ont., N6A 5B9 (office); 1836 Richmond Street, London, Ont., N5X 4B9, Canada (home). *Telephone:* (519) 661-3106 (office); (519) 660-0178 (home). *Fax:* (519) 661-3676 (office). *E-mail:* pdavenpo@uwo.ca (office). *Website:* www.uwo.ca (office); www.uwo.ca/pvp.

DAVEY, Grenville, BA; British sculptor, artist and academic; *Visiting Professor, University of the Arts, London;* b. 28 April 1961, Launceston, Cornwall; ed Exeter Coll., Goldsmith's Coll., London; currently Visiting Prof., Univ. of the Arts, London; Turner Prize, Tate Gallery 1992, Art and Architecture Award, Royal Soc. of Arts 1995. *Leisure interests:* work, walking. *Address:* University of East London, 4–6 University Way, London, E16 2RD, England (office). *Telephone:* (20) 8223-3433 (office).

DAVEY, Kenneth George, OC, PhD, FRSC; Canadian academic and scientist; *Distinguished Research Professor Emeritus of Biology, York University;* b. 20 April 1932, Chatham, Ont.; s. of William Davey and Marguerite Davey (née Clark); m. Jeannette Isabel Evans 1959 (separated 1989); one s. two d.; ed McKeough Public School, Chatham, Chatham Collegiate Inst., Univ. of Western Ontario, Univ. of Cambridge, UK; NRC Fellow (Zoology), Univ. of Toronto 1958–59; Drosier Fellow, Gonville and Caius Coll., Cambridge 1959–63; Assoc. Prof. of Parasitology, McGill Univ., Montréal 1963–66, Dir Inst. of Parasitology 1964–74, Prof. of Parasitology and Biology 1966–74; Prof. of Biology, York Univ., Toronto 1974–84, Chair. of Biology 1974–81, Dean of Science 1982–85, Distinguished Research Prof. of Biology 1984–2000, Prof. Emer. 2000–, Vice-Pres. (Academic Affairs) 1986–91; Ed. International Journal of Invertebrate Reproduction and Development 1979–85, Canadian Journal of Zoology 1995–2004; Assoc. Ed. Encyclopedia of Reproduction 1996–; mem. Bd of Dirs Huntsman Marine Lab. 1978–80, 1982–85, Pres. and Chair. of Bd 1977–80; Pres. Biological Council of Canada 1979–82, Canadian Soc. of Zoologists 1981–82; Sec. Acad. of Science, Royal Soc. of Canada 1979–85; mem. Council, Royal Canadian Inst. 1996– (Pres. 2000–02), mem. Nat. Council on Ethics in Human Research (Pres. 2002–03); Fellow, Entomological Soc. of Canada 1997; Hon. Fellow, Royal Entomological Soc. 2004; Queen's Jubilee Medal 1977, 2002; Hon. DSc (Western Ontario) 2002; Gold Medal, Entomological Soc. of Canada 1981, Fry Medal, Canadian Soc. of Zoologists 1987, Gold Medal, Biological Council of Canada 1987, Distinguished Biologist Award, Canadian Council of Univ. Biology Chairs 1992, Hitschfeld Award, Canadian Asscn Univ. Research Admins 1997, Wigglesworth Medal, Royal Entomological Soc., London 2004. *Publications:* Reproduction in Insects 1964; 200 articles on insect endocrinology. *Leisure interests:* handweaving, food and wine. *Address:* Department of Biology, York University, 4700 Keele Street, Toronto, ON M3J 1P3 (office); 96 Holm Crescent, Thornhill, ON L3T 5J3, Canada (home). *Telephone:* (416) 736-2100 (office); (905) 882-5077 (home). *Fax:* (416) 736-5698 (office). *E-mail:* davey@yorku.ca (office). *Website:* www.biol.yorku.ca (office).

DAVID, Adelino Castelo; São Tomé and Príncipe economist, central banker and government official; Gov. Banco Central de São Tomé e Príncipe 1992–94; Minister of Planning and Finance 1999–2001, 2004–05, Co-ordinator Centre De Recherche et d'Analyse des Politiques de Développement de Sao Tome et Principe, Ministry of Planning and Finance 2007–. *Address:* Ministry of Planning and Finance, Largo Alfândega, BP 168, São Tomé, São Tomé e Príncipe (office). *Telephone:* 225467 (office). *E-mail:* adelinocd@yahoo.com (office).

DAVID, Cristian, PhD; Romanian politician; b. 26 Dec. 1967; ed Univ. of Bucharest and Romanian Nat. Defence Coll.; with TMUCB Bucharest (eng co.) 1986–90, Designer 1990–91; Co-ordinator Nat. Liberal Univ. Youth Org. 1990–93, Sec.-Gen. 1993–97; Advisor, Ministry of Youth and Sport 1997–98; mem. Standing Cttee, Nat. Liberal Party—Partidul Naţional Liberal 1991–93, Dir Foreign Relations Dept 1997–2004, mem. Nat. Rep. Del. 2002–04, Chair. Foreign Affairs Comm. 2004–05, mem. Cen. Standing Cttee 2005–06, mem. Cen. Political Bureau 2006–; Dir Van Soestbergen Import Export SRL 1992–94, Team Int. Import Export SRL 1995–96, Team Int. Consult SRL 1999–2004; Assoc. Lecturer, Dept of Statistics and Econ. Forecasting, Acad. of Econ. Studies 2001–04; mem. Senate 2004–, mem. Senate Human Rights, Cults and Minorities Comm. 2004–; Minister-Del. responsible for internationally financed projects 2004–07; Minister of the Interior and Admin. Reform 2007–08; mem. Romanian Asscn for Liberty and Devt 1997–2000; Founding mem. Liberal Studies Inst. 2006. *Publications include:* various articles on econs and statistics. *Address:* National Liberal Party (NLP), 011866 Bucharest, Bd. Aviatorilor 86, Romania (office). *Telephone:* (21) 2310795 (office). *Fax:* (21) 2310796 (office). *E-mail:* dre@pnl.ro (office). *Website:* www .pnl.ro (office).

DAVID, François Paul; French civil servant; *Chairman, Coface;* b. 5 Dec. 1941, Clermont-Ferrand; s. of Jean David and Rose David (née Cabane); m. Monique Courtois 1967; two s.; ed French Lycée, London, Faculté de Lettres, Paris, Ecole nat. d'admin.; mem. staff Dept of Foreign Econ. Relations, Ministry of Finance 1969–73, Head Agric. Policy Office 1976–78; Commercial Counsellor, Embassy in the UK 1974–76; Tech. Adviser Office of Minister of Foreign Trade 1978–80; Asst Dir Ministry of Economy, Finance and Budget 1981–84, Deputy Dir 1984–86, Dir Office of Jr Minister in charge of Foreign Trade at Ministry of Economy, Finance and Privatization 1986–87, Dir Dept of Foreign Econ. Relations 1987–89; Dir-Gen. Int. Affairs, Aérospatiale 1990–94; Chair. Compagnie française d'assurance pour le commerce extérieur (Coface) 1994–; mem. Bd Dirs Eads & Vinci; Censor of Rexel; Commdr, Légion d'honneur; Chevalier, Ordre nat. du Mérite; Officier du Mérite agricole; Officier, Ordre de Saint-Charles (Monaco). *Publications:* Le Mythe de l'exportation 1971, Autopsie de la Grande-Bretagne 1976, Le Commerce international à la dérive 1982, La Guerre de l'export 1987, Relations économiques internationales: La politique commerciale des grandes puissances face à la crise 1989, Jacques Cœur, l'aventure de l'argent 1990. *Leisure interests:* tennis, karate. *Address:* Coface, 12 cours Michelet, La Défense 10, 92065 Paris -la-Défense Cedex (office). *Telephone:* 1-49-02-13-00 (office). *Fax:* 1-49-02-14-21 (office). *E-mail:* francois_david@coface.com (office). *Website:* www.coface.com (office).

DAVID, George Alfred Lawrence, MBA; American business executive; *Chairman, United Technologies Corporation;* b. 7 April 1942, Bryn Mawr, Pa; s. of Charles Wendell David and Margaret Simpson; m. Barbara Osborn 1965; one s. two d.; ed Harvard Univ. and Univ. of Virginia; Asst Prof. Univ. of Va, Charlottesville 1967–68; Vice-Pres. Boston Consulting group 1968–75; Sr Vice-Pres. (Corp. Planning and Devt) Otis Elevator Co., New York 1975–77, Sr Vice-Pres. and Gen. Man. Latin American Operations, West Palm Beach, Fla 1977–81, Pres. N American Operations, Farmington, Conn. 1981–85, Pres. and CEO Otis Elevator Co. 1985–89; Exec. Vice-Pres. and Pres. (Commercial/ Industrial) United Technologies Corpn (parent co.) 1989–92, Pres. and COO 1992–94, CEO 1994–2008, Chair. 1997–; mem. Bd of Dirs Citigroup Inc., Nat. Acad. Foundation, Inst. Int. Econs, Washington 1996–; mem. The Business Council, The Business Roundtable; Trustee, Carnegie Hall Corpn, Inc.; Order of Friendship (Russia) 1999, Légion d'honneur 2002. *Address:* United Technologies Corporation, 1 Financial Plaza, Suite 22, Hartford, CT 06103-2608, USA (office). *Telephone:* (860) 728-7000 (office). *Fax:* (860) 728-7979 (office). *E-mail:* invrelations@corphq.utc.com (office). *Website:* www.utc.com (office).

DÁVID, Ibolya, LLD, JD; Hungarian politician and lawyer; *Chairperson, Hungarian Democratic Forum;* b. 12 Aug. 1954, Baja; m.; two c.; ed Tóth Kálmán Grammar School and Vocational School for Water Man., Baja, Janus Pannonius Univ., Pécs; lawyer 1985–; mem. Hungarian Democratic Forum (MDF) 1989–, Tolna County Pres. 1993–97, mem. Nat. Exec. 1996–, Chair. 1999–, under Dávid's leadership party united with Hungarian Democratic People's Party (MDNP) which had previously broken away; mem. Tolna County Ass. 1990–94; mem. of Parliament 1990–, Deputy Parl. Group Leader 1994–98, 2004–; Minister of Justice 1998–2002; Del. to European Parl. 2002–04; Deputy Speaker Hungarian Nat. Ass. and mem., Council of Elders 2002–06; head of alliance between MDF, MDNP and Ind. Smallholder's Party (FKGP) at 2004 EU parl. elections, relinquished seat following victory; mem. Cttee on Immunity, Incompatibility and Mandate 2006–. *Address:* Hungarian Democratic Forum (Magyar Demokrata Fórum), 1026 Budapest, Szilágyi Erzsébet fasor 73 (office); Hungarian National Assembly, 1357, Budapest, Kossuth tér 1–3, Hungary (office). *Telephone:* (1) 441-5188 (office). *Fax:* (1) 441-441-5180 (office). *E-mail:* David.Ibolya@mkogy.hu; ibolya.david@ parlament.hu (office). *Website:* www.parlament.hu (office); www.mdf.hu (office).

DAVID, Jacques-Henri; French business executive; *Chairman, Deutsche Bank (France);* b. 17 Oct. 1943, Ygrande (Allier); s. of André David and Suzanne Dupeyrat; m. Isabelle Lamy 1967; one d.; ed Lycée Louis-le-Grand, Paris, Ecole Polytechnique, Inst. d'Etudes Politiques, Paris and Ecole Nat. Supérieure de la Statistique et des Études Économiques (Insee), Paris; Admin. Insee 1967–68; Head, econometric studies service, Banque de France 1969–75; Deputy Sec.-Gen. Conseil Nat. du Crédit 1973–75; Prof. Inst. d'Etudes Politiques 1975; Insp. des Finances, Ministry of Econ. and Finance 1975–79; Adviser, Office of Minister of Econ. 1979, Deputy Dir 1980, Dir 1980–81; Sec.-Gen. Conseil Nat. du Crédit 1981–84; Finance Dir Cie Saint-Gobain 1984–86,

Dir-Gen. 1986–89; Pres. Banque Stern 1989–92; Pres. Centre de Recherche pour l'expansion de l'économie (Rexecode) 1989–96; Dir-Gen. Compagnie Gen. des Eaux 1993–95; Pres. CEPME 1995–99, Sofaris 1996–99, Bank for Devt of Small and Medium-Sized Businesses (BDPME) 1997–99; mem. Deutsche Bank Group Social and Econ. Council 1996–1999; Chair. Deutsche Bank in France 1999–; Vice-Chair. Global Corporate Finance; Officier Légion d'honneur, Commdr Ordre du Mérite. *Publications:* La Politique monétaire 1974, Réévaluation et verité des bilans 1977, La Monnaie et la politique monétaire 1983, Crise financière et relations monétaires internationales 1985, Le Financement des opérations à risque dans les PME 1997. *Leisure interests:* skiing, yachting, golf. *Address:* Deutsche Bank, 3 avenue de Friedland, 75008 Paris, France (office). *Telephone:* 1-44-95-65-65 (office). *E-mail:* jacques-henri .david@db.com (office).

DAVID, Peter; Grenadian/Canadian politician; *Minister of Foreign Affairs;* mem. House of Reps for St George 2003–; Gen. Sec., Nat. Democratic Congress Party; Minister of Foreign Affairs 2008–. *Address:* Ministry of Foreign Affairs, Ministerial Complex, 4th Floor, Botanical Gardens, St St George's, Grenada (office). *Telephone:* 440-2640 (office). *Fax:* 440-4184 (office). *E-mail:* foreignaffairs@gov.gd (office).

DAVID-WEILL, Michel; French business executive; *Chairman of the Supervisory Board, EURAZEO;* b. 23 Nov. 1932, Paris; s. of late Pierre David-Weill and of Berthe Haardt; m. Hélène Lehideux 1956; four d.; ed Lycée français, New York and Inst. d'études politiques, Paris; Lazard Frères & Co. LLC, NY 1961–65, Chair. and Sr Pnr 1977–2005; Gen. Pnr Lazard Frères & Cie, Paris 1965, Maison Lazard & Cie 1976–2005; Gen. Pnr and Chair. Lazard Pnrs Ltd Partnership 1984–2005; Chair. Lazard Brothers & Co. Ltd, London 1990–92, Deputy Chair. 1992, Chair. Lazard LLC (after merger of Lazard Bros. Paris, London and NY offices) 2000–05; mem. Bd of Dirs EURAZEO 1972, now Chair. of Supervisory Bd; mem. Man. Bd, Sovac 1972–, Chair. 1982–95; mem. Bd of Dirs, Danone, later Vice-Chair.; mem. Man. Bd Publicis; Dir La France SA, La France IARD, La France-Vie, La France Participations et Gestion, SA de la Rue Impériale de Lyon, Fonds Partenaires-Gestion (FPG), Fiat SpA, Euralux, Exor Group, ITT Corp., The Dannon Co. Inc.; fmr Dir Pearson PLC, NY Stock Exchange; Chair. Artistic Council, Réunion des Musées Nationaux, Paris, Metropolitan Museum Council, New York, New York Hosp. Morgan Library; mem. Inst. (Acad. des Beaux Arts, Paris); Grand Officier, Légion d'honneur, Officier, Ordre Nat. du Mérite, Commdr des Arts et des Lettres. *Publication:* L'esprit en fête 2007. *Address:* Institut de France, 23 quai Conti, 75006 Paris, France. *Telephone:* 1-44-15-89-34 (office). *Fax:* 1-47-66-43-72 (office). *E-mail:* staff@md-w.com (office). *Website:* www.eurazeo.com (office).

DAVIDE, Hilario G., Jr, BSc, BL; Philippine chief justice; *Permanent Representative, United Nations;* b. 20 Dec. 1935, Colawin, Argau, Cebu; s. of Hilario P. Davide, Sr and Virginia Jimenea Perez; ed Univ. of the Philippines; Pvt. Sec. to Vice-Gov. then to Gov. of Cebu 1959–63; Faculty Mem. Coll. of Law, Southwestern Univ., Cebu City 1962–68; Del. to Constitutional Convention 1971, Chair. Cttee on Duties and Obligations of Citizens and Ethics of Public Officials; Minority Floor Leader 1978–79; mem. interim Batasang Pambansa Ass. representing Region VII 1978–84; Chair. Comm. on Elections 1988–90, Presidential Fact Finding Comm. 1990–91; Assoc. Justice of the Supreme Court 1991–98, Sr Assoc. Justice Oct.–Nov. 1998, Chief Justice 1998–2005; Perm. Rep. to UN 2007–; Hon. Pres. World Jurist Asscn of the World Peace Through Law Centre; mem. Advisory Council of Eminent Jurists, UNEP, Regional Office for Asia and the Pacific; Hon. LLD (Southwestern Univ.) 1999, (Far Eastern Univ.) 2001, (Univ. of the Philippines) 2001, (Angeles Univ. Foundation) 2001, (De La Salle Univ.) 2001; Hon. DH (Univ. of Cebu) 2000, (Ateneo de Manila Univ.) 2001, (Univ. of the Visayas) 2001; Service to the Nation Award 1987, Outstanding Kts of Columbus Award 1995, Nat. Maagap Award, Organized Response for the Advancement of Soc. (ORAS) 1998, Millennium Medal of Merit, Order of the Kts of Rizal 2000, Rajah Humabon Award 2001, Grand Perlas Award, Philippine Foundation Inc. 2001, Rule of Law Award, Chief Justice Techankee Foundation 2001, Chino Roces Foundation Freedom Award 2001, Rizal Peace Award, Univ. of S Philippines 2001. *Address:* Permanent Mission of the Philippines to the United Nations, 556 Fifth Avenue, 5th Floor, New York, NY 10036, USA (office). *Telephone:* (212) 764-1300 (office). *Fax:* (212) 840-8602 (office). *E-mail:* misunphil@aol.com (office). *Website:* www.un.int/phillipines (office).

DAVIDOVICH, Bella; American (b. Azerbaijan) pianist; b. 16 July 1928, Baku, Azerbaijan; d. of Mikhail Davidovich and Lucia Ratner; m. Julian Sitkovetsky 1950 (died 1958); one s.; ed Moscow Conservatory; studied with Konstantin Igumnov and Jakob Flier; First Prize, Chopin Competition, Warsaw 1949; soloist with Leningrad and Moscow Philharmonics for 28 consecutive seasons; taught piano at Moscow Conservatory 1962–78; toured Europe; went to USA 1978; mem. faculty Juilliard School, NY 1983–2003; became US citizen 1984; has performed with world's leading conductors in USA, Russia, Europe and Japan; juror, several int. piano competitions; Prof. Emer., Music Acad. of Baku, Azerbaijan; Distinguished Artist of the Russian Soviet Federative Socialist Repub. *Recordings:* numerous recordings on major int. labels. *Leisure interest:* literature. *Address:* c/o Tennant Artists, Unit 2, 39 Tadema Road, London SW10 0PZ, England (office); c/o KünstlerSekretariat am Gasteig, Elisabeth Ehlers/Lothar Schacke, Rosenheimer Strasse 52, 81669 Munich, Germany (office). *Telephone:* (20) 7376-3758 (office); (89) 4448879-2 (office). *Fax:* (20) 7351-0679 (office); (89) 4489522 (office). *E-mail:* info@ tennantartists.com (office); verena.vetter@ks-gasteig.de (office). *Website:* www.tennantartists.com (office); www.ks-gasteig.de (office).

DAVIDS, Willibrord Jacob Maria, LLM; Dutch judge; b. 17 Oct. 1938, Rotterdam; m. Marianne Baan; ed Roman Catholic Univ. of Nijmegen; worked at civil law notary office in Hilversum, Curaçao (Netherlands Antilles) and

Groningen 1965; lectured in civil law, Groningen Univ. 1975–80; apptd judge, dist court, Assen 1980, Vice-Pres. 1984; apptd Justice, Supreme Court of the Netherlands 1986, Vice-Pres. 1998–2004, Pres. 2004–08; Pres. Benelux Court, Court of Appeal for Supervision of Standards of Certified Architects, Asscn of Dutch Architects; mem. Coll. of Appeal, Benelux Asscn of Trade Mark Lawyers and Counsellors. *Publications:* several books and articles on real estate law, corpn law and criminal law. *Address:* c/o De Hoge Raad der Nederlanden, PO Box 20303, 2500 EH The Hague, Netherlands (office).

DAVIDSON, Basil Risbridger, MC; British historian and academic; b. 9 Nov. 1914, Bristol; s. of Thomas Davidson and Jessie Davidson; m. Marion Ruth Young 1943; three s.; served British Army 1940–45, Lt-Col 1945; journalist with The Economist, The Star, The Times, New Statesman, Daily Herald, Daily Mirror, 1938–62; Visiting Prof. in African History, Univ. of Ghana 1964, UCLA 1965; Regent's Lecturer in African History, UCLA 1971; Montague Burton Visiting Prof. of Int. Relations, Univ. of Edin. 1972; Simon Sr Research Fellow, Univ. of Manchester 1975–76; Agnelli Visiting Prof., Univ. of Turin 1990; Freeman City of Genoa 1945; Hon. Research Fellow, Univ. of Birmingham 1974; Hon. Fellow, SOAS (Univ. of London) 1989; Mil. Cross, Bronze Star, US Army, Zasluge za Narod, Yugoslav Army, Grand Officer, Order of Prince Henry the Navigator (Portugal) 2002; Hon. DLitt (Univ. of Ibadan) 1975, (Dar es Salaam) 1985, (Univ. of Western Cape, SA) 1997; Hon. DUniv (Open Univ.) 1980, (Edin.) 1981, (Bristol) 1999; Haile Selassie Award for African Research 1970, Medalha Amílcar Cabral 1976. *Publications:* principal works: Old Africa Rediscovered 1959, Black Mother—The African Slave Trade 1961 (revised 1980), The African Past 1964, History of West Africa to 1800 1965, History of East and Central Africa to the Late Nineteenth Century 1967, Africa in History: Themes and Outlines 1967, The Africans: A Cultural History 1969, The Liberation of Guiné 1969 (revised 1981), In the Eye of the Storm: Angola's People 1972, Black Star 1973, Can Africa Survive? 1975, Africa in Modern History, The Search for a New Society 1978, Special Operations Europe – Scenes from the Anti-Nazi War 1980, The People's Cause: A History of Guerrillas in Africa 1981, Modern Africa 1982, Africa (TV series) 1984, The Story of Africa 1984, The Fortunate Isles 1988, The Black Man's Burden 1992, The Search for Africa—History, Politics, Culture 1994, West Africa Before the Colonial Era: A History to 1850 1998. *Leisure interests:* planting trees, watching wild birds. *Address:* 21 Deanery Walk, Avonpark Village, Limpley Stoke, Bath, BA2 7JQ, England (home).

DAVIDSON, Janet Marjorie, ONZM, FRSNZ, MA, DSc; New Zealand archaeologist and ethnologist; b. 23 Aug. 1941, Lower Hutt; d. of Albert Dick Davidson and Christine Mary Davidson (née Browne); m. Bryan Foss Leach 1979; one d.; ed Hutt Valley High School and Univ. of Auckland; Field Assoc., Bernice P. Bishop Museum, Honolulu 1964–66; E. Earle Vaile Archaeologist, Auckland Inst. and Museum 1966–79; Hon. Lecturer in Anthropology, Univ. of Otago 1980–86; ethnologist, Nat. Museum of NZ 1987–91; Curator (Pacific Collections) Museum of NZ Te Papa Tongarewa 1991–2002; extensive archaeological field work in NZ and the Pacific; Rhodes Visiting Fellow, Lady Margaret Hall, Oxford 1974–76. *Publications:* Archaeology on Nukuaro Atoll 1971, The Prehistory of New Zealand 1984, Archaeology on Taumako: a Polynesian Outlier in the Eastern Solomon Islands (with B.F. Leach) 2008, numerous articles on the archaeology and prehistory of New Zealand and various Pacific Islands. *Leisure interests:* music, theatre, opera, ballet, cooking.

DAVIDSON, John Macdonald, AM, BArch, LFRAIA, RIBA; Australian architect; *Director, Architecture, Catalyst Design Group;* b. 21 Oct. 1926, Sydney; s. of the late John H. Davidson and of Daisy Macdonald; m. Helen M. King 1954; two s. one d.; ed Geelong Coll. and Univ. of Melbourne; Assoc. Godfrey and Spowers (architects) 1954–61, Pnr, later Dir 1961, Chair. Godfrey and Spowers Australia Pty Ltd 1979–91; Pres. Royal Australian Inst. of Architects 1978–79; mem. Expert Panel in Architecture (COPQ) 1978–; mem. Int. Council, Int. Union of Architects (UIA) 1981–85, Vice-Pres. UIA 1985–87; Chair. Metropolitan Strategy Consultative Cttee 1984–89, South Yarra Collaborative Pty Ltd 1983–89; co-founder (with son Hugo Davidson) and Dir, Architecture, Catalyst Design Group 1989–; Hon. FAIA. *Publication:* The Awarding and Administration of Architectural Contracts 1961. *Leisure interests:* music, art, writing, fly fishing. *Address:* Catalyst Design Group, 252 Church Street, Richmond, Vic. 3121 (office); 4/6 Lennox Street, Hawthorn, Vic. 3122, Australia. *Telephone:* (3) 9428-6352 (office). *Fax:* (3) 9428-6897 (office). *E-mail:* info@catalyst.net.au (office). *Website:* www.catalyst.net.au (office).

DAVIDSON, Ogunlade R., BEng, PEng, CEng; Sierra Leonean engineer, academic and international organization official; *Vice-Chairman, Intergovernmental Panel on Climate Change (IPCC);* ed Univ. of Sierra Leone, UMIST (now Univ. of Manchester) and Univ. of Salford, UK; chartered engineer 1993; Lecturer, Univ. of Sierra Leone 1978–83, Sr Lecturer 1983–93, first Dir of Research 1985–92, Head of Dept of Mechanical and Maintenance Eng 1993–2000, Prof. of Mechanical Eng 1993–, Dean of Faculty of Eng 1996–2000, 2003–05, currently Dean of Post-Grad. Studies; Prof. and Dir Energy and Devt Research Centre, Univ. of Cape Town, South Africa 2000–03; Sr Fulbright Scholar, Univ. of California, Berkeley, USA 1987; MacArthur Scholar, Princeton Univ. and Lawrence Berkeley Lab., USA 1990–92; Visiting Prof., Univ. of Gothenburg, Sweden, ENDA-TM, Senegal, Riso Nat. Lab., Denmark; Co-Chair. Working Group III, Intergovernmental Panel on Climate Change (IPCC) 1997–2008, Vice-Chair. IPCC 2008–; Co-Chair. Steering Cttee of Global Network on Energy for Sustainable Devt; has worked as consultant in energy, tech., climate change and environment for several nat. and int. bodies, including UNESCO, UNIDO, ILO, UN Econ. Comm. for Africa, UNDP, UNEP, Global Environment Facility, UN Framework Convention on Climate Change, New Partnership for Africa's Devt (NEPAD), Arab Devt Bank, World

Bank, Batelle Labs and Carnegie Corpn, New York; Corp. mem. Sierra Leone Inst. of Engineers 1979, Nigerian Soc. of Engineers 1985, Inst. of Energy (UK) 1993; Fellow, Univ. Research Council 1987, African Acad. of Sciences 1991, Sierra Leone Inst. of Engineers 2001. *Publications:* more than 300 publs, including books, book chapters, journal articles and conf. papers on African energy systems and policies, power sector reform, renewable energy policy, climate change-greenhouse gas mitigation and nat. climate change strategy. *Address:* Intergovernmental Panel on Climate Change, World Meteorological Organization, 7 bis, avenue de la Paix, CP 2300, 1211 Geneva 2, Switzerland (office). *Telephone:* (22) 730-82-08 (office). *E-mail:* IPCC-Sec@wmo.int (office); IPCC-Media@wmo.int (office). *Website:* www.ipcc.ch (office).

DAVIDSON, Richard K., BS; American business executive (retd); b. 1942, Allen, Kan.; m. Trish Davidson; three c.; ed Washburn Univ., Harvard Univ.; Conductor, Missouri Pacific Railroad 1960, Asst Trainmaster, Shreveport, LA 1966, later various operating positions in Fort Worth, Kansas City and N Little Rock, becoming Asst to Vice-Pres., Operations, St Louis 1975, Vice-Pres., Operations, 1976; joined Union Pacific Railroad (following merger with Missouri Pacific and Western Pacific) 1982, Vice-Pres., Operations 1986, Exec. Vice-Pres. 1989–91, Pres. and CEO 1991–2006, Chair. 1991–2006 (retd), Chair. Union Pacific Corpn 1997–2007; fmr Chair. Pres.'s Nat. Infrastructure Advisory Cttee; mem. Bd of Dirs Chesapeake Energy Corpn 2006–; Trustee and Dir Malcolm Baldrige Nat. Quality Award Foundation; fmr mem. US Strategic Command Consultation Cttee; mem. Horatio Alger Asscn; mem. Bd of Advisors Thayer Capital Pnrs; fmr Trustee, Boy Scouts of America, Washburn Univ. Endowment Asscn, Strategic Air and Space Museum, Omaha; Dr hc (Washburn Univ.) 1984, (Bellevue Univ.) 2003, (Univ. of Neb. at Kearney) 2003; Kan. Business Hall of Fame 2001, Horatio Alger Asscn of Distinguished Americans 2002, Light of Wellness Award 2003, Railway Age Railroader of the Year 2003, Neb. Business Hall of Fame 2004, Omaha Business Hall of Fame 2006. *Address:* c/o Board of Directors, Chesapeake Energy Corporation, PO Box 18496, Oklahoma City, OK 73154-0496, USA.

DAVIE, Alan, CBE, DA, HRSA, RWA; British painter, jazz musician, jeweller and print maker; b. 1920, Grangemouth, Stirlingshire; s. of James W. Davie and Elizabeth Turnbull; m. Janet Gaul 1947; one d.; ed Edinburgh Coll. of Art, Edinburgh Moray House Coll. of Educ.; Gregory Fellowship, Leeds Univ. 1956–59; Sr Fellow RCA Lectures Colour Conf. Bristol 1991; Visiting Prof. Univ. of Brighton 1993–; Hon. mem. Royal Scottish Acad. 1977; Hon. DLitt (Heriot-Watt Univ.) 1994, (Univ. of Herts.) 1995, (Edin.) 2003; Saltire Award, Mosaic Scotland 1976. *Work includes:* first public music recital, Tate Gallery and Gimpel Fils, London 1971; four recordings 1972–86; music concerts 1972, concerts and broadcasts 1974; various recitals of piano improvisations 1971–2003. *Television includes:* Alan Davie Painting 1961, Alan Davie (German TV) 1985, Talking Pictures (Scottish TV) 1992. *Publications:* Monograph: Alan Davie 1992, The Quest for the Miraculous, Alan Davie 1993, Alan Davie Drawings 1997, Alan Davie 2000. *Leisure interests:* gliding, music, photography, underwater swimming. *Address:* Gamels Studio, Rush Green, Hertford, SG13 7SB, England. *Telephone:* (1920) 463684. *Fax:* (1920) 484406.

DAVIES, A. Michael, MA, FCA; British business executive; b. 23 June 1934; s. of Angelo Henry Davies and Clarice Mildred Davies; m. Jane Priscilla Davies 1962; one s. (deceased) one d.; ed Shrewsbury School, Queens' Coll., Cambridge; Chair. Tozer Kemsley & Millbourne 1982–86, Bredero Properties 1986–94, Worth Investment Trust 1987–95, Calor Group 1989–97 (Dir 1987–97), Perkins Foods 1987–2001, Berk 1988–95, Wiltshier 1988–95, Nat. Express Group PLC 1991–2004, Simon Group 1993–2003, Corporate Services Group 1999–2002; Deputy Chair. T.I. Group 1990–93 (Dir 1984–93), Man-power 1987–91, AerFi 1993–2000; Dir Imperial Group 1972–82, Littlewoods Org. 1982–88, TV-am 1982–88, British Airways 1983–2002, Worcester Group 1991–92. *Address:* Little Woolpit, Ewhurst, Cranleigh, Surrey, GU6 7NP, England. *Telephone:* (1483) 277344. *Fax:* (1483) 277899. *E-mail:* amdavies@btinternet.com.

DAVIES, Sir David E. N., Kt, CBE, PhD, DSc, FRS, FIEE, FREng; British electrical engineer; *Chairman, Hazards Forum;* b. 28 Oct. 1935, Cardiff; s. of D. E. Davies and Sarah Samuel; m. 1st Enid Patilla 1962 (died 1990); two s.; m. 2nd Jennifer E. Rayner 1992; ed Univ. of Birmingham; Lecturer, then Sr Lecturer in Electrical Eng, Univ. of Birmingham 1961–67; Asst Dir Research Dept, British Railways Bd 1967–71; Visiting Industrial Prof. of Electrical Eng, Univ. of Loughborough 1969–71; Prof. of Electrical Eng, Univ. Coll. London 1971–88, Pender Prof. of Electrical Eng 1985–88, Vice-Provost Univ. Coll. 1986–88; Vice-Chancellor Loughborough Univ. of Tech. 1988–93; Chief Scientific Adviser, Ministry of Defence 1993–99; Chair. Defence Scientific Advisory Council 1992–93; Pres. IEEE 1994–95; Vice-Pres. Royal Acad. of Eng 1995–96, Pres. 1996–2001; Chair. Railway Safety 2000–03; currently Chair. Hazards Forum; Dir Strategy Ltd 1974–79, Gaydon Tech. 1986–88, Lough-borough Consultants 1988–93, Inst. Consumer Ergonomics 1988–93, ERA Tech. 1997–, Lattice PLC 2000–02; Adviser to Bd, Nat. Grid plc 2003–; mem. Defence Acad. Advisory Bd; mem. Bd ERA Foundation 2002–; Foreign mem. Russian Acad. of Sciences 2004; Hon. Fellow Univ. of Wales, Coll. of Cardiff 2001, Univ. Coll. London 2006; Hon. DSc (Birmingham) 1994, (Loughborough) 1994, (South Bank) 1994, (Bradford) 1995, (Surrey) 1996, (Warwick) 1997, (Bath) 1997, (Heriot-Watt) 1999, (UMIST) 2000, (Wales) 2002; Rank Prize for Optoelectronics 1984; IEEE Centennial Medal 1984, IEE Faraday Medal 1987 and other awards. *Publications:* about 120 publs on antennas, radar and fibre optics. *Address:* Hazards Forum, One Great George Street, Westminster, London, SW1P 3AA, England (office). *Telephone:* (20) 7665-2230 (office). *Website:* www.hazardsforum.co.uk (office).

DAVIES, David Reginald Howel, DPhil; American (b. Welsh) X-ray crystallographer and researcher; *Chief, Section on Molecular Structure,*

Laboratory of Molecular Biology, National Institutes of Diabetes, Digestive and Kidney Diseases, National Institutes of Health; b. 22 Feb. 1927, Camarthen, Wales; s. of Theophilus Howel Davies and Gwladys Evelyn Evans Davies (née Hodges); m. 1st Cynthia Margaret Seaman 1951 (divorced 1981); two d.; m. 2nd Monica Walters 1985; ed Magdalen Coll., Oxford, England, Calif. Inst. of Tech., Pasadena; Research Assoc., Albright & Wilson Ltd, Birmingham, England 1954–55; Visiting Scientist, NIH, Bethesda, Md 1955–61, Chief, Section on Molecular Structure, Lab. of Molecular Biology, Nat. Insts of Diabetes, Digestive and Kidney Diseases 1961–; Visiting Scientist, MRC Lab. Molecular Biology 1963–64, Max Planck Inst., Heidelberg 1972–73; mem. American Acad. of Arts and Sciences, NAS, American Soc. of Biological Chemists, American Crystallographic Asscn, Biophysical Soc. (Council 1960–65, 1973–78), Protein Soc.; Presidential Meritorious Exec. Award 1982, Presidential Rank Award 1988, Stein and Moore Award, Protein Soc. 1998. *Publications:* articles in scientific journals. *Leisure interests:* tennis, sailing. *Address:* Laboratory of Molecular Biology, Building 5, Room 338, NIDDK, National Institutes of Health, 9000 Rockville Pike, Bethesda, MD 20892 (office); 4224 Franklin Street, Kensington, MD 20895, USA (home). *Telephone:* (301) 496-4295 (office). *Fax:* (301) 496-0201 (office). *E-mail:* david .davies@nih.gov (office). *Website:* www-mslmb.niddk.nih.gov (office).

DAVIES, Edward Brian, BA, DPhil, FRS; British mathematician and academic; *Professor of Mathematics, King's College London;* b. 13 June 1944, Cardiff; m. Jane Christine Phillips 1968; one s. one d.; ed Oxford Univ.; Lecturer in Math., Oxford Univ. 1970–81; Prof. of Math., King's Coll., London 1981–; Fellow King's Coll. 1996; Sr Berwick Prize, London Math. Soc. 1998. *Publications:* Science in the Looking Glass 2003; four other academic books and more than 180 research papers. *Leisure interests:* philosophy, science. *Address:* Room 420, Strand Bldg, Department of Mathematics, King's College, Strand, London, WC2R 2LS, England (office). *Telephone:* (20) 7848-2698 (office). *Fax:* (20) 7848-2017 (office). *E-mail:* e.brian.davies@kcl.ac.uk (office). *Website:* www.mth.kcl.ac.uk/staff/eb_davies.html (office).

DAVIES, Emrys Thomas, CMG; British diplomatist (retd); b. 8 Oct. 1934, London; s. of Evan William Davies and Dinah Davies (née Jones); m. Angela Audrey May 1960; one s. two d.; ed Parmiter's Foundation School, London, Univs of Tours and Grenoble, France, School of Slavonic Studies, Cambridge Univ., SOAS, London Univ., Inst. of Fine Arts, Hanoi; served in RAF 1953–55; joined HM Diplomatic Service 1955, Attaché, Chargé d'Affaires Office, Peking 1956–59, Northern Dept (Soviet and E European Affairs), FCO 1959–60, Third Sec. British Political Residency, Bahrain 1960–62, mem. UK Del. UN Gen. Ass. (Econ. Cttee) 1962, Desk Officer, Econ. Affairs, UN Dept, FCO 1962–63, Asst Political Adviser Govt of Hong Kong 1963–68, First Sec. (Political), High Comm., Ottawa 1968–72, Asst Head N American Dept, FCO 1972–74, Asst Head Financial Relations Dept, FCO 1974–76, Commercial Counsellor, Embassy Peking (Chargé 1976 and 1978) 1976–78, NATO Defense Coll., Rome 1979, Deputy High Commr, Ottawa 1979–82, Overseas Inspector HM Diplomatic Service 1982–84, Deputy Head UK Del. (and Counsellor Econ. and Financial Affairs) OECD Paris 1984–87, Amb. to Vietnam 1987–90, High Commr in Barbados, Grenada, St Vincent, St Lucia, Dominica, Antigua and St Kitts 1990–94; Head UK Del. to EC Monitor Mission to fmr Yugoslavia, Zagreb 1995, Sarajevo 1998–99; Sec.-Gen. Tripartite Comm. for Restitution of Monetary Gold, Brussels 1995–98, Appointments Adviser to Welsh Office 1997–2002, Political Adviser to EU Police Mission, Sarajevo 2003. *Leisure interests:* golf, visual arts, walking, reading. *Address:* Edinburgh House, 8 Alison Way, Winchester, Hampshire, SO22 5BT, England.

DAVIES, E(van) Mervyn, CBE, JP, FCIB; British banking executive and government official; *Minister for Trade Promotion and Investment, Department for Business, Enterprise and Regulatory Reform;* b. 1952; s. of Richard Aled Davies and Margaret Davies; m. Jeanne Marie Gammie 1979; one s. one d.; ed Rydal School, North Wales, Harvard Business School; Man. Dir UK Banking and Sr Credit Officer, Citibank 1983–93; joined Standard Chartered Bank PLC with responsibility for Global Account Man. 1993, Head of Corp. and Investment Banking, Singapore –1997, mem. Bd Dirs 1997–2009, Group Exec. Dir responsible for Group-wide Tech. and Operations in Hong Kong, China and NE Asia 1997–2001, Group Chief Exec., London 2001–06, Chair. 2006–09 (resgnd); Minister for Trade Promotion and Investment 2009–, also Labour Whip in House of Lords 2009–; Chair. Fleming Family & Partners, Nordic Windpower Ltd; Dir (non-exec.) Tesco PLC 2003–, Breakingviews Ltd, Tottenham Hotspur Football Club, Trinity Ltd; mem. Advisory Cttee Corsair Capital LLC, UK India Business Council; Chair. Interim Exec. Cttee of Int. Centre for Financial Regulation 2007–, Business Council for Britain 2007–; mem. Mayor of London's Int. Business Advisory Council, London; JP Hong Kong 2000; mem. Hong Kong Exchange Fund Cttee, Singapore British Business Council, UK-India Forum; mem. Exec. Cttee Hong Kong Community Chest –2001; fmr Chair. Hong Kong Youth Arts Festival, Hong Kong Asscn of Banks, Asia Youth Orchestra; Chair. Council of the Univ. of Wales; Dir Visa Int. Asia Pacific Regional Bd –2001; Chair. British Chamber of Commerce, Hong Kong 2000–01 (also fmr Chair.), The Roundhouse's Major Projects Bd, Corp. Bd of Royal Acad. of Arts; mem. Bd of Dirs Hong Kong Asscn 2007–; Gov. LSE; Trustee, Royal Acad. Trust, Sir Kyffin Williams Trust; Fellow, Inst. of Bankers. *Leisure interests:* sport, Welsh art, antiques, opera, music, reading. *Address:* Department for Business, Enterprise and Regulatory Reform, 1 Victoria Street, London, SW1H 0ET, England (office). *Telephone:* (20) 7215-5000 (office). *Fax:* (20) 7215-0105 (office). *E-mail:* enquiries@berr.gsi.gov.uk (office). *Website:* www.berr.gov.uk (office).

DAVIES, Gavyn, OBE, BS; British economist and business executive; *Founding Partner, Active Private Equity Advisory LLP;* b. 27 Nov. 1950; s. of W. J. F. Davies and M. G. Davies; m. Susan Jane Nye 1989; two s. one d.; ed St John's Coll., Cambridge and Balliol Coll., Oxford; Econ. Adviser, Policy

Unit, 10 Downing Street 1974–79; economist, Phillips and Drew 1979–81; Chief UK Economist Simon & Coates 1981–86, Goldman Sachs 1986–93, Pnr 1988–2001, Head of Investment Research (London) 1991–93, Chief Int. Economist and Head of European Investment Research 1993–97, Chair. Investment Research Dept 1999–2001, Advisory Dir 2001–; Vice-Chair. BBC 2001, Chair. 2001–04 (resgnd); Founding Pnr, Active Private Equity Advisory LLP; Founder and Advisory Pnr, Prisma Capital Partners; Chair. Fulcrum Asset Management; Visiting Prof. of Econs, LSE 1988–98; Prin. Econs Commentator, The Independent 1991–99; mem. HM Treasury's Ind. Forecasting Panel 1993–97; Chair. Govt Inquiry into the Future Funding of the BBC 1999; Hon. Fellow, Aberystwyth Univ. 2002; Hon. DScS (Southampton) 1998; Hon. LLD (Nottingham) 2002; Dr hc (Middlesex). *Leisure interest:* Southampton Football Club. *Address:* Active Private Equity Advisory LLP, 5th Floor, 6 Chesterfield Gardens, London, W1J 5BQ, England (office). *Telephone:* (20) 7016-6480 (office). *Fax:* (20) 7016-6490 (office). *Website:* www.apeq.co.uk (office); www.prismapartners.com.

DAVIES, Sir Graeme John, Kt, BE, MA, PhD, ScD, FRSE, FREng; British (b. New Zealand) university vice-chancellor; *Vice-Chancellor, University of London;* b. 7 April 1937, Auckland, NZ; s. of Harry J. Davies and Gladys E. Davies; m. Florence I. Martin 1959; one s. one d.; ed Univ. of Auckland; Lecturer, Univ. of Cambridge 1962–77, Fellow, St Catharine's Coll. 1967–76; Prof., Dept of Metallurgy, Univ. of Sheffield 1977–86; Vice-Chancellor Univ. of Liverpool 1986–91; Chief Exec. Univs' Funding Council 1991–93, Polytechnics' and Colls' Funding Council 1992–93, Higher Educ. Funding Council for England 1992–95; Prin. and Vice-Chancellor Univ. of Glasgow 1995–2003; Vice-Chancellor Univ. of London 2003–; Freeman, City of London, Freeman and Burgess Holder, City of Glasgow; Hon. FRSNZ; Hon. Fellow, Trinity Coll. of Music 1995; Hon. DSc (Nottingham) 1995, (Edin.) 2003, (Ulster) 2004, (London South Bank) 2006; Hon. DMet (Sheffield) 1995; Hon. LLD (Liverpool) 1991, (Strathclyde) 2000; Hon. DEng (Manchester Metropolitan) 1996, (Auckland) 2003; Hon. DUniv (Glasgow, Paisley) 2004. *Publications:* Solidification and Casting 1973, Textures and Properties of Materials 1976, Hot Working and Forming Processes 1980, Superplasticity 1981, Essential Metallurgy for Engineers 1985. *Leisure interests:* cricket, birdwatching, The Times crossword. *Address:* The Coach House, Fosse Road, Farndon, Newark, NG24 3SF, England (home). *Telephone:* (20) 7862-8006 (office); (1636) 673117 (home). *E-mail:* graeme.davies@lon.ac.uk (office). *Website:* www.london.ac.uk/vice_chancellor.html (office).

DAVIES, Sir Howard John, Kt, MA, MSc; British academic administrator and business executive; *Director, London School of Economics;* b. 12 Feb. 1951; s. of Leslie Davies and Marjorie Davies; m. Prudence Keely 1984; two s.; ed Manchester Grammar School, Merton Coll., Oxford and Stanford Grad. School of Business; Foreign Office 1973–74; Pvt. Sec. to British Amb. in Paris 1974–76; HM Treasury 1976–82; McKinsey & Co. Inc. 1982–87; Controller, Audit Comm. 1987–92; Dir GKN PLC 1990–95; Dir-Gen. Confed. of British Industry (CBI) 1992–95; Deputy Gov., Bank of England 1995–97, Dir (non-exec.) 1998–2003; Chair. Financial Services Authority (fmrly Securities and Investments Bd) 1997–2003; Dir LSE 2003–; mem. NatWest Int. Advisory Bd 1992–95; mem. Bd Morgan Stanley 2004–, Paternoster UK Ltd 2006–; Deputy Chair. Rowntree Cttee Enquiry 1993; Pres. Age Concern England 1994–98; Chair. Employers' Forum on Age 1996–2004; Chair. panel of judges Man Booker Prize 2007; Trustee, Tate 2002–; Gov. RAM 2004–. *Leisure interests:* cricket, writing for publication. *Address:* London School of Economics, Houghton Street, London, WC2A 2AE, England. *Telephone:* (20) 7405-7686 (office). *Website:* www.lse.ac.uk (office).

DAVIES, John Arthur, MA, PhD, FRSC; Canadian research scientist and academic; *Emeritus Professor, Department of Engineering Physics, McMaster University;* b. 28 March 1927, Prestatyn, Wales; s. of Francis J. Davies and Doris A. Edkins; m. Florence Smithson 1950; three s. three d.; ed Ratcliff Coll., UK, St Michael's Coll. High School, Univ. of Toronto; Asst, later Assoc. Research Officer, Atomic Energy of Canada 1950–65, Sr Research Officer 1965–70, Prin. Research Officer 1970–85; Part-time Prof. of Eng Physics, McMaster Univ. 1970–92, Dir McMaster Accelerator Lab. 1989–92, Prof. Emer. 1992–; Adjunct Prof., Dept of Electrical Eng, Univ. of Salford, UK 1972–92; Visiting Prof., Nobel Inst. of Physics, Stockholm, Sweden 1962, Univ. of Aarhus, Denmark 1964–65, 1969–70, 1994, Univ. of Osaka, Japan 1972; mem. Royal Danish Acad. of Arts and Sciences, Böhmische Physical Soc., Chemical Inst. of Canada; Hon. DSc (Royal Roads Mil. Coll.) 1984, (Univ. of Salford) 1993; Noranda Award, Chem. Inst. of Canada 1965, First T.D. Callinan Award, Electrochem. Soc. 1968, W.B. Lewis Medal, Canadian Nuclear Soc. 1998. *Publications:* co-author of over 250 research articles and five books in the fields of ion implantation, ion channelling and ion beam analysis. *Leisure interests:* canoeing, cross-country skiing, curling. *Address:* Box 224, 7 Wolfe Avenue, Deep River, ON K0J 1P0, Canada (home). *Telephone:* (613) 584-2301 (home). *E-mail:* davies@magma.ca (home).

DAVIES, Jonathan, MBE; British sports commentator and fmr rugby player (rugby union and rugby league); b. 24 Oct. 1962, Trimsaran, Carmarthenshire; s. of the late Leonard Davies and of Diana Davies (née Rees); m. 1st Karen Marie Davies 1984 (died 1997); two s. one d.; m. 2nd Helen Jones 2002; ed Gwendraeth Grammar School; rugby union outside-half; played for the following rugby union clubs: Trimsaran, Neath, Llanelli; turned professional in 1989; with Cardiff 1995–97; played for Welsh nat. team (v. England) 1985, World Cup Squad (6 appearances) 1987, Triple Crown winning team 1988, tour NZ (2 test appearances) 1988, 29 caps, sometime Capt.; also played for Barbarians Rugby Football Club; rugby league career: played at three-quarters; Widnes (world record transfer fee) 1989, Warrington 1993–95 (free transfer); for Welsh nat. team; British nat. team, tour NZ 1990, 6 caps, fmr Capt.; reverted to rugby union 1995; retd from playing 1997; commentator on rugby union and league for Channel 4 Wales. *Publication:* Jonathan (autobiog.) 1989. *Leisure interest:* all sports. *Address:* c/o S4C, Parc Tŷ Glas, Llanishen, Cardiff, CF14 5DU, Wales.

DAVIES, Dame Kay Elizabeth, DBE, CBE, MA, DPhil, FRS, FRCPath, MRCP, FMedSci; British geneticist and academic; *Dr Lee's Professor of Anatomy and Head of Department, University of Oxford;* b. (Kay Elizabeth Partridge), 1 April 1951, Stourbridge; d. of Harry Partridge and Florence Partridge; m. Stephen Graham Davies 1973 (divorced); one s.; ed Somerville and Wolfson Colls, Oxford; Guy Newton Jr Research Fellow, Wolfson Coll., Oxford 1976–78; Royal Soc. European Postdoctoral Fellow, Service de Biochimie, Centre d'études nucléaires de Saclay, Gif-sur-Yvette, France 1978–80; Cystic Fibrosis Research Fellow, Biochem. Dept, St Mary's Hosp. Medical School, London 1980–82, MRC Sr Research Fellow, 1982–84; MRC Sr Research Fellow, Nuffield Dept of Clinical Medicine, John Radcliffe Hosp., Oxford 1984–86, MRC External Staff 1986–89, Molecular Genetics Group, Inst. of Molecular Medicine 1989–92, MRC Research Dir, Royal Postgraduate Medical School 1992–94, Head of Molecular Genetics Group, Inst. of Molecular Medicine 1994–95; Prof. of Molecular Genetics, Univ. of London 1992–94; Prof. of Genetics, Dept of Biochem., Univ. of Oxford 1995–97, Dr Lee's Prof. of Anatomy 1998–; Hon. Dir MRC Functional Genetics Unit, Oxford 1999–; Co-Dir Oxford Centre for Gene Function 2001–; Univ. Research Lecturer, Nuffield Dept of Clinical Medicine, John Radcliffe Hosp. 1989–92; Fellow, Green Coll., Oxford 1989–92, 1994–95, Keble Coll., Oxford 1995–, Hertford Coll., Oxford 1997–; mem. Bd of Govs Wellcome Trust 2008–; Wellcome Trust Award 1996, SCI Medal 1999, Feldberg Foundation Prize 1999, Gaetano Conte Prize in Basic Myology 2002. *Publications:* more than 300 papers in scientific journals. *Leisure interests:* tennis, music, general keep-fit. *Address:* Department of Physiology, Anatomy and Genetics, University of Oxford, South Parks Road, Oxford, OX1 3PT, England (office). *Telephone:* (1865) 285880 (office). *Fax:* (1865) 285878 (office). *E-mail:* kay.davies@dpag.ox.ac.uk (office). *Website:* www.dpag.ox.ac.uk (office).

DAVIES, Nicholas Barry, BA, DPhil, FRS; British biologist and academic; *Professor of Behavioural Ecology, Department of Zoology, University of Cambridge;* b. 23 May 1952, Liverpool; s. of Anthony Barry Davies and Joyce Margaret Davies; m. Jan Parr 1979; two d.; ed Merchant Taylors' School, Crosby, Pembroke Coll., Cambridge, Wolfson Coll., Oxford; Demonstrator in Zoology, Edward Grey Inst., Univ. of Oxford 1976–79; Jr Research Fellow, Wolfson Coll., Oxford 1977–79; Demonstrator, Dept of Zoology, Univ. of Cambridge 1979–84, Lecturer 1984–92, Reader 1992–95, Prof. of Behavioural Ecology 1995–, Fellow, Pembroke Coll. Cambridge 1979–; Pres. Int. Soc. for Behavioural Ecology 2000–02; Corresp. Fellow, American Ornithologists' Union 1999, German Ornithological Soc. 2000; Hon. mem. Spanish Ornithological Soc. 2004; Scientific Medal, Zoological Soc. of London 1987, Cambridge Univ. Teaching Prize 1995, William Bate Hardy Prize, Cambridge Philosophical Soc. 1995, Medal of Assn for Study of Animal Behaviour 1996, Frink Medal, Zoological Soc. of London 2001. *Publications:* Dunnock Behaviour and Social Evolution 1992, An Introduction to Behavioural Ecology (co-author) 1981, Behavioural Ecology: an Evolutionary Approach (co-ed.) 1978, Cuckoos, Cowbirds and Other Cheats (Best Book of the Year Award, British Trust for Ornithology 2000) 2000. *Leisure interests:* bird-watching, mountains, music. *Address:* Department of Zoology, University of Cambridge, Downing Street, Cambridge, CB2 3EJ, England (office). *Telephone:* (1223) 334405 (office). *Fax:* (1223) 336676 (office). *E-mail:* nbd1000@cam.ac.uk (office); n.b.davies@zoo.cam.ac.uk (office). *Website:* www.zoo.cam.ac.uk (office).

DAVIES, Omar, DEcon; Jamaican economist and academic; b. 28 May 1947, Clarendon; m.; three c.; ed Univ. of the West Indies, Northwestern Univ., USA; Asst Prof., Stanford Univ. 1973–76; Sr Lecturer, Univ. of the West Indies 1981–89; Dir-Gen. Planning Inst. of Jamaica 1989–93; mem. People's Nat. Party; with Office of the Prime Minister April–Aug. 1993; Minister without Portfolio responsible for Planning Devt Project Implementation Aug.–Nov. 1993; mem. Parl. 1993–, Chair. Public Accounts Cttee 2007–; Minister of Finance and Planning 1993–2007. *Address:* Houses of Representative, Gordon House, 81 Duke St, POB 636, Kingston, Jamaica (office). *Telephone:* 922-0202 (office). *Fax:* 967-0064 (office).

DAVIES, Sir Peter Maxwell, Kt (see MAXWELL DAVIES, Sir Peter).

DAVIES, Rodney Deane, CBE, FRS, DSc, CPhys; British radio astronomer and academic; *Professor Emeritus of Radio Astronomy, University of Manchester;* b. 8 Jan. 1930, Balaklava, S Australia; s. of Holbin James Davies and Rena Irene Davies (née March); m. Valda Beth Treasure 1953; two s. (one deceased), two d.; ed Univs of Adelaide and Manchester; Research Officer, Radio Physics Div., CSIRO Sydney 1951–53; Lecturer, Univ. of Manchester 1953–63, Sr Lecturer 1963–67, Reader 1967–76, Prof. of Radio Astronomy 1976–97, Prof. Emer. 1997–; Sec., Royal Astronomical Soc. 1978–86, Pres. 1987–89; Dir Nuffield Radio Astronomy Labs, Jodrell Bank 1988–97. *Publications:* Radio Studies of the Universe (with H.P. Palmer) 1959, Radio Astronomy Today (with H.P. Palmer and M.I. Large) 1963. *Leisure interests:* fell-walking, gardening. *Address:* University of Manchester, Jodrell Bank Observatory, Jodrell Bank, Macclesfield, Cheshire SK11 9DL; Park Gate House, Fulshaw Park South, Wilmslow, Cheshire SK9 1QG, England. *Telephone:* (1477) 571321 (office); (1625) 523592 (home). *Fax:* (1477) 571618 (office). *E-mail:* rdd@jb.man.ac.uk (office). *Website:* www.jb.man.ac.uk (office).

DAVIES, Rt Hon. Ron(ald), PC; British politician; b. 6 Aug. 1946; s. of the late Ronald Davies; m. 1st Anne Williams; m. 2nd Christina Elizabeth Rees 1981; one d.; m. 3rd Lynne Hughes 2002; ed Bassaleg Grammar School, Portsmouth Polytechnic, Univ. Coll. of Wales, Cardiff; schoolteacher 1968–70; Workers' Educ. Assn Tutor/Organizer 1970–74; Further Educ. Adviser, Mid-Glamorgan Local Educ. Authority 1974–83; mem. Rhymney Valley Dist

www.worldwhoswho.com

Council 1969–84 (fmr Vice-Chair.); MP (Labour) for Caerphilly 1983–2001, Opposition Whip 1985–87, Labour Spokesman on Agric. and Rural Affairs 1987–92, on Wales 1992–97, Sec. of State for Wales 1997–98; elected leader of Labour Group in Nat. Ass. for Wales Sept. 1998, resgnd Oct. 1998; mem. Nat. Ass. for Wales for Caerphilly 1999–2003 (resgnd), Chair. Econ. Devt Cttee 1999–2003; joined Forward Wales party 2004, currently Policy Dir; Highest Order, Gorsedd of the Bards 1998. *Publications:* pamphlets on Welsh devolution. *Leisure interests:* walking, gardening, sport. *Address:* c/o Forward Wales HQ, 67 Regent Street, Wrexham, LL11 1PG, Wales (office). *Telephone:* (1978) 314085 (office).

DAVIES, Ryland; British singer (tenor); b. 9 Feb. 1943, Cwm Ebbw Vale, Monmouthshire (now Gwent); s. of Gethin and Joan Davies; m. 1st Anne Howells 1966 (divorced 1981); m. 2nd Deborah Jane Rees 1983; one d.; ed Royal Manchester Coll. of Music (Fellow 1971); voice teacher Royal Northern Coll. of Music (RNCM) 1987–94, Royal Coll. of Music, London 1999–, also Royal Acad. of Music; Dir Opera Productions RNCM Mananan Festival, Clonter Opera Trust; début as Almaviva in The Barber of Seville, Welsh Nat. Opera 1964, subsequent appearances including Tamino in The Magic Flute 1974, Yenick in Bartered Bride 1989; Glyndebourne Festival Chorus 1964–66, taking parts including Belmonte in The Abduction from the Seraglio, Ferrando in Così fan tutte, Flamand in Capriccio, Lysander in A Midsummer Night's Dream, The Prince in Love of Three Oranges, Lensky in Eugene Onegin, Tichone in Katya Kabanova, Basilio/Curzio in Le nozze di Figaro, Auctioneer in The Rake's Progress; appearances with Scottish Opera as Ferrando and as Fenton in Falstaff, Tamino in The Magic Flute and as Nemorino in L'Elisir d'Amore; with Sadler's Wells Opera as Almaviva, Essex in Britten's Gloriana; with Royal Opera as Hylas in The Trojans, Don Ottavio in Don Giovanni, Ferrando, Cassio in Otello, Nemorino in L'Elisir d'Amore, Ernesto in Don Pasquale, Lysander in A Midsummer Night's Dream and Almaviva; with English Nat. Opera as Eisenstein in Die Fledermaus, Basilio in Le nozze di Figaro, Rev. H. Adams in Peter Grimes, Albazar in Turk in Italy, L'Aumonier in Dialogues des Carmélites, Gaudenzio in La Bohème; overseas appearances include Salzburg Festival, at San Francisco, Chicago, Paris, at Metropolitan Opera, New York, Hollywood Bowl, Paris Opera, Geneva, Brussels, Lyons, Amsterdam, Mannheim, Israel, Buenos Aires, Stuttgart, Nice, Nancy, Philadelphia, Berlin, Hamburg; returned to Covent Garden 1994, 2002, Welsh Nat. Opera 1994, New York Metropolitan Opera 1994, 1995, 2001, Glyndebourne 1997, New Israeli Opera 1997, Chicago Lyric Opera 1998, 2003, Santa Fe Opera 1998, 1999, New Israeli Opera 1998, Netherlands Opera 1998, 1999, 2002, English Nat. Opera 1999, Houston Grand Opera 2002, Japan 2002, Florence 2002, Zauberflote/Monastatos Netherlands 2003, Covent Garden Monostatos 2003, Basilio, Chicago Lyric Opera 2003, Peter Grimes, London Symphony, Barbican and New York, Colin Davis 2004, A Midsummer Night's Dream, La Fenice, Venice 2004, Ein Hurt, La Scala, Milan 2007, 2009; Boise Mendelsohn Foundation Scholarship 1964; Fellow Welsh Coll. of Music and Drama 1996; Hon. Fellow Royal Manchester Coll. of Music 1971; Ricordi Opera Prize, Royal Manchester Coll. of Music 1963, Imperial League of Opera Prize, Royal Manchester Coll. of Music 1963, First John Christie Award, Glyndebourne 1965. *Recordings include:* The Abduction from the Seraglio, L'Amore dei Tre Re (Montemezzi), La Navarraise (Massenet), The Trojans, Saul, Così fan tutte, Thérèse (Massenet), Monteverdi Madrigals, Idomeneo, The Seasons (Haydn), Messiah, L'Oracolo (Leone), Judas Maccabaeus, Pulcinella, Il Matrimonio Segreto, Lucia di Lammamoor, Otello, Mozart's Requiem, C Minor Mass, Credo Mass, Coronation Mass, Messe Solonelle; Oedipus Rex (Shepherd), Il Trovatore (Ruiz), Don Carlo (Conte di Lerma), Le nozze di Figaro (Basilio/Curzio), Esclarmonde (Massenet). *Video films include:* Don Pasquale, A Midsummer Night's Dream, Die Entführung aus dem Serail, Love of Three Oranges, Trial by Jury, Katya Kabanova. *Television:* Merry Widow, Capriccio (BBC, Glyndebourne), A Goodly Manner for a Song (STV), On Wenlock Edge (BBC Wales), Dido and Aeneas (BBC), Mass in C Minor (BBC Wales). *Achievements:* played rugby for Wales Schoolboys, 2 caps 1957–58, Wales Boys Clubs under-18s 1959–60. *Leisure interests:* art, cinema, sport, reading. *Address:* Hazard Chase Ltd, 25 City Road, Cambridge, CB1 1DP, England (office); Elm Cottage, Loseberry Road, Claygate, Surrey, KT10 9DQ, England (home). *Telephone:* (1223) 213400 (office). *Fax:* (1223) 460827 (office). *E-mail:* info@hazardchase.co.uk (office); rylandtenore@hotmail.com (home). *Website:* www.hazardchase.co.uk (office); www.rylanddavies.info.

DAVIES, Stephen Graham, MA, DPhil; British research chemist and academic; *Waynflete Professor of Chemistry, University of Oxford;* b. 24 Feb. 1950; s. of Gordon W.J. Davies and June M. Murphy; m. Kay E. Partridge 1973; one s.; ICI Postdoctoral Fellow, Oxford 1975–77; NATO Postdoctoral Fellow, Oxford 1977–78; Attaché de Recherche, CNRS, Paris 1978–80; Fellow, New Coll. Oxford 1980–; Univ. lecturer in Chem. Univ. of Oxford 1980–, currently Chair. of Chemistry and Waynflete Prof. of Chemistry; Dir Oxford Asymmetry Ltd 1991–; mem. of various cttees, editorial bds; Hickinbottom Fellowship 1984; Pfizer Award for Chem. 1985, 1988, Corday Morgan Medal 1984, Royal Soc. of Chem. Award for Organometallic Chem. 1989, Bader Award, Royal Soc. of Chem. 1989, Tilden Lecture Award 1996, Royal Soc. of Chemistry Award in Stereochemistry 1997, Prize Lectureship, Soc. of Synthetic Organic Chemistry, Japan 1998. *Publications:* Organometallic Chemistry: Applications to Organic Chemistry 1982; more than 250 papers in learned journals. *Leisure interest:* chemistry. *Address:* Dyson Perrins Laboratory, University of Oxford, South Parks Road, Oxford, OX1 3QY, England (office). *Telephone:* (1865) 275695 (office). *Fax:* (1865) 275633 (office). *E-mail:* steve.davies@chem.ox.ac.uk (office). *Website:* www.chem.ox.ac.uk/researchguide/sgdavies.html (office); www.chem.ox.ac.uk/oc/sgdavies/index.html (office).

DAVIES, (Stephen) Howard, FRSA; British theatre and film director; b. 26 April 1945; s. of the late Thomas Davies and of the late (Eileen) Hilda Bevan; m. Susan Wall (divorced); two d.; ed Christ's Hosp. and Univs of Durham and Bristol; Theatre Dir, Assoc. Dir Bristol Old Vic 1971–73; founder mem. Avon Touring Co.; Asst Dir RSC 1974, Assoc. Dir 1976–86; Founder and Dir The Warehouse RSC (productions include Piaf, Good, Les Liaisons Dangereuses) 1977–82; freelance Dir 1974–76; Assoc. Dir Nat. Theatre 1989–. *Productions include:* RSC: Troilus and Cressida 1977, Bandits 1977, Bingo 1977, The Jail Diary of Albie Sachs 1979, Much Ado About Nothing 1980, Piaf 1983, Henry VIII 1983, Les Liaisons Dangereuses 1986; Nat. Theatre: The Shaughraun 1988, Cat on a Hot Tin Roof 1988, The Secret Rapture 1989, Hedda Gabler 1989, The Crucible 1990, A Long Day's Journey Into Night 1996, Mary Stuart 1996, Chips With Everything 1997, Flight 1998, Battle Royal 1999, All My Sons (Olivier Award for Best Dir 2001) 2000, Private Lives 2001, The Talking Cure 2003, Mourning Becomes Electra 2003, Cyrano de Bergerac 2004, The House of Bernarda Alba 2005, The Life of Galileo 2006, Philistines 2007, Present Laughter 2007; Almeida: Who's Afraid of Virginia Woolf 1996, The Iceman Cometh (Evening Standard and Olivier Awards for Best Dir) 1998, Conversations After a Burial 2000, Period of Adjustment 2006; other: Vassa (Albery) 1999, Private Lives (Albery) 2001, The Breath of Life (Haymarket) 2002, A Moon for the Misbegotten (Old Vic) 2006. *Film:* The Secret Rapture (dir) 1993. *Television:* Tales from Hollywood 1992, Armadillo (BBC TV) 2001, Copenhagen 2002, Blue/Orange 2005. *Leisure interests:* travel, hill-walking, watching rugby, film, painting. *Address:* c/o Royal National Theatre, South Bank, London, SE1 9PX, England. *Telephone:* (20) 7452-3333. *Fax:* (20) 7620-1197. *Website:* www.nationaltheatre.org.uk.

DAVIES, Susan Elizabeth, OBE; British gallery director (retd); b. 14 April 1933, Iran; d. of the late Stanworth Adey and Joan Charlsworth; m. John R. T. Davies 1954 (deceased); two d.; ed Nightingale Bamford School, New York, Eothen School, Surrey and Triangle Secretarial Coll.; Municipal Journal 1953–54; Artists' Placement Group 1966–67; ICA 1967–70; Founder and Dir The Photographers' Gallery, London 1971–91; photography consultant and writer 1991–; Hon. FRPS 1986; Progress Medal, Royal Photographic Soc. 1982, Kulturpreis, German Photographic Soc. 1990. *Leisure interests:* jazz, gardening, grandchildren, great-grandchildren. *Address:* 57 Sandilands Road, Fulham, London SW6 2BD, England (home). *Telephone:* (20) 7731-7262 (home). *E-mail:* sue.ristic@btinternet.com (home).

DAVIES, Terence; British screenwriter and film director; b. 1945, Liverpool; ed Coventry Drama School and Nat. Film School; articled clerk in shipping office; later worked for 12 years in an accountancy practice. *Films:* Children 1977, Madonna and Child 1980, Death and Transfiguration 1983, Distant Voices, Still Lives (Int. Critics Prize, Cannes Film Festival) 1988, Movie Masterclass 1990, The Long Day Closes 1992, The Neon Bible 1995, The House of Mirth 2000, Of Time and the City 2008. *Radio:* Travels in Celluloid (BBC Radio 4 Book of the Week) 2000, The Walk to the Paradise Garden (BBC Radio 3) 2001. *Publications:* Hallelujah Now, A Modest Pageant.

DAVIGNON, Viscount Etienne, LLD; Belgian diplomatist and business executive; *Vice-Chairman, Suez-Tractebel SA;* b. 4 Oct. 1932, Budapest, Hungary; m. Françoise de Cumont 1959; one s. two d.; joined Ministry of Foreign Affairs 1959, Attache then Head of Office of Minister of Foreign Affairs Paul–Henri Spaak 1961–65; Political Dir 1969–76; Chair. Governing Bd, Int. Energy Agency 1974–77; Commr for Industry and Int. Markets, Comm. of European Communities 1977–81, Vice-Pres. for Industry, Energy and Research Policies 1981–85; joined Société Générale de Belgique 1985, 1988–2001, Exec. Chair. Bd of Dirs 1989–2001, Vice-Chair. 2001–03, Vice-Chair. Suez-Tractebel SA (susidiary) 2003–; Co-founder Brussels Airlines 2006–; Chair. Palais des Beaux-Arts, Brussels, Compagnie Maritime Belge, Institut Catholique des Hautes Etudes Commerciales, Spaak Foundation; Vice-Chair. Union Minière 1993–; Pres. Friends of Europe (think tank), Brussels, CSR Europe, Brussels; mem. Bd of Dirs Accor, Suez, Sofina, Cumerio, Real Software, Royal Sporting Club d'Anderlecht; Hon. DHumLitt (American Coll. in Paris) 1988. *Leisure interests:* golf, skiing, tennis. *Address:* Suez-Tractebel SA, place du Trône 1, 1000 Brussels (office); 12 avenue des Fleurs, 1150 Brussels, Belgium. *Telephone:* (2) 507-03-82 (office). *Fax:* (2) 507-03-00 (office). *E-mail:* etienne.davignon@suez.com (office). *Website:* www.tractebel.be (office).

DAVIS, Sir Andrew, Kt, CBE; British conductor; *Musical Director, Chicago Lyric Opera;* b. 1944; m. Gianna Rolandi 1989; one s.; ed Royal Coll. of Music, King's Coll., Cambridge, studied conducting with Franco Ferrara, Rome; continuo player with Acad. of St Martin-in-the-Fields and English Chamber Orchestra; Festival Hall debut conducting BBC Symphony Orchestra 1970; Asst Conductor Philharmonia Orchestra 1973–77; Prin. Guest Conductor Royal Liverpool Philharmonic Orchestra 1974–77; Music Dir Toronto Symphony 1975–88, Conductor Laureate 1988–; Musical Dir Glyndebourne Festival Opera 1988–2002; Chief Conductor BBC Symphony Orchestra 1989–2000, Conductor Laureate 2000–, tours with orchestra to Far East 1990, Europe 1992, Japan 1993, 1997, USA 1995, 1998, South America 2001, Far East and Australia 2002; Prin. Guest Conductor Royal Stockholm Philharmonic 1995–99; Musical Dir. Chicago Lyric Opera 2000–; has conducted London Philharmonic, London Symphony, Royal Philharmonic, Boston, Chicago, Cleveland, Los Angeles Philharmonic, New York Philharmonic, Pittsburg Symphony, Orchestre Nat. de France, Frankfurt Radio Orchestra, Royal Concertgebouw Orchestra, Tonhalle Orchestra, Stockholm Philharmonic Orchestra, Israel Philharmonic, Bavarian Radio Symphony and Berlin Philharmonic orchestras, London Sinfonietta, Dallas Symphony and Dresden Staatskapelle orchestras; has conducted at Glyndebourne Festival Opera, Covent Garden Opera, Metropolitan Opera, Washington, DC, Chicago Lyric Opera, Bavarian State Opera, Paris Opéra, La Scala, Milan, Sir Henry

DAV THE INTERNATIONAL WHO'S WHO 2010 DAV

Wood Promenade Concerts, maj. British and European music festivals; tours of People's Republic of China 1978, Europe 1983 with Toronto Symphony Orchestra. *Recordings include:* Duruflé's Requiem (Grand Prix du Disque 1978), cycle of Dvořák symphonies, Tippett's The Mask of Time (Gramophone Record of the Year Award 1987, Grand Prix du Disque 1988), Vaughan Williams symphony cycle. *Leisure interest:* medieval stained glass. *Address:* Columbia Artist Management Inc., 1790 Broadway, New York, NY 10019-1412, USA (office). *Telephone:* (212) 841-9500 (office). *Fax:* (212) 841-9744 (office). *E-mail:* cami@cami.com (office). *Website:* www.cami.com (office); www.lyricopera.org (office).

DAVIS, Carl, BA; American composer and conductor; *Principal Guest Conductor, Munich Symphony Orchestra;* b. 28 Oct. 1936, New York; s. of Isadore Davis and Sara Davis; m. Jean Boht 1971; two d.; ed New England Conservatory of Music, Bard Coll.; Asst Conductor, New York City Opera 1958; Assoc. Conductor London Philharmonic Orchestra 1987–88; Prin. Conductor Bournemouth Pops 1984–87; Prin. Guest Conductor Munich Symphony Orchestra 1990–; Artistic Dir and Conductor Royal Liverpool Philharmonic Orchestra, Summer Pops 1993–2000; Guest Conductor Hallé Orchestra, Birmingham Symphony Orchestra, Scottish Symphony Orchestra; Hon. Fellowship (Liverpool Univ.) 1992; Chevalier, Ordre des Arts et des Lettres 1983, Hon. CBE 2005; Hon. Dr of Arts (Bard, New York) 1994, Hon. DMus (Liverpool) 2002; Special Achievement Award for Music for Television and Film 2003. *Musical theatre:* Diversions (Obie Prize Best Review) 1958, Twists (Arts Theatre London) 1962, The Projector and Cranford (Theatre Royal Stratford East), Pilgrim (Edinburgh Festival), The Wind in the Willows, Peace (Opera North), Alice in Wonderland (Hammersmith) 1987, The Vackees (Haymarket) 1987, The Mermaid. *Incidental music for theatre includes:* Prospect Theatre Co., Nat. Theatre, RSC. *Ballet:* A Simple Man 1987, Lipizzaner 1988, Liaisons Amoureuses (Northern Ballet Theatre) 1988, Madly, Badly, Sadly, Gladly, David and Goliath, Dances of Love and Death (London Contemporary Dance Theatre), The Picture of Dorian Gray (Sadler's Wells Royal Ballet), A Christmas Carol (Northern Theatre Ballet) 1992, The Savoy Suite (English Nat. Ballet) 1993, Alice in Wonderland (English Nat. Ballet) 1995, Aladdin (Scottish Ballet) 2000, Pride and Prejudice: First Impressions (Central Ballet School Tour) 2002. *Music for TV includes:* The Snow Goose 1971, The World at War (Emmy Award) 1972, The Naked Civil Servant 1975, Our Mutual Friend 1978, Hollywood 1980, Churchill: The Wilderness Years 1981, Silas Marner 1985, Hotel du Lac 1986, The Accountant (BAFTA Award) 1989, The Secret Life of Ian Fleming 1989, Separate but Equal 1991, The Royal Collection 1991, A Year in Provence 1992, Fame in the 20th Century: Clive James 1992, Ghengis Cohn 1993, Thatcher: The Downing Street Years 1993, Pride and Prejudice 1995, Oliver's Travels 1995, Eurocinema: The Other Hollywood 1995, Cold War 1998–99, Good Night Mr Tom 1998, The Great Gatsby 2000, The Queen's Nose, An Angel for May, Book of Eve 2003, Promoted to Glory 2003. *Operas for TV:* The Arrangement, Who Takes You to The Party?, Orpheus in the Underground, Peace. *Film music:* The Bofors Gun 1969, The French Lieutenant's Woman (BAFTA Award) 1981, Champions 1984, The Girl in a Swing 1988, Rainbow 1988, Scandal 1988, Frankenstein Unbound 1989, The Raft of the Medusa 1991, The Trial 1992, Voyage 1993, Widow's Peak 1994, Topsy Turvy 2000; series of Thames Silents including Napoleon 1980, 2000, The Wind, The Big Parade, Greed, The General, Ben Hur, Intolerance, Safety Last, The Four Horsemen of the Apocalypse 1992, Wings 1993, Waterloo 1995, Phantom of the Opera 1996, 6 Mutuals (Chaplin Shorts) 2004. *Concert works:* Music for the Royal Wedding, Variations on a Bus Route, Overture on Australian Themes, Clarinet Concerto 1984, Lines on London Symphony 1984, Fantasy for Flute and Harpsichord 1985, The Searle Suite for Wind Ensemble, Fanfare for Jerusalem 1987, The Glenlivet Fireworks Music 1988, Norwegian Brass Music 1988, Variations for a Polish Beggar's Theme 1988, Pigeons Progress 1988, Jazz Age Fanfare 1989, Everest 1989, Landscapes 1990, The Town Fox (text by Carla Lane) 1990, A Duck's Diary 1990, Paul McCartney's Liverpool Oratorio (with Paul McCartney) 1991. *Recordings include:* Napoleon 1983, Christmas with Kiri (with Kiri Te Kanawa) 1986, Beautiful Dreamer (with Marylin Horne) 1986, The Silents 1987, Ben Hur 1989, A Simple Man 1989, The Town Fox and Other Musical Tales (text by Carla Lane) 1990, Paul McCartney's Liverpool Oratorio 1991, Leeds Castle Classics, Liverpool Pops at Home 1995. *Publications:* sheet music of television themes. *Leisure interests:* reading, gardening, playing chamber music, cooking. *Address:* c/o Hazard Chase, 72 Charlotte Street, London, W1T 4QQ, England (office). *Telephone:* (20) 3355-4535 (office). *Fax:* (20) 3355 4525 (office). *E-mail:* admin@threefoldmusic.co.uk; jeremy.woods@hazardchase.co.uk. *Website:* www.carl-davis.com (office).

DAVIS, Clive; American music company executive and producer; *Chief Creative Officer, Sony BMG Worldwide;* b. New York, NY; lawyer, CBS 1960, Vice-Pres. and Gen. Man. 1966; with Columbia Records –1973, joined Bell Records 1974, founder Arista Records 1975, later Pres.; founder, Chair. and CEO J Records (jt project with RCA Music Group) 2000–08; Chair. and CEO RCA Music Group 2000–08; Chair. and CEO BMG North America 2000–08; Chief Creative Officer Sony BMG Worldwide 2008–; producer for Dido, Aretha Franklin, Sarah McLachlan, Whitney Houston, Billy Joel, Janis Joplin, Alicia Keys, Carlos Santana, Patti Smith and Bruce Springsteen. *Publication:* Clive – Inside the Record Business (autobiog.) 1974. *Address:* Sony BMG, 550 Madison Avenue, New York, NY 10022-3211, USA (office). *Telephone:* (212) 833-8000 (office). *Website:* www.sonybmg.com (office).

DAVIS, Sir Colin Rex, Kt, CBE, CH; British conductor and musician; *President, London Symphony Orchestra;* b. 25 Sept. 1927, Weybridge, Surrey; s. of Reginald George Davis and Lilian Colbran; m. 1st April Cantelo 1949 (dissolved 1964); one s. one d.; m. 2nd Ashraf Naini 1964; three s. two d.; ed Christ's Hospital and Royal Coll. of Music; Asst Conductor, BBC Scottish Orchestra 1957–59; Conductor, Sadler's Wells Opera House 1959, Musical Dir 1961–65; Chief Conductor, BBC Symphony Orchestra 1967–71, Chief Guest Conductor 1971–75; Artistic Dir Bath Festival 1969; Musical Dir Royal Opera House, Covent Garden 1971–86; Prin. Guest Conductor, Boston Symphony Orchestra 1972–84; Prin. Guest Conductor, London Symphony Orchestra 1975–95, Prin. Conductor 1995–2007, Pres. 2007–; Prin. Guest Conductor, New York Philharmonic Orchestra 1998–2003; Music Dir and Prin. Conductor, Bavarian State Radio Orchestra 1983–92; Hon. Conductor Dresden Staatskapelle 1990–; Hon. Freedom of the Worshipful Co. of Musicians 2005; Commendatore of the Repub. of Italy 1976, Commdr.'s Cross of the Order of Merit, Fed. Repub. of Germany 1987, Commdr Ordre des Arts et des Lettres 1990, Order of the Lion of Finland (Commdr 1st Class) 1992, Bayerischen Verdienstorden 1993, Officier, Légion d'honneur 1999, Maximiliansorden (Bavaria) 2000; Hon. DMus (Keele) 2002, (RAM) 2002, Dr hc (Sorbonne, Univ. of Paris) 2006; Grosser Deutscher Schallplattenpreis 1978, Grammy Award 'Opera Recording of the Year' 1980, Freedom of the City of London 1992, Royal Philharmonic Soc. Gold Medal 1995, Pipe Smoker of the Year 1995, Distinguished Musician Award (ISM) 1996, Grammy Award 'Best Orchestral Recording' 1997, Sibelius Birth Place Medal 1998, Grammy Awards 'Best Classical Album' and 'Best Opera Recording' (for Les Troyens) 2002, South Bank Show Award 2004. *Recent recordings include:* Mendelssohn Symphonies Nos 3 & 5 2006, Sibelius Kullervo (BBC Music Magazine Choral Award 2007) 2006. *Leisure interests:* reading, tree-planting, knitting. *Address:* c/o Alison Glaister, 39 Huntingdon Street, London, N1 1BP, England. *Telephone:* (20) 7609-5864 (home). *Fax:* (20) 7609-5866 (home). *E-mail:* aglaister@rexx.demon.co.uk (office). *Website:* lso.co.uk.

DAVIS, Sir Crispin Henry Lamert, Kt, MA; British business executive; b. 19 March 1949; s. of the late Walter Patrick Davis and of Jane Davis (née Lamert); m. Anne Richardson 1970; three d.; ed Charterhouse, Oriel Coll., Oxford; joined Procter & Gamble 1970; Man. Dir Procter & Gamble Co., Germany 1981–84; Vice-Pres. Food Div., Procter & Gamble USA 1984–90; European Man. Dir United Distillers 1990–92, Group Man. Dir 1992–94; CEO Aegis PLC 1994–99; Chief Exec. Reed Elsevier 1999–2009; mem. Finance Cttee, National Trust 2000–. *Leisure interests:* sport, gardening, art. *Address:* Hills End, Titlarks Hill, Sunningdale, Berks., SL5 0JD, England (home). *Telephone:* (1344) 291233 (home).

DAVIS, D. Scott, BSc, CPA; American business executive; *Chairman and CEO, UPS Inc.;* b. 1952, Medford, Ore.; s. of Darrell Davis and Rose Davis; ed Portland State Univ., Univ. of Pennsylvania Wharton School; began career with Arthur Andersen Accountants; fmr Chief Financial Officer and later CEO II Morrow Inc., Oregon –1986, joined UPS Inc. (following UPS purchase of II Morrow) 1986, Chief Financial Officer and mem. Man. Cttee 2001–, Dir 2006–, Vice-Chair. 2006–07, Chair. and CEO 2008–; CEO Overseas Partners Ltd, Bermuda 1998–2000; Deputy Chair. Fed. Reserve Bank of Atlanta 2007; mem. Bd Dirs Honeywell International Inc.; Chair. Georgia Council on Econ. Educ.; mem. Bd Trustees Annie E. Casey Foundation. *Address:* UPS Inc., 55 Glenlake Parkway NE, Atlanta GA 30328, USA (office). *Telephone:* (404) 828-6000 (office). *Fax:* (404) 828-6562 (office). *E-mail:* info@ups.com (office). *Website:* www.ups.com (office).

DAVIS, Rt Hon. David (Michael), PC, MSc; British politician and business executive; b. 23 Dec. 1948; s. of Ronald Davis and Elizabeth Davis; m. Doreen Margery Cook 1973; one s. two d.; ed Warwick Univ., London Business School and Harvard Univ.; joined Tate & Lyle Transport 1974, Man. Dir Tate and Lyle 1980–82, Strategic Planning Dir Tate and Lyle PLC 1984–87, Dir (non-exec.) 1987–90; Conservative MP for Boothferry 1987–97, for Haltemprice and Howden 1997–; Asst Govt Whip 1990–93; Parl. Sec. Office of Public Service and Science, Cabinet Office 1993–94; Minister of State, FCO 1994–97; Chair. House of Commons Public Accounts Cttee 1997–; cand. Conservative Party leadership election 2001, 2005; Chair. Conservative Party 2001–02; Shadow Sec. of State for the Office of the Deputy Prime Minister 2002–03; Shadow Sec. of State for Home, Constitutional and Legal Affairs, Shadow Home Sec. 2003–08; Chair. Fed. of Conservative Students 1973–74; Chair. Financial Policy Cttee, Confed. of British Industry 1977–79. *Publications:* BBC Guide to Parliament, How to Turn Round a Business; numerous articles on business and politics. *Leisure interests:* writing, mountaineering. *Address:* House of Commons, London, SW1A 0AA, England (office). *Telephone:* (20) 7219-4710 (office). *E-mail:* davisd@parliament.uk (office). *Website:* www.daviddaviesmp.org.

DAVIS, Don H., Jr., MBA; American business executive (retd); ed Texas A&M Univ.; joined Allen-Bradley Co. 1963, Pres. 1989; fmrly Exec. Vice-Pres., COO Rockwell Automation and Semiconductor Systems, Pres. Automation, Rockwell Int. Corpn (later Rockwell Automation) 1993, Sr Vice-Pres. 1993, Pres., COO 1995–97, Pres. and CEO 1997–98, Chair. and CEO 1998–2004, Chair. 2004–05 (retd); mem. Bd of Dirs Illinois Tool Works, Inc. 2000–. *Address:* 4780 North Lake Drive, Milwaukee, WI 53211, USA (office).

DAVIS, Geena, BFA; American actress; b. 21 Jan. 1957, Wareham, Mass.; m. 1st Richard Emmolo 1981 (divorced 1983); m. 2nd Jeff Goldblum (q.v.) (divorced 1990); m. 3rd Renny Harlin 1993 (divorced); m. 4th Reza Jarrahy 2001; one d. two s.; ed Boston Univ.; mem. Mount Washington Repertory Theatre Co.; worked as a model; f. Dads and Daughters - See Jane program. *Films include:* Tootsie 1982, Fletch 1984, Transylvania 6-5000 1985, The Fly 1986, Beetlejuice 1988, The Accidental Tourist 1988 (Acad. Award for Best Supporting Actress), Earth Girls are Easy 1989, Quick Change 1990, The Grifters, Thelma and Louise 1991, A League of Their Own 1992, Hero 1992, Angie 1994, Speechless (also producer) 1994, Cutthroat Island 1995, The Long Kiss Goodnight 1996, Stuart Little 1999, Stuart Little 2 2002, Stuart Little 3: Call of the Wild (vioce) 2005. *TV appearances include:* Buffalo Bill (series) 1983, Sara (series) 1985, Secret Weapons 1985, The Geena Davis Show (series) 2000, Commander-in-Chief (series) 2005–06 (Golden Globe Award for Best

508

www.worldwhoswho.com

Actress in a Drama TV Series 2006), Exit 19 2008. *Address:* 2401 Main Street, Santa Monica, CA 90405-3515; c/o Dads & Daughters - See Jane, 2 West 1st Street, Suite 101, Duluth, MN 55802, USA. *E-mail:* ayavor@caa.com.

DAVIS, Glyn, AC, BA, PhD, DUniv, FASSA; Australian university administrator; *Vice-Chancellor and Principal, University of Melbourne;* ed Univ. of New South Wales and Australian Nat. Univ.; Lecturer in Politics and Public Policy, Griffith Univ., Queensland 1985, Australian Research Council QE II Research Fellow 1988, Prof. 1998–2005, Vice-Chancellor 2002–04; Commr for Public Sector Equity in Queensland Public Sector Man. Comm. 1990–93, Dir Gen. Office of Cabinet 1995–96, Queensland Dept of Premier and Cabinet 1998–2002; Vice-Chancellor and Prin. Univ. of Melbourne 2005–, Foundation Chair. Australia and New Zealand School of Govt (ANZSOG) 2002–05; Dir Australia 21; mem. Sesquicentenary Cttee for Queensland; Harkness Fellowship to Univ. of Calif., Berkeley, Brookings Inst., Washington, DC and John F. Kennedy School of Govt, Harvard Univ. 1987–88. *Publications:* The Future of Australian Governance: Policy Choices (co-ed.) 2000, Are You Being Served? State, Citizens and Governance (co-ed.) 2001, The Australian Policy Handbook (fourth edn, with Catherine Althaus and Peter Bridgman) 2007. *Address:* Office of the Vice-Chancellor, The University of Melbourne, Melbourne, Vic. 3010, Australia (office). *Telephone:* (3) 8344-6134 (office). *Fax:* (3) 9341-6060 (office). *E-mail:* vc@unimelb.edu.au (office). *Website:* www.unimelb.edu.au (office).

DAVIS, Gray, BA, JD; American lawyer and fmr politician; *Of Counsel, Loeb & Loeb LLC;* b. 26 Dec. 1942; m. Sharon Ryer 1983; ed Stanford Univ. and Columbia Univ. Law School; Chief of Staff to Gov. of California 1974–81, State Rep. 1982–86, State Controller 1986–94, Lt Gov. 1994–99, Gov. of California 1999–2003 (recalled); Of Counsel, Loeb & Loeb LLC, Los Angeles 2004–; mem. Southern Calif. Leadership Council; Distinguished Policy Fellow, UCLA School of Public Policy; f. Calif. Foundation for the Protection of Children. *Address:* Loeb & Loeb LLC, 10100 Santa Monica Boulevard, Suite 2200, Los Angeles, CA 90067-4120, USA (office). *Telephone:* (310) 282-2206 (office). *Fax:* (310) 510-6727 (office). *E-mail:* gdavis@loeb.com (office). *Website:* www.loeb.com/gdavis (office); www.gray-davis.com.

DAVIS, Ian, MA; British business executive; *Worldwide Managing Director, McKinsey & Company;* b. 1951, Kent; brother of Crispin Davis; m. Penny Davis; one s. one d.; ed Charterhouse, Balliol Coll., Oxford; began career with Bowater (paper manufacturing co.) 1972–79; joined McKinsey & Co. 1979, variety of positions in several countries with focus on consumer-related and retail industries, Head of London Office (with responsibility for Ireland and the Middle E) 1996–2003, Man. Dir 2003–; mem. World Econ. Forum Int. Business Council; Trustee Conference Bd; mem. Advisory Bd Judge Inst. of Man., Univ. of Cambridge, City of Beijing. *Leisure activities:* tennis, cricket, opera. *Address:* McKinsey & Company, No. 1 Jermyn Street, London, SW1Y 4UH, England (office). *Telephone:* (20) 7839-8040 (office). *Fax:* (20) 7339-5000 (office). *Website:* www.mckinsey.com (office).

DAVIS, James Othello, MD, PhD; American physician and academic; *Professor Emeritus, Department of Physiology, School of Medicine, University of Missouri;* b. 12 July 1916, Tahlequah, Okla; s. of Zemry Davis and Villa (Hunter) Davis; m. Florrilla L. Sides 1941; one s. one d.; ed Univ. of Missouri and Washington Univ. School of Medicine, St Louis, Mo.; Intern and Fellow, Barnes Hospital, St Louis 1946; Investigator, Gerontology Unit, Nat. Heart Inst., Bethesda, Md and Baltimore City Hosp. 1947–49; Investigator, Lab. of Kidney and Electrolyte Metabolism 1949–57; Chief, Section on Experimental Cardiovascular Disease, Nat. Heart Inst., Bethesda, Md 1957–66; Prof. and Chair. Dept of Physiology, Univ. of Mo. School of Medicine 1966–82, Prof. Emer. 1982–; discovered and defined the important relationship of the renin-angiotensin system to the control of aldosterone secretion; mem. NAS and numerous other professional socs and orgs; James O. Davis Distinguished Lecturership in Cardiovascular Science est. in his honour 1995; several awards and honours. *Publications:* more than 260 scientific publications. *Leisure interests:* trout fishing, travel, tennis. *Address:* 612 Maplewood Drive, Columbia, MO 65203-1764, USA. *Telephone:* (573) 443-7878.

DAVIS, John Horsley Russell, PhD, FBA; British social anthropologist and academic; *Honourary Fellow, All Souls College, University of Oxford;* b. 9 Sept. 1938; s. of William Russell Davis and Jean Davis (née Horsley); m. Dymphna Gerarda Hermans 1981; three s.; ed Univ. Coll., Oxford and Univ. of London; Lecturer, Sr Lecturer, Reader in Social Anthropology, then Prof. Univ. of Kent 1966–90, f. Centre for Social Anthropology and Computing 1983; Prof. of Social Anthropology, Univ. of Oxford 1990–95; Fellow, All Souls Coll. Oxford 1990–95, Warden 1995–2008, Hon. Fellow 2008–; Chair. European Asscn of Social Anthropologists 1993–94; Pres. Royal Anthropological Inst. 1997–2001. *Publications:* Land and Family in Pisticci 1973, People of the Mediterranean 1977, Libyan Politics: Tribe and Revolution 1987, Exchange 1992. *Leisure interests:* gardens, music. *Address:* c/o All Souls College, Oxford, OX1 4AL, England.

DAVIS, Judy; Australian actress; b. 23 April 1956, Perth; m. Colin Friels; one s. one d. *Films include:* My Brilliant Career, High Tide, Kangaroo, A Woman Called Golda, A Passage to India, Impromptu, Alice, Barton Fink, Where Angels Fear To Tread, Naked Lunch, Husbands and Wives, The Ref, The New Age, Children of the Revolution, Blood and Wine, Absolute Power, Deconstructing Harry, Celebrity, Gaudi Afternoon, The Man Who Sued God 2001, Swimming Upstream 2003, Marie Antoinette 2006, The Break-Up 2006,. *Television includes:* Life with Judy Garland: Me and My Shadows (Golden Globe Award) 2001, The Reagans 2003, Coast to Coast 2004, The Starter Wife (Emmy Award for Best Supporting Actress in a Mini-series 2007) 2007–08, Diamonds (mini-series) 2008. *Address:* c/o Shanahan Management Pty Ltd, PO Box 478, King's Cross, NSW 2011, Australia.

DAVIS, Leonard (Leon) Andrew, AO; Australian engineer and business executive; *President, Walter and Eliza Hall Institute of Medical Research;* b. 3 April 1939, Port Pirie; s. of Leonard Harold Davis and Gladys Davis; m. Annette Brakenridge 1963; two d.; ed S Australian Inst. of Tech.; Man. Dir Pacific Coal 1984–89; Group Exec. CRA Ltd 1989–91; Mining Dir RTZ Corpn 1991–94; Man. Dir, Chief Exec. CRA Ltd 1994–95; Deputy Chief Exec., COO RTZ–CRA 1996; CEO Rio Tinto 1996–2000, Deputy Chair. 2000–05; Chair. Westpac Banking Corpn 2000–07 (retd); mem. Bd Dirs Huysmans Pty Ltd, Trouin Pty Ltd; Pres. Walter and Eliza Hall Inst. of Medical Research; Hon. DSc (Curtin) 1998, (Queensland) 2004, (S Australia) 2005; Centenary Medal (Australia) 2004. *Address:* c/o Walter and Eliza Hall Institute of Medical Research, 1G Royal Parade, Parkville, Vic. 3050, Australia.

DAVIS, Michael (Mick) L.; South African mining executive; *CEO, XStrata PLC;* b. 1958, Port Elizabeth, Eastern Cape; m. Barbara Davis; three c.; ed Theodor Herzl School, Port Elizabeth, Rhodes Univ.; fmr teacher, Witwatersrand; fmr accountant; Exec. Dir Eskom, Johannesburg –1994; with Gencor Ltd 1994; Exec. Chair. Ingwe Coal Corpn Ltd, Marshalltown 1995–97; Chief Financial Officer and Exec. Dir Billiton PLC 1997–2001; CEO Xstrata PLC 2001–, mem. Bd Dirs 2002–; Chair. United Jewish Israel Appeal; mem. Jewish Leadership Council; fmr Exec. Union of Orthodox Synagogues, SA; Chair. Euro Chai SA Charity Trust. *Address:* Xstrata PLC, Bahnhofstrasse 2, PO Box 102, 6301 Zug, Switzerland (office). *Telephone:* (41) 726-60-70 (office). *Fax:* (41) 726-60-89 (office). *E-mail:* info@xstrata.com (office). *Website:* www.xstrata.com (office).

DAVIS, Nathaniel, PhD; American diplomatist and academic; *Alexander and Adelaide Hixon Professor of Humanities Emeritus, Harvey Mudd College;* b. 12 April 1925, Boston, Mass.; s. of Harvey Nathaniel Davis and Alice Marion Rohde; m. Elizabeth Kirkbride Creese 1956; two s. two d.; ed Phillips Exeter Acad., Brown Univ., Fletcher School of Law and Diplomacy, Cornell Univ., Middlebury Coll., Columbia Univ., Univ. Central de Venezuela; Asst in History, Tufts Univ. 1947; Lecturer in History, Howard Univ. 1962–65, 1966–68; Third Sec., US Embassy, Prague 1947–49; Vice-Consul, Florence 1949–52; Second Sec., Rome 1952–53, Moscow 1954–56; Deputy Officer-in-Charge, Soviet Affairs, Dept of State 1956–60; First Sec., Caracas 1960–62; Special Asst to Dir of Peace Corps 1962–63, Deputy Assoc. Dir 1963–65; Minister to Bulgaria 1965–66; Sr Staff, Nat. Security Council, White House 1966–68; Amb. to Guatemala 1968–71, to Chile 1971–73; Dir-Gen. US Foreign Service 1973–75; Asst Sec. of State for African Affairs April–Dec. 1975; Amb. to Switzerland 1975–77; State Dept Adviser, Naval War Coll. 1977–83; Alexander and Adelaide Hixon Prof. of Humanities, Harvey Mudd Coll., Claremont, Calif. 1983–, now Emer.; Lecturer Naval War Coll., San Diego 1991–2003; Del., Democratic Nat. Convention 1988, 1992, 1996, 2000; Fulbright Scholar 1996–97; mem. Exec. Bd Calif. Democratic Party; mem. American Acad. of Diplomacy 1990–; Hon. LLD (Brown Univ.) 1970; Hartshorn Premium 1942, Caesar Misch Premium 1942; Cinco Aguilas Blancas Alpinism Award 1962, US Navy's Distinguished Public Service Award 1983, Elvira Roberti Award for Outstanding Leadership, LA County Democratic Party 1995, Prism Award for Public Service, Claremont Democratic Club 1999. *Film appearance:* The War on Democracy 2007. *Publications:* The Last Two Years of Salvador Allende 1985, Equality and Equal Security in Soviet Foreign Policy 1986, A Long Walk to Church: A Contemporary History of Russian Orthodoxy 1995 (2nd Edition 2003). *Leisure interests:* skiing, mountain climbing, white water canoeing, water-colour painting. *Address:* Harvey Mudd College, 301 E 12th Street, Claremont, CA 91711-5990 (office); 1783 Longwood Avenue, Claremont, CA 91711, USA (home). *Telephone:* (909) 621-8022 (office); (909) 624-5293 (home). *Fax:* (909) 607-7600 (office); (909) 621-8360.

DAVIS, Sir Peter (John), Kt, FRSA; British business executive; *Chairman, Marie Curie Cancer Care;* b. 23 Dec. 1941, Heswall, Cheshire; s. of John Stephen Davis and Adriaantje Davis (née de Baat); m. Susan J. Hillman 1968; two s. one d.; ed Shrewsbury School, Inst. of Marketing; man. trainee, The Ditchburn Org., Lytham, Lancs. 1959–65; Gen. Foods Ltd, Banbury, Oxon. 1965–72; Marketing Dir Key Markets 1973; Man. Dir David Grieg and Group Man. Dir Key Markets, David Grieg 1975–76; Departmental Dir (non-foods) J. Sainsbury PLC 1976, mem. Bd responsible for marketing 1977, Asst Man. Dir Buying and Marketing 1979–86; Dir then Deputy Chair. Homebase Ltd 1983–86; Group CEO J. Sainsbury PLC 2000–04, Chair. 2004; Dir Shaws Supermarkets, USA 1984–86, Chair. 2000–03; Deputy Chief Exec. Reed Int. PLC 1986, Chief Exec. 1986–94, Chair. 1990–94, CEO and Deputy Chair. of Reed Elsevier 1993 (following merger Jan. 1993), Co-Chair. 1993–94; Vice-Pres. Chartered Inst. of Marketing 1991–; Chair. Nat. Advisory Council for Educ. and Training Targets 1993–97, Basic Skills Agency 1991–97, New Deal Task Force 1997–2000; mem. Bd Business in the Community 1991–2005, Deputy Chair. 1991–97, Chair. 1997–2001; Founder and Bd mem. Marketing Council 1994–2002; Trustee, Marie Curie Cancer Care Jan.–Sept. 2006, Chair., Sept. 2006–; also currently Sr Adviser and mem. Advisory Bd Permira Advisers (pvt. equity co.); Dir (non-exec.) Granada Group 1987–91, British Satellite Broadcasting (BSB) 1988–90, Boots Co. 1991–2000, Prudential Corpn 1994–95 (Group Chief Exec. 1995–2000), UBS AG 2001–07; fmr mem. Supervisory Bd Aegon, Elsevier; mem. Bd of Dirs Royal Opera House 1999–2005, Trustee 1994–2005, also Chair. Royal Opera House Foundation –2005; Chair. Basic Skills Agency 1989–97, Nat. Advisory Council for Educ. and Training Targets 1993–97, Welfare to Work New Deal Task Force 1997–2000; apptd mem. Curry Comm. on the Future of Farming and Food 2001, Implementation Group for food and farming strategy 2002; Chair. Govt's Employer Task Force on Pensions –2005; Trustee, Victoria and Albert Museum 1994–96; Fellow, Marketing Soc., City & Guilds 2004; Hon. LLD (Exeter) 2000; Gold Medal, Chartered Man. Inst. 2003. *Leisure interests:* sailing, opera, reading, wine. *Address:* Marie Curie Cancer Care, 89 Albert

Embankment, London, SE1 7TP, England. *Telephone:* (20) 7599-7777. *Website:* www.mariecurie.org.uk (office).

DAVIS, Richard K.; American banking executive; *Chairman, President and CEO, U.S. Bancorp;* has held man. positions with U.S. Bancorp since joining Star Banc Corpn (a predecessor) as Exec. Vice-Pres. 1993, Vice-Chair. U.S. Bancorp (following merger of Firstar Corpn and U.S. Bancorp 2001) 2001–04, responsible for Consumer Banking, including Retail Payment Solutions (card services), assumed additional responsibility for Commercial Banking 2003–04, Pres. U.S. Bancorp 2004–, COO 2004–06, mem. Bd of Dirs and CEO 2006–Chair. 2007–; mem. Bd of Dirs Xcel Energy. *Address:* U.S. Bancorp, U.S. Bancorp Center, 800 Nicollet Mall, Minneapolis, MN 55402-7014, USA (office). *Telephone:* (651) 466-3000 (office). *Fax:* (612) 303-0782 (office). *E-mail:* info@usbank.com (office). *Website:* www.usbank.com (office); www.usbancorp.com (office).

DAVIS, Roger J., MA, MPhil, PhD, FRS; British biologist/biochemist and academic; *H. Arthur Smith Chair and Professor, Program in Molecular Medicine, University of Massachusetts Medical School and Howard Hughes Medical Institute;* b. 26 March 1958; ed Queens' Coll., Cambridge; Research Fellow, Univ. of Cambridge 1983; Damon Runyon-Walter Winchill Cancer Fund Fellow, Dept of Biochemistry and Molecular Biology, Univ. of Massachusetts Medical School, Worcester, MA, USA 1984–85, Asst Prof. 1985–90, Assoc. Prof., Program in Molecular Medicine 1990–93, Prof. 1993–, H. Arthur Smith Chair, Molecular Medicine 2002–; Asst Investigator, Howard Hughes Medical Inst., Chevy Chase, MD 1990–93, Assoc. Investigator 1993–97, Investigator 1997–; Established Investigator, American Heart Assn 1990–95; mem. AAAS 1990–, Soc. for Microbiology 1990–; Open Entrance Scholarship Queens' Coll. 1976–78, Foundation Scholarship 1978–81, Science and Eng Research Council Scholarship 1979–82, Munro Studentship 1981–82, ranked 1st by Citation Index Inst. for Scientific Information 1996. *Publications:* more than 180 publs in scientific journals. *Address:* Program in Molecular Medicine, University of Massachusetts Medical School, Biotech II-Suite 309, 373 Plantation Street, Worcester, MA 01605, USA (office). *Telephone:* (508) 856-6054 (office). *Fax:* (508) 856-3210 (office). *E-mail:* Roger.Davis@umassmed.edu (office). *Website:* www.umassmed.edu (office); www.hhmi.org (office).

DAVIS, Steve, OBE; British professional snooker player; b. 22 Aug. 1957, Plumstead, London; s. of Harry George Davis and Jean Catherine Davis; m. Judith Lyn Greig 1990; two s.; ed Alexander McLeod Primary School, Abbey Wood School, London; became professional snooker player 1978; has won 75 titles; in 99 tournament finals; in list of top 16 players for record 22 seasons; major titles include: UK Professional Champion 1980, 1981, 1984, 1985, 1986, 1987; Masters Champion 1981, 1982, 1988, 1997; Int. Champion 1981, 1983, 1984; World Professional Champion 1981, 1983, 1984, 1987, 1988, 1989; winner Asian Open 1992, European Open 1993, Welsh Open 1994; mem. Bd World Professional Billiards and Snooker Assn 1993–; regular snooker presenter on BBC TV; BBC Sports Personality of the Year 1989, BBC TV Snooker Personality of the Year 1997. *Television:* Steve Davis and Friends (chat show); They Think It's All Over (presenter) 2003–. *Publications:* Steve Davis, World Champion 1981, Frame and Fortune 1982, Successful Snooker 1982, How to Be Really Interesting 1988, Steve Davis Plays Chess 1996. *Leisure interests:* collecting R & B and soul records, chess, Tom Sharpe books. *Address:* 10 Western Road, Romford, Essex, RM1 3JT; Mascalls, Mascalls Lane, Brentwood, CM14 8LJ, England. *Telephone:* (1277) 359911 (office). *Fax:* (1277) 359935 (office). *E-mail:* sharron.tokley@matchroom.com (office). *Website:* matchroomsport.com (office).

DAVIS, Terence (Terry), PC, LLB, MBA; British politician and international organisation official; *Secretary General, Council of Europe;* b. 5 Jan. 1938; m. Anne Davis 1963; one s. one d.; ed Univ. Coll., London, Univ. of Michigan, USA; Internal Auditor, Esso Oil Co. 1962–65; Man. Clarks Shoes 1965–68; Man. Chrysler Parts UK 1968–71; Sr Man. Leyland Cars 1974–79; joined Labour Party 1965; fmr local govt councillor; MP 1971–74, 1979–83, 1983–2004, Opposition Whip 1979–80, Opposition Spokesman for Health, Finance and Economic Affairs, then for Trade and Industry 1980–87, mem. Public Accounts Cttee 1987–94, Public Records Advisory Cttee, Special Cttee of PCs; mem. WEU Ass. 1992–2004, Leader British Del. 1997–2002, Vice-Pres. 1997–2001; mem. Parl. Ass. of Council of Europe 1992–2004, Leader British Del. 1997–2002, Vice-Pres. Ass., mem. Bureau, Pres. Socialist Group 2002–04, Sec.-Gen. Council of Europe 2004–; fmr Rapporteur, EBRD, North South Centre, OECD, Georgia's admission to Council of Europe; fmr Leader and mem. UK Del. to WEU Ass., fmr Vice-Pres. Ass., fmr Pres. Socialist Group, Rapporteur for several reports on defence and security issues; fmr mem. UK Del. to OSCE Ass., Leader of UK Del. to Parl. Ass.; fmr mem. Exec. Cttee of UK Br., IPU; fmr mem. UK Del. to UN Gen. Ass.; fmr Visiting Lecturer, Civil Service Coll.; Chair. Ind. Comm. of Inquiry into the Treatment of Elderly People in Birmingham 2001–02; attended two Parl. Confs for South East Europe Stability Pact; observed elections in Albania, Georgia, Latvia and Ukraine; mem. Amnesty International, UNA, Links Europa. *Address:* Office of the Secretary General, Council of Europe, 67075 Strasbourg Cedex, France (office). *Telephone:* (3) 88-41-20-50 (office). *Fax:* (3) 88-41-27-99 (office). *E-mail:* private.office@coe.int (office). *Website:* www.coe.int (office).

DAVISON, Alan, BSc, PhD, DIC, FRS; British chemist and academic; *Professor of Chemistry, Massachusetts Institute of Technology;* b. 24 March 1936, Ealing; ed Univ. Coll. of Swansea, Imperial Coll. of Science and Tech.; lecturer in chem., Harvard Univ. 1962–64; Asst Prof. MIT 1964–67, Assoc. Prof. 1967–74, Prof. of Inorganic Chem. 1974–; Alfred P. Sloan Foundation Fellow 1967–69; Hon. Fellowship, Univ. Coll. of Swansea 1990; maj. research interests include Technetium and Rhenium chem., radiopharmaceutical chem. and bioinorganic chem.; Herbert M. Stauffer Award for Outstanding Laboratory Paper 1990, Paul C. Aebersold Award for Outstanding Achievement in Basic Science applied to Nuclear Medicine 1993. *Publications include:* numerous articles and papers in professional journals. *Address:* Department of Chemistry, Room 6-435, Massachusetts Institute of Technology, Cambridge, MA 02139 (office); 80 Cass Street, West Roxbury, MA 02132, USA (home). *Telephone:* (617) 253-1794 (office). *Fax:* (617) 258-6989 (office). *E-mail:* adavison@mit.edu (office). *Website:* www.mit.edu/chemistry (office).

DAVISON, Edward Joseph, BASc, MA, PhD, ScD, FIEEE, FRSC, ARCT, FCAE, P.Eng; Canadian electrical engineer and academic; *University Professor, Department of Electrical Engineering, University of Toronto;* b. 12 Sept. 1938, Toronto; s. of Maurice J. Davison and Agnes E. Quinlan; m. Zofia M. Perz 1966; four c.; ed Royal Conservatory of Music, Toronto and Univs of Toronto and Cambridge, UK; Asst Prof. Dept of Electrical Eng, Univ. of Toronto 1964–66, 1967–68, Assoc. Prof. 1968–74, Prof. 1974–2001, Univ. Prof. Dept of Electrical and Computer Eng 2001–; Asst Prof. Univ. of Calif., Berkeley 1966–67; Pres. IEEE Control Systems Soc. 1983 (Distinguished mem. 1984–); Chair. Int. Fed. of Automatic Control (IFAC) Theory Cttee 1987–90, mem. IFAC Council 1991–93, 1993–96, Vice-Chair. IFAC Tech. Bd 1991–93, Vice-Chair. IFAC Policy Cttee 1996–99, Fellow, IFAC 2005; Dir Electrical Eng Assocs Ltd, Toronto 1977–, Pres. 1997–; Consulting Engineer Assn of Professional Engineers of Prov. of Ont. 1979–; Killam Research Fellowship 1979, 1981, E.W.R. Steacie Research Fellowship 1974, Athlone Fellowship 1961; mem. Russian Acad. of Nonlinear Sciences 1998–; Hon. Prof. Beijing Inst. of Aeronautics and Astronautics 1986; IEEE Centennial Medal 1984, IFAC Quazza Medal 1993, IFAC Outstanding Service Award 1996, Hendrik W Bode Lecture Prize (IEEE Control Systems Soc.) 1997, Killam Prize in Eng 2003, Canada Council 2003, inducted into Univ. of Toronto Eng Alumni Hall of Fame 2003. *Publications:* more than 450 research papers in numerous journals. *Leisure interests:* backpacking, skiing. *Address:* Department of Electrical Engineering, University of Toronto, Toronto, ON, M5S 1A4, Canada (office). *Telephone:* (416) 978-6342 (office); (416) 444-9381 (home). *Fax:* (416) 978-0804 (office). *E-mail:* ted@control.utoronto.ca (office). *Website:* www.control.utoronto.ca/people/profs/ted/ted.htm/ (office).

DAVISON, Ian Frederic Hay, CBE, BSc (Econ.), FCA; British business executive and accountant (retd) and financial services regulator; *Chairman, Ruffer LLP;* b. 30 June 1931, Hillingdon, Middx; s. of the late Eric Hay Davison and Inez Davison; m. Maureen Patricia Blacker 1955; one s. two d.; ed Dulwich Coll., LSE and Univ. of Michigan, USA; mem. Inst. of Chartered Accountants (mem. Council 1975–99); Man. Partner Arthur Andersen & Co., Chartered Accountants 1966–82; Ind. mem. NEDC for Bldg Industry 1971–77; mem. Price Comm. 1977–79; Chair. Review Bd for Govt Contracts 1981; Chief Exec. and Deputy Chair. Lloyd's 1983–86; Dept of Trade Insp., London Capital Securities 1975–77; Insp. Grays Bldg Soc. 1978–79; Chair. Accounting Standards Cttee 1982–84; Chair. The Nat. Mortgage Bank PLC 1992–2000, Roland Berger Ltd 1996–98; Chair. Dubai Financial Services Authority 2002–04; Chair. Ruffer LLP 2002–; Chair. (non-exec.) Northgate plc (fmrly McDonnell Information Systems) 1993–99, Newspaper Publrs 1993–94 (Dir 1986–94); Chair. Monteverdi Trust 1979–84, Sadler's Wells Foundation 1995–2003, Pro Provost RCA 1996–2007, Crédit Lyonnais Capital Markets 1988–91, Charterail 1991–92; Pres. Nat. Council for One-Parent Families 1991–2004; Dir Morgan Grenfell Asset Man. 1986–88, Midland Bank PLC 1986–88, Storehouse PLC 1988–96 (Chair. 1990–96), Chloride PLC 1988–98, Cadbury Schweppes PLC 1990–2000, CIBA PLC 1991–96; Trustee, Victoria and Albert Museum 1984–93; Dir and Trustee, Royal Opera House, Covent Garden 1984–86; Trustee, SANE 1996– (Chair. 2000–02); Gov. LSE 1982–2006; Chair. Railway Heritage Cttee 1999–2004; Chair. of Council, Exeter Cathedral 2002–08; Hon. Fellow (LSE) 2004; Hon. DSc (Aston) 1985, Hon. LLD (Bath) 1998. *Publication:* Lloyd's: A View of the Room 1987. *Leisure interests:* music, theatre, bell-ringing. *Address:* North Cheriton Manor, Templecombe, Somerset, BA8 0AE, England (home). *Telephone:* (1963) 32100 (home); (7932) 160482. *Fax:* (1963) 34225 (home). *E-mail:* ihdavison@aol.com (home).

DAVISON, Rt Hon. Sir Ronald Keith, GBE, CMG, PC, LLB; New Zealand judge and lawyer; b. 16 Nov. 1920, Kaponga; s. of the late Joseph James Davison and Florence Minnie Davison; m. Jacqueline May Carr 1948; two s. (one deceased) one d.; ed Te Kuiti Dist High School, Auckland Univ.; served in Army, reaching rank of Lt, 1940–46; Flying Officer, RNZAF, Europe; called to bar 1948; Pnr, Milne, Meek and Davison 1948–53; est. pvt. law practice 1953; QC 1963–; Chief Justice of NZ 1978–89; Chair. Legal Aid Bd 1969–78; Chair. Environmental Council 1969–74; Chair. Aircrew Industrial Tribunal 1971–78; Chair. Montana Wines Ltd 1972–78; mem. Auckland Dist Law Soc. Council 1959–65, Pres. 1965–66; Dir, NZ Insurance Co. Ltd 1975–78; mem. Auckland Electric Power Bd 1958–71; mem. NZ Law Soc. Council 1964–66; fmr mem. Torts and Gen. Law Reform Cttee; Church Advocate, Auckland Diocese 1973–78; Vicar's Warden, St Mark's Church, Remuera 1974–78; mem. Privy Council of UK 1978–. *Leisure interests:* golf, fishing. *Address:* 1 Lichfield Road, Parnell, Auckland, New Zealand. *Telephone:* (9) 3020493.

DAVUTOGLU, Ahmed, PhD; Turkish academic and government official; *Minister of Foreign Affairs;* b. 1959, Konya; ed Bosphorus Univ.; fmr Chair. Dept of Int. Relations, Beykent Univ., Istanbul; began working at Marmara Univ. 1993, Prof. 1999–2003; Foreign Policy Adviser to the Prime Minister of Turkey 2003–09; Minister of Foreign Affairs 2009–. *Address:* Ministry of Foreign Affairs, Dişişleri Bakanlığı, Dr Sadık Ahmet Cad. 12, 06100 Balgat, Ankara, Turkey (office). *Telephone:* (312) 2921000 (office). *Fax:* (312) 2873869 (office). *E-mail:* webmaster@mfa.gov.tr (office). *Website:* www.mfa.gov.tr (office).

DAVYDOV, Mikhail Ivanovich, DrMed; Russian clinical oncologist; *Regional Co-ordinator for Russia and CIS, N.N. Blokhin Russian Cancer Research Center, Russian Academy of Siences;* b. 11 Oct. 1947, Konotop, Sumy region, Ukraine; s. of Ivan Ivanovich Davydov and Asmar Tamrazovna Davydova; m. Irina Borisovna Zborovskaya; one s.; ed Moscow 1st Sechenov Inst. of Medicine; researcher, Sr Researcher, Head of Lab., Head of Div., Deputy Dir Moscow Blokhin Oncological Scientific Center (now N.N. Blokhin Russian Cancer Research Center), Russian Acad. of Medicine, Dir Research Inst. of Clinical Oncology 1980, Prof. 1986, now Regional Co-ordinator for Russia and CIS; mem. Int. Soc. of Surgeons, American and European Soc. of Surgeons, New York Acad. of Sciences; Corresp. mem. Russian Acad. of Medicine; numerous decorations including Merited Worker of Science of Russia 1996. *Publications:* over 300 scientific publs on oncological surgery, including three monographs and six methodical films. *Leisure interests:* boxing, sports, hunting, classical and retro music. *Address:* N.N. Blokhin Russian Cancer Research Center, Russian Academy of Medical Sciences, 115478 Moscow, Kashirskoye shosse 24, Russia (office). *Telephone:* (495) 324-11-14 (office). *Fax:* (495) 323-57-77 (office). *E-mail:* davydov@eso.ru (office). *Website:* www.eso.ru (office).

DAWE, Donald Bruce, AO, MLitt, PhD; Australian writer; b. 15 Feb. 1930, Geelong; s. of Alfred James Dawe and Mary Ann Matilda Dawe; m. Gloria Desley Dawe (née Blain) 1964 (died 1997); two s. two d.; ed Northcote High School, Univs of Melbourne, New England and Queensland; Educ. Section, RAAF 1959–68; teacher, Downlands Sacred Heart Coll., Toowoomba, Queensland 1969–71; Lecturer, Sr Lecturer, Assoc. Prof., Faculty of Arts, Univ. of Southern Queensland 1971–93; Hon. Prof. (Univ. of Southern Queensland) 1995; Hon. DLitt (Univ. of Southern Queensland) 1995, (Univ. of NSW) 1997; Myer Poetry Prize 1965, 1968, Patrick White Award 1980, Christopher Brennan Award 1984, Paul Harris Fellowship, Rotary Int. 1990, Philip Hodgins Memorial Medal for Literary Excellence 1997, Australia Council for the Arts Emer. Writers Award 2001, Centenary Medal 2003. *Publications:* poetry: No Fixed Address 1962, A Need of a Similar Name (Ampol Arts Award 1966) 1964, An Eye for a Tooth 1968, Beyond the Subdivisions 1969, Condolences of the Season: Selected Poems 1971, Over Here, Hark! and Other Stories 1983, Speaking in Parables 1987, The Side of Silence: Poems 1987–90 1990, Mortal Instruments: Poems 1990–95 1995, Sometimes Gladness: Collected Poems 1954–97 1997, A Poet's People 1999, Towards a War 2003; non-fiction: Essays and Opinions 1990; children's fiction: No Cat – and That's That 2002, The Chewing Gum Kid 2002, Luke and Lulu 2004, Smarty-Cat 2007. *Leisure interests:* gardening, watching Australian Rules football. *Address:* Authors, c/o Penguin Group (Australia), PO Box 701, Hawthorn 3122, Vic., Australia (office). *Website:* www.penguin.com.au (office).

DAWES, Kwame Senu Neville, BA, PhD; American/Ghanaian/Jamaican poet, playwright, critic and novelist; *Distinguished Poet in Residence and Louise Frye Scudder Professor of Humanities, University of South Carolina;* b. 28 July 1962, Accra, Ghana; s. of Neville Agustus Dawes and Sophia Dawes (née Tevi); m. Lorna Marie; three c.; ed Univ. of the West Indies, Univ. of New Brunswick; moved to Jamaica 1971; Chair. of the Division of Arts and Letters 1993–96; Asst Prof. in English, Univ. of S Carolina (USC) at Sumter 1992–96, Guest Lecturer, USC at Columbia 1994, Assoc. Prof. of English, USC 1996–2001, Prof. of English 2002–, currently Distinguished Poet in Residence and Louise Frye Scudder Prof. of Humanities, Dir MFA/Creative Writing program 2001–03; Series Ed. Caribbean Play Series, Peepal Tree Books, UK 1999–, Assoc. Poetry Ed. Peepal Tree Books 2006–; Criticism Ed. Obsidian II literary journal, Raleigh, NC 2000–05; programmer of annual Calabash Int. Literary Festival, Jamaica 2000–; Dir USC English Dept Spring Writers Festival 2002–03, S Carolina Poetry Initiative (founder) 2003–; Exec. Dir USC Arts Inst. 2005–; Faculty Mem., Pacific Univ. MFA program; mem. Nat. Book Critics' Circle, S Carolina Humanities Council (Bd mem.) 2000–07, S Carolina Book Festival (mem. Advisory Bd); Assoc. Fellow, Univ. of Warwick 1996; Hon. Fellow Univ. of Iowa Int. Writing Program 1986; Forward Poetry Prize for Best First Collection 1994, S Carolina Arts Comm. Individual Artist Fellowship 1996, Winner Poetry Business Chapbook Competition 2000, Ohio Univ. Press Hollis Summers Poetry Prize 2000, Pushcart Prize 2001, Hurston Wright Legacy Award for Fiction. *Plays:* In the Warmth of the Cold, And the Gods Fell, In Chains of Freedom, The System, The Martyr, It Burns and it Stings, Charity's Come, Even Unto Death, Friends and Almost Lovers, Dear Pastor, Confessions, Brown Leaf, Coming in from the Cold, Song of an Injured Stone (musical), In My Garden, Charades, Passages, A Celebration of Struggle, Stump of the Terebinth, Valley Prince, One Love 2001. *Writing for radio:* Salut Haiti (poem/drama), Samaritans (play), New World A-Comin' (play). *Publications:* poetry: Progeny of Air 1994, Resisting the Anomie 1995, Prophets 1995, Jacko Jacobus 1996, Requiem 1996, Shook Foil 1998, Wheel and Come Again: Reggae Anthology (ed.) 1998, Mapmaker (chapbook) 2000, Midland 2001, Selected Poems 2002, Bruised Totems 2004, Wisteria: Twilight Songs from The Swamp Country 2005, Brimming 2006, Gomer's Song 2007, Impossible Flying 2007; fiction: A Place to Hide (short stories) 2002, She's Gone (novel) 2007; non-fiction: Natural Mysticism: Towards a New Reggae Aesthetic (literary criticism) 1998, Talk Yuh Talk: Interviews with Caribbean Poets 2000, Bob Marley: Lyrical Genius 2002, A Far Cry from Plymouth Rock (memoir) 2007; contrib. to numerous journals and periodicals, including Beat Magazine, Black Issues, Black Warrior Review, Bristol Evening Post, Calabash, Caribbean Writer, Dagens Nyheter (Sweden), Globe and Mail, Impact, Library Journal, Lines, Morning Star, Poetry London Newsletter, Poetry Review, Publishers Weekly, The Atlanta Journal/Constitution, The Brunswickan, The Courier, The Daily Gleaner, The Daily News, The English Review, The Guardian, The Herald, The London Times, The Observer, The State, The Sumter Item, The Telegraph Journal, The Voice, Time Out London, Venue, Wasafiri, Western Daily Press, World Literature Today, World Literature Written in English, Granta. *Address:* English Department, University of South Carolina, Columbia, SC 29208 (office); Alison Granucci, Blue Flower Arts LLC, PO Box 1361, Millbrook NY 12545, USA (office). *Telephone:* (803) 777-2096 (office). *Fax:* (803) 777-9064 (office). *E-mail:* alison@blueflowerarts.com (office); dawesk@mailbox.sc.edu (office). *Website:* www.kwamedawes.com (home); www.blueflowerarts.com (office).

DAWKINS, Hon. John Sydney, BEc, RDA; Australian politician, economist and business consultant; *Director, Government Relations Australia;* b. 2 March 1947, Perth; m. 1st (divorced); one s. one d.; m. 2nd Maggie Dawkins 1987; one d. one step-s.; ed Scotch Coll., Roseworthy Agricultural Coll.; fmr mem. Senate, Univ. of W Australia; worked for Bureau of Agricultural Econs and Dept of Trade and Industry 1971–72; MP, House of Reps., Seat of Tangney, WA 1974–75, Seat of Fremantle, WA 1977–94; Minister for Finance and Minister Assisting the Prime Minister for Public Service Matters 1983–84, Minister for Trade and Minister Assisting the Prime Minister for Youth Affairs 1984–87, for Employment, Educ. and Training 1987–91, Treasurer 1991–93; Chair. Cairns Group of Agricultural Exporting Countries 1985–87, OECD Ministerial Council 1993, John Dawkins and Co. 1994–, Medical Corpn of Australasia 1997–, Elders Rural Services Ltd 1998–, mem. Bd Sealcorp Holdings, Fred Hollows Foundation, Indian Ocean Centre; fmr mem. Nat. Exec., Australian Labor Party, Party Vice-Pres. 1982–83; Australian Govt Special Investment Rep. 1994–95; Press Officer, WA Trades and Labor Council 1976–77; currently Dir Government Relations Australia (lobbying firm), Adelaide; Hon. DUniv (Univ. of S Australia, Queensland Univ. of Tech.) 1997. *Leisure interests:* farming, viticulture, travel. *Address:* Government Relations Australia, Level 2, 60 Hindmarsh Square, Adelaide, SA 5034, Australia (office). *Telephone:* (8) 8232-0344 (office). *Fax:* (8) 8359-3377 (office). *E-mail:* jdawkins@govrel.com.au (office). *Website:* www.govrel.com.au (office).

DAWKINS, (Clinton) Richard, MA, DSc, FRS, FRSL; British biologist, academic and author; *Professorial Fellow, New College, University of Oxford;* b. 26 March 1941, Nairobi, Kenya; s. of Clinton John Dawkins and Jean Mary Vyvyan Dawkins (née Ladner); m. 1st Marian Stamp 1967 (divorced 1984); m. 2nd Eve Barham 1984; one d.; m. 3rd Hon. Lalla Ward 1992; ed Balliol Coll., Oxford; Asst Prof. of Zoology, Univ. of Calif., Berkeley, USA 1967–69; Lecturer, Univ. of Oxford 1970–89, Reader in Zoology 1989–96, Charles Simonyi Reader in the Public Understanding of Science 1995–96, Charles Simonyi Prof. 1996–2008 (retd), Professorial Fellow, New College, Oxford 1970–; Ed. Animal Behaviour 1974–78, Oxford Surveys in Evolutionary Biology 1983–86; Gifford Lecturer, Univ. of Glasgow 1988, Sidgwick Memorial Lecturer, Newnham Coll., Cambridge 1988; Kovler Visiting Fellow, Univ. of Chicago 1990; Nelson Lecturer, Univ. of Calif., Davis 1990; f. Richard Dawkins Foundation for Reason and Science 2006; Hon. Fellow, Regent's Coll., London 1988, Balliol Coll. 2004, Hon. Patron, Philosophical Soc., Trinity Coll. Dublin 2004; Hon. DLitt (St Andrews) 1995, (ANU Canberra) 1996; Hon. DSc (Westminster) 1997, (Hull) 2001, (Sussex) 2005, (Durham) 2005, (Brussels) 2005; Hon. DUniv (Open Univ.) 2003; numerous awards including Silver Medal, Zoological Soc. 1989, Michael Faraday Award, Royal Soc. 1990, Nakayama Prize 1994, Int. Cosmos Prize 1997, Kistler Prize 2001, Bicentennial Kelvin Medal, Royal Soc. of Glasgow 2002, Shakespeare Prize for contribution to British Culture, Hamburg 2005, British Book Award for Author of the Year 2007. *Television includes:* Nice Guys Finish First, BBC 1985, The Blind Watchmaker, BBC 1986, Break the Science Barrier, Channel 4 1994, Royal Institution Christmas Lectures, BBC 1992, Big Ideas in Science, Channel 5 2004, The Root of All Evil?, Channel 4 2005. *Publications include:* The Selfish Gene 1976, The Extended Phenotype 1982, The Blind Watchmaker (RSL Prize 1987, LA Times Literature Prize 1987) 1986, The Tinbergen Legacy (ed with M. Dawkins and T. R. Halliday) 1991, River Out of Eden 1995, Climbing Mount Improbable 1996, Unweaving the Rainbow: Science, Delusion and the Appetite for Wonder 1998, A Devil's Chaplain (essays) 2003, The Ancestor's Tale: A Pilgrimage to the Dawn of Life 2004, The God Delusion 2006, The Oxford Book of Modern Science Writing (ed) 2008; numerous articles in scientific journals. *Leisure interest:* human intercourse. *Address:* New College, Holywell Street, Oxford, OX1 3BN; Richard Dawkins Foundation for Reason and Science, Suite 184, 266 Banbury Road, Oxford, OX2 7DL, England. *E-mail:* contact@richarddawkins.net. *Website:* richarddawkins.net; www.richarddawkinsfoundation.org.

DAWOOD, Mohammad Hussain; Pakistani business executive; s. of the late Ahmad Dawood; Chair. Dawood Group of Industries, Chair. and CEO Dawood Hercules Chemicals Ltd, Dawood Cotton Mills and other cos within group; mem. Bd of Dirs Dawood Bank Ltd; Hon. Consul of Italy in Punjab 2002. *Address:* Dawood Group of Industries, 35A Shahrah-e-Abdul Hameed Bin Baadees (Empress Road), Lahore 54000, Pakistan. *Telephone:* (42) 6301601. *Fax:* (42) 6360343. *E-mail:* mhd@dgi.com.pk. *Website:* www.dawoodgroup.com.

DAWSON, Sir Daryl Michael, Kt, AC, KBE, CB, LLM; Australian judge; *Adjunct Professor, Monash University;* b. 12 Dec. 1933, Melbourne; s. of Claude Charles Dawson and Elizabeth May Dawson; m. Mary Louise Thomas 1971; ed Canberra High School and Melbourne Univ. and Yale Univ., USA; admitted to Bar, Vic. 1957; Lecturer, Council of Legal Educ. 1962–74; mem. Ormond Coll. Council 1965–73 (Chair. 1992–93); QC 1971; mem. Victoria Bar Council 1971–74; admitted to Tasmania Bar 1972; Solicitor-Gen. State of Vic. 1974–82; mem. Australian Motor Sport Appeal Court 1974–86; Judge, High Court of Australia 1982–97; Judge, Hong Kong Court of Final Appeal 1997–2003; Chair. Longford Royal Comm. 1998–99, Trade Practices Act Review Cttee 2002–03; Adjunct Prof., Monash Univ. 1998–; Professorial Fellow, Univ. of Melbourne 1998–; mem. Council Menzies Foundation (fmr Chair.); Fulbright Scholar 1955; Hon. LLD (Monash) 2006. *Leisure interest:*

gardening. *Address:* c/o Menzies Foundation, Clarendon Terrace, 210 Clarendon Street, East Melbourne, Vic. 3002; PO Box 147, East Melbourne, Vic. 3002, Australia. *Telephone:* (3) 9417-2818. *Fax:* (3) 9417-4499. *E-mail:* dawson@netlink.com.au.

DAWSON, Jill Dianne, BA, MA; British writer, poet, editor and teacher; b. 1962, Durham, England; pnr Meredith Bowles; two s.; ed Univ. of Nottingham, Sheffield Hallam Univ.; mem. Nat. Asscn of Writers in Education, Soc. of Authors; Eric Gregory Award 1992, second prize, London Writers Short Story Competition 1994, Blue Nose Poet of the Year 1995, London Arts Board New Writers 1998. *Publications:* School Tales (ed.) 1990, How Do I Look? (non-fiction) 1991, Virago Book of Wicked Verse (ed.) 1992, Virago Book of Love Letters (ed.) 1994, Wild Ways (ed. with Margo Daly), White Fish with Painted Nails (poems) 1994, Trick of the Light (novel) 1996, Magpie (novel) 1998, Fred and Edie (novel) 2001, Gas & Air (ed. with Margo Daly), Wild Boy (novel) 2003, Watch Me Disappear 2006, The Great Lover 2009; contrib. to anthologies and periodicals. *Address:* United Agents, 12–26 Lexington Street, London, W1F 0LE, England (office). *Telephone:* (20) 3214-0800 (office). *Fax:* (20) 3214-0801 (office). *E-mail:* info@unitedagents.co.uk (office). *Website:* unitedagents.co.uk (office); www.jilldawson.co.uk.

DAWSON, Dame Sandra June Noble, DBE, BA, MA, FIPH, FCGI, CIMgt; British college principal and professor of management studies; *KPMG Professor of Management, Judge Business School and Master, Sidney Sussex College, University of Cambridge;* b. 4 June 1946, Bucks.; d. of Wilfred Denyer and Joy Denyer (née Noble); m. Henry R. C. Dawson 1969; one s. two d.; ed Dr Challoner's Grammar School, Amersham, Univ. of Keele; research officer, Govt Social Survey 1968–69; research officer, then Lecturer, Sr Lecturer, Industrial Sociology Unit, Dept of Social and Econ. Studies, Imperial Coll. of Science, Tech. and Medicine 1969–90, Deputy Dir Man. School 1987–94, Prof. of Organizational Behaviour, Man. School 1990–95; KPMG Prof. of Man. Studies, Univ. of Cambridge1995–, Dir Judge Business School, 1995–2006, Fellow, Jesus Coll., Cambridge 1995–99; Master, Sidney Sussex Coll., Cambridge 1999–; Chair. Riverside Mental Health Trust 1992–95, Exec. Steering Cttee, Advanced Inst. of Man. 2007–; mem. Bd of Dirs (non-exec.) Riverside Health Authority 1990–92, Cambridge Econometrics 1996–2006, Fleming Claverhouse Investment Trust 1996–2003, Rand Europe (UK) 2002–03; Barclays PLC 2003–, Oxfam 2006–; mem. Research Strategy Bd, Offshore Safety Div., Health and Safety Exec. 1991–95, Strategic Review Group, Public Health Lab. Service 1994–99, Sr Salaries Review Body 1997–2003, Econ. and Social Research Council Research Priorities Bd 2000–03, UK–India Round Table; Fellow, City & Guilds of London Inst. 1999; Hon. Fellow, Jesus Coll. Cambridge; Hon. DSc (Keele Univ.), Hon. DLitt (Keele) 2000; Anglian Businesswoman of the Year 2000. *Publications include:* Analysing Organisations 1986, Safety at Work: The Limits of Self Regulation 1988, Managing the NHS 1995, Policy Futures for UK Health 2000, Future Health Organisations and Systems 2005, Engaging with Care (jtly) 2007; papers on man. in learned journals. *Leisure interests:* music, walking, family. *Address:* Judge Business School, University of Cambridge, Trumpington Street, Cambridge, CB2 1AG (office); Sidney Sussex College, Sidney Street, Cambridge, CB2 3HU, England. *Telephone:* (1223) 766331 (office); (1223) 338800 (office). *Fax:* (1223) 766332 (office). *E-mail:* s.dawson@jbs.cam.ac.uk (office). *Website:* www.jbs.cam.ac.uk (office); www.sid.cam.ac.uk.

DAWSON, Thomas C., II, AB (Econs), MBA; American economist; b. 9 March 1948, Washington, DC; s. of Allan Duval Dawson and Jane Dodge Dawson; m. Moira Jane Haley 1974; two s. one d.; ed Stanford Univ., Woodrow Wilson School of Public and Int. Affairs, Princeton Univ.; Financial Economist, Office of Investment Affairs, US Dept of State 1971–72, Staff Asst to Asst Sec. for Econ. Affairs 1972–73, Staff Asst to Under-Sec. for Econ. Affairs 1973–74, Economist, US Consulate Gen., Rio de Janeiro 1974–78; Consultant, McKinsey and Co. 1978–80; Deputy Asst Sec. for Developing Nations, US Treasury Dept 1981–84, Asst Sec. for Business and Consumer Affairs 1984–85; Deputy Asst to the Pres. and Exec. Asst to Chief of Staff, White House 1985–87; Exec. Vice-Pres. Regdon Associates 1987–89; Special Asst to Asst Sec. for Int. Affairs, US Treasury Dept 1989; US Exec. Dir IMF 1989–93, Dir External Relations Dept 1999–2006; First Vice-Pres. Merrill Lynch and Co. 1993–94, Dir Financial Insts Group 1993–99. *Address:* 50 Portland Road, Summit, NJ 07901, USA (home).

DAY, Catherine, MA; Irish EU official; *Secretary-General, European Commission;* b. Dublin; ed Univ. Coll., Dublin; loan officer, Investment Bank of Ireland 1974–75; EC Information Officer, Confed. of Irish Industry 1975–79; Admin., Directorate Gen. (DG) III 1979–82, mem. Cabinet of Richard Burke, in charge of Personnel and Admin 1982–84, Cabinet of Peter Sutherland, in charge of Competition 1985–89, Cabinet of Sir Leon Brittan, in charge of Competition and External Relations 1989–95, Deputy Chef de Cabinet to Sir Leon Brittan, in charge of External Relations 1995–96, Dir DG IA responsible for relations with the Balkans, Turkey and Cyprus 1996–97, Dir DG IA, subsequently DG Enlargement, responsible for relations with cand. countries of Cen. and Eastern Europe 1997–2000, Deputy Dir-Gen. DG for External Relations, responsible for relations with the Western Balkans, NIS, Mediterranean including the Middle East 2000–02, Dir-Gen. DG Environment 2002–05, Sec.-Gen. EC 2005–; Hon. LLD (Nat. Univ. of Ireland) 2003. *Address:* Secretariat-General, European Commission, 1049 Brussels, Belgium (office). *Telephone:* (2) 2958312 (office). *Fax:* (2) 2993229 (office). *E-mail:* catherine.day@ec.europa.eu (office). *Website:* (office).

DAY, Sir Derek (Malcolm), Kt, KCMG; British diplomatist; b. 29 Nov. 1927, London; s. of late Alan W. Day and Gladys Day; m. Sheila Nott 1955; three s. one d.; ed Hurstpierpoint Coll. and St Catharine's Coll. Cambridge; RA 1946–48; entered diplomatic service 1951; served Tel Aviv 1953–56, Rome 1956–59, Washington, DC 1962–66, Nicosia 1972–75; Amb. to Ethiopia 1975–78; Asst Under-Sec. of State FCO 1979, Deputy Under-Sec. of State 1980, Chief Clerk 1982–84; High Commr in Canada 1984–87; Commr Commonwealth War Graves Comm. 1987–92; Vice-Chair. British Red Cross 1988–94; Dir Monenco Ltd, Canada 1988–92; Chair. Crystal Palace Sports and Leisure Ltd 1992–97; mem. Defence Medical Services Clinical Research Cttee 1995–2003 (Chair. 1999); Gov. Hurstpierpoint Coll. 1987–97; Gov. Bethany School 1987–2000. *Address:* Pedlar's End, Goudhurst, Kent, TN17 1AD, England (home). *Telephone:* (1580) 211114 (home). *E-mail:* dands.day@virgin.net (home).

DAY, Doris; American actress and singer; b. (Doris Mary Anne von Kappelhoff), 3 April 1924, Cincinnati, OH; d. of Frederick Wilhelm and Alma Sophia von Kappelhoff; m. 1st Al Jorden 1941 (divorced 1943); one s.; m. 2nd George Weilder 1946 (divorced 1949); m. 3rd Marty Melcher 1951 (died 1968); m. 4th Barry Comden 1976 (divorced 1981); professional dancing appearances, Doherty and Kappelhoff, Glendale, Calif.; singer Karlin's Karnival, radio station WCPO; singer with bands, Barney Rapp, Bob Crosby, Fred Waring, Les Brown; singer and leading lady, Bob Hope radio show (NBC) 1948–50; Laurel Award, Leading New Female Personality in Motion Picture Industry 1950, Top Audience Attractor 1962, American Comedy Lifetime Achievement Award 1991, Grammy Award for Lifetime Achievement 2008. *Recordings:* albums: You're My Thrill 1949, Tea for Two 1950, Lullaby of Broadway 1951, On Moonlight Bay 1951, I'll See You in My Dreams 1951, By the Light of the Silvery Moon 1953, Young Man with a Horn 1954, Day Dreams 1955, Day in Hollywood 1955, Young at Heart 1955, Love Me or Leave Me 1955, Most Happy Fella 1956, Day by Day 1957, Hooray for Hollywood Vols I and II 1959, Cuttin' Capers 1959, Day by Night 1959, Boys and Girls Together 1959, Hot Canaries 1959, Lights Cameras Action 1959, Listen to Day 1960, Show Time 1960, What Every Girl Should Know 1960, I Have Dreamed 1961, Bright and Shiny 1961, You'll Never Walk Alone 1962, Duet 1962, The Best of Doris Day 2002; singles: Day by Day 1949, Sugarbush 1952, Secret Love 1954, The Black Hills of Dakota 1954, If I Give My Heart to You 1954, Ready Willing and Able 1955, Whatever Will Be Will Be (Que Sera Sera) 1956, Move Over Darling 1964. *Films include:* Romance on the High Seas 1948, My Dream is Yours 1949, Young Man with a Horn 1950, Tea for Two 1950, West Point Story 1950, Lullaby of Broadway 1951, On Moonlight Bay 1951, I'll See You in My Dreams 1951, April in Paris 1952, By the Light of the Silvery Moon 1953, Calamity Jane 1953, Lucky Me 1954, Yankee Doodle Girl 1954, Love Me or Leave Me 1955, The Pajama Game 1957, Teacher's Pet 1958, The Tunnel of Love 1958, It Happened to Jane 1959, Pillow Talk 1959, Please Don't Eat the Daisies 1960, Midnight Lace 1960, Lover Come Back 1962, That Touch of Mink 1962, Jumbo 1962, The Thrill of It All 1963, Send Me No Flowers 1964, Do Not Disturb 1965, The Glass Bottom Boat 1966, Caprice 1967, The Ballad of Josie 1968, Where Were You When the Lights Went Out? 1968, With Six You Get Egg Roll 1968, Sleeping Dogs, Hearts and Souls 1993, That's Entertainment III 1994. *Television includes:* Doris Day Show (CBS) 1952–53, 1968–72, The Pet Set 1972, Doris Day and Friends 1985–86, Doris Day's Best 1985–86. *Address:* c/o Doris Day Animal League, 227 Massachusetts Avenue, NE, Washington, DC 20002; c/o Columbia Records, 550 Madison Avenue, New York, NY 10022, USA (office).

DAY, Sir (Judson) Graham, Kt, LLB; Canadian/British lawyer and business executive; *Of Counsel, Stewart McKelvey;* b. 3 May 1933; s. of Frank C. Day and Edythe G. (née Baker) Day; m. L. Ann Creighton 1958; one s. two d.; ed Queen Elizabeth High School, Halifax, NS and Dalhousie Univ., Halifax; pvt. law practice, Windsor, NS 1956–64; Canadian Pacific Ltd, Montréal and Toronto 1964–71; Deputy Chair. Org. Cttee for British Shipbuilders and Deputy Chair. and Chief Exec. desig., British Shipbuilders 1975–76; Prof. of Business Studies and Dir Canadian Marine Transportation Centre, Dalhousie Univ. 1977–81; Vice-Pres. Shipyards and Marine Devt, Dome Petroleum Ltd 1981–83; Chair. and CEO British Shipbuilders 1983–86; Chair. The Rover Group (fmrly BL) PLC 1986–91, CEO 1986–88; Dir Cadbury Schweppes PLC 1988–93, Chair. 1989–93 (retd); Deputy Chair. MAI 1989–93; Chair. British Aerospace 1991–92; Chair. PowerGen 1990–93 (retd); Chair. Sobeys Inc. 2001–04; Of Counsel Stewart McKelvey LLP (law firm); Herbert Lamb Chair in Business Education, Dalhousie Univ. Graduate Business School; Special Consultant to Ashurst Morris Crisp 1994–96; mem. Bd of Dirs Jacques Whitford, Extendicare Canada Inc., The Laird Group PLC 1985–98, Bank of NS (Canada) 1989–2004, NOVA Corpn of Alberta 1990–2000; Pres. Inc. Soc. of British Advertisers 1991–93; Dir (non-exec.) Ugland Int. Holdings (Deputy Chair. 1997–2000); Lead Dir DHX Media Ltd 2006; Dir (non-exec.) Scotia Investments Ltd 2004– (Chair. 2008–), The CSL Group Inc. 2000–; Hon. Fellow Cardiff Univ. 1990, Hon. Col West Nova Scotia Regt 2005–; Dr hc (Humberside) 1992 and numerous other hon. degrees. *Leisure interests:* reading, lakeside chalet in Canada. *Address:* Stewart McKelvey, Suite 900, Purdy's Wharf Tower One, 1959 Upper Water Street, POB 997, Halifax, NS, B3J 2X2, Canada (office). *Telephone:* (902) 420-3376 (office). *Fax:* (902) 684-3880 (office). *E-mail:* sirgraham@win.eastlink.ca (office). *Website:* www.smss .com (office).

DAY, Julian, MA, MBA; British retail executive; m.; two s.; ed Univ. of Oxford, London Business School; began career providing man. services for a variety of cos including Kohlberg, Kravis and Roberts (KKR); fmr Dir European Devt Chase Manhattan Bank; Pres. and CEO Bradley Printing Co. –1992; Exec. Vice-Pres. and Chief Financial Officer Safeway Inc. 1992–98; Exec. Vice-Pres. and Chief Financial Officer Sears, Roebuck and Co. 1999–2000, Exec. Vice-Pres. and COO 2000; Pres. and COO Kmart Holding Co. 2002–03, Pres. and CEO 2003–04; mem. Bd of Dirs; mem. Bd of Dirs Petco Inc. 2000–. *Leisure interests:* running, surfing, fitness. *Address:* c/o Kmart Corporation, 3100 West Big Beaver Road, Troy, MI 48084-3163, USA (office).

DAY, Peter, MA, DSc, DPhil, FRS; British chemist and academic; *Fullerian Professor of Chemistry Emeritus, The Royal Institution of Great Britain;* b. 20 Aug. 1938, Wrotham, Kent; s. of Edgar Day and Ethel Hilda Day (née Russell); m. Frances Mary Elizabeth Anderson 1964; one s. one d.; ed Maidstone Grammar School, Wadham Coll., Oxford; Cyanamid European Research Inst., Geneva 1962; Jr Research Fellow, St John's Coll., Oxford 1963–65, Tutor 1965–91; Departmental Demonstrator Univ. of Oxford 1965–67, Lecturer in Inorganic Chem. 1967–89; Oxford Univ. Prof. Associé de Paris-Sud 1975; Guest Prof., Univ. of Copenhagen 1978, Visiting Fellow, ANU 1980; Du Pont Lecturer, Indiana Univ. 1988; Sr Research Fellow, SRC 1977–82; mem. Neutron Beam Research Cttee Science and Eng Research Council 1983–88, Chem. Cttee 1985–88, Molecular Electronics Cttee 1987–88, Nat. Cttee on Superconductivity 1987–88, Materials Comm. 1988–90, Medicines Comm. 1998–2005; Vice-Pres. Dalton Div., Royal Soc. of Chem. 1986–88; Dir Inst. Laue-Langevin, Grenoble 1988–91; Dir Royal Inst. and Davy Faraday Research Lab. 1991–98, Fullerian Prof. of Chem. 1994–2008, Prof. Emer. 2008–; Visiting Prof., Univ. Coll., London 1991, Royal Inst. Research Fellow 1995–200, Emer. Prof. of Chem., Univ. of London; mem. Academia Europaea, Treas. 2000–09; Royal Soc. Blackett Memorial Lecturer 1994, Bakerian Lecturer 1999, Humphry Davy Lecturer 2002; Hon. Foreign mem. Indian Acad. of Science, Materials Research Soc. of India, Hon. Fellow, Wadham Coll., Oxford 1991, St John's Coll., Oxford 1996, Univ. Coll. London 2003; Hon. DSc (Newcastle) 1994, (Kent) 1999; Royal Soc. of Chem. Corday-Morgan Medal 1971, Solid State Chem. Award 1986, Daiwa Adrian Prize 1999. *Publications:* Physical Methods in Advanced Inorganic Chemistry (jtly) 1968, Electronic States of Inorganic Compounds 1974, Emission and Scattering Techniques 1980, Electronic Structure and Magnetism of Inorganic Compounds (Vols 1–7) 1972–82, The Philosopher's Tree 1999, Nature Not Mocked 2005, Molecules Into Materials 2007; numerous papers on inorganic chem. in learned journals. *Leisure interest:* driving slowly through rural France. *Address:* Chemistry Department, University College London, 20 Gordon Street, London, WC1H 0AJ (office); 16 Dale Close, Oxford, OX1 1TU, England (home). *Telephone:* (20) 7679-7466 (office); (20) 7679-0072 (office). *Fax:* (20) 7670-29587 (office). *E-mail:* pday@ri.ac.uk (office). *Website:* www.chem.ucl.ac.uk/people/day/index.html (office).

DAY, Peter Rodney, PhD; American (b. British) agricultural scientist; b. 27 Dec. 1928, Chingford, Essex; s. of Roland Percy Day and Florence Kate (née Dixon); m. Lois Elizabeth Rhodes 1950; two s. one d.; ed Chingford County High School and Birkbeck Coll., Univ. of London; John Innes Inst. 1946–63; Assoc. Prof., Ohio State Univ., Columbus, USA 1963–64; Chief, Genetics Dept, Conn. Agricultural Experiment Station, New Haven 1964–79; Dir Plant Breeding Inst., Cambridge, UK 1979–87; Prof. of Genetics and Dir Biotechnology Center for Agriculture and the Environment, Rutgers Univ. 1987–2001; Special Professorship, Univ. of Nottingham 1981–87; Sec. Int. Genetics Fed. 1984–93; Pres. British Soc. for Plant Pathology 1985; Chair. Cttee on Managing Global Genetic Resources, NAS, USA 1986–94; mem. Exec. Cttee, Norfolk Agricultural Station 1980–1987, Cttee on Genetic Experimentation, Int. Council of Scientific Unions 1984–93, Bd of Trustees, Int. Centre for Maize and Wheat Improvement, 1986–92, panel mem. Int. Food Biotechnology Council 1988–90; Fellow, American Phytopathological Soc.; Commonwealth Fund Fellow, Univ. of Wis. 1954–56; John Simon Guggenheim Memorial Fellow, Univ. of Queensland 1972; non-resident Fellow, Noble Foundation, Ardmore, Okla 1991–97; Visiting Fellow, Japan Soc. for the Promotion of Science 1998–; Frank Newton Prize, Birkbeck Coll., Univ. of London 1950. *Publications:* Fungal Genetics (with J. R. S. Fincham) 1963, Genetics of Host-Parasite Interactions 1974, Plant-Fungal Pathogen Interaction: A Classical and Molecular View (with Hermann Prell) 2001; more than 100 scientific papers. *Leisure interests:* music, Scottish country dancing, bird watching. *Address:* 8200 Tarsier Avenue, New Port Richey, FL 34653-6559, USA (home). *Telephone:* (727) 372-6382 (home). *Fax:* (727) 372-6382 (home). *E-mail:* p1rd@verizon.net (home).

DAY, Stockwell Burt; Canadian politician; *Minister for International Trade;* b. 16 Aug. 1950, Barrie, Ont.; s. of Stockwell Day and Gwendolyn Day (née Gilbert); m. Valorie Martin 1971; three s.; auctioneer, Alberta 1972–74; Dir Teen Challenge Outreach Ministries, Edmonton, Alberta 1974–75; contractor, Commercial Interiors, Alberta 1976–78; School Admin., Asst Pastor, Bentley (Alberta) Christian Centre 1978–85; mem. Legis. Ass. Alberta, Legislature, Edmonton 1986–, Govt Whip 1989–92, Govt House Leader 1994–97; Minister of Labour 1992–96, of Family and Social Services 1996–97; Prov. Treas., Acting Premier 1997–2000; Leader Canadian Alliance (Canadian Reform Conservative Alliance, fed. opposition party) 2000–02 (merged with Progressive Conservative Party of Canada to become Conservative Party of Canada 2003), Minister for Public Safety and Emergency Preparedness Canada 2006–08, for Int. Trade 2008–. *Leisure interests:* tennis, roller blading, backpacking, reading. *Address:* Foreign Affairs and International Trade, Lester B. Pearson Building, 125 Sussex Drive, Ottawa, ON K1A 0G2, Canada (office). *Telephone:* (613) 944-4000 (office). *Fax:* (613) 996-9709 (office). *E-mail:* enqserv@dfait-maeci.gc.ca (office). *Website:* www.international.gc.ca (office).

DAY-LEWIS, Daniel; Irish actor; b. 29 April 1957, London; s. of the late Cecil Day-Lewis and of Jill Balcon; m. Rebecca Miller 1996; two s.; one s. by Isabelle Adjani; ed Sevenoaks School, Sherington, SE London, Bedales and Bristol Old Vic Theatre School; Berlinale Camera Award, Berlin Film Festival 2005. *Films include:* My Beautiful Laundrette, A Room with a View, Stars and Bars, The Unbearable Lightness of Being, My Left Foot 1989 (Acad. Award for Best Actor, BAFTA Award, Best Actor), The Last of the Mohicans 1991, The Age of Innocence 1992, In the Name of the Father 1993, The Crucible 1995, The Boxer 1997, Gangs of New York (Screen Actors Guild Award for Best Actor 2003, BAFTA Award for Best Actor in a Leading Role 2003) 2002, The Ballad of Jack and Rose 2005, There Will Be Blood (Golden Globe for Best Actor in a

Drama 2008, Outstanding Performance by a Male Actor in a Leading Role, Screen Actors Guild 2008, Acad. Award for Best Actor 2008) 2007. *Plays include:* Class Enemy, Funny Peculiar, Bristol Old Vic; Look Back in Anger, Dracula, Little Theatre, Bristol and Half Moon Theatre, London; Another Country, Queen's Theatre; Futurists, Nat. Theatre; Romeo, Thisbe, RSC, Hamlet 1989. *Television includes:* A Frost in May, How Many Miles to Babylon?, My Brother Jonathan, Insurance Man. *Address:* c/o Julian Belfrage Associates, 46 Albemarle Street, London, W1S 4DF, England.

DAYAN, Edouard; French international organization official; *Director-General, Universal Postal Union;* Head of Air Transport Bureau 1984–86; held positions successively as Head Int. Mail Man. Dept, Int. Accounting Dept and Int. Partnership Strategy Dept, La Poste 1986–92, Deputy Dir of European and Int. Affairs 1993–97, Dir 1998–2005; Postal Expert, European Comm. 1992–93; Dir-Gen. UPU 2005–; Chair. European Social Dialogue Cttee 1994–; Chair. Tech. Cooperation Action Group, UPU 2001, also Chair. Quality of Service Fund Cttee and Bd of Trustees; fmr mem. Bd of Man. PostEurop; Chevalier, Légion d'honneur, Ordre nat. du Mérite. *Address:* Universal Postal Union, International Bureau, CP 13, 3000 Berne 15, Switzerland (office). *Telephone:* (31) 3503111 (office). *Fax:* (31) 3503110 (office). *E-mail:* edouard.dayan@upu.int (office). *Website:* www.upu.int (office).

DAYANANDA, Mahendra; Sri Lankan business executive; Exec. Dir 1872 Clipper Tea Co. Ltd, B. P. De Silva Holdings Ltd; Dir Capital Suisse Asia, Risis Ltd, De Silva (Ceylon) Ltd; Chair. Tea Tang Ltd; Vice-Chair., then Chair. Colombo Tea Traders' Asscn; Deputy Chair. Ceylon Chamber of Commerce, fmr Chair.; Vice-Pres. Sri Lanka Japan Business Cttee; mem. Nat. Bd of Arbitrators. *Address:* c/o Ceylon Chamber of Commerce, 50 Navam Mawatha, PO Box 274, Colombo 2 (office); B.P. De Silva Investments Ltd., 18, Charles Drive, Colombo 3, Sri Lanka (office). *Telephone:* (2) 576757 (office); (1) 380150 (office). *Fax:* (2) 576869 (office); (1) 449352 (office).

DAYTON, Mark; American fmr politician; b. 26 Jan. 1947, Minneapolis; two s.; ed Yale Univ.; science teacher, New York City Public Schools 1969–71; counsellor and admin. for a social service agency, Boston 1971–75; legis. asst to Walter Mondale, Senator from Minn. 1975–77; mem. staff Office of Gov. Rudy Perpich 1977–78; Commr of Econ. Devt, State of Minn. 1978–82, Commr of Energy and Econ. Devt 1982–86; cand. for Senate 1982; elected Minn. State Auditor 1990–94; held key positions in election campaign of Senator Paul Wellstone 1995–96; Senator from Minn. 2001–07, mem. Agric. Cttee, Armed Services Cttee, Rules Cttee, Governmental Affairs Cttee. *Address:* c/o SR-123, Russell Office Building, Washington, DC 20510, USA (office).

DÉ, Shobha; Indian writer and journalist; b. 7 Jan. 1948, Satara, India; m. 1st (divorced); m. 2nd Dilip Dé 1984; four d. two s.; ed Queen Mary's School, Bombay; fmr model; later copy-writer; launched India's first gossip magazine Stardust; also launched magazines Society, Celebrity and TV soap-opera Swabhimaan 1995; currently columnist, The Times of India, the Statesman, the Sunday Observer. *Publications include:* Socialite Evenings 1989, Strange Obsessions 1993, Sisters 1992, Uncertain Liaisons 1993, Shooting From the Hip: Selected Writings 1994, Sultry Days 1994, Snapshots 1995, Small Betrayals (short stories) 1995, Second Thoughts 1996, Surviving Men 1998, Selective Memory: Stories From My Life 1998, Speedpost 1999, Socialite Evenings 2005, Sisters 2005, Starry Nights 2005, Spouse: The Truth about Marriage 2005, Superstar India 2008; articles and columns in newspapers and magazines. *Leisure interests:* music, dancing, movies, reading. *Address:* c/o Marketing and Promotions Department, Penguin Books India Pvt. Ltd, 11 Community Centre, Panchsheel, Park, New Delhi 110017, India (office). *E-mail:* publicity@in.penguingroup.com (office). *Website:* www.penguinbooksindia.com; shobhaade.blogspot.com.

DE AGUIAR PATRIOTA, Antonio; Brazilian diplomatist; *Ambassador to USA;* b. 27 April 1954, Rio de Janeiro; m. Tania Cooper Patriota; two s.; ed Univ. of Geneva, Switzerland and Rio Branco Inst.; Adviser to Head UN Div., Ministry of Foreign Affairs 1980–82; mem. Perm. Mission to Int. Orgs, Geneva 1983–86; Political Counsellor, Embassy in Beijing 1987–88; Head Econ. Section, Embassy in Caracas 1988–90; Adviser to Sec.-Gen. for Political Affairs, Ministry of Foreign Affairs 1990–92; Deputy Diplomatic Advisor to Pres. of Brazil 1992–94; Political Counsellor, Perm. Mission to UN, New York 1994–99, mem. Brazilian delegation to UN Security Council 1995, 1998–99; Minister Counsellor, Perm. Mission to Int. Orgs, Geneva 1999–2003; Deputy Perm. Rep. to WTO 2001–02; Sec. for Diplomatic Planning, Office of the Minister of Foreign Affairs 2002–04, Chief of Staff 2004–05, Under-Sec.-Gen. for Political Affairs, 2005–07; Amb. to USA 2007–; several decorations from Brazil, France, Norway and Morocco. *Address:* Brazilian Embassy, 3006 Massachusetts Avenue, NW, Washington DC 20008, USA (office). *Telephone:* (202) 238-2700 (office). *Fax:* (202) 238-2827 (office). *E-mail:* ambassador@brasilemb.org (office). *Website:* www.brasilemb.org (office).

DE ARAUJO, Fernando; Timor-Leste politician and acting head of state; *Leader, Democratic Party;* fmr youth resistance leader; arrested for subversion 1991, imprisoned (with collaborator Xanana Gusmao) for six years in Cipinang Prison, Jakarta; f. Resistencia Nacional dos Estudantes de Timor-Leste (RENETIL); Founder and Leader Democratic Party (PD); current Pres. Nat. Parl.; Acting Pres. Feb.–April 2008. *Address:* Partido Democrático, 1 Rua Democracia, Pantai Kelapa, Dili, Timor-Leste (office). *Telephone:* 3608421 (office). *E-mail:* flazama@hotmail.com (office).

DE ARAÚJO SALES, HE Cardinal Eugénio; Brazilian ecclesiastic; *Archbishop Emeritus of São Sebastião do Rio de Janeiro;* b. 8 Nov. 1920, Acari, Rio Grande do Norte; s. of Celso Dantas and D. Josefa de Araújo Sales; ordained 1943; Bishop 1954; Apostolic Administrator, See of São Salvador da Bahia –1968; Archbishop of São Sebastião do Rio de Janeiro 1971–2001, Archbishop Emer. 2001–; cr. Cardinal-Priest of Gregorio VII 1969. *Leisure* *interest:* reading. *Address:* Rua Visconde de Pirajá 339, 22410-003 Rio de Janeiro, RJ, Brazil. *Telephone:* 2224-7516. *Fax:* 2267-1233.

DE BEAUCÉ, Thierry; French government official; b. 14 Feb. 1943, Lyon; s. of Bertrand Martin de Beauce and Simone de la Verpillère; two d.; ed Univ. of Paris and Ecole Nat. d'Admin; civil admin., Ministry of Cultural Affairs 1968–69; seconded to Office of Prime Minister 1969–73; Tech. Adviser, Pvt. Office of Pres. of Nat. Ass. 1974; seconded to Econ. Affairs Directorate, Ministry of Foreign Affairs 1974–76; Cultural Counsellor, Japan 1976–78; Second Counsellor, Morocco 1978–80; Vice-Pres. for Int. Affairs Société Elf Aquitaine 1981–86; Dir-Gen. of Cultural, Scientific and Tech. Relations, Ministry of Foreign Affairs 1986–87; State Sec. attached to Minister of Foreign Affairs 1988–91; Adviser to Pres. on African Affairs 1991–94; Vice-Pres. Conf. on Yugoslavia 1992; Amb. to Indonesia 1995–97; Dir of Int. Affairs, Vivendi 1997–; Chevalier, Légion d'honneur. *Publications:* Les raisons dangéreuses (essay) 1975, Un homme ordinaire (novel) 1978, L'Ile absolue (essay) 1979, Le désir de guerre 1980, La chute de Tanger (novel) 1984, Nouveau discours sur l'universalité de la langue française 1988, Le livre d'Esther 1989, La République de France 1991, La Nonchalance de Dieu 1995. *Address:* Vivendi, 52 rue d'Anjou, 75008 Paris (office); 73 avenue F. D. Roosevelt, Paris 8, France (home). *Telephone:* 1-45-63-22-37 (home).

DE BELOT, Jean Marie Louis, MA; French journalist and editor; *Partner, Euro RSCG;* b. 15 Dec. 1958, Neuilly-sur-Seine; s. of Philippe de Belot and Claude de Belot (née Vimal-Dessaignes); m. Frédérique Brunet 1983; two s. three d.; ed Univ. of Paris II-Panthéon Assas.; journalist, La Tribune de l'economie 1984; journalist then Chief Econ. Reporter, Le Figaro 1985, Chief Reporter, Expansion Group 1987, Chief of Financial Services 1990, Editorial Dir 2000–04; Jt Chief Ed. Les Echos 1992, Chief Econ. Ed. 1998; Pnr Euro RSCG 2005–. *Address:* Euro RSCG, 2 allée du Longchamp, 92281 Suresnes Cedex, France (office). *Telephone:* 1-58-47-93-93 (office). *Fax:* 1-58-47-93-99 (office). *E-mail:* contact.co@eurorscg.fr (office). *Website:* www.eurorscgco.com (office).

DE BENEDETTI, Carlo; Italian business executive; *Chairman, Compagnia Industriali Riunite;* b. 14 Nov. 1934, Turin; m. Margherita Crosetti 1960; three s.; ed Turin Polytechnic; with Compagnia Italiana Tubi Metallici Flessibili 1959; Chair. and CEO Gilardini 1972–76; Dir Euromobiliare Finance Co. 1973–, Vice-Chair. 1977–; f. Compagnia Industriali Riunite (CIR) 1976, Vice-Chair. and CEO 1976–95, Chair. 1995–; f. Finco 1976 (renamed Cofide–Compagnia Finanziaria De Benedetti 1985), Vice-Chair. and CEO 1976–91, Chair. 1991–; Vice-Chair. and CEO Olivetti & Co. SpA 1978–83, Chair. and CEO 1983–96, Hon. Chair. 1996–99; Dir SMI SpA 1983–; Chair. Cerus (Paris) 1986–; Chair. Sogefi; f. CDB Web Tech 2000, Exec. Chair. 2000–; f. Rodolfo Debenedetti Foundation 1998, Chair. 1998–; Vice-Chair. European Round Table of Industrialists, Brussels; Vice-Pres. Confindustria 1984–; mem. Int. Council, Morgan Guaranty Trust 1980–; Chair. Fondiara 1989–; controlled Editore Arnoldo Mondadori 1990, half-share 1991–; Co-Chair. Council for USA and Italy; mem. Bd of Dirs Valeo, Pirelli, Gruppo Editoriale L'Espresso; mem. European Advisory Cttee, NY Stock Exchange, Int. Council, Centre for Strategic and Int. Studies, Int. Advisory Council, China Int. Trust and Investment Corpn, Beijing, Royal Swedish Acad. of Eng Science, Italian Council, European Inst. of Business Admin; under house arrest after questioning on corruption charges Nov. 1993, released Nov. 1993; sentenced to six years and four months' imprisonment, sentence reduced to four and a half years July 1996; cleared of fraud charges connected with collapse of Banco Ambrosiano Veneto Aug. 1998; Hon. LLD (Wesleyan Univ., Conn., USA) 1986; Cavaliere del Lavoro 1983, Officier, Légion d'honneur 1987. *Publications:* L'Avventura della Nuova Economia 2000, lectures and articles in business journals. *Address:* CIR SpA, Via Ciovassino 1, 20121 Milan, Italy. *Telephone:* 02722701. *Fax:* 0272270200 (office).

DE BERNARDIS, Paolo, BSc, PhD; Italian astrophysicist and academic; *Professor, Università di Roma 'La Sapienza';* b. 1 Feb. 1959, Florence; ed Università di Roma 'La Sapienza'; Researcher, Università di Roma 'La Sapienza' 1984–92, Assoc. Prof. 1992–2001, Full Prof. 2001–; Co-investigator int. experiments Archeops, MAXIMA and BOOMERanG on the Cosmic Microwave Background; Co-investigator High Frequency Instrument, ESA Planck Satellite, in charge of cryogenic pre-amplifiers of all Planck-HFI detectors; mem. ESA Astronomy Working Group 2002–04; fmr referee, Astrophysical Journal, Astronomy and Astrophysics, Nature; Ed. Journal of Cosmology and Astroparticle Physics, Memorie della Società Astronomica Italiana; Premio Feltrinelli, Accad. dei Lincei 2001, Balzan Prize for Observational Astronomy and Astrophysics 2006. *Publications:* more than 100 papers in scientific journals on experimental astrophysics and cosmology, especially the Cosmic Microwave Background. *Address:* Laboratori di fisica, Edificio E. Fermi, stanza 6, piano 1, Gruppi/Servizi G31, Università degli Studi di Roma 'La Sapienza', P. le Aldo Moro 5, Rome, 00185, Italy (office). *Telephone:* (06) 49914271 (office). *Fax:* (06) 4957697 (office). *E-mail:* debernardis@roma1.infn.it (office). *Website:* www.uniroma1.it (office); oberon .roma1.infn.it/boomerang/b2k (office).

DE BERNIÈRES, Louis, MA; British writer; b. (Louis Henry Piers de Bernière-Smart), 8 Dec. 1954, London; s. of Maj. Reginald Piers Alexander de Bernière-Smart; ed Bradfield Coll., Berkshire, Univ. of Manchester, Leicester Polytechnic, Inst. of Educ., Univ. of London; landscape gardener 1972–73; teacher and rancher, Colombia 1974; philosophy tutor 1977–79; car mechanic 1980; English teacher 1981–84; bookshop asst 1985–86; supply teacher 1986–93; mem. Antonius Players 2003–; mem. PEN; Hon. Fellow, Trinity Coll. of Music; Dr hc (Univ. of East Anglia, Deree Univ. of Athens, Univ. of Aberdeen, Inst. of Educ., London); Granta Best of Young British Novelists 1994, Author of the Year Award 1997, Whittaker Platinum Award, Millepages Prize for Best Foreign Novel (France) 2006. *Publications:* The War of Don Emmanuel's Nether Parts 1990, Señor Vivo and the Coca Lord 1991, The Troublesome Offspring of Cardinal Guzman 1992, Captain Corelli's Mandolin 1994, Labels 1997, The Book of Job 1999, Gunter Weber's Confession 2001, Sunday Morning at the Centre of the World 2001, Red Dog 2001, Birds Without Wings 2004, A Partisan's Daughter 2008, Notwithstanding 2009; contrib. to Second Thoughts, Granta. *Leisure interests:* music, literature, golf, fishing, carpentry, gardening, cats. *Address:* Lavinia Trevor Agency, 29 Addison Place, London W11 4RJ, England (office). *Telephone:* (1986) 788665 (office).

DE BOER, Yvo; Dutch UN official; *Executive Secretary, United Nations Framework Convention on Climate Change;* b. 1954, Vienna, Austria; s. of a Dutch diplomatist; m.; three c.; ed boarding school in UK, tech. degree in social work in the Netherlands; involved in climate change policies since 1994; worked for UN Centre for Human Settlements (UN-HABITAT); served as Deputy Dir-Gen. for Environmental Protection, Ministry of Housing, Spatial Planning and Environment, as Head of Climate Change Dept; Dir for Int. Affairs, Ministry of Housing, Spatial Planning and Environment –2006; apptd by UN Sec.-Gen. as Exec. Sec. UN Framework Convention on Climate Change (UNFCCC) 2006–; helped prepare EU position in lead-up to negotiations on Kyoto Protocol, assisted in design of internal burden sharing of EU and led dels to UNFCCC negotiations; fmr Vice-Pres. Conf. of Parties to UNFCCC; fmr Vice-Chair. Comm. on Sustainable Devt; fmr mem. China Council for Int. Cooperation on Environment and Devt, Bureau of the Environment Policy Cttee of OECD, Advisory Group of the Community Devt Carbon Fund of the World Bank; fmr mem. Bd of Dirs Centre for Clean Air Policy. *Address:* UNFCCC, PO Box 260124, 53153 Bonn, Germany (office). *Telephone:* (228) 815-1000 (office). *Fax:* (228) 815-1999 (office). *E-mail:* ydeboer@unfccc.int (office); secretariat@unfccc.int (office). *Website:* unfccc.int (office).

DE BOER-BUQUICCHIO, Maud, LLD; Dutch lawyer and international organization official; *Deputy Secretary General, Council of Europe;* b. 28 Dec. 1944, Hoensbroek; m. Gianni Buquicchio; two s.; ed Leiden Univ.; mem. Legal Secr., Applications Div., European Comm. on Human Rights (ECHR) 1970–71; mem. Pvt. Office of Sec.-Gen. of Council of Europe 1972–77; Prin. Legal Officer, Case Law and Research Div., ECHR Secr. 1977–90, Head of Div. 1990–92; Sec. to First Chamber of ECHR 1992–98; Deputy Registrar, European Court of Human Rights 1998–2002; Deputy Sec.-Gen. Council of Europe 2002–. *Publications include:* Informationsfreiheit und die audiovisuelle Revolution (co-author) 1989, The Impact of the European Convention on Human Rights and the Rights of Children 1996; articles in professional journals and chapters in books on human rights and EU orgs. *Address:* Council of Europe, 67075 Strasbourg Cedex, France (office). *Telephone:* 3-88-41-23-82 (office). *Fax:* 3-88-41-27-40 (office). *E-mail:* maud.deboer -buquicchio@coe.int (office). *Website:* www.coe.int (office).

DE BONO, Edward Francis Charles Publius, DPhil, PhD; British author and academic; b. 19 May 1933; s. of the late Prof. Joseph de Bono and of Josephine de Bono (née O'Byrne); m. Josephine Hall-White 1971; two s.; ed St Edward's Coll., Malta, Royal Univ. of Malta and Christ Church, Oxford; Research Asst, Univ. of Oxford 1958–60, Jr Lecturer in Medicine 1960–61; Asst Dir of Research, Dept of Investigative Medicine, Univ. of Cambridge 1963–76, Lecturer in Medicine 1976–83; Dir Cognitive Research Trust, Cambridge 1971–; Sec.-Gen. Supranational Independent Thinking Org. 1983–; f. Edward de Bono Nonprofit Foundation; Chair. Council, Young Enterprise Europe 1998–; creator of two TV series: The Greatest Thinkers 1981, de Bono's Thinking Course 1982; apptd EU Amb. for Thinking for the Year of Creativity 2009; Hon. Registrar St Thomas' Hosp. Medical School, Harvard Medical School; Hon. Consultant Boston City Hosp. 1965–66; planet DE73 named edebono after him. *Publications:* The Use of Lateral Thinking 1967, The Five-Day Course in Thinking 1968, The Mechanism of Mind 1969, Lateral Thinking: A Textbook of Creativity 1970, The Dog Exercising Machine 1970, Technology Today 1971, Practical Thinking 1971, Lateral Thinking for Management 1971, Children Solve Problems 1972, Po: Beyond Yes and No 1972, Think Tank 1973, Eureka: A History of Inventions 1974, Teaching Thinking 1976, The Greatest Thinkers 1976, Wordpower 1977, The Happiness Purpose 1977, The Case of the Disappearing Elephant 1977, Opportunities: A Handbook of Business Opportunity Search 1978, Future Positive 1979, Atlas of Management Thinking 1981, de Bono's Thinking Course 1982, Conflicts: A Better Way to Resolve Them 1985, Six Thinking Hats 1985, Letter to Thinkers 1987, I Am Right You Are Wrong 1990, Positive Revolution for Brazil 1990, Six Action Shoes 1991, Serious Creativity 1992, Teach Your Child to Think 1992, Water Logic 1993, Parallel Thinking 1994, Teach Yourself to Think 1995, Mind Pack 1995, Edward de Bono's Textbook of Wisdom 1996, How to be More Interesting 1997, Simplicity 1998, New Thinking for the New Millennium 1999, Why I Want to be King of Australia 1999, The Book of Wisdom 2000, The de Bono Code 2000, H+ (Plus) A New Religion 2006, Tactics: The Art and Science of Success 2007, How to Have Creative Ideas 2007, Six Frames for Looking at Information, Think–Before it is too late, Reversed Quotations; numerous publs in Nature, Lancet, Clinical Science, American Journal of Physiology. *Leisure interests:* travel, toys, thinking. *Address:* Cranmer Hall, Fakenham, Norfolk, NR21 9HX, England (home); L2 Albany, Piccadilly, London, W1V 9RR. *Website:* www.edwarddebono.com (office).

DE BONT, Jan; Dutch cinematographer, film director and film producer; b. 22 Oct. 1943, Netherlands; ed Amsterdam Film Acad. *Cinematography:* Turkish Delight, Keetje Tippel, Max Heuelaar, Soldier of Orange, Private Lessons (American debut) 1981, Roar, I'm Dancing as Fast as I Can, Cujo, All the Right Moves, Bad Manners, The Fourth Man, Mischief, The Jewel of the Nile, Flesh and Blood, The Clan of the Cave Bear, Ruthless People, Who's That Girl, Leonard Part 6, Die Hard 1988, Bert Rigby—You're A Fool 1989, Black Rain 1989, The Hunt for Red October 1990, Flatliners 1990, Shining Through

1992, Basic Instinct 1992, Lethal Weapon 3, 1992. *TV (photography):* The Ray Mancini Story, Split Personality (episode of Tales from the Crypt). *Films directed:* Speed (debut) 1994, Twister, Speed 2: Cruise Control (also screen-play and producer), The Haunting (also producer), Lara Croft Tomb Raider: The Cradle of Life 2003. *Address:* c/o David Gersh, The Gersh Agency, 232 North Canon Drive, Beverly Hills, CA 90210, USA.

DE BORTOLI, Ferruccio; Italian journalist; *CEO, RCS Libri;* b. 20 May 1953, Milan; s. of Giovanni De Bortoli and Giancarla Soresini; m. Elisabetta Cordani 1982; one s. one d.; ed Univ. of Milan; journalist 1973–; mem. editorial staff, Corriere d'Informazione 1975–78; Econs Corresp. Corriere della Sera 1978–85; Ed.-in-Chief, L'Europeo (magazine) 1985–86; Ed.-in-Chief, Econs Section, Corriere della Sera 1987–93; Deputy Ed. Corriere della Sera 1993–96, Ed. 1997–2003; CEO RCS Libri 2003–; Pres. Flammarion 2003–; Dir Il Sole 24 Ore 2005–. *Leisure interests:* reading, music, skiing. *Address:* RCS Libri SpA, Via Mecenate 91, 20138 Milan (office); Via Donatello 36, 20131 Milan, Italy (home). *Telephone:* (02) 50951 (office). *Fax:* (02) 50952647 (office). *Website:* www.rcslibri.it (office); www.ilsole24ore.com (office).

DE BOTTON, Alain; Swiss writer; b. 20 Dec. 1969, Zürich; ed Gonville and Caius Coll., Cambridge; Chevalier, Ordre des Arts et des Lettres 2003. *Publications:* Essays in Love (aka On Love) 1993, The Romantic Movement: Sex, Shopping, and the Novel 1994, Kiss and Tell 1995, How Proust Can Change Your Life: Not a Novel 1997, The Consolations of Philosophy 2000, The Art of Travel (Charles Veillon European Essay Prize, Switzerland 2003) 2002, Status Anxiety 2004; The Architecture of Happiness 2006, The Pleasures and Sorrows of Work 2009; contrib. articles, book and television reviews to various periodicals. *Address:* United Agents, 12–26 Lexington Street, London, W1F 0LE, England (office). *Telephone:* (20) 3214-0800 (office). *Fax:* (20) 3214-0801 (office). *E-mail:* info@unitedagents.co.uk (office). *Website:* unitedagents.co.uk (office).

DE BREE, Simon, Jr; Dutch business executive; b. 14 April 1937, Koudekerke; s. of Cornelis de Bree and Leintje Minderhoud; m. Judith Rijkée 1963; one s. one d.; ed Univ. of Tech. Delft; research scientist, DSM NV 1966–69, Acquisition Dept 1969–73, Sales and Marketing, Plastics Div. 1973–80, Man. Polymers Group 1980–83, Pres. Polymers Group 1983–86; mem. Man. Bd DSM NV 1986–93, Chair. Man. Bd 1993–99; Chair. Supervisory Bds Stork NV, Koninklijke Boskalis Westminster NV, Parenco B.V.; mem. Bd Dirs Entergy Corpn; Kt, Order of Netherlands Lion; Society of Chemical Industry International Award 2000. *Leisure interests:* skiing, skating, cycling. *Address:* c/o DSM NV, PO Het Overloon 1, 6411 TE Heerlen, Netherlands.

DE BRICHAMBAUT, Marc Perrin; French international organization executive; *Secretary General, Organization for Security and Co-operation in Europe;* b. 29 Oct. 1948, Rabat, Morocco; m.; two c.; ed Ecole Normale Supérieur de Saint-Cloud, Institut d'Etudes Politiques and Ecole Nationale d'Admin, Paris; began his career at Conseil d'Etat, first as admin. judge, later as Conseiller d'Etat; posted to New York as Special Asst to UN Under-Sec.-Gen. for Int. Econ. and Social Affairs 1978; adviser to French Foreign Minister 1981–83; Chief of Staff, Ministry of European Affairs 1983–86, Ministry of Foreign Affairs 1984–86; Counsellor, French Embassy, Washington, DC, USA 1986–88; Prin. Adviser to Minister of Defence 1988–91; Head of French Del., CSCE (later became OSCE), Vienna 1991–94; Head, Legal Div., Ministry of Foreign Affairs 1994–98; Dir for Strategic Affairs, Ministry of Defence 1998–2005; Sec. Gen. OSCE 2005–. *Address:* OSCE, Kärtner Ring 5–7, 1010 Vienna, Austria (office). *Telephone:* (1) 514-36-180 (office). *Fax:* (1) 514-36-105 (office). *E-mail:* info@osce.org (office). *Website:* www.osce.org/secretariat (office).

DE BROGLIE, Prince Gabriel Marie Joseph Anselme; French administrator; b. 21 April 1931, Versailles; s. of Prince Edouard de Broglie and Princess Hélène Le Bas de Courmont; m. Diane de Bryas 1953; one s. one d.; ed Ecole Saint-Martin de France, Faculté de droit de Paris and Inst. d'études politiques; Auditor Conseil d'Etat 1960, Counsel 1967; Legal Adviser to Sec.-Gen., Interdepartmental Cttee on matters of European econ. co-operation 1964; Tech. Adviser, Ministry of Social Affairs 1966–68, to Prime Minister 1968–69, Minister of State for Cultural Affairs 1970; Sec.-Gen. Office de Radiodiffusion-Télévision Française 1971, Asst Dir-Gen. 1973; Dir Radio-France 1975–77, Dir-Gen. 1977–79; Pres. Inst. nat. de l'audiovisuel 1979–1981; mem. Haut Conseil de l'Audiovisuel 1972; Pres. Univ. Radiophonique et Télévisuelle Int. 1976–87, Hon. Pres. 1987; Vice-Pres., later Pres. TV Historical Cttee, Haute Autorité de l'Audiovisuel 1981–86 1980; Pres. Comm. Nat. de la Communication et des Libertés 1986–89; Pres. Soc. des Bibliophiles Français; mem. Acad. des Sciences Morales et Politiques 1997, Acad. française 2001–; Commdr, Légion d'honneur, Ordre nat. du Mérite; Commdr des Arts et Lettres. *Publications include:* Le Général de Valence ou l'insouciance et la gloire 1972, Ségur sans cérémonie, ou la gaieté libertine 1977, L'histoire politique de la Revue des Deux Mondes 1979, L'Orléanisme, la ressource libérale de la France 1981, Une image vaut dix mille mots 1982, Madame de Genlis (Gobert Prize) 1985, Le français, pour qu'il vive 1986, Guizot (Amb.'s Prize) 1990, Le XIX^{e}siècle, l'éclat et le déclin de la France 1995, Mac Mahon 2000. *Leisure interest:* books. *Address:* Institut de France, 23 quai Conti, 75006 Paris (office); 96 rue de Grenelle, 75007 Paris, France (home). *Telephone:* 1-44-41-43-30 (office). *Fax:* 1-44-41-44-34 (office). *E-mail:* secretariat_chancelier@institut-de-france.fr (office).

DE BRUM, Tony A.; Marshall Islands business executive and politician; *Minister of Foreign Affairs;* b. 1945, Likiep Atoll; ed Xavier High School, Micronesia; fmr mem. Ralik-Ratak Democratic Party; mem. Parl. for Majuro 1984–2000; fmr Minister of Health and Environment; Minister of Finance 1998–99; mem. Aelon Kein Ad (AKA) coalition 2007–; Senator for Kwajalein Atoll 2007–; Minister of Foreign Affairs 2008–. *Address:* Ministry of Foreign Affairs, POB 1349, Majuro MH 96960, Marshall Islands (office). *Telephone:* (625) 3181 (office). *Fax:* (623) 4979 (office).

DE BURGH, Chris; British singer and songwriter; b. (Christopher John Davison), 15 Oct. 1948, Argentina; m. Diane Patricia Morley; two s. one d.; ed Trinity Coll. Dublin; solo artist 1974–; numerous concerts world-wide; first Western artist to perform in Iran since the Islamic Revolution 2008; ASCAP Awards 1985, 1987, 1988, 1990, 1991, 1997, IRMA Awards (Ireland) 1985–90, Beroliner Award (Germany), BAMBI Award (Germany), Midem Trophy (France). *Recordings include:* albums: Far Beyond These Castle Walls 1975, Spanish Train And Other Stories 1975, At The End Of A Perfect Day 1977, Crusader 1979, Eastern Wind 1980, Best Moves 1981, The Getaway 1982, Man On The Line 1984, Into The Light 1986, Flying Colours 1988, High On Emotion – Live From Dublin 1990, Power Of Ten 1992, This Way Up 1994, Beautiful Dreams 1995, The Love Songs 1997, Quiet Revolution 1999, Notes From Planet Earth 2001, Timing Is Everything 2002, The Road to Freedom 2004, The Storyman 2006, Now and Then 2008, Footsteps 2009. *Address:* Kenny Thomson Management, 754 Fulham Road, London, SW6 5SH, England (office). *Telephone:* (20) 7731-7074 (office). *Fax:* (20) 7736-8605 (office). *E-mail:* ktmuk@dircon.co.uk (office). *Website:* www.cdeb.com.

DE CAROLIS, Patrick; French broadcasting executive, television producer, journalist and author; *CEO, France Televisions;* b. Arles; m.; four c.; positions with several TV channels including TFI, M6, France 5; joined France 3 1974, fmr Presenter Des racines et des ailes programme; fmr Gen. Dir Figaro magazine; CEO France Televisions 2005–. *Publication:* Conversation (co-author) 2001. *Address:* France Televisions, 7 esplanade Henri de France, 75907 Paris cedex 15, France (office). *Telephone:* 1-56-22-60-00 (office). *Website:* www.francetelevisions.fr (office).

DE CASTELLA, (François) Robert, MBE, BSc; Australian company director and fmr athlete; *Managing Director, SmartStart Pty Ltd;* b. 27 Feb. 1957, Melbourne; s. of Rolet François de Castella and Ann M. Hall; m. Gayelene J. Clews 1980 (divorced 1998); two s. one d.; m. Theresa de Castella 2003; one d.; ed Xavier Coll., Kew, Monash Univ. and Swinburne Inst. of Tech.; winner, Fukuoka Marathon (world's fastest for out-and-back course) 1981; Marathon Champion, Commonwealth Games, Brisbane 1982; winner Rotterdam Marathon 1983; World Marathon Champion, Helsinki 1983; winner Boston Marathon 1986; winner Commonwealth Games 1986; Dir Australian Inst. of Sport 1990–95; Chair. Health Promotions Bd ACT (Healthpact) 1996–; Man. Dir SmartStart (Australia) Pty Ltd 1997–; Chair. Leisure Australia Foundation 1999–; mem. Bd of Dirs Decorp Pty Ltd 1995–, Action Potential 1996–98, RWM Publs 1996–, Your Bread Co. Pty Ltd 2003–, Deeks Bakery & Cafes; mem. Bd Australian Sports Comm. –1999, Bd Sports Australian Hall of Fame 1997–; Dr hc (Univ. of Sunshine Coast) 2008, (Univ. of Canberra) 2008; Australian of the Year 1983, Sports Australia Hall of Fame, Athletics Australia Hall of Fame 2008. *Publications:* de Castella on Running 1984, Deek, Australia's World Champion 1984, Smart Sport 1996. *Leisure interests:* motorcycling, scuba diving, traditional Okinawian karate. *Address:* Smart-Start (Australia) Pty Ltd, PO Box 6127, Phillip DC, ACT 2606, Australia; IMG, Level 3/480, St Kilda Road, Melbourne, Vic., 3004, Australia (office). *Telephone:* (2) 6260-5750; (3) 9864-1111 (office). *Fax:* (2) 6260-5799. *E-mail:* deek@smartstart.com.au (office). *Website:* smartstart.com.au (office); www.imgworld.com (office).

DE CASTRO, Manuel (Noli) Leuterio, Jr, BCom; Philippine politician and broadcaster; *Vice-President;* b. 6 July 1949, Pola, Oriental Mindoro; s. of Inay Nene; ed Pola Cen. School, Pola Catholic High School, Univ. of the E (UE); began career in broadcasting as field reporter for Johnny de Leon 1976; radio anchorman, DWW 1982–86; joined ABS-CBN 1986, hosted TV programmes Good Morning, Philippines, At Your Service 1986, Magandang Umaga 1987–98, Overseas Limited 1988, TV Patrol, Magandang Gabi...Bayan (Good Evening...Nation) 1998; hosted radio programme Kabayan, My Fellow Filipinos, DZMM (radio station of ABS-CBN); apptd Vice-Pres. DZMM and Head of Production TV Patrol 1999–2001; elected to Senate 2001; Vice-Pres. of the Philippines 2004–, also Chair. Housing and Urban Devt Coordinating Council. *Address:* Office of the Vice-President, 7th Floor, PNB Financial Center, President Diosdado Macapagal Boulevard, Pasay City 1300, Metro Manila, Philippines (office). *Telephone:* (2) 8333311 (office). *Fax:* (2) 8316676 (office). *E-mail:* gma@easy.net.ph (office). *Website:* www.ovp.gov.ph (office).

DE CECCO, Marcello, BA, LLB; Italian economist; *Professor of Monetary Economics, University of Rome 'La Sapienza';* b. 17 Sept. 1939, Rome; s. of Vincenzo de Cecco and Antonietta de Cecco; m. Julia Maud Bamford; two s.; ed Univ. of Parma, Univ. of Cambridge, UK; Asst Lecturer, Univ. of East Anglia, England 1967–68; Prof. of Econs, Univ. of Siena 1968–79, European Univ. Inst., Florence 1979–86, Univ. of Rome 'La Sapienza' 1986–, Prof. of Monetary Econs 1989–; Exec. Dir Monte dei Paschi di Siena 1978–83; Dir Crediop, Rome 1979–81, Italian Int. Bank, London 1980–83; Visiting Scholar, IMF 1994; fmr mem. Inst. for Advanced Study, Princeton Univ., Center for Int. Affairs and Center for European Studies, Harvard Univ. *Publications:* Money and Empire: International Gold Standard, 1890–1914 1975, International Economic Adjustment: Small Countries and the European Monetary System 1983, The International Gold Standard 1983, Changing Money 1985, Monetary Theory and Economic Institutions: Proceedings of a Conference Held by the International Economic Association at Fiesole, Florence, Italy (co-author) 1987, Changing Money 1987, A European Central Bank: Perspectives on Monetary Unification After Ten Years of the E.M.S. (co-author) 1989, Managing Public Debt: Index-linked Bonds in Theory and Practice 1997, Markets and Authorities: Global Finance and Human Choice (co-author) 2002. *Address:* Dipartimento di Economia Pubblica, Via Castro Laurenziano 9, 00161 Rome, Italy (office). *Telephone:* (06) 49766358 (office).

DE CHALENDAR, Pierre-André; French business executive; *CEO, Compagnie de Saint-Gobain;* b. April 1958; ed École supérieure des sciences économiques et commerciales, École nat. d'admin; Finance Insp., later Deputy Dir-Gen. of Energy and Raw Materials, Ministry of Industry and Regional Devt –1989; Vice-Pres., Corp. Planning, Cie de Saint-Gobain 1989–92, Head of European Abrasives Div. 1992–96, also CEO Norton Abrasifs Europe (subsidiary co.) 1992–96, Pres. Worldwide Abrasives Div., N America 1996–2000, Gen. Del. for Saint-Gobain UK and Ireland 2000–02, CEO Meyer International (following acquisition by Saint-Gobain) 2000, Pres. Building Distribution Sector 2003–05, COO Cie de Saint-Gobain 2005–07, CEO 2007–. *Address:* Compagnie de Saint-Gobain, Les Miroirs, 18 avenue d'Alsace, 92400 Courbevoie, France (office). *Telephone:* 1-47-62-30-00 (office). *Fax:* 1-47-62-50-62 (office). *E-mail:* info@saint-gobain.com (office). *Website:* www.saint-gobain.com (office).

DE CHASTELAIN, Gen. Alfred John Gardyne Drummond, OC, CMM, CH, CD, BA; Canadian army officer and diplomatist; *Chairman, Independent International Commission on Decommissioning (Northern Ireland);* b. 30 July 1937, Bucharest, Romania; emigrated to Canada 1955, naturalized 1962; s. of Alfred George Gardyne de Chastelain and Marion Elizabeth de Chastelain (née Walsh); m. Mary Ann Laverty 1961; one s. one d.; ed Fettes Coll., Edin., UK, Mount Royal Coll., Calgary, Royal Mil. Coll. of Canada, Kingston, British Army Staff Coll., Camberley; commissioned 2nd Lt, 2nd Bn, Princess Patricia's Canadian Light Infantry (PPCLI) 1960, Capt., aide-de-camp to Chief of Gen. Staff, Army HQ 1962–64, Co. Commdr, 1st Bn, PPCLI, FRG 1964–65, Co. Commdr, Edmonton, rank of Maj., later with 1st Bn, UN Force, Cyprus 1968; Brigade Maj., 1st Combat Group, Calgary 1968–70, Commdg Officer, 2nd Bn, PPCLI, Winnipeg 1970–72, rank of Lt-Col, Sr Staff Officer, Quartier Gen. Dist, Québec 1973–74, rank of Col, Commdr Canadian Forces Base, Montréal 1974–76, Deputy Chief of Staff, HQ UN Forces, Cyprus and Commdr Canadian Contingent 1976–77, rank of Brig.-Gen. and apptd Commdt Royal Mil. Coll. of Canada, Kingston 1977–80, command of 4th Canadian Mechanized Brigade Group, FRG 1980–82, Dir.-Gen. Land Doctrine and Operations, Nat. Defence Headquarters, Ottawa 1982–83, rank of Maj.-Gen. 1983, Deputy Commdr Mobile Command, St Hubert, Québec 1983–86, rank of Lt-Gen. and apptd Asst Deputy Minister (Personnel) Nat. Defence HQ, Ottawa 1986–88, Vice-Chief, Defence Staff 1988–89, rank of Gen. and apptd Chief of the Defence Staff 1989–93; Amb. to USA 1993; reapptd Chief of the Defence Staff 1994–95; mem. Int. Body on the Decommissioning of Arms in NI 1995–96, Chair. Business Cttee and Co-Chair. Strand Two Talks, NI Peace Process (leading to the Good Friday Agreement) 1996–98, Chair. Independent Int. Comm. on Decommissioning, 1997–; Col of the Regt PPCLI 2000–03; Pres. Dominion of Canada Rifle Asscn 1986–93; mem. Royal Canadian Legion, Royal Canadian Mil. Inst.; Past First Nat. Vice-Pres. Boy Scouts of Canada; mem. St Andrews Soc. of Montreal, Royal Scottish Country Dance Soc.; Hon. Fellow, Lady Margaret Hall, Univ. of Oxford 2006; Canadian Forces Decoration 1968, Commdr Order of Mil. Merit 1985, Commdr OSJ 1991, US Legion of Merit 1995, Companion of Honour, UK 1998; Hon. DMilSc (Royal Mil. Coll. of Canada) 1996, Hon. LLD (Royal Roads Univ.) 2002, (Nipissing) 2006, (Carleton) 2006, (Queen's Univ., Kingston) 2007; Commendation Medal of Merit and Honour (Greece) 1991, Vimy Award 1992. *Publications:* articles on mil. affairs and int. diplomacy. *Leisure interests:* bagpipes, Scottish country dancing, fishing and painting. *Address:* Independent International Commission on Decommissioning, Block 1, Knockview Buildings, Stormont Estate, Belfast, BT4 3SL, Northern Ireland (office); 170 Acacia Avenue, Ottawa, ON K1M 0R3, Canada (home). *Telephone:* (28) 9048-8600 (office). *Fax:* (28) 9048-8601 (office); (613) 744-0777 (home). *E-mail:* chairman@iol.ie (office).

DE CLERCK, Stefaan; Belgian politician; *Mayor of Kortryk;* b. 12 Dec. 1951, Kortryk; two s. three d.; mem. Parl. 1991, 1998–2001; Minister of Justice 1995; Pres. Christelijke Volksparteit (CVP) (renamed Christen-Democratisch en Vlaams Partij—CD&V 2001) 1999–2004; Mayor of Kortryk 2001–. *Address:* Damkaai, 8500 Kortryk, Belgium (home). *Telephone:* (56) 20-46-33 (home). *Fax:* (56) 25-89-99 (home). *E-mail:* stefaan.d.clerck@pandora.be (home). *Website:* www.stef-kortryk.com (home).

DE CONCINI, Dennis, LLB; American fmr politician and lawyer; *Vice President and Partner, Parry, Romani, De Concini & Symms Associates;* b. 8 May 1937, Tucson, Ariz.; s. of Evo and Ora De Concini; one s. two d.; ed Univ. of Ariz. and Univ. of Ariz. Coll. of Law; Committeeman, Pima County 1958–76; worked with family law practice 1963–65; special counsel to Gov. of Ariz. 1965, Admin. Asst to Gov. 1965–67; Partner, DeConcini & McDonald, law firm 1968–73; Pima County Attorney 1972–76; Admin., Ariz. Drug Control District 1975–76; fmr mem. Ariz. Democratic Exec. Cttee, Vice-Chair. 1964, 1970; Senator from Arizona 1977–95, mem. Judiciary Cttee, Appropriations Cttee, Rules Cttee, Special Select Cttee on Indian Affairs, Veterans' Affairs Cttee; mem. Select Cttee on Intelligence, Senate Caucus on Int. Narcotics Control; Vice Pres. and Pnr Parry, Romani, De Concini & Symms Assocs., Washington, DC 1995–, DeConcini, McDonald, Yetwin & Lacy, Tuscon 1995–; Dir Nat. Center for Missing and Exploited Children 1995–; mem. Académie Française 1993–; Chair. Comm. on Security and Co-operation in Europe; served US Army 1959–60, Judge Advocate Gen. Corps. 1964–67; mem. or fmr mem. Pima County Bar Asscn, Ariz. Bar Asscn, American Bar Asscn, American Judicature Soc., American Arbitration Asscn, Nat. District Attorneys' Asscn; mem. Ariz. County Attorneys' and Sheriffs' Asscn, Sec.-Treas. 1975, Pres. 1976. *Leisure interests:* golf, boating, jogging. *Address:* Parry, Romani, De Concini & Symms Associates, 517 C Street, NE, Washington, DC 20002 (office); 2525 E Broadway, Suite 111, Tucson, AZ 85716, USA. *Telephone:* (202) 547-4000 (Washington) (office); (520) 325-9600 (Tucson) (office); (858) 459-5460 (LaJolla) (office). *Fax:* (202) 543-5044 (Washington) (office); (520) 327-9744 (Tucson) (office); (858) 459-5471 (LaJolla) (office). *E-mail:* prdands@aol.com (office); d.deconcini@atl.net (office). *Website:* www.lobbycongress.com (office).

DE CORTE, Frans; Belgian physicist and academic; *Professor, Department of Analytical Chemistry, Institute for Nuclear Sciences, University of Ghent;* currently Prof., Dept of Analytical Chem., Inst. for Nuclear Sciences, Univ. of Ghent; mem. Int. Advisory Bd, Radiochemical Conf. (RadChem), Mariánské Lázně, Czech Repub. 2002; mem. Int. Union of Pure and Applied Chem.; Hevesy Medal 2000. *Address:* Instituut voor Nucleaire Wetenschappen, Laboratorium voor Analytische Scheikunde, Proetuinstraat 86, 9000 Ghent, Belgium (office). *Telephone:* (9) 264-65-79 (office). *Fax:* (9) 264-66-99 (office). *E-mail:* frans.decorte@rug.ac.be (office). *Website:* www.analchem.ugent.be/ICPMS (office).

DE CREM, Pieter Frans Norbert Jozef Raymond; Belgian politician; *Minister of Defence;* b. 22 July 1962, Aalter; m. Caroline Bergez; three c.; ed Univ. Catholique de Louvain, Univ. Libre de Bruxelles; worked for Roularta Media Group 1987–89; Pres. youth section of CVP (Christelijke Volkspartij), Gand-Eeklo 1989–95; Attaché, Cabinet of Prime Minister Wilfried Martens 1989–92, Cabinet of Minister of Defence 1992–93; Adviser to De fabrieken van de Gebroeders De Beukelaar 1993–94; elected Mayor of Aalter 1995, re-elected 2000, 2006; elected to Chamber of Reps for Gand-Eeklo (CVP) 1995, re-elected 1999, elected to Chamber of Reps for Flanders East (party renamed Christen-Democratisch en Vlaams—CD&V) 2003, re-elected 2007, Head, CD&V parl. group 2003–07, Pres. Interior Comm. 2007, mem. OSCE parl. cttee; Minister of Defence 2007–; Officier, Ordre de Léopold. *Address:* Office of the Minister of Defence, Lambermont straat 8, 1000 Brussels, Belgium (office). *Telephone:* (2) 25-50-28-11 (office). *E-mail:* info@mod.mil.be (office). *Website:* www.pieterdecrem.be (office).

DE CUENCA Y CUENCA, Luis Alberto; Spanish philologist, poet, translator and writer; b. 1950, Madrid; ed Universidad Autónoma de Madrid; Prof. Philology Inst. of Council for Scientific Research; then Publs Dir; literary critic for several publs including El País; Dir Biblioteca Nacional (Nat. Library) 1996–2000; Premio Nacional de Literatura Infantil y Juvenil 1989. *Publications include:* Los Retratos 1971, Elsinore 1972, scholia 1978, Necrofilia 1983, Breviora 1984, La Caja de Plata 1985, Seis poemas por amor 1986, El otro sueño 1987, Poesía 1970–89 1990, Nausícaa 1991, El héroe y sus máscaras 1991, 77 Poemas 1992, Willendorf 1992, El hacha y la rosa 1993, El desayuno y otros poemas 1993, Los gigantes de hielo 1994, Animales domésticos 1995, Tres poemas 1996, Por fuertes y fronteras 1996, El bosque y otros poemas 1997, En el país de las maravillas 1997, Los mundos y los días 1998, Alicia 1999, Insomnios 2000, Mitologías 2001, Vamos a ser felices y otros poemas de humor y deshumor 2003, El enemigo oculto 2003, El puente de la espada: poemas inéditos 2003, Diez poemas y cinco prosas 2004, Ahora y siempre 2004, Su nombre era el de todas las mujeres y otros poemas de amor y desamor 2005, La vida en llamas 2006, Poesía 1979-1996 2006, A quemarropa 2006, Manantial 2007, Los mundos y los días : poesía 1970-2002 2007, Héroes y villanos del cómic 2007. *Address:* c/o Biblioteca Nacional, Paseo de Recoletos 20, 28071 Madrid, Spain.

DE DEO, Joseph E. (Joe), BA; American advertising executive; b. 18 Sept. 1937, Newark; s. of Joseph De Deo and Clara Veneziano; m. Esther Ellen Dadigan 1969; one s.; ed The Delbarton School, Princeton Univ.; joined Young and Rubicam (Y & R) as man. trainee, New York 1961, Account Exec. 1963, Account Supervisor 1967, Vice-Pres. 1968, Chair. Australian operations, opening agencies Sydney, then Adelaide and Melbourne 1969–79, Sr Vice-Pres. and Area Dir for Asia/Pacific Region 1971, set up Y & R cos Tokyo 1972, Hong Kong 1974, Chair. UK group, London and Regional Dir for UK, France, Belgium and Netherlands 1974–77, Area Dir for Europe and the Middle East 1977–80, Pres. Y & R Europe 1980–90, Pres. and CEO Young and Rubicam Advertising Worldwide 1990–92, Vice-Chair., Chief Creative Officer Young & Rubicam Inc., NY 1992–93, Corp. Vice-Chair. 1993–. *Leisure interests:* skiing, reading, antique collecting. *Address:* Young & Rubicam Inc., 285 Madison Avenue, New York, NY 10017, USA.

DE DUVE, Christian René, MD, MSc; Belgian cytologist and biochemist; *Professor Emeritus of Biochemical Cytology, Rockefeller University;* b. 2 Oct. 1917, Thames Ditton, England; s. of Alphonse de Duve and Madeleine Pungs; m. Janine Herman 1943; two s. two d.; ed Univ. of Louvain; Prof. of Physiological Chem., Univ. of Louvain Medical School 1947–85, Prof. Emer. 1985–; Prof. of Biochemical Cytology, Rockefeller Univ., New York City 1962–88, Prof. Emer. 1988–; Founder-mem. and Pres. Int. Inst. of Cellular and Molecular Pathology, Brussels 1974–91; mem. Royal Acad. of Medicine (Belgium), Royal Acad. of Belgium, ACS, Biochemical Soc., American Soc. of Biological Chem., Pontifical Acad. of Sciences, American Soc. of Cell Biology, Deutsche Akad. der Naturforschung, Leopoldina, Koninklijke Akad. voor Geneeskunde van België, etc.; Foreign mem. American Acad. of Arts and Sciences, Royal Soc., London, RSC; Foreign Assoc. NAS, USA; Hon. DSc (Keele Univ.) 1981; Dr hc (Rockefeller) 1997 and numerous other hon. degrees; Prix des Alumni 1949, Prix Pfizer 1957, Prix Francqui 1960, Prix Quinquennal Belge des Sciences Médicales 1967, Gairdner Foundation Int. Award of Merit (Canada) 1967, Dr H. P. Heineken Prijs (Netherlands) 1973, Nobel Prize for Medicine (shared) for discovery of lysosomes (digestive organelles of the cell) and peroxisomes (organelles that are the site of metabolic processes involving hydrogen peroxide) 1974. *Leisure interests:* tennis, skiing, bridge. *Address:* c/o Rockefeller University, 1230 York Avenue, New York, NY 10021, USA (office); ICP, 75 Avenue Hippocrate, 1200 Brussels, Belgium.

DE ESCOBAR, Ana Vilma Albanez; Salvadorean economist and politician; *Vice-President;* b. 2 March 1954; m. Carlos Patricio Escobar; one d.; ed Universidad Centroamericana "José Simeón Cañas"; fmr Project Man. USAID; fmr Prof. of French; Pres. Salvadorean Inst. of Social Security 1999–2003; Vice-Pres. of El Salvador 2004–. *Address:* Ministry for the Presidency, Avenida Cuba, Calle Darió González 806, Barrio San Jacinto,

San Salvador, El Salvador (office). *Telephone:* 221-8483 (office). *Fax:* 771-0950 (office). *Website:* www.casapres.gob.sv (office).

DE FERRANTI, Sebastian Basil Joseph Ziani, DL; British electrical engineer; b. 5 Oct. 1927, Alderley Edge, Cheshire; s. of the late Sir Vincent de Ferranti and Lady Dorothy H. C. de Ferranti (née Wilson); brother of the late Basil Ziani de Ferranti, MP, MEP; m. 1st Mona Helen Cunningham 1953 (died 2008); one s. two d.; m. 2nd Naomi Angela Rae 1983 (died 2001); ed Ampleforth Coll.; served 4th/7th Dragoon Guards 1947–49; Brown Boveri, Switzerland and Alsthom, France 1948–50; Transformer Dept, Ferranti Ltd 1950, Dir 1954–82, Man. Dir 1958–75, Chair. 1963–82; Dir GEC PLC 1982–97; Pres. BEAMA 1969–70, Manchester and Region Centre for Educ. in Science, Educ. and Tech. 1972–78; Chair. Int. Electrical Asscn 1970–73; Vice-Pres. RSA 1980–84; Commr Royal Comm. for Exhbn of 1851 1984–97; Dir Nat. Nuclear Corpn 1984–88; mem. Nat. Defence Industries Council 1969–77; Trustee, Tate Gallery 1971–78; Chair. North-West Civic Trust 1978–83; Chair. Hallé Concerts Soc. 1988–96, Pres. 1997–; High Sheriff of Cheshire 1988–89; Hon. mem. Royal Northern Coll. of Music 1997, mem. Bd of Govs 1988–2000; Hon. Fellow, UMIST; Granada Guildhall Lecture 1966; Royal Inst. Discourse 1969; Louis Blériot Lecture, Paris 1970; Faraday Lecture 1970, 1971; DL; Hon. DSc (Cranfield Inst. of Tech.) 1973, (Salford Univ.), Hon. LLD (Manchester) 1998. *Address:* Henbury Hall, Macclesfield, Cheshire, SK11 9PJ, England (home). *Telephone:* (1625) 422101.

DE FONBLANQUE, John, CMG, MA, MSc,; British diplomatist; *Director, Office of High Commissioner on National Minorities, Organization for Security and Co-operation in Europe;* b. 20 Dec. 1943, Fleet, Hants; s. of Maj.-Gen. E. B. De Fonblanque and Elizabeth De Fonblanque; m. Margaret Prest 1984; one s.; ed Ampleforth School, King's Coll., Cambridge, London School of Econs; joined FCO 1968, Second Sec. Jakarta 1969–72, Second, later First Sec. to EC, Brussels 1972–77; Prin. HM Treasury 1977–80; FCO 1980–83; Asst Sec. Cabinet Office 1983–86; Head of Chancery, New Delhi 1986, Counsellor (Political and Institutional) Mission to EC, Brussels 1988, Asst Under-Sec. of State Int. Orgs, then Dir Global Issues 1994–98, Dir (Europe) FCO 1998–99, Head Del. to OSCE with rank of Amb. 1999–2003; Dir Office of OSCE High Commr on Nat. Minorities 2004–. *Leisure interest:* mountain walking. *Address:* Office of High Commissioner on National Minorities, Organisation for Security and Co-operation in Europe Secretariat, Kärntner Ring 5–7, 4th Floor, 1010 Vienna (office); Van Moersselestraat 5, 2596 PD The Hague, Netherlands (home). *Telephone:* (70) 3125512 (office); (70) 3249081 (home). *E-mail:* john.defonblanque@osce.org (office); jdefonblanque@hotmail.com (home). *Website:* www.osce.org (office).

DE GELSEY, William, MA; British (b. Austrian) investment banker; *Chairman, Gedeon Richter Ltd;* b. 17 Dec. 1921, Vienna; s. of Henry Alexander de Gelsey and Marguerite Constance de Gelsey (née Lieser); ed Trinity Coll., Cambridge; Man., ICI, Manchester 1942–52; Man. Consultant, The Vilmos Co., London 1952–60; Exec. Dir, Hill Samuel & Co., London 1960–71; Exec. Dir, Orion Bank Ltd, London 1971–76, Man. Dir 1976–80, Deputy Chair., Orion Royal Bank Ltd, Japan 1980; mem. Bd, Gedeon Richter Ltd, Budapest, Hungary 1995–, Chair. 1999–; Sr Adviser to Man. Bd, CA IB Corporate Finance Beratungs GmbH, Vienna; Dir, China Investment and Finance Ltd, Hong Kong, Compagnie Générale de Developpement Immobilier, Paris. *Address:* Richter Gedeon Rt., Gyömröi út 19–21, 1103 Budapest, Hungary (office). *Telephone:* (1) 4314000 (office). *Fax:* (1) 2606650 (office). *E-mail:* (office). *Website:* www.richter.hu (office).

DE GEUS, Aart; Dutch lawyer and international organization executive; *Deputy Secretary-General, Organisation for Economic Co-operation and Development;* m.; three c.; ed Erasmus Univ., Rotterdam, Nijmegen Univ.; worked as lawyer in industry sector of Christian Trade Union –1988; mem. Exec. Bd Nat. Fed. of Christian Trade Unions 1988–98, Vice-Chair. Exec. Bd 1993–98; pnr in Amsterdam-based co. for strategy and man. 1998–2002; Minister of Social Affairs and Employment 2002–07; Chair. OECD Social Policy Ministerial Meeting 2005, has served in various functions at local, nat. and int. level, Deputy Sec.-Gen. OECD 2007–, in charge of Political Economy of Reform, and preparations for Ministerial Council Meeting and Exec. Cttee in Special Session. *Address:* OECD, 2 rue André Pascal, 75775 Paris Cedex 16, France (office). *Telephone:* 1-45-24-82-00 (office). *Fax:* 1-45-24-85-00 (office). *E-mail:* webmaster@oecd.org (office). *Website:* www.oecd.org (office).

DE GIORGI, HE Cardinal Salvatore; Italian ecclesiastic; *Archbishop of Palermo;* b. 6 Sept. 1930, Vernole; ordained priest 1953; Bishop 1973, Archbishop, See of Oria 1978, of Foggia 1981, of Taranto 1987, of Palermo 1996; elevated to Cardinal Priest of S. Maria in Ara Coeli 1998. *Address:* Curia Arcivescovile, Corso Vittorio Emanuele 461, 90134 Palermo, Italy (office). *Telephone:* (091) 6077248 (office). *Fax:* (091) 581069 (office). *E-mail:* arcivescovo@diocesipa.it (office). *Website:* www.diocesipa.it (office).

DE GOEIJ, Jeroen J. M., PhD; Dutch chemist and academic; *Professor of Radiochemistry, Eindhoven University of Technology;* Prof. of Radiochemistry, Eindhoven Univ. of Tech.; Prof. Emer., Interfaculty Reactor Inst. (IRI), Tech. Univ., Delft; Fellow, Int. Union of Pure and Applied Chem. (IUPAC); Kt, Order of the Lion of the Netherlands 2002; Hevesy Medal 2003. *Address:* Eindhoven University of Technology, Applied Physics, Physics and Applications of Accelerators, POB 513, CYC b 2.09, 5600 MB, Eindhoven, Netherlands (office). *Telephone:* (40) 247-4355 (office). *E-mail:* j.j.m.de.goeij@tue.nl (office). *Website:* web.phys.tue.nl (office).

DE GRAAF, Thom Carolus; Dutch politician and fmr civil servant; *Mayor of Nijmegen;* b. 11 June 1957, Amsterdam; m.; two c.; ed Catholic Univ. of Nijmegen; fmr Lecturer in Constitutional Law, Catholic Univ. of Nijmegen; civil servant, Ministry of Interior 1985–94; Deputy Dir for Police Affairs 1991–94; fmr Municipal Councillor, Leiden; mem. De Koning Cttee on Constitutional Reform 1992–93; joined Democraten 66 (D66) 1977, Sec. Nat. Bd 1986–90, Chair. D66 Parl. Group 1997; mem. Parl. 1994–2003; Deputy Prime Minister 2003–05, Minister of Govt Reform and Kingdom Relations 2003–05; Mayor of Nijmegen 2007–. *Leisure interests:* history, poetry, tennis, ice skating. *Address:* Municipality of Nijmegen, PO Box 9105, 6500 HG Nijmegen, Netherlands (office). *Telephone:* (24) 3292408 (office). *E-mail:* openhuis@nijmegen.nl (office). *Website:* www2.nijmegen.nl (office).

DE GRAVE, Franciscus (Frank) Hendrikus Gerardus, DJur; Dutch politician; b. 27 June 1955, Amsterdam; m.; two c.; ed Univ. of Groningen; Int. Sec. JOVD youth org. 1977–78, Nat. Pres. 1978–80; mem. Volkspartij voor Vrihoid en Democratie (VVD) Parl. group 1977–81; Asst Sec. to Man. Bd AMRO bank 1980–82; Amsterdam City Councillor 1982–86; mem. First Chamber of Parl. 1982–90; Councillor for Finances and Deputy Mayor, Amsterdam City Council 1990–94, Acting Mayor Jan.–June 1994; Sec. of State for Social Security and Employment 1996–98; Minister of Defence 1998–2002; mem. Vaste Comm. for Defence 1982–86, Bd Vereniging Nederlandse Gemeenten; Commr RAI, Bank Nederlandse Gemeenten and Amsterdam Arena. *Address:* c/o Ministry of Defence, Plein 4, PO Box 20701, 2500 ES The Hague, Netherlands (office). *Telephone:* (70) 3187320 (office). *Fax:* (70) 3187264 (office). *Website:* www.mindef.nl (office).

DE GUCHT, Karel; Belgian politician; *Minister of Foreign Affairs;* b. 27 Jan. 1954, Overmere; m. Mireille Schreurs; two s.; ed Koninlijk Atheneum Aalst, Free Univ. Brussels; Chair. Liberal Students' Union Brussels 1974–75, Nat. Chair. 1975–77; MEP 1980–94; Vice-Chair. PVV party 1985–88; Senator 1994–95; Nat. Chair. Flemish Liberals and Democrats–Citizens' Party (VLD) 1999; Minister of State 2002–04, Minister of Foreign Affairs 2004–07 (resgnd), reappointed Dec. 2007. *Publications:* De Tijd Wacht op Niemand (co-author; trans. Time and Tide Wait for No Man) 1990, Er Zijn Geen Eilanden Meer: Over Democratie, Vrijheid en Mensenrechten (co-author) 1999, Het Einde der Pilaren: Een Toscaans Gesprek (co-author) 2001, De Toekomst is Vrij 2002. *Address:* Federal Public Service of Foreign Affairs, Foreign Trade and Development Co-operation, 15 rue des Petits Carmes, 1000 Brussels, Belgium (office). *Telephone:* (2) 501-81-11 (office). *Fax:* (2) 501-81-70 (office). *E-mail:* info@diplobel.fed.be (office). *Website:* www.diplomatie.be (office).

DE GUILLENCHMIDT, Jacqueline; French lawyer; *Member, Conseil Constitutionnel;* b. 25 Sept. 1943, Beijing, People's Repub. of China; d. of Robert Barbara de de Labelotterie and France Pasquet du Bousquet de Lauriere; m. Michel de Guillenchmidt 1966; ed Institut d'études politiques de Paris; barrister, Paris 1972–82; Magistrate High Court of Pontoise 1982–85; Judge Dept of Justice 1985; Bureau Chief of the Commercial Law 1989–92, then in regulation in the conduct of civil affairs and Seal of the Dept of Justice 1992–93; Tech. Advisor to Minister of Justice 1993–94, Deputy Dir of cabinet of Minister of Justice 1994–95; State Councilor 1995; Chair. Comm. for Supervision and Control of Publications for Children and Adolescents 1995–99; Chair. Comm.for Support Fund for Expression Radio 1995–99; mem. Conseil supérieur de l'audiovisuel 1999–2004; Mem. Conseil Constitutionnel 2004–; Chevalier de la Légion d'Honneur, de l'ordre national du Mérite, des Palmes académiques et du Mérite agricole. *Address:* Conseil Constitutionnel, 2 rue de Montpensier, 75001 Paris, France (office). *Telephone:* 1-40-15-30-00 (office). *Fax:* 1-40-20-93-27 (office). *E-mail:* relations-exterieures@conseil-constitutionnel.fr (office). *Website:* www.conseil-constitutionnel.fr (office).

DE HAAN, Hendrik, PhD; Dutch academic; *Professor of International Economics, University of Groningen;* b. 8 April 1941, Nijmegen; m. Adriana Annie Kramer 1966; two s. one d.; ed Univ. of Groningen, Netherlands, Catholic Univ. of Louvain, Belgium; Prof. of Int. Econs, Univ. of Groningen 1971–; consultant to UNCTAD 1975; consultant-expert to UN on econ. and social consequences of the arms race 1977, 1982, 1987; consultant to UN on relationship between disarmament and devt 1985–87; Foreign Policy Adviser to Christian Democratic Party 1989–. *Publications:* Het Moderne Geldwezen (Modern Money), several other books on econ. topics, numerous articles in scientific journals. *Address:* Department of Economics, PO Box 800, 9700 AV Groningen (office); Hoofdstraat 173, 9827 PB Lettelbert, Netherlands (home). *Telephone:* (50) 633710 (office). *Fax:* (50) 637337.

DE HAVILLAND, Olivia Mary; American (b. British) actress; b. 1 July 1916, Tokyo, Japan; d. of Walter Augustus de Havilland and Lilian Augusta Ruse (stage name Lilian Fontaine); m. 1st Marcus Aurelius Goodrich 1946 (divorced 1953); one s.; m. 2nd Pierre Paul Galante 1955 (divorced 1979); one d.; ed Saratoga Grammar School, Notre Dame Convent, Los Gatos Union High School; stage debut in A Midsummer Night's Dream 1934, film debut in screen version 1935; Pres. Cannes Film Festival 1965 (first woman); on lecture tours in USA 1971–80; Acad. of Motion Picture Arts and Sciences tribute to her career, Los Angeles 2006; mem. Bd of Trustees of American Coll. in Paris 1970–71, of American Library in Paris 1974–81; mem. Altar Guild, Lay Reader, American Cathedral in Paris 1971–81; Hon. Bd mem. American Library in Paris; DHumLitt (American Univ. of Paris) 1994; Hon. DLitt (Univ. of Hertfordshire) 1998; numerous awards include Acad. Award 1946, 1949, New York Critics Award 1948, 1949, Look Magazine Award 1942, 1948, 1949, Exhibitor Laurel Award 1948, Winged Victory Award 1950, Women's Nat. Press Club Achievement Award for Outstanding Accomplishment in the Theatre 1950, Prix Femina Belge du Cinéma 1957, American Legion Humanitarian Medal 1967, Filmex Tribute 1978, American Acad. of Achievement Award 1978, American Exemplar Medal 1980, American Acad. of Achievement 25th Anniversary Salute to Excellence Statuette 1986, Golden Globe 1988, Birmingham Southern Coll. Gala XIV Women of Achievement Award 1999, John F. Kennedy Center for the Performing Arts Gold Medal 2005, Los Angeles County Museum Tribute 2006, Viennale: Vienna Int. Film Festival Tribute 2006, Nat. Medal of Arts 2008. *Films include:* Midsummer

Night's Dream 1935, Captain Blood 1935, Anthony Adverse 1936, The Adventures of Robin Hood 1938, Gone with the Wind 1939, Hold Back the Dawn 1941, Princess O'Rourke 1942, To Each His Own (Acad. Award, Ciné-Revue Award, Belgium) 1946, The Dark Mirror 1946, The Snake Pit 1947 (Nat. Bd of Review of Motion Pictures Best Actress Award 1948, Brazilian Film Critics' Award 1948, New York Film Critics' Award 1948, Box Office Blue Ribbon Award 1948, San Francisco Film Critics' Award 1948, Silver Mask, Italian Film Critics' Award 1950), The Heiress (Acad. Award 1949, Golden Globe Award 1949, Venice Film Festival Award 1949, New York Film Critics' Award 1949, San Francisco Film Critics' Award 1949, Cité-Revue Award 1950) 1949, My Cousin Rachel 1952, Not as a Stranger 1954, The Proud Rebel 1957, The Light in the Piazza 1961, Lady in a Cage 1963, Hush Hush Sweet Charlotte 1964, The Adventurers 1968, Airport '77 1976, The Swarm 1978, The Fifth Musketeer. *Plays include:* Romeo and Juliet 1951, Candida 1951–52, A Gift of Time 1962. *Television includes:* Noon Wine 1966, Screaming Woman 1972, Roots, The Next Generations 1979, Murder is Easy 1981, Charles and Diana: A Royal Romance 1982, North and South II 1986, Anastasia (Golden Globe Award) 1986, The Woman He Loved 1987. *Publications:* Every Frenchman Has One 1962, Mother and Child (contrib.) 1975. *Leisure interests:* crossword puzzles, reading tales of mystery and imagination, painting on Sunday. *Address:* BP 156-16, 75764 Paris Cedex 16, France.

DE HOOP, Adrianus Teunis, PhD; Dutch professor of electromagnetic theory and applied mathematics; *Lorentz Chair Emeritus Professor, Delft University of Technology;* b. 24 Dec. 1927, Rotterdam; ed Delft Univ. of Tech.; Research Asst, Delft Univ. of Tech. 1950–52, Asst Prof. 1953–56, Assoc. Prof. 1957–60, Prof. 1960–96, Lorentz Chair Prof. Emer. 1996–; Reserve Officer, Royal Netherlands Navy 1952–53; Research Asst, Univ. of Calif., Los Angeles 1956–57; Visiting Research Scientist, Philips Research Labs, Eindhoven 1976–77; Consultant 1977–89; mem. Royal Netherlands Acad. of Arts and Sciences 1989, Royal Flemish Acad. of Arts and Sciences of Belgium 1998, Visiting Scientist Schlumberger Oilfield Services, Ridgefield, USA 1982–; Hon. PhD (Ghent) 1982, (Vaxjo) 2008; Kt in the Order of the Netherlands Lion 2003; awards from Stichting Fund for Science, Tech. and Research 1986, 1989, 1990, 1993, 1994, Gold Research Medal, Royal Inst. of Eng 1989, Heinrich Hertz Medal, IEEE 2001, URSI Balthasar van der Pol Gold Research Medal 2002. *Publications:* Handbook of Radiation and Scattering of Waves 1995; numerous articles in journals. *Leisure interest:* playing the piano. *Address:* Faculty of Electrical Engineering, Mathematics and Computer Science, Delft University of Technology, Mekelweg 4, 2628 CD Delft (office); Korenmolen 17, 2661 LE Bergschenhoek, Netherlands (home). *Telephone:* (15) 2785203 (office); (10) 5220049 (home). *Fax:* (15) 2786194 (office). *E-mail:* a.t.dehoop@its.tudelft.nl (office). *Website:* www.atdehoop.com (office).

DE HOOP SCHEFFER, Jaap; Dutch politician and international organization official; b. 3 April 1948; m. Jeannine de Hoop Scheffer-van Oorschot; two c.; ed Leiden Univ.; fmr Reserve Officer in Air Force; fmr Sec. Del. of Netherlands to NATO, Brussels; Deputy Parl. Leader Christen-Democratisch Appèl (CDA – Christian Democrats) 1995–97, Leader 1997–2001; Minister of Foreign Affairs 2002–03; Sec.-Gen. NATO 2004–09. *Address:* c/o NATO Headquarters, Boulevard Leopold III, 1110 Brussels, Belgium (office).

DE IRALA, Xabier; Spanish business executive; *CEO, Bilbao Bizkaia Kutxa (BBK) Bank;* b. 1946, New York; ed La Salle Univ., Philippines; CEO and other positions, Gen. Electric, Spain 1971–86, CEO Gen. Electric, Portugal 1986–87, Financial Dir Gen. Electric, England 1987–88, Vice-Pres. Gen. Electric, CGR, France 1988–90; Exec. Vice-Pres., CEO, Asea Brown Boveri España 1990–96; Chair., CEO Iberia 1996–2003 (resgnd); CEO Bilbao Bizkaia Kutxa (BBK) Bank 2005–; Chair. Bd of Govs IATA; Chair. Fitur; Pres. Spain-Philippines Jt Business Cttee; Pres. Exceltur; mem. Advisory Bd, ESC Bordeaux, Bd of Dirs, Italtel, Italy; Officier, Légion d'honneur. *Leisure interests:* chess, mountaineering. *Address:* Bilbao Bizkaia Kutxa (BBK), Gran Via 30–32, Bilbao, Bizkaia, 48009, Spain (office). *Telephone:* (94) 4017000 (office). *Fax:* (94) 4017800 (office). *Website:* portal.bbk.es (office).

DE JAGER, Cornelis; Dutch astrophysicist; *Professor Emeritus of Space Research;* b. 29 April 1921, Den Burg, Texel; s. of Jan de Jager and Cornelia Kuyper; m. Duotje Rienks 1947; two s. two d.; ed Univ. of Utrecht; Asst in Theoretical Physics, Univ. of Utrecht 1946; Asst in Astronomy, Univ. of Leiden; Asst Astronomy Inst., Utrecht; Assoc. Prof. of Stellar Astrophysics, Univ. of Utrecht 1957, Ordinary Prof. in Gen. Astrophysics 1960–86; Extraordinary Prof., Univ. of Brussels and founder, Space Research Lab., Utrecht Astronomy Inst., Brussels 1961; Man. Dir Utrecht Astronomy Inst. 1963–78, Chair. Inst. Council 1978–83; Asst Gen. Sec. Int. Astronomical Union 1967–70, Gen. Sec. 1970–73; Pres. Netherlands Astronomy Comm. 1975–83; mem. Exec. Council Cttee on Space Research (COSPAR) 1970–72, Pres. 1972–78, 1982–86; mem. Exec. Council, ICSU 1970–82, Vice-Pres. 1976–78, Pres. 1978–80; Chair. Skepsis (for critical evaluation of the paranormal) 1987–97, European Council of Sceptical Orgs 1995–2001, Council of Chancellors of Global Foundation 2001–; Aggregate Prof., Univ. of Brussels 1970–86; currently Prof. Emer. of Space Research; mem. Royal Netherlands Acad. of Art and Sciences (Foreign Sec. 1985–90), Royal Belgium Acad. of Art and Sciences, Acad. Europe (Paris and London); Assoc. mem. Royal Astronomical Soc. (London); Corresp. mem. Soc. Royale de Science, Liège; mem. Int. Acad. Astronautics, Chair. Basic Sciences Section 1984–92; Foreign mem. Deutsche Akademie Leopoldina, Halle; Foreign Fellow Indian Nat. Scientific Acad.; hon. mem. Netherlands Soc. of Astronomy and Meteorology 1996; Kt, Order of the Dutch Lion 1983; Dr hc (Univ. of Wrocław, Poland) 1975, (Observatoire de Paris) 1976; Karl Schwarzschild Medal 1974, Yuri Gagarin Medal (USSR) 1984, J. Janssen Medal (France) 1984, Ziolkowski Medal, USSR Acad. of Sciences, Gold Medal Royal Astro-

nomical Soc., London 1988, Hale Medal, American Astronomical Soc. 1988, COSPAR Medal for Int. Co-operation in Space Science 1988, Silver Medal Royal Netherlands Acad. Arts and Sciences, Gold Medal Netherlands Soc. Astronomy and Meteorology, In Praise of Reason Award CSICOP, Buffalo, NY 1990, Von Karman Award of Int. Acad. of Astronautics 1993, Hon. Silver Medal, City of Utrecht 2003. *Publications:* about 550 publs including: The Hydrogen Spectrum of the Sun 1952, Structure and Dynamics of the Solar Atmosphere 1959, The Solar Spectrum 1965, Solar Flares and Space Research (with Z. Svestka) 1969, Sterrenkunde 1969, Reports on Astronomy 1970, 1973, Highlights in Astronomy 1970, Ontstaan en Levensloop van Sterren (with E. van den Heuvel) 2nd edn 1973, Image Processing Techniques in Astronomy (with H. Nieuwenhuyzen) 1975, The Brightest Stars 1980, Instabilities in evolved super- and hyper-giants 1992, Bolwerk van de Sterren 1993, Tien Opmerkelijke Sterrekundige Ontdekkingen 1995, Kannibalen bij de grenzen van het heelal 1996, Solar Flares and Collisions Between Current-carrying Loops (jtly) 1996, Van het Clijf tot Den Hoorn (jtly) 1998. *Leisure interests:* birds, plants, jogging, history. *Address:* Molenstraat 22, 1791 DL Den Burg, Texel, Netherlands (home). *Telephone:* (620) 420611 (office); (222) 320816 (home). *E-mail:* cdel@planet.nl (office). *Website:* www.nioz.nl (office).

DE JESUS CASTELHANO MAURICIO, Amadeu; Angolan central banker; *Governor, Banco Nacional de Angola;* fmr Chair. Unipetrol; Gov. Banco Nacional de Angola 2006–; Gov Alternate IMF 2006–. *Address:* Banco Nacional de Angola, CP 1243, Av. 4 de Fevereiro 151, Luanda, Angola (office). *Telephone:* (222) 335775 (office). *Fax:* (222) 335766 (office). *E-mail:* sec.gvb@bna.ao (office). *Website:* www.bna.ao (office).

DE JONGH, Eduard S.; Dutch art historian and academic; *Professor Emeritus of Art History, University of Utrecht;* b. 7 June 1931, Amsterdam; m. Lammijna Oosterbaan 1977; two s. one d.; ed Baarns Lyceum and Univ. of Utrecht; journalist and art critic, Het Parool and Vrij Nederland 1954–74; Librarian, Inst. for Art History, Univ. of Utrecht 1963–66; Ed. Openbaar Kunstbezit (radio course) 1963–73; Ed. Simiolus (art history quarterly) 1966–77; mem. staff, Centrum Voortgezet Kunsthistorisch Onderzoek, Univ. of Utrecht 1966–73; Asst Prof., Inst. for Art History, Univ. of Utrecht 1973–76, Prof. of Art History 1976–89, Prof. Emer. 1989–; Ed. Kunstschrift 1990–; Visiting Scholar, Getty Center for History of Art and Humanities 1987; mem. Royal Netherlands Acad.; Foreign mem. Royal Belgian Acad.; Dr hc (Amsterdam) 2002; Karel van Mander Award 1987. *Publications:* Zinne- en minnebeelden in de schilderkunst van de zeventiende eeuw 1967, Tot Lering en Vermaak: Betekenissen van Hollandse genrevoorstellingen uit de zeventiende eeuw 1976, Still Life in the Age of Rembrandt 1982, Portretten van echt en trouw: Huwelijk en gezin in de Nederlandse kunst van de zeventiende eeuw 1986, Kunst en het vruchtbare misverstand 1993, Faces of the Golden Age: Seventeenth-Century Dutch Portraits 1994, Kwesties van betekenis: Thema en motief in de Nederlandse schilderkunst van de zeventiende eeuw 1995, Mirror of Everyday Life: Genre Prints in The Netherlands 1550–1700 (with Ger Luijten) 1997, Questions of Meaning: Theme and Motif in Dutch Seventeenth-Century Painting 2000, Dankzij de tiende muze: 33 Opstellen uit Kunstschrift 2000, Charles Donker, etser (with Peter Schatborn) 2002, Muziek aan de muur: Muzikale voorstellingen in de Nederlanden 1500–1700 2008; many articles on iconological and art theoretical subjects. *Address:* Frederik Hendrikstraat 29, 3583 VG Utrecht, Netherlands.

DE JONGH-ELHAGE, Emily Saïdy; Netherlands Antilles politician; *Prime Minister and Minister of General Affairs and Foreign Relations;* b. 7 Dec. 1946; Commr of Public Works and Public Housing of Curaçao 1998–99; Commr of Educ., Sport and Cultural Affairs 1999–2002; Minister of Educ. and Culture 2002–03; Commr of Public Enterprises and Public Housing of Curaçao 2004–05; Prime Minister and Minister of Gen. Affairs and Foreign Relations 2006–; Leader Partido Antia Restrukturá (Party for the Restructured Antilles—PAR) 2005–. *Address:* Ministry of General Affairs and Foreign Relations, Plasa Horacio Hoyer 9, Willemstad, Curaçao, Netherlands Antilles (office). *Telephone:* (9) 461-1866 (office). *Fax:* (9) 461-1268 (office).

DE KEERSMAEKER, Baroness; Anne Teresa; Belgian choreographer; b. 11 June 1960, Wemmel; one s. one d.; ed Mudra, School of Maurice Béjart, Brussels and Tisch School of the Arts, New York Univ.; presented first work, Asch, in Brussels 1980; Founder and Artistic Dir Rosas Dance Co. 1983–; Rosas became co.-in-residence, Théâtre de la Monnaie, Brussels with herself as resident choreographer 1992; directed opera Bluebeard (Bartók) 1997; Artistic Dir at PARTS school 1995–; has also directed work for video; Officier, Ordre des Arts et des Lettres 2000; Dr hc (Flemish Univ. of Brussels) 1995; Eugène Baie Prize 1996, City of Paris Médaille de Vermeil 2002, Gabriella Moortgat Stichting Award 2002, Flemish Govt Erepenning Medal 2002, Oost Vlaanderen Keizer Karelprijs 2004. *Choreographic works:* Asch 1981, Fase: four movements to music of Steve Reich 1982, Rosas danst Rosas (Bessie Award 1988) 1983, Elena's Aria 1984, Bartók/Aantekeningen 1986, Verkommenes Ufer/Medeamaterial/Landschaft mit Argonauten 1987, Mikrokosmos-Monument/Selbstporträt mit Reich und Riley (und Chopin ist auch dabei)/Im zart fliessender Bewegung-Quatuor Nr. 4 (Japanese Dance Award for Best Foreign Production 1989) 1987, Ottone, Ottone 1988, Stella (London Dance and Performances Award 1989) 1989, Achterland 1990, Erts 1992, Mozart/Concert Arias, un moto di gioia 1992, Toccata 1993, Kinok 1994, Amor Constante más allá de la muerte 1994, Erwartung/Verklärte Nacht 1995, Woud 1996, Just Before 1997, Three Solos for Vincent Dunoyer 1997, Duke Bluebeard's Castle 1998, Drumming (Golden Laurel Wreath, Sarajevo 1998) 1998, Quartett 1999, I Said I 1999, In Real Time 2000, Rain 2001, Small Hands (out of the lie of no) 2001, (but if a look should) April Me 2002, Repertory Evening 2002, Once 2002, Bitches' Brew/Tacoma Narrows 2003, Kassandra – Speaking in Twelve Voices 2004, Desh 2005, Raga for the Rainy

Season/A Love Supreme 2005, D'un soir un jour 2006, Bartók/Beethoven/ Schönberg Repertory Evening 2006, Steve Reich Evening 2007, Keeping Still 2007. *Films:* Hoppla! 1989, Achterland 1994, Rosas danst Rosas 1997, Tippeke 2000. *Address:* Rosas VZW, Van Volxemlaan 164, 1190 Brussels, Belgium (office). *Telephone:* (2) 344-55-98 (office). *Fax:* (2) 343-53-52 (office). *E-mail:* mail@rosas.be (office). *Website:* www.rosas.be (office).

DE KLERK, F(rederik) W(illem), LLB; South African politician and lawyer; b. 18 March 1936, Johannesburg; s. of J. de Klerk; m. 1st Marike Willemse 1959 (divorced 1998); two s. one d.; m. 2nd Elita Georgiadis 1998; ed Monument High School, Krugersdorp, Potchefstroom Univ.; in law practice 1961–72; mem. House of Ass. 1972; Information Officer Nat. Party, Transvaal 1975; Minister of Posts and Telecommunications and of Social Welfare and Pensions 1978, subsequently Minister of Posts and Telecommunications and of Sport and Recreation 1978–79, of Mines, Energy and Environmental Planning 1979–80, of Mineral and Energy Affairs 1980–82, of Internal Affairs 1982–85, of Nat. Educ. and Planning 1984–89; Acting State Pres. of South Africa Aug.–Sept. 1989, State Pres. of South Africa 1989–94; Exec. Deputy Pres., Govt of Nat. Unity 1994–96; Leader of the Official Opposition 1996–97; mem. Nat. Party, Transvaal Leader 1982–89, Leader 1989–97; also fmr Chair. of the Cabinet and C-in-C of the Armed Forces; fmr Chair. Council of Ministers; seven hon. doctorates; shared Nobel Prize for Peace with Nelson Mandela (q.v.) 1993; jt winner Houphouet Boigny Prize (UNESCO) 1991; Asturias Prize 1992, Liberty Medal (SA) 1993, Order of Mapungubwe Gold 2002. *Publications:* The Last Trek: A New Beginning (autobiog.) 1999, various articles and brochures. *Leisure interests:* golf, reading. *Address:* PO Box 15785, 7506 Panorama, Cape Town, South Africa (office). *Telephone:* (21) 4182202 (office). *Fax:* (21) 4182626 (office). *E-mail:* fwdklerk@mweb.co.za (home). *Website:* www.fwdklerk.org.za (office).

DE KORTE, Rudolf Willem, Dr rer. nat; Dutch politician; b. 8 July 1936, The Hague; m.; two c.; ed Maerlant Gymnasium, The Hague, Leiden Univ., Harvard Business School, USA; employed in industry, Hong Kong 1964–66, Ethiopia 1967–68; Gen. Sales Man. Unilever-Emery NV 1969–71, Dir 1972–77; Sec. People's Party for Freedom and Democracy (VVD) 1971–78; mem. Parl. 1977, Minister for Home Affairs March–July 1986, Deputy Prime Minister and Minister for Econ. Affairs 1986–89; mem. (VVD) Lower House of Parl. 1989–; mem. Wassenaar Municipal Council 1978–82. *Address:* c/o Tweede Kamer der Staten-Generaal, PO Box 20018, 2500 EA The Hague, Netherlands.

DE LA BILLIÈRE, Gen. Sir Peter (Edgar de la Cour), Kt, KCB, KBE, DSO, MC, DL; British army officer (retd) and banker (retd); b. 29 April 1934, Plymouth; s. of Surgeon Lt-Commdr Claude Dennis Delacour de Labillière and Frances Christing Wright Lawley; m. Bridget Constance Muriel Goode 1965; one s. two d.; ed Harrow School, Staff Coll., Royal Coll. of Defence Studies; joined King's Shropshire Light Infantry 1952; commissioned, Durham Light Infantry; served Japan, Korea, Malaya (despatches 1959), Jordan, Borneo, Egypt, Aden, Gulf States, Sudan, Oman, Falkland Islands; Commdg Officer, 22 Special Air Service (SAS) Regt 1972–74; Gen. Staff Officer 1 (Directing Staff), Staff Coll. 1974–77; Commdr British Army Training Team, Sudan 1977–78; Dir SAS and Commdr SAS Group 1978–83; Commdr British Forces, Falkland Islands and Mil. Commr 1984–85; Gen. Officer Commdg Wales 1985–87; Col Comdt. Light Div. 1986–90; Lt-Gen. Officer commanding SE Dist 1987–90; Commdr British Forces in Middle East Oct. 1990–91; rank of Gen. 1991 after Gulf War, Ministry of Defence Adviser on Middle East 1991–92; retd from army June 1992; Pres. SAS Asscn 1991–96, Army Cadet Force 1992–99; mem. Council Royal United Services Inst. 1975–77; Chair. Jt Services Hang Gliding 1986–88; Cdre Army Sailing Asscn 1989–90; Commr Duke of York's School 1988–90; Freeman City of London 1991; Hon. Freeman Fishmongers' Co. 1991; Pres. Harrow School Asscn 2002–; Trustee Imperial War Museum 1992–99; Dir (non-exec.), Middle East and Defence Adviser, Robert Fleming Holdings 1992–99; Chair. Meadowland Meats 1994–2002; Jt Chair. Dirs FARM Africa 1995–2001 (mem. Bd 1992–2001); DL Hereford and Worcester 1993; Trustee Naval and Mil. Club 1999–2003, mem. Bd 1999–2003; Pres. Friends of Imperial War Museum 2003; Pres. Harrow Asscn 2002–; Hon. DSc (Cranfield) 1992; Hon. DCL (Durham) 1993; Legion of Merit Chief Commdr (USA), Order of Abdul Aziz 2nd Class (Saudi Arabia), Meritorious Service Cross (Canada), Kuwait Decoration of the First Class, Order of Qatar Sash of Merit. *Television:* Discovery: Clash of the Generals 2004. *Publications:* Storm Command: a personal story of the Gulf War 1992, Looking for Trouble (autobiog.) 1994, Supreme Courage: Heroic Stories from 150 Years of the Victoria Cross 2004. *Leisure interests:* family, squash, apiculture, farming, sailing.

DE LA CROIX DE CASTRIES, Henri René Marie Augustin; French insurance business executive and fmr civil servant; *Chairman of the Management Board and CEO, AXA;* b. 15 Aug. 1954, Bayonne (Basses-Pyrénées); s. of François de La Croix de Castries and Gisèle de La Croix de Castries (née de Chevigné); m. Anne Millin de Grandmaison 1984; one s. two d.; ed Ecole Saint-Jean-de-Passy, Coll. Stanislas, Faculté de droit, Paris, Ecole nat. d'admin.; Deputy Insp., then Insp. of Finance 2nd class, Treasury 1984, Deputy Sec.-Gen. Interministerial Cttee on Industrial Restructuring 1984–85, Head Office of Capital Goods 1985–88, of Foreign Exchange and Balance of Payments 1988–89; Man. Finance Dept, AXA (insurance group) 1989–90, Sec.-Gen. 1991–93, Man. Dir 1993–2000, SEVP, mem. Exec. Cttee AXA 2000–, CEO 2000–; Chair. Bd of Dirs Equitable Cos (USA); mem. Bd Asscn pour l'Aide aux Jeunes Infirmes; Chevalier, Ordre nat. du Mérite 1996, Chevalier, Légion d'honneur 2001. *Address:* AXA, 25 avenue Matignon, 75008 Paris (office); 17 rue du Cherche-Midi, 75006 Paris (home); Château de Gastines, 49150 Fougères, France (home). *Telephone:* 1-40-75-57-00 (office). *Fax:* 1-40-75-46-96 (office). *E-mail:* henri.decastries@axa.com (office). *Website:* www.axa.com (office).

DE LA HOYA, Oscar; American boxer; b. 4 Feb. 1973, Los Angeles; s. of Joel De La Hoya and the late Cecilia De La Hoya; m. Millie Corretjer; fmr amateur boxer, 223 victories (163 knockouts), only 5 losses; turned professional after winning gold medal lightweight Barcelona Olympics 1992; Int. Boxing Fed. (IBF) lightweight title 1995; World Boxing Council (WBC) super lightweight title (over Julio César Chávez) 1996; WBC welterweight title (over Pernell Whitaker) 1997; lost WBC welterweight belt to Felix Trinidad in a majority decision in 1999; lost to Sugar Shane Mosley in 2000 in his 2nd career defeat; has won major titles in six weight divisions: 130, 135, 140, 147, 154 and 160 pounds; lost super welterweight title to Mosley 2003; won World Boxing Org. middleweight title June 2004 defeating Felix Sturm, lost it when defeated by Bernard Hopkins Sept. 2004; defeated WBC jr middleweight champion Ricardo Mayorga 2006, lost title to Floyd Mayweather, Jr. 2007; lost to Manny Pacquiao 2008; retd from boxing 2009; f. Oscar de la Hoya Foundation; Owner, Golden Boy Promotions LLC; WBC Boxer of the Decade 2001. *Album:* Oscar (topped Billboard's Latin Dance charts for several weeks). *Publication:* American Son (autobiography) 2008. *Address:* c/o Golden Boy Promotions, 626 Wilshire Blvd, Suite 350, Los Angeles, CA 90017, USA (office). *Telephone:* (213) 489-5631 (office). *Fax:* (213) 489-9048 (office). *E-mail:* info@goldenboyllc.com (office). *Website:* www.goldenboypromotions.com (office); www.oscardelahoya.com.

DE LA MADRID HURTADO, Miguel; Mexican politician and lawyer; b. 1934, Colima; m. Paloma C. de la Madrid; five c.; ed Harvard Univ., USA; successively with Bank of Mexico, Petróleos Mexicanos (PEMEX) (Asst Dir of Finances 1970–72); Dir Public Sector Credit, later Under-Sec., Ministry of Finance; Sec. for Planning and Fed. Budget, Govt of Mexico 1979–80; Institutional Revolutionary Party (PRI) cand. to succeed López Portillo as Pres. of Mexico Sept. 1981; Pres. of Mexico 1982–88; Pres. Nat. Asscn of Lawyers 1989–, Mexican Inst. of Culture 1989–; Dir-Gen. Fondo de Cultura Económica 1990–2000. *Publications:* Elementos de Derecho Constitucional, La Politica de la Renovación, El Ejercicio de las Facultades Presidenciales, Una Visión de America Latina. *Leisure interests:* music, reading, films, golf. *Address:* Parras 46, Barrio Sta Catarina, Deleg. Coyoacán, 04010 México, DF, Mexico. *Telephone:* (55) 5658-4459. *Fax:* (55) 5658-7979 (office).

DE LA NUEZ RAMÍREZ, Raúl; Cuban politician; *Minister of Foreign Trade;* fmr Vice-Minister, Basic Industry Ministry; Minister of Foreign Trade 2000–. *Address:* Ministry of Foreign Trade, Infanta 16, esquina 23, Vedado, Havana, Cuba (office). *Telephone:* (7) 55-0428 (office). *Fax:* (7) 55-0376 (office). *E-mail:* cepecdir@infocex.cu (office). *Website:* www.infocex.cu/cepec (office).

DE LA PEÑA, Javier, MS; Spanish petrochemical industry executive; b. 13 May 1940, Cortés, Navarra; s. of Juan-Jesús de la Peña and Julia de la Peña; m. Katherine Zegarra 1969; one s. three d.; ed Univ. of Valencia and Univ. of Kansas, USA; joined Phillips Petroleum Group 1965, Dept of Eng, Okla and Int. Dept, New York, USA 1965–67, Marketing, Phillips Calatrava Ventas, Madrid 1967–68, Man. in charge of Projects for Latin America, New York 1968–70, Marketing Man. Phillips Calatrava Ventas, Madrid 1970–72, Gen. Man. 1972–74, Devt Man. Phillips Petroleum Chemicals, Brussels 1975–77, Vice-Pres., Devt and Licensing 1978–82, Vice-Pres. and Man. Dir for Petrochemicals (Olefins and Aromatics) of Phillips Petroleum Chemicals 1982–85; Vice-Pres. REPSOL PETROLEO SA, in charge of Petrochemical Group; REPSOL Rep. in Asscn of European Petrochemical Producers 1985; Pres. REPSOL QUIMICA SA 1986; Fulbright Scholar 1963–64. *Leisure interests:* sports, piano and music.

DE LA QUADRA-SALCEDO Y FERNANDEZ DEL CASTILLO, Tomás, PhD; Spanish politician; b. 1946, Madrid; m.; two c.; ed Univ. Complutense of Madrid; Asst Lecturer in Admin. Law, Faculty of Law, Univ. Complutense of Madrid 1977–81 (Temporary Lecturer 1968), in Audiovisual Media, Information Sciences Faculty 1981–; mem. Lawyers' Asscn of Madrid 1968–; Minister of Territorial Admin. 1982–85, of Justice 1985–93; Pres. Council of State 1985. *Publications:* various articles and books. *Address:* c/o PSOE, Ferraz 68 y 70, 28008 Madrid, Spain. *Telephone:* (1) 582 0444. *Fax:* (1) 582 0422.

DE LA RENTA, Oscar; Dominican Republic fashion designer; b. 22 July 1932, Santo Domingo; m. 1st Françoise de Langlade 1967 (died 1983); one adopted s.; m. 2nd Anne E. de la Renta 1989; ed Santo Domingo Univ., Academia de San Fernando, Madrid; staff designer, under Cristobal Balenciaga, AISA couture house, Madrid; Asst to Antonio Castillo, Lanvin-Castillo, Paris 1961–63; designer, Elizabeth Arden couture and ready-to-wear collection, New York 1963–65; designer and partner, Jane Derby Inc. New York 1965; after her retirement firm evolved into Oscar de la Renta, Inc. which was purchased by Richton Int. 1969; Chief Exec. Richton's Oscar de la Renta Couture, Oscar de la Renta II, Oscar de la Renta Furs, Oscar de la Renta Jewelry and mem. Bd of Dirs Richton Int. 1969–73; f. Oscar de la Renta, Ltd 1973, CEO 1973–; couturier for Balmain, Paris Nov. 1993–; produces about 80 different product lines including high-fashion clothing, household linens, accessories and perfumes for shops in USA, Canada, Mexico and Japan; owner, Oscar de la Renta shop, Santo Domingo 1968–; recipient of numerous fashion awards; Caballero, Order of San Pablo Duarte, Order of Cristobal Colon. *Address:* Oscar de la Renta Ltd, 550 7th Avenue, 8th Floor, New York, NY 10018, USA.

DE LA RÚA, Fernando; Argentine politician; b. 15 Sept. 1937, Córdoba; s. of Antonio de la Rúa and Eleonora Bruno de la Rúa; m. Inés Pertiné; two s. one d.; ed Liceo General Paz, Córdoba, Universidad Nacional de Córdoba; joined Unión Cívica Radical (UCR) as a student; mem. staff Ministry of Interior 1963–66; cand. for Vice-Pres. 1973, Senator for Fed. Capital 1973–76, 1983–96; visiting lecturer univs in USA, Mexico and Venezuela during mil.

www.worldwhoswho.com

dictatorship; f. Centro de Estudios Para la República (now Fundación de estudios sobre temas políticos), Buenos Aires 1982; Mayor of Buenos Aires 1996–99; Leader ALIANZA coalition; Pres. of Argentina 1999–2001; Prof. of Criminal Law, Univ. of Buenos Aires; Founder mem. Consejo Argentino para las Relaciones Internacionales. *Leisure interests:* gardening, birds, nature, reading. *Address:* c/o Casa de Goberniero, Balcarce 50, 1064 Buenos Aires, Argentina (office).

DE LA TOUR, Frances; British actress; b. 30 July 1944, Bovingdon, Herts.; d. of Charles de la Tour and Moyra de la Tour (née Fessas); m. Tom Kempinski 1972 (divorced 1982); one s. one d.; ed Lycée français de Londres, Drama Centre, London; Hon. Fellow, Goldsmiths Coll., Univ. of London 1999. *Stage appearances include:* with RSC: As You Like It 1967, The Relapse 1969, A Midsummer Night's Dream 1971, The Man of Mode 1971, Antony and Cleopatra 1999; Small Craft Warnings (Best Supporting Actress, Plays and Players Award) 1973, The Banana Box 1973, As You Like It (Oxford Playhouse) 1974, The White Devil 1976, Hamlet (title role) 1979, Duet for One (Best Actress, New Standard Award, Best Actress, Critics Award, Best Actress, Soc. of West End Theatres—SWET Award) 1980, Skirmishes 1981, Uncle Vanya 1982, Moon for the Misbegotten (Best Actress, SWET Award) 1983, St Joan (Royal Nat. Theatre) 1984, Dance of Death (Riverside Studios) 1985, Brighton Beach Memoirs (Royal Nat. Theatre) 1986, Lillian 1986, Façades 1988, King Lear 1989, When She Danced (Olivier Award) 1991, The Pope and the Witch 1992, Greasepaint 1993, Les Parents Terribles (Royal Nat. Theatre) 1994, Three Tall Women 1994–95, Blinded by the Sun (Royal Nat. Theatre) 1996, The Play About the Baby (Almeida Theatre) 1998, The Forest (Royal Nat. Theatre) 1998–99, Fallen Angels (Apollo) (Best Actress, Royal Variety Club) 2000–01, The Good Hope and Sketches by Harold Pinter (Royal Nat. Theatre) 2001–02, Dance of Death (Lyric) 2003, The History Boys (Nat. Theatre) 2004–05, (Broadway) (Tony Award for Best Supporting Actress) 2006. *Films include:* Rising Damp (Best Actress, Standard Film Award) 1980, The Cherry Orchard 1998, Love Actually 2002, Harry Potter and the Goblet of Fire 2005, The History Boys 2006, Nutcracker: The Untold Story 2009. *Television appearances include:* Rising Damp 1974, 1976, Flickers 1980, Skirmishes 1982, Duet for One 1985, Clem 1986, A Kind of Living (series) 1987–88, Cold Lazarus 1996, Tom Jones 1997, The Egg 2002, Waking the Dead 2004, Poirot: Death on the Nile 2004, Sensitive Skin 2005, Agatha Christie: The Moving Finger 2005. *Address:* c/o Claire Maroussas, ICM, Oxford House, 76 Oxford Street, London, W1N 0AX, England (office). *Telephone:* (20) 7636-6565 (office). *Fax:* (20) 7323-0101 (office).

DE LADOUCETTE, Philippe, MA, DScS, DrSc (Econ); French company executive and fmr government official; *Chief Executive Officer, Charbonnages de France;* b. 15 March 1948, Paris; s. of Charles de Ladoucette; ed Ecole Nationale des Ponts et Chaussées; fmr civil engineer with Ministry of Equipment (responsible for state contracts with medium-sized towns) 1974–77; Commr for Industrialization, Ardennes 1977–83; responsible for industrial devt, DATAR 1983–86; tech. adviser, Ministry of Industry, Posts and Telecommunications and Tourism 1986–88; responsible for industrial matters, Secr.-Gen. of Channel Tunnel 1988–93; Asst Dir Office of Minister of Enterprise and Econ. Devt 1993–94; Chair. Houillères du Bassin du Centre et du Midi 1994–; CEO SNET 1996–2000; CEO Charbonnages de France 1996–; Chevalier, Légion d'honneur, Officier Ordre Nat. du Mérite. *Leisure interests:* swimming, jogging, cycling. *Address:* Charbonnages de France, 100 avenue Albert 1er, BP 220, 92503 Rueil-Malmaison Cedex (office); 40 avenue Marceau, 75008 Paris, France (home). *Telephone:* 1-47-52-37-00 (office). *Fax:* 1-47-51-31-33 (office). *E-mail:* philippe.deladoucette@charbonnagesdefrance.fr (office); www.charbonnagesdefrance.fr (office).

DE LARROCHA, Alicia; Spanish pianist; b. 23 May 1923, Barcelona; d. of Eduardo de Larrocha and Teresa de Larrocha (née de la Calle); m. Juan Torra 1950; one s. one d.; ed studied with Frank Marshall in Barcelona; first public recital, Barcelona 1928; debut with Madrid Symphony Orchestra under Fernández Arbós, Madrid 1935; British debut Wigmore Hall 1953; US debut with the Los Angeles Philharmonic 1955; formed duo with cellist, Gaspar Cassado 1956; solo recitals and concerts with major orchestras in Europe, USA, Canada, Central and South America, South Africa, New Zealand, Australia and Japan; Dir Academia Marshall, Barcelona 1959–; mem. bd dirs Musica en Compostela 1968; corresp. mem. Hispanic Soc. of America, New York 1972; Hon. Pres. Int. Piano Archives, New York 1969; Orders of Civil Merit 1962, Isabel la Católica 1972; Academia Marshall Gold Medal 1943, Harriet Cohen Int. Music Award 1956, Grand Prix du Disque Acad. Charles Cros, Paris 1960, 1974, 1991, Paderewski Memorial Medal 1961, Edison Awards, Amsterdam 1968, 1978, First Gold Medal, Mérito a la Vocación 1973, Musician of the Year (Musical America Magazine) 1978, Deutsche Schallplatten Prize 1979, Gold Medal, Spanish Int. (USA) 1980, Medalla d'Oro, Barcelona 1982, Príncipe de Asturias Prize 1994. *Recordings include:* Albeniz Iberia (Grammy Award) 1974, (Grammy Award) 1989, Ravel Concertos (Grammy Award) 1975, Granados Goyescas (Grammy Award) 1991, Mozart Piano Sonatas, Mozart Piano Concerto No. 22, Mozart Piano Concertos Nos 23 and 24, Mozart Concerto for Two Pianos, Schumann Piano Concerto and Piano Quinter, Beethoven Piano Concertos Nos 1–5, Serenata Andalu/Works by Montsalvage and Falla, Khachaturian Piano Concerto, Musica Para Piano I–IV/Works by Granado, Soler, Albeniz, Falla, Mompou, Turina, Montsalvatge, Halffter and Surinach. *Address:* c/o Christa Phelps, Merchant House, 174 Sutherland Avenue, Little Venice, London, W9 1HR, England (office). *Telephone:* (20) 7286-7134 (office). *Fax:* (20) 7286-8499 (office). *E-mail:* info@christaphelps.com (office). *Website:* www.christaphelps.com (office).

DE LAURENTIIS, Dino; Italian film producer; b. (Agostine De Laurentiis), 8 Aug. 1919, Torre Annunziata, Naples; s. of Aurelio De Laurentiis and Giuseppina De Laurentiis (née Salvatore); m. 1st Silvana Mangano 1949; one s. (deceased) three d.; m. 2nd Martha Schumacher; two d.; f. Real Ciné, Turin 1941; Exec. Producer Lux Film 1942; acquired Safir Studios and f. Teatri della Farnesina 1948; Co-founder Ponti-De Laurentiis SpA 1950; Prin. De Laurentiis Entertainment Group Inc. 1986–88, Prin. and Founder Dino De Laurentiis Co. 1988–95, now consultant to co.; Cavaliere del Lavoro; numerous awards and prizes, including Irving Thalberg Memorial Award 2001, Venice Golden Lion Hon. Award 2003. *Films produced include:* Il Bandito 1946, La Figlia del Capitano 1947, Molti Sogni per la Strada 1948, Riso amaro (Bitter Rice) 1949, Anna 1951, Europa '51 (Venice Silver Lion 1952) 1952, La tratta delle bianche (Girls Marked For Danger) 1953, La strada (Acad. Award 1957, Silver Ribbon, Italian Film Critics 1957, Venice Golden Lion 1957) 1954, L'oro di Napoli (The Gold of Naples) 1954, Ulisse (Ulysses) 1955, Le notti di Cabiria (Acad. Award 1958, Golden David Award 1958, Cannes Palme d'Or 1958) 1957, War and Peace (Golden Globe Award 1956) 1956, La tempesta (The Tempest) (Golden David Award 1959) 1958, This Angry Age 1958, La grande guerra (The Great War) (Golden David Award 1960, Venice Golden Lion 1960) 1959, Tutti a casa (Everybody Go Home) (Golden David Award 1961) 1960, Io amo, tu ami (I Love, You Love) 1960, Una vita difficile (A Difficult Life 1962) 1961, The Best of Enemies (exec. producer) 1962, Barabbas 1962, Il Diavolo (The Devil, aka To Bed… Or Not to Bed) 1963, Best of Enemies (Golden Globe Award 1963), The Bible (Golden David Award 1966) 1966, I tre volti (Three Faces of a Woman) 1965, Banditi a Milano (Bandits in Milan) (Golden David Award 1968) 1968, Barbarella 1968, A Man Called Sledge 1970, Waterloo 1970, Io non vedo, tu non parli, lui non sente 1971, La spina dorsale del diavolo (The Devil's Backbone) 1971, The Valachi Papers 1972, Causa di divorzio (Cause of Divorce) 1972, Boccaccio 1972, Lo Scopone scientifico (The Scopone Game) 1972, Valdez, il mezzosangue (Valdez the Halfbreed) (uncredited) 1973, Serpico (exec. producer) 1973, Porgi l'altra guancia (Turn the Other Cheek) 1974, Neveroyatnye priklyucheniya italyantsev v Rossii (Unbelievable Adventures of Italians In Russia) 1974, Crazy Joe 1974, Uomini duri (Tough Guys) 1974, Death Wish 1974, Mandingo 1975, Three Days of the Condor 1975, Drum 1976, King Kong 1976, Lipstick 1976, The White Buffalo (exec. producer) 1977, Orca (exec. producer) 1977, The Shootist 1976, The Serpent's Egg 1977, King of the Gypsies (exec. producer) 1978, The Brink's Job (exec. producer) 1978, The Great Train Robbery 1978, Hurricane 1979, Flash Gordon 1980, Ragtime 1981, Conan the Barbarian (exec. producer, uncredited) 1982, Amityville II: The Possession 1982, The Dead Zone (exec. producer, uncredited) 1983, Firestarter 1984, The Bounty (exec. producer) 1984, Conan the Destroyer (exec. producer) 1984, Dune (exec. producer) 1984, Cat's Eye 1985, Year of the Dragon 1985, Silver Bullet 1985, Maximum Overdrive (exec. producer) 1986, Manhunter (aka Red Dragon: The Pursuit of Hannibal Lecter) 1986, Tai-Pan (exec. producer) 1986, Blue Velvet 1986, Trick or Treat 1986, King Kong Lives (exec. producer) 1986, Crimes of the Heart 1986, Weeds 1987, Dracula's Widow 1987, Adult Education 1987, The Desperate Hours 1990, Kuffs, Once Upon a Crime 1992, Army of Darkness (exec. producer) 1993, Body of Evidence 1993, Assassins (exec. producer) 1995, Unforgettable 1996, Bound, Breakdown 1997, U-571 2000, Hannibal 2001, Red Dragon 2002, Decameron: Angels and Virgins 2006. *Television:* Sometimes They Come Back (exec. producer) 1991, Slave of Dreams 1995, Solomon and Sheba 1995. *Address:* Dino de Laurentiis Company, 100 Universal City Plaza, Universal City, CA 91608, USA (office). *Telephone:* (818) 777-2111 (office). *Fax:* (818) 866-5566 (office). *Website:* www.dinodelaurentiis.it (office).

DE LIMA NETO, Antônio Francisco, BEcons, MBA; Brazilian banker; *President and CEO, Banco do Brasil SA;* b. 13 June 1965; ed Univ. Fed. de Pernambuco; joined Banco do Brasil SA as apprentice 1979, becoming Dir of Int. and Wholesale Business 2004–05, Man. Dir BB Leasing SA and BB Securities, Vice-Pres., Retail Div. 2006–07, Pres. 2007–, Interim CEO 2006–07, CEO 2007–, also Counsellor, BB Securities Ltd; Regional Dir Associação Brasileira das Empresas de Leasing; Embassy of Brazil and Brazilian Chamber of Commerce in GB Personality of the Year 2007. *Address:* Banco do Brasil SA, SBS Edifício, Sede III, 24° Andar, 70073-901 Brasília DF, Brazil (office). *Telephone:* (61) 3310-3400 (office); (61) 3310-5920 (office). *Fax:* (61) 3310-3735 (office). *E-mail:* presidencia@bb.com.br (office). *Website:* www.bb.com.br (office).

DE LUCCHI, Michele; Italian designer; b. 8 Nov. 1951, Ferrara; s. of Alberto De Lucchi and Giuliana Zannini; ed Liceo Scientifico Enrico Fermi, Padua, Faculty of Architecture, Univ. of Florence; founder mem., Cavart (avant-garde design and architecture group) 1973–76; Asst Prof., Univ. of Florence 1976–77; worked with Gaetano Pesce, Superstudio, Andrea Branzi, Ettore Sottsass 1977–80; Consultant, Centrokappa Noviglio, Milan 1978; Consultant, Olivetti Synthesis, Massa 1979–, Olivetti SpA, Ivrea 1984–; freelance designer, several furniture mfrs 1979–; founder mem., Int. Designer Group Memphis 1981. *Publication:* Architetture Verticali 1978. *Leisure interest:* travel photography. *Address:* 31 via Giorgio Pallavicino, 20154 Milan, Italy (office). *Telephone:* (02) 430081 (office). *Fax:* (02) 43008222 (office).

DE LUCÍA, Paco; Spanish musician (flamenco guitar) and composer; b. (Francisco Sánchez Gómez), 21 Dec. 1947, Algeciras; debut on Radio Algeciras 1958; mem., Paco de Lucía Sextet (with brothers, including flamenco guitarist Ramón de Algeciras and vocalist Pepe de Lucía); accompanied many flamenco singers in the 1960s before long-term association with Camaron de le Isla 1968–; worked with dancer José Greco and flamenco troupe Festival Flamenco Gitano; live debut at Carnegie Hall 1970; experimented with mixing musical elements in the 1970s, laying the foundations of Nuevo Flamenco; collaborations with jazz musicians, including Chick Corea, John McLaughlin, Larry Coryell, Al DiMeola; also performs Spanish classical guitar repertoire; Jerez Flamenco Competition Special Prize 1958. *Compositions for film:* La Nueva Costa del Sol 1976, Deprisa, deprisa 1981, La Sabina 1981, Carmen 1983, The Hit 1984. *Recordings include:* albums: Los Chiquitos De Algeciras 1961, Dos

Guitarras Flamencas (with Ricardo Mondrego) 1965, 12 Canciones de García Lorca Para Guitarra (with Ricardo Mondrego) 1965, Dos Guitarras Flamencas En América Latina (with Ramón de Algeciras) 1967, La Fabulosa Guitarra de Paco de Lucía 1967, Hispanoamerica 1969, Fantasia Flamenca 1969, Recital De Guitarra 1971, El Duende Flamenco 1972, En Vivo – Desde El Teatro Real 1975, Fuente Y Caudel 1975, Almoraima 1976, Interpreta A Manuel De Falla 1978, Castro Marin 1981, Friday Night In San Francisco (with John McLaughlin and Al DiMeola) 1981, Solo Quiero Caminar 1981, Passion Grace And Fire (with Al DiMeola and John McLaughlin) 1983, Live... One Summer Night 1984, Entre Dos Aguas 1986, Siroco 1987, Zyryab 1990, Concierto De Aranjuez 1991, Antología Del Cante Flamenco 1991, Live in America 1993, Guitar Trio (with Al DiMeola and John McLaughlin) 1996, Luzia 1998, Alcazar De Sevilla 1998, Flamenco Romántico 2000, España En Una Guitarra 2000, Guitarra Flamenca 2002, Guitar And Song 2002, Cositas Buenas (Billboard Latin Music Award for Best Latin Jazz Album 2005) 2004. *E-mail:* juan@pacodelucia.org (office). *Website:* www.pacodelucia.org.

DE MADARIAGA, Isabel, PhD, FBA, FRHistS; British historian, academic and writer; *Professor Emerita of Russian Studies, School of Slavonic and East European Studies, University of London;* b. 27 Aug. 1919, Glasgow, Scotland; d. of Salvador de Madariaga and Constance Archibald; m. Leonard B. Schapiro 1943 (divorced 1976); ed Ecole Internationale, Geneva, Switzerland, Headington School for Girls, Oxford, Instituto Escuela, Madrid, Univ. of London; with BBC Monitoring Service 1940–43; with Cen. Office of Information London 1943–47, Econ. Information Unit, Treasury 1947–48; Editorial Asst, Slavonic and East European Review 1951–64; Part-time Lecturer in History, LSE 1953–66; Lecturer in History, Univ. of Sussex 1966–68; Sr Lecturer in Russian History, Univ. of Lancaster 1968–71; Reader in Russian Studies, School of Slavonic and East European Studies, Univ. of London 1971–81, Prof. 1981–84, Prof. Emer. 1984–; Corresp. mem. Royal Spanish Acad. of History. *Publications:* Britain, Russia and the Armed Neutrality of 1780 1963, Opposition (with G. Ionescu) 1965, Russia in the Age of Catherine the Great 1981, Catherine II: A Short History 1990, Politics and Culture in Eighteenth-Century Russia 1998, Ivan the Terrible 2005; books translated into many languages including Turkish and Russian; many scholarly articles. *Leisure interest:* music. *Address:* 25 Southwood Lawn Road, London, N6 5SD, England (home). *Telephone:* (20) 8341-0862 (home).

DE MAIZIÈRE, Lothar; German politician and lawyer; b. 2 March 1940, Nordhausen; m.; three d.; mem. Christian Democratic Union, Leader 1989–90; Deputy Prime Minister and Spokesman on Church Affairs 1989–90; Prime Minister German Democratic Republic and Minister of Foreign Affairs March–Oct. 1990; Minister without Portfolio 1990–91, Deputy Chair. CDU, Chair Brandenburg CDU Oct.-Dec. 1990, 1991; leader Lutheran Church Council; resgnd as CDU deputy 1991. *Publication:* Anwalt der Einheit 1996. *Address:* Am Kupfergraben 6/6A, 10117 Berlin, Germany.

DE MAIZIÈRE, Gen. Ulrich; German army officer (retd); b. 24 Feb. 1912, Stade; s. of Walther de Maizière and Elisabeth Dückers; m. Eva Werner 1944 (died 2003); two s. two d.; ed Humanistisches Gymnasium, Hanover; army service 1930, commissioned 1933; Bn and Regimental Adjutant, 50th Infantry Regt; Gen. Staff Coll., Dresden 1940; during World War II, Gen. Staff Duties with 18th Motorized Infantry Div., G3 and Chief of Staff of 10th Mechanized Div., wounded 1944, at end of war Deputy Chief of Operations Div., Army Gen. Staff; POW 1945–47; dealer in books and sheet music 1947–51; Office of Fed. Commr for Nat. Security Affairs 1951; Col and Chief of Operations Br., Fed. Armed Forces Staff 1955; Commdr of Combat Team A1 and Commdr 2nd Brigade 1958; Deputy Commdr 1st Armoured Infantry Div. 1959; Commdt Fed. Armed Forces School for Leadership and Character Guidance 1960–62, Fed. Armed Forces Command and Staff Coll. 1962–64; Chief of Army Staff 1964–66; Chief of Fed. Armed Forces Staff 1966–72; Hon. Pres. Clausewitz Gesellschaft; Commdr Legion of Merit 1965, 1969, Grand Officier, Légion d'honneur 1969, two Iron Crosses (Second Class) 1939 and (First Class) 1944, Grosses Bundesverdienstkreuz mit Stern und Schulterband 1970; Freiherr-von-Stein-Preis 1964, Hermann-Ehlers-Preis 1986. *Publications:* Die Landesverteidigung im Rahmen der Gesamtverteidigung 1964, Soldatische Führung heute 1966, Bekenntnis zum Soldaten 1971, Führen im Frieden 1974, Verteidigung in Europa – Mitte 1975, In der Pflicht (autobiog.) 1989. *Leisure interests:* classical music, literature, contemporary history. *Address:* Tulpenbaumweg 20, 53177 Bonn, Germany (home). *Telephone:* (228) 9524459 (home). *Fax:* (228) 9524459 (home).

DE MARCO, Guido, KUOM, BA, LLD; Maltese fmr head of state; b. 22 July 1931, Valletta; s. of Emmanuele de Marco and Giovanna Raniolo; m. Violet Saliba; one s. two d.; ed St Aloysius Coll. and Royal Univ. of Malta; Crown Counsel 1964–66; MP (Nationalist Party) 1966–99; Deputy Prime Minister 1987–96, Minister for Internal Affairs and Justice 1987–91, of Foreign Affairs 1991–96, 1998–99; Shadow Minister and Opposition Spokesman on Foreign Affairs 1996–98; Pres. of Malta 1999–2004; Pres. Gen. Ass. of UN 1990–91; Lecturer, later Prof. of Criminal Law, Univ. of Malta 1967–; Medal Order of Diplomatic Service Merit 1991, Grand Cross Order of Merit (Portugal) 1994, Chevalier Grand Cross Order of Merit (Italy) 1995, Hon. mem. Most Distinguished Order of St Michael and St George 2000, Collare dell'Ordine al Merito Melitense, Order Stara Planina with Ribbon (Bulgaria) 2001, Collar Estoniani Order of the Cross of Terra Mariana 2001, Grand Cross Special Class Order of Merit (FRG) 2001. *Publications:* A Presidency With a Purpose 1991, A Second Generation United Nations 1995, Malta's Foreign Policy in the Nineties 1996, Momentum I 2002, Momentum II 2004. *Leisure interests:* reading and travel. *Address:* c/o Office of the President, The Palace, Valletta CMR 02, Malta (office). *Telephone:* 21221221 (office). *Fax:* 21241241 (office).

DE MARGERIE, Christophe Gabriel Jean Marie Jacquin; French oil industry executive; *CEO, Total Group;* b. 6 Aug. 1951, Mareuil-sur-Lay-Dissais (Vendée); s. of Pierre Rodocanachi and Colette Taittinger (remarried to Pierre-Alain Jacquin de Margerie); m. Bernadette Prud'homme; one s. two d.; ed Ecole Supérieure de Commerce, Paris; began career with Total Trading (later Totalfina, then TotalFinaElf, then Total Group) in 1974 in Finance Div., responsible for Budget and Exploration-Production Depts, Group Treas. 1987–90, roles in Middle East Div. including Financial Dir, Asst Dir, Asst Dir-Gen. 1990–95, Dir-Gen. 1995–99, mem. Group Man. Cttee 1995–99, Exec. Cttee 1999–, Dir-Gen. Exploration-Production Div. 1999–2007, CEO 2007–. *Address:* Total Group, 2 place de la Coupole, La Défense 6, 92400 Courbevoie, France (office). *Telephone:* 1-47-44-46-99 (office). *Fax:* 1-47-44-68-21 (office). *Website:* www.total.com (office).

DE MARIA, Walter, MFA; American artist; b. 1 Oct. 1935, Albany, Calif.; ed Univ. of Calif., Berkeley; participated in Happenings and theatrical productions in San Francisco area 1959–60; moved to NY, made first wooden box sculptures 1961; co-f. 9 Great Jones Street Gallery, NY 1963, presented first solo exhbn of sculpture 1963; drummer for rock group The Velvet Underground 1963; began 'invisible drawings' and composed music 1964; began making pieces from metal 1965; solo show at Cordier & Ekstrom, NY 1966; participated in Primary Structures, Jewish Museum, NY 1966; became leader of Earthworks Movt upon filling Galerie Heiner Friedrich with dirt, Munich, Germany 1968; created The Mile Long Drawing in the Desert in the Mojave Desert 1968; participated in Documenta, Kassel 1968; sculpture exhbn, Kunstmuseum Basel, Switzerland 1972; completed Three Continent Project 1972, Lightening Field, New Mexico 1977; recreated Earth Room, Heiner Friedrich Gallery, NY; Mather Sculpture Prize of Art Inst. of Chicago 1976, Baden-Württemberg Int. Fine Art Prize 1987. *Public Collections include:* Museum für Moderne Kunst (MKK), Frankfurt am Main (Germany), Museum für Gegenwartskunst, Basel (Switzerland), Dia Art Foundation, Chelsea, NY, Solomon R. Guggenheim Museum, NY, Gagosian Galleries in London, UK and USA. *Public Exhibitions include:* Walter de Maria – The 2000 Sculpture, Kunsthaus Zürich (Switzerland) 1999, Fernsehgalerie Gerry Schum, Kunsthalle Düsseldorf (Germany) 2003. *Publications:* essays on art, chapters in books. *Address:* c/o Gagosian Gallery, 980 Madison Avenue, New York, NY 10021, USA (office).

DE MARIA Y CAMPOS, Mauricio, MA; Mexican diplomatist and economist; b. 13 Oct. 1943, Mexico DF; s. of Mauricio de María y Campos and Teresa Castello; m. Patricia Meade 1981; two s. one d.; ed Nat. Univ. of Mexico, Univ. of Sussex, UK; Head Planning and Policy Unit Mexican Nat. Science and Tech. Council 1971–72; Deputy Dir Evaluation Dept Tech. Transfer Ministry of Trade and Industry 1973–74, Dir Gen. Foreign Investment 1974–77, Vice-Minister Industrial Devt 1982–89; Dir Gen. Tax Incentives and Fiscal Promotion Ministry of Finance 1977–82; Exec. Vice-Pres. Banco Mexicano SOMEX 1989–92; Deputy Dir Gen. UNIDO 1992–93, Dir Gen. 1993–97; Amb. at Large and Special Adviser on UN Affairs, Ministry of Foreign Affairs 1998–2001; Amb. to Southern Africa 2002–07; mem. Int. Club of Rome 1998– (Pres. of Mexican Chapter 1998–); Grand Commendateur Ordre nat. du Mérite, Order of Francisco de Miranda (Venezuela); Great Decoration in Gold on the Sash (Austria); Grand Ordre du Mono (Togo). *Publications:* Challenges and Opportunities for Scientific and Technological Collaboration between the EEC and Mexico 1990, The Transformation of the Mexican Automobile Industry during the 1980s 1992; various publs on industrial and technological policy and on regional devt. *Leisure interests:* classical music, writing, reading, swimming, jogging, dancing, journalism. *Address:* c/o Secretariat of State for Foreign Affairs, Avenida Ricardo Flores Magón 2, Col. Guerrero, Del. Cuauhtémoc, 06995 México, DF, México.

DE MELLO BRANDÃO, Lázaro; Brazilian economist and banking executive; *Chairman, Banco Bradesco SA;* b. 15 June 1926; joined Casa Bancária Almeida & Cie (renamed Banco Brasileiro de Descontos SA, then Banco Bradesco SA) 1942, various positions including Exec. Officer 1963–77, Deputy CEO 1977–81, Pres. 1981–99, Deputy Chair. Bd Dirs 1982–1990, Chair. 1990–; Chair. Bd Dirs Companhia Brasileira de Securitação (CIBRASEC) 1997–99, Bradespar 2004; mem. Bd Dirs Banco Espírito Santo SA, Lisbon, Portugal, Nat. Housing Bank 1984–85; Pres. Credit Guarantor Fund (FGC) 1999–2001; Exec. Officer Banking Asscn of States of São Paulo, Paraná, Mato Grosso and Mato Grosso do Sul 1966–74, CEO 1974–83; Vice-Pres. Bd of Exec. Officers, Nat. Fed. of Banks (FENABAN) 1971–76, 1980–83; mem. Bd Fed. of Brazilian Banking Asscns (FEBRABAN) 1983–91, 1994–2001; Hon. Citizen of Joinville. *Address:* Banco Bradesco SA, Avenida Ipiranga 282, 10 andar, CEP 01046-920 São Paulo, Brazil (office). *Telephone:* (11) 3235-9566 (office). *Fax:* (11) 3235-9161 (office). *Website:* www.bradesco.com.br (office).

DE MEURON, Pierre, DipArch; Swiss architect; b. 1950, Basel; ed Swiss Fed. Tech. Univ. (ETH), Zurich; Asst to Prof. Dolf Schnebli, ETH, Zurich 1977; f. architectural practice Herzog & De Meuron (with Jacques Herzog q.v.) 1978; Prof. of Architecture and Design, ETH 1999–; Visiting Prof. Harvard Univ., Cambridge, Mass. 1989, Tulane Univ., New Orleans 1991; (all jtly with Jacques Herzog) Architecture Prize, Berlin Acad. of Arts 1987, Andrea Palladio Int. Prize for Architecture, Vicenza, Italy 1988, Pritzker Architecture Prize 2001, RIBA Gold Medal (for work on Tate Modern) 2007. *Principal works include:* Blue House, Oberwil 1979–80, Photostudio Frei, Weil am Rhein 1981–82, Sperrholz Haus, Bottmingen 1984–85, Apartment Bldg, Hebelstr. 11, Basel 1984–88, Wohn- und Geschäftshaus Schwitter, Basel 1985–98, Goetz Art Gallery, Munich 1989–92, Wohn- und Geschäftshaus Schützenmattstr., Basel 1992–93, Dominus Winery, Napa Valley, Yountville, Calif. 1995–97, Tate Gallery Extension (Tate Modern), Bankside, London 1995–99, Cultural Centre and Theatre, Zurich 1996, Ricola Marketing Bldg, Laufen 1998, Laban Centre for Contemporary Dance (Stirling Prize) 2003. *Works in progress include:* Prada Headquarters, NY, De Young Museum, San Francisco, Walker Art Center Extension, Minneapolis; projects in England,

France, Germany, Italy, Spain and Japan. *Address:* Herzog & De Meuron Architekten, Rheinschanze 6, Basel, 4056, Switzerland (office). *Telephone:* (61) 3855758 (office). *Fax:* (61) 3855757 (office). *E-mail:* hdemarch@access.ch (office).

DE MEYER, Jan Carl Hendrika Oswald, DJur; Belgian judge; b. 21 Feb. 1921, Malines; s. of Oswald De Meyer and Anna Maria Gysbrechts; m. Rita Smets 1949 (died 1986); one s. four d.; ed St Rombout's Coll. Malines, Faculté St Louis, Brussels and Univ. of Louvain; mem. Bar at Malines 1944–48, 1952–86; Substitute Auditor, Council of State 1948–49, mem. Coordination Office 1949–52, Assessor 1962–80; Lecturer, Univ. of Louvain 1951–56, Ordinary Prof. 1956–86, Prof. Emer. 1986–, Head, Dept of Political and Social Sciences 1964–67, Dean, School of Law 1971–74; mem. Belgian Senate 1980–81; Judge, European Court of Human Rights 1986–98. *Address:* Kerselarenweg 1, 3020 Herent; Faculteit Rechtsgeleerdheid, Tiensestraat 41, 3000 Louvain, Belgium. *Telephone:* (32) 16226384.

DE MICHELIS, Gianni; Italian politician and professor of chemistry; b. 26 Nov. 1940, Venice; Prof. of Chem., Univ. of Padua; Lecturer in Chem., Univ. of Venice; Nat. Chair. Unione Goliardica Italiana 1962–64; Councillor, Venice 1964–76; mem. Cen. Cttee Italian Socialist Party (PSI) 1969–76, mem. Nat. Exec. 1976–; mem. Parl. for Venice 1976–; fmr Minister for State-owned Industries; Minister of Labour and Social Security 1986–87; Deputy Prime Minister 1988–89; Minister of Foreign Affairs 1989–92; Deputy Leader PSI 1992; charged with fraud May 1995; sentenced to 4 years' imprisonment for corruption July 1995; on trial for siphoning cash from Third World projects 1996. *Address:* c/o Socialisti Italiani, Via del Corso 476, 00186 Rome, Italy.

DE MIRANDA, João Bernardo; Angolan politician; b. 18 July 1951; m.; Dir of Information, Rádio Nacional de Angola 1977–80; Ed.-in-Chief Jornal de Angola newspaper 1980–84; Sec. Movimento Popular de Libertação de Angola (MPLA) Ideological Area (Prov. of Luanda); Head of Political and Legal Affairs Div., MPLA Cen. Cttee 1985–89, Head of Information and Propaganda Dept 1989–91; Vice-Minister of Information 1991; Vice-Minister of Foreign Relations 1991–99, Minister of Foreign Affairs 1999–2008. *Publications include:* Nambuangongo. *Address:* Movimento Popular de Libertação de Angola (MPLA), Luanda, Angola (office). *E-mail:* mpla@ebonet.net (office). *Website:* www2.ebonet.net/MPLA (office).

DE MISTURA, Stefan; Swedish UN official; *Special Representative of the Secretary-General for Iraq, United Nations;* b. 1947, Stockholm; m.; two d.; ed Univ. of Rome; joined UN 1970; Deputy Chef de Cabinet, FAO 1976–85; Dir WFP Operations in Sudan 1987; Dir of Fund-Raising and External Relations, UN Office of the Co-ordinator for Afghanistan 1988–91; Special Envoy of UN Sec.-Gen. to Albania 1990; UN Humanitarian Co-ordinator for Iraq 1997; Dir UN Information Centre, Rome –2000; Personal Rep. of UN Sec.-Gen. in South Lebanon 2001–05; Deputy Special Rep. of UN Sec.-Gen. in Iraq 2005–06, Special Rep. 2007–; Dir UN Systems Staff Coll., Turin, Italy 2006–07. *Address:* United Nations Assistance Mission for Iraq (UNAMI), c/o Office of the Secretary-General, United Nations, New York, NY 10017, USA (office). *Telephone:* (212) 963-1234 (office). *Fax:* (212) 963-4879 (office). *Website:* www.uniraq.org (office).

DE MITA, Luigi Ciriaco; Italian politician; b. 2 Feb. 1928, Fusco, Avellino; fmr mem. Catholic Action; mem. Chamber of Deputies for Benevento-Avellino-Salerno 1963, 1972–; Nat. Counsellor Partito Democrazia Cristiana (Christian Democrats) (DC) 1964, later Political Vice-Sec.; Under-Sec. for the Interior; Minister of Industry and Commerce 1973–74, of Foreign Trade 1974–76; Minister without Portfolio with responsibility for the Mezzogiorno 1976–79; Sec.-Gen. DC 1982–88, Pres. 1989, 1991–92; Prime Minister of Italy 1988–89; Head Parl. Comm. for Constitutional Reform –1993. *Address:* c/o Partito Democrazia Cristiana, Piazza del Gesù 46, 00186 Rome, Italy.

DE MOLINA, Alvaro G., BA, MBA; Cuban/American business executive; *CEO, GMAC Financial Services;* b. 13 July 1957, Cuba; ed Fairleigh Dickinson Univ., Rutgers Business School; began career with PriceWaterhouse 1979; later served in lead financial role for emerging markets at J.P. Morgan; spent 17 years at Bank of America, served as Chief Financial Officer, also served as CEO Bank of America Securities, Pres. Global Corp. and Investment Banking, and Corp. Treas.; with Cerberus Capital Management June–Aug. 2007; COO GMAC Financial Services Aug. 2007–08, CEO 2008–; mem. Bd Duke Univ. Fuqua School of Business, Foundation for the Carolinas, Florida International Univ., Financial Services Volunteer Corps. *Address:* GMAC Financial Services, 200 Renaissance Center, Detroit, MI 48265-2000, USA (office). *Telephone:* (313) 556-5000 (office). *Fax:* (815) 282-6156 (office). *E-mail:* info@gmacfs.com (office). *Website:* www.gmacfs.com (office).

DE MONTEBELLO, Comte Philippe, BA; French art historian and museum director; b. 16 May 1936, Paris; m. Edith Bradford Myles 1961; ed Harvard Univ., Inst. of Fine Arts, New York Univ., USA; Curatorial Asst, later Asst Curator, Assoc. Curator, Dept of European Paintings, Metropolitan Museum of Art, New York 1963–69, Vice-Dir for Curatorial and Educational Affairs 1974–77, Acting Dir 1977–78, Dir. 1978–99, Dir and CEO 1999–2008 (retd); Dir Museum of Fine Arts, Houston, Tex. 1969–74; Gallatin Fellow, New York Univ. 1981; Kt Commdr, Pontifical Order of St Gregory the Great 1984, Commendatore, Order of Merit (Italy) 1988, Orden de Isabel la Catolica (Spain) 1992, Officier de l'Ordre de Léopold (Belgium) 1994, Commdr de l'Ordre des Arts et Lettres 2001, Officier, Légion d'honneur 2005; Hon. LLD (Lafayette Coll.) 1979, (Dartmouth Coll.) 2004, Hon. DHumLitt (Bard Coll., New York) 1981, Hon. DFA (Iona Coll., New Rochelle) 1982, (Harvard) 2006, (New York) 2007; Nat. Inst. of Social Sciences Gold Medal 1989, Spanish Inst. Gold Medal Award 1992, National Council of Jewish Women, Rebekah Kohut Award 1993, Distinguished Alumnus Award, New York Univ. 1998, Mayoral Proclamation 2002, Celebration of twenty-five years as Dir of the Metropolitan Museum of Art, Nat. Endowment for the Arts, Nat. Medal of Arts 2003, Amigos del Museo del Prado Prize 2004, Conféd. Int. des Négociants en Oeuvres d'Art Prize 2005, and other awards. *Publications:* Peter Paul Rubens (monograph) 1968, articles in the Metropolitan Museum of Art Bulletin and the Bulletin, Museum of Fine Arts, Houston on topics from the Renaissance to the contemporary, more than 200 entries in the McGraw Hill Dictionary of Art 1967, including those on Velasquez, Murillo and Goya; The High Cost of Quality Museum News August 1984, The Met and the New Millennium: A Chronicle of the Past and a Blueprint for the Future 1994, introductions to numerous exhibition catalogues published by the Metropolitan Museum of Art. *Leisure interests:* chess, tennis, music. *Address:* 25 East 86th Street, 3E, New York, NY 10028, USA (home). *Telephone:* (212) 289-4475 (home).

DE MORAES, Antônio Ermírio; Brazilian business executive; *President, Grupo Votorantim;* b. 4 June 1928, São Paulo; s. of José Ermírio de Moraes; m. Maria Regina de Moraes; nine c.; ed Univ. of Colorado, USA; joined Grupo Votorantim 1949, Pres. Admin. Council 1962–; f. Companhia Brasileira de Alumínio 1955, Pres. 1962–; regular contrib. Folha de São Paulo (newspaper) 1991–; Pres. Red Cross Brazil 1962–66; Pres. Brazilian Asscn of Ceramics 1963, 1966, 1969; Pres. Real e Benemérita Sociedade Potuguesa de Beneficência, São Paulo 1969–; mem. São Paulo Acad. of Letters; Admin. Emer., Regional Admin. Council of São Paulo 1999; Grand Cross of the Nat. Order of Scientific Merit 2002; Engineer of the Year, São Paulo Inst. of Eng 1980, Personality of the Year in Agronomics, Instituto Agronômico de Campinas 2002. *Plays include:* Brasil S.A. 1996, Educação, pelo amor de Deus 1996, S.O.S. Brasil 2000, Acorda Brasil!. *Publications:* numerous newspaper articles. *Address:* Grupo Votorantim, Rua Amauri 255, 01448-000 São Paulo, Brazil (office). *E-mail:* antonio.ermirio@antonioermirio.com.br (office). *Website:* www.votorantim.com.br (office); www.antonioermirio.com.br (office).

DE MORNAY, Rebecca; American film and television actress; b. 29 Aug. 1961, Los Angeles, Calif.; m. Bruce Wagner 1989 (divorced 1991); ed in Austria and at Lee Strasberg Inst. in Los Angeles; apprenticed at Zoetrope Studios. *Theatre includes:* Born Yesterday 1988, Marat/Sade 1990. *Films include:* One from the Heart 1982, Risky Business 1983, Testament 1983, The Slugger's Wife 1985, Runaway Train 1985, The Trip to Bountiful 1985, Beauty and The Beast 1987, And God Created Woman 1988, Feds 1988, Dealers 1989, Backdraft 1991, The Hand that Rocks the Cradle (Best Actress, Cognac Crime Film Festival 1992), Guilty as Sin 1993, The Three Musketeers 1993, Never Talk to Strangers 1995, The Winner 1996, Thick as Thieves 1998, Table for One 1998, The Right Temptation 2000, Identity 2003, Raise Your Voice 2004, Lords of Dogtown 2005, Wedding Crashers 2005, Music Within 2007, American Venus 2007,. *Television appearances include:* The Murders in the Rue Morgue 1986, By Dawn's Early Light 1990, An Inconvenient Woman 1992, Blind Side 1993, Getting Out 1994, The Shining 1996, The Con 1997, Night Ride Home 1999, The Conversion (Dir) 1996, ER 1999, Night Ride Home 1999, Range of Motion 2000, A Girl Thing 2001, Salem Witch Trials 2002, Law and Order 2006, John from Cincinnati 2007–09. *Address:* 1990 South Bundy Drive, Suite 200, Los Angeles, CA 90025-5248, USA.

DE NIRO, Robert; American actor; b. 1943, New York; s. of the late Robert De Niro and of Virginia Admiral; m. 1st Diahnne Abbott 1976; one s. one d.; two s. by Toukie Smith; m. 2nd Grace Hightower 1997; one s.; f. and Pres. TriBeCa Productions 1989–; co-owner Nobu restaurants; co-cr. We Will Rock You (musical) 2002; Commdr Ordre des Arts et des Lettres; Chevalier, Légion d'Honneur; Lifetime Achievement Award, Gotham Awards 2001, American Film Inst. Lifetime Achievement Award 2003. *Films include:* The Wedding Party 1969, Jennifer On My Mind 1971, Bloody Mama, Born to Win 1971, The Gang That Couldn't Shoot Straight 1971, Bang the Drum Slowly 1973, Mean Streets 1973, The Godfather, Part II 1974 (Acad. Award for Best Supporting Actor), The Last Tycoon, Taxi Driver 1976, New York, New York, 1900 1977, The Deer Hunter 1978, Raging Bull (Acad. Award Best Actor) 1980, True Confessions 1981, The King of Comedy 1982, Once Upon a Time in America 1984, Falling in Love 1984, Brazil 1984, The Mission 1985, Angel Heart 1986, The Untouchables 1987, Letters Home from Vietnam, Midnight Run 1988, We're No Angels 1989, Stanley and Iris 1989, Goodfellas 1989, Jacknife 1989, Awakenings 1990, Fear No Evil 1990, Backdraft 1990, Cape Fear 1990, Guilty of Suspicion 1991, Mistress 1992, Night and the City 1992, Mad Dog and Glory 1992, This Boy's Life 1993, Mary Shelley's Frankenstein 1993, A Bronx Tale (also dir, co-produced) 1993, Sleepers 1996, The Fan 1996, Marvin's Room 1996, Great Expectations 1997, Jackie Brown 1998, Ronin 1998, Analyze This 1999, Flawless 1999 (also producer), The Adventures of Rocky and Bullwinkle (also producer) 1999, Meet the Parents (also producer) 2000, Men of Honor 2000, 15 Minutes 2001, The Score 2001, Showtime 2002, City By the Sea 2002, Analyze That 2002, Godsend 2004, Shark Tale (voice) 2004, The Bridge of San Luis Rey 2004, Meet the Fockers 2004, Hide and Seek 2005, Arthur and the Invisibles (voice) 2006, The Good Shepherd (also dir) 2006, Stardust 2007, What Just Happened? 2008, Righteous Kill 2008; as producer Thunderheart 1992, Entrophy 1999, Conjugating Niki 2000, Prison Song 2001, About a Boy 2002, Stage Beauty 2004, Meet the Fockers 2004, Rent 2005. *Address:* Tribeca Productions, 375 Greenwich Street, 8th Floor, New York, NY 10013; c/o CAA, 9830 Wilshire Boulevard, Beverly Hills, CA 90212, USA. *Telephone:* (212) 941-2000. *Fax:* (212) 941-2012. *E-mail:* contactus@tribecafilm.com. *Website:* www.tribecafilm.com.

DE NOINVILLE, Guillaume, LLM, MEcons, MBA; French business executive; *President-Director General, Electrolux France SAS;* b. 8 May 1960, Paris; s. of Christian Durey de Noinville and Béatrice Gallimard; m. Claire de Laguiche; three s. one d.; ed Inst. d'Etudes Politiques, Paris; Finance and Control Dept, Bull Group, Paris 1984–86; Treas. Electrolux France, Senlis 1986–92, Man. Dir Electrolux Financement (leasing co.), Senlis 1992–96, Chief Finance

Officer Electrolux France 1994–2002, Electrolux Belgium 1998–2002, Pres.-Dir Gen. Electrolux France SA 2001–, Chief Admin. Officer, Western Europe, Electrolux Group 2003–. *Address:* Electrolux France SAS, BP 20139, 43 avenue Félix Louat, 60307 Senlis Cedex (office); 29 avenue de la Grande Armée, 75116 Paris, France (home). *Telephone:* (3) 44-62-26-39 (office). *Fax:* (3) 44-62-21-89 (office). *E-mail:* guillaume.de-noinville@electrolux.fr (office). *Website:* www.electrolux.com (office).

DE OLIVEIRA, Constantino, Jr; Brazilian business executive; *President, Gol Linhas Aéreas Inteligentes;* b. 1969, Patrocínio, Minas Gerais; s. of Nenê Constantino de Oliveira; ed Univ. of the Fed. Dist, Brasília; Dir Grupo Áurea 1994–2000; mem. Admin. Council, GOL 2001–, Pres. 2001–; mem. Admin. Council, Gol Linhas Aéreas Inteligentes 2004–, Pres. 2004–; Admin. Emer., Regional Admin. Council of São Paulo 2006–; Exec. of Value, Valor Econômico 2001, 2002, Exec. Leader, Gazeta Mercantil 2003, Federico Bloch Prize, Int. Asscn of Latin-American Air Transport 2005, Business Leader of the Year, Latin Trade Awards 2006. *Address:* Gol Linhas Aéreas Inteligentes S.A., Rua Gomes de Carvalho, 1629, Vila Olímpia, 05457-006 São Paulo, Brazil (office). *Website:* www.voegol.com.br (office).

DE OLIVEIRA MACIEL, Marco Antônio, LLB, MA; Brazilian politician and lawyer; *Minority Leader in Senate;* b. 21 July 1940, Recife; s. of José do Rego Maciel and Carmen Sylvia Cavalcanti de Oliveira Maciel; m. Anna Maria Ferreira; one s. two d.; ed Catholic Univ. of Pernambuco, Pernambuco Univ.; adviser to Pernambuco State Govt 1964–66; Prof. of Public and Int. Law, Catholic Univ. of Pernambuco 1966–; State Deputy, Pernambuco Legis. Ass., Govt Leader 1967–71; Regional Sec. ARENA Party 1969–70, Second Nat. Sec. 1972, First Sec. 1974–75; Fed. Deputy 1971–79, Pres. Chamber of Deputies 1977–79; Gov. Pernambuco State 1979–82; Fed. Senator for PDS Party 1982; Minister for Educ. 1985–86; Minister Chief of Staff of Pres. 1986; Pres. Provisional Nat. Comm. Partido da Frente Liberal (PFL) 1984–85, Nat. Pres. 1987, Fed. Senator for PFL 1990, mem. Nat. Council, Leader PFL in Senate 1990; Minority Leader in Senate 1990–, Govt Leader 1991–92; Vice-Pres. of Brazil 1994–2003; mem. Pernambuco Section Brazilian Bar Asscn, Brazilian Acad. of Political and Moral Sciences 1993–, Argentinian Law Asscn; numerous honours including Grand Cross, Order of Rio Branco, Brasilia Order of Merit, Légion d'honneur (France), Grand Cross, Order of Infante Dom Henrique (Portugal), Grand Cross, Order of May (Argentina) 1979, Cross of Merit (FRG), Ordre nat. du Mérite (France), City of Recife Medal of Merit. *Publications:* numerous publs on politics and educ. *Address:* c/o Office of the Vice-President, Palácio do Planalto, 4° andar, 70150-900 Brasília, DF, Brasil (office). *Telephone:* (61) 411-1573 (office). *Fax:* (61) 323-1461 (office). *E-mail:* vpr@planalto.gov.br.

DE ORIOL E YBARRA, Iñigo, LicenDer; Spanish business executive; *Chairman, Iberdrola SA;* b. 6 Aug. 1935, Madrid; s. of the late José María de Oriol y Urquijo; ed Univ. Complutense; began career as legal consultant, Hidroeléctrica Española (HE) 1959, mem. Supervisory Bd 1975, Chair. Man. Cttee, Pres. 1985–91; Chair. Iberdrola SA (following merger of HE and Iberduero 1991) 1991–; mem. Advisory Bd Cementos Molins –2004; Pres. Chamber of Commerce and Industry of Madrid 1968–78, UNESA (Employers' Asscn of Electric Cos) 1987–89, 1996–98, 2002–; fmr Pres. Spanish-Portuguese Chamber of Commerce; mem. Superior Council of Chambers of Spain; Hon. Pres. Asscn of Latin American Chambers of Commerce (AICO), Chamber of Commerce and Industry of Madrid; Gran Cruz de Alfonso X; Enterprise Leader of the Year, Spain-USA Chamber of Commerce 2001. *Address:* Iberdrola SA, Cardenal Gardoqui 8, 48008 Bilbao, Spain (office). *Telephone:* 944151411 (office). *Fax:* 944154579 (office). *Website:* www.iberdrola.com (office).

DE PADT, Guido, LenD; Belgian politician; *Minister of the Interior;* b. 23 May 1954, Geraardsbergen; mem. Vlaamse Liberalen en Demokraten (VLD); Prov. Counsellor for E Flanders 1982–2003; Deputy Mayor of Geraardsbergen 1982–94, 2007–08, Mayor of Geraardsbergen 2001–06; Deputy for E Flanders 1994–2000; mem. Chamber of Reps 2003–; Minister of the Interior 2008–; Chair. Centre-Publique-d'Aide-Sociale for Geraardsbergen 2007–08. *Address:* Federal Public Service of the Interior, 1 rue de Louvain, 1000 Brussels, Belgium (office). *Telephone:* (2) 500-20-50 (Flemish) (office); (2) 500-20-48 (French) (office). *Fax:* (2) 500-20-39 (office). *E-mail:* info@ibz.fgov.be (office). *Website:* www.ibz.be (office).

DE PALMA, Brian, MA; American film director; b. 11 Sept. 1940, Newark, NJ; s. of Anthony Fredrick De Palma and Vivienne De Palma (née Muti); m. 1st Nancy Allen 1979 (divorced 1983); m. 2nd Gale Ann Hurd 1991 (divorced); one d.; m. 3rd Darnell Gregorio-De Palma 1997 (divorced) one c.; ed Sarah Lawrence Coll., Bronxville and Columbia Univ. *Films include:* (short films) Icarus 1960, 660124: The Story of an IBM Card 1961, Wotan's Wake 1962; (feature length) The Wedding Party 1964, The Responsive Eye (documentary) 1966, Murder à la Mode 1967, Greetings 1968, Dionysus in '69 (co-Dir) 1969, Hi Mom! 1970, Get to Know Your Rabbit 1970, Sisters 1972, Phantom of the Paradise 1974, Obsession 1975, Carrie 1976, The Fury 1978, Home Movies 1979, Dressed to Kill 1980, Blow Out 1981, Scarface 1983, Body Double 1984, Wise Guys 1985, The Untouchables 1987, Casualties of War 1989, Bonfire of the Vanities 1990, Raising Cain 1992, Carlito's Way 1993, Mission Impossible 1996, Snake Eyes 1998, Mission to Mars 2000, Femme Fatale 2002, The Black Dahlia 2006, Redacted (Silver Lion, Venice Film Festival 2007) 2007, Capone Rising 2008. *Address:* Paramount Pictures, 5555 Melrose Avenue, W Hollywood, CA 90038, USA.

DE PALMA, Rossy; Spanish actress; b. (Rosa Elena García), Palma de Mallorca; two s.; fmrly singer with punk band Peor Imposible; fashion model in Spain and for John-Paul Gaultier, Paris; launched fragrance Rossy de Palma Eau de Protection 2007. *Films include:* Law of Desire 1986, Women on the Verge of a Nervous Breakdown 1988, Don Juan, My Love 1990, Tie Me Up! Tie Me Down! 1990, Kika 1994, Ready to Wear 1994, The Flower of My Secret 1995, Las Hetairas, Prêt à Porter, Talk of Angels 1998, Foul Play 1998, The Loss of Sexual Innocence 1999, Va Savoir 2001, Dead Weight (Le Boulet) 2002, Laisse tes mains sur mes hanches 2003, People 2004, Double zéro 2004, Tu la conosci Claudia? 2004, 20 centímetros 2005, Mes copines 2006, Les Aristos 2006, La Edad ideal 2006.

DE PERETTI, Jean-Jacques; French politician; *Conseiller d'Etat, Conseil d'Etat;* b. 21 Sept. 1946, Clermont-Ferrand; three c.; ed Inst. des Hautes Etudes Internationales; Asst Lecturer, St-Maur Faculty of Law and Univs of Orléans and Paris I 1969–84; Chargé de Mission, Cabinet of Pierre Messmer 1972; Dir de Cabinet to Pres. of Paris Region 1974; Chargé de Mission to André Bord, Sec.-Gen. of Union des Démocrates pour la République (UDR) 1976; Chargé de Mission, Cabinet of Antoine Rufenacht, Sec. of State to Prime Minister; Sec. of State to Minister for Industry, Trade and Craft Trades; Man. Exec. IBM until 1986; Adviser to Prime Minister Jacques Chirac 1986; Mayor of Sarlat 1989–; fmr mem. Regional Council and Deputy to Nat. Ass. for Dordogne Dept's 4th constituency; Departmental Councillor for Dordogne 1992–; Nat. Sec. Rassemblement pour la République (RPR) 1990–93, Deputy Sec.-Gen. 1994–95; Minister for Overseas France May–Nov. 1995; Minister-Del. to Prime Minister with responsibility for Overseas France 1995–97; mem. Regional Council of Aquitaine; mem. Hudson Inst. 1969–; Legion d'Honneur. *Publications:* L'envol de la France dan les anées 80 (with Herman Khan and the Hudson Inst.) 1979, Gagner les Municipales 1988. *Address:* Mairie, 24200 Sarlat-la-Canéda, France (home). *Telephone:* (5) 53-31-53-30 (office); 1-47-53-80-53 (office). *Fax:* (5) 53-31-08-04 (office); 1-47-53-80-53 (office). *E-mail:* jjpc@wanadoo.fr (office). *Website:* jean-jacques.de-peretti@conseil-etat.fr (office).

DE PEYER, Gervase Alan, FRCM; British clarinettist and conductor; b. 11 April 1926, London; s. of Esme Everard Vivian de Peyer and Edith Mary Bartlett; m. 1st Sylvia Southcombe 1950 (divorced 1971); one s. two d.; m. 2nd Susan Rosalind Daniel 1971 (divorced 1979); m. 3rd Katia Perret Aubry 1980; ed King Alfred's School, London, Bedales School and Royal Coll. of Music, London; served HM Forces 1945, 1946; studied in Paris 1949; int. soloist 1949–; Founder mem. Melos Ensemble 1950–72; Prin. Clarinet, London Symphony Orchestra 1955–72; Founder and Conductor Melos Sinfonia of Washington 1992; Dir London Symphony Wind Ensemble; fmr Assoc. Conductor Haydn Orchestra of London; solo clarinettist, Chamber Music Soc. of Lincoln Center, NY 1969–89; fmr Resident Conductor Victoria Int. Festival, BC, Canada; Co-founder and Artistic Dir Innisfree Music Festival, Pa, USA; mem. Faculty, Mannes Coll. of Music, NY; also conductor; recording artist with all major companies (most recorded solo clarinettist in the world); gives recitals and master classes throughout the world; Gold Medallist Worshipful Co. of Musicians 1948, Charles Gros Grand Prix du Disque 1961, 1962, Plaque of Honor for Acad. of Arts and Sciences of America for recording of Mozart concerto 1962. *Leisure interests:* theatre, good food, anything dangerous, travel, sport. *Address:* 42 Tower Bridge Wharf, St Katherine's Way, London, E1W 1UR, England (home). *Telephone:* (20) 7265-1110. *Fax:* (20) 7265-1110. *E-mail:* gdepeyer@aol.com (office). *Website:* www.gervasedepeyer.com (office).

DE PURY, Simon; Swiss auctioneer and art dealer; *Chairman, Phillips de Pury & Company;* b. 1951, Basel; ed Acad. of Fine Arts, Tokyo, Japan; worked at the Bern auctioneers, Kornfeld & Klipstein, and subsequently studied at Sotheby's Inst. before joining Sotheby's, working in London, Geneva and Monte Carlo; Curator Thyssen-Bornemisza collection, Lugano 1979–86; returned to Sotheby's first as Chair. Sotheby's Switzerland and then as Chair. of Sotheby's Europe and the co.'s Prin. Auctioneer 1986, conducted all of Sotheby's major sales in Europe which included the Thurn und Taxis sale in Geneva and Regensburg, the Margrave sales in Baden-Baden and, from 1994, all the major Impressionist sales in New York; co-f. (with Daniella Luxembourg) de Pury & Luxembourg Art (art advisory co.), Geneva 1997, merged with Phillips Auctioneers to become Phillips, de Pury and Luxembourg 2001, Chair. and majority shareholder of Phillips de Pury & Company 2004–. *Address:* Phillips de Pury & Company, 450 West 15th Street, New York, NY 10011, USA (office). *Telephone:* (212) 940-1200 (office). *Fax:* (212) 924-3306 (office). *E-mail:* info@phillipsdepury.com (office). *Website:* www.phillipsdepury.com (office).

DE QUEIROZ DUARTE, Sergio; Brazilian diplomatist and UN official; *Under-Secretary-General and High Representative for Disarmament Affairs, United Nations;* b. Rio de Janeiro; ed Fed. Fluminense Univ., Rio de Janeiro, Brazilian School of Public Admin (Getúlio Vargas Foundation), Rio de Janeiro, Brazilian Diplomatic Acad. (Instituto Rio Branco), Rio de Janeiro; career diplomat with rank of Amb. in Brazilian Foreign Service, apptd Third Sec. 1957, diplomatic appointments have included Embassies in Rome 1961–63, in Buenos Aires 1963–66, in Washington, DC 1970–74, Perm. Mission to UN, Geneva 1966–68 (mem. Brazilian del. to 18-nation Disarmament Cttee); Alt. Rep., Office of Special Rep. of Brazil for Disarmament Affairs, Geneva 1979–86, Amb. to Nicaragua 1986–91, to Canada 1993–96, to People's Repub. of China 1996–99, to Austria 1999–2002 (also accred to Slovakia, Slovenia and Croatia and as Rep. to Int. Orgs, Vienna); Gov. for Brazil at Bd Govs, IAEA, Chair. Bd Govs 1999–2000; Head of Personnel, Ministry of Foreign Affairs, Brasilia 1975–79, Sec.-Gen. for Budget Control and Insp.-Gen. 1991, Exec. Sec.-Gen. 1991–92, Under-Sec.-Gen. for Foreign Service 1992–93, Amb.-at-Large for Disarmament and Non-Proliferation 2003–04; UN Under-Sec.-Gen. and High Rep. for Disarmament Affairs 2007–; elected Pres. Review Conf. of Parties to Treaty Prohibiting the Emplacement of Nuclear Weapons on the Seabed and the Subsoil Thereof, Geneva 1988, VII Review Conf. of Parties to Treaty on the Non-proliferation of Nuclear Weapons, New York 2005. *Address:* Office of the High Representative for Disarmament Affairs, Room

S-3170, United Nations, New York, NY 10017, USA (office). *E-mail:* ddaweb@ un.org (office). *Website:* disarmament.un.org (office).

DE RAAD, Ad, MSc; Dutch UN official; *Executive Coordinator, United Nations Volunteers;* b. 7 Dec. 1952; ed Delft Univ. of Tech.; sr positions, UNDP Country Offices in Bangladesh 1980–84, Tanzania 1984–87; various posts, Bureau for Finance and Admin, UNDP, New York 1987–93; Dir of Budget, UNDP, New York 1993–98; Deputy Exec. Coordinator UN Volunteers (UNV) programme, Bonn, Germany 1998–2003, Acting Exec. Coordinator 2003–04, Exec. Coordinator 2004–. *Address:* United Nations Volunteers, Postfach 260 111, 53153 Bonn, Germany (office). *Telephone:* (228) 8152000 (office). *Fax:* (228) 8152001 (office). *E-mail:* information@unvolunteers.org (office). *Website:* www.unvolunteers.org (office).

DE RACHEWILTZ, Igor, PhD, FAHA; Italian historian, philologist and academic; *Emeritus Fellow, Australian National University;* b. 11 April 1929, Rome; s. of Bruno Guido and Antonina Perosio; m. Ines Adelaide Brasch 1956; one d.; ed St Gabriel's Coll., Rome Univ. and Australian Nat. Univ.; Research Scholar, ANU 1956–60, Sr Lecturer, Faculty of Asian Studies 1963–65, Fellow, Inst. of Advanced Studies 1965–67, Sr Fellow 1967–94, Visiting Fellow 1995–; Lecturer in Asian Civilization, Canberra Univ. Coll. 1960–62; Visiting Prof., Bonn Univ. 1979, Rome Univ. 1996, 1999, 2001, 2002; mem. Sonderforschungsbereich 12, 1979–; Vice-Pres. Int. Asscn for Mongol Studies 1992–2002; Hon. Pres. Int. Centre for Genghis Khan Studies, Mongolia; Kt Order of Merit of Italian Repub. 1998; Hon. DLitt (Univ. Rome La Sapienza) 2001; Centenary Medal for Service to Australian Soc. and the Humanities in Asian Studies 2003; Gold Medal of the Perm. Int. Altaistic Conf. (PIAC) 2004. *Publications:* The Hsi-yu lu by Yeh-lü Ch'u-ts'ai 1962, Papal Envoys to the Great Khans 1971, Index to the Secret History of the Mongols 1972, The Preclassical Mongolian Version of the Hsiao-ching 1982, Repertory of Proper Names in Yüan Literary Sources 1988–96, text edn and word-index of Erdeni-yin tobci 1990–91, In the Service of the Khan 1993, Le matériel mongol du Houa ii iu de Houng-ou (1389): Commentaires 1995, The Mongolian Tanjur version of the Bodhicaryāvatāra 1996, The Secret History of the Mongols (new edn) 2004, (2nd edn 2006); over 100 articles on Sino-Mongolian topics, medieval history and Altaic philology. *Leisure interests:* botany, travel. *Address:* c/o Division of Pacific and Asian History, Australian National University, Canberra ACT 0200; 9 Ridley Street, Turner, ACT 2612, Australia (home). *Telephone:* (2) 6125-3171 (office); (2) 6248-0557 (home). *Fax:* (2) 6125-5525 (office). *E-mail:* ider@coombs.anu.edu.au (office). *Website:* rspas.anu.edu.au/pah (office).

DE RIBEROLLES, Dominique, BEcons, MBA; Spanish business executive; *CEO and General Manager, Compañía Española de Petróleos SA (CEPSA);* ed Polytechnic Univ. of Paris, Univ. of Washington, USA; began career as Admin. and Financial Man. of Lubricants Area, ELF Group, in charge of coordinating relations in Madrid between ELF and Compañía Española de Petróleos SA (CEPSA) 1990–96, Vice-Pres. CEPSA's Corp. Planning and Control Div. 1996–98, Sr Vice-Pres. 1998–2003, Exec. Dir 2003–06, CEO and Gen. Man. CEPSA 2006–. *Address:* Compañía Española de Petróleos SA, Campo de las Naciones, Avenida del Partenón 12, 28042 Madrid, Spain (office). *Telephone:* (91) 3376000 (office). *Fax:* (91) 7211613 (office). *E-mail:* webcepsa@cepsa.com (office). *Website:* www.cepsa.com (office).

DE ROBIEN, Gilles, LenD; French politician; b. 10 April 1941, Cocquerel, Somme; began career as gen. insurance agent, Amiens 1965; Deputy in Nat. Ass. for 2nd Somme constituency 1986–, mem. Finance Cttee, Cttee of Enquiry into Causes, Consequences and Prevention of Floods, Vice Pres. Nat. Ass. 1993–98, architect of Robien Act on reform of working hours 1996; Mayor of Amiens 1989–2008; Minister for Capital Works, Transportation, Housing, Tourism and Maritime Affairs 2002, for Nat. Educ., Higher Educ. and Research –2007; Chair. Communauté d'Agglomération Amiens-Métropole; mem. Picardie Regional Council 1992; mem. Exec. Bureau and Steering Cttee, Republican Party 1990–; mem. Nat. Council and Political Cttee, Union pour la démocratie française (UDF) 1991–, Chair. UDF Group in Nat. Ass. 1995–97, mem. Political Bureau and Vice-Chair. UDF 1998–. *Address:* Union pour la Démocratie Française (UDF), 133 bis rue de l'Université, 75007 Paris, France. *Telephone:* 1-53-59-20-00. *Fax:* 1-53-59-20-59. *E-mail:* internet@udf.org. *Website:* www.udf.org.

DE ROMANET DE BEAUNE, Augustin; French financial industry executive; *Chairman and CEO, Caisse des Dépôts;* b. 2 April 1961, Boulogne-Billancourt; s. of Luc de Romanet de Beaune and Anne-Marie de Romanet de Beaune (née Lafont); m. Florence Burin des Roziers 1986; three c.; ed Inst. of Political Studies, Paris, Ecole Nationale d'Administration; began career in Budget Dept, Ministry of the Economy and Finance; Financial Attaché, Perm. Mission of France to EC, Brussels 1990–93, Head, Budget Office 1993–95; Chief of Staff to State Sec. for Budget and Special Adviser to Minister of Economy, Finance and Planning 1995–2002; Chief of Staff to the Minister responsible for Budget and Budget Reform and Deputy Chief of Staff to Minister of Economy, Finance and Industry 2002–04; Chief of Staff to the Minister of Employment, Work and Social Cohesion and Deputy Chief of Staff to Prime Minister 2004–05; Deputy Sec.-Gen. to the Presidency 2005; Deputy Dir for Finance and Strategy and mem. Exec. Cttee, Crédit Agricole SA 2006; Chair. and CEO Caisse des Dépôts 2007–; mem. Bd of Dirs Oddo et Compagnie 1999–, Man. Pnr, Oddo Pinatton Corp. 2000–; mem. Bd of Dirs Dexia SA 2007, Soc. Nat. Immobilière (SNI), Accor, Veolia, Icade, CNP Assurance 2007–; Prof., Inst. of Political Studies, Paris 1986–90, Ecole Nationale d'Administra-tion 1990–93; Chevalier, Légion d'honneur; Nat. Defence Medal. *Address:* Caisse des Dépôts, 56 rue de Lille, 75356 Paris 07 SP, France (office). *Telephone:* 1-58-50-00-00 (office). *Website:* www.caissedesdepots.fr (office).

DE ROMILLY, Jacqueline, DèsSc; French professor of Ancient Greek; *Professor Emerita, College de France;* b. 26 March 1913, Chartres; d. of Maxime David and Jeanne Malvoisin; m. Michel Worms de Romilly 1940 (divorced 1973); ed Ecole Normale Supérieure, Univ. of Paris; Prof. of Ancient Greek, Univ. of Lille 1949–57, Univ. of Paris-Sorbonne 1957–73; Prof., Coll. de France 1973–84, Emer. Prof. 1984–; mem. Acad. des Inscriptions et Belles Lettres, Inst. de France 1975–, Acad. Française 1988–; Corresp. mem. of eight acads; Grand Croix de la Légion d'honneur, des Palmes académiques, Ordre des Arts et Lettres; Grand-Croix Ordre nat. du mérite; Commdr Order of the Phoenix (Greece); Insignia of Honour for Science and Art (Austria); Dr hc (several). *Publications:* L'enseignement en détresse 1984, Sur les chemins de Ste. Victoire 1987, Ouverture à coeur 1990, Pourquoi la Grèce? 1992, Les Oeufs de Pâques 1993, Lettres aux Parents sur les Choix Scolaires 1993, Tragédies grecques au fil des ans 1995, Rencontres avec la Grèce antique 1995, Alcibiade ou les dangers de l'ambition 1995, Jeux de lumière sur l'Hellade 1996, Hector 1997, Le Trésor des savoirs oubliés 1998, Laisse flotter les rubans 1999, La Grèce antique contre la violence 2000, Héros tragiques, héros lyriques 2001, Sous des dehors si calmes 2002, La Grèce antique 2003, Une certaine idée de la Grèce 2003, De la flûte à la lyre 2004, L'élan démocratique dans l'Athènes ancienne 2005; approx. 20 books on classical Greek literature including many on Thucydides, also on the history of moral and political ideas in ancient Greece. *Address:* 12 rue Chernoviz, 75016 Paris, France. *Telephone:* 1-42-24-59-07.

DE ROSNAY, Joël, DèsSc; French biologist; b. 12 June 1937, Mauritius; s. of Gaëtan de Rosnay and Natacha Koltchine; m. Stella Jebb 1959; one s. two d.; ed MIT; Dir of Applied Research, Inst. Pasteur 1975–84; Dir of Devt and Int. Relations, Cité des sciences et de l'industrie de La Villette 1988–97, Dir of Strategy 1996–99, Dir of Evaluation 1999–; Columnist Europe 1 1987–95; Officier Légion d'honneur, Officier Ordre nat. du Mérite; Prix de l'Information Scientifique, Acad. des Sciences 1990. *Publications:* Les origines de la vie 1965, Le macroscope 1975, La révolution biologique 1982, Branchez-vous 1985, L'avenir du vivant 1988, L'avenir en direct 1989, Les rendez-vous du futur 1991, L'homme symbiotique 1995, La plus belle histoire du monde (contrib.) 1996. *Leisure interests:* skiing, surfing. *Address:* 146 rue de l'Université, 75007 Paris; Cité des Sciences et de l'Industrie de la Villette, 30 avenue Corentin Cariou, 75019 Paris, France.

DE RUITER, Hendrikus; Dutch business executive; b. 3 March 1934, The Hague; m. Theodora O. van der Jagt 1957; one s. two d.; ed Technological Univ. of Delft; Research Chemist, Koninklijke/Shell Laboratorium Amster-dam (KSLA) 1956; Chief Technologist, Berre Refinery, Compagnie de Raffinage Shell-Berre 1965–67; returned to KSLA 1967; joined Shell Int. Petroleum Co. Ltd (SIPC), London 1969; Man. Dir Shell Co. of Thailand and Pres. Société Shell du Laos 1972; Coal Production and Trading Co-ordinator, SIPC 1975; Pres. Shell Int. Trading Co. 1979; Dir Shell Internationale Petroleum Maatschappij BV 1981; Man. Dir NV Koninklijke Nederlandsche Petroleum Maatschappij; mem. Presidium, Bd of Dirs, Shell Petroleum NV and Man. Dir The Shell Petroleum Co. Ltd 1983–1994; mem. Supervisory Bd AEGON NV (Vice-Chair. 1993–2004, Heineken NV 1993–2004, Koninklijke Ahold NV (Chair.) 1994–2003, Wolters Kluwer NV (Chair.) 1994–, Royal Dutch Petroleum Co. 1994–2004, Beers NV (Chair) 1995–2002, Coris Group PLC (fmrly Hoogovens Group BV) (Vice-Chair.) 1995–2002, Koninklijke Vopak NV (fmrly Koninklijke Pakhoed NV) 1995–2002; Dir Shell Petroleum NV 1994–2004, The Shell Petroleum Co. Ltd 1994–2004, Chair. Univar NV (fmrly part of Koninklijke Vopak) 2002–04; Kt Order of the Netherlands Lion 1987. *Address:* c/o Royal Dutch Petroleum Company, Carel van Bylandtlaan 30, PO Box 162, 2501 AN The Hague, Netherlands. *Telephone:* (70) 3774504.

DE SANCTIS, Roman William, MD; American cardiologist; b. 30 Oct. 1930, Cambridge Springs, Pa; s. of Vincent De Sanctis and Marguerita De Sanctis; m. Ruth A. Foley 1955; four d.; ed Univ. of Arizona, Harvard Medical School; Resident in Medicine, Mass. Gen. Hosp. 1958–60, Fellow in Cardiology 1960–62, Dir Coronary Care Unit 1967–80, Dir Clinical Cardiology 1980–98, Dir Emer. 1998–; Physician 1970–; mem. Faculty of Medicine, Harvard Medical School 1964–, Prof. 1973–98, James and Evelyn Jenks and Paul Dudley White Prof. of Medicine 1998–; Consultant to USN and Asst to Attending Physician to US Congress 1956–58; Master, American Coll. of Physicians 1995; Fellow, American Coll. of Cardiology, Inst. of Medicine; Hon. DSc (Wilkes Coll., Univ. of Ariz.); Distinguished Clinical Teaching Award, Harvard Medical School 1980; Gifted Teacher Award (American Coll. of Cardiologists), Glozny-Reisbeck Award, NY Acad. of Medicine 2003. *Publica-tions:* author and co-ed. of over 130 scientific papers. *Leisure interests:* travel, music, golf. *Address:* Yawkey Building, Suite 5700, 55 Fruit Street, Boston, MA 02114 (office); 5 Thoreau Circle, Winchester, MA 01890, USA (home). *Telephone:* (781) 726-2889 (office); (617) 729-1453 (home). *Fax:* (617) 643-1615.

DE SARAM, John Henricus; Sri Lankan lawyer and diplomatist; b. 27 June 1929; m.; ed Yale Univ. School of Law, USA; univ. law lecturer 1952; Pvt. Sec. and Aide-de-Camp to Chief Justice of Sri Lanka 1952–58; Asst and Assoc. Legal Officer, Gen. Legal Div., UN Office of Legal Affairs 1958–62, Legal Officer 1962–68, Sr Legal Officer 1968–77, Deputy Dir Legal Div. 1977–84, Codification Div. 1984–86, Dir Office of Legal Affairs 1986–89; Legal Consultant of UNDP to Indian Ocean Marine Affairs Co-operation 1989–91; Rep. of Sri Lanka, 6th Cttee of the UN Gen. Ass. 1991–96; mem. Int. Law Comm. 1992–96, Gen. Rapporteur 1993, Rep. to Inter-American Juridicial Cttee of OAS 1995; Legal Consultant of UN to Hangzhou Int. Centre on Small Hydro Power, China 1997; Perm. Rep. to UN, New York 1998–2002; mem. Int. Law and Human Rights Faculty, Univ. of Peace, Costa Rica; currently Consultant, D. L. & F. DE SARAM (law firm), Colombo. *Address:* D. L. & F. DE SARAM, 47 Alexandra Place, Colombo 7, Sri Lanka (office). *Telephone:* (11)

2695782 (office). *Fax:* (11) 2695410 (office). *E-mail:* desaram@desaram.com (office). *Website:* www.desaram.com (office).

DE SAVARY, Peter John; British business executive; b. 11 July 1944, Essex; m. 3rd Lucille Lana Paton; three d. (and two d. from previous m.); ed Charterhouse; commercial activities in finance, energy, leisure and property; British challenger for The Americas Cup 1983, 1987; Chair. The Carnegie Club, Scotland 1994–; Chair. Carnegie Abbey, Rhode Island; Chair. Cherokee Plantation, SC; owner and Chair. Millwall Football Club 2005–; Tourism Personality of the Year (English Tourist Bd) 1988. *Leisure interests:* sailing, carriage driving, riding. *Address:* Skibo Castle, Dornoch, Sutherland, IV25 3RQ, Scotland; Millwall Football Club, The Den, Zampa Road, London, SE16 3LN, England. *Telephone:* (20) 7232-1222 (London). *Website:* www.millwallfc.co.uk.

DE SCHOUTHEETE DE TERVARENT, Baron Philippe; Belgian diplomatist; *Representative of Order of Malta, European Commission;* b. 21 May 1932, Berlin, Germany; m. Bernadette Joos de ter Beerst 1956; two s.; ed Beaumont Coll., UK, Univ. of Louvain, Belgium; joined Belgian diplomatic service; served in Paris 1959–61, Cairo 1962–65, Madrid 1968–72, Bonn 1972–76; Chef de Cabinet to Minister of Foreign Affairs 1980–81; Amb. to Spain 1981–85; Political Dir 1985–87; Perm. Rep. to EU 1987–97; Guest Prof., Univ. of Louvain la Neuve 1990–2000; Rep. of Order of Malta to EC 2000–; Special Adviser EC 2000–04; Dir European Studies, Royal Inst. for Int. Relations, Brussels; Pres. Fund Inbev Baillet Latour 1999–; mem. Bd of Dirs Centre for European Policy Studies, Acad. Royale de Belgique; Grand Officer, Order of Leopold; Adolphe Bentinck Prize 1997, European Parl. Medal 1997. *Publications:* La coopération politique européenne 1986, Une Europe pour tous 1997, The Case for Europe 2000. *Address:* Avenue de Broqueville 99, 1200 Brussels, Belgium. *E-mail:* deschoutheete@skynet.be (home).

DE SILGUY, Yves-Thibault Christian Marie; French construction industry executive and fmr diplomatist; *Chairman, Vinci;* b. 22 July 1948, Rennes; s. of Raymond de Silguy and Claude de Pompery; m. Jacqueline de Montillet de Grenaud; one s. one d.; ed Inst. Saint-Martin, Faculté de Droit et des Sciences Economiques, Rennes, Univ. de Paris I, Inst. d'Etudes Politiques de Paris and Ecole Nat. d'Admin; worked at Ministry of Foreign Affairs 1976–81; Deputy Chef de Cabinet to François-Xavier Ortoli, Vice-Pres. of EC Comm. 1981–85; Second Counsellor, Washington, DC 1985–86; Adviser on European Questions and Int. Econs, Office of Prime Minister Chirac 1986–88; Dir, Int. Affairs Dept, Usinor-Sacilor 1988–90, Dir for Int. Affairs 1990–93; Sec.-Gen. Interdepartmental Cttee for Questions of Econ. Cooperation in Europe and Adviser for European Affairs and Adviser on European Affairs to Prime Minister Balladur 1993–95; Commr for Econ. and Monetary Union, EC 1995–99; mem. Exec. Bd Suez Group 2000–, CEO 2001–02, Sr Exec. Vice Pres. in charge of Int. Affairs and Relations 2001–06; Chair. Vinci 2006–; Pres. Algeria Cttee Mouvement des entreprises de France (MEDEF) 2000–; Officier, Légion d'honneur, Officier du Mérite agricole, Officier des Arts et des Lettres. *Publications:* Le syndrome du diplodocus 1996, L'euro 1998, L'economie, fil d'Ariane de l'Europe 2000. *Leisure interests:* sailing, hunting, tennis. *Address:* Vinci, 1 cours Ferdinand-de-Lesseps, 92851 Rueil-Malmaison Cedex, France (office). *Telephone:* 1-47-16-35-00 (office). *Fax:* 1-47-51-91-02 (office). *E-mail:* contact.internet@vinci.com (office). *Website:* www.vinci.com (office).

DE SILVA, C. R.; Sri Lankan lawyer and government official; *Attorney-General;* ed Royal Coll.; joined Attorney-Gen.'s Dept as State Counsel 1976, promoted to Sr State Counsel 1983, Deputy Solicitor-Gen. 1992–96, Additional Solicitor-Gen. 1996–99, took silk 1997, Solicitor-Gen. 1999–2007, Attorney-Gen. 2007–. *Address:* Chamber 48, Attorney-General's Department, Colombo, Sri Lanka (office). *Telephone:* (11) 440239 (office); (11) 323595 (office). *Fax:* (11) 329992 (office). *E-mail:* attorneygen@mail.ewisl.net (office); attorney@sri.lanka.net (office); counsel@sri.lanka.net (office). *Website:* www.attorneygeneral.gov.lk (office).

DE SOTO, Alvaro; Peruvian diplomatist; b. 16 March 1943, Argentina; divorced; two s. one d.; ed Int. School, Geneva, Catholic Univ. Lima, San Marcos Univ. Lima, Diplomatic Acad. Lima and Inst. of Int. Studies, Geneva; Acting Dir Maritime Sovereignty Div. Ministry of Foreign Affairs 1975–78; Deputy Perm. Rep. of Peru at UN, Geneva 1978–82; Special Asst to UN Sec.-Gen. 1982–86; Asst Sec.-Gen. and Exec. Asst to UN Sec.-Gen. 1987–91; Personal Rep. of UN Sec.-Gen. in El Salvador Peace Negotiations 1990–91; Asst Sec.-Gen. UN Office for Research and Collection of Information 1991; Sr Political Adviser to UN Sec.-Gen. 1992–94; Asst Sec.-Gen. for Political Affairs 1995–99, Under-Sec.-Gen., Special Adviser to Sec.-Gen. on Cyprus 1999–2000; UN Special Envoy for Myanmar 1997–99; Special Rep. of the Sec.-Gen. for Cyprus and Chief of Mission UNFICYP (UN Peace-Keeping Force in Cyprus) 2000–03; Special Rep. of the Sec.-Gen. for Western Sahara and Chief of the UN Mission for the Referendum in Western Sahara (MINURSO) 2003–05; UN Special Coordinator for the Middle East Peace Process and Personal Rep. of the Sec.-Gen. to the Palestine Liberation Org. and the Palestinian Authority 2005–07. *Address:* c/o Executive Office of the UN Secretary-General, United Nations Plaza, New York, NY 10017, USA (office).

DE SOTO, Guillermo Fernández; Colombian politician and international organization official; b. 1956; ed Univ. of Bogotá, Georgetown Univ., USA; Under-Minister of Foreign Affairs 1980, Minister 1998–2002; f. Groupe de Contadora; Intermediate Sec. Groupe de Rio; Dir Chamber of Commerce, Bogotá 1993–98; Sec.-Gen. Andean Community of Nations 2002–03. *Address:* c/o Andean Community of Nations, Avda Paseo de la República 3895, esq. Aramburú, San Isidro, Lima 27, Peru (office).

DE SOTO, Hernando; Peruvian economist; *President, Institute for Liberty and Democracy;* b. 2 June 1941, Arequipa; ed Institut Universitaire de Hautes Etudes Internationales, Geneva, Switzerland; fmr economist for GATT; fmr Pres. Exec. Cttee, Copper Exporting Countries Org. (CIPEC); fmr Man. Dir Universal Eng Corpn; fmr Prin. Swiss Bank Corpn Consultant Group; fmr Gov. Cen. Reserve Bank, Peru; Personal Rep. and Chief Adviser to Pres. Alberto Fujimori; currently Pres. Inst. for Liberty and Democracy, Lima; apptd rep. of Pres. to USA on free trade agreement 2006; Co-Chair. UN High Level Comm. on Legal Empowerment for the Poor; Downey Fellow, Yale Univ., USA 2003; Most Admirable Order of the Direkgunabhorn (Fifth Class), Thailand 2004; Hon. DLitt (Buckingham, UK) 2005; Sir Antony Fisher Int. Memorial Award – Atlas 1990, 2001, one of five Leaders for the New Millennium chosen by Time magazine 1999, The Freedom Prize (Switzerland), Goldwater Award (USA) 2002, Adam Smith Award, Asscn of Pvt. Enterprise Educ. (USA) 2002, CARE Canada Award for Outstanding Devt Thinking 2002, inducted into Democracy Hall of Fame Int., Nat. Grad. Univ. 2003, Templeton Freedom Prize (USA) 2004, Milton Friedman Prize for Advancing Liberty (USA) 2004, Deutsche Stiftung Eigentum prize for Property Rights Theory 2004, IPAE Award, Peruvian Inst. of Business Admin 2004, Americas Award 2005, Acad. of Achievement Golden Plate Award, USA 2005, Forbes' Compass Award for Strategic Direction 2005. *Publications:* The Other Path 1986, The Mystery of Capital: Why Capitalism Triumphs in the West and Fails Everywhere Else 2000. *Address:* Instituto Libertad y Democracia, Av. Las Begonias 441, Piso 9, San Isidro, Lima 27, Peru (office). *Telephone:* (1) 222-6800 (office). *Fax:* (1) 221-6949 (office). *E-mail:* hds@ild.org.pe (office). *Website:* www.ild.org.pe (office).

DE SOUZA, Wilfred Anthony, MB, BS, FRCS, FRCSE; Indian politician and surgeon; b. 23 April 1927, Anjuna, Bardez; s. of the late Tito Fermino and Alina Anamaria; m. Grace Goodwin; two c.; ed Grant Medical Coll. Univ. of Bombay; surgeon, Goa Medical Coll. Hosp. 1963–67; Consulting Surgeon, Hospicio Hosp., Margao and Asilo Hosp., Mapusa 1963–67; Consulting Surgeon, CMM Hosp., Panjim and Holy Cross Hosp., Mapusa 1969–96; elected to Goa, Daman and Diu Ass. 1974, 1980; elected to Legis. Ass. (after Goa became State in Repub. of India) 1989, 1994, 1999, 2002; Pres. Goa Pradesh Congress Cttee 1977–80; Minister for Public Health, Public Works Dept, Govt of Goa 1981–83, Science and Tech. Planning 1990; Leader of Opposition 1990–91; Deputy Chief Minister, Govt of Goa 1991–93, Chief Minister 1993–94, 1998; currently Deputy Chair., Planning Bd, Chair. Cttee on Public Undertakings, mem. Public Accounts Cttee; Pres. Goa unit of Nationalist Congress Party; Fellow Asscn of Surgeons of India; Hon. Fellow Int. Coll. of Surgeons; Commdr Grand Cross of the Order of Infante Dom Henrique (Portugal); Dr B. C. Roy Award for Eminent Medical Man and Statesman (India), Silver Elephant Award (India), Son of India Award. *Leisure interests:* stamp collecting, numismatics. *Address:* c/o Dias Bldg, Ormuz Road, Panjim, Goa (office); 359 Muddavaddi, Saligao, Bardez, Goa, India (home). *Telephone:* (832) 2224964 (office); (832) 2278000 (home); (832) 2409523. *Fax:* (832) 2409782 (home). *E-mail:* willie_goa@sancharnet.in.

DE THÉ, Guy Blaudin, MD, PhD; French cancer research specialist and academic; *Professor Emeritus, Institut Pasteur;* b. 5 May 1930, Marseilles; s. of François Blaudin de Thé and Madeleine du Verne; m. Colette Pierrard de Maujouy 1958 (died 1991); one s. two d.; ed Faculty of Medicine, Marseilles, Univ. of Paris, Sorbonne; Research Asst Duke Univ. Medical Center, USA 1961–63; Visiting Scientist, Laboratory of Viral Oncology, Nat. Cancer Inst., NIH, USA 1963–65; Head of Unit of Electron Microscopy, CNRS 1965–67; Chief, Unit of Biological Carcinogenesis, WHO Int. Agency for Research on Cancer, Lyons 1967–78; Dir of Research Faculty of Medicine Alexis Carrel, Lyon and Cancer Research Inst., Villejuif, Paris 1979–90, CNRS 1990–; Head Unit of Epidemiology of Oncogenic Viruses and Prof. Pasteur Inst., Paris 1990–97, Prof. Emer. 1998–; Visiting Prof. Faculty of Public Health, Harvard Univ. 1981–85; Fogarty Scholar-in-Residence, NIH, Bethesda USA 1992–96; Gen. Sec., then Pres. Int. Asscn of Retrovirology 1998–99; mem. Scientific Council, Ligue nat. française contre le cancer 1972–74; mem. Nat. Acad. Médecine, Soc. française de Microbiologie, American Soc. for Cell Biology, American Asscn for Cancer Research, AAAS, European Asscn for Cancer Research; Corresp. mem. Inst. de France Acad. des Sciences; Scientific Prize, Acad. of Sciences 1971, Medical Research Foundation 1979, Collège de France 1981, Silver Medal, CNRS 1981, Life Sciences Inst. Paris 1991; Commandeur, Ordre National du Mérite. *Publications:* many publs on the cell virus relationship in avian and murine leukaemia viruses and role of viruses in human tumours (Burkitt's lymphoma in Africa, Nasopharyngeal carcinoma in South-East Asia); Retroviruses and Central Nervous Degenerative Diseases; Sur la piste du cancer (popular scientific book) 1984, Modes de vie et cancers 1988. *Leisure interest:* arts. *Address:* Institut Pasteur, Département des rétrovirus, 28 rue Dr Roux, 75015 Paris (office); 14 rue Le Regrattier, 75004 Paris, France (home). *Telephone:* 1-45-68-89-30 (office); 1-43-54-01-22 (home). *Fax:* 1-45-68-89-31 (office); 1-40-51-05-15 (home). *E-mail:* dethe@pasteur.fr (office).

DE TRICORNOT DE ROSE, Comte François Jean-Baptiste Hubert Edouard Marie; French diplomatist (retd); b. 3 Nov. 1910; s. of Carlo de Tricornot de Rose and Madeleine Tavernier; m. Yvonne Daday 1933 (deceased); two d.; ed Ecole Libre des Sciences Politiques, Paris; Sec. French Embassy, London, UK 1937–40; liaison officer with Allied Forces in Tunisia 1943, Normandy, Belgium and Holland 1944; Sec. French Embassy, Italy 1945–46; mem. French del. to UN 1946–50; Minister-Counsellor, Spain 1952–56; Ministry of Foreign Affairs, Paris 1956–60; mem. Atomic Energy Comm. (Paris) 1950–64; Pres. European Nuclear Research Org. (CERN) 1958–60; Asst to Chief of Staff, Nat. Defence 1961–62; Amb. to Portugal 1964–69; Amb. and Perm. Rep. to NATO Council 1970–75; Vice-Pres. Council of Int. Inst. of Strategic Studies (London) 1980–2002; mem. Trilateral Comm. (European Group) 1976–90; Officier, Légion d'honneur, Commdr Ordre nat. du Mérite, Croix de Guerre. *Achievements:* Guinness Book of Records Award for playing 90 holes of golf (5 rounds) to celebrate his 90th birthday.

Publications: La France et la défense de l'Europe 1976, European Security and France 1984, La paix. Pourquoi pas? (with J. D. Remond and Chantal Ruiz-Barthélémy) 1986, Defendre la Défense 1989, La Troisième Guerre Mondiale n'a pas eu lieu, L'Alliance Atlantique et la Paix 1995. *Leisure interest:* golf. *Address:* 5 rue du Faubourg Saint-Honoré, 75008 Paris, France (home). *Telephone:* 1-42-65-70-75 (office); 1-42-65-70-60 (home). *Fax:* 1-40-17-02-56 (office).

DE VABRES, Renaud Donnedieu; French politician; b. 13 March 1954, Neuilly-sur-Seine, Haut de Seine; grandson of Prof. Henri Donnedieu de Vabres; ed Institut d'Etudes Politiques, Paris and Ecole Nationale d'Admin; nat. service in navy on board patrol ship La Paimpolaise; Prin. Pvt. Sec. to Préfet of Indre-et-Loire; Sec.-Gen. Centre Region Police Admin 1980–81, Alpes de Hautes Provence 1981–82; Sous-Préfet Château-Thierry 1982–85; Sr Lecturer, Institut d'Etudes Politiques, Paris 1984–; mem. Conseil d'Etat 1985–; Deputy to Assemblé Nationale for Indre-et-Loire 1997–, Vice-Pres. Comm. for Foreign Affairs; mem. Tours Municipal Council 2001–; mem. Centre Regional Council 1986–2001, Chair. Union pour la démocratie française (UDF) Group and Gen. Rapporteur on the Budget and Planning 1986–93, Vice-Chair. and Gen. Rapporteur on the Budget 1993–98; Delegate-Gen. of Parti Républicain (PR) as mem. Political Bureau 1986–96; Special Asst to François Léotard, Minister of State, Minister of Defence 1993–95; Delegate-Gen. of UDF 1996–98, of Nouvelle UDF 1998–2002, and concurrently Prin. Pvt. Sec. to François Léotard (PR) 1986 and UDF 1996–98; fmr Minister Del. for European Affairs; Spokesman for Union pour un Mouvement Populaire 2003–; Minister of Culture and Communication 2003–07. *Address:* c/o Union pour un Mouvement Populaire (UMP), 55 rue La Boétie, 75384 Paris Cedex 08, France (office). *E-mail:* ump@u-m-p.org (office). *Website:* www.u-m-p.org (office); www.rdonnedieudevabres.com.

DE VASCONCELOS LIMA, José Jorge, MS; Brazilian politician; b. 18 Nov. 1944, Recife, Pernambuco; m.; two d.; ed Universidade Federal de Pernambuco, Universidade Católica de Pernambuco, Univesidade Fed. do Rio de Janeiro, Universidad de Madrid, Spain; Prof., Universidade Fed. de Pernambuco in 1970s; Educ. Sec., Pernambuco 1975–79, Housing Sec. 1979–82; joined Partido da Frente Liberal (PFL) 1982, mem. Câmara dos Deputados 1982–98; Pres. PFL 1989–90, 1993–94; mem. Senado Fed. for Pernambuco 1999–2006, Minister of Mines and Energy 2001–02; PFL cand. for Vice Pres. 2006. *Address:* Partido da Frente Liberal (PFL), Senado Federal, Anexo 1, 26° andar, 70165-900 Brasília, DF, Brazil. *Telephone:* (61) 3311-4305. *Fax:* (61) 3224-1912. *E-mail:* pfl25@pfl.org.br. *Website:* www.pfl.org.br.

DE VAUCLEROY, Baron Gui, LLD, MEconSc; Belgian business executive; b. 28 Sept. 1933, Dendermonde; ed Univ. of Louvain; Research Asst Centre for Social Studies 1957–59; joined Delhaize Le Lion (later Delhaize Group) 1960, mem. Exec. Cttee 1967, Vice-Pres. Exec. Cttee 1984, CEO and Pres. Exec. Cttee 1990–98, Chair. Bd of Dirs 1999–2004; Chair. Fed. of Enterprises in Belgium 1999–2002; Vice-Pres. Union of Industrial Employers Europe 2000–02; Commdr de l'Ordre de Léopold, Grand Officier de l'Ordre de Léopold II. *Address:* Avenue Baron Albert d'Huart 137, 1950 Kraainem (home); c/o Delhaize Group, Rue Osseghem 53, PO Box 60, Molenbeek-Saint-Jean, Brussels 1080, Belgium (office).

DE VICENZO, Roberto; Argentine fmr golfer; b. 14 April 1923, Buenos Aires; professional golfer since 1938; won more than 230 tournaments worldwide; won Argentine PGA and Open 1944; subsequently won Argentine PGA six more times by 1952 and Open eight more times by1974; represented Argentina in numerous World Cups, twice individual winner; also winner, Chilean, Colombian, Brazilian and Panama Opens; first appeared in Britain 1948; winner, British Open, Hoylake 1967; Hon. mem. St Andrews World Golf Hall of Fame 1989.

DE VIDO, Julio Miguel; Argentine politician; *Minister of Planning, Public Investment and Services;* b. 26 Dec. 1949, Buenos Aires; ed Universidad de Buenos Aires; qualified architect; Dir-Gen. of Public Works, Inst. of Urban Devt, Santa Cruz 1988–90; Minister of Economy and Public Works of Santa Cruz 1991–99, Minister of Govt 1999–2003; elected Prov. Deputy, Santa Cruz 1997; adviser to presidential cand. Néstor Kirchner during election campaign 2003; Minister of Planning, Public Investment and Services 2003–. *Address:* Ministerio de Planificación Federal, Inversión Pública y Servicios, H. Yrigoyen 250, Piso 11 of. 1112 (1109), Buenos Aires, Argentina (office). *Telephone:* (11) 4349-5000 (office). *Website:* www.minplan.gov.ar (office).

DE VIRION, Tadeusz Józef; Polish lawyer and diplomatist; b. 28 March 1926, Warsaw; s. of Jerzy de Virion and Zofia de Virion; m. Jayanti de Virion 1985; one d.; ed Warsaw Univ.; served in Home Army during Nazi occupation 1943–45, took part in Warsaw Uprising 1944; qualified as judge 1948; qualified as attorney 1950, since then practising at Warsaw Bar, counsel for the defence in criminal cases; judge, State Tribunal 1989–90 (resgnd), 1993–2002; Amb. to UK 1990–93 (also accred to Ireland until Oct. 1991); Hon. and Devotional Kt of Sovereign Order of Kts of Malta 1980 and Commdr, Cross with Star 'Pro Merito Meliteusi'; Commdr Cross of Polonia Restituta; Gold Cross of Merit; Home Army's Cross. *Address:* ul. Zakopiańska 17, 03-934 Warsaw, Poland. *Telephone:* (22) 6178880.

DE VIRVILLE, Michel, PhD; French business executive and fmr civil servant; *Executive Vice-President and Corporate Secretary General, Renault SA;* b. 13 May 1945, Paris; Research Engineer, Centre Nat. de la Recherche Scientifique 1968–75, Adviser to Dir of Studies and Qualifications 1975–84; Tech. Adviser to Prime Minister's Office 1984–86; Adviser, Auditor-Gen.'s Office, Ministry of Labour 1986; Head of Cabinet, Ministry of Employment and Professional Training 1988–91; joined Renault SA 1993, Man. Human Resources Div. 1996, Corp. Sec.-Gen. 1998–, Human Resources Dir 1998–, mem. Exec. Cttee Renault Group, also currently Exec. Vice-Pres.; Chair. Unedic Jan.–March 2008; mem. Comm. pour la Libération de la Croissance Française. *Address:* Renault SA, 1967 rue du Vieux Pont de Sèvres, 92109 Boulogne-Billancourt Cedex, France (office). *Telephone:* 1-76-84-04-04 (office). *Website:* www.renault.com (office).

DE VRIES, Bert, DEcon; Dutch politician; b. 29 March 1938; ed Groningen Univ. and Amsterdam Free Univ.; fmrly worked in tax service, with Philips and as lecturer, Erasmus Univ. Rotterdam; mem. Parl. 1982–; Parl. Leader, Christian Democratic Appeal 1982; Minister of Social Affairs and Employment 1989–94. *Address:* c/o Christian Democratic Appeal, Dr. Kuyperstraat 5, 2514 BA The Hague, Netherlands.

DE VRIES, Gijs, MA; Dutch politician; *Counter-Terrorism Co-ordinator, European Union;* b. 1956, New York; m.; ed Leiden Univ.; Netherlands envoy, Convention for an EU Constitution 2000–03; MEP 1984–98, Leader, Liberal and Democratic Group 1994–98; Deputy Minister of Interior Affairs 1998–2002; Counter-Terrorism Co-ordinator, EU 2004–; Commdr, Hellenic Order of Merit 1996. *Address:* c/o European Union General Secretariat, Council of the European Union, rue de la Loi 175, 1048 Brussels, Belgium (office).

DE WAAL, Marius Theodorus, BSc, B.ING.; South African business executive; *Chairman, Transnet Limited;* b. 12 March 1925, Paarl Dist; s. of Pieter de Waal; m. Kitty du Plessis 1949; three s. one d.; ed Univs of Stellenbosch, Delft and Harvard Advanced Man. Programme, Swansea; town engineer, Bellville 1947–60; with Industrial Devt Corpn of SA Ltd 1961–90; Chair. Iscor Ltd 1988–95, Transnet 1990–, Siemens Ltd; Dir SA Reserve Bank, BMW; Hon. DEng, Hon. DComm, Hon. DBA. *Leisure interest:* tennis. *Address:* Transnet Ltd, PO Box 72501, Parkview 2122, South Africa.

DE WAART, Edo; Dutch conductor; *Artistic Director, Hong Kong Philharmonic Orchestra;* b. 1 June 1941, Amsterdam; s. of M. de Waart and J. Rose; one s. one d.; ed Amsterdam Music Lyceum with Haakon Stotijn, Hilversum with Franco Ferrara; Co-Prin. Oboe, Amsterdam Philharmonic 1961, Concertgebouw Orchestra 1963; Asst Conductor, New York Philharmonic 1965–66, Concertgebouw Orchestra, Amsterdam 1966; Musical Dir Netherlands Wind Ensemble 1966; Conductor Rotterdam Philharmonic 1967, Musical Dir and Prin. Conductor 1973–79; Prin. Guest Conductor San Francisco Symphony Orchestra 1975–77, Music Dir 1977–85; Music Dir Minn. Orchestra 1986–95; Artistic Dir, Nederlandse Omroep Stichtung (Dutch radio organization); Chief Conductor Netherlands Radio Philharmonic Orchestra 1989–; Prin. Guest Conductor Santa Fe Opera 1991–92; Artistic Dir and Chief Conductor Sydney Symphony Orchestra 1993–2003; Artistic Dir Hong Kong Philharmonic Orchestra 2004–; Chief Conductor Santa Fe Opera 2007–09; Music Dir Milwaukee Symphony Orchestra 2009–; Artistic Partner, St Paul Chamber Orchestra (2010–); guest conductor with leading orchestras and at venues in USA and Europe and at festivals including Spoleto, Bayreuth and Holland; First Prize, Dimitri Mitropoulos Competition, New York 1964; Hon. AO 2005. *Address:* Harrison Parrott, 5–6 Albion Court, London, W6 0QT, England (office); c/o Hong Kong Philharmonic Orchestra, Level 8 Administration Building, Hong Kong Cultural Centre, Tsim Sha Tsui, Kowloon, Hong Kong (office). *Telephone:* (20) 7229-9166 (office); 2721 2030 (office). *Fax:* (20) 7221-5042 (office); 2311 6229 (office). *E-mail:* info@harrisonparrott.com (office). *Website:* www.harrisonparrott.com (office); www.hkpo.com (office).

DE ZOYSA, Tilak; Sri Lankan business executive; *Chairman, Carson Cumberbatch & Company Ltd;* Deputy Chair. and Man. Dir Associate Motorways Ltd 1993–; Chair. Carson Cumberbatch & Co. Ltd 2001–; fmr Pres. Nat. Chamber of Commerce; fmr Chair. Ceylon Chamber of Commerce; Dir Bukit Darah Co. Ltd 2004–; Vice-Pres. Sri Lanka–France Business Council 2004–; mem. Monetary Bd of Sri Lanka; mem. Bd Dirs Taj Lanka Hotels Ltd; mem. Tariff Advisory Council; Hon. Consul for Croatia 1999–; Order of the Rising Sun, Gold Rays with Neck Ribbon, Japan. *Address:* Carson Cumberbatch & Co. Ltd, 61 Janadhipathi Mawatha, Colombo 1, Sri Lanka (office). *Telephone:* (11) 4739200 (office). *Fax:* (11) 4739300 (office). *E-mail:* carsons@carcumb.com (office). *Website:* www.carsoncumberbatch.com (office).

DEACON, Richard, CBE, RA, MA; British sculptor; b. 15 Aug. 1949, Bangor, Wales; s. of the late Group Capt. Edward William Deacon and the late Joan Bullivant Winstanley; m. Jacqueline Poncelet 1977 (divorced 2001); one s. one d.; ed Somerset Coll. of Art, St Martin's School of Art, RCA, Chelsea School of Art; toured S America 1996–97; Prof., Ecole Nat. Supérieure des Beaux-Arts, Paris 1998–; Vice-Chair. Baltic Centre for Contemporary Art Trust 1999–2005; mem. British Council, Arts Council of England Architecture Advisory Group 1996–99; Visiting Prof., Chelsea School of Art 1992–; Trustee Tate Gallery 1992–97; Chevalier Ordre des Arts et des Lettres 1997; Turner Prize 1987, Robert Jacobsen Prize 1995; Hon. DLitt (Leicester) 2005. *Works include:* What Could Make Me Feel This Way?, Struck Dumb, Doubletalk, Body of Thought No 2, The Back of My Hand, Distance No Object No 2, Dummy, Under My Skin, Breed, Skirt, Laocoon, After, Moor, Let's Not Be Stupid, No Stone Unturned, Building From the Inside, Can't See the Wood for the Trees, Out of Order, The Same But Different, Mountain, Another Mountain, Dead Leg, Nosotros Tres, Water Under The Bridge. *Leisure interests:* swimming, walking. *Address:* c/o Lisson Gallery, 67 Lisson Street, London, NW1 5DA, England (home). *Website:* www.richarddeacon.net (office).

DEAN, Christopher, OBE; British fmr ice skater; b. 27 July 1958, Nottingham; s. of the late Colin Dean and Mavis (née Pearson) Dean; m. 1st Isabelle Duchesnay 1991 (divorced 1993); m. 2nd Jill Ann Trenary 1994; two s.; police constable 1974–80; British Ice Dance Champion (with Jayne Torvill q.v., 1978–83, 1994; European Ice Dance Champion (with Jayne Torvill) 1981, 1982, 1984, 1994; World Ice Dance Champion (with Jayne Torvill) 1981–84, World Professional Champions 1984–85, 1990, 1995–96; Olympic Ice Dance gold medal (with Jayne Torvill) 1984, Olympic Ice Dance bronze medal (with

Jayne Torvill) 1994; choreographed Encounters for English Nat. Ballet 1996, Stars on Ice in USA 1998–99, 1999–2000; Hon. MA (Nottingham Trent) 1994, BBC Sports Personality of the Year (with Jayne Torvill) 1984, Figure Skating Hall of Fame (with Jayne Torvill) 1989. *Ice Dance:* World tours with own and int. companies of skaters 1985, 1988, 1994, 1997, also tours of Australia and New Zealand 1984, 1991, UK 1992, 1997–98, Japan 1996, USA and Canada 1997–98. *Television:* Path to Perfection (ITV video) 1984, Fire & Ice (also video) 1986, Bladerunners (BBC documentary), The Artistry of Torvill & Dean (ABC TV) 1994, Face the Music 1995, Torvill & Dean, The Story So Far (biographical video) 1996, Bach Sixth Cello Suite (with Yo-Yo Ma) 1996, Dancing on Ice 2007, 2008, 2009 (followed by nat. tours). *Publications:* Torvill and Dean's Face the Music and Dance (with Jayne Torvill) 1993, Torvill and Dean: An Autobiography (with Jayne Torvill) 1994, Facing the Music (with Jayne Torvill) 1995. *Leisure interests:* theatre, ballet, fast cars. *Address:* c/o Sue Young, PO Box 32, Heathfield, East Sussex, TN21 0BW, England (office). *Telephone:* (1435) 867825 (office); (1273) 330798.

DEAN, Graham, BA; British artist; b. 5 Dec. 1951, Birkenhead; s. of Leslie Dean and Dorothy Dean; m. Denise Warr 1989; one s. one d.; ed Laird School of Art, Birkenhead, Bristol Polytechnic Faculty of Art and Design; artist since 1974; Abbey Award in Painting, British School, Rome 1992; Int. Fellowship, Vermont Studio Center, USA 2003. *Dance:* collaborations with Darshan Singh Bhuller, including No Go Zone, White Picket Fence. *Radio:* Painting by Radio (series), BBC Radio 4, 1984. *Films:* several independent shorts and videos, including Solsbury Hill (with Peter Gabriel). *Publications:* The Green Room and Other Paintings 1995, Straight to Red 1999, Light Sweet Crude 2001, Shimmer 2004. *Leisure interests:* tennis, supporting Liverpool football club. *Address:* 17 Norfolk Road, Brighton, East Sussex, BN1 3AA, England (home); Waterhouse and Dodd, 26 Cork Street, London, W1S 3ND; Voc Palombaro, 32/37 San Vito, 05010 San Venanzo Terne, Umbria, Italy. *Telephone:* (20) 7734-7800 (office). *E-mail:* jsa@modbritart.com (office); graham.dean1@virgin.net (home). *Website:* www.grahamdean.com (home); www.modbritart.com.

DEAN, Howard, BA, MD; American politician; b. 17 Nov. 1948; s. of Howard Brush Dean and Andrea Maitland; m. Judith Steinberg; one s. one d.; ed Yale Univ. and Albert Einstein Coll. of Medicine; Intern, then resident in internal medicine, Medical Center Hosp. Vermont 1978–82; internal medicine specialist medical practice in Shelburne, Vt; mem. Vermont House of Reps 1983–86, Asst minority leader 1985–86; Lt Gov. State of Vermont 1986–91; Gov. of Vermont 1991–2003; sought Democratic Party presidential candidacy 2004; Chair. Democratic Nat. Cttee 2005–09. *Address:* 325 South Cove Road, Burlington, VT 05401-5447, USA. *Website:* www.democrats.org (office).

DEAN, Hon. John Gunther, PhD; American diplomatist; b. 24 Feb. 1926, Germany; s. of Dr Joseph Dean and Lucy Dean (née Aschkenazy); m. Martine Duphénieux 1952; two s. one d.; ed Harvard Coll., Harvard Univ. Graduate School and Univ. of Paris Law School, France; entered govt service 1950; diplomatic posts in France, Belgium, Viet Nam, Laos, Togo, Mali and in US Dept of State; Dir Pacification Program in Mil. Region 1, Viet Nam 1970–72; Deputy Chief Mission, American Embassy, Laos 1972–74; Amb. to Khmer Repub. 1974–75, to Denmark 1975–78, to Lebanon 1978–81, to Thailand 1981–85, to India 1985–88; mem. bd of dirs of corp. and academic insts in USA, Europe and Asia 1990–; Personal Rep. of Dir-Gen. of UNESCO for Cambodia 1989–90; mem. bd Petroleum Inst. of Thailand 1991–, Inst. Supérieur de Gestion 1991–, General Mediterranean Holdings 1992–, Maersk Line Shipping 1992–2007; numerous US and foreign decorations. *Publications:* The Oral History of John Gunther Dean, The Donation of Documents by Ambassador John Gunther Dean to the National Archives 2004, 2005. *Address:* 29 boulevard Jules Sandeau, 75116 Paris, France (office); BP 1318, Chalet Crettaz-Cô, 1936 Verbier, Valais, Switzerland (home). *Telephone:* 1-45-04-71-84 (office); 277712917 (home). *Fax:* 1-45-04-78-57 (office). *E-mail:* johnmartinedean@aol.com (home).

DEAN, Stafford Roderick; British singer (bass); b. 20 June 1937, Surrey; s. of Eric E. Dean and Vera S. Bathurst; m. 1st Carolyn J. Lambourne 1963; four s.; m. 2nd Anne E. Howells 1981; one s. one d.; ed Epsom Coll., Royal Coll. of Music and privately with Howell Glynne and Otakar Kraus; Opera for All 1962–64; Glyndebourne Chorus 1963–64, Prin. début as Lictor in L'Incoronazione di Poppea 1963; under contract to Sadler's Wells Opera/English Nat. Opera 1964–70; Royal Opera House, Covent Garden 1969–, début as Masetto in Don Giovanni; int. début as Leporello in Don Giovanni, Stuttgart 1971; guest appearances with Metropolitan Opera, New York, Chicago Lyric, San Francisco, Berlin, Munich, Hamburg, Cologne, Frankfurt, Vienna, Paris, Turin operas etc.; specializes in Mozart bass repertoire; bass soloist in world premiere of Penderecki Requiem, Stuttgart 1984; concert appearances in choral works by Beethoven, Shostakovich, Verdi. *Leisure interests:* family life, garden.

DEAN, Winton Basil, MA, FBA; British musicologist and author; b. 18 March 1916, Birkenhead; s. of Basil Dean and Esther (née Van Gruisen) Dean; m. Hon. Thalia Mary Shaw 1939 (died 2000); one s. (two d. deceased) one adopted d.; ed Harrow, King's Coll., Cambridge; mem. Music Panel, Arts Council of GB 1957–60; Ernest Bloch Prof. of Music, Univ. of Calif., Berkeley, USA 1965–66, Regent's Lecturer 1977; mem. Council, Royal Musical Asscn 1965–98 (Vice-Pres. 1970–98, Hon. mem. 1998–); mem. Vorstand, GF Händel-Gesellschaft, Halle 1980– (Vice-Pres. 1991–99, Hon. mem. 1999), Kuratorium, Göttinger Händel-Gesellschaft 1982–97, Hon. mem. 1997–; Hon. mem. RAM; Corresp. mem. American Musicological Soc.; Hon. MusDoc (Cambridge) 1996; City of Halle Handel Prize 1995. *Publications:* Bizet 1948, Carmen 1949, Handel's Dramatic Oratorios and Masques 1959, Shakespeare and Opera 1964, Georges Bizet, his Life and Work 1965, Handel and the Opera Seria 1969, The New Grove Handel 1982, Handel's Operas 1704–1726 (with J. M. Knapp) 1987, Essays on Opera 1990, (co-ed.) Handel's Opera Giulio Cesare in Egitto

1999, Handel's Operas 1726–1741 2007; maj. contribs to New Oxford History of Music, vol. VIII 1982 and Grove's Dictionary of Music and Musicians, 5th and 6th edns 1954, 1980. *Leisure interests:* shooting, naval history. *Address:* Hambledon Hurst, Godalming, Surrey GU8 4HF, England (home). *Telephone:* (1428) 682644 (home). *E-mail:* dean584@aol.com (home).

DEANE, Derek, OBE; British ballet dancer and choreographer; b. (Derek Shepherd), 18 June 1953, Cornwall; s. of William Gordon Shepherd and Margaret Shepherd; ed Royal Ballet School; with Royal Ballet Co. 1972–89, reaching rank of Premier Dancer; Asst Dir Rome Opera 1990–92; Artistic Dir English Nat. Ballet 1993–2001. *Leisure interests:* tennis, gardening, reading, dinner parties, theatre, performing arts, travel. *Address:* c/o English National Ballet, Markova House, 39 Jay Mews, London, SW7 2ES, England.

DEANE, Phyllis Mary, MA, FBA; British economic historian and academic; *Professor Emerita, University of Cambridge;* b. 13 Oct. 1918; d. of John Edward Deane and Elizabeth Jane Brooks; ed Chatham County School, Hutcheson's Girls' Grammar School, Glasgow and Univ. of Glasgow; Carnegie Research Scholar 1940–41; Research Officer, Nat. Inst. of Econ. and Social Research 1941–45; Colonial Research Officer 1946–48; Research Officer, Colonial Office 1948–49; Dept of Applied Econs, Univ. of Cambridge 1950–61, Lecturer, Faculty of Econs and Politics 1961–71, Reader in Econ. History 1971–81, Prof. 1981–83, Prof. Emer. 1983–; Fellow, Newnham Coll. 1961–83, Hon. Fellow 1983; Ed. Economic Journal 1968–75; Pres. Royal Econ. Soc. 1980–82; Hon. DLitt (Glasgow) 1989. *Publications:* The Future of the Colonies (with Julian Huxley) 1945, The Measurement of Colonial National Incomes 1948, Colonial Social Accounting 1953, British Economic Growth 1688–1959 (with W. A. Cole) 1962, The First Industrial Revolution 1965, The Evolution of Economic Ideas 1978, The State and the Economic System 1989, The Life and Times of J. Neville Keynes 2001, papers and reviews in econ. journals. *Leisure interests:* walking, gardening. *Address:* c/o Newnham College, Sidgwick Avenue, Cambridge, CB3 9DF, England (home).

DEANE, Seamus Francis, PhD; Irish academic, poet and novelist; *Donald and Marilyn Keough Emeritus Professor of Irish Studies, University of Notre Dame;* b. 9 Feb. 1940; s. of Winifred Deane and Frank Deane; m. Marion Treacy 1963; three s. one d.; ed Queen's Univ., Belfast, Univ. of Cambridge; Fulbright and Woodrow Wilson Scholar, Visiting Lecturer, Reed Coll., Portland, Ore. 1966–67; Visiting Lecturer, Univ. of Calif., Berkeley 1967–68, Visiting Prof. 1978; Lecturer, Univ. Coll., Dublin 1968–77, Sr Lecturer 1978–80, Prof. of English and American Literature 1980–93; Visiting Prof., Univ. of Notre Dame, Indiana 1977, Donald and Marilyn Keough Prof. of Irish Studies 1993–2005, now Emer. Prof.; Walker Ames Prof., Univ. of Washington, Seattle 1987, Jules Benedict Distinguished Visiting Prof., Carleton Coll., Minn. 1988; Dir Field Day Theatre Co. 1980–; mem. Royal Irish Acad. 1982; Hon. DLitt (Ulster) 1999; AE Memorial Award for Literature 1972; Ireland/America Fund Literary Award 1988; Guardian Fiction Prize 1996; Irish Times Int. Fiction Prize 1997, Irish Times Irish Literature Prize 1997; Ruffino Antico Fattore Int. Literary Award (Florence, Italy) 1998. *Publications:* Celtic Revivals 1985, Short History of Irish Literature 1986, Selected Poems 1988, The French Revolution and Enlightenment in England 1789–1832 1988, Field Day Anthology of Irish Writing 550–1990 1991, Reading in the Dark 1996, Strange Country 1997, Foreign Affections: Essays on Edmund Burke 2005. *Address:* Field Day Publications, c/o Newman House, 86 St. Stephen's Green, Dublin, 2, Ireland (office). *E-mail:* deane.4@nd.edu (office).

DEANE, Hon. Sir William Patrick, AC, KBE, BA, LLB, QC; Australian fmr Governor-General and judge; b. 4 Jan. 1931, St Kilda; s. of the late C.A. Deane, MC and Lillian Hussey; m. Helen Russell 1965; one s. one d.; ed St Joseph's Coll. Sydney, Sydney Univ. and Trinity Coll. Dublin, Ireland; Teaching Fellow in Equity, Univ. of Sydney 1956–61; barrister 1957; Justice, Supreme Court, NSW 1977, Fed. Court of Australia 1977–82; Pres. Australian Trade Practices Tribunal 1977–82; Justice, High Court of Australia 1982–95; Gov.-Gen. of Australia 1996–2001; KStJ; Hon. LLD (Sydney, Griffith, Notre Dame, Trinity Coll., Univ. of NSW, Univ. of Tech. of Sydney, Univ. of Queensland); Hon. DUniv (Southern Cross, Australian Catholic Univ., Queensland Univ. of Tech., Univ. of W Sydney); Hon. DSacredTheol (Melbourne Coll. of Divinity). *Address:* c/o PO Box 4168, Manuka 2603, Australia. *Telephone:* (2) 6239-4716 (office). *Fax:* (2) 6239-4916 (office).

DEARLOVE, Sir Richard (Billing), Kt, KCMG, OBE, MA; British diplomatist; *Master, Pembroke College, Cambridge;* b. 23 Jan. 1945; m. Rosalind McKenzie 1968; two s. one d.; ed Monkton Combe School, Kent School, Conn., USA, Queens' Coll., Cambridge; joined the Foreign Office 1966, postings to Nairobi 1968–71, Prague 1973–76, FCO, London 1971–73, 1976–80, 1984–87, First Sec. Paris 1980–84, Counsellor UK Mission to the UN (UKMIS), Geneva 1987–91, Washington 1991–93; Dir of Personnel and Admin., Secret Intelligence Service (SIS) 1993–94, Dir of Operations 1994–99, Asst Chief 1998–99, Chief 1999–2004; Master of Pembroke Coll., Cambridge 2004–; mem. Int. Advisory Bd AIG 2005–; Sr Adviser Monitor Group 2004–; Chair. Ascot Underwriting 2006–; Chair. of Trustees, Cambridge Union Soc. 2007–; Gov. English Speaking Union 2008–; Hon. Fellow, Queens' Coll. Cambridge 2004; Hon. LLD (Exeter) 2007. *Leisure interests:* painting, fly fishing, the future of Cornwall. *Address:* The Master's Lodge, Pembroke College, Cambridge, CB2 1RF, England (office). *Telephone:* (1223) 338129 (office). *Fax:* (1223) 766395 (office).

DEARY, Terry; British children's writer; b. 3 Jan. 1946, Sunderland; m. Jenny Deary 1975; one d.; fmr actor, theatre dir and drama teacher; Patron Single Homeless Action Initiative in Derwentside, Macmillan Cancer Relief Sunderland Appeal, Grace House Children's Hospice Appeal, Burnhope Asscn of Rural Crafts; Hon. DEduc (Sunderland) 2000; Books for Keeps magazine

Outstanding Children's Non-Fiction Author of the 20th Century 1999. *Radio:* Terrible Tales of Wales (series, BBC Radio Wales) 2005. *Theatre:* The Terry Deary History Roadshow (one-man show). *Publications include:* juvenile fiction: Calamity Kate 1980, Hope Street 1980, The Lambton Worm 1981, Twist of the Knife 1981, The Custard Kid 1982, The Wishing Well Ghost 1983, The Silent Scream 1984, The Windmill of Nowhere 1984, I Met her on a Rainy Day 1985, A Witch in Time 1986, Treasure of Skull Island 1986, Spine Chilling Stories 1987, The Ghosts of Batwing Castle 1988, The Dream Seller 1988, Bad Bart and Billy the Brave 1989, Magic of the Mummy 1990, Treasure of Grey Manor 1990, Two in to One Won't Go 1991, The Great Father Christmas Robbery 1991, Shadow Play 1992, Ghost Town 1992, Durham Tales 1993, The Spark Files (series) 1998–, Ghost for Sale 1999, Hat Trick 2000, Pitt Street Pirates 2001, Footsteps in the Fog 2003, War Games 2004, Dirty Little Imps 2004, Egyptian Tales (series) 2004–, The Boy who Haunted Himself 2004, The Last Viking 2005, The Fire Thief 2005, Flight of the Fire Thief 2006; juvenile non-fiction: True Monster Stories 1992, True Horror Stories 1993, True Shark Stories 1995, Shivers: Mysteries 1995, Terror 1995, Disasters 1995, Spooks 1995, The Magic of the Mummy 1995, The Truth About Guy Fawkes? 1996, True Detective Stories 1996, Who Killed Kit Marlowe? 1996, The Real Joan of Arc? 1996, Who Shot Queen Victoria? 1996, Encounter on the Moon 1996, The Philadelphia Experiment 1996, The Discovery at Roswell 1996, Alien Landing 1996, Vanished! 1996, Break Out! 1996, The Nuclear Winter Man 1996, True UFO Stories 1997, Explorers 1997, Inventors 1997, Scientists 1997, Writers 1997, Tudor Terror (series) 1997–, True War Stories 1998, Top Ten Shakespeare Stories 1998, Top Ten Greek Legends 1998, Bloody Scotland 1998, True Disaster Stories 1999, Potty Politics 1999, The Time Detectives (series) 2000–, Read-It! Chapter Books: Historical Tales (series) 2005–, Terry Deary's Terribly True Stories (series) 2006–, Dick Turpin: Legends and Lies 2007; Horrible Histories series: The Terrible Tudors (Blue Peter Book Award 2001) 1993, The Awesome Egyptians 1993, The Vile Victorians 1994, The Rotten Romans (Blue Peter Book Award 2002) 1994, The Vicious Vikings 1994, The Blitzed Brits 1995, Cruel Kings and Mean Queens 1995, The Groovy Greeks 1995, The Slimy Stuarts 1996, Wicked Words 1996, Dreadful Diary 1996, The Twentieth Century 1996, The Measly Middle Ages 1996, Poisonous Postcards 1997, Cut-throat Celts 1997, Dark Knights and Dingy Castles 1997, The Angry Aztecs 1997, The Gorgeous Georgians 1998, Even More Terrible Tudors 1998, The Frightful First World War 1998, Rowdy Revolutions 1999, Mad Millennium Play 1999, The Savage Stone Age 1999, The Woeful Second World War 1999, The Smashing Saxons 2000, Ireland 2000, The Incredible Incas 2000, Horrible Christmas 2000, The Stormin' Normans 2001, The USA 2001, The Barmy British Empire 2002, France 2002, Cruel Crimes and Painful Punishments 2002, Ruthless Romans 2003, The Wicked History of the World 2003, The Mad Miscellany 2004, Loathsome London 2005, Rotten Rulers 2005, Edinburgh 2005, York 2005, Dublin 2006, Stratford-Upon-Avon 2006, Pirates 2006, Awesome Annual 2006, Monstrous Miscellany 2006, Knights 2006, The Horrible History of the World 2006, Oxford 2007. *Address:* Terry-Deary.net Ltd, The Board Inn, Burnhope, County Durham DH7 0DP, England (office). *E-mail:* teryy@terry-deary.net. *Website:* www.terry-deary .net.

DEASY, Austin, TD; Irish politician (retd); b. 26 Aug. 1936, Dungarvan, Co. Waterford; s. of Michael Deasy and Geraldine Deasy; m. Catherine Keating 1961; two s. two d.; ed Dungarvan Christian Brothers' School and Univ. Coll., Cork; fmr secondary school teacher; mem. Waterford Co. Council and Dungarvan Urban Council 1967–2002; mem. Seanad Éireann 1973–77; mem. Dáil Éireann (Parl.) 1977–2002, Vice-Chair. Foreign Affairs Cttee 1997–2002; Minister for Agric. 1982–87; Leader, Irish Del. to Council of Europe 1997–2002; mem. Fine Gael. *Leisure interests:* golf, gardening, horse-racing. *Address:* Kilrush, Dungarvan, Co. Waterford, Ireland. *Telephone:* (58) 20760. *Fax:* (58) 45315.

DEBBASCH, Charles, DenD; French legal scholar and academic; *Professor of Law, Université d'Aix-Marseille III;* b. 22 Oct. 1937, Tunis, Tunisia; s. of Max Debbasch; m. Odile Peyridier 1959; three s. two d.; tutorial asst 1957; Jr Lecturer, Law Faculty, Université d'Aix-Marseille III 1959–62; Prof. of Law, Grenoble Univ. 1962–63; Prof. of Law, Université d'Aix-Marseille II 1963–67, Chair of Public Law, Faculty of Law and Econ. Sciences 1967, Dir Centre of Research into Legal Admin. 1966–, Centre of Research and Study on Mediterranean Societies 1969–71; Head of Research Comm., Ministry of Educ. 1968–69; Dir Teaching and Research Unit attached to faculty of Law and Political Sciences, Aix-Marseille Univ. 1966, Dean, Faculty of Law and Political Sciences 1971–73; Pres. Nat. Asscn of Pres. of Univs Specializing in Law and Politics and Deans of Law Faculties 1971–78; Prof. Coll. of Europe, Bruges 1975–81; Pres. Consultative Cttee Public Law Univs 1978; tech. adviser, Gen. Secr. French presidency 1978–81; Pres. Fondation Vasarely 1981–91; Dir and Dir-Gen. of Press Group, Dauphiné Libéré 1984–89; Pres. Agence générale d'information 1985–89; Pres. Supervisory Council of Dauphiné Libéré 1989–94, Observatoire int. de la démocratie 1994–; Dir Inst. Int. du droit des médias 1989–; Officier, Ordre nat. du Mérite, Chevalier, Légion d'honneur, Chevalier des Palmes Académiques, Grand Officer of the Aztec Eagle (Mexico), Commdr Order of Tunisian Repub., Officer of Merit, Senegal. *Publications:* Procédure administrative contentieuse et procédure civile 1962, La République tunisienne 1962, Institutions administratives 1975, Traité du droit de la radio-diffusion 1967, Le Droit de la radio et de la télévision 1970, L'Administration au pouvoir 1970, L'Université désorientée 1971, Droit administratif 1973, Science administrative 1980, la France de Pompidou 1974, Introduction à la politique 1982, Contentieux administratif 1985, Les Chats de l'émirat 1976, Institutions et droit administratifs (three vols, 1980–99), L'Etat civilisé 1979, L'Elysée dévoilé 1982, Lexique de politique 1984, Les constitutions de la France 1983, Droit constitutionnel 1986, Les Associations 1985, La Ve République 1985, La Disgrace du

socialisme 1985, La réussite politique 1987, La Cohabitation froide 1988, Le Droit de l'audiovisuel 1988, La société française 1989, Les grands arrêts du droit de l'audiovisuel 1991, Mémoires du Doyen d'Aix-en-Provence 1996, Droit des médias 1999, Droit administratif des biens 1999, La Constitution de la Ve République 2000, contrib. to numerous other works. *Address:* Centre de recherches administratives, Université de Droit, d'Economie et des Sciences, 3 avenue Robert Schuman, 13628 Aix-en-Provence (office); 25 avenue Mozart, 75116 Paris, France (office). *Telephone:* 4-42-17-29-29 (Aix); 1-45-20-45-72 (Paris). *E-mail:* debbasch.charles@wanadoo.fr (home).

DEBONO, Giovanna, BA; Maltese politician; *Minister for Gozo;* b. (Giovanna Attard), 25 Nov. 1956, Gozo; d. of the late Coronato Attard and of Anna Attard (née Tabone); m. Anthony Debono; one s. one d.; ed Univ. of Malta; teacher Educ. Dept 1981–87; MP, Nationalist Party 1987–; Parl. Sec. Ministry for Social Devt 1995–96; Minister for Gozo 1998–. *Address:* Ministry for Gozo, St Francis Square, Victoria, Gozo, Malta (office). *Telephone:* (21) 561482 (office). *Fax:* (21) 559360 (office). *E-mail:* giovanna.debono@gov.mt (office). *Website:* www.gozo.gov.mt (office).

DEBRAY, (Jules) Régis; French writer and government official; b. 2 Sept. 1940, Paris; s. of Georges Debray and Janine Alexandre; m. Elisabeth Burgos 1968; one d.; ed Ecole normale supérieure de la rue d'Ulm; colleague of Che Guevara, imprisoned in Bolivia 1967–70; Co-Ed., Comité d'études sur les libertés 1975; adviser on foreign affairs to François Mitterrand; responsible for Third World Affairs, Secr.-Gen. of Presidency of Repub. 1981–84; Office of Pres. of Repub. 1984–85, 1987–88; Maître des requêtes, Conseil d'Etat 1985–93; Sec.-Gen. Conseil du Pacifique Sud 1986–; Prix Fémina 1977. *Publications:* La Critique des armes 1973, La Guerilla du Che 1974, Entretiens avec Allende 1971, Les Epreuves du fer 1974, L'Indésirable 1975, La Neige brûle 1977, Lettre aux communistes français et á quelques autres 1978, Le Pouvoir intellectuel en France 1979, Le Scribe 1980, Critique de la raison politique 1981, La Puissance et les rêves 1984, Les Empires contre l'Europe 1985, Comète, ma comète 1986, Eloges 1986, Les Masques 1987, Que vive la République 1988, A demain de Gaulle 1990, Cours de médiologie générale 1991, Christophe Colomb, le visiteur de l'aube: les traités de Tordesillas 1992, Vie et mort de l'image: une histoire du regard en Occident 1992, Contretemps: Eloge des idéaux perdus 1992, Ledannois 1992, L'Etat séducteur 1993, L'Oeil naïf 1994, Manifestes médiologiques 1994, Par amour de l'art 1998, L'Abus monumental 1999, Croire, voir, faire 1999, L'Emprise 2000, i.f. suite et fin 2000, Introduction à la médiologie 2000, Loués soient les seigneurs 2000, L'Enseignement du fait religieux dans l'école laïque 2002, L'Edit de Caracalla ou plaidoyer pour les Etats-Unis d'occident 2002, L'Ancien Testament à travers 100 chefs-d'œuvre de la peinture 2003, Le Nouveau Testament à travers 100 chefs-d'œuvre de la peinture 2003, Dieu, un itinéraire 2003, Haïti et la France: Rapport à Dominique de Villepin, ministre des Affaires étrangères 2004, Le siecle et la règle 2004, Ce que nous voile le voile 2004, La Mythologie gréco-latine à travers 100 chefs-d'oeuvres de la peinture 2004, L'Histoire ancienne à travers 100 chefs-d'oeuvres de la peinture 2004, Chroniques de l'idiotie triomphante 2004, Journal D'Un Petit Bourgeois Entre Deux Feux Et Quatre Murs 2004, Le Plan Vermeil 2004, Le Feu Sacré 2005, Julien Le Fidèle Ou Le Banquet Des Démons 2005, Aveuglantes Lumières 2006, Supplique Aux Nouveaux Progressistes Du Xxie Siècle 2006. *Address:* Editions Gallimard, 5 rue Sébastien Bottin, 75007 Paris, France.

DEBRÉ, Bernard André Charles Robert, DenM; French politician and surgeon; b. 30 Sept. 1944, Toulouse; s. of the late Michel Debré and Anne-Marie Lemaresquier; m. Véronique Duron 1971; three s. one d.; ed Lycée Janson de Sailly and Faculté de Médecine, Paris; hosp. doctor 1965–1980; hosp. surgeon 1980; Prof. Faculté de Médecine, Paris 1985; Head of Urology, Hôpital Cochin 1990; other professional appointments; Deputy (RPR) to Nat. Assembly 1986–94, 2004– (joined UMP 2007); Mayor of Amboise 1992–2001; Minister of Cooperation 1994–95; mem. of French Cttee of Ethics 1986–88; f. Pour Paris Asscn (cr. to oppose policies of incumbent Mayor of Paris, Betrand Delanoë) 2005; Chevalier, Légion d'Honneur and numerous foreign decorations. *Publications:* La France malade de sa santé 1983, Un traité d'urologie (4 vols) 1985, Le voleur de vie (la bataille du Sida) 1989, L'illusion humanitaire 1997, Le retour de Mwami 1998, La grande transgression 2000 (Prix Louis Pauwels 2001), Le suicide de France (jtly) 2002, Avertissement aux Malades, aux Médicins et aux Elus (ed.) 2002, De la mauvaise conscience en général et de l'Afrique en particulier 2003, Tant que nous t'aimerons (L'Euthanasie la loi impossible) 2004, Le Roman de Shangai 2005, La revanche du serpent ou la fin de l'homo sapiens 2005, La Véritable Histoire des génocides rwandais 2006, Et si l'on parlait d'elle? 2007, articles in French and foreign journals. *Leisure interests:* travel, collecting antique plates, sports. *Address:* Assemblée nationale, 126 rue de l'Université, 75355 Paris 07 SP (office); 30 rue Jacob, 75006 Paris, France (home). *Telephone:* 1-43-25-51-41 (home); 6-85-30-45-73. *Fax:* 1-58-41-27-55 (office). *E-mail:* bdebre@assemblee-nationale.fr (office). *Website:* www.assemblee-nationale.fr (office).

DEBRÉ, Jean-Louis, DenD; French magistrate and politician; *President, Conseil Constitutionnel;* b. 30 Sept. 1944, Toulouse; s. of the late Michel Debré (fmr Prime Minister of France) and of Anne-Marie Lemaresquier; m. Ann-Marie Engel 1971; two s. one d.; ed Lycée Janson-de-Sailly, Inst. d'Etudes Politiques, Faculté de Droit, Paris and Ecole Nat. de la Magistrature; Asst Faculté de Droit, Paris 1972–75; Adviser, Office of Jacques Chirac 1974–76; Deputy Public Prosecutor, Tribunal de Grande Instance, Evry 1976–78; Magistrate, Cen. Admin. of Ministry of Justice 1978; Chef de Cabinet to Minister of Budget 1978; Examining Magistrate, Tribunal de Grande Instance, Paris 1979; RPR Deputy to Nat. Ass. 1986–95, 1997–2002, Pres. RPR Group 1997–2002; Town Councillor, Evreux 1989; Conseiller Général, Canton de Nonancourt 1992–2001; Deputy Sec.-Gen. and Spokesman for

Gaullist Party 1993; Minister of the Interior 1995–97; Vice-Pres. Gen. Council of the Euro 1998–; Mayor of Evreux 2001–07; Pres. Nat. Ass. 2002–07; Pres. Conseil Constitutionnel 2007–; Chevalier du Mérite Agricole, Grand-Croix l'Ordre d'Isabelle la catholique (Spain), Prix du Trombinoscope 2003, Marianne d'Or 2004,. *Publications:* Les idées constitutionnelles du Général de Gaulle 1974, La constitution de la Ve République 1974, Le pouvoir politique 1977, Le Gaullisme 1978, La justice au XIXe 1981, Les républiques des avocats 1984, Le curieux 1986, En mon for intérieur 1997, Pièges 1998, Le Gaulisme n'est pas une nostalgie 1999, Qu'est-ce que l'Assemblée nationale? 2006. *Leisure interests:* riding, tennis. *Address:* Conseil Constitutionnel, 2 Rue de Montpensier, 75001 Paris (office); 126 rue de l'Université, 75007 Paris, France (home). *Telephone:* 1-40-15-30-00 (office). *Fax:* 1-40-20-93-27 (office). *E-mail:* administration@conseil-constitutionnel.fr (office). *Website:* www.conseil-constitutionnel.fr (office).

DÉBY ITNO, Gen. Idriss; Chadian head of state; *President;* b. 1952, Zaghawa community; served in Army, trained as helicoptor pilot; fmr C-in-C of Armed Forces; fmr mil. adviser to Pres. Hissène Habré (q.v.), overthrew him in coup Dec. 1990; Chair. Interim Council of State, Head of State 1990–91; Pres. of Chad March 1991–, also C-in-C of Armed Forces; mem. Mouvement patriotique du salut (MPS). *Address:* Office of the President, Palais rose, BP 74, N'Djamena, Chad (office). *Telephone:* 51-44-37 (office). *Fax:* 51-45-01 (office). *E-mail:* presidence@tchad.td (office).

DECAUX, Alain; French historian and television producer; b. 23 July 1925, Lille; s. of Francis Decaux and Louise Tiprez; m. 1st Madeleine Parisy 1957; one d.; m. 2nd Micheline Pelletier 1983; one s. one d.; ed Lycée Faidherbe, Lille, Lycée Janson-de-Sailly, Paris and Univ. of Paris; journalist 1944–; historian 1947–; cr. radio programme La tribune de l'histoire with André Castelot, Colin-Simard and later Jean-François Chiappe 1951; cr. TV programmes: La caméra explore le temps, with Stellio Lorenzi and André Castelot 1956, Alain Decaux raconte 1969, L'histoire en question 1981, Le dossier d'Alain Decaux 1985; f. magazine L'histoire pour tous 1960; Pres. Groupement syndical des auteurs de télévision 1964–66, 1971–72; Vice-Chair. Société des auteurs et compositeurs dramatiques 1965–67, 1969–71, Chair. 1973–75; Dir Société Técipress 1967–91; Vice-Chair. Syndicat nat. des auteurs et compositeurs 1968–73; Admin. Librairie Plon 1969–72; Dir Historia Magazine 1969–71; worked on various periodicals, including Les nouvelles littéraires, Le Figaro littéraire, Historia, Histoire pour tous, Miroir de l'histoire, Lecture pour tous; Chair. Centre d'animation culturelle des Halles et du Marais (Carré Thorigny) 1971–73; mem. Conseil supérieur des lettres 1974; mem. Man. Cttee, Centre nat. des lettres 1974–75; Minister of Francophone Affairs 1988–91; Policy Co-ordinator, French Overseas TV 1989; elected to Académie Française 1979; Chair. Centre d'action culturelle de Paris 1981–; Chair. Société des amis d'Alexandre Dumas 1971; Pres. Coll. des conservateurs du Château de Chantilly 1998–2009; Prix d'histoire, Académie Française 1950, Grande médaille d'or, Ville de Versailles 1954, Grand prix du disque for Révolution française 1963, Prix Plaisir de lire 1968, Oscar de la télévision et de la radio 1968, 1973, Prix de la Critique de Télévision 1972, médaille de vermeil de la Ville de Paris 1973, Prix littéraire de la Paulée de Meursault 1973; Grand Officier, Légion d'honneur, Grand Croix, Ordre National du Mérite, Commdr Ordre des Arts et des Lettres. *Publications:* Louis XVII 1947, Letizia, mère de l'empereur 1949, La conspiration du général Malet 1952, La Castiglione, dame de cœur de l'Europe 1953, La belle histoire de Versailles 1954, De l'Atlantide à Mayerling 1954, Le prince impérial 1957, Offenbach, roi de Second Empire 1958, Amours Second Empire 1958, L'énigme Anastasia 1960, Les heures brillantes de la Côte d'Azur, Les grands mystères du passé 1964, Les dossiers secrets de l'histoire 1966, Grands secrets, grandes énigmes 1966, Nouveaux dossiers secrets 1967, Les Rosenberg ne doivent pas mourir (play) 1968, Grandes aventures de l'histoire 1968, Histoire des Françaises (2 vols) 1972, Histoire de la France et des Français (with André Castelot, 13 vols) 1970–74, Le cuirassé Potemkine (co-writer, play) 1975, Blanqui 1976, Les face à face de l'histoire 1977, Alain Decaux raconte (4 vols) 1978, 1979, 1980, 1981, L'Histoire en question (2 vols) 1982–83, Notre-Dame de Paris (co-writer, play) 1978, Danton et Robespierre (co-writer, play) 1979, Un homme nommé Jésus (co-writer, play) 1983, Victor Hugo (biog.) 1984, Les Assassins 1986, Le Pape pèlerin 1986, Destins fabuleux 1987, Alain Decaux raconte l'Histoire de France aux enfants 1987, L'Affaire du Courrier de Lyon 1987, Alain Decaux raconte la Révolution Française aux enfants 1988, La Liberté ou la mort (co-writer) 1988, La Révolution racontée aux enfants 1988, Alain Decaux raconte Jésus aux enfants 1991, Jésus était son nom 1991 (play), Le Tapis rouge 1992, Je m'appelais Marie-Antoinette (co-writer, play) 1993, Histoires Extraordinaires 1993, Nouvelles histoires extraordinaires 1994, L'abdication 1995, C'était le XXe siècle 1996, Alain Decaux raconte la Bible aux enfants 1996, Monaco et ses princes 1997, La course à l'abîme 1997, La Guerre absolue 1998, De Staline à Kennedy 1999, De Gaulle, celui qui a dit non (co-writer) 1999, Morts pour Vichy 2000, L'Avorton de Dieu: une vie de Saint Paul 2003, Tous les personnages sont vrais (Prix Saint-Simon 2005) 2004, La Révolution de la Croix – Néron et les Chrétiens 2007, Coup d'Etat à l'Elysée 2008. *Address:* 86 boulevard Flandrin, 75116 Paris, France. *Telephone:* 1-44-05-90-95 (office). *Fax:* 1-44-05-91-09 (office).

DECAUX, Jean-Claude; French advertising executive; *Chairman of the Supervisory and Executive Boards, JC Decaux;* b. 1937; Founder and Chair. of Supervisory and Exec. Bds JC Decaux SA 1955–, Co-CEO 1955– 2002; Prix France-Italie 2001. *Achievements include:* pioneered concept of street furniture providing cities with free bus shelters in return for advertising revenue 1964. *Address:* JC Decaux SA, Sainte Apelline, 78373 Plaisir Cedex, France (office). *Telephone:* 1-30-79-79-79 (office). *Fax:* 1-30-79-77-91 (office). *Website:* www.jcdecaux.com (office).

DECKER, Susan L., BSc, MBA; American business executive and accountant; *President, Yahoo! Inc.;* ed Tufts Univ. and Harvard Business School; Chartered Financial Analyst; Publishing & Advertising Equity Securities Analyst, Donaldson, Lufkin & Jenrette 1986–98, Global Dir Equity Research 1998–2000; Chief Financial Officer, Yahoo! Inc. 2000–, Sr Vice-Pres. Finance and Admin 2000–02, Exec. Vice-Pres. Finance and Admin 2002–07, Pres. 2007–; mem. Bd Dirs Costco Wholesale 2004–, Pixar Animation Studios 2004–06, Stanford Inst. for Econ. Policy Research 2005–07, Berkshire Hathaway, Intel Corpn; mem. Financial Accounting Standards Advisory Council 2000–04; ranked by Fortune magazine amongst 50 Most Powerful Women in Business in the US (48th) 2004, (40th) 2005, (20th) 2007, ranked by Forbes magazine amongst 100 Most Powerful Women (50th) 2008. *Address:* Yahoo! Inc., 701 1st Avenue, Sunnyvale, CA 94089, USA (office). *Telephone:* (408) 349-3300 (office). *Fax:* (408) 349-3301 (office). *Website:* www.yahoo.com (office).

DECQ, Odile; French architect; *Partner, Odile Decq Benoit Cornette Architects;* b. 1955; ed School of Architecture, Rennes, Univ. of Paris School of Architecture at La Villette, Inst. of Political Studies, Paris; Founding Pnr (with Benoit Cornette), Odile Decq Benoit Cornette Architects 1985–; teacher, Ecole d'Architecture de Paris—La Villette 1984–86; Guest Prof., Univ. of Montréal, Canada 1992, Univ. of Kansas 1997, 2000, Technische Universität, Vienna 1998, University College, London, UK 1998–2000; Prof. of Architecture and Head of Dept, Ecole Spéciale d'Architecture, Paris 1992–99, Dir 2007–; taught at Columbia Univ., New York 2001–03, Akademie Künst, Vienna 2003, Kunst Akademie, Dusseldorf, Germany 2004, Southern California Inst. of Architecture, Los Angeles 2006; jury mem. Westminster Univ. and Bartlett School, London, UK; elected mem. Acad. d'Architecture; Int. Fellow, RIBA 2007–; Hon. mem. Nat. Soc. of Architects, Czech Repub. 2007–; Commdr, Ordre des Arts et Lettres, Chevalier de la Légion d'Honneur; The Golden Lion Award, Architecture Biennale, Venice, Oscar du Design, Le Nouvel Economiste, Paris, Prix Plus Beaux Ouvrages de Construction Metallique, USINOR, Paris, Premier Award, Ninth Int. Prize for Architecture, London, DuPont Benedictus Commercial Award for Innovation in Architectural Laminated Glass, Premio Il Principe e l'Architetto, Museum of Contemporary Art, Rome 2003, Int. Architecture Award 2006. *Architectural works include:* Banque Populaire de L'Ouest, Rennes (received ten nat. and int. awards) 1990, Parc d'activités aéroportuaires, St Jacques de la Lande, Rennes 1994, Métafort, Aubervilliers 1995, Cité des Arts de Fort d'Aubervilliers 1995, Viaduct of Highway A14 and Highway Man. Centre, Nanterre 1996, French Pavilion, Venice Biennale 1996, A Third Bridge City, Rotterdam 1998, School of Econ. Sciences and Law Library, Univ. of Nantes 1998, Port de Gennevilliers 1999, Multiplex, Cambridge 1999, Collective Housing Project, Clichy 1999, Social Housing Complex, Paris 1999, Banque de France Office HQ, Montpellier, Vanishing black holes, (installation) Venice, Italy, 2000, Ice skating rink, Bordeaux 2000, 2001, Renovation of the Conf. Hall, UNESCO, Paris 2001, Client Centre, Dunkerque, France 2001, Flat unlimited (installation), Beijing, China 2004, Lillle Italy (restaurant), Paris 2004, Il Tre (restaurant), Paris 2005, Boat Wally 141, Fano, Italy 2006 (Int. Show Boats Award 2007), social housing, Paris 2006. *Publications include:* The Architect's Journal 1997, 100 Red Candles for Reading 2007; articles in professional journals, exhibition catalogues, monologues. *Address:* Odile Decq Benoit Cornette Architects, 11 rue des Arquebusiers, 75003 Paris, France (office). *Telephone:* 1-42-71-27-41 (office). *Fax:* 1-42-71-27-42 (office). *E-mail:* odbc@odbc-paris.com (office). *Website:* www.odbc-paris.com (office).

DeCRANE, Alfred C., Jr; American lawyer and business executive; b. 11 June 1931, Cleveland, Ohio; s. of Alfred Charles DeCrane and Verona DeCrane (née Marquard); m. Joan Elizabeth Hoffman 1954; one s. five d.; ed Notre Dame and Georgetown Univs; attorney, Texaco Inc., Houston and New York 1959, Asst to Vice-Chair. 1965, to Chair. 1967, Gen. Man. Producing Dept, Eastern Hemisphere 1968, Vice-Pres. 1970, Sr Vice-Pres. and Gen. Counsel 1976, mem. Bd of Dirs 1977–96, Exec. Vice-Pres. 1978–83, Pres. 1983–86, Chair. of Bd 1987–96, CEO 1993–96; Hon. Dir American Petroleum Inst.; mem. Bd of Dirs, Corn Products Int., Harris Corpn; mem. Advisory Bd Morgan Stanley Int.; mem. Bd of Trustees Univ. of Notre Dame; Hon. DHL (Manhattanville Coll.) 1990, Hon. JD (Univ. of Notre Dame) 2002. *Address:* c/o Texaco Inc., Two Greenwich Plaza, PO Box 1247, Greenwich, CT 06836, USA.

DEECH, Baroness (Life Peer), cr. 2005, of Cumnor in the County of Oxfordshire; **Ruth Lynn Deech,** DBE, MA; British university administrator and lawyer; b. (Ruth Fraenkel), 29 April 1943, London; d. of Josef Fraenkel and Dora Rosenfeld; m. John Deech 1967; one d.; ed St Anne's Coll., Oxford and Brandeis Univ. USA; called to Bar, Inner Temple 1967; Legal Asst Law Comm. 1966–67; Asst Prof., Univ. of Windsor Law School, Canada 1968–70; Fellow and Tutor in Law, St Anne's Coll., Oxford 1970–91, Vice-Prin. 1988–91, Prin. 1991–2004; mem. Univ. of Oxford Hebdomadal Council 1986–2000; Chair. Univ. of Oxford Admissions Cttee 1993–97, 2000–03; Gov. Oxford Centre for Hebrew and Jewish Studies 1994–2000; Chair. Human Fertilization and Embryology Authority 1994–2002; Pro-Vice-Chancellor Univ. of Oxford 2001–04; mem. Human Genetics Comm. 2000–02, European Acad. of Sciences and Arts 2001–; Rhodes Trustee 1997–2006; Visiting Prof., Osgoode Hall Law School, Canada 1978; Gov. BBC 2002–06; Ind. Adjudicator for Higher Educ. 2004–08; Freeman of the Drapers' Co. 2003, of the City of London 2003; Hon. Fellow, Soc. for Advanced Legal Studies 1997, Hon. Bencher, Inner Temple 1996–; Hon. LLD (Richmond American Int. Univ.) 2000, (Strathclyde) 2003. *Publications:* Divorce Dissent 1994; articles on family law, property law, autobiog. etc. *Leisure interests:* music, after-dinner speaking. *Address:* House of Lords, London, SW1A 0PW, England (office). *Telephone:* (20) 7219-3562 (office). *E-mail:* deechr@parliament.uk (office).

DEEN, Mohamed Waheed; Maldivian government official; *Minister of Youth and Sports;* b. 3 March 1947, Malé; m. Aisha Sayed Mohamed; four s. eight d.; ed attended coll. in Sri Lanka; ; Vice-Pres. Maldives Chamber of Commerce and Industries; mem. Human Rights Comm. of the Maldives; Minister of Atolls Devt 2005–07, of Youth and Sports 2007–; exec. mem. Maldives Tourism Advisory Bd; exec. mem. Maldives Tourism Promotion Bd; exec. mem. Sports Tourism Cttee; Exec. Vice-Pres. Commonwealth Body-building Fed.; Exec. Vice-Pres. Asian Bodybuilding Fed.; founder mem. and Chair. Diabetes and Cancer Soc.; mem. Exec. Bd Maldives Asscn of Tourism Industry; founder Maldives Bodybuilding Fed.; founder and Pres. Maldives Surfing Asscn; Man. Dir Orchid Holdings; Dir Thulhagiri Development, HPL Resorts; CEO Orchid Resorts; Man. Dir Deens Orchid Agency; Presidential Commemoration for Nat. Service in recognition of service rendered to the nation during terrorist attack of November 1988, Nat. Award in recognition of service to the tourism industry 1993, Nat. Award in recognition of service to community devt 1997, Hon. Award from Ministry of Tourism in recognition of 25 years of distinguished service rendered towards sustainable devt of tourism in Maldives. *leisure interests* football, cricket, squash, badminton, health and fitness. *Address:* Ministry of Youth and Sports, PA Complex, 5th Floor, Hilaalee Magu, Malé 20-307, Maldives (office); Deens Villa, Mihelli Goathé, Henveinu, Malé, The Maldives (home). *Telephone:* 3326986 (office); 6640088 (home). *Fax:* 3327162 (office). *E-mail:* info@youthsports.gov.mv (office). *Website:* www.youthsports.gov.mv (office); www.bandos.com.mv (home).

DEFAR, Meseret; Ethiopian athlete; b. 19 Nov. 1983, Addis Ababa; Silver Medal, 3000m, World Youth Championships 1999; Silver Medal, 5000m, African Championships 2000, World Jr Championships 2000; Gold Medal, 3000m, 5000m., World Jr Championships 2002; Gold Medal, 5000m All-African Games, Afro-Asian Games 2003; Bronze Medal, 3000m, World Indoor Championships, Birmingham 2003; Gold Medal, 5000m, Athens Olympics 2004; Gold Medal, 3000m, World Indoor Championships, Budapest 2004, Moscow 2006, Valencia 2008; Silver Medal, 5000m, World Championships, Helsinki 2005; Gold Medal, 5000m, World Championships, Osaka 2007; Bronze Medal, 5000m, Beijing Olympics 2008; Women's 5,000m Best Year Performance 2005–07, Women's 3,000m Best Year Performance 2006–07, Women's Track & Field Athlete of the Year 2007. *Address:* c/o Ethiopian Athletics Federation, PO Box 3241, Addis Ababa, Ethiopia. *Telephone:* (1) 152495. *Website:* www.ethiosports.com.

DEFLASSIEUX, Jean Sébastien; French banker; *Honorary Chairman, Crédit Lyonnais;* b. 11 July 1925, Cap d'Ail; s. of Alexis Deflassieux and Thérèse Dalmasso; m. 1st Christiane Orabona 1950 (deceased); one s.; m. 2nd Huguette Dupuy 2000; ed HEC, Law Faculty, Paris, London School of Econs, Ecole d'organisation scientifique du travail; analyst, Div. of financial studies, Crédit Lyonnais 1948–54; attached to Cabinet of Jean Filippi (Sec. of State for the Budget) 1956–57 and of Arthur Conte (Sec. of State for Industry) 1957; Insp. of Paris br. offices, Crédit Lyonnais 1958; Sub-Dir Haute Banque 1959–69, Dir of External Commerce 1969–72, of Int. Affairs 1972, in charge of the Cen. Man. of Int. Affairs 1978–82; Adviser to Prime Minister Pierre Mauroy 1981–84; Gen. Admin. 1982, Chair. and CEO Crédit Lyonnais 1982–86, Hon. Chair. 1986–; Chair. Banque des Echanges Internationaux, Paris 1987–96, Monacrédit (Monaco) 1980–99, Banque AIG, Paris 1991–94; Dir Arab Banking Corpn Int. Bank PLC, London 1991–, and of other banks and cos; Del. Gen. Radio Alpazur NRJ Menton 1998; Pres. European League for Econ. Co-operation (French Section) 1983; Pres. (French Section) Int. Vienna Council (East–West) 1985–96; Commdr, Légion d'Honneur, Commdr Ordre Nat. du Mérite, Croix de Guerre 1939–45, Palmes Académiques. *Leisure interests:* history, economics, political philosophy. *Address:* 9 boulevard du Jardin exotique, 98000 Monaco (home); 41 rue Vineuse, 75116 Paris (home); Crédit Lyonnais, 19 boulevard des Italiens, 75002 Paris, France. *Telephone:* 7-93-50-06-28 (Monaco) (home); 1-47-04-37-10 (Paris) (home); 1-42-95-11-11 (Paris) (office).

DEFORD, Frank, BA; American writer and editor; b. 16 Dec. 1938, Baltimore, Md; m. Carol Penner 1965; one s. two d.; ed Princeton Univ.; Contributing Ed., Sports Illustrated 1962–69, 1998–, Vanity Fair 1993–96; writer and commentator, Cable News Network 1980–86, Nat. Public Radio 1980–89, 1991–, NBC 1986–89, ESPN 1992–96, HBO 1996–; Ed.-in-Chief, The National 1989–91; writer, Newsweek Magazine 1991–93, 1996–98; Nat. Asscn of Sportswriters and Sportscasters Sportswriter of the Year 1982–88, Emmy Award 1988, Cable Ace 1996, Peabody Award 1999. *Film screenplays:* Trading Hearts 1986, Four Minutes 2005. *Publications:* Five Strides on the Banked Track 1969, Cut 'N' Run 1971, There She Is 1972, The Owner 1974, Big Bill Tilden: The Triumphs and the Tragedy 1977, Everybody's All-American 1981, Alex: The Life of a Child 1982, Spy in the Deuce Court 1987, World's Tallest Midget 1988, Casey on the Loose 1989, Love and Infamy 1993, The Other Adonis 2001, An American Summer 2002, The Old Ball Game 2005; contrib. to numerous magazines. *Address:* Sterling Lord Literistic Inc., 65 Bleecker Street, New York, NY 10012, USA (office).

DEGENERES, Ellen; American comedienne and actress; b. 26 Jan. 1958, New Orleans. *Films include:* Wisecracks 1991, Coneheads 1993, Mr Wrong 1996, Doctor Doolittle (voice) 1998, Goodbye Lover 1999, EdTV 1999, The Love Letter 1999, Reaching Normal 1999, If These Walls Could Talk 2 (also exec. producer) 2000, Finding Nemo (voice) 2003, My Short Film 2005. *TV includes:* (series) Duet 1988–89, Open House 1989, Laurie Hill 1992, Ellen 1994–98 (also producer), The Ellen Show 2001–02, host Emmy Awards 2001, 2005, Ellen: The Ellen DeGeneres Show (Daytime Emmy Award for best talk show 2005) 2003–, host Acad. Awards ceremony 2007. *Publication:* My Point...And I Do Have One 1995. *Address:* c/o ICM, 8942 Wilshire Boulevard, Beverly Hills, CA 90211, USA. *Telephone:* 310-550-4000. *E-mail:* comedy@icmtalent.com. *Website:* www.icmtalent.com.

DEGHATI, Reza; French (b. Iranian) photojournalist; *Founder, Webistan Photo Agency;* b. 26 July 1952, Tabriz, Iran; ed Univs of Tabriz and Tehran; photographer with Agence France Presse during Iranian revolution 1978; corresp. with Newsweek, Iran 1978–81, with Time Magazine 1983–88; consultant to UN Humanitarian Programme, Afghanistan 1989–91; Reporter for UNICEF 1989–95, for Nat. Geographic Magazine 1990–; f. Webistan Photo Agency 1991–; photographs have appeared in numerous int. magazines, including Der Spiegel, Paris-Match, Le Nouvel Observateur, The Observer, El País, Oggi, Newsweek, Life, etc.; regular corresp. for BBC Radio Persia and Radio France Int. Persia; Founder and Pres. Aïna (nonprofit org.); fmr teacher Ecole d'Art, Paris, Univ. of Georgetown, Washington, DC; lecturer, George Washington Univ., Washington, DC, Stanford Univ., Beijing Univ., Sorbonne, Paris; Sr Fellow, Ashoka Foundation 2008; Honor Medal, Univ. of Missouri (Columbia School of Journalism) 2006, Award of Recognition, Chicago Univ. 2006, Hon. Degree, American Univ. of Paris 2009; UNICEF Hope Prize for "Portraits of Lost Children in Rwanda" 1996, Pictet Prize, Paris 2008; Chevalier, Ordre Nat. du Merite 2005, Prince of Asturias Humanitarian Medal (Spain) 2006. *Films:* Nat. Geographic films: Into forbidden zone (Emmy Award 2002), Inside Mecca 2003, Reza: Shooting Back 2008. *Publications:* Paix en Galilee 1983, Bayan Ko! 1986, Paris-Pekin-Paris'87 1987, Around the world 1992, Kurdes: Les Chants Brules 1995, Massoud, des Russes aux Talibans 2001, Plus loin sur la Terre 2002, Le pinceau de Bouddha 2002, Eternités Afghanes 2002, Crossing destinies 2003, Insouciances 2004, The Silk Road 2007, War Peace 2008, Reporters without Borders 2008. *Leisure interests:* horse-riding, mountain biking. *Address:* Ainaworld, 22, rue Haxo, 75019 Paris, France (office). *Telephone:* (1) 53-19-83-83 (office). *Fax:* (1) 53-19-83-02 (office). *E-mail:* reza@ainaworld.org (office); reza@webistan.com (office). *Website:* www.ainaworld.org (office). *www.webistan.com* (office).

DEGUARA, Louis, MD; Maltese politician and doctor; *Minister of Health, the Elderly and Community Care;* b. 18 Sept. 1947, Naxxar; m. Maria Fatima Mallia; one s. one d.; ed St Aloysius Coll., Birkikara, Univ. of Malta; medical practitioner 1973; fmrly houseman, St Luke's, Sir Paul Boffa and Gozo Gen. Hosps, Prin. Medical Officer of Health, Northern Region; Gen. Practitioner 1977–; MP, Nationalist Party 1981–; Parl. Sec. Ministry for Social Devt 1995–96; Shadow Minister and Opposition Spokesman for Health 1996–98; Minister of Health 1998–. *Address:* Ministry of Health, the Elderly and Community Care, Palazzo Castellania, 15 Merchant Street, Valletta, CMR 02, Malta. *Telephone:* 21224071. *Fax:* 21252574.

DEHAENE, Jean-Luc; Belgian (b. French) politician; *Chairman, Board of Directors, Dexia Group;* b. 7 Aug. 1940, Montpellier, France; m. Celie Verbeke 1965; four c.; ed Univ. of Namur; adviser to various govt ministries 1972–81; Minister of Social Affairs and Institutional Reforms 1981–88; Deputy Prime Minister and Minister of Communications and Institutional Reforms 1988–92; Prime Minister of Belgium 1992–99; Vice-Pres. of EU Special Convention on a European Constitution 2001–08; Chair. Bd of Dirs Dexia Group 2008–; cand. (Christen-Democratisch en Vlaams Partij—CD&V) in 2003 Belgian elections. *Address:* Dexia Group, Square de Meeûs 1, 1000 Brussels, Belgium (office). *Telephone:* (2) 213-57-00 (office). *Fax:* (2) 213-57-01 (office). *Website:* www .dexia.com (office).

DEHECQ, Jean-François; French pharmaceuticals industry executive; *Chairman, Sanofi-Aventis SA;* b. 1 Jan. 1940, Nantes; ed Ecole Nat. Supériere des Arts et Métiers, Lille; began career as math. teacher, Lycée catholique Saint-Vincent de Senlis, Oise 1964; Man. Dir Sanofi (subsidiary of Elf-Aquitaine Group) 1973–98, Chair. and Man. Dir Sanofi-Synthélabo (following merger of Sanofi and Synthélabo 1998) 1999–2004, Chair. Sanofi-Aventis (following merger of Sanofi-Synthélabo and Aventis) 2004–; Pres. European Fed. of Pharmaceutical Industries and Asscns (EFPIA) 2001–02; Commdr, Légion d'honneur, Officier, Ordre nat. du Mérite agricole, Commdr du Mérite de l'Ordre souverain de Malte; Nessim Habif Prize, Congrès des Ingénieurs Arts et Métiers 2003. *Address:* Sanofi-Aventis, 174 Avenue de France, 75013 Paris, France (office). *Telephone:* 1-53-77-40-00 (office). *Fax:* 1-53-77-42-96 (office). *E-mail:* info@sanofi-synthelabo.com (office). *Website:* www.sanofi -synthelabo.com (office).

DEHEM, Roger Jules, PhD, FRSC; Belgian economist and academic; *Professor Emeritus of Economics, Laval University;* b. 24 July 1921, Wemmel; s. of Charles Dehem and Elise (née Masschelein) Dehem; m. Gertrude Montbleau 1950; two s. four d.; ed Univ. of Louvain; Lecturer, McGill Univ., Canada 1947–49, Prof., Univ. of Montréal, Canada 1948–58; Prin. Admin. OEEC 1958–59; Economist Adviser, Fabrimétal, Brussels 1959–60; Prof. of Econs, Laval Univ., Québec 1961–95, Prof. Emer. 1995–; Fellow Rockefeller Foundation 1946–48; Pres. Canadian Econ. Asscn 1973–74. *Publications:* L'efficacité sociale du système économique 1952, Traité d'analyse économique 1957, L'utopie de l'économiste 1969, L'équilibre économique international 1970, De l'étalon sterling à l'étalon dollar 1972, Précis d'économique internationale 1982, Histoire de la pensée économique 1984, Les Economies capitalistes et socialistes 1988, Capitalismes et Socialismes 1989. *Address:* 2000 rue Chapdelaine, Ste-Foy, Québec, G1V 1M3, Canada (home). *Telephone:* (418) 681-9593 (home). *Website:* www.ecn.ulaval.ca/EN/index.html (office).

DEHENNIN, Baron Herman, LLD; Belgian diplomatist; b. 20 July 1929, Lier; s. of Alexander Dehennin and Flora Brehmen; m. Margareta-Maria Donvil 1954; two s.; ed Catholic Univ. of Leuven; Lt in Royal Belgian Artillery 1951–53; entered Diplomatic Service 1954, Second Sec., The Hague 1956–59, First Sec., New Delhi 1960–63, Commercial Counsellor, Madrid 1964–65, Chargé d'Affaires, Congo 1965–66, Amb. to Rwanda 1966–70, EC Minister of Belgium in Washington, DC 1970–74, Deputy Admin. to Dir-Gen. Foreign Econ. Relations, Brussels 1974–77, Grand Marshal of the Belgian Royal Court 1981–85; Amb. to Japan 1978–81, to USA 1985–90, to UK 1991–94; Pres. Special Olympics 1995–; Grand Cross of Order of Leopold, Grand Cross of

Order of the Crown. *Leisure interests:* jogging, hiking, tennis, fishing, hunting, reading (history and philosophy).

DEHMELT, Hans Georg, Dr rer. nat; American physicist and academic; *Professor of Physics, University of Washington;* b. 9 Sept. 1922, Görlitz, Germany; s. of Georg Dehmelt and Asta Klemmt; m. Diana Dundore 1989; one s. from a previous m.; ed Gymnasium Zum Grauen Kloster, Berlin, Breslau Tech. Univ., Göttingen Univ. and Inst. of Hans Kopfermann; served as private in German army 1940–45, POW 1945–46; Deutsche Forschungs-Gemeinschafts Fellow, Inst. of Hans Kopfermann 1950–52; co-discovered nuclear quadrupole resonance 1949; postdoctoral work in microwave spectroscopy lab., Duke Univ., USA 1952–55; Visiting Asst Prof., Univ. of Washington, Seattle 1955–56, Asst Prof. 1956–58, Assoc. Prof. 1958–61, Prof. 1961–, also research physicist; with others, achieved the most precise electron magnetic moment determination to date, through work on geonium 1976–; became US citizen 1961; Fellow American Physical Soc.; mem. NAS, American Acad. of Arts and Sciences; Dr rer. nat hc (Ruprecht Karl Univ., Heidelberg) 1986, Hon. DSc (Chicago) 1987; Davisson-Germer Prize, American Physical Soc. 1970, Alexander von Humboldt Prize 1974, Award in Basic Research, Int. Soc. of Magnetic Resonance 1980, Count Rumford Prize, American Acad. of Arts and Sciences 1985, Nobel Prize in Physics 1989 for measurement on isolated subatomic particle and atomic particle at rest, Nat. Medal of Science 1995. *Publication:* Radiofrequency Spectroscopy of Stored Ions 1967. *Address:* Department of Physics, PO Box 35-1560, University of Washington, Seattle, WA 98195-1560; 1600 43rd Avenue E, Seattle, WA 98112-3205, USA (home). *Website:* www.phys.washington.edu/~dehmelt (office).

DEIGHTON, Len; British writer; b. 1929, London. *Publications:* The Ipcress File 1962 (also film), Horse under Water 1963, Funeral in Berlin 1964 (also film), Où est le Garlic 1965, Action Cook Book 1965, Cookstrip Cook Book (USA) 1966, Billion Dollar Brain 1966 (also film), An Expensive Place to Die 1967, Len Deighton's London Dossier (guide book) 1967, The Assassination of President Kennedy (co-author) 1967, Only When I Larf 1968 (also film), Bomber 1970 (also radio dramatization), Declarations of War (short stories) 1971, Close-Up 1972, Spy Story 1974 (also film), Yesterday's Spy 1975, Twinkle, Twinkle, Little Spy 1976, Fighter: the True Story of the Battle of Britain 1977, SS-GB 1978, Airshipwreck (co-author) 1978, Blitzkrieg 1979, Battle of Britain (co-author) 1980, XPD 1981, Goodbye Mickey Mouse 1982, Berlin Game 1983, Mexico Set 1984, London Match 1985, Winter: a Berlin Family 1899–1945 1987, Spy Hook 1988, ABC of French Food 1989, Spy Line 1989, Spy Sinker 1990, Basic French Cookery Course 1990, Mamista 1991, City of Gold 1992, Violent Ward 1993, Blood, Tears and Folly 1993, Faith 1994, Hope 1995, Charity 1996. *Address:* c/o Jonathan Clowes Ltd, 10 Iron Bridge House, Bridge Approach, London, NW1 8BD, England (office). *Telephone:* (20) 7722-7674 (office). *Fax:* (20) 7722-7677 (office). *E-mail:* jonathanclowes@aol.com (office).

DEINEKIN, Gen. Piotr Stepanovich, DrMilSc; Russian army officer; b. 14 Dec. 1937, Morozovsk, Rostov Region; m.; three c.; ed Balashov Military Aviation School, Yuri Gagarin Air Force Acad., Gen. Staff Acad.; pilot, army air force 1957–69, Commdr aviation regt, div. 1969–82, Deputy Commdr Army Air Force 1982–85, Commdr 1985–90, First Vice-C-in-C of USSR Air Force 1990, C-in-C and Deputy Minister of Defence of USSR (now Russia) 1991–97; Head Pres.'s Admin. Dept on the Cossack Problem 1998–; Hero of Russian Fed. 1997. *Address:* Staraya pl. 4, entr. 1, Moscow, Russia. *Telephone:* (495) 206-35-73 (office).

DEISS, Joseph; Swiss politician; b. 18 Jan. 1946, Fribourg; m. Elizabeth Mueller; three s.; ed Coll. Saint-Michel, Fribourg, Univ. of Fribourg, King's Coll., Cambridge, UK; Lecturer (part-time) in Political Economy, Univ. of Fribourg 1973–83, Prof. Extraordinary 1984–99, Sr Faculty mem. Dept of Social and Econ. Science 1996–98; Deputy, Great Council of Fribourg 1981–91, Pres. 1991, Nat. Adviser 1991–99; Vice-Pres. Comm. on Foreign Policy, Nat. Council 1995–96; Pres. Comm. on Revision of the Fed. Constitution 1996; Head of Fed. Dept of Foreign Affairs 1999–2002; Head of Fed. Dept of Econ. Affairs 2003–06 (resgnd); Pres. of the Swiss Confed. 2004; Pres. Banque Raiffaisen du Haut-Lac 1996–99; Chair. of Bd Schuhmacher AG, Schmitten 1996–99. *Address:* c/o Federal Department of Economic Affairs, Bundeshaus Ost, 3003 Bern, Switzerland (office).

DEITCH, Jeffrey, MBA; American art dealer, art critic and exhibition organizer; *Owner, Deitch Projects;* ed Wesleyan Univ., Harvard Business School; art critic and exhbn curator since mid-1970s; fmr Asst Dir John Weber Gallery, New York; fmr Curator De Cordova Museum, Lincoln, Mass; Vice-Pres. Citibank, responsible for developing and managing the bank's art advisory and art finance businesses 1979–88; f. own art advisory firm 1988; first American Ed. Flash Art; first important curatorial project was Lives, a 1975 exhbn about artists who used their own lives as an art medium, presented in vacant office bldg in Tribeca, lower Manhattan; opened a public gallery, Deitch Projects 1996; mem. Art Dealers Assen of America; mem. Bd Trustees Wesleyan Univ. 1982–85; Art Critic's Fellowship, Nat. Endowment for the Arts 1979. *Publications include:* numerous catalogue essays, including projects for the Museum of Modern Art, Paris, Stedelijk Museum, Amsterdam, Whitney Museum, New York; essay The Art Industry was included in catalogue for the Metropolis exhbn, Martin-Gropius-Bau, Berlin 1991; contrib. to Arts, Art in America, Artforum, and numerous other publs. *Address:* Deitch Projects, 76 Grand Street, New York NY 10012, USA (office). *Telephone:* (212) 343-7300 (office). *Fax:* (212) 343-2954 (office). *E-mail:* info@deitch.com (office). *Website:* www.deitch.com (office).

DEKKER, Cees, MSc, PhD; Dutch physicist and academic; *Professor of Molecular Biophysics, Delft University of Technology;* b. 7 April 1959, Haren; ed Univ. of Utrecht; Research Asst, Univ. of Utrecht 1984–88, Perm. Scientific Staff 1988–93; Visiting Researcher, IBM Research, Yorktown Heights, USA 1990–91; Perm. Scientific Staff, Delft Univ. of Tech. 1993–99, Antoni van Leeuwenhoek Prof. 1999–2000, Prof. of Molecular Biophysics 2000–, Leader of Molecular Biophysics Group; European Physical Soc. Agilent Technologies Europhysics Prize 2001 (jt recipient), Netherlands Org. for Scientific Research Spinoza Prize 2004. *Address:* Kavli Inst. of NanoScience and Molecular Biophysics, Delft University of Technology, Lorentzweg 1, 2628 CJ Delft, Netherlands (office). *Telephone:* (15) 2786094 (office). *Fax:* (15) 2781202 (office). *E-mail:* dekker@mb.tn.tudelft.nl.html (office). *Website:* www.mb.tn.tudelft.nl/user/dekker/index.html.

DEKKER, W.; Dutch business executive; b. 26 April 1924, Eindhoven; joined Philips, SE Asia Regional Bureau 1948, Man. 1956–59, with Indonesian Philips co. 1948–66, Man. Far East Regional Bureau 1959–66, Gen. Man. Philips in Far East, Tokyo 1966–72, mem. Bd British Philips 1972, Chair. and Man. Dir 1972–76, mem. Bd of Man. NV Philips' Glœilampenfabrieken 1976–82, Pres. 1982, Chair. 1982–94; mem. Supervisory Bd Dresdner Bank, Germany, AMRO Bank, Netherlands; mem. Int. Advisory Bd Allianz Versicherungs AG, Germany, Volvo, Sweden; mem. Bd Fiat, Italy; mem. Int. Advisory Cttee Chase Manhattan Bank, New York; mem. Advisory Bd Montedison, Italy; mem. Advisory Cttee for Investments of Foreign Cos in the Netherlands to Minister of Econ. Affairs; mem. Atlantic Advisory Council, United Technologies Corp., USA; Chair. Supervisory Bd Maatschappij voor Industriële Projecten; mem. European Advisory Cttee New York Stock Exchange; mem. Special Advisory Group, UNIDO; Prof. of Int. Man., Univ. of Leiden; mem. Tinbergen Inst., Rotterdam; Co-Founder European Roundtable of Industrialists 1983, Chair. 1988–; Hon. LLD (Univ. of Strathclyde) 1976; Dr hc (Tech. Univ. of Delft) 1987; Hon. CBE; Goldenes Ehrenzeichen für Verdienste um das Land Wien (Vienna); Commdr, Order of Orange Nassau; Commdr, Order of Belgian Crown; Kt, Order of Dutch Lion; Commdr Légion d'honneur; Cavaliere di Gran Croce dell'Ordine al Merito, Italy.

DEL CASTILLO GÁLVES, Jorge Alfonso Alejandro; Peruvian lawyer and politician; b. 2 July 1950, Lima; ed Nat. Univ. of San Marcos, Lima, Pontifical Catholic Univ. of Peru; Mayor of Barranco Ward, Lima 1984–86, apptd Prefect of Lima 1985; mem. Partido Aprista Peruano—PAP, Sec.-Gen. PAP 1999–, Rep. of PAP before OAS; Mayor of Metropolitan Lima Co. 1987–89; elected to Peruvian Congress of the Repub. for Lima 1995–, re-elected 2000, 2001, 2006; Pres. Council of Ministers (Prime Minister of Peru) 2006–08 (resgnd). *Address:* Partido Aprista Peruano, Avda Alfonso Ugarte 1012, Lima, Peru (office). *Telephone:* (1) 4281736 (office). *Website:* www.apra.org.pe (office).

DEL CID DE BONILLA, María Antonieta; Guatemalan central banker and government official; *President, Banco de Guatemala;* Exec. Dir for Guatemala, IDB 1998; Minister of Public Finance 2004–08; fmr Vice-Pres. Banco de Guatemala (cen. bank), Pres. 2008–. *Address:* Office of the President, Banco de Guatemala, 7a Avda 22-01, Zona 1, Apdo 365, Guatemala City, Guatemala (office). *Telephone:* 2230-6222 (office). *Fax:* 2253-4035 (office). *E-mail:* webmaster@banguat.gob.gt (office). *Website:* www.banguat.gob.gt (office).

DEL GENIO, Anthony D., BS, MS, PhD; American atmospheric scientist and academic; *Physical Scientist, Goddard Institute for Space Studies, National Aeronautics and Space Administration;* b. 21 Feb. 1952, New York, NY; m.; one c.; ed Cornell Univ., Univ. of California, Los Angeles; Scientific Programmer/Analyst, Climate Group, GTE Information Systems, NASA/Goddard Inst. for Space Studies (GISS), New York June–Sept. 1976, Consultant 1976–77, Nat. Research Council (NRC) RRA 1978–80, Man. Planetary Group, Sigma Data Services 1980–85, Physical Scientist, NASA/GISS 1985–; Grad. Research Asst, Dept of Earth and Space Sciences, UCLA 1973–76, 1976–78; Coordinator, Columbia Univ. Grad. Program in Atmospheric and Planetary Science 1984–; Lecturer, GISS/Columbia Univ. Summer Inst. on Planets and Climate 1980–85; Adjunct Asst Prof., Dept of Physics, Queensborough Community Coll., CUNY 1982–85; Adjunct Assoc. Prof., Dept of Environmental Science, Barnard Coll. 1993–99; Lecturer, Dept of Earth and Environmental Sciences, Columbia Univ. 1983–89, Adjunct Asst Prof. 1989–92, Adjunct Assoc. Prof. 1992–, Adjunct Prof. 1997–, Adjunct Prof., Dept of Applied Physics 1995–; Invited Lecturer, NATO ASI, Energy and Water Cycles in the Climate System, Glücksburg, Germany 1991, Int. Research Inst. for Climate Prediction, Applications and Training Pilot Project 1993, NCAR Summer School on Clouds and Climate 1993, NATO ASI, Remote Sensing of Energy and Water Cycles, Plon, Germany 1995, Goddard Earth Science and Tech. Summer Program 2003–04; Co-Investigator, Pioneer Venus Orbiter Cloud Photopolarimeter Experiment 1978–92; Pioneer Venus Dynamics and Structure Working Group 1979–80; Organizer, GISS/Columbia Univ. Summer Inst. on Planets and Climate 1983, 1985, 1987; Science Advisory Group, NASA Lidar Atmospheric Sensing Experiment 1988–97; Co-Investigator/Interdisciplinary, Earth Observing System 1989–99; Science Steering Group, GEWEX Water Vapor Project 1990; Prin. Investigator, Atmospheric Radiation Measurement Program 1993–; Team mem. Cassini Saturn Orbiter Imaging Science Subsystem 1990–; Cassini/Huygens Atmospheric Working Group 1991–; mem. NASA/Goddard Space Flight Center (GSFC) Dir's Discretionary Fund Review Panel 1991–93; Science Team mem. NASA TRMM/GPM 1991–97, 1998–2001, 2003–; Prin. Investigator, First ISCCP Regional Experiment III 1995–98, Cttee 1995–98; mem. Science Team Exec. Cttee, Dept of Energy ARM Program 1996–2000, 2002–05, SGP Site Advisory Cttee 1995–98, Cloud Modeling Working Group Steering Cttee 2000–; Assoc. Ed. Journal of Climate 1996–2004, Ed. 2004–; mem. Drafting Panel, FIRE-IV: CRYSTAL Research Plan 1998–99; Prin. Investigator, Global Aerosol Climatology Project 1998–2002; Reviewer, NAS/NRC Report 'Understanding

Climate Change Feedbacks'; Science Team mem. NASA Aqua AMSR-E 2003–07, CloudSat/CALIPSO 2007–; mem. Writing Panel, American Meteorological Soc. Statement on Climate Change 2007; mem. American Geophysical Union 1978, American Astronomical Soc. (Div. for Planetary Sciences) 1981, American Meteorological Soc. 1987 (Fellow 2007); NASA GISS Peer Award 1986, NASA Certificate of Outstanding Performance 1987, 1988, 1989, 1990, 1992, 1994, 1995, 1998, 2007, 2008, NASA GISS Best Publication Award 1989, 1990, 1993, 1994, 1997, 2000, 2002, 2003, 2006, 2007, Citation for Excellence in Reviewing, Icarus 1992, 1998, Outstanding Teacher Award, Columbia Univ. Dept of Earth and Environmental Sciences 1994, 2001, 2006, NASA Group Achievement Award, Cassini Imaging Science Subsystem 1998, NASA GSFC Earth Sciences Directorate Special Act Award 2004, 2005, 2006, NASA Exceptional Scientific Achievement Medal 2008. *Publications:* more than 100 scientific papers in professional journals on stratiform and cumulus cloud parameterization in general circulation models, hydrologic cycle feedbacks on climate, comparative dynamics of planetary atmospheres. *Address:* NASA Goddard Institute for Space Studies, 2880 Broadway, New York, NY 10025, USA (office). *Telephone:* (212) 678-5588 (office). *Fax:* (212) 678-5552 (office). *E-mail:* adelgenio@giss.nasa.gov (office); anthony.d.delgenio@nasa.gov (office). *Website:* www.giss.nasa.gov (office).

DEL NINNO, Giulio, BEng; Italian business executive; *CEO, Edison SpA;* b. 12 June 1940, Milan; plant designer, Termosystem 1968–69; Researcher, Snia Viscose SpA 1969–73; Production Dir Garzanti SpA 1973–76; Tech. and Research Dir Montefibre (Montedison Group) 1976–79, Total Quality Dir 1986–88, Dir of Electrical Energy Sector, Edison SpA (Montedison Group) 1988–96, CEO Montedison SpA (now Edison) 2001–; Chair. Due Palme SpA 1979–86. *Address:* Edison SpA, Foro Buonaparte 31, 20121 Milan, Italy (office). *Telephone:* (02) 62221 (office). *E-mail:* infoweb@edison.it (office). *Website:* www.edison.it (office).

DEL PINO VEINTIMILLA, Eugenia Maria, PhD; Ecuadorean biologist and academic; *Professor of Biology, Pontifical Catholic University of Ecuador;* b. 19 April 1945, Quito; ed Pontifical Catholic Univ. of Ecuador, Quito, Vassar Coll., Emory Univ., Atlanta, Ga, USA; currently Prof. of Biology, Pontifical Catholic Univ. of Ecuador; Vice-Pres. for Ecuador, Darwin Foundation 1992–96, Vice-Pres. Gen. Ass. 1998–2001; Alexander von Humboldt Foundation Fellowship, Cancer Research Centre, Heidelberg, Germany 1984–85; mem. Latin American Acad. of Sciences, Third World Acad. of Sciences (TWAS); L'Oreal-UNESCO Award for Women in Science 2000, Sheth Distinguished Int. Alumni Award, Emory Univ. 2003, Medal of the Acad. of Science for the Developing World, TWAS 2005, Eugenio Espejo Award, City Council of Quito 2005. *Publications:* numerous publs in scientific journals. *Address:* Pontificia Universidad Católica del Ecuador, Quito, Ecuador (office). *Telephone:* (2) 299-1700 (office). *Fax:* (2) 299-1687 (office). *E-mail:* edelpino@puce.edu.ec (office). *Website:* www.puce.edu.ec (office).

DEL PONTE, Carla, LLM; Swiss lawyer, international organization official and diplomatist; *Ambassador to Argentina;* b. 9 Feb. 1947, Lugano; one s.; ed Univs of Berne and Geneva; in pvt. practice, Lugano 1975–81; Investigating Magistrate, then Public Prosecutor, Lugano 1981–94; Attorney-Gen. and Chief Prosecutor of Switzerland 1994–2000, mem. Fed. Comm. on White-Collar Crime 1994–99; Chief Prosecutor, Int. Criminal Tribunals of Rwanda 1999–2003, of the Fmr Yugoslavia 1999–2007; Amb. to Argentina 2008–; Dr hc (Liège) 2002, (Wales, Bangor) 2003, Hon. Dottore in Giurisprudenza (Genoa) 2004; 22nd Peace Prize, UNA (Spain) 2002, Goler T. Butcher Prize 2004. *Publications:* Madame Prosecutor (memoir) 2009. *Address:* Embassy of Switzerland, Santa Fe 846, 10°, C1059ABP, Buenos Aires, Argentina (office). *Telephone:* (11) 4311-6491 (office). *Fax:* (11) 4313-2998 (office). *E-mail:* carla .delponte@eda.admin.ch (office); vertretung@bue.rep.admin.ch (office). *Website:* www.eda.admin.ch/buenosaires_emb/s/home.html (office).

DEL TORO, Benicio; Puerto Rican actor, director and writer; b. 19 Feb. 1967, Santurce, Puerto Rico; s. of Gustavo Del Toro and the late Fausta Sanchez Del Toro; ed Univ. of California, San Diego, Circle in the Square Acting School, Stella Adler Conservatory. *Films include:* Big Top Pee-wee 1988, Christopher Columbus: The Discovery 1992, Fearless 1993, Money for Nothing 1993, China Moon 1994, The Usual Suspects 1995, Swimming With Sharks 1995, Cannes Man 1996, The Funeral 1996, Basquiat 1996, The Fan 1996, Joyride 1997, Excess Baggage 1997, Fear and Loathing in Las Vegas 1998, Snatch 2000, Traffic (Acad. Award for Best Supporting Actor) 2000, The Way of the Gun 2000, The Pledge 2001, Bread and Roses 2001, The Hunted 2002, 21 Grams 2003, Sin City 2005, Things We Lost in the Fire 2007, Che (Cannes Film Festival Best Actor Prize) 2008. *Address:* c/o IFA Talent Agency, 8730 Sunset Boulevard #490, Los Angeles, CA 90069, USA. *Website:* www .beniciodeltoro.com.

DEL TORO, Guillermo; Mexican film director and producer; b. 9 Oct. 1964, Guadalajara, Jalisco; spent 10 years as makeup supervisor; f. The Tequila Gang (production co.). *Films include:* Doña Lupe 1985, Doña Herlinda y su hijo (exec. producer) 1985, Geometria 1987, Un Embrujo (producer) 1988, Cronos (also writer) 1993, Mimic (also screenplay) 1997, Bullfighter (actor) 2000, El Espinazo del diablo (also writer and producer) 2001, Asesino en serio (exec. producer) 2002, Blade II 2002, Hellboy (also screenplay) 2004, Crónicas (producer) 2004, Caleuche: El llamado del mar (exec. producer) 2006, Pan's Labyrinth (also screenplay and producer, Best Film Nat. Soc. of Film Critics 2007, Goya Award for Best Original Screenplay 2007, BAFTA Award for Best Film not in the English Language 2007) 2006, The Orphanage (producer) 2008, Hellboy II: The Golden Army (also screenplay) 2008. *Television includes:* Hora Marcada 1988. *Publication:* The Strain (with Chuck Hogan) 2009. *Address:* c/o Robert Newman, The Endeavor Agency, 9601 Wilshire Blvd., 10th Floor, Beverly Hills, CA 90212, USA. *Telephone:* (310) 248-2000. *Fax:* (310) 248-2020.

DEL VALLE ALLIENDE, Jaime; Chilean politician and lawyer; b. 2 July 1931, Santiago; m. Paulina Swinburn Pereira; four c.; ed Escuela de Derecho de la Universidad Católica de Chile; taught at Catholic Univ. Law School from 1955, Dir 1969, Dean 1970; various posts in Supreme Court 1958–64; Public Prosecutor 1964–74; Pro-Rector, Pontificia Univ. Católica de Chile 1974; Dir-Gen. nat. TV channel 1975–78; mem. Bd Colegio de Abogados 1981–, Pres. 1982–83; Minister of Justice Feb.–Dec. 1983; Minister of Foreign Affairs 1983–87. *Address:* c/o Ministerio de Asuntos Exteriores, Palacio de la Moneda, Santiago, Chile. *Telephone:* 6982501.

DEL VECCHIO, Leonardo; Italian business executive; *Chairman and Chief Executive, Luxottica Group SpA;* b. 1935, Milan; m.; four c.; sent to orphanage aged seven; apprentice at factory that made moulds for automobile parts; opened his own moulding shop 1958; Founder and Chair. Luxottica (world's largest designer and manufacturer of high-quality eyeglass frames and sunglasses) 1961–; est. museum for one of world's oldest collection of spectacles, Agordo, Italy. *Leisure interests:* Medieval European antiques and paintings. *Address:* Luxottica Group SpA, Via C. Cantù 2, 20123 Milan, Italy (office). *Telephone:* (02) 863341 (office). *Fax:* (0437) 63223 (office). *Website:* www.luxottica.it (office).

DELACÔTE, Jacques; French conductor; s. of Pierre Delacôte and Renée Wagner Delacôte; m. Maria Lucia Alvares-Machado 1975; ed Music Conservatoire, Paris, Acad. of Music, with Prof. Hans Swarowsky, Vienna; was Asst to Darius Milhaud and Leonard Bernstein; among the orchestras conducted: Orchestre de Paris, Orchestre Nat. de France, New York Philharmonic, Vienna Philharmonic, Vienna Symphony, Israel Philharmonic, Orchestre Nat. de Belgique, London Symphony, San Francisco, Cleveland, Scottish Chamber, Scottish Nat. Opera, RIAS Berlin, WDR Cologne, SF Stuttgart, SWF Baden-Baden, Bavarian Radio, Munich, English Chamber, BBC, London, London Philharmonic, Royal Philharmonic, London, Japan Philharmonic, Yomiuri Symphony, Dresdner Staatskapelle, Royal Opera House, Covent Garden (including Far East tour, Korea and Japan), English Nat. Opera, Opernhaus Zürich, Teatro Real, Madrid, Teatro Liceo, Barcelona, La Fenice, Venice, Vienna State Opera, Deutsche Oper, Berlin, Pittsburgh Opera, Welsh Nat. Opera, Opéra de Paris, Teatro Colón, Buenos Aires, Canadian Opera Co., Royal State Opera, Copenhagen, State Opera, Hamburg, State Opera, Munich, Chicago Lyric Opera, Semper Oper, Dresden; also recordings with EMI, Philips London and Tring London; 1st Prize and Gold Medal Mitropoulos Competition, New York 1971. *Festivals include:* Flandernfestival, Macerata Festival, Klangbogen Vienna, Dresden Musiktage. *Leisure interest:* chess. *Address:* Paul Steinhauer Public Relations, Hermanngasse 3, 1070 Vienna, Austria (office); Praça Eugênio Jardim 34/602, Copacabana, 22061-040 Rio de Janeiro RJ, Brazil. *Telephone:* (1) 52496470 (office). *Fax:* (1) 52496475 (office). *E-mail:* office@paulsteinhauer.com (office). *Website:* www.paulsteinhauer.com (office); www.jacques-delacote.com.

DELANÖE, Bertrand Jacques Marie; French politician; *Mayor of Paris;* b. 30 May 1950, Tunis, Tunisia; s. of Auguste Delanöe and Yvonne Delanöe (née Delord); ed Institution Sainte-Marie, Rodez, Univ. of Toulouse; mem. Conseil de Paris 1977–, Socialist Deputy 1981–86, Senator 1995–2001, Mayor of Paris 2001–; Pres. of Paris Socialist Group 1993–2001; mem. Cttee of Dirs, Parti Socialiste 1979–, Party Spokesman 1981–83, mem. Exec. Bureau 1983–87, 1997–; Pres. France-Egypt Friendship Group 1981–86, Int. Asscn of French-speaking Mayors (AIMF) 2001–, World Org. of United Local Cities and Govts 2007–; Dr hc (Univ. of Quebec, Canada). *Publication:* Pour l'honneur de Paris 1999, La Vie, passionnément (autobiography) 2004. *Address:* Hôtel de Ville, 75196 Paris RP, France (office). *Fax:* 1-42-76-53-43 (office). *Website:* www .paris.fr (office).

DELAWARI, Nurollah, BA; Afghan central banker; ed UCLA, USA; spent 16 years at Lloyds Bank, LA, USA; fmr Pres. and CEO Afghan Investment Support Agency; Sr Adviser to Minister of Finance 2002; Gov. Da Afghanistan Bank (Cen. Bank of Afghanistan) 2004–08. *Address:* c/o Da Afghanistan Bank (Central Bank of Afghanistan), Ibne Sina Wat, Kabul, Afghanistan.

DELAY, Florence; French writer and university lecturer; b. 19 March 1941, Paris; d. of the late Jean Delay and of Marie Madeleine Delay (née Carrez); ed Lycée Jean de la Fontaine, Paris, Sorbonne; Lecturer in Gen. and Comparative Literature, Univ. of Paris III 1972–; Theatre Critic Nouvelle Revue française 1978–85; mem. Editorial Bd Critique magazine 1978–96, Reading Cttee Gallimard publrs 1979–86; mem. Acad. française 2000–; Commdr des Arts et des Lettres; Chevalier Légion d'honneur; Chevalier Ordre nat. du Mérite; Grand prix du roman de la Ville de Paris 1999. *Film:* Procès de Jeanne d'Arc 1962, Le Jouet criminel 1969, Mort de Raymond Roussel 1975, Écoute voir 1979. *Publications:* Minuit sur les jeux 1973, Le Aïe aïe de la corne de brume 1975, L'Insuccès de la fête 1980, Riche et légère (Prix Femina) 1983, Course d'amour pendant le deuil 1986, Petites formes en prose après Edison (essays) 1987, Les Dames de Fontainebleau (essays) 1987, Partition rouge 1989 (jtly), Hexaméron 1989, Etxemendi (Prix François Mauriac) 1990, Semaines de Suzanne 1991, Catalina 1994, La Fin des temps ordinaires 1996, La Séduction brève (essays) 1997, Dit Nerval 1999, L'Evangile de Jean (trans. of Gospel of John) 2001, Trois désobéissances 2004, Graal Theatre 2005, Mon Espagne or et ciel (essays) 2008; several trans of Spanish dramatists including Fernando de Rojas, Pedro Calderón, Lope de Vega. *Address:* c/o Gallimard, 5 rue Sébastien Bottin, 75007 Paris, France (office).

DELAY, Tom; American fmr politician; b. 1947, Laredo, Tex.; m. Christine DeLay; one d.; ed Baylor Univ., Univ. of Houston; owned and operated small business in Tex. 1970s; elected to Texas House of Reps 1978; mem. US Congress from 22nd Dist, Texas, held various positions in House of Reps including Republican Conf. Sec., Deputy Whip, Chair. Republican Study Cttee, Majority Whip –2003, Majority Leader 2003–05 (resgnd after indictment by Tex. grand jury), mem. Appropriations Cttee; mem. Advisory Bd Child Advocates of Fort Bend Co.; Founder Grassroots Action and Information Network (GAIN) 2006–; Taxpayers Friend Award, Nat. Taxpayers Union; Golden Bulldog Award, Watchdog of the Treasury; Nat. Security Leadership Award, Peace Through Strength Coalition. *Publication:* No Retreat, No Surrender: One American's Flight (with Stephen Mansfield) 2007. *Website:* www.tomdelay.com.

DELEBARRE, Michel Stéphane Henry Joseph; French politician; *Mayor of Dunkirk;* b. 27 April 1946, Bailleul (Nord); s. of Stéphane Delebarre and Georgette Deroo; m. Janine Debeyre 1969; one d.; Asst Sec.-Gen. Cttee for the Expansion of the Nord-Pas de Calais area 1968–71, Sec.-Gen. 1971–74; Cabinet Dir for Pres. of Nord-Pas de Calais Regional Council 1974–78; Gen. Del. for Devt for City of Lille 1977–80; Sec.-Gen. City of Lille 1980; Pres. regional fund for contemporary art 1982; mem. of Cabinet of Prime Minister 1981–82; Cabinet Dir 1982–84; unassigned prefect 1983; Minister of Labour, Employment and Professional Training 1984–86; Socialist mem. of Parl. for Nord 1986, 1988–93, 1997–98; mem. Exec. Bd Socialist Party 1987; Minister of Transport and Marine Affairs 1989; Minister of State, Minister of Town and Physical Planning 1990–91; Minister of State, Minister of Civil Service and Public Admin. Enhancement 1991–92; Adviser for Urban and Regional Planning; Chair. Cttee of Experts advising Lionel Jospin, Leader Socialist Party 1995; First Deputy Pres., Regional Council for Nord-Pas de Calais 1986–97, Pres. 1998–2001, regional counsellor 2001–02;; Mayor of Dunkirk 1989–; Pres. Urban Community of Dunkirk 1995–, L'Union nationale des fédérations d'organismes d'HLM 1999–; mem. Nat. Council of Evaluation 1999–; Pres. Regional Cttees of EU 2006–. *Address:* Hôtel de Ville, place Charles Valentin, 59140 Dunkirk, France. *Telephone:* 3-28-59-12-34 (office). *Website:* www.michel-delebarre.fr.

DELGADO, Alvaro; Spanish artist; b. 9 June 1922, Madrid; m. Mercedes Gal Orendain; one s.; ed pupil of Vazquez Diaz 1936–39, Benjamin Palencia 1939–42; mem. Real Acad. de Bellas Artes, Real Acad. de San Fernando; Acad. Delegado de la Calcografía; Commdr Order of Ethiopia; First Prize, Concurso Nacional de Carteles Para Teatro 1939; First Prize, Proyecto Para Figurines y Decorados 1940; Cuba Prize for Painting, IIa Bienal Arte Hispano Americano 1952; Grand Prize for Painting, Bienal de Arte Mediterraneo, Alexandria 1955; Grand Prize for Painting, Exposición Int., Alicante 1960; Primera Medalla de Dibujo, Exposición Nacional Bellas Artes 1960; Gold Medal, Salón Nacional del Grabado 1962; Vocal del Patronato del Museo del Prado, Madrid 1970. *Leisure interest:* constant travel. *Address:* Biarritz 5, Parque de las Avenidas, Madrid 28028, Spain.

DELGADO DURÁN, Norberto; Panamanian politician; ed Univ. of Panamá; Exec. Dir Multi Credit Bank 1990–98, fmr Vice-Pres. Commercial; Prof. Instituto de Microfinanzas 1998–; Vice-Minister of Finance 1999–2000, Minister of Finance and the Treasury 2000–04; mem. Bd of Dirs Panama Canal Authority (ACP) 2004–; Pres. Instituto Panameño Autónomo Cooperativo (IPACOOP) 1999; Pres. Bd of Dirs Fondo de Inversión Social 1999. *Address:* c/o Panama Canal Authority, PO Box 526725, Miami, FL 33152-6725, USA (office).

DELIBES, Miguel, DIur; Spanish writer and academic; b. 17 Oct. 1920, Valladolid; s. of Adolfo Delibes and María Delibes; m. Angeles de Castro 1946 (died 1974); seven c.; ed School of Higher Studies, Bilbao, Univ. of Valladolid, School of Journalism, Bilbao; Prof. Univ. of Valladolid 1945–85; Dir El Norte de Castilla (newspaper) 1956–62; mem. Real Acad. de la Lengua 1973; Dr hc (Madrid, Valladolid, Saarbrücken); recipient Premio Nacional de Narrativa 1955, 1999, Premio de la Crítica 1962, Premio Nadal, Premio Nacional de Literatura, Premio Príncipe de Asturias, Premio Nacional de las Letras 1991, Miguel de Cervantes Prize 1993. *Publications include:* La sombra del ciprés es alargada 1948, El camino 1950, Las ratas 1962, El libro de la caza menor 1964, Cinco horas con Mario 1966, Parábola del náufrago 1969, El disputado voto del señor Cayo 1978, Los santos inocentes 1981, El tesoro 1985, Madera de héroe 1987, Pegar la hebra 1990, El conejo 1991, Señora de rojo sobre fondo gris 1991, El último coto 1992, Diario de un jubilado 1995, El hereje 1998, Madera de héroe 2002. *Leisure interests:* hunting, fishing, tennis. *Address:* Calle Dos de Mayo 10, 47004 Valladolid, Spain. *Telephone:* (98) 3300250.

ĐELIĆ, Božidar, MBA, MPA; Serbian economist and politician; *Deputy Prime Minister, in charge of European Integration, and Minister of Science and Technological Development;* b. 1 April 1965, Belgrade; m. Marie-Laure Đelić (divorced 2003); two d.; ed Institut d'Etudes Politiques de Paris, Ecole des Hautes Etudes Commerciales, Paris, Ecole des Hautes Etudes en Sciences Sociales, Harvard Business School and Kennedy School of Govt, Harvard Univ., USA; worked as expert adviser to several East European transition govts on issues of privatization, banking reform and macro-econ. reform, adviser to Leszek Balcerowicz in Poland (also helped establish Warsaw Stock Exchange) 1991–92, to Anatoly Chubais in Russia 1992–93, in Romania 1996; Pnr, McKinsey & Co. (consulting firm) 1991, returned on unpaid leave to Belgrade Nov. 2000; served as main negotiator with IMF, Paris Club and other financial insts; mem. Democratic Party; Minister of Finance 2001–03; withdrew from politics 2003–06; Man. for Southeastern Europe, Crédit Agricole 2005–06; returned to politics and became active in Democratic Party's election campaign late 2006, cand. for Prime Minister; Deputy Prime Minister, in charge of European Integration, and Minister of Science and Technological Devt 2007–; won French nat. competitions for high-school students in history and econs 1980, 1981, named by Vreme as Person of the Year 2001, placed first on Blic's ranking list of politicians Dec. 2002, included in top 100 young leaders list of World EC Forum and Forbes magazine 2002. *Address:* Ministry of Science and Technological Development, 11000 Belgrade, Nemanjina 22–26, Serbia (office). *Telephone:* (11) 3616516 (office). *Fax:*

(11) 3616516 (office). *E-mail:* info@nauka.sr.gov.yu (office). *Website:* www.nauka.sr.gov.yu (office); www.djelic.net.

DELIGNE, Vicomte; Pierre R., PhD; Belgian mathematician and academic; *Professor Emeritus, School of Mathematics, Institute for Advanced Study;* b. 3 Oct. 1944, Etterbeek; ed Athénée Adolphe Max, Brussels, Univ. of Brussels, Université Libre de Bruxelles, Ecole Normale Supérieure, Paris, France; Jr Scientist, Fond Nat. de la Recherche Scientifique (FNRS), Brussels 1967–68; Guest Scientist, Institut des Hautes Etudes Scientifiques, Bures-sur-Yvette, France 1967–68, Visiting mem. 1968–70, Perm. mem. 1970–84; Prof., Inst. for Advanced Study, Princeton, NJ, USA 1984–; Foreign Assoc. mem. Acad. des Sciences, Paris 1978–; Assoc. mem. Acad. Royale de Belgique 1994–; Foreign mem. Accad. Nazionale dei Lincei 2003–; Foreign Assoc. NAS 2007–; Foreign Hon. mem. American Acad. of Arts and Sciences 1978; Dr hc (Flemish Univ. of Brussels) 1989, (Ecole Normale Supérieure) 1995; Francois Deruyts Prize, Acad. Royale de Belgique 1974, Henri Poincaré Medal, Acad. des Sciences (Paris) 1974, Quinquennal Prize 'Doctor A. De Leeuw-Damry-Bourlart', FNRS 1975, Fields Medal, Int. Congress of Mathematicians (Helsinki) 1978, Crafoord Prize (Stockholm) (jt recipient) 1988, Balzan Prize 2004, Wolf Prize 2008. *Publications:* more than 80 publs in math. journals. *Address:* Fuld Hall 210, School of Mathematics, Institute for Advanced Study, Einstein Drive, Princeton, NJ 08540, USA (office). *Telephone:* (609) 734-8391 (office). *E-mail:* deligne@ias.edu (office). *Website:* www.math.ias.edu (office).

DeLILLO, Don, BA; American writer; b. 20 Nov. 1936, New York, NY; m. Barbara Bennett 1975; ed Cardinal Hayes High School, Fordham Coll., New York; fmr advertising copywriter Ogilvy, Benson & Mather; American Acad. of Arts and Letters Award in Literature 1984, Jerusalem Prize for the Freedom of the Individual in Soc. 1999, William Dean Howells Medal 2000. *Plays:* The Day Room 1987, Valparaiso 1999. *Publications:* Americana 1971, End Zone 1972, Great Jones Street 1973, Ratner's Star 1976, Players 1977, Running Dog 1978, The Names 1982, White Noise 1985 (Nat. Book Award 1985), Libra 1988 (Irish Times Fiction Prize 1989), Mao II 1991 (PEN/Faulkner Award 1992), Underworld 1997, The Body Artist 2000, Cosmopolis 2003, Falling Man 2007. *Address:* Wallace Literary Agency, 177 E 70th Street, New York, NY 10021, USA (office).

DELL, Michael S.; American computer industry executive; *Chairman and CEO, Dell Inc.;* b. Feb. 1965, Houston, Tex.; s. of Alexander Dell and Lorraine Dell; m. Susan Lieberman 1989; four c.; ed Univ. of Texas; Founder, Chair. and CEO Dell Computer Corpn (fmrly PCs Ltd, now Dell Inc.), Austin, Tex. 1984–2004, Chair. 2004–, CEO 2007–; f. MSD Capital 1998; co-f., with his wife, The Michael & Susan Dell Foundation 1999; Vice-Chair. US Business Council; mem. Foundation Bd of World Econ. Forum, Exec. Cttee of Int. Business Council, US Business Council, US Pres.'s Council of Advisors on Science and Tech., Tech. CEO Council, Governing Bd of Indian School of Business, Hyderabad; Entrepreneur of the Year Award, Inc. magazine 1990, JD Power Customer Satisfaction Award 1991, 1993, CEO of the Year, Financial World magazine 1993. *Publication:* Direct from Dell: Strategies that Revolutionized an Industry 1999. *Address:* Dell Inc., 1 Dell Way, Round Rock, TX 78682-0001, USA (office). *Telephone:* (512) 338-4400 (office). *Fax:* (512) 728-3653 (office). *E-mail:* webmaster@dell.com (office). *Website:* www.dell.com (office).

DELLA CASA-DEBELJEVIC, Lisa (see CASA-DEBELJEVIC, Lisa Della).

DELLA VALLE, Diego; Italian fashion designer and art collector; *President and CEO, Tod's SpA;* b. 30 Dec. 1953, Sant'elpidio a Mare, Ascoli Piceno; s. of Dorino della Valle, founder of the original Della Valle shoe makers 1940s; studied law in Bologna; brief work experience in USA 1975; joined his father in family business, leading role in definition of co. strategies and brand creation, Pres. and CEO Tod's SpA 2000–; mem. Bd IRI SpA, Banca Commerciale Italiana SpA; mem. Bd of Dirs Assicurazioni Generali, Banca Nazionale del Lavoro, LVMH, Ferrari, Maserati, Compagnia Immobiliare Azionaria, Confindustria; mem. Fundraising Cttee Umberto Veronesi Cancer Research; Pres. Bd of Dirs Della Valle Onlus Foundation; Hon. Pres. AC Fiorentina; degree hc in Business and Econs (Univ. of Ancona) 2000; Cavaliere del Lavoro 1996. *Address:* Tod's SpA, Via Filippo Della Valle 1, Sant'elpidio a Mare, Ascoli Piceno, Italy (office). *Telephone:* (0734) 871671 (office). *Website:* www.todsgroup.com (office).

DELLER, Jeremy; British artist; b. 1966, London; ed Courtauld Inst. of Art; acts as curator, producer or dir of broad range of projects, including orchestrated events, films and publs. *Works include:* Acid Brass (ongoing project and collaboration with The Williams Fairey Brass Band) 1997–, Fig. 1 2000, Folk Archive (ongoing project with Alan Kane investigating UK folk and vernacular art) 2000–, The Battle of Orgreave: The English Civil War Part II (co-production by Artangel/Channel 4, film by Mike Figgis) 2001, Social Parade (video), Five Memorials, This is US (CD produced in asscn with Bard Coll., Red Hook, USA) 2003, Memory Bucket (video documentary about Crawford, Texas—home town of George W. Bush—and Branch Davidian siege in nearby Waco) (Turner Prize 2004) 2003. *Address:* c/o Gavin Brown's Enterprise, 620 Greenwich Street, New York, NY 10014, USA (office). *E-mail:* gallery@gavinbrown.biz (office).

DELL'OLIO, Louis; American fashion designer; b. 23 July 1948, New York; ed Parsons School of Design, New York; Asst designer to Dominic Rompello of Teal Traina, New York 1969–71; Chief Designer, Georgini div. of Originala, New York 1971–74; design collaborator with Donna Karan (q.v.), Anne Klein & Co. 1974–93; Chief Designer 1984–93; mem. Fashion Designers of America; Coty Awards 1977, 1981.

DELLY, HE Cardinal Emmanuel-Karim, MA, DTheol, DCL; Iraqi ecclesiastic; *Patriarch of Babylon and Archbishop of Baghdad;* b. 6 Oct. 1927, Telkaif ed Pontifical Urbanian Univ., Pontifical Lateran Univ.; ordained priest of Mossul 1952; Titular Bishop of Palaeopolis in Asia and Auxiliary Bishop of Babylon 1962–2002 (retd); apptd Titular Archbishop of Kaskar dei Caldie 1967; Patriarch of Babylon and Archbishop of Baghdad 2003–; cr. Cardinal 2007–. *Address:* Archdiocese of Babylon (Chaldean), Baghdad, Iraq (office).

DELON, Alain; French actor; b. 8 Nov. 1935, Sceaux; m. Nathalie Delon (divorced); one s.; one s. one d. by Rosalie Van Breemen; with French Marine Corps 1952–55; ind. actor-producer under Delbeau (Delon-Beaume) Productions 1964–; Pres. and Dir-Gen. Adel Productions 1968–87, Leda Productions 1987–; cr. Alain Delon Diffusion SA (specialising in luxury goods) 1978; Chevalier, Légion d'honneur, Commdr des Arts et des Lettres. *Films include:* Christine 1958, Faibles femmes 1959, Le chemin des écoliers 1959, Purple Noon 1959, Rocco and His Brothers 1960, Eclipse 1961, The Leopard 1962, Any Number Can Win 1962, The Black Tulip 1963, The Love Cage 1963, L'insoumis 1964, The Yellow Rolls Royce 1964, Once a Thief 1964, Les centurions 1965, Paris brûle-t-il? 1965, Texas Across the River 1966, Les adventuriers 1966, Le samourai 1967, Histoires extraordinaires 1967, Diaboliquement votre 1967, Adieu l'ami 1968, Girl on a motorcycle 1968, La piscine 1968, Jeff 1968, Die Boss, Die Quietly 1969, Borsalino 1970, Madly 1970, Doucement les basses 1970, Le cercle rouge 1971, L'assassinat de Trotsky 1971, La veuve Couderc 1971, Un flic 1972, Le professeur 1972, Scorpio 1972, Traitement de choc 1972, Les granges brûlées 1973, Deux hommes dans la ville 1973, Borsalino & Co. 1973, Les seins de glace 1974, Creezy 1975, Zorro 1975, Le gitan 1975, Mr. Klein 1975, Le gang 1977, Mort d'un pourri 1977, Armageddon 1977, L'homme pressé 1977, Attention, les enfants regardent 1978, Le toubib 1979, Trois hommes à abattre 1980, Pour la peau d'un flic 1981 (dir), Le choc 1982 (dir), Le battant 1983 (dir), Un Amour de Swann 1984, Notre Histoire (César, Best Actor 1985) 1984, Parole de flic 1985, Le passage 1986, Ne réveillez pas un flic qui dort, Nouvelle Vague 1989, Dancing Machine 1990, Le Retour de Casanova 1992, Un Crime 1993, L'Ours en peluche 1994, Le Jour et La Nuit 1996, Une Chance sur deux 1998, Les Acteurs 2000, Les Nouveaux refus 2004, Astérix at the Olympic Games 2008. *Stage performances:* 'Tis Pity She's a Whore 1961, 1962, Les yeux crevés 1967, Variations énigmatiques 1996. *Television:* Comme au Cinéma (series) 1988, Fabio Montale (series) 2001, Le Lion 2003, Frank Riva (series) 2003–4. *Leisure interests:* swimming, riding, boxing. *Address:* Alain Delon International Diffusion SA, 7 rue des Battoirs, 1205 Geneva, Switzerland (office). *Telephone:* 227021108 (office). *E-mail:* info@alaindelon.com (office). *Website:* www.alaindelon.com.

DELORS, Jacques Lucien Jean; French politician and economist; *President, Conseil de l'emploi, des revenus et de la cohésion sociale;* b. 20 July 1925, Paris; s. of Louis Delors and Jeanne Rigal; m. Marie Lephaille 1948; one s. (deceased) one d. (Martine Aubry (q.v.)); ed Lycée Voltaire, Paris, Lycée Blaise-Pascal, Clermont-Ferrand, Univ. of Paris, Centre d'Etudes Supérieur de Banque (IEP); Head of Dept, Banque de France 1945–62, attached to staff of Dir-Gen. of Securities and Financial Market 1950–62, mem. Gen. Council 1973–79; mem. Planning and Investments Section, Econ. and Social Council 1959–61; Head of Social Affairs Section, Commissariat général du Plan 1962–69; Sec.-Gen. Interministerial Cttee for Vocational Training and Social Promotion 1969–72; Adviser to Jacques Chaban-Delmas 1969, Chargé de mission 1971–72; Assoc. Prof. of Co. Man., Univ. of Paris IX 1973–79; f. Club Echange et Projets 1974; Dir Labour and Soc. Research Centre 1975–79; Parti Socialiste Nat. Del. for int. econ. relations 1976–81; elected mem. European Parl. 1979, Chair. Econ. and Monetary Cttee 1979–81; Minister for the Economy and Finance 1981–84, for the Economy, Finance and Budget 1983–84; Mayor of Clichy 1983–84; Pres. Comm. of the European Communities (now European Commission) 1985–94; Pres. EMU Comm. 1988–89, Int. Comm. on Educ. for the Twenty-First Century, UNESCO 1992–99; Pres. Conseil d'admin. Collège d'Europe, Bruges 1995–99, Conseil de l'emploi, des revenus et de la cohésion sociale (CERC) 2000–08; f. Notre Europe 1996–2004; Officier, Légion d'honneur; hon. degrees from 24 univs in Europe, USA and Canada. *Publications:* Les indicateurs sociaux 1971, Changer 1975, En sortir ou pas (jtly) 1985, La France par l'Europe (jtly) 1988, Le Nouveau concert Européen 1992, Our Europe 1993, L'Unité d'un homme 1994, Combats pour l'Europe 1996, Mémoires 2004; numerous articles; reports for UN on French planning (1966) and long-term planning (1969). *Address:* Conseil de l'emploi, des revenus et de la cohésion sociale, 113 rue de Grenelle, 75007 Paris, France (office). *Telephone:* 1-53-85-15-16 (office). *Fax:* 1-53-85-15-21 (office). *E-mail:* jacques.delors@cerc.gouv.fr (office). *Website:* www.cerc.gouv.fr (office).

DELPY, Julie; French actress; b. 21 Dec. 1969, Paris; ed New York Univ. Film School. *Films include:* Detective 1985, Mauvais Sang 1986, La Passion Béatrice 1987, L'Autre Nuit 1988, La Noche Oscura 1989, Europa Europa 1991, Voyager 1991, Warszawa 1992, Young and Younger 1993, The Three Musketeers 1993, When Pigs Fly 1993, The Myth of the White Wolf 1994, Killing Zoe 1994, Mesmer 1994, Trois Couleurs Blanc 1994, Trois Couleurs Rouge 1994, Before Sunrise 1995, An American Werewolf in Paris 1997, The Treat 1998, LA Without a Map 1998, Blah, Blah, Blah (Dir), The Passion of Ayn Rand 1999, But I'm A Cheerleader 1999, Tell Me 2000, Sand 2000, Beginner's Luck 1999, Waking Life 2001, MacArthur Park 2001, Looking for Jimmy 2002, Cinemagique 2002, Notting Hill Anxiety Festival 2003, Before Sunset (Empire Film Award for Best Actress 2005) 2004, Frankenstein (TV) 2004, Broken Flowers 2005, 3 & 3 2005, The Legend of Lucy Keyes 2006, The Hoax 2006, The Air I Breathe 2007, Deux jours à Paris (Two Days in Paris) 2007, The Countess 2009. *Television includes:* ER 2001. *Address:* c/o The William Morris Agency, One William Morris Place, Beverly Hills, CA 90212, USA.

DELVALLE HENRIQUEZ, Eric Arturo; Panamanian politician; b. 2 Feb. 1937; m. Mariela Díaz de Delvalle; one s. two d.; ed Colegio Javier, Panama City, Louisiana State Univ. and Soulé Coll. of Accountancy; fmr Chair. and Dir of several pvt. commercial enterprises; mem. Bd of Dirs Inst. for Econ. Promotion 1963; mem. Games Control Bd 1960–64; Del. to Nat. Ass. 1968; Vice-Pres. Nat. Ass. 1968; Leader, Repub. Party; Vice-Pres. of Panama 1984, Pres. 1985–88 (removed from office for alleged drug-trafficking).

DELWAR HOSSAIN, Khandaker; Bangladeshi politician; *Secretary-General, Bangladesh Jatiyatabadi Dal (Bangladesh Nationalist Party);* Chief Whip of Parl. 1991–96, 2001–06, Chief Whip of the Opposition 1996–2001; mem. Bangladesh Jatiyatabadi Dal (Bangladesh Nationalist Party), mem. Standing Cttee, Sec.-Gen. 2007–. *Address:* Bangladesh Jatiyatabadi Dal (Bangladesh Nationalist Party), Banani Office, House 23, Rd 13, Dhaka, Bangladesh (office). *Telephone:* (2) 8819525 (office). *Fax:* (2) 8813063 (office). *E-mail:* bnpbd@e-fsbd.net (office). *Website:* www.bnpbd.com (office).

DELYAGIN, Mikhail G., DEcon; Russian economist; b. 18 March 1968, Moscow; ed Moscow State Univ.; mem. govt analytical expert group 1994–97; Head of Analytical Centre Kominvest, then Chief Analyst, Analytical Dept of the Presidency of the Russian Federation; adviser to the Deputy Chair. of the Govt 1997–99; adviser and Head of Motherland All-Russia 1997–99; Founder and Dir Inst. of Globalization Studies 1998–2002, Scientific Dir and Chair. Presidium 2002–06, Dir 2006–07; adviser to Prime Minister of Russian Fed. 2002–03; mem. Presidium Ideological Council of Rodina party 2004–06; mem. Presidium Congress of Russian Communities; mem. Political Conf., Drugaia Rossiya; mem. Council on Foreign and Defence Policy 1999–; mem. Bd of Dirs Russian Union of Taxpayers. *Publications include:* more than 350 publications in Russia and abroad, five monographs, including Economics of Nonpayments 1997, Ideology of Renaissance 2000, Practice of Globalization 2000. *Telephone:* (495) 510-57-71 (office). *E-mail:* info@iprog.ru (office). *Website:* deliagin.ru (office); www.iprog.ru/en (office).

DEMARCO, Richard, OBE, FRSA; British academic; *Professor Emeritus of European Cultural Studies, Kingston University;* b. 9 July 1930, Edinburgh; s. of Carmine Demarco and Elizabeth Valentine Fusco; m. Anne C. Muckle 1957; ed Holy Cross Acad., Edin. Coll. of Art, Moray House Coll. and Royal Army Educ. Corps; art master, Duns Scotus Acad., Edin. 1956–67; Vice-Chair. Founding Cttee and Vice-Chair. Bd Dirs Traverse Theatre, Edin. 1963–67; Dir Sean Connery's Scottish Int. Educ. Trust (SIET) 1972–74; Dir Richard Demarco Gallery 1966–, European Youth Parliament 1993–; Trustee Kingston-Demarco European Cultural Foundation 1993–95, Dir Demarco European Art Foundation 1993–; Prof. of European Cultural Studies, Kingston Univ. 1993–2000, Prof. Emer. 2001–; Artistic Adviser European Youth Parl. 1992–; Consultant to Ministries of the Environment and Culture, Malta 1999; mem. Royal Scottish Soc. of Painters in Watercolours; Hon. Fellow, Royal Incorporation of Architects; Hon. LLD (Dundee); Cavaliere della Repubblica Italiana, Chevalier des Arts et des Lettres (France). *Publications:* The Artist as Explorer 1978, The Road to Meikle Seggie 1978, A Life in Pictures 1994, Art = Wealth 1995. *Leisure interests:* exploring the road to Meikle Seggie in the footsteps of Roman legionnaires, Celtic saints and scholars, respectful of the Rule of St Benedict. *Address:* Demarco European Art Foundation, Building 2, New Parliament House, 5 Regent Road, Edinburgh, EH7 5BL; 23A Lennox Street, Edinburgh, EH4 1PY, Scotland (home). *Telephone:* (20) 8547-7027 (Kingston); (131) 557-0707 (Edinburgh); (131) 343-2124 (home). *Fax:* (20) 8547-8246 (Kingston); (131) 557-5972 (Edinburgh); (131) 343-3124 (home).

DEMBY, Albert Joe, PhD; Sierra Leonean politician; Vice-Pres. of Sierra Leone 1996–2002; Deputy Leader Sierra Leone People's Party. *Address:* Sierra Leone People's Party, 29 Rawdon Street, Freetown, Sierra Leone (office).

DEMEKSA, Kuma; Ethiopian politician; *Mayor of Addis Ababa;* fmr Minister of Internal Affairs; officially removed from presidency of Oromia State after he was dismissed from Oromo People's Democratic Org. for "abuse of power, corruption and anti-democratic practices"; absent from political scene until apptd State Minister of Capacity Building; Minister of Nat. Defence 2005–08; Mayor of Addis Ababa 2008–. *Address:* City Hall PO Box 9137, Addis Ababa, Ethiopia (office). *Telephone:* (11) 562391 (office). *E-mail:* addisababac@ethionet.et (office).

DEMEL, Herbert, PhD; Austrian business executive; b. 14 Oct. 1953, Vienna; ed Vienna Tech. Univ.; Robert Bosch GmbH, Stuttgart 1984–90; Audi AG, Ingolstadt 1990–, mem. Man. Bd in charge of Research and Devt 1993, Speaker of Man. Bd and CEO responsible for Research and Devt and Sales and Marketing 1994, Chair. Man. Bd 1995–97.

DEMERITTE, Richard C., CA, FAIA, FCGA, FBIM, FRSA, PhD; Bahamian diplomatist and chartered accountant; *Managing Partner, Richard C. Demeritte & Co;* b. 27 Feb. 1939, Nassau; s. of Richard and Miriam (née Whitfield) Demeritte; m. Ruth Smith 1966; one s. (deceased) two d.; ed Eastern Secondary School, Bahamas School of Commerce, Metropolitan Coll., London and Century Univ., USA; Deputy Treas. Treasury Dept 1956–79; Auditor-Gen. Commonwealth of the Bahamas 1980–84, 1988–96; High Commr in UK 1984–87; Amb. to EEC 1986–88, to Belgium, France, Fed. Repub. of Germany 1987–88; Man. Partner Richard C. Demeritte & Co., Chartered Accountants 1997–; Pres. Certified Gen. Accountants Asscn of the Bahamas (and mem. Council), Caribbean Asscn of Certified Gen. Accountants, Universal and Financial Business Consultants 1996–; fmr Pres. Asscn of Int. Accountants, now mem. Council; mem. Council Bahamas Inst. of Chartered Accountants; Fellow Certified Gen. Accountants, Canada 1996. *Leisure interests:* golf, chess, billiards, gardening, research, computer technology. *Address:* P.O. Box CB-11001, Cable Beach, West Bay Street, Nassau, Bahamas (home). *Telephone:* 327-5729 (office); 327-8193 (home). *Fax:* 327-0288 (office); 327-8861 (home). *E-mail:* demerite@bahamas.net.bs (office).

DEMETEROVÁ, Gabriela; Czech violinist; b. 17 May 1971, Prague; ed Prague Conservatory, Acad. of Fine Arts, Prague, Royal Acad. of Music, Denmark; soloist and Artistic Dir Czech Philharmonic Collegium ensemble 1995–; has performed with leading Czech orchestras in France, Germany, UK, USA; stringed Autumn Prague 2001, Int. Music Festival Čedeský Krumlov Honour to Baroque 2001; f. Collegium of Gabriela Demeterová chamber ensemble 2005; winner Jaroslav Kocián Competition, Yehudi Menuhin Competition 1993. *Recordings include:* selection from Biber's Biblical Sonatas 1996, Italian Baroque, W.A. Mozart – Sonatas for Piano and Violin 2003, Violin Magic, and numerous recordings for Czech Radio. *Leisure interests:* cycling, computer games, horse riding. *E-mail:* demeterova.agency@volny.cz (office). *Website:* www.gabrielademeterova.com.

DEMETRIOU, Andreas, BA, PhD; Cypriot psychologist, academic and politician; *Minister of Education and Culture;* b. 15 Aug. 1950, Strongylo, Famagusta; m. Julia Tsakalea; two s.; ed Aristotelian Univ. of Thessaloniki, Univ. of New South Wales, Australia; Research and Teaching Asst, Dept of Psychology and Educ., Aristotelian Univ. of Thessaloniki 1975–83, Lecturer in Developmental Psychology 1983–86, Asst Prof. of Developmental Psychology 1986–92, Prof. 1992–96, mem. Univ. Senate 1990–91, Head of Dept of Psychology 1991–92, Pres. School of Psychology 1993–95, mem. Research Cttee 1995–96; Visiting Asst Prof. of Psychology, Dept of Educ., Univ. of Thessaly 1988–90; Prof. of Psychology, Univ. of Cyprus 1996–, Head of Dept of Educational Science 1996–98, Vice-Rector 1999–2002, Acting Rector 2003, Dean of School of Humanities and Social Sciences 2004–06; Visiting Scholar, Univ. of New South Wales, Australia 1978, Stanford Univ. 1991; Consultant Visitor at Harvard, Yale, and Pittsburgh Univs 1985; Visiting Research Fellow, Univ. of Melbourne 1988; Visiting Prof., Univ. of Ljubljana 1995, Univ. of Porto 1998, Univ. of Marribor, Slovenia 2003; Distinguished Visiting Prof., Univ. of Fribourg 2001; Pres. First Conf. for Psychological Research 1989, Greek Psychological Soc. 1989–91, Sec.-Gen. 1991–93; Pres. Seventh Conf., Hellenic Psychological Soc. 1998, Interim Governing Bd, Technological Univ. of Cyprus 2004–08, Conf. of Rectors of the Univs of Cyprus 2007–08; Founding Ed. Psychology: The Journal of Greek Psychological Society 1992–96, mem. Editorial Bd 1997–; mem. Editorial Bd The European Journal of the Psychology of Education 1985–, Newsletter of the European Association for Research on Learning and Instruction 1987–91, Adult Development Series 1989–, Bulletin of the Didactics of Mathematics 1990–96, Developmental Science 1998–, The Child and the Adolescent: A Journal of Mental Health and Psychopathology 1999–, The Child and the Adolescent: The Journal of the Greek Association of Psychoanalytic Psychotherapy of Children 2001, MountainRise: An Electronic Journal Dedicated to Scholarship of Teaching and Learning 2004–; mem. Int. Programme Cttee, Third Conf. of European Asscn for Research on Learning and Instruction 1989, mem. Exec. Cttee 1989–93, Cttee for Oeuvre Award 2001, Conf. Pres. 2003–05; mem. Psychology Cttee, Inter-Univ. Center for Recognition of Foreign Degrees (Diapanepistimiako Kentro Anagnorisis Titlon Spoudon Allodapis—DIKATSA) 1989–92; mem. Psychological Practice Licencing Cttee, Ministry of Health and Social Services 1994–95; mem. Ad Hoc Cttee for Evaluation of Integrated Lyceum, Ministry of Educ.; mem. Governing Bd, Research Promotion Foundation 2000–03; Rep. to European Science Foundation 2001–03; Fellow, Int. Acad. of Educ. 2004–; Minister of Educ. and Culture 2008–. *Publications:* numerous contribs to academic journals. *Address:* Ministry of Education and Culture, Kimonos & Thoukydidou, Akropolis, 1434 Nicosia, Cyprus (office). *Telephone:* 22800600 (office). *Fax:* 22305974 (office). *E-mail:* registry@moec.gov.cy (office). *Website:* www.moec.gov.cy (office).

DEMIDOVA, Alla Sergeyevna; Russian actress; b. 29 Sept. 1936, Moscow; d. of S. Demidov and A. Kharchenko; m. Vladimir Valutsky 1961; ed Moscow Univ. and Shchukin Theatre School; acted with Taganka Theatre, Moscow 1964–; has appeared in films since 1957; f. Little Theatre "A" 1993; USSR State Prize 1977, People's Artist of RSFSR 1984, President's Prize 2001. *Film roles include:* Olga (Day Stars) 1968, Maria Spiridonova (The Sixth of July) 1968, Zhenya (A Degree of Risk) 1969, Julia von Meck (Tchaikovsky) 1970, Lesya Ukrainka (I Come to You) 1972, Arkadina (The Seagull), 1975, Liza (The Mirror) A. Tarkovsky, 1975, The Soothsayer (The Little Scarlet Flower) 1978, Pashenka (Father Sergius) 1978, Duchess of Marlborough (A Glass of Water) (TV) 1979, Lebiadkina (Demons) 1993, Empress (Invisible Travellers) 1999, Anna (Adjuster) (Nat. Acad. of Cinema Prize), Pisma k Elze 2002, Nastroyshchik (The Tuner) 2004. *Theatre roles include:* Elmira (Tartuf), Pani Bogenitskaya (Rush Hour), Ranevskaya (Cherry Orchard), Gertrude (Hamlet), Fedra (Fedra M. Tsvetaeva), Melentyeva (Wooden Horses), Masha (Three Sisters), Marina Mnishek (Boris Godunov, Donna Anna (The Feast During a Plague), Elektra (Elektra); has also performed Akhmatova's Requiem and Poem Without Hero. *Publications:* works on the art of theatre including The Second Reality, The Shadows behind the Mirrors, The Running Line of My Memory 2000, and numerous articles. *Leisure interests:* philosophy, painting, gardening, her animals (two dogs and a cat). *Address:* 125009 Moscow, Tverskaya str. 8, korp. 1 Apt. 83, Russia (home). *Telephone:* (495) 629-04-17 (home). *Fax:* (495) 629-04-17 (home). *E-mail:* demidowa@mtu-net.ru (home). *Website:* www.demidova.ru.

DEMIN, Col.-Gen. Yuri Georgiyevich, DJur Sc; Russian lawyer; b. 1945, Voronezh; m.; one d.; ed Higher KGB School, USSR Council of Ministers; involved in drafting of Fed. Security Service law 1994–95; Head of Legal Dept, Fed. Security Service of Russian Fed. 1995–97; Deputy Prosecutor-Gen., Chief Mil. Prosecutor 1997–2000; First Deputy Minister of Justice 2000–. *Publications:* (monographs) Diplomatic Missions 1995, Status of Diplomatic Missions and their Personnel 1995 and numerous articles. *Address:* Ministry of Justice, B. Karetny per. IDA, 101434 Moscow, Russia (office). *Telephone:* (495) 209-77-44 (office). *Fax:* (495) 209-66-95 (office).

DEMING, Claiborne P., BA, JD; American lawyer and business executive; *President and CEO, Murphy Oil Corporation;* m. Elaine Deming; four c.; ed Tulane Univ.; joined Murphy Oil Corpn as staff attorney 1979, held numerous exec. positions, including Pres. Murphy Oil USA, Inc. 1989–93, Exec. Vice-Pres. and COO 1993–94, mem. Bd of Dirs 1993, Pres. and CEO 1994–; mem. Bd of Dirs Entergy Corpn 2002–06; mem. Ark. State Bd of Educ. 1999–2002; Vice-Chair. Nat. Petroleum Council; Pres. El Dorado Educ. Foundation; Past Pres. 25 Year Club of the Oil and Gas Industry, South Ark. Symphony, United Way of Union Co.; mem. Tulane Law School Bd of Advisors, A.B. Freeman School of Business of Tulane Univ. Bd of Advisors; mem. Bd of Dirs American Petroleum Inst.; mem. ABA, Ark. Bar Asscn, La Bar Asscn. *Address:* Murphy Oil Corporation, PO Box 7000, El Dorado, AR 71731-7000 (office); Murphy Oil Corpn, 200 Peach Street, El Dorado, AR 71730, USA (office). *Telephone:* (870) 862-6411 (office). *Fax:* (870) 864-6373 (office). *E-mail:* info@murphyoilcorp.com (office). *Website:* www.murphyoilcorp.com (office).

DEMINT, Jim, AB, MBA; American politician; *Senator from South Carolina;* m.; four c.; ed Univ. of Tennessee, Clemson Univ.; est. marketing co.; mem. US House of Reps from S Carolina, 4th Dist 1998–2004, served as mem. House Educ. and Workforce Cttee, Transportation and Infrastructure Cttee, Small Business Cttee, Vice-Chair. Sub-Cttee on Employer and Employee Relations; Senator from S Carolina 2005–, mem. Senate Cttee on Commerce, Science and Transportation, Environment and Public Works, Economics, Aging, Sub-Cttee on Disaster Prediction and Prevention (Chair.); Republican; Friend of the Taxpayer Award, American for Tax Reform, Spirit of Enterprise Award, US Chamber of Commerce, 'A' Rating, Nat. Rifle Asscn. *Address:* 340 Russell Senate Office Building, Washington, DC 20510, USA (office). *Telephone:* (202) 224-6121 (office). *Fax:* (202) 228-5143 (office). *Website:* demint.senate.gov (office).

DEMIRCHIAN, Stepan; Armenian politician; *Chairman, People's Party of Armenia;* b. 1959, Yerevan; s. of Karen Demirchian (died 1999); m.; three d.; ed Yerevan Polytechnic Inst.; began career working at electrical eng plant; fmr dir of industrial machinery co.; elected Chair. People's Party of Armenia 1999, confirmed in post 2001–; Cand. in Presidential Election 2003; Head of Justice (Artarutiun) bloc (alliance of opposition parties) to contest legis. elections 2003. *Address:* People's Party of Armenia (Hayastani Zhoghovrdakan Kusaktsutyun—HzhK), Yerevan, Armenia (office). *E-mail:* hzhk@freenet.am (office). *Website:* www.ppa.am (office).

DEMIREL, Süleyman; Turkish fmr head of state and engineer; b. 1924; ed Istanbul Tech. Univ.; researcher in irrigation and electrification, Bureau of Reclamation 1949–50; Engineer, Electrical Survey Admin.; Head of Dams Dept 1954–55; Exchange Fellowship scholar, several pvt. cos and public depts, USA 1954–55; Dir-Gen. Hydraulic Works, Turkey 1955–60; pvt. contractor, engineer and Lecturer, Middle East Tech. Univ. 1962–64; Chair. Justice Party (AP) 1965–80; Isparta Deputy 1965–80; Deputy Prime Minister Feb.–Oct. 1965; Prime Minister (led AP Govt) 1965–71, (four coalition govts) 1977–78; Opposition Leader 1978–80; Prime Minister 1979–80; banned from politics 1980–87; Chair. True Path Party (DYP) 1987–93; Deputy for Isparta 1987–93; Prime Minister 1991–93; Pres. of Turkey 1993–2000; Honoured Mem. Azerbaijan Nat. Acad. of Sciences. *Address:* c/o Office of the President, Cumhurbaş-Kanlığı Köşkü, Cankaya, Ankara, Turkey.

DEMJÁN, Sándor; Hungarian business executive; *President, National Association of Entrepreneurs and Employers (VOSZ);* b. 14 May 1943, Börvely; m.; ed Coll. for Trading and Catering, Budapest; Sr Man. Sales Dept. ÁFÉSZ Gorsium, Székesfehérvár 1968–73; f. SKÁLA Dept Store Chain and SKÁLA-COOP, CEO SKÁLA Jt Venture 1973–86; Founder and Chair. Magyar Hitel Bank, CEO 1986–90; Founder and Partner Cen. European Devt Corpn (CEDC) 1990–91; Founder and Pres. Polus Investment Co. Inc., Toronto, Canada 1991–; f. Gránit Pólus Investment & Devt Co.; Founder and co-Chair. Bd Trigranit Devt Co. 1997–; f. WestEnd City Centre, Budapest 1999; co-Founder and co-Chair. (with George Soros), Int. Man. Centre 1988; Chair. Bd United Way 1995–98; Co-Chair. Nat. Asscn of Entrepreneurs and Employers (Vosz) 1997, now Pres.; est. first Corpn in fmr USSR (KAMAZ); adviser to Govt of Tatarstan; Pres. MLL Professional Football Sub-Alliance 2000; Man of the Year 1986, 1988, Entrepreneur of the Year 1996, Most Influential Businessman of the Decade 2000, Most Successful Real Estate Developer of the Year 2002, State of Hungary Award 1980, Planetary Consciousness, Hungarian Business Award 1998. *Leisure interests:* fishing, playing chess. *Address:* TriGranit Development Corporation, Váci út 3, 1062 Budapest (office); National Association of Entrepreneurs and Employers (VOSZ), Mázsa tér 2-6, 1107 Budapest, Hungary. *Telephone:* (1) 374-6502 (office); (1) 414-2181. *Fax:* (1) 374-6505 (office); (1) 414-2180. *E-mail:* info@trigranit.com (office); center@vosz.hu. *Website:* www.trigranit.com (office); www.vosz.hu.

DEMME, Jonathan; American director, producer and writer; b. 22 Feb. 1944, Rockville Center, NY; m. Joanne Howard; two c.; ed Univ. of Florida; worked in publicity Dept United Artists, Embassy Pictures, Pathe Contemporary Films; writer for Film Daily 1966–68. *Films directed:* Hot Box (also co-screenwriter), Caged Heat 1974, Crazy Mama 1975, Fighting Mad 1976, Citizens Band 1977, Last Embrace 1979, Melvin and Howard 1980, Swing Shift 1983, Something Wild 1986, Married to the Mob 1988, Swimming to Cambodia, The Silence of the Lambs (Acad. Award for Best Film 1992), Cousin Bobby 1992, Philadelphia 1993, Mandela 1996, That Thing You Do 1996, Beloved 1998, Storefront Hitchcock 1998, The Truth About Charlie 2002, The Agronomist 2003, Neil Young Heart of Gold 2006, Jimmy Carter Man from Plains 2007; exec. producer Devil in a Blue Dress 1995; Who am I this Time (for TV) 1982, Stop Making Sense (documentary) 1984, Konbir (video) 1989, Konbir: Burning Rhythms of Haiti (recording) 1989; producer Miami Blues 1990. *Address:* c/o Bob Bookman, Creative Artists Agency, 9830 Wilshire

Boulevard, Beverly Hills, CA 90212-1804; Clinica Estetico, 127 W 24th Street #7, New York, NY 10011-1914, USA.

DEMPSEY, Noel, BA; Irish politician; *Minister for Communications, Marine and Natural Resources;* b. 6 Jan. 1953, Trim, Co. Meath; m. Bernadette Rattigan; two s. two d.; ed St Michael's Christian Brothers' School, Trim, Univ. Coll., Dublin, St Patrick's Coll., Maynooth; fmr career guidance counsellor; Nat. Sec. Local Authority Mems Asscn 1984–89; Chair. Meath Co. Council 1986–87; fmr mem. numerous local govt cttees; mem. Dáil Éireann 1987–; mem. Dáil Public Accounts Cttee 1987–89, 1990–92; fmr Chair. Backbench Cttee on Tourism, Transport and Communications; fmr Sec. Backbench Cttee on the Environment; fmr Dir Midland East Regional Tourism Org.; Minister of State at Depts of Taoiseach, Defence and Finance, Govt Chief Whip 1992–94; fmr Opposition Spokesperson on Environment; Fianna Fáil Co-ordinator on Forum for Peace and Reconciliation; Nat. Treasurer Fianna Fáil; Minister for the Environment and Local Govt 1997–2002; Minister for Educ. and Science 2002–04, for Communications, Marine and Natural Resources 2004–. *Leisure interests:* Gaelic football, reading, golf. *Address:* Department of Communications, Marine and Natural Resources, Adelaide Road, Dublin 2 (office); Newtown, Trim, County Meath, Ireland (home). *Telephone:* (1) 6782004 (office); (46) 9431146 (home). *Fax:* (1) 6782029 (office); (46) 9436643 (home). *E-mail:* Minister.Dempsey@dcmnr.gov.ie (office). *Website:* www.dcmnr.gov.ie (office).

DEMSZKY, Gábor; Hungarian politician, journalist, editor and sociologist; *Mayor of Budapest;* b. 4 Aug. 1952, Budapest; s. of Rudolf Demszky and Irén Király; m. Vera Révai (divorced); m. Anikó Németh; four c.; ed Eötvös Loránd Univ.; contrib. to periodical Világosság (Lucidity) 1977; founding mem. SZETA (fund to support poor) 1979; founder AB Független Kiadó (independent publr) 1981; Ed. illegal Hirmondó (Courier) 1983; founding mem. Network of Free Initiative and SZDSZ 1988; founding mem. Alliance of Free Democrats, mem. Exec. Bd 1989; mem. Parl. 1990 (resgnd), 1998; Chair. Cttee of Nat. Security 1990; mem. Exec. Bd Alliance of Free Democrats 1994–, Pres. of Alliance 2000–01; Founder Children's Rescue Soc.; negotiator in Moscow talks on Soviet troops withdrawal and on Hungary's leaving the Warsaw Pact; Mayor of Budapest 1990–; Vice-Pres. Standing Conf. of Local and Regional Authorities, Council of Europe 1992–94; Congress of Local and Regional Authorities 1994–96; mem., European Parliament 2004 (resgnd due to conflict of interest); founding mem. and Dir Asscn to Save the Children; Co-Pres. Budapest Bank for Budapest Foundation; Pres. Budapest Sports Asscn; Freedom to Publish Prize, Int. Asscn of Publishers, Vienna 1984. *Leisure interests:* jogging, sailing, riding, water-skiing, fishing. *Address:* Városház utca 9/11, 1052 Budapest, Hungary. *Telephone:* (1) 327-1022 (office). *Fax:* (1) 327-1819 (office). *E-mail:* demszkyg@budapest.hu (office). *Website:* www.budapest.hu (office).

DEMUS, Jörg; Austrian concert pianist; b. 2 Dec. 1928, St Pölten, Lower Austria; s. of Dr Otto and Erika (Budik) Demus; ed Vienna State Acad. of Music and studies with various musicians; début at age 14; mem. Gesellschaft der Musikfreunde, Vienna; débuts in London and Switzerland 1950, tour of Latin America 1951, Paris 1953, New York 1955, Japan 1961; has composed music for piano, songs, chamber music, opera; has performed in almost all important musical centres; has made over 450 LP records and CDs; Dr hc (Amherst Univ.) 1981; Premier Busoni at Int. Piano Competition, Bolzano 1956; Harriet Cohen Bach-Medal 1958; Hon. Prof. of Austria 1977; Beethoven Ring, Vienna Beethoven Soc. 1977; Mozart Medal, Mozartgemeinde, Vienna 1979; several Edison Awards and Grand Prix du Disque; Schumann Award, Zwickau, E Germany, 1986. *Publications:* Abenteuer der Interpretation (essays), co-author of a book on Beethoven's piano sonatas. *Leisure interests:* antiques, nature, collecting and restoring historic keyboard instruments. *Address:* c/o Mr Roland Sölder, Lyra Artists Management, Döblinger Hauptstrasse 77A/10, 1190 Vienna, Austria (office); Aria's di Novella Partacini & Alexandra Plaickner, Rappresentanza Artisti, Via Josef Weingartner, 4, 39022 Lagundo, Italy (office). *Telephone:* (1) 3687472 (office); (1) 3681226 (home); (0473) 200200 (office). *Fax:* (1) 3687473 (office); (0473) 222424 (office). *E-mail:* info@arias.it (office). *Website:* www.arias.it (office).

DENAT DE GUILLEBON, Jeanne-Claude, (Christo and Jeanne-Claude); French/American artist; b. 13 June 1935, Casablanca, Morocco; m. Christo (Christo Javacheff); one s.; ed France, Switzerland, Univ. of Tunis, Tunisia; works with Christo 1961–: Iron Curtain Wall of Oil Barrels blocking rue Visconti, Paris, Wrapping a Girl, London 1962, Showcases 1963, Store Front 1964, Air Package and Wrapped Tree, Eindhoven, Netherlands 1966, 42,390 cu. ft. Package, Walker Art Center, Minneapolis School of Art 1966, Wrapped Kunsthalle, Bern 1968, 5,600 cu. m. Package for Kassel Documenta 4 1968, Wrapped Museum of Contemporary Art, Chicago 1969, Wrapped Coast, Little Bay, Sydney, Australia, 1 m. sq. ft. 1969, Valley Curtain, Grand Hogback, Rifle, Colorado, suspended fabric curtain 1970–72, Running Fence, Calif. 1972–76, Wrapped Roman Wall, Rome 1974, Ocean Front, Newport 1974, Wrapped Walk-Ways, Kansas City 1977–78, Surrounded Islands, Biscayne Bay, Miami, Florida 1980–83, The Pont Neuf Wrapped, Paris 1975–85, The Umbrellas, Japan-USA 1984–91, Wrapped Reichstag, Berlin 1971–95, Wrapped Trees, Fondation Beyeler and Berower Park, Riehen, Switzerland 1997–98, The Wall, 13,000 oil barrels, Gasometer, Oberhausen, Germany, indoor installation 1999, The Gates, Central Park, New York City 1979–2005; Praemium Imperiale 1995. *Website:* www.christojeanneclaude.net.

DENCH, Dame Judith (Judi) Olivia, CH, DBE; British actress; b. 9 Dec. 1934, York; d. of Reginald Arthur and Eleanora Olave (née Jones) Dench; m. Michael Williams 1971 (died 2001); one d.; ed The Mount School, York, Central School of Speech Training and Dramatic Art; performed in Old Vic seasons 1957–61, appearing in parts including Ophelia (Hamlet), Katherine (Henry V), Cecily (The Importance of Being Earnest), Juliet (Romeo and Juliet), appeared with Old Vic Co. at two Edin. Festivals, Venice, on tour to Paris, Belgium and Yugoslavia and on tour to USA and Canada; appearances with RSC 1961–62, including parts as Anya (The Cherry Orchard), Titania (A Midsummer Night's Dream), Dorcas Bellboys (A Penny for a Song), Isabella (Measure for Measure); on tour to W Africa with Nottingham Playhouse 1963; mem. Bd Nat. Theatre 1988–91; subsequent roles include Irina (The Three Sisters) and Doll Common (Alchemist), Oxford Playhouse 1964–65, title-role in Saint Joan and Barbara (The Astrakhan Coat), Nottingham Playhouse 1965, Amanda (Private Lives), Lika (The Promise) 1967, Sally Bowles (Cabaret) 1968, Grace Harkaway (London Assurance) 1970, 1972, Barbara Undershaft (Major Barbara) 1970; Assoc. mem. RSC 1969–, appearing as Bianca (Women Beware Women), Viola (Twelfth Night), Hermione and Perdita (Winter's Tale), Portia (Merchant of Venice), Duchess (Duchess of Malfi), Beatrice (Much Ado About Nothing), Lady Macbeth (Macbeth), Adriana (Comedy of Errors), also on tour with RSC to Japan and Australia 1970, Japan 1972; other performances include Vilma (The Wolf), Oxford and London 1973, Miss Trant (The Good Companions), 1974, Sophie Fullgarney (The Gay Lord Quex) 1975, Nurse (Too True to be Good) 1975, 1976, Millament (Way of the World) 1978, Cymbeline 1979, Juno and the Paycock 1980–81, Lady Bracknell (The Importance of Being Earnest) 1982, Deborah (A Kind of Alaska) 1982, Pack of Lies 1983, Mother Courage 1984, Waste 1985, Mr and Mrs Nobody 1986, Antony and Cleopatra 1987, Entertaining Strangers 1987, Hamlet 1989, The Cherry Orchard 1989, The Sea 1991, The Plough and the Stars 1991, Coriolanus 1992, The Gift of the Gorgon 1993, The Seagull (Royal Nat. Theatre) 1994, The Convent 1995, Absolute Hell (Royal Nat. Theatre) 1995, A Little Night Music (Royal Nat. Theatre) 1995, Amy's View (Royal Nat. Theatre) 1997, (New York) 1999, Filumena 1998, The Royal Family 2001, The Breath of Life (Theatre Royal, Haymarket) 2002, All's Well that Ends Well (Theatregoers' Award for Best Supporting Actress 2005) 2003–04; Dir Much Ado About Nothing 1988, Look Back in Anger 1989, The Boys from Syracuse 1991; mem. Bd, Nat. Theatre 1988–; Prin. Royal Scottish Acad. of Music and Drama 2001–; Hon. Fellow Royal Holloway Coll. London; Hon. DLitt (Warwick) 1978, (York) 1983, (Keele) 1989, (Birmingham) 1989, (Loughborough) 1991, (Open Univ.) 1994, (London) 1994, (Oxford) 2000; Dr hc (Surrey) 1996; numerous awards including Paladino d'Argentino (Venice Festival Award for Juliet) 1961, Best Actress of Year (Variety London Critics for Lika in The Promise) 1967, Most Promising Newcomer (British Film Acad. for Four in the Morning) 1965, Best Actress of the Year (Guild of Dirs for Talking to a Stranger) 1967, Soc. West End Theatre Award (for Lady Macbeth) 1977, Best Actress New Standard Drama Awards (for Juno and the Paycock) 1980, (for Lady Bracknell in The Importance of Being Earnest and Deborah in A Kind of Alaska) 1983, (for Cleopatra in Antony and Cleopatra) 1987, Olivier Award for Best Actress in Antony and Cleopatra 1987; BAFTA Award for Best Television Actress 1981, for Best Supporting Actress (for A Room with a View) 1987 and (for A Handful of Dust) 1988, Golden Globe and BAFTA Best Actress Award for Mrs Brown, Olivier Award for Outstanding Contrib. to Theatre 2004, Evening Standard Special Award for Outstanding Contrib. to British Theatre 2004. *Films include:* A Study in Terror 1965, He Who Rides a Tiger 1966, Four in the Morning 1966, A Midsummer Night's Dream (RSC Production) 1968, The Third Secret 1978, Dead Cert, Wetherby 1985, Room with a View 1986, 84 Charing Cross Road 1987, A Handful of Dust 1988, Henry V 1989, Goldeneye 1995, Mrs Brown 1996, Tea with Mussolini 1998, Shakespeare in Love (Acad. Award for Best Supporting Actress) 1998, The World is Not Enough 1999, Chocolat 2000, Iris (BAFTA Award for Best Actress 2002) 2001, The Shipping News 2001, The Importance of Being Earnest 2002, Die Another Day 2002, The Chronicles of Riddick 2004, Ladies in Lavender 2004, Mrs Henderson Presents 2005, Doogal (voice) 2006, Casino Royale 2006, Notes on a Scandal (Evening Standard British Film Award for Best Actress 2007) 2006, Quantum of Solace 2008. *TV appearances in:* Major Barbara, Pink String and Sealing Wax, Talking to a Stranger, The Funambulists, Age of Kings, Jackanory, Hilda Lessways, Luther, Neighbours, Parade's End, Marching Song, On Approval, Days to Come, Emilie, Comedy of Errors, Macbeth, Langrishe Go Down, On Giants' Shoulders, Love in a Cold Climate, A Fine Romance, The Cherry Orchard, Going Gently, Saigon – Year of the Cat 1982, Ghosts 1986, Behaving Badly 1989, Absolute Hell, Can You Hear Me Thinking?, As Time Goes By, Last of the Blonde Bombshells (BAFTA Best Actress). *Publications:* Judi Dench: A Great Deal of Laughter (biog.), Judi Dench: With a Crack in Her Voice 1998, Scenes from My Life (autobiog.) 2005. *Leisure interests:* painting, drawing, swimming, sewing, catching up with letters. *Address:* c/o Julian Belfrage Associates, 46 Albemarle Street, London, W1X 4PP, England.

DENCKER, Nils, BSc, PhD; Swedish mathematician and academic; *Professor of Mathematics, Lund University;* b. 14 March 1953, Lund; m. Anna Dencker; two s. two d.; ed Lund Univ.; C.L.E. Moore Instructor, MIT, USA 1981–83; returned to Lund Univ. as Prof. of Math. 1983–, Dir of Studies, Dept of Math. 2001–03; Chair. Swedish Math. Soc. 2007–09; mem. Royal Swedish Acad. of Sciences, Swedish Nat. Cttee for Math.; Gaarding Prize, Royal Physiographic Soc., Lund 2003, Clay Research Award, Clay Math. Inst. (co-recipient) 2005. *Achievement:* complete resolution of a conjecture made by F. Treves and L. Nirenberg in 1970. *Publications:* numerous papers in professional journals on micro-local analysis of partial differential equations and calculus of pseudo-differential operators. *Address:* Room 507, Center for Mathematical Sciences, Faculty of Science, Lund University, Box 118, 221 00 Lund, Sweden (office). *Telephone:* (46) 222-44-62 (office). *Fax:* (46) 222-42-13 (office). *E-mail:* dencker@maths.lth.se (office). *Website:* www.maths.lth.se (office).

DENDIAS, Nikolaos, LLM; Greek politician; *Minister of Justice;* b. 7 Oct. 1959, Corfu; m.; two c.; ed Univ. of Athens, Univ. Coll. London, London School of Econs; called to Corfu Bar 1986; mem. Nea Dimokratia 1978–, mem. Parl. Group for the Control of Tourism 2002, Cttee for the Revision of the Constitution 2006; mem. Parl. for Corfu 2004–, mem. Perm. Cttee on Finance,

Special Perm. Cttee on Nat. Budget and Cttee of Deontology 2007–, Vice-Pres. fact-finding Cttee for the Vatopedi Case 2008; Minister of Justice 2009–; mem. Centre for Political Research and Educ. 2006–; mem. Hellenic Cancer Soc. 2006–; currently Pres. Eptanission Politia Cultural Asscn. *Address:* Ministry of Justice, Odos Mesogeion 96, 115 27 Athens, Greece (office). *Telephone:* (210) 7711019 (office). *Fax:* (210) 7759879 (office). *E-mail:* minjust@otenet.gr (office). *Website:* www.ministryofjustice.gr (office).

DENENBERG, Herbert Sidney, PhD, JD, BS, LLM; American consumer affairs reporter, lawyer and academic; *Adjunct Professor of Information Science and Technology, Cabrini College;* b. 20 Nov. 1929, Omaha, Neb.; s. of David Aaron Denenberg and Fannie Molly (Rothenberg) Denenberg; m. Naomi Glushakow 1958; ed Omaha Cen. High School, Johns Hopkins and Creighton Univs, Harvard Law School and Univ. of Pennsylvania; lawyer, Denenberg & Denenberg, Attorneys-at-Law 1954–55; lawyer, US Army Judge Advocate Gen. Corps. 1955–58; Prof., Wharton School, Univ. of Pa 1962–71; Insurance Commr, State of Pa 1971–74; Special Adviser to Gov. of Pa on Consumer Affairs 1974; Commr, Pa Public Utilities Comm. 1974–75; Consumer Reporter, WCAU-TV (NBC), Philadelphia 1975–98; Consumer Columnist Philadelphia Daily News 1979–81, Philadelphia Journal 1981–82, Delaware Co. Daily and Sunday Times 1987–89, Burlington Co. Daily Times 1987–89, Reading Eagle 1989–, Doylestown Patriot 1987–89 and other newspapers; Consumer and Investigative Reporter Harron Cable Update, 2nd Tri-State Media Network Cable System 1999–2000, WLVT (PBS) 2001–; Adjunct Prof. of Information Science and Tech., Cabrini Coll. 2000–; mem. Advisory Bd The People's Doctor 1988–91; Consultant to US Dept of Labor, Small Business Admin., US Dept of Transportation, Legislature of Nev. and Wis.; Trustee Center for Proper Medication Use; mem. Inst. of Medicine (NAS); Hon. LLD (Allentown Coll.) 1989, Hon. DHL (Spring Garden Coll.) 1992; 40 Emmy awards for investigative and consumer reports; numerous awards from Nat. Press Club, Consumer Fed. of America and Nat. Acad. of TV Arts and Sciences, B'nai B'rith Beber Award, Consumer Fed. of America Outstanding Media Service Award; American Bd of Trial Advocates Award of Achievement for Excellence in Legal Reporting and Analysis 1996. *Publications include:* Risk and Insurance (textbook) 1964, Insurance, Government and Social Policy (textbook) 1969, Herb Denenberg's Smart Shopper's Guide 1980, The Shopper's Guidebook 1974, Life Insurance And/Or Mutual Funds 1967, Mass Marketing of Property and Liability Insurance 1970, The Insurance Trap 1972, Getting Your Money's Worth 1974, Cover Yourself 1974, Shopper's Guide to Medical Equipment 1990, A Consumer's Guide to Herbal Medicines 1999, hundreds of articles, Govt reports and statutes. *Leisure interests:* reading, photography. *Address:* PO Box 7301, St David's, PA 19087-7301, USA (office). *Telephone:* (610) 687-0293 (office); (610) 687-0293 (home). *Fax:* (610) 687-0229. *E-mail:* hdenenberg@aol.com (office). *Website:* thedenenbergreport.org (office).

DENEUVE, Catherine; French actress; b. (Catherine Dorléac), 22 Oct. 1943, Paris; d. of Maurice Dorléac and Renée Deneuve; m. David Bailey (q.v.) 1965 (divorced); one s. by Roger Vadim; one d. by Marcello Mastroianni; ed Lycée La Fontaine, Paris; film début in Les petits chats 1959; Pres., Dir-Gen. Films de la Citrouille 1971–79; f. Société Cardeva 1983; UNESCO Goodwill Amb. for the Safeguarding of Film Heritage 1994–2003; Hon. Golden Bear, Berlin Film Festival, Arts de l'Alliance française de New York Trophy 1998, Bangkok Film Festival Lifetime Achievement Award 2006. *Films include:* Les portes claquent 1960, L'homme à femmes 1960, Le vice et la vertu 1962, Et Satan conduit le bal 1962, Vacances portugaises 1963, Les parapluies de Cherbourg 1963 (Palme d'Or, Festival de Cannes 1964), Les plus belles escroqueries du monde 1963, La chasse à l'homme 1964, Un monsieur de compagnie 1964, La Costanza della Ragione 1964, Repulsion 1964, Le chant du monde 1965, La vie de château 1965, Liebes Karusell 1965, Les créatures 1965, Les demoiselles de Rochefort 1966, Belle de jour 1967 (Golden Lion at Venice Festival 1967), Benjamin 1967, Manon 70 1967, Mayerling 1968, La chamade 1966, Folies d'avril 1969, Belles d'un soir 1969, La sirène du Mississippi 1969, Tristana 1970, Peau d'âne 1971, Ça n'arrive qu'aux autres 1971, Liza 1971, Un flic 1972, L'évènement le plus important depuis que l'homme a marché sur la lune 1973, Touche pas la femme blanche 1974, La femme aux bottes rouges 1975, La grande bourgeoisie 1975, Hustle 1976, March or Die 1977, Coup de foudre 1977, Ecoute, voir… 1978, L'argent des autres 1978, A nous deux 1979, Ils sont grands ces petits 1979, Le dernier métro 1980, Je vous aime 1980, Le choix des armes 1981, Hôtel des Amériques 1981, Le choc 1982, L'Africain 1983, The Hunger 1983, Le bon plaisir 1984, Paroles et musiques 1984, Le lieu du crime 1986, Pourvu que ce soit une fille 1986, Drôle d'endroit pour une rencontre 1989, La reine blanche 1991, Indochine 1992 (César award for Best Actress 1993), Ma saison préférée 1993, La Partie d'Echecs 1994, The Convent 1995, Les Cent et une nuits 1995, Les Voleurs 1995, Genéalogie d'un crime 1997, Place Vendôme 1998, Le Vent de la nuit 1999, Belle-Maman 1999, Pola x 1999, Time Regained 1999, Dancer in the Dark 2000, Je centre à la maison 2001, Absolument fabuleux 2001, 8 Femmes 2002, Au plus près du paradis 2002, Un film parlé 2003, Palais Royal! 2006, Le Concile de Pierre 2006, Le Héros de la famille 2006, Persepolis (voice) 2007, A Christmas Tale 2008. *Publication:* Close Up and Personal (autobiog.) 2005. *Address:* c/o Artmédia, 20 avenue Rapp, 75007 Paris, France.

DENG, Liqun; Chinese politician; b. 1914, Guidong Co., Hunan Prov.; m. Luo Liyun; one s.; ed Beijing No. 26 Middle School; mem. CCP 1936–; Dir Educ. Dept Marxism-Leninism Inst.; Dir Propaganda Dept CCP Jibei Pref. Cttee; Deputy Dir Gen. Office of Finance and Econ. Comm. of NE China; Dir Policy Research Office of CCP Liaoning Provincial Cttee; after founding of People's Repub. of China in 1949 served as Chair. Cultural and Educ. Cttee of Xinjiang Regional People's Cttee; Dir Propaganda Dept of Xinjiang Bureau under CCP Cen. Cttee; Ed. and Deputy Ed.-in-Chief, Red Flag; branded as counter-revolutionary revisionist and purged during Cultural Revolution; Vice-Pres. Acad. of Social Sciences 1978; Dir Policy Research Section under CCP Cen. Cttee 1981; Adviser to Soc. for Study of Econ. of Minority Areas 1981, to Soc. of Labour Science 1982, to Soc. for Study of Workers' Political and Ideological Work; Dir CCP Cen. Cttee Propaganda Dept 1982–85; mem. 12th CCP Cen. Cttee 1982–87, also mem. Secr. 1982–87; Vice-Chair. Nat. Cttee for Promoting Socialist Ethics 1983; Head, CCP Cen. Leading Group for Educ. of Cadres 1985; mem. CCP Cen. Advisory Comm. 1987; Deputy Head, CCP Cen. Cttee Party Bldg Group 1990–; Deputy Head, CCP Cen. Cttee Leading Group for Party History Work 1994–; Hon. Pres. Soc. for Studies on Party Mems 1991–. *Address:* c/o Central Committee of Chinese Communist Party, Beijing, People's Republic of China.

DENG, Nan; Chinese politician; *Vice-Chair, China Association for Science and Technology;* b. Oct. 1945, Guang'an, Sichuan Prov.; d. of the late Deng Xiaoping (fmr Gen. Sec., CCP and fmr Chair., Gen. Mil. Comm., CCP) and of Zhuo Lin; ed Beijing Univ.; worker, Semiconductor Research Inst., Chinese Acad. of Sciences 1973; fmr Deputy Div. Chief, Policy Dept, State Science and Tech. Comm., later Deputy Dir, later Deputy Dir Science and Tech. Policy Dept, Dir 1989–91, Vice-Minister in charge of State Science and Tech. Comm. 1991–98; Vice-Minister of Science and Tech. 1998–2005; fmr Deputy Dir Environmental Protection Cttee of the State Council; joined CCP 1978; Del., CCP Nat. Congress 1992–97; mem. 17th CCP Cen. Cttee 2007–; Vice-Chair. China Asscn for Science and Tech. 2005–; fmr Deputy Dir China Cttee of the Int. Decade for Natural Disaster Reduction; fmr mem. Exec. Cttee, All-China Women's Fed.; UN Boutros Boutros-Ghali Special Research Prize. *Address:* China Association for Science and Technology, 3 Fuxing Lu, Beijing 100032, People's Republic of China (office). *Website:* english.cast.org.cn (office).

DENG, Pufang; Chinese politician; *Vice-Chairman, 11th CPPCC National Committee;* b. 1943; s. of the late Deng Xiaoping and Zhuo Lin; ed Beijing Univ.; joined CCP 1965; fmr staff mem. Service Dept, Cen. Mil. Comm. of People's Repub. of China; Vice-Pres. Welfare Fund for Handicapped 1984, Pres. 1985–; Ed.-in-Chief Spring Breeze (Journal) 1984–; Vice-Chair. China Organizing Comm. of UN's Decade of Disabled Persons 1986–90, Chair. 1990–; Vice-Chair. Cttee for Coordination of Work for the Disabled; Chair. China Disabled Persons' Fed. 1988–; Adviser, China Asscn for Int. Friendly Contacts 1991–; Del., 14th CCP Nat. Congress 1992–97; Alt. mem. 15th CCP Cen. Cttee 1997–2002, 16th CCP Cen. Cttee 2002–07; mem. Standing Cttee, 9th CPPCC Nat. Cttee 1998–2003, Vice-Chair. 11th CPPCC Nat. Cttee 2008–; Exec. Pres. Chinese Olympic Cttee 2003–; Rehabilitation International (RI) Presidential Awards, 15th RI World Ass. 1990, 17th RI World Ass. 1992, recipient of Testimonial from UN Sec.-Gen. 1998, UN Human Rights Award 2003. *Address:* China Welfare Fund for Handicapped, Beijing, People's Republic of China.

DENG, Yaping, MA; Chinese table tennis player (retired); b. 5 Feb. 1973, Zhengzhou, He'nan Prov.; m. Lin Zhigang 2007; one s.; ed Tsinghua Univ., Beijing, Univ. of Nottingham; mem. of Chinese women's table tennis team 1988; won over 20 gold medals in various world championships including Barcelona Olympics 1992, Atlanta Olympics 1996; top-ranked female table tennis player 1991–98; retired 1997; mem. Sports Cttee of IOC; has co-chaired Chinese Olympic Cttee and Sports Asscn of China; Chinese Sports Personality of the Century 1999, mem. Laureus World Sports Acad. *Address:* c/o State General Bureau for Physical Culture and Sports, 9 Tiyuguan Road, Chongwen District, Beijing, People's Republic of China.

DENG, Youmei; Chinese writer; *Deputy Chairman, Chinese Writers' Association;* b. 1931, Tianjin; messenger in CCP-led New 4th Army 1945; entered Cen. Research Inst. of Literature 1952; in political disgrace 1957–77; Sec. Chinese Writers' Asscn 1985–96, Deputy Chair. 1996–. *Publications:* On the Precipice, Our Army Commander, Han the Forger, Tales of Taoranting Park, Snuff Bottles, Na Wu, Moon Over Liangshan Mountain. *Address:* Chinese Writers' Association, 25 Dongtucheng Road, Beijing 100013, People's Republic of China. *Telephone:* (10) 64261554.

DENHAM, Rt Hon. John, BSc, PC; British politician; *Secretary of State for Innovation, Universities and Skills;* b. 15 July 1953, Seaton; m. Ruth Eleanor Dixon (divorced); three c.; ed Univ. of Southampton; Head of Youth Affairs, British Youth Council 1979–83; responsible for public educ. and advocacy for War on Want (charity) 1984–88; Hants. Co. Councillor 1981–89; Southampton City Councillor 1989–93, Chair. Southampton City Housing Cttee 1989–93; MP (Labour) for Southampton Itchen 1992–; Minister of State at Home Office 2001–03, Chair. Home Affairs Select Cttee 2003–07, Sec. of State for Innovation, Univs and Skills 2007–; mem. AMICUS/MSF (trade union). *Leisure interests:* cookery, walking, music, Southampton Football Club. *Address:* Department for Innovation, Universities and Skills, 1 Victoria Street, London, SW1H 0ET, England (office). *Telephone:* (20) 7215-5555 (office). *E-mail:* info@dius.gsi.gov.uk (office). *Website:* www.dius.gov.uk (office); www.johndenham.org.uk (office).

DENHAM, Susan Jane, BA, LLB, LLM, SC; Irish judge; *Judge, Supreme Court of Ireland;* b. 22 Aug. 1945, Dublin; d. of R. J. D. Gageby and Dorothy Lester; m. Brian Denham 1970; three s. one d. (and one s. deceased); ed Alexandra Coll. Dublin, Trinity Coll. Dublin, King's Inns, Dublin and Columbia Univ. New York; called to Irish Bar 1971; mem. Midland Circuit 1971–91; called to Inner Bar 1987; Judge, High Court 1991–92, Supreme Court 1992–; Pro-Chancellor Univ. of Dublin Trinity Coll. 1996–; Chair. Working Group on a Courts Comm. 1995–98, Chair. Courts Service 2001–04; Chair. Finance Cttee 2001–04; mem., Courts Service Bd 2004–08; Chair. ISIS (Irish Sentencing Information System) 2006–; Chair. Comm. on Court Practice and Procedures; Chair. Cttee on Videoconferencing; Chair. Working Group on Court of Appeal 2006–; Bencher King's Inns 1991–; Hon. Bencher Middle Temple 2005; LLD hc (Queen's Univ., Belfast) 2002. *Leisure interests:* Connemara ponies, gardens. *Address:* The Supreme Court, The Four Courts, Dublin 7, Ireland (office). *Telephone:* (1) 8886533 (office). *E-mail:* SupremeCourt@courts.ie (office).

DENHARDT, David Tilton, PhD, FRSC; American biologist and academic; *Professor of Biological Sciences, Rutgers University;* b. 25 Feb. 1939, Sacramento, Calif.; s. of David B. Denhardt and Edith E. Tilton; m. Georgetta Louise Harrar 1961; one s. two d.; ed Swarthmore Coll., Pa and Calif. Inst. of Tech., Pasadena; Instructor Biology Dept, Harvard Univ. 1964–66, Asst Prof. 1966–70; Assoc. Prof. Biochemistry Dept, McGill Univ., Montréal 1970–76, Prof. 1976–80; Dir Cancer Research Lab. and Prof. of Biochem., Microbiology and Immunology, Univ. of W Ont. 1980–88; Chair. Biological Sciences, Rutgers Univ. 1988–95, Dir Bureau of Biological Research 1988–95, Prof. of Biological Sciences 1988–, Chair. Biology Dept 1988–95; ed. Journal Virology 1977–87, GENE 1985–93, Experimental Cell Research 1994–; Assoc. Ed. Journal of Cell Biochemistry 1994–; mem. numerous bds; Fellow American Acad. of Microbiology 1993. *Leisure interests:* travel, reading, canoeing, skiing, camping. *Address:* Nelson Biological Laboratories, Rutgers University, 604 Allison Road, Piscataway, NJ 08854-8000, USA (office). *Telephone:* (732) 445-4569 (office); (908) 704-0279 (home). *Fax:* (732) 445-0104. *E-mail:* denhardt@biology.rutgers.edu (office). *Website:* lifesci.rutgers.edu/~denhardt/lab.html (office).

DENHOLM, Sir Ian (John Ferguson), Kt, CBE, JP, DL; British shipowner; b. 8 May 1927, Glasgow; s. of Sir William and Lady Denholm (née Ferguson); m. Elizabeth Murray Stephen 1952; two s. two d.; ed Loretto School, Midlothian; Chair. Denholm Group of Companies 1974–98; Deputy Chair. P & O Steam Navigation Co. 1980–83; Pres. Chamber of Shipping of UK 1973–74; Chair. North of England Protecting & Indemnity Asscn 1976–78, Murray Group Investments Trusts 1985–93, Dir P & O 1974–83, Fleming Mercantile Investment Trust PLC 1984–94; Murray Man. Ltd 1985–92; Pres. Gen. Council of British Shipping 1988–89, BIFA 1990–91, BIMCO 1991–93; mem. Nat. Ports Council 1974–77, Scottish Transport Group 1975–82, London Bd of Bank of Scotland 1982–91, West of Scotland Bd of Bank of Scotland 1991–95; DL Renfrewshire 1980; Hon. Norwegian Consul in Glasgow 1975–97. *Leisure interest:* fishing. *Address:* Newton of Belltrees, Lochwinnoch, Renfrewshire, PA12 4JL, Scotland. *Telephone:* (1505) 842406.

DENISOV, Andrei Ivanovich; Russian politician and diplomatist; *First Deputy Minister of Foreign Affairs;* b. 3 Oct. 1952, Kharkov, Ukraine; m. Natalya Denisova; one d.; ed Moscow Inst. of Int. Relations; joined Ministry of Foreign Affairs 1992, various diplomatic posts in ministry and abroad, Dir Dept of Econ. Co-operation 1997–2000, Deputy Minister of Foreign Affairs responsible for int. econ. co-operation 2001–04; Amb. to Egypt 2000–01; Perm. Rep. to UN 2004–06; First Deputy Minister of Foreign Affairs 2006–. *Address:* Ministry of Foreign Affairs, 119200 Moscow, Smolenskaya-Sennaya pl. 32/34, Russian Federation (office). *Telephone:* (495) 244-16-06 (office). *Fax:* (495) 230-21-30 (office). *E-mail:* ministry@mid.ru (office). *Website:* www.mid.ru (office).

DENISSE, François-Jean; French astronomer; b. 16 May 1915, Saint-Quentin, Aisne; s. of Jean Julien Denisse and Marie Nicolas; m. Myriam Girondot 1948; two d.; ed Ecole Normale Supérieure; teacher, Lycée, Dakar 1942–45; Attaché at CNRS 1946–47; Guest Worker, Nat. Bureau of Standards, USA 1948–49; Head of Research of CNRS at Ecole Normale Supérieure 1950–51, Dir of Studies, Inst. des Hautes Etudes, Dakar 1952–53; Asst Astronomer, Paris Observatory 1954–56, Astronomer 1956–63, Dir 1963–68; Chair. of Bd of Nat. Space Research Centre 1968–73; Dir Institut Nat. d'Astronomie et de Géophysique 1968–71; Pres. Bureau des Longitudes 1974–75; mem. Atomic Energy Comm. 1970–75, Head of Research at the Ministry of Univs 1976–81; Pres. Council of the European Southern Observatory 1977–81; Pres. Cttee for Space Research (COSPAR) 1978–82; mem. Acad. des Sciences 1967, Int. Acad. of Astronautics 1968–, Royal Astronomical Soc.; Commdr, Légion d'honneur, Commdr, Ordre national du Mérite. *Leisure interest:* golf. *Address:* 48 rue Monsieur Le Prince, 75006 Paris, France (home). *Telephone:* 1-43-29-48-74.

DENKTAŞ, Rauf R.; Turkish Cypriot politician and barrister; b. 27 Jan. 1924, Baf; s. of Judge M. Raif Bey; m. Aydin Munir 1949; two s. (one deceased) two d.; ed The English School, Nicosia and Lincoln's Inn, London; law practice in Nicosia 1947–49; Jr Crown Counsel 1949, Crown Counsel 1952; Acting Solicitor-Gen. 1956–58; Pres. Fed. of Turkish Cypriot Asscns 1958–60; Pres. Turkish Communal Chamber 1960, re-elected 1970; Pres. 'Turkish Federated State of Cyprus' 1975–83; elected Pres. 'Turkish Repub. of Northern Cyprus' (TRNC) Nov. 1983–2005; radio and TV broadcasts on Cyprus; Dr hc (Middle East Tech. Univ., Ankara) 1984, (Southeastern Univ., Washington, DC) 1989, (Eastern Mediterranean Univ., TRNC) 1990, (Black Sea Tech. Univ., Turkey) 1991. *Publications:* Secrets of Happiness 1941, Hell Without Fire 1944, A Handbook of Criminal Cases 1955, Five Minutes to Twelve 1966, The AKRITAS Plan 1972, A Short Discourse on Cyprus 1972, The Cyprus Problem 1973, A Discourse with Youth 1981, The Cyprus Triangle 1982, Woman and the World 1985, Inspirations from the Koran 1986, Examination World 1986, For Tomorrows 1986, UN Speeches on Cyprus 1986, Cyprus, An Indictment and Defence 1987, Ataturk, Religion and Secularism 1989, A Challenge on Cyprus 1990, Denktas As A Photographer, Images from Northern Cyprus 1991, The Cyprus Problem and the Remedy 1992, Karkot Stream 1993, Those Days 1993, Lest Cyprus Becomes Crete 2005, 10 vols of memoirs 1963–74, The Cyprus Problem 2005. *Leisure interests:* reading, writing, sea sports, shooting, photography. *Address:* c/o The Office of the President, 'Turkish Republic of Northern Cyprus', via Mersin 10, Lefkoşa, Turkey (office). *Telephone:* (22) 83141 (office); (81) 53190 (home). *Fax:* (22) 75281 (office); (81) 58167 (home). *E-mail:* pressdpt@brimnet.com (office).

DENKTAŞ, Serdar; Turkish Cypriot politician; *Deputy Prime Minister and Minister of Foreign Affairs;* b. 1959, Lefkoşa; m.; three c.; ed Cardiff Coll., UK; est. Turkish Students Asscn of Cardiff Coll., N Cyprus Cultural Asscn 1986, Young Businessman Asscn 1989; Dir-Gen. Cyprus Credit Bank –1990; elected mem. of Parl. for Lefkoşa 1990; Minister of Interior, Rural Affairs and Environment 1990–92; Leader Nine Movt (now Democracy Party) 1992; Dist Chair. for Lefkoşa, then Sec.-Gen. of Democracy Party 1992–93, Leader 1996–2000, 2002–; elected mem. of Parl. for Lefkoşa (Democracy Party) 1993; Minister of Youth and Sports 1994–95; Minister of Tourism and Environment 2001–03; Deputy Prime Minister and Minister of Foreign Affairs 2003–. *Address:* Office of the Deputy Prime Minister, Selcuklu Road, Lefkoşa (Nicosia), Mersin 10, Turkey (office). *Telephone:* (22) 83241 (office). *Fax:* (22) 84290 (office). *E-mail:* pubinfo@trncinfo.org (office). *Website:* www.trncinfo.org (home).

DENNARD, Robert (Bob) Heath, MS, PhD; American electronic engineer; *IBM Fellow, IBM Research Division;* b. 1932, Terrell, Tex.; s. of Buford and Loma Dennard; m. Jane Bridges; ed Southern Methodist Univ., Carnegie Inst. of Tech. (now Carnegie Mellon Univ.); began career with IBM 1958, mem. research team on six-transistor memory cell, invented one-transistor dynamic random access memory (DRAM) 1967 and electronic device scaling theory 1972, currently IBM Fellow, IBM Research Div., Yorktown Heights, NY; mem. Nat. Acad. of Eng, American Philosophical Soc.; Fellow, IEEE; Nat. Medal of Tech. 1988, Industrial Research Inst. Achievement Award 1989, Harvey Prize, Technion, Israel 1990, inducted into Nat. Inventors Hall of Fame 1997, IEEE Edison Medal 2001, Aachener and Münchener Award for Tech. and Applied Natural Sciences 2001, Lifetime Achievement Award, Lemelson-MIT 2005, C&C Prize 2006, Benjamin Franklin Medal in Electrical Eng 2007. *Achievements include:* has been granted 45 US patents in semiconductors and microelectronics since 1965. *Publications:* Design of Ion-Implanted MOSFETs with Very Small Physical Dimensions 1974; over 100 technical papers. *Leisure interests:* choral singing, Scottish country dancing. *Address:* IBM Research, POB 218, Yorktown Heights, NY 10598, USA (office). *E-mail:* dennard@us.ibm.com (office). *Website:* www.research.ibm.com (office).

DENNEHY, Brian; American actor; b. 9 July 1939, Bridgeport, Conn.; m. 2nd Jennifer Dennehey; three c. (from previous marriage); ed Chaminade High School, Columbia and Yale Univs; served with US Marine Corps for five years; numerous stage appearances; Tony Award (Best Actor in a Drama for Death of a Salesman) 1999. *Films include:* Looking for Mr. Goodbar 1977, Semi-Tough 1977, F.I.S.T. 1978, Foul Play 1978, Butch and Sundance: the Early Days 1979, 10 1979, Little Miss Marker 1980, Split Image 1982, First Blood 1982, Never Cry Wolf 1983, Gorky Park 1983, Finders Keepers 1984, The River Rat 1984, Twice in a Lifetime 1985, Silverado 1985, Cocoon 1985, The Check Is in the Mail 1986, F/X 1986, Legal Eagles 1986, Best Seller 1987, The Belly of an Architect 1987, Return to Snowy River 1988, Miles from Home 1988, Cocoon: The Return 1988, Indio 1989, Georg Elser - Einer aus Deutschland 1989, The Last of the Finest 1990, Presumed Innocent 1990, FX2 1991, Gladiator 1992, Tommy Boy 1995, The Stars Fell on Henrietta 1995, Romeo + Juliet 1996, Out of the Cold 1999, Silicon Towers 1999, Summer Catch 2001, Stolen Summer 2002, She Hate Me 2004, Our Fathers 2005, Assault on Precinct 13 2005, 10th & Wolf 2006, The Ultimate Gift 2006, Welcome to Paradise 2007, Ratatouille (voice) 2007, War Eagle, Arkansas 2007, Righteous Kill 2008. *Television appearances include:* Big Shamus, Little Shamus, Star of the Family, Birdland 1993, numerous TV films. *Address:* c/o Susan Smith and Associates, 121 North San Vicente Boulevard, Beverly Hills, CA 90211, USA. *Telephone:* (213) 852-4777 (office).

DENNETT, Daniel Clement, DPhil; American philosopher, academic and author; *University Professor and Co-Director, Center for Cognitive Studies, Tufts University;* b. 28 March 1942, Boston; s. of Daniel C. Dennett, Jr and Ruth M. Leck; m. Susan Bell 1962; one s. one d.; ed Phillips Exeter Acad., Wesleyan Univ., Harvard Univ., Oxford Univ.; Asst Prof. of Philosophy, Univ. of Calif., Irvine 1965–70, Assoc. Prof. 1971; Assoc. Prof., Tufts Univ. 1971–75, Prof. 1975–85, Distinguished Arts and Sciences Prof. 1985–2000, Co-Dir Center for Cognitive Studies, Tufts 1985–, Univ. Prof. 2000–, also now Austin B. Fletcher Prof. of Philosophy; Visiting Prof., Harvard 1973–74, Pittsburgh 1975, Oxford 1979, Ecole Normale Supérieure, Paris 1985; Visiting Fellow, All Souls Coll. Oxford 1979; John Locke Lecturer, Oxford 1983, Gavin David Young Lecturer, Adelaide, Australia 1984; Woodrow Wilson Fellow 1963, Guggenheim Fellow 1973, 1986, Fulbright Fellow 1978; Fellow Center for Advanced Study in Behavioral Sciences 1979, American Acad. of Arts and Sciences 1987. *Publications:* Content and Consciousness 1969, Brainstorms 1978, The Mind's I (with Douglas Hofstadter) 1981, Elbow Room 1984, The Intentional Stance 1987, Consciousness Explained 1991, Darwin's Dangerous Idea 1995, Kinds of Minds 1996, Brainchildren 1998, Freedom Evolves 2003, Breaking the Spell: Religion as a Natural Phenomenon 2006; numerous articles in professional journals. *Leisure interests:* sculpture, farming, cider-making, sailing, choral singing. *Address:* Center for Cognitive Studies, Tufts University, Medford, MA 02155-7059, USA (office). *Telephone:* (617) 627-3297 (office). *Fax:* (617) 627-3952 (office). *E-mail:* daniel.dennett@tufts.edu (office). *Website:* ase.tufts.edu/cogstud/~ddennett.htm (office).

DENNIS, Bengt, MA; Swedish banker; *Managing Director, Bengt Dennis Consulting AB;* b. 5 Jan. 1930, Grengesberg; m. Turid Stroem 1962; one s. one d.; ed Columbia Univ., New York, USA; econ. journalist 1959–67; Head of Dept, Ministry of Finance 1967–70; Under-Sec. of State, Ministry of Commerce 1970–76; Amb., Ministry of Foreign Affairs 1977–80; Ed.-in-Chief, Dagens Nyheter 1981–82; Gov. Cen. Bank of Sweden 1982–92; Chair. Bd of Dirs BIS 1990–93; Sr Adviser Skandinaviska Enskilda Banken 1994–2001; Man. Dir Bengt Dennis Consulting AB 2002–. *Leisure interests:*

sailing, skiing, skating. *Address:* Vasagatan 36, 4 tr., Box 415, 101 28 Stockholm (office); Maria Sandels Gränd 3, 112 69 Stockholm, Sweden (home). *Telephone:* (8) 613-08-50 (office); (8) 651-04-32 (home). *Fax:* (8) 613-08-68 (office). *E-mail:* bengt.dennis@bdco.biz (office).

DENNIS, Donna Frances; American sculptor and teacher; b. 16 Oct. 1942, Springfield, Ohio; d. of Donald P. Dennis and Helen Hogue Dennis; ed Carleton Coll., Northfield, Minn., Paris and New York; teaching positions at Skowhegan School 1982, Boston Museum School (Visiting Artist) 1983, State Univ. of NY, Purchase Coll. 1984–86, 1988–, School of Visual Arts, New York 1983–90, Princeton Univ. (Visiting Artist) 1984, State Univ. of NY Purchase Coll. (Assoc. Prof.) 1990–96, Prof. 1996–; perm. comms: Dreaming of Faraway Places: The Ships Come to Washington Market, PS 234, New York, Klapper Hall, Queens Coll., CUNY 1995, American Airlines Terminal, JFK Int. Airport, NY 1996, I.S. 5, Queens, NY 1997, Terminal One, JFK Int. Airport, NY 2001; Fellow Nat. Endowment for the Arts 1977, 1980, 1986, 1994; recipient of several awards, including John Simon Guggenheim Fellowship 1979, Distinguished Achievement Award, Carleton Coll. 1989, Bard Award, City Club of New York 1989, Bessie Award for Set Design 1992, NEA Fellowship (4 times), Pollock-Krasner Award 2001, Karl Kempner Distinguished Professorship Award Purchase College SUNY 2001–03. *Publication:* 26 Bars (with Kenward Elmslie) 1987. *Leisure interest:* reading fiction. *Address:* 131 Duane Street, New York, NY 10013, USA. *Telephone:* (212) 233-0605. *E-mail:* tunnelsandtowers@att.net. *Website:* www.donnadennisart.com.

DENNIS, Michael Mark, LLM; Canadian business executive; *President and CEO, BC International Corporation;* b. 4 March 1942, Toronto; ed Osgoode Hall Law School, York Univ. and Univ. of Calif., Berkeley; Asst Prof., Osgoode Hall Law School 1965–67; Consultant, Nat. Planning Comm. Philippines 1968–69; Chair. Fed. Govt Task Force on Housing 1970–72; Special Asst to Mayor of Toronto 1973–74; Commr of Housing City of Toronto 1974–79; Exec. Vice-Pres. Olympia & York Properties (USA) 1985–95; Exec. Dir Olympia & York Canary Wharf Ltd 1987–90; CEO Azure Devt Group, NY 1995–2005; Pres. and CEO BC Int. Corpn 2005–. *Publication:* Programs in Search of a Policy (with Susan Fish) 1973. *Leisure interests:* literature, travel, sports, music. *Address:* BC International Corporation, 980 Washington Street, Dedham, MA 02026, USA (office). *Telephone:* (781) 461-5700 (office). *Website:* www.bcintlcorp.com (office).

DENNISON, Lisa, MA; American auction house executive and fmr art museum director; *Chairman, North and South America, Sotheby's;* m. Roderick Waywell 1983; two s.; ed Wellesley Coll., Wellesley, Mass and Brown Univ., Providence, RI; curatorial internships at Guggenheim Museum 1973, Fogg Art Museum, Harvard Univ. 1974–76, Museum of Fine Arts, Boston 1977–78; Exhbn Coordinator, Solomon R. Guggenheim Museum, New York 1978–81, Asst Curator 1981–90, Assoc. Curator 1990–91, Collections Curator 1991–94, Curator of Collections and Exhbns 1994–96, Deputy Dir and Chief Curator 1996–2005, Dir and Chief Curator 2005–07, played key role in building Museum's perm. collections in New York and Bilbao, Spain; Chair. North and South America, Sotheby's, New York 2007–; fmr mem. Bd of Dirs American Asscn of Museum Curators, Byrd-Hoffman Foundation; Founding mem. Creative Arts Advisory Bd, Brown Univ.; mem. New York Cttee, Wellesley Coll. Friends of Art, Nat. Advisory Council, Visual Arts, Wake Forest Univ., Int. Advisory Bd Louise T. Blouin Foundation; mem. ArtTable. *Publications:* more than 25 essays in exhbn catalogues. *Address:* Sotheby's, 1334 York Ave at 72nd Street, New York, NY 10021, USA (office). *Telephone:* (212) 606-7000 (office). *Fax:* (212) 606-7107 (office). *Website:* www.sothebys.com (office).

DENNISS, Tom, PhD; Australian oceanographer, mathematician and business executive; *Executive Director and Chief Technology Officer, Oceanlinx Ltd;* fmr Lecturer in Math. and Oceanography, Univ. of New South Wales; spent five years in an investment bank; Founder and CEO Energetech Australia Pty Ltd (now called Oceanlinx Ltd) 1997–2006, Exec. Dir and Chief Tech. Officer 2006–; contrib. to marine tech. industry over many years through both academia and industry confs and cttees world-wide; several awards for pioneering work in wave power. *Address:* Oceanlinx Ltd, PO Box 116, Botany, NSW 1455, Australia (office). *Telephone:* (2) 9549-6300 (office). *Fax:* (2) 9549-6399 (office). *E-mail:* tom.denniss@oceanlinx.com (office). *Website:* www.oceanlinx.com (office).

DENNISTON, Rev. Robin Alastair, MA, MSc, PhD; British publisher and ecclesiastic; b. 25 Dec. 1926, London; s. of the late Alexander Guthrie Denniston and Dorothy Mary Gilliat; m. 1st Anne Alice Kyffin Evans 1950 (died 1985); one s. two d.; m. 2nd Dr Rosa Susan Penelope Beddington 1987 (died 2001); ed Westminster School and Christ Church, Oxford; Ed. Collins 1950–59; Man. Dir Faith Press 1959–60; Ed. Prism 1959–61; Promotion Man. Hodder & Stoughton Ltd 1960–64, Editorial Dir 1966, Man. Dir 1968–72, also Dir Mathew Hodder Ltd and subsidiary cos; Deputy Chair. George Weidenfeld & Nicolson (and subsidiary cos) 1973; Chair. (non-exec.) A. R. Mowbray & Co. 1974–88; Chair. Sphere Books 1975–76, Thomas Nelson & Sons (and subsidiary cos) 1975, Michael Joseph Ltd 1975, George Rainbird Ltd 1975; Dir Thomson Publs Ltd 1975, Hamish Hamilton Ltd 1975, W. W. Norton 1989–; Academic Publr, Oxford Univ. Press 1978, Sr Deputy Sec. to the Dels. 1984–88, Oxford Publr 1984–88; Student of Christ Church 1978; ordained Deacon 1978, Priest 1979; Hon. Curate, Parish of Clifton-on-Teme 1978, New with S Hinksey 1985; Non-Stipendiary Minister, Great with Little Tew 1987–90, St Serfs, Burntisland and St Columba's Aberdour, Fife 1990–93; Priest-in-Charge, Great with Little Tew and Over Worton with Nether Worton 1995–2002. *Publications:* The Young Musicians 1956, Partly Living 1967, Part Time Priests? (ed.) 1960, Anatomy of Scotland (co-ed.) 1992, Churchill's Secret War: Diplomatic Decrypts, the Foreign Office and Turkey 1942–4 1997, Trevor Huddleston: A Life 1999, Thirty Secret Years: A. G. Denniston's Work in Signals Intelligence 1914–44 2007. *Leisure interests:* music, reading. *Address:* Davenham, 148 Graham Road, Malvern, Worcs., WR14 2HY, England (home). *Telephone:* (1684) 573141 (home).

DENNY, Robyn (Edward M. F.), ARCA; British artist; b. 3 Oct. 1930, Abinger, Surrey; s. of Sir Henry Denny, Bt and Joan, Lady Denny; m. 1st Anna Teasdale (divorced); m. 2nd Marjorie Abéla; two s. one d.; ed Clayesmore School, Dorset, St Martin's School of Art and Royal Coll. of Art, London; first one-man exhbns in London at Gallery One and Gimpel Fils 1958; has since given one-man exhbns throughout Europe and USA; retrospective exhbn Tate Gallery, London 1973; has represented Britain at Biennales in Paris, Tokyo, Milan, Brussels, USA and Australia and at 33rd Venice Biennale; works in numerous public collections; has received many public commissions for site specific works; teaching assignments have included Slade School, Univ. of London and Minn. Inst. of Fine Art; fmr adviser, Arts Council of GB, Inst. of Contemporary Arts, London; recipient of several awards and prizes. *Publications:* articles and criticism in int. publs. *Address:* Unit 4B, 24–28 Wilds Rents, London, SE1 4QG, England.

DENOIX DE SAINT-MARC, Renaud; French lawyer and civil servant; *Member, Conseil Constitutionnel;* b. 24 Sept. 1938, Boulogne-sur-Seine; s. of Henri Denoix de Saint-Marc and Marie du Cheyron du Pavilion; m. Marie-Christine de Buchére de l'Epinois 1964; two c.; ed Ecole nationale d'administration, Institut d'études politiques de Paris; Auditor Conseil d'État 1964, maître des requêtes 1972, Govt Commr Ass. of Conseil d'État 1974–78, 1983–86; Deputy Dir of Cabinet, Minister of Justice Alain Peyrefitte 1978–79; Dir of Civil Affairs and Seal 1979–82; State Councillor 1985; Secrétaire général du Gouvernement 1986–95; Vice-Pres. Conseil d'État 2005–06 (retd); mem. Académie des sciences morales et politiques 2005; Mem. Conseil Constitutionnel 2007–; Grand Officier de la Légion d'honneur 2002, Chevalier de l'ordre national du Mérite, Chevalier du Mérite agricole et des Palmes académiques; Croix de la Valeur militaire, Prix Edouard Bonnefous 2001. *Address:* Conseil Constitutionnel, 2 rue de Montpensier, 75001 Paris, France (office). *Telephone:* 1-40-15-30-00 (office). *Fax:* 1-40-20-93-27 (office). *E-mail:* relations-exterieures@conseil-constitutionnel.fr (office). *Website:* www.conseil-constitutionnel.fr (office).

DENT, Alberto; Costa Rican politician and banker; b. 11 Dec. 1945; m.; four c.; ed Calif. State Polytech. Univ., USA; Gen. Man. Dent and Sons Ltd 1973–84; Pres. Banex Bank Ltd 1980–84; Exec. Pres. BFA Financial Group 1984–96; Dir Costa Rican Bankers' Asscn 1985–96, Pres. 1986–90; Adviser to Pres. of Costa Rica 1998–2000; Vice-Pres. Cen. Bank of Costa Rica 1998–2000; Minister of Agric. and Livestock 2000–01; Minister of Finance 2001–02, 2003–04 (resgnd); Pres. Financial Supervision Council 2003. *Address:* c/o Ministry of Finance, Diagonal al Teatro Nacional, San José, Costa Rica (office).

DENTON, Charles Henry, BA, FRSA, FRTS; British television executive; b. 20 Dec. 1937; s. of Alan Charles Denton and Mary Frances Royle; m. Eleanor Mary Player 1961; one s. two d.; ed Reading School and Univ. of Bristol; worked as deckhand 1960; trainee advertising 1961–63; with BBC 1963–68; freelance TV producer Granada, ATV and Yorkshire TV cos 1969–70; Dir Tempest Films Ltd 1969–71; Man. Dir Black Lion Films 1979–81; Head of Documentaries ATV 1974–77, Controller of Programmes 1977–81; Dir of Programmes Cen. Ind. TV 1981–84; Dir Cen. Ind. Television PLC 1981–87; founder and Chief Exec. Zenith Productions 1984–93, Chair. Zenith North Ltd 1988–93; Head of Drama BBC 1993–96; Chair. Action Time Ltd 1988–93, Producers' Alliance for Cinema and TV (PACT) 1991–1993, Cornwall Film 2001; Gov. BFI 1992–99; mem. Arts Council of England 1996–98; mem. Bd Film Council 1999–2002; Fellow Royal TV Soc., Royal Soc. of Arts. *Leisure interests:* walking, music.

DENTON, Derek Ashworth, AC, MB, BS, FRS, FAA, FRACP, FRCP; Australian research physiologist; *Honorary Professor of Physiology, University of Melbourne;* b. 27 May 1924, Launceston, Tasmania; s. of A.A. Denton; m. Dame Margaret Scott 1953; two s.; ed Launceston Grammar School and Univ. of Melbourne; Haley Research Fellow, Walter & Eliza Hall Inst. of Medical Research 1948; Overseas Nat. Health and Medical Research Council (NH & MRC) Fellow, Cambridge 1952–53; Medical Research Fellow, later Sr Medical Research Fellow, Nat. Health and Medical Research Council 1949–63, Prin. Research Fellow, Admin. Head and Chief Scientist 1964–70; Dir and originating Bd mem. Howard Florey Inst. of Experimental Physiology and Medicine 1971–89, Emer. Dir 1990–; Visiting Prof., British Heart Foundation and Balliol Coll. Oxford, UK; Adjunct Scientist, Southwest Foundation for Biomedical Research, San Antonio, Tex., USA; Dir The David Syme Co. Ltd 1984–, Australian Ballet Foundation 1983–, Sydney Dance Co. 1994–; First Vice-Pres. Int. Union of Physiological Sciences 1983–89; Chair. Nominating Cttee of Council, Int. Union of Physiological Sciences 1986–89; Chair. Cttee to Review Comms of Int. Union of Physiological Sciences 1986–95; Foreign Medical mem. Royal Swedish Acad. of Sciences; mem. Jury of Basic and Clinical Medical Awards, Albert and Mary Lasker Foundation 1979–89; OECD Examiner of Science and Tech. Policy of Govt of Sweden; Foreign Assoc. NAS, French Acad. of Science, Inst. of France 2000; Hon. Prof. of Physiology, Univ. of Melbourne 2004; Hon. LLD (Melbourne) 2006; Hon. Foreign Fellow, American Acad. of Arts and Sciences 1986; Hon. Foreign mem. American Physiology Soc. *Publications:* The Hunger for Salt 1982, The Pinnacle of Life 1993, Primordial Emotions: The Dawning of Consciousness 2006; 400 articles and reviews. *Leisure interests:* tennis, fishing, ballet, music, wine. *Address:* Office of the Dean, Faculty of Medicine, Dentistry and Health Sciences, University of Melbourne, 766 Elizabeth Street, Melbourne, Vic. 3010 (office); 816 Orrong Road, Toorak, Vic. 3142, Australia (home). *Telephone:* (3) 8344-5639 (office); (3) 9827-2640 (home). *Fax:* (3) 9347-0846 (office); (3) 9826-5457 (home). *E-mail:* ddenton@unimelb.edu.au.

DENTON, Frank Trevor, MA, FRSC; Canadian economist and academic; *Professor Emeritus of Economics, McMaster University;* b. 27 Oct. 1930, Toronto; s. of Frank W. Denton and Kathleen M. Davies; m. 1st Marilyn J. Shipp 1953 (died 2002); three s. one d.; m. 2nd Helen R. Evans 2003; ed Univ. of Toronto; economist, Prov. Govt of Ont. 1953–54, Fed. Govt of Canada 1954–59, 1961–64, Philips Electronics Industries Ltd 1959–60, Senate of Canada Cttee staff 1960–61; Dir of Econometrics, Dominion Bureau of Statistics 1964–68; Consultant, Econ. Council of Canada 1964–68; Prof. of Econs, McMaster Univ. 1968–96, Prof. Emer. 1996–; Dir McMaster Program for Quantitative Studies in Econs and Population 1981–96; various other consulting appointments; Fellow, American Statistical Assen, Royal Statistical Soc.; mem. Int. Statistical Inst., Int. Union for Scientific Study of Population; Hon. LLD (McMaster) 2008. *Publications:* Growth of Manpower in Canada 1970; Co-author: Population and the Economy 1975, Working-Life Tables for Canadian Males 1969, Historical Estimates of the Canadian Labour Force 1967, The Short-Run Dynamics of the Canadian Labour Market 1976, Unemployment and Labour Force Behaviour of Young People: Evidence from Canada and Ontario 1980, Pensions and the Economic Security of the Elderly 1981, Independence and Economic Security in Old Age (co-ed.) 2000; numerous monographs, articles, technical papers in economics, statistics, demography. *Address:* Department of Economics, KTH 413, McMaster University, Hamilton, Ont., L8S 4M4 (office); 23 Pelham Drive, Ancaster, Ont., L9K 1L4, Canada (home). *Telephone:* (905) 525-9140 ext. 23820 (office); (905) 304-9395 (home). *Fax:* (905) 521-8232 (office). *E-mail:* dentonf@mcmaster.ca (office). *Website:* socserv.mcmaster.ca/econ (office).

DENTON, Richard Michael, MA, PhD, DSc, FMedSci, FRS; British biochemist and academic; *Professor of Biochemistry, University of Bristol;* b. 16 Oct. 1941, Sutton Coldfield; s. of the late Arthur Benjamin Denton and of the late Eileen Mary Denton (née Evans); m. Janet Mary Jones 1965; one s. two d.; ed Wycliffe Coll., Stonehouse, Glos., Christ's Coll., Cambridge; Lecturer in Biochemistry Univ. of Bristol 1973–78, Reader 1978–87, Prof. (Personal Chair) 1987–, Head of Biochemistry Dept 1995–2000, Chair. Medical Sciences 2000–04, Dean of Medical and Veterinary Sciences 2003–04; MRC Research Fellowship 1984–88, mem. Council MRC 1999–2004, Chair. MRC Training and Career Devt Bd 2002–04; Founder Fellow Acad. of Medical Sciences 1998. *Publications:* over 240 research papers in various int. research journals, with maj. topics the molecular basis of the control of metabolism by insulin and other hormones, and the role of calcium ions within mitochondria. *Leisure interests:* family, fell walking, keeping fit, cooking. *Address:* Department of Biochemistry, University of Bristol School of Medical Sciences, University Walk, Bristol, BS8 1TD, England (office). *Telephone:* (117) 3312184 (office). *Fax:* (117) 3312168 (office). *E-mail:* r.denton@bristol.ac.uk (office). *Website:* www.bch.bris.ac.uk (office).

DÉON, Michel; French writer; b. 4 Aug. 1919, Paris; s. of Paul Déon and Alice de Fossey; m. Chantal d'Arc 1963; one s. one d.; ed Lycée Janson-de-Sailly and Faculty of Law, Paris; journalist with Action française, Marie-Claire 1942–56; Publr 1954; writer 1956–; mem. Acad. française 1978–, Acad. of Sciences, Portugal; Commdr, Légion d'honneur 2002, Officier des Arts et des Lettres; Dr hc (Nat. Univ. of Ireland); Prix Interallié 1970, Grand Prix du Roman 1973, Grand Prix Jean Giono 1996. *Plays:* Ma vie n'est plus un Roman, Ariane ou L'oubli. *Publications:* novels: Je ne veux jamais l'oublier 1950, La Corrida 1952, Le Dieu pâle 1954, Les trompeuses espérances 1956, Les gens de la nuit 1957, Tout l'amour du monde 1959, Un parfum de jasmin 1966, Les poneys sauvages 1970, Un taxi mauve 1973, Le jeune homme vert 1976, Mes arches de Noé 1978, Un déjeuner de soleil 1981, Louis XIV par lui-même 1983, Je vous écris d'Italie 1984, Bagages pour Vancouver 1985, La Montée du Soir, Ma Vie n'est plus un Roman (drama) 1987, Un Souvenir 1990, Le Prix de l'amour 1992, Parlons en... 1993, Ariane ou L'oubli (drama) 1992, Pages grecques (essays) 1993, Une longue amitié 1995, Je me suis beaucoup promené 1995, La Cour des Grands 1996, Madame Rose, Pages françaises 1999, Taisez-vous... J'entends venir un ange 2001, La chambre de ton père 2004, Cavalier passe ton chemin 2005. *Leisure interests:* shooting, sailing, bibliophile. *Address:* The Old Rectory, Tynagh, County Galway, Ireland; 5 rue Sébastien Bottin, 75007 Paris, France. *Telephone:* (90) 9745143 (Ireland). *Fax:* (90) 9745376 (Ireland). *E-mail:* chantaldeon@eircom.net (home).

DEPARDIEU, Gérard; French actor and vintner; b. 27 Dec. 1948, Chateauroux; s. of René Depardieu and Alice Depardieu (née Marillier); m. Elisabeth Guignot 1970; one s. one d.; ed Ecole communale, Cours d'art dramatique de Charles Dullin and Ecole d'art dramatique de Jean Laurent Cochet; Pres. Jury, 45th Cannes Int. Film Festival 1992; Chevalier, Ordre nat. du Mérite, Chevalier Légion d'honneur, Chevalier des Arts et des Lettres; numerous nat. and int. awards. *Appeared in short films:* Le Beatnik et le minet 1965, Nathalie Granger 1971. *Films include:* Les gaspards 1973, Les valseuses 1973, Pas si méchant que ça 1974, 1900 1975, La dernière femme 1975, Sept morts sur ordonnance 1975, Maîtresse 1975, Barocco 1976, René la Canne 1976, Les plages de l'Atlantique 1976, Baxter vera Baxter 1976, Dites-lui que je l'aime 1977, Le camion 1977, Préparez vos mouchoirs 1977, Rêve de singe 1977, Le sucre 1978, Buffet froid 1979, Loulou 1979, Le dernier métro 1980 (César award Best Actor, France), Le choix des armes 1981, La femme d'à côté 1981, La chèvre 1981, Le retour de Martin Guerre 1981 (Best Actor Award, American Society of Film Critics), Danton 1981, Le grand frère 1982, La lune dans le caniveau 1983, Les compères 1983, Fort Saganne 1983, Tartuffe (also Dir) 1984, Rive Droite, Rive Gauche 1984, Police 1984, One Woman or Two 1985, Jean de Florette 1985, Tenue de soirée 1985, Rue du départ 1986, Les fugitifs 1986, Sous le Soleil de Satan 1986, Camille Claudel 1987, Drôle d'endroit pour une rencontre 1988, Je veux rentrer à la maison 1988, Trop belle pour toi 1988, Cyrano de Bergerac 1989 (César award Best Actor), Uranus 1990, Green Card (Golden Globe for Best Comedy Actor), Mon Père ce héros 1991, 1492: Conquest of Paradise 1991, Tous les matins du monde 1991, Germinal 1992, A Pure Formality 1993, Le Colonel Chabert 1993, La Machine 1994, Elisa, Les Cents et Une Nuits, Les Anges Gardiens, Le Garçu (all 1994), Bogus, Unhook the Stars, Secret Agent 1995, Vatel 1997, The Man in the Iron Mask 1997, Les Portes du Ciel 1999, Astérix et Obélix 1999, Un pont entre deux rives (also Dir) 1999, Vatel 1999, Les Acteurs 2000, Chicken Run 2000, Le Placard 2001, 102 Dalmatians 2001, Astérix et Obélix: Mission Cleopatra 2002, Nathalie 2003, Tais-toi 2003, Les Clefs de bagnole 2003, San Antonio 2004, Nouvelle France 2004, 36 Quai des orfèvres 2004, Last Holiday 2005, Paris, je t'aime (segment) 2006, The Singer 2006, La Môme 2007, Michou d'Auber 2007, La Vie en Rose 2007, Astérix at the Olympic Games 2008, Babylon A.D. 2008. *Plays include:* Boudu sauvé des eaux 1968, Les Garçons de la bande 1969, Une fille dans ma soupe 1970, Galapagos 1971, Saved 1972, Home 1972, Ismé 1973, Isaac 1973, La Chevauchée sur le lac de Constance 1974, Les Gens déraisonnables sont en voie de disparition 1977, Tartuffe (also Dir) 1983, Lily Passion 1986, Les portes du ciel 1999, Œdipus Rex 2001, Le Carnaval des animaux 2001. *Television includes:* L'Inconnu 1974, Le Comte de Monte Cristo 1998, Balzac 1999, Bérénice 1999, Les Misérables 2000. *Publication:* Lettres volées 1988. *Address:* Artmédia, 20 avenue Rapp, 75007 Paris, France.

DEPARDON, Raymond; French photographer; b. 6 July 1942, Villefranche-sur-Saône; s. of Antoine Depardon and Marthe Bernard; m. Claudine Nougaret 1987; two s.; ed primary school in Villefranche; apprentice to Louis Foucherand, Paris 1958, Asst 1959; copy then photographic reporter, Dalmas agency 1960; Co-founder Gamma agency 1967; mem. Magnum Agency, Paris and New York 1978; Artistic Dir Rencontres Int. d'Arles 2006; solo exhbn Correspondance new yorkaise, San Clemente, Paris 1984, Lausanne 1985. *Films include:* Jan Pallach, Tibesti Tou (short) 1974, Numéros zéro 1977, Reporters 1981, Faits divers: les Années déclic 1983, Empty Quarter 1985, Urgences 1987, La Captive du désert 1990, La Colline des Anges 1993, Délits flagrants 1994, Sida propos 1995, Afriques: Comment ça va avec la douleur 1995, Paris 1998, Muriel Leferle 1999, Profils paysans l'approche 2001, Un homme sans l'Occident 2002, Quoi de neuf au Garet? 2004, Dixieme chambre - Instants d'audiences (Gold Plaque) 2004, Profils paysans: le quotidien 2005, Profils paysans: la vie moderne 2007. *Publications include:* photographic albums: Tchad 1978, Notes 1979, Correspondance new yorkaise 1981, Le Désert américain 1983, San Clemente 1984, Les Fiancées de Saigon 1986, Hivers 1987, Depardon cinéma 1993, Return to Vietnam (with Jean-Claude Guillebaud) 1994, La Ferme du Garet 1995, La Porte des Larmes (with Jean-Claude Guillebaud) 1995, En Afrique 1995, Voyages 1998, Silence rompu 1998, Corse 2000, Détours (Nadar Prize) 2000, Errances 2000, Rêves de déserts 2000, À Tombeau Ouvert 2000, Désert: un Homme sans l'Occident 2002, Piemonte: Una Definizione Fotografica 2003, 06 Alpes Maritimes 2003, Paroles Prisonnières 2004, Jeux Olympiques 2004, Images politiques 2004, Paris Journal 2004, Afriques 2005, Photographies de Personnalités Politiques 2006, La Solitude Heureuse du Voyageur 2006, Depardon-New York 2006. *Address:* Magnum, 19 rue Hégésippe Moreau, 75018 Paris (office); 18 bis rue Henri Barbusse, 75005 Paris, France (home). *Telephone:* 1-53-42-50-00 (office). *Fax:* 1-53-42-50-01 (office). *E-mail:* magnum@magnumphotos.fr (office). *Website:* www.magnumphotos.com (office).

DEPP, John (Johnny) Christopher; American actor; b. 9 June 1963, Owensboro, Ky; m. Lori Anne Allison 1983 (divorced 1985); pnr, Vanessa Paradis; one s. one d.; fmr rock musician; Co-founder and CEO Infinitum Nihil (production co.) 2004–; La Grande médaille de Vermeil, France 2006. *Television:* Slow Burn 1986, 21 Jump Street (series) 1987–90, United States of Poetry (series) 1995. *Films include:* A Nightmare on Elm Street 1984, Private Resort 1985, Platoon 1986, Cry Baby 1990, Edward Scissorhands 1990, Freddy's Dead: The Final Nightmare 1991, Benny and Joon 1993, What's Eating Gilbert Grape 1993, Arizona Dream 1993, Ed Wood 1994, Don Juan de Marco 1994, Dead Man 1995, Nick of Time 1995, The Brave 1997 (also writer and dir), Donnie Brasco 1997, Fear and Loathing in Las Vegas 1998, The Astronaut's Wife 1999, The Source 1999, The Ninth Gate 1999, Sleepy Hollow 1999, The Man Who Cried 2000, Before Night Falls 2000, Chocolat 2000, Blow 2001, From Hell 2001, Pirates of the Caribbean: The Curse of the Black Pearl (Screen Actors Guild Award Best Actor 2004) 2003, Once Upon a Time in Mexico 2003, Secret Window 2004, Finding Neverland 2004, The Libertine 2004, And They Lived Happily Ever After 2004, Charlie and the Chocolate Factory 2005, Corpse Bride (voice) 2005, Pirates of the Caribbean: Dead Man's Chest 2006, Pirates of the Caribbean: At World's End 2007, Sweeney Todd The Demon Barber of Fleet Street (Golden Globe for Best Actor in a Musical or Comedy 2008) 2007. *Address:* Infinitum Nihil, 9100 Wilshire Blvd, #275W, Beverly Hills, CA 90212; United Talent Agency (UTA), 9560 Wilshire Blvd., Suite 500, Beverly Hills, CA 90212-2401, USA. *Telephone:* (310) 273-6700 (UTA). *Fax:* (310) 247-1111 (UTA).

DERANT LAKOUÉ, Enoch; Central African Republic politician; *President, Parti social-démocrate;* fmr mem. Mouvement pour la Libération du Peuple Centrafricain (MLPC—Liberation Movt of the Cen. African People's Party); Founder and Pres. Parti social-démocrate (PSD) early 1990s; Prime Minister of Cen. African Repub. March–Oct. 1993; presidential cand. 1993, 1999; Founder Co-ordination of Opposition Political Parties; Dir BERETEC/CENTRAFRIQUE, Bangui. *Address:* Parti social-démocrate (PSD), BP 543, Bangui, Central African Republic (office).

DERBEZ BAUTISTA, Luis Ernesto, PhD; Mexican politician and economist; b. 1 April 1947, Mexico City; ed San Luis Potosí Autonomous Univ., Univ. of Oregon and Iowa State Univ., USA; economist, IBRD (World Bank), responsible for regional areas including Chile 1983–86, Cen. America 1986–89, Africa 1989–92, Western and Cen. Africa 1992–94, India, Nepal and Bhutan 1994–97 (also dir multilateral econ. assistance and structural adjustment programmes in Chile, Costa Rica, Honduras and Guatemala); ind.

consultant, World Bank, Mexico City Office and IDB, Washington, DC 1997–2000; Econ. Adviser and Co-ordinator of Econ. Affairs to Pres.-Elect of Mexico 2000; fmr Sec. for Economy; Sec. of State for Foreign Affairs 2003–06; fmr Prof., Grad. School of Business Man., Instituto Tecnológico y de Estudios Superiores de Monterrey (also Dir Econometric Studies Unit and Econs Dept); fmr Vice-Rector Univ. of the Americas, Cholula, Mexico; fmr Visiting Prof., Johns Hopkins Univ. School of Int. Studies, USA. *Address:* c/o Secretariat of State for Foreign Affairs, Avda Ricardo Flores Magón 2, Col. Guerrero, Del. Cuauhtémoc, 06995, Mexico, Mexico (office).

DERBYSHIRE, Sir Andrew George, Kt, MA, AADip, FRIBA, FRSA; British architect; b. 7 Oct. 1923; s. of late Samuel Reginald and Helen Louise Puleston Derbyshire (née Clarke); m. Lily Rhodes (née Binns); three s. one d.; ed Chesterfield Grammar School, Queens' Coll., Cambridge, Architectural Asscn, London; Admiralty Signals Establishment and Bldg Research Station 1943–46; Farmer and Dark (Marchwood and Belvedere power stations) 1951–53; W Riding Co. Architect's Dept 1953–55; Asst City Architect, Sheffield 1955–61; mem. Research Team, RIBA Survey of Architects' Offices 1960–62; mem. Robert Matthew, Johnson-Marshall and Partners 1961–, Chair. 1983–89, Pres. RMJM Group 1989–98; involved with Devt of Univ. of York 1962–, Cen. Lancs. New Town, NE Lancs. Impact Study, Univ. of Cambridge, W Cambridge Devt and New Cavendish Lab., Preston Market and Guildhall, London Docklands Study, Hillingdon Civic Centre, Cabtrack and Minitram feasibility studies, Suez Master Plan Study, Castle Peak Power Station, Hong Kong, Harbour reclamation and urban devt, Hong Kong; mem. RIBA Council 1950–72, 1975–81, Sr Vice-Pres. 1980–81; mem. Bldg Industry Communications Research Cttee 1964–66; mem. Ministry of Transport Urban Research and Devt Group 1967; mem. Inland Transport Research and Devt Council 1968; mem. Dept of the Environment Planning and Transport Research Advisory Council 1971–76; mem. Comm. on Energy and the Environment 1978–81; mem. (part-time) Cen. Electricity Generating Bd 1973–84; mem. of Bd, Property Services Agency 1975–79; mem. Bd London Docklands Devt Corpn and Chair. of Planning Cttee 1983–88; mem. Construction Industry Sector Group of NEDC 1988–92; mem. Construction Industry Council, Chair. Research Cttee 1989–94; Chair. Art for Architecture Project, RSA 1994–98; Hoffman Wood Prof. of Architecture, Univ. of Leeds 1978–80; External Prof., Dept of Civil Eng, Univ. of Leeds 1981–85; Gresham Coll. Prof. of Rhetoric 1990–92; Hon. Fellow Inst. of Structural Eng 1992, Inst. of Advanced Architectural Studies, Univ. of York 1994; Hon. DUniv (York) 1972. *Publications:* The Architect and His Office 1962, and numerous articles on planning, energy conservation and scientific research, including from 1998 onwards papers on architecture, science and feedback, and the conservation of 20th centrury buildings. *Leisure interests:* family, garden. *Address:* 4 Sunnyfield, Hatfield, Herts., AL9 5DX, England (home). *Telephone:* (1707) 265903 (home); (1707) 265903 (office). *Fax:* (1707) 275874 (office). *E-mail:* andrewderby@mailme.co.uk (office).

DEREVYANKO, Anatoly Panteleyevich, Dr His.; Russian scientist and archaeologist; *Director, Institute of Archaeology and Ethnography, Siberian Branch, Russian Academy of Sciences;* b. 9 Jan. 1943, Kozmo-Demyanovka Amurskaya oblast; m.; two c.; ed Blagoveshchensk Pedagogical Inst.; jr researcher, head of museum, Deputy Dir, Inst. of History, Dialectics and Philosophy at the Siberian branch of the Russian Acad. of Sciences 1965–76; Sec. of the Central Cttee of Comsomol 1976–79; Prof., Rector Novosibirsk Univ. 1980–83; Dir Inst. of Archaeology and Ethnography at the Siberian branch of the Russian Acad. of Sciences 1983–, currently also Chair. United Academic Council of Humanitarian Studies; specialist in the archaeology and ancient history of Siberia and the Far East; mem. Russian Acad. of Sciences (corresp. mem. 1979–87). *Publications include:* more than 400 scientific publications on general history; monographs include Palaeolithic of the Far East and Korea 1983, Palaeolithic of Japan 1984, Foreign Archaeology 1986. *Address:* Institute of Archaeology and Ethnography, Siberian branch of Russian Academy of Sciences, Academika Lavretyeva prosp. 17, Novosibirsk 630090, Russia (office). *Telephone:* (3832) 30-27-91 (office); (3832) 35-05-37 (office). *Fax:* (3832) 30-11-91 (office); (3832) 35-52-37 (office). *E-mail:* derev@archaeology.nsc.ru (office). *Website:* www.sati.archaeology.nsc.ru (office).

DERIPASKA, Oleg Vladimirovich; Russian business executive; *CEO, United Company RUSAL;* b. 2 Jan. 1968, Dzerzhinsk, Gorkii (now Nizhnii Novgorod) Oblast; m. Polina Yumashev; two c.; ed Moscow State Univ., Plekhanov Acad. of Nat. Econs; Financial Dir Jt Stock Mil. Investment and Trade Co. 1990–92; Dir Gen. Rosaluminproduct 1992–93; Dir Krasnoyarskaluminproduct 1993; Dir-Gen. Aluminproduct 1993–94, Chief Financial Officer 1994–96; Dir Sayany Aluminium Plant 1996–2000; Pres. Sibizsky Aluminy Group 1997–2000; Dir-Gen. Russian Aluminium Corpn (RUSAL, formed from merger of aluminium smelters and alumina refineries of Sibirsky Aluminium Group and Sibneft oil co.) 2000–03, mem. Bd of Dirs 2006–, CEO United Company RUSAL (formed from merger of RUSAL, SUAL Group and alumina assets of Glencore International AG 2007) 2009–; Founder and Chair. Bd of Dirs Basic Element LLC (holding group for RUSAL), GAZ (automobile mfrs), Aviacor (aircraft mfrs), Ingosstrakh (insurance co.); Chair. Bd Russian Nat. Cttee of Int. Chamber of Commerce; mem. Entrepreneurship Council of Govt of Russian Fed.; mem. Business Advisory Council APEC 2004–, Chair. Russian section 2007–; Vice-Pres. Russian Union of Businessmen and Entrepreneurs 1999–; Trustee, Nat. Science Support Foundation, Bolshoi Theatre, Schools of Business Admin of Moscow State Univ. and St Petersburg State Univ.; Order of Friendship 1999; named by Vedomosti (business daily) Businessman of the Year 1999, 2006, 2007. *Address:* United Company RUSAL Corporate Headquarters, 109240 Moscow, ul. Nikoloyamskaya 13/1, Russia (office). *Telephone:* (495) 720-51-70 (office). *Fax:* (495) 745-70-46 (office). *E-mail:* Rusal@rusal.ru (office). *Website:* www.rusal.com (office).

DERN, Laura; American actress; b. 10 Feb. 1967, Los Angeles, Calif.; d. of Bruce Dern and Diane Ladd; ed Lee Strasberg Inst., Royal Acad. of Dramatic Art, London; film debut aged 11 in Foxes 1980. *Films include:* Teachers 1984, Mask 1985, Smooth Talk 1985, Blue Velvet 1986, Haunted Summer 1988, Wild at Heart 1990, Rambling Rose 1991, Jurassic Park 1993, A Perfect World 1993, Devil Inside, Citizen Ruth 1996, Bastard Out of Carolina 1996, October Sky 1999, Dr T and the Women 2000, Daddy and Them 2001, Focus 2001, Novocaine 2001, Jurassic Park III 2001, I Am Sam 2001, Novocaine 2001, We Don't Live Here Anymore 2004, Happy Endings 2005, The Prize Winner of Defiance, Ohio 2005, Lonely Hearts 2006, Inland Empire 2006, Year of the Dog 2007, Tenderness 2008, The Monday Before Thanksgiving 2008. *TV appearances include:* Happy Endings 1983, The Three Wishes of Billy Greer 1984, Afterburn 1992, Down Came a Blackbird 1995, The Siege at Ruby Ridge 1996, The Baby Dance 1998, A Season for Miracles 1999, Within These Walls 2001, The West Wing (episode) 2002, Damaged Care 2002, Recount (Golden Globe Award for Best Supporting Actress in a Series 2009) 2008; Dir The Gift 1994. *Address:* c/o Fred Specktor, CAA, 9830 Wilshire Blvd, Beverly Hills, CA 90212-1825 (office); c/o Wolf/kasteller, 132 South Rodeo Drive, #300, Beverly Hills, CA 90212, USA (office).

DERNESCH, Helga; Austrian singer (soprano, mezzo-soprano); b. 3 Feb. 1939, Vienna; two c.; ed Vienna Conservatory; sang many operatic roles in Berne 1961–63, Wiesbaden 1963–66, Cologne 1966–69; freelance guest appearances at all major opera houses in Europe 1969–; regular appearances at Bayreuth Festival 1965–69, at Salzburg Easter Festival 1969–73; since 1979 has sung as mezzo-soprano; regular appearances at San Francisco Opera 1982–; debut Metropolitan Opera, New York 1985; has sung in operas and concerts throughout Europe, N and S America, Japan; many recordings. *Leisure interests:* films, people, literature. *Address:* Salztorgasse 8/11, 1013 Vienna, Austria (home).

DERR, Kenneth T., MBA; American business executive; *Chairman, Calpine Corporation;* b. 1936; m. Donna Mettler 1959; three c.; ed Cornell Univ.; with Chevron Corpn (fmrly Standard Oil Co. of Calif.) 1960–1999, Vice-Pres. 1972–85, Pres. Chevron USA Inc. 1978–84, Head Merger Program, Chevron Corpn and Gulf Oil Corpn 1984–85, Vice-Chair. Chevron Corpn 1985–88, Chair. 1989–99, CEO 1989–99; Dir Calpine Corpn 2001–05, Chair. and Acting CEO 2005, Chair. 2005–; mem. Bd of Dirs Citigroup Inc., AT&T, Halliburton; Dir American Petroleum Inst., then Chair. *Address:* Calpine Corporation, 50 West San Fernando Street, San Jose, CA 95113, USA (office). *Telephone:* (408) 995-5115 (office). *Fax:* (408) 995-0505 (office). *Website:* www.calpine.com (office).

DERSHOWITZ, Alan Morton, LLB; American lawyer and academic; *Felix Frankfurter Professor of Law, Harvard University;* b. 1 Sept. 1938, New York, NY; s. of Harry Dershowitz and Claire Ringel; m. Carolyn Cohen; two s. one d.; ed Brooklyn Coll. and Yale Univ.; admitted to DC Bar 1963, Mass Bar 1968, US Supreme Court 1968; law clerk to Chief Judge David Bazelon, US Court of Appeal 1962–63, to Justice Arthur Goldberg, US Supreme Court 1963–64; mem. Faculty, Harvard Coll. 1964–, Prof. of Law 1967–, Felix Frankfurter Prof. of Law 1993–; Fellow, Center for Advanced Study of Behavioral Sciences 1971–72; consultant to Dir Nat. Inst. for Mental Health 1967–69, Pres.'s Comm. on Civil Disorders 1967, Pres.'s Comm. on Causes of Violence 1968, Nat. Asscn for Advancement of Colored People Legal Defense Fund 1967–68, Pres.'s Comm. on Marijuana and Drug Abuse 1972–73, Ford Foundation Study on Law and Justice 1973–76; rapporteur, Twentieth Century Fund Study on Sentencing 1975–76; Guggenheim Fellow 1978–79; mem. Comm. on Law and Social Action, American Jewish Congress 1978; Dir American Civil Liberties Union 1968–71, 1972–75, Asscn of Behavioral and Social Sciences, NAS 1973–76; Chair. Civil Rights Comm. New England Region, Anti-Defamation League, B'nai B'rith 1980; Hon. MA (Harvard Coll.) 1967; Hon. LLD (Yeshiva) 1989. *Publications:* Psychoanalysis, Psychiatry and the Law (with others) 1967, Criminal Law: Theory and Process 1974, The Best Defense 1982, Reversal of Fortune: Inside the von Bülow Case 1986, Taking Liberties: A Decade of Hard Cases, Bad Laws and Bum Raps 1988, Chutzpah 1991, Contrary to Popular Opinion 1992, The Abuse Excuse 1994, The Advocate's Devil 1994, Reasonable Doubt 1996, The Vanishing American Jew 1997, Sexual McCarthyism 1998, Just Revenge 1999, The Genesis of Justice 2000, Supreme Injustice: How the High Court Hijacked Election 2000 2001, Letters to a Young Lawyer 2001, Shouting Fire: Civil Liberties in a Turbulent Age 2002, Why Terrorism Works 2002, America Declares Independence 2003, The Case for Israel 2003, America on Trial 2004, Rights from Wrongs: A Seculat Theory of the Origins of Rights 2004, Preemption: A Knife That Cuts Both Ways 2006, What Israel Means to Me 2006, The Case for Peace: How the Arab-Israeli Conflict Can be Resolved 2006, Blasphemy 2007, Finding Jefferson 2007, Is There a Right to Remain Silent? 2008; contrib. articles to legal journals. *Address:* Harvard University Law School, Hauser Hall 520, 1575 Massachusetts Avenue, Cambridge, MA 02138-2801, USA (office). *Telephone:* (617) 495-4617 (office). *Fax:* (617) 495-7855 (office). *E-mail:* dersh@law.harvard.edu (office). *Website:* www.law.harvard.edu (office); www.alandershowitz.com.

DERVAN, Peter B, BS, PhD; American chemist and academic; *Bren Professor of Chemistry, California Institute of Technology;* b. 28 June 1945, Boston, Mass; ed Boston Coll., Yale Univ.; Postdoctoral Fellow, Stanford Univ. 1973; Asst Prof. of Chemistry, Calif. Inst. of Tech. 1973–79, Assoc. Prof. 1979–82, Prof. 1982–88, Bren Prof. of Chemistry 1988–, also Chair., Div. of Chemistry and Chemical Eng 1994–99; Visiting Prof. at several int. univs including Eidgenössische Technische Hochschule Zürich, Switzerland 1983, MIT 1987, Univ. of Cambridge, England 1989, Johann Walfgang Goethe Univ., Frankfurt, Germany 1993, Univ. Catholique de Louvain, Belgium 1994; co-founder Gilead Sciences 1987, Gensoft; mem. Scientific Advisory Bd several biotechnology cos including Xencor Inc., Fluidigm; mem. Editorial Bd several journals including Chemical Reviews 1984–89, Journal of the American Chemical Society 1986–92, Journal of Medicinal Chemistry 1991–93, Bioorganic and Medicinal Chemistry 1993–; mem. NAS, American Acad. of Arts and Sciences, NAS Inst. of Medicine, American Philosophical Soc.; mem. several NSF Advisory Cttees; foreign mem. French Acad. of Sciences; Hon. DrSci (Boston Coll.) 1997 numerous awards including Willard Gibbs Medal 1993, Nichols Medal 1994, Kirkwood Medal 1998, Richard C. Tolman Medal 1999, Linus Pauling Award 1999, Tetrahedron Prize 2000, Harvey Prize 2002. *Address:* 164–30, California Institute of Technology, Pasadena, CA 91125, USA (office). *Telephone:* (626) 395-4115 (office). *Fax:* (626) 5568-87443 (office). *E-mail:* dervan@caltech.edu (office). *Website:* www.its.caltech.edu/~pbdgroup/dervan.html (office).

DERVIŞ, Kemal, BA, MA, PhD; Turkish economist, politician and United Nations official; b. 10 Jan. 1949, Istanbul; m. Catherine Anne Derviş; ed London School of Econs, UK, Princeton Univ., USA; Lecturer in Econs, Middle Eastern Tech. Univ. 1973; adviser on issues of econ. and int. relations to Prime Minister Bülent Ecevit 1973–76; Lecturer in Int. Relations and Econs, Princeton Univ. 1977; mem. Research Dept, World Bank 1978–82, Head of Industrial Strategy and Policy, Global Industry Dept 1982–86, Sr Economist for Europe, Middle East and N African Affairs 1986–87, Head of Cen. Europe Div. 1987–96, Vice-Pres. in charge of Middle East and N Africa Region 1996–2000, Vice-Pres. in charge of Poverty Reduction and Econ. Man. 2000–01; returned to Turkey 2001; Minister of Econ. Affairs and the Treasury (without party affiliation) 2001–02 (resgnd); mem. Cumhuriyet Halk Partisi (CHP—Republican People's Party—centre-left) 2002–; mem. Parl. for Istanbul 2002–05, represented Turkish Parl. in Constitutional Convention on the Future of Europe, mem. Jt Comm. of Turkish and European Parls; Admin. UNDP 2005–09, Chair. UN Devt Group; was also active in Centre for Econ. and Foreign Policy Studies; active participant in various European and int. networks, including Global Progressive Forum, Progressive Governance Network; mem. Comm. on Growth and Devt (sponsored by World Bank and others), Comm. on the Measurement of Econ. Performance and Social Progress, Advisory Cttee Centre for Econ. and Foreign Policy Studies (EDAM), Advisory Cttee Turkish Econ. and Social Studies Foundation (TESEV); fmr mem. Int. Task Force on Global Public Goods, Special Comm. on the Balkans; adviser, Institut de Prospective Economique du Monde Mèditerranèen. *Publications include:* General Equilibrium Models for Development Policy (co-author) 1982, A Better Globalization 2005; numerous papers in academic journals as well as current affairs publs on topics ranging from math. models of growth and social mobility and quantitative models of trade, to European enlargement and transatlantic relations (in English, Turkish, French and German). *Address:* c/o United Nations Development Programme, One United Nations Plaza, New York, NY 10017, USA (office); Türkiye Büyük Millet Meclisi, 06543 Ankara, Turkey (home). *E-mail:* kdervis@chp.org.tr (home).

DERWENT, Henry; British civil servant and international organization official; *President and CEO, International Emissions Trading Association;* held several positions in Depts of Transport and Environment, covering roads, transport industries, vehicle licensing, finance, local government and other fields, also acted as Corp. Finance Exec. on loan to major int. investment bank; Dir Int. Climate Change, Energy and Environmental Risk, Dept for Environment, Food and Rural Affairs –2008, acted as Special Rep. to Prime Minister on Climate Change during UK Presidency of EU 2005; Pres. and CEO Int. Emissions Trading Asscn 2008–. *Address:* International Emissions Trading Association, 24 rue Merle d'Aubigné, 1207 Geneva, Switzerland (office). *Telephone:* (22) 737-05-09 (office); (78) 879-56-42 (mobile). *Fax:* (22) 737-05-08 (office). *E-mail:* derwent@ieta.org (office). *Website:* www.ieta.org (office).

DERYABIN, Yuri Stepanovich; Russian diplomatist (retd); *Director, Centre for North European Research, Institute of Europe, Russian Academy of Sciences;* b. 3 Jan. 1932, Karachelka, Kurgan Region; m.; two d.; ed Moscow Inst. of Int. Relations; diplomatic service 1954–; Third, then Second Sec., Dept of Scandinavian Countries, Ministry of Foreign Affairs 1959–62; Second Sec., Embassy in Oslo 1962–65, First Sec., Embassy in Finland 1968–73, Counsellor 1973–75; Counsellor-Envoy 1980–83; Deputy Chief Second, European Dept, Ministry of Foreign Affairs 1986–87; Chief Dept of Problems of Security and Cooperation in Europe 1987–90; Deputy Minister of Foreign Affairs 1991–92; Amb. to Finland 1992–96; Deputy Sec., Security Council of Russia 1997–98; Dir Centre for N European Research, Inst. of Europe, Russian Acad. of Sciences 1999–. *Publications:* various articles for newspapers and journals, mainly concerning the Northern European model of social-economic and socio-political devt. *Address:* Institute of Europe, Centre for North European Research, Mokhovaya Str. 11, Korp. 38, 103873 Moscow, Russia (office). *Telephone:* (095) 692-04-86 (office); (495) 203-41-87 (office); (095) 931-22-96 (home). *Fax:* (095) 299-42-98 (office); (495) 200-42-98 (office). *E-mail:* namiant@list.ru (office); europe@ieras.ru (office); deryabin@newolymp.net (home). *Website:* www.ieras.ru/centrseurope.htm (office).

DERYCKE, Erik, LLM; Belgian politician and lawyer; *Judge, Constitutional Court of Belgium;* b. 28 Oct. 1949, Waregem; m.; two c.; ed Rijksuniversiteit, Gent; barrister in Kortrijk 1972–; Provincial Councillor for W Flanders 1975–84; Rep. for Kortrijk, Belgian Chamber of Reps 1984; Municipal Councillor for Waregem 1989; Sec. of State for Science Policy 1990–91; Minister for Devt Aid and Deputy Minister for Science Policy 1991–92; Sec. of State for Devt Aid 1992–95; Minister for Foreign Affairs and Devt Cooperation March–June 1995; Minister for Foreign Affairs 1995–99; currently Judge, Constitutional Court of Belgium; Hon. Pres. Socialist Party of Waregem; mem. Socialist Party Bureau. *Address:* Constitutional Court of Belgium, 7 Place Royale, 1000 Brussels, Belgium.

DERZHAVIN, Mikhail Mikhailovich; Russian actor; b. 15 June 1936, Moscow; m. Roksana Babayan; one s.; ed Moscow Shchukin Theatre School; with Moscow Lenkom Theatre 1959–67; actor Malaya Bronnaya Theatre 1967–69; with Moscow Satire Theatre 1969–. *Films include:* Womanizer, Impotent. *Theatre roles include:* Master of Ceremonies in Goodbye, Master of Ceremonies, Bear in Ordinary Miracle, lead role in Tartuffe, A Piece for Two; two-man variety shows with A. Shirvindt (q.v.). *Leisure interest:* fishing. *Address:* Moscow Satire Theatre, Triumphalnaya pl. 2, 103050 Moscow, Russia (office). *Telephone:* (495) 299-63-05 (office).

DESAI, Anita, BA, FRSL; Indian writer and academic; *John E. Burchard Professor Emerita of Humanities, Massachusetts Institute of Technology;* b. 24 June 1937, Mussoorie; d. of Toni Nimé and D. N. Mazumdar; m. Ashvin Desai 1958; two s. two d.; ed Queen Mary's School, Delhi and Miranda House, Univ. of Delhi; Elizabeth Drew Visiting Prof., Smith Coll., Mass, USA 1987–88; Purington Prof. of English, Mount Holyoke Coll. 1988–92; John E. Burchard Prof. of Humanities, MIT, Cambridge, Mass 1993–2002, now Prof. Emer.; Gildersleeves Prof., Barnard Coll.; Visiting Scholar, Rockefeller Foundation, Bellagio, Italy; Sidney Harman Visiting Prof. and Writer-in-Residence, Baruch Coll. 2003; mem. American Acad. of Arts and Letters, PEN, Sahitya Akademi, India; Hon. Fellow, Girton Coll., Cambridge 1988, Clare Hall, Cambridge 1991, Hon. mem. American Acad. of Arts and Letters; Royal Soc. of Literature Winifred Holtby Prize 1978, Sahitya Acad. Prize 1978, Fed. of Indian Publishers Award 1978, Guardian Prize for Children's Fiction 1983, Hadassah Prize, New York 1988, Literary Lion, NY Public Library 1993, Alberto Moravia Prize for Literature, Italy 1999, Padma Sri 1989, Scottish Arts Council Neil Gunn Award for Int. Writing 1994. *Film screenplay:* In Custody 1994. *Television:* The Village By The Sea (BBC) 1994. *Publications:* Cry, The Peacock 1963, Voices in the City 1965, Bye-Bye, Blackbird 1971, Where Shall We Go This Summer? 1973, Fire on the Mountain 1978, Games at Twilight 1979, Clear Light of Day 1980, The Village by the Sea 1983, In Custody 1984, Baumgartner's Bombay 1988, Journey to Ithaca 1995, Fasting, Feasting 1999, Diamond Dust and Other Stories 2000, The Zigzag Way 2004; children's books: The Peacock Garden, Cat on a Houseboat. *Address:* Rogers, Coleridge & White Ltd, 20 Powis Mews, London, W11 1JN, England (office). *Telephone:* (20) 7221-3717 (office). *Fax:* (20) 7229-9084 (office).

DESAI, Baron (Life Peer), cr. 1991, of St Clement Danes in the City of Westminster; **Meghnad Jagdishchandra Desai,** PhD; British economist and academic; *Professor Emeritus of Economics, London School of Economics;* b. 10 July 1940, Baroda, India; s. of Jagdishchandra Desai and Mandakini Desai (née Majmundar); m. 1st Gail Wilson 1970 (divorced 2004); one s. two d.; m. 2nd Kishwar Rusha 2004; ed Univ. of Bombay, Univ. of Pennsylvania, USA; Assoc. Specialist, Dept of Agricultural Econs, Univ. of Calif., Berkeley, USA 1963–65; Lecturer, LSE 1965–77, Sr Lecturer 1977–80, Reader 1980–83, Prof. of Econs 1983–, now Prof. Emer., Head Devt Studies Inst. 1990–95, Dir Centre for the Study of Global Governance 1992–2003, Chair. Econ. Research Div. 1983–95; consultant at various times to FAO, UNCTAD, Int. Coffee Org., World Bank, UNIDO, Ministries of Industrial Devt and Educ., Algeria, British Airports Authority and other bodies; Co-Ed. Journal of Applied Econometrics 1984–; mem. Editorial Bds Int. Review of Applied Econs and several other journals; mem. Council, Royal Econ. Soc. 1988; mem. Exec. Cttee Asscn of Univ. Teachers in Econs 1987– (Pres. 1987–90); mem. Univ. of London Senate representing LSE 1981–89; mem. Nat. Exec. of Council for Academic Freedom and Democracy 1972–83, Speaker's Comm. on Citizenship 1989–, Berndt Carlson Trust; mem. or fmr mem. Governing Body of Courtauld Inst., British Inst. in Paris, Cen. School of Arts, Polytechnic of N London; Chair. Holloway Ward (Islington Cen.) Labour Party 1977–80; Chair. Islington S and Finsbury Labour Party 1986–92, Pres. 1992–; Dr hc (Kingston Univ.) 1992; Hon. DSc (Econs) (E London) 1994; Hon. DPhil (London Guildhall) 1996; Hon. LLD (Monash Univ.) 2005; Pravasi Phraskar (Distinguished Diaspora Indian Award) 2004, Distinguished Alumnus Award, Martin School of Finance 2004. *Publications:* Marxian Economic Theory 1974 (trans. in several languages), Applied Econometrics 1976, Marxian Economics 1979, Testing Monetarism 1981, Marx's Revenge 2001, Global Governance and Financial Crises 2003, Nehru's Hero: Dilip Kumar in the Life of India 2004, Development and Nationhood 2004, Nehru's Hero 2005, Development and Nationhood 2005, The Route of All Evil: Political Economy of Ezra Pound 2006, Rethinking Islamism 2006, Dead on Time (novel) 2009, The Rediscovery of India 2009; ed. several books; numerous papers and contribs to books and journals. *Leisure interests:* reading, politics. *Address:* House of Lords, London, SW1A 0AA (office); 3 Deepdene Road, London, SE5 8EG, England (home). *Telephone:* (20) 7219-5066 (office); (20) 7274-5561 (home). *Fax:* (20) 7219-5979 (office). *E-mail:* m.desai@lse.ac.uk (office). *Website:* www.lse.ac.uk/Depts/global (office).

DESAI, Nitin Dayalji, BA, MSc; Indian international official, economist and civil servant; *Under-Secretary-General of the Johannesburg Summit, United Nations;* b. 5 July 1941, Bombay; s. of Dayalji M. Desai and Shantaben Desai; m. Aditi Gupta 1979; two s.; ed Univ. of Bombay and London School of Econs, UK; Lecturer in Econs, Univ. of Liverpool, UK 1965–67, Univ. of Southampton, UK 1967–70; consultant, Tata (India) Econ. Consultancy Services 1970–73; consultant/adviser, Planning Comm. Govt of India 1973–85; Sr Adviser, Brundtland Comm. 1985–87; Special Sec. Planning Comm. India 1987–88; Sec./Chief Econ. Adviser, Ministry of Finance 1988–90; Deputy Under-Sec.-Gen. UNCED, Geneva 1990–92; UN Under-Sec.-Gen. for Econ. and Social Affairs 1992–2003, Under-Sec.-Gen. of Dept for Policy Co-ordination and Sustainable Devt 1993–97, Sec.-Gen. of Johannesburg Summit 2002, Sec.-Gen's Special Adviser for World Summit on the Information Society 2003–; Hon. Fellow LSE 2004. *Address:* United Nations, New York, NY 10017 (office); 330 East 33 Street Apt. 12M, New York, NY 10016, USA (home). *Telephone:* (212) 532-0028 (home). *E-mail:* dsd@un.org (office). *Website:* www.un.org/esa/sustdev/ (office).

DESAILLY, Marcel David; French professional footballer; b. 7 Sept. 1968, Nima-Accra, Ghana; defender with Nantes Atlantique 1986–92, with Olympique de Marseille 1992–93 (winner European Cup 1993), with AC Milan 1993–98 (winner European Super Cup 1994, European Cup 1995, Champion of Italy 1994, 1996), with Chelsea 1998–2004, Capt. 2001–04; Al-Gharafa, Qatar 2004–05, Qatar SC 2005–06; debut for French nat. team 1993, winner World Cup 1998, Euro 2000; Capt. of France 2000–04; retd from int. football 2004; Chevalier, Légion d'honneur; ranked by FIFA amongst 100 greatest living players 2004. *Address:* c/o Fédération Française de Football, 87 boulevard de Grenelle, 75738 Paris Cedex 15, France (office). *Website:* www.marceldesailly.sports.fr.

DESARIO, Vincenzo, BA; Italian banker; *Director-General, Banca d'Italia;* b. 11 June 1933, Barletta; m.; three c.; ed Univ. of Bari; joined Banca d'Italia (Bank of Italy), Foggia br. 1960; Banking Supervision Inspectorate, Bank of Italy head office, Rome 1968; Cen. Man. for Banking and Financial Supervision, Bank of Italy 1983; Bank of Italy Del. to Interbank Deposit Protection Fund 1991; Deputy Dir-Gen. Bank of Italy 1993–94, Dir-Gen. 1994–. *Address:* Banca d'Italia, Via Nazionale 91, 00184 Rome, Italy (office). *Telephone:* (06) 47921 (office). *Fax:* (06) 47922983 (office). *Website:* www.bancaditalia.it (office).

DESCHAMPS, Didier Claude; French fmr professional footballer; b. 15 Oct. 1968, Bayonne (Pyrénées-Atlantiques); m. Claude Deschamps; one s.; ed St Bernard private school, Bayonne, Nantes Football Acad.; amateur player Aviron Bayonnais; played for FC Nantes 1989, Olympique de Marseille (OM), FC des Girondins de Bordeaux, OM 1989–94, Juventus (Turin, Italy) 1994–99, Chelsea (UK) 1999–2000, Valencia (Spain) 2000–01; played for French nat. team 1989–2000, Capt. and player, Euro 92, Tournoi de France 1997, Capt. of winning team of World Cup 1998 and Euro 2000; most capped player (France) (103 appearances); fmr Man. Club de Football de Concarneau; Sports Dir and Coach AS Monaco 2001–2005, won Coupe de la Lique 2002, reached Champions' League final 2004; coach Juventus, Italy 2006–07; Chevalier Légion d'honneur; French Footballer of the Year 1996, Médaille de la ville de Bayonne 1998, ranked by FIFA amongst top 100 greatest living footballers 2004. *Address:* c/o Fédération Française de Football, 87 boulevard de Grenelle, 75738 Paris Cedex 15, France.

DESCOINGS, Richard; French civil servant and research institute director; *Chief Administrator, Fondation nationale des sciences politiques; Director, Institut d'Etudes Politiques de Paris;* b. 23 June 1958, Paris; ed Institut d'études politiques de Paris and École nationale d'admin; auditor in legal section of Conseil d'État 1985–89, Special Adviser to Alain Lancelot, Dir Institut d'études politiques de Paris 1987–89, Deputy Dir Institut d'études politiques de Paris 1989–91; Conseiller d'État 1991–; successively Tech. Advisor to cabinet of Minister for the Budget with responsibility for monitoring nat. educ. and higher educ. budget, then Special Advisor to Minister of Nat. Educ. with responsibility for budgetary issues 1991–93; Deputy Gen. Reporter on report and studies section of Conseil d'État and on task force on responsibilities and org. of State 1993–96; Govt Commr for Legal Training, Conseil d'État 1995–96; Chief Admin. Fondation nationale des sciences politiques (Nat. Foundation of Political Science) and Dir Institut d'Etudes Politiques de Paris (Paris Inst. of Political Studies) (collectively referred to as Sciences Po) 1996–; Chevalier, Ordre nat. du Mérite, Ordre des Palmes académiques; Commdr, Order of Rio Branco (Brazil); Dr hc from univs in USA, UK and continental Europe. *Address:* Sciences Po, 27 rue Saint-Guillaume, 75337 Paris Cedex 07, France (office). *Telephone:* 1-45-49-50-50 (office). *Fax:* 1-42-22-39-64 (office). *E-mail:* richard.descoings@sciences-po.fr (office). *Website:* www.sciences-po.fr (office).

D'ESCOTO BROCKMANN, Miguel; Nicaraguan politician and international organisation official; b. 5 Feb. 1933, Hollywood, USA; s. of Miguel D'Escoto Muñoz and Rita Brockmann Meléndez; ed Instituto Pedagógico La Salle, Managua, Nicaragua, St Mary's Coll., Moraga, Calif., Manhattan Coll., New York, State Univ. of New York, Columbia Univ., Sur la ligne de Feu, New York; Sub-Dir Dept of Social Communications, Maryknoll, New York, USA 1962–63; worked for Brazilian and Mexican Church in slums of Belo Horizonte, Rio de Janeiro, Brazil and Mexico DF 1963–69, Dir 1970–79; Founder and Pres. Fundación Nicaragüense Pro-Desarrollo Comunitario Integral, León, Nicaragua 1973; became involved with Frente Sandinista de Liberación Nacional from 1975; f. Grupo de los 12, a group of professionals and intellectuals supporting the Sandinista Front 1977; Minister of Foreign Affairs 1979–90; Sr Adviser on Foreign Affairs to Pres. Daniel Ortega 2007–; Pres. 63rd UN Gen. Ass. 2008–09; elected mem. of Sandinista Ass. 1980. *Address:* United Nations, New York, NY 10017, USA. *Telephone:* (212) 963-1234 (office). *Fax:* (212) 963-4879 (office). *Website:* www.un.org (office).

DESHMUKH, Vilasrao, BSc; Indian politician; b. 26 May 1945, Babhalgaon, Latur Dist; ed Pune Univ.; Pres. Osmanabad Dist Youth Congress 1975–78; Dir Maharashtra State Co-operative Bank 1979–; mem. Maharashtra Legis. Ass. 1980–95; Minister of State responsible for revenue, co-operation, agric., home affairs, industry, educ., transport, tourism and agric. 1982–95; mem. (Congress Party) Latur Ass., Latur Dist 1999–; Leader, Congress Legislature Party in Maharashtra 2004–; Chief Minister of Maharashtra 1999–2003, 2004–08 (resgnd); f. Manjra Charitable Trust. *Address:* c/o Office of the Chief Minister, Government of Maharashtra, Mantralaya, Mumbai 400 032, India (office).

DESHPANDE, Shashi, BA, MA, BL; Indian writer; b. 19 Aug. 1938, Dharwad; d. of Adya Rangacharya and Sharada Adya; m. D. H. Deshpande 1962; two s.; ed Univs of Mumbai and Mysore; fmrly worked for a law journal and magazine; full-time writer 1970–; mem. Sahitya Akademi Bd for English 1989–94; Thirumathi Rangammal Prize 1984, Sahitya Akademi Award for a Novel 1990, Nanjangud Thirumalamba Award 1991. *Film script:* Drishti 1990. *Publications:* The Dark Holds No Terrors 1980, If I Die Today 1982, Come Up and Be Dead 1982, Roots and Shadows 1983, That Long Silence 1988, The Binding Vine 1993, A Matter of Time 1996, Small Remedies 2000; short stories: The Legacy and Other Stories 1978, It Was Dark 1986, The Miracle and Other Stories 1986, It Was the Nightingale 1986, The Intrusion and Other Stories 1994, The Stone Women 2000, Collected Stories, Vol. I 2003, Vol. II 2004, Moving On 2004; non-fiction: Writing from the Margin and other essays 2003. *Leisure interests:* reading, music. *Address:* Alison M. Bond Agency, 155 W 72nd Street, New York, NY 10023, USA (office); 409 41st Cross, Jayanagar V Block, Bangalore 560041, India (home). *Telephone:* (80) 26636228 (home). *Fax:* (80) 26641137 (home). *E-mail:* shashid@vsnl.com (home).

DESJOYEAUX, Michel; French yachtsman; b. 16 July 1965; three c.; began racing at age 18; set fastest time ever and became first man to achieve a solo, non-stop navigation of the world in less than 100 days (93 days 4 hours approx.); Whitbread 1985–86, winner Triangle du Soleil 1986, Twostar (with Jean Maurel) 1992, Solitaire du Figaro 1992, 1998, 2007, Leg 2 of Mini Transat 1991, Transat AG2R 1992, Figaro French Championships 1996, 1998, Multihull Trophy 1994, Spi Ouest 1997, Leg 1 of Transat AG2R (with Frank Cammas) 1998, Grand Prix de Fécamp (with Alain Gautier) 1999, Grand Prix de la Trinité (with Alain Gautier) 2000, Vendée Globe 2001, 2009, transatlantic sprint Route du Rhum 2002, Transat 2004 and others; pioneered the swing keel early 1990s. *Publication:* L'enfant de la vallée des fous 2001. *Address:* Mer Agitée SARL, Port La Forêt, 29940 La Forêt Fouesnant, France (office). *Telephone:* 2-98-56-82-85 (office). *Fax:* 2-98-56-81-69 (office). *E-mail:* micheldesjoyeaux@meragitee.com (office). *Website:* www.meragitee.com (office).

DESKUR, HE Cardinal Andrzej Maria; Polish ecclesiastic; b. 29 Feb. 1924, Sancygniów; ordained priest 1950; Sec. Pontifical Council for Social Communications, Pres. 1980–84, Pres. Emer. 1984–; consecrated Bishop (Titular See of Thenae) 1974, Titular Archbishop of Thenae 1980; cr. Cardinal-Deacon of S. Cesareo in Palatio 1985, Cardinal-Priest of S. Cesareo in Palatio 1996–; Pres. Pontifical Acad. of the Immaculate Conception; mem. Congregation for Devotion to God and Discipline of Sacraments, Congregation for Canonization, Pontifical Council for Ministry of Health Service Staff, Pontifical Comm. of the Holy See. *Address:* Pontifical Council for Social Communications, Palazzo S. Carlo, 00120 Città del Vaticano, Rome, Italy (office). *Telephone:* (06) 69883197 (office); (06) 69883597 (office). *Fax:* (06) 69885373 (office).

DESLONGCHAMPS, Pierre, FCIC, OC, OQ, PhD, FRSC, FRS; Canadian chemist and academic; *Professor of Chemistry, Sherbrooke University;* b. 8 May 1938, St-Lin, Québec; s. of Rodolphe Deslongchamps and Madeleine Magnan; m. 1st Micheline Renaud 1960 (divorced 1975); two s.; m. 2nd Shirley E. Thomas 1976 (divorced 1983); m. 3rd Marie-Marthe Leroux 1987; ed Montréal Univ., Univ. of New Brunswick; Post-doctoral Fellow Harvard Univ. 1965–66; Asst Prof. Montréal Univ. 1966–67, Asst Prof., Sherbrooke Univ. 1967–68, Assoc. Prof. 1968–72, Prof. 1972–; A. P. Sloan Fellowship 1970–72, E. W. R. Steacie Fellowship 1971–74; mem. Canadian Cttee of Scientists and Scholars 1993–, Soc. française de Chimie 1995; Foreign Assoc. mem. Acad. des Sciences de Paris 1995; Fellow, AAAS and numerous other academic socs; Fellow, Guggenheim Foundation 1979, World Innovation Foundation (WIF), UK 2002; several hon. degrees; Scientific Prize of Québec 1971, E. W. R. Steacie Prize 1974, Médaille Vincent (ACFAS) 1975, Izaak Walton Killam Memorial Scholarships 1976–77, Merck, Sharp and Dohme Lectures Award (CIC) 1976, Médaille Parizeau (ACFAS) 1979, Marie-Victorin Prize 1987, Alfred Bader Award (CSC) 1991, Canada Gold Medal for Science and Eng 1993, R. U. Lemieux Award for Organic Chem. (Chemical Soc. for Chem.) 1994. *Publications:* Stereoelectronic Effects in Organic Chemistry 1983; more than 225 publs in the area of organic synthesis and devt of concept of stereoelectronic effects in organic chem. *Leisure interests:* reading, fishing, hunting, canoeing. *Address:* Département de chimie, Institut de Pharmacologie, Université de Sherbrooke, Sherbrooke, Québec, PQ J1H 5N4 (office); 161 de Vimy, Sherbrooke, Québec PQ J1J 3M6, Canada (home). *Telephone:* (819) 564-5300 (office); (819) 563-8788 (home). *Fax:* (819) 820-6823 (office). *E-mail:* pierre.deslongchamps@usherbrooke.ca (office). *Website:* callisto.si.usherb.ca:8080/pierre.deslongchamps (office).

DESMARAIS, André, OC; Canadian business executive; *President and Co-CEO, Power Corporation of Canada;* b. 1959; s. of Paul Desmarais, Sr; brother of Paul Desmarais, Jr (q.v.); m. France Chrétien; joined Power Corpn of Canada 1983, Pres. and Co-CEO 1996–; Deputy Chair. Power Financial Corpn 1996–; mem. Int. Council J.P. Morgan Chase & Co. Inc. 2003–; Dir Great West Life Co. Inc., Investors Group Inc. *Address:* Power Corporation of Canada, 751 Victoria Square, Montreal, PQ H2Y 2J3, Canada (office). *Telephone:* (514) 286-7425 (office). *Fax:* (514) 286-7484 (office). *E-mail:* info@powercorporation.com (office). *Website:* www.powercorporation.com (office).

DESMARAIS, Paul, Jr, OC, BComm, MBA; Canadian business executive; *Chairman and Co-CEO, Power Corporation of Canada;* b. 1957; s. of Paul Desmarais, Sr; brother of André Desmarais (q.v.); ed McGill Univ., Institut Européen d'Admin des Affaires (INSEAD), France; with S.G. Warburg & Co. Ltd, London 1979–80; Planning Man. Standard Brands Inc., NY 1980–81; Dir of Planning Power Corpn of Canada 1981–82, Vice–Pres. 1982-91, Vice–Chair. 1991–96; Vice-Pres. Power Financial Corpn 1984–86, Pres. and COO 1986–90, Vice-Chair. 1989–90, Chair. 1990–2005, Chair. Exec. Cttee 2005–; Chair. and Co-CEO, Power Corpn of Canada (financial services and communications co.) 1996–; Chair. and CEO Parfinance, France 1993–98 (co. dissolved 1998); Dir and mem. Exec. Cttee IGM Financial Inc., Investors Group Inc., Mackenzie Inc., Great-West Lifeco Inc., The Great-West Life Assurance Co., Great-West Life & Annuity Insurance Co., London Insurance Group Inc., London Life Insurance Co., Pargesa Holding SA, Groupe Bruxelles Lambert SA; Dir Gesca Ltd, La Presse Ltd, Les Journaux Trans-Canada Inc. 1996, Suez, Total, Lafarge; mem. Strategic Cttee Imerys, then Vice-Chair. of the Bd; Chair. Advisory Bd SAGARD Private Equity Partners; Chair. HEC Int. Advisory Bd; mem. Bd of Dirs and Int. Council INSEAD; mem. Global Advisory Council Merrill Lynch; Hon. Chair. Faculty of Man., Int. Advisory Bd McGill Univ.; Insigne d'Officier de l'Ordre de la Couronne (Belgium) 1994; Canada 125 Medal 1992, Queen's Golden Jubilee Medal 2002. *Leisure interests:* golf, skiing, hunting, fishing. *Address:* Power Corporation of Canada, 751 Victoria Square, Montreal, PQ H2Y 2J3, Canada (office). *Telephone:* (514) 286-7424 (office). *Fax:* (514) 286-7484 (office). *E-mail:* info@powercorporation.com (office). *Website:* www.powercorporation.com (office).

DESMAREST, Thierry Jean Jacques; French mining engineer and business executive; *Chairman, Total;* b. 18 Dec. 1945, Paris; s. of Jacques Desmarest and Edith Desmarest (née Barbe); m. Annick Geraux 1972; one s. two d.; ed Ecole Nat. Supérieure des Mines de Paris, Ecole Polytechnique; qualified mining engineer; worked as engineer with Mines Directorate, New Caledonia 1971–73, Dir of Mines and Geology 1973–75; Tech. Adviser Ministry of Industry 1975–78, of Econ. 1978–80; mem. Bd Dirs Total Algeria 1981–83, Dir for Latin America and W Africa 1983–87, for the Americas, France, Far East and Dir Man. and Econ. Div. 1988–89, CEO Total Exploration Production 1989–95, mem. Exec. Cttee 1989–95, Pres. 1995, CEO Total Group (later Total Fina Elf, now Total) 1995–2007, Chair. 2007–; Pres. Elf Aquitaine (merged with Total Fina Elf) 2000–03; mem. Supervisory Bd Paribas 1995; Dir Asscn française des entreprises privées 2001–; Légion d'honneur 2004; Man. of the Year 1999, Nouvel Economiste. *Leisure interest:* skiing. *Address:* Total, 2 place de la Coupole, La Défense 6, 92400 Courbevoie, France (office). *Telephone:* 1-47-44-46-99 (office). *Fax:* 1-47-44-68-21 (office). *Website:* www.total.com (office).

DESMEDT, John E., MD, PhD; Belgian neurologist and academic; b. 19 Feb. 1926, Wavre; Prof. and Dir Brain Research Unit, Univ. of Brussels 1962–, fmr Chair. Dept of Physiology and Pathophysiology Medical Faculty; Pres. Int. Fed. for Clinical Neurophysiology 1985–; mem. Acad. Royale de Médecine de Belgique, Acad. Royale de Belgique; Foreign mem. Accad. Nazionale dei Lincei, Italy, Acad. Nat. de Médecine, France; Fellow New York Acad. of Sciences, Royal Soc. of Medicine, AAAS and mem. or hon. mem. of numerous other professional socs and int. scientific orgs; Dr hc (Palermo) 1975, (Strasbourg) 1981; Francqui Prize 1972, Dautrebande Prize for Pathophysiology 1979, Maisin Prize (Fonds Nat. de la Recherche Scientifique) 1985; Grand Officier, Ordre de Léopold. *Publications:* New Developments in Electromyography and Clinical Neurophysiology (three vols) 1973, Motor Control Mechanisms in Health and Disease 1983. *Leisure interests:* horse-riding, jogging, fishing. *Address:* c/o Brain Research Unit, University of Brussels, 20 rue Evers, Brussels 1000, Belgium.

DESMOND, Richard Clive; British publishing and media executive; *Chairman, Northern & Shell PLC;* b. 8 Dec. 1951; s. of Cyril Desmond and Millie Desmond; m. Janet Robertson 1983; one s.; Advertisement Exec. Thomson Newspapers 1967–68; Group Advertisement Man. Beat Publs Ltd 1968–74; f. Northern & Shell Network 1974 (later Northern & Shell PLC) Chair. 1974–; launched Int. Musician (magazine) 1974; Demonde Advertising 1976–89; Publr Next, Fitness, Cook's Weekly, Venture, Penthouse, Bicycle, Stamps, Electric Blue, Rock CD, Guitar, For Woman, Attitude, Arsenal, Liverpool; f. Fantasy Channel 1995, OK! Magazine 1993–, OK! TV 1999–; owner Express Newspapers 2000–. *Leisure interest:* drums. *Address:* Northern & Shell PLC, 10 Lower Thames Street, London, EC3R 6EN, England (office). *Telephone:* (871) 434-1010 (office). *Website:* www.northernandshell.co.uk (office).

DESMOND-HELLMANN, Susan, MD, MPH; American business executive and medical scientist; *President, Product Development, Genentech Inc.;* b. Reno, Nev.; ed Univ. of Nevada, Reno and Univ. of Calif., Berkeley School of Public Health; Adjunct Assoc. Prof. of Epidemiology and Biostatistics, Univ. of Calif., San Francisco, fmr Asst Prof. of Hematology-Oncology; Assoc. Dir Clinical Cancer Research, Pharmaceutical Research Inst., Bristol-Myers Squibb –1995; Clinical Scientist, Genentech Inc. 1995, Chief Medical Officer 1996, Exec. Vice-Pres. Devt and Product Operations and mem. Exec. Cttee 1999–2004, Pres. Product Devt and mem. Exec. Cttee 2004–; mem. US Dept of Health and Human Services Advisory Cttee on Regulatory Reform 2002; mem. Bd of Dirs Biotechnology Industry Org. 2001–, American Asscn for Cancer Research 2005–; spent two years as visiting faculty mem., Uganda Cancer Inst. studying AIDS and cancer; also spent two years in pvt. practice; ranked by Fortune magazine amongst 50 Most Powerful Women in Business in the US 2001, 2003, (24th) 2004, (23rd) 2005, (17th) 2006, (21st) 2007, ranked by Forbes magazine amongst 100 Most Powerful Women (81st) 2005, (61st) 2007, (87th) 2008, listed by The Wall Street Journal as one of its Women To Watch 2004, 2005, named the Healthcare Businesswomen's Asscn's Woman of the Year 2006; numerous honours and awards for work in oncology and AIDS research. *Address:* Genentech Inc., 1 DNA Way, South San Francisco, CA 94080-4990, USA (office). *Telephone:* (650) 225-1000 (office). *Fax:* (650) 225-6000 (office). *Website:* www.gene.com (office).

DESOER, Barbara J., BA, MBA; American banking executive; *President, Mortgage, Home Equity and Insurance Services, Bank of America Corporation;* ed Mount Holyoke Coll. and Univ. of Calif., Berkeley; joined Bank of America in 1977, held several commercial lending and credit admin assignments, served as Exec. Asst to two CEOs, then held several retail banking assignments, Regional Exec., Calif. Retail Bank 1996–98, Pres. Northern Calif. banking 1998, Pres. Banking Group May–Sept. 1999, Dir of Marketing, Bank of America 1999–2001, Pres. Consumer Products 2001–04, Global Tech., Service and Fulfillment Exec. 2004–08, Pres. Mortgage, Home Equity and Insurance Services 2008–, Dir Bank of America, N.A. and Fleet National Bank, mem. Bank of America's Risk & Capital and Man. Operating Cttees; mem. Advisory Council Haas School of Business, Univ. of California, Berkeley, Business Advisory Council Belk Coll. of Business Admin, Univ. of North Carolina, Charlotte; Chair. United Way of Cen. Carolinas; mem. Bd of Dirs North Carolina Dance Theatre, Presbyterian Hosp.; Trustee Providence Day School, Charlotte; ranked by Fortune magazine amongst 50 Most Powerful Women in Business in the US (47th) 2005, ranked first by US Banker magazine amongst The 25 Women to Watch 2005. *Address:* Bank of America Corporate Center, 100 North Tryon Street, Charlotte, NC 28255, USA (office). *Fax:* (704) 386-6699 (office). *Website:* www.bankofamerica.com (office).

D'ESPAGNAT, Bernard, PhD; French theoretical physicist, academic, philosopher and author; b. 22 Aug. 1921, Fourmagnac, Lot; ed Institut Henri Poincaré, Univ. of the Sorbonne; spent most of his early years in Paris; researcher, CNRS 1947–57; worked with Enrico Fermi in Chicago, USA 1951–52, and on research project led by Niels Bohr at Inst. in Copenhagen, Denmark 1953–54; worked at CERN, Geneva and, as a theoretical physicist, at European Org. for Nuclear Research 1954–59; Sr Lecturer, Faculty of Sciences, Univ. of the Sorbonne 1959–87; Dir Lab. of Theoretical Physics and Elementary Particles, Univ. of Paris XI (Orsay) 1980–87; Visiting Prof., Univ. of Texas, Austin, USA 1977, Univ. of California, Santa Barbara, USA 1984; mem. Brussels Int. Acad. of the Philosophy of Science 1975, French Acad. of Moral and Political Sciences 1996; Templeton Prize for "work which acknowledges that science cannot fully explain the 'nature of being" 2009. *Achievements include:* best known for his work on the nature of reality; developed concept of 'veiled reality'. *Publications include:* Conceptions de la physique contemporaine: les interprétations de la mécanique quantique et de la mesure 1965, Conceptual Foundations of Quantum Mechanics 1971, A la recherche du réel, le regard d'un physicien (In Search of Reality) 1979, Un atome de sagesse, propos d'un physicien sur le réel voilé 1982, Nonseparability and the Tentative Descriptions of Reality 1984, Une incertaine réalité: le monde quantique, la connaissance et la durée 1985, Penser la science ou les enjeux du savoir 1990, Georges d'Espagnat 1990, Regards sur la matière des quanta et des choses (co-author) 1993, Le Réel voilé, analyse des concepts quantiques (Veiled Reality: An Analysis of Quantum Mechanical Concepts) 1994, Physique et réalité – un débat avec Bernard d'Espagnat 1997, Ondine et les feux du savoir – Carnets d'une petite sirène 1998, Traité de physique et de philosophie 2002 (translated as On Physics and Philosophy 2006), Candide et le physicien (Candide and the Physicist) (with Claude Saliceti) 2008. *Address:* 39 rue d'Assas, 75006 Paris, France.

DESPIĆ, Aleksandar R., DrPhysChem; Serbian electrochemist; b. 6 Jan. 1927, Belgrade; s. of Ranko Despić and Vukosava Despić (née Kalimančić); m. Zorica Vukadinović 1954 (died 2002); ed Belgrade Univ., Imperial Coll. of Science and Tech., London, UK; served World War II; Sr Teaching Asst, Belgrade Univ. 1953–59, Asst Prof. 1959–64, Assoc. Prof. 1964–71, Prof. of Physical Chem. 1971–92; worked in Univ. of Pennsylvania, USA 1957–59, 1967–68; Pres. Serbian Chemical Soc. 1973–77 (Hon. Pres. 1978–), Union of Chemical Socs of Yugoslavia 1978–81; Vice-Pres. Int. Soc. of Electrochemistry 1977–79; Pres. Governing Bd Inst. of Electrochemistry, Belgrade 1987, Bd Young Scientists and Artists Foundation 1987; Founder and Dir Museum of Science and Tech., Belgrade 1989–99; Chair. Foundation for Devt of Scientific and Artistic Youth; Head of Div. of Surface Tech. and Energy Inst. of Tech. Sciences, Serbian Acad. of Sciences; Ed.-in-Chief Bull. Soc. Chim. (now Journal of the Serbian Chemical Society) 1969–75; Founder and Ed.-in-Chief Yugoslav Chemical Papers 1977; mem. Editional Bd Journal of Applied Electrochemistry; mem. European Expert Cttee of Electrochemistry, UNESCO 1977; Corresp. mem. Serbian Acad. of Sciences and Arts 1965, mem. 1976, Vice-Pres. 1981–94, Pres. 1995–99; Corresp. mem. Slovenian Acad. of Sciences and Arts 1976–; mem. European Acad. on Surface Technologies, Schwabisch Gmund 1989–, European Acad. of Sciences and Arts, Salzburg 1992–; October Prize 1968, 7 July Prize 1990, Karić Award 1999. *Publications:* more than 180 scientific works, 22 invention patents, more than 15 monographs and textbooks including On Theory of Mechanisms of Chemical Reactions 1965, On Theory of Dendritic Growth 1968, Aluminium-Air Battery with Salt Solution 1976, Electrochemical Deposition of Alloys and Composites 1995, numerous articles in Yugoslavian and foreign scientific periodicals. *Address:* Vlajkovićeva 13, 11000 Belgrade (home); Serbian Academy of Sciences and Arts, Knez Mihailova Str. 35, 11000 Belgrade, Serbia. *Telephone:* (11) 323-9492 (home). *E-mail:* adespic@eunet.yu (home).

DESYATNIKOV, Leonid Arkadievich; Russian composer; b. 1955, Kharkov, Ukraine; ed Leningrad State Conservatory; mem. Composers' Union 1979–; Golden Sheep Prize 2000. *Works include:* opera: Poor Lisa; ballet: Love Song in Minor; tango-operetta: Astor Piazzola's Maria de Buenos Aires (Grammy Award); symphony: Sacred Winter; film scores: Sunset 1990, Lost in Siberia 1991, Capital Punishment 1992, Touch 1992, Moscow Nights 1994, Katia Izmailova 1994, Hammer and Sickle 1994, Giselle's Mania 1995, The Prisoner of the Mountains 1996, The One Who is More Tender 1996, Moscow 2000, His Wife's Diary 2000. *Address:* Nepokorennykh prosp. 16, korp. 1, apt 177, 195220 St Petersburg, Russia (home). *Telephone:* (812) 545-20-98 (home).

DETREKŐI, Ákos, DSc; Hungarian civil engineer and university rector; *UNESCO Chair in Continuing Engineering Education, Budapest University of Technology and Economics;* b. 27 Nov. 1939, Budapest; m.; two c.; ed Tech. Univ., Budapest; Asst Faculty of Civil Eng, Budapest Univ. of Tech. and Econs 1963–68, Sr Asst 1968–72, Lecturer, Dept of Geodesy 1963–78, Dept of

Photogrammetry 1978–, Assoc. Prof. 1972–80, Prof., Head of Dept 1980–, Dean Faculty of Civil Eng 1986–90, Rector 1997–, UNESCO Chair in Continuing Eng Educ. 2000–; Lecturer, Technische Univ., Dresden 1980–83; mem. Hungarian Acad. of Sciences (mem. Cttee of Geodesy 1975, Chair. 1990–97), Hungarian Council for Space Research 1995– (mem. Bd of Supervision); Hon. Pres. Hungarian Humboldt Soc., Hungarian Soc. of Surveying, Remote Sensing and Cartography 1994–; Fed. Decoration of Germany, 1st Class 2002, Order of the Hungarian Repub. 2003; Fasching Antal Medal 1988, Lazar Deák Medal 1993, Albert Szent-Györgyi Prize 1996, Humboldt Medal 1996, Peter Pázmány Prize 2000. *Publications:* one book and numerous contribs and articles. *Leisure interest:* music. *Address:* Department of Photogrammetry and Geoinformatics, Budapest University of Technology and Economics, Müegyetem rkp. 9, 1111 Budapest (office); Naybányai ut 43/b, 1025 Budapest, Hungary (home). *Telephone:* (1) 4632471 (office). *Fax:* (1) 4632470 (office). *E-mail:* adetrekoi@epito.bme.hu (office). *Website:* www.bme.hu (office).

DETTORI, Lanfranco (Frankie); Italian professional flat race jockey; b. 15 Dec. 1970, Milan; s. of 13-times Italian champion jockey Gianfranco Dettori and Iris Maria Niemen; m. Catherine Allen 1997; has ridden races in England, France, Germany, Italy, USA, Dubai, Australia, Hong Kong and other countries in the Far East 1992–; 1,000 rides and 215 wins in UK 1995; horses ridden include Lamtarra, Barathea, Vettori, Mark of Distinction, Balanchine, Moonshell, Lochsong, Classic Cliché, Dubai Millennium, Daylami, Sakhee; maj. race victories include St Leger (twice), The Oaks (twice), The Breeders Cup Mile, Arc de Triomphe (twice), French 2,000 Guineas (twice), English 1,000 Guineas, Queen Elizabeth II Stakes, Prix L'Abbaye, The Japan Cup (twice), The Dubai World Cup; rode winners of all seven races at Ascot on 28 Oct. 1996; survived air crash 2000; launched signature range of food 2001; Team Capt., A Question of Sport, BBC TV 2002–04; Hon. MBE, Commendatore, Italy 2005; Jockey of the Year 1994, 1995, 2004, BBC Sports Personality of the Year 1996, Int. Sports Personality of the Year, Variety Club 2000. *Publications:* A Year in the Life of Frankie Dettori 1996, Frankie: The Autobiography 2004, Frankie's: Recipes from an Italian Family (with Marco Pierre White) 2007. *Leisure interests:* golf, wine, cooking. *Address:* Peter Burrell, Classic Management, 5th Floor, 140 Brompton Road, London, SW3 1HY, England (office). *Telephone:* (20) 7808-0233 (office). *Fax:* (20) 7584-7933 (office). *E-mail:* info@classicmanagement.biz (office). *Website:* www.classicmanagement.biz (office).

DETWEILER, David Kenneth, VMD, MS; American physiologist and academic; *Professor Emeritus of Physiology, University of Pennsylvania;* b. 23 Oct. 1919, Philadelphia, Pa; s. of David Rieser Detweiler and Pearl I. (Overholt) Detweiler; two s. four d.; ed Univ. of Pennsylvania; Asst Instructor, Veterinary School, Univ. of Pennsylvania 1942–43, Instructor 1943–45, Assoc. Instructor 1945–47, Asst Prof. 1947–51, Assoc. Prof. 1951–62, Prof. of Physiology and Head of Physiology Lab. 1962–90, Dir Comparative Cardiovascular Studies Unit 1960–90, Prof. Emer. 1990–; Guggenheim Fellow 1955–56; mem. Nat. Acads of Practice 1989, Inst. of Medicine, NAS; Hon. DSc (Ohio State Univ.) 1966; Hon. MVD (Vienna) 1968; Hon. DMV (Turin) 1969; Guggenheim Fellowship Award 1955, Gaines Award and Medal, American Veterinary Asscn 1960, Distinguished Veterinarian Award, Pennsylvania Veterinary Medical Asscn 1989; elected to Hon. Roll American Veterinary Asscn 1990, David K. Detweiler Prize for Cardiology established by German-speaking group of World Veterinary Medicine Asscn 1982, David K. Detweiler Conf. Room dedicated in School of Veterinary Medicine, Univ. of Pennsylvania 1993, School's Centennial Medal, Inst. of Medicine, NAS 1994, Certificate of Appreciation for Drug Evaluation and Research Seminar Program, Food and Drug Admin. 1998. *Publications:* more than 170 publs on cardiology and cardiovascular physiology. *Leisure interests:* art, music, languages. *Address:* Waverly Heights, Apt A212, 1400 Waverly Road, Gladwyne, PA 19035, USA (home). *Telephone:* (610) 645-8964 (home). *Fax:* (610) 645-8719 (home).

DEUBA, Sher Bahadur, MA; Nepalese politician; b. 12 June 1946, Angra, Dadeldhura Dist; m. Arju Deuba; one s.; ed Tribhuvan Univ.; Chair. Far Western Students Cttee, Kathmandu 1965; served a total of nine years' imprisonment for political activities 1966–85; Founder-mem. Nepal Students' Union 1970; Research Fellow, LSE 1988–90; active in Popular Movt for Restoration of Democracy in Nepal 1991; mem. Parl. 1991–; Minister of Home Affairs; Leader Parl. Party, Nepali Congress 1994; Prime Minister 1995–97, 2001–02, 2004–05; Minister of Foreign Affairs and Defence 2001–02; sentenced to two-year jail term for graft July 2005, released Feb. 2006; fmr Pres. Nepali Congress Party (Democratic) (merged again with Nepali Congress under Girja Prasad Koirala as Nepali Congress 2007). *Address:* Parliament of Nepal, Singha Durbar, Kathmandu, Nepal (office). *Telephone:* (1) 227480 (office). *Fax:* (1) 4222923 (office). *E-mail:* nparl@ntc.net.np (office). *Website:* www.parliament.gov.np (office).

DEUKMEJIAN, George, JD; American fmr state governor; b. 6 June 1928, Albany, NY; s. of C. George Deukmejian and Alice Deukmejian (née Gairdan); m. Gloria M. Saatjian 1957; one s. two d.; ed Siena Coll. and St John's Univ.; admitted to NY State Bar 1952, Calif. Bar 1956, Supreme Court Bar 1970; partner Riedman, Dalessi, Deukmejian & Woods, Long Beach, Calif. –1979; mem. Calif. Ass. 1963–67, Calif. Senate (Minority Leader) 1967–79; Attorney-Gen., Calif. 1979–82; Gov. of California 1983–90; Partner, Sidley and Austin 1991–2000; Republican. *Address:* 5366 East Broadway, Long Beach, CA 90803-3549, USA (office).

DEUTCH, John M., PhD; American chemist and academic; *Institute Professor, Department of Chemistry, Massachusetts Institute of Technology;* b. 27 July 1938, Brussels, Belgium; s. of Michael J. and Rachel Fischer Deutch; m. Pat Lyons; three s.; ed Amherst Coll. and Massachusetts Inst. of Tech.; Systems Analyst, Office of Sec. for Defense 1961–65; Fellow NAS/NRC, Nat.

Bureau of Standards 1966–67; Asst Prof., Princeton Univ. 1967–70; mem. Faculty, MIT 1970–, Prof. of Chem. 1971–; Chair. Dept of Chem. 1976–77, Dean, School of Science 1982–85, Provost 1985–90, Inst. Prof. 1990–; Dir of Energy Research, Dept of Energy 1977–79, Acting Asst Sec. 1979, Under-Sec. 1979–80; UnderSec. for Acquisition and Tech. Dept of Defense 1993–94, Deputy Sec. 1994–95; Dir CIA 1995–96; mem. White House Science Council 1985–89; mem. Bd of Dirs Citicorp, CMS Energy, Parkin-Elmer Corpn, Schlumberger, Science Applications Inc.; other professional and public appointments; mem. ACS, American Physical Soc., American Acad. of Arts and Sciences, Council on Foreign Relations, President's Foreign Intelligence Advisory Cttee 1990–94, Trilateral Comm. 1991; Sloan Fellow 1969–71; Guggenheim Fellow 1974; Hon. DSc (Amherst Coll.) 1978; Hon. DPhil (Lowell) 1986; recipient of awards from Dept of State and Dept of Energy. *Publications:* research articles. *Address:* Department of Chemistry, Massachusett Institute of Technology, 77 Massachusetts Avenue, Room 6-208, Cambridge, MA 02139, USA (office). *Telephone:* (617) 253-1479 (office). *Fax:* (617) 258-5700 (office). *E-mail:* jmd@mit.edu (office). *Website:* web.mit.edu/chemistry/deutch (office).

DEUTSCH, David Elieser, MA, DPhil, FRS; British physicist, academic and author; *Non-stipendiary Visiting Professor, Centre for Quantum Computation, University of Oxford;* b. 1953, Haifa, Israel; with Centre for Quantum Computation, Clarendon Lab., Univ. of Oxford 1990–, becoming Non-stipendiary Visiting Prof.; Distinguished Fellow, British Computer Soc. 1998, Paul Dirac Prize and Medal, Inst. of Physics 1998, Fourth Int. Award on Quantum Communication for "theoretical work on Quantum Computer Science" 2002, Edge of Computation Science Prize, Edge Foundation, Inc. 2005. *Achievements include:* pioneered the field of quantum computers by being the first person to formulate a specifically quantum computational algorithm; proponent of the many-worlds interpretation of quantum mechanics and of the multiverse hypothesis. *Publications:* The Fabric of Reality 1997 (translated into German, Italian, Spanish, Japanese, Finnish, Brazilian Portuguese, Russian, Chinese, French and Polish); several scientific papers in professional journals on quantum computing, quantum theory and parallel universes. *Address:* Centre for Quantum Computation, The Clarendon Laboratory, Parks Road, Oxford, OX1 3PU, England (office). *Telephone:* (1865) 272205 (office). *Fax:* (1865) 272375 (office). *E-mail:* david.deutsch@qubit.org (office). *Website:* www.qubit.org/people/david (office).

DEUTSCH-FÜR, Tamás; Hungarian politician; b. 27 July 1966, Budapest; s. of György Deutsch and Julianna Takács; m. Ágnes Sarolta Für; four s. two d.; ed Eötvös Loránd Univ., Budapest; co-founder Alliance of Young Democrats (FIDESZ) 1988, mem. Nat. Steering Cttee 1988–90, campaign chief 1990 local elections and 1998 parliamentary elections, party Vice-Pres. 1993–2003, head FIDESZ Budapest org. 2001–04, leader Budapest FIDESZ-Hungarian Christian Democratic Alliance joint faction 2002–03, Deputy Leader Parl. Group 2006–; mem. Parliament 1990–; Vice-Chair. Hungarian Olympic Cttee 1999–2001; Minister for Youth and Sport 1999–2002; mem. Budapest Municipal Ass. 2002–03; Deputy Speaker of Nat. Ass. 2004–06. *Publications:* contributing author to Gyermekek a Jognak Asztalánál (Children at the Table of the Law) 1991. *Leisure interests:* film, football. *Address:* Hungarian National Assembly, 1357 Budapest, Kossuth tér 1–3, Hungary (office). *Telephone:* (1) 441-4000 (office); (1) 441-5843 (office). *Fax:* (1) 441-5408 (office). *E-mail:* tamas.deutsch@parlament.hu (office). *Website:* www.parlament.hu (office).

DEV, Kapil (see KAPIL DEV).

DEVANEY, John Francis, CEng, FIEE, FIMechE; British business executive; *Chairman, Tersus Energy PLC;* b. 25 June 1946; s. of the late George Devaney and Alice Ann Devaney; two s. one d.; ed St Mary's Coll., Blackburn and Univ. of Sheffield; worked for Perkins Engines 1968–69, mfg positions in Peterborough 1968–76, Project Man., Ohio, USA 1976–77, Pres. 1983–88, Group Vice-Pres. European Components Group, Peterborough 1988, Group Vice-Pres. Enterprises Group, Toronto, Canada 1988–89; Chair., CEO and Group Vice-Pres. Kelsey-Hayes Corpn, Detroit, Mich., USA 1989–92; Man. Dir Eastern Electricity PLC (later Eastern Group PLC) 1992, CEO 1993, Exec. Chair. 1995–98; Dir EXEL Logistics (formed from merger of Nat. Freight Corpn with Ocean Group) 1996, Chair. 2000–02; Chair. Marconi PLC (later Telent PLC) 2002–07; Founder and Chair. British Energy; Chair. Liberata –2002; Chair. Nat. Air Traffic Services (NATS) 2005–; Chair. Tersus Energy PLC 2005–; Dir and fmr Chair. EA Technology; Dir (non-exec.) HSBC (fmrly Midland Bank) 1994–, British Steel 1998–; Pres. Electricity Asscn 1994–95, Inst. for Customer Services 1998–; mem. Bd of Dirs Northern Rock 2007–. *Leisure interests:* skiing, golf, tennis, sailing. *Address:* Tersus Energy PLC, 343 Linen Hall, 162–168 Regent Street, London, W1B 5DT, England (office). *Telephone:* (20) 7038-0600 (office). *Fax:* (20) 7038-0605 (office). *E-mail:* power@tersusenergy.com (office). *Website:* www.tersusenergy.com (office).

DEVE GOWDA, Haradanahalli Dodde Gowda; Indian politician; *President, Janata Dal (Secular);* b. 18 May 1933, Haradan ahalli; m.; four s. two d.; ed Govt polytechnic inst.; trained as civil engineer; ran contracting business; elected to Karnataka State Legis. in 1960s; imprisoned during state of emergency in 1970s; Minister of Public Works and Irrigation, Karnataka –1980; Chief Minister of Karnataka 1995–96; fmr mem. Lok Sabha; Leader multiparty United Front 1996; Prime Minister, Minister of Home and Agric., Science and Tech., Personnel and Atomic Energy 1996–97; currently President Janata Dal (Secular). *Address:* Janata Dal (Secular), 5 Safdarjung Lane, New Delhi 110 003, India. *Telephone:* (11) 23794499.

DEVEDJIAN, Patrick; French lawyer and politician; *Secretary General, Union pour un Mouvement Populaire;* b. 26 Aug. 1944, Fontainebleau (Seine-et-Marne); ed Université Panthéon-Assas Paris II; fmr mem. Occident group; admitted to Paris Bar 1970; joined Gaullist movt 1971; helped establish RPR party 1976; elected Mayor of Antony (Hauts-de-Seine) 1983, re-elected 1989, 1995, 2001; mem. Assemblée Nat. for Hauts-de-Seine 1986, re-elected 1988, 1993, 1997, 2002, 2005; Vice-Pres. Mouvement européen (France) 2002; Minister for Local Liberties 2002–04, for Industry 2004–05; adviser to Nicolas Sarkozy during presidential bid 2007; Exec. Sec. Gen. Union pour un Mouvement Populaire (UMP) 2007–; Pres. Conseil général des Hauts-de-Seine 2007–; as a lawyer, was involved in several cases defending mems of Armenian Secret Army for the Liberation of Armenia. *Address:* Union pour un Mouvement Populaire, 55 rue La Boétie, 75384 Paris Cedex 08, France (office). *Telephone:* 1-40-76-60-00 (office). *E-mail:* webmaster@u-m-p.org (office); information@patrickdevedjian.fr. *Website:* www.u-m-p.org (office); www .patrickdevedjian.fr.

DEVERS, Gail, BA; American athlete; b. 19 Nov. 1966, Seattle; m. Ron Roberts 1988 (divorced 1992); ed Univ. of California, Los Angeles; holds record for most World Championship gold medals won by a woman (five): 100m., (1993), 100m. hurdles (1993, 1995, 1999), 4x100m. relay (1997); Olympic champion 100m. (1992, 1996); Olympic gold medal 4x100m. relay (1996); won IAAF Grand Prix final 100m. hurdles 2000, 2002; won World Cup 100m. hurdles 2002; US champion 100m. hurdles (seven times); est. Gail Devers Foundation. *Address:* c/o Gail Devers Foundation, 6555 Sugarloaf Parkway, Suite 307-137, Duluth, GA 30097, USA. *Website:* www.gaildevers.com.

DEVESI, Sir Baddeley, GCMG, GCVO; Solomon Islands politician and administrator; b. 16 Oct. 1941, East Tathiboko, Guadalcanal; s. of Mostyn Tagabasoe Norua and Laisa Otu; m. June Marie Barley 1969; four s. three d. (one d. deceased); ed St Mary's School, Maravovo, King George VI School, Solomon Islands, Ardmore Teachers' Training Coll., Auckland, New Zealand; Teacher, Melanesian Mission schools, Solomon Islands 1965–66; elected mem. British Solomon Islands Legis. and Exec. Councils 1967–68; Lecturer, Solomon Islands Teachers' Coll. 1970–72, Asst Sec. for Social Services 1972, Internal Affairs 1972; Dist Officer, S. Malaita 1973–75; Perm. Sec. Ministry of Works and Public Utilities 1976, Ministry of Transport and Communications 1977; Gov.-Gen. of Solomon Islands 1978–88; Minister for Foreign Affairs and Trade Relations 1989–91; Deputy Prime Minister and Minister for Home Affairs 1990–92, for Health and Medical Sciences 1992; Deputy Prime Minister and Minister for Transport, Works, Communications and Aviation 1996–2000; Chancellor, Univ. of S Pacific 1980–83; KStJ; Hon. DUniv. *Leisure interests:* swimming, lawn tennis, cricket, reading, snooker. *Address:* c/o Office of Deputy Prime Minister, Honiara, Solomon Islands.

DEVINSKY, Ferdinand, DSc; Slovak medicinal chemist and politician; b. 17 Aug. 1947, Bratislava; m.; two c.; ed Slovak Univ. of Tech., Bratislava; researcher, Slovakofoarma 1970–72; Lecturer, Comenius Univ., Bratislava 1972–2002, Rector 1997-2003, currently Rector Emer. and Head of Dept, Faculty of Pharmacy 1990–; research studies in UK 1986–87, 1991–2007, Belgium, USA, Germany 1991; currently mem. Parl., Chair. Cttee for Educ., Science, Sport, Youth, Culture and Media; mem. Slovak Democratic and Christian Union; mem. Steering Cttee European Univ. Asscn 2006–; Hon. Sr Research Fellow, King's Coll. London, UK; Stella Della Solidarieta Italiana (Commendatore) 2004; Jubilee Medal, Charles Univ., Prague 1998. *Publications include:* numerous scientific papers and textbooks. *Leisure interests:* tennis, any creative work. *Address:* Comenius University, Faculty of Pharmacy, Kalinciakova 8, 832 32 Bratislava, Slovakia (office). *Telephone:* (2) 50117331 (office). *Fax:* (2) 50117357 (office). *E-mail:* ferdinand.devinsky@ fpharm.uniba.sk (office). *Website:* www.uniba.sk (office).

DeVITO, Danny; American actor and director; b. 17 Nov. 1944, New Jersey; m. Rhea Perlman 1982; two s. two d.; ed American Acad. of Dramatic Arts, Wilfred Acad. of Hair and Beauty Culture; Co-founder and Co-Chair. Jersey Films (production co.); Golden Globe Award for Taxi 1979, Emmy Award 1981. *Stage appearances include:* The Man with a Flower in his Mouth, Down the Morning Line The Line of Least Existence, The Shrinking Bride, Call me Charlie, Comedy of Errors, Merry Wives of Windsor, Three by Pirandello, One Flew Over the Cuckoo's Nest. *Films include:* Dreams of Glass 1970, Lady Liberty 1971, Hot Dogs for Gauguin 1972, Scalawag 1973, Hurry Up or I'll be 30 1973, One Flew Over the Cuckoo's Nest 1975, Deadly Hero 1976, The Money 1976, Car Wash 1976, The Van 1977, The World's Greatest Lover 1977, Goin' South 1978, Swap Meet 1979, Going Ape 1981, Terms of Endearment 1983, Romancing the Stone 1984, Johnny Dangerously 1984, Head Office 1985, Jewel of the Nile 1985, Wiseguys 1986, Ruthless People 1986, My Little Pony (voice) 1986, Tin Men 1987, Throw Momma from the Train (also dir) 1987, Twins 1988, War of the Roses (also dir) 1989, Other People's Money 1991, Batman Returns 1992, Hoffa (also producer, dir) 1992, Jack the Bear 1993, Look Who's Talking Now (voice) 1993, Renaissance Man 1994, Junior 1994, Get Shorty (also co-producer) 1995, Matilda (also dir, co-producer) 1996, Space Jam (voice) 1996, Mars Attacks 1996, The Rainmaker 1997, LA Confidential 1997, Living Out Loud (also producer) 1998, Man on the Moon (also producer) 1999, The Virgin Suicides 1999, The Big Kahuna 1999, Drowning Mona (also producer) 2000, Screwed 2000, Heist 2001, What's the Worst That Could Happen? 2001, Death to Smoochy 2002 (also dir), Duplex (voice, also dir) 2003, Anything Else 2003, Big Fish 2003, Family of the Year 2004, Catching Kringle (voice) 2004, Christmas in Love 2004, Marilyn Hotchkiss' Ballroom Dancing and Charm School 2005, Be Cool (also producer) 2005, The OH in Ohio 2006, Bye Bye Benjamin (exec. producer) 2006, Even Money 2006, Relative Strangers (also producer) 2006, Deck the Halls 2006, The Good Night 2007, Reno 911!: Miami 2007, Just Add Water 2007, Nobel Son 2007. *Television includes:* Taxi (series, also dir), Mary (dir), Valentine, The Rating Game (dir), All the Kids Do It, A Very Special Christmas Party, Two Daddies? (voice), The Selling of Vince DeAngelo (dir), Amazing Stories (also dir), The Simpsons (voice), It's Always Sunny in Philadelphia (series) 2006–07. *Address:* c/o Fred Specktor, Creative Artists Agency, 9830 Wilshire Boulevard, Beverly Hills, CA 90212; Jersey Films, 10351 Santa Monica Blvd., Suite 200, Los Angeles, CA 90025, USA. *Telephone:* (310) 203-1000 (Jersey Films).

DEVLIN, Dean; American actor, screenwriter and producer; b. 27 Aug. 1962; George Pal Memorial Award 1998. *Film produced:* The Patriot 2000. *Films written and produced:* Stargate 1994 (Best Picture, Acad. of Science Fiction, Fantasy and Horror Films, Readers' Choice Award, Sci-Fi Universe magazine), Independence Day 1996 (Best Picture, Acad. of Science Fiction, Fantasy and Horror Films, People's Choice Best Picture), Godzilla 1998. *Film screenplay:* Universal Soldier 1992. *Films acted in:* My Bodyguard 1980, The Wild Life 1984, Real Genius 1985, City Limits 1985, Martians Go Home 1990, Moon 44 1990, Total Exposure 1991. *TV series:* The Visitor (creator, exec. producer) 1997. *TV appearances in:* North Beach 1985, Rawhide 1985, Hard Copy 1987, Generations 1989; guest appearances in: LA Law, Happy Days, Misfits of Science. *Address:* c/o Creative Artists Agency, 9830 Wilshire Boulevard, Beverly Hills, CA 90212; Astaire East, 3rd Floor, 10202 W Washington Boulevard, Culver City, CA 90232, USA (office). *Telephone:* (310) 244-4300 (office).

DEVLIN, Stuart Leslie, AO, CMG; Australian goldsmith, silversmith and designer; b. 9 Oct. 1931, Geelong; s. of Richard and Jesse Devlin; m. 1st Kim Hose 1962; m. 2nd Carole Hedley-Saunders 1986; ed Gordon Inst. of Tech., Geelong, Royal Melbourne Inst. of Tech. and Royal Coll. of Art; art teacher, Victoria Educ. Dept 1950–58, Royal Coll. of Art 1958–60; Harkness Fellow, New York 1960–62; Lecturer, Prahan Tech. Coll., Melbourne 1962; Inspector of Art in Tech. Schools, Victoria Educ. Dept 1964–65; working as goldsmith, silversmith and designer in London 1965–; exhbns of gold and silver in numerous cities in UK, USA, Australia, Middle East, etc.; has executed many commissions for commemorative coins in gold and silver for various countries; designed and made cutlery for State Visit to Paris 1972, Duke of Edinburgh Trophy for World Driving Championship 1973, silver to commemorate opening of Sydney Opera House 1973, Grand National Trophy 1975 and Regalia for Order of Australia 1975–76; Centrepiece for Royal Engineers to commemorate their work in Northern Ireland 1984; Bas-relief portrait HRH Princess of Wales for Wedgwood 1986; devised and executed Champagne Diamond Exhbn 1987; designed and made Sydney 2000 Olympic coins 1997; designed and made Millennium Commemorative dishes for Goldsmiths' Co. and Information Technologists' Co. 2000; granted Royal Warrant (goldsmith and jeweller to HM Queen Elizabeth II) 1982; mem. Court of Wardens, Goldsmiths' Co. 1992, Prime Warden, 1996–97; Vice-Chair. Intergraph Graphics Users' Group, UK 1996–98; Hon. Dr of Arts (Royal Melbourne Inst. of Tech.) 2000. *Leisure interests:* work, computer graphics, swimming. *Address:* Fordwych, 52 Angmering Lane, East Preston, West Sussex, BN16 2TA, England. *Telephone:* (1903) 858939. *E-mail:* stuart@stuart-devlin.co.uk.

DEVONSHIRE, 12th Duke of, cr. 1694, Baron Cavendish, Earl of Devonshire, Marquess of Hartington, Earl of Burlington, Baron Cavendish (UK) Peregrine Andrew Morny Cavendish, CBE; British horse racing executive and landowner; b. 27 April 1944; s. of 11th Duke of Devonshire and Hon. Deborah Vivian Freeman Mitford; m. Amanda Carmen Heywood-Lonsdale 1967; one s. two d.; ed Eton, Exeter Coll., Oxford; Sr Steward, Jockey Club 1989–94; Chair. British Horseracing Bd 1993–96; Dir Sotheby's Holdings Inc. 1994–, Deputy Chair. 1996–; HM's Rep. at Ascot 1997–; Trustee, Yorkshire Dales Nat. Park Millennium Trust. *Address:* Chatsworth, Bakewell, Derbyshire DE45 1PP, England (home). *Telephone:* (1246) 565300 (office). *Website:* www.chatsworth.org (office).

DEVRIES, William Castle, MD; American surgeon; b. 19 Dec. 1943, Brooklyn; s. of Hendrik Devries and Cathryn L. Castle; seven c.; ed Univ. of Utah, Army Medical Department Basic Officer program; intern, Duke Univ. Medical Center 1970–71; Resident in Cardiovascular and Thoracic Surgery 1971–79; Asst Prof. of Surgery, Univ. of Utah –1984; Chief of Thoracic Surgery, Salt Lake Hosp., Va –1984; Pres. De Vries & Assocs 1988–99; Surgeon Hardin Memorial Hosp., Elizabethtown, Ky 1999–; joined US Defense Department as medical contractor Walter Reed Army Medical Center, Washington, DC, joined US Army Reserve 2000–; mem. American Medical Asscn, Soc. of Thoracic Surgeons; implanted first permanent artificial heart 1982. *Address:* Walter Reed Army Medical Center, 6900 Georgia Avenue, NW, Washington, DC 20307, USA (office). *Website:* www.wramc .amedd.army.mil.

DEVROYE, Luc, BEng, PhD; Belgian/Canadian computer scientist and academic; *Professor of Computer Science, McGill University;* b. Tienen, Belgium; m. Bea Devroye; ed Univ. of Leuven, Osaka Univ., Japan, Univ. of Texas at Austin, USA; Asst Prof., McGill Univ. 1977–81, Assoc. Prof. 1981–87, Prof. of Computer Science and Assoc. mem. Dept of Math. and Statistics 1987–, James McGill Prof. 2003–; working at Computational Geometry Lab., Carleton Univ., Ottawa 2006–; fmr mem. editorial bds of numerous Canadian and int. math. and computer science journals; Hon. mem. Belgian Statistical Soc. 1997; Dr hc (Catholic Univ. of Louvain) 2002; E. W. R. Steacie Memorial Fellowship 1987, Research Award, Alexander von Humboldt Foundation (Germany) 2004, Killam Prize, Canada Council for the Arts 2005. *Publications:* Nonparametric Density Estimation: The L1 View 1985, Lecture Notes on Bucket Algorithms 1986, Non-Uniform Random Variate Generation 1986, A Course In Density Estimation 1987, A Probabilistic Theory of Pattern Recognition (co-author) 1996, Combinatorial Methods in Density Estimation (co-author) 2001; own book on random number generation on his website; numerous papers in scientific journals on applied math., including computer science, statistics and probability theory. *Address:* School of Computer Science, McGill University, Office MC300N, 3480 University Street, Montreal, PQ H3A 2K6, Canada (office). *Telephone:* (514) 398-3738 (office). *Fax:*

(514) 398-3883 (office). *E-mail:* luc@cs.mcgill.ca (office). *Website:* www.cs.mcgill.ca (office); cg.scs.carleton.ca/~luc (office).

DEWAEL, Patrick; Belgian politician; *Speaker, Chamber of Representatives;* b. 13 Oct. 1955, Lier; m. Marleen Van Doren; three c.; solicitor 1977–85; sec., House of Reps 1985; mem. Parl. (Vlaamse Liberalen en Demokraten—VLD) for Tongeren-Maaseik Dist 1985–95, for Hasselt-Tongeren-Maaseik Constituency 1995–, Leader Liberal Party Group (VLD) 1992–99; Community Minister for Culture 1985–92; Mayor of Tongeren 1995–99; Minister-Pres. of Govt of Flanders 1999–2001, Minister of Govt of Flanders for Finance, Budget, Foreign Policy and European Affairs, Minister-Pres. of Govt of Flanders 2001–03; Deputy Prime Minister and Minister of the Interior 2003–07 (resgnd), reappointed Minister of Interior Dec. 2007, resgnd March 2008; Pres. Chamber of Reps 2008–. *Publications:* De warme hand 1991, Wederzijds respect. De gevaren van het Blok 2001, Vooruitzien 2001. *Address:* Chambre des Représentants, Place de la Nation, 1008 Brussels, Belgium (office). *Telephone:* (2) 549-81-36 (office). *Fax:* (2) 549-83-02 (office). *E-mail:* PRI@lachambre.be (office). *Website:* www.lachambre.be (office).

DEWEY, John Frederick, MA, PhD, DSc, ScD, FRS, FGS; British professor of geology; *Distinguished Professor, University of California, Davis;* b. 22 May 1937, London; s. of John Edward Dewey and Florence Nellie Mary Dewey; m. Frances Mary Blackhurst 1961; one s. one d.; ed Bancroft's School, Univ. of London; lecturer, Univ. of Manchester 1960–64, Univ. of Cambridge 1964–70; Prof. Univ. of Albany, NY 1970–82; Prof. Univ. of Durham 1982–86; Prof. of Geology, Univ. of Oxford 1986–2000, Fellow Univ. Coll. 1986–, Sr Research Fellow 2001–; Prof. of Geology, Univ. of Calif., Davis 2000–, Distinguished Prof. 2001–; mem. Academia Europaea 1990; Foreign mem. NAS 1997; T.N. George Medal, Univ. of Glasgow 1983, Lyell Medal, Geological Soc. of London 1984, Penrose Medal, Geological Soc. of America 1992, Arthur Holmes Medal, European Union of Geosciences 1993, Wollaston Medal, Geological Soc. of London 1999, Fourmarier Medal, Belgian Acad. of Sciences 2000. *Publications:* 138 papers in scientific journals. *Leisure interests:* skiing, tennis, cricket, model railways, watercolour painting, British, Irish and American music 1850–1950. *Address:* University College, Oxford, OX1 4BH, England; Department of Geology, One Shields Avenue, University of California, Davis, CA 95616-8605 (office); 748 Elmwood Drive, Davis, CA 95616, USA (home). *Telephone:* (530) 754-7472 (office); (530) 757-7519 (home). *Fax:* (530) 752-0951 (office). *E-mail:* dewey@geology.ucdavis.edu (office). *Website:* www.geology.ucdavis.edu (office).

DeWINE, R. Michael (Mike), BS, JD; American politician and academic; *Visiting Scholar, Center for Political Studies, Cedarville University;* b. 5 Jan. 1947, Springfield, Ohio; s. of Richard DeWine and Jean DeWine; m. Frances Struewing 1967; four s. four d.; ed Miami Univ., Oxford, Ohio and Ohio Northern Univ.; admitted to Bar, Ohio 1972, US Supreme Court 1977; Asst prosecuting attorney, Green County, Xenia, Ohio 1973–75, prosecuting attorney 1977–81; mem. Ohio Senate 1981–82; mem. US House of Reps 1983–90; Lt-Gov. of Ohio 1991–94; Senator from Ohio 1995–2007; Visiting Scholar, Center for Political Studies, Cedarville Univ. 2007; Republican. *Address:* Center for Political Studies, Cedarville University, 251 North Main Street, Cedarville, OH 45314 (office); 2587 Conley Road, Cedarville, OH 45314-9525, USA (home). *Telephone:* (937) 766-2783 (office). *Fax:* (937) 766-7583 (office). *Website:* www.cedarville.edu/centerforpoliticalstudies (office).

DEWOST, Jean-Louis; French academic and government official; *President, Commission nationale de contrôle des interceptions de sécurité (CNCIS);* b. 6 Sept. 1937, Dunkirk; s. of Emmanuel Dewost and Colette Ruyssen; m. Agnès Huet 1967; one s. two d.; ed Univ. de Paris, Inst. d'Etudes Politiques de Paris and Ecole Nat. d'Admin; jr official, Conseil d'Etat 1967–69; Asst Man. Industrial Affairs, European Org. for Devt and Construction of Space Vehicle Launchers (CECLES/ELDO) 1962–72, Dir Finance and Econ. Planning 1972–73; Maître des Requêtes, Conseil d'Etat 1972, Conseiller d'Etat 1986, Pres. de la Section Sociale, 2001–03; legal adviser EC Council Legal Service 1973–85, Jurisconsulte 1986–87; Dir-Gen. EC Legal Service 1987–2001; Pres. Comm. Nat. de contrôle des interceptions de sécurité (govt. admin. authority) 2003–; Prof., Inst. d'Etudes Politiques (Sciences Po), Paris; Officier, Légion d'honneur, Officier, Ordre nat. du Mérite, Grand Officier, Order of White Rose of Finland, Grand Officier Order of the Falcon of Iceland. *Publications:* several publs on French public law and EU law. *Leisure interests:* swimming, opera. *Address:* Commission nationale de contrôle des interceptions de sécurité, 35 rue Saint-Dominique, 75007 Paris (office); Sciences Po, 27 rue Saint-Guillaume, 75337 Paris Cedex 07 (office); 11 rue Sainte Anne, 75000, Paris, France (home). *Telephone:* 1-45-55-70-20 (office); 1-45-49-50-50 (office). *Fax:* 1-45-55-71-15 (office); 1-42-22-31-26 (office).

DEXTER, (Norman) Colin, OBE, MA (Cantab.), MA (Oxon.); British author; b. 29 Sept. 1930, Stamford, Lincs.; s. of Alfred Dexter and Dorothy Dexter (née Towns); m. Dorothy Cooper 1956; one s. one d.; ed Stamford School, Christ's Coll., Cambridge; nat. service (Royal Signals) 1948–50; taught Classics 1954–66; Sr Asst Sec. Oxford Delegacy of Local Examinations 1966–88; Fellow, St Cross Coll., Oxford; Gold Dagger, Crime Writers' Asscn (twice), Silver Dagger (twice), Cartier Diamond Dagger, Freedom of the City of Oxford 2001. *Publications:* Last Bus to Woodstock 1975, Last Seen Wearing 1977, The Silent World of Nicholas Quinn 1977, Service of All the Dead 1979, The Dead of Jericho 1981, The Riddle of the Third Mile 1983, The Secret of Annexe 3 1986, The Wench is Dead 1989, The Jewel that Was Ours 1991, The Way through the Woods 1992, Morse's Greatest Mystery and Other Stories 1993, The Daughters of Cain 1994, Death is Now my Neighbour 1996, The Remorseful Day 1999. *Leisure interests:* reading, music, crosswords (fmr nat. crossword champion). *Address:* 456 Banbury Road, Oxford, OX2 7RG, England.

DHALIWAL, Daljit, MA; British journalist; b. London; m. Lee Patrick Sullivan (divorced); ed Univ. of East London, Univ. of London; reporter for BBC, London 1990, NI Corresp. and Anchor, BBC World –1995; reporter ITN, London 1995, Anchor, World News for Public TV, Channel 4 News and World Focus –2001; Anchor, Your World Today and World Report CNN (Cable Network News) Int., Atlanta, Ga USA 2002–04; Anchor, Wide Angle (Public Broadcasting System), New York, 2002, 2006–07, Anchor, Global Watch 2008, host, Foreign Exchange with Daljit Dhaliwal 2008–; moderator and host, UN confs in New York and The Hague; Judge, Amnesty Int. Media Awards, BAFTA Awards; Dr hc (Univ. of East London). *Address:* c/o Thirteen/WNET, 450 West 33rd Street, New York, NY 10001, USA (office). *E-mail:* info@foreignexchange.tv (office). *Website:* foreignexchange.tv (office).

DHANABALAN, Suppiah, BA; Singaporean company director and fmr government official; *Chairman, Temasek Holdings (Pte.) Ltd;* b. 8 Aug. 1937; m. Tan Khoon Hiap 1963; one s. one d.; ed Victoria School and Univ. of Malaya; Asst Sec. Ministry of Finance 1960–61; Sr Industrial Economist, Deputy Dir (Operations and Finance) Econ. Devt Bd 1961–68; Vice-Pres., Exec. Vice-Pres. Devt Bank of Singapore (now DBS Group Holdings Ltd) 1968–78, Chair. 1998–2005; mem. Parl. 1976–96; Sr Minister of State, Ministry of Nat. Devt 1978–79, Ministry of Foreign Affairs 1979–80; Minister of Foreign Affairs 1980–88, Culture 1981–84, Community Devt 1984–86, Nat. Devt 1987–92, of Trade and Industry 1992–93; Chair. Parameswara Holdings 1994–; Sr Adviser, Nuri Holdings (S) Pte. Ltd 1994–99; Chair. Singapore Airlines Ltd 1996–98; Chair. Temasek Holdings (Pte.) Ltd (govt-owned investment co.) 1996–. *Leisure interests:* reading, golf. *Address:* Temasek Holdings (Pte) Ltd, 60B Orchard Road, #06-18, Tower 2, The Atrium at Orchard, Singapore 238891, Singapore (office). *Telephone:* 68286828 (office). *Fax:* 68211188 (office). *Website:* www.temasekholdings.com.sg (office).

DHANAPALA, Jayantha, BA, MA; Sri Lankan diplomatist and consultant; *President, Pugwash Conferences on Science and World Affairs;* b. 30 Dec. 1938, Colombo; s. of James Angus and Kumarihamy Dhanapala Ratemahatmaya; m. Maureen Elhart; one s. one d.; ed Univ. of Peradeniya, Univ. of London, UK, American Univ., Washington, DC, USA; corp. exec. in pvt. sector 1962–65; joined Sri Lankan Foreign Service 1965, diplomatic appointments in People's Repub. of China, UK and USA 1965–77; Dir Non-Aligned Movt Div., Ministry of Foreign Affairs 1978–80, Additional Foreign Sec. 1992–95; Deputy High Commr to India 1981–83; Amb. and Perm. Rep. to UN, Geneva, Switzerland 1984-87, Dir UN Inst. for Disarmament Research 1987–92; Amb. to USA (also accred to Mexico) 1995–97; UN Under-Sec.-Gen. for Disarmament Affairs 1998–2003; Sec.-Gen. Secr. for Co-ordinating the Peace Process 2004–05 (resgnd); Chief Negotiator in talks with LTTE 2004–05, Sr Adviser to Pres. 2004–07; Visiting Simons Prof., Simon Fraser Univ., Vancouver, Canada 2008; Pres. Review and Extension Conf. of Treaty on the Non-Proliferation of Nuclear Weapons 1995, Pugwash Confs on Science and World Affairs 2007–; Rep. of UN to Conf. on Disarmament; mem. Canberra Comm., Australia; Diplomat-in-Residence, Center for Non-Proliferation Studies, Monterey Inst. of Int. Studies, Calif., USA; Chair. UN Univ. Council 2007–08; Chair., Governing Bd Stockholm Int. Peace Research Inst. (SIPRI); mem. Int. Weapons of Mass Destruction Comm., Int. Advisory Group ICRC, Geneva Centre for Democratic Control of Armed Forces, Advisory Council of Stanford Inst. for Int. Studies, Int. Bd of Bonn Int. Center for Conversion, Int. Advisory Bd Center for Nonproliferation Studies, Monterey Inst. of Int. Studies; Hon. Pres. Int. Peace Bureau; Dr hc (Univ. of Peradeniya) 2000, (Sabaragamuwa Univ.) 2003; Hon. DHumLitt (Monterey Inst. of Int. Studies) 2001; Hon. DSc in Social Sciences (Univ. of Southampton) 2003; 'Jit' Trainor Award for Distinction in the Conduct of Diplomacy, Sri Lankan of the Year, (Lanka Monthly Digest) 2006, Sean MacBride Peace Prize 2007. *Publications include:* China and the Third World 1984, Nuclear War, Nuclear Proliferation and Their Consequences (co-author) 1985, Multilateral Diplomacy and the NPT: An Insider's Account 2005. *Leisure interests:* reading, watching sports, theatre and film. *Address:* 25/6 Pepiliyana Road, Nugegoda, Sri Lanka (home). *Telephone:* (11) 2856297 (home). *E-mail:* jdhanapala@yahoo.co.uk (office). *Website:* www.jayanthadhanapala.com (home).

DHANARAJAN, Dato' Gajaraj (Raj), PhD; Malaysian educationist; ed Univ. of Madras, India, Univ. of London, Univ. of Aston, UK; Research Officer and Lecturer, School of Biological Sciences, Univ. of Science, Malaysia, Assoc. Prof. of Distance Educ. and Deputy Dir Centre for Off-Campus Studies; Assoc. Dir (Academic) Open Learning Inst. of Hong Kong (now Open Univ. of Hong Kong) 1989–91, Dir 1991–95, Prof. 1992–95, Prof. Emer. 1995–; Pres. and CEO The Commonwealth of Learning, Vancouver 1995–; fmr Sec.-Gen. Asian Asscn of Open Univs; fmr educational adviser, Int. Union for the Conservation of Nature; Hon. Fellow Coll. of Preceptors, London 1996–; several hon. degrees; Asian Asscn of Open Univs Meritorious Service Award 1997; Order of Chivalry, State of Penang 1994. *Address:* The Commonwealth of Learning, 1285 West Broadway, Suite 600, Vancouver, BC, V6H 3X8, Canada (office). *Telephone:* (604) 775-8200 (office). *Fax:* (604) 775-8210 (office). *E-mail:* gdhan@col.org (office). *Website:* www.col.org/gdhan (office).

DHAR, Bansi; Indian business executive; b. 7 March 1930, Delhi; s. of the late Murli Dhar and Swaroop Devi; m. 1st Urmila Bansidhar 1953 (deceased); m. 2nd Suman Bansidhar 1976; three s.; ed Delhi Univ., Harvard Univ., USA; trainee, Eng Dept DCM Ltd 1952, various man. appointments, Chair. of Bd and Man. Dir DCM Shriram Industries Ltd 1990–; Chair. Bd Daurala Organics Ltd, Indital Tintoria Ltd, DCM Hyundai Ltd, Hindustan Vacuum Glass Ltd, DCM Remy Ltd; mem. Bd Dirs of several cos; mem. Exec. Cttee, Fed. Indian Chambers of Commerce and Industry (and fmr Pres.), Indian Chemical Mfrs Asscn; Vice-Chair. Shriram Scientific and Industrial Research Foundation; Dir Indian Trade Promotion Org.; Chair. Delhi Asscn of the Deaf; Pres. Delhi Badminton Asscn; fmr Pres. All India Org. of Employers, Indian

Sugar Mills Asscn, Delhi Factory Owners Asscn, Indian Council of Arbitration; Fellow All India Man. Asscn Indian Inst. of Chemical Engineers; Hon. DLitt (Agra). *Leisure interests:* badminton, gardening, philately, photography, Indian classical music, theatre, bridge. *Address:* DCM Shriram Industries Ltd, Kanchenjunga Building, 18 Barakhamba Road, New Delhi 110001 (office); 27 Sardar Patel Marg., New Delhi 110021, India (home). *Telephone:* (11) 3314641 (office); (11) 6113472 (home). *Fax:* (11) 3315424 (office); (11) 6875715 (home). *E-mail:* shriram@del2.vsnl.net.in (office).

D'HAUTERIVES, Arnaud Louis Alain; French artist; b. 26 Feb. 1933, Braine (Aisne); s. of Louis and Germaine (née Hincelin) d'Hauterives; m. Renée Delhaye 1959; two s. one d.; ed Ecole des Beaux Arts, Reims, Ecole Supérieure des Beaux Arts, Paris; started painting as a career 1957; illustrator of some art books; Jt Pres. Soc. Int. des Beaux Arts 1985, Hon. Pres. La Critique Parisienne 1984–; Pres. Acad. des Beaux Arts 1987–92, Life Sec. 1996–; mem. Inst. de France (Vice-Pres. 1987), Acad. des Sciences d'outre mer, Russian Acad. of Fine Arts (Dir 1998–); exhbns in France, Belgium, USA, China, Japan, Italy, Spain, USSR; academician Académie Royale des Beaux Arts de San Fernando; mem. Académie de Marseille; Hon. mem. Cercle de Lamer; Officier Légion d'honneur, des Palmes Académiques, Officier Ordre nat. du Mérite, Ordre des Arts et des Lettres; Premier Grand Prix de Rome 1957, Prix de la Critique 1967. *Leisure interests:* lithography, gliding. *Address:* c/o Académie des Beaux Arts, 23 Quai de Conti, 75006 Paris, France.

DHLAKAMA, Afonso Macacho Marceta; Mozambican politician; *President, Resistência Nacional Moçambicana (Renamo);* b. 1 Jan. 1953, Magunde; Chief of Logistics for Sofala Prov. of Forças Populares de Libertaçao de Moçambique 1975–77; Vice-Pres. Resistência Nacional Moçambicana (Renamo) (also known as Movimento Nacional de Resistência de Moçambique, fmr guerrilla group founded in 1976, in conflict with Govt 1976–82, obtained legal status 1994) and Vice-C-in-C of its armed forces 1977–79, Pres. and C-in-C 1979–92, Pres. of Renamo 1992–; presidential cand. 2004. *Address:* Resistência Nacional Moçambicana (Renamo), Avda Julius Nyerere 2541, Maputo, Mozambique (office). *Telephone:* (1) 493107 (office).

DHLOMO, Oscar Dumisani, DEd; South African politician; b. 28 Dec. 1943, Umbumbulu, Natal; s. of the late Isaac Dhlomo; m. Nokukhanya V. Ntshingila 1966; three s. one d.; ed Sibusiswe Secondary School, Amanzimtoti Coll., Univ. of SA and Univ. of Zululand; teacher, Umlazi 1967–72; secondary school headmaster, Umlazi 1973–74; Lecturer in Educ., Univ. of Zululand 1974–77; mem. KwaZulu Legislative Ass. 1978–90; Sec.-Gen. Inkatha 1978–90; Minister of Educ. and Culture, KwaZulu Govt –1990; First Chair. KwaZulu Nat. Jt Exec. Authority 1988–89; Chair. Bd KwaZulu Training Trust, Emandleni-Matleng Training Camp; Co-Convenor, KwaZulu-Natal Indaba, Chair. 1988–90; Dir Devt Bank of Southern Africa 1990–; Founder, Exec. Chair. Inst. for Multiparty Democracy 1991–; Dir Standard Bank Investment Corpn 1991–, Anglovaal Ltd 1991–, The Natal Witness Printing and Publishing Co. (Pty) Ltd 1991–, Shell SA (Pty) Ltd 1992–, Southern Life 1994– and several other cos; mem. Buthelezi Comm. 1982. *Publications:* co-author of two books on social studies, educ. papers. *Leisure interests:* music, reading. *Address:* c/o Development Bank of Southern Africa, 1258 Lever Road, Midrand, PO Box 1234, Halfway House 1685 (office); Private Bag X04, Ulundi 3838, South Africa. *Website:* www.dbsa.org (office).

DHOLAKIA OF WALTHAM BROOKS, Baron (Life Peer), cr. 1997, of Waltham Brooks in the Co. of West Sussex Navnit Dholakia, OBE, DL, BSc; British politician; *Deputy Leader, Liberal Democrats Peers;* b. 4 March 1937, Tabora, Tanganyika (now Tanzania); m.; two d.; ed P. P. Inst., Bhavnagar, Gujerat, India, Brighton Tech. Coll., UK; fmr magistrate, mem. Bd of Visitors, HM Prison Lewes; mem. House of Lords 1997–, Asst Whip (Liberal Democrat) 1997–2002, Jt Deputy Leader, Liberal Democrat Peers 2004–; Deputy Lt W Sussex 1999; Pres. Liberal Democrat party 1999, 2002, Spokesperson on Home Affairs; Pres. Nat. Asscn for the Care and Resettlement of Offenders (NACRO); mem. Council, Howard League for Penal Reform; mem. Governing Body, Commonwealth Inst.; mem. Man. Bd, Policy Research Inst. on Ageing and Ethnicity; mem. House of Lord Appointments Comm.; Vice-Pres. Mental Health Foundation, Pallant House Gallery, Chichester, British Empire and Commonwealth Museum, Bristol; Asian of the Year 2000, Bhartiya Samman Award (India) 2003. *Publications:* various articles on criminal justice matters. *Leisure interests:* photography, cooking, gardening, walking. *Address:* House of Lords, London, SW1A 0PW, England (office). *Telephone:* (20) 7219-5203 (office); (20) 8686-0444 (home). *Fax:* (20) 7219-3423 (office). *E-mail:* dholakian@parliament.uk (office).

DHUMAL, Prem Kumar; Indian politician and government official; *Chief Minister of Himachal Pradesh;* b. 10 April 1944, Samirpur, Hamirpur; s. of Capt. Mahant Ram; m. Smt. Sheela Devi 1972; ed Punjab Univ., Chandigarh, Guru Nanak Dev Univ., Amritsar; lectured at pvt. coll. in Punjab before joining Bhartiya Janata Yuva Morcha (BJYM) and becoming its Vice-Pres. 1982; associated with many social orgs, including Bharat Vikas Parishad, Vivekanand Memorial Soc. and Himachal Hitkarini Sabha; State Sec. BJYM 1980, Vice-Pres. 1982–85; Gen. Sec. Bharatiya Janata Party (BJP) 1985–93, Pres. BJP 1993–98; contested parl. election 1984, elected MP to Lok Sabha (BJP) for Hamirpur constituency 1989, 1991, 2007, mem. Consultative Cttee Union Ministry of Communications 1989–96, Standing Cttee for Transport and Tourism and Railway Convention Cttee 1991–96, Nat. Council for Teachers' Educ. 1993–96, Alt. Chair. Estimates Cttee of Lok Sabha 1989–91; fmr Indian Rep. in Int. Parl. Union; Leader of Opposition in Himachal Pradesh State Legis. Ass. 2003–07; Chief Minister of Himachal Pradesh 1998–2003, 2007–. *Leisure interests:* reading, writing short stories and articles for newspapers and magazines, listening to music. *Address:* 301 Himachal Sadan, Sardar Patel Marg, New Delhi (office); Village and PO Samirpur, Teh. Bhoranj, Hamirpur Dist, 177601, Himachal Pradesh, India. *Telephone:* (11) 24108878 (office); (98) 68180104 (mobile); (1972) 275060. *Website:* himachal .gov.in (office); premkumardhumal.com.

DI MONTEZEMOLO, Luca Cordero, LLM; Italian automotive industry executive; *Chairman, Fiat SpA;* b. 31 Aug. 1947, Bologna; s. of Massimo and Clotilde Cordero Lanza dei Marchese di Montezemolo; m. 1st Sandra Monteleoni (divorced); one s.; one d. (with Barbara Parodi); m. 2nd Ludovica Andreoni 2000; two d.; ed Univ. of Rome, Columbia Univ., New York, USA; began career working with the Chiomenti law firm, Rome, later joined Bergreen & Bergreen, New York; Team Man., Ferrari Formula One Racing Team and Asst to Chair. Enzo Ferrari 1973–77; Dir Public Affairs Dept, Fiat Group 1977–81; CEO ITEDI SpA (holding co. for Fiat Group's publishing interests) 1981–83; CEO Cinzano Int. SpA 1984–86; Gen. Man. Italia '90 Football World Cup Organising Cttee 1986–90; CEO RCS Video and Chair. RCS Home Video 1990–91; Chair. and CEO Ferrari SpA 1991–2006, Chair. 2006–; Chair. and CEO Maserati SpA 1997–2005; Chair. Fiat SpA 2004–; Pres. Confindustria 2004–08; mem. Bd of Dirs Pinault-Printemps-Redoute, La Stampa, Tod's, Poltrona Frau; Chair. Italian Asscn of Newspaper Publrs 2001–, Confindustria (Italian Employers' Asscn) 2004–; Pres. Modena Business and Industry Asscn 1996–2002, Bologna Int. Fair Org.; Pres. LUISS (Libera Università Internazionale degli Studi Sociali— Ind. Int. Univ. of Social Sciences), NTV (Nuovo Trasporto Viaggiatori), Industrialists of the Prov. of Modena 1996–2002, FIEG (Federazione Italiana Editori Giornali—Italian Newspaper Publrs Asscn) –2004; Vice-Pres. UNICE; mem. Gen. Council and Exec. Cttee Assonime; mem. Int. Advisory Bd Citi Inc.; Founder Charme (financial-entrepreneurial fund); Cavaliere del Lavoro, Chevalier, Légion d'honneur 2005; Hon. BEng (Modena Univ.) 2001, hon. degree in Business Man. (Univ. of Genoa) 2001, hon. degree in Industrial Design (Politecnico of Milan) 2001; voted Man of the Year by The Automobile magazine (USA), by Autocar magazine 2002, named by The Financial Times as one of the 50 Best Managers in the World. *Address:* Fiat SpA, 250 Via Nizza, 10126 Turin, Italy (office). *Telephone:* (011) 0061111 (office). *Fax:* (011) 0063798 (office). *E-mail:* info@fiatgroup.com (office). *Website:* www.fiatgroup .com (office).

DI PAOLA, Adm. Giampaolo; Italian naval officer; *Chairman of the Military Committee, NATO;* b. 15 Aug. 1944, Torre Annunziata, Naples; m. Roberta di Paola; two d.; ed Naval Acad., Submarine School, NATO Defence Coll., Rome; served aboard conventional submarines Gazzana and Piomarta 1968–74; Commdr submarines Cappellini 1974–75, Sauro 1980–81; served as ASW and Undersea Warfare Programme Officer, Long Term Planning Br., SACLANT, Norfolk, Va, USA 1981–84; CO frigate Grecale 1984–86; Plans and Programmes Br. Chief, Gen. and Financial Planning Div., Navy Staff, Rome 1986–89; Capt. CO aircraft carrier Garibaldi 1989–90; Exec. Asst. to Deputy Chief of Staff 1990–91; Chief of Naval Plans and Policy Br., Plans and Operations Div. 1991–92; Asst Chief of Staff for Plans and Operations 1993–94; Chief of Mil. Policy Div. 1994–98; Chief of the Cabinet, Ministry of Defence 1998–2001; Sec.-Gen. of Defence and Nat. Armaments Dir 2001–04; Chief of Defence Staff March 2004–08; Chair. NATO Mil. Cttee, Brussels 2008–; apptd Rear Adm. 1997, Adm. 2004; Kt Grand Cross Order of Merit (Italy), Commdr Ordre Nat. du Mérite (France), Kt Commdr Order of St Gregory the Great, Grand Cross with Swords Order of Merit of Malta, Kt of the Grand Cross of Merit of the Sacred Constantine Mil. Order of San Giorgio, Grand Officer Order of Infante Don Enrico (Portugal), Commdr Legion of Merit (USA), Commdr de la Légion d'honneur (France); Medal of the Order of St Maurice, Meritorious Long Command Gold Medal, Distinguished Award for Submariners, Sr Service Gold Cross, Bronze Medal for Sea-Duty Service in the Navy, Commemorative Medal of Sovereign Mil. Hospitaller Order of St John of Jerusalem, of Rhodes and of Malta, UN Medal for UN Peacekeeping Mission in Kosovo. *Address:* Office of the Chairman of the Military Committee, NATO Headquarters, Blvd Leopold III, 1110 Brussels, Belgium (office). *Telephone:* (2) 707-41-11 (office). *Fax:* (2) 707-45-79 (office). *E-mail:* natodoc@ hq.nato.int (office). *Website:* www.nato.int (office).

DI PIETRO, Antonio; Italian lawyer and politician; *President, Italia dei Valori;* b. 2 Oct. 1950, Montenero di Bisaccia; m. 1st Isabella Ferrara; one s.; m. 2nd Susanna Mazzoleni 1995; ed Statale Univ. Milan, Pavia Univ.; studied law at evening classes; fmr factory hand, Germany; fmr police officer; fmr magistrate, Bergamo; Prosecutor, Milan 1984–94; uncovered bribery of officials in Milan 1992, led Operation Clean Hands exposing high levels of political corruption in Italy 1992–94; Chair. Penal Rights in Economy, Libero Istituto Universitario di Castellanza 1995–96; consultant, Parl. Comm. on Slaughter, on Co-operation with Developing Countries 1995–96; Minister of Public Works 1996–97; elected to Senate 1997; mem. European Parl. 1999–, Chair. Euro Parl. Del. for relations with S America, Cen. Asia and SA; Founder and Exec. Pres. Italia dei Valori party 2000–; Minister of Infrastructures 2006–08; i p Dr hc (Thrace Univ., Greece) 1995. *Publications:* Memoria 1999, Intervista su Tangentopoli 2000, Mani Pulite–La Vera Storia 2002. *Address:* Sede Nazionale, Italia dei Valori, Via Santa Maria in Via 12, 00187 Rome, Italy. *Telephone:* (06) 97848144 (office). *E-mail:* antoniodipietro@ antoniodipietro.com (office). *Website:* www.antoniodipietro.com (office); italiadeivalori.antoniodipietro.com (office).

DI ROSA, Antonio, BSc; Italian journalist; *Editor, La Gazzetta;* b. 17 April 1951, Messina; s. of Calogero Rossetti and Anna Rossetti; partner; one s. two d.; began career at Giornale di Calabria 1974–78; moved to Gazzetta del Popolo 1978, Deputy Head Home News 1979–81, Head 1981–84; joined La Stampa 1984, Head Home News April–July 1988; Deputy Cen. Ed.-in-Chief Corriere della Sera 1988–93, Cen. Ed.-in-Chief 1993–96, Deputy Ed. 1996–2000; Ed. Il Secolo XIX 2000; Ed. La Gazzetta dello Sport 2004–; Premio Senigallia 1983. *Leisure interests:* books, cinema, travel. *Address:* Gazzetta dello Sport, Via Solferino 28, 20121 Milan (office); Via G. Morelli 1,

Milan, Italy (home). *Telephone:* (02) 62828024 (office). *Fax:* (02) 62827917 (office). *E-mail:* adirosa@rcs.it (office). *Website:* www.gazzetta.it (office).

DI RUPO, Elio, DSc; Belgian politician; *President, Socialist Party and Minister-President of Wallonia;* b. 1951, Morlanwelz; ed Univ. of Mons; researcher, Chef de Cabinet, Budget and Energy Minister, Walloon Region 1982–85; Communal Councillor, Mons 1982–2000; MP 1987–89, MEP 1989–1991; Pres. of Energy Comm.; Senator 1991–95; Minister of Educ. 1992–94, Deputy Prime Minister and Minister of Communications and Public Enterprises 1994–95, Deputy Prime Minister and Minister for Economy and Telecommunications 1995–99; Minister-Pres. of Wallonia 1999–2000, 2005–; Mayor of Mons 2001–; Pres. Socialist Party (PS) 2000–. *Address:* Parti Socialiste, 13 boulevard de l'Empereur, 1000 Brussels, Belgium (office). *Telephone:* (2) 548-32-11 (office). *Fax:* (2) 548-33-90 (office). *E-mail:* elio@dirupo.net (office). *Website:* www.ps.be (office).

DIAB, Rashid, MFA, PhD; Sudanese artist and gallery director; *Director, Medani Galeria;* b. 1957, Wad Medani, Gezira Prov.; ed School of Fine and Applied Arts, Khartoum, Complutense Univ., Madrid, Spain; currently Owner and Dir, Medani Galería, Madrid; has participated in over twenty solo exhbns in Africa, Europe, and Middle E; f. and Dir Dara Art Gallery, Khartoum 1999–; toured northern deserts of Sudan 2000; artistic adviser for presidential palace and govt offices, Sudan; winner of art prizes in Cuba and Taiwan. *Address:* Medani Galería, Madrid, Spain (office).

DIABRÉ, Zéphirin, MBA, PhD; Burkinabè international civil servant; b. 26 Aug. 1959, Ouagadougou; ed Ecole Supérieure de Commerce, Bordeaux, France, Univ. of Bordeaux; Prof. of Business Admin. 1987–89; Man. Dir Burkina Brewery 1989–92; Minister for Trade, Industry and Mining 1992–94, for Economy, Finance and Planning 1994–96; Chair. Council of Econ. and Social Affairs 1996–97; Visiting Scholar, Harvard Inst. for Int. Devt, Fellow of Weatherhead Center for Int. Affairs, USA 1997–98; Assoc. Admin. UNDP, New York 1999–2006; Officier, Ordre nat. du Mérite, Burkina Faso, Chevalier, Légion d'honneur. *Address:* c/o Ministry of Foreign Affairs and Regional Co-operation, rue 988, blvd du Faso, 03 BP 7038, Ouagadougou 03, Burkina Faso.

DIACK, Lamine; Senegalese international sports official and politician; *President, International Association of Athletics Federations (IAAF);* b. 7 June 1933; m.; 15 c.; long jump record holder, France and W Africa 1957–60; football coach, Foyer France Senegal football team 1963–64; Pres. African Amateur Athletic Confed. (AAAC) 1963–64; Technical Dir Senegal Nat. Football Team 1964–68; Gen. Commr for State Sport 1969–70, Sec. of State for Youth and Sport 1970–73; mem. Exec. Cttee Supreme Council for Sport in Africa (SCSA) 1973–87; Pres. ASC DIARAAF football team 1974–78, 1994–; mem. Nat. Olympic Cttee of Senegal 1974–, Pres. 1985–; Gen. Sec. Senegalese Athletic Fed. 1974–78, Pres. 1974–78, Hon. Pres. 1978–; mem. Int. Olympic Cttee 1999–; Vice-Pres. Int. Asscn of Athletics Feds (IAAF) 1976–91, Sr Vice-Pres. 1991–99, Pres. 1999–; Chair. City Council (Mayor) of Dakar 1978–80; mem. Nat. Ass. of Senegal (Parl.) 1988–93, Sr Vice-Pres. (Deputy Speaker) 1988–93; Chief Insp. of Taxes and State Property 1995–2001; Chair. Bd Soc. Nat. des Eaux (SONES) 1995–2001; numerous honours, including Grand Cordon of the Order of the Rising Sun (Japan), Grand Officier de l'Etoile Equatoriale (Gabon), Commdr Order of Good Hope (S. Africa), Chevalier, Légion d'honneur, Chevalier de l'Ordre Nat. du Lion (Senegal), Officiale di Grancroce (Italy), Officier de la Médaille de la Reconnaissance Centrafricaine, Médaille de l'Ordre du Nil de la République Arabe d'Egypte, Bernardo O'Higgins Medal, 1st Degree (Chile), Order of the Officer Cross Budapest (Hungary), Olympic Order, IAAF Order of Merit, ACNO Order of Merit, SCSA Order of Merit, CAF Order of Merit. *Address:* Office of the President, International Association of Athletics Federations, 17 rue Princesse Florestine, BP 359, MC 98007, Monaco (office). *Telephone:* 9310888 (office). *Fax:* 93159515 (office). *E-mail:* president@iaaf.org (office). *Website:* www.iaaf.org (office).

DIACONESCU, Cristian, LLB; Romanian judge and politician; *Minister of Foreign Affairs;* b. 2 July 1959, Bucharest; m.; one c.; ed Univ. of Bucharest; judge, Court of Ilfov Agricultural Sector 1983–1985, Court of Bucharest Fourth Dist and Tribunal of Bucharest 1985–1989; Inspector, Ministry of Justice 1989–90; mem. Perm. Mission to OSCE, then Perm. Mission to Int. Orgs, Vienna 1990–96; mem. OSCE Directorate, Ministry of Foreign Affairs 1996–97, Dir 1997, Gen. Dir, Gen. Directorate for Judicial and Consular Affairs 1998; Deputy Sec. Black Sea Org. for Econ. Cooperation 2000; Sec. of State for Bilateral Affairs, Ministry of Foreign Affairs 2000–04; mem. Senate 2004–; Minister of Justice 2004, of Foreign Affairs 2008–; Assoc. Prof., Chair of Int. Public Law, Hyperion Univ. 1993; mem. Nat. Defence Coll. Foundation 1995–, Prof. 1997–; Prof., Human Rights Inst. 1998–2000. *Address:* Ministry of Foreign Affairs, 011822 Bucharest, Al. Alexandru 31, Romania (office). *Telephone:* (21) 3192108 (office). *Fax:* (21) 3196862 (office). *E-mail:* mae@mae.ro (office). *Website:* www.mae.ro (office).

DIALLO, Cellou Dalein; Guinean economist and politician; b. 1953; worked at Cen. Bank of Guinea before joining ministerial cabinet of Pres. Lansan Conté in 1995; served for several years as Minister of Public Works, later Minister of Fisheries –2004; Prime Minister of Guinea 2004–06. *Address:* c/o Office of the Prime Minister, Conakry, Guinea (office).

DIALLO, Claude Absa, BA; Senegalese diplomatist; *Secretary-General, Ministry of Foreign Affairs;* b. 21 March 1942, Hanoi, Viet Nam; ed Univ. of Dakar and Nat. School of Admin., Senegal; Head of Geographical Div. Office of Political, Cultural and Social Affairs, Ministry of Foreign Affairs 1964; Adviser, Office of Minister for Foreign Affairs 1965–72; Minister-Counsellor, Bonn (also accred to Austria and Switzerland) 1972–77; Perm. Del. of Senegal at UNESCO 1977–80; roving Amb. 1980–81; Dir of Political and Cultural Affairs, Ministry of Foreign Affairs 1981–88; Perm. Rep. to UN, New York 1988–91, to UN Security Council 1988–89; Chair. UN Cttee on the Exercise of the Inalienable Rights of the Palestinian People 1988–91; UN ad hoc Cttee on Cambodia 1988–90; Amb. to Sweden 1992–93, to Norway 1993, to Russia 1993–95 (also accred to Bulgaria, Romania, Hungary, Ukraine, Poland, Czech Repub., Slovakia); Amb. and Perm. Rep. to UN and Other Int. Orgs, Geneva 1996–2002; Sec.-Gen. Ministry of Foreign Affairs 2006–; Chair. Bureau, World Conference Against Racism 2000. *Address:* Ministry of Foreign Affairs, place de l'Indépendance, BP 4044, Dakar, Senegal (office). *Telephone:* 33-889-1300 (office). *Fax:* 33-823-5496 (office). *E-mail:* maeuase@senegal.diplomatie.sn (office). *Website:* www.diplomatie.gouv.sn (office).

DIALLO, Gen. Mamadou Bailo; Guinean army officer; fmr Head of Ground Forces, Nat. Army of Guinea; Minister of Nat. Defence 2007–08. *Address:* c/o Ministry of National Defence, Camp Samory-Touré, Conakry, Guinea (office).

DIALLO NANDIGNA, Adiato; Guinea-Bissau politician; *Minister of Foreign Affairs;* Minister of Culture, Youth and Sport 2007–09, of Foreign Affairs 2009–. *Address:* Ministry of Foreign Affairs, International Co-operation and Communities, Rua Gen. Omar Torrijo, Guinea, Guinea-Bissau (office). *Telephone:* 204301 (office). *Fax:* 202378 (office).

DIAMANTOPOULOU, Anna; Greek politician and EU official; b. 1959, Kozani; m.; one c.; ed Aristotle Univ. of Thessaloniki, Panteion Univ. of Athens; civil engineer 1981–85; Lecturer, Insts of Higher Technological Educ. 1983–85; Man. Dir of regional devt co.; Prefect of Kastoria 1985–86; Sec.-Gen. for Adult Educ. 1987–88; Sec.-Gen. for Youth 1988–89; mem. Cen. Cttee of PASOK 1991–99; Pres. of Hellenic Org. of Small and Medium-Sized Enterprises and Handicrafts (EOMMEX); Sec.-Gen. for Industry 1994–96; mem. of Parl. 1996–99, 2004–; Deputy Minister for Devt 1996–99; EU Commr for Employment and Social Affairs 1999–2004; mem. Forum for Co-operation of Balkan Peoples, Int. Women's Network; Chevalier, Légion d'Honneur 2002. *Address:* Parliament Building, Syntagma Square, 101 80 Athens, Greece (office). *Telephone:* (21) 03288434 (office). *Fax:* (21) 03310013 (office). *E-mail:* infopar@parliament.gr (office). *Website:* www.parliament.gr (office).

DIAMOND, Abel J. (Jack), OC, MArch, DEng, FRAIC, ARIBA, RCA, MCIP, MAIP,; Canadian architect; *Principal and Founding Partner, Diamond and Schmitt Architects Inc.;* b. S. Africa; s. of Jacob Diamond and Rachel Zipporah Diamond (née Werner); m. Gillian Mary Huggins 1959; one s. one d.; ed Univs of Cape Town, Oxford, UK and Pennsylvania, USA; Asst Prof. of Architecture and Architectural Asst to Louis Kahn, Philadelphia 1963–64; Assoc. Prof., Univ. of Toronto 1964–69; Prof., Univ. of York 1969–72; Adjunct Prof., Univ. of Texas at Arlington 1980–81; Sr Pnr, A. J. Diamond, Donald Schmitt and Co. (now Diamond and Schmitt Architects Inc.) 1975–; Chair. Nat. Capital Comm., Design Advisory Comm., Ottawa; mem. Advisory Bd, School of Architecture, Univ. of Toronto 1987–; Commr Ont. Human Rights Comm. 1986–89; mem. Bd of Govs, Mount Sinai Hosp., Toronto 1987–; Graham Prof. of Architecture, Univ. of Pa 1996–; mem. Royal Acad. of Arts, Canada, RIBA, Canadian Inst. of Planners, American Inst. of Planners; Hon. FAIA; Hon. DEng (Dalhousie) 1996, Hon. LLD; numerous design prizes including Toronto Arts Award 1990, Royal Architectural Inst. Gold Medal 2001; Order of Ont. 1998. *Works include:* Ontario Medical Asscn HQ 1970, Univ. of Alberta Long Range Plan 1970, Alcan HQ Office, Toronto 1972, Montreal 1978, Cleveland 1982, Queen's Univ. Housing, Kingston, Ont. 1976, Citadel Theatre, Edmonton, Alberta 1976 (with B. Myers and R. L. Wilkin), Nat. Ballet School Stage Training Facility, Toronto 1983, Burns Bldg Renovation, Calgary 1983, Berkeley Castle Renovation, Toronto 1983, Metro Toronto Central YMCA 1984, Ont. Arts Council HQ Offices, Toronto 1985, Four Seasons HQ Offices, Toronto 1985, Imperial Theatre, St John, NB 1988, Earth and Sciences Center, Univ. of Toronto 1988, Curtiss Hall, Toronto 1988, Sunny Brook Hosp., Newcastle Town Hall 1989, York Univ. Student Centre 1991, Lois Hancsey Aquatic Center 1991, Jerusalem City Hall 1992, Richmond Hill Cen. Library 1992, HQ Toronto Historic Bd 1993, Israeli Foreign Ministry, Jerusalem 1996, 'Alumbrera', Mustique 2000, Garland House, Toronto. *Leisure interest:* watercolour painting. *Address:* Diamond and Schmitt Architects Inc., 384 Adelaide Street West, Suite 300, Toronto, ON, M5V 1R7, Canada (office). *Telephone:* (416) 862-8800 (office). *Fax:* (416) 862-5508 (office). *E-mail:* ajd@dsai.ca (office). *Website:* www.dsai.ca (office).

DIAMOND, Jared Mason, BA, PhD; American biologist, physiologist, academic and writer; *Professor of Geography and Physiology, David Geffen School of Medicine, University of California, Los Angeles;* b. 10 Sept. 1937, Boston, Mass; s. of Louis K. Diamond and Flora K. Diamond; m. Marie Nabel Cohen 1982; two s.; ed Harvard Coll., Univ. of Cambridge, UK; Fellow, Trinity Coll., Cambridge 1961–65, Jr Fellow, Soc. of Fellows, Harvard Univ. 1962–65; Assoc. in Biophysics, Harvard Medical School 1965–66; Assoc. Prof. of Physiology, David Geffen School of Medicine, Univ. of California Medical School, Los Angeles 1966–68, Prof. of Geography, UCLA 1968–; Research Assoc., Dept of Ornithology American Museum of Natural History 1973–; US Regional Dir World Wide Fund for Nature; mem. Editorial Bd Skeptic Magazine; mem. NAS; Fellow, American Acad. of Arts and Sciences, American Physiological Soc., Biophysics Soc., American Philosophical Soc., American Soc. of Naturalists, American Ornithologists Union 1978; Hon. DLitt (Sejong Univ., S Korea) 1995; Hon. PhD (Katholieke Universiteit Leuven, Belgium) 2008; Prize Fellowship in Physiology, Trinity Coll., Cambridge 1961–65, Lederle Medical Faculty Award 1968–71, Distinguished Teaching Award, UCLA Medical Class 1972, 1973, Distinguished Achievement Award, American Gastroenterological Asscn 1975, Kaiser Permanente/Golden Apple Teaching Award 1976, Nathaniel Bowditch Prize, American Physiological Soc. 1976, Franklin L. Burr Award, Nat. Geographic Soc. 1979, MacArthur Foundation 'Genius' Grant 1985, Archie Carr Medal 1989, MacArthur Foundation Fellow 1990, Tanner Lecturer, Univ. of Utah (and many other endowed lectureships) 1992, Royal Soc. Prizes for Science Books (Rhone-Poulenc Prize) 1992, 1998,

Science Book Prize, New Scientist London 1992, Los Angeles Times Science Book Prize 1992, Zoological Soc. of San Diego Conservation Medal 1993, Randi Award, Skeptics Soc. 1994, Faculty Research Lecturer, UCLA 1996, Phi Beta Kappa Science Book Prize 1997, Elliott Coues Award, American Ornithologists' Union 1998, Gold Medal in nonfiction, California Book Awards 1998, Nat. Medal of Sciences 1999, Lannan Literary Award for Nonfiction 1999, Tyler Prize for Environmental Achievement 2001, Lewis Thomas Prize for Writing about Science 2002, Dickson Prize in Science 2006. *Television:* Guns, Germs and Steel (three-part PBS documentary) 2005. *Publications:* The Avifauna of the Eastern Highlands of New Guinea 1972, Ecology and Evolution of Communities (co-ed.) 1975, Birds of Karkar and Bagabab Islands, New Guinea (co-author) 1979, The Avifaunas of Rennell and Bellona Islands. The Natural History of Rennell Islands, British Solomon Islands 1984, Community Ecology (co-author) 1985, Birds of New Guinea (co-author) 1986, The Third Chimpanzee: The Evolution and Future of the Human Animal 1992, 2006, Why is Sex Fun? – The Evolution of Human Sexuality 1997, Guns, Germs, and Steel: The Fates of Human Societies (Pulitzer Prize 1998, Cosmos Prize 1998) 1998, The Birds of Northern Melanesia: Speciation, Ecology, & Biogeography (co-author) 2001, Guns, Germs, and Steel Reader's Companion 2003, Collapse: How Societies Choose to Fail or Succeed 2004; several hundred research papers on physiology, ecology and ornithology; contribs to Discover, Natural History, Nature. *Address:* 1251A Bunche Hall, University of California at Los Angeles, Los Angeles, CA 90095-1524, USA (office). *Telephone:* (310) 825-6177 (office). *Fax:* (310) 206-5976 (office). *E-mail:* jdiamond@geog.ucla.edu (office). *Website:* 149.142.237.180/faculty/diamond .htm (office); www.geog.ucla.edu (office).

DIAMOND, Neil Leslie; American singer and composer; b. 24 Jan. 1941, Brooklyn, NY; m. Marcia Murphey 1975, two c. (and two c. from previous m.); ed New York Univ.; fmr songwriter for publishing co.; numerous tours worldwide, television and radio broadcasts; mem. SESAC. *Film scores:* Jonathan Livingston Seagull (Grammy Award) 1973, Every Which Way but Loose 1978, The Jazz Singer 1980; songs for many other films. *Film appearance:* The Jazz Singer 1980. *Recordings include:* albums: The Feel of Neil Diamond 1966, Just For You 1967, Velvet Gloves and Spit 1968, Brother Love's Travelling Salvation Show 1969, Touching You Touching Me 1969, Tap Root Manuscript 1970, Shilo 1970, Gold (live) 1970, Stones 1971, Hot August Night (live) 1972, Moods 1972, Serenade 1974, Beautiful Noise 1976, Love At The Greek (live) 1977, I'm Glad You're Here With Me Tonight 1977, Carmelita's Eyes 1978, You Don't Bring Me Flowers 1978, September Morn 1979, Voices Of Vista: Show # 200 1979, On The Way To The Sky 1981, Heartlight 1982, Song Sung Blue 1982, Primitive 1984, Headed For The Future 1986, Hot August Night II (live) 1987, The Best Years Of Our Lives 1989, Lovescape 1991, The Christmas Album 1992, Up On the Roof: Songs From The Brill Building 1993, The Christmas Album Vol. II 1994, Live In America 1994, Tennessee Moon 1996, Live In Concert 1997, The Movie Album: As Time Goes By 1998, Three Chord Opera 2001, 12 Songs 2005, Home Before Dark 2008. *Address:* c/o Columbia Records, Sony BMG, 550 Madison Avenue, New York, NY 10022, USA. *Website:* www.neildiamond.com.

DIANOV, Yevgeniy Mikhailovich; Russian physicist; *Director, Fibre Optics Research Centre, General Physics Institute, Russian Academy of Sciences;* b. 31 Jan. 1936, Tula; m. Helen Zagorovskaya 1968; one s. one d.; ed Moscow State Univ.; researcher, Lebedev Inst. USSR (now Russian) Acad. of Sciences 1960–72, Sr researcher 1972–80, Head of Lab. 1980–83; Head of Lab. Gen. Physics Inst. of USSR (now Russian) Acad. of Sciences 1983–85, Head of Dept of Gen. Physics 1985–88; Prof. Physical-Technical Inst. 1985–88; Deputy Dir of Gen. Physics Inst., Russian Acad. of Sciences 1988–93, Dir Fibre Optics Research Centre, Gen. Physics Inst. 1993–; Corresp. mem. USSR (now Russian) Acad. of Sciences 1987, mem. 1994; USSR State Prize 1974, Popov Prize, USSR Acad. of Sciences 1988, Russian Fed. State Prize 1998. *Publications:* over 500 papers on quantum electronics, fibre and integrated optics. *Leisure interests:* jogging, reading. *Address:* Fibre Optics Research Centre, General Physics Institute, RAS, 38 Vavilova Street, 119333 Moscow (office); Leninsky Prospekt 13, Apt. 139, 117071 Moscow, Russia (home). *Telephone:* (495) 135-74-49 (office); (495) 237-32-76 (home). *Fax:* (495) 135-81-39 (office); (502) 224-71-34. *E-mail:* dianov@fo.gpi.ru (office). *Website:* www .forc.gpi.ru (office).

DIARRA, Cheick Sidi; Malian diplomatist and UN official; *Under-Secretary-General and High Representative for the Least Developed Countries, Landlocked Developing Countries and Small Island Developing States, United Nations;* b. 31 May 1957, Kayes; m.; two c.; ed Dakar Univ.; joined civil service in 1981, assigned to Ministry of Foreign Affairs and Int. Co-operation, Legal Adviser 1987–88; First Counsellor, Perm. Mission to UN, New York 1989–93, Perm. Rep. to UN, New York 1993–2007; UN Under-Sec.-Gen. and High Rep. for the Least Developed Countries, Landlocked Developing Countries and Small Island Developing States; Chevalier de l'Ordre Nat. du Mali. *Address:* Office of the High Representative for the Least Developed Countries, Landlocked Developing Countries and Small Island Developing States, United Nations, Room S-770, New York, NY 10017, USA (office). *Telephone:* (212) 963-7778 (office). *Fax:* (917) 367-3415 (office). *E-mail:* OHRLLS-UNHQ@ un.org (office). *Website:* unohrlls.expressiondev.com (office).

DIARRA, Fatoumata Dembele, LLB; Malian judge and professor of law; *Judge, International Criminal Court;* b. 15 Feb. 1949, Koulikoro; m.; six c.; ed Ecole Nat. de la Magistrature, Paris, France, Ecole Nat. d'Admin, Bamako, Dakar Univ., Senegal; Investigative Judge, Jr Admin. Office, First Instance Tribunal of Bamako 1977–80; Trial Attorney, Office of the Prosecutor, Tribunal of Bamako 1980–81; Vice-Pres. Labour Court of Bamako 1981–82; Investigative Judge, Sr Investigation Office, Bamako 1984–86; Legis. Sec. Nat. Ass. of Mali 1986–91; Legal Adviser to Transition Cttee for the

Reinstallation of Republican Inst., Office of the Head of State 1991; Gen.-Dir Malian Office for Intellectual Property and Copyright 1991–93; Official Rep. of Office of the Commr for the Promotion of Women 1993–94; Appeal Court Adviser, Criminal Chamber 1994–96; Pres. Criminal Chamber, Bamako Appeal Court 1996–99; Nat. Dir Justice Admin 1999–2001; elected Judge Int. Criminal Tribunal for the Fmr Yugoslavia (ICTY) 2001; elected Judge Int. Criminal Court (ICC) 2003–; Prof. of Constitutional Law, Civil Law and Criminal Law, Cen. School for Industry, Trade and Admin (ECICA) 1986–91; Gen.-Sec. Asscn of Malian Women Lawyers 1986–88, Pres. 1988–95; Founding Pres. Legal Clinic for Women and Children Without Means 1993; Pres. Support Group for Legal Reform 1994, Observatory for the Rights of Women and Children (ODEF) 1995–, Legal Br. of Int. Council for French-speaking Women (CIFF) 1996–, Malian Electoral Support Network 1997–; Vice-Pres. Int. Fed. of Women with Legal Careers (FIFCJ) 1994–97, Fed. of African Women Lawyers (FJA) 1995–; mem. numerous working groups and parl. cttee on legal reform; Officier, Ordre nat. du Mali 2001. *Publications include:* numerous articles in professional journals on women's rights and int. law. *Address:* International Criminal Court, Maanweg 174, 2516 AB, The Hague, The Netherlands (office). *Telephone:* (70) 5158515 (office). *Fax:* (70) 5158555 (office). *E-mail:* pio@icc-cpi.int (office). *Website:* www.icc-cpi.int (office).

DIARRA, Seydou Elimane; Côte d'Ivoirian politician and diplomatist; b. 23 Nov. 1933; m.; ed Lycée Fénelon, La Rochelle, France; won scholarship to study agric. in France; researcher, Office de la recherche scientifique et technique d'outre-mer (Orstom) 1961; apptd Dir Centre national de la mutualité agricole 1962; Commercial Dir Caisse de stabilisation du café et du cacao (Caistab) 1965, Rep. of Caistab in London; fmr head of state-run agric. co-operation and insurance body, Abidjan; Pres., Dir-Gen. Saco et Chocodi 1985; fmr head of govt org. in charge of cocoa; fmr African Rep. to Int. Coffee Org.; fmr Amb. to Brazil, EU and UK; Chair. Chamber of Commerce and Industry, Côte d'Ivoire 1992; Minister of State, responsible for Governmental Co-ordination and the Planning of Devt Jan.–May 2000; Prime Minister of Côte d'Ivoire May–Oct. 2000 (resgnd), Jan. 2003–05. *Address:* c/o Office of the Prime Minister, Blvd Angoulvant, 01 BP 1533, Abidjan 01, Côte d'Ivoire (office).

DIAS, HE Cardinal Ivan; Indian ecclesiastic; *Prefect, Congregation for the Evangelization of Peoples;* b. 14 April 1936, Mumbai; ordained priest 1958; Bishop of Rusubisir with title of Archbishop 1982; Archbishop of Mumbai (fmrly Bombay) 1996–2006; cr. Cardinal 2001; Prefect, Congregation for the Evangelization of Peoples, Vatican City 2006–. *Address:* Congregation for Evangelization of Peoples, 48 Piazza di Spagna, 00187 Rome, Italy (office). *Telephone:* (06) 69879299 (office). *Fax:* (06) 69880118 (office). *E-mail:* cepsegreteria@evangel.va (office); bombaydiocese@vsnl.com (office). *Website:* www.vatican.va/roman_curia/congregations/cevang (office).

DIAS DA SILVA, Marluce; Brazilian business executive; Exec. at Mesbla SA 1986–91; joined TV Globo 1991, Dir Gen. Rede Globo de Televisão 1997–2002, returned as consultant to TV Globo; ranked by Fortune magazine amongst 50 Most Powerful Women in Business outside the US (38th) 2002. *Address:* c/o Net Serviços de Comunicação SA, Rua Verbo Divino 1356, 04719-002 São Paulo, Brazil. *Telephone:* (11) 51862606 (office). *Website:* www.globo.com (office).

DIAS DIOGO, Luisa, MEconSc; Mozambican politician; *Prime Minister;* b. 11 April 1958, Dist of Mágoè, Tete; d. of Luís João Diogo and Laura Atanásia Dias; m. António Albana Silva; two s. one d.; ed Univ. Eduardo Mondlane, Univ. of London, UK; joined Ministry of Planning and Finance 1980, with Dept of Econs and Investment 1980–84, Assoc. Head of Dept 1984–86, Programme Officer Study Dept 1986–89, Head, Dept of Budget 1989–92, Nat. Dir of Budget 1993–94; Programme Officer IBRD, Maputo 1994; Vice-Minister of Planning and Finance 1994–2000; Minister of Planning and Finance 2000–05; Prime Minister of Mozambique 2004–; mem. Comm. on Political Information 2000–; Alt. Gov. for the IMF and World Bank 1991; del. to numerous int. confs; ranked by Forbes magazine amongst 100 Most Powerful Women (73rd) 2004, (96th) 2005, (83rd) 2006, (89th) 2007. *Leisure interests:* reading, listening to music, spending time with family and friends. *Address:* Office of the Prime Minister, Praça da Marinha Popular, Maputo, Mozambique (office). *Telephone:* (1) 426861 (office). *Fax:* (1) 426881 (office). *E-mail:* dgpm.gov@teledata.mz (office). *Website:* www.mozambique.mz/governo/dnpo (office).

DIAS FERREIRA LEITE, Maria Manuela, BEcons; Portuguese economist and politician; b. 3 Dec. 1940, Lisbon; d. of Carlos Eugénio Dias Ferreira and de Julieta de Carvalho; ed Instituto Superior de Ciências Económicas e Financeiras, Tech. Univ. of Lisbon; researcher, Calouste Gulbenkian Foundation 1964–73; asst, Public Finance and Econs, Instituto Superior de Economia e Gestão 1966–79; Dir Dept of Statistics, Inst. of State Holdings 1975–77; Co-ordinator Finance Group, Research Bureau, Banco de Portugal 1977–86; Dir-Gen. Public Accounting, Ministry of Finance 1986–90; Sec. of State of Budget 1990–91; Sec. of State attached to Minister of Budget 1991–93; with Ministry of Educ. 1993–95; mem. Parl. 1991–95, 1995–2000; Vice-Pres. of Parl. Group, Social Democratic Party 1996–2001, Pres. Sept. 2001; Minister of State and of Finance 2002–04; consultant to Banco de Portugal 2004–; mem. Admin. Council, Banco Santander Totta 2006–. *Address:* c/o Banco de Portugal, Rua do Ouro 27, 1100-150 Lisbon; c/o Administrative Council, Banco Santander Totta, Rua de Ouro 88, 1100-061 Lisbon, Portugal. *E-mail:* info@bportugal.pt. *Website:* www.bportugal.pt; www.santandertotta.pt.

DIAZ, Cameron; American actress; b. 30 Aug. 1972, Long Beach, Calif.; d. of Emilio Diaz and Billie Diaz; fmr model; Boston Soc. of Film Critics Best Supporting Actress 2001, Chicago Film Critics Best Supporting Actress 2002.

Films include: The Mask 1994, The Last Supper 1995, Feeling Minnesota 1996, She's the One 1996, Head Above Water 1996, Keys to Tulsa 1997, My Best Friend's Wedding 1997, A Life Less Ordinary 1997, Fear and Loathing in Las Vegas 1997, There's Something About Mary 1998, Very Bad Things 1998, Being John Malkovich 1999, Invisible Circus 1999, Any Given Sunday 1999, Charlie's Angels 2000, Things You Can Tell Just by Looking at Her 2000, Shrek (voice) 2001, Vanilla Sky 2001, The Sweetest Thing 2002, Gangs of New York 2002, Charlie's Angels: Full Throttle 2003, Shrek II (voice) 2004, In Her Shoes 2005, The Holiday 2006, Shrek the Third (voice) 2007, What Happens in Vegas 2008. *Address:* c/o Creative Artists Agency, 2000 Avenue of the Stars, Los Angeles, CA 90067, USA.

DÍAZ, Francisco Gil, BSc, PhD; Mexican economist and government official; b. 2 Sept. 1943, Mexico City; ed Instituto Tecnológico Autónomo de México (ITAM), Univ. of Chicago, USA; Prof. and Co-ordinator, ITAM Econs Program 1970–76; Prof., Colegio de México 1970–84; 20 years as economist, Bank of Mexico, becoming Asst Dir and later Dir of Econ. Research; fmr Chief of Econ. Projections, Pres.'s Secr.; fmr Under-Sec. for Revenue and later Gen. Man. for Econ. and Financial Studies, Finance and Public Credit Secr., then Gen. Dir of Revenue Policy; fmr Gen. Man. Avantel SA (telecommunications co.); Sec. of State for Finance and Public Credit –2006. *Address:* c/o Secretariat of State for Finance and Public Credit, Palacio Nacional, Primer Patio Mariano, 3°, Of. 3045, Col. Centro, Del. Cuauhtémoc, 06000 Mexico DF, Mexico (office).

DÍAZ, Nelson Merentes, PhD; Venezuelan politician and banker; ed Central Univ. of Venezuela and Univ. of Budapest, Hungary; Minister of Science and Tech. Feb.–Nov. 2002, of State for Devt and Econs 2002–04, of State for Financial Devt Sept.–Dec. 2004, of Finance 2004–07; Pres. Nat. Bank for Econ. and Social Devt 2002–04; fmr Gov. for Venezuela World Bank, IMF, Caribbean Devt Bank; mem. Bd of Dirs, Venezuela Cen. Bank 2007–. *Address:* c/o Board of Directors, Banco Central de Venezuela, Apartado 2017, Carmelitas, Caracas 1010, Venezuela (office). *Telephone:* (212) 801-5111 (office). *Fax:* (212) 861-1649 (office). *Website:* www.bcv.org.ve (office).

DIBA, Farah (see PAHLAVI, Farah Diba).

DIBABA, Tirunesh; Ethiopian athlete; b. 1 June 1985, Bekoji, Arsi; long distance track athlete; began athletics running aged 14; moved to Addis Ababa 2000; competed in and finished 5th, aged 15, in women's jr race at Int. Asscn of Athletics Feds (IAAF) World Cross Country Championships 2001; Gold Medal, 5,000m, World Championships, Paris 2003, 5,000m and 10,000m, Helsinki 2005, 10,000m, Osaka 2007; Gold Medal, Jr Race, World Cross Country Championships, Lausanne 2003, Short Course, Saint-Galmier 2005, Long Course, Saint-Galmier 2005, Long Course, Fukuoka 2006, Sr Race, Edinburgh 2008; Gold Medal, 5,000m and 10,000m (Olympic record), Olympic Games, Beijing 2008; Silver Medal, Jr Race, World Cross Country Championships, Dublin 2002, Short Race, Brussels 2004, Sr Race, Mombasa 2007; Silver Medal, 5,000m, World Jr Championships, Kingston 2002; Bronze Medal, 5,000m, Olympic Games, Athens 2004; first woman to win 10,000m/5,000m double at same championships, Helsinki 2005; won five out of six Golden League events (5,000m) in same season 2006; set a new 5,000m world record of 14 minutes 11.15 seconds at Oslo Golden League 2008; first ever woman to win both 5,000m and 10,000m at same Olympics 2008. *Address:* c/o Ethiopian Athletics Federation, PO Box 3241, Addis Ababa, Ethiopia. *Telephone:* (11) 152495. *E-mail:* eth.ath.fed@telecom.net.et. *Website:* www.ethiosports.com.

DIBANGO, Manu; Cameroonian musician (saxophone, piano); b. 12 Dec. 1934, Douala; ed piano lessons; moved to Paris 1949, then Brussels, Belgium 1956; residency at Black Angels Club, Brussels; joined band led by Joseph Kabsele, African Jazz 1960, played with African Jazz in Zaire –1963; returned to Cameroon to form own band 1963–65; studio musician, Paris 1965; backed musicians, including Peter Gabriel, Sinead O'Connor, Angélique Kidjo, Geoffrey Oryema, Ray Lema, Touré Kunda; solo artist 1968–; Pres., Francophone Diffusion; Grammy Award for Best R&B Instrumental Performance of the Year 1973, Ronnie Scott Award for Services to Jazz 2007. *Compositions:* commissioned by President Ahidjo to write song for Africa Cup football match 1971. *Recordings include:* albums: O Boso 1971, Soma Loba 1972, Soul Makossa 1973, Super Kumba 1974, Manu 76 1976, Afrovision 1976, Big Blow 1976, A L'Olympia 1977, Ceddo 1978, Gone Clear 1980, Ambassador 1980, Waka Juju 1982, Deliverence 1983, Sweet and Soft 1983, Melodies Africaines vols 1 and 2 1983, Deadline 1984, Electric Africa 1985, Afrijazzy 1986, Negropolitains Vol. 2 1993, Wakafrika 1994, Bao Bao 1996, Mboa' Su 2000, Voyage Anthologique 2004, Essential Recordings 2006. *Publications:* Trois Kilos de Café (autobiog.) 1990. *Address:* c/o Francophone Diffusion, 33 rue du Fbg St Antoine, 75011 Paris, France.

DIBELA, Sir Kingsford, GCMG; Papua New Guinea politician and teacher; b. 16 March 1932; s. of Norman Dibela and Edna Dalauna; m. Winifred Tomalarina 1952; two s. four d.; ed St Paul's Primary School, Dogura; qualified as primary school teacher, teacher 1949–63; Pres. Weraura Local Govt Council 1963–77; mem. Parl. 1975–82, Speaker of Nat. Parl. 1977–80; Gov.-Gen. 1983–89; KStJ. *Leisure interests:* golf, sailing and cricket. *Address:* PO Box 113, Port Moresby, Papua New Guinea.

DIBIAGGIO, John A., DDS, MA; American dentist and university administrator; *President Emeritus, Tufts University;* b. 11 Sept. 1932, San Antonio; s. of Ciro DiBiaggio and Acidalia DiBiaggio; m. Nancy Cronemiller 1989; one s. two d. (from previous marriage); ed E Mich. Univ., Univ. of Detroit and Univ. of Mich.; gen. dentistry practice, New Baltimore, Mich. 1958–65; Asst Prof., School of Dentistry, Univ. of Detroit 1965–67; Asst Dean Student Affairs, Univ. of Ky 1967–70; Prof., Dean School of Dentistry, Va Commonwealth Univ. Richmond 1970–76; Vice-Pres. for Health Affairs, Exec. Dir Health Center, Univ. of Conn. Farmington 1976–79; Pres. Univ. of Conn. Storrs 1979–85, Mich. State Univ., E Lansing 1985–92, Tufts Univ., Medford, Mass. 1992–2001, now Pres. Emer.; mem. Bd American Automobile Asscn, Kaman Corpn; mem. numerous comms and professional socs; Trustee American Cancer Soc. Foundation 1993– (Pres. 1999); 11 hon. degrees; Pierre Fauchard Gold Medal Award 1987, 1989; Order of Merit (Italy). *Publications:* Applied Practice Management: A Strategy for Stress Control (with others) 1979; articles in professional journals. *Leisure interest:* tennis. *Address:* c/o Tufts University, Office of the President, Medford, MA 02155, USA (office).

DIBY, Charles Koffi; Côte d'Ivoirian economist and politician; *Minister of the Economy and Finance;* b. 7 Sept. 1957, Bouaké; m.; five c.; ed Nat. School of Man. and Int. Inst. of Public Admin, Paris; began career at Treasury 1984, responsible for Nat. Inst. for the Youth and Sports 1985–90, for Nat. Inst. for Professional Training 1990–91, Rep. for Cen. Agency for Public Spending 1991–93, Treasurer for Bondoukou Prov. 1993–94, Treas. for Daoukro Prov. 1994–97, Accountant, Central Agency for Public Spending 1997–98, Paymaster-Gen. 1998–99, Deputy Dir-Gen. of the Treasury 1999–2000, Dir-Gen. 2001–07; Counsellor to Minister of the Economy and Finance 2000–01; Minister Del. of the Economy and Finance 2006–07; Minister of the Economy and Finance 2007–. *Address:* Ministry of the Economy and Finance, 16e étage, Immeuble SCIAM, avenue Marchand, PO Box V163, Abidjan, Côte d'Ivoire (office). *Telephone:* 20-20-08-42 (office). *Fax:* 20-21-32-08 (office).

DICAPRIO, Leonardo; American actor; b. 11 Nov. 1974, Hollywood; s. of George DiCaprio and Irmelin DiCaprio; f. Appian Way production co.; Commandeur de l'Ordre des Arts et Lettres; Platinum Award, Santa Barbara Int. Film Festival 2005. *Films include:* Critters III 1991, Poison Ivy 1992, This Boy's Life 1993, What's Eating Gilbert Grape 1993, The Quick and the Dead 1995, The Basketball Diaries 1995, Total Eclipse 1995, Marvin's Room 1996, William Shakespeare's Romeo and Juliet 1996, Titanic 1997, Man in the Iron Mask 1998, Celebrity 1998, The Beach 2000, Don's Plum 2001, Gangs of New York 2002, Catch Me If You Can 2002, The Aviator 2004, The Departed (Best Int. Actor, Irish Film and Television Awards 2007) 2006, Blood Diamond 2006, The 11th Hour (voice, producer) 2007, Body of Lies 2008. *TV series include:* Parenthood 1990, Growing Pains 1991. *Address:* Appian Way, 9255 Sunset Blvd., Suite 615, West Hollywood, CA 90069; Special Artists Agency, 9465 Wilshire Blvd, Suite 890, Beverly Hills, CA 90212; c/o Birken Productions Inc., PO Box 291958, Los Angeles, CA 90029, USA (office). *Telephone:* (310) 300-1390 (Appian Way). *Website:* www.leonardodicaprio.com (office).

DICCIANI, Nance K., MBA, PhD; American business executive; ed Villanova Univ., Univs of Virginia and Pennsylvania, Wharton School of Univ. of Pennsylvania; held leadership roles in Divs of Chemical Groups, Industrial Chemicals and Specialty Chemicals with Air Products and Chemicals, Inc. 1977–91; Dir European Region, Rohm and Haas, later Sr Vice-Pres. and Business Group Exec. of Chemical Specialties, later Vice-Pres. and Gen. Man. Petroleum Chemicals Div. and Head, Worldwide Monomers Business 1991–2001; Pres. and CEO, Specialty Materials, Honeywell International, Inc. 2001–08 (retd); fmr Vice-Pres. Soc. of Chemical Industry and mem. Exec. Cttee; mem. Pres.'s Council of Advisors on Science and Tech. 2006–08; fmr mem. Exec. Cttee American Chem. Council (Chair. Bd Research Cttee); mem. Bd of Dirs Praxair Inc. 2008–, Rockwood Holdings, Inc. 2008–; fmr mem. Bd of Advisors CEFIC, Bd of Dirs PP&L Resources, Inc., Bd of Trustees Villanova Univ.; fmr adviser, Eng Schools of Villanova Univ., Univ. of Virginia, Univ. of Pennsylvania; Warren K. Lewis Lecturer in Chemical Eng, MIT 2003; fmr Special Olympics coach; honoured by Girl Scouts of America, ranked by Forbes magazine amongst 100 Most Powerful Women (32nd) 2004, (84th) 2005. *Address:* c/o Honeywell International, Inc., 101 Columbia Road, Morristown, NJ 07962-1219, USA (office).

DICHAND, Hans; Austrian journalist and editor; *Editor, Kronen Zeitung;* b. 29 Jan. 1921, Graz; served in mil. and was captured during World War II; began career as ed. in British news service in Graz; Ed.-in-Chief and Exec. Ed. Murtaler Zeitung, Judenburg 1946–47; Foreign Affairs Ed., Steirer Blatt, Graz 1947–48; with Wiener Tageszeitung 1948–49; Ed.-in-Chief Kleinen Zeitung Graz and Klagenfurt 1949–54; left Styria and moved to Kurier in Vienna as Ed.-in-Chief 1954–59; Ed. Kronen Zeitung 1959–; made several TV films. *Publications:* Begegnungen mit Paris (An Encounter with Paris) 1982, Die Künstler der klassischen Modernen in Österreich (The Artists of the Modern Classics in Austria) 1989, Im Vorhof der Macht (In the Forecourt of Power) 1996. *Address:* Kronen Zeitung, Muthgasse 2, 1190 Vienna, Austria (office). *Telephone:* (1) 360-10 (office). *Fax:* (1) 369-83-85 (office). *E-mail:* chefredaktion@kronenzeitung.at (office). *Website:* www.krone.at (office); www.krone.at/index.php?http%3A//blog.krone.at.

DICHTER, Avraham (Avi), BA, MBA; Israeli government official; *Minister of Public Security;* b. 1952; ed Bar Ilan Univ., Tel-Aviv Univ.; mil. service 1971–90, served in Sayeret Matkal commando unit; Head, Southern Dist (ISA), Israel Security Agency—ISA (Shabak) 1992–96, Head, Security and Protection Div. 1996–99, Deputy Dir ISA 1999–2000, Dir 2000–05; elected to Knessett 2006, Minister of Public Security 2006–; Research Fellow, Brookings Inst., Washington, DC 2005; mem. Kadima party. *Address:* Ministry of Public Security, POB 91181, Bldg 3, Kiryat Hamemshala (East), Jerusalem 91181, Israel (office). *Telephone:* 2-5308003 (office). *Fax:* 2-5847872 (office). *E-mail:* sar@mops.gov.il (office). *Website:* www.mops.gov.il (office).

DICHTER, Misha, BS; American concert pianist; b. 27 Sept. 1945, Shanghai, China; s. of Leon Dichter and Lucy Dichter; m. Cipa Dichter 1968; two s.; ed Juilliard School under Rosina Lhevinne; winner, Silver Medal, Tchaikovsky Int. Competition, Moscow 1966; since then has performed with leading orchestras and at festivals and given recitals worldwide; also performs with wife as piano duo; winner, Tchaikovsky Competition 1966, Grand Prix du Disque Liszt 1999. *Recordings include:* Beethoven Sonatas, Brahms Variations, music by Gershwin, Liszt, Mussorgsky, Stravinsky, Schumann,

Tchaikovsky. *Publications:* articles in New York Times, Ovation and Keyboard magazines. *Leisure interests:* tennis, jogging, drawing, sketching. *Address:* Shuman Associates, 120 West 58th Street, New York, NY 10019, USA (office). *Telephone:* (212) 315-1300 (office). *Fax:* (212) 757-3005 (office). *E-mail:* shumanpr@cs.com (office). *Website:* www.thedichters.com.

DICKERSON, Vivian M., MD; American physician and professor of obstetrics and gynaecology; *Executive Medical Director, Hoag Memorial Hospital Presbyterian;* one s.; ed Univ. of California, Santa Barbara, Univ. of California, San Diego School of Medicine; joined Peace Corps and worked in Togo, West Africa 1970s; completed residency training at UCLA Cedars-Sinai Medical Center; fmr Sr Research Analyst, Susan Samueli Center for Complementary and Alternative Medicine, Irvine, Clinical Prof. of Obstetrics and Gynecology, Univ. of California, Irvine (UCI) Medical Center –2006; Exec. Medical Dir of Women's Health Programs and Care, Hoag Memorial Hosp. Presbyterian, Newport Beach, Calif. 2006–; held numerous positions with American Coll. of Obstetricians and Gynaecologists (ACOG), including Chair. Dist IX (Calif.), Council of Dist Chairs, Cttee on Int. Relations, Grievance Cttee and Admin. Comm. 1984–2004, Pres. ACOG 2004–05; Chair. California Family Health Council 2000–04; Ed. in Chief The Female Patient (journal); mem. Advisory Bd Esprit Pharma Inc., Mirabel Medical Systems Ltd, Neomatrix LLC Inc.; ACOG Outstanding Dist Service Award, American Medical Women's Asscn Gender Equity Award 2000, UCI Coll. of Medicine, Golden Apple Award 2002. *Leisure interests:* hiking, skiing, scuba diving. *Address:* Hoag Hospital, One Hoag Drive, Newport Beach, CA 92663 (office); 615D E West View Drive, Orange, CA 92869, USA. *Telephone:* (949) 764-4624 (office). *Website:* www.hoaghospital.org (office).

DICKIE, Brian James; British opera director; *General Director, Chicago Opera Theater;* b. 23 July 1941; s. of the late Robert Kelso and of Harriet Elizabeth (née Riddell) Dickie; m. 1st Victoria Teresa Sheldon (née Price) 1968; two s. one d.; m. 2nd Nancy Gustafson 1989; ed Trinity Coll., Dublin; Admin. Asst Glyndebourne Opera 1962–66; Admin. Glyndebourne Touring Opera 1967–81; Opera Man. Glyndebourne Festival Opera 1970–81, Gen. Admin. 1981–89; Artistic Dir Wexford Festival 1967–73; Artistic Adviser Théâtre Musical de Paris 1981–87; Gen. Dir Canadian Opera Co. 1989–93; Artistic Counsellor Opéra de Nice 1994–97; Gen. Dir EU Opera 1997–99, Chicago Opera Theater 1999–; Chair. London Choral Soc. 1978–85, Theatres Nat. Cttee Opera Cttee 1976–85; Vice-Chair. Theatres Nat. Cttee 1980–85; Vice-Pres. Theatrical Man. Asscn 1983–85; mem. Bd Opera America 1991–93. *Address:* Chicago Opera Theater, 70 East Lake Street, Suite 815, Chicago, IL 60601 (office); 405 Edgemere Way North, Naples, FL 33999 (home); 2000 N Lincoln Park West, Apt 412, Chicago, IL 60614, USA (home). *Telephone:* (312) 7048420 (office); (773) 3276471 (home). *Fax:* (312) 7048421 (office). *E-mail:* briandickie@mac.com (home). *Website:* www.chicagooperatheater.org (office); briandickie.typepad.com.

DICKIE, Lloyd M., PhD, FRSC; Canadian ecologist; *Research Scientist Emeritus, Department of Fisheries and Oceans;* b. 6 March 1926, Kingsport, NS; s. of Ebenezer Cox Dickie and Pearl (née Sellars) Dickie; m. Marjorie C. Bowman 1952; one s. two d.; ed Acadia Univ., Yale Univ., Univ. of Toronto; research scientist, Fisheries Research Bd, NB 1951–62, Great Lakes Inst., Toronto 1962–65; Dir Marine Ecology Lab., Bedford Inst. Oceanography, Dartmouth, NS 1965–74; Chair. and Prof. of Oceanography, Dalhousie Univ., Halifax 1974–77, Dir Inst. of Environmental Studies, Dalhousie Univ. 1974–76; Research Scientist, Marine Ecology Lab. and Marine Fish Div., Bedford Inst. of Oceanography, Dartmouth, NS 1976–87; Sr Research Scientist, Biological Sciences Br., Dept of Fisheries and Oceans 1987–93, Research Scientist Emer. 1994–; participant in Ocean Production Enhancement Network 1991–92; mem. SPICES (Sr People of Int. Council for the Exploration of the Sea) Network; Oscar-Sette Memorial Award, American Fish Soc. 1991. *Publications:* Ad Mare: Canada Looks to the Sea (with R. W. Stewart) 1971, The Biomass Spectrum: A Predator-Prey Theory of Aquatic Production (co-author) 2001; more than 80 scientific papers. *Address:* 7 Lakewood Court, Dartmouth, NS, B2X 2R6, Canada (home). *Telephone:* (902) 435-1545 (home). *E-mail:* lloyd.dickie@ns.sympatico.ca (home).

DICKINSON, Angie; American actress; b. (Angeline Brown), 30 Sept. 1931, Kulm, ND; ed Immaculate Heart Coll., Glendale Coll. *Films include:* Lucky Me 1954, Man With the Gun, The Return of Jack Slade, Tennessee's Partner, The Black Whip, Hidden Guns, Tension at Table Rock, Gun the Man Down, Calypso Joe, China Gate, Shoot Out at Medicine Bend, Cry Terror, I Married a Woman, Rio Bravo, The Bramble Bush, A Fever in the Blood, The Sins of Rachel Cade, Jessica, Rome Adventure, Captain Newman MD, The Killers, The Art of Love, Cast a Giant Shadow, The Chase, The Poppy is Also a Flower, Last Challenge, Point Blank, Sam Whiskey, Some Kind of a Nut, Young Billy Young, Pretty Maids All in a Row, The Resurrection of Zachary Wheeler, The Outside Man, Big Bad Mama, Klondike Fever, Dressed to Kill, Charlie Chan and the Curse of the Dragon Queen, Death Hunt, Big Bad Mama II, Even Cowgirls Get the Blues, The Maddening, Sabrina, The Sun, The Moon and The Stars, Pay It Forward, Sealed with a Kiss 1999, The Last Producer 2000, Duets 2000, Pay it Forward 2000, Big Bad Love 2001, Elvis Has Left the Building 2004. *Television series:* Police Woman, Cassie & Co. *Television films:* The Love War, Thief, See the Man Run, The Norliss Tapes, Pray for the Wildcats, A Sensitive Passionate Man, Overboard, The Suicide's Wife, Dial M for Murder, One Shoe Makes it Murder, Jealousy, A Touch of Scandal, Stillwatch, Police Story: The Freeway Killings, Once Upon a Texas Train, Prime Target, Treacherous Crossing, Danielle Steel's Remembrance; mini-series: Pearl, Hollywood Wives, Wild Palms. *Address:* 1715 Carla Ridge, Beverly Hills, CA 90210-1911, USA.

DICKSON, Jennifer, CM, RA, LLD; Canadian artist, photographer and academic; b. 17 Sept. 1936, Piet Retief, S Africa; d. of the late John L. Dickson and Margaret J. (Turner) Dickson; m. Ronald A. Sweetman 1962; one s.; ed Goldsmith's Coll. School of Art, Univ. of London; Assoc., Atelier 17 (graphic workshop), Paris 1960–65; teacher, Brighton Coll. of Art 1961–68, Univ. of West Indies, Jamaica 1968, Univ. of Wisconsin 1972, Saidye Bronfman Centre, Montréal 1970–71, 1982–83, Ohio Univ., Athens 1973, 1979, Univ. of Southern Illinois 1973, California State Univ., Sacramento 1974, Denison Univ. 1976, Univ. of Ottawa 1980–83 (Sessional Instructor 1980–85); Lecturer, History of Art, Montréal Museum of Fine Arts 1988–91; visiting artist at many univs and colls; has held more than 55 solo exhbns in six countries and participated in more than 350 group exhbns; works in numerous public collections in Canada, USA, UK, Europe, New Zealand, Australia and S Africa including Nat. Gallery of Canada, Metropolitan Museum, New York, British Museum, London and Hermitage Museum, Leningrad; Fellow, Royal Soc. of Painter-Etchers and Engravers 1970–; Hon. LLD (Univ. of Alberta) 1988; awards include Prix de Jeunes Artistes pour Gravure, Biennale de Paris 1963, Special Purchase Award, World Print Competition, San Francisco Museum of Art 1974, Biennale Prize, 5th Norwegian Int. Print Biennale 1981, Victor Tolgesy Award, Ottawa Council for the Arts 2002. *Publications:* The Hospital for Wounded Angels 1987, The Royal Academy Gardener's Journal 1991, Water Song 1997, Garden Capricci 1999, Sanctuary: A Landscape of the Mind 2000 and suites of original prints and photographs, Nature and Artifice 2003. *Leisure interests:* historic gardens, opera, films. *Address:* c/o Wallack Galleries, 203 Bank Street, Ottawa, ON K2P 1W7; 20 Osborne Street, Ottawa, ON K1S 4Z9, Canada (home). *Telephone:* (613) 233-2315 (studio); (613) 730-2083 (home). *Fax:* (613) 730-1818 (home). *E-mail:* info@wallackgalleries.com; ronsweetman@canada.com.

DIDDY (see COMBS, Sean).

DIDION, Joan, BA; American writer; b. 5 Dec. 1934, Sacramento, Calif.; d. of Frank Reese Didion and Eduene Didion (née Jerrett); m. John Gregory Dunne 1964 (died 2003); one d. (died 2005); ed Univ. of Calif., Berkeley; Assoc. Features Ed. Vogue magazine 1956–63; fmr columnist Esquire, Life, Saturday Evening Post, fmr contributor Nat. Review; freelance writer 1963–; mem. American Acad. of Arts and Letters, American Acad. of Arts and Sciences, Council on Foreign Relations; First Prize Vogue's Prix de Paris 1956, American Acad. of Arts and Letters Morton Dauwen Zabel Prize 1978, Edward McDowell Medal 1996, George Polk Award 2001, American Acad. of Arts and Letter Gold Medal for Belles Lettres 2005, Medal for Distinguished Contrib. to American Letters, Nat. Book Foundation 2007. *Screenplays:* The Panic in Needle Park 1971, Play It as It Lays 1972, A Star is Born 1976, True Confessions 1981, Hills Like White Elephants 1991, Broken Trust 1995, Up Close and Personal 1996. *Publications include:* novels: Run River 1963, Play It as It Lays 1970, A Book of Common Prayer 1977, Telling Stories 1978, Democracy 1984, The Last Thing He Wanted 1996; essays: Slouching Towards Bethlehem 1969, The White Album 1978, After Henry 1992; non-fiction: Salvador 1983, Miami 1987, After Henry 1992, Political Fictions 2001, Where I Was From: A Memoir 2003, The Year of Magical Thinking (Nat. Book Award for Non-fiction; also screenplay) 2005. *Address:* Janklow & Nesbit, 445 Park Avenue, New York, NY 10022-2606, USA (office).

DIDO; British singer, musician (piano, violin) and songwriter; b. (Dido Florian Cloud de Bounevialle Armstrong), 25 Dec. 1971, London; sister of Rollo Armstrong; ed Guildhall School of Music, London; toured UK with classical music ensemble before joining pop groups aged 16; toured with brother Rollo's band, Faithless; signed solo deal with Arista Records, New York; BRIT Award for Best Female Solo Artist 2002, 2004, Ivor Novello Songwriter of the Year Award 2002, BAMBI Award for Best International Pop Act 2003, ASCAP Award for Songwriter of the Year 2008. *Recordings:* albums: No Angel (BRIT Award for Best Album 2002) 1999, Life for Rent 2003, Safe Trip Home 2008; singles: The Highbury Fields (EP) 1999, Here With Me 2001, Thank You 2001, Hunter 2001, All You Want 2002, Life for Rent 2003, White Flag (BRIT Award for Best British single 2004) 2003. *Address:* Nettwerk Music Group, 59–65 Worship Street, London EC2A 2DU, England (office). *Telephone:* (20) 7456-9500 (office). *E-mail:* eleanor@nettwerk.com (office). *Website:* nettwerk.com (office); www.didomusic.com.

DIEKMANN, Kai; German newspaper executive; *Editorial Director, Bild Group;* b. 1965, Ravensburg; Parl. Corresp., Bild and Bild am Sonntag, Bonn 1987; Chief Reporter Bunte magazine, Munich 1989–91; Deputy Ed. B.Z., Berlin 1991–92, Deputy Ed. and Chief Political Corresp. Bild, Hamburg 1992–97; Chief Ed. Welt am Sonntag, Berlin 1998–2000, Ed.-in-Chief Bild and Publr Bild and Bild am Sonntag, Hamburg 2001–, Content Exec. bild.de 2007–; Editorial Dir Bild Group 2007–; Head, Bild hilft e.V. – Ein Herz für Kinder (charity org.) 2001–; External Bd mem. Hürriyet 2004–; Goldene Feder 2000, 2005, World Media Award 2002. *Publications include:* Rita Süssmuth im Gespräch (co-author) 1994, Die neue Bundespräsident im Gespräch (co-author) 1994, Helmut Kohl. Ich wollte Deutschlands Einheit (co-author) 1996, Der große Selbstbetrug 2007. *Address:* Bild, Axel Springer AG, Axel-Springer-Straße 65, 10888 Berlin, Germany (office). *Telephone:* (30) 2591-0 (office). *Fax:* (30) 2591-76009 (office). *Website:* www.bild.de (office).

DIEKMANN, Michael; German business executive; *Chairman of the Board of Management, Allianz SE;* b. 23 Dec. 1954, Bielefeld; m.; three c.; ed Göttingen Univ.; Financial Dir Diekmann/Thieme GBR 1983–86, Pres. 1987–88; Exec. Asst to Head of Hamburg Regional Office, Allianz Versicherungs-AG 1988–89, Head of Sales, Hamburg Harburg Office 1990, Head of Hanover Office 1991–92, Head of Customer Relationship Man. for pvt. customers, Munich 1993, mem. Exec. Bd of Man. of regional office for N Rhine-Westphalia as Head of Sales 1994–95, Dir Allianz Insurance Man. Asia Pacific Pte Ltd, Singapore 1996–97, mem. Bd of Man. Allianz AG, Munich responsible for Asia-Pacific region 1998, responsible for Asia-Pacific, Cen. and Eastern Europe, Middle East, Africa and Group Man. Devt 2000, responsible for the

Americas and Group Human Resources 2002–03, Chair. Bd of Man., Allianz AG (renamed Allianz SE 2006) 2003–, also Chair. Allianz Deutschland AG, Allianz Global Investors AG, Dresdner Bank AG; Deputy Chair. BASF SE, Linde AG; Vice-Pres. Assurances Générales de France, Allianz SpA; mem. Bd Dirs Siemens AG. *Address:* Allianz SE, Königinstrasse 28, 80802 Munich, Germany (office). *Telephone:* (89) 3800-0 (office). *Fax:* (89) 3800-3425 (office). *E-mail:* info@allianz.com (office). *Website:* www.allianz.com (office).

DIEMU, Chikez; Democratic Republic of the Congo politician; *Minister of Defence, Demobilization and War Veterans' Affairs;* mem. Parl. 1997–; Sec. for Strategic Planning 1997–99; Vice-Pres. in charge of organization of Govt 1999–2001; Vice-Minister of Interior 2001–04; Gen.-Sec. People's Party for Reconstruction and Democracy 2001–05; Vice-Gov. Katanga Prov. 2004–07; Minister of Defence, Demobilization and War Veterans' Affairs 2007–. *Address:* Ministry of Defence, Demobilization and War Veterans' Affairs, BP 4111, Kinshasa-Gombe, Democratic Republic of the Congo (office). *Telephone:* (12) 59375 (office).

DIENER, Theodor Otto, DSc; American plant virologist and academic; *Distinguished University Professor Emeritus, Center for Biosystems Research, University of Maryland;* b. 28 Feb. 1921, Zürich, Switzerland; s. of Theodor E. Diener and Hedwig R. Baumann; m. Sybil Mary Fox 1968; three s. (from previous m.); ed Swiss Fed. Inst. of Tech., Zürich; Plant Pathologist, Swiss Fed. Agricultural Research Station, Waedenswil 1948–49; Asst Prof. of Plant Pathology, Rhode Island State Univ., Kingston, USA 1950; Asst-Assoc. Plant Pathologist, Wash. State Univ., Prosser 1950–59; Research Plant Pathologist, Plant Virology Lab., Agricultural Research Service, US Dept of Agric., Beltsville, Md 1959–88; Collaborator, Agricultural Research Service, US Dept of Agric., Beltsville, Md 1988–97; Prof., Center for Agric. Biotech. and Dept of Botany, Univ. of Md, College Park 1988–, Acting Dir Center for Agric. Biotech. 1991–92; Distinguished Univ. Prof. 1994–; Distinguished Prof., Univ. of Md Biotech. Inst. 1998–99, Distinguished Univ. Prof. Emer. 1999–; discovered and named viroids, smallest known agents of infectious disease; mem. NAS, American Acad. of Arts and Sciences, Leopoldina (German Acad. of Natural Scientists); Fellow, New York Acad. of Sciences, American Phytopathological Soc.; Campbell Award, American Inst. of Biological Sciences 1968, Superior Service Award, US Dept of Agric. 1969, Distinguished Service Award, US Dept of Agric. 1977, Alexander von Humboldt Award (FRG) 1975, Wolf Prize (Israel) 1987, E. C. Stakman Award, Univ. of Minn. 1988, Nat. Medal of Science (USA) 1987, Science Hall of Fame, Agricultural Research Service, US Dept of Agric. 1989. *Publications:* Viroids and Viroid Diseases 1979, Ed. The Viroids 1987; ed. numerous chapters in scientific books and more than 200 scientific papers. *Leisure interest:* private pilot. *Address:* University of Maryland Biotechnology Institute, Center for Biosystems Research, 5115 Plant Sciences Building, College Park, MD 20742-4450 (office); 11711 Battersea Drive, PO Box 272, Beltsville, MD 20705, USA (home). *Telephone:* (301) 405-7659 (office). *Fax:* (301) 504-5449 (office). *E-mail:* diener@umbi.umd .edu (office); todiener@verizon.net (home). *Website:* www.umbi.umd.edu/~cbr (office).

DIENSTBIER, Jiří; Czech politician, journalist and writer; *Ambassador-at-Large and Director and Trustee, Reuters Founders Share Company;* b. 20 April 1937, Kladno; s. of Jiří Dienstbier and Anna Dienstbierová; m. 4th J. Melenová 1999; one s. three d.; ed Charles Univ., Prague; Czechoslovak Broadcasting 1959, foreign correspondent in Far East, USSR, Germany, France, UK, Yugoslavia 1960–68, USA 1968–69; dismissed from broadcasting 1970; worked in archives of an eng company; expelled from Czechoslovak CP and Journalists' Union 1969; signed Charter 1977, spokesman 1979; sentenced to three years in prison 1979–82; boilerman 1982–89; spokesman for Charter 77 1985–86; ed. of Čtverec (The Square), a periodical on int. politics 1979–; Co-Founder of Lidové Noviny (The People's Newspaper) 1988–; Czechoslovak Minister for Foreign Affairs 1989–92; mem. Council of State 1990–92, Deputy Prime Minister CFSR 1990–92, Deputy to House of People Fed. Ass. 1990–92, Chair. Council of the Civic Movt 1991–; Chair. Free Democrats Party (fmrly Civic Movt) 1993–95 (merged with Liberal Nat. Social Party 1995); Chair. Liberal Nat. Social Party 1995–96 (left Party 1997); Chair. Czech Council on Foreign Relations; mem. Comm. on Global Governance; mem. UN Cttee for Solving Global Problems 1995–; Special Envoy to Gen. Ass. of UN 1995; lecturer 1998–; Special Rapporteur of the UN Comm. on Human Rights for Bosnia and Herzegovina, Croatia and Yugoslavia 1998–2001; Dir and Trustee, Reuters Founders Share Co. 2005–; Visiting Prof., Claremont Grad. Univ., Calif. 1997–98, Univ. of North Carolina, Chapel Hill 1999, Charles Univ., Prague 2001, 2003, Watson Inst., Brown Univ. 2003; Grand Cross of Order for Merit (Order of Kts of Malta) 1990; Das Grosse Verdienstkreuz mit Stern und Schulterband (Germany) 2002, Officier Légion d'honneur 2005; Dr hc (Univ. de Bourgogne) 1993; Humanist of the Year (USA) 1979, Francesco Cossiga Medal (Italy) 1991, Pro Merito Medal, Parl. Ass. Council of Europe 1991, Hero of Freedom of the Press in the World, IPI (Boston, USA) 2000. *Publications include:* The Night Began at Three in the Morning 1967, Before We Roast Young Pigs 1976, Christmas Present 1977, Guests 1978, Charter 77 – Human Rights and Socialism 1981, Radio Against Tanks 1988, Dreaming of Europe 1990, From Dreams to Reality 1999; Kosovo Shades over Balkans 2002, Tax on Blood 2002, stage plays, articles and essays in Samizdat. *Leisure interests:* reading, music, history. *Address:* Rytířská 31, 11000 Prague (office); Apolinářská 6, 12800 Prague 2, Czech Republic (home). *Telephone:* (2) 2161-0109; (2) 2492-3321 (home). *E-mail:* jiri_dienstbier@mzv .cz (office); j@dienstbier.cz (home).

DIEPGEN, Eberhard; German politician; *Senator for Justice;* b. 13 Nov. 1941, Berlin; m. Monika Adler 1975; one s. one d.; ed Free Univ. of Berlin; joined CDU 1962, later Chair., W Berlin CDU; mem. Berlin Chamber of Deputies 1971–81; mem. Bundestag (Parl.) as W Berlin Rep. 1980–81; Mayor of Berlin 1984–89, 1991–2001; Senator for Justice 2000–; Chair. Supervisory Bd Berlin Brandenburg Flughafen Holding GmbH 1996–; Grosses Bundesverdienstkreuz mit Stern 1994. *Leisure interests:* soccer, European history. *Address:* c/o Berliner Rathaus, 10173 Berlin, Germany.

DIETRICH, Siegfried, PhD; German chemist; *Director, Max-Planck-Institut für Metallforschung;* b. 1954, Singen; ed Univ. of Konstanz, Univ. of Munich; Research Assoc., Univ. of Wash., Seattle, USA 1982–83; Research Assoc., Ludwig-Maximilians-Universität, Munich 1983–86; Assoc. Prof., Univ. of Würzburg 1987–88, also Univ. of Mainz 1988; Full Prof., Univ. of Wuppertal 1989–90; Scientific mem. and Dir, Max-Planck-Institut für Metallforschung 2000–; Chair. for Theoretical Solid State Physics, Univ. of Stuttgart; Fellow Japan Soc. for the Promotion of Science 1997; mem. Int. Union of Pure and Applied Chem. (IUPAC); German Physical Soc. Walter-Schottky-Preis 1985, Max Born Medal and Prize 2002. *Address:* Max-Planck-Institut fur Metallforschung, Heisenbergstr. 3, 70569 Stuttgart, Germany (office). *Telephone:* (711) 689-1920 (office). *Fax:* (711) 689-1922 (office). *E-mail:* dietrich@mf.mpg .de (office). *Website:* www.mf.mpg.de/de/organisation/p_dietrich.html (office).

DIEWERT, Walter Erwin, BA, MA, PhD, FRSC; Canadian economist and academic; *Professor of Economics, University of British Columbia;* b. 4 Dec. 1941, Vancouver, BC; s. of Ewald Diewert and Linda Diewert; m. Virginia Diewert; ed Univ. of British Columbia, Univ. of California, Berkeley; mem. Faculty of Econs, Univ. of Chicago 1968–70; mem. Faculty of Econs, Univ. of British Columbia 1970–, currently Prof. of Econs; Research Assoc., Nat. Bureau of Econ. Research; Chair. Statistics Canada Advisory Cttee on Prices, mem. Statistics Canada Services Advisory Cttee, Statistics Canada Advisory Group on Science and Tech.; mem. NAS Panel on Conceptual, Measurement and Other Statistical Issues in Developing Cost of Living Indexes, Washington, DC 1999–2000; Assoc. Ed. Macroeconomic Dynamics; Fellow, Econometric Soc., World Acad. of Productivity Science; Distinguished Fellow, American Economic Soc.; mem. UN Canberra Group on Capital Measurement, UN Ottawa Group on Price Measurement; consultant for OECD, ILO, IMF, World Bank, US Bureau of Econ. Analysis, US Bureau of Labor Statistics, NZ Treasury, Australian Bureau of Statistics; Killam Prize, Canada Council for the Arts 2003, Doug Purvis Memorial Prize, Canadian Econs Assen 2005, Julius Shiskin Memorial Award for Econ. Statistics 2005. *Publications:* more than 260 publs in econ journals and books; numerous reports, including the report to NZ Business Roundtable, major contributor to 2004 Consumer Price Index Manual, 2004 Producer Price Index Manual and 2009 Export Import Price Index Manual. *Leisure interest:* tennis. *Address:* Department of Economics, University of British Columbia, Buchanan Tower 1009, #997-1873 East Mall, Vancouver, BC V6T 1Z1, Canada (office). *Telephone:* (604) 266-7300 (office). *Fax:* (604) 822-5915 (office). *E-mail:* diewert@econ.ubc.ca (office). *Website:* www.econ.ubc.ca/diewert/hmpgdie.htm (office).

DIEZ CANSECO TERRY, Raúl; Peruvian politician; b. 23 Jan. 1948, Lima; ed San Ignacio de Loyola Univ.; fmr Pres. Foptur, Dir Corpac; elected Frente Democrático mem. Parl. for Lima 1990; cand. for Mayor of Lima 1993; Acción Popular Party cand. for Pres. 1995; fmr Vice-Minister of Tourism; First Vice-Pres. 2001–04, concurrently Minister of Industry, Tourism, Integration and Int. Trade Negotiations 2001–03. *Address:* c/o Ministry of Industry, Tourism, Integration and International Trade Negotiations, Calle 1 Oeste, Urb. Corpac, San Isidro, Lima 27, Peru (office).

DIFORIO, Robert G., BA; American publishing executive; *Principal, D4EO Literary Agency;* b. 19 March 1940, Mamaroneck, NY; s. of Richard John Diforio Sr and Mildred Kuntz; m. Birgit Rasmussen 1983; one s. one d.; ed Williams Coll., Williamstown, Mass and Harvard Business School's Advanced Man. Program; Vice-Pres. Kable News Co. 1970; Vice-Pres. and Sales Man. New American Library (NAL) 1972, Sr Vice-Pres. and Marketing Dir 1976, Pres. and Publr 1980–82, CEO and Chair. Bd NAL/E. P. Dutton 1983–89; Prin. D4EO Literary Agency 1991–. *Leisure interest:* golf. *Address:* 7 Indian Valley Road, Weston, CT 06883, USA (office). *Telephone:* (203) 544-7180 (office); (203) 544-7182 (home). *Fax:* (203) 544-7160 (office). *E-mail:* bbo@d4eo .com (office). *Website:* www.d4eo.com (office).

DIJKGRAAF, Henk G.; Dutch energy industry executive; *CEO, Gasunie Trade and Supply BV;* b. 1946; ed Univ. of Delft, MIT, Boston, USA; began career with Royal Dutch/Shell 1972, various positions in Borneo, Kuala Lumpur, Gabon, Syria, London and The Hague; Dir Nederlandse Aardolie Maatschappij (NAM) 1992–95; CEO Shell Int. Gas and Shell Coal Int. 1995–99; Pres. Shell Nederland BV 1999–2003; Group CEO NV Nederlandse Gasunie 2004–05, CEO Gasunie Trade and Supply BV (after restructuring) 2005–. *Address:* NV Nederlandse Gasunie, Rozenburglaan 11, 9727 DL Groningen, The Netherlands (office). *Telephone:* (50) 52-12-271 (office). *Fax:* (50) 52-11-921 (office). *Website:* 212.83.207.146/tradesupply/en (office).

DIJOUD, Paul Charles Louis; French politician; *Conseiller d'Enterprises;* b. 25 July 1938, Neuilly-sur-Seine; s. of Jules-Raoul Dijoud and Andrée Claquin; m. Catherine Cochaux 1968 (divorced 1983); one s. one d.; m. 2nd Maryse Dolivot 1988; ed Lycée Condorcet, Faculté de Droit de Paris, Ecole Nat. d'Admin, Inst. d'Etudes politiques de Paris; commercial attaché, Dept of External Econ. Relations in Ministry of Econ. and Finance; elected to Nat. Ass. 1967, 1968, 1973, 1978, defeated 1981; Asst Sec.-Gen. Ind. Republican Party 1967–69; Conseiller Général for Canton of Embrun 1968–88; Pres. Ind. Republican Exec. Cttee for Provence-Côte d'Azur 1968–88; Mayor of Briançon 1971–83; Sec. of State attached to Prime Minister's Office 1973–74, later to Minister of Cultural Affairs and the Environment, to Minister of Employment with Responsibility for Immigrant Workers 1974, Secretary of State for Sport 1977, for Overseas Depts and Territories 1978; Commercial Adviser to Cen. Admin., Ministry of Economy and Finance 1981; Man. Dir Cie Commerciale Sucres et Denrées 1982–84; Pres. Comidex 1984; Pres. Conseil d'admin du parc nat. des Ecrins 1973; Plenipotentiary Minister 1988; Amb. to Colombia 1988–91, to Mexico 1992–94; Minister of State with responsibility for the principality of Monaco 1994–97; Amb. to Argentina 1997–2003; Conseiller d'Enterprises 2003–; Officier de la Légion d'honneur. *Address:* 27 Rue de la Ferme, 92200 Neuilly, France (office). *Telephone:* 1-46-40-06-68 (office); (06) 21725701 (mobile). *Fax:* 1-46-40-06-68 (office). *E-mail:* pauldijoudfr@hotmail .com (office).

DIKSHIT, Sheila, MA; Indian politician; *Chief Minister of Delhi;* b. 31 March 1938; m. Vinod Dikshit (deceased); one s. one d.; ed Convent of Jesus and Mary School and Delhi Univ.; mem. Parl. 1984–89; Minister of Parl. Affairs, Minister of State in the Prime Minister's Office 1986–89; Pres. Delhi Pradesh Congress Cttee 1998; Chief Minister, Govt of Nat. Capital Territory of Delhi 1998–; Sec. Indira Gandhi Memorial Trust. *Address:* Office of the Chief Minister, Delhi Secretariat, IP Estate, New Delhi 110002 (office); 3 Motilal Nehru Place, New Delhi, India (home). *Telephone:* (11) 23392020 (office); (11) 23018998 (home). *Fax:* (11) 23392111 (office); (11) 23018726 (home). *E-mail:* cmdelhi@nic.in (office). *Website:* delhigovt.nic.in (office).

DILEITA, Dileita Mohamed; Djibouti politician and diplomatist; *Prime Minister;* b. 12 March 1958, Tadjourahle; ed Centre for Vocational Training (CFA), Médéa, Algeria; fmr Amb. to Ethiopia; Prime Minister of Djibouti 2001–. *Address:* Office of the Prime Minister, BP 2086, Djibouti (office). *Telephone:* 351494 (office). *Fax:* 355049 (office).

DILENSCHNEIDER, Robert, MA; American business executive; *Principal, The Dilenschneider Group;* b. 21 Oct. 1943, New York; s. of Sigmund J. Dilenschneider and Martha Witucki; m. Janet Hennessey 1969; two s.; ed Univ. of Notre Dame and Ohio State Univ.; Account Supervisor, Hill and Knowlton Inc., New York 1967–70, Vice-Pres. 1970–73, Sr Vice-Pres. 1973–80, Exec. Vice-Pres., Chicago 1980–84, Pres. and COO, Chicago 1984–86, Pres. and CEO Hill and Knowlton, New York 1986–91; Prin. The Dilenschneider Group Inc., New York 1991–; mem. US–Japan Business Council, Public Relations Soc. of America, Int. Public Relations Asscn; mem. Advisory Bd New York Hosp., Cornell Medical Center, Coll. of Business Admin. at Univ. of Notre Dame; New York's Big Apple Award. *Publications:* Power and Influence: A Briefing for Leaders 1991, On Power 1993. *Address:* The Dilenschneider Group Inc., 200 Park Avenue, New York, NY 10166, USA.

DILIBERTO, Oliviero; Italian politician and academic; *Professor of Roman and Levantine Law, University of Rome 'La Sapienza';* b. 13 Oct. 1956, Cagliari; s. of Marco Diliberto and Mariadonella Reale; m. Gabriella Serrenti 1997; ed in Cagliari, Rome, Frankfurt and Paris; Prov. Sec. Juvenile Fed. of Italian Communist Party 1978; mem. Prov. Sec.'s Office, Italian CP 1982; mem. Nat. Sec.'s Office, Reconstructed CP 1994, Dir Liberazione (party journal) 1994, Leader Parl. Group 1995, now Pres. Progressive Parl. Group; fmrly mem. Third Perm. Cttee on Foreign and EC Affairs, Ninth Perm. Cttee on Transport, Post and Telecommunications; Minister of Justice 1998–2001; Prof. of Roman Law, Univ. of Cagliari; currently Prof. of Roman and Levantine Law, Univ. of Rome 'La Sapienza'. *Address:* Piazzale Aldo Moro 5, 00185 Rome, Italy.

DILKS, David Neville, BA, FRSL, FCGI; British historian, academic and university administrator; b. 17 March 1938, Coventry; s. of Neville Ernest and Phyllis Dilks; m. Jill Medlicott 1963; one s.; ed Royal Grammar School, Worcester, Hertford Coll. and St Antony's Coll., Oxford; Asst Lecturer, then Lecturer LSE 1962–70; Prof. of Int. History, Univ. of Leeds 1970–91, Chair. School of History 1974–79, Dean Faculty of Arts 1975–77; Vice-Chancellor Univ. of Hull 1991–99; Visiting Fellow, All Souls' Coll., Oxford 1973; Chair. and Founder Commonwealth Youth Exchange Council 1968–73; mem. Advisory Council on Public Records 1977–85, Inst. of Contemporary British History 1986–, Univs Funding Council 1988–91; Trustee Edward Boyle Memorial Trust 1982–96, Imperial War Museum 1983–91, Lennox-Boyd Trust 1984–91, Royal Commonwealth Soc. Library Trust 1987–91; Pres. Int. Cttee for the History of the Second World War 1992–2000; Freeman, Goldsmiths' Co. 1979, Liveryman 1984; Fellow, City and Guilds of London Inst.; Dr hc (Russian Acad. of Sciences) 1996; Curzon Prize, Univ. of Oxford 1960, Prix du rayonnement de la langue française 1994, Médaille de Vermeil, Acad. Française 1994. *Television:* historical adviser, The Gathering Storm (HBO/BBC) 2002, Winston Churchill at War (HBO/BBC) 2009. *Publications:* Curzon in India (Vols 1 & 2) 1969, 1970, The Diaries of Sir Alexander Cadogan (ed.) 1971, Retreat from Power (two vols, ed.) 1981, The Missing Dimension: Government and Intelligence Communities in the Twentieth Century (ed.) 1984, Neville Chamberlain: Pioneering & Reform, 1869–1929 1984, Barbarossa 1941, The Axis, The Allies and World War: Retrospect, Recollection, Revision (jtly), Grossbritannien und der deutsche Widerstand (jtly) 1994, The Great Dominion: Winston Churchill in Canada 1900–1954 2005; and numerous articles in learned journals. *Leisure interests:* ornithology, steam railways, organ music, Bentley cars. *Address:* Wits End, Long Causeway, Leeds, LS16 8EX, West Yorks., England (home). *Telephone:* (113) 267-3466 (home). *Fax:* (113) 261-1240 (home).

DILLANE, Stephen; actor; b. 1957, London; pnr Naomi Wirthner; one c.; ed Univ. of Exeter, Bristol Old Vic Drama School; early career as journalist for Croydon Advertiser newpaper; attended drama school, then worked in repertory Coventry, Manchester and Chester; Tony Award for Best Leading Actor (The Real Thing) 2000. *Films include:* Business as Usual 1987, La Chance 1994, Two If by Sea 1996, Welcome to Sarajevo 1997, Firelight 1997, Déjà Vu 1997, Love and Rage 1998, The Darkest Light 1999, Ordinary Decent Criminal 2000, The Parole Officer 2001, Spy Game 2001, The Gathering 2002, The Truth About Charlie 2002, The Hours 2002, King Arthur 2004, Haven 2004, Nine Lives 2005, Goal! 2005, The Greatest Game Ever Played 2005, Klimt 2005, Goal II: Living the Dream 2006, Savage Grace 2007. *Television:*

Comeback 1987, The Secret Garden 1987, The One Game 1988, An Affair in Mind 1988, Christabel 1988, The Yellow Wallpaper 1989, Heading Home 1991, Achilles Heel 1991, Frankie's House 1992, Hostages 1993, You Me + It 1993, The Rector's Wife 1994, The Widowing of Mrs. Holroyd 1995, Anna Karenina (miniseries) 2000, The Cazalets (series) 2001. *Plays:* (Royal Nat. Theatre) The Beaux's Strategem, Dancing at Lughnasa, Long Day's Journey into Night, Angels in America, Millennium Approaches, Perestroika; Hush (Royal Court); Endgame (Donmar Warehouse); Hamlet (Gielgud Theatre).

DILLARD, Annie, MA; American author; b. 30 April 1945, Pittsburgh, Pa; d. of Frank Doak and Gloria Lambert; m. 1st R. H. W. Dillard 1965; m. 2nd Gary Clevidence 1979 (divorced); m. 3rd Robert D. Richardson, Jr 1988; one d. two step-d.; ed Hollins Coll.; Contributing Ed. Harper's Magazine 1974–85; Distinguished Visiting Prof., Wesleyan Univ. 1979–83, Adjunct Prof. 1983–, Writer in Residence 1987–; mem. Bd of Dirs Writers' Conf. 1984– (Chair. 1991–); mem. Nat. Cttee on US–China Relations 1982–; Nat. Endowment for the Arts (Literature) Grant 1981, John Simon Guggenheim Memorial Grant 1985, Gov. of Connecticut's Award 1993, Campion Award 1994, Milton Prize 1994, American Arts and Letters Award in Literature 1998. *Publications:* Tickets for a Prayer Wheel (poetry), Pilgrim at Tinker Creek (Pulitzer Prize 1975) 1974, Holy the Firm 1978, Living by Fiction 1982, Teaching a Stone to Talk 1982, Encounters with Chinese Writers 1984, An American Childhood 1987, The Writing Life 1989, The Living (novel) 1992, The Annie Dillard Reader 1994, Mornings Like This (poetry) 1995, For the Time Being 1999, The Maytrees (prose) 2007. *Leisure interests:* soup kitchens in Key West, Fla and Chapel Hill, NC. *Address:* c/o Timothy Seldes, Russell and Volkening, 50 W 29th New York, NY 10001-4227, USA.

DILLER, Barry; American entertainment executive; *Chairman, IAC/Inter-Active Corporation;* b. 2 Feb. 1942, San Francisco; s. of Michael Diller and Reva (née Addison) Diller; Asst to Vice Pres. in charge of programming ABC-TV 1966–68, Exec. Asst to Vice Pres. in programming and dir of feature films, ABC, 1968, Vice Pres. Feature Films and Program Devt 1969–71, Vice Pres. Feature Films Circle Entertainment, div. of ABC) 1971–73, created TV movies of the week and miniseries, Vice-Pres. of prime-time TV, ABC network 1973; Chair. Bd and CEO Paramount Pictures Corpn 1974–84 (resgnd); Chair. and CEO 20th Century Fox Inc. 1984, Chair. and CEO Fox Inc. 1985–92 (resgnd); Chair. and CEO QVC Network 1992–95; Chair. and CEO Silver King Communications 1995–98, Chair. Home Shopping Network (HSN) 1995–98, Chair. and CEO USA Interactive (later IAC/InterActive Corpn) including USA Networks Inc., New York 1998–2001, Chair. 2001–; Chair. and CEO Vivendi Universal Entertainment (VUE) 2002–03; mem. Bd of Dirs Washington Post Co., Coca-Cola Co., Conservation Int., Channel 13/WNET, Museum of TV and Radio; fmr mem. Bd of Dirs News Corpn Ltd; Trustee, New York Univ.; mem. Bd of Councilors Univ. of Southern Calif. School of Cinema-TV, Dean's Council Tisch School of the Arts, Exec. Bd for Medical Sciences UCLA, American Film Inst., Variety Clubs Int., Hollywood Radio and TV Soc., Acad. of Motion Picture Arts and Sciences. *Address:* IAC/InterActive Corporation, 152 West 57th Street, 42nd Floor, New York, NY 10019, USA (office). *Telephone:* (212) 314-7300 (office). *Fax:* (212) 314-7379 (office). *Website:* www .iac.com (office).

DILLER, Elizabeth, BArch; American architect and academic; *Principal, Diller Scofidio + Renfro;* b. Łodz, Poland; ed The Cooper Union School of Architecture; co-f. (with Ricardo Scofidio q.v., Diller & Scofidio (now Diller Scofidio + Renfro), New York 1979, cr. installations and electronic media projects; taught at The Cooper Union School of Architecture 1981–90; Assoc. Prof. of Architectural Design, Princeton Univ. 1990, currently Prof. of Architectural Design, Dir Grad. Studies 1993–; Jt recipient (with Ricardo Scofidio) fellowships from Graham Foundation for Advanced Study in the Fine Arts 1986, New York Foundation for the Arts 1986, 1987, 1989, Chicago Inst. for Architecture and Urbanism 1989, Tiffany Foundation Award for Emerging Artists 1990, Progressive Architecture Award (for Slow House) 1991, Chrysler Award for Achievement and Design 1997, National Design Award in Architecture from the Smithsonian 2005,. *Publications:* (with Ricardo Scofidio) Flesh 1995, Back to the Front: Tourisms of War. *Address:* 601 West 26th Street, Suite 1815, New York, NY 10001 (office); Princeton University School of Architecture, 5116 Architecture, Princeton, NJ 08544-0001, USA (office). *Telephone:* (212) 260-7971 (home). *Fax:* (212) 260-7924 (office). *E-mail:* ediller@dillerscofidio.com (office). *Website:* www.dillerscofidio .com (office).

DILLMAN, Linda M.; American retail executive; *Executive Vice-President, Risk Management and Benefits Administration, Wal-Mart Stores Inc.;* b. Fort Wayne, Ind.; ed Univ. of Indianapolis; with Hewlett-Packard 1987–92; joined Wal-Mart in 1992, served in several key information services man. positions including Applications Devt Man. for SAM'S CLUB and Applications Devt Man. for Wal-Mart Store Systems, Dir Applications Devt 1997–98, Vice-Pres. Applications Devt 1998, later Vice-Pres. Int. Systems, Sr Vice-Pres. Information Systems Div. 2002, Exec. Vice-Pres. and Chief Information Officer Wal-Mart Stores Inc. 2002–06, Exec. Vice-Pres. Risk Man. and Benefits Admin 2006–; mem. Bd Network of Exec. Women, GS1 Global, Nat. Center for Women and Information Tech.; mem. Advisory Bd Univ. of Indianapolis; ranked by Fortune magazine amongst 50 Most Powerful Women in Business in the US (28th) 2003, (32nd) 2004, (29th) 2005, (29th) 2006, (33rd) 2007, Univ. of Indianapolis Distinguished Alumni Award 2003, David D. Lattanze Center at Loyola Coll. Information Systems Exec. of the Year 2004, Univ. of Michigan Stephen M. Ross School of Business Women in Leadership Award 2005, EMC Information Leadership Award, Computerworld 2006. *Leisure interests:* skiing, watching Formula 1 racing, travelling with college friends. *Address:* Wal-Mart Stores Inc. 702 SW 8th Street, Bentonville, AR 72716-

8611, USA (office). *Telephone:* (479) 273-4000 (home). *Fax:* (479) 273-4053 (office). *Website:* www.walmartstores.com (office).

DILLON, David Brian, BA, LLB; American retail executive; *Chairman and CEO, The Kroger Company;* b. 30 March 1951, Hutchinson, Kan.; m. Dee A. Ehling 1973; one s. two d.; ed Hutchinson High School, Univ. of Kansas, Southern Methodist Univ.; various positions with family-owned business Dillon Cos including Head of Supermarket, Convenience Store and Mfg Operations, Vice-Pres. 1983–86, Pres. 1986–90; Exec. Vice-Pres. The Kroger Co. 1990–95, mem. Bd of Dirs 1995–, Pres. 1995–2000, Pres. and COO 2000–03, CEO 2003–04, Chair. and CEO 2004–; mem. Bd of Dirs Convergys Corpn 2000–02. *Address:* The Kroger Co., 1014 Vine Street, Cincinnati, OH 45202-1100, USA (office). *Telephone:* (513) 762-4000 (office). *Fax:* (513) 762-1160 (office). *E-mail:* info@kroger.com (office). *Website:* www.kroger.com (office); www.thekrogerco.com (office).

DILLON, Matt; American actor; b. 18 Feb. 1964, New Rochelle, NY; s. of Paul Dillon and Mary Ellen Dillon. *Films include:* Over the Edge 1979, Little Darlings 1980, My Bodyguard 1980, Liar's Moon 1982, Tex 1982, The Outsiders 1983, Rumble Fish 1983, The Flamingo Kid 1984, Target 1985, Rebel 1985, Native Son 1986, The Big Town (The Arm) 1987, Kansas 1988, Drugstore Cowboy 1989, A Kiss Before Dying 1991, Singles 1992, The Saint of Fort Washington, Mr. Wonderful 1993, Golden Gate 1994, To Die For 1995, Frankie Starlight 1995, Beautiful Girls 1996, Grace of My Heart 1996, Albino Alligator 1996, In and Out 1997, Wild Things 1998, There's Something About Mary 1998, One Night at McCool's 2000, Deuces Wild 2000, City of Ghosts (also Dir) 2002, Employee of the Month 2004, Loverboy 2004, Crash 2005, Factotum 2005, Herbie Fully Loaded 2005, You, Me and Dupree 2006. *Address:* c/o CAA, 2000 Avenue of the Stars, Los Angeles CA 90067, USA. *Telephone:* (424) 288-2000. *Fax:* (424) 288-2900.

DILNOT, Andrew, CBE, BA; British economist and university administrator; *Principal, St. Hugh's College, Oxford;* ed Olchfa Comprehensive School, Swansea, St. John's Coll., Oxford; joined Inst. of Fiscal Studies 1981, Dir 1991–2002; Prin. St. Hugh's Coll., Oxford Oct. 2002–; visiting lecturer numerous univs in UK and abroad; regular contrib. to broadcast and printed media, including BBC Radio 4 programmes Analysis and More or Less; mem. Social Security Advisory Cttee, Govt Evidence-Based Policy Panel; mem. Council, Royal Econ. Soc.; mem. Council, Queen Mary and Westfield Coll. *Publication:* The Tiger That Isn't: Seeing Through a World of Numbers (with Michael Blastland) 2007. *Address:* Office of the Principal, St Hugh's College, Oxford, OX2 6LE, England (office). *Telephone:* (1865) 274900 (office). *Fax:* (1865) 274912 (office). *E-mail:* andrewdilnot@st-hughs.ox.ac.uk (office). *Website:* www.st-hughs.ox.ac.uk (office).

DIMAS, Pyrros; Greek weightlifter; b. (Pirro Ohima), 13 Oct. 1971, Himarra, Albania; m. Anastasia Sdougkou; two d. one s.; light-heavyweight lifter; emigrated to Greece 1991; gold medal Barcelona Olympic Games 1992, Atlanta Olympic Games 1996, Sydney Olympic Games 2000; World Championship title 1993, 1995, 1998; European Championship title 1995; world record in the snatch (85kg category); major in the Greek army; Greek Athlete of the Year 1992, 1993, 1995, 1996; Top Athlete in the 1995 World Championship. *Leisure interests include:* video games, backgammon, cinema. *Address:* c/o The Hellenic Weightlifting Federation, 43 Sygrou Av., 117 43 Athens, Greece (office). *Website:* www.pyrros.gr (office).

DIMBLEBY, David, MA; British broadcaster and journalist; b. 28 Oct. 1938, London; s. of the late Richard Dimbleby and of Dilys Thomas; m. 1st Josceline Gaskell 1967 (divorced 2000); one s. two d.; m. 2nd Belinda Giles 2000; one s.; ed Charterhouse, Christ Church, Oxford, Univs of Paris and Perugia; presenter and interviewer, BBC Bristol 1960–61; Chair. Dimbleby and Sons Ltd 1986–2001, fmrly Man. Dir 1967; Richard Dimbleby Award, BAFTA 1998. *Broadcasts include:* Quest (religious programme), What's New? (children's science), People and Power 1982–83; General Election Results Programmes 1979, 1983, 1987, 2001, various programmes for the Budget, by-elections, local elections etc.; presenter Question Time BBC 1993–. *Documentary films include:* Ku-Klux-Klan, The Forgotten Million, Cyprus: The Thin Blue Line 1964–65, South Africa: The White Tribe (Royal TV Soc. Supreme Documentary Award) 1979, The Struggle for South Africa (US Emmy Award, Monte Carlo Golden Nymph) 1990, US –UK Relations: An Ocean Apart 1988, David Dimbleby's India 1997; live commentary on many public occasions including: State Opening of Parliament, Trooping the Colour, Wedding of HRH Prince Andrew and Sarah Ferguson, HM The Queen Mother's 90th Birthday Parade (Royal TV Soc. Outstanding Documentary Award), Funeral of Diana, Princess of Wales 1997, Memorial services including Lord Olivier (Royal TV Soc. Outstanding Documentary Award), How We Built Britain (and book) 2007. *Publication:* An Ocean Apart (with David Reynolds) 1988. *Address:* c/o Rosemary Scoular, United Agents, 12–26 Lexington Street, London, W1F 0LE, England (office). *Telephone:* (20) 3214-0800 (office). *Fax:* (20) 3214-0801 (office). *E-mail:* info@unitedagents.co.uk (office). *Website:* unitedagents.co.uk (office).

DIMBLEBY, Jonathan, BA; British broadcaster, journalist and writer; b. 31 July 1944, Aylesbury, Bucks.; s. of the late Richard Dimbleby and of Dilys Thomas; m. Bel Mooney 1968 (divorced); one s. one d.; m. Jessica Ray 2007; one d.; ed Univ. Coll. London; reporter BBC Bristol 1969–70, World at One (BBC Radio) 1970–71, This Week (Thames TV) 1972–78, 1986–88, TV Eye 1979, Jonathan Dimbleby in Evidence series (Yorkshire TV) 1980–84; Assoc. Ed./Presenter First Tuesday 1982–86; Presenter/Ed. Jonathan Dimbleby on Sunday (TV-am) 1985–86, On the Record (BBC TV) 1988–93, Charles: the Private Man, the Public Role (Central TV) 1994, weekly political programme Jonathan Dimbleby (ITV) 1995–; presenter Any Questions? and Any Answers? (both BBC Radio 4) 1987–; main presenter of Gen. Election coverage (ITV); Pres. Voluntary Service Overseas 1999–, Soil Asscn 1997–, Royal Soc. for the Protection of Birds 2001–04, Bath Festivals Trust 2003–06; Vice-Pres. Council for Protection of Rural England 1997–; Trustee Richard Dimbleby Cancer Fund, Dimbleby Cancer Care and the Susan Chilcott Scholarship; Richard Dimbleby Award 1974. *Publications:* Richard Dimbleby 1975, The Palestinians 1979, The Prince of Wales: A Biography 1994, The Last Governor 1997, Russia: A Journey to the Heart of a Land and its People 2008. *Leisure interests:* tennis, riding, music, rural life. *Address:* David Higham Associates, Ltd, 5 Lower John Street, Golden Square, London, W1R 4HA, England (office). *Telephone:* (20) 7437-7888 (office).

DIMÉNY, Imre, DR.AGR.SC.; Hungarian agropolitician and agronomist; *Professor Emeritus, Corvinus University of Budapest;* b. 3 Aug. 1922, Komolló; s. of János Dimény and Anna Illyés; m. Margit Erzsébet Buzgó 1947; one d.; agronomic engineer; rural, county and ministry official 1945–55; Dept Head, later Vice-Pres. Nat. Planning Bureau 1955–62; Alt. mem. Cen. Cttee and Leader Agricultural Dept Hungarian Socialist Workers' Party 1962–66; Minister of Agric. and Food 1967–75; Prof., Univ. of Horticulture, Corvinus Univ. of Budapest 1975–95, Rector 1975–86, Prof. Emer. 1995–; mem. Hungarian Acad. of Sciences 1982–; Dr hc (Univ. of Agricultural Sciences Gödöllő) 1994, (Univ. of Horticulture and Food Industry, Pannon Univ. of Agric.) 1997, (Univ. of Agricultural Sciences, Debrecen) 1999. *Leisure interests:* reading, gardening. *Address:* Corvinus University, Faculty of Food Sciences, Villányi út 35–41, 1118 Budapest XI (office); Szilágyi Erzsébet fasor 79, 111/2, 1026 Budapest, Hungary (home). *Telephone:* (1) 482-6254 (office); (1) 356-6580 (home).

DIMITROV, Aleksander; Macedonian politician and lawyer; b. 29 Nov. 1949, Skopje; ed Skopje Univ.; mem. Man. Bd, Air Service Skopje, Sec. Forum for Int. Relations; ed. Forum (newspaper) 1969–72; ed. Mlad Borac (newspaper) 1972–78; Sec. Council for Foreign Relations 1979–82; Under-Sec. Cttee for Int. Relations 1982–92; Dir for Int. Affairs, Dir Office of Palair 1993–96; Minister of Foreign Affairs 1998–2001. *Address:* c/o Ministry of Foreign Affairs, Dame Grueva 14, 9100 Skopje, Macedonia.

DIMITROV, Petar, DEcon; Bulgarian politician; *Minister of the Economy and Energy;* b. 27 Jan. 1949, Klisura; ed Moscow Inst. of Econs and Statistics, Nottingham Trent Univ., UK 1994; Lecturer, Varna Univ. of Econs 1976–93, Deputy Rector 1989–93, Assoc. Prof. in Social Man. 1988, Head of Higher School of Man. 1990; mem. Nat. Ass. 1994–, Chair. Parl. Comm on Budget and Finance 2005–07, mem. Comm on Educ. and Science, on Econ. Policy, Budget and Finance; Minister of Economy and Energy 2007–. *Address:* Ministry of the Economy and Energy, 1000 Sofia, ul. Slavyanska 8, Bulgaria (office). *Telephone:* (2) 940-71-00 (office). *Fax:* (2) 987-21-90 (office). *E-mail:* public@mi.government.bg (office). *Website:* www.mi.government.bg (office).

DIMITROV, Philip, JD; Bulgarian lawyer, politician, diplomatist, academic and author; *Deputy Speaker, National Assembly;* b. 31 March 1955, Sofia; s. of Dimitar Vassilev Dimitrov and Katherine Philipova Dimitrova; m. Elena Valentinova Gueorgieva-Dimitrova 1988; ed St Kliment Ohridsky Univ., Sofia; attorney 1979–1991, 2002–05;Vice-Pres. Union of Democratic Forces 1990, Pres. 1990–94; Prime Minister of Bulgaria 1991–92; mem. Parl. 1991–97; Vice-Chair. Jt Parl. Cttee, EU–Bulgaria 1995–97; Perm. Rep. to UN, New York 1997–98; Amb. to USA 1998–2002; Special Envoy of OSCE Pres. for Armenia and Azerbaijan 2004; Deputy Speaker, Nat. Ass. (Parl.) 2005–; MEP 2007–; Woodrow Wilson Center Public Policy Scholar, Washington, DC 2003; Adjunct Prof., American Univ. in Bulgaria 2003–; mem. Sofia Bar Asscn; Truman-Reagan Freedom Award for contrib. to overcoming communism 1999; Dimitrov Scholarships and Lectures, American Univ. in Bulgaria, Sofia inaugurated 2002. *Publications include:* The Myths of the Bulgarian Transition 2003, The New Democracies and the Transatlantic Link 2003; three historical novels, For They Lived, O Lord 1991, The True Story of the Round Table Knights 1996, Light of Men 2003. *Leisure Interest:* history. *Address:* Bulgarian National Assembly, 1 Batemberg Square, Sofia 1000 (office); American University in Bulgaria, 2700 Blagoevgrad, Bulgaria. *Telephone:* (2) 9873238 (office); (73) 888456. *Fax:* (2) 9805358 (office). *E-mail:* phd@parliament.bg (office). *Website:* www.parliament.bg (office).

DIMMELER, Stefanie, BSc, PhD; German biologist, biochemist and academic; *Professor of Experimental Medicine and Head of Section of Molecular Cardiology, University of Frankfurt;* b. 18 July 1967, Ravensburg; ed Univ. of Konstanz; completed a fellowship in Experimental Surgery at Univ. of Cologne; completed a fellowship in Molecular Cardiology at Univ. of Frankfurt, Prof. of Experimental Medicine and Head of Section of Molecular Cardiology 2001–; mem. Editorial Bd Circulation, Circulation Research, Basic Research in Cardiology, Journal of Molecular and Cellular Cardiology; mem. Advisory Bd Lifeboat Foundation; Preis des Stifterverbandes für die Deutsche Wissenschaft 1991, Fritz Külz Prize, Deutschen Gesellschaft für Pharmakologie und Toxikologie 1994, Research Prize, Deutschen Stiftung für Herzforschung 1998, Herbert and Hedwig Eckelmann Foundation Prize 1999, Fraenkel Prize, Deutschen Gesellschaft für Kardiologie 2000, Alfried-Krupp-Förderpreis für junge Hochschullehrer 2002, Forßmann Prize, Ruhr-Universität Bochum 2004, Leibniz Prize 2005, Ernst Jung Prize, Jung-Stiftung für Wissenschaft und Forschung (co-recipient) 2007. *Achievements include:* responsible, together with Dr Zeiher, for scientific discoveries culminating in current clinical trial of human progenitor cells for cardiac repair. *Publications:* more than 120 scientific papers in professional journals on endothelial biology, including signal transduction, apoptosis, and renewal by circulating endothelial progenitor cells in health and disease. *Address:* University of Frankfurt, Theodor-Stern-Kai 7, 60596 Frankfurt am Main, Germany (office). *Telephone:* (69) 6301-7440 (office). *Fax:* (69) 6301-7113 (office). *Website:* www.uni-frankfurt.de (office).

DIMON, James (Jamie) L., MBA; American financial services industry executive; *Chairman and CEO, JPMorgan Chase & Company;* b. 13 March 1956, New York, NY; m. Judy Kent; three d.; ed The Browning School, New York, Tufts Univ., Harvard Univ.; Asst to Pres., American Express 1982–85; Pres. and COO Travelers Group 1991–98, also COO Smith Barney Inc. (subsidiary co.) –1996, Chair. and CEO 1996–97, Chair. and Co-CEO, Salomon Smith Barney Holdings Inc. (following merger) 1997–98; Pres. Citigroup 1998–2000; Chair. and CEO Bank One Corpn March 2000–04, Pres., COO and Dir JPMorgan Chase & Co. (after merger between Bank One Corpn and JPMorgan Chase & Co.) 2004–05, CEO and Pres. 2005–, Chair. 2006–; Vice-Chair. NYU School of Medicine Foundation Bd; Dir Tricon Global Restaurants Inc., Center on Addiction and Substance Abuse; Trustee, Mount Sinai-NYU Medical Center; mem. Council on Foreign Relations. *Address:* JPMorgan Chase & Co., 270 Park Avenue, New York, NY 10017-2070, USA (office). *Telephone:* (212) 270-6000 (office). *Fax:* (212) 270-1648 (office). *E-mail:* joseph.evangelisti@jpmchase.com (office). *Website:* www.jpmorganchase.com (office).

DIMOVSKA, Dosta; Macedonian politician; b. 17 Feb. 1954, Skopje; ed Skopje Univ.; teacher, Georgi Dimitrov School, Skopje 1980–98; Asst, Asst Prof., Faculty of Philosophy, Skopje Univ. 1981–91; mem. Parl. 1991–95; mem. of staff, BS Stock Holding Co. 1995–97, Kisela Voda, Skopje 1998; Chair. Cttee on Inter-Ethnic Relations; Deputy Prime Minister, Minister of Internal Affairs 1998–2001; Vice-Pres. Internal Macedonian Revolutionary Org.-Democratic Party for Macedonian Nat. Unity (IMRO-DPMNU) 1991, 1995. *Publications:* two vols of poetry, essays and political reviews. *Address:* IMRO-DPMNU, 1000 Skopje, Petar Drapshin br. 36, Macedonia (office). *Telephone:* (2) 111441 (office). *Fax:* (2) 211586 (office).

DINARDO, HE Cardinal Daniel Nicholas, BA, MA, LicTheol; American ecclesiastic; *Archbishop of Galveston-Houston;* b. 23 May 1949, Steubenville, OH; ed Catholic Univ. of America, Washington, DC, Pontifical Gregorian Univ. and the Augustinianum, Rome; ordained priest in Pittsburgh 1977; staff mem. Vatican Congregation for Bishops 1984–90; also served as Dir of Villa Stritch (residence for American priests working at the Vatican); taught a theology seminar in methodology at Gregorian Univ.; held pastoral posts in Pittsburgh Diocese, where he taught in the ongoing formation programme for priests and was Asst Spiritual Dir at St Paul Seminary 1990–97; Coadjutor Bishop of Sioux City, Ia 1997–98, Bishop of Sioux City 1998–2004; Coadjutor Bishop of Galveston-Houston, Tex. Jan.–Dec. 2004, Coadjutor Archbishop of Galveston-Houston Dec. 2004–06, Archbishop of Galveston-Houston 2006–; cr. Cardinal 2007–; mem. Bd Trustees Catholic Univ. of America. *Address:* Chancery Office, Archdiocese of Galveston-Houston, PO Box 907, 1700 San Jacinto Street, Houston, TX 77001-0907, USA (office). *Telephone:* (713) 659-5461 (office). *Fax:* (713) 759-9151 (office). *E-mail:* info@diogh.org (office). *Website:* www.diogh.org (office).

DINCERLER, M. Vehbi; Turkish politician; b. 2 Aug. 1940, Gaziantep; s. of Esat and Şefika Dincerler; m.; three s. one d.; ed Depts of Eng, Istanbul Tech. Univ., Business Inst., Istanbul Univ., Grad. School, Univ. of Syracuse, NY; worked for State Planning Org.; joined Project Studies for Turkey at World Bank, studied economy of Ireland; academic at Middle East Tech. Univ., Gaziantep Campus; mem. Nat. Ass. 1983–, Minister of Educ., Youth and Sports 1983–85, Minister of State 1985–87; Chair. Nat. Ass. Foreign Relations Cttee 1988–90; Minister of State 1989–91; mem. Constitutional Cttee 1991–, N Atlantic Ass.; Motherland Party. *Leisure interests:* music, social activities. *Address:* Ahmet Hasim Cad. 67/U Dikmen, Ankara 06460, Turkey. *Telephone:* (312) 4415361. *Fax:* (312) 4381555.

DINDAR, Mohammad Naim, BS, Dip.Agric.; Afghan banker; *Chief Executive, Banke Millie Afghan;* b. 29 Sept. 1947; s. of Mohammad Yasin and Zohra Begum; ed American Univ. of Beirut, Lebanon; Exchange Student, American Field Service 1964–65; Pres. Afghan Students' Asscn 1968–69; fmr Chief of Staff, Ministry of Finance; fmr Pres., Int. Relations, Antinarcotic Comm.; Sr Agriculture Analyst, Office of Agricultural Affairs; Chair. and CEO Banke Millie Afghan 2005–; Vice-Chair. Afghan Banking Asscn; mem. Bd Afghan Telecom, Ariana, Afghan Red Crescent. *Publications:* Afghan Marketing (co-author) 1975; contribs to Journal of Agriculture; several translations. *Address:* Banke Millie Afghan, PO Box 522, Jade Ibne Sina, Kabul, Afghanistan (office). *Telephone:* (20) 2102221 (office). *Fax:* (20) 2101801 (office). *E-mail:* info@bma.com.af (office). *Website:* www.bma.com.af (office).

DINE, James; American artist; b. 16 June 1935, Cincinnati, Ohio; m. Nancy Minto 1957; three s.; ed Cincinnati Art Acad.; first one-man exhbn Reuben Gallery, New York 1960; work appears in many public collections including Guggenheim Museum, Moderna Museet, Stockholm, Museum of Modern Art, New York, Dallas Museum of Fine Arts, Tate Gallery and Whitney Museum of Modern American Art. *Publications:* Welcome Home, Lovebirds 1969 (also illustrator); co-author and illustrator The Adventures of Mr. and Mrs. Jim & Ron 1970; illustrator The Poet Assassinated 1968, Drawing from the Glypothek 1993. *Address:* c/o The Pace Gallery, 32 East 57th Street, New York, NY 10022, USA.

DING, Fengying; Chinese party official; *Vice-Chairman, Hubei Provincial Committee, Chinese People's Political Consultative Conference;* b. 1943, Luotian Co., Hubei Prov.; ed Huazhong Teachers Coll., Cen. China Teachers' Coll.; Sec. CCP CYLC and Chair. Women's Fed., Beifeng Commune, Luotian Co. 1960–69; Deputy Sec. and Sec. CCP Party Cttee, Beifeng Commune Fourth Brigade, Luotian Co. 1960–69; joined CCP 1961; Deputy Dir CCP Revolutionary Cttee, Luotian Co. 1969–71, Deputy Sec. CCP Co. Cttee 1969–71; Chair. Hubei Branch, Chinese Women's Fed. 1973; Vice-Chair. Revolutionary Cttee, Hubei Prov. 1978–79; Alt. mem. 12th CCP Cen. Cttee 1982–87; First Sec. CCP Cttee, Huangguang Pref. 1983–; Deputy Sec. CCP Cttee, Hubei Prov. 1986, mem. CCP 5th Hubei Prov. Cttee 1988–, Sec. Comm. for Discipline Inspection, Hubei Prov. 1988–; mem. CCP Cen. Discipline Inspection Comm. 1992–, 9th CPPCC Nat. Cttee 1998–2003; Vice-Chairman CPPCC Hubei Prov. Cttee 2003–. *Address:* Hubei Dangwei, 1 Beihuanlu Road, Shuiguohu, Wuchang City, Hubei Province, People's Republic of China. *Telephone:* 813351.

DING, Guangen; Chinese state official; b. Sept. 1929, Wuxian Co., Jiangsu Prov.; ed Jiaotong Univ. of Shanghai; joined CCP 1956; held posts in Ministry of Railways as engineer, Gen. Transport Bureau, Dir Educ. Bureau, Sec. of Gen. Office; Deputy Sec.-Gen. Standing Comm. NPC 1983–85; Minister of Railways 1985–88; Vice-Minister State Planning Comm. 1988; apptd Dir Taiwan Affairs Office of the Council of State 1988; apptd Vice-Minister, State Devt and Reform Comm. 1988; mem. 12th CCP Cen. Cttee 1982–87, 13th CCP Cen. Cttee 1987–92 (also co-opted mem. Secr. of Politburo—4th Plenum), 14th CCP Cen. Cttee 1992–97 (also mem. Secr. of Politburo—1st Plenum), 15th CCP Cen. Cttee 1997–2002 (also mem. Secr. of Politburo); Alt. mem. 13th CCP Cen. Cttee Politburo 1987–92; Head of CCP United Front Work Dept 1990–92; apptd Head of CCP Propaganda Dept 1992; apptd Head of Cen. Leading Group for Propaganda and Thought 1994; apptd Dir Cen. Guidance Cttee on Ethical and Cultural Construction, CCP Cen. Cttee 1997. *Address:* Central Committee of the Chinese Communist Party, Zhongnanghai, Beijing, People's Republic of China.

DING, Gen. Henggao; Chinese politician and scientist; b. 1931, Nanjing Co., Jiangsu Prov.; m. Nie Lili (d. of Marshal Nie Rongzhen); ed Nanjing Univ., Leningrad Inst. of Precision Machinery and Optical Instruments, USSR; joined CCP 1953; held posts of Section Chief, Deputy Inst. Dir, Deputy Bureau Dir and Research Fellow, Ministry of Defence 1960s–70s; Minister of State Comm. of Science, Tech. and Industry for Nat. Defence 1985–96, Party Cttee Sec. 1989–; rank of Lt-Gen. PLA 1988–94, Gen. 1994–; Alt. mem. 12th CCP Cen. Cttee 1982–87, mem. 13th CCP Cen. Cttee 1989–92, 14th CCP Cen. Cttee 1992–97; mem. State Leading Group for Science and Tech.; mem. Standing Cttee, 9th CPPCC Nat. Cttee 1998–2003; Pres. Chinese Soc. of Inertial Tech. 1995–; mem. Chinese Acad. of Eng 1994–; Hon. Pres. Chinese Astronautics Soc.; State Special Class Award for scientific and technological achievements for nat. defence 1994. *Address:* 1 South Building, Aimin Street, Xicheng District, Beijing 100034, People's Republic of China. *Telephone:* (10) 66056357. *Fax:* (10) 66738111. *E-mail:* engach@mail.cae.ac.cn (office).

DING, Jieyin; Chinese sculptor; b. 4 Feb. 1926, Yinxian, Zhejiang; d. of Ding Yong-sen and Gao Yu-ding; m. Hong Bo 1952; one d.; ed Cen. Acad. of Fine Arts, Beijing; Asst Researcher, Sculpture Studio, Cen. Acad. of Fine Arts; Ed. China Sculpture; Chief Ed. supplement Chinese Art, New Evening newspaper, Hong Kong; Vice-Dir Longshan Art Acad., Rizhao 1992–; mem. China Artists' Asscn; about 60 pieces of sculpture; works exhibited at China Art Gallery, Beijing 1991, 1992 and commissioned by various cities. *Publications:* Clay Figures in the Temples of Da Tong 1982, The Art of Colour Clay Sculpture in Jin Ancestral Temple 1988; articles in Meishu, Art Research, People's Daily and Chinese Art supplement, New Evening (Hong Kong). *Leisure interests:* literature, basketball. *Address:* Xiao-Wei-Hu-Tong 68, Beijing 100005, People's Republic of China. *Telephone:* 5136377.

DING, Shisun; Chinese university administrator and mathematician; b. 5 Sept. 1927, Shanghai; s. of Ding Rounong and Liu Huixian; m. Gui Linlin 1956; two s.; ed Tsinghua Univ.; Asst Tsinghua Univ. 1950–52; joined China Democratic League 1952; joined staff Beijing Univ. 1952, promoted to Lecturer then Prof. of Math. 1979, Vice-Chair. Math. Dept 1978–80, Chair. 1981–82, Pres. Beijing Univ. 1984–89; Pres. Math. Soc. of Beijing 1986–88; Vice-Pres. Chinese Math. Soc. 1988–91; fmr Chair. Jiang Zehan Scholarship Fund Cttee; fmr Vice-Chair. Zhou Peiyuan Fund Cttee; fmr Vice-Pres. Chinese Educ. Asscn for Int. Exchanges; fmr Deputy Head, Math. Examination and Appraisal Group, Nat. Natural Science Foundation of China; fmr mem. 2nd Panel of Judges of State Academic Degrees Cttee, Exec. Council of China Overseas Exchanges Asscn, Exec. Council of China Soc. of Higher Educ., Council of Chinese People's Inst. of Foreign Affairs; visited Math. Dept, Harvard Univ., USA 1983; Exec. Vice-Chair. China Democratic League Cen. Cttee 1988–96, Chair. 1996–; mem. 7th CPPCC Nat. Cttee 1988–93, Standing Cttee of 8th CPPCC Nat. Cttee 1993–98; Vice-Chair. Educ. and Culture Cttee; Vice-Chair. Standing Cttee of 9th NPC 1998–2003, Standing Cttee of 10th NPC 2003–; Chair. Advisory Cttee American Studies Center, Peking Univ.; Pres. Western Returned Students' Asscn 1999–; mem. Macao Special Admin. Region Preparatory Cttee, Govt Del., Macao Hand-Over Ceremony 1999; Dr hc (Soka, Japan) 1985; Hon. DSc (Nebraska) 1988. *Publications:* Concise Textbook of Higher Algebra, Analytic Geometry and Orders of Linear Displacement Register; numerous math. papers on algebra and number theory. *Leisure interest:* classical music. *Address:* c/o Advisory Committee, American Studies Center, Main Library, 5th Floor, Peking University, Beijing, 100871, People's Republic of China.

DING, Gen. Wenchang; Chinese party official and army officer; b. 1933, Suxian Co., Anhui Prov.; ed PLA High Infantry School, Air Force Aviation School; joined CCP 1956; Chief, Political Dept, Air Force, PLA Services and Arms, Dir 1988, Political Commissar 1992–99, Party Cttee Sec.; rank of Maj.-Gen. 1988–90, Lt-Gen. of Air Force 1990–96, Gen. 1996–; Deputy, 7th NPC 1988–93; mem. 14th CCP Cen. Cttee 1992–97, 15th CCP Cen. Cttee 1997–2002. *Address:* Political Department of Air Force, Beijing, People's Republic of China.

DING, William, BSc; Chinese internet executive; *Chairman and Chief Technology Officer, NetEase.com Inc.;* b. (Ding Lei), Oct. 1971, Ningbo City, Zhejiang Prov.; ed China Electronic Science and Tech. Univ., Chengdu; tech. engineer, Ningbo Telecom 1993–95; tech. support engineer, Sybase Guangzhou Co. 1995–96, Guangzhou Feijie Co. 1996–97; Founder and CEO

NetEase.com Inc. (introduced first free e-mail service, online community and personalized information service in China) 1997–2000, Chief Tech. Officer 2000–01, Acting CEO and COO June–Sept. 2001, Chair. and Chief Tech. Officer 2001–; named one of the 10 most influential Internet celebrities in China 1999, named one of China's Top Ten IT Figures 2001, 2002. *Address:* NetEase.com, SP Tower D, 26th Floor, Tsinghua Science Park, Building 8, No. 1 Zhongguancun East Road, Haidian District, Beijing 100084 (office); 2nd Floor, Tower B, Keeven International R&D Centre, Beijing 100086, People's Republic of China. *Telephone:* (10) 82558163 (office). *Fax:* (10) 82618163 (office). *E-mail:* ir@service.netease.com (office). *Website:* (office).

DING, Xiaqi; Chinese mathematician and research professor; *Professor, Center of Mathematical Sciences, Zhejiang University;* b. 25 May 1928, Yiyang Co., Hunan Prov.; m. Luo Peizhu 1957; three d.; ed Dept of Math., Wuhan Univ.; Research Asst, Assoc., Assoc. Prof., Prof., Inst. of Math., Acad. Sinica 1951–79; Research Prof., Inst. of Systems Sciences, Acad. Sinica 1979–91; Research Prof., Inst. of Applied Math., Academia Sinica 1991–; Prof. and Dir Wuhan Inst. of Math., Acad. Sinica 1985–94, Dr Wuhan Inst. of Math. Physics; Academician, Chinese Acad. of Sciences 1991–; currently Prof. Center of Mathematical Sciences, Zhejiang Univ. Hangzhou; mem. Cttee Math. Soc. of China; Standing mem. Cttee of Chinese Soc. of Systems Eng; Prize Award, Nat. Science Conf., Beijing 1978, Prize of Chinese Acad. of Sciences 1978, 1st Class Prize, Chinese Acad. of Science 1988, 2nd Class Prize Natural Science Prize of People's Repub. of China 1989, Hua Loo-Keng Mathematics Prize. *Publications:* more than 80 papers on PDE, functions spaces, number theory and numerical analysis; 4 monographs. *Leisure interest:* mathematics. *Address:* Center of Mathematical Sciences, Zhejiang University, Hangzhou 310027, People's Republic of China (office). *Telephone:* (571) 87953030 (office). *Fax:* (571) 87953035 (office). *Website:* www.cms.zju.edu.cn (office).

DING GUANGXUN, Bishop K. H.; Chinese theologian and church leader; *Vice-Chairman, 10th National Committee, Chinese People's Political Consultative Conference;* b. 20 Sept. 1915, Shanghai; ed St Johns Univ., Shanghai, Columbia Univ. and Union Theological Seminary, New York, USA; ordained 1942; Sec. Student Christian Movt of Canada, Student World Christian Fed., Geneva; returned to China 1951; Pres. Nanjing Theological Seminary 1952, consecrated Bishop 1955; Vice-Chair. Three-Self Patriotic Cttee Movt of the Protestant Churches of China 1961, Chair. 5th Cttee 1980–97, Hon. Chair. 1997–; apptd Vice-Pres. Nanjing Univ. 1979; Founder, China Amity Foundation 1984; Pres. Christian Council of China 1985, Hon. Pres. 1997–; mem. 3rd CPPCC Nat. Cttee 1959–64, Standing Cttee 5th CPPCC Nat. Cttee 1978–83, Vice-Chair. 7th CPPCC Nat. Cttee 1989–93, Religious Cttee 1991–, Vice-Chair. 8th CPPCC Nat. Cttee 1993–98, 9th CPPCC Nat. Cttee 1998–2003, 10th CPPCC Nat. Cttee 2003–; Chair. Chinese Religious Peace Cttee 1994–; Sec. of Secr. CCP Cen. Cttee 1992–; Deputy, 3rd NPC 1964–75, 4th NPC 1975–78, 5th NPC 1978–83, mem. 6th Standing Cttee of NPC 1983–88, 7th Standing Cttee of NPC 1988–93; Vice-Chair. CPPCC Jiangsu Prov. Cttee; Hon. Pres. Chinese People's Asscn for Peace and Disarmament 1985–. *Publications:* Testimony of Chinese Christianity, Chinese Christianity Today and Voice of Chinese Christians. *Address:* Nanjing Theological Seminary, Nanjing 210029; 378 Mo Chou Road, Nanjing 210004, People's Republic of China.

DINGWALL, Bruce; British petroleum executive; *CEO, Venture Production;* b. 1959; began career as geophysicist with Exxon working in North Sea; Business Devt Man. for Asia, Vice-Pres. of Exploration for Indonesia and Exploration Man. for Pakistan, LASMO PLC –1997; CEO Venture Production (petroleum co.) 1997–; Pres. UKOOA (UK Offshore Petroleum Operators Asscn) 2002–. *Address:* Venture Production, First Floor, Crimon Place Wing, King's Close, 62 Huntly Street, Aberdeen, AB10 1RS (office); UK Offshore Operators Association, 9 Albyn Terrace, Aberdeen, AB10 1YP, Scotland (office). *Telephone:* (1224) 619000 (Venture) (office); (1224) 626652 (UKOOA) (office). *Fax:* (1224) 658151 (Venture) (office); (1224) 626503 (UKOOA) (office). *E-mail:* enquiries@vpc.co.uk (office). *Website:* www.vpc.co.uk (Venture) (office); www.ukooa.co.uk (UKOOA) (office).

DINI, Lamberto; Italian politician and banker; *Deputy Speaker of Senate;* b. 1 March 1931, Florence; m.; one d.; ed Univ. of Florence, Univs of Minnesota and Michigan, USA; economist, IMF, Washington DC, then various posts to Deputy Dir Africa Dept 1959–76, mem. Bd Exec. Dirs 1976–78, now Alt. Gov. for Italy; joined Banca d'Italia (cen. bank) as Asst Gen. Man. 1979, later Gen. Man.; mem. Monetary Cttee of EU, Bd Dirs BIS; Minister of the Treasury 1994–95; Prime Minister of Italy 1995–96; Minister of Foreign Affairs 1996–2001; Deputy Speaker of Senate 2001–; Leader Rinnovamento Italiano; Vice-Pres. European Liberal, Democrat and Reform Party; Fulbright Scholar. *Address:* Senate of the Italian Republic, Palazzo Madama Piazza Madama, 00186 Rome; Rinnovamento Italiano, Via di Ripetta 142, 00186 Rome, Italy (office). *Telephone:* (06) 67062208 (Senate) (office). *Fax:* (06) 67063611 (Senate) (office). *E-mail:* l.dini@senato.it (office). *Website:* www.senato.it (office); www.rinnovamento.it (office).

DINI AHMED, Ahmed; Djibouti politician; b. 1932, Obock; Vice-Pres., Territorial Ass., French Somaliland (now Repub. of Djibouti) 1959–60; Minister of Production 1963–64, of the Interior 1967–72; joined Ligue Populaire Africaine pour l'Indépendance 1972; Pres. Nat. Ass. of French Territory of the Afars and the Issas May–June 1977, of Repub. of Djibouti June–July 1977; Prime Minister July–Dec. 1977; Pres. Front pour la restauration de l'unité et de la démocratie (insurgent movt) 1992–94, split into two factions March 1994; leader of faction favouring a continuation of mil. activities.

DINKIĆ, Mlađan, BA, MA; Serbian economist, academic, government official and fmr central banker; *Deputy Prime Minister and Minister of the Economy and Regional Development;* b. 20 Dec. 1964; m.; ed Univ. of Belgrade; research asst, Faculty of Econs, Univ. of Belgrade 1990–93, Prof. 1994–; f. G17 (political party, later G17 Plus), Co-ordinator 1997–2001, Vice-Pres. 2001–06, Pres. 2006–; Gov. Nat. Bank of Yugoslavia 2000–03, Gov. Nat. Bank of Serbia 2003–04; fmr econ. adviser to govt; Minister of Finance 2004–06 (resgnd), of the Economy and Regional Devt 2007–, Deputy Prime Minister 2008–. *Publications:* Measuring Economic Efficiency 1994, The Economy of Destruction 1995, Final Account: Economic Consequences of NATO Bombing 1999. *Leisure interests:* music, guitar, piano. *Address:* Ministry of the Economy and Regional Development, 11000 Belgrade, bul. Kralja Aleksandra 15, Serbia (office). *Telephone:* (11) 3347231 (office). *Fax:* (11) 3346770 (office). *E-mail:* officemprov@mpriv.sr.gov.yu (office). *Website:* www.mpriv.sr.gov.yu (office).

DINKINS, David, BS; American fmr politician and lawyer; *Professor in the Practice of Public Affairs and Senior Fellow, Center for Urban Research and Policy, School of International and Public Affairs, Columbia University;* b. 10 July 1927, Trenton, NJ; m. Joyce Burrows 1953; one s. one d.; ed Howard Univ., Washington, DC and Brooklyn Law School; joined Harlem law firm 1956; elected to New York State Ass. 1965; Pres. Bd of Elections, New York 1972; City Clerk, New York 1975–85; Manhattan Borough Pres. 1986; contested Democratic Primary, defeating Mayor Edward Koch Sept. 1989; Mayor of New York 1990–93; Prof. in Practice of Public Affairs and Sr Fellow, Center for Urban Research and Policy, Columbia Univ.'s School of Int. and Public Affairs 1993–; host Dialogue with Dinkins radio public affairs program; mem. Council on Foreign Relations; mem. Bd of Govs American Stock Exchange. *Leisure interest:* tennis. *Address:* School of International and Public Affairs, Columbia University, 420 West 118th Street, New York, NY 10027, USA. *Telephone:* 212-854-4253. *E-mail:* dd98@columbia.edu. *Website:* www.sipa.columbia.edu.

DINWIDDY, Bruce Harry, CMG, MA; British diplomatist; b. 1 Feb. 1946, Epsom; s. of the late Thomas Lutwyche Dinwiddy and Ruth Dinwiddy (née Abbott); m. Emma Victoria Llewellyn 1974; one s. one d.; ed Winchester Coll., New Coll. Oxford; economist, Govt of Swaziland, Overseas Devt Inst. (ODI) Nuffield Fellow 1967–70, Research Officer 1970–73; entered FCO 1973, Cen. and Southern African Dept 1973–4, Second Sec. Mission CSCE, Geneva 1974, Hong Kong and Indian Ocean Dept 1974–75; Del. to Mutual and Balanced Force Reductions (MBFR) negotiations, Vienna 1975–77; Perm. Under Sec.'s Dept, FCO London 1977–81, Personnel Operations Dept 1983–84, Asst Head, Personnel Policy Dept 1985–86, 2001–02; Head of Chancery in Cairo, Egypt 1981–83; Counsellor on loan to Cabinet Office 1986–88; CDA/SWP, Ebenhausen 1989; Embassy Counsellor in Bonn, Germany 1989–91; Deputy High Commr in Ottawa, Canada 1992–95; Head of African Dept (Southern) FCO 1995–98; Commr (non-resident) British Indian Ocean Territory 1996–98; High Commr in Dar es Salaam, Tanzania 1998–2001; secondment to Standard Chartered Bank 2001–02; Gov. of Cayman Islands 2002–05. *Publication:* Promoting African Enterprise 1974. *Leisure interests:* golf, lawn tennis, music, travel.

DION, Céline, CC, OQ; Canadian singer; b. 30 March 1968, Charlemagne, Québec; d. of Adhémar Dion and Thérèse Dion; m. René Angélil 1994; one s.; recording artist 1979–; winner, Eurovision song contest, Dublin 1988; performed anthem The Power of the Dream at opening ceremony of Olympic Games, Atlanta 1996; Las Vegas show, A New Day 2002–07; Medal of Arts (France) 1996; Gala de L'ADISQ Awards for Pop Album of the Year 1983, for Best Selling Record 1984, 1985, for Best Selling Single 1985, for Pop Song of the Year 1985, 1988, for Female Artist of Year 1983–85, 1988, for Discovery of the Year 1983, for Best Québec Artist Outside Québec 1983, 1988, Journal de Québec Trophy 1985, Spectrel Video Award for Best Stage Performance 1988, Juno Awards for Album of the Year 1991, for Single of the Year 1993, for Female Vocalist of the Year 1991–93, Acad. Award for Best Song Written for a Motion Picture or TV (for Beauty and The Beast duet with Peabo Bryson) 1992, Grammy Award (for Beauty and the Beast) 1993, (for My Heart Will Go On, from film Titanic) 1999, American Music Award for Best Adult Contemporary Artist 2003, World Music Diamond Award 2004. *Recordings include:* albums: Tellement J'ai D'Amour, Incognito, Unison 1990, Dion chante Plamondon 1991, Céline Dion 1991, The Colour of My Love 1993, Les Premières Années 1994, Des Mots Qui Sonnent 1995, Power Of Love 1995, The French Album 1995, D'eux 1995, Falling Into You 1996, Live à Paris 1996, Let's Talk About Love 1997, A l'Olympia 1998, Chansons En Or 1998, Céline Dion Vol. 2 1998, S'il Suffisait D'Aimer 1998, These Are Special Times (Grammy and Juno Awards 1999) 1998, Amour 1998, Au Coeur Du Stade 1999, Tout En Amour 2002, Let's Talk About Love 1999, All The Way – A Decade of Song 1999, A New Day Has Come 2002, One Heart 2003, 1 Fille & 4 Types 2003, Miracle 2004, Taking Chances 2007. *Publications:* All the Way 2000, My Story, My Dreams 2001, Miracle (with Anne Geddes) 2004. *Leisure interests:* skiing, water-skiing, roller-blading, miniature cups, crystal objects, teapots, cuddly frogs, looking after son, golf. *Address:* Les Productions Feeling, 2540 boulevard Daniel-Johnson, Bureau 755, Laval, PQ H7T 2S3, Canada (office). *Telephone:* (450) 978-9555 (office). *Fax:* (450) 978-1055 (office). *E-mail:* info@feelingprod.com (office). *Website:* www.celinedion.com (home).

DION, Hon. Stéphane, PC, BA, MA, PhD; Canadian politician and academic; b. 28 Sept. 1955, Quebec City; m. Janine Krieber; one d.; ed Laval Univ., Inst. d'études politiques de Paris, France; Asst Prof. of Political Science, Univ. of Moncton Jan.–May 1984; Asst Prof. of Political Science, Univ. of Montreal 1984–89, Assoc. Prof. 1989–95, Prof. 1995; MP (Liberal Party of Canada) for St-Laurent/Cartierville 1996–; Minister of Intergovernmental Affairs and Pres. Queen's Privy Council for Canada 1996–2003, Minister of Environment 2004–06, Leader Liberal Party of Canada 2006–08 (resgnd), also Leader of the

Opposition; Pres. UN Climate Change Conference, Montreal 2005; Guest Scholar, Brookings Inst., Washington, DC 1990–91, Laboratoire d'économie publique de Paris 1994–95; Research Fellow, Canadian Centre for Man. Devt 1990–91; Co-Ed. Canadian Journal of Political Science 1990–93; mem. Aid to Scholarly Publs Cttee of Social Sciences Fed. of Canada, Advisory Council of Inst. of Intergovernmental Relations, Queen's Univ.; Dr hc (Carlos III Univ. of Madrid) 2002. *Address:* House of Commons, Room 301, Justice Building, Ottawa, ON, K1A 0A6, Canada (office). *Telephone:* (613) 996-5789 (office). *Fax:* (613) 996-6562 (office). *E-mail:* dions@parl.gc.ca (office). *Website:* www.stephanedion.parl.gc.ca (office).

DIOP, Abdoulaye; Senegalese politician; *Minister of State, Minister of the Economy and Finance;* ed Lycée El Hadj Malick Sy de Thiès, Univ. of Dakar and Ecole Nat. d'Admin et de Magistrature; asst to Prin. Paymaster, Thiès 1980–81; rate collector, Commune de Fatick 1981–84, Commune de Mbour 1984–87, Commune de Pikine 1987–90; tax collector, Dakar Centre 1990–93; tax and rate collector, Ville de Dakar 1993–95, Dakar Urban Community 1993–95; Sr Banking Exec., Treasurer-Gen. and Dir of Treasury and Public Finance 1995–98; Minister Del., Ministry of Economy and Finance 2000; Minister of State, Minister of Economy and Finance 2001–; mem. Observatoire des finances locales de Cotonou 1996–, Comm. de réforme des textes de la décentralisation; Pres. Tech. Cttee responsible for Reform of Local Finance in Senegal; Chevalier, Ordre nat. du Lion de la République du Sénégal 1996. *Address:* Ministry of the Economy and Finance, rue René Ndiaye, BP 4017, Dakar, Senegal (office). *Telephone:* 822-11-06 (office). *Fax:* 822-41-95 (office). *E-mail:* cthiam@minfinances.sn (office). *Website:* www.finances.gouv.sn (office).

DIOP, Bécaye; Senegalese politician; *Minister of the Armed Forces;* b. 1945; m.; six c.; Minister Del. to the Minister of Educ. for Tech. Educ., Vocational Training, Adult Literacy and Nat. Languages 2000–01; Minister of the Armed Forces 2002–; mem. Parti Démocratique Sénégalais (PDS). *Address:* Ministry of the Armed Forces, Bldg Administratif, avenue Léopold Sédar Senghor, BP 4041, Dakar, Senegal (office). *Telephone:* 849-75-44 (office). *Fax:* 823-63-38 (office). *Website:* www.forcesarmees.gouv.sn (office).

DIOP, Iba Mar; Senegalese professor of medicine; b. 17 May 1921, St Louis; m.; six c.; ed African School of Medicine and Pharmacy, Univ. of Bordeaux; Head of Clinic, Dakar Faculty of Medicine and Pharmacy 1965, Asst Prof. 1970, Prof. 1975, Dean 1976; specialist in infectious diseases; Pres. Asscn of African Faculties and Schools of Medicine 1977–81; Fellow Islamic Acad. of Sciences, mem. Council and Vice-Pres. 1994–98, Acting Pres. 1999; mem. Medical Comm., IOC, Acad. Nat. de Médecine, France, African Acad. of Sciences 1988, Founding Mem. and Sec. Senegal Acad. of Sciences and Techniques; Founding Pres. then Hon. Pres. Int. Union Against Venereal Diseases; Sec. Medical Soc. of French-speaking Black Africa 1962, Vice-Pres. 1963, Pres. 1977, now mem.; mem. French-speaking Soc. for Infectious Pathology 1971, Int. Therapeutic Union 1975; Fellow Third World Acad. of Sciences, mem. Council 1992; Hon. Dean UCAD; UNO Medal (Congo) 1961, Commdr, Ordre des Palmes Académiques 1985, Officier, Légion d'honneur 1983, Médaille Orange, Croix Rouge Française 1968, Officier, Ordre des Palmes Académiques (Togo) 1980, Commdr, Ordre Nat. de la Côte d'Ivoire 1982, Chevalier, Ordre Nat. du Cameroun 1983, Officer, Nat. Order of Cen. Africa 1983, Médaille de la Ville de Paris 1985, Commdr, Congo Order of Merit 1985, First Laureate Alfred Quenum Prize for Africa, WHO, First Laureate Mohamed El Fasi Prize, Laureate Third World Acad. of Sciences. *Publications:* over 300 publs on infectious and tropical diseases. *Address:* Clinique Fann Hock, Rue 70 x 55, BP 15504, Dakar-Fann, Senegal (office).

DIOP, Majmout; Senegalese politician and pharmacist; *Secretary-General, Parti africain de l'indépendance;* b. 30 Sept. 1922, St Louis; ed Ecole Africaine de Médecine et de Pharmacie, Dakar, Paris Univ. and African Inst., Univ. of Moscow; hosp. pharmacist, Senegal and Gabon 1947–50; Pres. Senegalese Students' Asscn in France 1951; studied Marxism at Bucharest 1953–56; Sec.-Gen. Parti africain de l'indépendance (PAI) 1957–; exiled from Senegal 1961–76; engaged in research in political sociology at Inst. of Human Sciences, Mali 1968–76; dispensary pharmacist, Dakar 1977–. *Publications:* Contribution à l'Etude des problèmes politiques en Afrique Noire 1959, Classes et idéologies de classe au Sénégal 1963, Notes sur la classe ouvrière sénégalaise 1965, Histoire des classes sociales dans l'Afrique de l'Ouest (Vol. I) 1971, (Vol. II) 1972, Etude sur le Salariat 1975, Essai sur l'esclavage en Afrique de l'Ouest (to be published); and many articles in reviews and journals. *Address:* Parti africain de l'indépendance (PAI), PO Box 820, Maison du Peuple Guediewaye, Dakar (office); 153 Avenue du Président Lamine Gueye, Dakar (office); 210 HCM, Guediawaye, Dakar, Senegal (home). *Telephone:* 837-01-36 (office).

DIOP, Pape Bouba; Senegalese professional footballer; b. 28 Jan. 1978, Dakar; began career as midfielder with Espoir Dakar, then Diaraaf Dakar 1997–98, Vevey-Sports 1999–2000, Neuchâtel Xamax July–Dec. 2000, Grasshoppers Zurich, Switzerland Jan.–Dec. 2001, Racing Club de Lens, France Jan. 2002–04, Fulham UK 2004–; mem. Senegal nat. football team June 2000–, took part in African Nations Cup, Feb. 2002, top scorer for Senegal nat. football team in World Cup 2002. *Address:* Fulham FC, Training Ground, Motspur Park, New Malden Surrey, KT3 6PT, England (office). *Telephone:* (20) 8336-0514 (office). *Website:* www.fulhamfc.com (office).

DIOUF, Abdou, LenD, LèsL; Senegalese fmr head of state; *Secretary-General, La Francophonie;* b. 7 Sept. 1935, Louga; m. 1963; ed Lycée Faidherbe, St Louis, Dakar and Paris Univs; Dir of Tech. Co-operation and Minister of Planning Sept.–Nov. 1960; Asst Sec.-Gen. to Govt 1960–61; Sec.-Gen. Ministry of Defence June–Dec. 1961; Gov. Sine-Saloum Region 1961–62; Dir de Cabinet of Minister of Foreign Affairs 1962–63, of Pres. of Repub. 1963–65; Sec.-Gen. to Pres.'s Office 1964–68; Minister of Planning and Industry 1968–70; Prime Minister 1970–80; Pres. of Senegal 1981–2000, of Confed. of Senegambia 1982–89; Chair. OAU 1985–86; mem. Nat. Ass. for Longa Département 1973–; mem. Senegalese Progressive Union (UPS) 1961–, later Asst Sec.-Gen.; fmr Asst Sec.-Gen. Parti socialiste sénégalais (PS), now Chair.; currently Sec.-Gen. La Francophonie, Paris; Jt Winner Africa Prize for Leadership 1987. *Address:* La Francophonie, 28 rue de Bourgogne, 75007 Paris, France (office). *Telephone:* 1-44-11-12-50 (office). *Fax:* 1-44-11-12-76 (office). *E-mail:* oif@francophonie.org (office). *Website:* www.francophonie.org (office).

DIOUF, Jacques, PhD; Senegalese international civil servant and agronomist; *Director-General, United Nations Food and Agriculture Organization;* b. 1 Aug. 1938, Saint-Louis; m. Aïssatou Seye 1963; one s. four d.; ed Lycée Faidherbe, Saint-Louis, Ecole Nat. d'Agriculture, Paris/Grignon, Ecole Nat. d'Application d'Agronomie Tropicale, Paris/Nogent and Sorbonne, Paris; Exec. Sec. African Groundnut Council, Lagos 1965–71; Exec. Sec. West African Rice Devt Asscn, Monrovia 1971–77; Sec. of State for Science and Tech., Govt of Senegal, Dakar 1978–83; mem. Nat. Ass., Chair. Foreign Relations Cttee and elected Sec., Dakar 1983–84; Sec.-Gen. Banque centrale des états de l'Afrique de l'ouest, Dakar 1985–90; Perm. Rep. of Senegal to UN 1991–93; Dir-Gen. FAO 1994–; led Senegalese dels to UN Confs on Science and Tech., Vienna 1979 (Chair. of 1st Comm.), Industrial Devt, New Delhi 1980, New and Renewable Energy Sources, Nairobi (Vice-Chair.) 1981, Peaceful Use of Space, Vienna 1982; African Rep., Consultative Group on Int. Agricultural Research, Washington; mem. Bd of Dirs ISNAR, The Hague, IITA Lagos, IIRSDA Abidjan, ICRAF, Nairobi, Int. Foundation for Science, Stockholm, African Capacity Building Foundation, Harare, World Inst. for Devt Econs Research, Helsinki, Council of African Advisers of the World Bank, Washington DC; Chair. SINAES, Dakar; mem. Consultative Cttee on Medical Research, WHO, Geneva; Grand Commdr, Order of the Star of Africa (Liberia) 1977, Commdr, Order of Agricultural Merit (Canada) 1995, Grand Cross, Order of Merit in Agric., Fisheries and Food (Spain) 1996, Order of Solidarity (Cuba) 1998, Commdr, Légion d'honneur 1998, Grand Cross, Order of May for Merit (Argentina) 1998, Two Niles Decoration (Sudan), 2000, Nat. Order of Merit for Co-Operation and Devt (Guinea Bissau) 2001, Distinguished Cross, Order of the Quetzal (Guatemala) 2001, Commdr, Order of St Charles (Monaco) 2002, Distinguished Cross (Peru) 2002, Kt Grand Cross (First Class) of the Most Exalted Order of the White Elephant (Thailand) 2003, Order of the Golden Fleece (Georgia) 2003, Golden Fortune Saint George Award 'Honour, Eminence, Labour' (First Grade) (Ukraine) 2003, Medal of Commdr, Nat. Order of Merit (Mauritania) 2003, Congressional Medal of Achievement (Philippines) 2004, Order of Vasco Nuñez de Balboa (Panama) 2004, Order of Ulises Rojas (Guatemala) 2004, Order of the Golden Heart, Rank of Grand Cross (Philippines) 2004, Grand Master Nat. Order (Madagascar) 2005, Order of Malta 2006, Commdr Grand Cross, Order of Merit of Repub. of Hungary 2007; numerous hon. doctorates; Award for Services to Educ. (France) 1979, Hilal Award (Pakistan) 2005. *Publications:* La détérioration du pouvoir d'achat de l'Arachide 1972, Les fondements du dialogue scientifique entre les civilisations Euro-occidentale et Négro-Africaine 1979, The Challenge of Agricultural Development in Africa 1989. *Leisure interests:* reading, music, sports. *Address:* Food and Agriculture Organization of the United Nations, Viale delle Terme di Caracalla, 00153 Rome, Italy (office). *Telephone:* (06) 57051 (office). *Fax:* (06) 57053152 (office). *E-mail:* fao-hq@fao.org (office). *Website:* www.fao.org (office).

DIPICO, Manne Emsley, BA; South African civil servant and trade union official; *Regional Chairman, African National Congress, Northern Cape;* b. 21 April 1959, Kimberley; ed Univ. of Fort Hare; joined African Nat. Congress (ANC) 1982; Nat. Educ. Co-ordinator Nat. Union of Mineworkers; Azanian Students' Org. (AZASO) rep. for United Democratic Front (UDF) Exec. Border Region, AZASO Treas. Univ. of Fort Hare; mem. UDF N Cape 1985–86; detained Ciskei 1984, detained under state of emergency Kimberley 1986, arrested and sentenced to five years for furthering the aims of a banned org. through terrorist activities 1987–90, released before end of sentence; Regional Sec. ANC 1991–92, Regional Chair. N Cape 1992–; Regional Elections Co-ordinator 1993–94; Premier N Cape Prov. Legislature 1994–2004. *Address:* c/o Private Bag X5016, Kimberley 8301 (office); 5248 Magashula Street, PO Mankurwane, Galeshawe-Kimberley 8345, South Africa (home). *Telephone:* (53) 8309300 (home). *Fax:* (53) 8332122 (office). *E-mail:* cmatlhacko@pancmail.ncape.gov.za (office).

DIPU, Moni, MBBS, MPH, LLB, LLM; Bangladeshi politician; *Minister of Foreign Affairs;* d. of the late M.A. Wadud; m. Tawfique Nawaz; one s. one d.; ed Dhaka Medical Coll., Johns Hopkins Univ. School of Public Health, USA, Univ. of London, UK; mem. Bangladesh Awami League, Sec. for Women's Affairs –2009, mem. Sub–cttee on Foreign Affairs; mem. Jatiya Sangsad (Parl.) for Chadnpur-3 2008–; Minister of Foreign Affairs 2009–. *Address:* Ministry of Foreign Affairs, Segunbagicha, Dhaka 1000, Bangladesh (office). *Telephone:* (2) 9562862 (office). *Fax:* (2) 9555283 (office). *E-mail:* info@mofabd.org (office). *Website:* www.mofa.gov.bd (office); www.dipumoni.com.

DIRCEU DE OLIVEIRA E SILVA, José; Brazilian politician and lawyer; b. 16 March 1946, Passa Quatro; m. 1st Clara Becker (divorced); m. 2nd Maria Rita Garcia de Andrade; one s. two d.; ed Pontifical Catholic Univ. of São Paulo; fmr student leader; organized protest of 100,000 people against Brazilian mil. dictatorship 1967; jailed 1968, released 1969 in exchange for kidnapped US Amb. Charles Elbrick; went into exile in Cuba where he underwent plastic surgery to change his appearance and received guerrilla training; returned permanently to Brazil 1975; assumed false identity (Carlos Henrique Gouveia de Melo) in Cruzeiro do Oeste, Paraná, became a shopkeeper; amnestied 1979; co-founder (with Luiz Inácio Lula da Silva) Workers' Party (PT), later Gen. Sec., Leader 1994, Pres. 1995–; elected State

Deputy 1986, Deputy Fed. Parl. 1990, 1997, 1999, 2001–; Gov. State of São Paulo 1994; Chief Adviser to Pres.-elect Luiz Inácio Lula da Silva (q.v.); Chief of Cabinet 2003–05 (resgnd); facing trial on charges of conspiracy and corruption 2007. *Address:* c/o Office of the Civilian Cabinet, Palácio do Planalto, 4° Andar, Praça dos Três Poderes, 70150 Brasília, DF, Brazil (office).

DIRKSEN, Gebhard, DJur; German banker and lawyer; b. 29 June 1929, Göttingen; s. of Wilhelm and Magdalene (née Güthenke) Dirksen; m. Renate Pöhl 1971; one s. two d.; ed at schools in Gutersloh/Westfalen and Univs of Mainz, Freiburg and Göttingen; articled in Göttingen, Hanover and Celle; Deputy Chair. Bd of Dirs Norddeutsche Landesbank Girozentrale 1959–94. *Address:* Westpreussenufer 4, 30659 Hannover, Germany. *Telephone:* 6478746.

DISANAYAKA, Heen Banda, BA; Sri Lankan banker; b. 28 Aug. 1937, Talawa; m. Wasantha Wijekoon 1963; one s. two d.; ed Univ. of Sri Lanka; Dir-Gen. of Customs 1976; Alt. Exec. Dir Asian Devt Bank 1987; Deputy Sec. to Treasury 1989; Gov. Cen. Bank of Sri Lanka 1992–95, also fmr Chair. of Monetary Bd; Alt. Dir IMF, Washington DC 1996–98. *Leisure interest:* organic farming. *Address:* 84/1 Old Kottawa Road, Mirihana, Nugegoda, Sri Lanka. *Telephone:* 2399091-7 (office); 2852199 (home). *Fax:* 2399098 (office). *E-mail:* ndtfmd@sltnet.lk (office).

DISKIN, Yuval, BA, MA; Israeli state security official; *Director, Shin Bet;* b. 1956; m. 1st; four c.; m. 2nd; one d.; ed Bar Ilan Univ., Haifa Univ.; joined Shin Bet (Israel Security Agency) 1978, Co-ordinator Nablus Dist 1979–84, Dist Co-ordinator Nablus, Jenin, Tulkarm 1984–89, Dir Dept for Counter-terrorism, Arab Affairs Br. 1990, Deputy Dir Arab Affairs Br., Dir 1994, Dir Jerusalem, Judea and Samaria Region 1997–2000, Deputy Dir Shin Bet 2000–03, Dir 2005–. *Address:* c/o Ministry of Public Security, PO Box 18182, Building 3, Rinjat Hamemshala, Jerusalem 91181, Israel (office).

DISNEY, Anthea; British media executive; *Executive Vice-President for Content, News Corporation;* b. 13 Oct. 1946, Dunstable; d. of Alfred Leslie and Elsie Wale; m. Peter Robert Howe 1984; ed Queen's Coll.; New York corresp. London Daily Mail 1973–75, Features Ed. 1975–77, New York Bureau Chief 1977–79; columnist London Daily Express, New York 1979–84; Managing Ed. New York Daily News 1984–87; Ed. Sunday Daily News 1984–87; Ed. US magazine 1987–88; Ed.-in-Chief Self magazine 1988–89; magazine developer Murdoch magazines 1989–90; exec. producer A Current Affair, Fox TV 1990–91; Ed.-in-Chief TV Guide magazine 1991–95; Editorial Dir Murdoch Magazines 1994–95; Pres. and CEO HarperCollins Publrs 1996–97; Chair., CEO News America Publishing 1997–99; Exec. Vice-Pres. of Content, News Corpn 1999–. *Address:* 50 East 89th Street, New York, NY 10128-1225; News Corporation, Suite 300, 1211 Avenue of the Americas, New York, NY 10036, USA (office). *Telephone:* (212) 852-7017 (office). *Fax:* (212) 852-7145 (office). *Website:* www.newscorp.com (office).

DITTUS, Peter, DEcon; German economist; *Secretary-General, Bank for International Settlements;* m., three c.; ed Saarbrücken Univ., Univ. of Mich.; worked as economist at World Bank and OECD; joined BIS as economist 1992, apptd Deputy Sec.-Gen. 2000, Sec.-Gen. 2005–, mem. Exec. Cttee. *Publications include:* Die Wahl der Geldverfassung 1987, A Macroeconomic Model for Debt Analysis of the Latin America Region and Debt Accounting Models for the Highly Indebted Countries (jtly) 1991, Trade and Employment: Can We Afford Better Market Access for Eastern Europe? (jtly) 1994, Corporate Governance in Central Europe: The Role of Banks 1994, Corporate Control in Central Europe and Russia: Should Banks Own Shares? (jtly) 1995, numerous papers on int. econs. *Address:* Bank for International Settlements, Central-bahnplatz 2, Basel 4002, Switzerland (office). *Telephone:* (61) 2808080 (office). *Fax:* (61) 2809100 (office). *E-mail:* peter.dittus@bis.org (office). *Website:* www.bis.org (office).

DITZ, Johannes; Austrian industrial executive and fmr politician; fmr mem. Austrian People's Party; CEO Österreichische Industrieholding AG (Govt holding co.); Chair. Austrian Airlines, Telekom Austria; Chair. Supervisory Bd OMV (oil and gas co.); Vice-Chair. Supervisory Bd Böhler-Uddeholm AG. *Address:* c/o Austrian Airlines, Fontanastr. 1, 1107 Vienna, Austria (office). *Telephone:* (1) 176-6 (office). *Fax:* (1) 688-55-05. *E-mail:* public.relations@aua.com (office). *Website:* www.aua.com (office).

DIVUNGUI-DI-N'DINGE, Didjob; Gabonese engineer and politician; *Vice-President;* b. 5 May 1946, Alombié; m.; six c.; ed Ecole Nat. Supérieure des Arts et Métiers, Paris, France, Institut Nat. Polytechnique, Grenoble, France; fmr employers' rep. and Vice-Chair. Perm. Comm. to the Econ. and Social Council; Dir-Gen. Soc. d'Energie et d'Eau du Gabon 1974; Adviser to Pres. of Gabon for Electrical Energy and Water Resources 1975; Minister of Energy and Water Resources 1983; presidential cand. 1993; currently Vice-Pres. of Gabon; Grand Croix de l'Ordre National de l'Etoile Equatoriale, Grand Croix de l'Ordre National du Mérite Gabonais, Grand Officer dans l'Ordre National du Mérite Français, Commandeur dans l'Ordre National de Côte d'Ivoire. *Address:* Office of the Vice-President, Libreville, Gabon (office).

DIXIT, Avinash Kamalakar, BSc, BA, PhD; American economist and academic; *John J. F. Sherrerd '52 Professor of Economics, Princeton University;* b. 8 June 1944, Bombay (now Mumbai), India; s. of Kamalakar Ramachandra Dixit and Kusum Dixit; ed Bombay Univ., Univ. of Cambridge, UK, Massachusetts Inst. of Tech.; Research Asst, MIT 1965–67; Acting Asst Prof., Univ. of California, Berkeley 1968–69; Lord Thomson of Fleet Fellow and Lecturer in Econs, Balliol Coll., Oxford 1970–74; Prof. of Econs, Univ. of Warwick 1974–80; Prof. of Econs and Int. Affairs, Princeton Univ. 1981–85, Prof. of Econs 1985–89, John J.F. Sherrerd '52 Prof. of Econs 1989–; Visiting Research Assoc., MIT 1972, Visiting Prof. 1977, 1994; Visiting Scholar, IMF 1990, 2000; Visiting Scholar, Russell Sage Foundation 2002–03; Vice-Pres.

American Econ. Asscn 2002, Pres. 2008; Fellow, Econometric Soc. 1977, Vice-Pres. 2000, Pres. 2001; Guggenheim Fellowship 1992; Fellow, American Acad. of Arts and Sciences 1992; mem. NAS. *Publications:* Theory of International Trade (co-author) 1980, Thinking Strategically (co-author) 1991, Investment under Uncertainty (co-author) 1994, Lawlessness and Economics 2004, The Art of Strategy (co-author) 2008. *Address:* Department of Economics, 212 Fisher Hall, Princeton University, Princeton, NJ 08544 (office); 36 Gordon Way, Princeton, NJ 08540, USA (home). *Telephone:* (609) 258-4013 (office). *Fax:* (609) 258-6419 (office). *E-mail:* dixitak@princeton.edu (office). *Website:* www.princeton.edu/~dixitak/home (office).

DIXIT, Kamal Mani, BA; Nepalese business executive; b. 2 Sept. 1929, Kathmandu; s. of Kedermani Dixit and Vidyadevi Dixit; m. Aniu Dixit; two s. one d.; mem. of Bd Salt Trading Corpn 1967–71, Vice-Chair. 1971–95, Chair. 1995–; Chair. Nepal Vegetable Ghee Industries Ltd; acted in Adikabi Shanubhakta Ltd; GDB by King of Nepal 2004. *Publications:* nearly 50 books. *Leisure interest:* writing. *Address:* Salt Trading Corporation Ltd, Kalimati, PO Box 483, Kathmandu, Nepal (office). *Telephone:* (1) 4271418 (office); (1) 5536338 (home). *Fax:* (1) 4271704 (office); (1) 5536390 (home). *E-mail:* salt@stcnepal.com (office); kmldxt@gmail.com (home). *Website:* www.stcnepal.com (office).

DIXON, Sir (David) Jeremy, Kt, RIBA; British architect; *Principal, Dixon Jones Ltd;* b. 31 May 1939; s. of the late Joseph L. Dixon and Beryl M. Braund; m. Fenella Clemens 1964 (separated 1990); one s. two d., partner Julia Somerville; ed Merchant Taylors' School and Architectural Asscn School of Architecture; Prin. in pvt. practice with Fenella Dixon 1975–90; formed partnership of Jeremy Dixon/BDP with William Jack (for extension to Royal Opera House, Covent Garden), Prin. 1983–90; Prin. Jeremy Dixon, Edward Jones 1990–; other projects include Piazzale Roma, Venice, grove of fountains Somerset House (with Edward Jones); Tate Gallery restaurant; Nat. Portrait Gallery extension; shop for Clifton Nurseries; Northants. county offices; housing projects in London; study centre for Darwin Coll., Cambridge; work for J. Sainsbury PLC, Henry Moore Foundation, Magna Carta Bldg, Salisbury Cathedral 2001, Exhibition Road Project 2004; Chair. RIBA Regional Awards Group 1991–. *Leisure interests:* walking in English landscape, contemporary sculpture and painting, music. *Address:* Unit 6c, The Courtyard, 44 Gloucester Avenue, London, NW1 8JD, England (office). *Telephone:* (20) 7483-8888. *E-mail:* jeremydixon@dixonjones.co.uk.

DIXON, Kenneth Herbert Morley, CBE, DL, BA (Econs), FRSA; British business executive; b. 19 Aug. 1929, Stockport; s. of Arnold Morley Dixon and Mary Jolly; m. Patricia Oldbury Whalley 1955; two s.; ed Cranbrook School, Sydney, Univ. of Manchester, Harvard Business School, USA; joined Rowntree & Co. Ltd 1956, Dir 1970, Chair. UK Confectionery Div. 1973–78, Deputy Chair. Rowntree Mackintosh Ltd 1978–81, Group Chair. Rowntree Mackintosh PLC (now Rowntree PLC) 1981–89; Vice-Chair. Legal and General Group 1986–94; Deputy Chair. Bass PLC 1990–96; mem. Council Inc. Soc. of British Advertisers 1971–79, Council Cocoa, Chocolate and Confectionery Alliance 1972–79, Council Advertising Asscn 1976–79, CBI Cos Cttee 1979–84, Council CBI 1981–90, BIM Econ. and Soc. Affairs Cttee 1980–84, Food and Drink Fed. Exec. Cttee 1986–89 (mem. Council 1986–87); mem. Council York Univ. 1983–2001, Pro-Chancellor 1987–2001, Chair. 1990–2001; Trustee, Joseph Rowntree Foundation 1996–, Deputy Chair. 1998–2001, Chair. 2001–04; Morrell Fellow Univ. of York 2007; DUniv hc (York) 1993, (Open) 1997. *Leisure interests:* reading, music, fell walking. *Address:* Joseph Rowntree Foundation, The Homestead, Water End, York, YO30 6WP, England. *Telephone:* (1904) 615901. *Fax:* (1904) 620072. *E-mail:* info@jrf.org.uk. *Website:* www.jrf.org.uk.

DIXON, Richard Newland, PhD, ScD, FRS, CChem, FRSC; British chemist and academic; *Professor Emeritus of Chemistry and Senior Research Fellow, University of Bristol;* b. 25 Dec. 1930, Borough Green; s. of Robert T. Dixon and Lilian Dixon; m. Alison M. Birks 1954; one s. two d.; ed Judd School, Tonbridge, King's Coll. London and St Catharine's Coll. Cambridge; Scientific Officer, UKAEA, Aldermaston 1954–56; Postdoctoral Fellow, Univ. of Western Ont., Canada 1956–57; Nat. Research Council, Ottawa 1957–59; ICI Fellow, Univ. of Sheffield 1959–60, Lecturer in Chem. 1960–69; Prof. of Chem., Univ. of Bristol 1969–96, Alfred Capper Pass Prof. of Chem. 1990–96, Prof. Emer. 1996–, Leverhulme Fellow Emer. 1996–99, Univ. Sr Research Fellow 1996–, Dean, Faculty of Science 1979–82, Pro-Vice Chancellor 1989–92; Dir (non-exec.) United Bristol Healthcare NHS Trust 1994–2003, Vice-Chair. 1995–2003; Trustee, Charitable Trusts for United Bristol Hospitals 2003–, Chair. 2006–; Sorby Research Fellow, Royal Soc. 1964–69; mem. Council, Faraday Div. Royal Soc. of Chem. 1985–98 (Vice-Pres. 1989–98), Cttees of Science and Eng Research Council 1980–83, 1987–90; Corday Morgan Medal, Royal Soc. of Chem. 1968, Spectroscopy Medal, Royal Soc. of Chem. 1985; Hallam Lecturer, Univ. of Wales 1988, Liversidge Lecturer, Royal Soc. of Chem. 1993, Harkins Lecturer, Univ. of Chicago, USA 1993, Rumford Medal, Royal Soc. 2004. *Publications:* Spectroscopy and Structure 1965, Theoretical Chemistry, Vol. I 1972, Vol. II 1974, Vol. III 1977; numerous research articles in scientific journals. *Leisure interests:* mountain walking, photography, gardening, theatre-going. *Address:* School of Chemistry, University of Bristol, Cantock's Close, Bristol, BS8 1TS (office); 22 Westbury Lane, Coombe Dingle, Bristol, BS9 2PE, England (home). *Telephone:* (117) 9287661 (office); (117) 9681691 (home). *Fax:* (117) 9251295 (office). *E-mail:* r.n.dixon@bris.ac.uk (office). *Website:* www.chm.bris.ac.uk/staff/rdixon.htm (office).

DIZ, Adolfo César, CPA, DEcon, MA, DPhil; Argentine economist; *Professor of International Finance, University of Cema;* b. 12 May 1931, Buenos Aires; s. of Agustín Diz and Elisa Aristizábal; m. Martha Solari 1959; five s.; ed Univ. de Buenos Aires and Univ. of Chicago; Instructor of Statistics, Univ. de Buenos Aires 1951–55, 1958–59; Prof. of Statistics, Univ. Nacional de Tucumán

1959–60, Dir Inst. of Econ. Research 1959–65, Prof. of Statistics and Econometrics 1960–61, 1964, Prof. of Monetary Theory 1962, 1965–66; Exec. Dir Int. Monetary Fund (IMF) 1966–68; Envoy extraordinary and Minister plenipotentiary, Argentine Financial Rep. in Europe 1969–73; Dir Center for Latin American Monetary Studies 1973–76; Pres. Banco Central de la República Argentina 1976–81; Dir Per Jacobsson Foundation 1976–; Econ. Consultant 1981–; Prof. of Int. Finance, Univ. of CEMA 2000–; mem. Nat. Acad. of Econ. Sciences; mem. of Argentine Socs., American Econ. Asscn and Econometric Soc. *Publications:* Money and Prices in Argentina 1935–62, in Varieties of Monetary Experience (Ed. D. Meiselman), Money Supply Models (in Spanish), The Money Supply and its Instruments (in Spanish) and numerous economic articles. *Address:* Callao Avenida 2049-P6 (1024), Buenos Aires, Argentina. *Telephone:* (11) 4815-2418 (office); (11) 4813-6036. *Fax:* (11) 4815-2418. *E-mail:* acdiz@overnet.com.ar (home).

DJADALLAH, Bichara Issa; Chadian government official; Minister of Nat. Defence –2007. *Address:* c/o Ministry of National Defence, BP 916, N'Djamena, Chad (office).

DJAFFAR, Ahmed Ben Saïd; Comoran politician; *Minister of Foreign Affairs;* fmr head of local devt charity funded by EU; Minister of Foreign Affairs 2006–. *Address:* Ministry of Foreign Affairs, Co-operation, the Francophonie and Comorans Abroad, BP 428, Moroni, The Comoros (office). *Telephone:* (74) 4100 (office). *Fax:* (74) 4111 (office).

DJALIL, Matori Abdul; Indonesian politician; b. 11 July 1942, Semarang, Jawa Tengah; ed Satya Wacana Christian Univ., Salatiga; previously Chair. Nat. Awakening Party; Sec. Gen. United Devt Party 1989–94; Deputy Chair. MPR RI 1999–2004; Minister of Defence 2001–04. *Address:* c/o Jalan Medan Merdeka Barat 13–14, Jakarta Pusat, Indonesia (office).

DJANGONÉ-BI, Djessan Philippe, MA, PhD; Côte d'Ivoirian academic and diplomatist; *Ambassador to UK and Ireland;* b. 1 Jan. 1946; m. Martine Djangoné-Bi; two c.; ed Brandeis Univ., USA, Univ. of Abidjan, Sorbonne Univ., Paris, Univ. of Paris III, France; Second Asst to Dean of Faculty of Arts and Humanities, Nat. Univ. of Côte d'Ivoire 1979–82, Dir of English Dept 1980–82; currently Sr Lecturer, Dept of English, Univ. of Cocody, Abidjan; Head of Int. Co-operation Div., Ministry of Higher Educ. and Scientific Research 2000–01; Perm. Rep. to UN, New York 2001–07, Amb. to UK 2007– (also accred to Ireland 2008–). *Address:* Embassy of Côte d'Ivoire, 2 Upper Belgrave Street, London, SW1X 8BJ, England (office). *Telephone:* (20) 7235-6991 (office). *Fax:* (20) 7259-5320 (office).

DJEBAR, Assia; Algerian novelist, poet, dramatist, filmmaker and academic; *Silver Chair Professor of Francophone Literature and Civilization, New York University;* b. (Fatima-Zohra Imalhayène), 30 June 1936, Cherchell; d. of the late Tahar Imalhayène and Bahia Sahraoui; m. 1st Ahmed Ould-Rouïs 1958 (divorced 1975); m. 2nd Malek Alloula 1981 (divorced 2005); one d.; ed Lycée Fénélon, Paris and École Normale Supérieure de Sèvres, France; taught history at Univ. of Algiers 1962–65, 1974–84; Foundation Distinguished Prof. and Dir Center for French and Francophone Studies, Louisiana State Univ., USA 1995–2001; Silver Chair Prof. of Francophone Literature and Civilization, New York Univ. 2002–; mem. Acad. Royale de Langue Française de Belgique 2000–, Acad. Française 2005–; Dr hc (Concordia Univ., Montréal) 2002, (Osnabrück Univ.) 2005; Venice Film Festival Int. Critics' Prize 1979, Prix Maurice Maeterlinck 1995, Neustadt Int. Prize for Literature (USA) 1996, Yourcenar Prize 1997, Friedenspreis des Deutschen Buchhandels, Frankfurt 2000, Pablo Neruda Prize, Italy 2005, Grinzane Cavour Prize, Italy 2006. *Films:* La Nouba des femmes du Mont Chenoua 1979, La Zerda ou les chants d'oubli 1982. *Publications:* La Soif (trans. as The Mischief) 1957, Les Impatients 1958, Women of Islam 1961, Les Enfants du nouveau monde 1962, Les Alouettes naïves 1967, Poèmes pour l'Algérie heureuse 1969, Rouge l'aube (with Walid Garn) 1969, La Nouba des femmes du Mont Chenoua 1969, Les Femmes d'Alger dans leur appartement (trans. as Women of Algiers in their Apartment) 1980 (new edn 2002), L'Amour la fantasia (trans. as Fantasia: An Algerian Cavalcade) 1985, Ombre sultane (trans. as A Sister to Scheherazade) 1987, Loin de Médine (trans. as Far from Medina) 1991, Chronique d'un été algérien 1993, Le Blanc de l'Algérie (trans. as Algerian White) 1995, Vaste est la prison (trans. as So Vast the Prison) 1995, Oran, langue morte 1997, Les Nuits de Strasbourg 1997, Ces voix qui m'assiègent 1999, Filles d'Ismaël dans le vent et la tempête (musical drama in five acts) 2002, La Femme sans sepulture 2002, La Disparation de la langue française-roman 2004. *Address:* Department of French, New York University, 13 University Place, Office 621, New York, NY 10003-4556, USA (office). *Telephone:* (212) 992-9509 (office). *E-mail:* assia.djebar@nyu.edu (office). *Website:* french.as.nyu.edu/object/assiadjebar.html (office); www.assiadjebar.net (home).

DJERASSI, Carl, AB, PhD; American/Austrian chemist, academic and author; *Professor Emeritus of Chemistry, Stanford University;* b. 29 Oct. 1923, Vienna; s. of Dr Samuel Djerassi and Dr Alice Friedmann; m. 1st Virginia Jeremiah (divorced 1950); m. 2nd Norma Lundholm (divorced 1976); one s. one d. (deceased); m. 3rd Diane W. Middlebrook 1985 (died 2007); ed Kenyon Coll. and Univ. of Wisconsin; Research Chemist, Ciba Pharmaceutical Co., Summit, NJ 1942–43, 1945–49; Assoc. Dir of Research, Syntex, SA, Mexico City 1949–51, Research Vice-Pres. 1957–60, Pres. Syntex Research 1968–72; Assoc. Prof. of Chem., Wayne State Univ., Detroit 1952–54, Prof. 1954–59; Prof. of Chem., Stanford Univ. 1959–2002, Prof. Emer. 2002–; Pres. Bd Zoecon Corpn (renamed Sandoz Crop Protection Corpn) 1968–83, Chair. 1968–88; f. Djerassi Foundation Resident Artists Program; Royal Chemical Soc. Centenary Lecturer 1964; Royal Swedish Acad. of Eng Sciences thirteenth Chemical Lecturer 1969; Swedish Pharmaceutical Soc. Scheele Lecturer 1972; mem. Editorial Bd Journal of the American Chemical Society 1968–76, Journal of Organic Chemistry 1955–58, Tetrahedron 1958–92, Steroids 1963–, Proceedings of NAS 1964–70; mem. NAS Bd on Science and Tech. for Int. Devt 1967–76, Chair. 1972–76; mem. American Pugwash Cttee 1967–1981; mem. NAS, NAS Inst. of Medicine, Brazilian Acad. of Sciences, American Acad. of Arts and Sciences; Foreign mem. German Acad. of Natural Scientists (Leopoldina), Royal Swedish Acad. of Sciences 1973, Bulgarian Acad. of Sciences 1979, Royal Swedish Acad. of Eng Sciences 1984, Acad. Europaea; Hon. Fellow, Royal Chemical Soc. 1968, American Acad. of Pharmaceutical Science; Austrian Cross for Culture and Science 1999, Great Merit Cross of Germany 2003, Great Merit Cross for Services to Austria 2008, Gold Honour Ring of Austrian Acad. of Sciences 2008; numerous hon. degrees; Award in Pure Chem. 1958, Baekeland Medal 1959, Fritzsche Medal 1960, Creative Invention Award 1973, Award in the Chem. of Contemporary Technological Problems 1983, Esselen Award for Chem. in the Public Interest 1989, ACS; Intra-Science Research Award 1969, Freedman Foundation Patent Award 1971, Chemical Pioneer Award 1973, Perkin Medal 1975, American Inst. of Chemists; Nat. Medal of Science 1973 (for synthesis of first oral contraceptive), Wolf Prize in Chem. 1978, Bard Award in Medicine and Science 1983, Roussel Prize (Paris) 1988, NAS Award for the Industrial Application of Science 1990, Nat. Medal of Tech. 1991, Priestley Medal (ACS) 1992, Nevada Medal 1992, Thomson Gold Medal (Int. Mass Spectrometry Soc.) 1994, Prince Mahidol Award (Thailand) 1996, Willard Gibbs Medal 1997, Othmer Gold Medal, Chem. Heritage Foundation 2000, Erasmus Medal, Academia Europaea 2003, Gold Medal, American Inst. of Chemists 2004, on postage stamp, Austrian Post Office 2005, Serono Prize for Fiction, Rome 2005, Lichtenberg Medal of Göttingen Acad. of Sciences 2005. *Radio:* five radio plays, BBC World Service, West German Radio (WDR), Austrian Radio (ORF), NPR (USA). *Plays:* An Immaculate Misconception 1998, Oxygen (with Roald Hoffman) 2000, Calculus 2003, EGO 2003, Three on a Couch 2004, Phallacy 2005, Taboos 2006; numerous broadcasts. *Publications:* (author or co-author) Optical Rotatory Dispersion 1960, Steroid Reactions 1963, Interpretation of Mass Spectra of Organic Compounds 1964, Structure Elucidation of Natural Products by Mass Spectrometry (two vols) 1964, Mass Spectrometry of Organic Compounds 1967, The Politics of Contraception 1979, 1981, The Futurist and Other Stories (fiction) 1988, Cantor's Dilemma (novel) 1989, Steroids Made It Possible (autobiog.) 1990, The Clock Runs Backward (poetry) 1991, The Pill, Pygmy Chimps and Degas' Horse (autobiog.) 1992, Bourbaki Gambit (novel) 1994, From the Lab into the World (collected essays) 1994; Marx, deceased (novel) 1996, Menachem's Seed (novel) 1997, NO (novel) 1998, This Man's Pill (memoir) 2001, Newton's Darkness: Two Dramatic Views (with David Pinner) 2003, Sex in an Age of Technological Reproduction 2008, Four Jews on Parnassus: A Conversation 2008; numerous scientific articles, also poems, memoirs and short stories. *Leisure interests:* skiing, modern art, opera, theatre. *Address:* Department of Chemistry, Stanford University, Stanford, CA 94305-5080, USA (office). *Telephone:* (650) 723-2783 (office). *E-mail:* djerassi@stanford.edu (office). *Website:* www.djerassi.com (office).

DJOKOVIC, Novak; Serbian professional tennis player; b. 22 May 1987, Belgrade; s. of Srđan and Dijana Djokovic; ed trained at Nikola Pilić's tennis acad., Munich, Germany; turned professional 2003; Winner, Dutch Open, Amersfoort 2006, Open de Moselle, Metz 2006, Next Generation Adelaide Int., Asscn of Tennis Professionals Tour, Adelaide 2007, Miami Masters, Asscn of Tennis Professionals Masters Series 2007, Estoril Open 2007, Masters Series Rogers Cup, Montreal 2007,BA-CA Tennis Trophy, Vienna 2007, Grand Slam singles title, Australian Open 2008, Masters Series Pacific Life Open, Indian Wells, Calif. 2008, Masters Series singles title, Internazionali d'Italia, Rome 2008,Winner, Tennis Masters Cup, Shanghai 2008. *E-mail:* contact@novak-djokovic.com (office). *Website:* www.novakdjokovic.rs (home).

DJOUDI, Karim, BSc, MSc; Algerian banker and government official; *Minister of Finance;* b. 13 July 1958, Montpellier, France; ed Louis Pasteur Univ., Strasbourg and Univ. of Paris, Sorbonne, France; joined Cen. Bank of Algeria 1988, Cen. Dir 1990; Dir-Gen. of the Treasury, Ministry of Finance 1999–2003; Minister Del. responsible for Promotion of Investment 2003–05, responsible for Financial Reform 2005–07; Minister of Finance 2007–. *Address:* Ministry of Finance, Immeuble Maurétania, place du Pérou, Algiers, Algeria (office). *Telephone:* (21) 71-13-66 (office). *Fax:* (21) 73-42-76 (office). *E-mail:* algeriafinance@multimania.com (office). *Website:* www.finances-algeria.org (office).

DLAMINI, Absalom Themba; Swazi politician; *Prime Minister;* Prime Minister of Swaziland 2003–. *Address:* Office of the Prime Minister, Government House, POB 395, Mbabane, Swaziland (office). *Telephone:* 4042251 (office). *Fax:* 4043943 (office). *E-mail:* ppcu@realnet.co.sz (office).

DLAMINI, Barnabas Sibusiso; Swazi politician; *Prime Minister;* Minister of Finance 1984–93; fmr Exec. Dir IMF; Prime Minister of Swaziland July 1996–2003, 2008–. *Address:* Office of the Prime Minister, Government House, PO Box 433, Mbabane, Swaziland (office). *Telephone:* 4042251 (office). *Fax:* 4043943 (office). *Website:* www.gov.sz (office).

DLAMINI, Lutfo Ephraim; Swazi politician; *Minister of Foreign Affairs;* Minister of Enterprise and Employment 1998–2008, of Foreign Affairs 2008–; Chair. World Cup Faciliatory Cttee. *Address:* Ministry of Foreign Affairs, POB 518, Mbabane, Swaziland (office). *Telephone:* 4042661 (office). *Fax:* 4042669 (office).

DLAMINI, Mabili, BA; Swazi politician and diplomatist; b. 10 April 1957, Mankayane; m.; three s.; ed Univ. of Botswana and Swaziland; fmr Amb. to Malaysia and Singapore; Minister of Foreign Affairs and Trade 2003–06. *Leisure interests:* golf, soccer. *Address:* c/o Ministry of Foreign Affairs and Trade, PO Box 518, Mbabane, Swaziland (office).

DLAMINI, Moses Mathendele; Swazi politician and diplomatist; fmr Amb. to Taiwan; fmr Pres. of the Senate; fmr Chair. Parl. Del. to UN; Minister of

Foreign Affairs and Trade 2006–08; Order of Brilliant Star with Grand Cordon (Taiwan). *Address:* c/o Ministry of Foreign Affairs and Trade, POB 518, Mbabane, Swaziland (office).

DLAMINI, Obed Mfanyana; Swazi politician; *President, Ngwane National Liberatory Congress;* b. 4 April 1937, Mhlosheni Area, Shiselweni Dist; ed Swaziland Nat. High School, UNISA; teacher and Boarding Master, Manzini Nazarene High School 1961–64; cost clerk, later Asst Personnel Officer, Roberts Construction (Swaziland) (Pty) Ltd 1964–66; clerk, Standard Chartered Bank of Swaziland 1966, Asst Man. Admin. –1981; fmr Training and Ind. Relations Man. Swaziland Fruit Canners (Pty) Ltd; fmr Gen. Sec. Swaziland Fed. of Trade Unions, mem. Labour Advisory Bd, Training and Localization Council, Wages Advisory Bd, Man. Training Council, Regional Educ. Advisory Bd, Workers' Educ. Group; Prime Minister of Swaziland 1989–93; Senator 1993–; Pres. Ngwane Nat. Liberatory Congress (CNNLC); Chair. Swazi Democratic Alliance 1999–. *Leisure interests:* soccer, wrestling, tug-of-war, jazz, music. *Address:* Ngwane National Liberatory Congress, Ilanga Centre, Martin Street, Manzini; The Senate, Mbabane, Swaziland. *Telephone:* 5053935 (office).

DLAMINI, Sotsha; Swazi politician; b. 1940; fmr Asst Police Commr –1984; Prime Minister of Swaziland 1986–89. *Address:* c/o Office of the Prime Minister, Mbabane, Swaziland.

DLAMINI-ZUMA, Nkosazana C., MB, ChB; South African politician and medical doctor; *Minister of Foreign Affairs;* b. 27 Jan. 1949; m. Jacob Zuma (divorced); four c.; ed Amanzintoti Training Coll., Univ. of Zululand, Univ. of Natal, Univ. of Bristol, Univ. of Liverpool; Research Technician Medical School, Univ. of Natal 1972; Vice-Pres. SA Students Org. 1975–76; Chair. ANC Youth Section GB 1977–78; House Officer Frenchay Hosp. Bristol 1978–79; House Officer Canadian Red Cross Memorial Hosp., Berks. 1979–80; Medical Officer-Pediatrics Mbabane Govt Hosp. Swaziland 1980–85; Pediatric attachment Wittington Hosp. 1987–89; Vice Chair. Regional Political Cttee of ANC GB 1978–88, Chair. 1988–89; ANC Health Dept Lusaka 1989–90; Research Scientist Medical Research Council, Durban 1991–94; Minister of Health 1994–99, of Foreign Affairs 1999–; Dir Health Refugee Trust, Health and Devt Org., England 1988–90; Chair. S Natal Region Health Cttee of ANC 1990–92; mem. Exec. Cttee S Natal Region of ANC 1990–93; Chair. S Natal Region ANC Women's League 1991–93; Pres. World Conf. Against Racism 2001; mem. Steering Cttee Nat. AIDS Co-ordinating Cttee 1992–; mem. Bd Centre for Social Devt Studies Univ. of Natal, Durban 1992–; Trustee Health Systems Trust 1992–; Dr hc (Natal) 1995, (Bristol) 1996. *Address:* 602 Stretten Bay, St Andrews Street, Durban 4001 (home); Department of Foreign Affairs, Union Buildings, East Wing, Government Avenue, Pretoria 0002, South Africa (office). *Telephone:* (12) 3511000 (office). *Fax:* (12) 3510253 (office). *E-mail:* minister@foreign.gov.za (office). *Website:* www.dfa.gov.za (office).

DLOUHÝ, Vladimír, CSc; Czech politician and economist; b. 31 July 1953, Prague; m. 1st (divorced 1999); m. 2nd Eliška Břízoá 2001; one s. one d.; ed Prague School of Econs, Charles Univ. Prague and Catholic Univ., Louvain; fmr teacher, Prague School of Econs; scientist, Inst. of Econ. Forecasting, Czechoslovak Acad. of Sciences 1983–89, latterly Deputy Dir; Deputy Prime Minister and Chair. State Planning Comm. 1989–90; Minister of the Economy 1990–92; Minister of Trade and Industry of Czech Repub. 1992–97; Int. Adviser, Goldman Sachs 1997–; Adviser to Exec. Man., ABB 1997–; mem. Civic Democratic Alliance 1991–98, Vice-Pres. March–Oct. 1992, Deputy Chair. 1993–97; mem. State Defence Council 1993; Chair. Council of Customs Union 1994–97, Bd of Supervisors Stock Co. Unipetrol 1996–97; Deputy Chair. Bd of Supervisors, Volkswagen-Skoda Group, Mladá Boleslav 1994–95; mem. Parl. 1996–98; mem. Bd of Supervisors, Foundation Bohemiae 1992–2001; mem. Bd of Dirs Cofinec 1997–2000; Grand-Croix, Ordre de Léopold II (Belgium). *Publications:* Ekonometrický model čs. obchodní bilance 1985, Models of Disequilibrium and Shortage in Centrally Planned Economies 1989; articles in Czechoslovak and int. econ. journals. *Leisure interest:* music. *Address:* Pachtův palác, Anenské náměstí 4, 110 00 Prague 1, Czech Republic. *Telephone:* (2) 2163-5351. *Fax:* (2) 2163-5350.

DMITRIEV, Alexander Sergeevich; Russian conductor; b. 19 Jan. 1935, Leningrad; m.; one s.; ed Leningrad Choir School, Leningrad State Conservatory, Vienna Akad. für Musik und darstellende Kunst; Conductor Karelian Radio and TV Symphony Orchestra 1961, Prin. Conductor 1962–71; Prin. Conductor Maly Opera and Ballet Theatre, Leningrad (now St Petersburg) 1971–77, and Music Dir Symphony Orchestra of St Petersburg Philharmonia 1977–; Prin. Conductor Stavanger Symphony Orchestra (Norway) 1990–98; Merited Worker of Arts of Karelian ASSR 1967, People's Artist of Russia 1976, USSR People's Artist; Prize 2nd USSR Competition for Conductors 1966. *Recordings include:* Handel's Messiah, Haydn's Creation, Schubert's Symphony Nos. 1–9, Tchaikovsky's Symphonies 4, 5, 6, Rachmaninov's Symphony No. 2, Debussy's 3 Nocturnes, Ravel's Valses nobles et sentimentales, Ma Mère l'Oye, Saeverud's Peer Gynt, Symphony dolorosa, Balakirev's Piano Concerto, Medtner's Piano Concerto No. 1, Rachmaninov's Piano Concerto No. 3, Britten's Violin concerto, Sibelius Violin Concerto, Shostakovich and Tchaikovsky Violin Concertos, Shostakovich Symphony No. 7, Scriabin Symphony No. 3. *Address:* Symphony Orchestra, St Petersburg Philharmonic Society, Mikhailovskaya str. 2, St Petersburg 091011, Russia (office). *Telephone:* (812) 714-64-17 (home). *Fax:* (812) 571-21-26 (office). *E-mail:* dmitriev@mail.spbnit.ru (home). *Website:* www.philharmonia.spb.ru (office).

DMITRIEV, Andrey Viktorovich; Russian diplomatist; *Ambassador to Cuba;* b. 10 April 1941, Moscow; m.; one s. one d.; ed Moscow State Pedagogic Inst. of Foreign Languages, Diplomatic Acad.; mem. staff UN Secr., New York 1969–76, USSR Embassy, Brazil 1978–82, Peru 1987–89, USSR then Russian Embassy, Nicaragua 1989–92, Amb. to Nicaragua 1995–99, Dir Latin

American Dept Ministry of Foreign Affairs, Moscow 1999–2001, Amb. to Cuba (also accred to Barbados) 2000–. *Address:* Embassy of Russia, 5A Avenida, N6402, entre 62–66, Miramar, Havana, Cuba (office). *Telephone:* (7) 204-10-85 (office). *Fax:* (7) 204-10-38 (office). *E-mail:* embrusia@ceniai.inf.cu (office). *Website:* www.cuba.mid.ru (office).

DMITRIYEVA, Tatyana Borisovna, MD, DMedSc; Russian psychiatrist and politician; *Director, Serbsky National Research Centre;* b. 21 Dec. 1951, Ivanovo; d. of Boris Alexandrovich Gareyev and Julia Fedorovna Gareyeva; m. Andrey Sergeyevich Dmitriyev; ed Ivanovo Inst. of Medicine; psychiatrist Ivanovo Region Psychiatric Hosp. 1975–76; Jr, later Sr Researcher All-Union Serbsky Nat. Research Centre for Social and Forensic Psychiatry 1976–86, Head of Clinical Dept, Deputy Dir 1986–90, Dir 1990–; concurrently Prof., Head of Chair. Moscow Sechenov Acad. of Medicine; Minister of Public Health of Russian Fed. 1996–98; Chair. Psychiatric Section, Academic Council of the Ministry of Health; mem. Russian Acad. of Medical Sciences; Order Merit to Fatherland Fourth Degree 2001, Third Degree 2006; Russian Acad. of Medical Sciences V. S. Gulevich Prize for the Best Medical Work on Medical Biological Chemistry 2001. *Publications:* Mental Health of the Population of Russia 2001, Manual on Social Psychiatry 2001, Social Stress and Mental Health 2001, Alliance of Law and Mercy: On Human Rights Protection in Psychiatry 2001, Handbook of Legal Psychiatry (ed.) 2004; 350 academic works, including 22 monographs, 11 handbooks for doctor and psychologists and six textbooks. *Leisure interests:* reading fiction, horse riding, travel. *Address:* Serbsky Research Centre, Kropotkinsky per. 23, 119992 Moscow (office); 113191 Moscow, Apt 21, Bldg 2, house 2/1, Malaya Tulskaya ul., Russia. *Telephone:* (495) 201-52-62 (office). *Fax:* (495) 201-72-31 (office). *E-mail:* center@serbsky.ru (office).

DMITRIYEVSKY, Anatoly Nikolayevich; Russian engineer; b. 6 May 1937; m.; one s. one d.; ed Gubkin Moscow Inst. of Oil and Gas; Sr teacher Gubkin Moscow Univ. of Oil and Gas; Pro-rector, Chair Algerian Nat. Inst. of Oil, Gas and Chem.; Dir Oil and Gas Research Inst., Russian Acad. of Sciences 1987–; Pres. Union of Scientific and Eng Org. of Russia; mem. of Bd Int. Gas Union; mem. Russian Acad. of Sciences 1991; USSR State Prize 1986, State Prize of Russia 1998. *Publications include:* Lithological System and Genetic Analysis of Oil and Gas Sedimentary Basins 1982, Fundamental Basis of Oil and Gas Geology 1991. *Leisure interests:* tennis, mountain skiing, photography. *Address:* Oil and Gas Research Institute, Gubkina str. 3, 117701 Moscow, Russia (office). *Telephone:* (495) 135-73-71 (office). *Fax:* (495) 135-54-65 (office). *E-mail:* a.dmitrievsky@ogri.ru (office).

DO, Thich Quang; Vietnamese Buddhist leader; in exile in India and Sri Lanka; taught Buddhist philosophy in Saigon in the 1960s and 1970s; fmr leader Unified Buddhist Church of Vietnam; imprisoned by Communist authorities; released 1998. *Address:* Thanh Zinh Zen Monastery, Ho Chi Minh City, Vietnam (office).

DO NASCIMENTO, HE Cardinal Alexandre; Angolan ecclesiastic; b. 1 March 1925, Malanje; s. of Antonio André do Nascimento and Maria Ana Alves da Rocha; ed Gregoriana Univ., Rome, Faculty of Laws, Lisbon; ordained priest 1952; Bishop of Malanje 1975; Archbishop of Lubango 1977–86, of Luanda 1986–2001; Archbishop Emer. of Luanda 2001–; Apostolic Admin. of Onjiva; mem. Sacred Congregation for the Propagation of the Faith and the Evangelization of the People; cr. Cardinal 1983; Pres. Caritas Internationalis; Preacher, Retreat of the Holy Father and the Roman Curia 1984; mem. Sacred Congregation Pro Culto Divino 1985, Congregation Pro Institutione Catholica; Hon. mem. Acad. das Ciéncias (Lisbon), Acad. da Historia; Dr hc (Lisbon) 2000; Golden Medal for Human Rights Portuguese Ass. *Publications:* Caminhos da Esperança 1992, Livro de Ritmos (poetry), Discursos e Mensagens 2002. *Leisure interests:* reading, music. *Address:* Rua Américo Júlio Carvalho 97–99, Bairro Azul, Luanda, Angola. *Telephone:* (2) 350755. *Fax:* (2) 351751. *E-mail:* dalexnascimento@snet.co.ao.

DO NASCIMENTO, Edson Arantes (see PELÉ).

DO SACRAMENTO E SOUSA, Lt-Col. Óscar Aguiar; São Tomé and Príncipe politician; Vice-Pres. Chamber of Commerce 2002; Minister of Defence and Internal Order 2003–08; Minister of Foreign Affairs 2004, 2006. *Address:* c/o Ministry of Defence and Internal Order, Av. 12 de Julho, CP427, São Tomé (office).

DOAN, Nguyen Thi, PhD; Vietnamese economist and politician; *Vice President;* b. 11 Jan. 1951, Ha Nam Prov.; ed Sofia Economic Univ., Bulgaria; mem. Nat. Ass. representing Ha Nam Prov; mem. 10th Cen. Cttee, CP of Viet Nam 2006; fmr Deputy Sec.Party Cttee of Block-I Cen. Agencies; mem. Party Cen. Cttee's Comm. for Inspection 1998, Deputy Perm. Head –2007; Vice Pres. of Viet Nam 2007–. *Address:* Dang Cong San Viet Nam (Communist Party of Viet Nam), 1 Hoang Van Thu, Hanoi, Viet Nam (office). *E-mail:* cpv@hn.vnn.vn (office). *Website:* www.cpv.org.vn (office).

DOBBINS, James F., BA; American diplomatist; *Director, International Security and Defense Policy Center, RAND Corporation;* b. 1942, New York; m. Toril Kleivdal; two s.; ed Georgetown Univ. School of Foreign Service; US naval officer; mem. Policy Planning Staff, State Dept, Washington DC 1969–71, Deputy Asst Sec. 1982–85, Prin. Deputy Asst Sec. 1989–90, Acting Asst Sec. for European and Canadian Affairs 1991, Special Asst to Pres., Nat. Security Council Staff 1996–99, Special Adviser to Pres. for Kosovo and Dayton Implementation 1999–2000, Asst Sec. of State for European Affairs 2000–01; mem. US Mission to OECD 1967–68, US Del. to Vietnam Peace Talks 1968; Political Officer, US Embassy, Paris 1969; mem. US Mission to UN 1973–75, Political-Mil. Officer US Embassy, London 1978–81; Deputy Chief of Mission, Bonn, FRG 1985–89; Amb. to the EC 1991–93; Special Envoy to Afghanistan 2001–03; Sr Fellow, RAND Corpn 1993, Dir Int. Security and

Defense Policy Center 2003–; mem. Council on Foreign Relations 1995–96; two Superior Honor Awards, three Presidential Awards, six Sr Performance Awards, Dept of the Army Decoration for Dist Civilian Service, Armed Forces Expeditionary Medal, Nat. Defense Service Medal, Expeditionary Medal, Repub. of Viet Nam. *Publication:* America's Role in Nation-Building: From Germany to Iraq (co-author) 2003, The UN's Role in Nation-Building: From the Congo to Iraq (co-author) 2005, The Beginner's Guide to Nation-Building (co-author) 2007. *Address:* International Security and Defense Policy Center, RAND Corporation, 1200 South Hayes Street, Arlington, VA 22202, USA (office). *Telephone:* (703) 413-1100, ext. 5286 (office). *E-mail:* James_Dobbins@rand.org (office). *Website:* www.rand.org (office).

DOBBS, Michael John, PhD, MALD, MA; British writer; b. 14 Nov. 1948; m. Rachel Dobbs; four s.; ed Christ Church, Oxford and Fletcher School of Law and Diplomacy, USA; UK Govt Special Adviser 1981–87; Chief of Staff, UK Conservative Party 1986–87, Jt Deputy Chair. 1994–95; Deputy Chair. Saatchi & Saatchi 1983–91; BBC TV presenter 1999–2001. *Publications:* House of Cards 1989, Wall Games 1990, Last Man to Die 1991, To Play the King 1992, The Touch of Innocents 1994, The Final Cut 1995, Goodfellowe MP 1997, The Buddha of Brewer Street 1998, Whispers of Betrayal 2000, Winston's War 2002, Never Surrender 2003, Churchill's Hour 2004, Churchill's Triumph 2005, First Lady 2006, The Lords' Day 2007, The Edge of Madness 2008. *Address:* Newton House, Wylye, Wilts. BA12 0QS, England (office). *Telephone:* 7836 201967 (mobile). *E-mail:* michldobbs@aol.com (office).

DOBESCH, Gerhard, DPhil; Austrian academic; *Professor of Roman History, Archaeology and Epigraphy, University of Vienna;* b. 15 Sept. 1939, Vienna; s. of Dr Carl Dobesch and Gustave Dobesch; ed Univ. of Vienna; Lecturer in Ancient History 1967–73; Prof. of Greek and Roman History, Univ. of Graz 1973–76; Prof. of Roman History, Archaeology and Epigraphy, Univ. of Vienna 1976–; Corresp. mem. Austrian Archaeological Inst. 1972–98 (mem. 1998–), Austrian Acad. of Sciences 1980–84 (mem. 1984–). *Publications:* Caesars Apotheose zu Lebzeiten und sein Ringen um den Königstitel 1966, Der Panhellen: Gedanke und der Philippos des Isokrates 1968, Wurde Caesar zu Lebzeiten in Rom als Staatsgott anerkannt? 1971, Nochmals zur Datierung des grossen Senatskonsultes 1971, Nikolaos von Damaskus und die Selbstbiographie des Augustus 1978, Die Kelten in Österreich nach den ältest 1980, Die Kimbern in den Ostalpen und die Schlacht bei Noreia 1982, Zu Caesars Sitzenbleiben vor dem Senat 1988, Zur Einwanderung die Kelten in Oberitalien 1989, Caesar als Ethnograph 1989, Zu zwei Daten d. Gesch. Galliens 1989, Europa in d. Reichskonzeption 1989, Autonomie des Menschen und Werthaftigkeit in der Antike 1990, Die Kelten als Nachbarn der Etrusker 1992, J. K. Newman u. Catull 1992, 100 Jahre Kleinasiat. Komm. 1993, Principis dignationem 1993; Vom äusseren Proletariat zum Kulturträger 1994, Phokion und der Korinthische Bund 1994, Aus der Vor-und Nachgeschichte der Markomannenkriege 1994, Das europäische 'Barbaricum' und die Zone der Mediterrankultur 1995, Der Ostalpenraum als Kultur- und Machtgrundlage in keltischer und römischer Zeit 1996, Würdigung Fritz Schachermeyr 1996, Die römische Kaiserzeit–eine Fortsetzung des Hellenismus? 1996; Zu Virunum als Namen der Stadt auf dem Magdalensberg 1997, Ende und Metamorphose des Etruskertums 1998, Der Weltreichsgedanke bei Caesar 1998, Mitherausgeber: Adolf Wilhelm, Kleine Schriften: Abt. II, Teil III 2000 Teil IV 2002, Teil V 2003, Einige merkwürdige Überlieferungen über Caesar 2000, Urgeschichtliches Eisen in der Sicht des Althistorikers 2000, Caesars monarchische Ideologie 2000, Ausgewählte Schriften (two vols) 2001, Caesars Volcae Tectosages in Mitteleuropa 2001, Caesar, Commentarii über den gallischen Krieg, Buch 1, Kapitel 1: eine Sensation, Wiener Humanistische Blätter 42 2001, Caesars Urteil über Ciceros Bedeutung – Gedanken über Cic. Brut. 253 und Plin. n. h., 117 2003, Caesar und der Hellenismus 2004, Zentrum, Peripherie und 'Barbaren' in der Urgeschichte und der Alten Geschichte 2004, Einige Beobachtungen zu Politik und Tod des Haeduers Diviciacus und seines Bruders Dumnorix 2005, Wassergrenzen under Wasserwege aus urgeschichtlicher und römischer Sicht 2005; numerous specialist articles. *Leisure interests:* literature, art history. *Address:* Universität Wien, Institut für Alte Geschichte, Dr. Karl Lueger-Ring 1, 1010 Vienna (office). Spitalgasse 29/10, 1090 Vienna, Austria (home). *Telephone:* 4277-40520 (office); 407 95 22 (home). *Fax:* 4277-9405 (office). *E-mail:* gerhard.dobesch@univie.ac.at (office).

DOBRETSOV, Nikolai Leontyevich, DGeol; Russian geologist; *Director-General, United Institute of Geology, Geophysics and Mineralogy and Chairman, Siberia Branch, Russian Academy of Sciences;* b. 15 Jan. 1936; m.; five c.; ed Leningrad Inst. of Mines; chief Altai Mining expedition, Jr then Sr Researcher; Head of Lab. Inst. of Geology and Geophysics, Siberian br. of USSR (now Russian) Acad. of Sciences in Novosibirsk; Head of Lab. Inst. of Tectonics and Geophysics, USSR Acad. of Sciences in Khabarovsk; Dir Buryat Inst. of Geology, Chair. Presidium of Buryat Research Cen. Siberian br. of USSR Acad. of Sciences, Dir-Gen. United Inst. of Geology, Geophysics and Mineralogy; Corresp. mem. USSR (now Russian) Acad. of Sciences 1984, mem. 1987, mem. Presidium 1991–, Pres. of Siberian br. 1997–, Vice-Pres. Russian Acad. of Sciences; Pres. Asscn of Acads of Sciences in Asia (AASA); Labourer of the Red Banner 1986, State Prize of the Russian Fed. 1997. *Publications include:* Introduction to Global Petrology 1980, Global Petrological Processes 1981, Deep-level Geodynamics 1994; papers on tectonics and petrography. *Leisure interests:* books, fishing. *Address:* Siberian Branch, Russian Academy of Sciences, Prosp. Akademika Lavrentieva, 17, Novosibirsk 630090; United Institute of Geology, Geophysics and Mineralogy, Prospect Acad. Koptyuga 3, 630090 Novosibirsk, Russia (office). *Telephone:* (3832) 30-05-67 (office); (383) 333-26-00 (office). *Fax:* (3832) 30-18-62 (office); (383) 333-27-92 (office). *E-mail:* dobr@sbras.nsc.ru (office). *Website:* www.sbras.ru (office); geology.uiggm.nsc.ru (office).

DOBRIANSKY, Paula J., MA, PhD, BSFS; American diplomatist; *Under-Secretary for Democracy and Global Affairs;* b. 14 Sept. 1955, Alexandria, VA; ed Harvard Univ., Georgetown Univ. School of Foreign Service; early career positions include Dir European and Soviet Affairs, Nat. Security Council, The White House; Deputy Asst Sec. of State, Human Rights and Humanitarian Affairs; Assoc. Dir Policy and Programs, US Information Agency; Co-Chair Int. TV Council, Corpn for Public Broadcasting Sr Int. Affairs and Trade Advisor, Hunton and Williams; Sr Vice-Pres. and Dir, George F. Kennan Sr Fellow for Russian and Eurasian Studies, Washington Office, Council of Foreign Relations; Under-Sec. for Democracy and Global Affairs 2001–, Special Envoy for NI 2007–; mem. Bd Western NIS Enterprise Fund, Nat. Endowment for Democracy (NED) (also Vice-Chair.), Freedom House, American Council of Young Political Leaders, ABA Cen. and E European Law Initiative, US Advisory Comm. on Public Diplomacy; Host, Freedom's Challenge (three years); Co-host Worldwise (Nat. Empowerment TV); Ford and Rotary Foundation Fellow; Poland's Highest Medal of Merit, Grand Cross, Commdr of Order of Lithuanian Grand Duke Gediminas; Dr hc (Fairleigh Dickinson Univ.), (Flagler Coll.); State Dept Superior Honor Award, Dialogue on Diversity's Int. Award 2001, NED Service Medal, Georgetown Univ. Annual Alumni Achievement Award. *Address:* US Department of State, Office 7250, 2201 Central Street, NW, Washington, DC 20520, USA (office). *Telephone:* (202) 647-6240 (office). *Website:* www.state.gov (office).

DOBRODEYEV, Oleg Borisovich, CandHistSc; Russian television producer; *Chairman, All-Russian State Television-Radio Company (VGTRK);* b. 28 Nov. 1959, Moscow; m.; one s.; ed Moscow State Univ.; mem. of staff Inst. of USA and Canada 1982–83; Ed. TV programme Vremya, USSR Cen. TV, later Deputy Ed.-in-Chief 1983–90; Ed.-in-Chief news programme Vesti; Ed.-in-Chief Information TV Agency (ITA) 1990–91, Ostankino Co. 1991–93; Ed.-in-Chief Information Service, NTV Co., later Vice-Pres. 1993–2000, Dir-Gen. NTV Co. 1997–2000; Chair. All-Russian State TV-Radio Co. (VGTRK) 2000–; Order of Honour 1999. *Leisure interest:* reading people's memoirs. *Address:* All-Russian State TV-Radio Co., Yamskogo Polya 5th str. 19/21, 125040 Moscow, Russia (office). *Telephone:* (495) 234-8600 (office); (495) 214-4978 (office). *Fax:* (495) 214-2347 (office). *E-mail:* info@rfn.ru (office); vgtrk2@space.ru (office). *Website:* www.vgtrk.com (office).

DOBRYNIN, Anatoliy Fedorovich, MSc; Russian diplomatist (retd); b. 16 Nov. 1919, Krasnaya Gorka, Moscow Region; m.; one d.; ed S. Ordzhonikidze Moscow Aviation Inst., Higher Diplomatic School, Ministry of Foreign Affairs; engineer at aircraft plant, World War II; joined diplomatic service 1946; Counsellor, later Minister-Counsellor, Soviet Embassy, Washington 1952–55; Asst Minister of Foreign Affairs 1955–57; Under-Sec.-Gen. for Political and Security Council Affairs UN 1957–59, Head American Dept, USSR Ministry of Foreign Affairs 1959–61; Amb. to USA 1962–86; Adviser to Pres. Gorbachev (q.v.) 1988–91; Consultant to Russian Ministry of Foreign Affairs 1995–; mem. CPSU 1945–, Cand. mem., CPSU Cen. Cttee 1966–71, mem. 1971–90, Sec. Cen. Cttee for Foreign Affairs 1986–88; Head Int. Dept 1986–88; Deputy of USSR Supreme Soviet 1986–89; Hero of Socialist Labour 1982, Order of Lenin (five times). *Publication:* In Confidence: Moscow's Ambassador to Six Cold War Presidents (memoirs) 1995. *Address:* c/o Ministry of Foreign Affairs, Smolenskaya Sennaya 32/34, 119200 Moscow, Russia.

DOBRZAŃSKI, Stanisław; Polish business executive and politician; *President, Polskie Sieci Elektroenergetyczne SA;* b. 22 March 1949, Hrubieszów; m.; two c.; ed Maria Skłodowska-Curie Univ., Lublin; Deputy Dir Polish Nat. Library, Warsaw 1982–85; Dept Dir, Ministry of Culture and Art; Dir agency of Wschodni Bank Cukrownictwa; Under-Sec. of State, Office of the Council of Ministers 1993–96; Minister of Nat. Defence 1996–98; Pres. Man. Bd Polskie Sieci Elektroenergetyczne SA (Polish Power Grid Co.) 2001–. *Address:* Polskie Sieci Elektroenergetyczne SA, ul. Mysia 2, 00-456 Warsaw, Poland (office). *Telephone:* (22) 693-15-80 (office); (22) 621-49-04 (office). *Fax:* (22) 628-59-64 (office). *E-mail:* stanislaw.dobrzanski@pse.pl (office). *Website:* www.pse.pl (office).

DOBSON, Rt Hon. Frank (Gordon), PC, BSc (Econs); British politician; b. 15 March 1940; s. of the late James William Dobson and Irene Shortland Dobson; m. Janet Mary Alker 1967; two s. one d.; ed Archbishop Holgate Grammar School, York, LSE; admin. appointments with Cen. Electricity Generating Bd 1962–70, Electricity Council 1970–75; mem. Camden Borough Council 1971–76, Leader 1973–75; Asst Sec. Comm. for Local Admin. 1975–79; MP for Holborn and St Pancras South 1979–83, for Holborn and St Pancras 1983–; Opposition Spokesman on Educ. 1981–83, on Health 1983–87, on Energy 1989–92, on Employment 1992–93, on Transport and London 1993–94, on Environment and London 1994–97; Sec. of State for Health 1997–99; Labour candidate for Mayoralty of London 2000; Shadow Leader of the House of Commons 1987–89; Gov. LSE 1986–2003, Inst. of Child Health 1987–92; Gov. Royal Veterinary Coll. 2004–; mem. of Court, Univ. of York 2004–; mem. of Court, London School of Hygiene and Tropical Medicine 2009–. *Address:* House of Commons, London, SW1A 0AA (office); 22 Great Russell Mansions, Great Russell Street, London, WC1B 3BE, England (home). *Telephone:* (20) 7219-4452 (office); (20) 7242-5760 (home). *Fax:* (20) 7219-6956 (office).

DOBSON, Michael William Romsey, MA; British banking and finance executive; *CEO, Schroders PLC;* b. 13 May 1952, London; s. of Sir Denis (William) Dobson; m. Frances de Salis 1998; two d.; ed Eton Coll., Trinity Coll. Cambridge; joined Morgan Grenfell 1973, banker Morgan Grenfell New York 1978–80, Man. Dir 1984–85, Chief Exec. Morgan Grenfell Asset Management 1987–88, Deputy CEO Morgan Grenfell Group (now Deutsche Morgan Grenfell) 1988–89, CEO 1989–96; mem. Bd of Man. Dirs Deutsche Bank AG 1996–2000 (responsible for investment banking 1996–98, for asset man. 1998–2000), mem. Advisory Bd; f. Beaumont Capital Man. Ltd 2000 (acquired by Schroders PLC 2001); Dir (non-exec.) Schroders PLC April–Nov. 2001, CEO 2001–. *Address:* Schroders PLC, 31 Gresham Street, London, EC2V 7QA, England (office). *Telephone:* (20) 7658-6962 (office). *Fax:* (20) 7658-3476 (office). *E-mail:* michael.dobson@schroders.com (office). *Website:* www.schroders.com (office).

DOCHANASHVILI, Guram; Georgian writer; b. 1939, Tbilisi, Georgia; s. of Petre Dochanashvili and Gulnara Emukhvari; m.; one d.; ed Tbilisi State Univ.; worked in Dept of Archaeology Inst. of History Georgian Acad. of Sciences 1962–75; Head. Div. of Prose Mnatobi (magazine) 1975–85; Deputy Dir Gruzia Film Studio 1985–; Ivane Dzhavakhishvili Medal, Tbilisi State Univ. 1984, State Prize of Georgia 1994. *Publications include:* Besame 1989, Havaiuri valsi 1990. *Publications include:* There, Behind the Mountain 1966. *Address:* c/o Georgian Union of Writers, Machabeli str. 13, 380000 Tbilisi, Georgia.

DOCHERTY, David, BA, PhD; British broadcasting executive; *Group Chief Executive, YooMedia PLC;* b. 10 Dec. 1956, Scotland; s. of David Docherty and Anna Docherty; m. Kate Stuart-Smith 1992; two d.; ed Univ. of Strathclyde, London School of Econs; Research Fellow Broadcasting Research Unit, London 1984–88; Dir of Research Broadcasting Standards Council 1988–89; Head of Broadcasting Analysis BBC TV 1990–92, Head of TV Planning and Strategy BBC Network TV 1992–96, Dir of Strategy and Channel Devt, BBC Broadcast 1996–97, Deputy Dir of TV BBC Broadcast 1997, Dir New Services, BBC Bd of Man. 1999; Man. Dir of Broadband Content, Telewest Communications 2000–2002; CEO YooMedia PLC's iPublic div. 2003–2004, Group Chief Exec. YooMedia PLC 2004–; Chair. Living Health; Chair. Bd of Govs Univ. of Luton 2001–; mem. Bd BBC America UKTV. *Publications:* The Last Picture Show?: Britain's Changing Film Audience 1987, Keeping Faith?: Channel 4 and Its Audience 1988, Running the Show: 21 Years of London Weekend Television 1990, Violence in Television Fiction 1991, The Spirit Death 2000, The Killing Jar 2002, The Fifth Season 2003. *Leisure interest:* writing. *Address:* YooMedia PLC, 155-157 Great Portland Street, London, W1W 6QP (office); Serge Hill, Abbots Langley, Herts., WD5 0RY, England (home). *Telephone:* (20) 7462-0870 (office). *Fax:* (20) 7462-0871 (office). *E-mail:* inquiries@yoomedia.com (office). *Website:* www.yoomedia.com (office).

DOCTOROW, Edgar Lawrence (E.L.), AB; American novelist, dramatist and academic; *Lewis and Loretta Gluckman Professor of American and English Letters, New York University;* b. 6 Jan. 1931, New York; s. of David Richard and Rose Doctorow (née Levine); m. Helen Esther Setzer 1954; one s. two d.; ed Kenyon Coll., Gambier, Ohio, Columbia Univ.; served with US army 1953–55; script reader, Columbia Pictures 1959; Ed. New American Library, New York 1960–64; Ed.-in-Chief Dial Press., New York 1964–69, Publr 1969; Writer-in-Residence, Univ. of Calif., Irvine 1969–70; mem. faculty, Sarah Lawrence Coll., Bronxville, NY 1971–78; Creative Writing Fellow, Yale School of Drama 1974–75; Creative Artists Program Service Fellow 1973–74; Visiting Sr Fellow, Council on Humanities, Princeton Univ. 1980–81, Prof. of English 1982–87; Lewis and Loretta Gluckman Prof. of American and English Letters, New York Univ. 1987–; mem. Authors Guild (dir), American PEN, Writers Guild of America East, Century Asscn; Guggenheim Fellow 1973; Hon. LHD (Kenyon Coll.) 1976, (Hobart Coll.) 1979; Hon. DLitt (William Smith Coll.) 1979; Hon. DHL (Brandeis Univ. 1989; Arts and Letters Award (American Acad. and Nat. Inst. of Art) 1976, Nat. Book Critics Circle Award 1976, 1990, 2005, Guggenheim Fellow 1973, Nat. Book Award 1986, William Dean Howells Medal, American Acad. of Arts and Letters 1990, PEN/Faulkner Prize 1990, 2005, Nat. Humanities Medal 1998, Commonwealth Award 2000. *Publications:* Welcome to Hard Times 1960, Big as Life 1966, The Book of Daniel 1971, Ragtime 1975, Drinks before Dinner (play) 1975, Loon Lake 1980, Lives of the Poets: Six Stories and a Novella 1984, World's Fair 1985, Billy Bathgate 1988, Jack London, Hemingway and the Constitution: Selected Essays 1977–92 1993, The Waterworks 1994, Poets and Presidents: Selected Essays 1994, The Best American Short Stories (ed. with Katrina Kenison) 2000, City of God 2000, Sweet Land Stories 2004, Reporting the Universe 2004, The March 2006, Creationists: Selected Essays 1993–2006 2006. *Address:* c/o International Creative Management, 825 8th Avenue, New York, NY 10019, USA (office); English Department, New York University, 19 University Place, Second Floor, New York, NY 10003; c/o Random House Publishers, 1745 Broadway, New York, NY 10019, USA (office). *E-mail:* eld1@nyu.edu.

DODANGODA, Amarasiri; Sri Lankan politician; *Minister of Justice and Law Reforms;* fmr Minister of Vocational Training and Rural Industries; apptd Minister of Human Resources Devt, Tech. and Vocational Educ. 2001; Minister of Public Admin and Home Affairs 2004–05; Minister of Justice and Law Reforms 2005–. *Address:* Ministry of Justice and Law Reforms, Superior Courts Complex Bldg, Colombo 12, Sri Lanka (office). *Telephone:* (11) 2323022 (office). *Fax:* (11) 2320785 (office). *E-mail:* Secmoj@srilanka.net (office). *Website:* www.justiceministry.gov.lk (office).

DODD, Christopher J., BA, JD; American politician; *Senator from Connecticut;* b. 27 May 1944, Willimantic, Conn.; s. of Thomas J. and Grace (Murphy) Dodd; ed Providence Coll., RI and Univ. of Louisville, Ky; Volunteer with Peace Corps, Dominican Repub. 1966–68; admitted to Conn. Bar 1973; mem. House of Reps 1975–81 from 2nd Dist Conn.; Senator from Conn. 1980–, mem. Foreign Relations Cttee., ranking mem. Sub-Cttee. on W Hemisphere, Peace Corps and Narcotics Affairs; Democrat; numerous awards. *Address:* 448 Russell Senate Building, Washington, DC 20510-0001, USA. *Telephone:* (202) 224-2823 (office). *Website:* dodd.senate.gov (office).

DODD, Lois; American artist; b. 22 April 1927, Montclair, NJ; d. of Lawrence Dodd and Margaret Vanderhoff; one s.; ed Montclair High School, Cooper Union; co-founder, Tanager Gallery 1952–62; mem. Bd of Govs Skowhegan School of Painting and Sculpture 1980– (Chair. 1986–88); mem. Nat. Acad. of Design 1988–, American Acad. of Arts and Letters 1998–; Hon. degree (Old Lyme Acad., Conn.); American Acad. and Inst. of Arts and Letters Award 1986, Hassam, Speicher, Betts and Symons Purchase Prize 1991, Nat. Acad. of Design Leonilda S. Gervas Award 1987, Henry Ward Ranger Purchase Award 1990, 2005, Augustus St Gaudens Award for Achievement from Cooper Union 2005. *Address:* Alexandre Gallery, 41 East 57th Street, New York, NY 10022; 30 East 2nd Street, New York, NY 10003, USA (home). *Telephone:* (212) 755-2828; (212) 254-7159 (home).

DODGE, David A., BA PhD; Canadian banker; b. Toronto; ed Queen's Univ., Princeton Univ., USA; fmr Asst Prof. of Econs, Queen's Univ.; Assoc. Prof. of Canadian Studies and Int. Econs, School of Advanced Int. Studies, Johns Hopkins Univ., USA; Dir Int. Econs Programme, Inst. for Research on Public Policy 1979–80; fmr fed. public servant, sr positions in Cen. Mortgage and Housing Corpn, Anti-Inflation Bd, Dept of Employment and Immigration, Dept of Finance; fmr Deputy Minister of Finance; mem. Bd of Dirs Bank of Canada 1992–97, Gov. and Chair. 2001–08; Sr Fellow Faculty of Commerce, Univ. of BC; Visiting Prof. Dept of Econs, Simon Fraser Univ. 1997–98; Deputy Minister of Health 1998–2001. *Address:* c/o Bank of Canada, 234 Wellington Street, Ottawa, ON K1A 0G9, Canada (office).

DODIK, Milorad; Bosnia and Herzegovina politician; *Prime Minister, Republika Srpska;* b. 12 March 1959, Banja Luka; m.; two c.; ed Univ. of Belgrade; Pres. of Exec. Bd, Municipal Ass. of Laktaši 1986–90; mem. Parl. Socialist Repub. of Bosnia and Herzegovina 1990; Rep. Nat. Ass. of Republika Srpska; Prime Minister 1998–2001, 2006–; Founder and Chair. Alliance of Ind. Social Democrats. *Address:* Office of the Prime Minister of Republika Srpska, 78000 Banja Luka, trg Republike Srpske 1, Bosnia and Herzegovina (office). *Telephone:* (51) 331333 (office). *Fax:* (51) 331366 (office). *E-mail:* kabinet@vladars.net (office). *Website:* www.vladars.net (office).

DODIN, Lev Abramovich; Russian theatre director; *Artistic Director and General Manager, Maly Drama Theatre;* b. 14 May 1944, Leningrad; m. Tatyana Borisovna Shestakova (q.v.) 1972; ed Leningrad Theatre Inst.; lecturer in drama, Leningrad Theatre Inst., 1963–83; with Leningrad Youth Theatre 1967– (now Chief Dir), Artistic Dir and Gen. Man., Leningrad Maly Drama Theatre 1983–; Prof., St Petersburg Acad. of Dramatic Art; mem. Gen. Ass. of the Union of Theatres of Europe; USSR State Prize 1986, State Prize of Russia 1992, Triumph Prize 1992, Ubu Prize, Italy 1993, 1995, Stanislavsky Prize 1996, RSFSR Merited Artist 1986, People's Artist of Russian Fed., Golden Sofit Saint Petersburg Theatre Award 1996, Golden Mask National Theatre Award 1997, 1999, 2004, Abbiati Italian Critics' Award "for best opera staging" 1998, European Theatre Award 2000, Russian Presidential Award "for excellent service" in 2001, Tovstonogov's Award "for outstanding achievements in the art of theatre" 2002, Russian State Prize 2003, Chayka Moskow Theatre Award 2003, Pro Cultura Hungarica Hugary State Prize 2005; Order of Literature and Arts, France 1994. *Productions include:* The Robber (K. Čapek) 1974, The Gentle One (Dostoyevsky) 1980, The House (F. Abramov) 1980, Brothers and Sisters (F. Abramov) 1985, Lord of the Flies 1986, Stars in the Morning Sky (A. Galin) 1988, Gaudeamus 1990, The Demons (Dostoyevsky) 1992, Claustrophobia (V. Yerofeev) 1994, The Cherry Orchard (A. Chekhov) 1994, Play With No Title (A. Chekhov) 1966, Chevengur (A. Platonov) 1999, Molly Sweeney (Brian Friel) 2000. *Operas include:* Elektra (R. Strauss) 1995, Lady Macbeth of Mtsensk (Franco Abbiati Prize for best musical performance, Italy 1998) (D. Shostakovich) 1998, Mazeppa (Tchaikovsky) 1999, The Queen of Spades (Tchaikovsky) 1998–2001. *Address:* Maly Drama Theatre, Rubinstein Str. 18, St Petersburg, Russia. *Telephone:* (812) 113-21-08. *Fax:* (812) 113-33-66 (office). *E-mail:* levdodin@mdt.sp.ru (office). *Website:* www.mdt-dodin.ru (office).

DODON, Igor, DEcon; Moldovan economist, academic and government official; *First Deputy Prime Minister and Minister of the Economy and Trade;* b. 18 Feb. 1975, Sadova, Straseni Dist; m.; one c.; ed Agrarian Univ. of Moldova, Acad. of Econ. Studies, Int. Inst. of Man.; worked at Moldovan Stock Exchange 1997–2005, positions included Sr Specialist in Clearing and Listing Depts, Man. of Electronic Systems of Negotiation, Dir of Marketing, Listing and Quotations Dept; Chair. Nat. Securities Depository 2001–05; Chair. Moldovan Commodity Exchange 2003–05; Deputy Minister of Economy and Trade 2005–06, Minister of Economy and Trade 2006–08, First Deputy Prime Minister and Minister of Economy and Trade 2008–; fmr Prof., Acad. of Econ. Studies, Free Int. Univ. of Moldova, Int. Inst. of Man., State Univ. of Moldova. *Address:* Ministry of the Economy and Trade, 2033 Chişinău, Piaţa Marii Adunări Naţionale 1, Moldova (office). *Telephone:* (22) 25-01-07 (office). *Fax:* (22) 23-40-64 (office). *E-mail:* mineconcom@mec.gov.md (office). *Website:* www.mec.gov.md (office).

DOER, Gary Albert; Canadian politician; *Premier of Manitoba;* b. 31 March 1948, Winnipeg, Man.; m. Ginny Devine; two d.; first elected to Manitoba Legis. Ass. as MP for Concordia 1986, Minister of Urban Affairs 1986–88, Minister of Crown Investments 1987–88, Minister of Man. Telephone Systems 1987–88, also Minister responsible for Man. Liquor Control Comm.; Leader New Democrats 1988–, Leader of the Opposition 1988–99, Premier of Man., Pres. Exec. Council and Minister of Fed. –Prov. Relations 1999–; fmr Pres. Man. Govt Employees' Asscn; fmr Deputy Supt, Vaughan Street Detention Centre; Vice-Pres. Man. Special Olympics, Pres. Boys' and Girls' Club of Winnipeg; mem. Bd Winnipeg Blue Bombers, Prairie Theatre Exchange, Niagara Inst., Univ. of Man. *Leisure interest:* waterskiing. *Address:* Office of the Premier, Legislative Building, 204 Broadway, Winnipeg, Man. R3C 0V8, Canada (office). *Telephone:* (204) 945-3714 (office). *Fax:* (204) 949-1484 (office). *Website:* www.gov.mb.ca (office).

DOERING, William von Eggers, PhD; American chemist and academic; *Professor Emeritus of Chemistry, Harvard University;* b. 22 June 1917, Fort Worth, Tex.; s. of Carl Rupp Doering and Antoinette Mathilde von Eggers; m. 1st Ruth Haines 1947 (divorced 1954); two s. one d.; m. 2nd Sarah Cowles 1969 (divorced 1981); ed Shady Hill School, Mass., Belmont Hill School, Mass. and Harvard Univ.; with Office of Scientific Research and Devt 1941, Nat. Defense Research Cttee 1942, Polaroid Corpn 1943 (all in Cambridge, Mass.); Instructor, Columbia Univ. 1943–45, Asst Prof. 1945–48, Assoc. Prof. 1948–52; Prof., Yale Univ. 1952–56, Whitehead Prof. of Chem. 1956–67; Prof., Harvard Univ. 1967–68, Mallinckrodt Prof. of Chem. 1968–86, Prof. Emer. 1986–; Chair. Council for a Liveable World, Washington, DC 1964–73, Pres. 1973–78; US Dir People's Repub. of China-USA Chem. Grad. Program 1982–86; mem. NAS, American Acad. of Arts and Sciences; Hon. Prof., Fudan Univ., Shanghai 1980; Hon. DSc (Texas Christian Univ.); Hon. DNatSci (Karlsruhe) 1987; John Scott Award 1945, ACS Award in Pure Chem. 1953, A. W. von Hoffman Medal (Gesellschaft Deutscher Chemiker) 1962, William C. DeVane Medal 1967, Theodore William Richards Medal 1970, James Flack Norris Award 1989 and other awards from ACS; Robert A. Welch Award in Chem. 1990; Kosolapoff Award, Auburn Univ. 1995. *Publications:* Quinine 1944, Tropolone 1950, Tropylium Ion 1954, Carbenes 1954, Bullvalene 1962, Thermal Rearrangements 1966. *Leisure interests:* music, theatre, tennis, hiking. *Address:* Harvard University, Dept of Chemistry, 12 Oxford Street, Cambridge, MA 02138 (office); 53 Francis Avenue, Cambridge, MA 02138, USA (home). *Telephone:* (617) 495-4263 (office). *Fax:* (617) 495-1792 (office). *E-mail:* doering@chemistry.harvard.edu (office). *Website:* www.chem.harvard .edu (office).

DOERR, L. John, BS, MS, MBA; American inventor and investment company executive; *Partner, Kleiner Perkins Caufield & Byers;* b. 29 June 1951, St Louis, Mo.; m. Ann Howland Doerr; two c.; ed Rice Univ., Harvard Univ.; joined Intel Corpn 1974, became one of Intel's most successful salespeople; Pnr, Kleiner Perkins Caufield & Byers, Menlo Park, Calif. 1980–, has directed venture capital funding to several tech. cos, including Compaq, Netscape, Symantec, Sun Microsystems, drugstore.com, Amazon.com, Intuit, Google, Friendster, Go.com, myCFO; currently mem. Bd of Dirs Google, Amazon.com, Intuit, Homestore, Sun Microsystems (all public cos), Zazzle, Good Technology, Miasole, Purkinje, Segway Inc., Spatial Photonics (all pvt. ventures); helped found TechNet (lobbying org.); has also invested heavily in 'carbon trading'; listed in Forbes magazine's Midas List. *Publications:* holds patents for computer memory devices. *Leisure interests:* kids' stuff (trampolines and rock concerts), cycling, hiking, skiing, photography, surfing (the web), travelling, reading, music, messing around with computers/technology. *Address:* Kleiner Perkins Caufield & Byers, 2750 Sand Hill Road, Menlo Park, CA 94025, USA (office). *Telephone:* (650) 233-2750 (office). *Fax:* (650) 233-0300 (office). *E-mail:* johnd@kpcb.com (office). *Website:* www.kpcb.com (office).

DOGAN, Akhmed, PhD; Bulgarian politician; *President, Movement for Rights and Freedoms;* b. 29 March 1954, Pchelarovo, Varna region; m. 2nd; two c.; ed Univ. of Sofia, Bulgarian Acad. of Sciences; worked for Bulgarian communist intelligence service 1974–88; founded organized resistance against so-called revival process (forcible re-naming of ethnic Turks in Bulgaria) 1985; prosecuted for championing rights of ethnic Turks 1986, arrested and sent to Cen. Investigation Bureau for six months and 15 days 1986; arrested and sentenced to 10 years in prison for founding and leading anti-state org. Movt for Rights and Freedoms (MRF) June 1989, amnestied Dec. 1989; elected Deputy, 7th Grand Nat. Ass. (GNZ) under name Medi Doganov 1990–, Pres. MRF Parl. Group (Chair. Central Council and Central Operative Bureau of MRF), Deputy to 36th Nat. Ass. 1991–94, 37th Nat. Ass. 1994–97, Deputy and Co-Chair. Nat. Salvation Alliance in 38th Nat. Ass. 1997–2001, 40th Nat. Ass. 2001–; First Pres. Liberal Democratic Union 1998–99; was disclosed as a State Security agent under the name 'Sava' 1997; Chair. Inst. for Integration Studies 1999; Dir Prava i Svobodi (Rights and Liberties) newspaper. *Address:* Movement for Rights and Freedoms (Dvizhenie za prava i svobodi), 1301 Sofia, bul. A. Stamboliyski 45A, Bulgaria (office). *Telephone:* (2) 811-44-66 (office). *Fax:* (2) 811-44-60 (office). *E-mail:* dr .ahmeddogan@dps.bg (office). *Website:* www.dps.bg (office).

DOĞAN, Aydın; Turkish media executive; b. 1936, Kelkit; m.; ed Istanbul High Economy and Commerce Acad.; started business operations while still at school, f. his first industrial co. 1974; Pres. Doğan Group; owner eight newspapers including Hürriyet and Milliyet and two TV stations; fmr mem. Ass. and Admin. Bd Istanbul Chamber of Commerce; fmr Bd mem. Union of Chambers and Stock Markets; Chair. Newspaper Owners' Union 1986–96; f. Aydın Doğan Foundation 1996; Hon. DHumLitt (Girne American Univ.) 1999, Dr hc (Aegean Univ.) 2000; State Superior Services Medal 1999. *Address:* Aydın Doğan Vakfi, Hürriyet Medya Towers, 34544 Güneşli, Istanbul, Turkey (office). *Telephone:* (212) 677-0760 (office). *Fax:* (212) 677-0762 (office). *E-mail:* advakfi@hurriyet.com.tr (office).

DOGAR, Hon. Abdul Hameed, BSc, LLB; Pakistani judge; *Chief Justice of the Supreme Court;* b. 22 March 1944, Gaarhi Mori, Khairpur Dist, Sindh Prov.; ed Int. Islamic Univ. Islamabad, Al-Azhar Univ., Cairo, Egypt, Macca and Madina Univ., Saudi Arabia; joined judicial service with appointment to High Court 1995, elevated to Supreme Court 2000, Chief Justice of Pakistan 2007– (took oath on Prov. Constitution Order which replaced the Constitution 3 Nov. 2007, later took fresh oath according to Article 178 of the Constitution 15 Nov. 2007); Sec., Dist Bar Asscn, Khairpur 1973–74, Pres. 1987–88, 1989–90, 1991–92, 1993–94, 1994–95; Vice-Chair. Dist Council, Khairpur 1979–83; Jt Sec., High Court Bar Asscn, Sukkur Bench 1984–85; Chair. Bd Govs IBA March–April 2000; mem. Sindh Madresah Bd, Karachi 1980–83, Syndicate, Shah Abdul Latif Univ., Khairpur 1996–2000; mem. Bd Govs, Bd of Intermediate and Secondary Educ., Sukkur 1988–90, Nat. Univ. of Modern Languages, Islamabad 2003; Judge-in-Charge, Supreme Court Employees' Co-operative Housing Soc., Islamabad 2004; Acting Chief Election Commr July–Aug. 2004, Nov.–Dec. 2004, 2005–06; Chair. Supreme Judicial Council, Law and Justice Comm., Fed. Judicial Acad., Nat. Judicial Policy-making Cttee, Governing Body, Access to Justice Devt Fund; Hon. Sec. Dist Red Crescent Soc., Khairpur 1980–85. *Address:* Supreme Court of Pakistan, Constitution Avenue, Islamabad, Pakistan (office). *Telephone:* (51) 9220581 (office). *Fax:* (51) 9213452 (office). *E-mail:* info@supremecourt.gov.pk (office). *Website:* www.supremecourt.gov.pk (office).

DOĞRAMACI, İhsan, MD, LLD, LHD, FRCP, FAAP; Turkish paediatrician, academic and university administrator; *Chairman, Board of Trustees and President, Bilkent University;* b. 3 April 1915, Erbil; s. of Ali Doğramacı and Ismet Kirdar; m. Ayser Hikmet Suleyman 1941; two s. one d.; ed Istanbul, Harvard and Washington Univs; Asst Prof. of Paediatrics, Ankara Univ. 1947–49, Assoc. Prof. 1949–54, Prof. and Head of Dept 1954–63; Dir Inst. of Child Health, Ankara 1958–81; Prof. of Paediatrics and Head of Dept, Hacettepe Faculty of Medicine 1963–81, Dean of Faculty June–Nov. 1963; Pres. Ankara Univ. 1963–65; Chair. Bd of Trustees Middle East Tech. Univ. 1965–67; Pres. Hacettepe Children's Medical Centre, Ankara 1965–81; Rector, Hacettepe Univ. 1967–75; Pres. UNICEF Exec. Bd 1967–70; Pres. Int. Paediatric Asscn 1968–77, Dir-Gen. 1977–93, Hon. Pres. 1992–; Pres. and Chair. Bd of Trustees, Bilkent Univ. 1985–, Pres. Bilkent Univ. 1992–; Pres. Union of Middle Eastern and Mediterranean Paediatric Socs 1971–73, Int. Children's Center, Ankara 1980–2006 (Hon. Pres. 2006–), Higher Educ. Council of Turkey 1981–92; Ed. Turkish Journal of Pediatrics; mem. of Standing Conf. of Rectors and Vice-Chancellors of the European Univs 1969–81; Corresp. mem. Acad. Nat. de Médecine, France 1973; Hon. Pres. Int. Conf. for Higher Educ. 1992–; Hon. Fellow, American Acad. of Pediatrics 1959; Hon. mem. American Pediatric Soc., Deutsche Gesellschaft für Kinderheilkunde 1973, Soc. de Pédiatrie de Paris 1958, British Paediatric Asscn 1964, Finnish Paediatric Asscn 1971; Founding Hon. Fellow, Royal Coll. of Paediatrics and Child Health London 1996, Hon. Pres. Turkish Nat. Cttee for UNICEF 2003–; Grand Officier, Duarte, Sánchez y Mella (Dominican Repub.) 1976, Officier, Légion d'honneur 1978, Order of Homayoun First Class (Iran) 1978, Commdr, Order of the Lion of Finland (First Class), Commdr, Order of Merit of Poland 1989, Gran Cruz Placa de Plata de la Orden Heráldica de Cristóbal Colón (Dominican Repub.) 1990, First Rank Order of Independence (Azerbaijan) 1998, Order of the Cross of St Mary's Land (Estonia) 1999, Order of Haydar Aliyev (Azerbaijan) 2004; Hon. LLD (Nebraska) 1965; Dr hc (Nice) 1973, (Glasgow, Anatolia, Bosporus, Baghdad, Marmara, Ain Shams, Soka, Devlet Tib (Baku), E Mediterranean, De Montfort, Istanbul, Nice, Osmangazı, Rome La Sapienza); Nat. Award for Distinguished Service in Scientific and Technical Research 1978, Christopherson Award 1986, Léon Bernard Foundation Prize, WHO 1981, Maurice Pate Award, UNICEF 1995, State Medal for Outstanding Merit 1995, State Medal (Romania) 1997, Health-For-All Gold Medal, WHO 1997, Peace Justice and Tolerance Prize Council of Europe 1998, Distinguished Service Award Turkish Ministry of Foreign Affairs 2000, Sevda Cenap and Music Foundation Honor Award Gold Medal 2005. *Publications:* Annenin Kitabi – Mother's Handbook on Child Care 1952–2000, Premature Baby Care 1954; more than 100 articles in professional journals on paediatrics, public health and medical educ. *Address:* Board of Trustees, Bilkent University, 06800 Ankara, Turkey (office). *Telephone:* (312) 2664596 (office). *Fax:* (312) 2664678 (office). *E-mail:* vicepres@bilkent.edu.tr (office). *Website:* www.bilkent.edu.tr (office).

DOHERTY, Peter Charles, AC, MVSc, PhD; Australian immunologist; *Laureate Professor, Department of Microbiology and Immunology, University of Melbourne;* b. 15 Oct. 1940, Oxley; s. of Eric Doherty and Linda Doherty; m. Penelope Stephens 1965; two s.; ed Indooroopilly High School, Univ. of Queensland and Univ. of Edinburgh, UK; following graduation, worked as rural veterinary officer in Queensland Dept of Agric. and Stock, later worked in Animal Research Inst., Yeerongpilly; worked in CSIRO and Serum Labs; Sr Scientific Officer, Dept of Experimental Pathology, Moredun Research Inst., Edinburgh 1967–71; Assoc. Prof., then Prof. Wistar Inst., Philadelphia, USA 1975–82; Head of Dept of Experimental Pathology, John Curtin School of Medical Research, Canberra, 1982–88; Michael F. Tamer Endowed Chair for Immunology Biomedical Research, Co-Leader of Infection and Host Defense Program and Chair. Dept of Immunology, St Jude Children's Research Hosp., Memphis, Tenn., USA 1988–2002; Adjunct Prof. of Pediatrics and Pathology, Univ. of Tennessee, Memphis 1992–2002; Laureate Prof., Dept of Microbiology and Immunology, Univ. of Melbourne 2002–; mem. Bd Int. Lab. for Research in Animal Diseases, Nairobi, Kenya 1987–92; mem. Scientific Review Bd, Howard Hughes Medical Inst. 1997–; Hon. DVSc (Queensland), Hon. DSc (Australian Nat. Univ., Edin., Tufts, Warsaw), Hon. DMSc (Rhodes), Hon. DPh (Kyorin); Paul Ehrlich Prize for Medicine, Germany 1983, Gairdner Int. Award for Medical Science, Canada 1986, Albert Lasker Basic Medical Research Award 1995, Nobel Prize in Medicine (jt recipient) 1996, Australian of the Year 1997. *Publications:* numerous publs in scientific journals, chapters in books and review articles. *Leisure interests:* walking, reading. *Address:* Department of Microbiology and Immunology, University of Melbourne, Victoria 3010, Australia (office). *Telephone:* (3) 8344-5689 (office). *Fax:* (3) 9347-1540 (office). *Website:* www.microbiol.unimelb.edu.au (office).

DOI, Takeo; Japanese psychiatrist; b. 1920, Tokyo; pioneered concept of amae (dependency) associated with social and psychological characteristics of the Japanese people; research draws from wide range of material from psychoanalysis, anthropological and literary theory; first published book Amae no Kōzo became best-seller in Japan 1971. *Publications:* Amae no Kōzo (Anatomy of Dependence) 1971, Psychological World of Natsume Soseki 1976, The Anatomy of Self: Individual versus Society 1986, Petals Falling in the

Night (co-author) 1991,. *Address:* c/o Kodansha International, Otowa YK Building, 1-17-14 Otowa, Bunkyo-ku, Tokyo 112-8652, Japan (office).

DOIG, Peter, MA; British painter; b. 1959, Edinburgh; ed Chelsea School of Art, Wimbledon School of Art, St Martin's School of Art; grew up in Canada; moved to Trinidad 2002; Trustee Tate Gallery; Prof., Düsseldorf State Acad. of Art. *Works include:* Blotter 1993, Olin MKIV Part II 1995–96, Daytime Astronomy 1997–98, 100 Years Ago 2001, Almost Grown 2001, Country Rock 2001, Black Orpheus 2003, Curious 2005. *Address:* c/o Victoria Miro Gallery, 16 Wharf Road, London N1 7RW, England (office). *Telephone:* (20) 7336-8109 (office). *E-mail:* info@victoria-miro.com (office). *Website:* www.victoria-miro.com (office).

DOJE, Cedain; Chinese government official; b. 1924; m. Gesang Zhuoga; ed Beijing Normal Univ.; Gov. of Xizang (Tibet) Autonomous Region 1983–85; Researcher, Inst. of Research on World Religions, Chinese Acad. of Social Sciences 1985–; adviser, United Front Work Dept under CCP Cen. Cttee 1986–; mem. Standing Cttee 6th NPC 1986–88, Standing Cttee 7th NPC 1988–93, 8th NPC 1993–97; Vice-Chair. Educ., Science, Culture and Public Health Cttee under the NPC 1986; Deputy Head China-Spain Friendship Group 1986; Gen. Sec. China Nat. Center for Tibetan Studies; Chair. Tibetan Folk Arts Asscn. *Publications:* Education in Tibet 1995, Tibet's Feudal Serfdom Society 2005. *Address:* c/o China National Center for Tibetan Studies, 3/F A2 Building (Rongfeng 2008), Blk 8, 305 Guang An Men Wai Street, Xuanwu District, Beijing, People's Republic of China.

DOJE, Cering; Chinese government official; *Chairman, Ethnic Affairs Committee, 10th National People's Congress;* b. 1939, Xiahe Co., Gansu Prov.; worked as clerk in Tibet 1959; joined CCP 1960; magistrate, Co. (Dist) People's Court, Nagarze Co. and Gyaca Co., Tibet 1962; mem. Tibet Autonomous Region CCP 1974–90; mem. Standing Cttee Tibet CCP 1977–90; First Sec. Xigaze Municipality CCP 1979–82; Vice-Chair. Tibet Autonomous Region 1983–85, Acting Admin. Head 1986–88, Chair. 1988–90; Deputy for Tibet Autonomous Region, 7th NPC 1988–; Vice-Minister of Civil Affairs 1990–93, Minister 1993–2003; Chair. 10th NPC Ethnic Affairs Cttee 2003–; Vice-Chair. China Cttee Int. Decade for Nat. Disaster Reduction 1998–; mem. 8th NPC 1993–97; mem. 14th CCP Cen. Cttee 1992–97, 15th CCP Cen. Cttee 1997–2002, 16th CCP Cen. Cttee 2002–07. *Address:* c/o Ministry of Civil Affairs, 147 Beiheyan Dajie, Dongcheng Qu, Beijing 100721, People's Republic of China (office). *Telephone:* (10) 65135333 (office). *Fax:* (10) 65135332 (office).

DOKLE, Namik; Albanian politician; b. 1946, Durres; mem. Albanian Socialist Party (SP); Ed.-in-Chief Zeri Popullit (SP newspaper) 1991; Deputy Chair. of Parl. 1997–2001; Speaker of Parl. 2001–02; Deputy Prime Minister 2003–05.

DOKTOR, Mgr Martin; Czech canoeist; b. 21 May 1974, Polička; s. of Josef Doktor and Zuzana Doktorová; m. Kateřina Svobodová 2000; one s.; ed Charles Univ., Prague; silver medals 500m and 1000m Canoeing World Championships, Duisburg, Germany; gold medals 500m and 1000m Olympic Games, Atlanta, USA 1996; silver medals 200m and 1000m, gold medal 500m Canoeing World Championships, Dartmouth, Canada 1997; silver medal 500m, gold medal 1000m European Championships, Plovdiv, Bulgaria 1997; World Cup winner 1998; gold medal 200m World Championships, Szeged, Hungary 1998, silver medal 1000m; World Cup winner 1999; silver medals 200m, 500m and 1000m European Championships, Zagreb, Croatia 1999; silver medal 200m and 500m, bronze medal 1000m Canoeing World Championships, Milan, Italy 1999; gold medal 1000m, bronze medal 200m European Championships 2000; World Cup winner 2000; bronze medal 1000m European Championships, Italy 2001; silver medal 1000m World Championships, Poland 2001; World Cup winner 2002, silver medal C1 200m and bronze medal C1 500m, World Championships, Gainesville, USA 2003; World Cup winner 2003, 2004; Best Czech Sportsman of the Year 1996. *Publications:* Story of the Defeated Champion 2000, Technique and Tactics of Paddling in Flat Water Canoes 2001. *Leisure interests:* skiing, music, cycling, golf. *Address:* Sluneční 627, 533 04 Sezemice, Czech Republic (home); Račice 64, 411 08 Štětí. *Telephone:* (46) 6931717 (office); (41) 6811872 (home). *Fax:* (46) 6931717 (office); (41) 6810400 (home). *E-mail:* prosport@pce.cz (office); md@martindoktor.cz (home). *Website:* www.martindoktor.cz (home).

DOLAN, Charles F.; American cable television executive; *Chairman, Cablevision Systems Corporation;* b. 16 Oct. 1926, Cleveland, Ohio; m. Helen Burgess; three s. three d.; ed John Carroll Univ.; served in USAF; jtly with wife est. co. producing and distributing sports and industrial films; subsequently f. Teleguide Inc. (providing information services via cable to New York hotels) and Sterling Manhattan Cable (first urban cable TV co. in USA), Home Box Office Inc.; Founder and Chair. Cablevision Systems Corp. 1985–; co-owner Madison Square Garden Properties 1995–; Dir Cold Spring Harbor Lab., St Francis Hosp., Long Island; Chair. Nat. Acad. of TV Arts and Sciences; a Man. Dir of Metropolitan Opera, New York; Trustee Fairfield Univ., Conn.; mem. Bd of Govs Nat. Hockey League. *Address:* Cablevision Systems Corporation, 1111 Stewart Avenue, Bethpage, NY 11714-3581, USA. *Telephone:* (516) 803-2300. *Fax:* (516) 803-2273. *Website:* www.cablevision.com.

DOLAN, James; American business executive; *President and CEO, Cablevision Systems Corporation;* m.; five c.; fmrly Asst Gen. Man. Cablevision Chicago, Vice-Pres. for Advertising Sales Cablevision; Man. WKNR-AM radio station, Cleveland; Corpn Dir Advertising Rainbow Programming Holdings, CEO 1992–95; CEO, Pres. Cablevision Systems Corpn 1995–; Chair. Madison Square Garden, NY. *Leisure interests:* yachting, music. *Address:* Cablevision Systems Corporation, 1111 Stewart Avenue, Bethpage, NY 11714, USA (office). *Telephone:* (516) 803-2300 (office). *Fax:* (516) 803-2273 (office). *Website:* www.cablevision.com (office).

DOLAN, Peter Robert, BA, MBA; American business executive; b. 6 Jan. 1956, Salem, Mass; m. Katherine Lange 1981; two s.; ed Tufts Univ., Tuck School of Business, Dartmouth Coll.; with Gen. Foods 1980–88; Vice-Pres. of Marketing Bristol-Myers Products Div. 1988–90, Sr Vice-Pres. of Marketing and Sales 1990–91, Sr Vice-Pres. of Marketing, Sales and Operations 1991–92, Exec. Vice-Pres. 1992, Pres. 1993–94, Group Pres. Nutritionals and Medical Devices, Bristol-Myers Squibb Co. 1997–98, Pres. Europe and Worldwide Medicines 1998, Sr Vice-Pres. of Strategy 1998–2000, Pres. 2000–05, Chair. 2001–05, CEO 2001–06 (resgnd); mem. Bd of Dirs New York Botanical Garden, Nat. Center on Addiction and Substance Abuse, Columbia Univ.; Trustee Tufts Univ. *Address:* 4 Beach Avenue, Larchmont, NY 10538, USA (office).

DOLBY, Ray M., BS, PhD; American engineer and inventor; *Chairman, Dolby Laboratories Inc.;* b. 1933, Portland, Ore.; m. Dagmar Dolby; ed Stanford Univ., Univ. of Cambridge, UK; mem. staff Ampex Corpn 1949–57; consultant, UKAEA 1961; UN adviser in India 1963–65; Founder and Chair. Dolby Laboratories Inc., London 1965–, opened further offices and labs in San Francisco 1976, inventor Dolby noise-reduction units, Dolby 'A' system sold to recording studios, work on noise-reduction for tape cassettes and 8-track cartridge led to Dolby 'B' system 1971, now adopted world-wide, developed Dolby Stereo optical cinema soundtrack process 1975, inventor Dolby SR (Spectral Recording) for professional audio recording, also adapted for cinema 1986; holder of more than 50 US patents; Fellow, Audio Eng Soc. (also Past Pres.), British Kinematograph, Sound and TV Soc.; Hon. mem. Soc. of Motion Picture and TV Engineers; Hon. Fellow, Pembroke Coll. Cambridge 1983; Hon. OBE 1986; Hon. DSc (Cambridge); Dr hc (York) 1999; Silver Medal, Audio Eng Soc. 1971, Gold Medal 1992; Soc. of Motion Picture and TV Engineers Samuel L. Warner Memorial Award 1978, Alexander M. Poniatoff Medal for Tech. Excellence, and Progress Medal 1983, Acad. of Motion Picture Arts and Sciences Progress Medal, Scientific and Eng Award 1979, Acad. of Motion Picture Arts and Sciences Scientific and Eng Award 1989, Emmy Award, Acad. of TV Arts and Sciences 1989, US Nat. Medal of Tech. 1997, IEEE Masaru Ibuka Consumer Electronics Award 1997, Asscn Medal of Honor, American Electronic 1997, Charles F. Jenkins Lifetime Achievement Award, Acad. of TV Arts and Sciences 2003. *Publications include:* contribs to papers on videotape recording, long wavelength X-ray analysis and noise reduction. *Address:* Dolby Laboratories, Inc., 100 Potrero Avenue, San Francisco, CA 94103-4813, USA (office). *Telephone:* (415) 558-0200 (office). *Fax:* (415) 863-1373 (office). *Website:* www.dolby.com (office).

DOLCE, Domenico; Italian fashion designer; *CEO, Dolce & Gabbana;* b. 13 Aug. 1958, Polizzi Generosa, nr Palermo, Sicily; s. of Saverio Dolce; designer, father's atelier, then Asst in a Milan atelier; with Stefano Gabbana opened fashion consulting studio 1982, selected to take part in New Talents show, Milano Collezioni 1985; co-f. Dolce & Gabbana 1985, first maj. women's collection 1985, knitwear 1987, beachwear, underwear 1989, men's wear 1990, women's fragrance 1992, D&G line, men's fragrance 1994, eyewear 1995; est. Dolce and Gabanna Industria production units 1999–2000; acquired and renovated Cinema Metropol in Milan for fashion shows and exhibitions 2005; opened boutiques in major cities in Europe, America and Asia; with Steffano Gabanna, Woolmark Award 1991, Perfume Acad. Int. Prize for Best Feminine Fragrance of Year 1993, Best Masculine Fragrance of Year 1995, French "Oscar des Parfums", UK FHM Designers of the Year 1996, Footwear News Designers of the Year 1997, Russian Harper's Bizarre Style Award 1999, T de Telva Award for Best Designers of the Year 2002, US GQ Best Designers of the Year 2003, UK Elle Best Int. Designers 2004, Premio Resultati 2004, Russian GQ Best Int. Designers 2005. *Publications:* with Stefano Gabbana, 10 Years Dolce and Gabbana 1996, Wildness 1997, Dolce and Gabbana Mémoires de la Mode 1998, Holllywood 2003, Calcio 2004, Music 2004, 20 years Dolce and Gabbana 2005. *leisure interests:* gym, travel, modern art. *Address:* Dolce & Gabbana, Via San Damiano 7, 20122 Milan, Italy (office). *Telephone:* (02) 774271 (office). *Fax:* (02) 76020600 (office). *Website:* www.dolcegabbana.it (office).

DOLE, Elizabeth Hanford, MA, JD; American fmr politician; b. 29 July 1936, Salisbury, N Carolina; d. of John Van Hanford and Mary E. Cathey; m. Robert J. Dole (q.v.) 1975; ed Duke and Harvard Univs and Univ. of Oxford, UK; called to DC Bar 1966; Staff Asst to Asst Sec. for Educ., US Dept of Health, Educ. and Welfare, Washington, DC 1966–67; practising lawyer, Washington, DC 1967–68; Assoc. Dir Legis. Affairs, then Exec. Dir Pres.'s Comm. for Consumer Interests 1968–71; Deputy Asst Office of Consumer Affairs, The White House, Washington, DC 1971–73; Commr Fed. Trade Comm. 1973–79; Asst to Pres. for Public Liaison 1981–83; Sec. of Transportation 1983–87; Sec. of Labor 1989–90; Pres. American Red Cross 1991–98; cand. for Republican presidential nomination 1999; Senator from N Carolina 2003–09; Trustee Duke Univ. 1974–88; mem. Visiting Comm., John F. Kennedy School of Govt 1988–; mem. Comm. Harvard School of Public Health 1992–, Bd of Overseers, Harvard Univ. 1989–95; recipient of hon. doctorates from 40 colls and univs; Radcliffe Coll. Medal, Distinguished Service Award, Nat. Safety Council 1989, N Carolina Award 1991, Lifetime Achievement Award, Women Execs in State Govt 1993, named N Carolinian of the Year by NC Press Asscn 1993, Leadership Award, League of Women Voters 1994, Raoul Wallenburg Award for Humanitarian Service 1995, Churchwoman of the Year, Religious Heritage of America 1995, named one of the world's three most admired women in Gallup Poll 1998, inducted into Safety and Health Hall of Fame Int. 1998, Humanitarian Award, Nat. Comm. Against Drunk Driving 1998, Nat. Religious Broadcasters' Bd of Dirs Award 1999, Foreign Policy Asscn Medal, ranked by Forbes magazine amongst 100 Most Powerful Women (30th) 2004,

(58th) 2005. *Address:* c/o 555 Dirksen Office Building, Washington, DC 20510, USA (office).

DOLE, Robert J. (Bob); American fmr politician and lawyer; *Special Counsel, Alston & Bird LLP;* b. 22 July 1923, Russell, Kan.; s. of Doran R. Dole and Bina Dole; m. 2nd Elizabeth Hanford Dole (q.v.) 1975; one d.; ed Russell public schools, Univ. of Kansas and Washbourn Municipal Univ.; mem. Kansas Legislature 1951–53; Russell Co. Attorney 1953–61; mem. House of Reps 1960–68; US Senator from Kansas 1969–96; Senate Majority Leader 1995–96; Senate Republican Leader 1987–96; House Majority Leader 1985–87, Minority leader 1987; Chair. Republican Nat. Cttee 1971–72; Vice-Presidential Cand. 1976, Presidential Cand. 1996; mem. of counsel Verner, Liipfert, Bernhard, McPherson and Hand; Special Counsel Alston and Bird LLP 2003–; Chair. Senate Finance Cttee 1981–84; Pres. Dole Foundation 1983–99; Dir Mainstream Inc.; Adviser, US Del. to FAO Conf., Rome 1965, 1974, 1977; mem. Congressional del. to India 1966, Middle East 1967; mem. US Helsinki Comm., del. to Belgrade Conf. 1977; Chair. International Comm. on Missing Persons 1997–; Trustee, William Allen White Foundation, Univ. of Kan.; mem. Nat. Advisory Cttee, The John Wesley Colls; mem. American Bar Asscn; mem. Nat. Advisory Cttee on Scouting for the Handicapped, Kan. Asscn for Retarded Children, Advisory Bd of United Cerebral Palsy, Kan.; Republican; Hon. mem. Advisory Bd of Kidney Patients Inc.; Presidential Medal of Freedom 1997; Distinguished Service Award 1997. *Publications:* Great Political Wit (co.ed.) 1999, Great Presidential Wits 2001. *Leisure interests:* politics, watching the news. *Address:* Alston & Bird LLP, 10th Floor, North Building, 601 Pennsylvania Avenue, NW, Washington, DC 20004-2601, USA (office). *Telephone:* (202) 654-4848 (office). *Fax:* (202) 654-4850 (office). *E-mail:* bdole@alston.com (office). *Website:* www.alston.com (office); www.bobdole.org.

DOLGEN, Jonathan L., JD; American film executive; b. 27 April 1945, NY; ed Cornell Univ., New York. Univ. Law School; lawyer Fried, Frank, Harris, Shriver & Jacobson 1969–76; Asst Gen. Counsel then Deputy Gen. Counsel Columbia Pictures Industries 1976–85, Sr Vice-Pres. World Business Affairs 1979, Exec. Vice-Pres. 1980; Pres. Columbia's Pay Cable & Home Entertainment Group 1983; Sr Exec. Vice-Pres. Fox Inc. 1985–90; Pres. TV Div. Twentieth Century Fox Inc. 1985–88, Pres. 1988–93; Chair. Twentieth TV 1988–90; Pres. Columbia Pictures 1990–94, Pres. Columbia Pictures, Culver City 1991–94; Chair. and CEO Viacom Entertainment Group 1994–2004; Sr Consultant ARTISTdirect Inc. 2006–; f. Friends of Cornell Univ. Arts Center, founder mem. Educ. First; mem. Alumni Council New York Univ. Law School; mem. City of Los Angeles Advisory Council, Los Angeles County Homeland Security Advisory Council, Cornell Univ. Major Gifts Cttee; Bd Dirs Sony Pictures, Charter Communications Inc., Expedia Inc.; Fellow Claremont Univ. Center and Grad. School. *Address:* ARTISTdirect Inc., 1601 Cloverfield Blvd S, Ste. 400, Santa Monica, CA 90404, USA (office). *Website:* www.ARTISTdirect.com.

DOLGUSHIN, Nikita Aleksandrovich; Russian dancer, choreographer, teacher and set and costume designer; *Artistic Director and Chief Ballet Master, State Opera and Ballet Theatre of St Petersburg Rimsky-Korsakov Conservatoire;* b. 8 Nov. 1938, Leningrad; s. of Aleksandr Pavlovich and Vera Ivanovna Kazanskaya; m. Alexsandra Anatolievna Baranova; ed School of Choreography (Russian Ballet Acad. named after A. Vaganova); soloist, Kirov (now Mariinsky) Opera and Ballet Theatre, Leningrad (now St Petersburg) 1959–61; leading dancer, Novosibirsk Theatre of Opera and Ballet 1961–66; soloist, Igor Moiseyev Young Ballet Ensemble 1966–68; soloist Leningrad Maly Opera and Ballet Theatre 1969–83; Head of Ballet, St Petersburg Conservatoire (SPB) 1983–2000, Artistic Dir, head of ballet co., State Theatre of SPB Conservatoire; fmr Prof., Paris Univ. of Dance; Chevalier Order of Catherine the Great, Knight Order's Master of Saint Rus, Order of Civil Honour and Advantage; Dr hc (Univ. of Towson, USA); USSR People's Artist, Kt of Ballet (Spirit of Dance), Laureate of Int. Competition (Varna), Person of the Year 2003, Honoured Worker of Russia. *Leading roles include:* Satire (Spartacus), Albert (Giselle), Romeo, Troubadour, Paris (Romeo and Juliet), Nutcracker, Prince, Drosselmeier (Nutcracker), Prince Igor (Yaroslavna), Young Man (Les Sylphides), Smith (On Thunder's Path), Ferhard (Legend of Love), Young Man (Leningrad Poem), Siegfried (Swan Lake), Bahram (Seven Beauties), Prince (Cinderella), Corsaire, Slave, Conrad (Le Corsaire), Mephistopheles (Masquerade), Troubadour (Raymond), Solore (Le Baydere), Soloist (Bolero), Prince Desire (The Sleeping Beauty), Chevalier (Paquita), Soloist (Concert in White), Hamlet (Reflections), Chevalier (Mozartine), Soloist (Chamber Suite), Colen (Vain Precaution), Torero (Carmen-suite), Franz (Coppelia), James (La Sylphide), Poet (Crossroad), Man (Fulfilment), Tutor (Pedagogical Poem), Boris (Tsar Boris), Feb (Esmeralda), Basil (Don Quixote), Carl (Robbers), Narcissi, Pierrot, Judas (Monolog of Judas), Moor (Moor's Pavane), Don Juan, Armand Duvall (Dream), Eugene (Onegine), Solilst (Humoresque), Ponti Pillatus (Master and Margarita), Faune (L'Apres-midi d'un Faune), Soloist (Song of the Dead Children). *Ballets produced:* Tchaikovsky's Andante sostenuto, Reflections, Mozartiana, Romeo and Juliet, The Nutcracker, The Dreams, Chausson's Dream, Nasidze's King Lear (with G. Aleksidze), Russian Ballet of the Golden Century, Mahler's Adagietto, Gershwin's We Do Care!, Borodin's Dances of Polovets, Bizet/Schredrin's Carmen-suite; set and costume designer of 27 ballet performances. *Films:* Nikita Dolgushin Philosophy of Dance, How the Heart to Express Itself, The Magic, The Place in History, Masqueradel. *Publications:* articles in Ballet magazine 1960–2005. *Leisure interests:* collecting. *Address:* St Petersburg State Conservatoire, Teatralnaya pl. 3, St Petersburg 190000, Russia. *Telephone:* (812) 571-66-74 (office); (812) 314-56-44 (home). *Fax:* (812) 311-81-65 (office). *E-mail:* info@bolshoy-kamenny.spb.ru (office). *Website:* www.bolshoy-kamenny.spb.ru (office).

DOLLÉ, Guy; French steel industry executive; b. 1942; ed Ecole Polytechnique; began career with IRSID Steel Research Centre, Metz; Head of Plates and Tubes Div., Usinor 1980, Chair. GTS (subsidiary co.) 1985, Exec. Vice-Pres. Usinor Aciers 1986, Head of Production, Sollac N Region (following merger wih Usinor), Vice-Pres. Industrial Affairs 1987, Chair. and CEO Unimétal 1993-95, Exec. Vice-Pres. for Strategy, Usinor 1995–97, Head of Stainless Steel and Alloys Div. 1997–99, Sr Exec. Vice-Pres., Usinor 1999–2002, Chair. and CEO Arcelor S.A. (following merger of Aceralia, Arbed and Usinor groups) 2002–06. *Address:* c/o Arcelor S.A.19 avenue de la Liberté, 2930 Luxembourg, Luxembourg (office).

DOLLERY, Sir Colin (Terence), Kt, BS, MB, ChB, FRCP, FMedSci; British physician; b. 14 March 1931; s. of Cyril Robert Dollery and Thelma Mary Dollery; m. Diana Myra Stedman 1958; one s. one d.; ed Lincoln School and Univ. of Birmingham; House Officer, Queen Elizabeth Hosp. Birmingham, Hammersmith Hosp. and Brompton Hosp. 1956–58; Medical Registrar, Hammersmith Hosp. 1958–60, Sr Registrar and Tutor in Medicine 1960–62; Consultant Physician 1962–2000; Lecturer in Medicine, Royal Post grad. Medical School, Univ. of London 1962–65, Prof. of Clinical Pharmacology 1965–87, Prof. of Medicine 1987–91, Dean 1991–96, Pro-Vice-Chancellor for Medicine 1992–96; Sr Consultant Research and Devt, SmithKline Beecham PLC 1996–2000, GlaxoSmithKline 2001–; Dir (non-exec.) Larson-Davis, Inc. 1998–99, Discovery Partners, Inc. 2001–, Predict, Inc. 2001–; mem. MRC 1982–84, Univ. Funding Council (fmrly Univ. Grants Cttee) 1984–91; Fellow Imperial Coll. London 2003; fmr Pres. Int. Union of Pharmacology; Hon. mem. Asscn of American Physicians; Chevalier, Ordre Nat. du Mérite; British Pharmacological Soc. Wellcome Gold Medal. *Publications:* The Retinal Circulation 1971, Therapeutic Drugs 1991; papers in scientific journals. *Leisure interests:* travel, amateur radio, work. *Address:* c/o GlaxoSmithKline plc, 3rd Avenue, Harlow CM19 5AW (office); 101 Corringham Road, London, NW11 7DL, England (home). *Telephone:* ((1279) 646154 (office). *E-mail:* colin-dollery-1@gsk.com (office).

DOLLFUS, Audouin, DèsSc; French astronomer; *Astronomer Emeritus, Observatoire de Paris;* b. 12 Nov. 1924, Paris; s. of Charles Dollfus and Suzanne Soubeyran; m. Catherine Browne 1959; four c.; ed Univ. de Paris; joined Observatoire de Meudon (astrophysical div. of Observatoire de Paris) 1946, Head of Lab. for Physics of the Solar System; Astronomer, Observatoire de Paris 1965, now Emer.; Pres. Observatoire de Triel 1994–; mem. Int. Acad. of Astronautics (Trustee 1975–81), Soc. Astronomique de France (Pres. 1979–81), Aéro-club de France (Trustee, Hon. Vice Pres. 1995–99), French Asscn for the Advancement of Science (Pres. 1993–95); Assoc. Royal Astronomical Soc., London, Soc. French Explorers, Explorers Club USA, Soc. Philomatique de Paris, New York Acad. of Science; Hon. mem. Royal Astronomical Soc. of Canada, Astronomy and Geophysics Soc. of USSR; Officier des Palmes académiques; Médaille de l'Aeronautique, Grand Prix Acad. des Sciences (Paris), Int. Award Galabert for Astronautics, Diploma Tissandier (Int. Fed. Astronautics), Gold Medal Jaussen, Soc. Astronomique de France. *Achievements:* pioneered balloon astronomy, discovered Janus (10th satellite of planet Saturn) 1966. *Publications:* seven books and 350 scientific publs on astrophysics. *Leisure interests:* ballooning (holds three official world records with gas balloons: duration, distance, altitude), history of astronomy. *Address:* Observatoire, 92195 Meudon (office); 77 rue Albert Perdreaux, 92370 Chaville, France. *Telephone:* 1-45-07-77-47 (office); 1-47-50-97-43 (home). *E-mail:* audouin.dollfus@obspm.fr (office).

DOLOGUELE, Anicet G.; Central African Republic politician; *Chairman, Banque de Développement des Etats de l'Afrique Centrale;* b. 17 April 1957, Bozoum; m.; three c.; ed Univ. de Bangui, Bordeaux Univ., France; fmr Finance and Budget Minister; Prime Minister, Minister of the Economy, Finance, Planning and Int. Co-operation 1999–2001; currently Chair. Banque de Développement des Etats de l'Afrique Centrale; Grand Officier Ordre du Mérite Centrafricain, Commdr Ordre du Mérite Centrafricain, Médaille d'or Ordre du Mérite Centrafricain. *Address:* Banque de Développement des Etats de l'Afrique Centrale, Place du Gouvernement, BP 1177, Brazzaville, Republic of the Congo (office). *Telephone:* (242) 81-18-85 (office). *Fax:* (242) 81-18-80 (office). *E-mail:* bdeac@bdeac.org (office). *Website:* www.bdeac.org (office).

DOLZHENKO, Irina Igorevna; Russian singer (mezzo-soprano); b. 23 Oct. 1955, Tashkent, Uzbekistan; m.; one d.; mem. children's troupe, Stanislavsky and Nemirovich-Danchenko Music Theatre, Moscow –1996; soloist, Bolshoi Theare 1996–; sang with Swedish Royal Opera, Deutsche Oper, Berlin, Teatro Colón, Buenos Aires, New Israeli Opera, Tel-Aviv; recitals in Japan, South Korea, USA, Australia, Europe; People's Artist of Russia. *Operatic roles include:* Amneris in Aida, Adalgisa in Norma, Amelfa in The Golden Cockerel, Morozova in Oprichnik, Cherubino in Marriage of Figaro, Azucena in Il Trovatore, Ulrica in Un Ballo in Maschera. *Address:* Robert Gilder and Co., 91 Great Russell Street, London, WC1B 3PS, England (office). *Telephone:* (20) 7580-7758 (office). *Fax:* (20) 7580-7739 (office). *E-mail:* rgilder@robert-gilder.com (office). *Website:* www.robert-gilder.com (office).

DOMARKAS, Juozas; Lithuanian conductor; *Artistic Director and Chief Conductor, Lithuanian National Symphony Orchestra;* b. 28 July 1936, Varkaliai, Plunge Dist; m. (wife deceased); two s.; ed Klaipeda Simkus Coll. of Music, Lithuanian Acad. of Music, Leningrad State Conservatory; Asst Conductor, Vilnius Band 1957–60; Artistic Dir and Chief Conductor Lithuanian Nat. Symphony Orchestra 1964–; participated in numerous nat. and int. festivals; teacher, sr teacher, Assoc. Prof. Lithuanian Acad. of Music 1968–93, Chair and Prof. 1993–; numerous recordings; Grand Duke Gediminas First Order and Award 1998. *Address:* Lietuvos Nacionaline Filharmonija, Ausros Vartu 5, 2001, Vilnius (office); Jogalios 16-5, 2001 Vilnius, Lithuania (home). *Telephone:* (2) 62-70-47 (office); (2) 62-84-61 (home). *Fax:* (2) 62-28-59 (office).

DOMB, Cyril, MA, PhD, FRS; British/Israeli academic; *Professor Emeritus of Physics, Bar Ilan University;* b. London; s. of Joel Domb and Sarah Domb (née Wulkan); m. Shirley Galinsky 1957; three s. three d.; ed Hackney Downs School, London, Pembroke Coll., Cambridge; Fellow, Clarendon Lab., Oxford 1949–52; Univ. Lecturer in Mathematics, Univ. of Cambridge 1952–54; Prof. of Theoretical Physics, Univ. of London 1954–81; Prof. of Physics, Bar Ilan Univ., Israel 1981–89, Prof. Emer. 1989–; Academic Pres. Jerusalem Coll. of Tech. 1985–94; Fellow King's Coll. London; Rayleigh Prize 1947, Max Born Prize 1981. *Publications:* Co-operative Phenomena in Crystals, in Advances in Physics 1960, Clerk Maxwell and Modern Science (ed.) 1963, Phase Transitions and Critical Phenomena, Vols 1–6 (co-ed. with M.S. Green), Vols 7–20 (ed. with J.L. Lebowitz), Memories of Kopul Rosen (ed.) 1970, Challenge – Torah Views on Science and its Problems (ed. with A. Carmell) 1976, The Critical Point 1996; over 160 scientific papers. *Leisure interests:* walking, swimming. *Address:* c/o Department of Physics, Bar Ilan University, 52 900 Ramat Gan, Israel (office); 32 Cumberland Gardens, London, NW4 1LD, England.

DOMBROVSKIS, Valdis; Latvian economist and politician; *Prime Minister;* b. 5 Aug. 1971, Riga; ed Univ. of Latvia, Riga Univ. of Tech., Maincas Univ. and Merilendas Univ.; lab. asst, Inst. of Solid-State Physics, Univ. of Latvia 1991–93 (Asst 1997), Dept of Semiconductor Physics 1993–95, Inst. of Physics, Mainz Univ., Germany 1995–96; Research Asst, Faculty of Electrical Eng, Maryland Univ., USA 1998; Macroeconomic Analyst, Monetary Policy Dept, Bank of Latvia 1998–99, Sr Economist 1999–2001, Chief Economist 2001–02; mem. Jaunais Laiks Party, mem. Bd 2002–04; mem. Parl. 2002–04; Observer, Council of the EU 2003–04; Minister of Finance 2002–04, Gov. for Latvia World Bank and IMF; mem. European Parl. (Group of the European People's Party (Christian Democrats) and European Democrats) 2004–09, Cttee on Budgets, Del. to ACP-EU Jt Parl. Ass., Substitute mem. Cttee on Econ. and Monetary Affairs, Cttee on Budgetary Control, Temporary Cttee on Policy Challenges and Budgetary Means of the Enlarged Union 2007–13, Del. to EU-Kazakhstan, EU-Kyrgyzstan and EU-Uzbekistan Parl. Cooperation Cttees, and for Relations with Tajikistan, Turkmenistan and Mongolia; Prime Minister of Latvia 2009–; mem. New Era (Jaunais laiks). *Address:* Office of the Cabinet of Ministers, Brīvības bulv. 36, Rīga 1520, Latvia (office). *Telephone:* 6708-2800 (office). *Fax:* 6728-0469 (office). *E-mail:* vk@mk.gov.lv (office). *Website:* www.mk.gov.lv (office).

DOMENICI, Pete V., BS, LLB; American fmr politician; b. 7 May 1932, Albuquerque; s. of Cherubino Domenici and Alda Domenici; m. Nancy Burk 1958; two s. six d.; ed Univs of Albuquerque, New Mexico, Denver; elected to Albuquerque City Comm. 1966, Chair. 1967; mem. Nat. League of Cities Revenue and Finance Steering Cttee and the Resolutions Cttee of 1969 Annual Conf. of Mayors; served on Gov.'s Policy Bd for Law Enforcement and on Middle Rio Grande Conf. of Govts; Senator from New Mexico 1972–2009 (retd), Chair. Senate Budget Cttee 1981, 1995–2001, Senate Indian Affairs Cttee; Republican; several hon. degrees; numerous awares including Public Sector Leadership Award 1996. *Leisure interests:* hunting, fishing.

DOMINGO, Plácido, FRCM; Spanish singer (tenor); *General Director, Los Angeles Opera;* b. 21 Jan. 1941, Madrid; s. of the late Plácido Domingo and Pepita Domingo (née Embil); m. Marta Ornelas; three s.; ed Nat. Conservatory of Music, Mexico City; operatic debut at Monterrey, Mexico 1961; with Israel Nat. Opera for over two years; debut at Metropolitan Opera, New York 1968; British debut in Verdi's Requiem at Festival Hall 1969; Covent Garden debut in Tosca 1971, returned to sing in Aïda, Carmen 1973, La Bohème 1974, Un Ballo in Maschera 1975, La Fanciulla del West; has taken leading roles in about 120 operas; with New York City Opera 1965–; Artistic Dir Washington Nat. Opera 1994–2003, Gen. Dir 2003–; Artistic Dir Los Angeles Opera 2000–03, Gen. Dir 2003–; Artistic Adviser and Prin. Guest Conductor Los Angeles Opera; Fellow, Royal N Coll. of Music; engagements include Tosca (conducting), Romeo and Juliet at Metropolitan Opera, New York, Aïda, Il Trovatore in Hamburg, Don Carlos in Salzburg, I vespri siciliani and La forza del destino in Paris, Turandot in Barcelona, Otello in Paris, London, Hamburg and Milan, Carmen in Edin., Turandot at the Metropolitan; New York stage debut in My Fair Lady 1988 (213 performances by 2000); Luigi in Il Tabarro at the Met 1989; Otello at Covent Garden 1990, Lohengrin at Vienna Staatsoper, Don José at Rio de Janeiro, Otello at the Met and Barcelona; Don Carlos at Los Angeles, Dick Johnson at Chicago, Riccardo in Un Ballo in Maschera at the 1990 Salzburg Festival; debut as Parsifal at the Met 1991 and 2001, Otello at Covent Garden 1992, Siegmund in Die Walküre at the Vienna Staatsoper 1992; 1997 season included Don José and Siegmund at the Met and Gabriele Adorno in Simon Boccanegra at Covent Garden; 1999 season Herman in the Queen of Spades at the Met, and at Covent Garden 2002; concert performance of Verdi's Battaglia di Legnano with the Royal Opera 2000; Canio in Pagliacci at Covent Garden 2003; Nero in premiere of Monteverdi's Poppea in Los Angeles 2003; Rasputin in premiere of Deborah Drattell's Nicholas and Alexandra, Los Angeles 2003; opened 2002/03 Los Angeles Opera Season in Puccini's Fanciulla del West; Maurizio in Adriana Lecouvreur, Metropolitan Opera 2009; announced intention to sing baritone title role in Verdi's Simon Boccanegra at Berlin Staatsoper 2009; Commdr Légion d'honneur, Hon. KBE 2002, Medal of Freedom, Star of the Order of Merit (Hungary) 2005; Dr hc (Royal Coll. of Music) 1982, (Univ. Complutense de Madrid) 1989; Hon. DMus (Univ. of Oxford) 2003; nine Grammy Awards, European Culture Foundation Culture Prize 2003, Classic FM Gramophone Listeners' Choice Award 2005, Opera News Award 2005, Classic BRIT Award for Lifetime Achievement 2006, Birgit Nilsson Prize 2009. *Films include:* Madama Butterfly with von Karajan, La Traviata 1982, Carmen 1984, Otello 1986. *Recordings:* has made well over 100 recordings, including Aïda, Un Ballo in Maschera, Tosca, Tannhäuser 1989, Die Frau ohne Schatten 1993, Gounod's Roméo et Juliette 1996, Merlin by Albeniz 2000, Tristan and Isolde (Classical Brit Awards Critic's Choice Award 2006), Pasión Española (Latin Grammy Award for Best Classical Album) 2008; has made more than 50 videos. *Publications:* My First Forty Years (autobiog.) 1983, My Operatic Roles 2000. *Address:* Vincent and Farrell Associates, Suite 740, 481 8th Avenue, New York, NY 10001, USA (office); c/o Los Angeles Opera, 135 N Grand Avenue, Los Angeles, CA 90012 (office); c/o Washington National Opera, 2600 Virginia Avenue NW, Suite 104, Washington, DC 20037, USA (office). *Website:* www.placidodomingo.com; www.losangelesopera.com; www.dc-opera.org.

DOMINGO SOLANS, Eugenio, DEcon; Spanish international banker, economist and university professor; b. 26 Nov. 1945, Barcelona; ed Univ. of Barcelona, Autonomous Univ. of Madrid; Prof. of Public Finance, Univ. of Barcelona 1968–70, Autonomous Univ. of Madrid 1970–; economist, Banco Atlántico 1970, 1973–77, 1978–79; economist, Research Group, Econ. and Social Devt Plan 1970–73; Econ. Adviser, Ministry of Econs 1977–78; Man. Research Dept, Inst. of Econ. Studies 1979–86; Asst Pres. Banco Zaragozano 1986–91; mem. Bd BZ Gestión 1987–91, Banco Zaragozano 1988–94, Banco de Toledo 1988–94 (Sec. Bd 1990–94); mem. Governing Council and Exec. Comm., Banco de España 1994–98; Prof. of Monetary Policy and Spanish Tax System, Univ. Coll. of Financial Studies, Madrid 1996–; mem. Exec. Bd and Governing Council, European Cen. Bank 1998–; Businessmen's Soc. Award 1994. *Address:* Universidad Autónoma de Madrid, Carretera de Colmenar Km. 15, Cantoblanco, 28049 Madrid, Spain (office). *Telephone:* (91) 3975000 (office). *Fax:* (91) 3974123 (office). *Website:* www.uam.es (office).

DOMINI, Amy, BA; American mutual fund company executive; *CEO and President, Domini Social Investments LLC;* b. 25 Jan. 1950, New York, NY; d. of Enzo Vice Domini and Margaret Cabot Domini (née Colt); m. Peter D. Kinder 1980 (divorced); two s.; ed Boston Univ.; stockbroker, Tucker Anthony & RL Day, Cambridge, Mass 1975–80, Moseley Securities, Cambridge 1980–85; portfolio man., Franklin R & D Corpn, Boston 1985–87; pvt. trustee, Loring, Wolcott & Coolidge 1987–; Chair. Bd Linder, Lydenberg, Domini & Co., Cambridge 1991–; f. Domino Social Equity Fund 1991; Founder, CEO and Pres. Domini Social Investments LLC, Boston 1996–; Chair. Pension Fund Episcopal Church, New York 1994–; mem. Governing Bd, Interfaith Center on Corp. Responsibility, New York 1985–95, Bd of Dirs, Social Investment Forum, Washington, DC 1994–, Bd Progressive Govt Inst. 2003–; mem. Nat. Community Capital Asscn, Boston Security Analysis Soc.; Hon. DHumLitt (Berkeley Divinity School at Yale) 2007, Hon. DBA (Northeastern Univ. Law School) 2007; Accioniste Award, Accion Int. 1992, SRI (Socially Responsible Investing) Service Award 1996, Best Mutual Funds Award, Money Magazine 1998, Theodore M. Hesburgh Award for Business Ethics, Notre Dame Univ. 2005, citation from Pres. Bill Clinton for work with UN Foundation, 2005, ranked by Time Magazine amongst 100 Most Influential People in the World 2005. *Publications include:* Ethical Investing 1984, Challenges of Wealth 1988, The Social Investment Almanac 1992, Investing for Good 1993, Socially Responsible Investing: Making a Difference and Making Money 2001; several articles on ethical investment in professional journals. *Leisure interests:* day-sailing, gardening. *Address:* c/o Loring, Wolcott & Coolidge, 230 Congress Street, Floor 12, Boston, MA 02110-2437 (office); 7 Dana Street, Cambridge, MA 02138, USA (home). *Telephone:* (617) 622-2240 (home); (617) 547-3236 (home). *Fax:* (617) 523-6531 (office). *E-mail:* adomini@domini.com (office). *Website:* domini.com (office).

DOMINIAN, Jacobus (Jack), MBE, DSc, FRCPE, FRCPsy; British psychiatrist; b. 25 Aug. 1929, Athens, Greece; s. of Charles Dominian and Mary Scarlato; m. Edith Mary Smith 1955; four d.; ed St Mary's School, Bombay, Stamford Grammar School, England, Fitzwilliam Coll., Cambridge, Exeter Coll., Oxford and Inst. of Psychiatry, London; Sr House Officer United Oxford Hosps 1955–58; Registrar Maudsley Hosp., London 1958–61, Sr Registrar 1961–64; Sr Consultant Psychiatrist Cen. Middx Hosp., London 1965–88, Hon. Consultant 1988–; Dir One Plus One (Marriage and Partnership Research) 1971–; Hon. DSc (Lancaster) 1976. *Publications:* Christian Marriage 1967, Marital Breakdown 1968, Depression 1976, Proposals for a New Sexual Ethic 1976, Authority 1976, Marital Pathology 1980, Marriage, Faith and Love 1981, The Capacity to Love 1985, Sexual Integrity: The Answer to AIDS 1987, Passionate and Compassionate Love – A Vision for Christian Marriage 1991, The Everyday God (with Edmund Flood) 1993, Marriage 1995, One Like Us: a psychological interpretation of Jesus 1998, Let's Make Love 2001. *Leisure interests:* swimming, theatre, music and reading. *Address:* 1 Benjamin Street London, EC1M 5QG, England (office). *Telephone:* (20) 7553-9530.

DOMINO, Fats; American blues singer; b. (Antoine Domino), 26 Feb. 1928, New Orleans, La.; fmr factory worker; began singing career in local clubs; Hall of Fame Grammy Award 1997, Lifetime Achievement Grammy Award 1997, Nat. Medal of Arts 1998. *Singles include:* The Fat Man, Goin' Home, Going To The River, Please Don't Leave Me, Don't You Know, Ain't That A Shame, Bo Weevil, I'm In Love Again, My Blue Heaven, Blueberry Hill, Walking to New Orleans, My Girl Josephine, Let The Four Winds Blow, Red Sails In The Sunset. *Recordings include:* albums: Here Comes Fats Domino 1963, Southland USA 1965, Fats Domino 1966, Trouble in Mind, Fats is Back 1968, Sleeping on the Job 1978, The Fat Man 1995, Live at Gilleys 1999, Live! Collector's Edition 2000.

DOMLJAN, Žarko; Croatian politician; b. 14 Sept. 1932, Imotski; m. Iva Marijanovic; one d.; ed Zagreb Univ., Music Coll.; mem. Croatian Nat. Theatre Orchestra 1955–57; Ed.-in-Chief, Deputy Dir, Editorial Dept of Lexicographical Inst. 1968–86; Ed.-in-Chief Yugoslav Encyclopedia of Art and Encyclopedia of Croatian Art 1985–96, Life of Art Journal 1967–73; research adviser, Inst. of Art History 1987–90; mem. and Pres. Sabor (Parl. of Croatian Repub.) 1990–92; mem. Chamber of Reps of Croatian Parl. 1992, apptd Vice-Pres. 1992; Chair. Foreign Policy Bd; mem. State Council of Defence and Nat. Security and of Presidential Council. *Publications:* Architect Hugo Erlich

1979, Modern Architecture in Yugoslavia 1986, Umjetnička topografija Hrvatske, Križevci – grad i okolica (Art Topography of Croatia, Križevci – The Town and its Environs) (co-ed.) 1993. *Leisure interests:* tennis, mountain trekking. *Address:* Kukuljevićeva 32, 10000 Zagreb, Croatia (home). *Telephone:* (1) 4851011 (office).

DOMMISSE, Ebbe, BA, MSc; South African newspaper editor; b. 14 July 1940, Riversdale; s. of Jan Dommisse and Anna Dommisse; m. Daléne Laubscher 1963; two s. one d.; ed Paarl Boys High School, Univ. of Stellenbosch and Grad. School of Journalism, Columbia Univ., New York, USA; reporter, Die Burger, Cape Town 1961, Chief Sub-Ed. 1968, News Ed. 1971; Asst Ed. and Political Commentator, Beeld, Johannesburg (Founder-mem. of new Johannesburg daily) 1974; Asst Ed. Die Burger 1979, Sr Asst Ed. 1984, Ed. 1990–2000; Exec. mem. Nasionale Koerante; Trustee Helpmekaarfonds; mem. Akad. vir Wetenskap en Kuns; Nieman Travel Fellowship 1987. *Publications:* with Alf Ries: Broedertwis 1982, Leierstryd 1990, Anton Rupert 2005. *Leisure interests:* reading, the arts, ecology, tennis. *Address:* c/o Die Burger, PO Box 692, Cape Town 8000, South Africa (office).

DOMOTO, Hisao; Japanese painter; b. 1928; ed Kyoto Municipal Special School of Art; studied Nihonga (Japanese-style painting); studied in France, Italy and Spain 1952, settled in Paris 1955; abandoned traditional Japanese style and exhibited abstract paintings at Salon des Indépendants, Salon de Mai, Paris 1956, 1957; rep. at Rome/New York Art Foundation, first Exhbn Rome, 'Otro Arte' Exhbn Madrid, Facchetti and Stadler Galleries, Paris 1957; one-man Exhbn Martha Jackson Gallery, New York 1959, Toward the Abyss of Painting, Tokyo 2005; First Prize, Acad. of Japan 1951 and 1953; First Prize of Musée d'Art Moderne for foreign painters in Paris 1958.

DON MALAVO, Estanislao; Equatorial Guinean politician; Deputy Minister of Finance and the Budget 2006–08, Minister of Finance and the Budget 2008–. *Address:* Ministry of Finance and the Budget, Malabo, Equatorial Guinea (office). *Website:* www.ceiba-guinea-ecuatorial.org/guineees/indexbienv1.htm (office).

DONAGHY, Rita, CBE, BA, FRSA; British public servant; b. 9 Oct. 1944, Bristol; d. of William Scott Willis and Margaret Brenda Howard; m. 1st James Columba Donaghy 1968 (divorced 1985); m. 2nd Ted (Edward) Easen-Thomas; ed Univ. of Durham; Asst Registrar, then Perm. Sec. of Students' Union, Univ. of London Inst. of Educ. 1968–2000; Pres. Nat. and Local Govt Officers' Asscn (NALGO) 1989–90, TUC 2000; mem. Low Pay Comm. 1997–2000; Chair. Advisory, Conciliation and Arbitration Service (ACAS) 2000–07; Dir (non-exec.) King's Coll. Hospital 2005–; mem. Cttee on Standards in Public Life (Kelly Cttee) 2000–07, Acting Chair. 2007; Chair., Dept of Work & Pensions Inquiry on Fatalities in Construction; conducted Review of Women's Nat. Comm. for Dept of Commerce & Local Govt 2007; Fellow Chartered Inst. of Personnel and Devt 2002–; Hon. DUniv (Open Univ.) 2002, Dr hc (Keele Univ.) 2004, Hon. DBA (Greenwich) 2005. *Leisure interests:* theatre, gardening, reading. *Address:* 35 Lyndhurst Grove, London, SE15 5AN, England (home). *Telephone:* (20) 7703-4573 (home). *Fax:* (20) 7703-4573 (home). *E-mail:* r.donaghy@btinternet.com (home).

DONAHUE, Timothy M., BA; American telecommunications industry executive; ed John Carroll Univ.; Pres. Paging Div., McCaw Cellular Communications (now AT&T Wireless) 1986–89, Pres. US Cen. Region 1989–91, Pres. Northeast Region and Gen. Man. AT&T Wireless 1991–96; Pres. and COO Nextel Communications Inc. 1996–99, Pres. and CEO 1999–2005, Exec. Chair. Sprint Nextel Corpn 2005–06; Dir NII Holdings, Nextel Pnrs, Eastman Kodak Co., John Carroll Univ., Tyco Healthcare 2007–. *Address:* c/o Board of Directors, Tyco Healthcare, 15 Hampshire Street, Mansfield, MA 02048, USA (office).

DONALD, Sir Alan (Ewen), Kt, KCMG, BA, LLM; British diplomatist (retd); b. 5 May 1931, Inverurie, Aberdeenshire, Scotland; s. of Robert T. Donald and Louise Turner; m. Janet H.T. Blood 1958; four s.; ed Aberdeen Grammar School, Fettes Coll. Edinburgh and Trinity Hall, Cambridge; mil. service 1949–50; joined Foreign (later Diplomatic) Service 1954; Third Sec., Beijing 1955–57; Pvt. Sec. to Parl. Under-Sec. of State, Foreign Office 1958–61; UK Del. to NATO, Paris 1961–64; First Sec. Beijing 1964–66; Counsellor, Athens 1971–73; Political Adviser to Gov. of Hong Kong 1974–77; Amb. to Zaire, Rwanda and Burundi 1977–80, to People's Repub. of the Congo 1978–80, to Indonesia 1984–88, to People's Repub. of China 1988–91; Asst Under-Sec. (Asia/Pacific), FCO 1980–84; Adviser on Chinese Affairs, Rolls-Royce 1991–99; Dir Fleming Far Eastern Investment Co. 1991–97, China Fund Inc. 1992–2003, Batey, Burn Ltd 1992–98, HSBC China Fund Ltd 1994–2004, Fleming Asian Investment Co. 1997–2001; Hon. LLD (Aberdeen) 1991. *Leisure interests:* music, military history, water colour sketching, films. *Address:* Applebys, Chiddingstone Causeway, nr Tonbridge, Kent, TN11 8JH, England (home). *Telephone:* (1892) 870598 (home). *Fax:* (1892) 870490 (home). *E-mail:* alan.donald@chiddingstone.net (home).

DONALD, Athene Margaret, PhD, FRS; British physicist and academic; *Professor of Experimental Physics, University of Cambridge;* b. (Athene Margaret Griffith), 15 May 1953, London; d. of Walter Griffith and Annette Marian Tylor; m. Matthew J. Donald 1976; one s. one d.; ed Camden School for Girls, London and Girton Coll., Cambridge; postdoctoral researcher, Cornell Univ., USA 1977–81; Fellow, Robinson Coll., Univ. of Cambridge 1981–, Science and Eng Research Council Research Fellow 1981–83, Royal Soc. Research Fellow 1983–85, Lecturer 1985–95, Reader 1985–98, Prof. of Experimental Physics 1998–; mem. Governing Council, Inst. of Food Research 1999–2003; mem. Biotechnology and Biological Sciences Research Council Strategy Bd 2003–04; mem. Royal Soc. Council 2004–06; mem. RAE panel E19 (2007 exercise); Samuel Locker Award in Physics, Univ. of Birmingham 1989, Charles Vernon Boys Prize, Inst. of Physics 1989, Rosenhain Medal and Prize,

Inst. of Materials 1995, William Hopkins Prize, Cambridge Philosophical Soc. 2003, Mott Prize, Inst. of Physics 2005, Bakerian Lecturer, Royal Soc. 2006. *Publications:* Liquid Crystalline Polymers (jtly) 1992, Starch: Structure and Function (jtly) 1997, Starch: Advances in Structure and Function (jtly) 2001; numerous articles in scientific journals. *Leisure interests:* music, walking. *Address:* Department of Physics, Cavendish Laboratory, University of Cambridge, JJ Thomson Avenue, Cambridge, CB3 0HE, England (office). *Telephone:* (1223) 337382 (office). *Fax:* (1223) 337000 (home). *E-mail:* amd3@cam.ac.uk (office). *Website:* www.bss.phy.cam.ac.uk/~amd3 (office).

DONALDSON, Charles Ian Edward, MA, FBA, FRSE, FAHA; British/Australian professor of English; *Director, Centre for Research in the Arts, Social Sciences and Humanities, King's College, University of Cambridge;* b. 6 May 1935, Melbourne, Australia; s. of Dr William Edward Donaldson and Elizabeth Donaldson (née Weigall); m. 1st Tamsin Jane Procter 1962 (divorced 1990); one s. one d.; m. 2nd Grazia Maria Therese Gunn 1991; ed Melbourne Grammar School, Melbourne Univ., Magdalen Coll., Oxford, Merton Coll., Oxford; Sr Tutor in English, Melbourne Univ. 1958; Fellow and Lecturer in English, Wadham Coll., Oxford 1962–69; CUF Lecturer in English, Oxford Univ. 1963–69; Prof. of English, ANU 1969–91, Dir, Humanities Research Centre 1974–90; Regius Prof. of Rhetoric and English Literature, Edin. Univ. 1991–95; Grace 1 Prof. of English and Fellow, King's Coll., Cambridge Univ. 1995–2002, Convenor King's Coll. Research Centre 1997–2000, Dir Centre for Research in the Arts, Social Sciences and Humanities 2001–; visiting appointments at Univ. of Calif., Santa Barbara 1967–68, Gonville and Caius Coll., Cambridge 1985, Cornell Univ. 1988, Folger Shakespeare Library 1988, Melbourne Univ. 1991. *Publications:* The World Upside Down: Comedy From Jonson to Fielding 1970, Ben Jonson: Poems (ed.) 1975, The Rapes of Lucretia: A Myth and its Transformations 1982, Jonson and Shakespeare (ed.) 1982, Transformations in Modern European Drama 1983, Seeing the First Australians (ed., with Tamsin Donaldson) 1985, Ben Jonson 1985, Shaping Lives (co-ed.) 1992, Jonson's Walk to Scotland 1993, The Death of the Author and the Life of the Poet 1995, Jonson: Selected Poems (ed.) 1995, Jonson's Magic Houses 1997. *Address:* King's College, Cambridge, CB2 1ST (office); 11 Grange Road, Cambridge, CB3 9AS, England (home). *Telephone:* (1223) 765275 (office); (1223) 321683 (home). *Fax:* (1223) 765276 (office). *E-mail:* id202@cus.cam.ac.uk (office). *Website:* www.crassh.cam.ac.uk (office).

DONALDSON, Roger; New Zealand (b. Australian) film director; b. 15 Nov. 1945, Ballarat, Australia; emigrated to NZ aged 19; established still photography business, then started making documentary films. *Television:* Winners and Losers (series of short dramas). *Films include:* Sleeping Dogs (also producer) 1977, Nutcase (1980, Smash Palace (also producer and writer) 1981, The Bounty 1984, Marie 1985, No Way Out 1987, Cocktail 1988, Cadillac Man (also producer) 1990, White Sands 1992, The Getaway 1994, Species 1995, Dante's Peak 1997, Thirteen Days 2000, The Recruit 2003, The World's Fastest Indian (also producer and writer) 2005, The Bank Job 2007. *Address:* c/o Creative Artists Agency, Inc. (CAA), 9830 Wilshire Blvd., Beverly Hills, CA 90212-1825, USA.

DONALDSON, Samuel (Sam) Andrew, BA; American broadcast journalist; b. 11 March 1934, El Paso, Tex.; s. of Samuel A. Donaldson and Chloe Hampson; m. 1st Billie K. Butler 1963; three s. one d.; m. 2nd Janice C. Smith 1983; ed Univ. of Texas, El Paso and Univ. of Southern Calif.; radio/TV news reporter/anchorman, WTOP, Washington, DC 1961–67; Capitol Hill/corresp., ABC News, Washington, DC 1967–77, White House Corresp. 1977–89, Chief White House Corresp. 1998–99, Anchor, Prime Time Live 1989–98; Co-anchor 20/20 Live, ABC 1998; Anchor, SamDonaldson@abcnews.com 1999, The Sam Donaldson Show, ABC Radio Network 2001–; panellist, This Week With David Brinkley 1981–96; Co-anchor, This Week with Sam Donaldson and Cokie Roberts 1996–2002; currently panelist This Week and co-host Politics Live, ABC News Now; Pres. Wilson Council (pvt sector advisory group to Woodrow Wilson Int. Center for Scholars), Washington, DC; Broadcaster of the Year Award, Nat. Press Foundation 1998 and numerous other awards. *Publication:* Hold on Mr President 1987. *Address:* ABC, 1717 Desales Street, NW, Washington, DC 20036, USA (office). *E-mail:* samdonaldson@abcnews.com (office).

DONALDSON, Simon Kirwan, DPhil, FRS; British mathematician and academic; *Professor of Pure Mathematics, Imperial College London;* b. 20 Aug. 1957, Cambridge; s. of Peter Donaldson and Jane Stirland; m. Ana Nora Hurtado 1986; two s. one d.; ed Sevenoaks School, Kent, Pembroke Coll., Cambridge, Worcester Coll., Oxford; Jr Research Fellow, All Souls Coll., Oxford 1983–85; Wallis Prof. of Math., Univ. of Oxford 1985–98; Fellow, St Anne's Coll., Oxford 1985–98; Prof. of Pure Math., Imperial Coll., London 1998–, Pres. Inst. of Math. Sciences 2003–; Hon. Fellow, Pembroke Coll., Cambridge 1992, St Anne's Coll., Oxford 1999; Fields Medal 1986, Crafoord Prize (with S-T Yau) 1994, King Faisal International Prize (with M.S. Narasimhan) 2006, Nemmers Prize 2008. *Publications:* The Geometry of Four-manifolds (with P. B. Kronheimer) 1990, Floer Homology Groups in Yang-Mills Theory 2002; numerous papers in math. journals. *Leisure interest:* sailing. *Address:* Room 674, Huxley Building, Department of Mathematics, Imperial College, 180 Queen's Gate, London, SW7 2BT, England (office). *Telephone:* (20) 7594-8559 (office). *Fax:* (20) 7594-8517 (office). *E-mail:* s.donaldson@ic.ac.uk (office). *Website:* www.ma.ic.ac.uk (office).

DONALDSON, William H., MBA; American business executive and government official; ed Yale Univ., Harvard Business School; rifle platoon Commdr and later aide-de-camp to Commanding Gen. 1st Provisional Marine Air Ground Task Force, US Marine Corps 1953–55; Co-Founder Donaldson, Lufkin & Jenrette 1959, CEO 1959–73; Under-Sec. of State 1973–75; fmr Counsel to Vice-Pres. Rockefeller; Co-Founder Grad. School of Man., Yale Univ. 1975, first Dean and William S. Beinecke Prof. of Man. 1975–80; f.

Donaldson Enterprises investment co. 1981, Chair. 2001–; Chair. and CEO New York Stock Exchange 1990–95; Chair., Pres. and CEO Aetna Inc. –2001; Commr and Chair. Securities and Exchange Comm. 2002–05. *Address:* c/o Securities and Exchange Commission, 450 Fifth Street, NW, Washington, DC 20001, USA (office).

DONATH, Helen; American singer (soprano); b. 10 July 1940, Corpus Christi, Tex.; d. of Jimmy Erwin and Helen Hamauei; m. Klaus Donath 1965; one s.; ed Roy Miller High School, Del Mar Coll., Texas; studied with Paola Novikova, later with husband Klaus Donath (by whom all song-recitals are accompanied); début at Cologne Opera House 1962, at Hanover Opera House 1963–68, Bayerische Staatsoper, Munich 1968–72; guest appearances in London (Covent Garden), Vienna, Milan, San Francisco, Lisbon, New York, etc.; has given concerts in all maj. European and American cities; over 100 recordings 1962–; Pope Paul Medal, Salzburg 50 Year Anniversary Medal, Bratislava Festival Award, Deutscher Schallplattenpreis and Grosses Lob for her first song recital recording, Lower Saxony Prize for Culture 1990. *Major roles include:* Pamina in Die Zauberflöte, Zerlina in Don Giovanni, Eva in Die Meistersinger, Sophie in Der Rosenkavalier, Susanna in Le Nozze di Figaro, Anne Trulove in The Rake's Progress, Ilia in Idomeneo, Micaela in Carmen. *Leisure interests:* family, gardening, cooking, swimming, filming. *Address:* Artists Management Vienna, Bernd Schimickl, Rainergasse 35/2/4, 1050 Vienna, Austria (office). *Telephone:* (1) 5816271 (office). *E-mail:* bschmickl@hotmail.com (office). *Website:* www.artistsmanagementvienna.net (office).

DONDELINGER, Albert Marie Joseph, DJur; Luxembourg banker; b. 22 March 1934, Redange, Attert; s. of Jean Dondelinger and Simone Lamborelle; m. Francine Dondelinger-Gillen; three d.; ed Coll. St Michel, Brussels, Catholic Univ. of Louvain, Belgium; Alt. Gov. for Luxembourg, IBRD 1967–76; mem. European Monetary Cttee 1971–76, Bd of Belgium-Luxembourg Exchange Inst. 1972–76; Adviser to Group of Twenty and Assoc. mem. IMF Interim Cttee 1972–76; mem. Bd European Monetary Co-operation Fund and mem. Govs' Cttee, EEC Cen. Banks 1973–76; Govt Commr to State Savings Bank 1974–76; Co-Chair. Comm. for Financial Affairs of Conf. for Int. Econ. Co-operation (North-South Dialogue, Paris) 1975–76; Chair. Luxembourg Bankers' Asscn 1977–78; Man. Dir and Chair. Exec. Bd, Banque Internationale à Luxembourg 1977–90, Hon. Chair. 1990–; ind. economic and business man. consultant 1990–; Pres. European League for Econ. Co-operation (Luxembourg Bureau); Vice-Pres. Foundation Prince Henri-Princesse Maria Teresa; Vice-Chair. SOS-Sahel; Pres. Cercle Artistique de Luxembourg; mem. Bd Inst. Régional Intracommunautaire; mem. Inst. Int. d'Etudes Bancaires 1978–; Commdr Order of Couronne de Chêne (Luxembourg), Commdr Order of the Crown (Belgium), the Nat. Order (Ivory Coast), Officier, Ordre Nat. du Mérite, Order of Merit (Luxembourg). *Publication:* Le secret bancaire au Grand-Duché de Luxembourg 1972. *Leisure interests:* photography, bibliophily, golf, skiing, swimming.

DONDUKOV, Alexander Nikolayevich, DTechSc; Russian politician and engineer; *Member, Federation Council;* b. 29 March 1954, Kuybyshev (now Samara); engineer, Sr engineer, leading constructor Moscow Machine Construction Bureau (designers' office), Moscow 1977–85; Deputy Chief Constructor 1985, Chief Constructor 1991, Head, Gen. Constructor Moscow Machine Construction factory Skorost' 1991–93; Chair. Bd of Dirs, Gen. Constructor A. S. Yakovlev Machine Designers' Office 1993–2000, 2001–; mem. Govt Council for Industrial Policy 1994–; mem. Congress of Russian Intelligentsia 1994–; Minister of Industry, Science and Tech., Russian Fed. 2000–02; mem. Fed. Council (representing Belgorod) 2002–. *Address:* A. S. Yakovlev Machine Designers' Bureau, Leningradsky prosp. 68, 123315 Moscow A-47 (office); Federation Council, ul. B. Dmitrovka 26, 103426 Moscow, Russia. *Telephone:* (495) 157-57-37 (office); (495) 203-90-74 (office). *Fax:* (495) 203-46-17 (office). *E-mail:* post_sf@gov.ru (office). *Website:* www.council.gov.ru (office).

DONE, Kenneth Stephen, AM; Australian artist; b. 29 June 1940, Sydney; s. of Clifford Wade Done and Lillian Maureen Done; m. Judith Ann Walker; one s. one d.; ed Katoomba and Mosman High Schools, Nat. Art School, Sydney; Creative Dir Advertising Samuelson Talbot, Sydney, J. Walter Thompson 1960–78; Chair. Ken Done Group of Cos 1979–; Goodwill Amb. UNICEF Australia; Paul Harris Fellow, Rotary Int; Hon. Fellow Design Inst. of Australia 1999; NSW Tourism Award 1986, Rotary Award for Excellence 1993, Spirit of Australia Award 1993, Cannes Gold Lion Award, Export Hero Award, Westpac Banking Corpn 1999, Life Fellow Medal Powerhouse Museum 2002. *Publications:* Ken Done: Paintings and Drawings 1975–87, Craftsman House 1992, Ken Done Paintings (1990–94) 1994, Ken Done: The Art of Design 1994, Ken Done's Sydney, 20 Years of Painting 1999, The Art of Ken Done, Craftsman House 2002. *Leisure interests:* golf, swimming, diving, travelling. *Address:* 1 Hickson Road, The Rocks, NSW 2000, Australia (office). *Telephone:* (2) 9247-2740 (office). *Fax:* (2) 9251-4884 (office). *E-mail:* kate@done.com.au (office). *Website:* www.done.com.au (office).

DONEN, Stanley; American film producer and director; b. 13 April 1924, Columbia, SC; s. of Mortie and Helen Donen; ed Univ. of South Carolina; Lifetime Achievement Award, Acad. of Motion Picture Arts and Sciences 1998, Golden Eddie Award, American Cinema Eds 1988, Lifetime Achievement Award, Palm Beach Int. Film Festival 1999. *Films include:* On the Town 1949, Royal Wedding 1951, Love Is Better Than Ever 1952, Singin' in the Rain 1952, Fearless Fagan 1952, Give a Girl a Break 1953, Seven Brides for Seven Brothers 1954, Deep in My Heart 1954, It's Always Fair Weather 1955, Funny Face 1957, The Pajama Game 1957, Kiss Them for Me 1957, Indiscreet 1958, Damn Yankees! 1958, Once More, with Feeling! 1960, Surprise Package 1960, The Grass Is Greener 1960, Charade 1963, Arabesque 1966, Two for the Road 1967, Bedazzled 1967, Staircase 1969, The Little Prince 1974, Lucky Lady 1975, Movie Movie 1978, Saturn 3 1980, Blame It on Rio 1984. *Television includes:* Love Letters 1999. *Address:* c/o LaGrange Group, 11828 La Grange Avenue, Los Angeles CA 90025, USA.

DONG, Jichang; Chinese party official; b. 1930, Hancheng Co., Shaanxi Prov.; joined CCP 1949; Alt. mem. 12th CCP Cen. Cttee 1982–87, mem. 13th Cen. Cttee 1987–92; Deputy Sec. CCP Cttee, Shaanxi Prov. 1983–90, a Vice-Chair. 1990–; Sec. CCP Cttee, Xian 1984; Vice-Chair. Shaanxi Prov. Cttee. of CPPCC 1990–; Pres. Econ. Promotion Asscn for Lonhai-Lanxin Area 1987–. *Address:* Shaanxi Provincial Chinese Communist Party, Xian, Shaanxi, People's Republic of China.

DONG, Kejun; Chinese woodcut artist; b. 18 Feb. 1939, Chongqing, Sichuan; s. of Dong Xueyuan and Gue Ximing; m. Lü Hengfen 1969; one s.; Dir of Chinese Artistic Asscn; Standing Dir Chinese Woodcut Asscn; Vice-Chair. Guizhow Artistic Asscn; Chair. Guiyang Artistic Asscn; Vice-Pres. Acad. of Painting and Calligraphy; mem. Standing Cttee of Guizhou Br. of CPPCC; Vice-Chair. Guizhou Prov. Br. Artists' Assoc. 1988–; Chair. Artists' Assoc. Guiyang Br. 1988–; Council mem. Artists' Assoc. 1988–; works on view at nat. exhbns 1965–, also in Japan, USA, France, Sweden, Germany, Africa and Australia; Prizewinner, 9th Nat. Woodcut Exhbn 1986; First Grade Nat. Artist. *Works include:* Spring Returns to the Miao Mountain 1979, A Close Ball 1979, An Illustration of the Continuation of Feng Xuefeng's Fables (a hundred pieces) 1980, Company 1981, Go Back Drunkenly 1982, Lively Spring 1983, The Miao Nat Sisters in Their Splendid Costume 1985, Contemporary Totem-1 1986, Mountain Breath 1986, A White Cottage 1987, Sunny Rain 1988, A Hundred Pieces of Coloured Inkwash Drawings 1991–92, The Big Sleep 1993, The Bird Market 1993, Illusion 1993, Eagle 1994, Man and Horse 1995, Going to Market 1995. *Publications:* Dong Kejun Woodcut Works, Selected Paintings of Dong Kejun 1992, Selected Chinese Coloured Inkwash Paintings 1995. *Leisure interests:* literature, music, film and dance. *Address:* Guiyang Artistic Asscn, 27 Road Shizi, Guiyang, Guizhou Prov., People's Republic of China.

DONG, Mingzhu; Chinese business executive; *President, Gree Electric Appliances Inc.;* joined Gree Electric Appliances Inc. (then called Haili), Zhuhai 1990, later Business Man., later Departmental Man. of Business Dept, later Vice-Gen. Man., Gen. Man. 2001, currently Pres.; Chair. Female Asscn of Entrepreneurs, Zhuhai City 2002–; Deputy Dir Chinese Household Appliances Asscn; mem. Female Asscn of Entrepreneurs, Guangdong, currently Vice-Chair.; mem. Standing Cttee Zhuhai Political Consultative Conf.; Del., 10th NPC 2003–; Nat. Excellent Woman Worker 1998, Guangdong Prov. Excellent Female Man. 1999, Nat. May 1 Labour Medal, elected one of Home Electric Appliance Top 10 Famous Individuals of the Year by Beijing Youth magazine 1999, received title of Excellent Woman in Guangdong Prov. 2000, Chinese Outstanding Woman 2001, elected one of Female Entrepreneurs of All Time in China 2002, one of Top 10 Businesswoman of China 2002, named as Excellent Woman and one of Nat. Successful Female Models by Nat. Women's Union 2003, named by first Global Chinese Women Conf. one of 10 Most Powerful Chinese Women 2003, named by MBA one of 10 Most Respected Innovative Entrepreneurs 2004, ranked by Fortune magazine amongst 50 Most Powerful Women in Business outside the US (42nd) 2004, (48th) 2005, (48th) 2007, named as one of Top 10 Chinese Marketing People 2004, named one of 10 Excellent Business Leaders and one of "10 Innovation People that influence the future development trend of Chinese household appliances" 2005, named one of Guangdong Top Ten Economically Influential People 2005, ranked by Forbes magazine amongst 100 Most Powerful Women (93rd) 2007. *Publication:* Lay Out in the World (autobiog.; adapted for TV by China-Central TV Station). *Address:* Gree Electric Appliances Inc., 6 West Jinji Road, Qianshan, Zhuhai 519070, Guangdong Province, People's Republic of China (office). *Telephone:* (756) 8614883 (office). *Fax:* (756) 8614998 (office). *Website:* www.gree.com.cn (office).

DONG, Zheng; Chinese research professor and physician; b. 3 Nov. 1926, Gaoyang Co., Hebei Prov.; s. of Dong Mingxun and Dong Wangshi; m. Li Qun 1953; two s.; ed Bethune Medical Univ., Northwest China Univ.; Chief Physician, Inst. of Acupuncture and Moxibustion 1955–70; 2nd Nat. Training Course of Traditional Medicine 1958–59; Research Prof. and Dir Dept of Medicine, Guanganmen Hosp. 1983–95; Research Prof. Tung Shin Hosp., Malaysia 1993; mem. Acupunture and Moxibustion Asscn, Traditional Chinese Medicine Research Asscn, Specialist Group, China Scientific and Tech. Asscn; specializes in use of combined Chinese traditional medicine and Western medicine; has conducted studies of asthma, eczema, emphysema, bronchitis, allergic diseases, immunopathy, diseases of connective tissues and nerve system, multiple sclerosis, polymyositis, dermatomyositis, myotonic muscular dystrophy; Advanced Worker Medal 1977. *Publications:* Male Sex Disorders 1959, A Short Course in Acupuncture and Moxibustion 1960, A Short Course in Traditional Chinese Herbs 1960, The Surface of the Body connects with the Viscera 1992, External Qigong in the Treatment of Disease, Smoking is Harmful to Health; and numerous articles concerning connection between Yinyang theory and modern medicine, effect of external Qigong on human body. *Leisure interests:* traditional Chinese painting, Chinese qigong and taiji box. *Address:* Guanganmen Hospital, Academy of Traditional Medicine, Bei-xin-Ge, Guang An Men, Beijing 100053 (office); Apt 1301, 78 Maliandou Road, Xuan Wu area, Beijing, People's Republic of China. *Telephone:* (10) 8800-1137 (office); (10) 6335-5009 (home).

DONG, Zigang, MD, DrPH; biologist and academic; *Hormel-Knowlton Professor and Executive Director, Hormel Institute, University of Minnesota;* Guest Prof., The First Mil. Medical Univ., Guangzhou, China 2000–; Hon. Prof., The Fourth Mil. Univ., Xian, Shanxi, China 2000–; Hormel-Knowlton Prof. and Exec. Dir Hormel Inst., Univ. of Minn., USA; mem. NIG Reviewer Reserve 1997–, Study Section of Cancer Centers for NIH 2000–, Grant Review Panel of American Inst. for Cancer Research 2000–, Working Group for RAPID (Rapid

Access for Preventive Intervention Devt) programme of Nat. Cancer Inst. 2002, Special Emphasis Study Section of NIH 2002; Hon. Prof., The Fourth Mil. Univ., Xian, China 2000–. *Publications:* numerous articles in scientific journals. *Address:* Hormel Institute, University of Minnesota, 801 16th Avenue NE, Austin, MN 55912, USA (office). *Telephone:* (507) 433-8804 (office). *Fax:* (507) 437-9606 (office). *Website:* www.hi.umn.edu (office).

DONIGI, Peter Dickson, CBE, LLB; Papua New Guinea diplomatist and lawyer; b. 19 Dec. 1950; m.; five c.; ed Univ. of Papua New Guinea; pvt. legal practice 1981–98; Amb. and Special Envoy to UN 1991–92, apptd Perm. Rep. to UN 1998; Amb. to Germany (also accred to Holy See) 1992–95; mem. Council Commonwealth Lawyers' Asscn 1991–; fmr Pres. Papua New Guinea Law Soc.; Commonwealth Fellow 1991. *Publications:* Indigenous or Aboriginal Rights to Property: A Papua New Guinea Experience. *Address:* c/o Permanent Mission of Papua New Guinea to the United Nations, 201 East 42nd Street, Suite 405, New York, NY 10017, USA (office).

DONLEAVY, James Patrick; Irish author; b. 23 April 1926, New York City; s. of Patrick Donleavy and Margaret Donleavy; m. 1st Valerie Heron (divorced 1969); one s. one d.; m. 2nd Mary Wilson Price (divorced 1989); one s. one d.; ed Preparatory School, New York and Trinity Coll., Dublin; served in USN during World War II; Evening Standard Drama Award 1960, Brandeis Univ. Creative Arts Award 1961–62, Citation, American Acad. and Nat. Inst. of Arts and Letters 1975, Worldfest Houston Gold Award 1992, Cine Golden Eagle Writer and Narrator 1993. *Publications:* (novels) The Ginger Man 1955, A Singular Man 1963, The Beastly Beatitudes of Balthazar B 1968, The Onion Eaters 1971, A Fairy Tale of New York 1973, The Destinies of Darcy Dancer, Gentleman 1977, Schultz 1979, Leila 1983, Wrong Information is Being Given Out at Princeton 1998; (short stories and sketches) Meet My Maker the Mad Molecule 1964, An Author and His Image 1997; (novella) The Saddest Summer of Samuel S. 1966; also: The Unexpurgated Code: A Complete Manual of Survival and Manners 1975, De Alfonce Tennis, The Superlative Game of Eccentric Champions: Its History, Accoutrements, Rules, Conduct and Regimen, A Legend 1984, J. P. Donleavy's Ireland: In All Her Sins and in Some of Her Graces 1986, A Singular Country 1989, The History of the Ginger Man 1993, The Lady Who Liked Clean Rest Rooms 1995; (plays) The Ginger Man 1959, Fairy Tales of New York 1960, A Singular Man 1964, The Saddest Summer of Samuel S. 1968, The Plays of J. P. Donleavy 1972, The Beastly Beatitudes of Balthazar B. 1981, Are You Listening Rabbi Löw? 1987, That Darcy, That Dancer, That Gentlemen 1990. *Leisure interests:* De Alfonce Tennis, dry stone walling. *Address:* Levington Park, Mullingar, Co. Westmeath, Ireland. *Telephone:* (44) 9348903. *Fax:* (44) 9348351.

DONNELLAN, Declan; British theatre and opera director; b. 4 Aug. 1953, Manchester; ed Univ. of Cambridge; called to Bar (Middle Temple) 1978; freelance theatre productions include Don Giovanni (Scottish Opera Go Round), A Masked Ball (Opera 80), Rise and Fall of the City of Mahagonny (Wexford Festival), Macbeth and Philoctetes (Nat. Theatre of Finland); co-f. Cheek By Jowl (production co.) 1981, Artistic Dir 1981–; productions with Cheek By Jowl include Racine's Andromache, Corneille's The Cid, Twelfth Night, A Midsummer Night's Dream, Hamlet, As You Like It, Measure for Measure, Much Ado About Nothing 1998 and his own trans. of Musset's Don't Fool With Love and The Blind Men; also wrote and directed Lady Betty and Sara Sampson; Assoc. Dir Nat. Theatre (NT) 1989–97; work for NT includes Fuente Ovejuna 1989, Peer Gynt, Sweeney Todd 1993, Angels in America, Perestroika 1993, School for Scandal 1998; Dir Falstaff, Salzburg Festival 2001; Dir Le Cid by Corneille, Avignon Festival; Dir Boris Godunov and Twelfth Night, Russian Theatre Confed.; recipient of six Olivier Awards, Time Out Award (with Nick Ormerod) for Angels in America 1992, Observer Award for Outstanding Achievement, as well as awards in Paris, New York and Moscow. *Publications:* The Actor and The Target. *Address:* Cheek by Jowl Theatre Company, Alford House, Aveline Street, London, SE11 5DQ, England. *Telephone:* (20) 7793-0153 (office). *Fax:* (20) 7735-1031 (office). *Website:* www.cheekbyjowl.com (office).

DONNELLY, Christopher Nigel, CMG, TD, BA; British defence, security and foreign affairs specialist; *Senior Fellow, Defence Academy of the United Kingdom;* b. 10 Nov. 1946, Rochdale, Lancs.; s. of the late Anthony Donnelly and Dorothy M. Morris; m. Jill Norris 1971; one s. one d.; ed Cardinal Langley School, Middleton, Lancs. and Univ. of Manchester; Instructor, Royal Mil. Acad. Sandhurst (RMAS) 1969–72; Sr Lecturer, Soviet Studies Research Centre, RMAS 1972–79, Dir 1979–89; TA (Int. Corps) 1970–93; Adjunct Prof., Carnegie Mellon Univ. 1985–89, Georgia Tech. Univ. 1989–93; Special Adviser for Cen. and E European Affairs to Sec.-Gen. of NATO 1989–2003; Sr Fellow, Defence Acad. of the UK, Founder and Head of Advanced Research and Assessment Group 2003–07; currently Dir Inst. for Statecraft and Governance, Oxford; Dir Atlantic Council of the UK; Grand Cross of Commdr, Order of the Lithuanian Grand Duke Gediminas. *Publications:* Red Banner 1989, War and the Soviet Union 1990, Gorbachev's Revolution 1991, Nations, Alliances and Security 2004; numerous articles on Russian and Eastern European defence and security issues. *Leisure interests:* shooting, fishing. *Address:* Headquarters, Defence Academy of the United Kingdom, Shrivenham, Swindon, Wilts., SN6 8LA, England (office). *Telephone:* (1793) 785075 (office). *Fax:* (1793) 785072 (office). *E-mail:* cdonnelly.hq@da.mod.uk (office). *Website:* www.defac.ac.uk (office); www.tandf.co.uk/journals/titles/13518046 .asp.

DONNER, Clive; British film and theatre director; b. 21 Jan. 1926, London; s. of Alex Donner and Deborah Donner (née Taffel); m. Jocelyn Rickards 1971; asst film editor, Denham Studios 1942; freelance film director 1956–; work has included feature films and documentary films for British television and direction of theatrical productions in London and New York. *Films include:* (as ed.) Scrooge 1951, Genevieve 1952, The Purple Plain 1955; (as Dir) The Secret Place 1952, Some People (Best Film, Barcelona Festival) 1962, The Caretaker (Silver Bear, Berlin Film Festival) 1963, Nothing but the Best (Best Film, Barcelona Festival) 1963, What's New Pussycat? (Jean Georges Auroil/Paul Gibson Award) 1965, Here We Go Round the Mulberry Bush 1967, Alfred the Great 1969, Best Kept Secret (Silver Award, Motor Neurone Asscn) 1986, Stealing Heaven 1988, Bohème. *Plays directed include:* The Formation Dancers 1964, plays by Shakespeare and Pinter, Nottingham Playhouse 1970–71, The Front Room Boys, Royal Court Theatre 1971, Kennedy's Children, King's Head Theatre, Arts Theatre, Golden Theater, New York 1975. *TV programmes directed:* Rogue Male (Int. Emmy Award) 1976, She Fell Among Thieves 1977, Oliver Twist 1981, The Scarlet Pimpernel 1982, A Christmas Carol 1984, Charlemagne 1994. *Leisure interests:* classical music (particularly opera), popular music, reading, walking anywhere from the streets of London to the Australian sea shore. *Address:* 20 Thames Reach, 80 Rainville Road, London, W6 9HS, England. *Telephone:* (20) 7385-5580. *Fax:* (20) 7385-2423 (home).

DONNER, Jörn Johan, BA; Finnish film director, writer, politician and diplomatist; b. 5 Feb. 1933, Helsinki; s. of Dr Kai Donner and Greta von Bonsdorff; m. 1st Inga-Britt Wik 1954 (divorced 1962); m. 2nd Jeanette Bonnier 1974 (divorced 1988); m. 3rd Bitte Westerlund 1995; five s. one d.; ed Helsinki Univ.; worked as writer and film dir in Finland and Sweden, writing own film scripts; contrib. and critic to various Scandinavian and int. journals; CEO Jörn Donner Productions 1966–; Dir Swedish Film Inst., Stockholm 1972–75, Exec. Producer 1975–78, Man. Dir 1978–82; Chair. Bd Finnish Film Foundation, 1981–83, 1986–89, 1992–95; mem. Bd Marimekko Textiles and other cos; mem., Helsinki City Council 1969–1972, 1984–92; mem. Parl. 1987–95; Vice-Chair. Foreign Affairs Cttee 1991–95; Chair. Finnish EFTA Parliamentarians 1991–95; Consul-Gen. of Finland, Los Angeles 1995–96; mem. European Parl. 1996–99; Opera Prima Award Venice Film Festival 1963, Vittorio de Sica Prize, Sorrento 1978, Acad. Award for Producer of Best Foreign Language Picture (Fanny and Alexander) 1984. *Films:* A Sunday in September 1963, To Love 1964, Adventure Starts Here 1965, Rooftree 1967, Black on White 1968, Sixty-nine 1969, Portraits of Women 1970, Anna 1970, Images of Finland 1971, Tenderness 1972, Baksmalla 1974, Three Scenes (with Ingmar Bergman), The Bergman File 1975–77, Men Can't Be Raped 1978, Dirty Story 1984, Letters from Sweden 1987, Ingmar Bergman, a Conversation 1998, The President 2000. *Television:* host of talk show (Sweden and Finland) 1974–95. *Publications:* 52 books including: Report from Berlin 1958, The Personal Vision of Ingmar Bergman 1962. *Leisure interest:* fishing. *Address:* POB 214, 00171 Helsinki (office); Pohjoisranta 12, 00170 Helsinki, Finland (home). *Telephone:* (9) 1356060 (home); (9) 1357112 (office). *E-mail:* j.donner@surfnet.fi (home).

DONNER, Richard; American director and producer; b. 24 April 1930, New York; actor off-Broadway; collaborated with dir Martin Ritt on TV adaptation of Somerset Maugham's Of Human Bondage; moved to Calif. and began directing commercials, industrial films and documentaries. *Films include:* X-15 1961, Salt and Pepper 1968, Twinky 1969, The Omen 1976, Superman 1978, Superman II 1980, Inside Moves 1981, The Toy 1982, Ladyhawke 1985, The Goonies 1985, Lethal Weapon 1987, Scrooged 1988, Lethal Weapon 2 1989, Radio Flyer 1991, The Final Conflict (exec. producer) 1991, The Lost Boys (exec. producer) 1991, Delirious (exec. producer) 1991, Lethal Weapon 3 1992, Free Willy (co-exec. producer) 1993, Maverick 1994, Assassins 1995, Free Willy 3: The Rescue, Conspiracy Theory 1997, Double Tap (producer) 1997, Lethal Weapon 4 1998 (also producer), Made Men (producer) 1999, Any Given Sunday (producer) 1999, X-Men (producer) 2000, Blackheart (producer) 1999, Timeline (also producer) 2003, 16 Blocks 2006. *Television includes:* (films) Portrait of a Teenage Alcoholic, Senior Year, A Shadow in the Streets, Tales from the Crypt presents Demon Knight (co-exec. producer), Any Given Sunday 1999, X-Men 2000 (exec. producer); (series episodes) Have Gun Will Travel, Perry Mason, Cannon, Get Smart, The Fugitive, Kojak, Bronk, Lucas Tanner, Gilligan's Island, Man From U.N.C.L.E., Wild Wild West, Twilight Zone, The Banana Splits, Combat, Two Fisted Tales, Conspiracy Theory. *Address:* The Donners Company, 9465 Wilshire Boulevard, #420, Beverly Hills, CA 90212; c/o CAA, 9830 Wilshire Boulevard, Beverly Hills, CA 90212, USA. *Telephone:* (310) 777-4600 (office). *Fax:* (310) 777-4610 (office).

DONOGHUE, Denis, PhD; Irish literary critic; b. 1 Dec. 1928; ed Univ. Coll., Dublin; Admin. Office, Irish Dept of Finance 1951–54; Asst Lecturer, Univ. Coll., Dublin 1954–57, Coll. lecturer 1957–62, 1963–64, Prof. of Modern English and American Literature 1965–79; Visiting Scholar, Univ. of Pa 1962–63; Univ. Lecturer, Cambridge Univ. and Fellow, King's Coll. 1964–65; Henry James Prof. of Letters, New York Univ. 1979–; mem. Int. Cttee of Asscn of Univ. Profs of English; BBC Reith Lecturer 1982; Hon. DLitt. *Publications:* The Third Voice 1959, Connoisseurs of Chaos 1965, The Ordinary Universe 1968, Emily Dickinson 1968, Jonathan Swift 1969, Yeats 1971, Thieves of Fire 1974, Sovereign Ghost: Studies in Imagination 1978, Ferocious Alphabets 1981, The Arts Without Mystery 1983, We Irish: Essays on Irish Literature and Society 1987, Walter Pater: Lover of Strange Souls 1995, The Practice of Reading 1998, Words Alone: The Poet T. S. Eliot 2000, Adam's Curse: Reflections on Literature and Religion 2001, The American Classics: A Personal Essay 2005; contribs to reviews and journals and ed. of three vols. *Address:* English Department, New York University, 726 Broadway (7th Floor), New York, NY 10003, USA; Gaybrook, North Avenue, Mount Merrion, Dublin, Ireland. *E-mail:* dd1@nyu.edu (office).

DONOHOE, Amanda; British actress; b. 29 June 1962, London; ed Francis Holland School for Girls, London, Cen. School of Speech & Drama, London; mem. Royal Exchange Theatre, Manchester; Broadway debut, Uncle Vanya 1995. *Films include:* Foreign Body 1986, Castaway 1986, The Lair of the White Worm 1988, Tank Malling 1989, Diamond Skulls 1989, The Rainbow

1989, The Laughter of God 1990, Paper Mask 1990, The Madness of King George 1994, Liar Liar 1997, One Night Stand 1997, Stardust 1998, The Real Howard Spitz 1998, I'm Losing You 1998, Glory Glory 2000, Circus 2000, Wild About Harry 2000, Phoenix Blue 2001, Starship Troopers 3: Marauder 2008. *Television includes:* Star Quality 1985, Frankie and Johnnie 1985, An Affair in Mind 1988, Game, Set, and Match (series) 1988, L.A. Law (series) 1990–92, Shame 1992, It's Nothing Personal 1993, Briefest Encounter 1993, The Substitute 1993, A Woman's Guide to Adultery 1993, Shame II: The Secret 1995, Deep Secrets 1996, The Thorn Birds: The Missing Years 1996, A Knight in Camelot 1998, Batman Beyond: The Movie 1999, Rock the Boat 2000, In the Beginning 2000, Lucky Day 2002, Murder City (series) 2004, Bad Girls (series) 2006, Love Trap (series) 2007, Emmerdale Farm (series) 2009. *Plays include:* The Graduate 2001.

DONOHOE, Peter Howard, BMus, ARCM, FRNCM; British pianist; b. 18 June 1953, Manchester; s. of Harold Donohoe and Marjorie Donohoe (née Travis); m. Elaine Margaret Burns 1980; one d.; ed Chetham's School of Music, Royal Manchester Coll. of Music, Univ. of Leeds, studied with Derek Wyndham and Yvonne Loriod, Paris; professional solo pianist 1974–; appears several times each season with major symphony orchestras in London and rest of UK and performs regularly at the Promenade Concerts 1979–; performances with the LA Philharmonic, Chicago, Boston, Pittsburgh, Cincinnati, Dallas, Detroit and Cleveland orchestras and in Europe with Berlin Philharmonic and Symphony, Leipzig Gewandhaus, Dresden Philharmonic, Vienna Symphony, Czech Philharmonic, Swedish Radio and Radio France Philharmonic orchestras and Maggio Musicale Fiorentino; has also performed at Edin. Festival, Schleswig-Holstein Music Festival, La Roque d'Anthéron, France, and Festival of the Ruhr; Founder and Artistic Dir British Piano Concerto Foundation; Vice-Pres. Birmingham Conservatoire of Music; Hon. DMus (Birmingham) 1992, (Univ. of Cen. England), Hon. DLitt (Warwick) 1996; jt winner, Moscow Int. Tchaikovsky Competition 1982, Grand Prix Int. du Disque (Liszt), Gramophone Concerto Award (Tchaikovsky). *Recordings include:* Messiaen's Turangalila Symphony 1986, Dominic Muldowney Piano Concerto 1986, Tchaikovsky's Piano Concerto No. 2 (Gramophone magazine's Concerto of the Year 1988) 1986, Brahms Piano Concerto No. 1, Liszt, Berg and Bartok Sonatas, Beethoven, Diabelli Variations and Sonata Opus 101, Rachmaninov Preludes, Four British Concertos with Northern Sinfonia, Foulds' Dynamic Triptych, pieces by Rawsthorne, Bliss, Darnton, Rowley, Ferguson, Gerhard, Alwyn, Pitfield and Harty. *Leisure interests:* golf, helping young musicians, jazz. *Address:* c/o Askonas Holt Ltd, Lincoln House, 300 High Holborn, London, WC1V 7JH, England (office). *Telephone:* (20) 7400-1743 (office). *Fax:* (20) 7400-1799 (office). *Website:* www.askonasholt.co.uk (office).

DONOHUE, Craig S.; American business executive; *CEO, CME Group Inc. (Chicago Mercantile Exchange);* Vice-Pres. and Assoc. Gen. Counsel Chicago Mercantile Exchange (CME) Holdings 1995–97, Vice-Pres. Div. of Market Regulation 1997–98, Sr Vice-Pres. and Gen. Counsel CME 1998–2000, Man. Dir Business Devt and Corp./Legal Affairs, CME 2000–01, Man. Dir and Chief Admin. Officer CME 2001–, CME Holdings Aug. 2001, Exec. Vice-Pres. and Chief Admin. Officer, Office of the CEO, CME Holdings and of CME 2002–03, mem. Bd of Dirs and CEO CME Holdings and of CME 2004–06, CEO CME Group Inc. (following merger with Chicago Bd of Trade) 2006–; Vice-Chair. and Chair.-Elect Nat. Council on Econ. Educ.; mem. Bd of Dirs Execs' Club of Chicago, Chicagoland Chamber of Commerce; mem. Global Markets Advisory Cttee Commodity Futures Trading Comm., Advisory Council Youth Services of Glenview/Northbrook. *Address:* CME Group Inc., 20 South Wacker Drive, Chicago, IL 60606, USA (office). *Telephone:* (312) 930-1000 (office). *E-mail:* info@cme.com (office). *Website:* www.cme.com (office).

DONOVAN, Shaun L., BA, MA, MPA; American architect and government official; *Secretary of Housing and Urban Development;* b. 24 Jan. 1966, New York City; m. Liza Donovan (née Gilbert); two s.; ed Harvard Univ.; worked as an architect in New York and Italy; Asst Dir Community Preservation Corpn, New York City; Special Asst US Dept of Housing and Urban Devt, Washington, DC 1998–2000, Deputy Asst Sec. for Multifamily Housing 2000–01; acting Fed. Housing Admin Commr during the presidential transition 2000–01; Visiting Scholar, New York Univ.; consultant to Millennial Housing Comm., Washington, DC 2001–02; Man. Dir of FHA lending and affordable housing investments, Prudential Mortgage Capital Co. 2002–04; Commr New York City Dept of Housing Preservation and Devt 2004–08; US Sec. of Housing and Urban Devt, Washington, DC 2009–. *Address:* Department of Housing and Urban Development, 451 Seventh St, SW, Washington, DC 20410, USA (office). *Telephone:* (202) 708-1112 (office). *Fax:* (202) 708-0299 (office). *Website:* www.hud.gov (office).

DOODY, Margaret Anne, BA, MA, PhD; Canadian academic and writer; *John and Barbara Glynn Family Professor of Literature, University of Notre Dame;* b. 21 Sept. 1939, St John, NB; d. of Rev. Hubert Doody and Anne Ruth Cornwall; ed Centreville Regional High School, NB, Dalhousie Univ., Halifax, Lady Margaret Hall, Oxford, UK; Instructor in English 1962–64; Asst Prof., English Dept, Vic. Univ. 1968–69; Lecturer, Univ. Coll. of Swansea, UK 1969–77; Visiting Assoc. Prof. of English, Univ. of California, Berkeley 1976–77, Assoc. Prof. 1977–80; Prof. of English, Princeton Univ., NJ 1980–89; Andrew W. Mellon Prof. of Humanities and Prof. of English, Vanderbilt Univ., Nashville, Tenn. 1989–99, Dir Comparative Literature 1992–99; John and Barbara Glynn Family Prof. of Literature, Univ. of Notre Dame, Ind. 2000–, Dir PhD Program in Literature 2001–07; Stanley Kelley Jr Visiting Prof. for Distinguished Teaching, Princeton Univ. 2008–09; Commonwealth Fellowship 1960–62, Canada Council Fellowship 1964–65, Imperial Oil Fellowship 1965–68, Guggenheim Foundation Fellowship 1978, Nat. Endowment for the Humanities Fellowship 2007; Hon. LLD (Dalhousie) 1985; Rose Mary

Crawshay Prize 1986. *Play:* Clarissa (co-writer), New York 1984. *Publications:* non-fiction: A Natural Passion: A Study of the Novels of Samuel Richardson 1974, The Daring Muse 1985, Frances Burney: The Life in the Works 1988, Samuel Richardson: Tercentenary Essays (ed. with Peter Sabor) 1989, The True Story of the Novel 1996, Anne of Green Gables (co-ed. with Wendy Barry and Mary Doody Jones) 1997, Tropic of Venice 2007; Aristotle detective series: Aristotle Detective 1978, Aristotle and the Fatal Javelin (short story) 1980, Aristotle and the Poetic Justice 2002, Aristotle and the Secrets of Life 2003, Poison in Athens (novel) 2004, Mysteries of Eleusis (novel) 2005, Annello di Bronzo (novella); other fiction: The Alchemists (novel) 1980. *Leisure interests:* travel, looking at ancient buildings, paintings and mosaics, reading detective fiction, visiting Venice, swimming in the sea, music (Mozart, bluegrass). *Address:* English Department, 356 O'Shaughnessy Hall, University of Notre Dame, Notre Dame, IN 46556 (office); 435 Edgewater Drive, Mishawaka, IN 46545, USA (home). *Telephone:* (574) 257-7927 (home). *E-mail:* mdoody@nd.edu (office); margaret.doody.1@nd.edu (office). *Website:* www.nd.edu/~mdoody (office).

DOOGE, James Clement Ignatius, ME, MSc; Irish engineer, politician and academic; *Professor Emeritus, University College Dublin;* b. 30 July 1922, Birkenhead, England; s. of Denis Patrick and Veronica Catherine (née Carroll) Dooge; m. Veronica O'Doherty 1946 (died 1991); two s. three d.; ed Christian Brothers' School, Dún Laoghaire, Univ. Coll., Dublin, Iowa, USA; Jr Civil Engineer, Irish Office of Public Works 1943–46; Design Engineer, ESB 1946–58; Prof. of Civil Eng, Univ. Coll., Cork 1958–70, Univ. Coll., Dublin 1970–81, 1982–84, now Prof. Emer.; Minister for Foreign Affairs 1981–82; Leader Irish Senate 1983–87; consultant UN specialized agencies, EC; Pres. Royal Irish Acad. 1987–90, Int. Asscn for Hydrological Sciences 1975–79; mem. Exec. Bureau Int. Union for Geodesy and Geophysics 1979–87; Pres. ICSU 1993–96; mem. Royal Acad. of Eng; Hon. Agric. Science Degree 1978, Hon. DTech 1980, Hon. DSc (Birmingham), Hon. ScD (Dublin) 1988, Hon. D Eng (Edin.) 2000, Hon. Dr (Kraków) 2000, (Madrid) 2001; Horton Award 1959, Bowie Medal (American Geophysical Union) 1986; Kettle Plaque 1948, 1985 and Mullins Medal 1951, 1962 (Inst. of Engineers of Ireland), John Dalton Medal 1998, Int. Prize for Meteorology 1999. *Address:* Centre for Water Resources Research, University College, Earlsfort Terrace, Dublin 2 (office); 2 Belgrave Road, Monkstown, Co. Dublin, Ireland (home). *Telephone:* 7167499 (office); 2805515 (home). *Fax:* 7167399 (office); 2806583 (home).

DOOKERAN, Winston, BA, MSc; Trinidad and Tobago economist; *Leader, Congress of the People;* b. 24 June 1943, Trinidad and Tobago; m. Shirley Dookeran; one s.; ed Univ. of Manitoba, Canada, London School of Econs; Lecturer in Econs, Univ. of the West Indies 1971–81, 1981–86; MP for Chaguanas constituency 1981–91, MP for St Augustine 2002–; Minister of Planning and Mobilization, Vice-Chair. Nat. Planning Comm. 1986–91; Dir Price-Waterhouse Man. Consultants and to the Caribbean Govs 1992–95; Fellow, Center for Int. Affairs, Harvard Univ. 1993–95; Sr Economist UN ECLAC 1995–97; fmr Gov. Cen. Bank of Trinidad and Tobago 1997–2002; Visiting Scholar, Weatherhead Center for Int. Affairs Harvard Univ. 2002–03; Leader, United Nat. Congress 2005–06, Congress of the People 2006–; Hon. LLD (Univ. of Manitoba) 1991. *Publications:* Choices and Change: Reflections on the Caribbean (ed.) 1996, The Caribbean Quest: Directions for Structural Reforms in a Global Economy (co-ed.) 1999, Uncertainty, Stability and Challenges 2006. *Address:* Systematics Studies Ltd, St Augustine, Trinidad (office). *Telephone:* (868) 645-8466 (office); (868) 640-5694 (home). *Fax:* (868) 645-8467 (office). *E-mail:* wdookeran@tstt.net.tt (home). *Website:* www.winstondookeran.com (home).

DÖPFNER, Mathias, MA, PhD; German publishing executive; *CEO and Chairman, Axel Springer AG;* b. 15 Jan. 1963, Bonn; m.; journalist, Frankfurter Allgemeine Zeitung 1982; dir public relations agency 1988–90; fmr Asst to CEO, Gruner & Jahr, Hamburg; Ed.-in-Chief Wochenpost, Berlin 1994–96, Hamburger Morgenpost 1996–98; joined Axel Springer AG 1998, Ed.-in-Chief Die Welt 1998–2000, mem. Man. Bd, Multimedia Div. 2000–, Head of Newspapers Div. 2000–02, Chair. and CEO 2002–; mem. Bd of Dirs Time Warner 2006–; Axel Springer Prize for Young Journalists 1992, Golden Pen Award, Bauer Verlagsgruppe 2000, Journalism Award of German medium-sized businesses 2000, World Econ. Forum Global Leader of Tomorrow 2001, Berlin Order of Merit 2007, Leo Baeck Medal 2007, Jerusalem Award 2008, Global Leadership Award, American Inst. for Contemporary German Studies, New York 2008. *Publications:* Neue Deutsche Welle: Kunst oder Mode 1983, Erotik in der Musik 1986, Musikkritik in Deutschland seit 1945 1991, Brüssel: das Insider-Lexikon 1992, Axel Springer: Neue Blicke auf den Verleger (ed.) 2005, Ernst Cramer: Ich habe es erlebt (ed.) 2008. *Address:* Axel Springer AG, Axel-Springer-Straße 65, 10888 Berlin, Germany (office). *Telephone:* (30) 2591-0 (office). *Website:* www.axelspringer.com (office).

DORAKUMBURE, Wijeratne Bandara; Sri Lankan diplomatist; High Commr to Pakistan 2007–. *Address:* High Commission of Sri Lanka, 2c, St 55, F-6/4, Islamabad, Pakistan (office). *Telephone:* (51) 2828723 (office). *Fax:* (51) 2828751 (office). *E-mail:* srilanka@isb.comsats.net.pk (office).

DORAN, Seán; Irish/Australian theatre director; b. 1958, Derry, Northern Ireland; ed Univ. of East Anglia and Goldsmiths Coll., London; dir music-theatre co., Bloomsbury, London 1988; Chief Exec. UK Year of Literature and Writing, NI 1995; Artistic Dir Belfast Festival, NI 1997–99; Dir Perth Int. Arts Festival, Australia 1999–2003; Artistic Dir and Chief Exec. ENO, London 2003–05.

DORDA, Abuzed Omar, BA; Libyan politician and diplomatist; b. 4 April 1944, Rhebat; m.; six c.; ed Benghazi Univ.; teacher 1965–70; Gov. Misurata Prov. 1970–72; Minister of Information and Culture 1972–74, Under-Sec., Ministry of Foreign Affairs 1974–76, Minister of Municipalities 1976–79, Sec.-

Gen. People's Cttee for Economy 1979–82, for Agric. 1982–86, for the Municipality of Al-Jabal Al-Gharbi 1986–90, Sec. of the Gen. People's Cttee (Prime Minister) 1990–94, Asst Sec. 1994–95; Perm. Rep. to UN 1997–2003. *Address:* c/o Permanent Mission of Libya to the UN, 309–315 East 48th Street, New York, NY 10017, USA (office).

DORDAIN, Jean-Jacques; French international organization official and professor of fluid mechanics; *Director-General, European Space Agency;* b. 14 April 1946; ed Ecole Centrale; researcher, Office nat. d'études et de recherches aérospatiales (ONERA) 1970–76, Co-ordinator of Space Activities 1976–86, Dir of Fundamental Physics 1983–86; joined ESA 1986, Head of Space Station and Platforms Promotion and Utilisation Dept 1986, later Head of Microgravity and Columbus Utilization Dept, Assoc. Dir for Strategy, Planning and Int. Policy 1993–99, Dir Directorate of Strategy and Tech. Assessment 1999–2001, Dir of Launchers 2001–03, Dir-Gen. ESA 2003–. *Address:* European Space Agency, 8–10 rue Mario Nikis, 75738 Paris Cedex 15, France (office). *Telephone:* 1-53-69-76-54 (office). *Fax:* 1-53-69-75-60 (office). *Website:* www.esa.int (office).

DORÉ, Ousmane; Guinean economist and politician; *Minister of the Economy, Finance and Planning;* fmr Sr Economist, IMF Africa Dept, fmr IMF Rep. to Senegal and Guinea-Bissau; Minister of the Economy, Finance and Planning 2007–. *Address:* Ministry of the Economy and Finance, Boulbinet, BP 221, Conakry, Guinea (office). *Telephone:* 30-45-17-95 (office). *Fax:* 30-41-30-59 (office).

DORE, Ronald Philip, CBE, BA; British university professor; *Research Associate, London School of Economics;* b. 1 Feb. 1925, Bournemouth; s. of Philip H. B. Dore and Elsie C. King; m. Nancy MacDonald 1957; one s. one d.; one s. with Maria Paisley; ed School of Oriental and African Studies, London Univ.; Asst Prof. then Assoc. Prof., Univ. of BC 1956–60; Reader, LSE 1961, Hon. Fellow 1980; Prof., LSE and SOAS 1964–69; Prof. and Fellow, Inst. of Devt Studies, Sussex Univ. 1970–81; Tech. Change Centre, London 1982–86; Dir Japan-Europe Industry Research Centre, Imperial Coll., London 1986–91; Research Assoc., Centre for Econ. Performance, LSE and Political Science 1991–; Visiting Prof. Imperial Coll. of Science, Tech. and Medicine, London Univ. 1982, of Sociology, Harvard Univ. 1987; Adjunct Prof., MIT 1989–94; mem. British Acad. 1975–; Foreign Hon. Fellow, American Acad. of Arts and Sciences 1978, Hon. Foreign Fellow Japan Acad. 1986–; Order of the Rising Sun (Third Class) Japan; Japan Foundation Prize 1977. *Publications:* City Life in Japan 1958, Land Reform in Japan 1959, Education in Tokugawa Japan 1965, British Factory/Japanese Factory 1973, The Diploma Disease 1976, Shinohata Portrait of a Japanese Village 1978, Flexible Rigidities, Industrial Policy and Structural Adjustment in Japanese Economy 1986, Taking Japan Seriously: A Confucian Perspective on Leading Economic Issues 1987, Japan and World Depression, Then and Now (Essays) (Jt Ed.) 1987, How the Japanese Learn to Work (with Mari Sako) 1988, Corporatism and Accountability: Organized Interests in British Public Life (Jt Ed.) 1990, Will the 21st Century be the Age of Individualism? 1991, The Japanese Firm: the Source of Competitive Strength (Jt Ed.) 1994, Japan, Internationalism and the UN 1997, Stockmarket Capitalism, Welfare Capitalism: Japan and Germany versus the Anglo-Saxons 2000, Social Evolution, Economic Development and Culture 2001, Selected Writings of Ronald Dore 2002, New Forms and Meanings of Work in an Increasingly Globalised World 2004, Dare No Tame No Kaisha Ni Suru Ka? (Whom Should Corporations Serve?) 2006, Finanza Pigliatutto (Finance Takes All) 2009. *Address:* 157 Surrenden Road, Brighton, East Sussex, BN1 6ZA, England. *Telephone:* (1273) 501-370 (home).

DORENSKY, Sergey Leonidovich; Russian pianist and piano teacher; b. 3 Dec. 1931, Moscow; m. Nina Tserevitinova; one s.; ed Moscow State Conservatory (pupil of Grigory Ginzburg); winner Int. Competitions Warsaw 1955, Rio de Janeiro 1958; concert tours in USSR, Brazil, Japan, Italy, Germany, Australia, New Zealand, S Korea; teacher Moscow Conservatory 1957–, Prof. 1981, Dean Piano Faculty 1978–97; Vice-Pres. Russian Chopin Soc., Russian Rachmaninov Soc.; mem. jury of more than 75 maj. int. competitions, including Tchaikovsky (Moscow), Van Cliburn (Fort Worth), Mozart (Salzburg), UNISA (Pretoria); mem. Russian Acad. of Arts 1995; People's Artist of Russia 1988, Order of Friendship 1997. *Address:* Bryusov per. 8/10, Apt. 75, 103009 Moscow, Russia (home). *Telephone:* (495) 229-22-24 (home).

DORFF, Stephen; American actor; b. 29 July 1973, Atlanta, Georgia; started acting aged 9. *Films:* The Gate 1987, The Power of One 1992, An Ambush of Ghosts 1993, Judgment Night 1993, Rescue Me 1993, BackBeat 1993, S.F.W. 1994, Reckless 1995, Innocent Lies 1995, I Shot Andy Warhol 1996, The Audition 1996, Space Truckers 1997, City of Industry 1997, Blood and Wine 1997, Blade 1998, Entropy 1999, Quantum Project 2000, Cecil B. Demented 2000, The Last Minute 2001, Zoolander 2001, All For Nothin' 2002, Deuces Wild 2002, Riders 2002, FearDotCom 2002, Den of Lions 2003, Cold Creek Manor 2003, Alone in the Dark 2005, Tennis, Anyone? 2005, Shadowboxer 2005, World Trade Center 2006, .45 2006, Botched 2006. *Television films:* In Love and War 1987, Hiroshima Maiden 1988, The Absent-Minded Professor 1988, I Know My First Name is Steven 1989, Always Remember I Love You 1989, Do You Know the Muffin Man? 1989, A Son's Promise 1990, Earthly Possessions 1999, Covert One: The Hades Factor 2006. *Television series:* What a Dummy 1990. *Address:* c/o ICM, 8942 Wilshire Boulevard, Beverly Hills, CA 90211, USA.

DORFMAN, (Vladimiro) Ariel; Chilean/American writer and academic; *Walter Hines Page Distinguished Professor of Literature and Latin American Studies, Duke University;* b. 6 May 1942, Buenos Aires, Argentina; s. of Adolfo Dorfman; m. Angélica Dorfman 1966; two s.; ed Univ. of Chile, Santiago; Teaching Asst, Univ. of Chile 1963–65, Asst Prof. of Spanish Literature and Journalism 1965–68, Assoc. Prof. 1968–70, Prof. 1970–73; exiled after Chilean coup 1973; Maître des Conférences Spanish-American Literature, Sorbonne Paris IV 1975–76; Head Scientific Research, Spanns Seminarium, Univ. of Amsterdam 1976–80; Visiting Prof., Univ. of Maryland 1983; Post-Doctoral Fellow and Consultant Latin American Council, Duke Univ., NC 1984, Visiting Prof. of Literature and Latin American Studies 1985–89, Research Prof. of Literature and Latin American Studies, 1989–96, Walter Hines Page Distinguished Prof. of Literature and Latin American Studies, Center for Int. Studies and Romance Studies 1996–; Research Scholar Univ. of Calif., Berkeley 1968–69; Friedrich Ebert Stiftugn Research Fellow 1974–76; Fellowship at Woodrow Wilson Int. Center for Scholars 1980–81; Visiting Fellow, Inst. for Policy Studies 1981–84; Fellow, American Acad. of Arts and Sciences; Dr hc (Ill. Wesleyan Univ.) 1989, (Wooster Coll.) 1991, (Bradford Coll.) 1993, (American Univ.) 2001; Time Out Award 1991, New York Public Library Literary Lion 1992, Dora Mavor Award 1994, Int. Poetry Forum Charity Randall Citation 1995, Writers' Guild of Great Britain Best Film for Television 1995, ALOA Prize, Denmark 2002, Lowell Thomas Silver Award for Travel Book 2004. *Plays:* Widows (Kennedy Center New American Plays Award) 1988, Death and the Maiden (Olivier Award for Best Play, London 1992) 1991, Reader (Kennedy Center Roger L. Stevens Award) 1992, Who's Who (with Rodrigo Dorfman) 1998, Speak Truth to Power: Voices from Beyond the Dark 2000, Manifesto from Another World: Voices from Beyond the Dark 2004, Purgatorio 2005, Picasso's Closet 2006, The Other Side 2006, Dancing Shadows (with Eric Woolfson) 2007. *Film screenplays:* Death and the Maiden 1994, Prisoners in Time 1995, My House is on Fire 1997. *Publications:* fiction: Hard Rain 1973, My House is On Fire 1979, Widows 1983, Dorando la pildora 1985, Travesía 1986, The Last Song of Manuel Sendero 1987, Máscara 1988, Konfidenz 1995, The Nanny and the Iceberg 1999, Blake's Therapy 2001, The Rabbit's Rebellion 2001, The Burning City (with Joaquin Dorfman) 2003; poetry: Missing 1982, Last Waltz in Santiago and Other Poems of Exile and Disappearance 1988, In Case of Fire in a Foreign Land: New and Collected Poems from Two Languages 2002; non-fiction: How to Read Donald Duck (with Armand Mattelart) 1971, The Empire's Old Clothes 1983, Some Write to the Future 1991, Heading South, Looking North: A Bilingual Journey 1998, Exorcising Terror: The Incredible Ongoing Trial of General Augusto Pinochet 2002, Desert Memories: Journeys Through the Chilean North 2004, Other Septembers, Many Americas: Selected Provocations, 1980–2004 2004. *Address:* c/o Center for International Studies, Duke University, PO Box 90404, Durham, NC 27708, USA. *Fax:* (919) 684-8749 (office). *E-mail:* adorfman@duke.edu (office). *Website:* www.adorfman.duke.edu (office).

DORGAN, Byron Leslie, MBA; American politician; *Senator from North Dakota;* b. 14 May 1942, Dickinson, ND; s. of Emmett P. Dorgan and Dorothy (Bach) Dorgan; m. Kimberly Olsen Dorgan; four c. (one deceased); ed Univ. of North Dakota, Univ. of Denver; Exec. Devt trainee, Martin Marietta Corpn, Denver 1966–67; Deputy Tax Commr, then Tax Commr, State of ND 1967–80; Democrat mem. 97th–101st Congress from N Dakota 1981–93, mem. Ways and Means Cttee 1981–93; Senator from N Dakota 1993–, Asst Democratic Floor Leader 1996–99; Chair. Democratic Policy Cttee 1999–; mem. Cttee on Commerce, Science and Transportation, Cttee on Indian Affairs. *Publication:* Reckless! How Debt, Deregulation and Dark Money Nearly Bankrupted America... And How We Can Fix It 2009. *Address:* 713 Hart Senate Office Bldg, Washington, DC 20510-0001, USA. *Telephone:* (202) 224-2551 (office). *E-mail:* senator@dorgan.senate.gov. *Website:* dorgan.senate.gov (office).

DÖRIG, Rolf, LLD; Swiss business executive; *CEO, Swiss Life Group;* b. 1957; m.; three s.; ed Univ. of Zürich, Harvard Business School, USA; called to the Bar, Zürich; joined Credit Suisse 1986, several exec. positions and in different geographical markets, Chief of Staff and Chief Communications Officer, Credit Suisse Group 1997–2000, mem. Exec. Bd responsible for Swiss corp. and retail banking 2000–02, also Chair. Switzerland, Credit Suisse Group 2002, Exec. Vice-Pres. Swiss Life Group (fmrly Swiss Life/Rentenanstalt), CEO 2002–; Vice-Pres. Kaba Holding Ltd, Rümlang; Vice-Chair. Danzer AG, Baar; Chair. Zürich Chamber of Commerce; mem. Bd of Dirs Swiss Insurance Asscn, Adecco Management & Consulting SA, Kaba Holding AG, economiesuisse, Zürich, SA, Grasshopper-Club Zürich. *Address:* Swiss Life, General Guisan-Quai 40, 8022 Zürich, Switzerland (office). *Telephone:* (43) 284-33-11 (office). *Fax:* (43) 281-20-80 (office). *E-mail:* info.com@swisslife.ch (office). *Website:* www.swisslife.com (office).

DORIN, Sir Bernard J., GCVO; French diplomatist; b. 25 Aug. 1929, Beauvais; s. of Gen. Robert Dorin and Jacqueline Dorin (née Goumard); m. Christine du Bois de Meyrignac 1971; two s. two d.; ed Univs of Paris and Lyon, Harvard Univ., USA, Institut d'Etudes Politiques, Paris, Ecole Nat. d'Admin; Attaché Embassy, Ottawa 1957–59; Political Directorate Ministry of Foreign Affairs 1959–63; Adviser to Sec.-Gen. 1963–64; Tech. Adviser to Pvt. Office of Minister of Information 1964–66, of Minister Del. with responsibility for Scientific Research and Nuclear and Space Questions 1966–67, of Minister of Nat. Educ. 1967–68, of Minister with responsibility for Scientific Research 1968–69; Chargé de Mission responsible to the Personnel and Gen. Admin. Dir Ministry of Foreign Affairs 1970–71; Amb. to Haiti 1972–75; Head Francophone Affairs Dept Ministry of Foreign Affairs 1975–78, of American Div. 1981–84; Amb. to S Africa 1978–81, to Brazil 1984–87, to Japan 1987–90, to UK 1991–93; Ambassadeur de France dignitaire 1992–; Conseiller d'Etat 1993–97; Officier Légion d'honneur, Ordre nat. du Mérite; Chevalier Order of Malta. *Publications:* Appelez-moi Excellence, Les Kurdes: destin tragique, destin héroïque 2005. *Leisure interests:* mountaineering, heraldry, naive painting. *Address:* 59 rue Michel Ange, 75016 Paris, France (home). *Telephone:* 1-44-49-95-95 (home).

DORIN, Françoise Andrée Renée; French actress, novelist, playwright and songwriter; b. 23 Jan. 1928, Paris; d. of late René Dorin and of Yvonne

Guilbert; m. Jean Poiret (b. Poiré) (divorced); one d.; at Théâtre des Deux-Ânes, then du Quartier Latin (Les Aveux les plus doux 1957), then La Bruyère (Le Chinois 1958); Presenter TV programme Paris-Club 1969; playwright and author 1967–; Chevalier, Légion d'honneur, Officier, Ordre nat. du Mérite, Arts et Lettres; trophée Dussane 1973, Grand Prix du théâtre (for L'Etiquette) 1981. *Songs include:* Que c'est triste Venise 1965, La danse de Zorba 1965, Qu'est-ce que vous voulez que j'en fasse 1965, La bourse et la vie 1966, C'est ton nom 1966, C'est pas croyable 1966, Au coin de mes rêves 1966, Dieu que ça lui ressemble 1966, Une chanson comme on n'en fait plus 1967, Mais mon coeur est vide 1968, Il n'y a en que pour la rose 1968, Il a fallu 1968, Depuis le temps 1968, Quand on a notre âge 1968, Le reconnais-tu? 1968, Pourquoi je t'aime 1968, Les souvenirs que l'on a pas eus, Les filles et les roses, Mourir de soif, Pourquoi pas nous, Téléphoner à Sylvie, Les Fans de Mozart, Tout était pareil, Dis-moi, Oh non, ce n'est pas toi 1976, Tous les chemins mènent à l'homme, Le tournant, L'humour ensemble, Ma dernière chanson, N'avoue jamais, Faisons l'humour ensemble, Les miroirs truqués 1982, Et s'il n'en restait qu'une, je serai celle-là 2006, On s'est aimé à cause 2006. *Plays include:* Comme au théâtre 1967, La Facture 1968, Un sale égoiste, Les Bonshommes 1970, Le Tournant 1973, Le Tube 1974, L'Autre Valse 1975, Si t'es beau, t'es con 1976, Le Tout pour Le tout 1978, L'Intoxe 1980, La valise en carton 1986, Les Cahiers Tango 1987, Et s'il n'en restait qu'un 1992; lyrics for Vos gueules les mouettes 1971, Monsieur Pompadour 1972, L'Etiquette 1983, Les jupes-culottes 1984, La valise en carton (musical comedy) 1986, L'âge en question 1986, La Retour en Toupaine 1993, Monsieur de Saint-Futile (Vaudeville) 1996, Soins intensifs 2001. *Publications:* novels include Virginie et Paul, La Seconde dans Rome, Va voir Maman, Papa travaille 1976, Les lits à une place 1980, Les miroirs truqués 1982, Les jupes-culottes 1984, Les corbeaux et les renardes 1988, Nini patte-en-l'air 1990, Au nom du père et de la fille 1992, Pique et Coeur 1993, La Mouflette 1994, Les Vendanges tardives 1997, La Courte paille 1999, Les Julottes 2001, La mouflette 2001, Le rêve party 2002, Tout est toujours possible 2004, Et puis...après 2005, En avant toutes 2007. *Address:* c/o Artmédia, 20 avenue Rapp, 75007 Paris, France.

DORIS, Ennio; Italian business executive; *Founder and CEO, Mediolanum SpA;* b. 3 July 1940, Tombolo; began career as salesman for Fideuram 1969; worked for Dival SpA 1971–82; started own fund man. co. Programma Italia 1982, expanded operations into banking and insurance, renamed co. Mediolanum SpA 1996. *Address:* Mediolanum SpA, Palazzo Meucci, Via Francesco Sforza, 15, 20080 Milan 3, Italy (office). *Telephone:* (2) 90491 (office). *Fax:* (2) 90493434 (office). *E-mail:* info@mediolanum.it (office). *Website:* www.mediolanum.it (office).

DORJE, Dasho Ugen; Bhutanese politician; b. 1969; fmr Speaker of the Tshogdu Chenmo (Nat. Ass.). *Address:* Tshogdu Chenmo Secretariat, Gyelyong Tshokhang, PO Box 139, Thimphu, postcode, Bhutan (office). *Telephone:* (2) 322729 (office). *Fax:* (2) 324210 (office). *E-mail:* lobzangdorji@nab.gov.bt (office). *Website:* www.nab.gov.bt (office).

DORJI, Lyonpo Chenkyab, MSc; Bhutanese diplomatist and international organization official; b. 1943, Haa Dist, western Bhutan; m.; three c.; ed Forestry Research Inst., Dehra Dun, Swiss Technical Inst., Zurich, Switzerland, Wood Tech. and Transport, Austria; joined Dept of Forests 1961, Dir –1984; Dir Bd of Int. Center for Integrated Mountain Devt (ICIMOD), Kathmandu, Nepal 1983–85; Jt Sec. Dept of Trade, Commerce, and Industry and Mines 1984–85; Sec. Ministry of Trade, Industries and Forests 1985–86; Sec. Nat. Planning Comm. 1986–88; Sec. Dept of Agric. 1986–88; Vice-Chair. and Deputy Minister of Planning Comm. (ind. charge) 1988–91; Cabinet Minister for Planning 1991, Chair. 1991–98; Chair. Nat. Environment Comm. 1992–98; served as mem. of several key insts of Royal Govt of Bhutan; Amb. to Thailand (also accred to Singapore and Australia, and responsible for Bhutan's relations with other SE Asian countries) –2005; Sec.-Gen. South Asian Asscn for Regional Cooperation (SAARC) 2005–08. *Publications:* The Bhutan Forest Act 1969, The National Forest Policy 1974. *Address:* c/o Ministry of Foreign Affairs, Convention Centre, PO Box 103, Thimphu, Bhutan. *Telephone:* (2) 321413.

DORJI, Damcho, BA, LLB, LLM; Bhutanese barrister; b. 1965, Chholing village, Gasa; ed Punakha Public School, Sherubtse Coll., Bombay Univ., India, int. legal studies in USA; joined High Court 1990; Drangpon in Gelephu, Mongar, Wangduephodrang and Punakh 2000–06; Dir Office of Legal Affairs May–Aug. 2006, Attorney-Gen. Aug. 2006–07. *Address:* c/o Office of the Attorney-General, PO Box 1045, Thori Lam, Lower Motithang, Thimphu, Bhutan (office).

DORJI, Lt-Gen. Goongloen Gongma Lam; Bhutanese military officer (retd); Inspector-Gen. Royal Bhutan Police; Chief of Operations Royal Bhutan Army –2005; Drakpoi Wangyel Medal. *Address:* c/o Royal Bhutan Army Headquarters, Lungtenphu, Bhutan.

DORJI, Dasho Karma; Bhutanese civil servant; *Secretary, Ministry of Trade and Industry*; *Chairman, State Trading Corporation of Bhutan;* ed St Joseph's Coll., Darjeeling, India, State Univ. of New York, USA; joined Ministry of Foreign Affairs 1974, various posts at missions to UN, USA and India, Amb. to Bangladesh (also accred to Maldives, Thailand and Repub. of Korea) 1989–93; Dir Dept of Power 1993–96, Jt Sec. for Power 1996–2000, Sec. Ministry of Trade, Industry and Power 2000–; currently Chair. State Trading Corpn of Bhutan; Man.-Dir Karma Group Org.; mem. Bd Bank of Bhutan, Bhutan Devt Finance Corpn, Bhutan Board Products Ltd; Pres. Bhutan Table Tennis Fed.; Nyekemship with Red Scarf and Sword of Honour 1998. *Address:* Ministry of Trade and Industry, Tashichhodzong, PO Box 141, Thimphu, Bhutan (office). *Telephone:* (2) 322211 (office). *Fax:* (2) 323617 (office). *E-mail:* kdorjee@druknet.bt (office). *Website:* www.mti.gov.bt (office).

DORJI, Lyonpo Kinzang, BA; Bhutanese politician, government official and central banker; *Chairman, Royal Monetary Authority;* b. 1951, Chali, Mongar Dist; ed Kolkata, India; Zonal Admin. for Sarpang, Zhemgang, Trongsa and Bumthang 1989–1991; Dir Gen. Ministry of Agric. 1991–93, Jt Sec. 1993–94, Sec. 1994–98, Deputy Minister 1998, Minister 1998–2003; elected Speaker Nat. Ass. 1997; Prime Minister, Chair. 2002–03; Minister of Works and Human Settlements 2003–07; Interim Prime Minister 2007–08; Chair. Royal Monetary Authority (cen. bank) 2008–, Dept of Planning, Tourism Council of Bhutan 2008–; Coronation Medal 1999. *Address:* Office of the Chairman, Royal Monetary Authority of Bhutan, PO Box 154, Thimphu (office); Tourism Council of Bhutan, PO Box 126, Thimphu, Bhutan. *Telephone:* (2) 323111 (office); (2) 323251. *Fax:* (2) 322847 (office); (2) 323695. *E-mail:* rma@rma.org.bt (office); dot@tourism.gov.bt. *Website:* www.rma.org.bt (office); www.tourism.gov.bt.

DORJI, Lyonpo Leki, BA; Bhutanese government official; b. 31 Dec. 1944, Rukubji, Wangduephodrang; ed Nanital Public School, India, Coll. of Mil. Eng, India, Victoria Univ. of Wellington, NZ; Third Sec. New York mission 1973–74; Second Sec., New Delhi mission 1974–75; Officer on Special Duty, Royal Secr. 1975–77; Head, Registration Dept 1978–80; Sec., Royal Secr. and to Ministry of Agric. 1980; Deputy Minister, Ministry of Agric. 1991–94; Deputy Minister, Ministry of Communications 1994, Minister of Information and Communications 2003–08; Red Scarf 1983, Orange Scarf 1991. *Address:* c/o Ministry of Information and Communications, POB 278, Thimphu, Bhutan. *Telephone:* (2) 327976. *Fax:* (2) 324860. *E-mail:* moic@druknet.bt. *Website:* www.moic.gov.bt.

DORJI, 'Rongthong' Kunley; Bhutanese politician; *President, Druk National Congress;* b. 7 Jan. 1939, Wangdicholing, Bhumthang; fmr businessman; moved to Nepal 1991; Founder-Pres. Nepal-based Druk Nat. Congress 1994–; currently battling extradition case in New Delhi since 1998. *Publications:* Silent Suffering in Bhutan Part I, Silent Suffering in Bhutan Part II, Call of the Drum (booklet), The Main Points Behind The Unhealthy Politics Being Played In The Democractic Process That Is Unfolding In Bhutan (booklet). *Address:* Druk National Congress, B-125, 1st Floor, Dayanand Colony, Lajpat Nagar IV, New Delhi, 110 024, India (office). *Telephone:* (11) 65641453 (office); (11) 26472636 (office). *Fax:* (11) 26472636 (office). *E-mail:* dnc@bhutandnc.com (office); dnc2006@gmail.com (office). *Website:* www.bhutandnc.com (office).

DORJI, Lyonpo Sangye Ngedup, BA; Bhutanese politician and fmr diplomatist; *Leader, People's Democratic Party;* b. 1953, Nobgang, Punakha Dist; m.; four c.; ed Dr Graham's Homes School, Kalimpong, St Stephen's Coll., New Delhi, India; joined Bhutanese Foreign Service 1976, served at Perm. Mission to UN, New York 1977, First Sec., New Delhi 1986, Amb. to Kuwait 1986–89; Dir of Trade and Industry, Ministry of Commerce and Industry 1989–92; Jt Sec., Planning Comm. 1991; Sec. of Health 1994–95, of Health and Educ. 1995–98, Deputy Minister of Health and Educ. 1998–99, Minister of Health and Educ. 1999–2003; Chair. Council of Ministers 1999–2000, Prime Minister 2005–06; Minister of Agric. 2001–05; Leader, People's Democratic Party 2007–; Chair. Exec. Cttee WHO 1996–99; mem. Bd of Dirs Global Alliance for Vaccines and Immunization (GAVI); responsible for establishing Health Trust Fund, Nat. Tech. Training Authority, Nat. Employment Bd, Royal Univ. of Bhutan, Inst. for Zorig Chusum, Trashiyangtse, Be Somebody movt, Educ. Staff Welfare Fund, Youth Counselling, Scouts Programme, Land Man. Campaign; Red Scarf 1987, Orange Scarf 1998, Druk Thuksay Medal (Heart Son of Bhutan) 1999, Coronation Medal 1999. *Address:* People's Democratic Party, Drizang Lam, Lower Motithang, Thimphu, Bhutan (office). *Telephone:* (2) 335557 (office). *Fax:* (2) 335757 (office). *E-mail:* secretary@pdp.bt (office). *Website:* www.pdp.bt (office).

DORMAN, David W., BA; American telecommunications executive; b. 1954; ed Georgia Inst. of Tech.; began career in software devt, sales and marketing; joined Sprint Business 1981, Pres. 1990–94; CEO Pacific Bell 1994–96, later becoming Exec. Vice-Pres. SBC Communications; Chair., Pres. and CEO PointCast Network 1996–99; CEO Concert (global jt venture between AT&T Corpn and British Telecom) 1999–2000; Pres. AT&T Corpn 2000–02, mem. Bd of Dirs Feb. 2002–, Chair. and CEO July 2002–05 (after acquisition of AT&T by SBC Communications, now AT&T Inc.), now consultant; mem. Bd 3Com Corpn, ETEK Dynamics Ltd, Sabre, Science Applications Int. Corpn (SAIC), Scientific-Atlanta Inc., Int. Advisory Bd, British American Business Council; mem. Bd of Dirs Atlanta Symphony Orchestra; mem. Pres. Clinton's Advisory Cttee on High Performance Computing and Communications, Information Tech. and Next Generation Internet.

DORMANDY, John Adam, MD, DSc, FRCS; British surgeon; *Consultant Vascular Surgeon, St. George's Hospital;* b. 5 May 1937, Hungary; s. of Paul Szeben and Clara Szeben; m. Klara Dormandy 1982; one s. one d.; ed St Paul's School, London and Univ. of London; Resident in Surgery, St George's Hosp. Medical School 1963–65, Lecturer in Applied Physiology 1970–74, Sr Lecturer in Surgery 1975–80, Prof. of Vascular Sciences 1995–; Consultant Vascular Surgeon, St James' and St George's Hosp. 1973–; Pres. of Section of Clinical Medicine, Royal Soc. of Medicine 1978; Pres. Venous Forum 1984; Chair. Int. Soc. of Haemorheology 1982; Examiner in Physiology, Royal Coll. of Surgeons 1984, Hunterian Prof. 1970; Hamilton Bailey Prize in Surgery 1973, Fahreus Medal 1983. *Publications:* numerous articles in books and scientific journals. *Leisure interests:* tennis, skiing. *Address:* Department of Vascular Surgery, St George's Hospital, Ingleby House, Blackshaw Road, London, SW17 0QT (office); 82 East Hill, London, SW18 2HG, England (home). *Telephone:* (20) 8767-8346. *E-mail:* dormandyjohn@aol.com (home).

DORMANN, Jürgen; German business executive; *Chairman, Adecco;* b. 1940; ed Heidelberg Univ.; began career with Hoechst AG 1963, Finance and

Accounting Dir 1987–94, Chair. Man. Bd 1994–2002, apptd Chair. Bd of Dirs 1999, oversaw merger of Hoechst AG with Rhône-Poulenc SA to create Aventis SA, CEO Aventis SA 1994–99, Chair. Man. Bd 1999–2002, Chair. Group Supervisory Bd 2002–04, Vice-Chair. Sanofi-Aventis 2004; Dir ABB (Asea Brown Boveri) Ltd 1998–, Chair. 2001–07, CEO 2002–04; Dir Adecco 2004–, Chair. 2007–; Dir IBM 1996– (mem. Audit Cttee), BG Group (UK); mem. Supervisory Bd Allianz AG 1999–; mem. European Chemical Industry Council 2000–. *Address:* Adecco, Sägereistrasse 10, PO Box, 8152 Glattbrugg, Switzerland (office). *Telephone:* (44) 878-8888 (office). *Fax:* (44) 829-8888 (office). *E-mail:* info@adecco.com (office). *Website:* www.adecco.com (office).

DORMENT, Richard, MA, MPhil, PhD; British art critic; b. 15 Nov. 1946, Montclair, NJ; s. of James Dorment and Marguerite Dorment (née O'Callaghan); m. 1st Kate S. Ganz 1970 (divorced 1981); one s. one d.; m. 2nd Harriet Mary Waugh 1985; ed Georgetown Prep. School, Princeton and Columbia Univs; Asst Curator European Painting Phila Museum of Art 1973–76; Curator Alfred Gilbert: Sculptor and Goldsmith Exhbn, RA, London 1985–86; art critic Country Life 1986; Co-Curator James McNeill Whistler Exhbn, Tate Gallery 1994–95; art critic Daily Telegraph 1986–; reviewer for New York Review of Books; contrib. to Burlington Magazine, Times Literary Supplement, Literary Review; Trustee, Watts Gallery 1996–, Wallace Collection, London 2004–; mem. British Council Advisory Cttee 1996–, Govt Art Collection Advisory Cttee 1996–; mem. Reviewing Cttee on Export of Works of Art 1996–2002; mem. Judging Panel, Turner Prize 1989; Hawthornden Prize for Art Criticism in Britain 1992; Critic of the Year, British Press Awards 2000. *Publications:* Victorian High Renaissance (exhbn catalogue contrib.) 1976, Alfred Gilbert 1985, British Painting 1750–1900: A Catalogue of British Paintings in the Philadelphia Museum of Art 1986, Alfred Gilbert: Sculptor and Goldsmith 1986, James McNeill Whistler (with Margaret MacDonald) 1994, Manet and the Sea (exhbn catalogue contrib.) 2003, Pre-Raphaelite and Other Masters: The Andrew Lloyd Webber Collection (exhbn catalogue contrib.) 2003. *Address:* 10 Clifton Villas, London, W9 2PH, England (home).

DORN, Dieter; German theatre director; *Manager, Bayerisches Staatsschauspiel;* b. 31 Oct. 1935, Leipzig; ed Theaterhochschule, Leipzig and Max-Reinhardt-Schule, Berlin; actor, producer and dir in Hanover 1958–68; Dir in Essen and Oberhausen 1968–70; Dir at Deutsches Schauspielhaus, Hamburg 1971, Burgtheater, Vienna 1972, 1976; Dir at Staatliche Schauspielbühnen, Berlin 1972–75, Salzburg Festival 1974, 1982, 1986; Chief Dir Münchner Kammerspiele (producing works by Lessing, Goethe, Büchner, Shakespeare etc.) 1976–83, Man. (Intendant) 1983–2001; Man. (Intendant) Bayerisches Staatsschauspiel 2001–; has also directed opera productions in Vienna, Munich, Kassel, New York and at Salzburg, Bayreuth and Ludwigsburg festivals; mem. Akademie der Künste, Berlin, Bayerische Akademie der Schönen Künste. *Address:* Bayerisches Staatsschauspiel, Max-Joseph-Platz 1, 80539 Munich, Germany (office). *Telephone:* (21) 852000 (office). *Fax:* (21) 852005 (office). *Website:* www.bayerischesstaatsschauspiel.de (office).

DORN, Ludwik, MA; Polish politician; b. 5 June 1954, Warsaw; m.; three c.; ed Warsaw Univ.; involved in anti-communist opposition; participated in ind. meetings of 1st Warsaw Scout's Czarna Jedynka; activist Workers' Defence Cttee; mem. editorial team underground newspaper Głos, Solidarity, KSR; f. Documentation and Analysis Centre; Ed. Wiadomości underground newspaper; mem., then Deputy Chair. Centre Accord party; Head of Analysis Team Chancellery of Pres. of Repub. of Poland 1991; co-f. Law and Justice party, currently Deputy Chair.; Deputy III and IV Sejm (Parl.); Chair. Parl. Club of Law and Justice Party 2002–; Deputy Prime Minister 2005–07; Minister of Interior and Admin 2005–07 (resgnd); Marshal Sejm (Parl. Ass.) 2007. *Publications:* translated novels by John Le Carré and Len Deighton; O śpiochu tłuściochu i psie Sabie (About the Fat Sleepyhead and Saba the Dog); numerous literary essays. *Leisure interests:* roller blading, connoisseur of fine wines and cuisine. *Address:* c/o Sejm, ul. Wiejska 4/6/8, 00-902 Warsaw, Poland. *E-mail:* zjablon@sejm.gov.pl.

DORONINA, Tatyana Vasiliyevna; Russian actress; *Artistic Director, Moscow Gorky Arts Theatre;* b. 12 Sept. 1933, Leningrad; d. of Vasiliy Ivanovich Doronin and Anna Ivanovna Doronina; m. Robert Dimitrievich Takhnenko; ed Studio School of Moscow Art Theatre; Leningrad Lenin Komsomol State Theatre 1956–59; Leningrad Maxim Gorky State Bolshoi Drama Theatre 1959–66; Moscow Art Theatre 1966–71; Moscow Mayakovski Theatre 1971–83; Moscow Arts Theatre 1983–, Artistic Dir Moscow Gorky Arts Theatre 1987–; works as actress and stage dDir; People's Artist of the USSR 1981. *Theatre roles include:* Zhenka Shulzhenko (Factory Girl by Volodin), Lenochka (In Search of Happiness by Rozov), Sophia (Wit Works Woe by Griboyedov), Nadya Rozoyeva (My Elder Sister by Volodin), Nadezhda Polikarpovna (The Barbarians by Gorky), Lushka (Virgin Soil Upturned by Sholokov), Nastasya Filippovna (The Idiot by Dostoyevsky), Valka (Irkutsk Story by Arbuzov), Oxana (Loss of the Squadron by Korneichuk), Masha (Three Sisters by Chekhov), Grushenka (Brothers Karamazov by Dostoyevsky), Arkadina (The Seagull by Chekhov). *Films include:* Pereklichka 1965, Starshaya Sestra 1966, Yeshche Raz Pro Lyubov 1968, Tri Topolya Na Plyushchikhe 1969, Chudnyy Kharakter 1970, Machekha 1973, Kakaya U Vas Ulybka 1974, Na Yasnyy Ogon 1975, Kapel 1981, Valentin I Valentina 1985. *Address:* Moscow Gorky Arts Theatre, 119146 Moscow, 22 Tverskoi Blvd, Russia. *Telephone:* (495) 203-74-66.

DORR, Noel, MA, BComm; Irish diplomatist; b. 1 Nov. 1933, Limerick; s. of John Dorr and Bridget Clancy; m. Caitríona Doran 1983; ed St Nathy's Coll., Ballaghderreen, Nat. Univ. of Ireland, Georgetown Univ., Washington, DC, USA; Third Sec., Dept of Foreign Affairs, Dublin 1960–62, Embassy, Brussels 1962–64, First Sec., Embassy, Washington, DC 1964–70, Dept of Foreign Affairs, Dublin 1970–72, Counsellor (Press and Information) 1972–74, Asst Sec. and Political Dir 1974-77, Deputy Sec. and Political Dir 1977–80, Perm. Rep. to UN 1980–83; Amb. to UK 1983–87; Sec. Dept of Foreign Affairs 1987–95; Personal Rep. of Minister for Foreign Affairs, EU Intergovernmental Conf. 1996–97, 2000. *Leisure interests:* reading, swimming. *Address:* 19 Whitebeam Avenue, Clonskeagh, Dublin 14, Ireland (home). *Telephone:* (1) 2694086 (home). *Fax:* (1) 2603430 (home). *E-mail:* ndorr@eircom.net (home).

DORRELL, Rt Hon. Stephen James, PC, BA; British politician; b. 25 March 1952; s. of Philip Dorrell; m. Penelope Anne Wears Taylor 1980; three s. one d.; ed Uppingham School, Brasenose Coll. Oxford; Conservative MP for Loughborough 1979–97, for Charnwood 1997–, Parl. Pvt. Sec. to Sec. of State for Energy 1983–87, Asst Govt Whip 1987–88, a Lord Commr of Treasury 1988–90, Parl. Under-Sec. of State, Dept of Health 1990–92, Financial Sec. to Treasury 1992–94; Sec. of State for Nat. Heritage 1994–95, for Health 1995–97; Shadow Sec. for Educ. and Employment 1997–98. *Leisure interests:* aviation, reading. *Address:* House of Commons, London, SW1A 0AA, England. *Telephone:* (20) 7219-4472. *Fax:* (20) 7219-5838 (office). *E-mail:* dorrells@parliament.uk (office).

DORSAINVIL, Daniel, PhD; Haitian economist and government official; *Minister of the Economy and Finance;* b. 25 Aug. 1959, Port-au-Prince; ed Univ. of Pennsylvania, USA; fmr official, USAID; Econ. Advisor to Pres. Préval –2006; Minister of the Economy and Finance 2006–. *Address:* Ministry of Economy and Finance, Palais des Ministères, rue Monseigneur Guilloux, Port-au-Prince, Haiti (office). *Telephone:* 2227113 (office). *Fax:* 2231247 (office).

DORSEN, Norman, BA, LLD; American professor of law, civil libertarian and educator; *Frederick I. and Grace A. Stokes Professor of Law and Counselor to the President, New York University;* b. 4 Sept. 1930, New York; s. of Arthur Dorsen and Tanya Stone; m. Harriette Koffler 1965; three d.; ed Bronx High School of Science, Columbia Coll., Harvard Law School and London School of Econs, UK; law clerk to Chief Judge Calvert Magruder, US Court of Appeals, First Circuit 1956–57, to Justice John M. Harlan, US Supreme Court 1957–58; pvt. law practice, New York 1958–60; Assoc. Prof. of Law, New York Univ. Law School 1961–65, Prof. 1965–78, Frederick I. and Grace A. Stokes Prof. of Law 1978–, Counselor to the Pres.; Co-Dir Arthur Garfield Hays Civil Liberties Program; mem. Bd of Dirs American Civil Liberties Union 1965–91, Gen. Counsel 1969–76, Pres. 1976–91; Founding Pres. Soc. of American Law Teachers 1972–74, Pres. US Assn of Constitutional Law; Vice-Chair. US Dept of Health, Educ. and Welfare Review Panel on New Drug Regulation 1975–76, Chair. 1976–77; mem. Bd of Dirs Lawyers Comm. for Human Rights 1978–, Chair. 1995–2000, Thomas Jefferson Center for Protection of Free Expression 1990–; Dir Global Law School Program 1994–, Chair. 1996–2002; mem. Council on Foreign Relations; Chair., US Treasury Citizens' Panel on Allegations regarding Good O'Boys Round-up; consultant Americans for Religious Liberty; Fellow, American Acad. of Arts and Sciences; Founder and Editorial Dir I.CON, The Int. Journal of Constitutional Law; mem. Bd of Govs Int. Assn of Law Schools; Hon. LLD (Ripon Coll., John Jay Coll. of Criminal Justice); Minister of Justice's Medal (France) 1983, Eleanor Roosevelt award for Human Rights, various awards for civil rights and as legal educator. *Publications include:* books: Political and Civil Rights in the US (with others) 1967, Frontiers of Civil Liberties 1968, ACLU Handbooks Series (Gen. Ed.) 1971–95, Disorder in the Court (co-author) 1973, The Evolving Constitution 1987, Human Rights in Northern Ireland (with others) 1991, Democracy and the Rule of Law (co-ed.) 2001, The Unpredictable Constitution (co-ed.) 2002, Comparative Constitutionalism 2003; articles on constitutional law and civil liberties. *Leisure interests:* country living, aerobics. *Address:* New York University School of Law, Vanderbilt Hall, 40 Washington Square South, Room 308, New York, NY 10012-1099 (office); 146 Central Park West, New York, NY 10023, USA (home). *Telephone:* (212) 998-6233 (office). *Fax:* (212) 995-4030 (office). *E-mail:* dorsenn@juris.law.nyu.edu (office). *Website:* www.law.nyu.edu (office).

DORST, Tankred; German writer; b. 19 Dec. 1925, Sonneberg; s. of Max Dorst and Elisabeth Dorst; m. Ursula Ehler-Dorst; dir production of Ring, Bayreuth Festival 2006; mem. German PEN Centre, Bayerische Akad. der schönen Künste, Deutsche Akad. der darstellenden Künste, Deutsche Akad. für Sprache und Dichtung; several prizes including Gerhart Hauptmann Prize, Georg-Büchner Prize 1990. *Film as director and screenwriter:* Eisenhans. *Plays:* around 40 plays including Toller, Eiszeit, Merlin oder das wüste Land, Herr Paul, Was sollen wir tun, Fernando Krapp hat mir diesen Brief geschrieben, Die Legende vom Armen Heinrich, Karlos, Korbes, Ich bin nur vorübergehend hier 2007, Künstler 2008; several opera libretti; four plays for children. *TV films (writer and director):* Klaras Mutter, Mosch, Eisenhaus. *Publications:* Plays (vols 1–7), Merlins Zauber, Die Reise nach Stettin, Der schöne Ort, Sich im Ordischen zü uben, Plays (vol 8) 2008. *Address:* Karl Theodor Strasse 102, 80796 Munich, Germany (home). *Fax:* (89) 3073256.

DORUK, Mustafa, PhD; Turkish engineer and academic; *Professor of Metallurgical Engineering, Middle East Technical University;* b. 23 Feb. 1932; ed School of Eng, Yildiz, Technische Hochschule, Darmstadt, Germany; Asst Prof., Dept of Metallurgical Eng, Middle East Tech. Univ., Turkey 1963–70, Assoc. Prof. 1970–76, Prof. 1976–, Chair. of Dept 1965–69, of Dept of Metallurgical and Materials Eng 1988–97; Asst Pres. and Acting Pres. Middle East Tech. Univ. 1974–77, Dean Faculty of Eng 1978–85; UN Scholar, UCLA, USA 1972–73; Visiting Prof. Technische Hochschule, Darmstadt 1979; mem. Structure and Materials Panel of NATO/AGARD, Int. Congress on Corrosion, Founding mem. Corrosion Assn of Turkey; mem. Chamber of Turkish Metallurgical Engineers; Fellow Islamic Acad. of Sciences; Hon. Senator, Technical Univ. Darmstadt. *Publications:* over 50 publs. *Address:* Middle East Technical University, Metallurgical and Materials Engineering Department, Room D-106, Ankara, Turkey (office); Islamic Academy of Sciences, PO Box

830036, Amman, Jordan (office). *Telephone:* (312) 2102516 (office). *Fax:* (312) 2101267 (office). *E-mail:* doruk@rorqual.cc.metu.edu.tr (office). *Website:* www.mete.metu.edu.tr/People/Faculty/doruk/index.html (office).

DOS ANJOS, Carlos Gustavo; São Tomé and Príncipe government official and diplomatist; b. 1956; fmr foreign affairs adviser to Pres.; Minister of Foreign Affairs, Co-operation and Communities 2006–07. *Address:* c/o Ministry of Foreign Affairs, Co-operation and Communities, Av. 12 de Julho, CP 111, São Tomé, São Tomé and Príncipe (office).

DOS SANTOS, HE Cardinal Alexander José Maria, OFM; Mozambican ecclesiastic; b. 18 March 1924, Inhambane; ordained priest 1953, elected to Church in Lourenço Marques (now Maputo) 1974, consecrated Bishop 1975; Archbishop of Maputo 1976–2003 (retd); cr. Cardinal 1988. *Address:* c/o Paço Arquiepiscopal, Avenida Eduardo Mondlane 1448, CP 258, Maputo, Mozambique.

DOS SANTOS, Fernando (Nandó) da Piedade Dias; Angolan politician; *Speaker, National Assembly;* b. 1952, Luanda; ed Instituto Industrial de Luanda; involved with Grupo Boa Esperança from 1970 (pro-independence); nat. service, Portuguese colonial army 1973–74, deserted to join guerilla forces of Movimento Popular de Libertação de Angola (MPLA); mem. staff FAPLA (Armed Forces of MPLA), rank of Maj. 1984, Col 1986, Maj.-Gen. 1992; Insp., Corpo do Polícia Popular de Angola—CPPA (People's Police Force of Angola) 1976–78, Head of 1st Command Div. 1978–79, Head of Political Dept and Personnel Section in Nat. Directorate 1979–81, Nat. Dir of People's Police 1984–86; Deputy Head Nat. Political Directorate, Ministry of the Interior 1981–84, Nat. Dir of Personnel 1982–84, Deputy Minister of State Security 1984, Deputy Minister of the Interior 1984, also Head of Information Services 1990, Deputy Minister of the Interior responsible for Internal Order 1995–99, Minister of the Interior 1999–2002; elected Deputy People's Ass. 1986–; Commdr-Gen. and Gen. Commr of Nat. Police (Polícia Nacional) 1995–; Co-ordinator Exec. Cttee of Inter-Ministerial Comm. of Process of Peace and Reconciliation 2001, Nat. Comm. for Social and Productive Reintegration of Demobilized Troops and Displaced Persons 2002; Prime Minister of Angola 2002–08; Speaker, Nat. Ass. 2008–. *Address:* Assembléia Nacional, CP 1204, Luanda, Angola (office). *Telephone:* 222334021 (office). *Fax:* 222331118 (office). *E-mail:* assembleianacional@parlamento.ebonet.net (office). *Website:* www.parlamento.ao (office).

DOS SANTOS, José Eduardo; Angolan head of state; *President;* b. 28 Aug. 1942, Luanda; s. of the late Eduardo Avelino dos Santos and Jacinta José Paulino; ed Liceu Salvador Correia; joined Movimento Popular de Libertação de Angola (MPLA) 1961; went into exile 1961 and was a founder mem. and Vice-Pres. of MPLA Youth based in Léopoldville, Congo (now Kinshasa, Democratic Repub. of Congo); first Rep., MPLA, Brazzaville 1961; sent with group of students for training in Moscow 1963; graduated as Petroleum Engineer, Inst. of Oil and Gas, Baku 1969; then mil. course in telecommunications; returned to Angola and participated in war against Portuguese 1970–74; Second in Command of Telecommunications Services, MPLA Second Politico-Military Region, Cabinda; mem. Provisional Readjustment Cttee, Northern Front 1974; mem. MPLA Cen. Cttee and Political Bureau 1974–; Chair. MPLA; Minister of Foreign Affairs, Angola 1975; Co-ordinator, MPLA Foreign Relations Dept 1975; Sec. Cen. Cttee for Educ., Culture and Sport, then for Nat. Reconstruction, then Economic Devt and Planning 1977–79; First Deputy Prime Minister, Minister of Planning and Head of Nat. Planning Comm. 1978–79; Pres. of Angola 1979– and Chair. of Council of Ministers 1979–, also Prime Minister 1999–2002; C-in-C of FAPLA (Armed Forces of MPLA). *Address:* Office of the President, Protocolo de Estado, Futungo de Belas, Luanda, Angola (office). *Telephone:* 222370150 (office). *Fax:* 222370366 (office).

DOS SANTOS, Manuel, BSc (Econs); Mozambican politician and diplomatist; b. 7 May 1944; s. of Armando Augusto dos Santos and Luisa Chapassuca; m. Dabanga Diana dos Santos 1966; mem. Mozambique Liberation Front Exec. Cttee 1967–77, Nat. Treasurer, Sec. for Econ. Affairs 1967–73; mem. Frente de Libertação de Moçambique (FRELIMO) Cen. Cttee 1967–91; Public Relations Officer to Prime Minister's Office 1974–75; Dir Foreign Trade at Ministry for Industry and Trade 1975–76; Gen. Sec. Ministry of Foreign Affairs 1977–78; Minister for Internal Trade 1978–80; Amb. to Tanzania 1980–83; Amb. and Perm. Rep. of Mozambique to UN 1983–89; Pres. Econ. and Soc. Council UN 1986; mem. Nat. Ass. 1972–; Deputy Minister for Foreign Affairs 1989. *Address:* c/o Ministry for Foreign Affairs, Avda Julius Nyerere 4, Maputo, Mozambique (office). *Telephone:* 744061 (office).

DOS SANTOS DINIZ, Abílio; Brazilian retail executive; *President, Companhia Brasileira de Distribuição;* b. 28 Dec. 1936, São Paulo; s. of Valentim Diniz; m.; two s. two d.; ed Getúlio Vargas Business Foundation, Columbia Univ., Ohio Univ., USA; joined Companhia Brasileira de Distribuição – Pão de Açúcar 1956, Vice Pres. 1989–96, CEO 1996–2002, Pres. Admin. Council 2000–; Admin. Emer. Regional Admin. Council of São Paulo 1983; f. São Paulo Supemarket Asscn; mem. Nat. Monetary Council 1979–89; mem. Superior Council Portuguese–Brazilian Community of São Paulo 2006–; Personality of the Year, Brazilian Asscn of Retail Mans 1971. *Address:* Grupo Pão de Açúcar, Avenida Brigadeiro Luís Antônio, 3126, Jardim Paulista, 01402-901 São Paulo, Brazil. *Website:* www.cbdri.com.br.

DOSBOL, Nur uulu, PhD; Kyrgyzstani politician; *Chairman, Jany Kyrgyzstan (New Kyrgyzstan) party;* b. 26 April 1948; ed Kyrgyz State Univ.; Jr Research Asst, History Inst. of Kyrgyz SSR Acad. of Sciences 1972–81, Intern-Researcher 1981–83, Sr Research Asst 1983–89, doctorate degree study 1989–92, Head of Dept, History Inst. 1993–95; Deputy of Zhogorku Kenesh (Parl.) 1995–2000; Minister of Educ., Science and Youth Policy 2005–07; Deputy Prime Minister 2007–08; State Sec. of Kyrgyzstan 2008–; Chair. Jany Kyrgyzstan (New Kyrgyzstan) party; fmr mem. Agrarian-Labor Party. *Address:* Jany Kyrgyzstan, 720000 Bishkek, Kiyevskaya 120, Kyrgyzstan (office). *Telephone:* (312) 21-19-61 (office). *Fax:* (312) 21-65-04 (office).

DOSHI, Balkrishna Vithaldas, ARIBA; Indian architect; b. 26 Aug. 1927, Pune; s. of Vithaldas Gokuldas and Radhaben Vithaldas; m. Kamala Savailal Parikh 1955; three d.; ed Sir J.J. Coll. of Arts, Bombay; Sr Designer, Le Corbusier Studio, Paris 1951–55; Prin., Vastu-Shilpa Architecture and Planning Firm, Ahmedabad 1956–77; founding mem. and First Hon. Dir School of Architecture, Ahmedabad 1962–72, School of Planning, Ahmedabad 1972–81; Dean, Centre for Environmental Planning and Tech. 1972–79, Dean Emer. 1981–; founder and Hon. Dir Kanoria School of Arts Ahmedabad 1984–; Vice-Pres. Council of Architecture, Govt of India 1973–74; mem. Advisory Bd, Architecture and Urbanism Publishing Co., Tokyo 1972–, Bldg Inst., London 1972–76, Int. Jury Panel, Competition for Urban Environment in Developing Countries, Manila 1975–76; Sr Partner, Messrs. Stein Doshi & Bhalla, New Delhi, Ahmedabad 1977–; f. mem.-trustee and Dir Vastu-Shilpa Foundation for Studies and Research in Environmental Design, Ahmedabad 1978–; Chair. Centre for Environmental Planning and Tech., Study Cell 1978–81; Chair. Panel of Juries, Int. Architectural Design Competition for the Indira Gandhi Nat. Centre for Arts 1987–; Fellow, Indian Inst. of Architects; Hon. Fellow, AIA 1971, Acad., Int. Acad. of Architecture 1989; awards include Padmashree award, Govt of India 1976; Pan Pacific Architectural Citation award, Hawaii Chapter of AIA 1981, Baburao Mhatre Gold Medal (Indian Inst. of Architects) 1988, Architect of the Year Award 1991. *Major works include:* Campus for Centre for Environmental Planning and Tech., Ahmedabad 1966, townships for Gujarat State Fertilizer Co. Ltd, Baroda 1968, Electronics Corpn of India Ltd, Hyderabad 1972, Dept of Atomic Energy, Govt of India, Kota 1972, Indian Farmers' Fertilizer Co-op. Ltd, Kalol 1973, Indian Inst. of Man., Bangalore 1977, Nat. Inst. of Fashion Tech., New Delhi 1989, Kharghar Node, New Bombay 1992, Office Complex for Bharat Diamond Bourse, Bombay, Husain-Doshi Gufa Museum 1992. *Publications:* numerous articles and contributions to architectural journals. *Leisure interests:* photography, studies of philosophy. *Address:* 14, Shree Sadma Society, Navrangpura, Ahmedabad 380009, India. *Telephone:* (79) 491610 (office); (79) 429344 (home).

DOSHI, Vinod, MSc (Eng); Indian business executive; b. 20 March 1932; s. of Lalchand Hirachand and Lalitabai Doshi; ed Albion Coll., Mich., USA and Univ. of Mich.; man. trainee, Cooper Eng Ltd (now amalgamated with Walchandnagar Industries Ltd) 1958, Dir in charge of operations 1960, Man. Dir 1970–75; Vice-Chair. and Man. Dir Walchandnagar Industries Ltd 1975, now Chair.; mem. Bd of Dirs, The Premier Automobiles Ltd 1972–, Chair. of Bd 1982–; Chair. and Dir numerous cos; mem. or fmr mem. of numerous Govt bodies etc. *Leisure interests:* colour photography, music and sound recording, amateur theatre and commercial cinema. *Address:* L. B. Shastri Marg, Kurla, Mumbai, 400070, India (office). *Telephone:* (22) 5115190 (office). *Fax:* (22) 5144000 (office).

DOST, Shah Mohammad; Afghan politician; b. 1929, Kabul; ed Kabul Univ.; mem. People's Democratic Party of Afghanistan 1963, mem. Cen. Cttee 1979; fmr Deputy Foreign Minister and Foreign Minister of the Democratic Rep. of Afghanistan; mem. Revolutionary Council; Minister of State for Foreign Affairs 1986–88; Perm. Rep. to UN 1988–90; Order of People's Friendship. *Address:* c/o Ministry of Foreign Affairs, Shah Mahmoud Ghazi Street, Shar-i-Nau, Kabul, Afghanistan.

DOSTAM, Gen. Abdul Rashid; Afghan politician and military leader; *Chief of Staff to Commander-in-Chief of Armed Forces;* b. 1954, Khowja Dokoh, Juzjan Prov.; fmr plumber; with Oil and Gas Exploration Enterprise 1979; undertook mil. training in USSR 1980; Commdr pro-Soviet Jozjani Dostum Militia, N Afghanistan 1980–92; Defence Minister in Pres. Najibullah's Govt (1986–92); allied with Gulbuddin Hekmatyar's Pashtun warriors and Shi'a guerrillas following transition of power 1992; est. Itehad Shamal/Northern Unity org. which controlled most N Afghanistan provs 1993–97; fled to Turkey when Taliban occupied Mazar-i-Sharif 1997; returned to fight with Northern Alliance (NA) against Taliban 2001; Deputy Minister of Defence 2001–04; presidential cand. 2004; Chief of Staff to C-in-C of Armed Forces 2005–; Leader, Junbesh-i Melli-i Islami (Nat. Islamic Movt), Uzbek mil. wing of NA –2005; mem. Jabhe-ye-Motahed-e-Milli (United Nat. Front) 2007–; f. Balkh Air (airline); awarded Hero of the Repub. of Afghanistan Medal by Pres. Najibullah. *Address:* c/o Ministry of Defence, Shash Darak, Kabul, Afghanistan.

DOTÉ, Elie, PhD; Central African Republic politician and government official; b. Bangui; m.; six c.; with Ministry of Agric. and Animal Husbandry 1974–80; fmr mem. staff African Devt Bank (ADB), Chief of Agric. and Rural Devt 2001; Prime Minister and Head of Govt of Central African Repub. 2005–08 (resgnd), Minister of Finance 2006–08 (resgnd). *Address:* c/o Office of the Prime Minister, Bangui, Central African Republic (office). *Website:* www.kodro.net (office).

DOTRICE, Roy, OBE; British actor; b. 26 May 1925, Guernsey, Channel Islands; s. of Louis Dotrice and Neva Wilton; m. Kay Newman 1946; three d.; ed Dayton and Intermediate Schools, Guernsey; air gunner, RAF 1940; POW 1942–45; acted in repertory 1945–55; formed and directed Guernsey Theatre Co. 1955; TV Actor of the Year Award 1968. *Stage appearances include:* Royal Shakespeare Co. 1957–65 (playing Caliban, Julius Caesar, Hotspur, Firs, Puntila, Edward IV, etc.); World War 2½, New Theatre, London 1966; Brief Lives (one-man play), Criterion (over 400 performances, world record for longest-running solo performance) 1969, toured England, Canada, USA 1973, Mayfair (over 150 performances) 1974; Broadway season 1974; Australian tour 1975; Peer Gynt, Chichester Festival 1970; One At Night, Royal Court 1971; The Hero, Edinburgh 1970; Mother Adam, Arts 1971; Tom Brown's

Schooldays, Cambridge 1972; The Hollow Crown, seasons in USA 1973 and 1975, Sweden 1975; Gomes, Queen's 1973; The Dragon Variation, Duke of York's 1977; Australian tour with Chichester Festival 1978; Passion of Dracula, Queen's 1978; Oliver, Albery 1979; Mr. Lincoln (one-man play), New York 1980, Fortune 1981, A Life, New York 1981, Henry V, Stratford, Conn. 1981, Falstaff (American Shakespeare Co.) 1982, Kingdoms, Broadway 1982, Churchill, Washington and Los Angeles 1983, The Genius, Los Angeles 1984, Enemy of the People, New York 1985, Hay Fever, New York and Washington 1985–86, The Homecoming 1991, New York, The Best of Friends, New York 1993, The Woman In Black, USA 1995, Moon for the Begotten (Tony Award) 2000. *Films include:* The Heroes of Telemark 1965, A Twist of Sand 1968, Lock up Your Daughters 1969, Buttercup Chain, Tomorrow, One of Those Things 1971, Nicholas and Alexandra 1971, Amadeus, The Corsican Brothers 1983, The Eliminators 1985, Shaka Zulu 1985, Young Harry Houdini 1986, Camila, L-Dopa, The Lady Forgets, The Cutting Edge, The Scarlet Letter, Swimming with Sharks, These Foolish Things 2006, Played 2006, Go Go Tales 2007, Hellboy II: The Golden Army 2008. *TV appearances include:* Dear Liar, Brief Lives, The Caretaker (Emmy Award), Imperial Palace, Misleading Cases, Clochemerle, Dickens of London, Stargazy on Zummerdown, Casualty 2005, Life Begins 2005–06, The Afternoon Play 2006, Heartbeat 2006; numerous American TV appearances including Remington Steel, Hart to Hart, Family Reunion, Magnum P.I., Fairy Tale Theatre, Beauty and the Beast, Tales of Gold Monkey, The Wizard, A Team, Tales from the Dark Side, Going to Extremes, The Good Policeman, Madigan Man. *Leisure interests:* baseball, fishing, riding. *Address:* 98 St Martin's Lane, London, WC2, England. *Telephone:* (20) 7836-7054.

DOTY, Paul Mead, BS, MA, PhD; American biochemist and academic; *Mallinckrodt Professor Emeritus of Biochemistry and Director Emeritus, International Security Program, John F. Kennedy School of Government, Harvard University;* b. 1 June 1920, Charleston, WV; s. of Paul Mead and Maud Stewart Doty; m. 1st Margaretta Elenor Grevatt 1942 (divorced 1953); one c.; m. 2nd Helga Boedtker 1954 three d.; ed Pennsylvania State Coll., Columbia Univ. and Univ. of Cambridge, UK; Instructor and Research Assoc., Polytechnic Inst., Brooklyn 1943–45, Asst Prof. of Chem. 1945–46; Asst Prof. of Chem., Univ. de Notre Dame 1947–48; Asst Prof., Harvard Univ. 1948–50, Assoc. Prof. of Chem. 1950–56, Prof. 1956, Pres. Science Advisory Cttee 1961–65, Mallinckrodt Prof. of Biochemistry 1968–88, Prof. Emer. 1988–, Prof. of Public Policy and Dir Int. Security Program 1988–90, Dir Emer. 1990–; Sr Fellow Harvard 1973–91; Dir of Center for Science and Int. Affairs, Harvard Univ. 1973–85; Consultant to the Arms Control and Disarmament Agency, Nat. Security Council; mem. Gen. Advisory Cttee on Arms Control 1977–81; mem. Bd MITRE Corpn 1975–92, Int. Science Foundation 1993–97; Founder, Ed. Int. Security 1975–85; Sr Fellow, Aspen Inst. Berlin (mem. Bd 1973–); Fellow American Acad. of Arts and Science, NAS, Philosophical Soc., Rockefeller Fellow, Univ. of Cambridge 1946–47. *Leisure interests:* reading, travel, computing. *Address:* Belfer Center for Science and International Affairs, Littauer-P-28, John F. Kennedy School of Government, Harvard University, 79 JFK Street, Cambridge, MA 02138 (office); 4 Kirkland Place, Cambridge, MA 02138, USA (home). *Telephone:* (617)495-1401 (office); (617) 864-6679 (home). *Fax:* (617) 495-8963 (office); (617) 864-3739 (home). *E-mail:* paul_doty@harvard.edu (office). *Website:* www.ksg.harvard.edu (office).

DOUANGCHAI, Maj.-Gen. Phichit; Laotian army commander and politician; *Deputy Prime Minister and Minister of National Defence;* fmr Mil. Chief of Staff; currently Deputy Prime Minister and Minister of Nat. Defence; mem. Politburo. *Address:* Ministry of National Defence, rue Phone Kheng, Ban Phone Kheng, Vientiane, Laos (office). *Telephone:* (21) 412803 (office). *Fax:* (21) 412801 (office).

DOUGAN, Brady W., BA (Econs), MBA; American banking executive; *CEO, Credit Suisse Group;* b. 1959; ed Univ. of Chicago, Ill.; began career in derivatives group of Bankers Trust; with Credit Suisse First Boston 1990–, fmr Co-Head, Global Debt Capital Markets Group and of Credit Suisse Financial Products marketing effort in the Americas, Head of Equities Div. 1996–2001, Global Head, Securities Div. 2001–02, Co-Pres. Institutional Securities 2002–04, mem. Exec. Bd, Chair. Man. Council and CEO, mem. Exec. Bd Credit Suisse Group 2004–07, CEO Credit Suisse Investment Bank 2004–07, CEO Credit Suisse Group 2007–. *Address:* Credit Suisse Group, PO Box 1, 8070 Zurich (office); Credit Suisse Group, Paradeplatz 8, 8001 Zurich, Switzerland (office). *Telephone:* (44) 212-16-16 (office). *Fax:* (44) 333-25-87 (office). *E-mail:* info@credit-suisse.com (office). *Website:* www.credit-suisse .com (office).

DOUGLAS, Barry, OBE; Irish pianist and conductor; b. 23 April 1960, Belfast, Northern Ireland; s. of Barry Douglas and Sarah Jane Douglas (née Henry); m. Deirdre O'Hara; two s. one d.; ed Royal Coll. of Music, London with John Barstow; pvt. study with Maria Curcio; London debut, Wigmore Hall 1981; toured Europe 1986–; regularly performs in USA; other concerts in Japan, USSR, Australia, Iceland, Czechoslovakia; recital debut in Carnegie Hall, New York 1988; Artistic Dir Camerata Ireland; winner of Tchaikovsky Piano Competition, Moscow 1986; tours USA, S America, Russia, Europe, Australia; has given numerous premieres of contemporary music by Buckley, Wilson, McCabe, Penderecki and O'Leary; Hon. FRCM; Hon. DMus (Belfast); Diploma Royal Coll. of Music, Emmy Award for Concerto, (Channel 4 TV programme) 1993, Diapason d'Or for Reger/Strauss recording 1998. *Recordings include:* Tchaikovsky Concertos Nos 1, 2 and 3, Sonata in G, Brahms Concerto No. 1, Piano Quintet in F Minor, Liszt concertos and Sonata in B Minor, Beethoven, Mussorgsky, Prokofiev, Rachmaninov Concerto No. 2, Berg, Reger, Strauss, Debussy, Britten, Corigliano, Penderecki Piano Concerto (with composer conducting), Beethoven Piano Concertos. *Television:* Rhapsody in Belfast (BBC documentary) 1978, After the Gold (ITV) 1987,

Playing for Peace Sky Artsworld) 2001. *Leisure interests:* driving, reading, food, wine, theatre. *Address:* IMG Artists, The Light Box, 111 Power Road, London, W4 5PY, England (office); Opus 3 Artists, 470 Park Avenue South, 9th Floor North, New York, NY 10016, USA (office). *Telephone:* (20) 7957-5800 (office); (212) 584-7500 (office). *Fax:* (20) 7957-5801 (office); (646) 300-8200 (office). *E-mail:* labrahams@imgartists.com (office); info@opus3artists.com (office). *Website:* www.imgartists.com (office); www.opus3artists.com (office); www.camerata-ireland.com (office); www.barrydouglas.com (home).

DOUGLAS, Denzil Llewellyn; Saint Christopher and Nevis politician; *Prime Minister and Minister of Finance, Sustainable Development, Information and Technology and Minister of Tourism, Sports and Culture;* Leader Saint Kitts-Nevis Labour Party; Prime Minister of Saint Christopher and Nevis, Minister of Finance, of Nat. Security, of Information, of Planning and of Foreign Affairs 1995–2001; Prime Minister and Minister of Finance, Devt Planning and Nat. Security 2001–04; Prime Minister, Minister of Finance, Sustainable Development, Information and Technology and Minister of Tourism, Sports and Culture 2004–; Chair. Bd Caribbean Devt Bank 2002–. *Address:* Office of the Prime Minister, Basseterre, Saint Christopher and Nevis (office).

DOUGLAS, James H. (Jim), BA; American state official; *Governor of Vermont;* b. 21 June 1951, Springfield, Mass; m. Dorothy Douglas; two s.; ed Middlebury Coll.; mem. Vt House of Reps 1972–79, Majority Whip 1975–77, Majority Leader 1977–79; Exec. Asst to Gov. of Vt 1979–80; Vt Sec. of State 1980–93; State Treas. 1994–2002; Gov. of Vt 2003–; fmr Pres. Nat. Asscn of Secs of State, Addison Co. Chamber of Commerce, Porter Medical Center; mem. Republican Town Cttee. *Address:* Office of the Governor, Pavilion Office Building, 109 State Street, Montpelier, VT 05609, USA (office). *Telephone:* (802) 828-3333 (office). *Fax:* (802) 828-3339 (office). *Website:* www.vermont .gov/governor (office).

DOUGLAS, Kirk, AB; American actor; b. 9 Dec. 1916, Amsterdam, NY; s. of Harry and Bryna (née Sanglel) Danielovitch; m. 1st Diana Dill (divorced 1950); two s. including Michael Kirk Douglas (q.v.); m. 2nd Anne Buydens 1954; two s. (one deceased); ed St Lawrence Univ. and American Acad. of Dramatic Arts; Pres. Bryna Productions 1955–; Dir Los Angeles Chapter, UN Asscn; Acad. Awards 1948, 1952, 1956; Commdr des Arts et Lettres 1979, Légion d'honneur 1985, Presidential Medal of Freedom 1981; New York Film Critics' Award, Hollywood Foreign Press Award, American Film Inst.'s Lifetime Achievement Award 1991, Kennedy Center Honors 1994, Hon. Acad. Award 1996, Lifetime Achievement Award Screen Actors' Guild 1999, Golden Bear, Berlin Film Festival 2000, Nat. Medal of Arts 2002. *Stage appearances include:* Spring Again, Three Sisters, Kiss and Tell, The Wind is Ninety, Alice in Arms, Man Bites Dog, The Boys of Autumn, Before I Forget. *Films include:* The Strange Love of Martha Ivers 1946, Out of the Past (aka Build My Gallows High) 1947, Mourning Becomes Electra 1947, I Walk Alone 1948, The Walls of Jericho 1948, My Dear Secretary 1949, A Letter to Three Wives 1949, Champion 1949, Young Man With a Horn 1950, The Glass Menagerie 1950, Along the Great Divide 1951, Ace in the Hole 1951, Detective Story 1951, The Big Trees 1952, The Big Sky 1952, The Bad and the Beautiful 1952, The Story of Three Loves 1953, The Juggler 1953, Un acte d'amour (Act of Love) 1953, 20,000 Leagues Under the Sea 1954, The Racers 1955, Ulisse (Ulysses) 1955, Man Without a Star 1955, The Indian Fighter 1955, Lust for Life 1956, Top Secret Affair 1957, Gunfight at the O.K. Corral 1957, Paths of Glory (also producer) 1957, The Vikings 1958, Last Train from Gun Hill 1959, The Devil's Disciple 1959, Spartacus (also exec. producer) 1960, Town Without Pity 1961, The Last Sunset 1961, Lonely Are the Brave 1962, Two Weeks in Another town 1962, The Hook 1963, The List of Adrian Messenger 1963, For Love or Money 1963, Strangers When We Meet, Seven Days in May 1964, In Harms Way 1965, Cast a Giant Shadow 1966, Paris brûle-t-il? (Is Paris Burning?) 1966, Grand Prix (producer) 1966, The Way West 1967, The War Waggon 1967, A Lovely Way to Die 1968, The Brotherhood (also producer) 1968, The Arrangement 1969, There Was a Crooked Man 1970, To Catch a Spy 1971, The Light at the Edge of the World (also producer) 1971, Gunfight 1971, Summertree (producer) 1971, The Special London Bridge Project 1972, Un uomo da rispettare (A Man to Respect) 1972, Cat and Mouse, Scalawag (also dir) 1973, Once Is Not Enough 1975, Posse (also dir and producer) 1975, Holocaust 2000 1977, The Fury 1978, The Villain 1979, Home Movies 1979, Saturn 3 1980, The Final Countdown 1980, The Man from Snowy River 1982, Eddie Macon's Run 1983, Tough Guys 1986, Oscar 1991, Welcome to Veraz 1991, Greedy 1994, Diamonds 1999, Family Jewels 2002, It Runs in the Family 2003, Illusion 2004. *Television work includes:* Tales of the Vikings (series, producer) 1960, Dr. Jekyll and Mr. Hyde 1973, Mousey 1974, The Moneychangers (mini-series) 1976, Victory at Entebbe 1976, Remembrance of Love 1982, Draw! 1984, Amos 1985, Queenie (mini-series) 1987, Inherit the Wind 1988, Two-Fisted Tales 1991, The Secret 1992, Take Me Home Again 1994, Touched by an Angel (series) 2000. *Publications:* The Ragman's Son: An Autobiography 1988, Dance with the Devil (novel) 1990, The Secret (novel) 1992, The Gift (novel) 1992, Last Tango in Brooklyn (novel) 1994, Climbing the Mountain: My Search for Meaning 1997, The Broken Mirror (novel) 1997, My Stroke of Luck 2002, Let's Face It 2007. *Address:* Warren Cowan Associates, 8899 Beverly Boulevard, Suite 412, Beverly Hills, CA 90048-2427 (office); The Bryna Company, 141 S El Camino Drive, Beverly Hills, CA 90212, USA (office). *Telephone:* (310) 274-5294 (office). *Fax:* (310) 274-2537 (office).

DOUGLAS, Michael Kirk, BA; American actor and film producer; b. 25 Sept. 1944, New Brunswick, NJ; s. of Kirk Douglas (q.v.) and Diana Douglas; m. 1st Diandra Mornell Luker 1977 (divorced); one s.; m. 2nd Catherine Zeta-Jones (q.v.) 2000; one s. one d.; appeared in TV series Streets of San Francisco; f. Further Films (production co.); Hon. DLit (Univ. of St Andrews, Scotland) 2006 Spencer Tracy Award 1999, UN Messenger of Peace 2000, Golden Globe

Cecil B. DeMille Award 2004, Career Achievement Award, Nat. Bd of Review 2007, Lifetime Achievement Award, American Film Institute 2009, David O. Selznick Achievement Award, Producers Guild of America 2009. *Film appearances:* It's My Turn, Hail Hero! 1969, Summertime 1971, Napoleon and Samantha 1972, Coma 1978, Running 1979, Star Chamber 1983, Romancing the Stone (also producer) 1984, A Chorus Line 1985, Jewel of the Nile 1985, Fatal Attraction 1987, Wall Street (Acad. Award for Best Actor 1988) 1987, Heidi 1989, Black Rain 1989, The War of the Roses 1990, Shining Through 1990, Basic Instinct 1992, Falling Down 1993, Disclosure 1994, The American President 1995, The Ghost and the Darkness (also exec. producer) 1996, The Game 1997, A Perfect Murder 1998, One Day in September (voice) 1999, Traffic 2000, Wonder Boys 2000, One Night at McCool's 2000, Don't Say a Word 2001, A Few Good Years 2002, It Runs in the Family 2003, Monkeyface 2003, The In-Laws 2003, The Sentinel 2006, You, Me and Dupree 2006, King of California 2007. *Films produced include:* One Flew Over the Cuckoo's Nest (Academy Award for Best Film 1975), The China Syndrome, Starman (exec. producer), Flatliners 1990, Stone Cold 1991, Eyes of an Angel (exec. producer) 1991, Radio Flyer 1992, Made in America (co-exec. producer) 1993, Face/Off (exec. producer) 1997, The Rainmaker 1997, One Night at McCools 2000, Godspeed, Lawrence Mann 2002. *Address:* c/o Creative Artists Agency Inc., 9830 Wilshire Boulevard, Beverly Hills, CA 90212; Furthur Films, 100 Universal City Plaza, Bldg. 507-4G, Universal City, CA 91608, USA. *Telephone:* (818) 777-6700 (Further Films). *Website:* www.michaeldouglas .com (office).

DOUGLAS, Hon. Sir Roger Owen, Kt; New Zealand politician and accountant; b. 5 Dec. 1937, Auckland; s. of Norman V. Douglas and Jennie Douglas; m. Glennis June Anderson 1961; one s. one d.; ed Auckland Grammar School, Auckland Univ.; entered House of Reps as Labour mem. for Manukau 1969 (now Manurewa); Minister of Broadcasting 1973–75, of the Post Office 1973–74, of Housing (with State Advances, Housing Corpn) 1974–75; Minister of Finance and Minister in Charge of the Inland Revenue Dept and of Friendly Socs 1984–87, of Finance 1988, of Police and Immigration 1989–90; MP for ACT Party List 2008–; Dir Brierley Investments 1990–98 (Chair. (interim) 1998); John Fairfax Ltd 1997–99, Aetna Health (NZ) Ltd 1997–99, Tasman Inst. 1997–; fmr Pres. Auckland Labour Regional Council, Manukau Labour Cttee; Finance Minister of the Year, Euromoney Magazine 1985, Max Schmidheiny Freedom Prize, Switzerland 1995, Ludwig Erhard Foundation Prize, Germany 1997, Friedrich von Hayek Medal, Austria 2002, Turgot Freedom Prize, Paris 2008. *Publications:* There's Got to be a Better Way 1980, Toward Prosperity 1987, Unfinished Business 1993, Completing the Circle 1996; several papers on int. and econ. affairs. *Leisure interests:* cricket, rugby, rugby league, reading, grandchildren. *Address:* 411 Redoubt Road, Manukau City 2016, Auckland, New Zealand (home). *Telephone:* (9) 2636928 (office); (9) 2639596 (home). *Fax:* (9) 2636938 (office). *E-mail:* rdouglas@xtra.co.nz (office). *Website:* www.rogerdouglas.org.nz (home).

DOUSTE-BLAZY, Philippe Jean Georges Marie, DenM; French politician and physician; b. 1 Jan. 1953, Lourdes; s. of Louis Douste-Blazy and Geneviève Béguère; m. Marie-Yvonne Calazel 1977; ed Lycée Pierre de Caousou, Toulouse and Univ. Paul Sabatier, Toulouse; Intern, Toulouse hosps 1976–82; Head of Cardiology Clinics and Asst to Toulouse hosps 1982–86; Univ. Prof. 1988–; Dir Arcol 1988–; Mayor of Lourdes 1989–2000, of Toulouse 2001–; mem. European Parl. 1989; Regional Councillor for Midi-Pyrénées 1992; Deputy to Nat. Ass. (Union pour la démocratie française) 1993, 1997–2001; Minister of Social Affairs, of Health and the City 1993–95, of Culture 1995–97, of Health and Social Protection 2004–05, of Foreign Affairs 2005–07; Pres. Union pour la démocratie française group, Nat. Ass. 1998–; mem. New York Acad. of Sciences and numerous medical orgs. *Leisure interests:* classical music, golf. *Address:* Assemblée nationale, 75355 Paris (office); Hôtel de ville, 31000 Toulouse (office); 1 rue de Bagnères, 65100 Lourdes, France (home).

DOUVILLE, Jean; Canadian business executive and lawyer; *Chairman of the Board of Directors, National Bank of Canada;* called to Quebec Bar 1968; joined UAP Inc. 1971, Pres. 1981, CEO 1982, Chair. 1994–; mem. Bd of Dirs Nat. Bank of Canada 1991–, fmr Chair. Audit and Risk Man. Cttee, Conduct Review and Corp. Governance Cttee, Chair. Nat. Bank of Canada 2004–; mem. Bd of Dirs Genuine Parts Co., Richelieu's Hardware Ltd 2005–; fmr Dir Leroux Steel Inc., Van Houtte Inc. *Address:* National Bank of Canada, National Bank Tower, 600 de la Gauchetière West, Montreal, PQ H3B 4L2, Canada (office). *Telephone:* (514) 394-5000 (office). *Fax:* (514) 394-8434 (office). *Website:* www.nbc.ca (office).

DOVE, Rita Frances, BA, MFA; American writer, poet and academic; *Commonwealth Professor of English, University of Virginia;* b. 28 Aug. 1952, Akron, OH; d. of Ray Dove and Elvira Dove (née Hord); m. Fred Viebahn 1979; one d.; ed Miami Univ., Ohio, Univ. of Tübingen, Germany and Univ. of Iowa; Asst Prof., Ariz. State Univ., Tempe 1981–84, Assoc. Prof. 1984–87, Prof. of English 1987–89; Prof., Univ. of Va, Charlottesville 1989–93, Commonwealth Prof. of English 1993–; Poet Laureate of the USA 1993–95, of the Commonwealth of Virginia 2004–06; Consultant in Poetry, Library of Congress 1993–95; Special Consultant in Poetry, Library of Congress Bicentennial 1999–2000; Assoc. Ed., Callaloo 1986–98, adviser and Contributing Ed. 1998–; adviser and Contributing Ed. Gettysburg Review 1987–, TriQuarterly 1988–, Meridian 1989–, Ploughshares 1992–, Georgia Review 1994–, Bellingham Review 1996–, Poetry Int. 1996–, Int. Quarterly 1997–, Mid-American Review 1998–, Hunger Mountain 2003–, American Poetry Review 2005–; Writer-in-Residence, Tuskegee Inst., Ala 1982; poetry panellist, Nat. Endowment for Arts, Washington, DC 1984–86 (Chair. 1985); judge, Pulitzer Prize in Poetry 1991 (Chair. of Jury 1997); mem. Bd of Dirs

Associated Writing Programs 1985–88, Pres. 1986–87; mem. jury Anisfield-Wolf Book Awards; Chancellor The Acad. of American Poets 2006–; mem. Acad. of American Poets, Associated Writing Programs, Poetry Soc. of America, Poets and Writers; Fulbright Fellow 1974–75, Nat. Endowment for the Arts grants 1978, 1989, Portia Pittman Fellow, Tuskegee Inst. 1982, Guggenheim Fellowship 1984, Rockefeller Foundation Residency in Bellagio, Italy 1988, Mellon Fellow, Nat. Humanities Center 1989, Fellow, Center for Advanced Studies, Univ. of Virginia 1989–92; 22 hon. degrees; Acad. of American Poets Peter I. B. Lavan Younger Poets Award 1986, Callaloo Award 1986, General Electric Foundation Award for Younger Writers 1987, Ohio Gov.'s Award 1988, Ohioana Library Book Award 1990, New York Public Library Literary Lion Award 1990, Nat. Book Award in Poetry 1991, NAACP Great American Artist Award 1993, Glamour Woman of the Year Award 1993, American Acad. of Achievement Golden Plate Award 1994, Folger Shakespeare Library Renaissance Forum Award 1994, Ohioana Library Book Award 1994, Charles Frankel Prize/Nat. Humanities Medal 1996, Heinz Award in the Arts and Humanities 1996, New York Public Library Literary Lion Award 1996, Sara Lee Frontrunner Award 1997, Barnes and Noble Writers Award 1997, Levinson Prize 1998, Ohioana Library Book Award 2000, New York Public Library Library Lion Award 2000, Duke Ellington Lifetime Achievement Award in the Literary Arts, Ellington Fund in Washington, DC 2001, Emily Couric Leadership Award 2003, Commonwealth Award of Distinguished Service 2006, Library of Virgina Lifetime Achievement Award 2008, Fulbright Asscn Lifetime Achievement Medal 2009. *Publications:* poetry: Ten Poems 1977, The Only Dark Spot in the Sky 1980, The Yellow House on the Corner 1980, Mandolin 1982, Museum 1983, Thomas and Beulah (Pulitzer Prize in Poetry 1987) 1986, The Other Side of the House 1988, Grace Notes 1989, Selected Poems 1993, Lady Freedom Among Us 1994, Mother Love 1995, Evening Primrose 1998, On the Bus with Rosa Parks 1999, Best American Poetry (ed.) 2000, American Smooth 2004, Sonata Mulattica 2009; prose: Fifth Sunday (short stories) 1985, Through the Ivory Gate (novel) 1992, The Darker Face of Earth (verse play) 1994, The Poet's World (essays) 1995. *Leisure interests:* playing the viola da gamba, classical voice training, ballroom dancing. *Address:* 219 Bryan Hall, University of Virginia, POB 400121, Charlottesville, VA 22904-4121, USA (office). *Telephone:* (434) 924-6618 (office). *Fax:* (434) 924-1478 (office). *E-mail:* rfd4b@virginia.edu (office). *Website:* www.people.virginia.edu/~rfd4b (office).

DOVER, Sir Kenneth James, Kt, MA, DLitt, FRSE, FBA; British classical scholar; b. 11 March 1920, Croydon; s. of Percy Henry James and Dorothy Valerie Anne (Healey) Dover; m. Audrey Ruth Latimer 1947; one s. one d.; ed St Paul's School, Balliol and Merton Colls, Oxford; served Royal Artillery 1940–45; Fellow and Tutor of Balliol Coll., Oxford 1948–55; Prof. of Greek, Univ. of St Andrews 1955–76, Chancellor 1981–2005; Pres. Corpus Christi Coll. Oxford 1976–86, Hon. Fellow 1986–; Visiting Lecturer, Harvard Univ. 1960; Visiting Prof. Univ. of Calif., Berkeley 1967; Prof.-at-Large Cornell Univ. 1983–88; Prof. Stanford Univ. 1987–92; FBA 1966–, Pres. 1978–81; Hon. Fellow, Balliol Coll. 1977–, Merton Coll. 1980–, Pres. Hellenic Soc. 1971–74, Classical Asscn 1975; Foreign mem. Royal Netherlands Acad. 1979–; Foreign Hon. mem. American Acad. of Arts and Sciences 1979–, also Royal Netherlands Acad.; Hon. LLD (Birmingham) 1979, Hon. DLitt (Bristol and London) 1980, (Liverpool) 1983, (Durham) 1984, Hon. LLD and DLitt (St Andrews) 1981, Hon. DHL (Oglethorpe) 1984; Kenyon Medal, British Acad. 1993. *Television:* main contrib. to The Greeks (BBC One) 1980. *Publications:* Greek Word Order 1960, Clouds (Aristophanes) 1968, Lysias and the Corpus Lysiacum 1968, (with A. W. Gomme and A. Andrewes) Historical Commentary on Thucydides, vol. IV 1970, vol. V 1981, Theocritus, Select Poems 1971, Aristophanic Comedy 1972, Greek Popular Morality in the Time of Plato and Aristotle 1974, Greek Homosexuality 1978, The Greeks 1980, Ancient Greek Literature (with M. L. West and others) 1980, Greek and the Greeks 1987, The Greeks and their Legacy 1989, Frogs (Aristophanes) 1993, Marginal Comment 1994, The Evolution of Greek Prose Style 1997. *Leisure interests:* gardening, historical linguistics. *Address:* 49 Hepburn Gardens, St Andrews, Fife, KY16 9LS, Scotland (home). *Telephone:* (1334) 473589 (home).

DOWELL, Sir Anthony James, Kt, CBE; British director, producer and fmr ballet dancer; b. 16 Feb. 1943, London; s. of Arthur H. Dowell and Catherine E. Dowell; ed Hampshire School, Royal Ballet School; Prin. Dancer, The Royal Ballet 1966, Sr Prin. Dancer 1967–84, Asst to the Dir 1984, Assoc. Dir 1985–86, Dir 1986–2001 (retd); joined American Ballet Theatre 1978; cr. roles in the following ballets: The Dream 1964, Romeo and Juliet 1965, Shadow Play 1967, Monotones 1969, Triad 1972, Manon 1974, A Month in the Country 1976; narrator in Oedipus Rex, Metropolitan Opera House, New York 1981; cr. role of Prospero in Nureyev's The Tempest, Royal Opera House, London 1982; dir new productions of Swan Lake and The Sleeping Beauty for Royal Ballet; designed costumes for Thaïs pas de deux (Frederick Ashton), In the Night (Jerome Robbins) and Symphony in C (George Balanchine) for Royal Ballet; Queen Elizabeth II Coronation Award, Royal Acad. of Dancing 1994, Critics' Circle Award 2001, De Valois Award for Outstanding Achievement in Dance 2002. *Address:* c/o The Royal Ballet, Covent Garden, London, WC2E 7QA, England. *Telephone:* (20) 212-9712 (office).

DOWELL, John Derek, PhD, CPhys, FInstP, FRS; British physicist and academic; *Professor Emeritus of Physics, University of Birmingham;* b. 6 Jan. 1935, Ashby-de-la-Zouch; s. of William E. Dowell and Elsie D. Dowell; m. Patricia Clarkson 1959; one s. one d.; ed Coalville Grammar School, Leics. and Univ. of Birmingham; Research Fellow, Univ. of Birmingham 1958–60; Research Assoc. CERN, Geneva 1960–62; Lecturer, Univ. of Birmingham 1962–70, Sr Lecturer 1970–74, Reader 1974–80, Prof. of Elementary Particle Physics 1980–97, Poynting Prof. of Physics 1997–2002, Emer. Prof. 2002–; Visiting Scientist, Argonne Nat. Lab. USA 1968–69; Scientific Assoc. CERN 1973–74, 1985–87; Chair. SERC Particle Physics Cttee 1981–85; mem. CERN

Scientific Policy Cttee 1982–90, 1993–96; mem. European Cttee for Future Accelerators 1989–93, BBC Science Consultative Group 1992–94, DESY Extended Scientific Council 1992–98; Chair. CERN LEP Cttee 1993–96; mem. CERN Research Bd 1993–96; Chair. ATLAS Collaboration Bd 1996–98; mem. UK Particle Physics and Astronomy Research Council 1994–97; mem. Court of Univ. of Warwick 1993–2001; mem. Council, Royal Soc. 1997–98, also Vice-Pres.; Fellow American Physical Soc.; mem. RAE Physics Panel, Higher Educ. Funding Council 2001; Rutherford Medal and Prize, Inst. of Physics 1988. *Publications:* numerous papers in physics journals. *Leisure interests:* piano, amateur theatre, golf. *Address:* School of Physics and Astronomy, University of Birmingham, Birmingham, B15 2TT (office); 57 Oxford Road, Moseley, Birmingham, B13 9ES, England (home). *Telephone:* (121) 414-4658 (office); (121) 449-3332 (home). *Fax:* (121) 414-6709 (office). *E-mail:* jdd@hep.ph.bham.ac.uk (office).

DOWLING, John Elliott, AB, PhD; American professor of neuroscience and neurobiologist; *Gordon and Llura Gund Professor of Neurosciences, Harvard University;* b. 31 Aug. 1935, Rhode Island; s. of Joseph Leo Dowling and Ruth W. (Tappan) Dowling; m. 1st Susan Kinney (divorced 1974); two s.; m. 2nd Judith Falco 1975; one d.; ed Harvard Coll., Harvard Univ.; Instructor, Harvard Univ. 1961, Asst Prof. 1961–64; Assoc. Prof., Johns Hopkins Univ. 1964–71; Prof. of Biology, Harvard Univ. 1971–87, Assoc. Dean 1980–84, Master, Leverett House 1981–98, Prof. of Ophthalmology, Harvard Medical School 1986–, Maria Moors Cabot Prof. of Natural Science 1987–2001, Harvard Coll. Prof. 1999–2001, Pres., Corp. Marine Biological Lab. 1998–2007, Gordon and Llura Gund Prof. of Neurosciences 2001–, Head Tutor, Neurobiology, Harvard Univ. 2006–; mem. NAS, American Acad. of Arts and Sciences, American Philosophical Soc.; Hon. MD (Lund, Sweden) 1982; Friedenwald Medal 1970, Retinal Research Award 1981, Prentice Medal 1991, Von Sallman Prize 1992, Helen Keller Prize 2000, Llura Liggett Gund Award 2001, Paul Kayser Int. Eye Research Award 2008. *Publications:* The Retina: An Approachable Part of the Brain 1987, Neurons and Networks 1992, Creating Mind: How the Brain Works 1998, The Great Brain Debate: Nature or Nurture? 2004; over 300 publs in professional journals and ed. of five vols. *Leisure interests:* sailing, squash, golf and music. *Address:* The Biological Laboratories, Harvard University, 16 Divinity Avenue, Cambridge, MA 02138 (office); 135 Charles Street, Boston, MA 02114, USA (home). *Telephone:* (617) 495-2245 (office); (617) 720-4522 (home). *Fax:* (617) 496-3321 (office). *E-mail:* dowling@mcb.harvard.edu (office). *Website:* www.mcb.harvard.edu (office).

DOWLING, Patrick Joseph, CBE, BE, PhD, FICE, FCGI, FREng, FRS; Irish university administrator; *Vice-Chancellor, University of Surrey;* b. 23 March 1939, Dublin; s. of John Dowling and Margaret McKittrick; m. Grace Lobo 1966; one s. one d.; ed Christian Bros. School, Dublin, Univ. Coll. Dublin and Imperial Coll. London; Sr Demonstrator in Civil Eng, Univ. Coll. Dublin 1960–61; Bursar in Structural Steelwork, Imperial Coll. London 1961–62, research on Steel Bridge Decks 1962–65; bridge engineer, British Constructional Steelwork Asscn 1965–68; Research Fellow, Imperial Coll. London 1968–74, Reader in Structural Steelwork 1974–79, Prof. of Steel Structures 1979–94, British Steel Prof. and Head, Dept of Civil Eng 1985–94; Vice-Chancellor and Chief Exec., Univ. of Surrey 1994–; Pnr, Chapman and Dowling Consulting Engineers 1981–94; Chair. Surrey Satellite Tech. Ltd 1994–; Chair. Eng Council 2001–; Pres. Inst. of Structural Engineers 1994–95; Fellow, Imperial Coll., London 1997; DL Surrey 1999; Hon. LLD (Nat. Univ. of Ireland) 1995; Dr hc (Vilnius Tech. Univ., Lithuania) 1996, (Ulster) 1998; Telford Premium, ICE 1976, Gustave Trasenster Medal, Asscn des Ingénieurs Sortis de l'Univ. de Liège 1984; several awards from Inst. of Structural Engineers. *Publications:* Steel Plated Structures 1977, Buckling Shells in Offshore Structures 1982, Structural Steel Design 1988, Constructional Steel Design 1992; over 200 refereed papers. *Leisure interests:* travelling, sailing, reading, good company, modern art, theatre. *Address:* Office of the Vice-Chancellor, University of Surrey, Guildford, Surrey, GU2 7XH, England (office). *Telephone:* (1483) 689249 (office). *Fax:* (1483) 689518 (office). *E-mail:* p.dowling@surrey.ac.uk (office). *Website:* www.surrey.ac.uk (office).

DOWLING, Vincent; American (b. Irish) actor, director, producer and playwright; *Founding Director and President-for-Life, Miniature Theatre of Chester;* b. 7 Sept. 1929, Dublin; s. of Mai Kelly Dowling and William Dowling; m. 1st Brenda Doyle 1952 (deceased); m. 2nd Olwen Patricia O'Herlihy 1975; one s. four d.; ed St Mary's Coll., Rathmines, Dublin, Rathmines School of Commerce, Brendan Smith Acad. of Acting; with Standard Life Insurance Co., Dublin 1946–50; Brendan Smith Productions, Dublin 1950–51; Roche-David Theatre Productions 1951–53; actor, Dir, Deputy Artistic Dir, Lifetime Assoc., Abbey Theatre, Dublin 1953–76, Artistic Dir 1987–89; Producing Dir Great Lakes Shakespeare Festival, Cleveland, Ohio 1976–84; Artistic and Producing Dir Solvang Theaterfest 1984–86; Prof. of Theatre, Coll. of Wooster, Ohio 1986–87; Producing Dir, Abbey Theatre 1989–90; Founding Dir and Pres.-for-Life, Miniature Theatre of Chester 1990–; residency Tyrone Guthrie Arts Centre, Annamackerrig, Ireland 2005; host Shooting from the Hip WXOT Northampton Valley Free Radio 2005–06; Co-Founder, Jacob's Ladder Trail Business Asscn; several distinguished visiting professorships at univs in USA; Hon. DFA (Westfield State Coll., Mass. John Carroll Univ., Cleveland, Ohio, Coll. of Wooster, Ohio 1999), DHumLitt (Kent State Univ.) 2003; European Artist's Prize, Loyola Univ. 1969; Outstanding Producer, Cleveland Critics Circle Award 1982 for The Life and Adventures of Nicholas Nickelby; Irishman of the Year 1982; Wild Geese Award 1988, Loyola Mellon Humanitarian Award 1989, Walks of Life Award, Irish American Archives Soc. of Cleveland 2000, Amb. (of Ireland to USA) Award 2005. *Film appearances:* My Wife's Lodger 1953, Boyds Shop 1959, Johnny Nobody 1963, Young Cassidy 1965. *Original plays:* The Fit-Ups 1978, Acting is Murder 1986, A Day in the Life of an Abbey Actor 1990, Wilde About Oscar, Another Actor at the White House (one-man show), The Upstart Crow (A Two-Person Play about Will Shakespeare) 1995, 4 P's (one-man autobiographical), The Miraculous Revenge (adapted; played, produced and co-directed) 2004. *Plays:* as producer: Arthur Miller's The Price 2005, Solomon 2005. *Radio:* role of Christy Kennedy (for 17 years) in The Kennedys of Castlerosse, Radio Éireann; writer, narrator Festival Scrapbook, Radio WCLV, Cleveland, Ohio 1980-84. *Television:* dir and producer The Playboy of the Western World (Emmy Award) Public Broadcasting Service, USA 1983, One Day at a Time, ABC Television 1998. *Publication:* Astride the Moon (autobiog.) 2000, My Abbey (Theatre), articles for Irish Echo Newspaper, 75th Anniversary Issue, Irish Sunday Independent Magazine. *Leisure interests:* fly-fishing, collecting paintings and sculpture, canoeing, travel abroad on house-swaps, old films. *Address:* 322 East River Road, Huntington, MA 01050, USA (home). *Telephone:* (413) 667-3906 (home). *Fax:* (413) 667-3906 (home). *E-mail:* newlo@compuserve.com (home). *Website:* www.miniaturetheatre.org (office).

DOWNE, William (Bill) A., BA, MBA; Canadian banking executive; *President and CEO, BMO Financial Group (Bank of Montreal);* b. 1952, Montreal; m. Robin Downe; three s.; ed Wilfrid Laurier Univ., Univ. of Toronto; joined Bank of Montreal (BMO) 1983 as credit analyst, has held numerous sr man. positions in Corp. and Govt Banking, Houston and Denver, Sr Vice-Pres. US Corp. Banking 1992–96, Exec. Vice-Pres. North American Corp. Banking 1996–98, Head of Global Fixed Income Treasury 1998–99, Vice-Chair. Bank of Montreal 1999–2001, Deputy Chair. BMO Financial Group and CEO BMO Nesbitt Burns 2001–06, COO BMO Financial Group 2006–07, Pres. and CEO 2007–; Chair. Bd of Dirs St Michael's Hosp., Toronto; Rotman Distinguished Business Alumni Award, Joseph L. Rotman School of Man. 2003, Arbor Award, Univ. of Toronto 2005. *Address:* Bank of Montreal, 1 First Canadian Place, 100 King Street, West Toronto, ON M5X 1A1, Canada (office). *Telephone:* (416) 867-5000 (office). *Fax:* (416) 867-6793 (office). *E-mail:* info@bmo.com (office). *Website:* www.bmo.com (office).

DOWNER, Alexander John Gosse, BA; Australian politician and diplomatist; *Special Advisor to the Secretary General on Cyprus, United Nations;* b. 9 Sept. 1951; s. of Sir Alexander Downer; m. Nicola Robinson 1978; one s. three d.; ed Geelong Grammar School, Victoria, Radley Coll. and Univ. of Newcastle-upon-Tyne, UK; mem. Australian Diplomatic Service 1976–81, Australian Mission to European Communities, Embassy in Belgium and Luxembourg 1977–80; Sr Foreign Affairs Rep., S Australia 1981; Political Adviser to Prime Minister 1982–83; Dir Australian Chamber of Commerce 1983–84; mem. House of Reps (Liberal) for Mayo, S Australia 1984–; Shadow Minister for Arts, Heritage and Environment 1987, for Housing, Small Business and Customs 1988–89, for Trade and Trade Negotiations 1990–92, for Defence 1992–93; Fed. Shadow Treas. 1993–94; Leader Liberal Party 1994–95; Shadow Minister for Foreign Affairs 1995–96; Minister for Foreign Affairs 1996–2007; Special Advisor to UN Sec.-Gen. on Cyprus 2008–; Hon. DCL. *Leisure interests:* reading, music, tennis, golf. *Address:* Office of the Special Representative for Cyprus, United Nations Peacekeeping Operation in Cyprus (UNFICYP), 1590 Nicosia, Cyprus (office). *Website:* www.unficyp.org (office); www.alexanderdowner.com.au (office).

DOWNEY, Sir Gordon (Stanley), Kt, KCB, BScEcon; British public servant; b. 26 April 1928, London; s. of Stanley William Downey and Winifred Downey; m. Jacqueline Goldsmith 1952; two d.; ed Tiffin's School, London School of Econs; commissioned Royal Artillery 1946–48; Ministry of Works 1951; entered Treasury 1952; Asst Pvt. Sec. to Chancellor of Exchequer 1955–57; Asst Sec. 1965, Under-Sec. 1972; Head of Cen. Unit., Treasury 1975; Deputy Sec. 1976; Deputy Head of Cen. Policy Review Staff (on secondment) 1978–81; Comptroller and Auditor-Gen. 1981–87; Special Adviser to Ernst and Young 1988–90; Complaints Commr for Securities Asscn 1989–90; Chair. Delegacy, King's Coll. Medical and Dental School 1989–91; Chair. Financial Intermediaries, Mans and Brokers Regulatory Asscn 1990–93, Personal Investment Authority 1992–93; Parl. Commr for Standards 1995–98; Readers' Rep., The Independent 1990–95; Fellow, King's Coll. London 2002; mem. Bd, Business Performance Group, LSE 1989–94. *Leisure interests:* reading, tennis, visual arts. *Address:* 137 Whitehall Court, London, SW1A 2EP, England (home). *Telephone:* (20) 7321-0914 (home). *Fax:* (20) 7321-0914 (home). *E-mail:* downey137@hotmail.com (home).

DOWNEY, James, OC, PhD; Canadian academic and university administrator; *Professor of English, University of Waterloo;* b. 20 April 1939; s. of Ernest and Mimy Ann (née Andrews) Downey; m. Laura Ann Parsons 1964; one s. one d.; ed Memorial Univ. of Newfoundland, Univ. of London, UK; Asst Prof. of English, Carleton Univ. 1966–69, Assoc. Prof. 1969–75, Prof. 1975–80, Chair. Dept of English 1972–75, Acting Dean, Faculty of Arts 1975, Dean 1976–78, Vice-Pres. (Acad.) 1978–80, Pres. pro tempore 1979; Pres. and Vice-Chancellor Univ. of New Brunswick 1980–90, Prof. of English 1980; Pres. and Vice-Chancellor Univ. of Waterloo 1993–99, now Prof. of English; Co-Chair. Comm. on Excellence in Educ. in NB 1991–92; Dir, Centre for the Advancement of Co-operative Educ. 2002–05; Fellow Univ. of Georgia 1985; Hon. DHumLitt (Maine) 1987, Hon. DLitt (Newfoundland) 1991, Hon. LLD (New Brunswick) 1991, Hon. LLD (Toronto) 1998, (McMaster) 1999, (Carleton) 2000; Symons Medal 2001, David Smith Award 2003;Officer of the Order of Canada 1997. *Publications:* The Eighteenth Century Pulpit 1969, Fearful Joy 1974 (co-ed.), Schools for a New Century 1993, Innovation: Essays by Leading Canadian Researchers 2002 (co-ed.). *Address:* Department of English Language and Literature, HH 245, University of Waterloo, 200 University Avenue West, Waterloo, Ont., N2L 3G1 (office); 272 Mary Street, Waterloo, Ont., N2J 1S6, Canada (home). *Telephone:* (519) 885-1211, ext. 6766 (office). *E-mail:* jdowney@uwaterloo.ca (office). *Website:* english.uwaterloo.ca (office).

DOWNEY, Robert, Jr; American actor and singer; b. 4 April 1965, New York, NY; s. of Robert Downey and Elsie Ford; m. 1st Deborah Falconer (divorced 2004); one s.; m. 2nd Susan Levin 2005; first movie role in his father's film Pound 1970; joined cast of tv show Saturday Night Live for one season 1985–86; sentenced to probation for possession of cocaine; imprisoned for further drugs offence breaching terms of probation Dec. 1997; released to serve six months at rehabilitation centre 1998; imprisoned again Aug. 1999, freed Aug. 2000, charged with drugs possession Dec. 2000; began singing career April 2005–. *Films include:* Pound (debut) 1970, Up the Academy (uncredited) 1980, Baby It's You 1983, Firstborn 1984, Deadwait 1985, Tuff Turf 1985, Weird Science 1985, To Live and Die in LA, America 1986, Back to School 1986, The Pick-up Artist 1987, Less Than Zero 1987, Johnny Be Good 1988, Rented Lips 1988, 1969 1988, That's Adequate 1989, True Believer 1989, Chances Are 1989, Air America 1990, Too Much Sun 1991, Soapdish 1991, Chaplin (BAFTA Award) 1992, Heart and Souls 1993, Short Cuts 1993, Hail Caesar 1994, Back to School, Soapdish, The Last Party (also writer) 1993, Natural Born Killers 1994, Only You 1994, Richard III 1995, Restoration 1995, Home for the Holidays 1995, Danger Zone 1996, One Night Stand 1997, Bliss Vision 1997, Two Girls and a Guy (also composed song 'Snakes') 1997, Hugo Pool (aka Pool Girl) 1997, The Gingerbread Man 1998, U.S. Marshals 1998, In Dreams 1999, Friends & Lovers (also composed song 'Carla') 1999, Bowfinger 1999, Black and White 1999, Wonder Boys 2000, Auto Motives 2000, Lethargy 2002, Whatever We Do 2003, The Singing Detective (also singer of 'In My Dreams') 2003, Gothika 2003, Eros 2004, Game 6 2005, Kiss, Kiss, Bang, Bang 2005, The Shaggy Dog 2006, A Scanner Darkly 2006, Goodnight, and Good Luck 2006, Fur: An Imaginary Portrait of Diane Arbus 2006, A Guide to Recognizing Your Saints 2006, Zodiac 2007, Lucky You 2007, Charlie Bartlett 2007, Iron Man 2008, Tropic Thunder 2008. *Television includes:* Mussolini: The Untold Story (mini-series) 1985, Mr. Willowby's Christmas Tree 1995, as Larry Paul in Ally McBeal (series) 2000–01. *Recording:* album: The Futurist 2005. *Address:* Creative Artists Agency (CAA), 9830 Wilshire Blvd, Beverly Hills, CA 90212-1825; c/o Sony Classical, 550 Madison Avenue, New York, NY 10022, USA. *Telephone:* (310) 288-4545 (CAA). *Fax:* (310) 288-4800 (CAA). *Website:* www.robertdowneyjrmusic.com.

DOWNIE, Leonard, Jr, MA; American newspaper executive; *Vice-President at Large, The Washington Post Company;* b. 1 May 1942, Cleveland, Ohio; s. of Leonard Downie Sr and Pearl Evenheimer; m. 1st Barbara Lindsey 1960 (divorced 1971); two s.; m. 2nd Geraldine Rebach 1971 (divorced 1997); one s. one d.; m. 3rd Janice Galin 1997; ed Ohio State Univ.; joined The Washington Post 1964, became investigative reporter in Washington, specializing in crime, housing and urban affairs; helped to supervise coverage of Watergate affair; Asst Man. Ed. Metropolitan News 1974–79; London Corresp. Washington Post 1979–82, Nat. Ed. 1982–84, Man. Ed. 1984–91, Exec. Ed. 1991–2008, Vice-Pres. at Large, The Washington Post Co. 2008–; Dir LA Times–Washington Post News Service 1991–, Int. Herald Tribune 1996–2002; Alicia Patterson Foundation Fellow 1971–72; Hon. LLD, Ohio State Univ.; two Washington-Baltimore Newspaper Guild Front Page Awards, American Bar Asscn Gavel Award for legal reporting, John Hancock Award for business and financial writing. *Publications:* Justice Denied 1971, Mortgage on America 1974, The New Muckrakers 1976, The News About the News (with Robert G. Kaiser) 2002. *Leisure interests:* ballet, classical music, travel, sports. *Address:* The Washington Post Company, 1150 15th Street, NW, Washington, DC 20071, USA (office). *Telephone:* (202) 334-6000 (office). *E-mail:* twpcoreply@washpost.com (office). *Website:* www.washpostco.com (office).

DOWNIE, Robert Silcock, MA, BPhil, FRSE, FRSA; British academic; *Professor Emeritus of Moral Philosophy, University of Glasgow;* b. 19 April 1933, Glasgow; s. of Robert M. Downie and Margaret M. Brown; m. Eileen Dorothea Flynn 1958; three d.; ed Univ. of Glasgow, Queen's Coll., Oxford; Tutor, Worcester Coll., Oxford 1958–59; Lecturer in Moral Philosophy, Univ. of Glasgow 1959–68, Sr Lecturer 1968–69, Prof. 1969, now Prof. Emeritus; Visiting Prof., Syracuse Univ., USA 1963–64, Dalhousie Univ., Nova Scotia, Canada 1976, Univ. of Durham 2000. *Publications:* Government Action and Morality 1964, Respect for Persons 1969, Roles and Values 1971, Education and Personal Relationships 1974, Caring and Curing 1980, Healthy Respect 1987, Health Promotion: Models and Values 1990, The Making of a Doctor 1992, The Healing Arts 1994, Francis Hutcheson: Selected Writings 1994, Palliative Care Ethics 1996, Medical Ethics 1996, Clinical Judgement 2000, The Philosophy of Palliative Care 2006. *Leisure interest:* music. *Address:* Department of Philosophy, University of Glasgow, Glasgow, G12 8QQ, Scotland (office). *Telephone:* (141) 339-8855 (office). *Fax:* (141) 330-4112 (office). *E-mail:* r.downie@philosophy.arts.gla.ac.uk (office). *Website:* www.gla.ac.uk/Acad/Philosophy (office).

DOWSON, Duncan, CBE, FRS, FEng, FIMechE, FRSA, FCGI; British mechanical engineer and academic; *Professor Emeritus, School of Mechanical Engineering, University of Leeds;* b. 31 Aug. 1928, Kirbymoorside,York; s. of Wilfrid Dowson and Hannah Dowson; m. Mabel Strickland 1951; one s. (and one s. deceased); ed Lady Lumley's Grammar School, Pickering and Univ. of Leeds; Research Eng Sir W.G. Armstrong Whitworth Aircraft Co. 1953–54; lecturer in Mechanical Eng, Univ. of Leeds 1954, Sr Lecturer 1963–65, Reader 1965–66, Prof. of Eng Fluid Mechanics and Tribology 1966–93, now Prof. Emer. 1993–, Hon. Fellow and Research Prof. 1998–2001; Hon. Prof. Univ. of Hong Kong 1992–, Univ. of Bradford 1996–; External Prof. Univ. of Loughborough 2001–; Dir Inst. of Tribology, Dept of Mech. Eng 1967–87, Head, Dept of Mech. Eng 1987–93, Pro-Vice-Chancellor 1983–85, Dean for Int. Relations 1987–93; Pres. Inst. of Mechanical Engineers 1992–93; Chair. Yorks. Region, Royal Soc. of Arts 1992–97; Foreign mem. Royal Swedish Acad. of Eng Sciences; Life Fellow, American Soc. of Mechanical Eng (ASME); Hon. Fellow American Soc. of Lubrication Engineers (ASLE), Inst. of Mechanical Engineers; James Clayton Memorial Lecturer, Inst. of Mechanical Engineers 2000; Hon. D Tech (Chalmers Univ. of Tech. Göteborg) 1979; Hon. DSc (Inst. Nat. des Sciences Appliquées, Lyon) 1991, (Liège) 1996; Hon. DEng (Waterloo, Canada) 2001; James Clayton Fund Prize, Thomas Hawksley Gold Medal,

Tribology Gold Medal 1979, James Alfred Medal 1988, Sarton Medal (Belgium) 1998; recipient of numerous awards from Inst. of Mech. Eng, ASME, ASLE etc. *Publications:* Elastohydrodynamic Lubrication: the fundamentals of roller and gear lubrication (jtly) 1966, History of Tribology 1979, An Introduction to the Biomechanics of Joints and Joint Replacement (jtly) 1981, Ball Bearing Lubrication: The Elastohydrodynamics of Elliptical Contacts (jtly) 1981; papers in professional journals. *Leisure interest:* genealogy. *Address:* School of Mechanical Engineering, University of Leeds, Leeds, LS2 9JT (office); Ryedale, 23 Church Lane, Adel, Leeds, LS16 8DQ, England. *Telephone:* (113) 233-2153 (office); (113) 267-8933. *Fax:* (133) 242-4611 (office); (113) 281-7039 (home). *E-mail:* d.dowson@leeds.ac.uk (office); DDRyedale@aol.com (home). *Website:* leva.leeds.ac.uk (office).

DOWSON, Sir Philip (Manning), Kt, CBE, PPRA, RIBA; British architect; b. 16 Aug. 1924, Johannesburg, S Africa; s. of Robert Dowson and Ina Cowen; m. Sarah Crewdson 1950; one s. two d.; ed Gresham's School, Univ. Coll., Oxford, Clare Coll., Cambridge; Lt, RNVR 1943–47; Cambridge 1947–50; Architectural Asscn 1950–53; joined Ove Arup & Partners 1953; Founder, Architectural Partner, Arup Assocs 1963; Sr Partner, Ove Arup Partnership 1969–90, Consultant 1990–; Pres. Royal Acad. of Arts 1993–99; mem. Royal Fine Art Comm. 1971–97, Craft Advisory Cttee 1972–75; Hon. FAIA; Hon. Fellow, Duncan of Jordanstone Coll. of Art 1985, RCA 1989, Clare Coll., Cambridge 1992; Gov. St Martin's School of Art 1975–80; Trustee, Thomas Cubitt Trust 1978–98, Royal Botanic Gardens, Kew 1983–95, The Armouries, HM Tower of London 1984–89, Nat. Portrait Gallery 1993–99, Coram Foundation 1993–99; Hon. Dr of Art (De Montfort Univ.) 2000; Royal Gold Medal for Architecture 1981. *Works include:* urban and univ. devt and coll. bldgs: Oxford, Cambridge, Birmingham, Leicester; housing; schools; new uses for old bldgs; bldgs for music and industrial and office devts. *Publications:* articles in technical press. *Leisure interest:* sailing. *Address:* c/o Royal Academy of Arts, Burlington House, Piccadilly, London, W1V 0DS, England.

DOYLE, Frederick Bernard, BSc, MBA, CEng, FICE, FIWEM, CIM; British civil engineer and business executive; *Director, KPMG Search & Selection;* b. 17 July 1940, Manchester; s. of James Hopkinson and Hilda Mary (née Spotsworth) Doyle; m. Ann Weston 1963; two s. one d.; ed St Bede's Coll., Manchester, Victoria Univ. of Manchester, Harvard Business School; Resident Civil Engineer, British Rail 1961–65; Man. Consultant, Arthur D. Little Inc. 1967–72; with Booker McConnell Ltd 1973–81, Sec. to Exec. Cttee 1973, Dir Eng Div. 1974, Chair. Gen. Eng Div. 1976, Chair. and Chief Exec. Booker McConnell Eng Ltd 1979, Dir of parent co. 1979; Chief Exec. Social Democratic Party 1981–83, Welsh Water Authority 1983–87; Dir Public Sector Operations, MSL Int. 1988–90, Dir 1994–96, Man Dir 1997–99; Man. Dir Hamptons 1990–92; Gen. Man. Bristol and West Bldg Soc. 1992–94; Head of Public Sector Practice, Hoggett Bowers Exec. Search and Selection 1999–2000; Dir KPMG Search and Selection 2001–; crew member Times Clipper Round the World Yacht Race 2000; NATO Fellowship 1965. *Leisure interests:* walking, theatre, reading, travel, sailing. *Address:* KPMG Search & Selection, 2 Cornwall Street, Birmingham, B3 2DL (office); 38A West Road, Bromsgrove, Worcs., B60 2NQ, England (home). *Telephone:* (121) 232-3000 (office); (1527) 873565 (home). *Fax:* (121) 232-3609 (office). *E-mail:* bernard.doyle@kpmg.co.uk (office); aandbdoyle@aol.com (home). *Website:* www.kpmg.co.uk (office).

DOYLE, James Edward, JD; American state official and lawyer; *Governor of Wisconsin;* b. 23 Nov. 1945, Washington, DC; s. of James E. Doyle and Ruth Doyle (née Bachhuber); m. Jessica Laird 1966; two s.; ed Stanford Univ., Univ. of Wisconsin, Harvard Univ. Law School; volunteer Peace Corps, Tunisia 1967–69; Attorney DNA Legal Services, Navajo Indian Reservation, Chinie, Ariz. 1972–75; Partner Jacobs & Doyle, Madison, Wis. 1975–77; Dist Attorney Dane Co. 1977–83; Partner Doyle & Ritz, Madison 1983–90; Counsel Lawton & Cates, Madison 1990–91; Attorney-Gen. State of Wis. 1991–2002; Gov. of Wis. 2002–; mem. ABA, Wis. Bar Asscn, 7th Circuit Bar Asscn; Democrat. *Address:* Office of the Governor, 115 East State Capitol, Madison, WI 53702, USA (office). *Telephone:* (608) 266-1212 (office). *Fax:* (608) 267-8983 (office). *E-mail:* governor@wisconsin.gov (office). *Website:* www.wisgov.state.wi.us/index.asp (office).

DOYLE, Noreen, BA, MBA; American/Irish banker and international finance official; b. 1949; ed Coll. of Mount St Vincent, Tuck School of Business, Dartmouth Coll.; began career with Morgan Guaranty Trust; joined Bankers Trust 1974, Client Man., New York and Houston, Div. Man. for multinat. cos, New York, Man. Dir for distribution of structured financings, New York, responsible for European affairs, London 1990–92; joined EBRD and set up syndication business 1992, responsible for credit and market risks 1997–2001, First Vice-Pres. and Head of Banking 2001–05 (retd), fmr mem. Exec. Cttee; mem. Bd of Dirs Credit Suisse 2004–, Newmont Mining Corpn of Canada Ltd 2005–, QinetiQ 2005–, Rexam PLC 2005–. *Address:* c/o Board of Directors, Credit Suisse Group, Paradeplatz 8, 8070 Zurich, Switzerland.

DOYLE, Roddy; Irish writer and playwright; b. 1958, Dublin; m. Belinda Doyle; two s.; lecturer at universities. *Play:* Brown Bread 1992, USA 1992. *Publications:* The Commitments 1987, screenplay (with Dick Clement and Ian La Frenais) 1991, The Snapper 1990, screenplay 1992, The Van 1991, Paddy Clarke Ha Ha Ha (Booker Prize) 1993, The Woman Who Walked into Doors 1996, A Star Called Henry 1999, The Giggler Treatment 2000, Rory and Ita 2002, Oh, Play That Thing 2004, Paula Spencer 2006, Wilderness 2007, The Deportees (short stories) 2007. *Address:* c/o Patti Kelly, Viking Books, 375 Hudson Street, New York, NY 10014, USA (office).

DRABBLE, Dame Margaret, DBE, BA; British author; b. 5 June 1939, Sheffield; d. of the late J. F. Drabble and Kathleen Drabble (née Bloor); sister of A. S. Byatt; m. 1st Clive Swift 1960 (divorced 1975); two s. one d.; m. 2nd

Michael Holroyd (q.v.) 1982; ed Newnham Coll., Cambridge; Chair., Nat. Book League 1980–82; Ed. The Oxford Companion to English Literature 1979–2000; Chair., Soc. of Authors 2008–09; Hon. Foreign mem. American Acad. of Arts and Letters 2002; Hon. Fellow, Sheffield City Polytechnic 1989; Hon. DLitt (Sheffield) 1976, (Bradford) 1988, (Hull) 1992, Hon. doctorates (Manchester) 1987, (Keele) 1988, (East Anglia) 1994, (York) 1995, (Cambridge) 2006; James Tait Black Memorial Prize 1968, Book of the Year Award, Yorkshire Post 1972, E. M. Forster Award, American Acad. of Arts and Letters 1973, St Louis Literary Award 2003. *Publications:* fiction: A Summer Bird-Cage 1963, The Garrick Year 1964, The Millstone (John Llewelyn Rhys Memorial Prize 1966) 1965, Jerusalem the Golden 1967, The Waterfall 1969, The Needle's Eye 1972, The Realms of Gold 1975, The Ice Age 1977, The Middle Ground 1980, The Radiant Way 1987, A Natural Curiosity 1989, The Gates of Ivory 1991, The Witch of Exmoor 1996, The Peppered Moth 2001, The Seven Sisters 2002, The Red Queen 2004, The Sea Lady 2006; plays: Laura 1964, Isadora 1968, Thank You All Very Much 1969, Bird of Paradise 1969; non-fiction: Wordsworth 1966, Arnold Bennett: A Biography 1974, The Genius of Thomas Hardy (ed.) 1976, For Queen and Country: Britain in the Victorian Age 1978, A Writer's Britain 1979, The Oxford Companion to English Literature (co-ed.) 1985, 2000, The Concise Oxford Companion to English Literature (co-ed. with Jenny Stringer) 1987, Angus Wilson: A Biography 1995. *Leisure interests:* walking and talking. *Address:* c/o Viking Publicity, Penguin, 80 Strand, London, WC2R 0RL, England (office). *Website:* www.penguin.co.uk (office).

DRACH, Ivan Fyodorovich; Ukrainian politician and writer; b. 17 Oct. 1936, Telizhentsy, Kiev Oblast; m. Mariya Drach; one s. one d.; ed Univ. of Kiev, Moscow State Univ.; worked as school teacher; Corresp. for Literaturnaya Ukraina and Witczyna newspapers 1961–87; scriptwriter Dovzheniev Studio 1964–87; mem. Bd, Sec. Union of Ukrainian Writers 1989–92; joined CP 1959, resgnd 1990; Founder mem. Narodny Rukh (Ukrainian nationalist opposition Movt), Leader, then co-Chair. 1989–92; Chair. Bd Ukraina Soc. 1992–; mem. Ukrainian Supreme Soviet 1990–; mem. Ukrainian World Coordination Council 1992–99; Chair. State Cttee of Information Policy, TV and Radio 2001; Ukrainian State Prize 1976, USSR State Prize 1983, Yaroslav Mudry Order 1996. *Publications include:* Sun Flower 1962, Ballads of Everyday Life 1967, I Come to You 1970, Poems 1972, The Kievan Sky 1976, The Sun and the Word (poetry) 1978, Green Gates 1980, Dramatic Poems 1982, Grigory Skovoroda 1984, Temple of Sun 1988. *Address:* Gorky str. 18, Apt 7, 252005 Kiev, Ukraine. *Telephone:* (44) 228-87-69.

DRACHEVSKY, Leonid Vadimovich; Russian diplomatist and politician; b. 5 April 1942, Alma-Ata; m.; three c.; ed Mendeleyev Inst. of Chemical Tech., Diplomatic Acad., Ministry of Foreign Affairs; Deputy Chair. State Cttee of Sport, RSFSR 1986–90, First Deputy Chair. Cttee of Sport, USSR 1990–91; on staff Ministry of Foreign Affairs since 1992; Consul (rank of Counsellor) Gen. Consulate of Russian Fed., Barcelona, Spain 1992; Head of Div., Dir Dept on Problems of CIS 1993–94; Dir First Dept of CIS Countries 1994–96; Amb. to Poland 1996–98; Deputy Minister of Foreign Affairs 1998–99; Minister for Relations with CIS Cos 1999–2000; Plenipotentiary Rep. of Russian Pres. to Siberian Fed. Dist 2000–04; Chair. Russian Part of Russian-Chinese Cttee of Friendship, Peace and Devt 2002. *Address:* Office of the Plenipotentiary Representative of the President, Derzhavina str. 18, 630091 Novosibirsk, Russia (office). *Telephone:* (3832) 21-95-31 (Novosibirsk) (office); (495) 206-72-71 (Moscow) (office). *Fax:* (3832) 17-06-31 (office). *E-mail:* sfo@sfo.nso.ru (office). *Website:* www.sfo.nsk.su (office).

DRAGHI, Mario, PhD; Italian civil servant, EU official and international banker; *Governor, Bank of Italy;* ed Univ. of Rome, Mass Inst. of Tech., USA; Prof. of Econs, Florence Univ., Italy 1981–91; Exec. Dir IBRD 1984–90; Adviser to Bank of Italy 1990; Dir-Gen. Ministry of the Treasury and of the Budget 1991–2001; mem. Econ. and Financial Cttee EEC (now EU) 1991– (Chair. 2000–); Chair. Italian Cttee for Privatizations 1993; Dir ENI –2001; Vice-Chair. and Man. Dir Goldman Sachs Int., London UK 2002–06; Gov. Bank of Italy 2006–; Chair. Financial Stabilities Forum 2006–; mem. Group of Seven deputies 1991–; mem. Bd of Trustees, Princeton Inst. for Advanced Study, USA; IOP Fellow, Kennedy School of Government, Harvard Univ., USA; Trustee The Brookings Inst., Washington, DC 2003–; chaired cttee that drafted legislation governing Italian financial markets ('Draghi Law'). *Publications:* Produttività del lavoro, salari reali, e occupazione (Collana di economia: Sezione 4; 17) 1979, Public Debt Management: Theory & History (co-author) 1990, Transparency, Risk Management and International Financial Fragility: Geneva Reports on the World Economy 4 (co-author) 2004. *Address:* Bank of Italy, Via Nazionale 91, Rome 00184, Italy (office). *Telephone:* (3) 90647921 (office). *Website:* www.gs.com (office).

DRAGUTINOVIĆ, Diana, MSc, PhD; Serbian economist and politician; *Minister of Finance;* b. 6 May 1958, Belgrade; m.; two c.; ed Univ. of Belgrade; Lecturer in Econs, Univ. of Belgrade 1999–; Special Adviser to Ministry of Finance and Economy 2001–02, to IMF 2002–04; Vice-Gov. Nat. Bank of Serbia 2004–08; Minister of Finance 2008–; fmr Co-Ed. Economic Thought (journal); fmr mem. Int. Editorial Bd Economic Annals. *Publications:* numerous textbooks, articles and journal contribs. *Address:* Ministry of Finance, Kneza Miloša 20, 11000 Belgrade, Serbia (office). *Telephone:* (11) 3619900 (office). *Fax:* (11) 3618914 (office). *E-mail:* informacije@mfin.sr.gov.yu (office). *Website:* www.mfin.sr.gov.yu (office).

DRAKE, Frank Donald, BEng (Phys), MA, PhD; American astronomer; *Chairman, Board of Trustees, Search for Extraterrestrial Intelligence (SETI) Institute;* b. 28 May 1930, Chicago; s. of Richard C. Drake and Winifred Thompson Drake; m. 1st Elizabeth B. Bell 1953 (divorced 1977); three s.; m. 2nd Amahl Shakhashiri 1978; two d.; ed Cornell and Harvard Univs; USN 1952–55; Harvard Radio Astronomy Project 1955–58; Ewen-Knight Corpn

1957–58; scientist, Head Scientific Services and Telescope Operations on Nat. Radio Astronomy Observatory 1958–63; Chief, Lunar and Planetary Science Section, Jet Propulsion Lab. 1963–64; Prof. of Astronomy, Cornell Univ. 1964–85, Goldwin Smith Prof. of Astronomy 1976–85; Dir Arecibo Ionospheric Observatory 1966–68; Assoc. Dir Center for Radiophysics and Space Research, Cornell Univ. 1967–75; Chair. Dept of Astronomy, Cornell Univ. 1968–71; Dir Nat. Astronomy and Ionosphere Center 1971–81; Prof. of Astronomy, Univ. of Calif., Santa Cruz 1984–95, Prof. Emer. 1995–, Dean Div. of Natural Sciences 1984–88; Pres. Astronomical Soc. of the Pacific 1988–90; mem. AAAS, NAS 1972, The Explorers Club, Advisory Bd The World Book Encyclopedia, Int. Astronomical Union, Int. Scientific Radio Union, American Astronomical Soc.; Fellow American Acad. of Arts and Sciences; Pres. SETI (Search for Extraterrestrial Intelligence) Inst. 1984–2000, Chair. Bd of Trustees 2000–. *Publications:* Intelligent Life in Space 1962, Murmurs of Earth 1979, (with Dava Sobel) Is Anyone Out There? 1992; and over 135 papers and articles. *Leisure interests:* snorkelling, horticulture, lapidary. *Address:* SETI Institute, 2035 Landings Drive, Mountain View, CA 94043, USA (office). *Telephone:* (650) 961-6633 (office). *Fax:* (650) 961-7099 (office). *E-mail:* drake@seti.org (office).

DRAKE, Michael V.; American university chancellor and physician; *Chancellor, University of California, Irvine;* m. Brenda Drake; served as clinician, physician-scientist and teacher; fmr Steven P. Shearing Prof. of Ophthalmology and Sr Assoc. Dean for Admissions and Extramural Academic Programs, Univ. of Calif., San Francisco School of Medicine; fmr Univ. of Calif. Vice-Pres. for Health Affairs, also oversaw the Univ. of Calif. Special Research Programs, including tobacco-related disease research, breast cancer research and HIV/AIDS research, the Calif./Mexico Health Initiative and Calif. Health Benefits Review Program; Chancellor Univ. of Calif., Irvine 2005–; mem. NAS Inst. of Medicine 1998; mem. several nat. scientific and scholarly socs; fmr Nat. Pres. Alpha Omega Alpha Honor Medical Soc.; Chair.-elect Bd of Trustees Asscn of Academic Health Centers; several awards for teaching, public service, mentoring and research, including the UCSF School of Medicine's Clinical Teaching Award and the UCSF Chancellor's Award for Public Service, inducted into Gold Headed Cane Soc. 2003, Herbert W. Nickens Award, American Asscn of Medical Colls 2004. *Publications:* co-author of four books; numerous scholarly articles and book chapters. *Address:* The Chancellor's Office, 510 Administration, University of California, Irvine, Irvine, CA 92697-1900, USA (office). *Telephone:* (949) 824-5111 (office). *Fax:* (949) 824-2087 (office). *E-mail:* chancellor@uci.edu (office). *Website:* www.uci.edu (office).

DRAPER, Kenneth, MA, RA; British painter and sculptor; b. 19 Feb. 1944, Killamarsh, Sheffield; s. of Albert Draper and Dorothy Rosa Anne Lamb; m. 1st Heather Lieven Beste 1965 (divorced); one s.; m. 2nd Nadiya Jinnah 1972 (divorced); m. 3rd Jean Macalpine; ed Chesterfield Coll. of Art, Kingston School of Art, RCA; solo exhbns include Redfern Gallery, London 1969, Warwick Arts Trust, London 1981, Galerie Nouvelles Images, Den Haag, Holland 1984, Austin Desmond, London 1991, Adelson Gallery, New York 1993, Friends Room, RA 1993, Hart Gallery, London 1994, 1996, 1998, Peter Bartlow Gallery, Chicago 1995; group exhbns include: British Sculptors 1972, RA 1972, Silver Jubilee Exhbn Contemporary British Sculpture, Battersea Park 1977, The British Art Show, Mappin, Sheffield 1980, British Sculpture in the Twentieth Century, Whitechapel Art Gallery 1981; work in public collections of Arts Council of GB, Contemporary Arts Soc., Courtauld Inst., London, Ashmolean Museum, Oxford, Usher Gallery, Lincoln; Mark Rothko Memorial Award 1971. *Leisure interests:* reading, chess, sport, travel. *Address:* Carrer Gran 55A, 07720 Es Castell, Minorca, Balearic Islands, Spain. *Telephone:* (971) 353457. *Fax:* (971) 353457. *E-mail:* drapermacalpine@terra.es (office). *Website:* www.kennethdraper.com.

DRAPER, William Henry, III, BA, MBA; American fmr government official; *General Partner, Draper Richards L.P.;* b. 1 Jan. 1928, White Plains, NY; s. of William Henry Draper and Katherine Baum; m. Phyllis Culbertson 1953; one s. two d.; ed Yale and Harvard Univs; with Inland Steel Co., Chicago 1954–59; Draper, Gaither & Anderson, Palo Alto, Calif. 1959–62; Pres. Draper & Johnson Investment Co. Palo Alto 1962–65; Founder and Gen. Pnr, Sutter Hill Capital Co., Palo Alto 1965–70, Sutter Hill Ventures, Palo Alto 1970–81; Pres. and Chair. Export-Import Bank US, Washington, DC 1981–86; Admin., CEO UNDP 1986–93; Man. Dir Draper Int., San Francisco 1994; currently Gen. Pnr Draper Richards L.P.; Trustee Yale Univ. 1991–98, George Bush Library Foundation 1993–; Chair. World Affairs Council, N Calif. 2000–02; Republican; Hon. LLD (Southeastern Univ.); SD Forum Vision Award, Dow Jones VC Hall of Fame 2005, Silicon Valley Fast 50 Lifetime Achievement Award 2006, Distinguished Service Award (IIE). *Address:* Draper Richards L.P., 50 California Street, Suite 2925, San Francisco, CA 94111 (office); 91 Tallwood Court, Atherton, CA 94027-6431, USA (home). *Telephone:* (415) 616-4050 (office). *Fax:* (415) 616-4060 (office). *E-mail:* bill@draperrichards.com (office). *Website:* www.draperrichards.com (office).

DRAŠKOVIĆ, Vuk; Serbian politician, journalist and writer; *President, Serbian Renewal Movement;* b. 29 Nov. 1946, Central Banat Region, Vojvodina; m. Danica Drašković (née Bošković); ed Belgrade Univ.; moved to Herzegovina; as student took part in demonstrations 1968; mem. staff Telegraph Agency of Yugoslavia TANJUG 1969–78, worked in Lusaka, Zambia; dismissed from post of correspondent for disinformation 1978; Adviser Council of Trade Unions of Yugoslavia 1978–80; Ed. Rad (newspaper) 1980–85; freelance journalist and writer 1985–; Founder and Pres. Serbian Renewal Movt (Srpslei pokret obnove) 1990–; cand. for Presidency of Yugoslavia 1990, 1992, of Serbia 1997; mem. Nat. Ass.; detained, released from detention July 1993; leader of mass protests against Pres. Milošević from Nov. 1996; Deputy Prime Minister of Yugoslavia 1998–99 (resgnd); Minister of Foreign Affairs 2004–06. *Publications include:* novels: Judge, Knife, Prayer 1,

Prayer 2, Russian Consul, Night of the General, Target, Polemics, Answers; numerous articles and collections of articles. *Address:* Serbian Renewal Movement (Srpski pokret obnove), 11000 Belgrade, Kneza Mihailova 48, Serbia (office). *Telephone:* (11) 3283620 (office). *Fax:* (11) 2628170 (office). *E-mail:* vuk@spo.org.yu (office). *Website:* www.spo.org.yu (office).

DRASKOVICS, Tibor, LLB; Hungarian banking and finance executive and fmr government official; b. 26 June 1955, Budapest; ed Eötvös Lóránd Univ. of Budapest; started career as legal expert Ministry of Finance 1979–84, Sec. to Minister 1984–86, Head of Legal Dept 1986, Head of Legal Div. 1988, Deputy State Sec. 1990–91, Admin. State Sec. 1994–98; Man. Dir Concordia Biztosítási (insurance brokers) 1991–93; tax consulting man. Arthur Andersen Ltd 1993–94; mem. Monetary Council, Nat. Bank of Hungary 1995–98; CEO ABN-AMRO 1999; Deputy CEO K&H Bank 2001; Chief of Cabinet of the Prime Minister 2002; Minister of Finance 2004–05; Order of Merit of the Hungarian Republic's Middle Cross.

DRAVINS, Dainis, PhD; Swedish astronomer and academic; *Professor of Astronomy, Lund University;* b. 10 Sept. 1949, Lund; m. Christina Dravins (née Hedqvist) 1982; one s.; ed Lund and Uppsala Univs and Calif. Inst. of Tech., USA; Prof. of Astronomy, Lund Univ. 1984–; mem. Royal Swedish Acad. of Sciences 1987; Foreign mem. Latvian Acad. of Sciences 1992. *Publications:* numerous articles on astronomy. *Address:* Lund Observatory, Box 43, 22100 Lund, Sweden (office). *Telephone:* (46) 2227297 (office); (46) 2227000 (office). *Fax:* (46) 2224614 (office). *E-mail:* dainis@astro.lu.se (office). *Website:* www.astro.lu.se/~dainis (office).

DRAY, William Herbert, MA, DPhil, LLD, FRSC; Canadian academic; *Professor Emeritus of Philosophy, University of Ottawa;* b. 23 June 1921, Montreal, PQ; s. of William J. Dray and Florence E. Jones; m. Doris K. Best 1943; one s. one d.; ed Univ. of Toronto and Balliol and Nuffield Coll., Oxford, UK; RCAF 1941–46, Active Reserve (Wing Commdr, retd) 1956–66; Lecturer in Philosophy, Univ. of Toronto 1953–55, Asst Prof. to Prof. 1955–68; Prof., Trent Univ. 1968–76, Chair. Dept of Philosophy 1968–73; Prof. of Philosophy with cross-appointment to History, Univ. of Ottawa 1976–86, Prof. Emer. 1986–; visiting appointments at Ohio State Univ. 1959, Case Inst. 1966, Harvard Univ. 1967, 1973, Stanford Univ. 1962, Duke Univ. 1973; ACLS Fellowship 1960–61, Canada Council Fellowship 1971, 1978, Killam Research Fellowship 1980–81, Nat. Humanities Center Fellowship 1983–84; elected Fellow, Royal Soc. of Canada 1967; Molson Prize of the Canada Council 1986, Lifetime Achievement Award The R. G. Collingwood Soc. 2005. *Publications:* Laws and Explanation in History 1957, Philosophy of History 1964, 1993, Philosophical Analysis and History (ed.) 1966, Perspectives on History 1980, Substance and Form in History (co-ed. with L. Pompa) 1981, La philosophie de l'histoire et la pratique historienne d'aujourd'hui (co-ed. with D. Carr *et al.*) 1982, On History and Philosophers of History 1989, History as Re-enactment 1995, The Principles of History: R. G. Collingwood (ed. with W. J. van der Dussen) 1999. *Address:* Apt 818, 32 Clarissa Drive, Richmond Hill, Ont., L4C 9R7, Canada. *Telephone:* (905) 883-1995. *E-mail:* whdray@aol.com (home).

DRAZEN, Jeffrey M., BS, MD; American writer; *Editor-in-Chief, New England Journal of Medicine;* b. 19 May 1946, St Louis, MO; Prof. in the Dept of Environmental Health, Harvard School of Public Health; Distinguished Parker B. Francis Prof. of Medicine, Dept of Medicine, Brigham and Women's Hospital; Ed.-in-Chief, New England Journal of Medicine. *Publications:* Five Lipoxygenase Products in Asthma (ed.) 1998; contrib. to Genomic Medicine: Articles from the New England Journal of Medicine 2001. *Address:* New England Journal of Medicine, 10 Shattuck Street, Boston, MA 02115-6094, USA (office). *Telephone:* (617) 734-7870 (office). *Fax:* (617) 739-9864 (office). *E-mail:* jdrazen@nejm.org (office). *Website:* www.nejm.org (office).

DRÉ (see ANDRE 3000).

DREIFUSS, Ruth; Swiss politician; *Chairperson of Commission on Intellectual Property Rights, Innovation and Public Health, World Health Organization;* b. 9 Jan. 1940, St Gall; ed Ecole d'Etudes Sociales, Geneva and Univ. of Geneva; Sec. 1958–59; Ed. Coopération, Swiss Union of Cooperatives, Basle 1961–64; Asst Sociologist, Centre Psycho-Social Universitaire, Geneva 1965–68; Asst in Nat. Accounting, Faculty of Econ. and Social Sciences, Univ. of Geneva 1970–72; civil servant, Swiss Devt Agency Fed. Ministry of Foreign Affairs 1972–81; Sec. Swiss Fed. of Trade Unions 1981–93; elected to Swiss Fed. Council 1993, Vice-Pres. 1998, Pres. of Swiss Confed. 1999; Head, Fed. Dept of Home Affairs 1994–2002; Chair. Comm. on Intellectual Property Rights, Innovation and Public Health, WHO; mem. Social Democratic Party; Dr hc (Haifa) 1999, (Jerusalem) 2000. *Address:* Secretariat for the Commission on Intellectual Property Rights, Innovation and Public Health, World Health Organization, 20 avenue Appia, 1211 Geneva 27, Switzerland (office). *Telephone:* (22) 7912764 (office). *Fax:* (22) 7914852 (office). *E-mail:* cipih@who.int (office). *Website:* www.who.int (office).

DRELL, Sidney David; American physicist and academic; *Professor Emeritus, Stanford Linear Accelerator Center;* b. 13 Sept. 1926, Atlantic City, NJ; s. of Tulla and Rose White Drell; m. Harriet Stainback 1952; one s. two d.; ed Princeton Univ. and Univ. of Illinois; Research Assoc. Univ. of Illinois 1949–50; Research Assoc. MIT 1952–53, Asst Prof. 1953–56; Physics Instructor, Stanford Univ. 1950–52, Assoc. Prof. 1956–60, Prof. of Physics 1960–63, Lewis M. Terman Prof. and Fellow 1979–84, Prof. Stanford Linear Accelerator Center 1963–98, Prof. Emer. 1998–, Deputy Dir 1969–98, Exec. Head of Theoretical Physics 1969–86, Co-Dir Stanford Center for Int. Security and Arms Control 1984–89; Sr Fellow, Hoover Inst. 1998–; Adjunct Prof., Dept of Eng and Public Policy, Carnegie Mellon Univ. 1989–96; Visiting Scientist and Guggenheim Fellow, CERN 1961–62; Visiting Prof. and Loeb Lecturer, Harvard Univ. 1962, 1970; consultant to Los Alamos Scientific Lab. 1956–, Office of Science and Tech., Exec. Office of the Pres. 1960–73; consultant Arms Control and Disarmament Agency 1969–81, Office of Tech. Assessment, US Congress 1975–91, Office of Science and Tech. Policy 1977–82, Nat. Security Council 1973–81; Consultant, Senate Select Cttee on Intelligence 1978–83; consultant to House Armed Services Cttee 1990–91, Senate Select Cttee on Intelligence 1990–93; Chair. Int. Advisory Bd Inst. of Global Conflict and Cooperation, Univ. of Calif. 1990–93; mem. High Energy Physics Advisory Panel to DOE 1974–86 (Chair. 1974–82); mem. JASON Div. (Mitre Corpn) 1960–; mem. Bd The Arms Control Asscn, Washington, DC 1971–93; mem. Council on Foreign Relations 1980–; mem. Advisory Cttee MIT Physics Dept 1974–90; mem. Pres.'s Science Advisory Cttee 1966–70; Visiting Schrodinger Prof., Theoretical Physics, Univ. of Vienna 1975; mem. Bd of Trustees, Inst. for Advanced Study, Princeton, NJ 1974–83; Bd Gov. Weizmann Inst. of Science, Rehovoth, Israel 1970–; Bd Dir Annual Reviews Inc. 1976–97; mem. numerous advisory cttees and editorial bds including MIT Lincoln Lab. Advisory Bd 1985–90, Aspen Strategy Group 1984–91, Carnegie Comm. on Science, Tech. and Govt 1988–93, Scientific and Academic Advisory Cttee on Nat. Labs, Univ. of Calif. 1988–92, Pres.'s Foreign Intelligence Advisory Bd 1993–2001, Comm. on Maintaining US Nuclear Weapons Expertise 1999; Chair. Pres.'s Council on the Nat. Labs 1992–99; Fellow American Physical Soc. (Pres. 1986); mem. NAS, American Acad. of Arts and Sciences, American Philosophical Soc. 1987–, Academia Europaea 1995; Guggenheim Fellow, Rome 1972; Richtmeyer Memorial Lecturer to American Asscn of Physics Teachers 1978; Visiting Fellow, All Souls Coll., Oxford Univ. 1979; Danz Lecturer, Univ. of Washington 1983; I. I. Rabi Visiting Prof. Columbia Univ. 1984; Hans Bethe Lecturer, Cornell Univ. 1988, Brickwedde Lecturer, Johns Hopkins Univ.; Sr Advisory Group LANL 2003–; Hon. DSc (Univ. of Ill., Chicago Circle) 1981; E. O. Lawrence Memorial Award 1972, Univ. of Ill. Alumni Award for Distinguished Service in Eng 1973, Leo Szilard Award for Physics in the Public Interest 1980, MacArthur Fellowship Award 1984–89, Univ. of Ill. Achievement Award 1988, Hilliard Roderick Prize in Science, Arms Control and Int. Security (AAAS) 1993, Co-recipient Ettore Majorana-Erice Science for Peace Prize 1994, Woodrow Wilson Award for Distinguished Achievement in the Nation's Service, Princeton Univ. 1994, Gian Carlo Wick Commemorative Award ICSC World Lab. 1996, Distinguished Assoc. Award of US Dept of Environment 1997, I. Ya. Pomeranchuk Prize (Moscow) 1998, Linus Pauling Lecturer and Medallist, Stanford Univ. 1999–2000, Presidential Medal, Univ. of Calif. 2000, one of 10 scientists honoured by U.S. Reconnaissance Office as Founders of National Reconnaissance as a Space Discipline 2000, Enrico Fermi Award 2000, Nat. Intelligence Distinguished Service Medal 2001, William O. Baker Award, Security Affairs Support Asscn 2001, Heinz R. Pagels Human Rights of Scientists Award 2001, Heinz Award for Public Policy 2005. *Publications:* Relativistic Quantum Mechanics, Relativistic Quantum Fields (both with J. D. Bjorken) and numerous papers on theoretical physics; Facing the Threat of Nuclear Weapons 1983 (updated 1989), The Reagan Strategic Defense Initiative: A Technical, Political and Arms Control Assessment (co-author) 1984, Sidney Drell on Arms Control 1988, Reducing Nuclear Danger (co-author) 1993, In the Shadow of the Bomb: Physics and Arms Control 1993, The New Terror: Facing the Threat of Biological and Chemical Weapons (co-ed.) 1999, New Mission for Nuclear Weapons? (co-author) 2003, The Gravest Danger: Nuclear Weapons (co-author) 2004, Nuclear Weapons, Scientists, and the Post-Cold War Challenge: Selected Papers on Arms Control; contrib. Wall Street Journal 2007. *Leisure interests:* music, reading. *Address:* Stanford Linear Accelerator Center, 2575 Sand Hill Road, Mail Stop 80, Menlo Park, CA 94025 (office); 620 Sand Hill Road, Apt 420–D, Palo Alto, CA 94304, USA (home). *Telephone:* (650) 926-2664 (office). *Fax:* (650) 926-4500 (office). *E-mail:* drell@slac.stanford.edu (office). *Website:* www.slac.stanford.edu (office).

DRENTH, Pieter Johan Diederik, PhD; Dutch academic; *Professor Emeritus of Psychology, Vrije University;* b. 8 March 1935, Appelscha; s. of Gerrit Drenth and Froukje Wouda; m. Maria Annetta Elizabeth de Boer 1959; three s.; ed Vrije Univ., Amsterdam; served in Royal Dutch Navy 1955–60; Research Fellow, Social Science Research Div., Standard Oil Co., New York 1960–61; Sr Lecturer in Psychometrics and Industrial Psychology, Vrije Univ., Amsterdam 1962–67, Prof. of Work and Organizational Psychology and Psychodiagnostics 1967–2000, Prof. Emer. 2000–, Vice-Chancellor 1983–87, Dean Faculty of Psychology and Educ. 1998–2000; Visiting Prof., Washington Univ., St Louis 1966, Univ. of Washington, Seattle 1977; Pres. Royal Netherlands Acad. of Arts and Sciences 1990–96, ALLEA (European Network of Acads of Science) 2000–; mem. Royal Netherlands Acad. of Arts and Sciences 1980; mem. Supervisory Bd Shell-Nederland BV; Kt Order of the Lion 1991; Commdr Order of Oranje-Nassau 1996; Dr hc (Ghent) 1980, (Paris V) 1996; Heymans Award for Outstanding Contrib. to Psychology 1986, Aristotle Award for outstanding Contribs to European psychology 1995. *Publications:* Mental Tests and Cultural Adaptation (Ed.) 1972, Inleiding in de testtheorie 1976, Decisions in Organizations 1988, Advances in Organizational Psychology (Ed.) 1988, New Handbook Work and Organizational Psychology (Ed.) 1989, Testtheorie 1990, Gardening in Science 1996; numerous scientific papers and psychological tests. *Leisure interests:* cycling, music, literature. *Address:* Royal Netherlands Academy of Arts and Sciences, Kloveniersburgswal 27-29, 1000 GC Amsterdam (office); Pekkendam 6, 1081 HR Amsterdam, Netherlands (home). *Telephone:* (20) 5510754 (office); (20) 6449109 (home). *Fax:* (20) 6447938 (home); (20) 6204941. *E-mail:* president@allea.org (office); pjdd@xs4all.nl (home).

DRESE, Claus Helmut, DPhil; German theatre director; b. 25 Dec. 1922, Aachen; s. of Karl Drese and Helene Drese; m. Helga Lautz 1950; two c.; studied German studies, philosophy and history in Cologne, Bonn and Marburg; Theatre Literary Man., Mannheim 1952–59; Theatre Dir, Heidelberg 1959–62, Wiesbaden 1962–68, Cologne 1968–75, Zurich 1975–86; Dir

Vienna State Opera 1986–91. *Publications:* various contribs to newspapers, radio and television.

DRETSKE, Frederick Irwin, BSEE MA, PhD; American philosopher and academic; *Senior Research Scholar, Duke University;* b. 9 Dec. 1932, Ill.; s. of Hattie Walschlager and Frederick E Dretske; m. 1st Virginia Lord 1954; m. 2nd Brenda Peters 1965; m. 3rd Judith Fortson 1988; one s. one d.; ed Purdue Univ., Univ. of Minnesota; Asst Prof. to Prof., Univ. of Wisconsin 1960–90; Fellow, Center for Advanced Study in the Behavioral Sciences, Stanford Univ., Calif. 1988, Prof. of Philosophy 1990–98; Sr Research Scholar, Duke Univ., Durham, NC 1999–; American Council of Learned Socs Fellowship 1965; Nat. Endowment for the Humanities Fellowships 1975, 1985; Pres. American Philosophical Asscn (Cen. Div.) 1984–85; elected Fellow, American Acad. of Arts and Sciences 2003; Alexander von Humboldt Prize 2007. *Publications:* Seeing and Knowing 1969, Knowledge and the Flow of Information 1981, Explaining Behavior 1988, Naturalizing the Mind 1995, Perception, Knowledge and Belief 2000. *Leisure interests:* carpentry, travel, clock repair. *Address:* 1410 Bivins Street, Durham, NC 27707, USA (home). *Telephone:* (919) 490-4641 (home). *E-mail:* fred.dretske@mindspring.com (home).

DREW, John Sydney Neville, MA, AM, MBA; British academic; *John Monnet Professor of European Business and Management, European Business School, London;* b. 7 Oct. 1936, Hornchurch; s. of late John Drew and Kathleen Wright; m. Rebecca Usher 1962; two s. one d.; ed King Edward's School, Birmingham, St John's Coll. Oxford, Tufts Univ. and London Business School; served in HM Diplomatic Service, First Sec. in Paris, MECAS (Middle East Center for Arabic Studies), Kuwait, Bucharest 1960–73; Dir of Marketing and Exec. Programmes, London Business School 1973–79; Dir of Corp. Affairs, Rank Xerox 1979–84; Dir of European Affairs, Touche Ross Int. 1984–86; Head, UK Offices, Comm. of EC 1987–93; Dir Durham Inst., Visiting Prof. of European Business, Univ. of Durham 1995–2003; currently John Monnet Prof. of European Business and Man., European Business School, London; Dir Europa Times 1993–94, Change Group Int. 1996–2003; Deputy Chair. Enterprise Support Group 1993–94; Pres. Inst. of Linguists 1993–99, EUROTAS 1998–2003; Trustee Thomson Foundation 1993–2007; Assoc. Fellow, Templeton Coll. Oxford 1982–86; Visiting Prof., Imperial Coll. London 1987–91, Open Univ. 1992–2001; Hon. ed. European Business Journal 1987–2002; Hon. MBA (Northumbria) 1991. *Publications:* Doing Business in the European Community 1979, Networking in Organizations 1986, Developing an Active Company Approach to the European Market 1988, Readings in International Enterprise (Ed.) 1995, Ways Through the Wall (Ed.) 2005; articles on European integration and personal devt. *Leisure interests:* travel, golf, personal and inner development. *Address:* 49 The Ridgeway, London, NW11 8QP, England (home). *Telephone:* (20) 8455-5054 (office). *E-mail:* profdrew@eurotas.org (office).

DREWS, Juergen, MD; German physician and business executive; *Managing Partner, Bear Stearns Health Innoventures Management LLC;* b. 16 Aug. 1933, Berlin; s. of Walter Drew and Lotte Grohnert; m. Dr Helga Eberlein 1963; three d.; ed Univs of Berlin, Innsbruck, Austria, Heidelberg and Yale Univ., USA; Prof. of Medicine, Univ. of Heidelberg 1973–; Head Chemotherapy Section, Sandoz Research Inst., Vienna 1976–79, Head Sandoz Research Inst. 1979–82, Int. Pharmaceutical R&D, Sandoz, Basel 1982–85; Dir Pharmaceutical Research, F. Hoffmann-La Roche Ltd, Basel 1985–86, Chair. Research Bd and mem. Exec. Cttee 1986–90, Pres. Int. R&D and mem. Exec. Cttee Roche Group, Hoffmann-La Roche Inc., Nutley, NJ 1991–95, Pres. Global Research, mem. Exec. Cttee 1996–97; Chair. Int. Biomedicine Man. Partners, Basel 1998–2001; Chair., Genaissance Pharmaceuticals Inc –2005; currently Man. Pnr, Bear Stearns Health Innoventures Man. LLC; fmr Chair., Supervisory Bd Tegenero Immuno Therapeutics AG; mem. Dean's Council, Yale Univ. School of Medicine 1993; mem. Bd of Dirs Protein Design Labs, Inc., Calif., MorphoSys GmbH, Munich, Genomics Pharmaceutical Company, Munch, Human Genome Sciences, Md;. *Publications:* Chemotherapie 1979, Immunpharmakologie, Grundlagen und Perspektiven 1986, Immunopharmacology 1990, Die verspielte Zukunft 1998, In Quest of Tomorrow's Medicines 1999; more than 200 scientific papers. *Leisure interests:* skiing, climbing, literature, piano. *Address:* Bear Stearns Health Innoventures LLC, 83 Madison Avenue, 28th Floor, New York, NY 10179, USA (office). *Telephone:* (212) 272-2253 (office). *Fax:* (212) 881-1378 (office). *E-mail:* jdrews@bear.com (office). *Website:* www.healthinnoventures.com (office).

DREXLER, Millard (Mickey) S.; American business executive; *Chairman and CEO, J. Crew Group, Inc.;* b. 1944, Bronx, New York; m.; worked part-time in garment industry, New York; Pres., CEO Ann Taylor Co.; Exec. Vice-Pres. Merchandising, Pres. Gap Stores Div. Gap Inc., San Bruno, Calif. 1983–, now Pres., mem. Bd of Dirs. The Gap Inc., San Bruno, Pres., CEO The Gap Inc., San Francisco 1995–2002; Chair. and CEO J. Crew Group Inc. 2003–. *Leisure interest:* novels by John Grisham. *Address:* J. Crew Group Inc., 770 Broadway, New York, NY 10013, USA (office). *Telephone:* (212) 209-2500. *Fax:* (212) 209-2666. *Website:* www.jcrew.com.

DREYFUS, George, AM; Australian composer; b. 22 July 1928, Wuppertal, Germany; two s. one d.; ed Vienna Acad. of Music; Composer-in-Residence, Tienjin, China 1983, Shanghai 1987, Nanjing 1991; Grosses Bundesverdienstkreuz (Germany); Henry Lawson Award 1972, Prix de Rome 1976, 2004, Mishkenot Sha'ananim, Jerusalem 1980, Don Banks Fellowship 1992. *Compositions include:* Garni Sands, The Gilt-Edged Kid (operas); Symphonies Nos. 1 & 2; Symphonie Concertante 1977; Jingles ... & More Jingles; Reflections in a Glasshouse; The Illusionist; The Grand Aurora Australis Now Show; Galgenlieder; Songs Comic & Curious; Music in the Air; From within Looking out; The Seasons; Ned Kelly Ballads; Quintet after the Notebook of J.-G. Noverre; Sextet for Didjeridoo & Wind Instruments; Old Melbourne; several pieces for young people; The Sentimental Bloke (musical) 1985, Lifestyle 1988, Song of Brother Sun 1988 (choral pieces), Rathenau (opera) 1993, Die Marx Sisters (opera) 1994; more than 100 scores for film and TV including The Adventures of Sebastian the Fox 1963, Rush 1974, Great Expectations 1986. *Television:* The Gilt-Edged Kid (Australian Broadcasting Corpn —ABC) 1975, Didjeridu in Deutschland (SBS) 1988, Bicycles and Bassoons (SBS) 1989, Life is Too Serious (ABC) 2000. *Publications:* The Last Frivolous Book (autobiog.) 1984, Being George – And Liking It! 1998; numerous commercial CDs on the Move label. *Leisure interests:* swimming, gardening. *Address:* 3 Grace Street, Camberwell, Vic. 3124, Australia (home). *Telephone:* (3) 9809-2671 (home). *Fax:* (3) 9809-2671 (home). *E-mail:* gdreyfus@bigpond.net.au (home).

DREYFUS, Gilles D., MD; French cardio-thoracic surgeon and academic; *Professor of Cardiac Surgery, Royal Brompton & Harefield NHS Trust;* b. 24 May 1951, Paris; ed Paris V Universite, Rene Descartes Medical School; began career as intern, Paris Hospitals 1978; Chef de Clinique, assistant des hopitaux 1982–86; univ. prof. 1989; Chief of Cardiothoracic Unit, Foch Hospital, Paris 1996–2001; Prof. of Cardiac Surgery, Dept of Cardiac Surgery, Royal Brompton & Harefield NHS Trust 2001–; Prof., Imperial Coll. London; mem. European Asscn for Cardio-Thoracic Surgery, French Soc. for Thoracic and Cardiovascular Surgery, French Soc. for Cardiology, Soc. for Heart Valve Disease, American Asscn for Thoracic Surgery, Soc. of Thoracic Surgeons, Int. Soc. for Heart and Lung Transplantation, British Cardiac Soc.; Chevalier de la Légion d'honneur. *Leisure interests:* skiing, golf. *Address:* Harefield Hospital, Hill End Road, Harefield, Middlesex, UB9 6JH (office); 34 Queen's Gate Gardens, London SW7 5RR, England (home). *Telephone:* (1895) 828665 (office). *Fax:* (1895) 828666 (office). *E-mail:* g.dreyfus@rbht.nhs.uk (office); g.dreyfus@btinternet.com (home). *Website:* www.rbht.nhs.uk (office).

DREYFUSS, Richard Stephan; American actor; b. 29 Oct. 1947, New York; s. of Norman Dreyfuss and Gerry D. Student; m. Jeramie Dreyfuss 1983; two s. one d.; ed San Fernando Valley State Coll.; alternative mil. service Los Angeles County Gen. Hosp. 1969–71; mem. American Civil Liberties Union Screen Actors Guild, Equity Asscn, American Fed. of TV and Radio Artists, Motion Picture Acad. Arts and Sciences; Golden Globe Award 1978, Acad. Award for Best Actor in The Goodbye Girl 1978. *Stage appearances include:* Julius Caesar 1978, The Big Fix (also producer) 1978, Othello 1979, Death and the Maiden 1992, The Prisoner of Second Avenue 1999, Complicit 2008. *Films include:* American Graffitti 1972, Dillinger 1973, The Apprenticeship of Duddy Kravitz 1974, Jaws 1975, Inserts 1975, Close Encounters of the Third Kind 1976, The Goodbye Girl 1977, The Competition 1980, Whose Life Is It Anyway? 1981, Down and Out in Beverly Hills 1986, Stakeout 1988, Moon over Parador 1989, Let it Ride, Always 1989, Rosencrantz and Guildernstern are Dead, Postcards from the Edge 1990, Once Around 1990, Randall and Juliet 1990, Prisoners of Honor 1991, What About Bob? 1991, Lost in Yonkers 1993, Another Stakeout 1993, The American President, Mr Holland's Opus 1995, Mad Dog Time 1996, James and the Giant Peach (voice) 1996, Night Falls on Manhattan 1997, The Call of the Wild 1997, Krippendorf's Tribe 1998, A Fine and Private Place 1998, The Crew 2000, The Old Man Who Read Love Stories 2000, Who is Cletis Tout? 2001, Silver City 2004, Poseidon 2006, Signs of the Time 2008, W 2008, My Life in Ruins 2009. *Television includes:* Nuts 1987 (dir, producer) Oliver Twist 1997, Fail Safe 2000, Education of Max Bickford 2001–02, Day Reagan Was Shot 2001, Coast to Coast 2003, Copshop 2004, Ocean of Fear 2007, Tin Man 2007. *Publication:* The Two Georges (with Harry Turtledove) 1996. *Address:* William Morris Agency, 1 William Morris Place, Beverly Hills, CA 90212, USA (office). *Telephone:* (310) 859-4000 (office). *Fax:* (310) 859-4462 (office). *Website:* www.wma.com (office).

DRÈZE, Jacques H., PhD; Belgian economist and academic; *Professor Emeritus, Center for Operations Research and Econometrics (CORE);* b. Verviers; m.; five s.; ed Univ. de Liège, Columbia Univ., USA; Visiting Asst. Prof., Carnegie Inst. of Tech. 1957–58; Lecturer, Univ. Catholique de Louvain 1958–62, Prof. 1962–89; Visiting Assoc. Prof., Northwestern Univ. 1962; Ford Foundation Prof., Univ. of Chicago 1963–64, Prof. 1964–68; Titulaire de la Chaire Francqui Belge, Univ. de Bruxelles 1970–71, Katholieke Univ. Leuven 1982–83; Andrew D. White Prof.-at-Large, Cornell Univ. 1971–77; Research Fellow, Carnegie Inst. of Tech. 1954; Chargé de recherche Univ. Libre de Bruxelles 1958–60; Research Assoc., Purdue Univ. 1957, Northwestern Univ. 1962, 1963, Univ. of Wisconsin 1964, MIT 1966, Stanford Univ. 1979; Research Dir Center for Operations Research and Econometrics (CORE) 1966–71, Pres. 1971–83, now Prof. Emer.; mem. CEPS Macroeconomic Policy Group 1984–85, Chair. 1986–87; Chair. Bd Inst. of Man. Science 1961; Dir Int. Centre for Man. Science, Louvain 1966–71; Assoc. Ed. Econometrica 1963–64, Co-Ed. 1964–69; Vice-Pres. Econometric Soc. 1969, Pres. 1970; Pres. European Econ. Asscn. 1985–86, Int. Econ. Asscn. 1996–99; Co-ordinator European Unemployment Programme 1985–88; Corresp Fellow, British Acad. 1990; Foreign Assoc. US NAS 1993; Corresp. mem. Acad. Royale des Sciences, des Letters et de Beaux-Arts de Belgique 2000; Hon. mem. American Econ. Asscn 1976, Asociacion Argentina di Economica Politica 1998, Latin American and Caribbean Econ. Asscn. 1999; Foreign Hon. mem. American Acad. of Arts and Science 1978; Foreign mem. Royal Netherlands Acad. of Arts and Science 1980; mem. Academica Europaea 1989 Dr hc (Essex) 1980, (Sorbonne) 1980, (Montréal) 1982, (Liège) 1983, (Antwerp) 1985, (Norges Handelshoyskole, Bergen) 1986, (Bologna) 1988, (Geneva) 1988, (Basel) 1988, (Chicago) 1991, (Aix-Marseille) 1992, (Cergy-Pontoise) 1000, (Bolzano) 2000 Prix des Alumni, Fondation Universitaire, Brussels 1964, Prix Emile De Laveleye, Acad. Royale des Sciences, des Lettres et des Beaux-Arts de Belgique 1993, Prix, Acad. dei Lincei, Rome 1999. *Publications include:* numerous books and articles on econ. policy including contribs. to: Economic Essays: A Festschrift for Werner Hildenbrand 2001, Monetary Theory as Basis for Monetary Policy 2001, On the Macroeconomics of Uncertainty and Incomplete Markets 2001. *Address:*

Centre for Operations Research and Econometrics (CORE), Université Catholique de Louvain, Voie du Roman Pays, 34, 1348 Louvain-la-Neuve, Belgium (office). *Telephone:* (10) 474347 (office). *Fax:* (10) 474301 (office). *E-mail:* dreze@core.ucl.ac.be (office). *Website:* www.core.ucl.ac.be (office).

DRINFELD, Vladimir Gershonovich, PhD; Ukrainian mathematician; *Researcher, B. Verkin Institute for Low Temperature Physics and Engineering;* b. 14 Feb. 1954, Kharkov (now Kharkiv); ed Moscow Univ., Steklov Inst., Moscow; B. Verkin Inst. for Low Temperature Physics and Eng, Nat. Acad. of Sciences of the Ukraine 1981–; mem. Nat. Acad. of Sciences of the Ukraine 1992–; Fields Medal, Int. Congress of Mathematicians, (Kyoto, Japan) 1990. *Publications:* numerous publs on quantum groups and number theory. *Address:* B. Verkin Institute for Low Temperature Physics and Engineering, 47 Lenin Avenue, Kharkov 61103, Ukraine (office). *Telephone:* (57) 340-22-23 (office). *Fax:* (57) 340-33-70 (office). *E-mail:* ilt@ilt.kharkov.ua (office). *Website:* www.ilt.kharkov.ua (office).

DRISS, Rachid; Tunisian diplomatist and journalist; *President, Association des études internationales;* b. 27 Jan. 1917, Tunis; m. Jeanine Driss 1953; one s.; ed Sadiki Coll., Tunis; joined Neo-Destour party 1934; journalist exiled in Cairo and, with Pres. Bourguiba, Founder mem. Bureau du Maghreb Arabe; returned to Tunisia 1955; Ed. El Amal; Deputy, Constitutional Ass. 1956; Minister of Posts, Telegraph and Telephones 1957–64; mem. Nat. Ass. 1959, 1969; Amb. to USA and Mexico 1964–69; mem. Political Bureau of Council of the Repub. 1969–; Perm. Rep. to UN 1970–76; Vice-Pres. Econ. and Soc. Council 1970, Pres. 1971, 1972; mem. Conseil Constitutionnel 1987–92; Special Emissary of Arab League to Kuwait and Iraq 1992; Founder, Pres. Asscn des études internationales 1981–, Arab Bd for Child Devt; Pres. Higher Comm. on Human Rights and Fundamental Freedoms 1991–2000; Dir Etudes Internationales (quarterly); Grand Cordon de l'Ordre de l'Indépendance de la République Tunisienne and many foreign decorations. *Publications:* From Bab Souika to Manhattan 1980, Diaries from the Maghreb Office in Cairo 1981, A l'aube la lanterne 1981, From Djakarta to Carthage 1985, Errances (poems) 1990, Feuilles d'insomnie (novel) 1990, Report on Human Rights in Tunisia 1992, Au gré du Calame (poems) 1996, Reflets d'un combat (history of Tunisian Nat. Movt) 1997. *Address:* Rue St Cyprien, 2016 Carthage, Tunisia (home). *Telephone:* (71) 791663 (office); (71) 746846 (home). *Fax:* (71) 796593 (office). *E-mail:* aeitunis@planet.tn (office).

DRIVER, Minnie (Amelia); British actress; b. 31 Jan. 1970, London; d. of Charles Driver and Gaynor Churchward (née Millington); ed Bedales School, Hants.; Best Newcomer, London Circle of Film Critics 1997, Best Actress, London Circle of Film Critics 1998. *Television appearances include:* God on the Rocks 1990, Mr Wroe's Virgins 1993, The Politician's Wife 1995, The Riches (series) 2007. *Films include:* Circle of Friends 1995, Goldeneye 1995, Baggage 1996, Big Night 1996, Sleepers 1996, Grosse Pointe Blank 1997, Good Will Hunting 1997, The Governess 1998, Hard Rain 1998, At Sachem Farm 1998, Trespasser (voice) 1998, An Ideal Husband 1999, Tarzan (voice) 1999, South Park: Bigger, Longer and Uncut 1999, Slow Burn 2000, Beautiful 2000, Return to Me 2000, The Upgrade 2000, High Heels and Lowlifes 2001, D.C. Smalls 2001, Owning Mahoney 2003, Hope Springs 2003, Ella Enchanted 2004, Portrait 2004, The Phantom of the Opera 2004, The Virgin of Juarez 2006, Delirious 2006. *Play:* Sexual Perversity in Chicago, Comedy Theatre, London 2003. *Recordings:* album: Everything I've Got in My Pocket 2004, Seastories 2008. *Address:* c/o Lou Coulson, First Floor, 37 Berwick Street, London, W1V 3LF, England. *Telephone:* (20) 7734-9633.

DRONKE, (Ernst) Peter (Michael), MA, FBA; British medieval Latin scholar and author; *Professor Emeritus of Medieval Latin Literature, University of Cambridge;* b. 30 May 1934; s. of A. H. R. Dronke and M. M. Dronke (née Kronfeld); m. Ursula Miriam Brown 1960; one d.; ed Victoria Univ., NZ and Magdalen Coll., Oxford; Research Fellow, Merton Coll., Oxford 1958–61; Lecturer in Medieval Latin, Univ. of Cambridge 1961–79, Reader in Medieval Latin Literature 1979–89, Prof. 1989–2001, Prof. Emer. 2001–, Fellow, Clare Hall 1964–2001; Visiting Prof. of Medieval Studies, Westfield Coll. London 1981–86; Carl Newell Jackson Lecturer, Harvard Univ., USA 1992; Corresp. Fellow, Real Academia de Buenas Letras, Royal Dutch Acad., Medieval Acad. of America, Austrian Acad. of Sciences, Fondazione Lorenzo Valla, Istituto Lombardo Acad. of Sciences and Letters; Co-ed. Mittellateinisches Jahrbuch 1977–2002; Hon. Pres., Int. Courtly Literature Soc.; Premio Internazionale Ascoli Piceno 1988. *Publications:* Medieval Latin and the Rise of European Love-Lyric (2 Vols) 1965–66, The Medieval Lyric 1968, Poetic Individuality in the Middle Ages 1970, Fabula 1974, Abelard and Heloïse in Medieval Testimonies 1976, Barbara et antiquissima carmina (with Ursula Dronke) 1977, Bernardus Silvestris, Cosmographia (ed.) 1978, Introduction to Francesco Colonna, Hypnerotomachia 1981, Women Writers of the Middle Ages 1984, The Medieval Poet and his World 1984, Dante and Medieval Latin Traditions 1986, Introduction to Rosvita, Dialoghi Drammatici 1986, A History of Twelfth-Century Western Philosophy (ed.) 1988, Hermes and the Sibyls 1990, Latin and Vernacular Poets of the Middle Ages 1991, Intellectuals and Poets in Medieval Europe 1992, Verse with Prose: From Petronius to Dante 1994, Nine Medieval Latin Plays 1994, Hildegard of Bingen, Liber divinorum operum (co-ed.) 1996, Sources of Inspiration 1997, Dante's Second Love (lectures) 1997, Introduction to Alessandro nel medioevo occidentale 1997, Growth of Literature: the Sea and the God of the Sea (with Ursula Dronke) 1998, Etienne Gilson's Letters to Bruno Nardi (ed.) 1998, Hildegard of Bingen: The Context of Her Thought and Art (co-ed.) 1998, Imagination in the Late Pagan and Early Christian World 2003, Forms and Imaginings 2007, The Spell of Calcidius 2008; essays in learned journals and symposia. *Leisure interests:* music, film and Brittany. *Address:* 6 Parker Street, Cambridge, CB1 1JL, England (home).

DROSDICK, John G. (Jack), BEng; American business executive; *Chairman, Sunoco Inc.;* b. 1944, W Hazelton, Pa; ed Villanova Univ., Univ. of Mass; began career with Exxon Corpn 1968, various man. positions in NJ, Tex. and La; Pres. Tosco Corpn 1987–92; Pres. Ultramar Corpn 1992–96; Pres. and COO Sunoco Inc. 1996–2000, Chair., CEO and Pres. 2000–08, Chair. (non-exec.) July–Dec. 2008; Chair. Sunoco Partners LLC; Dir United States Steel (USS) Corpn 2003–; Dir Lincoln Nat. Corpn; Chair. Bd of Trustees, Villanova Univ.; Trustee, Kimmel Center for the Performing Arts, Philadelphia Museum of Art (also Chair. Exec. Bd). *Address:* Sunoco Inc., 1735 Market Street, Suite LL, Philadelphia, PA 19103-7583, USA (office). *Telephone:* (215) 977-3000 (office). *Fax:* (215) 977-3409 (office). *E-mail:* info@sunocoinc.com (office). *Website:* www.sunocoinc.com (office).

DROZDOVA, Margarita Sergeyevna; Russian ballerina; b. 7 May 1948, Moscow; ed Moscow Choreographic School, State Inst. of Theatre Art (GITIS); danced with Stanislavsky Musical Theatre Ballet Co., Moscow 1967–87, apptd teacher/repetiteur and balletmaster 1987; mem. CPSU 1980–91; Int. Competitions for Ballet Dancers in Varna 1972, in Moscow 1973, Anna Pavlova Award, Paris 1968; RSFSR State Prize 1980, People's Artist of USSR 1986. *Roles include:* Odette-Odile, Gayané, The Commissar (M. Bronner's 'Optimistic Tragedy'), Medora (A. Adam's 'Corsaire'), Swanilda (Delibes' 'Coppélia'), Cinderella (Prokofiev). *Address:* c/o Stanislavsky and Nemirovich Danchenko Musical Theatre, Bolshaya Dmitrovka 17, Moscow, Russia. *Telephone:* (495) 629-83-88; (495) 299-31-36 (home).

DRUBICH, Tatyana Lusienovna; Russian actress; b. 7 June 1960, Moscow; m. Sergey Soloviev (divorced); one d.; ed Third Moscow Medical Inst.; worked as a nurse then as a physician; actress 1972–; Head of Russian Rep. of German chemical factory Dr Weigert 1992–. *Films include:* 15th Spring (debut) 1972, 100 Days after Childhood 1975, Disarray 1978, Particularly Dangerous 1978, The Rescuer 1979, The Direct Heiress 1982, Selected 1983, Tester 1984, Black Monk 1986, Keep Me, My Talisman 1986, Assa 1987, Black Rose – an Emblem of Sorrow, White Rose – an Emblem of Love 1989, Hey, Fools 1996, Moscow 2000, O lyubvi (About Love) 2003, Gololed (Slippery Ice), Anna Karenina 2007, 2-Assa-2, ili vtoraya smert' Anny Kareninoy (2-Assa-2, or The Second Death of Anna Karenina) 2007. *Address:* Seleznevskaya str. 30, korp. 3, Apt 77, 103473 Moscow, Russia. *Telephone:* (495) 281-60-82.

DRUCKER, Michel; French television journalist; b. 12 Sept. 1942, Vire (Calvados); s. of Abraham Drucker and Lola Schafler; m. Danielle Savalle (Dany Saval) 1973; ed Lycée Emile-Maupas, Vire; sports reporter, ORTF 1964, presenter variety programmes 1966, producer and presenter Sport en Fête, football commentator 1969; commentator World Cup Football Championships 1970, 1974, 1978; presenter (Radio-Télé-Luxembourg – RTL) C'est vous 1974–, Les Rendez-vous du dimanche 1975–1981, Stars 1981, Champs-Elysées 1982–85, (Europe 1) Studio 1 1983, (Antenne 2) Champs-Elysées, 1987–90, (TF1) Stars 90 1990–94, Ciné Stars 1991–94, (France 2) Studio Gabriel 1994–97, Faites la fête 1994–98, Drucker & Co., Stars & Co. 1997–98, Vivement dimanche, Vivement dimanche prochain, Tapis rouge 1998–2001, Tenue de soirée 2006–; Founder Production DMD 1998; Chevalier Légion d'honneur, des Arts et Lettres; Sports Journalist of the Year, Télémagazine 1971, 1972, 1973, Prix Triomphe de la télévision à la Nuit du cinéma 1973, 1987, 7 d'Or Award for Best Variety Programme Presenter, Prix Gémeaux de la francophonie, Quebec, Canada 2000. *Publications:* La Balle au bond (autobiog.) 1973, La Coupe du monde de football 1974, La Chaîne (novel) 1979, Novembre des amours 1984, Hors antenne, conversation avec Maurice Achard 1987, Les Numéros 1. Tous les grands du football français 1987, Stars 90 2000, Mais Qu'est-ce qu'on va faire de toi? 2007. *Leisure interests:* tennis, cycling, football, skiing, flying. *Address:* Production DMD, 21 rue Jean Mermoz, 75008 Paris (office); Pavillon Gabriel, 9 avenue Gabriel, 75008 Paris, France (home). *Telephone:* 1-40-76-00-89 (office). *Fax:* 1-45-63-61-42 (office).

DRURY, Very Rev. John Henry, MA; British ecclesiastic and university administrator; *Chaplain and Fellow, All Souls College, Oxford;* b. 23 May 1936, Clacton; s. of Henry Drury and Barbara Drury; m. Clare Nineham 1972 (died 2004); two d.; ed Bradfield Coll. and Trinity Hall, Cambridge; Curate, St John's Wood Church, London 1963; Chaplain, Downing Coll. Cambridge 1966; Chaplain and Fellow, Exeter Coll. Oxford 1969; Canon of Norwich Cathedral 1973; lecturer, Univ. of Sussex 1979; Dean, Kings Coll. Cambridge 1981; Dean, Christ Church, Oxford 1991–2003; Hussey Lecturer Univ. of Oxford 1997; Chaplain and Fellow, All Souls Coll., Oxford 2003–; Hon. Fellow, Exeter Coll., Oxford 1992, Trinity Hall, Cambridge 1997, Hon. Student of Christ Church, Oxford 2003. *Television:* Painting the Word, Channel 5 (UK), 2002. *Publications:* Angels and Dirt 1972, Luke 1973, Tradition and Design in Luke's Gospel 1976, Parables in the Gospels 1985, Critics of the Bible 1724–1873 1989, The Burning Bush 1990, Painting the Word 1999. *Leisure interests:* drawing, walking, carpentry. *Address:* All Souls College, Oxford, OX1 4AL, England. *Telephone:* (1865) 279368. *Fax:* (1865) 279299. *E-mail:* john.drury@all-souls.ac.uk.

DRUT, Guy Jacques; French politician and fmr athlete; b. 6 Dec. 1950, Oignies (Pas de Calais); s. of Jacques Drut and Jacqueline Wigley; m. 2nd Véronique Hardy 1984; one d. and one d. by first m.; ed Lycée de Douai, Lycée d'Henin-Liétard, Lycée Roubaix, Ecole Normale Supérieure d'Educ. Physique et Sportive and Inst. Nat. des Sports; French Jr record-holder, 110m hurdles, pole vault and decathlon; French 110m hurdles champion 1970–76, 1981; European 100m hurdles champion, Rome 1974; European 110m hurdles record, Rome 1974, world record, Berlin 1975; silver medal, 110m hurdles, Munich Olympics 1972, gold medal, Montreal Olympics 1976; bronze medal, 50m hurdles, European Championships 1981; retd from competition 1981; Chief of Staff to Prime Minister Jacques Chirac 1975–76; mem. Nat. Council UDR, Cen. Cttee RPR; Deputy Mayor of Paris responsible for Youth and Sport 1985–89; Deputy (RPR) from Seine-et-Marne to Nat. Ass. 1986–95; Town

Councillor, Meaux 1989–92; Regional Councillor, Ile-de-France 1992–; Mayor of Coulommiers 1992–; Minister of Youth and Sport May–Nov. 1995, Minister del. 1995–97; elected Deputy for Seine-et-Marne (Groupe du Rassemblement pour la République) 1997, re-elected (Groupe Union pour un Mouvement Populaire) 2002–; mem. IOC 1996–2005 (resgnd); Chevalier, Ordre Nat. du Mérite. *Publications:* L'or et l'argent 1976, Jacques Chirac: la victoire du sport (co-author) 1988, J'ai deux mots à vous dire 1997. *Leisure interests:* golf, hunting. *Address:* Mairie, 77120 Coulommiers; Assemblée nationale, 75355 Paris, France. *Telephone:* 1-64-75-80-02 (office). *Fax:* 1-64-75-03-53 (office). *E-mail:* gdrut@assemblee-nationale.fc (office). *Website:* www.assemblee -nationale.fc (office).

DRYSDALE, Andrew; South African journalist; b. 19 Oct. 1935, Duiwelsk-loof, Transvaal; s. of Andrew Patarson Drysdale; ed Parktown High School; fmr Ed. The Argus; Fellow Harvard Univ., USA. *Leisure interests:* golf, tennis. *Address:* PO Box 56, Cape Town 8000, South Africa.

DRYUKOV, Anatoly Matveyevich; Russian diplomatist; b. 4 Sept. 1936, Voronezh; m.; two d.; ed Moscow Inst. of Int. Relations; diplomatic service 1960–; Attaché, Embassy in Karachi 1962–64; mem. Dept of S East Asia, USSR Ministry of Foreign Affairs 1964–66; mem. Secr. of Deputy Minister 1966–69; First Sec., Embassy in Lusaka 1969–73; Asst Deputy Minister 1973–78, expert, Deputy Chief Dept of S East Asia 1978–86, Deputy Chief Dept of Socialist Countries of Asia 1986–87; with Embassy in Singapore 1987–90; Chief, Main Dept of Staff and higher educ. establishments of USSR Ministry of Foreign Affairs 1990–91; Amb. to India 1991–96; Gen. Insp., Ministry of Foreign Affairs 1996–98; Amb. to Armenia 1998–2005. *Address:* c/o Ministry of Foreign Affairs, 119200 Moscow, Smolenskaya-Sennaya pl. 32/34, Russian Federation.

DU, Daozheng; Chinese journalist; *Publisher, Yanhuang Chunqiu;* b. Nov. 1923, Dingxiang Co., Shanxi Prov.; s. of Du Xixiang and Qi Luaying; m. Xu Zhixian 1950; one s. four d.; ed Middle School, Dingxiang, Shanxi and Beijing Marx-Lenin Coll.; joined CCP 1937; Chief of Hebei and Guangdong Bureau, Xinhua News Agency 1949–56; Ed.-in-Chief Yangchen Wanbao 1956–69; Dir Home News Dept, Xinhua News Agency 1977–82; Ed.-in-Chief Guangming Daily 1982; Dir Media and Publs Office 1987–88; Deputy 7th NPC 1988–92; Dir State Press and Publs Admin. 1988–89; Founder and Publisher, Yanhuang Chunqiu (liberal journal) 1991–; Hon. Pres. Newspaper Operation and Man. Asscn 1988–; Nat. News Prize 1979. *Publications:* Explore Japan (co-author), Interviews with Famous Chinese Journalists. *Leisure interest:* photography. *Address:* Yanhuang Chunqiu, Beijing, People's Republic of China (office).

DU, Ming-xin; Chinese composer and music editor; b. 19 Aug. 1928, Qianjiang Co., Hubei Prov.; m. 1966; one s. one d.; ed Yu Cai Music School and Tchaikovsky State Conservatoire, USSR; debut solo piano concert, Shanghai 1948; Prof. of Composition, Cen. Conservatory of Music 1978–; participated in the Asian Composers' Conference and Music Festival, Hong Kong 1981; travelled to USA for performance of Violin Concerto No. 1, John F. Kennedy Center 1986, and gave lectures in music insts; Exec. Dir Chinese Musicians' Asscn; mem. 11th CPPCC 1997–2002. *Compositions include:* Violin Concerto No. 1, Violin Concerto No. 2, Piano Concerto No. 1, Piano Concerto No. 2, Great Wall Symphony, Luoshen Symphony, Youth Symphony, The South Sea of My Mother Land (symphonic picture), The Goddess of the River Luo (symphonic fantasia), Flapping! the Flags of Army, The Mermaid (ballet suite), The Red Detachment of Women (ballet suite), Wonderful China (film soundtrack) 1982, piano trio, string quartet. *Address:* Central Conservatory of Music, 43 Baojia Street, Beijing 100031, People's Republic of China.

DU, Qinglin, MA; Chinese politician; *Vice-Chairman, 11th CPPCC National Committee;* b. Nov. 1946, Panshi Co., Jilin Prov.; ed Northeast China Teachers' Univ., Jilin Univ.; joined CCP 1966; mem. Young Cadres Class, CCP Jilin City Cttee 1964–66; mem. and Deputy Group Leader Socialist Educ. Work Team, CCP Liuhe Co. Cttee, Jilin Prov., Yongji Co. Cttee, Jilin Prov., Shulan Co. Cttee, Jilin Prov. 1964–66; clerical worker, Publicity Dept, CCP Jilin City Cttee 1967–68; Sec. CCP Communist Youth League and Head of Workshop, No. 1 Automobile Works 1968–74, Deputy Chair. CCP Revolutionary Cttee 1974–78, Deputy Dir No. 1 Automobile Works 1974–78, Deputy Sec. CCP Party Br. 1974–78; Sec. CCP Communist Youth League, Jilin City Cttee 1978–79; Deputy Sec. Communist Youth League Jilin Prov. Cttee, mem. Communist Youth League Cen. Cttee 1979–84; Deputy Sec. CCP Changchun City Cttee 1984–85; Deputy Sec. CCP Jilin Prov. Cttee 1988–92; Deputy Sec. CCP Hainan Prov. Cttee 1992–98, Sec. 1998–2001; Alt. mem. 14th CCP Cen. Cttee 1992–97, mem. 15th CCP Cen. Cttee 1997–2002, 16th CCP Cen. Cttee 2002–07, 17th CCP Cen. Cttee 2007–; Chair. Standing Cttee, Hainan Prov. People's Congress 1993–2001; Minister of Agric. 2001–06; Sec. Sichuan CCP Prov. Cttee 2006–07; Head CCP Cen. Cttee United Front Work Dept 2007–; Vice-Chair. 11th CPPCC Nat. Cttee 2008–. *Address:* Chinese People's Political Consultative Conference, Beijing, People's Republic of China (office).

DU, Runsheng; Chinese politician and economist (retd); b. 8 Aug. 1913, Taigu, Shanxi; ed Beijing Teachers' Univ.; involved in revolutionary activities in early 1930s; Commdr guerrilla forces, Taihang Mountains; mem. of a border region govt, Deputy Gov. Taihang Pref. 1937–45; Sec.-Gen. Cen.-Plains Bureau, CCP 1946–49; Sec.-Gen. Cen.-South Bureau, CCP, Vice-Chair. Land Reform Cttee of Cen.-South Region 1949; Sec.-Gen. Cen. Dept of Rural Work, CCP and Deputy Dir Agric. and Forestry Office of State Council 1953; Sec.-Gen. Acad. of Sciences 1956–79; in disgrace during Cultural Revolution 1967–76; Deputy Dir State Agric. Comm. in charge of Policy Study on Rural Reform 1979–82; Dir Rural Policy Research Office of Secr., CCP and Pres. Rural Devt Research Centre, State Council; in charge of Policy Study on Rural Econ. Reform and Devt 1982; Pres. Soc. of Land Econ. 1994–; mem. Cen.

Advisory Cttee, CCP 1983–, Deputy Head Leading Group for Educ. of Cadres, CCP Cen. Cttee 1985, Deputy to NPC, mem. Finance and Econ. Cttee, NPC 1983–88; mem. Leading Group for Finance and Economy of CCP Cen. Cttee 1988–89; Pres. China Agricultural Econs Soc. 1988; Vice-Chair. Nat. Agricultural Zoning Cttee 1983–; Deputy Head Leading Group for Devt of Rural Energy 1984–; Dir Rural Policy Research Centre of CCP Cen. Cttee 1988; Pres. Friendship Asscn for the Mentally Handicapped 1993; a Vice-Pres. Chinese Fed. for the Disabled 1993–; Guest Prof. Chinese People's Univ.; Hon. Prof., Beijing Agricultural Univ. 1949–. *Publications:* Rural Economic Reform in China (collection of articles) 1985, many articles on rural devt in China. *Leisure interest:* tennis. *Address:* State Council's Research Center for Rural Development, 9 Xihuangchenggen Nanjie, Beijing 100032, People's Republic of China (office). *Telephone:* 665254 (office).

DU, Shuanghua; Chinese business executive; *Chairman, Hengshui Jinghua Steel Pipe Co;* b. Hebei Prov.; Man. Hengshui Jinghua Steel Pipe Co. Ltd, Rizhao Steel. *Address:* Hengshui Jinghua Pipe Co. Ltd, Lizhuang, Nanjiao, Hengshui, Hebei Province, People's Republic of China (office). *Telephone:* (318) 6018009 (office). *Fax:* (318) 6018188 (office). *E-mail:* jhhg@jhhg.net (office). *Website:* www.jhhg.net (office).

DU, Gen. Tiehuan; Chinese army officer; b. 1938, Anshan City, Liaoning Prov.; ed PLA Mil. Acad.; Asst Dir PLA Gen. Political Dept 1993–94; Political Commissar Ji'nan Mil. Region 1994–96; Political Commissar, Beijing Mil. Area Command 1996–97; mem. 15th CCP Cen. Cttee 1997–2002; rank of Lt-Gen. 1997, Gen. 2000. *Address:* c/o Political Commissar's Office, Beijing Military Area Command, Beijing, People's Republic of China (office).

DU, Yuzhou; Chinese government official; *Director, State Administration for the Textile Industry;* b. 1942, Qiqihar, Heilongjiang; ed Tsinghua Univ.; joined CCP 1965; technician, Changde Textile Machinery Plant, Hunan 1968–70, Deputy Workshop Head, then Deputy Section Chief 1970–73; engineer, Deputy Dir then Dir Design Inst. of Ministry of Textile Industry 1978–85; Vice-Minister of Textiles 1985–93; Vice-Chair., Chair. Chinese Gen. Asscn of Textile Industry, Dir State Admin. for the Textile Industry 1993–; Pres. China Nat. Garment Asscn; Chair. of China Nat. Fed. of Textile Manufacturers. *Address:* State Administration for the Textile Industry, 12 East Changan Street, Beijing 100742, People's Republic of China (office). *Telephone:* (10) 85229207 (office). *Website:* www.ctei.gov.cn (office).

DU CANN, Rt Hon. Sir Edward Dillon Lott, PC, KBE, MA, FRSA; British politician and business executive; b. 28 May 1924, Beckenham; s. of C. G. L. du Cann and Janet du Cann (née Murchie); m. 1st Sallie Murchie 1962 (divorced 1989); one s. two d.; m. 2nd Jenifer Patricia Evelyn (Lady Cooke) née King 1990 (died 1995); ed Woodbridge School, Suffolk and St John's Coll., Oxford; served with RNVR 1943–46; MP 1956–87; Founder and Chair. Unicorn Group of Unit Trusts 1957–62, 1964–72; Founder-mem. Asscn Unit Trust Mans. 1961, Chair. 1961; Econ. Sec. to the Treasury 1962–63; Minister of State, Bd of Trade 1963–64; Chair. of Conservative Party 1965–67, Pres. 1981–82; Chair. 1922 Cttee 1972–84; First Chair. Select Cttee on Public Expenditure 1971–73, Public Accounts Cttee 1974–79; mem. Cttee of Privileges 1972–87; First Chair. Treasury and Civil Service Cttee 1979–83, Liaison Cttee of Select Cttee Chairs 1979–83; Vice-Chair. British-American Parl. Group 1977–81; Pres. Conservative Parl. EC Reform Group 1985–87; Founder-Chair. All-Party Maritime Affairs Parl. Group 1984–87; Chair. Public Accounts Comm. 1984–87; led Parl. del. to USA 1978, 1979, first British Parl. del. to China 1982; Chair. Keyser Ullmann Ltd 1972–75, Cannon Assurance Ltd 1972–80, Lonrho PLC 1984–91 (Dir 1972–92), Sunshine Technology Group (China) 2006–; Dir Martins Bank 1967–69, Barclays Bank (London Bd) 1969–72; Visiting Fellow, Univ. of Lancaster Business School 1970–82; Patron Asscn of Insurance Brokers 1973–77, Human Ecology Foundation 1987; Gov. Hatfield Coll., Univ. of Durham 1988–92; Master Fruiterers Co. 1990; Pres. Inst. of Freight Forwarders 1988–89, Pres. Royal Naval Asscn (Cyprus Br.) 2004–, Oxford Univ. Rugby League Club 2004–06, Oxford Soc. (Cyprus Br.) 2005–; Vice-Pres. St Margarets Hospice, Taunton 1984–, Limassol Hospice 2003–; Hon. Vice-Pres. British Insurance Brokers Asscn 1978–; Chair. Templeton Foundation Awards Ceremony 1984 (mem. Panel of Judges 1984); mem. of Man. Council of the GB-SasaKawa British-Japanese Foundation 1984–93; Adm., House of Commons Yacht Club 1974–87; Hon. Col 155 Regiment (Wessex) Volunteers 1972–82; First Hon. Freeman Borough of Taunton Deane 1977; Hon. Life Mem. Inst. of RCT, Commonwealth Parl. Asscn, Taunton Racecourse. *Publications:* Investing Simplified 1959, The Case for a Bill of Rights 1975, How to Bring Government Expenditure under Parliamentary Control 1979, A New Competition Policy 1984, Hoist the Red Ensign 1987, Two Lives 1995, The Wellington Caricatures 2000. *Leisure interests:* sailing, gardening, walking the dog. *Address:* Flat 7, 42 Great Smith Street, London, SW1P 3BU, England; Pervolia, Lemona, 8545 Paphos, Cyprus. *E-mail:* edwardducann@btinternet.com.

DU PLESSIS, Christian; British singer (baritone); b. 2 July 1944, Vryheid, South Africa; ed Potchefstroom and Bloemfontein Univs, studied with Teasdale Griffiths and Esme Webb in South Africa, Otakar Kraus in London; debut with the PACT Opera in Johannesburg as Yamadori in Madama Butterfly 1967; British debut in Andrea Chénier at Theatre Royal, Drury Lane 1970; Valentin in Faust at Barcelona 1971; Prin. Baritone, ENO 1973–81, notably as Cecil in Maria Stuarda and Verdi's Germont and Posa; USA debut in Les Pêcheurs de Perles, Texas 1984; Covent Garden debut in Rigoletto 1984; recipient, Ernest Oppenheimer Bursary 1968, 1969, 1970; major roles with cos in UK, USA, France, Netherlands, Hong Kong, Ireland; retd 1988. *Leisure interest:* dir of fine arts gallery.

DU PLESSIS, Daniel Jacob, MB, MCh, FRCS; South African surgeon and university vice-chancellor; b. 17 May 1918, Paarl; s. of Daniel J. du Plessis and

Louisa M. (Carstens) du Plessis; m. Louisa S. Wicht 1946; two s.; ed Paarl Boys' High School, Univs of Cape Town and the Witwatersrand; Capt. South African Medical Corps 1942–46; postgraduate studies, Cape Town, Johannesburg, Oxford and London 1946–52; Surgeon, Univ. of Cape Town and Groote Schuur Hosp. 1952–58; Prof. of Surgery, Univ. of the Witwatersrand, Johannesburg 1958–77, Vice-Chancellor 1978–83; Nuffield Scholarship 1951–52, Carnegie Fellowship 1963; Hon. Fellowship American Coll. of Surgeons 1974, American Surgical Asscn 1981, Asscn of Surgeons of GB and Ireland 1979, Coll. of Surgeons of SA 1982; Pres. Southern Transvaal Br., Medical Asscn of SA 1986–87; mem. Advisory Council for Univs and Technikons 1984–92; Hon. Life Vice-Pres. Surgical Research Soc. of SA, Asscn of Surgeons of SA 1984; Chair. of Council, B. G. Alexander Nursing Coll. 1985–95; Natalspruit (now Bonalesedi) Nursing Coll. 1986–92; mem. Council, Medical Univ. of Southern Africa 1986–94, Johannesburg Coll. of Educ. 1986–92, Univ. of Transkei 1989–92; mem. Bd of Govs, American Coll. of Surgeons 1988–(94); Trustee South African Blood Transfusion Service 1985–; Hon. LLD (Witwatersrand) 1984; Hon. MD (Cape Town) 1986; Hon. PhD (Medical Univ. of Southern Africa) 1995; Paul Harris Rotary Award 1983; Order for Meritorious Service (Gold) 1989. *Publications:* Principles of Surgery 1968, Synopsis of Surgical Anatomy 1975; and articles in professional journals. *Leisure interests:* walking, reading. *Address:* 17 Chateau Road, Richmond, Johannesburg 2092, South Africa (home).

DU PLESSIS, Jan, LLB, BCom; South African chartered accountant and tobacco industry executive; *Non-Executive Chairman, British American Tobacco;* b. Cape Town; m.; two s. one d.; ed Univ. of Stellenbosch; qualified as chartered accountant; joined Rembrandt Group 1981, moved to England 1982, held various positions before co-founding Compagnie Financière Richemont SA (Swiss public co. formed following demerger of Rembrandt's non-South African interests 1988), Group Finance Dir 1988–2004; Finance Dir Rothmans Int. 1990–96; Dir (non-exec.) British American Tobacco (BAT) PLC 1999–, mem. Audit, Nominations and Remuneration Cttees, Chair. (non-exec.) BAT 2004–, Chair. Nominations Cttee; Chair. (non-exec.) RHM PLC 2005–07; Dir (non-exec.) Lloyds TSB 2005–, Rio Tinto 2008–, Marks & Spencer 2008–. *Address:* British American Tobacco PLC, Globe House, 4 Temple Place, London, WC2R 2PG, England (office). *Telephone:* (20) 7845-1936 (office). *Fax:* (20) 7845-2184 (office). *E-mail:* info@bat.com (office). *Website:* www.bat.com (office).

DUARTE, Cristina; Cape Verde politician, economist and international banker; *Minister of Finance and Public Administration;* Co-ordinator World Bank Growth and Competitiveness Project 2005–06; Minister of Finance and Public Admin 2006–. *Address:* Ministry of Finances and Public Administration, 107 Av. Amílcar Cabral, CP 30, Praia, Santiago, Cape Verde (office). *Telephone:* 2607400 (office). *E-mail:* aliciab@gov1.gov.cv (office). *Website:* www.mf.cv (office).

DUARTE FRUTOS, Oscar Nicanor, LicenFil, PhD; Paraguayan politician and fmr head of state; b. 11 Oct. 1956, Coronel Oviedo; m. María Gloria Penayo; six c.; ed Nat. Univ. of Asunción, Catholic Univ. of Asunción; journalist, Ultima Hora newspaper 1981–91; Minister of Educ. and Culture 1993–97, 1999–2001; Leader, Partido Colorado 2001–; Pres. of Paraguay 2003–08; fmr Prof. of Sociology and Ethics, Faculty of Philosophy, Nat. Univ. of Asunción. *Address:* Asociación Nacional Republicana—Partido Colorado, Casa de los Colorados, 25 de Mayo 842, Asunción, Paraguay (office). *Telephone:* (21) 44-4137 (office). *Fax:* (21) 49-7857 (office). *Website:* www.anr.org.py (office).

DUBAI, Ruler of (see MAKTOUM, Rashid al-).

DUBENETSKY, Yakov Nikolayevich; Russian banker and economist; *Head of Centre of Investments, Institute of National Economic Forecasting;* b. 26 Oct. 1938, Stayki, Belarus; m.; one s.; ed Moscow State Univ.; Deputy Chair. Stroybank of the USSR 1985–87; First Deputy Chair. Bank for Industry and Construction of the USSR (Pomstroybank of the USSR) 1987–91; Chair. Bd Russian Jt Stock Investment and Commercial Bank for Industry and Construction (Pomstroybank of Russia) 1991–99; apptd Chair. Bank Asscn of Russia 1995; currently Head of Centre of Investments, Inst. of Nat. Econ. Forecasting, Russian Acad. of Sciences; Vice-Pres. Asscn of Russian Banks 1995–; Co-Chair. Round Table of Russian Business 2000–; mem. Political Consultative Council of Pres. of Russian Fed. 1996–, Nat. Banking Council 1996–, Int. Acad. of Man. 1997–, Bd for finance and economy, Rosneftegazstroi 2001–. *Address:* Institute of National Economic Forecasting, Russian Academy of Sciences, 47 Nakhimovskii prospect, 117418 Moscow, Russia (office). *Telephone:* (045) 129-34-22 (office). *Fax:* (045) 310-70-71 (office). *E-mail:* office@mail.ecfor.rssi.ru (office). *Website:* www.ecfor.rssi.ru (office).

DUBININ, Sergey Konstantinovich, DEcon; Russian business executive; *Financial Director, RAO UES;* b. 10 Dec. 1950, Moscow; m.; two c.; ed Moscow State Univ.; Docent, Researcher and Prof., Moscow State Univ. 1974–91; mem. Pres. Mikhail Gorbachev's admin 1991; Deputy Chair. Russian State Cttee for co-operation with CIS 1992–93; First Deputy Minister of Finance, Acting Minister of Finance 1993–94; First Deputy Chair. Exec. Bd Commercial Bank Imperial 1994–95; mem. Exec. Bd Jt Stock co. Gazprom 1995, Deputy Chair. Bd Gazprom Co. 1998–2001; Deputy CEO Unified Power Grids of Russia (RAO ES) 2001–, currently mem. Man. Bd and Financial Dir; Chair. Cen. Bank of Russia 1995–98; Russian Rep. to IBRD 1996–98; Chair. Interstate Monetary Cttee CIS 1996–98, Supervisory Bd Sberbank and Vneshtorgbank; 850th Anniversary of Moscow Govt Award 1998. *Publications:* books on public, int. and corp. finance and finance markets; numerous articles on scientific research. *Leisure interests:* art, classical music, theatre, sports. *Address:* RAO UES, 101-3 Vernadskogo Prosp, 119526 Moscow, Russia (office). *Telephone:* (495) 710-44-45 (office). *Fax:* (495) 625-29-52 (office). *E-mail:* baldihina@rao.elektra.ru (office). *Website:* www.rao-ees.ru (office).

DUBININ, Yuri Vladimirovich, DHistSc; Russian diplomatist (retd) and academic; *Professor of International Politics, Moscow State Institute of International Relations, Ministry of Foreign Affairs;* b. 7 Oct. 1930, Nalchik; m. Liana Khatchatrian 1953; three d.; ed Moscow Inst. for Int. Relations; mem. CPSU 1954–91; Asst at Embassy in Paris 1955–56; with UNESCO Secr., Paris 1956–59; mem. Apparat USSR Ministry of Foreign Affairs 1959–63, 1969–78; First Sec., Embassy Counsellor, Embassy in Paris 1963–69; Amb. to Spain 1978–86, to USA 1986–90, to France 1990–91; Perm. Rep. to UN, New York 1986; Prof. of Political Science, George Washington Univ., USA 1991; Visiting Prof. of Politics and History, Washington and Lee Univ. 1993; Amb.-at-Large 1991–94; Deputy Minister of Foreign Affairs 1994–99; Amb. to Ukraine 1996–99; Head of Russian Del. on negotiations with Estonia 1991, with Ukraine 1992–94; mem. Int. Ecological Acad. Kiev 1997, Int. Acad. of Spiritual Unity of Peoples of the World 2001; currently Prof. of Int. Politics, Moscow State Inst. of Int. Relations, Ministry of Foreign Affairs; also currently Prof. of Int. Politics, Moscow Int. Higher Business School (MIRBIS) Inst.; Hon. Prof., Slaviansky Univ., Kiev, Ukraine 1999; numerous honours and awards including Orders of the Red Banner 1971, 1980, 1988, Order of Honour 1996, Order of Merit (Ukraine); planet named Dubinin by Int. Astronomical Soc. 1999. *Publications:* USSR–France: Experience of Co-operation 1979, Soviet-Spanish Relations 1983, Representing Perestroika in the West 1989, Diplomatic Truth: Memoirs of the Ambassador to France 1997, Ambassador, Ambassador!: Memoirs of the Ambassador to Spain 1999, Time of Change: Notes of the Ambassador to the US 2003. *Address:* Moscow State Institute for International Affairs, 119454 Moscow, prospekt Vernadskogo, 76 (office); Bolshoi Palashevsky per. 3, App. 34, 123104 Moscow, Russia. *Telephone:* (495) 434- 00-89 (office); (495) 203-27-49. *Fax:* (495) 434-90-66 (office); (495) 203-27-49 (office). *Website:* www.mgimo.ru (office).

DUBOWITZ, Victor, MD, PhD, FRCP, FRCPCH, DCH; British paediatrician and academic; *Professor Emeritus of Paediatrics, Royal Postgraduate Medical School, University of London;* b. 6 Aug. 1931, Beaufort West, S. Africa; s. of the late Charley Dubowitz and Olga Schattel; m. Lilly M. S. Sebok 1960; four s.; ed Cen. High School, Beaufort West and Univs of Cape Town and Sheffield; intern, Groote Schuur Hospital, Cape Town 1955; Sr House Officer, Queen Mary's Hosp. for Children 1957–59; Research Assoc., Royal Postgraduate Medical School, Univ. of London 1958–59, Prof. of Paediatrics 1972–96, Prof. Emer. 1996–, Dir Jerry Lewis Muscle Research Centre 1975–96; Lecturer in Clinical Pathology, Nat. Hosp. for Nervous Diseases, London 1960; Lecturer in Child Health, Univ. of Sheffield 1961–65, Sr Lecturer 1965–67, Reader 1967–72; Research Assoc., Inst. for Muscle Disease and Asst Paediatrician, Cornell Medical Coll., New York 1965–66; Consultant Paediatrician, Hammersmith Hosp. 1972–96; Pres. European Paediatric Neurology Soc. 1994–97, World Muscle Soc. 1995–, Medical Art Soc. 1996–2000; Curator of Art, Royal Coll. of Paediatrics and Child Health; Dir of Therapeutic Studies, European Neuromuscular Centre, Netherlands 2000–03; Ed.-in-Chief Neuromuscular Disorders 1990–, European Journal of Paediatric Neurology 1996–2003; several awards. *Publications:* The Floppy Infant 1969, Muscle Biopsy: A Modern Approach (with M. Brooke) 1973, 1985, Gestational Age of the Newborn (with L. M. S. Dubowitz) 1977, Muscle Disorders in Childhood 1978, The Neurological Assessment of the Pre-term and Full-term Newborn Infant (with L. M. S. Dubowitz) 1981, 1999, A Colour Atlas of Muscle Disorders in Childhood 1989, A Colour Atlas of Brain Disorders in the Newborn (with L. de Vries, L. Dubowitz and J. Penock) 1990, Ramblings of a Peripatetic Paediatrician 2005, Muscle Biopsy: A Practical Approach (with Caroline Sewry) 2006. *Leisure interests:* sculpting, hiking, photography, antique glass. *Address:* 25 Middleton Road, Golders Green, London, NW11 7NR, England (home). *Telephone:* (20) 8455-9352 (home). *Fax:* (20) 8905-5922 (home). *E-mail:* v.dubowitz@imperial.ac.uk (home).

DUBRULLE, Christophe; French retail executive; *Chairman, Groupe Auchan;* Man. Dir Leroy Merlin 1982, later Chair., Bd of Admin.; Chair. Groupe Auchan 1999–, also Man. Dir Hypermarkets; Dir La Rinascente SpA. *Address:* Groupe Auchan, 200 rue de la Recherche, 59650 Villeneuve d'Ascq, France (office). *Telephone:* 3-28-37-67-00 (office). *Fax:* 3-20-67-55-20 (office). *E-mail:* info@auchan.com (office). *Website:* www.auchan.com (office).

DUBY, Jean Jacques, PhD; French mathematician and scientist; *President, Observatoire des Sciences et des Techniques;* b. 5 Nov. 1940, Paris; s. of Jean Duby and Lucienne Duby (née Lacomme); m. Camille Poli 1963; one d.; ed Ecole Normale Supérieure, Paris; research staff mem., Thomas J. Watson Research Center, USA 1963–64; Systems Engineer, IBM France 1965–66, Man. Application Systems, IBM Mohansic Lab. 1974–75, Exec. Asst to Vice-Chair. IBM Corpn 1975–76, Br. Office Man. IBM France 1977–78, special assignment, IBM Communications Div. 1979, Dir Switching Systems IBM Europe 1980–82, Dir Science and Tech., IBM France 1986–88, Group Dir Science and Tech., IBM Europe 1988–91; Man. Grenoble Scientific Centre 1967–69; Assoc. Prof., European Systems Research Inst. and Univ. of Geneva 1970–71; Project Man., Paris Stock Exchange 1972–73; Scientific Dir CNRS 1982–86; Scientific Dir Union d'assurances de Paris 1991–97; Pres. Inst. Nat. de recherche sur les transports et leur securité 1992–96; Chair. Bd of Dirs Ecole Normale Supérieure de Cachan 1994–2000; Dir-Gen. Ecole Supérieure d'Electricité 1995–2005; Professeur des universités 1999–; Chair. Scientific Council of Bouygues Telecom 2001–; Pres. Observatoire des Sciences et des Techniques 2002–; Scientific Council, Schneider Electric 2004–; Officier, Ordre nat. du Mérite, Chevalier, Ordre Nat. de la Côte d'Ivoire. *Leisure interests:* skiing, mountaineering. *Address:* Observatoire des Sciences et des Techniques, 93 rue de Vaugirard, 75006 Paris, France (office). *E-mail:* jean-jacques.duby@obs-ost.fr (office). *Website:* www.obs-ost.fr (office).

DUBYNA, Oleh; Ukrainian politician and engineer; *President, Ukrainian National Energy Company (Ukrenergo);* b. 20 March 1959, Elizavetovka, Dniepropetrovsk region; m.; one s.; ed Dnieprodzerzhinsk Industrial Inst., Dnieprodzerzhinsk State Tech. Univ.; employee Dniepr Metallurgic plant 1976, master, Sr master, then engineer 1986–93, Head of Bureau, Deputy Head of Div., First Deputy Dir-Gen. 1996–98; teacher Dnieprodzerzhinsk Polytechnical Higher School 1985–86; Asst to Dir, then Deputy Dir-Gen. Dniepr br. of Intermontage Kam – Soviet-Swiss Joint Venture DEMOS 1993–96; Deputy Head, Chair. Bd of Dirs, Dir-Gen. Alchevsk Metallurgic plant 1998–99; Dir-Gen. Kryvoy Rog State Ore-Metallurgic plant, Krivorozhstal 1999–; Deputy Prime Minister for Econ. Policy 2000–01; First Deputy Prime Minister 2001–02; Adviser to Pres. Leonid Kuchma 2002–04; Pres. Ukrainian Nat. Energy Co. (Ukrenergo) 2004–. *Address:* Ukrainian National Energy Company (Ukrenergo), Kiev, Ukraine (office). *Website:* www.ukrenergo.energy.gov.ua (office).

DUC, Nguyen Phu, LLD, DJur; Vietnamese diplomatist; b. 13 Nov. 1924, Son-Tay; m.; two s.; ed Univ. of Hanoi, Harvard Law School, USA; Perm. Observer to UN 1964–65; Special Asst for Foreign Affairs to Pres. Thieu 1968; Envoy to Thailand, Khmer Repub., Laos, Indonesia, USA 1972; Minister of Foreign Affairs 1973; Amb. to Belgium 1974–75; attended confs on Viet Nam 1966, 1967, 1968, 1969, 1973, active in negotiations leading to Paris Conf. 1968 and to Paris Agreement 1973. *Publications:* The Viet-Nam Peace Negotiations: Saigon's Side of the Story 2005. *Address:* c/o Dalley Book Service, 90 Kimball Lane, Christianburg, VA 24073, USA.

DUCA, Gheorghe, DSci; Moldovan academic; *President, Academy of Sciences of Moldova;* b. 29 Feb. 1952, Sîngerei; ed State Univ. of Moldova, Inst. of Chemical Physics, Russian Acad. of Sciences, Univ. of Odessa; Head of Physical Chem. Dept, State Univ. of Moldova 1988–92, Dir Research Centre of Ecological and Applied Chem. 1991–98, Head of Industrial and Ecological Chem. Dept 1992–98, Dean of Faculty of Ecology 1992–95; Pres. Republican Cttee for awarding prizes to young researchers in science and tech. 1992–2006, Scientific Specialised Council for nomination of DrSci degree 1994–2006; Chair. Parl. Comm. for Culture, Science, Educ., and Mass Media 1998–2001; Pres. Moldovan Research and Devt Asscn 2000–06; Minister of Ecology, Construction and Territory Devt 2001–04; Pres. Acad. of Sciences of Moldova 2004–; Ed.-in-Chief Environment Journal 2002–04; Head of Editorial Bd Chemistry Journal of Moldova 2005–06; mem. Int. Editorial Bd Chemistry and Technology of Water Journal 2001–06, Editorial Advisory Bd Environmental Engineering and Management Journal 2002–06; Co-Pres. Moldo-Polish Intergovernmental Mixed Comm. for Commercial, Econ., Scientific and Tech. Co-operation 2001–05, Danube Convention 2003–04; Pres. Admin. Council of Concession Agreement of Redeco 2005–06, Admin. Council of Nat. Science Foundation of Moldova 2005–06; mem. ACS 1997–, Cen. European Acad. of Sciences and Arts 1999–, Int. Acad. of Informatics 1999–, Pedagogical Acad. of Russia 1999–; Commdr, Cross of Honour (Poland) 2004; Dr hc (Gh. Asachi Univ., Romania) 2000; State Prize for Youth in Science and Tech. 1983, State Prize for Science, Tech. and Production 1995, 2000, Scientist of the Year, Acad. of Sciences of Moldova 2005, Medail d'Or 2005. *Address:* Academy of Sciences of Moldova, 2001 Chisinau, 1 Bd.Stefan cel Mare, Moldova (office). *Telephone:* (22) 27-14-78 (office). *Fax:* (22) 27-60-14 (office). *E-mail:* duca@mrda.md (office); duca@asm.md (office). *Website:* www.duca.md (office).

DUCEPPE, Gilles, BA; Canadian politician; *Leader, Bloc Québécois;* b. 22 July 1947, Montréal; s. of Jean Duceppe and Hélène Rowley; m. Yolande Brunelle; two c.; ed Collège Mont-Saint-Louis, Université de Montréal; Vice-Pres. Union générale des étudiants et étudiantes du Québec (UGEQ) 1968–69; Dir Quartier Latin journal 1970–71; with Company of Young Canadians –1977; Union Negotiator Confed. of Nat. Trade Unions 1977; elected MP for Montreal's Laurier-Sainte-Marie riding (Bloc Québécois) 1990–, Interim Leader Bloc Québécois 1996, Leader 1997–; Leader of the Opposition 1997. *Address:* Bloc Québécois, 3750 Cremazie Est, bureau 307, Montréal, PQ H2A 1B6, Canada (office). *Telephone:* (514) 526-3000 (office). *Fax:* (514) 526-2868 (office). *E-mail:* infobloc@bloc.org (office). *Website:* www.blocquebecois.org (office).

DUCH-PEDERSEN, Alf, MSc; Danish banking executive; *Chairman and General Manager, Danske Bank Aktieselskab;* b. 15 Aug. 1946; began career with Danish Turnkey Dairies A/S 1973–84; various positions with APV Anhydro A/S 1984–87, APV Pasilac A/S 1987–91, APV PLC, London 1989–91; with Tryg-Baltica Forsikring, Skadesforsikringsselskab A/S 1991–97; mem. Bd Dirs Danisco 1994–97, CEO and Pres. Exec. Bd 1997–2006; apptd mem. Bd Dirs Danske Bank A/S 1999–, Chair. 2003–; Deputy Chair. (non-exec.) Group 4 Securicor PLC, Group 4 Falck A/S; mem. Bd Dirs Tech. Univ. of Denmark, Denmark-America Foundation; mem. Cen. Bd Confed. of Danish Industries. *Address:* Danske Bank Aktieselskab, 2–12 Holmens Kanal, 1092 Copenhagen K, Denmark (office). *Telephone:* 33-44-00-00 (office). *E-mail:* info@danskebank.com (office). *Website:* www.danskebank.com (office).

DUCHESNEAU, François, Docteur d'état ès-lettres et sciences humaines; Canadian philosopher and academic; *Professor of Philosophy, University of Montreal;* ed Univ. of Paris-I, France; taught at Univ. of Ottawa; Prof. of Philosophy, Univ. of Montreal 1979–; Visiting Prof., Catholic Univ. of Louvain, Belgium (Pulpit Draper) 1995, Univ. of Alberta 1997, École des Hautes Études en sciences sociales, Paris 1999; mem. RSC 1984–; Prix des sciences humaines, Asscn canadienne française pour l'avancement des sciences 1992, Killam Research Fellowship 1995–97, Killam Prize for Humanities, Canada Council for the Arts 2003. *Publications:* L'Empirisme de Locke 1973, La physiologie des lumières – Empirisme, modèles et théories 1982, Genèse de la théorie cellulaire 1987, Leibniz et la méthode de la science 1993, La dynamique de Leibniz 1994, Philosophie de la biologie 1997, Les modèles du vivant de Descartes à Leibniz 1998; more than 160 articles on the history of modern philosophy, the history and philosophy of science, empiricist theories of knowledge and the philosophy and scientific work of Leibniz. *Address:* Département de philosophie, Université de Montréal, CP 6128, succ. Centre-ville, Montréal, PQ H3C 3J7, Canada (office). *Telephone:* (514) 343-7373 (office). *Fax:* (514) 343-2098 (office). *E-mail:* francois.duchesneau@umontreal.ca (office). *Website:* www.philo.umontreal.ca/prof/francois.duchesneau.html (office).

DUCHOVNY, David; American actor; b. 7 Aug. 1960, New York; s. of Amram Duchovny and Meg Duchovny; m. Tea Leoni (q.v.) 1997; ed Yale and Princeton Univs; stage appearances include off-Broadway plays, The Copulating Machine of Venice, California and Green Cockatoo; writer and dir of various episodes of The X-Files; Golden Globe for Best Actor in Drama Series 1996. *Films include:* Working Girl 1988, New Year's Day 1989, Bad Influence 1990, Julia Has Two Lovers 1990, The Rapture 1991, Don't Tell Mom the Babysitter's Dead 1991, Denial 1991, Beethoven 1992, Chaplin 1992, Red Shoe Diaries 1992, Ruby 1992, Venice, Venice 1992, Kalifornia 1993, Apartment Zero, Close Enemy, Loan, Independence Day, Playing God 1997, The X-Files 1998, Return To Me 2000, Evolution 2001, Zoolander 2001, Red Shoe Diaries 15: Forbidden Zone (video) 2002, Full Frontal 2002, XIII (voice) 2003, Connie and Carla 2004, House of D (also dir and writer) 2004, The X Files: Resist or Serve (voice) 2004, Area 51 (voice) 2005, Trust the Man 2005, The TV Set 2006, Queer Duck: The Movie (voice) 2006, Things We Lost in the Fire 2007, The X Files: I Want to Believe 2008. *Television includes:* Twin Peaks 1990, The X-Files 1993–2002, The X-Files: The Truth 2002, Life With Bonnie 2002, The TV Set 2006, Californication (series) 2007–. *Address:* ICM, 8942 Wilshire Blvd, Beverly Hills, CA 90211, USA. *Telephone:* (310) 550-4000.

DUCKWORTH, Marilyn, OBE; New Zealand writer; b. (Marilyn Rose Adcock), 10 Nov. 1935, Auckland; d. of Cyril John Adcock and Irene Robinson; sister of Fleur Adcock (q.v.); m. 1st Harry Duckworth 1955 (divorced 1964); m. 2nd Ian Macfarlane 1964 (divorced 1972); m. 3rd Daniel Donovan 1974 (died 1978); m. 4th John Batstone 1985; four d.; ed Queen Margaret Coll., Wellington and Victoria Univ., Wellington; 10 writers' fellowships 1961–96 including Katherine Mansfield Fellowship, Menton 1980, Fulbright Visiting Writer's Fellowship, USA 1987, Victoria Univ. Writing Fellowship 1990, Hawthornden Writing Fellowship, Scotland 1994, 2001, Sargeson Writing Fellowship, Auckland 1995, Auckland Univ. Literary Fellowship 1996; NZ Literary Fund Award for Achievement 1963, NZ Book Award for Fiction 1985. *Plays:* Home to Mother, Feet First. *Television:* Close to Home (series). *Publications:* 15 novels including A Gap in the Spectrum 1959, A Barbarous Tongue 1963, Disorderly Conduct 1984, Married Alive 1985, Pulling Faces 1987, A Message from Harpo 1989, Unlawful Entry 1992, Seeing Red 1993, Leather Wings 1995, Studmuffin 1997, Swallowing Diamonds 2003, Playing Friends 2007; short stories: Explosions on the Sun 1989; poems: Other Lovers' Children 1975; memoir: Camping on the Faultline 2000. *Leisure interest:* playing the violin. *Address:* 41 Queen Street, Mt Victoria, Wellington 6011, New Zealand (home). *Telephone:* (4) 384-9990 (home). *Fax:* (4) 384-9990 (home). *E-mail:* marilynduckworth@paradise.net.nz (home).

DUCORNET, Erica (Rikki) Lynn, BA; American/French writer, artist and teacher; b. 19 April 1943, New York; d. of Gerard De Gré and Muriel Harris; m. Jonathan Cohen; one s.; Novelist-in-Residence, Univ. of Denver 1988–; has taught writing at Writers at Work, Bard Coll., Brown Univ., Naropa Univ., Vermont Studio Center, Centrum Writer's Workshop, Univ. of Trento; mem. PEN; Lannan Literary Award in Fiction 1993, 2004, Critics Choice Award 1995, Charles Flint Kellogg Award in Arts and Letters 1998, Lannon Literary Fellowship 1998. *Publications:* The Stain 1984, Entering Fire 1986, The Fountains of Neptune 1989, Eben Demarst 1990, The Jade Cabinet 1993, The Butcher's Tales 1994, Phosphor in Dreamland 1995, The Word 'Desire' 1997, The Fan Maker's Inquisition (LA Times Book of the Year) 2000, Gazelle 2004; two books of short stories The Word Desire, The Complete Butcher's Tales; six collections of poetry including The Cult of Seizure; two children's books; essays The Monstrous and the Marvelous; Dimsumzoo (drama). *Address:* c/o Department of English, University of Denver, 2000 East Asbury, Denver, CO 80208, USA.

DUCZMAL JAROSZEWSKA, Agnieszka; Polish conductor; *Artistic Director and Conductor, Amadeus Chamber Orchestra of Polish Radio;* b. 7 Jan. 1946, Krotoszyn; d. of Henryk Duczmal and Leokadia Surdyk Duczmal; m.; one s. two d.; ed Acad. of Music, Poznań; Founder, Artistic Dir land Conductor, Amadeus Chamber Orchestra of Polish Radio 1968–; Asst Conductor Poznań Nat. Philharmonic 1971–72, Conductor Poznań Opera 1972–81; performs in Europe, N and S America and Asia; over 46 recordings including live concerts for TV and performances for radio; Commdr's Cross, Order of Polonia Restituta 1998; won award at first Nat. Competition for Conductors, Katowice 1970, distinction, 4th Int. Herbert von Karajan Competition 1975, Silver Medal of Herbert von Karajan at the Meeting of Young Orchestras, West Berlin 1976, La Donna del Mondo Award of St Vincent Int. Culture Centre, Rome 1982. *Recordings:* J. S. Bach/Józef Koffler, Goldberg Variations (world premiere recording), Knittel, The Passion of Our Lord according to St Matthew, Op. 20 (world premiere recording), Alexandre Tansman, Chamber Music (world premiere recording). *Leisure interests:* dogs, literary classics, gardening, mountaineering. *Address:* Amadeus Chamber Orchestra of Polish Radio, al. Marcinkowskiego 3, 61-745 Poznań, Poland (office). *Telephone:* (61) 851-66-86 (office). *Fax:* (61) 851-66-87 (office). *E-mail:* agnieszka.duczmal@amadeus.pl (office). *Website:* www.amadeus.pl (office).

DUDA-GRACZ, Jerzy; Polish painter; b. 20 March 1941, Częstochowa; s. of Adam Duda-Gracz and Pelagia Stepniewska; m. Wilma Dudek 1969; one d.; ed Acad. of Fine Arts in Kraków 1968; lecturer, Acad. of Fine Arts in Kraków, Silesian Univ. and European Acad. of Arts, Warsaw; mem. Union of Polish Artists and Designers 1979–90; Prof. Silesian Univ., Katowice; about 180 one-man and about 360 group exhbns in Poland, Europe, America and Asia; perm. exhbn Duda-Gracz Author's Gallery, Częstochowa; works in perm. collections include: Nat. Museum Warsaw, Kraków, Poznań, Wrocław, Gdańsk, Uffizi Gallery Florence, A. Pushkin Museum Moscow; Grand Cross Order of Polonia Restituta 2000; numerous awards including Silver Cross of Merit 1977, Prime Minister Prize (2nd Class) 1979, Minister of Culture and Art Prize (1st Class) 1985, Minister of Foreign Affairs Prize (1st Class) 1988. *Leisure interest:* reading books (especially diaries). *Address:* ul. Daszyńskiego 24, 40-834 Katowice, Poland (home).

DUDAU, Nicolae; Moldovan politician and diplomatist; *Ambassador to Italy;* b. 19 Dec. 1945, Grineuts; m. Galina Dudau; one d.; ed Higher CPSU School, Moscow, Chişinău Tech. Univ.; employee Chişinău tractor mfg factory 1963–75; army service 1964–67; various admin. posts in orgs in Chişinău 1975–90; Deputy Chair. Chişinău City Planning Cttee 1990–91; First Sec. Chişinău City CP Cttee 1990–91; Exec. Dir Int. Charity Foundation 1991–93; Minister-Counsellor Moldovan Embassy in Russia 1993–94; First Deputy Minister of Foreign Affairs 1997–98, Minister of Foreign Affairs 2001–04; Amb. to Belarus 1998–2001, to Italy 2004–. *Address:* Embassy of the Republic of Moldova, 8 Strada Monte Bello Rome, Italy (office).

DUDBRIDGE, Glen, PhD, FBA; British academic; *Shaw Professor of Chinese, University of Oxford;* b. 2 July 1938, Clevedon, Somerset; s. of George Victor Dudbridge and Edna Kathleen Dudbridge (née Cockle); m. Sylvia Lo Fung-young 1965; one s. one d.; ed Bristol Grammar School, Magdalene Coll. Cambridge and New Asia Inst. of Advanced Chinese Studies, Hong Kong; Research Fellow, Magdalene Coll. 1965; Lecturer in Modern Chinese, Oxford Univ. 1965–85; Prof. of Chinese, Cambridge Univ. 1985–89; Shaw Prof. of Chinese, Oxford Univ. 1989–; Fellow, Wolfson Coll. Oxford 1966–85, Emer. Fellow 1985–; Fellow, Magdalene Coll. Cambridge 1985–89; Fellow, Univ. Coll. Oxford 1989–; Visiting Prof., Yale Univ., USA 1972–73, Univ. of Calif., Berkeley, USA 1980, 1998; Hon. mem. Chinese Acad. of Social Sciences 1996. *Publications:* The Hsi-yu chi (a study of antecedents to the sixteenth-century Chinese novel) 1970, The Legend of Miao-shan 1978, The Tale of Li Wa (study and critical edition of a Chinese story from the ninth century) 1983, Religious Experience and Lay Society in T'ang China (A reading of Tai Fu's Kuang-I Chi) 1995, Sanguo Dian Lüe Ji Jiao 1998, Lost Books of Medieval China 2000. *Address:* University College, Oxford, OX1 4BH, England (office).

DUDDY, Patrick Dennis; American diplomatist; *Ambassador to Venezuela;* b. Bangor, Maine; m. Mary Huband; two c.; ed Colby Coll., Northeastern Univ., Nat. War Coll.; career diplomatist, has served in embassies in Chile, Dominican Repub., Costa Rica, Paraguay and Panama, fmr Deputy Chief of Mission, La Paz, fmr Consul Gen., São Paulo, Deputy Asst Sec., Bureau of Western Hemisphere Affairs, Dept of State –2007, Amb. to Venezuela 2007–. *Address:* US Embassy, Calle F con Calle Suapure, Urb. Colinas de Valle Arriba, Caracas 1080, USA (office). *Telephone:* (212) 975-6411 (office). *Fax:* (212) 975-6710 (office). *E-mail:* embajada@state.gov (office). *Website:* caracas.usembassy.gov (office).

DUDERSTADT, James (Jim) Johnson, BEng, MS, PhD; American scientist, academic and university administrator; *President Emeritus and University Professor of Science and Engineering, University of Michigan;* b. 5 Dec. 1942, Madison, Iowa; s. of Mack Henry Duderstadt and Katharine Sydney Johnson Duderstadt; m. Anne Marie Lock 1964; two d.; ed Yale Univ., California Inst. of Tech.; US Atomic Energy Comm. Postdoctoral Fellow, California Inst. of Tech. 1968; Asst Prof. of Nuclear Eng, Univ. of Mich. 1969, Assoc. Prof. 1972, Prof. 1976–81, Dean Coll. of Eng 1981, Provost and Vice-Pres. for Academic Affairs 1986, Pres. 1988–96, Pres. Emer. and Prof. of Science and Eng 1996–, Dir Millennium Project 1996–; mem. US Nat. Science Bd 1985–96 (Chair. 1991–94), Nat. Acad. of Eng Council 1997–2002, Advisory Councils of US Dept of Energy, Dept of Educ., NSF, Nat. Acads, MIT, Caltech, Georgia Tech; Co-Chair. Glion Colloquium; Dir Unisys; numerous hon. degrees and lectureships; Compton Award, American Nuclear Soc. 1985, E. O. Lawrence Award, US Dept of Energy 1986, Reginald Wilson Award, Nat. Medal of Tech., Nat. Acad. of Eng, American Acad. of Arts & Sciences, Duderstadt Center at Univ. of Mich. *Publications:* Nuclear Reactor Analysis (with L. J. Hamilton) 1976, Transport Theory (with W. R. Martin) 1979, Inertial Confinement Fusion (with G. A. Moses) 1982, Intercollegiate Athletics and the American University 2000, A University for the 21st Century 2000, Higher Education in the Digital Age (co-author) 2003, Beyond the Crossroads: The Future of the Public University in America (co-author) 2003, Engineering Research and America's Future 2005, View from the Helm 2006, Globalization of Higher Education (co-author) 2008, Engineering for a Changing World 2008; numerous tech. publs on nuclear reactor theory, radiation transport, statistical mechanics and kinetic theory, plasma physics and computer simulation. *Address:* Millennium Project, 2001 Duderstadt Center, University of Michigan, 2281 Bonisteel Boulevard, Ann Arbor, MI 48109-2094, USA (office). *Telephone:* (734) 647-7300 (office). *Fax:* (734) 647-6814 (office). *E-mail:* jjd@umich.edu (office). *Website:* www.milproj.dc.umich.edu/home (office).

DUDLEY, Hugh Arnold, CBE, ChM, FRCS, FRACS; British surgeon and academic; *Professor Emeritus of Surgery, St Mary's Hospital, London;* b. 1 July 1925, Dublin; s. of Walter Dudley and Ethel Smith; m. Jean Bruce Lindsay Johnston 1947; two s. one d.; ed Edin. and Harvard Univs; Lecturer in Surgery, Edin. Univ. 1954–58; Sr Lecturer in Surgery, Aberdeen Univ. 1958–63; Foundation Prof. of Surgery, Monash Univ., Melbourne 1963–72; Prof. of Surgery, St Mary's Hosp., London 1973–88, Prof. Emer. 1988–; Ed. Operative Surgery 1976–94, Consulting Ed. 1994–; Chair. Ethics Cttee, Army Personnel Research Establishment 1989–94, Chemical and Biological Research Establishment, Porton Down 1988–96 (mem. Council 1992–94); fmr Pres. of Surgical Research Soc. of Australasia and of GB and Ireland, of Biological Eng Soc. and of British Journal of Surgery Soc.; Hon. Fellow

American Surgical Asscn 1986, SA Coll. of Surgeons 1987. *Publications:* Principles of General Surgical Management 1958, Communication in Medicine and Biology 1977; Ed. Emergency Surgery 1979, 1986, Guide for House Surgeons 1974, 1982, 1987, Practical Procedures for House Officers 1988, The People's Hosp. of North East Scotland (jtly) 1992. *Leisure interest:* surgical history. *Address:* Glebe Cottage, Haughs of Glass, Huntly, Aberdeenshire, AB54 4XH, Scotland (home). *Telephone:* (1466) 700376. *E-mail:* hugh.dudley@aol.com (home).

DUDLEY, William C., BA, PhD; American financier and economist; *President and CEO, Federal Reserve Bank of New York;* b. 1952; m. Ann E. Darby; ed New Coll., Sarasota, Fla; Univ. of California, Berkeley; Economist, Fed. Reserve Bd, Washington, DC 1981–83; Vice-Pres. Morgan Guaranty Trust Co. 1983–86; joined Goldman Sachs and Co. 1986, Chief US Economist 1995–2005, Pnr and Man. Dir 1996–2006, Advisory Dir 2006; Exec. Vice-Pres. and Head of Markets Group, Fed. Reserve Bank of New York 2007–09, Pres. and CEO 2009–; Vice-Chair. Fed. Open Market Cttee 2009–; mem. Tech. Consultants Group to Congressional Budget Office 1999–2005. *Address:* Federal Reserve Bank of New York, 33 Liberty Street, New York, NY 10045, USA (office). *Telephone:* (212) 720-5000 (office). *Website:* www.newyorkfed.org (office).

DUERR, Hans-Peter Emil, PhD; German physicist and academic; *Emeritus Professor, Max-Planck-Institut für Physik, University of Munich;* b. 7 Oct. 1929, Stuttgart; s. of Dr Rupert Duerr and Eva Duerr (née Kraepelin); m. Carol Sue Durham 1956; two s. two d.; ed Univs of Stuttgart and California, Berkeley; Research Asst Dept of Physics, Univ. of California, Berkeley 1956–57, Max-Planck Inst. für Physik, Göttingen and Munich 1958–62; Visiting Assoc. Prof., Univ. of California, Berkeley and Inst. of Math. Sciences, Madras, India 1962–63; Visiting Prof., University of California, Berkeley 1968–69; Prof., Univ. of Munich 1969; mem. Directorate Max-Planck Inst. für Physik, Munich, Chair. 1971–72, 1977–80, 1987–92, Vice-Chair. 1981–86, 1993–95, Prof. Emer. 1997–; Man. Dir Max-Planck-Inst. für Physik und Astrophysik 1978–80; mem. Bd Vereinigung Deutscher Wissenschaftler 1980–86, mem. Advisory Bd 1986–91, Chair. Bd 1991–; Chair. Advisory Cttee Wissenschaftszentrum Munich 1984–; mem. Bd Greenpeace Germany 1985–91, Co-Chair. Exec. Cttee 1988–89; Chair. Bd Global Challenges Network 1987–; mem. Pugwash Council 1987–, Club of Rome 1991–; mem. Bd Int. Foundation for the Survival and Devt of Humanity 1988–93, Moscow, Chair. Bd German br., Munich 1988–93; mem. Bd and Scientific Advisory Cttee Internationale Akademie für Zukunftsfragen, Vienna 1990–; Chair. Kuratorium Umweltakademie-Umwelt und Man., Oberpfaffenhofen, 1990–; mem. Kuratorium E.F.-Schumacher-Gesellschaft 1980–, City Energy Cttee, Munich 1983–, Int. Advisory Council Econ. Devt of Hainan, China 1990–93, Council Int. Network of Engineers and Scientists for Global Responsibility, Hamburg 1991–, Ständiges Wissenschaftsforum der Sozialdemokratie, Bonn 1994–, Scientific Advisory Cttee Institut für Zukunftsstudien und Technologiebewertung, Berlin 1995– and other cttees and advisory bds; Pres. Bd of Trustees European Trust for Natural and Cultural Wealth, Prague; mem. Bd Dirs Bulletin of Atomic Scientists, Chicago 1993–, Academia Scientarium et Artium Europaea, Salzburg; Advisory Cttee Int. Judicial Org. for Environment and Devt (IJO) 1991–, Advisory Council Int. Center of Integrative Studies, New York 1993–, Scientific Advisory Bd Potsdam Inst. for Climate Impact Research; Trustee Muhammad Abdus Salam Foundation, London 1994–, Comm. on Globalization 2001; mem. Deutsche Akademie der Naturforscher Leopoldina Halle; Dr hc (Oldenburg) 2002; Award of Merit, Oakland 1956, Right Livelihood Award 1987, Waldemar von Knoeringen Award 1989, Ecology Prize Goldene Schwalbe 1990, Natura Obligat Medal 1991, Elise and Walter Haas Int. Award 1993, Peace Nobel Prize (Councillor Pugwash) 1995, 'München leuchtet' Gold Medal 1996. *Publications:* more than 300 publs on nuclear physics, elementary particle physics, gravitation, epistemology, peace and disarmament, energy, ecology, econs, politics. *Address:* Max-Planck-Institut für Physik, Foehringer Ring 6, 80805 Munich (office); Grasmeierstrasse 14C, 80805 Munich, Germany (home). *Telephone:* (89) 32354280 (office); (89) 32197844 (home). *Fax:* (89) 32354304 (office); (89) 32197845 (home). *E-mail:* hpd@mppmu.mpg.de (office). *Website:* www.mppmu.mpg.de (office); www.gcn.de (office).

DUESBERG, Peter H., PhD; American (b. German) molecular biologist and academic; *Professor of Molecular and Cell Biology, University of California, Berkeley;* b. 2 Dec. 1936, Münster, Germany; s. of Richard Duesberg and Hilde Saettele; m. Sigrid Duesberg; one s. three d.; ed Univ. of Würzburg, Univ. of Basel, Switzerland, Univ. of Munich, Univ. of Frankfurt; Postdoctoral Fellow, Dept of Molecular Biology and Virus Lab., Max Planck Inst. for Virus Research, Tübingen, Germany 1963; Postdoctoral Fellow and Asst Research Virologist, Univ. of California, Berkeley 1964–68, Asst Prof. in Residence 1968–70, Asst Prof. 1970–71, Assoc. Prof. 1971–73, Prof. 1973–, Prof. of Molecular and Cell Biology 1989–; Fisher Distinguished Prof., Univ. of North Texas, Denton 1992; Guest Prof., Univ. of Heidelberg at the Medical School, Mannheim 1997, Aug.–Dec. 1998, July–Dec. 2000; mem. NAS 1986; mem. Int. Panel of Scientists invited by Pres. Thabo Mbeki and South African Govt to discuss the AIDS crisis, Pretoria 6–7 May 2000, Johannesburg 3–4 July 2000; Fogarty Scholar-in-Residence, NIH, Bethesda, Md 1986–87, Lichtfield Lecturer, Univ. of Oxford, UK 1988, C. J. Watson Lecturer, Abbott Northwestern Hosp., Minneapolis, Minn. 1990, Shaffer Alumni Lecturer, Tulane Univ., New Orleans, La 1992, Constance Ledward Rollins Lecturer, Univ. of New Hampshire, Durham, Distinguished Speaker, Dept of Biology, Univ. of Louisville, Ky; Merck Award 1969, Calif. Scientist of the Year Award 1971, First Annual American Medical Center Oncology Award 1981, NIH Outstanding Investigator Grant 1985–92, Wissenschaftspreis, Hanover, Germany 1988. *Achievement:* isolated the first cancer gene through work on retroviruses in 1970, and mapped the genetic structure of these viruses; came to public attention with claim that HIV is not the cause of AIDS 1987; based on experience with retroviruses, challenged virus-AIDS hypothesis in numerous medical and scientific journals and instead proposed hypothesis that various AIDS diseases are brought on by long-term consumption of recreational drugs and anti-HIV drugs; developed theory that cancers originate from normal cells with individual karyotypes, much like new species. *Publications:* AIDS: The Good News Is… (with John Yiamouyiannis) 1995, Infectious AIDS: Have We Been Misled? (collection of 13 articles published in scientific journals 1987–96) 1995, AIDS: Virus or Drug Induced? (collection of 27 articles by scientists, independent scholars and investigative journalists from Australia, Europe and USA) 1996, Inventing the AIDS Virus 1996; numerous scientific papers in professional journals on genetic structure of retroviruses and aneuploidy of cancers. *Address:* Department of Molecular and Cell Biology, 353 Donner Lab #3206, University of California at Berkeley, 16 Barker Hall, Berkeley CA 94720-3206, USA (office). *Telephone:* (510) 642-6549 (office). *Fax:* (510) 643-6455 (office). *E-mail:* duesberg@berkeley.edu (office). *Website:* mcb.berkeley.edu/labs/duesberg (office); mcb.berkeley.edu/faculty/BMB/duesbergp.html (office); www.duesberg.com (office).

DUFF, Michael James, PhD; British physicist and academic; *Abdus Salam Professor of Theoretical Physics, Imperial College London;* b. 28 Jan. 1949, Manchester; s. of Edward Duff and Elizabeth Duff (née Kaylor); m. Lesley Yearling 1984; one s. one d.; ed De La Salle Coll., Salford, Queen Mary Coll. and Imperial Coll., London; Post-doctoral Fellowships in Theoretical Physics, Int. Centre for Theoretical Physics, Trieste, Italy, Univ. of Oxford, King's Coll. and Queen Mary Coll., London Univ., Brandeis Univ., USA 1972–79; Faculty mem. Imperial Coll. London 1979–88, Sr Physicist, CERN, Geneva 1984–87; Prof. of Physics, Texas A&M Univ., USA 1988–92, Distinguished Prof. of Physics 1992–99; Oskar Klein Prof. of Physics, Univ. of Mich. 1999–2005, Dir Mich. Center for Theoretical Physics 2000–05; Prin. of Physical Sciences, Imperial Coll. London 2005–06, Abdus Salam Prof. of Theoretical Physics 2006–; Fellow, American Physical Soc., Inst. of Physics; Meeting Gold Medal, El Colegio Nacional, Mexico City 2004. *Publications:* Observations on Conformal Anomalies 1977, Kaluza-Klein Supergravity 1986, Strings Solitons 1994, The World in Eleven Dimensions 1999; numerous articles on unified theories of the elementary particles. *Leisure interests:* soccer, watercolours, golf. *Address:* Blackett Laboratory, Imperial College London, Prince Consort Road, London SW7 2AZ (office); Yew Tree House, Church Lane, Milton, Oxfordshire OX14 4BL, UK (home). *Telephone:* (20) 7594-8571 (office); (1235) 833-511 (home). *Fax:* (20) 7594-7844 (office). *E-mail:* m.duff@imperial.ac.uk (office). *Website:* www3.imperial.ac.uk/people/m.duff (office).

DUFFEY, Joseph Daniel, PhD; American fmr government official, academic and business executive; *Senior Vice-President, Laureate Education Inc.;* b. 1 July 1932, Huntington, W Va; s. of Joseph I. Duffey and Ruth Wilson Duffey; m. Anne Wexler 1974; four s.; ed Marshall Univ., Andover Newton Theological School, Yale Univ. and Hartford Seminary Foundation; Assoc. Prof. and Acting Dean, Hartford Seminary Foundation 1960–70; Adjunct Prof. and Fellow, Calhoun Coll. 1970–74; Gen. Sec. and Spokesman American Asscn of Univ. Prof., Washington, DC 1974–76; Asst Sec. of State, US Dept of State 1977; Chair. Nat. Endowment for the Humanities, US Govt 1977–82; Chancellor Univ. of Mass. 1982–91, also Pres. 1990–91; Pres. American Univ. Washington 1991–93; Head US Information Agency 1993–98; Sr Exec. Chair. Int. Univ. Project, Sylvan Learning Systems (now Laureate Education Inc.), Washington 1999, now Sr Vice-Pres.; Order of Leopold II (Belgium) 1979, Tree of Life Award, American Jewish Congress 1984. *Publications:* Lewis Mumford's Quest 1979, US Global Competitiveness 1988, Looking Back and Looking Forward: The US and the World Economy 1989. *Address:* Laureate Education Inc., 2801 New Mexico Avenue, NW, Washington, DC 20007, USA. *Telephone:* (202) 965-1044 (office). *Fax:* (202) 965-1098 (office). *E-mail:* www.jduffey@earthlink.net (office). *Website:* www.laureate-inc.com (office).

DUFFIELD, Dame Vivien Louise, CBE, DBE, MA; British philanthropist; *Campaign Chair, University of Oxford;* b. 26 March 1946; d. of Sir Charles Clore and Francine Halphen; m. John Duffield 1969 (divorced 1976); one s. one d.; ed Cours Victor Hugo, Paris, Lycée Français de Londres, Heathfield School, Lady Margaret Hall, Oxford; Dir Royal Opera House Trust 1985–2001, Royal Opera House 1990–2001; Vice-Chair. Great Ormond Street Hosp. Wishing Well Appeal 1987, Royal Marsden Hosp. Cancer Appeal 1990; currently Campaign Chair., Univ. of Oxford; mem. NSPCC Centenary Appeal Cttee 1983, Financial Devt Cttee 1985; mem. Royal Ballet Bd 1990–, Gov. Royal Ballet 2002–; Trustee Dulwich Collection Picture Gallery 1993–2002; Gov. South Bank Bd 2002–; Chair. Clore Duffield Foundation (after merger with Clore Foundation); Hon. DLitt (Buckingham) 1990; Hon. DPhil (Weizmann Inst.) 1985, (Hebrew Univ.) 1998;; Hon. RCM 1987. *Leisure interests:* skiing, opera, ballet, shooting. *Address:* c/o Clore Duffield Foundation, Studio 3, Chelsea Manor Studios, Flood Street, London, SW3 5SR, England. *Telephone:* (20) 7351-6061. *Fax:* (20) 7351-5308. *Website:* www.cloreduffield.org.uk.

DUFFUOR, Kwabena, BSc, MBA, MA, PhD; Ghanaian banking executive and politician; *Minister of Finance and Economic Planning;* ed Univ. of Ghana, Syracuse Univ., USA; with Ghana Commercial Bank 1969–1995, positions included Special Asst to Man. Dir, Chief Economist and Head of Research Dept; Deputy Gov. Bank of Ghana 1995–97, Gov. 1997–2001; Lecturer in Econs, Finance and Banking, Univ. Ghana 1982–91, mem. Advisory Bd Inst. of Social Statistical and Econ. Research; Minister of Finance and Econ. Planning 2009–; fmr Chair. Bd of Dirs UniBank Ghana Ltd; mem. Bd of Dirs Accra Brewery Ltd 1983–94, State Gold Mining Corpn 1984–91, Shell Ghana Ltd 1986–91, Ecobank, Cote d'Ivoire 1989–95, Ashanti Goldfields Co. Ltd 2000–01; mem. Econs Soc.; Fellow, Chartered Inst. of Bankers, Ghana. *Address:* Ministry of Finance and Economic Planning, POB M40, Accra, Ghana (office). *Telephone:* (21) 686100 (office). *Fax:* (21) 666205 (office). *E-mail:* promofep@mofep.gov.gh (office). *Website:* www.mofep.gov.gh (office).

DUFFY; British singer and songwriter; b. (Amy Ann Duffy), 1984, Nefyn, Wales; d. of John Duffy and Joyce Duffy (née Williams); solo artist 2007–; MOJO Award for Song of the Year (for Mercy) 2008, Q Award for Best Breakthrough Act 2008, BRIT Awards for Best British Breakthrough Act, for Best British Female Solo Artist 2009. *Recordings include:* album: Rockferry (Grammy Award for Best Pop Vocal Album 2009, BRIT Award for Best British Album 2009) 2008. *Address:* c/o Rough Trade Records, 66 Golborne Road, London, W10 5PS, England (office). *Website:* www.roughtraderecords.com (office); www.iamduffy.com.

DUFFY, Carol Ann, CBE, BA, FRSL; British poet and dramatist; *Poet Laureate;* b. 23 Dec. 1955, Glasgow, Scotland; d. of Frank Duffy and May Black; one d.; ed St Joseph's Convent, Stafford and Univ. of Liverpool; Poetry Ed. Ambit 1983–; Lecturer in Creative Writing, then Prof. of Contemporary Poetry, Manchester Metropolitan Univ. 1996–; Poet Laureate 2009–; mem. Poetry Soc. (Vice-Pres.); C. Day-Lewis Fellowships 1982–84, Eric Gregory Award 1985, Cholmondeley Award 1992, Lannan Award (USA) 1995, Signal Poetry Award 1997. *Plays:* Take My Husband 1984, Cavern Dreams 1986, Grimm Tales 1994, More Grimm Tales 1997. *Publications include:* poetry: Fleshweathercock 1973, Standing Female Nude (Scottish Arts Council Award) 1985, Selling Manhattan (Scottish Arts Council Award, Somerset Maugham Award 1988) 1987, Home and Away 1988, The Other Country (Dylan Thomas Award) 1990, Mean Time (Whitbread Poetry Award, Forward Poetry Prize, Scottish Arts Council Book Award) 1993, Selected Poems 1994, The Pamphlet 1998, The World's Wife 1999, Time's Tidings 1999, Feminine Gospels 2001, Underwater Farmyard 2002, Out of Fashion (ed.) 2004, Rapture (T. S. Eliot Prize 2006) 2005, Another Night Before Christmas 2005, Selected Poems 2006, The Lost Happy Endings (with Jane Ray) 2006, The Hat (for children) 2007, Answering Back (ed.) 2008. *Leisure interest:* holidays. *Address:* Rogers, Coleridge and White, 20 Powis Mews, London W11 1JN, England (office); c/o Pan Macmillan Ltd, 20 New Wharf Road, London, N1 9RR, England (office). *Telephone:* (20) 7221-3717 (office). *Fax:* (20) 7229-9084 (office). *E-mail:* info@rcwlitagency.com (office). *Website:* www.rcwlitagency.co.uk (office).

DUFFY, Francis (Frank) Cuthbert, CBE, PhD, MArch, AADipl(Hons); British architect; *Senior Consultant with title of Founder, DEGW plc;* b. 3 Sept. 1940, Berwick-upon-Tweed; s. of the late John Austin Duffy and Annie Margaret Duffy (née Reed); m. Jessica Duffy; three d.; ed Architectural Asscn School, London, Univ. of California, Berkeley and Princeton Univ., USA; Asst Architect Nat. Bldg Agency 1964–67; consultant to JFN Assocs, New York 1968–70, est. JFN Assocs in London 1971–74; co-f. DEGW plc 1974, Partner 1974–89, Chair. 1989–99, Sr Consultant with title of Founder 1999–; Harkness Fellow 1967–71; Visiting Prof., MIT 2001–04, Univ. Coll. London and Univ. of Reading; Pres. RIBA 1993–95, Architects' Council of Europe 1994; est. DEGW's combination of major interior design and architectural work (e.g. Boots The Chemists, Nottingham, Apicorp, Saudi Arabia) and strategic workplace consultancy to int. corp. clients (e.g. BBC, BP, Google, GSK, Microsoft) as well as govt clients (e.g. UN, GSA, UK Treasury, Ministry of Defence, Home Office) and cultural insts (e.g. British Museum, Design Museum, Somerset House Trust, South Bank Centre); mem. Advisory Cttee on Restoration of Windsor Castle; Pres.'s Award for Lifetime Achievement from British Council of Offices 2004. *Publications:* Office Landscaping 1965, Planning Office Space 1966, The ORBIT Studies 1981–85, The Changing Workplace 1982, The Changing City 1989, RIBA Strategic Study 1992–95, The New Office 1997, Design for Change 1998, New Environments for Working 1998, Architectural Knowledge 1998, Work and the City 2008; numerous articles and papers in professional journals. *Leisure interests:* reading, writing, talking, drawing. *Address:* DEGW plc, The Merchant Centre, 1 New Street Square, London, EC4A 3BF (office); Threeways, The Street, Walberswick, nr Southwold, Suffolk, IP18 6UE, England (home). *Telephone:* (20) 7239-7777 (office); (1502) 723814 (home). *Fax:* (20) 7278-3613 (office). *E-mail:* fduffy@degw.com (office). *Website:* www.degw.com (office).

DUFFY, Maureen Patricia, BA, FRSL, FKC; British writer and poet; b. 21 Oct. 1933, Worthing, Sussex; d. of Grace Rose Wright; ed Trowbridge High School for Girls, Sarah Bonnell High School for Girls, King's Coll., London; staged pop art exhbn with Brigid Brophy 1969; Chair. Greater London Arts Literature Panel 1979–81, Authors Lending and Copyright Soc. 1982–94, Copyright Licensing Agency 1996–99 (Vice-Chair. 1994–96); Pres. Writers' Guild of GB 1985–88 (Jt Chair. 1977–78); Co-founder Writers' Action Group 1972–79; Vice-Pres. European Writers Congress 1992–2003 (Pres. 2003–05), Beauty without Cruelty 1975–, British Copyright Council 1998–2003 (Vice-Chair. 1981–86, Chair. 1989–98, Hon. Pres. 2003); Fellow, King's Coll., London 2002; Hon. Pres. Authors Lending and Copyright Soc. 2002; CISAC Gold Medal for Literature 2002, Benson Medal RSL 2004. *Radio:* The Passionate Shepherdess, Only Goodnight. *Television:* Upstairs Downstairs (Episode 11). *Plays:* Pearson (London Playwrights' Award), Rites (Nat. Theatre) 1969, A Nightingale in Bloomsbury Square (Hampstead Theatre) 1974, The Masque of Henry Purcell (Southwark Theatre) 1995. *Publications:* That's How It Was 1962, The Single Eye 1964, The Microcosm 1966, The Paradox Players 1967, Lyrics for the Dog Hour (poems) 1968, Wounds 1969, Love Child 1971, The Venus Touch 1971, The Erotic World of Faery 1972, I Want to Go to Moscow 1973, Capital 1975, Evesong (poems) 1975, The Passionate Shepherdess 1977, Housespy 1978, Memorials of the Quick and the Dead (poems) 1979, Inherit the Earth 1980, Gorsaga 1981, Londoners: An Elegy 1983, Men and Beasts 1984, Collected Poems 1949–84 1985, Change 1987, A Thousand Capricious Chances: Methuen 1889–1989 1989, Illuminations 1991, Occam's Razor 1992, Henry Purcell (biog.) 1994, Restitution

1998, England: The Making of a Myth from Stonehenge to Albert Square 2001, Alchemy 2004, Family Values 2008, The Orpheus Trail 2009. *Address:* 18 Fabian Road, London, SW6 7TZ, England. *Telephone:* (20) 7385-3598. *Fax:* (20) 7385-2468. *Website:* www.maureenduffy.co.uk.

DUFFY, Terrence A.; American business executive; *Executive Chairman, CME (Chicago Mercantile Exchange);* ed Univ. of Wisconsin-Whitewater; Pres. TDA Trading, Inc. 1981–; mem. Chicago Mercantile Exchange Inc. (CME) 1981–, mem. Bd of Dirs CME 1995–, Vice-Chair. CME 1998–2002, served on exec., compensation, nominating, strategic planning and regulatory oversight cttees, Chair. 2002–06, Vice-Chair. Chicago Mercantile Exchange Holdings Inc. (CME Holdings) 2001–, Chair. 2002–06, Exec. Chair. CME Inc. (following merger with Chicago Bd of Trade) 2006–; mem. Nat. Saver Summit on Retirement Savings 2002–, Fed. Retirement Thrift Investment Bd 2003–; mem. Bd of Dirs World Business Chicago, Ill. Agricultural Leadership Foundation; mem. Bd of Regents, Mercy Home for Boys and Girls; Co-Chair. Mayo Clinic Greater Chicago Leadership Council; mem. Econ. Club of Chicago, Execs' Club of Chicago, Pres.'s Circle of Chicago Council on Global Affairs; Trustee Saint Xavier Univ.; recognized by Irish America Magazine as one of Top 100 Irish Business Leaders 2003–. *Address:* CME, 20 South Wacker Drive, Chicago, IL 60606, USA (office). *Telephone:* (312) 930-1000 (office). *E-mail:* info@cme.com (office). *Website:* www.cme.com (office).

DUFOIX, Georgina, DèsSc Econ; French politician; b. (Georgina Nègre), 16 Feb. 1943, Paris; d. of Alain Nègre and Antoinette Pallier; m. Antoine Dufoix 1963; two s. two d.; ed Lycée de Nîmes and Univs of Montpellier and Paris-Sorbonne; mem. Man. Cttee Parti Socialiste 1979; Sec. of State for Family Affairs 1981–83, for Family Affairs, Population and Immigrant Workers 1983–84; Govt Spokeswoman and Minister for Social Affairs and Nat. Solidarity 1984–86; Conseiller-gén. for Gard 1982, Socialist Deputy 1986–88; Sec. of State for Family Affairs, for Women's Rights and for Repatriates May–June 1988; Chargée de mission auprès du Président 1988–92; Pres. Admin. Council, French Red Cross 1989–92; Del. Fight against Drugs 1989–93; mem. Governing Bd UN Research Inst. for Social Devt, Geneva 1990–2000, Communications Co. Vera, Governing Bd War-torn Soc. Project, Geneva 1998–2008, Governing Bd InterPeace International, Geneva; Woman of the Year (France) 1989. *Leisure interest:* her vineyard. *Address:* Domaine de Montroche, Route de Saint Gilles, 30900 Nîmes, France (home). *Telephone:* (4) 66-29-80-00 (office). *E-mail:* gdufoix@free.fr (home).

DUFOUR, Bernard, MSc; French aviation official (retd); b. 14 Feb. 1933, France; s. of Jean Dufour and Denise Dufour (née Penot); m. Bernadette de Villepin 1956; five c.; ed Ecole Ozanam, Limoges, Lycée Janson de Sailly, Paris, Ecole Ste Geneviève, Ecole Polytechnique, Calif. Inst. of Tech., USA; Engineer Sud Aviation 1956–61, Dir helicopter production 1961–64, St Nazaire 1964–65, Toulouse 1965–76, Usine Belfort Alsthom 1977–89, GEC Alsthom (Electromechanical Div.) 1989–94; Dir Gen. ALSTOM Electroméca-nique 1989–94; Pres., CEO SNECMA 1994–96; Phare (EU pre-accession programme) expert in Romania 1997–98; Chevalier, Ordre nat. du Mérite, Légion d'honneur, Tudor Vladiminescu (Romania); Médaille Aéronautique. *Leisure interests:* cycling, riding, sailing, skiing. *Address:* 4 rue Henri Heine, 75016 Paris, France (home). *Telephone:* 1-45-25-22-78 (home). *Fax:* 1-45-25-22-78 (home). *E-mail:* dufourbern@wanadoo.fr (home).

DUFOUR, Jean-Marie, BSc, MSc, MA, PhD, FRSC; Canadian economist and academic; *Professor of Economics, University of Montreal;* ed McGill Univ., Univ. of Montreal, Concordia Univ., Univ. of Chicago; Lecturer in Statistics, Univ. of Québec at Trois-Rivières 1972–73; Prof. of Math., Collège Édouard-Montpetit, Longueuil, Montréal 1973–75; Research Assoc., Inst. of Applied Econ. Research, Concordia Univ. 1978–79; Lecturer in Econs (full-time), Dept of Econ. Sciences, Univ. of Montreal 1978–79, Asst Prof. of Econs 1979–83, Assoc. Prof. of Econs 1983–88, Prof. of Econs 1988–, Chair. Dept of Econ. Sciences 1995–97, Holder of Canada Research Chair in Econometrics, Research Fellow, CIREQ (Centre interuniversitaire de recherche en economie quantitative, mem. research staff, Centre for Research in Econ. Devt 1979–85, Sr mem. research staff ('Chercheur régulier') and Dir research programme in econometrics and macroeconomics 1985–90, Dir Centre 1988–95, 1997–99; Lecturer in Econometrics, Univ. of Sherbrooke 1979, 1981; Lecturer in Quantitative Methods (Time Series), École des Hautes Études Commerciales, Montréal 1980, 1981; Fellow, CIRANO (Centre for Interuniversity Research and Analysis on Orgs, Montreal); Dir Canadian Econometrics Study Group; Project Leader Math. and Statistical Methods for Financial Modelling and Risk Man., MITACS (Math. of Information Tech. and Complex Systems) (Canadian network of centres of excellence); Consultant in Econs, Econ. Council of Canada 1981, Office de Planification et de Développement économique du Québec 1982, Royal Comm. on the Econ. Union and Devt Prospects for Canada (McDonald Comm.), Ottawa 1983–84; Research Fellow, CORE (Centre for Operations Research and Econometrics), Université Catholique de Louvain, Belgium 1985–86; Invited Prof. of Econs, Université de Toulouse I, France 1983; Visiting Prof. of Econs, Univ. of Pennsylvania 1992, Stanford Univ. 1999, Univ. of Toronto 2000; Visiting Prof. of Econometrics, Univ. of Lausanne, Switzerland 1995, Institut d'Économie Industrielle, Université des sciences sociales de Toulouse, France 2002, École Nationale de la Statistique et de l'Admin Économique, Paris, France 2004; Visiting Prof. of Econometrics and Statistics, Institut Supérieur de Gestion, Université de Tunis III, Tunisia 1998; Visiting Scholar, Center for Computational Research in Econs and Man. Science, MIT 1980, Queen's Univ. 1986, CEPREMAP, Paris 1986, Université Libre de Bruxelles (Institut de statistique), Belgium 1988, 1989, 1990, 1993, Institut d'Économie Industrielle, Université des Sciences Sociales de Toulouse, France 1992, 1994, Institut für Statistik und Ökonometrie, Humboldt-Universität zu Berlin, Germany 1994, Institut Nat.Nat. de Statistique et d'Économie Appliquée, Rabat, Morocco 1997, École Nationale de la Statistique et de l'Admin Économique, Centre de Recherche en Économie et Statistique, Paris 1990, 1991, 1993, 1995, 1997, 2000, 2001, Centre for Econ. Research, Kaltholieke Universiteit Tilburg, Netherlands 2000, Faculty of Econs, Technische Universität Dresden, Germany 2000, Tinbergen Inst. and Dept of Actuarial Science and Econometrics, Universiteit van Amsterdam, Netherlands 1996, 1997, 1999, 2001, 2003, 2004, Deutsche Bundesbank, Frankfurt, Germany 2001, 2004, Institut für Wirtschaftsforschung, Halle, Germany 2005, 2006, 2007; mem. Bd Dirs Soc. canadienne de science économique 1984–87, Pres.-Elect 1998–99, Pres. 1999–2000; Vice-Pres. Canadian Econs Asscn 2000–01, Pres.-Elect 2001–02, Pres. 2002–03; mem. Int. Statistical Inst. 1990–; Assoc. Ed. Canadian Journal of Economics 1984–88, Cahiers du Centre d'Études de Recherche Opérationnelle 1989–, Econometric Theory 1991–93, Annales d'Économie et de Statistique 1990–, Econometric Reviews 1991–96, 1998–2003, Journal of Econometrics 1994–, Econometrica 1996–2002; Guest Ed. Empirical Economics 1993–94; mem. Editorial Bd Empirical Economics 1994–2003; Fellow, Centre for Operations Research and Econometrics, Université Catholique de Louvain, Belgium 1985–86; Benjamin Meaker Visiting Prof. of Econs, Univ. of Bristol, UK 1993, 1999; Killam Research Fellow, Canada Council for the Arts 1998–2000; Netherlands Org. for Scientific Research (Nederlandse Organisatie voor Wetenschappelijk Onderzoek, NWO) Visitor's Fellowship 2003–04; mem. American Econ. Asscn, Canadian Econs Asscn, Inst. of Math. Statistics, Int. Statistical Inst., Soc. Canadienne de Science Économique, Statistical Soc. of Canada; Fellow, Journal of Econometrics 1996–, Econometric Soc. 1998–, American Statistical Asscn 2005–; Officier, Ordre nat. du Québec 2006; Govt of Québec Doctoral Fellowship 1975–78, Canada Council Doctoral Fellowship 1975–78, Leave Fellowship from Social Sciences and Humanities Research Council of Canada 1985–86, Prize for Excellence in Research, Soc. Canadienne de Science Économique 1988, John Rae Prize for Outstanding Research, Canadian Econs Asscn 1994, Marcel Dagenais Prize for Excellence in Research, Soc. Canadienne de Science Économique 2000, Marcel-Vincent Prize pour les sciences sociales, Asscn francophone pour le savoir 2005, Konrad Adenauer Research Award, Alexander von Humboldt Foundation (Germany) 2005, Radio-Canada Personality of the week, La Presse/Radio-Canada 2006, Killam Prize for Social Sciences, Killam Trust and Canada Council for the Arts 2006, Guggenheim Fellow 2006–07. *Publications:* L'aide publique au financement des exportations (co-author) 1983, Government Assistance to Export Financing (English trans. of previous title) 1983, New Developments in Time Series Econometrics (co-ed.) 1993, Recent Developments in the Econometrics of Structural Change (co-ed.) 1996, Resampling Methods in Econometrics (co-ed.) 2006, Heavy Tails and Stable Paretian Distributions in Econometrics (co-ed.) 2007; more than 110 articles in professional journals on econometrics and statistics, macroeconomics, finance and public finance. *Address:* Université de Montréal, Département de sciences économiques 3150, rue Jean-Brillant, Room C-6030, bureau G6088 CP 6128, succursale Centre-ville Montréal, PQ H3C 3J7, Canada (office); 1060 Bernard Ouest, Apt. 5 Outremont (Québec) Canada H2V 1V2 (home). *Telephone:* (514) 343-2400 (office); (514) 273-0497 (home). *Fax:* (514) 343-5831 (office). *E-mail:* jean.marie.dufounr@umontreal.ca (office). *Website:* www.fas.umontreal.ca/SCECO/Dufour (office).

DUFOURCQ, Bertrand Charles Albert, LenD; French diplomatist; *President, Centre de Musique Baroque de Versailles;* b. 5 July 1933, Paris; s. of Norbert Dufourcq and Marguerite-Odette Latron; m. Elisabeth Lefort des Ylouses 1961; two s. two d.; ed Lycées Montaigne and Louis-le-Grand, Paris, Faculté de Droit, Paris, Inst. d'Etudes Politiques, Paris and Ecole Nat. d'Admin; Sec. for Foreign Affairs 1961; Chef de Cabinet to Prefect/Admin.-Gen. of City of Algiers 1961; Ministry of Foreign Affairs 1962; Cultural Counsellor, Tokyo 1964; Counsellor for Foreign Affairs 1967; various posts at Ministry of Foreign Affairs and Ministry of Industrial and Scientific Devt 1967–69; Head of Cultural, Scientific and Tech. Service, Embassy, Moscow 1969–72; Ministry of Foreign Affairs 1972–76, 1978–79; Amb. to People's Repub. of Congo 1976–78; European Dir Ministry of External Relations 1979–84; Dir Office of M. Claude Cheysson 1984; special attachment to Minister of External Relations 1984–85; Admin. Ecole Nat. d'Admin. 1980–83; Amb. to Vatican 1985–88; Dir of Political Affairs, Ministry of Foreign Affairs 1988–91; Amb. to USSR 1991, to Russia 1992 (also accred to Mongolia 1991–92), to Germany 1992–93; Sec.-Gen. Ministry of Foreign Affairs 1993–98; Pres. Fondation de France 2000–2007; Pres. Centre de Musique Baroque de Versailles 1998–; Commdr Légion d'honneur, Ordre nat. du Mérite, Amb. de France. *Address:* Centre de Musique Baroque de Versailles, Hôtel des Menus-Plaisirs, 22 avenue de Paris, BP 353, 78003 Versailles Cedex (office); 48 rue Madame, 75006 Paris, France (home). *Telephone:* 1-39-20-78-10 (office). *Fax:* 1-39-20-78-01 (office). *Website:* www.cmbv.com (office).

DUGAS, Richard J., Jr., BSc; American construction industry executive; *CEO and President, Pulte Homes Inc.;* ed Louisiana State Univ.; held marketing and customer service postions with Exxon Co. 1986–89; worked in process improvement and plant operational efficiency, PepsiCo 1990–94; joined Pulte Homes Inc., Bloomfield Hills, Mich. 1994, has held numerous exec. positions including Vice-Pres. Process Improvement, City Pres. and Market Man., Atlanta Div., Coastal Region Pres., Exec. Vice-Pres. and COO –2003, Pres. and CEO 2003–. *Address:* Pulte Homes Inc., 100 Bloomfield Hills Parkway, Suite 300, Broomfield Hills, MI 48304, USA (office). *Telephone:* (248) 647-2750 (office). *Fax:* (248) 433-4598 (office). *Website:* www.pulte.com (office).

DUGGER, John Scott; American artist and designer; b. 18 July 1948, Los Angeles, Calif.; s. of Dr James Attwood Dugger and Julian Marie Riddle; ed Loy Norrix High School, Kalamazoo, Mich., Gilmore Inst. of Art, Mich., School of the Art Inst. of Chicago, Ill.; created Perennial (first Ergonic Sculpture), Paris 1970; Leader Soc. for Anglo-Chinese understanding Del. to China 1972; Founder-Dir Banner Arts, London 1976; mem. Exec. Cttee Art Services

Grants Ltd (Artists' Housing Charity) 1980–85; Chair. Asscn of Space Artists, London 1984, 1985; Vice-Chair. Int. Artists Asscn, UK Cttee 1986–87; major works include Documenta 5, People's Participation Pavilion, Kassel, FRG 1972, Monumental Strip-Banner Installation, Trafalgar Square, London 1974, Sports Banner Exhbn, Inst. of Contemporary Arts, London 1980; Original Art Banners commissioned for HM the Queen's 60th Birthday, Buckingham Palace 1986, Tibet Mountainscape Banner for His Holiness the XIV Dalai Lama— Int. Year of Tibet 1991; Int. Certified Master Fabric Craftsman, IFAI (Industrial Fabric Asscn) 1992; works on display at Arts Council of GB, Tate Gallery, London; Major Award, Arts Council of GB 1978, Calouste Gulbenkian Foundation Awards 1979, 1980, Int. Achievement Award 1993. *Leisure interests:* oriental art, mountaineering, martial arts.

DUHALDE MALDONADO, Eduardo Alberto; Argentine fmr head of state; b. 5 Oct. 1941, Lomas de Zamora, Prov. of Buenos Aires; s. of Tomás Duhalde and María Esther Maldonado; m. Hilda Beatriz González 1971; one s. four d.; fmr mem. staff Legal Dept Lomas de Zamora Town Council; Pres. Exec. Cttee Partido Justicialista of Lomas de Zamora 1973; Mayor Lomas de Zamora 1974–76, removed from post following mil. coup, re-elected 1983; elected Nat. Deputy for Prov. of Buenos Aires 1987, First Vice-Pres. Chamber of Deputies 1987–89; Vice-Pres. of Argentina, Pres. Senate 1989–91; Gov. Prov. of Buenos Aires 1991–99; Partido Justicialista cand. presidential elections 1999; Pres. Congreso Nacional del Partido Justicialista; Pres. of Argentina 2002–03; f. Office for Drug Addiction Prevention and Assistance, Lomas de Zamora 1984, Comm. on Drug Addiction, Chamber of Deputies; Orden de Boyacá, Colombia, Orden Cruceiro do Sul, Brazil, Orden del Quetzal, Guatemala, Orden de Bernardo O'Higgins, Chile; Dr hc (Genoa) 1992, (Universidad Hebrea Argentina) 1999, (Universidad del Salvador) 1999. *Publications:* La revolucıón productiva (with Carlos Saúl Menem q.v.) 1987, Los políticos y las drogas 1988, Hacía un mundo sin drogas 1994, Política, familia, sociedad y drogas 1997. *Leisure interests:* fishing, chess, folk music, reading, watching football. *Address:* c/o Office of the President, Balcarce 50, 1064 Buenos Aires, Argentina (office).

DUHAMEL, Olivier, LLD; French academic and politician; *Professor of Law and Political Science, University of Paris (Sciences Po);* b. 2 May 1950, Neuilly-sur-Seine; ed Inst. of Political Studies, Paris; Founder and Ed. Pouvoirs magazine 1977–; Ed. TNS Sofres 1984–; currently Prof. of Law and Political Science, Univ. of Paris (Sciences Po); Adviser to Pres. of Constitutional Council 1983–95; mem. Consultative Comm. for the Revision of the Constitution 1992–93; Founder and Pres. REVE (Réflexion-Engagement-Vision pour l'Europe) 1994; founder mem. AGIR 1995–, SOS Europe (inter-parliamentary group) 1997–; Pres. Europartenaires 1997–2000; MEP (Socialist Party) June 1997–2004, mem. Cttee on Constitutional Affairs, Cttee on Citizens' Freedoms and Rights 1994–2001, on Justice and Home Affairs; mem. Bureau Party of European Socialists 2001–04; mem. Convention on Future of Europe 2002–03; fmr Visiting Prof., Univ. of Washington, New York Univ.; columnist La Marseillaise 1997–; contrib. Le Monde, France Culture (TV) 2004–, European Art Forum 2004–. *Publications:* Chili ou la tentative révolution 1974, Changer le PC? 1979, La Gauche et la 5ème République 1980, Histoire des idées politiques (co-author) 1982, Le nouveau Président (co-author) 1987, Le pouvoir politique en France 1991, Droit constitutionnel et politique 1994, Les Démocraties 1993, Histoire constitutionnelle de la France 1995, Petit Dictionnaire de l'Euro (co-author) 1998, Le Quinquennat 2000, La 5ème République (1958–2001) (co-author) 2001, Présidentielles: les surprises de l'historique (1965–95) 2001, Vive la VIème République 2002, Pour l'Europe 2003, La Constitution européene 2004, La Ve République (1985–2004) 2004, Pour Europe: Le texte intégral de la constitution expliqué et commenté 2005, Des raisons du Non 2005, Matins d'un Européen 2005. *Address:* Sciences Po, 27 rue Saint-Guillaume, 75007, Paris (office); 59 boulevard Raspail, 75006 Paris, France (home). *Telephone:* 1-45-49-50-50 (office); 1-42-84-11-64 (home). *Fax:* 1-42-22-31-26 (office). *E-mail:* lolivier.d@wanadoo.fr (home). *Website:* www.sciences-po.fr (office).

DUIGAN, John, MA; Australian film director, screenwriter and author; b. 19 June 1949, Hartley Wintney, Hampshire, England; ed Univ. of Melbourne; fmr Lecturer, Univ. of Melbourne and Latrobe Univ.; Co-Dir Vietnam (TV mini-series); wrote and directed TV documentaries: Fragments of War: The Story of Damien Parer 1988, Bitter Rice 1989. *Films include:* The Firm Man (1975), Trespassers 1976, Mouth to Mouth 1978, Dimboola 1979, Winter of Our Dreams 1981, Far East 1982, One Night Stand 1984, The Year My Voice Broke 1987 (Australian Acad. Award for Best Dir), Romero 1989, Flirting 1991, Wide Sargasso Sea 1993, Sirens 1994, The Journey of August King 1995, The Leading Man 1996, Lawn Dogs 1997, Molly 1999, Paranoid 2000, The Parole Officer 2001, Head in the Clouds 2004. *Publications:* novels: Badge, Players, Room to Move. *Address:* c/o Creative Artists Management (CAA), 9830 Wilshire Blvd., Beverly Hills, CA 90212-1825, USA.

DUKAKIS, Michael Stanley; American fmr politician and academic; *Distinguished Professor, Department of Political Science, Northeastern University;* b. 3 Nov. 1933, Brookline, Mass.; s. of Dr. Panos Dukakis and Euterpe Dukakis; m. Katharine Dickson; one s. two d.; ed Brookline High School, Swarthmore Coll., Harvard Law School; Army service in Korea 1955–57; mem. Town Meeting, Brookline 1959, Chair. Town Cttee 1960–62; Attorney Hill & Barlow, Boston 1960–74; alt. Del. Democratic Nat. Convention 1968; mem. Mass. House of Reps for Brookline 1962–70, later Chair. Cttee on Public Service and mem. Special Comm. on Low Income Housing; f. a research group for public information 1970; moderator of TV public affairs debate programme The Advocates; Gov. of Massachusetts 1975–79, 1983–91; teacher Fla Atlantic Univ., Boca Raton 1992; Democratic Cand. for Pres. 1988; lecturer and Dir of Inter-Governmental Studies, John F. Kennedy School of Govt, Harvard Univ. 1979–82; Distinguished Prof. Northeastern Univ., Boston; Vice Chair. AmTrack Reform Bd 1998–; Gold Medal, City of Athens, Greece 1996. *Publication:* Creating the Future: Massachusetts comeback and its promise for America (with Rosabeth Moss Kanter) 1988. *Address:* Department of Political Science, Northeastern University, 327 Meserve Hall, Boston, MA 02115 (office); 650 Kelton Avenue, Apartment 302, Los Angeles, CA 90024, USA (home). *Telephone:* (617) 373-4396 (home). *Fax:* (617) 373-5311 (office). *E-mail:* m.dukakis@neu.edu (home). *Website:* www.polisci.neu.edu (office).

DUKAKIS, Olympia, MA; American actress; b. 20 June 1931; m. Louis Zorich; three s.; ed Boston Univ.; teacher of drama at New York Univ. grad. program for 15 years; Founding mem. The Charles Playhouse, Boston, Whole Theatre, Montclair, NJ; appeared in more than 100 regional theatre productions; subsequently appeared in off-Broadway shows including Mann Ish Mann, The Marriage of Bette and Boo, Titus Andronicus, Peer Gynt, The Memorandum, The Curse of the Starving Class, Electra; has appeared in Broadway productions of Abraham Cochrane, The Aspern Papers, The Night of the Iguana, Who's Who in Hell, Mike Nichols' Social Security; mem. Bd Nat. Museum of Women in the Arts, Washington, DC and other arts orgs; recipient of two Obie Awards. *Films include:* John and Mary 1969, Rich Kids 1979, The Idolmaker 1980, Moonstruck (Acad. Award for Best Supporting Actress 1988) 1987, Working Girl 1988, Dad 1989, Look Who's Talking 1989, Steel Magnolias 1989, In the Spirit 1990, Look Who's Talking Too 1990, The Cemetery Club 1993, Digger 1993, Look Who's Talking Now 1993, I Love Trouble 1994, Jeffrey 1995, Mighty Aphrodite 1995, Mr Holland's Opus 1995, Picture Perfect 1997, My Beautiful Son 2001, Ladies and The Champ 2001, And Never Let Her Go 2001, The Intended 2002, Jesus, Mary and Joey 2003, The Event 2003, Charlie's War 2003, The Great New Wonderful 2005, The Thing About My Folks 2005, 3 Needles 2005, Whiskey School 2005, Away from Her 2006, Day on Fire 2006, In the Land of Women 2007, Hove (The Wind) 2009. *Television includes:* Nicky's World 1974, The Seagull 1975, King of America 1982, Lucky Day 1991, The Last Act Is a Solo 1991, Fire in the Dark 1991, Sinatra 1992, Tales of the City (miniseries) 1993, A Match Made in Heaven 1997, Scattering Dad 1998, The Pentagon Wars 1998, More Tales of the City (miniseries) 1998, The Last of the Blonde Bombshells 2000, And Never Let Her Go 2001, Ladies and the Champ 2001, My Beautiful Son 2001, Further Tales of the City (miniseries) 2001, Guilty Hearts (miniseries) 2002, Center of the Universe (series) 2004, Jesus, Mary and Joey 2006, Numb3rs 2006. *Address:* c/o William Morris Agency, One William Morris Place, Beverly Hills, CA 90212; 222 Upper Mountain Avenue, Montclair, NJ 07043, USA (home).

ĐUKANOVIĆ, Milo; Montenegrin politician and economist; *Prime Minister;* b. 15 Feb. 1962, Nikšić; m. Lidija Kuč; one s.; ed Faculty of Econs, Univ. of Montenegro, Podgorica; joined League of Communists of Yugoslavia (LCY) 1979 (mem. Cen. Cttee 1986–89) later named Democratic Party of Socialists (Demokratska Partija Socijalista Crne Gore), Deputy Chair. 1994–98, Chair. 1998–; Prime Minister of Repub. of Montenegro 1991–98, 2003–06, 2008–; Pres. of Repub. of Montenegro 1998–2002; mem. Skupština Crne Gore (Ass. of Montenegro) 2006–; Hon. mem. The Int. Raoul Wallenberg Foundation. *Address:* Office of the Prime Minister, Jovana Tomaševića bb, 81000 Podgorica (office); Democratic Party of Socialists of Montenegro (Demokratska Partija Socijalista Crne Gore), 81000 Podgorica, Jovana Tomaševića bb, Montenegro. *Telephone:* (81) 242530 (office). *Fax:* (81) 242329 (office). *E-mail:* kabinet .premijera@mn.yu (office); predsjednik@dps.cg.yu. *Website:* www.vlada.cg.yu (office); www.dpscg.org.

DUKE, Michael (Mike) Terry, BEng; American business executive; *President and CEO, Wal-Mart Inc.;* b. 1950; m. Susan Duke; one s. two d.; ed Georgia Inst. of Tech.; spent 23 years working for various retailers including Federated Dept Stores and May Dept Stores; joined Wal-Mart Inc. 1995, Sr Vice-Pres. of Logistics 1995–2000, Sr Vice-Pres. of Distribution and Exec. Vice-Pres. of Logistics 2000, Exec. Vice-Pres. of Admin 2000–03, Pres. Wal-Mart Stores USA 2003–05, Vice-Chair. and Head of Int. Div. Wal-Mart Inc. 2005–09, Pres. and CEO Wal-Mart Inc. 2009–, mem. Bd of Dirs 2008–; mem. Bd of Dirs US-China Business Council, CIES–The Food Business Forum; mem. Exec. Bd Conservation Int. Center for Environmental Leadership in Business; mem. Bd of Advisors, Univ. of Arkansas. *Address:* Wal-Mart Stores, Inc., 702 SW 8th Street, Bentonville, AR 72716-8611, USA (office). *Telephone:* (479) 273-4000 (office). *Fax:* 479) 277-1830 (office). *Website:* www .walmartstores.com (office).

DUKE, Robin Chandler; American diplomatist; b. 1923; m. Angier Biddle Duke (deceased); writer, New York Journal American newspaper 1940s; fmr mem. Bd of Dirs American Home Products, Rockwell Int., Int. Flavors and Fragrances; mem. Bd of Trustees US–Japan Foundation; mem. Bd of Dirs Lucile and David Packard Foundation, UN Asscn of USA 2000–, The Worldwatch Institute 2005–; fmr Vice-Chair. and mem. Advisory Bd Inst. of Int. Educ.; Chair. Del. to 21st Session of UNESCO 1980, Amb. 1980; Amb. to Norway 2000–01; fmr Pres. NARAL Pro-Choice America; mem. Council on Foreign Relations; Fellow, Acad. of Arts and Social Sciences; f. Population Action Int. *Address:* 435 East 52nd Street, Apt 2E, New York, NY 10022-6445, USA.

DUKES, Alan M., MA; Irish politician; *Director-General, Institute of European Affairs;* b. 22 April 1945, Dublin; s. of James Dukes and Margaret Moran; m. Fionnuala Corcoran 1968; two d.; ed Scoil Colmcille and Colaiste Mhuire, Dublin and Univ. Coll., Dublin; Chief Econ., Irish Farmers Asscn 1967–72; Dir Irish Farmers Asscn, Brussels 1973–76; Personal Adviser to Commr of EEC 1977–80; TD (Fine Gael) for Kildare 1981–2002; Opposition Spokesperson on Agric. March–Dec. 1982; Minister of Agric. 1981–82, for Finance 1982–86, for Justice 1986–87; Leader and Pres. Fine Gael 1987–90; mem. Council of State 1987–90; Minister for Transport, Energy and Communications 1996–97; Opposition Spokesperson on Environment and Local Govt; Pres. Irish Council of the European Movt 1987–91, Chair. 1997–2000; Vice-Pres. Int. European Movt 1991–96; Adjunct Prof. of Public Admin, Man. Univ. of Limerick 1991–; Dir-Gen. Inst. of European Affairs 2003–; Public Affairs Consultant, WHPR, Dublin; Vice-Pres. European People's Party 1987–96; Chair. Jt Oireachtas Cttee on Foreign Affairs 1995–96; Officier de la Légion d'honneur 2004, Commdr's Cross of the Order of Merit (Poland) 2004. *Leisure interests:* reading, music, walking, horse-riding, motor sport. *Address:* Institute of European Affairs, Europe House, 8 North Great Georges Street, Dublin 1, Ireland (office). *Telephone:* (1) 8746756 (office); 876846274 (mobile) (home). *Fax:* (1) 8786880 (office); (45) 520306 (home). *E-mail:* info@iiea.com (office); alandukes@eircom.net (home). *Website:* www.iiea.com (office).

ĐUKIĆ-DEJANOVIĆ, Slavica, MA PhD; Serbian psychiatrist and politician; *President, National Assembly;* b. 4 July 1951, Rača Kragujevačka; ed Medical Faculty, Univ. of Belgrade; joined Medical Faculty, Univ. of Kragujevac 1982, currently Prof. and Assoc. Dean for Int. Collaboration; Dir KBC Kragujevac Hosp. 1995–2001; Dir Centrum Neuropsychiatrii, Kragujevac; Minister for the Family 2000–01; mem. Socialist Party of Serbia (Socijalistička partija Srbije) 1990–, Vice Pres. 1996–97, 2002–; mem. Nat. Ass., Pres. 2008–; Vice-Pres. Asscn of Psychiatrists of Serbia. *Publications include:* more than 160 articles published in medical journals. *Address:* Office of the President, Narodna skupština Republike Srbije (National Assembly of the Republic of Serbia), 11000 Belgrade, Kralja Milana 14, Serbia (office). *Telephone:* (11) 3222001 (office). *E-mail:* webmaster@parlament.sr.gov.yu (office); slavica1@eunet.yu (office). *Website:* www.parlament.sr.gov.yu (office).

DULAIMI, Saadoun ad-, PhD; Iraqi government official, psychologist and statistician; b. 1954, Ramadi; ed Univ. of Keele, UK; fmr army reserve officer; emigrated 1980s; has taught in Jordan and USA; returned to Iraq 2003; est. Centre for Research and Strategic Studies; Minister of Defence 2005–06. *Address:* c/o Ministry of Defence, Baghdad, Iraq (office).

DULBECCO, Renato; American virologist; b. 22 Feb. 1914, Cantanzaro, Italy; s. of Leonardo and Maria Dulbecco; m. 1st Giuseppina Salvo 1940 (divorced 1963); m. 2nd Maureen Muir 1963; two d. (and one s. deceased); ed Univ. of Turin; Asst Prof. of Pathology, Univ. of Turin 1940–46, of Experimental Embryology 1947; Research Assoc. Dept of Bacteriology, Indiana Univ. 1947–49; Sr Research Fellow Calif. Inst. of Tech. 1949–52, Assoc. Prof. 1952–53, Prof. 1954–63; Sr Fellow, Salk Inst. for Biological Studies 1963–72; Asst Dir of Research, Imperial Cancer Research Fund Labs (London) 1972–74, Deputy Dir 1974–77; Distinguished Research Prof., Salk Inst., La Jolla, Calif. 1977–, Pres. 1989–92, Pres. Emer. 1993–; Chair. Int. Physicians for Prevention of Nuclear War Inst., American-Italian Foundation for Cancer Research; mem. American Asscn for Cancer Research, NAS, American Acad. of Arts and Sciences; Foreign mem. Royal Soc., London 1974, Accad. Nazionale dei Lincei; Hon. mem. Accademia Ligure di Scienze e Lettere; Trustee, La Jolla Co. Day School; Hon. LLD (Glasgow) 1970, Hon. DSc (Yale) 1968, Dr hc (Vrije Univ., Brussels) 1978; several awards, including Ehrlich Prize, Lasker Award 1964, Ludovic Gross Horwitz Prize 1973, Selman A. Waksman Award in Microbiology, NAS, 1974, Nobel Prize in Medicine (Physiology) 1975; Mandel Gold Medal (Czechoslovak Acad. of Sciences) 1982. *Address:* Salk Institute, PO Box 85800, San Diego, CA 92186-5800 (office); 7525 Hillside Drive, La Jolla, CA 92037-3941, USA (home). *Telephone:* (858) 453-4100 (office). *Fax:* (858) 458-9741 (office). *E-mail:* Dulbecco@salk.edu (office).

DULIĆ, Oliver, MD; Serbian physician and politician; *Minister of the Environment and Spatial Planning;* b. 21 Jan. 1975, Belgrade; m. Andrea Dulić; ed Univ. of Belgrade; trained as orthopaedic surgeon, Belgrade; mem. Democratic Party (Demokratska Stranka) 1997–, Pres. Subotica br. 1997–2000, Vice-Pres. Vojvodina Prov. br. 2000–06, now mem. Exec. Cttee; mem. Narodna skupština Republike Srbije (Parl.) 2003–, Speaker 2007–08; Minister of the Environment and Spatial Planning 2008–. *Address:* Ministry of the Environment and Spatial Planning, Nemanjina 11, 11000 Belgrade, Serbia (office). *Telephone:* (11) 3617717 (office). *Fax:* (11) 3617722 (office). *E-mail:* info@ekoplan.gov.rs (office). *Website:* www.ekoplan.gov.rs (office).

DULLOO, Madan Murlidhar, LLB, DCL, SC, HSC; Mauritian lawyer and politician; b. 20 Sept. 1949, Port Louis; s. of Balram Bholanath Dulloo and Belwantee Lutchmee Gangaram; m. Indira Priyadarshani Dookun; three c.; ed Univ. of London, Inns of Court School of Law, Middle Temple, London, Univ. of Paris (Sorbonne); teacher 1970–71; lawyer 1976–86, 1994–2005; fmr Minister of Foreign Affairs and Emigration, Minister of Agric., Minister of Fisheries and Natural Resources; Minister of Justice and Attorney-Gen. 1986–94; Minister of Foreign Affairs, Int. Trade and Co-operation 2005–08; Leader, Mouvement Militant Socialiste Mauricien. *Leisure interests:* sports, yoga, religion, sun, sea, nature, anthropology. *Address:* c/o Ministry of Foreign Affairs, International Trade and Co-operation, New Government Centre, 5th Floor, Port Louis, Mauritius (office). *E-mail:* madan@wanadoo.mu (home).

DUMAS, Jean-Louis Robert Frédéric, LenD; French business executive (retd); b. 2 Feb. 1938, Paris; s. of Robert Dumas and Jacqueline Hermès; m. Rena Gregoriadès 1962; one s. one d.; ed Lycée Janson-de-Sailly, Faculté de Droit de Paris and Inst. d'Etudes Politiques, Paris; asst buyer, Bloomingdales, New York 1963; joined gen. man. Hermès 1964, Dir, Gen. Man. 1971–78, Chair. and Man. Dir Hermès, Holding Hermès 1978–95, Pres. Groupe Hermès (later Hermès Int.) 1995–2006, Man., Artistic Dir Hermès Int. 1995–2006; Pres. Castille Investissements 1997; Pres. Sport-Soie 1978; Vice-Pres. Comité Colbert 1978–88, Pres. 1988–91; Dir Orfèvrerie Christofle 1988, Gaumont 1991; nat. adviser on foreign trade 1973–; Officier, Légion d'honneur, Officier des Arts et des Lettres. *Leisure interests:* photography, watercolour paintings. *Address:* Hermès, 24 rue du Faubourg St Honoré, 75008 Paris, France (office). *Telephone:* 1-40-17-49-20 (office). *Fax:* 1-40-17-49-21 (office). *Website:* www.hermes.com (office).

DUMAS, Marlene; South African painter; b. 1953, Cape Town; ed Univ. of Cape Town; with Atelier '63, Haarlem, Netherlands 1976–78, Psychological Inst., Univ. of Amsterdam 1979–80; Coutts Contemporary Art Foundation Coutts Award, Prince Bernard Fund David Roell Prize. *Address:* c/o Frith Street Gallery, 59–60 Frith Street, London, W1D 3JJ, England (office). *Telephone:* (20) 7494-1550 (office). *Fax:* (20) 7287-3733 (office). *E-mail:* info@frithstreetgallery.com (office). *Website:* www.frithstreetgallery.com (office).

DUMAS, Rhetaugh Etheldra Graves, MS, PhD, RN, FAAN; American nurse, psychologist, academic and university administrator; *Vice Provost Emerita, Dean Emerita and Lucille Cole Professor of Nursing, School of Nursing, University of Michigan;* b. 26 Nov. 1928, Natchez, Miss.; d. of Rhetaugh Graves and Josephine (Clemmons) Graves Bell; sister of Wade H. Graves and Norman Bell, Jr; m. A. W. Dumas, Jr 1950; one d.; ed Dillard Univ., New Orleans, Yale Univ. School of Nursing and Union Grad. School, Yellow Springs, Ohio; Dir Student Health Center, Dillard Univ. 1957–59; Yale-New Haven Hosp. 1960; Instructor in Psychiatric Nursing, Dillard Univ. 1961; Research Asst and Instructor Yale Univ. School of Nursing 1962–65, Asst Prof. 1965–66, Assoc. Prof. 1966–72; Dir of Nursing, Conn. Medical Health Center, Yale-New Haven Medical Center 1966–72; Chief, Psychiatric Nursing Educ. Br., Div. of Manpower and Training 1972–75; Deputy Dir Div. of Manpower and Training Programs, Nat. Inst. of Mental Health 1976–79; Deputy Dir Nat. Inst. of Mental Health, Alcohol, Drug Abuse and Mental Health Admin., US Public Health Service 1979–81; Dean Univ. of Mich. School of Nursing, Ann Arbor 1981, Prof. 1981, Vice-Provost for Health Affairs, Univ. of Mich. 1994–97, Cole Prof., School of Nursing 1994–, Vice-Provost Emer. 1997–, Dean Emer. 1997–; Pres. American Acad. of Nursing 1987–89; Pres. Nat. League of Nursing 1997–99; mem. NAS Inst. of Medicine; Hon. Doctor of Public Service (Simmons Coll.) 1976, (Cincinnati) 1981, (Florida International Univ.) 1996; Hon. DHumLitt (Yale) 1989, (San Diego) 1993, (Georgetown) 1996; Hon. LLD (Dillard) 1990, (Bethune-Cookman Coll.) 1997, (Massachusetts-Dartmouth) 1997; Hon. DSc (Indiana Univ., Gary) 1996. *Publications:* The Dilemmas of Black Females in Leadership; numerous articles in professional journals and book chapters. *Leisure interests:* reading, music, singing. *Address:* 400 N Ingalls Street, Room 4320, University of Michigan, Ann Arbor, MI 48109-0482 (office); 6 Eastbury Court, Ann Arbor, MI 48105, USA (home). *Telephone:* (734) 936-6213 (office); (734) 668-6103 (home). *Fax:* (734) 764-4546 (office); (734) 761-6195 (home). *E-mail:* rhetaugh@umich.edu (office). *Website:* www.nursing.umich.edu/faculty/dumas_rhetaugh.html (office).

DUMAS, Roland, LenD; French fmr government minister, politician, lawyer and journalist; b. 23 Aug. 1922, Limoges; s. of Georges Dumas and Elisabeth Dumas (née Lecanuet); m. 2nd Anne-Marie Lillet 1964; two s. one d.; ed Lycée de Limoges, Univ. of Paris and Univ. of London, UK; called to the Bar, Paris 1950 and has practised as a lawyer ever since; journalist with AGEFI, Socialiste Limousin; Political Dir La Corrèze républicaine et socialiste 1967–; mem. Nat. Ass. 1956–58, 1967–68, 1981–83, 1986–93, Vice-Pres. 1968; Minister for European Affairs 1983–84, for Foreign Affairs 1984–86, 1988–93; Govt spokesman July–Dec. 1984; Pres. Nat. Ass. Comm. on Foreign Affairs 1986–87; Chair. Constitutional Court 1995–99, resgnd March 2000; involved in 'Elf Affair' (financial scandal) May 2001, acquitted Jan. 2003; Officier, Légion d'honneur, Croix de guerre, Croix du combattant volontaire, Grand-Croix de l'Ordre d'Isabelle la Catholique (Spain), Order of Merit (Germany). *Publications:* J'ai vu vivre la Chine, Les avocats, Le droit de l'information et de la presse, Plaidoyer pour Roger-Gilbert Lecomte, Le droit de la propriété littéraire et artistique, Le droit de la presse, Le peuple assemblé 1989, Le fil et la pelote – Mémoires 1996, L'epreuve 2003, Affaires etrangeres (Tome 1) 2007. *Address:* 19 quai de Bourbon, 75004 Paris, France (office). *Telephone:* 1-4354-3663 (office). *Fax:* 1-5310-8566 (office).

DUMASY, Lise, DèsL; French academic; *President, University Stendhal Grenoble III;* b. 18 June 1954, Taza, Morocco; m. J.P. Dumasy; two s.; ed Ecole Normale Supérieure, Sèvres; Visiting Asst, Princeton Univ., USA 1977–78; schoolteacher, 1978–80; Research Engineer CNRS 1980, seconded to Inst. de France 1984; teacher, Mannheim Univ. 1987–88; Sr Lecturer, Univ. Stendhal (Grenoble-III) then Prof. 1992–, Head of Dept of French Language, Literature and Civilization 1992–95, mem. Scientific Council 1997, Prin. 1999–2004, Pres. 2007–; Chevalier de l'Ordre des Palmes Académiques. *Publications:* La querelle du roman-feuilleton 1999, Pamphlet, Utopie, Manifeste, XIX-XX (with C. Massol) 2001, Tocqueville, de la démocratie en Amérique, étude littéraire 2004, Stendhal, Balzac, Dumas: un récit romantique? (with C. Massol) 2007. *Leisure Interests:* music, travel. *Address:* Office of the President, Université Stendhal (Grenoble-III), BP 25, 38040 Grenoble Cedex 9, France (office). *Telephone:* (4) 76-82-43-01 (office). *E-mail:* presidence@u-grenoble3.fr (office). *Website:* www.u-grenoble3.fr (office).

DUMMETT, Sir Michael Anthony Eardley, Kt, MA, DLitt; British academic; b. 27 June 1925, London; s. of George Herbert Dummett and Mabel Iris Dummett (née Eardley-Wilmot); m. Ann Chesney 1951; three s. two d.; ed Sandroyd School, Winchester Coll., Christ Church, Oxford; mil. service 1943–47; Asst Lecturer in Philosophy, Univ. of Birmingham 1950–51; Prize Fellow, All Souls Coll., Oxford 1950–57, Research Fellow 1957–61; Harkness Foundation Fellow, Univ. of Calif., Berkeley 1955–56; Reader in Philosophy of Mathematics, Univ. of Oxford 1961–74; Sr Research Fellow, All Souls Coll., Oxford 1974–79, Sub-Warden 1974–76; Visiting Lecturer, Univ. of Ghana 1958, Stanford Univ., Calif., USA 1960–66, Univ. of Minn. 1968, Princeton Univ. 1970, Rockefeller Univ., New York 1973; William James Lecturer in Philosophy, Harvard Univ. 1976; Wykeham Prof. of Logic, Univ. of Oxford 1979–92; Fellow, New College, Oxford 1979–92, Emer. Fellow 1992–98, Hon. Fellow 1998–; Fellow, British Acad. 1967–84 (resgnd), Sr Fellow 1995–; Emer. Fellow, All Souls College, Oxford 1979–; Chair. Jt Council for the Welfare of

Immigrants 1970–71, unofficial cttee of inquiry into events in Southall, 1979–80; mem. Shadow Bd Barclays Bank 1981; Foreign Hon. mem. American Acad. of Arts and Sciences; Dr hc (Nijmegen) 1983, Hon. DLitt (Caen) 1993, (Aberdeen) 1993, (Stirling) 2003, (Athens) 2005, Hon. DUniv (Stirling) 2002; Lakatos Award 1994, Rolf Schock Prize in Philosophy and Logic 1995. *Publications:* Frege: Philosophy of Language 1973, The Justification of Deduction 1973, Elements of Intuitionism 1977, Truth and other Enigmas 1979, Immigration: Where the Debate Goes Wrong 1978, Catholicism and the World Order 1979, The Game of Tarot 1980, Twelve Tarot Games 1980, The Interpretation of Frege's Philosophy 1981, Voting Procedures 1984, The Visconti-Sforza Tarot Cards 1986, Ursprünge der Analytischen Philosophie 1988, The Logical Basis of Metaphysics 1991, Frege and other Philosophers 1991, Frege: Philosophy of Mathematics 1991, Grammar and Style 1993, The Seas of Language 1993, Origins of Analytical Philosophy 1993, Il Mondo e l'Angelo 1993, I Tarocchi Siciliani 1995, A Wicked Pack of Cards 1996, Principles of Electoral Reform 1997, La Natura e il Futuro della Filosofia 2001, On Immigration and Refugees 2001, A History of the Occult Tarot 1870–1970 2002, Truth and the Past 2004, A History of Games Played with the Tarot Pack (with J. McLeod) 2003, Thought and Reality 2006. *Leisure interests:* history of card games and playing cards. *Address:* 54 Park Town, Oxford, OX2 6SJ, England (home). *Telephone:* (1865) 558698 (home). *Fax:* (1865) 558698 (home).

DUNAWAY, (Dorothy) Faye; American actress; b. 14 Jan. 1941, Bascom, Florida; d. of John Dunaway and Grace Dunaway; m. 1st Peter Wolf 1974; m. 2nd Terry O'Neill 1981; one s.; ed Univ. of Florida and Boston Univ.; spent three years with Lincoln Center Repertory Co. in New York, appearing in A Man For All Seasons, After the Fall and Tartuffe; Off-Broadway in Hogan's Goat 1965; appeared at the Mark Taper Forum, LA in Old Times, as Blanche du Bois in A Streetcar Named Desire 1973, The Curse of an Aching Heart 1982. *Films include:* Hurry Sundown 1967, The Happening 1967, Bonnie and Clyde 1967, The Thomas Crown Affair 1968, A Place For Lovers 1969, The Arrangement 1969, Little Big Man 1970, Doc 1971, The Getaway 1972, Oklahoma Crude 1973, The Three Musketeers 1973, Chinatown 1974, Three Days of the Condor 1975, The Towering Inferno 1976, Voyage of the Damned 1976, Network (Acad. Award Best Actress) 1976, The Eyes of Laura Mars 1978, The Champ 1979, The First Deadly Sin 1981, Mommie Dearest 1981, The Wicked Lady 1982, Supergirl 1984, Barfly 1987, Burning Secret 1988, The Handmaid's Tale 1989, On a Moonlit Night 1989, Up to Date 1989, Scorchers 1991, Faithful 1991, Three Weeks in Jerusalem, The Arrowtooth Waltz 1991, Double Edge, Arizona Dream, The Temp, Dun Juan DeMarco 1995, Drunks, Dunston Checks In, Albino Alligator, The Chamber, Fanny Hill 1998, Love Lies Bleeding 1999, The Yards 1999, Joan of Arc 1999, The Thomas Crown Affair 1999, The Yards 2000, Stanley's Gig 2000, Yellow Bird 2001, Changing Hearts 2002, The Rules of Attraction 2002, Mid-Century 2002, The Calling 2002, Blind Horizon 2003, Last Goodbye 2004, El Padrino 2004, Jennifer's Shadow 2004, Ghosts Never Sleep 2005, Cut Off 2006, Love Hollywood Style 2006, Rain 2006, Cougar Club 2007, Say It in Russian 2007, The Gene Generation 2007, Flick 2008, The Bait 2008, La Rabbia 2008, The Seduction of Dr. Fugazzi 2009. *Television includes:* After the Fall 1974, The Disappearance of Aimee 1976, Hogan's Goat, Mommie Dearest 1981, Evita! – First Lady 1981, 13 at Dinner 1985, Beverly Hills Madame 1986, The Country Girl, Casanova, The Raspberry Ripple, Cold Sassy Tree, Silhouette, Rebecca, Gia 1998, Running Mates 2000, The Biographer 2002, Anonymous Rex 2004, Back When We Were Grownups 2004. *Publication:* Looking For Gatsby (autobiog., with Betsy Sharkey) 1995. *Address:* ICM, 10250 Constellation Blvd, Los Angeles, CA 90067, USA.

DUNAYEV, Arman G., PhD; Kazakhstani politician and economist; b. 1967; ed Kazakh State Univ.; economist for various financial and investments cos; joined Ministry of Finance 2000, Vice-Minister of Finance 2001–04, Minister 2004–06. *Address:* c/o Ministry of Finance, pl. Respubiliki 60, 473000 Astana, Kazakhstan (office).

DUNBAR, Adrian; British actor; b. Enniskillen, Northern Ireland; m. Anna Nygh 1986; one d.; one step s.; ed Guildhall School of Music and Drama, London. *Films include:* Sky Bandits 1986 Unusual Ground Floor Conversion 1987, The Dawning 1988, A World Apart 1988, My Left Foot 1989, Dealers 1989, Hear My Song 1991 (also writer), Force of Duty 1992, The Playboys 1992, The Crying Game 1992, Pleasure 1994, Widows' Peak 1994, Innocent Lies 1995, Richard III 1995, The Near Room 1995, The General 1998, The Wedding Tackle 2000, Wild About Harry 2000, How Harry Became a Tree 2001, Shooters 2002, Triggerman 2002, The Measure of My Days 2003, Monkey's Blood (dir) 2004, Tma 2005, Mickybo and Me 2005. *Stage appearances include:* Ourselves Alone (Royal Court Theatre) 1985, King Lear (Royal Court). *Television appearances include:* After You've Gone 1984, The Englishman's Wife 1990, Drowning in the Shallow End 1990, Children of the North 1991, Force of Duty 1992, A Statement of Affairs (miniseries) 1993, A Woman's Guide to Adultery 1993, Pleasure 1994, The Blue Boy 1994, Cruel Train 1995, Melissa (miniseries) 1997, The Jump 1998, The Officer from France 1998, Relative Strangers (miniseries) 1999, Tough Love (series) 2000, Murphy's Law: Manic Munday 2003, Suspicion 2003, The Quatermass Experiment 2005, Child of Mine 2005.

DUNCAN, Andy, BSc; British broadcasting executive; *CEO, Channel 4;* b. 31 July 1962; ed Univ. of Manchester Inst. of Science and Tech.; joined Unilever in 1984, Chair. Van Den Bergh Foods Business Unit 1995–97, Van Den Bergh Foods Marketing Dir 1997–99, European Category Dir for Food and Beverages Div. and mem. Global Category Bd 1999–2001; Dir of Marketing and Communications, BBC 2001–03, Dir of Marketing, Communications and Audiences 2003–04, mem. Exec. Cttee BBC, Bd of Dirs BBC Commercial Holdings Ltd; CEO Channel 4 2004–; Chair. Tea Council 1999, Freeview; Grocer Magazine Overall Grand Prix Advertising Prize 1998, 1999, Marketer of the Year, Marketing Week Effectiveness Awards 2003, numerous IPA Effectiveness and other industry awards. *Address:* Channel 4 Television, 124 Horseferry Road, London, SW1P 2TX, England (office). *Telephone:* (20) 7396-4444 (office). *Website:* www.channel4.com (office).

DUNCAN, Arne, BA; American school administrator and government official; *Secretary of Education;* b. 6 Nov. 1964, Chicago; s. of Starkey Duncan and Sue Duncan (née Morton); m. Karen Duncan; two c.; ed Harvard Univ.; professional basketball player in Australia 1987–91; Dir Ariel Educ. Initiative, Chicago 1991–98; dir of magnet schools and Deputy Chief of Staff to CEO of Chicago Public Schools 1998–2001, CEO Chicago Public Schools 2001–08; US Sec. of Educ., Washington, DC 2009–; mem. Bd of Dirs Ariel Educ. Initiative, Chicago Cares, The Children's Center, Golden Apple Foundation, Illinois Council Against Handgun Violence, Jobs for America's Graduates, Junior Achievement, Nat. Asscn of Basketball Coaches' Foundation, Renaissance Schools Fund, Scholarship Chicago, South Side YMCA; mem. Bd of Overseers, Harvard Univ.; mem. Visiting Cttee Harvard Univ. Grad. School of Educ., Univ. of Chicago School of Social Service Admin; Fellow, Leadership Greater Chicago 1995; mem. Aspen Inst. Henry Crown Fellowship Program 2002; Dr hc (Illinois Inst. of Tech.), (National-Louis Univ.); Hon. LLD (Lake Forest Coll.) 2003; Citizen of the Year, City Club of Chicago 2006. *Achievements include:* was Co-captain of Harvard Univ. basketball team and was named first team Academic All-American. *Address:* Department of Education, 400 Maryland Ave, SW, Washington, DC 20202, USA (office). *Telephone:* (202) 401-2000 (office). *Fax:* (202) 401-0596 (office). *Website:* www.ed.gov (office).

DUNCAN, Dan L.; American business executive; *Chairman, Enterprise GP Holdings LP;* b. 2 Jan. 1933; m. Jan Ellis Duncan; four c.; ed Massey Business Coll.; served in US Army 1953–55; with Wanda Petroleum 1957–69; joined EPCO Inc., Houston, Tex. 1969, Pres. 1970–79, CEO 1970–95, Chair. 1979, bought out pnrs to form Enterprise Products Pnrs LP, mem. Bd of Dirs and Chair. Enterprise Products GP 1998–, EPE Holdings LP 2005–; mem. Bd of Dirs and Chair. Gen. Pnr of Operating Partnership 2003–; Trustee Baylor Univ. Coll. of Medicine 2002–; elected to Tex. Business Hall of Fame. *Address:* Enterprise GP Holdings LP, PO Box 4323, Houston, TX 77002 (office); Enterprise GP Holdings LP, 1100 Louisiana Street, Houston, TX 77210-4323, USA (office). *Telephone:* (713) 381-6500 (office). *E-mail:* info@enterprisegp.com (office). *Website:* www.enterprisegp.com (office).

DUNCAN, Daniel Kablan; Côte d'Ivoirian politician; b. 1943, Ouelle; ed Inst. Commercial, Nancy and Inst. de Commerce Int. Paris; Ministry of Economy and Finance 1970; in-house training, IMF, Washington, DC 1973; joined Cen. Bank of W African States (BCEAO); with Caisse Nat. de Prévoyance Sociale; returned to BCEAO HQ, Dakar 1989; Minister Del. responsible for Econ., Finance and Planning, Office of Prime Minister 1990–93; Prime Minister of Côte d'Ivoire 1993–2000; also fmr Minister of Economy, Finance and Planning, Minister of Planning and Industrial Devt; mem. Parti démocratique de la Côte d'Ivoire—Rassemblement démocratique africain (PDCI—RDA). *Address:* c/o Office of the Prime Minister, boulevard Angoulvant, 01 BP 1533, Abidjan 01, Côte d'Ivoire.

DUNCAN, Sam K.; American retail executive; *Chairman and CEO, OfficeMax Inc.;* b. Blytheville, Ark.; joined Albertson's Inc. 1969, positions including courtesy clerk, store man., Dir of Operations; Vice-Pres. Grocery Dept, Fred Meyer Inc. 1992–97, Exec. Vice-Pres. Food Div. 1997–98, Pres. 2001–02, Pres. Ralph's Supermarkets Div. 1998–2001, Pres. Fred Meyer Inc. 2001; CEO and Pres. Shopko Stores Inc. 2002–05; Chair. and CEO OfficeMax Inc. 2005–. *Address:* Office Max Corporate Headquarters, 150 East Pierce Road, Itasca, IL 60143, USA (office). *Telephone:* (630) 438-7800 (office). *Website:* www.officemax.com (office).

DUNCAN, Tim, BA; American professional basketball player; b. 25 April 1976, St Croix, US Virgin Islands; s. of William and the late Ione Duncan; m. Amy Duncan 2001; one c.; ed Wake Forest Univ.; as a youth trained as swimmer; began playing organized basketball age 14; played college basketball at Wake Forest Univ. where he was elected All-American; selected by San Antonio Spurs in first round (first pick overall) in 1997 Nat. Basketball Asscn (NBA) draft; named NBA Finals Most Valuable Player 1999, 2003, 2005 as Spurs won NBA championship in those seasons; NBA Most Valuable Player 2002, 2003; named to both All-NBA First Team and All-Defensive Team in each of his first eight seasons; chosen for Team USA Team 1999, played 2004 Olympics (Athens) winning Bronze Medal; co-MVP NBA All-Star Game 2000; founder and Pres. The Tim Duncan Foundation (educational charity) 2001–; Trustee Children's Bereavement Center, Children's Center of San Antonio, Cancer Therapy and Research Center; NBA Rookie of the Year 1998; Home Team Community Service Award, Fannie Mae Foundation 2001. *Leisure interests:* video games, swimming, collecting knives and swords. *Address:* San Antonio Spurs, One SBC Center, San Antonio, TX 78219, USA (office). *Telephone:* (210) 444-5000 (office). *Website:* www.nba.com/spurs; www.slamduncan.com.

DUNCAN SMITH, Rt Hon. (George) Iain, PC; British politician; b. 9 April 1954; s. of the late Group Capt. W. G. G. Duncan Smith and of Pamela Mary Duncan Smith (née Summers); m. Elizabeth Wynne Fremantle; two s. two d.; ed HMS Conway (Cadet School), Royal Mil. Acad. Sandhurst; served in Scots Guards 1975–81; Dir GEC (later Marconi) 1981–88, Bellwinch PLC 1988–89; Marketing and Development Dir Jane's Defence Weekly, Jane's Fighting Ships 1989–92; Conservative Party cand. for Bradford W, gen. election 1987; Vice-Chair. Fulham Conservative Asscn 1991; MP for Chingford 1992–97, for Chingford and Woodford Green 1997–; mem. Select Cttee on Health 1994–95, on Standards and Privileges 1996–97; Vice-Chair. Conservative European Affairs Cttee 1996–97; Shadow Sec. of State for Social Security 1997–99, for

Defence 1999–2001; Leader Conservative Party and Leader of the Opposition 2001–03; Chair. Centre for Social Justice 2004–; mem. Bd of Dirs Global DataCenter Man. Ltd 2007–; Freeman City of London. *Publications:* The Devil's Tune 2003, pamphlets on social security, European and defence issues. *Leisure interests:* family, painting, fishing, cricket, tennis, shooting, opera, reading. *Address:* House of Commons, London, SW1A 0AA, England (office). *Telephone:* (20) 7219-3000 (office). *Fax:* (20) 7219-4867 (office). *Website:* www.iainduncansmith.org (office).

DUNG, Nguyen Tan, LLB; Vietnamese politician; *Prime Minister;* b. 17 Nov. 1949, Ca Mau Town; m.; one d. one s.; served in Viet Nam People's Army 1961–81; mem. Communist Party of Viet Nam 1967–, mem. Central Police Party Cttee 1995–96, mem. Politburo 1997–; Deputy Interior Minister 1995–96; First Deputy Prime Minister of Viet Nam 1997–2006, Prime Minister 2006–; Gov. State Bank of Viet Nam 1998–06. *Address:* Office of the Prime Minister, Hanoi (office); c/o State Bank of Viet Nam, 47–49 Ly Thai To, Hanoi, Viet Nam (office). *Telephone:* (4) 9342524 (State Bank) (office). *Fax:* (4) 8268765 (State Bank) (office). *E-mail:* sf-sbv@hn.hnn.vn (office).

DUNHAM, Archie W., BEng, MBA; American business executive; b. 1938; m. Linda Dunham; three c.; ed Univ. of Oklahoma; with US Marine Corps 1960–64; Pres. and CEO Conoco Inc. 1996–2002, Chair. 1999–2002, Chair. ConocoPhillips (following merger between Conoco and Phillips) 2002–04 (retd); mem. Bd of Dirs Union Pacific Corpn 2000–, Louisiana-Pacific Corpn, Phelps Dodge Corpn; fmr mem. Bd of Dirs American Petroleum Inst., Energy Inst. of the Americas, Nat. Bd, Smithsonian Inst., US–Russia Business Council, Greater Houston Partnership, Memorial Hermann Healthcare System; fmr Chair. Nat. Assen of Mfrs; Chair. and fmr Pres. Houston Grand Opera; mem. Bretton Woods Cttee, Business Round Table, The Business Council; Gov. The Houston Forum; mem. Bd of Visitors M.D. Anderson Cancer Center; mem. Texas Gov.'s Business Council, Comm. on Nat. Energy Policy, Nat. Infrastructure Advisory Council, Marine Corps Heritage Foundation; Trustee George Bush Presidential Library Foundation, Houston Symphony, United Way of the Texas Gulf Coast; Dr hc (Oklahoma) 1999; B'nai B'rith Int. Achievement Award 2000, Ellis Island Medal of Honor 2001, Horatio Alger Award 2001. *Address:* c/o Board of Directors, Union Pacfic Corporation, 1400 Douglas Street, Omaha, NE 68179, USA (office).

DUNHAM, John L., BA; American business executive; *Chairman and CEO, May Department Stores Company;* m. Mary Jane Beadles; ed US Air Force Acad.; Divisional Vice-Pres. Merchandise Processing, Ohio Div., May Dept Stores Co. 1976–78, Vice-Pres. Operations, D & F Div. 1978–83, Sr Vice-Pres. Operations, Calif. Div. 1983–87, Chair. Sibley's Div. 1987–89, G. Fox Div. 1989–93, Merchandising Co. 1993–96, Exec. Vice-Pres. and Chief Financial Officer 1996–2001, mem. Bd of Dirs 1997–, Vice-Chair. 1999–2001, Pres. 2001–05, Chair. and CEO 2005–; mem. Bd of Dirs YMCA of Greater St Louis. *Address:* May Department Stores Company, 611 Olive Street, St Louis, MO 63101, USA (office). *Telephone:* (314) 342-6300 (office). *Fax:* (314) 342-3064 (office). *Website:* www.mayco.com (office).

DUNLOP, Frank, BA, CBE; British theatre director and festival director; *Director, Piccolo Theatre Company;* b. 15 Feb. 1927, Leeds; s. of Charles Norman Dunlop and Mary Aarons; ed Kibworth Beauchamp Grammar School, Univ. Coll. London, Old Vic School, London; served in RAF 1946–49; f. and Dir Piccolo Theatre Co. 1954–; Assoc. Dir Bristol Old Vic 1955–59; theatre dir West End of London and Mermaid Theatre 1959–; theatre dir Brussels, including Theatre Nat. Belge 1959–; Dir Nottingham Playhouse 1961–64; f. Dir Pop Theatre 1966–; Assoc. Dir and Admin. Nat. Theatre London 1967–71; Founder and Dir Young Vic Theatre 1970–78, 1980–83; theatre dir USA (Broadway, LA) 1974–; Dir Edin. Festival 1983–91; Fellow, Univ. Coll., London 1979; Hon. DUniv (Heriot-Watt) 1989, (Edin.) 1990. *Publication:* Scapino 1975. *Leisure interests:* work and doing nothing. *Address:* c/o Piccolo Theatre Co., 13 Choumert Square, London, SE15 4RE, England; c/o Miracle Management, Suite 417, 1775 Broadway, New York, NY 10019, USA. *Telephone:* (212) 265-8787 (USA). *Fax:* (212) 265-8873 (USA).

DUNMORE, Helen, BA; British poet and novelist; b. 1952, Yorkshire; m.; one s. one d. one step-s.; ed York Univ.; cttee mem. Soc. of Authors (Chair. 2005–); Hon. FRSL. *Publications include:* poetry: The Apple Fall 1983, The Sea Skater (Poetry Soc. Alice Hunt Bartlett Award) 1986, The Raw Garden (Poetry Book Soc. Choice) 1988, Short Days, Long Nights: New & Selected Poems 1991, Secrets (Signal Poetry Award 1995) 1994, Recovering a Body 1994, Bestiary 1997, Out of the Blue: New and Selected Poems 2001; fiction: Going to Egypt 1992, Zennor in Darkness (McKitterick Prize 1994) 1993, In the Money 1993, Burning Bright 1994, A Spell of Winter (Orange Prize for Women Writers of Fiction 1996) 1995, Talking to the Dead 1996, Your Blue-Eyed Boy 1998, With Your Crooked Heart 1999, The Siege 2001, The Silver Bead 2003, Ingo 2005, House of Orphans 2006, The Tide Knot 2006, The Deep 2007, Counting the Stars 2008; short stories: Love of Fat Men 1997, Ice Cream 2000, Mourning Ruby 2003. *Leisure interests:* family life and friendships. *Address:* Caradoc King, A. P. Watt Ltd, 20 John Street, London, WC1N 2DR, England (office). *Telephone:* (20) 7405-6774 (office). *Fax:* (20) 7831-2154 (office). *Website:* helendunmore.com (office).

DUNN, Douglas Eaglesham, OBE, BA, FRSL; Scottish poet and academic; *Professor of Creative Writing, University of St Andrews;* b. 23 Oct. 1942, Inchinnan; s. of William D. Dunn and Margaret McGowan; m. 1st Lesley B. Wallace 1964 (died 1981); m. 2nd Lesley Jane Bathgate 1985; one s. one d.; ed Univ. of Hull; full-time writer 1971–91; Writer-in-Residence, Duncan of Jordanstone Coll. of Art and Dundee Dist Libraries 1986–88; Fellow in Creative Writing, Univ. of St Andrews 1989–91, Prof. 1991–, Head School of English 1994–99; Dir St Andrews Scottish Studies Inst. 1992–; Hon. Visiting Prof., Dundee Univ. 1987–89; mem. Scottish PEN; Hon. Fellow, Humberside Coll. 1987; Hon. LLD (Dundee) 1987; Hon. DLitt (Hull) 1995; Cholmondley Award 1989. *Publications:* Terry Street 1969 (Somerset Maugham Award 1972), The Happier Life 1972, New Poems 1972–73 (ed.) 1973, Love or Nothing 1974 (Faber Memorial Prize 1976), A Choice of Byron's Verse (ed.) 1974, Two Decades of Irish Writing (criticism) 1975, The Poetry of Scotland (ed.) 1979, Barbarians 1979, St Kilda's Parliament 1981 (Hawthornden Prize 1982), Europa's Lover 1982, A Rumoured City: New Poets from Hull (ed.) 1982, To Build a Bridge: A Celebration of Humberside in Verse (ed.) 1982, Elegies 1985 (Whitbread Poetry Award and Whitbread Book of the Year 1986), Secret Villages (short stories) 1985, Selected Poems 1986, Northlight 1988, New and Selected Poems 1989, Poll Tax: The Fiscal Fake 1990, Andromache 1990, The Essential Browning (ed.) 1990, Scotland. An Anthology (ed.) 1991, Faber Book of Twentieth Century Scottish Poetry (ed.) 1992, Dante's Drum-Kit 1993, Boyfriends and Girlfriends (short stories) 1995, Oxford Book of Scottish Short Stories (ed.) 1995, The Donkey's Ears, The Year's Afternoon 2000, 20th Century Scottish Poems (ed.) 2000, The Faber Browning 2004. *Leisure interests:* playing the clarinet and saxophone, listening to jazz, gardening, philately. *Address:* School of English, The University of St Andrews, St Andrews, Fife, KY16 9AL, Scotland (office). *Telephone:* (1334) 462666 (office). *Fax:* (1334) 462655 (office). *E-mail:* ded@st-andrews.ac.uk (office). *Website:* www.st-andrews.ac.uk/~www_se (office).

DUNN, John Montfort, BA, FBA, FSA; British political theorist; *Professor of Political Theory, University of Cambridge;* b. 9 Sept. 1940, Fulmer; s. of Brig. Henry G. M. Dunn and Catherine M. Kinloch; m. 1st Susan D. Fyvel 1965; m. 2nd Judith F. Bernal 1971; m. 3rd Ruth Ginette Scurr 1997; two s. (one deceased) two d.; ed Winchester Coll., Millfield School, King's Coll., Cambridge and Harvard Univ., USA; Grad. School of Arts and Sciences; Official Fellow in History, Jesus Coll., Cambridge 1965–66; Fellow, King's Coll., Cambridge 1966–, Coll. Lecturer, Dir of Studies in History 1966–72; Lecturer in Political Science, Univ. of Cambridge 1972–77, Reader in Politics 1977–87, Prof. of Political Theory 1987–; Visiting Lecturer, Univ. of Ghana 1968–69; Chair. Section P. (Political Studies), British Acad. 1994–97, Bd of Consultants, Kim Dae-Jung Peace Foundation for the Asia-Pacific Region 1994–; Distinguished Visiting Prof., Univs of Tulane, Minnesota, Yale; mem. Council of British Acad. 2004–07; hon. foreign mem. American Acad. of Arts and Sciences 1991. *Publications:* The Political Thought of John Locke 1969, Modern Revolutions 1972, Dependence and Opportunity (with A. F. Robertson) 1973, Western Political Theory in the Face of the Future 1979, Political Obligation in its Historical Context 1980, Locke 1984, The Politics of Socialism 1984, Rethinking Modern Political Theory 1985, The Economic Limits to Modern Politics (ed.) 1990, Interpreting Political Responsibility 1990, Storia delle dottrine politiche 1992, Democracy: The Unfinished Journey (ed.) 1992, Contemporary Crisis of the Nation State? (ed.) 1994, The History of Political Theory 1995, Great Political Thinkers (21 vols, co-ed.) 1997, The Cunning of Unreason 2000, Pensare la Politica 2002, Locke: A Very Short Introduction 2003, Setting the People Free: The Story of Democracy 2005. *Leisure interests:* watching birds and animals, opera, travel. *Address:* King's College, Cambridge, CB2 1ST (office); The Merchant's House, 31 Station Road, Swavesey, Cambridge, CB4 5QJ, England (home). *Telephone:* (1223) 331258 (office); (1954) 231451 (home). *Fax:* (1223) 331315 (office). *E-mail:* jmd24@cam.ac.uk (office).

DUNN, Baroness (Life Peer), cr. 1990, of Hong Kong Island in Hong Kong and of Knightsbridge in the Royal Borough of Kensington and Chelsea; **Lydia Selina Dunn;** British business executive; *Executive Director, John Swire & Sons Ltd;* b. 29 Feb. 1940; d. of Yenchuen Yeh Dunn and Chen Yin Chu; m. Michael David Thomas, CMG, QC 1988; ed St Paul's Convent School, Coll. of Holy Names, Oakland, Calif., USA and Univ. of California, Berkeley; Exec. Dir John Swire & Sons Ltd 1996–; Dir John Swire & Sons (HK) Ltd 1978–2003, Swire Pacific Ltd 1981–, Cathay Pacific Airways Ltd 1985–97 (Adviser to Bd 1997–2002), Volvo 1991–93 (mem. Int. Advisory Bd 1985–91), Christie's Int. PLC 1996–98, Christie's Fine Art 1998–2000, Marconi PLC (fmrly GEC) 1997–2002; Deputy Chair. Hong Kong & Shanghai Banking Corpn 1992–96 (Dir 1981–96), HSBC Holdings PLC (fmrly Hong Kong and Shanghai Banking Corpn) 1992–2008 (Dir 1990–2008); mem. Hong Kong Legis. Council 1976–88 (Sr mem. 1985–88); mem. Hong Kong Exec. Council 1982–95 (Sr mem. 1988–95); Chair. Lord Wilson Heritage Trust 1993–95; mem. Hong Kong/Japan Business Co-operation Cttee 1983–95, Chair. 1988–95; mem. Hong Kong/US Econ. Co-operation Cttee 1984–93; Chair. Hong Kong Trade Devt Council 1983–91; Hon. Fellow, London Business School 2000; Hon. LLD (Chinese Univ. of Hong Kong) 1984, (Univ. of Hong Kong) 1991, (Univ. of BC, Canada) 1991, (Leeds) 1994; Hon. DSc (Buckingham) 1995; Prime Minister of Japan's Trade Award 1987, US Sec. of Commerce's Award to Peace and Commerce 1988. *Publication:* In the Kingdom of the Blind 1983. *Leisure interests:* study of antiques, theatre, music, opera, ballet. *Address:* House of Lords, London, SW1A 0PW; John Swire & Sons Ltd, Swire House, 59 Buckingham Gate, London, SW1E 6AJ, England (office). *Telephone:* (20) 7219-5353 (House of Lords); (20) 7834-7717 (office). *Fax:* (20) 7828-9029 (office).

DUNNING, Thom H., BS, PhD; American chemist and academic; *Director, Oak Ridge National Laboratory Joint Institute for Computational Sciences and Distinguished Professor of Chemistry, University of Tennessee;* b. 3 Aug. 1943, Jeffersonville, IN; ed Univ. of Mo., Calif. Inst. of Tech., Pasadena; Research Fellow, Battelle Memorial Inst., Columbus, OH 1970–71; Scientist III, Jet Propulsion Lab., La Cañada, CA 1971; Research Fellow, Calif. Inst. of Tech., Pasadena 1971–73; Staff Mem., Laser Theory Group, Los Alamos Nat. Lab. 1973–78, Assoc. Group Leader 1975–76; Sr Scientist, Argonne Nat. Lab. 1978–89, Group Leader, Theoretical and Computational Chemistry Group 1978–79; Visiting Prof., Univ. of Colo 1989; Assoc. Dir Pacific Northwest Nat. Lab. 1989–94, Dir 1994–97, Battelle Fellow 1997–2001; Adjunct Prof.,

Washington State Univ. 1990–2001; Winslow Fellow, Univ. of Melbourne, Australia 1996; Asst Dir for Scientific Simulation, Office of Science, Washington, DC 1999–2001; Prof. of Chemistry, Univ. of NC Chapel Hill 2001–02; Vice Pres., High Performance Computing and Communications Div., MCNC Research 2001–02; Distinguished Scientist, Oak Ridge Nat. Lab., Computer Science and Mathematics Div. 2002–; Distinguished Prof. of Chemistry, Univ. of Tenn. 2002–, Dir Univ. of Tenn. –Oak Ridge Nat. Lab. Jt Inst. for Computational Sciences 2002–; mem. Editorial Bd Journal of Chemical Physics 1998–2001; mem. numerous advisory cttees; mem. American Physical Soc. (Fellow 1992–), AAAS (Fellow 1992–), American Chemical Soc.; US Dept of Energy E. O. Lawrence Award in Chemistry 1996. *Address:* Joint Institute for Computational Sciences – University of Tennessee – Oak Ridge National Laboratory, MS 6008, 1 Bethel Valley Road, Oak Ridge, TN 37831–6008, USA (office). *Telephone:* (865) 576-0750 (office). *Fax:* (865) 576-4368 (office). *E-mail:* dunning@jics.utk.edu (office). *Website:* www.chem.utk.edu/dunning.html (office).

DUNST, Kirsten Caroline; American actress; b. 30 April 1982, Point Pleasant, NJ; d. of Klaus Dunst and Inez Dunst; ed Notre Dame High School; began career aged four as model, Elite agency; first roles in TV commercials; has appeared in more than 40 films and 10 TV guest appearances; Female Star of the Year, ShoWest Awards 2007. *Films include:* The Bonfire of the Vanities 1990, High Strung 1991, Interview with the Vampire 1994 (MTV Award for Best Breakthrough Performance, Saturn Award for Best Young Actress), Little Women 1994, Jumanji 1995, Mother Night 1996, Wag the Dog 1997, Small Soldiers 1998, Strike! 1998, The Virgin Suicides 1999, Drop Dead Gorgeous 1999, Luckytown Blues 2000, Bring It On 2000, Crazy/Beautiful 2001, The Cat's Meow 2001, Spider-Man 2002, Mona Lisa Smile 2003, Levity 2003, Eternal Sunshine of the Spotless Mind 2004, Spider-Man 2 2004, Wimbledon 2004, Elizabethstown 2005, Marie Antoinette 2006, Spider-Man 3 2007, How to Lose Friends & Alienate People 2008. *TV appearances include:* Sisters 1991, Star Trek: The Next Generation 1993, ER (several episodes) 1996, The Outer Limits 1997, Stories From My Childhood 1998. *Address:* William Morris Agency, One William Morris Place, Beverly Hills, CA 90212, USA (office). *Telephone:* (310) 859-4000 (office). *Fax:* (310) 859-4462 (office). *Website:* www.wma.com (office).

DUNSTAN, (Andrew Harold) Bernard, RA; British artist; b. 19 Jan. 1920, Teddington; s. of the late Dr A. E. Dunstan; m. Diana M. Armfield 1949; three s.; ed St Paul's School, Byam Shaw School and Slade School; has exhibited at Royal Acad. since 1945; exhibits regularly at Agnews, London; numerous solo exhbns; works in many public and pvt. collections including Museum of London, Nat. Portrait Gallery, Nat. Gallery of NZ; Past Pres. Royal West of England Acad.; mem. New English Art Club; Chair. Artists' Gen. Benevolent Inst. 1987–91; Trustee RA 1989–95. *Publications:* Learning to Paint 1970, Painting in Progress 1976, Painting Methods of the Impressionists 1976, The Paintings of Bernard Dunstan 1993, Ruskin's Elements of Drawing (ed.) 1991. *Leisure interest:* music. *Address:* 10 High Park Road, Kew, Richmond, Surrey, TW9 4BH, England (home). *Telephone:* (20) 8876-6633 (home).

DUNWOODY, (Thomas) Richard, MBE; British fmr professional jockey and business executive; b. 18 Jan. 1964, Belfast, Northern Ireland; s. of George Dunwoody and Gillian Dunwoody (née Thrale); m. (divorced); ed Rendcomb Coll.; rode winner of Grand Nat. (West Tip) 1986, (Minnehoma) 1994, Cheltenham Gold Cup (Charter Party) 1988, Champion Hurdle (Kribensis) 1990; Champion Nat. Hunt Jockey 1992–93, 1993–94, 1994–95; at retirement in 1999 held record for most wins (1,699, record later broken); Group Man. Partner, Dunwoody Sports Marketing 2002; Nat. Hunt Jockey of the Year 1990, 1992–95, Champion of Champions 2001. *Publications:* Hell For Leather (with Marcus Armytage), Dual (with Sean Magee), Hands and Heels (with Marcus Armytage), Obsessed. *Leisure interests:* motor sport, rugby, football, running. *Address:* c/o Dunwoody Sports Marketing, The Litten, Newtown Road, Newbury, Berks., RG14 7BB, England (office). *Telephone:* (1635) 582880 (office). *Fax:* (1635) 845811 (office). *E-mail:* richard.d@du-mc.co.uk (home).

DUPLAT, Jean-Louis; Belgian judge; Pres. Tribunal de Commerce –1989; Chair. Belgian Banking and Finance Comm. 1989–2000. *Address:* Commission Bancaire et Financière, 99 avenue Louise, 1050 Brussels, Belgium.

DUQUESNE, Antoine; Belgian politician and barrister; b. 3 Feb. 1941, Ixelles; ed Athénée Royal of Liège, Univ. of Liège; Asst Lecturer in Law, State Univ. of Liège 1965–71; barrister in Liège 1965–75; Chef de Cabinet for various ministers 1973–87; Asst Gen. Sec. of Comité Nat. de Formation et de Perfectionnement Professionel dans les Métiers et Négoces 1975–77; Gen. Admin. of Comité Nat. de Coordination et de Concertation de la Formation Permanente des Classes moyennes 1977–82; Man. of Caisse Nat. de Crédit Professionel (CNCP) 1983–88; Minister of Nat. Educ. 1987–88; Barrister in Marche-en-Famenne 1988–; Senator and mem. Comms on Social Affairs, Educ. and Science and Chair. Comm. of Agric. and the Self-Employed 1988–91; town councillor, Manhay 1989–, Mayor 1995–; Chair. Parti Réformateur Libéral (PRL) 1990–92; Deputy and mem. of Comms of Revision of the Constitution and of Justice 1991–99; Prov. Chair. PRL for Luxembourg 1994–; Vice-Chair. of House of Reps 1995–99; Chair. Comm. of Justice 1996–98; Chair. Comm. for Foreign Relations 1999; Minister of the Interior 1999–2004; mem. Conseil régional wallon 1991–95, Conseil de la Communauté française 1991–95; Grand Officer, Order of Leopold 1999. *Publications:* numerous legal articles. *Address:* c/o Ministry of the Interior, 60–62 rue Royale, 1000 Brussels, Belgium (office); Al Maison 3, 6960 Harre-Manhay, Belgium (home). *Telephone:* (2) 504-85-11 (office). *Fax:* (2) 504-85-00 (office).

DUQUESNE, Jacques Henri Louis, LenD; French journalist and writer; b. 18 March 1930, Dunkerque; s. of Louis Duquesne and Madeleine Chevalier; m. Edith Dubois 1954; one s. one d.; ed Coll. Jean-Bart, Dunkirk and Faculté de Droit, Paris; reporter, La Croix 1957–64; Deputy Dir Panorama Chrétien 1964–70, head of investigations 1967; Asst Ed.-in-Chief, L'Express 1970–71; Co-founder and Asst Ed.-in-Chief, Le Point 1972–74, Ed.-in-Chief 1974–77, Pres.-Dir-Gen. 1985–90; Dir-Gen. La Vie Catholique group of publs 1977–79; news reporter, Europe No. 1 1969–97, La Croix 1983–, Midi Libre 1997–; Chair. Bd L'Express 1997–2005; mem. Jury, Prix Interallié 1986–; Chevalier, Légion d'honneur. *Publications:* L'Algérie ou la guerre des mythes 1959, Les 16–24 ans 1964, Les prêtres 1965, Les catholiques français sous l'occupation 1966, Demain une Eglise sans prêtres 1968, Dieu pour l'homme d'aujourd'hui 1970, La gauche du Christ 1972, Les 13–62 ans 1974, La grande triche 1977, Une voix, la nuit 1979, La rumeur de la ville 1981, Maria Vadamme 1983, Alice Van Meulen 1985, Saint-Eloi 1986, Au début d'un bel été 1988, les Vents du Nord m'ont dit 1989, Catherine Courage 1990, Jean Bart 1992, Laura C. 1994, Jésus 1994, Théo et Marie 1996, les Années Jean-Paul II 1996 (jtly), Le Dieu de Jésus 1997, Le Bonheur en 36 vertus, Romans du Nord 1999, Les Héritières 2000, Pour comprendre la guerre d'Algérie 2001, Et pourtant nous étions heureux 2003, Marie 2004, Dieu malgré tout 2005, Judas, le deuxieme jour 2007. *Address:* 13 rue de Poissy, 75005 Paris, France (home). *Telephone:* 1-43-54-32-41.

DURACK, David Tulloch, MB, DPhil, FRCP, FRACP, FACP; American medical scientist and academic; *Vice-President of Corporate Medical Affairs, Becton Dickinson Technologies;* b. 18 Dec. 1944, W Australia; s. of Reginald W. Durack and Grace E. Tulloch; m. Carmen E. Prosser 1970; three s. one d.; ed Scotch Coll. Perth and Univs of W Australia and Oxford; Rhodes Scholar; intern Radcliffe Infirmary, Oxford; further training at Royal Postgrad. Medical School, London; fmr Chief, Div. of Infectious Diseases and Int. Health, Duke Univ., NC 1977, Prof. 1982, now Consulting Prof.; Chair. Dept of Medicine and Chief, Div. of Infectious Diseases, Health Care Int. (Scotland) 1994–95; now Vice-Pres., Corp. Medical Affairs, Becton Dickinson Technologies 1999–. *Publications:* co-ed. of medical textbooks; more than 200 articles and 30 textbook chapters. *Leisure interest:* flying (multi-engine, instrument-rated pilot). *Address:* Becton Dickinson Technologies, PO Box 12016, RTP, NC 27709–2016 (office); 1700 Woodstock Road, Durham, NC 27705–5232, USA (home). *Telephone:* (919) 597-6492 (office); (919) 401-4848 (home). *Fax:* (919) 549-7572 (office). *E-mail:* david.durack@bd.com (office); dtd@daviddurack.com (home). *Website:* www.bd.com (office).

DURAFOUR, Michel André François, Diplôme de l'Ecole libre des Sciences Politiques; French politician and writer; b. 11 April 1920, Saint-Etienne, Loire; s. of Antoine Durafour and Olga Durafour (née Gaillard); m. Maryse Forissier 1973; one s. one d.; ed Lycée de Saint-Etienne, Law Faculty of Paris Univ., Ecole des Sciences Politiques; assignment in office of Minister of Information 1944–46; journalist, writer, Deputy Mayor 1947–65, Mayor of Saint-Etienne 1965–77; mem. Senate for Loire (Ind.) 1965–67; Deputy to Nat. Ass. for Saint-Etienne NE, NW 1967–68, 1973–74, 1978–81; Minister of Labour 1974–76, Minister attached to Prime Minister with responsibility for Econ. and Finance 1976–77, of the Civil Service and Admin. Reform 1988–91, of State 1989–91; mem. Secr. Parti Radical-Socialiste; mem. Nat. Bureau of Mouvement Réformateur 1971–; Chair. Groupe des Réformateurs (Social Democratic group) in Nat. Ass. 1973–74; Pres. Comm. de la Production et des Échanges de l'Assemblée Nat.; Assoc. Prof., Univ. of Paris IX 1980–81; Prof., Univ. of Lyon III 1981; Pres. Conseil Régional (Rhône-Alpes) 1980–81, Regional Councillor and Gen. Chair. Budget 1986–88; mem. Senate for Loire, Social Democratic group 1983–88; Vice-Pres. de la Comm. des Affaires Culturelles du Sénat 1985, de la Comm. des Finances du Sénat 1986–88; Ministre d'Etat in charge of civil service and admin. reforms 1988–91; Conseiller d'Etat (on special service) 1992–96. *Publications:* Les Démoniaques (Grand Prix du Théâtre for Les Démoniaques) 1950, Notre rêve qui êtes aux cieux (film entitled Les fruits sauvages), Bettina Colonna, Les hommes sont comme ça, Le juif du ciel, Les moutons du ciel, Agnès et les vilains Messieurs (under pseudonym Pierre Jardin) (Grand Prix du Roman d'Aventure for Agnès et les vilains Messieurs) 1963, Dites-le avec des pastèques, Pascaline, La Baïonnette de Mirabeau and others. *Address:* 13 rue Elisée Reclus, 42000 Saint-Etienne, France (home).

DURÁN, José Luis; Spanish business executive; *CEO, Carrefour SA;* with Arthur Andersen 1987; Man. Auditor Pryca (subsidiary of Carrefour) 1991–94, Man. Auditor Southern Europe 1994–96, Americas 1996–97, Chief Financial Officer (CFO) Pryca 1997–99, CFO Carrefour Spain 1999–2001, CFO and Man. Dir of Org. and Systems, Carrefour SA 2001–05, mem. Exec. Cttee, Group Man. Dir 2005, Chair. Bd of Man. 2005–08, CEO 2008–. *Address:* Carrefour SA, 6 avenue Raymond Poincaré, 75016 Paris, France (office). *Telephone:* 1-53-70-19-00 (office). *Fax:* 1-53-70-86-16 (office). *E-mail:* info@carrefour.com (office). *Website:* www.carrefour.com (office).

DURÁN, Roberto; Panamanian fmr professional boxer; b. 16 June 1951, Chorrillo; m. Felicidad Durán; four c.; professional boxer March 1967–2002; first fighter to win world titles at four different weights; won world lightweight title from Ken Buchanan June 1972; equalled the record number of championship defences (12) before relinquishing title to box as welterweight from Feb. 1979; won World Boxing Council version of world welterweight title from Ray Leonard, Montreal June 1980: lost it to Leonard, New Orleans Nov. 1980, retained it 1989; won WBC version of world middleweight title against Ian Barkley, Atlantic City Feb. 1989, relinquished it to challenge Ray Leonard to WBC super-middleweight title: lost to Leonard, Las Vegas Dec. 1989; exempt from all taxes, receives monthly pension for life from govt. *Leisure interest:* cars. *Address:* Nuevo Reperto El Carmen, Panama.

DURÁN-BALLÉN, Sixto; Ecuadorean fmr head of state and diplomatist; *Leader, Partido Conservador;* b. 14 July 1921, Boston, Mass, USA; s. of Sixto E. Durán Ballén and Maria E. Durán Ballén; m. Josephine Villa Lobos 1945; three s. six d.; ed Sturens Inst. of Tech., NJ, Columbia Univ. and Univ. of Wisconsin; practised as architect; Sub-Dir of Regional Planning for Tungurahua 1949–68; fmr Mayor of Quito; official of Inter-American Devt Bank, Washington, DC 1956; mem. Chamber of Deputies 1984–; f. Partido Unidad Republicana 1992; Pres. of Ecuador 1992–96; mem. Partido Conservador Ecuatoriano (PCE), mem. Parl. 1998–; Amb. to UK 2001–03; Leader Partido Conservador; Chevalier Légion d'honneur, Commdr Order of Orange-Nassau (Netherlands), Order of San Carlos (Colombia), Order of Tidor Vladimirescu (First Class) (Romania), Order of Francisco Miranda (Venezuela). *Address:* Partido Conservador, Wilsón 578, Quito, Ecuador (office). *Telephone:* (2) 250-5061 (office).

DURAND, Claude; French publisher; *Chairman and CEO, Librairie Arthème Fayard;* b. 9 Nov. 1938, Livry-Gargan (Seine-et-Oise); s. of Félix Durand and Suzanne Durand (née Thuret); m. Carmen Perea 1965; two s.; ed Ecole normale d'instituteurs de Versailles; fmr schoolteacher; Literary Dir Editions du Seuil 1965–78; Gen. Man. Editions Grasset 1978–80; Chair. and CEO Librairie Arthème Fayard 1980–, Librairie Stock 1991–98; Chair. Bd of Dirs Inst. Mémoire de l'édition contemporaine 1990–93, Deputy Chair. 1993–; Pres. Pre-Production Revenues Comm., Centre National de la Cinématographie 2005–; Officier, Légion d'honneur, Chevalier, Ordre nat. du Mérite, Commdr des Arts et des Lettres. *Publication:* La Nuit zoologique (novel, Prix Médicis) 1979. *Address:* Librairie Fayard, 13 rue du Montparnasse, 75006 Paris (office); 46 rue de Naples, 75008 Paris, France (home). *Telephone:* 1-45-49-82-00 (office). *E-mail:* presse@editions-fayard.fr (office). *Website:* www.fayard.fr (office).

DURANT, Isabelle; Belgian politician; b. 4 Sept. 1954, Brussels; ed Univ. Coll. London; registered nurse; teacher 1981–89; mem. of Ecologist Party (ECOLO) 1989–, Attaché of Ecologist Party Parl. Group at Regional Council of Brussels 1992–94, Fed. Sec. and Spokeswoman for ECOLO 1994–99, mem. Fed. Office of ECOLO-AGALEV 1995–99, Co-Pres. ECOLO 2004–; Co-ordinator of Etats généraux de l'Ecologie politique (EGEP) 1996–; Deputy Prime Minister and Minister for Mobility and Transport 1999–2003 (resgnd); Senator 2003–. *Address:* Maison des Parlementaires, 21 rue de Louvain, Bureau 3213, 1009 Brussels, Belgium (office). *Telephone:* (2) 5499059 (office). *E-mail:* isabelle.durant@ecolo.be (home). *Website:* www.isabelledurant.be (office).

DURANTE, Viviana Paola; Italian ballerina; b. 8 May 1967, Rome; joined Royal Ballet Co., London 1984, became soloist 1987, prin. 1989, guest artist 1997, 1999; guest ballerina American Ballet Theater, Teatro della Scala Milan, K-Ballet Japan; Premio Positano Award (Italy) 1991, Evening Standard Award, Time Out Award. *Principal parts include:* Ondine, Juliet, Nikiya (La Bayadère), Odette-Odile (Swan Lake), Aurore (Sleeping Beauty), Cinderella, Princess Rose (Prince of Pagodas), Anastasia, Marie Vetsera (Mayerling), Excelsior 2001; also roles in My Brother and My Sisters, Requiem, Don Quixote, Manon, Nutcracker, Rhapsody, Capriccio, Anna Karenina, Carmen, Symphonic Variations. *Video Films:* Mayerling, Sleeping Beauty. *Leisure interests:* yoga, reading, life. *Address:* c/o Royal Ballet Company, Royal Opera House, Covent Garden, London, WC2E 9DD, England. *E-mail:* vivian@viviandurante.com. *Website:* www.viviandurante.com.

DURÃO BARROSO, José Manuel, MPolSci; Portuguese politician; *President, European Commission;* b. 23 March 1956, Lisbon; m. Margarida Sousa Uva; three s.; ed Univs of Lisbon and Geneva; mem. Maoist party after revolution in Portugal 1974; Lecturer, Faculty of Law, Univ. of Lisbon, Dept of Political Science, Univ. of Geneva; mem. Parl. 1985–; fmr Sec. of State for Home Affairs and for Foreign Affairs and Co-operation; Minister of Foreign Affairs 1992–95; mem. Nat. Council Social Democratic Party (PSD), Leader 1999–; Vice-Pres. EPP 1999–; Prime Minister of Portugal 2002–04 (resgnd); Chair. Comm. for Foreign Affairs 1995–96; Pres. European Comm. 2004–; Head, Dept of Int. Relations, Univ. Lusíada 1995–99; Visiting Scholar, Georgetown Univ., Washington, DC, Visiting Prof. 1996–98; decorations from Brazil, Germany, Japan, Morocco, Netherlands, Portugal, Spain, UK; Hon. DUniv (Rhode Island) 2005, Hon. DH (Georgetown Univ.) 2006, Hon. Dr rer. pol (Genoa Univ.) 2006, Hon. DIur (Kobe Univ.) 2006. *Publications:* Governmental System and Party System (co-author) 1980, Le Système Politique Portugais face à l'Intégration Européenne 1983, Política de Cooperação 1990, A Política Externa Portuguesa 1992–93, A Política Externa Portuguesa 1994–95, Uma Certa Ideia de Europa 1999, Uma Ideia para Portugal 2000; several studies on political science and constitutional law in collective works, encyclopaedias and int. journals. *Address:* European Commission, 200 rue de la Loi, 1049 Brussels, Belgium (office); Social Democratic Party, Rua de São Caetano 9, 1249-087 Lisbon Codex, Portugal (office). *Telephone:* (2) 298-18-00 (office); (21) 3952140 (Lisbon) (office). *Fax:* (2) 295-01-38 (office); (21) 3976967 (Lisbon) (office). *E-mail:* psd@psd.pt (office). *Website:* europa.eu (office); www.psd.pt (office).

DURBIN, Richard (Dick) Joseph, JD; American politician; *Senator from Illinois;* b. 21 Nov. 1944, East St Louis, Ill.; s. of William Durbin and Ann Durbin; m. Loretta Schaefer 1967; one s. two d.; ed Georgetown Univ.; called to Bar, Ill. 1969; legal practice 1969–; Chief legal counsel to Lt Gov. Paul Simon of Ill. 1969; mem. staff, minority leader, Ill. State Senate 1972–77, parliamentarian 1969–77; Assoc. Prof. Medical Humanities, S Ill. Univ. 1978–; mem. 98th–103rd Congress 1983–97; Senator from Ill. 1997–; mem. Select Cttee on Ethics 1999 and numerous other cttees; Democrat. *Address:* 332 Dirksen Senate Office Building, Washington, DC 20510-0001, USA (office). *Telephone:* (202) 224-2152 (office). *Fax:* (202) 228-0400 (office). *E-mail:* dick@durbin.senate.gov (office). *Website:* durbin.senate.gov (office).

DURDYNETS, Gen. Vasyl Vasylyevich; Ukrainian lawyer and army officer; b. 27 Sept. 1937, Romochevytsya; m.; one d.; ed Lvov State Univ.; Sec., First Sec. Lvov Regional Comsomol Cttee, Deputy Head of Section Central Comsomol Cttee, Moscow, Head of Section Central Cttee of Lviv Regional CP 1960–73; Deputy Head of Dept of Admin., CP Cen. Cttee 1973–78; Deputy Minister, then First Deputy Minister of Internal Affairs 1978–91; People's Deputy 1991–94, Head Cttee of Defence and Nat. Safety 1991–92, mem. 1997–, First Deputy Speaker of Parl. 1992–94; First Deputy Head Co-ordination Cttee for Fighting Corruption and Organized Crime 1994–95, Head 1995–99; Vice-Prime Minister, First Vice-Prime Minister 1995–99, Acting Prime Minister June–July 1997; Dir Nat. Bureau of Investigations 1997–99; Minister for Emergency Situations and Protection of the Population from the Consequences of the Chernobyl Catastrophe 1999–2002; mem. Supreme Econ. Council 1997; Hon. Prof. Acad. of Internal Affairs 1997; ICDO Medal, Int. Civil Defence Org. (Switzerland) 2000, 14 nat. awards. *Address:* c/o Ministry for Emergency Situations and Protection of the Population from the Consequences of Chernobyl, 01030 Kiev, 55 O. Gonchara Str., Ukraine (office). *Telephone:* (44) 247-30-01 (office). *Fax:* (44) 226-34-37 (office).

DURIE, Sir David Robert Campbell, Kt, KCMG, KStJ, KCFO, MA, CCMI, FRSA; British fmr public servant and diplomatist; b. 21 Aug. 1944, Glasgow, Scotland; s. of the late F. R. E. Durie; m. Susan Frances Weller; three d.; ed Univ. of Oxford; served in various British Govt depts 1966–91; Minister and Deputy UK Perm. Rep. to EU 1991–95; Dir-Gen. for Enterprise and Regions, Dept Trade and Industry 1995–2000; Gov. and C-in-C Gibraltar 2000–03; Ind. Chair. Responsibility in Gambling Trust (fmrly Gambling Industry Charitable Trust) 2004–07; mem. Lord Chancellor's Advisory Council on Nat. Records and Archives 2006–; Ind. Mem. Greater London Authority Standards Cttee 2008–. *Leisure interests:* exercise, culture, family.

DURKAN, Mark; Irish politician; b. 26 June 1960, Derry; s. of Brendan Durkan and Isobel Durkan (née Tinney); m. Jackie Durkan; one d.; ed St Columb's Coll., Derry, Queen's Univ., Belfast, Magee Coll., Derry; Deputy Pres. Union of Students in Ireland 1982–84; Asst to John Hume, MP 1984–98; Chair. Social Democratic and Labour Party (SDLP) 1990–95, Leader 2001–; Derry City Council 1993–2002; mem. Forum for Peace and Reconciliation, Dublin 1994–96; SDLP Negotiator in inter-party discussions 1996–98; mem. NI Ass. 1998–2002; Minister of Finance 1999–2001, Deputy First Minister 2001–02; MP for Foyle 2005–; mem. NI Housing Council 1993–95, Western Health and Social Services Council 1993–2000. *Address:* Constituency Office, 2nd floor, 23 Bishop Street, Derry, BT48 6PR, Northern Ireland (office). *Telephone:* (28) 7136-0700 (office). *Fax:* (28) 7136-0808 (office). *E-mail:* durkanm@parliament.uk (office); m.durkan@sdlp.ie (office). *Website:* www.markdurkan.ie.

DURLACHER, Nicholas John, CBE, BA; British business executive; *Chairman, Elexon Ltd;* b. 20 March 1946, Plaxtol; s. of John Sidney Durlacher and Alma Gabriel Adams; m. Mary McLaren 1971; one s.; ed Stowe School, Buckingham, Magdalene Coll., Cambridge; fmrly Chair. London Int. Financial Futures and Options Exchange; Chair. Securities and Futures Authority 1995–2001; Ennismore European Smaller Companies Fund 1998–; Chair. FFastFill PLC 2000–02; Chair. Elexon Ltd 2000–, Quilter Global Enhanced Income Trust PLC 2000–05; Dir UFJ Int. PLC 2002–04; Trustee Brain and Spine Foundation 2000–. *Leisure interests:* skiing, golf, tennis. *Address:* Elexon Ltd, 4th Floor, 350 Euston Road, London, NW1 3AW (office); 10 Rutland Street, London, SW7 1EH, England (home). *Telephone:* (20) 7380-4251 (office). *Fax:* (20) 7380-0407 (office). *E-mail:* nick.durlacher@elexon.co.uk (office). *Website:* www.elexon.co.uk (office).

DURLEŞTEANU, Mariana; Moldovan economist and diplomatist; *Minister of Finance;* b. 5 Sept. 1971; m.; two c.; ed Babeş-Bolyai Univ., Cluj-Napoca, Romania; fmr nat. gymnast; economist, later leading economist, Foreign Financing and External Debt Dept, Ministry of Finance 1995–96, Chief of External Debt Service Div. 1996–97, Head of Foreign Financing and External Debt Directorate 1997–2001, Deputy Minister of Finance 2001–02, First Deputy Minister of Finance 2002–05, Minister of Finance 2008–; Gov. for Moldova, Black Sea Trade and Devt Bank (BSTDB) 2001–04; Alt. Gov. for Moldova, IMF 2001–04; Deputy Chair. Moldovagaz (jt venture) 2004–05; Chair. Savings Bank (Banca de Economii) 2004–05; Amb. to UK 2004–08; Labour Glory Decoration. *Address:* Ministry of Finance, 2005 Chişinău, str. Cosmonauţilor 7, Moldova (office). *Telephone:* (22) 23-35-75 (office). *Fax:* (22) 22-13-07 (office). *E-mail:* protocol@minfin.moldova.md (office). *Website:* www.minfin.md (office).

DURON, Willy; Belgian insurance executive; *Managing Director and Group CEO, KBC Group NV;* b. 1945; ed Univs of Ghent and Louvain; joined ABB-Insurance (later KBC Insurance), promoted to Pres.; Man. Dir and Group CEO KBC Group NV 2000–, also Pres. Exec. Cttee, mem. Agenda Cttee, Nomination Cttee; Dir KBC Asset Man. *Address:* KBC Group NV, Havenlaan 2, 1080 Brussels, Belgium (office). *Telephone:* (2) 429-4916 (office). *Fax:* (2) 429-4416 (office). *Website:* www.kbc.be (office).

DUROV, Lev Konstantinovich; Russian actor; b. 23 Dec. 1931, Moscow; m. Irina Nikolayevna Kirichenko; one d.; ed Studio School of Moscow Art Theatre; actor and stage dir, Cen. Children's Theatre 1954–63, Lenkom Theatre 1963–67, Malaya Bronnaya Theatre 1967–; Theatre-School of Contemporary Plays 1993–; as stage dir produced over 20 theatre productions; People's Artist of Russian Fed. 1982, USSR People's Artist 1990, laureate, Pegas Prize (Ne poslat li nam gontsa?), laureate, Khrustalnaya Turandot For Honour and Achievement 2006. *Plays include:* Chebutykin, Medvedenko, Molière, Sganarelle, Yago, Zhevakin, Alyosha. *Films include:* Visokosnyy god 1961, 9 dney odnogo goda 1961, Ya shagayu po Moskve 1963, Ko mne, Mukhtar! 1964, Lebedev protiv Lebedeva 1965, Na polputi k lune 1966, Chyort s portfelem 1966, Zhitiye i vozneseniye Yurasya Bratchika 1968, Spokoynyy den v kontse voyny 1970, Sluchay s Polyninym 1970, Starikirazboyniki 1971, Zemlya, do vostrebovaniya 1972, Zayachiy zapovednik 1972, Ekhali v tramvaye Ilf i Petrov 1972, Chetvyortyy 1972, Chelovek na svoyom meste 1972, Moskva-Kassiopeya 1973, Kalina krasnaya 1973, Tsimbireli papa 1973, Vesenniye perevyortyshi 1974, Posledniy den zimy 1974, Otroki vo vselennoy 1974, Georgiy Sedov 1974, Shag navstrechu 1975, Potryasayushchiy Berendeev 1975, Okovani soferi 1975, Na yasniy ogon 1975, Brillianty dlya diktatury proletariata 1975, Suse, liebe Suse 1975, ...I drugie offitsialnye litsa 1976, Doverie 1976, Vooruzhyon i ochen opasen 1977, Veter 'Nadezhdy' 1977, Po semeynym obstoyatelstvam 1977, Alenkiy tsvetochek 1977, Troye iz Prostokvashino (voice) 1978), Veroy i pravdoy 1979, Pyos v sapogakh (voice) 1981, 34-y skoryy 1981, Skazka stranstviy 1982, Kolybelnaya dlya brata 1982, Shyol chetvyortyy god voyny 1983, Proshchanie s Matyoroy 1983, Zachem cheloveku krylya 1984, Uspekh 1984, Tufli s zolotymi pryazhkami 1984, Kak stat schastlivym 1985, Detstvo Bambi 1985, Yunost Bambi 1986, Kapitan 'Piligrima' 1986, God telyonka 1986, Dzhek Vosmyorkin, amerikanets 1987, Chelovek s bulvara Kaputsinov 1987, Esperanza 1988, Smirennoye kladbishche 1989, Bespredel 1989, Dinozavry XX veka 1990, Lyubov 1991, Gangstery v okeane 1991, Au, ograblenie poezda - Za vsyo nado platit 1991, Zvezda sherifa 1992, Ubiystvo v Sunshine Menor 1992, Tayna villy 1992, Sem sorok 1992, Gardemariny III 1992, Davayte bez fokusov! 1992, Serye volki 1993, Master i Margarita 1994, Gospoda artisty 1994, Bulvarnyy roman 1994, Tsvety provincyi 1994, Meshcherskie 1995, Koroli i kapusta 1996, Tango nad propastyu 1997, Noch pered Rozhdestvom (voice) 1997, Ne valyai duraka 1997, Na zare tumannoy yunosti 1997, Akh, zachem eta noch 1997, Sirota kazanskaya 1997, Afinskie vechera 1999, Lunoi byl polon sad (two times laureate, Int. Moscow Cinema Festival 2000) 2000, Zhizn dlinoyu v pesnyu, Rannyaya lyubov 2003, Vesegonskaya volchitsa 2004, Poslednii boi mayora Pugacheva 2005, Angel-khranitel 2007. *Television includes:* Bumbarash 1971, Neschastnyy sluchay 1972, Bolshaya Peremena (miniseries) 1972, Semnadtsat mgnoveniy vesny (miniseries) 1973, Strannye vzroslye 1974, Kashtanka 1975, Nos 1977, Krasavets-muzhchina 1978, D'Artanyan i tri mushketyora 1978, Ne boysya, ya s toboy 1981, Ne zhdali, ne gadali 1982, Etyud dlya domino s royalem 1982, Gori, gori yasno 1983, Gde-to v gubernskom sadu (Koe-chto iz gubernskoy zhizni) 1983, Russia (miniseries) 1986, Klad 1988, Syn klouna 1989, Selo Stepanchikovo i yego obitateli 1989, Detstvo Nikity (Iz russkoy zhizni) (miniseries) 1992, Stranitsy teatralnoy parodii (miniseries) 1996, Grafinya de Monsoro (series) 1998, Banditskiy Peterburg: Krakh Antibiotika (miniseries) 2001, Russkie v Gorode Angelov (series) 2003, Operativnyy psevdonim (series) 2003. *Address:* Frunzenskaya nab. 3B, Apt 206, 119146 Moscow, Russia (home). *Telephone:* (495) 242-43-46 (home). *E-mail:* editor@levdurov.ru (home). *Website:* www.levdurov.ru (home).

ĐUROVIĆ, Dragan; Montenegrin politician; b. 31 Oct. 1959, Danilovgrad; m.; three c.; Legal Adviser and Sec., Agro-Econ. Inst. 1982–92; Dir Directorate for Regional Agricultural Devt 1992–93; Chair. Exec. Bd, Danilovgrad Municipality Ass. 1993–95; Dir Pobjeda publishing co. 1995–2001; Deputy Prime Minister of Montenegro with Responsibility for Political System and Internal Policy 2001–06, Minister of Interior Affairs 2003–06; acting Minister of Foreign Affairs 2002–03; acting Prime Minister 2002–03; currently Deputy, Parl. of Repub. of Montenegro, apptd Deputy, House of Citizens of Fed. Parl. twice, Deputy, Parl. of Repub. of Montenegro three times; fmr mem. Presidency of Democratic Party of Socialists; Chief Deputy, Democratic Party of Socialists Club; Pres. Danilovgrad basketball club. *Television:* Bjelopavlici (co-writer). *Address:* Democratic Party of Montenegrin Socialists (Demokratska Partija Socijalista Crne Gore), 81000 Podgorica, Jovana Tomaševića 33 (office); 104/20 Bulevar Sv. Petar Cetinjski, 8100 Podgorica, Montenegro (home). *Telephone:* (82) 243735 (office); (82) 202060 (home). *Fax:* (82) 242101 (office). *E-mail:* webmaster@dps.cg.yu (office); dragandj@cg.yu (office). *Website:* www.dps.cg.yu (office).

ĐUROVIĆ, Gordana, MA, PhD; Montenegrin (b. Serbian) academic and politician; *Deputy Prime Minister, responsible for European Integration;* b. 1964, Novi Kneevac, Vojvodina; m.; two c.; ed Herceg-Novi Secondary School of Econs, Faculty of Econs, Univ. of Belgrade and Univ. of Montenegro, Podgorica; Assoc. Prof., Faculty of Econs, Univ. of Montenegro, Podgorica, Assoc. Vice-Dean for scientific research 1998–2000, Head Dept of Econ. Policy 2000–; project manager and assoc., Regional Devt in Montenegro 1998, Programme on Utility Services Usurpation in Montenegro 1999, Devt Strategy and Poverty Reduction in Montenegro 2000; Minister for Int. Econ. Relations and European Integration, Ass. of the Repub. of Montenegro 2004–06; Deputy Prime Minister with responsibility for European Integration 2006–. *Publications:* Economic Development 1996, Alternative Development Draft Lines of the Economy of Montenegro (co-author) 2002; more than 40 articles and 15 research papers. *Address:* Office of the Deputy Prime Minister, Government of Montenegro, 81000 Podgorica, Jovana Tomaševića bb, Montenegro (office). *Telephone:* (81) 242552 (office). *Fax:* (81) 224552 (office). *E-mail:* gordana.djurovic@gov.me (office). *Website:* www.vlada.cg.yu (office).

DÜRR, Heinz; German business executive; *Chairman of the Supervisory Board, Dürr AG;* b. 16 July 1933, Stuttgart; s. of Otto Dürr; m. Heide Dürr; three d.; ed Tech. Hochschule, Stuttgart; Man. and Man. Dir Dürr AG (fmrly Otto Dürr GmbH), Stuttgart 1957–80, Chair. Supervisory Bd 1980–; Chair. Exec. Bd AEG AG, Berlin and Frankfurt 1980–90; mem. Exec. Bd Daimler-Benz AG, Stuttgart 1986–90; Chair. Exec. Bd Deutsche Bundesbahn, Deutsche Reichsbahn 1991–94, Deutsche Bahn AG 1994–97, Supervisory Bd Deutsche Bahn AG 1997–99, Carl-Zeiss-Stiftung (Commr) 1999–, Krone GmbH 1999–; Chair. Fed. of Metal Working Industries in Baden-Württemberg and mem. Presidium Fed. of Metal and Electrical Industry Employers' Asscns 1975–80; mem. European Advisory Bd, Schroder, Salomon, Smith Barney 2001 and seven supervisory bds; Hon. DrIng (Rhine-Westphalian Tech. Univ., Aachen) 1996. *Leisure interests:* tennis, golf, theatre, jazz, cross-country skiing. *Address:* Dürr AG, Otto-Dürr-Strasse 8, 70435 Stuttgart (office); Charlottenstrasse 57, 10117 Berlin, Germany. *Telephone:* (711) 1360 (office). *Fax:* (711) 1361455 (office). *Website:* www.durr.com (office).

DURR, Hon. Kent D. Skelton; South African fmr politician, fmr diplomatist and business executive; b. 28 March 1941, Cape Town; s. of Dr John M. Durr and Diana Skelton; m. Suzanne Wiese 1966; one s. two d.; ed SA Coll. School, Cape Town Univ.; Dir family publishing co. 1966–68; Founder and later Man. Dir Durr Estates 1968–84; Chair. Clean Diesel Technologies Inc. 1995–97, Fuel-Tech NV 1995–97; Exec. Chair. Commonwealth Investment Guarantee Agency Ltd 1997; elected to Prov. Council of Cape 1974, MP for Maitland 1977–91, Deputy Minister (Trade and Industry) 1984–86, (Finance) 1984–88; Minister of Budget and Public Works 1988–89; Cabinet Minister of Trade and Industry and Tourism 1989–91; Amb. to UK 1991–94, High Commr in UK 1994–95; Chair. Commonwealth Investment Guarantee Agency 1995–99, Nasdaq Listed Cos, USA 1995–99; mem. Parl. and Senate (African Christian Democratic Party) 1999–; Chair. Darling Wildlife (Cattle and Game) 1999–2004; Freeman City of London 1995. *Leisure interests:* field sports, mountaineering, conservation, game farming. *Address:* Houses of Parliament, PO Box 15, Cape Town 8000 (office); Darling Wildlife, PO Box 289, Yzerfontein 7351, Cape; Sonquasfontein Private Nature Reserve, Darling, Western Cape 7345, South Africa (home). *Telephone:* (21) 4033803 (office); (21) 6853908 (home). *Fax:* (21) 4619690 (office); (2245) 12352 (home); (21) 6853908. *E-mail:* kdurr@acdp.co.za (office).

DURRANI, Akram Khan, BA, LLB; Pakistani politician; b. 2 March 1960, Bannu Dist; s. of Ghulam Qadir Khan Durrani and Kalam Bibi; three s. one d.; ed Govt Coll., Nowshera; mem. NW Frontier Prov. (NWFP) Prov. Ass. 1990–93, 1997–99, 2002–; Chief Minister of NWFP 2002–07; mem. Nat. Security Council; mem. Jamiat-e-Ulema-e-Islam. *Address:* c/o Chief Minister's Secretariat, Peshawar, North West Frontier Province; Frontier House, SAQ Road, Peshawar, North West Frontier Province, Pakistan (home). *Telephone:* (91) 9211719; (91) 9211074 (home). *Fax:* (91) 9210409 (home).

DURRANT, Jennifer Ann; British artist; b. 17 June 1942, Brighton; d. of Caleb John Durrant and Winifred May Durrant (née Wright); m. William A. H. Henderson 1964 (divorced 1976); m. 2nd Richard Alban Howard Oxby 2000; ed Varndean Grammar School for Girls, Brighton, Brighton Coll. of Art and Crafts, Slade School of Fine Art, Univ. Coll., London; part-time art teacher various colls 1965–74 including St Martin's School of Art, London 1974–87, Chelsea School of Art 1987–89; part-time Lecturer on Painting, RCA 1979–2000, Royal Acad. Schools 1991–98; external assessor at various colls; Exhbn Selector, Northern Young Contemporaries, Whitworth Gallery, Manchester, TV SW Arts; Painting Faculty mem. The British School at Rome 1979–83; Artist-in-Residence, Somerville Coll., Oxford 1979–80; works in collections of Arts Council of GB, British Council, Contemporary Art Soc., Tate Gallery, Museum of Fine Arts, Boston, USA, Neue Galerie, Aachen and in pvt. collections; Abbey Minor Travelling Scholarship British School at Rome 1964, Arts Council Award 1976, Arts Council Major Award 1977, Greater London Arts Asscn Award 1980, Athena Art Award 1988, Independent on Sunday Artist of the Year 1996. *Commissions:* Newham Hosp. (in asscn with Greater London Arts Asscn and King Edward's Hosp. Fund), R. P. Scherer 50th Anniversary, Swindon UK, Thomas Neal floor mosaics Covent Garden, London, Glaxo UK, Stevenage. *Leisure interests:* classical music, including opera, archaeology, visiting museums, looking at paintings and sculpture, the natural world. *Address:* La Vigna, Via Bondi 14, 06069 Tuoro sul Trasimeno, Italy. *Telephone:* 75829010.

DURRANT, (Mignonette) Patricia, CD, OJ, BA; Jamaican diplomatist and UN official; *Ombudsman, United Nations;* b. 30 May 1943; ed Univ. of West Indies, Univ. of Cambridge, UK; Admin. Officer, Ministry of Agric. 1964–70; First Sec. Ministry of Foreign Affairs 1971–72, Prin. Asst Sec. 1972–74; Minister-Counsellor, Mission to OAS, Washington, DC 1974–77; Asst Dir Political Div., Ministry of Foreign Affairs 1977–81, Deputy Dir 1981–83; Deputy Perm. Rep. to UN, New York 1983–87, Perm. Rep. 1995–2002, Pres. UN High-Level Cttee on Tech. Co-operation among Developing Countries 1999–2001, Rep. of Jamaica to UN Security Council 2000–01, UN Ombudsman 2002–; Chair. UN Preparatory Cttee for the Special Session on Children, Chair. Consultative Cttee for the UN Devt Fund for Women (UNIFEM), Vice-Chair. Preparatory Cttee for Special Session on Population and Devt 1999 and Vice-Chair. Open-Ended Working Group on the Reform of the UN Security Council; Amb. to FRG (and non-resident Amb. to Israel, the Netherlands, Switzerland and the Holy See) 1987–92; Dir-Gen. Ministry of Foreign Affairs and Foreign Trade 1992–95; Distinguished Grad. Award, Univ. of West Indies 1998, Distinguished Achievement Award, World Asscn of fmr UN Interns and Fellows (WAFUNI). *Address:* Permanent Mission of Jamaica to the United Nations, 767 Third Avenue, 9th Floor, New York, NY 10017, USA (office). *Telephone:* (212) 935-7509 (office). *Fax:* (212) 935-7607 (office). *E-mail:* jamaica@un.int (office). *Website:* www.un.int/jamaica (office).

DUSSAULT, René, LLL, PhD, FRSC; Canadian judge; *Judge, Québec Court of Appeal;* b. 23 Nov. 1939, Québec; s. of Daniel Dussault and Madeleine Pelletier; m. Marielle Godbout 1967; two s.; ed Laval Univ. and London School of Econs and Political Science; lecturer in Law, Laval Univ. 1966–70; legal counsel, Québec Health and Welfare Inquiry Comm.; Special Adviser to Minister of Social Affairs of Québec 1970–73; Chair. Québec Professions Bd 1973–77; Deputy Minister of Justice, Québec 1977–80; Prof. Nat. School of Public Admin. 1981–89; Laskin Chair in Public Law, Osgoode Hall Law School 1983–84; legal consultant, Kronström, McNicoll & Assocs., Québec City; Judge, Québec Court of Appeal 1989–; Co-Chair. Royal Comm. on Aboriginal Peoples 1991–96; Hon. LLD (York) 1992, (Dalhousie) 1997; Québec Interprofessional Council Prize 1991; Québec Bar Asscn Medal 1987, Vanier Medal, Inst. of Public Admin. of Canada 1998, Touchstone Award, Canadian Bar Asscn 2001,. *Publications:* Le contrôle judiciaire de l'administration au

Québec 1969, Traité de droit administratif, Vols I & II 1974 (also co-author of subsequent vols), Administrative Law: A Treatise, Vols I-V 1985–90. *Address:* Office of the Court, Québec Courthouse, 300 Jean-Lesage blvd, suite 4.27, Québec, PQ G1K 8K6 (office); 1332 James-LeMoine Avenue, Sillery, PQ G1S 1A3, Canada (home). *Telephone:* (418) 649-3425 (office); (418) 527-6332 (home). *Fax:* (418) 643-4154 (office). *E-mail:* rdussault@justice.gouv.qc.ca (office). *Website:* www.tribunaux.qc.ca (office).

DUTHEILLET DE LAMOTHE, Olivier; French lawyer; *Member, Conseil Constitutionnel;* b. 10 Nov. 1949, Neuilly; s. of Alain Dutheillet de Lamothe and Suzanne Garnier; m. Marie-Caroline Sainsaulieu 1981; one s. one d.; ed Institut d'Etudes Politiques de Paris, Ecole Nationale d'Administration; held several posts at Council d'Etat, including Auditor 1975, Rapporteur Litagation Section 1975–77, Head Documentation Centre and Coordination 1977–79, Maitre des requetes 1979, Govt Commr Ass. of Litigation and other judicial panels 1981–86; Tech. Adviser to Minister of Health and Social Security 1979–81; Legal Adviser to Directorate Gen. of Civil Aviation 1985–86; Adviser to Minister of Social Affairs and Employment 1986–87; Dir of Labour Relations Ministry of Labour, Employment and Vocational Training 1987–95; State Councillor 1992; Social Adviser Presidency of the Repub. 1995–97, Deputy Sec.-Gen. of the Presidency 1997–2000; Rapporteur Litigation Section 2000–01; Prof., Institut d'Etudes Politiques de Paris 2001; Mem. Conseil Constitutionnel 2001–; Global Distinguished Fellow, Hauser Global Law School Program, New York Univ. School of Law; Chevalier de l'Ordre national de la Légion d'Honneur, de l'Ordre national du Mérite. *Leisure interests:* cinema, skiing. *Address:* Conseil Constitutionnel, 2 rue de Montpensier, 75001 Paris, France (office). *Telephone:* 1-40-15-30-00 (office). *Fax:* 1-40-20-93-27 (office). *E-mail:* relations-exterieures@conseil-constitutionnel.fr (office). *Website:* www.conseil-constitutionnel.fr (office).

DUTILLEUX, Henri; French composer; b. 22 Jan. 1916, Angers; s. of Paul Dutilleux and Thérèse Dutilleux (née Koszul); m. Geneviève Joy 1946; ed Conservatoire Nat. de Musique, Paris; Dir Service Créations Musicales Radiodiffusion Française 1945–63; Prof. of Composition Ecole Normale de Musique, Paris 1961–, Pres. 1969–74; Assoc. Prof. Conservatoire Nat. Supérieur de Musique, Paris 1970–71; fmr mem. UNESCO Music Council; assoc. mem. Royal Acad. of Music, Belgium; hon. mem. American Acad. and Inst. of Arts and Letters, Accad. di Santa Cecilia, Rome, RAM, London; Grand Prix de Rome 1938, Grand Prix du Disque 1957, 1958, 1966, 1968, 1976, 1978, 1984, Grand Prix Nat. de la Musique 1967, Prix de la Ville de Paris 1974, Koussevitzky Int. Recording Award 1976, World Record Award (Montreux) 1983; Prix Int. Maurice Ravel 1987, Grand Prix, Music Council UNESCO 1987, Praemium Imperiale Japan 1994, Ernst von Siemens Music Prize for outstanding contribution to int. music life 2005, Honour for Lifetime Achievement Midem Classical Awards 2007; Grand-Croix de la Légion d'honneur 2004, Commdr Ordre Nat. du Mérite, des Arts et des Lettres, du Mérite Culturel de Monaco. *Compositions:* Sonata for Piano 1948, First Symphony 1951, Le Loup (Ballet) 1953, Second Symphony (Le Double) 1959, Métaboles (for orchestra) 1964, Cello Concerto: Tout un monde lointain 1970, Figures de Résonances (for two pianos) 1971, Preludes for Piano 1974, Ainsi la Nuit (for string quartet) 1976, Timbres, Espace, Mouvement (for orchestra) 1978, 3 Strophes sur le nom de Sacher (for cello) 1981, L'Arbre des Songes (violin concerto) 1985, Le Jeu des contraires (for piano) 1988, Mystère de l'instant (for 24 strings and cimbalom) 1989, Les Citations (for oboe, harpsichord, double-bass and percussion) 1991, The Shadows of Time (for orchestra) 1997, Sur le même accord for violin and orchestra 2002, Correspondances for song and orchestra 2003, Le Temps l'horloge 2007–09. *Publications:* Mystère et Mémoire des sons 1997 (trans. by Roger Nichols as Mystery and Memory). *Address:* 12 rue St-Louis-en-l'Isle, 75004 Paris, France (home). *Telephone:* 1-43-26-39-14 (home).

DUTKOWSKY, Robert M., BS; American computer industry executive; *CEO, Tech Data Corporation;* b. 2 Jan. 1955, Endicott, NY; m. Lorraine Dutkowsky; two c.; ed Cornell Univ., Ithaca, NY; worked at IBM 1977–97, served in sr man. positions including Exec. Asst to fmr CEO Lou Gerstner, Vice-Pres. for Distribution, Asia/Pacific; Exec. Vice Pres. Sales and Marketing EMC Corpn 1997–2000; Chair., Pres. and CEO GenRad Inc. 2000–02; Pres. Assembly Test Div. Teradyne Inc. 2001–02; Chair., Pres. and CEO JD Edwards Inc. 2002–03; Chair., Pres. and CEO Egenera Inc. 2004–06; CEO Tech Data Corpn 2006–. *Address:* Tech Data Corpn, 5350 Tech Data Drive, Clearwater, FL 33760-3122, USA (office). *Telephone:* (727) 539-7429 (office). *Fax:* (727) 538-7803 (office). *E-mail:* info@techdata.com (office). *Website:* www.techdata.com (office).

DUTOIT, Charles E.; Swiss conductor and music director; *Artistic Director and Principal Conductor, Royal Philharmonic Orchestra, London;* b. 7 Oct. 1936, Lausanne; s. of Edmond Dutoit and Berthe Dutoit (née Laederman); one s. one d.; ed Conservatoire of Lausanne and Geneva, Accademia Musicale Chigiana, Siena, Italy, Conservatorio Benedetto Marcello, Venice, Italy and Berks. Music Center, Tanglewood, USA; Assoc. Conductor Berne Symphony Orchestra 1964, Principal and Artistic Dir 1966–78; Assoc. Conductor Tonhalle Orchestra Zurich 1966; Conductor and Artistic Dir Zurich Radio Orchestra 1964; Artistic Dir Nat. Symphony Orchestra of Mexico and Göteborg Symphony Orchestra 1977–2002; Artistic Dir Montréal Symphony Orchestra 1977–2002; operatic debut Covent Garden (conducting Faust) 1983; Prin. Guest Conductor Minn. Orchestra 1983–84, 1985–86; Artistic Dir and Prin. Conductor Philadelphia Orchestra summer season, Mann Music Center 1991–2001, Saratoga Springs 1991–; Music Dir Orchestre Nat. de France 1990–2001; Prin. Guest Conductor NHK Symphony Orchestra, Tokyo 1996–, Music Dir 1998–2003; Chief Conductor and Artistic Adviser Philadelphia Orchestra 2007–; Artistic Dir and Principal Conductor, Royal Philharmonic Orchestra 2009–; guest conductor of all major orchestras in USA, Europe,

South America, Far East Asia, Australia and Israel; Hon. Citizen of the city of Philadelphia 1991; Commdr Ordre des Arts et Lettres 1996, Hon. OC; Hon. PhD (Montreal) 1984, (Laval) 1985, (McGill); two Grammys, Grand Prix de l'Académie du disque français, High Fidelity Int. Record Critics' Award, Montreux Record Award, Japan Record Acad. Award, Musician of the Year (Canada Music Council) 1982, two awards from Canadian Conf. of the Arts, Grand Prix du Président de la République (France). *Recordings:* over 125 recordings with various orchestras since 1980, winning over 40 int. awards and including Falla's Three Cornered Hat and El amor Brujo, The Planets, Tchaikovsky's 1st Piano Concerto, Saint-Saëns 3rd Symphony, Bizet's L'Arlesienne and Carmen Suites, Gubaidulina Offertorium with Boston Symphony, Symphonies by Honegger, Roussel's Symphonies with French Nat. Orchestra, Saint-Saëns Piano Concertos, Suppé Overtures, Berlioz' Les Troyens. *Address:* Royal Philharmonic Orchestra, 16 Clerkenwell Green, London EC1R 0QT, England (office). *Website:* www.rpo.co.uk (office).

DUTRA, José Eduardo de Barros, BSc; Brazilian oil and gas executive and politician; b. 11 April 1957, Rio de Janeiro; s. of José Araújo Dutra and Clóvis de Barros Dutra; m. (separated); ed Univ. Fed. Rural do Rio de Janeiro; geologist, Geologia Sondagens (Geosol) Ltda 1980–81; geologist, Petrobrás Mineradora (Petromisa) 1983–90, Companhia Vale do Rio Doce 1990–94; elected Senator for state of Sergipe 1995–2003; Pres. and CEO Petróleo Brasileiro SA (Petrobras) 2003–05; Leader Partido dos Trabalhadores (PT – Workers' Party) 1996–97; unsuccessful candidate Senator for Sergipe 2006, also mem. PT Nat. Bd; Pres. Sindimina (regional miners' union) 1989–94; fmr mem. numerous parl. cttees; mem. Geologist Asscn of Sergipe; Geologist Asscn of Sergipe Geologist of the Year 1988. *Address:* c/o Sede Nacional do Partido dos Trabalhadores, Rua Silveira Martins, 132, Centro, 01019–000 São Paulo, Brazil (office).

DUTREIL, Renaud; French politician and business executive; *Chairman, LVMH Inc.;* b. 12 June 1960, Chambéry; ed École Normale Supérieure, Institut d'Études Politiques de Paris, Ecole Nationale d'Admin; Auditor Council of State 1989, later Govt Commr; elected Deputy 1993, 1997, 2002; mem. Council Castle-Thierry (Aisne) 1995–2001, Charly-on-Marne, (Aisne) 2001–08; Sec. of State 2002–04; Minister for the Civil Service and Reform of the State 2004–05; Minister of Small and Medium-Sized Enterprises, Trade, Crafts and the Liberal Professions 2005–07; Pres. Union en Mouvement, Union pour la Majorité Présidentielle 2002; Chair. LVMH Inc. 2008–. *Publications:* Le coq sur la paille 1993, La République des Ames mortes 2001. *Address:* LVMH Inc., 19 East 57th Street, New York, NY 10022, USA (office). *Telephone:* (212) 931-2700 (office). *Fax:* (212) 931-2730 (office). *Website:* www.lvmh.com (office).

DUVAL, Charles Gaëtan Xavier Luc, BA, FCA; Mauritian chartered accountant and politician; *Deputy Prime Minister and Minister of Tourism, Leisure and External Communications;* b. 28 Jan. 1958, ; m.; three c.; ed Univ. of Leeds, UK; Audit Man., Casson Beckman, UK 1980–86; Founding Pnr, Coopers & Lybrand (Mauritius); fmr pnr and business consultant, De Chazal Du Mée (Chartered Accountants); Sr Pnr, Nexia, Baker & Arenson 2000–05; Minister of Industry and Tourism 1994–95; Founder and Leader Parti Mauricien Xavier-Luc Duval 1989–; mem. Nat. Ass. 1999–; Minister of Industry, Commerce, Corp. Affairs and Financial Services 1999–2000, of Tourism, Leisure and External Communications 2005–, Deputy Prime Minister 2005–. *Address:* Ministry of Tourism, Leisure and External Communications, Air Mauritius Centre, Level 12, John F. Kennedy Street, Port Louis, Mauritius (office). *Telephone:* 211-7930 (office). *Fax:* 208-6776 (office). *E-mail:* mtou@mail.gov.mu (office). *Website:* tourism.gov.mu (office).

DUVAL, David Robert; American professional golfer; b. 9 Nov. 1971, Jacksonville, Fla; s. of senior PGA Tour golfer Bob Duval; ed Georgia Tech.; turned professional 1993; mem. Walker Cup team 1991, Pres.'s Cup team, 1996, 1998, Ryder Cup team 1999; winner Nike Wichita Open 1993, Nike Tour Championship 1993, Michelob Championship at Kingsmill 1997, 1998, Walt Disney World/Oldsmobile Classic 1997, the Tour Championship 1997, Tucson Chrysler Classic 1998, Shell Houston Open 1998, NEC World Series of Golf 1998, Mercedes Championship 1999, Bob Hope Chrysler Classic 1999, the Players Championship 1999, BellSouth Classic 1999, Ryder Cup 1999, Open Championship, Royal Lytham, UK 2001; f. Duval Designs (golf design and architectural firm) 2005; Collegiate Player of the Year 1993, Dave Williams Award 1993, Jasper Award, Jacksonville 1996. *Leisure interests:* reading, fly fishing, surfing, skiing, baseball. *Address:* c/o IMG Golf, IMG Center, 1360 East 9th Street, Suite 100, Cleveland, OH 44114, USA (office).

DUVALIER, Jean-Claude; Haitian politician; b. 3 July 1951, Port-au-Prince; s. of late Pres. François Duvalier and late Simone (née Ovide) Duvalier; m. Michele Bennett 1980 (divorced 1990); one s.; ed Coll. of St Louis de Gonzague, Port-au-Prince and faculty of law, Univ. of Haiti; named political heir to Pres. François Duvalier Jan. 1971; Life Pres. 1971–86 (overthrown in coup); now living in Mougins, France.

DUVALL, Robert; American actor; b. 5 Jan. 1931, San Diego, Calif.; s. of William H. Duvall; m. 1st Gail Youngs (divorced); m. 2nd Sharon Brophy 1991; ed Principia Coll. Ill.; student, Neighborhood Playhouse, New York; f. Butchers Run Films (production co.) 1992. *Films include:* To Kill a Mockingbird 1963, Captain Newman, MD 1964, The Chase 1965, Countdown 1968, The Detective 1968, Bullitt 1968, True Grit 1969, The Rain People 1969, M*A*S*H 1970, The Revolutionary 1970, The Godfather 1972, Tomorrow 1972, The Great Northfield, Minnesota Raid 1972, Joe Kidd 1972, Lady Ice 1973, The Outfit 1974, The Conversation 1974, The Godfather Part II 1974, Breakout 1975, The Killer Elite 1975, Network 1976, The Eagle Has Landed 1977, The Greatest 1977, The Betsy 1978, Apocalypse Now 1979, The Great Santini 1980, True Confessions 1981, Angelo My Love (actor and dir) 1983,

Tender Mercies (Acad. Award for Best Actor 1984) 1983, The Stone Boy 1984, The Natural 1984, The Lightship 1986, Let's Get Harry 1986, Belizaire the Cajun 1986, Colors 1988, Convicts, Roots in a Parched Ground, The Handmaid's Tale 1990, A Show of Force 1990, Days of Thunder 1990, Rambling Rose 1991, Newsies 1992, The New Boys 1992, Stalin 1992, The Plague, Geronimo, Falling Down 1993, The Paper 1994, Wrestling Ernest Hemingway 1994, Something To Talk About, The Stars Fell on Henrietta, The Scarlet Letter, A Family Thing (also co-producer), Phenomenon 1996, The Apostle 1997, Gingerbread Man 1997, Deep Impact, A Civil Action 1999, Gone In Sixty Seconds 2000, A Shot at Glory (also producer) 2000, The 6th Day 2000, Apocalypse Now: Redux 2001, John Q 2002, Assassination Tango (also producer and dir) 2002, Secondhand Lions 2003, Gods and Generals 2003, Open Range 2003, Kicking & Screaming 2005, Thank You for Smoking 2005, Lucky You 2007, We Own the Night 2007; dir We're Not the Jet Set. *Television includes:* Lonesome Dove (mini-series) 1989, Broken Trail (miniseries; Emmy Award for Best Actor in a Mini-series 2007) 2006. *Stage appearances include:* A View from the Bridge 1965 (Obie Award), Wait Until Dark 1966, American Buffalo. *Address:* c/o William Morris Agency, 151 S. El Camino Drive, Beverly Hills, CA 90212,; Butchers Run Films, 100 Universal City Plaza Building 507, Suite 2D, Universal City, CA 91608, USA. *Telephone:* (818) 777-7333 (Butchers Run).

DUVALL, Shelley; American actress and producer; b. 7 July 1949, Houston, Tex.; f. TV production co. Think Entertainment. *Films include:* (actress): Brewster McCloud 1970, McCabe and Mrs. Miller 1971, Thieves Like Us 1974, Nashville 1975, Buffalo Bill and the Indians 1976, Three Women (Cannes Festival Prize 1977) 1977, Annie Hall 1977, The Shining 1980, Popeye 1980, Time Bandits 1981, Frankenweenie 1984, Roxanne 1987, Suburban Commando 1991, Underneath 1995, Portrait of a Lady 1996, Twilight of the Ice Nymphs 1997, Changing Habits 1997, Tale of the Mummy 1998, Home Fries 1998, The 4th Floor 1999, Dreams in the Attic 2000, Big Monster on Campus 2000, Manna From Heaven 2002. *Television includes:* (actress): Bernice Bobs Her Hair, Lily, Twilight Zone, Mother Goose Rock 'n' Rhyme, Faerie Tale Theatre (Rumpelstiltskin, Rapunzel), Tall Tales and Legends (Darlin' Clementine); (exec. producer): Faerie Tale Theatre, Tall Tales and Legends, Nightmare Classics, Dinner at Eight (film), Mother Goose Rock 'n' Rhyme, Stories from Growing Up, Backfield in Motion (film), Bedtime Stories, Mrs. Piggle-Wiggle. *Address:* POB 1660 Blanco, TX 78606, USA.

DUVERGER, Maurice; French political scientist; *Professor Emeritus of Political Sociology, University of Paris;* b. 5 June 1917, Angoulême; s. of Georges and Anne (née Gobert) Duverger; m. Odile Batt 1949; ed Bordeaux Univ.; contrib. to Le Monde 1946–, El País (Spain), Il Corriere della Sera (Italy); Prof. of Political Sociology, Univ. of Paris 1955–85, Prof. Emer. 1985–; Founder and Pres. Inst. of Research into Insts and Cultures of Europe (IRICE); mem. European Parl. 1989–95; mem. American Acad. of Arts and Sciences, Finnish Acad. of Sciences; Grand Officier Légion d'honneur, Commdr ordre nat. du Mérite; Dr hc (Siena, Geneva, New Jersey, Milan, Barcelona, Warsaw, Sofia, Prague, Athens). *Publications:* Les partis politiques 1951, Demain, la république... 1959, De la dictature 1961, La Sixième république et le régime présidentiel 1961, Introduction to the Social Sciences 1964, Introduction à la politique 1964, La démocratie sans le peuple 1967, Institutions politiques 1970, Janus: les deux faces de l'Occident 1972, Sociologie de la politique 1973, La monarchie républicaine 1974, Lettre ouverte aux socialistes 1976, L'autre coté des choses 1977, Echec au roi 1978, Les orangers du lac Balaton 1980, La République des Citoyens 1982, Bréviaire de la cohabitation 1986, La Cohabitation des Français 1987, La nostalgie de l'impuissance 1988, Le Lièvre libéral et la tortue européenne 1990, Europe des hommes 1994, L'Europe dans tous ses Etats 1995, A la recherche du droit perdu 2001. *Leisure interest:* theatre. *Address:* Presses universitaires de France, 6 avenue Reille, 75014 Paris (office); IRICE, 1 rue Descartes, 75005 Paris; Mas du Grand Côté, 13100 Le Tholonet, France (home); 24 rue des Fossés-Saint-Jacques, 75005 Paris (home).

DUWAISAN, Khalid Abdulaziz ad-, BA (Comm); Kuwaiti diplomatist; *Ambassador to UK;* b. 15 Aug. 1947; s. of Abdulaziz Saud Al-Duwaisan and Sabeka Abdullah Al-Duwaisan; m. Dalal Al-Humaizi 1980; one s. one d.; ed Cairo Univ., Univ. of Kuwait; joined Ministry of Foreign Affairs 1970, Diplomatic Attaché 1974, Embassy, Washington, DC 1975; Amb. to Netherlands 1984 (also accred to Romania 1988); Chair. Kuwaiti del. for supervision of demilitarized zone between Iraq and Kuwait and Chief Co-ordinator Comm. for Return of Stolen Property 1991; Amb. to UK (also accred to Ireland, Norway, Sweden and Denmark) 1993–; Hon. GCVO (UK). *Leisure interests:* tennis, swimming. *Address:* Kuwaiti Embassy, 2 Albert Gate, London, SW1X 7JU (office); 22 Kensington Palace Gardens, London, W8, England (home). *Telephone:* (20) 7590-3400 (office); (20) 7221-7374 (home). *Fax:* (20) 7823-1712 (office). *E-mail:* Kuwait@dircon.co.uk (office); enquiries@kuwaitinfo.org.uk (office). *Website:* www.kuwaitinfo.org.uk (office).

DUYET, Pham The; Vietnamese trade union official, economist and fmr politician; fmr mine man.; fmr Pres. Viet Nam Gen. Confed. of Labour; Leader CP of Hanoi, Viet Nam 1987. *Address:* Communist Party of Viet Nam, 1 Hoang Van Thu, Hanoi, Viet Nam.

DVOŘÁK, Tomás; Czech professional athlete; b. 11 May 1972, Zlín; s. of Petr Dvořák and Hana Dvořák; m. Gabriela Dvořák; two d.; decathlete; bronze medal, Olympic Games, Atlanta 1996, gold medal, European Cup 1995, 1999 (world record of 8,994 points, since broken), gold medal, World Championships, Athens 1997, Seville 1999, Edmonton 2001; Athlete of the Year, Czech Repub. 1999, Jim Thorpe All-Around Award. *Leisure interests:* cooking, gardening, family, music. *Address:* Stadion Juliska, 160 00 Prague 6, Czech Republic (office). *Telephone:* (2) 20203812 (office).

DVORKIN, Maj.-Gen. Vladimir, PhD; Russian naval officer (retd), defence and foreign affairs specialist and academic; *Principal Researcher, Institute of World Economy and International Relations, Russian Academy of Sciences;* b. 12 Jan. 1936, Leningrad (now St Petersburg); ed High Mil. Naval Coll.; worked at State Cen. Naval Testing Site; took part in first Soviet tests of nuclear-powered ballistic missile submarines and in first underwater test launches; worked in 4th Cen. Research Inst., Russian Defence Ministry 1962–2001, Head of Inst. 1993–2001; Sr Advisor at PIR Center and Carnegie Moscow Center; Prof. and Full mem. Russian Acad. of Missile and Artillery Sciences, Acad. of the Mil. Sciences, Russian Eng Acad., Int. Eng Acad., Acad. of Astronautics; made significant contrib. to formulating Soviet and Russia's position at negotiations on strategic offensive arms control and reduction; participating for many years as an expert in preparing SALT II, the INF Treaty, START I and START II; Merits marked with orders: 'For Merits to the Fatherland' (Fourth Degree), 'For Military Merits', 'Labor Red Banner', 'Red Star'; numerous medals; Honoured Worker of Science and Tech. of Russian Fed. *Publications:* co-author of all major documents related to Strategic Nuclear Forces and Strategic Missile Forces; more than 350 publs. *Address:* Institute of World Economy and International Relations (IMEMO), Profsoyushaya Str. 23, Moscow, B-71, GSP-7, 117997 (office); PIR Center, Na Trekhprudnom, Trekhprudny Per. 9, Bldg 1B, Moscow 103001, Russia. *Telephone:* (495) 120-52-36 (office); (495) 234-05-25. *Fax:* (495) 234-95-58. *E-mail:* imemoran@imemo.ru (office); info@pircenter.org. *Website:* www.imemo.ru (office); www.pircenter.org.

DVORKOVICH, Arkady V., MA; Russian economist and politician; *Head, Presidential Experts Directorate, President's Executive Office;* b. 26 March 1972, Moscow; ed Moscow State Univ., New Econ. School, Moscow, Duke Univ., USA; worked for Econ. Expert Group, Ministry of Finance 1994–2000, Head of Economic Expert Group 1997–2000; Adviser to Minister of Econ. Devt and Trade 2000–, Expert of the Strategic Research Centre 2000–01; Deputy Minister of Econ. Devt and Trade 2001–04; Head of Presidential Experts Directorate, Pres.'s Exec. Office 2004–; Pres. Russian Investment and Finance Analysts' Guild; mem. Nation Banking Council; First Vice-Pres. Russian Chess Fed. 2007–. *Publications:* various articles on econs. *Address:* Office of the President, Staraya pl. 4, 103132 Moscow, Russian Federation (office). *Telephone:* (495) 925-35-81 (office). *Fax:* (495) 206-07-66 (office). *E-mail:* president@gov.ru (office). *Website:* www.kremlin.ru (office).

DVORSKÝ, Peter; Slovak singer (tenor); b. 25 Sept. 1951, Partizánske, Topol'čany Dist; s. of Vendelín Dvorský and Anna Dvorská; m. Marta Varšová 1975; two d.; ed State Conservatoire, Bratislava; studied with R. Carossi and M. di Luggo, Milan 1975–76; opera soloist, Slovak Nat. Theatre, Bratislava 1972–96, 1999; sang at Metropolitan Opera, New York 1977, Covent Garden, London 1978, Bolshoi Theatre, Moscow 1978, La Scala, Milan 1979; performs regularly at Bratislava, Vienna State Opera, Covent Garden, La Scala, New York Metropolitan Opera, Munich, Berlin, Prague, Geneva, Paris, Buenos Aires, Tokyo and in many other cities throughout the world; numerous radio and TV performances; many recordings; Chair. Council of Slovak Music Union 1991–; Pres. Harmony Foundation 1991–; Dir State Opera Košice, Slovakia 2006–; performed charity concerts after floods in Czech Repub. 2002; Pres. Dvořak Competition, Karlovy Vary, Czech Repub.; awards include Tchaikovsky Competition, Geneva (5th Prize 1974, 1st Prize 1975), Leoš Janáček Memorial Medal 1978, Giuseppe Verdi Medal 1979, Artist of Merit 1981, Nat. Artist 1984, Kammersänger, Vienna 1986, Francisco Cilea Prize 1991, Wilhelm Furtwängler Prize 1992. *Leisure interests:* hunting, music, piano, family. *Address:* J. Hronca 1A, 841 02 Bratislava, Slovakia. *Fax:* (2) 64287626.

DWEK, Raymond Allen, DPhil, DSc, FRS, FRSC, CBiol, FIBiol; British scientist and academic; *Director, Glycobiology Institute, University of Oxford;* b. 10 Nov. 1941, Manchester; s. of Victor Joe Dwek and Alice Liniado; m. Sandra Livingstone 1964; two s. two d.; ed Carmel Coll., Univ. of Manchester, Lincoln Coll., Oxford, Exeter Coll., Oxford; Research Lecturer in Physical Chem., Christ Church, Oxford 1966–68, in Biochemistry 1975–76; Lecturer in Inorganic Chem., Christ Church, Oxford 1968–75, in Biochemistry, Trinity Coll., Oxford 1976–84; Fellow Exeter Coll., Oxford 1974–88, Professorial Fellow 1988–; Dir Glycobiology Inst., Univ. of Oxford 1988–, Prof. of Glycobiology 1988–, Head of Dept of Biochemistry 2000–; Dir for Grad. Training 1998–; mem. Oxford Enzyme Group 1971–88; Founder-mem. Oxford Oligosaccharide Group 1983; Univ. of Oxford Dir (non-exec.) and Founder Glycosciences Ltd (fmrly Glycosystems Ltd); Dir and Founding Scientist, IgX, Oxford 1998; Dir United Therapeutics 2002–; Visiting Royal Soc. Research Fellow, Weizmann Inst., Rehovot, Israel 1969; Royal Soc. Locke Research Fellow 1974–76; Visiting Prof., Duke Univ., NC; Hon. Life/Founder mem. Swedish Biophysical Soc. 1979–; Kluge Chair of Tech. & Soc., Kluge Center of the Library of Congress, Washington 2007; Biomedical Research Council Distinguished Visitor, Singapore 2005; mem. European Molecular Biological Org. (EMBO) 1988–, Scientific Advisory Bd, Hepatitis Foundation USA 1994–, Inst. for Applied Biosciences, Ben-Gurion Univ. of the Negev, Israel (chair.) 2001–05, Commonwealth Project for Hepatitis Outreach, Pa USA 2002–, Bd of Scientific Govs Scripps Research Inst., La Jolla USA 2003– (Inst. Prof. 2008–), European Lipidonics Initiative, Europe 2004–, Bd of Govs Exec. Cttee, Ben-Gurion Univ., Israel 2005–, Int. Advisory Bd of NIBN, Israel 2005–; Pres. Inst. of Biology, London 2008–; Judge, Millennium Fund Competition, The Daily Telegraph 1994; Boyce Thompson Distinguished Lecturer, Cornell Univ., USA 1997; Scientific Adviser to the Pres., Ben Gurion Univ., Negev, Israel; Hon. mem. Inst. of Biochemistry, Bucharest 2000–, Hon. Fellow, Lincoln Coll., Oxford 2004; Hon. Fellow, Royal Soc. of Physicians 2007; Foreign mem. American Philosophical Soc. 2006; Commdr Nat. Romanian Order for Merit 2000; Dr hc (Catholic Univ. of Louvain) 1996, (Cluj, Romania) 2005, Hon. PhD (Ben-Gurion Univ., Israel) 2001, Hon. DSc (Scripps Research Inst., La Jolla, Calif.) 2004; Wellcome Trust Award for Research in Biochem. Related to

Medicine 1994, Scientific Leadership Award Hepatitis B Foundation, Philadelphia, Delaware Valley Coll. Centennial Award 1997, Lemieux Lecture, Univ. of Alberta, Canada 2003, Huxley Medal 2007. *Publications:* books: Nuclear Magnetic Resonance (NMR) in Biochemstry 1973, Physical Chemistry Principles and Problems for Biochemists (jtly) 2002, NMR in Biology (jtly) 1977, Biological Spectrosocopy (jtly) 1984; numerous scientific articles and patents. *Leisure interests:* family, patent law, sport, listening to music. *Address:* Glycobiology Institute, South Parks Road, Oxford, OX1 3QU (office); Exeter College, Oxford, OX1 3DP, England. *Telephone:* (1865) 275344 (office). *Fax:* (1865) 275771. *E-mail:* raymond.dwek@exeter.ox.ac.uk (office). *Website:* www.bioch.ox.ac.uk/glycob (office).

DWORKIN, Ronald Myles, FBA; American legal scholar, philosopher and writer; *Professor of Law, New York University;* b. 11 Dec. 1931; s. of David Dworkin and Madeline Talamo; m. Betsy Celia Ross 1958 (died 2000); one s. one d.; ed Harvard Coll., Oxford Univ., UK, Harvard Law School; Legal Sec. to Judge Learned Hand 1957–58; Assoc., Sullivan & Cromwell, New York 1958–62; Assoc. Prof. of Law, Yale Law School 1962–65, Prof. 1965–68, Wesley N. Hohfeld Prof. of Jurisprudence 1968–69; Prof. of Jurisprudence, Oxford Univ. 1969–98, now Emer., Fellow, Univ. Coll. 1969–98, now Emer.; Quain Prof. of Jurisprudence, Univ. Coll., London 1998–2004, Bentham Prof. of Law and Philosophy 2004–; Visiting Prof. of Philosophy, Princeton Univ. 1974–75; Prof. of Law, New York Univ. Law School 1975–; Prof.-at-Large, Cornell Univ. 1976–80; Visiting Prof. of Philosophy and Law, Harvard Univ. 1977, of Philosophy 1979–82; mem. Council, Writers and Scholars Educational Trust 1982–, Programme Cttee, Ditchley Foundation 1982–; Co-Chair. US Democratic Party Abroad 1972–76; Fellow, American Acad. of Arts and Sciences 1979; Hon. Queen's Counsel;; Hon. LLD (Williams Coll.) 1981, (John Jay Coll. of Criminal Justice) 1983, (Claremont Coll.) 1987, (Kalamazoo Coll.) 1987; Holberg Int. Memorial Prize 2007. *Publications:* Taking Rights Seriously 1977, The Philosophy of Law (Ed.) 1977, A Matter of Principle 1985, Law's Empire 1986, Philosophical Issues in Senile Dementia 1987, A Bill of Rights for Britain 1990, Life's Dominion 1993, Freedom's Law 1996, Sovereign Virtue 2000, Justice in Robes 2006; articles in legal and philosophical journals. *Address:* New York University School of Law, 4111 Vanderbilt Hall, 40 Washington Square South, New York, NY 10012, USA (office); 17 Chester Row, London, SW1W 9JF, England. *Telephone:* (212) 998-6248 (office). *Fax:* (212) 995-4526 (office). *E-mail:* ronald.dworkin@nyu.edu (office). *Website:* www.nyu.edu/gsas/dept/philo/faculty/dworkin (office).

DWURNIK, Edward; Polish painter and illustrator; b. 19 April 1943, Radzymin; m.; one d.; ed Acad. of Fine Arts, Warsaw; over 150 one-man exhbns (retrospective) including Warsaw 1971, 1974, 1975, 1977, 1980, 1990, 1994–95, 1997, 1999, 2000, The Zacheta Gallery of Contemporary Art, Warsaw 2001, Toruń 1980, Wrocław 1987, Bydgoszcz 1997, Bytom 1997, PGS, Sopot 1999, Kraków 2000; exhbns abroad: Darmstadt 1977, Moscow 1978, Göteborg 1981, Kassel 1982, Fifth Biennale of Sydney 1984, Nouvelle Biennale de Paris 1985, Eindhoven 1986, Lingen 1986, Cologne 1986, London 1987, 1991–92, 19th Art Biennale, São Paulo 1987, Olympic Art Festival, Seoul 1988, Leipzig 1991, Vienna 1993, 1999–2000, Stuttgart (retrospective) 1994, Fassbender Gallery, Chicago 1996, Nevin Kelly Gallery, Washington, DC 2004; Cyprian Kamil Norwid Art Critics' Award for Exhbn Summer 80, Warsaw 1981, Solidarity Labour Union Cultural Award (for paintings from Warsaw series 1981) 1983, Coutts Contemporary Art Foundation Award, Zurich 1992; numerous Polish and int. awards. *Leisure interests:* driving, travelling, opera, films, music (heavy metal). *Address:* ul. Podgorska 5, 02-921 Warsaw, Poland. *Telephone:* (22) 8429879. *Fax:* (22) 8429879.

DYACHENKO, Tatyana Borisovna; Russian politician; b. 17 Jan. 1960, Sverdlovsk; d. of fmr Pres. Boris Yeltsin and Naina Yeltsin; two s.; m. 2nd Valentin Borisovich Yumashev; one d.; ed Moscow State Univ.; engineer, Construction Bureau Salut 1982–94, Construction Bureau Zarya Urala, Moscow 1994–95; mem. Boris Yeltsin Election Campaign 1996; counsellor to Pres. Yeltsin 1997–99; adviser to Chair. of Admin of Pres. of Russian Fed. 1999–2001; Dir Fund of the First Pres. of Russia B. N. Yeltsin. *Leisure interest:* tourism. *Address:* Str. 3, 23 Bolshaya Polyanka str., 119180 Moscow, Russian Federation (office). *Telephone:* (495) 729-41-51 (office). *Fax:* (495) 729-54-52 (office). *E-mail:* fond@fonde.ru (office). *Website:* www.yeltsin.ru (office).

DYADKOVA, Larissa; Russian singer; b. 9 March 1952, Zelenodolsk; m. Alexandre Kogan 1985; one d.; ed Leningrad Conservatory class of J. Levando; joined the Kirov Opera Company, making debut as Valvya in Glinka's Ivan Susanin; guest soloist Metropolitan Opera, La Scala, Communale Theatre, Florence, Deutsche Oper Berlin, Arena di Verona, San Francisco Opera, New Israeli Opera, Chicago Lyric Opera. *Concert appearances:* performs Verdi's Requiem in concerts, vocal series by Mussorgsky and Mahler, cantatas by Prokofiev; works with conductors Levine, Rostropovich, Mehta, Abbado, Temirkanov, Gergiev. *Address:* IMG Artists, Carnegie Hall Tower, 152 West 57th Street, 5th Floor, New York, NY 10019 USA (office). *Telephone:* (212) 994-3500 (office). *Fax:* (212) 994-3550 (office). *E-mail:* atreuhaft@imgartists.com (office). *Website:* www.imgartists.com (office).

DYAKOV, Dumitru; Moldovan politician and journalist; *Chairman, Democratic Party of Moldova (Partidul Democrat din Moldova);* b. 10 Feb. 1952, Kargopole, Kurgan Region, Russia; m.; two d.; ed Belarus State Univ.; Sec. Comsomol Cttee, Moldovan State TV and Radio; corresp., Komsomolskaya Pravda in Moldova –1976; on Comsomol Cen. Cttee, on Moldovan CP Cen. Cttee; Head TASS Bureau in Romania 1989–93; Sec. Moldovan Embassy, Moscow 1993–94; mem. Parl. 1994–; Chair. Parl. Comm. on Foreign Policy 1994–95; Deputy Speaker 1995–97, Speaker 1998–2000; f. Alliance for Democratic and Flourishing Moldova 1998; Founder Chair. Democratic Party of Moldova 2000–. *Address:* Democratic Party of Moldova (Partidul Democrat din Moldova), 2001 Chişinău, str. Tighina 32, Moldova (office). *Telephone:* (22)

27-82-29 (office). *Fax:* (22) 27-82-30 (office). *E-mail:* pdm@mtc.md (office). *Website:* www.pdm.md (office).

DYBKJAER, Lone, MChemEng; Danish politician and fmr EU official; b. (Lone Vincents), 23 May 1940, Copenhagen; m. Poul Nyrup Rasmussen (q.v.); two d.; ed Rungsted Statsskole, Tech. Univ. of Denmark; Sec., Acad. of Tech. Sciences 1964–66, Medico-Tech. Cttee 1966–70; Head Information Secr., Tech. Univ. of Denmark 1970–77; Adviser, Geotechnical Inst. 1978–79; mem. Folketing (Parl.) 1973–77, 1979–94; Chair. Parl. Energy Cttee, 1984–87, Tech. Cttee 1984–88, Parl. nine-mem. Cttee on Tech. Bd 1986–88; Social Liberal Party Spokesperson on Energy, Labour Market and Environmental Questions 1979–87, 1990–94, on Foreign Affairs 1987–88; Minister of the Environment 1988–90; mem. European Parl. 1994–2004, First Vice-Chair. Cttee on Devt and Co-operation (responsible for human rights) 1999–2002, mem. Cttee on Women's Rights and Equal Opportunities 1999–2004, Cttee on Constitutional Affairs 2002–04, ACP-EU Ass. 2002–04; Bird Life Prize 1993, Cyclist of the Year 1989, Gold Medal for Conservation of Bldgs 1991. *Publications:* Tête à tête with a Modern Politician 1998, Peculiar Parliament 1999, Digital Denmark 1999. *Leisure interests:* tennis, reading, family life. *Address:* Christiansborg, 1240 KBHK, Denmark (office); Allégade 6A, 2000 Frederiksberg, Denmark (home). *Telephone:* 33212585 (office). *Fax:* 33253960 (office). *E-mail:* rvlody@ft.dk (office). *Website:* www.lonedybkjaer.dk (office).

DYDUCH, Marek; Polish politician and lawyer; *Secretary-General, Democratic Left Alliance;* b. 27 Aug. 1957, Świdnica; s. of Hipolit Dyduch and Krystyna Dyduch; m. Dorota Dyduch; one d. one s.; ed Wrocław Univ.; Chair. Local Council 1982–83; Chair. City-Communal Exec. Bd Union of Polish Socialist Youth (ZSMP), Żarów 1982–83, Vice-Chair. Prov. Exec. Bd, Wałbrzych 1983–86, Chair. 1986–91; mem. Polish United Workers' Party (PZPR) 1982–; mem. Prov. Nat. Council, Wałbrzych 1984–88; Deputy to Sejm (Parl.) 1993–, Vice-Chair. Comm. of Justice, Co-Pres. Comm. of Codification for Penal Codes, mem. Social Policy Comm., Comm. for Health Insurance, Comm. for Social Insurance, Justice and Human Rights Comm., Extraordinary Comm. for the Reform of Public Admin, Extraordinary Comm. for Social Insurance; mem. Social Democracy of the Repub. of Poland (SdRP) 1990–99, Democratic Left Alliance (SLD, after party reorganization) 1999–, Chair. Lower-Silesian Prov. Bd, SLD, Wrocław 1999–2002, Sec.-Gen. SLD 2002–, currently mem. Nat. Exec. Bd SLD; Sec. of State, Ministry of the Treasury 2001–02; Founder Ferdinand Lassal Foundation, Wrocław; Bronze Cross of Merit 1989. *Leisure interests:* tennis, skiing, local and global social phenomena, history, science-fiction. *Address:* National Council of Democratic Left Alliance, ul. Rozbrat 44A, 00-419 Warsaw, Poland (office). *Telephone:* (22) 629-25-54 (office). *Fax:* (22) 621-25-92 (office). *E-mail:* mdyduch@sld.org.pl (office); marek@dyduch.pl (office). *Website:* www.sld.org.pl (office); www.dyduch.pl (office).

DYER, Alexander Patrick, BS, MBA; American business executive; *Deputy Chairman, Bunzl PLC;* b. 30 Aug. 1932, Santa Rosa, Calif.; s. of John Dyer and late Amie M. Moore; m. Shirley Shine 1954; one s. (and one s. deceased); ed US Mil. Acad. and Harvard Business School; Exec. Vice-Pres. Air Products and Chemicals, BOC Group PLC 1987–89, Man. Dir Gases and CEO 1989–93, Deputy Chair. 1993–95, CEO 1993–96; Deputy Chair. Bunzl PLC 1996– (Chair. 1993–96); Dir BWAY Corpn. *Leisure interests:* golf, skeet, antique collecting. *Address:* Bunzl PLC, 110 Park Street, London, W1K 6NX, England (office); 1803 Apple Tree Lane, Bethlehem, PA 18105, USA (home). *Telephone:* (20) 7495-4950 (office); (610) 691-5522 (home). *Fax:* (20) 7495-2527 (office); (610) 866-5102 (home). *E-mail:* apdyer1954@aol.com (home).

DYKE, Gregory (Greg), BA; British media executive; *Chairman, Sunshine Acquisition Ltd.;* b. 20 May 1947; s. of David Dyke and Denise Dyke; partner Sue Howes; one s. one d.; one step-s. one step-d.; ed Hayes Grammar School, Univ. of York and Harvard Business School; reporter on local paper; researcher, London Weekend Television (LWT) 1977, later founding producer, The Six O'Clock Show; joined TV-AM 1983; Dir of Programmes, TVS 1984–87; Dir of Programmes, LWT 1987–90, Man. Dir 1990; Group Chief Exec. LWT (Holdings) PLC 1991–94; Chair. Ind. TV Asscn 1992–94; Chair. GMTV 1993–94; Chair. CEO Pearson TV 1995–99; Chair. Channel 5 Broadcasting 1997–99; Dir Gen. BBC 2000–04 (resgnd); Dir BSkyB 1995, Phoenix Pictures Inc., New York, Pearson PLC 1996–99 and others; Dir (non-exec.) Manchester United Football Club 1997–99; mem. Supervisory Bd ProSiebenSat.1 Media 2004–; adviser Apax Partners Inc. 2004–, Chair. Sunshine Acquisition Ltd (acquisition vehicle formed by Apax) 2005–, BFI 2008–; Trustee Science Museum 1996–, English Nat. Stadium Trust 1997–99; Royal TV Soc. Lifetime Achievement Award, Broadcasting Press Guild Award 2004. *Publication:* Memoirs 2004. *Leisure interests:* tennis, theatre, football, cinema. *Address:* c/o Apax Partners, 15 Portland Place, London, W1B 1PT, England (office).

DYKHOVICHNY, Ivan Vladimirovich; Russian film director; b. 16 Oct. 1947, Moscow; m.; ed Shchukin Higher Theatre School and Acad. of Cinematography; actor, Taganka Theatre 1970–81; film dir, Mosfilm Studios 1984–96; Chief Dir All-Russian TV 1998–2000; winner, All-Union Film Festival, All-European Festival of Cameramen's Art. *Films include:* Moskva, Lyubov Moya (actor) 1974, Cherni Monakh 1989, Prorva 1992, Zhenskaya Rol 1995, Muzyka dlya Dekabrya 1995, Kopeyka 2002, Rokovaya voyna. Fotografiya bezdny (documentary) 2005, Vdokh-vydokh 2006. *Television scriptwriting includes:* Catch 22. *Address:* Stary Petrovsko-Razumovsky proyezd 6/8, korp. 3, Apt 110, 125083 Moscow, Russia. *Telephone:* (495) 214-48-61.

DYLAN, Bob; American composer, musician (guitar, piano, harmonica, autoharp) and singer; b. (Robert Allen Zimmerman), 24 May 1941, Duluth, Minn.; m. Sarah Lowndes (divorced 1978); four c. one adopted d.; ed Univ. of Minn.; best known for composition and interpretation of pop, country and folk music; performer, numerous tours and concerts; devised and popularized folk-rock 1965; performed with The Band; f. new group The Traveling Wilburys 1988; host, Theme Time Radio Hour with Your Host Bob Dylan (XM Satellite Radio) 2006–; Commdr, Ordre des Arts et des Lettres; Hon. DMus (Princeton Univ.) 1970, (Univ. of St Andrews) 2004; Acad. Award for Best Theme Song (for Things Have Changed, from The Wonder Boys) 2002, Grammy Award for Best Solo Rock Vocal Performance (for Someday Baby) 2007, Premio Príncipe de Asturias 2007, Pulitzer Prize Special Citation 2008. *Films appearances:* Eat the Document, Pat Garrett and Billy the Kid, Renaldo and Clara (also directed), Hearts of Fire 1986, Concert for Bangladesh, Masked and Anonymous 2003. *Radio:* presenter weekly music programme (Deep Tracks Channel, XM) 2006–. *Recordings include:* albums: The Freewheelin' Bob Dylan 1964, Bringing It All Back Home 1965, Highway 61 Revisited 1965, Blonde On Blonde 1966, John Wesley Harding 1968, Nashville Skyline 1969, Self Portrait 1970, New Morning 1970, Planet Waves (with The Band) 1974, Before The Flood 1974, Blood On The Tracks (with The Band) 1975, Hard Rain 1976, Desire 1976, Street Legal 1978, Slow Train Coming 1979, Infidels 1983, Empire Burlesque 1985, Knocked out Loaded 1986, Down in the Groove 1988, Traveling Wilburys (with Traveling Wilburys) 1988, Dylan and the Dead (with Grateful Dead) 1989, Oh Mercy 1989, Under The Red Sky 1990, Vol. 3 (with Traveling Wilburys) 1990, The Bootleg Series 1990, Good as I Been to You 1992, World Gone Wrong 1993, Unplugged 1995, Time Out of Mind (Grammy Award 1998) 1997, Love and Theft 2001, Modern Times (Grammy Award for Best Contemporary Folk/Americana Album 2007) 2006, Together Through Life 2009. *Publications:* Tarantula 1966, Writings and Drawings 1973, The Songs of Bob Dylan 1966–1975 1976, Lyrics 1962–1985 1986, Drawn Blank 1994, Highway 61 Revisited (interactive CD-ROM), Chronicles: Volume One (memoir) (Quill Book Award for Best Biography or Memoir 2005) 2004, Lyrics 1962–2001 2005, Dylan's Inspirations 2006. *Address:* c/o Jeff Rosen, PO Box 870, Cooper Station, New York, NY 10276, USA (office); c/o Columbia Records, 550 Madison Avenue, New York, NY 10022; c/o XM Satellite Radio Holdings Inc., 1500 Eckington Place, NE, Washington, DC 20002-2194, USA. *Website:* www.bobdylan.com.

DYSON, Freeman John, FRS; American physicist and academic; *Professor Emeritus of Physics, Institute for Advanced Study;* b. 15 Dec. 1923, Crowthorne, England; s. of late Sir George Dyson and Lady Mildred (Atkey) Dyson; m. 1st Verena Huber 1950 (divorced 1958); one s. one d.; m. 2nd Imme Jung 1958; four d.; ed Cambridge and Cornell Univs; Fellow of Trinity Coll., Cambridge 1946; Warren Research Fellow, Birmingham Univ. 1949; Prof. of Physics, Cornell Univ. 1951–53; Prof., Inst. for Advanced Study, Princeton 1953–94, Prof. Emer. 1994–; Chair. Fed. of American Scientists 1962; mem. NAS 1964–; Foreign Assoc. Acad. des Sciences, Paris 1989; Hon. DSc (City Univ., UK) 1981, (Oxford) 1997; Gifford Lecturer, Aberdeen 1985, Heineman Prize, American Inst. of Physics 1965, Lorentz Medal, Royal Netherlands Acad. 1966, Hughes Medal, Royal Soc. 1968, Max Planck Medal, German Physical Soc. 1969, Harvey Prize, Israel Inst. of Tech. 1977, Wolf Prize (Israel) 1981, Matteucci Medal, Rome 1990, Fermi Award (USA) 1994, Templeton Prize 2000. *Publications:* Disturbing the Universe 1979, Weapons and Hope 1984, Origins of Life 1986, Infinite in All Directions 1988, From Eros to Gaia 1992, Imagined Worlds 1997, The Sun, The Genome and the Internet 1999, The Scientist as Rebel 2006, A Many-colored Glass 2007; papers in The Physical Review, Journal of Mathematical Physics, etc. *Address:* Institute for Advanced Study, Princeton, NJ 08540 (office); 105 Battle Road Circle, Princeton, NJ 08540, USA (home). *Telephone:* (609) 734-8055 (office). *Fax:* (609) 951-4489 (office). *E-mail:* dyson@ias.edu (office). *Website:* www.sns.ias.edu/~dyson (office).

DYSON, Sir James, Kt, CBE, FCSD, MDes; British designer and inventor; *Chairman, Dyson Appliances Ltd;* b. 2 May 1947; s. of Alec Dyson and Mary Dyson (née Bolton); m. Deirdre Hindmarsh 1967; two s. one d.; ed Gresham's School, Royal Coll. of Art; Dir Rotork Marine 1970–74; Man. Dir Kirk Dyson 1974–79; developed and designed Dyson Dual Cyclone vacuum cleaner 1979–93; Founder and Chair. Prototypes Ltd (now Dyson Research) 1979–, Dyson Appliances Ltd 1992–; Chair. Bath Coll. of Higher Educ. 1990–92, Design Museum 1999–2004; mem. Design Council 1997–, Council RCA 1998–; Founder and Pres. James Dyson Foundation 2002–; est. Dyson School of Design Innovation, Bath 2006; Fellow, Royal Acad. of Eng 2005; Hon. Fellow, Liverpool John Moores Univ., MEID (Inst. of Eng Designers) 1997; numerous hon. doctorates including Hon. DSc (Oxford Brookes) 1997, (Bath, Imperial College London, RCA); numerous design awards and trophies; Royal Designer for Industry Royal Soc. of Arts 2005. *Publications include:* Doing a Dyson 1996, Against the Odds (autobiog.) 1997. *Leisure interests:* running, garden design, music, fishing, cricket, tennis. *Address:* Dyson Ltd, Tetbury Mill, Malmesbury, Wilts., SN16 0RP, England (office). *Telephone:* (1666) 827200 (office). *Fax:* (1666) 827321. *E-mail:* laura.brock@dyson.com (office). *Website:* www.dyson.com (office).

DYVIK, Helge Julius Jakhelln, DPhil; Norwegian academic; *Professor of General Linguistics, University of Bergen;* b. 23 Dec. 1947, Bodø; s. of late Einar Dyvik and Harriet Dyvik (née Jakhelln); m. 1st Eva Sætre 1973 (divorced 1994); one s. one d.; m. 2nd Martha Thunes 2001; one s.; ed Univ. of Bergen, Univ. of Durham, UK; Research Asst (Old Norse), Univ. of Bergen 1974–75, Lecturer 1976, Project Asst (Old Norwegian syntax) 1976–81, Research Fellow (Vietnamese syntax project) 1981–83, Prof. of Gen. Linguistics 1983–; Pres. Nordic Asscn of Linguists 1993–1998; mem. Norwegian Language Council 2000–, Programme Cttee for Nordic Council of Ministers' Research Programme on Language Tech. 2000–05 (Chair. 2002–); Chair. Expert Cttee for Standardisation and Language Observation under the Norwegian Language Council 2007–; Fridtjof Nansen Award for Eminent Research, Norwegian Acad. of Letters and Science 1987. *Publications:* Grammatikk og Empiri 1981, Categories and Functions in Vietnamese Classifier Constructions 1983, Semantic Mirrors 1998. *Leisure interests:* play reading, choral singing. *Address:* Department of Linguistic, Literary and Aesthetic Studies, Linguistic Studies Section, University of Bergen, Sydnespl. 7, 5007 Bergen (office); Straumevn. 3A, 5151 Straumsgrend, Bergen, Norway (home). *Telephone:* 55-58-22-61 (office). *E-mail:* helge.dyvik@lili.uib.no (office). *Website:* www.hg.uib.no/i/lili/slf/ans/Dyvik (office).

DZAIDDIN BIN HAJI ABDULLAH, Rt Hon Tun Sri Dato' Seri Mohamed; Malaysian judge; *Chairman, Bursa Malaysia Berhad;* b. 16 Sept. 1937, Arau, Perlis; m. Puan Noriah Binti Tengku Ismael; two c.; ed Sultan Abdul Hamid Coll. Alor Setar; journalist The Malay Mail 1956; joined police service as Insp.; called to Bar, Middle Temple, London, UK 1966; admitted as advocate and solicitor in Kota Bharu and Kuala Lumpur 1967; juridical commr (part-time) 1979–82; apptd High Court Judge, Criminal Div. of Kuala Lumpur High Court 1982–84, Penang High Court 1984–92; Supreme Court Judge (renamed Fed. Court Judge) 1992–2000; Chief Justice of the Fed. Court 2000–03; Chair. Bursa Malaysia Berhad (fmrly Kuala Lumpur Stock Exchange) 2004–; apptd Dir (non-exec.) and Public Interest Dir by Minister of Finance 2004–; fmr Chair. Kelantan Bar Cttee; Vice-Pres. Malaysian Bar 1981–82; Chair. Tun Mohamad Suffian Foundation, Deutsche Bank (Malaysia), Advisory Council Business Ethics Inst. of Malaysia, Royal Comm. to Enhance the Operation and Man. of the Royal Police Force; Life mem. ASEAN Law Asscn of Malaysia, Pres. 1994–97; Pres. ASEAN Law Asscn 1997–; Hon. LLD (San Beda Coll.) 2002; several awards including Seri Paduka Baginda Yang DiPertuan Agong of the Most Esteemed Order of Seri Setia Mahkota Malaysia. *Address:* The Special Commission to Enhance the Operation and Management of The Royal Police Force, PO Box 10840, 50726 Kuala Lumpur, Malaysia (office). *E-mail:* dzaiddin@suruhanjayakhaspolis.gov.my (office). *Website:* www.suruhanjayakhaspolis.gov.my (office).

DZASOKHOV, Aleksandr Sergeyevich, CandHistSc; Russian politician; b. 3 April 1934, Ordzhonikidze, North Ossetian ASSR; m. Farisa Borissovna 1959; two s.; ed North Caucasian Mining-Metallurgical Inst. and CPSU Higher Party School; mem. CPSU 1957–91; First Sec. Ordzhonikidze Komsomol City Cttee 1957–61; Sec. of USSR Cttee of Youth Orgs 1961–64; leader of young Soviet specialists to Cuba 1964–65; First Sec., Pres. of USSR Youth Orgs 1965–67; Deputy Chair., Chair. of Soviet Cttee for Solidarity with Countries of Asia and Africa 1965–86; USSR Amb. to Syria 1986–88; First Sec. of North Ossetian CPSU Dist Cttee (Obkom) 1988–90; USSR People's Deputy 1989–91; Chair. Cttee of USSR Supreme Soviet on Int. Affairs 1990–91; mem., Sec. of Cen. Cttee CPSU, mem. of CPSU Politburo 1990–91; People's Deputy of Russia, mem. Supreme Soviet of Russian Fed. 1992–93; Chair. Sub-Cttee on Asia and the Pacific; mem. State Duma (Parl.) 1993–98; elected Pres. of Repub. of North Ossetia-Alania 1998–2005; Deputy Chair. Inter-Parl. Group of Russian Fed. 1993, Chair. 1996–2001; mem. Acad. of Creative Endeavours; mem. Bd Dirs Pervyi Kanal. *Publications:* several books on problems of post-colonialism in third-world countries, including Formation and Evolution of the Post-colonial World 1999. *Address:* c/o House of Soviets, Office of the President, Svobody pl. 1, 362038 Vladikavkaz, North Ossetia-Alania, Russia. *Telephone:* (8672) 53-35-24.

DZHANIBEKOV, Maj.-Gen. Vladimir Aleksandrovich; Russian cosmonaut (retd); b. 13 May 1942, Iskander, Tashkent Region, Uzbekistan; m. Lilya Munirovna Dzhanibekova; two d.; ed Yeisk High Mil. Aviation School; mem. CPSU 1970–91; mil. pilot-instructor 1965–70; selected mem. Cosmonauts' team 1970; Commdr Soyuz 27 1978, Soyuz 39 1981, Soyuz T-6 1982, Soyuz T-12 1984, Soyuz T-13 1985; Commdr Cosmonauts' team Yuriy Gagarin Centre of Cosmonauts' Training 1985–88; Head Dept of Theoretical and Research Educ. of Cosmonauts 1988–98; Hero of Soviet Union 1978, 1981; Hero of Mongolian Repub. 1981; Officier Légion d'honneur 1982. *Leisure interest:* painting. *Address:* c/o Yuriy Gagarin Centre for Cosmonauts' Training, Zvezdny Gorodok, Moscow Region, Russia.

DZHEMILEV, Mustafa (Abdul-Dzhemil); Ukrainian activist; b. 14 Nov. 1943, Ayserez, Crimea; m. Safinar Dzhemileva; two s. one d.; suffered continual harassment from Soviet authorities when he attempted to form a youth movt in Tashkent 1962–; subsequently, imprisonment or exile for activity: 1966–67, 1969–72, 1974–75, 1975–77, 1979–82, 1983–86; continued to organize Crimean Tatar protest actions in Cen. Asia and Moscow; returned to Crimea 1989; Chair. Crimean Tatar Majlis 1991–; Pres. Crimea Foundation 1991–; mem. Ukrainian Parl. 1998–, Chair. Council of Reps 1999–; political observer Business magazine; Dr hc (Seljuk Univ., Higher Tech. Inst. Gebze, Turkey); Nansen Medal UNHCR 1998, Pylyp Orlyk Int. Award 2000, Yaroslav Mudryi Medal 2001, Hon. Prize of Parliament of Ukraine 2002. *Leisure interest:* studying informative websites. *Address:* ul. Shmidta 25, Simferopol, Crimea (office); 6th Microrayon 100, Bakhchesaray, Crimea, Ukraine (home). *Telephone:* (652) 2275259 (office); (652) 5443758 (home). *Fax:* (652) 2274372 (office). *E-mail:* MCemiloglu@ttt.Crimea.com (home).

DZHIGARKHANIAN, Armen Borisovich; Armenian/Russian actor; b. 3 Oct. 1935, Yerevan; m. Tatiana Vlasova 1967; one s.; ed Yerevan Theatre Inst.; actor with Stanislavsky Russian Drama Theatre in Yerevan 1955–67; with Moscow Lenin Komsomol Theatre 1967–69, with Mayakovsky Theatre 1969–96, with Dzhigarkhanian Theatre 1996–; Armenian SSR State Prize 1975, 1979; RSFSR People's Artist 1973, USSR People's Artist 1985, Stanislavsky Award 2001. *Films:* has appeared in a number of films. *Roles include:* Levinson in Fadeev's Thunder, Stanley in Tennessee Williams' Streetcar Named Desire, Socrates and Nero in Radzinsky's Chats with Socrates and the Theatre in the time of Nero and Seneca, Big Daddy in Tennessee Williams' Cat on a Hot Tin Roof, Max in Pinter's Homecoming, Krapp in Beckett's Krapp's Last Tape, Domenic in E. D. Phillippo's Philoumena Marturano. *Leisure interests:* reading, listening to classical music, playing with pet Siamese cat. *Address:* 121002 Moscow, 37 Starokonysheny per., Apt. 9, Russia. *Telephone:* (495) 930-23-07 (office); (495) 203-30-79 (home); (214) 772-7464 (Dallas, USA). *Fax:* (495) 930-03-47 (office).

DZHORBENADZE, Avtandil Khristoforovich, DrMed; Georgian politician; b. 1951, Chibati, Lanchkhut region; s. of Khristophor Dzhorbenadze and Mariam Kamaladze; m. Nino Vepkhadze; two s.; ed Tbilisi State Inst. of Med. 1974; intern, Tbilisi Clinical Hosp. #1 1975, roentgenologist, Sec. CP Cttee, Deputy Chief Doctor 1978–86; therapeutist, Tbilisi Polyclinic #29 1975–76; practitioner mil. unit in Georgia 1976–78; First Deputy Head, then Head Tbilisi City Dept of Public Health 1986–92; Deputy Minister of Public Health and Social Security 1992–93; Minister of Public Health 1993–99, of Labour, Public Health and Social Security 1999–2001; Minister of State and Head of the State Chancellery of Georgia 2001–03; Chair. Citizens' Union of Georgia. *Publications:* over 30 scientific publs. *Address:* c/o Office of State Minister, Ingorkva 7, 380034 Tbilisi, Georgia (office).

DZHUMALIYEV, Kubanychbek; Kyrgyzstani politician; First Deputy Prime Minister and Minister of Transport and Communications 2005–06 (resgnd). *Address:* c/o Ministry of Transport and Communications, 42 Isanova Street, 720017 Bishkek, Kyrgyzstan (office).

DZIUBA, Andrzej Franciszek, (Franciszek Wieczyński), DD; Polish ecclesiastic and academic; *Bishop of Łowicz;* b. 10 Oct. 1950, Pleszew; s. of Stanisław Dziuba and Ludwika Slachciak; ed Primatial Priests' Seminary, Gniezno, Pontifical Theological Faculty, Poznań, Catholic Univ. Lublin, Acad. Alfonsiana, Rome and Univ. Italiana per Stranieri, Perugia; ordained priest, Gniezno 1975; Asst Parish Priest and Catechist, Łobżenica 1975–76; studies in Lublin 1976–79, Rome 1979–81; Sec. to Primate of Poland 1981–98, Dir Secr. 1984–98; Asst Parish Priest, St Martin's Church, Warsaw 1981–98, St Barbara's Church, Warsaw 1998, Bishop of Łowicz 2004–; Prof., Catholic Univ. Lublin 1989–, Acad. of Catholic Theology, Warsaw 1995–99, Primatial Priest's Seminary, Gniezno 1998–, Cardinal S. Wyszyński Univ. 1999–; Hon. Chaplain to Pope John Paul II 1990, Prelate 1996; Primate of Poland Foundation in GB 1991; Canon Metropolitan Chapter of Warsaw 1998; Theological Counsellor to Primate of Poland 1998–; Hon. Conventual Chaplain of Order of Malta 1998, Grand Cross 2005; Kt Commdr of Equestrian Order of Holy Sepulchre of Jerusalem 1996, Cross with Gold Star of Merit of Holy Sepulchre of Jerusalem 1996, Kt Ecclesiastical Grace of Sacred Mil. Constantinian Order 1999. *Publications:* Mikołaj z Mościsk, teolog moralista XVII w. 1985, Jan Azor, teolog-moralista 1988, Informator Katolicki 89/90 1990, Droga Krzyżowa 1991, Różaniec święty 1992, Kościół katolicki w Polsce. Informator 1993, Jezus nam przebacza. Przygotowanie do sakramentu pojednania 1994, Matka Boża z Guadalupe 1995, Kościół katolicki w Polsce. Informator 1995, Orędzie moralne Jezusa Chrystusa 1996 Dynamika wiary 1997, Kościół katolicki w Polsce. Informator 1997, Droga krzyżowa 1998, Biography of Cardinal Józef Glemp 1998, Cardinal Stefan Wyszyński Primate of Poland. A Life-Sketch 2000, U źródeł Bożej Madrości. Życie i nauka Jezusa Chrystusa 2000, Spowiedź małżeńska. Życie małżeńskie a sakramentalna posługa pokuty i pojednania 2002, Prestamé spoteczne karolynats Stefana Wyczyniskiego, Prymosa Polski 2004; numerous articles on moral theology, church history, Catholic social sciences. *Address:* Diocese of Łowicz, Stary Rynek 20, 99-400 Łowicz, Poland (office). *Telephone:* (46) 8376615 (office). *Fax:* (46) 8374349 (office). *E-mail:* kuria@diecezja.lowicz.pl (office). *Website:* www .diecezja.lowicz.pl.

DZIUBA, Ivan Mykhailovych; Ukrainian literary critic; b. 26 July 1931, Mykolaivka, Ukraine; s. of Mykhailo Dzyuba and Olga Dzyuba; m. Marta Lenets 1963; one d.; ed Donetsk Pedagogical Inst.; ed. various journals and publs published by Ukrainian State Publishing House; published An Ordinary Man or a Petit Bourgeois as well as numerous samizdat articles in 1960s; expelled from Writers' Union 1972 after publication of Internationalism or Russification? (numerous edns); arrested 1972, sentenced to 5 years' imprisonment 1973; recanted and released Nov. 1973; Writers' Union membership restored 1980s; mem. Ukrainian Acad. of Sciences 1992–, mem. Presidium 1997–; Academician-Sec. Dept of Literature, Language and Arts 1996–2004; Minister of Culture Dec. 1992–94; Sr Researcher, T. Shevchenko Inst. of Literature 1994–; Ed.-in-Chief Suchasnist (magazine) 1991–2003, Encyclopaedia of Modern Ukraine 1998–; Head of Cttee Tazas Shevchenko Nat. Ukrainian Award; freelance literary corresp. 1982–; O. Biletski Prize 1987, Laureate, Shevchenko's Award 1991, Int. Antonovich Prize 1992, V. Zhabotinsky Prize 1996, Vernadsky Prize 2001. *Publications:* 25 books including Between Politics and Literature 1998, Thirst 2001, Trap 2003; numerous articles on history and devt of Ukrainian literature and writers of former USSR. *Leisure interests:* gardening, mushrooming. *Address:* 54 Volodymyrska str., Kiev 01030 (office); Antonova str. 7, Apt 60, Kiev 03186, Ukraine (home). *Telephone:* (44) 235-09-81 (office); (44) 248-41-77 (home). *Fax:* (44) 228-11-93 (office). *E-mail:* shevcom@ukr.net (office).

DZIWISZ, Cardinal Stanisław, ThD; Polish ecclesiastic; *Archbishop of Kraków;* b. 27 April 1939, Raba Wyżna; ed Primatial Priest Seminary, Kraków, Metropolitan Ecclesiastic Seminary, Kraków, Pontifical Acad. of Theology, Kraków; ordained priest, Kraków 1963; Asst Parish Priest, Maków

Podhalański 1963–65; Chaplain to Archbishop of Kraków Karol Wojtyła (later Pope John Paul II) 1966–78; Lecturer, Higher Inst. of Catechism, Kraków 1966–78; ed. Kraków Curie Notificationes e Curia Metropolitana Cracoviensi 1966–78; Personal Sec. to Pope John Paul II 1978–2005, Prelate 1985, Apostolic Protonotary, Canon of Cathedral Chapter, Lviv and Metropolitan Chapter, Kraków 1997; Titular Bishop of San Leone and Prefetto aggiunto (Prefecture of the Sacred Household) 1998–2005; Titulare Archbishop of San Leone 2003–05; Archbishop of Kraków 2005–; elevated to Cardinal (Cardinal-Priest of S. Maria del Popolo) 2006; Vice-Chair. John Paul II Foundation 1985. *Publications include:* Kult św. Stanisława biskupa w Krakowie do Soboru Trydenckiego (Cult of Saint Stanislaus, Bishop of Kraków until Council of Trent) 1997. *Address:* Archdiocese of Kraków, ul. Franciszkanska 3, 31 004 Kraków, Poland (office). *Telephone:* (12) 6288100 (office). *Fax:* (12) 4294617 (office). *E-mail:* kuria@diecezja.krakow.pl (office). *Website:* www.diecezja.pl (office).

DZOMBIĆ, Aleksandar; Bosnia and Herzegovina banking executive and government official; *Minister of Finance, Republika Srpska;* b. 1968, Banja Luka; m.; one s.; ed Univ. of Banja Luka, Belgrade Univ.; worked in Banja Luka City Admin; Head, Dept and Project Man., Kristal Bank, Banja Luka; Dir Agroprom Bank, Banja Luka; Exec. Dir Nova Banka, Bijeljina; Minister of Finance 2006–. *Address:* Ministry of Finance of Republika Srpska, Banja Luka, trg Republike Srpske 1, 78000 Bosnia and Herzegovina (office). *Telephone:* (51) 331350 (office). *Fax:* (51) 331351 (office). *E-mail:* mf@mf .vladars.net (office). *Website:* www.vladars.net (office).

DZUMAGULOV, Apas Dzumagulovich; Kyrgyzstani politician and diplomatist; b. 19 Sept. 1934, Arashan, Kyrgyz SSR; m.; three s.; ed Moscow Gubkin Inst. of Oil; mem. CPSU 1962–91; worked at Complex S., Geological Expedition USSR Acad. of Sciences 1958–59; Sr geologist oil field Changar-Tash, Head. Cen. Research Lab., Chief Geologist Drilling Div., Chief Engineer Oil Co. Kyrghizneft Osh Dist 1959–73; Head Industrial-Transport Div. Cen. Cttee CP of Kyrgyz SSR 1973–79; Sec. Cen. Cttee CP of Kirgyzia 1979–85; First Sec. Issyk-Kul Dist Cttee 1985–86; Chair. Council of Ministers Kyrgyz SSR 1986–91; Chair. Org. Cttee, then Chair. Regional Soviet of Deputies, Head of Admin. Chuysk Region 1991–93; Deputy to USSR Supreme Soviet 1984–89; USSR People's Deputy 1989–91; People's Deputy of Kyrgyzstan; mem. Revision Comm. CPSU 1986–91; Prime Minister of Kyrgyz Repub. 1993–97; Amb. to Germany, Scandinavian countries and the Holy See 1998–2003. *Address:* c/o Ministry of Foriegn Affairs, 59 Razzakov str., Bishkek 720040, Kyrgyzstan (office). *Telephone:* (312) 620545 (office). *Fax:* (312) 660501. *E-mail:* gendep@mfa.gov.kg (office).

DŽUNOV, Todor, DSc; Macedonian professor of law and jurist; *President of Constitutional Court;* b. 11 Oct. 1931, Vatasha, Kavadarci; m. Granka Džunov 1958; ed Univ. of Cyril and Methodius, Skopje; Asst, Faculty of Law, Skopje 1956, Reader 1964, Assoc. Prof. 1969, Prof. 1974–94, Dean, Faculty of Law 1981–83; Rector, Univ. of 'Cyril and Metodius', Skopje 1985–88; Justice of the Constitutional Court 1994, Pres. 2000–; Pres. Research Council of Macedonia 1973–80; mem. and Chief of dels of interstate bodies for scientific and tech. co-operation with Greece, USA and UK; mem. del. on succession issues on Fmr Repub. of Yugoslavia; 11th of October Award 1980, Gold Award, Faculty of Law, Skopje 2001, Gold Award, Faculty of Philosophy, Univ. of Cyril and Methodius, Skopje, State Medal for Labour, State Medal for People Merit. *Publications:* more than 100 titles including Private International Law (textbook), International Legal Regulation of the Use of Rivers and Lakes of Common Interest Out of Navigation 1964, International Regulation of the Use of Waters 1979, Collection of Laws on the Private International Law 1984, Foreign Policy of SFRY and Non-Alignment 1989. *Address:* Constitutional Court, 12 Udarka brig. 2, 1000 Skopje (office); Partizanski odredi No. 8/25, 1000 Skopje, Republic of Macedonia (home). *Telephone:* (2) 163063 (office); (2) 130163 (home). *Fax:* (2) 119355 (office). *E-mail:* tdzunov@usud.gov.mk (office).

DZURINDA, Mikuláš, PhD; Slovak politician; *Chairman, Slovak Democratic and Christian Union-Democratic Party;* b. 4 Feb. 1955, Spišský Štvrtok; m.; two d.; ed Univ. of Transport and Communications, Žilina, econ. researcher Transport Research Inst., Žilina 1979–80; information tech. officer Czechoslovak Railways Regional Directorate, Bratislava 1980–88, Head of Automated Control Systems Dept 1988–91; Deputy Minister of Transport and Postal Service of Slovak Repub. 1991–92, 1994; Vice-Chair. for Econ. Christian Democratic Movt 1993–2000; spokesman of Slovak Democratic Coalition 1997–98, Chair. 1998–; Prime Minister of Slovak Repub. 1998–2002, 2002–06; f. Slovak Democratic and Christian Union (SDKÚ, merged with Democratic Party 2006) 2000, Chair. 2000–; mem. Nat. Council of Slovak Repub. (NCSR) 1992–; Vittorino Colombo Award (Italy) 2000. *Publication:* Where There's a Will There's a Way. *Leisure interests:* family, sport, running a marathon. *Address:* Slovenská demokratická a krestanská únia-Demokratická strana (SDKÚ-DS), Ružinovská 28, 827 35 Bratislava, Slovakia (office). *Telephone:* (2) 4341-4102 (office). *Fax:* (2) 4341-4106 (office). *E-mail:* sdku@sdkuonline.sk (office). *Website:* www.sdkuonline.sk (office).

E

EAGLEBURGER, Lawrence Sidney, BS, MS; American lawyer and fmr government official; *Senior Public Policy AdvisEr, Baker, Donelson, Bearman, Caldwell & Berkowitz PC;* b. 1 Aug. 1930, Milwaukee, Wis.; s. of late Dr Leon S. and Helen M. Eagleburger; m. Marlene Ann Heinemann 1966; three s.; ed Univ. of Wis.; joined US foreign service 1957; Third Sec., Tegucigalpa, Honduras 1957–59; Dept of State 1959–62; Second Sec., Belgrade, Yugoslavia 1962–65; Dept of State 1965–66; mem. Nat. Security Council staff 1966–67; Special Asst to Under-Sec. of State 1967–68; Exec. Asst to Asst to Pres. for Nat. Security Affairs 1969; Politicial Adviser, US Mission to NATO 1969–71; Deputy Asst Sec. of Defense, Internal Security Affairs 1971–72, Acting Asst Sec. of Defense, Internal Security Affairs 1973, Exec. Asst to Sec. of State 1973–77; Deputy Asst to Pres. for Nat. Security Operations 1973; Deputy Under-Sec. of State for Man., Exec. Asst to Sec. of State 1975–77; Amb. to Yugoslavia 1977–81; Asst Sec. of State for European Affairs 1981–82, Under-Sec. of State for Political Affairs 1982–84; Deputy Sec. of State 1989–92 (Envoy to Israel during Gulf Conflict 1991); Acting Sec. of State Aug.–Dec. 1992, Sec. of State Dec. 1992–Jan. 1993; Prof. (part-time) Univ. of S Carolina 1984 (Distinguished Visiting Prof. of Int. Studies 1984), Univ. of Va (part-time) 1993–; Sr Public Policy Adviser, Baker, Donelson, Bearman, Caldwell & Berkowitz PC (law firm) 1993–; Pres. Kissinger Assoca Inc. 1984–89; mem. Iraq Study Group, US Inst. of Peace 2006; mem. Bd of Dirs Halliburton Co., Phillips Petroleum Co., Universal Corpn, Comsat; Hon. KBE 1995; Hon. LLD (S Carolina) 1985, (George Washington Univ.) 1986; President's Award for Distinguished Civil Service, Dept of Defense Distinguished Service Medal. *Address:* Baker, Donelson, Bearman, Caldwell & Berkowitz PC, 555 11th Street, NW, Washington, DC 20004, USA (office). *Telephone:* (202) 508-3450 (office). *Fax:* (202) 220-2250 (office). *E-mail:* leagleburger@bakerdonelson.com (office). *Website:* www.bakerdonelson.com (office).

EAGLETON, Terence (Terry) Francis, PhD, FBA; British academic; *John Edward Taylor Professor of English Literature, University of Manchester;* b. 22 Feb. 1943, Salford, Lancs.; s. of Francis Paul Eagleton and Rosaleen Riley; m. 1st Elizabeth Rosemary Galpin 1966 (divorced 1976); two s.; m. 2nd Willa Murphy 1996; one s. one d.; ed Trinity Coll., Cambridge; Fellow in English, Jesus Coll., Cambridge 1964–69; Tutorial Fellow, Wadham Coll., Oxford 1969–89; Lecturer in Critical Theory and Fellow of Linacre Coll., Oxford 1989–92; Thomas Warton Prof. of English Literature and Fellow of St Catherine's Coll., Oxford 1992–2001; fmr Prof. of Cultural Theory, Univ. of Manchester, currently John Edward Taylor Prof. of English Literature; Hon. DLitt (Salford) 1994; Dr hc (Nat. Univ. of Ireland) 1995, (Santiago di Compostela) 1997; Irish Sunday Tribune Arts Award 1990. *Film:* screenplay for Wittgenstein. *Plays:* St Oscar 1989, Disappearances 1998. *Publications:* Criticism and Ideology 1976, Marxism and Literary Criticism 1976, Literary Theory: an Introduction 1983, The Function of Criticism 1984, The Rape of Clarissa 1985, Against the Grain 1986, William Shakespeare 1986, The Ideology of the Aesthetic 1990, Ideology: An Introduction 1993, The Crisis of Contemporary Culture 1993, Heathcliff and the Great Hunger 1995, The Illusions of Postmodernism 1996, Literary Theory 1996, Crazy John and the Bishop and Other Essays on Irish Culture 1998, Scholars and Rebels in Ireland 1999, The Idea of Culture 2000, The Gatekeeper (autobiog.) 2001, Sweet Violence: The Idea of the Tragic 2002, Figures of Dissent (essays) 2003, After Theory 2003, The English Novel: An Introduction 2004, Holy Terror 2005, The Meaning of Life 2007; contribs to periodicals incl. London Review of Books. *Leisure interest:* Irish music. *Address:* Department of English and American Studies, University of Manchester, Manchester, M13 9PL, England (office). *Telephone:* (161) 275-3146 (office). *Fax:* (161) 275-3256 (office). *E-mail:* english@man.ac.uk (office). *Website:* www.art.man.ac.uk/english (office).

EAGLING, Wayne John; Canadian ballet dancer and choreographer; s. of Eddie Eagling and Thelma Eagling; ed P. Ramsey Studio of Dance Arts, Royal Ballet School; Sr Prin., Royal Ballet 1975–91; Artistic Dir Dutch Nat. Ballet 1991–2003; freelance choreographer 2003–. *Ballet roles include:* danced lead roles in Sleeping Beauty, Swan Lake, Cinderella and other major classics; created roles include: Young Boy in Triad, Solo Boy in Gloria, Ariel in The Tempest, Woyzeck in Different Drummer; choreographed The Hunting of the Snark and Frankenstein, The Modern Prometheus, Ruins of Time 1993, Symphony in Waves 1994, Alma Mahler (for La Scala, Milan) 1994, Duet 1995, Lost Touch 1995, Nutcracker and Mouseking (with Toer van Schayk) 1996, The Last Emperor (for Hong Kong Ballet) 1998, Magic Flute (with Toer van Schayk) 1999, Le Sacré du Printemps 2000, Mary Stuart (Rome Opera) 2004. *Publication:* The Company We Keep (with Ross MacGibbon and Robert Jude) 1981. *Leisure interests:* golf, scuba diving, tennis. *Address:* Overtoom 21, Apt #4, 1054 HA Amsterdam, Netherlands (home). *Telephone:* (20) 6168164 (home). *Fax:* (20) 6168164 (home). *E-mail:* weagling@xs4all.nl (home).

EAMES, Baron (Life Peer), cr. 1995, of Armagh in the County of Armagh; **Most Rev. Robert Henry Alexander Eames,** LLD, PhD, OM, DD; British ecclesiastic; b. 27 April 1937; s. of William E. Eames and Mary E. T. Eames; m. Ann C. Daly 1966; two s.; ed Methodist Coll., Belfast, Queen's Univ., Belfast and Trinity Coll., Dublin; Research Scholar and Tutor, Faculty of Laws, Queen's Univ., Belfast 1960–63; Asst Curate, Bangor Parish Church 1963–66; Rector, St Dorothea's, Belfast 1966–74; Examining Chaplain to Bishop of Down 1973; Rector, St Mark's, Dunelda 1974–75; Bishop of Derry and Raphoe 1975–80; Bishop of Down and Dromore 1980–86; Archbishop of Armagh and Primate of All Ireland 1986–2006 (retd); Select Preacher, Oxford Univ. 1986–87, Cambridge Univ. 1989; Irish Rep., Anglican Consultative Council 1984, mem. Standing Cttee 1985; Chair. Archbishop of Canterbury's Comm. on Communion and Women in the Episcopate 1988–, Comm. on Inter-Anglican Relations 1988–, Anglican Int. Doctrinal Comm. (USA) 1991; Chair. Consultative Group on the Past (NI) 2007–08; Gov. Church Army 1985–; Hon. LLD (Queen's Univ. Belfast) 1989, (Trinity Coll. Dublin) 1992, (Lancaster) 1994; Dr hc (Cambridge) 1994, (Open Univ.) 2008; Hon. DD (Exeter) 1999. *Publications:* A Form of Worship for Teenagers 1965, The Quiet Revolution: Irish Disestablishment 1970, Through Suffering 1973, Thinking through Lent 1978, Through Lent 1984, Chains to be Broken 1992; contribs to New Divinity, Irish Legal Quarterly, Criminal Law Review, Northern Ireland Legal Quarterly, Univ. Review and The Furrow. *Leisure interests:* sailing, rugby, football, reading. *Address:* House of Lords, London SW1A 0PW, England (office); 3 Downshire Crescent, Hillsborough, Co. Down, BT26 6DD, Ireland (home). *Telephone:* (28) 9268-9913.

EANES, Gen. António dos Santos Ramalho; Portuguese politician and army officer; b. 25 Jan. 1935, Alcains; s. of Manuel dos Santos Eanes and Maria do Rosario Ramalho; m. Maria Manuela Duarte Neto Portugal 1970; two s.; ed High School, Castelo Branco, Higher Inst. of Applied Psychology, Lisbon Faculty of Law; enlisted in Army School 1953; Commissioned to Portuguese India 1958–60, Macao 1960–62, Mozambique 1962–64, Operations Officer of Light Infantry Battalion, Mozambique 1966–67, Information Officer, Portuguese Guinea (Guinea-Bissau) 1969–73, Angola 1973–74; Physical Education Instructor, Mil. Acad. 1968; Dir of Dept of Cultural and Recreational Affairs 1973; rank of Second Lt 1957, Lt 1959, Capt. 1961, Maj. 1970, Gen. 1978; involved in leadership of mil. movts finally contesting mil. apparatus and colonial wars 1968–74; after April Revolution named to first 'Ad-hoc' Cttee for mass media June 1974; Dir of Programmes of Portuguese TV June–Sept. 1974, Chair. of Bd of Dirs of TV co., resigned after accusation of 'probable implication' in abortive counter-coup March 1975, cleared after inquiry; rank of Lt-Col; mem. Cttee restructuring 5th Div., Gen. Staff Armed Forces; Army Chief of Staff (with temporary rank of Gen.) 1975–76; mem. of Mil. Cttee of Council of Revolution; responsible for Constitutional Law approved Dec. 1975; Col 1976; Pres. of Portugal 1976–86; Chair. of Council of Revolution; C-in-C of Armed Forces 1976–80, 1980–81; Leader, Portuguese Democratic Renewal Party 1986–87; mem. Council of State; War Cross 2nd class, Silver Medal for Distinguished Services with Palm, Silver Medal for Exemplary Behaviour, Commemorative Medal of the Portuguese Armed Forces, Degree of Kt of Mil. Order of Avis. *Leisure interests include:* playing bridge. *Address:* c/o Círculo Português de Bridge, Avenida 5 Outobro, 4, 1200 Lisbon, Portugal. *Website:* www.circulobridge.pt.

EARL, Belinda Jane, BSc; British retail executive; *Group CEO, Jaeger Group Ltd;* b. 20 Dec. 1961, Plymouth; d. of the late Colin Lee and of Diana Lee; m. David Mark Earl 1985; two s.; ed Univ. of Wales, Aberystwyth; Controller, Fashion Div., Harrods 1983–85; Buying and Merchandising Dir, Debenhams 1985–97, Trading Dir 1997–2000, mem. Exec. Cttee 1998, mem. Bd of Dirs 1999, CEO 2000–03; Group CEO Jaeger Group Ltd 2004–; Chair. Skillsmart 2002, Patron 2005–; Fellow, City and Guilds 2006–. *Address:* Jaeger, 57 Broadwick Street, London, W1F 9QS, England (office). *Telephone:* (20) 7200-4000 (office). *Fax:* (20) 7200-4004 (office). *Website:* www.jaeger.co.uk (office).

EARL, Robert I.; American business executive; *Chairman and CEO, Planet Hollywood International Inc.;* b. 1952; f. President Entertainment (theme restaurants) 1977, sold co. to Pleasurama PLC, joined Pleasurama man. team, Man. Hard Rock Cafe PLC 1987–93; CEO and Dir Planet Hollywood Int. 1993–2000, Chair. Bd 1998–. *Address:* Planet Hollywood International Inc., 7598 West Sand Lake Road, Orlando, FL 32819, USA (office). *Telephone:* (407) 903-5500 (office). *Fax:* (407) 352-7310 (office). *E-mail:* general_information@planethollywood.com (office). *Website:* www.planethollywood.com (office).

EARNHARDT, Dale, Jr; American racing driver; b. 10 Oct. 1974, Kannapolis, NC; s. of the late Dale Earnhardt (died 2001); grand s. of Ralph Earnhardt; began driving career age 17; competed in street stock div., Concord (NC) Speedway; drives Budweiser No. 8 Chevrolet; winner of two Championships and 13 races in Busch Series 1998–2000; became first third-generation NASCAR Champion after winning Busch Series Title 1998, 1999; moved into NASCAR Nextel Cup circuit 2000; raced Winston Cup circuit with father 2000; opened Daytona Speedweeks with father as mems of same team 2001; 15 victories in 183 Cup starts 2000–04; winner Atlanta, Bristol, Daytona and Tex. NASCAR Nextel Cups 2004, Budweiser Shootout 2004, The Winston 2004, USG Sheetrock 400 2005; co-Owner Chance2 Team, winning Busch Series Championships 2004; f. JR Motorsports LLC; appeared in music videos for Sheryl Crow, Three Doors Down; named one of Top 100 Celebrities, Forbes Magazine. *Publications:* Driver No. 8 2002. *Leisure interests:* collecting street cars and race cars, computer games. *Address:* JR Motorsports LLC, Mooresville, NC 28115, USA (office). *Telephone:* (704) 799-4800 (office). *Fax:* (704) 799-4801 (office). *E-mail:* Info@jrmotorsport.com (office). *Website:* www.jrmotorsport.com (office).

EASLEY, Michael F., JD, BA; American state official; b. 23 March 1950, Rocky Mount, NC; m. Mary Pipines; one s.; ed Univ. of NC, NC Cen. Univ. School of Law; Dist Attorney, 13th Dist, NC 1982–91; pvt. practice, Southport, NC 1991–92; NC Attorney-Gen. 1993–2000; Gov. of NC 2000–09; Pres. NC Conf. of Dist Attorneys; mem. NC Dist Attorneys Asscn; Democrat; Public Services Award, US Dept of Justice 1984. *Leisure interests:* hunting, sailing, woodwork. *Address:* Democratic National Committee, 430 South Capitol Street, SE, Washington, DC 20003, USA (office). *Telephone:* (202) 863-8000 (office). *Fax:* (202) 863-8174 (office). *Website:* www.democrats.org (office).

EAST, Rt Hon. Paul Clayton, PC, QC, LLM; New Zealand politician, lawyer and diplomatist; b. 1946, Opotiki; s. of Edwin Cuthbert East and Edith Pauline Addison East; m. Marilyn Therese Kottmann 1972; three d.; ed Univ. of Virginia School of Law, Univ. of Auckland School of Law, King's Coll.; law clerk, Morpeth Gould & Co., Auckland 1968–70; Pnr, East Brewster Solicitors, Rotorua 1974–; fmr Rotorua City Councillor and Deputy Mayor; Nat. Party MP for Rotorua 1978–96; Attorney-Gen., Minister responsible for Serious Fraud Office and Audit Dept 1990–97, Leader of the House 1990–93, Minister of Crown Health Enterprises 1991–96, for State Services 1993–97, for Defence and War Pensions 1996–97, for Corrections 1996–97; High Commr in UK (also accred to Nigeria and Ireland) 1999–2002. *Leisure interests:* fishing, skiing, golf. *Address:* 23 Sophia Street, PO Box 608, Rotorua, New Zealand. *E-mail:* pauleastnz@hotmail.com (home).

EASTCOTT, Harry Hubert Grayson, MS, FRCS, FRCOG; British surgeon; *Consultant Surgeon Emeritus, St Mary's Hospital London;* b. 17 Oct. 1917, Montreal, Canada; s. of Henry George Eastcott and Gladys Eastcott (née Tozer); m. Doreen Joy Mittell 1941; four d.; ed Latymer School, London and Medical Schools at St Mary's Hosp., London, Middlesex Hosp., London and Harvard Medical School USA; Jr resident appointments 1941–43; Surgeon Lt RNVR 1944–46; Sr Surgical Registrar St Mary's Hosp., London 1947–50, Asst Dir Surgical Unit of Medical School 1950–54, Consultant Surgeon 1955–82, Emer. 1982–; Consultant Surgeon Royal Masonic Hosp., London 1964–80; King Edward VII Hosp. for Officers, London 1965–87; in Surgery and Vascular Surgery RN 1957–82; Pres. Medical Soc., London 1976 (Sec. 1963, Trustee 1987), Section of Surgery, Royal Soc. of Medicine 1977 (Sec. 1963), United Services Section 1980–82, Int. Vascular Symposium, London 1981; Sr Vice-Pres. Royal Coll. of Surgeons 1982 (mem. Ct. of Examiners 1964–70, mem. Council 1971–83, Jr Vice-Pres. 1981–83, mem. Court of Patrons 1997); fmr Examiner in Surgery Univs. of London, Cambridge, Lagos and Queen's, Belfast; Hunterian Professorship R.C.S. 1953; Editorial Sec. British Journal of Surgery 1972–78; Hon. FACS 1977; Hon. FRACS 1978; Hon. Fellow American Surgical Asscn 1981; Hon. mem. Soc. for Vascular Surgery, USA 1974, Purkinje Soc., Czechoslovakia 1984, Int. Union of Angiology 1995, European Soc. for Vascular Surgery 1995; Hon. mem. and Hippocratic Orator, Hellenic Medical Soc. 1986; Fothergillian Gold Medal, Medical Soc. of London 1974, Cecil Joll Prize, Royal Coll. of Surgeons 1983, Galen Medal of Worshipful Soc. of Apothecaries 1993, Leriche Prize, Int. Surgical Soc. 2001; several memorial lectures. *Achievements:* first successful repair of obstructed internal carotid artery for recurring strokes. *Publications:* Arterial Surgery 1969, 1973, 1993, A Colour Atlas of Operations upon the Internal Carotid Artery 1984; contrib. to Lancet. *Leisure interests:* music, travel, aeronautics, gardening. *Address:* 16 White Cross Road, Haddenham, Bucks., HP17 8BA, England. *Telephone:* (1844) 290629.

EASTMAN, Dean Eric, PhD; American physicist, science policy consultant, data processing executive and academic; *Professor, Department of Physics and James Franck Institute, University of Chicago;* b. 21 Jan. 1940, Oxford, Wis.; m. Ella Mae Staley 1979; Research Staff mem. IBM, Yorktown Heights, NY 1963–74, Man. Surface Physics and Photo-emission 1971–82, Dir Advanced Packaging Tech. Lab. and Sr Man. III-V Semi-conductor Packaging Tech. & Systems Dept and GaAs Devices and Tech. Dept 1982–85, STD Dir of Devt and Product Assurance 1985–86, IBM Research Vice-Pres. of System Tech. and Science 1986–94, IBM Dir Hardware Devt Re-Eng 1994–95, IBM Server Group Vice-Pres. Devt Re-Eng and Tech. Strategy 1996–98; Prof., Dept of Physics and James Franck Inst., Univ. of Chicago 1998–; Govt Adviser to numerous science orgs.; Fellow American Physical Soc.; mem. NAS, Nat. Acad. of Eng; IBM Fellow 1974–; APS Oliver E. Buckley Prize 1980. *Publications:* numerous articles on solid state physics in professional journals. *Address:* Department of Physics, JFI Box 15 - RI 231, University of Chicago, 5801 S. Ellis Avenue, Chicago, IL 60637 (office); 806 Pines Bridge Road, Ossining, NY 10562, USA (home). *Telephone:* (773) 834-0988 (office). *Fax:* (773) 834-3444 (office). *E-mail:* d-eastman@uchicago.edu (office). *Website:* physics.uchicago.edu (office).

EASTMAN, Ernest, MIA; Liberian politician and diplomatist; b. 27 March 1930, Monrovia; s. of H. Nathan Eastman and Adeline Payne; m. Salma Mohammedali; four s. five d.; ed Coll. of West Africa, Oberlin Coll., Ohio, Columbia Univ., New York; Dir Bureau of Afro-Asian Affairs (Dept of State) 1957–64; Under-Sec. of State for Admin. 1964–67; Under-Sec. of State 1968–72; Amb. to East Africa (Kenya, Lesotho, Madagascar, Tanzania, Uganda, Zambia) 1972–74; Amb. to the Far East (Japan, Repub. of Korea, Democratic People's Repub. of Korea, Philippines, Indonesia, India) 1974–77; Sec.-Gen. Mano River Union (Economic and Customs Union for the Repubs of Liberia, Sierra Leone and Guinea) 1977–83; Minister of Foreign Affairs 1983–85; mem. special missions to the Presidents of Dahomey, Niger, Guinea, Ivory Coast, Gambia and USA; mem. official del. to several int. confs of the OAU, UN and Non-Aligned Movt; several decorations including Kt Great Band, Humane Order of African Redemption, several European and African decorations. *Publications:* A History of the State of Maryland in Liberia 1957; many newspaper articles on int affairs. *Address:* c/o Ministry of Foreign Affairs, POB 9002, Monrovia, Liberia.

EASTMAN, John; American lawyer; *CEO, MPL Communications, Inc.;* b. 1940, New York; s. of late Lee Eastman; brother of Linda McCartney (died 1998); m. Jodie Eastman; three c.; ed Stanford Univ. and New York Univ.; worked for Senate Commerce Cttee 1963; Office of US Attorney, New York; took part in Robert Kennedy's 1968 presidential election campaign; with father founded Eastman & Eastman (law firm); specializes in contract and copyright law; represents many leading showbusiness and media personalities; currently CEO MPL Communications (McCartney Productions Ltd); fmr Dir Apple Corps Ltd Linda McCartney Foods; Trustee American Museum of Natural History; fmr Trustee Smith Coll. *Leisure interests:* collecting pictures, 19th-century English literature. *Address:* MPL Communications, Inc., 41 West 54th Street, New York, NY 10019, USA (office). *Telephone:* (212) 246-5881 (office). *Fax:* (212) 246-7852 (office). *Website:* www.mplcommunications .com (office).

EASTON, David, MA, PhD, FRSC; Canadian political scientist and academic; *Distinguished Research Professor of Political Science, University of California, Irvine;* b. 24 June 1917, Toronto; s. of Albert Easton and Mary Easton; m. Sylvia Johnstone 1942 (died 1990); one s.; ed Univ. of Toronto and Harvard Univ.; Teaching Fellow, Dept of Govt, Harvard Univ. 1944–47; Asst Prof., Dept of Political Science, Univ. of Chicago 1947–53, Assoc. Prof. 1953–55, Prof. 1955–, Andrew MacLeish Distinguished Service Prof. 1969–82, Prof. Emer. 1982–; Sir Edward Peacock Prof. of Political Science, Queen's Univ., Kingston, Ont. 1971–80; Distinguished Prof. of Political Science, Univ. of California, Irvine 1981–, Distinguished Faculty Lectureship for Research 1997; Ford Rotating Research Prof., Univ. of California, Berkeley 1960–61; Pres. American Political Science Asscn 1968–69; mem. Int. Cttee on Social Science Documentation 1969–71; Chair. Bd Trustees Acad. of Ind. Scholars 1979–81; Co-Chair. Western Center, American Acad. of Arts and Sciences 1984–90, Vice-Pres. of Acad. 1984–90; Fellow, Center for Advanced Study in the Behavioral Sciences, Stanford 1957–58, American Acad. of Arts and Sciences 1962–; Hon. LLD (McMaster) 1970, (Kalamazoo) 1972; Hon. DPhil (Freie Universität, Berlin) 2001; Int. Alexander von Humboldt Research Prize 1995, Lauds and Laurels Distinguished Research Award, Univ. of Calif., Irvine 1995, David Easton Award est. by American Political Science Foundation (Foundations of Political Theory Section) 1996, Public Policy Studies Org. Thomas R. Dye Service Award 1997, Panunzio Award, Univ. of Calif. 2005–06. *Publications:* The Political System: An Inquiry into the State of Political Science 1953, A Framework for Political Analysis 1965, A Systems Analysis of Political Life 1965, Varieties of Political Theory (ed.) 1966, Children in the Political System: Origins of Political Legitimacy (with J. Dennis) 1969, The Analysis of Political Structure 1990, Divided Knowledge: Across Disciplines, Across Cultures (co-ed.) 1991, The Development of Political Science (co-ed.) 1991, Regime and Discipline (co-ed.) 1995; plus several reports of educ. cttees chaired by him. *Address:* University of California, Department of Political Science, 4251 Social Sciences Plaza B, Mail Code 5100, Irvine, CA 92697, USA (office). *Telephone:* (949) 824-6132 (office). *Fax:* (949) 824-8762 (office); (949) 824-5180 (office). *E-mail:* d2easton@oac.uci.edu (office). *Website:* www.polisci .uci.edu (office).

EASTON, Sheena; British singer and actress; b. (Sheena Shirley Orr), 27 April 1959, Bellshill, Scotland; m. 1st Rob Light 1985; m. 2nd Tim Delarm 1997; two c.; ed Royal Scottish Acad. of Music and Drama; singer Glasgow club circuit 1979; career launched by appearance on TV show, The Big Time (BBC 1) 1980; solo recording artist 1980–; numerous concerts and tours worldwide, TV appearances; Grammy Award for Best New Artist 1981, for Best Mexican/ American Performance (with Luis Miguel) 1985, Emmy Award (for Sheena Easton... Act 1) 1983. *Television appearances include:* Miami Vice (series) 1987–88, Body Bags 1993, The Highlander 1993, The Adventure of Brisco County Jr 1993, TekWar 1995, Gargoyles 1995–96, Outer Limits 1996, Road Rovers 1996, All Dogs go to Heaven 1996–97, Duckman 1997, Chicken Soup for the Soul 1999, The Legend of Tarzan 2001, Young Blades 2005. *Stage appearance:* Man of La Mancha (Chicago, then Broadway) 1991–92, The Colors of Christmas 2001. *Recordings include:* albums: Take My Time 1981, You Could Have Been With Me 1981, Madness, Money And Music 1982, Best Kept Secret 1983, A Private Heaven 1985, Do You 1985, The Lover In Me 1989, The Collection 1989, What Comes Naturally 1991, No Strings 1993, My Cherie 1995, Body And Soul 1997, Freedom 2000, Fabulous 2000. *Address:* Harriet Wasserman Management, 15250 Ventura Blvd, Suite 1215, Sherman Oaks, CA 91403-3201, USA (office). *Website:* www.sheenaeaston.com.

EASTWOOD, Clint; American actor and film director; b. 31 May 1930, San Francisco; s. of Clinton Eastwood and Ruth Eastwood; m. 1st Maggie Johnson 1953 (divorced); one s. one d.; one d. by Frances Fisher 1993; m. 2nd Dina Ruiz 1996; one d.; ed Los Angeles City Coll.; worked as lumberjack in Ore.; served in US Army; appeared in TV series Rawhide 1959–65; Owner Malpaso Productions 1969–; Owner Mission Ranch Resort, Carmel, Calif.; Co-Chair. UNESCO Campaign to protect the world's film heritage; mem. Nat. Arts Council 1973; Mayor of Carmel, Calif. 1986–88; Co-founder and Pnr, Tehama Inc. (sportswear co.) 1997–; Vice-Chair. Calif. State Parks and Recreation Comm.; Fellow, BFI 1993; Légion d'honneur, Commdr des Arts et des Lettres; Hon. DFA (Wesleyan) 2000, Hon. DLit (Univ. of Southern California) 2007; numerous awards including Irving G. Thalberg Award 1995, Lifetime Achievement Award, American Film Inst. 1996, Kennedy Center Honors, John F. Kennedy Center Performing Arts 2000, Lifetime Achievement Award, Screen Actors Guild 2003, Broadcast Film Critics Asscn 2004, Lifetime Achievement Award, Dirs Guild of America 2006, Jack Valenti Humanitarian Award, Motion Picture Asscn of America 2007. *Films include:* Revenge of the Creature 1955, Francis in the Navy 1955, Lady Godiva 1955, Tarantula 1955, Never Say Goodbye 1956, The First Travelling Saleslady 1956, Star in the Dust 1956, Escapade in Japan 1957, Ambush at Cimarron Pass 1958, Lafayette Escadrille 1958, A Fistful of Dollars 1964, For a Few Dollars More 1965, The Good, the Bad and the Ugly 1966, The Witches 1967, Hang 'Em High 1968, Coogan's Bluff 1968, Where Eagles Dare 1969, Paint Your Wagon 1969, Kelly's Heroes 1970, Two Mules for Sister Sara 1970, The Beguiled 1971, Play Misty for Me (also dir) 1971, Dirty Harry 1971, Joe Kidd 1972, High Plains Drifter (also dir) 1973, Magnum Force 1973, Breezy (dir) 1973, Thunderbolt and Lightfoot 1974, The Eiger Sanction (also dir) 1975, The Outlaw Josey Wales (also dir) 1976, The Enforcer 1976, The Gauntlet (also dir) 1978, Every Which Way But Loose 1978, Escape from Alcatraz 1979, Bronco Billy (also dir) 1980, Any Which Way You Can 1980, Firefox (also dir) 1982, Honky Tonk Man (also dir) 1982, Sudden Impact (also dir) 1983, Tightrope 1984, City Heat 1984, Pale Rider 1985 (also dir), Heartbreak Ridge 1986 (also dir), Bird 1988 (Golden Globe Award for Best Dir 1989), The Dead Pool 1988, Pink Cadillac 1989, White Hunter, Black Heart (also dir) 1989, The Rookie (also dir) 1990, Unforgiven (also dir) (Acad. Awards for Best Film and Best Dir 1993) 1992, In the Line of Fire 1993, A Perfect World (also dir) 1993, The Bridges of Madison County (also dir, producer) 1995, The Stars Fell on Henrietta (co-producer), Absolute Power (also dir) 1997, True Crime 1998, Midnight in the Garden of Good and Evil (dir) 1997, Space Cowboys (dir) 2000, Bloodwork (also dir and producer) 2002, Mystic River (dir) 2003, Million Dollar Baby (also dir and composer) (Special Filmmaking Achievement Award, Nat. Bd of Review of Motion Pictures, Best Dir, Golden Globe Awards, Dirs Guild of America Awards 2005, Best Film, Best Dir, Acad. Awards 2005) 2004, Flags of Our Fathers 2006, Letters from Iwo Jima (Nat. Bd of Review of Motion Pictures Best Film 2006, Los Angeles Film Critics Asscn Best Film 2006) 2006, Changeling 2008, Gran Torino (also dir) 2008. *Address:* c/o Leonard Hirshan, William Morris Agency, 1 William Morris Place, Beverly Hills, CA 90212; Malpaso Productions, c/o Warner Bros, 4000 Warner Blvd., Bldg 81, Burbank CA 91522, USA. *Telephone:* (818) 954-3367 (Malpaso).

EASTWOOD, Trevor, AM, BEng; Australian business executive; *Chairman, Wesfarmers Ltd;* ed Univ. of Western Australia, Advanced Man. Program at Harvard Business School, USA; began career with Westralian Farmers Co-operative Ltd 1963, held several man. positions until retirement in 1992, including Man. Dir Wesfarmers Ltd 1984–92, mem. Bd of Dirs 1994–, Chair. (non-exec.) 2002–; mem. Bd of Dirs The WCM Group Ltd; fmr Chair. West Australian Newspapers Holdings Ltd; fmr mem. Bd of Dirs Qantas Airways Ltd. *Address:* Wesfarmers Ltd, 11th Floor, Wesfarmers House, 40 The Esplanade, Perth 6000, WA, Australia (office). *Telephone:* (8) 9327-4211 (office). *Fax:* (8) 9327-4216 (office). *E-mail:* info@wesfarmers.com.au (office). *Website:* www.wesfarmers.com.au (office).

EATON, Fredrik Stefan, OC, BA, LLD; Canadian business executive and fmr diplomatist; *Chairman, White Raven Capital Corporation;* b. 26 June 1938, Toronto; s. of the late John David Eaton and Signy Hildur Stephenson; m. Catherine Martin 1962; one s. one d.; ed New Brunswick Univ.; joined The T. Eaton Co. Ltd and held various positions in Victoria, London, Toronto 1962–67, Dir 1967–69, Chair., Pres., CEO 1977–88, Chair. 1988–91; Pres., Dir Eaton's of Canada (parent co. of the other Eaton cos) 1969–77, Chair. Exec. Cttee 1994–97; High Commr in UK 1991–94; Chancellor Univ. of New Brunswick 1993–2003; currently Chair. White Raven Capital Corpn; Chair. Bd of Trustees, Canadian Museum of Civilization Corpn 2007–; Order of Canada 1990, Order of Ontario 2001; Hon. LLD (New Brunswick) 1983; Man. Award, McGill Univ. 1987. *Leisure interests:* art, music, reading, shooting, yachting. *Address:* White Raven Capital Corporation, 55 St Clair Avenue West, Suite 260, Toronto, ON M4V 2Y7, Canada (office). *Telephone:* (416) 929-3942 (office). *Fax:* (416) 925-4339 (office).

EATON, George, FCA; Irish chartered accountant; *Senior Partner, Eaton Neary;* b. 11 Jan. 1942, Cork; s. of Thomas J. V. Eaton and Catherine Hannon; m. Ellen Patricia O'Grady 1966; one d.; ed Christian Brothers Coll., Cork, Inst. of Chartered Accountants, Ireland; with Touche Ross, Chartered Accountants, Cork 1960–66; Chief Accountant, Seafield Fabrics, Youghal 1966–67; Deputy Man. Dir General Textiles 1967–75; Sr Pnr, Eaton Dowd (later Eaton Neary) 1976–; Chair. Portuguese Irish Chamber of Commerce 1987–89; Pres. Chambers of Commerce of Ireland 1985–87; Hon. Consul of Hungary 1990–. *Publication:* Introducing Ireland 1989. *Leisure interests:* history, genealogy, reading, book collecting. *Address:* Custume Place, Athlone, Ireland (office). *Telephone:* (9064) 78531 (office). *Fax:* (9064) 74691 (office). *E-mail:* companies@eatonneary.ie (office).

EATON, Robert J., BS; American automobile industry executive and engineer; *Chairman Emeritus, Chrysler Corporation;* b. 13 Feb. 1940, Arkansas City, Kansas; s. of Gene Eaton and Mildred Eaton; m. Connie Drake 1964; two s.; ed Univ. of Kansas; joined Gen. Motors (Chevrolet Motor Div.) 1963, transferred to eng staff 1971, Exec. Engineer 1974, Chief Engineer, Corp. Car Programs 1976, Asst Chief Engineer and Dir of Reliability at Oldsmobile 1979, Vice-Pres. in charge of Tech. Staffs 1986, Pres. Gen. Motors Europe 1988–92; COO Chrysler Motors Corpn 1992–93, Chair., CEO 1993–1998 (now Chair. Emer.), Co.-Chair., Co.-CEO Daimler Chrysler 1998–2000 (after 1998 merger of Chrysler with Daimler Benz); mem. Bd of Dirs Group Lotus 1986–, ChevronTexaco Corpn 2000–, Int. Paper Co.; mem. Industrial Advisory Bd Stanford Univ.; Fellow, Soc. of Automotive Engineers, Eng Soc. of Detroit; mem. Nat. Acad. of Eng; Contemporary Honors Award, Kansas Business Hall of Fame 2005 Chevalier du Tastevin 1989. *Leisure interests:* skiing, golf, hunting. *Address:* c/o Board of Directors, ChevronTexaco Corporation, 6001 Bollinger Canyon Road, San Ramon, CA 94583, USA.

EATWELL, Baron (Life Peer), cr. 1992, of Stratton St Margaret in the County of Wiltshire; **John Leonard Eatwell,** PhD; British academic; *President, Queens' College, Cambridge;* b. 2 Feb. 1945; s. of Harold Jack Eatwell and Mary Eatwell; m. 1st Hélène Seppain 1970 (divorced); two s. one d.; m. 2nd Elizabeth Digby 2006; ed Headlands Grammar School, Swindon, Queens' Coll. Cambridge, Harvard Univ., USA; Teaching Fellow, Grad. School of Arts and Sciences, Harvard Univ. 1968–69; Research Fellow, Queens' Coll. Cambridge 1969–70; Fellow, Trinity Coll. Cambridge 1970–96, Asst Lecturer, Faculty of Econs and Politics, Cambridge Univ. 1975–77, Lecturer 1977, currently Prof. of Financial Policy, Pres. Queens' Coll. 1997–; Visiting Prof. of Econs, New School for Social Research, New York 1982–96; Econ. Adviser to Neil Kinnock, Leader of Labour Party 1985–92; Opposition Spokesman on Treasury Affairs and on Trade and Industry, House of Lords 1992–93, Prin. Opposition Spokesman on Treasury and Econ. Affairs 1993–97; Trustee Inst. for Public

Policy Research 1988–95, Sec. 1988–97, Chair. 1997–; Dir (non-exec.) Anglia TV Group 1994–2001, Cambridge Econometrics Ltd 1996–2007; Chair. Extemporary Dance Theatre 1990, Crusaid 1993–98, British Screen Finance Ltd 1997–2000 and assoc. cos; Gov. Contemporary Dance Trust 1991–95; Dir Arts Theatre Trust, Cambridge 1991–98, Bd, Securities and Futures Authority 1997–2001; mem. Bd Royal Opera House 1998–2006; Chair. Royal Ballet 1998–2001, Commercial Radio Cos Asscn 2000–04, British Library Bd 2001–06, Royal Opera House Pension Scheme 2008–, Classic FM Consumer Panel 2008–; mem. Regulatory Decisions Cttee, FSA 2001–05; Dir Cambridge Endowment for Research in Finance 2002–; Gov. Royal Ballet School 2003–06; Dir (non-exec.) Rontech Ltd 2003–06, Artsworks Ltd 2007–, SAV Credit Ltd 2008–. *Publications:* An Introduction to Modern Economics (with Joan Robinson) 1973, Whatever Happened to Britain? 1982, Keynes's Economics and the Theory of Value and Distribution (ed. with Murray Milgate) 1983, The New Palgrave: A Dictionary of Economics, 4 Vols 1987, The New Palgrave Dictionary of Money and Finance, 3 Vols 1992 (both with Murray Milgate and Peter Newman), Transformation and Integration: Shaping the Future of Central and Eastern Europe (jtly) 1995, Global Unemployment: Loss of Jobs in the '90s (ed.) 1996, Not "Just Another Accession": The Political Economy of EU Enlargement to the East (jtly) 1997, Global Finance at Risk: Case for International Regulation (with L. Taylor) 2000, Hard Budgets, Soft States 2000, Social Policy Choices in Central and Eastern Europe 2002, International Capital Markets (with L. Taylor) 2002; articles in scientific journals. *Leisure interests:* classical and contemporary dance, Rugby Union football. *Address:* The President's Lodge, Queens' College, Cambridge, CB3 9ET, England (home). *Telephone:* (1223) 335556 (home). *Fax:* (1223) 335555 (home). *E-mail:* president@queens.cam.ac.uk (office).

EBADI, Shirin; Iranian lawyer, human rights activist and academic; b. 1947, Hamadan; d. of Mohammad Ali Ebadi; m.; two d.; ed Univ. of Tehran; apptd Judge (first and only woman) and Pres. of Tehran City Court 1974, forced to step down from bench after 1979 revolution, retd 1984; currently runs own law practice specializing in human rights; arrested on charges of "disturbing public opinion" 2000, received suspended sentence Sept. 2000; mem. Cttee for the Defence of Rights of the Victims of Serial Murders; Founder Society for Protecting the Rights of the Child, Centre for Defence of Human Rights; Lecturer in Law, Univ. of Tehran; Hon. LLD (Brown Univ.) 2004, (Univ. of British Columbia) 2004; Dr hc (Univ. of Maryland, College Park) 2004, (Univ. of Toronto) 2004, (Simon Fraser Univ.) 2004, (Univ. of Akureyri) 2004, (Australian Catholic Univ.) 2005, (Univ. of San Francisco) 2005, (Concordia Univ.) 2005, (Univ. of York) 2005, (Université Jean Moulin, Lyon) 2005, (Loyola Univ., Chicago) 2007, (New School Univ.) 2007; Human Rights Watch Award 1996, Rafto Prize 2001, Nobel Peace Prize (first Iranian and first Muslim woman) 2003, International Democracy Award 2004, Lawyer of the Year Award 2004, ranked 99th by Forbes magazine amongst 100 Most Powerful Women 2004, UCI Citizen Peacebuilding Award 2005, The Golden Plate Award, Academy of Achievement 2005. *Publications include:* The Rights of the Child: A Study of Legal Aspects of Children's Rights in Iran 1994, History and Documentation of Human Rights in Iran 2000, Iran Awakening 2006, Refugee Rights in Iran 2008; numerous other books and journal articles. *Address:* Society for Protecting the Rights of the Child, 26 Tenth Street, Nobakht Street, Tehran, Iran. *Website:* www.irsprc.org.

EBASHI, Setsuro, MD, PhD; Japanese biophysicist, pharmacologist and academic; *Professor Emeritus, National Institute for Physiological Sciences;* b. 31 Aug. 1922, Tokyo; s. of Haruyoshi Ebashi and Hisaji Ebashi; m. Fumiko Takeda 1956; ed Univ. of Tokyo; Prof. of Pharmacology, Faculty of Medicine, Univ. of Tokyo 1959–83, Prof. of Biophysics, Faculty of Science 1971–83, Prof. Emer. 1983–; Prof. Nat. Inst. for Physiological Sciences 1983–86, Dir-Gen. 1985–91, Prof. Emer. 1993–; Prof. Grad. Univ. for Advanced Studies 1988, Prof. Emer. 1993–; Pres. Okazaki Nat. Research Inst. 1991–93; Visiting Prof. Univ. of Calif. 1963, Harvard Univ. 1974; Pres. Int. Union of Pure and Applied Biophysics 1978–81, Int. Union of Pharmacology 1990–94; mem. Japan Acad., Sec.-Gen. 2000; Foreign Mem. Royal Soc., Academia Europaea; Foreign Assoc. NAS; Ed. Emer., Japan Acad. (PJA) Series B, Physical and Biological Sciences; Asahi Prize 1968; Imperial Prize, Japan Acad. 1972; Int. Prize for Biology 1999, Peter Harris Award 1986, Order of Cultural Merit (Bunka-Kunsho) 1975, Grand Cordon of Order of the Sacred Treasure 1995. *Publications:* articles in scientific journals. *Address:* 17-503, Nagaizumi Myodaiji, Okazaki 444-0864, Japan (home). *Telephone:* (564) 53-7345. *Fax:* (564) 52-3719. *E-mail:* ebashi@nips.ac.jp (home).

EBDANE, Hermogenes, Jr., BSc, MSc, PhD; Philippine politician; *Minister of Public Works and Highways;* b. 30 Dec. 1948, Candelaria, Zambales; m. Alma Cabanayan; three c.; ed Philippine Mil. Acad.; fmr Nat. Security Advisor and Dir Gen., Nat. Security Council; fmr Vice-Chair. Anti-Terrorism Task Force; fmr Nat. Anti-Terrorism Coordinator; fmr Dir Human Resources, Philippine Nat. Police, fmr Deputy Chief of Admin, Chief 2002–04; Sec. of Public Works and Highways 2004–07, 2008–, of Nat. Defense (acting) 2007; Philippine Legion of Honor, Distinguished Conduct Star, Bronze Cross Medal, numerous military honours. *Address:* Department of Public Works and Highways, DPWH Bldg, Bonifacio Drive, Port Area, Metro Manila, Philippines (office). *Telephone:* (2) 3043000 (office). *Fax:* (2) 5275635 (office). *E-mail:* pid@dpwh .gov.ph (office). *Website:* www.dpwh.gov.ph (office).

EBERHARTER, Stephan; Austrian skier; b. 24 March 1969, Brixlegg; Gold Medal, Super-G and Combined, World Championships, Saalbach 1991, Super-G, St Moritz, Switzerland 2003; Silver Medal, Super-G, World Champion-ships, St Anton 2001; Silver Medal, Giant Slalom, Olympic Games, Nagano, Japan 1998; Gold Medal, Giant Slalom, Olympics Games, Salt Lake City, USA 2002, Silver Medal, Super-G, Bronze Medal, Downhill; World Cup ranking (Gen.): Third 1998, Fourth 1999, Sixth 2000, Second 2001, First 2002, 2003,

Second 2004. *Leisure interests:* music, golf. *Address:* Stephan Eberharter, Dorfstrasse 21, 6272 Stumm i.Z., Austria. *E-mail:* wcroad@hotmail.com; designskiwcorg@hotmail.com. *Website:* www.skiworldcup.org.

EBERLE, Adm. Sir James Henry Fuller, GCB; British naval officer (retd); b. 31 May 1927, Bristol; s. of Victor Fuller Eberle, MC and Joyce Mary Eberle; m. Ann Patricia Thompson 1950 (died 1988); one s. two d.; ed Clifton Coll. and Royal Naval Coll., Dartmouth; served in Second World War at home, East Indies and Pacific 1944–45; served in Korean War, HMS Belfast and Fleet Staff Officer 1952–53; Sr officer, 100 Minesweeping Squadron 1958–59; Capt. HMS Intrepid 1968–70; Defence Fellow, Univ. Coll., Oxford 1970; promoted Rear-Adm. 1971; Flag Officer, Carriers and Amphibious Ships and Commdr NATO Striking Group Two 1975–76; mem. Admiralty Bd 1977–78; Commdr-in-Chief Fleet, Allied C-in-C Eastern Atlantic, C-in-C Channel 1979–80; C-in-C Naval Home Command 1981–82; retd 1983, rank of Adm.; Dir Royal Inst. of Int. Affairs 1984–90; Dir UK-Japan 2000 Group 1986–98; Chair. UK Asscn of Harriers and Beagles 1998–; mem. Bd Countryside Alliance 2002–; Hon. DLit (Bristol) 1989, (Sussex) 1992;Freeman of Bristol 1946, London 1982. *Publications:* Management in the Armed Forces 1972, Jim, First of the Pack 1982, Britain's Future in Space 1988. *Leisure interests:* tennis, field sports. *Address:* Homestead Farm, Houghton, Stockbridge, Hants., SO20 6LG, England (home). *Telephone:* (1264) 821659 (home). *E-mail:* admiraljim@lineone.net (home).

EBERT, Peter; British (naturalized) opera director; b. 6 April 1918, Frankfurt am Main, Germany; s. of the late Carl Ebert and Lucie Oppenheim; m. 1st Kathleen Havinden 1944; two d.; m. 2nd Silvia Ashmole 1951; five s. three d.; ed Salem School, Germany and Gordonstoun, Scotland; Intendant, Stadttheater Bielefeld, Germany 1973–75, Wiesbaden State Theatres 1975–77; Dir of Productions, Scottish Opera 1965–76, Gen. Admin. 1977–80; Producer, Guild Opera Co., Los Angeles 1962–76; Hon. DMus (St Andrews) 1979. *Television includes:* dir: As You Like It 1953, The Barber of Seville 1961; actor: Die Bombe tickt 1993, Sperling und das Loch in der Wand 1996. *Leisure interest:* building walls. *Address:* Col di Mura, 06010 Lippiano, Italy. *Telephone:* (075) 8502102. *Fax:* (075) 8502102.

EBERT, Tibor, BA; Hungarian writer, poet and dramatist; b. 14 Oct. 1926, Bratislava, Czechoslovakia; m. Eva Gati 1968; one d.; ed Ferenc Liszt Acad. of Music, Eötvös Lórand Univ., Budapest; Dramaturg József Attila Theatre, Budapest 1984–85; Ed.-in-Chief Agora Publrs, Budapest 1989–92; Ed. Hirvivo Literary Magazine 1990–92; mem. PEN Club, Asscn of Hungarian Writers, Literary Asscn Berzsenyi; Hon. mem. Franco-Hungarian Soc. 1980–; Order of Hungarian Repub. 1996; Bartók Prize 1987, Commemorative Medal, City of Pozsony-Pressburg-Bratislava 1991, Esterházy Prize 1993. *Plays:* Les Escaliers, Musique de Chambre, Demosthenes, Esterhaźy, Bartók, Attila, Le Rout Casimir et Olivier, Le Tableau. *Publications:* Mikrodrámák 1971, Rosarium 1987, Kobayashi 1989, Legenda egy fúvószenekarról 1990, Jób könyve 1991, Fagyott Orpheusz (poems) 1993, Esö 1996, Egy város glóriája 1997, Bartók 1997, Eredök 1998, Eltem 1998, Drámák 2000, Bolyongás 2001, Vecseruye 2001, Kaleidoszkóp 2002, Álmomban 2002, Feljegyzcśek 2004, Tüzfalau 2006, Vár 2006; contrib. numerous short stories, poems, dramas and essays to several leading Hungarian literary journals and magazines. *Address:* Csévi u 15c, 1025 Budapest, Hungary.

EBISAWA, Katsuji; Japanese broadcasting executive; *President, NHK (Japan Broadcasting Corporation);* b. 1934; joined NHK (Japan Broadcasting Corpn) 1957, held positions successively as political news reporter, Dir of Political News, Head of News Dept, Pres. NKH Enterprises 1991, Gen. Man.-Dir, Exec. Vice-Pres., Pres. 1997–; currently Pres. Asia–Pacific Broadcasting Union (ABU); mem. Bd of Dirs, Int. Council of the Nat. Acad. of TV Arts and Sciences (NATAS); hosted regional semi-finals for Int. Emmy Awards, Tokyo 1999; Int. Emmy Directorate Award, NATAS 2002. *Address:* NHK, 2-2-1 Jinnan, Shibuya, Tokyo 150-8001, Japan (office). *Telephone:* (3) 3465-1111 (office). *Fax:* (3) 3469-8110 (office). *Website:* www.nhk.or.jp (office).

EBTEKAR, Massoumeh, MSc, PhD, DSc; Iranian scientist, academic and politician; *Associate Professor of Immunology, Tarbiat Modares University;* b. 21 Sept. 1960, Tehran; d. of the late Prof. Taghi Ebtekar and Fatima Barzegar; m.; two c.; ed Shahid Beheshti Univ. and Tarbiat Modares Univ., Tehran; Ed.-in-Chief Keyhan Int. (English daily newspaper) 1981–83; Editorial Dir Farzaneh Journal of Women's Studies and Research; Founding mem. Centre for Women's Studies and Research 1986–; Dir Women's NGO Co-ordination Office, Tehran 1994–; Pres. Network of Women's NGOs in the Islamic Repub. of Iran 1995–; Faculty mem. School of Medical Science, Tarbiat Modares Univ. 1989–95, Asst Prof. of Immunology 1995–2006, Assoc. Prof. 2006–; Vice-Pres. of Iran and Head of Dept of the Environment (first female Vice-Pres.) 1997–2005; Founder and Head, Centre for Peace and the Environment, Tehran 2005–; mem. Tehran City Council 2007–, est. and Head of Environment Cttee, currently runs 20 working groups on environmental issues; del., vice-chair. or chair. numerous int. confs on women; Champion of the Earth Award, UNEP 2006, Distinguished Researcher 2007. *Publications include:* book: Natural Peace and Ethics; contribs to Farzaneh Journal of Women's Studies and numerous int. journals. *Leisure interests:* swimming, reading, blogging. *Address:* Faculty of Medical Sciences, Tarbiat Modares University, Intersection of Chamran and Ale-Ahmad Highways, PO Box 14115-331, Tehran (office); City Council, Behesht Avenue, Tehran, Iran (office). *Telephone:* (21) 82883891 (office); (21) 55893613 (home). *Fax:* (21) 88013030 (office). *E-mail:* Ebtekarm@modares.ac.ir (office); ebtekarm@gmail.com (home). *Website:* www.modares.ac.ir/med/Ebtekarm (office); ebtekarm .blogspot.com (home).

ECCLESTON, Christopher; British actor; b. 16 Feb. 1964, Salford; s. of Joseph Ronald Eccleston and Elsie Lavinia Eccleston. *Films include:* Let Him Have It 1991, Shallow Grave 1995, Jude 1996, Elizabeth 1998, A Price Above Rubies 1998, Heart 1999, Old New Borrowed Blue 1999, Existenz 1999, Gone in 60 Seconds 2000, The Invisible Circus 2001, The Others 2001, I am Dina 2002, 28 Days Later 2002, The Seeker: The Dark Is Rising 2007. *Theatre includes:* Miss June 2000. *Television appearances:* Cracker 1993–94, Hearts and Minds 1995, Our Friends in the North 1996, Hillsborough 1996, Strumpet 2001, Flesh and Blood (Best Actor, Royal TV Soc. Awards 2003) 2002, The Second Coming (TV film) 2003, Doctor Who (BBC) 2005, Perfect Parents 2006, Heroes 2007. *Leisure interest:* supporting Manchester United Football Club. *Address:* c/o Claire Maroussas, Independent Talent Group, Oxford House, 76 Oxford Street, London, W1D 1BF, England (office). *Website:* www .independenttalent.com (office).

ECCLESTONE, Bernard (Bernie), BSc; British business executive; *CEO, Formula One Management Ltd;* b. Oct. 1930; m. 1st; one d.; m. 2nd Slavica Ecclestone; two d.; ed Woolwich Polytechnic, London; est. car and motorcycle dealership, Midweek Car Auctions, Bexley, Kent; racing-car driver for short period (Formula 3); owner Connaught racing team 1957; Man. Jochen Rindt; purchased Brabham racing team 1970 (sold 1990); CEO Formula One Admin. Ltd, CEO Formula One Management Ltd; Vice-Pres. Fed. Int. de l'Automobile (FIA) (racing's int. governing body); Grand Decoration of Honour, Austria, Medal of the First Degree, Bahrain, Keys to the Cities of Sao Paulo and Rio de Janeiro, Bandeirante Medal, Sao Paulo, Order of Merit of the Medium Cross, Hungary, Grand Officier of the Order of Merit, Italy, Silver gilt and Silver grade medals, Monaco, Motorsport Industry Asscn Business Achievement Award, British Racing Driver's Club inaugural Gold Medal, Grand Officer of the Equestrian Order of Saint Agata, Republic of San Marino. *Address:* c/o Formula One Management Limited, 6 Prince's Gate, London, SW7 1QJ, England. *Telephone:* (20) 7584-6668. *Fax:* (20) 7589-0311. *E-mail:* ckai@fomltd .com. *Website:* www.formula1.com.

ECHANDI JIMÉNEZ, Mario, LLD; Costa Rican politician and diplomatist; b. 1915, San José; s. of Alberto Echandi and Josefa Jiménez; ed Univ. de Costa Rica; legal career 1938–47; Sec.-Gen. Partido Unión Nacional 1947; Amb. to USA 1950–51, 1966–68; Minister for Foreign Affairs 1951–53; Pres. of Costa Rica 1958–62; defeated cand. in presidential election 1970. *Address:* San José, Costa Rica.

ECHÁVARRI, Luis Enrique, MSc; Spanish business executive and international organization official; *Director-General of Nuclear Energy Agency, Organisation for Economic Co-operation and Development;* b. 17 April 1949, Bilbao; m.; two c.; ed Univ. of Basque Country, Univ. of Madrid; Project Man. for Lemóniz, Sayago and Almaraz nuclear power plants, Westinghouse Electric, Madrid; Tech. Dir and Commr, Consejo de Seguridad Nuclear (Spanish nuclear regulatory comm.); Dir-Gen. OECD Nuclear Energy Agency (NEA) 1997–; rep. of Spain at int. fora on nuclear energy, including Int. Atomic Energy Agency and EU; mem. INSAG-IAEA; represents NEA at Int. Energy Agency Governing bd. *Address:* OECD Nuclear Energy Agency, Le Seine Saint-Germain, 12 boulevard des Iles, 92130 Issy-les-Moulineux, France (office). *Telephone:* 1-45-24-10-01 (office). *Fax:* 1-45-24-11-15 (office). *E-mail:* nea@nea.fr (office). *Website:* www.nea.fr (office).

ECHENOZ, Jean Maurice Emmanuel; French writer; b. 26 Dec. 1947, Orange, Vaucluse; s. of Marc Echenoz and Annie Languin; one s.; ed Univ. of Aix-en-Provence, Sorbonne and Univ. of Paris; professional writer 1979–; Grand Prix du roman de la Ville de Paris 1997. *Film:* Le Rose et le blanc (Prix Georges Sadoul) 1979. *Publications:* Le Méridien de Greenwich (Prix Fénéon 1980) 1979, Cherokee (Prix Médicis Étranger) 1983, L'Equipée malaise (trans. as Double Jeopardy) 1986, L'Occupation des sols 1988, Lac (Grand Prix du Roman de la Société des Gens de Lettres 1990, European Literature Prize, Glasgow 1990) 1989, Nous trois 1992, Les Grandes blondes (trans. as Big Blondes) (Prix Novembre) 1995, Un An 1997, Je m'en vais (trans. as I'm Gone) (Prix Goncourt) 1999, Jérôme Lindon 2001, Samuel (trans. of bible, jtly) 2001, Au piano (trans. as Piano) 2003, Ravel 2006, Courir 2008. *Address:* c/o Editions de Minuit, 7 rue Bernard-Palissy, 75006 Paris, France (office). *Website:* www.leseditionsdeminuit.com (office).

ECHEVARRIA, Most Rev. Javier, PhD; Spanish ecclesiastic; *Prelate, Opus Dei;* b. 14 June 1932; ed Univ. of Madrid, Pontifical Univ. of St Thomas, Rome, Pontifical Lateran Univ., Rome; moved to Rome 1950; ordained priest 1955; Lecturer in Moral Theology, Collegio Romano della Santa Croce 1960, Collegio Romano di Santa Maria 1964; apptd. personal sec. to Josemaría Escrivá (Founder of Opus Dei) 1957, mem. Gen. Council Opus Dei 1966–75, Sec.-Gen. 1975–82, Vicar-Gen. 1982–94, Prelate of Opus Dei 1994–; consecrated Bishop 1995; Consultant, Sacred Congregation for the Clergy 1995–; mem. Supreme Tribunal of the Apostolic Signatura 2001–, Sacred Congregation for the Causes of Saints 2002–. *Publications:* Memoria del Beato Josemaría Escrivá 2000, Itinerarios de vida cristiana 2001, Para servir a la Iglesia 2001, Getsemaní 2005, Eucaristía y Vida Cristiana 2005, Por Cristo: con Él y en Él 2007. *Address:* Curia of the Prelature, 73 Viale Bruno Buozzi, 00197 Rome, Italy (home). *Telephone:* (06) 808961 (home). *Fax:* (06) 80896420 (home). *Website:* www.opusdei.org (office).

ECKHARDT, Sándor, MD, PhD, DSc; Hungarian oncologist; *Professor of Clinical Oncology, Postgraduate University Medical School, University of Budapest;* b. 14 March 1927, Budapest; s. of Sándor Eckhardt and Irén Huszár; m. Mária Petrányi; three s.; ed Semmelweis Medical Univ. Budapest; began his career at Uzsoki Hosp., Budapest; worked at Nat. Inst. of Oncology, Budapest from 1953, Dir 1971–92, now Prof. Emer.; specialist in internal medicine 1955; training course of malignant diseases in children, Villejuif, France 1969; MRC Fellow, Chester Beatty Inst., London, 1961; Eleanor Roosevelt Cancer Research Fellow, Bethesda 1964–65; Chair. Drug Devt Program, Hungary 1966–70; Prof. Clinical Oncology, Postgraduate Univ.

Medical School, Univ. of Budapest 1977–; mem. Hungarian Acad. of Sciences 1985–; Chair. Trial Centre of East European countries and Program Co-ordinator of drug research 1979–98; mem. Union Int. Contre le Cancer (UICC) Exec. Cttee 1978–86, Treas. 1986–90, Pres. 1990–94, Past Pres. 1994–98; Sec. Gen. 14th Int. Cancer Congress 1982–86; adviser WHO Cancer Unit 1971–98; mem. Medical Advisory Cttee WHO Euro Office, Copenhagen 1974–82; mem. Scientific Council Int. Agency for Research on Cancer 1976–80, Chair. 1979–82; mem. American Asscn of Cancer Research 1976–, Medical Acad. of Moscow 1979–, European Soc. of Medical Oncology 1985–; American Soc. of Clinical Oncology 1987–, Chief Ed. Antitumour Drug Therapy, Budapest 1977–86; Clinical Ed. Oncology 1978–84, Onkologie 1980–86, Current Medical Chem. 2002; Labour Order of Merit 1975; State Prize 1985, Széchenyi Prize 1994. *Publications:* include Drug Therapy of Cancer (WHO Geneva) 1973, Dibromodulcitol 1982, Drug Development in Eastern Europe 1987, Co-Ed. Proceedings of the 14th International Cancer Congress, Budapest (13 vols) 1986, Cancer Surveys 1994, Ann. Oncol. 1999, 7 Surg. Oncol. 2000, Current Medical Chemistry 2002. *Address:* National Institute of Oncology, Ráth György utca 7/9, 1525 Budapest, Hungary (office). *Telephone:* (1) 224-8751 (office). *Fax:* (1) 224-8620 (office); (1) 224-8741 (office). *E-mail:* eckhardt@oncol.hu (office).

ECKRODT, Rolf, DipEng; German automotive executive; b. 25 Feb. 1942, Gronau, Westphalia; ed Univ. of Bochum; Quality Assurance Passenger Cars Dept, Daimler Benz AG 1966–68, Man., Passenger Cars 1968, Project Leader, Production Components 1981–83, Vice-Pres. Axle Production 1983–86, Exec. Asst to Head of Mercedes-Benz Passenger Car Div. 1986–87, Dir Planning and Production, Passenger Cars and Components 1987–90, Dir Worldwide Planning and Production 1990–92, Pres. Mercedes Benz do Brasil 1992–96, Exec. Vice-Pres. and Deputy CEO, Adtranz 1996–98, Pres. and CEO 1998–2001; Exec. Vice-Pres. and COO Mitsubishi Motors Corpn 2001–02, Pres. and CEO 2002–04 (resgnd); Chair. Union of European Railway Industries (UNIFE) 193–96; Vice-Pres. German-Brazil Chamber of Commerce, São Paulo; Hon. Consul of Brazil, Potsdam 1999–2000. *Address:* 16-4 Konan 2-chome, Minato-ku, Tokyo 108-8410, Japan (office).

ECO, Umberto, PhD; Italian writer and academic; *Professor, University of Bologna;* b. 5 Jan. 1932, Alessandria, Piedmont; s. of Giulio Eco and Giovanna Bisio; m. Renate Ramge 1962; one s. one d.; ed Liceo Plana, Alessandria, Univ. degli Studi, Turin; cultural ed. Italian TV (RAI), Milan 1954–59; mil. service 1958–59; Sr Non-fiction Ed., Bompiani, Milan 1959–75; Asst Lecturer in Aesthetics, Univ. of Turin 1956–63, Lecturer 1963–64; Lecturer, Faculty of Architecture, Univ. of Milan 1964–65; Prof. of Visual Communications, Univ. of Florence 1966–69; Prof. of Semiotics, Milan Polytechnic 1970–71; Assoc. Prof. of Semiotics, Univ. of Bologna 1971–75, Prof. 1975–, Dir Inst. of Communications Disciplines 1993–, f. School of Arts 2000; Visiting Prof. New York Univ. 1969–70, 1976, Northwestern Univ. 1972, Yale Univ. 1977, 1980, 1981, Columbia Univ. 1978, 1984; Columnist on L'Espresso 1965; Ed. VS 1971–; mem. Academia Europaea 1998–; Chevalier de la Légion d'honneur, Ordre pour le Mérite, Cavaliere di Gran Croce (Italy); Hon. DLitt (Glasgow) 1990, (Kent) 1992 and numerous other hon. degrees; Medici Prize 1982, McLuhan Teleglobe Prize 1985, Crystal Award (World Econ. Forum) 2000; Prince of Asturias Prize for Communication and the Humanities 2000, Manzoni Prize 2008. *Publications:* Il Problema Estetico in San Tommaso (trans. as The Aesthetics of Thomas Aquinas) 1956, Sviluppo dell'Estetica Medioevale (trans. as Art and Beauty in the Middle Ages) 1959, Opera Aperta 1962, Diario Minimo 1963, Apocalittici e Integrati 1964, L'Oeuvre Ouverte 1965, La Struttura Assente 1968, Il Costume di Casa 1973, Trattato di Semiotica Generale 1975, A Theory of Semiotics 1976, The Role of the Reader 1979, Il Nome della Rosa (novel, trans. as The Name of the Rose) 1981, Semiotics and the Philosophy of Language 1984, Sette anni di desiderio 1977–83 1984, Faith in Fakes 1986, Il pendolo di Foucault 1988, The Open Work 1989, The Limits of Interpretation 1990, Misreadings 1993, How to Travel with a Salmon and Other Essays 1994, L'isola del giorno prima (novel, trans. as The Island of the Day Before) 1995, The Search for the Perfect Language 1995, Serendipities 1997, Kant and the Platypus 1999, Baudolino (novel) 2000, Experiences in Translation 2000, Five Moral Pieces 2001, Mouse or Rat?: Translation as Negotiation 2003, On Beauty: A History of a Western Idea (ed.) 2004, The Mysterious Flame of Queen Loana 2005, Turning Back the Clock: Hot Wars and Media Populism (essays) 2007, On Ugliness 2007. *Address:* Scuola Superiore Studi Umanistici, Via Marsala 26, Bologna, Italy. *Telephone:* (051) 2917111 (office). *E-mail:* sssub@dsc.unibo.it (office).

EDBERG, Stefan; Swedish fmr professional tennis player; b. 19 Jan. 1966, Vastervik; m. Annette Edberg; one s. one d.; won Jr Grand Slam 1983, Milan Open 1984, San Francisco, Basle and Memphis Opens 1985, Gstaad, Basle and Stockholm Opens 1986, Australian Open 1986, 1987, Wimbledon 1988, 1990, finalist 1989, US Open 1991, Masters 1989, German Open 1992, US Open 1992; winner (with Anders Jarryd) Masters and French Open 1986, Australian and US Opens 1987; semi-finalist in numerous tournaments; mem. Swedish Davis Cup Team 1984, 1987; retd in 1996 having won 60 professional titles and more than US $20 million in prize money; f. Stefan Edberg Foundation to assist young Swedish tennis players; Adidas Sportsmanship Award (four times), inducted into Int. Tennis Hall of Fame 2004. *Leisure interest:* golf. *Address:* c/o ATP Tour, 200 ATP Tour Boulevard, Ponte Vedra Beach, FL 32082, USA.

EDDERY, Patrick James John, OBE; Irish fmr professional jockey and race horse trainer; b. 18 March 1952, Newbridge, Co. Galway; s. of Jimmy Eddery and Josephine Eddery; m. Carolyn Jane (née Mercer) 1978; one s. two d.; winner of 4,632 races in UK (second only to Gordon Richards); first win on Alvaro at Epsom 1969; has ridden 100 winners in a year 28 times 1973–; first jockey in Britain to ride seven winners in a day 1992; rode for Peter Walwyn 1972–80; Champion Jockey 1974–77, 1986, 1988–91, 1996; Champion Jockey in Ireland 1982; rode winner of the Oaks 1974, 1979, 1996, 2002, the Derby, on Grundy 1975, on Golden Fleece 1982, Quest for Fame 1990, Prix de l'Arc de Triomphe 1980, 1985–87, St Leger (four times); retd 2003; owner of stud farm; racehorse trainer 2003–; Flat Jockey of the Year 1990, 1991, 1996. *Leisure interests:* tennis, golf, snooker, swimming. *Address:* Musk Hill Farm, Nether Winchendon, Aylesbury, Bucks., HP18 0DT, England (home). *Telephone:* (1844) 296153 (office); (1844) 291980 (home). *Fax:* (1844) 290280 (office). *E-mail:* simon@patedderyracing.com; ceddery@waitrose.com (home). *Website:* patedderyracing.com.

EDDINGTON, Sir Roderick (Rod) Ian, Kt, MEngSc, DPhil; Australian fmr airline executive; b. 2 Jan. 1950, Perth; s. of Gilbert Maxwell Eddington and April Mary Eddington; m. Young Sook Park 1994; one s. one d.; ed Christ Church Grammar School, WA, Univ. of Western Australia, Univ. of Oxford, UK; taught at University of Oxford, UK for two years; joined Cathay Pacific Airways Ltd 1979, various positions Hong Kong, Korea and Japan, Deputy Man. Dir 1990–92, Man. Dir and CEO 1992–96; Dir News Ltd (Australian arm of News Corpn) 1997–2000, Deputy Chair. 1998–2000; Exec. Chair. Ansett Australia 1997–2000; CEO British Airways (BA) 2000–05, also mem. Bd of Dirs; Chair. Victorian Major Events Co. 2005–; Chair. for Australia and New Zealand, JPMorgan 2006–; mem. Bd of Dirs John Swire & Sons Pty Ltd 1997–, News Corpn, Rio Tinto; apptd UK Treasury and Department for Transport to write report on the future of Britain's transport system 2006; mem. Bd of Man. Fremantle Dockers Football Club 1998–2000; business adviser to Labor Party of Australia 2007–; Deputy Chair. Growing Victoria Together Summit 2000; mem. Victorian Govt's Innovation Economy Advisory Bd 2002–; Rhodes Scholar 1974. *Leisure interests:* cricket, bridge, football. *Address:* c/o British Airways, Waterside, PO Box 365, Harmondsworth, UB7 0GB, England (office).

EDDY, Don, MFA; American artist; b. 4 Nov. 1944, Long Beach, Calif.; m. Leigh Behnke 1995; one d.; ed Fullerton Jr Coll., Univ. of Hawaii, Honolulu, Univ. of California at Santa Barbara; represented in numerous public collections; subject of two monographs and an electronic book about his work. *Address:* 543 Broadway, New York, NY 10012, USA (office). *Telephone:* (212) 925-3124 (office). *Fax:* (212) 925-2302 (office). *E-mail:* doneddyart@aol.com (office).

EDELMAN, Eric S., PhD; American diplomatist; *Under-Secretary of Defense for Policy;* m. Patricia Davis; two s. two d.; ed Cornell Univ., Yale Univ.; mem. US Del. to West Bank/Gaza Autonomy Talks 1980–81; Watch Officer, State Dept Operations Center 1981–82; Staff Officer, Secr. Staff 1982; Special Asst to Sec. of State 1982–84; with Office of Soviet Affairs, Dept of State 1984–86; Head, External Political Section, Embassy in Moscow 1987–89; Special Asst (European Affairs) to Under-Sec. of State for Political Affairs 1989–90; Asst Deputy Under-Sec. of Defense for Soviet and East European Affairs, Office of Sec. of Defense 1990–93; Deputy Chief of Mission, Prague 1994–96; Exec. Asst to Deputy Sec. of State; Amb. to Finland 1998–2001, to Turkey 2003–05; Under-Sec. of Defense for Policy 2005–; Prin. Deputy Asst to Vice-Pres. for Nat. Security Affairs 2001–03; Award for Distinguished Civilian Service 1993, Superior Honor Award 1989, 1990, 1995. *Address:* Office of the Under-Secretary of Defense for Policy, 2000 Defense Pentagon, Washington, DC 20301-2000, USA (office). *Telephone:* (703) 428-0711 (office). *Fax:* (703) 428-1982 (office). *Website:* www.defenselink.mil/policy (office).

EDELMAN, Gerald Maurice, MD, PhD; American molecular biologist, neuroscientist and academic; *Professor and Chairman, Department of Neurobiology, Scripps Research Institute;* b. 1 July 1929, New York; s. of Edward Edelman and Anna Freedman Edelman; m. Maxine Morrison 1950; two s. one d.; ed Ursinus Coll., Univ. of Pennsylvania and The Rockefeller Univ.; Medical House Officer, Mass Gen. Hosp. 1945–55; Capt., US Army Medical Corps 1955–56; Asst Physician, Hosp. of The Rockefeller Univ. 1957–60; Asst Prof. and Asst Dean of Grad. Studies, The Rockefeller Univ, 1960–63, Assoc. Prof. and Assoc. Dean of Grad. Studies 1963–66, Prof. 1966–74, Vincent Astor Distinguished Prof. 1974–92, Assoc. Neurosciences Research Program, Scientific Chair. 1980, Dir Neurosciences Inst., Neurosciences Research Program 1981–; Prof., Scripps Research Inst., La Jolla, Calif., Chair. Dept of Neurobiology 1992–; mem. Biophysics and Biophysical Chemistry Study Section, NIH 1964–67, Scientific Council, Center for Theoretical Studies 1970–72, The Harvey Society 1974– (Pres. 1975–76); mem. NAS, American Acad. of Arts and Sciences, American Philosophical Soc., Genetics Soc., ACS, American Soc. of Biological Chemists, American Asscn of Immunologists, American Soc. for Cell Biology, Soc. for Developmental Biology, Alpha Omega Alpha Hon. Medical Soc., Council on Foreign Relations, AAAS; mem. Bd of Overseers Faculty of Arts and Sciences, Univ. of Pa; mem. Bd Scientific Overseers, Jackson Lab.; mem. Bd of Trustees, Carnegie Inst. of Washington, also mem. Advisory Cttee; mem. Advisory Bd, The Basel Inst. for Immunology 1970–77 (Chair. 1975–77); mem. Bd of Govs, Weizmann Inst. of Science, Israel; Trustee, Rockefeller Brothers Fund 1972–82; Fellow, New York Acad. of Sciences, New York Acad. of Medicine; Non-Resident Fellow and mem. Bd of Trustees, Salk Inst. for Biological Studies; Foreign mem. Acad. des Sciences; Hon. mem. Japanese Biochemical Soc., Pharmaceutical Soc. of Japan; Hon. DSc (Univ. of Pa) 1973, (Adolphus Coll., Minn.) 1975, (Georgetown) 1989, (Tulane) 1991, (Miami) 1995, (Adelphi) 1995; Hon. ScD (Ursinus Coll.) 1974, (Williams Coll.) 1976; Hon. MD (Siena) 1974; Dr hc (Paris, Cagliari) 1989, (Naples) 1990; Annual Alumni Award, Ursinus Coll. 1969, Eli Lilly Award in Biological Chem., American Chemical Soc. 1965, Spencer Morris Award, Univ. of Pa 1954, Nobel Prize for Physiology or Medicine 1972 (with R. Porter), Albert Einstein Commem. Award of Yeshiva Univ. 1974, Buchman Memorial Award, Calif. Inst. of Tech. 1975, Rabbi Shai Shaknai Memorial Prize in Immunology and Cancer Research,

Hebrew Univ.-Hadassah Medical School, Jerusalem 1977, Regents Medal of Excellence, New York 1984, Cécile and Oskar Vogt Award (Düsseldorf) 1988, Distinguished Grad. Award, Univ. of Pa 1990, Medal of the Presidency of the Italian Repub. 1999 and many other awards and prizes. *Publications:* Neural Darwinism 1987, Topobiology 1988, The Remembered Present 1989, Bright Air, Brilliant Fire 1992, A Universe of Consciousness 2000, Second Nature: Brain Science and Human Knowledge 2007; over 500 articles in professional journals. *Leisure interests:* violin, chamber music. *Address:* Department of Neurobiology, SBR 14, The Scripps Research Institute, 10550 North Torrey Pines Road, La Jolla, CA 92037-1000, USA (office). *Telephone:* (858) 784-2600 (office). *Fax:* (858) 784-2646 (office). *Website:* www.scripps.edu/nb (office).

EDELMAN, Marek; Polish politician and doctor; b. 1921, Warsaw; ed Acad. of Medicine; mem. Jewish Socialist Party (Bund) and Jewish Fighting Org. (ŻOB); participant, then Commdr Warsaw Ghetto Uprising 1943; soldier Home Army, participant Warsaw Uprising 1944; co-f. Cttee for Defence of Workers 1976; interned 1981–82; mem. Solidarity Self-governing Ind. Trade Union, Civic Cttee attached to Lech Wałęsa (q.v.), Democratic Union (UD), later Freedom Union (UW); Order of the White Eagle 1998; Citizen of the Year, Łódź 1999. *Publications:* The Bund's Role in the Defence of the Warsaw Ghetto 1945, The Ghetto is Fighting 1946. *Address:* Regionalna Rada Unii Wolności, ul. Piotrkowska 157, 90-440 Łódź, Poland (office).

EDELSTEIN, Victor Arnold; French couturier and artist; b. 10 July 1945, London; m. Anna Maria Succi 1973; trainee designer Alexon 1962, Asst Designer and Pattern Cutter to Biba 1967, designer Salvador 1971, Christian Dior 1975; f. Victor Edelstein Ltd 1978–93; designed ballet of Rhapsody in Blue for Rambert Dance Co. 1989; pantomime Cinderella, Richmond Theatre 1991, black pas de deux, Swan Lake, Covent Garden 1991; exhbns include Sotheby's, London 1996, Hopkins Thomas Gallery, Paris 1999. *Leisure interests:* opera, gardening, collecting old master drawings, skiing.

EDELSTEIN, Yuli; Israeli (b. Ukrainian) politician; b. 1958, Chernovitz, Ukraine; m.; two c.; ed Moscow Inst. for Teacher Training; fmr Hebrew teacher, Moscow; emigrated to Israel 1987; fmr teacher Melitz Centre for Jewish-Zionist Educ., School for Educational Inst., Jerusalem; Adviser to Opposition Leader Benjamin Netanyahu 1993–94; a founder of Yisrael Ba-Aliya Party 1996; headed party's election campaign; mem. Knesset (Parl.) 1996–, Minister of Immigrant Absorption 1996–99, Deputy Minister 2001–03; Deputy Speaker Knesset 1999–2001. *Address:* c/o Ministry of Immigration and Absorption, PO Box 883, 2 Rehov Kaplan, Kiryat Ben-Gurion, Jerusalem 91006 (office); Alon Shvut, Israel (home). *Telephone:* (2) 6752691 (office). *Fax:* (2) 5669244 (office).

EDELSTENNE, Charles; French aviation industry executive; *Chairman and CEO, Dassault Aviation;* b. 9 Jan. 1938, Paris; s. of Simon Edelstenne and Ida Edelstenne (née Brutman); m. Adèle Edelhertz 1963; one s. one d.; Chief Financial Officer Avions Marcel Dassault-Bréguet Aviation 1960–71, Deputy Sec.-Gen. 1971–75, Sec.-Gen. 1975–86, Vice-Pres. 1986–89, Dir 1989–2000, Chair. and CEO Dassault Aviation 2000–, f. Dassault Systèmes 1981, Man. Dir 1981–93, Chair. and CEO 1993–2002, Pres. Dassault Systèmes America 1992–2002, Chair. Dassault Falcon Jet Corpn 1978–, Pres. Dassault International USA 2001–; Dir Société Anonyme Belge de Constructions Aéronautiques, Belgium, Groupe Industriel Marcel Dassault, Paris, Sogitec Industries, Thales Systems Aéroportes, Dassault Réassurance; Pres. Groupement des Industries Françaises Aéronautiques et Spatiales (GIFAS) 2005–; Dir French Aircraft Mfrs Assen (Chair. Econ. Cttee 1981–87); fmr Vice-Pres. Foundation for Defence Studies; Chair. French Defence Industries Council 2006–; Pres. AeroSpace and Defence Industries Asscn Europe 2006–07. *Address:* Dassault Aviation, 9 Rond-Point des Champs-Elysées, 75008 Paris, France (office). *Telephone:* 1-53-76-93-00 (office). *Fax:* 1-53-76-93-20 (office). *Website:* www.dassault-aviation.com (office).

EDGAR, David Burman, BA; British writer; b. 26 Feb. 1948, Birmingham; s. of Barrie Edgar and Joan Edgar (née Burman); m. Eve Brook 1979 (died 1998); two step-s.; pnr Stephanie Dale; ed Oundle School, Manchester Univ.; Fellow in Creative Writing, Leeds Polytechnic 1972–74; Resident Playwright, Birmingham Repertory Theatre 1974–75, Bd mem. 1985–; Lecturer in Playwriting, Univ. of Birmingham 1975–78, Dir of Playwriting Studies 1989–, Prof. 1995–99; Founder Writers' Union 1970s; UK/US Bicentennial Arts Fellow resident in USA 1978–79; Literary Consultant, RSC 1984–88; Fellow Birmingham Polytechnic 1991, Judith E. Wilson Fellow, Clare Hall, Cambridge 1996; Hon. Sr Research Fellow, Univ. of Birmingham 1988–92, Hon. Prof. 1992–; Hon. MA (Bradford) 1986; DUniv (Surrey) 1993, (Birmingham) 2002; Soc. of West End Theatres Best Play Award 1980, Tony Award for Best Play 1981, Plays and Players Award for Best Play 1983, Evening Standard Award for Best Play 1995. *Plays:* Two Kinds of Angel 1970, Rent or Caught in the Act 1972, State of Emergency 1972, The Dunkirk Spirit 1974, Dick Deterred 1974, O Fair Jerusalem 1975, Saigon Rose 1976, Blood Sports 1976, Destiny (for RSC) 1976, Wreckers 1977, The Jail Diary of Albie Sachs (for RSC) 1978, Mary Barnes 1978–79, Teendreams 1979, The Adventures of Nicholas Nickleby (adaptation for RSC) 1980, Maydays (for RSC) 1983, Entertaining Strangers 1985, That Summer 1987, The Shape of the Table 1990, Dr Jekyll and Mr Hyde (adaptation for RSC) 1991, Pentecost 1994, Other Place 1994, Young Vic 1995, Albert Speer (adaptation for Nat. Theatre) 2000, The Prisoner's Dilemma 2001, Continental Divide 2003, Playing with Fire (Nat. Theatre, London) 2005. *TV Plays:* I Know What I Meant 1974, Baby Love 1974, Vote for Them 1989, Buying a Landslide 1992, Citizen Locke 1994. *Radio:* Ecclesiastes 1977, A Movie Starring Me 1991. *Film:* Lady Jane 1986. *Publications:* Destiny 1976, Wreckers 1977, Teendreams 1979, Maydays 1983, Plays One 1987, The Second Time as Farce 1988, Heartlanders 1989, Plays Two 1990, Plays Three 1991, Pentecost 1995, State of Play (ed.) 1999, Albert Speer 2000, The Prisoner's Dilemma 2001, Continental Divide 2004, Playing With Fire 2005. *Leisure interests:* fine art, cookery, writing letters. *Address:* 6th Floor, Fairgrove House, New Oxford Street, London, WC1A 1HB, England (office). *Telephone:* (20) 7079-7990 (office). *Fax:* (20) 7079-7999 (office).

EDGAR, James; American fmr politician; *Distinguished Fellow, Institute of Government and Public Affairs, University of Illinois;* b. 22 July 1946, Vinita, Okla; m. Brenda Smith; one s. one d.; ed Eastern Ill. Univ., Univ. of Ill. and Sangamon State Univ.; key Asst to Speaker, Ill. House of Reps. 1972–73; aide to Pres. Ill. Senate 1974, to House Minority Leader 1976; mem. Ill. House of Reps. 1977–91; Dir Legis. Affairs, Gov. of Ill. 1979–80; Sec. of State of Ill. 1981–91; Gov. of Illinois 1991–99; Chair. Nat. Govt's Asscn Comm. Econ. Devt and Tech. Innovation 1991, Strategic Planning Review Task Force 1991; Distinguished Fellow, Inst. of Govt and Public Affairs, Univ. of Ill. 1999–; Republican. *Address:* University of Illinois Institute of Government and Public Affairs, 1007 W Nevada Street, Apartment MC-037, Urbana, IL 61801, USA (office). *Telephone:* (217) 333-3340 (office). *Website:* www.igpa.uiuc.edu (office).

THE EDGE; Irish musician (guitar) and songwriter; b. (David Howell Evans), 8 Aug. 1961, Barking, Essex, England; ed Mount Temple School; founder mem. and guitarist, the Feedback 1976, renamed the Hype, finally renamed U2 1978–; major concerts include Live Aid Wembley 1985, Self Aid Dublin, A Conspiracy of Hope (Amnesty Int. Tour) 1986, Smile Jamaica (hurricane relief fundraiser) 1988, Very Special Arts Festival, White House, Washington, DC 1988; numerous tours worldwide; Grammy awards for Album of the Year and Best Rock Performance by a Duo or Group with Vocal (for The Joshua Tree) 1987, Grammy awards for Best Rock Performance by a Duo or Group with Vocal (for Desire) and Best Performance Video, short form (for Where the Streets Have No Name) 1988, BRIT Awards for Best Int. Act 1988–90, 1992, 1998, 2001, Best Live Act 1993, Outstanding Contribution to the British Music Industry 2001, JUNO Award 1992, World Music Award 1992, Grammy Award for Best Rock Vocal by a Duo or Group (for Achtung Baby) 1992, Grammy Award for Best Alternative Music Album (for Zooropa) 1993, Grammy Award for Best Music Video, long form (for Zoo TV Live from Sydney) 1994, Grammy Award for Song of the Year, Record of the Year, Best Rock Performance by a Duo or Group with Vocal (all for Beautiful Day) 2000, Grammy Awards for Best Pop Performance by a Duo or Group with Vocal (for Stuck In A Moment You Can't Get Out Of), for Record of the Year (for Walk On), for Best Rock Performance by a Duo or Group with Vocal (for Elevation), for Rock Album of the Year (All That You Can't Leave Behind) 2001, American Music Award for Favorite Internet Artist of the Year 2002, Ivor Novello Award for Best Song Musically and Lyrically (for Walk On) 2002, Golden Globe for Best Original Song (for The Hands That Built America, from film Gangs of New York) 2003, Grammy Awards for Best Rock Performance by a Duo or Group with Vocal, Best Rock Song, Best Short Form Music Video (all for Vertigo) 2004, TED Prize 2004, Nordoff-Robbins Silver Clef Award for lifetime achievement 2005, Q Award for Best Live Act 2005, Digital Music Award for Favourite Download Single (for Vertigo) 2005, Meteor Ireland Music Award for Best Irish Band, Best Live Performance 2006, Grammy Awards for Song of the Year, for Best Rock Performance by a Duo or Group with Vocal (both for Sometimes You Can't Make it on Your Own), for Best Rock Song (for City of Blinding Lights), for Album of the Year and Best Rock Album of the Year (both for How to Dismantle an Atomic Bomb) 2006; Portuguese Order of Liberty 2005. *Films:* Rattle and Hum 1988. *Recordings include:* albums: Boy 1980, October 1981, War 1983, Under a Blood Red Sky 1983, The Unforgettable Fire 1984, Wide Awake In America 1985, The Joshua Tree (Grammy Award for Album of the Year, Best Rock Performance by a Duo or Group with Vocal) 1987, Rattle and Hum 1988, Achtung Baby (Grammy Award for Best Rock Performance by a Duo or Group with Vocal 1992) 1991, Zooropa (Grammy Award for Best Alternative Music Album) 1993, Passengers (film soundtrack with Brian Eno) 1995, Pop 1997, The Best Of 1980–90 1998, All That You Can't Leave Behind (Grammy Award for Best Rock Album 2001) 2000, The Best Of 1990–2000 2002, How To Dismantle An Atomic Bomb (Meteor Ireland Music Award for Best Irish Album 2006, Grammy Awards for Album of the Year, for Best Rock Album 2006) 2004, No Line on the Horizon 2009; solo: Captive 1987. *Address:* Principle Management, 30–32 Sir John Rogersons Quay, Dublin 2, Ireland (office). *E-mail:* candida@numb.ie (office). *Website:* www.u2.com.

EDGLEY, Michael Christopher, MBE; Australian entrepreneur; *Chairman, Edgley Ventures Pty Ltd.;* b. 17 Dec. 1943, Melbourne; s. of the late Eric Edgley and of Edna Edgley (née Luscombe); divorced; two s. three d.; ed Trinity Coll., Perth; Chair. Edgley Ventures Pty Ltd 1962–, promoting a wide range of cultural, artistic and sporting events throughout Australia, NZ, UK, Asia and S Africa; Citizen of the Year Award for WA 1976. *Leisure interests:* jogging, tennis. *Address:* Edgley International, POB 4500, Richmond, Vic. 3121, Australia (office). *Telephone:* (3) 9428-7711 (office). *Fax:* (3) 9428-7712 (office). *E-mail:* headoffice@edgley.com.au (office). *Website:* www.edgley.com.

EDINBURGH, HRH The Duke of; (Prince Philip), (Prince of the United Kingdom of Great Britain and Northern Ireland, Earl of Merioneth, Baron Greenwich), KG, KT, OM, GBE; b. 10 June 1921, Corfu, Greece; s. of Prince Andrew of Greece and Denmark and Princess Alice of Battenberg; m. 20 Nov. 1947 HRH Princess Elizabeth (HM Queen Elizabeth II q.v.); children: Prince Charles Philip Arthur George, Prince of Wales (q.v.), b. 14 Nov. 1948, Princess Anne Elizabeth Alice Louise, The Princess Royal (q.v.), b. 15 Aug. 1950, Prince Andrew Albert Christian Edward, Duke of York (q.v.), b. 19 Feb. 1960, Prince Edward Antony Richard Louis, Earl of Wessex (q.v.), b. 10 March 1964; ed Cheam, Salem and Gordonstoun Schools, Royal Naval Coll., Dartmouth; renounced right of succession to thrones of Greece and Denmark, naturalized British subject 1947, adopting surname Mountbatten; served Royal Navy 1939–51, served in Indian Ocean, Mediterranean, North Sea, Pacific Ocean during Second World War; Personal ADC to King George VI 1948–52; PC

1951–; ranks of Adm. of the Fleet, Field Marshal, Marshal of the Royal Air Force, Captain-Gen. Royal Marines 1953–; Chancellor, Univs. of Wales 1948–76, Edinburgh 1952–, Salford 1967–91, Cambridge 1977–; Pres., Patron or Trustee numerous orgs including: Nat. Playing Fields Asscn 1948–, Nat. Maritime Museum 1948–, London Fed. of Clubs for Young People (now called London Youth) 1948–, City & Guilds of London Inst. 1951–, Cen. Council of Physical Recreation 1951–, Design Council 1952–, RSA 1952–, English-Speaking Union of the Commonwealth 1952–, Outward Bound Trust 1952–, Trinity House 1952–, Guild of Air Pilots and Air Navigators 1952–, RCA 1955–, Commonwealth Games Fed. 1955–90, Duke of Edinburgh's Award Scheme 1956–, Duke of Edinburgh's Commonwealth Study Confs 1956–, Royal Agric. Soc. of the Commonwealth 1958–, Voluntary Service Overseas 1961–, World Wildlife Fund UK 1961–82, Int. Equestrian Fed. 1964–86, Maritime Trust 1969–, Royal Commonwealth Ex-Services League 1974–, Royal Acad. of Eng 1976–, British Trust for Ornithology 1987–; Pres. World Wide Fund for Nature 1981–96, Pres. Emer. 1997–; numerous awards, decorations and hon. degrees world-wide. *Publications:* 14 publications 1957–2004. *Address:* Buckingham Palace, London, SW1A 1AA, England. *Website:* www.royal.gov.uk.

EDLEY, Christopher, Jr; American professor of law, university dean and civil rights scholar; *Dean of School of Law (Boalt Hall), University of California, Berkeley;* ed Swarthmore Coll., Pa, John F. Kennedy School of Government, Harvard Univ., Harvard Law School, Cambridge, Mass; Asst Dir White House Domestic Policy Staff (Carter Admin) –1981; taught at Harvard Law School 1981–2004, later Prof. and Founding Co-Dir The Civil Rights Project; Dean, School of Law (Boalt Hall), Univ. of Calif., Berkeley 2004–; served in Dukakis presidential campaign as Nat. Issues Dir; Sr Adviser on Econ. Policy for Clinton–Gore Presidential Transition 1992; served two years as sr budget and policy official in Clinton Admin; Special Counsel to Pres. Clinton and Dir White House Review of Affirmative Action 1995; Sr Adviser to Pres. Clinton for Race Initiative 1997–99; Sr Policy Adviser to Al Gore and mem. Democratic Policy Drafting Cttee during presidential campaign 2000; mem. US Civil Rights Comm., Task Force on the Future of the Common School (Century Foundation), Nat. Comm. on Fed. Electoral Reform, Council on Foreign Relations, Nat. Acad. of Public Admin; mem. Bd Nat. Immigration Forum, Bd on Testing and Assessment of the Nat. Research Council (NAS); founding mem. Advisory Bd for the Madison Soc.; mem. Exec. Cttee of Bd of People for the American Way; Adjunct Scholar at the Urban Inst.; fmr Vice-Chair. Bd of Congressional Black Caucus Foundation; fmr Ed. Harvard Review; fmr mem. Editorial Bd Washington Post. *Publications include:* Administrative Law: Rethinking Judicial Control of Bureaucracy, Not All Black and White: Affirmative Action, Race and American Values. *Address:* School of Law (Boalt Hall), University of California, Berkeley, CA 94720-7200 (office); The Civil Rights Project, 125 Mount Auburn Street, 3rd Floor, Cambridge, MA 02138, USA (office). *Telephone:* (510) 642-1741 (Berkeley) (office); (617) 496-6367 (Cambridge) (office). *Fax:* (617) 495-5210 (Cambridge) (office). *E-mail:* cedley@law.berkeley.edu (office).

EDMONDS, David, CBE, BA; British business executive; *Chairman, NHSDirect;* b. 6 March 1944, Grapenhall; s. of Albert Edmonds and Gladys Edmonds; m. Ruth Edmonds (née Beech) 1964; two s. two d.; ed Helsby Co. Grammar School, Univ. of Keele; with Ministry of Housing 1966–70, with Dept of the Environment 1970–84; Chief Exec. The Housing Corpn 1984–91; Man. Dir Group Services NatWest Group 1991–98; Dir-Gen. Oftel (Office of Telecommunications) 1998–2004; Chair. NHSDirect 2004–; mem. Bd English Partnerships 2000–, Chair. Property, Planning and Projects Cttee 2000–; mem. Council and Treasurer Keele Univ. 1997–; Dir-Gen. Oftel 1998–2003, mem. Bd Office of Communications (Ofcom) 2004–. *Leisure interests:* opera, golf, art, walking. *Address:* Department of Health, Richmond House, 79 Whitehall, London SW1A 2NS, England (office). *Telephone:* (20) 7210-4850 (office). *Website:* www.nhsdirect.uk (office).

EDMONDS, John Walter, MA; British academic and fmr trade union official; *Visiting Senior Research Fellow, King's College London;* b. 28 Jan. 1944, London; s. of Maude Rose Edmonds and Walter Edgar Edmonds; m. Janet Linden 1967; two d.; ed Oriel Coll. Oxford; Research Asst, GMB (fmrly Gen., Municipal and Boilermakers' Union) Trade Union 1965, Deputy Research Officer 1967, Regional Organizer 1968, Nat. Officer 1972, Gen. Sec. 1986–2003; fmr mem. Royal Comm. on Environmental Pollution, Council Advisory, Conciliation and Arbitration Service (ACAS), Forestry Comm.; mem. Nat. Employment Panel (fmrly New Deal Task Force) –2002; Dir (non-exec.) Carbon Trust 2002–, Environment Agency 2003–, Salix Finance 2005–; Visiting Sr Research Fellow, King's Coll. London 2003–; Chair. Inland Waterways Advisory Council 2006–; Hon. Trustee Nat. Soc. for the Prevention of Cruelty to Children; Hon. Fellow, Society for the Environment 2006; Hon. DIur (Sussex) 1993. *Leisure interests:* cricket, carpentry. *Address:* 50 Graham Road, Mitcham, Surrey, CR4 2HA, England (home). *Telephone:* (20) 8648-9991 (home). *E-mail:* johnedmonds1@hotmail.com (home).

EDSTRÖM, Jan-Erik, MD; Swedish professor of molecular genetics; *Research Associate, Karolinska Institute, Stockholm;* b. 21 April 1931; s. of Erik Edström and Vera (née Henriksson) Edström; m. 1st Karin Ivarsson 1955 (divorced 1968); three s.; m. 2nd Elisabet Ericson 1980; two s. two d.; Assoc. Prof. of Histology, Univ. of Gothenburg 1962–64; Prof. of Histology, Univ. of Umeå 1964–65, Karolinska Inst., Stockholm 1965–79, Research Assoc. 2000–; Sr Scientist, European Molecular Biology Lab., Heidelberg 1979–85; Prof. of Molecular Genetics, Univ. of Lund 1985–2000; mem. Royal Acad. of Science 1986; MD hc (Karolinska Inst.) 1968. *Publications:* publs on molecular genetics. *Address:* Karolinska Institutet, CMB, Box 285, 171 77 Stockholm (office); Nybodagatan 7, X, 17142 Solna, Sweden. *Telephone:* (8) 7287558 (office). *Fax:* (8) 313529 (office). *E-mail:* Jan-Erik.Edstrom@cmb.ki.se (office). *Website:* info.ki.se/index_en.html (office).

EDWARD, Sir David Alexander Ogilvy, Kt, KCMG, QC, MA, FRSE; British judge; b. 14 Nov. 1934, Perth; s. of John O.C. Edward and Margaret I. MacArthur; m. Elizabeth Young McSherry 1962; two s. two d.; ed Sedbergh School, Univ. Coll., Oxford and Univ. of Edinburgh; advocate 1962–, Clerk Faculty of Advocates 1967–70, Treas. 1970–77; Pres. Consultative Cttee, Bars and Law Socs of the EEC 1978–80; Salvesen Prof. of European Insts and Dir Europa Inst., Univ. of Edin. 1985–89, Hon. Prof. 1990, now Chair.; Judge of the Court of First Instance of the European Communities 1989–92, Judge, Court of Justice of the EC 1992–2003; Pres. Scottish Council for Int. Arbitration; fmr Specialist Adviser to House of Lords Select Cttee on the EEC; fmr Chair. Continental Assets Trust PLC; fmr Dir Adam & Co. PLC, Harris Tweed Asscn Ltd; fmr mem. Law Advisory Cttee British Council, Panel of Arbitrators, Int. Centre for Settlement of Investment Disputes; fmr mem. Gründungssenat, Europa-Univ. Viadrina, Frankfurt/Oder; fmr Trustee, Nat. Library of Scotland; Trustee Trier Acad. of European Law, Industry and Parl. Trust, Hopetoun House Trust, Carnegie Trust for the Univs of Scotland; Hon. Bencher, Gray's Inn; Hon. Fellow Univ. Coll. Oxford; Hon. LLD (Univ. of Edin.) 1993, (Aberdeen) 1997, (Napier) 1998; Hon. DIur (Saarland) 2001, (Münster) 2001. *Publications:* The Professional Secret: Confidentiality and Legal Professional Privilege in the EEC 1976, European Community Law: an introduction (with R.C. Lane) 1995; articles in legal journals. *Address:* 32 Heriot Row, Edinburgh EH3 6ES, Scotland (home).

EDWARDES, Sir Michael (Owen), Kt, BA, FBIM; British business executive; *Group Deputy Chairman, Carvill Group;* b. 11 Oct. 1930, South Africa; s. of Denys Owen Edwardes and Audrey Noel Edwardes (née Copeland); m. 1st Mary Margaret Finlay 1958 (divorced, died 1999); three d.; m. 2nd Sheila Ann Guy 1988; ed St Andrew's Coll., Grahamstown, SA, Rhodes Univ., SA; joined Chloride Group in SA as management trainee 1951, mem. Man. Bd 1969, Chief Exec. 1972, Exec. Chair. 1974–77, Deputy Chair. (non-exec.) 1977–82, Chair. (non-exec.) 1982–88 (acting Chief Exec. 1985–87); Chair. and Chief Exec. British Leyland Ltd. 1977–82; Dir (non-exec.) Hill Samuel Group PLC 1980–87, Standard Securities 1984–87, Minerals and Resources Corpn 1984–, Flying Pictures Ltd 1987–; Chair. Mercury Communications Ltd 1982–83, ICL PLC 1984; Chair. and Chief Exec. Dunlop Holdings 1984–85; Chair. Charter Consolidated PLC 1988–96, Tryhorn Investments Ltd 1987–, Porth Group PLC 1991–95, ARC Int. Ltd 1991–93; Exec. Dir Minorco 1984, Strand Partners 1994–, Syndicated Services Co. Inc. 1995–; Group Deputy Chair. R. K. Carvill Int. Holdings Ltd (now Carvill Group) 1988–; Dir (non-exec.) Int. Man. Devt Inst., Washington 1978–94, Hi-Tec Sports 1993–; Pres. Comité des Constructeurs d'Automobiles du Marché Commun 1979–80; Trustee Thrombosis Research Inst. 1991–; mem. Nat. Enterprise Bd 1975–77, CBI Council 1974 (mem. President's Cttee 1981–), Review Cttee for Queen's Award for Industry; Hon. Fellow, Inst. of Mechanical Engineers; Hon. DIur (Rhodes Univ., SA) 1980; Young Businessman of the Year 1975. *Publication:* Back From the Brink 1983. *Leisure interests:* water skiing, sailing, squash, tennis. *Address:* R.K. Carvill & Co., Ltd, St. Helen's, 1 Undershaft, London EC3A 8JT, England (office). *Telephone:* (20) 7929-2800 (office). *Fax:* (20) 7929-1604 (office). *Website:* www.carvill.com (office).

EDWARDS, Anthony; American actor; b. 19 July 1962, Santa Barbara, Calif.; ed Royal Acad. of Dramatic Art, London; joined Santa Barbara Youth Theatre, in 30 productions aged 12–17; working in commercials aged 16; stage appearance in Ten Below, New York 1993; Screen Actors Guild Award 1996, 1998, 1999, Golden Globe 1998. *Films include:* Fast Times at Ridgemont High 1982, Heart Like a Wheel 1982, Revenge of the Nerds 1984, The Sure Thing 1985, Gotcha! 1985, Top Gun 1985, Summer Heat 1987, Revenge of the Nerds II 1987, Mr. North 1988, Miracle Mile 1989, How I Got into College 1989, Hawks 1989, Downtown 1990, Delta Heat, The Client 1994, Us Begins with You 1998, Don't Go Breaking My Heart 1999, Jackpot 2001, Northfork 2003, Thunderbirds 2004, The Forgotten 2004, Zodiac 2007. *Television includes:* (series) It Takes Two 1982–83, Northern Exposure 1992–93, ER 1994–2002, Soul Man, Rock Story 2000; (films) The Killing of Randy Webster 1981, High School USA 1983, Going for the Gold: The Bill Johnson Story 1985, El Diablo 1990, Hometown Boy Makes Good 1990, In Cold Blood 1996; (specials) Unpublished Letters, Sexual Healing. *Address:* c/o United Talent Agency, 9560 Wilshire Boulevard, Suite 500, Beverly Hills, CA 90212, USA.

EDWARDS, Blake; American film director and screenwriter; b. (William Blake McEdwards), 26 July 1922, Tulsa, Okla; m. Julie Andrews (q.v.) 1969; ed high school; served US Coast Guard Reserve World War II; wrote for radio shows Johnny Dollar, Line-Up; writer and creator of Richard Diamond; creator TV shows Dante's Inferno, Peter Gunn, Mr. Lucky; Academy Awards Lifetime Achievement Award 2004. *Writer:* All Ashore 1952, Sound Off 1952, Cruisin' Down the River 1953, Drive a Crooked Road 1954, My Sister Eileen (musical version) 1955, Operation Mad Ball 1957, Notorious Landlady 1962, The Pink Panther 2005. *Writer and co-producer:* Panhandle 1947, Stampede 1948. *Writer and director:* Bring Your Smile Along 1955, He Laughed Last 1955, Mr Cory 1956, This Happy Feeling 1958. *Co-writer and director:* The Great Race 1964. *Films directed:* Operation Petticoat 1959, High Time 1960, Breakfast at Tiffany's 1961, Days of Wine and Roses 1962, The Carey Treatment 1972. *Producer and director:* Experiment in Terror 1962. *Producer, co-writer, director:* The Soldier in the Rain 1963, The Pink Panther 1964, A Shot in the Dark 1964, What Did You Do in the War, Daddy? 1966, Peter Gunn 1967, The Party 1968, Darling Lili 1969, Wild Rovers 1971, The Tamarind Seed 1974, The Return of the Pink Panther 1975, The Pink Panther Strikes Again 1976, Revenge of the Pink Panther 1978, 10 1979, S.O.B. 1980, Victor/Victoria 1981, Trail of the Pink Panther 1982, Curse of the Pink Panther 1983, The Man Who Loved Women 1983, Micki and Maude 1984, That's Life 1986,

Blind Date 1986, Sunset 1988, Skin Deep 1989, Switch 1991, Son of the Pink Panther 1993. *Writer, director and co-producer:* Victor/Victoria (stage musical), Broadway 1995. *Address:* Creative Artists Agency, 9830 Wilshire Boulevard, Beverly Hills, CA 90212-1825 (office); Blake Edwards Co., Suite 501, 10520 Wilshire Boulevard, Apt 1002, Los Angeles, CA 90024, USA (office). *Telephone:* (310) 288-4545 (office). *Fax:* (310) 288-4800 (office).

EDWARDS, Sir Christopher Richard Watkin, Kt, MD, FRCP, FRCPE, FMedSci, FRSE; British physician and university vice-chancellor; b. 12 Feb. 1942; s. of Thomas Archibald Watkin Edwards and Beatrice Elizabeth Ruby Watkin Edwards; m. Sally Amanda Kidd 1968; two s. one d.; ed Marlborough Coll., Christ's Coll. Cambridge; lecturer in Medicine, St Bartholomew's Hosp., London 1969–75, Sr Lecturer and MRC Sr Research Fellow 1975–80, Hon. Consultant Physician 1975–80; Moncrieff Arnott Prof. of Clinical Medicine, Univ. of Edin. 1980–95, Dean Faculty of Medicine 1991–95, Provost Faculty Group of Medicine and Veterinary Medicine 1992–95; Prin. and Prof. of Medicine Imperial Coll. of Science and Medicine, Univ. of London 1995–2000; Vice-Chancellor Univ. of Newcastle 2001–07; mem. MRC 1991–95; Gov. Wellcome Trust 1994–; Co-founder FMedSci 1998; Hon. DSc (Aberdeen) 2000, Fellowship of Imperial Coll. London 2003. *Publications:* Clinical Physiology (Ed.) 1984, Essential Hypertension as an Endocrine Disease 1985, Endocrinology 1986, Recent Advances in Endocrinology and Metabolism, Vol. 3 (Ed.) 1989, Davidson's Principles and Practice of Medicine (Ed.) 1995; over 400 scientific papers and communications. *Leisure interests:* running, reading, golf, skiing, painting. *Address:* c/o University of Newcastle upon Tyne, 6 Kensington Terrace, Newcastle upon Tyne, NE1 7RU, England (office).

EDWARDS, Edwin Washington, LLD; American politician; b. 7 Aug. 1927, Marksville, La.; s. of Clarence W. Edwards and Agnes Brouillette Edwards; m. 1st Elaine Schwartzenburg 1949 (divorced 1989); two d. two s.; m. 2nd Candace Picou 1994; ed Louisiana State Univ.; naval cadet 1945–46; practised law in Crowley, La. 1949–80, Sr Pnr Edwards, Edwards and Broadhurst (law firm); practised in Baton Rouge, La. 1980s; mem. Crowley City Council 1954–62, La. State Senate 1964–66; House of Reps 1965–72, Public Works Cttee 1965–68, Whip to La. and Miss. Dels, Judiciary Cttee and Cttee on Internal Security; Gov. of Louisiana 1972–80, 1984–88, 1992–96; convicted of racketeering, conspiracy and extortion May 2000; sentenced to 10 years' imprisonment 2001; fmr Chair. Interstate Oil Compact Comm. 1974, Ozarks Regional Comm. 1974, Educ. Comm. of Task Force on State, Institutional and Fed. Responsibilities 1975; fmr mem. Nat. Resources and Environmental Man. Cttee of Southern Govs' Conf., Rural and Urban Devt Cttee of Nat. Govs' Conf.; fmr mem. Crowley Chamber of Commerce, Crowley Industrial Foundation, American Legion; Democrat.

EDWARDS, Gareth Owen, MBE, CBE; British business executive and fmr rugby union player; b. 12 July 1947; s. of Thomas Granville Edwards and Annie-Mary Edwards; m. Maureen Edwards 1972; two s.; ed Pontardawe Tech. School, Millfield School, Cardiff Coll. of Educ.; Welsh Secondary Schools Rugby int. 1965–66; English Schools 200 yards hurdles champion 1966 (UK under-19 record-holder); Welsh nat. team: 53 caps 1967–78, Capt. 13 times, youngest captain (aged 20) 1968; played with following clubs: Cardiff 1966–78, Barbarians 1967–78, British Lions 1968, 1971, 1974; Jt Dir Euro-Commercials (South Wales) Ltd 1982–, Players (UK) Ltd 1983–88; Chair. Hamdden Ltd 1991–; Chair. Regional Fisheries Advisory Cttee, Welsh Water Authority 1983–89. *Publications:* Gareth – An Autobiography 1978, Rugby Skills 1979, Rugby Skills for Forwards 1980, Gareth Edwards on Fishing 1984, Gareth Edwards on Rugby 1986, Gareth Edwards' 100 Great Rugby Players 1987. *Leisure interests:* fishing, golf. *Address:* 211 West Road, Nottage, Porthcawl, Mid-Glamorgan, CF36 3RT, Wales. *Telephone:* (1656) 785669 (Porthcawl).

EDWARDS, (James) Griffith, CBE, FMedSci; British psychiatrist and academic; *Emeritus Professor of Addiction Behaviour, Institute of Psychiatry, University of London;* b. 3 Oct. 1928, India; s. of the late J. T. Edwards and Constance Amy Edwards (née McFadyean); m. 1st 1969 Evelyn Morrison (divorced 1981); one s. two d. (one deceased); m. 2nd Frances Susan Stables 1981; ed Andover Grammar School, Balliol Coll., Univ. of Oxford; served RA 2nd Lt 1948–49; Jr Hosp. appointments, King George Ilford, St Bartholomew's, the Maudsley Hosp. 1956–62; worker 1962, Lectr 1966, Sr Lectr 1967 Inst. of Psychiatry; Dir Addiction Research Unit 1967–94; fmrly Chair. Nat. Addiction Centre; Prof. of Addiction Behaviour, Inst. of Psychiatry, Univ. of London 1979–94, Emer. Prof. 1994–; Ed. Addiction (formerly British Journal of Addiction) 1978–96, Ed.-in-Chief 1996–2004, Commissioning Ed. 2005–; Series Ed. Int. Monographs on the Addictions 1995–; Hon. Prof. Univ. of Chile 1992–; Jellinek Memorial Prize (international award for alcohol research) 1981, Nathan B. Eddy Gold Medal (international award for drug misuse research) 1996, Auguste Forrell Prize (European award for alcohol research) 1998. *Publications:* Alcohol: the Ambiguous Molecule 2000, Matters of Substance: Drugs and Why We Use Them 2004; papers on scientific and clinical aspects of addiction. *Address:* c/o National Addiction Centre, Institute of Psychiatry, King's College London, De Crespigny Park, London, SE5 8AF (office); 32 Crooms Hill, London, SE10 8ER, England (home). *Telephone:* (20) 8858-5631 (home). *E-mail:* p.davis@iop.kcl.ac.uk (office); grifsu@crooms .freeserve.co.uk (home).

EDWARDS, Huw, BA; British news broadcaster and journalist; *Presenter, Ten O'Clock News, British Broadcasting Corporation;* b. 1961, Bridgend, Wales; m.; five c.; ed Univ. of Wales, Cardiff; began career as reporter with local radio station Swansea Sound; joined BBC training scheme 1984, becoming parl. reporter, Political Corresp. BBC News, London 1988, Chief Political Corresp., London 1997–99, BBC News 24, Presenter BBC One O'Clock, Six O'Clock and Breakfast News 1994–99, Six O'Clock News 1999–2003, Ten O'Clock News (BAFTA Award for News Coverage – Madrid Bombing 2004, BAFTA Award for News Coverage 2005, Royal TV Soc. Award 2005) 2003–; Hon. Fellow (Univ. of Wales, Cardiff) 2003, (Lampeter) 2006, (Swansea) 2007, (Newport) 2007, (Swansea Metropolitan) 2007, Paul Harris Fellow, Rotary Int., Hon. Prof. of Journalism, Cardiff Univ. 2006; BAFTA Wales Presenter of the Year 2001, 2002, 2003, 2004. *Other TV and radio work includes:* Newsnight, Panorama, Songs of Praise, classical music programmes on BBC Two, BBC Radio 3 and Radio 4, Bread of Heaven (BBC Wales) 2004, State Opening of Parliament, Trooping the Colour, Festival of Remembrance (all for BBC 1). *Address:* BBC Television Centre, Wood Lane, London, W12 7RJ, England (office). *Website:* www.bbc.co.uk (office).

EDWARDS, James Burrows, BS, DMD, FACD, FICD; American oral and maxillofacial surgeon and fmr university president; *President Emeritus, Medical University of South Carolina;* b. 24 June 1927, Hawthorne, Fla; s. of O. M. Edwards and Bertie R. Hieronymus Edwards; m. Ann Norris Darlington 1951; one s. one d.; ed Coll. of Charleston, Univ. of Louisville and Univ. of Pa Graduate Medical School, Henry Ford Hosp.; oral surgery residency, Henry Ford Hosp., Detroit, Mich. 1958–60; dentistry practice, specializing in oral and maxillofacial surgery, Charleston, SC 1960–; Clinical Assoc. in Oral Surgery, Coll. of Dental Medicine, Medical Univ., SC 1967–77, Clinical Prof. of Oral Surgery and Community Dentistry 1977-82, Prof. of Oral and Maxillofacial Surgery 1982, Pres. of Univ. 1982–99, Pres. Emer. 1999–; Fellow American Coll. of Dentists, Int. Coll. of Dentists; mem. Federation Dentaire Internationale, British Assn of Oral and Maxillofacial Surgeons, Int. Soc. of Oral and Maxillofacial Surgeons and numerous dental orgs in US; Chair. of Charleston County Republican Cttee 1964–69; Chair. of First Congressional District Republican Cttee 1970; mem. SC Statewide Steering Cttee for Republican Party; mem. SC State Senate 1972–74; Governor of South Carolina 1975–78; US Sec. of Energy 1981–82; mem. Bd of Dirs Wachovia Bank of SC, Phillips Petroleum Co., William Benton Foundation, Brendle's Inc., SCANA Corpn, Encyclopaedia Britannica Inc., Imo Delaval Inc., Harry Frank Guggenheim Foundation and numerous others; twelve hon. degrees. *Leisure interests:* hunting, fishing, sailing, water skiing. *Address:* 100 Venning Street, Mount Pleasant, SC, 29464, USA (home). *Telephone:* (843) 884-3493 (home). *Fax:* (843) 849-5456 (home).

EDWARDS, John Coates, MA, CMG; British diplomatist; b. 25 Nov. 1934, Tunbridge Wells, Kent; s. of Herbert J. Edwards and Doris M. Edwards (née Starzacher); m. Mary Harris 1959 (died 2006); one s. one d.; ed Skinners' Company School, Tunbridge Wells and Brasenose Coll. Oxford; Lt RA 1953–55; Colonial Office 1960–62; Nature Conservancy Council 1962–64; Ministry of Overseas Devt 1965–68, 1976–78; First Sec. Bangkok and Perm. Rep. to ECAFE 1968–71; Head, E Africa Devt Div. British High Comm. Nairobi 1972–75; Head, British Devt Div. in the Caribbean, Barbados and UK; Dir Caribbean Devt Bank 1978–81; Head, W Indian and Atlantic Dept FCO 1981–84; Deputy High Commr in Kenya 1984–88; High Commr in Lesotho 1988–91, in Botswana 1991–94; Head UK Del., EC Monitoring Mission in fmr Yugoslavia 1995–99; JP, Kent 2000–04; Chair. Kenya Soc.; mem. council Royal Overseas League. *Leisure interests:* birdwatching, fishing, visual arts, walking, local history. *Address:* Fairways, Back Lane, Ightham, Sevenoaks, Kent, TN15 9AU, England (home). *Telephone:* (1732) 883556 (home).

EDWARDS, John Reid, BS, JD; American politician and lawyer; b. 10 June 1953; s. of Wallace R. Edwards and Catherine Edwards; m. Mary Elizabeth Anania; one s. (deceased) two d.; ed N Carolina Univ., Univ. of N Carolina at Chapel Hill; called to Bar, NC 1977, Tenn. 1978; Assoc., Dearborn and Ewing, Nashville 1978–81; trial lawyer, Wade Smith 1981; Assoc., Tharrington Smith and Hargrove, Raleigh 1981–83, Pnr 1984–92; Pnr, Edwards and Kirby, Raleigh 1993–99; Senator from N Carolina 1999–2005; f. One America Cttee (political action cttee) 2001; unsuccessful pursuit of Democratic nomination for US presidency 2004, Democratic cand. for Vice-Pres. 2004; Dir, Center on Poverty, Work and Opportunity, Univ. of N Carolina School of Law 2005–06; Sr Advisor Fortress Investment Group LLC 2005; unsuccessful cand. for Democratic nomination for Pres. of US 2007–08; Dir Urban Ministries, Raleigh 1996–97; mem. NC Acad. of Trial Lawyers (Vice-Pres. Bd of Govs), NC Bar Assn, Banking, Housing and Urban Affairs, Governmental Affairs, Small Business and Y2K Cttees; Fellow, American Coll. of Trial Lawyers. *Publications include:* Four Trials 2003, Home: The Blueprints of Our Lives 2006, Ending Poverty in America 2007. *Address:* c/o 410 Market Street, Suite 400, Chapel Hill, NC 27516, USA (office). *Website:* johnedwards.com (office).

EDWARDS, Jonathan, CBE; British fmr athlete; b. 10 May 1966, London; s. of Andrew David Edwards and Jill Caulfield; m. Alison Joy Briggs 1990; two s.; ed West Buckland, Devon; bronze medal, World Championships 1993; gold medal, Fifth Athletics World Championships, Gothenburg 1995 (twice breaking own world record for triple jump, clearing 18.29m), Edmonton 2001; silver medal, Olympic Games, Atlanta 1996, World Championships 1997, 1999; gold medal European Championships 1998, European Indoor Championships 1998, Goodwill Games 1998, Olympic Games 2000, World Championships 2001, Commonwealth Games 2002; retd after World Championships 2003; currently athletics commentator BBC; Sports Fellowship, Univ. of Durham 1999; British Sportsman of the Year 1995, IAAF Athlete of the Year 1995, BBC Sports Personality of the Year 1995, British Male Athlete of the Year 1995, 2000, 2001. *Publication:* A Time to Jump 2000. *Address:* c/o Jonathan Marks, MTC, 20 York Street, London, W1U 6PU, England. *Telephone:* (20) 7935-8000. *Fax:* (20) 7935-8066. *E-mail:* info@mtc-uk.com (office). *Website:* www.mtc-uk.com (office).

EDWARDS, Jorge; Chilean writer and diplomatist; b. 29 July 1931, Santiago; ed Univ. of Chile, Princeton Univ., USA; diplomatist 1957–73, Amb. to Cuba 1970, Advisory Minister in Paris 1971–73; Literary Prize of the City of Santiago 1961, 1991, Atenea Prize of Univ. of Concepción (Chile), Essay Prize of the City of Santiago 1991, Cervantes Prize 1999. *Publications:*

(novels) El patio 1952, Gente de la ciudad 1962, Las máscaras 1967, Temas y variaciones 1969, Fantasmas de carne y hueso 1992, El peso de la noche 1965, Las máscaras 1967, Temas y variacones 1969, Persona non grata 1973, Desde la cola del dragón 1977, Los convidados de piedra 1978, El museo de cera 1981, La mujer imaginaria 1985, El anfitrión 1988, Cuentos completos 1990, Adiós poeta 1990, El regalo 1991, Fantasmas de carne y hueso 1993, El whisky de los poetas 1994, El origen del mundo 1996, El sueño de la Historia 2000, Diálogos en un tejado 2003, El inútil de la familia 2005, La casa de Dostoievsky (Premio Iberoamericano Planeta–Casa de América de Narrativa) 2008. *Address:* c/o Alfaguara, Torrelaguna 60, 28043 Madrid, Spain.

EDWARDS, Kenneth John Richard, PhD; British university vice-chancellor (retd); b. 12 Feb. 1934; s. of John Edwards and Elizabeth M. Edwards; m. Janet M. Gray 1958; two s. one d.; ed Market Drayton Grammar School, Univ. of Reading and Univ. Coll. of Wales, Aberystwyth; Fellow, Univ. of Calif. 1961–62; ARC Fellow, Welsh Plant Breeding Station, Aberystwyth 1962–63, Sr Scientific Officer 1963–66; Lecturer in Genetics, Univ. of Cambridge 1966–84, Head, Dept of Genetics 1981–84; Lecturer, St John's Coll. Cambridge 1971–84, Fellow 1971–87, Tutor 1981–84; Sec.-Gen. of Faculties, Univ. of Cambridge 1984–87; Vice-Chancellor, Univ. of Leicester 1987–99; Chair. Cttee of Vice-Chancellors and Prins 1993–95; mem. Marshall Aid Commemoration Comm. 1991–98, Council ACU 1994–99; Chair. Governing Body, Inst. of Grassland and Environmental Research 1994–99; Pres. Asscn of European Univs 1998–2001; Visiting Lecturer, Birmingham 1965; Visiting Prof., Buenos Aires 1973; Leverhulme Research Fellow, Univ. of Calif. 1973; Hon. LLD (Belfast) 1994, (Leicester) 1999; Hon. DSc (Reading) 1995, (Loughborough) 1995, (Warwick) 2000; Dr hc (Cluj, Romania) 1997, (Maribor, Slovenia) 1999, (Olomouc, Czech Repub.) 2002. *Publications:* Evolution in Modern Biology 1977; articles on genetics in scientific journals. *Leisure interests:* music, gardening. *Address:* 10 Sedley Taylor Road, Cambridge, England. *Telephone:* (1223) 245680 (home). *E-mail:* kenneth.edwards@ntlworld.com (home).

EDWARDS, N. Murray, BComm, LLB (Hons), JD; Canadian lawyer and business executive; *Owner and President, Edco Financial Holdings Ltd;* b. Regina, Sask.; m. Heather Bala; one s.; ed Univs of Saskatchewan and Toronto; moved to Calgary in 1983 and became lawyer and later Pnr, Burnet, Duckworth & Palmer; Owner and Pres. Edco Financial Holdings Ltd (merchant bankers) 1988–; leading investor in and Man. Dir and Exec. Chair. of numerous publicly traded cos, including Canadian Natural Resources Ltd (CNRL), Ensign Resource Service Group Inc., Magellan Aerospace Corpn, Penn West Petroleum Ltd and Resorts of the Canadian Rockies Inc.; Dir and Co-owner of Nat. Hockey League's Calgary Flames; Dir of Business Devt, Bank of Canada; mem. Bd Govs The Canadian Unity Council; mem. Council of Champions, Calgary Children's Initiatives, Banff Centre; mem. Bd of Dirs Canadian Council of Chief Execs, Canada West Foundation. *Address:* Edco Financial Holdings Ltd, Suite 2500, 350 7th Avenue SW, Calgary, AB T2P 4N1 (office); Canadian Natural Resources Ltd, 2500, 855 – 2 Street SW, Calgary, AB Canada (office). *Telephone:* (403) 261-4850 (Edco) (office); (403) 517-6700 (CNRL) (office). *Fax:* (403) 517-7350 (CNRL) (office). *E-mail:* info@cnrl.com (office). *Website:* www.cnrl.com (office).

EDWARDS, Peter Philip, PhD, FRS, FRSC; British scientist and academic; *Professor of Inorganic Chemistry, University of Birmingham;* b. 30 June 1949; s. of the late Ronald Goodlass and of Ethel Mary Edwards; m. Patricia Anne Clancy 1970; two s. one d.; ed Univ. of Salford; Fulbright Scholar and NSF Fellow, Baker Lab. of Chem., Cornell Univ. 1975–77; Science and Eng Research Council/NATO Fellow and Ramsay Memorial Fellow, Inorganic Chem. Lab., Oxford Univ. 1977–79; demonstrator in Inorganic Chem., Jesus Coll., Cambridge Univ. 1979–81, Dir of Studies in Chem. 1979–91, lecturer, Univ. Chem. Labs. 1981–91; Visiting Prof. Cornell Univ. 1983–86; Nuffield Science Research Fellow 1986–87; Co-Founder and Co-Dir. Interdisciplinary Research Centre in Superconductivity 1988; BP Venture Research Fellow 1988–90; Prof. of Inorganic Chem. Univ. of Birmingham 1991–, of Chem. and of Materials 1999–, Head of School of Chemistry 1996–99; Royal Soc. Leverhulme Trust Sr Research Fellow 1996–97; Vice-Pres. Dalton Division Royal Soc. of Chem. 1995; Corday Medal 1985, Tilden Medal 1992, Liversidge Medal 1999. *Publications:* The Metallic and Non-Metallic States of Matter (jtly) 1985, Metal-Insulator Transitions Revisited 1995. *Leisure interests:* exercise, sports. *Address:* School of Chemistry, University of Birmingham, Edgbaston, Birmingham, B15 2TT, England (office). *Telephone:* (121) 414-4379 (office). *Fax:* (121) 414-4442. *E-mail:* p.p.edwards@bham.ac.uk (office). *Website:* www.chem.bham.ac.uk.

EDWARDS, Philip Walter, PhD, FBA; British academic; b. 7 Feb. 1923, Barrow-in-Furness; s. of the late R. H. Edwards and B. Edwards; m. 1st Hazel Valentine 1947 (died 1950); m. 2nd Sheila Wilkes 1952; three s. one d.; ed King Edward's High School, Birmingham, Univ. of Birmingham; Lecturer in English, Univ. of Birmingham 1946–60; Prof. of English Literature, Trinity Coll. Dublin 1960–66; Visiting Prof., Univ. of Mich. 1964–65; Prof. of Literature, Univ. of Essex 1966–74; Visiting Prof., Williams Coll., Mass. 1969; Visiting Fellow, All Souls Coll., Oxford 1970–71; King Alfred Prof. of English Literature, Univ. of Liverpool 1974–90; Visiting Prof., Univ. of Otago, New Zealand 1980, Int. Christian Univ., Tokyo 1989. *Publications:* Sir Walter Ralegh 1953, The Spanish Tragedy (ed.) 1959, Shakespeare and the Confines of Art 1968, Massinger, Plays and Poems (ed. with C. Gibson) 1976, Pericles Prince of Tyre (ed.) 1976, Threshold of a Nation 1979, Hamlet Prince of Denmark (ed.) 1985, Shakespeare: A Writer's Progress 1986, Last Voyages 1988, The Story of the Voyage 1994, Sea-Mark: The Metaphorical Voyage, Spenser to Milton 1997, The Journals of Captain Cook (ed.) 1999, Pilgrimage and Literary Tradition 2005. *Leisure interest:* calligraphy. *Address:* High Gillinggrove, Gillinggate, Kendal, Cumbria, LA9 4JB, England (home). *Telephone:* (1539) 721298 (home).

EDWARDS, Robert Geoffrey, CBE, MA, PhD, FRS; British medical scientist and academic; *Professor Emeritus of Human Reproduction, University of Cambridge;* b. 27 Sept. 1925; s. of Samuel Edwards and Margaret Edwards; m. Ruth Eileen Fowler 1956; five d.; ed Manchester Cen. High School and Univs of Wales and Edinburgh; Research Fellow, Calif. Inst. of Tech. 1957–58; scientist, Nat. Inst. of Medical Research, Mill Hill 1958–62; Glasgow Univ. 1962–63; Dept of Physiology, Univ. of Cambridge 1963–89; Ford Foundation Reader in Physiology 1969–85; Prof. of Human Reproduction, Univ. of Cambridge 1985–89, Prof. Emer. 1989–; Fellow, Churchill Coll. Cambridge, now Extraordinary Fellow; Scientific Dir Bourn Hallam Clinics, Cambs. and London; Chair. European Soc. of Human Reproduction and Embryology 1984–86; Visiting Scientist, Johns Hopkins Univ. 1965, Univ. of NC 1966, Free Univ. Brussels 1984; Hon. Pres. British Fertility Soc. 1988–; Life Fellow, Australian Fertility Soc.; Chief Ed. Human Reproduction 1986–; Hon. mem. French Soc. for Infertility; Hon. Citizen of Bordeaux; Hon. FRCOG; Hon. MRCP; Hon. DSc (Hull, York, Free Univ. Brussels); Gold Medal, Spanish Fertility Soc. 1985, King Faisal Award 1989, Albert Lasker Award for Clinical Medical Research 2001. *Publications:* A Matter of Life (with P. C. Steptoe) 1980, Conception in the Human Female 1980, Mechanisms of Sex Differentiation in Animals and Man (with C. R. Austin), Human Conception in Vitro (with J. M. Purdy) 1982, Implantation of the Human Embryo (with J. M. Purdy and P. C. Steptoe) 1985, In Vitro Fertilization and Embryo Transfer (with M. Seppälä) 1985, Life Before Birth 1989; numerous articles in scientific and medical journals. *Leisure interests:* farming, politics, music. *Address:* Duck End Farm, Dry Drayton, Cambridge, CB3 8DB, England. *Telephone:* (1954) 780602.

EDWARDS, Robert John, CBE; British journalist; b. 26 Oct. 1925, Farnham, Surrey; s. of Gordon Edwards and Margaret Edwards (née Grain); m. 1st Laura Ellwood 1952 (dissolved 1972); two s. two d.; m. 2nd Brigid Segrave 1977; ed Ranelagh School; Ed. Tribune 1951–55; Deputy Ed. Sunday Express 1957–59; Ed. Daily Express 1961–62, 1963–65; Ed. Evening Citizen (Glasgow) 1962–63; Ed. Sunday People (fmrly The People) 1966–72; Ed. Sunday Mirror 1972–84; Dir Mirror Group Newspapers 1976–86, Sr Group Ed. 1984–85, Deputy Chair. (non-exec.) 1985–86; Chair. London Press Club Scoop of the Year Awards Panel 1990–2003; Ombudsman to Today newspaper 1990–95. *Publication:* Goodbye Fleet Street 1988. *Leisure interests:* walking, reading newspapers. *Address:* Tregeseal House, Nancherrow, St Just, Penzance, TR19 7PW, England (home). *Telephone:* (1736) 787060 (home). *Fax:* (1736) 786617 (home). *E-mail:* edwardsrj@aol.com (home).

EDWARDS, (Roger) Nicholas (see Crickhowell, Baron).

EDWARDS, Sir Samuel (Sam) Frederick, Kt, FRS, FInstP, FIMA, FRSC, CChem, CPhys, CMath; British physicist and administrator; *Cavendish Professor Emeritus of Physics, University of Cambridge;* b. 1 Feb. 1928, Swansea; s. of Richard and Mary Jane Edwards; m. Merriell E. M. Bland 1953; one s. three d.; ed Swansea Grammar School, Gonville and Caius College, Cambridge, Harvard Univ.; member, Inst. for Advanced Study, Princeton 1952–53; staff mem. Univ. of Birmingham 1953–58, Univ. of Manchester 1958–72; Prof. of Theoretical Physics, Univ. of Manchester 1963–72; John Humphrey Plummer Prof. of Physics, Univ. of Cambridge 1972–84, Cavendish Prof. 1984–95, Prof. Emer. 1995–, Pro Vice-Chancellor 1992–95; mem. Council, Inst. of Physics 1967–73, Vice-Pres. of Inst. 1970–73, Chair. Publ Div. 1970–73; mem. Science Bd, Science Research Council 1970–73, mem. Physics Cttee 1968–70, Polymer Science Cttee 1968–73, Chair. Physics Cttee 1970–73, Science Research Council 1973–77; Dir Lucas Industries 1981–93, Steetley PLC 1985–92; mem. Council European Physical Soc. 1969–71, Univ. Grants Cttee 1971–73, Scientific Advisory Council, Min. of Defence 1973–81, 1988– (Chair. 1978–81), Advisory Bd for the Research Councils, Dept of Ed. and Science 1973–77, Metrology and Standards Requirements Bd, Dept of Industry 1974–77, Advisory Council on Research and Devt, Dept of Energy 1974–77 (Chair. 1983–88), UK Del. NATO Science Cttee 1974–78, Senatsausschuss für Forschungspolitik und Forschungsplanung der Max Planck Gesellschaft 1975–77, Council Inst. of Math. and its Applications 1976– (Pres. 1980–81), European Council for Research and Devt 1975–79, Scientific Advisory Cttee Allied Corpn 1980–84; Chair. Council BAAS 1977–82, Pres. 1988–89, Council Royal Soc. 1981–83 (Vice-Pres. 1982–83); Chief Scientific Adviser, Dept of Energy 1983–88; Chair. Sr Advisory Group of Unilever PLC 1992–96; mem. Research Advisory Group BP 1993–97; Fellow, Gonville and Caius Coll., Cambridge 1972–; Foreign mem. Acad. des Sciences 1989, NAS 1996; Hon. Fellow, Inst. of Physics, French Physical Soc., BAAS 2002; Hon. mem. European Physical Soc.; Hon. DTech (Loughborough) 1975; Hon. DSc (Edin., Salford, Bath, Birmingham, Wales, Strasbourg, Sheffield, Dublin, Leeds), (Swansea) 1994, (E Anglia) 1995, (Cambridge) 2001, (Mainz) 2002, (Tel-Aviv) 2006; Maxwell, Guthrie Medals and Prizes, Inst. of Physics 1974, 1987, Founders' Polymer Prize 2001, American Physical Soc. Prize for High Polymer Physics 1982, Davy Medal, Royal Soc. 1984, Gold Medallist, Inst. of Math. 1986, Gold Medallist Rheology Soc. 1990, LVMH Science pour l'Art Prize 1993, Boltzmann Medal, IUPAP 1995, Royal Medal, Royal Soc. 2001, Dirac Medal 2005. *Publications:* Technological Risk 1980, Theory of Polymer Dynamics (with M. Doi) 1986, Networks of Liquid Crystal Polymers (with S. Aharoni) 1994. *Address:* Cavendish Laboratory, Cambridge, CB3 9LU (office); 7 Penarth Place, Cambridge, CB3 9LU, England (home). *Telephone:* (1223) 337259 (office); (1223) 366610 (home). *Fax:* (1223) 337000 (office). *E-mail:* sfe11@phy.cam.ac.uk (office). *Website:* www.poco.phy.cam.ac.uk/~sfe11/Welcome.htm (office).

EDWARDS, Sian; British conductor; b. 27 Aug. 1959; ed Royal Northern Coll. of Music, Manchester; studied with Sir Charles Groves, Norman Del Mar and Neeme Järvi and with Prof. I.A. Musin, Leningrad Conservatoire 1983–85; won first Leeds Conductors' Competition 1984; has worked with many leading orchestras in UK including London Philharmonic (LPO), Royal Liverpool Philharmonic, Royal Scottish Orchestra, City of Birmingham Symphony, Hallé, BBC Philharmonic, English Chamber orchestras and London Sinfonietta; also with LA Philharmonic Orchestra, The Cleveland Orchestra, The Ensemble Modern, Rotterdam Philharmonic Orchestra and other orchestras; operatic debut, Mahagonny, Scottish Opera 1986; other operatic productions include La Traviata and L'Heure Espagnole (Glyndebourne) 1987–88, Katya Kabanova, New Year (Glyndebourne Touring Opera) 1988–90, The Knot Garden, Rigoletto, Il Trovatore (Royal Opera House, Covent Garden) 1988–91, world premiere Greek (Mark Anthony Turnage), Munich Biennale 1988, Edin. Festival 1988, The Gambler (ENO) 1990, Khovanshchina (ENO) 1994, Mahagonny 1995, La Clemenza di Tito 1998, Eugene Onegin 2000, Peter Grimes (ENO) 2001, Don Giovanni, Danish Royal Opera 2001, The Death of Klinghoffer, La Damnation de Faust, Finnish Nat. Opera 2001; Music Dir ENO 1993–95. *Recordings include:* Tchaikovsky orchestral music (Royal Liverpool Philharmonic Orchestra) and Peter and the Wolf, Young Person's Guide to the Orchestra, Tchaikovsky's Fifth symphony (LPO). *Address:* c/o Ingpen & Williams, 7 St George's Court, 131 Putney Bridge Road, London, SW15 2PA, England (office). *Telephone:* (20) 8874-3222 (office). *Fax:* (20) 8877-3113 (office). *E-mail:* info@ingpen.co.uk (office).

EELSEN, Pierre Henri Maurice, LenD; French administrator and company executive; b. 12 July 1933, Montmorency, Val-d'Oise; s. of Maurice Eelsen and Jacqueline Robert; m. 1st; two s. one d.; m. 2nd Danièle Mesle, 1980; one s.; ed Lycée Jacques-Decour, Paris, Univ. de Paris; at Renault 1958–84, responsible for econ. studies Renault Eng 1959, attached to Dir of Relations 1965, Head Dept Agric. Machinery 1967, attached to Gen. Secretariat 1969, Asst to Sec.-Gen. 1971, Jt Sec.-Gen. 1975, Gen. Del. 1979, mem. Exec. Cttee 1981; Head Dept Int. Affairs Chambre syndicale des constructeurs d'automobiles 1962; mem. European Econ. and Social Cttee 1982–84; Pres. Nat. Asscn for Devt of Overseas depts 1982–85; Admin. Ecole nat. d'admin. 1983; Pres.-Dir-Gen. Air Inter 1984–90; Pres. Agence Nationale pour le Développement de l'Education Permanente (ADEP) 1985–91, Centre national d'enseignement à distance 1988–, Admin. council Institut régional d'admin. de Nantes 1988, French Div. of Centre européen de l'entreprise publique 1989, Chambre Syndicale des Transporteurs Aériens 1986–90; Pres. Nord-Pas de Calais Développement 1991–94, Observatoire Nat. du Tourisme 1991–96, L'Institut européen de recherche et de formation supérieure du tourisme 1992–94; Man. Ed Consultants 1994–; Vice-Pres. Airport Div. SEN (Vinci Group) 1999–2002; Chair. Sogindo 2002–06; Commdr, Ordre nat. du Mérite, Officier, Légion d'honneur. *Address:* c/o Sogindo, 52 rue Guynemer, 92404 Courbevoie Cedex (office); 33 rue Lhomond, 75005 Paris (home); Domaine de Camarat, 83350 Ramatuelle, France (home). *Fax:* 1-43-31-20-37 (home).

EFI, HH Tuiatua Tupua Tamasese, (O le Ao o le Malo of Samoa); b. 1938; s. of Tupua Tamasese Mea'ole; m. Filia; ed St Joseph's Coll., Apia, Western Samoa and Victoria Univ., Wellington, NZ; elected to Western Samoan Parl. 1965–91; Minister of Works, Civil Aviation, Marine and Transport 1970–73; Prime Minister (as the Hon. Ta'isi Tupuola Tufuga Efi) 1976–82, fmr Minister of Foreign Affairs, Local and Dist Affairs and Police; Deputy Prime Minister 1985–88; Jt Leader Samoa Nat. Devt Party (SNDP); mem. Council of Deputies 2007; elected Head of State (O le Ao o le Malo) of Samoa 15 June 2007. *Address:* Government House, Vailima, Apia, Samoa (office). *Website:* www.govt.ws (office).

EFIMOV (see YEFIMOV).

EFSTATHIOU, George Petros, BA, PhD, FRS; British astrophysicist; *Professor of Astrophysics, University of Cambridge;* b. 2 Sept. 1955, London; s. of Petros Efstathiou and Christina Parperi; m. 1st Helena Jane Smart 1976 (divorced 1997); m. 2nd Yvonne Nobis 1998; three s. one d.; ed Somerset Comprehensive School, London, Keble Coll., Oxford, Univ. of Durham; Research Asst, Univ. of Calif., Berkeley 1979–80; Research Asst, Univ. of Cambridge 1980–83, Jr Research Fellow, King's Coll. Cambridge 1980–84, Sr Research Fellow 1984–88, Asst Dir of Research, Inst. of Astronomy, Cambridge 1984–88, Prof. of Astrophysics and Fellow, King's Coll. Cambridge 1997–, Dir Inst. of Astronomy 2004–08; Savilian Prof. of Astronomy and Fellow, New Coll. Oxford 1988–97; Bappu Medal and Prize, Astronomical Soc. of India 1988, Maxwell Medal and Prize, Inst. of Physics 1990, Bodossaki Foundation Prize for Astrophysics 1994, Robinson Prize in Cosmology, Royal Soc. 1997, Heineman Prize for Astrophysics (jtly), American Inst. of Physics 2005. *Publications:* articles in astronomical journals. *Leisure interests:* running, playing guitar. *Address:* Institute of Astronomy, Madingley Road, Cambridge, CB3 0HA, England (office). *Telephone:* (1223) 337530 (office); (1223) 574001 (home). *Fax:* (1223) 339910 (office). *E-mail:* gpe@ast.cam.ac.uk (office). *Website:* www.ast.cam.ac.uk (office).

EFUMAN, Santiago Nsobeya; Equatorial Guinean politician; Minister of Foreign Affairs, Int. Co-operation and Francophone Affairs 2001–03; Govt Spokesman, Ministry of Information, Culture and Tourism 2006–. *Address:* Ministry of Information, Culture and Tourism, Malabo, Equatorial Guinea (office).

EGAN, HE Cardinal Edward Michael, DD, JCD; American ecclesiastic; *Cardinal Archbishop of New York;* b. 2 April 1932, Oak Park, Ill.; s. of Thomas J. Egan and Genevieve Costello Egan; ed St Mary of the Lake Seminary, Mundelein, Ill., Pontifical N American Coll., Vatican City, Pontifical Gregorian Univ., Rome, Italy; ordained priest 1957; curate at Holy Name Cathedral Parish 1958, later Asst Chancellor Archdiocese of Chicago and Sec. to HE Cardinal Albert Meyer; Asst Vice-Rector and Repetitor of Moral Theology and Canon Law, Pontifical N American Coll., Vatican City 1960; Sec. to HE Cardinal John Cody 1964, later Co-Chancellor Archdiocese of Chicago; Judge, Tribunal of the Sacred Roman Rota 1971–85; fmr Prof. of Canon Law, Vatican

City, Pontifical Gregorian Univ., Rome; fmr Prof. of Civil and Criminal Procedure, Studium Rotale; fmr Commr Congregation for the Sacraments and Divine Worship; fmr Consultor Congregation of the Clergy; consecrated Bishop 1985; Auxiliary Bishop of New York and Vicar for Educ. 1985; Third Bishop of Bridgeport 1988–2000; Archbishop of New York 2000–; cr. Cardinal 2001; Pres. and Chair. Bd Trustees Catholic Near East Welfare Asscn; Trustee Ratisbonne Inst., Jerusalem, Israel, St Thomas More Coll., NH, Sacred Heart Univ., Fairfield, CT, Nat. Shrine of the Immaculate Conception, Washington, DC, Catholic Univ. of America, Washington, DC 2000–(09); Dr hc (St John's Univ., New York, Thomas More Coll., Western Connecticut State Univ.). *Address:* Archdiocese of New York, 1011 First Avenue, New York, NY 10022-4134, USA (office). *Telephone:* (212) 371-1000 (office). *Fax:* (212) 826-6020 (office). *Website:* www.ny-archdiocese.org (office).

EGAN, Sir John Leopold, Kt, MSc Econ, DL, FRAeS, FIC, FIMI, FCIT, FCIPS; British business executive; *Chairman, Severn Trent PLC;* b. 7 Nov. 1939, Rawtenstall, Lancs.; s. of James Edward Egan; m. Julia Emily Treble 1963; two d.; ed Bablake School, Coventry, Imperial Coll., London, London Business School; petroleum engineer, Shell Int. 1962–66; Gen. Man. AC-Delco Replacement Parts Operation, Gen. Motors Ltd 1968–71; Man. Dir Unipart, Parts and Service Dir, Leyland Cars 1971–76; Corp. Parts Dir Massey Ferguson 1976–80; Chair. Jaguar Cars Ltd 1980–84, Chair and Chief Exec., Chief Exec. and Man. Dir Jaguar PLC 1984–85, Chair. and Chief Exec. Jaguar PLC 1985–90; Chief Exec. BAA PLC 1990–99, Dir 1990–; Dir Legal & Gen. Group 1987–97, Vice-Chair. 1993–97, Pres. 1998–; Chair. MEPC PLC 1998–2000, Inchcape PLC 2000–05, Harrison Lovegrove Ltd 2000–05, Qinetiq 2001–02, Asite 2001–05, Severn Trent PLC; Deputy Pres. CBI 2001–02, Pres. 2002–2004; mem. Bd of Dirs Foreign and Colonial Investment Trust 1985–97, British Tourist Authority 1994–97, Governance for Owners 2006–; Pres. Inst. of Man. 2000–01; Sr Fellow, RCA; Hon. Prof., Dept of Eng, Univ. of Warwick 1990; Dr hc (Cranfield Inst.) 1986, Hon. DTech (Loughborough) 1987, Hon. LLD (Bath) 1988; Castrol Gold Medal, Inst. of Motor Industry Award 1982, Int. Gold Medal, Inst. of Production Engineers, City and Guilds of London Hon. Insignia Award for Tech. 1987 and several other awards. *Leisure interests:* skiing, squash, walking, music. *Address:* Severn Trent PLC, 2297 Coventry Road, Birmingham, B26 3PU, England (office). *Telephone:* (121) 722-4265 (office). *Fax:* (121) 722-4777 (office). *E-mail:* john.egan@stplc.com (office). *Website:* www.severntrent.com.

EGASHIRA, Toshiaki; Japanese insurance industry executive; *President and Representative Director, Mitsui Sumitomo Insurance Company Ltd;* fmr Dir in Pres.'s Office, fmr Chief Dir of China, Chief Dir of Kanagawa & Shizuoka, later Man. Exec. Officer and CEO Mitsui Sumitomo Insurance Co. Ltd, later Pres., Exec. Pres. and Rep. Dir, Pres. and Rep. Dir Mitsui Sumitomo Insurance Group Holdings, Inc. 2008–. *Address:* Mitsui Sumitomo Insurance Co. Ltd, 27-2 Shinkawa 2-chome, Chuo-ku, Tokyo 104-8252, Japan (office). *Telephone:* (3) 3297-1111 (office). *Fax:* (3) 3297-6888 (office). *E-mail:* info@ms-ins.com (office). *Website:* www.ms-ins.com (office).

EGELAND, Jan, MA; Norwegian UN official; *Special Advisor to the Secretary-General, United Nations;* m. Anne Kristin Sydnes; two d.; ed Univ. of Oslo, Univ. of Calif., Berkeley, USA; State Sec., Ministry of Foreign Affairs 1990–97; Special Adviser to UN Sec.-Gen. on Colombia 1999–2002; Sec.-Gen. Norwegian Red Cross 2002–03; UN Under-Sec.-Gen. for Humanitarian Affairs and Humanitarian Relief Coordinator 2003–07; Special Advisor to Sec.-Gen. 2007–; co-organized Norwegian channel between Israel and Palestinian Liberation Organisation leading to Oslo Accord 1993; directed Norwegian facilitation of UN-led peace talks leading to ceasefire agreement between Guatemalan govt and Unidad Revolucionaria Nacional Guatemalteca guerrillas 1996; fmr Dir Int. Dept Norwegian Red Cross; fmr Chair. Amnesty Int. (AI) Norway and Vice-Chair. AI Int. Exec. Cttee; fmr Head of Devt Studies, Henry Dunant Inst., Geneva; fmr Fellow, Int. Peace Research Inst., Oslo and Truman Inst. for the Advancement of Peace, Jerusalem; fmr radio and TV int. news reporter, Norwegian Broadcasting Corpn. *Publications include:* reports, studies and articles on conflict resolution, humanitarian affairs and human rights. *Address:* United Nations, New York, NY 10017, USA (office). *Telephone:* (212) 963-1234 (office). *Fax:* (212) 963-4879 (office). *Website:* www.un.org (office).

EGELUND, Niels; Danish diplomatist; *Ambassador to France;* b. 4 July 1946, Copenhagen; ed Coll. of Europe, Bruges, Belgium, Univ. of Århus; joined Foreign Service 1972, First Sec., Embassy in Washington, DC 1976–80, Deputy Chief of Mission, Bonn 1985–87; Amb., Under-Sec. of State, Political Dir 1992–93; Diplomatic Counsellor to Prime Minister 1993–99; Perm. Rep. to NATO 1999–2003; Amb. to France 2003–; Commdr, Order of Dannebrog and various other decorations. *Address:* Embassy of Denmark, 77 avenue Marceau, 75116 Paris, France (office). *Telephone:* 1-44-31-21-21 (office). *Fax:* 1-44-31-21-88 (office). *E-mail:* paramb@um.dk (office). *Website:* www.amb-danemark.fr (office).

EGGERS, Dave; American writer; m. Vendela Vida 2003; Ed. Might magazine 1994–97, Timothy McSweeney's Quarterly Concern, or 'McSweeney's,' journal and publishers 1998–. *Publications:* A Heartbreaking Work of Staggering Genius (memoir) 2000, You Shall Know Our Velocity (novel) 2003, The Future Dictionary of America (with Jonathan Safran Foer and Nicole Krauss) 2004, The Best of McSweeney's: Volume 1 (ed.) 2004, Volume 2 (ed.) 2005, How We Are Hungry 2005, What is the What: The Autobiography of Valentino Achak Deng: A Novel 2006; contrib. to periodicals. *Address:* McSweeney's, 826 Valencia Street, San Francisco, CA 94110, USA (office). *E-mail:* letters@mcsweeneys.net (office). *Website:* www.mcsweeneys.net.

EGGLESTON, William; American photographer and academic; b. 27 July 1939, Memphis, Tenn.; Lecturer in Visual and Environmental Studies,

Carpenter Center, Harvard Univ. 1974; Researcher in Color Video, MIT 1978; Guggenheim Fellow 1974; Photographic Soc. of Japan Master Photographers of 1960–1979 Award 1989, Univ. of Memphis Distinguished Achievement Award 1996, Hasselblad Award 1998, Nat. Arts Club Gold Medal for Photography, New York 2003, Getty Images Lifetime Achievement Award 2004, Photoespana Award 2004. *Address:* Eggleston Artistic Trust, 3251 Poplar Avenue #110, Memphis TN 38111, USA (office). *Telephone:* (901) 323-7575 (office). *Fax:* (901) 323-7557 (office). *E-mail:* info@egglestontrust.com (office). *Website:* www.egglestontrust.com (office).

EGGLETON, Arthur C. (Art); Canadian politician; b. 29 Sept. 1943, Toronto; fmr accountant; mem. Toronto City Council and Metropolitan Toronto Council 1969–93; Mayor of Toronto 1980–91; MP for York Centre 1993–2004; Pres. Treas. Bd and Minister responsible for Infrastructure 1993–96; Minister for Int. Trade 1996–97, of Nat. Defence 1997–2002; mem. Bd of Dirs Luxell Technologies Inc. 2005–, Skylink Group; mem. Senate 2005–, Chair. Standing Cttee on Social Affairs, Science and Tech., mem. Standing Cttee on Nat. Finance; Voluntary Chair. Rebuilding Lives Campaign, St John's Rehabilitation Hosp.; Civic Award of Merit, Toronto 1992. *Address:* The Senate of Canada, Ottawa, ON K1A 0A4, Canada. *Telephone:* (613) 995-4230 (office). *Fax:* (613) 995-4237 (office). *E-mail:* egglea@sen.parl.gc.ca (office). *Website:* www.seatorarteggleton.ca (office).

EGILSSON, Ólafur; Icelandic diplomatist and lawyer; *Ambassador to Cambodia, Indonesia, Malaysia, Thailand and Singapore;* b. 20 Aug. 1936, Reykjavik; s. of Egill Kristjánsson and Anna Margrjet Thurídur Ólafsdóttir Briem; m. Ragna Sverrisdóttir Ragnars 1960; one s. one d.; ed Commercial Coll. of Iceland and Iceland Univ.; journalist with newspapers Vísir 1956–58, Morgunbladid 1959–62; Publishing Exec. 1963–64; Head, NATO Regional Information Office, Reykjavik 1964–66; Gen.-Sec. Icelandic Asscn for Western Co-operation 1964–66; Political Div., Icelandic Foreign Ministry 1966–69; First Sec., then Counsellor, Icelandic Embassy, Paris 1969–71; Deputy Perm. Rep. OECD, UNESCO and Council of Europe 1969–71; Deputy Perm. Rep. N Atlantic Council, Deputy Head, Icelandic Del. to EEC, Counsellor, Embassy in Brussels 1971–74; Counsellor, then Minister Counsellor, Political Div. of Foreign Ministry 1974–80; Chief of Protocol (with rank of Amb.) 1980–83; Acting Prin. Pvt. Sec. to Pres. of Iceland 1981–82; Deputy Perm. Under-Sec. and Dir-Gen. for Political Affairs, Foreign Ministry 1983–87; Amb. to UK (also accred to Ireland, Netherlands and Nigeria) 1986–89; Amb. to USSR, later Russia 1990–94; Amb. to Denmark (also accred to Japan, Italy, Israel, Lithuania and Turkey) 1994–96; in charge of Arctic co-operation 1996–98 (also accred to Holy See, Turkey, Australia and NZ); Amb. to China (also accred to Australia, Japan, Repub. of Korea, NZ and Viet Nam) 1998–2002, to Cambodia, Indonesia, Malaysia, Thailand and Singapore (non-resident) 2002–; Chair. Bd of Govs Icelandic Int. Devt Agency 1982–87; Exec. mem. Bible Soc. of Iceland 1977–87, History Soc. 1982–88; Commdr Icelandic Order of the Falcon 1981 and decorations from Finland, France, Norway, Spain, Sweden and Luxembourg. *Publications:* Co-author: Iceland and Jan Mayen 1980, NATO's Anxious Birth – The Prophetic Vision of the 1940s 1985; Ed. Bjarni Benediktsson 1983. *Leisure interests:* history, walking, music (classical, opera). *Address:* c/o Ministry of Foreign Affairs, Raudararstigur 25, PO Box 1000, Reykjavik 150 (office); Valhúsabraut 35, 170 Saltjarnarnes, Iceland (home). *Telephone:* (354) 545-9900 (office); (354) 551 5411 (home). *Fax:* (354) 562-2373 (office); (354) 551 5411 (home). *E-mail:* olafur.egilsson@utn.stjr.is (office); olegice@simnet.is (home). *Website:* www.mfa.is (office).

EGLI, Alphons, DJur; Swiss politician; b. 8 Oct. 1924, Lucerne; s. of Gotthard Egli; m.; three c.; ed legal studies in Zurich, Berne and Rome; private legal practice in Lucerne 1952–82; mem. Lucerne Municipal Council 1963–67, Lucerne Cantonal Parl. 1967–75; mem. Council of States 1975; Leader, Christian Democratic Group 1979; Fed. Councillor 1982–; Head, Fed. Dept of the Interior 1982–85, 1986, Pres. of Swiss Confed. and Head of State Jan.–Dec. 1986. *Address:* c/o Federal Chancellery, Bundeshaus-West, Bundesgasse, 3003 Berne, Switzerland.

EGLIN, Colin Wells, BSc; South African fmr politician and quantity surveyor; b. 14 April 1925, Cape Town; s. of Carl Eglin and Elsie May Wells; m. 1st Joyce Eglin 1949 (died 1997); three d.; m. 2nd Raili Eglin 2000; ed De Villiers Graaff High School and Univ. of Cape Town; army service in Egypt and Italy 1943–45; mem. Pinelands Municipal Council 1951–54, Cape Prov. Council 1954–58; mem. Parl. 1958–61, 1974–2004; Leader Progressive Party 1970–75, Progressive Reform Party 1975–77, Progressive Fed. Party 1977–79, 1986–88; Official Opposition Leader 1977–79, 1986–87; Chief DP Constitutional Negotiator 1991–96; Co-Chair. Transitional Exec. Council 1993–94; mem. Man. Cttee Constitutional Ass. 1994–96; Vice-Pres. Liberal Int. 1990–2003; Sec.-Gen. Org. of African Liberal Parties 1995–99; Democratic Party Spokesman on Foreign Affairs 1989–2004; Pnr, Bernard James and Pnrs (Quantity Surveyors) 1952–2004; consultant on parl. and constitutional matters 2004–; Officer of the Order of the Disa (Prov. of Western Cape) 2005; Hon. LLD (Cape Town) 1997; Parliamentarian of the Century, Leadership Magazine Jan. 2000, Ramon Trias Fargas Memorial Award 2002, St Dunstans Achievers Award 2003, Asscn of SA Quantity Surveyors Achievers Award 2004. *Publications:* Betrayal of Coloured Rights, Forging Links in Africa, Priorities for the Seventies, New Deal for the Cities, Africa – A Prospect of Reconciliation, Pacesetter for Political Change, Security Through Negotiation, Crossing the Borders of Power (memoirs) 2007. *Leisure interests:* golf, travel, reading. *Address:* 4th Floor, 183 Sir Lowry Road, Cape Town 8001, South Africa (office). *Telephone:* (21) 4618707 (office); (21) 7940584 (home). *Fax:* (21) 4618717 (office); (21) 7940584 (home). *E-mail:* coleglin@netactive.co.za (home).

EGLINTON, Geoffrey, PhD, DSc, FRS; British organic geochemist and academic; *Senior Research Fellow, University of Bristol;* b. 1 Nov. 1927, Cardiff; m. Pamela J. Coupland 1955; two s. one d. (deceased); ed Sale Grammar School and Univ. of Manchester; Post-doctoral Fellow, Ohio State Univ. 1952; Lecturer in Organic Chem., Univ. of Glasgow 1954–64; Visiting Fellow, Univ. of Calif., Berkeley 1964; Sr Lecturer in Organic Chem., Univ. of Glasgow 1964–67, Reader 1967; Sr Lecturer in Organic Geochem. and Head, Organic Chem. Unit, Univ. of Bristol 1967, Reader in Organic Geochem. 1968–73, Prof. and Head of Organic Geochem. Unit 1973–93, Prof. Emer. 1993–2004, Dir Biogeochemistry Centre 1991–97, Sr Research Fellow 1995–; H. Burr Steinbach Visiting Scholar, Woods Hole Oceanographic Inst., Mass 1986, Adjunct Scientist 2000–; Adjunct Prof. Dartmouth Coll., NH 2003, Visiting Prof. 2006–; Melvin Calvin Lectureship (Univ. of Calif., Berkeley) 1985; Geochemistry Fellow, Geochemical Soc. and European Asscn for Geochemistry 1996; NASA Gold Medal 1973, Hugo Muller Silver Medal, Chem. Soc. 1974, Alfred E. Treibs Medal Geochemical Soc. 1981, Major Edward Fitzgerald Coke Medal of the Geological Soc. 1986, Harold C. Urey Award, European Asscn of Geochemists 1997, Royal Medal, Royal Soc. 1997, Martin Gold Medal, Chromatographic Soc. 1999, Goldschmidt Medal, Geochemical Soc. 2000, Wollaston Medal, Geological Soc. 2004, Dan David Prize 2008. *Publications:* over 500 articles and books. *Leisure interests:* hiking, sailing.

EGON, Nicholas; British painter; b. 15 Nov. 1921, Brno, Czechoslovakia; m. 1st Diana Horton 1948; m. 2nd Matti Xylas 1980; ed pvt. tutors, Birkbeck Coll., London Univ., Oxford Univ.; served with army in Middle East 1942–46; taught painting and history of art, Sir John Cass Coll., lectured at Nat. Gallery, London and Oxford and Cambridge 1946–50; portraits, landscapes and abstracts in nat., royal and pvt. collections, USA, UK, France, Italy, Greece, Spain, Jordan, Saudi Arabia, Morocco, Oman and Switzerland; Chair. of Patrons, Centre for Hellenic Studies, King's Coll., London Univ. 1989–. *Solo exhibitions:* 10 exhbns in London 1950–86, Nat. Gallery of Jordan 1984, Benaki Museum, Athens 2007. *Publications:* Some Beautiful Women (portraits) 1952, Paintings of Jordan 1986. *Leisure interests:* travel, history, music, archaeology. *Address:* Villa Aëtos, Katakali, 20100 Corinthia (Studio) (home); Deinokratous 81, 115 21 Athens, Greece (home); 34 Thurloe Square, London, SW7 2SR, England (home). *Telephone:* (27410) 33442 (Corinthia) (home); (210) 7291774 (Athens) (home); (20) 7589-0700 (London) (home). *Fax:* (27410) 33640 (Corinthia) (home); (210) 7294748 (Athens) (home); (20) 7589-0620 (London) (home). *E-mail:* egon@faroship.com (office); egon@astronship.gr (home).

EGOYAN, Atom, OC, BA; Canadian film director; b. 19 July 1960, Cairo, Egypt; s. of Joseph Egoyan and Shushan Devletian; m. Arsinée Khanjian; one c.; ed Univ. of Toronto; Dir Ego Film Arts, Toronto 1982–; Chevalier, Ordre des Arts et des Lettres; Dr hc (Trinity Coll., Univ. of Toronto, Univ. of Victoria, Brock Univ., Ont., Coll. of Art and Design, Univ. of British Columbia); Best Dir, Irish Times 2007, Dan David Prize for Creative Rendering of the Past 2008. *Exhibitions:* Return to the Flock, Irish Museum of Modern Art 1996, Early Development, Le Fresnoy, USA 1997, Notorious, Museum of Modern Art, Oxford 1999, Venice Biennale, Close, Venice Biennale 2001, Steenbeckett, Museum of Mankind, London 2002, Hors d'Usage, Musée d'Art Contemporain de Montréal 2002. *Films:* writer, dir and producer feature films: Next of Kin (Gold Ducat award, Mannheim Int. Film Week 1984) 1984, Family Viewing (Int. Critics Award 1988, Best Feature Film Award, Uppsala, Prix Alcan, Festival du Nouveau Cinéma, Montreal) 1987, Speaking Parts (Best Screenplay Prize, Vancouver Int. Film Festival) 1989, The Adjuster (Special Jury Prize, Moscow Film Festival, Golden Spike Award, Valladolid Film Festival) 1991, Calendar (prize at Berlin Int. Film Festival) 1993, Exotica (Int. Film Critics Award, Cannes Film Festival 1994, Prix de la Critique award for Best Foreign Film 1994) 1994, The Sweet Hereafter (Grand Prix, Int. Critics Prize, Cannes Film Festival 1997) 1997, Elsewhereless 1998, Dr Ox's Experiment 1998, Felicia's Journey 1999, Krapp's Last Tape 2000, Ararat 2002, Where the Truth Lies 2005, Adoration 2008. *Operas:* Salome, Canadian Opera Co. 1996, Houston Grand Opera 1997, Elsewhereless 1998, Dr Ox's Experiment 1998, Salome (new production), Canadian Opera Co. 2002, Die Walküre, Canadian Opera Co. 2004, 2006. *Play:* Eh Joe (interpretation of Samuel Beckett's teleplay for the stage, Dublin and London) 2006. *Leisure interest:* classical guitar. *Address:* Ego Film Arts, 80 Niagara Street, Toronto, ON M5V 1C5, Canada. *Telephone:* (416) 703-2137 (office). *Fax:* (416) 504-7161 (office). *E-mail:* questions@egofilmarts.com (office). *Website:* www.egofilmarts.com (office).

EGUIAGARAY UCELAY, Juan Manuel, BA, PhD; Spanish politician; b. 25 Dec. 1945, Bilbao; m.; one s.; ed Univ. of Deusto, Univ. of Nancy, France; mem. PSE-PSOE (Workers' Socialist Party of Spain) 1977–; councillor, Town Council, Bilbao 1979, Prov. Deputy, Vizcaya 1979–81, mem. Juntas Generales Vizcaya 1979–83, Deputy and Spokesman for Socialist Party of Basque Parl. 1980–88, mem. Exec. Cttee PSE-PSOE 1979–, Vice-Sec. Gen. Basque Socialists 1985–88, Govt Del. for Autonomous Community of Murcia, then for Autonomous Community of the Basque Country 1988–89; Exec. Sec. PSOE Fed. Exec. Comm. 1990; Minister for Public Admin 1991–93, of Industry and Energy 1993–96; Nat. Deputy for Murcia 1996–; Fed. Sec. for the Economy (34th Fed. Congress of PSOE), fmrly PSOE Nat. Parl. Spokesman and PSOE Nat. Parl. Spokesman for Econ. Affairs; Vice-Chair. Cttee on Econ., Trade and Tax Affairs; Prof. of Econs, Univ. de Deusto. *Address:* Congreso de los Diputados, Plaza de las Cortes 9, 28014 Madrid, Spain. *Telephone:* (1) 3907639. *Fax:* (1) 4201648 (office). *E-mail:* juan.eguiagaray@diputado.congreso.es (office).

EHLE, Jennifer; British/American actress; b. 29 Dec. 1969, Winston-Salem, NC; d. of John Ehle and Rosemary Harris; ed N. Carolina School of the Arts, Cen. School of Speech and Drama. *Plays include:* Summerfolk (Royal Nat. Theatre), The Relapse (RSC), The Painter of Dishonour (RSC), Richard III

(RSC) 1996, Tartuffe (Playhouse), The Real Thing (Albery) 1999, (Broadway) 2000 (Tony Award for Best Actress 2000), The Philadelphia Story (Old Vic, London) 2005, The Coast of Utopia (Lincoln Centre, New York) (Tony Award for Best Performance by a Featured Actress in a Play 2007) 2006. *Television:* The Camomile Lawn (mini series) 1992, Micky Love (film) 1993, The Maitlands (film) 1993, Self Catering (film) 1994, Pleasure (film) 1994, Beyond Reason (film) 1995, Pride and Prejudice (mini series) (BAFTA Award for Best Actress) 1995, Melissa (mini series) 1997. *Films:* Backbeat 1994, Paradise Road 1997, Wilde 1997, Bedrooms and Hallways 1998, This Year's Love 1999, Sunshine 1999, Possession 2002, The River King 2005, Alpha Male 2006, Michael Clayton 2006, Before the Rains 2007, Pride and Glory 2008. *Address:* c/o Independent Talent Group, 76 Oxford Street, London, W1N 0AX, England. *Telephone:* (20) 7636-6565.

EHLERMANN, Claus-Dieter, DrIur; German lawyer; *Chairman, Appellate Body of the World Trade Organization;* b. 15 June 1931, Scheessel; s. of Kurt Ehlermann and Hilde (née Justus) Ehlermann; m. Carola Grumbach 1959; two d.; ed Univs of Marburg/Lahn and Heidelberg, Univ. of Michigan Law School, Ann Arbor; Research Asst Fed. Constitutional Court, Karlsruhe 1959–61; Legal Adviser, Legal Service of the Comm. of European Communities 1961–73, Dir and Deputy Financial Controller 1973–77, Dir-Gen. of the Legal Service 1977–87; Spokesman of the Comm. of the European Communities and of its fmr Pres. Jacques Delors (q.v.) 1987–90, Dir-Gen. of Directorate-Gen. for Competition 1990–95; Prof. of Econ. Law, European Univ. Inst., Florence; fmr mem. Appellate Body of WTO, Geneva 1995–2000, Chair. Appellate Body of WTO 2001–, Senior Counsel, Wilmer, Cutler & Pickering; Hon. Prof. Univ. of Hamburg; Hon. Bencher, Gray's Inn, London; Hon. DrIur 1999. *Publications:* numerous documents on the European Community and its legal order. *Leisure interests:* reading, skiing. *Address:* Istituto Universitario Europeo, Badia Fiesolana, Via dei Roccettini 9, 50016 San Domenico di Fiesole (Firenze), Italy; Centre William Rappard, Rue de Lausanne 154, Case postale, 1211 Geneva 21, Switzerland; 51 avenue du Val des Seigneurs, 1150 Brussels, Belgium (home). *Telephone:* (055) 4685798 (Italy); (2) 7622127 (home). *Fax:* (055) 4685776 (Italy); (2) 7711993 (home). *E-mail:* claus.ehlermann@iue.it (office); carola.ehlermann@planetinternet.be (home). *Website:* www.iue.it/rsc/eco-pol/competition.htm (office); www.iue.it/law/ehlermann/index.htm (home).

EHLERS ZURITA, Freddy; Ecuadorean journalist, politician and international organization official; *Secretary-General, Andean Community of Nations;* b. 1945, Quito; ed Cen. Univ. of Ecuador; fmr host, TV programme La Televisión; Dir Bd of Cartagena Agreement's Andean TV Program 1980–88; unsuccessful cand. for Pres. of Ecuador 1996, 1998; mem. Andean Parl. for Ecuador 2002–06, Vice-Pres. 2003–04, mem. Cttee on Educ., Culture, Science, Tech. and Communication; Sec.-Gen. Andean Community of Nations (Comunidad Andina de Naciones) 2007–. *Address:* Comunidad Andina de Naciones, Paseo de la República 3895, San Isidro, Lima 27, Peru (office). *Telephone:* (1) 4111400 (office). *Fax:* (1) 2213329 (office). *E-mail:* contacto@comunidadandina.org (office). *Website:* www.comunidadandina.org (office).

EHRLICH, Paul Ralph, MA, PhD; American entomologist, population biologist and academic; *Bing Professor of Population Studies and President, Center for Conservation Biology, Stanford University;* b. 29 May 1932, Philadelphia, Pa; s. of William Ehrlich and Ruth Ehrlich (née Rosenberg); m. Anne Fitzhugh Howland 1954; one d.; ed Univs of Pennsylvania and Kansas; Field Officer, Northern Insect Survey (Canadian Arctic and Subarctic) summers of 1951 and 1952; Research Asst, DDT Resistance Project, Dept of Entomology, Univ. of Kansas 1952–54, Kansas Univ. Fellow 1954–66, NSF Pre-Doctoral Fellow 1955–57, Assoc. Investigator, USAF research project, Alaska and Univ. of Kansas 1956–57, Research Assoc., Chicago Acad. of Sciences and Univ. of Kansas Dept of Entomology 1957–59; Asst Prof. of Biological Sciences, Stanford Univ. 1959–62, Assoc. Prof. of Biological Sciences 1962–66, Prof. of Biological Studies 1966–, Dir Grad. Studies, Dept of Biological Sciences 1966–69, 1974–76, Bing Prof. of Population Studies 1977–, Pres. Center for Conservation Biology 1988–; NSF Sr Post-Doctoral Fellow, Univ. of Sydney 1965–66; Assoc., Center for the Study of Democratic Insts, Santa Barbara, Calif. 1969–72; Sec. Lepidopterists' Soc. 1957–63, mem. Exec. Council 1968; Corresp. NBC News 1989–92; Pres. Zero Population Growth 1969–70 (Hon. Pres. 1970–), Zero Population Growth Fund 1972–73, The Conservation Soc. 1972–73, American Inst. of Biological Sciences 1989, Asscn for Tropical Lepidoptera 2001; Vice-Pres. Soc. for the Study of Evolution 1970; Co-Chair. Research Cttee, Rocky Mountain Biological Lab. 1973–75, Trustee 1971–86; Mem.-at-Large, Governing Bd American Inst. of Biological Sciences 1969–70; mem. Advisory Council, Friends of the Earth 1970–, Scientific Advisory Cttee, Sierra Club 1972–, Council, Soc. for the Study of Evolution 1974–76; mem. and Active Cttee mem., Int. Asscn for the Study of Ecology 1969–70; mem. Bd Dirs Common Cause 1972; mem. Bd of Consultants, Lizard Island Research Station 1975–78; mem. Bd of Govs Soc. for Conservation Biology 1986–88; mem. Editorial Bd Systematic Zoology 1964–67, International Journal of Environmental Sciences 1969–71, American Naturalist 1974–76, Oecologia 1981–85, 1991–, Revista de Biologia Tropical, Universidad de Costa Rica 1996–; Sr Assoc. Ed. American Naturalist 1984; Advisory Ed. Human Nature 1977–79; mem. NAS 1985, American Philosophical Soc. 1990, European Acad. of Sciences and Arts 1992; Elective mem. American Ornithologists' Union 1989; Foreign mem. Russian Acad. of Natural Sciences 1997–; Fellow, California Acad. of Sciences 1961, AAAS 1978, American Acad. of Arts and Sciences 1982, Entomological Soc. of America 1987; Hon. Life mem. American Humanist Asscn 1989, British Ecological Soc. 1989, Int. Soc. for Philosophical Enquiry 1991; Sigma Xi-Resa Grant-in-Aid of Research done in Alaska and NW Canada 1955, First Prize, Mitchell Foundation 1979, John Muir Award, Sierra Club 1980, Humanist Distinguished Service Award, American Humanist Asscn 1985, First Distinguished Achievement Award, Soc. for Conservation Biology 1987, Gold Medal, World Wildlife Fund Int. 1987, AAAS/Scientific American Gerard Piel Award for Service to Science in the Cause of Humankind 1989, UN Global 500 Roll of Honour 1989, Crafoord Prize in Population Biology and the Conservation of Biological Diversity, Royal Swedish Acad. of Sciences 1990, Distinguished Service Citation, Univ. of Kansas 1991, MacArthur Prize Fellowship 1990–95, Major Achievement Award, New York City Audubon Soc. 1991, Volvo Environment Prize 1993, World Ecology Medal, Int. Center for Tropical Ecology 1993, UNEP Sasakawa Environment Prize 1994, Heinz Award for the Environment 1995, Distinguished Peace Leader, Nuclear Age Peace Foundation 1996, Tyler Prize for Environmental Achievement 1998, Dr A.H. Heineken Prize for Environmental Sciences 1998, Nat. Audubon Soc., One Hundred Champions of Conservation 1998, Blue Planet Prize, Asahi Glass Foundation (Japan) 1999, Distinguished Scientist Award, American Inst. of Biological Sciences 2001, Eminent Ecologist Award, Ecological Soc. of America 2001. *Publications include:* How to Know the Butterflies 1960, Process of Evolution 1963, The Population Bomb 1968, 1971, Population Resources, Environment: Issues in Human Ecology (with A. H. Ehrlich) 1970, 1972, How to Be a Survivor (with R. L. Harriman) 1971, The Race Bomb (with S. Feldman) 1977, Extinction: The Causes and Consequences of the Disappearance of Species (with A. H. Ehrlich) 1981, The Golden Door: International Migration, Mexico and the United States (with D. L. Bilderback and A. H. Ehrlich) 1981, The Cold and the Dark: The World After Nuclear War (with Carl Sagan, Donald Kennedy and Walter Orr Roberts) 1984, Earth (with A. H. Ehrlich) 1987, Science of Ecology (with Joan Roughgarden) 1987, New World, New Mind (with R. Ornstein) 1988, The Birder's Handbook: A Field Guide to the Natural History of North American Birds (with David S. Dobkin and Darryl Wheye) 1988, The Cassandra Conference: Resources and the Human Predicament 1988, The Population Explosion (with A. H. Ehrlich) 1990, Healing the Planet: Strategies for Resolving the Environmental Crisis (with A. H. Ehrlich) 1991, Birds in Jeopardy: The Imperiled and Extinct Birds of the United States and Canada, Including Hawaii and Puerto Rico (with David S. Dobkin and Darryl Wheye) 1992, The Stork and the Plow (with A. H. Ehrlich and G. C. Daily) 1995, A World of Wounds: Ecologists and the Human Dilemma 1997, Betrayal of Science and Reason: How Anti-Environment Rhetoric Threatens Our Future (with A. H. Ehrlich) 1998, Human Natures: Genes, Cultures, and the Human Prospect 2002, One With Nineveh: Politics, Consumption and the Human Future (with A. H. Ehrlich) 2004, The Dominant Animal: Human Evolution and the Environment (with A. H. Ehrlich) 2008; co-ed.: Man and the Ecosphere: Readings from Scientific American (with J. P. Holdren and R. W. Holm) 1971, Global Ecology (with J. P. Holdren) 1971, Human Ecology: Problems and Solutions (with A. H. Ehrlich and J. P. Holdren) 1973, Introductory Biology 1973, Ark II (with D. Pirages) 1974, The Process of Evolution (with R. W. Holm and D. R. Parnell) 1974, The End of Affluence (with A. H. Ehrlich) 1974, Biology and Society (with R. W. Holm and I. Brown) 1976, Ecoscience: Population, Resources, Environment (with A. H. Ehrlich and J. P. Holdren) 1977, Introduction to Insect Biology and Diversity (with H. V. Daly and J. T. Doyen) 1978, Machinery of Nature 1986, Wild Solutions 2001, Butterflies: Ecology and Evolution taking Flight (with Carol Boggs and Ward Watt) 2003, On the Wings of Checkerspots: A Model System for Population Biology (with Ilkka Hanski) 2004; more than 950 scientific and popular articles. *Leisure interest:* collecting primitive art. *Address:* Department of Biology, HERRIN 409, Stanford University, Stanford, CA 94305-5020, USA (office). *Telephone:* (650) 723-3171 (office). *Fax:* (650) 723-5920 (office). *Website:* www.stanford.edu/group/CCB/Staff/Ehrlich.html (office).

EHRLICH, Robert L., Jr, BA, JD; American lawyer and fmr state official; *Attorney at Law, Womble Carlyle Sandridge & Rice PLLC;* b. 25 Nov. 1957, Arbutus, Md; s. of Bob Ehrlich and Nancy Ehrlich; m. Kendel Sibiski; one c.; ed Gilman School, Princeton Univ., Wake Forest Univ. Law School; Assoc., Ober, Kaler, Grimes and Shriver (law firm) 1982–92, Of Counsel 1992–94; mem. Md House of Dels 1987–95; mem. US House of Reps 1995–2003; Gov. of Md 2003–07; Attorney at Law, Womble Carlyle Sandridge & Rice PLLC, Baltimore 2007–; co-host (with wife) radio talk show on WBAL; Republican; Outstanding Young Marylander, Md Jaycees 1995, Legislator of the Year, Biotechnology Industry Org., Spirit of Enterprise Award, US Chamber of Commerce, Guardian of Small Business, Nat. Fed. of Ind. Business 1987–90, Fed. Official of the Year, Nat. Industries for the Blind. *Address:* Womble Carlyle Sandridge & Rice PLLC, 1302 Concourse Drive, Linthicum, MD 21090, USA (office). *Telephone:* (410) 691-5590 (office). *Fax:* (410) 694-0872 (office). *E-mail:* Robert.Ehrlich@wcsr.com (office). *Website:* www.wcsr.com (office).

EHRLICH, Thomas, LLB; American lawyer, academic and fmr university president; *Senior Scholar, Carnegie Foundation for the Advancement of Teaching;* b. 4 March 1934, Cambridge, Mass; s. of William Ehrlich and Evelyn Seltzer; m. Ellen Rome Ehrlich 1957; two s. one d.; ed Harvard Coll. and Harvard Law School, Cambridge, Mass; law clerk, US Court of Appeals, New York 1959–60; Assoc., Foley, Sammond & Lardner (law firm), Milwaukee, Wis. 1960–62; Special Asst to Legal Adviser, US Dept of State, Washington, DC 1962–65, to Under-Sec. of State George W. Ball 1964–65; Prof., Stanford Univ. Law School, Stanford, Calif. 1965–71, Dean and Richard E. Lang Prof. 1971–75; Pres. Legal Services Corpn, Washington, DC 1976–79; Dir Int. Devt Co-operating Agency, Washington, DC 1979–80; Guest Scholar, The Brookings Inst. 1981; Provost and Prof. of Law, Univ. of Pa, Phila 1982–87; Pres. Ind. Univ. 1987–94; Visiting Prof., Stanford Law School 1994–99; Distinguished Univ. Scholar, Calif. State Univ., San Francisco 1995–2000; Sr Scholar Carnegie Foundation for the Advancement of Teaching 1997–; Arbitrator, US–France Int. Aviation Dispute, Geneva, Switzerland; fmr mem. American Asscn for Higher Educ., Council of Ten (Council of Pres., Big Ten Univs); mem. Council on Foreign Relations, ABA Special Comm. on

Professional Standards, Exec. Cttee American Soc. of Int. Law, Bd of Dirs Center for Law and Social Policy and many other bodies; Hon. LLD (Villanova) 1979, (Notre Dame) 1980, (Univ. of Pa) 1987, (Indiana). *Publications:* The International Legal Process (with Abram Chayes and Andreas F. Lowenfeld), (three vols) 1968, Supplement 1974, New Directions in Legal Education (with Herbert L. Packer) 1972, International Crises and the Role of Law, Cyprus 1958–67 1974, International Law and the Use of Force (with Mary Ellen O'Connell) 1993, The Courage to Inquire 1995, The Future of Philanthropy and the Nonprofit Sector in a Changing America (co-ed. with Charles T. Clotfelter) 1999, Higher Education and Civic Responsibility 2000, Educating Citizens (with Anne Colby, Elizabeth Beaumont and Jason Stephens) 2003; numerous articles, reviews and other publs. *Address:* Carnegie Foundation for the Advancement of Teaching, 51 Vista Lane, Stanford, CA 94305, USA (office). *Telephone:* (650) 566-5137 (office). *E-mail:* ehrlich@carnegiefoundation.org (office). *Website:* www.carnegiefoundation.org (office).

EHRLING, Marie, BSc (Econs); Swedish business executive; m.; one s.; ed Stockholm School of Econs; Deputy CEO and COO SAS Airlines, responsible for Ground and Station Services Divs, Int. Traffic Routes and establishment of Star Alliance –2002; Pres. TeliaSonera Sweden 2003–06; mem. Bd of Dirs Securitas AB 2006–, Nordea AB 2007–, Oriflame Cosmetic SA 2007–, HomeMaid AB 2007–, Safegate AB, World Childhood Foundation; ranked by Fortune magazine amongst 50 Most Powerful Women in Business outside the US (27th) 2003, (21st) 2004, (21st) 2005, ranked by Forbes magazine amongst 100 Most Powerful Women (85th) 2006, ranked by the Financial Times amongst Top 25 Businesswomen in Europe (18th) 2005, (15th) 2006. *Address:* c/o Board of Directors, Safegate AB, Stenåldersg. 2 A, 213 76 Malmö, Sweden. *E-mail:* marie.ehrling@myme.se.

EHRMAN, Sir William, KCMG; British diplomatist; *Ambassador to People's Republic of China;* b. 28 Aug. 1950; m. Penelope Anne Ehrman; three d. one s.; joined FCO 1973; Third Sec., later Second Sec. Beijing 1976–78; First Sec. Perm. Mission to UN, New York 1979–83; First Sec. Beijing 1983–84; Hong Kong and Security Policy Depts, FCO 1985–89, Political Adviser Hong Kong 1989–93, Head Near East and North Africa Dept, FCO 1993–94; mem. Bosnia Contact Group 1994–95; Prin. Pvt. Sec. to Foreign Sec. 1995–97; with Unilever China 1997–98; Amb. to Luxembourg 1998–2000; Dir of Int. Security, FCO 2000–02, Dir-Gen. of Defence and Intelligence 2002–04; Chair. Jt Intelligence Cttee, Cabinet Office 2004–05; Amb. to People's Repub. of China 2006–. *Address:* Embassy of the United Kingdom, 11 Guang Hua Lu, Jian Guo Men Wai, Beijing 100600, People's Republic of China (office). *Telephone:* (10) 51924000 (office). *Fax:* (10) 65321937 (office). *Website:* www.britishembassy.org.cn (office).

EHSAS, Mohammad Qasim; Afghan trade union official; *President of the Central Council, National Union of Afghanistan Employees;* fmr mem. Parcham (leftist party); fmr Deputy Minister of Commerce; cand. in elections 2005; currently Pres. of Cen. Council Nat. Union of Afghanistan Employees; adviser to Workers' Del., 95th Session of ILO Conf., Geneva 2006. *Address:* Central Council of National Union of Afghanistan Employees, Aryana Square in front of Urdu Puplication Department, Shashdarak, PO Box 756, Kabul, Afghanistan (office). *Telephone:* (20) 01959 (office).

EIBL-EIBESFELDT, Irenäus, DPhil; Austrian zoologist and academic; *Head, Human Ethology Film Archive, Max-Planck Institute, Andechs;* b. 15 June 1928, Vienna; s. of Anton Eibl-Eibesfeldt and Maria Eibl-Eibesfeldt (née von Hauninger); m. Eleonore Siegel 1950; one s. one d.; ed Univ. of Vienna and Univ. of Munich, Germany; Research Assoc., Biology Station, Wilhelminenberg, nr Vienna 1946–48, Max Planck Inst. of Behavioural Physiology 1951–69; Head of ind. research unit on human ethology, Max Planck Inst. 1970–96, Emer. Researcher and Head Human Ethology Film Archive 1996–; Lecturer, Univ. of Munich 1963, Prof. 1970; Hon. Scientific Dir Int. Inst. for Submarine Research, Vaduz 1957–70; Head Ludwig-Boltzmann-Inst. for Urban Ethology, Vienna 1992–; mem. Humanwissenschaftliches Zentrum, Ludwig-Maximilians-Univ., Munich 1997, Deutsche Akad. der Naturforscher 1977; Founding mem. and Pro-Dekan European Acad. of Arts and Sciences; Pres. Int. Soc. for Human Ethology 1985–93; Corresp. mem. Deutsche Akad. der Naturforscher Leopoldina, Fellow Animal Behavior Soc.; Dr hc (Salamanca) 1994; Wilhelm Bölsche Gold Medal 1971, Burda Prize for Communications Research 1980, Philip Morris Research Prize 1988, Gold Medal of Honour (City of Vienna) 1989, Bundesverdienstkreuz (Germany) 1995, Schwenk'scher Umweltpreis 1996, Haackert Medal for Research on Human Ethology 1997, Bayerischer Verdienstorden 1997, Jahrespreis von STAB, Zurich 1997, Österreichisches Ehrenkreuz für Wissenschaft und Kunst 1998 and many others. *Publications:* Galapagos, die Arche Noah im Pacific 1960, Im Reich der tausend Atolle 1964, Grundriss der vergleichenden Verhaltensforschung 1967, Liebe und Hass 1970, Die ko-Buschmanngesellschaft 1972, Der vorprogrammierte Mensch 1973, Menschenforschung auf neuen Wegen 1976, Der Hai: Legende eines Mörders (with H. Hass) 1977, Die Malediven. Paradies im Indischen Ozean 1982, Die Biologie des menschlichen Verhaltens, Grundriss der Humanethologie 1984, Der Mensch – das riskierte Wesen 1988, Human Ethology 1989, Das verbindende Erbe 1991, Und grün des Lebens goldner Baum 1992, Im Banne der Angst (co-author) 1992, Wider die Misstrauensgesellschaft 1994, In der Falle des Kurzzeitdenkens 1998. *Leisure interests:* skin diving, skiing, arts. *Address:* Humanethologisches Filmarchiv der Max Planck Gesellschaft, Von-der-Tann-Strasse 3-5, 82348 Andechs (office); Fichtenweg 9, 82319 Starnberg, Germany (home). *Telephone:* (8152) 373157 (office); (8152) 373159 (office); (8151) 746607 (home). *Fax:* (8152) 373170 (office). *E-mail:* eibl@orn.mpg.de (office). *Website:* erl.ornithol.mpg.de/~fshuman/index.html (office).

EICHEL, Hans; German politician; b. 24 Dec. 1941, Kassel; m.; two c.; ed Univs of Marburg and Berlin; fmr schoolmaster; mem. Kassel City Council 1968–75, Chair. Social Democratic Party (SDP) Group 1970–75; mem. Nat. Exec. of Young Socialists 1969–72; Chief Mayor of Kassel 1975–91; mem. SDP Nat. Exec. and Spokesman on Local Govt 1984; Chair. SDP Asscn Hesse 1989; Minister-Pres. of Hesse 1991–99; Federal Minister of Finance 1999–2005. *Address:* c/o Sozialdemokratische Partei Deutschlands (SPD), Wilhelmstr. 141, 10963 Berlin, Germany (office).

EICHELBAUM, Rt Hon. Sir (Johann) Thomas, GBE, PC; New Zealand judge; *Judge of Appeal, Fiji;* b. 17 May 1931, Koenigsberg, Germany; s. of Dr Walter Eichelbaum and Frida M. Eichelbaum; m. Vida Beryl Franz 1956; three s.; ed Hutt Valley High School and Victoria Univ. Coll.; admitted solicitor 1953, barrister 1954; Partner, Chapman Tripp & Co. 1958–78; QC 1978; barrister 1978–82; Pres. NZ Law Soc. 1980–82; Judge, High Court of NZ 1982; Chief Justice of NZ 1989–99; Judge of Appeal, Fiji 1999–; Non-Perm. Judge, Court of Final Appeal Hong Kong 2000–; Privy Councillor 1989–; Chair. Royal Comm. on Genetic Modification 2000–01; Hon. LLD (Vic. Univ. of Wellington) 1998. *Publications:* Mauet's Fundamentals of Trial Techniques (Ed.-in-Chief) 1989, Introduction to Advocacy (Consulting Ed.) 2000. *Leisure interests:* reading, walking. *Address:* Raumati Beach, New Zealand. *E-mail:* thoseich@actrix.gen.nz (home).

EICHHORN, Lisa; American actress; b. 2 April 1952, Glen Falls, NY; ed Queen's Univ. Ontario, St Peter's Coll. Oxford and Royal Acad. of Dramatic Art. *Films include:* Yanks 1979, The Europeans 1979, Why Would I Lie? 1980, Cutter and Bone (Cutter's Way) 1981, The Weather in the Streets 1983, Wildrose 1984, Opposing Force (Hell Camp) 1986, Grim Prairie Tales 1990, Moon 44 1990, Grim Prairie Tales 1990, King of the Hill 1993, The Vanishing 1993, Mr 247 1994, A Modern Affair 1995, Sticks and Stones 1996, First Kid 1996, Judas Kiss 1998, The Talented Mr Ripley 1999, Goodbye Lover 1999, Boys and Girls 2000, Things Left Unsaid 2000. *Television includes:* Diana: A Tribute to the People's Princess 1998, My Neighbor's Daughter 1998, Kenneth Tynan: In Praise of Hardcore 2005. *Stage appearances include:* roles in British Shakespearean productions, A Doll's House, A Golden Boy, The Speed of Darkness, The Summer Winds, The Common Pursuit, The Hasty Heart, Pass/Fail, Arms and the Man, Misfits 1996. *Address:* 1719 Friedensburg Road, Reading, PA 19606, USA.

EICHLER, Ralph, PhD; Swiss physicist, academic and university administrator; *President, Swiss Federal Institute of Technology (ETH Zürich);* b. 31 Dec. 1947, Guildford, England; m.; three c.; ed Swiss Federal Inst. of Tech. (ETH Zürich); Postdoctoral Fellow, Stanford Univ., USA 1977–79; Scientist, Deutsches Elektronen Synchrotron (DESY), Hamburg 1979–82; Scientist, Inst. for Medium-Energy Physics, ETH Zürich 1982–86, Prof. 1986–89, Assoc. Prof. of Physics 1989–93, Prof. 1993–, Deputy Dir 1998–2002, Dir Paul Scherrer Inst. 2002–, Pres. ETH Zürich 2007–. *Address:* Office of the President, ETH Zürich, HG F 59, Rämistrasse 101, 8092 Zürich, Switzerland (office). *Telephone:* (44) 632-20-17 (office). *Fax:* (44) 632-10-01 (office). *E-mail:* ralph.eichler@sl.ethz.ch (office). *Website:* www.ethz.ch (office).

EIDE, Kai, BA; Norwegian diplomatist; *Special Envoy of the Secretary-General to Afghanistan, United Nations;* b. 28 Feb. 1949, Sarpsborg; m. Gro Holm; two d.; ed Univ. of Oslo; entered Norwegian Foreign Service 1975, mem. Del. to CSCE Follow-up Meeting in Belgrade 1977–78, Madrid 1980–82, Sec., Embassy in Prague 1977–78, First Sec. 1979–82, First Sec. Del. to Conf. on Disarmament in Europe, Stockholm 1983–84, First Sec. Del. to NATO, Brussels 1984–87; Deputy Dir Pvt. Office of NATO Sec.-Gen. 1987–89; State Sec., Office of the Prime Minister, Oslo 1989–90; Minister Counsellor and Deputy Perm. Rep. to NATO 1991–93, Amb. to Int. Conf. on the Fmr Yugoslavia (ICFY) 1993–95, Amb. and Special Adviser on Balkan Area, Ministry of Foreign Affairs 1996, Special Rep. of UN Sec.-Gen. and Head of UN Mission in Bosnia and Herzegovina, Sarajevo 1997–98, Amb. and Del. to OSCE, Vienna 1998–2002, Chair. OSCE Perm. Council 1999, mem. Mitchell Cttee Staff (Sharm el Sheikh Fact Finding Mission) 2000–01, Perm. Rep. to NATO, Brussels 2002–06, Special Envoy of UN Sec.-Gen. to Kosovo 2005, to Afghanistan 2008–; Political Dir, Ministry of Foreign Affairs 2006–08; Special Adviser, Planning Div., STATOIL 1991. *Publications:* several publs on foreign and security matters. *Address:* United Nations Assistance Mission in Afghanistan (UNAMA), PO Box 5858, Grand Central Station, New York, NY 10163-5858, USA (office); UNAMA, PO Box 1428, Islamabad, Pakistan (office); UNAMA, Peace Street, Kabul, Afghanistan. *Telephone:* (0831) 246000 (Brindisi, Italy) (office). *Fax:* (212) 963-2669 (New York) (office); (0831) 246069 (Brindisi, Italy) (office). *E-mail:* spokesperson-unama@un.org (office). *Website:* www.unama-afg.org (office).

EIFMAN, Boris Yakovlevich; Russian choreographer; *Artistic Director, St Petersburg Ballet Theatre Boris Eifman;* b. 22 July 1946, Rubtsovsk, Altai Region; s. of Yankel Borisovich Eifman and Klara Markovna Kuris; m. Valentina Nikolayevna Morozova; one s.; ed Kishinev School of Choreography, Leningrad State Conservatory; Balletmaster, Leningrad School of Choreography 1970–77; concurrently ballet productions in professional theatres including Firebird (Kirov Theatre 1975); Founder and Artistic Dir Leningrad Ensemble of Ballet (now St Petersburg Ballet Theatre Boris Eifman) 1977; Chevalier des Arts et des Lettres 1999; People's Artist of Russia 1995, Golden Baton Prize 1995, 1996, 1997, 2001, 2005, Triumph Prize 1996, Golden Mask Prize 1996, 1999, Russian State Prize 1999, Best Choreographer, Benois de la Dance 2006. *Ballets include:* Before Firebird – Gayaney 1972, Idiot (Tchaikovsky's 6th Symphony) 1980, Marriage of Figaro 1982, The Legend 1982, Twelfth Night 1984, The Duel (after Kuprin) 1986, Master and Margarita (after Bulgakov) 1987, Thérèse Raquin 1991, Requiem (Mozart) 1991, Tchaikovsky 1993, Don Quixote or Madman's Fantasy (Minkus) 1994, Brothers Karamazov (after Dostoyevsky) 1995, Red Giselle 1997, My Jerusalem 1998, Russian Hamlet 1999, Don Juan 2001, Who is Who? 2003, Musageie 2004, Anna Karenina 2005, The Seagull 2007. *Address:* St

Petersburg Ballet Theatre Boris Eifman, ul. Liza Chaikina 2, 197198 St Petersburg, Russia. *Telephone:* (812) 232-23-70 (office). *Fax:* (812) 232-18-62 (office). *E-mail:* eifman@inbox.ru. *Website:* eifmanballet.ru.

EIGEN, Manfred, Dr rer. nat; German physical chemist; b. 9 May 1927, Bochum; s. of Ernst Eigen and Hedwig Feld; m. Elfriede Müller; one s. one d.; ed Georg-August-Univ. zu Göttingen; Max-Planck Inst. of Physical Chem., Göttingen, as Asst, later as Head of Dept 1953–, Dir 1964; Hon. Prof. Technical Univ., Braunschweig 1965–; Pres. Studienstiftung des Deutschen Volkes 1983–; mem. Akad. der Wissenschaften, Göttingen; Foreign Assoc. mem. Nat. Acad. of Sciences, USA; Foreign mem. Royal Soc., UK, Acad. Française 1978; Hon. Dr Univ. of Washington, St Louis Univ., Harvard Univ. and Cambridge Univ. and numerous other hon. degrees; Foreign hon. mem. American Acad. of Arts and Sciences; Otto Hahn Prize 1967; Nobel Prize for Chem. (jt recipient) for investigation of extremely rapid chemical reactions by means of disturbing the (molecular) equilibrium by the action of very short energy pulses 1967. *Address:* Max Planck Inst. for Biophysical Chemistry, Am Fassberg 11, 37077 Göttingen, Germany. *Telephone:* 5512011433 (office). *Fax:* 5512011435 (office).

EIKENBERRY, Lt-Gen. Karl W., BS, MS, PhD; American army officer and international organization official; *Deputy Chairman of the Military Committee, NATO;* b. 1951; ed US Mil. Acad., West Point, Harvard Univ., Stanford Univ.; mil. operational assignments included service as commdr and staff officer with mechanized, light, airborne and ranger infantry units in US, South Korea and Europe; has served in numerous admin.-political positions, including Dir. for Strategic Planning and Policy for US Pacific Command, US Security Coordinator and Chief of Office of Mil. Cooperation, Kabul, Afghanistan, Asst Army Attaché and later Defense Attaché, Embassy in Beijing, Sr Country Dir for China, Taiwan, Hong Kong and Mongolia in Office of the US Sec. of Defense, and Deputy Dir. for Strategy, Plans, and Policy on Army Staff; Commdr Combined Forces Command–Afghanistan 2005–07; Deputy Chair. Mil. Cttee, NATO, Brussels 2007–; Defense Superior Service Medal, Legion of Merit, Bronze Star, Ranger Tab, Combat and Expert Infantryman badges, and master parachutist wings, US Dept of State Superior Honor Award, Dir of Cen. Intelligence Award, Akbar Khan Award (Afghanistan) presented by Pres. Hamid Karzai. *Address:* North Atlantic Treaty Organization, blvd Léopold III, 1110 Brussels, Belgium (office). *Telephone:* (2) 707-41-11 (office). *Fax:* (2) 707-45-79 (office). *E-mail:* natodoc@hq.nato.int (office). *Website:* www.nato.int (office).

EINARSSON, Sveinn, PhD; Icelandic theatre director and author; b. 18 Sept. 1934, Reykjavik; s. of Einar Ól Sveinsson and Kristjana Thorsteinsdóttir; m. Thora Kristjánsdóttir 1964; one d.; ed Univ. of Stockholm, Univ. of Paris, Sorbonne, Univ. of Iceland; Artistic Dir Reykjavik Theatre Co. 1963–72 (Hon. mem. 1991); Prin. Reykjavik Theatre School 1963–70; Gen. Man. and Artistic Dir Nat. Theatre of Iceland 1972–83; Head of Programme Production, Icelandic State TV 1989–93; Counsellor, Ministry of Culture 1983–89, 1993–2004; Chair. Icelandic Nat. Comm. for UNESCO 1995–; Artistic Dir Reykjavik Arts Festival 1998–2001; Vice-Pres. Int. Theatre Inst. 1979–81; mem. (part-time) Faculty, Univ. of Iceland 1970–; now freelance director and author; has directed over 90 productions (including opera) on stage and TV in Iceland, the Nordic countries, UK and Germany; productions also presented in Venezuela, Canada, the Baltic States and Korea (Theatre of Nations); several appointments with the Council of Europe: Chair. several cultural cttees; Vice-Pres. Nordic Theatre Union 1975–82; mem. Exec. Bd UNESCO 2001–05; hon. mem. of several socs etc.; Paul Harris Fellow Rotary Club of Reykjavik 2004, Hon. mem. The Nordic Theatre Union 2008; Officer, Order of White Rose of Finland, Order of Merit (Norway), Commdr, Swedish Nordstjärnan, Commdr, Ordre des Arts et Lettres (France) 2004; Children's Book of Year Award 1986, Clara Lachmann Prize 1990, First Prize, Short Story Competition, 50th Anniversary of Repub. of Iceland 1994, Jón Sigurdsson Prize 1997, Best Theatre Production Award 2003, Hon. Award for Lifetime Achievement in the Theatre 2003. *Plays:* Egg of Life 1983, I'm Gold and Treasures 1984, Bukolla 1991, Bandamannasaga 1992, The Amlodi Saga 1996, The Daughter of the Poet 1998, Edda 2000. *Television:* (plays) A Stop on My Way 1971, Time is in No Harmony with Me 1993. *Publications include:* on theatre: Theatre By the Lake 1972, My Nine Years Down There 1987, Íslensk Leiklist (History of Icelandic Theatre) Vol. I 1991, Vol. II 1996, My Eleven Years Up There 2000, A People's Theatre Comes of Age 2007, Leiklisten i veröldinni (The Theatre in the World) 2007; novel: The Electricity Man 1998; children's books: Gabriella in Portugal 1985, Dordingull 1994. *Leisure interests:* music, skiing, forestry. *Address:* Ministry of Culture, Solvholsgata 4, 101 Reykjavik (office); Tjarnargata 26, 101 Reykjavik, Iceland (home). *Telephone:* 551-4032 (home); 545-9500 (office). *Fax:* 562-3068 (office). *E-mail:* sveinn.einarsson@mrn.stjr.is.

EINAUDI, Luigi R., BA, PhD; American international organization official, diplomatist and academic; ed Harvard Univ.; researcher RAND Corpn, Santa Monica, Calif. 1964–74; staff mem. Policy Planning Staff, Office of Sec. of State 1974–77, 1993–97; Dir of Policy Planning, Bureau of Inter-American Affairs, Dept of State 1977–89; Amb. to OAS 1989–93; US Special Envoy to Ecuador–Peru Peace Talks 1995–98; worked on multilateral governance and conflict resolution at Inter-American Dialogue, Washington, DC 1998–2000; Special Rep. of OAS Sec.-Gen. in Honduras–Nicaragua boundary dispute 1999; Asst Sec.-Gen. OAS 2000–04, Sec.-Gen. 2004–05; teacher at UCLA, Harvard, Wesleyan and Georgetown Univs; lecturer in numerous univs in USA, Latin American and Europe; mem. Council on Foreign Relations; recipient of decorations from Presidents of Ecuador and Peru; recipient of awards from Presidents Jimmy Carter, Ronald Reagan, George Bush and Secretaries of State Henry Kissinger, Madeleine Albright, Frasure Award for Peace-keeping 1997, seven other medal citations from Depts of State and Defense; Terry Woods Memorial Award, OAS 2005. *Publications include:* Beyond Cuba, Latin America Takes Charge of Its Future 1974; numerous articles and monographs. *Address:* c/o Organization of American States, 17th and Constitution Avenue, NW, Washington, DC 20006, USA (office).

EINHORN, Jessica P., MA, PhD; American academic and fmr government official; *Dean, Paul H. Nitze School of Advanced International Studies (SAIS), Johns Hopkins University;* b. 1948; ed Barnard Coll., Columbia Univ., Paul H. Nitze School of Advanced Int. Studies (SAIS), Princeton Univ. LSE, London, Brookings Inst., Harvard Univ.; various roles with US Treasury, US State Dept and Int. Devt Cooperation Agency of USA –1992; Vice-Pres. and Treasurer, World Bank 1992–96, Man. Dir 1996-98; Visiting Fellow, IMF 1998–99; Consultant, Clark & Weinstock, Washington 1999–2002; Dean, Paul H. Nitze School of Advanced Int. Studies (SAIS), Johns Hopkins Univ. 2002–; Trustee Rockefeller Brothers Fund; Dir Council on Foreign Relations, Inst. for Int. Econs, Center for Global Devt; Dir Pitney Bowes Inc. 1999–; Chair. Global Advisory Bd J.E. Robert Cos; mem. Exec. Cttee Trilateral Comm.; fmr Trustee German Marshall Fund. *Publications:* Expropriation Politics 1974; various articles. *Address:* Paul H. Nitze School of Advanced International Studies, 1740 Massachusetts Avenue, NW, Washington, DC 20036, USA (office). *Telephone:* (202) 663-5624 (office). *Fax:* (202) 663-5621 (office). *E-mail:* jeinhorn@jhu.edu (office). *Website:* www.sais-jhu.edu (office).

EINIK, Michael, MBA; American diplomatist; *Executive Director, Project on Ethnic Relations Regional Center for Central, Eastern and Southeastern Europe;* b. 1949, New York; ed Univ. of Miami, George Washington Univ., Washington, DC; joined Dept of State 1972; Econ./Commercial Officer Brasilia, then San Salvador; with Bureau of Econ. and Business Affairs, Dept of State; staff Asst to Asst Sec. of State; worked in Office of Fuels and Energy during 1970s oil crisis; Petroleum Officer, Embassy, Nigeria 1981; served in Econ. Section, Moscow; Prin. Officer, Consulate-Gen., Zagreb representing US in both Croatia and Slovenia 1988–92; Chief of Personnel, European Bureau 1992–94; Deputy Chief of Mission, Bucharest; Amb. to Macedonia 1999–2002; Pres. Netcare Healthcare Central Europe (Netcare CE) 2004; Exec. Dir Project on Ethnic Relations (PER) Regional Center for Cen., Eastern and Southeastern Europe, Bucharest, Romania 2006–. *Address:* c/o Project on Ethnic Relations, 15 Chambers Street, Princeton, NJ 08542-3707 USA (office). *Telephone:* (609) 683-5666 (office). *Fax:* (609) 683-5888 (office). *E-mail:* per@per-usa.org (office). *Website:* www.per-usa.org/romania.htm (home).

EIRÍKSSON, Gudmundur, BS, AB, LLB, LLM; Icelandic diplomatist, judge and academic; b. 26 Oct. 1947, Winnipeg, Canada; s. of Rev. Eirikur Sverrir Brynjolfsson and Gudrun Gudmundsdottir; m. Thorey Vigdis Ólafsdóttir 1973; one s. three d.; ed Rutgers Univ., USA, King's Coll., Univ. of London, UK, Columbia Univ., USA; Law of the Sea Officer and Consultant, UN, New York 1974–77; Asst Legal Adviser, Legal Adviser, Ministry for Foreign Affairs, Iceland 1977–96, Amb. 1988–; Rep. of Iceland to Third UN Conf. on Law of the Sea 1978–82; mem. UN Int. Law Comm. 1987–96; Judge, Int. Tribunal for the Law of the Sea 1996–2002 (Pres. Chamber of Fisheries Disputes 1999–2002); Dean for Cooperative Programmes, Sec. of Council, Prof. and Dir of Int. Law and Human Rights Studies, Univ. for Peace, Costa Rica (UPEACE) 2001; Amb. to Canada (also accred to Colombia, Costa Rica, Ecuador, Nicaragua, Panama, Peru and Venezuela) 2003–05, to South Africa 2008–09; Visiting Scholar Univ. of Va Law School, USA 1984–85; Lecturer, Univ. of Iceland 1987–96; Visiting Prof. of Law, Univ. of New Mexico School of Law 1994–95; Pres. Council of N Atlantic Salmon Conservation Org. 1984–88; mem. Panel of Conciliators and Arbitrators, Center for Arbitrations, Mediation and Conciliation, Dakar, Panel of Conciliators and Panel of Arbitrators, Int. Centre for the Settlement of Investment Disputes, Washington, DC; Grand Kt, Order of the Icelandic Falcon; Jelf Memorial Medal, King's Coll., Univ. of London 1973. *Publications:* The International Tribunal for the Law of the Sea 2000; numerous articles on the law of the sea, legal educ., int. criminal law, int. orgs, disarmament and human rights. *Address:* Ministry for Foreign Affairs, Reykjavík, Iceland (office). *Telephone:* 545-9021 (office). *Fax:* 249-1929 (office). *E-mail:* eiriks@racsa.co.cr (office).

EISELE, Lt-Gen. Manfred S.; German army officer; b. 17 March 1938, Wilhelmshaven; s. of Wilhelm Eisele and Gertrud Eisele-Meyer; m. Elke Krümpelmann 1962; two d.; ed Blankenese High School, Mil. Acad., Gen. Staff Acad., Hamburg, USA Command and Gen. Staff Coll. and Royal Coll. of Defence Studies; Commdg Officer, Artillery-Bn 125, Bayreuth 1977–78; Chef de Cabinet/Chief of Gen. Staff, Bonn 1978–80; Head of Public Information, Ministry of Defence 1980–81; Commdg Officer, Mechanized Infantry Brigade 17, Hamburg 1984–88; Chief, Combat Requirements Brigade, Supreme HQ Allied Forces Europe (SHAPE), Mons, Belgium 1988–91; Dir Politico-Military Affairs, Ministry of Defence, Bonn 1991–92; Commdg Officer, 12th Panzer Div. Würzburg 1992–94, Armed Forces Office, Bonn 1994; Asst Sec.-Gen. UN Dept of Peace-Keeping Operations 1994; Bundesverdienstkreuz, Legion of Merit, USA, Grand Cross, Rider of Vadar, Bulgaria; Dag Hammarskjöld Medal. *Publications:* Die Vereinten Nationen und das Internationale Krisenmanagement (preface by Kofi Annan) 2000. *Leisure interests:* international politics, history, music, sport. *Address:* Ravensburgstrasse 2B, 97209 Veitshöchheim, Germany. *Telephone:* (931) 9500055. *Fax:* (931) 9500042. *E-mail:* E.u.M.Eisele@t-online.de (home).

EISEN, Herman Nathaniel, AB, MD; American immunologist, microbiologist and academic; *Professor Emeritus of Immunology, Massachusetts Institute of Technology;* b. 15 Oct. 1918, Brooklyn, NY; s. of Joseph M. Eisen and Lena M. Eisen (née Karush); m. Natalie Aronson 1948; three s. two d.; ed New York Univ., Washington Univ. in St Louis; Prof. of Medicine (Dermatology), Washington Univ., St Louis 1955–61, Prof. of Microbiology and Head of Dept 1961–73; Dermatologist-in-Chief, Barnes Hosp. 1955–61; Prof. of Immunology, MIT 1973–89, Whitehead Inst. Prof. of Immunology 1982–89, Prof.

Emer. 1989–; mem. Bd Scientific Advisers Mass Gen. Hosp., Boston 1977–, Boston Children's Hosp. 1976–, Howard Hughes Medical Inst., Merck Sharp & Dohme Research Labs, Rahway 1976–; Harvey Lecturer 1964; Consultant to Surgeons-Gen. of Public Health Service, Dept of the Army; Chair. Study Section for Allergy and Immunology, NIH 1964–68; mem. Editorial Bd Journal of Immunology, Bacteriological Reviews, Physiological Reviews, Proceedings of the NAS; mem. American Soc. for Clinical Investigation (Vice-Pres. 1963–64), American Asscn of Immunologists (Pres. 1968–69), American Soc. for Biological Chemists, American Asscn of Physicians, Inst. of Medicine, NAS, American Acad. of Arts and Sciences; Hon. ScD (Washington Univ.) 2003; New York Univ. Medical Science Achievement Award 1978, Dupont Award, Clinical Ligand Soc. 1987, Outstanding Investigator Award, Nat. Cancer Inst. 1986, Lifetime Achievement/Service Award, American Asscn of Immunologists 1991, Behring-Heidelberger Award, American Asscn of Immunologists 1993. *Publications:* Methods in Medical Research Vol. 10 (ed.) 1964, Microbiology (co-author) 1967–90, Immunology 1974–90 (four edns), Contemporary Topics in Molecular Immunology Vol. 5 (ed.) 1976; more than 230 scientific articles. *Leisure interest:* landscape gardening. *Address:* Center for Cancer Research, Massachusetts Institute of Technology, Room E17-128, 77 Massachusetts Avenue, Cambridge, MA 02139-4307 (office); 9 Homestead Street, Waban, MA 02168, USA (home). *Telephone:* (617) 253-6406 (office). *Fax:* (617) 258-6172 (office). *E-mail:* hneisen@mit.edu (office). *Website:* mit.edu/biology/www/facultyareas/facresearch/eisen.html (office).

EISENBERG, Leon, MD, MA; American physician, psychiatrist and academic; *Presley Professor of Social Medicine and Professor of Psychiatry Emeritus, Harvard Medical School;* b. 8 Aug. 1922, Philadelphia; s. of Morris Eisenberg and Elizabeth Sabreen; m. 1st Ruth Bleier 1947 (divorced 1967); m. 2nd Carola Guttmacher 1967; one s. one d.; ed Univ. of Pennsylvania, Mt. Sinai Hosp., New York, Sheppard Pratt Hosp., Baltimore, Johns Hopkins Hosp., Baltimore; Capt. Army Medical Corps 1948–50; Instructor in Psychiatry and Pediatrics, Johns Hopkins Medical School 1954, Asst Prof. 1955–58, Assoc. Prof. 1958–61, Prof. of Child Psychiatry 1961–67; Chief of Psychiatry Massachusetts Gen. Hosp. 1967–74; Prof. of Psychiatry, Harvard Medical School 1967–93, Chair. of Exec. Cttee, Dept of Psychiatry 1974–80, Presley Prof., Dept of Social Medicine and Health Policy 1980–93, Prof. Emer. 1993–; Royal Soc. of Medicine Visiting Prof. 1983; Queen Elizabeth II Lecturer, Canadian Pediatric Soc. 1986; Consultant, Div. of Mental Health, WHO 1980; Lilly Lecturer, Royal Coll. of Psychiatrists 1986; Dir WHO/Harvard Collaborating Center for Research and Training in Psychiatry 1986–; mem. Inst. of Medicine NAS 1974–; WHO expert advisory panel on Mental Health 1984–; Consultant, Child Mental Health, Pan American Health Org., Uruguay 1991; William Potter Lecturer, Thomas Jefferson Univ. 1992; mem. American Acad. of Arts and Sciences; Hon. Fellow, Royal Coll. of Psychiatrists 1985; Hon. DSc (Manchester) 1973, (Mass.) 1991; numerous awards including Theobald Smith Award 1979, Aldrich Award American Acad. of Pediatrics 1980, Dale Richmond Award, American Acad. of Pediatrics 1989, Special Presidential Commendation, American Psychiatric Asscn 1992, Thomas W. Salmon Medal New York Acad. of Medicine 1995, Rhoda and Bernard Sarnat Prize for outstanding contrib. to mental health Inst. of Medicine of the Nat. Acads of Sciences 1996, Diversity Lifetime Achievement Award Harvard Medical School 2001, Award for Distinguished Contrib. to Public Policy Soc. for Research in Child Devt 2003, Distinguished Service Award American Psychiatric Asscn 2003, Ruane Prize for Child and Adolescent Psychiatric Research Nat. Alliance for Research in Schizophrenia and Depression, Human Right Award American Psychiatric Asscn 2005. *Publications:* more than 240 articles in journals, 130 chapters in books and 11 edited or co-edited books including World Mental Health: Problems and Priorities in Low-Income Countries 1995, The Best Intentions: Unintended Pregnancy and the Well-Being of Children and Families 1995, The Implications of Genetics for Health Professional Education 1999, Bridging Disciplines in the Brain, Behavioral and Clinical Sciences 2000. *Leisure interests:* classical music, theatre, reading. *Address:* Harvard Medical School, Department of Global Health and Social Medicine, 641 Huntington Avenue, Boston, MA 02115-6019 (office); University Green, Suite # 310, 130 Mt. Auburn Street, Cambridge, MA 02138-5757, USA. *Telephone:* (617) 432-1710 (office); (617) 868-0112 (home). *Fax:* (617) 432-3721 (office); (617) 432-2565 (home). *E-mail:* leon_eisenberg@hms.harvard.edu (home).

EISENHOWER, John Sheldon Doud, BS, MA; American author and diplomatist; b. 3 Aug. 1922, Denver, Colo; s. of the late Gen. Dwight D. Eisenhower (Pres. of USA 1953–61) and Mamie Eisenhower (née Doud); m. 1st Barbara Jean Thompson 1947 (divorced 1986); one s. three d.; m. 2nd Joanne Thompson 1990; ed Stadium High School, Tacoma, Wash., US Mil. Acad., West Point, Columbia Univ. and Armored Advance Course and General Staff Coll., US Army; 2nd Lt, US Army 1944, assigned to First Army, World War II; Instructor in English, US Mil. Acad., West Point 1948–51; served as Battalion Operations Officer, Div. Asst Operations Officer and Div. Intelligence Officer, 3rd Div., Korea; Jt War Plans Div., Army Staff, Pentagon 1957–58; Asst Staff Sec. in White House 1958–61; researcher and editor on Eisenhower memoirs The White House Years; Amb. to Belgium 1969–71; Consultant to Pres. Nixon; Chair. Interagency Classification Review Cttee 1972–73; Brig.-Gen. US Army Reserve 1974; mem. Nat. Archives Advisory Cttee 1974–77; Chair. Pres.'s Advisory Cttee on Refugees 1975; Order of the Crown (Belgium); Legion of Merit, Bronze Star, Army Commendation Ribbon, Combat Infantry Badge, Grand Cross. *Publications:* The Bitter Woods 1969, Strictly Personal 1974, Allies 1981, So Far From God 1989, Intervention! 1993, Agent of Destiny 1997, Yanks 2001, General Ike 2003. *Leisure interest:* military history. *E-mail:* dyentz@nni.com (office).

EISENMAN, Peter David, PhD, MS, FAIA; American architect; b. 11 Aug. 1932, Newark; s. of Herschel I. Eisenmann and Sylvia H. Heller; m. 1st

Elizabeth Henderson 1963 (divorced 1990); one s. one d.; m. 2nd Cynthia Davidson 1990; one c.; ed Cornell Univ., Columbia Univ., Cambridge Univ.; Founder Inst. of Architecture and Urban Studies, New York 1967, Dir 1967–82; Architect-in-Residence American Acad., Rome 1976; with Eisenmann/Robertson Architects, New York 1980–88; Eisenmann Architects 1988–; commissioned to design Berlin Holocaust Memorial; Kea Prof. Univ. of Md 1978; Charlotte Davenport Prof., Yale Univ. 1980, Louis I. Kahn Prof. of Architecture 2001–; Arthur Rotch Prof., Harvard Univ. 1982–85; Irwin Chanin Distinguished Prof. 1986–; Louis H. Sullivan Research Prof. of Architecture, Univ. of Ill. 1987–93; John Williams Prof. of Architecture, Univ. of Ark. 1997; Frank H.T. Rhodes Class of '56 Prof., Cornell Univ. 2008–; Arnold W. Brunner Memorial Prize in Architecture, American Acad. and Inst. of Arts and Letters 1984, Golden Lion for lifetime achievement, Venice Biennale 2004. *Principal works include:* Pvt. Residences Princeton, NJ, Hardwick, Vt, Lakeville and Cornwall, Conn. 1968–76, Housing, Koch-Friedrichstrasse, Berlin 1980–86, Wexner Center for Visual Arts, Columbus, Ohio 1983–89, Columbus Convention Centre 1988–93, Univ. of Cincinnati Coll. of Design, Art, Architecture and Planning 1988–96, Koizumi Sangyo Bldg, Tokyo 1989–90, Emory Univ. Art Centre 1991–95, Rebstock Park, Frankfurt, Germany 1991–95, Max Reinhardt Haus, Berlin 1992–, Haus Immendorff, Düsseldorf, Germany 1993–94, Jewish Museum, San Francisco 1996–, Library UN Complex, Geneva 1996–, Staten Island Inst. of Arts and Sciences 1997–, Holocaust Memorial, Berlin 1998–, City of Culture, Santiago de Compostela, Spain 1999–. *Address:* Eisenmann Architects, 41 W 25th Street, New York, NY 10010-2021, USA (office).

EISENSTADT, Shmuel Noah, MA, PhD; Israeli sociologist and academic; *Rose Isaacs Professor Emeritus of Sociology, Hebrew University of Jerusalem;* b. 10 Sept. 1923, Warsaw, Poland; s. of Michael Eisenstadt and Rosa Baruchin; m. Shulamit Yaroshevski 1948; two s. one d.; ed Hebrew Univ. of Jerusalem and London School of Econs and Political Science; Chair. Dept of Sociology, Hebrew Univ., Jerusalem 1951–69, Prof. of Sociology 1959, currently Rose Isaacs Prof. Emer. of Sociology; Dean, Faculty of Social Sciences 1966–68; Fellow, Center for Advanced Studies in Behavioral Sciences, Stanford Univ., USA 1955–56; Visiting Prof., Univ. of Oslo 1958, Univ. of Chicago 1960, 1971, Harvard Univ. 1966, 1968–69, 1975–80, Univ. of Michigan 1970, Univ. of Zürich 1975, Stanford Univ. 1984, 1986, 1987, 1988; Carnegie Visiting Prof., MIT 1962–63, Simon Visiting Prof., Univ. of Manchester, UK 1977; Research Fellow, Hoover Inst. 1986; Tanner Lecturer on Human Values, Univ. of Calif. 1988; Distinguished Visiting Prof., Univ. of Alberta, Canada 1989; Prof., Univ. of Chicago Cttee on Social Thought 1990–93; Max Weber Prof., Univ. of Heidelberg, Germany; Visiting Prof., Univ. of Erfurt, Germany 1998–2000; Chair. Council on Community Relations, Israel 1962–64, Israeli Sociological Soc. 1969–72; mem. Advisory Bd Int. Encyclopedia of the Social Sciences; mem. Scientific Cttee Centro Gino Germani, Rome; Sr Fellow, Wilson Center for Int. Exchange, Washington, DC 1996, 1998; Fellow, Netherlands Inst. of Advanced Studies (SCASSS) 1973, Van Leer Jerusalem Inst.; Hon. Research Fellow, Inst. of Sociology, Chinese Acad. of Social Sciences 2000; Foreign Assoc. NAS; mem. Israel Acad. of Sciences and Humanities, Int. Sociological Soc., American Sociological Asscn; Foreign mem. American Philosophical Soc.; Foreign Hon. mem. American Acad. of Arts and Sciences; Sr Fellow, Cultural Center, Yale Univ. 2004; Corresp. Fellow British Acad. 2006; Hon. Research Fellow, ANU 1977; Hon. Fellow, Open Univ. Tel-Aviv, LSE 2003, Israeli Sociological Soc.; Hon. mem. Polish Sociological Soc. 2004; Dr hc (Helsinki) 1986, (Duke) 2002, (Central European Univ., Budapest) 2003, (Warsaw) 2005, (Haifa) 2007; Hon. LLD (Harvard), Hon. DHumLitt (Hebrew Union Coll., Jewish Inst. of Religion); Hon. DPhil (Tel-Aviv); Hon. Dr (Haifa) 2007; McIver Award, American Sociological Asscn 1964, Kaplun Prize in Social Sciences 1969, Rothschild Prize in Social Sciences 1970, Israel Prize in Social Sciences 1973, Int. Balzan Prize in Sociology 1988, Max Planck Research Award (with W. Schluchter) 1994, Amalfi Prize in European Sociology 2001, Humboldt Research Award 2002, Amb. of Cultural Dialogue Award, Polish Asia Pacific Council, Warsaw 2003, EMET Prize in Sociology 2005, Holberg Int. Memorial Prize 2006. *Publications:* The Absorption of Immigrants 1954, From Generation to Generation 1956, Essays on Sociological Aspects of Economical and Political Development 1961, The Political Systems of Empires 1963, Essays on Comparative Institutions 1965, Modernization, Protest and Change 1966, Israeli Society 1968, The Protestant Ethic and Modernization 1968, Political Sociology of Modernization (in Japanese) 1968, Comparative Perceptives on Social Change (ed.) 1968, Charisma and Institution Building: Selections from Max Weber (ed.) 1968, Ensayos sobre el Cambio social y la Modernización (Spanish) 1969, Modernização e Mudança Social (Portuguese) 1969, Political Sociology (ed.) 1970, Social Differentiation and Stratification 1971, Collection of Essays in Japanese 1971, Tradition, Change and Modernity 1973, Collection of Essays in Spanish 1973, Post-traditional Societies (ed.) 1974, The Form of Sociology: Paradigms and Crises (with M. Curelaru) 1976, Macrosociology (with M. Curelaru) 1977, Revolutions and Transformation of Societies 1978, Patrons, Clients and Friends (with L. Roniger) 1984, Transformation of Israeli Society 1985, Origins and Diversity of Axial Age Civilizations (ed.) 1986, Society, Culture and Urbanization (with A. Shachar) 1987, The Origins of the State Reconsidered (with M. Abitbol and N. Chazan) 1986, European Civilization in Comparative Perspective 1987, Center Formation, Protest Movements and Class Structure in Europe and the US (with L. Roniger and A. Seligman) 1987, Patterns of Modernity I and II 1987, Kulturen der Achsenzeit (trans.) 1987, The Early State in African Perspective 1988, Knowledge and Society: Studies in the Sociological Culture, Past and Present (co-ed. with I. Silber) 1988, Japanese Models of Conflict Resolution (co-ed. with Eyal Ben-Ari) 1990, Martin Buber on Intersubjectivity and Cultural Creativity (ed.), Jewish Civilization: The Jewish Historical Experience in a Comparative Perspective 1992, The Political Systems of Empires

1993, Power, Trust and Meaning 1995, Japanese Civilization: A Comparative View 1996, Modernità, Modernizzazione e Oltré 1997, Paradoxes of Democracy: Fragility, Continuity and Change 1999, Fundamentalism, Sectarianism and Revolutions 2000, Die Vielfalt der Moderne 2000, Public Spheres and Collective Identities (co-ed. with W. Schluchter and B. Wittrock), Multiple Modernities (ed.) 2002, Fundamentalism and Modernity (in Hebrew) 2002, Jewish Civilization: The Jewish Historical Experience in a Comparative Perspective and Its Manifestations in Israeli Society 2003, Japanese Civilization 2003, Comparative Civilizations & Multiple Modernities (essays, two vols) 2003, Explorations in Jewish Historical Experience: The Civilizational Dimension 2004, Axial Civilizations and World History (co-ed.) 2005, The Great Revolutions and Modernity 2006, Reflections on Modernity: Collection of Essays 2006, Civilizations (essay, in Blackwell Encyclopedia of Sociology) 2007, Las Grandes Revoluciones y las civilizaciones de la modernidad 2007. *Address:* The Van Leer Jerusalem Institute, POB 4070, Jerusalem 91040 (office); 30 Radak Street, Jerusalem 92186, Israel (home). *Telephone:* 2-5605235 (office); 2-5632467 (home). *Fax:* 2-5619293 (office); 2-5617620 (home). *E-mail:* miriamb@vanleer.org.il (office). *Website:* www.vanleer.org.il (office).

EISNER, Michael Dammann, BA; American business executive; b. 7 March 1942, Mount Kisco, NY; s. of Lester Dammann and Margaret Dammann; m. Jane Breckenridge 1967; three s.; ed Lawrenceville School, Denison Univ.; Sr Vice-Pres. Prime-Time Production and Devt, ABC Entertainment Corpn 1973–76; Pres. and COO Paramount Pictures Corpn 1976–84; Chair. and CEO The Walt Disney Co. 1984–2004, CEO 2004–05, mem. Bd of Dirs 2005–06; fmr mem. Bd of Dirs Calif. Inst. of the Arts, Denison Univ., American Hosp. of Paris Foundation, UCLA Exec. Bd for Medical Sciences, Nat. Hockey League (ice hockey); mem. Business Steering Cttee of the Global Business Dialogue on Electronic Commerce, The Business Council; est. Eisner Foundation; host, Conversations with Michael Eisner (CNBC) 2006; Founder Tomante LLC 2005–, Dir Veoh Networks Inc. 2006–; Chevalier, Légion d'honneur. *Address:* Tornante LLC, 233 South Beverly Drive, Beverly Hills, CA 90212-3896; c/o Veoh Networks, Inc., 7220 Trade Street, Suite 115, San Diego, CA 92121, USA (office). *Telephone:* (310) 274-2550 (Tornante). *E-mail:* admin@tornante.com. *Website:* www.tornante.com; www.veoh.com (office).

EISNER, Thomas, BA, PhD; American scientist and academic; *Jacob Gould Schurman Professor of Chemical Ecology Emeritus, Cornell University;* b. 25 June 1929, Berlin, Germany; s. of Hans E. Eisner and Margarete Heil-Eisner; m. Maria L. R. Löbell 1952; three d.; ed High School and Preparatory School, Montevideo, Uruguay, Champlain Coll., Plattsburgh, NY and Harvard Univ; Research Fellow in Biology, Harvard Univ. 1955–57; Asst Prof. of Biology, Cornell Univ. 1957–62, Assoc. Prof. 1962–66, Prof. of Biology 1966–76, Jacob Gould Schurman Prof. of Chemical Ecology 1976, currently Prof. Emer., Dir Cornell Inst. for Research in Chemical Ecology 1993–2006; Sr Fellow, Cornell Center for the Environment 1994–; Consultant, World Environment and Research Programme MacArthur Foundation 1987–92; Lalor Fellow 1954–55, Guggenheim Fellow 1964–65, 1972–73; mem. Nat. Council for Nature Conservancy 1969–74, Council Fed. American Scientists 1977–81, External Scientific Advisory Cttee, MBL, Woods Hole 1989–91, 1996–99; Foreign mem. Royal Soc. 1997; Dir National Audubon Soc. 1970–75; Pres. American Soc. of Naturalists 1988; mem. NAS 1969, American Philosophical Soc. 1986, Akademie Naturforscher Leopoldina 1986; Fellow, American Acad. of Arts and Sciences 1969, Animal Behavior Soc. 1971, American Entomological Soc. 1987, Zero Population Growth (Dir 1969–70); Chair. Biology Section, AAAS 1980–81, mem. Cttee for Scientific Freedom and Responsibility 1980–87, Chair. Sub cttee on Science and Human Rights 1981–87; mem. Steering Cttee on Consequences of Nuclear War 1983–87, Scientific Advisory Council, World Wildlife Fund 1983–90, NAS Cttee on Human Rights 1987–90, Advisory Council, Monell Chemical Senses Center 1988–2000, World Resources Inst. 1988–95; mem. Task Force for the 90s, AIBS 1990–99, Scientific Advisory Council, Xerces Soc. (Pres. 1992–2006), Scientific Advisory Cttee, Cttee for Nat. Inst. for the Environment 1991–, Entomology Soc. of America Standing Cttee on Fellows 1993–94, Bd of Dirs Union of Concerned Scientists 1993–, Nat. Museum of Natural History 1995–2000; Chair. Advisory Council, Center for Biodiversity and Conservation, American Museum of Natural History 1995–99; mem. Int. Advisory Bd Encyclopedia of Biodiversity 1997–98, INBio 1997–98, FUNDAQUIN 1997–2007, American Philosophical Soc. Council 1999-2005, Science Adv Xerces Soc. 2006–; Hon. PhD (Würzburg) 1982, (Zürich) 1983, (Göteborg) 1989, (Drexel) 1992; Newcomb-Cleveland Prize (with E. O. Wilson) of AAAS 1967, Founders Memorial Award of Entomological Soc. of America 1969, Prof. of Merit, Cornell Univ. 1973, Archie F. Carr Medal 1983, four awards for film Secret Weapons, BBC TV 1984, Procter Prize 1986, Karl Ritter von Frisch Medal 1988, Centennial Medal, Harvard Univ. 1989, Tyler Prize 1990, Esselen Award 1991, Silver Medal, Int. Soc. of Chemical Ecology 1991, Nat. Medal of Science 1994, Green Globe Award 1997, John Wiley Jones Award 1999, Lewis Thomas Award 2005, Grand Prix de la Fondation de la Chimie 2006, John J. Carty Award 2008; numerous other awards. *Publications:* seven books, including For Love of Insects 2004, Secret Weapons 2005; more than 400 technical papers on animal behaviour, chemical ecology, comparative physiology, chemical communication in animals, conservation. *Leisure interests:* photography, cinematography, orchestra conducting, piano. *Address:* Department of Neurobiology and Behavior, Division of Biological Sciences, W347 Seely G. Mudd Hall, Cornell University, Ithaca, NY 14853, USA (office). *Telephone:* (607) 255-4464 (office). *E-mail:* te14@cornell.edu (office). *Website:* www.nbb.cornell.edu/neurobio/eisner/eisner (office).

EITEL, Bernhard, PhD; German professor of geography and university administrator; *Rector, Ruprecht Karls University;* b. 1959, Karlsruhe; ed Univ. of Karlsruhe, Univ. of Stuttgart; Lecturer, Dept of Geography, Univ. of Stuttgart 1989–95; Prof. of Physical Geography, Univ. of Passau 1995–2001; Prof. of Physical Geography, Ruprecht Karls Univ., Heidelberg 2001–, also Head of Geography Dept, Rector, Ruprecht Karls Univ. 2007–. *Address:* Office of the Rector, Ruprecht Karls University, Grabengasse 1, 69117 Heidelberg, Germany (office). *Telephone:* (6221) 54-23-156 (office). *Fax:* (6221) 54-21-47 (office). *E-mail:* rektor@rektorat.uni-heidelberg.de (office). *Website:* www.rektorat.uni-heidelberg.de/rector.html (office).

EIZENSTAT, Stuart Elliot, AB, JD; American diplomatist, lawyer and fmr government official; *Director of International Trade and Finance, Covington & Burling;* b. 15 Jan. 1943, Chicago; s. of Leo Eizenstat and Sylvia Eizenstat; m. Frances Taylor 1967; two s.; ed Univ. of North Carolina and Harvard Univ.; admitted Ga Bar 1967, DC Bar 1981; mem. White House staff 1967–68; mem. nat. campaign staff for Hubert M. Humphrey 1968; law clerk, US Dist Court, Ga 1968–70; Pnr, Powell, Goldstein, Frazer & Murphy (law firm), Washington, DC 1970–77, 1981–93, Chair. Washington Office 1991–93; Asst to Pres. of USA for Domestic Affairs and Policy 1977–81, Dir Domestic Policy Staff 1977–81; Amb. to EU 1993–96; Under-Sec. of Commerce for Int. Trade 1996–97; Special Envoy for Property Restitution in Cen. Europe 1993–96, Dept of State Property Claims in Cen. Europe 1995–97; Under-Sec. of Econ., Business and Agricultural Affairs 1997–99; Deputy Sec. of Treasury 1999–2001; Alt. Gov. IBRD 1998–99; State Dept Special Envoy on Property Claims in Cen. Europe; Special Rep. of Pres. and Sec. of State on Holocaust Issues 1999–2001; Adjunct Lecturer, Kennedy School of Govt, Harvard Univ. 1981–93; Guest Scholar, Brookings Inst. Washington 1981; Dir of Int. Trade and Finance, Covington & Burling 2001–; Co-Chair. European American Business Council; mem. Presidential Task Force on US Int. Broadcasting 1991; mem. Bd of Dirs Hercules Inc. Wilmington, Israel Discount Bank of New York, P.S.I. Holdings Inc. Indianapolis; numerous other public appointments; Democrat; hon. degrees (Yeshiva Univ.) 1996, (North Carolina) 2000, (Jewish Theological Seminary) 2000; numerous awards including Leadership Award, Secr. of State 1999, B'nai B'rith Leadership Award 2000, Washington Inst. for Jewish Leadership and Values award for leadership 2001; Légion d'honneur 2004. *Publications include:* The Path to History (with A. Young) 1973, Environmental Auditing Handbook 1984, The American Agenda: Advice to the 41st President (co-ed.) 1988; articles in newspapers and professional journals. *Leisure interest:* tennis. *Address:* Covington & Burling, 1201 Pennsylvania Avenue, NW, Washington, DC 20004-2401 (office); 9107 Brierly Road, Chevy Chase, MD 20815-5654, USA (home). *Telephone:* (202) 662-5745 (office). *E-mail:* seizenstat@cov.com (office). *Website:* www.cov.com (office); www.eabc.org.

EKEUS, Carl Rolf; Swedish diplomatist; *High Commissioner on National Minorities, Organization for Security and Co-operation in Europe;* b. 7 July 1935, Kristinehamn; m. Christina C. Oldfelt 1970; three s. three d.; ed Univ. of Stockholm; law practice, Karlstad 1959–62; Legal Div. Ministry of Foreign Affairs 1962–63; Sec. Swedish Embassy, Bonn 1963–65; First Sec. Nairobi 1965–67; Special Asst to Minister of Foreign Affairs 1967–73; First Sec., Counsellor, Perm. Mission to UN, New York 1974–78; Counsellor, The Hague 1978–83; Amb. and Perm. Rep. to Conf. on Disarmament, Geneva 1983–89, Chair. Cttee on Chemical Weapons 1984, 1987; Amb. and Head of Swedish Del. to CSCE, Vienna 1989–93; Chair. Cttee on Principles Chapter of Charter of Paris 1991; Exec. Chair. UN Special Comm. on Iraq 1991–97; Amb. to USA 1997–2000; Chair. Stockholm Int. Peace Research Inst. 2000–; OSCE High Commr on Nat. Minorities 2001–; mem. Canberra Comm. on the Elimination of Nuclear Weapons, advisory Bd Center for Non-Proliferation, Monetary Inst., Tokyo Forum on Non-Proliferation and Disarmament; mem. advisory Bd of UN Sec.-Gen. on Disarmament Matters 1999–2004, Bd Dirs Nuclear Threat Initiative 2001, Bd Axel and Margaret Ax:son Johnson Foundation 2001–; mem. Royal Acad. of War Science, Stockholm 2001; Hon. LLD (California Lutheran Univ.) 1999; Wateler Peace Prize, Carnegie Foundation 1997. *Publications:* reports as Special Investigator on the submarine question 1980–2001, Sweden's security policy 1969–89 2002; several articles on foreign policy, int. economy, nuclear non-proliferation, disarmament and arms control, chemical weapons, European security, Iraq and weapons of mass destruction. *Leisure interests:* piano playing, tennis. *Address:* High Commission on National Minorities, Prinsessegracht 22, 2514 AP The Hague, Netherlands (office); Stockholm International Peace Research Institute, Signalistgatan 9, 169 70 Solna (office); Rådmansgatan 57, 11360 Stockholm, Sweden (home). *Telephone:* (70) 3125500 (The Hague) (office); (8) 312653 (home). *Fax:* (70) 3635910 (The Hague) (office). *E-mail:* rekeus@hcnm.org (office). *Website:* www.sipri.se (office); www.osce.org/hcnm (office).

EKREN, Nazim, PhD; Turkish politician; b. 1956, Istanbul; m.; two c.; ed Uludağ and Marmara univs, Manchester Business School, UK; fmr Dir Türkiye Vakiflar Bankasi; fmr Dir Banking and Insurance Inst., Univ. of Marmara; mem. of Grand Nat. Ass., representing Istanbul 2002–; Deputy Prime Minister and State Minister for Economy 2007–09; Co-founder, Bd Mem. and Deputy Chair. (Econ. Affairs), AKP (Adalet ve Kalkinma Partisi/Justice and Devt Party). *Address:* c/o Deputy Prime Ministers' Office, Başbakan Yard, ve Devlet Bakani, Bakanliklar, Ankara, Turkey (office).

EKSTEEN, Jacobus Adriaan, MA; South African diplomatist and broadcasting executive (retd) and political consultant; b. 31 Oct. 1942, Volksrust; s. of Jacobus Adriaan and Helena Barendina Hendrika (née Baard) Eksteen; m. Ria Hofmeyr 1991; three s. (previous marriage); ed Univs of Pretoria and South Africa; entered Civil Service 1961; mem. SA legal team at Int. Court of Justice in South West Africa (Namibia) 1966; Third Sec., Second Sec., then First Sec., Embassy, USA 1968–73; served in Head Office of Dept of Foreign Affairs as Head of UN and South West Africa sections 1973–76; Counsellor and Deputy Perm. Rep. at SA Perm. Mission to UN 1976, Minister 1978, Acting Perm. Rep. 1977–79, Perm. Rep. and Amb. 1979–81; Head of Planning

Div., Ministry of Foreign Affairs 1981–83; mem. SA Del. to Patent Cooperation Treaty, Washington 1970, to INTELSAT Conf., Washington 1971, to UN Gen. Assembly 1972, 1979, 1981; involved in all discussions on Namibia 1977–83; presented South Africa's case in UN Security Council Aug. 1981; Dir-Gen. (desig.) South African Broadcasting Corp. 1983, Dir-Gen. 1984–88; SA Rep. in Namibia 1990–91; Amb. and Perm. Rep. to UN and Special Agencies in Geneva 1992–95; Amb. to Turkey (also accred to Azerbaijan, Kyrgyzstan, Turkmenistan, Uzbekistan) 1995. *Leisure interests:* reading, walking, stamp collecting, hunting. *Address:* c/o Ministry of Foreign Affairs, Union Buildings, East Wing, Government Avenue, Pretoria 0002, South Africa.

EKWUEME, Alex Ifeanyichukwu, BArch, LLB, MA, PhD; Nigerian politician, architect and lawyer; b. 21 Oct. 1932, Oko; s. of the late Lazarus Ibeabuchi Ekwueme and Agnes Nkwodumma Ekwueme; ed King's Coll., Lagos, Univ. of Washington, Seattle, Univ. of Strathclyde, Glasgow, Nigerian Law School, Lagos; est. Ekwueme Associates (architects) 1958; fmr Pres. Nigerian Inst. of Architects, Architectural Registration Council of Nigeria; Vice-Pres. candidate with Alhaji Shehu Shagari in Presidential elections Aug. 1979; Vice-Pres. of Nigeria 1979–83; detained 1983, released July 1986; fmr mem. Nat. Exec. of banned Nat. Party of Nigeria; mem. Nat. Constitutional Conf. 1994–95; Chair. All-Nigeria Politicians Summit Conf. 1995; Founding Chair. and Chair. Bd of Trustees People's Democratic Party 1998–; Fulbright Scholar 1952; Grand Commdr Order of the Niger 1988–; several hon. doctorates. *Leisure interests:* reading, lawn tennis. *Address:* Oko, Anambra State, Nigeria. *Telephone:* (42) 454815. *Fax:* (42) 456667; (42) 254757 (office).

EL-BADRI, Abdalla Salem, BS; Libyan oil industry executive and international organization official; *Secretary-General, Organization of the Petroleum Exporting Countries (OPEC);* b. 1940, Ghemmines; ed Univ. of Florida, USA; began career at Esso-Libya 1965; seconded by state-owned Nat. Oil Corpn (NOC) to become mem. Umm Al-Jawaby Man. Bd 1977; Chair. Waha Oil Co. 1980–83; Chair. NOC 1983–90, 2000–02, Sec. Man. Cttee 2004–06; Sec., Gen. People's Cttee of Petroleum 1990–93, Gen. People's Cttee of Energy 1993–2002, Under-Sec., Gen. People's Cttee 2002–04; Sec.-Gen. OPEC 2007–. *Address:* Organization of the Petroleum Exporting Countries (OPEC), Obere Donaustrasse 93, 1020 Vienna, Austria (office). *Telephone:* (1) 21-11-20 (office). *Fax:* (1) 216-43-20 (office). *Website:* www.opec.org (office).

EL-BAZ, Farouk, BS, MS, PhD; Egyptian/American scientist and academic; *Director, Center for Remote Sensing, Boston University;* b. 1 Jan. 1938, Zagazig; s. of the late El-Sayed El-Baz and of Zahia Hammouda; m. Catherine Patricia O'Leary 1963; four d.; ed Ain Shams Univ., Cairo, Asyut Univ., Missouri School of Mines and Metallurgy, Univ. of Missouri, Massachusetts Inst. of Tech., Heidelberg Univ., Germany; Demonstrator, Geology Dept, Asyut Univ. 1958–60; Lecturer, Mineralogy-Petrography Inst., Univ. of Heidelberg 1964–65; exploration geologist, Pan-American UAR Oil Co., Cairo 1966; Supervisor, Lunar Science Planning and Operations, BellComm, Bell Telephone Labs., Washington, DC for Apollo Program, NASA HQ 1967–72; Research Dir, Center for Earth and Planetary Studies, Nat. Air and Space Museum, Smithsonian Inst., Washington, DC 1973–82; Science Adviser to Pres. Anwar Sadat of Egypt 1978–81; Vice-Pres. for Science and Tech. and for Int. Devt, Itek Optical Systems, Lexington, Mass. 1982–86; Dir Center for Remote Sensing, Boston Univ. 1986–; Adjunct Prof., Faculty of Science, Ain Shams Univ., Cairo, Egypt; pioneering work in the applications of space photography to understanding of arid terrain; Pres. Arab Soc. of Desert Research; mem. US Nat. Acad. of Eng, Academia Bibliotheca Alexandrina, the African, Arab, Islamic, Palestine, Hassan II (Moroccan) Acad. of Science, Third World Acad. of Science; Order of Merit, First Class (Arab Repub. of Egypt); Hon. DSc (New England Coll., NH) 1989; Hon. PhD (Mansoura Univ.); Hon. LLD (American Univ. of Cairo); Hon. DEng (Univ. of Missouri-Rolla); numerous honours and awards, including from NASA: Apollo Achievement Award, Certificate of Merit for Contribs to Manned Space Flight, Exceptional Scientific Achievement Medal and Special Recognition Award; from AAAS: Award for Public Understanding of Science and Tech. 1992, Apollo-Soyuz Test Project Experiment Team Award 1992; Golden Door Award, Int. Inst. of Boston, Nevada Medal, Arab Thought Foundation Pioneer Award, Texas Dawa Award. *Publications:* Say It in Arabic 1968, Astronaut Observations from the Apollo-Soyuz Mission 1977, Egypt as Seen by Landsat 1979, Desert Landforms of Southwest Egypt 1982, Deserts and Arid Lands 1984, The Geology of Egypt 1984, Physics of Desertification 1986, The Gulf War and the Environment 1994, Atlas of Kuwait from Satellite Images 2000, Wadis of Oman: Satellite Image Atlas 2002, Development Corridor: Securing a Better Future for Egypt 2007, Remote Sensing in Archaeology 2007. *Leisure interests:* reading history, travel, swimming. *Address:* Center for Remote Sensing, Boston University, 725 Commonwealth Avenue, Boston, MA 02215-1401, USA (office). *Telephone:* (617) 353-9709 (office). *Fax:* (617) 353-3200 (office). *E-mail:* farouk@bu.edu (office). *Website:* www.bu.edu/remotesensing/faculty/el-baz/index.html (office).

ELACHI, Charles, MS, PhD, FIEEE; American (b. Lebanese) electrical engineer and academic; *Director, Jet Propulsion Laboratory;* b. 18 April 1947, Rayak, Lebanon; m. Valerie Gifford; two d.; ed Univ. of Grenoble and Polytechnic Inst., Grenoble, France, Calif. Inst. of Tech. (Caltech), Pasadena, Univ. of Southern Calif., UCLA; taught The Physics of Remote Sensing at Caltech 1982–2000, now Prof. of Electrical Eng and Planetary Science, Vice-Pres. Caltech 2001–; Dir Space and Earth Science, Jet Propulsion Lab. late 1980s–90s, Dir Jet Propulsion Lab. 2001–; Principal Investigator or Co-Investigator on numerous research and devt studies and flight projects sponsored by NASA including Shuttle Imaging Radar series (SIR-A 1981, SIR-B 1984, SIR-C 1994), Magellan Imaging Radar, Rosetta Comet Nucleus Sounder Experiment; currently Team Leader Cassini Titan Radar Experiment; mem. Univ. of Arizona Eng School Advisory Cttee, Boston Univ. Center of Remote Sensing Advisory Council, UCLA Science Bd of Visitors; fmr Chair. several nat. and int. cttees that developed NASA road-maps for exploration of neighbouring solar systems 1995, our solar system 1997, Mars 1998; mem. Nat. Acad. of Eng (NAE) 1989–, NAE 4th Decadal Cttee 1993–95, NAE Membership Cttee 1995; mem. Int. Acad. of Astronautics; Fellow, AIAA; participated in several archeological expeditions in Egyptian Desert, Arabian Peninsula and Western Chinese Desert in search of old trading routes and buried cities using satellite data; lecturer and keynote speaker at numerous nat. and int. confs and univs in China, Japan, Australia, France, UK, Netherlands, Denmark, Austria, Switzerland, Norway, Germany, Italy, Greece, Egypt, Kenya, India, Morocco, and Brazil; ASP Autometric Award 1980, 1982, NASA Exceptional Scientific Medal 1982, W.T. Pecora Award 1985, IEEE Geoscience and Remote Sensing Distinguished Achievement Award 1987, selected by LA Times newspaper as one of "Southern California's rising stars who will make a difference in L.A." 1988, Asteroid 1982 SU was renamed 4116 Elachi in recognition of his contrib. to planetary exploration 1989, IEEE Medal of Eng Excellence 1992, NASA Outstanding Leadership Medal 1994, Nevada Medal 1995, COSPAR Nordberg Medal 1996, NASA Distinguished Service Medal 1999, Dryden Award 2000, UCLA Dept of Earth and Space Science Distinguished Alumni Award 2002, Wernher Von Braun Award 2002, NASA Outstanding Leadership Medal 2002, Takeda Award 2002. *Publications:* three textbooks and over 230 publs and patents in the fields of remote sensing, planetary exploration, Earth observation from space, electromagnetic theory and integrated optics. *Leisure interests:* skiing, woodworking, history, travel. *Address:* Jet Propulsion Laboratory, 4800 Oak Grove Drive, Pasadena, CA 91109, USA (office). *Telephone:* (818) 354-4321 (office). *Website:* www.jpl.nasa.gov (office).

ELAHI, Chaudhry Pervez; Pakistani politician; *President, Pakistan Muslim League (Q) in Punjab;* b. 1 Nov. 1945; s. of Chaudhry Manzoor Elahi; ed Forman Christian Coll., Univ. of London, UK; mem. Punjab Prov. Ass. 1985–, Deputy Leader, then Leader of the Opposition 1993–96, Speaker 1997–99; Minister of Local Govt and Rural Devt, Punjab 1985–86, 1988–1990, 1990–93; Chief Minister of Punjab 2002–07; Pres. Pakistan Muslim League (Q) party in Punjab; mem. Nat. Security Council. *Address:* 30C, Ch. Zahur Elahi Road, Gulberg-II, Lahore, Pakistan (home). *E-mail:* info@pml.org.pk (office). *Website:* www.pml.org.pk (office).

ELARABY, Nabil A., JSD, LLM; Egyptian diplomatist and international arbitrator; b. 15 March 1935; m.; two s. one d.; ed Cairo Univ., New York Univ. Law School, USA; fmr Rep. of Egypt to various UN bodies, including Gen. Ass., Security Council, ECOSOC, Comm. on Human Rights, Conf. on Disarmament; Legal Adviser to Egyptian del. to UN Middle East Peace Conf., Geneva 1973–75; Dir Legal and Treaties Dept, Ministry of Foreign Affairs 1976–78, 1983–87; Amb. to India 1981–83; led Egyptian del. to Taba talks 1986–89; Deputy Perm. Rep. to UN, New York 1978–81, Perm. Rep. 1991–99; Perm. Rep., UN Office at Geneva 1987–91; Judge, Judicial Tribunal of Org. of Arab Petroleum Exporting Countries (OAPEC) 1990–; mem. Int. Law Comm. 1994–2001; Partner Zaki Hashem and Partners 1998; mem. International Court of Justice 2001–05; apptd by ICC as Arbitrator in a dispute concerning Suez Canal 1989; mem. Governing Bd Stockholm Int. Peace Research Inst.; Commr UN Compensation Comm., Geneva 1999–2001; Visiting Scholar, Robert F. Wagner Grad. School of Public Service, New York Univ. 1992–93; fmr chair. numerous UN cttees and working groups; Kt of Italian Repub. 1962, Order of the Repub. (Egypt) 1976. *Publications:* several articles on UN Charter, peacekeeping and various int. issues. *Leisure interest:* tennis. *Address:* c/o International Court of Justice, Peace Palace, Carnegieplein 2, 2517 KJ The Hague, Netherlands (office).

ELBAZ, Alber; Israeli designer; *Designer, Rive Gauche, Yves Saint Laurent;* b. 1961, Casablanca, Morocco; ed Shenkar Coll. of Textile Tech. and Fashion, Tel-Aviv; moved to New York, USA 1980s; worked for cheap fashion firm for two years; worked for Geoffrey Beene, New York 1989–96; joined Guy Laroche, Paris, France 1997–98; designer of ready-to-wear, Yves Saint Laurent, Paris 1998–2000, Designer, Rive Gauche 2003–; designer for Krizia 2000–01; Creative Dir Lanvin 2001–03; Chevalier, Légion d'honneur 2007. *Address:* Rive Gauche, Yves Saint Laurent, 38 rue du Faubourg, Saint-Honoré, 75008 Paris, France (office). *Telephone:* 1-42-65-74-59 (office). *Fax:* 1-42-65-23-16 (office). *Website:* www.ysl.com (office).

ELBEGDORJ, Tsakhiagiin, MA; Mongolian politician; b. 30 March 1963, Zereg Som, Hovd Prov.; m.; two c.; ed Harvard Univ., USA; machinist, Erdenet copper mine 1981–82; army service 1982; mil. reporter, Mil. School, Lvov, Ukraine 1983–88; journalist, Ulaan-Od (Ministry of Defence newspaper) 1988–90; mem. Co-ordinating Council of Mongolian Democratic Union (MDU) 1989, Leader 1990; Deputy to People's Great Hural 1990–92, also mem. State Little Hural; mem. State Great Hural 1992–94, 1996, Vice-Chair. 1996–; mem. Gen. Council Mongolian Nat. Democratic Party 1994, Leader 1996–, also Leader Democratic Union coalition in State Great Hural; Prime Minister of Mongolia April–Dec. 1998, 2004–06. *Address:* c/o Prime Minister's Office, State Palace, Sükhbaataryn Talbai 1, Ulan Bator 12 (office); Mongolian National Democratic Party, Chingisiyn Örgön Chölöö 1, Ulan Bator, Mongolia (office).

ELDER, Sir Mark Philip, Kt, BA, MA (Hons), CBE; British conductor; *Music Director, Hallé Orchestra;* b. 2 June 1947, Hexham; s. of John Elder and Helen Elder; m. Amanda Jane Stein 1980; one d.; ed Bryanston School and Corpus Christi Coll., Cambridge; music staff, Wexford Festival 1969–70; Chorus Master and Asst Conductor Glyndebourne 1970–71; music staff, Royal Opera House, Covent Garden 1970–72; Staff Conductor, Australian Opera 1972–74; Staff Conductor, ENO 1974–77, Assoc. Conductor, 1977–79, Music Dir 1979–93; Prin. Guest Conductor London Mozart Players 1980–83, BBC Symphony Orchestra 1982–85, City of Birmingham Symphony Orchestra

1992–95; Music Dir Rochester Philharmonic Orchestra, NY 1989–94, Hallé Orchestra, Manchester, UK 2000–; Hon. FRNCM; Dr hc (RAM) 1984, (Manchester) 2003, (Sheffield) 2006; Olivier Award for Outstanding Contrib. to Opera 1990, Royal Philharmonic Soc. Award for Conductor 2006. *Address:* c/o Ingpen & Williams, 7 St George's Court, 131 Putney Bridge Road, London, SW15 2PA (office); Hallé Concerts Society, The Bridgewater Hall, Manchester, M1 5HA, England (home). *Telephone:* (20) 8874-3222 (office). *E-mail:* info@ingpen.co.uk (office). *Website:* www.ingpen.co.uk (office); www.halle.co.uk (office).

ELDER, Murdoch George, DSc, MD, FRCS, FRCOG; British physician and academic; *Emeritus Professor of Obstetrics and Gynaecology, Imperial College London;* b. 4 Jan. 1938, Kolkata, India; s. of the late A. J. Elder and L. A. C. Elder; m. Margaret McVicker 1964; two s.; ed Edinburgh Acad. and Edinburgh Univ.; lecturer, Royal Univ. of Malta 1969–71; Sr Lecturer and Reader, Univ. of London, Charing Cross Hosp. Medical School 1971–78; Prof. of Obstetrics and Gynaecology, Univ. of London at Hammersmith Hosp. 1978–98; Dean, Royal Postgrad. Medical School Inst. of Obstetrics and Gynaecology 1985–95; Chair. Div. of Paediatrics, Obstetrics and Gynaecology, Imperial Coll. School of Medicine, Univ. of London 1996–98, Emer. Prof. 1998–; Visiting Prof. UCLA 1984, 1986, 1997, Univ. of Singapore 1987, Univ. of Natal 1988; consultant to WHO and other int. orgs etc.; mem. WHO Scientific and Ethics Research Group; External Examiner to Univs of Edin., Cambridge, Oxford, London, Leeds, Bristol, Glasgow, Dundee, Malta, Malaya, Malaysia, Helsinki, Rotterdam, Cape Town, Singapore; Hon. Fellow Imperial Coll. School of Medicine; Silver Medal, Hellenic Obstetrical Soc. 1984, Bronze Medal, Helsinki Univ., 1996. *Publications include:* Human Fertility Control (co-author) 1979, Preterm Labor (co-ed.) 1981 and 1996, Obstetrics and Gynaecology 2002; more than 240 original publs in field of biochemistry of reproduction and clinical high-risk obstetrics. *Leisure interests:* travel, golf. *Address:* Easter Calzeat, Broughton, Biggar, ML12 6HQ, Scotland. *Telephone:* (1899) 830359. *E-mail:* melder@eastercalzeat.fsnet.co.uk (home).

ELDERFIELD, John, PhD; American art historian and museum curator; ed Courtauld Inst. of Art, UK; various positions with Museum of Modern Art, New York 1975–, Chief Curator at Large –2003, Chief Curator of Painting and Sculpture 2003–08 (retd), organizer of exhbns including The Wild Beasts: Fauvism and Its Affinities 1976, Kurt Schwitters 1985, Henri Matisse 1992, Bonnard 1998, Matisse Picasso 2003; Chevalier des Arts et des Lettres; Eric Mitchell Prize, Time Magazine 100 Most Influential People 2005. *Publications:* Modern Painting and Sculpture: 1880 to Present at the Museum of Modern Art, Henri Matisse: A Retrospective, Helen Frankenthaler, Language of the Body. *Address:* c/o Museum of Modern Art, 11 West 53rd Street, New York, NY 10019-5497, USA (office).

ELDIN, Gérard; French civil servant and banker; b. 21 March 1927, Cannes; s. of Charles and Elise Eldin; m. Marie-Cécile Bergerot 1960; two s. two d.; ed Bethany Coll., USA, Univ. d'Aix-en-Provence and Ecole Nat. d'Admin, Paris; Insp. of Finances 1954–58; served in the Treasury 1958–63; Adviser to Minister of Finance and Econ. Affairs 1963–65; Deputy Dir Dept of Planning 1965–70; Deputy Sec.-Gen. OECD 1970–80; Deputy Gov. Crédit Foncier de France 1980–86; Chair. Foncier-Investissement 1982–86, Crédit-Logement 1986–87, 1995–96; Chair. Banque centrale de compensation 1987–90; Chair. Foncier-court terme Sicav 1988–96; Chair. and CEO Soc. d'études immobilières et d'expertises foncières (Foncier-Expertise) 1990–96; Dir Compagnie foncière de France 1980–93, Soc. immobilière Paix-Daunou 1987–93, Soc. des Immeubles de France 1993–2000; Chevalier Légion d'honneur, Commdr Ordre nat. du Mérite. *Leisure interests:* singing, local history. *Address:* 32 rue des Archives, 75004 Paris, France (home). *Telephone:* 1-44-54-09-83 (home).

ELDON, David Gordon, CBE, JP, FCIB; British business executive; *Chairman, Noble Group Ltd;* with HSBC Group, based in Middle and Far East 1968–2005, mem. Bd of Dirs HSBC Holdings and Chair. Hongkong and Shanghai Banking Corpn Ltd –2005 (retd); currently Sr Adviser, PricewaterhouseCoopers, Hong Kong; mem. Bd of Dirs Noble Group Ltd 2007–, currently Ind. Chair. (non-exec.); Chair. (non-exec.) Dubai Int. Financial Centre Authority; Deputy Chair. Hong Kong Jockey Club; mem. Bd of Dirs Mass Transit Railway Corpn, Hong Kong, Eagle Asset Man. Ltd, China Central Properties Ltd; fmr Chair. Hong Kong Gen. Chamber of Commerce; Founding mem. and Past Chair. Seoul Int. Business Advisory Council; Int. Council mem. Bretton Woods Cttee; Adviser to Unisys; Hon. Citizenship of Seoul 2005; Gold Bauhinia Star, Govt of Hong Kong Special Admin. Region 2004; Hon. DBA (City Univ. of Hong Kong); named DHL/SCMP Hong Kong Business Person of the Year 2003, Asian Banker Lifetime Achievement Award 2006. *Address:* Noble Group Ltd, 18th Floor, MassMutual Tower, 38 Gloucester Road, Hong Kong Special Administrative Region, People's Republic of China (office). *Telephone:* 2861-3511 (office). *Fax:* 2527-0282 (office). *E-mail:* noble@thisisnoble.com (office). *Website:* www.thisisnoble.com (office).

ELDON, Stewart Graham, CMG, OBE, MSc; British diplomatist; *Permanent Representative, NATO;* b. 18 Sept. 1953, Accra, Ghana; m. Christine Mason 1978; one s. one d.; ed Pocklington School, Yorks. and Christ's Coll., Cambridge; entered FCO 1976, UK Mission New York 1976, Asst Desk Officer, UN Dept, FCO 1977–78, Third (later Second) Sec., British Embassy, Bonn 1978–82, Head of Section, Repub. of Ireland Dept, FCO 1982–83, Minister of State, FCO 1983–86, First Sec., Chancery, UK Mission, New York 1986–90, Deputy Head, Middle East Dept, FCO 1990–91, seconded to Cabinet Office 1991–93, Centre for Int. Affairs, Harvard Univ. 1993–94, Political Counsellor, UK Del. to NATO/WEU 1994–97, Dir of Confs, FCO 1997–98, Deputy Perm. Rep. UK Mission, New York 1998–2002; Visiting Fellow, Yale Univ. 2002; Amb. to Ireland 2003–06; Perm. Rep., NATO 2006–. *Leisure interests include:* travel, science fiction. *Address:* North Atlantic Treaty Organization (NATO), blvd Léopold III, 1110 Brussels, Belgium (office). *Telephone:* (2) 707-41-11 (office). *Fax:* (2) 707-45-79 (office). *E-mail:* natodoc@hq.nato.int (office). *Website:* www.nato.int (office).

ELENOVSKI, Lazar, BA; Macedonian politician; b. 19 March 1971, Skopje; s. of Akeksandar Elenovski and Mirusha Elenovski; m.; one s.; ed Faculty of Econs, Skopje; fmr Deputy CEO JSP (public transport co.); joined Social Democratic Alliance of Macedonia, f. Social Democratic Youth of Macedonia 1992, Sec.-Gen. 1996–99, Pres. 1999–2001; f. Young Europeans for Security (YES Macedonia) 1995; mem. Presidency, Social-Democratic Union of Macedonia 1997–2003; Sec.-Gen. Euro-Atlantic Club of Macedonia 2001–05; Pres. Euro-Atlantic Council of Macedonia 2005–06; Co-founder Cen. and South Eastern European Security Forum (Balkan Mosaic); Minister of Defence 2006–08; mem. New Social Democratic Party 2006–; mem. Atlantic Treaty Asscn. *Publications:* numerous articles on the Euro-Atlantic integration process, the Balkan region, and security sector reforms. *Leisure interest:* philosophy. *Address:* New Social Democratic Party (NSDP), Dame Gruev 5, 1000 Skopje, Former Yugoslav Republic of Macedonia (office). *Telephone:* (2) 3238775 (office). *Fax:* (2) 3290465 (office). *E-mail:* nsdp@nsdp.org.mk (office). *Website:* www.nsdp.org.mk (office).

ELEWA, Gen. Abdullah Ali, MSc; Yemeni army officer and politician; career in Yemeni Armed Forces, sr positions include Commdr of Air Force in S Lebanon, Chief of Staff 1994; fmr Gov. of Al-Gawf; Minister of Defence –2006. *Address:* c/o Ministry of Defence, POB 4131, San'a, Yemen (office).

ELFMAN, Danny; American film music composer and musician (guitar); b. 29 May 1953, Amarillo, Tex.; lead singer, rhythm guitarist and songwriter eight-piece rock band, Oingo Bongo; numerous songs and scores for films, TV programmes and computer games. *Music for film:* Forbidden Zone 1980, Fast Times at Ridgemont High 1982, Bachelor Party 1984, Surf II 1984, Beverly Hills Cop 1984, Weird Science 1985, Pee-Wee's Big Adventure 1985, Wisdom 1986, Something Wild 1986, Back to School 1986, Summer School 1987, Hot to Trot 1988, Big Top Pee-Wee 1988, Beetlejuice 1988, Midnight Run 1988, Scrooged 1988, Batman 1989, Ghostbusters II 1989, Dick Tracy 1990, Nightbreed 1990, Darkman 1990, Edward Scissorhands 1990, Pure Luck 1991, Batman Returns 1992, Article 99 1992, Army of Darkness 1993, Sommersby 1993, The Nightmare Before Christmas 1993, Black Beauty 1994, Dolores Claiborne 1995, To Die For 1995, Dead Presidents 1995, Mission: Impossible 1996, The Frighteners 1996, Freeway 1996, Extreme Measures 1996, Mars Attacks! 1996, Men In Black 1997, Flubber 1997, Good Will Hunting 1997, Scream 2 1997, A Simple Plan 1998, A Civil Action 1998, My Favorite Martian 1999, Instinct 1999, Anywhere But Here 1999, Sleepy Hollow 1999, The Family Man 2000, Proof of Life 2000, Spy Kids 2001, Planet of the Apes 2001, Heartbreakers 2001, Mazer World 2001, Novocaine 2001, Spider-Man 2002, Men in Black II 2002, Red Dragon 2002, Chicago 2002, Hulk 2003, Big Fish 2003, Spider-Man 2 2004, Charlie and the Chocolate Factory 2005, Charlotte's Web 2006, Spider-Man 3 2007, Hellboy II: The Golden Army 2008, Wanted 2008, Standard Operating Procedure 2008. *Music for television:* Amazing Stories 1985, Alfred Hitchcock Presents 1985, Fast Times 1986, Sledge Hammer! 1986, Pee-Wee's Playhouse 1986, Tales from the Crypt 1989, The Simpsons 1989, Beetlejuice 1989, The Flash 1990, Batman 1992, Family Dog 1993, Weird Science 1994, Perversions of Science 1997, Dilbert 1999, Desperate Housewives 2004. *Recordings:* albums with Oingo Boingo: Only A Lad 1981, Nothing To Fear 1982, Good For Your Soul 1983, Dead Man's Party 1985, Boingo 1986, Skeletons In The Closet 1989, Dark At The End Of The Tunnel 1990, Article 99 1992. *Address:* Blue Focus Management, 15233 Ventura Boulevard, Suite 200, Sherman Oaks, CA 91403, USA (office).

ELIAS, Rt Hon. Dame Sian, LLB, JSM, QC; New Zealand lawyer; *Chief Justice;* ed Auckland Univ., Stanford Univ., USA; worked for Turner Hopkins & Partners 1972–75; barrister 1975–88; QC 1988; Law Commr and Chair. ICI Cttee of Inquiry 1989–90; apptd High Court Judge 1995; involved in litigation concerning Treaty of Waitangi 1987; sat on Court of Appeal 1998–99; Chief Justice of NZ 1999–; mem. Motor Sports Licensing Appeal Authority 1984–88, Working Party on the Environment 1984; Commemorative Medal for Services to the Legal Profession 1990. *Address:* Chief Justice's Chambers, PO Box 1091, Wellington, New Zealand (office). *Telephone:* (4) 9143641 (office). *Fax:* (4) 9143636 (office). *E-mail:* lynette.maru@courts.govt.nz (office). *Website:* www.justice.govt.nz (office).

ELIASSON, Jan, MA; Swedish diplomatist and UN official; b. 17 Sept. 1940, Göteborg; s. of John H. Eliasson and Karin Eliasson (née Nilsson); m. Kerstin Englesson 1967; one s. two d.; ed School of Econs, Göteborg; entered Swedish Foreign Service 1965; Swedish OECD Del., Paris 1967; at Swedish Embassy, Bonn 1967–70; First Sec. Swedish Embassy, Washington 1970–74; Head of Section, Political Dept, Ministry for Foreign Affairs, Stockholm 1974–75; Personal Asst to the Under-Sec. of State for Foreign Affairs 1975–77; Dir Press and Information Div., Ministry for Foreign Affairs 1977–80, Asst Under-Sec., Head of Div. for Asian and African Affairs, Political Dept 1980–82; Foreign Policy Adviser, Prime Minister's Office 1982–83; Under-Sec. for Political Affairs, Stockholm 1983–87; Perm. Rep. of Sweden to UN, New York 1988–92; Chair. UN Trust Fund for SA 1988–92; Personal Rep. to UN Sec.-Gen. on Iran-Iraq 1988–92; Vice-Pres. ECOSOC 1991–92; Under-Sec.-Gen. for Humanitarian Affairs, UN 1992–94; Chair. Minsk Conf. on Nagornyi Karabakh 1994; State Sec. for Foreign Affairs 1994–2000; Amb. to USA 2000–05; Pres. UN General Ass. 2005–06; Minister of Foreign Affairs 2006; Special Envoy of the UN Sec.-Gen. for Darfur 2006–08; Sec. to Swedish Foreign Policy Advisory Bd 1983–87; Expert, Royal Swedish Defence Comm. 1984–86; Dir Inst. for East-West Security Studies, New York 1989–93, Int. Peace Acad. 1989–2001; Dr hc (American Univ. Washington, DC) 1994, (Gothenburg) 2001, (Bethany Coll., Kansas) 2005, (Uppsala) 2006. *Leisure interests:* art, literature, sports.

Address: c/o Ministry for Foreign Affairs, Gustav Adolfs torg 1, 103 39 Stockholm, Sweden (office).

ELIASSON, Olafur; Danish artist; b. 1967, Copenhagen; ed Royal Acad. of Arts, Copenhagen; lives and works in Berlin; Edstrand Foundation Prize, Sweden 1998. *Address:* c/o Royal Academy of Arts, School of Visual Arts, Kgs. Nytorv 1, Postboks 3014, 1021 Copenhagen K, Denmark (office); c/o Tate Modern, Bankside, London, SE1 9TG, England (office). *Telephone:* 33-74-46-00 (Copenhagen) (office). *Fax:* 33-74-46-66 (Copenhagen) (office). *E-mail:* bk@kunstakademiet.dk (office). *Website:* www.kunstakademiet.dk (office).

ELINSON, Jack, MA, PhD; American sociomedical scientist and academic; *Professor Emeritus of Sociomedical Sciences and Special Lecturer, Department of Sociomedical Sciences, Columbia University;* b. (Israel Jacob Elinson), 30 June 1917, New York; s. of Sam Elinson and Rebecca Block Elinson; m. May Gomberg 1941; three s. one d.; ed Coll. of the City of New York and George Washington Univ.; scientific aide, US Govt Food and Drug Admin., Soil Conservation Service, Nat. Bureau of Standards 1937–41; statistician, War Dept 1941–42; Social Science Analyst, Dept of Defense, Armed Forces Information and Educ. Div., Attitude Research Br. 1942–51; Sr Study Dir Nat. Opinion Research Center, Univ. of Chicago 1951–56; Prof. of Sociomedical Sciences, Columbia Univ. 1956–86, Prof. Emer. and Special Lecturer 1986–; Visiting Prof. of Behavioral Sciences, Univ. of Toronto 1969–75, Distinguished Visiting Prof., Inst. for Health Care Policy, Rutgers Univ. 1986–89, Distinguished Sr Scholar 1990–; Visiting Prof. Grad. Program in Public Health, Robert Wood Johnson Medical School 1986–; Consultant, Medical and Health Research Asscn of New York City 1986–96; Service Fellow, Nat. Center for Health Statistics, US Public Health Service 1977–81; mem. Inst. of Medicine, NAS 1990; numerous professional appointments; Exceptionally Distinguished Achievement Award, American Asscn for Public Opinion Research 1993, and many other honours and distinctions. *Publications:* Chronic Illness in a Rural Area (with R. E. Trussell) 1959, Family Medical Care under Three Types of Health Insurance (with J. J. Williams and R. E. Trussell) 1962, Public Image of Mental Health Services (with E. Padilla and M. E. Perkins) 1967, Health Goals and Health Indicators (with A. Mooney and A. E. Siegmann) 1977, Sociomedical Health Indicators (with A. E. Siegmann) 1979, Assessment of Quality of Life in Clinical Trials of Cardiovascular Therapies (with N. K. Wenger, M. E. Mattson and C. D. Furberg) 1984; articles in professional journals. *Leisure interests:* grandchildren, genealogy. *Address:* Columbia University, Mailman School of Public Health, Department of Sociomedical Sciences, 722 West 168th Street, New York, NY 10032 (office); 1181 E Laurelton Parkway, Teaneck, NJ 07666, USA (home). *Telephone:* (212) 305-4027 (office); (201) 836-9222 (home). *Fax:* (212) 305-0315 (office); (212) 836-5758 (home). *E-mail:* je7@columbia.edu (office); jelinson@juno.com (home). *Website:* www.sms.mailman.columbia.edu/faculty/elinson.html (office).

ELIZABETH II, HM Queen (Elizabeth Alexandra Mary), (Queen of Great Britain and Northern Ireland and of Her other Realms and Territories), (see Reigning Royal Families section for full titles); b. 21 April 1926, London; d. of HRH Prince Albert, Duke of York (later HM King George VI) and Duchess of York (later HM Queen Elizabeth The Queen Mother); succeeded to The Throne following Her father's death 6 Feb. 1952; married 20 Nov. 1947, HRH The Prince Philip, The Duke of Edinburgh (q.v.), b. 10 June 1921; children: Prince Charles Philip Arthur George, Prince of Wales (q.v.) (heir apparent), b. 14 Nov. 1948; Princess Anne Elizabeth Alice Louise, The Princess Royal (q.v.), b. 15 Aug. 1950; Prince Andrew Albert Christian Edward, Duke of York (q.v.), b. 19 Feb. 1960; Prince Edward Antony Richard Louis, Earl of Wessex, b. 10 March 1964. *Address:* Buckingham Palace, London, SW1A 1AA; Windsor Castle, Berkshire, SL4 1NJ, England; Balmoral Castle, Aberdeenshire, AB35 5TB, Scotland; Sandringham House, Norfolk, PE35 6EN, England; Palace of Holyroodhouse, Edinburgh, Scotland. *Website:* www.royal.gov.uk.

ELIZONDO BARRAGÁN, Fernando, LicenDer, MJ; Mexican lawyer, politician and business executive; *Secretary of Energy; Chairperson, Petróleos Mexicanos (PEMEX);* b. Monterrey, Nuevo León; ed Centro Univ. Monterrey (CUM), Univ. of Nuevo León, New York Univ., USA; laywer, Monterrey 1972–79, 1986–94; various positions in legal div., Grupo Industrial Alfa 1979–89; Co-ordinator CANACO Monterrey, CAINTRA Nuevo León and COPARMEX Nuevo León 1988–92; mem. Civic Council of Nuevo León 1988–92; Exec. Pres. Grupo Salinas y Rocha 1995–97; Sec. of Finance and the Treasury, State of Nuevo León 1997–2003; Gov. (interim) of State of Nuevo León 2003–04; Sec. of Energy of Mexico and Chair. Petróleos Mexicanos (PEMEX) 2004–; del. to numerous int. confs and orgs. *Address:* Secretariat of State for Energy, Insurgentes Sur 890, 17°, Del Valle, Benito Juárez, 03100 México, DF (office); Petróleos Mexicanos, Avenida Marina Nacional 329, Colonia Huasteca, 11311 México, DF, Mexico (office). *Telephone:* (55) 5000-6000, ext. 1000 (office). *Fax:* (55) 5000-6222 (office). *E-mail:* secretario@energia.gob.mx (office); elevin@dcf.pemex.com (office). *Website:* www.energia.gob.mx (office); www.pemex.com (office).

ELKANN, John Jacob Philip; American/Italian automotive industry executive; *Vice-Chairman, Fiat Group;* b. 1 April 1976, New York City; s. of Alain Elkann and Margherita 'Daisy' Agnelli de Pahlen; grandson of the late Gianni Agnelli, Chair. of Fiat; m. Donna Lavinia Borromeo 2004; two s.; ed Victor Duruy Lycée, Paris, France, Politecnico di Torino; spent his childhood travelling with his parents and siblings between UK, Brazil and France; mem. Bd of Dirs Fiat 1997–; analyst, Gen. Electric Co. 2000, later mem. Corp. Audit Group 2001–02; returned to Turin to work with Fiat family business 2002, Vice-Chair. Fiat Group 2004–, Investment Man. IFIL SpA (investment co., one of Agnelli-family holding cos) 2003–06, Vice-Chair. 2006–; Chair. IFI SpA 2007–, EXOR Group SA; mem. Council of Admin, RCS MediaGroup, Gruppo Banca Leonardo SpA; Pres. Fondazione Italia-Giappone; Vice-Pres. Fondazione Italia-Cina, Fondazione Giovanni Agnelli, Italian Aspen Inst., Consigliere della Pinacoteca Giovanni e Marella Agnelli; mem. Bd of Dirs Le Monde. *Leisure interest:* Juventus football team. *Address:* Fiat SpA, Via Nizza 250, 10126 Turin (office); EXOR, Corso Matteotti 26, 10121 Turin, Italy (office). *Telephone:* (011) 006-1111 (office). *Fax:* (011) 006-3798 (office). *Website:* www.fiatgroup.com (office); www.ifil.it (office).

ELLEMANN-JENSEN, Uffe, MA; Danish politician; b. 1 Nov. 1941; s. of Jens Peter Jensen; m. Alice Vestergaard 1971; two s. two d.; ed Univ. of Copenhagen; Danish Defence staff 1962–64; Sec., Meat Producers' Asscn 1964–67; journalist on Berlingske Aftenavis 1967–70; econ. and political corresp. Danish TV 1970–75; Ed.-in-Chief and mem. Bd daily newspaper Borsen 1975–76; mem. Parl. 1977–2001 (Liberal), Party Spokesperson, Political Affairs 1978–82, Chair. Parl. Market Cttee 1978–79; mem. Exec. Cttee Liberal Party 1979, Chair. 1984–98; mem. Bd Cen. Bank 1978–81, 1996–99, Index Figures' Bd 1979–81, Inter-Parl. Union 1979–82; Minister of Foreign Affairs 1982–93; Vice-Pres. European Liberal Party 1985–95, Pres. 1995–2000; Adjunct Prof., Copenhagen Business School 2006–; Chair. Foreign Policy Soc., Denmark 1993–, Baltic Devt Forum 1998–, Danish Centre for Int. Studies and Human Rights 2002–; Dir Reuters Founders Share Co. Ltd 2000–; Trustee Int. Crisis Group 1999–; Chair. Bankinvest 2003; mem. Bd Royal Theatre 2004, The Vaccine Fund 2005; Dr hc (Univ. of Gadansk) 2002; Robert Schuman Prize 1987. *Publications:* De nye millionaerer (The New Millionaires) 1971, Det afhaengige samfund (The Dependent Society) 1972, Hvad gør vi ved Gudenåen (We Ought to Do Something About Gudenåen) 1973, Den truede velstand (The Threatened Wealth) 1974, Økonomi (Economy) 1975, Da Danmark igen sagde ja til det falles (When Denmark Repeated its Yes to Europe) 1987, Olfert Fischer 1991, Et lille land – og dog (A Small Country – And Yet) 1991, Din egen dag er kort (Short is Your Own Day) 1996, Ude med snøren (Going Fishing) 2001, Østen for solen (East of the Sun) 2002, Fodfejl (Foot Fault) 2004; numerous articles in newspapers and periodicals. *Leisure interests:* fishing, hunting, opera. *Address:* PO Box 56, 1002 Copenhagen K, Denmark. *Telephone:* 7020-9394 (office). *Fax:* 7020-9395 (office). *E-mail:* bdf@bdforum.org (office); uffe@ellemann.dk (home). *Website:* www.bdforum.org (office).

ELLER, Timothy, BS; American construction industry executive; *Chairman and CEO, Centex Corporation;* b. 1948; ed Univ. of Neb.; joined Centex Homes, Ill. 1973, Project Man. 1975, Vice-Pres. Minn. Div. 1977, Pres. 1981, Exec. Vice-Pres. Centex Real Estate Corpn/Centex Homes 1985–90, Pres. and COO 1990–91, Pres. and CEO Centex Homes 1991–98, Chair. 1998–2003, Exec. Vice-Pres. Centex Corpn 1998, Pres. and COO 2002, mem. Bd of Dirs 2002–, Chair. and CEO 2004–; Chair. High Production Home Builders Council; mem. Exec. Cttee Jt Center for Housing Studies, Harvard Univ.; Life Trustee Nat. Housing Endowment; mem. Bd of Trustees Nature Conservancy of Tex. *Address:* Centex Corporation, 2728 North Harwood Street, Dallas, TX 75201-1516, USA (office). *Telephone:* (214) 981-5000 (office). *Fax:* (214) 981-6859 (office). *Website:* www.centex.com (office).

ELLINGSRUD, Geir, CandReal, PhD; Norwegian mathematician and university rector; *Rector, University of Oslo;* b. 29 Nov. 1948; ed Univ. of Oslo, Stockholm Univ., Sweden; Asst Lecturer, Univ. of Oslo 1973–80, Assoc. Prof. 1985–89, Prof. of Math. 1992–, Rector Univ. of Oslo 2006–; Guest Prof., Univ. of Strasbourg, France 1980–81, Univ. of Nice, France 1982–83; Lecturer, Stockholm Univ. 1983–84; Prof. of Math., Univ. of Bergen 1989–92. *Address:* University of Oslo, PO Box 1072, Blindern, 0316 Oslo, Norway (office). *Telephone:* 22-85-63-03 (office). *Fax:* 22-85-44-42 (office). *E-mail:* ellingsr@math.uio.no (office). *Website:* www.uio.no (office).

ELLIOTT, Rev. Charles Middleton, MA, DPhil; British ecclesiastic; *Dean Trinity Hall, Cambridge;* b. 9 Jan. 1939, Wakefield; s. of Joseph William Elliott and Mary Evelyn Elliott; m. Hilary Margaret Hambling 1962; three s. one d. (deceased); ed Repton, Lincoln and Nuffield Colls Oxford and Scholae Cancellarii, Lincoln; lecturer in Econs Univ. of Nottingham 1962–65; Reader in Econs Univ. of Zambia 1965–69; Asst Sec. Jt Cttee on Soc., Devt and Peace, Vatican/WCC, Geneva 1969–72; Sr Lecturer in Econs Univ. of E Anglia 1972–77; Prof. of Devt Studies, Univ. of Wales 1977–82; Dir Christian Aid 1982–84; Benjamin Meaker Prof. Univ. of Bristol 1985–86; Visiting Prof. King's Coll. London 1987–88; Prebendary of Lichfield Cathedral 1987–96; Fellow, Chaplain and Dean, Trinity Hall, Cambridge 1990–, Affiliated Lecturer in Theology, Univ. of Cambridge 1991–, in Social and Political Sciences 1993–; Sec. Inst. of Contemporary Spirituality 1988–92; Pres. Feed the Minds 1991–; Chair. Univ. Bd of Electors to Livings 1997–; Collins Religious Book Prize 1985. *Publications:* Patterns of Poverty in the Third World 1975, Praying the Kingdom 1985, Praying through Paradox 1987, Comfortable Compassion 1987, Signs of Our Times 1988, Sword and Spirit: Christianity in a Divided World 1989, Memory and Salvation 1995, Strategic Planning for Churches: An Appreciative Approach 1997, Locating the Energy for Change: An Introduction to Appreciative Inquiry 1999; numerous articles in learned journals. *Leisure interests:* walking, gardening, fly-fishing, sailing. *Address:* Trinity Hall, Cambridge, CB2 1TJ (office); 11 Perowne Street, Cambridge, CB1 2AY, England (home). *Telephone:* (1223) 332525 (office); (1223) 69233 (home). *Fax:* (1223) 332537 (office). *E-mail:* cme13@hermes.cam.ac.uk (office). *Website:* www.trinhall.cam.ac.uk.

ELLIOTT, Sir John Huxtable, Kt, FBA; British historian and academic; b. 23 June 1930, Reading, Berks.; s. of Thomas Charles Elliott and Janet Mary Payne; m. Oonah Sophia Butler 1958; ed Eton Coll. and Trinity Coll., Cambridge; Asst Lecturer in History, Univ. of Cambridge 1957–62, Lecturer 1962–67; Prof. of History, King's Coll., Univ. of London 1968–73; Prof., School of Historical Studies, Inst. for Advanced Study, Princeton, NJ 1973–90; Regius Prof. of Modern History, Univ. of Oxford and Fellow, Oriel Coll., Oxford 1990–97; Fellow, Trinity Coll., Cambridge 1954–67, Fellow, Royal

Acad. of History, Madrid, American Acad. of Arts and Sciences, American Philosophical Soc, King's Coll., Univ. of London 1998, Accad. Naz. dei Lincei 2003; mem. Scientific Cttee, Prado Museum 1996; Hon. Fellow, Trinity Coll., Cambridge 1991, Oriel Coll., Oxford 1997; Commdr, Order of Alfonso X El Sabio 1984, Commdr, Order of Isabel la Católica 1987, Grand Cross of Order of Alfonso X, El Sabio 1988, Grand Cross of Order of Isabel la Católica 1996, Cross of Sant Jordi (Catalonia) 1999; Dr hc (Universidad Autónoma de Madrid) 1983, (Genoa) 1992, (Portsmouth) 1993, (Barcelona) 1994, (Warwick) 1995, (Brown) 1996, (Valencia) 1998, (Lleida) 1999, (Madrid Complutense) 2003, (Coll. of William and Mary) 2005, (London) 2007, (Carlos III, Madrid) 2008; Visitante Ilustre of Madrid 1983, Leo Gershoy Award, American Historical Asscn 1985, Wolfson Literary Award for History and Biography 1986, Medal of Honour, Universidad Int. Menéndez y Pelayo 1987, Gold Medal for Fine Arts (Spain) 1991, Eloy Antonio de Nebrija Prize (Univ. of Salamanca) 1993, Prince of Asturias Prize in Social Sciences 1996, Gold Medal, Spanish Inst., New York 1997, Balzan Prize for History 1500–1800 1999. *Publications:* Imperial Spain, 1469–1716 1963, The Revolt of the Catalans 1963, Europe Divided, 1559–1598 1968, The Old World and the New, 1492–1650 1970, The Diversity of History (co-ed. with H. G. Koenigsberger) 1970, A Palace for a King (with J. Brown) 1980 (revised edn 2003), Memoriales y Cartas del Conde Duque de Olivares 1978–80, Richelieu and Olivares 1984, The Count-Duke of Olivares 1986, Spain and Its World 1500–1700 1989, The Hispanic World (ed.) 1991, The World of the Favourite (co-ed.) 1999, The Sale of the Century (with J. Brown) 2002, Empires of the Atlantic World (Francis Parkman Prize 2007) 2006, Spain, Europe and the Wider World 1500–1800 2009. *Leisure interest:* looking at paintings. *Address:* 122 Church Way, Iffley, Oxford, OX4 4EG, England. *Telephone:* (1865) 716703.

ELLIOTT, Marianne, OBE, DPhil, FRHistS, FBA; Irish historian and academic; *Professor of Modern History and Director, Institute of Irish Studies, University of Liverpool;* b. 25 May 1948, N Ireland; d. of Terence J. Burns and Sheila O'Neill; m. Prof. Trevor Elliott 1975; one s.; ed Dominican Convent, Fort William, Belfast, Queen's Univ. Belfast and Lady Margaret Hall, Oxford; French Govt research scholar in Paris 1972–73; other research in Ireland, UK, France, Netherlands and USA; Lecturer in History, West London Inst. of Higher Educ. 1975–77; Research Fellow, Univ. Coll. Swansea 1977–82; Visiting Prof., Iowa State Univ. 1983, Univ. of South Carolina 1984; Research Fellow, Univ. of Liverpool 1984–87; Simon Fellow, Univ. of Manchester 1988–89; Lecturer, Birkbeck Coll., Univ. of London 1991–93; Andrew Geddes and John Rankin Prof. of Modern History, Univ. of Liverpool 1993–, Dir Inst. of Irish Studies 1997–; mem. Opsahl Comm. on NI 1993, Encounter 1998–; Fellow, British Acad. 2002; Leo Gershoy Award for History 1983, Sunday Independent/Irish Life Award for Biography 1989, James Donnelly Sr Award for History (American Conf. for Irish Studies) 1991, Ford's Lecturer, Univ. of Oxford 2005. *Publications:* Partners in Revolution: The United Irishmen and France 1982, Watchmen in Sion: The Protestant Idea of Liberty 1985, The People's Armies (translation) 1987, Wolfe Tone: Prophet of Irish Independence 1989, A Citizens' Inquiry: The Report of the Opsahl Commission on Northern Ireland 1993, The Catholics in Ireland: A History 2000, The Long Road to Peace in Northern Ireland (ed.) 2001, Robert Emmet: The Making of a Legend 2003. *Leisure interests:* running, swimming, hill-walking, gardening. *Address:* Institute of Irish Studies, University of Liverpool, 1 Abercromby Square, Liverpool, L69 7WY, England (office). *Telephone:* (151) 794-3831 (office). *Fax:* (151) 794-3836 (office). *E-mail:* melliott@liverpool.ac.uk (office); irishstudies@liv.ac.uk (office). *Website:* www.liv.ac.uk/irish (office).

ELLIOTT, Missy 'Misdemeanour'; American hip-hop and rap artist and producer; b. 1971, Portsmouth, Va; joined vocal group, Sista, obtained record deal; began collaborating with Tim Mosley on singles with Aaliyah; guest rapper on various releases; obtained solo record deal; CEO Goldmind Inc. production co. 1996–, signed numerous successful acts; began releasing solo records as vocalist and rapper; supervised and guest on soundtrack of film, Why Do Fools Fall in Love 1998; live appearances include Lilith Fair travelling festival, 1998; started own lipstick line with Iman Bowie's cosmetics line; five Soul Train Lady of Soul Awards, Grammy Awards for Best Female Rap Solo Performance 2002, Best Rap Solo Performance 2001, MTV Video of the Year 2003, American Music Award for Favorite Rap/Hip-Hop Female 2003, Grammy Award for Best Female Rap Solo Performance (for Work It) 2004, MTV Video Award for Best Hip Hop Video, for Best Dance Video 2005, Lady of Soul Award for Best R&B/Soul Video (for Lose Control) 2005, American Music Award for Favorite Female Rap/Hip-Hop Artist 2005, BET Award for Best Female Hip Hop Artist 2006. *Recordings include:* albums: Supa Dupa Fly 1997, Da Real World 1999, Miss E... So Addictive 2001, Under Construction 2002, This is Not a Test! 2003, The Cookbook 2005, Respect M.E. 2006, Block Party 2008. *Address:* c/o Elektra Records, 75 Rockefeller Plaza, New York, NY 10019, USA. *Website:* www.missy-elliott.com.

ELLIOTT, Sir Roger James, Kt, MA, DPhil, FRS; British physicist and publisher; b. 8 Dec. 1928, Chesterfield; s. of James Elliott and Gladys Elliott (née Hill); m. Olga Lucy Atkinson 1952; one s. two d.; ed Swanwick Hall School, Derbyshire and New Coll., Oxford; Research Assoc. Univ. of Calif., Berkeley 1952–53; Research Fellow, Atomic Energy Research Est., Harwell 1953–55; Lecturer, Univ. of Reading 1955–57; Lecturer, Univ. of Oxford 1957–65, Reader 1965–74, Fellow, St John's Coll. 1957–74 (now Hon. Fellow), New Coll. 1974–96 (now Hon. Fellow), Wykeham Prof. of Physics 1974–89, Prof. of Physics 1989–96, Prof. Emer. 1996–; Del. Oxford Univ. Press 1971–88, Sec. to Dels and Chief Exec. 1988–93, Chair. Computer Bd 1983–87; mem. Bd Blackwell Ltd 1996–, Chair. 1999–2002; Visiting Prof., Univ. of Calif., Berkeley 1960–61; Miller Visiting Prof., Univ. of Ill., Urbana 1966; Visiting Distinguished Prof., Fla State Univ. 1981, Mich. State Univ. 1997–2000; Physical Sec. and Vice-Pres. Royal Soc. (London) 1984–88; Treas. Publrs Asscn 1990–92, Pres. 1992–93; Chair. ICSU Press 1997–2002, Disability Information Trust 1998–2001; mem. Bd (part-time) UKAEA 1988–94, British Council 1990–98, Mexican Acad. of Science 2003; Fellow, Inst. of Physics; Treas. ICSU 2002; Hon. DSc (Paris) 1983, (Bath) 1991, (Essex) 1993; Maxwell Medal (Physical Soc.) 1968, Guthrie Medal 1989. *Publications:* Magnetic Properties of Rare Earth Metals 1972, Solid State Physics and its Applications 1973; articles in learned journals. *Address:* 11 Crick Road, Oxford, OX2 6QL, England (home). *Telephone:* (1865) 273997 (home). *Fax:* (1865) 273947 (home). *E-mail:* r.elliott1@physics.ox.ac.uk (office).

ELLIS, Bret Easton, BA; American writer; b. 7 March 1964, Los Angeles; ed Bennington Coll.; mem. Authors' Guild. *Publications:* Less Than Zero 1985, The Rules of Attraction 1987, American Psycho 1989, The Informers 1994, Glamorama 1998, Lunar Park 2005; contrib. to Rolling Stone, Vanity Fair, Elle, Wall Street Journal, Bennington Review. *Address:* c/o Amanda Urban, International Creative Management, 40 W 57th Street, New York, NY 10019, USA (office).

ELLIS, Gavin Peter; New Zealand journalist; *Editor-in-Chief, New Zealand Herald;* b. 6 March 1947, Auckland; s. of Peter Fisher Dundass Ellis and Catherine Ellis (née Gray); m. 1st Janine Laurette Sinclair 1969; m. 2nd Jennifer Ann Lynch 1991; one s.; ed Mount Roskill Grammar School and Auckland Univ.; on staff of Auckland Star paper 1965–70; public relations consultant 1970–71; joined New Zealand Herald 1972, Asst Ed. 1987–96, Ed. 1996–99, Ed.-in-Chief 1999–; Harry Brittain Memorial Fellow 1980; Chair. NZ Section, Commonwealth Press Union; mem. New Zealand Knowledge Wave Trust; mem. NZ Council for Security Co-operation Asia-Pacific. *Leisure interests:* medieval history, opera. *Address:* 46 Albert Street, Auckland, New Zealand. *Telephone:* (9) 379-5050. *Fax:* (9) 373-6406. *E-mail:* gavin_ellis@herald.co.nz (office); gavin.ellis@xtra.co.nz (home). *Website:* www.nzherald.co.nz (office).

ELLIS, George Francis Rayner, FRAS, PhD; British/South African professor of astrophysics and applied mathematics; b. 11 Aug. 1939, Johannesburg; s. of George Rayner Ellis and Gwen Hilda (née MacRobert) Ellis; m. 1st Sue Parkes 1963; one s. one d.; m. 2nd Mary Wheeldon 1978; ed Michaelhouse, Univ. of Cape Town and Cambridge Univ.; Fellow Peterhouse, Cambridge 1965–67; Asst Lecturer, lecturer Cambridge 1967–73; Prof. of Applied Math., Univ. of Cape Town 1974–88, 1990–; Prof. of Cosmic Physics, SISSA, Trieste 1988–92; G. C. MacVittie Visiting Prof. of Astronomy, Queen Mary Coll., London 1987–; Chair. GR10 Scientific Cttee 1988; mem. Int. Cttee on Gen. Relativity and Gravitation; Pres., Int. Soc. of Gen. Relativity and Gravitation 1989–92; mem. Cttee (and Vice-Pres.) Royal Soc. of SA 1990–, Pres. 1992–96; Founding mem., mem. Council, Acad. of Science of SA 1995–97, 2000–; Fellow Inst. of Maths and its Applications; Chair. Quaker Service, West Cape 1976–86, Quaker Peacework Cttee 1978–86, 1990–95, SA Inst. of Race Relations, West Cape 1985–87; Clerk SA Yearly Meeting of Quakers 1986–88; Fellowship of Univ. of Cape Town; Hon. DSc (Haverford Coll.) 1996, (Natal Univ.) 1998; Herschel Medal of Royal Soc. of SA, Gravity Research Foundation 1st Prize 1979, Star of South Africa Medal 1999. *Publications:* The Large Scale Structure of Space-Time (with S. W. Hawking) 1973, The Squatter Problem in the Western Cape (with J. Maree, D. Hendrie) 1976, Low Income Housing Policy (with D. Dewar) 1980, Flat and Curved Space-Times (with R. Williams) 1988, Before the Beginning 1993, The Renaissance of General Relativity and Cosmology (co-ed.) 1993, The Dynamical Systems Approach to Cosmology (co-ed.) 1996, The Density of Matter in the Universe (with P. Coles) 1996, On the Moral Nature of the Universe: Cosmology, Theology and Ethics (with N. Murphy) 1996. *Leisure interests:* climbing, gliding. *Address:* Department of Mathematics and Applied Mathematics, University of Cape Town, Rondebosch 7701, Cape Town (office); 3 Marlow Road, Cape Town 7701, South Africa (home). *Telephone:* (21) 6502339 (office); (21) 7612313 (home). *Fax:* (21) 6502334 (office); (21) 7976349 (home). *E-mail:* ellis@maths.uct.ac.za (office); mmellis@iafrica.com (home).

ELLIS, Adm. James O., Jr, MSc; American military officer (retd); *President and CEO, Institute of Nuclear Power Operations (INPO);* b. Spartanburg, SC; ed US Naval Test Pilot School, US Naval Acad., Georgia Inst. of Tech., Univ. of West Florida, Harvard Univ.; Naval Aviator 1971, tours with Fighter Squadron 92, USS Constellation (CV 64) and Fighter Squadron l, USS Ranger (CV 61); first CO of Strike/Fighter Squadron 131, USS Coral Sea (CV 43); served as experimental/operational test pilot, in Navy Office of Legis. Affairs, and F/A-l8 Program Coordinator, Deputy Chief of Naval Operations (Air Warfare); served as Exec. Officer of USS Carl Vinson (CVN 70) and CO of USS LaSalle (AGF 3); assumed command of USS Abraham Lincoln (CVN 72) and participated in Operation Desert Storm while deployed during her maiden voyage 1991; Inspector Gen. US Atlantic Fleet, served as Dir for Operations, Plans and Policy on staff of C-in-C US Atlantic Fleet 1993; Commdr Carrier Group Five/Battle Force Seventh Fleet 1995–96; Deputy Commdr and Chief of Staff, Jt Task Force Five (counter-narcotics force for US C-in-C in the Pacific); Deputy Chief of Naval Operations (Plans, Policy and Operations) 1996–98; C-in-C US Naval Forces, Europe, London, UK and C-in-C Allied Forces, Southern Europe, Naples, Italy 1998; C-in-C US Strategic Command, Offutt Air Force Base, Neb. 1998–2004; Pres. and CEO Inst. of Nuclear Power Operations (INPO) 2005–; mem. Bd of Dirs Lockheed Martin Corpn, America First Cos LLC, The Burlington Capital Group, LLC, Level 3 Communications, Inc. 2005–; Advisor to Bd, Inmarsat 2004–; Defense Distinguished Service Medal, Navy Distinguished Service Medal, Legion of Merit (four awards), Defense Meritorious Service Medal, Meritorious Service Medal (two awards), Navy Commendation Medal; numerous campaign and service awards. *Address:* Institute of Nuclear Power Operations, 700 Galleria Parkway, SE, # 100, Atlanta, GA 30339, USA. *Telephone:* (770) 644-8000. *Fax:* (770) 644-8549.

ELLIS, John Martin, BA, PhD; American academic; *Professor Emeritus of German Literature, University of California, Santa Cruz;* b. 31 May 1936,

London, England; s. of John Albert Ellis and Emily Ellis; m. Barbara Rhoades 1978; two s. two d. one step-d.; ed City of London School and Univ. Coll., London; Royal Artillery 1954–56; Tutorial Asst in German, Univ. of Wales, Aberystwyth 1959–60; Asst Lecturer in German, Univ. of Leicester 1960–63; Asst Prof. of German, Univ. of Alberta, Canada 1963–66; Assoc. Prof. of German Literature, Univ. of Calif., Santa Cruz 1966–70, Prof. 1970–94, Prof. Emer. 1994–, Dean Graduate Div. 1977–86; Literary Ed. Heterodoxy 1992–2000; Sec.-Treas. Asscn of Literary Scholars and Critics 1994–2001; Pres. Calif. Asscn of Scholars 2007–; Guggenheim Fellowship, Nat. Endowment for the Humanities Sr Fellowship; Nat. Asscn of Scholars' Peter Shaw Memorial Award (for Literature Lost). *Publications include:* Narration in the German Novelle 1974, The Theory of Literary Criticism: A Logical Analysis 1974, Heinrich von Kleist 1979, One Fairy Story Too Many: The Brothers Grimm and Their Tales 1983, Against Deconstruction 1989, Language, Thought and Logic 1993, Literature Lost: Social Agendas and the Corruption of the Humanities 1997. *Leisure interests:* birdwatching, golf. *Address:* 144 Bay Heights, Soquel, CA 95073, USA (home). *Telephone:* (831) 476-1144 (home). *Fax:* (831) 476-1188 (home). *E-mail:* john.ellis@earthlink.net (office).

ELLIS, Jonathan Richard (John), MA, PhD, FRS, FInstP; British physicist; *Senior Staff Physicist, CERN;* b. 1 July 1946, Hampstead; s. of Richard Ellis and Beryl Lilian Ellis (née Ranger); m. Maria Mercedes Martinez Rengifo 1985; one s. one d.; ed Highgate School, King's Coll., Univ. of Cambridge; Postdoctoral Research Fellow, Stanford Linear Accelerator Center 1971–72; Richard Chase Tolman Fellow, Calif. Inst. of Technology 1972–73; Research Fellow, CERN 1973–74, Staff mem. 1974–, Leader, Theoretical Physics Div. 1988–94, Sr Staff Physicist 1994–, now Adviser to CERN Dir.-Gen. on relations with non-member states; Hon. Fellow King's Coll., Cambridge 2006; Dr hc (Southampton) 1994; Maxwell Medal (Royal Soc.) 1982, Dirac Medal and Prize (Inst. of Physics) 2005. *Publications:* over 800 scientific publs. *Leisure interests:* literature, music, travel, hiking, cinema. *Address:* Theory Division, CERN, CH- 1211 Geneva 23 (office); 5 Chemin du Ruisseau, Tannay, 1295 Mies, Vaud, Switzerland (home). *Telephone:* (22) 7674142 (office); (22) 7764858 (home). *Fax:* (22) 7673850 (office); (22) 7764858 (home). *E-mail:* john.ellis@cern.ch (office). *Website:* www.cern.ch.

ELLIS, Osian Gwynn, CBE, FRAM; British harpist; b. 8 Feb. 1928, Ffynnongroew, Flintshire, Wales; s. of Rev. T. G. Ellis; m. Rene Ellis Jones 1951; two s.; ed Denbigh Grammar School, Royal Acad. of Music; Prin. Harpist London Symphony Orchestra 1960–94; mem. Melos Ensemble; Prof. of Harp Royal Acad. of Music 1959–89; recitals and concerts worldwide; radio and TV broadcasts; works written for him include harp concertos by Hoddinott 1957, Mathias 1970, Jersild 1972, Robin Holloway 1985, Rhian Samuel 2000, solos and chamber music by Gian Carlo Menotti 1977, William Schuman 1978 and music by Britten: Suite for Harp 1969, Canticle V 1974, Birthday Hansel 1975, Folk Songs for voice and harp 1976; Hon. DMus (Wales) 1970; Grand Prix du Disque, French Radio Critics' Award and other awards. *Publication:* Story of the Harp in Wales 1991. *Address:* Arfryn, Ala Road, Pwllheli, Gwynedd, LL53 5BN, Wales. *Telephone:* (1758) 612501.

ELLIS, Reginald John, PhD, FRS; British biologist and academic; *Professor Emeritus of Biological Sciences, University of Warwick;* b. 12 Feb. 1935, Newcastle-under-Lyme; s. of Francis Gilbert Ellis and Evangeline Gratton Ellis; m. Diana Margaret Warren 1963; one d.; ed Highbury Grove Grammar School, London and King's Coll., Univ. of London; Agricultural Research Council Fellow, Dept of Biochemistry, Univ. of Oxford 1961–64; Lecturer, Depts of Botany and Biochemistry, Univ. of Aberdeen 1964–70; Sr Lecturer, Univ. of Warwick 1970–73, Reader 1973–76, Prof. of Biological Sciences 1976–96, Prof. Emer. 1996–, f. Molecular Chaperone Club; Sr Research Fellow, Science and Eng Research Council 1983–88; mem. European Molecular Biology Org. 1986–; Sr Visiting Research Fellow, St John's Coll. Oxford 1992–93; Academic Visitor, Oxford Centre for Molecular Sciences 1996–2000; Tate & Lyle Award 1980, International Gairdner Foundation Award 2004. *Publications:* 165 papers on plant and microbial biochemistry; Chloroplast Biogenesis (ed.) 1984, Molecular Chaperones (ed.) 1990, The Chaperonins (ed.) 1996, Molecular Chaperones Ten Years On (ed.) 2000, Protein Misfolding and Human Disease (ed.) 2004. *Leisure interests:* landscape photography, fell walking. *Address:* Department of Biological Sciences, University of Warwick, Gibbet Hill Road, Coventry, West Midlands, CV4 7AL (office); 44 Sunningdale Avenue, Kenilworth, Warwicks. CV8 2BZ, England (home). *Telephone:* (2476) 523509 (office); (1926) 856382 (home). *Fax:* (2476) 523701 (office). *E-mail:* jellis@bio.warwick.ac.uk (office). *Website:* www.bio.warwick.ac.uk (office).

ELLIS, Richard Salisbury, CBE, DPhil, FRS, FInstP; British astronomer and academic; *Steele Professor of Astronomy, California Institute of Technology;* b. 25 May 1950, Colwyn Bay, Wales; s. of the late Capt. Arthur Ellis and of Marion Ellis; m. Barbara Williams 1972; one s. one d.; ed Univ. Coll. London, Univ. of Oxford; researcher, Univ. of Durham 1974–81, Lecturer 1981–83, Prof. of Astronomy 1985–93, Visiting Prof. 1994–; Plumian Prof., Univ. of Cambridge 1993–99, Visiting Prof. 2000–03, Dir Inst. of Astronomy 1994–99, Professorial Fellow, Magdalene Coll. Cambridge 1994–99; Prof. of Astronomy, California Inst. of Tech. 1999–2002, Steele Prof. of Astronomy 2002–, Dir Palomar Observatory 2000–02, Caltech Optical Observatories 2002–05; Royal Soc. Regius Prof., Univ. of Oxford 2008–, Professorial Fellow, Merton Coll. Oxford 2008–; Sr Research Fellow, Royal Greenwich Observatory 1983–85; Visiting Prof., Univ. Coll. London 2004–; Fellow, Univ. Coll. London 1998, Royal Astronomical Soc.; mem. American Astronomical Soc., Astronomical Soc. of the Pacific; Hon. DSc (Durham) 2002; Bakerian Prize, Royal Soc. 1998, Gruber Cosmology Prize 2007. *Publications:* numerous articles in scientific journals; Observational Tests of Cosmological Inflation 1991, Large Scale Structure in the Universe 1999. *Leisure interests:* skiing, photography, travel. *Address:* Astronomy Department, Mail Stop 105-24, California Institute of

Technology, Pasadena, CA 91125, USA (office); Department of Astrophysics, Keble Road, Oxford, OX1 3RH, England. *Telephone:* (626) 395-2598 (office); (626) 676-5530 (home). *Fax:* (626) 568-9352 (office). *E-mail:* rse@astro.caltech.edu (office). *Website:* www.astro.caltech.edu/~rse.

ELLISON, Harlan Jay; American author and screenwriter; b. 27 May 1934, Cleveland, OH; s. of Louis Laverne Ellison and Serita (née Rosenthal) Ellison; m. 1st Charlotte Stein 1956 (divorced 1959); m. 2nd Billie Joyce Sanders 1961 (divorced 1962); m. 3rd Lory Patrick 1965 (divorced 1965); m. 4th Lori Horwitz 1976 (divorced 1977); m. 5th Susan Toth 1986; ed Ohio State Univ.; part-time actor, Cleveland Playhouse 1944–49; f. Cleveland Science-Fiction Soc. 1950 and Science-Fantasy Bulletin; served US Army 1957–59; ed. Rogue magazine, Chicago 1959-60, Regency Books, Chicago 1960–61; lecturer at colls and univs; voice-overs for animated cartoons; book critic, LA Times 1969–82; Editorial Commentator Canadian Broadcasting Co. 1972–78; Instructor Clarion Writers Workshop, Michigan State Univ. 1969–77; Pres. The Kilimanjaro Corpn 1979–; TV writer for Alfred Hitchcock Hour, Outer Limits, The Man from U.N.C.L.E., Burke's Law; film writer for The Dream Merchants, The Oscar, Nick the Greek, Best By Far, Harlan Ellison's Movie; scenarist: I, Robot 1978, Bug Jack Barron 1982–83; creative consultant, writer and dir The Twilight Zone 1984–85; conceptual consultant, Babylon 5 1993–98; mem. American Writers' Guild and American Science Fiction Writers; Hugo Awards 1967, 1968, 1973, 1974, 1975, 1977, 1986, Special Achievement Awards 1968–72, Certificate of Merit, Trieste Film Festival 1970, Edgar Allan Poe Award, Mystery Writers 1974, 1988, American Mystery Award 1988, Bram Stoker Award, Horror Writers Asscn 1988, 1990, 1994; World Fantasy Award 1989, Georges Méliès Award for cinematic achievement 1972, 1973, PEN Award for journalism 1982; Americana Annual American Literature: Major Works 1988, World Fantasy 1993 Life Achievement Award, two Audie Awards, Audio Publishers Asscn 1999 and numerous other awards. *Publications include:* Web of the City 1958, The Deadly Streets 1958, Sex Gang 1959, A Touch of Infinity 1960, The Sound of a Scythe 1960, Spider Kiss 1961, Children of the Streets 1961, Gentleman Jackie 1961, Ellison Wonderland 1962, Paingod 1965, I Have no Mouth and I must Scream 1967, From the Land of Fear 1967, Dangerous Visions (ed.) 1967, Doomsman 1967, Love ain't Nothing but Sex Mispelled 1968, The Beast that Shouted Love at the Heart of the World 1969, Over the Edge 1970, The Glass Teat 1970, De Helden van de Highway 1973, Approaching Oblivion 1974, Deathbird Stories 1975, No Doors, No Windows 1975, The Other Glass Teat 1975, A Boy and His Dog 1975, Strange Wine 1978, Shatterday 1980, Stalking the Nightmare 1982, An Edge in My Voice 1985, Demon with a Glass Hand 1986, Night and the Enemy 1987, The Essential Ellison 1987, Angry Candy 1988, Harlan Ellison's Watching 1989, Vic and Blood 1989, The Harlan Ellison Hornbook 1990, Harlan Ellison's Movie 1990, All the Lies that are my Life 1991, Run for the Stars 1991, Mefisto in Onyx 1993, Mind Fields (33 stories inspired by the art of Jacek Yerka) 1994, Robot: The Illustrated Screenplay 1994, City on the Edge of Forever (screenplay) 1995, Jokes without Punchlines 1995, Slippage 1996, Harlan Ellison's Dream Corridor 1996, Edgeworks: The Collected Ellison (four vols) 1996–97, Repent, Harlequin 1997, Troublemakers 2001. *Leisure interests:* shooting pool, supporting progressive and environmental agendas and causes. *Address:* c/o The Harlan Ellison Rrcording Collection, PO Box 55548, Sherman Oaks, CA 91413-0548, USA (office). *Website:* harlanellison.com (office).

ELLISON, Lawrence (Larry) J.; American software industry executive; *CEO, Oracle Corporation;* b. 1944, Bronx, New York; divorced; two c.; ed Univs of Illinois and Chicago; started as technician with Firemans' Fund, Wells Fargo Bank; with Ampex built databases; co-f. Software Devt Labs (later Oracle Corpn) 1977, CEO 1977–, Pres. 1978–96, mem. Bd of Dirs and Chair. 1990–92, 1995–2004; mem. Bd of Dirs Apple Computer Inc. 1997. *Leisure interests:* racing sail boats, flying aeroplanes, playing tennis and guitar. *Address:* Oracle Corpn, 500 Oracle Parkway, Redwood City, CA 94065-1675, USA (office). *Telephone:* (650) 506-7000 (office). *Fax:* (650) 506-7200 (office). *E-mail:* info@oracle.com (office). *Website:* www.oracle.com (office).

ELLMAN, Michael, MSc(Econ), PhD; British economist and academic; *Professor of Economics, University of Amsterdam;* b. 27 July 1942, Ripley, Surrey; m. Patricia Harrison 1965; one s. one d.; ed Cambridge Univ. and London School of Econs; lecturer Glasgow Univ. 1967–69; Research Officer then Sr Research Officer, Dept of Applied Econs, Cambridge Univ. 1969–75; Assoc. Prof. Amsterdam Univ. 1975–78, Prof. of Econs 1978–; Fellow Tinberg Inst.; Kondratieff Prize 1998. *Publications:* Planning Problems in the USSR 1973, Socialist Planning 1989, The Destruction of the Soviet Economic System (ed. with V. Kontovovich) 1998, Russia's Oil and Natural Gas: Bonanza or Curse? (ed.) 2006. *Leisure interests:* walking, cycling. *Address:* Department of Economics, Universiteit van Amsterdam, Roetersstraat 11, 1018 WB Amsterdam, Netherlands (office). *Telephone:* (20) 5254235 (office). *Fax:* (20) 5254254 (office). *E-mail:* m.j.ellman@uva.nl (office).

ELLROY, James; American writer; b. (Lee Earle Ellroy), 4 March 1948, Los Angeles, Calif.; m. 1st Mary Doherty 1988 (divorced 1991); m. 2nd Helen Knode 1991; ed John Burroughs Junior High School and Fairfax High School, Los Angeles. *Films include:* Dark Blue 2002, Street Kings (screenplay and story) 2008. *Publications:* Brown's Requiem 1981, Clandestine 1982, Blood on the Moon (Lloyd Hopkins series) 1983, Because the Night (Lloyd Hopkins series) 1984, Killer on the Road 1986, Silent Terror 1986, Suicide Hill (Lloyd Hopkins series) 1986, The Black Dahlia (LA series) 1987, The Big Nowhere (LA series) 1988, LA Confidential (LA series) 1990, White Jazz (LA series) 1992, Hollywood Nocturnes (essays and stories) 1994, American Tabloid (Underworld USA series) (Time Magazine Novel of the Year) 1995, My Dark Places (memoir) (Salon.com Book of the Year) 1996, LA Noir 1998, Crime Wave (essays and stories) 1999, The Cold Six Thousand (Underworld USA series) 2001, Destination: Morgue (essays and stories) 2003. *Address:* Sobel Weber Associates Inc, 146 East 19th Street, New York, NY 10003, USA (office); c/o Warner Books Publicity Dept, 1271 Avenue of the Americas, New York, NY 10020, USA (office).

ELLWOOD, David T., PhD; American economist and academic; *Scott M. Black Professor of Political Economy and Dean, John F. Kennedy School of Government, Harvard University;* b. Minnesota; m. Marilyn Ellwood; two d.; ed Harvard Univ.; Research Asst, Cttee on Costs and Benefits of Auto Air Emission Controls, Nat. Bureau of Econ. Research 1974, Research Asst 1978–80, Research Assoc. 1988–; Research Asst to A. Mitchell Polinsky, Harvard Univ. 1974–75, to Prof. Martin S. Feldstein 1974–75, 1977, Teaching Fellow, Labor Econs 1977–79; Research Assoc., Health Policy Program, Univ. of California, San Francisco 1975–76; Asst Prof. of Public Policy, John F. Kennedy School of Govt, Harvard Univ. 1980–84, Assoc. Prof. of Public Policy 1984–88, Prof. of Public Policy 1988–92, Co-Dir Malcolm Wiener Center for Social Policy 1992–93, Academic Dean, 1992–93, 1995–97, Malcolm Wiener Prof. of Public Policy 1992–93, 1995–98, Dir Multidisciplinary Program in Inequality and Social Policy 1998–99, Lucius N. Littauer Prof. of Political Economy 1998–2003, Scott M. Black Prof. of Political Economy 2003–, Dean John F. Kennedy School of Govt 2004–; Asst Sec. for Planning and Evaluation, US Dept of Health and Human Services, Washington, DC 1993–95; Faculty Affiliate, Jt Center for Poverty Research, Northwestern Univ. and Univ. of Chicago 1997–; Sr Research Affiliate, Nat. Poverty Center, Gerald R. Ford School of Public Policy, Univ. of Michigan 2003–; mem. Nat. Acad. of Social Insurance 1990–, Nat. Acad. of Public Admin 2000–; mem. of Review Panel, Work and Welfare Demonstration, Manpower Demonstration Research Corpn 1985–; mem. Bd of Dirs Malcolm Hewitt Wiener Foundation 2000–, Abt Assocs 2001–; Morris and Edna Zale Award for Outstanding Distinction in Scholarship and Public Service, Stanford Univ., David Kershaw Award for Outstanding Contribution to Policy Analysis and Man., Asscn of Public Policy Analysis and Man. *Publications:* A Working Nation?: Workers, Work and Government in the New Economy (co-ed.) 2000; contribs to The Economic Journal, Harvard Business Review, New England Economic Review, Bulletin of the New York Academy of Medicine, The American Prospect, Journal of Economic Perspectives, The New York Times, Washington Post, Los Angeles Times, Boston Globe; books: Poor Support: Poverty and the American Family 1988. *Address:* Office of the Dean, John F. Kennedy School of Government, Harvard Kennedy School, 79 John F. Kennedy Street, Cambridge, MA 02138, USA (office). *Telephone:* (617) 495-1122 (office). *Fax:* (617) 495-9118 (office). *E-mail:* david_ellwood@Harvard.edu (office). *Website:* www.hks.harvard.edu (office).

ELLWOOD, Peter Brian, CBE, FCIB, FRSA; British business executive; *Chairman, ICI PLC;* b. 15 May 1943, Bristol; s. of the late Isaac Ellwood and Edith Ellwood (née Trotter); m. Judy Ann Windsor 1968; one s. two d.; ed King's School, Macclesfield; joined Barclays Bank 1961; worked in London and Bristol; Chief Exec. Barclaycard 1985; Dir Barclays Bank (UK) Ltd; Chief. Exec. Retail Banking, TSB Bank PLC; Dir TSB Group PLC 1990–95, Chief Exec. 1992–95; Deputy Chief Exec. Lloyds TSB Group PLC 1995–97, Chief Exec. 1997–2003; Chair. ICI PLC 2004–; Chair. Royal Parks Advisory Board 2003, Chair. Royal Parks Foundation 2003; Deputy Chair. Royal Coll. of Music 2003; Chair. Visa Europe, Middle East and Africa 1992–96, Visa Int. 1994–99; Dir (non.-exec.) Sears PLC 1994–96, Royal Philharmonic Orchestra 1996–; mem. Court Univ. Coll. Northampton (fmrly Nene Coll.) 1989–; Hon. LLD (Leicester) 1994; Dr hc (Univ. of Cen. England) 1995. *Leisure interests:* music, theatre. *Address:* ICI PLC, 20 Manchester Square, London, W1U 3AN, England (office). *Telephone:* (20) 7009-5000 (office). *Fax:* (20) 7009-5001 (office). *Website:* www.ici.com (office).

ELMAN, Richard Samuel; British business executive; *CEO, Noble Group Ltd;* arrived in Asia from England mid-1960s; Regional Dir of Asia Operations, Phibro, New York, USA 1976–86, mem. Bd of Dirs for two years; Founder and CEO Noble Group Ltd (global commodity merchant) 1986–, mem. Bd of Dirs 1994–; mem. Hong Kong Inst. of Dirs. *Address:* Noble Group Ltd, 18th Floor, MassMutual Tower, 38 Gloucester Road, Hong Kong Special Administrative Region, People's Republic of China (office). *Telephone:* 2861-3511 (office). *Fax:* 2527-0282 (office). *E-mail:* richard@thisisnoble.com (office). *Website:* www.thisisnoble.com (office).

ELMANDJRA, Mahdi, PhD; Moroccan academic; *Professor, University Mohamed V;* b. 13 March 1933, Rabat; s. of M'Hamed Elmandjra and Rabia Elmrini; m. Amina Elmrini 1956; two d.; ed Lycée Lyautey, Casablanca, Putney School, Vermont, USA, Cornell Univ., London School of Econs and Faculté de Droit, Univ. de Paris; Head of Confs, Law Faculty, Univ. of Rabat 1957–58; Adviser, Ministry of Foreign Affairs and to Moroccan Del. to UN 1958–59; Dir-Gen. Radiodiffusion Télévision Marocaine 1959–60; Chief of African Div., Office of Relations with Mem. States, UNESCO 1961–63; Dir Exec. Office of Dir-Gen. of UNESCO 1963–66; Asst Dir-Gen. of UNESCO for Social Sciences, Human Sciences and Culture 1966–69; Visiting Fellow, Centre of Int. Studies, LSE 1970; Asst Dir-Gen. of UNESCO for Pre-Programming 1971–74; Special Adviser to Dir-Gen. of UNESCO 1975–76; Prof., Univ. Mohamed V, Rabat 1977–; Co-ordinator, Conf. on Tech. Co-operation between Developing Countries (UNDP) 1979–80; Sr Adviser, UN Int. Year of Disabled Persons 1980–81; mem. Consultative Cultural Council of the Inst. of the Arab World (Paris); fmr Pres. World Future Studies Fed. (WFSF), Futuribles Int.; mem. Club of Rome, Acad. of the Kingdom of Morocco; Vice-Pres. Asscn Maroc-Japon; mem. World Acad. of Art and Science, Exec. Cttee, Soc. for Int. Devt, Exec. Cttee, African Acad. of Sciences, Pugwash Confs, Founding Pres. Moroccan Asscn of Human Rights, Acad. of the Kingdom of Morocco; Officier des Arts et des Lettres (France), Order of the Rising Sun (Japan) and numerous other decorations; Master Jury Aga Khan Award for Architecture 1986, Albert Einstein Int. Foundation Medal for Peace 1990. *Television:* various programmes for French, Moroccan, Spanish, Japanese and Arab channels. *Publications:* Africa 2000 1980, The New Age of Culture and Communication 1981, The Future of Humor 1982, Maghreb 2000 1982, L'Interpellation du Tiers Monde 1982, Les Aspects économiques du dialogue Euro-Arabe 1982, Information and Sovereignty 1983, The Conquest of Space: Political, Economic and Socio-Cultural Implications 1984, Casablanca 2000 1984, Development and Automation 1985, Communications, Information and Development 1985, Tomorrow's Habitat 1985, Learning Needs in a Changing Society 1986, Media and Communications in Africa 1986, The Future of International Cooperation 1986, The Financing of Research and Development in the Third World 1986, Maghreb et Francophonie 1988, Three Scenarios for The Future of International Cooperation 1988, The Place of Arab Culture in the World of Tomorrow 1988, Social Change and Law 1988, China in the 21st Century 1989, Fusion of Science and Culture: Key to the 21st Century 1989, Human Rights and Development 1989, How to Construct a Positive Vision of the Future 1990, Gulf Crisis: Prelude to the North-South Confrontation 1990, Western Discrimination in the Field of Human Rights 1990, Africa: The Coming Upheaval 1990, La Première Guerre Civilisationnelle 1991, Retrospective des Futurs 1992, Nord-Sud: Prélude à l'Ere Postcoloniale 1992, The Agreements Concerning Gaza and Jericho 1993, Biodiversity: Cultural and Ethical Aspects 1994, Cultural Diversity: Key to Survival in the 21st Century 1994, The New Challenges Facing the United Nations 1995, Dialogue de la Communication 1996, Al Quds (Jerusalem): Symbole et mémoire 1996, La décolonisation culturelle: défi majeur du 21e siècle 1996, Immigration as a Cultural Phenomenon 1997, The Path of a Mind 1997, Communication Dialogue 2000, Reglobalization of Globalization 2000, Intifadate 2000, Humiliation 2003. *Leisure interests:* reading, swimming, music, writing. *Address:* BP 53, Rabat, Morocco (office). *Telephone:* (37) 774-258 (office). *Fax:* (37) 757-151 (office). *E-mail:* elmandjra@elmandjra.org (home). *Website:* www.elmandjra.org (home).

ELMER, Michael B.; Danish lawyer; *Vice-President, Danish Maritime and Commercial Court;* b. 26 Feb. 1949, Copenhagen; s. of Poul Chr. B. Elmer and Etly Elmer (née Andersson); pnr Annette Andersen; one d.; ed Univ. of Copenhagen; civil servant, Ministry of Justice 1973–76, 1977–82, Head of Div. 1982–87, 1988–91, Deputy Perm. Sec., Head of Community Law and Human Rights Dept 1991–94; Assoc. Prof., Univ. of Copenhagen 1975–85; Deputy Judge, Hillerød 1976–77; Asst Public Prosecutor 1980–81; Judge, Court of Ballerup 1981–82; external examiner Danish law schools 1985–; High Court Judge (a.i.), Eastern High Court, Copenhagen 1987–88; Vice-Pres. (a.i.) Danish Maritime and Commercial Court, Copenhagen 1988, Vice Pres. 1997–; Rep. EC Court of Justice, Luxembourg 1991–94; Advocate-Gen. EC Court of Justice 1994–97; mem. governing council UNIDROIT, Rome 1999–; int. commercial arbitrator; Chair. and mem. numerous govt and int. orgs and cttees; Kt, Order of Dannebrog, Grand Cross, Order of Merit (Luxembourg). *Publications:* several books and articles on civil law (especially property law), penal law and community law. *Leisure interests:* travelling, collecting antiques, Leica photography. *Address:* Sø-og Handelsretten, Bredgade 70, 1260, Copenhagen (office); Skovalléen 16, 2880 Bagsvaerd, Denmark (home). *Telephone:* 33-47-92-22 (office); 35-55-49-63 (home). *Fax:* 33-47-92-82 (office). *E-mail:* elmer@shret.dk (office); michael.elmer@tdcadsl.dk (home).

ELRINGTON, Wilfred, SC; Belizean lawyer and politician; *Attorney-General and Minister of Foreign Affairs and Foreign Trade;* mem. United Democratic Party; contested Pickstock constituency as an ind. 2002; Attorney-Gen. and Minister of Foreign Affairs and Foreign Trade 2008–. *Address:* Ministry of the Attorney-General, General Office, Belmopan (office); Ministry of Foreign Affairs and Foreign Trade and of Tourism, Information and NEMO, New Administration Building, PO Box 174, Belmopan, Belize (office). *Telephone:* 822-2504 (Ministry of the Attorney-Gen.) (office); 822-2167 (Ministry of Foreign Affairs) (office). *Fax:* 822-3390 (Ministry of the Attorney-Gen.) (office); 822-2854 (Ministry of Foreign Affairs) (office). *E-mail:* scregistry@btl.net (office); belizemfa@btl.net (office). *Website:* www.belizelaw.org (office); www.mfa.gov.bz (office).

ELS, Theodore Ernest (Ernie); South African professional golfer; b. 17 Oct. 1969, Johannesburg; s. of Nils Els and Hettie Els; m. Leizl Els; one s. one d.; wins include South African Open 1992, 1996, US Open, 1994, 1997, Toyota World Matchplay Championships 1994, 1995, 1996, South African PGA Championship 1995, Byron Nelson Classic 1995, Buick Classic 1996, 1997, Johnnie Walker Classic 1997, Bay Hill Invitational 1998, Nissan Open 1999, Int. presented by Quest 2000, Standard Life Loch Lomond 2000, Open Championship 2002, Genuity Championship 2002, British Open 2002, sixth World Match Play title 2004, Mercedes Championship 2003; mem. Dunhill Cup Team 1992–2000, World Cup Team 1992, 1993, 1996, 1997, 2001; mem. President's Cup 1996, 1998, 2000; f. Ernie Els Foundation to help disadvantaged children 1999; South African Sportsman of the Year 1994, Lifetime Membership European Tour 1998. *Leisure interests:* movies, reading, sport. *Address:* 46 Chapman Road, Klippoortjie 1401, South Africa.

ELSASSER, Hans Friedrich, Dr rer. nat; German economic geographer and astronomer; b. 29 March 1929, Aalen/Württemberg; s. of Jakob Elsasser and Margarete Elsasser-Vogelgsang; m. Ruth Abele 1953; two s. one d.; ed Univ. of Tübingen; Asst Prof., Univ. of Tübingen 1957, Univ. of Göttingen 1959; Prof. of Astronomy, Univ. of Heidelberg 1962; Dir State Observatory, Heidelberg-Königstuhl 1962–75; Dir Max Planck Inst. for Astronomy, Heidelberg-Königstuhl 1968, Calar Alto Observatory, Spain; currently Prof. of Econ. Geography, Mathematisch-naturwissenschaftliche Fakultät, Universität Zürich; mem. Acad. of Sciences of Heidelberg, Halle, Helsinki and Vienna; planet Elsasser named after him; Comendador de la Orden de Isabel la Católica (Spain), Bundesverdienstkreuz. *Publications:* about 150 articles in astronomical journals and three textbooks, two with H. Scheffler. *Leisure interest:* tennis.

ELSENHANS, Lynn Laverty, BA, MBA; American business executive; *President and CEO, Sunoco Inc.;* ed Rice Univ., Harvard Business School; joined Shell Oil 1980s, later Pres. and CEO Shell Oil Products East, Singapore, Dir of Strategic Planning, Sustainable Devt and External Affairs for Shell Int. Ltd, London, UK 2002–03, served concurrently as Pres. Shell Oil Co. and Pres. and CEO Shell Oil Products USA 2003–05, Exec. Vice-Pres. of Global Manufacturing, Shell Downstream, Inc. (subsidiary of Royal Dutch/ Shell Group) 2005–08; mem. Bd of Dirs, Pres. and CEO Sunoco, Inc., Philadelphia 2008–; mem. Bd of Dirs International Paper Co.; mem. Bd of Trustees, Rice Univ., Council of Overseers for Jesse H. Jones Grad. School of Man.; ranked by Forbes magazine amongst 100 Most Powerful Women (39th) 2008. *Address:* Sunoco Inc., 1735 Market Street, Suite LL, Philadelphia, PA 19103-7583, USA (office). *Telephone:* (215) 977-3000 (office). *Fax:* (215) 977-3409 (office). *E-mail:* info@sunocoinc.com (office). *Website:* www.sunocoinc.com (office).

ELSON, Bill; American music agent; Head of Music Div. Int. Creative Man. (ICM); clients have included Janis Joplin, the Doors, Jefferson Airplane, Def Leppard, Paul McCartney, Bob Dylan, Metallica. *Address:* ICM New York, 40 W 57th Street, New York, NY 10019, USA.

ELSTEIN, David Keith, MA; British broadcasting executive; *Chairman, Luther Pendragon Holdings;* b. 14 Nov. 1944; ed Haberdashers' Aske's School, Gonville and Caius Coll. Cambridge; producer (BBC) The Money Programme, Panorama, Cause for Concern, People in Conflict 1964–68; (Thames TV) This Week, The Day Before Yesterday, The World At War 1968–72; (London Weekend) Weekend World 1972; Ed. This Week (Thames TV) 1974–78; f. Brook Productions 1982; Exec. Producer A Week in Politics 1982–86, Concealed Enemies 1983; Man. Dir Primetime TV 1983–86; Dir of Programmes, Thames TV 1986–92; Head of Programmes BSkyB 1993–96; Chief Exec. Channel 5 Broadcasting 1996–2000; Chair. Nat. Film and TV School 1996–2002, British Screen Advisory Council 1997–2008, Broadcasting Policy Group 2003–, Commercial Radio Cos Asscn 2004–06, Screen Digest 2004–, XSN PLC 2004–08, Sparrowhawk Investments Ltd 2004–07, DCD Media PLC 2005–, Luther Pendragon Holdings 2006–; Vice-Chair. Kingsbridge Capital Advisors Ltd 2004–; Dir Virgin Media Inc. 2003–08; Visiting Prof. Stirling Univ. 1995–. *Publications:* The Political Structure of UK Broadcasting 1949–1999 (Oxford Lectures) 1999, Beyond The Charter: The BBC After 2006 (Broadcasting Policy Group) 2004. *Leisure interests:* theatre, cinema, bridge, politics, reading. *Address:* c/o Luther Pendragon Holdings, Priory Court, Pilgrim Street, London, EC4V 6DR, England (office). *E-mail:* elsteindavid@aol.com (home).

ELSTONE, Robert G., BA (Hons), MA (Econ), MCom; Australian investment banker and business executive; *Managing Director and CEO, Australian Stock Exchange Ltd (ASX);* ed Univs of London and Manchester, UK and Univ. of Western Australia, Sr Exec. Devt Programs at Harvard and Stanford Grad. Schools of Business, USA; career has spanned investment banking in 1980s, public co. CFO roles in 1990s, aviation and global resource materials sectors, and wholesale financial markets and risk man. in 2000s; managed Australian office of Paribas' int. capital markets activities in Paris, London and New York 1980s; Man. Dir and CEO SFE Corpn (holding co. for Sydney Futures Exchange prior to its merger with Australian Stock Exchange Ltd (ASX)) 2000–06, Man. Dir and CEO ASX 2006–; Dir (non-exec.) Nat. Australia Bank (also Chair. Risk Cttee of the Bd); mem. Bd Guardians Commonwealth Govt's Future Fund; mem. Bd of Dirs SFE Clearing Corpn Ltd, Austraclear Ltd, Australian Clearing House Pty Ltd, ASX Settlement and Transfer Corpn Pty Ltd; Chair. Financial Sector Advisory Council; Adjunct Chair (Professorial Fellow), Finance Faculty, School of Econs and Business, Univ. of Sydney; Hon. Fellow, Finance and Treasury Asscn. *Address:* ASX Ltd, Exchange Centre, 20 Bridge Street, Sydney, NSW 2000, Australia (office). *Telephone:* (2) 9338-0000 (office). *Fax:* (2) 9227-0885 (office). *E-mail:* info@asx.com.au (office). *Website:* www.asx.com.au (office).

ELTIS, Walter Alfred, MA, DLitt; British economist; *Fellow Emeritus, Exeter College, Oxford;* b. 23 May 1933, Warnsdorf, Czechoslovakia; s. of Rev. Martin Eltis and Mary Schnitzer; m. Shelagh M. Owen 1959; one s. two d.; ed Wycliffe Coll., Emmanuel Coll. Cambridge and Nuffield Coll. Oxford; Research Fellow in Econs, Exeter Coll., Oxford 1958–60; Lecturer in Econs, Univ. of Oxford 1961–88; Fellow and Tutor in Econs, Exeter Coll. Oxford 1963–88, Fellow Emer. 1988–; Econ. Dir Nat. Econ. Devt Office 1986–88, Dir-Gen. 1988–92; Chief Econ. Adviser to the Pres. of Bd of Trade 1992–95; Visiting Reader in Econs, Univ. of Western Australia 1970–71; Visiting Prof., Univ. of Toronto 1976–77, European Univ. Florence 1979, Univ. of Reading 1992–2004; Gresham Prof. of Commerce, Gresham Coll. London 1993–96; mem. Reform Club (Chair. 1994–95), Political Economy Club, European Soc. for the History of Econ. Thought (Vice-Pres. 2000–04). *Publications:* Growth and Distribution 1973, Britain's Economic Problem: Too Few Producers (with R. Bacon) 1976, The Classical Theory of Economic Growth 1984, Keynes and Economic Policy (with P. Sinclair) 1988, Classical Economics, Public Expenditure and Growth 1993, Britain's Economic Problem Revisited 1996, Condillac: Commerce and Government (co-ed. with S. M. Eltis) 1998, Britain, Europe and EMU 2000. *Leisure interests:* chess, music. *Address:* Danesway, Jarn Way, Boars Hill, Oxford, OX1 5JF, England (home). *Telephone:* (1865) 735440 (home).

ELTON, Sir Arnold, Kt, KB, CBE, MS, FRCS, FRSM, FICS; British surgeon; *Health Adviser, Wellington Hospital;* b. 14 Feb. 1920; s. of the late Max Elton and Ada Elton; m. Billie Pamela Briggs 1952; one s.; ed Univ. Coll., London, Univ. Coll. Hosp. Medical School, London; House Surgeon, House Physician, Casualty Officer, Univ. Coll. Hosp. 1943–45; Sr Surgical Registrar, Charing Cross Hosp. 1947–51; Consultant Surgeon, Harrow Hosp. 1951–70, Mount Vernon Hosp. 1960–70, Wellington Hosp.; Consultant Surgeon, Northwick Park Hosp. and Clinical Research Centre 1970–85 (now Consulting Surgeon); Surgeon Emer. Clementine Churchill Hosp.; First Chair. Medical Staff Cttee Northwick Park Hosp., Chair. Surgical Div. and Theatre Cttee; Health Adviser, Wellington Hosp. 2000–; mem. Ethical Cttee Northwick Park Hosp., Govt Working Party on Breast Screening for Cancer 1985–; Surgical Tutor, Royal Coll. of Surgeons 1970–82; Nat. Chair. Conservative Medical Soc. 1975–92, Chair. European Group and Pres. 1992–97, Pres. Emer. 1997–; European Rep. 1994–, Ed. European Bulletin 1994–, also Chair. Educ. and Research Div.; Examiner, Gen. Nursing Council, Royal Coll. of Surgeons 1971–83; Medical Adviser Virgin Fitness Clubs, Adviser, H.C.A. Group of Hosps; Exec. Dir Healthy Living (UK) Ltd, Healthy Living (Durham) Ltd, Universal Lifestyle Ltd, Medical Consulting Services Ltd; Chair. Int. Medical and Scientific Fundraising Cttee, British Red Cross, Medical and Science Div., World Fellowship Duke of Edinburgh Award; Fellow, Asscn of Surgeons of GB, Int. Coll. of Surgeons; Founding mem. British Asscn of Surgical Oncology; mem. Court of Patrons Royal Coll. of Surgeons 1986–, Int. Medical Parliamentarians Org. (Chair UK Div.), European Soc. of Surgical Oncology, World Fed. of Surgical Oncological Socs (adviser on int. affairs), European Fed. of Surgeons, Tricare Europe Preferred Provider Network (US Armed Forces and Families), Breast and Thyroid Surgery 1997–; Devt Consultant, Ridgeford Properties Ltd 2001; Health Exec. Bovis Lend Lease Ltd 2000–; Medical Consultant and Adviser, Keltbray Ltd 2003–; Health Consultant and Adviser, Clipfine, BDL; mem. Nat. Events Cttee of Imperial Cancer Research Fund; Gosse Research Scholarship; Health Consultant and Adviser to Sir Robert McAlpine Ltd; mem. Apothecaries and Carmen Liveries; Queen's Jubilee Medal for Community Services; Freeman, City of London. *Publications:* various medical publs. *Leisure interests:* tennis, music, cricket. *Address:* The Consulting Rooms, Wellington Hospital, Wellington Place, London, NW8 9LE (office); 58 Stockleigh Hall, Prince Albert Road, London, NW8 7LB, England (home). *Telephone:* (20) 7483-5275 (office). *Fax:* (20) 7722-6638 (office).

ELTON, Benjamin (Ben) Charles, BA; British writer and performer; b. 3 May 1959; s. of Prof. Lewis Richard Benjamin Elton and Mary Elton (née Foster); m. Sophie Gare 1994; ed Godalming Grammar School, S Warwicks. Coll. of Further Educ., Univ. of Manchester; first professional appearance Comic Strip Club 1981; numerous tours as stand-up comic 1986–; British Acad. Best Comedy Show Awards 1984, 1987, Best New Comedy Laurence Olivier Award 1998. *Film:* Maybe Baby (writer and dir) 2000, Much Ado About Nothing (actor) 1993. *Television:* writer: Alfresco 1982–83, The Young Ones (jtly) 1982–84, Happy Families 1985, Filthy Rich and Catflap 1986, Blackadder II (jtly) 1986, Blackadder the Third (jtly) 1987, Blackadder Goes Forth (jtly) 1989, The Thin Blue Line (jtly) 1995–96; writer and performer: South of Watford (jtly, documentary series) 1984–85, Friday Night Live 1988, Saturday Live 1985–87, Ben Elton Live 1989, 1993, 1997, The Man from Auntie 1990, 1994, Stark 1993, The Ben Elton Show (jtly) 1998. *Theatre:* Gasping 1990, Silly Cow 1991, Popcorn 1996, Blast from the Past 1998, The Beautiful Game (musical, book and lyrics) 2000, We Will Rock You (story to musical) 2002, Tonight's the Night (story to musical) 2003. *Recordings:* albums: Motormouth 1987, Motorvation 1989. *Publications:* novels: Bachelor Boys 1984, Stark 1989, Gridlock 1992, This Other Eden 1993, Popcorn 1996, Blast from the Past 1998, Inconceivable 1999, Dead Famous 2001, High Society 2002, Past Mortem 2004, The First Casualty 2005, Chart Throb 2006. *Leisure interests:* walking, reading, socializing. *Address:* c/o Phil McIntyre, Second Floor, 35 Soho Square, London, W1D 3QX, England (office).

ELTON, 2nd Baron, cr. 1934, of Headington; **Rodney Elton,** MA, TD; British politician and company director; *Deputy Speaker and Deputy Chairman of Committees, House of Lords;* b. 2 March 1930, Oxford; s. of the late Godfrey Elton, 1st Baron and Dedi Hartmann; m. 1st Anne Frances Tilney 1958 (divorced 1979); one s. three d.; m. 2nd Susan Richenda Gurney 1979; ed Eton Coll. and New Coll., Oxford; fmr Capt. Queen's Own Warwicks. and Worcs. Yeomanry; fmr Maj. Leics. and Derbyshire Yeomanry; farming 1957–73; Asst Mastership in History Loughborough Grammar School 1962–67, Fairham Comprehensive School for Boys 1967–69; contested Loughborough div. of Leics. 1966, 1970; Lecturer Bishop Lonsdale Coll. of Educ. 1969–72; Opposition Whip House of Lords 1974–76, a Deputy Chair. of Cttees. 1997–; Deputy Speaker 1999–; an Opposition Spokesman 1976–79; Parl. Under-Sec. of State for N Ireland 1979–81, Dept of Health and Social Security 1981–82, Home Office 1982–84, Minister of State 1984–85; Minister of State Dept of Environment 1985–86; Chair. Financial Intermediaries' Mans' and Brokers' Regulatory Asscn (FIMBRA) 1987–90; Dir Andry Montgomery Ltd 1977–79, Deputy Chair. 1978–79, 1986–99; Dir Overseas Exhbns Ltd 1977–79, Bldg Trades Exhbn Ltd 1977–79; mem. Panel on Takeovers and Mergers 1987–90; Chair. Independent Enquiry into Discipline in Schools (Report 1989); Chair. Intermediate Treatment Fund 1990–93; Chair. DIVERT Trust 1993–2000, Pres. 2000–2002; Quality and Standards Cttee, City and Guilds of London Inst. 1999–2004; Deputy Chair. Asscn of Conservative Peers 1986–93; Vice-Pres. Inst. of Trading Standards Admins 1990–; mem. House of Lords Select Cttee on the Scrutiny of Delegated Powers 1994–97; mem. Select Cttee on the Constitution 2003–, Ecclesiastical Cttee (of both houses) 2002–; mem. council Rainer Foundation 1990–96, City and Guilds of London Inst. 1991–97; Licensed Lay Minister, Church of England 1998–; fmr Trustee City Parochial Foundation and Trust for London; Conservative; Hereditary Peer 1999; Hon. Vice-Pres. Inst. of Trading Standards Officers. *Leisure interest:* painting. *Address:* House of Lords, London SW1A 0PW, England (office). *Telephone:* (20) 7219-3165 (office). *Fax:* (20) 7219-5979 (office). *E-mail:* eltonr@parliament.uk (office).

ELWES, Cary; British actor; b. 26 Oct. 1962, London; s. of Dominic Elwes and Tessa Kennedy; ed Harrow School; stage debut in Equus 1981. *Films include:* Another Country 1984, Oxford Blues 1984, The Bride 1985, Lady Jane 1986, Maschenka 1987, The Princess Bride 1987, Glory 1989, Days of Thunder 1990, Hot Shots! 1990, Leather Jackets 1991, Bram Stoker's Dracula 1992, Robin Hood: Men in Tights 1992, The Crush 1993, Rudyard Kipling's Jungle Book 1994, The Chase 1994, Twister 1996, Liar Liar 1997, Kiss the Girls 1997, The Informant 1997, Quest for Camelot (voice) 1998, Cradle Will Rock 1999, Shadow of the Vampire 2000, Wish You Were Dead 2000, Saw 2004, Ella Enchanted 2004, The Bard's Tale (voice) 2004, Neo Ned 2005, Edison 2005, Pucked 2006, Walk the Talk 2007, Georgia Rule 2007. *Television includes:* Race Against Time 2000, The X Files (series) 2001–02, The Riverman 2004, Pope John Paul II 2005, Haskett's Chance 2006, Law & Order 2007. *Address:* c/o Michael Gruber, William Morris Agency, 1 William Morris Place, Beverly Hills, CA 90212, USA.

EMAN, Jan Hendrik Albert (Henny); Aruban politician and lawyer; *Leader, Arubaanse Volkspartij;* Leader Arubaanse Volkspartij (AVP); Prime Minister of Aruba and Minister of Gen. Affairs 1986–89, 1993–2001. *Address:* Arubaanse Volkspartij, Oranjestad, Aruba (office). *Telephone:* (8) 33500 (office). *Fax:* (8) 37870 (office).

EMANUEL, Elizabeth Florence, MA, DesRCA, FCSD; British fashion designer; b. 5 July 1953, London; d. of Samuel Charles Weiner and Brahna Betty Weiner; m. David Leslie Emanuel 1975 (separated 1990); one s. one d.; ed City of London School for Girls, Harrow Coll. of Art, Royal Coll. of Art; opened London salon 1978; designed wedding gown for HRH Princess of Wales 1981, costumes for Andrew Lloyd Webber's Song and Dance 1982, sets and costumes for ballet Frankenstein, The Modern Prometheus, Royal Opera House London, La Scala Milan 1985, costumes for Stoll Moss production of Cinderella 1985, costumes for film The Changeling 1995, Ros Beef 2004, uniforms for Virgin Atlantic Airways 1990, Britannia Airways 1995; launched int. fashion label Elizabeth Emanuel 1991; launched Bridal Collection for Berkertex Brides UK Ltd 1994; launched bridal collection in Japan 1994; opened new shop and design studio 1996; launched own brand label (with Richard Thompson) 1999; f. Art of Being (couture label) 2005. *Publication:* Style for All Seasons (with David Emanuel) 1982, A Dress for Diana (with David Emanuel) 2006. *Leisure interests:* ballet, cinema, writing, environmental and conservation issues. *Address:* Garden Studio, 51 Maida Vale, Little Venice, London, W9 1SD, England (home). *Telephone:* (20) 7289-4545 (home). *Fax:* (20) 7289-7584 (home). *E-mail:* info@elizabethemanuel.co.uk (home). *Website:* www.elizabethemanuel.co.uk.

EMANUEL, Kerry Andrew, PhD; American meteorologist and academic; *Professor of Meteorology, Massachusetts Institute of Technology;* b. 21 April 1955, Cincinnati; ed Massachusetts Inst. of Tech.; Adjunct Asst Prof. then Asst Prof., UCLA 1978–81; Postdoctoral Fellow, Univ. of Oklahoma Cooperative Inst. for Mesoscale Meteorological Studies 1979; Asst Prof., Dept of Meterology and Physical Oceanography, MIT 1981–83, Asst Prof. then Assoc. Prof. Center for Meteorology and Physical Oceanography and Dept of Earth, Atmospheric and Planetary Sciences 1983–87, Prof. 1987–, Dir 1989–97; mem. NAS 2007–; Carl-Gustaf Rossby Research Medal, named one of Time 100 influential people of 2006. *Achievements include:* researcher in atmospheric dynamics, has specialized in atmospheric convection and mechanisms acting to intensify hurricanes. *Publications:* Atmospheric Convection 1994, Divine Wind: The History and Science of Hurricanes 2005, What We Know About Climate Change 2007; numerous scientific papers in professional journals. *Address:* Room 54-1620, Department of Earth, Atmospheric and Planetary Sciences, Massachusetts Institute of Technology, 77 Massachusetts Avenue, Cambridge, MA 02139-4307, USA (office). *Telephone:* (617) 253-2462 (office). *Fax:* (617) 253-6208 (office). *E-mail:* emanuel@texmex.mit.edu (office). *Website:* wind.mit.edu/~emanuel/home.html (office).

EMANUEL, Rahm Israel, BA, MA; American banking executive and politician; *White House Chief of Staff;* b. 29 Nov. 1959, Chicago; ed Sarah Lawrence Coll., Northwestern Univ.; mem. campaign team for Paul Simon's election to US Senate 1984; nat. campaign dir for Democratic Congressional Campaign Cttee 1988; Sr Adviser and chief fundraiser for Richard M. Daley's campaign for Mayor of Chicago 1988–89; Nat. Financial Dir Clinton/Gore Campaign 1991–92; Asst to Pres. Bill Clinton, also Dir of Political Affairs and Deputy Dir of Communications, The White House, Washington, DC 1993–95, Dir of Special Projects and Sr Adviser for Policy and Strategy 1995–98; Man. Dir Wasserstein Perella (now Dresdner Kleinwort), Chicago 1999–2002; mem. US House of Reps from Fifth Illinois Dist 2003–09, Chair. Democratic Congressional Campaign Cttee 2005–07, House Democratic Caucus 2007–08; Chief of Staff, The White House, Washington, DC 2009–; mem. Bd of Dirs Fed. Home Loan Mortgage Corpn (Freddie Mac) 2000–01. *Publication:* The Plan: Big Ideas for Change in America (with Bruce Reed) 2009. *Address:* Office of the Chief of Staff, The White House, 1600 Pennsylvania Avenue, NW, Washington, DC 20500, USA (office). *Telephone:* (202) 456-1414 (office). *Fax:* (202) 456-2461 (office). *Website:* www.whitehouse.gov/president (office).

EMBUREY, John Ernest; British professional cricket coach and fmr professional cricketer; *Head Coach, Middlesex County Cricket Club;* b. 20 Aug. 1952, Peckham, London; s. of John Emburey and Rose (née Roff) Emburey; m. 2nd Susan Elizabeth Ann Booth 1980; two d.; ed Peckham Manor Secondary School; right-hand late-order batsman, off-break bowler, slip or gully fielder; teams: Middx 1973–95, Western Prov. 1982–84, Northants. 1996–98 (player/chief coach and man.); 64 Tests for England 1978–1995, two as capt., scored 1,713 runs (average 22.5) and took 147 wickets (average 38.4); scored 12,021 runs (seven hundreds) and took 1,608 wickets in first-class cricket; toured Australia 1978–80, 1986–87, West Indies 1981, 1986, India 1981/82, 1992/93, Pakistan 1987, New Zealand 1988, Sri Lanka 1982, 1993; 61

one-day ints (seven as capt.); mem. seven County Championship winning teams with Middx (1976, 1977, 1980, 1982, 1985, 1990, 1993), Gillette Cup 1977, 1980, Benson and Hedges Cup 1983, 1986, Sunday League Winners' trophy 1991, Natwest Trophy 1994, 1998; retd from playing 1997; Coach Middx Co. Cricket Club 2001–; Sky TV commentator; Wisden Cricketer of the Year 1984. *Publications:* Emburey – A Biography 1987, Spinning in a Fast World 1989. *Leisure interests:* golf, fishing, reading. *Address:* c/o Middlesex County Cricket Club, Lord's Cricket Ground, London, NW8 8QN, England. *Telephone:* (20) 7289-1300 (office).

EMERSON, David L., PhD; Canadian politician; b. 1944, Montreal; m. Theresa Emerson; ed Univ. of Alberta, Queen's Univ.; Researcher, Econ. Council of Canada, Ottawa 1972; Deputy Minister of Finance, BC 1984, 1990, later Deputy Minister to Premier and Pres. BC Trade Devt Corpn; Pres. and CEO Western and Pacific Bank of Canada, Vancouver 1986–90; Head, Vancouver Int. Airport Authority 1992; Pres. and CEO Canfor Corpn 1998; mem. Conservative Party of Canada; MP (Vancouver Kingsway) 2004–, Minister of Industry 2004, of Int. Trade and Minister for the Pacific Gateway and the Vancouver-Whistler Olympics 2006–2008, acting Minister for Foreign Affairs May–June 2008, Minister of Foreign Affairs 2008. *Address:* Conservative Party of Canada, 130 Albert Street, Suite 1204, Ottawa, ON K1P 5G4, Canada (office). *Telephone:* (613) 755-2000 (office). *Fax:* (613) 755-2001 (office). *Website:* www.conservative.ca (office).

EMERSON, E. Allen, BS, PhD; American computer scientist and academic; *Endowed Professor, Department of Computer Sciences, University of Texas at Austin;* ed Univ. of Texas at Austin, Harvard Univ.; currently Endowed Prof., Dept of Computer Sciences, Univ. of Texas at Austin; mem. editorial bds of leading formal methods journals and conf. programme cttees; Kanellakis Prize, Asscn for Computing Machinery (ACM) 1998, CMU Newell Prize, IEEE LICS'06 Test-of-Time Award, ACM A.M. Turing Award 2007, an Information Sciences Inst. Highly Cited Researcher. *Publications:* Methods for Mu-calculus Model Checking: A Tutorial 1995; several book chapters and numerous scientific papers in professional journals on model checking, decision procedures and algorithmic methods of program synthesis. *Address:* Department of Computer Sciences, Taylor Hall 2.124, University of Texas at Austin, Austin, TX 78712, USA (office). *Telephone:* (512) 471-9537 (office); (512) 471-7316 (Sec.) (office). *Fax:* (512) 471-8885 (office). *E-mail:* emerson@cs .utexas.edu (office). *Website:* www.cs.utexas.edu/~emerson (office).

EMERTON, Rev. John Adney, MA, DD, FBA; British ecclesiastic and academic; *Regius Professor Emeritus of Hebrew, University of Cambridge;* b. 5 June 1928, Winchmore Hill; s. of Adney Spencer Emerton and Helena Mary Emerton (née Quin); m. Norma Elizabeth Bennington 1954; one s. two d.; ed Minchenden Grammar School, Southgate, Corpus Christi Coll., Oxford and Wycliffe Hall, Oxford; ordained deacon 1952, priest 1953; Asst Lecturer in Theology, Univ. of Birmingham 1952–53; curate, Birmingham Cathedral 1952–53; Lecturer in Hebrew and Aramaic, Univ. of Durham 1953–55; Lecturer in Divinity, Univ. of Cambridge 1955–62; Visiting Prof., Trinity Coll., Univ. of Toronto 1960; Fellow, St Peter's Coll. and Reader in Semitic Philology, Univ. of Oxford 1962–68; Regius Prof. of Hebrew, Univ. of Cambridge 1968–95, Prof. Emer. 1995–; Fellow, St John's Coll. Cambridge 1970–; Sec. Int. Org. for Study of Old Testament 1971–89, Pres. 1992–95; Hon. Canon, St George's Cathedral, Jerusalem 1984–; mem. Ed. Bd Vetus Testamentum 1971–97; Visiting Fellow, Inst. for Advanced Studies, Hebrew Univ. of Jerusalem 1983; Corresp. mem. Göttingen Akad. der Wissenschaften 1990; Hon. DD (Edin.) 1977; Burkitt Medal for Biblical Studies, British Acad. 1991. *Publications:* The Peshitta of the Wisdom of Solomon 1959, The Old Testament in Syriac – The Song of Songs 1966; articles in journals. *Address:* St John's College, Cambridge CB2 1TP (office); 34 Gough Way, Cambridge, CB3 9LN, England (home). *Telephone:* (1223) 363219 (home).

EMERY, Alan Eglin Heathcote, MD, PhD, DSc, FRCP, FRCPE, FLS, FRSE, FRSA; British physician and professor of human genetics; *Chief Scientific Adviser, European Neuromuscular Centre;* b. 21 Aug. 1928, Manchester; s. of Harold Heathcote Emery and Alice Eglin; m. 2nd Marcia Lynn Miller 1988; three s. three d. from previous m.; ed Manchester Grammar School, Chester Coll., Manchester Univ. and Johns Hopkins Univ., USA; Postdoctoral Research Fellow, Johns Hopkins Univ., Baltimore 1961–64; Lecturer, then Reader in Medical Genetics, Manchester Univ. 1964–68; Foundation Prof. and Chair., Dept of Human Genetics, Univ. of Edin. 1968–83, Prof. Emer. and Hon. Fellow 1983–; Hon. Visiting Fellow, Green Coll., Oxford 1985–; Research Dir European Neuromuscular Centre and Chair. Research Cttee 1990–99, Chief. Scientific Adviser 1999–; Pres. British Clinical Genetics Soc. 1980–83; Visiting Prof., Univs of New York, Heidelberg, UCLA, Padua, Beijing, Duke, Cape Town, Warsaw, Royal Postgrad. Medical School, London, etc.; Harveian, Boerhave, Jenner Lecturer, etc.; mem. Scientific Cttee Int. Congress on Neuromuscular Diseases 1990, 1994, 1998, 2000; mem. Exec. Cttee Research Group on Neuromuscular Diseases of World Fed. of Neurology 1996–, Exec. Bd World Muscle Soc. 1999–; Adviser, Asian and Oceanian Myology Centre, Tokyo 2000–; Vice-Pres. Muscular Dystrophy Campaign of Great Britain 1999–; Pres. Section Medical Genetics, Royal Soc. of Medicine 2001–04; mem. Royal Soc. of Literature; Hon. FRS (SA); Hon. Fellow Univ. of Edin. 1990–, Gaetano Conte Acad. (Italy) 1991; Hon. mem. Dutch Soc. of Genetics 1999, Asscn of British Neurologists 1999; Hon. MD (Naples, Würzburg); Int. Award for Genetic Research (USA), Gaetano Conte Prize for Clinical Research 2000, Pro Finlandiae Gold Medal for contribs to Neuroscience 2000, Lifetime Achievement Award, WFN 2002. *Publications:* Psychological Aspects of Genetic Counselling 1984, Introduction to Recombinant DNA (2nd edn with S. Malcolm) 1995, Methodology in Medical Genetics (2nd edn) 1986, Principles and Practice of Medical Genetics (2nd edn) 1991, Elements of Medical Genetics (8th edn) 1992, The History of a Genetic Disease: Duchenne

Muscular Dystrophy or Meryon's Disease 1995, Diagnostic Criteria for Neuromuscular Disorders (2nd edn) 1997, Neuromuscular Disorders: Clinical and Molecular Genetics 1998, Muscular Dystrophy: The Facts (2nd edn) 2000, The Muscular Dystrophies 2001, Medicine and Art (with M. L. H. Emery) 2003, Duchenne Muscular Dystrophy (3rd edn) 2003, Surgical & Medical Treatment in Art (with M. L. H Emery) 2006; 300 scientific papers. *Leisure interests:* marine biology, oil painting, fly fishing. *Address:* Green College, Oxford, OX2 6HG (office); 2 Ingleside Court, Upper West Terrace, Budleigh Salterton, Devon, EX9 6NZ, England (home); European Neuromuscular Centre (ENMC), Lt.Gen. van Heutszlaan 6, 3743 JN, Baarn, Netherlands. *Telephone:* (1395) 445847 (home). *Fax:* (1395) 443855 (home). *E-mail:* enmc@euronet.nl (office). *Website:* www.enmc.org (office).

EMERY, Lin; American sculptor; b. New York City; d. of Cornell Emery and Jean Weill; m. S. B. Braselman 1962 (deceased); one s.; ed Univs of Chicago and Sorbonne, Paris; worked in studio of Ossip Zadkine, Paris 1950; 54 solo exhbns in US museums and galleries 1957–2006; int. exhbns in Tokyo, Hong Kong, Manila, Sofia, Paris, London, Berlin, Brisbane, Kyoto and Frankfurt 1961–98; public sculpture erected in Civic Center, New Orleans 1966–70, Fidelity Center, Oklahoma City 1972, Humanities Center, Columbia, SC 1974, Federal Plaza, Houma, La. 1997, Marina Centre, Singapore 1986, City of Oxnard, Calif. 1988, Osaka Dome, Japan 1997, Mitre Corpn, Alexandra, Va 2001, Schiffer Publishing Co., Atglen, Pa 2002, Sterling Corpn, Las Colinas, Tex. 2002, etc.; Visiting Prof., Tulane School of Architecture, New Orleans 1969–70, Newcomb School of Art, New Orleans 1980; Visiting Artist and Lecturer, Art Acad. of Cincinnati, La. State Univ., Univ. of New Orleans, Univ. of Tex. at Austin, Univ. of Maine 1985–88; Chair. 9th Int. Sculpture Conf. 1976, Co-Chair. Mayor's Steering Cttees, New Orleans 1979–80; Studio Chair. Coll. Art Asscn 1979; Chair. Int. Sculpture Symposium, New Orleans 2004; mem. Bd Contemporary Arts Center, New Orleans 1997–; mem. Loyola Univ. Visiting Cttee 1996–99; adviser, Artists Guild, New Orleans 1997–99; mentor, Center for Creative Arts, New Orleans 1998; mem. Nat. Acad. of Design 2003–, Int. Women's Forum 2003–, Century Asscn, New York; Order of St Lazarus Companionate of Merit 2004; Hon. LHD (Loyola Univ.) 2004; Mayor's Award for Achievement in the Arts, La. 1980, Lazlo Aranyi Award for Public Art, Va 1990, Delgado Award for Artistic Excellence, La. 1997, Grand Prix for Public Sculpture (Japan) 1997, Gov.'s Arts Award, La. 2001, S. Simon Award Nat. Acad. 2005. *Address:* 7520 Dominican Street, New Orleans, LA 70118, USA (home). *Telephone:* (504) 866-7775 (home). *Fax:* (504) 866-0144 (home). *E-mail:* lin@linemery.com (office).

EMIN, Tracey, RA; British artist; b. 1964, Margate; ed John Cass School of Art, London, Maidstone Coll. of Art, Royal Coll. of Art; f. Tracey Emin Museum, London 1996; Int. Award for Video Art, Baden-Baden 1997, Video Art Prize, Südwest Bank, Stuttgart 1997. *Art work:* 'The Roman Standard' (commissioned by the BBC for Art05 Festival, Upper Duke Street, Liverpool) 2005. *Films include:* Why I Never Became a Dancer, Top Spot (dir) 2004. *Publications:* Exploration of the Soul 1995, Always Glad to See You 1997, Tracey Emin: Holiday Inn 1998, Tracey Emin on Pandaemonium 1998, Absolute Tracey 1998, Strangeland 2005. *Leisure interests:* writing poetry, watching sunsets. *Address:* c/o White Cube, 48 Hoxton Square, London, N1 6PB, England (office). *Telephone:* (20) 7930-5373 (office). *Website:* www.whitecube.com/artists/emin (office).

EMINEM, (Slim Shady); American rap artist and musician; b. (Marshall Bruce Mathers III), 17 Oct. 1972, St Joseph, MO; m. Kim Mathers (divorced); one d.; moved to Detroit aged 12; dropped out of high school to join local rap groups Basement Productions, D12; released debut album The Infinite on ind. label FBT; after releasing Slim Shady EP, made guest appearances with Kid Rock and Shabbam Shadeeq, leading to deal with Dr Dre's Aftermath Records; collaborations with artists, including Dr Dre, D12, Missy Elliott, Dido; founder and owner Slim Shady record label 1999–, Eight Mile Style publishing co.; MTV Annual American Music Awards Best Hip Hop Artist 2000, 2002, three Grammy Awards 2001, Best Pop/Rock Male Artist 2002, MTV Europe Music Awards Best Male Act, Best Hip Hop Act 2002, BRIT Award for Best Int. Male Solo Artist 2003, 2005, American Music Awards for Best Male Pop/Rock Artist, Best Male Hip Hop/R&B Artist 2003, Acad. Award for Best Music (for Lose Yourself, from film 8 Mile) 2004, Grammy Award for Best Male Rap Solo Performance (for Lose Yourself) 2004, Grammy Award for Best Rap Song (for Lose Yourself) 2004, Echo Award for Best Int. Hip Hop Artist, Germany 2005, Smash Hits Award for Best Hip-Hop Act 2005, American Music Award for Favorite Male Rap/Hip-Hop Artist 2005, 2006. *Film:* 8 Mile 2002. *Recordings include:* albums: The Infinite 1997, The Slim Shady LP 1999, The Marshall Mathers LP (MTV Award for Best Album) 2000, The Eminem Show (MTV Award for Best Album 2002, Grammy Award for Best Rap Album, BRIT Award for Best Int. Album, American Music Awards for Best Pop/Rock Album, Best Hip Hop/R&B Album 2003) 2002, Eminem Is Back 2004, Encore 2004, Curtain Call 2005, Eminem Presents The Re Up 2006, Relapse 2009. *Publication:* Angry Blonde 2000, The Way I Am (auto-biog.) 2008. *Address:* c/o Paul Rosenberg, Goliath Artists, 151 Lafayette Street, New York, NY 10013, USA (office). *Telephone:* (212) 324-2410 (office). *Fax:* (212) 324-2415 (office). *Website:* www.shadyrecords.com; www.eminem.com.

EMMANUELLI, Henri Joseph; French politician; *Chairman, Conseil général des Landes;* b. 31 May 1945, Eaux-Bonnes, Pyrénées-Atlantiques; s. of the late Louis Emmanuelli and of Julie Chourre; m. Antonia Gonzalez 1967; one s. one d.; ed Lycée Louis-Barthou, Pau, Institut d'études politiques de Paris; mem. staff Banque de l'Union Parisienne, then Compagnie financière de banque 1969–78; Deputy for Landes 1978–82, 1986–93, 1993–97, 2000–; Chair. Conseil général, Landes 1982–98, 2000–; Sec. of State for Overseas Territories and Depts 1981–83, for Budget 1983–86; Chair. Finance Comm. of Nat. Ass. 1991–93, Pres. Nat. Ass. 1992–93, Pres. Comm. for Finances, Gen.

Econs and Planning 1997, 2000–; mem. Nat. Secr. Parti Socialiste 1987–, Leader 1994–95. *Publications:* Plaidoyer pour l'Europe 1992, Citadelles interdites 2000. *Leisure interests:* skiing, swimming. *Address:* Assemblée nationale, 75355 Paris; Parti Socialiste, 10 rue de Solférino, 75333 Paris Cedex, France; 22–24 rue Victor Hugo, 40000 Mont-de-Marsan (office). *E-mail:* presidence@cg40.fr (office); hemmanuelli@assemblee-nationale.fr (office).

EMMERICH, Roland; film director, screenwriter and film producer; b. 10 Nov. 1955; film produced as student Das Arche Noah Prinzip (The Noah's Ark Principle) shown at 1984 Berlin Film Festival and sold to more than 20 countries; f. Centropolis Film Productions. *Films include:* Franzmann 1979, Das Arche Noah Prinzip 1984, Joey 1985, Hollywood-Monster 1987, Moon 44 1990, Eye of the Storm (producer) 1991, Universal Soldier 1992, Stargate 1994, The High Crusade (producer) 1994, Independence Day 1996, Godzilla 1998, The Thirteenth Floor (producer) 1999, The Patriot 2000, Eight Legged Freaks (producer) 2002, The Day After Tomorrow 2004, 10,000 BC 2008, 2012 2009. *TV:* (series) The Visitor (producer) 1997. *Address:* c/o Creative Artists Agency, 9830 Wilshire Boulevard, Beverly Hills, CA 90212, USA.

EMMERT, Mark A., BA, MPA, PhD; American university administrator, political scientist and academic; *President, University of Washington;* b. 16 Dec. 1952, Tacoma, Wash.; m. DeLaine S. Emmert; one s. one d.; ed Univ. of Washington, Maxwell School, Syracuse Univ.; various public service roles 1976–80; Univ. Fellow and Research Asst, Maxwell School, Syracuse Univ. 1980–83; Research Assoc., Center for Governmental Studies, then Asst Prof., Dept of Political Science, Northern Illinois Univ. 1983–85; held faculty and admin. positions at Univ. of Colorado, including Assoc. and Asst Prof., Grad. School of Public Affairs, Assoc. Dean Grad. School of Public Affairs, Assoc. Vice-Chancellor for Academic Affairs, Univ. of Colorado, Denver and Pres.'s Office, Boulder and Denver Campuses 1985–92; Prof. of Political Science, Provost and Vice-Pres. for Academic Affairs, Montana State Univ. 1992–95; Prof. of Political Science, Chancellor and Provost Univ. of Connecticut 1995–99; Prof., E. J. Ourso Coll. of Business Admin and Chancellor Louisiana State Univ. 1999–2004; Prof., Evans School of Public Affairs and Pres. Univ. of Washington 2004–, mem. Univ. of Washington Medicine Bd; Guest of Ministry of Educ., People's Repub. of China; Visiting Scholar and Guest of Monash Univ., Melbourne, Australia; lectured and conducted training programs in Hong Kong, Okinawa, Panama City, Guam, US Micronesia, Germany, France and Mexico; consultant and trainer, Asscn of Governing Bds, San Antonio Art Inst., Colorado State Univ., Vision Hispanica, Colorado Gov.'s Business-Educ. Summit, Educ.-Policy Fellowship Program for the Inst. for Educational Leadership, Univ. of Oklahoma, Minnesota State Univ. System, Rochester Inst. of Tech.; Chair. Louisiana Univs Marine Consortium 2002; Chair. Pres.'s Council Southern Univs Research Asscn 2001–02; Co-Chair. Prosperity Partnership 2005–; mem. New England Council of Pres 1994–99, New England Asscn of Schools and Colls 1998–99, Educ. Comm. of the States, Commr for Louisiana 2000–04, Univ. Research Asscn (Pres Council 2000–04), Cttee Exec. Southeastern Conf. 2002–04, Exec. Council Southern Asscn of Schools and Colls 2000–04, Nat. Visiting Cttee Arizona State Univ. 2004–, American Asscn of Colls and Univs 2005–, Asscn of American Univs, Nat. Security Higher Educ. Advisory Bd 2005–, Asscn of Governing Bds of Univs and Colls Council of Pres 2005–, Nat. Asscn of State Univs and Land-Grant Colls (Co-Chair. Bd on Oceans and Atmosphere), American Council on Educ., Council of Fellows, Comm. on Leadership and Institutional Effectiveness, Nat. Collegiate Athletic Asscn Presidential Task Force on the Future of Intercollegiate Athletics Fiscal Responsibility Sub-cttee, Pac-10 Conf. of CEOs 2005–; Charter mem. Asscn of Pacific Rim Univs 2005–; fmr Dir Josephson Inst. of Ethics Bd, Louisiana Research Park Corpn, Shaw Center for the Arts, Baton Rouge Chamber of Commerce; Leadership mem. and Campaign Cabinet, Capital Area United Way; mem. Organizing Cttee Summer Nat. Sr Games 2001; mem. Advisory Bd Policy Consensus Center, Seattle Community Devt Roundtable 2005–, Gov.'s Global Competitiveness Council 2005– (mem. Research and Innovation Sub-cttee), Puget Sound Partnership; fmr mem. Bd of Dirs Baton Rouge Center for World Affairs; Trustee Greater Seattle Chamber of Commerce 2006–; mem. Conn. Acad. of Arts and Sciences; American Council on Educ. Fellow, J. W. Fulbright Admin. Fellow, Germany 1991, J. W. Fulbright Sr Admin. Seminar, Germany 1994, Gambit Magazine Baton Rouge Citizen of the Year 2000, Good Growth Award, Baton Rouge Business Report and Growth Council 2003, Marketer of the Year, Sales and Marketing Execs Asscn 2003. *Publications:* numerous journal articles, monographs, book chapters and tech. reports. *Leisure interests:* boating, golf, scuba diving, fly-fishing, skiing, reading. *Address:* Office of the President, University of Washington, 301 Gerberding Hall, Box 351230, Seattle, WA 98195-1230, USA (office). *Telephone:* (206) 543-5010 (office). *Fax:* (206) 616-1784 (office). *E-mail:* pres@u.washington.edu (office). *Website:* www.washington.edu (office).

EMMOTT, William (Bill) John, BA; British journalist; b. 6 Aug. 1956; s. of Richard Emmott and Audrey Emmott; m. 1st Charlotte Crowther 1982 (divorced); m. 2nd Carol Barbara Mawer 1992; ed Latymer Upper School, Hammersmith and Magdalen and Nuffield Colls, Oxford; Brussels Corresp., The Economist 1980–82, Econs Corresp. 1982–83, Tokyo Corresp. 1983–86, Finance Ed. 1986–89, Business Affairs Ed. 1989–93, Ed.-in-Chief 1993–2006, Editorial Dir Economist Intelligence Unit May–Dec. 1992; Hon. Fellow, Magdalen Coll., Oxford 2002; Hon. LLD (Warwick) 1999; Hon. DLitt (City) 2001. *Publications:* The Pocket Economist (with R. Pennant-Rea) 1983, The Sun Also Sets 1989, Japanophobia 1993, Kanryo no Taizai 1996, 20:21 Vision: The Lessons of the 20th Century for the 21st 2003. *Leisure interests:* cricket, dog-walking, journalism. *Address:* c/o The Economist, 25 St James's Street, London, SW1A 1HG, England (office).

EMOTO, Kanji; Japanese steel industry executive; *Chairman, Co-CEO and Representative Director, JFE Holdings Incorporated;* Chair., Co-CEO and Rep. Dir JFE Holdings Inc.; Chair. Kawasaki Steel Corpn (KSC) –2003; Dir Energy Conservation Center (ECC), Tokyo. *Address:* JFE Holdings Incorporated, 1-1-2 Marunouchi, Chiyoda-ku, Tokyo 100-0005, Japan (office). *Telephone:* (3) 3217-4049 (office). *Fax:* (3) 3214-6110 (office). *Website:* www.jfe-holdings.co.jp (office).

EMOVON, Emmanuel Uwumagbuhunmwun, PhD; Nigerian professor of chemistry and government minister; b. 24 Feb. 1929, Benin City; s. of late Gabriel A. Emovon and Oni Emovon; m. Princess Adesuwa C. Akenzua 1959; three s. three d.; ed Baptist School, Benin City, Edo Coll., Benin City, Univ. Coll., Ibadan, Univ. Coll., London Univ., UK; Lecturer in Chem., Univ. Coll. Ibadan 1959; Prof. of Chem., Univ. of Benin 1971; Vice-Chancellor Univ. of Jos 1978; Fed. Minister of Science and Tech. 1985–89; Co-ordinator, Sheda Science and Tech. Complex 1990, now retd; invested Chief Obayagbona of Benin 1991; fmr mem. numerous govt cttees and bds; fmr external examiner; Fellow Science Asscn of Nigeria, Nigerian Acad. of Science; nat. mem. ICSU 1986. *Publications:* numerous scientific papers. *Leisure interests:* photography, gardening, tennis, table tennis, cricket and football. *Address:* c/o Sheda Science and Technology Complex, Ministry of Science and Technology, P.M.B. 186, Garki, Abuja, Nigeria.

EMPEY, Sir Reginald Norman Morgan, BSc, OBE; British politician; *Leader, Ulster Unionist Party;* b. 26 Oct. 1947; s. of Samuel Frederick Empey and Emily Winifred Empey (née Morgan); m. Stella Ethna Donnan 1977; one s. one d.; ed The Royal School, Armagh, Queen's Univ., Belfast; Publicity Officer, Ulster Young Unionist Council 1967–68, Vice-Chair. 1968–72; Chair. Vanguard Unionist Party 1974–75; mem. E Belfast NI Constitutional Convention 1975–76; Deputy Lord Mayor 1988–89, Lord Mayor of Belfast 1989–90, 1993–94; mem. Belfast East, NI Ass. 1998–2002 (Ass. suspended Oct. 2002); Minister of Enterprise, Trade and Investment 1999–2002; mem. Belfast City Council 1985–, Ulster Unionist Council 1987– (Hon. Sec. 1990–96, Vice-Pres. 1996–); Bd mem. Police Authority for NI 1992–, European Cttee of the Regions for NI 1994–; mem. Ulster Unionist Party, Leader 2005–. *Leisure interests:* gardening, walking. *Address:* Ulster Unionist Party, 1st Floor, 174 Albertbridge Road, Belfast, BT5 4GS, Northern Ireland (office). *Telephone:* (28) 9046-3200 (office). *Fax:* (28) 9045-6899 (office). *E-mail:* uup@uup.org (office). *Website:* www.uup.org (office).

EMSIS, Indulis, PhD; Latvian politician and biologist; b. 2 Jan. 1952, Salacgrīva, Limbazi Dist; m.; one d.; ed Riga First Secondary School, Univ. of Latvia, Moscow Scientific Research Inst.; Head, Lab. of Environmental Protection 1978–89; Deputy Chair. Nature Preservation Cttee 1989–90; mem. Supreme Council, Chair. Latvian Environmental Protection Cttee 1990–93; Minister of State, Ministry for Environmental Protection and Regional Devt 1993–98; Deputy Chair. SIA Eirokonsultants 1998–2000, Dir-Gen. SIA Eiroprojekts 2000–02; mem. Riga City Council 2000–02, Deputy Chair. Devt Cttee; mem. 6th Saeima (Parl.) 1993–98, 8th Saeima 2002–04, 9th Saeima 2006–, Speaker 2006–07; Prime Minister of Latvia March–Dec. 2004; mem. Latvian Green Party (part of Greens' and Farmers' Union) 1990–, currently Co-Chair.; Three Star Order (Third Degree) 1996; Award of the Baltic Sea Foundation for Outstanding Contribs to Protection of the Marine Environment, Certificate of Merit of the Cabinet of Ministers of the Repub. of Latvia. *Address:* c/o Office of the Speaker, Saeima, Jekaba iela 11, Rīga 1811, Latvia. *Telephone:* 7087-111. *E-mail:* Indulis.Emsis@saeima.lv (office). *Website:* www.saeima.lv (office).

ENAHORO, Chief Anthony, C.FR.; Nigerian politician, journalist, newspaper publisher and company director; b. 22 July 1923, Uromi Ishan, Bendel State; s. of late Chief Okotako Enahoro and Princess Inibokun Okoje; m. Helen Ediae 1954; four s. one d.; ed Govt Schools Uromi and Owo, King's Coll. Lagos; journalist 1942–52; Ed. Southern Nigerian Defender 1944–45, Daily Comet 1945–49; Assoc. Ed. West African Pilot; Ed.-in-Chief Nigerian Star 1950–52; foundation mem. Action Group Party, later Acting Gen. Sec. and Fed. Vice-Pres.; Chair. Uromi Dist Council and Ishan Div. Council; mem. Western House of Assembly and Fed. House of Reps and Party Chief Whip 1951–54; Dir Nat. Coal Bd 1953–56; Minister of Home Affairs, Transport, Information and Midwest Affairs and Leader of the House (Western Region) 1954–59; Fed. MP and Opposition Spokesman on Foreign Affairs, Internal Affairs and Legislature Affairs 1959–63; moved motion for self-govt and attended all constitutional talks preceding independence in 1960; detained during Emergency period Western Region 1962, fled to Britain, extradited and imprisoned in Nigeria for treasonable felony; released by mil. govt 1966; Leader, Midwest State del. to Constitutional Conf. and mem. Constitutional Cttee 1966; Fed. Commr for Information, Culture, Youth, Sports, Co-operatives and Labour 1967–75; mem. Nat. Democratic Coalition (NADECO); Fed. Commr for Special Duties 1975; Pres. World Black and African Festival of Arts and Culture 1972–75; State Chair. Nat. Party of Nigeria 1978–80; Chair. Cttees Edo State Movt 1981–, Nigerian Shippers Council 1982; detained Aug.–Dec. 1994; Hon. DSc (Benin) 1972. *Publication:* Fugitive Offender (autobiog.). *Leisure interests:* golf, reading, travel. *Address:* Rainbow House, 144 Upper Mission Road, P.M.B. 1425, Benin City, Nigeria. *Telephone:* 200803 (office); 243770 (home).

ENCINAS RODRÍGUEZ, Alejandro, BEcons; Mexican politician; *President, Partido de la Revolución Democrática;* b. 13 May 1954, Mexico City; ed Univ. Nacional Autónoma de México; mem. Cámara Federal de Diputados (Partido Revolucionario Institucional— PRI) 1985–88, mem. (Partido de la Revolución Democrática— PRD) 1991–94; adviser, ECLAC 1990, Inter-American Inst. for Co-operation on Agric. 1991; Head, Mexico City Govt 2005–06; Pres. PRD 2008–. *Address:* Partido de la Revolución Democrática, Avda Benjamín Franklin 84, Col. Escandón, 11800 México DF, Mexico (office). *Telephone:*

(55) 1085-8000 (office). *Fax:* (55) 1085-8144 (office). *E-mail:* comunicacion@prd .org (office). *Website:* www.prd.org.mx (office).

ENDARA GALIMANY, Guillermo; Panamanian politician and lawyer; b. 12 May 1936, Panamá; m. 1st (died 1989); m. 2nd Ana Mae Díaz 1990; ed Tulane Univ., Univ. of Panamá, New York Univ. School of Law; labour lawyer; fmr Prof. of Business Law, Univ. of Panamá; aide to fmr Pres. of Panamá, Arnulfo Arias Madrid; leader Alianza Democrática Oposicionista y Civilista (ADOC); mem. Nat. Democratic Coalition (NADECO); Pres. of Panamá 1989–94. *Address:* c/o Oficina del Presidente, Palacio Presidencial, Valija 50, Panamá 1, Panama.

ENDERBY, Sir John Edwin, Kt, KB, CBE, FRS, DSc, PhD; British scientist and academic; *Chairman, Melys Diagnostics Ltd;* b. 16 Jan. 1931, Grimsby; s. of late Thomas Edwin Enderby and Rheita Rebecca Hollinshead Enderby; m. Susan Bowles; one s. two d.; one s. (deceased) one d. from previous marriage; ed Chester Grammar School, Westminster Coll., Birbeck Coll., Univ. of London; lecturer then Reader Univ. of Sheffield 1960–69; Prof. and Head of Dept Univ. of Leicester 1969–76; Prof. of Physics Univ. of Bristol 1976–81; H. H. Wills Prof. 1981–96, Prof. Emer. 1996–, Head of Dept, Dir H. H. Wills Lab. 1981–94; Directeur-Adjoint Inst. Laue-Langevin, Grenoble, France (on secondment) 1985–88; Ed. Proc. of the Royal Soc. 'A' 1989–93; Ed.-in-Chief Journal of Physics: Condensed Matter 1997–2001; Physical Sec. and Vice-Pres. of the Royal Soc. 1999–2004; Pres. Inst. of Physics 2004–06; Chair. Melys Diagnostics Ltd 2004–; mem. Council PPARC 1994–98; Chief Scientific Adviser, Inst. of Physics Publishing 2002; Distinguished Argonne Fellow (USA); Hon. Fellow, Birbeck Coll., Univ. of London 2001, Foreign Mem. Royal Holland Acad. of Science and Humanities 2001; Hon. DSc (Loughborough) 1998, (Leicester) 2006, (Bristol) 2006, (Sheffield) 2007, (East Anglia) 2007; Guthrie Medal and Prize, Inst. of Physics 1995. *Publications:* numerous papers on liquids in learned journals. *Leisure interests:* travel, woodwork, music, reading. *Address:* Melys Diagnostics Ltd, Whitland Abbey, Whitland, Carmarthenshire, SA34 0LG, Wales (office); H. H. Wills Physics Laboratory, University of Bristol, Tyndall Avenue, Bristol, BS8 1TL (office); 7 Cotham Lawn Road, Bristol BS6 6DU, England (home). *Telephone:* (1994) 240265 (Wales) (office); (117) 928-8737 (office); (117) 973-3411 (home). *Fax:* (1994) 241176 (Wales) (home); (117) 925-5624. *E-mail:* dawoodp@aol.com. *Website:* www.iop.org; www.melysdiagnostics.com (office).

ENDERS, Thomas, PhD; German aeronautics industry executive; *CEO, Airbus SAS;* b. 21 Dec. 1958; ed Univ. of Bonn, UCLA, USA; served with 1st Airborne Div., Bundeswehr 1977–78, completed officer training, Maj. in Army Reserve Forces 1978–83; Asst. Fed. Parl., Bonn 1982–85; Research Assoc., Research Inst. of Konrad Adenauer Foundation, St Augustin 1985–87, Research Inst. of German Council on Foreign Affairs, Bonn 1988–89; Sr Research Assoc., IISS, London, UK 1989–90; mem. Planning Staff, Minister of Defence 1989–91; joined aeronautics mfr MBB (later Dasa and now part of EADS) 1991, served in various marketing posts 1991–95, Corp. Sec. and Head of Office of Chair. 1995–96, Dir of Corp. Devt and Tech. 1996–2000, apptd Head of Defence and Security Systems Div. 2000; mem. Exec. Cttee and CEO Defence and Security Systems Div., European Aeronautic Defence and Space Co. (EADS) NV 2000–05, Co-CEO EADS 2005–07; CEO Airbus SAS 2007–; Pres. German Aerospace Industries Asscn (BDLI) 2005–; Chair. Atlantik-Brücke e.V. 2005–. *Address:* Airbus SAS, 1, Rond Point Maurice Bellonte, 31707 Blagnac, France (office). *Telephone:* 5-61-93-33-33 (office). *Fax:* 5-61-93-49-55 (office). *Website:* www.airbus.com (office).

ENDICOTT, Timothy Andrew Orville, AB, MPhil, LLB, DPhil; Canadian lawyer and academic; *Professor of Legal Philosophy and Dean, Faculty of Law,, University of Oxford;* ed Harvard Coll., USA, Univ. of Oxford, Univ. of Toronto, Canada; barrister and solicitor, Osler, Hoskin & Harcourt LLP (law firm), Toronto 1988–91; Tutor in Law, Univ. of Oxford 1994–, Stipendiary Lecturer, Jesus Coll. 1994–95, Stipendiary Lecturer, St Anne's Coll. 1995–96, Lecturer, St Catherine's Coll. 1996–99, Fellow, 1998–99, Fellow, Balliol Coll. 1999–, Examiner 2001–03, Dir of Grad. Studies, Faculty of Law 2004–, Prof. of Legal Philosophy 2006–, Dean, Faculty of Law 2007–; fmr External Examiner, Univ. Coll., London; fmr Examiner for Research Degrees, Univ. of London, Univ. of Toronto, Univ. of Birmingham, Univ. of Melbourne; currently External Examiner, King's Coll., Univ. of London; Rhodes Scholar, Univ. of Oxford 1983–85. *Publications:* Vagueness in Law 2000, Properties of Law (co-ed.) 2006, Administrative Law 2009. *Address:* Balliol College, University of Oxford, Oxford, OX1 3BJ, England (office). *Telephone:* (1865) 277754 (office). *E-mail:* timothy.endicott@law.ox.ac.uk (office). *Website:* www.law.ox.ac.uk (office).

ENDO, Akira, PhD; Japanese scientist and academic; *Director, Biopharm Research Laboratories, Inc.;* b. 1933, Akita; ed Faculty of Agric., Tohoku Univ.; joined Sankyo Co. Ltd 1957, later Head of Lab. of Fermentation Research Labs; fmr Research Assoc., Albert Einstein Coll. of Medicine; fmr Prof., Dept of Agricultural Chem., Faculty of Agric., Tokyo Univ. of Agric. and Tech.; Dir Biopharm Research Laboratories, Inc. 1997–; Japan Prize, The Science and Tech. Foundation of Japan 2006, Albert Lasker Award for Clinical Medical Research, Lasker Foundation 2008. *Achievements include:* discovered first cholesterol-lowering statin drug. *Publications:* numerous scientific papers in professional journals. *Address:* Biopharm Research Laboratories, Inc., 3-41-3, 501 Shimorenjaku, Mitaka, Tokyo, Japan (office). *E-mail:* info@biopharmgroup.com (office). *Website:* www.biopharmgroup.com (office).

ENDZIŅŠ, Aivars, DrIur; Latvian lawyer; *Chairman, Constitutional Court of Latvia;* b. 8 Dec. 1940, Rīga; m.; two s.; ed Univ. of Latvia, Moscow State Univ.; lecturer, Assoc. Prof., Univ. of Latvia 1972–90, 1996–97; Assoc. Prof. Police Acad. 1998–, Prof. 2002–; mem. Supreme Council, Presidium Supreme Council 1990–93; mem. Saeima (Parl.), Vice-Chair. Legal Affairs Cttee

1993–96; Acting Chair., then Chair. Constitutional Court 1996–; mem. Parl. Ass., Council of Europe 1995–96; Assoc. mem. Democracy Through Law Comm. (Venice Comm.) 1992–95, mem. 1995–, mem. Bureau 1991–2001; Order of Three Stars 2001, Grand Officer Repub. of Italy 2004. *Publications:* more than 60 academic publs. *Leisure interests:* fishing, hunting. *Address:* Constitutional Court, J. Alunāna iela 1, Rīga 1010 (office); No. 31 Drustu St, Rīga 1002, Latvia (home). *Telephone:* 7830750 (office); 793-4654 (home). *Fax:* 7830770 (office). *E-mail:* aivars.e@satv.tiesa.gov.lv (office). *Website:* www.satv.tiesa.gov.lv (office).

ENESTAM, Jan-Erik, MPolSci; Finnish politician; *Secretary-General, Nordic Council;* b. 12 March 1947, Västanfjärd; m. Solveig V. Dahlqvist 1970; three c.; tourism researcher, Åland Provincial Govt 1972–74; researcher, Finnish Tourist Bd 1974; Head of Office, Åland Provincial Govt 1974–78; Municipal Man. Västanfjärd 1978–83; Project Man. Nordic Council of Ministers 1983–91; mem. Regional Policy Advisory Bd 1987–91; mem. Parl. 1991–; Chair. Västanfjärd Municipal Council 1989–96; Special Adviser to Minister of Defence 1990–91; Minister of Defence and Minister at Ministry of Social Affairs (Equality) and Health Jan.–April 1995; Minister of the Interior 1995–99, Minister of Defence, Nordic Co-operation and Foreign Affairs (Adjacent Areas) 1999–2003, of the Environment and Foreign Affairs (Nordic Co-operation) 2003–07; Deputy Chair. Cen. Fed. of Fishing Industry 1986–94; Vice-Pres. Svenska Folkpartiet – SFP (Swedish People's Party) Parl. Group 1991–94, Chair. SFP 1998–2006; Sec.-Gen. Nordic Council 2007–; Commdr, Order of the White Rose of Finland 1996, Kt (Third Class), Order of Grand Duke Gediminas (Lithuania) 1997, Cross of Merit with Clasp, Armour Guild; Medal for Mil. Merit 1995, Medal of Merit, Cen. Chamber of Commerce of Finland. *Leisure interests:* literature, cross-country skiing, swimming, football, canoeing, cooking. *Address:* Nordic Council, Store Strandstræde 18, 1255 Copenhagen K, Denmark (office). *Telephone:* 33-96-04-00 (office). *Fax:* 33-11-18-70 (office). *E-mail:* jee@norden.org (office). *Website:* www.norden.org (office).

ENGEL, Johannes K.; German journalist and editor; b. 29 April 1927, Berlin; s. of Karl and Anna (née Helke) Engel; m. Ruth Moter 1951; one s. one d.; journalist, Int. News Service and Der Spiegel magazine 1946–, office man., Frankfurt am Main 1948, Dept Head 1951, Ed.-in-Chief, Hamburg 1961, co-Ed.-in-Chief Der Spiegel (with Erich Böhme) 1973–86. *Address:* Kirchenredder 7, 22339 Hamburg, Germany. *Telephone:* 30071 (office).

ENGELBRECHT, Jüri; Estonian physicist, mathematician and academic; *Professor, Institute of Cybernetics, Tallinn Technical University;* b. 1 Aug. 1939, Tallinn; m.; two c.; ed Tallinn Tech. Univ.; Sr lecturer Tallinn Tech. Univ.; Sr researcher, head of Dept, Deputy Dir Inst. of Cybernetics Estonian Acad. of Sciences 1968–94; part-time assoc., then Prof. Tallinn Tech. Univ. 1974–92, 1994–; Adjunct Prof. Helsinki Univ. of Tech.; mem. Estonian Acad. of Sciences 1990, Pres. 1994–; Chair. Estonian Cttee for Mechanics 1991–; mem. numerous socs and cttees; Ed.-in-Chief Proc. of the Estonian Acad. of Sciences 1991–95; Ed. Research Reports in Physics 1988–93; mem. Ed. Bd Prikladnaya Mekhanika and several other journals; mem. Estonian Soc. for Physics, New York Acad. of Sciences, European Acad. of Sciences and Arts, Accad. Peloritana dei Pericolanti, Italy, Latvian Acad. of Sciences, Hungarian Acad. of Sciences, Gothenburg Royal Soc. of Sciences and Arts, World Innovation Foundation; Kt White Rose 1st Class (Finland), Coat of Arms 4th Class (Estonia), Lion Grand Cross (Finland); Dr hc (Budapest); Estonian Science Prize, Humboldt Research Award 1993. *Publications:* Nonlinear Deformation Waves 1981, Nonlinear Wave Processes of Deformation in Solids 1983, Nonlinear Evolution Equations 1986, An Introduction to Asymmetric Solitary Waves 1991, Nonlinear Dynamics and Chaos 1993, Nonlinear Wave Dynamics: Complexity and Simplicity 1997, and more than 200 scientific articles. *Address:* Institute of Cybernetics, Tallinn Technical University, Akadeemia tee 21, Tallinn EE12617, Estonia (office). *Telephone:* (2) 644-21-29 (office). *Fax:* (2) 645-18-05. *Website:* www.akadeemia.ee (office).

ENGELL, Hans; Danish politician, columnist, author and newspaper editor; b. 8 Oct. 1948, Copenhagen; s. of Knud Engell Andersen; ed Coll. of Journalism; journalist for Berlingske newspaper consortium 1968–78; Head of Press Service of Conservative People's Party 1978–82; mem. Parl. 1984–, Minister for Defence 1982–87, of Justice 1989–93; Chair. Conservative Parl. Group 1987–89; Leader Conservative People's Party 1995–97; Ed.-in-Chief Ekstra Bladet 2000–07; Commdr Order of Dannebrog, Grand Commdr Order of Benemerencia. *Address:* Puggaardsgade 13, 1573 Copenhagen, Denmark (home). *Telephone:* 33-13-09-13 (office). *E-mail:* hans.engell@eb.dk (office).

ENGEN, Travis, BS; American business executive (retd); *Chairman, The Prince of Wales International Business Leaders Forum (IBLF);* b. 1944, Calif.; m.; one d.; ed MIT; held various man. positions at Bell Aerospace including dir of electronics; Dir Marketing Republic Electronic Industries Group 1976–79; Dir Govt Avionics, Bendix Avionics Div. 1980–83; Vice-Pres. and Gen. Man., Bendix Gen. Aviation Avionics Div. 1983–85; Pres. and Gen. Man. ITT Avionics 1985–1986, Pres. and CEO ITT Defence, Exec. Vice-Pres. ITT Corpn 1991–94, CEO ITT Industries, 1995; Dir Alcan Inc. 1996–2006, Pres. and CEO 2001–06 (retd); Dir Lyondell Chemical Co., Int. Aluminium Inst., Canadian Council of Chief Execs; mem. US Govt Defense Business Practice Implementation Bd; Chair. World Business Council for Sustainable Devt, Prince of Wales Int. Business Leaders Forum 2005–. *Leisure interest:* racing vintage cars. *Address:* c/o The Prince of Wales International Business Leaders Forum (IBLF), 15-16 Cornwall Terrace Regent's Park, London, NW1 4QP, England (office). *Website:* www.iblf.org.

ENGHOLM, Björn, DIPL.-POL.; German politician; b. 9 Nov. 1939, Lübeck; m.; two d.; ed Acad. of Econs and Politics, Hamburg and Univ. of Hamburg; apprentice printer 1959–62, Journeyman's Certificate 1962; joined SPD 1962, mem. governing Bd 1984–; lecturer and freelance journalist 1964–69; mem. Bundestag 1969–82; Parl. State Sec. Ministry of Educ. and Science 1977–81, Minister 1981–82, Opposition Leader Landstag of Schleswig-Holstein 1983–88, Minister-Pres. 1988–93; Chair. SDP 1990–93. *Address:* Jürgen-Wullenwever-Str. 9, 23566 Lübeck, Germany.

ENGIBOUS, Thomas (Tom) J., MSc; American electronics industry executive; *Chairman, Texas Instruments Inc.;* ed Purdue Univ.; joined Texas Instruments Inc. (TI) 1976, Exec. Vice-Pres. 1993–96, Pres. Semiconductor group 1993–96, Pres. and CEO TI 1996–2004, mem. Bd of Dirs 1996–, Chair. 2004–; Chair. Catalyst org.; Dir J. C. Penney Co. Inc., Dallas Citizens Council, Southwest Medical Foundation, US–Japan Business Council, Nat. Center for Educational Accountability; mem. Eng Visiting Cttee, Purdue Univ.; mem. Nat. Acad. of Eng, Inst. of Electrical and Electronics Engineers; Trustee Southern Methodist Univ.; Hon. DEng (Purdue Univ.) 1997. *Address:* Texas Instruments Inc., 12500 TI Boulevard, Dallas, TX 75266-4136, USA (office). *Telephone:* (972) 995-2011 (office). *Website:* www.ti.com (office).

ENGL, Walter L., Dr rer. nat, FIEEE; German professor of engineering; b. 8 April 1926, Regensburg; ed Technical Univ. of Munich; Siemens Instrument and Control Div. 1950–63, latterly Head of Research Div.; Prof., Tech. Univ. of Aachen 1963–91, Dean Faculty of Eng 1968–69; Visiting Prof., Univ. of Arizona 1967, Stanford Univ. 1970, Univ. of Tokyo 1972, 1980; Hon. Prof. Univ. of Kiel 1992; mem. Acad. of Science of North Rhine-Westphalia; mem. Int. Union of Radio Science; Foreign Assoc. mem. Eng Acad. of Japan; VDE-Ehrenring (highest award of German Electrical Engineers Soc.). *Publications:* 100 publs. *Address:* Zum Heider Busch 5, 52134 Herzogenrath, Germany (home). *E-mail:* w.l.engl@web.de (home).

ENGLAND, Philip Christopher, DPhil, FRS; British geophysicist and academic; *Professor of Geology, Department of Earth Sciences, University of Oxford;* b. 30 April 1951, Lancaster; ed Univ. of Bristol, Univ. of Oxford; NATO Postdoctoral Fellow, Norwegian Seismic Array, Kjeller, Norway 1976; NERC Research Fellow, Dept of Geodesy and Geophysics, Univ. of Cambridge 1977–79, Jr Research Fellow, Darwin Coll. 1978–80, IBM Research Fellow, Dept of Earth Sciences 1979–81; Asst and Assoc. Prof., Dept of Geological Sciences, Harvard Univ., USA 1981–86; Lecturer in Geophysics, Dept of Earth Sciences, Univ. of Oxford 1986–, Tutorial Fellow, Exeter Coll. 1986, Prof. of Geology 2000–, currently also Head of Dept of Earth Sciences; Visiting Prof., Univ. Joseph Fourier, Grenoble, France 1990, Univs de Paris Sud, Paris VI, Paris VII, Ecole Normale Superieure, Paris 1990, 1992, Div. of Geological and Planetary Sciences, Calif. Inst. of Tech. 1996; Fellow, Univ. Coll. Oxford. *Publications:* co-author of articles for Journal of Geophysical Research, Nature, Earth and Planetary Science Letters, Geophysical Research Letters. *Address:* Department of Earth Sciences, University of Oxford, Parks Road, Oxford, OX1 3PR, England (office). *Telephone:* (1865) 272018 (office). *E-mail:* philip.england@earth.ox.ac.uk (office). *Website:* www.earth.ox.ac.uk (office).

ENGLAND, Richard, BArch; Maltese architect, academic, artist and poet; *Director, England & England, Architects;* b. 3 Oct. 1937, Sliema; s. of Edwin England Sant Fournier and Ina Desain; m. Myriam Borg Manduca 1962; one s. one d.; ed St Edward's Coll., Univ. of Malta, Politecnico, Milan, Italy; student-architect in Gio Ponti's studio, Milan 1960–62; Dir England & England, Architects 1962–; Dean Faculty of Architecture, Head, Dept of Architecture, Univ. of Malta 1987–89; Prof., Int. Acad. of Architecture 1987–, Academician 1991–; subject of several monographs; Fellow, Inst. of Professional Designers (London), Foundation for Int. Studies, Malta; Hon. Prof. Univ. of Ga, Inst. of Advanced Studies, New York Univ., Univ. of Malta, Univ. of Buenos Aires; Hon. Fellow, Univ. of Bath (UK), AIA 1999; Hon. mem. World Forum of Young Architects, Colegio de Arquitectos, Jalisco, Mexico; Officer, Nat. Order of Merit (Malta) 1993; Dr hc (Univ. of Architecture, Civil Eng and Geology, Sofia, Bulgaria); Interarch 1985, 1989, 1991, 1993 and 1995 Laureate Prizes, Commonwealth Architects Regional Awards 1985, 1987, Gold Medal City of Toulouse 1985, Comité des Critiques d'Architecture Silver Medal 1987, USSR Biennale Laureate Prize 1988, IFRAA Prize (USA) 1991, Int. Prize, Costa Rica Biennale 1996, Gold Medal, Belgrade Architectural Biennale 2000, Grand Prix, Int. Acad. of Architecture 2006. *Works include:* Manikata Church, Univ. of Malta Extension, Cen. Bank of Malta, Malta Parl., Millenium Chapel, St James Cavalier Centre for Creativity, Valletta; various commercial bldgs, hotels and banks in Malta and the Middle East. *Publications:* Walls of Malta 1973, White is White 1973, Contemporary Art in Malta 1974, Carrier-Citadel Metamorphosis 1974, Island: A Poem for Seeing 1980, Uncaged Reflections: Selected Writings 1965–80, In Search of Silent Spaces 1983, Octaves of Reflection (with Charles Camilleri) 1987, Eye to I (selected poems) 1994, Sacri Luogi 1995, Mdina, Citadel of Memory (with Conrad Thake) 1996, Fraxions 1996, Gozo – Island of Oblivion 1997, Transfigurations: Places of Prayer (with Linda Schubert) 2000, Viaggio in Italia: Travel Sketches 2000, Gabriel Caruana Ceramics 2001, The Palette, Paintings of John Borg Manduca 2005, Norbert Attard 2007, Sanctuaries: Collected Poems 2007, Clavichords: Collected Poems 2009. *Leisure interests:* music and art in general. *Address:* England & England Architects, 26/1 Merchants Street, Valletta, VLT10 (office); 8 Oleander Street, The Gardens, St Julians, STJ 1912, Malta (home). *Telephone:* 21240894/21245187 (office); 21350171 (home). *Fax:* 21241174 (office); 21354263 (home). *E-mail:* richardengland@onvol.net (office). *Website:* www.richardengland.com (office).

ENGLE, Robert F., BA, MS, PhD; American economist and academic; *Michael Armellino Professor in the Management of Financial Services, Leonard Stern School of Business, New York University;* b. 1942; ed Williams Coll., Cornell Univ.; Asst Prof., MIT 1969–74, Assoc. Prof. 1974–77; Assoc. Prof. Univ. of Calif., San Diego (UCSD) 1975–77, Prof. 1977–, Chair. Dept of Econs 1990–94, Chancellor's Assocs. Chair. in Econs 1993–; Michael Armellino Prof. in the Man. of Financial Services, NY Univ. Stern School of Business 2000–; Prin.

Robert F. Engle Econometric Services; Nat. Bureau of Econ. Research (NBER) Research Assoc. 1987–; Fellow Econometric Soc. 1981– (mem. Council 1994–), AAAS 1995–; Roger F. Murray Prize, Inst. for Quantitative Research in Finance 1991, Nobel Prize in Econs 2003 (jt recipient). *Publications include:* more than 100 academic papers and three books. *Address:* Kaufman Management Center, 44 West 4th Street, KMC 9-62, New York, NY 10012-1126, USA (office). *Telephone:* (212) 998-0710 (office). *Fax:* (212) 995-4220 (office). *E-mail:* rengle@stern.nyu.edu (office). *Website:* www.stern.nyu.edu/~rengle (office).

ENGLER, John Mathias, JD; American lawyer, politician, fmr state official and association executive; *President and CEO, National Association of Manufacturers;* b. 12 Oct. 1948, Mount Pleasant, Mich.; s. of Mathias Engler and Agnes Neyer; m. Michele Engler; three d.; ed Mich. State Univ. and Thomas M. Cooley Law School; mem. Mich. House of Reps 1971–78; mem. Mich. Senate 1979–90, Republican leader 1983, majority leader 1984–90; Gov. of Mich. 1990–2003; Pres. and CEO Nat. Asscn of Mfrs 2004–; Hon. LLD (Alma Coll.) 1984, (W Mich.) 1991. *Address:* National Association of Manufacturers, 1331 Pennsylvania Avenue, NW, Washington, DC 20004-1790, USA (office). *Telephone:* (202) 637-3106 (office). *Fax:* (202) 637-3460 (office). *E-mail:* john.m.engler@nam.org (office). *Website:* www.nam.org (office).

ENGLERT, François, DèsSc; Belgian physicist and academic; *Professor Emeritus of Physics, Université Libre de Bruxelles;* b. 6 Nov. 1932; m. Mira Nikomarow; one s. one d.; ed Université Libre de Bruxelles; Asst, Université Libre de Bruxelles 1959–60, Chargé de cours 1961–64, Prof. of Physics 1964–, Co-Dir Theoretical Physics Group 1980–98, Prof. Emer. 1998–; Research Assoc., Cornell Univ., Ithaca, NY, USA 1959–60, Asst Prof. 1960–61; Perm. Sackler Fellow and Sr Prof. by Special Appointment, Tel-Aviv Univ., Israel 1992–; Prix de Sciences Mathematiques et Physiques, Acad. Royale de Belgique 1977, First Award of the Int. Gravity Contest (with R. Brout and E. Gunzig) 1978, Prix Franqui 1982, European Physical Soc. High Energy and Particle Physics Prize (with R. Brout and P. W. Higgs) 1997, Wolf Prize in Physics (with R. Brout and P.W. Higgs) 2004. *Publications:* more than 115 articles in scientific journals. *Address:* Service de physique théorique, Université Libre de Bruxelles, Campus de la Plaine, CP 225, 1 Boulevard du Triomphe, 1050 Brussels, Belgium (office). *Telephone:* (2) 650-55-80 (office); (2) 375-46-49 (home). *Fax:* (2) 650-59-51 (office). *E-mail:* fenglert@ulb.ac.be (office). *Website:* www.ulb.ac.be/sciences/physth (office).

ENGLISH, Hon. Bill, BA, BComm; New Zealand politician; *Deputy Prime Minister, Minister of Finance and Minister of Infrastructure;* b. 1961; m.; six c.; ed Otago Univ., Victoria Univ. of Wellington; fmr policy analyst and farmer; MP for Wallace 1990–93, for Clutha-Southland 1993–; Parl. Under-Sec. for Health and Crown Health Enterprises 1993–96, Minister of Crown Health Enterprises, Assoc. Minister of Educ., Minister of Health 1996–99 and Assoc. Minister of Revenue 1997–99, Minister of Finance (including Responsibility for Govt Superannuation Fund) and of Revenue 1999, Assoc. Treas. 1998–99; Leader New Zealand Nat. Party 2001–03, Deputy Leader 2006–, Leader of the Opposition 2001–03, Nat. Party Spokesman for Education 2003–08; Deputy Prime Minister, Minister of Finance and Minister of Infrastructure 2008–. *Leisure interests:* rugby, running, cycling. *Address:* The Treasury, 1 The Terrace, Wellington 6011; Parliament Buildings, Wellington, New Zealand (office). *Telephone:* (4) 472-2733 (office); (4) 471-9057 (office). *Fax:* (4) 473- 0982 (office); (4) 472-4169 (office). *E-mail:* info@treasury.govt.nz (office); bill .english@national.org.nz (office). *Website:* www.treasury.govt.nz (office); www .national.org.nz (office).

ENGLISH, Edmond J., BA; American business executive; b. 1954; ed Northeastern Univ. Coll. of Business Admin; joined TJC Companies Inc. 1983, various merchandising positions 1983–95, Sr Vice-Pres., Merchandising 1995–97, Exec. Vice-Pres., Merchandising, Planning and Allocation, Marmaxx Group 1997–98, Sr Vice-Pres. and Group Exec. 1998–99, COO TJX 1999–2000, Chair. Marmaxx Group 2000–01, Pres. 1999–2005, CEO 2000–05 (resgnd); mem. Bd of Dirs Citizens Financial Group; Hon. Dr of Law, Framingham State Coll. 2002; Sir Ernest Shackleton Award, Shackleton Schools 2002, named Business Leader of the Year, MetroWest Chamber of Commerce 2003, named one of America's Most Powerful People, Forbes 2000. *Address:* c/o Board of Directors, Citizens Financial Group, Inc., 1 Citizens Plaza, Providence, RI 02903; c/o TJX Companies Incorporated, 770 Cochituate Road, Framingham, MA 01701, USA (office).

ENGLISH, Joseph Thomas, MD; American psychiatrist; *Professor and System Chairman, Department of Psychiatry and Behavioral Sciences, St. Vincent Catholic Medical Centers of New York;* b. 21 May 1933, Philadelphia, Pa; s. of Thomas J. English and Helen Gilmore English; m. Ann Carr Sanger 1969; two s. one d.; ed Jefferson Medical Coll.; Resident in Psychiatry, Inst. of Pa Hospital, Philadelphia 1959–61, Nat. Inst. of Mental Health, Bethesda, Md 1961–62; Chief Psychiatrist, US Peace Corps. 1962–66; Dir Office of Econ. Opportunity, Office of the Pres. 1966–68; Admin., Health Services and Mental Health Admin. US Dept of Health, Educ. and Welfare 1968–70; Pres. New York City Health and Hosps Corpn 1970–73; Adjunct Prof. Cornell Univ. School of Medicine 1975–; Assoc. Dean and Prof. of Psychiatry, New York Medical Coll. 1979–, now also Chair.; Professor and System Chair. Dept of Psychiatry and Behavioral Sciences, St. Vincent Catholic Medical Centers of New York 1973–; Visiting Fellow, Woodrow Wilson Nat. Fellowship Foundation 1979–; Trustee Sarah Lawrence Coll. 1986–90, Menninger Foundation 1993–; Pres. American Psychiatric Asscn 1992–93, mem. World Psychiatric Soc. (Chair. section on religion and psychiatry 1994–); mem. Joint Comm. Accreditation Hosps 1984–86, Vice-Chair. 1986–88, Chair. 1988–89, Commr 2002–; numerous awards. *Address:* Department of Psychiatry and Behavioral Sciences, St Vincent's Hospital and Medical Center, 203 West 12th Street,

New York, NY 10011-7762, USA. *Telephone:* (212) 604-8252. *Fax:* (212) 604-8794. *Website:* www.svcmc.org.

ENGLISH, Sir Terence Alexander Hawthorne, Kt, KBE, MA, FRCS, FRCP; British surgeon; b. 3 Oct. 1932, Pietermaritzburg, South Africa; s. of Arthur Alexander English and the late Mavis Eleanor Lund; m. 1st Ann Margaret Smart Dicey; two s. two d.; m. 2nd Judith Milne 2002; ed Witwatersrand Univ. and Guy's Hosp. Medical School, London; Intern, Demonstrator in Anatomy, Jr Surgical Registrar, Guy's Hosp. 1962–65; Resident Surgical Officer, Bolingbroke Hosp. 1966; Surgical Registrar, Brompton Hosp. 1967; Sr Surgical Registrar, Nat. Heart and London Chest Hosps 1968–72; Research Fellow, Cardiac Surgery, Univ. of Ala 1969; Consultant Cardiothoracic Surgeon to Papworth and Addenbrooke's Hosps 1973–95; Dir British Heart Foundation Heart Transplant Research Unit, Papworth Hosp. 1980–89; Consultant Cardiac Adviser, Humana Hosp. Wellington, London 1983–89; Master of St Catharine's Coll. Cambridge 1993–2000; Pres. Int. Soc. for Heart Transplantation 1984–85, Royal Coll. of Surgeons 1989–92; mem. Jt Consultants Cttee 1989–92, Standing Medical Advisory Cttee 1989–92, Audit Comm. 1993–99; Pres. BMA 1995–96; Gov. The Leys School 1993–2001; Hon. Fellow, St Catharine's Coll., Cambridge, St Hugh's Coll., Cambridge, Worcester Coll., Oxford, King's Coll., London; Hon. FRCP and Hon. FRCS (Canada); Hon. FRACS; Hon. FRCA; Hon. FACS; Hon. FRCS (Ireland); Hon. FRCS (Glasgow); Hon. DSc (Sussex, York); Hon. MD (Nantes), (Mahidol, Bangkok); Man. of the Year, Royal Asscn for Disability and Rehabilitation 1980, Clement Price Thomas Award, Royal Coll. of Surgeons 1986. *Achievement:* performed Britain's first successful heart transplant in 1979. *Publications:* over 100 articles in scientific journals. *Leisure interests:* reading, hill walking, South African history. *Address:* 28 Tree Lane, Oxford, OX4 4EY, England (home). *Telephone:* (1865) 717708 (home). *E-mail:* tenglish@doctors.org.uk (home).

ENGSTRÖM, Odd, BA; Swedish politician; b. 20 Sept. 1941, Skillingmark, Värmland Co.; m. Gunilla Engström; one s. one d.; ed Univ. of Uppsala; Admin. Officer, Cabinet Office 1965–67, Ministry of Finance 1967–68; Prin. Admin. Officer, Nat. Bd of Health and Welfare 1968–70; Deputy Asst Under-Sec., Asst Under-Sec. Ministry of Finance 1970–77; Sec. to Parl. Group, Social Democratic Party 1977–82; Under-Sec. of State, Cabinet Office 1982–84; Dir of Finance, Stockholm City Admin. 1984–86; Dir-Gen. Nat. Audit Bureau 1986; Political Adviser, Cabinet Office 1986–88; Minister with responsibility for the Budget, Ministry of Finance 1988–89; Deputy Prime Minister 1989–91, MP 1991–93; Chair. Bank Support Group 1993; Dir-Gen. Ministry of Finance 1993.

ENHSAYHAN, Mendsayhany, PhD; Mongolian politician; fmrly worked as economist; fmr Chief of Staff to Pres. Ochirbat; Prime Minister of Mongolia 1996–98; Pres. Premier Int. Inc. 1998–; mem. Democratic Alliance. *Address:* Pease Avenue 11A, Ulan Bator 210648, Mongolia (office); c/o Great Hural, Ulan Bator, Mongolia. *Telephone:* (1) 312635 (office); (1) 321733 (home). *Fax:* (1) 312608 (office). *E-mail:* premier@magicnet.mn (office). *Website:* www .premiermongolia.com (office).

ENKHBAYAR, Nambaryn; Mongolian politician, writer and head of state; *President;* b. 1 June 1958, Ulan Bator; s. of Baljinnyam Nambar and Radnaa Budkhand; m. Onon Tsolmon 1986; four c.; ed High School No. 23, Ulan Bator, Literature Inst., Moscow, Leeds Univ., UK; Ed. and Interpreter, Exec. Sec. and Head of Dept, Asscn of Mongolian Writers' 1980–90; Vice-Pres. and Ed., Mongolian Interpreters' Union 1990–92; First Vice-Chair. Culture and Art Devt Cttee 1990–92; Minister of Culture 1992–96; Leader of the Opposition 1997–2000; mem. Great Hural (Parl.) 1992–; Speaker 2004–05; President 2005–, also C-in-C of Armed Forces; Leader, Mongolian People's Revolutionary Party (MPRP) 1997–; Prime Minister of Mongolia 2000–04; World Bank Adviser on Asian Culture and Buddhist Religion 1998–; Chair. Mongolia-India Friendship Asscn; Head Nat. Council of Museums 1995–; Int. Pres. Alliance of Religions and Conservation 2003–; Govt of Mongolia Polar Star 1996; MPRP Politician of the Year 1997; Govt of Mongolia Star of the Flag for Work Achievements 2001. *Publications:* translated several classic Russian novels; About Mongolian Arts, Literature and Emptiness 1989, On the Indicators of Development from the Buddhist Point of View 1998, Some Thoughts on the Relationship between Buddhist Philosophy and Economics 1998, To Develop or Not to Develop 1998. *Leisure interests:* reading, tennis, basketball, volleyball. *Address:* State Palace, Ulan Bator 12 (office); Ikh Tenger, Suite 50-3, Ulan Bator, Mongolia (home). *Telephone:* (1) 323252 (office). *Fax:* (1) 329281 (office). *E-mail:* president@pmis.gov.mn (office). *Website:* www.pmis.gov.mn/president (office).

ENKHBOLD, Mieyeegombo; Mongolian politician; *Deputy Prime Minister;* b. 1964; ed Mongolian Nat. Univ.; joined Mongolian People's Revolutionary Party (MPRP) 1990, Chair. MPRP Council, Ulan Bator 1997–, Chair. MPRP 2005–07; elected Mayor of Ulan Bator 1999; Prime Minister of Mongolia 2006–07 (resgnd); Deputy Prime Minister 2007–. *Address:* Mongolian People's Revolutionary Party (MPRP), Baga Toiruu 37/1, Ulan Bator, Mongolia (office). *Telephone:* (11) 320432 (office). *Fax:* (11) 320432 (office). *E-mail:* contact@mprp.mn (office). *Website:* www.mprp.mn (office).

ENKHBOLD, Nyamaa, MA; Mongolian politician; *Head of Government Affairs Directorate;* b. 1957; m.; two c.; ed Press Inst. of Moscow, Russia, Political Inst., Moscow, Univ. of Sydney, Australia; mem. Mongolian People's Revolutionary Party; Economist Ministry of Culture 1979–80, Expert, Planning Dept 1980–86, Deputy Dir State Printing House 1986–90; Gen. Dir Mongol Hevlel Corpn 1990–93; Adviser to Deputy Prime Minister 1993–95; Head Press and Public Relations Dept, Office of the Pres. 1997–2000; mem. State Great Hural (Parl.) 2000–; Minister of Foreign Affairs 2006–07; Head of Govt Affairs Directorate 2007–. *Address:* Government Affairs Directorate,

State Palace, Sükhbaataryn Talbai 1, Ulan Bator, Mongolia (office). *Telephone:* (11) 323501 (office). *Fax:* (11) 310011 (office).

ENKHSAIKHAN, Jargalsaihany, PhD; Mongolian diplomatist; b. 4 Sept. 1950, Ulan Bator; m. 1st Tuul Myagmarjavyn 1976 (divorced 1993); m. 2nd Batgerel Budjavyn 1994; two s. four d.; ed Moscow State Inst. for Int. Relations; Sec. of Legal Dept, Ministry of Foreign Affairs 1974–79; Mongolian Rep. at UN Conf. on Law of the Sea 1976–82; Sec. Mongolian Mission to UN, NY 1979–86; Acting Head Legal and Policy Planning Depts Ministry of Foreign Affairs 1986–88; Minister-Counsellor Mongolian Embassy, Moscow 1988–92; Adviser to Pres. of Mongolia 1992–93; Exec. Sec. to Mongolian Nat. Security Council, Nat. Security Adviser to Pres. of Mongolia 1994–96; apptd Perm. Rep. to UN 1996; Rapporteur Legal (Sixth) Cttee of UN Gen. Ass. 1983, Vice-Chair. 1984, Chair. 1998; Vice-Chair. Special Cttee on Non-Use of Force in Int. Relations 1983; Chair. Group of Land-Locked States at UN 1997–; Vice-Pres. 52nd session UN Gen. Ass. 1997; Vice-Chair. Disarmament Comm. 1997; Mongolian State Order of the Polar Star 1991. *Publications:* articles on int. relations and int. law. *Leisure interest:* reading. *Address:* c/o Permanent Mission of Mongolia to the UN, 6 East 77th Street, New York, NY 10021, USA (office).

ENNACEUR, Mohamed, PhD; Tunisian diplomatist, politician and lawyer; b. 21 March 1934, El Djem; m. Siren Möenstre; three s. two d.; ed Univ. of Tunis, Univ. of Paris (Sorbonne); fmrly practised as lawyer; Gov. of Sousse 1972–73; Minister of Labour and Social Affairs 1974–77, 1979–85; Pres. Econ. and Social Council of Tunisia 1985–91; Amb., Perm. Rep. of Tunisia to UN and other int. orgs, Geneva 1991–96; barrister 1997–; Chair. World Employment Conf. (ILO) 1976, 71st session of Int. Labour Conf. (ILO) 1985, 49th session of Human Rights Comm. (UN) 1993; Pres. Inst. Social-Consult; Ed. Tunisian Social Law Review; Hon. KBE, Grand Cordon of Order of Independence, Grand Cordon of Order of the Repub.; several awards and decorations from France, Britain, Germany, Belgium, Netherlands, Luxembourg, Ivory Coast. *Publications:* Human Rights after the Vienna Conference 1993; articles on labour law, human rights and social policy in Int. Studies Review, Tunisian Social Law Review, Int. Review of the Red Cross and other publs. *Leisure interests:* sports, music. *Address:* 10 rue du Mali, 1002 Tunis (office); 15 rue Othman Kaak, 2026 Sidi Bou Said, Tunisia (home). *Telephone:* (1) 848439 (office); (1) 741127 (home). *Fax:* (1) 847943 (office). *E-mail:* social.consult@planet.tn (office); med.ennaceur@planet.tn (home).

ENO, Brian Peter George St John Baptiste de la Salle; British composer, artist, keyboard player and producer; b. 15 May 1948, Woodbridge, Suffolk; s. of the late William Arnold Eno and of Maria Alphonsine Eno (née Buslot); m. 1st Sarah Grenville 1967; one d.; m. 2nd Anthea Norman-Taylor 1988; two c.; ed St Mary's Convent, St Joseph's Coll., Ipswich School of Art, Winchester Coll. of Art; founder mem. Roxy Music 1971–73; worked with guitarist Robert Fripp 1975–76; invented 'ambient music' 1975; Visiting Prof., RCA 1995–; Hon. Prof. of New Media, Berlin Univ. of Art 1998–; f. Long Now Foundation 1996; mem. PRS, BAC&S; Hon. DTech (Plymouth) 1995; Q Magazine Award for Best Producer (with others) 1993, BRIT Awards for Best Producer 1994, 1996, Inspiration Award (with David Bowie) 1995, Grammy Award for Producer of Best Record of the Year 2000. *Recordings:* albums: Here Come The Warm Jets 1974, Taking Tiger Mountain (By Strategy) 1974, Another Green World 1975, Discreet Music 1975, Before and After Science 1977, Music For Films 1978, Ambient 1: Music For Airports 1978, After the Heat 1978, My Life in the Bush of Ghosts (with David Byrne) 1981, Ambient 3: Day of Radiance 1981, Empty Landscapes 1981, Ambient 4: On Land 1982, Music For Films Vol. 2 1983, Apollo: Atmospheres and Soundtracks 1983, Begegnungen 1984, Thursday Afternoon 1985, Begegnungen II 1985, Music For Films Vol. 3 1988, Wrong Way Up 1990, Nerve Net 1992, The Shutov Assembly 1992, Neroli 1993, Headcandy 1994, Spinner 1995, The Drop 1997, Extracts from Music for White Cube 1997, Kite Stories 1999, I Dormienti 1999, Music for Onmyo-Ji 2000, Music for Civic Recovery Center 2000, Drawn From Life 2001, January 07003: Bell Studies for The Clock 2003, Another Day on Earth 2005; with Robert Fripp: No Pussyfooting 1975, Evening Star 1976, The Equatorial Stars 2004, The Cotswold Gnomes 2006, Beyond Even 1992–2006 2007, Everything that Happens will Happen Today (with David Byrne) 2008; numerous albums as producer, co-producer, collaborations, guest appearances on albums, and remixes. *Publications include:* A Year with Swollen Appendices 1995, The Margin: A Canongate Diary for 2007 (ed.). *Address:* c/o Opal Ltd, 4 Pembridge Mews, London, W11 3EQ, England (office). *Telephone:* (20) 7221-4933 (office). *Fax:* (20) 7727-5404 (office). *E-mail:* opal@opaloffice.com (office). *Website:* www.enoshop.co.uk (office).

ENOKSEN, Hans; Greenlandic politician; *Prime Minister, Greenland Home Rule Government;* b. 1956; mem. Siumut Party, Chair. 2001; mem. Parl. 1995–; Minister for Fisheries, Hunting and Settlements 2001–; Prime Minister, Greenland Home Rule Govt Dec. 2002–; Greenland Home Rule Nersonaat in Gold 2003. *Address:* Greenland Home Rule Government, POB 1015, 3900 Nuuk, Greenland (office). *Telephone:* 345000 (office). *Fax:* 325002 (office). *E-mail:* info@gh.gl (office). *Website:* www.nanoq.gl (office).

ENOKSEN, Odd Roger; Norwegian politician; b. 25 Sept. 1954, Andøy; m. 1st Turid Pettersen; m. 2nd Anne Kari Spjelkavik; four c.; ed Kleiva Coll. of Agric.; Leader of Andøy Centre Party 1975–78; Manager Enoksen Torvprodukter (peat producer) A/S 1985–90; Manager Andøytorv (peat supplier) 1990–93; mem. Centre Party's Exec. Cttee 1993–95, Leader Nordland Branch 1996–98, First Deputy Leader 1997–99, Leader 1999–2003; mem. Storting (Parl.) 1993–, Leader Cttee of Industry 1997–99, mem. Extended Foreign Policy Cttee 1997–99; Minister of Local Govt and Regional Devt 1999–2000, of Petroleum and Energy 2005–07; Man. Dir Andøya Rocket Range 2005–. *Address:* Senterpartiet (Centre Party), Akersgt. 35, 3rd Floor, POB 1191 Sentrum, 0107 Oslo, Norway (office). *Telephone:* 23-69-01-00 (office). *Fax:* 23-69-01-01 (office). *E-mail:* epost@senterpartiet.no (office). *Website:* www.senterpartiet.no (office).

ENQUIST, Per Olov, MA; Swedish novelist, playwright, journalist and poet; b. 1934, Hjoggböle; m. 2nd Lone Bastholm; ed Univ. of Uppsala; Visiting Prof. UCLA 1973; Nordic Council literary prize 1968, August Award 1999, Independent Foreign Fiction Prize 2003, Augustpriset 2008. *Publications:* Kristallögat 1961, Färdvägen 1963, Magnetisörens Femte Vinter 1964, Bröderna Casey 1964, Hess 1966, Sextiotalskritik 1966, Legionärerna 1968, Sekonden 1971, Katedralen i München 1972, Berättelser Från de Inställda Upprorens Tid (short stories) 1974, Tribadernas Natt 1975, Chez Nous (with Anders Ehnmark) 1976, Musikanternas Uttåg 1978, Mannen På Trottoaren 1979, Till Fedra 1980, Från Regnormarnas Liv 1981, En Triptyk 1981, Doktor Mabuses Nya Testamente (with Anders Ehnmark) 1982, Strindberg Ett Liv 1984, Nedstörtad Ängel 1985, Två Reportage om Idrott 1986, I Lodjurets Timma 1988, Kapten Nemos Bibliotek 1991, Hamsun (screenplay) 1996, Bildmakarna (play) 1998, Livläkarens Besök (The Visit of the Ryal Physician) 1999, Systrarna (play) 2000, Lewis Resa (Lewi's Journey) 2001, Boken om Blanche och Marie (The Story of Blanche and Marie) 2004, Et Annat Liv 2008; contrib. to literary criticism in newspapers, including Uppsala Nya Tidning, Svenska Dagbladet, Expressen. *Address:* c/o Norstedts, Tryckerigatan 4, Box 2052, 103 12 Stockholm, Sweden (office). *Website:* www.panorstedt.se (office).

ENRILE, Juan Ponce (see PONCE ENRILE, Juan).

ENSIGN, John E., DMV; American politician and fmr veterinarian; *Senator from Nevada;* b. 25 March 1958, Roseville, Calif.; s. of Mike Ensign and Sharon Ensign; m. Darlene Sciaretta; one s.; ed Ore. State Univ., Colo State Univ.; owner of animal hosp. in Las Vegas; Gen. Man. Gold Strike Hotel and Casino 1991, Nevada Landing Hotel and Casino 1992; mem. US Congress from 1st Dist, Nev. 1994–98, mem. Ways and Means Cttee, Sub-Cttee on Health, Sub-Cttee on Human Resources, Comm. on Resources 1995–98; cand. for Senate 1998–99; Senator from Nevada 2000–. *Address:* 364 Russell Senate Office Building, Washington, DC 20510, USA (office). *Telephone:* (202) 224-6244 (office). *Fax:* (202) 228-2193 (office). *Website:* ensign.senate.gov (office).

ENTHOVEN, Marius, MSc; Dutch civil servant and international official; *Executive Director, Research Institute, NIB Capital Bank;* b. 23 Nov. 1940, Baarn; s. of Emil S. Enthoven and Anna G. Schouten; m. Lidwine Kolfschoten 1965; four d.; ed Delft Tech. Univ., Princeton Univ., USA; scientist with Dutch Aerospace Labs (NLR) 1967–72; Head, Noise Abatement Dept, Ministry for Environment 1972–77, Dir Scientific Affairs 1977–80, Chief Insp. Environmental Protection 1980–88, Dir-Gen. Environmental Protection 1988–94; Dir-Gen. Environment, Nuclear Safety and Civil Protection, Directorate-Gen. XI, European Comm. 1994–97; Special Adviser to Sec.-Gen., European Comm. 1997–98; Dir NIB Capital Bank NV, Netherlands 1998–, currently Exec. Dir Research Inst.; Kt Order of the Dutch Lion. *Publications:* books and articles on environmental man. issues. *Leisure interests:* literature, theatre, music, tennis. *Address:* NIB Capital Bank, PO Box 380, 2501 The Hague BH, Netherlands. *Telephone:* (70) 3425496 (office). *Fax:* (70) 3657269 (office). *E-mail:* marius.enthoven@nibcapital.com (office). *Website:* www.nibcapital.com.

ENTOV, Revold Mikhailovich, PhD; Russian economist; *Professor, University of Moscow;* b. 23 March 1931, Kiev; m. Galina Gorvitz 1962; one s. one d.; ed Kharkov Univ. and Inst. for World Econ. and Int. Relations (IMEMO); Asst Prof., Bashkirian Agricultural School 1954–57; research worker, IMEMO 1961, now Head of Section; Prof., Univ. of Moscow 1970–; mem. Comm. Evaluating Projects of Econ. Reform in USSR (now Russia) 1990–91; mem. Russian Acad. of Sciences 1994; mem. Editorial Bd Mirovaya ekonomika i mezhdunarodnye otnosheniya (The World Economy and International Relations), Ekonomika i matematicheskie metody (The Economy and Mathematical Methods); USSR State Prize 1977, Adam Smith Prize 1999, Zolotaya Vyshka Prize 2004. *Publications include:* Public Credit of the U.S. 1967, Theories of Prices 1982, Movements of Capital and the Profit Rate 1987, The Distribution of Wealth 1992, Corporate Management and the Protection of Property Rights: Empirical Analysis and Actual Reform Tendencies (with A. D. Radygin) 2001; numerous articles on econ. theory and the US economy. *Leisure interest:* history of psychology. *Address:* Institute for World Economy and International Relations, Profsoyuznaya 23, 117859 Moscow (office); Azovskaya 4, Apt 44, 113149 Moscow, Russia (home). *Telephone:* (495) 128-29-07 (office); (495) 310-17-67 (home).

ENTRECANALES DOMECQ, José Manuel, Licenciado en Ciencias Económicas; Spanish business executive; *Chairman, Endesa SA;* b. 1 Jan. 1963, Madrid; ed Universidad Complutense de Madrid; Assoc., Merrill Lynch Europe Ltd Capital Markets, London and New York 1986–90; mem. Bd of Dirs Sefinco Ltd New York 1990–92; Finance Dir ACCIONA, SA 1992–2004, Chair. 2004–; Man. Dir Vodafone España 1994–2000, Chair. 2000–07, also Chair. Vodafone Foundation; Chair. Endesa SA 2007–; mem. Bd of Dirs Agropecuaria El Cijaral, SA, Grupo Entrecanales, SA, Tivafen, SA, Servicios Urbanos Integrales, SA, Osmosis Internacional, SA; mem. Bd Conferencia Española de Fundaciones, Guggenheim Foundation, Spanish Red Cross, Universal Library, Cotec Foundation for Technological Innovation, Reina Sofía Higher School of Music, Business and Society Foundation, Inst. of Family Business, Spain-US Chamber of Commerce, Spanish Institutional Foundation; Patron Pro CNIC Foundation, Carolina Foundation, Prince of Asturias Foundation, Family Enterprise Inst. *Address:* Endesa SA, Ribera de Loira 60, 28042 Madrid, Spain (office). *Telephone:* (91) 2131000 (office). *Fax:* (91) 5645496 (office). *E-mail:* info@endesa.es (office). *Website:* www.endesa.es (office).

ENTREMONT, Philippe; French pianist and conductor; b. 7 June 1934, Reims; s. of Jean Entremont and Renée Entremont (née Monchamps); m. Andrée Ragot 1955; one s. one d.; ed Inst. Notre-Dame à Reims, Conservatoire

Nat. Supérieur de Musique de Paris; has performed with all major orchestras of world 1953–; Pres. of Acad. Int. de Musique Maurice Ravel, Saint-Jean-de-Luz 1973–80; Musical Dir and Permanent Conductor, Vienna Chamber Orchestra 1976–; Dir New Orleans Symphony Orchestra 1980–86; Prin. Conductor Denver Symphony Orchestra 1986–88, Paris Orchestre Colonne 1987–90, Netherlands Chamber Orchestra 1993–2002, Israel Chamber Orchestra 1995–; Dir American Conservatory Fontainebleau 1994; f. Santo Domingo Biennial Festival 1997; Prin. Guest Conductor Shanghai Broadcasting Symphony Orchestra 2001–; Prin. Guest Conductor Munich Symphony Orchestra 2005–6, Prin. Conductor 2006; Conductor Super World Orchestra, Tokyo 2006; Officier Ordre nat. du Mérite, Officier, Légion d'honneur, Commdr des Arts et Lettres, Österreichisches Ehrenkreuz für Wissenschaft und Kunst (Arts and Sciences Cross of Honour, Austria); Harriet Cohen Piano Medal 1951, Grand Prix Int. Concours Marguerite Long-Jacques Thibaud 1953, four Grand Prix du Disque Awards, Edison Award 1960, Grammy Award 1972;. *Leisure interest:* golf. *Address:* c/o Tim Fox, Columbia Artists Management Inc., 1790 Broadway, New York, NY 10019-1412, USA; c/o Bureau de concerts Dominique Lierner, 17 rue du 4 septembre, 75002 Paris (office); 10 rue de Castiglione, 75001 Paris, France. *Telephone:* 1-42-86-06-08. *Fax:* 1-42-86-86-61 (home).

ENTWISTLE, John Nicholas McAlpine, OBE; British solicitor and consultant; *Immigration Judge;* b. 16 June 1941, Southport, Lancs.; s. of Sir Maxwell Entwistle and Lady (Jean) Entwistle; m. Phillida Burgess; one s. one d.; ed Uppingham School, Rutland; qualified as solicitor 1963; Asst Attorney, Shearman & Sterling, New York, USA 1963–64; partner, Maxwell Entwistle & Byrne 1966–91; mem. Liverpool City Council 1968–71; Nat. Vice-Chair. The Bow Group 1967–68; Parl. cand. (Conservative) for Huyton 1970; Consultant Solicitor, Davies Wallis Foyster 1992–2004; Lloyds underwriting mem. 1971–2000; Founder Dir Merseyside TEC 1990–91; Dir (non-exec.) Rathbone Brothers PLC 1992–98; Deputy Dist Chair. Appeals Service 1992–; Chair. Liverpool Chamber of Commerce & Industry 1992–94; Founder Chair. NW Chambers of Commerce Assen 1993–97; Pres. British Chambers of Commerce 1998–2000; mem. Chancellor of Exchequer's Standing Cttee on preparation for EMU 1998–2000; mem. Council, Britain in Europe 1999–2004; Home Sec.'s rep. for appointments to Merseyside Police Authority 1994–2000; Chair. several pvt. property cos; Trustee Nat. Museums & Galleries on Merseyside 1990–97; mem. Nat. Trust NW Regional Cttee 1992–98, Parole Bd 1994–2000, Disciplinary Cttee, Mortgage Compliance Bd 1999–2004, Criminal Injuries Compensation Appeals Panel 2000–; part-time asylum adjudicator 2000–05; Immigration Judge 2005–; DL for Merseyside 1992–2002. *Leisure interests:* collecting and painting pictures, gardening, shooting. *Address:* Low Crag, Crook, nr Kendal, Cumbria, LA8 8LE, England (home). *Telephone:* (15395) 68715 (office); (15395) 68268 (home). *Fax:* (15395) 68769 (office). *E-mail:* jentwistle@onetel.net (office).

ENYA; Irish singer, composer and musician (piano); b. (Eithne Ní Bhraonáin), 17 May 1961, Gweedore, Donegal; d. of Leon Ó Braonáin and Máire Bean Uí Bhraonáin; keyboard and background vocals with family group, Clannad (traditional Irish music) 1980–82; formed Aigle Music (with producer and sound engineer Nicky Ryan and man. and lyricist Roma Ryan) 1982; performed at the Queen's 50th Wedding Anniversary, birthday celebrations of King Gustav of Sweden and privately for Pope John Paul II; numerous other live appearances, including the Acad. Awards 2002; Ivor Novello Int. Achievement Award 1998, six World Music Awards including Best-Selling Artist in the World 2001, Japanese Grand Prix Award for New Artist of the Year, Hot Press Best Irish Solo Artist, Academy of Achievement of America Golden Plate Award, Billboard Artist Award, Echo Award (for Only Time), BMI Special Citation of Achievement (for Only Time, for Orinoco Flow, I Don't Wanna Know), Las Vegas Film Critics' Soc. Award for Best Original Song (for May It Be), Phoenix Film Critics' Award for Best Original Song (for May It Be), Broadcast Film Critics' Award for Best Song (for May It Be). *Recordings include* albums: with Clannad: Crann Ull 1980, Fuaim 1982; as Enya: Enya 1987, Watermark (IFPI Platinum European Award) 1988, Shepherd Moons (IFPI Platinum European Award, Grammy Award, Billboard Music Award, NARM Best-Selling Album Award) 1991, The Celts 1992, The Memory of Trees (Grammy Award) 1995, Paint the Sky with Stars (Japanese Grand Prix Album of the Year) 1997, A Day Without Rain (Grammy Award, Japanese Grand Prix Album of the Year) 2000, Amarantine (Grammy Award for Best New Age Album 2007) 2005, And Winter Came 2008. *Address:* Treesdale, Church Road, Killiney, Co. Dublin, Ireland (office). *Website:* www.enya.com.

ENZENSBERGER, Hans Magnus, (Andreas Thalmayr), DPhil; German poet and writer; *Artistic Director, Renaissance Theatre Berlin;* b. 11 Nov. 1929, Kaufbeuren; m. 1st Dagrun Averaa Christensen; one d.; m. 2nd Maria Alexandrowna Makarowa 1986; m. 3rd Katharina Bonitz; one d.; ed Univs of Erlangen, Freiburg im Breisgau, Hamburg and Paris; Third Programme Ed., Stuttgart Radio 1955–57; Lecturer, Hochschule für Gestaltung, Ulm 1956–57; Literary Consultant to Suhrkamp's (publrs), Frankfurt 1960–; mem. 'Group 47', Ed. Kursbuch (review) 1965–75, Publr 1970–90; Ed. TransAtlantik (monthly magazine) 1980–82; Publr and Ed., Die Andere Bibliothek 1985–2005; Artistic Dir Renaissance Theatre Berlin 1995–; Ordre pour le Mérite 2000; Hugo Jacobi Prize 1956, Kritiker Prize 1962, Georg Büchner Prize 1963, Premio Pasolini 1982, Heinrich Böll Prize 1985, Kultureller Ehrenpreis der Stadt München 1994, Heinrich Heine Prize, Düsseldorf 1997, Príncipe de Asturias 2002, and others. *Publications:* poetry: Verteidigung der Wölfe 1957, Landessprache 1960, Blindenschrift 1964, Poems for People Who Don't Read Poems (English edn) 1968, Gedichte 1955–1970 1971, Mausoleum 1975; essays: Clemens Brentanos Poetik 1961, Einzelheiten 1962, Politik und Verbrechen 1964; also: Deutschland, Deutschland unter Anderen 1967, Das Verhör von Habana (play) 1970, Freisprüche 1970, Der kurze Sommer der Anarchie (novel) 1972, Gespräche mit Marx und Engels 1973, Palaver 1974; Ed. Museum der Modernen Poesie 1960, Allerleirauh 1961, Andreas Gryphius Gedichte 1962, Edward Lears kompletter Nonsense (trans.) 1977, Raids and Reconstruction (essays, English edn), Der Untergang der Titanic (epic poem) 1978, Die Furie des Verschwindens 1980, Politische Brosamen 1982, Critical Essays 1982, Der Menschenfreund 1984, Ach Europa! 1987, Mittelmass und Wahn 1988, Requiem für eine romantische Frau 1988, Der Fliegende Robert 1989, Zukunftsmusik (poems) 1991, Die grosse Wanderung 1992, Aussichten auf den Bürgerkrieg 1993, Diderots Schatten 1994, The Palace (libretto) 1994, Civil War (English edn) 1994, Selected Poems (English edn) 1994, Kiosk (poems) 1995 (English edn 1997), Voltaires Neffe (play) 1996, Der Zahlenteufel 1997, The Number Devil (English edn) 1998, Zickzack 1997, Wo warst du, Robert? (novel) 1998, Where were you, Robert? (English edn) 2000, Leichter als Luft (poems) 1999 (English edn 2001), Mediocrity and Delusion (English edn) 1992, Die Elixiere der Wissenschaft (essays and poems) 2002, Nomaden im regal (essays) 2003, Die Geschichte der Wolken (poems) 2003, Dialoge (prose) 2005; as Andreas Thalmayr: Heraus mit der Sprache 2005. *Leisure interests:* early 17th century Flemish art, mathematics. *Address:* c/o Suhrkamp-Verlag, Lindenstr. 29, 60325 Frankfurt am Main, Germany.

ENZI, Michael Bradley, MBA; American politician; *Senator from Wyoming;* b. 1 Feb. 1944, Bremerton, Wash.; s. of Elmer Enzi and Dorothy Bradley; m. Diana Buckley 1969; one s. two d.; ed George Washington Univ. and Denver Univ.; Pres. NZ Shoes Inc., Gillette, WY 1969–96, NZ Shoes of Sheridan Inc., WY 1983–91; Acting Man. Dunbar Well Services, Gillette 1985–97; Chair. Bd Dirs First Wyoming Bank, Gillette 1978–88; Dir Black Hill Corpn 1992–96; Mayor of Gillette 1975–82; mem. WY House of Reps, Cheyenne 1987–91, WY State Senate 1991–96; Senator from WY 1997–, mem. Foreign Relations Cttee.; Republican; Distinguished Eagle Scout. *Publication:* Harvard Journal on Legislation 1998. *Leisure interests:* fishing, fly tying, canoe making, reading. *Address:* 379A Senate Russell Office Building, Washington, DC 20510, (office); 431 Circle Drive, Gillette, WY 82716, USA (home). *Telephone:* (202) 224-3424 (office). *Fax:* (202) 228-0359 (office). *E-mail:* senator@enzi.senate.gov (office). *Website:* www.enzi.senate.gov (office).

EÖRSI, Mátyás, PhD; Hungarian lawyer and politician; *Chairman, European Affairs Committee, Hungarian National Assembly;* b. 24 Nov. 1954, Budapest; m.; three c.; ed Eötvös Loránd Univ., Budapest; founding mem. Alliance of Free Democrats (SZDSZ) and mem. Nat. Cttee, also Legal Rep. 1988, mem. Nat. Governing Cttee 1991, 2003–, Chair. SZDSZ Goodwill and Ethics Cttee 1993–98, Foreign Affairs Spokesman 1994–, Deputy Leader Parl. Group 2002–06, Leader Parl. Group 2007–; mem. Exec. Office Liberal Int. 1997–, Vice-Pres. 2002–; foreign trade lawyer 1981 and worked as legal advisor and at int. trading co.; est. Eörsi and Pnrs 1987; following regime change became regular mem. Council of Europe Parl. Ass.; Head, Hungarian del. with observer status Ass. of WEU and Head, del. to Parl. Ass. of Cen. European Initiative; mem. Parl. 1990–; Chair. Foreign Affairs Cttee, Nat. Ass. 1994–97; State Sec. for Policy, Ministry of Foreign Affairs 1997–98; mem. Hungarian Parl. del. to Council of Europe 1998–; Leader, Liberal faction, Council of Europe Parl. Ass. 2001–; Vice-Chair. Nat. Ass. Foreign Affairs Cttee 2002–06; mem. OSCE Parl. Ass. 2002–; Chair. Nat. Ass. European Affairs Cttee 2004–, Foreign Affairs and Hungarian Minorities Abroad Cttee, Nat. Ass., 2006–. *Address:* Hungarian National Assemby, 1357 Budapest, Kossuth tér 1–3, Hungary (office). *Telephone:* (1) 441-5000 (office); (1) 441-5765 (office). *Fax:* (1) 441-5952 (office). *Website:* www.parlament.hu (office).

EÖTVÖS, Peter; German (b. Hungarian) composer, conductor and academic; b. 2 Jan. 1944, Székelyudvarhely, Hungary; s. of László Eötvös and Ilona Szücs; m. 1st Piroska Molnár 1968; one s.; m. 2nd Pi-Hsien Chen 1976; one d.; m. 3rd Maria Mezei 1995; ed Budapest Acad. and Musikhochschule, Cologne; played in Stockhausen's Ensemble, Cologne 1968–76; composer and producer at WDR Electronic Music Studio, Cologne 1971–79; Conductor and Musical Dir Ensemble Intercontemporain, Paris 1979–91; Prin. Guest Conductor BBC Symphony Orchestra, London 1985–88; First Guest Conductor, Budapest Festival Orchestra 1992–95; Chief Conductor Netherlands Radio Chamber Orchestra 1994–2005; Prof., Musikhochschule Karlsruhe, Germany 1992–98, 2002–08, Cologne 1998–2001; f. Int. Eötvös Inst. for Young Conductors 1991; mem. Akad. der Künste, Berlin, Szechenyi Acad. of Art, Budapest, Sächsische Akad. der Künste, Dresden; Commdr, Ordre des Arts et Lettres 2003; Bartok Award, Budapest 1997, Stephan Kaske Prize, Munich 2000, Kossuth Prize, Hungary 2002, Midem Classical Award 'Living Composer', Cannes 2004, European Composing Prize 2004, Frankfurt Music Prize 2007. *Compositions include:* for orchestra: Chinese Opera, Shadows, Psychokosmos, Atlantis, Ima, Jet Stream, CAP-KO, Zeropoints, Two Monologues, Replica, Konzert für zwei Klaviere, Levitation; for ensemble: Intervalles-Intérieures, Windsequenzen, Steine, Triangel, Octet, Sonata per sei; for string quartet: Korrespondenz, Encore; for vocal ensemble: Three comedy madrigals; for percussion: Psalm 151; for violin: Seven (Prix de Composition Musicale, Fondation Prince Pierre de Monaco 2008); for musical theatre/opera: Radames, Harakiri, Three Sisters, As I Crossed a Bridge of Dreams, Le Balcon, Angels in America, Lady Sarashina, Love and Other Demons. *Leisure interests:* pipe, jazz, walking. *Address:* Harrison Parrott, 5–6 Albion Court, Albion Place, London, W6 0QT, England (office); Cseppkő u. 53, 1025 Budapest, Hungary (home). *Telephone:* (20) 7229-9166 (office); (1) 3259273 (home). *Fax:* (20) 7221-5042 (office); (1) 3355961 (home). *E-mail:* info@harrisonparrott.co.uk (office); eotvospeter@hotmail.com (home). *Website:* www.harrisonparrott.com (office); www.eotvospeter.com (home).

EPERON, Alastair David Peter, FRSA; British corporate affairs consultant; *Director, Group Corporate Affairs, The Boots Company PLC;* b. 17 Nov. 1949, Kent; s. of Stanley A. Eperon and Patricia Woodrow; m. Ruth Tabbenor 1976; two d.; ed Ramsden School for Boys, Orpington, Kent; worked as journalist; Press Officer, Surrey Co. Council 1972–74; Head of Public Affairs, The

www.worldwhoswho.com

Housing Corpn 1974–78; Sr Consultant, Shandwick 1978–80; Dir, then Deputy Man. Dir Ogilvy & Mather Public Relations, then Chief Exec. Ogilvy & Mather Corp. Financial 1980–86; Dir McAvoy Wreford Bayley 1986–, Man. Dir 1988–89, Chief Exec. McAvoy Bayley 1989–91; Dir Valin Pollen Int. 1989–90; Dir Group Corp. Affairs, The Boots Co. PLC 1991–; Deputy Chair. British Retail Consortium; Chair. CBI Distributive Trades Panel, Advisory Bd, The Foundation; Dir Business in the Community; Fellow, Inst. of Public Relations. *Leisure interests:* gardening, countryside. *Address:* The Boots Company PLC, Group Headquarters, Nottingham, NG90 4HQ, England (office). *Telephone:* (115) 968-7023 (office). *Fax:* (115) 968-7161 (office). *E-mail:* alastair.eperon@boots-plc.com (office).

EPHREM, Gen. Sebhat; Eritrean politician and army officer; *Minister of Defence;* served in Eritrean Armed Forces, rank of Gen.; currently Minister of Defence. *Address:* Ministry of Defence, POB 629, Asmara, Eritrea (office). *Telephone:* (1) 165952 (office). *Fax:* (1) 124990 (office).

EPHRON, Nora, BA; American writer and scriptwriter; b. 19 May 1941, New York; d. of Henry Ephron and Phoebe Ephron (née Wolkind); sister of Delia Ephron; m. 1st Dan Greenburg (divorced); m. 2nd Carl Bernstein (divorced); two s.; m. 3rd Nicholas Pileggi; ed Wellesley Coll.; reporter, New York Post 1963–68; freelance writer 1968–; Contributing Ed. and columnist, Esquire Magazine 1972–73, Sr Ed. 1974–78; Contributing Ed., New York Magazine 1973–74; mem. American Writers' Guild, Authors' Guild, PEN, Acad. of Motion Picture Arts and Sciences; BAFTA for Best Screenplay 1989. *Film appearances:* Crimes and Misdemeanors, Husbands and Wives. *Screenplays:* Silkwood (with Alice Arlen) 1983, Heartburn 1986, When Harry Met Sally… 1989, Cookie 1989 (co-exec. producer, co-screenwriter), My Blue Heaven 1990, This is My Day 1992 (dir, screenwriter, with Delia Ephron), Sleepless in Seattle (also dir) 1993, Mixed Nuts (also dir), Michael (also dir) 1996, You've Got Mail (also dir) 1998, Red Tails in Love: a Wildlife Drama in Central Park (also producer and dir) 2000, Lucky Numbers 1999, Hanging Up (also producer) 2000, Bewitched (also dir) 2005. *Publications:* Wallflower at the Orgy 1970, Crazy Salad 1975, Scribble, Scribble 1978, Heartburn 1983, Nora Ephron Collected 1991, Big City Eyes 2000, I Feel Bad About My Neck 2006. *Address:* 136 East 79th Street, New York, NY 10075 (office); c/o Sam Cohn, International Creative Management, 40 West 57th Street, New York, NY 10019, USA (office).

EPSTEIN, Emanuel, BS, MS, PhD; American professor of plant nutrition and plant physiologist; *Edward A. Dickson Emeritus Professor, University of California, Davis;* b. 5 Nov. 1916, Duisburg, Germany; s. of Harry Epstein and Bertha Epstein (née Löwe); brother of Gabriel Epstein (q.v.) and Theodor Epstein; m. Hazel M. Leask 1943; two c. (one deceased); ed Univ. of California (Davis and Berkeley); served in US Army 1943–46; Plant Physiologist, US Dept of Agric., Beltsville, Md 1950–58; Lecturer and Assoc. Plant Physiologist, Univ. of California, Davis 1958–65, Prof. of Plant Nutrition and Plant Physiologist 1965–87, Research Prof. 1987–, Prof. of Botany 1974–87, Research Prof. 1987–, Edward A. Dickson Emer. Prof. 2009; Faculty Research Lecturer 1980; Consultant to govt agencies, private orgs and publrs at various times; Guggenheim and Fulbright Fellowships; mem. NAS; Pres. Pacific Div., AAAS 1990–91; Gold Medal, Pisa Univ. (Italy) 1962, Charles Reid Barnes Life Membership Award, American Soc. of Plant Physiologists 1986, Univ. of Calif., Davis Coll. of Agricultural and Environmental Sciences Award of Distinction 1999, Cal Aggie Alumni Asscn Citation for Excellence 1999. *Publications:* Mineral Nutrition of Plants: Principles and Perspectives 1972, 2nd edn (with A. J. Bloom) 2005, The Biosaline Concept: An Approach to the Utilization of Underexploited Resources (co-ed.) 1979, Saline Agriculture: Salt-Tolerant Plants for Developing Countries (co-ed.) 1990; research papers, reviews and articles. *Leisure interests:* hiking, photography and history. *Address:* Department of Land, Air and Water Resources, Soils and Biogeochemistry, University of California, Davis, CA 95616-3630, USA (office). *Telephone:* (530) 752-0197 (office). *Fax:* (530) 752-1552 (office). *E-mail:* eqepstein@ucdavis.edu (office). *Website:* lawr.ucdavis.edu (office).

EPSTEIN, Gabriel, AADip (Hons), FRIBA, SADG; British architect, planning consultant and teacher; *Professor Emeritus, University of Stuttgart;* b. 25 Oct. 1918, Duisburg, Germany; s. of Harry Epstein and Bertha Epstein (née Löwe); brother of Emanuel Epstein (q.v.); m. Josette A. Glonneau 1955; two s. one d.; ed schools in Germany, Belgium and Israel and Architectural Asscn School of Architecture, London; officer in Royal Engineers in World War II; Partner, Shepheard, Epstein & Hunter 1955–86; Prof. of Architecture and Dir Inst. of Public Bldgs and Design, Univ. of Stuttgart 1978–88, Prof., Centre for Infrastructure Planning, Univ. of Stuttgart 1984–2006, Prof. Emer. 2006–; consultant and mem. competition juries London, Stuttgart, Paris, Brussels, Leipzig, Berlin, Munich, etc. 1992–96; Pres. Architectural Asscn, London 1963–64, Franco-British Union of Architects 1976–77; mem. Berlin Acad. of Arts and Letters, Soc. Française des Architectes; Hon. DLitt (Lancaster); four Civic Trust Awards for Univ. and Housing Work 1966–82, two Ministry Medals for Good Design in Housing 1968, 1976, Int. Prize for Architecture for London Housing 1983. *Works include:* master plan and bldgs, Univ. of Lancaster; master plans and bldgs for Open Univ. (UK), Univ. of Tlemcen (Algeria) and Univ. of Ghana; town-planning consultant for London Docks (Wapping) 1976–81, for New Univ., Paris Region 1992, for European Parl. Complex, Brussels 1992, 2003; many housing projects in London and schools and colleges in England 1950–85; School of Architecture and Eng, Library and several faculty and auditoria bldgs for Univ. of Louvain-la-Neuve, Belgium 1970–80. *Publications:* Planning Forms for Twentieth Century Cities 1976, Well-Being In Cities: The Low Energy City 1979, Energy Use and City Form 1981, Living-Places 2004. *Leisure interest:* sketching/painting. *Address:* 3 rue André Mazet, 75006 Paris, France. *Telephone:* 1-43-25-89-59. *Fax:* 1-43-26-57-42.

EPSTEIN, Matthew A., BA; American opera administrator and academic; b. 23 Dec. 1947, New York, NY; ed Univ. of Pennsylvania; Vice-Pres. Columbia Artists Man. 1973–99; Artistic Dir Brooklyn Acad. of Music 1987–90; consultant Santa Fe Opera 1980–; Artistic Dir Welsh Nat. Opera 1991–94; mem. Faculty, Voice and Vocal Piano, Music Acad. of the West, Santa Barbara, Calif. 1997–; Artistic Dir Lyric Opera of Chicago 1999–2005; Artistic Dir Kennedy Center Gala honoring George London (televised by PBS, recorded by RCA) 1981; Dir Rossini 200th Birthday Celebration Gala, Lincoln Center (televised and recorded by EMI) 1990; Artistic Consultant 'Celebration of the American Musical', Lincoln Center (televised) 1997. *Address:* Music Academy of the West, 1070 Fairway Road, Santa Barbara, CA 93108-2899, USA. *Telephone:* (805) 969-4726. *Fax:* (805) 969-0686. *Website:* www .musicacademy.org.

EPSTEIN, Sir (Michael) Anthony, Kt, CBE, MD, DSc, PhD, FRCPath, FRS; British virologist and academic; *Professor, Nuffield Department of Clinical Medicine, University of Oxford;* b. 18 May 1921, London; ed St Paul's School, London, Trinity Coll., Cambridge and Middlesex Hosp. Medical School, London; House Surgeon, Middlesex Hosp. and Addenbrooke's Hosp., Cambridge 1944; commissioned RAMC 1945–47; Asst Pathologist, Bland Sutton Inst., Middlesex Hosp. Medical School 1948–65; Berkeley Travelling Fellow and French Govt Exchange Scholar, Inst. Pasteur, Paris 1952–53, Visiting Investigator, Rockefeller Inst., New York 1956; Reader in Experimental Pathology, Middlesex Hosp. Medical School and Hon. Consultant in Experimental Virology, Middlesex Hosp. 1965–68; Prof. of Pathology, Univ. of Bristol 1968–85, Head of Dept and Hon. Consultant Pathologist, Avon Area Health Authority (Teaching) 1968–82; Emer. Prof. of Pathology, Univ. of Bristol; Prof., Nuffield Dept of Clinical Medicine, Univ. of Oxford 1985–; Extraordinary Fellow, Wolfson Coll., Oxford 1986–2001, Hon. Fellow 2001–; mem. MRC Cell Bd 1979–84, Chair. 1982–84; Chair. CRC/MRC Jt Cttee for Inst. of Cancer Research 1982–87; mem. MRC 1982–86, Chair. MRC Tropical Medicine Research Bd 1985–88, Medical and Scientific Advisory Panel, Leukaemia Research Fund 1982–85, Council of Royal Soc. 1983–85, 1986–91; mem. UK Co-ordinating Cttee on Cancer Research 1983–87, Scientific Advisory Cttee, The Lister Inst. of Preventive Medicine 1984–86; Scientific Adviser, Charing Cross Medical Research Centre 1984–87; Foreign Sec. and Vice-Pres. Royal Soc. 1986–91, MRC Assessor 1987–91; mem. Expert Working Party on Bovine Spongiform Encephalopathy, Dept of Health 1988, mem. Exec. Bd Int. Council of Scientific Unions 1990–93, Chair. Cttee for Science in Cen. and Eastern Europe 1992–95; mem. Exec. Council European Science Foundation 1990–93; Special Rep. of Dir-Gen., UNESCO, for Science in Russia, Moscow 1992; mem. Programme Advisory Group, World Bank China Key Studies Project 1992–96; Jt Founder Ed. Int. Review of Experimental Pathology 1962–86; Fellow Univ. Coll. London 1991; Hon. Prof., Zhongshan Medical Univ., People's Repub. of China 1981, Chinese Acad. of Preventive Medicine 1988; Hon. Fellow Queensland Inst. of Medical Research 1983, Royal Coll. of Pathologists of Australasia 1995, Cancer Research UK 2004, Univ. of Bristol 2006; Hon. mem. Belgian Soc. for Study of Cancer 1979, Pathological Soc. 1987; Hon. FRSE 1991; Hon. FRCP 1986; Hon. MD (Edin.) 1986, (Charles Univ., Prague) 1998; Hon. DSc (Birmingham) 1996; Leeuwenhoek Prize Lecturer, Royal Soc. 1983; Markham Skerritt Prize (Univ. of Bristol) 1977, Paul Ehrlich and Ludwig Darmstaedster Prize and Medal (Frankfurt) 1973, Bristol-Myers Award (New York) 1982, Prix Griffuel (Paris) 1986, Gairdner Foundation Int. Award (Toronto) 1988, S. Weiner Distinguished Visitor Award (Univ. of Manitoba) 1988, Royal Medal, The Royal Soc. 1992. *Scientific achievement:* discovered Epstein-Barr virus (EBV) (first human cancer virus) 1964. *Publications:* over 240 scientific papers in int. journals; numerous studies on EBV and other viruses; author and ed. of five scientific books. *Address:* Nuffield Department of Clinical Medicine, Oxford University, John Radcliffe Hospital, Headington, Oxford, OX3 9DU, England (office). *Telephone:* (1865) 221334 (office). *Fax:* (1865) 222901 (office). *Website:* www.ndm.ox.ac.uk (office).

ERAKAT, Saeb, BA, MA, PhD; Palestinian politician and journalist; b. 1955, East Jerusalem; m. two s. two d.; ed San Francisco State Univ., USA and Bradford Univ., UK; fmr journalist Al Quds daily; Lecturer in Political Science An-Najah Univ. 1983, fmr Sec.-Gen. Arab Studies Soc.; mem. negotiating team Oslo Peace Process 1995; Head Palestinian Negotiation Steering and Monitoring Cttee 1996, currently Chief Palestinian Peace Negotiator; elected mem. Palestinian Legis. Council, Jericho 1996; Minister of Negotiation Affairs, Palestinian Nat. Authority (PNA) 2004–06; Hon. PhD (Peru) 2004. *Publications include:* eight books and numerous articles on foreign policy. *Address:* c/o Fatah, Ramallah, Palestinian Autonomous Areas (office). *E-mail:* fateh@fateh.org. *Website:* www.fateh.net.

ERBAKAN, Necmettin; Turkish politician; b. 1926, Sinop; ed Inst. of Mechanics, Tech. Univ. of Istanbul and Technische Universität, Aachen, Germany; Asst Lecturer, Inst. of Mechanics, Tech. Univ. of Istanbul 1948–51, Prof. 1954–66; Engineer, Firma Deutz 1951–54; Chair. Industrial Dept, Turkish Asscn of Chambers of Commerce 1966–68, Chair. of Asscn 1968; mem. Nat. Ass. 1969–80; f. Nat. Order Party 1970 (disbanded 1971); Chair. Nat. Salvation Party Oct. 1973 (disbanded 1981); Deputy Prime Minister and Minister of State Jan.–Sept. 1974; Deputy Prime Minister 1975–77, July–Dec. 1977; detained 1980–81; now leader Refah Partisi (Welfare Party, f. 1983); Prime Minister of Turkey 1996–98; sentenced to 28 months' imprisonment for fraud March 2002. *Address:* c/o Office of the Prime Minister, Basbakanlik, Ankara, Turkey.

ERBSEN, Claude Ernest, BA; American journalist; *Director, Innovation International Media Consultancy Group;* b. 10 March 1938, Trieste, Italy; s. of Henry M. Erbsen and Laura Erbsen; m. 1st Jill J. Prosky 1959; m. 2nd Hedy M. Cohn 1970; two s. one d.; ed Amherst Coll. Mass.; reporter and printer, Amherst Journal Record 1955–57; staff reporter, El Tiempo, Bogotá 1960;

with Associated Press (AP) in New York and Miami 1960–65; reporter to Chief of Bureau, AP Brazil 1965–69; Exec. Rep. for Latin America, AP 1969–70; Business Man. and Admin. Dir AP-Dow Jones Econ. Report, London 1970–75; Deputy Dir AP World Services, New York 1975–80, Vice-Pres., Dir 1987–2003; Vice-Pres., Dir AP-Dow Jones News Services 1980–87; currently Dir, Innovation Int. Media Consultancy Group; mem. Bd Dirs World Press Inst. St Paul; mem. Int. Press Inst., Council on Foreign Relations; San Giusto d'Oro award, City of Trieste 1995. *Leisure interests:* reading, travel, folk art. *Address:* Innnovation, 27 Stratton Road, Scarsdale, NY 10583-7556, USA (office). *Telephone:* (914) 725-1809 (office). *E-mail:* erbsen@innovation-mediaconsulting.com (office). *Website:* www.innovation-mediaconsulting.com (office).

ERÇEL, Gazi; Turkish banker; b. 20 Feb. 1945, Gelibolu; m. Zeynel Erçel; one d.; ed Ankara Univ., Vanderbilt Univ., Tenn.; bank examiner, Ministry of Finance 1967–77; Deputy Dir-Gen. of Treasury 1977–82; Asst to Exec. Dir IMF, Washington DC 1982–86; Dir-Gen. of Treasury and Foreign Trade 1987–89; Gov. Cen. Bank of Turkey 1996–2001; Cen. Banker of the Year Award, Global Finance, Prague 2000. *Address:* c/o Türkiye Cumhuriyet Merkez Bankasi AS, Istiklal Cad. 10, 06100 Ulus, Ankara, Turkey. *Website:* www.tcmb.gov.tr (office).

ERDEI, Tamás; Hungarian banker; *Chairman and CEO, Hungarian Foreign Trade Bank;* b. 1954; one c.; fmr Gen. Man. Br. Office Nat. Savings Bank; Chief Officer in Banking Supervision, Ministry of Finance 1981–83; Chief Accountant Hungarian Foreign Trade Bank (MKB) 1983–85, Exec. Dir 1985–90, Deputy Chief Exec. 1990–94, CEO 1994–97, Chair. and CEO 1997–; Pres. Hungarian Banking Asscn 1997–. *Address:* Hungarian Foreign Trade Bank MKB, Váci u. 38, Budapest V, Hungary (office).

ERDEM, Kaya; Turkish government official; b. 1928, Zonguldak; s. of Hilmi and Pakize Erdem; m. Sevil Şibay 1956; two d.; ed High School of Commerce, Univ. of Marmara; mem. faculty, Anatolian Univ. 1959–65; Finance Dir Sugar Corpn 1960–62; Asst Dir-Gen. State Treasury 1963–72; mem. Cttee for Reorganization of State Econ. Enterprises 1971–72; Dir-Gen. State Treasury 1972–73; Chief Financial Counsellor, Turkish Embassy, London 1973–76; Sec.-Gen. Ministry of Finance 1978–80; Minister of Finance 1980–82, Deputy Prime Minister, Minister of State 1983–89; prominent in drafting and implementation of econ. stabilization programme 1980. *Publications:* State Economic Enterprise 1966; and numerous articles on cost and managerial accountancy. *Leisure interests:* bridge, tennis. *Address:* c/o Office of the Deputy Prime Minister, Basbakan yard. ve Devlet Bakani, Bakanlıklar, Ankara, Turkey.

ERDENEBAT, Badarchiin, DEcon; Mongolian politician; b. 1959, Hövsgöl prov.; m. Sergelen; ed Novosibirsk Higher School of Geodesy and Cartography, Mongolian State Univ., Inst. of Econ. and Political Studies, Russian Acad. of Sciences; f. Erel Group (interests in banking, investment, mining and construction) 1989, Dir-Gen. –2000; f. Mongolian Democratic New Socialist Party (now Motherland Party) 1998, currently Chair.; mem. Mongolian Great Khural (Parl.) 2000–; Minister of Defence 2004–06, of Fuel and Power 2006–07. *Address:* Motherland Party, Erel Co, Bayanzürkh District, Ulan Bator, Mongolia (office).

ERDENECHULUUN, Luvsangiin; Mongolian diplomatist and politician; b. 10 Oct. 1948, Ulan Bator; s. of Sonomyn Luvsan and Lhamsurengiin Baimanhand; m. Sukh-Ochiryn Solongo 1969; two s. one d.; ed State Inst. of Int. Relations, Moscow and Diplomatic Acad. Moscow; officer, Dept of Int. Relations, Ministry of Foreign Affairs 1972–80; First Sec. Perm. Mission of Mongolia at UN 1980–84; Head, Press and Information Dept Ministry of Foreign Affairs 1985–86, Head, Dept of Int. Orgs 1988–90; Deputy Perm. Rep. to UN 1990, Perm. Rep. 1992–96; Adviser to Pres. of Mongolia 1996–97; Minister of Foreign Affairs 2000–04; Distinguished Service Medal, Order of Polar Star. *Address:* c/o Ministry of Foreign Affairs, Peace Avenue Building 7A, Ulan Bator, Mongolia (office).

ERDŐ, HE Cardinal Péter, DCL, DTheol; Hungarian ecclesiastic; *Archbishop of Esztergom-Budapest and President, Hungarian Catholic Bishops' Conference;* b. 25 June 1952, Budapest; ed Seminary of Esztergom, Theological Acad. of Budapest, Pontifical Lateran Univ., Rome; ordained priest by Bishop László Lékai 1975; parish priest, Parish of Dorog; Prof. of Theology and Canon Law, Seminary of Esztergom 1980–88; Prof., Faculty of Canon Law, Pontifical Gregorian Univ., Rome 1986–2002; Prof., Faculty of Theology, Peter Pazmany Catholic Univ., Budapest 1988–2003, Dean of Faculty 1997, Rector 1998–2007; auxiliary Bishop of Szekesfekhervar 1999; Titular Bishop of Puppi 1999; consecrated by Pope John Paul II, Vatican City 2000; Archbishop of Esztergom-Budapest 2002–; cr. Cardinal 2003, Cardinal-Priest of St Balbina 2003–; Pres. Hungarian Catholic Bishops' Conf. 2005–, Consilium Conferentiarum Episcopalian Europae; mem. Hungarian Acad. of Sciences 2007; Galileo Galilei Prize, Italian Rotary Club 1999. *Publications:* 30 books, 500 articles. *Address:* Archdiocese of Esztergom-Budapest, Primasi es Erseki Hivatal, Mindszenty hercegprimas ter 2, Pf. 25, 2501 Esztergom, Magyarorszag, Hungary (office). *Telephone:* (33) 411-288 (office). *Fax:* (33) 411-085 (office).

ERDOES, Mary Callahan, BS, MBA; American business executive; *CEO, JPMorgan Private Bank;* b. 13 Aug. 1967, Winnetka, Ill.; m. Philip Erdoes; two d.; ed Georgetown Univ. and Harvard Business School; worked at Bankers Trust; Vice-Pres. with Meredith, Martin & Kaye –1996; Head of Fixed Income Group, JPMorgan Private Bank 1996–2002, apptd Head of Global Investments 2002, currently CEO and mem. JPMorgan Chase Exec. Cttee; mem. Bd of Dirs US Fund for UNICEF 2005–; ranked 100th by Forbes magazine amongst 100 Most Powerful Women 2005. *Leisure interests:* running, Dora the Explorer games, Ring Around the Rosie or whatever her two daughters request. *Address:* 41 River Terrace, New York, NY 10282-1113; JPMorgan Private Bank, 345 Park Avenue, New York, NY 10154-1002, USA (office). *Website:* www.jpmorgan.com (office).

ERDOGAN, Recep Tayyip, BA; Turkish politician; *Prime Minister;* b. 1954, Rize; m.; four c.; ed Marmara Univ., Istanbul; professional footballer 1969–80; elected Chair. Nat. Salvation Party Youth Org. early 1970s; Chair. Istanbul Br. Welfare Party 1985; Mayor of Metropolitan Istanbul 1994–98, tenure of office ended by court decree 1998, convicted of having read a provocative poem in public, imprisoned for four months and banned for life from holding public office; mem. Virtue Party 1998–2001; Founder and Chair. AK Partisi – AKP (Justice and Development Party), ruling party in Turkey following 2002 elections, constitutional ban preventing him from holding public office overturned Jan. 2003; Prime Minister of Turkey March 2003–; Founder Democratization and Action Movt; European of the Year 2004, Agricola Medal, UN Food and Agric. Org. 2007. *Address:* Office of the Prime Minister, Başbakanlik, Bakanliklar, Ankara (office); AK Partisi, Genel Merkezi Ceyhun Atif Kansu Cad., No. 202 Balgat, Ankara, Turkey (office). *Telephone:* (312) 4189056 (office). *Fax:* (312) 4180476 (office). *E-mail:* info@basbakanlik.gov.tr (office). *Website:* www.basbakanlik.gov.tr (office); www.akparti.org.tr (office).

ERDŐS, André; Hungarian diplomatist; *Senior Adviser, International Centre for Democratic Transition (ICDT), Budapest;* b. 18 May 1941, Algiers, Algeria; s. of Gusztáv Erdős and Márta Czeichner; m. Katalin Pintér 1965; one d.; ed Moscow State Inst. for Int. Relations, Budapest School of Political Sciences; joined Hungarian Ministry of Foreign Affairs 1965; attaché, Morocco 1968–72; staff mem., CSCE Dept Ministry of Foreign Affairs 1972–78; assigned to Perm. Mission of Hungary at UN, New York 1978–83; del. to UN Gen. Ass. 1984, 1985, 1989; Adviser to Minister of Foreign Affairs of Hungary 1984–86; Head of Hungary's del. to Vienna CSCE follow-up meeting 1986–89; Perm. Rep. to UN 1990–94, 1997–2001; Pres. UN Disarmament and Int. Security Comm. 2001–02; Hungarian Rep., UN Security Council 1992–93; Deputy State Sec. for Multilateral Affairs, Ministry of Foreign Affairs 1994–97; Amb. to France 2002–06; currently Sr Adviser Int. Centre for Democratic Transition, Budapest; Prof., Corvinus Univ., Budapest; mem. Prime Minister's Council on Foreign and Security Policy; Hon. Prof., Budapest Inst. for Grad. Int. and Diplomatic Studies 1999; Commdr's Cross, Order of Merit (Hungary), Order of Duke Branimir with Ribbons (Croatia), Commdr, Légion d'honneur (France), Grand Croix, Ordre nat. du Mérite (France). *Publications:* Co-operation in the United Nations between Socialist and Developing Countries 1981, Soviet-German Relations 1939–41 1984, The Circumstances of the Birth of the 1941 Soviet-German Non-Aggression Pact 1987, Geography vs. Political Reality at the United Nations 2001, Sorsfordító Esztendök (Crucial Years) 2004, Additions to the history of Hungarian foreign policy during the system change 2009; numerous articles on int. affairs. *Leisure interests:* philately, numismatics, collecting postcards, making video movies. *Address:* International Centre for Democratic Transition, Arvacska u.12, Budapest 1022, Hungary (office). *Telephone:* (1) 438-0820 (office). *Fax:* (1) 438-0821 (office). *E-mail:* andreerdos@yahoo.com (office). *Website:* www.icdt.hu (office).

ERDRICH, (Karen) Louise, MA; American writer and poet; b. 7 June 1954, Little Falls, MN; d. of Ralph Louis Erdrich and Rita Joanne (Gourneau) Erdrich; m. Michael Anthony Dorris 1981 (died 1997); six c. (one s. deceased); ed Dartmouth Coll., Johns Hopkins Univ.; Visiting Poetry Teacher, ND State Arts Council 1977–78; Teacher of Writing, Johns Hopkins Univ., Baltimore 1978–79; Communications Dir, Ed., Circle-Boston Indian Council 1979–80; Textbook Writer Charles Merrill Co. 1980; mem. PEN (mem. Exec. Bd 1985–90); Guggenheim Fellow 1985–86; Nelson Algren Award 1982, Pushcart Prize 1983, Nat. Magazine Fiction Award 1983, 1987, First Prize O. Henry Awards 1987. *Publications include:* fiction: Love Medicine (Nat. Book Critics' Circle Award for best work of fiction) 1984, The Beet Queen 1986, Tracks 1988, The Crown of Columbus (with Michael Anthony Dorris) 1991, The Bingo Palace 1994, The Bluejay's Dance 1995, Tales of Burning Love 1996, The Antelope Wife 1998, The Birchbark House 1999, The Last Report on the Miracles at Little No Horse 2001, The Master Butcher's Singing Club 2003, Four Souls 2004, The Painted Drum 2005, The Plague of Doves 2008, The Red Convertible: Selected and New Stories 1978–2008 2009; poetry: Jacklight 1984, Baptism of Desire 1989; non-fiction: Imagination (textbook) 1980; contrib. short stories, children's stories, essays and poems to anthologies and journals, including American Indian Quarterly, Atlantic, Frontiers, Kenyon Review, Ms, New England Review, New York Times Book Review, New Yorker, North American Review, Redbook. *Address:* The Wylie Agency, 250 West 57th Street, Suite 2114, New York, NY 10107, USA (office). *Telephone:* (212) 246-0069 (office). *Fax:* (212) 586-8953 (office). *E-mail:* mail@wylieagency.com (office). *Website:* www.wylieagency.com (office).

EREDIAUWA, Omo N'Oba N'Edo Uku-Akpolokpolo, Oba of Benin, BA; Nigerian traditional monarch; *Member, Council of State;* b. 24 June 1923; ed Edo Coll., Benin, Govt Coll., Ibadan, Yaba Coll., Lagos, Cambridge Univ., England; followed career in Civil Service; retd 1973 as Perm. Sec. in Fed. Ministry of Health; Civil Commr for Bendel State 1975–77; succeeded to throne of Benin March 1979–99; mem. Council of State 1979–. *Address:* The Palace, Box 1, Benin City, Bendel State, Nigeria. *Telephone:* (52) 240001.

EREN, Halıt, MA, PhD; Turkish institute director and academic; *Director-General, Research Centre for Islamic History, Art and Culture (IRCICA);* b. 1953, Gümülcine (Komotini); ed Inst. of Social Sciences and Inst. of Turkic Studies, Marmara Univ., Istanbul; apptd Sr Researcher and Head of Library and Documentation Dept, Research Centre for Islamic History, Art and Culture (IRCICA) 1981, Deputy Dir-Gen. 1984–2005, Co-ordinator/mem. Organizing Cttee of IRCICA's congresses and symposiums relating to Caucasia, Cen. Asia and the Balkans, participated in Islamic Summit Confs,

Islamic Confs of Ministers of Foreign Affairs, Culture, and Information, and other confs and cttees of OIC, Dir-Gen. IRCICA 2005–; Founder and Admin. Turkish-Islamic Asscn of England 1979–81; mem. Exec. Bd Cen. Office of the Solidarity Asscn of Western Thrace Turks, Istanbul 1984–94, Pres. 1992–94; Sec.-Gen. Foundation for Research on Islamic History, Art and Culture, Istanbul 1990–; Founding mem. Turkish Soc. for the History of Science 1989–, Rumeli (Eastern Europe) Foundation for Educ., Istanbul 1993–; mem. Preparatory Cttee Seventh Devt Plan of Turkey 1993; Founding mem. Western Thrace Foundation for Educ., Culture and Health, Istanbul 1996, Vice-Pres. 1996–98, 2002–04; Second Pres. Cultural and Solidarity Asscn of East European Turks 1997–2001; mem. Exec. Bd and Second Chair. Cultural and Solidarity Foundation of East European Turks 2001–; Advisor on Balkan Affairs to Minister of State of Repub. of Turkey 1997; Founder and Ed.-in-Chief Bati Trakya'nin sesi (The Voice of Western Thrace) journal 1987–94, Gen. Co-ordinator 1994–97; Ed. Rumeli kültürü journal 2002–. *Publications include:* World Bibliography of Translations of the Meanings of the Holy Quran: 1515–1980 (compiler, jtly with Ismet Binark) 1986, Bati Trakya Türkleri (Western Thrace Turks) 1997; numerous articles in professional journals. *Address:* Research Centre for Islamic History, Art and Culture (IRCICA), PO Box 24, Beşiktaş, 80692 İstanbul, Turkey (office). *Telephone:* (212) 2591742 (office). *Fax:* (212) 2584365 (office). *E-mail:* ircica@ircica.org (office). *Website:* www.ircica.org (office).

ERESMAN, Randall K. (Randy), BSc; Canadian petroleum engineer and energy industry executive; *President and CEO, EnCana Corporation;* b. Medicine Hat, Alberta; m. Shelly Eresman; two c.; ed Northern Alberta Inst. of Tech., Edmonton, Univ. of Wyoming; joined Alberta Energy Co. (AEC) 1980, Vice-Pres. AEC Oil and Gas 1996–99, Pres. AEC Oil and Gas Partnership 1999–2002, Exec. Vice-Pres. EnCana Corpn (after merger of AEC and PanCanadian Energy Corpn), responsible for Onshore N America Div. Jan.–Dec. 2002, COO 2002–06, Pres. and CEO 2006–; mem. Asscn of Professional Engineers, Geologists and Geophysicists of Alberta, Young Pres' Org., Canadian Council of Chief Execs; mem. Nat. Advisory Bd of Univ. of Wyoming's Coll. of Eng, Nat. Petroleum Council (an Oil and Natural Gas Advisory Cttee to US Sec. of Energy). *Address:* EnCana Corpn, 1800 855 2nd Street SW, PO Box 2850, Calgary, Alberta, T2P 2S5, Canada (office). *Telephone:* (403) 645-2000 (office). *Fax:* (403) 645-3400 (office). *E-mail:* info@encana.com (office). *Website:* www.encana.com (office).

ERGEN, Charles (Charlie) W., BS, MBA; American business executive; *Chairman and CEO, EchoStar Communications Corporation;* m.; ed Univ. of Tenn., Babcock Grad. School, Wake Forest Univ.; f. EchoStar Communications Corpn 1980, now Chair. and CEO, f. Dish Network (subsidiary of EchoStar Communications Corpn) 1996, Chair. and CEO 1998–; Home Satellite TV Asscn Star Award 1988, Rocky Mountain News Business Person of the Year 1996, 2001. *Address:* EchoStar Communications Corporation, 9601 South Meridian Boulevard, Englewood, CO 80112, USA (office). *Telephone:* (303) 723-1000 (office). *Fax:* (303) 723-1399 (office). *Website:* www.dishnetwork.com (office).

ERGIN, Mehmet, PhD; Turkish professor of physical chemistry; *Fellow and Secretary General, Islamic Academy of Sciences;* b. 25 May 1936, Yozgat; m.; two c.; ed Ankara Gazi High School, Ankara Univ., Univ. of Glasgow, UK; researcher, Nuclear Chem. Lab., Atomic Energy Comm., Acting Dir 1963–66, fmr Pres.; research and training at IAEA Labs, Vienna; researcher, Inst. for Physics and Chem., Asscn for Meat Research, FRG, then Dept of Chem., Univ. of Glasgow; Lecturer, Asst Prof., then Prof. of Physical Chem., Dept of Chem., Hacettepe Univ.; Exec. Sec. Turkish Scientific and Research Council (TUBITAK) 1974, Deputy Sec. Gen. for Planning and Coordination 1985–87, Pres. 1987–90; Fellow, Islamic Acad. of Sciences, Vice-Pres. 1986–99, Sec. Gen. 1999–; mem. Bd of Trustees and Visiting Lecturer, Faith Univ., Istanbul. *Address:* Islamic Academy of Sciences, PO Box 830036, Amman, Jordan (office). *Telephone:* 5522104 (office). *Fax:* 5511803 (office). *E-mail:* secretariat@ias-worldwide.org (office). *Website:* www.ias-worldwide.org (office).

ERGMA, Ene, PhD, DrSci; Estonian politician and astrophysicist; *Speaker of Parliament;* b. 29 Feb. 1944, Rakvere; ed Viljandi Secondary School, Moscow State Univ., Russia, Tartu Univ.; jr research assoc., Inst. of Physics and Astronomy, Estonian Acad. of Sciences 1972–74; jr research assoc., Exec. Sec., Sr and Leading Research Assoc., Astronomical Council, USSR Acad. of Science 1974–88; Prof. of Theoretical Physics and Astrophysics, Tartu Univ. 1988–92, Prof. of Astrophysics 1992–, Head of Theoretical Physics Inst. 1993–96, Head of Physics Dept 1993–98; Vice-Pres. Estonian Acad. of Sciences 1999–; fmr Vice-Chair. Educ. and Culture Cttee, Tartu City Council; Speaker Parl. of Estonia (Riigikogu) (first woman in position) 2003–06, Deputy Speaker 2006–07, Speaker 2007–; Guest Prof., Amsterdam Univ. 1997; Guest Researcher, Helsinki Univ. 2000; mem. European Astronomical Union, Int. Astrophysical Union, Estonian Astronomical Cttee, Tartu Observatory Science Council, Estonian Physical Soc. Cttee, Estonian Acad. of Sciences, Euroscience; Assoc. mem. Royal Astronomical Soc.; foreign mem. Royal Swedish Acad. of Eng Sciences; Grand Cross, Order of Orange-Nassau (Netherlands), Grand Cross, Order of Crown (Belgium), Order of the Nat. Coat of Arms, 2nd class (Estonia), Royal Order of the North Star, 1st class (Sweden), Grand Decoration of Honour (Austria), Commdr's Cross, Order of Repub. of Poland, Grand Cross, Order of Merit of the Italian Repub., Grand Officer, Order of Infante Dom Henrique (Portugal), Order of the White Star, 4th class, Estonia 2001; Estonian Repub. Science Award in Exact Sciences 2002, Medal of Estonian Acad. of Sciences. *Publications include:* over 100 scientific articles in professional journals. *Leisure interests:* tennis. *Address:* Estonian Parliament, Lossi plats 1a, 15165 Tallinn, Estonia (office). *Telephone:* 631-6301 (office). *E-mail:* ene.ergma@riigikogu.ee (office). *Website:* www.riigikogu.ee (office); www.parlament.ee (office).

ERICKSON, Arthur Charles, CC, BArch, FRAIC, ARCA; Canadian architect; *President and Chief Executive Officer, Arthur Erickson Architectural Corporation;* b. 14 June 1924, Vancouver; s. of the late Oscar and of Myrtle Erickson (née Chatterson); ed Univ. of British Columbia, McGill Univ.; travel study in Mediterranean countries and N Europe on McGill Scholarship 1950–53; private practice 1953–62; Asst Prof. Univ. of Oregon 1955–56; Instructor and Asst Prof. Univ. of British Columbia 1957–60, Assoc. Prof. 1961; Canada Council Fellowship for architectural research in Asia 1961; with Erickson, Massey 1963–72; Prin. Arthur Erickson Architects 1972–91, Pres. and CEO Arthur Erickson Architectural Corpn 1991–; mem. many architectural insts and asscns; mem. Science Council of Canada Cttee on Urban Devt 1971, Bd Canadian Conf. of the Arts 1972, Canadian Council on Urban Research, Bd of Trustees, Inst. for Research on Public Policy, fmr mem. Design Council of Portland Devt Comm.; mem. Int. Council of Museum of Modern Art, Americas Soc.; Life mem. Vancouver Art Gallery; Hon. Fellow, Royal Architectural Inst. of Scotland 1987; Hon. FCAE; Hon. Fellow, CAM Foundation; Hon. FAIA 1978; Hon. FRIBA 2001; Hon. DEng, (Nova Scotia Technical Coll.) 1971; Hon. LLD (Simon Fraser Univ.) 1973, (McGill Univ.) 1975, (Univ. of Manitoba) 1978, (Lethbridge Univ.) 1981; Hon. DLitt (British Columbia) 1985; won First Prize in competition for Simon Fraser Univ., First Prize for design of Canadian Pavilion at Expo '70, Osaka, Pan Pacific Citation, American Inst. of Architects, Hawaiian Chapter 1963, Molson Prize, Canada Council for the Arts 1967, Architectural Inst. of Japan Award for Best Pavilion Expo '70, Royal Bank of Canada Award 1971, American Architectural Fraternity 1973, Auguste Perret Award, Int. Union of Architects 1974, Canadian Housing Design Council Awards for Residential Design 1975, President's Award of Excellence, American Soc. of Landscape Architects 1979, Grande Médaille d'Or Académie d'Architecture de France 1984, Gold Medal, Royal Architectural Inst. of Canada 1984, Gold Medal, American Inst. of Architects 1986. *Publications:* The Architecture of Arthur Erickson 1975, Seven Stones by Edith Iglauer. *Leisure interests:* reading, writing, music, skiing, scuba. *Address:* 1672 West 1st Avenue, Vancouver, BC, V6J 1G1, Canada. *Telephone:* (604) 737-9801 (office). *Fax:* (604) 737-9092 (office). *E-mail:* atelier@lynx.bc.ca (office). *Website:* arthurerickson.com (office).

ERIKSSON, Göran Olof, MA; Swedish theatre director, author and translator; b. 7 March 1929; s. of Walfrid Eriksson and Ebba Renck; m. 1st Lill-Inger Ingman 1953; m. 2nd Jane Friedmann 1982; one s. one d.; ed Uppsala Univ.; Literary Ed. Göteborgs Handels-och Sjöfarts-Tidning 1956–62; Chief Cultural Ed. Stockholms-Tidningen 1962–66; theatre critic, Dagens Nyheter 1966–68; Dir Stockholms Stadsteater 1967–69, 1975–90; Prin. Dramatiska Institutet 1969–73; Artistic Leader, Ländsteatern i Dalarna 1974–77; now freelance author and dir; Swedish Theatre Critics' Award 1985, Elsa Thulin Prize 1990. *Publications:* I samma plan (essays) 1966; plays: Volpone 1969, Pariserliv 1975, En Skandal i Wien 1978, Freden 1987; essays; radio plays; trans. of about 100 plays by Shakespeare, Molière, Racine, Beckett, etc.

ERIKSSON, Per, MSc, PhD; Swedish telecommunications engineer and university administrator; *Vice-Chancellor, Lund University;* ed Lund Univ.; Pres. and Chair. of several consultancies in signal processing and acoustics 1980–79; Asst Prof. of Telecommunications and Signal Processing, Faculty of Eng, Lund Univ. 1981, Dir of Undergraduate Studies in Electrical Eng 1981–87, Dean and Chair. of Undergraduate Studies 1983–88, Vice-Chancellor Lund Univ. 2009–; Founding Pres. Blekinge Inst. 1989–2000; Dir Gen. Swedish Govt Agency for Innovation Systems (Vinnova) 2000–08; mem. Royal Swedish Acad. of Eng Sciences; Royal Inst. of Tech. Janne Carlsson Prize for Academic Leadership 1999, Telecom City Prize of Honour 2001. *Address:* Office of the Vice-Chancellor, Lund University, PO Box 117, 221 00 Lund, Sweden (office). *Telephone:* (222) 00-00 (office). *Fax:* (222) 47-20 (office). *E-mail:* per.eriksson@rektor.lu.se (office). *Website:* www.lu.se (office).

ERIKSSON, Per-Olof, MSc (Eng); Swedish business executive; b. 1 March 1938, Seglora; s. of Gunhild Eriksson and Herbert Eriksson; m. Helena Eriksson Joachimsson 1962; two s. one d.; ed Royal Inst. of Tech., Stockholm; Dir and Head of Production and Materials Control, Sandvik Coromant 1975; Pres. Seco Tools AB 1976; Pres. and CEO Sandvik AB 1984–94; Chair. Callans Trä AB, Country Systems AB, Odlander,Fredriksson & Co. AB; mem. Bd Biotage AB, Kamstrup-Senea AB, Öresund Investment AB; Hon. DTech. *Leisure interests:* orienteering, skiing, hunting and sailing. *Address:* Hedåsvägen 57, 811 61 Sandviken, Sweden (home). *Telephone:* 26-27-02-02 (home). *Fax:* 26-27-02-06 (home).

ERIKSSON, Sven-Goran; Swedish professional football manager; b. 5 Feb. 1948, Torsby; m. Ann-Christine Petterson 1977 (divorced); two c.; player with Degerfors 1975, Asst Coach 1976, Coach 1977–78; Coach, IFK Gothenburg 1979–82 (won Swedish Cup 1979, Swedish League Champions 1981 1982, UEFA Cup 1982), Benfica 1982–84, 1989–92 (won Portuguese League Championship and Cup 1983, Portuguese League Championship 1984), AS Roma 1982–87 (won Italian Cup 1986), AC Fiorentina 1987–89, Sampdoria 1992–97 (won Italian Cup 1994), Lazio 1997–2001 (won Italian Cup 1998, Italian Super Cup 1998, UEFA Cup 1999, UEFA Super Cup 1999, Italian League Champions 2000); Coach, England Nat. Team 2001–06; Man. Manchester City Football Club 2007–08; Head Coach, Mexican Nat. Team 2008–09; Prince's Plaque (Swedish Govt Award) 2001, BBC Sports Coach of the Year 2001. *Publication:* Sven-Goran Eriksson on Football 2001. *Address:* c/o Athole Still, Athole Still International, Foresters Hall, 25-27 Westow Street, London, SE19 3RY, England (office). *Telephone:* (20) 8771-5271 (office). *Fax:* (20) 8771-8172 (office).

ERJAVEC, Karl Viktor; Slovenian politician and government official; *Minister of the Environment and Physical Planning;* b. 21 June 1960, Aiseau, Belgium; m.; two d.; ed Univ. of Ljubljana; worked in pvt. business sector –1990; mem. Kranj Urban Municipality Ass. Exec. Council 1990–95, apptd

Sec. for Gen. Admin and other Legal Affairs 1990; fmr Head, Office of Human Rights Ombudsman, Repub. of Slovenia 1995–2000, fmr Dir Expert Service; State Sec. for Judicial Admin, Ministry of Justice 2001–04; Minister of Defence 2004–08, of the Environment and Physical Planning 2008–; Pres. Democratic Party of Pensioners of Slovenia 2005–. *Publications:* numerous articles on human rights and judicial system functions. *Leisure interests:* painting, sports. *Address:* Ministry of the Environment and Physical Planning, 1000 Ljubljana, Dunajska cesta 48, Slovenia (office). *Telephone:* (1) 4787400 (office). *Fax:* (1) 4787422 (office). *E-mail:* gp.mop@gov.si (office). *Website:* www.mop.gov.si (office).

ERKEBAYEV, Abdygany Erkibayevich, DPhilSci; Kyrgyzstani politician; b. 9 Sept. 1953, Kara-Tent, Osh Region; m.; two s. one d.; ed Kyrgyz State Univ.; jr researcher, Inst. of World Literature USSR Acad. of Sciences 1976–82; sr teacher, Kyrgyz Women's Pedagogical Inst. 1982–85; Deputy Ed. Kyrgyzstan Madanyaty (newspaper), Dir Inst. of Language and Literature Kyrgyz Acad. of Sciences 1985–90; Deputy Supreme Soviet Kyrgyz SSR 1990–91; Minister of Press and Information Kyrgyz Repub. 1991–92; Vice-Prime Minister 1992–93; Head, Osh Region Admin. 1993–95; mem. Zhogorku Kenesh (Parl.), Chair. Cttee on Social Problems 1995–, Chair. Zhogorku Kenesh 2000–05; Chair. Interparl. Cttee of Russia, Belarus, Kazakhstan, Kyrgyzstan (Union of Four); Co-Chair. Union of Democratic Forces; mem. Nat. Acad. of Sciences Kyrgyz Repub.; Dank Medal. *Publications:* eight books and more than 150 articles and reviews on problems of literature, arts and politics. *Leisure interest:* reading. *Address:* Zhogorku Kenesh, ul. Abdymomunov 207, 720003 Bishkek, Kyrgyzstan (office). *Telephone:* (312) 61-16-04 (office); (312) 550408 (home). *Fax:* (312) 62-50-12 (office). *E-mail:* zs@kenesh.gov.kg (office). *Website:* www.kenesh.kg (office).

ERLANDE-BRANDENBURG, Alain; French museum curator; *Curator, Musée Nationale de la Renaissance;* b. 2 Aug. 1937, Luxeuil-les-Bains; s. of Gilbert Erlande and Renée Pierra; m. Anne-Bénédicte Mérel 1980; four c.; Curator Musée de Cluny and Musée d'Ecouen 1967, Chief Curator 1981; Dir of Studies Ecole pratique des hautes études 1975; Prof. Ecole du Louvre; Assoc. Prof. Ecole Nationale des Chartes 1991–2000; Asst Dir Musées de France 1987–92; Head Musée Nat. du Moyen-Age 1991–94; Curator Musée Nat. de la Renaissance, Château d'Ecouen 2000–05; Pres. Soc. française d'archéologie; Dir French Archives, Ministry of Culture and the French Language 1994–98; Pres. French Soc. of Archaeology 1985–94, Nat. Soc. of French Antique Dealers 1995; Commdr, Ordre nat. du Mérite, Officier, Légion d'honneur, Commdr des Arts et des Lettres. *Publications:* Paris monumental 1974, Le roi est mort 1975, Les rois retrouvés 1977, La dame à la licorne 1978, La cathédrale d'Amiens 1982, L'abbaye de Cluny 1982, L'art gothique 1984, Chartres 1986, La conquête de l'Europe 1260–1380 1987, La cathédrale 1989, Notre-Dame de Paris 1991, Quand les cathédrales étaient peintes 1993, Histoire de l'architecture française: Du Moyen Age à la Renaissance 1995, De pierre, d'or et de felu: la création artistique au Moyen Age 1999, Trois abbayes cisterciennes en Provence, Senanque, Silvacane, Le Thoronet, Paris, le 8ejour 2000, Le Sacre de l'artiste. La création au Moyen Age 2000, Royaumont 2004, L'art gothique 2004. *Address:* 10 bis rue du Pré-aux-clercs, 75007 Paris (home); Impasse de l'abbaye, 77120 Beautheil, France (home). *Telephone:* 1-44-45-95-38 (home). *Fax:* 1-34-38-38-78 (office); 1-45-44-95-38 (home). *E-mail:* alain.erlande_brandenburg@culture.gouv.fr (office). *Website:* www.musee-renaissance.fr (office).

ERLEN, Hubertus, Dr-Ing; German business executive; *Vice-Chairman, Supervisory Board, Bayer Schering Pharma AG;* b. 7 June 1943, Troppau; ed Tech. Univ., Berlin; joined pharmaceutical manufacturing arm of Schering AG 1972, moved to Electroplating Div. 1981, Tech. Dir Feucht plant, Nuremberg 1981–84, mem. Div. Bd 1984–85, mem. Bd 1986–, CEO Schering AG 2001–06, Vice-Chair. Supervisory Bd Bayer Schering Pharma AG 2006–; mem. Supervisory Bd Celesio AG, Invest in Germany GmbH; Chair. Robert Koch Foundation; Vice-Chair. Schering Foundation. *Address:* Supervisory Board, Bayer Schering Pharma AG, Friedrichstr. 81–82, 10117 Berlin, Germany (office). *Telephone:* (30) 46814041 (office). *Website:* www.bayerscheringpharma.de (office).

ERLO, Louis Jean-Marie, (pseudonym of Louis Camerlo); French theatre director; b. 26 April 1929, Lyons; one s.; ed Ecole de la Martinière and Ecole Nat. Professionnelle, Lyons; Asst Producer, Opéra de Lyon 1951, Producer 1953, Dir 1969–; Dir Opéra-Studio, Paris 1973–79; mem. Conseil de développement culturel 1971–73; Dir Aix-en-Provence Festival 1982; has produced operas in many of the major houses of Europe and in San Francisco and Buenos Aires and also for TV (especially works by Wagner); Chevalier, Légion d'honneur, Ordre nat. du Mérite, Commdr des Arts et Lettres. *Address:* Théâtre de l'Opéra, Place de la Comédie, 69001 Lyons, France.

ERMITA, Eduardo; Philippine politician and fmr army officer; *Executive Secretary;* b. 13 July 1935, Balayan, Batangas; m. Elivra Ermita (née Ramos); one s. three d.; ed Naval Postgraduate School, Monterey, Calif., Kennedy Center, Fort Bragg, N Calif., Airborne School, Fort Benning, Ga, USA; Sr Mil. Asst, Office of the Under-Sec. of Nat. Defence 1976–85; Commdg Gen., Civil Relations Service, Armed Forces of the Philippines (AFP) 1985–86; Deputy Chief of Staff, AFP 1986–88, Vice Chief of Staff 1988; Under-Sec., Dept of Nat. Defence 1988–92; Vice-Chair. Govt Peace Panel Negotiations with Moro Nat. Liberation Front 1992–96; Acting Sec. of Nat. Defence 2001; Presidential Adviser on Peace Process 2001–03; Chair. Govt Peace Negotiating Panel in Talks with Moro Islamic Liberation Front 2003; resgnd from AFP, rank of Gen. 2003; Sec. of Nat. Defence 2003–04; Exec. Sec. 2004–; Prov. Chair. LAKAS-NUCD, Prov. of Batangas 1992–; Regional Chair. LAKAS-NUCD, Region IV 1992–; Chair. Inter-Agency Cttee for the Relief, Rehabilitation and Devt 2001; Chair., Vice-Chair. or mem. numerous Govt and Legis. Cttees 1992–2001; mem. Nat. Unification Comm. 1993–94; Pres. Repub. of Philippines Golf Asscn (RPGA) 1994–2000; Commdr, Legion of Honour (Philippines) 1988; Mil. Merit Medals, Outstanding Achievement Medal 1986, Distinguished Service Star 1986, Gold Cross Medal 1987, Distinguished Conduct Star 1988. *Address:* c/o Secretariat of National Defence, DND Building, 3rd Floor, Camp Aguinaldo, Quezon City, Metro Manila, Philippines (office).

ERNAUX, Annie; French writer; b. (Annie Duchesne), 1 Sept. 1940, Lillebonne, Seine-Maritime; d. of the late Alphonse Duchesne and Blanche Dumenil; m. Philippe Ernaux 1964 (divorced); two s.; ed Lycée Jeanne-d'Arc, Rouen, Univs of Rouen, Bordeaux and Grenoble; teacher of literature 1966–2000; Prix Renaudot 1984. *Publications:* Les armoires vides 1974, Ce qu'ils disent ou rien 1977, La femme gelée 1981, La place 1984, Une femme 1988, Passion simple 1992, Journal du dehors 1993, La honte 1997, Je ne suis pas sortie de ma nuit 1997, L'événement 2000, La Vie Extérieure 2000, Se perdre 2001, L'occupation 2002, L'écriture comme un couteau 2003, L'usage de la photo 2005, Les Années 2008. *Address:* 23 rue des Lozères, 95000 Cergy, France (home). *E-mail:* annie.ernaux@tiscali.fr (home).

ERNI, Hans; Swiss painter; b. 21 Feb. 1909, Lucerne; m. Doris Kessler 1949; one s. two d.; ed Académie Julien, Paris and Vereinigte Staatsschulen für freie und angewandte Kunst, Berlin; mem. Groupe Abstraction-Création, Paris; mem. SWB; abstract mural picture, Swiss section, Triennale Milan, frescoes Lucerne; Mural in Bernese Hosp. Montana; mem. Alliance Graphique Int.; great mural at the Musée Ethnographique, Neuchâtel 1954; has illustrated bibliophile edns of classics by Plato, Pindar, Sophocles, Virgil, Buffon, Renard, Valéry, Homer (Odyssey), Albert Schweitzer (La Paix), Voltaire (Candide), Paul Eluard, etc.; murals for int. exhbn in Brussels 1958; mosaics for the Abbey of St Maurice 1961, for Swiss TV and Radio bldg, Berne 1964; engraved glass panels 'Day and Night' and 'Towards a Humanistic Future' for the Soc. des Banques Suisses, Geneva, 1963; Pro Juventute stamps 1965; murals in Rolex Foundation, Union de Banques Suisses, Sion 1966, for Swissair Zürich and La Placette Geneva 1967; Int. Prize at the Biennale del Mare 1953. *Publications:* Wo steht der Maler in der Gegenwart? 1947, Erni en Valais 1967, Israel Sketchbook 1968. *Leisure interest:* art. *Address:* 6045 Meggen, Lucerne, Switzerland. *Telephone:* (41) 371382. *Website:* www.hans-erni.ch.

ERNST, Richard R., DrScTech; Swiss chemist and academic; *Professor Emeritus, Laboratory of Physical Chemistry, Eidgenössischen Technischen Hochschule (ETH) Zürich;* b. 14 Aug. 1933, Winterthur; s. of Robert Ernst and Irma Brunner; m. Magdalena Kielholz 1963; one s. two d.; ed Edgenössische Technische Hochschule, Zürich; Scientific Collaborator, Physical-Chem. Lab., ETH, Zürich 1962–63; Scientist, Varian Associates, Palo Alto, Calif., USA 1963–68; tutor, then Asst Prof., Assoc. Prof., ETH, Zürich 1968–76, Prof. of Physical Chem. 1976–98, now Prof. Emer.; mem. editorial bd various journals on magnetic resonance; Pres. Research Council of ETH, Zürich 1990–94; Vice-Pres. Bd Spectrospin AG, Fällanden 1989–; Fellow American Physical Soc.; mem. Schweizer Chemikerverband, Int. Soc. of Magnetic Resonance, Schweizerische Chemische Gesellschaft, Deutsche Akad. der Naturforscher Leopoldina, Academia Europaea, Schweizerische Akad. der Technischen Wissenschaften, NAS, Royal Soc. London; Dr hc (ETH-Lausanne) 1985, (Zürich) 1994, (Antwerp) 1997, (Babes-Bolyai) 1998, (Montpellier) 1999, (Allahabad) 2000, (Prague) 2002; Hon. Dr rer. nat (Munich Tech. Univ.) 1989; several awards including Benoist Prize 1986, John Gamble Kirkwood Medal, Yale Univ. 1989, Ampere Prize 1990, Wolf Prize for Chem., Jerusalem 1991, Nobel Prize for Chem. 1991. *Leisure interests:* music, Tibetan art. *Address:* Laboratorium für Physikalische Chemie, ETH Zürich, Wolfgang Paulistr. 10, HCI, 8093 Zürich (office); Kurlistr. 24, 8404 Winterthur, Switzerland (home). *Telephone:* (52) 2427807 (home); (1) 6324368 (office). *Fax:* (1) 6321257 (office). *E-mail:* ernst@nmr.phys.chem.ethz.ch (office). *Website:* www.chab.ethz.ch (office).

EROĞLU, Derviş, PhD; Turkish-Cypriot politician; *Chairman, Ulusal Birlik Partisi (National Unity Party);* b. 1938, Ergazi Magosa Dist; m.; four c.; ed Univ. of Istanbul; fmr urologist, Ankara; mem. Parl. 1976–; Chair. Ulusal Birlik Partisi (Nat. Unity Party) 1981–; Prime Minister 'Turkish Repub. of Northern Cyprus' 1985–93, 1996–2003. *Address:* National Unity Party, 9 Atatürk Meydanı, Lefkoşa (Nicosia), Mersin 10, 'Turkish Republic of Northern Cyprus' (office). *Telephone:* (22) 73972.

EROPKIN, Dmitriy P.; Russian economist and banker; *President, Rossiyskiy Kredit Bank;* b. 1970, Moscow; ed Moscow Aviation Univ., Financial Acad. to Govt of Russian Fed.; economist, JSC Rossiyskiy Kredit Bank 1994–95, Man. Int. Transfers Area, Int. Settlement Dept April–June 1995, Deputy Head of Int. Settlement Dept June–Sept. 1995, Deputy Dir Int. Settlement Div. and Head of Int. Settlement Dept Sept. 1995–, also Head of Financial Trade and Documentary Business Dept March 1996–, Dir Int. Settlement and Corresp. Relations Div. and Vice-Pres. JSC Rossiyskiy Kredit Bank responsible for devt programmes of rep. offices and subsidiary banks in UK, Switzerland, Hungary, China, Viet Nam and Bahrain 1996–97, Deputy Chair. and Dir Int. Div. 1997–2001, Chair. and Pres. Rossiyskiy Kredit Bank 2006–07, Pres. 2007–; Chair. JSC Impexbank 2001–04, Chair. and Pres. 2004–06; Pres. and Chair. Supervisory Bd Unicor man. co.; mem. Presidium of Council of Asscn of Russian Banks; mem. Cttee on Financial Markets and Credit Orgs, Chamber of Trade and Industry of Russian Fed.; Hon. Diploma, Asscn of Russian Banks 2004. *Address:* Rossiyskiy Kredit Bank, 26/9 Smolenskii Blvd, Moscow 119002, Russia (office). *Telephone:* (495) 967-34-43 (office). *Fax:* (495) 247-39-39 (office). *E-mail:* web-adm@roscredit.ru (office). *Website:* www.roscredit.ru (office).

ERRÁZURIZ OSSA, HE Cardinal Francisco Javier; Chilean ecclesiastic; *Archbishop of Santiago;* b. 5 Sept. 1933, Santiago; ed German School of the Congregation of the Divine Word, Catholic Univ., Univ. of Fribourg, Switzerland; ordained priest 1961; first Superior of Secular Inst. of Schoenstatt (German-based Marian movt) in Chile, Spain and Ecuador 1965, Superior Gen. in Germany 1971–87; Sec. Vatican Congregation for Consecrated Life and Socs of Apostolic Life, Rome 1990; granted personal title of Archbishop 1990; Archbishop of Valparaíso 1996–98, of Santiago 1998–; Pres. Chilean Bishops' Conf. 1998; cr. Cardinal 2001. *Address:* Casilla-30 D, Erasmo Escala 1884, Santiago, Chile (office). *Telephone:* (2) 6963275 (office); (2) 2744830 (home). *Fax:* (2) 6989137 (office); (2) 2092251 (home).

ERRERA, Gérard, CVO; French diplomat; *Secretary General, Ministry of Foreign Affairs;* b. 30 Oct. 1943, Brive; s. of Paul Errera and Bella Montekio; m. Virginie Bedoya; three c.; ed Inst. d'Etudes Politiques and Ecole Nat. d'Admin. Paris; First Sec. Washington, DC 1971–75; Special Adviser to Minister of Foreign Affairs 1975–77, 1980–81; Political Counsellor, Madrid 1977–80; Special Adviser to the Minister of Foreign Affairs 1980–81; Consul-Gen. San Francisco 1982–85; Dir of Int. Relations, French Atomic Energy Comm. and Gov. for France, IAEA 1985–90; Amb. to Conf. on Disarmament, Geneva 1991–95; Amb. and Perm. Rep. to NATO, Brussels 1995–98; Deputy Sec.-Gen. and Dir-Gen. of Political Affairs, Ministry of Foreign Affairs 1998–2002; Amb. to UK 2002–07; Sec.-Gen. Ministry of Foreign Affairs 2007–; Chevalier, Légion d'honneur; Officier de l'Ordre nat. du Mérite. *Leisure interests:* skiing, tennis, guitar. *Address:* Ministry of Foreign Affairs, 37 quai d'Orsay, 75351 Paris 07, France (office). *Telephone:* 1-43-17-53-53 (office). *Fax:* 1-43-17-52-03 (office). *E-mail:* gerard.errera@diplomatie.gouv.fr (office). *Website:* www.diplomatie.gouv.fr (office).

ERRINGTON, Stuart Grant, CBE, MA, JP, DL; British financier and business executive; b. 23 June 1929, Liverpool; s. of Sir Eric Errington Bt and of the late Lady (Marjorie) Errington; m. Anne Baedeker 1954; two s. one d.; ed Rugby School, Trinity Coll., Oxford; nat. service 1947–49; Man., Ellerman Lines Ltd 1952–59; various positions, to Jt Man. Dir, Astley Industrial Trust Ltd 1959–70; various positions, to Chair. and Chief Exec., Mercantile Credit Co. Ltd (now Mercantile Group PLC) 1970–89; Dir Barclays Merchant Bank (Barclays Bank UK) 1979–86, Kleinwort Overseas Investment Trust PLC 1982–98, Municipal Mutual Insurance 1989–, Northern Electric PLC 1989–96, Nationwide Bldg Soc. (mem. 1989–97, Vice-Chair. 1995–97), Associated Property Owners 1998–; Chair. Equipment Leasing Asscn 1976–78, Finance Houses Asscns 1982–84, Europe Fed. of Leasing Asscns 1978–80, Sportsmatch 1992–2005; Chair. Nat. Asscn of Citizens' Advice Bureaux 1989–94; Chair. Berks. and Oxfordshire Magistrates' Courts Cttee 1999–; mem. Council Royal Holloway, London Univ. 1989– (Vice-Chair. 1995–). *Leisure interests:* fishing, golf, reading. *Address:* Earleywood Lodge, Ascot, Berks., SL5 9JP, England. *Telephone:* (1344) 621977. *Fax:* (1344) 625778.

ERRÓ, Gudmundur, (pseudonym of Gudmundsson); Icelandic artist; b. 19 July 1932, Olafsvik; s. of Gudmundur Einarsson and Soffia Kristiansdottir; m. Bat Yosef 1958 (divorced 1969); one c.; ed Reykjavik, Oslo, Ravenna and Florence Art Acads; painter since 1956, over 135 personal exhbns worldwide (six retrospective including Jeu de Paume, Paris 1999) and has participated in over 250 group exhbns; works in perm. public collections in Betzalel Museum, Jerusalem, Tel-Aviv Museum of Modern Art, Moderna Museet, Stockholm, Samlung Ludwig, Aachen, Musée Nat. d'Art Moderne, Centre Georges Pompidou, Paris, Musée d'Art Moderne de la Ville de Paris, Nat. Museum of Iceland, Reykjavik, Musée Municipal, Reykjavik, Museo Nacional, Havana, Luisiana Museum, Denmark, Museum of Modern Art, New York, Nat. Gallery, Berlin, Kunstmuseum, Berne, Hara Museum, Tokyo, Stadische Galerie im Lenbachhaus, Munich, Nat. Air and Space Museum, Washington, DC, Musée des Deux Guerres Mondiales aux Invalides, Paris, Musée de Grenoble, Musée Hedendaagse Kunst, Utrecht, Bibliothèque Nationale, Paris, Fandation Maeght, St Paul de Vence, Musée de Dunkerque, Musée Cantini, Marseille, La Donation Lintas, Musée de Nîmes, FRAC Rhône-Alpes, FRAC, Ile de la Réunion, Musée Bertrand, Chateauroux, Musée d'Art Moderne, Saint-Etienne, Fonds Nat. d'Art Contemporain, Musée Picasso, Antibes, Konstmuseet Arkiv for Decorativ Kunst, Lund, Sweden, Randes Kunstmuseum, Denmark, Hôtel de Ville, Lille, La Villette, Cité des Sciences et de l'Industrie, Paris, Göteborg Kunstmuseum, Museum of Contemporary Art, Seoul, Fondation Van Gogh, Arles, FDAC Val-de-Merne, Conseil Géné; public comms include Angoulême (Ma campagne) 1982, Ministère de la Culture, ADEA 1982, Hommage à la Bande Dessinée 1982, Réalisation d'un autobus peint 1985, Commande de Samurval, Valencienne 1985, Hôtel de Ville, Lille, salle de Conseil Municipal (L'Histoire de Lille, Commande de la Mairie de Lille) 1988, La Cité des Sciences et de l'Industrie la Villete, Paris (La science et les ingénieurs, Commande de la Cité des Sciences et du Ministère de la Culture) 1989, Réalisation d'une sérigraphie pour le Bicentenaire de la Révolution Française (Commande du Ministère de la Culture) 1989, Auditorium Des Halles, Paris (Music Scape, Commande de la Ville de Paris) 1997; Officier des Arts et Lettres; Gold Medal (Sweden), Falcon Medal (Iceland). *Publications:* Sjalfsdadledsla (Mecapoème 1959) 1991, Easy is Interesting 1993, The Discontinued Story: Se Non E Vero E Ben Trovato (catalogue) 1996. *Leisure interests:* travelling (Far East), food, Cuban cigars, wine. *Address:* 39 rue Fondary, 75015 Paris, France. *Telephone:* 1-45-75-26-33. *Fax:* 1-45-75-26-33.

ERSBØLL, Niels, LLM; Danish diplomatist; b. 9 April 1926, Copenhagen; m. Birgitte Ullerup; two s. five d.; joined Ministry of Foreign Affairs 1955, Head of Div. 1964–67, Dir Secr. for Econ. Affairs 1967–73, State-Sec. for Econ. Affairs 1977–78; Embassy Sec. Del. to NATO, Paris 1958–60, Mission to EFTA and GATT, Geneva 1963–64, Amb. Perm. Rep. to EC, Brussels 1973–77; served in the EFTA Secr., Geneva 1960–63; Chair. Govt Bd Int. Energy Agency 1978–80; Sec.-Gen. EU (fmrly EC) Council, Brussels 1980–94; Hon. KCMG; numerous mil. awards. *Address:* Rungstedvej 36, 2970 Hørsholm, Denmark; Gachard, Montfaucon, 46240 La Bastide Murat, France.

ERSHAD, Lt-Gen. Hossain Mohammad; Bangladeshi politician and fmr army officer; b. 1 Feb. 1930, Rangpur; s. of the late Maqbul Hussain and of Begum Majida Khatun; m. Raushan Ershad 1956; one s. one adopted d.; ed Univ. of Dhaka, Officers' Training School, Kohat, Pakistan; first appointment in 2nd E Bengal Regt 1952; several appointments in various units including Adjutant, E Bengal Regt Centre, Chittagong 1960–62; completed staff course, Quetta Staff Coll. 1966; promoted Lt-Col 1969; Commdr 3rd E Bengal Regt 1969–70, 7th E Bengal Regt 1971–72; Adjutant-Gen. Bangladesh Army; promoted Col 1973; attended Nat. Defence Coll., New Delhi, India 1975; promoted Brig. 1975, Maj.-Gen. 1975; Deputy Chief of Army Staff 1975–78, Chief 1978–86; rank of Lt-Gen. 1979; led mil. takeover in Bangladesh March 1982; Chief Martial Law Admin. and Pres. Council of Ministers 24 March 1982, adopted title of Prime Minister Oct. 1982, of Pres. of Bangladesh Dec. 1983, elected Pres. of Bangladesh Oct. 1986, resigned Dec. 1990; also Minister of Defence 1986–90, of Information 1986–88; fmrly in charge of several ministries including Home Affairs; Chief Adviser Bangladesh Freedom Fighters' Asscn; Chair. Bangladesh Olympic Asscn, Bangladesh Lawn Tennis Fed.; UN Population Award 1987; sentenced to ten years' hard labour on charges of keeping unlicensed firearms, acquitted after appeal 1995; sentenced to a further ten years' imprisonment for illegally amassing money 1992, to seven years' imprisonment for graft 1993, to five years' imprisonment for misappropriation of funds 2000, to six months' imprisonment for attempting to influence the proceedings in a corruption case 2002, to two years' imprisonment for corruption 2006, acquitted of several corruption charges from the previous decade 2006, sentenced to two years' imprisonment on corruption charges 2006, sentence suspended due to time already served 2007. *Leisure interests:* golf, writing poems, art, literature, oriental music.

ERSKINE, Peter; British telecommunications executive; fmr European Vice-Pres. of Sales and Customer Service, Mars; fmr Sr Vice-Pres. of Sales and Marketing, UNITEL; sr positions with British Telecommunications (BT) 1993–, including Dir BT Mobile, Pres. and CEO Concert and Man. Dir BT Cellnet 1998–2001; CEO mmO2 2001–08, mem. Bd of Dirs Telefónica 02 Europe plc (parent co.). *Address:* c/o O2 UK Ltd, Wellington Street, Slough, SL1 1YP, England (office).

ERTL, Gerhard, Dr rer. nat, Dipl.Phys; German chemist and academic; *Professor Emeritus, Department of Physical Chemistry, Fritz-Haber-Institut der Max-Planck-Gesellschaft, Berlin;* b. 10 Oct. 1936, Stuttgart; ed Tech. Univ. of Stuttgart, Univ. of Paris, Ludwig-Maximilians Univ., Munich; Asst and Lecturer, Tech. Univ. of Munich 1965–68; Prof. and Dir, Inst. for Physical Chemistry, Tech. Univ., Hanover 1968–73; Prof. and Dir, Inst. for Physical Chemistry, Ludwig-Maximilians Univ., Munich 1973–86; Visiting Prof., Dept of Chemical Eng, Calif. Inst. of Tech., Pasadena, CA, USA 1976–77; Visiting Prof., Dept of Physics, Univ. of Wis., Milwaukee 1979; Visiting Prof., Dept of Chemistry, Univ. of Calif., Berkeley 1981–82; Dir, Dept Physical Chemistry, Fritz-Haber-Institut der Max-Planck-Gesellschaft, Berlin 1986–2004, Prof. Emer. 2004–; mem. German Acad. of Sciences Leopoldina 1986–, Academia Europaea 1992–, Berlin-Brandenburg Acad. of Sciences 1998–; Foreign Hon. Mem. American Acad. of Arts and Sciences 1993–; Foreign Assoc. NAS (USA) 2002–; Hon. Fellow Royal Soc. of Edinburgh 1985–; Dr hc (Ruhr Univ. of Bochum) 1992, (Univ. of Münster) 2000, (Aarhus Univ.) 2003, (Univ. of Leuven) 2003, (Chalmers Univ. of Tech.) 2003; numerous awards including Univ. of Wis., Milwaukee E. W. Muller Award 1979, Scientific Soc. of Braunschweig C. F. Gauss Medal 1985, Royal Soc. of Chemistry Centenary Medal 1985, American Chemical Soc. Langmuir Lecture 1986, German Chemical Soc. Liebig Medal 1987, Royal Soc. of Chemistry Bourke Medal 1991, Science and Tech. Foundation of Japan Prize 1992, Wolf Prize in Chemistry 1998, Nobel Prize in Chemistry 2007. *Address:* Physical Chemistry Department, Fritz-Haber-Institut der Max-Planck-Gesellschaft, Faradayweg 4–6, 14195 Berlin, Germany (office). *Telephone:* (30) 8413-5100 (office). *Fax:* (30) 8413-5106 (office). *E-mail:* ertl@fhi-berlin.mpg.de (office). *Website:* www.rz-berlin.mpg.de/pc/Ertl.html (office).

ERTUĞRULOĞLU, Tahsin; Turkish-Cypriot politician; *Chairman, National Unity Party;* b. 1953, Lefkosa (Nicosia); m.; two c.; ed Univs. of Arizona and Minnesota; joined Ministry of Foreign Affairs and Defence 1983, Head of Political Affairs, 'Turkish Repub. of Northern Cyprus' London Rep.'s Office 1986–91; Under-Sec. to Prime Minister 1991–94, re-apptd 1996; Counsellor, Office of Prime Minister, Legis. Ass. 1994–96; mem. Parl. for Lefkosa 1998–2004; Minister of Foreign Affairs and Defence 1998; Chair. Bayrak Radio and TV Exec. Cttee; Chair. Nat. Unity Party 2006–. *Address:* National Unity Party, Lefkosa, 'Turkish Republic of Northern Cyprus' (office). *Telephone:* 2285033 (office). *Website:* www.ubp-kktc.org (office).

ERWA, Lt-Gen. Elfatih Mohamed; Sudanese diplomatist; b. 11 May 1950, Khartoum; m. Kawther Amin Mohamed 1973; seven c.; ed Sudan Military Coll.; fmr pilot; Adviser to Pres. of Repub. 1989–90; State Minister in the Presidency for Nat. Security 1990–95, for Nat. Defence 1995–96; Perm. Rep. to UN 1996–2006; Order of Bravery. *Leisure interests:* flying, reading, computers. *Address:* c/o Ministry of Foreign Affairs, POB 873, Khartoum, Sudan (office). *Website:* www.sudanmfa.com (office).

ERWIN, Alexander (Alec), BEcons; South African politician, academic and trade union official; b. 17 Jan. 1948; m.; ed Durban High School, Univ. of Natal; Lecturer, Dept of Econs, Univ. of Natal 1971–78; visiting lecturer, Centre of Southern African Studies, Univ. of York 1974–75; Gen. Sec. Trade Union Advisory and Co-ordinating Council 1977–79; Gen. Sec. Fed. of SA Trade Unions 1979–81; Br. Sec. Nat. Union of Textile Workers 1981–83; Educ. Sec. Fed. of SA Trade Unions 1983–85; Educ. Sec. Congress of SA Trade Unions 1986–88; Nat. Educ. Officer Nat. Union of Metalworkers 1988–93; Interim Exec. mem. ANC S Natal Region 1989; Exec. mem. ANC Western Areas Br. 1990–91; fmr mem. Devt and Reconstruction Cttee, Natal Peace

Accord; fmr Congress of SA Trade Unions rep. at Nat. Econ. Forum; fmr Ed. ANC Reconstruction and Devt Programme; Deputy Minister of Finance 1994; Minister of Trade and Industry 1996–99, 1999–2004, of Public Enterprises 2004–08 (resgnd); Dr hc 1997. *Address:* African National Congress, 54 Sauer Street, Johannesburg 2001, South Africa. *Telephone:* (11) 3761000 (office). *Fax:* (11) 3761134 (office). *E-mail:* nmtyelwa@anc.org.za (office). *Website:* www.anc.org.za (office).

ERZAN, Ayse, BA, PhD; Turkish physicist; *Professor of Physics, Istanbul Technical University;* b. 2 May 1949, Ankara; m. Orhan Silier; ed Bryn Mawr Coll. and State Univ. of NY at Stony Brook, USA; worked at univs and research inst. in Switzerland, Portugal, Germany, the Netherlands and Italy –1990; currently Prof. of Physics, Istanbul Tech. Univ.; specialization in condensed matter physics, phase transitions and scaling behaviour in complex systems; recently involved in investigating math. models of evolution and biological networks; mem. Turkish Acad. of Sciences, Palestinian Acad. for Science and Tech., TWAS (fmrly Third World Acad. of Sciences); L'Oréal UNESCO Award for Women in Science 2003. *Address:* Department of Physics, Faculty of Sciences and Letters, Istanbul Technical University, Maslak, 34 469 Istanbul, Turkey (office). *Telephone:* (212) 285 3277 (office). *Fax:* (212) 285 6386 (office). *E-mail:* erzan@itu.edu.tr (office). *Website:* atlas.cc.itu.edu.tr/ ~erzan (office).

ERZEN, Jale Nejdet, MFA, PhD; Turkish art historian, artist and writer; *Professor of History of Art and Aesthetics, Middle East Technical University;* b. 12 Jan. 1943, Ankara; d. of Necdet Erzen and Selma Erzen; ed Art Center Coll. of Design, LA, Istanbul Tech. Univ.; taught part-time at various univs in Turkey; lectured widely in USA, Italy and France; mem. staff, Faculty of Architecture, Middle East Tech. Univ. 1974–, Prof. of History of Art and Aesthetics 1992–; visiting Prof., Univ. Bologna 1999–; Founder and Ed. Boyut Fine Arts Journal 1980–85; Founder, Pres. SANART Asscn of Aesthetics and Visual Culture; Gen. Sec. Int. Asscn of Aesthetics 1995–98; adviser, Int. Asscn for Applied Aesthetics 1998–2001; works in pvt. and state collections in Turkey and Europe; Consultant Istanbul Biennale 1992, Istanbul Contemporary Museum 1992–93, Ankara Contemporary Museum 2000–01; Fullbright Fellow, Lawrence Univ., Wis. 1985; Japan Soc. for the Promotion of Science Fellowship 2003–; also consultant for various architectural journals; Chevalier, Ordre des Arts et des Lettres 1991; Best Critic Award, Istanbul Art Fair 2000. *Video:* Exhbn of Suleiman the Magnificent, Grand Palais, Paris (with Stephane Yerasimos) 1989. *Publications include:* books on Ottoman architect Sinan, and Turkish artists Sabri Berkel, Erol Akyavas, Mehmet Aksoy; various articles on aesthetics, modern art, Ottoman architecture, environmental aesthetics, competitive aesthetics. *Leisure interests:* gardening, horseriding, poetry. *Address:* Faculty of Architecture, Middle East Technical University, Inönu blvd, 06531 Ankara (office); Sanart, Kenedi Cad. 42, Kavaklidere, 06660 Ankara, Turkey (home). *Telephone:* (312) 2102215 (office); (312) 4464761 (home). *Fax:* (312) 2101249 (office). *E-mail:* erzen@arch.metu.edu.tr (office). *Website:* www.metu.edu.tr (office).

ESAKI, Leo, PhD; Japanese scientist and academic administrator; *President, Shibaura Institute of Technology;* b. 12 March 1925, Osaka; s. of Soichiro Esaki and Niyoko Ito; m. 1st Masako Araki 1959; one s. two d.; m. 2nd Masako Kondo 1986; ed Univ. of Tokyo; with Sony Corpn 1956–60, conducted research on heavily-doped germanium and silicon which resulted in the discovery of tunnel diode; with IBM Corpn, USA 1960–92, IBM Fellow 1967–92, IBM T. J. Watson Research Center, New York, 1960–92, Man. Device Research 1962–92; Dir IBM-Japan 1976–92, Yamada Science Foundation 1976–; Pres. Univ. of Tsukuba, Ibaraki, Japan 1992–98; Chair. Science and Tech. Promotion Foundation of Ibaraki 1998–; Dir-Gen. Tsukuba Int. Congress Center 1999–; Pres. Shibaura Inst. of Tech. 2000–; Sir John Cass Sr Visiting Research Fellow, London Polytechnic 1981; at IBM pioneered (with co-workers) research on superlattices and quantum wells, triggering wide spectrum of experimental and theoretical investigations leading to emergence of new class of transport and optoelectronic devices; mem. Japan Acad. 1975, American Philosophical Soc. 1991, Max-Planck Gesellschaft 1984; Foreign Assoc. NAS 1976, American Nat. Acad. of Engineering 1977; Nishina Memorial Award 1959, Asahi Press Award 1960, Toyo Rayon Foundation Award 1961, Morris N. Liebmann Memorial Prize 1961, Stuart Ballantine Medal, Franklin Inst. 1961, Japan Acad. Award 1965, Nobel Prize for Physics 1973, Order of Culture, Japanese Govt 1974, US-Asia Inst. Science Achievement Award 1983, American Physical Soc. Int. Prize for New Materials (with others) 1985, IEEE Medal of Honor 1991, Japan Prize 1998, Grand Cordon Order of Rising Sun (First Class) 1998. *Publications:* numerous articles in professional journals. *Address:* Shibaura Institute of Technology, 3-9-14 Shibaura, Minato-ku, Tokyo 108 (office); 12-6 Sanban-cho, Chiyoda-ku, Tokyo 102, Japan (home). *Telephone:* (3) 5476-3137 (office); (3) 3262-1788 (home). *Fax:* (3) 5476-3175 (office). *E-mail:* leoesaki@sic.shibaura-it.ac.jp (office). *Website:* www.shibaura-it.ac.jp/english/index.html (office).

ESAW, Kofi; Togolese diplomatist and politician; *Minister of Foreign Affairs and Regional Integration;* Amb. to Ethiopia 2004–08, concurrently Amb. to African Union; Minister of Foreign Affairs and Regional Integration 2008–. *Address:* Ministry of Foreign Affairs and Regional Integration, place du Monument aux Morts, BP 900, Lomé, Togo (office). *Telephone:* 221-36-01 (office). *Fax:* 221-39-74 (office). *E-mail:* diplo@republicoftogo.com (office).

ESBER, Ali Ahmad Said, (Adonis), PhD; Syrian poet and academic; b. 1930, Kassabin, nr Latakia; ed Univ. of Damascus, Univ. of St Joseph, Beirut; Prof. of Arabic Literature, Lebanese Univ., Beirut 1971–85; PhD Adviser, Univ. of St Joseph, Beirut 1971–85; Visiting Lecturer, Collège de France, Paris 1983, Georgetown Univ., Washington, DC 1985; Assoc. Prof. of Arab Poetry, Univ. of Geneva 1989–95; mem. Acad. Stéphane Mallarmé, Paris, Haut Conseil de Réflexion du Collège Int. de Philosophie, Paris; Officier, Ordre des Arts et des

Lettres 1993; Prix des Amis du Livre, Beirut 1968, Syria-Lebanon Award, Int. Poetry Forum 1971, Nat. Prize for Poetry, Lebanon 1974, Grand Prix des Biennales Internationales de la Poésie de Liège, Belgium 1986, Prix Jean Malrieu-Etranger, Marseille 1991, Feronia-Cita di Fiano, Rome 1993, Nazim Hikmat Prize, Istanbul 1994, Prix Méditerranée-Etranger, France 1995. *Publications include:* Songs of Mihyar, the Damascene 1961, The Book of Changes and Migration to the Regions of Day and Night 1965, A Time Between Ashes and Roses 1970, Introduction to Arab Poetry 1971, A Tomb for New York 1971, The Blood of Adonis 1971, Singular in the Form of Plural 1974, Further Songs of Mihyar, the Damascene 1975, The Shock of Modernity 1978, The Book of Five Poems 1980, Manifesto of Modernity 1980, Transformations of the Lover 1982, Mémoire du Vent 1991, La Prière et L'Épée 1992, Soleils Seconds 1994, The Pages of Day and Night 2001, Chants de Mihyar le Damascène 2002, If Only the Sea Could Sleep 2003, Commencement du Corps, Fin de l'Océan 2004, Histoire qui se Déchire sue le Corps d'une Femme 2008. *Address:* 1 sq Henri Regnault, 92400 Courbevoie, France (home).

ESCHENBACH, Christoph; German conductor and concert pianist; *Music Director, Orchestre de Paris;* b. 20 Feb. 1940, Breslau (now Wrocław, Poland); ed Musikhochschulen, Cologne and Hamburg; Musical Dir of Philharmonic Orchestra, Ludwigshafen 1979–83; Chief Conductor Tonhalle Orchestra, Zürich 1982–86; Co-Artistic Dir Pacific Music Festival 1992–98; Artistic Dir Schleswig-Holstein Music Festival 1999–2002; Musical Dir Houston Symphony Orchestra 1988–99 (Conductor Laureate 1999–), Ravinia Festival 1994–2003; Prin. Conductor NDR Symphony Orchestra 1998–2004; Musical Dir Orchestre de Paris 2000–(10), Philadelphia Orchestra 2003–08; Music Dir designate, Nat. Symphony Orchestra, includes role as Music Dir, Kennedy Center (2010–); has appeared as conductor Boston Symphony, Chicago Symphony, Houston Symphony, LA Philharmonic, New York Philharmonic, Philadelphia Orchestra, San Francisco Symphony (US conducting debut 1975), Berlin Philharmonic, Danish Nat. Radio Orchestra, Hamburg NDR Symphony Orchestra, Kirov Orchestra, all five London orchestras, Orchestre de Paris, Vienna Philharmonic; as pianist with Atlanta Symphony, Radio Orchestras of Munich and Stuttgart, Israel Philharmonic and Israel Chamber Orchestras, NHK Orchestra Tokyo; operatic engagements include Bayreuth, Houston Grand Opera, NY Metropolitan Opera, Hessian State Theatre, Darmstadt (operatic conducting debut 1978); festivals include Bayreuth, Ravinia Festival and Schleswig-Holstein Musical Festival; Officer's Cross with Ribbon, German Order of Merit 1990, Commdr's Cross 1993, Officer's Cross with Star of the German Order of Merit 2002, Chevalier de la Légion d'honneur 2002; 1st Prize, Steinway Piano Competition 1952, Munich Int. Competition 1962, Clara Haskil Competition 1965, Leonard Bernstein Award 1993. *Address:* Opus 3 Artists, 470 Park Avenue South, 9th Floor North, New York, NY 10016, USA (office). *Telephone:* (212) 584-7500 (office). *Fax:* (646) 300-8200 (office). *E-mail:* info@opus3artists.com (office). *Website:* www .opus3artists.com (office); www.christoph-eschenbach.com.

ESCHENMOSER, Albert, DrScNat; Swiss chemist and academic; *Professor, Skaggs Institute for Chemical Biology;* b. 5 Aug. 1925, Erstfeld; s. of Alfons Eschenmoser and Johanna Eschenmoser (née Oesch); m. Elizabeth Baschnonga 1954; two s. one d.; ed Collegium Altdorf, Kantonsschule St Gallen, Swiss Federal Inst. of Tech. (ETH), Zürich; Privatdozent, Organic Chem., ETH 1956, Assoc. Prof. of Organic Chem. 1960, Prof. of Organic Chem. 1965, now Prof. Emer.; Prof., Skaggs Inst. for Chemical Biology, La Jolla, Calif., USA 1996–; mem. Deutsche Akad. der Naturforscher Leopoldina (Halle) 1976; Foreign Assoc. NAS 1973; Foreign mem. Royal Soc. (London) 1986, Pontifical Acad. (Vatican) 1986, Akad. der Wissenschaften (Göttingen) 1986, Academia Europaea (London) 1988, Croatian Acad. of Sciences and Arts 1994; Foreign Hon. Mem. American Acad. of Arts and Sciences 1966, Pharmaceutical Soc. for Japan 1999; Hon. FRSC (London) 1981; Hon. mem. Gesellschaft Oesterreichischer Chemiker, Vienna 1997; Orden pour le mérite für Wissenschaften und Künste (Bonn) 1992, Österreich. Ehrenzeichen für Wissenschaft und Kunst (Vienna) 1993; Hon. Dr rer. nat (Fribourg) 1966; Hon. DSc (Chicago) 1970, (Edin.) 1979, (Bologna) 1989, (Frankfurt) 1990, (Strasbourg) 1991, (Harvard) 1993, (TSRI La Jolla, Calif.) 2000; ETH Kern Award 1949, Werner Award, Swiss Chemical Soc. 1956, ETH Ruzicka Award 1958, ACS Fritzsche Award 1966, Marcel Benoist Prize (Switzerland) 1973, R.A. Welch Award in Chem., Houston, Texas 1974, Kirkwood Medal, Yale 1976, A.W.v. Hofmann-Denkmünze, GDCh 1976, Dannie-Heinemann Prize, Akad. der Wissenschaften, Göttingen 1977, Davy Medal, Royal Soc., London 1978, Cliff S. Hamilton Award and Medal, Lincoln 1980, Tetrahedron Prize, Pergamon Press 1981, G. Kenner Award, Univ. of Liverpool 1982, ACS Arthur C. Cope Award 1984, Wolf Prize in Chem. (Israel) 1986, M.-M. Janot Medal (France) 1988, Cothenius Medal, Akad. Leopoldina 1991, Ciba-Drew Award, Madison 1994, H.H. Inhoffen Medal, Braunschweig 1995, Nakanishi Prize, Chemical Soc. of Japan 1998, Paracelsus Prize, New Swiss Chemical Soc. 1999, Grande Médaille d'Or, Acad. des Sciences, Paris 2001, A.I. Oparin Medal, Int. Soc. for the Origin of Life 2002, ACS Roger Adams Award 2003, Kitasato Microbial Chemistry Medal, Tokyo 2003, F.A. Cotton Medal, Texas A&M Univ. 2004, F. Westheimer Medal, Harvard Univ. 2004, D.H.R. Barton Medal, Royal Soc. of Chem. 2004. *Publications:* numerous articles on organic synthesis in professional journals. *Address:* Laboratorium für Organische Chemie, ETH Hönggerberg HCI-H309, 8093 Zürich (office); Bergstrasse 9, 8700 Küsnacht (ZH), Switzerland (home). *Telephone:* (44) 6322893 (office); (44) 9107392 (home). *Fax:* (44) 6321043 (office). *E-mail:* eschenmoser@org.chem.ethz.ch (office).

ESCHWEY, Helmut Ludwig, DSc; German business executive; *Chairman, Board of Management, Heraeus Holding GmbH;* b. 25 July 1949, Heidenheim/ Brenz; m.; two s.; ed Freiburg Univ.; various man. roles with Henkel KGaA, Düsseldorf, Veith Pirelli AG, Höchst/Odenwald and Freudenberg Group,

Weinheim 1975–92; mem. Man. Bd Battenfeld Holding 1992, Chair. 1993; mem. Man. Bd SMS Kunststofftechnik AG 1994, Pres. Plastics Tech. Group 1994–2003, currently mem. Advisory Bd; Chair. Bd of Man. Heraeus Holding GmbH 2003–; Dir Inst. of Plastics Processing (IKV), Rheinish-Westphalian Tech. Univ. (RWTH); mem. Supervisory Bd Altana AG; fmr Chair. Plastics and Rubber Machinery Div., Verband Deutscher Maschinen- und Anlagenbau eV (VDMA, German Eng Fed.). *Address:* Heraeus Holding GmbH, Heraeusstrasse 12-14, 63450 Hanau, Germany (office). *Telephone:* (61) 81350 (office). *Fax:* (61) 81353550 (office). *E-mail:* pr@heraeus.com (office). *Website:* www.heraeus.com (office).

ESCOBAR CERDA, Luis, MPA; Chilean economist and academic; *Professor of Economics, University of Chile;* b. 10 Feb. 1927; m. 2nd Helga Koch 1973; five c.; ed Univ. de Chile and Harvard Univ.; Dir School of Econs, Univ. de Chile 1951–55, Dean of Faculty of Econs 1955–64; Minister of Econ. Devt and Reconstruction 1961–63; mem. Inter-American Cttee for Alliance for Progress 1964–66; Exec. Dir IMF 1964–66, 1968–70, IBRD 1966–68; Special Rep. for Inter-American Orgs IBRD 1970–75; Trustee of Population Reference Bureau 1968–73; mem. Advisory Cttee on Population and Devt OAS 1968–73, Council Soc. for Int. Devt 1969–72; Deputy Exec. Sec. Jt Bank/Fund Devt Cttee 1975–79; Prof., Georgetown Univ. 1975–79, George Washington Univ. 1977, Dept of Econs, American Univ. 1978–79; CEO private banks 1979–84; Minister of Finance 1984–85; Amb. to UN and Int. Orgs in Geneva 1986–90; Consultant on econ. and financial matters 1990–; Prof., Univ. of Chile 1990–, Dean, Faculty of Business Admin., Iberoamerican Univ. for Sciences and Tech. 1997–2001; Prof. Univ. del Pacifico 2002–, Acad. Mem. for Life and Extraordinary Prof., Univ. of Chile; Vice-Pres. Partido Radical Social Demócrata 1994–95; Gold Medal for Best Graduate in Econs and Honor Medal, Univ. of Chile; recognition for contribution to teaching and research in econs 1996. *Publications:* The Stock Market 1959, Organization for Economic Development 1961, A Stage of the National Economic Development 1962, Considerations on the Tasks of the University 1963, Organizational Requirements for Growth and Stability 1964, The Role of the Social Sciences in Latin America 1965, The Organization of Latin American Government 1968, Multinational Corporations in Latin America 1973, International Control of Investments 1974, External Financing in Latin America 1976, 1978, Mi Testimonio 1991, Financial Problems of Latin American Economic Integration 1992, Globalization and Challenges of Globalization 2000–01; articles in newspapers. *Leisure interests:* reading, tennis, skiing. *Address:* 1724 Sánchez Fontecilla, Santiago 10, Chile (home). *Telephone:* (2) 2080227 (home). *Fax:* (2) 2286367 (home). *E-mail:* escobarcerda@yahoo.com (home).

ESCOBEDO, Helen (Elena), ARCA; Mexican sculptor; b. 28 July 1934, Mexico City; d. of Manuel G. Escobedo and Elsie Fulda Escobedo; m. 1st Fredrik Kirsebom (divorced 1982); one s. one d.; m. 2nd Hans-Jürgen Rabe 1995; ed Univ. of Motolinia, RCA, London; Dir of Fine Arts Nat. Univ. of Mexico 1961–74, Dir of Museums and Galleries 1974–78; Tech. Dir Nat. Museum of Art, Mexico 1981–82; Dir Museum of Modern Art, Mexico 1982–84; mem. Espacio Escultórico design team 1978–79; Guggenheim Fellowship; Assoc. mem. Acad. Royale de Belgique; Fonca Stipendium 2000–03; Order of the Lion (Finland); Tlatilco Prize for Sculpture, Int. Water Sculpture Competition Prize, New Orleans World Fair 1983. *Designs include:* Gateway to the Wind, Olympic Highway 68, Mexico City, 1968, Signals, Auckland Harbour 1971, Rain Towers, New Orleans 1984, The Great Cone, Jerusalem 1986, Seaview, Arlington House, London 1989. *Publication:* Mexican Monuments, Strange Encounters 1989. *Leisure interests:* reading, writing. *Address:* Weinheimerstrasse 24, 14193 Berlin, Germany (March–Sept.) (home); Primera Cerrada de San Jerónimo 19, Mexico 10200 DF, Mexico (Oct.–Feb.) (home). *Telephone:* (30) 89542148 (Berlin) (home); (55) 5595-0941 (Mexico) (home). *Fax:* (30) 89542149 (Berlin) (home); (55) 5683-4699 (Mexico) (home). *E-mail:* helenescobedo@yahoo.com (home). *Website:* www.helen-escobedo.com (home).

ESCOVAR SALOM, Ramón; Venezuelan politician and fmr diplomatist; b. 1926, Lara State; mem. Nat. Congress 1947; Minister of Justice; Rep. to Lara State Legis. Ass.; mem. Senate; Sec.-Gen. of the Presidency 1974–75; Minister of Foreign Affairs 1975–77; Amb. to France 1986–89; Attorney-Gen. of Venezuela 1989–93; Prosecutor Int. Tribunal investigating crimes committed in Fmr Yugoslavia 1993–94; Minister of the Interior 1994; Perm. Rep. to UN 1999–2001. *Address:* c/o Ministry of Foreign Affairs, Edif. MRE, Avda Urdaneta, Esq. Carmelitas, Caracas 1010, Venezuela.

ESCUDERO DURÁN, Lorena, PhD; Ecuadorean academic and politician; *Secretary for Migration;* b. 1965; ed Univ. of Cuenca, Nat. Autonomous Univ. of Mexico and Univ. of Alicante, Spain; Dir Centre for Latinamerican Social and Political Studies, Univ. of Cuenca 2002–07, Coordinator of Postgraduate Studies 2003–07; Minister of National Defence Feb.–Aug. 2007; Sec. for Migration 2007–. *Publications:* numerous articles in professional journals. *Address:* Secretariat for Migration, Palacio Nacional, García Moreno 1043, Quito, Ecuador (office). *Telephone:* (2) 221-6300 (office). *Website:* www.presidencia.gov.ec (office).

ESHAQ, Mohammad; Afghan radio and television administrator and engineer; *Director-General, Radio-Television Afghanistan;* fmr Man. Dir Afghan News (English-language daily); fmr Man. Dir Payam-e Mojahed (weekly publ. of Jamiat-e Eslami—Islamic Society); fmr Deputy Minister of Aviation and Tourism; fmr rep. of Northern Alliance in Washington, DC; Dir-Gen. Radio-TV Afghanistan 2002–; mem. Bd Int. Acad. of TV Arts and Sciences 2003–. *Address:* Radio-Television Afghanistan, St 10, Lane 2, Wazir Akbar Khan, PO Box 544, Kabul, Afghanistan (office). *Telephone:* (20) 2101086 (office). *E-mail:* rtakabul@hotmail.com (office); mohammadeshaq@hotmail.com (home).

ESKÉNAZI, Gérard André, MBA; French business executive; b. 10 Nov. 1931, Paris; s. of Roger Eskénazi and Léone Blanchard; m. Arlette Gravelin 1964; three s. one d.; ed studies in law and business admin; joined Banque de Paris et des Pays-Bas (now Banque Paribas) 1957, Pres. Cie Financière de Paribas 1978–82; Chair. of Bd and Chair. Exec. Cttee of Pargesa SA 1985–90; Deputy Chair. and Pres. Groupe Bruxelles Lambert SA 1982–90; Chair. Parfinance 1986–90; Deputy Chair. Banque Bruxelles Lambert 1982–90; Deputy Chair. Banque Internationale à Luxembourg 1984–90; Chair. Compagnie Industrielle Pallas (COMIPAR) 1991–95; now Chair. Naviter 1999–; mem. Bd Schneider 1981–97, Petrofina 1986–90, Cie Financière Paribas 1988–90; Chevalier, Légion d'honneur and Ordre nat. du mérite. *Leisure interest:* horse riding. *Address:* Naviter, 68 rue de Faubourg Saint-Honoré, 75008 Paris (office); 7 rue Maurice Ravel, 92210 St Cloud, France (home). *Telephone:* 1-53-05-28-30 (office).

ESKEW, Michael L., BEng; American business executive; ed Purdue Univ.; joined UPS 1972, Industrial Eng Man., Ind. 1972, various man. positions including roles with UPS Germany and UPS Airlines, Corp. Vice-Pres., Industrial Eng 1994–96, Group Vice-Pres. for Eng 1996–99, Dir UPS 1998–, Exec. Vice-Pres. 1999–2002, also Vice-Chair. 2000–02, Chair. and CEO 2002–07 (retd); Dir 3M Corpn; Trustee The UPS Foundation, The Annie E. Casey Foundation; mem. Pres.'s Export Council, Business Roundtable. *Address:* c/o UPS Corporate Headquarters, 55 Glenlake Parkway Northeast, Atlanta, GA 30328, USA (office).

ESKIN, Alex, BS, PhD; American mathematician and academic; *Professor of Mathematics, University of Chicago;* b. 19 May 1965, Moscow; ed UCLA, MIT, Stanford Univ., Princeton Univ.; Dickson Instructor, Univ. of Chicago 1994–96, Assoc. Prof. of Math. 1997–98, Prof. 1998–; research interests include lie groups, ergodic theory, geometric group theory, rational billiards; DOE Scholarship 1991, Sloan Fellowship 1992, Packard Fellowship 1997–2002, Clay Research Prize 2007. *Publications:* numerous papers in academic journals. *Address:* Department of Mathematics, University of Chicago, 5734 University Avenue, Chicago, IL 60637-1514, USA (office). *Telephone:* (773) 702-7380 (office). *Fax:* (773) 702-9787 (office). *E-mail:* eskin@math.uchicago.edu (office). *Website:* www.math.uchicago.edu (office).

ESKINDAROV, Mikhail A., DEcon; Russian economist, academic and university rector; *Rector, Finance Academy of the Government of the Russian Federation;* currently Rector, Finance Acad. of Govt of Russian Fed.; co-f. Earmarked Capital Endowment; mem. Bd of Dirs VTB group. *Address:* The Finance Academy, Moscow 125993, 49–55 Leningradsky Prospect, Russia (office). *Telephone:* (495) 943-98-55 (office). *Fax:* (495) 157-70-70 (office). *E-mail:* academy@fa.ru (office). *Website:* www.fa.ru (office).

ESKOLA, Antti Aarre, PhD; Finnish academic; *Professor Emeritus of Social Psychology, University of Tampere;* b. 20 Aug. 1934, Urjala; m. Riti Laakso 1958; one s. one d.; ed Univ. of Helsinki; Prof. of Sociology, Univ. of Turku 1965; Prof. of Social Psychology, Univ. of Tampere 1966–97, Prof. Emer. 1997–; Research Prof., Acad. of Finland 1982–87; mem. Finnish Acad. of Science and Letters 1983; Hon. DScS (Lapland) 2004. *Publications:* Social Influence and Power in Two-Person Groups 1961, Blind Alleys in Social Psychology 1988; several other studies, textbooks, essay collections and a novel. *Address:* Tammelan puistokatu 30–32 A 16, 33100 Tampere, Finland (home).

ESMAHAN D'AUBUISSON, Ricardo; Salvadorean politician; *Minister of the Economy;* Exec. Sec., Inter-party Comm. to Support the Peace Process 1989–92; Dir-Gen. Directorate Gen. for Consumer Protection 1994–95; Pres. El Savador Chamber of Agric. and Agro-industry (CAMAGRO) 2003–08, Cen. American Fed. of Agric. and Agro-industry (FECAGRO) 2003–07; adviser to Exec. Cttee Nat. Assсn of Pvt. Enterprise (ANEP) 2004–08; Minister of the Economy 2008–. *Address:* Ministry of the Economy, Edif. C1–C2, Centro de Gobierno, Alameda Juan Pablo II y Calle Guadalupe, San Salvador, El Salvador (office). *Telephone:* 2231-5600 (office). *Fax:* 2221-5446 (office). *E-mail:* webmaster@minec.gob.sv (office). *Website:* www.minec.gob.sv (office).

ESMATI, Zabiullah; Afghan airline executive; *President, Ariana Afghan Airlines;* fmrly lived in Calif., USA; Dir Gen. Ind. Admin of Anti-Bribery and Corruption (GIAAC) –2007; Pres. Ariana Afghan Airlines 2007–. *Address:* Ariana Afghan Airlines, PO Box 76, Ansari Watt, Kabul, Afghanistan (office). *Telephone:* (20) 2100351 (office). *Fax:* (873) 762523846 (office). *E-mail:* afghanairlines@yahoo.com (office); flyariana@mail.com (office); info@flyariana.com (office). *Website:* www.flyariana.com (office).

ESMENARD, Francis; French publisher; b. 8 Dec. 1936, Paris; s. of Robert Esmenard and Andrée Michel; one s.; Pres. and Dir-Gen. Editions Albin Michel 1982–, Paris; Vice-Pres. Nat. Publishing Syndicat 1979–; Prés. du Directoire 1999–. *Leisure interests:* tennis, golf, skiing. *Address:* Editions Albin Michel, 22 rue Huyghens, 75014 Paris, France (office). *Telephone:* 1-42-79-10-00. *Fax:* 1-43-27-21-58. *Website:* www.albin-michel.fr (office).

ESPADA, Rafael, MD; Guatemalan/American cardiac surgeon, academic and politician; *Vice-President of Guatemala;* b. 14 Jan. 1944, Guatemala City; ed Universidad San Carlos, Guatemala City, Baylor Coll. of Medicine, Tex., specialist training from LeClub Mitrale, France; performed surgery internship residency training in gen. and thoracic surgery at Baylor Coll. of Medicine, Houston 1970–76, Instructor, Asst and Assoc. Prof. of Surgery 1977–97, Prof. of Cardiothoracic Surgery 1997–, joined Methodist DeBakey Heart Center, Houston 1977, Deputy Chief of Cardiothoracic Surgery 2005–07; Founder and Medical Dir Unidad de Cirugía Cardiovascular de Guatemala (UNICAR) (cardiovascular hosp.), Guatemala City 1995–; Vice-Pres. of Guatemala 2008–; mem. Unidad Nacional de la Esperanza (UNE); Hon. Prof., Universidad LaSalle, Mexico; Dr hc (Univ. of Francisco Marroquin,

Guatemala) 1992; Chest Foundation Gov.'s Award, Int. Rotary Soc. Paul Harris Award, Methodist Hosp. Humanitarian Award 2006, among others. *Achievements include:* believed to have been one of first surgeons ever to perform successfully a cardiac autotransplant. *Address:* Vicepresidencia de la República de Guatemala, 6 Avenida, 4-19, Zona 1, Casa Presidencial, Guatemala City (office); c/o UNICAR, 9 avenida, 8-00, Zona 11, Guatemala City, Guatemala. *Telephone:* 2238-0106 (office). *E-mail:* webmasterservice@vicepresidencia.gob.gt (home). *Website:* www.vicepresidencia.gob.gt (office).

ESPERSEN, Lene, MSc; Danish politician; *Minister of Economic and Business Affairs;* b. 26 Sept. 1965, Hirtshals, N Jutland; d. of Ole Peter Espersen and Inger Tanggaard Espersen; m.; two s.; ed Hirtshals Municipal School, Hjørring Upper Secondary School, Lester B. Pearson United World Coll., Canada, Århus Univ.; Vice-Chair. Denmark Conservative Students 1986–88; market analyst Aarhuus Stiftsbogtrykkerie 1991–92; systems designer Bankernes EDB Cen., Roskilde 1992–94; cand. for Conservative People's Party (DKF) in Ringkjøbing constituency 1993, Sæby constituency 1994; cand. for European Parl. 1994; mem. of Folketing (Parl.) for N Jutland Co. constituency 1994–; Political Spokesperson and mem. Parl. Party, DKF 1999–2001, Leader 2008–; Minister of Justice 2001–08, of Econ. and Business Affairs 2008–. *Address:* Ministry of Economic and Business Affairs, Slotsholmsgade 10–12, 1216 Copenhagen K, Denmark (office). *Telephone:* 33-92-33-50 (office). *Fax:* 33-12-37-78 (office). *E-mail:* oem@oem.dk (office). *Website:* www.oem.dk (office).

ESPERT ROMERO, Nuria; Spanish actress and director; b. 11 June 1935, Hospitalet (Barcelona); m. Armando Moreno 1955; two d.; professional actress since 1947; first maj. success in Medée aged 19; created her own co. 1959; has appeared in works by Calderón, Shakespeare, O'Neill, Lope De Vega, Genet, Lorca, Espriu, Valle Inclán, Sartre etc.; Dir The House of Bernarda Alba (Lorca) with Glenda Jackson and Joan Plowright, London 1986 (Evening Standard Drama Award); has also directed operas Madame Butterfly, Elektra, Rigoletto, La Traviata and Carmen at Covent Garden and in Scotland, Brussels, Israel and Japan; Artistic Dir Turandot, Liceo Theater, Barcelona 1999; more than 100 Spanish honours and awards; 17 int. awards. *Theatre includes:* The Seagull 1997, Master Class 1998, Who's Afraid of Virginia Woolf 1999, 2000, Medée 2002. *Publications:* numerous int. theatre publications. *Leisure interests:* resting, thinking, reading. *Address:* Pavia 2, 28013 Madrid, Spain. *Fax:* (91) 3511177 (office); (91) 5474501 (home). *E-mail:* interludio@portalatino.net (home).

ESPINASSE, Jacques Paul, MBA; French business executive; b. 12 May 1943, Alès; s. of Gustave Espinasse and Andrée Bernadel; m. Daniele Samat 1964; one s. one d.; ed Univ. of Michigan, USA; financial analyst, London and Brussels 1967–70; Consultant, Science Man. Int. 1970–73; Head, Control Dept Renault Véhicules Industriels 1973–78, Commercial Man. in charge of export in Europe 1979; Head, Int. Treasury Dept Régie Renault 1980; Financial Officer, Sommer Allibert 1981–82; Chief Financial Officer CEP Communication 1982–85; Chief Financial Officer Havas 1985–87, Exec. Vice-Pres. 1987–93; Consultant 1994–; Dir-Gen. Télévision par satellite (TPS) 1999–2002; Chief Financial Officer Vivendi Universal (now Vivendi) 2002–07, mem. Man. Bd 2005–; mem. Supervisory Bd Canal+ Group; mem. Bd of Dirs SFR, Vivendi Games, Inc., Veolia Environnement, Vivendi Universal Net, Hammesson, AXA Belgium, SES Global, Maroc Telecom, LBPAM; Chevalier Ordre nat. du Mérite; Chevalier Ordre nat. de la Légion d'Honneur. *Leisure interest:* golf, skiing. *Address:* Avenue Louise 541, 1050 Brussels, Belgium (home). *Telephone:* (2) 649-47-10 (home). *Fax:* (2) 649-48-10 (home). *E-mail:* j.espinasse@skkynet.be. *Website:* www.vivendi.com (office).

ESPINOSA, Maria Fernanda, PhD; Ecuadorean anthropologist, government official, poet and diplomatist; *Permanent Representative, United Nations;* b. 7 Sept. 1964, Quito; m. Galo Mora; ed Catholic Univ. of Ecuador, Facultad Latinoamericana de Ciencias Sociales (FLACSO) and Rutgers Univ., USA; fmr Adjunct Prof. of Politics and Political Ecology, FLACSO; Sr Adviser on Biodiversity and Indigenous Peoples, Int. Union for the Conservation of Nature (IUCN) 1995–2005, Regional Dir for South America 2005–07; Minister of Foreign Affairs 2007 (resgnd); Perm. Rep. to UN, New York 2008–; research fellowships from Ford Foundation, Latin American Studies Assen, Int. Soc. of Women Geographers, Rockefeller Foundation, Natura Foundation; Premio Nacional de Poesía 1990. *Publications:* Poetry: Caymándote, 1990; Tatuaje de Selva, 1992; Loba Triste, 2000; numerous newspaper and journal articles on environmental, cultural and political issues. *Address:* Permanent Mission of Ecuador to the United Nations, 866 United Nations Plaza, Room 516, New York, NY 10017, Ecuador (office). *Telephone:* (212) 935-1680 (office). *Fax:* (212) 935-1835 (office). *E-mail:* ecuador@un.int (office). *Website:* www.un.int/ecuador (office).

ESPINOSA CANTELLANO, Patricia, MA; Mexican government official, politician and diplomatist; *Secretary of Foreign Affairs;* ed Ibero-American Univ.; mem. Nat. Action Party (PAN) 1987–, Head Secr. of Political Promotion of Women, mem. Nat. Exec. Cttee, Head of Sub-coordination for Culture, Educ. and Information, PAN Parl. Group; mem. 57th Legislature, Chamber of Deputies 1997–2000, mem. Equity and Gender Cttee; Chair. Querétaro Municipal Directive Cttee, Head State Secr. of Political Promotion of Women, Head Secr. of Social Devt, Municipality of Querétaro 2000–01; Pres. Nat. Women's Inst. of Mexico (Inmujeres) 2001–06; Sec. of Foreign Affairs 2006–; participated in Non-Governmental Org. (NGO) Forums, Fourth World Conf. on Women, Beijing; Chair. Bd, Regional Conf. on Women of Latin America and the Caribbean; mem. Mexican Assen for the Integral Advancement of the Family. *Address:* Secretariat of State for Foreign Affairs, Avda Ricardo Flores Magón 2, Col. Guerrero, Del. Cuauhtémoc, 06995 México, DF, Mexico (office). *Telephone:* (55) 5063-3000 (office). *Fax:* (55) 5063-3195 (home). *E-mail:* comentario@sre.gob.mx (office). *Website:* www.sre.gob.mx (office).

ESPINOZA VENEGAS, Samuel; Mexican ecclesiastic; *Anglican Bishop of Western Mexico and Primate of Mexico;* ed St Andrew's Seminary and Universidad Autónoma de Baja Calif., Mexico; teacher of sociology and history; Anglican Bishop of Western Mexico 1980–, Primate of Mexico 1997–. *Leisure interest:* reading. *Address:* Fco. J. Gamboa 255, Guadalajara, Jalisco (office); Apdo 2-366, 44280 Guadalajara, Jalisco (office); Av. Ley 2735, Lire, Vallarta, S.H. Guadalajara, Jalisco, Mexico (home). *Telephone:* (36) 16-44-13 (office); (36) 15-20-73 (home). *Fax:* (36) 16-44-13 (office). *E-mail:* diocte@vianet.com.mx (office).

ESQUIVEL, Manuel, PC; Belizean politician and teacher; b. 2 May 1940, Belize City; s. of John Esquivel and Laura Esquivel; m. Kathleen Levy 1971; one s. two d.; ed Loyola Univ., USA, Univ. of Bristol, England; teacher at St John's Jr Coll., Belize City –1984; f. United Democratic Party 1973, Chair. 1976–82; fmr Councillor, Belize City Council; mem. Senate 1979–84; Prime Minister of Belize 1984–89, 1993–98, also Minister of Finance, fmrly of Defence and of Econ. Devt; Leader of the Opposition 1989–93; Dr hc (Loyola Univ., USA) 1986. *Address:* c/o United Democratic Party, 19 King Street, P.O. Box 1143, Belize City, Belize.

ESSAAFI, M'Hamed; Tunisian diplomatist; b. 26 May 1930, Kelibia; m. Hedwige Klat 1956; one s. one d.; ed Sorbonne, Paris; First Sec., London 1956; Counsellor, then Minister Plenipotentiary, Ministry of Foreign Affairs 1960–64; Amb. to UK 1964–69; Sec.-Gen. Ministry of Foreign Affairs 1969–70, 1976–78; Amb. to USSR 1970–74, to FRG 1974–76, to Belgium, Luxembourg and EEC 1978–79; Perm. Rep. to UN Jan.–Aug. 1980; UN Sec.-Gen.'s Special Rep. for Humanitarian Affairs in SE Asia 1980–81; Chef de Cabinet of UN Sec.-Gen. Jan.–June 1982; UN Under-Sec.-Gen. and Disaster Relief Co-ordinator 1982–92; Grand Officier, Ordre de la République tunisienne; Chevalier, Ordre de l'Indépendance. *Address:* 41 Chemin Moise, Duboule, 1209 Geneva, Switzerland (home); rue de la Mosquée BH20, La Marsa, Tunis, Tunisia (home). *Telephone:* (71) 746-442 (Tunisia) (home); 227886462 (Switzerland) (home).

ESSENHIGH, Adm. Sir Nigel, Kt, KCB; British naval officer; b. 1944; m. Susie Essenhigh; ed Royal Coll. of Defence Studies; joined Royal Navy 1963, qualified as Prin. Warfare Officer, specializing in navigation 1972, served in variety of ships, Commdr Type 42 Destroyers HMS Nottingham and HMS Exeter; Hydrographer of the Navy, Chief Exec. UK Hydrographic Office, with rank of Rear Adm.; several appointments at Ministry of Defence including Asst Chief of Defence Staff (Programmes); promoted to Adm., C-in-C Fleet; C-in-C E Atlantic (NATO) and Commdr Allied Naval Forces N (NATO); First Sea Lord and Chief of Naval Staff 2001–02; Fellow Nautical Inst., Royal Inst. of Navigation; mem. Hon. Co. of Master Mariners; Younger Brother Trinity House; ADC. *Address:* c/o Ministry of Defence, Main Building, Whitehall, London, SW1A 2HB, England (office).

ESSEX, David, OBE; British singer, actor and composer; b. (David Albert Cook), 23 July 1947, London; s. of Albert and Doris Cook (née Kemp); m. Maureen Annette Neal 1971; one s. one d.; ed Shipman Secondary School, E London; started in music industry 1965; TV debut on Five O'Clock Club; has since made numerous TV appearances in UK, Europe and USA, including own BBC series 1977, The River BBC1 Series 1988; appeared on stage in repertory and later in Godspell 1971, Evita 1978, Childe Byron, Mutiny! (also wrote music) 1985, with Sir Peter Hall's Co. in She Stoops to Conquer tour and Queen's Theatre, London 1993–94; wrote score for Russian All Stars Co.'s Beauty and the Beast 1995–96; first concert tour of UK 1974, subsequent tours 1975 (including Europe, USA and Australia), 1976, 1977, 1978, 1979 (including Europe and USA), 1980, 1987, 1988, 1989/90 (World Tour); Amb. for Voluntary Service Overseas 1990–92; Pres. Stanstead Park Cricket Club; numerous gold and silver discs for LP and single records in Europe and USA; voted Best Male Singer and Outstanding Music Personality in Daily Mirror poll 1976; Variety Club of GB Award for Show Business Personality of the Year (joint) 1978 ASCAP Award 1989, BASCA Award for Composer 1994. *Films include:* Assault, All Coppers Are . . . 1971, That'll Be The Day (Variety Club Award) 1973, Stardust 1974, Silver Dream Racer 1979, Shogun Mayeda 1991. *Albums include:* Rock On 1974, All the Fun of the Fair 1975, Out on the Street 1976, Gold and Ivory 1977, Imperial Wizard 1979, Hot Love 1980, Be Bop the Future 1981, Stage Struck 1982, The Whisper 1983, This One's For You 1984 (all solo); Under Different Skies (album of musicians from developing countries); War of the Worlds (with Jeff Wayne, Richard Burton and others), From Alpha to Omega (with Cat Stevens) 1978, Silver Dream Racer (film soundtrack: composer/producer) 1979, Centre Stage 1986, Touching the Ghost 1989, David Essex Greatest Hits 1991, Cover Shot 1993, Back to Back 1994. *Publication:* A Charmed Life 2003. *Leisure interests:* motorcycling, cricket, squash, flying helicopters. *Address:* c/o London Management, 2–4 Noel Street, London, W1V 3RB, England. *Telephone:* (20) 7287-9000. *Fax:* (20) 7287-3036.

ESSIMI MENYE, Lazare; Cameroonian government official; *Minister of Finance and Economy;* b. Mfomakap; m.; four c.; ed Institut des Statistiques et d'Économie Appliquée, Morocco, Institut National des Sciences et Techniques Nucléaires, Saclay, France; UNDP adviser for Rwanda 1990–92; adviser to World Bank 1994; fmr govt adviser for IMF, Washington, DC; fmr Minister-Del. in charge of the budget, Ministry of Finance and Economy, Minister of Finance and Economy 2007–. *Address:* Ministry of Economy and Finance, BP 13750, Quartier Administratif, Yaoundé, Cameroon (office). *Telephone:* 7723-2099 (office). *Website:* www.camnet.cm/investir/minfi.

ESSNER, Robert Alan, BA, MA; American pharmaceutical industry executive; b. 26 Oct. 1947; s. of Arthur Essner and Charlotte E. Levy; m. 1st Rosalind Essner (divorced); two c.; m. 2nd Anne Essner; three c.; ed Miami Univ., Oxford, Ohio and Univ. of Chicago; with Sandoz Pharmaceutical Corpn

1978–86, Vice-Pres. 1986–87; Pres. Sandoz Consumer HealthCare Group 1987; joined American Home Products (AHP) 1989, Pres. Wyeth-Ayerst Labs 1993–97, Pres. Wyeth-Ayerst Pharmaceuticals 1997–2000, Exec. Vice-Pres., mem. Bd of Dirs, AHP (now Wyeth) 1997–2007, Pres. and COO 2000–01, CEO 2001–07, Chair. 2003–08; mem. Bd Dirs Massachusetts Mutual Life Insurance Co.; Chair. Children's Health Fund Corp. Council; mem. Business Roundtable, Business Council; fmr Chair. Pharmaceutical Research & Mfrs of America. *Address:* c/o Wyeth, 5 Giralda Farms, Madison, NJ 07940-0874, USA. *Telephone:* (973) 660-5000.

ESSO, Laurent; Cameroonian politician; b. 1942; fmr Minister of Justice, of Public Health; fmr Minister Del. at the Presidency in charge of Defence; Minister of State in charge of External Relations 2004–06. *Address:* c/o Ministry of External Relations, Yaoundé, Cameroon (office).

ESSWOOD, Paul Lawrence Vincent, ARCM; British singer (countertenor) and conductor; b. 6 June 1942, Nottingham; s. of Alfred W. Esswood and Freda Garatt; m. 1st Mary L. Cantrill 1966 (divorced 1990); two s.; m. 2nd Aimée Désirée Blattmann 1990; one s. one d.; ed West Bridgford Grammar School and Royal Coll. of Music; Lay Vicar, Westminster Abbey 1964–71; Prof. Royal Coll. of Music 1973–85, Royal Acad. of Music 1985–; Co-founder, Pro Cantione Antiqua – A Cappella 1967; opera debut, L'Erismena, Univ. of Calif., Berkeley 1968; debut at La Scala, Milan with Zürich Opera in L'Incoronazione di Poppea and Il Ritorno d'Ulisse 1978; Scottish opera debut in Dido and Aeneas 1978; world premiere, Penderecki's Paradise Lost, Chicago Lyric Opera 1979, Philip Glass's Akhnaton, Stuttgart 1984, Herbert Will's Schlafes Bruder, with Zurich Opera 1996; world première, Schnittke's Faust Cantata, Vienna, 1986; Handel's Riccardo Primo, Covent Garden, 1991; has appeared at many maj. int. festivals; specialist in performance of baroque music and has made many recordings of works by Bach, Handel, Purcell, Monteverdi, Cavalli, Britten (Abraham and Isaac), folksongs etc.; Prof. at 'Maîtrise de Notre Dame', Paris, conducting debut at Chichester Festival with Purcell's The Fairy Queen 2000, Kraków, Poland 2001; Hon. RAM 1990; Handel Prize (Germany) 1992. *Leisure interests:* gardening, apiculture. *Address:* Jasmine Cottage, 42 Ferring Lane, Ferring, West Sussex, BN12 6QT, England (home). *Telephone:* (1903) 504480 (home). *Fax:* (1903) 504480 (home). *Website:* www.themusickecompanye.com; www.esswood.co.uk.

ESSY, Amara, LLM; Côte d'Ivoirian diplomatist; b. 20 Dec. 1944, Bouake; m. Lucie Essy 1971; three s. three d.; Chief of Div. of Econ. Relations 1970; First Counsellor, Ivory Coast Embassy, Brazil 1971–73, Ivory Coast Mission to the UN 1973–75; Perm. Rep. to the UN Office, Geneva 1975–81, to UNIDO, Vienna 1975–81; Amb. to Switzerland 1978–81; Perm. Rep. to the UN (and non-resident Amb. to Argentina and Cuba), New York 1981–91; Pres. UN Security Council 1990–91; Minister of Foreign Affairs 1990–98; Pres. 49th Session UN Gen. Ass. 1994–95; Minister of State, Minister of Foreign Affairs in charge of Int. Co-operation 1998–99; Sec.-Gen. OAU Sept. 2001–02; Chair. (interim) African Union July 2002–03; fmr UN Special Envoy for Countries Affected by the War in the Democratic Repub. of the Congo (DRC); participated in the following UN confs: Law of the Sea (Caracas, Geneva, New York), Int. Women's Year (Mexico City), Econ. Co-operation among Developing Countries, UNCTAD (Nairobi, Manila) and of the codification of int. law; meetings of the Econ. and Social Council and Comm. on Human Rights. *Address:* c/o Ministry of Foreign Affairs, Bloc Ministériel, blvd Angoulvand, BP V109, Abidjan, Côte d'Ivoire.

ESTEFAN, Gloria Maria; American singer and songwriter; b. 1 Sept. 1957, Havana, Cuba; d. of Jose Fajardo and Gloria García; m. Emilio Estefan 1979; one s. one d.; ed Univ. of Miami; went to USA 1959; f. Gloria Estefan Foundation 1997; American Music Award 1987, Billboard Latin Music Award for Best Female Tropical Airplay Track (for Tu Fotografía) 2005, Latin Grammy Award for Best Tropical Song (for Pintame de Colores) 2008. *Recordings include:* albums: Primitive Love 1986, Let it Loose 1987, Anything For You 1988, Cuts Both Ways 1989, Coming Out of the Dark 1991, Greatest Hits 1992, Mi Terra 1993, Hold Me, Thrill Me, Kiss Me 1994, Destiny 1996, Gloria! 1998, Santo Santo 1999, Alma Caribeño: Caribbean Soul 2000, Greatest Hits: Vol. 2 2001, Unwrapped 2003, 90 Millas (Latin Grammy Award for Best Traditional Tropical Album 2008) 2007. *Address:* Estefan Enterprises Inc., 6205 Bird Road, Miami, FL 33155, USA. *Website:* www.gloriaestefan.com.

ESTERHÁZY, Péter; Hungarian writer and essayist; b. 14 April 1950; s. of Mátyás Esterházy and Lili Mányoky; m. Gitta Reén; two s. two d.; ed Budapest Univ.; worked as a system supervisor; full-time writer 1978–; Füst Milán, Déry, Kossuth Prize 1996, József Attila, Krúdy, Aszu, Márai, Magyar Irodalini Díj, Vilenica awards, Österreichische Staatspreis für europäische Literatur, Frankfurt Book Fair Peace Prize 2004. *Publications:* short stories: Fancsikó és Pinta 1976, Pápai vizeken ne kalózkodj! 1977; novels: Termelési regény 1979, Függő 1981, Ki szavatol a lady biztonságáért? 1982, Fuharosok 1983, Kis magyar pornográfia (translated as A Little Hungarian Pornography) 1984, A sziv segédigéi 1985, Bevezetés a szépirodalomba 1986, Tizenhét hattyúk (as Csokonai Lili) 1987, Hrabal könyve (translated as The Book of Hrabal) 1990, Hahn-Hahn grófnő pillantása (The Glance of Countess Hahn-Hahn Down the Danube) 1991, Egy nő (She Loves Me) 1995, Harmonia caelistis (translated as Celestial Harmonies) 2000; essays: A kitömött hattyú 1988, Az elefántcsonttoronyból 1991, A halacska csodálatos élete 1991, Egy kékharisnya följegyzéseiből 1994, Egy kék haris 1996. *Leisure interests:* football, mathematics. *Address:* c/o Hungarian Writers' Federation, Bajza-utca 18, 1062 Budapest, Hungary. *Telephone:* (1) 322-8840.

ESTES, Richard; American painter; b. 14 May 1932, Kewanee, Ill.; s. of William Estes and Maria Estes; ed Chicago Art Inst.; began career as commercial artist working in publishing and advertising 1956; moved to Spain 1962; began to paint full-time 1966; currently living and working in New York and Maine; MECA Award for Achievement as a Visual Artist, Maine Coll. of Art 1996. *Address:* c/o Marlborough Gallery, 40 West 57th Street, New York, NY 10019, USA (office). *Telephone:* (212) 541-4900 (office). *Fax:* (212) 541-4948 (office). *E-mail:* mny@marlboroughgallery.com (office). *Website:* www.marlboroughgallery.com (office).

ESTES, William K., PhD; American behavioural scientist and academic; *Distinguished Scholar and Professor of Psychology, Indiana University;* b. 17 June 1919, Minneapolis, Minn.; s. of Dr George D. Estes and Mona Kaye; m. Katherine Walker 1942; two s.; ed Univ. of Minnesota; medical admin. officer, US Army 1944–46; Faculty mem., Indiana Univ. 1946–62; Prof. of Psychology, Stanford Univ. 1962–68; Ed. Journal of Comparative and Physiological Psychology 1962–68, Psychological Review 1977–82, Psychological Science 1990–94; Prof., Rockefeller Univ. 1968–79; Prof., Harvard Univ. 1979–89, Prof. Emer. 1989–; Prof. and Distinguished Scholar Indiana Univ. 1999–; Pres. Experimental Div., American Psychological Asscn 1958; Chair. Office of Scientific and Eng Personnel, Nat. Research Council 1982–85; Chair., Cttee on Contribs of the Behavioral and Social Sciences to the Prevention of Nuclear War, NAS 1985–89; Guggenheim Fellow 1985–86; Chair. Psychonomic Soc. 1972, Soc. for Math. Psychology 1984; mem. Soc. of Experimental Psychologists, NAS, American Acad. of Arts and Sciences, etc.; Distinguished Scientific Contrib. Award, American Psychological Asscn 1962, Warren Medal for Psychological Research 1963, Gold Medal for Lifetime Achievement in Psychological Science, American Psychological Foundation 1992, Nat. Medal of Science (USA) 1997. *Publications:* An Experimental Study of Punishment 1944, Modern Learning Theory (with S. Koch and others) 1954, The Statistical Approach to Learning Theory 1959, Studies in Mathematical Learning Theory (with R. R. Bush) 1959, Stimulus Sampling Theory (with E. Neimark) 1967, Learning Theory and Mental Development 1970, Handbook of Learning and Cognitive Processes (ed.) 1975, Models of Learning, Memory and Choice 1982, Statistical Models in Behavioral Research 1991, Classification and Cognition 1994. *Leisure interest:* music. *Address:* Psychology Building, Indiana University, Bloomington, IN 47405, USA (office). *Telephone:* (812) 856-5780 (office). *E-mail:* wkestes@indiana.edu (office). *Website:* www.indiana.edu/~psych/faculty/estes.html (office).

ESTEVE-COLL, Dame Elizabeth, DBE, BA, FRSA; British university chancellor and fmr museum director; *Chancellor, University of Lincoln;* b. 14 Oct. 1938; d. of P. W Kingdon and Nora Kingdon; m. José Alexander Timothy Esteve-Coll 1960 (died 1980); ed Birkbeck Coll., Univ. of London; librarian, London Borough of Merton, Kingston Coll. of Art, Kingston Polytechnic 1968–77; Head, Dept of Learning Resources, Kingston Polytechnic 1977–82; Univ. Librarian Univ. of Surrey, Chair. Arts Cttee 1982–85; Chief Librarian, Nat. Art Library, Victoria & Albert Museum 1985–87; Dir Victoria & Albert Museum 1988–95; Vice-Chancellor Univ. of E Anglia 1995–97; Chancellor, Univ. of Lincoln 2001–; Assoc. Library Asscn; Hon. LittD (E Anglia) 1997; Hon. DLitt (Hull) 1998. *Publication:* The Victoria and Albert Museum (with others) 1992. *Address:* c/o Coldham Hall, Tuttington, Aylsham, Norfolk NR11 6TA, England (office). *Telephone:* (1263) 735465 (office). *Fax:* (1263) 735465 (office).

ESTEVEZ, Emilio; American actor and film director; b. 12 May 1962, New York; s. of Martin Sheen (q.v.); m. Paula Abdul (q.v.) 1992 (divorced 1994); one s. one d. *Television:* The West Wing (actor episode, Twenty Five) 2003, The Guardian (dir episodes, Hazel Park 2003, All is Mended 2004, The Watchers 2004), Cold Case (dir episodes, The Sleepover 2004, Wishing 2005), CSI:NY (dir episodes, The Closer, The Dove Commission 2005), Close to Home (dir episode, Baseball Murder 2005). *Films include:* Seventeen Going on Nowhere (actor) 1980, To Climb a Mountain (actor) 1981, In the Custody of Strangers (actor) 1982, Tex (actor) 1982, The Outsiders (actor) 1983, Nightmares (actor) 1983, Repo Man (actor) 1984, The Breakfast Club (actor) 1984, St Elmo's Fire (actor) 1984, That was Then, This is Now (actor, writer) 1985, Maximum Overdrive (actor) 1986, Wisdom (dir, actor, writer) 1986, Stakeout (actor) 1987, Young Guns (actor) 1988, Nightbreaker (actor) 1989, Young Guns II (actor) 1990, Men at Work (dir, actor, writer) 1989, Freejack (actor) 1992, The Mighty Ducks (actor) 1992, Loaded Weapon (actor) 1993, Another Stakeout (actor) 1993, Judgement Night (actor) 1993, D2: The Mighty Ducks (actor) 1994, Mission Impossible (actor) 1996, The War at Home (dir, actor, prod.) 1996, D3: Mighty Ducks (actor) 1996, Dollar for the Dead (actor) 1998, Late Last Night (actor) 1999, Rated X (dir, actor) 2000, Sand (actor) 2000, Los Reyes magos (voice) 2003, Culture Clash in AmeriCCa (dir) 2005, LA Riot Spectacular (actor) 2005, Bobby (dir, actor, writer) 2006, Arthur and the Invisibles (voice) 2006. *Address:* c/o UTA, 5th Floor, 9560 Wilshire Boulevard, Beverly Hills, CA 90212, USA.

ESTIER, Claude; French journalist, politician and writer; b. 8 June 1925, Paris; s. of Henri Ezratty and Lucie Bernerbe; ed Lycée Carnot and Ecole des Sciences Politiques, Paris; Political Ed. Le Populaire 1947; Ed. L'Observateur, France-Observateur, then Le Nouvel Observateur 1950–; Ed. Le Monde 1955–58; Ed.-in-Chief Libération 1958–64, Dir 1968; mem. Nat. Assembly 1967–68, 1981–86; Pres. Comm. for Foreign Affairs 1983–86; mem. Paris City Council 1971–89; Nat. Press Sec. Socialist Party 1971–79; Editorial Dir L'Unité (Socialist Party Weekly) 1972–86; MEP 1979–81; Senator 1986; Chair. Senate Socialist Group 1988–2004; Officier Légion d'honneur. *Publications:* Pour l'Algérie 1963, L'Egypte en révolution 1965, Journal d'un Fédéré 1969, La plume au poing 1977, Mitterrand Président 1981, Véridique histoire d'un Septennat (with Véronique Neiertz) 1987, De Mitterand à Jospin: Trente ans de campagnes présidentielles 1995, Dix ans qui ont changé le monde 2000, Un combat centenaire 2005, J'ai tant vu (Memoires) 2008. *Address:* Palais du Luxembourg, 75291 Paris Cedex 06, France (office). *Telephone:* 1-42-34-45-12 (office).

ESTLEMAN, Loren Daniel, BA; American writer; b. 15 Sept. 1952, Ann Arbor, Mich.; s. of Leauvett C. Estleman and Louise A. Estleman; m. Deborah Ann Green 1993; one step-s. one step-d.; ed Eastern Mich., Univ.; police reporter, Ypsilanti Press 1972–73; Ed.-in-Chief, Community Foto News 1975–76; Special Writer, Ann Arbor News 1976; staff writer, Dexter Leader 1977–80; full-time novelist 1980–; Vice-Pres. Western Writers of America 1998–2000, Pres. 2000–02; Western Writers of America Spur Award, Best Historical Novel 1981, Spur Award, Best Short Fiction 1986, 1996, Private Eye Writers of America Shamus Award, Best Novel 1984, Shamus Award, Best Short Story 1985, 1988, Mich. Foundation of the Arts Award for Literature 1987, Mich. Library Asscn Authors Award 1997, Spur Award, Best Western Novel 1999, Western Heritage Award, Outstanding Western Novel 1998, 2001, Western Heritage Award, Outstanding Short Story 2000, Western Heritage Award for Outstanding Western Novel 2001, Shamus Award for Best Short Story 2003; Dr hc of Humane Letters, Eastern Mich. Univ. 2002. *Publications:* novels: The Oklahoma Punk 1976, The Hider, Sherlock Holmes vs. Dracula 1978, The High Rocks 1979, Dr. Jekyll and Mr. Holmes, Stamping Ground, Motor City Blue 1980, Aces and Eights, Angel Eyes, The Wolfer 1981, Murdock's Law, The Midnight Man 1982, Mister St John, The Glass Highway 1983, This Old Bill, Sugartown, Kill Zone, The Stranglers 1984, Every Brilliant Eye, Roses Are Dead, Gun Man 1985, Any Man's Death 1986, Lady Yesterday 1987, Bloody Season, Downriver 1988, Silent Thunder, Peeper 1989, Sweet Women Lie, Whiskey River 1990, Sudden Country, Motown 1991, King of the Corner 1992, City of Widows 1994, Edsel 1995, Stress 1996, Never Street, Billy Gashade 1997, The Witchfinder, Journey of the Dead, Jitterbug 1998, The Rocky Mountain Moving Picture Association 1999, The Hours of the Virgin 1999, White Desert 2000, The Master Executioner 2001, Sinister Heights 2002, Something Borrowed, Something Black 2002, Black Powder, White Smoke 2002, Poison Blonde 2003, Port Hazard 2004, Retro 2004, Little Black Dress 2005, The Undertaker's Wife 2005, Nicotine Kiss 2006, The Adventures of Johnny Vermillion, 2006, American Detective 2007, Amos Walker's Detroit 2007, Frames 2008, Gas City 2008; non-fiction: The Wister Trace 1987, Writing the Popular Novel 2004; collections: General Murders 1988, The Best Western Stories of Loren D. Estleman 1989, People Who Kill 1993; anthologies: P.I. Files 1990, Deals with the Devil 1994, American West 2001. *Leisure interests:* collecting books, antiques, typewriters, records and old films on tape and DVD, movie posters. *Address:* 5552 Walsh Road, Whitmore Lake, MI 48189, USA. *Website:* www.lorenestleman.com (office).

ESTRADA, Joseph Marcelo Ejercito (Erap); Philippine fmr politician; b. 19 April 1937, Tondo, Manila; film actor 1960–89; Mayor of San Juan 1969–85; mem. Senate 1987, Vice-Pres. 1992; Chair. Partido ng Masang Pilipino (PMP); Pres. of the Philippines 1998–2001; impeached for corruption by Congress Nov. 2000, on trial in Senate 2002, sentenced to life imprisonment Sept. 2007, officially pardoned and released Oct. 2007.

ESZTERHAS, Joseph (Joe) A.; American scriptwriter; b. 23 Nov. 1944, Csakanydoroszlo, Hungary; s. of Stephen Eszterhas and Maria Biro; m. 1st Geraldine Javer 1972 (divorced 1994); one s. one d.; m. 2nd Naomi Baka 1994; one s.; ed Ohio State Univ.; reporter, Plain Dealer, Cleveland; staff writer, Man. Ed. Rolling Stone, San Francisco 1971–75; screenwriter 1975–; writer and producer, Checking Out 1980, Betrayed 1989; recipient of various awards. *Film screenplays:* FIST 1978, Flashdance 1983, Jagged Edge 1985, Big Shots 1987, Betrayed 1988, Checking Out 1989, Music Box 1990, Hearts of Fire 1990, Basic Instinct 1992, Nowhere to Run 1993, Sliver 1993, Showgirls 1995, Jade 1995, Telling Lies in America 1997, An Alan Smithee Film: Burn Hollywood Burn 1997, Basic Instinct 2 2006, Szabadság, szerelem 2006. *Publications:* novels: Thirteen Seconds: Confrontation at Kent State 1970, Charlie Simpson's Apocalypse 1974, Nark! 1974, Fist 1977; non-fiction: Hollywood Animal: A Memoir 2004, The Devil's Guide to Hollywood: The Screenwriter as God! 2006, Crossbearer: A Memoir of Faith 2008. *Leisure interest:* reading. *Address:* c/o St Martin's Press, 175 Fifth Avenue, New York, NY 10010, USA. *Website:* www.joeeszterhas.com.

ETAIX, Pierre; French film director and actor; b. 23 Nov. 1928, Roanne; s. of Pierre and Berthe (née Tacher) Etaix; m. 2nd Annie Fratellini 1969 (deceased); ed Lycée de Roanne; apprenticed as stained-glass designer; asst film producer 1949–55; Chevalier, Ordre nat. du Mérite, Ordre des Arts et des Lettres. *Films include:* Pickpocket 1959, Une grosse tête 1961, Rupture (also dir and writer) 1961, Le Pèlerinage 1962, Heureux anniversaire (also dir, writer, producer, Acad. Award ('Oscar') for best short film 1963) 1962, Le Soupirant (also dir and writer) 1962, Yoyo (also dir and writer) 1965, Tant qu'on a la santé (also dir and writer) 1966, Le Grand amour (also dir and writer) 1969, Pays de cocagne (dir) 1971, The Day the Clown Cried 1972, Sérieux comme le plaisir 1975, Max mon amour 1986, L'Âge de Monsieur est avancé (also dir and writer) 1987, Nuit docile 1987, Henry & June 1990. *Television includes:* Show Pierre Etaix 1974, Lundi 1980, La Métamorphose 1983, L'Étrange château du docteur Lerne 1983, L'Aide-mémoire 1984, Les Idiots 1987, Souris noire (series writer and dir) 1987, Méliès 88: Rêve d'artiste (dir) 1988, Bouvard et Pecuchet 1989, J'écris dans l'espace (dir and writer) 1989. *Achievement:* creator (with Amie Fratellini) of the first circus school in France 1973. *Publications:* Le carton à chapeau 1981, Dactilographisme 1982, Croquis de Jerry Lewis 1983, Stars System (jtly) 1986, Criticons la caméra 2001. *Address:* Editions du Seuil, 27 rue Jacob, 75261 Paris cedex 06, France (office).

ETAYO MIQUEO, José Javier; Spanish mathematician and academic; *Professor Emeritus, Universidad Complutense of Madrid;* b. 28 March 1926, Pamplona; s. of Nicolás Etayo and María Miqueo; m. Laura Gordejuela 1956; four s.; ed Univs of Valladolid, Zaragoza and Madrid; Prof. Univ. of Madrid 1952–61; Full Prof. Univ. of Zaragoza 1961–63; Full Prof. of Math. Univ. Complutense of Madrid 1963–91, Prof. Emer. 1991–; Vice-Dean Faculty of Sciences, Univ. of Madrid 1971–75; Pres. Real Soc. Matemática Española 1976–82; mem. Consejo Superior de Investigaciones Científicas 1969, Spanish Cttee Int. Math. Union 1979–85; mem. Real Acad. de Ciencias Exactas, Fisicas y Naturales de Madrid 1983–, Gen. Sec. 1992–2008. *Publications:* gen. math. and geometry textbooks, various math. research papers, especially in differential geometry, essays, critical reviews of science books. *Leisure interests:* reading, music, theatre, cinema. *Address:* Real Academia de Ciencias Exactas, Fisicas y Naturales, Calle Valverde 22, 28004 Madrid (office); Avenida Reina Victoria 70, 4B, 28003 Madrid, Spain (home). *Telephone:* (91) 7014230 (office); (91) 5541173 (home). *Fax:* (91) 7014232 (office). *E-mail:* secretaria@rac.es (office).

ETCHEGARAY, HE Cardinal Roger, DIurUtr; French ecclesiastic; b. 25 Sept. 1922, Espelette; s. of Jean-Baptiste Etchegaray and Aurélie Dufau; ed Petit Séminaire, Ustaritz and Grand Séminaire, Bayonne; ordained priest 1947, served diocese of Bayonne 1947–60; Asst Sec., then Sec.-Gen. French Episcopal Conf. 1961–70, Pres. 1975–81; Archbishop of Marseilles 1970–84; Pres. Council of European Episcopal Confs 1971–79; Prelate, Mission of France 1975–81; Titular Bishop of Porto-Santa Rufina; cr. Cardinal 1979; Pres. Pontifical Council for Justice and Peace 1984, now Pres. Emer.; Vice Dean Coll. of Cardinals 2005–; Pres. Council Cor Unum 1984–95; Special Papal Emissary to Togo 1993, to Bethlehem totry to help end standoff between Israeli forces and Palestinian gunmen in Church of the Nativity 2002; Pres. Cttee for Grand Jubilee of Year 2000; Officier, Légion d'honneur, Commdr, Ordre nat. du Mérite, Grand Cross Nat. Order (FRG), Grand Cross Nat. Order of Hungary. *Publications:* Dieu à Marseille 1976, J'avance comme un âne 1984, L'évangile aux couleurs de la vie 1987, Jésus, vrai homme, vrai Dieu 1997. *Address:* Piazza San Calisto, Rome 00153, Italy.

ETCHEGARAY AUBRY, Alberto; Chilean politician and civil engineer; b. 5 May 1945; s. of Alberto Etchegaray and Odette Etchegaray; m.; five s., two d.; Univ. Prof. of Business Admin.; Dir Dept of Studies, Unión Social de Empresarios Cristianos; co-ordinator of visit of Pope John Paul II to Chile; Dir Hogar de Cristo; mem. Council, Semanas Sociales de Chile (initiative of Episcopal Conf. of Chile); Minister of Housing and Urban Devt 1990–94; Pres. Nat. Council against Poverty 1994–98; Dir Cía. Seg. de Vida la Construcción SA; Pres. Fundación Nacional para la Superación de la Pobreza 1997–2000, Dir 2000–; Dir Banco del Desarollo. *Publication:* Poverty in Chile: The Challenge of Equity and Social Intergration. *Address:* Canada 185-A, Providencia, Santiago, Chile. *Telephone:* (2) 204-1917 (office). *Fax:* (2) 269-0718 (office). *E-mail:* domet@ctcreuna.cl (office).

ETEKI MBOUMOUA, William-Aurélien, LicenDroit; Cameroonian politician; *President, Red Cross (Cameroon);* b. 20 Oct. 1933, Douala; s. of Joseph Mboumoua and Mana Katta; m. Naimi Bessy Eyewe; one s. one d.; ed Ecole Nat. de la France d'Outre-mer, Paris; Prefect for Nkam 1959, for Sanage Maritime 1960–61; Minister of Educ., Youth and Culture 1961–68; mem. Exec. Council, UNESCO 1962–68, Pres. of Conf., UNESCO 1968–70; Special Adviser, with rank of Minister, to Pres. of United Republic of Cameroon 1971–74, 1978–80; Minister charged with Special Functions at the Presidency 1978; Co-Minister in charge of Missions 1980–84, Minister of Foreign Affairs 1984–87; Sec.-Gen. OAU 1974–78; Special Rep. of UN Sec.-Gen. on Small Arms Proliferation in West Africa, mem. Eminent Persons Group on curbing illicit trafficking in Small Arms and Light Weapons 1999; Nat. Pres. Cameroon Red Cross Soc. 1994–; mem. Ind. Comm. for implementation of proposals in UNDP document Proposals for Africa in this Millennium 1999, Jury du Prix UNESCO Ville pour la Paix; Commdr des Palmes académiques, Grand Officier de l'Ordre de la Valeur and many other decorations. *Publications:* Un certain humanisme 1970, Démocratiser la culture 1974; and many articles on education and African culture. *Leisure interests:* literature, poetry, painting, tennis, football, swimming. *Address:* PO Box 631, Yaoundé (office); PO Box 1155, Yaoundé, Cameroon (home). *Telephone:* 2224177 (office); 2202592 (home). *Fax:* 2224177 (office); 2202592 (home). *E-mail:* crol-Rcam@ iccnet_cm (office).

ETHERINGTON, William (Bill) A., BEE; Canadian banking executive; *Chairman, Canadian Imperial Bank of Commerce (CIBC);* b. 1942; ed Univ. of Western Ont.; joined IBM Canada 1964, held several sales, services and staff positions 1964–80, served successively as Vice-Pres. Western Region, Vice-Pres. Sales, Vice-Pres. Finance and Chief Financial Officer 1980–88, Asst Gen. Man. IBM Latin America 1988–91, Pres. and CEO IBM Canada Ltd 1991–95, Global Gen. Man., Large Enterprise Sales, IBM Corpn 1995–97, Gen. Man. IBM Europe, Middle E and Africa 1997–98, Sr Vice-Pres. and Group Exec., Sales and Distribution, IBM Corpn and Chair., Pres. and CEO IBM World Trade Corpn 1998–2001; currently Chair. Canadian Imperial Bank of Commerce (CIBC); mem. Bd of Dirs Canadian Imperial Bank (USA) 1994–, Allstream Inc., Dofasco Inc., MDS Inc., AT&T Canada, The Relizon Co., Celestica Inc. 2001–; Head United Way Campaign of Greater Toronto 1993; Hon. LLD (Univ. of Western Ont.). *Address:* Canadian Imperial Bank of Commerce, Commerce Court, Toronto, Ont. M5L 1A2, Canada (office). *Telephone:* (416) 980-2211 (office). *Fax:* (416) 980-5028 (office). *Website:* www.cibc.com (office).

ETIANG, Paul Orono, BA; Ugandan politician and diplomatist; *Director, Cairo International Bank;* b. 15 Aug. 1938, Tororo; s. of Kezironi Orono and Mirabu Adacat Adeke Achom; m. Zahra A. Foum 1967; two s. two d.; ed Busoga Coll. and Makerere Univ. Coll.; Dist Officer, Prov. Admin 1962–64; Asst Sec., Ministry of Foreign Affairs 1964–65, Third Sec., Uganda Embassy, Moscow 1965–66, Second Sec. 1966–67; First Sec., Uganda Perm. Mission to UN, New York 1967–68; High Commr to UK 1968–71; Chief of Protocol and Marshal of Diplomatic Corps, Uganda 1971; Perm. Sec., Ministry of Foreign Affairs 1971–73, Acting Minister of Foreign Affairs May–Oct. 1973; Minister of State for Foreign Affairs 1973–76, of Transport, Works and Communications 1976–78, for Regional Co-operation 1988–89, for Commerce 1989–91, for Information 1991–96, Third Deputy Prime Minister and Minister of Labour and Social Services 1996–97, Third Deputy Prime Minister and Minister for Disaster Preparedness and Refugees 1997–98; mem. Parl. 1998–2001; Asst Sec.-Gen. OAU, Addis Ababa 1978–87; Chair. Tororo Rock FM Radio 2001–, Uganda Railways Corpn 2003–06; Dir Cairo Int. Bank 2004–. *Leisure interests:* billiards, badminton, music, theatre. *Address:* PO Box 7089, Kampala, Uganda (office).

ETIENNE, Winter; Haitian government official; *Head, National Port Authority;* b. Port-au-Prince; trained paramilitary forces loyal to Duvalier family 1990, took part in mil. coup that overthrew Pres. Jean-Bertrand Aristide who later returned to power 1990; Leader, Front pour la Libération et la Reconstruction Nationales (fmrly Front de Résistance de l'Artibonite) rebel group whose activities led to overthrow and exile of Pres. Aristide Feb. 2004; apptd himself regional Dir of Police, Mayor of Gonaïves and Police Commr; Head, Nat. Port Authority 2004–. *Address:* National Port Authority, Port-au-Prince, Haiti (office). *Telephone:* 222-1942 (office).

ETO'O FILS, Samuel; Cameroonian footballer; b. 10 March 1981, Nkon; forward; teams played for include Real Madrid, Spain 1996–2004, Leganes, Spain 1996–98 (on loan), Espanyol, Spain 1998–99 (on loan), Real Mallorca, Spain 1999–2004 (initially on loan and then part-owned by Real Madrid), FC Barcelona, Spain 2004–; played for Cameroon in World Cups 1998, 2002, gold medal Sydney Olympic Games 2000, winner African Nations Cup 2000, 2002; leading scorer for Real Mallorca in 2003–04 Primera Liga season, won Copa del Rey 2003; Confed. of African Football Footballer of the Year 2003. *Address:* c/o Futbol Club Barcelona, Avenida Arístides Maillol, 08028 Barcelona, Spain (office). *Website:* www.fcbarcelona.com (office).

ETOUNGOU, Simon Nko'o; Cameroonian diplomatist and politician; b. 14 Feb. 1932; ed secondary and post-secondary schools and diplomatic training in France; Head of Office in Ministry of Econ. Planning 1956–57; Cabinet Attaché, Ministry of Finance 1958–59; First Sec., Cameroon Embassy, Paris 1960; Minister-Counsellor 1960–61; Amb. to Tunisia 1961–64; led numerous Cameroon dels 1963–64; concurrently Amb. to Algeria July–Nov. 1964, to USSR 1964–65; Minister of Foreign Affairs 1965–66, 1968–70, Minister of Finance 1966–68; Amb. to Belgium, Netherlands and Luxembourg and Perm. Rep. to EEC 1971–79; Amb. to Algeria 1985–88, to France 1988–96; Kt of Nat. Order of Merit (Cameroon) and decorations from Senegal, Tunisia, FRG and Gabon. *Address:* c/o Ministry of Foreign Affairs, Yaoundé, Cameroon.

ETROG, Sorel, OC; Canadian sculptor; b. 29 Aug. 1933, Jassy, Romania; s. of Moshi Etrog and Toni Etrog; ed Jassy High School and Tel Aviv Art Inst.; Brooklyn Museum Art School Scholarship 1958; first one-man show 1958; Canadian rep. Venice Biennale 1966; comms. include Los Angeles Co. Museum 1966, Canadian Pavilion, Expo 67, Olympic Centre, Toronto 1972, Bow Valley Square, Calgary 1975, SunLife Canada, Toronto 1984, Olympic Park, Seoul 1988; works now in numerous public collections including Nat. Gallery of Canada, Tate Gallery, London, Musée d'Art Moderne, Paris, Museum of Modern Art, New York, Stratford Shakespeare Festival Theatre, Stratford, Ont., etc.; designer and illustrator of books; wrote and directed film Spiral (CBC) 1975; mem. Royal Canadian Acad., Arts and Letters Club; Hon. Fellow, Univ. Coll. of Swansea 1990; Chevalier des Arts et des Lettres. *Publications:* Dream Chamber 1982, Hinges (play) 1983, The Kite 1984, Images from the Film Spiral 1987. *Address:* Box 67034, 2300 Yonge Street, Toronto, Ont., M4P 1E0, Canada. *Telephone:* (416) 480-0109. *Fax:* (416) 480-2914.

ETTL, Harald; Austrian trade union official and politician; *Member, European Parliament;* b. 7 Dec. 1947, Gleisdorf, Styria; m.; three c.; ed Higher Fed. Teaching and Experimental Coll. for Textile Industry, Vienna; Asst to Works Man., Eybl carpet factory, Ebergassing; Sec. Textile, Clothing and Leather Workers' Union 1971–73, Cen. Sec. 1973–84, Pres. 1984–2000; Vice Pres. Metal-Textile Trade Union 2000–; Vice-Pres. Int. Textile, Clothing and Leather Workers' Asscn 2004–; Chair. Consumer Information Asscn 1993–; Minister for Health and the Civil Service 1989–92; MEP 1996–; Chair. Gen. Accident Insurance Scheme 1978–89; Pres. Accident Insurance Cttee, Fed. of Austrian Social Insurance Bodies 1978–89; Chair. Working Group for Integration in Austrian Trade Union Confed.; mem. Social Democratic Party. *Address:* c/o Metal-Textile Trade Union, Plössglasse 15, 1041 Vienna, Austria (office). *Telephone:* (1) 501-46-402 (office). *Fax:* (1) 501-46-400 (office). *E-mail:* harald.ettl@metaller.at (office). *Website:* www.metaller.at (office); www .harald-ettl.at.

ETZWILER, Donnell Dencil, BA, MD; American paediatrician; *Clinical Professor Emeritus, University of Minnesota School of Medicine;* b. 29 March 1927, Mansfield, Ohio; s. of Donnell S. Etzwiler and Berniece J. Etzwiler; m. Marion Grassby Etzwiler 1952; one s. three d.; m. 2nd Helen B. Etzwiler 1989; ed Indiana and Yale Univs; service in USNR 1945–46; Intern, Yale-Grace New Haven Community Hosp. 1953–54; Resident, New York Hosp., Cornell Medical Center 1954–55, NIH Fellowship in Metabolism 1955–56; Instructor, Cornell Univ. Medical Coll., New York 1956–57; Clinical Prof., Univ. of Minn. School of Medicine 1957–98, Prof. Emer. 1998–; Paediatrician, Park Nicollet Medical Center, Minn. 1957–96; Medical Dir, Camp Needlepoint 1960–85; Paediatrician, Project Hope, Peru 1962; Founder, Pres. Int. Diabetes Center 1967–96, Pres. Emer. 1996–; Vice-Pres. Int. Diabetes Fed. 1979–85; Commr, Nat. Comm. on Diabetes 1975–76; Pres. American Diabetes Asscn 1976–77; Dir Diabetes Collaborating Center, WHO 1985–, Chair. 1988–94; Founder and mem. Bd Compass Project Foundation, Pres. 1998–; mem. Bd, Park Nicollet Medical Foundation 1960–96, Diabetes Research Educational Foundation 1983–93, Inst. Research and Educ. 1996–2000; Co-Dir Int. Diabetes Programme (Russia) 1989–; Fellow, All India Inst. of Diabetes, Bombay 1979, Inst. of Medicine, NAS 1982; Hon. mem. American Dietetic Asscn 1980, American Asscn of Diabetes Educators 1993, Russian Nat. Diabetes Fed. 1995; Banting Medal 1977, Upjohn Award 1983, Beckton Dickinson Camp Award 1979, Diabetes in Youth Award, American Diabetes Asscn 1976, NIH Certificate of Approval 1993, Peace Award (Russia) 1994, Charles H. Best Medal for Distinguished Service (American Diabetes Asscn) 1994, Circle of Leadership Award (American Diabetes Asscn) 1998, Shotwell Award 2000. *Publications:* Education and Management of the Patient with Diabetes 1973, Diabetes Manual; Health Education for Living Program 1976, Living Well With Diabetes 1985; Ed. First International Workshop on Diabetes and Camping 1974, How to Live with Diabetes (in Russian) 1991, Staged Diabetes Management 1999, Detection and Treatment of Type 2 Diabetes and Dysmetabolic Syndrome X in Children and Adolescents 2002; over 200 scientific articles in medical journals. *Leisure interests:* tennis, photography, travel. *Address:* 7611 Bush Lake Drive, Minneapolis, MN 55438, USA. *Telephone:* (952) 942-8489. *Fax:* (952) 944-2537. *E-mail:* dretzwiler@aol.com (office).

EUBANK, Chris; British fmr professional boxer; b. 8 Aug. 1966, Dulwich; m.; four c.; WBC Int. Middleweight Boxing Champion March–Nov. 1990 two defences; WBO Middleweight Boxing Champion Nov. 1990–Aug. 1991 three defences; WBO World Super-Middleweight Boxing Champion Sept. 1991–March 1995 fourteen defences, lost title to Steve Collins, Cork Sept. 1995, failed to regain title against Joe Calzaghe, Sheffield Oct. 1997; unsuccessful fights for WBO Cruiserweight title against Carl Thompson, Manchester April 1998, Sheffield July 1998; Patron Breakthrough; numerous UK television appearances; Amb. for the Int. Fund for Animal Welfare; spokesperson for the Nat. Soc. for the Prevention of Cruelty to Children.

EUGENIDES, Jeffrey, BA, MA; American novelist; b. 1960, Detroit, Mich.; m.; one d.; ed Brown Univ., Stanford Univ.; Fellow, Berliner Künstlerprogramm 2002; Guggenheim Foundation Fellowship, Nat. Foundation for the Arts Fellowship, American Acad. in Berlin Prize Fellowship 2000–01; teacher in Creative Writing Program, Princeton Univ. 1999–2000, 2007–; Whiting Writers' Award, American Acad. of Arts and Letters Harold D. Vursell Memorial Award. *Publications:* The Virgin Suicides 1993, Middlesex (Pulitzer Prize for Fiction 2003) 2002, My Mistress's Sparrow is Dead (Ed.) 2008; contrib. to The New Yorker, The Paris Review, The Yale Review, The Gettysburg Review, Best American Short Stories, Granta's Best of Young American Novelists. *Address:* Creative Writing Program, Princeton University, 185 Nassau Street, Princeton, NJ 08544, USA. *Telephone:* (609) 258-8561. *Fax:* (609) 258-2230. *Website:* www.princeton.edu/~visarts/cwr.

EUH, Yoon-dae, BA, MA, MBA, PhD; South Korean academic; *Professor of International Business and Finance, Korea University;* ed Korea Univ., Asian Inst. of Man., Univ. of Michigan, USA; Prof. of Int. Business and Finance, Korea Univ. 1979–, Chair. Dept of Int. Business and Trade 1982–86, Assoc. Dean Coll. of Business Admin 1986–89, Dean Academic Affairs 1991–93, Dir Inst. for Business Research and Educ. 1993–97, Dean Grad. School of Business Admin 1996–98, Pres. Korea Univ. 2003–06; Research Fellow, Inst. for Int. Commerce, Univ. of Michigan 1976–78; Visiting Prof., PAMI (Summer Program) Coll. of Business Admin, Univ. of Hawaii, USA 1982–87, Faculty of Commerce and Business Admin, Univ. of British Columbia, Canada 1989; Visiting Scholar, Inst. of Developing Economies, Japan 1985–86; Scholar, Faculty of Econs, Univ. of Tokyo, Japan 1990–91; adviser, Korea Inst. for Int. Econ. Policy 1997–, Korea Devt Inst. 1997–; Policy Advisor, Ministry of Foreign Affairs and Trade 1993–2004; Chair. Advisory Bd Ministry of Educ. and Human Resources 2003–05, Cttee for Future Korea, Ministry of Information and Communication 2006–; Co-Chair. Nat. Fed. for Cooperation between Univ. and Industry 2006–; Vice-Chair. Nat. Econ. Advisory Council 2005–; Founding Pres. Korea Center for Int. Finance 1999–2000; Dir (non-resident) Korea Inst. for Public Finance 1996–99; mem. Monetary Bd Bank of Korea 1992–95; mem. Bd of Dirs Korea Devt Bank 1996–97, Korea First Bank 1998–99, Hyundai Corpn 1998–2002, CJ Home Shopping 1999–2003; mem. (Minister) Public Fund Oversight Comm. 2001–03; Pres. Korean Acad. of Int. Business 1992–93, Korea Money and Finance Asscn 1995–96, Korean Academic Soc. of Business Admin 2002–03; Hon. Prof., Jilin Univ. 2005, Nanjing Univ. 2006; Hon. Fellow, Royal Holloway, Univ. of London 2005,; Hon. LLD (Weseda Univ.) 2005; Hon. PhD (Yonsei Univ.) 2006; Hon. DUniv (Griffith Univ.); Asian Inst. of Man. Triple A Award, A Merit, Les Insignes de Chevalier de l'Ordre nat. du Mérite, Global CEO Award 2006. *Address:* College of Business Administration, University of Korea, Anam-dong, Sungbuk-gu, Seoul 136-701, South Korea (office). *Telephone:* (2) 3290-1916 (office). *Fax:* (2) 395-1976 (office). *E-mail:* ydeuh@korea.ac.kr (office). *Website:* www.korea.ac.kr (office).

EUSTACE, Arnhim; Saint Vincent and the Grenadines politician and economist; *President, New Democratic Party;* b. 1946; economist specializing in fiscal man.; fmr Minister of Finance; Prime Minister of Saint Vincent and the Grenadines 2000–01; Pres. New Democratic Party (NDP) 2000–. *Address:* New Democratic Party, Murray Road, PO Box 1300, Kingstown, Saint Vincent and the Grenadines.

EUSTACE, Dudley Graham (D. G.), BA; British business executive; *Chairman of the Supervisory Board, AEGON NV;* b. 3 July 1936; m. Carol Diane Zakrajsek; two c.; ed Univ. of Bristol; with John Barrit & Son, Hamilton, Bermuda 1962; with Int. Resort Facilities 1963; exec. positions with Alcan Aluminium Ltd in various locations including Montreal, Vancouver, Buenos Aires, Rio de Janeiro, Madrid and UK 1964–87; joined British Aerospace plc 1987, Financial Dir 1988–92; mem. Group Cttee, Royal Philips Electronics NV 1992–2001, Exec. Vice Pres. and Chief Financial Officer 1993–97, Vice-Chair. Bd of Man. 1997–99; Chair. Smith & Nephew PLC 2000–06; mem. Supervisory Bd AEGON NV 1997–, currently Chair.; Chair.

Supervisory Bd The Nielsen Company; Vice-Chair. Supervisory Bd KPN NV 2001–, Hagemeyer NV; mem. Export Guarantees Advisory Council, UK 1988, European Advisory Council for Rothschilds; mem. Council of Univ. of Surrey. *Address:* Supervisory Board, AEGON NV, PO Box 202, 2501 The Hague, The Netherlands (office). *Telephone:* (70) 3443210 (office). *E-mail:* info@aegon.com (office). *Website:* www.aegon.com (office).

EVAN, Gerard, BA, PhD, FRS, FMedSci; British medical scientist and academic; *Gerson and Barbara Bass Bakar Distinguished Professor of Cancer Research, Cancer Research Institute, University of California, San Francisco;* b. 1955, London; s. of Robert Evan and Gwendoline Evan (née Groom); m.; one s. one d.; ed Univs of Oxford and Cambridge, Univ. of California, USA; MRC Dept of Microbiology and Immunology, Univ. of California at San Francisco (UCSF) 1982–84; Research Fellowship, Downing Coll. Cambridge 1984–88; Asst Prof., Ludwig Inst. for Cancer Research, Cambridge 1984–88; Prin. Scientist, Imperial Cancer Research Fund 1988–99; Royal Soc. Napier Research Prof., Univ. Coll. London 1996–99; Gerson and Barbara Bass Bakar Distinguished Prof. of Cancer Biology, UCSF 1999–; mem. Scientific Advisory Bd EISAI London Research Labs 1994–, Oxagen Inc. 1997–, ESBA Tech 1998–; Consultant Cantab Pharmaceuticals Ltd 1994–99, Ontogeny Inc., Boston 1998–, Cambridge Antibody Tech. Inc. 1998–, Amersham/Nycomed 1998–; mem. Scientific Review Bd DNAX 1998–; Pfizer Prize in Biology 1995, Royal Soc. Napier Research Prof. of Cancer Biology 1996, Joseph Steiner Prize, Swiss Oncological Soc. 1997. *Radio includes:* participation in numerous science programmes for BBC. *Publications:* numerous academic publs. *Leisure interests:* sailing, music, white water rafting, hiking, skiing. *Address:* UCSF Cancer Center and Cancer Research Institute, Box 0875, University of California, 2340 Sutter Street, San Francisco, CA 94143-0875 (office); 728 Marin Drive, Mill Valley, CA 94941, USA (home). *Telephone:* (415) 514-0438 (office); (415) 514-0878 (office). *Fax:* (415) 514-0878 (office). *E-mail:* gevan@cc .ucsf.edu (office). *Website:* cancer.ucsf.edu/people/evan_gerard.php (office).

EVANGELISTA, Linda; Canadian model; b. St Catharines, Ont.; m. Gerald Marie (divorced 1993); face of Yardley Cosmetics; numerous catwalk fashion shows. *Address:* dna Model Management, 520 Broadway, 11th Floor, New York, NY 10012, USA. *Telephone:* (212) 226-0080, ext. 4. *E-mail:* info@ dnamodels.com. *Website:* www.dnamodels.com.

EVANGELOU, Alecos C.; Cypriot politician and lawyer; *Senior Partner, Alecos Evangelou and Co., Advocates;* b. 23 July 1939, Kato Lakatamia; s. of Costas Evangelou and Theano A. Tsiappa; m. Nicoulla Protopapa 1965; one s. two d.; ed English School, Nicosia and Gray's Inn, London; called to the Bar, Gray's Inn, London 1967; worked in Nicosia Dist Admin., later at Ministry of Finance 1957–72; law officer, Attorney, Office of Attorney-Gen. 1972–93; fmr Chair. Appropriate Authority for Intellectual Property; fmr Pres. Supreme Sports Tribunal; fmr Chair. Cyprus Radio-Television Authority; Minister of Justice and Public Order 1993–97; now Sr Partner Alecos Evangelou and Co. (law firm); del. to several UN, European and Commonwealth confs; Chair. two Commonwealth Ministerial Confs; Chair. Cyprus Radio-TV Authority 1998–; Deputy Gov. American Biographical Inst., Inc. *Leisure interest:* gardening. *Address:* PO Box 29238, Nicosia 1623, Cyprus (office). *Telephone:* (22) 879999 (office). *Fax:* (22) 879990 (office). *E-mail:* evangelou.advocates@cytanet.com.cy (office).

EVANS, Anthony G., BSc, PhD; British physicist and academic; *Professor, Department of Mechanical Engineering and Department of Materials, University of California, Santa Barbara;* ed Imperial Coll., London; mem. Tech. Staff, Atomic Energy Research Establishment, Harwell 1968–72; mem. Tech. Nat. Bureau of Standard, Washington, DC, USA 1972–74; Group Leader, Rockwell Int. Science Center, Thousand Oaks, CA 1974–78; Prof., Dept of Materials Science and Mineral Eng, Univ. of Calif., Berkeley 1978–85, Alcoa Prof. and Chair., Materials Dept 1985–91, Alcoa Prof. and Co-Dir, High Performance Composites Center 1985–97; Gordon McKay Prof. of Materials Eng, Div. of Applied Sciences, Harvard Univ. 1994–98; Prof. and Dir, Princeton Materials Inst., Princeton Univ. 1998–2002, Gordon Wu Prof. of Mechanical and Aerospace Eng 1998–2002; currently Prof. Dept of Mechanical Eng and Dept of Materials, Univ. of Calif. Santa Barbara; Vice Pres., American Ceramic Soc. 1984–88, Distinguished Life Mem. 2000–; mem. Defense Sciences Research Council 1974–, Chair. 1997–2001; mem. Nat. Acad. of Eng 1997–; Fellow, Acad. of Arts and Sciences 2000–; Imperial Coll. Matthey Prize 1967, American Ceramic Soc. Ross Coffin Purdy Award 1974, American Ceramic Soc. Richard M. Fulrath Award 1979, American Ceramic Soc. Robert Sosman Award 1980, American Ceramic Soc. Hobart N. Kraner Award 1986, American Ceramic Soc. John Jepsson Medal 1988, Inst. of Materials Griffith Medal and Prize 1994, Materials Research Soc. Turnbull Award 2000. *Publications:* Over 370 technical articles on topics concerned with the mechanical properties and processing of advanced structural materials. *Address:* Department of Mechanical Engineering and Department of Materials, Engr II, Room 2361A, University of California, Santa Barbara, Santa Barbara, CA 93106-5070, USA (office). *Telephone:* (805) 893-7839 (office). *Fax:* (805) 893-8651 (office). *E-mail:* agevans@engineering.ucsb.edu (office). *Website:* www.me.ucsb.edu/dept_site/people/evans_page.html (office).

EVANS, (Christopher) Paul, PhD; British civil servant; b. 25 Dec. 1948, Newport; s. of Colwyn Evans and Margery Evans; m. Margaret Beckett 1971; two d.; ed St Julian's High School, Newport, Trinity Coll., Cambridge; with Dept of the Environment, subsequently of the Environment, Transport and the Regions, then Dept for Transport, Local Govt and the Regions, now Office of the Deputy Prime Minister 1975–; Private Sec. to Perm. Sec. 1978–80, Prin. 1980, Asst Sec. 1985, Under-Sec. 1993; Dir Urban Policy Unit 1997–2001; Strategic Dir of Regeneration, London Borough of Southwark 2001–. *Address:* Regeneration Department, Council Offices, Chiltern House, Portland Street, London, SE17 2ES, England (office). *Telephone:* (20) 7525-5501 (office). *Fax:* (20) 7525-5484 (office). *E-mail:* paul.evans@southwark.gov.uk (office).

EVANS, Daniel Jackson, MS; American politician; *Chairman, Daniel J. Evans Associates;* b. 16 Oct. 1925, Seattle, Wash.; s. of Daniel Lester and Irma Evans (née Ide); m. Nancy Ann Bell 1959; three s.; ed Roosevelt High School, Seattle and Univ. of Washington; USNR 1943–46; Lt on active duty Korean War 1951–53; Asst Man. Mountain Pacific Chapter, Assoc. Gen. Contractors 1953–59; State Rep. King County 1956–64; Pnr, Gray and Evans, structural and civil engineers 1959–64; Gov. Washington State 1965–77; Chair. Western Govs Conf. 1968–69, Nat. Govs Conf. 1973–74; Senator from Washington 1983–89; now involved with environmental work; mem. Advisory Comm. on Intergovernmental Relations 1972, Trilateral Comm. 1973; Keynote Speaker Republican Nat. Convention 1968; mem. Pres.'s Vietnamese Refugee Comm. 1974; mem. Nat. Center for Productivity and Quality of Working Life 1975–76; mem. Carnegie Council on Policy Studies in Higher Educ. 1977; mem. Univ. of Washington Bd of Regents 1993-2005 (Pres. 1996-97); Trustee Urban Inst. 1977, The Carnegie Foundation for the Advancement of Teaching 1977; Pres. Evergreen State Coll. 1977–83; Chair. Daniel J. Evans Assocs ., Seattle 1998–; Dir Puget Sound Power and Light, Tera Computer Co., Burlington Northern/ Santa Fe, Inc., Flow Int., WA Mutual Bank; Republican; several hon. degrees; Nat. Municipal League Distinguished Citizen Award 1977. *Leisure interests:* skiing, sailing, mountain climbing. *Address:* Daniel J. Evans Assocs., 1111 3rd Avenue, Suite 3400, Seattle, WA 98101, USA.

EVANS, David (see (The) Edge).

EVANS, David A., AB, PhD, FRSC; American chemist and academic; *Arthur and Ruth W. Sloan Research Professor of Chemistry, Harvard University;* b. 11 Jan. 1941, Washington, DC; ed Oberlin Coll., OH, Calif. Inst. of Tech., Pasadena, CA; Asst Prof. of Chemistry, Univ. of Calif. 1967–72, Assoc. Prof. 1972–73, Prof. 1974; Consultant, Upjohn Co. Kalamazoo, MI 1972–74; Prof. of Chemistry, Calif. Inst. of Tech. 1974–83; Consultant, Eli Lilly Co., IN 1974–89; Prof. of Chemistry, Harvard Univ. 1983–90, Abbott and James Lawrence Prof. of Chemistry 1990–, Chair. Dept of Chemistry and Chemical Biology 1995–98, Arthur and Ruth W. Sloan Research Prof. 1999–; Consultant, Oxford Asymmetry Ltd, Oxford, England 1994–2001, DuPont Pharmaceuticals Co., Wilmington, DE 1994–; visiting lecturer at numerous int. univs; mem. NAS 1984–, American Acad. of Arts and Sciences 1988–; mem. Editorial Bd Journal of the American Chemical Soc. 1983–88, Topics in Sterochemistry 1989–, Chemical Reviews 1993–96, Organic Letters 1999–; Fellow Alfred P. Sloan Foundation 1972–74, AAAS 1992–; Hon. MA (Harvard Univ.) 1983 numerous awards including Phila Organic Chemists Club Allen R. Day Award 1984, American Chemical Soc. Arthur C. Cope Scholar Award 1988, OH State Univ. Mack Award 1992, Univ. of Neb. C. S. Hamilton Award 1992, American Chemical Soc. Remsen Award 1996, Univ. of Tokyo Yamada Prize 1997, Royal Soc. of Chemistry Robert Robinson Award 1998, Tetrahedron Prize 1998, Eidgenossische Technische Hochschule Prelog Medal 1999, American Chemical Soc. Arthur C. Cope Award 2000, Willard Gibbs Award 2005. *Address:* Department of Chemistry and Chemical Biology, Harvard University, 12 Oxford Street, Converse 301, Cambridge, MA 02138, USA (office). *Telephone:* (617) 495-2948 (office). *Fax:* (617) 495-1460. *E-mail:* evans@chemistry .harvard.edu (office). *Website:* daecr1.harvard.edu (office).

EVANS, Donald L., BEng, MBA; American politician and oil executive; b. 27 July 1946, Houston; m. Susie Marinis; three c.; ed Univ. of Tex.; joined Tom Brown Inc. 1975, Pres. 1979, later Chair. and CEO; Advisor to George W. Bush's political campaigns 1978–, Nat. Finance Chair. 1999, Chair. Bush/ Cheney campaign 2000; Sec. of Commerce 2001–05 (resgnd); mem. Univ. of Tex. System Bd of Regents 1995–2001, Chair. 1997–2001; Chair. United Way of Midland 1981, Pres. 1989; Chair. Beefeaters Ball, Midland Cerebral Palsy Center; mem. YMCA of Midland Metropolitan Bd 1988–94, Bd of Govs, Bynum School, Bd The Gladney Fund, Midland Chamber of Commerce, Exec. Cttee Young Life, Bd Scleroma Research Foundation, Young Presidents Org., Omicron Delta Kappa Soc., Texas Cowboys; Trustee Memorial Hosp. and Medical Center; driving force behind Native Vision programme for 10,000 Native American children; Hon. DHumLitt (Univ. of S Carolina) 2001; Midland Jaycees Distinguished Service Award and Boss of the Year 1980, Univ. of Texas at Austin Distinguished Alumni Awards (School of Eng) 1997, 2002, (McCombs School of Business) 2002, Nat. Foreign Trade Council World Trade Award 2002. *Leisure interest:* golf. *Address:* 900 Whann Avenue, McLean, VA 22101, USA (home).

EVANS, Hon. Gareth John, AO, QC, LLB, MA; Australian international organization official and fmr politician; *President and Chief Executive, International Crisis Group;* b. 5 Sept. 1944, Melbourne; s. of the late Allan O. Evans and Phyllis Evans (née Le Boeuf); m. Merran Anderson 1969; one s. one d.; ed Univ. of Melbourne, Magdalen Coll., Oxford; Lecturer and Sr Lecturer in Law, Univ. of Melbourne 1971–76; mem. Australian Reform Comm. 1975; Barrister-at-Law 1977–; Senator for Victoria 1978–96; Shadow Attorney-Gen. 1980–83; Attorney-Gen. 1983–84; Minister for Resources and Energy, Minister Assisting the Prime Minister and Minister Assisting the Minister for Foreign Affairs 1984–87; Minister for Transport and Communications 1987–88, for Foreign Affairs 1988–96; Deputy Leader of Govt in the Senate 1987–93, Leader 1993–96; MP for Holt, Vic. 1996–99; Deputy Leader of Opposition, Shadow Treas. 1996–98; Pres. and Chief Exec. Int. Crisis Group 2000–; Co-Chair. Int. Comm. on Intervention and State Sovereignty 2000–; mem. UN Sec. –Gen.'s High Level Panel on Threat, Challenges and Change 2003–04, Weapons of Mass Destruction Comm. 2004–06; Hon. LLD (Melbourne Univ.) 2002, (Carleton Univ., Canada) 2005; Hon. Fellow, Magdalen Coll., Oxford 2004–; Australian Humanist of the Year 1990, ANZAC Peace Prize 1994, Grawemeyer Award for Ideas Improving World Order 1995; Chilean Order of Merit (Grand Cross) 1999. *Publications:* Labor and the

Constitution 1972–75 (ed.) 1977, Law, Politics and the Labor Movement (ed.) 1980, Labor Essays 1980, 1981, 1982 (co-ed.), Australia's Constitution: Time for Change? (co-author) 1983, Australia's Foreign Relations (co-author) 1991, Co-operating for Peace 1993, The Responsibility to Protect 2008. *Leisure interests:* reading, football, travel. *Address:* International Crisis Group, 149 avenue Louise, 1050 Brussels, Belgium (office). *Telephone:* (2) 536-00-74 (office). *Fax:* (2) 502-50-38 (office). *E-mail:* gevans@crisisgroup.org (office). *Website:* www.crisisgroup.org (office).

EVANS, Sir Harold Matthew, Kt, MA; American (b. British) publisher, fmr newspaper editor and writer; *Editor at Large, The Week and Contributing Editor, US News & World Report;* b. 28 June 1928, Manchester, England; s. of the late Frederick and Mary Evans; m. 1st Enid Parker 1953 (divorced 1978); one s. two d.; m. 2nd Tina Brown (q.v.) 1982; one s. one d.; ed Durham Univ.; Commonwealth Fund Fellow, Univ. of Chicago 1956–57; Ed. Sunday Times, London 1967–81, The Times 1981–82; mem. Bd Times Newspapers Ltd, Dir 1978–82; Int. Press Inst. 1974–80; Dir Goldcrest Films and Television 1982–85; Ed.-in-Chief Atlantic Monthly 1984–86, Contributing Ed. 1986–, Editorial Dir and Vice-Chair. 1998–; Ed. Dir U.S. News and World Report 1984–86, Contributing Ed. 1986–, Editorial Dir and Vice-Chair. 1998–; Vice-Pres. and Sr Ed. Weidenfeld and Nicolson 1986–87; Adviser to Chair. Condé Nast Publications 1986–; Founding Ed.-in-Chief, Condé Nast Traveler 1986–90; Pres. and Publr Random House Adult Trade Group 1990–97; Editorial Dir Mortimer Zuckerman's media properties 1997–; Editorial Dir and Vice-Chair. New York Daily News Inc. 1998–99, Fast Co. 1998–; author Little, Brown and Co., NY 2000–; writer and presenter A Point of View (BBC Radio 4) 2005–; Fellow, Soc. Industrial Artists, Inst. of Journalists; Hon. Visiting Prof. of Journalism City Univ. 1978–; Hon. DCL (Durham) 1998; Dr hc (Stirling) 1982, (Teesside, London Inst.), Hon. DCL (Durham) 1998; Journalist of the Year Prize 1973, Int. Ed. of the Year Award 1975, Inst. of Journalists Gold Medal Award 1979; Design and Art Dir, Pres.'s Award 1981, Ed. of Year Award, Granada 1982, Hood Medal, Royal Photographic Soc. 1981, Press Photographers of GB Award 1986; Gold Award for Achievement, British Press Awards 2000, World Press Freedom Hero, Int. Press Inst. 2000. *Publications:* Active Newsroom 1964, Editing and Design, Newsman's English 1970, Newspaper Design 1971, Newspaper Headlines 1973, Newspaper Text 1973, We Learned to Ski (co-author) 1974, Freedom of the Press 1974, Pictures on a Page 1978, Suffer the Children (co-author), How We Learned to Ski 1983, Good Times, Bad Times 1983, Front Page History 1984, The American Century 1998, They Made America 2004. *Leisure interests:* music, table tennis, skiing. *Address:* Little, Brown and Co., 1271 Avenue of the Americas, New York, NY 10020, USA (office). *Telephone:* (212) 302-9671 (office); (212) 371-1193 (home). *Fax:* (212) 302-9671 (office); (212) 754-4273 (home). *E-mail:* cindyquillinan@gmail.com (office); harold371@aol.com (home).

EVANS, John David Gemmill, MA, PhD, MRIA; British academic; *Professor of Logic and Metaphysics, Queen's University, Belfast;* b. 27 Aug. 1942, London; s. of John Desmond Evans and Babette Evans; m. Rosemary Ellis 1974; ed St Edward's School, Oxford, Queen's Coll., Cambridge; Research Fellow, Sidney Sussex Coll., Cambridge 1964–65, Fellow and Lecturer 1965–78; Visiting Prof., Duke Univ., NC 1972–73; Dean of Arts Faculty, Queen's Univ., Belfast 1986–89; Prof. of Logic and Metaphysics 1978–, Head of School of Philosophical Studies 2004–05; Dir of School of Philosophical and Anthropological Studies 1987–95; Bd mem. Arts Council of NI 1991–94; Council mem. Royal Inst. of Philosophy 1991–98; Chair. UK Nat. Cttee for Philosophy 1994–2003; mem. Exec. Cttee Int. Fed. of Philosophical Socs (FISP) 1988–, Aristotelian Soc. 1998–2001, Exec. Cttee British Philosophical Asscn 2003–05, Bureau Centrale, Asscn Int. des Professeurs de Philosophie 2000–. *Publications:* Aristotle's Concept of Dialectic 1977, Aristotle 1987, Moral Philosophy and Contemporary Problems 1987, Teaching Philosophy on the Eve of the Twenty-First Century 1997, Philosophy of Education (Proceedings of 21st World Congress of Philosophy vol. 4) 2006. *Leisure interests:* mountaineering, astronomy, travel, gardening. *Address:* School of Philosophical Studies, Queen's University, Room 101, 15 University Square, Belfast, BT7 1NN, Northern Ireland (office). *Telephone:* (28) 9097-3624 (office). *Fax:* (28) 9024-7895 (office). *E-mail:* jdg.evans@qub.ac.uk (office). *Website:* www.qub.ac.uk/phil (office).

EVANS, Jonathan; British government official; *Director General, Security Service (MI5);* b. 1958; ed Univ. of Bristol; joined Security Service (MI5) 1980, worked on counter-espionage investigations 1980–85, moved to Protective Security Policy Dept serving in posts related to Irish-related counter terrorism, Head Security Service's Secr. and attachment to Home Office 1985–99, moved to Int. Terrorism Dept 1999, Dir of Int. Counter Terrorism 2001–05, Deputy Dir Gen. MI5 2005–07, Dir Gen. 2007–. *Address:* Office of the Director General, Security Service, PO Box 3255, London, SW1P 1AE, England (office). *Website:* www.mi5.gov.uk (office).

EVANS, Leo Henry (Rusty), BA, BAdmin; South African diplomatist; b. 12 Dec. 1943, Durban; s. of John Evans and Dorothy Redstone; m. 1st Kathleen Barbour 1967 (divorced 1989); three s. one d.; m. 2nd Gerda van Tonder 1989; one d.; ed Christian Brothers' Coll. Kimberley and Univs of Natal and S Africa; entered Dept of Foreign Affairs 1966; Third Sec. Lisbon 1967–70; Consul, Rio de Janeiro 1972; Consul-Gen. São Paulo 1976–78; Minister, Washington, DC 1980, London 1982; Dir Ministry of Foreign Affairs 1986, Chief Dir 1988, Deputy Dir-Gen. Africa 1989, Deputy Dir-Gen. Overseas Countries 1991; Dir-Gen. Dept of Foreign Affairs 1992–97; Dir Int. Govt Relations and Public Affairs Consultancy, Karoo Oranje Landbou Kooperasie 1998–; Order of Dom Infante Henriques (Portugal). *Leisure interests:* yachting, hunting. *Address:* PO Box 1846, Groenloof 0027, South Africa (office). *E-mail:* gevans@fort.co.za (home).

EVANS, Lloyd Thomas, AO, MAgrSci, DPhil, DSc, FRS; Australian botanist and agriculturist; b. 6 Aug. 1927, Wanganui, New Zealand; s. of Claude Evans and Gwendolyn Fraser; m. Margaret Newell 1954; two s. two d. (one deceased); ed Wanganui Collegiate School, Univ. of Canterbury, New Zealand and Brasenose Coll., Oxford; Rhodes Scholar 1951–54; Commonwealth Fund Fellow, Calif. Inst. of Tech. 1954–56; Research Scientist, Div. of Plant Industry, Commonwealth Scientific and Industrial Research Org. (CSIRO) 1956–, Chief 1971–78, now Hon. Research Scientist; NAS Pioneer Research Fellow, US Dept of Agric. 1963–64; Overseas Fellow, Churchill Coll., Cambridge 1969–70; Visiting Fellow, Wolfson Coll., Cambridge 1978; Pres. Australian Soc. of Plant Physiologists 1971–73, Australian and New Zealand Asscn for the Advancement of Science 1976–77, Australian Acad. of Science 1978–82 (Fellow); mem. Bd of Trustees, Int. Foundation for Science, Stockholm 1982–87, Int. Rice Research Inst., Philippines 1984–89, Int. Centre for Improvement of Wheat and Maize 1990–95; mem. Norwegian Acad. of Science and Letters; Foreign Fellow Indian Nat. Acad. of Agricultural Science;; Hon. mem. Royal Soc., NZ, Royal Agric. Soc., England, Hon. Research Fellow, CSIRO Div. of Plant Industry 1992–; Hon. LLD (Canterbury) 1978; Bledisloe Medal 1974, Farrer Medal 1979, Adolph E. Gude Award and other awards and prizes. *Publications:* Environmental Control of Plant Growth 1963, The Induction of Flowering 1969, Crop Physiology 1975, Day-length and the Flowering of Plants 1975, Wheat Science – Today and Tomorrow 1981, Policy and Practice: Essays in Honour of Sir John Crawford 1987, Crop Evolution, Adaptation and Yield 1993, Feeding the Ten Billion: Plants and Population Growth 1998; over 200 research papers. *Leisure interests:* chopping wood, Charles Darwin, tennis. *Address:* 3 Elliott Street, Campbell, Canberra, ACT 2612, Australia. *Telephone:* (2) 477815. *E-mail:* Lloyd.Evans@csiro.au.

EVANS, Sir Martin John, Kt, PhD, ScD, FRS, FMedSci; British scientist and academic; *Director, Cardiff School of Biosciences;* b. 1 Jan. 1941, Stroud, Glos.; s. of Leonard Wilfred Evans and Hilary Joyce Evans (née Redman); m. Judith Clare Williams 1966; two s. one d.; ed St Dunstan's Coll. Catford and Christ's Coll. Cambridge; Research Asst Dept of Anatomy and Embryology, Univ. Coll. London 1963–66, Asst Lecturer 1966–69, Lecturer 1969–78; Univ. Lecturer, Dept of Genetics, Univ. of Cambridge 1978–91, Reader in Mammalian Genetics 1991, Prof. of Mammalian Genetics 1994–99; Dir, School of Biosciences and Prof. of Mammalian Genetics, Univ. of Cardiff 1999–; Hon. Fellow, St Edmund's Coll., Cambridge 2002; Hon. DSc (Mt Sinai School of Medicine) 2002; March of Dimes Prize in Developmental Biology 1999, Albert Lasker Award for Basic Medical Research 2001, Miami Nature Biotechnology Winter Symposium Special Achievement Award 2003, Nobel Prize for Medicine (with Mario Capecchi and Oliver Smithies) 2007 for the discovery of principles for introducing specific gene modifications in mice by the use of embryonic stem cells. *Publications:* more than 140 scientific publs. *Leisure interests:* family, golf. *Address:* Cardiff School of Biosciences, Biomedical Sciences Building, Cardiff University, Museum Avenue, PO Box 911, Cardiff, CF10 3US, Wales (office). *Telephone:* (29) 2087-4120 (office). *Fax:* (29) 2087-4117 (office). *E-mail:* EvansMJ@cardiff.ac.uk (office). *Website:* www.cardiff.ac.uk/biosi (office).

EVANS, Nicholas, BA; British author; b. Bromsgrove, Worcs.; m. 2nd Charlotte Gordon Cumming; three s. one d.; ed Univ. of Oxford; previously journalist for Evening Chronicle, Newcastle upon Tyne and producer documentaries for London Weekend TV, writer and producer films for TV and cinema; now novelist. *Publications:* The Horse Whisperer 1995, The Loop 1998, The Smoke Jumper 2001, The Divide 2005. *Leisure interests:* tennis, skiing, books, cinema. *Address:* c/o AP Watt Ltd, 20 John Street, London, WC1N 2DR, England (office). *Telephone:* (20) 7405-6774 (office). *Fax:* (20) 7831-2154 (office). *E-mail:* apw@apwatt.co.uk (office); nicholas@nicholasevans .com (office). *Website:* www.apwatt.co.uk (office); www.nicholasevans.com.

EVANS, Paul, BSc; British insurance executive; *CEO, AXA Sun Life;* b. 1965; m.; three c.; ed Imperial Coll., London; Dir PricewaterhouseCooper Insurance Div., London and Toronto, 1985–2000; joined AXA 2000, Group Finance Dir and mem. Bd AXA UK 2001–03, CEO AXA Sun Life 2003–; mem. Inst. of Chartered Accountants, Asscn of British Insurers. *Address:* AXA Centre, POB 1810, Bristol BS99 5SN, England (office). *Website:* www.axa.co.uk (office).

EVANS, Richard B., BEng, MMan.; American aluminium industry executive; *CEO and President, Alcan Inc.;* ed Oregon State Univ., Stanford Univ.; held sr man. positions with Kaiser Aluminum and Chemical Corpn –1997; Sr Advisor, Corporate Devt, Alcan Aluminium Ltd, Montreal 1997, Exec. Vice-Pres., Fabricated Products, N America and Pres. Alcan Aluminum Corpn 1997–99, Pres. Global Fabrication 1999–2000, Head Fabrication, Alcan Inc. Europe 2000–05, Exec. Vice-Pres. and COO Alcan Inc. 2005–06, CEO and Pres. 2006–; Chair. Int. Aluminium Inst.; mem. Bd of Dirs Bowater Inc.; fmr Chair. US Aluminium Asscn; fmr Vice-Chair. European Aluminium Asscn. *Address:* Alcan Inc., 1188 Sherbrooke Street West, Montreal, PQ H3A 3G2, Canada (office). *Telephone:* (514) 848-8000 (office). *Fax:* (514) 848-8115 (office). *Website:* www.alcan.com (office).

EVANS, Richard John, MA, DPhil, LittD, FBA, FRSL; British historian and academic; *Regius Professor of Modern History, University of Cambridge;* b. 29 Sept. 1947, Woodford, Essex; s. of the late Ieuan Trefor Evans and of Evelyn Evans (née Jones); m. 1st Elín Hjaltadóttir 1976 (divorced 1993); m. 2nd Christine L. Corton 2004; two s.; ed Forest School, London, Jesus Coll., Oxford, St Antony's Coll., Oxford; Lecturer in History, Stirling Univ. 1972–76; Lecturer in European History, Univ. of E Anglia 1976–83, Prof. 1983–89; Prof. of History, Birkbeck Coll., Univ. of London 1989–98; Vice-Master Birkbeck Coll. Univ. of London 1993–98, Acting Master 1997; Prof. of Modern History, Cambridge Univ. 1998–, Regius Prof. of Modern History 2008–, Chair., Faculty of History 2008–; Fellow, Gonville and Caius Coll., Cambridge 1998–; Visiting Assoc. Prof. of European History, Columbia Univ., New York 1980;

Fellow, Royal Historical Soc.; Fellow, Alexander von Humboldt Foundation, Free Univ. of Berlin 1981; Fellow, Humanities Research Centre, ANU, Canberra, Australia 1986; Hon. Fellow, Jesus Coll., Oxford 1998, Birkbeck Coll. 1999; Stanhope Historical Essay Prize 1969, Wolfson Literary Award for History 1987, William H. Welch Medal, American Asscn for the History of Medicine 1988, Hamburg Civic Medal for Arts and Sciences 1993, Fraenkel Prize in Contemporary History 1994. *Publications:* The Feminist Movement in Germany 1894–1933 1976, The Feminists 1977, Society and Politics in Wilhelmine Germany (ed.) 1978, Sozialdemokratie und Frauenemanzipation im deutschen Kaiserreich 1979, The German Family (co–ed.) 1981, The German Working Class (co–ed.) 1982, The German Peasantry (co–ed.) 1986, The German Unemployed (co–ed.) 1987, Death in Hamburg 1987, Comrades and Sisters 1987, Rethinking German History 1987, In Hitler's Shadow 1989, Kneipengespräche im Kaiserreich 1989, Proletarians and Politics 1990, Rituals of Retribution 1996, Rereading German History 1997, In Defence of History 1997, Tales from the German Underworld 1998, Lying about Hitler 2001, The Coming of the Third Reich 2003, The Third Reich in Power 2005, The Third Reich at War 2008; contrib. to scholarly journals, newspapers, magazines, radio and TV. *Leisure interests:* gardening, music (playing the piano), reading, travelling. *Address:* Gonville and Caius College, Cambridge, CB2 1TA, England (office). *Telephone:* (1223) 332495 (office). *E-mail:* rje36@cam.ac.uk (office); chairman@hist.cam.ac.uk (office). *Website:* www .richardjevans.com (office).

EVANS, Sir Richard Mark, Kt, KCMG, KCVO, MA; British diplomatist (retd); b. 15 April 1928, British Honduras (now Belize); s. of the late Edward Walter Evans and Anna Margaret Kirkpatrick Evans; m. 1st Margaret Elizabeth Sessinger 1960 (divorced 1970); m. 2nd Rosemary Grania Glen Birkett 1973; two s.; ed Dragon School, Oxford, Repton School and Magdalen Coll., Oxford; Third Sec., Peking 1955–57, Second Sec., London 1958–62, First Sec., Peking 1962–64, First Sec. (Commercial), Berne 1964–68, First Sec., London 1968–70, Head of Near Eastern Dept, FCO 1970–72 and Far Eastern Dept 1972–74, Counsellor (Commercial), Stockholm 1975–77, Minister (Econ.), Paris 1977–79, Asst, then Deputy Under-Sec., FCO 1979–83, Amb. to People's Repub. of China 1984–88; Fellow Emer., Wolfson Coll., Oxford 1995–. *Publication:* Deng Xiaoping and the Making of Modern China 1993. *Leisure interests:* music, reading, travel. *Address:* Sevenhampton House, Sevenhampton, Highworth, Wilts., SN6 7QA, England (home).

EVANS, Robert; American actor and film producer; b. 29 June 1930, Harlem, New York; s. of Josh Evans; m. 1st Ali McGraw (divorced); one s.; m. 2nd Phyllis George 1978 (divorced); child radio actor in more than 300 radio productions; partner women's clothing firm Evan-Picone 1952–67; ind. producer at 20th Century-Fox 1966–76; Vice-Pres. (Production) Paramount Pictures Corpn 1966–69, Vice-Pres. (Worldwide Production) 1969–71, Exec. Vice-Pres. 1971–76; resgnd to be ind. producer. *Films include:* (actor) The Man of 1000 Faces 1957, The Sun Also Rises 1957, The Fiend Who Walked the West 1958, The Best of Everything 1959, (producer) Chinatown 1974, Marathon Man 1976, Black Sunday 1977, Players 1979, Popeye 1980, Urban Cowboy 1980, Cotton Club 1984, The Two Jakes 1989, Sliver 1993, Jade, The Phantom, The Saint, The Out of Towners, The Kid Stays in the Picture 2003. *Publication:* The Kid Stays in the Picture 1994. *Address:* 242 North Beverly Drive, Beverly Hills, CA 90210, USA.

EVANS, Robert John Weston, PhD, FBA; British historian and academic; *Regius Professor of History, University of Oxford;* b. 7 Oct. 1943, Leicester; s. of T. F. Evans and M. Evans; m. Kati Robert 1969; one s. one d. (deceased); ed Dean Close School, Cheltenham and Jesus Coll., Cambridge; Research Fellow, Brasenose Coll. Oxford 1968–97; Univ. Lecturer in Modern History of East-Central Europe, Univ. of Oxford 1969–90, Reader 1990–92, Prof. of European History 1992–97, Regius Prof. of History 1997–; Ed. English Historical Review 1985–95; Fellow Hungarian Acad. of Sciences 1995, Austrian Acad. of Sciences 1997; Fellow, Learned Soc. of Czech Repub. 2004; Wolfson Literary Award for History 1980, Anton Gindely-Preis (Austria) 1986, František Palacký Medal (Czechoslovakia) 1991. *Publications:* Rudolf II and His World 1973, The Wechel Presses 1975, The Making of the Habsburg Monarchy 1979, The Coming of the First World War (co-ed) 1988, Crown, Church and Estates (co-ed) 1991, The Revolutions in Europe 1848–9 (ed.) 2000, Austria, Hungary, and the Habsburgs, c. 1683-1867 2006, Curiosity and Wonder from the Renaissance to the Enlightenment (co-ed) 2007, Czechoslovakia in a Nationalist and Fascist Europe 1918-48 (co-ed) 2007. *Address:* Oriel College, Oxford, OX1 4EW (office); Rowan Cottage, 45 Sunningwell, Abingdon, Oxon., OX13 6RD, England (home). *Telephone:* (1865) 615038 (office). *E-mail:* robert.evans@history.ox.ac.uk (office). *Website:* www.history.ox.ac.uk (office).

EVANS, Ronald M., PhD; American biologist and academic; *Professor, Gene Expression Laboratory, The Salk Institute for Biological Studies;* ed Univ. of California, Los Angeles; worked in Dept of Molecular Cell Biology, The Rockefeller Univ., New York 1975–78; Asst Research Prof., Tumor Virology Lab., The Salk Inst. for Biological Studies, La Jolla, Calif. 1978–83, Assoc. Prof., Molecular Biology and Virology Lab. 1983–84, Sr Mem. 1984–86, Prof., Gene Expression Lab. 1986–, mem. Bd Trustees 1990–94, 1996–99, Chair. Faculty 1993–94, 1997–98; Adjunct Prof., Dept of Biology, Univ. of California, San Diego 1985–, Adjunct Prof., Dept of Biomedical Sciences, School of Medicine 1989–, Adjunct Prof., Dept of Neurosciences 1995–; Investigator, Howard Hughes Medical Inst., Chevy Chase, MD 1985–; Chair of Molecular and Developmental Neurobiology, March of Dimes, White Plains, NY 1998–; S. Richard Hill, Jr Visiting Prof., Univ. of Alabama 1995; Woodward Visiting Prof., Memorial Sloan-Kettering 1996; First Alvin Taurog Lectureship in Pharmacology, Southwestern Medical Center 1996; Burroughs Wellcome Visiting Prof., Univ. of Massachusetts 1998; Founder and Chair. Scientific Advisory Bd Ligand Pharmaceuticals 1988–; Chair. Cancer Research Cttee, American Asscn for Cancer Research-Pezcoller Int. Award 2001; mem. NAS 1989–90, Endocrine Soc., Soc. for Developmental Biology, Soc. for Neuroscience, The Harvey Soc. 1995; mem. Scientific Advisory Bd SIBIA 1983–, Nat. Advisory Cttee Pew Scholars Program in the Biomedical Sciences 1987–2000, External Scientific Advisory Bd Massachussets Gen. Hosp. 1996–, Scientific Advisory Bd Dana Farber Cancer Inst. 1996–, Scientific Advisory Bd Osaka Bioscience Inst. 1999–; Assoc. Ed. Molecular Brain Research 1985–93, Journal of Neuroscience 1985–90, Neuron 1987–93; Co-Ed. Current Opinion in Cell Biology 1993; Ed. Molecular Endocrinology 1993–97; mem. Editorial Bd Genes and Development 1992–, Hormones and Signalling (Academic Press series) 1996–; NIH Fellowship 1975–78; Fellow, American Acad. of Microbiology 1993, American Acad. of Arts and Sciences 1997; Gregory Pincus Medal, Laurentian Soc. 1988, The Louis S. Goodman and Alfred Gilman Award, American Soc. for Pharmacology and Experimental Therapeutics 1988, Van Meter/Rorer Pharmaceuticals Prize, American Thyroid Asscn 1989, Eleventh C. P. Rhoads Memorial Award, American Asscn for Cancer Research 1990, Gregory Pincus Memorial Award, Worcester Foundation for Experimental Biology 1991, Rita Levi Montalcini Award, Fidia Research Foundation Neuroscience 1991, Osborne and Mendel Award, American Inst. of Nutrition 1992, Robert J. and Claire Pasarow Foundation Award for Cancer Research 1993, Edwin B. Astwood Lectureship Award, The Endocrine Soc. 1993, Transatlantic Medal, Soc. for Endocrinology 1994, California Scientist of the Year, California Museum of Science 1994, Dickson Prize in Medicine, Univ. of Pittsburgh 1994–95, Morton Lecture and Award, Biochemical Soc., Univ. of Liverpool, UK 1996, Gerald Aurbach Memorial Award, Asscn for Bone and Mineral Research 1997, Fred Conrad Koch Award, The Endocrine Soc. 1999, Bristol-Myers Squibb Award for Distinguished Achievement in Metabolic Research 2000, Lya and Harrison Latta Lecturer, UCLA 2000. *Publications:* more than 260 publs in scientific journals. *Address:* Salk Institute for Biological Studies, Howard Hughes Medical Institute, 10010 N Torrey Pines Road, La Jolla, CA 92037, USA (office). *Telephone:* (858) 453-4100 ext. 1302 (office). *Fax:* (858) 455-1349 (office). *E-mail:* evans@salk.edu (office). *Website:* www.salk.edu (office).

EVANS, Stephen Nicholas, CMG, OBE, BA, MPhil; British diplomatist; *High Commissioner to Bangladesh;* b. 29 June 1950; s. of Vincent Morris Evans and Doris Mary Evans (née Braham); m. Sharon Ann Holdcroft 1975; one s. two d.; ed King's Coll., Taunton, Bristol Univ., Corpus Christi Coll., Univ. of Cambridge; Lt in Royal Tank Regt 1971–74; Third Sec., FCO 1974–75, language student (Vietnamese), SOAS, London 1975, Second Sec., FCO 1976–78, First Sec., Hanoi 1978–80, FCO 1980–82, language training (Thai), Bangkok 1982–83, First Sec., Bangkok 1983–86, FCO 1986–90, First Sec. (Political), Ankara 1990, Counsellor (Econ., Commercial, Aid), Islamabad 1993–96, seconded to UN Special Mission to Afghanistan 1996–97, Counsellor and Head of OSCE and Council of Europe Dept, FCO 1997–98, Counsellor and Head of South Asian Dept 1998–2001, Chargé d'affaires, Kabul 2001–02, High Commr in Sri Lanka 2002–06, Amb. to Afghanistan 2006–07, Dir Afghanistan Information Strategy, FCO 2007–08, High Commr to Bangladesh 2008–. *Leisure interests:* military, naval and South Asian history, cycling, golf. *Address:* British High Commission, PO Box 6079, United Nations Road, Baridhara, Dhaka 1212, Bangladesh (office). *Telephone:* (2) 8822705 (office). *Fax:* (2) 8823437 (office). *E-mail:* Dhaka.Chancery@fco.gov.uk (office). *Website:* www.ukinbangladesh.org (office).

EVANS, Ted, AC, BEcon (Hons); Australian banking executive; *Chairman, Westpac Banking Corporation;* ed Queensland Univ.; began career in Postmaster-Gen.'s Dept, Ipswich, Queensland; joined Australian Treasury 1969, Deputy Sec. 1984–89, Sec. to Treasury 1993–2001, mem. Australian Perm. Del. to OECD, Paris 1976–79, Exec. Dir representing Australia, IMF 1989–93; Dir Westpac Banking Corpn 2001–, Chair. 2007–, Chair. Nominations Cttee; Dir Commonwealth Bank of Australia 1993–96, Reserve Bank of Australia 1993–2001, IBT Education Ltd 2004–08, Navitas Ltd; Hon. DUniv (Griffith). *Address:* Westpac Banking Corpn, Level 20, 275 Kent Street, Sydney 2000, Australia (office). *Telephone:* (2) 8253-0390 (office). *Fax:* (2) 8253-1888 (office). *E-mail:* info@westpac.com.au (office). *Website:* www.westpac.com.au (office).

EVANS OF PARKSIDE, Baron (Life Peer), cr. 1997, of St Helens in the County of Merseyside; **John Evans;** British politician and engineer; b. 19 Oct. 1930; s. of the late James Evans and Margaret Evans (née Robson); m. Joan Slater 1959; two s. one d.; ed Jarrow Cen. School; apprentice marine fitter 1946–49, 1950–52; nat. service, Royal Engineers 1949–50; engineer, Merchant Navy 1952–55; joined Amalgamated Union of Eng Workers (later Amalgamated Eng Union) 1952; joined Labour Party 1955; worked as fitter in shipbuilding, steel and eng industries 1955–65, 1968–74; mem. Hebburn Union Dist Council 1962, Leader 1969, Chair. 1972; Sec./Agent Jarrow Co-operative Labour Party 1965–68; Labour MP for Newton 1974–83, for St Helens, North 1983–97; Asst Govt Whip 1978–79; Opposition Whip 1979–80; Parl. Pvt. Sec. to Leader of Labour Party 1980–83; Opposition Spokesman on Employment 1983–87; MEP 1975–78; Chair. Regional Policy, Planning and Transport Cttee 1976–78; mem. Labour Party Nat. Exec. Cttee 1982–96. *Leisure interests:* watching football, reading, gardening. *Address:* House of Lords, Westminster, London, SW1 0PW (office); 6 Kirkby Road, Culcheth, Warrington, Cheshire, WA3 4BS, England (home). *Telephone:* (20) 7219-6541 (office).

EVANS OF TEMPLE GUITING, Baron (Life Peer), cr. 2000, of Temple Guiting in the County of Gloucestershire; **Matthew Evans,** CBE, BSc Econs, FRSA; British publishing executive; b. 7 Aug. 1941; s. of the late George Ewart Evans and Florence Ellen Evans; m. 1st Elizabeth Amanda Mead 1966 (divorced 1991); two s.; m. 2nd Caroline Michel 1991; two s. one d.; ed Friends' School, Saffron Walden and LSE; bookselling 1963–64; with Faber & Faber 1964–, Man. Dir 1972–93, Chair. 1981–; Chair. Nat. Book League 1982–84,

English Stage Co. 1984–90; mem. Council, Publishers' Asscn 1978–84; Gov. BFI 1982–97, Vice-Chair. 1996–97; Chair. Library and Information Comm. 1995–99; Chair. Museums, Libraries and Archives Council 2000–02; Dir Which? Ltd 1997–; mem. Arts Council Nat. Lottery Advisory Panel 1997–99, Univ. for Industry Advisory Group 1997, Royal Opera House Working Group 1997, Arts and Humanities Research Bd 1998–; mem. Franco-British Soc. 1981–; founder mem. Groucho Club (Dir 1982–97); Hon. FRCA 1999; Hon. FLA 1999. *Leisure interest:* cricket. *Address:* c/o House of Lords, London SW1A 0PW, England (office). *Telephone:* (20) 7219-6631 (office). *E-mail:* evansm@parliament.uk (office).

EVATT, Elizabeth Andreas, AC, LLM; Australian lawyer, human rights expert and academic; b. 11 Nov. 1933, Sydney; d. of Clive R. Evatt and Marjorie M. Evatt (née Andreas); m. Robert Southan 1960; one d.; ed Univ. of Sydney and Harvard Univ.; called to Bar, Inner Temple; Chief Judge Family Court of Australia 1976–88; Deputy Pres. Conciliation and Arbitration Comm. 1973–89, Australian Industrial Relations Comm. 1989–94; Pres. Australian Law Reform Comm. 1988–93, mem. 1993–94; mem. UN Cttee on Elimination of Discrimination Against Women 1984–92, Chair. 1989–91; Chancellor, Univ. of Newcastle 1988–94; reviewed Aboriginal and Torres Strait Islander Heritage Protection Act 1984; Hearing Commr (part-time), Human Rights and Equal Opportunity Comm. 1995–98; mem. UN Human Rights Cttee 1993–2000, World Bank Admin. Tribunal 1998–2006, Commr Int. Comm. of Jurists 2003–; currently Hon. Visiting Prof., Univ. of New South Wales Law School; fmr Chair. Public Interest Advocacy Centre, Sydney; Australian Human Rights Medal 1995. *Address:* Unit 2003, 184 Forbes Street, Darlinghurst, NSW 2010, Australia. *Fax:* (2) 9331-6734 (home). *E-mail:* eevatt@bigpond.net.au (office).

EVE, Trevor John; British actor; b. 1 July 1951; s. of Stewart Frederick Eve and Elsie Eve (née Hamer); m. Sharon Patricia Maughan 1980; two s. one d.; ed Bromsgrove School, Kingston Art Coll., Royal Acad. of Dramatic Art; Patron Childhope International. *Theatre includes:* Children of a Lesser God (Olivier Award for Best Actor 1982) 1981, The Genius 1983, High Society 1986, Man Beast and Virtue 1989, The Winter's Tale 1991, Inadmissible Evidence 1993, Uncle Vanya (Olivier Award for Best Supporting Actor 1997) 1996. *Television includes:* Shoestring 1979–80, Jamaica Inn, A Sense of Guilt 1990, Parnell and the Englishwoman 1991, A Doll's House 1991, The Politician's Wife 1995, Black Easter 1995, Under the Sun 1997, Evilstreak 1999, David Copperfield 1999, Waking The Dead 2000–04. *Films include:* Hindle Wakes, Dracula, A Wreath of Roses, The Corsican Brothers, Aspen Extreme, Psychotherapy, The Knight's Tale, The Tribe, Appetite, Possession, Troy 2004; (producer for Projector Productions): Alice Through the Looking Glass 1998, Cinderella, Twelfth Night 2002. *Leisure interests:* golf, tennis. *Address:* c/o ICM Ltd, Oxford House, 76 Oxford Street, London, W1N 0AX, England (office). *Telephone:* (20) 7434-1110 (office); (20) 7636-6565 (office). *Fax:* (20) 7323-0101 (office).

EVENO, Bertrand; French publishing executive; b. 26 July 1944, Egletons; s. of Jean-Jacques Eveno and Suzanne Gavoille; m. 2nd Brigitte Pery 1984; five d. (three d. from previous m.); ed Lycée Condorcet and Law Faculty, Paris; Treasury Inspector 1973–77; Tech. Consultant to Health Minister 1977–78; Cabinet Dir for Minister of Culture and Communication 1978–81; mem. Atomic Energy Comm. Control Bd 1981–83; Deputy Gen. Man. André Shoe Co. 1984–86; Chair. Editions Fernand Nathan 1987–2000; Pres. Conseil d'admin., Fondation nationale de la photographie 1981–95, Gens d'Image 1986–2000; Chair. Larousse-Nathan Int. 1988–90, Le Robert dictionaries 1989–2000, Editions Masson 1995–98; Dir-Gen. Groupe de la Cité 1988–2000, Presses de la Cité 1991–95; Pres., Dir-Gen. Larousse-Bordas 1996–2000; Pres., Dir-Gen. Havas Educ. et Référence 1999–2000; Dir Anaya Groupe 1999–2000; Pres. Agence France Presse 2000–05; Dir-Gen. Hachette Filipacchi Photos (Eyedea from 2007) 2005–; Zellidja Scholarship 1961. *Publication:* monograph on Willy Ronis in Les grands photographes 1983. *Address:* Eyedea, 13 rue d'Enghien, 75010 Paris (office); 80 rue de Rennes, 75006 Paris, France (home). *Telephone:* 1-44-79-30-79 (office). *Fax:* 1-44-79-30-56 (office). *E-mail:* presse@eyedea.fr (office). *Website:* www.hoaqui.com (office).

EVERED, David Charles, MD, FRCP, FIBiol; British scientific administrator and physician; b. 21 Jan. 1940, Beaconsfield; s. of the late Thomas C. Evered and Enid C. Evered; m. 1st Anne Lings 1964 (died 1998); one s. two d.; m. 2nd Sheila Pusinelli 2000; ed Cranleigh School, Surrey and Middlesex Hosp. Medical School; jr hosp. appointments London and Leeds 1964–70; First Asst in Medicine, Wellcome Sr Research Fellow and Consultant Physician, Univ. of Newcastle-upon-Tyne and Royal Vic. Infirmary 1970–78; Dir The Ciba Foundation, London 1978–88; Second Sec., MRC, London 1988–96, Consultant 1996–; mem. Council Int. Agency for Research into Cancer 1988–96, Royal Post grad. Medical School 1994–96, Bd Hammersmith Hosps Nat. Health Service (NHS) Trust 1995–96, numerous cttees, socs and other professional bodies; Chair. NOC NHS Trust 1998–2001; Special Adviser Int. Agency for Research on Cancer, WHO, Lyon, France 2001–03. *Publications:* Diseases of the Thyroid 1976, Atlas of Endocrinology (with R. Hall and R. Greene) 1979, Collaboration in Medical Research in Europe (with M. O'Connor) 1981; numerous papers in professional journals. *Leisure interests:* reading, history, tennis, music. *Address:* Old Rectory Farm, Rectory Road, Padworth Common, Berks., RG7 4JD, England (home). *E-mail:* david_evered@hotmail.com (home).

EVERETT, Rupert; British actor; b. 29 May 1960, Norfolk; ed Ampleforth School and Cen. School for Speech and Drama, London; apprenticed with Glasgow Citizen's Theatre 1979–82; has modelled for Versace, Milan; sometime image of Opium perfume for Yves Saint Laurent. *Stage appearances include:* Another Country 1982, The Vortex 1989, Private Lives, The Milk Train Doesn't Stop Here Anymore, The Picture of Dorian Gray 1993, The Importance of Being Earnest 1996, Some Sunny Day 1996. *Films include:* A Shocking Accident 1982, Another Country 1984, Dance with a Stranger 1985, The Right Hand Man 1985, Duet for One 1986, Chronicle of Death Foretold 1987, Hearts of Fire 1987, Haunted Summer 1988, The Comfort of Strangers 1990, Inside Monkey Zetterland 1992, Pret à Porter 1994, The Madness of King George 1995, Dunston Checks In 1996, My Best Friend's Wedding 1997, A Midsummer Night's Dream 1998, B Monkey 1998, An Ideal Husband 1999, Inspector Gadget 1999, The Next Best Thing 2000, Unconditional Love 2002, The Importance of Being Earnest 2002, To Kill a King 2003, Stage Beauty 2004, Separate Lies 2005, The Chronicles of Narnia: The Lion, the Witch and the Wardrobe (voice) 2005, Shrek the Third (voice) 2007, Stardust 2007, St Trinian's 2007. *Television includes:* Arthur the King, The Far Pavilions 1982, Princess Daisy 1983, Mr. Ambassador 2003. *Publications:* Hello Darling, Are You Working? 1992, The Hairdressers of St Tropez 1995, Red Carpets and Other Banana Skins (autobiog.) 2006. *Address:* c/o William Stein, ICM, 8942 Wilshire Boulevard, Beverly Hills, CA 90211-1934, USA (office). *Telephone:* (310) 550-4000 (office). *E-mail:* film@icmtalent.com (office).

EVERITT, Anthony Michael, BA; British writer, academic and fmr arts organization administrator; b. 31 Jan. 1940; s. of the late Michael Everitt and Simone de Vergriette; ed Cheltenham Coll. and Corpus Christi Coll. Cambridge; Lecturer, Nat. Univ. of Iran, SE London Coll. of Further Educ., Birmingham Coll. of Art, Trent Polytechnic 1963–72; Art Critic, The Birmingham Post 1970–75, Drama Critic 1974–79, Features Ed. 1976–79; Dir Midland Group Arts Centre, Nottingham 1979–80, E Midlands Arts Asscn 1980–85; Chair. Ikon Gallery, Birmingham 1976–79, Birmingham Arts Lab. 1977–79; Vice-Chair. Council of Regional Arts Asscns 1984–85; mem. Drama Panel, Arts Council of GB 1974–78, Regional Cttee 1979–80; mem. Cttee for Arts and Humanities, Council for Nat. Academic Awards 1986–87, Performing Arts Cttee 1987–92; mem. Gen. Advisory Council, IBA 1987–90; Deputy Sec.-Gen. Arts Council of GB 1985–90, Sec.-Gen. 1990–94; Visiting Prof. in Visual and Performing Arts, Nottingham Trent Univ.; Hon. Fellow, Dartington Coll. of Arts 1995; Companion, Liverpool Inst. of Performing Arts 2003. *Publications:* Abstract Expressionism 1974, In from the Margins 1997, Joining In 1997, The Governance of Culture 1997, The Creative Imperative 2001, Citizens – Towards a Citizenship Culture (contrib.) 2001, Cicero – A Turbulent Life 2000, Cicero – The Life and Times of Rome's Greatest Politician (USA), New Voices 2004, The First Emperor – Caesar Augustus and the Triumph of Rome 2006, Augustus – The Life of Rome's First Emperor (USA) 2006; contribs to newspapers and journals. *Address:* Westerlies, Anchor Hill, Wivenhoe, Essex, CO7 9BL, England (home).

EVERLING, Ulrich, DJur; German judge; *Honorary Professor of European Law, University of Bonn;* b. 2 June 1925, Berlin; s. of Emil Everling; m. Lore Schwerdtfeger 1953; two s. two d.; ed Zehlendorfer Gymnasium, Berlin and Univ. of Göttingen; lawyer, Fed. Ministry of Econs 1953–80, Dept of European Policy 1970–80; Lecturer, Hon. Prof. of European Law, Univ. of Münster 1971–80, Univ. of Bonn 1981–; Judge, Court of Justice of the European Communities 1980–88; Dr hc 2001. *Publications:* Die europäische Wirtschaftsgemeinschaft: Kommentar zum Vertrag (co-author) 1960, Das Niederlassungsrecht im Gemeinsamen Markt 1964, Das europäische Gemeinschaftrecht im Spannungsfeld von Politik und Wirtschaft, Ausgewählte Aufsätze 1964–1984 1986, Buchpreisbindung im deutschen Sprachraum und Europäisches Gemeinschaftrecht 1997, Unterwegs zur Europäischen Union, Ausgewählte Aufsätze 1985–2000 2001; numerous articles on European law and policy. *Address:* Dahlienweg 5, 53343 Wachtberg, Germany (home). *Telephone:* (228) 324177 (home). *Fax:* (228) 324898 (home).

EVERT, Christine (Chris) Marie; American fmr professional tennis player; b. 21 Dec. 1954, Fort Lauderdale, Fla; d. of James Evert and Colette Evert; m. 1st John Lloyd 1979 (divorced 1987); m. 2nd Andy Mill 1988 (divorced 2006); m. 3rd Greg Norman 2008; three s.; ed St Thomas Aquinas High School, Fort Lauderdale; amateur player 1970–72; professional 1972–1989; Wimbledon Singles Champion 1974, 1976, 1981; French Champion 1974, 1975, 1979, 1980, 1983, 1985, 1986; US Open Champion 1975, 1976, 1977, 1978, 1980, 1982; Italian Champion 1974, 1975, 1980; South African Champion 1973; Colgate Series Champion 1977, 1978; World Champion 1979; played Wightman Cup for USA 1971–73, 1975–82, 1984–85; won 1,000th singles victory (first ever player) Australian Open Dec. 1984; played Federation Cup for USA 1977–82; ranked No. 1 in the world for seven years; won 1,309 matches in her career; won 157 singles titles and 18 Grand Slam titles (third best in history); Pres. Women's Tennis Asscn (WTA) 1975–76, 1983–91; Founder Chris Evert Charities for needy and drug-abusive mothers and their children 1989; Host and Organizer Annual Chris Evert Pro-Celebrity Tennis Classic 1989–; Pnr and coach, Evert Tennis Acad., Boca Raton, Fla; owner, Evert Enterprises/IMG, Boca Raton, Fla 1989–; Dir and mem. Bd Pres.'s Council on Physical Fitness and Sports 1991–; NBC TV sports commentator and host for numerous TV shows; mem. Bd Ounce of Prevention Fund of Florida, Make-A-Wish Foundation of S Florida, Florida Sports Foundation, United Sports Foundation of America, Save the Children, American AIDS Asscn, Women's Sports Foundation, The Don Shula Foundation, Nat. Cttee to Prevent Child Abuse, The Buoniconti Fund, Palm Beach Co. Sports Authority; Sports Illustrated Sportsman of the Year Award 1976, WTA Sportsmanship Award 1979 and Player Service Award 1981, 1986, 1987, named Greatest Woman Athlete of the Last 25 Years (Women's Sports Foundation) 1985, voted by Korbel One of Top 10 Romantic People of 1989, Flo Hyman Award 1990, Providencia Award 1991, Nat. High School Hall of Fame 1992, March of Dimes Lifetime Achievement Award 1993, Madison Square Garden Walk of Fame 1993, Int. Tennis Hall of Fame 1995, bi-colour hybrid tea rose named for her by Spring Hill Nurseries Co. 1996, Int. Tennis Fed. Chartrier Award 1997, named by ESPN as One of Top 50 Athletes of the 20th Century 1999.

Publications: Chrissie (autobiog.) 1982, Lloyd on Lloyd (with John Lloyd) 1985. *Leisure interests:* Visiting Paris and the Great Barrier Reef in Hamilton Island. *Address:* Evert Enterprises/IMG, 7200 West Camino Real, Suite 310, Boca Raton, FL 33433; Evert Tennis Academy, 10334 Diego Drive South, Boca Raton, FL 33428, USA. *Telephone:* (561) 394-2400 (office); (561) 488-2055 (office). *Website:* www.evertacademy.com (office).

EVERT, Militiades; Greek politician; b. 1939, Athens; m. Lisa Evert (née Vanderpool); two d.; ed Econ. Univ. of Athens; mem. Parl. 1974–; Mayor of Athens 1986–90; Minister of Health and Welfare 1989–90, to the Prime Minister 1990–91; Leader New Democracy Party 1993–96 (resgnd). *Address:* c/o New Democracy Party, Odos Rigillis 18, 10674 Athens, Greece (office). *Website:* www.nd.gr (office).

EVES, Ernie, QC; Canadian politician; b. 1946, Windsor; m.; one s. (deceased) one d.; ed Univ. of Toronto, Osgoode Hall Law School, York Univ.; first elected as MPP for Parry Sound, Ont. Legislature 1981, fmr Vice-Chair. Priorities, Policy and Communications Bd of Cabinet, fmr Vice-Chair. Man. Bd of Cabinet, fmr Govt House Leader, fmr Minister of Community and Social Services, fmr Minister of Skills Devt, Deputy Premier and Minister of Finance, Ont. 1995–2001, Leader Ont. Progressive Conservative Party March 2002–Sept. 2004, MPP for Dufferin-Peel-Wellington-Grey 2002–05 (resgnd), Premier of Ont. April 2002–Oct. 2003; Leader of the Official Opposition Oct. 2003–Sept. 2004; Chair. Ont. Advisory Council on Int. Trade and Investment 2006–; Founder and Sec. Treas. Big Brothers' Asscn of Parry Sound; mem. Advisory Bd Embassy of Hope; Co-founder and Chair. Justin Eves Foundation 1995–. *Address:* c/o Justin Eves Foundation, 40 Dundas Street West, Suite 220, Toronto, ON M5G 2C2, USA. *Telephone:* (416) 586-0085. *Fax:* (416) 586-0050. *Website:* www.justinevesfoundation.com.

EVIN, Claude, DIur; French politician; b. 29 June 1949, Le Cellier, Loire-Atlantique; s. of André Evin and Adrienne Lecommandeur; m. Françoise Guillet 1971; three d.; Sec. St-Nazaire Section, Parti Socialiste 1975–77, mem. Loire-Atlantique Fed. Cttee of Socialist Party 1975–, mem. Nat. Cttee 1991–; Mun. Councillor and Deputy Mayor of St-Nazaire 1977–; Deputy to Nat. Ass. 1978–88, 1997–; MP Ass. of Council of Europe; Chair. Nat. Ass. Cultural, Family and Social Affairs Cttee 1981–86; mem. Social Security Audit Comm. 1985; Vice-Pres. Nat. Ass. 1986–88; Minister-Del. attached to Minister of Social Affairs and Employment with responsibility for Social Protection May–June 1988; Minister of Solidarity, Health and Social Protection 1988–91; Conseiller régional Pays de la Loire 1992–98; mem. Econ. and Social Council 1994–97, Parl. Ass., Council of Europe. *Address:* 30 rue du Bois Savary, 44600 St-Nazaire, France. *Telephone:* (2) 51-10-10-51. *Fax:* (2) 51-10-10-50.

EVORA, Cesaria; Cape Verde singer and songwriter; b. 27 Aug. 1941, Mindelo, Sao Vicente; two c.; sang in bars in Mindelo from late teens; travelled to Lisbon, Portugal to record two tracks for a compilation of Cape Verdean singers; later went to Paris to record first solo album; first large-scale US tour 1995, continues to tour internationally; Chevalier, Légion d'Honneur 2009. *Recordings include:* albums: La Diva aux pieds nus 1988, Distino di Belita 1990, Mar Azul 1991, Miss Perfumado 1992, Sodade, les plus belles mornas de Cesaria 1994, Cesaria 1995, Cabo Verde 1997, Best of Cesaria Evora 1998, Café Atlantico 1999, Cesaria Evora Remixes 1999, Sao Vicente de Longe 2001, Voz de Amor (Grammy Award for Best Contemporary World Music Album 2004) 2003, Rogamar 2006. *Address:* c/o Lusafrica, 13 rue Auger, 93500 Pantin, France (office). *Website:* www.lusafrica.fr (office); www.cesaria-evora.com.

ÉVORA, Nelson; Portuguese (b. Côte d'Ivoire) athlete; b. 20 April 1984, Côte d'Ivoire; triple jumper and long jumper; triple jump Olympic and World Champion; relocated to Portugal aged five; represented Cape Verde until June 2002, when became Portuguese citizen; still holds Cape Verdean records in both long jump (7.57m) and triple jump (16.15m); first coached by João Ganço; Gold Medal, triple and long jump, European Athletics Jr Championships, Tampere, Finland 2003; competed in triple jump at Athens Olympics 2004; Bronze Medal, triple jump, European Under-23 Championships 2005; finished first in long jump and second in triple jump, European Cup in Athletics, Thessaloniki 2006; finished sixth at Int. Asscn of Athletics Feds (IAAF) World Indoor Championships 2006; finished fourth in triple jump and sixth in long jump at European Athletics Championships, Gothenburg 2006 (set Portuguese triple jump record of 17.23m during qualification); finished fifth at European Athletics Indoor Championships, Birmingham 2007; finished first in triple jump, European Cup in Athletics, Milan 2007; Gold Medal, World Championships, Osaka 2007 (set personal best, Portuguese nat. record and second-best world mark of the year at 17.74m); Bronze Medal, triple jump (17.27m), IAAF World Indoor Championships, Valencia 2008; Gold Medal, triple jump (17.67m), Olympic Games, Beijing 2008; competes for S.L. Benfica (sports club), Lisbon. *Address:* c/o Federação Portuguesa de Atletismo, 15-B Largo da Lagoa, 2799-538 Linda a Velha, Portugal. *Telephone:* (21) 4146020. *Fax:* (21) 4146021. *E-mail:* comunicacao@fpatletismo.pt. *Website:* www.fpatletismo.pt.

EVREN, Gen. Kenan; Turkish army officer and fmr Head of State; b. 1918, Alaşehir, Manisa; s. of Naciye Evren and Hayrullah Evren; m.; three d.; ed Military Acad., War Coll.; Artillery Officer 1938; served in Korea; Chief of Staff of the Land Forces, then Deputy Chief of Staff of the Armed Forces; Commdr Fourth Army (Aegean Army), Izmir 1976; rank of Gen. 1974; Chief of the Land Forces 1977; Chief of Staff of the Armed Forces 1978; led coup deposing civilian Govt Sept. 1980; Head of State and Chair. Nat. Security Council 1980–82, Pres. of Turkey 1982–89; Head, Turkish mil. del. to USSR 1975; est. cultural foundation; numerous decorations. *Achievements:* building Marmaris High School, opened 2000. *Leisure interests:* oil painting, education. *Address:* Beyaz Ev Sokak 27, Armutalan, Marmaris, Turkey (home).

Telephone: (252) 4171300 (home). *Fax:* (252) 4171313 (home). *E-mail:* kev@marmariskoleji-kiz.com (office).

EWALD, François, PhD; French insurance expert and academic; *Professor, Conservatoire national des arts et métiers;* b. 29 April 1946, Boulogne-Billancourt; ed Sorbonne, Paris; Asst to Michel Foucault, Coll. de France 1975–84; expert on issues of risk and responsibility, the formation of an insured soc. and the devt of the French Social Security System; Professorial Chair. of Insurance, Conservatoire nat. des arts et métiers (CNAM) 1997–; Distinguished Visitor, Univ. of Connecticut Law School 2003; Founder and Pres. Michel Foucault Centre; mem. Acad. des Technologies. *Publications include:* L'Etat providence 1986, Naissance du Code civil 1989, Le problème français des accidents thérapeutiques 1992, Le principe de précaution (jtly) 2001. *Address:* c/o Fédération française des sociétés d'assurances, 26 boulevard Haussmann, 75 311 Paris, Cedex 09, France (office). *Telephone:* 1-42-47-93-51 (office). *E-mail:* ewald@academie-technologies.fr. *Website:* www.ffsa.fr (office).

EWANGO, Corneille E. N., BSc, MSc; Democratic Republic of the Congo botanist and conservationist; *Senior Botanist Researcher and Head of Botanical and Forest Ecology Program, Democratic Republic of the Congo Program, Wildlife Conservation Society;* ed Univ. of Kisangani, Univ. of Missouri, St Louis, USA, Wageningen Univ., the Netherlands; staff mem. Congolese Inst. for the Conservation of Nature and Wildlife Conservation Soc. (WCS)'s Democratic Repub. of Congo (DRC) programme, responsible for Okapi Faunal Reserve's botany programme, Ituri Rainforest 1996–2003; extensive research experience in DRC, Rwanda, Uganda and Cameroon; Dir WCS and Centre de Formation et de Recherche en Conservation Forestière (CEFRE-COF), Ituri Landscape, DRC Program 2006–07; Sr Botanist Researcher and Head of Botanical and Forest Ecology Program, WCS-DRC Program 2006–; PhD student, Forest Ecology and Forest Man. Group, Wageningen Univ., the Netherlands 2007–; Goldman Environmental Prize 2005, Emerging Explorers Award—Africa, Nat. Geographic Soc. 2007, Invited Speaker, TEDGlobal 2007 Conf., Africa: The Next Chapter, Arusha, Tanzania 2007. *Achievements include:* helped lead effort to protect and preserve Okapi Reserve during civil war in DRC; uncovered 270 species of lianas and 600 tree species in the area. *Publications:* several scientific papers in professional journals on forest dynamics, tropical forest structure and functional ecology, lianas, biodiversity conservation, biology of epiphytes, and plant taxonomy and systematics. *Address:* WCS Site Manager, 1725 Avenue Col. Mondjiba, Chanic Building, PO Box 240, Ngaelima, Kinshasa I, Democratic Republic of the Congo (office). *E-mail:* ewango_corneille@yahoo.com (office). *Website:* www.wcs.org/drcongo (office).

EWING, Maria Louise; American singer (soprano); b. 27 March 1950, Detroit; d. of Norman I. Ewing and Hermina M. Veraar; m. Sir Peter Hall 1982 (divorced 1989); one d.; ed Cleveland Inst. of Music; debut at Metropolitan Opera, New York singing Cherubino in The Marriage of Figaro 1976, closely followed by debuts with major US orchestras, including New York Philharmonic and at La Scala Milan; performs regularly at Glyndebourne including the Barber of Seville, L'Incoronazione di Poppea and Carmen; repertoire also includes Pelléas et Mélisande, The Dialogues of the Carmelites, Così fan Tutte, La Perichole, La Cenerentola, The Marriage of Figaro (Susanna); performed Salome, Covent Garden 1988, Carmen, Earl's Court, London 1989, Tosca, Los Angeles 1989, Salome, Washington 1990, Madame Butterfly, Los Angeles, Tosca, Seville, Salome, Covent Garden 1992, Tosca, Los Angeles, Chicago, Salome, San Francisco, The Trojans, Metropolitan New York 1993, Madame Butterfly, Tosca, Vienna, The Trojans, Metropolitan, New York 1993/94; also appears as concert and recital singer; debut Promenade Concerts, London 1987, Lady Macbeth of Mtsensk with Metropolitan Opera 1994. *Leisure interests:* home and family. *Address:* c/o David Godfrey, Mitchell-Godfrey Management, 48 Gray's Inn Road, London, WC1X 8LT, England (office); c/o Herbert Breslin, 119 West 57th Street, Room 1505, New York, NY 10019, USA (office).

EWING, Rodney Charles, BS, MS, PhD; American geologist and academic; *Donald R. Peacor Collegiate Professor, Department of Geological Sciences, University of Michigan;* ed Texas Christian Univ., Stanford Univ. (NSF Fellowship); mem. Faculty, Dept of Earth and Planetary Sciences, Univ. of New Mexico 1974–97, Chair. Dept 1979–84, Regents' Prof. Emer. 1997–; Prof., Dept of Nuclear Eng and Radiological Sciences, Univ. of Michigan 1997–, responsible for programme in radiation effects and nuclear waste man., also holds appointments in Geological Sciences and Materials Science and Eng, currently Donald R. Peacor Collegiate Prof., Dept of Geological Sciences; Adjungeret Prof., Univ. of Århus, Denmark; Councillor, Materials Research Soc. 1983–85, 1987–89, Sec. 1985–86; Pres. Mineralogical Soc. of America 2002, Int. Union of Materials Research Socs 1997–98, New Mexico Geological Soc. 1981; mem. Bd Dirs Caswell Silver Foundation 1980–84, Energy, Exploration, Education, Inc. 1979–84; Guest Scientist or Faculty mem. Battelle Pacific Northwest Labs, Oak Ridge Nat. Lab., Hahn-Meitner-Institut, Berlin, Dept of Nuclear Eng, Technion Univ., Haifa, Israel, Centre d'Études Nucléaires de Fontenay-Aux-Roses, Commissariat à l'Énergie Atomique (France), Charles Univ., Prague, Japan Atomic Energy Research Inst., Institut für Nukleare Entsorgungstechnik of Kernforschungszentrum Karlsruhe, Århus Univ., Mineralogical Inst., Tokyo Univ., Khlopin Radium Inst., St Petersburg, Russia; mem. Bd of Radioactive Waste Man., Nat. Research Council, Nat. Research Council cttees for NAS that reviewed Waste Isolation Pilot Plant in NM 1984–96, Remediation of Buried and Tank Wastes at Hanford, Wash. and INEEL, Ida 1992–95, INEEL High-Level Waste Alternative Treatments 1998–99, sub-cttee on WIPP for the Environmental Protection Agency's Nat. Advisory Council on Environmental Policy and Tech. 1992–98; has served as invited expert to Advisory Cttee on Nuclear Waste of

Nuclear Regulatory Comm.; fmr consultant to Nuclear Waste Tech. Review Bd; mem. Program Cttee, Materials Research Soc., Ed. or Assoc. Ed. proceedings vols for symposia on the 'Scientific Basis for Nuclear Waste Management', Berlin 1982, Boston 1984, Stockholm 1985, Berlin 1988, Strasbourg 1991, Kyoto 1994, Boston 1998, Sydney 2000; Fellow, Geological Soc. of America, Mineralogical Soc. of America; Guggenheim Fellowship 2002, Lomonosov Gold Medal, Russian Acad. of Sciences 2006. *Publications:* Radioactive Waste Forms for the Future (co-ed. and contributing author) 1988; ed. or co-ed. of seven monographs, proceedings vols or special issues of journals; author or co-author of more than 400 research publs on radiation effects caused by heavy-particle interactions with crystalline materials, the structure and crystal chemistry of complex Nb-Ta-Ti oxides, the crystal chemistry of actinide and fission product elements, the application of 'natural analogues' to the evaluation of the long-term durability of radioactive waste forms and the release and transport of radionuclides, the low-temperature corrosion of silicate glasses, the neutronics and geochemistry of the natural nuclear reactors in Gabon, Africa; holds patent for the development of a highly durable material for the immobilization of excess weapons plutonium. *Address:* Department of Geological Sciences, University of Michigan, 2534 C.C. Little Building, 1100 N University Avenue, Ann Arbor, MI 48109-1005, USA (office). *Telephone:* (734) 763-9295 (office). *Fax:* (734) 647-8531 (office). *E-mail:* rodewing@engin.umich.edu (office). *Website:* www.geo.lsa.umich.edu/relw/groupmembers/ewing/ewing.htm (office).

EYCKMANS, Luc A. F., MD, PhD; Belgian fmr professor of medicine; *Executive Director, Francqui Foundation;* b. 23 Feb. 1930, Antwerp; s. of Robert Eyckmans and Alice van Genechten; m. Godelieve Cornelissen 1957; four s. three d.; ed Univ. of Leuven; Fellowship in Tropical Medicine, Antwerp 1956–57; Hosp. Physician, Kisantu (fmr Belgian Congo) 1957–60; Fellowship in Infectious Diseases, Dallas and Cornell, New York 1961–64, in Tropical Medicine, Bahia, Brazil 1964; Lector in Infectious Diseases and Physician, Univ. of Leuven 1965–72; Prof. of Medicine (Infectious Diseases), Univ. of Antwerp 1973–76, Dir Inst. of Tropical Medicine "Prince Leopold" 1976–95; Visiting Prof. Univ. of Antwerp 1977–95, Univ. of Leuven 1989–95; Exec. Dir and mem. Bd Francqui Foundation 1992–; mem. Royal Acad. of Overseas Sciences (Belgium), Acad. Europaea; Corresp. mem. Acad. Nat. de Médicine, Paris; Grand Officer, Order of the Crown (Belgium); Dr hc (Lille). *Publications:* 130 contributions to professional journals and chapters in scientific publs. *Leisure interest:* hiking. *Address:* Francqui Foundation, Rue Defacqz 1, B 1000 Brussels (office); Wildenhoge 26, B 3020 Winksele, Belgium (home). *Telephone:* (2) 539-33-94 (office); (16) 22-05-96 (home). *Fax:* (2) 537-29-21 (office). *E-mail:* francquifoundation@skynet.be (office). *Website:* www.francquifoundation.be (office).

EYLER, John H., BCom, MBA; American retail executive; ed Univ. of Wash., Harvard Univ. Graduate School of Business; began retail career with The May Dept Stores Co., becoming Pres. and CEO May D&F, Denver; fmr Chair. and CEO MainStreet; CEO Hartmarx, Chicago –1992; Chair. and CEO FAO Schwarz, NY 1992–2000; Pres. and CEO Toys 'R' Us 2000–05, Chair. 2001–05; fmr Dir The Toys 'R' Us Children's Fund Inc. *Address:* c/o Toys 'R' Us Inc., One Geoffrey Way, Wayne, NJ 07470-2030, USA (office).

EYRAUD, Francis Charles, LenD, DES; French business executive; b. 16 Aug. 1931, Saint-Bonnet, Hautes Alpes; s. of Charles Eyraud and Francine Villaron; m. Simone Desmé 1967; two s. one d.; ed Coll. du Rondeau Montfleury, Grenoble, Faculté de Droit, Lettres, IEP, Paris; ENA promotion, Alexis de Tocqueville 1958; civil admin. of finance 1960; Prof. Centre de Formation des Finances 1961; in charge of practical studies, Faculté de Droit 1962; special mission to USA 1965; Chef de Bureau 1967; civil admin. 1968; Deputy Dir 1973; judicial agent of Treasury 1979–; Prés.-Dir Gén. Société Nationale d'Exploitation Industrielle des Tabacs et Allumettes (SEITA) 1981–87; Man. Dir CORESTA 1982, Vice-Pres. 1984–86, Pres. 1986; Paymaster of Seine-Maritime and of Haute-Normandie 1988–96, of Yvelines 1996–98; Officier Légion d'honneur, Commdr Ordre nat. du Mérite, Officier des Palmes académiques; Commdr des Arts et des Lettres and other decorations. *Publications:* Cours de Législation Financière 1965. *Address:* 33 rue Saint-Augustin, 75002 Paris, France (home). *Telephone:* 1-47-42-50-67 (home).

EYRE, Ivan; Canadian artist and academic; *Professor Emeritus of Drawing and Painting, University of Manitoba;* b. 15 April 1935, Tullymet, Sask.; s. of Thomas Eyre and Kay Eyre; m. Brenda Fenske 1957; two s.; mem. Faculty, Univ. of Manitoba, Winnipeg 1959–93, Head, Drawing Dept 1974–78, Prof. of Drawing and Painting 1975–93, Prof. Emer. 1994–; works represented in permanent collections at Winnipeg Art Gallery, Nat. Gallery, Ottawa, Edmonton Art Gallery, Montreal Museum of Fine Arts, Assiniboine Park Pavilion Gallery, Winnipeg, Man. etc.; Canada Council Sr Fellow 1966–77; Founder mem. Winnipeg Art Gallery 1996; mem. Royal Canadian Acad. of Arts; subject of books 'Ivan Eyre' by George Woodcock, 'Ivan Eyre Drawings' by Tom Lovatt and of various documentary films; Queen's Silver Jubilee Medal 1977, Academic of Italy with Gold Medal 1980, Jubilee Award, Univ. of Manitoba Alumni Asscn 1982, Queen's Golden Jubilee Medal 2002, Order of Manitoba 2007. *Publications:* Ivan on Eyre (auto-biog.). *Address:* 1098 Des Trappistes Street, Winnipeg, Manitoba, R3V 1B8, Canada (home). *Fax:* (204) 275-6650 (home).

EYRE, Sir Richard, Kt, CBE, DLit; British theatre, film and television director; b. 28 March 1943, Barnstaple, Devon; m. Sue Birtwistle 1973; one d.; ed Sherborne School and Univ. of Cambridge; directed his first production, The Knack, at Phoenix Theatre, Leicester 1965; Asst Dir Phoenix Theatre 1967; Assoc. Dir Royal Lyceum, Edinburgh 1967–70, Dir of Productions 1970–72; Artistic Dir Nottingham Playhouse 1973–78; Producer-Dir Play for Today for BBC 1978–80; Assoc. Dir Nat. Theatre (now called Royal Nat. Theatre) 1980–86, Artistic Dir 1988–97; BBC Gov. 1995–; Cameron Mackin-

tosh Visiting Professorship, St Catherine's Coll. Oxford 1997; Visiting Prof. of Drama, Univ. of Warwick 1999, Univ. of Sheffield 2000; Hon. Fellow Goldsmiths Coll. 1993, King's Coll. London 1994; Hon. mem. Guildhall School of Music and Drama 1996; Officier des Arts et des Lettres 1998; Hon. DLitt (Nottingham Trent) 1992, (S Bank) 1994; Hon. BA (Surrey) 1998; Dr hc (Royal Scottish Acad. of Drama) 2000, DUniv (Oxford Brookes Univ.) 2003, (Liverpool Univ.) 2003; Patricia Rothermere Award 1995, STV Award for Best Dir 1969, 1970, 1971, Vittorio de Sica Award 1986, Special Award, Evening Standard Awards for Drama 1988, for Best Dir 1997, Special Award for running Nat. Theatre 1997, Critics Circle Award 1996/97, Laurence Olivier Award for Outstanding Achievement 1997, South Bank Show Award for Outstanding Achievement 1997, Director's Guild Award for Outstanding Achievement 1997. *Plays directed include:* Hamlet (Royal Court) 1980, Guys and Dolls (Olivier 1982, Soc. of West End Theatres and Evening Standard Awards for Best Dir 1982), The Beggar's Opera, Schweyk in the Second World War (Nat. Theatre) 1982, The Government Inspector (Nat. Theatre) 1985, Futurists (Nat. Theatre) (Time Out Award for Best Dir) 1986, Kafka's Dick (Royal Court) 1986, High Society (W End) 1987, The Changeling 1988, Bartholomew Fair 1988, Hamlet 1989, The Voysey Inheritance 1989, Racing Demon 1990, Richard III (Nat. Theatre, also nat. and int. tour) 1990, Napoli Milionaria 1991, Murmuring Judges 1991, White Chameleon 1991, The Night of the Iguana 1992, Macbeth 1993, The David Hare Trilogy – Racing Demon, Murmuring Judges, The Absence of War 1993 (Racing Demon, New York 1995), Johnny on a Spot 1994, Sweet Bird of Youth 1994, Skylight 1995, 1996 (New York 1996), La Grande Magia 1995, The Prince's Play 1996, John Gabriel Borkman 1996, Guys and Dolls 1996, 1997, King Lear 1997, Amy's View 1997 (New York 1999), The Invention of Love 1997, The Judas Kiss 1998 (New York 1998), The Novice 2000, The Crucible (New York) 2002, Vincent in Brixton 2002, Mary Poppins 2004, Hedda Gabler (London 2005), Mary Poppins (New York) 2006, The Reporter Nat. Theatre) 2007. *Films:* The Ploughman's Lunch (Evening Standard Award for Best Film) 1983, Loose Connections 1984, Laughterhouse (Venice Film Festival Award for Best Film) 1984, Iris (Special Mention for Excellence in Filmmaking Award, Nat. Bd of Review 2001, Humanitas Screenwriting Award for screenplay 2002) 2001, Stage Beauty 2004, Notes on a Scandal 2006. *Radio:* Macbeth (BBC Radio 3) 2000, Angel (BBC Radio 4) 2001. *Television:* Waterloo Sunset, Comedians 1974, The Imitation Game 1980, Pasmore 1981, The Cherry Orchard, Country 1982, Past Caring, The Insurance Man (Tokyo World TV Festival Special Prize 1986) 1986, "V", Tumbledown (Italia RAI Prize 1988, BAFTA Award for Best TV Single Drama, Royal TV Soc. Award for Best Single Drama 1989) 1987, Suddenly Last Summer 1993, The Absence of War (BBC) 1995, King Lear (BBC) (Peabody Award 1998) 1998, Changing Stages: A Personal View of 20th-Century Theatre (writer and presenter on BBC 2) 2000. *Opera:* La Traviata, Covent Garden 1994, Le Nozze di Figaro, Aix-en-Provence, France 2001. *Publication:* Utopia and Other Places (memoirs) 1993, The Eyre Review 1998, Changing Stages (with Nicholas Wright) 2000, Angel (radio play) 2001, Iris (screenplay) 2002, National Service 2003, Hedda Gabler 2005. *Address:* c/o Judy Daish Associates Ltd, 2 St Charles Place, London, W10 6EG, England (office). *Telephone:* (20) 8964-8811 (office). *Fax:* (20) 8964-8966 (office).

EYRE, Richard Anthony, MA; British media executive; b. 3 May 1954; s. of Edgar Gabriel Eyre and Marjorie Eyre (née Corp); m. Sheelagh Colquhoun 1977; one s. one d.; ed King's Coll. School, Wimbledon, Lincoln Coll., Oxford Univ.; media buyer Benton & Bowles 1975–79, media planner 1980–84; TV airtime salesman Scottish TV 1979–80; Media Dir Aspect 1984–86, Bartle Bogle Hegarty 1986–91; Chief Exec. Capital Radio PLC 1991–97, ITV 1997–2000, Pearson TV 2000–01; Dir of Strategy and Content, RTL Group 2000–01; Non-Exec. Chair. RDF Media 2001; Adviser to 19 Group 2002–; fmr bd mem., Guardian Media Group; Non-Exec. Chair. GCap Media PLC 2007–08. *Address:* c/o GCap Media PLC, 30 Leicester Square, London, WC2H 7LA, England (office).

EYSKENS, Viscount Mark, LLD, DEcon; Belgian politician; *Minister of State;* b. 29 April 1933, Louvain; m. Ann Rutsaert 1962; two s. three d.; ed Catholic Univ. of Louvain, Columbia Univ.; Prof. Catholic Univ. of Louvain; Econ. Adviser, Ministry of Finance 1962–65; mem. of Parl. 1977–; Sec. of State for the Budget and Regional Economy and Minister of Co-operation 1976–80; Minister of Finance 1980–81; Prime Minister 1981; Minister for Econ. Affairs 1981–85, for Finance 1985–88, of Foreign Affairs 1989–92, Minister of State 1998–; Chair. Council of EC Ministers of Finance 1987; Gov. IMF, IBRD 1980–81, 1985–88; mem. Council of Europe 1995–; Pres. Royal Acad. of Sciences, Letters and Fine Arts, Centre for European Culture, Inst. for European Policy; Vice-Pres. Royal Inst. for Int. Relations, Ass. of WEU 1995–; Observer European Convention 2002–, Pres. of Francqui Foundation; mem. of bd, Int. Crisis Group (ICG); numerous Belgian and foreign awards including Benelux-Europe Prize, J.M/ Huyghe Prize, Scriptores Christiani Prize. *Publications:* author of 40 books including Algemene economie 1970, Economie van nu en straks 1975, Ambrunise 1976, Une planète livrée à deux mondes 1980, La source et l'horizon, Le redressement de la société européenne 1985, Economie voor iedereen 1987, Vie et mort du Professeur Mortal 1989, Buitenlandse zaken 1992, Affaires étrangères 1992, Le Fleuve et l'océan 1994, De Reis naar Dabar 1996, De lust van de verbeelding 1996, L'Affaire Titus 1998, Democratie tussen Spin en Web 1999, Het verdriet van het werelddorp 2000, Leven in tijden van Godsverduistering 2001, Het hijgen van de geschiedenis 2003, Omdat wij van de avond nooit genzen 2004, De oude prof en de zee 2005, Le vieux prof et la mer 2006, Mijn levens 2008; has written more than 1000 articles, columns and contribs. *Leisure interests:* painting, literature, music. *Address:* Royal Academy of Sciences and Arts, Hertogsstraat 1, 1000 Brussels, Belgium (office). *Telephone:* (2) 550-23-23 (office). *Fax:* (1) 640-60-18 (home). *E-mail:* m.eyskens@skynet.be (office). *Website:* www.eyskens.com (home).

EYTON, Anthony John Plowden, RA, RWS, R.W.A.; British artist; b. 17 May 1923, Teddington, Middx; s. of the late Capt. John Seymour Eyton and Phyllis Annie Tyser; m. Frances Mary Capell 1960 (divorced); three d.; ed Twyford School, Canford School and Camberwell School of Art; part-time teacher, Camberwell Art School 1955–86, Royal Acad. Schools 1963–99; mem. Royal Cambrian Acad., Royal Inst. Oil Painters (ROI); Hon. mem. Pastel Soc.; several awards and prizes. *Publications:* Indian Memories, Journal of P A Eyton, RA Publications 1996. *Leisure interest:* gardening. *Address:* c/o Browse and Darby Ltd, 19 Cork Street, London, W1X 1HB, England (office). *Telephone:* (20) 7734-7984 (office).

EYZAGUIRRE GUZMAN, Nicolás, PhD; Chilean international organization official and politician; b. 1952; ed Harvard Univ., USA; Exec. Dir IMF 1998; Minister of Finance 2000–06; mem. Partido Por la Democracia—PPD. *Publication:* The Macroeconomy of Quasi-Fiscal Operations in Chile (with Osvaldo Larrañaga) 1990. *Address:* c/o Ministry of Finance, Teatinos 120, 12° Santiago, Chile (office).

EZRA, Baron (Life Peer), cr. 1983, of Horsham in the County of West Sussex; **Derek Ezra,** Kt, MA, MBE; British business executive; b. 23 Feb. 1919, Australia; s. of David and Lillie Ezra; m. Julia Elizabeth Wilkins 1950; ed Monmouth School and Magdalene Coll., Cambridge; mil. service 1939–47; rep. of Nat. Coal Bd at Cttees of OEEC and ECE 1948–52; mem. UK Del. to High Authority of European Coal and Steel Community 1952–56; Regional Sales Man. Nat. Bd 1958–60, Dir-Gen. of Marketing 1960–65; mem. Nat. Coal Bd 1965, Deputy Chair. 1965–71, Chair. 1971–82; Chair. British Inst. of Man. 1976–78, Vice-Chair. 1978; Chair. British Coal Int.; Chair. British National-ised Industries Chairmen's Group 1980–81, Pres. Nat. Materials Handling Centre 1978; Pres. Coal Industry Soc. 1981–86, British Standards Inst. 1983–86, Econ. Research Council 1985–2000, Inst. of Trading Standards Admin. 1987–92; Dir Redland PLC 1982–89; Chair. Associated Heat Services PLC 1966–2000, British Iron and Steel Consumers Council 1983–86, Petrolex PLC 1982–85, Sheffield Heat and Power Ltd 1985–2000, Associated Gas Supplies Ltd 1987–95, Energy and Tech. Services Group 1990–2000, Micro-power Ltd 2000–; Industrial Adviser to Morgan Grenfell 1982–88; Chair. Throgmorton Trust 1984–90; mem. British Overseas Trade Bd 1972–82, Bd, Solvay, Belgium; Hon. Fellow Inst. of Civil Engineers 1986; Hon. LLD (Leeds) 1982; Order of Merit, Italy, Commdr Order of Merit, Luxembourg, Officier, Légion d'honneur. *Publications:* Coal and Energy 1978, The Energy Debate 1983. *Address:* House of Lords, Westminster, London, SW1A 0PW, England. *Telephone:* (20) 7219-3180.

EZRA, Gideon; Israeli politician; *Minister of Environment Protection;* b. 30 June 1937, Jerusalem; m.; three c.; ed Haifa Univ.; served with Nahal paratroops; with Gen. Security Services 1962–95, achieved rank equivalent to Maj. Gen., fmr Deputy Head; Adviser to Minister of Internal Security 1995; mem. Knesset 1996–, fmr mem. Econs Cttee, Foreign Affairs and Defense Cttee, Internal Affairs and Environment Cttee, Educ., Culture, and Sports Cttee; Deputy Minister of Public Security 2001–03; Minister in the Prime Minister's Office, responsible for Co-ordination between Govt and Knesset (Parl.) 2003–04; Acting Minister of Tourism July–Aug. 2004, Minister of Tourism 2004–05; Acting Minister of Internal Security Sept.–Nov. 2004, Minister of Internal Security 2004–06, of Environment Protection 2006–; fmr mem. Likud party; joined Kadima 2006. *Address:* Ministry of Environment Protection, PO Box 34033, 5 Kanfei Nesharim Street, Givat Shaul, Jerusalem 95464 (office); c/o The Knesset, HaKiryah, Jerusalem 91950, Israel (office). *Telephone:* (2) 6553745 (Ministry) (office); (2) 6753333 (Ministry) (office); (2) 6753800 (Knesset) (office). *Fax:* (2) 6553752 (Ministry) (office); (2) 6753510 (Knesset) (office). *E-mail:* ori@sviva.gov.il (office); gezra@knesset.gov.il (office). *Website:* www.sviva.gov.il (office); www.environment.gov.il (office); www.knesset.gov.il/mk/eng/mk_eng.asp?mk_individual_id_t=96 (office).

F

FABBRI, Fabio; Italian politician, lawyer and journalist; b. 15 Oct. 1933, Ciano d'Enza, Reggio Emilia; s. of Nello Fabbri and Gisella Brechi; m. Minnie Manzini 1959; one s. one d.; ed Univ. of Parma; fmr journalist with Il Mondo and contrib. to Nord e Sud, Itinerari, Mondo Operario; now contrib. to L'Avanti and other political and cultural magazines; Chair. Parma Provincial Transport Authority 1968–70; Socialist Senator for Borgotaro Salsomaggiore, Emilia Romagna 1976; fmr Under-Sec., Ministry of Agric. and Forestry; Minister for Regional Affairs 1982–83, for EEC Affairs 1986–87, of Defence 1993–94; Chair. of Socialist Parl. Group; Pres. Istituto per il dialogo e la cooperazione internazionale. *Leisure interests:* reading, trekking, skiing. *Address:* Piazza Garibaldi 17, 431000 Parma, Italy.

FABIANI, Simonetta (see Simonetta).

FABIUS, Laurent; French politician; b. 20 Aug. 1946, Paris; s. of André Fabius and Louise Mortimer; ed Lycées Janson-de-Sailly and Louis-le-Grand, Paris, Ecole normale supérieure, Ecole Nat. d'Admin; Auditor, Council of State 1973; First Deputy Mayor of Grand-Quevilly 1977–, Mayor 1995–; Deputy (Seine-Maritime) to Nat. Ass. 1978–81, 1986–, Pres. 1988–92, 1997–2000, 2002–07, 2007–; Nat. Sec. Parti Socialiste, in charge of press 1979–81, 1991–92, First Sec. 1992–93, Pres. Groupe Socialiste in Nat. Ass. 1995–97; Minister-Del. for the Budget, attached to Minister of Econ. and Finance 1981–83; Minister of Industry and Research 1983–84, Minister of Econs, Finance and Industry 2000–02; Prime Minister 1984–86; Pres. Regional Council, Haute Normandie 1981–82; Pres. Syndicat intercommunal à vocations multiples (Sivom) 1989–2000; mem. Gen. Council, Seine-Maritime 2000–; Grand Croix de l'Ordre nat. du Mérite. *Publications:* La France inégale 1975, Le coeur du futur 1985, C'est en allant vers la mer 1990, Les blessures de la vérité (Prize for Best Political Book 1996) 1995, Cela commence par une balade 2003, Une certaine idée de l'Europe 2005. *Address:* Assemblée Nationale, Casier de la Poste, Palais Bourbon, 75355 Paris 07 (office); Mairie, Esplanade Tony Larue, 76120 Grand-Quevilly, France (office). *Telephone:* 2-35-68-93-00 (Grand-Quevilly) (office). *Fax:* 2-35-67-27-39 (Grand-Quevilly) (office). *E-mail:* lfabius@assemblee-nationale.fr (office). *Website:* www.laurent-fabius.net (office).

FABRE, Jan; Belgian artist, playwright and stage designer; b. 1958, Antwerp; ed Decorative Arts Inst., Royal Acad. of Fine Arts; began career as decorator and set designer; wrote a series of plays and produced black and white films 1970s; became active in the field of performance art 1976–81; became engaged in theatrical, operatic and dance performances 1980–; produced a series of chamber plays 1980s; est. Troublyn (creative work asscn); fmr artist-in-residence Museum of Natural History, London; decorated the Hall of Mirrors at the Royal Palace at the invitation of the Queen of Belgium 2003; productions have been staged in Europe, the USA, Japan and Australia; contrib. to numerous European museums and galleries including deSingel arts centre, Antwerp, Centre for Contemporary Art, Warsaw, Gallery of Modern and Contemporary Art, Bergamo. *Drawings include:* The Flying Cock, The Road from the Earth to the Stars is not Smooth, Hour of the Blue. *Sculptures include:* House of Flames III, Scissors' House. *Stage works include:* Body, Body on a Wall. *Stage performances include:* This is the theatre one should have awaited and expected 1982, The power of theatrical frenzy (staged at Venice Biennial) 1984, Sweet Temptations, Universal Copyrights 1 & 9, Luminous Icons, The end comes a little bit earlier this century. But business as usual 1998, The values of night 1999. *Opera includes:* Glass in the head will be made of glass (Flemish Opera House, Antwerp) 1990. *Ballet includes:* Sound of one clapping hand 1989, The Four Temperaments 1997. *Address:* c/o Galleria d'Arte Moderna e Contemporanea (GAMeC), Via San Tomaso 82, 24121 Bergamo, Italy (office). *Telephone:* 035-399528/9 (office). *E-mail:* info@gamec.it (office). *Website:* www.gamec.it (office).

FÁBREGA, Jorge, ML; Panamanian professor of law and judge; *Justice, Supreme Court;* b. (Jorge Fábrega Ponce), 19 April 1922, Santiago; s. of Luis Ramon Fábrega and Maria Fábrega; m. Gloria de Fábrega 1960; two s. two d.; ed Univ. of Southern California, Univ. of Pennsylvania, Univ. of Panama; Alt. Justice Court of Appeals 1960–68, Supreme Court of Panama 1970–80, 1989, 1999–2005; Prof. of Law, Univ. of Panama 1967; Pres. Govt Comm. drafting Labour Code 1969–71, Constitutional Comm. 1983, Panamanian Bar Asscn 1983–85; mem. Govt Comm. drafting new Judicial Code 1970–74; Hon. mem. Spanish Bar; Brazilian Labour Judicial Order. *Publications:* Enriquecimiento sin causa 1960, Institutes of Civil Procedure 1972, Casación 1978, Estudios Procesales 1984, Código de Trabajo Anotado 1970, 1971, 1986, Estudios Procesales 1988, Instituciones de Derecho Procesal 1998, Procesos Civiles 1999, Medios de Prueba, Casación Civil, Teoría General de la Prueba 2000, Judges and Lawyers in the World Literature 2001. *Leisure interests:* reading, travel. *Address:* Edicicio P.H. Plaza 54, Segundo Piso, Oficina 2A, Aveni da Samuel Lewis, Urbanización Obarrio, Panamá (office); PO Box 0816-02883, Panamá; Las Cumbres, Vía El Peñón, Panamá, Republic of Panama (home). *Telephone:* 269-6412 (office); 269-6621 (home). *Fax:* 264-3933 (office). *E-mail:* fabregam@morenoyfabrega.com (office).

FABRIZI, Pier Luigi, BEcons; Italian banker and professor of finance; *Professor of Financial Markets, Bocconi University;* b. 23 April 1948, Siena; s. of Francesco Fabrizi and Bianca Corradeschi; m. Patrizia Vaselli; two c.; ed Siena Univ.; Asst Prof. of Banking Parma Univ. 1974–82, Assoc. Prof. 1982–87, Prof. of Financial Insts 1987–93, Dean Faculty of Econs 1990–97; Prof. of Financial Markets, Bocconi Univ., Milan 1993–; Chair. Banca Monte dei Paschi di Siena SpA 1998–; mem. Bd Dirs S. Paolo IMI, Turin 1998–99, Ing. C. Olivetti SpA, Ivrea 1999, Banca Agricola Mantovana, Mantova 1999, Banco Nazionale del Lavoro SpA, Rome 2001, Unipol Assiarrazioni SpA, Bologna 2001; Grande Ufficiale, Ordine al Merito. *Publications:* L'attività in titoli con clientela nelle banche di deposito 1986, La gestione dei flussi finanziari nelle aziende di credito 1990, La gestione integrata dell'attivo e del passivo nelle aziende di credito 1991, Nuovi modelli di gestione dei flussi finanziari nelle banche 1995, Le banche nell' intermediazione mobiliare e nell'asset management 1996, La formazione nelle banche e nelle assicurazioni-bancaria (ed.) 1998, Il futuro del sistema bancario italiano: Strategie e modelli organizzativi 2000; La gestione del risparmio privato (ed.) 2000. *Address:* c/o Banca Monte Paschi Siena SpA, P.za Salimbeni 3, 53100 Siena (office); c/o Università Bocconi, Via Sarfatti 25, 20136 Milan (office); Via Adelaide Coari 11, 20141 Milan, Italy. *Telephone:* (0577) 294211 (Siena) (office); (02) 58365910 (Milan) (office); (02) 55210884 (Milan). *Fax:* (0577) 294017 (Siena) (office); (02) 58365909 (Milan) (office). *E-mail:* pierluigi.fabrizi@banca.mps.it (office); pierluigi.fabrizi@uni.bocconi.it (office).

FADDEYEV, Ludvig Dmitriyevich; Russian mathematician and physicist; *Director, International Mathematical Institute, St Petersburg Branch of V.A. Steklov Mathematical Institute;* b. 23 March 1934, Leningrad; m.; two d.; ed Leningrad Univ.; Sr Research Fellow, Leningrad Br., Inst. of Math., USSR (now Russian) Acad. of Sciences 1965–; mem. staff, Leningrad State Univ. 1967–, Prof. at Math.-Mechanical Faculty 1969–; currently Dir Int. Math. Inst., St Petersburg Br. of V.A. Steklov Math. Inst.; Pres. Int. Math. Union 1986–; mem. USSR (now Russian) Acad. of Sciences 1976, mem. Presidium 1976–, Acad.-Sec. Dept of Math.; mem. American Acad. of Arts and Sciences, Boston 1979; specialist in quantum mechanics; D. Heinemann Prize, American Physical Soc. 1975, USSR State Prize 1971, Max Planck Gold Medal 1995. *Address:* International Mathematical Institute, St Petersburg Branch of V.A. Steklov Mathematical Institute, Nab. Fontanki 27, D-11, 191023 St Petersburg, Russia (office). *Telephone:* (812) 571-43-95 (office); (812) 310-53-77 (home). *E-mail:* admin@pdmi.ras.ru (office). *Website:* eimi.imi.ras.ru (office).

FADEYECHEV, Alexei Nikolayevich; Russian ballet dancer; b. 16 Aug. 1960, Moscow; s. of Nikolay Fadeyechev (q.v.) and Nina Fetisova; m. Rastozguyeva Tatyana; ed Bolshoi Choreographic School; Prin. Dancer, Bolshoi Ballet 1978, Artistic Dir 1998–2000; co-f. (with Nina Ananiashvili q.v.) ballet co. Moscow Theatre of Dance 2000; has performed with Mariinsky (fmrly Kirov) Ballet, Royal Danish Ballet, Royal Swedish Ballet, Nat. Ballet of Netherlands, Nat. Ballet of Finland, Nat. Ballet of Portugal, Birmingham Royal Ballet, Boston Ballet, Tokyo Ballet and numerous others; People's Artist of Russia. *Performances as a dancer include:* Frantz in Coppelia, Prince Siegfried in Swan Lake, Prince Desire in The Sleeping Beauty, Prince in The Nutcracker, Jean de Brienne in Raimonda, Basil in Don Quixote, Albrecht in Giselle, title roles in Spartacus, Ivan the Terrible, Macbeth, Romeo and Juliet, Cyrano de Bergerac, Prince of the Pagodas, leading roles in Les Sylphides, Paquita. *Address:* Karetny Ryad str. 5/10, Apt 20, 103006 Moscow, Russia (office). *Telephone:* (495) 419-35-31 (home).

FADEYECHEV, Nikolay Borisovich; Russian ballet dancer; b. 27 Jan. 1933; m. 1st Nina Fetisova; m. 2nd Irina Kholina; two s.; ed Bolshoi Theatre Ballet School; Bolshoi Theatre Ballet Co. 1952–76, coach, Bolshoi Theatre 1971–; People's Artist of USSR 1976. *Chief roles:* Siegfried (Swan Lake), Albert (Giselle), Jean de Brienne (Raimonde), Harmodius (Spartacus), Frondoso (Laurensia), Danila (Stone Flower), Romeo (Romeo and Juliet), Prince Desire (Sleeping Beauty), José (Carmen Suite), Karenin (Anna Karenina), Prince (Nutcracker), Illiys (Giselle), Vatslav. *Address:* Viktorenko str. 2/1, Apt 19, 125167 Moscow, Russia (home). *Telephone:* (495) 157-33-22 (home).

FADIAH, João Aladje Mamadu; Guinea-Bissau politician; Minister of the Economy and Finance 2004–05. *Address:* c/o Ministry of the Economy and Finance, CP 67, Avda 3 de Agosto, Bissau, Guinea-Bissau (office).

FADUL, Francisco; Guinea-Bissau politician; fmr adviser to Gen. Ansumane Mane; Prime Minister of Guinea-Bissau 1998–99; currently Leader Partido Unido Social Democrático (PUSD). *Address:* Partido Unido Social Democrático (PUSD), Bissau, Guinea-Bissau (office).

FAECKE, Peter; German journalist, writer and editor; b. 3 Nov. 1940, Grunwald, Silesia; ed Univs of Göttingen, Berlin, Hamburg, Paris; Lecturer, Univ. of Texas, Austin, USA; Dir Edition Köln, PEN-Centre Germany; awards include stipend of Villa Massimo, Rome and literature prizes of Lower Saxony, North-Rhine-Westphalia and City of Cologne. *Publications:* Die Brandstifter (novel) 1962, Der Rote Milan (novel) 1965, Postversand-Roman (novel) (with Wolf Vostell) 1970, Gemeinsam gegen Abriss: Ein Lesebuch aus Arbeitersiedlungen 1974, Das Unaufhaltsame Glück der Kowalskis 1982, Flug ins Leben (novel) 1988, Der Mann mit den besonderen Eigenschaften (novel) 1993, Grabstein für Fritz (documentary film) 1993, Als Elizabeth Arden Neunzehn war (novel) 1994, Eine Liebe zum Land (film script) 1994, Ankunft eines Schüchternen im Himmel (novel) 2000, Das Kreuz des Südens (reports) 2001, Vom Überfliessen der Anden, Reportagen aus Peru 2001, Hochzeitsvorbereitungen auf dem Lande (novel) 2003, Die geheimen Videos des Herrn Vladimiro (novel) 2004, Lima die Schöne-Lima die Schreckliche (reports) 2005, Wenn bei uns ein Gratis stirbt ... (reports) 2005, Der Kardinal, ganz in Rot und frisch gebügelt (novel) 2007, Die Tango-Sängerin (novel) 2008, Dem alten Mann seine Kiste (novel) 2009. *Address:* Pohlstadtsweg 414, 51109 Cologne, Germany (home). *Telephone:* (221) 726207 (home). *Fax:* (221) 1794149 (office). *E-mail:* edition.koeln@t-online.de (office); peterfaecke@t-online.de (home). *Website:* www.peterfaecke.de (office).

FAGERNÄS, Peter, LLM; Finnish investment banker and business executive; *Chairman, Fortum Corporation;* b. 1952; Chair., Pres. and CEO Hermitage & Co. Oyj (investment bank); Founder and Chair. Conventum Oyj (investment bank); Chair. Fortum Corpn, Pohjola Group PLC; mem. Supervisory Bd Finnlines PLC; fmr mem. Bd Dirs Merita Bank, Kansallis-Osake-Pankki; Vice-Pres. and mem. Bd, Helsinki Stock Exchange. *Address:* Fortum Corporation, Keilaniemi, 00048 Espoo, Finland (office). *Telephone:* 10-45-11 (office). *Fax:* 10-45-24798 (office). *Website:* www.fortum.com (office).

FAGIN, Claire Mintzer, PhD, RN; American nurse and academic; b. 25 Nov. 1926, New York; d. of Harry Mintzer and Mae Mintzer (née Slatin); m. Samuel Fagin 1952; two s.; ed Wagner Coll., Teachers' Coll., Columbia Univ. and New York Univ.; Staff Nurse, Sea View Hosp., Staten Island, New York 1947, Clinical Instructor 1947–48; Bellevue Hosp., New York 1948–50; Psychiatric Mental Health Nursing Consultant, Nat. League for Nursing 1951–52; Asst Chief, Psychiatric Nursing Service Clinical Center, NIH 1953–54, Supt 1955; Research Project Co-ordinator, Children's Hosp., Dept of Psychiatry, Washington, DC 1956; Instructor in Psychiatric-Mental Health Nursing, New York Univ. 1956–58, Asst Prof. 1964–67, Dir Grad. Programs in Psychiatric-Mental Health Nursing 1965–69, Assoc. Prof. 1967–69; Prof. and Chair. Nursing Dept, Herbert H. Lehman Coll. 1969–77; Dir Health Professions Inst., Montefiore Hosp. and Medical Center 1975–77; Dean, School of Nursing, Univ. of Pa, Philadelphia 1977–92, Prof. 1992–96, interim Pres. 1993–94, Dean Emer., Prof. Emer. 1996–; mem. Task Force Jt Cttee on Mental Health of Children 1966–69, Gov.'s Cttee on Children, New York 1971–75, Inst. of Medicine, NAS (Governing Council 1981–83), Comm. on Human Rights 1991–94, American Acad. of Nursing (Governing Council 1976–78), Expert Advisory Panel on Nursing, WHO 1974, Nat. Advisory Mental Health Council, Nat. Inst. of Mental Health 1983–87, Bd of Health Promotion and Disease Prevention 1990–94; Pres. American Orthopsychiatric Asscn 1985; Dir Salomon Inc. 1994–97; mem. Bd of Dirs Radian 1994–2002, Visiting Nurse Service of NY; Program Dir, Building Academic Geriatric Nursing Capacity Program, John A. Hartford Foundation 2000–05; Pres. Nat. League for Nursing 1991–93; consultant to many foundations, public and pvt. univs, health-care agencies; speaker on radio and TV; Hon. Fellow, Royal College of Nursing 2002; Hon. DSc (Lycoming Coll., Cedar Crest Coll., Univ. of Rochester, Medical Coll. of Pennsylvania, Univ. of Maryland, Loyola Univ., Wagner Coll., Case Western Reserve 2002); Hon. LLD (Pennsylvania); Hon. DHumLitt (Hunter Coll., Rush Univ., Johns Hopkins 2003), Hon. DrIur (Toronto) 2004; numerous awards and distinctions including American Acad. of Nursing Living Legend 1998, NY Univ. Pres.'s Medal 1998, American Nurses Foundation Nightingale Lamp Award 2002. *Publications:* numerous books including Nursing Leadership: Global Strategies (ed.) 1990, Essays in Nursing Leadership 2000, When Care Becomes a Burden 2001, and over 100 articles on nursing and health policy. *Leisure interests:* theatre, opera, art, sailing, snorkeling, gardening. *Address:* 200 Central Park South, Apartment 12E, New York, NY 10019-1415, USA (home).

FAGIOLO, Silvio, LLB; Italian diplomat and academic; *Professor of International Relations, Libera Università Internazionale degli Studi Sociali Guido Carli in Roma;* b. 15 July 1938, Rome; m. Margret Klauth; two c.; ed Univ. La Sapienza, Rome; joined diplomatic service 1969; foreign missions to Moscow, USSR 1972–76, Detroit, USA 1976–79, Bonn, W Germany 1982–86; Deputy Chief Italian Embassy, Washington, DC 1991–95; Amb. to Germany 2001; Adviser for European and Security Affairs, Ministry of Foreign Affairs, Head of Cabinet 1997–2000; mem. EU Group that organized Intergovernmental Conf. that led to Maastricht Treaty; Personal Rep. of Italian Foreign Minister at Intergovernmental Confs. that led to Treaty of Amsterdam 1996, Treaty of Nice 2002; Perm. Rep. to EU 2001; currently mem. Faculty of Political Science and Prof. of Int. Relations, Libera Università Internazionale degli Studi Sociali Guido Carli in Roma. *Publications:* I gruppi di pressione in URSS 1977, L'operaio americano 1980, La Russia di Gorbaciov 1987, La pace fredda 1998. *Leisure interests:* sports, music. *Address:* Faculty of Political Science, Libera Università Internazionale degli Studi Sociali Guido Carli in Roma, Viale Pola 12, 00198 Rome (office); Via Casolvecchio Sicuro 4, 00133 Rome, Italy (home). *Telephone:* (6) 45472990 (home). *Fax:* (6) 45472990 (home). *E-mail:* silviofagiolo@hotmail.com (home). *Website:* www.luiss.it/scienzepolitiche (office).

FAHEY, Hon. John Joseph, AC; Australian politician and lawyer; b. 10 Jan. 1945, New Zealand; s. of Stephen Fahey and Annie Fahey; m. Colleen McGurran 1968; one s. two d.; ed St Anthony's Convent, Picton and Chevalier Coll. Bowral, Sydney Univ. Law Extension; mem. Parl. of NSW 1984–95; Minister for Industrial Relations and Employment and Minister Assisting Premier of NSW 1988–90; Minister for Industrial Relations, Further Educ., Training and Employment, NSW 1990–92; Premier and Treas. of NSW 1992; Premier and Minister for Econ. Devt of NSW 1993–95; Fed. mem. for Macarthur and Minister for Finance 1996–2001, for Admin. 1997–2001; consultant, adviser, dir 2002–; Chair. Sydney 2000 Olympic Bid Co. 1992–93. *Leisure interest:* keen sports follower. *Address:* c/o J.P. Morgan Australia Ltd, Level 26, Grosvenor Place, 225 George Street, Sydney, NSW (office); Ashford, 39 Hurlingham Avenue, Burradoo, NSW 2576, Australia (home). *Telephone:* (2) 9220-1649 (office). *Fax:* (2) 4861-4113 (office). *E-mail:* faheyj@bigpond.com (home).

FAHIM, Makhdoom Amin; Pakistani politician; b. Hala Taluka; Vice-Chair. Pakistan People's Party (PPP), Leader PPP Parliamentarians faction to contest elections 2002, currently Leader Parl. Group; Acting Chair. Alliance for the Restoration of Democracy 2003, currently Chair. *Address:* Pakistan People's Party (PPP), 8, St 19, F-8/2, Islamabad (office); 11-A, 2nd Sun Set Street, DHA, Karachi, Pakistan (home). *Telephone:* (51) 2255264 (office). *Fax:*

(51) 2282741 (office). *E-mail:* csppp@comsats.net.pk (office). *Website:* www.ppp.org.pk (office).

FAHIM, Sulaiman al-, MBA, PhD; United Arab Emirates business executive; *CEO, Hydra Properties;* b. 1978; ed American Univ., Washington, DC; Founder and CEO Hydra Properties (real estate co.) 2005–; Rep., Abu Dhabi United Group for Devt and Investment (sovereign wealth fund); owner of Manchester City Football Club; creator and host Hydra Executives (reality TV series) 2008–; Pres. UAE Chess Asscn; ranked by Arabian Business Magazine amongst 100 Most Powerful Arabs 2006, Visionary Award, Middle East CEO magazine 2007. *Address:* Hydra Properties, Banyas Road, Essa Saleh Al Gurg Office Tower, 6th Floor, United Arab Emirates (office). *Telephone:* (4) 2294499 (office). *Fax:* (4) 2294447 (office). *E-mail:* ceo@hydraproperties.com (office). *Website:* www.hydraproperties.com (office).

FAHIM KHAN, Marshal Mohammad Qassim; Afghan politician and fmr guerrilla leader; b. 1957, Omarz Dist, Panjshir Valley; m.; three c.; ed Kabul Islamic Inst., Kabul Univ.; qualified doctor; joined troops fighting USSR occupation forces 1979–89; joined Northern Alliance (NA), led NA forces into Kabul 1992, Head of Intelligence, Chief of Staff, Leader 2001–02; Vice-Pres. and Minister of Defence, Afghan Interim Authority Dec. 2001–June 2002, Afghan Transitional Authority 2002–04; currently mem. Meshrano Jirga (upper house of parl.) and Sr Adviser to Pres. Karzai. *Address:* c/o Office of the President, Gul Khana Palace, Presidential Palace, Kabul, Afghanistan (office).

FAHIYE, Husayn Elabe; Somali politician; Minister of Nat. Planning 2000–07, of Human Rights 2004–07, of Foreign Affairs 2007, of Trade, Industry and Tourism 2008–. *Address:* Ministry of Trade, Industry and Tourism, Mogadishu, Somalia.

FAHMY, M. Nabil, BSc, MA; Egyptian diplomatist; *Ambassador to USA;* m. Mrs M. Nabil Fahmy (née Nermin); one s. two d.; ed American Univ., Cairo; mem. Cabinet of Sec. of Pres. for External Communications 1974; Political Officer Cabinet of Vice-Pres. 1975–76; mem. Cabinet, Ministry of Foreign Affairs 1976–78; Second Sec. Mission to UN for Conf. on Disarmament 1978–82, First Sec. then Counsellor to UN 1986–91; Sr Disarmament Official, Dept for Int. Orgs, Ministry of Foreign Affairs 1991, Counsellor –1995; Amb. to Japan 1997–99, to USA 1999–; mem. UN Sec.-Gen.'s Advisory Bd on Disarmament Matters 1999–. *Publications include:* numerous publs on nuclear proliferation. *Address:* Embassy of Egypt, 3521 International Court, NW, Washington, DC 20008, USA (office). *Telephone:* (202) 895-5400 (office). *Fax:* (202) 244-4319 (office). *E-mail:* embassy@egyptembassy.net (office). *Website:* www.egyptembassy.net (office).

FAHRHOLZ, Bernd, LLB; German banking executive; joined Dresdner Bank as legal adviser 1977, with Domestic Corp. Customer Div. 1985–89, Man. Corp. Finance Div. 1989, later Co-Head, Int. Activities, Sr Gen. Man. 1996, Head of Global Finance, Investment Banking Div. 1997, mem. Bd of Man. Dirs 1998–2003, Chair. 2000–01, also Man. Dir Corp. Centre, Corp. Communications, Econs, Gen. Secr., Group Devt, Group Strategy, Human Resources and Legal Services, CEO 2000–03 (after acquisition of Dresdner Bank by Allianz AG forming Allianz-Dresdner AG). *Address:* c/o Allianz-Dresdner AG, Königinstrasse 28, 80802 Munich, Germany (office).

FAHRNI, Fritz, PhD; Swiss professor and business executive; *Chairman of the Board, Institut für Technologiemanagement (ITEM-HSG), Universität St Gallen;* b. 7 Sept. 1942; two d.; ed Swiss Fed. Inst. of Tech. (ETH), Zürich, Ill. Inst. of Tech., Chicago and Harvard Business School; research worker, Ill. Inst. of Tech., NASA 1967–70; Team Leader, Research, Eng, Devt and Production Processes, CIBA-GEIGY 1971–76; Head, Research and Devt Gas Turbine Dept Sulzer Brothers 1976–80, Head, Gas Turbine Dept 1980–82, Head, Textile Machinery Group 1982–87, Pres. and CEO Sulzer Corpn 1988–99; Chair. Bd, Universität St Gallen, Institut für Technologiemanagement (ITEM-HSG) 1999–, Prof. of Practice in Tech. Man. and Entrepreneurship, ETH Zürich and Universität St Gallen 2000–; Int. Entrepreneurial Leadership Award, Ill. Inst. of Tech. 2000; several times winner of "Entrepreneur of the Month" and "E of the Year" awards, Switzerland. *Leisure interests:* sport, mountaineering, reading, music, garden. *Address:* Universität St Gallen, Institut für Technologiemanagement, Dufourstrasse 40a, 9000 St Gallen (office); ETH – Swiss Federal Institute of Technology, D-MTEC, Kreuzplatz 5, 8032 Zürich, Switzerland (office). *Telephone:* (71) 2247201 (office); (1) 3902595 (home). *Fax:* (71) 2247321 (office). *E-mail:* fritz.fahrni@unisg.ch (office); ffahrni@ethz.ch (office). *Website:* www.item.unisg.ch (office); www.tmu.ethz.ch (office).

FAINI, Riccardo, PhD; Italian economist and international organization official; *Professor of Political Economy, University of Rome Tor Vergata;* b. 12 April 1957, Lausanne, Switzerland; m. Lauri Faini; three s.; ed Laurea Università Bocconi, Massachusetts Inst. of Tech.; Lecturer, Univ. of Essex, UK 1980–83; Researcher, Univ. of Venezia 1983–85; Assoc. Prof., Bologna Center of Johns Hopkins Univ. 1988–90; Prof. of Econs, Univ. of Brescia 1990–; currently Prof. of Political Economy, Univ. of Rome Tor Vergata; Economist, World Bank Trade Policy Div. 1985–88; Exec. Dir IMF 1998–2001; apptd Dir-Gen. Ministry of the Economy and Finance 2000; Research Fellow Human Resources and Int. Trade Programs, Centre for Econ. and Policy Research; Research Dir Centro Studi Luca d'Agliano; Research Fellow, IZA research inst. 2001–. *Publications:* Non-Traded Inputs and Increasing Returns 1999, Trade and Migration: The Controversies and the Evidence (co-ed.) 1999, Labour Markets, Poverty and Development (co-ed.). *Leisure interests:* Latin American literature, tennis. *Address:* Università di Roma Due Tor Vergata – IZA and CEPR, Centro Studi Luca D'Agliano, via Sarfatti 25, 20136 Milano, Italy. *Telephone:* (02) 58363390 (office). *Fax:* (02) 58363399 (office). *E-mail:* centro.dagliano@uni-bocconi.it (office).

FAINSILBER, Adrien, DPLG; French architect and urban designer; b. 15 June 1932, Le Nouvion; s. of Fanny Moscovici and Sigismond Fainsilber; m. Julia Berg 1961; two s. one d.; ed Ecole Nationale Supérieure des Beaux Arts; architect Univ. of Villetaneuse 1969–70, Univ. of Tech. of Compiègne 1973, Evry Hosp. 1980, La Géode, Parc de la Villette, Paris 1984, Cité of Science and Industry, Paris 1985, Water Treatment Plant, Valenton 1987, Museum of Beaux Arts, Clermont-Ferrand 1992, Town Hall, La Flèche 1994, HQ Unedic, Paris 1994, master plan and housing for Zac Richter, Port Marianne, Montpellier 1995, Montsouris Mutual Inst. Psychiatric Centre for Adolescents, Paris 1996, Museum of Modern and Contemporary Art, Strasbourg 1997, Children's Hosp., Purpan, Toulouse 1998, Courthouse Avignon 2000, Municipal Library, Marseille 2003; county seat for Haut-Rhin 2004; mem. Int. Acad. of Architecture; Chevalier Légion d'honneur 1987, Officier des Arts et des Lettres 1997Bronze Medal Soc. d'Encouragement à l'Art et à l'Industrie 1973, Silver Medal Acad. of Architecture 1986, U.I.A. Prix Auguste Perret 1990, Prix de Construction Metallique 2004. *Publications:* La Virtualité de l'Espace: Projets et Architecture 1962–1988, Adrien Fainsilber & Associés 1986–2002. *Leisure interests:* swimming, windsurfing, travel. *Address:* 7 rue Salvador Allende, 92000 Nanterre (office); 9 cité de l'Alma, 75007 Paris, France (home). *Telephone:* 1-55-69-36-20 (office); 1-45-51-34-33 (home). *Fax:* 1-55-69-36-21 (office). *E-mail:* agence@fainsilber.com (office). *Website:* www.fainsilber.com (office).

FAIRBANK, Richard (Rich) D., BEcons, MBA; American banking executive; *Chairman and CEO, Capital One Financial Corporation;* b. 1950, Northampton, Mass; m.; four c.; ed Stanford Univ., Stanford Grad. School of Business; consultant, Strategic Planning Assocs (later Mercer Management) 1981–87; Chair. and CEO Capital One Financial Corpn 1994–; mem. US Region Bd of Dirs MasterCard 1995–2004 (Chair. 2002–04), mem. MasterCard International Global Bd of Dirs 2004–; Washingtonian Magazine Business Leader of the Year, Institutional Investor magazine Best CEO in specialty finance, American Banker magazine Banker of the Year Award 2006. *Address:* Capital One Financial Corporation, 1680 Capital One Drive, McLean, VA 22102-3407, USA (office). *Telephone:* (703) 720-1000 (office). *Fax:* (703) 720-2306 (office). *E-mail:* info@capitalone.com (office). *Website:* www.capitalone.com (office).

FAIRCLOUGH, Anthony John, CMG, MA, FRSA; British environmental protection/sustainable development consultant; b. 30 Aug. 1924, Birmingham; s. of Wilfrid Fairclough and Lillian Anne Fairclough (née Townshend); m. Patricia Monks 1957; two s.; ed St Philip's Grammar School, Birmingham and St Catharine's Coll., Cambridge; Ministry of Aircraft Production and Ministry of Supply 1944–48; Colonial Office 1948–64; Sec. Nyasaland Comm. of Inquiry 1959; Private Sec. to Minister of State for Commonwealth Relations and for the Colonies 1963–64; Head, Pacific and Indian Ocean Dept, Commonwealth Office 1964–68; Head, W Indian Dept, FCO 1968–70; Head, New Towns 1 Div., Dept of Environment 1970–72, Under-Sec., Head of Planning, Minerals and Countryside Directorate 1973–74; Dir Cen. Unit on Environmental Pollution 1974–78; Dir Int. Transport, Dept of Transport 1978–81; Dir for the Environment, Comm. of the EC 1981–85; Acting Dir-Gen. for the Environment, Consumer Protection and Nuclear Safety, Comm. of the European Communities 1985–86, Deputy Dir-Gen. for Devt, 1986–89, Special Adviser 1989–94, Hon. Dir-Gen. European Comm. 1989–; Dir (later Sr Adviser) Environmental Resources Man. 1989–97; Capacity 21 Adviser UNDP 1992–; consultant on sustainable devt and environmental protection. *Publications:* numerous papers on sustainable devt, environmental policy and man., and devt policy. *Leisure interests:* travel, gardening, reading, photography. *Address:* 6 Cumberland Road, Kew, Richmond, Surrey, TW9 3HQ, England (home); Apt 12, Résidence Balderic, 32 Quai aux Briques, 1000 Brussels, Belgium (home). *Telephone:* (20) 8940-6999 (Richmond) (home). *E-mail:* tony.fairclough@googlemail.com (home).

FAIREY, Michael Edward, A.C.I.B.; British banker; *Deputy Group Chief Executive, Lloyds TSB Group PLC;* b. 17 June 1948, Louth, Lincs.; s. of Douglas Fairey and Marjorie Fairey; m. Patricia Ann Dolby 1973; two s.; ed King Edward VI Grammar School; Asst Dir, Watford Group, Barclays Bank 1967–86, Operations Dir Barclaycard 1986–88, Exec. Dir Barclays Card Services 1988–92; Dir Retail Credit and Group Credit Dir, TSB Group 1992, Group Dir Credit Operations 1993–96, Information Tech. and Operations Dir 1996–97, Group Dir, Cen. Services, Lloyds TSB Group 1997–98, Deputy Group Chief Exec. 1998–. *Leisure interests:* tennis, opera, football. *Address:* Lloyds TSB Group PLC, 25 Gresham Street, London, EC2V 7HN (office); Churchfields House, Hitchin Road, Codicote, Herts., SG4 8TH, England (home). *Telephone:* (20) 7356-1410 (office); (1438) 821710 (home). *Fax:* (20) 7356-2080 (office); (1438) 821079 (home). *E-mail:* mike.fairey@lloydstsb.co.uk (office).

FAIRHEAD, Rona, BL, MBA; British business executive; *Chief Executive, Financial Times Group;* m. Tom Fairhead; three c.; ed Univ. of Cambridge, Harvard Business School, USA; worked for Bain & Co. and Morgan Stanley; sr exec. in aerospace industry, working for Bombardier/Shorts Aerospace and British Aerospace –1995; Exec. Vice-Pres. Strategy and Group Financial Control and mem. Exec. Bd ICI PLC 1995–2001; Deputy Finance Dir Pearson 2001–02, Chief Financial Officer 2002–06, Chief Exec. Financial Times Group 2006–, mem. Pearson Bd and Pearson Man. Cttee; Chair. Interactive Data Corpn 2007–; Dir (non-exec.) HSBC Holdings plc 2004–. *Address:* The Financial Times Group, One Southwark Bridge, London, SE1 9HL, England (office). *Telephone:* (20) 7873-3000 (office). *Website:* www.ft.com (office).

FAIRWEATHER, Sir Patrick (Stanislaus), KCMG; British diplomatist; b. 17 June 1936; s. of John George Fairweather and Dorothy Jane Fairweather (née Boanus); m. Maria Merica 1962; two d.; ed Ottershaw School, Surrey and Trinity Coll. Cambridge; entered FCO 1965; served Rome 1966–69, Paris 1970–73, Vientiane 1975–76, First Sec., UK Representation to EEC, Brussels 1976–78; Amb. to Angola 1985–87; Asst Under-Sec. of State, FCO 1987–90, Deputy Under-Sec. of State 1990–92; Amb. to Italy and (non-resident) to Albania 1992–96; retd from HM Diplomatic Service 1996; Sr Adviser, Schroders 1996–; Dir The Butrint Foundation 1997–. *Leisure interests:* travel, gardening, photography, sailing. *Address:* c/o The Butrint Foundation, 14 St James's Place, London, SW1A 1NP, England.

FAISAL, Ameen; Maldivian politician; *Minister of Defence and National Security;* mem. Maldivian Democratic Party (MDP), mem. MDP Nat. Council and Pres. of MDP Male' Dhaairaa constituency 2007–08; Shadow Defence Minister –2008; Minister of Defence and Nat. Security 2008–. *Address:* Ministry of Defence and National Security, Ameer Ahmed Magu, Malé 20126, Maldives (office). *Telephone:* 3322607 (office). *Fax:* 3332689 (office). *E-mail:* admin@defence.gov.mv (office). *Website:* www.defence.gov.mv (office).

FAITHFULL, Marianne; British singer; b. 29 Dec. 1946, Ormskirk, Lancs.; d. of Glynn Faithfull and Eva Faithfull; m. 1st John Dunbar; one s.; m. 2nd Ben Brierley; m. 3rd Giorgio della Terza; made first recording (As Tears Go By) aged 17. *Films:* I'll Never Forget Whatsisname 1967, Girl on a Motorcycle 1968, Hamlet 1969, Lucifer Rising 1972, Ghost Story 1974, Assault on Agathon 1975, When Pigs Fly 1993, The Turn of the Screw 1994, Shopping 1994, Moondance 1995, Crimetime 1996, Intimacy 2001, Far From China 2001, Alone in the Dark 2003, A Letter to True 2003, Nord-Plage 2004, Paris, je t'aime 2006, Marie Antoinette 2006, Irina Palm 2007. *Television:* Anna 1967, The Door of Opportunity 1970, The Stronger 1971. *Stage appearances:* Three Sisters (London) 1967, Seven Deadly Sins (St Ann's Cathedral, New York) 1990, The Threepenny Opera (Gate Theatre, Dublin) 1992. *Recordings include:* albums: Come My Way 1965, Marianne Faithfull 1965, Go Away From My World 1966, North Country Maid 1966, Faithfull Forever 1966, Love in a Mist 1967, Dreaming My Dreams 1977, Faithless (with the Grease Band) 1978, Broken English 1979, Dangerous Acquaintances 1981, A Child's Adventure 1983, Summer Nights 1984, Music for the Millions 1985, Strange Weather 1987, Rich Kid Blues 1988, Blazing Away 1990, A Secret Life 1995, 20th Century Blues 1997, The Seven Deadly Sins 1998, Vagabond Ways 1999, Stranger On Earth 2001, Kissin' Time 2002, Before the Poison 2004, Easy Come Easy Go 2009. *Publications:* Faithfull (autobiog.) 1994, Marianne Faithfull Diaries 2002. *E-mail:* assistante@mac.com (office). *Website:* www.mariannefaithfull.org.uk.

FAIVRE d'ARCIER, Bernard, LèsL; French civil servant and culture consultant; *CEO, BFA-Conseil;* b. 12 July 1944, Albertville; s. of Guy Faivre d'Arcier and Geneviève Teilhard de Chazelles; m. 1st Sylvie Dumont 1966; one s.; m. 2nd Madeleine Lévy 1991; ed Hautes études commerciales, Inst. d'études politiques and Ecole nat. d'admin; Civil Admin. Ministry of Culture 1972–79; Dir Festival d'Avignon 1979–84, Artistic Dir 1992–2003; Tech. Adviser to the Prime Minister's Cabinet 1984–86; Pres. la SEPT (TV Channel) 1986; Consultant, UNESCO 1987–88; Adviser to the Pres. of the Nat. Ass. 1988; Head of Dept of Theatre, Ministry of Educ. and Culture 1992–; Dir Nat. Centre for Theatre 1992; CEO BFA-Conseil (Man. Consultants); Commdr des Arts et des Lettres, Officier, Ordre du Mérite, Chevalier, Légion d'honneur. *Leisure interests:* art, theatre. *Address:* 27 rue Michel Le Comte, 75003 Paris, France (home). *Telephone:* 1-42-78-72-13 (home). *E-mail:* bernard.faivre-darcier@orange.fr.

FAIZULLAEV, Alisher Omonullaevich, PhD; Uzbekistan diplomatist and social scientist; *First Vice-Rector, University of World Economy and Diplomacy;* b. 10 Jan. 1957, Tashkent; s. of Omonulla Faizullaev and Nasiba Ashrapkhanova; m. Shakhnoz Faizullaeva; two s. two d.; ed Tashkent State Univ. and Inst. of Psychology, USSR Acad. of Sciences, Moscow; Lecturer, Uzbekistan Acad. of Sciences, Tashkent 1979–80, Sr Lecturer 1983–86; Visiting Fellow, Inst. of Psychology, USSR Acad. of Sciences 1986–87; Sr Lecturer, Tashkent State Univ. 1987–88; Head of Dept, Exec. Training Inst., Tashkent 1988–91; Intern, City Council of San Diego, CA 1989; Head of Dept, Inst. of Political Sciences and Man., Tashkent 1991–92; Distinguished Visiting Scholar, Western Washington Univ., Bellingham, USA 1992; Dir Inst. of Man., Univ. of World Economy and Diplomacy, Tashkent 1992–93, currently First Vice-Rector; Consultant on Political Affairs, then Chief Consultant on Int. Affairs and Foreign Econ. Relations, Office of the Pres. of Uzbekistan 1993–94; Deputy Minister of Foreign Affairs 1994–95; Amb. to Belgium and Head of Missions to EU and Euro-Atlantic Partnership Council/NATO 1995–98, concurrently Amb. to the Netherlands and Luxembourg with residence in Brussels 1997–98; State Adviser to Pres. of Uzbekistan on Int. Affairs and Foreign Econ. Relations 1998–99; First Deputy Minister of Foreign Affairs Feb.–Dec. 1999; Amb. to UK 1999–2003; Dir Centre for Political Studies, Tashkent 2003–; Visiting Scholar, Centre of Int. Studies and Visiting Fellow, Jesus Coll., Cambridge 2007; USSR Young Social Scientists Prize 1987. *Publications:* Motivational Self-Regulation of Personality (in Russian) 1987, Human Being, Politics, Management (in Russian and Uzbek) 1995; several papers on behavioural, social and political sciences in learned journals. *Leisure interests:* tennis, fencing. *Address:* University of World Economy and Diplomacy, Buyuk Ipak Yuli 54, Tashkent 100137, Uzbekistan (office). *Telephone:* (71) 2676769 (office). *Fax:* (71) 2670900 (office). *E-mail:* uwed@uwed.freenet.uz (office). *Website:* uwed.freenet.uz (office).

FAIZULLAYEV, Ravshanbek; Uzbekistan politician; First Deputy Prime Minister 2004–05. *Address:* c/o Office of the Cabinet of Ministers, Government House, 100008 Tashkent, Uzbekistan (office). *Telephone:* (71) 139-82-95 (office). *Fax:* (71) 139-86-01 (office).

FAKHFAKH, Mokhtar, BS; Tunisian banker; b. 10 Aug. 1930, Sfax; s. of Ahmed B. Abdessalem Fakhfakh and Fatouma Hamouda; m. Samira Fakhfakh; one s. one d.; ed law studies; Pres. and Gen. Man. Soc. Hotelière et Touristique de Tunisie 1961–67; Dir of Commerce, Ministry of Finance and Commerce 1967–69; Pres. and Gen. Man. Banque du Sud 1969–71; Gen. Man. Banque de Développement Economique de Tunisie 1971–78; Pres. and Gen. Man. Cie Financière Immobilière et Touristique de Tunisie 1978–80, Banque Int. Arabe de Tunisie 1980, now Pres.; African Banker of Year 1994; Commdr Ordre de la République. *Address:* Banque International Arabe de Tunisie, 70–72 Avenue Habib Bourguiba, BP 520, 1080 Tunis, Tunisia. *Telephone:* (1) 340-733. *Fax:* (1) 340-680. *E-mail:* abderrazak.lahiani@biat.com.tn (office). *Website:* www.biat.com.tn (office).

FAKHR, Maj.-Gen. Ahmed Ismail, BA, MA, MBA; Egyptian national security expert and strategic analyst; b. 5 April 1931, Cairo; m. Bahiga Bahgat Helmy 1956; two s.; ed Nat. Defence Coll. Cairo, air defence studies in Moscow, Royal Coll. of Defence Studies, London and Nat. Defence Univ. Washington, DC; Dir Nat. Defence Coll. Cairo 1980–82, Nasser Higher Mil. Acad. Cairo 1982–84; Ed.-in-Chief, Defence Magazine, Al-Ahram Asscn Cairo 1985; Adviser on Foreign Aid to Prime Minister 1986–89; Rep. of UNIMEG (pvt. business consortium), Moscow 1990; fmr Dir Nat. Center for Middle East Studies; elected Chair. of local people's council, Cairo Governate; mem. Egyptian del. to Madrid Peace Conf. 1992; other government appointments; Fellowship Royal Coll. of Defense Studies, London 1987; Mil. Medal and other decorations. *Publications:* Defence of Egypt (classified) 1981, Arms Control Series 1992, Egypt and the 21st Century 1994, Conflict: Prevention and Resolution 1994, The Future of the Military in Egypt 1995, U.S.–Egyptian Relations 1995, The Middle East: Technological Edge 1995. *Leisure interests:* reading on int. affairs and nat. security, classical music, ballet. *Address:* 27 Dr Khalil Abdel Khalek Street, Heliopolis, Cairo, Egypt. *Telephone:* 2454551.

FAKI, Moussa Mahamat; Chadian politician; *Minister of Foreign Affairs;* b. 21 June 1960; early career as Prof. of Law, Chad Univ.; Dir-Gen. Nat. Sugar Soc. 1996–99; Minister of Transport and Public Works 2002; Prime Minister of Chad 2003–05; Minister of Foreign Affairs 2008–. *Address:* Ministry of Foreign Affairs, BP 746, N'Djamena, Chad (office). *Telephone:* 51-80-50 (office). *Fax:* 51-45-85 (office).

FALCAM, Leo A.; Micronesian fmr head of state; b. 20 Nov. 1935; fmr Vice-Pres. of Micronesia, Pres. 1999–2003. *Address:* c/o Office of the President, PO Box PS-53, Palikir, Pohnpei, Eastern Caroline Islands, FM 96941, Micronesia (office). *Telephone:* 320-2228 (office). *Fax:* 320-2785 (office).

FALCO, Edith (Edie); American actress; b. 5 July 1963, Brooklyn, NY; d. of Frank Falco and Judith Loney; one adopted s.; ed State Univ. of NY at Purchase. *Television includes:* The Sunshine Boys (film) 1995, Oz (series) 1997–99; The Sopranos (series – Emmy Award for Outstanding Lead Actress in A Drama Series 2000, 2003, Golden Globe Award for Best Performance by an Actress in a Drama Series 2000, SAG Award for Outstanding Performance by a Female Actor in a Drama Series 2000, 2008) 1999–2007, Jenifer (film) 2001, Fargo (film) 2003. *Films include:* The Unbelievable Truth 1989, Trust 1990, Laws of Gravity 1992, Time Expired 1992, Bullets Over Broadway 1994, Rift 1995, The Addition 1995, Breathing Room 1996, Hurricane 1997, Private Parts 1997, Cop Land 1997, Trouble on the Corner 1997, Cost of Living 1997, A Price above Rubies 1998, Judy Berlin 1999, Stringer 1999, Random Hearts 1999, Overnight Sensation 2000, Death of a Dog 2000, Sunshine State 2002, Family of the Year 2004, The Girl from Monday 2005, The Great New Wonderful 2005, The Quiet 2005, Freedomland 2006. *Plays:* 'night, Mother 2005. *Address:* c/o ICM, 825 Eighth Avenue, New York, NY 10019, USA (office). *Telephone:* (212) 556-5600.

FALCO, Randel (Randy) E., MBA; American business executive; *Chairman and CEO, AOL LLC;* m. Susan; three c.; ed Iona Coll.; joined NBC 1975, several positions in Finance, Tech. Operations, Corp. Strategic Planning, Vice-Pres. Finance and Admin, NBC Sports 1986–91, Pres. Broadcast and Network Operations Div., NBC 1993–98, COO Olympics, Barcelona Olympics 1992, Atlanta Olympics 1996, Sydney Olympics 2000, Salt Lake City Olympics 2002, Pres. NBC TV Network 1998–2003, Group Pres. 2003–04, Pres. NBC Universal TV Networks Group 2004–06; Chair. and CEO AOL LLC (div. of Time Warner) 2006–; mem. Bd of Dirs Ronald McDonald House; Dr hc (Iona Coll.) 2001; six Emmy Awards. *Address:* AOL LLC, 22000 AOL Way, Dulles, VA 20166, USA (office). *Telephone:* (703) 265-1000 (office). *Fax:* (703) 433-7283 (office). *Website:* www.corp.aol.com (office).

FALCONER OF THOROTON, Baron (Life Peer), cr. 1997, of Thoroton in the County of Nottinghamshire; **Charles Leslie Falconer,** QC; British lawyer and politician; b. 19 Nov. 1951; s. of the late John Falconer and Anne Falconer; m. Marianna Hildyard 1985; three s. one d.; ed Trinity Coll., Glenalmond, Queen's Coll., Cambridge; called to the Bar 1974, took silk 1991; Solicitor-Gen. 1997–98; Minister of State Cabinet Office 1998–2001; Minister with responsibility for Millennium Dome 1998–2001; Minister of State for Housing and Planning 2001, for the Criminal Justice System 2002–03; Lord Chancellor 2003–07; also Sec. of State for Justice May–June 2007; Labour. *Address:* House of Lords, London, SW1A 0PW, England (office). *Telephone:* (20) 7219-3000 (office). *Website:* www.parliament.uk (office).

FALCONES JAQUOTOT, Baldomero, MBA; Spanish business executive; *Chairman and Managing Director, Fomento de Construcciones y Contratas SA;* b. 1946, Majorca; ed IESE Business School of Univ. of Navarra; Founding Pnr, Magnum Industrial Partners; mem. Bd of Dirs MasterCard International Worldwide 1997–2007, Vice-Chair. 2001–03, Chair. 2003–07; fmr Chair. Santander Central Hispano, Seguros y Reaseguros SA; Exec. Vice-Chair. and CEO Fomento de Construcciones y Contratas SA 2007–08, Chair. and Man. Dir 2008–; mem. Bd of Dirs Unión Fenosa; fmr Dir for Spain at RWE; fmr Gen. Man. and mem. Exec. Cttee, Banco Santander Central Hispano; Chair. Plan Foundation (Spain); mem. Econ. Cttee, Fundación Albéniz. *Address:* Fomento de Construcciones y Contratas SA, Calle Federico Salmón, Madrid 28010 (office); Fomento de Construcciones y Contratas SA, Balmes 36, 08007 Barcelona, Spain (office). *Telephone:* (93) 496-4900 (office). *Fax:* (93) 487-8892 (office). *E-mail:* info@fcc.es (office). *Website:* www.fcc.es (office).

FALCONÍ BENÍTEZ, Fander, MSc, PhD; Ecuadorean economist, academic and politician; *Minister of External Relations, Trade and Integration;* ed Pontifical Catholic Univ. of Ecuador, Latin-American Faculty of Social Sciences, Autonomous Univ. of Barcelona; econs ed. for Punto de Vista newspaper 1987–91; econs analyst for Hoy newspaper 1987–89; adviser to Nat. Energy Inst. 1989–91; Tech. Asst Dept of Energy Planning and Dept for Subregional Andean Oil Integration Project, Latin American Energy Org. 1991–93; researcher, Ecuador Chamber of Commerce and Industry, Germany 1993–96; consultant to Petróleos del Ecuador SA 1995; Financial Man. Petróleos y Servicios 1995–96; Presidential adviser to Nat. Telecommunications Council 1996; UNDP adviser, Ministry of the Environment 2001; adviser to Fundación Natura 2001–02; Prof., Latin-American Faculty of Social Sciences 2001–; Prof. of Agricultural Econs and Rural Devt, Central Univ. of Ecuador 2001–04; Prof., Nat. Polytechnic School 2002–04; Nat. Sec. for Planning and Devt 2007–08; Minister of External Relations, Trade and Integration 2008–; Visiting Prof., San Simón Univ. 2003, Centro Bartolomé de las Casas 2004, Univ. of Guadalajara, Mexico 2004. *Address:* Ministry of External Relations, Trade and Integration, Avda 10 de Agosto y Carrión, Quito, Ecuador (office). *Telephone:* (2) 299-3200 (office). *Fax:* (2) 256-4873 (office). *E-mail:* webmast@mmrree.gov.ec (office). *Website:* www.mmrree.gov.ec (office).

FALDO, Nicholas (Nick) Alexander, MBE; British professional golfer, golf course designer and television commentator; b. 18 July 1957, Welwyn Garden City; m. 1st Melanie Faldo (divorced); m. 2nd Gill Faldo 1986 (divorced); one s. two d.; m. 3rd Valerie Bercher; one d.; ed Sir Francis Osborne School, Welwyn Garden City; won England Boys' Int. 1974, England Youth Int. 1975, Herts. Co. Championship, Berkshire Trophy, Scrutton Jug, S African Golf Union Special Stroke Championship, was Co. Champion of Champions, mem. GB Commonwealth team, Sr England Int. 1975–; became professional 1976; won Skol Lager Int., Rookie of the Year (Best British Newcomer) 1977, Colgate PGA Championship 1978, 1980, 1981, five titles on PGA European Tour, Golf Writers' Asscn Trophy and Harry Vardon Trophy 1983, Open Championship, Muirfield 1987, French Open and Volvo Masters, Valderrama 1988, Masters, Augusta, Ga, USA 1989, French Open 1989, US Masters 1989, 1990, 1996, Open Championship, St Andrew's 1990, Irish Open 1991, 1992, 1993, Open Championship, Muirfield 1992, Toyota World Match Play Championship 1992, Scandinavian Masters 1992, European Open 1992, Johnnie Walker World Championship 1992, (seven tournament victories 1992), Alfred Dunhill Belgian Open 1994, Doral Ryder Open, USA 1995; World No. 1 1992–94, Johnnie Walker Asian Classic 1993, Los Angeles Open, USA 1997, World Cup 1998; involved in Faldo Design, an int. golf course architectural co. 1991–; named Capt. European Ryder Cup team beginning 2008; lead analyst for Golf Channel and CBS TV PGA tour coverage; BBC Sports Personality of the Year 1989, PGA Award for Outstanding Services to Golf 2003. *Publications:* In Search of Perfection (with Bruce Critchley) 1995, Faldo – A Swing for Life 1995, Life Swings: The Autobiography 2004. *Leisure interests:* fly fishing, helicopter flying, golf course design. *Address:* c/o Faldo Enterprises, 18-20 Sheet Street, Windsor, Berks., SL4 1BG, England (office). *Telephone:* (1753) 829711 (office). *Fax:* (1753) 829712 (office). *Website:* www.nickfaldo.com (office).

FALIK, Yuri Aleksandrovich; Russian composer and conductor; b. 30 July 1936, Odessa; s. of Aleksander Yefimovich Falik and Yevgeniya Mikhailovna Bochko; m. Valentina Alexandrovna Papkova; one s. one d.; ed Odessa Specialized School, Leningrad State Conservatory as cellist (teachers A. Shtrimer and M. Rostropovich), as composer (B. Arapov); teacher, Leningrad (now St Petersburg) Conservatory 1965–88, Prof. of Composition and Instrumentation 1988–; toured as conductor with orchestras in Russia and USA; First Prize, Int. Cellists Competition Helsinki 1962, Merited Worker of Arts of Russia 1981, People's Artist of Russia 2002. *Compositions:* for musical theatre: Orestea (choreographic tragedy) 1968, Scapin Antics (opera) 1981; comic opera: Plutin Skapena 1984; ballet: Oresteya 1968; for symphony orchestra: Symphony No. 1 1963, No. 2 (Kaddish) 1993, Light Symphony 1971, Concertos 1967, 1977, Mass over Igor Stravinsky 1975, Symphonietta for strings 1984, Canto in memoria: Symphony No. 3 2005; for instruments with orchestra: Concertino for oboe 1961, Violin Concerto 1971, Chamber Concerto for three flutes 1983, Concertino for bassoon 1987, Concerto della Passione for cello 1988, Lyrical Concertino for viola and orchestra 2005; vocal-symphony works: Five Poems by Anna Akhmatova for soprano and chamber orchestra 1978, Ringaday for mezzo-soprano and orchestra 1986, Polly and Dinosaurs (musical fairy-tale over Geraldine Freund) 1989, Mass 1996; works for choir a cappella, including Liturgy Chants 1992; chamber ensembles, including, "Buffoons", a Concerto for Winds and Percussion 1966, Eight Quartets 1955–2001, Brass quintet 2003; romances, instrumental pieces; Four Concertos for chorus a capella 1979–98, Elegies: Concerto for soprano solo and chorus a capella 2001, Miraculous images, cycle for chorus a capella 2004. *Address:* Finlyandsky prospekt 1, Apt 54, 194044 St Petersburg, Russia (home). *Telephone:* (812) 542-63-06 (home). *Fax:* (812) 311-58-11 (home). *E-mail:* afalik2000@mail.ru (home).

FALISE, Michel, DenD, DèsScEcon; French economist and academic; b. 11 March 1931, Marcinelle; s. of A. Falise and L. Falise; m. Marie-Françoise de Gheldere 1957; three s. three d.; ed Facultés Universitaires de Namur, Univ. Catholique de Louvain, Harvard Univ., USA; Econ. Adviser, Banque de Bruxelles 1958–60; Prof., Univ. Catholique de Lille 1960, Dean, Faculty of Social Sciences 1965–79, Pres.-Rector 1979–91, Pres. Conseil Supérieur 1991–95; Deputy Mayor of Lille 1995–2002, Pres. délégué du Conseil

Communal de Concertation de la Ville de Lille 1996–; Consultant to OECD, WHO, EC and French Govt offices; Pres. Int. Fed. of Catholic Univs 1980–91, Fed. des Universités Catholiques Européennes 1991–97, Habitat et Humanisme 1994–2001; mem. Asscn Int. des Universités 1990–2000, Nat. Observatory of Poverty and Exclusion 1999–2001; Officier, Légion d'honneur, Chevalier des Palmes académiques, Commdr Ordre de la Couronne (Belgium), Officier de l'Ordre de Léopold (Belgium); Dr hc (Leuven, Belgium), (Sacred Heart, USA), (Catholique de Rio de Janeiro); Prix Asscn Française des Sciences Econs, Grand Prix de la Société Industrielle (Lille). *Publications:* La demande de monnaie 1960, L'équilibre macro-économique 1976, Une pratique chrétienne de l'économie 1985, Repères pour une éthique d'entreprise 1992, Economie et foi 1993, La démocratie participative: promesses et ambiguïtés 2003, Combattre les Exclusions 2005, Acteurs dans un Monde en Mutation 2008. *Address:* Mairie de Lille, POB 667, 59033 Lille Cedex (office); 9 allée Raoul Dufy, 59510 Hem, France (home). *Telephone:* (3) 20-49-50-05 (office); (3) 20-75-65-17 (home).

FALK, Thomas J., BCom, MSc; American business executive; *Chairman and CEO, Kimberly-Clark Corporation;* b. 1958, Waterloo, Ia; m. Karen Falk; one s.; ed Univ. of Wisconsin, Stanford Univ. Grad. School of Business; accountant, Alexander Grant & Co. –1983; joined Audit Dept, Kimberly-Clark Corpn 1983, various man. positions, including Sr Auditor 1984, Sr Financial Analyst 1986, Dir of Corp. Strategy Analysis 1987, Operations Man. for Infant Care, Beech Island, SC 1989, Vice-Pres. Operations Analysis and Control 1990, Sr Vice-Pres. of Analysis and Admin 1991–93, Group Pres., Infant and Child Care 1993–95, Group Pres. N America Consumer Products 1995–98, Group Pres. Global Tissue and Paper 1998–99, COO 1999, Pres. 1999–2002, Dir 1999–, CEO 2002–, Chair. 2003–; mem. Bd Dirs Centex Corpn; mem. Dallas Regional Advisory Bd, J. P. Morgan Chase; Nat Trustee, Boys and Girls Clubs of America. *Address:* Kimberly-Clark Corpn, PO Box 619100, Dallas TX 75261-9100, USA (office). *Telephone:* (972) 281-1478 (office). *Fax:* (972) 281-1490 (office). *E-mail:* info@kimberly-clark.com (office). *Website:* www.kimberly-clark.com (office).

FALKENGREN, Annika; Swedish business executive; *President and Group CEO, SEB AB;* m.; one c.; ed Univ. of Stockholm; joined SEB (Skandinaviska Enskilda Banken) AB as trainee in Stockholm br. 1987, Head, Corp. & Insts Div. 2001–05, Deputy CEO SEB AB 2005, Pres. and Group CEO 2005–; mem. Bd of Dirs Securitas AB; ranked by Fortune magazine amongst 50 Most Powerful Women in Business outside the US (13th) 2006, (11th) 2007, ranked by the Financial Times amongst Top 25 Businesswomen in Europe (20th) 2005, (tenth) 2006, (ninth) 2007. *Leisure interests:* golf, reading. *Address:* SEB AB, Kungsträdgårdsg 8, 106 40 Stockholm, Sweden (office). *Telephone:* (771) 62-10-00 (office). *E-mail:* seb@seb.se (office). *Website:* www.seb.se (office).

FALL, Sir Brian James Proetel, GCVO, KCMG, MA, LLM; British diplomatist (retd); *British Government Special Representative for South Caucasus;* b. 13 Dec. 1937; s. of John William Fall and Edith Juliette Fall (née Proetel); m. Delmar Alexandra Roos 1962; three d.; ed St Paul's School, Magdalen Coll. Oxford, Univ. of Michigan Law School, USA; joined HM Foreign (now Diplomatic) Service 1962, UN Dept, Foreign Office 1963, Moscow 1965, Geneva 1968, Civil Service Coll. 1970, Eastern European and Soviet Dept and Western Orgs Dept, Foreign Office 1971, New York 1975, Harvard Univ. Center for Int. Affairs 1976, Counsellor Moscow 1977–79, Head of Energy, Science and Space Dept, FCO 1979–80, Head of Eastern European and Soviet Dept, FCO 1980–81, Prin. Pvt. Sec. to Sec. of State for Foreign and Commonwealth Affairs 1981–84, Dir Cabinet Sec.-Gen. of NATO 1984–86, Asst Under-Sec. of State (Defence), FCO 1986–88, Minister, Washington 1988–89, High Commr in Canada 1989–92; Amb. to Russia (also accred to several mems of CIS) 1992–95; Prin. Lady Margaret Hall, Oxford 1995–2002; British Govt Special Rep. for S Caucasus 2002–; Chair. MC Russian Market Fund 1996–2002; Adviser, Rio Tinto 1996–; Gov. St Mary's School, Calne 1996–; Hon. Fellow, Lady Margaret Hall 2002; Hon. LLD (York Univ., Toronto) 2002. *Leisure interests:* France. *Address:* 2 St Helena Terrace, Richmond, Surrey, TW9 1NR, England (home).

FALL, Cheikh Ibrahima, MSc (Econ), MBA; Senegalese international civil servant and banker; b. 1 Oct. 1947, Louga; m. Marième Diouma Faye 1972; two s. one d.; financial analyst, Operations Dept Banque Ouest-Africaine de Développement (BOAD) 1978–79, Rural Devt and Infrastructural Operations Dept 1979–81, Officer-in-Charge of Dept 1981, Dir of Dept 1981–85, Dir Loans and Equity Dept 1985–86; Dir Office of Pres. of African Devt Bank (ADB) 1986–92, Dir Co. Programmes, S Region Dept 1992–95, Officer-in-Charge of Admin. and Gen. Services and ADB restructuring exercise 1995–96, Sec.-Gen. ADB 1996–99, 2004–06; Vice-Pres. and Corp. Sec. World Bank (IBRD) 1999–2004. *Leisure interests:* music, golf, reading. *Address:* c/o African Development Bank, rue Joseph Anoma, 01 BP 1387, Abidjan 01, Côte d'Ivoire. *Telephone:* 20-20-44-44.

FALL, François Lonseny, LLM; Guinean politician and diplomatist; *Secretary-General's Special Representative for Somalia and Head, Political Office for Somalia (UNPOS), United Nations;* b. 21 April 1949; m.; four c.; ed Conakry Univ.; First Counsellor, Embassyn in Cairo 1982–85, Abuja 1985–89, Paris 1989–90, Mission to UN, New York 1990–93; Head, Div. of Consular Affairs, Ministry of Foreign Affairs 1993, Deputy Dir of Legal and Consular Affairs 1995–96, Dir 1996–2000; Perm. Rep. to UN, New York 2000–02; Minister at the Presidency, in charge of Foreign Affairs 2002–04; Prime Minister Feb.–April 2004 (resgnd); mem. UN Cttee for the Elimination of Racial Discrimination 2000–02, Econ. Community of W African States (ECOWAS) Ministerial Cttee for Security and Mediation 2002–04; UN Sec.-Gen.'s Special Rep. for Somalia and Head, UN Political Office for Somalia (UNPOS) 2005–. *Address:* Political Office for Somalia, United Nations, PO Box 67578, Nairobi, Kenya 00200 (office). *Telephone:* (20) 7621234.

FALL, Ibrahima D., LLM, PhD; Senegalese international organization official, politician and academic; *Resident Coordinator and Resident Representative, Deputy Special Representative of the Secretary-General and Humanitarian Coordinator for Burundi, United Nations Development Programme (UNDP);* b. 1942, Tivaouane, Thies; s. of Momar Khoudia Fall and Seynabou (Diakhate) Fall; m. Déguène Fall; five c.; ed Univ. of Dakar, Inst. of Political Science, Paris, Faculty of Law, Univ. of Paris, Acad. of Int. Law, The Hague, Netherlands; Prof. of Int. Law and Int. Relations, Cheikh Anta Diop Univ., Dakar 1972–81, Dean of Faculty of Law 1975–81; Minister of Higher Educ. 1983–84, of Foreign Affairs 1984–90; Adviser, Supreme Court of Senegal; Asst Sec.-Gen. for Human Rights and Dir UN Centre for Human Rights, Geneva 1992–97; Sec.-Gen. UN World Conf. on Human Rights, Vienna 1993; Asst Gen. Sec. UN Dept of Political Affairs 1997–2000, Special Envoy of UN Sec.-Gen. to Côte d'Ivoire 2000–02, Special Rep. for the Great Lakes Region 2002–08, currently Resident Coordinator and Resident Rep., Deputy Special Rep. of UN Sec.-Gen. and UNDP Humanitarian Coordinator for Burundi, Bujumbura; consultant, UNESCO; Founding-mem. and Hon. Pres. Senegalese Asscn for African Unity; mem. African Council for Higher Educ. *Publications:* articles on int. public law, constitutional law and political science in professional journals. *Address:* UNDP Office in Burundi, Bujumbura, Burundi (office); Sicap Fenêtre Mermoz, Dakar, Senegal (home). *Telephone:* 228108 (office). *Fax:* 215213 (office). *E-mail:* ibrahima.fall@undp.org (office); fall5@un.org (office). *Website:* www.undp.org (office).

FÄLLDIN, (Nils Olof) Thorbjörn; Swedish politician and farmer; b. 24 April 1926, Högsjö; s. of Nils Johan Fälldin and Hulda Katarina Fälldin (née Olsson); m. Solveig Rut Oberg 1956; two s. one d.; ed secondary school; mem., Second Chamber of Parl. 1958–64, First Chamber 1967–70; mem. Riksdag (Parl.) 1971–85; Chair. Centre Party 1971–85; Prime Minister 1976–78, 1979–82; Chair. Bd Nordic Museum 1986–96, Swedish Telecom/Telia 1988–95, Föreningen Norden 1988–2000, Föreningsbanken AB 1992–97; The King's Medal (12th Class with Chain) 1986; Grand Cross, Order of the White Rose (Finland) 1990; Grand Officer, Royal Norwegian Order of Merit 1999; Hon. PhD (Mitthögskolan) 2001. *Leisure interests:* fishing, athletics. *Address:* Ås, 870 16 Ramvik, Sweden (home). *Telephone:* (612) 43-097 (home). *E-mail:* solveigfalldin@hotmail.com (home).

FALLON, Ivan Gregory, FRSA; Irish journalist; *CEO, UK Group, Independent News and Media PLC;* b. 26 June 1944; s. of Padraic Fallon and Dorothea Maher; m. 1st Susan Mary Lurring 1967 (divorced 1997); one s. two d.; m. 2nd Elizabeth Rees-Jones 1997; ed St Peter's Coll., Wexford, Trinity Coll. Dublin; on staff of Irish Times 1964–66, Thomson Prov. Newspapers 1966–67, Daily Mirror 1967–68, Sunday Telegraph 1968–70; Deputy City Ed., Sunday Express 1970–71, Sunday Telegraph 1971–84, City Ed. 1979–84; Deputy Ed. Sunday Times 1984–94; Group Editorial Dir, Argus Group, SA 1994–; Chief Exec. Ind. Newspapers Holdings Ltd, South Africa 1997–2002; Exec. Chair. iTouch PLC 2000–05; CEO UK Group, Independent News and Media Group PLC 2002–; mem. Council, Univ. of Buckingham 1982–, Council of Govs, United Medical and Dental Schools of Guy's and St Thomas' Hosps 1985–94; Trustee Project Trust 1984–94, Generation Trust, Guy's Hosp. 1985–; Dir N. Brown Holdings 1994–. *Publications:* DeLorean: The Rise and Fall of a Dream-maker (with James L. Srodes) 1983, Takeovers 1987, The Brothers: The Rise of Saatchi and Saatchi 1988, Billionaire: The Life and Times of Sir James Goldsmith 1991, The Player: The Life of Tony O'Reilly 1994. *Leisure interests:* tennis, walking. *Address:* Independent News & Media PLC, Independent House, 2023 Bianconi Avenue, Citywest Business Campus, Naas Road, Dublin 24, Ireland (office). *Telephone:* (1) 4663200 (office). *Fax:* (1) 4663222 (office). *E-mail:* mail@inplc.com (office). *Website:* www.inmplc.com (office).

FALLON, Martin (see Patterson, Harry).

FALLON, Adm. William Joseph, MA; American military officer (retd); b. 30 Dec. 1940, East Orange, NJ; ed Naval War Coll., Newport, RI, Nat. War Coll., Washington, DC, Old Dominion Univ., Norfolk, Va, Villanova Univ., Pa; received comm. through USN ROTC Program, designated naval flight officer upon completion of training 1967; began Naval Aviation service flying RA-5C Vigilante with a combat deployment to Viet Nam; served in flying assignments with Attack Squadrons and Carrier Air Wings with deployment to the Mediterranean Sea, Atlantic, Pacific and Indian Oceans, in USS Saratoga, USS Ranger, USS Nimitz, USS Dwight D. Eisenhower, USS Theodore Roosevelt; Commdr Carrier Air Wing Eight, Operation Desert Storm 1991, Battle Force Sixth Fleet, Operation Deliberate Force, Bosnia 1995, other command posts included Attack Squadron Sixty Five on USS Dwight D. Eisenhower, Medium Attack Wing One at NAS Oceana, Va, Carrier Group Eight, Theodore Roosevelt Battle Group; Commdr, Second Fleet and Commdr, Striking Fleet Atlantic 1997–2000; shore duties have included Deputy Dir for Operations, Jt Task Force, Southwest Asia, Deputy Dir, Aviation Plans and Requirements, Staff of the Chief of Naval Operations, Washington, DC; flag officer assignments included Asst Chief of Staff, Plans and Policy, NATO Supreme Allied Commdr, Atlantic, Deputy and Chief of Staff, US Atlantic Fleet, Deputy C-in-C and Chief of Staff, US Atlantic Command; Vice-Chief of Naval Operations 2000–03; Commdr US Fleet Forces Command and US Atlantic Fleet 2003–05; Commdr US Pacific Command 2005–07; Commdr US Cen. Command (first naval officer to hold the position) 2007–08 (resgnd); Defense Distinguished Service Medal, Distinguished Service Medal, Defense Superior Service Medal, Legion of Merit, Bronze Star, Meritorious Service Medal, Air Medal, Navy Commendation Medal. *Address:* c/o US Central Command, 7115 South Boundary Boulevard, MacDill AFB, Tampa, FL 33621-5101, USA (office).

FALOTTI, Pier Carlo; business executive; b. 1942; began career as tech. salesman 1960; Pres. and CEO Digital EMEA 1983–92; CEO The Ask Group

1992–94; head non-USA operations AT&T 1994-96; Exec. Vice-Pres. and head, Oracle Europe, Middle East, Africa 1996–2000; Chair. Icon MediaLab 2001; mem. Bd of Dirs First Virtual Corpn, Logitech SA, Linkvest, Centric Software Inc. 2000–, Acer Inc. 2005–. *Address:* c/o Board of Directors, Acer, Inc., 9F, 88 Hsin Tai Wu Road, Sec 1 Hsichih, Taipei 221, Taiwan.

FÄLTHAMMAR, Carl-Gunne, PhD; Swedish scientist and academic; *Professor Emeritus of Plasma Physics, Alfvén Laboratory, Royal Institute of Technology;* b. 4 Dec. 1931, Markaryd; s. of Oskar Fälthammar and Ingeborg Fälthammar; m. Ann-Marie Sjunnesson 1957; one s. one d.; ed Royal Inst. of Tech. (KTH), Stockholm; Asst Prof. KTH 1966–69, Assoc. Prof. 1969–75, Chair. Dept of Plasma Physics 1967–97, Prof. of Plasma Physics 1975–, now Emer.; mem. Swedish Nat. Cttee for Radio Science 1970–96, Swedish Nat. Cttee for Geodesy and Geophysics 1973–96; Chair. Swedish Geophysical Soc. 1978–80; mem. Royal Swedish Acad. of Sciences, Int. Acad. of Astronautics, Academia Europaea; other professional affiliations; Hon. PhD (Oulu) 1989; Basic Sciences Award, Int. Acad. of Astronautics 1996, Golden Badge Award, European Geophysical Union 1996, Hannes Alfvén Medal, European Geophysical Soc. 1998. *Publications:* Cosmical Electrodynamics (with H. Alfvén) 1963, Magnetospheric Physics (with B. Hultqvist) 1990; papers in plasma physics and space physics. *Address:* Division of Plasma Physics, Alfvén Laboratory, The Royal Institute of Technology, 100 44 Stockholm, Sweden (office). *Telephone:* (8) 790-76-85 (office). *Fax:* (8) 24-54-31 (office). *E-mail:* carl-gunne.falthammar@alfrenlab.kth.se (office). *Website:* www.plasma.kth.se (office).

FALTINGS, Gerd, PhD; German mathematician and academic; *Professor and Member of the Board of Scientific Members, Max-Planck-Institut für Mathematik;* b. 28 July 1954, Gelsenkirchen-Buer; ed Westphalian Wilhelm Univ. of Münster; Postdoctoral Research Fellow, Harvard Univ., Cambridge, Mass, USA 1978–79; Prof. of Math., Univ. of Wuppertal 1979–85; mem. Faculty, Princeton Univ., NJ, USA 1985; currently Prof. and mem. Bd Scientific Mems, Max-Planck-Institut für Mathematik, Bonn; Danny Heineman Prize, Akad. der Wissenschaften, Göttingen 1983, Fields Medal, Int. Congress of Mathematicians, Berkeley, Calif. 1986, Leibniz Prize, Germany 1996, von Staudt Prize, Erlangen 2008. *Publications:* numerous publs in math. journals. *Address:* Max-Planck-Institut für Mathematik, PO Box 7280, 53072 Bonn (office); Max-Planck-Institut für Mathematik, Vivatsgasse 7, 53111 Bonn, Germany (office). *Telephone:* (228) 402228 (office). *Fax:* (228) 402277 (office). *E-mail:* gerd@mpim-bonn.mpg.de (office). *Website:* www.mpim-bonn.mpg.de (office).

FALTLHAUSER, Kurt, BEcons, Dr rer. pol; German politician; b. 13 Sept. 1940, Munich; m.; two c.; ed Univ. of Munich; leader, Gen. Student Council, Univ. of Munich 1964–65; mem. Bavarian Landtag 1974–80, 1998–2008; State Minister and Head, Bavarian State Chancellery 1995–98, State Minister of Finance 1998–2007; mem. Bundestag 1980–95; Chair. Finance and Budget Committee, Christian Social Union (CSU); Financial Spokesman CDU/CSU Parl. Group., also Deputy Chair.; Parl. State Sec. to the Fed. Minister of Finance; Chair. Bd of Admin Bayerische Landesbank; Lecturer and Hon. Prof., Faculty of Econs, Univ. of Munich. *Address:* Maximilianeum, 81627 Munich, Germany (home). *Telephone:* (89) 41260 (home). *E-mail:* info@faltlhauser.de (home).

FÄLTSKOG, Agnetha Åse; Swedish singer and actress; b. 5 April 1950, Jönköping; m. 1st Björn Ulvæus 1971 (divorced 1979); m. 2nd Tomas Sonnenfeld; solo recording artist aged 17; actress, Jesus Christ Superstar, Sweden; mem. pop group ABBA 1973–82; winner, Eurovision Song Contest 1974; world-wide tours; concerts include Royal Performance, Stockholm 1976, Royal Albert Hall, London 1977, UNICEF concert, New York 1979, Wembley Arena 1979; reunion with ABBA, Swedish TV This Is Your Life 1986; solo artist 1982–90, 2004–; World Music Award, Best Selling Swedish Artist 1993. *Films:* ABBA: The Movie 1977, Rakenstam 1983. *Recordings:* albums: with Abba: Waterloo 1974, Abba 1976, Greatest Hits 1976, Arrival 1976, The Album 1978, Voulez-Vous 1979, Greatest Hits Vol. 2 1979, Super Trouper 1980, The Visitors 1981, The Singles: The First Ten Years 1982, Thank You For The Music 1983, Absolute Abba 1988, Abba Gold 1992, More Abba Gold 1993, Forever Gold 1998, The Definitive Collection 2001; solo: Eleven Women In One Building 1975, Wrap Your Arms Around Me 1983, Eyes of a Woman 1985, I Stand Alone 1987, My Colouring Book 2004; singles include: with Abba: Ring Ring 1973, Waterloo 1974, Mamma Mia 1975, Dancing Queen 1976, Fernando 1976, Money Money Money 1976, Knowing Me Knowing You 1977, The Name Of The Game 1977, Take A Chance On Me 1978, Summer Night City 1978, Chiquitita 1979, Does Your Mother Know? 1979, Angel Eyes/Voulez-Vous 1979, Gimme Gimme Gimme (A Man After Midnight) 1979, I Have A Dream 1979, The Winner Takes It All 1980, Super Trouper 1980, On and On and On 1981, Lay All Your Love On Me 1981, One Of Us 1981, When All Is Said and Done 1982, Head Over Heels 1982, The Day Before You Came 1982, Under Attack 1982, Thank You For The Music 1983; solo: I Was So In Love, The Heat Is On, Can't Shake You Loose, I Wasn't The One (Who Said Goodbye), If I Thought You'd Ever Change Your Mind 2004. *Address:* c/o Warner Music Sweden AB, PO Box 1228, 164 28 KISTA, Sweden. *E-mail:* webmaster@agnetha.net (office). *Website:* www.abbasite.com; agnetha.net.

FALUSI, Adeyinka Gladys, PhD; Nigerian geneticist and academic; *Professor of Haematology, Genetic and Bioethics Research Unit, Institute for Medical Research and Training, College of Medicine, University of Ibadan;* has served as Visiting Scientist at numerous hosps including Hammersmith Hosp., London, UK 1983–84, John Radcliffe Hosp., Oxford, Memorial Sloan Kettering Cancer Center, New York, USA 1994–95, Humboldt Univ. Inst. for Tropical Medicine, Berlin 1998; currently Prof., Inst. for Medical Research and Training, Coll. of Medicine, Univ. of Ibadan; Country Coordinator for Nigeria, Networking for Ethics of Biomedical Research in Africa 2005–06;

Founder and Vice-Pres. Sickle Cell Asscn of Nigeria; Founding Chair. Nigerian Bioethics Initiative; L'Oréal-UNESCO Women in Science Award 2001, CEDPA/Nigerian News Rare Gems Award 2003, Vocational Excellence Award for Impact in Science 2004. *Address:* U.I.P.O.Box 22772, Ibadan, Nigeria (office). *Telephone:* (3) 7864468 (office). *Fax:* (2) 2411171 (office). *E-mail:* gfalusi@yahoo.com (office). *Website:* www.comui.edu.ng/research/IMRAT/Falusi (office).

FALZON, Michael, BArch; Maltese politician and architect; *Chairman, Water Services Corporation;* b. 17 Aug. 1945, Gzira; m. Mary Anne Aquilina; one s.; ed the Lyceum and Univ. of Malta; in practice as architect; mem. Nat. Exec. Nationalist Party 1975; Sec. of Information of the Party; Ed. The Democrat (weekly paper) 1975; MP 1976–96; Shadow Minister for Information and Broadcasting 1976–81; for Industry 1981–87; Minister for Devt of Infrastructure 1987–92, for Environment 1992–94, for Educ. and Human Resources 1994–96; Ed. The People and People on Sunday newspapers 1997–98; Chair. Water Services Corpn 1998–. *Address:* Water Services Corporation, Qormi Road, Luqa, LQA 05, Malta. *Telephone:* 22443309 (office). *Fax:* 22443900 (office). *E-mail:* water@wsc.com.mt (office); micfal@maltanet.net (home). *Website:* www.wsc.com.mt (office).

FAN, Jingyi; Chinese journalist; *President, China Society of News Photography;* b. 1931, Suzhou City, Jiangsu Prov.; ed St John's University, Shanghai; joined CCP 1978; Ed., later Ed.-in-Chief, Deputy Dir, later Dir and mem. Editorial Bd Liaoning Daily 1979–84; Dir Foreign Languages Publ. and Distribution Bureau 1984–86; Ed.-in-Chief Economic Daily 1986–93, People's Daily 1993–98; Del., 13th CCP Nat. Congress 1987–92, 14th CCP Nat. Congress 1992–97; mem. 8th CPPCC Nat. Cttee 1993–98 (Vice-Chair. Economy Cttee); mem. Standing Cttee of 9th NPC 1998–2003 (Vice-Chair. Educ., Science, Culture and Public Health Cttee); Pres. China Soc. of News Photography 1995–; currently also Prof. of Journalism, Tsinghua Univ.; Hon. Pres. Photo-Journalism Soc. 1994–; honoured as one of the excellent journalists of China 1991. *Address:* Omnicom Building, School of Journalism and Communication, Tsinghua University, Beijing 100084, People's Republic of China (office). *Telephone:* (10) 62781145 (office). *Fax:* (10) 62771410 (office). *E-mail:* tsjc@tsinghua.edu.cn. *Website:* www.tsjc.tsinghua.edu.cn (office).

FAN, Maj.-Gen. Zhilun; Chinese army official; b. 1935, Fushun Co., Sichuan Prov.; s. of Fan Ximing and Fan Zhougshi; m. Ding Xin 1966; one s. one d.; Deputy Commdr and Chief of Staff Chinese People's Armed Police Force 1985; Deputy Pres. Mil. Educ. Coll. and Mil. Staff Coll. 1991–; Deputy Chief of Staff, Beijing Mil. Region of PLA 1993–. *Leisure interests:* climbing, swimming, calligraphy. *Address:* Headquarters of the Beijing Military Region, No. Jia 1, Badachu, Western Hill, Beijing, People's Republic of China.

FAN HSU, Rita, CBE, JP, BA, MScS; Hong Kong politician; *President of Legislative Council, Hong Kong Special Administrative Region;* b. 20 Sept. 1945, Shanghai, People's Repub. of China; m. Stephen Fan Sheung-tak; two c.; ed St Stephen's Girls' Coll., Univ. of Hong Kong; mem. Legis. Council 1983–92, Exec. Council 1989–92; Chair. Bd of Educ. 1986–89, Educ. Comm. 1990–92; mem. Preliminary Working Cttee of the Preparatory Cttee for the Hong Kong Special Admin. Region (HKSAR) 1993–95, Preparatory Cttee for the HKSAR 1995–97; Hong Kong Deputy to the 9th NPC, People's Repub. of China 1998–2003, 10th NPC 2003–08; Pres. Provisional Legis. Council 1997–98, First Legis. Council of HKSAR 1998–2000, Second Legis. Council 2000–04, Third Legis. Council 2004–08; Supervising Adviser, Hong Kong Fed. of Women; Hon. Advisor, Jr Chamber Int. Hong Kong; Grand Bauhinia Medal, Gold Bauhinia Star; Hon. LLD (China Univ. of Political Science and Law); Hon. DScS (City Univ. of Hong Kong). *Address:* Office of the President of the Legislative Council, Legislative Council Building, 8 Jackson Road, Central, Hong Kong Special Administrative Region, People's Republic of China (office). *Telephone:* 28699461 (office). *Fax:* 28779600 (office). *E-mail:* wlam@legco.gov.hk (office). *Website:* www.ritafan.org (office).

FANG, Lizhi; Chinese astrophysicist; *Head Theoretical Astrophysics Group, Beijing Astronomical Observatory;* b. 12 Feb. 1936, Beijing; s. of Cheng Pu and Peiji (née Shi) Fang; m. Li Shuxian 1961; two s.; ed Univ. of Peking; asst teacher, Univ. of Science and Tech. of China 1958–63, Lecturer 1963–78, Prof. of Physics 1978–87, Vice-Pres. of Univ. 1984–87; Prof. and Head Theoretical Astrophysics Group, Beijing Astronomical Observatory, Chinese Acad. of Sciences 1987–; Sr Visiting Fellow Inst. of Astronomy, Univ. of Cambridge, UK 1979–80; Visiting Prof., Research Inst. of Fundamental Physics, Kyoto Univ. 1981–82, Physics Dept, Univ. of Rome 1983; mem. Inst. for Advanced Study, Princeton 1986; Assoc. mem. Int. Centre for Theoretical Physics, Trieste 1984–89; lived in asylum in US Embassy, Beijing 1989–90, to London, then to USA 1990–; Prof. of Physics and Astronomy, Univ. of Ariz., Tucson 1991–; mem. Chinese Acad. of Sciences 1981–89, New York Acad. of Sciences 1986–; mem. of Council Chinese Soc. of Physics 1982–87, Chinese Soc. of Astronomy 1982–85, Asscn pro Centro Int. de Fisica 1983–87, Int. Centre for Theoretical Physics 1984–89, Int. Centre for Relativistic Astrophysics 1985–89, Chinese Soc. of History of Science and Tech. 1987–89; Pres. Chinese Soc. of Gravitation and Relativistic Astrophysics 1983–89; Vice-Pres. Chinese Soc. of Astronomy 1985–89; mem. various Int. Astronomical Union and IUPAP comms, etc.; Ed. Scientia Sinica 1978–89, Acta Physica Sinica 1979–89, Acta Astronomica Sinica 1980–83, Acta Astrophysica Sinica 1982–83, Journal of Modern Physics, etc.; Dr hc (Rome Univ.) 1990; Nat. Award for Science and Tech. 1978, Chinese Acad. of Sciences Award 1982, New York Acad. of Sciences Award 1988, Robert F. Kennedy Human Rights Award 1989 etc. *Publications:* Modern Cosmology Review (ed.) 1978, Astrophysics Today (ed.) 1980, Basic Concepts in Relativistic Astrophysics (with R. Ruffini) 1981, English ed. 1987, Cosmology of the Early Universe (ed. with R. Ruffini) 1984, Galaxies, Quasars and Cosmology (ed. with R. Ruffini) 1985, Advances in Science of China: Physics (ed. with others) 1986, Introduction to

Mechanics (with S. Li) 1986, Observational Cosmology (co-ed.) 1987, Creation of the Universe (with S. X. Li) 1987, Quantum Cosmology (ed. with R. Ruffini) 1987, Collection of History of Sciences (ed.) 1987, Philosophy as a Tool of Physics 1988, Origin, Structure and Evolution of Galaxies (ed.) 1988. *Leisure interest:* swimming. *Address:* Department of Physics, University of Arizona, Tucson, AZ 85721, USA (office); Beijing Observatory, Zhongguancun, Beijing 100080, People's Republic of China (office). *E-mail:* fanglz@physics.arizona.edu (office). *Website:* www.arizona.edu (office); www.physics.arizona.edu/~fanglz/ (office).

FANG, Shouxian; Chinese nuclear physicist; *Director, Beijing Electron Positron Collider National Laboratory;* b. 27 Oct. 1932, Shanghai City; m. 1st Run Moyin (died 1965); m. 2nd Yao Mayli 1968, two d.; ed Fudan Univ., Shanghai; Prof. of Research, Nuclear Physics Inst., Academia Sinica 1982–; Project Dir, Beijing Electron Positron Collider (BEPC) 1986, Dir Inst. of High Energy Physics 1988, Dir BEPC Nat. Lab. 1992–; mem. Chinese Acad. of Sciences 1991–; Hon. Nat. Natural Science Award 1990. *Address:* c/o PO Box 918, Beijing 100039, People's Republic of China. *Telephone:* 8219574. *Fax:* 8213374.

FANG, Weizhong; Chinese economist; *Chairman, Chinese Macroeconomics Society;* b. 11 March 1928, Dongfeng Co., Jilin Prov.; three s.; ed Dongbei Univ., Northeast China Univ., Northeast China Teachers' Univ.; joined CCP 1950; Sec. Publicity Dept, CCP Northeast Bureau 1950–52; Deputy Dir Research and Editing Div., State Devt and Reform Comm. 1952–61; Researcher, General Office, CCP Cen. Cttee 1961–65; Vice-Minister, State Devt and Reform Comm. 1977–93; Prof., Beijing Univ., People's Univ. of China, Beijing; Deputy Ed. China Econ. Yearbook; Chief Ed. Chronicle of Major Econ. Events; Alt. mem. 12th CCP Cen. Cttee 1982–87; mem. 13th CCP Cen. Cttee 1987–92; Alt. mem. 14th CCP Cen. Cttee 1992–97; mem. CPPCC 8th Nat. Cttee 1993–98, 9th Nat. Cttee 1998–2003, Chair. Economy Sub-Cttee 1993–2003; Chair. Chinese Macroeconomics Soc. 1995–; Vice-Chair. China Planning Soc., China Enterprise Man. Asscn; mem. Council of People's Bank of China 1974–; Chief Ed. Chronicle of Major Economic Events. *Leisure interest:* calligraphy. *Address:* Chinese Macroeconomics Society, 18th Floor B, Hua Zun Mansion, 29 Beisanhuan Zhonglu, Xicheng District, Beijing 100029, People's Republic of China (office). *E-mail:* Eng@macrochina.com.cn.

FANG, Gen. Zuqi; Chinese army officer; *Political Commissar, Nanjing Military Region, People's Liberation Army;* b. 1935, Jingjiang, Jiangsu Prov.; joined PLA 1951, took part in Korean War 1952; joined CCP 1956; worked as Asst, Cadre Dept, Army (or Ground Force), PLA Services and Arms, later Deputy Chief of Div. Org. Section; Deputy Regt Political Commissar, Army (or Ground Force), PLA Services and Arms 1969–70; fmr Dir Political Dept, PLA Shenyang and Beijing Mil. Area Command; Political Commissar, Nanjing Mil. Region 1994–; rank of Maj.-Gen. Group Army, PLA Services and Arms 1988–93, Lt-Gen. 1993–98, Gen. 1998–; mem. 15th CCP Cen. Cttee 1997–2002. *Address:* Political Commissar's Office, Nanjing Military Region, Nanjing, Jiangsu Province, People's Republic of China.

FANJUL, Oscar, PhD; Spanish economist; b. 1949, Santiago, Chile; ed Univ. Complutense de Madrid; Visiting Scholar, Harvard Univ. and MIT, Prof. Univ. Autónoma de Madrid; served as Sec.-Gen. and Under-Sec. Dept of Industry and Energy 1983–84; mem. team which negotiated Spain's entry to EC; has also served in Instituto Nacional de Industria (INI) and at Confederación Española de Cajas de Ahorros; Chair. Instituto Nacional di Hidrocarburos (INH) 1985–, Repsol SA 1986–; mem. Bd Argentaria (Corporación Bancaria Española) 1991–, Teneo 1992–, London Stock Exchange, Unilever (non-exec.) The Marsh & McLennan, Acerinox, Técnicas Reunidas; mem. Int. Bd The Chubb Corpn, European Advisory Bd, Carlyle Group; Int. advisor to Goldman Sachs; mem. Trilateral Comm. 1991–, Group of Econ. Analysis of the European Comm.; Vice Chair. Omega Capital; Orden de Isabel la Católica, Order of Belgian Crown. *Publications:* several articles and books on industrial and financial matters. *Address:* P° de la Castellana, 278–280, 28046 Madrid, Spain. *Telephone:* (91) 3488100. *Fax:* (91) 3142821.

FAOURI, Refaat al-, PhD; Jordanian university rector, international organization executive and academic; *Director-General, Arab Administrative Development Organization (ARADO);* ed Saint Louis Univ., Mo., USA; occupied several positions at Yarmouk Univ., including researcher and teaching asst, School of Econs, Asst Teacher, Public Relations Div., Co-teacher in Public Relations Div., Asst Dean of Faculty of Economy and Admin. Sciences, mem. Bd of Dirs Consulting and Community Service Centre, Refugees and Immigrants Centre, Dean of Faculty of Economy and Admin. Sciences, Vice-Chair. Admin. Affairs, Chair. Refugees, Immigrants and Expatriation Centre, Chair. Jordanian Studies Centre, currently Deputy Rector Yarmuk Univ. for Quality Affairs; fmr Lecturer, Saint Univ.; has held numerous admin. posts, including mem. Bd of Dirs Public Admin Inst., Amman-Jordan, Dir Trust Council, Ministry of Higher Educ. and Scientific Research, Dir at Distinction Centre for Jordanian Office Services, mem. Informative Cttee for the Creativity and Distinction Fund Program, Ministry of Admin. Devt, Jordan; Dir-Gen. Arab Admin. Devt Org. (ARADO) 2007–. *Publications:* several books, including Management of Organizational Innovation; 36 research papers on business admin. *Address:* Arab Administrative Development Organization, 2 El Hegaz Street, PO Box 2692 al-Horreia, Heliopolis, Cairo, Egypt (office). *Telephone:* (2) 4175410 (office). *Fax:* (2) 4175407 (office). *E-mail:* arado@idsc.gov.eg (office); info@arado.org.eg (office). *Website:* www.arado.org.eg (office).

FARACI, John V.; American forest products industry executive; *Chairman and CEO, International Paper Company;* b. 1950; joined International Paper 1974 as financial analyst, various positions in Planning, Gen. Man. and Finance Depts, Vice-Pres. 1989, CEO and Man. Dir Carter Holt Harvey (subsidiary co.) 1995–99, Sr Vice-Pres. and Chief Financial Officer, International Paper 1999–2000, Exec. Vice-Pres. and Chief Financial Officer 2000–03, Pres. Feb.–Nov. 2003, Chair. and CEO Nov. 2003–; mem. Bd of Dirs United Technologies Corpn 2005–, Grand Teton Nat. Park Foundation, Nat. Park Foundation; mem. Citigroup Int. Advisory Council; mem. Business Round Table, Sustainable Forestry Bd; Trustee, Denison Univ. *Address:* International Paper Company, 6400 Poplar Avenue, Memphis, TN 38197, USA (office). *Telephone:* (901) 419-9000 (office). *Fax:* (901) 214-9682 (office). *E-mail:* info@internationalpaper.com (office). *Website:* www.internationalpaper.com (office).

FARAH, former Empress of Iran (see Pahlavi).

FARAH, Ali Abdi; Djibouti politician; b. 16 Feb. 1947; mem. Rassemblement Populaire pour le Progrès (RPP); fmr Minister for Industry, Energy and Minerals and Acting Minister for Public Works and Housing; Minister of Foreign Affairs, Int. Co-operation and Parl. Relations 1999–2005. *Address:* c/o Ministry of Foreign Affairs and International Co-operation, BP 1863, Djibouti (office).

FARAH, Col. Hassan Abshir; Somali politician and diplomatist; *Minister of Fishery and Marine Resources;* b. 20 June 1945; fmr Mayor of Mogadishu; fmr Gov. of Middle Shabelle and Bakol; fmr Amb. to Austria, Repub. of Korea, Japan, Germany; Minister of Internal Affairs and Security, Puntland State –2000; Minister of Mineral Resources and Water 2000–01; Chair. Somali Peace Conf. 2000; Prime Minister of Somalia 2001–03; Minister of Fishery and Marine Resources 2007–. *Address:* Ministry of Fishery and Marine Resources, Mogadishu, Somalia (office).

FARAH, Nuruddin; Somali novelist; b. 24 Nov. 1945, Baidoa; s. of Farah Hassan and Fatuma Aleli; m. Amina Mama 1992 (divorced 2007); one s. one d.; ed Panjab Univ., Chandigarh, India, Univs of London and Essex, UK; Lecturer, Nat. Univ. of Somalia, Mogadishu 1971–74; Assoc. Prof., Univ. of Jos, Nigeria 1981–83; Writer-in-Residence, Univ. of Minn. 1989, Brown Univ. 1991; Prof., Makerere Univ., Kampala 1990; Rhodes Scholar St Antony's Coll., Oxford 1996; Visiting Prof., Univ. of Texas at Austin 1997; now full-time novelist; mem. Union of Writers of the African People, PEN Int., Somali-Speaking PEN Centre; Hon. DLitt (Univ. of Kent at Canterbury) 2000; English-speaking Union Literary Prize 1980, Tucholsky Award 1991, Premio Cavour Award 1992, Zimbabwe Annual Award 1993, Neustadt Int. Literary Prize 1998, Festival Étonnant Voyageur St Malo, France 1998. *Plays include:* The Offering 1976, Yussuf and his Brothers 1982. *Publications:* From a Crooked Rib 1970, A Naked Needle 1976, Sweet and Sour Milk 1979, Sardines 1981, Close Sesame 1983, Maps 1986, Gifts 1992, Secrets 1998, Yesterday, Tomorrow: Voices from the Somali Diaspora 1999, Links 2004, Knots 2007; contrib. to Guardian, New African, Transition Magazine, New York Times, Observer, TLS, London Review of Books. *Address:* c/o Deborah Rogers, Rogers, Coleridge & White, 20 Powis Mews, London, W11 1JN, England (office).

FARELL CUBILLAS, Arsenio, PhD; Mexican politician; b. June 1921, Mexico City; ed Nat. Univ of Mexico; Lecturer in Civil Law and Gen. Theory of Process, Nat. Univ. of Mexico and in Civil Law, Iberoamerican Univ., Mexico City; Pres. Nat. Chamber of Sugar and Alcohol Industries 1973; Dir-Gen. Fed. Electricity Comm. 1973–76; Dir-Gen. Social Security Inst. 1976–82; Sec. of State for Employment 1982–85, for Labour and Social Welfare 1985–95; now Comptroller Gen. *Publications:* essays and articles on legal matters. *Address:* Office of Comptroller General, Avenida Insurgentes 1775, 10 Piso, Mexico City 01020, Mexico (office).

FAREMO, Grete, LLB; Norwegian lawyer, business executive and fmr politician; b. 16 June 1955, Byglandsfjord, Setesdal; d. of Osmund Faremo and Tora Aamlid; pnr, Magne Lindholm; one d.; ed Univ. of Oslo; with Ministry of Finance, Norwegian Agency for Devt Co-operation; Head of Div. Ministry 1984, Minister of Devt Co-operation 1990–92, of Justice and Police 1992–96, of Oil and Energy 1996; mem. Parl. (Stortinget) 1993–97; Dir Storebrand Insurance Co. 1997–98, Pres. 1997–2003; Dir of Legal and Corp. Affairs, Microsoft Northern Europe 2003–08; mem. Bd Labour Party Forum for Art and Culture 1989–90, Int. Analysis 1997; mem. Bd of Dirs Norsk Hydro 2006–; Chief Negotiating Officer Aker Eiendom 1986; fmr Dir (of Cultural Affairs) Aker Brygge (business and leisure complex), Norsk Arbeiderpresse; Chair. Norsk Folkehjelp 2003–08; mem. European Group, Trilateral Comm. 1998–2002. *Address:* c/o Board of Directors, Norsk Hydro ASA, Drammensveien 264, 0283 Oslo, Norway.

FARES, Farouk Saleh, BAgr, DEA, PhD; Syrian soil scientist, institute director and academic; *Director-General, Arab Centre for the Study of Arid Zones and Dry Lands (ACSAD);* b. 1945; m.; three c.; ed Damascus Univ., Paris Univ. VI in cooperation with the Nat. Agricultural Inst.-Nat. Higher School for Agric., Paris, INA-ENSA and ORSTOM, Nancy Univ. (France) in cooperation with Soil Research Centre (CNRS), Nancy, Nuclear Studies Centre (France), Nat. Inst. for Polytechnic, Lorraine and Biological Soil Research Centre (CNRS), Nancy, Pennsylvania State Univ., USA (Fulbright Scholarship), Environmental Resources Research Inst.; Dir-Gen. Arab Centre for the Study of Arid Zones and Dry Lands (ACSAD), Damascus, Syria 2004–. *Address:* Arab Centre for the Study of Arid Zones and Dry Lands (ACSAD), PO Box 2440, Damascus, Syria (office). *Telephone:* (11) 5743039 (office). *Fax:* (11) 5743063 (office). *E-mail:* acsad@net.sy (office). *Website:* www.acsad.org (office).

FARES, Issam M.; Lebanese politician and business executive; b. 1937, Bayno, Akkar; m. Hala Fares; four c.; ed Tripoli Coll.; began as businessman in Arabian Gulf, then moved to investment; f. numerous major business corpns in USA, Europe and Middle E including The Wedge Group; f. The Fares

Foundation; mem. Parl.; Deputy Prime Minister –2005; Chair. numerous governmental cttees; serves on bds of int. orgs, major business corpns and univs and insts of higher learning; lectures frequently at home and abroad; Order of the Prince Yaroslav the Wise, Second Rank (Ukraine), Grand Officer of the Nat. Order (Lebanon), Grand Cordon de Jean Baptiste (Antiochian Orthodox Church), Grand Cordon of Archon Depoutatos (Patriarchate of Constantinople), Grand Cordon of St Daniel (Patriarchate of Moscow and All Russia), Grand Officier de la Légion d'honneur (France), Grand Cross of the Phoenix (Greece), Grand Commdr Makarios the Third (Cyprus), Order of 'Stara Platina', First Rank (Bulgaria); Dr hc (Diplomatic Acad., Moscow, Tufts Univ., Mass, USA); Medal of Sts Peter and Paul (Antiochian Orthodox Patriarchate), World Maronite Foundation Gold Decoration, Antiochian Orthodox Christian Archdiocese of NY and N America Gold Medal of Merit, Maronite Cen. Council Gold Medal (Lebanon), Prize of the Int. Foundation for the Unity of Orthodox Nations (Patriarchate of Moscow and All Russia), UNESCO Gold Medal of Acropole, Alahd Nat. Merit (Algeria), Ministry of Youth and Sports Hon. Golden Medal (Bulgaria). *Address:* Sofil Center, Charle Malek Avenue, Achrafieh, Beirut (office); POB 16-5169, Beirut, Lebanon. *Telephone:* (1) 201755 (office). *Fax:* (1) 203999 (office). *E-mail:* dpmissam@fares.org.lb (office). *Website:* www.issam-fares.org (office).

FARHÂDI, Ravan A. G.; Afghan diplomatist and academic; b. 23 Aug. 1929, Kabul; m.; three c.; ed Istiqlal Coll., Kabul, Inst. d'Etudes Politiques de Paris, Inst. des Hautes Etudes Int., Univ. of Paris, Ecole Pratique des Hautes Etudes, Univ. of Paris; Lecturer in History of Political Thought, School of Law and Political Science, Univ. of Kabul 1955–58; First Sec. Embassy, Karachi 1958–61, Dir of UN Affairs, Ministry of Foreign Affairs 1961–62, Counsellor and Deputy Chief of Mission, Embassy, Washington, DC 1962–64, Dir.-Gen. for Political Affairs, Ministry of Foreign Affairs 1964–70, Deputy Foreign Minister 1970–72, also Sec. Council of Ministers 1965–71; Amb. to France 1973–74; mem. Advisory Scientific Comm. of Ministry of Culture 1975–78; political prisoner of Communist regime, Pol-e Charkhi prison, Kabul 1978–80; Assoc. Prof., Univ. of Paris (Panthéon-Sorbonne) 1981–85, Dept of Near Eastern Studies, Univ. of Calif. at Berkeley, USA 1985–92; Prof., Inst. of Islamic Thought and Civilisation, Kuala Lumpur, Malaysia 1992–93; Perm. Rep. to UN 1993–2006; Visiting Fellow, ANU, Canberra 1985. *Publications:* Abdullâh Ansâri of Herât: An Early Sufi Master 1996. *Address:* c/o Ministry of Foreign Affairs, Malak Azghar Road, Kabul, Afghanistan (office).

FARHANG, Mohammad Amin, PhD; Afghan government official and economist; *Minister of Commerce and Industry;* b. 1940, Kabul; s. of Mir Mohammad Sediq Farhang; ed Esteqlal High School, Kabul Univ., Köln Univ., Germany; Prof. of Econs, Kabul Univ. and Dir Nat. Economy Inst. 1974–78; imprisoned because of opposition to Communist regime 1978–82; emigrated to Germany 1982; fmr Prof. Ruhr Univ., Co-ordinator Afghanistan Archive; returned to Afghanistan 2001; Minister of Reconstruction 2001, of Economy 2005–06, of Commerce and Industry 2006–. *Publications:* numerous articles. *Address:* Ministry of Commerce and Industry, Darulaman Wat, Kabul, Afghanistan. *Telephone:* (20) 2290090. *Fax:* (20) 2500356. *E-mail:* info@commerce.gov.af. *Website:* www.commerce.gov.af.

FARINA, HE Cardinal Raffaele, PhD, SDB; Italian ecclesiastic; *Archivist of the Vatican Secret Archives;* b. 24 Sept. 1933, Buonalbergo; ed Pontifical Gregorian Univ.; professed as mem. of Salesians of Saint John Bosco 1954; ordained priest of Salesians of Saint John Bosco 1958; Prof., Pontifical Salesian Univ., Rome for several years before becoming Dean of the Theology Faculty, Rector Pontifical Salesian Univ. 1977–83, 1992–97; Under-Sec. Pontifical Council for Culture 1983–92; Prefect of Vatican Library 1997–2007, Librarian of the Vatican Library and Archivist of the Vatican Secret Archives 2007–; Titular Bishop of Opitergium 2007–; cr. Cardinal 2007. *Address:* Vatican Secret Archives, 00120 Città del Vaticano, Italy (office). *Telephone:* (06) 6988-3314 (office). *Fax:* (06) 6988-5574 (office). *E-mail:* info@vatican.va (office). *Website:* www.vatican.va/library_archives/vat_secret_archives/index .htm (office).

FARISH, William; American business executive, race horse owner and fmr diplomatist; b. 1938, Houston, Tex.; m. Sarah Sharp; one s. three d.; ed Univ. of Virginia; f. investment firm W. S. Farish & Co.; f. Lane's End Farm, Versailles, Ky (thoroughbred horse farm) 1978; Chair. Exec. Cttee Breeders Cup Ltd; Vice-Chair. US Jockey Club; Dir Thoroughbred Breeders and Owners Asscn; Chair. Bd Churchill Downs Inc., Ky; US Amb. to UK 2001–04; Trustee Keeneland Asscn 2006–. *Leisure interests:* horse breeding, hunting quail, polo. *Address:* c/o Lane's End, POB 626, Versailles, KY 40383 Washington, DC 20006-3307; W.S. Farish & Co., Houston, Texas, USA (office). *E-mail:* bfarish@aol.com.

FARIZ, Ziad, PhD; Jordanian government official and economist; ed Arab Inst. for Planning, Kuwait, Keele Univ., UK; Minister of Planning 1989, 1991, of Industry and Trade 1989–91; Chair. Bd Bank of Export and Finance 1995; Gov. Cen. Bank of Jordan –2000; fmr CEO Arab Banking Corpn; Deputy Prime Minister and Minister of Finance 2005–07 (resgnd); fmr mem. Advisory Bd, UNDP Regional Bureau for Arab States, Arab Human Devt Report. *Address:* c/o Ministry of Finance, POB 85, Amman 11118, Jordan (office).

FARLEY, Carole, MusB; American singer (soprano); b. 29 Nov. 1946, Le Mars, IA; d. of Melvin Farley and Irene Farley (née Reid); m. José Serebrier 1969; one d.; ed Indiana Univ. and Hochschule für Musik, Munich (Fulbright Scholar); operatic debut in USA in title role of La Belle Hélène, New York City Opera 1969; debut at Metropolitan Opera as Lulu 1977; now appears regularly in leading opera houses of the world and in concert performances with major orchestras in USA and Europe; Metropolitan Opera première of Shostakovich's Lady Macbeth of Mtsensk (Katerina Ismailova); Wozzeck (Marie), Toulouse Opera; mem. American Guild of Musical Artists; numerous awards

and prizes including Grand Prix du Disque for Les Soldats Morts (by A. Lemeland) 1995 and Diapason d'Or (France) 1997. *Recordings include:* Le Pré aux Clercs, Behold the Sun, French songs by Chausson, Duparc, Satie and Fauré, Prokofiev songs, Poulenc's The Human Voice, Menotti's The Telephone, Britten's Les Illuminations, Prokofiev's The Ugly Duckling, Kurt Weill songs, Milhaud songs (with John Constable), Tchaikovsky opera arias, Delius songs with orchestra, Les Soldats Morts 1995 (Grand Prix du Disque), Grieg songs with orchestra, Ned Rorem Songs with Ned Rorem, Piano, Der Wampyr by Marschner, Songs of William Bolcom. *Roles include:* Monteverdi's Poppea, Massenet's Manon, Mozart's Idomeneo, Verdi's La Traviata, Offenbach's Tales of Hoffmann and Strauss's Salome, Shostakovich's Lady Macbeth of Mtsensk, Wagner's Parsifal; (videos) Poulenc's La Voix Humaine, Menotti's The Telephone, Strauss's Four Last Songs and Songs with orchestra. *Leisure interests:* skiing, jogging, swimming, dancing, cooking, entertaining, reading. *Address:* Robert Lombardo Associates, Suite 6F, 61 West 62nd Street, New York, NY 10023, USA (office). *Telephone:* (212) 586-4453 (office). *Fax:* (212) 581-5771 (office). *Website:* www.rlombardo.com (office); www.carolefarley.com . *E-mail:* caspi123@aol.com (home).

FARMER, Paul, MD, PhD; American physician, medical anthropologist and academic; *Maude and Lillian Presley Professor of Medical Anthropology, Department of Social Medicine, Harvard Medical School;* ed Harvard Medical School and Harvard Univ.; worked amongst disposed peasants in Haiti 1990s; currently Maude and Lillian Presley Prof. of Medical Anthropology, Dept of Social Medicine, Harvard Medical School, Co-dir Program in Infectious Diseases and Social Change; divides his clinical time between Brigham and Women's Hosp. (Div. of Infectious Disease), where he is an attending physician, and Clinique Bon Sauveur charity hosp. in rural Haiti, where he serves as Medical Co-dir; Founding Dir Partners in Health 1987; visiting prof. at insts throughout USA as well as in France, Canada, Peru, Netherlands, Russia and Central Asia; has worked in communicable disease control in Americas for over a decade and is an authority on tuberculosis treatment and control; mem. Int. Scientific Cttee's Int. Conf. on AIDS, AIDS DOTS-Plus Working Group for the Global Tuberculosis Programme of WHO, Scientific Cttee of WHO Working Group on DOTS-Plus for MDR-TB, Commonwealth of Mass Bureau of Communicable Disease Control; Coordinator Int. Working Group on Multidrug-Resistant Tuberculosis; Chief Advisor, Tuberculosis Programs of the Open Soc. Inst.; Chief Medical Consultant, Tuberculosis Treatment Project in the Prisons of Tomsk (Siberia) for Public Health Research Inst.; has served on Scientific Review Bds of ten Int. Confs on AIDS; Duke Univ. Humanitarian Award, Margaret Mead Award, American Anthropological Asscn, Outstanding Int. Physician Award, American Medical Asscn, Heinz Humanitarian Award, John D. and Catherine T. MacArthur Foundation Genius Award 1993. *Publications:* more than 75 publs including AIDS and Accusation 1992, The Uses of Haiti 1994, Infections and Inequalities 1998, Pathologies of Power 2003; Co-Ed.: Women, Poverty, and AIDS 1996, The Global Impact of Drug-Resistant Tuberculosis 1999. *Address:* Department of Social Medicine, Harvard Medical School, 641 Huntington Avenue, Boston MA 02115, USA (office). *Telephone:* (617) 432-1707 (office). *Website:* www.hms.harvard.edu/dsm (office).

FARMER, Richard Gilbert, MS, MD, M.A.C.P., F.A.C.G; American physician and professor of medicine; *Clinical Professor of Medicine, Division of Gastroenterology, Georgetown University Hospital;* b. 29 Sept. 1931, Kokomo, Ind.; s. of Oscar I. Farmer and Elizabeth J. Gilbert Farmer; m. Janice M. Schrank 1958; one s. one d.; ed Indiana Univ., Univ. of Maryland, Milwaukee Co. Hosp. (Marquette Univ.), Mayo Foundation, Rochester, Minn. and Univ. of Minnesota; mil. service 1960–62; staff, Cleveland Clinic Foundation and Cleveland Clinic Hosp. 1962–91, Chair. Dept of Gastroenterology 1972–82, Chair. Div. of Medicine 1975–91; Asst and Assoc. Clinical Prof., Case Western Reserve Univ. School of Medicine 1972–91; Sr Medical Adviser, Bureau for Europe, US Agency for Int. Devt 1992–94; consultant in health care, Eastern Europe and Soviet Union 1994–96; Clinical Prof. of Medicine, Georgetown Univ. Medical Center 1992–; Medical Dir Quality Health Int. 1997–98, Eurasian Medical Educ. Program 1997–; medical consultant Scandinavian Care Consultants, Stockholm 1998–; mem. Inst. of Medicine, Nat. Advisory Bd, Nat. Foundation for Ileitis and Colitis, Nat. Comm. on Digestive Diseases 1977–79; Gov. for Ohio, American Coll. of Physicians 1980–84, Regent 1985–91; Chair. Health and Public Policy Comm. 1986–88; Pres. American Coll. of Gastroenterology 1978–79, Asscn of Program Dirs in Internal Medicine 1977–79; Interstate Postgrad. Medical Asscn 1983–84; mem. council to assess quality of care in the Medicare program, Gen. Accounting Office, US House of Reps. 1986–89; Special Citation, American Coll. of Physicians 1984, Mastership American Coll. of Gastroenterology 1991, American Coll. of Physicians 1993, mem. Int. Org. for Study of Inflammatory Bowel Disease (Deputy Chair. 1982–86); Founder's Award, Asscn of Program Dirs in Internal Medicine 1993; Jubilee Medal, Charles Univ. of Prague, Czech Republic 1998. *Publications:* author or co-author of 260 publs in the medical literature, primarily relating to digestive diseases with a specific interest in inflammatory bowel disease and health care in Eastern Europe and the fmr Soviet Union; of six books and contrib. to others. *Leisure interests:* squash, tennis, running and reading (history and current events). *Address:* Georgetown University Hospital, 3800 Reservoir Road, NW, Washington, DC 20007 (office); Eurasian Medical Education Program, 1150 18th Street, NW, Suite 275, Washington, DC 20036 (office); 9126 Town Gate Lane, Bethesda, MD 20817, USA (home). *Telephone:* (202) 444-6649 (office); (301) 365-5828 (home). *Fax:* (202) 463-8203 (office); (301) 365-6202 (home). *E-mail:* rgfarmer@emep -online.org (office); rg.jm.farmer@worldnet.att.net (home). *Website:* www .georgetown.edu/departments/medicine/gastroenterology (office).

FARNELL-WATSON, Peter; British business executive; *Managing Director, Nijkamp & Nijboer;* b. 8 Feb. 1947, Royston, Herts.; m. Bunny Farnell-

Watson; one s. one d.; ed schools in SA, UK and New Zealand, Colchester School of Art and Cen. School of Art, London; industrial designer, Unimark Int. 1970; Corp. Identity Man. Rennies Consolidated, SA 1972, Dir of Corp. Communications 1974; seconded to Jardine Matheson, Hong Kong 1977; Account Dir Corp. Identity, Landor Assocs. San Francisco 1984, Vice-Pres. responsible for Consulting and Account. Man., Corp. and Product Branding 1986, Group Dir responsible for Corp. and Retail Branding Operations in San Francisco 1988, Man. Dir San Francisco office and mem. Bd of Dirs Landor Assocs 1990, Exec. Dir Worldwide Accounts 1991, Co-Man. Dir Landor Assocs Europe 1992–96, apptd Man. Dir 1996; Man. Dir Nijkamp & Nijboer 2003–. *Address:* c/o Nijkamp & Nijboer, De Haer, Haerstraat 125, 7573 PA Oldenzaal, Netherlands.

FARNHAM, John Peter, AO; Australian (b. British) singer and entertainer; b. 1 July 1949, Essex, UK; m. Jillian Farnham 1973; two s.; ed Lyndale High School; settled in Australia 1959; apprenticed as plumber; lead singer for Strings Unlimited 1965; began recording 1967; television appearances including nature series Survival with Johnny Farnham for ABC; f. John Farnham Band 1978; lead singer for Little River Band 1982–85; 12 Gold Record Awards; Australian of the Year, Bicentennial 1998. *Recordings include:* Sadie the Cleaning Lady 1967 (3 Gold Records), Friday Kind of Monday 1968, Rose Coloured Glasses 1968, One 1969, Raindrops Keep Falling on My Head 1969, Comic Conversation 1970, Rock Me Baby 1972, Don't You Know It's Magic 1973, Everything is Out of Season 1973, Uncovered 1980, The Net 1982, Playing to Win 1984, Whispering Jack 1986, Chain Reaction 1990, Full House 1991, Jesus Christ Superstar: The Album 1992, Then Again 1992, Romeo's Heart 1996, Anthology Series I, II and III 1997, 33⅓ 2001, The Last Time 2002, I Remember When I was Young 2005. *Address:* c/o Sony BMG Australia, PO Box 88, Darlinghurst, NSW 1300, Australia (office). *Website:* www.sonybmg.com.au (home); www.johnfarnham.com.au.

FARNISH, Christine, BSc; British financial executive; *Director of Public Policy and Sustainability, Barclays PLC;* b. 21 April 1950; m. 1st; three s.; m. 2nd John Hayes; one d.; ed Ipswich High School, Univ. of Manchester; with Countryside Comm. 1972–76; London Borough of Lewisham 1983–86; London Research Centre 1986–88; joined Cambridge City Council 1988, Asst Chief Exec. –1994; Dir Consumer Affairs, Oftel 1994–98, Deputy Dir-Gen. 1998; Dir Consumer Div., Financial Services Authority (FSA) 1998–2002; Chief Exec. Nat. Assn of Pension Funds 2002–06; Dir of Public Policy, Barclays PLC 2006–; Dir (non-exec.) Office of Fair Trading 2003–; mem. Council Advertising Standards Authority; Dir (non-exec.) Papworth NHS Trust 1998–2002; Trustee, FSA Pension Plan –2002. *Address:* Barclays PLC, 1 Churchill Place, London, E14 5HP, England (office). *Telephone:* (20) 7116-1000 (office). *Fax:* (20) 7116-7542 (office). *E-mail:* christine.farnish@barclays.com (office). *Website:* www.barclays.com (office).

FAROOK, M. L. Mohamed Ali; Sri Lankan diplomatist; currently High Commr to the Maldives. *Address:* High Commission of Sri Lanka, H. Sakeena Manzil, Medhuziyaaraiyh Magu, Malé 20-05, The Maldives (office). *Telephone:* 3322845 (office). *Fax:* 3321652 (office). *E-mail:* highcom@dhivehinet .net.mv (office).

FAROOQ, Qazi Muhammad, BL; Pakistani judge (retd) and government official; *Chief Election Commissioner;* b. 6 Jan. 1938, Abbottabad; ed Dennys High School, Rawalpindi, Gordon Coll., Rawalpindi, Univ. Law Coll., Lahore, Nat. Inst. of Public Admin, Lahore, Inst. of Shariah and Legal Profession, Islamabad, Islamic Univ., Madina Munawwara; lawyer in Abbottabad –1967; joined PCS (Judicial Br.) 1967, worked as Civil Judge in Charsadda, Lakki Marwat, Bannu and as Sr Civil Judge, Mardan 1967–74, promoted as Additional Dist and Session Judge 1974, served at Haripur, Abbottabad and Mansehra 1974–77, promoted as Dist and Session Judge 1977, served at Mansehra, Bannu and Peshawar 1977–82; Prov. Election Commr NW Frontier Prov. 1982–88; Registrar Peshawar High Court 1988–91, Judge of Peshawar High Court 1991–99, Chief Justice Peshawar High Court 1999–2000; Judge, Supreme Court of Pakistan 2000–03; Judge-in-Charge, Fed. Judicial Acad., Islamabad 2000–03; Chief Election Commr 2006–; Chair. Cttee of Admin, Al-Mizan Foundation 2005–; mem. Law Reforms Comm. 2000–03, Law and Justice Comm. of Pakistan 2005–. *Address:* Election Commission of Pakistan Secretariat, Election House, Constitution Avenue G-5/2, Islamabad, Pakistan (office). *Telephone:* (51) 9201915 (office). *Fax:* (51) 9205300 (office). *E-mail:* cec@ecp.gov.pk (office). *Website:* www.ecp.gov.pk (office).

FAROOQI, Hamidullah; Afghan banker, economist and academic; fmr Prof. of Econs, Kabul Univ., continues to lecture; Pres. and CEO Afghanistan Int. Chamber of Commerce; Founder and Prin. Int. Model School (pvt. primary school teaching exclusively through English) 2005–; fmr Chair. Banke Millie Afghan (Afghan Nat. Bank), currently Chair. Supervisory Bd. *Address:* Banke Millie Afghan (Afghan National Bank), Jade Ibne Sina, PO Box 522, Kabul, Afghanistan (office). *Telephone:* (20) 2100311 (office). *Fax:* (20) 2101801 (office). *E-mail:* bankemillie_kabul@hotmail.com (office); info@bmakabul.com .af (office). *Website:* www.bmakabul.com.af (office).

FAROOQI, Khaled; Afghan politician; *Leader, Hizb-i Islami Afghanistan (Islamic Party of Afghanistan);* Leader of Hizb-i Islami (Islamic Party) in Paktika Prov., led breakaway faction that claimed to renounce violence and support US-trained Afghan Nat. Army, higher educ. for women, free elections and moves to disarm pvt. militias 2001, Leader, Hizb-i Islami Afghanistan (Islamic Party of Afghanistan) 2006–; mem. Parl. (Paktika Prov.) 2005–, Chair. Cttee on Communication, Urban Devt, Water, Power and Municipal Affairs 2005–. *Address:* Hizb-i Islami Afghanistan (Islamic Party of Afghanistan), Area A, Khushal Mena, Kabul, Afghanistan. *Telephone:* (79) 9421474.

FAROOQUI, Dewan M. Yousuf; Pakistani business executive; *Chairman, Pakistan Textile City;* Sindh Prov. Minister for Local Govt, Transport, Labour, Industries, Housing and Town Planning 2000–03; currently CEO Dewan Farooqui Motors Ltd; Group Man.-Dir and Pres. Dewan Mushtaq Group (DMG), responsible for overseeing Dewan Motorcycles, Dewan Sugar Mills Ltd, Dewan Textile Mills Ltd, Dewan Salman Fiber Ltd; Chair. Bd of Dirs, Pakistan Textile City 2004–; Co-Chief Patron Pakistan-Korea Business Forum; mem. Bd of Dirs Pakistan Industrial Tech. Assistance Center (PITAC); mem. Pakistan Automotive Mfrs Assn, Pakistan-France Business Alliance, Young Pres. Org., Int. Chamber of Commerce, Pakistan-India Business Forum; Pres. Sindh Squash Assn; Sitari-i-Imtiaz Award for Public Service (Highest Industrial Investor), Pres. of Pakistan. *Address:* Dewan Farooqui Motors Ltd, Dewan Centre, 3-A, Lalazar, Beach Hotel Road, Karachi, Pakistan (office). *Telephone:* (21) 5857862 (office); (21) 111313786 (office). *Fax:* (21) 5611345 (office). *E-mail:* dewanyousuf@dewangroup.com.pk (office). *Website:* www.dewangroup.com.pk (office).

FARQUHAR, John William, AB, MD, FAHA; American/Canadian physician and academic; *Professor Emeritus of Medicine, Stanford University;* b. 13 June 1927, Winnipeg, Canada; s. of John Giles Farquhar and Marjorie Victoria Roberts; m. Christine Louise Johnson 1968; one s. one d. (and two s. from previous m.); ed Univ. of California, Berkeley and San Francisco, London School of Hygiene and Tropical Medicine; Intern Univ. of Calif. Hosp., San Francisco 1952–53, Resident 1953–54, 1957–58; Postdoctoral Fellow 1955–57; Resident, Univ. of Minn. 1954–55; Research Assoc., Rockefeller Univ., New York 1958–62; Asst Prof. of Medicine, Stanford Univ. 1962–66, Assoc. Prof. 1966–73, Prof. 1973–97, C. F. Rehnborg Prof. in Disease Prevention 1989–99, Prof. Emer. 1999–, Dir Stanford Center for Research in Disease Prevention (now Stanford Prevention Research Center) 1973–98, Assoc. Chief of Staff for Health Promotion, Stanford Univ. Hosp. 1994–97; Dir Collaborating Center for Chronic Disease Prevention, WHO 1985–99; Pres. Soc. of Behavioral Medicine 1990–92; mem. NAS Inst. of Medicine, American Soc. of Clinical Investigation, Acad. of Behavioral Medicine, American Soc. of Preventive Cardiology; mem. NAS Inst. of Medicine Cttee on Preventing the Global Epidemic of Cardiovascular Disease; Order of St George for Service to Autonomous Govt of Catalonia 1996; James D. Bruce Award 1983, Myrdal Prize 1986, Charles A. Dana Foundation Award for Pioneering Achievements in Health 1990, Nat. Cholesterol Award for Public Educ. 1991, Research Achievement Award, American Heart Assn 1992, Joseph Stokes Preventive Cardiology Award, American Soc. Preventive Cardiology 1999, American Heart Assn Ancel Keys Lectureship 2000, Fries Award for the person who most improved the public's health 2005. *Publications:* The American Way of Life Need Not Be Hazardous to Your Health 1978, The Last Puff (with Gene Spiller) 1990, The Victoria Declaration for Heart Health 1992, The Catalonia Declaration: Investing in Heart Health 1996, Worldwide Efforts to Improve Heart Disease 1997, Diagnosis: Heart Disease (with Gene Spiller) 2000; contribs to professional journals. *Leisure interests:* 20th century history, classical music, ornithology, Scottish history, Canadian history, languages. *Address:* 649 Cabrillo Street, Stanford, CA 94305 (home); School of Medicine, Stanford Prevention Research Center, MSOB, 251 Campus Drive, Stanford, CA 94305-5411, USA. *Telephone:* (650) 723-6051 (office); (650) 327-1177 (home). *Fax:* (650) 498-4828 (office); (650) 498-7623 (office). *E-mail:* john .farquhar@stanford.edu (office). *Website:* www.prevention.stanford.edu (office).

FARQUHAR, Robin Hugh, PhD; Canadian academic and university administrator; *Professor Emeritus, School of Public Policy and Administration, Carleton University;* b. 1 Dec. 1938, Victoria, BC; s. of Hugh E. Farquhar and Jean MacIntosh; m. Frances Caswell 1963; three d.; ed Victoria High School, Victoria Coll., Univ. of British Columbia, Univ. of Chicago; teacher, Counsellor and Coach, Edward Milne Secondary School, Sooke, BC 1962–64; Assoc. Dir and Deputy Dir Univ. Council for Educational Admin 1966–71; Chair. Dept of Educational Admin and Asst Dir Ont. Inst. for Studies in Educ. and Assoc. Prof., then Prof., School of Grad. Studies, Univ. of Toronto 1971–76; Dean of Educ. and Prof. Univ. of Sask., Saskatoon 1976–81; Pres., Vice-Chancellor and Prof., Univ. of Winnipeg 1981–89; Pres., Vice-Chancellor and Prof., Carleton Univ., Ottawa 1989–96, Prof. of Public Policy and Admin 1996–2004, now Prof. Emer.; int. consultant, higher educ. policy and man. 2004–; Hon. mem. World Innovation Foundation, Fellow Commonwealth Council for Educational Admin, Hon. Citizen City of Winnipeg, Hon. Scout; 125th Anniversary of the Confederation of Canada Commemorative Medal; Hon. Diploma in Adult Educ.;; Award of Merit, Canadian Bureau for Int. Education, Ottawa–Carleton Partnership Award of Excellence for Leadership. *Publications:* numerous books and articles on educational admin. *Leisure interests:* jogging, golf, music. *Address:* 64 Queen Elizabeth Drive, Ottawa, ON K2P 1E3, Canada (home). *Telephone:* (613) 230-4735 (home). *Fax:* (613) 230-1094 (home). *E-mail:* rfarquha@connect.carleton.ca (home).

FARR, David N., BS, MBA; American business executive; *Chairman, President and CEO, Emerson Electric Company;* b. 1955; m.; two c.; ed Wake Forest Univ., Vanderbilt Univ.; joined Corp. Staff Dept, Emerson Electric Co. (later Emerson) 1981, becoming Man., Investor Relations, Vice-Pres., Corp. Planning and Devt, Pres. Ridge Tool Div., Group Vice-Pres. for Industrial Components and Equipment, Pres. Emerson Electric Asia-Pacific, Hong Kong 1994–97, Exec. Vice-Pres. Emerson 1997–99, Sr Exec. Vice-Pres. and COO 1999–2000, CEO 2000–, Chair. 2004–, Pres. 2005–, mem. Bd of Dirs; mem. Bd of Dirs Delphi Corpn, United Way of Greater St Louis (Chair. annual fund-raising campaign 2007); mem. Exec. Bd The Muny at Forest Park, Boy Scouts of America (Greater St Louis Area Council); mem. Civic Progress, The Business Council, Washington DC; Trustee, Webster Univ. *Address:* Emerson Electric Co., PO Box 4100, 8000 West Florissant Avenue, St Louis, MO 63136-8506, USA (office). *Telephone:* (314) 553-2000 (office). *Fax:* (314) 553-3527 (office). *E-mail:* info@emerson.com (office). *Website:* www.emerson.com (office).

FARRAKHAN, Louis; American religious leader; *Leader, Nation of Islam;* b. (Louis Eugene Wolcott), 11 May 1933, New York City; m. Betsy Wolcott; nine c.; ed Winston-Salem Teachers Coll.; fmrly Leader and Nat. Spokesman, Nation of Islam Mosque, Harlem; f. reorganized org. Nation of Islam 1977, Leader 1977–; organizer 'Million Man March' 1995, Washington, DC, 'Million Family March' 2000; barred from entering UK on grounds that his opinions would provoke disorder April 2002. *Address:* Nation of Islam, 7351 South Stony Island Avenue, Chicago, IL 60649, USA. *Telephone:* (773) 324-6000 (office). *Website:* www.noi.org (office).

FARRELL, Andrew, OBE; British rugby football player (rugby league); b. 30 May 1975, Wigan, Lancashire; s. of Peter Farrell; m. to Colleen Farrell; loose forward, second row, prop forward or stand off; signed for Wigan Warriors 1992 (senior debut versus Keighley in Nov. 1991); became youngest player to win a Wembley final in 1993 aged 17 years and 11 months; won Harry Sunderland Trophy for Man of the Match in the 1996 and 1997 Premiership finals (both against St Helens)—only Wigan player to have won the award twice; Super League record of 11 goals in a match versus St Helens 1997, repeated feat versus Paris St Germain 1997; highest Super League point scorer 1997; passed 3,000 points for Wigan in 2004 (second-highest total for the club); five caps for GB Acad., one cap for GB Under-21s, full GB debut versus Australia 1993 (youngest forward to win GB cap), 34 caps in total (fifth-highest figure); GB Capt. 1998– on 29 occasions (record); five caps for England; rep. Lancashire in 2003 Origin Match; awarded Wigan testimonial season 2001; Man of Steel 1995, 2004, selected for Super League Dream Team 2003, 2004, Rugby League World Golden Boot Award 2004 (only second British player to win prize). *Address:* c/o Wigan Warriors, JJB Stadium, Loire Drive, Wigan, Lancashire, WN5 0UH, England. *Telephone:* (1942) 774000. *Fax:* (1942) 214880. *E-mail:* wrlfc@wiganrl.com. *Website:* www.wigan-warriors.com.

FARRELL, Colin; Irish actor; b. 31 May 1976, Castleknock, Dublin; s. of Eamon Farrell and Rita Farrell (née Monaghan); ed Gaiety School of Drama, Dublin. *Films include:* Drinking Crude 1997, Falling for a Dancer (TV) 1998, The War Zone 1999, Ordinary Decent Criminal 2000, Tigerland (Boston Soc. of Film Critics Best Actor Award) 2000, American Outlaws 2001, Hart's War 2002, Minority Report 2002, Phone Booth 2002, The Recruit 2003, Daredevil 2003, Veronica Guerin 2003, S.W.A.T. 2003, Intermission 2003, A Home at the End of the World 2004, Alexander 2004, The New World 2005, Ask the Dust 2006, Miami Vice 2006, Cassandra's Dream 2007, In Bruges (Golden Globe Award for Best Actor in a Musical or Comedy 2009) 2008, Pride and Glory 2007. *Television includes:* Ballykissangel 1996, Love in the 21st Century 1999. *Address:* c/o Creative Artists Agency, 9830 Wilshire Boulevard, Beverly Hills, CA 90212-1825, USA (office). *Telephone:* (310) 288-4545 (office). *Fax:* (310) 288-4800 (office). *Website:* www.caa.com (office).

FARRELL, Patrick M.; Irish politician; b. 30 Aug. 1957, Leitrim; s. of Bill Farrell and Mamie Casey; m. Margaret Logan 1988; one s. one d.; ed Man. College, Carrick-on-Shannon, Inst. of Public Admin.; Hosp. Admin. Sligo 1981–86; CEO Galvia Hosp., Galway 1986–91; Gen. Sec. Fianna Fáil 1991–98; fmr Chair. Irish Council of the European Movt; mem. of Senate 1992; mem. Bd of Friends of Fianna Fáil Inc., USA. *Leisure interests:* current affairs, reading, writing. *Address:* c/o Aras De Valera, 13 Upper Mount Street, Dublin 2, Ireland. *Telephone:* (1) 6761551. *Fax:* (1) 6785960.

FARRELL, Suzanne; American ballerina; *Artistic Director, Suzanne Farrell Ballet;* b. 16 Aug. 1945; ed School of American Ballet; fmr Prin. Dancer with New York City Ballet –1989; also danced with Béjart Ballet, Brussels; appeared in numerous Balanchine ballets choreographed for her including Mozartiana, Chaconne, Meditation, Vienna Waltzes; staged seven Balanchine ballets at John F. Kennedy Center for Performing Arts, Washington, DC 1995 and many other stagings of Balanchine's works; Artistic Dir Suzanne Farrell Ballet co. at Kennedy Center 2000–; repetiteur for Balanchine Trust, including Kirov Ballet, Royal Danish Ballet and Paris Opéra Ballet; mem. Advisory Panel Princess Grace Foundation, Sr Advisory Bd of Arthritis Foundation; EPPES Prof. of Dance,. Florida State Univ.; trains ballet dancers in camp in The Adirondacks; several hon. degrees; Nat. Medal of the Arts 2003, Kennedy Center Honor 2005, Capezio Dance Award 2005. *Television:* Suzanne Farrell: Elusive Muse (documentary). *Publication:* Holding On To The Air (autobiog.) 1990. *Address:* Suzanne Farrell Ballet, Kennedy Center for the Performing Arts, Washington, DC 20566, USA. *Website:* www.kennedy-center.org/programs/ballet/farrell.

FARRELL, Sir Terence (Terry), Kt, CBE, MCP, MArch, MRTPI, RIBA, FCSD, FRSA; British architect; *Principal, Terry Farrell & Partners;* b. 12 May 1938; s. of Thomas Farrell and Molly Farrell (née Maguire); m. 1st Angela Rosemarie Mallam 1960; two d.; m. 2nd Susan Hilary Aplin 1973; two s. one d.; ed St Cuthbert's Grammar School, Newcastle-upon-Tyne, Newcastle Univ., Univ. of Pennsylvania, USA; Harkness Fellow, Commonwealth Fund, USA 1962–64; Partner, Farrell Grimshaw Partnership 1965–80, Terry Farrell Partnership 1980–87; Prin. Terry Farrell & Partners 1987–; Visiting Prof., Univ. of Westminster 1998–2001; Hon. FAIA; Hon. DCL (Newcastle) 2000; Hon. DArts (Lincoln) 2003. *Major projects include:* Vauxhall Cross (MI6 Bldg), London, The Peak, Hong Kong, Kowloon Station, Hong Kong, Charing Cross Station Redevelopment, Edinburgh Int. Conf. Centre, British Consulate and British Council Bldgs, Hong Kong, Dean Centre Art Gallery, Edin., Int. Centre for Life, Newcastle, Transportation Centre for Inchon Int. Airport, Seoul, The Deep 'Submarium', Hull. *Publications:* Architectural Monograph 1985, Urban Design Monograph 1993, Ten Years, Ten Cities: The work of Terry Farrell and Partners, 1991–2001 2002, Place 2005; articles in numerous journals. *Leisure interests:* walking, swimming. *Address:* Terry Farrell & Partners, 7 Hatton Street, London, NW8 8PL, England (office). *Telephone:* (20) 7258-3433 (office). *Fax:* (20) 7723-7059 (office). *E-mail:* tfarrell@terryfarrell.co.uk (office). *Website:* www.terryfarrell.com (office).

FARRELL, Thomas Francis, II, BA, JD; American lawyer and business executive; *Chairman, President and CEO, Dominion Resources, Inc.;* b. 1954; m. Anne Garland Farrell (neé Tullidge); two s.; ed Univ. of Va; Pnr, McGuire Woods Beatle & Booth (law firm) 1981–95; joined Dominion Resources Inc., Richmond 1995, Sr Vice Pres. and Gen. Counsel 1995–97, Sr Vice Pres. for Corp. Affairs 1997–99, Exec. Vice Pres. 1999–2003, Pres. and COO 2002–05, Pres. and CEO 2006–07, Chair., Pres. and CEO 2007–, also CEO Va Power, Dominion Generation Inc., Pres. and COO Consolidated Natural Gas Co. (subsidiaries of Dominion Resources); mem. Bd of Dirs Va Electric and Power Co., Inst. of Nuclear Power Operations; mem. Va Bar Assen, Va Law Foundation; Rector, Bd of Visitors, Univ. of Va 2005–. *Address:* Dominion Resources, Inc., 120 Tredegar Street, Richmond, VA 23219, USA (office). *Telephone:* (804) 819-2000 (office). *Fax:* (804) 819-2233 (office). *E-mail:* thomas_farrell@dom.com (office). *Website:* www.dom.com (office).

FARRINGTON, David Philip, OBE, MA, PhD, FBA, FMedSci; British psychologist, academic and criminologist; *Professor of Psychological Criminology, Institute of Criminology, University of Cambridge;* b. 7 March 1944, Ormskirk, Lancs.; s. of William Farrington and Gladys Holden Farrington; m. Sally Chamberlain 1966; three d.; ed Univ. of Cambridge; mem. staff, Inst. of Criminology, Univ. of Cambridge 1969–, Prof. of Psychological Criminology 1992–; Pres. European Assen of Psychology and Law 1997–99; Visiting Fellow, US Nat. Inst. of Justice 1981; Chair. Div. of Criminological and Legal Psychology, British Psychological Soc. 1983–85; mem. Parole Bd for England and Wales 1984–87; Vice-Chair. US Nat. Acad. of Sciences Panel on Violence 1989–92; Visiting Fellow US Bureau of Justice Statistics 1995–98; Co-Chair. US Office of Juvenile Justice and Delinquency Prevention Study Group on Serious and Violent Juvenile Offenders 1995–97; Pres. British Soc. of Criminology 1990–93, Pres. American Soc. of Criminology 1998–99; Co-Chair. US Office of Juvenile Justice and Delinquency Prevention Study Group on Very Young Offenders 1998–2000; Chair. UK Dept of Health Advisory Cttee for the Nat. Programme on Forensic Mental Health 2000–03; mem. Bd of Dirs Int. Soc. of Criminology 2000–; Pres. Acad. of Experimental Criminology 2001–03; Co-Chair. Campbell Collaboration Crime and Justice Group 2000–; Sellin-Glueck Award of American Soc. of Criminology 1984, Sutherland Award of American Soc. of Criminology 2002, Joan McCord Award, Acad. of Experimental Criminology 2005, Beccaria Gold Medal, Criminology Soc. of German-Speaking Countries 2005. *Publications:* 27 books and over 420 articles on criminology and psychology. *Address:* Institute of Criminology, University of Cambridge, Sidgwick Avenue, Cambridge, CB3 9DT (office); 7 The Meadows, Haslingfield, Cambridge, CB3 7JD, England (home). *Telephone:* (1223) 335360 (office); (1223) 872555 (home). *Fax:* (1223) 335356 (office). *E-mail:* enquiries@crim.cam.ac.uk (office). *Website:* www.crim.cam.ac.uk (office).

FARROW, Mia Villiers; American actress; b. 9 Feb. 1945, Calif.; d. of John Villiers Farrow and Maureen O'Sullivan; m. 1st Frank Sinatra 1966 (divorced 1968); m. 2nd André Previn 1970 (divorced 1979); 14 c.; Stage début in The Importance of Being Earnest, New York 1963; French Acad. Award for Best Actress 1969, David Donatello Award (Italy) 1969, Rio de Janeiro Film Festival Award 1969, San Sebastian Award. *Stage appearances in London:* Mary Rose, The Three Sisters, House of Bernarda Alba 1972–73, The Marrying of Ann Leete (RSC) 1975, The Zykovs 1976, Ivanov (RSC) 1976; appeared in Romantic Comedy (Broadway) 1979. *Films include:* Guns at Batasi 1964, Rosemary's Baby 1968, Secret Ceremony 1969, John and Mary 1969, See No Evil 1970, The Great Gatsby 1973, Full Circle 1978, A Wedding 1978, Death on the Nile 1978, The Hurricane 1979, A Midsummer Night's Sex Comedy 1982, Zelig 1983, Broadway Danny Rose 1984, Purple Rose of Cairo 1985, Hannah and Her Sisters 1986, Radio Days 1987, September 1988, Another Woman 1988, Oedipus Wrecks 1989, Crimes and Misdemeanors 1989, Alice 1990, Shadows and Fog 1992, Husbands and Wives 1992, Widow's Peak 1994, Miami Rhapsody 1995, Private Parts 1997, Reckless 1995, Coming Soon 2000, Purpose 2002, The Omen 2006, Arthur and the Invisibles 2006, The Ex 2007, Be Kind Rewind 2007. *Television appearances:* Peyton Place 1964–66; Johnny Belinda 1965, Peter Pan 1975, Goodbye Raggedy Ann (film), Miracle at Midnight, The Secret Life of Zoey (film) 2002, Samantha: An American Girl Holiday (film) 2004. *Publication:* What Falls Away (autobiog.) 1996. *Leisure interests:* reading, mind wandering, listening to music and certain people. *Address:* International Creative Management, c/o Sam Cohn, 40 West 57th Street, New York, NY 10019, USA. *Website:* www.mia-farrow.com.

FARULLI, Piero; Italian academic; *Teacher, Scuola di Musica di Fiesole;* b. 13 Jan. 1920, Florence; s. of Lioniero Farulli and Maria (née Innocenti) Farulli; m. Antonia Parisi 1945; ed Conservatorio Statale Luigi Cherubini, Florence (under Gioacchino Maglioni); Prof. of Viola 1957–77; for thirty years a mem. of Quartetto Italiano; has also collaborated with Amadeus and Berg Quartets; appeared with Trio di Trieste 1978; has lectured at Accad. Chigiana di Siena and at Salzburg Mozarteum; mem. of judging panel at several int. competitions and is active in many aspects of musical life and education in Italy, notably at the Scuola di Musica di Fiesole, which he founded in 1974; Medaglia della Cultura e dell'Arte; Grand 'Ufficiale della Repubblica 1994. *Address:* Scuola di Musica di Fiesole, Via delle Fontanelle, 24, 50016 S. Domenico di Fiesole, Florence, Italy (office); Via G. d'Annunzio 153, Florence, Italy. *Telephone:* (055) 597851 (office); (055) 608007 (office). *Fax:* (055) 599686 (office). *Website:* www.scuolamusica.fiesole.fi.it (office).

FARUQUE, Mohammad, BEng; Pakistani industrialist; *Chairman, Ghulam Faruque Group;* b. 14 Jan. 1930, Magpur, India; s. of the late Ghulam Faruque and Zulfara Faruque; one d. two s.; ed Univ. of Southern Calif.; Chair. Ghulam Faruque Group, conglomerate which includes Cherat Cement Co. Ltd, Mirpurkhas Sugar Mills Ltd, Greaves Pakistan (Pvt.) Ltd. *Leisure interests:* cricket, golf, reading. *Address:* Ghulam Faruque Group, Modern Motors House, Beaumont Road, Karachi 75530, Pakistan (office). *Telephone:* (21) 5682565 (office); (21) 5888889 (home). *Fax:* (21) 5682839 (office). *E-mail:* faruque@fascom.com (office).

FASCETTO, Jorge E.; Argentine journalist and fmr international organization official; ed La Plata Nat. Univ.; apptd. Gen. Man. El Día newspaper, La Plata 1967, Chair. Bd of Dirs. 1980–; Vice-Pres. Exec. Cttee Asociacíon de Diarios del Interior de la República Argentina (ADIRA) 1985, Asociacíon de Entidades Periodísticas Argentinas (ADEPA) 1986; Dir and mem. Exec. Cttee and Advisory Council Inter-American Press Asscn (IAPA), Pres. IAPA Tech. Center 1989; Chair. Int. Press Inst. 2002–04. *Address:* c/o El Día, Avda A. Diagonal 80 817–21, 1900 La Plata, Argentina (office).

FASE, Martin M. G., PhD; Dutch banker, economist and academic; *Emeritus Professor of Monetary Economics, University of Amsterdam;* b. 28 Dec. 1937, Boskoop; s. of A. P. Fase and G. J. M. de Groot; m. Lida E. M. Franse 1965; two s.; ed Univ. of Amsterdam; Research Assoc., Inst. of Actuarial Sciences and Econometrics, Amsterdam 1965–69; Ford Foundation Fellow, Dept of Econs, Univ. of Wis., Madison, USA 1969–71; with De Nederlandsche Bank 1971–2001, Deputy Dir 1985–2001; Extraordinary Prof. of Business Statistics, Erasmus Univ., Rotterdam 1978–86; Extraordinary Prof. of Monetary Econs, Univ. of Amsterdam 1986–2003; Fellow Royal Netherlands Acad. of Arts and Sciences 1987, Hollandsche Maatschappij der Wetenschappen 1989, mem. Maatschappi der Nederlandse Letterhunau 2001; Officier Order of Orange Nassau 1995; N. G. Pierson Medal 1996. *Publications:* An Econometric Model of Age-Income Profiles: a Statistical Analysis of Dutch Income Data 1970, The Monetary Sector of the Netherlands in 50 Equations: a Quarterly Monetary Model for the Netherlands 1970–79, in Analysing the Structure of Econometric Models (ed. J.P. Ancot) 1984, Seasonal Adjustment as a Practical Problem 1991, Demand for Money and Credit in Europe 1999, Tussen behoud en vernieuwing 2000; articles in European Econ. Review, Journal of Int. Econs and other journals; several monographs. *Leisure interests:* Dutch literature, hiking. *Address:* Ruysdaelweg 3B, 2051 EM Overveen, Netherlands (home). *Telephone:* (23) 527 1700 (home). *E-mail:* mmg.fase@wxs.nl (home).

FASQUELLE, Jean-Claude; French publisher; *Chairman of the Board, Éditions Grasset et Fasquelle;* b. 29 Nov. 1930, Paris; s. of Charles Fasquelle and Odette Cyprien-Fabre; m. 1st Solange de la Rochefoucauld; one d.; m. 2nd Nicola Jegher 1966; ed Ecole des Roches, Verneuil-sur-Avre, Sorbonne and Faculté de Droit, Paris; Pres.-Dir-Gen. Société des Editions Fasquelle 1953–60, Editions du Sagittaire 1958–; Admin.-Dir-Gen. Editions Grasset et Fasquelle 1960, Pres.-Dir-Gen. 1980–2000, Chair. of Bd 2000–; Dir Le Magazine littéraire (monthly) 1970–2004. *Address:* Éditions Grasset et Fasquelle, 61 rue des Saintes-Pères, 75006 Paris (office); 13 Square Vergennes, 75015 Paris, France (home). *Telephone:* 1-44-39-22-00 (office). *Fax:* 1-44-39-22-18 (office).

FASSBAENDER, Brigitte, FRNCM; German singer (mezzo-soprano) and artistic director; *Intendantin, Tiroler Landestheater;* b. 3 July 1939, Berlin; d. of the late Willi Domgraf-Fassbaender and Sabine Peters; ed Nuremberg Conservatoire and studied with father; debut at Bavarian State Opera, Munich 1961; has appeared at La Scala Milan, Vienna State Opera, Covent Garden London, Metropolitan Opera, New York, San Francisco and Salzburg; Teacher of Solo Vocal Music Musikhochschule, Munich; soloist, Dir of Opera, Brunswick 1995–97; Intendantin (Artistic Dir), Tiroler Landestheater, Innsbruck 1999–; Bundesverdienstkreuz am Bande, Bayerischer Verdienstorden. *Recordings:* over 100 recordings since 1964. *Address:* Tiroler Landestheater und Orchester GmbH, Rennweg 2, 6020 Innsbruck, Austria (office). *Telephone:* (512) 52-07-4 (office). *E-mail:* tiroler@landestheater.at (office). *Website:* www.landestheater.at (office).

FASSI, Abbas al-; Moroccan politician; *Prime Minister;* b. 18 Sept. 1940, Berkane; m.; four c.; ed Univ. Mohammed V, Rabat; apptd Sec.-Gen. Moroccan Human Rights League 1972; mem. Exec. Cttee Istiqlal Party 1974–, Gen. Sec. 1998–; Minister of Housing 1977–81, of Handicrafts and Social Affairs 1981–85, of Social Devt, Solidarity, Employment and Professional Training 2000–02, Minister of State 2002–07; Prime Minister of Morocco 2007–; Amb. to Tunisia and Perm. Rep. to League of Arab Nations 1985–90; Amb. to France 1990–94; mem. Bd of Dirs Caisse Nat. de Sécurité Sociale, Entraide Nationale, Social Devt Agency; Grand Officier, Order National de Mérite (France), Commandeur, Ordre de la République (Tunisia). *Address:* Office of the Prime Minister, Palais Royal, Touarga, Rabat, Morocco (office). *Telephone:* (3) 7219400 (office). *Fax:* (3) 7769995 (office). *E-mail:* courrier@pm.gov.ma (office). *Website:* www.pm.gov.ma (office).

FASSI-FIHRI, Ahmed, LenD; Moroccan civil servant and diplomatist; b. 6 Aug. 1936, Oujda; m. Touria El Ouazzani; two s. two d.; pvt. sec. of Minister of Interior 1956; Head of Office, Dept of Minerals and Geology 1958; Head, Office of Minister of Foreign Affairs 1959; Chargé d'affaires, Moroccan Embassy, Berne 1960; Pres. Melnes Municipality 1963; founder and Dir Nat. Documentation Centre 1967–, Information Science School 1974, Multimedia Centre 1993; Order of Ridha. *Publications:* articles in field of information science in Arabic and French. *Leisure interests:* listening to Arabic and classical music; reading of the Arabic intellectual literary productions. *Address:* Centre National de Documentation, Boulevard Hadj Ahmed Cherkaoui, Rabat, Morocco. *Telephone:* (3) 774944; (3) 773139. *Fax:* (3) 773134.

FASSI-FIHRI, Taieb, PhD; Moroccan government official; *Minister of Foreign Affairs and Co-operation;* b. 9 April 1958, Casablanca; m.; two c.; ed Lycée Descartes, Rabat, Institut Nat. de la Statistique et d'Economie Appliquée, Rabat, Université Panthéon-Sorbonne, Paris, Institut d'Etudes Politiques, Paris; Lecturer, Univ. of Paris VII, as well as Chargé d'Etudes at Institut Français des Relations Internationales 1983–84; attached to Dept of Planning, Ministry of Planning 1984, in charge of special duties in Cabinet of Minister in Charge of Relations with the EEC 1985–86; Chief of Div., Ministry of Foreign Affairs and Co-operation in charge of relations with EC 1986–89; Dir Office of the Minister of State in charge of Foreign Affairs and Co-operation 1989–93; Sec. of State for Foreign Affairs and Co-operation 1993–98; Head of Mission at Royal Cabinet 1998–99; Sec. of State for Foreign Affairs 1999–2000, for Foreign Affairs and Co-operation 2000–02, Coordinator, responsible for negotiation of free trade agreement with Morocco and USA 2002, Minister Del. for Foreign Affairs and Co-operation 2002–07, Minister of Foreign Affairs and Co-operation 2007–; Officer, Wissam Al Arch Order 2001. *Address:* Ministry of Foreign Affairs and Co-operation, avenue Franklin Roosevelt, Rabat, Morocco (office). *Telephone:* (3) 7761583 (office). *Fax:* (3) 7765508 (office). *E-mail:* mail@maec.gov.ma (office). *Website:* www.maec.gov.ma (office).

FASSINO, Piero Franco Rodolfo, BSc; Italian politician; *Shadow Minister for Foreign Affairs;* b. 7 Oct. 1949, Avigliana; m.; local councillor Turin 1975–80, 1985–90, Prov. Councillor 1980–85; various posts within Turin Fed. of Partito Comunista Italiano (PCI) 1971–83, Prov. Sec. 1983–87, elected to PCI Exec. 1983, Co-ordinator Nat. Secr. 1987, then Head of party org. during transition to Partito Democratico della Sinistra (PDS), mem. Nat. Secr. and Int. Sec. PDS 1991–96, PDS Rep. to Socialist Int. 1992, PDS re-named Democratici di Sinistra (DS) 1998, Leader (Nat. Sec.) DS 2001–07, mem. Partito Democratico (formed after merger between Democratici di Sinistra, Democrazia è Libertà—La Margherita and other left-wing and centrist parties); Pres. Cen. and Western Europe Cttee Socialist Int. 1993, Chair. Cttee for Peace, Democracy and Human Rights 2004–; fmr Vice-Pres. Socialist Group, Council of Europe; mem. Chamber of Deputies from Liguria (PDS) 1994–96, from Piedmont 1996–; Under-Sec. Ministry for Foreign Affairs 1996–98; Minister for Foreign Trade 1998–2000, for Justice 2000–01; Shadow Minister for Foreign Affairs 2008–; mem. Parl. Asscn for Cen. Europe Initiative; Vice-Pres. Italian–Israeli Parl. Friendship Asscn 1995. *Publications:* Per Passione 2003. *Address:* Partito Democratico, Piazza Saint'Anastasia 7, 00186 Rome, Italy. *Telephone:* (06) 675471. *Fax:* (06) 67547319. *E-mail:* info@partitodemocratico.it. *Website:* www.partitodemocratico.it.

FATTOUH, Rawhi, (Abu Wisam), BA; Palestinian politician; b. 23 Aug. 1949; m.; one d. two s.; ed Damascus Univ.; Speaker of Palestinian Parl. 2004–06; Acting Exec. Pres. Palestinian (Nat.) Authority 2004–05; aide to Pres. Mahmoud Abbas –2008. *Publications:* several articles in Arabic about the Middle East. *Address:* c/o Office of the President, Ramallah, Palestinian Autonomous Areas, via Israel (office).

FAU, Yamandú; Uruguayan academic and politician; mem. Parl. 1984–2000; Minister of Educ. and Culture 2000; elected Senator 2000; Minister of Nat. Defence 2002–05; mem. Partido Colorado de Uruguay. *Address:* c/o Ministry of National Defence, Edif. General Artigas, Avda 8 de Octubre 2628, Montevideo, Uruguay (office).

FAUCI, Anthony Stephen, MD; American medical researcher; *Director, National Institute of Allergy and Infectious Diseases;* b. 24 Dec. 1940, Brooklyn, New York; s. of Stephen Fauci and Eugenia Fauci; m. Christine Grady 1985; three d.; ed Coll. of the Holy Cross, Cornell Univ. Medical Coll.; Instructor in Medicine, Cornell Medical Coll. 1971–72; Medical Dir US Public Health Service 1968–70, 1972; Clinical Assoc. Lab. of Clinical Investigation, Nat. Inst. of Allergy and Infectious Diseases (NIAID) 1968–71, Sr Staff Fellow, Lab. of Clinical Investigation 1970–71, Sr Investigator 1972–74, Head Physiology Section 1974–80, Deputy Clinical Dir NIAID 1977–84, Dir 1984–; Chief Resident in Medicine, New York Hosp., Cornell Univ. Medical Center 1971–72; Chief Lab. of Immunoregulation 1980–; Dir Office of AIDS Research and Assoc. Dir Nat. Inst. of Health (NIH) for AIDS Research 1988–94; Consultant Naval Medical Center, Bethesda 1972–; Bristol Award of the Infectious Diseases Soc. of America (IDSA) 1999, Int. Prize for Scientific Research, Fondazione PISO 1999, Frank Berry Prize in Fed. Medicine 1999, Timely Topics Award Lecture of the US and Canadian Acad. of Pathology 1999; ed. of numerous learned journals on immunlogy. *Leisure interests:* jogging, tennis. *Address:* NIAID/NIH, 31 Center Drive MSC 2520, Bethesda, MD 20892-0001 (office); 3012 43rd Street, NW, Washington, DC 20016, USA (home). *Telephone:* (301) 496-2263 (office). *Fax:* (301) 496-4409 (office). *E-mail:* afauci@niaid.nih.gov (office). *Website:* www.niaid.nih.gov (office).

FAUCON, Bernard; French photographer; b. 12 Sept. 1950, Apt; ed Lycée d'Apt, Univ. of Aix en Provence, Sorbonne, Paris; Grand Prix Nat. de la Photographie 1989. *Publications:* Les grandes vacances 1980, Summer Camp 1980, Les Papiers qui volent 1986, Les Chambres d'amour 1987, Tables d'amis 1991, Les Idoles et les sacrifices 1991, Les Ecritures 1993, Jours d'images 1995, La Fin de l'Image 1997, La peur du voyage 1999, Le plus beau jour de ma jeunesse 2000, La plus belle route du monde 2000, Une singulière Gourmandise 2004, Bernard Faucon Catalogue Raisonné 2006, Été 2550 Actes Sud 2009. *Leisure interest:* cookery, travelling. *Address:* 6 rue Barbanègre, 75019 Paris, France (home). *Telephone:* 1-40-05-99-70 (home). *E-mail:* info.contact@bernardfaucon.net (office). *Website:* www.bernardfaucon.net (home).

FAULKNER, John, BA, DipEd; Australian politician; *Special Minister of State, Cabinet Secretary and Vice-President of the Executive Council;* b. 12 April 1954, Leeton, NSW; ed Macquarie Univ.; mem. NSW Admin. Cttee,

Australian Labor Party (ALP) 1978–89, Asst Gen. Sec. 1980–89, mem. ALP Nat. Exec. 1989–, Nat. Pres. ALP 2007–08; research officer for NSW Minister for Sport and Recreation 1980; mem. Senate 1989–, Man. of Govt Business 1993–96, Leader of Opposition 1996–2004; Minister for Veterans' Affairs and Minister for Defence Science and Personnel 1993–94, for Sport and Territories March 1994, for Environment, Sport and Territories 1994–96; Shadow Minister for Social Security 1996–97, for Public Admin and Govt Services 1997–2001, for Territories 1997–98, for Olympic Coordination and Centenary of Fed. 1998–2001, for Public Admin and Home Affairs 2001–03, for Public Admin and Accountability 2003–04; Special Minister of State, Cabinet Sec. and Vice-Pres. of the Exec. Council 2007–; mem. Macquarie Univ. Council 1984–92. *Address:* Department of the Prime Minister and Cabinet, 1 National Circuit, Canberra, ACT 2600, Australia (office). *Telephone:* (2) 6277-7600 (office). *Website:* www.smos.gov.au (office).

FAULKS, Sebastian, CBE, MA, FRSL; British writer; b. 20 April 1953, Newbury, Berks.; s. of Peter Faulks and Pamela Lawless; m. Veronica Youlten 1989; two s. one d.; ed Wellington Coll. and Emmanuel Coll., Cambridge; reporter, Daily Telegraph newspaper 1979–83, feature writer, Sunday Telegraph 1983–86; Literary Ed. The Independent 1986–89, Deputy Ed. The Independent on Sunday 1989–90, Assoc. Ed. 1990–91; columnist, The Guardian 1992–97, Evening Standard 1997–99, Mail on Sunday 1999–2000; invited to write new James Bond 007 novel to celebrate centenary of Ian Fleming's birth 2008; Hon. Fellow, Emmanuel Coll., Cambridge 2007; Hon. DLitt (Tavistock Clinic, Univ. of E London). *Radio:* Panelist, The Write Stuff, BBC Radio 4 1998–. *Television:* Churchill's Secret Army 2000. *Publications:* A Trick of the Light 1984, The Girl at the Lion d'Or 1989, A Fool's Alphabet 1992, Birdsong 1993, The Fatal Englishman 1996, Charlotte Gray 1998, On Green Dolphin Street 2001, Human Traces 2005, Pistache 2006, Engleby 2007, Devil May Care (writing as Ian Fleming) (British Book Award for Popular Fiction 2009) 2008. *Leisure interests:* wine, sport. *Address:* Aitken Alexander Associates Ltd, 18–21 Cavaye Place, London, SW10 9PT, England (office). *Telephone:* (20) 7373-8672 (office). *Fax:* (20) 7373-6002 (office). *E-mail:* reception@aitkenalexander.co.uk (office). *Website:* www.aitkenalexander.co.uk (office); www.sebastianfaulks.com (office).

FAURE, Danny; Seychelles politician; *Minister of Finance and Designated Minister;* b. 1962; early career as teacher, Seychelles Polytechnic and Nat. Youth Service; fmr Chair. Seychelles People's Progressive Front; Leader of Govt Business, Nat. Ass. 1993–98; Minister for Educ. and Youth 1998–2006; Minister of Finance and Designated Minister 2006–. *Address:* Ministry of Finance, POB 313, Victoria, Mahé, Seychelles (office). *Telephone:* 382000 (office). *Fax:* 324248 (office).

FAURE, Maurice Henri, KCMG, DenD; French politician; b. 2 Jan. 1922, Azerat (Dordogne); s. of René Faure and Irène Joudinaud; m. Andrée Guillemain 1945; two s.; ed Lycée de Périgueux, Faculty of Law and Letters, Bordeaux and Toulouse Univs; Deputy for Lot (Radical-Socialist) 1951 (re-elected to Nat. Ass. 1956, 1958, 1962, 1967, 1968, 1973, 1978, 1981); Sec. of State for Foreign Affairs (Mollet Cabinet) 1956–57, (Bourgès-Manoury Cabinet) June–Nov. 1957, (Gaillard Cabinet) 1957–58; Minister for European Insts May–June 1958, for Justice May–June 1981; Minister of State for Equipment and Housing 1988–89; mem. Conseil Constitutionnel 1989–98; Pres. French del. Common Market and Euratom Conf., Brussels 1956; mem. del. 11th Session UN Gen. Ass., New York 1956; Special Asst Minister for Foreign Affairs on Morocco and Tunisia 1956–57; fmr mem. European Coal and Steel Community Ass.; mem. European Parl. 1959–67, 1973–81; Senator of Lot 1983–88; fmr Mayor of Prayssac (Lot), Mayor of Cahors 1965–90; Conseiller Général, Salviac canton (Lot) 1957–58, Montcuq canton 1963; Pres. Departmental Asscn of Mayors of Lot, Mouvement européen; Pres. Entente démocratique of the Nat. Ass. 1960–62; Pres., later Leader, Parti republicain radical et radical-socialiste 1961–65, 1969–71; fmr Pres. Rassemblement démocratique Group, Nat. Ass.; Pres. Econ. Devt Comm. for Midi-Pyrénées 1964–70; Pres. Conseil général du Lot 1970–94, Hon. Pres. 1994–; resigned from Rassemblement pour la République May 1977; Vice-Pres. Conseil de la région Midi-Pyrénées 1974–; Officier de la Légion d'honneur, Commdr, Mérite civil, and other awards. *Publications:* D'une république à l'autre, Entretiens sur l'histoire et la politique 1999. *Address:* 28 boulevard Raspail, 75007 Paris, France (home).

FAURE, Roland; French journalist; b. 10 Oct. 1926, Montelimar; s. of Edmond Faure-Geors and Jeanne Gallet; m. Véra Hitzbleck 1956; three s.; ed Enclos Saint-François, Montpellier and Faculté de Droit, Aix-en-Provence; journalist, Méridional-la France, Marseilles 1947; del. in America, Asscn de la presse latine d'Europe et d'Amerique 1951, Sec.-Gen. 1954–; Founder and Ed.-in-Chief, Journal français du Brésil, Rio de Janeiro 1952–53; Diplomatic Ed. L'Aurore 1954, Head of Diplomatic Service 1959, Ed.-in-Chief 1962, Dir and Ed.-in-Chief 1968–78; attached to Cabinet of Minister of Public Works 1957–58; Dir Toutes les nouvelles de Versailles 1954–86; mem. Admin. Bd Antenne 2 1975–79; Dir of Information, Radio-France 1979–81; Founder and Dir Radio CVS 1982; Pres. Dir-Gen. Société Nat. de programme Radio France 1986–89, Société Nat. de Radiodifffusion; Pres. Université radiophonique et télévisuelle int. (URTI) 1987–97, Communauté des radios publiques de langue française (CRPLF) 1987; Pres. Admin. Council Fondations Marguerite Long-Jacques Thibaud 1991–2007; Pres. Club DAB 1991–; mem. Conseil Supérieur de l'Audiovisuel (CSA) 1989–97, mem. numerous professional asscns. etc.; Officier, Légion d'honneur; Officier, Ordre Nat. du Mérite, des Arts et des Lettres. *Publications:* Brésil dernière heure 1954; articles in newspapers and journals. *Address:* La Radio numérique, 40 rue Guynemer, 92130 Issy-les-Moulineaux (office); 94 boulevard de la Tour Maubourg, Paris 7e, France (home). *Telephone:* 1-49-55-01-15 (office).

FAUROUX, Roger, LèsL; French business executive; *Président d'honneur de Saint-Gobain;* b. 21 Nov. 1926, Montpellier (Hérault); s. of Théo Fauroux and Rose Fauroux (née Ségu); m. Marie Le Roy Ladurie 1953; three s. three d.; ed Lycée de Besançon, Lycée Henri IV, Paris, Ecole normale supérieure, Ecole nationale d'admin; Asst Insp. of Finance 1956, Insp. 1958; Office of Minister of Educ. May–Nov. 1960; Admin. Dir Cie Pont-à-Mousson 1961, Finance Dir 1964–69; Finance Dir Cie de Saint-Gobain-Pont-à-Mousson 1970, Asst Dir-Gen. 1972–75, Admin. Dir-Gen. 1978–80, Pres., Dir-Gen. 1980–86, now Président d'honneur de Saint-Gobain; Dir Ecole nat. d'admin 1986–88; Pres. Soc. des Investisseurs du Monde (newspaper) 1986–88; Minister of Industry, also of Territorial Devt, then of Regional Planning 1988–91; Mayor of Saint-Girons 1989–95; Pres. Cerf Editions 1987, 1992–97; Pres. Haut Conseil à l'Integration 1999–; Dir Certain Teed Products, Fabbrica Pisana (Italy), Cristalería Española (Spain), Cie Générale des Eaux, Banque Nationale de Paris, Institut Pasteur, Petrofina (Belgique); mem. Admin. Council Eurotunnel 1991–92, Commercial Union 1992–97, MK2 1993–99; mem. Supervisory Bd Vereinigte Glaswerke Siemens 1993–97, Commercial Union France 1994, Usinor 1995–, France Télécom 2000–, Orange SA 2000–; Pres. Mission of SE European Integration 1999–2000; currently Président d'honneur de Saint-Gobain; Officier, Légion d'honneur, Officier, Ordre Nat. du Mérite. *Publication:* Etats de service 1998. *Address:* c/o Compagnie de Saint-Gobain, Les Miroirs, 92096 Paris-la-Défense Cedex, France.

FAUST, (Catharine) Drew Gilpin, BA, MA, PhD; American historian, academic and university president; *President, Harvard University;* b. 18 Sept. 1947, Clarke Co., Va; d. of McGhee Tyson Gilpin and Catharine Gilpin; m. 1st Stephen Faust (divorced); m. 2nd Charles E. Rosenberg; two d.; ed Concord Acad., Bryn Mawr Coll. and Univ. of Pennsylvania; Asst Prof. of History, Dept of American Civilization, Univ. of Pennsylvania 1976–80, Assoc. Prof. 1980–84, Prof. 1984–88, Stanley Sheerr Prof. of History 1988–89, Annenberg Prof. of History 1989–2000, Chair. Dept of American Civilization 1990–95, Dir Women's Studies Program 1996–2000; Dean, Radcliffe Inst. for Advanced Study, Harvard Univ. 2001–07, Lincoln Prof. of History 2003–07, Pres., Harvard Univ. (first woman) 2007–; Chair. Presidential Cttee on Univ. Life, Univ. of Pennsylvania 1988–90; mem. American Acad. of Arts and Sciences, American Philosphical Soc., Southern Historical Asscn (Pres. 1999–2000), American Historical Asscn (Vice-Pres. 1992–96), Exec. Bd Org. of American Historians 1999–2002, Exec. Bd Soc. of American Historians 1999–2002, Educational Advisory Bd, Guggenheim Foundation, Pulitzer Prize for History jury 1986, 1990, 2004 (Chair.); Trustee Bryn Mawr Coll. 1997–, Nat. Humanities Center 2002–, Andrew W. Mellon Foundation 2003–; ranked by Forbes magazine amongst 100 Most Powerful Women (47th) 2007, (76th) 2008. *Publications:* A Sacred Circle: The Dilemma of the Intellectual in the Old South 1977, The Ideology of Slavery: Proslavery Thought in the Antebellum South, 1830-1860 1981, James Henry Hammond and the Old South: A Design for Mastery 1985, The Creation of Confederate Nationalism: Ideology and Identity in the Civil War South 1989, Southern Stories: Slaveholders in Peace and War 1992, Mothers of Invention: Women of the Slaveholding South in the American Civil War (Soc. of American Historians' Francis Parkman Prize 1997) 1996, This Republic of Suffering 2008. *Address:* c/o Kasia Lundy, Office of the President, Harvard University, Massachusetts Hall, Cambridge, MA, 02138, USA (office). *Telephone:* (617) 495-1502 (office). *Fax:* (617) 495-8550 (office). *E-mail:* kasia_lundy@harvard.edu (office). *Website:* www.president.harvard.edu (office).

FAVIER, Jean, DèsL; French historian and academic; b. 2 April 1932, Paris; m. Lucie Calisti 1956; four s.; ed Faculté des Lettres, Paris and Ecole nationale des chartes; mem. Ecole française de Rome 1956–58; Curator, Nat. Archives 1956–61; Researcher, CNRS 1962–64; taught at Lycée d'Orléans 1961–62; Lecturer, Faculté des lettres, Univ. of Brest 1964–66, Rouen 1966–69; Dir of Studies, Ecole pratique des hautes études 1965–1997; Prof. of Medieval Econ. History, Univ. of Paris-Sorbonne 1969–97; Dir Inst. of History, Sorbonne 1971–75; Dir Revue Historique 1973–97; Dir-Gen. Archives de France 1975–94; Curator Château de Langeais 1995–; Hon. mem. Soc. of Antiquaries, London, Soc. Nat. des Antiquaires de France, Pres. 1993; Pres. Conseil d'admin, Ecole normale supérieure 1988–97; Pres. Nat. Library of France 1994–96, Asscn des lauréats du concours général 1990–2001, French Comm. for UNESCO 1997–; mem. Acad. des Inscriptions et Belles-Lettres, Medieval Acad. of America, Acad. Royale des Sciences, des Lettres et des Beaux-Arts, Belgium; mem. Cttee for Nat. Celebrations 1998–; Hon. mem. Belgium and Luxembourg Acad., Acads of Lyon, Reims and Rouen; Grand Officier, Légion d'honneur; Grand Croix, Ordre Nat. du Mérite; Commdr des Arts et des Lettres; Commdr des Palmes académiques, and decorations from Belgium, Germany, Luxembourg, Spain and Poland; several prizes including Prix des Ambassadeurs 1978 and Grand Prix Gobert (Acad. française) 1981. *Publications:* Un conseiller de Philippe-le-Bel: Enguerran de Marigny 1963, Les Finances pontificales à l'époque du grand schisme d'Occident 1966, De Marco Polo à Christophe Colomb 1968, Les contribuables parisiens à la fin de la guerre de cent ans 1970, Finance et fiscalité au bas moyen age 1971, Paris au XVe siècle 1974, Le trafic fluvial dans la région parisienne au XVe siècle 1975, Philippe-le-Bel 1978, La guerre de cent ans 1980, François Villon 1982, Le Temps des principautés 1984, Chronicle of the French Revolution 1788–1789 (co-ed.) 1988, L'univers de Chartres 1988, Les Grandes découvertes, d'Alexandre à Magellan 1991, les Archives de la France (ed.) 1992, Dictionnaire de la France médiévale 1993, Paris, deux mille ans d'histoire 1997, Charlemagne 1999, Louis XI 2001, De l'or et des épices: naissance de l'homme d'affaires au Moyen-Âge 2004, Les Plantagenêts 2004, Un roi de marbre 2005, Les papes d'Avignon 2006. *Leisure interests:* organ, photography. *Address:* Institut de France, 23 quai de Conti, 75006 Paris (office); 9 rue Reiter, 94100 St-Maur-des-Fossés, France (home).

FAVILA, Peter B., BSc; Philippine politician; *Secretary of Trade and Industry;* b. 27 Aug. 1948, Manila; m. Alice Arnaldo Favilo; two c.; ed Univ. of Santo Tomas; fmr positions include Sr Vice-Pres. Metropolitan Bank and Trust Co., Pres. Security Bank, Allied Bank, Philippine Nat. Bank; Chair. Philippine Stock Exchange –2005, Securities Clearing Corpn of the Philippines –2005; Presidential Adviser on Infrastructure Finance, Econ. Adviser to Speaker of House of Reps –2005; Sec. of Trade and Industry 2005–; fmr Dir ASEAN Chamber of Commerce and Industry, Philippine Airlines, Bankers Asscn of the Philippines; mem. Advisory Council, Asian Bankers Asscn; mem. Bd of Advisors, Asian Inst. of Man. Policy Forum, Bd of Trustees Alay sa Kawal Foundation; mem. Man. Asscn of the Philippines, Philippine Chamber of Commerce and Industry, Rotary Club of Makati South. *Address:* Department of Trade and Industry, Industry and Investments Building, 385 Sen. Gil J. Puyat Avenue, Buendia, Makati City, 3117 Metro Manila, Philippines (office). *Telephone:* (2) 8953611 (office). *Fax:* (2) 8956487 (office). *E-mail:* mis@dti.dti.gov.ph (office). *Website:* www.dti.gov.ph (office).

FAVORSKY, Oleg Nikolayevich; Russian expert on thermal technology; b. 27 Jan. 1929; m.; two d.; ed Moscow Aviation Inst.; engineer, sr engineer, leading engineer, sr researcher, First Deputy Dir of Div. Cen. Inst. of Aviation Engine 1953–73, Deputy Dir 1987–95; Dir-Gen. and Chief Constructor Sojuz Scientific-Production Unit, USSR Ministry of Aviation Industry 1973–87; Corresp. mem. USSR (now Russian) Acad. of Sciences 1982, mem. 1990; Acad.-Sec. Dept of Physical-Tech. Problems of Energy Consumption 1995–2002; Lenin Prize. *Publications:* author of scientific works and practical devt in the field of aviation gas-turbine engines, on thermal exchange in space and in high temperature devices, problems of space ecology. *Leisure interests:* tennis, stamp-collecting. *Address:* Russian Academy of Sciences, 32A Leninsky Prospekt, 117334 Moscow, Russia. *Telephone:* (495) 938-14-00 (office). *Fax:* (495) 938-13-54 (office).

FAVRE, Brett Lorenzo; American professional football player; b. 10 Oct. 1969, Gulfport, Miss.; s. of the late Irvin Favre and Bonita Favre; m. Deannam Favre (née Tynes); two d.; ed Hancock North Central High School, Univ. of Southern Miss.; quarterback; drafted out of coll. by Nat. Football League (NFL) Atlanta Falcons 1991 (33rd pick overall); traded to Green Bay Packers 1992–2008, retd but returned to play with New York Jets 2008 (retd); selected Nat. Football Conf. (NFC) Pro Bowl squad 1992–2007, youngest quarterback in Nat. Football League (NFL) history to play in a Pro Bowl; NFL Most Valuable Player (MVP) 1995, 1996, 1997 (jtly with Detroit Lions' Barry Sanders), first player to win three MVPs; set record of 38 touchdown passes 1995; led Green Bay to Super Bowl victory 1997; played 205 consecutive games (89 more than the next-highest total for a quarterback); holds NFL record for most career touchdown passes with 442, most career passing yards with 61,655, most career pass completions with 5,377; f. the Brett Favre Forward Foundation 1995; Green Bay Chamber of Commerce's Community Service Award 1997, Sports Illustrated Sportsman of the Year 2007. *Publications:* For the Record (with Chris Havel) 1997, Most Valuable Player (with Marc Serota) 1999, Favre (with Bonita Favre and Chris Havel) 2004. *Leisure interest:* golf. *Address:* c/o The Brett Favre Forward Foundation, 1 Willow Bend, Hattiesburg, MS 39402, USA. *E-mail:* info@officialbrettfavre.com. *Website:* www.officialbrettfavre.com.

FAVRHOLDT, David Cornaby, DPhil; Danish philosopher and academic; *Professor Emeritus, University of Southern Denmark;* b. 24 April 1931, Oregon, USA; s. of Elias Favrholdt and Bertha Cornaby; m. 1st Nina Fønss 1961; m. 2nd Anne Birch 1968; ed Copenhagen Univ.; Asst Prof. in Philosophy, Copenhagen Univ. 1961–66; Prof. of Philosophy and Head of Dept, Odense Univ. 1966–2001; currently Prof. Emer., Univ. of Southern Denmark; mem. Danish Research Council for Humanities 1985–91; mem. Royal Danish Acad. of Science and Letters, Academia Europaea; Århus Univ. Gold Medal 1958, Fyens Stiftstid Research Prize 1972. *Publications:* An Interpretation and Critique of Wittgenstein's Tractatus 1964, Philosophy and Society 1968, Chinese Philosophy 1971, The List of Sins 1973, Lenin: His Philosophy and World View 1978, Niels Bohr's Philosophical Background 1992, Studies in Niels Bohr's Philosophy 1994, Philosophical Codex 1999; trans. of Wittgenstein and John Locke; Niels Bohr: Collected Works, Vol. 10 Complementarity Beyond Physics (ed.) 1999, Aesthetics and Philosophy 2000; articles on Niels Bohr. *Leisure interests:* piano, classical music. *Address:* University of Southern Denmark, Campusvej 55, 5230 Odense M (office); Oehlenschlaegersvej 57, 5230 Odense M, Denmark (home). *Telephone:* 65-50-33-20 (office). *E-mail:* d.favrholdt@webspeed.dk (office). *Website:* www.sdu.dk (office).

FAWCETT, Amelia Chilcott, CBE, BA, JD; British/American investment banker and lawyer; *Chairman, Pensions First LLP;* b. Boston, Mass; d. of Frederick John Fawcett II and Betsey Sargent Chilcott; ed Wellesley, Univ. of Virginia School of Law; worked for Sullivan & Cromwell law firm, New York 1983–85, Paris 1986–87; joined Morgan Stanley 1987, Vice-Pres. 1990, Exec. Dir 1992, Man. Dir and Chief Admin. Officer for European Operations 1996–2002, Vice-Chair. Morgan Stanley International Ltd 2002–06; Chair. Pensions First LLP 2007–; mem. Bd of Dirs (non-exec.) State Street Corpn 2006–, Guardian Media Group 2006– (Chair. 2009–); Chair. London Int. Festival of Theatre; mem. Financial Services Practitioner Forum 1999–2001, Court of Dirs Bank of England (Chair. Audit Cttee) 2004–, Council of Univ. of London (Chair. Audit Cttee), Trustee and Deputy Chair. Nat. Portrait Gallery 2004– (Chair. Devt Bd); mem. London Employers Coalition 1998–2002, Competitiveness Council (Dept of Trade and Industry) 1999–2000, New Deal Task Force, Nat. Employment Panel 1999–2005; ranked by Fortune magazine amongst 50 Most Powerful Women in Business outside the US (43rd) 2003, (40th) 2004, (43rd) 2005, (49th) 2006, Prince of Wales Amb. Award 2004, ranked by the Financial Times amongst Top 25 Businesswomen in Europe (16th) 2005, (14th) 2006. *Leisure interests:* fly fishing, sailing, hill walking,

reading, farm in Wales. *Address:* 90 Long Acre, London, WC2E 9RZ, England (office). *Telephone:* (20) 7849-3496 (office). *Fax:* (20) 7225-5021 (office). *E-mail:* amelia.fawcett@pensionsfirst.com (office); amelia@acfawcett.com (home). *Website:* www.pensionsfirst.com (office).

FAWCETT, Don Wayne, MD; American anatomist and cell biologist; b. 14 March 1917, Springdale, Iowa; s. of Carlos J. Fawcett and Mary Mable Kennedy; m. Dorothy Secrest 1941; two s. two d.; ed Harvard Coll., Harvard Medical School; Capt., Medical Corps, US Army 1943–46; Research Fellow in Anatomy, Harvard Medical School 1946, Instructor 1946–68, Assoc. 1948–51, Asst Prof. 1951–55, Hersey Prof. of Anatomy and Head of Dept 1959–85, Prof. Emer.; Curator, Warren Anatomical Museum 1961–70, James Stillman Prof. of Comparative Anatomy 1962–85, Sr Assoc. Dean for Preclinical Affairs 1975–77; scientist Int. Laboratory for Research on Animal Diseases, Kenya 1980–85; Prof. and Chair. Dept of Anatomy, Cornell Medical Coll. 1955–59; Pres. American Asscn of Anatomists 1965–66, American Soc. for Cell Biology 1961–62, Int. Fed. of Socs for Electron Microscopy 1976–79; mem. NAS and numerous socs; eight hon. degrees. *Publications:* over 200 papers and three textbooks on histology, cell biology and reproductive biology. *Leisure interests:* photography of nature and wildlife, shell collecting. *Address:* 1224 Lincoln Road, Missoula, MT 59802, USA. *Telephone:* (406) 549-1415. *E-mail:* dfawc20586@aol.com.

FAXON, Roger, BA; American entertainment business executive; *Chairman and CEO, EMI Music Publishing;* ed Johns Hopkins Univ.; fmrly Sr Staff mem. US Congress; COO LUCASFILM Ltd 1980–84; Founding Pnr The Mount Company 1984–86; worked at Tri-Star and Columbia Pictures 1986–90, rising to Sr Exec. Vice-Pres. Columbia Pictures Entertainment; fmrly COO Sotheby's North and South America, CEO Sotheby's Europe, Man. Dir Sotheby's –1994; Sr Vice-Pres. of Business Devt and Strategy EMI Music 1994–99, Exec. Vice-Pres. and Chief Financial Officer EMI Music Publishing 1999–2002, Chief Financial Officer EMI Group PLC 2002–05, Bd mem. 2002–05, 2006–, Pres. and COO EMI Music Publishing 2005–06, Jt CEO 2006–07, Chair. and CEO 2007–; mem. Bd of Dirs ASCAP. *Address:* EMI Music Publishing, 75 Ninth Avenue, 4th Floor, New York, NY 10011, USA (office). *Telephone:* (212) 492-1200 (office). *Fax:* (212) 245-1865 (office). *E-mail:* rfaxon@emimusicpub.com (office). *Website:* www.emimusicpub.com (office).

FAYE, Jean Pierre; French writer; *President, European University of Research;* b. 19 July 1925, Paris; m. Marie-Odile Demenge 1952; one s. one d.; ed Univ. de Paris à la Sorbonne; teacher, Lycée de Reims 1951–54; Exchange Fellow, Univ. of Chicago 1954–55; Asst Prof., Univ. of Lille 1955–56, Univ. de Paris (Sorbonne) 1956–60; Research, CNRS 1960 (Dir of Research 1983); Founder of the Collectif Change and Centre d'Analyse et de Sociologie des Langages (CASL); Founder and Pres. High Council, Coll. Int. de Philosophie; Founder and Pres. The European Philosophical Univ.; Pres. European Univ. of Research, Paris 1985–90, 1993–, Inst. for Foundation of the European City of Culture 1997; Ed. Change (review) 1968–85; Hon. Pres. European City of Récollets, Paris 2004; Chevalier Légion d'honneur, Commdr des Arts et des Lettres; Prix Renaudot 1964, Int. Essay Prize, Weimar Cultural Capital of Europe 2000, Int. Literature Prize, Novi Sad 2007. *Artistic achievements:* art exhbns: paintings, books and catalogues of Titus-Carmel, Erro, Fromanger, Velickovic, Vieira da Silva, Henri Maccheroni, Kienholz, Arman; plays: Le Centre, directed by Polieri, Hommes et Pierres, directed by Roger Blin, Vitrine, directed by Jacques Mauclair; radio: 15 lectures on Nietzsche 2000; television: debate on Nietzsche 2002. *Publications:* novels: Entre les rues 1958, La cassure 1961, Battement 1962, Analogues 1964, L'écluse 1964, Les Troyens 1970, Inferno versions 1975, L'ovale 1975, Yumi, visage caméra 1983, La Grande Nap 1992; poems: Fleuve renversé 1959, Théâtre 1964 (produced at Odéon, Théâtre de France by Roger Blin and Jean-Louis Barrault 1965), Couleurs pliées 1965, Verres 1977, Syeeda 1984; essays: Le récit hunique 1967, Langages totalitaires, Théorie du récit 1972, La critique du langage et son économie 1973, Migrations du récit sur le peuple juif 1974, Les Grandes Journées du Père Duchesne 1981, Dictionnaire Politique, essai de Philosophie Politique 1982, La raison narrative 1990, Le livre de Lioube 1992, Ode Europe 1992, La déraison antisémite et son langage 1993, Le piège: La philosophie heideggerienne et le nationalsocialisme 1993, Didjla, le Tigre 1994, Le langage meurtrier 1995, le Siècle des idéologies 1996, Qu'est-ce que la philosophie? 1997, Guerre trouvée 1997, Le vrai Nietzsche 1998, Le livre du vrai 1998, Nietzsche et Salomé 2000, Court traité sur le transformat 2000, Introduction aux langages totalitaires 2003, Journal de voyage absolu 2003, La philosophie désormais 2004, Le transformat, le littoral, in Jean-Pierre Faye et la philosophie 2004, Eclat Rançon 2007, Les voies neuves de la philosophie 2008. *Address:* European University of Research, 1 rue Descartes, 75005 Paris (office); 1B rue Vaneau, 75007 Paris, France (home). *Telephone:* 1-4705-1803 (home).

FAYED, Mohamed al-; Egyptian business executive; *Chairman, Harrods Holdings;* b. 27 Jan. 1933, Alexandria; s. of Aly Aly Fayed; m. 1st Samira Khashoggi 1954 (divorced 1958); one s. (died 1997); m. 2nd Heini Wathen; four c.; f. co. in Alexandria 1956; involved in shipping, property, banking, oil and construction; Chair. and owner Ritz Hotel, Paris 1979–; Chair. Harrods Ltd, London 1985–, Harrods Holdings PLC 1994–; owner Fulham Football Club, London 1997–; Hon. mem. Emmanuel Coll., Cambridge; Commdr Order of Merit (Italy) 1990, Officier, Légion d'honneur 1993; La Grande Médaille de la Ville de Paris 1985, Plaque de Paris 1989. *Address:* Harrods Holdings, 87-135 Brompton Road, Knightsbridge, London, SW1X 7XL, England (office). *Telephone:* (20) 7730-1234 (office). *Fax:* (20) 7581-0470 (office). *Website:* www.harrods.com (office).

FAYEZ, Eid al-, BA; Jordanian politician; *Minister of the Interior;* b. 1945; ed Beirut Arab Univ.; Dir-Gen. Jordanian-Iraqi Transport Co. 1983–86; Dir-Gen. Jordanian Ports Corpn, Aqaba 1986–90; Sec.-Gen. Ministry of Youth 1990–93;

Adviser, Royal Hashemite Court 1993–99; Minister of Labour 1999, fmr Minister of Youth and State, Minister of the Interior 2007–. *Address:* Ministry of the Interior, POB 100, Amman, Jordan (office). *Telephone:* (6) 4638849 (office). *Fax:* (6) 5606908 (office). *E-mail:* info@moi.gov.jo (office). *Website:* www.moi.gov.jo (office).

FAYEZ, Faisal al-, BSc, MA; Jordanian politician; b. 1952; ed Univ. of Cardiff, UK, Boston Univ., USA; joined Ministry of Foreign Affairs upon graduation; fmr diplomat, Embassy of Jordan, Brussels; fmr Deputy Dir of Royal Protocol, Royal Court; Chief of Royal Protocol and Minister of the Royal Court 2003; Prime Minister and Minister of Defence 2003–05; Minister of the Royal Court of Jordan –Nov. 2005. *Address:* c/o Office of the Prime Minister, POB 80, Amman, Jordan (office).

FAYEZ, Mohamed Baha-Eldin, PhD; Egyptian chemist and academic; *Research Professor Emeritus, National Research Centre;* b. 4 Feb. 1927, Cairo; ed Alexandria and Glasgow Univs; scientist Nat. Research Centre (NRC), Cairo, f. Dept of Chem. of Natural Products, Dir NRC 1984–87, now Research Prof. Emer.; six industrial inventions including a urinary tract medicine; Science and Tech. Exec., Egyptian Acad. of Scientific Research and Tech., later Vice-Pres.; Founder and Dir UNDP Knowledge Transfer Programme in Egypt 1980; active in promoting tech. as essential part of econ. devt 1976–, maj. contrib. to formulation of a nat. tech. policy for Egypt 1984; Chair. UN Intergovernmental Cttee on Science and Tech. for Devt, UNCTAD Cttees on Transfer of Tech. and Reverse Transfer of Tech.; consultant to UN on tech. policies and tech. devt, adviser on tech. devt to UNCTAD in Zimbabwe; Egyptian del. int. and UN groups on tech. transformation and tech. transfer for developing countries; Founding Fellow Islamic Acad. of Sciences 1986; State Prize for Chem. (Egypt) 1966, Prize for Islamic Medicine, Kuwait Foundation for the Advancement of Science 1982, Prize for Outstanding Invention of the Year, WIPO 1984, State Prize of Merit in Sciences (Egypt) 1990. *Address:* National Research Center, Dokki- Cairo 12622, Egypt; Islamic Academy of Sciences, POB 830036, Amman, Jordan (office). *E-mail:* info@nrc.org.eg. *Website:* www.nrc.sci.eg; www.ias-worldwide.org (office).

FAYEZ, Nora bint Abdullah Al-, BA, MA; Saudi Arabian educationist, academic and politician; *Deputy Minister of Women's Education;* ed King Saud Univ., Utah State Univ., USA; served as Dir-Gen. of Girls' Schools at Kingdom Schools; Lecturer and Head of Training Techniques Centre, women's section of Inst. of Public Admin 1984–88, Dir-Gen. women's section 1993–2009; Assoc. Prof. in Educ. Techniques, Coll. of Educ., King Saud Univ. 1989–95; Controller of Educ. Techniques, Inst. of Pvt. Educ., Ministry of Educ. 1989–93, apptd to Council of Ministers (first woman) as Deputy Minister for Women's Educ. 2009–; Head of Women's Cttee of Human Resources Devt Forum under Human Resources Devt Fund, Riyadh 2004; mem. Women's Organizing Cttee of Janadriya Festival 1991, 1992, Bd of Dirs Coll. of Literature at Gen. Presidency of Girls Educ. 1994–2000, Cultural Advisory Cttee of Janadriya Festival 1995, Women's Cttee for King Abdul Aziz Museum (Darah) 1997–99, Consultative Council of Nat. Museum 1999–, Consultative Council of Supreme Comm. for Tourism 2001–03, Women's Cttee of King Abdul Aziz Foundation for Gifted Persons 2002–07, Women's Cttee of First Riyadh Econ. Forum 2003, Women's Science Cttee for the Cultural Season of the World Ass. of Muslim Youth 2005; adviser, Prince Salman Social Center 1998–2001, King Abdul Aziz Women's Charity Soc., Qassim 2000–03; has attended several nat. and int. seminars and courses, including The Effective Training Man. Workshop Course, Brussels, Belgium 1985, Man. Communication for Devt, Washington, DC, USA 1994, Distance Educ., Salzburg, Austria 1997, Man. Work Conf., Denver, USA 1997, Women in Man., Dubai 1998, The Art of Leadership, Advanced Management, Euromatech, Amsterdam, Netherlands 2003, Oxford Advanced Man. and Leadership Programme, Oxford Man. Centre, London, UK 2008. *Address:* Ministry of Education, PO Box 3734, Airport Road, Riyadh 11148, Saudi Arabia (office). *Telephone:* (1) 404-2888 (office). *Fax:* (1) 401-2365 (office). *E-mail:* webmaster@moe.gov.sa (office). *Website:* www.moe.gov.sa (office).

FAYMANN, Werner; Austrian politician; *Federal Chancellor;* b. 4 May 1960, Vienna; m.; two c.; ed Univ. of Vienna; consultant, Zentralsparkasse 1985–88; Prov. Chair. Socialistic Youth Vienna 1985–94; mem. State Parl. and Municipal Council of Vienna 1994–2007, Exec. City Councillor for housing, housing construction and urban renewal; fmr Pres. Viennese Fund for Provision of Property and Urban Renewal; fmr Vice-Pres. Viennese Business Agency; Fed. Minister for Transport, Innovation and Tech. 2007–08; Federal Chancellor 2008–; Exec. Chair. Social Democratic Party of Austria (SPÖ) 2008–. *Address:* Office of the Federal Chancellor, Ballhauspl. 2, 1014 Vienna (office); Social Democratic Party of Austria, Löwelstr. 18, 1014 Vienna, Austria (office). *Telephone:* (1) 531-15-0 (office); (1) 534-27-0 (SPÖ) (office). *Fax:* (1) 535-03-38-0 (office); (1) 535-96-83 (SPÖ) (office). *E-mail:* post@bka.gv.at (office); werner.faymann@spoe.at (office). *Website:* www.bka.gv.at (office); www.spoe.at (office); www.das-ist-faymann.at.

FAYYAD, Salam Khaled Abdullah, BSc, MBA, PhD; Palestinian economist and politician; *Prime Minister and Minister of Finance;* b. 1952, Tulkarm, West Bank; m.; three c.; ed American Univ. of Beirut, Lebanon, Univ. of Texas, USA; fmr Lecturer in Econs, Yarmuk Univ., Jordan; fmr official, US Fed. Reserve Bank, St Louis; joined IMF, Washington, DC 1987, various sr positions including Resident Rep. to Palestinian Authority (PA), Jerusalem 1995–2001; Regional Man. of West Bank–Gaza, Arab Bank 2001–02 (resgnd); Minister of Finance, PA 2002–05 (resgnd), March 2007–, also of Foreign Affairs June 2007–08; Prime Minister of Palestinian Autonomous Areas 2007–. *Publications:* numerous research papers on Palestinian economy. *Address:* Ministry of Finance, POB 795, Sateh Marhaba, Al-Birah/Ramallah (office); Ministry of Finance, POB 4007, Gaza, Palestinian Autonomous Areas (office). *Telephone:* (2) 2400650 (office); (8) 2826188 (office). *Fax:* (2) 2400595 (office); (8) 2820696 (office). *E-mail:* cbomof@palnet.com (office). *Website:* www.mof.gov.ps (office).

FAZIO, Antonio; Italian fmr central banker; b. 11 Oct. 1936, Alvito, Frosinone; s. of the late Eugenio Fazio and Maria Giuseppa Persichetti; m. Maria Cristina Rosati; one s. four d.; ed Univ. of Rome, Massachusetts Inst. of Tech., USA; Research Fellow, Research Dept, Banca d'Italia 1960, Consultant to Research Dept 1961–66, Deputy Head, then Head, Econometric Research Office 1966, Deputy Dir Research Dept's Monetary Section 1972, Head, Research Dept 1973–79, Cen. Man. for Econ. Research 1980, Deputy Dir-Gen. Banca d'Italia 1982–93, Gov. 1993–2005 (resgnd); Asst Prof. of Demography, Univ. of Rome 1961–66; Paul Harris Fellow, Rotary Int; Kt, Grand Gross Order of Merit (Italy); Hon. DEcon (Bari) 1994; Hon. DLitt (Johns Hopkins) 1995; Hon. Dr rer. pol (Macerata) 1996; Hon. LLB (Cassino) 1999; Hon. Dr Statistics and Econs (Milan) 1999; Hon. Dr Computer Eng (Lecce) 2000; Hon. Dr Banking Econs (Verona) 2002; Hon. LLD (St John's) 2002; Hon. PhD (Catania) 2002; Euromoney Cen. Banker of the Year 1996, St Vincent Prize for Econs 1997, 'Pico della Mirandola' Prize for Econs, Finance and Business 1997–98, Int. Award in the Humanities, Accad. di Studi Mediterranei 1999, Keynes Sraffa Prize (London) 2003. *Publications:* texts dealing mainly with monetary theory, econ. policy and monetary policy issues; Econometric Model of the Italian Economy. *Address:* Bank of Italy, Via Nazionale 91, 00184 Rome, Italy (office). *Telephone:* (6) 47921 (office).

FEARON, Douglas Thomas, BA, MD, FRCP, FAAS, FRS, FMedSci; American professor of immunology; *Professor, Wellcome Trust Immunology Unit;* b. 16 Oct. 1942, Brooklyn, New York; s. of the late Henry Dana Fearon and of Frances Fearon (née Eubanks); m. 2nd Clare M. Wheless 1977; one s. one d.; ed Williams Coll., Johns Hopkins Univ. School of Medicine; residency, Johns Hopkins Hosp. 1968–70; US Army Medical Corps 1970–72; Post-doctoral Fellowship, Harvard Medical School 1972–75, Instructor, Harvard Medical School 1975–76, Asst Prof. of Medicine 1976–79, Assoc. Prof. 1979–84, Prof. of Medicine 1984–87; Prof. of Medicine, Johns Hopkins Univ. School of Medicine 1987–93; Prof., Wellcome Trust Immunology Unit Univ. of Cambridge, UK 1993–, Fellow, Trinity Coll. Cambridge 2001–, Sheila Joan Smith Prof. of Immunology 2004–; Hon. Consultant, Addenbrooke's Hosp. Cambridge 1993–; Lee C. Howley Prize, Arthritis Foundation; Bronze Star (US Army). *Publications:* more than 100 articles in scientific journals. *Leisure interest:* golf. *Address:* Wellcome Trust Immunology Unit, MRC Centre, Hills Road, Cambridge, CB2 2QH, England (office). *Telephone:* (1223) 330528 (office). *Fax:* (1223) 336815 (office). *E-mail:* dtf1000@cam.ac.uk (office). *Website:* www.trin.cam.ac.uk (office).

FEAST, Michael William, PhD, DSc, FRAS, FRSSA, ARCS; South African astronomer; b. 29 Dec. 1926, Deal, England; s. of Frederick Feast and Dorothy Feast (née Knight); m. Elizabeth Constance Maskew 1962; one s. two d.; ed Imperial Coll., London; Postdoctoral Fellow, Nat. Research Council of Canada 1949–51; astronomer Radcliffe Observatory 1952–74; astronomer South African Astronomical Observatory 1974–92, Dir 1977–92; Hon. Prof. of Astronomy, Univ. of Cape Town 1983–; Royal Soc. Guest Fellow, Inst. of Astronomy, Cambridge 1992–93; Pres. Int. Astronomical Union Comm. on Stellar Spectra 1967–70, on Variable Stars 1970–76; Vice-Pres. Int. Astronomical Union 1979–85; Pres. Astronomical Soc. of SA 1957–58, 1979–80; Founder mem. S African Acad. of Science 1995–; Assoc. Royal Astronomical Soc.; Hon. DSc (Cape Town) 1993; Gill Medal, Astronomical Soc. of SA 1983, de Beers' Gold Medal (S African Inst. of Physics) 1992. *Publications:* over 300 astronomical and physics papers, mainly in Royal Astronomical Soc. monthly notices. *Address:* Astronomy Department, University of Cape Town, Rondebosch 7701, South Africa. *Telephone:* (21) 6502396. *Fax:* (21) 6503342. *E-mail:* mwf@artemisia.ast.uct.ac.za (office).

FEDDEN, (Adye) Mary, OBE, RA; British fmr painter; b. 14 Aug. 1915, Bristol; d. of Harry Vincent Fedden and Ida Margaret Fedden (née Prichard); m. Julian Trevelyan 1951 (died 1988); ed Badminton School, Bristol, Slade School of Art, London; taught painting at RCA 1956–64, Yehudi Menuhin School 1964–74; exhbns at Redfern, Beaux Arts, Christopher Hull and New Grafton Galleries, London and various prov. galleries 1948–; works purchased by HM The Queen, Tate Gallery, Crown Prince of Jordan; Pres. Royal West of England Acad. 1984–88; Hon. DLitt (Bath) 1996. *Publications:* illustrator: Motley the Cat 1997, The Green Man 1998, Birds 1999. *Leisure interest:* reading. *Address:* Durham Wharf, Hammersmith Terrace, London, W6 9TS, England (home). *Telephone:* (20) 8563-2391 (home).

FEDERER, Roger; Swiss professional tennis player; b. 8 Aug. 1981, Basel; s. of Robert Federer and Lynette Federer (née Durand); m. Mirka Vavrinec 2009; world rank No. 1 as jr 1998, won Wimbledon jr title that year; turned professional 1998; semi-finalist, men's singles, Olympic Games, Sydney 2000; singles titles: Milan 2001, Hamburg TMS 2002, 2005, Sydney 2002, Vienna 2002, 2003, Marseille 2003, Tennis Masters Cup, Houston 2003, 2004, 2006, 2007, Wimbledon 2003, 2004, 2005, 2006, 2007, Halle 2003, 2004, 2005, 2006, 2008, Vienna 2002, 2003, Munich 2003, Dubai 2003, 2004, 2005, 2007, Australian Open 2004, 2006, 2007, Bangkok 2004, 2005, Canada AMS 2004, Gstaad 2004, Hamburg AMS 2004, 2007, Indian Wells AMS 2004, 2005, 2006, Toronto 2004, 2006, US Open 2004, 2005, 2006, 2007, 2008, Cincinnati 2005, 2007, Doha 2005, 2006, Miami 2005, 2006, Rotterdam 2005, Basel 2006, 2007, 2008, Madrid 2006, Tennis Masters Cup, Shanghai 2006, 2007, Tokyo 2006, Estoril 2008; runner-up, French Open 2006, 2007, 2008, Wimbledon 2008, Australian Open 2009; eight doubles titles: Rotterdam 2001 (with Jonas Bjorkman), 2002 (with Max Mirnyi), Gstaad 2001 (with Marat Safin), Moscow 2002 (with Mirnyi), Vienna 2003 (with Yves Allegro), Miami TMS 2003 (with Mirnyi), Halle 2005 (with Yves Allegro), Beijing Olympics 2008 (with Stanislas Wawrinka); (as of 2 Feb. 2009): 626 career singles wins, 151 defeats; 112 career doubles wins, 71 defeats; 57 career singles titles, eight career doubles titles; career winnings of US $45,318,757; 16 Davis Cup ties 1999– (24 singles wins, six defeats; nine doubles wins, five defeats); first player to be ranked World No. 1 for four consecutive (non-calendar) years Feb. 2004–Feb. 2008; top ranked player on ATP computer for a record 237 consecutive weeks 2 Feb. 2004–17 Aug. 2008; first player to be ranked World No. 1 for 237 consecutive weeks, ranked World No. 2 since 18 Aug. 2008; coached by Peter Lundgren 1999–2003, Tony Roche (part-time) 2005–07, José Higueras 2008; Swiss Sportsman of the Year 2003, 2004, Swiss Personality of the Year 2003, ATP European Player of the Year 2004, BBC Sports Personality of the Year 2004, Laureus World Sportsman of the Year 2005, 2006, 2007, 2008. *Leisure interests:* golf, soccer, skiing, playstation, music, playing cards. *Address:* c/o Lynette Federer, PO Box 209, 4103 Bottmingen, Switzerland (office); IMG Tennis, IMG Center, 1360 East 9th Street, Suite 100, Cleveland, OH 44114, USA. *Telephone:* (61) 4215712 (office). *Fax:* (61) 4215719 (office). *E-mail:* management@rogerfederer.com (office). *Website:* www.rogerfederer.com (office).

FEDERMAN, Raymond; American academic and writer; b. 15 May 1928, Paris, France; m. Erica Hubscher 1960; one d.; ed Univ. Calif. at Los Angeles and Columbia Univ.; Asst Prof., Univ. of California at Santa Barbara 1959–64; Assoc. Prof., State Univ. of NY, Buffalo 1964–68, Prof. 1968–90, Distinguished Prof. of Literature 1990–99, Melodia E. Jones Distinguished Prof. 1992–99; Guggenheim Fellow 1966–67, Nat. Endowment for the Arts Fellow 1986; American Book Award 1987. *Publications:* novels: Double or Nothing 1971, Take It or Leave It 1976, The Voice in the Closet 1979, The Twofold Vibration 1982, Smiles on Washington Square 1985, To Whom It May Concern 1990; essays: Journey to Chaos 1965, Surfiction 1976, Critifiction 1992, The Supreme Indecision of the Writer 1996, La Fourrure de Ma Tante Rachel 1996, Loose Shoes 1999, The Precipice and Other Catastrophes 1999. *Leisure interests:* golf, tennis. *Address:* c/o Department of English, State University of New York, Clemens Hall, Buffalo, NY 14620, USA (office).

FEDEROVSKI, Vladimir; Russian/French diplomatist, writer and academic; *Professor of History, Hautes Etudes Commerciales;* b. 1950, Moscow; ed Inst. of Int. Relations, Moscow; attaché Soviet Embassy, Nouakchott, Mauritius 1972; interpreter for Leonid Brezhnev, Sec.-Gen. of CP 1970s; counsellor Soviet Embassy, Paris, France 1985; Spokesperson Movt for Democratic Reform, USSR 1985–91; acquired French citizenship 1995; currently Prof. of History, Hautes Etudes Commerciales (HEC), Paris; adviser on cold war history Mémorial de Caen. *Publications include:* Histoire de la diplomatie française 1985, Histoire secrète d'un coup d'État 1991, Les Égéries russes 1993, Les Egéries romantiques 1995, Le Département du diable 1996, Les Deux Soeurs ou l'art d'aimer 1997, Le Triangle russe 1999, Les Tsarines: Les Femmes qui ont fait la Russie 1999, L'Histoire secrète des ballets russes 2002, Le roman de Saint-Petersbourg 2002, Le Roman du Kremlin 2004. *Address:* Hautes Etudes Commerciales, Jouyen-Josas Cedex, 78351 Paris, France (office). *Telephone:* 1-39-67-7000 (office).

FEDERSPIEL, Thomas Holger, CBE; Danish lawyer; b. 25 Oct. 1935, Hellerup; s. of Per Torben Federspiel and Elin Federspiel (née Zahle); m. 1st Benedicte Buhl 1965 (divorced 1984); two s.; m. 2nd Bettina Hage 1997; ed Krebs Skole, Rungsted Statsskole, Copenhagen Univ.; Assoc. Jonas Bruun 1961–66, Slaughter and May, London, Davis Polk & Wardwell 1966–67; Partner Per Federspiel 1968, Gorrissen & Federspiel (now Gorrissen Federspiel Kierkegaard) 1989–2004; admitted to Court of Appeal 1964, Supreme Court 1969; F. Gorrissen & Federspiel 1989; Chair. Danish Bar Council Cttee on Pvt. Int. Law 1971–81; Pres. Int. Bar Asscn 1980–82; mem. Council Int. Bar Asscn 1971–84; mem. Bd Queen Margrethe's and Prince Henrik's Foundation; Chair. and mem. bd various cos and charitable foundations; Hon. mem. ABA 1981, Int. Bar Asscn 1984; Hon. Legal Adviser to the British Embassy; Kt of the Order of Dannebrog, Insignia of Honour of the Order of Dannebrog. *Leisure interests:* tennis, skiing, shooting, reading. *Address:* 12 H.C. Andersens Boulevard, 1553 Copenhagen (office); Rungsted Strandvej 22, 2950 Vedbaek, Denmark (home). *Telephone:* 33-41-41-41 (office); 45-86-13-42 (home). *Fax:* 33-41-41-33 (office). *E-mail:* tf@gfklaw.dk (office).

FEDIN, Vladimir, DChemSci; Russian chemist and academic; *Director, Nikolaev Institute of Inorganic Chemistry;* b. 5 Sept. 1954, Pensa; ed Russian Acad. of Sciences and Univ. of Moscow; currently Prof. and Dir Nikolaev Inst. of Inorganic Chem., Siberian Br. of Russian Acad. of Sciences; Fellow, Int. Union of Pure and Applied Chem.; mem. Program Cttee and Advisory Bd, Int. Siberian Workshop on Advanced Inorganic Fluorides ISIF-2006. *Publications include:* numerous articles in professional journals. *Address:* Nikolaev Institute of Inorganic Chemistry, Siberian Branch of Russian Academy of Sciences, 3 Acad. Lavrentiev Avenue, Novosibirsk 630090, Russia (office). *Telephone:* (383) 330-94-90 (office); (383) 330-58-42 (home). *Fax:* (383) 330-94-89 (office). *E-mail:* cluster@che.nsk.su (office). *Website:* www.che.nsk.su (office).

FEDOR, Martin, MEconSc; Slovak government official; b. 4 March 1974, Považská Bystrica; ed Comenius Univ., Dublin European Inst., Ireland; Head of Cabinet 1998; Dir Int. Relations Section, SDKU 2000–02, Head Dept of Foreign Policy and Integration 2000–, Deputy Chair. New Generation (SDKU Youth Org.) –2002; State Sec. Ministry of Defence 2003–06, Minister of Defence 2006. *Address:* c/o Ministry of Defence, Kutuzovova 7, 832 28 Bratislava, Slovakia (office).

FEDOROV, Alexey Innokentevich; Russian manufacturing executive; *President, Irkut Corporation;* b. 14 April 1952, Irkutsk; ed Oklahoma City Univ. Business School, USA; design engineer, Irkutsk Aviation Industrial Asscn, Irkutsk, Siberia, USSR 1974, Pres. 1998–2005, Chair. 2005–; Pres. Irkut Corpn (biggest producer of mil. and civilian aircraft in Russia) 2000–, outlets in Russia, USA, Europe, India, SE Asia, annual contracts exceed US $4 billion; Gen. Dir and Gen. Constructor Russian Aviation Construction Corpn MiG 2004–; Pres. United Aviation Construction Corpn 2004–; Order Merit to Fatherland (Fourth Degree), Badge of Honour, Peter the Great Golden Symbol. *Address:* Irkut Corporation, 68 Leningrad Prospect, 125315 Moscow, Russia (office). *Telephone:* (495) 777-21-01 (office). *Fax:* (495) 777-21-01 (office). *E-mail:* inbox@irkut.com (office). *Website:* www.irkut.com (office).

FEDOROV, Igor B., DrTech; Russian university administrator; *Rector, Moscow Bauman Technical University;* b. 1940; m.; one d.; ed Moscow Bauman Tech. Univ.; engineer, asst, Docent, Head of Dept, Prorector for Scientific Work, Moscow Bauman Tech. Univ. –1991, Rector 1991–; mem. Int. Acad. of Informatization, Int. Acad. of Eng, Asscn of Rectors of Europe, Eurasian Asscn of Univs, Russian Acad. of Natural Sciences, Int. Acad. of Higher Educ. Problems; Merited Worker of Science and Tech.; Prize of USSR Ministry of Educ. 1991. *Publications include:* more than 140 scientific papers on higher education problems; five monographs and 15 patents. *Address:* Moscow Bauman Technical University, 2nd Baumanskaya str. 5, 105005 Moscow, Russia (office). *Telephone:* (495) 261-17-43 (office). *E-mail:* bauman@bmstu.ru (office). *Website:* www.bmstu.ru (office).

FEDOROV, Valentin Petrovich, DEcon; Russian politician and manager; *Deputy Director, Institute of Europe;* b. 6 Sept. 1939, Zhatai, Yakutia; m.; two d.; ed G. Plekhanov Moscow Inst. of Nat. Econ., Inst. of World Econ. and Int. Relations, USSR Acad. of Sciences; worked in State Planning Cttee Yakutia 1964–78; jr researcher, Head of Div., Corresp. Journal of Inst. of World Econ. and Int. Relations in W Germany 1978–84; Prorector on Int. Relations, Prof. G. V. Plekhanov Moscow Inst. of Nat. Econ., 1987–90; Governor Sakhalin Region, opposed transfer of S Kuril Islands to Japan 1990–93; People's Deputy of Russia 1990–93; Deputy Minister of Econ. 1993–94; Prime Minister of Sakhá (Yakutia) Repub. 1997–98; mem. Political Council Movt for Democratic Reforms, Co-Chair. Duma of Russian Nat. Sobor; Vice-Pres. Russian Union of Industrialists and Entrepreneurs 1994–2001; Pres. Asscn of Road-Builders 1996–; Deputy Dir Inst. of Europe 2000–; mem. Russian Acad. of Natural Sciences, Russian Eng Acad. *Publications:* FRG: Country and People; several plays, collections of poems, monographs on econs. *Address:* Institute of Europe, Mokhovaya str. 11, 3B, 1038730 Moscow, Russia (office). *Telephone:* (495) 203-32-67 (office). *Fax:* (495) 200-42-98 (office). *E-mail:* vpfyodorov@mail.ru. *Website:* www.ieras.ru (office).

FEDOSEYEV, Vladimir Ivanovich; Russian conductor; *Artistic Director, Tchaikovsky Academy Symphony Orchestra;* b. 5 Aug. 1932, Leningrad; s. of Ivan Fedoseyev and Elena Fedoseyeva; m. Olga Dobrokhotova; two c.; ed conductors' class of Moscow Musical Pedagogical Inst., Moscow Conservatoire; mem. CPSU 1963–91; Artistic Dir and Chief Conductor Moscow Radio Symphony Orchestra of USSR Radio Network (now Tchaikovsky Acad. Symphony Orchestra) 1974–; concurrently Music Dir Vienna Symphony Orchestra 1997–; first Perm. Guest Conductor Tokyo Philharmonic Orchestra 1996–, Radio France Orchestra 2001–; Perm. Guest Conductor Zürich Opera 1997–; works with Bolshoi and Mariinsky Theatres, opera productions and concerts abroad, including Italy, France, Austria, Germany, Japan, Switzerland, Spain, UK, USA; People's Artist of USSR 1980, RSFSR State Prize 1989, Crystal Award of Asahi Broadcasting Corpn, Osaka 1989, Golden Orpheus, for recording of opera May Night, Gold Medal, Int. Gustav Mahler Soc. 2007. *Recordings:* Symphonies by Beethoven, Mahler, Shostakovich, Mussorgsky, Sviridov, Russian operas. *Address:* Malaya Nikitskaya 24, 121069 Moscow, Russia (home). *Telephone:* (495) 229-57-68 (Moscow) (home); (495) 690-64-52 (Moscow) (office); (1) 503-84-77 (Vienna) (home). *Fax:* (495) 291-82-43 (Moscow) (office). *E-mail:* tsom@fedoseyev.com (office); vdedyukhin@fedoseyev.com (office). *Website:* www.fedoseyev.com (office); www.bso.ru (office).

FEDOSOV, Yevgeny Aleksandrovich, DTechSc; Russian automation and avionics specialist; *Scientific Director, State Research Institute of Aviation Systems (GosNIIAS);* b. 14 May 1929, Moscow; s. of Alexander Yefimovitch Fedosov and Nadezhda Anempodistovna Smirnova; m. Lydia Petrovna Vasilyeva; one d.; ed Bauman Tech. Inst.; post-grad. work at Inst. 1953–56; mem. CPSU 1959–91; Research Fellow, Head of Dept, Deputy Dir State Research Inst. of Aviation Systems (GosNIIAS) 1956–70, Dir Research and Tech. 1970–2001, Gen. Dir GosNIIAS 2001–06, Scientific Dir 2006–; simultaneously Head of Dept of Physico-Tech. Inst. 1970–; Prof. 1969; Corresp. mem. USSR (now Russian) Acad. of Sciences 1979, mem. 1984–; Lenin Prize 1976, Hero of Socialist Labour 1983, B.N. Petrov Gold Medal, Acad. of Sciences 1989, Honoured Scientist of Russian Fed. 1996. *Publications:* works on analysis and synthesis of complex multi-level operational systems. *Leisure interests:* tennis, gardening. *Address:* State Research Institute of Aviation Systems (GosNIIAS), Viktorenko str. 7, 125319 Moscow, Russia (office). *Telephone:* (499) 157-70-47 (office). *Fax:* (499) 943-86-05 (office). *E-mail:* info@gosniias.re (office). *Website:* www.gosniias.ru (office).

FEDOTOV, Aleksei Leonidovich; Russian diplomatist; *Ambassador to Czech Republic;* b. 29 June 1949, Moscow; m. 1st Yelena Fedotova; one d.; m. 2nd Tatiana Fedotova; one s.; ed Moscow State Inst. of Int. Relations; attaché, USSR Embassy, Sri Lanka 1972–74, Counsellor Singapore 1983–85; Dept of S Asia, Ministry of Foreign Affairs 1974–78, adviser 1986; Third, Second, First Sec., Secr. of Deputy Minister, asst to Deputy Minister 1978–83; Counsellor, Deputy Head of Div., Sr Counsellor, Head of Div. 1986–92, Head of Dept, Deputy Exec. Sec., Deputy Dir of Dept, Deputy Exec. Sec. 1992–96, Dir, Dept of Personnel, mem. Bd of Dirs Ministry of Foreign Affairs 1996–2000; Deputy Minister of Foreign Affairs 2000–2004; Amb. to Czech Repub. 2004–; mem. Russian Acad. of Natural Sciences; several Russian state decorations. *Leisure interests:* literature, painting, history. *Address:* Embassy of the Russian Federation, Pod kaštany 1, 160 00 Prague, Czech Republic (office). *Telephone:*

(2) 33374100 (office). *Fax:* (2) 33377235 (office). *E-mail:* embrus@tiscali.cz (office). *Website:* www.czech.mid.ru (office).

FEDOTOV, Maxim Viktorovich; Russian violinist and academic; *Professor and Head, Violin and Viola Department, Russian Gnesin Academy of Music;* b. 24 July 1961, Leningrad (now St. Petersburg); s. of Viktor Andreyevich Fedotov and Galina Nikolayevna Fedotova; m. Galina Yevgenyevna Petrova, pianist; one d.; ed Specialized Music School for Gifted Children in Leningrad, Moscow State Conservatory (with D. Tsyganov and I. Bezrodny); concert tours since 1975; Prof. Moscow State Conservatory 1987–2001; Prof. and Head, Violin and Viola Dept, Russian Gnesin Acad. of Music 2003–; Artistic Dir and Chief Conductor, Russian Symphony Orchestra 2003–; as soloist plays with G. Petrova, regular recitals in Moscow and St Petersburg; performed in Madrid, Berlin, Leipzig, Frankfurt, Cologne, Milan, Chicago and other cities; took part in music festivals in Salzburg, Oakland, Bergen, Dresden, Klagenfurt; toured Australia, New Zealand, Korea, Turkey; Pres. Asscn of Laureates of P. I. Tchaikovsky Int. Competition 2002–; mem. Peter the Great's Arts and Sciences Acad., St. Petersburg; prize winner All-Union Music Competition Riga 1981, N. Paganini Competition Genoa 1982, Vercelli 1984, P. Tchaikovsky (Moscow 1986), Tokyo 1986 (First Prize); People's Artist of Russia. *Address:* Gnesin Academy of Music, Povarskaya, 38, 121069 Moscow (office); Tolbukhin str. 8, korp. 1, Apt. 6, 121596 Moscow, Russia. *Telephone:* (495) 291-3855 (office); (495) 447-25-60 (home). *Fax:* (495) 291-3102 (office). *E-mail:* gmu@gnesin.ru (office). *Website:* www.gnesin.ru (office).

FEDOTOV, Mikhail Aleksandrovich, DJur; Russian politician and lawyer; b. 18 Sept. 1949, Moscow; m. 3rd Maria Fedotova; one s. one d; ed Moscow State Univ., All-Union Inst. of Law; teacher of law, All-Union Inst. of Law 1973–90; Deputy Minister of Press and Mass Information of Russia 1991–92, Minister 1992–93; represented Pres. Yeltsin in Constitutional Court trial against CPSU 1992; Dir-Gen. Russian Agency of Intellectual Property (RAIS) Feb.–Dec. 1992; Russian rep. at UNESCO, Paris 1993–97; Sec. Russian Union of Journalists 1998–; Laureate Prize, Union of Journalists of the USSR 1990, UNESCO Medal in honour of the 50th anniversary of the Universal Declaration of Human Rights 1999. *Publications:* more than 100 books and essays on human rights and constitutionalism, intellectual property and int. humanitarian co-operation. *Address:* Russian Union of Journalists, Zubovskiy blvd 4, 119021 Moscow, Russia (office). *Telephone:* (495) 201-44-47 (office). *E-mail:* ruj@ruj.ru (office). *Website:* www.ruj.ru (office).

FEDOTOV, Yuri Victorovich; Russian diplomatist; *Ambassador to the Court of St James (UK);* b. 14 Dec. 1947, Moscow; m. Yelena Fedotova; one s. one d.; ed Moscow State Inst. of Int. Relations; entered diplomatic service 1971, different posts in Ministry of Foreign Affairs and abroad (Algeria 1974–80, India 1983–88); Deputy Head, Dept of Int. Relations, Ministry of Foreign Affairs 1991–93; Deputy Perm. Rep. and Acting First Deputy Perm. Rep. to UN, New York 1994–99; Dir Dept of Int. Orgs, Ministry of Foreign Affairs 1999–2002, Deputy Minister of Foreign Affairs 2002–05, mem. Bd of Dirs 2000–05; Amb. to the Court of St James (UK) 2005–. *Address:* 13 Kensington Palace Gardens, London W8 4QX, England (office). *Telephone:* (20) 7229-3620 (office). *Fax:* (20) 7229-5804 (office). *E-mail:* yfedotov@mid.ru (office); office@rusemblon.org (office). *Website:* www.great-britain.mid.ru (office).

FEFFER, Marc-André (Patrice), M.Droit pub; French television executive and lawyer; *Director General, La Poste;* b. 22 Dec. 1949, Neuilly-sur-Seine; s. of Jacques Feffer and Marie-Jeanne Thirlin; m. Hélène Cataix 1976; three d.; ed Lycée Condorcet and Faculté de Droit, Inst. d'Etudes Politiques and Ecole Nat. d'Admin, Paris; official Conseil d'Etat 1976, Counsel 1980, now mem.; Sec.-Gen. Comm. des Sondages 1980; Adviser Office of Pres. of EEC 1981–84; Dir Centre Mondial Informatique et Ressource Humaine 1984; Head of Information (Legal and Tech.), Prime Minister's Staff 1985–88, Sr Defence Counsel, Information 1986–88; Sec.-Gen. Canal+ 1988–94, Gen. Man. 1994–95, Dir Exec. Cttee 1994, Exec. Vice-Pres. 1995–2003, Deputy Chair. Exec. Bd and Gen. Council 2000–03; Dir-Gen. La Poste 2004–; Chair. Bd of Dirs Poste Immo 2007–; Chevalier, Légion d'honneur, Commdr Ordre des Arts et des Lettres. *Leisure interests:* sailing, windsurfing. *Address:* La Poste, 44 boulevard de Vaugirard, 75757 Paris Cedex 15, France (office). *Telephone:* 1-55-44-00-00 (office). *Fax:* 1-55-44-22-62 (office). *E-mail:* service.presse@laposte.fr (office). *Website:* www.laposte.fr (office).

FEFFERMAN, Charles, PhD; American mathematician and academic; *Herbert Jones University Professor of Mathematics, Princeton University;* b. 18 April 1949, Washington, DC; ed Univ. of Maryland and Princeton Univ.; child prodigy, graduated aged 17, doctorate aged 20, professor aged 22; Lecturer in Math., Priceton Univ. 1969–70, Prof. 1973–84, Herbert Jones Univ. Prof. of Math. 1984–, Chair. and Prof., Dept of Math. 1999–2002; Asst Prof. of Math., Univ. of Chicago 1970–71, Prof. 1971–73 (youngest full prof. ever appointed in USA); Wilson Elkins Visiting Professorship, Univ. of Maryland; Visiting Prof., Calif. Inst. of Tech., Courant Inst. of Math. Sciences, New York Univ., Univ. of Paris, France, Mittag-Leffler Inst., Djursholm, Sweden, Weitzmann Inst., Rehovot, Israel, Bar-Ilan Univ., Ramat-Gan, Israel Univ. of Madrid (Autónoma), Spain; mem. American Acad. of Arts and Sciences 1972, NAS 1979, American Philosophical Soc. 1989; mem. Editorial Bd Communications in Partial Differential Equations, Advances in Mathematics, Re-vista Mat. Iberoamericana, Journal of Fourier Analysis and Applications, Proceedings of the National Academy of Sciences, Journal d'Analyse; 1979 Hon. PhD (Univ. of Maryland) 1979, (Knox Coll.) 1981, (Bar-Ilan Univ.) 1985, (Univ. of Madrid (Autónoma)) 1990; NSF Fellowship 1966–69, Alfred P. Sloan Foundation Fellowship 1970, Nato Postdoctoral Fellowship 1971, Salem Prize 1971, First Recipient Alan T. Waterman Award 1976, Fields Medal, Int. Congress of Mathematicians, Helsinki 1978, American Math. Soc. Colloquium Lecturer 1983, Bergman Prize 1992. *Publications:* Renewing U.S. Mathematics – A Plan for the Nineties (co-author); more than 80 publs in math. journals on multivariable complex analysis, partial differential equations and harmonic analysis. *Address:* 1102 Fine Hall, Department of Mathematics, Washington Road, Princeton University, Princeton, NJ 08544-1000, USA (office). *Telephone:* (609) 258-4200 (office). *Fax:* (609) 258-1367 (office). *E-mail:* cf@math.princeton.edu (office). *Website:* www.math.princeton.edu (office).

FEGETA, Siraj; Ethiopian politician; *Minister of Defence;* Minister of Fed. Affairs 2005–08, of Defence 2008–. *Address:* Ministry of Defence, POB 1373, Addis Ababa, Ethiopia (office). *Telephone:* (11) 5511777 (office). *Fax:* (11) 5516053 (office).

FEHER, George, PhD; American physicist and academic; *Professor of Physics, University of California, San Diego;* b. 29 May 1924, Czechoslovakia; s. of Ferdinand Feher and Sylvia Feher (née Schwartz); m. Elsa Rosenvasser Feher 1961; three d.; ed Univ. of Calif., Berkeley; Research Physicist, Bell Telephone Labs, NJ 1954–60; Visiting Assoc. Prof., Columbia Univ., New York 1956–60; Prof. of Physics, Univ. of Calif., San Diego 1960–; Visiting Prof., MIT 1967–68; mem. American Physical Soc., Biophysical Soc. (Nat. Lecturer 1983), mem. Bd of Dirs Technion-Israel Inst. of Tech., Haifa, Israel 1968; mem. Bd of Govs Weizmann Inst. of Science, Rehovot 1988; Fellow, AAA, Int. EPR/ESR Soc. 1996, Biophysical Soc. 2000; mem. NAS, American Acad. of Arts and Sciences; Hon. DPhil (Hebrew Univ. of Jerusalem) 1994; American Physical Soc. Prize for origination and devt of Electron Nuclear Double Resonance (ENDOR) technique and for applying it to solid state and nuclear research problems 1960, Oliver E. Buckley Solid State Physics Prize 1976, Biophysics Prize 1982, Inaugural Annual Award, Int. Electron Spin Resonance Soc. 1991, Bruker Lectureship, Oxford Univ., UK 1992, Rumford Medal, American Acad. of Arts and Sciences 1992, Zavoiski Award 1996, Wolf Prize in Chemistry 2007. *Publications:* over 200 articles in numerous specialist scientific journals, reviews, symposia. *Leisure interests:* photography, sports. *Address:* Department of Physics 0319, University of California, San Diego, 9500 Gilman Drive, La Jolla, CA 92093-0319, USA (office). *Telephone:* (858) 534-4389 (office). *E-mail:* gfeher@physics.ucsd.edu (office). *Website:* physics.ucsd.edu/~raifeher (office).

FEHRENBACH, Charles Max, DèsSc; French astronomer and academic; *Professor Emeritus of Astronomy, University of Marseilles;* b. 29 April 1914, Strasbourg; s. of Charles Fehrenbach and Alma (née Holtkemper) Fehrenbach; m. Myriam Léonie Graff 1939 (deceased); two s. one d.; m. 2nd Reine Bonnaud 1989; ed Lycée Fustel-de-Coulanges and Univ. of Strasbourg; Asst Lecturer Univ. of Strasbourg 1934; Teacher Lycée Saint-Charles, Marseille 1939; Astronomer Strasbourg Observatory 1941; Asst Dir Haute Provence Observatory 1943, Dir 1948–83; Prof. of Astronomy, Univ. of Marseilles 1948–83, Prof. Emer. 1983–; Dir Marseille Observatory 1949–81; Pres. Comm. des instruments, Observatoire européen austral 1958–72, mem. Bd 1965–72; mem. Bd Canada France Hawaii Telescope 1975–79, Pres. 1979; mem. Int. Astronomical Union, Vice-Pres. 1973–79; mem. Bureau des Longitudes 1973, Pres. 1987; mem. Rotary Int.; mem. Acad. des Sciences Paris 1968, Int. Astronautical Acad. 1986, Acad. of New York 1991; Assoc. mem. Royal Astronomical Soc., London 1961, Acad. Royale des Sciences de Belgique 1973–, Acad. of Marseille 1979, Acad. of Athens 1980; Corresp. mem. Acad. of Coimbra 1953, Halle 1966, Vienna 1973, Royal Soc. Uppsala 1984; Hon. mem. SA Astronomical Soc. 1965; Dr hc (Geneva) 1982; Croix de guerre, Commdr Légion d'honneur, Palmes académiques, de Léopold II, Chevalier du Mérite agricole, Officier Ordre de Léopold de Belgique; Lauréat, Inst. de France, Acad. Royale de Belgique, Astron. Gesellschaft, Grand prix des sciences de la Ville de Paris 1976, Médaille d'or du CNRS 1978. *Publications:* Des hommes, des télescopes, des étoiles 1990; 280 publs in int. reviews on astronomy and related topics. *Leisure interests:* gardening, fishing. *Address:* Institut de France, 23 quai Conti, 75006 Paris (office); Les Magnanarelles, 84160 Lourmarin, France. *Telephone:* (4) 90-68-00-28. *Fax:* (4) 90-68-18-52 (home). *E-mail:* fehrenbach.charles@wanadoo.fr (home).

FEHRENBACH, Franz, BEng; German business executive; *Chairman of the Board of Management, Robert Bosch GmbH;* b. 1 July 1949, Kenzingen, Breisgau; m.; three s.; ed Univ. of Karlsruhe; trainee, Robert Bosch GmbH 1975–76, Man. Office of the Exec. Man., Electrical and Electronic Equipment Div. 1976–78, Dir Material Planning and Logistics Dept 1978–80, Commercial Plant Man., Hildesheim 1980–82, Vice-Pres., Corp. Dept Planning and Control 1982–85, Commercial Plant Man., Robert Bosch Corpn, Automotive Group, USA 1985–88, Exec. Vice-Pres. 1988–89, Exec. Vice-Pres., Finance and Admin, Starters and Alternators Div. 1989–94, Pres., Starters and Alternators Div. 1994–96, Exec. Vice-Pres., Finance and Admin, Diesel Systems Div. 1996–97, Pres. Diesel Systems Div. 1997–99, Deputy mem. Bd of Man. 1999–2001, mem. 2001–03, Chair. 2003–, also limited Partner, Robert Bosch Industrietreuhand KG 2003–; mem. Supervisory Bd BASF SE; mem. Man. Bd VDA (German Asscn of the Automotive Industry), US Bd of Presiding Cttee of BDI (Fed. of German Industries), Asia Pacific Cttee of German Business, BBUG (Baden-Baden Entrepreneurs' Conf.); mem. Senate of Max Planck Soc. *Address:* Robert Bosch GmbH, Robert-Bosch-Platz 1, 70839 Gerlingen-Schillerhohe, Germany (office). *Telephone:* (711) 8110 (office). *Fax:* (711) 8116630 (office). *E-mail:* info@bosch.com (office). *Website:* www.bosch.com (office).

FEI, Junlong; Chinese astronaut; b. 1965, Suzhou, Jiangsu; m. 1991; one s.; joined PLA Air Force 1982, served as fighter pilot; selected to be astronaut, Shenzhou Program 1998; shortlisted to fly on board Shenzhou 5, (China's first manned space mission) 2003; debut space flight on board Shenzhou 6, with astronaut Nie Haisheng, launched from Jiuquan Satellite Launch Centre, Gobi Desert (China's second space mission) 12 Oct. 2005; asteroid 9512

Feijunlong named after him. *Address:* c/o China National Space Administration, Beijing, People's Republic of China.

FEIFFER, Jules Ralph; American cartoonist, writer and dramatist; b. 26 Jan. 1929, New York, NY; s. of David Feiffer and Rhoda Davis; m. 1st Judith Sheftel 1961 (divorced 1983); one d.; m. 2nd Jennifer Allen 1983; two c.; ed Art Students' League, Pratt Inst.; asst to syndicated cartoonist Will Eisner 1946–51; cartoonist, author, syndicated Sunday page, Clifford, engaged in various art jobs 1953–56; contributing cartoonist Village Voice, New York 1956–97; cartoons published weekly in The Observer (London) 1958–66, 1972–82, regularly in Playboy (magazine); sponsor Sane; US Army 1951–53; mem. Dramatists' Guild (council 1970); currently Adjunct Prof., Program in Writing and Literature, Stony Brook Southampton Coll.; fmr teacher Yale School of Drama, Northwestern Univ.; fmr Sr Fellow, Columbia Univ. Nat. Arts Journalism Program; mem. American Acad. of Arts and Letters 1995–; Hon. Fellow, Inst. for Policy Studies 1987; Dr hc (Southampton Coll., Long Island Univ.) 1999; Acad. Award for Animated Cartoon (for Munro) 1961, Special George Polk Memorial Award 1962, Best Foreign Play, English Press (for Little Murders) 1967, Outer Critics Circle Award (Obie) 1969, (The White House Murder Case) 1970, Pulitzer Prize for Editorial Cartooning 1986, Writers Guild of America, East's Ian McLellan Hunter Award for Lifetime Achievement in Writing 2004, Nat. Cartoonist Soc. Milton Caniff Lifetime Achievement Award 2004, Benjamin Franklin Creativity Laureate Award 2006. *Plays:* Crawling Arnold 1961, Little Murders 1966, God Bless 1968, The White House Murder Case 1970, Feiffer on Nixon: The Cartoon Presidency 1974, Knock Knock 1975, Grown Ups 1981, A Think Piece 1982, Carnal Knowledge 1988, Anthony Rose 1989, Feiffer The Collected Works (vols 1, 2, 3) 1990, A Bad Friend 2003. *Screenplays:* Little Murders 1971, Carnal Knowledge 1971, Popeye 1980, I Want to Go Home (Best Screenplay, Venice Film Festival) 1989, I Lost My Bear 1998, Bark, George 1999. *Publications:* Sick, Sick, Sick 1959, Passionella and Other Stories 1960, The Explainers 1961, Boy, Girl, Boy, Girl, 1962, Hold Me! 1962, Harry, The Rat With Women (novel) 1963, Feiffer's Album 1963, The Unexpurgated Memoirs of Bernard Mergendeiler 1965, The Great Comic Book Heroes 1967, Feiffer's Marriage Manual 1967, Pictures at a Prosecution 1971, Ackroyd (novel) 1978, Tantrum 1980, Jules Feiffer's America: From Eisenhower to Reagan 1982, Marriage is an Invasion of Privacy 1984, Feiffer's Children 1986, Ronald Reagan in Movie America 1988, Elliott Loves (also play) 1990, The Man in the Ceiling (juvenile) 1993, A Barrel of Laughs, A Vale of Tears (juvenile) 1995, A Room with a Zoo (juvenile), The Daddy Mountain (juvenile), Explainers 2008. *Address:* Royce Carlton Inc., 866 United Nations Plaza, New York, NY 10017, USA (office). *Telephone:* (212) 355-7700 (office). *Fax:* (212) 888-8659 (office). *E-mail:* info@ roycecarlton.com (office); info@julesfeiffer.com (office). *Website:* www .roycecarlton.com (office); www.julesfeiffer.com.

FEINENDEGEN, Ludwig E., DrMed; German professor of nuclear medicine; *Professor Emeritus, Department of Nuclear Medicine, University Hospital, Heinrich Heine University, Düsseldorf;* b. 1 Jan. 1927, Garzweiler; s. of Ludwig Feinendegen and Rosa Klauth; m. Jeannine Gemuseus 1960; two s.; ed Univ. of Cologne; Asst Physician and Scientist, Medical Dept Brookhaven Nat. Lab., Upton, NY, USA 1958–63; Scientific Officer, Euratom, Brussels and Paris 1963–67; Dir Inst. of Medicine Research Center Jülich GmbH and Prof. for Nuclear Medicine, Heinrich Heine Univ, Dept of Nuclear Medicine, Univ. Hosp., Düsseldorf 1967–93, Prof. Emer. 1993–; Scientist, Brookhaven Nat. Lab., USA 1993–98, Research Collaborator 2000–; Assignee, OBER Dept of Energy, USA 1994–98; Fogarty Scholar NIH, Bethesda 1998–99; mem. Advisory Council, Fed. Ministries of Interior and Defence and other professional appts; mem. Cttee for meetings of Nobel Laureates 1978–2005; mem. Rhine Westfalian Acad. of Sciences (Vice-Pres. 1978–79); mem. Int. Comm. on Radiation Units and Measurements (ICRU) 1981–, Dist Gov. Rotary Int. 1992–93; numerous awards; Bundesverdienstorden. *Publications:* more than 600 publs in nat. and int. scientific journals and books on nuclear medicine and radiation biology. *Address:* Medical Department, Brookhaven National Laboratory, Upton, NY 11973, USA (office); Wannental 45, 88131 Lindau, Germany (home). *Telephone:* (8382) 277310 (Germany) (office); (631) 344-2837 (USA) (office); (8382) 75673 (home). *Fax:* (8382) 2773113 (Germany) (office); (631) 344-2653 (USA) (office); (8382) 947626 (home). *E-mail:* feinendegen@ gmx.net (home).

FEINGOLD, Russell Dana, BA, JD; American politician and lawyer; *Senator from Wisconsin;* b. 2 March 1953, Janesville, Wis.; s. of Leon Feingold and Sylvia Binstock; m. 1st Susan Levine 1977; two d.; m. 2nd Mary Speerschneider 1991; two step-c.; ed Univ. of Wisconsin, Madison, Magdalen Coll. Oxford, UK, Harvard Univ. Law School; practised as attorney 1979–85; Democrat State Senator 1983–92, US Senator from Wisconsin 1993–, mem. Foreign Relations Cttee., ranking mem. Sub-Cttee on African Affairs. *Address:* 506 Hart Senate Office Bldg, Washington, DC 20510-0001 (office); 8383 Greenway Boulevard, Middleton, WI 53562, USA. *Telephone:* (202) 224-5323 (office). *E-mail:* russell_feingold@feingold.senate.gov (office). *Website:* feingold.senate.gov (office).

FEINSTEIN, Dianne Goldman Berman; American politician; *Senator from California;* b. 22 June 1933, San Francisco, Calif.; d. of Leon Goldman and Betty Goldman (née Rosenburg); m. 1st Bertram Feinstein 1962 (deceased); one d.; m. 2nd Richard C. Blum 1980; ed Stanford Univ.; Intern in Public Affairs, Coro Foundation, San Francisco 1955–56; Asst to Calif. Industrial Welfare Comm., Los Angeles, also San Francisco 1956–57; Vice-Chair. Calif. Women's Bd Terms and Parole 1962–66; Chair. San Francisco City and Co. Advisory Comm. for Adult Detention 1967–69; Supervisor City and Co. of San Francisco 1970–78; Mayor of San Francisco 1978–88; served on Trilateral Comm. 1980s; Senator from California 1992–; mem. Council on Foreign Relations; Democrat; numerous hon. degrees; named by City and State Magazine the nation's "Most Effective Mayor" 1987, Woodrow Wilson Award for Public Service 2001, Nat. Distinguished Advocacy Award, American Cancer Soc. 2004, ranked by Forbes magazine amongst 100 Most Powerful Women (50th) 2004, (42nd) 2005. *Address:* 331 Senate Hart Office Building, Washington, DC 20510-0001, USA (office). *Telephone:* (202) 224-3841 (office). *Fax:* (202) 228-3954 (office). *Website:* feinstein.senate.gov (office).

FEIREISS, Kristin; German art gallery director and writer; *Director, Aedes West;* b. 1942; Founder and Dir (with pnr Hans-Jürgen Commercell) Aedes West Gallery (first pvt. forum for architecture in Germany), West Berlin 1980–, est. office in East Berlin 1995, over 250 exhbns shown including work of Peter and Alison Smithson, Peter Cook, Rem Koolhas, John Hejduk, over 200 catalogues published; Dir Netherlands Architecture Inst. 1996–2001; Bundesverdienstkreutz, Germany 1994; Literaturpreis für Baukultur, German Asscn of Architects and Engineers 1995. *Publications include:* Josef Paul Kleihues 1983, John Hejduk 1984, Fehling und Gogel 1986, Also Rossi 1989, Frank Gehry 1989, Nalbach und Nalbach 1990, Shin Takamatsu 1991, Syskowitz und Kowalski 1991, Zaha Hadid 1992, Hilde Léon Konrad Wohlhage 1992, Gustav Peichl: von der Skizze zum Bauwerk 1992, Sauerbruch und Hutton 1992, Daniel Libeskind: Erweiterung des Berlin Museums mit Abteilung Jüdisches Museum 1992, Ben van Berkel 1994, Christoph Mäckler 1995, Architekten Grüntuch/Ernst 1997, The Netherlands Architecture Institute 1999, Clorindo Testa 2001, Andre Poitiers 2002. *Address:* Aedes am Pfefferberg, Christinenstr. 18-19, 10119 Berlin, Germany. *Telephone:* (30) 282-7015 (office). *Fax:* (30) 2839-1466 (office). *E-mail:* aedes@ baunetz.de (office). *Website:* www.aedes-arc.de (office).

FEITH, Pieter Cornelius, LicenPolSci, MA; Dutch diplomatist and international organization official; *Special Representative in Kosovo, European Union;* b. 9 Feb. 1945, Rotterdam; m.; three d.; ed Univ. of Lausanne, Switzerland, Fletcher School of Law and Diplomacy, Medford, USA; performed mil. military service as reserve officer of Netherlands Marine Corps; with diplomatic service 1970–95, posted to Damascus, Bonn, New York (Mission to UN), Khartoum and Netherlands Mission to NATO and WEU, Brussels, also Chair. first UN Conf. of States Parties to the Chemical Weapons Convention, The Hague 1997; Personal Rep. of NATO Sec.-Gen. Lord Robertson for Yugoslavia, Dir of Crisis Man. and Operations Directorate, Head of NATO Balkans Task Force and Political Adviser to Commdr IFOR Bosnia-Herzegovina 1995–2001; Gen. Secr. of Council of EU, Deputy Dir-Gen. for Politico-Mil. Affairs 2001–; Personal Rep. of EU High Rep., Javier Solana, for Sudan/Darfur 2004; Head of EU Expert Team for Iraq 2005; Head of EU-led Aceh Monitoring Mission (AMM) in Indonesia 2005–06; Civilian Operations Commdr for all civilian ESDP Crisis Man. Operations, Acting Dir of EU Civilian Planning and Conduct Capability 2007; led team of EU officials and approved the Constitution of the Repub. of Kosovo April 2008, EU Special Rep. in Kosovo 2008–. *Leisure interest:* playing tennis. *Address:* Jüri Laas (Press Adviser), Council of the European Union, Rue de la Loi 175, 1048 Brussels, Belgium (office). *Telephone:* 486-79-80-55 (mobile) (office). *Fax:* (2) 281-69-34 (office). *E-mail:* juri.laas@consilium.europa.eu (office). *Website:* www .consilium.europa.eu (office).

FEKTER, Maria, DIur; Austrian politician; *Minister of the Interior;* b. 1 Feb. 1956; ed Linz Univ.; Municipal Counsellor, Attnang-Puchheim 1986–90; State Sec., Fed. Ministry of Econ. Affairs 1990–94; mem. Nat. Council (Parl.) 1994–2007; Fed. Minister of the Interior 2008–; mem. Exec. Cttee Österreichischer Wirtschaftsbund 1990–2002. *Address:* Federal Ministry of the Interior, Herrengasse 7, 1014 Vienna, Austria (office). *Telephone:* (1) 531-26-0 (office). *Fax:* (1) 531-26-10-86-13 (office). *E-mail:* post@bmi.gv.at (office). *Website:* www.bmi.gv.at (office).

FELBER, René; Swiss politician; b. 14 March 1933, Biel; m.; three c.; teacher, Boudevilliers 1953–55, Le Locle 1955–64; joined Social Democratic Party 1958; Mayor of Gen. Council, Le Locle 1960; Mayor of Le Locle 1964–80; mem. of Parl., Neuchâtel 1965–76; Nat. Councillor 1967–81; mem. Govt of Repub. and Canton of Neuchâtel; Head of Cantonal Dept of Finances 1981–87; Pres. Govt of Neuchâtel 1984; mem. Fed. Council 1988–93; Head Fed. Dept of Foreign Affairs 1988; Vice-Pres. Jan.–Dec. 1991, Pres. of Switzerland Jan.–Dec. 1992. *Address:* c/o Social Democratic Party, Spitalgasse 34, 3001 Bern, Switzerland.

FELCH, William Campbell, MD; American fmr physician; b. 14 Nov. 1920, Lakewood, Ohio; s. of Don H.W. Felch and Beth Campbell; m. Nancy Cook Dean 1945; two s. one d.; ed Phillips Exeter Acad., Princeton Univ. and Columbia Coll. of Physicians and Surgeons; served in US Army 1942–48; in pvt. practice, internal medicine 1951–88; Chief of Staff, United Hosp., Port Chester, New York 1975–77; Ed. The Internist 1975–86; Medical Dir Osborn Home, Rye 1979–88; Exec. Vice-Pres. Alliance for Continuing Medical Educ. 1979–91 (Distinguished Service Award 1991); mem. Inst. of Medicine, NAS; Fellow American Coll. of Physicians; Ed. ACME Almanac 1978–90, Journal of Continuing Educ. in the Health Professions 1992–94; Award of Merit, New York State Soc. of Internal Medicine 1976, Internist of Distinction, Soc. of Internal Medicine of New York 1973. *Publications:* Aspiration and Achievement 1981, Primer, Continuing Medical Education (co-ed.) 1986, Decade of Decisions 1989, Vision of the Future 1991, The Secrets of Good Patient Care 1996, Alliance for Continuing Medical Education: The First 20 Years 1996, A Chronical of Commitments: A Memoir 2001. *Leisure interest:* travel. *Address:* 8545 Carmel Valley Road, Carmel, CA 93923, USA (home). *Telephone:* (831) 625-6593 (home). *Fax:* (831) 624-4032 (home). *E-mail:* srfelch@comsat.net (home).

FELD, Eliot; American dancer and choreographer; b. 5 July 1942, Brooklyn, New York; s. of Benjamin Feld and Alice Posner; ed High School of Performing Arts, New York; debut as Child Prince in Nutcracker, New York City Ballet

1954; mem. cast, West Side Story, Broadway 1958 (also appeared in film), I Can Get It For You Wholesale, Broadway 1962 and Fiddler on the Roof, Broadway; dancer and choreographer, American Ballet Theater 1963–68; Founder, Prin. Dancer and Choreographer, American Ballet Co. 1968–71; freelance choreographer, N America and Europe 1971–73; Founder, Artistic Dir and Choreographer, Feld Ballets, NY; Founder, The New Ballet School 1977, The Joyce Theater 1982, Ballet Tech 1996; Co-founder, Lawrence A. Wien Center for Dance & Theater 1986; has choreographed over 100 ballets since 1967 including Nodrog Doggo 2000, Coup de Couperin 2000, Organon 2001, Pacific Dances 2001, Skandia 2002, Pianola 2002, Lincoln Portrait 2002, Behold the Man 2002; Guggenheim Fellow; Dance Magazine Award 1990; Dr hc (Juilliard) 1991. *Address:* c/o Ballet Tech., 890 Broadway, 8th Floor, New York, NY 10003-1211, USA (office). *Telephone:* (212) 777-7710 (office). *Fax:* (212) 353-0936.

FELDBAEK, Ole, MA, DPhil; Danish academic; *Professor of Economic History, University of Copenhagen;* b. 22 July 1936, Copenhagen; s. of Commdr Henri Feldbaek and Kathy Feldbaek; m. Inge Kjaergaard 1976; one s. one d.; ed Univ. of Copenhagen; Lecturer in Econ. History, Univ. of Copenhagen 1968, Prof. 1981–; Fellow, Royal Danish and Royal Norwegian Acads, Academia Europaea; Amalienborg Prize 2001. *Publications include:* The Battle of Copenhagen: Nelson and the Danes and numerous books and articles on 18th century European and Asian history (econ., political and mil.). *Address:* 12 Sagaparken, 2920 Charlottenlund, Denmark (home).

FELDMAN, Jerome Myron, MD; American physician, medical scientist and academic; *Professor Emeritus, Division of Endocrinology, Metabolism and Nutrition, Duke University Medical Center;* b. 27 July 1935, Chicago, Ill.; s. of Louis Feldman and Marian (Swichkow) Feldman; m. Carol B. Feldman; one s. two d.; ed Northwestern Univ., Michael Reese, Chicago and Duke Univ.; Chief, Endocrinology and Metabolism, Durham Veteran's Admin. Hosp. 1971–2000, Staff Internist 1971–; Assoc. Prof. of Medicine, Duke Univ. 1972–98, Prof. of Medicine 1998–, now Prof. Emer., Dir Clinical Research Unit Core Lab. 1984; mem. Duke Comprehensive Cancer Center 1982–; Ed. Journal of Clinical Endocrinology and Metabolism 1983–89. *Publications:* 218 research articles, book chapters and reviews dealing with hormone-secreting tumours, endocrinology and metabolism. *Leisure interests:* music, art. *Address:* Duke University Medical Center, Box 2963, Durham, NC 27710, USA. *Telephone:* (919) 286-0411. *E-mail:* feld002@duke.edu (office). *Website:* endocrine.duke.edu/home.asp?divisionID=46 (office).

FELDMAN, Michael, PhD; Israeli biologist and academic; *Professor Emeritus, Department of Immunology, Weizmann Institute of Science;* b. 21 Jan. 1926, Tel Aviv; m. Lea Noyfeld 1946; one s. one d.; ed Herzlia High School, Tel Aviv, Hebrew Univ., Jerusalem; British Council Scholar, Inst. of Animal Genetics, Edinburgh, Scotland 1953–55; joined Weizmann Inst. of Science, Rehovot 1955; Dept of Virology, Univ. of Calif., Berkeley, USA 1960–61; Visiting Scientist, Nat. Cancer Inst., NIH, Bethesda, Md, USA 1961; fmr Head, Dept of Cell Biology, Weizmann Inst. 1961–90, Chair. Scientific Council 1962–64, Dean, Feinberg Grad. School 1966–72, Dean, Faculty of Biology 1983–85, now Prof. Emer., Dept of Immunology; Visiting Prof., Stanford Medical School, Stanford, Calif., USA 1976–77; Scholar-in-Residence, John F. Fogarty Int. Center, NIH, Bethesda 1978–79; Visiting Prof., Memorial Sloan Kettering Cancer Inst., New York 1990–91; research activities include cancer research (in particular, control of tumour metastasis), cellular immunology and developmental biology; mem. Israel Acad. of Sciences and Humanities 1980–; Hon. Fellow Open Univ. of Israel 2000; Dr hc (Ben-Gurion Univ.) 1988; Griffuel Prize, Paris 1984, Rothschild Prize, Jerusalem 1986, San Marino Prize for Medicine 2000. *Publications:* numerous publs on cancer research immunology and developmental biology, in Scientific American, Nature, Nature Medicine, Journal of Experimental Medicine and other int. journals. *Leisure interests:* the arts, art history. *Address:* c/o The Weizmann Institute of Science, P.O. Box 26, Rehovot 76100, Israel. *Telephone:* 8-9344073 (office); 8-9472763 (home). *Fax:* 8-9344125 (office). *Website:* www.weizmann.ac.il/immunology (office).

FELDMANN, Marc, MB BS, PhD, FRS, FRCP, FRCPath, FMedSci, FAA; Australian immunologist and rheumatologist; *Head of Kennedy Institute of Rheumatology Division, Head of Department of Cytokine Biology and Cellular Immunology and Professor of Cellular Immunology, Faculty of Medicine, Imperial College London;* b. 2 Dec. 1944; ed Univ. of Melbourne, Walter and Eliza Hall Inst. of Medical Research; Resident Medical Officer, Professorial Dept of Medicine and Surgery, St Vincent's Hosp., Melbourne 1968; Postdoctoral C.J. Martin Fellow, Dept of Zoology, Imperial Cancer Research Fund Tumour Immunology Unit, Univ. Coll. London, UK 1972–73, Sr Staff Mem. 1974, Special Appointment Grade 1977; Deputy Dir and Head, Immunology Unit, Charing Cross Sunley Research Centre 1985–92; Prof. of Cellular Immunology, Univ. of London 1986; Wellesley Visiting Prof. and Distinguished Lecturer, Toronto, Canada 1988; mem. Scientific Advisory Bd and Consultant, Xenova PLC, Slough, UK 1989–99, Syntex Research (now Roche Bioscience), Palo Alto, Calif., USA 1991–, Centocor, Inc., Malvern, Pa, USA 1991–; Consultant, Sandoz, Basel, Switzerland 1991–98, Canji, Inc., La Jolla, Calif. 1994–, Alza Inc., Palo Alto 1994–, Ferring AS, Copenhagen, Denmark 1996–2000, Wyeth (fmrly Genetics Inst.), Boston, Mass, USA 1997–, Boehringer-Ingelheim 1999–, Novartis, Canfite, Inc., Receptor Biologix, Inc., Novo Nordisk 2003–; Head of Div., Imperial Coll. School of Medicine, Kennedy Inst. of Rheumatology 2000–, Head of Dept of Cytokine Biology and Cellular Immunology 2000–; Founder and Consultant, Synovis Ltd 2001–; Founder-mem. and Jr Councillor, Int. Cytokine Soc.; mem. British Soc. for Rheumatology (currently Pres), British Soc. of Immunologists, American Asscn of Immunologists, Autralian Immunology Soc.; mem. Research Subcttee, Arthritis Research Council, UK 1984–88 (mem. Scientific Consultative Cttee 2000–05), Oliver Bird Cttee, Nuffield Foundation 1991–96, Medical Research Advisory Cttee, Multiple Sclerosis Soc., UK 1991–2000 (Chair. 1999–2000), Scientific Advisory Bd, Jenner Inst. 2000–05, Scientific Advisory Cttee, Deutsches RheumaForschungsZentrum, Berlin, Germany 2002–06; Transmitting Ed. International Immunology 2001–; mem. Editorial Bd Journal of Experimental Pathology 1997–, Cytokines, Cytokine and Growth Factor Reviews, Journal of Autoimmunity, European Cytokine Network, Medical Immunology; mem. European Molecular Biology Org. 2005; Hon. mem. Scandinavian Soc. of Immunology, Polish Immunology Soc.; Hon. MD (Technical Univ., Munich) 2002; Univ. of Melbourne awards: Robert Gartley Healey Prize in Medicine, Hubert Sydney Jacobs Prize in Clinical Gynaecology, Sandoz Prize in Clinical Obstetrics, Fulton Scholarship, Clara Myers Prize in Surgical Pediatrics, Robert Garley Healey Prize in Surgery, Beaney Scholarship, Mead Johnson Prize in Pediatrics, Grieve Memorial Prize in Pediatrics; other awards: Margaret Ryan Prize in Surgery, Royal Australian Coll. of Surgeons, Marshall-Allen Prize in Obstetrics, Royal Coll. of Obstetricians and Gynaecologists, Michael Ryan Prize in Medicine Royal, Australian Coll. of Medicine, Watson-Smith Lecturer, Royal Coll. of Physicians (London) 1994, Canada Trust Distinguished Lecturer in Immunology (Toronto, Canada) 1998, Carol-Nachman Prize for Rheumatology Research (Germany) 1999, EULAR Prix Courtin-Clarins (jtly) 1999, Crafoord Prize (jtly), Royal Swedish Acad. 2000, Albert Lasker Clinical Medical Research Award (jtly) 2003, Cameron Prize, Univ. of Edinburgh (jtly) 2004, European Inventor of the Year, Lifetime Achievement Award, European Patent Office 2007, Curtin Medal, ANU 2008. *Publications:* 90 patents and more than 600 publs in scientific journals. *Leisure interests:* tennis, hiking. *Address:* Kennedy Institute of Rheumatology Division, Imperial College School of Medicine, 65 Aspenlea Road, Hammersmith, London, W6 8LH, England (office). *Telephone:* (20) 8383-4400 (office). *Fax:* (20) 8563-0399 (office). *E-mail:* m.feldmann@imperial.ac.uk (office). *Website:* www1.imperial.ac.uk/medicine/default.html (office).

FELDSTEIN, Martin Stuart, MA, DPhil; American economist and academic; *President and CEO, National Bureau of Economic Research;* b. 25 Nov. 1939, New York; s. of Meyer Feldstein and Esther Feldstein (née Gevarter); m. Kathleen Foley 1965; two d.; ed Harvard Univ. and Univ. of Oxford, UK; Research Fellow, Nuffield Coll., Oxford 1964–65, Official Fellow 1965–67, Lecturer in Public Finance 1965–67; Asst Prof. of Econs, Harvard Univ. 1967–68, Assoc. Prof. 1968–69, Prof. 1969–, George F. Baker Prof. of Econs 1984–; Pres. and CEO Nat. Bureau of Econ. Research 1977–82, 1984–2008; Chair. Pres.'s Council of Econ. Advisers 1982–84; mem. Pres.'s Foreign Intelligence Advisory Bd 2006–; mem. Advisory Bd Congressional Budget Office, New York Fed. Reserve Bank, Boston Fed. Reserve Bank; mem. J.P. Morgan Int. Council; mem. Bd of Contribs, Wall Street Journal; Fellow, American Philosophical Soc., American Acad. of Arts and Sciences, Econometric Soc., Nat. Asscn of Business Economists; mem. American Econ. Asscn, Vice-Pres. 1988, Pres. 2004; mem. Inst. of Medicine, NAS, Council on Foreign Relations (Dir 1998–, Trustee 1999–, (mem. Exec. Cttee 2002–), Trilateral Comm. 1984– (Exec. Cttee 1990–), Nat Cttee on US-China Relations (Dir) 2001–, Group of 30 2002–; Foreign mem. Austrian Acad. of Sciences; Corresp. Fellow, British Acad.; mem. Bd Dirs American Int. 1988–, Eli Lilly 2001–; Hon. Fellow, Nuffield Coll. Oxford 1998; Hon. LLD (Univ. of Rochester) 1984, (Marquette) 1985; Bernhard Harms Prize, Weltwirtschafts Institut, Distinguished Service Award, The Tax Foundation, John Bates Clark Medal, American Econ. Asscn 1977. *Address:* National Bureau of Economic Research, 1050 Massachusetts Avenue, Cambridge, MA 02138 (office); 147 Clifton Street, Belmont, MA 02478, USA (home). *Telephone:* (617) 868-3905 (office). *Fax:* (617) 868-7194 (office). *E-mail:* msfeldst@nber.org (office); mfeldstein@harvard.edu (office). *Website:* www.nber.org/feldstein (office).

FELDT, Kjell-Olof, PhD; Swedish politician; b. 18 Aug. 1931, Holmsund; m. Birgitta von Otter; three c.; ed Univs of Uppsala and Lund; Budget Sec., Ministry of Finance 1962–64, Budget Dir 1965, Under-Sec. 1967–70; Minister of Trade 1970–75, of Finance 1983–90; Minister without Portfolio 1975–76; mem. Parl. 1971–90; mem. Exec. Cttee Social Democratic Party 1978–90; Chair. Bank of Sweden 1967–70, 1994–99, Swedish Road Fed. 1992–, Vin & Sprit AB 1991–93; mem. Bd Dirs Nordbanken 1991–94, Sandrew Theatre Co. 1990–. *Publication:* Memoirs 1991.

FELL, Sir David, Kt, KCB, BSc, FIB, DUniv; British business executive, banker and government official; *Chairman, Northern Bank Ltd;* b. 20 Jan. 1943, Belfast; s. of Ernest Fell and Jessie McCreedy; m. Sandra J. Moore 1967; one s. one d.; ed Royal Belfast Academical Inst. and Queen's Univ. Belfast; Sales Man. Rank Hovis McDougall Ltd 1965–66; teacher 1966–67; Research Assoc. 1967–69; Dept of Agric. 1969–72, Asst Sec. 1971–81; Dept of Commerce 1972–82, Under-Sec. 1981–82; Deputy Chief Exec. Industrial Devt Bd 1982–84; Perm. Sec. Dept of Econ. Devt 1984–91; Second Perm. Under-Sec. NI Office and Head, NI Civil Service 1991–97; Chair. Northern Bank Ltd (subsidiary of Nat. Australia Bank) 1998–, Boxmore Int. PLC 1998–2000, Nat. Irish Bank Ltd 1999–; Dir Nat. Australia Group Europe Ltd 1998–, Dunloe Ewart PLC 1998–2002, Fred Olsen Energy ASA 1999–2003, Chesapeake Corpn. 2000–; Chair. Prince's Trust, NI 1999–, Harland & Wolff Group PLC 2001–02, Titanic Properties Ltd 2001–, Titanic Quarter Ltd 2001–. *Leisure interests:* music, reading, golf, rugby. *Address:* Northern Bank Ltd, Head Office, P.O. Box 183, Donegal Square, Belfast, BT1 6JS, Northern Ireland.

FELLAG, Mohamed Said; Algerian actor and comedian; b. 1950, Kabylie; began career as classical actor; fmr Dir Théâtre Régional, Bougie; moved to Paris 1995; Prince Claus Award 1999. *Films include:* Liberté, la nuit 1983, Le Gone du chaâba 1998, Inch'Allah dimanche 2001, Fleurs de sang 2002, Momo mambo 2003, Voisins, voisines 2005, Rue des figuiers (TV) 2005. *Shows* *include:* The Adventures of Tchop 1986, Khorotov Cocktail 1989, Djurdjurassic Bled 1998.

FELLNER, Eric, CBE; British film producer; b. 10 Oct. 1959; four s. one d.; ed London Guildhall; Co-Chair. Working Title Films; four Academy Awards and 18 BAFTA Awards, Empire Film Award for outstanding contribution to British cinema (jtly) 2005. *Films include:* Sid and Nancy 1986, Pascali's Island 1988, The Rachel Papers 1989, Hidden Agenda 1990, A Kiss Before Dying 1991, Liebstraum 1991, Wild West 1992, Posse 1993, Romeo is Bleeding 1993, Four Weddings and a Funeral 1994, The Hudsucker Proxy 1994, Loch Ness 1995, French Kiss 1995, Dead Man Walking 1995, Fargo 1996, Bean 1997, The Borrowers 1997, Elizabeth 1998, The Big Lebowski 1998, Notting Hill 1999, Plunkett & Macleane 1999, O Brother, Where Art Thou? 2000, Billy Elliot 2000, Bridget Jones's Diary 2001, Captain Corelli's Mandolin 2001, The Man Who Wasn't There 2001, About a Boy 2002, The Guru 2002, 40 Days and 40 Nights 2002, Ali G Indahouse 2002, Long Time Dead 2002, My Little Eye 2002, Love Actually 2003, Calcium Kid 2003, Ned Kelly 2003, Shape of Things 2003, Johnny English 2003, Thirteen 2003, Shaun of the Dead 2004, Thunderbirds 2004, Wimbledon 2004, Bridget Jones: The Edge of Reason 2004, Gettin' Square 2004, Inside I'm Dancing 2004, Mickybo and Me 2005, The Interpreter 2005, Pride and Prejudice 2005, Nanny McPhee 2005, Middle of Nowhere 2006, Smokin' Aces 2006, United 93 (Best British Producer, London Film Critics' Circle Awards 2007) 2006, Hot Fuzz 2007, Atonement 2007, Elizabeth: The Golden Age 2007, Definitely Maybe 2008, Wild Child 2008, Burn After Reading 2008, Frost/Nixon 2009. *Address:* Working Title Films, 76 Oxford Street, London, W1D 1BS, England (office); Working Title Films, 4th Floor, 9770 Wilshire Blvd, Beverly Hills, CA 90212, USA (office). *Telephone:* (20) 7307-3000 (London) (office); (310) 777-3100 (USA) (office). *Fax:* (20) 7307-3001 (London) (office); (310) 777-5243 (USA) (office). *Website:* www.workingtitlefilms.com (office).

FELLNER, Fritz, PhD; Austrian historian and academic; *Professor Emeritus of Modern History, University of Salzburg;* b. 25 Dec. 1922, Vienna; s. of Peter Fellner and Marie Obenaus; m. Liselotte Lamberg 1950; two s.; ed Realgymnasium, Matura, Univ. of Vienna and Inst. für Österreichische Geschichtsforschung; Research Fellow, Österreichisches Kulturinstitut, Rome 1951–52; Asst Lecturer, Univ. of Vienna 1954–64, Dozent 1960; Prof. of Modern History, Univ. of Salzburg 1964–93, Prof. Emer. 1993–. *Publications:* Schicksalsjahre Österreichs. Das pol. Tagebuch Josef Redlichs 1908 bis 1919 1953/54, Der Dreibund 1960, St Germain im Sommer 1919 1977, Dichter und Gelehrter. Hermann Bahr und Josef Redlich in ihren Briefen 1896–1934 1980, Vom Dreibund zum Völkerbund 1994, Ein wahrhaft patriotisches Werk: Die Kommission für neuere Geschichte Österreichs 1897–2000 2001, Geschichtsschreibung und nationale Identität: Probleme und Leistungen der Österreichischen Geschichtswissenschaft 2002, Österreichische Geschichtswissenschaft im 200 Jahrhundert: Ein biographisch-bibliographisches Lexikon (with Doris A. Corradini) 2006. *Address:* Neustiftgasse 47/5, 1070 Vienna, Austria. *Telephone:* (1) 5260827. *Fax:* (1) 5260827 (office).

FELLNER, Peter John, PhD; British pharmaceuticals and biotechnology executive; *Chairman, Vernalis PLC;* b. 31 Dec. 1943; s. of the late Hans Julius Fellner and essica Fellner (née Thompson); m. 1st Sandra Head (née Smith) 1969; one d. one step-s.; m. 2nd Jennifer Mary Zabel (née Butler) 1982; two step-s.; ed Univ. of Sheffield and Trinity Coll. Cambridge; Post-doctoral Research Fellow, Univ. of Strasbourg, France 1968–70, Assoc. Prof. 1970–73; Sr Research Investigator, Searle UK Research Labs 1973–77, Dir of Chem. 1977–80, Dir of Research 1980–84; Dir of Research Roche UK Research Centre 1984–86, Man. Dir Roche UK 1986–90; CEO Celltech PLC 1990–99, CEO Celltech Group (fmrly Celltech Chiroscience) PLC 1999–2003; Chair. Vernalis PLC (fmrly British Biotech PLC), Chair. (non-exec.) Celltech Group PLC 2003–, Ionix Pharmaceuticals Ltd, Astex Technology 2002–; Chair. Premier Research Group PLC 2007–; Dir (non-exec.) Colborn Dawes Ltd 1986–90, Synaptica Ltd 1999–2002, Qinetiq Group PLC 2004–, UCB SA 2005–, Evotec AG 2005–, Bespak PLC 2005–; mem. MRC 2000–07. *Leisure interest:* country walking. *Address:* Vernalis PLC, Oakdene Court, 613 Reading Road, Winnersh, RG41 5UA, England (office). *Telephone:* (118) 989-9312 (office). *Fax:* (118) 989-9369 (office). *Website:* www.vernalis.com (office).

FELLS, Ian, CBE, MA, PhD, FRSE, FREng, FIE, FIChemE; British professor of energy conversion; *Principal Consultant, Fells Associates;* b. 5 Sept. 1932, Sheffield; s. of Dr H. Alexander Fells and Clarice Fells; m. Hazel Denton Scott 1957; four s.; ed King Edward VII School, Sheffield and Trinity Coll. Cambridge; lecturer and Dir of Studies, Dept of Fuel Tech. and Chemical Eng, Univ. of Sheffield 1958–62; Reader in Fuel Science, King's Coll., Univ. of Durham 1962; Prof. of Energy Conversion, Univ. of Newcastle-upon-Tyne 1975–; mem. Science Consultative Group, BBC 1976–81, Electricity Supply Research Council 1979–90; Exec. David Davies Inst. of Int. Affairs 1975–; Pres. Inst. of Energy 1978–79; Scientific Adviser World Energy Council 1990–98; Dir and Trustee, Int. Centre for Life 1995–; Chair. New and Renewable Energy Centre, Northumberland 2002–05; Principal Consultant, Fells Associates; Adviser to House of Commons and House of Lords Select Cttee; numerous other professional appointments; Hatfield Memorial Prize 1974, Beilby Memorial Medal and Prize 1976, Royal Soc. Faraday Medal and Prize 1993, Melchett Medal 1999, John Collier Memorial Medal 1999, Kelvin Medal 2002. *Television series:* Young Scientist of the Year, The Great Egg Race, Men of Science, Earth Year 2050, Take Nobody's Word For It, What If the Lights Go Out?. *Radio:* extensive radio contribs. *Publications:* UK Energy Policy Post-Privatization 1991, Energy for the Future 1995, World Energy, 1923–1998 and Beyond 1998, Turning Point, An Independent Review of UK Energy Policy 2001. *Leisure interests:* cross-country skiing, sailing, swimming. *Address:* Fells Associates, 29 Rectory Terrace, Newcastle upon Tyne, NE3 1YB, England (office). *Telephone:* (8703) 211-661 (office); (191) 285-5343 (home). *Fax:* (191) 285-5343 (home). *E-mail:* ian@fellsassociates.com (office). *Website:* www.fellsassociates.com (office); www.narec.co.uk (office).

FELTHEIMER, Jon, BA; American entertainment industry executive; *CEO, Lions Gate Entertainment Corporation;* b. 2 Sept. 1951, Brooklyn, NY; m.; three c.; ed Wash. Univ., St Louis; moved to LA to become musician; joined New World Entertainment 1983, held various exec. positions including Pres. and CEO, Dir of Domestic and Int. Distribution Businesses, Man. New World TV Div., Marvel Productions and Learning Corpn of America Units; joined Sony Pictures Entertainment (SPE) 1991, launched interactive tv business 1996, cr. TriStar TV, Head of Columbia TriStar TV Group and Exec. Vice-Pres. SPE –2000; CEO Lions Gate Entertainment Corpn, Vancouver, Canada 2000–. *Address:* Lions Gate Entertainment Corporation, 555 Brooksbank Avenue, North Vancouver, BC V7J 355, Canada (office). *Telephone:* (604) 983-5555 (office). *Fax:* (604) 983-5554 (office). *Website:* www.lionsgatefilms.com (office).

FELTUS, Alan Evan, MFA; American artist and academic; b. 1 May 1943, Washington, DC; s. of Randolph Feltus and Anne Winter; m. Lani H. Irwin 1974; two s.; ed Tyler School of Fine Arts, Pa, Cooper Union for Advancement of Science and Art, NY, Yale Univ., Conn.; instructor, School of Dayton Art Inst., Ohio 1968–70; Asst Prof., American Univ., Washington, DC 1972–84; full-time artist 1984–, represented by Forum Gallery, New York 1973–; exhibits regularly in USA; occasional teaching workshops and lectures; resident in Italy since 1987; Rome Prize Fellowship, American Acad. in Rome 1970–72, Nat. Endowment for Arts Fellowship 1981, Louis Comfort Tiffany Foundation Grant in Painting 1980, Pollock-Krasner Foundation Grant in Painting 1992, 2005, Thomas B. Clarke Prize, Nat. Acad. of Design 1984, Benjamin Altman Prize 1990, Joseph S. Isidor Memorial Medal 1995, Raymond Neilson Prize 2001. *Address:* c/o Forum Gallery, 745 Fifth Avenue, New York, NY 10151, USA (office); Porziano 68, 06081 Assisi, Perugia, Italy (home). *Telephone:* (212) 355-4545 (office). *Fax:* (212) 355-4547 (office). *E-mail:* gallery@forumgallery.com (office); alan@feltus.com (home). *Website:* www.forumgallery.com (office); www.alanfeltus.com (home).

FENBY, Jonathan Theodore Starmer, CBE; British writer and journalist; *Director, China Research, Trusted Sources;* b. 11 Nov. 1942, London; s. of the late Charles Fenby and June Fenby (née Head); m. Renée Wartski 1967; one s. one d.; ed King Edward's School, Birmingham, Westminster School and New Coll. Oxford; corresp. and ed. Reuters World Service, Reuters Ltd 1963–77; corresp. (France and Germany), The Economist 1982–86; Home Ed. and Asst Ed. The Independent 1986–88; Deputy Ed. The Guardian 1988–93; Ed. The Observer 1993–95; Dir Guardian Newspapers 1990–95; Ed. South China Morning Post 1995–99; Ed. Netmedia Group; Assoc. Ed. Sunday Business 2000–01; Ed. Business Europe 2000–01; Ed. www.earlywarning.com 2004–06; currently Dir China Research, Trusted Sources; mem. Bd European Journalism Centre, Belgian–British Colloquium; Chevalier, Ordre du Mérite (France) 1992. *Radio:* broadcasts on BBC, CBC and French and Swiss radio. *Television:* broadcasts on BBC, CNN, CNBC, Channel Four, FR2, Sky, Bloomberg. *Publications:* The Fall of the House of Beaverbrook 1979, Piracy and the Public 1983, The International News Services 1986, On the Brink: The Trouble with France 1998 (new edn 2002), Comment peut-on être Français? 1999, Dealing With the Dragon: A Year in the New Hong Kong 2000, Generalissimo: Chiang Kai-shek and the China He Lost 2003, The Sinking of the Lancastria 2005, Alliance: The Inside Story of How Roosevelt, Stalin and Churchill Won One War and Began Another 2007; contrib. to newspapers and magazines in Europe, USA, Asia. *Leisure interests:* walking, jazz, belot. *Address:* Trusted Sources, 48 Charlotte Street, London, W1T 2NS (office); 101 Ridgmount Gardens, Torrington Place, London, WC1E 7AZ, England (home). *Telephone:* (20) 3008-5764 (office). *E-mail:* jtfenby@hotmail.com (home). *Website:* www.trustedsources.co.uk (office).

FENCHEL, Tom Michael, DPhil; Danish marine biologist and academic; *Professor of Marine Biology, University of Copenhagen;* b. 19 March 1940, Copenhagen; s. of W. Fenchel and Käte (née Sperling); m. 1st Anne Thane 1964; m. 2nd Hilary Adler 1978 (divorced 1989); one s. one d.; m. 3rd Ilse Duun 1995; ed Univ. of Copenhagen; Lecturer in Marine Biology, Univ. of Copenhagen 1964–70, Prof. of Marine Biology 1987–; Prof. of Ecology and Zoology, Univ. of Aarhus 1970–87; Gold Medal, Univ. of Copenhagen 1964, Ecology Prize 1987, Huntsmann Award for Oceanography 1987. *Publications:* Theories of Populations in Biological Communities (with F. B. Christiansen) 1977, Bacteria and Mineral Cycling (with T. H. Blackburn) 1979, Ecology of Protozoa 1987, Ecology and Evolution in Anoxic Worlds (with B. J. Finlay), Bacterial Biochemistry (jtly), Bacterial Biogeochemistry (with G. M. King and T. H. Blackburn) 1998, Origin and Early Evolution of Life 2002. *Address:* Marine Biological Laboratory, University of Copenhagen, Strandpromenaden 5, 3000 Helsingor, Denmark (office). *Telephone:* 35-32-19-60 (office). *Fax:* 35-32-19-51 (office). *E-mail:* tfenchel@bi.ku.dk (office). *Website:* www.mbl.ku.dk (office).

FENDER, Sir Brian Edward Frederick, Kt, PhD, CMG; British academic and business consultant; *President and Chairman, Institute of Knowledge Transfer;* b. 15 Sept. 1934, Barrow; s. of the late George Clements Fender and of Emily Goodwin; m. 1st 1956; one s. three d.; m. 2nd Ann Linscott 1986; ed Carlisle and Sale Grammar Schools, Imperial Coll., London; Research Instructor, Univ. of Washington, Seattle 1959–61; Sr Research Fellow, Nat. Chemical Lab. Teddington 1961–63; Fellow, St Catherine's Coll., Oxford 1963–84, Lecturer in Inorganic Chem. 1965–80; Asst Dir Inst. Laue-Langevin, Grenoble 1980–82, Dir 1982–85; Vice-Chancellor, Keele Univ. 1985–95; Chief Exec. Higher Educ. Funding Council for England 1995–2001; Chair. BTG PLC 2003–08; Pres. and Chair. Inst. of Knowledge Transfer 2005–; mem. Science and Eng Research Council 1985–90; Pres. Nat. Foundation for Educational Research 1999–2007; Hon. Fellow St Catherine's Coll. Oxford, Imperial Coll.

London, Cardiff Univ. *Publications:* scientific articles on neutron scattering and solid state chemistry. *Leisure interests:* modern art, cooking. *Address:* The Institute of Knowledge Transfer, 76 Portland Place, London, W1B 1NY (office); Bishops Offley Manor, Bishops Offley, Stafford, ST21 6ET, England (home). *Telephone:* (20) 7470-4912 (office). *E-mail:* fenderbrian@hotmail.com (home). *Website:* ikt.org.uk (office).

FENECH, Tonio, BCom, BA (Hons); Maltese accountant, auditor and politician; *Minister of Finance, Economy and Investment;* b. 5 May 1969; s. of the late Carmel V. Fenech and of Helen Fenech (née Zarb); m. Claudine Ellul 1998; one s. one d.; ed St Aloysius' Coll., Birkirkara, Manoel Theatre Acad. of Dramatic Arts, Univ. of Malta; gained early work experience during school summer holidays at Multi Packaging Ltd; mem. Youth Fellowship 1987–96; with Price Waterhouse (later PricewaterhouseCoopers) 1993–2004, later became man. in audit practice, subsequently Sr Consultant in man. consultancy practice, several int. work experiences in Italy and Libya, including Instituto per le Opere Religiose (IOR) Vatican Bank; mem. Partit Nazzjonalista (Nationalist Party), mem. Exec. Cttee Nationalist Party Coll. of Councillors 1998–99, Sec.-Gen. Nationalist Party Coll. of Councillors 1999–2003, mem. Nationalist Party Exec. Cttee 1999–; elected as local councillor for Birkirkara 1996–98, Mayor of Birkirkara 1998–2003; mem. Parl. from 8th Dist 2003–, apptd observer to European Parl. 2003–04; Parl. Sec., Ministry of Finance 2004–, participated in Malta's accession to EuroZone; Minister of Finance, Economy and Investment 2008–; mem. Housing Authority Bd 1998–2003, e-Malta Comm. 2001–03. *Address:* Ministry of Finance, Economy and Investment, Maison Demandols, 30 South Street, Valletta CMR 02, Malta (office). *Telephone:* 21249640 (office); 25998285 (office); 27327302; 79927302. *Fax:* 21233605 (office); 21251712 (office). *E-mail:* info.mfin@gov.mt (office); fenechtonio@gmail.com. *Website:* www.mfin.gov.mt (office); www.toniofenech.com.

FENECH-ADAMI, Edward, KUOM, BA, LLD; Maltese politician, lawyer and fmr head of state; b. 7 Feb. 1934, Birkirkara; s. of Luigi Fenech Adami and Josephine Pace; m. Mary Sciberras 1965; four s. one d.; ed St Aloysius Coll., Univ. of Malta; entered legal practice 1959; Ed. Il-Poplu (weekly) 1962–69; mem. Nat. Exec. Nationalist Party 1961, Asst Gen. Sec. 1962–75, Pres. Gen. and Admin. Councils 1975–77, Leader 1977–2004; mem. Parl. 1969–2004; Leader of Opposition 1977–82, 1983–87, 1996–98; Prime Minister 1987–96, 1998–2004; Pres. of Malta 2004–09; Vice-Pres. European Union of Christian Democrat Parties 1979–99; Nat. Order of Merit. *Address:* c/o President's Office, The Palace, Valletta CMR02, Malta (office).

FENEUILLE, Serge Jean Georges, PhD; French academic and company director; *Chairman, High Council of Science and Technology;* b. 16 Nov. 1940, Rheims; s. of Georges Feneuille and Marguerite Lemoine; m. Jeannine Large 1960; ed Coll. Moderne de Rheims, Ecoles Normales d'Instituteurs de Chalons-sur-Marne and Nancy, Ecole Normale Supérieure de St-Cloud; Maître-Asst, Univ. of Paris 1964–69; Maître de Recherche CNRS 1969–74, Dir of Research 1974–; Prof., Univ. Paris-Sud 1979–98; Dir of Research, Lafarge Coppée 1981–85, Scientific Dir and mem. Exec. Cttee 1985–86, Asst Dir-Gen. 1988–89, Dir-Gen. and Head of Research, Tech. and Strategy 1989–94, Special Adviser to Chair. and CEO 1995–2000; Man. Dir Centre Expérimental du Bâtiment et des Travaux Publiques 1998–2000; Dir-Gen. CNRS 1986–88; Pres. Admin. Council Ecole Normale Supérieure de Lyon 1986–94; Chair. Orsan (subsidiary of Lafarge Coppée) 1992–94, Innovation and Research Comm., Conseil Nat. du Patronat Français (CNPF) 1993–97; mem. Archaeological mission in Saggarah 2002–; mem. Sudanese Antiquities (French section) 2003–; Chair. High Council of Science and Tech. 2006–; mem. French Acad. of Tech. 2000–; Officier, Ordre nat. du Mérite, des Palmes académiques, Chevalier Légion d'honneur; Prix Daniel Guinier de la Soc. Française de Physique, Bronze Medal CNRS, Prix Servant de l'Acad. des Sciences, Prix Jaffé de l'Institut de France. *Publications:* numerous articles in scientific journals. *Leisure interests:* egyptology, painting, literature. *Address:* 1 rue Descartes, 75005 Paris (office); 25 avenue du Maréchal Maunoury, 75016 Paris, France (office). *Telephone:* 1-55-55-84-70 (office); 1-45-27-14-50 (office). *Fax:* 1-45-27-14-50 (office). *E-mail:* sfeneuille@wanadoo.fr (office); serge.feneuille@hcst.fr (home). *Website:* www.hcst.fr (office).

FENG, Duan; Chinese physicist; *Professor of Physics, Nanjing University;* b. 27 April 1923, Suzhou City, Jiangsu Prov.; s. of Feng Zhou-bai and Yan Su-qing; m. Chen Lian-fang 1955; three d.; ed Nat. Cen. Univ., Nanjing; Prof. of Physics, Nanjing Univ. 1978–; Dir of Grad. School of Nanjing Univ. 1984–88; Dir Nat. Lab. of Solid State Microstructures 1986–95; mem. Chinese Acad. of Sciences 1980–; Pres. Chinese Physical Soc. 1991–95; Fellow, the Third World Acad. of Sciences 1993–; State Prize for Natural Sciences 1982, 1995, 2003, 2004, State Prize for Progress of Science and Tech. 1997, 1998, Tan Kah Kee Prize in Math. and Physics 1999. *Publications:* Physics of Metals (Vols 1–4) 1987–99, New Perspective on Condensed Matter Physics 1992, Introduction to Condensed Matter Physics, Vol. I 2005. *Leisure interest:* literature. *Address:* Institute of Solid State Physics, Nanjing University, Nanjing 210008, Jiangsu Province, People's Republic of China. *Telephone:* (25) 83593705 (office); (25) 83592906 (home). *Fax:* (25) 83590535 (office); (25) 83300535. *E-mail:* duanf@netra.nju.edu.cn (home).

FENG, Gong; Chinese actor and director; b. Dec. 1957, Tianjin; joined China Railway Art Work Troupe 1980; actor, China Broadcasting Art Troupe 1984–; performs comic dialogues with Niu Qun; numerous prizes. *Films include:* Xiao po qing wang 1987, Li hun he tong 1990, Zhanzhi luo bie paxia 1993, Meishi touzhe le (Steal Happiness) 1998, Shui shuo wo bu zai hu (The Marriage Certificate) 2001, Eat Hot Tofu Slowly 2005. *Address:* China Broadcasting Art Troupe, Beijing, People's Republic of China.

FENG, He; Chinese sculptor; *Vice-Director, Sculpture Research Studio, Institute of Fine Arts;* b. 12 Nov. 1931, Peixian, Jiangsu Prov.; s. of Feng Zigu and Chen Jiechen; m. Zhou Ji 1965; one s.; ed Cen. Inst. of Fine Arts; mem. Sculpture Research Studio, Inst. of Fine Arts, Deputy Dir 1981–84, Vice-Dir 1988–; specialized in ceramics and animal sculpture; exhibited work China Art Gallery 1979, 1981, also in France and Burma. *Works include:* Woman's Head 1958, The Master of the Land 1964, Doe 1964, Bellicose Goat 1978, Buffalo 1979, You are Always in Our Hearts Dear Premier Zhou 1979, Ah Bing the Blind Man 1979, Buffalo and the Leopard 1985, Moonlight 1985, Winter 1986, Monument of Juvenile Heroes, The Song of the Young Pioneer 1990, Dream 1990, 12 Animals, Young Pioneer Park 1991. *Leisure interest:* drama. *Address:* Central Institute of Fine Arts, East Beijing 100730, People's Republic of China (office). *Telephone:* 55-4731 (ext. 391) (office).

FENG, Jicai; Chinese writer and artist; *Director, Feng Jicai Research Institute of Arts and Literature;* b. 9 Feb. 1942, Tianjin, Zhejiang Prov.; s. of Feng Jifu and Ge Changfu; m. Gu Tongzhao; ed Tianjin Middle School; painter, Tianjin Calligraphic and Painting Studio 1962; writer, Tianjin Municipal Writers' Asscn 1978; joined China Asscn for Promoting Democracy 1983, currently Vice-Chair. 10th Cen. Cttee; Exec. Vice-Chair. China Fed. of Literary and Art Circles 1988, 2001–, Chinese Writers' Asscn 1986 (mem. Council 1986), Chinese Soc. for the Study of Folk Literature and Art 1986, UNESCO Int. Folk Arts Org.; Chair. Fiction Soc. of China 2000–; Dir Feng Jicai Research Inst. of Arts and Literature and Hon. Dean School of Social Sciences and Foreign Languages, Tianjin Univ. 2001–; Ed.-in-Chief Free Forum on Literature 1986; Ed. Artists; mem. 6th CPPCC Nat. Cttee 1983–88, 7th CPPCC Nat. Cttee 1988–93, 8th CPPCC Nat. Cttee 1993–98, Standing Cttee 9th CPPCC Nat. Cttee 1998–2003. *Publications:* Magic Whip 1984, Gratitude to Life 1991, Legend of Magic Lamp, Tall Woman and Her Dwarf Husband, Sculpted Pipe, Crysanthemums and other stories. *Address:* Tianjin Municipal Federation of Literary and Art Circles, Tianjin, People's Republic of China (office).

FENG, Lanrui; Chinese economist; b. 17 Sept. 1920, Guiyang, Guizhou Province; d. of Feng Shaotang and Xie Guangyu; m. Li Chang 1946; two s. two d.; ed Senior Party School of the CCP Cen. Cttee; Sr Research Fellow, Inst. of Marxism-Leninism and Mao Zedong Thought, Chinese Acad. of Social Sciences 1980–, Deputy Dir 1980–82, Adviser 1983–86; mem. Editorial Cttee, Encyclopedia of People's Repub. of China, for vol. Scientific Socialism 1980–93, A Comprehensive Dictionary of Economics, for vol. Population, Labour and Consumption 1983–92; Sr Adviser, Economy in the Special Zone 1989–; mem. Cttee of Specialists, Social Security in China 2002–; Sec.-Gen. China Council of Econ. Asscns 1981–91; mem. Standing Cttee Chinese People's Friendship Asscn 1988–93; Sun Yefang Prize for econ. article of 1984, Xinhya Digests Prize for Most Impressive Article of the Year 1998. *Publications:* Labour: Payment and Employment (collected articles) 1982, Regarding the Principle – To Each According to his Work, Chinese Research on Employment Theory 1982, Urban Employment and Wages in China (co-author) 1982, On the Relationship between Employment and Economic Growth (co-author) 1983, The Worldwide New Industrialization and China's Socialist Modernization (co-author) 1984, On Letting Some People Get Rich Ahead of Others 1984, The Incomplete Form of Distribution According to Work at the Initial Stage of Socialism 1985, Overcome Egalitarianism and Let Some People Get Rich Ahead of Others 1985, More on Letting Some People Get Rich Ahead of Others 1986, The Double Hundred Policy Cannot be Separated from Democracy and Freedom 1986, The Double Hundred Policy and Science Associations 1986, Distribution According to Work, Wage and Employment 1988, Employment at the Initial Stage of Socialism (co-author) 1988, On the Ageing of the Chinese Population 1989, The Labour Market of China 1991, Social Security Must be Unified 1994, Actively Foster the Labour Market 1995, Can Inflation be Reduced under 10% for the Current Year?, Unemployment in China: 21% by the year 2000? 1996 (Impressive Article of the Year 1998), The Restructuring of China's Social Security System 1997, Selected Works on Economics of Feng Lanrui (two vols) 1999, Forward in the Same Ship: A Suggestion for Amending the PRC Constitution 2002, Living in the People's Heart 2006 and numerous articles on the market economy including contribs to China Economics Daily, Studies in the Market Economy, Hu Yaobong. *Leisure interest:* literature. *Address:* 34 Dongzongbu Hutong, Beijing 100005, People's Republic of China (home). *Telephone:* 65124654 (home).

FENG, Mengbo; Chinese pop artist; b. 1966, Beijing; ed Print-Making Dept, Cen. Acad. of Fine Arts, Beijing; work consists of computer animations and paintings which resemble video-game screens; has exhibited at galleries in Germany, London, Sydney, Taipei and Hong Kong and at 45th Venice Biennale; Interactive Art award, Prix Ars Electronica (Austria) 2004. *Works include:* Game Over: The Long March 1994, My Private Album (interactive installation) 1997, Q4U 2002, Taking Mount Doom by Strategy, Phantom Tales, Streetfighter (painting series), Built to Order 2005. *Leisure interest:* collecting industrial antiques. *Address:* c/o Art So Close, No 7, Tianwei 4th Street, Tianzhu Airport Industrial Zone A Shunyi, Beijing 101312, People's Republic of China.

FENG, Xiaogang; Chinese screenwriter, director and actor; b. 1958, Beijing; m. Xu Fan 1999; ed Beijing Broadcasting Acad.; art designer Beijing TV Art Centre 1985; began writing film and TV screenplays 1989; Hundred-Flower Award for Party A, Party B. *Films:* Zaoyu jiqing (Unexpected Passion) (writer) 1991, After Separation 1992, Yong shi wo ai (Lost My Love) (writer) 1994, The Funeral of a Famous Star, Living in Dire Strait, Jiafang yifang (The Dream Factory) (actor, dir) 1997, Bu jian bu san (Be There or Be Square) (writer, dir) 1998, Sorry, Baby 1999, Yi sheng tan xi (A Sigh) (writer, dir) 2000, Baba (Father) (actor) 2000, Da wan (Big Shot's Funeral) (writer, dir) 2001, Shui shuo wo bu zai hu (The Marriage Certificate) (actor) 2001, Shou ji (dir, producer) 2003, Ka la shi tiao gou (Cala, My Dog!) (exec. producer) 2003, Tian xia wu zei (A World Without Thieves) (writer, dir) 2004, Gong fu (actor) 2004, The Banquet 2006, The Assembly 2007, Trivial Matters (actor) 2007, The Nobles (writer, dir) 2008. *Television:* Lend Me a Little Love, A Beijing Man in New York (TV Gold Eagle Award). *Publications:* After Separation 1992, A Born Coward 1994, Stories in the Editorial Office. *Address:* Beijing Television Art Centre, Beijing, People's Republic of China (office).

FENG, Ying; Chinese ballet dancer; *Deputy Director, National Ballet of China;* b. 28 Feb. 1963, Harbin; m. James Y. Ho 1989; one d.; ed Beijing Dance Acad.; Paris Opera Ballet School 1982–83; apptd Prin. Dancer, Cen. Ballet of China 1980; leading role in many classical and Chinese ballets; Guest Artist, 2nd Paris Int. Ballet Competition 1986; toured USA, UK, Russia, Japan, Singapore, Hong Kong, Taiwan; Deputy Dir, Nat. Ballet of China 2004–; mem. Chinese Dancers' Asscn 1982, China Ballet Art Soc. 1992; Leader Cen. Corps de Ballet 2008; First Prize Pas de Deux, Nat. Ballet Competition 1987, award at 5th Japan World Ballet Competition 1987, First Class Dancer of the State 1987. *Address:* Central Ballet of China, 3 Taiping Street, Beijing 100050, People's Republic of China. *Website:* www.ballet.org.cn/en (office).

FENIC, František (Fero); Slovak producer, writer and media executive; *Director, FEBIO s.r.o.;* b. 20 March 1951, Nižná Šebastová; ed Comenius Univ., Bratislava, FAMU/Acad. of Musical Arts, Prague, Czech Repub.; mil. service 1978–79; Dir Studio of Short Films, Slovak Film Production, Bratislava 1979–83, 1985–86, Barrandov Film Studio Prague 1984; film-making interrupted for political reasons March 1984; freelance tourist guide Youth Travel Agency 1986–92; f. FEBIO s.r.o. 1991, Dir 1992–; '1 June 1953' Journalism Award. *Films include:* over twenty documentary films and full-length films including Vlak dospelosti, Praha slzám neverí, Noc, kdy se rospadl stát, Dzusový román (also screenwriter) 1984, Zvláštní bytosti (also screenwriter) 1990, Ceská soda 1998. *Television includes:* GEN, GENUS, OKO, VIP – Influential People, Czech Soda, The Way We Live. *Publication:* Encyclopedia of Slovak Dramatic Arts 1989. *Leisure interest:* travel. *Address:* FEBIO s.r.o., Ruzová 13, 11000 Prague 1, (office); Vejvodova 4, 11000 Prague 1, Czech Republic (home).

FENN, John B., AB, PhD; American chemist and academic; *Professor of Analytical Chemistry, Virginia Commonwealth University;* b. 1917, New York; ed Berea Coll., Yale Univ.; researcher in process devt, Monsanto Co., then Sharples Chemical, Michigan 1940–52, co. specializing in combustion engines, Richmond 1952–59; apptd Dir of Project SQUID (USN programme of basic and applied research in jet propulsion), Princeton Univ., Prof. of Aerospace and Mechanical Sciences; Prof. of Chemical Eng, Yale Univ. 1967–87, Prof. Emer. 1987–; Prof. of Analytical Chem., Virginia Commonwealth Univ., Richmond 1994–, Affiliate Prof. of Chemical Eng, School of Eng, Virginia Commonwealth Univ.; Visiting Prof. Trento Univ., Italy, Univ. of Tokyo, Japan, Indian Inst. of Science, Bangalore, Chinese Acad. of Science, Beijing; sole or co-inventor on 19 patents; Nobel Prize in Chem. for work in the field of mass spectrometry (jt recipient) 2002. *Address:* Department of Chemistry, Virginia Commonwealth University, 1001 West Main Street, POB 842006, Richmond, VA 23284-2006, USA (office). *E-mail:* jbfenn@vcu.edu (office). *Website:* www.has.vcu.edu (office).

FENN, Sir Nicholas M., GCMG, MA; British diplomatist; b. 19 Feb. 1936, London; s. of the late Rev. Prof. J. E. Fenn and Kathleen Fenn (née Harrison); m. Susan Clare Russell 1959; two s. one d.; ed Kingswood School, Bath and Peterhouse, Cambridge; Flying Officer, RAF 1954–56; Third Sec., Mandalay, then Rangoon 1959–63, Asst Pvt. Sec. to Sec. of State for Foreign Affairs 1963–67, First Sec. British Interests Section, Swiss Embassy, Algiers 1967–69, First Sec. and Spokesman, UK Mission to the UN, New York 1969–72, Deputy Head of Energy Dept FCO 1972–75, Counsellor, Embassy in Beijing 1975–77, Royal Coll. of Defence Studies 1978, Head of News Dept and Foreign Office Spokesman 1979–82; Amb. to Burma 1982–86, to Ireland 1986–91; High Commr in India 1991–96; Chief Exec. Marie Curie Cancer Care 1996–2000, Chair. 2000–06; Jt Chair. Encounter 1998–2003; Trustee Sight Savers Int. 1996–2005, Guide Dogs for the Blind 2002–06; Gov. Kingswood School, Bath 1996–2006, Jawaharlal Nehru Memorial Trust 1998–2006; Churchwarden, Parish Church of St Michael and St George, Marden, Kent 2001–06; Hon. Fellow, Peterhouse, Cambridge. *Leisure interest:* sailing. *Address:* c/o Oxford and Cambridge Club, 71 Pall Mall, London, SW1Y 5HD, England.

FENNER, Frank John, AC, CMG, MBE, MD, FAA, FRS, FRACP, FRCP; Australian research biologist; *Visiting Fellow, John Curtin School of Medical Research;* b. 21 Dec. 1914, Ballarat, Vic.; s. of Dr and Mrs Charles Fenner; m. E. M. Roberts 1944 (deceased); one d.; ed Thebarton Tech. High School, Adelaide High School, Adelaide Univ.; Medical Officer, Hosp. Pathologist, Australian Forces 1940–43, Malariologist 1943–46; Francis Haley Research Fellow, Walter and Eliza Hall Inst. for Medical Research, Melbourne 1946–48; Travelling Fellow, Rockefeller Inst. for Medical Research 1948–49; Prof. of Microbiology, ANU 1949–73, now Emer., Dir John Curtin School of Medical Research 1967–73, Visting Fellow 1982–, Dir Centre for Resource and Environmental Studies 1973–79; Foreign Assoc. NAS 1977; Chair. Global Comm. for the Certification of Smallpox Eradication, WHO 1977–80; Univ. Fellow, ANU 1980–82; Harvey Lecturer, Harvey Soc. of New York 1958; Overseas (Foundation) Fellow, Churchill Coll., Cambridge 1961–62; Dr hc (Univ. of Liege) 1992; Hon. DS (Oxford Brooks Univ.) 1995, (ANU) 1996; DUniv (Univ. of Adelaide) 2007; David Syme Prize, Melbourne Univ. 1949; Mueller Medal 1964; ANZAAS Medal 1980; Britannica Australia Award 1967; ANZAC Peace Prize 1980; Leeuwenhoek Lecture 1961; Flinders Lecture 1967, David Lecture 1973, Florey Lecture 1983, Burnet Lecture 1985; Stuart Mudd Award 1986, Japan Prize 1988, Advance Australia Award 1989, Copley Medal 1995, Albert Einstein World Award for Science 2000, Clunies Ross Nat. Science and Tech. Award for Lifetime Contrib. 2002, Prime Minister's Award for Science 2002, ACT Australian of the Year 2003, ACT Sr Australian of the Year 2006. *Publications:* The Production of Antibodies (with F. M. Burnet) 1949, Myxomatosis (with F. N. Ratcliffe) 1965, The Biology of Animal Viruses 1968, Medical Virology (with D. O. White) 1970, Classification and Nomenclature of Viruses, Second Report 1976, The Australian Academy of Science: The First Twenty-five Years (ed. with A. L. G. Rees) 1980, Veterinary Virology (with others) 1987, Smallpox and its Eradication (with others) 1988, Human Monkeypox (with Z. Jezek) 1988, The Orthopoxviruses (with others) 1988, Portraits of Viruses (ed. with A. Gibbs) 1988, History of Microbiology in Australia (ed.) 1990, The Australian Academy of Science: The First Forty Years (ed.) 1995, Biological Control of Vertebrate Pests (with B. Fantini) 1999, The John Curtin School of Medical Research: The First Fifty Years, 1948 to 1998 (with D. R. Curtis) 2001, The Australian Academy of Science: The First Fifty Years (ed) 2005; about 300 scientific papers, mainly on acidfast bacili, pox viruses, viral classification, environmental problems and the history of science. *Leisure interests:* gardening, tennis. *Address:* John Curtin School of Medical Research, GPO Box 334, Canberra, ACT (office); 8 Monaro Crescent, Red Hill, Canberra, ACT 2603, Australia (home). *Telephone:* (2) 6125-2526 (office); (2) 6295-9176 (home). *Fax:* (2) 6125-4712 (office). *E-mail:* Frank.Fenner@anu.edu.au (office). *Website:* jcsmr.anu.edu.au (office).

FENTENER VAN VLISSINGEN, Annemiek M.; Dutch business executive; *Chairman of the Supervisory Board, SHV Holdings NV;* b. 1961; ed Univ. of Groningen; fmr Man. of Strategy and Business Devt, SHV Holdings NV, currently Chair. Supervisory Bd; mem. Supervisory Bd Draka Holding NV 2001– (Deputy Chair. 2006–), Flint Holding NV, Heineken NV 2006–; fmr mem. Bd of Dirs Ubbink/Buco; mem. NPM Capital NV. *Address:* SHV Holdings NV, Rijnkade 1, 3511 LC Utrecht, Netherlands (office). *Telephone:* (30) 233-88-33 (office). *Fax:* (30) 233-83-04 (office). *E-mail:* info@shv.nl (office). *Website:* www.shv.nl (office).

FENTIE, Dennis G.; Canadian politician and business executive; *Premier of Yukon;* b. 8 Nov. 1950, Edmonton, Alberta; Owner and Man. Francis River Construction Ltd; elected MLA (New Democratic Party) for Watson Lake, Yukon Territory 1996–; joined Yukon Party May 2002–, Leader June 2002–; Premier of Yukon 2002–; fmr Dir Watson Lake Chamber of Commerce; fmr Commr Yukon Forest Comm.; fmr Dir Asscn of Yukon Forests. *Leisure interests:* baseball, hockey, history, current affairs. *Address:* Government of Yukon, Box 2703, Whitehorse, Yukon Y1A 2C6, Canada (office). *Telephone:* (867) 667-8660 (office). *Fax:* (867) 393-6252 (office). *E-mail:* dennis.fentie@gov.yk.ca (office). *Website:* www.gov.yk.ca (office).

FENTON, Alexander, CBE, MA, DLitt; British professor of Scottish ethnology; *Director, European Ethnological Research Centre;* b. 26 June 1929, Shotts, Lanarkshire; s. of Alexander Fenton and Annie S. Stronach; m. Evelyn E. Hunter 1956; two d.; ed Univs of Aberdeen, Cambridge and Edinburgh; Sr Asst Ed. Scottish Nat. Dictionary 1955–59; Dir Nat. Museum of Antiquities of Scotland 1978–85; Research Dir Nat. Museums of Scotland 1985–89; Dir European Ethnological Research Centre 1989–; Prof. of Scottish Ethnology and Dir School of Scottish Studies, Univ. of Edinburgh 1990–94, now Emer.; Ed. Review of Scottish Culture; Hon. Prof. of Antiquities, Royal Scottish Acad.; Hon. DLitt (Aberdeen) 1989. *Publications:* Scottish Country Life, The Northern Isles: Orkney & Shetland, Rural Architecture of Scotland, The Shape of the Past (two vols), Country Life in Scotland, Wirds An' Wark 'E Seasons Roon', The Turra Coo, The Island Blackhouse, Craiters – or Twenty Buchan Tales, Buchan Words and Ways. *Leisure interest:* languages. *Address:* European Ethnological Research Centre, c/o National Museums of Scotland, Chambers Street, Edinburgh, EH1 1JF (office); 132 Blackford Avenue, Edinburgh, EH9 3HH, Scotland (home). *Telephone:* (131) 247-4086 (office); (131) 667-5456 (home). *E-mail:* afenton@eerc.org.uk (office).

FENTON, James Martin, MA, FRSL, FRSA, FSA; British poet, writer and journalist; b. 25 April 1949, Lincoln; s. of Rev. Canon J. C. Fenton and Mary Hamilton Ingoldby; ed Durham Choristers School, Repton School, Magdalen Coll. Oxford; Asst Literary Ed., New Statesman 1971, Editorial Asst 1972, Political Columnist 1976–78; freelance corresp. in Indo-China 1973–75; German Corresp., The Guardian 1978–79; Theatre Critic, Sunday Times 1979–84; Chief Book Reviewer, The Times 1984–86; Far East Corresp. The Independent 1986–88, columnist 1993–95; Prof. of Poetry, Oxford Univ. 1994–99, Trustee Nat. Gallery London 2002, Visitor Ashmolean Museum 2003; Hon. Fellow, Magdalen Coll., Oxford 1999; Antiquary to the RA 2002; Queen's Gold Medal for Poetry 2007. *Publications include:* Our Western Furniture 1968, Terminal Moraine 1972, A Vacant Possession 1978, A German Requiem 1980, Dead Soldiers 1981, The Memory of War 1982, You Were Marvellous 1983, Children in Exile 1984, Poems 1968–83 1985, The Fall of Saigon (in Granta 15) 1985, The Snap Revolution (in Granta 18) 1986, Cambodian Witness: The Autobiography of Someth May (ed.) 1986, Partingtime Hall (poems, with John Fuller) 1987, All the Wrong Places: Adrift in the Politics of Asia 1989, Manila Envelope 1989, Underground in Japan, by Rey Ventura (ed.) 1992, Out of Danger (poems) 1993, Collected Stories by Ernest Hemingway (ed.), Leonardo's Nephew: Essays on Art and Artists 1998, The Strength of Poetry, Oxford Lectures, An Introduction to English Poetry 2002, A Garden from a Hundred Packets of Seed, The Love Bomb & Other Musical Pieces 2003, Selected Poems 2006; trans.: Verdi's Rigoletto 1982, Simon Boccanegra 1985. *Address:* United Agents, 12–26 Lexington Street, London, W1F 0LE, England (office). *Telephone:* (20) 3214-0800 (office). *Fax:* (20) 3214-0801 (office). *E-mail:* info@unitedagents.co.uk (office). *Website:* www.unitedagents.co.uk (office); www.jamesfenton.com (home).

FENTY, Adrian M., BA, JD; American politician; *Mayor of Washington, DC;* b. 7 Dec. 1970, Washington, DC; m. Michelle Fenty; twin s.; ed Mackin Catholic

High School, Oberlin Coll., Howard Univ. School of Law; passed DC Bar; worked as intern for Senator Howard Metzenbaum (Democrat-OH), Del. Eleanor Holmes Norton (Democrat-DC), and Rep. Joseph P. Kennedy II (Democrat-Mass) before becoming involved in local politics; served as ANC 4C Commr and Treas. and Pres. 16th Street Neighborhood Civic Asscn; lead attorney and Counsel for Washington, DC City Council's Cttee on Educ., Libraries and Recreation –2000; elected to Washington, DC City Council representing Ward 4 2000– (re-elected 2004), Chair. Cttee on Human Services, overseeing Dept of Youth Rehabilitation Services, Child and Family Services Agency, Dept of Human Services, and Office on Aging; Mayor of Washington, DC 2007– (youngest ever mayor); Democrat; has received community service awards from several groups, including DC Acorn for his "commitment to social justice" and from Fed. of Citizens for "courageous community service". *Address:* Office of the Mayor, John A. Wilson Building, 1350 Pennsylvania Avenue, NW, Washington, DC 20004, USA (office). *Telephone:* (202) 727-1000 (office). *Website:* dc.gov/mayor/index.shtm (office).

FEPULEA'I, Feesago Siaosi; Samoan diplomatist and government official; *Chairman, Public Service Commission;* High Commr to Belgium 1985–1989, to Australia 1990–1997, to NZ 1997–2005; Chair. Public Service Comm. 2005–. *Address:* Public Service Commission, Apia, Samoa (office).

FÉRAUD, Pierre; French retail executive; *President and CEO, Foncière Euris SA;* ed Ecole des Hautes Etudes Commerciales, Institut d'Etudes Politiques, Paris; fmrly with UIC-SOFAL (commercial bank) and GMF (insurance co.); joined Groupe Euris 1991, Pres. Foncière Euris SA 1991, currently Pres. and CEO, also Man. Dir Rallye Group. *Address:* Foncière Euris SA, 83 rue du Faubourg Saint-Honore, 75008 Paris, France (office). *Telephone:* 1-44-71-14-00 (office). *Fax:* 1-44-71-14-50 (office). *E-mail:* info@fonciere-euris.fr (office). *Website:* www.fonciere-euris.fr (office).

FERGUS-THOMPSON, Gordon; British pianist; b. 9 March 1952, Leeds; s. of the late George Thompson and Constance Webb; ed Temple Moor Grammar School, Leeds and Royal Northern Coll. of Music; debut at Wigmore Hall 1976; has appeared as soloist with orchestras, including Orchestra of the Hague, Gothenburg Symphony Orchestra, Royal Liverpool Philharmonic, The Philharmonia, City of Birmingham Symphony, Hallé, BBC Symphony; extensive tours in Europe, N America, Australia, Far East and S Africa; Prof. of Piano, Royal Coll. of Music 1996–; Gulbenkian Foundation Fellowship 1978; MRA Prize for Best Instrumental Recording of the Year 1991, 1992. *Recordings include:* The Rachmaninoff Sonatas 1987, Balakirev and Scriabin Sonatas 1987, Complete Works of Debussy (five vols), Complete Works of Scriabin (five vols) 1990–2001, Rachmaninoff's Etudes-Tableaux 1990, Bach Transcriptions 1990, Complete Works of Ravel (two vols) 1992, Headington: Piano Concerto 1997. *Leisure interests:* art, chess, cooking, tennis, humour. *Address:* 12 Audley Road, Hendon, London, NW4 3EY, England (home). *Telephone:* (20) 8202-5861 (home).

FERGUSON, Sir Alexander (Alex) Chapman, Kt, CBE; British professional football manager; b. 31 Dec. 1941, Glasgow; s. of the late Alexander Beaton Ferguson and Elizabeth Hardy; m. Catherine Ferguson 1966; three s.; ed Govan High School; player with Queen's Park 1958–60, St Johnstone 1960–64, Dunfermline Athletic 1964–67, Glasgow Rangers 1967–69, Falkirk 1969–73, Ayr United 1973–74 (two Scottish League caps); managed the following clubs: East Stirling 1974, St Mirren 1974–78 (First Div. Champions 1976–77), Aberdeen 1978–86 (winners European Cup Winners' Cup, Super Cup 1983, Premier Div. Champions 1980, 1982, 1984, winners Scottish FA Cup on four occasions, League Cup 1985), Scottish Nat. Team (Asst Man.) 1985–86, Manchester United 1986– (winners FA Cup 1990, 1994, 1996, 1999, 2004, League Cup 1992, 2006, European Cup Winners' Cup, Super Cup 1991, FA Premier League Championship 1992/93, 1993/94, 1995/96, 1996/97, 1998/99, 1999/2000, 2000/01, 2002/03, 2006/07, League and FA Cup double 1994 and 1996 (new record)), Champions League European Cup 1999; Freeman, Cities of Aberdeen, Glasgow and Manchester; Hon. MA (Salford) 1996; Hon. LLD (Robert Gordon) 1997; Hon. MSc (Manchester Metropolitan) 1998 (UMIST) 1998; Hon. DLitt (Glasgow Caledonian) 2001; Hon. DUniv (Glasgow) 2001; Man. of the Year Scotland 1983–85, Man. of the Year England 1993–94, 1996, voted Best Coach in Europe, UEFA Football Gala 1999. *Publications:* A Light in the North 1985, Alex Ferguson: Six Years at United 1992, Just Champion 1994, A Year in the Life 1995, A Will to Win (jtly) 1997, Managing My Life: My Autobiography (jtly) 1999, The Unique Treble 2000. *Leisure interests:* golf, snooker, horse racing, fine wine. *Address:* Manchester United FC, Old Trafford, Manchester, M16 0RA, England (office). *Telephone:* (161) 868-8103 (office). *Fax:* (161) 868-8807 (office). *Website:* www.manutd.com (office).

FERGUSON, C. David; American business executive (retd); ed Marietta Coll.; joined Engine Parts Div. Gould Inc. 1963, Foil Div. 1967; subsequently Group Vice-Pres. (Materials and Components); Exec. Vice-Pres. (Materials and Components); Chair., Pres. and CEO Gould Inc. (later Gould Electronics) 1988–2001; Pres. and Gen. Man. Foil Div., Gould Inc., Eastlake, O; mem. Bd Gould Foils Ltd, Nikko Gould Foil Co., Ltd, Gould Electronics (Canada) Ltd. *Address:* c/o Gould Electronics Inc., 34929 Curtis Boulevard, Eastlake, OH 44095, USA.

FERGUSON, David, BA; British composer; *Chairman, British Academy of Composers & Songwriters;* b. 24 May 1953, London, England; m.; one s.; ed School of Slavonic and East European Studies; mem. Random Hold 1978–83 (toured Europe and USA); film and TV composer 1985–; Chair. British Acad. of Composers & Songwriters 2003–; Chair. Creators' Rights Alliance 2000–. *Compositions for television (drama):* Moondial 1988, A Country Boy (series) 1989, Bathing Elizabeth 1990, Mug 1990, Dancing in the Dark 1990, Milking the Chocolate Man 1990, All About Laura 1990, Necklace 1990, The Final Frame 1990, A Fair & Easy Passage 1990, Killing Time 1990, A Dark Season 1991, Say Hello to the Real Dr Snide 1991, Bad Girl 1992, A Fatal Inversion 1992, Chalkface 1992, Century Falls 1993, Gallowglass 1993, A Dark Adapted Eye 1994, Cracker (series) 1994, Life After Life 1995, The Gambling Man 1995, Albert Camus: Combat contre l'absurde 1996, Some Kind of Life 1996, Breakout 1997, The Ice House 1997, The Woman in White 1997, Touch & Go 1998, Rebus: The Hanging Garden 2000, Rebus: Black and Blue 2000, Rebus: Dead Souls 2001, Rebus: Mortal Causes 2001, Lloyd & Hill: A Shred of Evidence 2001, Auf Wiedersehen Pet (series four) 2003. *Compositions for television (documentary):* Low-Tech 1985, The Longest Running Show on Earth 1985, Antenna 1986, Volunteers 1986, Spacecraft (series) 1986, The Sword of Islam 1987, Mail Order Brides 1987, Sounds of Surprise 1987, Sea Farmers 1988, A Matter of Life & Debt 1988, Building Sights: The Mellor Factory 1989, Forty Minutes: How Could She? 1990, Missionaries (series) 1990, Rough Justice: Slipping Through the Net 1990, The Energy Alternative 1990, Thawing of a Cold War Warrior 1990, A Planned Miracle 1991, Compass: The Marquesas 1991, Under the Sun: The Final Cut 1991, Horizon: Inside the Chernobyl Sarcophagus 1991, Everyman: Lifeline 1992, Fire in the Blood (series) 1992, Inside Story: Dogs of War 1992, Town Hall (series) 1992, Everyman: Samaritans 1993, The Skipper (series) 1993, Cutting Edge: Horse Detectives 1993, Who Killed Dixon 1993, Diamond Empire 1993, The Inside Track on Parenting 1993, Inside Story: Hostage 1993, Storm Chasers 1994, Witness 1994, Russian Bomb 1994, Horizon: Blueprint for Genocide 1994, The Death of Apartheid 1995, The Reagan Agenda 1996, Short Stories: Murder Trial 1996, Secret Lives: Jeremy Thorpe 1996, Black Box 1996, Horizon: Return to Chernobyl 1996, X Cars (series) 1996, American Visions (series) 1997, Crash 1997, The Provos 1997, Fraud Squad 1998, Quest for the Lost Civilisation 1998, Hostage 1999, Loyalists 1999, Agents of Change 1999, HMS Splendid 1999, Deaf Century 1999, Mudslide 1999, Brits 2000, Fergal Keane's Forgotten Britain 2000, Diana: Story of a Princess 2001, Bourne to Dance 2001, Falklands: Home Front 2001, The Fall of Milosovic 2002, Up for it (series) 2002, Secret State 2002, Action Adventure (series) 2003. *Compositions for film:* Coded Hostile 1989, Disaster at Valdez 1992, Hostile Waters 1997, Bravo 2 Zero 1998, Dr Jekyll and Mr Hyde 2002. *Recordings:* albums: with Random Hold: The View from Here 1979, Burn the Buildings 1981, Nine Ways to Win 1984; solo: The View from Now 1998. *Address:* British Academy of Composers & Songwriters, British Music House, 25–27 Berners Street, London, W1T 3LR, England (office). *E-mail:* ferguson@kbnet.co.uk (office). *Website:* www.davidferguson.com.

FERGUSON, Iain, CBE; British business executive; *CEO, Tate & Lyle PLC;* held positions at Unilever including Exec. Chair. Birds Eye Walls, Sr Vice Pres. Corp. Devt –2003; CEO Tate & Lyle PLC 2003–; fmr Commr Govt Comm. on the Future of Farming and Food; Pres. Inst. of Grocery Distribution; Vice Pres. Food and Drink Fed.; non-Exec. Dir Rothamsted Research Ltd, Sygen Int. PLC, British Nutrition Foundation; Forbes magazine European Businessman of the Year 2004. *Address:* Tate & Lyle PLC, Head Office, Sugar Quay, Lower Thames Street, London, EC3R 6DQ, England (office). *Telephone:* (20) 7626-6525 (office). *Fax:* (20) 7623-5213 (office). *Website:* www.tateandlyle.com (office).

FERGUSON, Niall Campbell Douglas, MA, DPhil; British historian, writer, academic and television presenter; *Laurence A. Tisch Professor of History, Harvard University;* b. 18 April 1964, Glasgow, Scotland; s. of James Campbell Ferguson and Molly Hamilton; m. Susan M. Douglas 1994; two s. one d.; ed Univ. of Oxford, Univ. of Hamburg; Fellow, Christ's Coll., Cambridge 1989–90, Peterhouse, Cambridge 1990–92, Jesus Coll. Oxford 1992–; Houblon Norman Fellowship, Bank of England 1998–89; Prof. of Political and Financial History, Univ. of Oxford 2000–02, Herzog Prof. of Financial History, Stern School of Business, New York Univ. 2002–04; Laurence A. Tisch Prof. of History, Harvard Univ. 2004–; William Ziegler Prof. of Business Admin, Harvard Business School 2006–; Sr Fellow, Hoover Inst., Stanford Univ. 2003–; mem. Bd Dirs Chimerica Media Ltd 2006–; consultant, GLG Pnrs (hedge fund) 2007–; Sr Adviser, Morgan Stanley 2007–; Wadsworth Prize for Business History 1998. *Television:* Empire: How Britain Made the Modern World 2003, American Colossus 2004, War of the World 2006, The Ascent of Money 2008. *Publications:* Paper and Iron: Hamburg Business and German Politics in the Era of Inflation 1897–1927 1995, (ed.) Virtual History: Alternatives and Counterfactuals 1997, The World's Banker: A History of the House of Rothschild, The Pity of War 1998, The Cash Nexus: Money and Power in the Modern World 1700–2000 2001, Empire: How Britain Made the Modern World 2003, Colossus: the Price of America's Empire 2004, The War of The World: History's Age of Hatred 2006, The Ascent of Money: A Financial History of the World 2008. *Leisure interests:* books, music, theatre, wine, hill walking. *Address:* Harvard University, Minda de Gunzberg Center for European Studies, Adolphus Busch Hall, 27 Kirkland Street, Cambridge, MA 02138, USA (office). *Telephone:* (617) 495-4303 (ext. 203) (office). *Fax:* (617) 496-9594 (office). *E-mail:* nfergus@fas.harvard.edu (office). *Website:* www.ces.fas.harvard.edu (office); www.niallferguson.org.

FERGUSON, Paul; South African stockbroker; b. 23 Aug. 1943, Johannesburg; s. of Ray Ferguson and Joy Ferguson; trained as chartered accountant; Dir Ferguson Bros, Hall Stewart & Co. Inc. 1973–, Chair. 1983–; Pres. Johannesburg Stock Exchange 1982–84, Cttee mem. 1979–, Chair. 1988–89, Vice-Chair. 1993–; Dir of various cos. *Leisure interest:* squash. *Address:* PO Box 691, Johannesburg 2000 (office); 60 Kent Road, Dunkeld, Johannesburg 2196, South Africa (home). *Telephone:* (11) 8335740 (office); (11) 7882227.

FERGUSON, Rodwell; Belizean politician; MP for Stann Creek West Area; fmr Minister of State for Tourism, Nat. Devt and Educ.; Minister of Defence, Youth and Sports 2007–08; fmr Vice-Pres. Belize Nat. Comm. for UNESCO; mem. People's United Party. *Address:* c/o People's United Party, 3 Queen

Street, Belize City, Belize. *Telephone:* 223-2428. *Fax:* 223-3476. *Website:* www.pupbelize.bz.

FERGUSON, Roger Walter, Jr, BA, PhD, JD; American business executive; *President and CEO, TIAA-CREF;* b. 28 Oct. 1951, Washington, DC; ed Harvard Univ.; attorney with Davis Polk & Wardwell, New York 1981–84; Assoc. and Pnr, McKinsey & Co. 1984–97; mem. Bd Govs US Fed. Reserve, Washington, DC 1997–2006, Vice-Chair. 1999–2006 (resgnd); Chair. America Holding Corpn and Head of Financial Services, Swiss Re 2006–08; Pres. and CEO TIAA-CREF (Teachers Insurance and Annuity Asscn — Coll. Retirement Equities Fund), New York 2008–; mem. Bd of Overseers, Harvard Univ.; mem. Bd Inst. for Advanced Study, Carnegie Endowment for Int. Peace, New America Foundation; Dr hc (Lincoln Coll.), (Webster Univ.). *Address:* TIAA-CREF, 730 Third Avenue, New York, NY 10017, USA (office). *Telephone:* (212) 916-6240 (office). *Fax:* (212) 916-6230 (office). *E-mail:* trustees@tiaa-cref.org (office). *Website:* www.tiaa-cref.org (office).

FERGUSON-SMITH, Malcolm Andrew, MBChB, MA, FRS, FRSE, FRCPath, FRCP(Glas), FRCOG, FMedSci; British professor of pathology; *Emeritus Research Professor, Centre for Veterinary Science, University of Cambridge;* b. 5 Sept. 1931, Glasgow, Scotland; s. of John Ferguson-Smith and Ethel May Ferguson-Smith (née Thorne); m. Marie Eva Gzowska 1960; one s. three d.; ed Stowe School, Univ. of Glasgow; Registrar in Lab. Medicine, Dept of Pathology, Western Infirmary, Glasgow 1958–59; Fellow in Medicine and Instructor, Johns Hopkins Univ. School of Medicine 1959–61; Lecturer, Sr Lecturer, then Reader in Medical Genetics, Univ. of Glasgow 1961–73, Prof. 1973–87; Prof. of Pathology, Univ. of Cambridge 1987–98, now Emer. Research Prof., Centre for Veterinary Science 1998–; Fellow, Peterhouse Coll., Cambridge 1987–98; Dir W of Scotland Medical Genetics Service 1973–87, East Anglian Regional Clinical Genetics Service 1987–95; Pres. Clinical Genetics Soc. 1979–81, European Soc. of Human Genetics 1997–98, Int. Soc. for Prenatal Diagnosis 1998–2002; Ed. Prenatal Diagnosis 1980–2006; mem. Johns Hopkins Univ. Soc. of Scholars; mem. BSE Inquiry Committee 1997–2000; Foreign mem. Polish Acad. of Science 1988, Nat. Acad. of Medicine Buenos Aires 2002; Pres. Asscn of Clinical Cytogeneticists 2003–05; Hon. Consultant in Medical Paediatrics, Royal Hosp. for Sick Children, Glasgow 1966–73, in Clinical Genetics, Yorkhill and Assoc. Hosps 1973–87, in Medical Genetics, Addenbrooke's Hosp., Cambridge 1987–98; Hon. Assoc. Royal Coll. of Veterinary Surgeons 2002; Hon. DSc (Strathclyde Univ.) 1992, (Glasgow) 2002; Bronze Medal, Univ. of Helsinki 1968, Makdougall-Brisbane Prize of Royal Soc. of Edinburgh 1984–86, San Remo Int. Prize for Research in Genetics 1990, Mauro Baschirotto Award for achievements in human genetics 1996, Sir James Y. Simpson Award 1998, J. B. S. Haldane Medal 2000, McLaughlin-Gallie Professorship, RCPS, Canada, 2001. *Publications:* Early Prenatal Diagnosis (ed.) 1983, Essential Medical Genetics (co-author) 1984, Prenatal Diagnosis and Screening (co-ed.) 1992; papers on cytogenetics, gene mapping, human genetics, comparative genomics, evolutionary biology and prenatal diagnosis in medical and scientific journals. *Leisure interests:* swimming, sailing, fishing. *Address:* Department of Veterinary Medicine, University of Cambridge, Madingley Road, Cambridge, CB3 0ES, England. *Telephone:* (1223) 766496. *Fax:* (1223) 766496 (office). *E-mail:* maf12@cam.ac.uk (office). *Website:* www.vet.cam.ac.uk/genomics (office).

FERGUSSON, Sir Ewen Alastair John, GCMG, GCVO, MA; British diplomatist (retd); b. 28 Oct. 1932, Singapore; s. of the late Sir Ewen MacGregor Field Fergusson and Lady (Winifred Evelyn) Fergusson; m. Sara Carolyn Montgomery Cuninghame (née Gordon Lennox) 1959; one s. two d.; ed Rugby and Oriel Coll., Oxford; 2nd Lt 60th Rifles (KRRC) 1954–56; Foreign (Diplomatic) Service 1956–92; Asst Pvt. Sec. to Minister of Defence 1957–59; British Embassy, Addis Ababa 1960; FCO 1963; British Trade Devt Office, New York 1967; Counsellor and Head of Chancery, Office of UK Perm. Rep. to EC 1972–75; Pvt. Sec. to Foreign and Commonwealth Sec. 1975–78, Asst Under-Sec. of State 1978–82; Amb. to SA 1982–84, to France 1987–92; Deputy Under-Sec. of State 1984–87; Chair. (non-exec.) Coutts & Co. 1993–99, Savoy Hotel Group 1995–98 (Dir 1993–98); Dir (non-exec.) BT 1993–99, Sun Alliance 1993–96; Chair. Rugby School 1995–2002 (Gov. 1985–2002); Trustee, Nat. Gallery 1995–2002, Henry Moore Foundation 1998– (Chair. 2001–); Hon. Fellow, Oriel Coll. Oxford 1988; Grand Officier, Légion d'honneur 1992; King at Arms, Most Distinguished Order of St Michael and St George 1996–2007; Hon. LLD (Aberdeen) 1995. *Achievements:* played rugby for Scotland (five caps) 1954. *Address:* 111 Iverna Court, London, W8 6TX (office); 22 Iverna Gardens, London, W8 6TN, England (home). *Telephone:* (20) 7937-2240 (office); (20) 7937-5545 (home). *Fax:* (20) 7938-1136 (office); (20) 7376-0418 (home). *E-mail:* sir.ewenfergusson@btinternet.com (office).

FERIANTO, Djaduk; Indonesian composer and musician; brother of Butet Kertaredjasa. *Compositions include:* Kompi Susu (Milk Brigade), Brigade Mailing (Thieves' Brigade).

FERLAND, E. James, BSc, MBA; American energy industry executive; *Chairman, President and CEO, Public Service Enterprise Group Inc.;* ed Univ. of Maine, Univ. of New Haven, Harvard Grad. School of Business Admin; began career as engineer, The Hartford Electric Light Co., CT 1964–67; mem. operating staff Millstone Nuclear Power Station 1967–76, Station Superintendent 1976–78; Dir of Rate Regulatory Project, Corp. HQ, Northeast Utilities 1978–80, Exec. Vice-Pres. and Chief Financial Officer 1980–83, Pres. and COO 1983–86; Chair., Pres. and CEO Public Service Enterprise Group Inc. (PSEG) 1986–; Chair. and CEO Public Service Electric and Gas Co. (PSE&G) 1986–, Pres. 1986–91; Chair. and CEO PSEG Energy Holdings LLC 1989–; fmr mem. Bd Dirs Vermont Yankee Nuclear Power Corpn, Yankee Atomic Electric Co., Maine Yankee Atomic Power Co., The HSB Group Inc., Foster Wheeler Corpn; currently mem. Bd Cttee for Econ. Devt; fmr Chair. NJ State Chamber of Commerce, Metro Newark Chamber of Commerce, Public

Affairs Research Inst. of NJ, Inst. of Nuclear Power Operations, Electric Power Research Inst.; fmr mem. Bd NJ Performing Arts Center, Edison Electric Inst., Nuclear Energy Inst., American Gas Asscn, Asscn of Edison Illuminating Cos, NJ Utilities Asscn, The United Way of Tri-State. *Address:* Public Service Enterprise Group Inc., 80 Park Plaza, Newark, NJ 07102, USA (office). *Telephone:* (973) 430-7000 (office). *Fax:* (973) 824-7056 (office). *Website:* www.pseg.com (office).

FERLINGHETTI, Lawrence, MA, PhD, DUniv; American writer and painter; b. 24 March 1920, Yonkers, New York; s. of Charles Ferlinghetti and Clemence Mendes-Monsanto; m. 1951; one s. one d.; ed Columbia Univ., Univ. of Paris; served as Lt Commdr in USNR in World War II; co-f. (with Peter D. Martin) the first all-paperback bookshop in USA, City Lights Bookstore, San Francisco 1953; f. City Lights publishing co. 1955; arrested on obscenity charges following publ. of Allan Ginsberg's 'Howl' 1956 (later acquitted); participant One World Poetry Festival, Amsterdam 1980, World Congress of Poets, Florence 1986; First Poet Laureate of San Francisco 1998–99; Ed. City Lights Books; mem. Nat. Acad. of Arts and Letters 2003; Commdr, French Acad. of Arts and Letters 2007; Poetry Prize, City of Rome 1993, Premio Internazionale Flaiano, Italy 1999, Premio Internazionale di Camaiore, Italy 1999, Premio Cavour, Italy 2000, LA Times Book Festival Lifetime Achievement Award 2001, Poetry Soc. of America Robert Frost Medal 2003, Nat. Book Foundation Literarian Award 2005. *Publications include:* Pictures of the Gone World (poems) 1955, Selections from Paroles by Jacques Prévert, A Coney Island of the Mind (poems) 1958, Berlin 1961, Her (novel), Starting from San Francisco (poems) 1961, Where is Vietnam? 1965, An Eye on the World 1967, After the Cries of the Birds 1967, Unfair Arguments with Existence (seven plays), Routines (plays), The Secret Meaning of Things (poems) 1969, Tyrannus Nix? (poem) 1969, The Mexican Night (travel journal) 1970, Back Roads to Far Places (poems) 1971, Open Eye, Open Heart (poems) 1973, Who Are We Now? 1976, Northwest Ecolog 1978, Landscapes of Living and Dying (poems) 1979, Literary San Francisco: A Pictorial History from the Beginnings to the Present (with Nancy J. Peters) 1980, Leaves of Life: Drawings from the Model 1983, The Populist Manifestos 1983, Over All the Obscene Boundaries (poems) 1984, Endless Life: Selected Poems 1984, Seven Days in Nicaragua Libre 1984, Inside the Trojan Horse 1987, Love in the Days of Rage (novel) 1988, When I Look at Pictures (poems and paintings) 1990, These Are My Rivers: New and Selected Poems 1993, A Far Rockaway of the Heart 1997, How to Paint Sunlight: New Poems 2001, Americus (Book One) 2004, Poetry as Insurgent Art (prose and poetry) 2007; also trans, film-scripts and phonograph records. *Address:* c/o City Lights Bookstore, 261 Columbus Avenue, San Francisco, CA 94133-4519, USA (office). *Telephone:* (415) 362-8193 (office). *Fax:* (415) 362-4921. *E-mail:* staff@citylights.com (office). *Website:* www.citylights.com.

FERM, Anders; Swedish diplomatist; b. 1938, Ockeldo; m.; one c.; ed Stockholm School of Econs; Special Political Asst to Minister of Transport 1965–69, Prime Minister's Chef de Cabinet 1969–73; Exec. Sec. of Ind. Comm. of Disarmament and Security Issues, Vienna 1980–83; Perm. Rep. to UN, New York 1983–88; Amb. to Denmark 1988–90; Ed.-in-Chief Arbetet 1990; exec. man. publishing 1973–80, fmr mem. numerous cttees and bds including PEN Club, Publrs Asscn, Swedish Television Corpn. *Address:* c/o Arbetet, P.O. Box 125, 201 21 Malmö, Sweden.

FERMOR, Sir Patrick Michael Leigh, Kt, DSO, OBE, CLit; British writer; b. 11 Feb. 1915, London; s. of the late Sir Lewis Leigh Fermor and Muriel Eileen Fermor (née Ambler); m. Hon. Joan Eyres-Monsell 1968 (died 2003); ed King's School, Canterbury; travelled for four years in Cen. Europe, Balkans and Greece in 1930s; enlisted in Irish Guards 1939; 'I' Corps 1940; Lt British Mil. Mission, Greece 1940; Liaison Officer, Greek GHQ, Albania; with Cretan Resistance for two years in German-occupied Crete; Team-Commdr Special Allied Airborne Reconnaissance Force, N Germany 1945; Deputy Dir British Inst. Athens 1945–46; travelled in Caribbean and Cen. America 1947–48; Corresp. mem. Athens Acad. 1980; Hon. Citizen of Heraklion, Crete 1947, Gytheion, Laconia 1966, Kardamyli, Messenia 1967; Chevalier, Ordre des Arts et des Lettres (France) 1995; Hon. DLitt (Kent) 1991, (American School of Greece) 1993, (Warwick) 1996; Int. PEN/Time Life Silver Pen Award 1986, Municipality of Athens Gold Medal of Honour 1988, Prix Jacques Audiberti, Ville d'Antibes 1992, British Guild of Travel Writers Lifetime Achievement Award 2004. *Publications:* The Traveller's Tree (Heinemann Foundation Prize for Literature 1950, Kemsley Prize 1951) 1950, Colette's Chance Acquaintances (trans.) 1952, A Time to Keep Silence 1953, The Violins of Saint Jacques 1953, The Cretan Runner (trans.) 1955, Mani (Duff Cooper Prize) 1958, Roumeli 1966, A Time of Gifts (WHSmith Award 1978) 1977, Between the Woods and the Water (Thomas Cook Award) 1986, Three Letters from the Andes 1991, Words of Mercury 2003. *Leisure interests:* travel, reading.

FERNALD, Ivan; Suriname government official; Minister of Defence 2005–. *Address:* Ministry of Defence, Kwattaweg 29, Paramaribo, Suriname (office). *Telephone:* 474244 (office). *Fax:* 420055 (office). *E-mail:* defensie@sr.net.

FERNANDES, Anthony (Tony) Francis; Malaysian airline executive and fmr music industry executive; *Group CEO, AirAsia;* b. 1964, Kuala Lumpur; ed boarding school in England, LSE; started as auditor London accountancy firm 1987; fmr Financial Analyst, Virgin, Financial Controller Virgin TV Div. 1987–89; joined Warner Music 1989, youngest ever Man. Dir Warner Music (Malaysia), Vice-Pres. ASEAN Region, 1999–2001; co-founder Tune Air; bought Air Asia Sept. 2001, CEO AirAsia (Asia's first 'no frills' airline) and Tune Air (parent co. of AirAsia) 2001–; awarded title Setia Mahkota Selangor by HRH King of Malaysia Sultan Salahuddin Abdul Aziz Shah 1999; Joint Winner CEO of the Year 2003 American Express Corp. Services/Business Times, Emerging Entrepreneur of the Year 2003 Ernst & Young. *Address:*

AirAsia Sdn Bhd, Lot N1, Level 4, Main Terminal Building, Kuala Lumpur International Airport, 64000 KLIA, Sepang, Selangor, Malaysia (office). *Telephone:* (3) 8660-4274 (office). *Fax:* (3) 8776-0222 (office). *E-mail:* tonyfernandes@airasia.com (office). *Website:* www.airasia.com (office).

FERNANDES, George; Indian trade union official and politician; *Leader, Janata Dal—United;* b. 3 June 1930, Bangalore, Karnataka; s. of John Fernandes and Alice Fernandes; m. Leila Kabir 1971; one s.; ed St Peter's Seminary, Bangalore; joined Socialist Party of India 1949, mem. Nat. Cttee 1955–77, Treas. 1964, Chair. 1971–77; Ed. Konkani Yuvak (Konkani Youth) monthly in Konkani language 1949, Raithavani weekly in Kannada language 1949, Dockman weekly in English 1952–53, also New Society; fmr Chief Ed. Pratipaksha weekly in Hindi; trade union work in S Kanara 1949, 1950, in Bombay (now Mumbai) and Maharashtra 1950–58; Founding Pres. All-India Radio Broadcasters and Telecasters Guild, Khadi Comm. Karmachari Union, All-India Univ. Employees' Confed.; Pres. All-India Railwaymen's Fed. 1973–77; organized nat. railways strike 1974; Treas. All-India Hind Mazdoor Sabha 1958; formed Hind Mazdoor Panchayat 1958, Gen. Sec. for over 10 years; Convenor, United Council of Trade Unions; fmr mem. Gen. Council of Public Services Int., Int. Transport Workers' Fed.; Founder-Chair. New India Co-operative Bank Ltd (fmrly Bombay Labour Co-operative Bank Ltd); Gen. Sec. Samyukta Socialist Party of India 1969–70; mem. Bombay Municipal Corpn 1961–68; mem. for Bombay City, Lok Sabha 1967–77; went underground on declaration of emergency 1975; mem. Janata Party 1977, Gen. Sec. 1985–86; mem. for Muzzafarpur, Bihar, Lok Sabha 1977–79, also elected to Lok Sabha 1980, 1989, 1991, 1996, 1998; Minister of Communications March–July 1977, of Industry 1977–79 (resgnd from Govt 1979), for Railways 1989–90, for Kashmir Affairs 1990–91, of Defence 1998–2001, 2001–04; Deputy Leader Lok Dal 1980–; mem. Standing Parl. Cttee on Finance 1993–96, also Consultative Cttee on Home Affairs, mem. Standing Parl. Cttee on External Affairs 1996, also Consultative Cttee on Human Resources Devt; Pres. Samata Party 1994–2000, 2002–04; fmr Pres. Janata Dal—United, currently Sr Leader; Chair. Editorial Bd Pratipaksh (Hindi monthly); Ed. The Other Side (English language monthly); Pres. Hind Mazdoor Kisan Panchayat; Chair. India Devt Group, London 1979, Schumacher Foundation 1979; fmr mem. Press Council of India; mem. Amnesty International, People's Union for Civil Liberties; involved in anti-nuclear and environmental campaigns. *Publications:* What Ails the Socialists: The Kashmir Problem, The Railway Strike of 1974, George Fernandes Speaks. *Leisure interests:* music, reading. *Address:* Janata Dal—United (People's Party—United), 7 Jantar Mantar Road, New Delhi 110 001 (office); 3 Krishna Menon Marg, New Delhi 110011 (home); 30 Leonard Road, Richmond Town, Bangalore, Karnataka 560025, India. *Telephone:* (11) 23368833 (office); (80) 22214143 (Bangalore); (11) 23793397 (New Delhi) (home); (11) 23015403 (New Delhi) (home). *Fax:* (11) 23368138 (office).

FERNANDES DE ARAÚJO, HE Cardinal Serafim; Brazilian ecclesiastic; b. 13 Aug. 1924, Minas Novas; ordained priest 1949; Titular Bishop of Verinopolis 1959; Coadjutor Archbishop of Belo Horizonte, Minas Gerais, Brazil 1982, Archbishop 1986–2004; Cardinal-Priest of S. Luigi Maria Grignion de Montfort 1998–. *Address:* c/o Cúria Metropolitana, Av. Brasil 2079, CP 494, 30140-002 Belo Horizonte, MG, Brazil. *Telephone:* (31) 261-3400. *Fax:* (31) 261-5713.

FERNÁNDEZ, Alberto Angel; Argentine politician; b. 2 April 1959, Buenos Aires; m.; one s.; ed Universidad de Buenos Aires; Prof., Dept of Penal Rights, Universidad de Buenos Aires; Pres. Asociacíon de Superintendentes de Seguros de América Latina 1989–92; Exec. Vice-Pres. Grupo Banco Provincia 1997; mem. Parl. for Buenos Aires 2000; Cabinet Chief 2003–08 (resgnd); Industrialist of the Year in Insurance 1997, Millennium Prize for Industrialist of the Century 2000. *Address:* c/o Avenida Pte Julio A. Roca 782, 1067 Buenos Aires, Argentina (office).

FERNÁNDEZ, Aníbal Domingo; Argentine accountant and politician; *Minister of Justice and Human Rights;* b. 9 Jan. 1957, Quilmes; m.; one s.; adviser to Budget Cttee, Buenos Aires Prov. Senate 1983–85, Admin. Sec., Peronista bloc 1985–91, Senator 1995–; Mayor of Quilmes 1991; Asst to Minister of Govt and Justice, Govt of Buenos Aires 1997–99; Sec. of Labour 1999–2001, Minister of Labour 2001–02; Sec.-Gen. to the Presidency Jan.–Oct. 2002; Minister of Production 2002–03, of the Interior 2003–07, of Justice and Human Rights 2007–; Senator of the Year 1996. *Address:* Ministry of Justice and Human Rights, Sarmiento 329, 1041 Buenos Aires, Argentina. *Telephone:* (11) 4328-3015 (office). *E-mail:* prensa@jus.gov.ar (office). *Website:* www.jus.gov.ar (office).

FERNÁNDEZ, Carlos Rafael, BEcons; Argentine economist and politician; *Minister of the Economy and Production;* b. 1954, Ciudad de la Plata; ed La Plata Nat. Univ.; Nat. Dir of tax coordination for provs 1989–97; Sub-Sec., tax coordination and policy for Buenos Aires prov. govt 1997, Under-Sec. for Fiscal Policy, Buenos Aires Prov. 2002–03, interim Prov. Minister of Economy 2007; Treasury Sec. 2006; Under-Sec. for Relations with the Provinces, Ministry of Economy 2007; Sub-Sec of the Budget Dec. 2007–March 2008; Dir Administración Fed. de Ingresos Públicos (tax agency) March–April 2008; Minister of Economy and Production 2008–. *Address:* Ministry of Economy and Production, Hipólito Yrigoyen 250, C1086AAB Buenos Aires, Argentina (office). *Telephone:* (11) 4349-5000 (office). *E-mail:* sagpya@mecon.gov.ar (office). *Website:* www.mecon.gov.ar (office).

FERNANDEZ, Dominique, DèsSc; French writer; b. 25 Aug. 1929, Neuilly-sur-Seine; s. of Ramon Fernandez and Liliane Chomette; m. Diane Jacquin de Margerie (divorced); one s. one d.; ed Lycée Buffon, Paris and Ecole Normale Supérieure; Prof. Inst. Français, Naples 1957–58; Prof. of Italian, Univ. de Haute-Bretagne 1966–89; literary critic, L'Express 1959–84, Le Nouvel Observateur 1985–; music critic, Diapason 1977–85, Opera International 1978, Classical Repertoire 2000–; elected mem. Académie française 2007; mem. Reading Cttee, Editions Bernard Grasset 1959–; Chevalier, Légion d'honneur, Commdr, Ordre nat. du Mérite, Cruzeiro do Sul (Brazil); Prix Médicis 1974, Prix Goncourt 1982, Grand Prix Charles Oulmont 1986, Prix Prince Pierre de Monaco 1986, Prix Méditerranée 1988, Prix Oscar Wilde 1988. *Publications:* Le roman italien et la crise de la conscience moderne 1958, L'écorce des pierres 1959, L'aube 1962, Mère Méditerranée 1965, Les Evènements de Palerme 1966, L'échec de Pavèse 1968, Lettre à Dora 1969, Les enfants de Gogol 1971, Il Mito dell'America 1969, L'arbre jusqu'aux racines 1972, Porporino 1974, Eisenstein 1975, La rose des Tudors 1976, Les Siciliens 1977, Amsterdam 1977, L'étoile rose 1978, Une fleur de jasmin à l'oreille 1980, Le promeneur amoureux 1980, Signor Giovanni 1981, Dans la main de l'ange 1982, Le volcan sous la ville 1983, Le banquet des anges 1984, L'amour 1986, La gloire du paria 1987, Le rapt de Perséphone (opera libretto) 1987, Le radeau de la Gorgone 1988, Le rapt de Ganymede 1989, L'Ecole du Sud 1991, Porfirio et Constance 1992, Séville 1992, L'Or des Tropiques 1993, Le Dernier des Médicis 1993, La Magie Blanche de Saint-Pétersbourg 1994, Prague et la Bohême (jtly) 1995, La Perle et le croissant 1995, Le Musée idéal de Stendhal 1995, Saint-Pétersbourg 1996, Tribunal d'honneur 1997, Le musée de Zola 1997, Le voyage d'Italie 1998, Rhapsodie roumaine 1998, Palerme et la Sicile 1998, Le loup et le chien 1999, Les douze muses d'Alexandre Dumas 1999, Bolivie 1999, Nicolas 2000, Errances solaires 2000, L'amour qui ose dire son nom 2001, Syrie 2002, La Course à l'abîme 2003, Dictionnaire amoureux de la Russie 2004, Rome 2004, Sentiment indien 2005, Sicile 2006, Jérémie! Jérémie! 2006, l'Art de raconter 2007, Place rouge 2008, Ramon 2009. *Leisure interest:* operatic music. *Address:* 14 rue de Douai, 75009 Paris (home); c/o Editions Bernard Grasset, 61 rue des Saints-Pères, 75006 Paris, France (office).

FERNÁNDEZ, Gonzalo; Uruguayan lawyer and politician; *Minister of Foreign Affairs;* Sec. of Presidency 2005–08; Minister of Foreign Affairs 2008–; mem. Partido Socialista del Uruguay. *Address:* Ministry of Foreign Affairs, Avda 18 de Julio 1205, 11100 Montevideo, Uruguay (office). *Telephone:* (2) 9022132 (office). *Fax:* (2) 9021349 (office). *E-mail:* webmaster@mrree.gub.uy (office). *Website:* www.mrree.gub.uy (office).

FERNANDEZ, Chief Oladeinde; Central African Republic business executive and diplomatist; *Ambassador to the United Nations;* b. 1937; m. 1st Barbara Fernandez (divorced); m. 2nd Aduke Fernandez 1982 (separated); Yoruba tribal chief; Central African Repub. Amb. to UN. *Address:* c/o Permanent Representative of the Central African Republic to the UN, 51 Clifton Avenue, Suite 2008, Newark, NJ 07104, USA (office).

FERNÁNDEZ BERMEJO, Mariano, LicenDer; Spanish lawyer, professor of law and politician; b. 10 Feb. 1948, Ávila; ed Complutense Univ.; Public Prosecutor, Prov. Court of Santa Cruz de Tenerife 1974–76, Territorial Court of Cáceres 1976–81; Deputy Chief Prosecutor, Prov. Court of Segovia 1981–84, Chief Prosecutor 1984–86; exec. adviser to Ministry of Justice 1986–89; Prosecutor, Tribunal Supremo (Supreme Court) 1989–92, Chief Prosecutor, Chamber for Admin. Proceedings 2004–07; Chief Prosecutor, Madrid High Court of Justice 1992–2003; Minister of Justice 2007–09 (resgnd); Interim Adjunct Prof. of Criminal Law, Extremadura Univ. 1977–80; Prof., Nat. Univ. of Distance Learning (UNED) 1980–81; San Raimundo de Penafort Cross of Honour, Silver Cross Order of Merit of the Civil Guard; Jesús Vicente Chamorro Prize 2003, Political Merit Medal. *Publications:* El concepto de desamparo 1987, Líneas generales de la Reforma del Derecho del Menor 1988, Adopción y acogimientos familiares 1988, El menor de edad en la legislación española 1994, La Mediación como solución alternativa al proceso y su significación respecto a la víctima 2000, La protección de los Derechos Humanos en los colectivos sociales marginales 2001, Contra la especulación del suelo 2003. *Address:* c/o Ministry of Justice, San Bernardo 45, 28015 Madrid, Spain (office).

FERNÁNDEZ DE KIRCHNER, Cristina Elisabeth; Argentine politician, lawyer and head of state; *President;* b. 19 Feb. 1953, La Plata, Buenos Aires; m. Néstor Carlos Kirchner; one s. one d.; ed Universidad Nacional de La Plata; began political career in Tendencia Revolucionaria faction of Partido Justicialista 1970s; elected prov. rep. in Patagonian prov. of Santa Cruz 1989–95, Chair. Constitutional Affairs, Authorities and Regulations Cttee, Santa Cruz House of Reps 1989–95, First Vice-Chair. 1990; elected to represent Santa Cruz in Senate 1995–97, 2001–05, in Chamber of Deputies 1997, Senator representing Prov. of Buenos Aires (Front for Victory faction of party) 2005–07; Pres. of Argentina 2007–; mem. Congress Partido Justicialista 1985, mem. Nat. Congress 1995, Pres. Congress Partido Justicialista 2004; ranked by Forbes magazine amongst 100 Most Powerful Women (13th) 2008. *Address:* General Secretariat to the Presidency, Balcarce 50, C1064AAB Buenos Aires, Argentina (home). *Telephone:* (11) 4344-3674 (office). *Fax:* (11) 4344-2647 (office). *E-mail:* dgi@presidencia.gov.ar (office). *Website:* www.secretariageneral.gov.ar (home).

FERNÁNDEZ DE LA VEGA, María Teresa; Spanish lawyer, judge and politician; *First Deputy Prime Minister and Minister of the Presidency and Government Spokesperson;* b. 15 June 1949, Valencia; ed Complutense Univ. of Madrid, Barcelona Univ.; started career as legal sec.; one of first women judges in Justicia Democrática movement during transition to democracy; served in Ministry of Justice 1980s; magistrate 1989; Sec. of State for Justice 1994; MP 1996–, fmr Sec.-Gen., Socialist Group in Congress, First Deputy Prime Minister, Minister of the Presidency and Govt Spokesperson 2004–; Assoc. Prof. Barcelona Central Univ., Complutense Univ. of Madrid; tutor, UNED. *Address:* Prime Minister's Chancellery and Ministry of the Presidency, Complejo de la Moncloa, 28071 Madrid, Spain (office). *Telephone:* (91) 3353535 (office). *Fax:* (91) 5492739 (office). *Website:* www.mpr.es (office).

FERNÁNDEZ MALDONADO SOLARI, Gen. Jorge; Peruvian politician and army officer; b. 29 May 1922, Ilo, Moquegua; s. of Arturo Fernández Maldonado Soto and Amelia Solari de Fernández Maldonado; m. Estela Castro Faucheux; two s. two d.; ed Chorillos Mil. School; Head of Army Intelligence Service; Dir of Army Intelligence School, also of Mariscal Ramon Castilla Mil. School, Trujillo; Mil. Attaché, Argentina; mem. Pres. Advisory Cttee (COAP); Minister of Energy and Mines 1968–75; Army Chief of Staff 1975–76; Prime Minister, Minister of War, Commdr-Gen. of Army Feb.–July 1976; Senator 1985–; Sec.-Gen. Intergovernmental Council of Copper Exporting Countries 1990–.

FERNÁNDEZ-MURO, José Antonio; Argentine painter; b. 1 March 1920; Dir Nat. School of Fine Arts, Buenos Aires 1957–58; travelled and studied in Europe and America on UNESCO Fellowship of Museology 1957–58; lives in New York 1962–; represented in numerous Group Shows including 50 ans de Peinture Abstraite, Paris and The Emergent Decade, Guggenheim Museum 1965; prizes include Gold Medal, Brussels World Fair 1958, Guggenheim Int. and Di Tella Int. Awards. *Major works:* Superimposed Circles 1958, In Reds, Di Tella Foundation, Buenos Aires 1959, Horizonte terroso, Museum of Modern Art, Caracas 1961, Círculo azogado, Museum of Modern Art, New York 1962, Lacerated Tablet, Rockefeller, New York 1963, Elemental Forms, MIT 1964, Silver Field, Guggenheim Museum 1965, Summit, Bonino Gallery, New York.

FERNÁNDEZ ORDÓÑEZ, Miguel Ángel, LicenDer, LicenCienEcon; Spanish politician, central banker and academic; *Governor, Banco de España;* b. 3 April 1945, Madrid; ed Universidad Complutense de Madrid; mem. Socialist Workers' Party; Prof. of Political Economy Universidad Complutense de Madrid 1970–72; Chief of Section, Coyuntura de la Comisaría del Plan de Desarrollo 1970–72; economist, Dept of Econ. Studies, OECD 1973; Chief of Co-ordination Service, Ministry of Planning and Devt 1974–75; econ. consultant, Ministry of Finance 1976; Deputy Dir-Gen. of Conjunctural Analysis, Ministry of the Economy 1977; consultant to Exec. Dir World Bank 1978–80; Sec. Cttee of Public Investments, Ministry of the Economy 1980–82; Sec. of State for the Economy and Planning 1982–86; elected Deputy for Madrid 1986–88; Sec. of State for Commerce 1987–88; Exec. Dir IMF 1988–90; Pres. Icopostal, Sociedad de Valores y Bolsa 1990–91; mem. Council of Admin Banco Argentaria and Pres. Fundación Argentaria 1991–92; Pres. Court of Defence of Competition 1992–95; Pres. Comm. of Nat. Electric System 1995–99; econ. columnist, El País y Cinco Días, collaborator on TV programme Economía a Fondo, CNN+ and Dir radio programme Economía de los Negocios, SER 2000–03; Sec. of State for Internal Revenue 2004–06; Counsellor, Banco de España and mem. Exec. Comm. March–July 2006, Gov. Banco de España July 2006–; mem. Cuerpo de Técnicos Comerciales and State Economists. *Publications:* La Competencia; numerous articles on political economy, regulation, liberalization, privatization, defence of competition and the financial system. *Address:* Banco de España, Alcalá 48, 28014 Madrid, Spain (office). *Telephone:* (91) 3385000 (office). *Fax:* (91) 5310059 (office). *E-mail:* bde@bde.es (office). *Website:* www.bde.es (office).

FERNÁNDEZ RETAMAR, Roberto, Dr en Fil; Cuban writer; b. 9 June 1930, Havana; s. of José M. Fernández Roig and Obdulia Retamar; m. Adelaida de Juan 1952; two d.; ed Univ. de la Habana, Univ. de Paris à la Sorbonne and Univ. of London; Prof. Univ. de la Habana 1955–; Visiting Prof. Yale Univ. 1957–58; Dir Nueva Revista Cubana 1959–60; Cultural Counsellor of Cuba in France 1960; Sec. Union of Writers and Artists of Cuba 1961–65; Ed. Casa de las Américas 1965–, now Pres.; Visiting Lecturer Columbia Univ. 1957, Univ. of Prague 1965; Felix Varela Order of first grade 1981, Orden de Mayo, Argentina 1998; Nat. Prize for Poetry, Cuba 1952, Rúben Dario Latin American Prize 1980, Int. Prize for Poetry Nikola Vaptsarov, Bulgaria 1989, Nat. Literary Award Cuban Book Inst. 1989, Int. Prize for Poetry Pérez Bonalde, Argentina 1989, Official Medal of Arts and Letters, France 1998. *Publications:* poetry: Elegía como un Himno 1950, Patrias 1952, Alabanzas, Conversaciones 1955, Vuelta de la Antigua Esperanza 1959, Con las Mismas Manos 1962, Poesía Reunida 1948–1965 1966, Buena Suerte Viviendo 1967, Que veremos arder 1970, A quien pueda interesar 1970, Cuaderno paralelo 1973, Juana y otros temas personales 1981, Aquí 1995; studies: La Poesía contemporánea en Cuba 1954, Idea de la Estilística 1958, Papelería 1962, Ensayo de otro mundo 1967, Introducción a Cuba: la historia 1968, Caliban 1971, Lectura de Martí 1972, El son de Vuelo popular 1972, Introducción a Martí 1978. *Leisure interests:* reading, swimming. *Address:* 508 H Street, Vedado, Havana, Cuba.

FERNÁNDEZ REYNA, Leonel, DIur; Dominican Republic politician and head of state; *President;* b. 26 Dec. 1953, Santo Domingo; s. of the late José Antonio Fernández Collado and of Yolanda Reyna Romero; m. Margarita Cedeño; one c. (two c. from previous m.); ed Universidad Autónoma de Santo Domingo; joined Partido de la Liberación Dominicana 1973, Pres. 2002–; cand. for Vice-Pres. 1994; Pres. 1996–2000, 2004–. *Address:* Administrative Secretariat of the Presidency, Palacio Nacional, Avda México, esq. Dr Delgado, Santo Domingo, DN, Dominican Republic. *Telephone:* 686-4771 (office). *Fax:* 688-2100 (office). *E-mail:* prensa@presidencia.gov.do (office). *Website:* www.presidencia.gov.do (office); www.leonelfernandez.com.

FERNANDO, Merrill Joseph; Sri Lankan tea planter and business executive; *Founder and Chairman, Dilmah Tea;* b. 6 May 1930, Negombo; s. of P. Harry Fernando and Lucy Fernando; m.; two s.; ed Maris Stella Colles, Negombo; selected for training as tea taster, travelled to Mincing Lane, London, UK; worked in UK tea co. before returning to Sri Lanka; joined A. F. Jones & Co., becoming Man. Dir within two years, bought out British shareholders and ran business with another pnr; supplied first ever consignment of Ceylon tea direct to then USSR 1950s; est. Merrill J. Fernando & Co. Ltd, supplied bulk tea to most of world's major tea brands 1960s–70s; lost tea plantation to nationalization 1970s, sold business with intention of emigrating from Sri Lanka, remained in Sri Lanka and est. M. J. F. Exports Ltd 1974; registered trademark DILMAH in face of opposition from bulk tea customers early 1980s; DILMAH Tea launched in Australia 1988, thereafter in NZ and to date in 94 countries world-wide; est. The Merrill J. Fernando Charitable Foundation. *Address:* Dilmah (MJF Group), PO Box 1630, Colombo 10, Sri Lanka (office). *Telephone:* (11) 2933070 (office). *Fax:* (11) 2933080 (office). *E-mail:* info@dilmahtea.com (office). *Website:* www.dilmahtea.com (office); www.mjffoundation.org.

FERNANDO, Most Rev. Nicholas Marcus, BA, PhL, STD; Sri Lankan ecclesiastic; b. 6 Dec. 1932; s. of W. Severinus Fernando and M. M. Lily Fernando; ordained priest 1959; Rector, St Aloysius Minor Seminary 1965–73; Archbishop of Colombo 1977–2002, Archbishop Emer. 2002–; mem. Sacred Congregation for the Evangelization of Peoples 1989; Pres. Catholic Bishops' Conf. of Sri Lanka 1989–95. *Address:* c/o Archbishop's House, 976 Gnanartha Pradeepaya Mawatha, Colombo 8, Sri Lanka. *Telephone:* 695471-2-3. *Fax:* (1) 692009.

FERNEYHOUGH, Brian John Peter, ABSM, ARAM, FRAM, FBC; British composer and academic; *William H. Bonsall Professor of Music, Stanford University;* b. 16 Jan. 1943, Coventry; s. of Frederick George Ferneyhough and Emily May Ferneyhough (née Hopwood); m. 4th Stephanie Hurtik 1990; ed Birmingham School of Music, RAM, Sweelinck Conservatory, Amsterdam, Music Acad., Basle; composition teacher, Musikhochschule, Freiburg, Germany 1973–78, Prof. of Composition 1978–86; Prin. Composition Teacher, Royal Conservatory of The Hague 1986; Prof. of Music, Univ. of California, San Diego 1987–99; Leader of Master Class in Composition, Civica Scuola di Musica, Milan 1982–86; Visiting Artist, DAAD Berlin 1976–77; Guest Prof., Musikhögskolan, Stockholm 1980, 1981, 1982, 1985; Visiting Prof., Univ. of Chicago 1986; Lecturer in Composition, Darmstadt Int. Courses 1976–96; Guest Prof. of Poetics, Mozarteum, Salzburg, Austria 1995; mem. Akad. der Künste, Berlin 1996; William H. Bonsall Prof. of Music, Stanford Univ. 2000–; Visiting Prof., Harvard Univ. 2007–08; Chevalier, Ordre des Arts et des Lettres 1984; Koussevitsky Prize 1979, Grand Prix du Disque 1978, 1984, Ernst von Siemens Prize for Music (Germany) 2007, and other awards and prizes. *Works include:* Sonatas for String Quartet 1967, Firecycle Beta 1969–71, Transit 1972–74, Time and Motion Study III 1974, La Terre Est Un Homme 1976–79, Second String Quartet 1979–80, Lemma-Icon-Epigram 1981, Carceri d'Invenzione 1981–86, 3rd String Quartet 1987, Kurze Schatten II 1988, La Chute d'Icare 1988, Fourth String Quartet 1989–90, Allgebrah 1991, Bone Alphabet 1991, Terrain 1992, On Stellar Magnitudes 1994, String Trio 1995, Incipits 1995–96, Allgebrah 1996, Flurries 1997, Unsichtbare Farben 1999, Doctrine of Similarity 2000, Opus Contra Naturam 2000, Stele for Failed Time 2001, Shadowtime (opera) 2004, Plötzlichkeit 2005, Fifth String Quartet 2006, Dum transisset I-IV 2007, Exordium 2008, Chronos-Aion 2008. *Publications:* Complete Writings on Music 1994, Collected Writings 1996; various articles published separately. *Leisure interests:* reading, cats, wife, wine (not in that order). *Address:* Office 231A, Department of Music, Braun Music Center, Stanford University, 541 Lasuen Mall, Stanford, CA 94305-3076, USA (office). *Telephone:* (650) 725-3102 (office). *Fax:* (650) 725-2686 (office). *E-mail:* brian.ferneyhough@stanford.edu (office). *Website:* www.stanford.edu/group/Music (office).

FERNIOT, Jean; French journalist; b. 10 Oct. 1918, Paris; s. of Paul Ferniot and Jeanne Ferniot (née Rabu); m. 1st Jeanne Martinod 1942 (divorced); one s. two d.; m. 2nd Christiane Servan-Schreiber 1959 (divorced); two s.; m. 3rd Béatrice Lemaître 1984; ed Lycée Louis-le-Grand; Head, Political Dept, France-Tireur 1945–57; political columnist, L'Express 1957–58; Chief Political Corresp., France-Soir 1959–63; Ed. L'Express 1963–66; with Radio Luxembourg 1967–83; political commentator, France-Soir 1967–70, Asst Chief Ed. 1969–70; Dir Éditions Grasset, in charge of Collection Humeurs 1978–83; Dir then Adviser Cuisine et Vins de France 1981; Pres. Fondation Communication Demain 1980–89, Terminology Comm., Nat. Council for Tourism 1991–97; Pres. (Supervisory Council) Evénement du Jeudi 1992; mem. jury, Prix Interallié 1970–; Commdr des Arts et des Lettres, Croix de Guerre, Chevalier du Mérite agricole, Commdr du Mérite (Italy); Prix Interallié 1961. *Publications:* Les ides de mai 1958, L'ombre porté 1961, Pour le pire 1962, Derrière la fenêtre 1964, De Gaulle et le 13 mai 1965, Mort d'une révolution 1968, Paris dans mon assiette 1969, Complainte contre X 1973, De de Gaulle à Pompidou 1972, Ça suffit! 1973, Pierrot et Aline 1973, La petite légume 1974, Les vaches maigres (with Michel Albert) 1975, Les honnêtes gens 1976, C'est ça la France 1977, Vous en avez vraiment assez d'être français 1979, Carnet de croûte 1980, Le Pouvoir et la sainteté 1982, Le Chien-loup 1983, Saint Judas 1984, Un mois de juin comme on les aimait 1986, Soleil orange 1988, Miracle au village 1989, Je recommencerais bien 1991, L'Europe à Table 1993, La France des Terroirs Gourmands 1993, Jérusalem, nombril du monde 1994, La Mouffe 1995, Morte saison 1996, Un temps pour aimer, un temps pour haïr 1999, Ce soir ou jamais 2002, Noces de Nuit 2003, C'était ma France 2004, L'enfant du miracle 2006, Vivre avec ou sans Dieu 2007. *Leisure interest:* history. *Address:* 11 bis rue d'Orléans, 92200 Neuilly-sur-Seine, France. *Telephone:* 1-46-24-25-30 (home).

FERRAGAMO, Ferruccio; Italian business executive; b. 9 Sept. 1945, Fiesole, Florence; m. Amanda Collingwood; five c.; began career working on production side of family business Salvatore Ferragamo Italia SpA, later involved in worldwide management of Ferragamo stores; finance and admin. from 1983; now CEO Salvatore Ferragamo SpA; Vice-Pres. Polimoda, Florence; mem. Bd Società Gaetano Marzotto & Fratelli, La Fondaria Assicurazioni, Banca Mercantile, Florence, Centro di Firenze per la Moda Italiana. *Leisure interests:* golf, shooting, sailing, tennis. *Address:* c/o

Salvatore Ferragamo Italia, SpA, Via di Tornabuoni 2, 50123 Florence, Italy. *Telephone:* (055) 33601.

FERRARA, Abel; American film director and actor; b. 12 May 1951, Bronx, NY; m. Nancy Ferrara; two d.; began making short films while at school; has used pseudonym Jimmy Laine; television work includes episodes of Miami Vice and pilot for NBC's Crime Story. *Films include:* Nicky's Film 1971, The Hold Up 1972, Could This Be Love? 1973, Nine Lives of a Wet Pussy 1976, Not Guilty: For Keith Richards 1977, Driller Killer (also acted) 1979, Ms.45 (also acted) 1981, Fear City 1984, China Girl 1987, Cat Chaser 1989, The King of New York 1990, Bad Lieutenant 1992, Body Snatchers 1993, Dangerous Game 1993, The Addiction 1995, The Funeral 1996, California 1996, The Blackout 1997, New Rose Hotel 1998, 'R Xmas 2001, Mary (Venice Film Festival Special Jury Prize) 2005. *Address:* c/o William Morris Agency, 151 S El Camino Drive, Beverly Hills, CA 90212, USA.

FERRARI BRAVO, Luigi; Italian legal scholar; *Professor of Law, University of Rome;* b. 5 Aug. 1933; ed Univ. of Naples; Asst Prof., Univ. of Naples 1956–61; Prof. of Int. Org., Univ. of Bari 1961–65, of Int. Law 1965–68, Full Prof. of Int. Law and Dir Inst. of Int. Law 1968–74; Prof. of Int. Law, Istituto Universitario Orientale, Naples 1962–68, Full Prof. of Int. Org. 1974–79, Dean, Dept of Political Science 1975–76; Prof. of EC Law, High School of Public Admin. Rome 1965–79, Full Prof. 1975; Full Prof. of EC Law, Faculty of Political Science, Univ. of Rome 1979–82, Full Prof. of Public Int. Law 1982–91; Full Prof. of EC Law, Faculty of Law, Univ. of Rome 1991–; Lecturer, Hague Acad. of Int. Law 1975, 1982 and many other univs and scientific insts; numerous professional appointments; mem. Italian Bar, Int. Law Asscn, American Soc. of Int. Law, Soc. Française de Droit Int. etc. *Publications:* articles in professional journals. *Address:* Faculty of Law, University of Rome, Piazzale Aldo Moro 5, 00185 Rome, Italy.

FERRARO, Geraldine Anne, JD; American politician and lawyer; *Of Counsel, Blank Rome LLP;* b. 26 Aug. 1935, Newburgh, NY; d. of Dominick Ferraro and Antonetta L. Ferraro (née Corrieri); m. John Zaccaro 1960; one s. two d.; ed Marymount Manhattan Coll., Fordham Univ. School of Law; lawyer in New York Bar 1961, US Supreme Court 1978; practised law in New York 1961–74, Asst Dist Attorney, Queens Co., New York 1974–78; mem. House of Reps 1979–84; first woman from a maj. party to be a cand. for US Vice-Pres. in 1984 presidential election; Man. Pnr Keck Mahin Cate & Koether, New York 1993–94; apptd. by Pres. Clinton as US Amb. to UN Human Rights Comm. 1994–96, World Conf., Vienna 1993, 4th World Conf. on Women 1995; Prof. Georgetown Univ. School of Public Policy; Founder and Pres. G & L Strategies; Sr Man. Dir and Chair. of Public Affairs Practice, The Global Consulting Group –2006; Prin., Blank Rome Govt Relations LLC, Washington, DC 2007, Of Counsel, Blank Rome LLP, NY 2008–; Fellow, Kennedy School of Govt, Harvard Univ. 1988; Pres. Int. Inst. of Women Political Leaders 1985–90; mem. Nat. Democratic Inst. for Int. Affairs; Democrat; hon. degrees from 14 colls and univs; numerous awards. *Television:* Co-host Crossfire, CNN 1996–98; currently political analyst for FOX News. *Publications:* My Story (with Linda Bird Francke) 1985, Changing History: Women, Power and Politics 1993, Framing a Life 1998. *Address:* Blank Rome LLP, 405 Lexington Avenue, New York, NY 10174, USA (office). *Website:* www.blankrome.com (office).

FERREIRA DE OLIVEIRA, Manuel, PhD; Portuguese engineer and business executive; *CEO, Galp Energia SGPS SA;* ed Faculdade de Engenharia da Universidade do Porto (FEUP), Univ. of Manchester, UK; Prof., Faculty of Eng, Univ. of Porto 1971–80; held several exec. positions in the oil industry in Venezuela and UK 1980–95; Chair. of the Bd and Exec. Cttee PETROGAL - Petróleos de Portugal SA 1995–2000; Chair. Supervisory Bd UNICE 2000–06; Exec. Dir Galp Energia SGPS SA 2006–, mem. Exec. Cttee and CEO 2007–; mem. Gen. Council Associação Empresarial de Portugal; Pres. Gen. Council EGP Univ. of Porto Business School; Vice-Pres. Forum for Competitiveness; mem. Bd of Dirs Business Council for Sustainable Devt Portugal; Vice-Pres. European Fed. of Beer Producers; Grand Master Confraternity of Beer; Ordem Francisco Miranda (Venezuela), Grau da Grã-Cruz da Ordem de Mérito. *Address:* Galp Energia SGPS SA, Rua Tomás da Fonseca, Torre A, Edifício Galp Energia, 1600-209 Lisbon, Portugal (office). *Telephone:* (21) 724-25-00 (office); (21) 724-19-69 (office). *Fax:* (21) 003 90 80 (office). *E-mail:* presidencia@galpenergia.com (office). *Website:* www.galpenergia.com (office).

FERRELL, John William (Will); American actor; b. 16 July 1967, Irvine, Calif.; s. of Lee Ferrell and Kay Ferrell; m. Viveca Paulin 2000; two s.; ed Univ. of Southern Calif. *Films include:* Men Seeking Women 1997, Austin Powers: International Man of Mystery 1997, The Thin Pink Line 1998, A Night at the Roxbury 1998, The Suburbans 1999, Austin Powers: The Spy Who Shagged Me 1999, Dick 1999, Superstar 1999, Drowning Mona 2000, The Ladies Man 2000, Jay and Silent Bob Strike Back 2001, Zoolander 2001, Old School 2003, Elf 2003, Anchorman: The Legend of Ron Burgundy 2004, Melinda and Melinda 2004, The Wendell Baker Story 2005, Kicking and Screaming 2005, Bewitched 2005, Winter Passing 2005, The Producers 2005, Wedding Crashers 2005, Curious George (voice) 2006, Talladega Nights: The Ballad of Ricky Bobby 2006, Stranger Than Fiction 2006, Blades of Glory 2007, Semi-pro 2008, Step Brothers 2008. *Stage performance:* You're Welcome America. A Final Night with George W. Bush (Broadway) 2009. *Television includes:* cast mem. Saturday Night Live 1995–2002. *Address:* Creative Artists Agency, Inc., 9830 Wilshire Blvd, Beverly Hills, CA 90212-1825, USA. *Telephone:* (310) 288-4545. *Fax:* (310) 288-4800. *Website:* www.caa.com.

FERRER SALAT, Carlos; Spanish banker and business executive; Chair. Banco de Europa, Ferrer Int. (pharmaceutical co.); Founder and first Chair. Spanish Employers' Fed. (CEOE); Pres. European Employers' Union (UNICE), Brussels 1991–; mem. Bds Volkswagen, IBM Europe and others.

FERRERO, Juan Carlos; Spanish professional tennis player; b. 12 Feb. 1980, Onteniente; s. of Eduardo and the late Rosario Ferrero; world ranked 1st as a junior 1998, won Wimbledon junior title that year; turned professional 1998; 11 singles titles: Mallorca 1999, Barcelona 2001, Dubai 2001, Estoril 2001, Rome Tennis Masters Series (TMS) 2001, Hong Kong 2002, Madrid TMS 2003, Monte Carlo TMS 2002, 2003, French Open 2003, Valencia 2003; runner-up French Open 2002, US Open 2003; 234 singles wins, 101 defeats; ranked 4th Champions Race 2002, ranked 3rd in 2003; career winnings of US $8,996,110; 9 Davis Cup ties 1999– (11 singles wins, three defeats); won Davis Cup with Spain in 2000; coached by Antonio Martinez and Samuel Lopez; f. Equalite J. C. Ferrero tennis school in 2001; Asscn of Tennis Professionals (ATP) Rookie of the Year 1999. *Leisure interests:* soccer, collecting cars and motor-cycles.

FERRERO, Molecule; Italian business executive; b. 1927, Alba; s. of Pietro Ferrero; m.; two s.; joined family confectionery co. Ferrero SpA in 1950, later took control of co. and expanded throughout Europe and worldwide eventually becoming one of Europe's largest confectionery manufacturers; products include Nutella, Ferrero Rocher, Kinder, Tic Tacs, turned over control of co. to his sons 1997; Founder Fondazione Ferrero 1983. *Address:* Ferrero SpA, Via Maria Cristina 47, 10025, Pino Torinese (office); Fondazione Ferrero, Strada di Mezzo 41, Alba 12051, Italy. *Telephone:* (173) 2951 (office). *Fax:* (173) 363034 (office). *E-mail:* info@fondazioneferrero.it. *Website:* www.ferrero.it (office); www.fondazioneferrero.it (office).

FERRERO COSTA, Carlos; Peruvian politician; b. 7 Feb. 1941, Lima; m. Nina Ghislieri.1968; four c.; Congressional Speaker 2000–03; Prime Minister of Peru 2003–05 (resgnd); currently mem. Congreso (Perú Posible). *Address:* c/o Perú Posible, Avda Faustino Sánchez Carrión, Lima, Peru (office). *Telephone:* (1) 4620303 (office). *E-mail:* carfecos@gmail.com (office). *Website:* /www.carlosferrero.org (office).

FERRERO-WALDNER, Benita Maria, DIur; Austrian politician and diplomatist; *Commissioner for External Relations and European Neighbourhood Policy, European Commission;* b. 5 Sept. 1948, Oberndorf, Salzburg; ed Univ. of Salzburg; export and sales managerial roles in German and US cos, Germany 1978–83; joined Diplomatic Service 1984, several posts Ministry of Foreign Affairs, Vienna 1984–86, First Sec., Dakar, Devt Aid Dept, Vienna; Counsellor for Econ. Affairs, Deputy Head of Mission, Chargé d'affaires, Paris 1986–93; Deputy Chief of Protocol, Ministry of Foreign Affairs 1993; UN Chief of Protocol, Exec. Office of Sec.-Gen., New York 1994–95; State Sec., Ministry of Foreign Affairs 1995–2000, Minister of Foreign Affairs 2000–04; EU Commr for External Relations and European Neighbourhood Policy 2004–; Mérite Europêen Gold Medal. *Publication:* The Future of Development Co-operation, Setting Course in a Changing World. *Leisure interests:* reading, yoga, cycling. *Address:* European Commission, 200 rue de la Loi, 1049 Brussels, Belgium (office). *Telephone:* (2) 2994900 (office). *Fax:* (2) 2981299 (office). *Website:* ec.europa.eu/commission_barroso/ferrero-waldner/index_en.htm (office).

FERRES, Veronica Maria; German actress; b. Oct. 1906, Cologne; m. Martin Krug 2001; one d.; ed Ludwig-Maximilian-Univ., Munich; several awards including Golden Camera Award, Germany 1998, 2002, Bavarian TV Award 2002. 2004, Romy Award, Austria 2002, Video Award, Germany 2004. *Films include:* The Mask of Desire (Bambi Best Actress Award) 1992, Lateshow, The Ladies Room, Schtonk 1992, Superwoman 1996, Rossini 1997, Honeymoon 1997, The Parrot 1997, The Second Homeland 1997, The Bride (Best Actress Award 9th Int. Film Festival, Pescara 1999) 1999, Klimt 2006, Die Wilden Hühner 2006, Bye Bye Harry! 2006, Die Wilden Hühner und die Liebe 2007, Adam Resurrected 2008, Die Wilden Hühner und das Leben 2009. *Plays include:* Gold 1998, The Casket 2000, The Geierwally 2000, Talking With 2000, The Bernauerin 2000, Ghostride 2000, Everyman 2002–04,. *Television includes:* Jack's Baby, The Chaos Queen, The Naughty Woman, Dr Knock, Catherine the Great, Tatort Fatal Motherlove, The Mountain Doctor, Bobby 2002, Sans Famille 2002, Les Misérables 2002, The Manns (Golden Grimme Award, Emmy Award) 2002, Forever Lost 2003, Anna's Return 2003, Stronger Than Death 2003, The Return of the Dancing Master 2004, Stars Even Shine At Day 2004, No Heaven Over Africa 2005, Neger, Neger, Schornsteinfeger 2006, Mein alter Freund Fritz 2007, Die Frau vom Checkpoint Charlie (mini-series) 2007, Das Wunder von Berlin 2008. *Leisure interests:* horseriding, skiing, fencing, golf, scuba diving, dancing. *Address:* Ferres Management, Kurfürstenstr. 18, 80801 Munich, Germany (office). *Telephone:* (89) 34020927 (office). *Fax:* (89) 38398689 (office); (89) 4702198 (office); (89) 399744 (home).

FERRETTI, Alberta; Italian fashion designer and retailer; b. 1951; m. 1968 (separated); two s.; made clothes and opened first boutique The Jolly Shop, Cattolica 1968, launched first collection under the name Alberta Ferretti 1974; began mfg clothes for other designers in 1970s; launched Alberta Ferretti line 1981, Philosophy line 1984, lingerie, accessories and beachwear lines 2001; Owner and Vice-Pres. Aeffe fashion design and mfg co.; Cavaliere del Lavoro 1998; Dr hc (Bologna); Alta Roma Career Awards 2005. *Leisure interests:* swimming, reading, sailing. *Address:* AEFFE Spa, via Delle Querce, 15, 47842 San Giovani in Marignana; Via Donizetti 48, 20122 Milan, Italy (office). *Telephone:* (2) 760591 (office). *Fax:* (2) 782373 (office). *E-mail:* ufficiostampa@aeffe.com (office). *Website:* www.aeffe.com (office); www.albertaferretti.com (office).

FERRIER, Johan Henri Eliza, PhD; Suriname politician; b. 12 May 1910, Paramaribo; mem. Suriname Parl. 1946–48; Dir Dept of Educ., Paramaribo 1951–55; Prime Minister, Minister of Gen. Affairs, of Home Affairs 1955–58; Counsellor, Ministry of Educ., Arts and Science, Netherlands 1959–65; Man.

Dir Billiton Mining Co., Suriname 1966–67; Gov. of Suriname 1968–75; Pres. Repub. of Suriname 1975–80.

FERRY, Bryan; British singer and songwriter; b. 26 Sept. 1945, Washington, Co. Durham; s. of the late Frederick Charles Ferry and Mary Ann Ferry (née Armstrong); m. Lucy Margaret Mary Helmore 1982 (divorced 2003); three s. one d.; ed Univ. of Newcastle-upon-Tyne; formed Roxy Music 1971; official debut, Lincoln Festival 1972; first US concerts 1972; first British and European tours 1973; Ivor Novello Award for Outstanding Contrib. to British Music 2003, BMI Icon Award 2008. *Recorgings include:* albums: with Roxy Music: Roxy Music 1972, For Your Pleasure 1973 (Grand Prix du Disque, Golden Rose Festival, Montreux 1973), Stranded 1973, Country Life 1974, Siren 1975, Viva Roxy Music 1976, Manifesto 1979, Flesh & Blood 1980, Avalon 1982, The Atlantic Years 1983, Street Life – 20 Great Hits 1986; solo: These Foolish Things 1973, Another Time Another Place 1974, Let's Stick Together 1976, In Your Mind 1977, The Bride Stripped Bare 1978, Boys And Girls 1985, Bete Noire 1987, The Ultimate Collection 1988, Taxi 1993, Mamouna 1995, Bryan Ferry and Roxy Music Video Collection 1996, Frantic 2002, Dylanesque 2007. *Address:* TCB Group, 24 Kimberley Court, Kimberley Road, Queens Park, London, NW6 7SL, England (office). *Telephone:* (20) 7328-7272 (office). *Fax:* (20) 7372-0844 (office). *E-mail:* info@tcbgroup.co.uk (office); info@bryanferry.com. *Website:* www.tcbgroup.co.uk (office); www.bryanferry.com.

FERRY, Luc, Dr rer. pol; French philosopher, politician and academic; b. 3 Jan. 1951, Colombes; s. of Pierre Ferry and Monique Faucher; m. Marie-Caroline Becq de Fouquières 1999; three d. (one from previous marriage); ed Lycée Saint-Exupéry, Centre nat. de télé-enseignement, Sorbonne, Univ. of Heidelberg; lecturer, Teacher Training Coll., Arras, Asst Lecturer, Univ. of Reims 1977–79; Asst Lecturer, Ecole Normale Supérieure, Paris 1977–79, 1980–82; Research Attaché Nat. CNRS 1980–82; Asst Lecturer, Univ. of Paris I-Panthéon Sorbonne and Paris X-Nanterre 1980–88; Prof. of Political Sciences, Inst. of Political Studies, Univ. of Lyon II–Lumière 1982–88; Prof. of Philosophy, Univ. of Caen 1989–97; Asst Lecturer, Paris I 1989; Prof. of Philosophy, Univ. of Paris VI-Jussieu 1996–; Founder-mem., Sec. Gen. College of Philosophy 1974–; responsible for Ideas section then Editorial Adviser, L'Express 1987–94; Pres. Nat. Curriculum Council (CNP) 1994–2002; Minister for Nat. Educ., Research and Technology 1997–2002; Minister of Youth, Nat. Educ. and Research 2002–04; mem. Comm. for UNESCO 1997–2002; Dir Editions Grasset collection of Coll. of Philosophy; fmr mem. Saint-Simon Foundation; columnist for Le Point 1995–; Chevalier Légion d'honneur, Ordre des Arts et des Lettres. *Publications include:* Philosophie politique (3 vols 1984–85), la Pensée 68, le Nouvel ordre écologique: l'arbre, l'animal et l'homme (Prix Jean-Jacques Rousseau) 1992, Homo aestheticus – L'Intervention du goût à l'âge démocratique 1990 (Prix Médicis 1992), l'Homme Dieu ou le sens de la vie (Prix Littéraire des Droits de l'Homme)1996, La Sagesse des Modernes 1998, Le Sens du Beau 1998, Philosopher à dix-huit ans (jtly) 1999, Qu'est-ce que l'homme? (jtly) 2000, Qu'est-ce qu-une vie réussie 2002, numerous articles on philosophy. *Address:* c/o Ministry of Youth, National Education and Research, 110 rue de Grenelle, 75357 Paris, France (office).

FERSHT, Sir Alan Roy, Kt, MA, PhD, FRS, FMedSci; British chemist and academic; *Herchel Smith Professor of Organic Chemistry, University of Cambridge;* b. 21 April 1943, London; s. of Philip Fersht and Betty Fersht; m. Marilyn Persell 1966; one s. one d.; ed Sir George Monoux Grammar School, Walthamstow and Gonville and Caius Coll., Cambridge; Research Fellow, Brandeis Univ., Waltham, Mass, USA 1968–69; Fellow, Jesus Coll., Cambridge 1969–72; mem. scientific staff, MRC Lab. of Molecular Biology, Cambridge 1969–77; Eleanor Roosevelt Fellow, Stanford Univ., Calif. 1978–79; Wolfson Research Prof. of Royal Soc. 1978–89; Prof. of Biological Chem., Imperial Coll., London 1978–88; Herchel Smith Prof. of Organic Chem., Univ. of Cambridge 1988–; Dir Cambridge Interdisciplinary Research Centre for Protein Eng 1989–; Dir MRC Unit for Protein Function and Design 1989–; Fellow, Gonville and Caius Coll., Cambridge 1988–, Imperial Coll. London 2004; Foreign Assoc. NAS (USA) 1993; Hon. Foreign mem. American Acad. of Arts and Sciences 1988; Hon. mem. Japanese Biochemical Soc. 2002; Hon. PhD (Uppsala) 1999, (Free Univ. of Brussels) 1999, (Weizmann Inst.) 2004, (Hebrew Univ.) 2006; Fed. of European Biochemical Socs Anniversary Prize 1980, Novo Biotech. Award 1986, Charmian Medal for Enzyme Chem., RSC 1986, Gabor Medal, Royal Soc. 1991, Max Tishler Prize, Harvard Univ. 1992, Harden Medal, Biochem. Soc. 1993, Feldberg Foundation Prize 1996, Davy Medal, Royal Soc. 1998, Anfinsen Award, The Protein Soc. 1999, Laureate, 'Chaire Bruylants', Louvain 1999, RSC Natural Products Award 1999, Stein and Moore Award, The Protein Soc. 2001, ACS Bader Award 2005, Linderstrøm-Lang Prize and Medal 2005, Bijvoet Medal 2008. *Publications:* Enzyme Structure and Mechanism 1977, Structure and Mechanism in Protein Science 1999: A Guide to Enzyme Catalysis and Protein Folding, Jaques Staunton Chess Sets 1849–1939: A Collectors Guide 2007; papers in scientific journals. *Leisure interests:* chess, horology. *Address:* Cambridge Centre for Protein Engineering, MRC Centre, Hills Road, Cambridge, CB2 0QH (office). *Telephone:* (1223) 402137 (office). *Fax:* (1223) 402140 (office). *E-mail:* arf25@cam.ac.uk (office). *Website:* www.mrc-cpe.cam.ac.uk (office); www.ch.cam.ac.uk/staff/arf.html (office).

FERT, Albert; French physicist and academic; *Scientific Director, Unité Mixte de Physique, CNRS-Thales;* b. 7 March 1938, Carcassonne; m.; two c.; ed Ecole Normale Supérieure, Paris, Université de Paris, Université Paris-Sud; Asst Université de Grenoble 1962–64; Asst Prof., Université Paris-Sud (Orsay) 1964–76; Prof. of Physics, Université Paris-Sud 1976–; Scientific Dir Unité Mixte de Physique, CNRS-Thales (Orsay) 1995–; one of the discoverers of giant magnetoresistance phenomenon, leading to new field of research, spintronics, which has led to enormous increase in storage capacity and reading speed of magnetic hard-disk drives; mem. French Acad. of Sciences 2004; American Physical Soc. New Materials Prize (jtly) 1994, IUPAP Magnetism Award (jtly) 1994, Grand Prix de Physique Jean Ricard, Société Française de Physique 1994, Hewlett-Packard Europhysics Prize (jtly) 1997, CNRS Gold Medal 2003, Wolf Foundation Prize for Physics (jtly) 2007, Nobel Prize for Physics (jtly) 2007. *Address:* CNRS Headquarters, 3 rue Michel-Ange, 75794 Paris Cedex 16, France (office). *Telephone:* 1-44-96-40-00 (office). *Fax:* 1-44-96-53-90 (office). *Website:* www2.cnrs.fr (office).

FERY, John Bruce, MBA; American business executive (retd); b. 16 Feb. 1930, Bellingham, Wash.; s. of Carl S. Fery and Margaret Fery; m. Delores L. Carlo 1953; three s.; ed Univ. of Washington and Stanford Univ. Grad. School of Business; Asst to Pres., Western Kraft Corpn 1955–56, Production Man. 1956–57; Asst to Pres., Boise Cascade Corpn 1957–58, Gen. Man. Paper Div. 1958–60, Vice-Pres. 1960–67, Exec. Vice-Pres. and Dir 1967–72, Pres. 1972–78, Chair, CEO 1978–94; Hon. Dr of Natural Resources (Idaho) 1983; Hon. LLD (Gonzaga) 1982; Stanford Univ. School of Business Ernest Arbuckle Award 1980. *Address:* 609 Wyndemere Drive, Boise, ID 83702, USA (home).

FETISOV, Vyacheslav Aleksandrovich; Russian professional ice hockey coach and fmr professional ice hockey player; *Head, Federal Agency for Physical Culture and Sports;* b. 20 April 1958, Moscow; m. Lada Fetisova; one d.; played with Cen. Army Sports Club 1975–89; USSR champion 1975, 1979–89; seven times world champion with USSR teams 1977–91; Olympic champion 1984, 1988; played with Nat. Hockey League (NHL) New Jersey Devils 1989–95, Detroit Red Wings 1995–98 (team won Stanley Cup 1997); Asst Coach New Jersey Devils 1998–2001; Gen. Man. and Coach Russian Olympic hockey team Salt Lake City 2002 (won bronze medal); Chair. Fed. Agency on Physical Culture and Sports 2002–; mem. Council of Founders of World Anti-Doping Agency (WADA), Head, Cttee of Sportsmen of WADA; Soviet Honoured Masters of Sport Award 1984, 1986, 1990, inducted into Hockey Hall of Fame 2001, UNESCO Champion for Sport 2004. *Address:* Federal Agency of Physical Culture and Sport, Kazakova str. 18, 105064 Moscow, Russia (office). *Telephone:* (495) 105-72-50 (office). *Fax:* (495) 267-34-40 (office). *E-mail:* info@rossport.ru (office). *Website:* www.rossport.ru (office).

FETSCHER, Iring, (Edler von Goldeck), DPhil; German political scientist and academic; *Professor Emeritus, J. W. Goethe Universität;* b. 4 March 1922, Marbach/Neckar; s. of Prof. Rainer Fetscher; m. Elisabeth Götte 1957; two s. two d.; ed König-George-Gymnasium, Dresden, Eberhard-Karls-Universität, Tübingen, Université de Paris and Johann Wolfgang Goethe-Univ., Frankfurt; Ed. Marxismusstudien 1956–; radio commentator on political, philosophical and sociological questions; Prof. of Political Science, Johann Wolfgang Goethe-Univ., Frankfurt 1963–88, Prof. Emer. 1988–; Theodor-Heuss Prof. New School for Social Research, New York 1968–69; Guest Prof. Tel Aviv Univ. 1972; Fellow, Netherlands Inst. for Advanced Study in the Humanities and Social Sciences 1972–73; Inst. for Advanced Studies, ANU, Canberra; Extraordinary Prof. for Social and Political Philosophy, Catholic Univ. of Nijmegen 1974–75; Chair. of the Expert Comm. for Criminal Prevention at the Govt of Hessen 1993–2004, Hon. Chair. 2004–; Bundesverdienstkreuz (First Class) 1993; Chevalier Ordre des Palmes Académiques 1993, Order of Merit, Hessen 2003; Hon. DPhil 2004; Goethe Plakette (Frankfurt) 1992. *Publications include:* Von Marx zur Sowjetideologie 1956, Über dialektischen und historischen Materialismus (Commentary of Stalin) 1956, 1962, Rousseaus politische Philosophie 1960, 1968, 1975, Der Marxismus, seine Geschichte in Dokumenten Vol. I 1962, Vol. II 1964, Vol. III 1965, 4th edn in one vol. 1983, Marx-Engels Studienausgabe (4 vols) 1966, Introduction to Hobbes' Leviathan 1966, Karl Marx und der Marxismus 1967, Der Rechtsradikalismus 1967, Der Sozialismus 1968, Der Kommunismus 1969, Hegel: Grösse und Grenzen 1971, Modelle der Friedenssicherung 1972, Wer hat Dornröschen wachgeküsst?—das Märchenverwirrbuch 1972, 1974, Marxistische Porträts Vol. I 1975, Herrschaft und Emanzipation 1976, Terrorismus und Reaktion 1981, Analysen zum Terrorismus, Ideologien und Strategien 1981, Vom Wohlfahrtsstaat zur neuen Lebensqualität, die Herausforderungen des demokratischen Sozialismus 1982, Der Nulltarif der Wichtelmänner, Märchen- und andere Verwirrspiele 1982, Arbeit und Spiel (essays) 1983, Handbuch der politischen Ideen (co-ed. with H. Münkler), Vols 1, 3, 4, 5 1985–93, Überlebensbedingungen der Menschheit zur Dialektik des Fortschritts 1986 (enlarged edn) 1991, Die Wirksamkeit der Träume, literarische Skizzen eines Sozialwissenschaftlers 1987, Utopien, Illusionen, Hoffnungen-Plädoyer für eine politische Kultur in Deutschland 1990, Toleranz—von der Unentbehrlichkeit einer kleinen Tugend für die Demokratie 1990, Neugier und Furcht: Versuch, mein Leben (autobiog.) 1995, Joseph Goebbels im Berliner Sportpalast: 'Wollt ihr den totalen Krieg?' 1988, Marx 1999, Bertolt Brecht: Die Dreigroschenoper—Dreigroschenroman Kommentar 2001. *Leisure interests:* collecting autographed letters and manuscripts and first edns of philosophers and writers. *Address:* J. W. Goethe Universität, PO Box 111932, 60054 Frankfurt-am-Main, Germany (office). *Telephone:* (69) 79822300 (office); (69) 521542 (home). *Fax:* (69) 7988383 (office); (69) 510034 (home). *E-mail:* iefetscher@jahoo.de (home). *Website:* www.iringfetscher.de (home).

FETTER, Trevor, BEcons, MBA; American healthcare industry executive; *President and CEO, Tenet Healthcare Corporation;* b. 1960; ed Stanford Univ., Harvard Business School; Investment Banker, Merrill Lynch Capital Markets –1988; Exec. Vice-Pres. and Chief Financial Officer Metro-Goldwyn-Mayer Inc. 1988–95; joined Tenet Healthcare Corpn 1995, Exec. Vice-Pres. and later Chief Financial Officer –2000, Pres. 2002–, CEO 2003–, mem. Bd of Dirs; Chair. Broadlane Inc. 2000–, also CEO 2000–02; Dir Fed. of American Hosps; fmr Dir Catalina Island Conservancy, Santa Barbara Zoological Gardens, Neighborhood Youth Asscn. *Address:* Tenet Dallas, 13737 Noel Road, Dallas,

TX 75240, USA (office). *Telephone:* (469) 893-2200 (office). *Fax:* (469) 893-1321 (office). *Website:* www.tenethealth.com (office).

FETTIG, Jeff M., BA, MBA; American business executive; *Chairman and CEO, Whirlpool Corporation;* b. 1957, Tipton, Ind.; ed Indiana Univ.; began career as Operations Assoc., Whirlpool Corpn 1981, various man. positions in sales, planning, operations and product devt 1981–89, Vice-Pres. Marketing, KitchenAid Appliance Group 1989–90, Vice-Pres., Marketing, Philips Whirlpool Appliance Group, Whirlpool Europe BV 1990–92, Vice-Pres., Group Marketing and Sales, N American Appliance Group 1992–94, Exec. Vice-Pres. Whirlpool Corpn and Pres. Whirlpool Europe and Asia 1994–99, apptd Dir Whirlpool Corpn 1999, Pres. and COO 1999–2004, Chair., Pres. and CEO 2004–06, Chair. and CEO 2006–; mem. Bd Dirs Dow Chemical Co.; mem. Dean's Advisory Council, Ind. Univ. Kelley School of Business; Trustee, Midwest Region, Boys and Girls Club of America. *Address:* Whirlpool Corporation, 2000 North M-63, Benton Harbor, MI 49022-2692, USA (office). *Telephone:* (269) 923-5000 (office). *Fax:* (269) 923-5443 (office). *E-mail:* info@ whirlpoolcorp.com (office). *Website:* www.whirlpoolcorp.com (office).

FETTING, Rainer; German painter and sculptor; b. 31 Dec. 1949, Wilhelmshaven; ed Hochschule der Künste, Berlin, with Prof. Jänisch; Co-founder Galerie am Moritzplatz with Helmut Middendorf, Salome, Bernd Zimmer, Anne Jud and Berthold Schepers, Luciano Castelli 1977; lived in New York and Berlin 1983–94, lives and works in Berlin 2006–; DAAD scholarship, Columbia Univ. New York 1978. *Works include:* Willy Brandt sculpture for Willy-Brandt-Haus, Berlin 1996. *Address:* Hasenheide 61/1, 10967 Berlin, Germany. *Telephone:* (30) 690-42-275. *Fax:* (30) 694-19-83. *E-mail:* privat@fetting.de.

FETTWEIS, Alfred Leo Maria, DèsSc Appl., FIEEE; German communications engineer and academic; *Professor Emeritus, University of Bochum;* b. 27 Nov. 1926, Eupen, Belgium; s. of Paul Fettweis and Helene Fettweis (née Hermanns); m. Lois J. Piaskowski 1957; two s. three d.; ed Catholic Univ. of Louvain, Belgium, Columbia Univ., Polytechnic Inst. of Brooklyn, NY, USA; Devt Engineer with Int. Telephone and Telegraph Corpn (ITT), Belgium 1951–54, 1956–63 and USA 1954–56; Prof. of Theoretical Electricity, Eindhoven Univ. of Tech. 1963–67; Prof. of Communications Eng Ruhr-Univ. Bochum 1967–92, Prof. Emer. 1992–; Visiting Distinguished Prof., Univ. of Notre Dame 1994–96; Vice-Pres. IEEE Circuits and Systems Soc., Region 8 1987–; mem. Rheinisch-Westfälische Akad. der Wissenschaften, Academia Europaea, Academia Scientiarum et Artium Europaea; invention and comprehensive theory of the wave-digital method for filtering and numerical integration; fundamental issues in physics; Dr hc (Linköping) 1986, (Mons) 1988, (Leuven) 1988, (Budapest) 1995, (Poznań) 2004; Prix Acta Technica Belgica 1963, Darlington Prize Paper Award 1980, Prix George Montefiore 1981, Verband der Elektrotechnik (VDE) Ehrenring 1984, IEEE Centennial Medal 1984, Tech. Achievement Award, IEEE Circuits and Systems Soc. (CASS) 1988, Karl-Küpfmüller-Preis of Informationstechnische Gesellschaft 1988, Basic Research Award of Eduard Rhein Foundation 1993, Peter-Johns Prize, International Journal of Numerical Modelling 1993, CASS Golden Jubilee Medal 1999, CASS Millennium Medal 2000, Van Valkenburg Award 2001, (first) CASS Belevitch Award 2003. *Publications:* two books, many tech. papers on circuits, systems, telecommunications, digital signal processing, relativity theory, numerical integration and related areas; about 30 patents. *Leisure interests:* hiking, music. *Address:* Lehrstuhl für Nachrichtentechnik, Ruhr-Universität Bochum, Universitätsstrasse 150, 44780 Bochum (office); Im Königsbusch 18, 44797 Bochum, Germany (home). *Telephone:* (234) 322-2497 (office); (234) 322-3063 (office); (234) 797922 (home). *Fax:* (234) 321-4100 (office). *E-mail:* fettweis@nt.rub.de (office); fettweis@nt.ruhr-uni-bochum.de (office). *Website:* www.nt.ruhr-uni-bochum .de (office).

FETTWEIS, Günter Bernhard Leo, DrIng; Austrian/German mining engineer and academic; *Professor Emeritus, Montanuniversität Leoben;* b. 17 Nov. 1924, Düsseldorf, Germany; s. of Ewald I. Fettweis and Aninhas M. (née Leuschner-Fernandes) Fettweis; m. Alice Y. Fettweis 1949; one s. three d.; ed Univ. of Freiburg and Tech. Univ. of Aachen; Scientific Asst Tech. Univ. of Aachen 1950–52; Jr Mining Inspector Nordrhein-Westfalen 1953–54; Ruhr coal-mining industry, then Production Man. of the Osterfeld, Sterkrade and Hugo Haniel coal mines, B.A.G. Neue Hoffnung, Oberhausen/Ruhr 1955–59; Prof. and Head Dept of Mining Eng and Mineral Econs, Montan Univ. Leoben 1959–93 (now Prof. Emer.), Rector (Vice-Chair.) 1968–70; Vice-Pres., later Pres. Mining Soc. of Austria 1963–93; Vice-Pres. Austrian Soc. of Rock Mechanics 1968–81, Int. Organizing Cttee World Mining Congress 1976–2001; mem. Supervising Bd ÖBAG (Austrian State Mining Industry) 1988–95; Chair. Bd Inst. for Research about Mineral Resources 1983–87; Corresp. mem. Austrian Acad. of Sciences 1977, mem. 1983; Foreign mem. Polish Acad. of Sciences 1991, European Acad. of Sciences, Salzburg 1990, Paris 1996, Russian Acad. of Natural Sciences 1997, Mining Sciences 1998; Hon. mem. Hungarian Acad. of Sciences 1990; Dr hc (Aachen), (Miskolc, Hungary), (Petrosani, Romania), (Moscow); Dr hc mit Laureate Assessor des Bergfachs; Austrian State Award of Energy Research; nat. and int. medals (Austria, Germany, Poland, The Vatican). *Publications:* World Coal Resources, Methods of Assessment and Results 1976–79, Atlas of Mining Methods (three vols, co-author) 1963–66, Mining in the Process of Change (ed.) 1988, Bergwirtschaft (mineral econs; co-author) 1990, Deponietechnik und Entsorgungsbergbau (waste disposal) (ed.) and about 250 other publs. *Leisure interests:* history, philosophy, cosmology, Africa, sailing. *Address:* Institut für Bergbaukunde, Borgtechnik und Bergwirtschaft der Montanuniversität Leoben, Franz-Josef-Strasse 18, A-8700 Leoben (office); Gasteigergasse 5, A-8700 Leoben, Austria (home). *Telephone:* (3842) 402/538 (office);

(3842) 21190 (home). *Fax:* (3842) 402/530 (office); (3842) 21190 (home). *E-mail:* fettweis@unileoben.ac.at (office).

FEULNER, Edwin J., PhD, MBA; American research institute administrator; *President, Heritage Foundation;* m. Linda Claire Leventhal; one s. one d.; ed Regis Univ., Georgetown Univ., Univ. of Edinburgh, LSE; Pres. The Heritage Foundation; Treasurer and Trustee, Mont Pelerin Soc. (also fmr Pres.); Trustee and fmr Chair. Intercollegiate Studies Inst.; Dir Nat. Chamber Foundation; adviser to several US govt depts and agencies; fmr Consultant for Domestic Policy to US Pres. Ronald Reagan; US Rep. to UN Special Session on Disarmament 1982; mem. numerous govt comms including Carlucci Comm. on Foreign Aid 1983, Pres.'s Comm. on White House Fellows 1981–83, Meltzer Comm. 1999–2000; mem. Bd of Visitors George Mason Univ.; Trustee Acton Inst., Int. Republican Inst.; fmr Pres. Philadelphia Soc.; fmr Dir Sequoia Bank, Regis Univ., Council for Nat. Policy; regular contrib. to several publs including Chicago Sun Times, Chicago Tribune, New York Times, Washington Post; Dr hc (Nichols Coll.) 1981, (Univ. Francisco Marroquin, Guatemala) 1982, (Bellevue Coll.) 1987, (Gonzaga Univ.) 1992, (Grove City Coll.) 1994, (Pepperdine Univ.) 2000, (St Norbert Coll.) 2002, (Hillsdale Coll.) 2004, (Thomas More Univ.) 2005, (Edin.) 2006, (Hanyang Univ., Korea); Presidential Citizen's Medal 1989. *Publications:* US–Japan Mutual Security: The Next Twenty Years (Ed.), China: The Turning Point (ed.), Looking Back 1981, Conservatives Stalk the House 1983, The March of Freedom 1998, Intellectual Pilgrims 1999, Leadership for America 2000, Getting America Right 2006. *Address:* The Heritage Foundation, 214 Massachusetts Avenue, NE, Washington, DC 20002, USA (office). *Telephone:* (202) 546-4400 (office). *Fax:* (202) 544-0904 (office). *E-mail:* president@heritage.org (office). *Website:* www .heritage.org (office).

FEYDER, Jean, DJur; Luxembourg diplomatist; *Director of Co-operation and Humanitarian Action, Ministry of Foreign Affairs;* b. 24 Nov. 1947; m.; two c.; joined Ministry of Foreign Affairs 1974, Head, UN Dept 1974–76, Deputy Perm. Rep. to UN, New York July–Dec. 1975, currently Dir Co-operation and Humanitarian Action (with title of Amb.); assigned to Luxembourg mission to EC, Brussels (with responsibility for accession negotiations) 1977; Deputy Perm. Rep. to EEC 1983; Perm. Rep. to UN, New York 1987–93; mem. Bd Dirs ATTF (Financial Technology Tech. Agency). *Address:* Direction de la Coopération et de l'Aide Humanitaire, 6 rue de la Congregation, 1352 Luxembourg, Luxembourg.

FFOWCS WILLIAMS, John Eirwyn, MA, PhD, ScD (Cantab.), CEng, FREng, FRAeS, FInstP, FIMA, FRSA; British professor of engineering; b. 25 May 1935; m. Anne Beatrice Mason 1959; two s. one d.; ed Derby Tech. Coll., Univ. of Southampton; eng apprentice, Rolls-Royce Ltd 1951–55; Spitfire Mitchell Memorial Scholar to Southampton Univ. 1955–60 (Pres. Students' Union 1957–58); joined Aerodynamics Div., Nat. Physical Lab. (NPL) 1960–62; with Bolt, Beranek & Newman, Inc. 1962–64; Reader in Applied Mathematics, Imperial Coll. of Science and Tech. 1964–69, Rolls-Royce Prof. of Theoretical Acoustics 1969–72; Rank Prof. of Eng, Cambridge Univ. 1972–2002; Master Emmanuel Coll., Cambridge 1996–2002 (Professorial Fellow 1972–96; Life Fellow 2002); Chair. Concorde Noise Panel 1965–75, Noise Research Cttee Airport Regions Conf. (ARC) 1969–76, Topexpress Ltd 1979–89; Dir VSEL Consortium PLC 1987–95; Foreign Assoc. Nat. Acad. of Eng (NAE) (USA) 1995; Fellow AIAA, Inst. of Acoustics, Acoustical Soc. of America; Hon. Prof. Beijing Inst. of Aeronautics and Astronautics 1992–; Foreign Hon. mem. American Acad. of Arts and Sciences 1989; Aero-Acoustics Medal, AIAA 1977, Rayleigh Medal, Inst. of Acoustics 1984, Silver Medal, Soc. Française d'Acoustique 1989, Gold Medal, RAeS 1990, Per Bruel Gold Medal, ASME 1997, Sir Frank Whittle Medal, Royal Acad. of Eng. 2002. *Publications:* Sound and Sources of Sound 1983 (with A. P. Dowling), numerous articles in professional journals; film on Aerodynamic Sound (jtly). *Leisure interests:* friends and cigars. *Address:* c/o Emmanuel College, Cambridge, CB2 3AP, England.

FFRENCH-DAVIS MUÑOZ, Ricardo, PhD; Chilean economist; *Principal Regional Adviser, Economic Commission for Latin America and the Caribbean;* b. 27 June 1936, Santiago; m. Marcela Yampaglia 1966; ed Catholic Univ. of Chile, Univ. of Chicago; Researcher and Prof. of Econs, Econ. Research Cen., Catholic Univ. 1962–64; Prof. of Econs, Univ. of Chile 1962–73, 1984–; Deputy Man. Research Dept, Cen. Bank of Chile 1964–70; Research Dir Cen. on Planning Studies, Catholic Univ. 1970–75; Vice-Pres. and Dir Centre for Latin American Econ. Research (CIEPLAN), Santiago 1976–90; Research Dir Cen. Bank of Chile 1990; mem. Acad. Council, Latin American Program, The Woodrow Wilson Center, Washington, DC 1977–80; mem. UN Cttee on Econ. Planning 1990–92; mem. Exec. Cttee Latin American Studies Asscn 1992–94; Visiting Fellow, Univ. of Oxford 1974, 1979; Visiting Prof., Boston Univ. 1976; Pres. Acad. Circle, Acad. de Humanismo Cristiano, Chile 1978–81; Co-ordinator Working Group on Econ. Issues of Inter-American Dialogue 1985–86; Prin. Regional Adviser, Econ. Comm. for Latin America and the Caribbean (ECLAC) 2000–; mem. Editorial Bds Latin American Research Review, El Trimestre Economico and Colección Estudios Cieplan; Ford Foundation Grants 1971, 1975, 2001, Social Science Research Council Grant 1976, Inter-American Dialogue Grant 1985–86. *Publications:* Políticas Económicas en Chile: 1952–70 1973, El cobre en el desarrollo nacional (co-ed.) 1974, Economía internacional: teorías y políticas para el desarrollo 1979, 1985, Latin America and a New International Economic Order (co-ed.) 1981, 1985, The Monetarist Experiment in Chile 1982, Relaciones financieras externas y la economía latinoamericana (ed.) 1983, Development and External Debt in Latin America (co-ed.) 1988, Debt-equity swaps in Chile 1990, Latin America and the Caribbean: Policies to Improve Linkages with the World Economy (ed.) 1998, Macroeconomics, Trade and Finance 2000, Financial Crisis in 'Successful' Emerging Economies (ed.) 2001, Economic Reforms in

Chile: From Dictatorship to Democracy 2002; over 100 articles on int. econs, Latin-American econ. devt and Chilean econ. policies in 8 languages. *Address:* Economic Commission for Latin America and the Caribbean, Santiago, Chile (office); Casilla 179-D, Santiago, Chile (home). *Telephone:* (562) 210-2555 (office). *Fax:* (562) 208-1801 (office). *E-mail:* ricardo.ffrenchdavis@cepal.org (office). *Website:* www.eclac.cl (office).

FICEAC, Bogdan; Romanian editor and newspaper executive; *Editor-in-Chief, România Liberă (Free Romania);* fmr Deputy Ed.-in-Chief, România Liberă (Free Romania), Bucharest, currently Ed.-in-Chief; Reuters Foundation Fellow, John S. Knight Fellowship, Stanford Univ. *Publications include:* Cenzura comunista 1999, Tehnici de manipulare 2004. *Address:* România Liberă, Piaţa Presei Libere 1, Corp. c, etaj 4, 013701 Bucharest, Romania (office). *Telephone:* (21) 2224770 (office). *Fax:* (21) 2232071 (office). *E-mail:* redactia@romanialibera.ro (office). *Website:* www.romanialibera.ro (office).

FICO, Robert, DIur; Slovak politician and lawyer; *Prime Minister;* b. 15 Sept. 1964, Topoľčany; m.; one c.; ed Comenius Univ., Bratislava; mem. staff Inst. of Laws, Ministry of Justice 1986–91; mem. Parl. 1992–; Head of Slovak del. to Parl. Meeting of European Council, Rep. to European Cttee for Human Rights and European Court for Human Rights 1994–2000; mem. Party of Democratic Left—SDL 1994–99, Vice-Chair. 1998–99; Founder and Chair. Direction Party—Smĕr 1999– (absorbed Party of Civic Understanding 2003, Social Democratic Alternative, Social Democratic Party of Slovakia and Party of Democratic Left 2004, renamed Direction-Social Democracy 2004), Pres. Parl. Mems Club 2002–; Observer on behalf of European Socialists' faction at European Parl. 2002–04; Prime Minister of Slovakia 2006–. *Publication:* Trest smrti (Punishment of Death). *Leisure interest:* sport. *Address:* Office of the Government, nám. Slobody 1, 813 70 Bratislava, Slovakia (office). *Telephone:* (2) 5729-5111 (office). *Fax:* (2) 5249-7595 (office). *E-mail:* urad@vlada.gov.sk (office). *Website:* www.vlada.gov.sk (office); www.strana-smer.sk (office).

FIDALGO, José María; Spanish trade union official and orthopaedic surgeon; *General Secretary, Confederación Sindical de Comisiones Obreras (CCOO)*b. 18 Feb. 1948, León; orthopaedic surgeon, Hosp. La Paz, Madrid; mem. trade union movt 1974–; mem. Confederación Sindical de Comisiones Obreras (CCOO) 1977–, Sec. of Institutional Policy 1987–2000, Gen. Sec. 2000–; Gen. Sec. Fed. of Health Workers 1981–87. *Address:* Confederación Sindical de Comisiones Obreras (CCOO), Fernández de la Hoz 12, 28010 Madrid, Spain (office). *Telephone:* (91) 7028011 (office). *Fax:* (91) 3104804 (office). *E-mail:* aida@ccoo.es (office). *Website:* www.ccoo.es (office).

FIELD, Helen; British singer (soprano); b. 14 May 1951, Wrexham, Clwyd, Wales; ed Royal Northern Coll. of Music, Manchester and Royal Coll. of Music, London, studied FRG; won triennial Young Welsh Singers' Competition 1976; roles with Welsh Nat. Opera include Musetta, Poppea, Kristina, Gilda, Marzelline, Mimi, Tatyana, Jenůfa, the Vixen, Marenka and Desdemona; has also appeared with Opera North and Scottish Opera; debut at Royal Opera House, Covent Garden as Emma in Khovanschina 1982; debut with ENO, as Gilda 1982, at Metropolitan Opera, New York, as Gilda; has also appeared with Netherlands, Cologne and Brussels opera cos; concert performances with several leading orchestras and regular radio and TV appearances; recordings include Rigoletto, A Village Romeo and Juliet and Osud. *Address:* Robert Gilder and Co., 91 Great Russell Street, London, WC2B 3PS, England (office). *Telephone:* (20) 7580-7758 (office). *Fax:* (20) 7580-7739 (office). *E-mail:* rgilder@robert-gilder.com (office). *Website:* www.robertgilder.com (office); www.helenfield.com.

FIELD, Sir Malcolm David, Kt; British business executive; *Chairman, Aricom PLC;* b. 25 Aug. 1937, London; m. (divorced 1982); one d.; m. 2nd Rosemary Anne Charlton 2001; ed Highgate School and London Business School; joined W.H. Smith 1963, Wholesale Dir 1970–78, Man. Dir Retail Group 1978–82, Man. Dir 1982–93; Group Chief Exec. 1994–96; Chair. Civil Aviation Authority (CAA) 1996–2001; Policy Adviser to Dept of Transport, London and the Regions 2000–; mem. Bd of Man. Navy, Army and Air Force Insts (NAAFI) 1973–93, Chair. 1986–93; mem. Bd of Dirs (non-exec.) Marine Environment Protection Cttee (MEPC) 1989–99, Scottish & Newcastle PLC 1993–98, Phoenix Group 1994–97, The Stationery Office 1996–2001, Walker Greenbank PLC 1997–2001, Sofa Workshop Ltd 1998–2002, Beeson Gregory 2000–04, Odgers 2002–; Chair. (non-exec.) Tubelines Ltd 2003–06; Chair. Aricom PLC 2004–; Sr non-exec. Dir Hochschild Mining 2006–. *Leisure interests:* watching cricket, tennis, ballet, modern art, reading biographies, recreating garden in Devon. *Address:* 21 Embankment Gardens, London, SW3 4LW, England (office). *Telephone:* (20) 7351-7455 (office); (7740) 433744 (home). *Fax:* (20) 7351-7452 (office). *E-mail:* mdfield@netcomuk.co.uk (office).

FIELDHOUSE, David Kenneth, MA, DLitt, FBA; British academic; *Emeritus Vere Harmsworth Professor of Imperial and Naval History, University of Cambridge;* b. 7 June 1925, India; s. of Rev. E. Fieldhouse and C. H. B. Fieldhouse (née Corke); m. Sheila Elizabeth Lyon 1952; one s. two d.; ed Dean Close School, Cheltenham, Queen's Coll. Oxford; war service as Sub. Lt, RNVR 1943–47; Sr History Master, Haileybury Coll. 1950–52; Lecturer in History, Canterbury Univ., NZ 1953–57; Beit Lecturer in Commonwealth History, Univ. of Oxford 1958–81; Vere Harmsworth Prof. of Imperial and Naval History, Univ. of Cambridge 1981–92, now Prof. Emer.; Fellow, Nuffield Coll. Oxford 1966–81, Jesus Coll. Cambridge 1981–92, Emer. 1992–. *Publications:* The Colonial Empires 1966, The Theory of Capitalist Imperialism 1967, Economics and Empire 1830–1914 1973, Unilever Overseas 1978, Black Africa 1945–1980 1986, Merchant Capital and Economic Decolonization 1994, The West and the Third World 1999, Kurds, Arabs and Britons 2001, Western Imperialism in the Middle East 1914–1958 2006. *Leisure interests:* golf, sailing, music. *Address:* Jesus College, Cambridge, CB5 8BL, England (office). *Telephone:* (1223) 339339 (office); (1223) 234425 (home). *E-mail:* dkf1000@cam.ac.uk (home).

FIELDING, Sir Leslie, Kt, KCMG, LLD, FRSA, FRGS; British fmr university vice-chancellor and diplomatist; b. 29 July 1932, London; s. of Percy Archer Fielding and Margaret Calder Horry; m. Sally Harvey 1978; one s. one d.; ed Emmanuel Coll., Cambridge, School of Oriental and African Studies, London, St Antony's Coll., Oxford; with HM Diplomatic Service (served Tehran, Singapore, Phnom Penh, Paris and London) 1956–73; Dir External Relations Directorate-Gen., European Comm., Brussels 1973–77; Visiting Fellow, St Antony's Coll., Oxford 1977–78; Head European Community Del., Tokyo 1978–82; Dir-Gen. for External Relations, Brussels 1982–87; Vice-Chancellor Univ. of Sussex 1987–92; mem. Japan–EC Asscn 1988–98, UK–Japan 2000 Group 1993–2000; mem. House of Laity of Gen. Synod of Church of England 1990–92; Hon. Pres. Univ. Asscn for Contemporary European Studies 1990–2000, Hon. Fellow, Emmanuel Coll. Cambridge 1990–, Hon. Fellow Sussex European Inst. 1993; Grand Officer's Star of Order of St Agatha of San Marino 1987, White Rose of Finland 1988, Silver Order of Merit (Austria) 1989. *Publications:* Travellers' Tales (contrib.)1999, More Tales from the Travellers' (contrib.) 2005, Before the Killing Fields: Witness to Cambodia and the Vietnam War 2008, Kindly Call Me God: The Misadventures of 'Fielding of the FO', Eurocrat Extraordinaire and Vice-Chancellor Semipotentiary 2009. *Leisure interests:* country life, theology. *Address:* Wild Cherry Farm, Elton, nr Ludlow, Shropshire, SY8 2HQ, England (home). *E-mail:* FieldingLeslie@aol.com (home).

FIELDS, Janice (Jan) L.; American business executive; *Executive Vice-President and Chief Operating Officer, McDonald's USA;* m. Doug Fields; two c.; joined McDonald's as restaurant crew mem. 1978, worked in all facets of restaurant business, apptd Regional Vice-Pres. Pittsburgh Region 1994, Pres. Cen. Div., McDonald's USA –2006, Exec. Vice-Pres. and COO McDonald's USA 2006–, Exec. Sponsor for Career Devt Program; mem. Bd Chicago Urban League, United Cerebral Palsy; mem. Advisory Bd Catalyst (women's org.); McDonald's Pres.'s Award 1988, McDonald's Golden Arch Partners Award 1988, McDonald's Women Operators Network Recognition Award 2001, McDonald's Women's Leadership Award 2002, ranked by Fortune magazine amongst 50 Most Powerful Women in Business (48th) 2007, ranked by Forbes magazine amongst 100 Most Powerful Women (67th) 2008. *Address:* McDonald's Corporation, 2111 McDonald's Drive, Oak Brook, IL 60523, USA (office). *Telephone:* (630) 623-3000 (office). *Fax:* (630) 623-5004 (office). *E-mail:* info@mcdonalds.com (office). *Website:* www.mcdonalds.com (office).

FIELDSEND, Sir John Charles Rowell, Kt, KBE, BA, LLB; British judge and barrister; b. 13 Sept. 1921, Lincoln; s. of Charles Fieldsend and Phyllis Fieldsend; m. Muriel Gedling 1945; one s. one d.; ed Michaelhouse, Natal, Rhodes Univ. Coll., Grahamstown, SA; served Royal Artillery 1943–45; called to the Bar, Southern Rhodesia 1947, QC 1959; advocate in pvt. practice 1947–63; Pres. Special Income Tax Court for Fed. of Rhodesia and Nyasaland 1958–63; High Court Judge, Southern Rhodesia 1963–68 (resgnd); Asst Solicitor, Law Comm. for England and Wales 1968–78; Sec. Law Comm. 1978–80; Chief Justice of Zimbabwe 1980–83; Chief Justice, Turks and Caicos Islands 1985–87; Pres., Court of Appeal, St Helena 1985–93; Judge, Court of Appeal, Falkland Islands and British Antarctic Territory 1985–96, Court of Appeal, Gibraltar 1985–97 (Pres. 1990); Prin. Legal Adviser, British Indian Ocean Territory 1984–87, Chief Justice 1987–98. *Leisure interest:* travel. *Address:* Great Dewes, Ardingly, Sussex, RH17 6UP, England (office).

FIENNES, Joseph Alberic; British actor; b. 27 May 1970, Salisbury; s. of Mark Fiennes and the late Jini Lash; brother of Ralph Fiennes (q.v.), Martha, Magnus, Sophie and Jacob Fiennes; ed Guildhall School of Music and Drama. *Theatre includes:* The Woman in Black, A Month in the Country, A View from the Bridge, Real Classy Affair, Edward II, Love's Labours Lost, Epitaph for George Dillon (Comedy Theatre, London) 2005–06. *RSC performances include:* Son of Man, Les Enfants Du Paradis, As You Like It, Troilus and Cressida, The Herbal Bed. *Television includes:* The Vacillations of Poppy Carew 1995, Animated Epics: Beowulf (voice) 1998. *Radio:* Romeo and Juliet, Keith Douglas Poems. *Films include:* Stealing Beauty 1996, Shakespeare in Love 1998, Martha – Meet Frank, Daniel and Laurence 1998, Elizabeth 1998, Forever Mine 1999, Rancid Aluminium 2000, Enemy at the Gates 2001, Killing Me Softly 2001, Dust 2001, Leo 2002, Sinbad: Legend of the Seven Seas 2003, Luther 2003, Merchant of Venice 2004, Man to Man 2005, The Great Raid 2005, The Darwin Awards 2006, Running with Scissors 2006, Goodbye Bafana 2007, The Escapist 2007. *Address:* c/o Ken McReddie, 2 Barrett Street, London, W1U 1BD, England (office). *Telephone:* (20) 7499-7448 (office).

FIENNES, Ralph Nathanial; British actor; b. 22 Dec. 1962; s. of Mark Fiennes and the late Jini Lash; brother of Joseph Fiennes (q.v.); ed St Kieran's Coll., Kilkenny, Ireland, Bishop Wordsworth's School, Salisbury, Chelsea School of Art, Royal Acad. of Dramatic Art, London. *Plays include:* Open Air Theatre, Regent's Park: Twelfth Night, Ring Round the Moon 1985, A Midsummer's Night Dream 1985, 1986, Romeo and Juliet 1986; Royal Nat. Theatre: Six Characters in Search of an Author, Fathers and Sons, Ting Tang Mine 1987; RSC: King John, Much Ado About Nothing, title role of Henry VI in The Plantagenets 1988, Playing with Trains 1989, Troilus and Cressida, King Lear 1990, The Man Who Came to Dinner, Love's Labours Lost 1991; Almeida Theatre: Hamlet 1995, Ivanov 1997, Richard II 2000, Coriolanus 2000, Brand 2003, Oedipus 2008. *TV appearances include:* A Dangerous Man: Lawrence after Arabia 1990, Prime Suspect 1991, The Cormorant 1993, The Great War and the Shaping of the 20th Century (voice) 1996, How Proust Can Change Your Life 2000, The Miracle Maker (voice) 2000. *Films include:* Wuthering Heights 1992, The Baby of Macon 1993, Schindler's List 1993, Quiz Show 1994, Strange Days 1995, The English Patient 1996, Oscar and Lucinda 1997, The Avengers 1998, The Prince of Egypt (voice) 1998, Onegin (also exec.

producer) 1999, Sunshine 1999, The End of the Affair 1999, Spider 2002, The Good Thief 2002, Red Dragon 2002, Maid in Manhattan 2002, The Chumscrubber 2005, Chromophobia 2005, Harry Potter and the Goblet of Fire 2005, The Constant Gardener 2005, The White Countess 2005, Wallace & Gromit in the Curse of the Were-Rabbit (voice) 2005, Land of the Blind 2006, Harry Potter and the Order of the Phoenix 2007, Bernard and Doris 2007, In Bruges 2008, The Duchess 2008. *Leisure interests:* swimming, reading, music. *Address:* c/o Dalzell Beresford Associates, 26 Astwood Mews, London, SW7 4DE, England (office). *Telephone:* (20) 7341-9411 (office). *Fax:* (20) 7341-9412 (office). *E-mail:* mail@dalzellandberesford.co.uk (office).

FIENNES, Sir Ranulph Twisleton-Wykeham-, 3rd Bt, cr. 1916, OBE, DLitt; British travel writer, lecturer and explorer; b. 7 March 1944, Windsor; s. of Lt-Col Sir Ranulph Twisleton-Wykeham-Fiennes, DSO, 2nd Bt and Audrey Newson; m. 1st Virginia Pepper 1970 (died 2004); m. 2nd Louise Millington 2005; one d.; ed Eton; Lt Royal Scots Greys 1966, Capt. 1968, retd 1970; attached 22 SAS Regt 1966, Sultan of Muscat's Armed Forces 1968; Leader, British Expeditions to White Nile 1969, Jostedalsbre Glacier 1970, Headless Valley, BC 1971, (Towards) North Pole 1977; Leader, Transglobe Expedition (first polar circumnavigation of world on its polar axis) 1979–82; led first unsupported crossing of Antarctic continent and longest unsupported polar journey in history Nov. 1992–Feb. 1993; first man to reach both poles on land; discovered lost city of Ubar in Oman 1993; ran seven marathons on seven continents in seven days 2003; climbed north face of Mount Eiger 2007; Exec. Consultant to Chair. of Occidental Petroleum Corpn 1984–90; Hon. mem. Royal Inst. of Navigation; Hon. DSc (Loughborough Coll.) 1986; Hon. DUniv (Univ. of Cen. England in Birmingham) 1995, (Univ. of Portsmouth) 2000, (Sheffield) 2005, (Univ. of Abertay, Dundee) 2007; Hon. DLitt (Glasgow Caledonian) 2002; Dhofar Campaign Medal 1969, Sultan's Bravery Medal 1970, Livingstone Medal, Royal Scottish Geographical Soc., Royal Inst. of Navigation 1977, Gold Medal of Explorers Club of NY 1983, Founders Medal Royal Geographical Soc. 1984, Polar Medal for Arctic and Antarctic, with Bars 1985, with clasp 1995, ITN Award for Int. Exploit of the Decade 1989, Explorers Club Millennium Award for Polar Exploration 2000, ITV1 Greatest Briton – Sportsman of the Year 2007. *Achievements include:* has raised £13.5 million for various charities. *Publications:* A Talent for Trouble 1970, Ice Fall in Norway 1972, The Headless Valley 1973, Where Soldiers Fear to Tread 1975, Hell on Ice 1979, To the Ends of the Earth 1983, Bothie – The Polar Dog (with Virginia Twisleton-Wykeham-Fiennes) 1984, Living Dangerously 1987, The Feather Men 1991, Atlantis of the Sands 1992, Mind over Matter 1993, The Sett 1996, Fit for Life 1998, Beyond the Limits 2000, The Secret Hunters 2001, Captain Scott 2003, Mad Bad and Dangerous to Know (autobiog.) 2007. *Leisure interests:* langlauf, photography. *Address:* Greenlands, Exford, Minehead, West Somerset, TA24 7NU, England. *Telephone:* (1643) 831350.

FIERSTEIN, Harvey Forbes; American actor and screenwriter; b. 6 June 1954, Brooklyn, New York; s. of Irving Fierstein and Jacqueline Harriet Gilbert; ed Pratt Univ.; began acting career as founding mem. The Gallery Players, Brooklyn; professional acting debut in Pork 1971; Fund for Human Dignity Award 1983, GLAAD Award for Visibility 1994, Humanitas Prize (in Children's Animation category) 2000; four Tony Awards, Best Actor (Play) and Author of Best Play for Torch Song Trilogy 1983, Book (Musical) Tony for writing the libretto of La Cage aux Folles 1984, Best Actor (Musical) Hairspray 2003; also three Drama Desk Awards, Drama League Award, New York Magazine Award, a special Obie, Theater World and LA Drama Critics Circle Award. *Films include:* Garbo Talks 1984, Torch Song Trilogy (also writer) 1988, The Harvest 1993, Mrs. Doubtfire 1993, Bullets Over Broadway 1994, Dr. Jekyll and Ms. Hyde 1995, White Lies 1996, Independence Day 1996, Everything Relative 1996, Kull the Conqueror 1997, Mulan (voice) 1998, Safe Men 1998, Jump 1999, Playing Mona Lisa 2000, Death to Smoochy 2002, Duplex 2003, Mulan II (voice) 2004, Farce of the Penguins (voice) 2007; narrator The Times of Harvey Milk. *TV appearances include:* The Demon Murder Case (voice) 1983, Apology 1986, Tidy Endings 1988, In the Shadow of Love: A Teen AIDS Story 1992, Daddy's Girls (series) 1994, Happily Ever After: Fairy Tales for Every Child (voice) 1995, Stories from My Childhood (series, voice) 1998, X-Chromosome (series, voice) 1999, Double Platinum 1999, The Sissy Duckling (also writer, voice) 1999, Common Ground (also writer) 2000. *Plays:* Fiddler on the Roof 2005, A Catered Affair (also co-author) 2007. *Leisure interests:* gay rights activist, painting, gardening, cooking. *Address:* c/o William Morris Agency, 1325 Avenue of the Americas, New York, NY 10019, USA.

FIGEĽ, Ján, MSc; Slovak politician and research scientist; *Commissioner for Education, Training, Culture and Multilingualism, European Commission;* b. 20 Jan. 1960, Vranov nad Topľou; m.; four c.; ed Košice Technical Univ., Georgetown Univ., USA, UFSIA, Antwerp, Belgium; Research and Devt Scientist, ZPA Prešov 1983–1992; mem. Parl. 1992–98, 2002–, mem. Foreign Affairs Cttee, Cttee for European Integration 1992–98, Chair. Foreign Affairs Cttee 2002–; mem. Party Presidium, Christian Democratic Movt 1992–98, Deputy Chair. for Foreign Policy 1994–98, 2000–; State Sec., Ministry of Foreign Affairs 1998–2002; Chief Negotiator for Slovakia's accession to EU 1998–2003; mem. Bd Slovak Democratic Coalition 1998–2000; Vice-Chair. European People's Party 1998; mem. Convention on the Future of Europe 2002–03; Head, Standing Del. of Observers of European Parl. 2003–; mem. European Parl. Cttee on Econ. Affairs and Devt 2003–, Vice-Chair. 2004–; EU Commr without Portfolio 2004, for Educ., Training, Culture and Multilingualism 2004–; mem. Cen. European Forum, Int. Cttee for Support of Democracy in Cuba; Pres. Pan-European Union Slovakia; mem. Bd Dirs Slovak Soc. for Foreign Policy, Anton Tunega Foundation, Foundation for the Support of Social Change; mem. Council Cen. European Inst. for Econ. and Social Reforms; Hon. Pres. Centre for European Policy, Kolping Work Slovakia. *Publications:* Slovakia on the Road to EU Membership (co-author) 2002. *Address:* European Commission, rue de la Loi 200, 1049 Brussels, Belgium (office). *Telephone:* (2) 298-87-16 (office). *Fax:* (2) 298-80-88 (office). *E-mail:* CAB-FIGEL@ec.europa.eu (office). *Website:* ec.europa.eu/commission_barroso/figel (office).

FIGES, Eva, BA; British writer; b. 15 April 1932, Berlin; d. of Emil Unger and Irma Unger; m. John Figes 1954 (divorced 1963); one s. one d.; ed Kingsbury Co. School, Queen Mary Coll., Univ. of London; Guardian Fiction Prize 1967. *Publications include:* Winter Journey 1967, Patriarchal Attitudes 1970, B 1972, Nelly's Version 1977, Little Eden 1978, Waking 1981, Sex and Subterfuge 1982, Light 1983, The Seven Ages 1986, Ghosts 1988, The Tree of Knowledge 1990, The Tenancy 1993, The Knot 1996, Tales of Innocence and Experience 2003, Light 2007, Journey to Nowhere 2008. *Leisure interests:* music, films, theatre, visual arts. *Address:* Rogers, Coleridge & White Ltd, 20 Powis Mews, London, W11 1JN, England (office). *Telephone:* (20) 7221-3717 (office). *Fax:* (20) 7229-9084 (office). *Website:* www.rcwlitagency.co.uk (office).

FIGES, Orlando, PhD; British historian, academic and writer; *Professor of History, Birkbeck College, London;* b. 20 Nov. 1959; s. of John Figes and Eva Figes (née Unger); m. Stephanie Palmer 1990; two d.; ed Gonville and Caius Coll., Cambridge, Trinity Coll., Cambridge; Fellow Trinity Coll., Cambridge 1984–89, Dir of Studies in History 1988–98, Lecturer in History, Univ. of Cambridge 1987–99; Prof. of History, Birkbeck Coll., Univ. of London 1999–. *Publications include:* Peasant Russia, Civil War: the Volga Countryside in Revolution 1917–21 1989, A People's Tragedy: the Russian Revolution 1891–1924 (Wolfson History Prize, WHSmith Literary Award, NCR Book Award, Los Angeles Times Book Prize) 1996, Interpreting the Russian Revolution (co-author) 1999, Natasha's Dance: a Cultural History of Russia 2002, The Whisperers: Private Life in Stalin's Russia 2007; numerous review articles and contribs to other published books. *Leisure interests:* football, wine, gardening. *Address:* School of History, Classics and Archaeology, Birkbeck College, Malet Street, London, WC1E 7HX, England (office). *Telephone:* (20) 7631-6299 (office). *Fax:* (20) 7631-6552 (office). *E-mail:* orlando.figes@ntlworld.com (office). *Website:* www.bbk.ac.uk/hca/staff/figes.shtml; www.bbk.ac.uk (office).

FIGGIS, Brian Norman, PhD, DSc, FAA; Australian chemist and academic; *Professor Emeritus of Inorganic Chemistry, University of Western Australia;* b. 27 March 1930, Sydney; s. of John N. E. Figgis and Dorice B. M. (née Hughes) Figgis; m. Jane S. Frank 1968; one s. one d.; ed Univs of Sydney and New South Wales; Research Fellow, then Lecturer, Univ. Coll., London, UK 1957–62; Reader, Univ. of Western Australia 1963–69, Prof. 1969, now Prof. Emer.; Visiting Prof., Univ. of Texas, USA 1961, Univ. of Arizona 1968, Univ. of Florence, Italy 1975, Univ. of Sussex, UK 1975; Visiting Scientist, Institut Laue-Langevin, France, Brookhaven Nat. Lab., Upton, NY, USA, Argonne Nat. Lab., Ill. 1984, 1991; Inorganic Award, Royal Australian Chemical Inst. 1985, Walter Burfitt Prize, Royal Soc. of NSW 1986, H.G. Smith Medal, Royal Australian Chemical Inst. 1989, Centenary Medal 2003. *Publications:* Introduction to Ligand Fields 1966, Ligand Field Theory and Its Applications 2000; Ed. Transition Metal Chemistry (Vols 8 and 9) 1984–85; 220 articles in scientific journals. *Leisure interest:* DIY. *Address:* 9 Hamersley Street, Cottesloe, WA 6011, Australia (home). *Telephone:* (8) 9384-3032 (home). *E-mail:* bnf@cyllene.uwa.edu.au.

FIGGIS, Mike; British film director, writer and musician; b. 28 Feb. 1949, Carlisle; studied music, performing in band Gas Board; musician in experimental theatre group The People Show in early 1970s; made ind. films including Redheugh, Slow Fade, Animals of the City; made film The House for Channel 4 (UK); Inst. of Film Professionals (IFP) Ind. Spirit Award 1996, Nat. Soc. of Film Critics Award. *Films include:* Stormy Monday (also screenplay and music) 1988, Internal Affairs (also music) 1990, Liebestraum (also screenplay and music) 1991, Mr. Jones 1993, The Browning Version 1994, Leaving Las Vegas (also screenplay and music) 1995, One Night Stand 1997, Flamenco Women 1997, Miss Julie 1999, The Loss of Sexual Innocence 1999, Time Code 2000, Hotel 2001, The Battle of Orgreave 2001, Cold Creek Manor 2003, Co/Ma 2004 (also writer). *Address:* c/o Robert Newman, The Endeavor Agency, 9601 Wilshire Blvd., 10th Floor, Beverly Hills, CA 90212, USA.

FIGO, Luis Filipe Madeira Caeiro; Portuguese professional footballer; b. 4 Nov. 1972, Lisbon; m. Helene Svedin; three d.; played for Sporting Lisbon 1990–96, Barcelona 1996–2000, Portugal nat. team 1991– (110 caps, currently taking break from int. football), signed by Real Madrid for then world record transfer fee 2000–05; with Inter Milan 2005–07, Al Ittihad, Saudi Arabia 2007–; Golden Ball for Best Player of the Year 2000, FIFA European Footballer of the Year 2000, FIFA World Player of the Year 2001. *Leisure interests:* the beach, rock music, spending time with friends. *Address:* c/o Al Ittihad, P.O.Box 5945, 21432 Jeddah, Saudi Arabia (office). *Telephone:* (1) 672-8888. *Fax:* (1) 672-0112. *E-mail:* alsanie-hamad@yahoo.com. *Website:* www.alittihadclub-sa.com/page.

FIGUERES OLSEN, José María, MPA; Costa Rican/Spanish international organization official, business executive and fmr politician; *CEO, Concordia 21;* b. 24 Dec. 1954, San José; s. of José Figueres Ferrer (fmr Pres. of Costa Rica); two c.; ed US Mil Acad., West Point NY, Kennedy School of Govt, Harvard Univ.; mem. Partido de Liberación Nacional (PLN); Minister of Agric. 1986–90; Pres. of Costa Rica 1994–98; Pres. Leadership for Environment and Devt (LEAD); Man. Dir World Econ. Forum 2000–03, Co-CEO 2003–04, CEO 2004; CEO Concordia 21, Madrid, Spain 2004–; Chair. Water Supply and Sanitation Collaborative Council 2004–; mem. Bd Global Fairness Initiative, BT Global Services Strategy & Marketing Advisory Bd, Abraaj Capital Advisory Bd, Grupo San Cristobal, Dubai Recycling Park, Talal Abu-Ghazaleh Org., Earth Council Geneva, DARA (non-profit org.), Fundación para las Relaciones Internacionales y el Diálogo Exterior (FRIDE); mem. Dean's

Alumni Council, Harvard Univ.; Bd Fellow, Thunderbird School of Man.; Int. Adviser, Global Environmental Action; Order of José Matías Delgado Grand Silver Cross (El Salvador) 1999; first recipient of Global Prize from World Bank's Global Environmental Fund 1988, Liberty Prize, Max Schmidheiny Foundation and St Gallen Univ. 1998, Award of the Climate Inst., Washington, DC 1998, Sustainability Award in Switzerland 2003. *Address:* Concordia 21, C/ Felipe IV, 9 – 1°, Derecha, 28014 Madrid, Spain (office). *Telephone:* (91) 531-52-32 (office). *E-mail:* info@josemariafigueres.org (office). *Website:* www.josemariafigueres.org (office).

FIGUEROA, Adolfo, PhD; Peruvian economist, academic and international consultant; *Emeritus Professor of Economics, Catholic University of Peru, Lima;* b. 14 April 1941, Carhuaz; s. of José Manuel Figueroa and Modesta Figueroa; m. Yolanda Vásquez 1965; one s. one d.; ed Colegio Guadalupe (High School), Lima, San Marcos Univ., Lima, Vanderbilt Univ., Nashville, Tenn., USA; Prof. of Econs, Catholic Univ. of Peru, Lima 1970–, Head, Dept of Econs 1976–79, 1987–90, 1996–98, Dean Faculty of Social Sciences 2002–05, Prof. Emer. 2008–; Dir Research Project on Productivity and Educ. in Agric. in Latin America, ECIEL Program 1983-85; Consultant to ILO, FAO, Inter-American Foundation, Ford Foundation, IFAD, IDB, World Bank; Visiting Prof., Univ. of Pernambuco, Brazil 1973, St Antony's Coll., Oxford 1976, Univ. of Ill., USA 1980, Econs Dept, Univ. of Nicaragua 1985, Univ. of Notre Dame, USA 1992, Univ. of Tex. 1997, Univ. of Wis. 2001; mem. Exec. Council Latin American Studies Asscn 1988–91, Editorial Advisory Bd, Journal of Int. Devt 1988–92, World Devt 1997–, European Review of Latin American Studies 1997–, Journal of Human Devt and Capabilities 2008–; mem. Int. Network for Econ. Method; Award of Excellence in Grad. Teaching Univ. of Ill., USA 1980, Winner, Collaborative Research Grant Competition, MacArthur Foundation 1999, Winner, Tinker Professorship Competition, Univ. of Wis. 2001. *Publications:* Estructura del Consumo y Distribución de Ingresos en Lima 1968–1969 1974, Distribución del Ingreso en el Perú (co-author) 1975, La Economía Campesina de la Sierra del Perú 1981, Capitalist Development and the Peasant Economy in Peru 1984, Educación y Productividad en la Agricultura Campesina de América Latina 1986, Teorías Económicas del Capitalismo 1992, Crisis Distributiva en el Perú 1993, Social Exclusion and Inequality in Peru 1996, Reformas en sociedades desiguales 2001, La sociedad sigma: una teoría del desarrollo económico 2003, Nuestro mundo social, una introducción a la ciencia económica 2008; articles in econ. journals on inequality and poverty, econ. growth, econ. devt, agric., labour markets, and econs of educ. *Leisure interests:* music, classical guitar. *Address:* CENTRUM, Universidad Católica del Perú, Apartado 1761, Lima 1 (office); Jirón Robert Kennedy 129, Lima 21, Peru (home). *Telephone:* (1) 313-3400 (office); (1) 261-6241 (home). *Fax:* (1) 313-3417 (home). *E-mail:* afiguer@pucp.edu.pe (office). *Website:* macareo.pucp.edu.pe/~afiguer/afiguer.htm (office).

FIGUEROA SERRANO, Carlos; Chilean politician and lawyer; b. 28 Nov. 1930, Angol; s. of Carlos Figueroa and Isabel Serrano; m. Sara Guzmán 1953; seven c.; ed Colegio de los Sagrados Corazones, School of Law, Universidad de Chile; practising lawyer 1957–, served at Appeals Court, Santiago 1971–72; Prof. of Procedural Law, Catholic Univ. of Chile 1960–76; joined Partido Demócrata Cristiano (PDC) 1957; Under-Sec. for Agric. 1967–69; Minister of Economy 1969–70; Acting Minister of Foreign Relations and of Finance, various occasions 1967–70; Pres. PDC Political Cttee 1980; Del. for Providencia to Prov. Bd of Eastern Santiago 1984–87; Head Communications and Publicity, Patricio Aylwin's Presidential Campaign 1989; Amb. to Argentina 1990–93; Dir Communications and Publicity, Eduardo Frei's Presidential Campaign 1993; Minister for Foreign Affairs March–Sept. 1994, for Interior 1994–99; Dir CIC SA 1971–, Financiera Condell 1986–90, Pesquera Guafo SA 1987–89; Gen. Man. VEEP SA (bldg contractors) 1980–86; Pres. Asociación Radiodifusoras de Chile 1972–78; Counsellor Asociación Iberamericana de Radiodifusión 1973–79, Sec. Bd of Dirs 1975–77. *Address:* c/o Ministro del Interior, Palacio de la Moneda, Santiago, Chile.

FIIL, Niels Peter, PhD; Danish business executive; b. 8 Feb. 1941; s. of Svend Rasmussen and Gerda Fiil Rasmussen; m. Berthe M. Willumsen 1978; one d.; ed Univ. of Copenhagen; Assoc. and Asst Prof., Univ. of Copenhagen 1970–81; Visiting Prof., Harvard Medical School 1978–79; Man. Molecular Biology R&D, Novo Industri A/S 1980–86, Vice-Pres. 1987–, Vice-Pres. Pharmaceutical Biotechnology, Novo Nordisk A/S 1989–; mem. European Molecular Biology Org. 1979, Royal Danish Acad. of Science and Letters 1982, Royal Swedish Acad. of Eng Science 1988. *Publications:* scientific papers in the field of microbial genetics and biotechnology. *Address:* Novo Nordisk A/S, Healthcare Chemistry, Novo Nordisk Park, 2760 Maalov (office); Fuglebakkevej 5, 2000 Frederiksberg, Denmark (home). *Telephone:* (45) 44-44-88-88 (office).

FIKENTSCHER, Wolfgang, LLM, DJur; German professor emeritus of law; *Chairman, Commission for Cultural-Anthropological Studies, Bavarian Academy of Sciences;* b. 17 May 1928, Nuremberg; s. of Erich Fikentscher and Elfriede (née Albers) Fikentscher; m. Irmgard van den Berge 1956; three s. one d.; ed Univs. of Erlangen, Munich and Mich., USA; teacher of Labour Law, Trade Union Schools 1952–56; Prof. of Law, Univ. of Münster 1958–65, Univ. of Tübingen 1965–71, Univ. of Munich 1971–, fmrly Law Director, Institute für Rechtsphilosophie und Rechtsinformatik; currently Chair. Comm. for Cultural-Anthropological Studies, Bavarian Acad. of Sciences; Visiting Prof. Univ. of Calif. Law School, Berkeley; Fellow Netherlands Inst. for Advanced Study in the Social Sciences 1971–72, Santa Fe Inst. 1991–92, 1995–96, 2003; Research Fellow, Gruter Inst. for Law and Behavioural Research 1992–; Bundesverdienstkreuz, Bayerischer Verdienstorden; Hon. DrJur (Zürich); Max-Planck Prize (jtly with Robert D. Cooter) 1995. *Publications:* Methoden des Rechts in vergleichender Darstellung, (5 vols) 1975–77, Wirtschaftsrecht (2 vols) 1983, Modes of Thought 1995, Schuldrecht 1997, Die Freiheit und ihr Paradox 1997, numerous books and articles on civil and commercial law, antitrust law, int. law, anthropology and ethology of law. *Address:* Institut für internationales Recht der Universität Munich, Ludwigstr. 29/II, 80539 Munich (office); Ringstrasse 15, 86911 Diessen-Riederau, Germany (home). *Telephone:* (8807) 206808 (home). *Fax:* (8807) 206808 (home). *E-mail:* fikentscher@jura.uni-muenchen.de (office). *Website:* www.gruterinstitute.org.

FILARDO, Leonor, MS; Venezuelan economist, banker and international finance official; b. 1944; d. of Jesus Filardo and Carmen Vargas de Filardo; m. (divorced); three d.; ed Caracas Catholic Univ., Surrey Univ.; worked for Cen. Bank of Venezuela 1970–75, Sr Vice-Pres. Int. Operations 1979–84; Sr Vice-Pres. of Int. Finance, Venezuelan Investment Fund 1975–79; Exec. Dir, World Bank Exec. Bd 1984–86; Alt. Exec. Dir IMF 1986–88, Exec. Dir 1988–90; Rep. Office, Washington DC 1990; Vice-Pres. Cen. Bank of Venezuela 1993–94; Minister Counsellor, Embassy in Washington, DC 1994; fmr Adviser to Cen. American and Venezuelan govts on stabilization and structural adjustment programmes, participant in negotiations with IMF for External Fund Facility for Venezuela; mem. Centro de Divulgación del Conocimiento Económico—CEDICE (think tank); mem. Exec. Cttee Youth Orchestra of the Americas; Francisco de Miranda Medal, (1st Class) Venezuela 1990. *Leisure interests:* art, music, opera, travel, workout. *Address:* CEDICE, Av. Andrés Eloy Blanco (Este 2), Edif. Cámara de Comercio de Caracas, Nivel Auditorio, Los Caobos, Caracas, Venezuela (office). *Telephone:* (212) 571-3357 (office). *E-mail:* cedice@cedice.org.ve (office). *Website:* www.cedice.org.ve (office).

FILARET (see Philaret).

FILARET, Denisenko M. A.; Ukrainian ecclesiastic; *'Patriarch of Kyiv and all Rus-Ukraine';* b. 1929, Donetsk Oblast; ed Odesa Seminary and Moscow Theological Acad.; monk and teacher from 1950; Rector Moscow Acad. 1954; moved to Saratov Seminary 1956, Kyiv Seminary 1957; fmr Chancellor Ukrainian Exarchate of Russian Orthodox Church–Moscow Patriarchate; apptd Bishop of Luga, Leningrad (now St Petersburg) Diocese 1962, Bishop of Vienna and Austria Nov. 1962, Bishop of Dmitrov, Moscow Diocese 1964; Rector Moscow's theological schools and Deputy Chair. Dept of External Church Relations 1964–66; Archbishop of Kyiv and Galicia 1966; Metropolitan of Kyiv 1968, dismissed May 1992; was instrumental in formation of self-styled 'Patriarchate of Kyiv and all Rus-Ukraine' June 1992; 'Patriarch of Kyiv and all Rus-Ukraine' 1995–. *Address:* Ukrainian Orthodox Church (Kyiv Patriarchate), 01004 Kyiv, vul. Pushkinska 36, Ukraine (office). *Telephone:* (44) 234-10-96 (office). *Fax:* (44) 234-30-55. *E-mail:* patz@ukrpack.net (office); pres_centr@i.ua (office). *Website:* www.cerkva.info (office).

FILATOV, Sergey Alexandrovich, C.TECH.SC.; Russian politician; b. 10 July 1936, Moscow; s. of Alexander Filatov and Maria Filatova; m.; two d.; ed Moscow Energy Inst.; constructor, head of project Dept "Serp i Molot" metallurgical plant 1957–66, engineer in Cuba 1966–68, chief engineer of project, leading constructor, Head of Lab., Head of Dept Tselikov All-Union Research Inst. of Metallurgic Machine Construction 1969–90; People's Deputy of Russia 1990–93; mem. Supreme Soviet 1990–91, Sec. Presidium of Supreme Soviet 1991, First Vice-Chair. Supreme Soviet of Russia 1991–93; Head of Staff of Russian Pres. 1993–96; Chair. Comm. of Pres. of Russian Fed. for State Prizes in Literature and Art 1993–; f. Union of Progressive Forces 1997, Chair. Co-ordination Bd in support of Russian Pres. 1996–, Organizing Cttee, Congress of Russian Intelligentsia 1997–; State Prize of USSR, State Prize Laureate, Order of Friendship, Medal for the Defender of Independent Russia 1987. *Publications:* On the Way to Democracy 1995, Full Non-secret 2000. *Leisure interests:* cycling, swimming. *Address:* Mira prospekt 49A, 129110 Moscow (office); 33-102 Garibaldi Street, Moscow, Russia (home). *Telephone:* (495) 208-26-65 (office); (495) 561-66-23 (home). *Fax:* (495) 971-15-00 (office). *E-mail:* jah@mail.cnt.ru (office).

FILIMON, Valeria; Romanian journalist; b. 29 May 1949, Butimanu; d. of Ion Dumitrescu and Maria Dumitrescu; m. Vasile Filimon 1984; ed Univ. of Bucharest; freelance journalist for various Romanian dailies and literary magazines 1967–90; Assoc. Prof. 1970–90; journalist 1990–93; Ed.-in-Chief Femeia Moderna (magazine) 1993–98, Regala 1998–, Olimp 1999–; Project Coordinator in Romania, Int. Fed. of Journalists 1996–; Vice-Pres. Asscn of Romanian Journalists; Romanian Writers' Union Prize. *Publications:* co-author of critical edn of Romanian novelist Liviu Rebreanu 1968–75; Lyceum (collection of literary criticism in two vols) 1974. *Address:* Societatea Ziaristilor din Romania, Piata Presei Libere 1, Oficial Postal 33, 71341 Bucharest (office). *Telephone:* (21) 2228351 (office). *Fax:* (21) 2224266 (office).

FILIPACCHI, Daniel; French journalist and publisher; *Honorary President, Hachette Filipacchi Médias;* b. 12 Jan. 1928, Paris; s. of Henri Filipacchi and Edith Besnard; typographer, Paris-Match 1944, photographer 1948, head of information and dir of photographic service 1953; fashion photographer, Marie-Claire 1957; producer of radio transmissions, Europe No. 1 1955, 1960; Owner and Dir Jazz Magazine 1955, Cahiers du cinéma 1961–70; Founder and Dir Salut les copains (became Salut 1976) 1961, Lui, Mlle Age tendre (became OK Age tendre 1976), Pariscope 1965, Photo 1967, Le Monde des Grands Musées 1968, Ski 1969, Union 1972, Playboy France 1973–84, Girls 1982; editorial adviser to Newlook 1982, Penthouse 1984; Pres.-Dir-Gen. WEA Filipacchi Music SA 1971–84, Cogedipresse; Owner and fmr Dir Paris-Match 1976; mem. editorial Cttee Elle 1981; Vice-Pres. Hachette 1981–93, Pres.-Dir-Gen. Hachette Magazines Inc. (USA) 1990; Pres.-Dir-Gen. Filipacchi Médias SA 1993–97; Jt Man. Cogédipresse 1994–97; Admin. and Hon. Pres. Hachette Filipacchi Médias 1997–. *Address:* c/o Lagardère Active Media, 149-151, rue Anatole France, 92534 Levallois-Perret, France.

FILIPOV, Grisha; Bulgarian politician (retd); b. 13 July 1919, Kadiyevka, Ukraine; one s. (died 2005); ed Moscow Univ., USSR; returned to Bulgaria

1936; joined Bulgarian CP 1940; arrested for political activities and sentenced to 15 years' imprisonment 1941; released after coup 1944; various posts in party, including Head of Inspectorate in Ministry of Industry 1947; Counsellor, Deputy Head and Deputy Chair. of Cttee on Planning 1951–58; Deputy Head of a Dept, Cen. Cttee of Bulgarian CP 1958; cand. mem. Cen. Cttee of Bulgarian CP 1962–66, mem. 1966–89, Sec. Cen. Cttee 1971–82, 1986–89; Deputy Chair. State Planning Comm. 1962–66; mem. Politburo 1974–89; mem. State Council 1986–89; Chair. Council of Ministers (Prime Minister of Bulgaria) 1981–86; fmr mem. Nat. Ass.; arrested and accused of misappropriation of state funds 14 July 1992.

FILIPOVIĆ, Karlo; Bosnia and Herzegovina politician; *Executive Board President, Social Democratic Party of Bosnia and Herzegovina;* b. 1954, Solakovicima; s. of Jozo Filipović and Mara Filipović; m.; one d.; ed Univ. of Sarajevo; Pres. Council of Municipalities, Sarajevo City Ass. 1987–89; mem. Cen. Cttee Communist League of Bosnia and Herzegovina 1988–91, elected mem. of presidency 1989; mem. of presidency Socialist Party of Bosnia and Herzegovina 1991–92; mem. of presidency of Social Democratic Party of Bosnia and Herzegovina (SDP BiH) 1992–95, Sec. 1995–97, Sec.-Gen. 1997–2001, Pres. Exec. Bd 2001–; mem. House of Reps (Parl.) 1998–2001; Pres. Fed. of Bosnia and Herzegovina 2001–02, Vice-Pres. 2002–04. *Address:* Social Democratic Party of Bosnia and Herzegovina, Alipašina 41, 71000 Sarajevo, Bosnia and Herzegovina (office). *Telephone:* (33) 664044 (office). *Fax:* (33) 644042 (office). *E-mail:* predssednik-glavnog-odbora@sdp-bih.org.ba (office). *Website:* www.sdp-bih.org.ba (office).

FILIPPENKO, Aleksander Georgyevich; Russian actor; b. 2 Sept. 1944, Moscow; m. 2nd Marina Ishimbayeva; one d.; ed Moscow Inst. of Physics and Tech., Moscow, Shchukin Higher School of Theatre; Sr Engineer Inst. of Geochemistry, USSR Acad. of Sciences 1967–69; actor Amateur Theatre Nash Dom 1967–69, Taganka Theatre 1969–75, Vakhtangov Theatre 1975–94; founder and actor Experimental One-Man Theatre 1995–; staged Train to Chatanooga, Dead Souls, Fanbala; Merited Artist of Russia. *Films include:* Star and Death of Joakin Murietta, My Friend Ivan Lapshin, Master and Marguerita; lead TV programme If 1997–98. *Address:* Spiridonyevsky per. 8, Apt. 17, 103104 Moscow, Russia (home). *Telephone:* (495) 202-77-15 (home).

FILIPPOV, Vladimir Mikhailovich, Dr Physics-Math; Russian government official, mathematician and academic; *Rector, People's Friendship University of Russia;* b. 1951; m.; one s. one d.; ed Patrice Lumumba Univ. of Friendship of Peoples, Steklov Math. Inst. USSR Acad. of Sciences; Asst, Chair of Higher Math., Chair. Council of Young Scientists, Head Dept of Science, Lumumba Univ. of Friendship of Peoples 1973–85; Prof., Head, Chair of Math. Analysis, Dean, Faculty of Physics, Math. and Natural Sciences, Lumumba Univ. 1985–93, Rector 1993–98; Minister of Gen. and Professional Educ. of Russian Fed. 1998–2000; Minister of Educ. 2000–04, First Deputy Minister of Educ. and Science 2004–05; Presidential Aide 2004–; Rector People's Friendship Univ. of Russia 2005–; Vice-Pres. Euro-Asian Asscn of Univs; mem. Russian Acad. of Natural Sciences, Int. Acad. of Informatization. *Publications:* more than 120 scientific works on problems of differential equations and functional analysis. *Address:* People's Friendship University of Russia, 6 Miklukho-Maklaya str., 117198 Moscow, Russia (office). *Telephone:* (495) 434-70-27 (office). *E-mail:* rector@rudn.ru (office). *Website:* www.rudn.ru (office).

FILIZZOLA SERRA, Rafael, LLB; Paraguayan lawyer, academic and politician; *Minister of the Interior;* b. 16 Feb. 1968, Asunción; ed Univ. Católica Nuestra Señora de la Asunción; Sec. Gen. Nat. Fed. of Univ. Students 1990–91; Founding mem. Asunción Para Todos (APT) and Constitución Para Todoa (CPT) (ind. political movts) 1991; Prof. of Political Law, Universidad Católica de Asunción; mem. Nat. Congress for Asunción 1998–2008; Founder and Pres. Partido Demcrática Progresista (PDP) 2007–; Minister of the Interior 2008–. *Address:* Ministry of the Interior, Estrella y Montevideo, Asunción, Paraguay (office). *Telephone:* (21) 49-3661 (office). *Fax:* (21) 44-6448 (office). *Website:* www.ministeriodelinterior.gov.py (office).

FILLIOUD, Georges, LenD; French politician and journalist; b. 7 July 1929, Lyon; s. of Marius Fillioud and Camille Metifiot; m. 1st Aimée Dieunet 1949; one s. one d.; m. 2nd Danielle Evennou 1996; ed Ecole nationale professionnelle de Lyon, Univ. of Paris and Lyon; journalist, Chief Reporter, then Sr Ed., Europe No.1 radio station 1956–66; Deputy (Drôme) to Nat. Ass. 1967–68, 1973–81; Asst Sec.-Gen. Convention des institutions républicaines 1970; Councillor, Romans 1970–77, Mayor 1977–81; Press Sec. Parti Socialiste 1971–; Sec.-Gen. Féd. des élus socialistes et républicains 1972–; mem. Parl. Del. for French broadcasting 1974; Vice-Pres. Nat. Ass. Socialist Group 1978–79; Minister of Communication 1981–83, Sec. of State 1983–86; Conseiller d'État 1986; Admin., Pres. Institut nat. de l'audiovisuel (Ina) 1990–94; Pres. Arte Gen. Ass. 1999–. *Publications:* Le dossier du Vercors 1965, L'affaire Lindemans 1966, la Mort d'un chien 1988, Homo Politicus 1996. *Address:* 30 passage Thière, 75011 Paris, France (home).

FILLON, François-Charles Amand; French politician; *Prime Minister;* b. 4 March 1954, Mans; s. of Michel Fillon and Annie Soulet; m. Penelope Clarke 1980; three s. one d.; ed Univ. of Maine, Univ. René-Descartes, Paris and Fondation Nationale des Sciences Politiques; Parl. Asst to Joël Le Theule 1976–77; served in Office of Minister of Transport 1978–80, Office of Minister of Defence 1980–81; Head of Legis. and Parl. Work, Ministry of Industry 1981; Town Councillor, Sablé-sur-Sarthe, Mayor 1983–2001; Pres. Conseil Général, Sarthe 1992–98, of Sablé-sur-Sarthe Dist 2001–; RPR Deputy to Nat. Ass. 1981–93; Pres. Comm. for Nat. Defence and Armed Forces 1986–88; Minister for Higher Educ. and Research 1993–95; Minister of Information Tech. and Posts May–Nov. 1995, Minister del. 1995–97; Spokesman, Exec. Comm. RPR 1998–, Political Adviser 1999–; Chair. Conseil Régional des Pays de la Loire 1998–; Municipal Councillor, Solesmes 2001–; Minister of Social Affairs, Labour and Solidarity 2002–04, Minister of Youth, National Education and Research 2004–05; Senator for Sarthe 2004–07; Prime Minister 2007–. *Address:* Office of the Prime Minister, Hôtel de Matignon, 57 rue de Varenne, 75007 Paris (office); Beaucé, 72300 Solesmes, France (home). *Telephone:* 1-42-75-80-00 (office). *Fax:* 1-42-75-78-31 (office). *E-mail:* premier-ministre@premier-ministre.gouv.fr (office). *Website:* www.premier-ministre.gouv.fr (office); www.blog-fillon.com (home).

FILMON, Gary Albert, PC, MSc; Canadian politician and business executive; *Vice-Chairman, Wellington West Capital;* b. 24 Aug. 1942, Winnipeg, Man.; s. of Albert Filmon and Anastasia Filmon (née Dosckocz); m. Janice Wainwright 1963; two s. two d.; ed Sisler High School, Univ. of Manitoba; consulting engineer, Underwood McLellan Ltd 1964–69; Pres. Success/Angus Commercial Coll. 1969–80; Winnipeg City Councillor 1975–79; mem. Legis. Ass. for River Heights 1979–81, for Tuxedo 1981–; Minister of Consumer and Corp. Affairs and Environment and Minister Responsible for Man. Housing and Renewal Corpn 1981; Leader Man. Progressive Conservative Party 1983–88; Premier of Man., Pres. Exec. Council, Minister of Fed. Prov. Relations 1988–99; Leader of the Opposition 1999–2002; headed govt task force to evaluate emergency response to forest fires in BC 2004; mem. Security Intelligence Review Cttee 2001–; currently Vice-Chair. Wellington West Capital Inc.; consultant, The Exchange Group. *Address:* Wellington West Capital, 200 Waterfront Drive, Suite 400, Winnipeg, MB, R3B 3P1, Canada (office). *Website:* www.wellingtonwest.com (office).

FILO, David, BS, MS; American internet executive; *Chief Yahoo!, Yahoo! Inc.;* b. Moss Bluff, La.; ed Tulane Univ. and Stanford Univ., Calif.; co-created Yahoo! internet navigational guide 1994, co-founder, Chief Exec. Yahoo! Inc. 1994–. *Address:* Yahoo! Incorporated, 701 1st Avenue, Sunnyvale, CA 94089, USA (home). *Telephone:* (408) 349-3300 (office). *Fax:* (408) 349-3301 (office). *Website:* www.yahoo.com (office).

FINCH, Jon Nicholas; British actor, writer and director; b. 2 March 1943, Caterham, Surrey; s. of Arthur Leonard Finch and Nancy Karen Houghton; m. Catriona MacColl 1981 (divorced 1989); one d. by Helen Elizabeth Drake; ed Caterham School; served 21 Special Air Service (SAS) Regt (Artists) Reserve 1960–63; theatre technician and dir etc. 1963–67, actor in TV 1967–70; Hon. Dr of Metaphysics; Most Promising Artiste, Variety Club of GB 1972. *Films include:* lead role in Roman Polanski's Macbeth, Alfred Hitchcock's Frenzy, Lady Caroline Lamb, The Final Programme, El hombre de la cruz verde, Die estandarte, La sabina, Gary Cooper que estas en los cielos, La amenaza, La più bella del reame, Une femme fidèle, Death on the Nile, Breaking Glass, Girocity, Doktor Faustus, Riviera, Paradiso, Plaza Real, Streets of Yesterday, The Voice, Beautiful in the Kingdom, Mirror, Mirror, Lurking Fear (USA), Darklands (UK), Lucan, Anazapta, The Kingdom of Heaven. *Television films:* The Rainbow, Unexplained Laughter, A Love Renewed, Beautiful Lies, Maigret, Sherlock Holmes: The Mazarin Stone, Merlin's Crystal Cave, Dangerous Curves (USA), The Acts of Peter and Paul (USA), White Men are Cracking Up, New Tricks. *Television includes:* Counterstrike (series), Steve, Ben Hall (series), Richard II, Henry IV Parts I and II, Much Ado About Nothing, Make or Break, The Odd Job Man (series), Mary Queen of Scots, Casualty. *Theatre:* Les Liaisons Dangereuses, King Lear, The Importance of Being Earnest, Music to Murder By, The Invisible Man. *Leisure interests:* reading, collecting hip flasks. *Address:* Unicorn House, Croft Road, Old Town, Hastings, E Sussex TN34 3HE, England. *Telephone:* (7905) 215030.

FINCHAM, John Robert Stanley, PhD, FRS; British geneticist and academic; *Professor Emeritus of Genetics, University of Cambridge;* b. 11 Aug. 1926, Southgate, Middx; s. of Robert Fincham and Winifred Emily Fincham (née Western); m. Ann Katherine Emerson 1950; one s. three d.; ed Peterhouse and Botany School, Univ. of Cambridge; Lecturer in Botany, Univ. Coll. Leicester 1950–54, Reader in Genetics, Univ. of Leicester 1954–60; Head, Dept of Genetics, John Innes Inst. 1960–66; Prof. and Head, Dept of Genetics, Univ. of Leeds 1966–76, Univ. of Edinburgh 1976–84; Arthur Balfour Prof. of Genetics, Univ. of Cambridge 1984–91, now Emer.; Professorial Fellow, Peterhouse, Cambridge 1984–91, now Emer. Fellow; Emil Christian Hansen Medal (Copenhagen) 1977; Hon. Fellow Div. of Biology, Univ. of Edinburgh 1992–. *Publications:* Fungal Genetics (with P. R. Day, later edns also with A. Radford) 1963, Microbial and Molecular Genetics 1965, Genetic Complementation 1966, Genetics 1983, Genetically Engineered Organisms 1991, Genetic Analysis 1994, numerous articles in professional journals. *Leisure interest:* books, walking, music. *Address:* 20 Greenbank Road, Edinburgh, EH10 5RY, Scotland (home). *Telephone:* (31) 447-3313 (home).

FINCHER, David; American film director; b. 28 Aug. 1962, Denver, Colo; s. of Jack Fincher; m. Donya Fiorentino 1990 (divorced); one d.; fmrly with Propaganda Films (video production co.); directed numerous music videos and commercials. *Films include:* Alien 3 1992, Se7en 1995, The Game 1997, Fight Club 1999, Panic Room 2002, Zodiac 2007, The Curious Case of Benjamin Button 2008. *Address:* Creative Artists Agency (CAA), 2000 Avenue of the Stars, Los Angeles, CA 90067, USA (office). *Telephone:* (424) 288-2000 (office). *Fax:* (424) 288-2900 (office). *Website:* www.caa.com (office).

FINCK, August von; German business executive; b. 11 March 1930; owner, Bankhaus Merck, Finck & Co., Munich, Deutsche Spar- & Kreditbank AG, Munich, Carlton Holdings (controller of Mövenpick restaurant chain); majority shareholder, Löwenbräu AG, Munich, Würzburger Hofbräu AG. *Address:* Pacellistrasse 4, 80333 Munich, Germany.

FINDLAY, Paul Hudson Douglas, BA; British opera director; b. 26 Sept. 1943, New Zealand; s. of the late John Niemeyer Findlay and Aileen May (née Davidson) Findlay; m. Françoise Christiane 1966; one s. one d.; ed Univ. Coll. School, London, Balliol Coll., Oxford, London Opera Centre; Production and

Technical Man. New Opera Co. 1967; Dir London Sinfonietta 1967–; Stage Man. Glyndebourne Touring Opera and English Opera Group 1968; Asst Press Officer Royal Opera House, Covent Garden 1968–72, Personal Asst to Gen. Dir 1972–76, Asst Dir 1976–87, Opera Dir 1987–93; Man. Dir Royal Philharmonic Orchestra 1993–95; Planning Dir European Opera Centre 1997–; Arts Man. Kirov Ballet; Chair. Opera 80 1987; currently Gen. Man. Mariinsky Theater, St Petersburg, Russia; Vice-Pres. Performing and Visual Arts, Global Music Network —2002; mem. Bd of Dirs English Touring Opera, Arts Educational Trust; Vice-Pres. GMN Europe 1998–2001; Dir Youth and Mind 2000–; Cavaliere Ufficiale del Ordine al Merito della Repubblica Italiana; Chevalier des Arts et des Lettres 1991. *Leisure interests:* tennis, gardening. *Address:* c/o Board of Directors, English Touring Opera, 52-54 Rosebery Avenue, London, EC1R 4RP, England.

FINE, Anne, OBE, BA, FRSL; British writer; b. (Anne Laker), 7 Dec. 1947, Leicester; d. of Brian Laker and Mary Baker; m. Kit Fine 1968 (divorced 1991); two d.; ed Northampton High School for Girls and Univ. of Warwick; Children's Laureate 2001–03; mem. Soc. of Authors; Dr hc; Scottish Arts Council Writer's Bursary 1986, Scottish Arts Council Book Award 1986, Publishing News' British Book Awards Children's Author of the Year 1990, 1993, Nasen Special Educational Needs Book Award 1996, Prix Sorcière 1998, Prix Versele 1999, 2000, Boston Globe Horn Book Award 2003. *Publications:* for older children: The Summer House Loon 1978, The Other Darker Ned 1978, The Stone Menagerie 1980, Round Behind the Icehouse 1981, The Granny Project 1983, Madame Doubtfire 1987, Goggle-Eyes (Guardian Children's Fiction Prize, Carnegie Medal 1990) 1989, The Book of the Banshee 1991, Flour Babies (Whitbread Children's Book of the Year, Carnegie Medal 1993) 1992, Step by Wicked Step 1995, The Tulip Touch (Whitbread Children's Book of the Year 1997) 1996, Very Different (short stories) 2001, Up on Cloud Nine 2002, Frozen Billy 2004, The Road of Bones 2006, Ivan the Terrible 2007; for younger children: Scaredy-Cat 1985, Anneli the Art Hater 1986, Crummy Mummy and Me 1988, A Pack of Liars 1988, Stranger Danger 1989, Bill's New Frock (Smarties Prize 1990) 1989, The Country Pancake 1989, A Sudden Puff of Glittering Smoke 1989, A Sudden Swirl of Icy Wind 1990, Only a Show 1990, Design-a-Pram 1991, A Sudden Glow of Gold 1991, The Worst Child I Ever Had 1991, The Angel of Nitshill Road 1991, Poor Monty (picture book) 1991, The Same Old Story Every Year 1992, The Chicken Gave It to Me 1992, The Haunting of Pip Parker 1992, The Diary of a Killer Cat 1994, Press Play 1994, How to Write Really Badly 1996, Countdown 1996, Jennifer's Diary 1996, Care of Henry 1996, Loudmouth Louis 1998, Charm School 1999, Roll Over Roly 1999, Bad Dreams 2000, Ruggles (picture book) 2001, Notso Hotso 2001, The Jamie and Angus Stories 2002, How to Cross the Road and Not Turn Into a Pizza 2002, The More the Merrier 2003, Eating Things on Sticks 2009; adult fiction: The Killjoy 1986, Taking the Devil's Advice 1990, In Cold Domain 1994, Telling Liddy 1998, All Bones and Lies 2001, Raking the Ashes 2005, Fly in the Ointment 2008, Our Precious Lulu 2009; non-fiction: Telling Tales: an Interview with Anne Fine 1999. *Leisure interests:* reading, walking. *Address:* c/o David Higham Associates, 5–8 Lower John Street, London, W1R 4HA, England (office). *Telephone:* (20) 7434-5900 (office). *Website:* www.annefine.co.uk (office). *Fax:* (1833) 690519 (home).

FINE, Kit, BA, PhD, FBA; British philosopher, mathematician and academic; *Silver Professor of Philosophy and Mathematics, New York University;* b. 26 March 1946, Farnborough; s. of Maurice Fine and Joyce Cicely Woolf; two d.; ed Cheltenham Grammar School for Boys, Balliol Coll. Oxford, Univ. of Warwick; Prof., Univ. of Michigan, Ann Arbor, USA 1978–88; Prof., UCLA 1988–97; Silver Prof. of Philosophy and Math., New York Univ. 1997–; Ed. Journal of Symbolic Logic 1978–87, Notre Dame Journal of Formal Logic 1984–87, Studies in Logic 1989–93; Guggenheim Fellow 1978–79; Fellow, American Council of Learned Socs 1981–82, American Acad. of Arts and Sciences; Corresponding Fellow, British Acad.; Dr hc (Bucharest). *Publications:* Worlds, Times and Selves (with A. N. Prior) 1977, Reasoning with Arbitrary Objects 1985, Limits of Abstraction 2002, Modality and Tense 2005, Semantic Relationism 2007. *Leisure interests:* music, gardening, cooking. *Address:* Department of Philosophy, New York University, 5 Washington Place, New York, NY 10003, USA (office). *Telephone:* (212) 998-3558 (office). *Fax:* (212) 995-4179 (office). *E-mail:* kf14@nyu.edu (office). *Website:* philosophy.fas.nyu.edu (office).

FINE, Leon Gerald, MB, ChB, FRCP, FACP, FRCP(Glas), FMedSci; American professor of medicine; *Dean, Faculty of Clinical Sciences, Royal Free and University College Medical School;* b. 17 July 1943, Cape Town, South Africa; s. of Matthew Fine and Jeanette Lipshitz; m. Brenda Sakinovsky 1966; two d.; ed Univ. of Cape Town; mem. staff Albert Einstein Coll. of Medicine 1972–76, Univ. of Miami 1976–78; Chief, Div. of Nephrology UCLA 1978–91; Head Dept of Medicine, Univ. Coll. London Medical School 1991–, Dean, Faculty of Clinical Sciences, Royal Free and Univ. Coll. Medical School 2002–; Ed.-in-Chief Nephron 2003–; numerous invited lectureships; Founding Fellow Acad. of Medical Sciences, UK. *Publications:* over 100 articles in the area of kidney disease and renal biology. *Leisure interest:* book collecting. *Address:* Royal Free and University College Medical School, Faculty of Clinical Sciences, Drayton House, 30 Gower Street, London, WC1E 6BT, England (office). *Telephone:* (20) 7679-5486 (office); (20) 8342-9680 (home). *Fax:* (20) 7679-5484 (office); (20) 8342-9680 (home). *E-mail:* l.fine@ucl.ac.uk (office). *Website:* www.ucl.ac.uk/medicalschool.

FINEBERG, Harvey Vernon, MD, PhD; American physician and professional society administrator; *President, Institute of Medicine;* b. 15 Sept. 1945; s. of Saul Fineberg and Miriam Fineberg (née Pearl); m. Mary Elizabeth Wilson 1975; ed Harvard Univ.; Intern, Beth Israel Hosp., Boston 1972–73; Asst Prof., School of Public Health, Harvard Univ., Boston 1973–78, Assoc. Prof. 1978–81, Prof. 1981–2002, Dean 1984–97; Provost, Harvard Univ.

1997–2001; physician at E Boston Health Center 1974–76, Harvard St Health Center 1976–84; Trustee, Newton Wellesley Hosp., Mass. 1981–86; mem. Public Health Council, Mass. 1976–79; mem. Bd of Dirs American Foundation for AIDS Research 1986–97; mem. Inst. of Medicine 1983– (Pres. 2002–); Jr Fellow, Harvard Univ. 1974–75, Mellon Fellow 1976. *Address:* Institute of Medicine, 500 5th Street NW, Washington, DC 20001-2721 (office); 1812 Kalorama Square NW, Washington, DC 20008-4022, USA (home). *Telephone:* (202) 334-3300 (office). *Fax:* (202) 334-3851 (office). *Website:* www.iom.edu (office).

FINEMAN, S. David, BA, LLB; American lawyer and business executive; *Chairman, United States Postal Service;* ed America Univ., George Washington Univ.; fmr Lecturer on Business Law, Temple Univ.; Co-Founder and Man.-Pnr Fineman & Bach, PC (law firm) then Fineman, Krekstein & Harris, PC, Phila; served as Special Counsel to Phila Parking Authority, Sec. of Banking of Commonwealth of Pa, Insurance Commr of Commonwealth of Pa; fmr mem. Phila Planning Comm., Phila Mayor Edward Rendell's Intergovernmental Task Force, Mayor W. Wilson's Transition Team 1987; apptd Gov. US Postal Service by Pres. Bill Clinton 1995, Vice-Chair. Bd Govs 2001–03, Chair. 2004–; fmr mem. Industry Policy Advisory Cttee, US Secr. of Commerce, Bd Dirs Phila Chamber of Commerce, Free Library of Phila; apptd to Center City Advisory Bd, Jefferson Bank 1999; currently mem. Bar Asscns of Phila, Pa and USA; mem. Defense Research Inst. *Address:* United States Postal Service, 475 L'Enfant Plaza SW, Washington, DC 20260-0010 (office); Fineman, Krekstein & Harris, 30 South 17th Street, Suite 1800, Philadelphia, PA 19103, USA (office). *Telephone:* (202) 268-2500 (office); (215) 893-9300 (office). *Fax:* (202) 268-4860 (office); (215) 893-8719 (office). *Website:* www.usps.com (office); www.finemanbach.com (office).

FINETTE, Jean Regis, LèsL; Mauritian politician; b. 8 July 1934; m.; three c.; ed Coll. Royal Curepipe and Port Louis, Univ. of Mauritius; Lecturer in Cooperative Studies, Univ. of Mauritius for 17 years; Deputy to Legis. Ass. 1982–; Minister for Local Govt 1988–93, of Health 1993–96; Officier des Palmes Académiques. *Address:* Lothar Koenig Street, Cité Rosray, Beau Bassin, Mauritius.

FINI, Gianfranco; Italian politician; *President, Camera dei Deputati;* b. Bologna; fmr journalist; mem. Movimento Sociale Italiano-Destra Nazionale (MSI) 1987–94, Alleanza Nazionale 1994–2008, Chair. 1994–2008; Vice-Pres. Council of Ministers (Deputy Prime Minister) 2001–04; Minister of Foreign Affairs 2004–06; Pres. Camera dei Deputati (Chamber of Deputies) 2008–; Rep. to EU Special Convention on Pan-European Constitution 2002–06. *Address:* Camera dei Deputati, Palazzo di Montecitorio, Rome, Italy. *Telephone:* (06) 67603316 (office). *Fax:* (06) 6892953 (office). *E-mail:* dlwebmast@camera.it (office). *Website:* www.camera.it (office).

FINIKASO, Taukelina T., LLB; Tuvaluan diplomatist and politician; *Minister of Communications, Transport and Tourism;* ed Univ. of Sydney, Australia; High Commr to Fiji (non-resident to Papua New Guinea and Samoa) 2001–06; Minister of Communications, Transport and Tourism 2006–. *Address:* Ministry of Works, Communications and Transport PMB, Vaiaku, Funafuti, Tuvalu (office). *Telephone:* 20052 (office). *Fax:* 20772 (office). *E-mail:* tuvmet@tuvalu.tv (office).

FINK, Bernarda; Slovenian singer (mezzo-soprano); b. 29 Aug. 1955, Buenos Aires; m.; two c.; ed Instituto Superio de Arte del Teatro Colón, Buenos Aires and studied with Michel Corboz in Europe; sang Rossini's Cenerentola at Buenos Aires 1986; concerts of Baroque music with Michel Corboz as conductor in Paris, Geneva, Berlin, Lisbon and Tokyo; sang Penelope in Monteverdi's Ulisse at Innsbruck 1993, Montpellier and Barcelona (also the Messenger in Orfeo); Amsterdam as Proserpina in Orfeo 1995; Cenerentola at the Berlin Staatsoper 1994; season 2000 as Dorabella at Aix-en-Provence and European tour as Gluck's Orpheus, with René Jacobs; recitals at Carnegie and Wigmore Halls, Paris, Vienna and Sydney Opera Houses; sang Cecilio in Lucio Silla at Theater an der Wien 2005–06, Sesto in a concert version of La Clemenza di Tito 2005; has worked with leading conductors including Blomstedt, Bychkov, Gardiner, Gergiev, Harnoncourt, Herreweghe, Jansons, Marriner, Minkowski, Muti, Norrington, Welser-Möst; festival appearances include Salzburg Festival and Mozartwochen, Wiener Festwochen, Schubertiade Schwarzenberg, Prague Spring Festival, Tokyo Summer Festival and the Montreux Festival. *Recordings include:* Caldara's Maddalena ai Piedi di Cristo (Gramaphone Award), Dvorák songs (solo recital) (Diapson d'Or), Rossini's Zelmira and Handel's Amadigi, Handel's Giulio Cesare and Flavio, Monteverdi's Orfeo and Ulisse, Messiah. *Address:* Impulse Art Management, PO Box 15401, MK Amsterdam, Netherlands (office). *Telephone:* (20) 626-69-44 (office). *Fax:* (20) 622-71-18 (office). *E-mail:* info@impulseartmanagement.nl (office). *Website:* www.impulseartmanagement.nl (office).

FINK, Gerald R., BA, MS, PhD; American geneticist and academic; *American Cancer Society Professor of Genetics, Massachusetts Institute of Technology;* b. 1 July 1940, Brooklyn, NY; s. of Rebecca Fink and Benjamin Fink; m. Rosalie Lewis 1961; two d.; ed Amherst Coll., Yale Univ.; Postdoctoral Fellow, NIH 1965–66, 1966–67; Instructor, NIH Grad. Program 1966; Instructor, Cold Spring Harbor Summer Program 1970–; Asst Prof. of Genetics, Cornell Univ. 1967–71, Assoc. Prof. 1971–76, Prof. 1976–79, Prof. of Biochemistry 1979–82; Prof. of Molecular Genetics, MIT 1982–; American Cancer Soc. Prof. of Genetics 1979–; mem. Whitehead Inst. for Biomedical Research 1982–, Dir 1990–2001; Sec. Genetics Soc. of America 1977–80, Vice-Pres. 1986–87, Pres. 1988–89; mem. NAS, American Acad. of Arts and Sciences, American Philosophical Soc., Inst. of Medicine 1996, American Acad. of Microbiology 1996; Hon. DSc (Amherst Coll.) 1982, (Cold Spring Harbor) 1999; NAS-US Steel Prize in Molecular Biology 1981, Genetics Soc. of America Medal 1982, Yale Science and Eng Award 1984, Emil Christian Hansen Foundation Award for Microbiological Research 1986, Wilbur Lucius Cross Medal, Yale Univ. 1992, Bristol-Myers Squibb Infectious Disease Research Award 1993, Ellison Medical Foundation Sr Scholar Award 2001, George W. Beadle Award, Genetics Soc. of America 2001, Yeast Genetics and Molecular Biology Lifetime Achievement Award 2002. *Publications:* numerous scientific publs. *Address:* Whitehead Institute for Biomedical Research, 9 Cambridge Center, Cambridge, MA 02142, USA (office). *Telephone:* (617) 258-5215 (office). *E-mail:* gfink@wi.mit.edu (office). *Website:* www.wi.mit.edu/research/faculty/fink.html (office); web.mit.edu/biology/www/facultyareas/facresearch/fink.html (office).

FINK, Jonathan, BA, PhD; American volcanologist and academic; *Julie A. Wrigley Director, Global Institute of Sustainability, Arizona State University;* ed Colby Coll., Stanford Univ.; has held post-doctoral appointments in Dept of Applied Math., Weizmann Inst., Israel, and in Planetary Geology group, Arizona State Univ.; Post-doctoral researcher in Geology, Stanford Univ.; joined Arizona State Univ. 1979, Prof., School of Earth and Space Exploration, Coll. of Liberal Arts and Sciences and School of Sustainability 1982–, Chair. Geology Dept (now part of School for Earth and Space Exploration) –1997, Vice-Pres. for Research and Econ. Affairs 1997–2007, Julie A. Wrigley Dir Global Inst. of Sustainability 2007–, also Univ. Sustainability Officer, Office of the Pres. 2007–; has held an adjunct faculty position in Dept of Chemical Eng, Univ. of Colorado; Dir Geochemistry and Petrology Program, NSF 1992–93; fmr Visiting Fellow, Research School of Earth Sciences, ANU; fmr Visiting Scientist, Nat. Museum of Natural History, Smithsonian Inst.; mem. Bd of Dirs The Nature Conservancy, Arizona; Fellow, Geological Soc. of America 1997, AAAS 2004. *Publications:* numerous scientific papers in professional journals on fluid mechanics, remote sensing, isotope geochemistry to study eruptions on Earth and other planets, and problems of urban sustainability. *Address:* GIOS Building, Room 476, 800 S. Cady Mall, Box 875402, Mail Code: 5402, Tempe AZ 85287-5502, USA (office). *Telephone:* (480) 965-4797 (office). *E-mail:* jonathan.fink@asu.edu (office). *Website:* www.asu.edu (office); schoolofsustainability.asu.edu (office).

FINK, Laurence Douglas, BA, MBA; American investment banker; *Chairman and CEO, BlackRock, Inc.;* ed Univ. of California, Los Angeles and UCLA Anderson School of Man.; began career in bond trading div. of The First Boston Corpn 1976, became one of first mortgage-backed securities traders on Wall Street, later Co-head, Taxable Fixed Income Div., started Financial Futures and Options Dept and headed Mortgage and Real Estate Products Group, mem. Man. Cttee and a Man. Dir The First Boston Corpn aged 28; f. BlackRock 1988, mem. Bd of Dirs 1999–, Chair. and CEO BlackRock, Inc. 1998–, Chair. Exec. Cttee, Man. Cttee, mem. Nominating and Governance Cttee, Chair. and CEO Blackrock Financial Management Inc., CEO and Dir BlackRock International Ltd, Chair. and CEO BlackRock Advisors, Chair. Nomura BlackRock Asset Man. (jt venture in Japan), Trustee and Pres. BlackRock Funds, Dir several of BlackRock's offshore funds and alternative investment vehicles; mem. Bd of Trustees New York Univ., Chair. Financial Affairs Cttee and mem. Exec. Cttee, Ad Hoc Exec. on Bd Governance, Cttee on Trustees; Co-Chair. and mem. Exec. Cttee Mount Sinai New York Univ. Health Bd of Trustees, New York Univ. Hosps Center Bd of Trustees (Chair. Devt/Trustee Stewardship Cttee and mem. Finance Cttee); mem. Bd Execs New York Stock Exchange (now NYSE Next), mem. an advisory panel 2003–. *Address:* BlackRock, Inc., 40 East 52nd Street, New York, NY 10022, USA (office). *Telephone:* (212) 810-5300 (office). *Fax:* (212) 409-3123 (office); (212) 935-1370 (office). *E-mail:* info@blackrock.com (office). *Website:* www1.blackrock.com (office).

FINLAY, B. Brett, OC, BSc, PhD, FRSC; Canadian microbiologist and academic; *Peter Wall Distinguished Professor, University of British Columbia;* ed Univ. of Alberta, Stanford Univ. School of Medicine; Assoc. Prof., Biotechnology Lab., Univ. of British Columbia 1989–96, Prof., Michael Smith Labs and Depts of Biochemistry and Molecular Biology, and Microbiology and Immunology 1996–, Peter Wall Distinguished Prof. 2002–; Dir SARS Accelerated Vaccine Initiative; Co-founder Inimex Pharmaceuticals, Inc.; mem. several editorial and advisory bds; mem. Canadian Centres of Excellence for Bacterial Diseases 1989; Fellow, American Acad. of Microbiology 2003, Canadian Acad. of Health Sciences 2005; Hon. mem. Univ. of British Columbia Golden Key Int. Honour Soc. 2001; Distinguished Scientist Seminar Award, Univ. of Southern Alabama 1991, Howard Hughes Medical Inst. Int. Research Scholar 1991, 1997, 2000, 2001, Fisher Scientific Award, Canadian Soc. of Microbiologists 1991, Killam Research Prize, Univ. of British Columbia 1993, Soc. Scientist Award 1996, 21st Annual Joseph E. Smadel Lecturer, Infectious Diseases Society of America 1997, E. W. R. Steacie Prize 1998, Howard Hughes Medical Inst. Holiday Lectures Presenter (first non-American) 1999, Dr Cam Coady Foundation Lectureship 2001, CIHR Distinguished Investigator Award 2001, 3M Distinguished Lectureship, Univ. of Western Ontario 2001, Distinguished Lecture in Biochemistry Award and Plaque, Univ. of Alberta 2001, Celebrate Research citation, Univ. of British Columbia 2001–04, James W. McLaughlin Distinguished Speaker, Univ. of Texas Medical Br. at Galveston 2002, Nat. Merit Award, Ottawa Life Sciences Council 2003, chosen by Time Canada as one of five Best in Medicine 2003, British Columbia Biotechnology Award for Innovation and Achievement 2003, featured in Maclean's The 2003 Watch List 2003, Solutions Through Research Award, British Columbia Innovation Council 2004, Squibb Award, Infectious Diseases Soc. of America 2004, Michael Smith Prize in Health Research 2004, CIHR Partnership Award for Sars Accelerated Vaccine Initiative 2005, awarded $5.7 million from Genome Canada for the PREPARE (Proteomics for Emerging Pathogen Response) project 2005, Gates Foundation Award in Global Disease Fight 2005, Jacob Biely Faculty Research Prize, Univ. of British Columbia 2006, Killam Prize, Canada Council for the Arts 2006, RSC Flavelle Medal 2006. *Publications:* numerous scientific papers in professional journals on host-pathogen interactions at the molecular level. *Address:* Room #331 East Mall, Michael Smith Building, University of British Columbia, Vancouver, BC V6T 1Z3, Canada (office). *Telephone:* (604) 822-2210 (office). *Fax:* (604) 822-9830 (office). *E-mail:* bfinlay@interchange.ubc.ca (office). *Website:* www.finlaylab.biotech.ubc.ca (office).

FINLAY, Frank, CBE; British actor; b. 6 Aug. 1926, Farnworth, Lancs.; s. of Josiah Finlay and Margaret Finlay; m. Doreen Joan Shepherd 1954; two s. one d.; ed St Gregory the Great, Farnworth, Royal Acad. of Dramatic Art, London; repertory 1950–52, 1954–57; Hon. Fellow (Bolton Inst.) 1992; Clarence Derwent Best Actor Award (for Chips with Everything) 1962, Best Actor Award, San Sebastian (for Othello) 1966, Soc. of Film and TV Arts Awards (for The Lie and Don Quixote), Best Actor Award (for Bouquet of Barbed Wire). *Stage appearances include:* Belgrade, Epitaph for George Dillon 1958, Sugar in the Morning, Sergeant Musgrave's Dance, Chicken Soup with Barley, Roots, I'm Talking About Jerusalem, The Happy Haven, Platonov, Chips with Everything 1958–62 (all at Royal Court), St Joan, The Workhouse Donkey, Hobson's Choice 1963, Othello, The Dutch Courtesan 1964, The Crucible, Much Ado About Nothing, Mother Courage 1965, Juno and the Paycock, The Storm 1966 (all at Nat. Theatre), After Haggerty (Aldwych, Criterion), Son of Man (Leicester Theatre, Round House) 1970, Saturday Sunday Monday, The Party 1973, Plunder, Watch It Come Down, Weapons of Happiness 1976, Amadeus 1982 (all at Nat. Theatre), Kings and Clowns (Phoenix), Filumena (Lyric) 1978, The Girl in Melanie Klein 1980, The Cherry Orchard 1983, Mutiny (Piccadilly) 1985, Beyond Reasonable Doubt 1987, Black Angel 1990, A Slight Hangover 1991, The Heiress 1992, The Woman in Black 1993–94, Capt. Hook/Mr Darling in Peter Pan 1994, Gaslight 1995, The Handyman 1996. *Film appearances include:* The Longest Day 1962, Private Potter 1962, Life for Ruth 1962, Loneliness of the Long Distance Runner 1962, The Comedy Man 1963, The Informers 1964, Hot Enough for June 1964, A Study in Terror 1965, Othello 1965, The Sandwich Man 1966, The Deadly Bees 1966, The Jokers 1967, I'll Never Forget What's'isname 1967, Robbery 1967, The Shoes of the Fisherman 1968, Inspector Clouseau 1968, Twisted Nerve 1968, Cromwell 1970, The Molly Maguires 1970, Assault 1971, Danny Jones 1971, Gumshoe 1971, Shaft in Africa 1973, Van Der Walk and the Dead, The Three Musketeers 1973, The Ring of Darkness, The Wild Geese, The Four Musketeers 1974, Murder by Decree 1979, The Return of the Soldier 1982, The Ploughman's Lunch 1982, Enigma 1983, The Key 1983, 1919 (voice) 1985, Life Force 1985, King of the Wind 1989, The Return of the Musketeers 1989, Cthulhu Mansion 1990, Sparrow 1993, Gospa 1995, Romance and Rejection 1996, Limited Edition 1996, For My Baby 1997, Stiff Upper Lips 1998, So This Is Romance? 1998, Dreaming of Joseph Lees 1999, Ghosthunter 2000, The Martins 2001, The Pianist 2002, Silent Cry 2002, The Statement 2003, Lighthouse Hill 2004, The Waiting Room 2007. *TV appearances include:* Target Luna (series) 1960, The Compartment 1961, The Murderer 1966, Much Ado About Nothing 1967, Oldenberg 1967, Never Mind the Quality, Feel the Width 1967, Les Misérables 1967, This Happy Breed 1969, Julius Caesar 1969, Blood of the Lamb 1969, The Lie 1970, Casanova (mini-series) 1971, The Merchant of Venice 1972, The Adventures of Don Quixote 1973, Candide 1973, Voltaire, Van Der Walk and the Girl 1972, Van Der Walk and the Rich 1973, The Death of Adolf Hitler 1973, Pas de frontières pour l'inspecteur: Le bouc émissaire 1975, 84 Charing Cross Road 1975, Bouquet of Barbed Wire (mini-series) 1976, Another Bouquet (mini-series) 1977, Count Dracula 1977, The Thief of Baghdad 1978, Saturday Sunday Monday, Sakharov 1984, A Christmas Carol 1984, In the Secret State 1985, Arc de Triomphe 1985, The Last Campaign, Napoleon in Betzi, Dear Brutus, Tales of the Unexpected, Tales from 1001 Nights, Aspects of Love—Mona, Casanova 1987, Verdict on Erebus, Mountain of Diamonds 1991, Encounters, The Other Side, Stalin 1992, Charlemagne (mini-series) 1993, An Exchange of Fire 1993, Common as Muck (series) 1994, A Mind to Murder 1995, How Do You Want Me? (series) 1998, The Magical Legend of the Leprechauns 1999, Longitude 2000, The Sins (mini-series) 2000, In The Beginning (voice, uncredited) 2000, Station Jim 2001, The Lost Prince 2003, Eroica 2003, Prime Suspect 6 2003, Life Begins (series) 2004, Heartbeat, Dalgliesh, Sherlock Holmes. *Leisure interests:* reading, walking, the countryside. *Address:* c/o Ken McReddie Ltd, Paurelle House, 91 Regent Street, London, W1R 7TB, England.

FINLAY, Thomas Aloysius, BA; Irish lawyer; b. 17 Sept. 1922; s. of Thomas A. Finlay and Eva Finlay; m. Alice Blayney 1948; two s. three d.; ed Xavier School, Dublin, Clongowes Wood Coll., Univ. Coll., Dublin; called to the Bar, King's Inn Dublin 1944; mem. Dail Eireann 1954–57; Sr Counsel 1961; Bencher 1972; Judge of the High Court 1972, Pres. 1974; Chief Justice 1985–94; Chair. Referendum Comm. 1998–2001; mem. Council of State; Hon. Bencher (Inn of Court, NI) 1985, (Middle Temple) 1986; Hon. LLD (Dublin, Nat. Univ. of Ireland) 1992. *Leisure interests:* fishing, shooting, conversation. *Address:* 22 Ailesbury Drive, Dublin 4, Ireland. *Telephone:* 2693395.

FINLAYSON, Chris, BA, LLM, LTCL; New Zealand lawyer and politician; *Attorney-General, Minister in Charge of Treaty of Waitangi Negotiations and Minister for Arts, Culture and Heritage;* b. 4 Dec. 1956, Wellington; ed Victoria Univ.; admitted to Bar 1981; Pnr, Brandon Brookfield (law firm) 1986–90; Lecturer in Law, Victoria Univ. 1987–2002; Law Soc. Rep., New Zealand Council of Law Reporting 1990–98, New Zealand Council of Legal Educ. 1992–98, High Court Rules Cttee 1999–2005; Pnr, Bell Gully 1991–2003; Barrister 2003–; mem. New Zealand Nat. Party 1974–, mem. Rules Cttee 1997–2001, Regional Chair. Lower North Island 2001–03, Electorate Chair. Mana Electorate 2003–05, Policy Chair. 2005–05; Assoc. Spokesman Treaty of Waitangi Issues and Maori Affairs 2005–06, Arts, Culture and Heritage 2005–06; Deputy Chair. Justice and Electoral Cttee 2005–08; Attorney-Gen., Minister in Charge of Treaty of Waitangi Negotiations and Minister for Arts, Culture and Heritage 2008–; Chair. Arts Board 1998–2001; Trustee Theatre Arts Charitable Trust, New Zealand Symphony Orchestra Foundation.

Address: Office of the Attorney-General, Department of the Prime Minister and Cabinet, Executive Wing, Parliament Buildings, Wellington, New Zealand (office). *Telephone:* (4) 817-9700 (office). *Fax:* (4) 472-3181 (office). *E-mail:* admin@dpmc.govt.nz (office). *Website:* www.dpmc.govt.nz (office).

FINLAYSON, Max, BSc, PhD; Australian ecologist, academic and international organization official; *Professor of Ecology and Biodiversity and Director, Institute for Land, Water and Society, Charles Sturt University;* b. Mt Barker, WA; ed Univ. of Western Australia, James Cook Univ., Townsville; worked with CSIRO Irrigation Research at Griffith on aquatic weed control and using water plants to treat waste water 1980–83; worked at Office of the Supervising Scientist, Alligator Rivers Region, Kakadu, Northern Territory researching effects of uranium mining on floodplain environment 1983–89, research/managerial job 1993–2000; worked with Int. Waterbird and Wetland Research Bureau, Slimbridge, Glos., UK 1989–93, worked on wetlands conservation projects and capacity building in USSR, Eastern Europe, Eastern Africa and the Mediterranean; worked in S Africa arguing against expansion of mineral sands mining into St Lucia Nature Reserve; Dir Environmental Research Inst. for Office of Supervising Scientists, Darwin 2000–05; Prin. Researcher (Ecology), Int. Water Man. Inst., Colombo, Sri Lanka 2005–07; Prof. of Ecology and Biodiversity and Dir Inst. for Land, Water and Society, Charles Sturt Univ. 2007–; Pres. Supervisory Council Wetlands International 2001–07; mem. Scientific Advisory Council to Biological Station Tour Du Valat, Camargue, France 2007–; Recognition of Excellence, Ramsar Wetland Conservation Awards 2002. *Publications:* more than 200 book chapters, journal articles, reports, guidelines and proceedings on wetland ecology and management. *Address:* Institute for Land, Water and Society, Charles Sturt University, Albury-Wodonga (Thurgoona) Campus, Elizabeth Mitchell Drive, PO Box 789, Albury, NSW 2640, Australia (office). *Telephone:* (2) 6051-9779 (office). *Fax:* (2) 6051-9797 (office). *E-mail:* mfinlayson@csu.edu.au (office). *Website:* www.csu.edu.au/research/ilws (office).

FINLEY, Diane, BA, MBA; Canadian politician; *Minister of Human Resources and Social Development;* b. 1957, Hamilton, Ont.; m. Doug Finley; ed Port Dover Composite School, Univ. of Western Ont.; fmr Admin. Univ. of Western Ont. French immersion school; positions in health care, transportation, agricultural equipment manufacturing, publishing, aviation; fmrly with Laidlaw Group of Cos; mem. Parl. 2004–; Official Opposition Critic for Agric. and Agri-food 2004; Minister of Human Resources and Skills Devt 2006–07, 2008–, of Citizenship and Immigration 2007–08. *Address:* Human Resources and Social Development, Phase IV, 140 promenade du Portage, Gatineau, QC K1A 0J9, Canada (office). *Telephone:* (819) 994-6313 (office). *Fax:* (819) 953-7260 (office). *Website:* www.hrsdc.gc.ca (office).

FINLEY, Gerald Hunter, MA, ARCM, FRCM; Canadian singer (baritone); b. 1960, Montreal; s. of Eric Gault Finley and Catherine; m. Louise Winter 1990; two s.; ed Glebe Collegiate Inst., Ottawa, Univ. of Ottawa, Royal Coll. of Music, London, UK, Nat. Opera Studio, London, King's Coll. Cambridge; chorister St Matthew's Church, Ottawa 1969–78; mem. Ottawa Choral Soc., Cantata Singers, Ont. Youth Choir 1977–78, Glyndebourne Festival Chorus, UK 1986–89; professional debut as opera soloist, Antonio in Le Nozze di Figaro, Ottawa 1987 and Papageno in The Magic Flute, London 1989; roles at Glyndebourne include Sid in Albert Herring 1989, Papageno, Guglielmo, Count Dominik in Arabella, Kuligin in Katya Kabanova 1990–93, Figaro in Marriage of Figaro at opening of new opera house 1994; Owen Wingrave, Olivier in Capriccio, Nick Shadow; Agamemnon in Iphigénie en Avlide, debut Canadian Opera Co., Sid in Albert Herring 1991; has sung Figaro at Covent Garden London and many other opera houses worldwide 1992–; other roles at Covent Garden include Pilgrim in Pilgrim's Progress, Achilla in Giulio Cesare, Creonte in L'Anima del Filosofo, Forester in Cunning Little Vixen, Don Giovanni, Count in Le Nozze di Figaro 2006; roles at Opéra de Paris include Valentin, Sharpless, Papageno, Figaro, Don Giovanni 2001; debut Metropolitan Opera, New York, Papageno in The Magic Flute 1998; Don Giovanni at Metropolitan Opera, Vienna, Prague, Budapest, Rome and Tel Aviv; role of Mr. Fox in Fantastic Mr. Fox, LA Opera 1998; debut ENO, Harry Heegan in The Silver Tassie 2000, Onegin in Eugene Onegin 2005; at San Francisco Opera J.Robert Oppenheimer in Dr Atomic 2005, also at Amsterdam, Chicago, Metropolitan Opera and ENO; concert soloist and lieder singer; Visiting Prof. Royal Coll. of Music (RCM) 2000; John Christie Award, Glyndebourne 1989; Juno Award for Best Vocal Peformance (Canada) 1998; Singer Award Royal Philharmonic Soc. 2001. *Films:* Owen Wingrave 2001, L'amour de loin 2006, Doctor Atomic 2008. *Recordings:* albums include: Papageno, Guglielmo, Sid, Masetto, Haydn's Creation, Brahms' Requiem, Silver Tassie, Pilgrim's Progress, Dido and Aeneas; Songs of Travel 1998, Schubert Complete Songs 1817–1821, Complete Songs of Henri Duparc 2002, Songs of Charles Ives 2005, 2008, Stanford – Orchestral Songs (Gramophone Awards Editor's Choice Award) 2006, Barber: Hermit Songs (Gramophone Award for Best Solo Vocal 2008) 2007. *Radio:* numerous recordings with BBC and CBC. *Leisure interests:* wine, reading, ice skating. *Address:* IMG Artists, The Light Box, 111 Power Road, London, W4 5PY, England (office); c/o IMG Artists, Carnegie Hall Tower, 152 West 57th Street, 5th Floor, New York, NY 10019, USA (office). *Telephone:* (20) 7957-5800 (London) (office); (212) 994-3500 (USA) (office). *Fax:* (20) 7957-5801 (London) (office); (212) 994-3550 (New York) (office). *E-mail:* salmansi@imgartists.com (office). *Website:* www.imgartists.com (office); www.geraldfinley.com.

FINN, Pavel Konstantinovich; Russian scriptwriter; b. (Pavel Finn-Halfin), 28 June 1940, Moscow; m. Irina Chernova-Finn; one s.; ed All-Union State Inst. of Cinematography; fmr journalist, documentary maker; freelance script writer 1968–; Head of Higher Workshop Course of Scriptwriters; Chair. Cinema Dramaturgy Council, Moscow Union of Cinematographers 2001; First Deputy Chair. Russian Union of Cinematographers 2001–; Distinguished Artist of the Russian SFSR 1991. *Films include:* Headless Horse Rider 1973, Armed and Very Dangerous 1977, 26 Days of Dostoyevsky's Life 1980, Icicle in a Warm Sea 1983, Witness 1985, Lady Macbeth of Mtsensk Region 1989, Accidental Waltz 1989, Sunset 1990, Myth about Leonid 1991, A Big Concert of Peoples 1991, Shylock 1993, Jester's Revenge 1994, For What 1995, Career of Arthur Whui 1996, Break Point, We Are Your Kids, Moscow, Eve's Gates, Death of Tairov or Princess Brambilla, Secrets of Court Coups: Film Two 2000, Miracles, or Pike in the Moscow Style 2001, Ravine 2007. *Leisure interests:* buying books, reading. *Address:* Union of Cinematographers, Vassil'yevskaya str. 13, 123825 Moscow (office); 4th Rostovsky per. 2/1, Apt 9, 119121 Moscow, Russia (home). *Telephone:* (495) 248-53-28 (home); (495) 334-59-34 (home). *Fax:* (495) 251-51-06 (office). *E-mail:* pavelfinn@mtu-net.ru (home).

FINN, Victor Konstantinovich, DrSc; Russian philosopher, logician and computer scientist; b. 15 July 1933, Moscow; m. Irina Yevgenyevna Yavchunovskaya-Belova; one d.; ed Moscow State Univ.; researcher, Head of Sector, Lab. of Electromodelling, USSR Acad. of Sciences 1957–59; Head of Lab. All-Union Inst. for Scientific and Tech. Information (VINITI) 1959–; Lecturer, Moscow State Univ. 1967–68; Prof., Head Dept of Artificial Intelligence, Moscow State Inst. of History and Archives (now Russian Humanitarian Univ.) 1979–; mem. Acad. of Natural Sciences; mem. Bd int. journals Studia Logica, Foundation of Science; mem. Council Russian Asscn of Artificial Intelligence; Honoured Science Worker 2007. *Publications:* over 100 scientific papers and books including Logical Problems of Information Search 1976, Epistemological and Logical Problems of History (with K. Khvostova) 1995, Intellectual Systems and Society 2001. *Address:* 1st Miusskaya str. 20, Apt. 19, 125047 Moscow, Russia (home). *Telephone:* (495) 155-43-65 (office); (495) 251-08-99 (home). *Fax:* (495) 152-54-47 (office). *E-mail:* finn@viniti.ru (office); ira-finn@mtu-net.ru (home).

FINNBOGADÓTTIR, Vigdís; Icelandic politician and fmr head of state; b. 15 April 1930, Reykjavík; d. of Finnbogi Rutur Thorvaldsson and Sigridur Eiriksdóttir; m. (divorced); one adopted d.; ed Junior Coll., Menntaskólinn i Reykjavik, Univs of Grenoble and Sorbonne, France, Univ. of Iceland; press officer, Nat. Theatre of Iceland 1954–57, 1961–64; teacher at Reykjavík Grammar School 1962–67, Hamrahlíð Grammar School 1967–72; taught French at Jr Colls, Menntaskólinn i Reykjavik, Menntaskólinn vid Hamrahlid; fmr Head of Guide Training, Iceland Tourist Bureau; Dir Reykjavík Theatre Co. 1972–80; taught French drama, Univ. of Iceland; worked for Icelandic State TV; fmr Chair. Alliance Française; mem. Advisory Cttee on Cultural Affairs in Nordic Countries 1976–80, Chair. 1978–80; Pres. of Iceland 1980–96; UNESCO Goodwill Amb. for Languages 1998–; mem. Club of Madrid; Hon. GCMG 1982; Dr hc (Grenoble) 1985, (Bordeaux) 1987, (Smith Coll., USA) 1988, (Luther Coll., USA) 1989, (Manitoba) 1989 (Nottingham) 1990, (Tampere) 1990, (Gothenburg) 1990, (Gashuin, Tokyo) 1991, (Miami) 1993, (St Mary's, Halifax) 1996), (Leeds) 1996, (Memorial, St John) 1997, (Guelph) 1998, (Iceland) 2000. *Leisure interest:* theatre. *Address:* c/o Office of the President, Stornarráðshúsið, v/Lækjarötu, 150 Reykjavík, Iceland (office).

FINNEGAN, John D., BA, MBA, DJur; American business executive; *Chairman, President and CEO, The Chubb Corporation;* b. 1949; ed Princeton, Rutgers and Fordham Univs; began career with Gen. Motors (GM) 1976, various positions including Vice-Pres. GM and Pres. GM Acceptance Corpn 1997–99, Exec. Vice-Pres. GM and Pres. and Chair. GM Acceptance Corpn 1999–2002; apptd Dir The Chubb Corpn 2002, Pres. and CEO 2002–03, Chair., Pres. and CEO 2003–; mem. Bd United Negro Coll. Fund. *Address:* The Chubb Corporation, 15 Mountain View Road, Warren, NJ 07061-1615, USA (office). *Telephone:* (908) 903-2000 (office). *Fax:* (908) 903-3402 (office). *Website:* www.chubb.com (office).

FINNEY, Albert; British actor; b. 9 May 1936; m. 1st Jane Wenham (divorced); one s.; m. 2nd Anouk Aimée 1970 (divorced 1978); m. 3rd Pene Delmage 2006; ed Salford Grammar School and Royal Acad. of Dramatic Art; Birmingham Repertory Co. 1956–58; Shakespeare Memorial Theatre Co. 1959; Nat. Theatre 1965, 1975; formed Memorial Enterprises 1966; Assoc. Artistic Dir English Stage Co. 1972–75; Dir United British Artists 1983–86; Hon. LittD (Sussex) 1966; Lawrence Olivier Award 1986; London Standard Drama Award for Best Actor 1986, Dilys Powell Award, London Film Critics Circle 1999; BAFTA Fellowship 2001. *Plays include:* Julius Caesar, Macbeth, Henry V, The Beaux' Stratagem, The Alchemist, The Lizard on the Rock, The Party 1958, King Lear, Othello 1959, A Midsummer Night's Dream, The Lily-White Boys 1960, Billy Liar 1960, Luther 1961, 1963, Much Ado About Nothing, Armstrong's Last Goodnight 1965, Miss Julie 1965, Black Comedy 1965, Love for Love 1965, A Flea in Her Ear 1966, A Day in the Death of Joe Egg 1968, Alpha Beta 1972, Krapp's Last Tape 1973, Cromwell 1973, Chez Nous 1974, Loot (Dir) 1975, Hamlet 1976, Tamburlaine the Great 1976, Uncle Vanya 1977, Present Laughter 1977, The Country Wife 1977–78, The Cherry Orchard 1978, Macbeth 1978, Has 'Washington' Legs? 1978, The Biko Inquest (Dir) 1984, Sergeant Musgrave's Dance (Dir) 1984, Orphans 1986, J.J. Farr 1987, Another Time 1989, Reflected Glory 1992, Art 1996. *Films acted in include:* The Entertainer 1959, Saturday Night and Sunday Morning 1960, Tom Jones 1963, Night Must Fall 1963, Two for the Road 1967, Charlie Bubbles (also Dir) 1968, Scrooge 1970, Gumshoe 1971, Murder on the Orient Express 1974, Wolfen 1979, Loophole 1980, Looker 1980, Shoot the Moon 1981, Annie 1982, Life of John Paul II 1983, The Dresser 1983, Under the Volcano 1983, Orphans (also Dir) 1987, Miller's Crossing 1989, The Image 1989, The Playboys 1992, Rich in Love 1992, The Browning Version 1993, The Run of the Country 1995, Washington Square, Breakfast of Champions 1999, Simpatico 1999, Delivering Milo 1999, Erin Brockovich 2000, Big Fish 2003, A Good Year 2006, Amazing Grace 2006, The Bourne Ultimatum 2007, Before the Devil Knows You're Dead 2007. *TV appearances include:* The Endless Game 1989, The Green Man (mini-series) 1990, Karaoke 1995, Nostromo 1997, My Uncle Silas 2001, 2003, The Lonely War 2002, The Gathering Storm (Emmy Award 2002, Golden Globe for Best Actor in a mini-series or TV movie 2003, BAFTA Award for Best Actor 2003) 2002. *Address:* c/o Michael Simkins LLP, Lynton House, 7–12 Tavistock Square, London, WC1H 9LT, England (office). *Telephone:* (20) 7874-5600 (office). *Fax:* (20) 7874-5601 (office).

FINNEY, David John, CBE, MA, ScD, FRS, FRSE; British professor of statistics (retd) and consultant biometrician; b. 3 Jan. 1917, Latchford, Warrington; s. of Robert George Stringer Finney and Bessie Evelyn Finney (née Whitlow); m. Mary Elizabeth Connolly 1950; one s. two d.; ed Univs of Cambridge and London; statistician, Rothamsted Experimental Station 1939–45; Lecturer in the Design and Analysis of Scientific Experiment, Univ. of Oxford 1945–54; Reader in Statistics, Univ. of Aberdeen 1954–64, Prof. of Statistics 1964–66; Prof. of Statistics, Univ. of Edin. 1966–84; Dir Agricultural Research Council's Unit of Statistics 1954–84; Dir Research Centre, Int. Statistical Inst., Netherlands 1987–88; Pres. Biometric Soc. 1964–65; Chair. Computer Bd for Univs 1970–74; Pres. Royal Statistical Soc. 1973–74; Visiting Scientist Int. Rice Research Inst. 1984–85; FAO Key Consultant to Indian Agricultural Statistics Research Inst. 1983–91; mem. Adverse Reactions Sub-cttee of Cttee on Safety of Medicines 1963–80; Weldon Memorial Prize 1956; Paul Martini Prize 1971; Hon. DèsSc Agronomiques (Gembloux); Hon. DSc (City Univ., Heriot-Watt Univ.); Hon. Dr Math. (Waterloo, Ont.) 1989. *Publications:* Probit Analysis 1947, 1952, 1971, Biological Standardization (with J.H. Burn and L. G. Goodwin) 1950, Statistical Method in Biological Assay 1952, 1964, 1978, Introduction to Statistical Science in Agriculture 1953, 1962, 1964, 1972, Experimental Design and its Statistical Basis 1955, Técnica y Teoría en el Diseño de Experimentos 1957, Introduction to the Theory of Experimental Design 1960, Statistics for Mathematicians 1968, Statistics for Biologists 1980; more than 290 papers. *Leisure interests:* music, travel, statistical biometry. *Telephone:* (131) 667-0135 (home). *E-mail:* david.finney@freeuk.com (home).

FINNEY, Sir Tom, Kt, CBE, OBE; British football official; b. 5 April 1922, Preston; s. of the late Alf Finney and Margaret Finney; m.; one s. one d.; ed Deepdale Modern School; joined Preston North End Football Club 1940, retd 1960, now Pres.; played 433 league games for Preston, scored 187 goals; 76 England caps, scored 30 goals; Hon. Freeman of Preston 1979; Hon. LLD (Lancaster) 1998; Football Writers' Asscn Footballer of the Year 1954, 1957; Professional Football Asscn Merit Award 1979. *Publications:* Football Around the World 1953, Finney on Football 1958, Finney: A Football Legend 1990, Tom Finney: My Autobiography 2003. *Leisure interests:* walking, golf, reading autobiographies. *Address:* Preston North End Football Club, Deepdale, Sir Tom Finney Way, Preston, PR1 6RU, England (office).

FINNIS, John Mitchell, LLB, DPhil, FBA; Australian/British academic and barrister; *Professor of Law and Legal Philosophy, University of Oxford;* b. 28 July 1940, Adelaide; s. of the late Maurice M. S. Finnis and of Margaret McKellar Stewart; m. Marie Carmel McNally 1964; three s. three d.; ed St Peter's Coll., Adelaide, Univ. of Adelaide, Oxford Univ.; Fellow and Praelector in Jurisprudence, Univ. Coll., Oxford 1966–, Stowell Civil Law Fellow 1973–, Vice-Master 2001–; Lecturer in Law, Oxford Univ. 1966–72, Rhodes Reader in the Laws of the Commonwealth and the United States 1972–89, Prof. of Law and Legal Philosophy 1989–, mem. Philosophy Sub-Faculty 1984–, Chair. Bd of Faculty of Law 1987–89; Prof. and Head of Dept of Law, Univ. of Malawi 1976–78; Biolchini Family Prof. of Law, Univ. of Notre Dame, Ind., USA 1995–, Adjunct Prof. of Philosophy 1999–; barrister, Gray's Inn 1970–; Gov., Plater Coll., Oxford 1972–92; Consultor, Pontifical Commission Iustitia et Pax 1977–89, mem. 1990–95; Special Adviser, Foreign Affairs Cttee, House of Commons, on role of UK Parl. in Canadian Constitution 1980–82; mem. Catholic Bishops' Jt Cttee on Bio-ethical Issues 1981–89, Int. Theological Comm. (Vatican) 1986–92; Gov. Linacre Centre for Medical Ethics 1981–96, 1998– (Vice-Chair. 1987–96, 1998–); Huber Distinguished Visiting Prof., Boston Coll. Law School 1993–94; mem. Pontifical Acad. Pro Vita 2001–. *Publications:* Halsbury's Laws of England (fourth edn), Vol. 6 (Commonwealth and Dependencies) 1974, 1990, 2003, Natural Law and Natural Rights 1980, Fundamentals of Ethics 1983, Nuclear Deterrence, Morality and Realism (with Joseph Boyle and Germain Grisez) 1987, Moral Absolutes 1991, Aquinas: Moral, Political and Legal Theory 1998; articles on constitutional law, legal philosophy, ethics, moral theology and late sixteenth-century history. *Address:* University College, Oxford, OX1 4BH, England (office); Notre Dame Law School, South Bend, IN 46556, USA (office). *Telephone:* (1865) 276641 (UK) (office); (574) 631-5989 (USA) (office); (1865) 558660 (UK) (home).

FINO, Bashkim Muhamet; Albanian politician and economist; b. 12 Oct. 1962, Gjirokaster; m.; two c.; ed Tirana Univ. and studies in USA; economist, Economic Data Inst., Gjirokaster Dist 1986–89, Dir 1989–92; Mayor of Gjirokaster (Socialist Party of Albania) 1992–96; Prime Minister of Albania March–July 1997; Deputy Prime Minister 1997–98. *Address:* c/o Council of Ministers, Këshilli i Ministrave, Tirana, Albania.

FINSCHER, Ludwig, PhD; German musicologist, lexicographer and academic (retd); b. 14 March 1930, Kassel; ed Univs of Göttingen and Saarbrücken; Asst Lecturer, Univ. of Kiel 1960–65, Univ. of Saarbrücken 1965–68; Ed. Die Musikforschung 1961–68, Co-Ed. 1968–74; Prof. of Musicology, Univ. of Frankfurt am Main 1968–81, Univ. of Heidelberg 1981–95; mem. Akad. der Wissenschaften, Heidelberg, Akad. der Wissenschaften und der Literatur, Mainz, Academia Europaea; Corresp. mem. American Musicological Soc.; Hon. mem. Int. Musicological Soc., Gesellschaft für Musikforschung; Hon. Foreign Mem. Royal Musical Asscn, London 1978; Ordre pour le Mérite 1994, Grand Order of Merit (Germany) 1997; Dr hc (Athens) 2002, (Zürich) 2003; Akademie der Wissenschaften Prize, Göttingen 1968, Balzan 2006. *Publications:* Collected Works of Gaffurius (ed., two vols) 1955, 1960, Collected Works of Compère (ed., five vols) 1958–72, Loyset Compère (*c.* 1450–1518): Life and Works 1964, Geschichte der Evangelischen Kirchenmusik (co-ed., second edn) 1965, Studien zur Geschichte des Streichquartetts: I, Die Entstehung des klassischen Streichquartetts: Von den Vorformen zur Grundlegung durch Joseph Haydn 1974, Collected Works of Hindemith (co-ed. with K. von Fischer) 1976–, Renaissance-Studien: Helmuth Osthoff zum 80. Geburtstag (ed.) 1979, Quellenstudien zu Musik der Renaissance (ed., two vols) 1981, 1983, Ludwig van Beethoven (ed.) 1983, Claudio Monteverdi: Festschrift Reinhold Hammerstein zum 70. Geburtstag (ed.) 1986, Die Musik des 15. und 16. Jahrhunderts: Neues Handbuch der Musikwissenschaft (ed., Vol. 3/1–2) 1989–90, Die Mannheimer Hofkapelle im Zeitalter Carl Theodors (ed.) 1992, Die Musik in Geschichte und Gegenwart (ed., second edn, 26 vols) 1994–2007, Joseph Haydn 2000, Geschichte und Geschichten: Ausgewählte Aufsätze zur Musikhistorie 2003; contrib. editorially to the complete works of Mozart and Gluck, contrib. to scholarly books and journals. *Address:* Am Walde 1, 38302 Wolfenbüttel, Germany (home). *Telephone:* (5331) 32713 (home). *Fax:* (5331) 33276 (home).

FIONDA, Andrew, MA, M.Design; British fashion designer; b. 8 Feb. 1967, Middlesbrough, Cleveland; s. of Frederick Fionda and of Sarah Park; ed Nottingham Trent Univ., Royal Coll. of Art; designer for fashion houses in UK and for John McIntyre, Hong Kong; launched Pearce Fionda collection with Reynold Pearce (q.v.) 1994; exhbns. include Design of the Times, RCA 1996, The Cutting Edge of British Fashion 1997; Man. Dir Pearce Fionda (London) Ltd; British Apparel Export Award for Best New Designer (with Reynold Pearce) 1994, New Generation Award Lloyds Bank British Fashion Award 1995, Int. Apparel Fed. World Young Designers Award 1996; Lloyds Bank British Fashion Award (Glamour Category) 1997. *Leisure interests:* cinema, gym, music, reading. *Address:* Pearce Fionda, 27 Horsell Road, Highbury, London, N5 1XL, England (office). *Telephone:* (20) 7609-6470 (office). *E-mail:* pearcef@dircon.co.uk (office).

FIORELLO, Rosario Tindario, (Fiorello); Italian singer and radio and television presenter; *Co-host, Viva Radio 2, Radiotelevisione Italiana SpA (RAI);* b. 16 May 1960, Catania; began career working in tourist villages, first as barman and then as singer, mimic and entertainer; spotted by talent scout Claudio Cecchetto late 1980s; began hosting show Viva Radio Deejay; host TV show Karaoke, went on to host various other shows, first on Mediaset networks, then with RAI with Stasera Pago Io 2001, 2002, 2004; Co-host, with Marco Baldini, Francesco Bozzi and Enrico Cremonesi, radio show Viva Radio 2 2002–. *Discography:* Veramente falso 1992, Nuovamente falso 1992, Spiagge e lune 1993, Karaoke 1993, Finalmente tu 1995, Sarò Fiorello 1996, Dai miei amici cantautori 1997, Batticuore (CD Bianco) 1998, Batticuore (CD Rosso) 1998, I miei amici cantautori 2000, Fiorello The Greatest 2002, Uno è famoso, l'altro no: Il meglio di Viva Radio 2 (CD and book) 2002, Viva Radio 2 (il meglio del 2003) 2003, A modo mio 2004, Viva Radio 2 (il meglio del 2005) 2005. *Address:* Viva Radio 2, Radiotelevisione Italiana SpA, Viale Mazzini 14, 00195 Rome, Italy (office). *Telephone:* (06) 38781 (office). *E-mail:* info@vivaradio2.it (office). *Website:* www.radio.rai.it/radio2/vivaradio2/index.cfm (office); www.rosariofiorello.it.

FIORENTINO, Linda; American actress; b. 9 March 1960, Philadelphia, Pa; ed Rosemont Coll., Circle in the Square Theatre School; mem. Circle in the Square Performing Workshops. *Films include:* Vision Quest 1985, Gotcha! 1985, After Hours 1985, The Moderns 1988, Queens Logic 1991, Shout 1991, Wildfire 1992, Chain of Desire 1993, The Desperate Trail 1994, The Last Seduction 1994, Bodily Harm 1995, Larger Than Life 1996, Jade 1995, Unforgettable 1997, The Split 1997, Men in Black 1997, Kicked in the Head 1997, Body Count 1998, Dogma 1999, Ordinary Decent Criminal 2000, Where the Money Is 2000, What Planet Are You From? 2000, Liberty Stands Still 2002, Once More with Feeling 2009. *Television films include:* The Neon Empire 1989, The Last Game 1992, Acting on Impulse 1993, Beyond the Law 1994, The Desperate Trail 1995. *Address:* c/o United Talent Agency, 9560 Wilshire Boulevard, Floor 5, Beverly Hills, CA 90212, USA.

FIORI, Publio; Italian politician and lawyer; *Leader, Rifondazione Democristiana;* b. 1938; elected Christian Democrat mem. Rome City Council 1971, Lazio Regional Council 1975; Christian Democrat Deputy 1979–94, Alleanza Nazionale Deputy 1994, Vice-Pres., Chamber of Deputies 2001; resgnd Alleanza Nazionale 2005, joined Democrazia Cristiana per le Autonomie but resgnd 2006; Founder and Leader Rifondazione Democristiana 2006–; fmr mem. Parl. Comm. on Finance, Under-Sec. for Posts and Telecommunications, for Health; Minister of Transport 1994–95. *Address:* Via Monte Zebio 32, 00195 Rome, Italy (office). *Telephone:* (06) 3227658 (office); (06) 3225931 (office). *Fax:* (06) 3612170 (office). *E-mail:* sedenazionale@rifondazionedc.it (office); ufficiostampa@rifondazionedc.it (office); studiolegalefiori@libero.it (office). *Website:* www.rifondazionedc.it (office); www.publiofiori.com (office).

FIORINA, Carleton (Carly) S., BA, MS, MBA; American computer industry executive; b. (Cara Carleton Sneed), 6 Sept. 1954, Austin, Tex.; m. Frank Fiorina; two step-d.; ed attended secondary schools in Ghana, UK, N Carolina, and Calif., Stanford Univ., Robert H. Smith School of Business at Univ. of Maryland, Sloan School of Man. at MIT; began career with entry-level job, Hewlett-Packard Shipping Dept; fmr English teacher in Italy and seller of telephone services to fed. agencies; spent nearly 20 years at AT&T Corpn and Lucent Technologies Inc., Exec. Vice-Pres. Computer Operations, oversaw formation and spin-off of Lucent Technologies from AT&T, served as Lucent's Pres. Global Service Provider Business and Pres. Consumer Products; Pres., CEO and Dir Hewlett-Packard Co. 1999–2000, Chair. and CEO 2000–05; mem. Bd Dirs US-China Bd of Trade, PowerUp, Revolution Health Group 2005–, Cybertrust 2005–, Taiwan Semiconductor Manufacturing Co. Ltd

2006–; Gen. Business News Contrib., Fox Business Network 2007–; econ. advisor to Sen. John McCain's campaign for US Pres. 2008; mem. Exec. Bd NY Stock Exchange; adviser, US Space Comm.; mem. Bd of Dirs Revolution Healthcare Group LLC, Taiwan Semiconductor Manufacturing; fmr mem. Bd of Dirs Cisco Systems, Kellogg Co., Merck & Co., Telecommunications Industry Asscn, USA-Repub. of China Econ. Council, Goldstar Information & Communications Inc., Seoul, S Korea, AT&T Taiwan Telecommunications, Taipei; Hon. Fellow, London Business School 2001; listed in Forbes' America's Most Powerful People, ranked by Fortune magazine amongst 50 Most Powerful Women in Business in the US (first) 1998–2003, (second) 2004, ranked by silicon.com amongst Top 50 Agenda Setters (22nd) 2002, (10th) 2003, Appeal of Conscience Award 2002, Concern Worldwide 'Seeds of Hope' Award 2003, Private Sector Council Leadership Award 2004, ranked tenth by Forbes magazine amongst 100 Most Powerful Women 2004. *Publication:* Tough Choices (memoir) 2006. *Leisure interests:* piano, gardening. *Address:* 3150 South Street, NW, No. 3B, Washington, DC 20007, USA (home). *Website:* www.carlyfiorina.com.

FIRE, Andrew Z., PhD; American microbiologist and academic; *Professor of Pathology and Genetics, School of Medicine, Stanford University;* b. 1959, Santa Clara Co., Calif.; ed Univ. of California, Berkeley and Massachusetts Inst. of Tech.; Researcher, Univ. of Cambridge, UK 1983–86; mem. staff, Dept of Embryology, Carnegie Inst. of Washington, Baltimore, Md 1986–2003, Carnegie Investigator 2003–; Prof. of Pathology and Genetics, Stanford Univ. School of Medicine 2003–; Adjunct Prof., Dept of Biology, Johns Hopkins Univ., Baltimore 2003–; Genetics Soc. of America Medal, Maryland Distinguished Young Scientist Award 1997, NAS Award in Molecular Biology (jtly) 2003, Wiley Prize in the Biomedical Sciences, Mellon Lecturer, Univ. of Pittsburgh 2003, Bernard Cohen Memorial Lecturer, Univ. of Pennsylvania School of Medicine 2004, Dr H.P. Heineken Prize for Biochemistry and Piophysics 2004, Nobel Prize in Medicine (with Craig C. Mello) 2006. *Publications:* numerous publs in scientific journals. *Address:* Departments of Pathology and Genetics, Stanford University School of Medicine, 300 Pasteur Drive, L235, Stanford, CA 94305-5324, USA (office). *Telephone:* (650) 723-2885 (office). *Fax:* (650) 725-6902 (office). *E-mail:* afire@stanford.edu (office). *Website:* genome-www.stanford.edu/group/fire (office).

FIRTASH, Dmitry; Ukrainian business executive; *Executive Chairman, Group DF;* m. Maria Firtash (divorced); expert in gas trading and distribution business in Eastern and Cen. Europe; secured gas deal with Turkmenistan Govt in exchange for supplies of fresh produce 1993; est. Highrock Holdings, partnership with gas trader Itera to oversee trade between Turkmenistan and Ukrainian state energy-provider Naftogaz 2001; f. Eural Trans Gas 2002 (replaced Highrock Holdings 2003); through his co. Centragas Holdings AG est. partnership with Russian energy corpn Gazprom to set up RosUkrEnergo 2004, which distributes gas from Cen. Asian states to Ukraine and EU; f. OSTCHEM Holding AG 2004, to consolidate his investments in titanium, soda ash, mineral fertilizers and other chemical products; f. Group DF 2007 to bring together business interests in energy, chemicals and property; other cos include Hungarian gas trader Emfesz, Estonian fertilizer mfr Nitrofert. *E-mail:* info@groupdf.com (office). *Website:* www.groupdf.com (office).

FIRTH, Colin; British actor; b. 10 Sept. 1960, Grayshott, Hampshire; s. of David Firth and Shirley Firth; one s. by Meg Tilly; ed Montgomery of Alamein School, Winchester and Drama Centre, London; Radio Times Best Actor Award for Tumbledown, 1996 Best Actor Award of Broadcasting Press Guild for Pride and Prejudice, Commdr of the Order of the Star of Italian Solidarity 2005. *Theatre includes:* Another Country 1983, Doctor's Dilemma 1984, The Lonely Road 1985, Desire Under the Elms 1987, The Caretaker 1991, Chatsky 1993, Three Days of Rain 1999. *Television appearances:* Dutch Girls 1984, Lost Empires (series) 1985–86, Robert Lawrence in Tumbledown 1987, Out of the Blue 1990, Hostages 1992, Master of the Moor 1993, The Deep Blue Sea 1994, Mr Darcy in Pride and Prejudice 1994, Nostromo 1997, The Turn of the Screw 1999, Donovan Quick 1999, Celebration 2006, Born Equal 2006. *Radio:* Richard II in Two Planks and a Passion 1986, Rupert Brooke in The One Before The Last 1987. *Films:* Another Country 1983, Camille 1984, A Month in the Country 1986, Apartment Zero 1988, Valmont (title role) 1988, Wings of Fame 1989, Femme Fatale 1990, The Hour of the Pig 1992, Good Girls 1994, Circle of Friends 1995, The English Patient 1996, Fever Pitch 1996, Shakespeare in Love 1998, The Secret Laughter of Women 1999, My Life So Far 1999, Relative Values 1999, Londinium 2000, Bridget Jones's Diary 2000, The Importance of Being Earnest 2002, Hope Springs 2003, Love Actually 2003, Trauma 2004, Bridget Jones: The Edge of Reason 2004, Where the Truth Lies 2005, Nanny McPhee 2005, The Last Legion 2007, And When Did You Last See Your Father? 2007, St Trinian's 2007, Then She Found Me 2007, The Accidental Husband 2008, Mamma Mia! 2008, Easy Virtue 2008. *Address:* c/o ICM Ltd, Oxford House, 76 Oxford Street, London, W1N 0AX, England. *Telephone:* (20) 7636-6565. *Fax:* (20) 7323-0101.

FIRTH, Peter; British actor; b. 27 Oct. 1953, Bradford; s. of Eric Firth and Mavis Firth; m. Lindsey Readman 1990; two s. one d.; has appeared with Nat. Theatre in Equus, Romeo and Juliet, Spring Awakening; Broadway appearances include role of Mozart in Amadeus; Acad. Award for Best Supporting Actor, Tony Award, Golden Globe for Best Supporting Actor (all for Equus) and numerous other awards. *Films include:* Fratello sole, sorella luna 1972, Daniele e Maria 1973, King Arthur, the Young Warlord 1975, Aces High 1976, Joseph Andrews 1977, Equus 1977, When You Comin' Back, Red Ryder? 1979, Tess 1979, Feuer und Schwert: Die Legende von Tristan und Isolde 1982, White Elephant 1983, Born of Fire 1983, Letter to Brezhnev 1985, Lifeforce 1985, A State of Emergency 1986, Prisoner of Rio 1988, Tree of Hands 1989, Trouble in Paradise 1989, The Laughter of God 1990, The Hunt for Red October 1990, Burndown 1990, The Rescuers Down Under (voice) 1990, The Pleasure Principle 1991, White Angel 1993, El Marido perfecto 1993, Shadowlands 1993, An Awfully Big Adventure 1995, Marco Polo: Haperek Ha'aharon 1996, Merisairas 1996, Gaston's War 1997, Amistad 1997, Woundings 1998, Mighty Joe Young 1998, Chill Factor 1999, Pearl Harbor 2001, The Greatest Game Ever Played 2005. *TV includes:* The Flaxton Boys (series) 1969, Here Come the Double Deckers (series) 1970, Her Majesty's Pleasure 1973, Diamonds on Wheels 1974, The Picture of Dorian Gray 1976, The Lady of the Camellias 1976, The Flipside of Dominick Hide 1980, Another Flip for Dominick 1982, The Aerodrome 1983, Northanger Abbey 1986, Blood Royal: William the Conqueror 1990, The Incident 1990, Children Crossing 1990, Murder in Eden (miniseries) 1991, Prisoner of Honor 1991, Heartbeat (series) 1994, Resort to Murder (miniseries) 1995, The Witch's Daughter 1996, And the Beat Goes On (series) 1996, The Garden of Redemption 1997, The Broker's Man (series) 1997, Holding On (miniseries) 1997, That's Life (series) 2000, Spooks (series) 2002, Me & Mrs Jones 2002, Hawking 2004. *Leisure interests:* cookery, sailing. *Address:* Susan Smith Associates, 121 North San Vicente Boulevard, Beverly Hills, CA 90211, USA. *Telephone:* (213) 852-4777. *Fax:* (213) 658-7170.

FISCHER, Adam; Austrian conductor; b. 9 Sept. 1949, Budapest, Hungary; m. Doris Fischer 1979; one s. one d.; ed Budapest School of Music; conducting and composition studies in Budapest and Vienna with Swarowsky; held posts at Graz Opera, Karlsruhe; Gen. Music Dir Freiburg; work with Bavarian State Opera; regular conductor with Vienna State Opera 1973–, and with Zurich Opera; major debuts Paris Opera 1984, La Scala 1986, Royal Opera House 1989, ENO 1991, San Francisco Opera 1991, Chicago Lyric Opera 1991, Metropolitan Opera, New York 1994; has conducted many world-class orchestras, particularly Helsinki Philharmonic, Boston and Chicago Symphony and LA Philharmonic and Vienna Chamber Orchestra; concert tours to Japan and USA; Music Dir Kassel Opera 1987–92, founder and Artistic Dir, first Gustav Mahler Festival, Kassel 1989; f. Austro-Hungarian Haydn Orchestra (AHHO) and Festival, Eisenstadt, Austria 1987, later Music Dir AHHO; Music Dir, Mannheim Opera 2000–; Conductor, Bayreuth Festival (Ring Cycle) 2001–; Chief Conductor, Danish Radio Sinfonietta; first prize (jtly) Milan Cantelli Competition 1973. *Film:* BBC TV film of Bartok's Bluebird's Castle with London Philharmonic Orchestra (Italia Prize 1989 and Charles Heidsieck Prize). *Recordings include:* complete Haydn symphonies, Lucio Silla and Des Knabaen Wunderhorn with Danish Radio Sinfonietta. *Address:* c/o Raab und Böhm Agentur, Plankengasse 7, 1010 Vienna, Austria (office). *Telephone:* (1) 5120-5010 (office). *Fax:* (1) 512-7743 (office). *E-mail:* office@rbartists.at (office). *Website:* www.rbartists.at (office).

FISCHER, Andreas, PhD; Swiss professor of philology and university administrator; *President, University of Zürich;* b. 1947; ed Univ. of Basel, Univ. of Durham; Prof. of English Philology, Univ. of Basel 1981; Visiting Prof., Univ. of Michigan 1984–85; Prof. of English Philology, Univ. of Zürich 1985–, Deputy Dean, Faculty of Arts 2002–04, Dean 2004–06, Pres. (Rector) Zürich Univ. 2008–; Ed. Swiss Papers in English Language and Literature; mem. Advisory Bd Journal of Historical Pragmatics; mem. Advisory Bd Inst. for Historical Study of Language, Dept of English Language, Univ. of Glasgow; mem. Zürich James Joyce Foundation. *Publications:* Dialects in the South West of England, Engagement, Wedding and Marriage in Old England. *Address:* Office of the President, University of Zürich, Künstlergasse 15, 8001 Zürich, Switzerland (office). *Telephone:* (44) 63-42211 (office). *E-mail:* rektor@uzh.ch (office). *Website:* www.uzh.ch (office).

FISCHER, August A.; Swiss fmr publishing executive; b. 7 Feb. 1939, Zürich; m. Gillian Ann Fischer 1961; one s. one d.; various positions E.I. Du Pont De Nemours & Co. 1962–78; Man. Dir European subsidiary of Napp Systems Inc. 1978–81, Exec. Vice-Pres., then Pres. and COO Napp Systems Inc., San Diego, Calif. 1981–89; Gen. Man. Devt, News Int. PLC 1989–90, Man. Dir 1990–95, mem. Bd and COO News Corpn Ltd 1991–95, Chief Exec. News Int. PLC (UK subsidiary of News Corpn) 1993–95; mem. Supervisory Bd Ringier AG, Zürich, consultant 1995–97; Chair. Bd and CEO Axel Springer Verlag AG 1998–2001; mem. Advisory Bd, RocSearch; mem. American Man. Asscn, The Pres.'s Asscn; Trustee St Katharine and Shadwell Trust. *Address:* c/o RocSearch Ltd, 36–40 Rupert Street, London W1D 6DW, England (office).

FISCHER, Edmond H., DèsSc; American biochemist and academic; *Professor Emeritus of Biochemistry, University of Washington;* b. April 1920, Shanghai, China; s. of Oscar Fischer and Renee C. Fischer (née Tapernoux); m. Beverley B. Bullock; two s.; ed Univ. of Geneva; Asst, Labs of Organic Chem., Univ. of Geneva 1946–47; Fellow, Swiss Nat. Foundation 1948–50; Research Fellow, Rockefeller Foundation 1950–53; Privat-dozent, Univ. of Geneva 1950; Research Assoc., Div. of Biology, Calif. Inst. of Tech., USA 1953; Asst Prof., Univ. of Washington, USA 1953–56, Assoc. Prof. 1956–61, Prof. of Biochemistry 1961–90, Prof. Emer. 1990–; mem. numerous cttees, professional orgs etc.; Gov. Basel Inst. for Immunology 1996–, Weizmann Inst. of Science, Rehovot, Israel 1997–; mem. NAS, AAAS, American Acad. of Arts and Sciences, Swiss Chem. Soc., British Biochemical Soc.; Dr hc (Montpellier) 1985, (Basel) 1988; shared Nobel Prize for Medicine 1992, several other awards and honours. *Leisure interests:* classical piano, flying (pvt. pilot). *Address:* Department of Biochemistry, University of Washington, 1959 NE Pacific Street, HSB J-405, Seattle, WA 98195-7350 (office); 5540 NE Windermere Road, Seattle, WA, USA (home). *Telephone:* (206) 523-7372 (home). *E-mail:* efischer@u.washington.edu (office). *Website:* depts.washington.edu/biowww (home).

FISCHER, Erik, MA; Danish art historian; b. 8 Oct. 1920, Copenhagen; s. of Adolf Fischer and Ellen Henius; ed Univ. of Copenhagen; Asst Keeper of Prints and Drawings, Royal Museum of Fine Arts, Copenhagen 1948–57, Keeper of Prints and Drawings 1957–90; Asst Prof. of Art History, Univ. of Copenhagen 1964–90; Chair. Danish State Art Foundation 1965–67, Bd,

Queen Margrethe and Prince Henrik Foundation 1970–2002; Pres. Int. Advisory Cttee of Keepers of Public Collections of Graphic Art 1971–76; Hon. mem. Germanisches Nationalmuseum, Nuremberg 1977; mem. Bd Politiken Foundation 1990–2001; Fellow, Royal Danish Acad.; Assoc. Ateneo Veneto; Hon. mem. Royal Danish Acad. of Fine Arts 2000; Kt, Order of Dannebrog, Order of Nordstjernen; Hon. DPhil (Copenhagen) 1991; Klein Prize 1973; Amalienborg Medal 1983, 2002, N.L. Høyen Medal, Royal Danish Acad. of Fine Arts 1989, Danish Literary Acad. Prize 1989, Ingenio et Arti Medal 1990. *Publications:* Moderne dansk Grafik 1957, Melchior Lorck Drawings 1962, Tegninger af C. W. Eckersberg 1983, Von Abildgaard bis Marstrand 1985, Billedtekster (anthology) 1988, C. W. Eckersberg–His Mind and Times 1993. *Address:* Agergårdsvej 5, Ammendrup, 3200 Helsinge, Denmark (home). *Telephone:* 48-79-44-04 (home). *Fax:* 48-79-44-04 (home). *E-mail:* erikfischer@mail.tele.dk (home).

FISCHER, Heinz, DIur; Austrian politician; *President;* b. 9 Oct. 1938, Graz; m. Margit Fischer; two c.; ed Univ. of Vienna; Assoc. Prof. of Political Science, Univ. of Innsbruck 1978–94, Prof. 1994–; Sec. Socialist Parl. Party 1963–75, Exec., Floor Leader 1975–83, 1987–90, Deputy Chair. Socialist Party 1979–2004; mem. Nationalrat (Parl.) for Vienna 1971–2004, Pres. Nationalrat 1990–2002, Second Pres. 2002–04; Fed. Minister for Science and Research 1983–87; Deputy Chair. European Socialist Party 1992–2004; Pres. of Austria 2004–; Co-Ed. Europäische Rundschau; fmr mem. Nat. Security Council and Foreign Affairs Council; Pres. Nat. Fund of the Repub. of Austria for Victims of Nat. Socialism 1995–2002; Vice-Pres. Inst. for Advanced Studies –2004; Pres. Austrian Friends of Nature –2005; Pres. Austrian Univ. Extension Asscn. *Publications:* Positions and Outlook 1977, The Kreisky Era 1993, Reflexionen 1999, Times of Change: An Austrian Interim Report 2003; numerous books and articles on law and political science. *Address:* Office of the Federal President, Hofburg, 1014 Vienna, Austria (office). *Telephone:* (1) 534-22-0 (office). *Fax:* (1) 535-65-12 (office). *Website:* www.hofburg.at (office).

FISCHER, Iván; Hungarian/Dutch conductor; *Music Director, Budapest Festival Orchestra;* b. 20 Jan. 1951, Budapest; s. of Sándor Fischer and Evelin Boschán; two s. two d.; ed B. Bartók Music Conservatory, Budapest and Wiener Hochschule für Musik under Hans Swarowsky, Mozarteum, Salzburg under Nikolaus Harnoncourt; Jt Music Dir Northern Sinfonia of England, Newcastle 1979–82; Music Dir and Artistic Dir, Kent Opera 1982–2000; Prin. Guest Conductor Cincinnati Symphony Orchestra 1989–96; Music Dir Lyon Opera House 2000–03; Prin. Conductor Nat. Symphony Orchestra, Washington, DC 2008–; Co-founder and Music Dir Budapest Festival Orchestra 1983–; debut in London with Royal Philharmonic Orchestra 1976; concerts with London Symphony Orchestra, Berlin Philharmonic Orchestra, Concertgebouw Orchestra etc.; main performances in USA: Los Angeles Philharmonic, Cleveland, Philadelphia, San Francisco Symphony and Chicago Symphony Orchestras; operas: Idomeneo, Don Giovanni, Julius Caesar, La Bohème, La Clemenza di Tito, Marriage of Figaro, Magic Flute in London, Paris, Vienna; Premio Firenze 1974, Rupert Foundation Award, BBC, London 1976, Gramophone Award for Best Orchestral Recording of the Year (for The Miraculous Mandarin) 1998, Golden Medal, Republic of Hungary 1998, Crystal Award, World Econ. Forum 1998, Kossuth Prize 2006, Gramophone Editor's Choice Award (for Mahler's Second Symphony) 2007. *Address:* c/o Edward Yim, IMG Artists, Carnegie Hall Tower, 152 West 57th Street, 5th Floor, New York, NY 10019, USA (office); Budapest Festival Orchestra, Alkotás utca 39/c., 1123 Budapest, Hungary (office). *Telephone:* (212) 994-3500 (New York) (office); (1) 489-4330 (Budapest) (office). *Fax:* (212) 995-3550 (New York) (office); (1) 355-4049 (Budapest) (office). *E-mail:* artistsny@imgartists.com (office); bfofound@mail.datanet.hu (office). *Website:* www.imgartists.com (office); www.bfz.hu (office).

FISCHER, Jan; Czech economist, statistician and politician; *Prime Minister;* b. 2 Jan. 1951, Prague; m.; two s. one d.; ed Univ. of Econs, Prague; joined Research Inst. of Socio-econ. Information as researcher 1974; Vice-Pres. Fed. Statistical Office 1990–93, Czech Statistical Office 1993–2000, Pres. 2003–09; Prime Minister 2009–; Production Dir Taylor Nelson Sofres Factum Co. 2000–02; mem. Czech Statistical Soc., Int. Statistical Inst.; mem. Academic Council and Bd of Dirs Univ. of Econs, Prague; mem. Academic Council J.E. Purkyne Univ., Usti nad Labem, North Bohemia. *Address:* Office of the Government, náb. E. Beneše 4, 118 01 Prague 1, Czech Republic (office). *Telephone:* 224002111 (office). *Fax:* 224003090 (office). *E-mail:* posta@vlada.cz (office). *Website:* www.vlada.cz (office).

FISCHER, Joseph (Joschka); German academic and fmr politician; b. 12 April 1948, Gerabronn; m. 1st 1967 (divorced 1984); m. 2nd (divorced); m. 3rd Claudia Bohm 1987 (divorced 1999); m. 4th Nicola Leske 1999 (divorced 2003); m. 5th Minu Barati 2005; joined Green Party 1982, fmr Leader; mem. German Bundestag 1983–85; Minister of the Environment and Energy, Hesse 1985–87, of the Environment, Energy and Fed. Affairs 1991–94; Deputy Bundesrat 1985–87, Chair. Green Parl. Group, Hesse Parl. 1987–91; Deputy Minister-Pres. of Hesse 1991–98; Speaker Parl. Group Alliance 90/Greens, Bundestag 1994–98; Vice-Chancellor and Minister of Foreign Affairs, Fed. Govt 1998–2005; Sr Fellow, Liechtenstein Inst. on Self-Determination, Princeton Univ. 2006–07, also Frederick H. Schultz Class of 1951 Prof. of Int. Econ. Policy, Woodrow Wilson School of Public and Int. Affairs and Fellow, European Union Program;. *Publication:* The Red-Green Years: German Foreign Policy from Kosovo to Sept. 11 2007. *Address:* c/o Bündnis 90/Die Grünen (Alliance 90/Greens), Pl. vor dem Neuen Tor 1, 10115 Berlin, Germany (office).

FISCHER, Paul Henning, DIur; Danish diplomatist; *Treasurer of the Royal Orders; Chamberlain;* b. 24 March 1919, Copenhagen; s. of Ernst Fischer and Ellen Dahl; m. Jytte Kalckar 1945; one s.; ed Lyceum Alpinum, Zuoz, Switzerland and Univ. of Copenhagen; Foreign Service 1944–89, Stockholm,

The Hague, Ministry of Foreign Affairs 1944–60; Asst Prof., Univ. of Copenhagen 1948–52; Del. Gen. Ass., UN 1959, 1961; Amb. to Poland 1960–61; Perm. Under-Sec. of State for Foreign Affairs 1961–71; Amb. to France 1971–80, to FRG 1980–89; mem. UN register for fact-finding experts in internal disputes; mem. Perm. Court of Arbitration, The Hague 1982; Judge ad hoc, Int. Court of Justice, The Hague 1988; mem. CSCE Dispute Settlement Mechanism; Treasurer of the Royal Orders; Chamberlain of HM Queen Margrethe; Grand Cross, Order of Dannebrog and foreign decorations. *Publications:* European Coal and Steel Community, International Law Studies on International Co-operation; numerous articles. *Leisure interests:* literature, music. *Address:* Amalienborg, 1257 Copenhagen (office); Straedet 8, Borsholm, 3100 Hornbaek, Denmark (home). *Telephone:* 49-75-01-51 (home).

FISCHER, Stanley, BSc, MSc, PhD; American/Israeli economist and central banker; *Governor, Bank of Israel;* b. 15 Oct. 1943, Lusaka, Zambia; s. of Philip Fischer and Ann Kopelowitz; m. Rhoda Keet 1965; three s.; ed London School of Econs, UK, Massachusetts Inst. of Tech.; Postdoctoral Fellow Univ. of Chicago 1969–70, Asst Prof. of Econs 1970–73; Assoc. Prof. MIT 1973–77, Prof. 1977–88, 1990, Killian Prof. 1992–94; Head of Dept 1993–94; Vice-Pres. and Chief Economist World Bank, Washington, DC 1988–90; Visiting Sr Lecturer Hebrew Univ., Jerusalem 1972, Fellow Inst. for Advanced Studies 1976–77, Visiting Prof. 1984; Visiting Scholar Hoover Inst. Stanford Univ. 1981–82; Consultant on Israeli Economy Dept of State 1984–87, 1991–94; First Deputy Man. Dir IMF 1994–2001; Vice-Chair. Citigroup 2002–05; Pres. Citigroup Int. 2002–05; Gov. Bank of Israel 2005–; Fellow, Econometric Soc., American Acad. of Arts and Sciences; Dr hc (Tbilisi State Univ.) 1996, (Ben Gurion Univ.) 1998, (Tel-Aviv Univ.) 2001, (Hebrew Univ.) 2006. *Publications:* Rational Expectations and Economic Policy (ed.) 1980, Indexing, Inflation and Economic Policy 1986, Macroeconomics and Finance: Essays in Honor of Franco Modigliani (ed.) 1987, Economics (with Dornbusch and Schmalensee) 1988, Lectures in Macroeconomics (jtly) 1989, Macroeconomics (with Dornbusch) 1994, ed. NBER Macroeconomics Annual and work on int. econ. and macroeconomic issues. *Address:* Bank of Israel, PO Box 780, Kiryat Ben-Gurion, Jerusalem 91007, Israel (office). *Telephone:* 2-6552211 (office). *Fax:* 2-6528805 (office). *E-mail:* webmaster@bankisrael.gov.il (office). *Website:* www.bankisrael.gov.il (office).

FISCHER, Thomas R., BEcons, PhD; German banker and business executive; *Chairman, RWE AG;* b. 6 Oct. 1947, Berlin; ed Univ. of Freiburg, Breisgau; fmr amateur boxer, employed in family-owned business 1965–68, 1973–76; Research Asst, Univ. of Freiburg, Breisgau 1980–81; Head of Controlling, VARTA Batterie AG 1981–85; Deputy Dir Group Devt Dept, Deutsche Bank AG, Hanover 1985–91; Man. Dir Deutsche Immobilien Anlagegesellschaft mbH (subsidiary of Deutsche Bank) 1991–92, Global Head of Derivatives Deutsche Bank AG, Frankfurt 1992–95, Chair. Risk Man. Cttee, mem. Bd Man. 1999–2002; Vice-Chair. Landesgirokasse, Stuttgart 1995–96, Chair. 1996–98; Chair. WestLB AG 2004–07; CEO –2007; Chair. RWE AG 2006–. *Address:* RWE AG, Opernplatz 1, 45128 Essen, Germany (office). *Telephone:* (201) 1200 (office). *Website:* www.rwe.com (office).

FISCHER, Timothy Andrew, AC; Australian politician; b. 3 May 1946, Lockhart, NSW; s. of J. R. Fischer and Barbara Mary Fischer; m. Judy Brewer 1992; two s.; ed Boree Creek School, Xavier Coll., Melbourne; joined Army 1966, officer with First Bn, Royal Australian Regt, Australia and Vietnam 1966–69; farmer, Boree Creek, NSW; mem. NSW Legis. Ass. 1970–84; MP for Farrer, NSW 1984–2002; Shadow Minister for Veterans' Affairs 1985–89 and Deputy Man. of Opposition Business 1989–90; Leader Nat. Party of Australia 1990–99; Shadow Minister for Energy and Resources 1990–93, for Trade 1993–96; Deputy Prime Minister and Minister for Trade 1996–99; Chair. Tourism Australia 2004–07; Royal Decoration for Service to the Kingdom of Thailand 1997 Hon. DLit (Australian Nat. Univ.) 2005. *Leisure interests:* chess, tennis, skiing, water skiing, bush-walking, mountaineering. *Address:* 520 Swift Street, Albury, NSW 2640; P.O. Box 10, Boree Creek, NSW 2652, Australia.

FISCHER, Václav; Czech business executive; b. 22 June 1954; m. (divorced); ed School of Econs, Prague; fmr tourist guide, Prague; emigrated to Germany 1978, f. Fischer Reisen (travel agents) 1980; returned to Czechoslovakia 1989, f. Czech br. Fischer Reisen; f. Fischer a.s. 1996; mem. Senate 1999–2002; Matěj Hrebenda Prize for contribution to prosperous relations between Czech Repub. and Slovakia 2001. *Publications:* I am Writing to You. *Leisure interests:* cycling, theatre, travel. *Address:* Fischer a.s., Provaznická 13, 110 00 Prague 1, Czech Republic (office). *Telephone:* (2) 21636501 (office). *Fax:* (2) 21636517 (office). *E-mail:* info@fischer.cz (office).

FISCHER-APPELT, Peter, DrTheol; German university administrator and educator; b. 28 Oct. 1932, Berlin; s. of Hans Fischer-Appelt and Margret Fischer-Appelt (née Appelt); m. Hildegard Zeller 1959; two s. one d.; ed Schubart-Oberschule, Aalen and Univs of Tübingen, Heidelberg and Bonn; Scientific Asst, Protestant Theology Faculty, Univ. of Bonn 1961–70; Pastor, Cologne-Mülheim 1964–65; Co-founder and Chair. Bundesassistentenkonferenz, Bonn 1968–69; Pres. Univ. of Hamburg 1970–91, Pres. Emer. 1991–, teaching assignment in Systematic Theology 1972–; Pres. 'Cyril and Methodius' Int. Foundation, Sofia 1992–98, Hon. Pres. 2002; mem. Exec. Cttee Inter-Univ. Centre for Postgrad. Studies, Dubrovnik 1974–81, Chair. of Council 1981–98, Hon. mem. 1998; mem. Standing Conf. on Univ. Problems, Council of Europe 1987–94, Deputy Chair. 1987–88, Chair. 1989–90; Chair. Steering Group, Higher Educ. Legislation Reform Programme for Cen. and Eastern Europe 1992–98; mem. and Chair. Bd of Trustees UNESCO Inst. for Educ., Hamburg 1992–96; mem. German Comm. UNESCO 1991–2002, Hon. mem. 2002; mem. Bd of Trustees, Deutscher Akad. Austauschdienst 1972–2007 and various other comms, etc.; mem. European Acad. of Sciences and Arts, Salzburg; Horseman of Madara (First Class), Order of Cyril and Methodius (First Class), Bulgaria, Order of the Croatian Star with the Effigy of Rudjer Bošković; numerous hon. degrees; Gold Medal, Bulgarian Acad. of Sciences, Pro Cultura Hungarica Medal, Medal of the Comm. of Nat. Educ., Poland 2000, Medal Pro Merito of the Council of Europe 2000. *Achievements:* annual Peter Fischer-Appelt Award for eminent achievements in acad. teaching, Univ. of Hamburg 1991, annual Prof. Dr Peter Fischer-Appelt Awards for best Bulgarian school teachers in Bulgarian, German, Spanish, Classic languages Cyril and Methodius Int. Foundation, Sofia 2004. *Publications:* Metaphysik im Horizont der Theologie Wilhelm Herrmanns 1965, Albrecht Ritschl und Wilhelm Herrmann 1968, Rechtfertigung 1968, Wissenschaft und Politik 1971, Zum Verständnis des Glaubens in der liberalen und dialektischen Theologie 1973, Zum Gedenken an Ernst Cassirer 1975, Integration of Young Scientists into the University 1975, Wilhelm Herrmann 1978, Hiob oder die Unveräusserlichkeit der Erde 1981, The Future of the University as a Research Institution 1982, Was darf ich hoffen? Erwartungen an das Musiktheater 1982, Die Oper als Denk- und Spielmodell 1983, Die Kunst der Fuge: Ein deutsches Forschungsnetz im Aufbau 1984, Dialogue and Co-operation for World Peace Today 1985, Die Universität zwischen Staatseinfluss und Autonomie 1986, The University in the 21st Century 1988, Die Ostpolitik der Universitäten 1992, Die Universität im Prozess der Humanisierung der Gesellschaft 1994, Wer hat Angst vor den Wandlungen der Universität 1994, Die Erhellung des Mythos durch die Sprache der Musik 1995, The University: Past, Present and Future 1996, Concepts of the University 1997, Die Buchstaben und Europa 1997, One Europe to Tend 2000, Gottes Sein im Werden des Wissens 2000, Hochschulpolitik als Sozialpolitik 2001, Wissenschaft in der Kaufmannsrepublik 2002, Das Modell Byzanz und seine Einflüsse auf die Lebenswelt Osteuropas 2003, Felix Mendelssohn Bartholdy und Arnold Schönberg 2003, Hermann Cohen und Arnold Schönberg 2003, Die "Göttlichen Stimmen" in Schönbergs Oper "Moses und Aron" 2003, Wie weit reicht Europa? 2004, The University of Reason 2004, Curt Kosswig, ein Wegbereiter der Türkei nach Europa 2004. *Leisure interests:* chess, skiing, music, opera, theatre. *Address:* Waldweg 22, 25451 Quickborn-Heide, Germany. *Telephone:* (4106) 71212 (home). *Fax:* (4106) 78637 (home).

FISCHER-DIESKAU, Dietrich; German singer (baritone) and conductor; b. 28 May 1925, Berlin; s. of Dr Albert Fischer-Dieskau and Dora Klingelhöffer; m. 1st Irmgard Poppen 1949 (died 1963); three s.; m. 2nd Ruth Leuwerik 1965 (divorced 1967); m. 3rd Kristina Pugell 1968; m. 4th Julia Varady 1978; ed high school in Berlin, singing studies with Profs Georg Walter and Hermann Weissenborn; mil. service 1943–45; POW in Italy until 1947; First Lyric and Character Baritone, Berlin State Opera 1948–; mem. Vienna State Opera Co. 1957–; Prof. of Singing Musikhochschule Berlin 1981–; numerous concert tours in Europe, USA and Asia; has appeared at a number of festivals: Bayreuth, Salzburg, Lucerne, Montreux, Edin., Vienna, Holland, Munich, Berlin, Coventry, etc.; best-known roles in Falstaff, Don Giovanni, The Marriage of Figaro, etc.; first performances of contemporary composers Britten, Henze, Tippett, etc.; mem. Akad. der Künste, Bayerische Akad. der Schönen Künste, Munich, Int. Mahler-Gesellschaft (Vienna) and German Section, Int. Music Council, High School for Music and Theatre, Munich 1999; Hon. mem. Wiener Konzerthausgesellschaft 1963, RAM (London), Royal Acad. (Stockholm), Deutschen Oper, Berlin 1978, Royal Philharmonic Soc.; Bundesverdienstkreuz 1st Class 1958, Grosses Verdienstkreuz des Verdienstordens der Bundesrepublik Deutschland 1974, Chevalier Légion d'honneur 1990; Hon. DUniv (Oxford) 1978, Hon. DMus (Paris-Sorbonne) 1980, (Yale) 1980; Int. Recording Prizes almost every year since 1955, Berlin Kunstpreis 1950, Mantua Golden Orpheus Prize 1955, Edison Prize 1960, 1962, 1964, 1965, 1967, 1970, President's Prize Charles Gros Acad., Paris 1980, Förderungspreis der Ernst-von-Siemens-Stiftung 1980, Mozart Medal 1962, Golden Orpheus 1967, Grammy Award (several times), Prix Mondial Montreux (several times), Ernst-Reuter-Plak 1993, Polar Music Prize 2004, Lotte Lehmann Foundation World of Song Award 2005, Midem Classical Music Award for Lifetime Achievement 2006. *Publications:* Texte deutscher Lieder 1968, Auf den Spuren der Schubert-Lieder 1971, Wagner und Nietzsche, der Mystagoge und sein Abtrünniger 1974, Franz Schubert, ein Portrait 1976, Robert Schumann—Wort und Musik 1981, Töne sprechen, Worte klingen-Zur Geschichte und Interpretation des Gesanges 1985, Nachklang 1987, Wenn Musik der Liebe Nahrung ist: Künstlerschicksale im 19 Jahrhundert 1990, Johann Friedrich Reichardt: Kapellmeister dreier Preussenkönige 1992, Claude Debussy und seine Welt 1994, Schubert und seine lieder 1998. *Leisure interest:* painting. *Address:* c/o Deutsche Verlanganstalt, Stüttgart, Germany (office).

FISCHL, Eric, BFA; American artist; b. 9 March 1948, New York City; ed Phoenix Junior Coll., Ariz., Ariz. State Univ., Tempe, Calif. Inst. of the Arts; moved to Chicago and worked as guard at Museum of Contemporary Art; taught painting Nova Scotia Coll. of Art and Design, Halifax 1974–78; moved to NY City 1978. *Address:* c/o Mary Boone Gallery, 745 Fifth Avenue, New York, NY 10151, USA. *E-mail:* ericfischl@mac.com. *Website:* www.ericfischl.com.

FISCHLER, Franz; Austrian fmr politician and consultant; b. 23 Sept. 1946, Absam, Tyrol; m.; two s. two d.; ed Franciscan secondary school, Tyrol and Agricultural Univ., Vienna; Asst Univ. of Vienna Dept of Agricultural Man. 1973–79; Dept Head, Tyrolean Prov. Chamber of Agric. 1979, Sec. 1982, Dir 1985–89; Minister of Agric. and Forestry 1989–94; EU Commr for Agric. and Rural Devt 1995–99, for Agric., Rural Devt and Fisheries 1999–2004; consultancy work, Franz Fischler Consult GmbH 2005–; Pres. EcoSocial Forum Europe. *Address:* Franz Fischler Consult GmbH, Doerferstrasse 30B, 6067 Absam, Austria. *Website:* www.franz-fischler-consult.co.at.

FISHBURNE, Laurence; American actor; b. 30 July 1961, Augusta, Georgia; s. of Laurence John Fishburne, Jr and Hattie Bell Crawford Fishburne; m. Hanja Moss 1985 (divorced); one s. one d. *Stage appearances include:* Short Eyes, Two Trains Running, Riff Raff (also writer and dir). *Television appearances include:* One Life to Live (series, debut aged 11), Peewee's Playhouse, Tribeca (Emmy Award 1993), A Rumour of War, I Take These Men, Father Clements Story, Decoration Day, The Tuskegee Airmen, Miss Ever's Boys, Always Outnumbered. *Film appearances include:* Cornbread Earl and Me 1975, Fast Break, Apocalypse Now, Willie and Phil, Death Wish II, Rumble Fish, The Cotton Club, The Color Purple, Quicksilver, Band of the Hand, A Nightmare on Elm Street 3: Dream Warriors, Gardens of Stone, School Daze, Red Heat, King of New York, Cadence, Class Action, Boyz 'N the Hood, Deep Cover, What's Love Got to Do With It? Searching for Bobby Fischer, Higher Learning, Bad Company, Just Cause, Othello, Fled, Hoodlums (also exec. producer), Event Horizon, Welcome to Hollywood, Once in the Life (also writer), The Matrix 1999, Michael Jordan to the Max 2000, Once in the Life 2000, Osmosis Jones 2001, The Matrix Reloaded 2003, The Matrix Revolutions 2003, Mystic River 2003, Assault on Precinct 13 2005, Akeelah and the Bee 2005, Mission: Impossible III 2006, Five Fingers 2006, Bobby 2006, TMNT (voice) 2007, The Death and Life of Bobby Z 2007, Fantastic Four: Rise of the Silver Surfer (voice) 2007. *Address:* c/o Sam Gores, Paradigm, 10100 Santa Monica Boulevard, 25th Floor, Los Angeles, CA 90067, USA.

FISHER, Carrie; American actress and author; b. 21 Oct. 1956, Beverly Hills; d. of Eddie Fisher and Debbie Reynolds (q.v.); m. Paul Simon 1983 (divorced 1984); one d.; ed Beverly Hills High School and Cen. School of Speech and Drama, London; appeared with her mother in nightclub act aged 13; appeared in chorus of Broadway production of Irene, starring Debbie Reynolds, aged 15; Broadway stage appearances in Censored Scenes from King Kong, Agnes of God; several TV credits; film début in Shampoo (Photoplay Award as Best Newcomer of the Year) 1974. *Films include:* Shampoo 1974, Star Wars 1977, The Empire Strikes Back 1980, The Blues Brothers 1980, Return of the Jedi 1983, Under the Rainbow, Garbo Talks, The Man With One Red Shoe 1985, Hannah and Her Sisters 1986, Amazing Women on the Moon 1987, Appointment With Death 1988, The 'Burbs 1989, Loverboy 1989, She's Back 1989, When Harry Met Sally… 1989, The Time Guardian 1990, Sibling Rivalry 1990, Drop Dead Fred 1991, Soapdish 1991, This is My Life 1992, Austin Powers: International Man of Mystery 2000, Scream 3 2000, Famous 2000, Heartbreakers 2001, Jay and Silent Bob Strike Back 2001, A Midsummer Night's Rave 2002. *Publications:* Postcards From the Edge (novel and screenplay, PEN Award for first novel 1987) 1987, Surrender the Pink 1990, Delusions of Grandma 1994 (novels), The Best Awful There Is 2003, Wishful Drinking (memoir) 2009; short stories. *Address:* c/o William Morris Agency, 1 William Morris Place, Beverly Hills, CA 90212, USA (office).

FISHER, Donald G., BS; American business executive; *Chairman Emeritus, The Gap Inc.;* b. 1928; m. Doris F. Fisher; three s.; ed Univ. of Calif.; with M. Fisher & Son 1950–57; fmr partner, Fisher Property Investment Co.; Co-Founder (with wife Doris F. Fisher), Pres. The Gap Stores Inc. (later The Gap Inc.), San Bruno, Calif., Chair. 1996–2004, now Chair. Emer. and Dir; mem. Bd of Dirs Charles Schwab Corpn. *Address:* The Gap Inc., 2 Folsom Street, San Francisco, CA 94105, USA (office). *Telephone:* (650) 952-4400 (office). *Fax:* (415) 427-2553 (office). *Website:* www.gap.com (office).

FISHER, Doris F., BS; American business executive; b. 1931; m. Donald G. Fisher; three s.; ed Stanford Univ.; Co-founder (with husband) Gap Inc., San Francisco 1969–, mem. Bd of Dirs; Dir Gap Foundation; Trustee Stanford Univ.; ranked on Mother Jones 400 (131st) 1998, (184th) 2001, ranked Forbes magazine amongst 100 Most Powerful Women (60th) 2005. *Address:* Gap Inc. Headquarters, 2 Folsom Street, San Francisco, CA 94105, USA (office). *Telephone:* (650) 952-4400 (office). *Website:* www.gapinc.com (office); www.gap.com (office).

FISHER, Joel, BA; American sculptor; *Head of Sculpture, Northumbria University;* b. 6 June 1947, Salem, Ohio; s. of James R. and Marye (née Giffin) Fisher; m. 1st Pamela Robertson-Pearce 1977 (divorced); one s.; m. 2nd Gabrielle Wambaugh 2003; one d.; ed Kenyon Coll., Ohio; lecturer numerous schools; Artist in Residence, Univ. of Auckland 2000; Kress Foundation Art History Award 1967, 1968, Gast der Berliner Kunstler Program des DAAD (German Academic Exchange Service) 1973–74, 1994, George A. and Eliza Gardner Howard Foundation Fellow 1987, Guggenheim Fellow 1993, Pollock-Krassner Foundation Award 1993, Henry Moore Fellowship (Newcastle upon Tyne) 2001–03, Phi Beta Kappa. *Publications:* A Shadow of the Earth 1968, Double Camouflage 1970, Berliner Book 1974, Instances of Change 1975, False History 1978, Between Two and Three Dimensions – Drawings and Objects Since 1979 1984, Little Buttercup: Happiest Bear in the World (photos) 2004. *Address:* 29 Goldspink Lane, Newcastle upon Tyne, NE2 1NQ England; P.O. Box 349, River Road, North, Troy, VT 05859, USA (home). *Telephone:* (191) 227-3140 (office); (191) 230-0370 (home); (802) 988-2870 (home). *E-mail:* joel.fisher@unn.ac.uk (office); jfisher@together.net (office).

FISHER, Kenneth (Ken) L., BA; American business executive and writer; *CEO and Chief Investment Officer, Fisher Investments Inc.;* b. 29 Nov. 1950, San Francisco; s. of Philip A. Fisher; m. Sherrilyn Fisher; three s.; ed Humboldt State Univ.; began career in father's investment firm; founder, CEO and Chief Investment Officer Fisher Investments Inc. 1978–, f. Fisher Investments Europe 2000, Gruner Fisher 2008; columnist, Forbes Magazine 1984–; est. Kenneth L. Fisher Chair in Redwood Forest Ecology, Humboldt State Univ. 2006; Bernstein Fabozzi/Jacobs Levy Award for outstanding published research article of the year 2000. *Publications include:* Super Stocks 1984, The Wall Street Waltz 1987, 100 Minds that Made the Market 1996, The Only Three Questions that Count 2006, The Ten Roads To Riches

2008; various research papers on investment and stocks. *Address:* Fisher Investments Inc., 13100 Skyline Boulevard, Woodside, CA 94062-4547, USA (office). *Telephone:* (800) 851-8845 (office). *Fax:* (650) 851-3514 (office). *E-mail:* webresponse@fi.com (office). *Website:* www.fi.com (office).

FISHER, Mark Andrew, BA, MBA; British banker; b. 29 April 1960; ed Warwick Business School; joined NatWest in 1981, joined Royal Bank of Scotland (RBS) (following its acquisition of NatWest in 2000), Chief Exec. RBS Manufacturing Div. 2000–07, mem. bd of Dirs RBS Group 2006–, Chair. Man. Bd and CEO ABN AMRO (bank partially owned by RBS) 2007–(09); Fellow, Chartered Inst. of Bankers in Scotland. *Address:* c/o ABN AMRO Holding NV, Gustav Mahlerlaan 10, 1082 PP Amsterdam, Netherlands (office). *Telephone:* (20) 628-9393 (office). *Fax:* (20) 629-9111 (office). *E-mail:* info@abnamro.com (office). *Website:* www.abnamro.com (office).

FISHER, Michael Ellis, BSc, PhD, FRS; British theoretical scientist and university teacher and researcher; *Distinguished University Professor and University System of Maryland Regents Professor, Institute for Physical Science and Technology, University of Maryland;* b. 3 Sept. 1931, Trinidad, West Indies; s. of Harold Wolf Fisher and Jeanne Marie Fisher (née Halter); m. Sorrel Castillejo 1954; three s. one d.; ed King's Coll., London; Lecturer in Math., RAF Tech. Coll. 1952–53; London Univ. Postgraduate Studentship 1953–56; Dept of Scientific and Industrial Research Sr Research Fellow 1956–58; Lecturer in Theoretical Physics, King's Coll., London 1958–62, Reader in Physics 1962–64, Prof. of Physics 1965–66; Prof. of Chem. and Math., Cornell Univ., USA 1966–73, Horace White Prof. of Chem., Physics and Math. 1973–89, Chair. Dept of Chem. 1975–78; Wilson H. Elkins Prof., Inst. for Science and Tech., Univ. of Md 1987–93, Distinguished Univ. Prof. and Univ. System of Md Regents Prof. 1993–; Guest Investigator, Rockefeller Inst., New York 1963–64; Visiting Prof. of Applied Physics, Stanford Univ., USA 1970–71; Walter Ames Prof., Univ. of Wash. 1977; Visiting Prof. of Physics, MIT 1979; Sherman Fairchild Distinguished Scholar, Caltech 1984; Visiting Prof. of Theoretical Physics, Oxford 1985; Lorentz Prof., Univ. of Leiden 1993; Visiting Prof., Nat. Inst. of Standards and Tech., Gaithersburg, Md 1993; George Fisher Baker Lecturer, Cornell Univ. 1997; Distinguished Lecturer in Theoretical Physics, The Technion 2004; John Simon Guggenheim Memorial Fellow 1970–71, 1978–79; Fellow, American Acad. of Arts and Sciences; Foreign Assoc., NAS, American Philosophical Soc.; Foreign mem. Brazilian Acad. of Sciences, Royal Norwegian Soc. of Sciences and Letters; Hon. FRSE, Hon. Fellow, Indian Acad. of Sciences (Bangalore); Hon. DSc (Yale) 1987; Hon. DPhil (Tel-Aviv) 1992; Jr Collectors Silver Cup, British Philatelic Exhbn 1946, Irving Langmuir Prize in Chemical Physics, American Physical Soc. 1970, Award in Physical and Math. Sciences, New York Acad. of Sciences 1978, Guthrie Medal, Inst. of Physics 1980, Wolf Prize in Physics, Israel 1980, Michelson-Morely Award, Case-Western Reserve Univ. 1982, James Murray Luck Award, NAS 1983, Boltzmann Medal, IUPAP 1983, Festschrift and Conf. in honour of 60th Birthday: Current Problems in Statistical Mechanics 1991, Lars Onsager Medal, Norwegian Inst. of Tech. 1993, Joel H. Hildebrand Award for Chem. of Liquids 1995, Hirschfelder Prize in Theoretical Chem., Univ. of Wis. 1995, First Lars Onsager Memorial Prize, American Physical Soc. 1995, G. N. Lewis Memorial Lecture Award, Univ. of Calif. 1995, American Physical Soc. Centennial Speaker 1998, Royal Medal Royal Soc. of London 2005, Queen's Medal, Royal Soc., London. *Publications:* Analogue Computing at Ultra-High Speed (with D. M. MacKay) 1962, The Nature of Critical Points 1964, also in Russian 1968; over 390 contribs to scientific journals, proceedings and reviews. *Leisure interests:* Flamenco guitar, travel. *Address:* Institute for Physical Science and Technology, University of Maryland, 4211 Computer and Space Science, College Park, MD 20742-2431, USA (office). *Telephone:* (301) 405-4819 (office). *Fax:* (301) 314-9404 (home). *E-mail:* xpectnil@ipst.umd.edu (office). *Website:* www.ipst.umd.edu/index.html (office).

FISHER, Robert (Bob) J.; American retail executive; b. 1955; s. of Donald G. Fisher (q.v.) and Doris F. Fisher; Man. The Gap, Inc. 1980–85, Exec. Vice Pres., Merchandise, Banana Republic 1985–89, Pres. 1989–90, mem. Bd of Dirs The Gap Inc. 1990–99, Exec. Vice-Pres. 1992–99, COO 1992–93, 95–97, CFO 1993–95, Pres. Gap Div. 1997–99 (resgnd), Chair. The Gap Inc. 2004–07, currently mem. Bd of Dirs; mem. Bd of Dirs Sun Microsystems Inc.; mem. Bd of Trustees, Golden Gate Nat. Park Asscn, Natural Resources Defense Council. *Address:* c/o Board of Directors, The Gap Inc., 2 Folsom Street, San Francisco, CA 94105, USA (office). *Telephone:* (650) 952-4400 (office). *Fax:* (415) 427-2553 (office). *Website:* www.gap.com (office).

FISHLOW, Albert, PhD; American economist, academic and fmr government official; *Professor of International and Public Affairs, Director of the Columbia Institute of Latin American Studies, and Director of the Center for the Study of Brazil, Columbia University;* b. 21 Nov. 1935, Philadelphia; m. Harriet Fishlow 1957; one s. two d.; ed Univ. of Pennsylvania, Harvard Univ.; Acting Asst Prof., Assoc. Prof., then Prof., Univ. of Calif., Berkeley 1961–77, Prof. of Econs 1983, Chair. Dept of Econs 1973–75, 1985–89, Dean Int. and Area Studies 1990, Dir Int. House 1990, now Prof. Emer.; currently Prof. of Int. and Public Affairs, Dir of Columbia Inst. of Latin American Studies, and Dir of Center for Study of Brazil, Columbia Univ., New York; mem. Berkeley Foundation Trustees Int. Cttee 1990–; Prof. of Econs, Yale Univ. 1978–83; Visiting Fellow, All Souls Coll. Oxford, UK (Guggenheim Fellow) 1972–73; Co-Ed. Journal of Devt Econs 1986–; Dir-at-Large, Bd of Social Science Research Council 1990–; Deputy Asst Sec. of State for Inter-American Affairs 1975–76; mem. Council on Foreign Relations 1975–, Paul A. Volcker Sr Fellow for Int. Econ. –1999; Consultant to Rockefeller, Ford and other foundations, fmr Consultant to World Bank, IDB, UNDP; Nat. Order of the Southern Cross (Brazil) 1999; David Wells Prize, Harvard 1963, Arthur H. Cole Prize, Econ. History Asscn 1966, Joseph Schumpeter Prize, Harvard 1971, Outstanding Service Award, Dept of State 1976. *Publications include:* American Railroads and the Transformation of the Ante Bellum Economy 1965, International Trade, Investment, Macro Policies and History: Essays in Memory of Carlos F. Diaz-Alejandro (co-ed.) 1987; numerous articles. *Address:* 834 International Affairs Building, Columbia University, Mail Code 3323, New York, NY 10027, USA (office). *Telephone:* (212) 854-1555 (office). *Fax:* (212) 864-4847 (office). *E-mail:* af594@columbia.edu (office). *Website:* www.sipa.columbia.edu (office).

FISHMAN, Jay S., MA; American insurance executive; *Chairman, President and CEO, The Travelers Companies Inc.;* b. NJ; ed Wharton School, Univ. of Pennsylvania; fmr Dir of Mergers and Acquisitions, American Can Co.; Sr Vice-Pres. of Merchant Banking, Shearson Lehman Brothers –1989; Exec. Vice-Pres. and Chief Financial Officer, then Sr Vice- and Treasurer, Primerica Corpn 1989–93; Chief Financial Officer, Travelers Insurance Group 1993, various positions including Chief Financial Officer, Chief Admin. Officer, Pres. and COO Commercial Lines, Travelers Property Casualty 1996–98, Pres. and CEO Travelers Property Casualty Corpn 1998–2000, Chair. and CEO Travelers Insurance 2000, Chair., Pres. and CEO The St Paul Co. –2004, CEO and Pres. The St Paul Travelers Cos Inc. (following merger of The St Paul Co. and Travelers Insurance Group 2004) 2004–, Chair. 2005– (renamed The Travelers Cos Inc. 2007); COO, Finance and Risk, Citigroup 2000–01; mem. Bd of Overseers Carlson School of Man. at Univ. of Minnesota; Trustee, Univ. of Pennsylvania. *Address:* The Travelers Companies Inc., 385 Washington Street, St Paul, MN 55102, USA (office). *Telephone:* (651) 310-7911 (office). *Fax:* (651) 310-3386 (office). *E-mail:* info@travelers.com (office). *Website:* www.travelers.com (office).

FISIAK, Jacek, OBE, PhD, DLitt; Polish philologist, linguist and academic; *Head, Department of the History of English, School of English, A. Mickiewicz University, Poznań;* b. 10 May 1936, Konstantynów Łódzki; s. of Czesław Fisiak and Jadwiga Fisiak; m. Liliana Sikorska; ed Warsaw Univ.; staff mem. Łódź Univ. 1959–67, Asst Prof. 1962–67; staff mem. Adam Mickiewicz Univ., Poznań 1965–, Head English Dept 1965–69, Head Dept of History of English, School of English 1969–, Extraordinary Prof. 1971–77, Prof. 1977–, Rector 1985–88; Chair. Comm. on Modern Languages and Literature, Ministry of Higher Educ. 1974–88; Minister of Nat. Educ. 1988–89; participant Round Table debates 1989; Visiting Prof. Univ. of Calif., LA 1963–64, Univ. of Kan. 1970, Univ. of Fla 1974, State Univ. of New York 1975, American Univ., Washington, DC 1979–80, 1991–92, Univ. of Kiel 1979–80, Vienna Univ. 1983, 1988–89, 1990–91, Univ of Zürich 1984, 1994, Univ. of Tromsø 1986, Univ. of Jyväskylä 1987, Univ. of Saarbrücken 1990, 1993, Univ. of Bamberg 1994; Ed. Studia Anglica Posnaniensia 1967–, Papers and Studies in Contrastive Linguistics 1972–, Ed.-in-Chief Folia Linguistic Historica 1978–; Pres. Int. Asscn of Univ. Profs of English 1974–77, Societas Linguistica Europaea 1982–83, Int. Soc. for Historical Linguistics 1981–83; Chair. Neophilological Cttee, Polish Acad. of Sciences 1981–93; mem. Finnish Acad. of Sciences and Humanities 1990, Academia Europaea 1990, Finnish Acad. of Arts and Sciences, Norwegian Acad. of Sciences 1996, New York Acad. of Sciences 1996, Medieval Acad. of America 2001, Polish Acad. of Sciences 2004; Pres. Polish-British Friendship Soc. 1989–; mem. editorial bds of numerous foreign and int. philological journals, numerous scientific socs; consultant Ford Foundation, IREX, Swedish Govt, Austrian Ministry of Higher Educ., Encyclopaedia Britannica (Chicago); Dr. hc (Jyväskylä) 1982, (Opole) 2005; Commdr.'s Cross of the Order Polonia Restituta with Star, Grand Cross of the Order Polonia Restituta, Officer's Cross of the Order of the British Empire (OBE), Nat. Educ. Comm. Medal, Commdr's Cross of Lion of Finland Order, Officier, Ordre des Palmes Académiques and numerous other decorations. *Publications:* 164 publs, 40 books including Morphemic Structure of Chaucer's English 1965, A Short Grammar of Middle English 1968, 1996, Recent Developments in Historical Phonology (ed.) 1978, Historical Syntax (ed.) 1983, A Bibliography of Writings for the History of English 1987, Historical Dialectology (ed.) 1990, An Outline History of English 1993, 2000, Medieval Dialectology 1995, Linguistic Change Under Contact Conditions 1995, Studies in Middle English Linguistics 1997, Typology and Linguistics Reconstruction 1997, East Anglia (co-author with P. Trudgill) 2001, The New Kościuszko Foundation Dictionary (English–Polish, Polish–English) 2003. *Leisure interests:* history, sport. *Address:* School of English, A Mickiewicz Univ., Al. Niepodleglosci 4, 61-874 Poznan (office). *Telephone:* (61) 8293506 (office); (61) 8293521 (office); (61) 8243153 (home). *Fax:* (61) 8523103 (office); (61) 9243153 (home). *E-mail:* fisiak@amu.edu.pl (office). *Website:* www.amu.edu.pl (office).

FISICHELLA, Domenico; Italian politician and university professor; *Vice President, Italian Senate;* b. 15 Sept. 1935, Messina, Sicily; m. Loredana Fisichella; two d.; Prof. of Political Science, Univ. of Florence, Università La Sapienza and Libera Università Internazionale degli Studi Sociali (LUISS), Rome; co-f. Alleanza Nazionale Party 1992, elected Senator 1994–; Minister of Culture 1994–95; Vice Pres. of Senate 1996–; Gold Medal for achievement in field of culture, education and art, Carlo Casalegno Journalism Prize 1985, Culture Prize for essays 1988, Guido and Roberto Cortese Prize for essays 1996. *Publications include:* Denaro e democrazia: Dall'antica Grecia all'economia globale (Money and Democracy: From Ancient Greece to Global Economy) 2000, Totalitarismo: Un regime del nostro tempo (Totalitarianism: A Regime of Our Times) 2002, Politica e mutamento sociale (Politics and Social Changes) 2002, La destra e l'Italia (The Right and Italy) 2003, Lineamenti di scienza politica: Concetti, problemi, teorie (Fundamentals of Political Science: Concepts, Problems, Theories) 2003, Contro il federalismo (Against Federalism) 2004, and numerous articles in nat. dailies. *Address:* Senato della Repubblica, Piazza Madama, 00186 Rome, Italy. *Telephone:* (6) 6706-2206 (office). *Fax:* (6) 6706-3667 (office). *E-mail:* d.fisichella@senato.it (office). *Website:* www.fisichella.it (home).

FISK, David John, CB, ScD, CEng, FREng, FInstP; British engineer and academic; *Royal Academy of England Professor of Engineering for Sustainable Development, Imperial College London; Chief Scientific Adviser, Office of the Deputy Prime Minister;* b. 9 Jan. 1947; s. of the late John Howard Fisk and of Rebecca Elizabeth Fisk (née Haynes); m. Anne Thoday 1972; one s. one d.; ed Stationers' Co. School, Hornsey, St John's Coll. Cambridge and Univ. of Manchester; joined Bldg Research Establishment, Sr Prin. Scientific Officer, Head, Mechanical and Electrical Eng Div. 1978–84; with Dept of Environment (then Dept of the Environment, Transport and the Regions, then Dept for Transport, Local Govt and the Regions, now Office of the Deputy Prime Minister—ODPM) 1984–, Asst Sec. Cen. Directorate of Environmental Protection 1984–87, Under-Sec. 1987, Deputy Chief Scientist 1987–88, Chief Scientific Adviser 1988– (Dir Air Climate and Toxic Substances Directorate 1990–95, Environment and Int. Directorate 1995–98, Cen. Strategy Directorate 1999–2002); Visiting Prof., Univ. of Liverpool 1988–2002; Dir Watford Palace Theatre 2000–; Royal Acad. of Eng Prof. of Eng for Sustainable Devt, Imperial Coll. of Science, London 2002–; Hon. Fellow Chartered Inst. of Bldg Service Engineers. *Publications:* Thermal Control of Buildings 1981; numerous papers on bldg science, systems theory and econs. *Leisure interests:* theatre, music. *Address:* c/o Office of the Deputy Prime Minister, Eland House, Bressenden Place, London, SW1E 5DU (office); Department of Civil and Environmental Engineering, Imperial College, London, SW7 2BU, England (office). *Telephone:* (20) 7944-6980 (ODPM) (office). *Fax:* (20) 7944-2168 (ODPM) (office). *E-mail:* david.fisk@odpm.gsi.gov.uk (office); d.fisk@imperial.ac.uk (office). *Website:* www.odpm.gov.uk (office); www.cv.ic.ac.uk (office).

FISMER, Christiaan Loedolff; South African politician; b. 1956, Pretoria; s. of William Fismer and Elizabeth Fismer; m. Linda Mills; twin d.; ed Univ. of Pretoria; mil. service; admitted to Pretoria Bar 1986; practised as advocate 1986–87; fmr Chair. Student Rep. Council, Univ. of Pretoria, Pres. Afrikaanse Studentebond (ASB – umbrella org. for univ. governing bodies); mem. Nat. Party; co-f. Nat. Party Youth Action; MP for Rissik 1987, Sr Transvaal Whip of Nat. Party 1989; apptd party rep. to Conf. for a Democratic S Africa (CODESA) working group on implementation of decisions 1991; Prov. Leader Nat. Party in Eastern Transvaal 1994; fmr Deputy Minister in Office of State Pres. F. W. de Klerk; Deputy Minister of Justice 1994–95; Minister of Gen. Services 1995–96, of Provincial and Constitutional Affairs March–May 1996; pvt. law practice 1996–; Univ. of Pretoria Gold Medal. *Address:* c/o National Party, Private Bag X402, Pretoria 0001, South Africa. *Telephone:* (12) 348-3100. *Fax:* (12) 348-5645.

FISZEL, Roland Henri Léon; French engineer; b. 16 July 1948, Paris; s. of Jean Fiszel and Marie Eber; m. Nadine Kohn 1974; one s. two d.; ed Lycée Pasteur, Neuilly-sur-Seine, Ecole polytechnique, Massachusetts Inst. of Tech., USA; Head of Housing Dept, Ministry of Construction 1974–77; Head of Studies and Planning Group, Infrastructure Div., Hauts-de-Seine 1977–81; Deputy Sec.-Gen. Codis-Cidise, in charge of Treasury 1981–82; Tech. Adviser, Office of Minister of Social Affairs and Nat. Solidarity 1983–84, then of Minister of the Economy and Finance 1984–86; Dir Nat. Printing Office 1986–92; Adviser to Chair. of Euris 1996; fmr Pres. and Dir-Gen. Société francaise de production; Ingénieur en chef des ponts et chaussées; Dir representing State, Agence Havas 1986–87; Dir Antenne 2 1988–92; fmr Sec.-Gen. Caisse nationale du Crédit agricole. *Leisure interests:* skiing, tennis. *Address:* 4 rue Jobbé Duval, 75015 Paris, France (home).

FITCH, Val Logsdon, BEng, PhD; American physicist and academic; *James S. McDonnel Distinguished University Professor of Physics, Princeton University;* b. 10 March 1923, USA; s. of Fred B. Fitch and Frances M. Fitch (née Logsdon); m. 1st Elise Cunningham 1949 (died 1972); two s. (one deceased); m. 2nd Daisy Harper Sharp 1976; ed McGill and Columbia Univs; US Army 1943–46; Instructor, Columbia Univ. 1953–54, Princeton Univ. 1954, Prof., Princeton Univ. 1960–, Chair. Dept of Physics 1976, Cyrus Fogg Brackett Prof. of Physics 1976–84, James S. McDonnel Distinguished Univ. Prof. of Physics 1984–; Pres. American Physical Soc. 1987–88; Sloan Fellow 1960–64; mem. NAS, American Acad. of Arts and Sciences, President's Science Advisory Cttee 1970–73, American Philosophical Soc.; three hon. degrees; Research Corpn Award 1968; Ernest Orlando Laurence Award 1968, John Witherill Medal, Franklin Inst. 1976; Distinguished Alumnus Award, Columbia Univ.; Nobel Prize for Physics jtly with J. W. Cronin for work on elementary particles 1980; Nat. Medal of Science 1993. *Publications:* major publs in area of elementary particles. *Leisure interest:* conservation. *Address:* PO Box 708, Princeton University, Department of Physics, Princeton, NJ 08544, USA (office). *Telephone:* (609) 258-4374 (office). *Fax:* (609) 258-6360 (office). *E-mail:* vfitch@princeton.edu (office). *Website:* www.princeton.edu (office).

FITERMAN, Charles; French politician; b. 28 Dec. 1933, St-Etienne; s. of Moszek Fiterman and Laja Rozenblum; m. Jeannine Poinas 1953; Departmental Sec. Jeunesse Communiste 1952; Sec. CGT, St-Etienne SFAC 1958–62; Dir Cen. School, Parti Communiste Français (PCF) 1963–65; elected to PCF Cen. Cttee 1972, to Political Bureau and Cen. Cttee Sec. 1976; Gen. Councillor, Head, Econ. Section and PCF Rep. to Liaison Cttee of Signatory Parties to Common Programme of the Left 1977; Deputy (Val-de-Marne) to Nat. Ass. 1978–81; Minister of State, Minister of Transport 1981–84; Deputy for Rhône 1986–88; Mayor of Tavernes 1989–; f. Refondations Movt 1990, Convention pour une alternative progressiste 1994; Pres. Forum Alternatives Européennes 1994–99; mem. Socialist Party 1998–, Conseil Economique et Socialde France; Chevalier Légion d'honneur. *Address:* CES, 9 Place d'Iéna, 75016 Paris, France (office). *Telephone:* 1-40-29-48-40. *Fax:* 1-40-29-48-39 (office). *E-mail:* charles.fiterman@wanadoo.fr (office).

FITOUSSI, Jean-Paul Samuel, DèsScEcon; French economist and academic; *President, Observatoire Français des Conjonctures Economiques (OFCE);* b. 19 Aug. 1942, La Goulette; s. of Joseph Fitoussi and Mathilde Cohen; m. Anne Krief 1964; one s. one d.; ed Acad. Commerciale, Paris and Univs of Paris and Strasbourg; Asst Lecturer 1968–71; Dir of Studies 1971–73; Maître de Conférence Agrégé 1974–75; Prof. 1975–78; Titular Prof. 1978–82; Dean. Faculty of Econ. Science and Dir Dept of Econ. Science, Strasbourg 1980–81; Prof. in charge of research prog. on foundation of macroeconomic policy, Inst. Universitaire Européen, Florence 1979–83; Prof. Inst. d'Etudes Politiques, Paris 1982–; Dir Dept of Studies Observatoire Français des Conjonctures Economiques (OFCE) 1982–89, Pres. 1990–; Chair. Scientific Council of Inst. d'Etudes Politiques, Paris 1997–; Sec.-Gen. Int. Econ. Asscn 1984–; consultant to EC Comm. 1978–; mem. Bd Ecole Normale Supérieure, Paris 1998–; External Prof. Univ. Européenne, Florence 1984–93, mem. Research Council, Universitaire Européen, Florence 2003–; mem. Econ. Comm. of the Nation 1996–, Council of Econ. Analysis of the Prime Minister 1997–; Expert, Comm. of the European Parl. 2000–; mem. UN Research Inst. for Social Devt 2001–; mem. Exec. Cttee Aspen Inst. Italia 2001–, Comité national d'évaluation de la politique de la ville 2002–, Comité national d'initiative et de proposition pour la recherche 2004–, Scientific Bd Austrian Inst. of Economic Research 2004–, Bd of Dirs École Normale Supérieure 2004–, Advisory Bd Centre on Capitalism and Soc., Columbia Univ. 2004–, Cttee for Evaluation of Research 2005–; columnist for Le Monde and La Repubblica; Hon. Prof., Univ. of Trento, Italy; Officier Ordre nat. du Mérite, Chevalier Légion d'honneur, Grand Officier de l'Ordre de l'Infant Henri (Portugal); Dr hc (Buenos Aires); Prix Asscn Française de Sciences Economiques, Prix Acad. des Sciences Morales et Politiques. *Publications:* Inflation, équilibre et chômage 1973, Le fondement macroéconomique de la théorie Keynesienne 1974, Modern Macroeconomic Theory 1983, Monetary Theory and Economic Institutions (with N. de Cecco) 1985, The Slump in Europe (with E. Phelps) 1988, Competitive Disinflation (with others) 1993, Pour l'emploi et la cohésion sociale 1994, Le débat interdit: monnaie, Europe, pauvreté 1995, Economic Growth, Capital and Labour Markets 1995, Le nouvel âge des inégalités (with Pierre Rosanvallon) 1996, Rapport sur l'état de l'Union européenne 1999, 2000, 2002, Réformes structurelles et politiques macroéconomique: les enseignements des modèles de pays (with O. Posset) 2000, contrib. to collected publs, L'enseignement supérieur de l'économie en question, Rapport au ministre de l'éducation nationale 2001, Rapport sur l'état de l'union européenne 2002; La Règle et le choix 2002, How to Reform the European Central Bank (with J. Creel) 2002, Il dilttatore benevolo 2003, Rapport sur l'état de l'union européene 2004, Les inégalités 2003, La démocratie et le marché 2004, L'ideologie du monde 2004, Ségrégation urbaine et intégration sociale (jtly) 2004, Macroeconomic Theory and Economic Policy 2004, La politique de l'impuissance 2005, Report on the State of the European Union 2005. *Leisure interests:* travel, cinema, guitar, scuba-diving. *Address:* Observatoire Français des Conjonctures Economiques, 69 quai d'Orsay, 75340 Paris Cedex 07 (office); 47 rue de boulainvilliers, 75016 Paris, France (home). *Telephone:* 1-44-18-54-01. *Fax:* 1-44-18-54-71. *E-mail:* presidence@ofce.sciences-po.fr (office). *Website:* www.ofce.sciences-po.fr (office).

FITRAT, Abdul Qadeer, BA, MA; Afghan central banker; *Governor and Chairman, Supreme Council (Supervisory Board), Da Afghanistan Bank (Central Bank of Afghanistan);* ed secondary school, Kabul, Int. Islamic Univ., Islamabad, Pakistan, Wright State Univ., Dayton, Ohio, USA; fmr Asst Research Coordinator for USAID-supported project, ESSP, Peshawar, Pakistan; fmr Chair. Bank–e-Millie Afghan, Kabul early 1990s; Consultant Economist, IMF, Washington, DC late 1990s; First Deputy Gov. Da Afghanistan Bank (Cen. Bank of Afghanistan) 1995, Gov. 1996, Gov. and Chair. Supreme Council (Supervisory Bd) 2007–; consumer banker to First Union Nat. Bank, northern Va 2000–01; Adviser to Exec. Dir, World Bank 2004–07. *Address:* Da Afghanistan Bank, Ibne Sina Wat, Kabul, Afghanistan (office). *Telephone:* (20) 2100301 (office); (20) 2102812 (office). *Fax:* (20) 2100305 (office). *E-mail:* governor.office@centralbank.gov.af (office). *Website:* www.centralbank.gov.af (office).

FITTIPALDI, Emerson; Brazilian fmr racing driver; b. 12 Dec. 1946, São Paulo; s. of Wilson Fittipaldi and Juze Fittipaldi; m. 1st Maria Helena Dowding 1970; one s. two d.; m. 2nd Teresa Hotte 1995; ed scientific studies; Brazilian champion Formula V and Go-Kart 1967; Formula 3 Lombard Championship 1969; Formula 1 world champion 1972 (youngest ever), 1974; second in World Championship 1973, 1975; won Indianapolis 500 1989, 1993; retd (following injury) 1996 with 17 Indy Car victories; owns Fittipaldi Motoring Accessories, 500,000-acre orange plantation and exports orange concentrate; has Mercedes Benz partnership in Brazil; partner Hugo Boss fashion retailer; set up the Fittipaldi Foundation to help impoverished children in Brazil; runs Fittipaldi-Dingman Racing; mem. Bd Laureus World Sports Acad. *Leisure interests:* sport, music, water skiing, flying. *Address:* c/o CMG Worldwide, Praia de Botafogo 228, Sala 1111, Rio de Janeiro, 22359-900, Brazil. *Website:* www.emersonfittipaldi.com.

FITZGERALD, Edmund Bacon, BSE; American business executive; *Managing Director, Woodmont Associates;* b. 5 Feb. 1926, Milwaukee; s. of Edmund Fitzgerald and Elizabeth Bacon Fitzgerald; m. Elisabeth McKee Christensen 1947; two s. two d.; ed Univ. of Michigan; fmr Chair. and CEO Cutler-Hammer Inc., Milwaukee; then Vice-Chair. and COO, Industrial Products, Eaton Corpn (following merger with Cutler-Hammer); Pres. Northern Telecom Inc., USA (subsidiary of Northern Telecom Ltd) 1980–82; CEO Northern Telecom Ltd 1984–89, Chair. 1985–90; Man. Dir Woodmont Assocs., Nashville 1990–; Adjunct Faculty, Strategy and Business Economics, Owen Graduate School of Man., Vanderbilt Univ. 1990–; Dir Ashland Oil Inc., Becton Dickinson and Co., GTI; mem. Pres. Reagan's Nat. Telecommunications Security Advisory Council; Trustee, Cttee for Econ. Devt, Washington, DC; fmr Pres. Nat. Electrical Mfrs Asscn; fmr Vice-Chair. Industry Advisory Council, Dept of Defense; mem. Korea-US Wisemen Council; Order of the

Rising Sun Gold and Silver Star (Japan) 1997. *Publications:* Globalizing Customer Solutions 2001, Edmund Fitzgerald: The Ship and the Man 2002, Lizzy's Curacao 2003. *Address:* Owen Graduate School of Management, 401 21st Avenue South, Nashville TN 37203; Woodmont Associates, 3434 Woodmont Blvd., Nashville, TN 37215-1422, USA. *Telephone:* (615) 385-9206 (Owen). *Fax:* (615) 383-5227 (Owen). *Website:* www.owen.vanderbilt .edu.

FITZGERALD, Frances; American writer; b. 1940; d. of Desmond Fitzgerald and Marietta Peabody Fitzgerald Tree; m. James Paul Sterba 1990; ed Radcliffe Coll.; author of series of profiles for Herald Tribune magazine; freelance author of series of profiles, Vietnam 1966; frequent contrib. to The New Yorker; Vice-Pres. PEN; mem. Editorial Bds The Nation, Foreign Policy; Overseas Press Club Award 1967, Nat. Inst. of Arts and Letters Award 1973, Sydney Hillman Award 1973, George Polk Award 1973, Bancroft Award for History 1973. *Publications include:* Fire in the Lake – The Vietnamese and the Americans in Vietnam (Pulitzer Prize 1973, Nat. Book Award 1973) 1972, America Revised – History Schoolbooks in the Twentieth Century 1979, Cities on a Hill – A Journey Through Contemporary American Cultures 1986, Way Out There in the Blue – Reagan, Star Wars and the End of the Cold War (New York Times Ed.'s Choice, New York Public Library Helen Bernstein Award) 2000; contribs to The New York Review of Books, The New York Times Magazine, Esquire, Architectural Digest, Islands, Rolling Stone. *Address:* 531 E 72nd Street, Apt 3B, New York, NY 10021-4017, USA (home).

FITZGERALD, Garret; Irish politician and economist; b. 9 Feb. 1926, Dublin; s. of the late Desmond Fitzgerald and Mabel McConnell; m. Joan O'Farrell 1947; two s. one d.; ed Belvedere Coll., Univ. Coll. and King's Inns, Dublin; called to the Bar 1946; Research and Schedules Man., Aer Lingus 1947–58; Rockefeller Research Asst, Trinity Coll., Dublin 1958–59; Lecturer in Political Economy, Univ. Coll., Dublin 1959–73; fmr Chair. and Hon. Sec. Irish Br., Inst. of Transport; mem. Seanad Éireann 1965–69; mem. Dáil Éireann for Dublin SE 1969–92; Leader and Pres. Fine Gael 1977–87; Minister for Foreign Affairs 1973–77; Taoiseach (Prime Minister) of Repub. of Ireland 1981–82, 1982–87; Pres. Council of Ministers of EEC Jan.–June 1975, European Council July–Dec. 1984, fmr Pres. Irish Council of European Movt; fmr Vice-Pres. European People's Party, European Parl.; mem. Senate Nat. Univ. of Ireland 1973–, Chancellor 1997–; fmr Man. Dir Economist Intelligence Unit of Ireland; mem. Trilateral Comm. 1987–; Dir GPA Group 1987–93, Int. Inst. for Econ. Devt, London 1987–95, Trade Devt Inst. 1987–, Comer Int. 1989–94, Point Systems Int. 1996–, Election Commr 1999–; mem. Radio Telefís Éireann Authority; fmr Irish Corresp. BBC, Financial Times, Economist, Columnist Irish Times; Order of Christ (Portugal) 1986, Order of Merit (Germany) 1987, Grand Cordon, Order of the Rising Sun (Japan) 1989, Commdr Légion d'honneur 1995; Hon. LLD (New York, St Louis, Keele, Boston Coll., Westfield Coll., Mass. Nat. Univ. of Ireland, Univ. of Dublin); Hon. DCL (St Mary's Univ., Halifax, Nova Scotia) 1985, (Oxford) 1987; Dr hc (Queen's Belfast) 2000. *Publications:* State-sponsored Bodies 1959, Planning in Ireland 1968, Towards a New Ireland 1972, Unequal Partners (UNCTAD) 1979, Estimates for Baronies of Minimum Level of Irish Speaking Amongst Successive Decennial Cohorts 1771–1781 to 1861–1871 1984, The Israeli/Palestinian Issue 1990, All in a Life (autobiog.) 1991. *Address:* 37 Annavilla, Dublin 6, Ireland. *Telephone:* (1) 496-2600. *Fax:* (1) 496-2126. *E-mail:* Garretfg@iol.ie (home).

FITZGERALD, Mgr Michael Louis, BA, DTheol; British ecclesiastic; *President, Pontifical Council for Inter-Religious Dialogue;* b. 1937, Walsall; ed Pontifical Gregorian Univ., School of Oriental and African Studies, London Univ.; ordained priest, Soc. of Missionaries of Africa (White Fathers) 1961; teacher, Makarere Univ., Kampala, Uganda and later Pontifical Inst. of Arabic and Islamic Studies, Rome; two years pastoral work, Sudan; mem. Gen. Council of Missionaries of Africa 1980–86; Sec. Secr. for Non Christians (now renamed Pontifical Council for Inter-Religious Dialogue) 1987–2002, Pres. Oct. 2002–; Titular Bishop of Nepte 1991–, Archbishop 2002–; presented von Hügel Lecture on Christian-Muslim Relations, Cambridge 2002. *Publications include:* Signs of Dialogue: Christian Encounter with Muslims (co-author) 1992; numerous specialist articles and lectures. *Address:* Pontifical Council for Inter-Religious Dialogue, Via dell'Erba 1, Rome, 00193, Italy (office). *Telephone:* (06) 69884321 (office). *Fax:* (06) 69884494 (office). *E-mail:* dialogo@interrel.va (office).

FITZGERALD, Niall, FRSA, BComm; Irish business executive; *Chairman, Reuters Group PLC;* b. 13 Sept. 1945; m.; two s. two d.; ed Univ. Coll., Dublin; joined Unilever 1967, various man. roles including CEO, Unilever Food Div., S Africa, early 1980s, later Treasurer, Unilever, London, Dir Unilever PLC and Unilever NV 1987–2004, Financial Dir 1987–89, Co-ordinator, Edible Fats and Dairy 1989–90, mem. Foods Exec. 1989–91, Co-ordinator, Detergents 1991–95, Vice-Pres. Unilever PLC 1994–96, Chair. 1996–2004, also becoming Vice-Chair. Unilever NV 1996–2004; Dir Reuters Group 2003–, Chair. 2004–; Pres. Advertising Asscn, S Africa Int. Investment Advisory Council, Shanghai Major's Int. Business Leaders' Council; Vice-Chair. The Conf. Bd; mem. World Econ. Forum, Int. Advisory Bd, Council on Foreign Relations, Trilateral Comm., EU–China Cttee, US Business Council; Gov. Nat. Inst. of Econ. and Social Research; Trustee, Leverhulme Trust; fmr Dir Merck, Ericsson, Bank of Ireland, Prudential Corpn; Hon. KBE. *Leisure interests:* jazz, opera, football, rugby, golf. *Address:* Reuters Group PLC, Reuters Building, Canary Wharf, London, E14 5EP, England (office). *Telephone:* (20) 7250-1122 (office). *Fax:* (20) 7542-4064 (office). *Website:* www.reuters.com (office).

FITZGERALD, Peter Gosselin, AB, JD; American banker, lawyer and fmr politician; *Chairman, Chain Bridge Bancorp Inc.;* b. 20 Oct. 1960, Elgin, Ill.; s. of Gerald Francis Fitzgerald and Marjorie (née Gosselin) Fitzgerald; m. C. Nina Kerstiens 1987; one s.; ed Dartmouth Coll., Univ. of Michigan; called to

Bar Ill. 1986; with US Dist Court Ill. 1986; Assoc. Isham, Lincoln & Beale 1986–88; Pnr, Riordan, Larson, Bruckert & Moore 1988–92; Counsel, Harris Bankmont Inc. 1992–96; mem. Ill. Senate 1993–98, Chair. State Govt Operations Cttee 1997–99, US Senator from Illinois 1999–2005 (retd), Chair. Senate Sub-Cttee on Consumer Affairs and Product Safety 2003–05, Sub-Cttee on Financial Man., the Budget and Int. Security 2003–05; Chair. Chain Bridge Bancorp Inc. 2006–; mem. various bds and asscns. *Address:* 1320 Old Chain Bridge Road, Suite 420, McLean, VA 22101, USA (office). *Telephone:* (703) 748-2005 (office). *Fax:* (703) 748-2007 (office). *E-mail:* dgumino@fitzgeraldpeter.com (office).

FITZGERALD, Peter Hanley, PhD, DSc, FRCPath, FRSNZ; New Zealand director of cancer research (retd); b. 10 Oct. 1929, Gore; s. of John J. Fitzgerald and Nora Eileen (née Hanley) Fitzgerald; m. Kathleen O'Connell 1955 (divorced 1988); three s. two d.; ed St Bede's Coll., Christchurch, Univ. of Canterbury, Univ. of New Zealand and Univ. of Adelaide; Dir Cancer Soc. of NZ Cytogenetic and Molecular Oncology Unit, Christchurch School of Medicine 1967–95; Pres. NZ Genetics Soc. 1978, NZ Soc. for Oncology 1973–74; mem. Nat. Scientific Cttee Cancer Soc. of NZ 1981–85, Int. Scientific Advisory Bd Cancer Congress, Seattle 1982, Canterbury Museum Trust Bd 1985–2001, Royal Soc. of NZ Council 1986–89; Hon. Cytogeneticist Canterbury Area Health Bd 1967–95; Prof. (Research Fellow), Christchurch School of Medicine, Univ. of Otago 1990–95; Sir George Grey Scholarship 1952; NZ Nat. Research Fellowship 1955–57; Human Genetics Soc. of Australasia Orator 1994 (Pres. NZ Branch 1990); Hon. Lecturer in Botany and Zoology Univ. of Canterbury 1971–95, in Pathology, Univ. of Otago 1979–90; Hon. Life mem. Cancer Soc. NZ 1995, NZ Soc. for Oncology 1995, Emer. mem. Human Genetics Soc. Australasia 2002. *Publications:* over 140 publs on cancer-related topics. *Leisure interests:* gardening, walking, music, literature, horology. *Address:* Cytogenetic and Molecular Oncology Unit, Christchurch Hospital, Christchurch (office); 115 Gardiners Road, Christchurch 5, New Zealand (home). *Telephone:* (3) 359-4244 (home). *Fax:* (3) 359-4104 (home).

FITZGERALD, Stephen Arthur, AO, BA, PhD; Australian scholar and diplomatist; b. 18 Sept. 1938, Hobart, Tasmania; s. of F. G. FitzGerald; m. Helen Overton; one s. two d.; ed Tasmania Univ., Australian Nat. Univ.; Dept of Foreign Affairs 1961–66; Research Scholar, ANU 1966–69, Research Fellow 1969–71, Fellow 1972–73, Professorial Fellow 1977–, Head Dept of Far Eastern History 1977–79, Head Contemporary China Centre, Research School of Pacific Studies 1977–79; Amb. to People's Repub. of China (also accred to Democratic People's Repub. of Korea) 1973–76; Ed. Australian Journal of Chinese Affairs; Deputy Chair. Australia–China Council 1979–86; mem. Australian Acad. of Science Sub-Cttee on Relations with China; Trustee, Australian Cancer Foundation 1985–99; Chair. Asian Studies Council 1986–91; Chair. and Man. Dir Stephen Fitzgerald and Co. Ltd; Chair. Asia-Australia Inst., also Prof. Univ. of NSW 1990–; Co-Chair. Jt Policy Cttee on Relations between Northern Territory and Indonesia; mem. council Musica Viva Australia; Dunlop Asia Medal 1999, Australia–China Council Award 1999. *Publications:* China and the Overseas Chinese 1972, Talking with China 1972, China and the World 1977, Immigration: A Commitment to Australia (jtly) 1988, A National Strategy for the Study of Asia in Australia (jtly) 1988, Asia in Australian Education (jtly) 1989, Australia's China (jtly) 1989, Ethical Dimension to Australia's Engagement with Asia 1993, Is Australia an Asian Country? 1997, East View-West View: Divining the Chinese Business Environment 1999. *Address:* Stephen Fitzgerald & Co., P.O. Box 620, Woollahra, NSW 2025, Australia. *Telephone:* (2) 9385-9111. *Fax:* (2) 9385-9221. *E-mail:* aai@unsw.edu.au (office). *Website:* www.aai@unsw.edu.au (office).

FITZGERALD, Tara; British actress; b. 18 Sept. 1969, Sussex; d. of the late Michael Callaby and of Sarah Geraldine Fitzgerald; stage debut in Our Song, London; appeared in London as Ophelia in Hamlet 1995, Antigone 1999. *Theatre:* Our Song, London, Hamlet (New York Critics Circle Best Supporting Actress Award 1995, Drama Desk Award Best Supporting Actress 1995) New York, A Streetcar Named Desire 1999, The Doll's House 2003, And Then There Were None, Gielgud Theatre, London 2005. *Films:* Hear My Song 1991, Galleria 1993, Sirens 1994, A Man of No Importance 1994, The Englishman Who Went up a Hill but Came Down a Mountain 1995, Brassed Off 1996, Conquest 1998, The Snatching of Bookie Bob 1998, Childhood 1999, New World Disorder 1999, Rancid Aluminium 2000, Dark Blue World 2001, I Capture the Castle 2003, Five Children and It 2004, Secret Passage 2004, In a Dark Place 2006. *Television includes:* The Black Candle 1991, Six Characters in Search of an Author 1992, The Camomile Lawn (miniseries) 1992, Anglo Saxon Attitudes 1992, Fall from Grace 1994, The Vacillations of Poppy Carew 1995, The Tenant of Wildfell Hall 1996, The Woman in White 1997, The Student Prince 1997, Little White Lies 1998, Frenchman's Creek (Best Actress Award, Reims Int. TV Festival 1999) 1998, In the Name of Love 1999, Love Again 2003, Marple: The Body in the Library 2004, Like Father Like Son 2005, The Virgin Queen (miniseries) 2005, Jane Eyre (miniseries) 2006, Waking the Dead (series) 2007–09, U Be Dead 2008. *Address:* c/o Lindy King, United Agents, 12–26 Lexington Street, London, W1F 0LE, England (office). *Telephone:* (20) 3214-0800 (office). *Fax:* (20) 3214-0801 (office). *E-mail:* info@unitedagents.co.uk (office). *Website:* www.unitedagents.co.uk (office).

FITZGIBBON, Joel; Australian politician; *Minister for Defence;* b. 16 Jan. 1962, Bellingen, NSW; m. Dianne Fitzgibbon; one s. two d.; ed Univ. of New England, NSW, Univ. of Newcastle; automotive electrician 1978–90; Dir Hunter-Manning Tourist Authority 1987–89; Deputy Mayor of Cessnock 1989–90; part-time Lecturer, Tech. and Further Educ. (TAFE); Del. Hunter Region Asscn of Councils 1994–95; MP (Australian Labor Party) for Hunter 1996–, various portfolios including Small Business, Tourism, Banking and Financial Services, Forestry, Mining and Energy, Asst Treas., Shadow

Minister for Defence; Minister for Defence 2007–. *Address:* Department of Defence, Russell Offices, Russell Drive, Campbell, Canberra, ACT 2600, Australia (office). *Telephone:* (2) 6265-9111 (office). *E-mail:* J.Fitzgibbon.MP@aph.gov.au (office). *Website:* www.defence.gov.au (office); www.joelfitzgibbon.com.

FITZPATRICK, Sean; New Zealand fmr rugby union player; b. 4 June 1963, Auckland; s. of Brian Fitzpatrick; ed Sacred Heart Coll., Auckland; hooker New Zealand All Blacks 1986–97, capt. 1992–97; int. debut 28 June 1986; final appearance before retirement 29 Nov. 1997; rugby consultant to NZ Rugby Football Union 1999–; Man. Auckland Blues Super 12 Team 2001–03; second-most capped NZ player of all time, most consecutive int. rugby union appearances (63 in 1986–95), missed only two test matches during his career; totals: 128 All Blacks games, including 92 tests (55 test points, including 12 tries). *Publication:* Turning Point – The Making of a Captain. *Address:* c/o International Rugby Academy, PO Box 12420, Wellington, New Zealand (office).

FITZWATER, Marlin, BA; American fmr government official; b. 24 Nov. 1942, Salina, Kan.; s. of Max Fitzwater and Phyllis Seaton; m.; two c.; ed Univ. of Kansas; served with USAF 1968–70; Sec. and speechwriter Dept of Transport, Washington 1970–72; with press relations dept, Environmental Protection Agency 1972–74, Dir Press Office 1974–81; Deputy Asst Sec. for Public Affairs, Dept of Treasury 1981–83; Deputy Press Sec. to Pres. 1983–85, Press Sec. to Vice-Pres. 1985–87; Prin. Deputy Press Sec. to Pres. 1987–89; Press Sec. to Pres. 1989–93; Advertising Pres. Fitzwater & Tutweiler, Inc. 1993; mem. Bd of Trustees Franklin Pierce Coll. 1999–, mem. of Advisory Board, Marlin Fitzwater Center for Communication; Presidential Merit Award 1982. *Publication:* Call the Briefing 1995. *Address:* c/o Marlin Fitzwater Center for Communication, Franklin Pierce College, 20 College Road, Rindge, NH 03461-0060, USA.

FIVE, Karin Cecilie (Kaci) Kullmann; Norwegian company director and fmr politician; b. 13 April 1951, Oslo; m.; two c.; ed Univ. of Oslo; mem. Baerum Municipal Council 1975–81; Chair. Young Conservatives 1977–79; Deputy mem. Storting (Parl.) 1977–81, mem. Storting 1981–97, mem. Finance and Foreign Affairs Cttee, Vice-Chair. Conservative Party Parl. Group 1985–89, Conservative Party Spokesperson for Foreign Affairs and EU 1994; Cabinet Minister of Trade, Shipping and European Affairs 1989–90; Deputy Chair. Conservative Party 1982–88, Chair. 1991–94; Deputy mem. Nat. Council on Youth Affairs 1979–81; Exec. Officer, Norwegian Employers' Fed. 1980–81; Sr Pnr, European Public Policy Advisers (EPPA) 1997–98; Sr Vice-Pres. Aker RGI 1998–2002, now adviser; mem. Bd of Dirs Asker og Baerums Budstikke ASA 1997–, Norsk Medisinaldepot AS 2001–, Bluewater Insurance ASA 2004–, Clavis Pharma ASA 2007–, AS J. Ludwig Mowinckels Rederi 2008–, Magda Müller Mowinckels Foundation 2002–, Statoil ASA 2002–07 (Deputy Chair. 2003–07); Chair. Norwegian Assen of Foundations 2003–; Vice-Chair. Scheiblers Foundation 1998–; Chair. Norwegian Export Council 2000–02; mem. Norwegian Nobel Cttee 2003–. *Address:* Lille Toppenhaug 4, 1353 Baerums Verk, Norway. *Telephone:* 916-300-40. *Fax:* 67-56-17-11. *E-mail:* kaci@kaci.no. *Website:* www.kaci.no.

FIXMAN, Marshall, PhD; American chemist and academic; *Distinguished Professor Emeritus, Colorado State University;* b. 21 Sept. 1930, St Louis, Mo.; s. of Benjamin Fixman and Dorothy Finkel; m. 1st Marian Beatman 1959 (died 1969); one s. two d.; m. 2nd Branka Ladanyi 1974; ed Univ. City High School, Mo., Washington Univ., Mo. and MIT; Postdoctoral Fellow, Yale Univ. 1953–54; served US Army 1954–56; Instructor in Chem., Harvard Univ. 1956–59; Sr Fellow, Mellon Inst., Pa 1959–61; Dir Inst. of Theoretical Science, Univ. of Ore. 1961–64, Prof. of Chem. 1961–65; Sloan Visiting Prof. of Chem., Harvard Univ. 1965; Prof. of Chem., Yale Univ. 1965–79; Prof. of Chem. and Physics, Colo State Univ. 1979–2000, Distinguished Prof. 1986–2000, Prof. Emer. 2000–; Fellow American Acad. of Arts and Sciences, American Physical Soc.; mem. NAS; Alfred P. Sloan Fellowship 1962–64; Assoc. Ed. Journal of Chemical Physics 1994–; mem. Editorial Bd Macromolecules, Journal of Physical Chem., Accounts of Chemical Research, Journal of Polymer Science; ACS Award in Pure Chem. 1964, American Physical Soc. High Polymer Physics Prize 1980, ACS Polymer Chem. Award 1991. *Leisure interests:* hiking and photography. *Address:* Department of Chemistry, Colorado State University, Fort Collins, CO 80523-0001, USA (office). *Telephone:* (970) 491-6037 (office). *Fax:* (970) 491-3361 (office). *Website:* www.chm.colostate.edu (office).

FJÆRVOLL, Dag Jostein; Norwegian politician; b. 20 Jan. 1947, Hadsel; s. of Edmund Fjærvoll; m.; two c.; fmr teacher; Head Teacher Melbu School 1984; mem. Hadsel Municipal Council 1975, mem. Exec. Bd 1980–, Mayor 1980–85; mem. Storting Nordland Co. 1985–87; mem. Standing Cttee on Local Govt and the Environment 1985–89, on Shipping and Fisheries 1989–93, on Scrutiny and the Constitution 1993–97; Vice-Pres. Lagting 1989–93, Odelsting 1993–97; Minister of Defence 1997–99; Christian Democratic Party. *Address:* c/o Ministry of Defence, Myntgt. 1, PO Box 8126 Dep., 0030 Oslo, Norway.

FLAHAUT, André, MA; Belgian politician; *Minister for Defence;* b. 18 Aug. 1955, Walhain; ed Université Libre de Bruxelles; Asst to Emile Vandervelde Inst. 1979, Man. 1989; Councillor of Walhain 1982–94; Chair. Parti Socialiste Fed. of Wallon Brabant 1983–95; Prov. Councillor of Brabant 1987–91; Chair. Office de la Naissance et de l'Enfance 1989–95; Vice-Chair. of Intercommunale des Oeuvres Sociales du Brabant Wallon 1993–95; Chair. Mutualité Socialiste du Brabant Wallon 1993; Parl. Rep. 1994; Minister for Civil Service 1995–99, for Defence 1999–. *Address:* Ministry of Defence, 8 rue Mont Lambert, 1000 Brussels, Belgium (office). *Telephone:* (2) 550-28-11 (office). *Fax:* (2) 550-29-19 (office). *E-mail:* cabinet@mod.mil.be (office). *Website:* www.mil.be (office).

FLAHERTY, Jim, LLB; Canadian politician; *Minister of Finance;* b. 30 Dec. 1949; m. Christine Flaherty; three s.; ed Princeton Univ., Osgoode Hall Law School; called to the bar, Ont. 1975; mem. Prov. Parl. for Whitby-Ajax 1995–2005; Attorney Gen. 1995; fmr Solicitor Gen.; fmr Critic for Public Infrastructure Renewal for the Official Opposition; fmr Minister Responsible for Native Affairs, Minister of Labour, of Enterprise, Opportunity and Innovation, of Finance, of Correctional Services, Deputy Premier; Co-Chair. Task Force on Safe Streets and Healthy Communities 2005; mem. Parl. 2006–; Minister of Finance 2006–. *Address:* Finance Canada, East Tower, 19th Floor, 140 O'Connor Street, Ottawa, ON K1A 0G5, Canada (office). *Telephone:* (613) 992-1573 (office). *Fax:* (613) 996-2690 (office). *E-mail:* jflaherty@fin.gc.ca (office); consltcomm@fin.gc.ca (office). *Website:* www.fin.gc.ca (office).

FLAMMARION, Charles-Henri, LèsL, LèsLet, MBA; French publishing executive; b. 27 July 1946, Boulogne-Billancourt; s. of the late Henri Flammarion and of Pierrette Chenelot; m. Marie-Françoise Mariani 1968; one s. two d.; ed Lycée de Sèvres, Sorbonne, Paris, Institut d'Etudes Politiques, Paris and Columbia Univ., USA; Asst Man. Editions Flammarion 1972–81, Gen. Man. 1981–85, Pres. Flammarion SA 1985–; Pres. Editions J'ai Lu 1982–, Audie-Fluide Glacial 1990–; mem. Bureau du Syndicat Nat. de l'Édition 1979–88, 1996–; Vice-Pres. Cercle de la Librairie 1988–94, Pres. 1994–2003; Pres. Casterman 1999–. *Leisure interests:* cooking, travel, skiing, walking. *Address:* Flammarion SA, 26 rue Racine, 75006 Paris (office); 5 avenue Franco-Russe, 75007 Paris, France (home).

FLANAGAN, Andrew Henry, CA; British business executive; b. 15 March 1956, Glasgow, Scotland; s. of Francis Desmond Flanagan and Martha Donaldson Flanagan; m. Virginia Walker 1972; one s. one d.; ed Univ. of Glasgow; chartered accountant with Touche Ross 1976–79, Price Waterhouse 1979–81; Financial Control Man. ITT 1981–86; Finance Dir PA Consulting Group 1986–91; Group Finance Dir and Chief Financial Officer BIS Ltd 1991–94; Finance Dir Scottish TV PLC 1994–96, Man. Dir 1996–97; Chief Exec. Scottish Media Group (later SMG PLC) 1997–2006; Dir ITV Network Ltd, Heart of Midlothian PLC, Scottish Rugby Union 2000–. *Leisure interests:* golf, cinema, reading, skiing.

FLANAGAN, Barry, OBE, RA; British sculptor; b. 11 Jan. 1941, Prestatyn, N Wales; ed Mayfield Coll., Sussex, Birmingham Coll. of Arts and Crafts and St Martin's School of Art, London; works in public collections including Art Inst., Chicago, Kunsthaus, Zurich, Museum of Modern Art, New York, Nagaoka Museum, Tokyo, Nat. Gallery of Canada, Ottawa, Stedelijk Museum, Amsterdam, Tate Gallery and Victoria and Albert Museum, London and Walker Art Gallery, Liverpool; outdoor sculpture commissioned by City of Ghent and by Camden Borough Council, London for Lincoln's Inn Fields, London, Equitable Life Tower West, NY, Stockley Park, Uxbridge, Kawakyo Co., Osaka; mem. Zoological Soc. of London. *Address:* c/o Waddington Galleries, 11 Cork Street, London, W1S 3LT, England.

FLANAGAN, Richard; Australian writer and film director; b. 1961, Tasmania; ed Univ. of Oxford, UK; fmr river guide; scriptwriter, author of history books, novelist; Rhodes Scholar. *Film:* The Sound of One Hand Clapping (dir). *Publications include:* non-fiction: A Terrible Beauty: A History of the Gordon River County, Codename Iago: The Story of John Friedrich, Parish-Fed Bastards: A History of the Politics of the Unemployed in Britain 1884–1939 1994; novels: Death of a River Guide (Victorian Premier's Award for Fiction) 1995, The Sound of One Hand Clapping 1998, Gould's Book of Fish (Commonwealth Writer's Prize) 2002, The Unknown Terrorist 2007, Wanting 2008. *Address:* Rogers, Coleridge and White, 20 Powis Mews, London, W11 1JN, England (office). *Telephone:* (20) 7221-3717 (office). *Fax:* (20) 7229-9084 (office). *E-mail:* info@rcwlitagency.com (office). *Website:* www.rcwlitagency.com (office).

FLANAGAN, William F., JD, DEA, LLM; Canadian professor of law; *Dean, Faculty of Law, Queen's University;* ed Univ. of Toronto, Columbia Univ., Univ. Paris I, France; began career as law clerk to Hon. Justice W. Z. Estey, Supreme Court of Canada, Ottawa 1986–87; joined Law Faculty, Queen's Univ., Kingston, Ont. 1991, Queen's Nat. Scholar 1996, becoming Prof. of Law, also Dir and Founder, Int. Law Spring Program, Queen's Univ. Int. Study Centre, Herstmonceux, UK 2001–05, Dean Faculty of Law 2005–, Co-Chair. Queen's Annual Business Law Symposium 1998–; Vice-Chair. Workplace Safety and Insurance Appeals Tribunal 1991–2003; Exec. Dir Canada AIDS Russia Project. *Publications:* several casebooks on property law, int. human rights, int. trade law and business law. *Address:* Office of the Dean, Faculty of Law, Queen's University, Kingston, ON K7L 3N6, Canada (office). *Telephone:* (613) 533-6000 (office). *Fax:* (613) 533-6509 (office). *E-mail:* w.flanagan@queensu.ca (office). *Website:* law.queensu.ca (office).

FLANIGEN, Edith Marie, MS; American chemist (retd); b. 1929, Buffalo, NY; ed Holy Angels Acad., D'Youville Coll., Buffalo, Syracuse Univ.; Research Chemist, Linde Div., Union Carbide 1952, Corp. Research Fellow 1973, Sr Research Fellow 1982, with UOP (jt venture of Union Carbide and Allied Signal, now subsidiary of Honeywell) 1988–94 (retd), now consultant; Fellow, American Acad. of Arts and Sciences; Perkin Medal (first female recipient) 1992, American Chemical Soc. Francis P. Garvan–John M. Olin Medal 1993, Int. Zeolite Assen Award 1994, Nat. Inventors Hall of Fame 2004, Lemelson-MIT Lifetime Achievement Award 2004.

FLANNERY, Joseph Patrick, BS, MBA; American business executive; *Chairman, President and CEO, Uniroyal Holding Inc.;* b. 20 March 1932, Lowell, Mass.; s. of Joseph Patrick Flannery and Mary Agnes Egan Flannery; m. Margaret Barrows 1957; three s. three d.; ed Lowell Tech. Inst., Harvard Grad. School of Business Admin.; Pres. Uniroyal Chemical Co. 1975–77; Exec. Vice-Pres. Uniroyal Inc., Middlebury, Conn. 1977; Pres. of parent co. and mem. Bd of Dirs. and Exec. Cttee 1977, CEO 1980, Chair. Uniroyal Inc. 1982; Chair., Pres. and CEO Uniroyal Holding, Inc. (investment man. firm) 1986–; fmr Pnr Clayton & Dubilier, Inc.; Dir Scotts Co., Newmont Mining Corpn,

Kmart Corpn, Ingersoll-Rand Co., The Kendall Co., APS Inc., Newmont Gold Co., ArvinMeritor. *Address:* Uniroyal Holding Inc., 70 Great Hill Road, Naugatuck, CT 06770-2224, USA.

FLANNERY, Timothy (Tim), BSc, MSc, PhD; Australian mammalogist, palaeontologist and academic; *Professor, Macquarie University;* b. 28 Jan. 1956; ed La Trobe Univ., Monash Univ., Univ. of New South Wales; fmr Prof., Univ. of Adelaide; fmr Dir South Australian Museum, Adelaide; fmr Prin. Research Scientist, Australian Museum; fmr Chair in Australian Studies, Harvard Univ., USA; fmr adviser on environmental issues to Australian Fed. Parl.; currently mem. Climate Risk Concentration of Research Excellence and Prof., Macquarie Univ. 2007–; Chair. Copenhagen Climate Council; mem. Wentworth Group of Concerned Scientists; surveyed mammals of Melanesia, discovered 16 new species 1990s; Greater Monkey-faced Bat (*Pteralopex flanneryi*) named after him 2005, named Australian of the Year 2007. *Publications:* Mammals of New Guinea 1990, The Future Eaters: An Ecological History of the Australasian Lands and People 1994, Mammals of the South-West Pacific & Moluccan Islands 1995, Throwim Way Leg: An Adventure 1998, The Eternal Frontier: An Ecological History of North America and Its Peoples 2001, A Gap in Nature (co-author) 2001, Astonishing Animals (co-author) 2004, Country: A Continent, a Scientist & a Kangaroo 2005, The Weather Makers: The History & Future Impact of Climate Change (Book of the Year, New South Wales Premier's Literary Awards 2006) 2006, Chasing Kangaroos: A Continent, a Scientist, and a Search for the World's Most Extraordinary Creature 2007; Ed.: The Birth of Melbourne, The Birth of Sydney, The Explorers, Watkin Tench, 1788, Terra Australis – Matthew Flinders' Great Adventures in the Circumnavigation of Australia, John Morgan – The Life and Adventures of William Buckley, John Nicol – Life and Adventures: 1776–1801, Joshua Slocum – Sailing Alone Around the World; more than 90 scientific papers in professional journals. *Address:* E8B 321, Faculty of Science, Macquarie University, Sydney, NSW 2109, Australia (office). *Telephone:* (2) 9850-8418 (office). *E-mail:* tflanner@els.mq.edu.au (office); tim.flannery@mq.edu.au (office). *Website:* www.mq.edu.au (office).

FLAVELL, Richard Anthony, PhD, FRS; British professor of immunobiology; *Sterling Professor and Chairman, Department of Immunobiology, School of Medicine, Yale University;* b. 23 Aug. 1945, Chelmsford; s. of John Trevor Flavell and Iris Flavell (née Hancock); m. Madlyn Nathanson 1987; one d.; two s. from previous m.; ed Univ. of Hull, Univ. of Amsterdam and Univ. of Zurich, Wetenschappelijk Medewerker, Univ. of Amsterdam, The Netherlands; Head Lab. of Gene Structure and Expression, Nat. Inst. for Medical Research, Mill Hill, London 1979–82; Pres. and Chief Scientific Officer Biogen NV 1982–88; Prof. and Chair. of Immunobiology, Yale Univ. School of Medicine and Investigator, Howard Hughes Medical Inst., Conn., USA 1988–; mem. NAS 2002, Inst. of Medicine 2006; Fed. of European Biochemical Socs Anniversary Prize 1980, Colworth Medal 1980, Darwin Trust Prize 1995. *Publications:* approx. 650 scientific articles. *Leisure interests include:* music, tennis, horticulture. *Address:* Department of Immunobiology, Yale University School of Medicine, 300 Cedar Street, TACS 569, New Haven, CT 06520, USA (office). *Telephone:* (203) 737-2216 (office). *E-mail:* richard.flavell@yale.edu (office). *Website:* www.info.med.yale.edu (office).

FLECKENSTEIN, Günther; German theatre director; b. 13 Jan. 1924, Mainz; m. Heike Kaase 1965; two d.; ed Realgymnasium, Mainz and Univ. Mainz; producer of plays and operas; Dir Deutsches Theater, Göttingen 1966–86, Hon. mem. 1990–; freelance producer 1986–; Guest Dir for theatres in Berlin, Hamburg, Stuttgart and Moscow; Guest Dir TV in Munich, Stuttgart and Berlin; Dir Hersfelde Festspiele 1976–81; has dramatized for stage and TV Der Grosstyrann und das Gericht (Bergengruen); stage production in German of Les jeux sont faits (Sartre), Im Räderwerk (Sartre); productions for children's and young people's theatre; Zückmayer Medal for services to the German language 1979, Hon. Plaque, Bad Hersfeld 1982, Hon. Plaque, Göttingen 1984, Polish Medal for Cultural Service 1986, Niedersachsen Verdienstkreuz 1990, Kolbenhoff Kulturpreis 1997. *Publications:* Norwegische Novelle, Gedichtband, Biographie: Lebensspüren, Ceterum censeo, Aphorismen und Commentare. *Address:* Sandstrasse 14, 82110 Germering, Germany.

FLEISCHER, Ari; American fmr government official; b. 1962; ed Middlebury Univ.; Press Sec. for Senator Pete Domenici 1989–1994; Deputy Communications Dir for Pres. George H. W. Bush's 1992 re-election campaign; fmr Communications Dir for Elizabeth Dole; White House Press Sec. for Pres. George W. Bush 2001–03; f. Ari Fleischer Communications 2003; sports marketing consultant with IMG 2004–; Spokesman Don't Take My Bat Away coalition. *Publications:* Taking Heat: The President, The Press And My Years In The White House 2005. *Address:* c/o IMG Center, 1360 East 9th Street, Suite 100, Cleveland, OH 44114, USA (office).

FLEISCHMANN, Peter; German film director and producer; b. 26 July 1937, Zweibrücken; s. of Alexander Fleischmann and Pascal Fleischmann; two c.; ed Inst. de Hautes Etudes Cinématographiques, Paris; fmrly asst to dir of short feature films, documentaries and animations; Co-founder Hallelujah Film with Volker Schlondorff; now produces and directs feature and documentary films; Consultant to Studio Babelsberg; Pres. Fédération Européene des Réalisateurs Audiovisuels; Chair. European Audiovisual Centre, Babelsberg; mem. EC Expert Council for reform of audiovisual politics. *Films include:* Alexander und das Auto ohne linken Scheinwerfer 1965 (animation), Herbst der Gammler 1967 (documentary), Jagdszenen aus Niederbayern (feature) 1968, Der Dritte Grad 1971 (feature), Hamburger Krankheit 1979 (feature), Frevel 1983 (feature), Al Capone von der Pfalz 1984 (documentary), Es ist nicht leicht ein Gott zu sein 1988 (feature), Deutschland, Deutschland 1991 (documentary), Mein Onkel, der Winzer 1993 (documentary). *Address:* Europäisches Filmzentrum Babelsberg, August-

Bebel-Strasse 26-53, 14482 Potsdam, Germany. *Telephone:* (331) 7062700 (office). *Fax:* (331) 7062710 (office).

FLEMING, Graham Richard, PhD, FRS; British chemist and academic; *Professor of Chemistry, University of California, Berkeley;* b. 3 Dec. 1949, Barrow; s. of Maurice N. H. Fleming and Lovima E. Winter; m. Jean McKenzie 1977; one s.; ed Univs of London and Bristol; Research Fellow, Calif. Inst. of Tech., USA 1974–75; Univ. Research Fellow, Univ. of Melbourne, Australia 1975, ARGC (Australian Research Grants Cttee) Research Asst 1976; Leverhulme Fellow, Royal Inst. 1977–79; Asst Prof., Univ. of Chicago, USA 1979–83, Assoc. Prof. 1983–85, Prof. 1985–87, Arthur Holly Compton Distinguished Service Prof. 1987–97; Prof. of Chem., Univ. of Calif., Berkeley 1997–, Melvin Calvin Distinguished Prof. of Chem. 2002–, Dir Physical Biosciences Div., Lawrence Berkeley Nat. Lab. 1997–2004, Assoc. Lab. Dir for Physical Sciences, Deputy Lab. Dir 2004–07; Dir Calif. Inst. for Quantitative Biosciencel Research 2001; Fellow, American Acad. of Arts and Sciences; A. P. Sloan Foundation Fellow, Guggenheim Fellowship; mem. NAS; Marlow Medal, Royal Soc. of Chem., Coblentz Award, Tilden Medal, ACS Nobel Laureate Signature Award for Grad. Educ. in Chem., ACS Peter Debye Award in Physical Chem., ACS Harrison Howe Award, Earle K. Pyler Prize, American Physical Soc. *Leisure interest:* climbing mountains. *Address:* Department of Chemistry, 221 Hildebrand, University of California, Berkeley, CA 94720, USA (office). *Telephone:* (510) 643-2735 (office). *Fax:* (510) 642-6340 (office). *E-mail:* fleming@cchem.berkeley.edu (office). *Website:* chemistry .berkeley.edu/index.shtml (office).

FLEMING, Osbourne Berrington; Anguillan/British politician and business executive; *Chief Minister and Minister of Home Affairs, Natural Resources, Lands and Physical Planning;* b. 18 Feb. 1940, East End; ed Valley Secondary School; Customs Officer, Saint Kitts 1959–64; lived in St Thomas, US Virgin Islands 1964–68, Saint Kitts 1968–81; f. Fleming's Transport (transport and shipping co.), St Croix 1974; MP (People's Progressive Party), Minister of Tourism, Agric. and Fisheries 1981–85; MP (Anguilla Nat. Alliance—ANA), Minister of Finance 1985–89; ind. MP, Minister of Finance and Econ. Devt 1989–94; rejoined ANA, apptd Leader Opposition in House of Ass. 1994–2000; mem. ANA/Anguilla Democratic Party United Front; Chief Minister 2000–, also Minister of Minister of Home Affairs, Tourism, Agric., Fisheries and Environment 2000–08, of Home Affairs, Natural Resources, Lands and Physical Planning 2008–. *Leisure interests:* playing draughts, dominoes and cards. *Address:* Office of the Chief Minister, The Secretariat, The Valley, Anguilla (office); Sea Feather's, East End, Anguilla, West Indies (home). *Telephone:* 497-2518 (office); 497-4783 (home). *Fax:* 497-3389 (office). *E-mail:* chief-minister@gov.ai (office). *Website:* www .gov.ai (office).

FLEMING, Renée, MMus; American singer (soprano); b. 14 Feb. 1959, Indiana, PA; d. of Edwin Davis Fleming and Patricia (Seymour) Alexander; m. Richard Lee Ross 1989 (divorced 2000); two d.; ed Potsdam State Univ., Eastman School of Music of Univ. of Rochester, Juilliard School American Opera Center; debuts Houston Grand Opera in Marriage of Figaro 1988, Spoleto Festival, Charleston and Italy 1987–90, New York City Opera in La Bohème 1989, San Francisco Opera, Metropolitan Opera, Paris Opera at Bastille, Teatro Colon, Buenos Aires all in Marriage of Figaro 1991, Glyndebourne in Così fan tutte 1992, La Scala Milan in Don Giovanni 1993, Vienna State Opera in Marriage of Figaro 1993, Lyric Opera of Chicago in Susannah 1993, San Diego Opera in Eugene Onegin 1994, Paris Opera 1996, Massenet's Thais at Nice and Gounod's Marguerite at the Met 1997, Floyd's Susannah at the Met 1999, Louise at Barbican Hall, London and the Marschallin at Covent Garden 2000; premiered Previn's A Streetcar Named Desire 1998; recital tour with Jean-Yves Thibaudet 2001–02; London Proms 2002, Dvořák's Rusalka in concert at Covent Garden 2003, Bellini's Il Pirata at the Met 2003; Fulbright Scholar to Germany 1984–85; Hon. mem. RAM 2003; Chevalier, Légion d'honneur 2005; Hon. doctorate Juilliard School, New York 2003; Fulbright Scholar 1984–85, George London Prize 1988, Richard Tucker Award 1990, Solti Prize, Acad. du Disque Lyrique 1996, Prix Maria Callas Acad. du Disque Lyrique 1997, 2004, Vocalist of the Year, (Musical America) 1997, Prize Acad. du Disque Lyrique 1998, Grammy Awards 1999, 2002, creation of the dessert 'La Diva Renée' by Master Chef Daniel Boulud 1999, Classical BRIT Awards for Top-selling Female Artist 2003, for Outstanding Contribution to Music 2004, LOTOS Medal of Merit 2005, Polar Music Prize 2008, Opera News Award 2008. *Recordings include:* Sacred Songs 2005, R. Strauss's Daphne (with Cologne Radio Chorus and Symphony Orchestra) 2005, Love Sublime (with Brad Mehldau) 2006, Homage: The Age of the Diva 2006, Four Last Songs 2008. *Publication:* The Inner Voice: The Making of a Singer (autobiog.) 2005. *Address:* M. L. Falcone Public Relations, 155 West 68th Street, Suite 1114, New York, NY 10023-5817, USA (office). *Telephone:* (212) 580-4302 (office). *Fax:* (212) 787-9638 (office). *Website:* www.renee -fleming.com.

FLEMING, Stephen Paul; New Zealand cricketer; *Captain, New Zealand National Cricket Team;* b. 1 April 1973, Christchurch, Canterbury; s. of Pauline Fleming; ed Waltham Primary School, Cashmere High School, Christchurch Teachers' Coll.; left-handed batsmen; teams: Canterbury 1991–2000, Wellington 2000–, Middlesex 2001, Yorkshire 2003 and New Zealand 1994– (retd as one-day side captain 2007); 89 tests for New Zealand, scored 5,663 runs (average 39.32, highest score 274 not out versus Sri Lanka 2003) with eight hundreds; scored 11,648 runs (average 41.89) with 23 hundreds in first-class cricket; 228 one-day internationals, scored 6,462 runs (average 32.14) with six hundreds; Capt. New Zealand Nat. Cricket Team 1997– (apptd versus England, youngest Capt. in New Zealand history); New Zealand's highest run-scorer in one-day internationals; holds New Zealand record for number of test caps, test runs and test catches. *Publications:*

Cricketing Safari (with Nathan Astle) 2000. *Leisure interests:* golf, computer games, reading. *Address:* c/o Cricket Wellington, Brierley Pavilion, Basin Reserve, Rugby Street, POB 578, Wellington, New Zealand (office). *Telephone:* (4) 384-3171 (office). *Fax:* (4) 384-3498 (office). *E-mail:* cricket@firebirds.co.nz (office).

FLETCHER, Ernie, BS; American fmr state official; b. 12 Nov. 1952, Mount Sterling, Ky; m. Glenna Foster; one d. one s.; ed Univ. of Kentucky Coll. of Eng and Coll. of Medicine; served in US Air Force as F-4E Aircraft Commdr and N American Aerospace Defense Command (NORAD) Alert Force Commdr 1980s; family practice physician 1983–95; elected to Ky Legislature as Rep. for 78th Congressional Dist 1995–99, mem. Ky Comm. on Poverty, Task Force on Higher Educ.; elected to US House of Reps from 6th Congressional Dist 1999–2003, mem. House Cttee on Energy and Commerce, Chair. Policy Sub-Cttee on Health; Gov. of Ky 2003–08, fmr CEO St Joseph Medical Foundation; Republican; Chair. Southern States Energy Bd; mem. Bd of Dirs Achieve, Inc. *Address:* c/o The Capitol Building, 700 Capital Avenue, Suite 100, Frankfort, KY 40601, USA (office).

FLETCHER, Hugh Alasdair, BSc, MCom, MBA; New Zealand business executive and university administrator; *Chancellor, University of Auckland;* b. 28 Nov. 1947, Auckland; s. of Sir James Muir Cameron Fletcher and Margery V. Fletcher (née Gunthorp); m. Rt Hon. Dame Sian Seerpoohi Elias (Chief Justice of NZ) 1970; two s.; ed Auckland Univ. and Stanford Univ.; CEO Fletcher Holdings Ltd 1980, Man. Dir Fletcher Challenge Ltd 1981, CEO 1987–97, Dir Fletcher Building 2002–; Chair. Air NZ 1985–89; mem. Prime Minister's Enterprise Council 1992–98, Asia-Pacific Advisory Cttee NY Stock Exchange 1995–2004; Chancellor Univ. of Auckland 2004–; Chair. Ministerial Inquiry into Telecommunications 2000–; mem. Bd of Dirs Rubicon 2002–, IAG NZ 2003–, Reserve Bank of NZ 2003–; Harkness Fellowship 1970–72; Distinguished Alumni Award, Univ. of Auckland 1996. *Leisure interest:* horse riding, hunting, breeding, racing. *Address:* PO Box 11468, Ellerslie, Auckland (office); 79 Penrose Road, Auckland, New Zealand (home). *Telephone:* (9) 579-4226 (office). *Fax:* (9) 579-8408 (office). *E-mail:* hugh.fletcher@xtra.co.nz (office). *Website:* www.auckland.ac.nz.

FLETCHER, John E.; Australian retail executive; b. 1952, Melbourne, Vic.; m. Nola Fletcher; three c.; accounting, operating and sr man. positions, Brambles Industries 1974–82, Gen. Man. Transport Div. 1982–84, Commercial Dir, Europe 1984–86, Man. Dir CHEP Australia 1986–88, Man. Dir Brambles Australia 1988–93, CEO Brambles Industries 1993–2001; CEO and Man. Dir Coles Myer Ltd (renamed Coles Group Ltd 2006) 2001–07; mem. Bd of Dirs Telstra Corpn 2001–06. *Leisure interests:* golf, tennis, skiing. *Address:* c/o Coles, 800 Toorak Road, Tooronga, Vic. 3146, Australia. *Telephone:* (3) 9829-5111.

FLETCHER, Neville Horner, AM, PhD, DSc, FAA, FTSE; Australian physicist and academic; *Visiting Fellow, Research School of Physical Sciences and Engineering, Australian National University;* b. 14 July 1930, Armidale, NSW; s. of Alleine Horner Fletcher and Florence Mabel Glass; m. Eunice M. Sciffer 1953; one s. two d.; ed Armidale High School, New England Univ. Coll., Univ. of Sydney, Harvard Univ.; Research Engineer, Clevite Transistor Products, USA 1953–55; Researcher, CSIRO Radiophysics Lab. 1956–59, Dir CSIRO Inst. of Physical Sciences 1983–88; Chief Research Scientist 1988–95; at Univ. of New England 1960–83, Sr Lecturer in Physics 1960–63, Prof. of Physics 1963–83, Dean, Faculty of Science 1963–65, mem. Univ. Council 1968–72, Chair. Professorial Bd 1970–72, Pro Vice-Chancellor 1969–72, Prof. Emer. 1983–; Adjunct Prof., ANU 1990–95, Visiting Fellow, Research School of Physical Sciences and Eng 1995–; Adjunct Prof., Univ. of NSW 1997–; Chair. Antarctic Science Advisory Cttee 1990–96; mem. Australian Research Grants Cttee 1974–78, 1995–98; Sec. for Physical Sciences, Australian Acad. of Science 1980–84; mem. Govt Meteorology Policy Cttee 1981–84, Int. Comm. on Acoustics 1985–90; Fellow, Australian Acad. of Science 1976, Australian Acad. of Technological Sciences and Eng 1987, Fellow Australian Inst. of Physics (Pres. 1981–83), Inst. of Physics (London), Australian Acoustical Soc., Acoustical Soc. of America; Univ. Medal, Sydney 1951, Frank Knox Fellowship, Harvard Univ. 1952, Edgeworth David Medal, Royal Soc. of NSW 1963, Lyle Medal, Australian Acad. of Science 1993, Distinguished Alumni Award, Univ. of New England 1994, Silver Medal in Musical Acoustics, Acoustical Soc. of America 1998. *Publications:* The Physics of Rainclouds 1962, The Chemical Physics of Ice 1970, Physics and Music 1976, The Physics of Musical Instruments 1990, Acoustic Systems in Biology 1992, Principles of Vibration and Sound 1995, Brief Candles (short stories) 2005; over 190 papers in scientific journals. *Leisure interests:* music (flute, bassoon and organ), writing. *Address:* Department of Electronic Materials Engineering, Research School of Physical Sciences and Engineering, Australian National University, Canberra, ACT 0200, Australia (office). *Telephone:* (2) 6125-4406 (office); (2) 6288-8988 (home). *Fax:* (2) 6215-0511 (office). *E-mail:* neville.fletcher@anu.edu.au (office). *Website:* www.rsphysse.anu.edu.au/eme/profile.php/34 (office); www.phys.unsw.edu.au/music/people/fletcher.html (office); www.science.org.au/scientists/nf.htm (office).

FLETCHER, Philip John, CBE, MA; British public servant; *Chairman, Water Services Regulation Authority (Ofwat);* b. 2 May 1946, London; s. of the late Alan Philip Fletcher and Annette Grace Fletcher (née Wright); m. Margaret Anne Boys; two d. (one deceased); ed Marlborough Coll., Trinity Coll., Oxford; joined Civil Service 1968, Under-Sec. of Housing, Water and Cen. Finance, Dept of the Environment 1986–90; Planning and Devt Control 1990–93; Chief Exec. PSA Services 1993–94; Deputy Sec. Cities and Countryside Group 1994–95; Receiver for the Metropolitan Police Dist 1996–2000; Dir-Gen. of Water Services 2000–06, Chair. Water Services Regulation Authority (Ofwat) 2006–; Reader, Church of England; mem. Archbishops' Council for the Church of England and Ofqual Cttee. *Leisure interest:* walking.

Address: Ofwat, Centre City Tower, 7 Hill Street, Birmingham, B5 4UA, England (office). *Telephone:* (121) 625-1300 (office). *Fax:* (121) 625-1348 (office). *E-mail:* philip.fletcher@ofwat.gsi.gov.uk (office). *Website:* www.ofwat.gov.uk (office).

FLEURY, Gen. Jean André; French air force officer and aeronautics industry executive; b. 1 Dec. 1934, Brest; s. of René Fleury and Blanche-Marie Marsille; Commdt, Saint Dizier Air Base 1977–78; Head, Office of Supply, Air Force Gen. Staff 1978–81; Deputy Chief of Planning, Armed Forces Gen. Staff 1983–85; Commdt, Strategic Air Forces 1985–87; Chief of Staff to Pres. of Repub. 1987–89; Chief of Staff of Air Force 1989–91; mem. Supreme Council of Army and Air Forces 1989; Pres. Aéroports de Paris 1992–99; Chair. Airports Council Int. 1998–99; aeronautics consultant 2000–; mem. Econ. and Social Regional Council of Britanny 2001–07; Grand Croix, Légion d'honneur, Commdr Ordre nat. du Mérite, Croix de la Valeur militaire, Commdr Legion of Merit (USA). *Publication:* Faire face: Memoires d'un chef d'état major 1996, Le Gènèral qui pensait comme un civil 2004, Le mystère de la Chesnaie 2007, Les guerres du Golfe 2009. *Address:* Les Mirages, La Combe de Haut, 56140 Pleucadeuc, France (office). *Telephone:* (2) 97-26-96-85 (office). *Fax:* (2) 97-26-98-22 (office). *E-mail:* fleurygeneral@wanadoo.fr (office).

FLIER, Jeffrey S., BS, MD; American endocrinologist and academic; *Dean, Faculty of Medicine, Harvard University;* b. 1948, New York; m. Dr Eleftheria Maratos-Flier; two c.; ed City Coll. of New York, Mount Sinai School of Medicine; intern, Mount Sinai Hosp., New York 1972–73, residency training in internal medicine 1973–74; Clinical Assoc., NIH, Bethesda, Md 1974–78; Asst Prof. of Medicine, Harvard Medical School 1978–82, Assoc. Prof. 1982–93, Prof. 1993–, George C. Reisman Prof. of Medicine 1999–, Chief of Endocrine Div. 1990, Chief Academic Officer, Beth Israel Deaconess Medical Center (BIDMC) 2002–07, also Carolyn Shields Walker Prof. of Medicine, Harvard Medical School, Dean, Faculty of Medicine 2007–; Chief of Diabetes Unit, Beth Israel Deaconess Medical Center 1998–2002; Visiting Scientist, Whitehead Inst., MIT 1985–86; Fellow, American Acad. of Arts and Sciences; mem. AAAS, NAS Inst. of Medicine (Pres. 2001); Hon. MD (Univ. of Athens) 1997; American Diabetes Asscn Eli Lilly Award, American Physiological Soc. Berson Lecture, American Diabetes Asscn Banting Medal 2005. *Publications:* over 200 scholarly papers and reviews. *Address:* Office of the Dean, Harvard Medical School, Gordon Hall, 25 Shattuck Street, Boston, MA 02115, USA (office). *Telephone:* (617) 432-1000 (office). *E-mail:* jflier@bidmc.harvard.edu (office). *Website:* hms.harvard.edu/hms (office).

FLIMM, Jürgen; German theatre director; *Artistic Director, Salzburg Festspiele;* b. 17 July 1941, Giessen; s. of Werner Flimm and Ellen Flimm; m. Susanne Ottersbach 1990; early work at the Munich Kammerspiele; Dir Nationaltheater, Mannheim 1972–73; Prin. Dir Thalia Theater, Hamburg 1973–74; directed plays in Munich, Hamburg, Bochum, Frankfurt 1974–79 and in Zürich, Amsterdam, Salzburg, Vienna, Milan; Dir Cologne Theatre 1979–85, Thalia Theatre, Hamburg 1985–2000, Salome at the Met, New York 2004, Monteverdi's Poppea Zürich Opera 2005; Pres. German Bühnenverein 1999–2003; Acting Dir Salzburg Festspiele 2001–06, Artistic Dir 2006–(11); Artistic Dir Festival Ruhrtriennale 2005–07; Gen. Man. designate, Deutsche Staatsoper, Berlin (2010–); Dr hc (Hildesheim) 2002; Bundesverdienstkreuz 1992, Konrad-Wolf-Preis, Berlin 1995. *Films:* Wer zu spät kommt – die letzten Tage des Politbüros 1990, Käthchens Traum 2004. *Publications:* Theatergänger 2004. *Address:* Salzburger Festspiele, Hofstallgasse 1, 5020 Salzburg, Austria (office). *Telephone:* (662) 8045-200 (office). *Fax:* (662) 8045-720 (office). *E-mail:* j.flimm@salzburgfestival.at (office). *Website:* www.salzburgfestival.at (office).

FLOCKHART, Calista; American actress; b. 11 Nov. 1964, Freeport, Ill.; d. of Ronald Flockhart and Kay Flockhart; one adopted s. *Films include:* Naked in New York 1993, Quiz Show 1994, Getting In 1994, Pictures of Baby Jane Doe 1995, Drunks 1995, The Birdcage 1996, Telling Lies in America 1997, Milk and Money 1997, A Midsummer Night's Dream 1999, Like a Hole in the Head 1999, Bash 2000, Things You Can Tell Just By Looking At Her 2000, The Last Shot 2004, Fragile 2005. *Plays on Broadway include:* The Glass Menagerie, The Three Sisters. *Television work includes:* The Guiding Light 1978, Darrow 1991, An American Story 1991, Life Stories: Families in Crisis 1992, Ally McBeal (Best Actress Award, Golden Globes 1998) 1997–2002, Bash: Latter-Day Plays 2000, Brothers and Sisters (ABC) 2006–09. *Address:* c/o The Gersh Agency, POB 5617, Beverly Hills, CA 90210, USA (office).

FLOOD, Philip James, AO, BEcons (Hons); Australian diplomatist; b. 2 July 1935, Sydney; s. of Thomas C. Flood and Maxine S. Flood; m. 2nd Carole Henderson 1990; two s. one d. from previous m.; ed North Sydney High School, Univ. of Sydney; mem. staff Mission to EEC and Embassy, Brussels 1959–62, Rep. to OECD Devt Assistance Cttee, Paris 1966–69, Asst Sec. Dept of Foreign Affairs 1971–73, High Commr in Bangladesh 1974–76, Minister, Embassy, Washington, DC 1976–77, CEO Dept Special Trade Representations 1977–80; First Asst Sec. Dept of Trade 1980–84, Deputy Sec. Dept of Foreign Affairs 1985–89, Amb. to Indonesia 1989–93, Dir-Gen. Australian Int. Devt Assistance Bureau (AUSAID) 1993–95, Dir-Gen. Office of Nat. Assessments 1995–96, Sec. Dept of Foreign Affairs and Trade 1996–98; High Commr in London 1998–2000; Head Inquiry into Immigration Detention 2000–01; Chair. Australia-Indonesia Inst. 2001–05; Head Inquiry into Australian Intelligence Agencies 2004; Chair. Inquiry into Plasma Fractionation 2006; Fellow, Royal Australian Inst. Public Admin.; Bintang Jasa Utama (Indonesian Order of Merit) 1993. *Publication:* Odyssey by the Sea 2005. *Leisure interests:* reading, theatre, walking, swimming.

FLOR, Claus Peter; German conductor; *Music Director, Malaysian Philharmonic Orchestra;* b. 16 March 1953, Leipzig; adopted s. of Richard Flor and Sigrid Langer; ed Music School, Weimar and High School of Music, Weimar/

Leipzig; studied under Rolf Reuter, Rafael Kubelik and Kurt Sanderling; learnt violin and clarinet before commencing conducting studies; Chief Conductor, Suhl Philharmonic 1981–84; Chief Conductor, Music Dir Berliner Sinfonie Orchester 1984–92; Artistic Adviser, Zürich Tonhalle Orchestra 1991–96; Prin. Guest Conductor, Philharmonia Orchestra, London 1991–94, Dallas Symphony Orchestra 1999–2008, Orchestra Sinfonica di Milano Giuseppe Verdi 2003–08; Music Dir, Malaysian Philharmonic Orchestra Aug. 2008–; debut with Los Angeles Philharmonic 1985; debut with Berlin Philharmonic 1988; regular appearances with Vienna Symphony, Orchestre de Paris, Royal Concertgebouw, Rotterdam Philharmonic and major German orchestras; frequent guest engagements with leading orchestras in UK, USA, Canada etc.; conductor of opera at many German opera houses including Berlin Staatsoper and Deutsche Oper, Berlin. *Recordings include:* Mendelssohn, Cherubini, Dvořák, Mozart, Shostakovich. *Leisure interests:* collecting red wines, history and genealogy of European nobility. *Address:* c/o IMG Artists, The Light Box, 111 Power Road, London, W4 5PY, England (office). *Telephone:* (20) 7957-5800 (office). *Fax:* (20) 7957-5801 (office). *E-mail:* amonsey@imgartists.com (office). *Website:* www.imgartists.com (office).

FLORES, Mario; Nicaraguan politician; Minister of Finance and Public Credit 2006–07; mem. Bd of Govs IDB. *Address:* c/o Ministry of Finance and Public Credit, Frente a la Asamblea Nacional, Apdo 2170, Managua, Nicaragua (office).

FLORES, Sylvia, BA; Belizean politician; *Minister of Human Development;* b. 27 Nov. 1951; one c.; ed Hunter Coll., NY, USA; career as coll. lecturer and community activist; fmr Mayor of Belize City; Speaker of the House of Reps 1998–2001; Pres. of the Senate 2001–03; Minister of Defence and Nat. Emergency Man. 2003–05; Minister of Human Devt 2005–, of Housing 2005–07. *Leisure interests:* reading novels, watching sports. *Address:* Ministry of Human Development and Housing, West Block, Independence Hill, Belmopan, Belize (office). *Telephone:* 822-2248 (office). *Fax:* 822–3175 (office). *E-mail:* mhd@btl.net (office).

FLORES BERMÚDEZ, Roberto, LLB; Honduran politician and diplomatist; *Ambassador to USA;* b. 15 Aug. 1949; m. Laura Flores; two c.; ed Univ. of Honduras; Dir-Gen. Diplomatic Protocol, Ministry of Foreign Affairs 1984–86, Dir-Gen. Foreign Politics 1986–87, Head of Cabinet 1988–89, Dir-Gen. Int. Orgs 1990, Minister of Foreign Affairs 2000–02, Amb. to UN, New York 1990–92, to USA 1994–98, to UK 1998–99, Minister of Foreign Affairs 2000–06, Amb. to USA 2006–; fmr mem. Honduran Del. to Cen. American Parl.; fmr Head of Tech. Del., Cen. American Peace Negotiation Process. *Address:* Embassy of Honduras, 3007 Tilden Street, NW, Suite 4M, Washington, DC 20008, USA (office). *Telephone:* (202) 966-7702 (office). *Fax:* (202) 966-9751 (office). *E-mail:* embassy@hondurasemb.org (office). *Website:* www.hondurasemb.org (office).

FLORES FACUSSÉ, Carlos Roberto, BEng, MIntEcon, PhD; Honduran fmr head of state; *President, Partido Liberal;* b. 1 March 1950, Tegucigalpa; s. of Oscar A. Flores and Margarita Facussé de Flores; m. Mary Carol Flake; one s. one d.; ed American School, Tegucigalpa and Louisiana State Univ.; Rep. for Francisco Morazan to Liberal Convention, Pres. Departmental Liberal Council, Francisco Morazan; Finance Sec. Nat. Directorate Movimiento Liberal Rodista; Congressman Nat. Ass. for Francisco Morazan 1980–97; Presidential Sec. 1982–83; Gen. Co-ordinator Movimiento Liberal Florista; Pres. Cen. Exec. Council Partido Liberal de Honduras; Pres. of Honduras 1998–2002; Co-owner, Man. and mem. editorial Bd La Tribuna, Co-owner and Man. Lithopress Industrial; fmr Man. CONPACASA; fmr Prof. School of Business Admin, Nat. Univ. of Honduras, Cen. American Higher School of Banking; fmr mem. Bd of Dirs Honduran Inst. of Social Security, Cen. Bank of Honduras, Inst. Nacional de Formación Profesional; mem. Industrial Eng Asscn of Honduras, Nat. Asscn of Industries, Consejo Hondureño de la Empresa Privada (COHEP), Honduran Inst. of Inter-American Culture. *Publication:* Forjemos Unidos el Destino de Honduras. *Address:* Partido Liberal, Col. Miramonte, No. 1, Tegucigalpa, Honduras.

FLORES NANO, Lourdes, PhD; Peruvian lawyer and politician; *President, Alianza Electoral Unidad Nacional;* b. 7 Oct. 1959; ed Pontifical Catholic Univ., Lima, Business Inst. of Madrid, Universidad Complutense de Madrid; fmr Lecturer in Commercial Law, Pontifical Catholic Univ. of Lima, Univ. of Lima; elected Deputy, Congress 1990, 1995–2000; mem. Constituent Democratic Congress 1993; Founder and Head Attorney, Lourdes Flores Nano Abogados, EIRL; Pres. Alianza Electoral Unidad Nacional, unsuccessful cand. for Pres. of Peru 2001, 2006; fmr mem. Council, Metropolitan Municipality of Lima; mem. Exec. Council Inter-American Dialogue, Christian Democrat Org. of America, Int. Christian Democrat Org.; mem. Bd Int. IDEA. *Address:* Unidad Nacional, Calle Ricardo Palma 1111, Miraflores, Lima, Peru (office). *Telephone:* (1) 2242773 (office). *Website:* www.unidadnacional.org (office).

FLORES PEREZ, Francisco; Salvadorean fmr head of state; b. 17 Oct. 1959; m. Lourdes Rodríguez de Flores; one s. one d.; ed Amherst Coll.; fmr lecturer; fmr Deputy and Pres. Legislative Ass.; fmr Vice-Minister of Planning, then Vice-Pres. and Adviser to Pres. Cristiani; Information Sec. to Pres. Armando Calderón Sol; Pres. of El Salvador 1999–2004; mem. Nat. Republican Alliance (ARENA). *Address:* c/o Ministry for the Presidency, Avda Cuba, Calle Darió González 806, Barrio San Jacinto, San Salvador, El Salvador (office).

FLOSSE, Gaston; French Polynesian politician; b. 24 June 1931, Rikitea (Gambier archipelago); m. Marie-Jeanne Mao 1994; Pres. City Council Pirae 1963–65, Mayor 1965–2000; Govt Councillor in charge of Agric. 1965–67; mem. French Polynesian Territorial Ass. for Windward Islands 1967–, Pres. 1972–77; Pres. Tahoeraa Huiraatira Party 1971–; Vice-Pres. Govt Council 1982–84, Pres. Governing Council 1984–87, 1991–2004, Pres. of French Polynesia Feb.–June 2004, Oct. 2004–05, 2008; mem. Cen. Cttee Union des Democrates pour la République (UDR), France, then Founding mem. RPR; Deputy for French Polynesia, Nat. Ass., France 1978–97; Sec. of State in charge of S Pacific Affairs, France 1986–88; Senator of French Repub. 1998–; Chevalier, Légion d'honneur, Ordre nat. du Mérite, First 'Grand Maître', Order of Tahiti Nui; Dr hc (Kyung Hee Univ., Korea) 1985. *Address:* Tahoera'a Huiraatira, rue du Commandant Destremeau, BP 471, Papeete, French Polynesia. *Telephone:* 429898 (office). *Fax:* 450004 (office). *E-mail:* courrier@tahoeraahuiraatira.pf (office). *Website:* tahoeraahuiraatira.pf (office).

FLOWERS, Baron (Life Peer), cr. 1979, of Queen's Gate in the City of Westminster; **Brian Hilton Flowers,** Kt, MA, DSc, FRS, FInstP, MRIA; British physicist; b. 13 Sept. 1924, Blackburn, Lancs.; s. of the late Rev. Harold J. Flowers and Marion V. Flowers (née Hilton); m. Mary Frances Behrens 1951; two step s.; ed Bishop Gore Grammar School, Swansea, Gonville and Caius Coll., Cambridge, Univ. of Birmingham; Anglo-Canadian Atomic Energy Mission (Tube Alloys) at Montreal and Chalk River, Canada 1944; joined staff AERE, Harwell 1946, Head of Theoretical Physics Div. 1952–58; Prof. of Theoretical Physics, Univ. of Manchester 1958–61, Langworthy Prof. of Physics 1961–72, Chancellor 1994–2001; Chair. Science Research Council 1967–73; Rector Imperial Coll. of Science and Tech., London 1973–85; Vice-Chancellor Univ. of London 1985–90; Chair. Computer Bd for Univs and Research Councils 1966–70; Pres. Inst. of Physics 1972–74, European Science Foundation 1974–80, Nat. Soc. for Clean Air 1977–79; Chair. Royal Comm. on Environmental Pollution 1973–76, Standing Comm. on Energy and the Environment 1978–81, Univ. of London Working Party on Future of Medicine and Dentistry Teaching Resources 1979–80, Cttee of Vice-Chancellors and Prins of the Univs of the UK 1983–85; Founder-mem. Academia Europaea 1988; Vice-Chair. Asscn of Commonwealth Univs 1987–90; Chair. House of Lords Select Cttee on Science and Tech. 1989–93, Nuffield Foundation 1987–98, Cttee on Org. of the Academic Year 1992–93; Pres. Asscn for Colleges 1993–95; Gov. Middlesex Univ. 1992–2001; Corresp. mem. Swiss Acad. of Eng Sciences 1986; Fellow, Physical Soc. 1956; Sr Fellow, RCA 1983; Hon. Fellow, Imperial Coll. 1972, Gonville and Caius Coll., Cambridge 1974, UMIST 1985; Hon. FIEE 1975; Hon. FRCP 1992; Chevalier, Légion d'honneur 1975, Officier 1981; Hon. DSc (Sussex) 1968, (Wales) 1972, (Leicester) 1973, (Manchester) 1973, (Liverpool) 1974, (Bristol) 1982, (Oxford) 1985, (Nat. Univ. of Ireland) 1990, (Reading) 1996, (London) 1997; Hon. ScD (Dublin) 1984; Hon. LLD (Dundee) 1985, (Glasgow) 1987, (Manchester) 1994; Hon. DEng (Nova Scotia) 1983; Rutherford Medal and Prize, Inst. of Physics and the Physical Soc. 1968, Chalmers Medal (Sweden) 1980, Glazebrook Medal, Inst. of Physics 1987. *Publications:* Properties of Matter (with E. Mendoza) 1970, An Introduction to Numerical Methods in C++ 1995; numerous scientific papers in the journals of learned socs on nuclear reactions and the structure of atomic nuclei, on science policy and on energy and the environment. *Leisure interests:* music, walking, computing, gardening. *Address:* 53 Athenaeum Road, London, N20 9AL, England (home). *Telephone:* (20) 8446-5993 (home). *E-mail:* FOFQG@clumsies.demon.co.uk (home).

FLOWERS, Matthew Dominic; British art dealer, musician and composer; *Managing Director, Angela Flowers Gallery PLC;* b. 8 Oct. 1956, London; s. of Adrian John Flowers and Angela Mary Flowers (née Holland); m. Huei Chjuin Hong (divorced); two s.; ed William Ellis School; worked with various bands including Sore Throat and Blue Zoo, appeared on TV programmes Top of the Pops and Old Grey Whistle Test 1974–83; joined Angela Flowers Gallery (now Angela Flowers Gallery PLC) as art gallery Asst 1975, Man. Dir 1988–. *Leisure interests:* soccer, chess, music. *Address:* Flowers East, 82 Kingsland Road, London E8 8DP, England (office). *Telephone:* (20) 7920 7777 (office). *Fax:* (20) 7920 7770 (office). *E-mail:* matt@flowerseast.com (office). *Website:* www.flowerseast.com (office).

FLYNN, Padraig; Irish politician; b. 9 May 1939, Castlebar; m. Dorothy Tynan; one s. three d.; ed St Patrick's Teacher Training Coll., Dublin; fmr school teacher and publican; mem. Mayo Co. Council 1967–86; mem. Dáil 1977–92; Minister of State, Dept of Transport and Power 1980–81; Minister for the Gaeltacht March–Oct. 1982, for Trade, Commerce and Tourism Oct.–Dec. 1982, for Environment 1987–91, for Justice Feb.–Dec. 1992, for Industry and Commerce Nov.–Dec. 1992; EU Commr for Employment and Social Affairs and for Relations with the Econ. and Social Cttee 1993–99; Fianna Fáil. *Leisure interests:* golf, reading, world affairs. *Address:* c/o Fianna Fáil, 65–66 Lower Mount Street, Dublin 2, Ireland.

FO, Dario; Italian playwright, clown, actor and painter; b. 24 March 1926, San Giano; m. Franca Rame 1954; one c.; ed Acad. of Fine Arts, Milan; comedian, Teatro di Rivista; co-founder theatre groups, Fo-Rame Co. 1957–68, Associazione Nuova Scena 1968–69, Collettivo Teatrale la Comune 1970–; cand. for Mayor of Milan 2006; Hon. DLitt (Westminster) 1997; Dr hc (Univ. La Sapienza, Rome) 2006; Univ. of Copenhagen Sonning Prize 1981, Associazione Torre Nat. Award Against Violence and the Camorra 1986, Obie Prize 1986, Campione d'Italia Agro Dolce Prize 1987, Nobel Prize for Literature 1997. *Film scripts:* Lo Svitato 1956, Musica per vecchi animali 1989. *Plays include:* Il dito nell'occhio (with Franco Parenti and Giustino Durano) 1953, I sani da legare (with Parenti and Durano) 1954, Ladri, manichini e donne nude 1957, Comica finale 1958, Gli arcangeli non giocano a flipper 1959, La storia vera di Piero d'Angera, che alla crociata non c'era 1960, Aveva due pistole con gli occhi bianchi e neri 1960, Chi ruba un piede è fortunato in amore 1961, Isabella, tre caravelle e un cacciaballe 1963, Settimo: ruba un po' meno 1964, La colpa è sempre del diavolo 1965, La signora è da buttare 1967, Grande pantomima per pupazzi piccoli, grandi e medi 1968, L'operaio conosce 300 parole, il padrone 1000, per questo lui è il padrone 1969, Legami pure, tanto spacco tutto lo stesso 1969, Il funeral e del padrone 1969, Mistero buffo 1969, Morte accidentale di un anarchico 1970, Fedayin 1971,

Basta con i fascisti 1973, Ci ragiono e canto N.3 1973, Guerra di popolo in Cile 1973, Non si paga, non si paga! 1974, Fanfani rapito 1975, La marijuana della mamma è la più bella 1975, Tutta casa, letto e chiesa 1977, La tragedia di Aldo Moro 1979, Storia della tigre e altre storie 1979, Una madre (with Franca Rame) 1981, Clacson, trombette e pernacchi 1981, L'Opera dello sghignazzo 1982, Il fabulazzo osceno 1982, Coppia aperta 1982, Patapunfete 1983, Quasi per caso una donna: Elisabetta 1983, Dio li fa poi li accoppa 1983, Lisistrata romana 1983, Hellequin, Harlekin, Arlecchino 1985, Diario di Eva 1985, Parti femminili (with Franca Rame) 1986, Il ratto della Francesca 1986, La rava e la fava (aka La parte del leone) 1987, Lettera dalla Cina 1989, Il braccato 1989, Il papa e la strega 1989, Zitti! Stiamo precipitando! 1990, Johan Padan a la descoverta de le Americhe 1991, Parliamo di donne (two one-act pieces, L'Eroina and Grassa è bello) 1991, Settimo: ruba un po' meno! n. 2 1992, Dario Fo incontra Ruzzante 1993, Mamma! I sanculotti! 1993, Un palcoscenico per le donne 1994, Sesso? Grazie, tanto per gradire! 1994, Bibbia dei villani 1996, Il diavolo con le zinne 1996, Lu Santo Jullare Francesco 1999, My First Seven Years (Plus a Few More) (memoir) 2005, L'Anomalo Bicefalo (on the Premier Silvio Berlusconi) 2006. *Radio:* Poer Nano 1950, Chicchirichì, Cocoricò, Ragazzi in Gamba, Non si vive di solo pane 1951. *Television:* Canzonissima 1962, Il teatro di Dario Fo 1976, Buona sera con Franca Rame 1980, Trasmissione forzata 1987. *Address:* C. So di Porta Romana 132, 20122 Milan, Italy (office). *Telephone:* (02) 58430506 (office). *E-mail:* francarame@iol.it (office). *Website:* www.francarame.it (office).

FOALE, Marion Ann, RCA; British designer; b. 13 March 1939, London; d. of S. D. Foale; one s. one d.; ed South West Essex Tech and School of Art, RCA; career fashion designer; designed Queen's mantle for OBE dedication ceremony 1960; Founding partner (with Sally Tuffin) Foale and Tuffin Ltd 1961–72; signed with Puritan Fashion Corps, NY 1965–70; designed clothes for films; Susannah York (q.v.) in Kaleidoscope 1966, Audrey Hepburn in Two for the Road 1966; f. own label Marion Foale–Knitwear Designer 1982. *Publication:* Marion Foale's Classic Knitwear 1987. *Leisure interest:* studying fine art. *Address:* Foale Ltd, The Cottage, 133A Long Street, Atherstone, Warwicks., CV9 1AD, England (office). *Telephone:* (1827) 720333 (office). *Fax:* (1827) 720444 (office). *E-mail:* foale@talk21.com (office). *Website:* www .marionfoale.com (office).

FODOR, Gen. Lajos; Hungarian army officer; b. 29 July 1947, Debrecen; m. Éva Kovács; one s. one d.; ed Lajos Kossuth Land Forces Military Acad., Szentendre, Frunze Military Acad., Moscow, Defence Language Inst., San Antonio, American Nat. Defence Univ.; infantry officer 1970; platoon leader 14th Mechanized Infantry Regt Nagykaniza 1971; Bn Commdr 63rd Mechanized Infantry Regt Nagyatád 1971–79, Deputy Commdr 1981–83, Regt Commdr 1983–85; Brig. 26th Mechanized Infantry Regt Lenti 1985–87; Deputy Chief and Chief of Mechanized Infantry and Armored Service, Gen. Dir of Training 1989; Deputy Commdr 5th Army, Székesfehérvár; Deputy Commdr and Maj.-Gen. of Hungarian Army 1992; Dir of Mil. Intelligence Office 1993; Deputy Chief of Defence Staff 1996–99, Chief 1999–; Under-Sec. for Policy, Ministry of Defence 1999–; Gen. and Commdr of Defence Forces 1999–2005. *Address:* c/o Honvédelmi Minisztérium, V. ker., Balaton u. 7–11, 1055 Budapest, Hungary (office). *Telephone:* (1) 236-5111 (office). *Fax:* (1) 447-1111 (office). *E-mail:* honvedelem@armedia.hu (office).

FOGARTY, Thomas J., BS, MD; American thoracic surgeon and academic; *Clinical Professor of Surgery, Stanford University;* b. 25 Feb. 1934, Cincinnati, OH; ed Xavier Univ., Univ. of Cincinnati; built and sold first invention, centrifugal clutch for scooters, as a boy; designed and raced soap-box derby cars 1940s; worked as scrub technician, Good Samaritan Hosp., Cincinnati; Peripheral Vascular Fellowship, Univ. of Cincinnati Coll. of Medicine 1962; Residency in Gen. Surgery, Univ. of Oregon Medical School 1965; Clinical Assoc. for NIH Surgery Br. 1967; Advanced Research Fellow in Cardiovascular Surgery, Stanford Univ. Medical Center 1969, Instructor of Surgery, Div. of Cardiovascular Surgery 1969–70, Asst Prof. of Surgery, Volunteer Clinical Faculty 1970–71, Asst Clinical Prof. of Surgery, Medical Center 1971–73, pvt. practice in Stanford Medical Center 1973–78, Pres. of Medical Staff 1977–79, Clinical Prof. of Surgery 1993–; Dir of Cardiovascular Surgery, Sequoia Hosp., Redwood City, Calif. 1980–93; holds 63 US patents for medical devices; founder or co-founder of over 30 start-up cos mfg medical devices; Pres. Fogarty Eng Lab.; co-founder Three Arch Pnrs (venture capital firm); f. Fogarty Medical Foundation 2000; est. Thomas Fogarty Winery and Vineyards, Santa Cruz, Calif. 1978; Co-Ed.-in-Chief Journal of Endovascular Therapy; mem. numerous professional socs including American Bd of Surgery, American Bd of Thoracic Surgery, American Coll. of Surgeons, American Medical Asscn, Calif. Medical Soc., San Francisco Surgical Soc., Soc. of Vascular Surgery; Hon. PhD (Xavier Univ.) 1987; San Francisco Patent and Trademark Asscn Inventor of the Year 1980, Lemelson-MIT Prize 2000. *Medical Inventions include:* Fogarty® Embolectomy Balloon Catheter 1961, Medtronic/AneuRx Endovascular Aortic Stent-Graft, Fogarty® Surgical Clips and Clamps, Hancock Tissue Heart Valve (with Warren Hancock). *Publications:* chapters in numerous surgical textbooks, over 150 articles in professional journals in fields of cardiac, vascular and gen. surgery. *Leisure interests:* fishing, model-building, wine-making, inventing, design. *Address:* Stanford University School of Medicine, 300 Pasteur Drive, Stanford, CA 94305 (office); Thomas Fogarty Winery & Vineyards, 3270 Alpine Road, Portola Valley, CA 94028, USA (office). *Telephone:* (650) 723-4000 (office); (650) 854-1822 (office). *E-mail:* tjf@fogartybusiness.com (office); info@ fogartywinery.com (office). *Website:* med.stanford.edu (office); www.ctsnet.org (office).

FOGEL, Robert William, PhD, FAAS; American historian, academic, economist and biodemographer; *Charles R. Walgreen Distinguished Service Professor and Director, Center for Population Economics, University of* Chicago; b. 1 July 1926, New York, NY; s. of Harry Gregory and Elizabeth (Mitnik) Fogel; m. Enid Cassandra Morgan 1949; two s.; ed Cornell, Columbia, Cambridge, Harvard and Johns Hopkins Univs; Instructor, Johns Hopkins Univ. 1958–59; Asst Prof., Univ. of Rochester 1960–64; Assoc. Prof., Univ. of Chicago 1964–65, Prof. of Economics 1965–75, Prof. of Economics and History 1970–75; Prof., Harvard Univ. 1975–81; Charles R. Walgreen Distinguished Service Prof. of American Insts, Univ. of Chicago 1981–, Dir Center for Population Econs 1981–; Chair. History Advisory Cttee of the Math. Social Science Bd 1965–72; Pres. Econ. History Asscn 1977–78; Social Science History Asscn 1980–81; American Econ. Asscn 1998; Nat. Bureau of Econ. Research Assoc.; Fellow Econ. Soc., American Acad. of Arts and Sciences, NAS, Royal Historical Soc., AAAS, American Philosophical Soc.; several hon. degrees, Nat. Science Foundation grants 1967, 1970, 1972, 1975, 1978, 1992–96, Fulbright Grant 1968; Arthur H. Cole Prize 1968, Schumpeter Prize 1971, Bancroft Prize in American History 1975, Gustavus Myers Prize 1990, shared Nobel Prize in Econs 1993. *Publications:* The Union Pacific Railroad: A Case in Premature Enterprise 1960, Railroads and American History (co-author) 1971, The Dimensions of Quantitative Research in History (co-author) 1972, Time on the Cross: The Economics of American Negro Slavery (with S. L. Engerman) 1974, Ten Lectures on the New Economic History 1977, Which Road to the Past?: Two Views of History (with G. R. Elton) 1983, Without Consent or Contract: The Rise and Fall of American Slavery (co-author), Vol. I 1989, Vols II–IV 1992, The Political Realignment of the 1850s: A Socio-economic Analysis 1996, The Fourth Great Awakening and the Future of Egalitarianism 2000, The Escape from Hunger and Premature Death 1700–2100: Europe, America and the Third World 2004, The Slavery Debates 1952–1990: a retrospective 2003; contrib. to numerous books and scholarly journals. *Leisure interests:* carpentry, photography. *Address:* Center for Population Economics, University of Chicago, Graduate School of Business, 5807 South Woodlawn Avenue, Chicago, IL 60637-1511 (office); 5321 S University Avenue, Chicago, IL 60615, USA (home). *Telephone:* (773) 702-7709 (office). *Fax:* (773) 702-2901 (office). *E-mail:* rwf@cpe.uchicago.edu (office). *Website:* www.cpe.uchicago.edu (office); gsb.uchicago.edu (office).

FOGELBERG, Graeme, MCom, MBA, PhD; New Zealand university administrator; b. 10 Dec. 1939, Wellington; s. of the late Frederick Edward Fogelberg and Evelyn Fogelberg (née Greenwell); m. (divorced); three s. two d.; ed Wellington Coll., Victoria Univ. of Wellington and Univ. of Western Ontario; Prof. of Business Admin. Victoria Univ. of Wellington 1970, Dean Faculty of Commerce Admin. 1977–82, Deputy Vice-Chancellor 1986–92; professorial appts at Univ. of Western Ont. 1975–76, 1986–87 and Pa State Univ. 1992–93; Vice-Chancellor Univ. of Otago, Dunedin 1994–2004; Chair. NZ Vice-Chancellors Cttee 1999–2000; fmr Chair. Asscn of Commonwealth Univs; Fellow NZ Inst. of Dirs; Pres. Rotary Club of Wellington 1988–89. *Publications:* several business study books and articles in accounting, business, man. and econs journals. *Leisure interests:* tennis, skiing and fine New Zealand wines. *Address:* c/o University of Otago, P.O. Box 56, Dunedin, New Zealand.

FOGELHOLM, Markus, MA; Finnish banker and business executive; *Managing Director, The Finnish Bankers' Association;* b. 11 March 1946, Helsinki; s. of Eila Fogelholm and Georg Fogelholm; m. Saara RI Suokas 1969; one s. one d.; ed Univ. of Helsinki; joined Bank of Finland 1972, Head Foreign Financing Dept 1984–87, Market Operations Dept 1992–2001; Special Asst to Exec. Dir of UN Centre on Transnat. Corpns 1978–81; Alt. Exec. Dir IMF 1987–89, Exec. Dir 1989–91; Man. Dir The Finnish Bankers' Asscn; mem. Bd Finnvera; Hon. mem. Forex Finland. *Leisure interests:* wine, music, tennis, hiking, skating. *Address:* The Finnish Bankers' Association, Museokatu 8A, POB 1009, SF-00101 Helsinki, Finland. *Telephone:* (9) 4056-1211 (office). *Fax:* (9) 4056-1291 (office). *E-mail:* markus.fogelholm@fba.fi (office). *Website:* www .fba.fi (office).

FOING, Bernard H., MS, PhD; French space scientist; *Chief Scientist and Senior Research Coordinator, SMART-1 Project, European Space Agency;* ed Lycee Louis-Le-Grand, Paris Ecole Normale Superieure, ENSET, Int. Acad. of Astronautics; Chief Scientist and Sr Research Coordinator, ESA Research and Scientific Support Dept (RSSD), Exec. Dir Int. Lunar Exploration Working Group (ILEWG), Head of Research Div., ESA RSSD, SMART-1 Lead Project Scientist; Convener EGS/EGU sessions 1997–, Cttee on Space Research (COSPAR) 1992–, ILEWG 2000–; numerous radio and TV interviews on space and lunar exploration. *Films:* Black Sun Highlights, documentaries on space and lunar exploration. *Music:* plays viola (superior studies), guitar and piano accompaniment (classical/jazz), performer in int. amateur orchestras, quartet and chamber music groups. *Publications:* more than 400 publs including 150 refereed papers on space science and tech., lunar and planetary exploration; main ed. 20 books on space science and exploration, including: Multi-Site Continuous Spectroscopy Workshops Proceedings (co-ed.) 1988, 1990, 1994, Helioseismology from Space (Advances in Space Research (ASR), Vol. 11, No. 4) 1991, Astronomy and Space Research, from the Moon (ASR Vol. 14, No. 6) 1994, Special Issue, Open Session on Solar & Heliospheric Physics, Journal of Physical Chemistry of Earth 1996, Missions to the Moon, Advances in Moon and Exploring the Cold Universe (ASR Vol. 18, No. 11) 1998, Solar Seismology and Variability (ASR Vol. 24, No. 2) 1999, The Moon and Mars (ASR Vol. 23, No. 11), Lunar Exploration 2000 (ASR Vol. 30, No. 8) in Special Issue on Lunar Exploration (Planetary and Space Science, Vol. 50, Issue 14–15) 2002, Earth-Like Planets and Moons 2002, ESA report to COSPAR 2002, The Next Steps in Exploring Deep Space 2003, The Moon and Near-Earth Objects (ASR Vol. 37, No. 1, co-ed.) 2006, 9th ILEWG ed. on Exploration and Utilisation of the Moon (abstracts) 2007, The Moon: Science, Exploration and Utilisation 2008; Organiser/Ed. Forum ed. Française des Spécialistes en Astronomie (1987): ESA Horizon 2000. *Address:* ESTEC/SRE-S, Postbus 299, Noordwijk 2200 AG, Netherlands (office). *Telephone:* (71) 565-5647 (office). *Fax:* (71) 565-4697 (office). *E-mail:* bfoing@rssd.esa.int (office); Bernard.Foing@esa.int (office).

Website: www.esa.int (office); sci.esa.int/smart-1 (office); sci.esa.int/ilewg (office).

FOK, Canning Kin-ning, BA, CA; Hong Kong telecommunications executive; *Group Managing Director and Executive Director, Hutchison Whampoa Ltd;* b. 1951; four c.; ed St John's Univ., Minn., USA, Univ. of New England, Australia; began career with Cheung Kong (real estate co.) 1979; joined Hutchison Whampoa Group 1984, Exec. Dir 1984–93, Group Man.-Dir and Exec. Dir Hutchison Whampoa Ltd 1993–, also Chair. Hutchison Telecom Int., Hutchison Harbour Ring Ltd, Hutchison Telecommunications (Australia) Ltd, Hutchison Global Communications Holdings Ltd; Partner and Co-Chair. Husky Energy Inc.; Deputy Chair. Cheung Kong Infrastructure Holdings Ltd, Hongkong Electric Holdings Ltd; Dir Cheung Kong (Holdings) Ltd; mem. Australian Inst. of Chartered Accountants.

FOK, Ian, BS, MBA; Hong Kong business executive; *Managing Director, Yau Wing Company Ltd;* b. (Fok Chun-wan), s. of the late Henry Fok; ed Univ. of British Columbia, Canada; Man. Dir Yau Wing Co. Ltd; Chair. Chinese Gen. Chamber of Commerce, Hong Kong; Vice-Chair. China Overseas Friendship Asscn, Guangdong Overseas Friendship Asscn; mem. Standing Cttee 9th Guangdong Prov. Cttee of CPPCC, All China Fed. of Industry and Commerce; mem. Bd of Dirs Fok Ying Tung Foundation Ltd; fmr Pres. Hong Kong Wushu Union, Vice-Chair. Wushu Fed. of Asia, mem. Exec. Cttee and Chair. of Marketing and Devt Cttee Int. Wushu Fed.; fmr mem. Hong Kong Trade and Devt Council, Council and Exec. Cttee of Hong Kong Man. Asscn, Bd of Dirs Boao Forum for Asia; Trustee Chinese Univ. of Hong Kong United Coll. 1996–2005; Hon. Citizen of Panyu and Guangzhou; Hon. Univ. Fellow, Open Univ. of Hong Kong; Life Hon. Pres. Hong Kong Chamber of Commerce in China; Silver Bauhinia Star 2005. *Address:* Yau Wing Co. Ltd, Units 1105–1112, West Tower Shun Tak Centre, 168–200 Connaught Road Central, Hong Kong Special Administrative Region, People's Republic of China (office). *Telephone:* 2522-7131 (office). *Fax:* 2810-4580 (office).

FOK, Timothy, JP; Hong Kong business executive; *Managing Director, Yau Wing Company Ltd;* b. (Fok Tsun-ting), 14 Feb. 1946, Hong Kong; s. of the late Henry Fok; m. Loletta Chu (divorced 2006); three s.; ed Millfield Coll., UK, Univ. of Southern California, USA; Man. Dir Yau Wing Co. Ltd, Chair. H.Y.T. Fok Group of Cos; mem. Legis. Council of Hong Kong, representing the Sports, Performing Arts, Culture and Publication functional constituency; mem. CPPCC; mem. IOC 2001–; Pres. Sports Fed. and Olympic Cttee of Hong Kong, Hong Kong Sports Writer Asscn, Hong Kong Football Asscn; Vice-Pres. Olympic Council of Asia, Organizing Cttee of 2008 Olympics and Paralympics Equestrian Events, Hong Kong East Asian Games Organizing Cttee; mem. 2008 Olympics Coordination Comm.; Gov. Fok Ying Tung Foundation; Grand Bauhinia Star. *Address:* Yau Wing Co. Ltd, Units 1105–1112, West Tower Shun Tak Centre, 168–200 Connaught Road Central, Hong Kong Special Administrative Region, People's Republic of China (office). *Telephone:* 2522-7131 (office). *Fax:* 2810-4580 (office).

FOKIN, Valery Vladimirovich; Russian theatre and film director; b. 28 Feb. 1946, Moscow; m. Tatiana Krivenko; two s.; ed Moscow Shchukin Theatre School; Stage Dir Moscow Sovremennik Theatre 1971–85; Chief Stage Dir Yermolova Theatre 1985–90; Artistic Dir M. Yermolova Theatre Centre 1990–2000; Founder, Artistic Dir and Dir-Gen. Meyerhold Artistic Centre 1990–; Theatre Prize, BITEF Prize, State's Prize, Honoured Art Worker of Poland, three Crystal Turandot awards including for Last Night of the Tsar. *Film:* The Metamorphosis. *Theatre includes:* (Stage Dir) Valentin and Valentina, I'll Go and Go, Inspector, Provincial Anecdotes, Lorenzacchio, Who's Afraid of Virginia Woolf, In Spring I Shall Come Back to You, Transformation, (Chief Stage Dir) Speak Up, Second Year of Freedom, Sports Scenes of 1980, Invitation to Punishment (Artistic Dir), Hotel Room in Town N (Best Dir), (Dir) Artand and His Double, The Queen of Spades (opera). *Television:* over 25 films and performances. *Publications:* Hotel Room in Town N, The Metamorphosis; numerous articles and speeches. *Address:* Vsevolod Meyerhold Centre, Novoslobodskaya str. 23, Moscow (office); Triohprudniy pereulok 13/11, 5, Moscow, Russia (home). *Telephone:* (495) 363-10-46 (office); (495) 299-16-76 (home). *Fax:* (495) 363 1041 (office). *E-mail:* meyerhold@meyerhold.ru (office). *Website:* www.theatre.ru/meyerholdcentre/ (office).

FOKIN, Vitold Pavlovych; Ukrainian politician; b. 25 Oct. 1932, Novomikolaivka, Zaporozhye region; m.; one s. one d.; ed m. Dnepropetrovsk Mining Inst.; fmr mem. CP; mining engineer 1954–71; Deputy Chair. Council of Ministers of Ukraine 1987–90; Chair. State Cttee for Econs Aug.–Nov. 1990; Chair. Council of Ministers (Prime Minister) of Ukraine 1990–92; Sr Researcher Inst. of World Econ. and Int. Relations 1993–, Pres. Int. Fund for Humanitarian and Econ. Relations with Russian Fed. 1993–; mem. Higher Econ. Council of Pres. of Ukraine 1997–; People's Deputy 1998–; Prof. Nat. Acad. of Mines; Chair. Supervisory Bd DEWON Inc. 2000–; Miner's Glory Order 1st, 2nd, 3rd class 1961–1963, Decoration of Honour 1967, 2 Orders of Working Red Banner 1970, 1975, Order of St Prince Volodymyr 2002, Order of Yaroslav the Wise 2002, Order of Honour 2004; Laureate of State Prize of Ukraine 1983, Medal for Services 2004, seven medals. *Publications:* about 30 published works and articles in social, political and technical journals and books. *Leisure interests:* hunting, fishing, tennis, tourism. *Address:* International Fund for Humanitarian and Economic Relations with Russian Federation, 19 Panasa Myrnogo Street, 01011 Kiev (office); Verkhovna Rada, M. Hrushevskoho rul 5, 252019 Kiev; Flat 266, 13 Suvorova Street, 01010 Kiev, Ukraine (home). *Telephone:* (44) 290-75-85 (office); (44) 290-52-55 (home). *Fax:* (44) 290-05-92 (office). *E-mail:* vitold.fokin@dewon.com.ua.

FOKIN, Yuri Yevgenyevich; Russian diplomatist; b. 2 Sept. 1936, Gorky (now Nizhny Novgorod); m.; one s.; one d.; ed Moscow Inst. of Int. Relations; on staff, USSR Ministry of Foreign Affairs 1960–; with USSR Mission in UN 1960–65, Secr. of Minister of Foreign Affairs 1966–73, Sr Adviser, Dept of Planning of Int. Events 1973–76; Deputy Perm. Rep. of USSR to UN 1976–79; Deputy Dir-Gen. Ministry of Foreign Affairs 1979–80, Dir-Gen. 1980–86; Amb. to Cyprus 1986–90, to Norway 1995–97, to UK 1997–2000; Head, Second European Dept, Russian Ministry of Foreign Affairs 1990–92, Dir Second European Dept 1991–95; on staff, Ministry of Foreign Affairs 1995–, Rector, Diplomatic Acad. of Ministry of Foreign Affairs –2006; decorations from Russia, Austria, Norway. *Publications:* Diplomatic Yearbook 2000, 2001, 2002, State & Diaspora: A Record of Interaction. *Leisure interests:* reading, ballet, theatre, tennis. *Address:* c/o Diplomatic Academy of the Ministry of Foreign Affairs, 53/2 Ostozhenka, 119992 Moscow, Russia. *Telephone:* (495) 245-33-86. *E-mail:* Yuri.Fokine@dipacademy.ru.

FOLBRE, Nancy, MA, PhD; American economist and academic; *Professor of Economics, University of Massachusetts;* ed Univ. of Texas, Univ. of Massachusetts; consultant, Maine Comm. for Women 1981, Kenya Fuelwood Project 1981, Beijer Inst. 1981, 1983, Royal Swedish Acad. of Science 1981, 1983, Zimbabwe Energy Planning Project, 1983, Int. Center for Research on Women 1989–90, The Population Council 1989–94, ILO 1992, World Bank 1994–95; Asst Prof. of Econs, Bowdoin Coll. 1980–83; Assoc. Prof. of Econs, Univ. of Mass 1984–91, Prof. of Econs 1991–, Chair. Dept of Econs 2003–04; Visiting Assoc. Prof., American Univ. 1991; Visiting Lecturer, Eugene Havens Center, Univ. of Wisconsin 1991; Visiting Scholar, Women's Research and Resource Center, Univ. of California, Davis 1992, Gender Inst., LSE, UK 1995; Visiting Chair. in American Studies, Ecole des Hautes Etudes en Sciences Sociales, Paris, France 1995–96; Visiting Research Fellow, ANU 2000, 2002, Adjunct Prof., Social and Political Theory Program 2003–; Phi Beta Kappa Visiting Scholar 2000–01; Visiting Fellow, Russell Sage Foundation 2005–06; Co-Founder and CEO The Dancing Monkey Project 1998–; Pres. Int. Asscn for Feminist Econs 2002–; Staff Economist, Center for Popular Econs 1979–; Consultant to UN Human Devt Office 2005; Assoc. Ed. Feminist Economics 1995–; mem. Bd Foundation of Child Devt; mem. NAS; French-American Foundation Fellow 1995–96, MacArthur Foundation Fellow 1998–2003; Olivia Schieffelin Nordberg Award 1999, Distinguished Visiting Scholar Award, Univ. of Mass 2002. *Publications include:* A Field Guide to the US Economy 1988, Issues in Contemporary Economics, Vol. 4 (co-ed.) 1991, Who Pays for the Kids? Gender and the Structures of Constraint 1994, The New Field Guide to the US Economy 1995, War on the Poor: A Defense Manual 1996, The Economics of the Family (ed.) 1996, De la différence des sexes en économie politique 1997, The Ultimate Field Guide to the US Economy 2000, The Invisible Heart: Economics and Family Values 2001, Family Time (co-ed.) 2003; numerous articles in professional journals, chapters in books and newspaper articles. *Address:* Department of Economics, Thompson Hall, University of Massachusetts, Amherst, MA 01003, USA (office). *Telephone:* (413) 545-3283 (office). *Fax:* (413) 545-2921 (office). *E-mail:* folbre@econs.umass.edu (office). *Website:* www.unix.oit.umass.edu/~folbre/folbre (office).

FOLEY, HE Cardinal John Patrick; American ecclesiastic; *Pro-Grand Master of the Equestrian Order of the Holy Sepulchre of Jerusalem;* b. 11 Nov. 1935, Darby, Pa; ed Columbia Univ., New York, studies in Rome; ordained priest in Philadelphia, Pa 1962; Asst Ed. The Catholic Standard & Times (Philadelphia's archdiocesan paper) 1960s, covered the Second Vatican Council 1963–65, Ed. 1970–84; Titular Archbishop of Neapolis in Proconsulari 1984–; Pres. Pontifical Council for Social Communications 1984–2 April 2005, 21 April 2005–; Pro-Grand Master Equestrian Order of the Holy Sepulchre of Jerusalem 2007–; cr. Cardinal 2007. *Address:* Equestrian Order of the Holy Sepulchre of Jerusalem, Borgo Spirito Santo 73, 00193 Rome, Italy (office). *Telephone:* (06) 6828121 (office); (06) 6877347 (office). *Fax:* (06) 6880-2298 (office). *E-mail:* info@holysepulchre.net (office). *Website:* www.holysepulchre.net (office).

FOLEY, Lt-Gen. Sir John Paul, Kt, KCB, OBE, MC, DL; British business executive and civil servant (retd) and fmr army officer; *High Sheriff of Herefordshire and Worcestershire;* b. 22 April 1939, London; s. of Henry Thomas Hamilton Foley and Helen Constance Margaret Foley (née Pearson); m. Ann Rosamond Humphries 1972; two d.; ed Bradfield Coll., Berks., Army Staff Coll., Camberley, Royal Coll. of Defence Studies, London; nat. service with Royal Green Jackets (RGJ) 1959–61, then Regimental Service 1962–70, attached Staff Coll. 1971; Brig.-Maj. 1974–75; instructor Staff Coll. 1976–78; CO 3 RGJ 1978–80, Commdt, Jr Div. Staff Coll. 1981–82, Dir SAS 1983–85, Royal Coll. of Defence Studies 1986; Chief British Mission to Soviet Forces, E Germany 1987–89; Deputy Chief Defence Intelligence 1989–91, Chief 1994–97; Commdr British Forces Hong Kong 1992–94, retd 1997; Lt-Gov. of Guernsey 2000–05; High Sheriff of Herefords. and Worcs. 2006–; mem. Security Comm.; Chair. British Greyhound Racing Bd 1999–2000, Defence Appointments, Defence Consultant Alpha Business Ventures Ltd 1998–2000; KStJ. *Leisure interests:* gardening, reading, walking, tennis, bird watching, golf.

FOLEY, Thomas Stephen, BA, LLB; American politician, diplomatist and lawyer; *Partner, Akin Gump Strauss Hauer & Feld LLP;* b. 6 March 1929, Spokane, Wash.; s. of Ralph E. Foley and Helen Marie Higgins; m. Heather Strachan 1968; ed Washington Univ.; Pnr, Higgins and Foley 1957–58; Deputy Prosecuting Attorney, Spokane Co. 1958–60; Instructor of Law, Gonzaga Univ. 1958–60; Asst Attorney Gen., Wash. State 1960–61; Interior and Insular Affairs Cttee, US Senate, Washington, DC 1961–64; mem. 89th–100th Congresses from 5th Dist Wash. 1965–94, Chair. Agric. Cttee 1975–81, Vice-Chair. 1981–86; Chair. House Democratic Caucus 1976–80, House Majority Whip 1981–87, Majority Leader 1987–89, Speaker House of Reps 1989–95; Pnr, Akin, Gump, Strauss, Hauer & Feld, Washington, DC 1995–98, rejoined firm 2001–; Amb. to Japan 1997–2001; Democrat. *Publication:* Measuring Lives (novel) 1996. *Address:* Akin Gump Strauss Hauer & Feld

LLP, Robert S. Strauss Building, 1333 New Hampshire Avenue, NW, Washington, DC 20036-1564, USA (office). *Telephone:* (202) 887-4170 (office). *Fax:* (202) 887-4288 (office). *E-mail:* tfoley@akingump.com (office). *Website:* www.akingump.com (office).

FØLLESDAL, Dagfinn, PhD; Norwegian academic; *Clarence Irving Lewis Professor of Philosophy, Stanford University;* b. 22 June 1932, Askim; s. of Trygve Føllesdal and Margit Teigen; m. Vera Heyerdahl 1957; five s. one d.; ed Univs of Oslo and Göttingen and Harvard Univ.; Research Asst in Ionospheric Physics, Norwegian Research Council 1955–57; Instructor and Asst Prof. of Philosophy, Harvard Univ. 1961–64; Prof. of Philosophy, Univ. of Oslo 1967–99; Prof. of Philosophy, Stanford Univ. 1968–76, Clarence Irving Lewis Prof. of Philosophy 1976–; Visiting Prof. Coll. de France 1977; Guggenheim Fellow 1978–79; Fellow, Center for Advanced Study in Behavioral Sciences 1981–82, American Council of Learned Socs 1983–84, Inst. for Advanced Study, Princeton 1985–86, Wissenschaftskolleg, Berlin 1989–90, Centre for Advanced Study, Oslo 1995–96, 2003–04; mem. American Acad. of Arts and Sciences, Academia Europaea and scientific acads in Norway, Denmark, Sweden and Finland; Pres. Norwegian Acad. of Science 1993, 1995, 1997; Univ. of Oslo Research Prize 1995, Alexander von Humboldt Research Award 1997, Lauener Prize 2006. *Publications:* Husserl und Frege 1958, Referential Opacity and Modal Logic 1966, Argumentasjonsteori språk og vitenskapsfilosofi (with L. Walløe and J. Elster) 1977; Ed. Journal of Symbolic Logic 1970–82, Philosophy of Quire, 5 vols 2000; numerous articles on philosophy of language, phenomenology, existentialism, action theory, educational and ethical issues. *Leisure Interests:* skiing, running. *Address:* Department of Philosophy, Building 90, Stanford University, Stanford, CA 94305-2155, USA (office); Filosofisk institutt, Universitetet i Oslo, PB 1024, Blindern 0317, Oslo (office); Staverhagan 7, 1314 Slependen, Norway (home). *Telephone:* (650) 723-2587 (office); (47) 67-55-00-01 (home). *Fax:* (47) 67-55-00-02 (home). *E-mail:* dagfinn@csli.stanford.edu (office). *Website:* www-philosophy.stanford .edu (office); www.hf.uio.no/filosofi/organisasjon/ansatte/follesdal.html (office).

FOLLETT, Kenneth (Ken) Martin, BA; British writer; b. 5 June 1949, Cardiff, Wales; s. of Martin D. Follett and Veenie Evans; m. 1st Mary Elson 1968 (divorced 1985); one s. one d.; m. 2nd Barbara Broer 1985; one step-s. two step-d.; ed Univ. Coll. London; trainee reporter, South Wales Echo, Cardiff 1970–73; reporter, London Evening News 1973–74; Editorial Dir Everest Books, London 1974–76, Deputy Man. Dir 1976–77; full-time writer 1977–; Fellow Univ. Coll. London 1994; mem. Council, Nat. Literary Trust 1996–; Chair. Nat. Year of Reading 1998–99; Pres. Dyslexia Inst. 1998–; Vice-Pres. Stevenage Borough Football Club 2000–, Stevenage Community Trust 2002–; Patron, Stevenage Home-Start 2000–; Chair. Govs, Roebuck Primary School and Nursery 2001–; Chair. of the Advisory Cttee, Reading is Fundamental UK 2003–; Bd mem., Nat. Acad. of Writing 2003–; Dir, Stevenage Leisure Ltd 1999–2004. *Publications:* The Shakeout 1975, The Bear Raid 1976, The Modigliani Scandal 1976, The Power Twins and the Worm Puzzle 1976, The Secret of Kellerman's Studio 1976, Paper Money 1977, Eye of the Needle (MWA Edgar Award 1979) 1978, Triple 1979, The Key to Rebecca 1980, The Man from St Petersburg 1982, On Wings of Eagles 1983, Lie Down with Lions 1986, The Pillars of the Earth 1989, Night Over Water 1991, A Dangerous Fortune 1993, A Place Called Freedom 1995, The Third Twin 1996, The Hammer of Eden 1998, Code to Zero 2000, Jackdaws (Corine Readers' Award, Germany 2003) 2001, Hornet Flight 2003, Whiteout 2004, World Without End 2007; screenplays; contrib. to book reviews and essays. *Leisure interests:* left-wing politics, bass guitarist in blues band Damn Right I Got The Blues, Shakespeare. *Address:* PO Box 4, Knebworth, Hertfordshire SG3 6UT, England (office). *Telephone:* (1438) 810400 (office). *Fax:* (1438) 810444 (office). *E-mail:* ken@ken-follett.com (office). *Website:* www.ken-follett.com (office).

FOMENKO, Anatoly Timofeevich; Russian mathematician and academic; *Professor, Department of Mathematics and Mechanics, Moscow State University;* b. 13 March 1945; m.; ed Moscow State Univ.; Asst, Sr Researcher, now Prof. Dept of Math. and Mechanics Moscow State Univ.; Corresp. mem. USSR (now Russian) Acad. of Sciences 1990, mem. 1994; research in theory of minimal surfaces, topology of multidimensional manifolds, simplectic geometry and theory of topological classifications of integrable differential equations; Chair. Moscow Math. Soc.; Award of Moscow Math. Soc. 1974, Award of Presidium of Russian Acad. of Sciences 1987, State Award of Russian Fed. 1996. *Publications include:* Simplectic Geometry: Methods and Applications 1988, The Plateau Problem 1990. *Leisure interests:* statistical analysis of historical texts, painting. *Address:* Department of Mathematics and Mechanics, Moscow State University, Vorobyevy gory, 119992 Moscow, Russia (office). *Telephone:* (495) 939-39-40 (office). *Website:* www.math.msu.su (office).

FOMENKO, Piotr Naumovich; Russian stage director; b. 13 July 1932, Moscow; m. Maya Andreyevna Tupikova; one s.; ed Ippolitov-Ivanov Higher School of Music, V. Lenin Pedagogical Inst., State Inst. of Theatre Art; stage dir in amateur clubs and studios of Moscow 1953–61; guest dir in Moscow theatres including Taganka, Na Maloy Bronnoy, Cen. Children's, Mayakovsky, Cen. Theatre of Soviet Army, Satire and others 1961–84; Stage Dir Theatre of Comedy, Leningrad 1972–78, Chief Stage Dir 1978–82; staged over 20 productions, some of which were banned; Dir Vakhtangov Theatre, Moscow 1985–; f. Little Stage (Under the Roof) Mossoviet Theatre; f. Theatre-Workshop of P. Fomenko 1991, toured throughout Europe; directed films and TV productions 1965–; Lecturer, State Inst. of Theatre Art 1982, Prof. 1989; masterclasses in Paris Conservatory, Cen. Reimschad (Germany); People's Artist of Russia, Crystal Turandot Prize, K. Stanislavsky Prize and others. *Plays include:* Death of Tarelkin (A. Sukhovo-Kobylin), Fruit of Education (L. Tolstoy), New Mysteria-Buff (after V. Mayakovsky), Interrogation (P. Weiss), As You Like It (William Shakespeare), Guilty Without Guilt

(A. Ostrovsky), The Queen of Spades (A. Pushkin), Caligula (A. Camus). *Television includes:* Childhood, Boyhood and Youth (trilogy by L. Tolstoy), Belkin's Stories (A. Pushkin), To the Rest of the Lifetime (four series). *Films include:* Almost Funny Story, About a Ride in an Old Car. *Address:* Theatre Workshop of Piotr Fomenko, Kutuzovskiy Prosp. 30/32, 121165 Moscow (office); Pobedy pl. 1, korp. A, Apt. 75, 121293 Moscow, Russia (home). *Telephone:* (495) 249-17-03 (office); (495) 148-07-73 (home).

FONDA, Bridget; American actress; b. 27 Jan. 1964, Los Angeles; d. of Peter Fonda (q.v.) and Susan Fonda; m. Danny Elfman 2003; one s.; ed New York Univ. theater programme; studied acting at Lee Strasberg Inst. and with Harold Guskin; workshop stage performances include Confession and Pastels. *Films:* Aria (Tristan and Isolde sequence) (début) 1987, You Can't Hurry Love 1988, Shag 1988, Scandal 1989, Strapless 1989, Frankenstein Unbound 1990, The Godfather: Part III 1990, Doc Hollywood 1991, Out of the Rain 1991, Single White Female 1992, Singles 1992, Bodies Rest and Motion 1993, Point of No Return 1993, Little Buddha 1994, It Could Happen To You 1994, Camilla 1994, The Road to Welville 1994, Rough Magic 1995, Balto (voice) 1995, Grace of My Heart 1996, City Hall 1996, Drop Dead Fred, Light Years (voice), Iron Maze, Army of Darkness, Touch, Jackie Brown, Finding Graceland, The Break Up, South of Heaven West of Hell, Lake Placid 1999, Delivering Milo, Monkey Bone 2001, Kiss of the Dragon 2001, The Whole Shebang 2001,. *Television includes:* Leather Jackets 1991, In the Gloaming 1997, After Amy 2001, The Chris Isaak Show 2002, Snow Queen 2002. *Address:* 114 Fremont Place, Los Angeles, CA 90005, USA.

FONDA, Jane; American actress and activist; b. 21 Dec. 1937, New York City; d. of the late Henry Fonda and of Frances Seymour; sister of Peter Fonda q.v.); m. 1st Roger Vadim 1967 (divorced 1973, died 2000); one d.; m. 2nd Tom Hayden 1973 (divorced 1989); one s.; m. 3rd Ted Turner 1991 (divorced 2001); ed Emma Willard School, Troy, NY, Vassar Coll.; studied with Lee Strasberg and became mem. Actors Studio, NY; founder and Chair. Georgia Campaign for Adolescent Pregnancy Prevention 1995–; est. Jane Fonda Center for Adolescent Reproductive Health, Emory Univ. School of Medicine 2002; produced 23 home exercise videos including Jane Fonda's Workout 1982 (top-grossing home video of all time); Acad. Award for Best Actress 1972, 1979, Golden Globe Award 1978. *Films include:* Tall Story 1960, A Walk on the Wild Side 1962, Period of Adjustment 1962, Sunday in New York 1963, The Love Cage 1963, La Ronde 1964, Cat Ballou 1965, Histoires extraordinaires 1967, Barefoot in the Park 1967, Hurry Sundown 1967, Barbarella 1968, They Shoot Horses Don't They? 1969, Klute 1970, Steelyard Blues 1972, Tout va bien 1972, A Doll's House 1973, The Blue Bird 1975, Fun with Dick and Jane 1976, Julia 1977, Coming Home 1978, California Suite 1978, The Electric Horseman 1979, The China Syndrome 1979, Nine to Five 1980, On Golden Pond 1981, Roll-Over 1981, Agnes of God 1985, The Morning After 1986, The Old Gringo 1988, Stanley and Iris 1990, Monster-in-Law 2005, Georgia Rule 2007; producer Lakota Woman 1994. *Plays include:* There Was a Little Girl, Invitation to a March, The Fun Couple, Strange Interlude, 33 Variations (Broadway) 2009. *Television:* The Dollmaker (ABC-TV) 1984 (Emmy Award). *Publications:* Jane Fonda's Workout Book 1982, Women Coming of Age 1984, Jane Fonda's New Workout and Weight Loss Program 1986, Jane Fonda's New Pregnancy Workout and Total Birth Program 1989, Jane Fonda Workout Video, Jane Fonda Cooking for Healthy Living 1996, My Life So Far (autobiography) 2005. *Address:* c/o Kim Hodgert, Creative Artists Agency, 9830 Wilshire Boulevard, Beverly Hills, CA 90212-1825 (office); Georgia Campaign for Adolescent Pregnancy Prevention, 100 Auburn Avenue, Suite 200, Atlanta, GA 30303, USA (office). *Telephone:* (310) 288-4545 (office). *Fax:* (310) 288-4800 (office).

FONDA, Peter; American film actor, director and producer; b. 23 Feb. 1939, New York; s. of the late Henry Fonda and of Frances Seymour; brother of Jane Fonda (q.v.); m. Susan Brewer (divorced 1974); two c.; ed Univ. of Omaha. *Films include:* Tammy and the Doctor 1963, The Victors 1963, Lilith 1964, The Young Lovers 1964, The Wild Angels 1966, The Trip 1967, Easy Rider (also co-screenplay writer, co-producer) 1969, The Last Movie 1971, The Hired Hand (also dir) 1971, Two People (also dir) 1973, Idaho Transfer (dir) 1973, Dirty Mary, Crazy Larry 1974, Race with the Devil 1975, 92 in the Shade 1975, Killer Force 1975, Fighting Mad 1976, Futureworld 1976, Outlaw Blues 1977, High Ballin' 1978, Wanda Nevada (also dir) 1979, Open Season, Smokey and the Bandit II 1980, The Cannonball Run (cameo) 1981, Split Image 1982, Spasms 1983, Dance of the Dwarfs (also known as Jungle Heat) 1983, Peppermint-Frieden 1983, Certain Fury 1985, Mercenary Fighters 1987, The Rose Garden 1989, Fatal Mission 1990, South Beach 1992, Deadfall 1993, Nadja 1994, Love and a 45 1994, Painted Hero 1996, Escape from LA 1996, Ulee's Gold 1997, Reckless, Diajobu My Friend, Family Spirit, Bodies Rest and Motion, Molly and Gina, The Limey 1999, South of Heaven, West of Hell 2000, Thomas and the Magic Railroad 2000, Second Skin 2000, Wooly Boys 2001, The Laramie Project 2002, The Heart Is Deceitful Above All Things 2004, Ghost Rider 2007, Wild Hogs 2007, 3:10 to Yuma 2007. *Television films:* The Hostage Tower 1980, Don't Look Back 1996, A Reason to Live, A Time of Indifference, Sound, Certain Honorable Men, Montana, The Maldonado Miracle 2003, Capital City 2004, A Thief of Time 2004, Back When We Were Grownups 2004, Supernova (mini-series) 2005. *Other work includes:* Grand Theft Auto: San Andreas (video game, voice) 2004. *Address:* IFA Talent Agency, 8730 West Sunset Boulevard, Suite 490, Los Angeles, CA 90069, USA (office).

FONSECA, Ralph H.; Belizean politician; *Minister of Home Affairs, Public Utilities and Housing;* b. 9 Aug. 1949; m.; three c.; ed St John's Coll.; fmr Asst Gen. Man. Texaco, Belize; fmr Area Gen. Man. Cardinal Distributors, Canada; fmr Research Engineer, Control Data; fmr Systems Analyst, Prescribe Data System; fmr gen. man. brewing co.; fmr Man. Dir Hillbank Agroindustry; fmr

Chair. Belize Electricity Co.; fmr Chair. Belize Telecommunications Authority Ltd; fmr Pres. Consolidated Electricity Services; mem. Parl. 1993–; Minister of Budget Man., Investment and Home Affairs 1999–2003, Minister of Finance and Home Affairs 2003–05; Minister of Home Affairs and Public Utilities 2005–, of Housing 2007–. *Address:* Ministry of Home Affairs and Public Utilities, Curl Thompson Building, Belmopan, Belize (office). *Telephone:* 822-2218 (office). *Fax:* 822-2195 (office). *E-mail:* investment@btl.net (office).

FONSECA, Rubem; Brazilian writer; b. 11 May 1925, Juiz de Fora, MG; ed Escola de Policia, Rio de Janeiro, Fundação Getúlio Vargas, New York Univ.; commissioner of police, São Cristóvão (RJ) 1952; Premio Camões 2003, Premio Juan Rulfo 2003. *Screenplays include:* Relatório de um homen casado, Stelinha, A grande arte. *Publications:* Os prisioneiros 1963, A coleira do cão 1965, Lucía McCartney 1967, O caso Morel 1973, O homen de fevereiro ou março 1973, Feliz ano novo 1975, O cobrador (Prêmio Estácio de Sá) 1979, A grande arte (trans. as High Art) (Prêmio Goethe, Prêmio Jabuti) 1983, Buffo & Spallanzani 1986, Vastas emoções e pensamentos imperfeitos (Prêmio Pedro Nava) 1988, Agosto 1990, Romance negro e outras histórias 1992, Contos reunidos 1994, O selvagem da ópera 1994, O buraco na parede (Prêmio Jabuti) 1995, Romance negro, Felis ano novo e outras histórias 1996, Histórias de amor 1997, E do meio do mundo prostitute só amores guardei ao meu charuto (Prêmio Machado de Assis) 1997, Confraria dos espadas (Prêmio Eça de Queiroz) 1998, O doente Molière (Prêmio de melhor romance do ano, Associação Paulista de Críticos de Arte) 2000, Secreções, excreções, desatinos 2001, Pequenas criaturas 2002, Diário de um fescenino 2003, 64 contos de Rubem Fonseca 2004, Ela e outras mulheres 2006; contrib. to numerous anthologies. *Address:* c/o Companhia das Letras, Rua Bandeira Paulista 702 cj. 32, 04532-002 São Paulo, SP, Brazil. *Telephone:* (11) 3707-3500. *Fax:* (11) 3707-3501. *Website:* www.ciadasletras.com.br.

FONTAINE, André; French journalist; b. 30 March 1921, Paris; s. of Georges Fontaine and Blanche Rochon-Duvigneaud; m. Isabelle Cavaillé 1943; two s. one d.; ed Coll. Ste. Marie de Monceau, Paris, Sorbonne and Faculty of Law, Paris Univ.; journalist 1946–; joined Le Monde 1947, Foreign Ed. 1951–69, Chief Ed. 1969–85, Ed.-in-Chief and Dir 1985–91, Consultant to Dir 1991–; mem. Bd French Inst. of Int. Relations –1992, Bank Indosuez 1983–85; Chair. Group on Int. Strategy for the Ninth French Plan 1982; Vice-Chair. Franco-British Council (French section) 1999–2002; Atlas Int. Ed. of the Year 1976. *Publications:* L'alliance atlantique à l'heure du dégel 1960, History of the Cold War (two vols) 1965, 1967, La guerre civile froide 1969, Le dernier quart du siècle 1976, La France au bois dormant 1978, Un seul lit pour deux rêves 1981, Sortir de l'hexagonie (with others) 1984, L'un sans l'autre 1991, Après eux le déluge 1995, La tache rouge 2004. *Address:* Le Monde, 80 boulevard Auguste-Blanqui, 75707 Paris Cedex 13, France (office). *Telephone:* 1-57-28-20-00 (office). *Fax:* 1-57-28-21-21 (office). *E-mail:* a.fontaine@lemonde.fr (office). *Website:* www.lemonde.fr (office).

FONTAINE, Maurice Alfred, DèsSc; French physiologist; b. 28 Oct. 1904, Savigny-sur-Orge; s. of Emile Fontaine and Lea Vadier; m. Yvonne Broca 1928; one s.; ed Lycée Henri IV, Paris and Faculty of Sciences and Faculty of Pharmacy, Univ. of Paris; various posts at Faculty of Sciences, Paris and Faculty of Pharmacy, Paris; Dir Lab. at Ecole pratique des hautes études 1946; Dir Inst. Océanographique, Paris 1957–68, 1975; Pres. Soc. Européenne d'Endocrinologie Comparée 1969; Dir of Musée Nat. d'Histoire Naturelle, Paris 1966–71; lectures on comparative and ecological physiology, particularly of marine animals; specializes in comparative endocrinology and fish migration; Dir of Research in these fields and also the study of ectocrine substances in sea water and marine pollution; fmr Pres. Acad. des Sciences; mem. Acad. Nat. de Médecine, Acad. d'Agric., New York Acad. of Sciences; Hon. Mem. Romanian Acad. 1991; Commdr, Légion d'honneur, Commdr, Ordre de Sahametrei (Cambodia), Commdr, Ordre de St Charles (Monaco). *Publications:* Physiologie (collection La Pléïade) 1969, Rencontres insolites d'un biologiste autour du monde 1999. *Leisure interests:* the sea, especially migrations of fish, thalasso-éthique. *Address:* 25 rue Pierre Nicole, 75005 Paris, France (home).

FONTAINE, Nicole; French lawyer and politician; b. 1942, Normandy; ed Inst. d'Etudes Politiques, Paris; admitted to Bar, Hauts-de-Seine; Legal Adviser Secrétariat général de l'Enseignement catholique, Deputy Sec.-Gen. 1972–81, Chief Rep. 1981–84; mem. Conseil supérieur de l'Educ. nationale 1975–81; mem. Standing Cttee 1978–81; mem. Conseil économique et social 1980–84; mem. European People's Party; MEP 1984–, Vice-Pres. 1989–94, First Vice-Pres. 1994–99, Pres. 1999–2002, mem. Parl. Cttee on Legal Affairs and Citizens' Rights, on Culture, Youth, Educ. and the Media, on Women's Rights 1984–89, apptd by European People's Party as perm. mem. Conciliation Cttee 1994–2002; fmr Vice-Pres. Union pour la Démocratie Française (UDF); mem. Union for a Popular Movt (UMP); Minister for Industry 2002–04. *Publications:* Les députés européens: Qui sont-ils? Que font-ils? 1994, l'Europe de vos initiatives 1997, Le traité d'Amsterdam 1998, My Battles at the Presidency of the European Parliament 2002. *Address:* European Parliament, Bât. Paul-Henri Spaak, 08B046, 60, rue Wiertz, 1047 Brussels, Belgium (office); 45 rue du Bois de Boulogne, 92200 Neuilly-sur-Seine; Villa Mirasol, Bd Napoléon III, 06320 Villefranche-sur-Mer, France. *Telephone:* (2) 284-52-25 (office). *Fax:* (2) 284-92-25 (office). *E-mail:* nfontaine@aol.com. *Website:* www.europarl.europa.eu (office).

FONTANA, Carlo; Italian opera house director and journalist; b. 15 March 1947, Milan; s. of Ciro Fontana; m. Roberta Cavallini; ed Univ. Statale di Milano; journalist 1968–77; responsible for youth activities, Piccolo Teatro di Milano 1968–71; Asst to Gen. Man. Teatro all Scala, Milan 1977–79, mem. Admin. Council 1980–84; Deputy Admin. Fonit Cetra 1979–84; Pres. Associazione Lirica Concertistica Italiana (AS.LI.CO.) 1980–83; Dir Music Section, Venice Biennale 1983–86; Dir Ente Autonomo Teatro Comunale di Bologna 1984–90; Sovrintendente, Teatro alla Scala, Milan 1990–2005; Prof., Univ. of Pavia; Pres. Associazione Nazionale Enti Lirici e Sinfonici 1986–; mem. Commissione Centrale Musica, Consiglio Nazionale dello Spettacolo; Grand 'Ufficiale della Repubblica Italiana; Ambrogino d'Oro, Milan 1999. *Leisure interests:* sport, music. *Address:* c/o Teatro alla Scala, Via Filodrammatici 2, 20121 Milan, Italy.

FONTANELLI, Paolo, MBA, PhD; Italian business executive; *CEO, Furla;* ed Classical Lyceum degree, Florence, Univ. of Florence (thesis work at Cornell Univ., USA), Bocconi Univ., Milan, Advanced Man. Program, Harvard Business School, USA; conducted research in astrophysics and achieved fellowships from Cornell Univ., Observatoire de Paris, Arecibo Observatory, Puerto-Rico and Nat. Radio Astronomy Observatory, Va, USA 1982–85; Payload Expert, Sax satellite project at Aeritalia SpA (Italian aerospace co.) 1986–88; Controller Eli Lilly Italia SpA 1988–89, Treasury Man. 1989–90; Chief Financial Officer, Industrie Puccioni SpA 1991–95; Asst to the CEO, Salvatore Ferragamo Italia SpA 1995–98, Group Chief Financial Officer 1998–99; Chief Financial Officer, Giorgio Armani Group 1999–2007, Pres. and CEO Giorgio Armani Hong Kong and Greater China 2000–07; CEO Furla 2007–. *Address:* Furla SpA, Via Bellaria 3/5, 40068 San Lazzaro di Savena, Bologna, Italy (office). *Telephone:* (051) 6202711 (office). *Fax:* (051) 450660 (office). *E-mail:* webmaster@furla.com (office). *Website:* www.furla.com (office).

FONTENEAU, Pascale; Belgian writer; b. 1963, Fougères, Ille-et-Vilaine; ed Université libre de Bruxelles; broadcast first story Chronique des polars on campus radio, Université libre de Bruxelles; works for Passa Porta (literary asscn); contrib. to Le Monde newspaper, Paris 2003–. *Publications include:* Confidences sur l'escalier 1992, Etats de lame 1993, Les Fils perdus de Sylvie Derijke 1995, Les Damnés de l'artère 1996, Otto 1997, La Puissance du désordre 1997, Curieux Sentiments 2000, La Vanité des pions 2000, Où est passé René (with Didier Lange) 2003, Trop c'est Trop 2003, TGV 2003, Croismoi 2005, Jour de gloire 2006, Contretemps 2007, Etats de Lame 2008. *Address:* c/o Les Éditions du Masque, 17, rue Jacob, 75006 Paris, France (office). *Website:* www.lemasque.com (office).

FONTES LIMA, Maria Cristina Lopes; Cape Verde lawyer and politician; *Minister of State Reform and National Defence;* b. 15 June 1958, Praia, Santiago; Minister of Local Admin 2001–02, Minister of Justice 2001–06, Minister of Interior 2002–04, Minister Adjunct to Prime Minister and Govt Spokesperson 2004–06, Minister of the Presidency of Council of Ministers 2006–08, Minister of State Reform and Nat. Defence 2006–; fmr Chair. Network of African Women Ministerial and Parliamentarian Bureau. *Address:* Ministry of State Reform and National Defence, Praia, Santiago, Cape Verde.

FOOT, Michael David Kenneth Willoughby, CBE, MA, FCIB; British financial regulator; *Inspector of Banks and Trust Companies, Central Bank of The Bahamas;* b. 16 Dec. 1946; s. of Kenneth Willoughby Foot and Ruth Joan Foot (née Cornah); m. Michele Annette Cynthia Macdonald 1972; one s. two d.; ed Pembroke Coll., Cambridge and Yale Univ.; joined Bank of England 1969, Man. 1978, Sr Man. 1985; seconded to IMF, Washington, DC as UK Alt. Exec. Dir 1985–87; Head Foreign Exchange Div., Bank of England 1988–90, European Div. 1990–93, Banking Supervision Div. 1993–94, Deputy Dir Supervision and Surveillance 1994–96, Exec. Dir 1996–98; Man. Dir Financial Services Authority 1998–2004; Inspector of Bank and Trust Cos, Central Bank of the Bahamas 2004–; Hon. Pres. ACI(UK) 2002–04. *Publications:* essays on monetary econs in various books and professional journals. *Leisure interests:* choral singing, tennis. *Address:* Central Bank of The Bahamas, Frederick Street, PO Box N-4868, Nassau, N.P., Bahamas (office). *Telephone:* 322-2193 (office). *Fax:* 322-4321 (office). *E-mail:* queries@centralbankbahamas.com (office). *Website:* www.centralbankbahamas.com (office).

FOOT, Rt Hon. Michael Mackintosh, PC, MP; British politician and journalist; b. 23 July 1913, Plymouth, Devon; s. of the late Isaac Foot; (brother of the late Lord Caradon); m. Jill Craigie 1949 (died 1999); ed Forres School, Swanage, Leighton Park School, Reading and Wadham Coll., Oxford; Pres. Oxford Union 1933; contested Monmouth 1935; Asst Ed. Tribune 1937–38, Jt Ed. 1948–52, Ed. 1952–59, Man. Dir 1952–74; mem. staff Evening Standard 1938, Acting Ed. 1942–44; political columnist Daily Herald 1944–64; MP (Labour) for Plymouth, Devonport 1945–55, for Ebbw Vale 1960–83, for Blaenau Gwent 1983–92; fmr Opposition Spokesman on European Policy; Sec. of State for Employment 1974–76; Lord Pres. of Council, Leader of House of Commons 1976–79, Shadow Leader 1979–80; Deputy Leader of Labour Party 1976–80, Leader 1980–83; Hon. Fellow, Wadham Coll., Oxford 1969; Hon. mem. Nat. Union of Journalists 1985; Spanish Republican Order of Liberation 1973; Hon. DLitt (Univ. of Wales) 1985, (Nottingham) 1990, (Plymouth) 1993; Hon. LLD (Exeter) 1990. *Publications:* Armistice 1918–1939 1940, Trial of Mussolini 1943, Brendan and Beverley 1944, part author Guilty Men 1940 and Who Are the Patriots? 1949, Still At Large 1950, Full Speed Ahead 1950, The Pen and the Sword 1957, Parliament in Danger 1959, Aneurin Bevan Vol. I 1962, Vol. II 1973, Harold Wilson: A Pictorial Biography 1964, Debts of Honour 1980, Another Heart and Other Pulses 1984, Loyalists and Loners 1986, The Politics of Paradise 1988, H.G.: The History of Mr. Wells 1995, Aneurin Bevan 1897–1960 1997, Dr. Strangelove I Presume 1999, The Uncollected Michael Foot 2003, Isaac Foot: A West Country Boy 2006. *Address:* c/o Tribune, 9 Arkwright Road, London, NW3 6AN, England.

FOOT, Philippa Ruth, MA, FBA; British academic; *Griffin Professor Emerita, University of California, Los Angeles;* b. 3 Oct. 1920, Owston Ferry, Lincs.; d. of W. S. B. Bosanquet and Esther Cleveland Bosanquet; m. M. R. D. Foot 1945 (divorced 1960); ed Somerville Coll., Oxford; Lecturer in Philosophy,

Somerville Coll. Oxford 1947–50, Fellow and Tutor 1950–69, Vice-Prin. 1967–69, Sr Research Fellow 1970–88, Hon. Fellow 1988–; Prof. of Philosophy, UCLA 1974–91, Griffin Prof. 1988–91, Prof. Emer. 1991–; fmr Visiting Prof., Cornell Univ., MIT, Univ. of California, Berkeley, Princeton Univ., CUNY; Pres. Pacific Div. American Philosophical Asscn 1983–84; mem. American Acad. of Arts and Sciences; Dr hc (Sofia Univ., Bulgaria) 2000. *Publications:* Theories of Ethics (ed.) 1967, Virtues and Vices 1978, Natural Goodness 2001, Moral Dilemmas 2002; articles and reviews in professional journals. *Leisure interests:* reading, walking, gardening. *Address:* 15 Walton Street, Oxford, OX1 2HG, England. *Telephone:* (1865) 557130.

FOOTE, Huger, BA; American photographer and artist; b. 13 Nov. 1961, Memphis, Tenn.; s. of Shelby Foote and Gwyn Foote; ed Sarah Lawrence Coll., New York; began photography aged 12; photo assistant, Paris 1983–87; freelance photographer, New York 1987–93; began working as professional artist, Memphis 1993–98; moved to London 1998; has held exhbns across Europe and the USA. *Solo exhibitions include:* Ledbetter Lusk Gallery, Memphis 1996, Gallery of Contemporary Photography, Santa Monica 1997, Dorothy de Pauw Gallery, Brussels 2000, Patrick de Brock Gallery, Knokke. *Group exhibitions include:* Ledbetter Lusk Gallery 1995, Memphis Coll. of Art 1996, Artfair Seattle 1997, Memphis Arts Council 1997, The Armory, New York 1998, River Gallery, Chatanooga 1999, Belgian Art Fair 1999, Hamiltons Gallery, Brussels 2000, Sotheby's, London 2000, Contemporary Art Center of Virginia 2000, Houldsworth Fine Art, London 2000, Hamiltons Gallery, London 2005. *Publications:* Seasons 1997, Sleep (photo essay) 2000, My Friend From Memphis (monograph) 2001; contribs to Wall Street Journal, Vanity Fair, Vogue etc. *Leisure interests:* cycling, travelling in Africa and Pakistan. *Address:* Hamiltons Gallery, 3 Carlos Place, London, W1 2TU, England (office). *Telephone:* (20) 7499-9493 (office). *Fax:* (20) 7629-9919 (office). *E-mail:* info@hamiltonsgallery.com (office). *Website:* www.hamiltonsgallery.com (office).

FORBES, Bryan, CBE; British film industry executive, film director, screenwriter and novelist; b. 22 July 1926, Stratford, London; m. Nanette Newman (q.v.) 1955; two d.; ed West Ham Secondary School, RADA; first stage appearance 1942; served in Intelligence Corps 1944–48; entered films as actor 1948; Head of Production, Assoc. British Picture Corpn 1969–71, subsequently named EMI Film Productions Ltd; mem. Gen. Advisory Council of BBC 1966–69, Experimental Film Bd of British Film Acad.; Govt Nominee BBC Schools Broadcasting Council 1972; mem. Beatrix Potter Soc. (Pres. 1982–96, now patron), Nat. Youth Theatre (Pres. 1984–2005), Writers Guild of GB (Pres. 1988–91); Founder and fmr Dir Capital Radio Ltd; Hon. DLitt (CNNA) 1987, (Sussex) 1999; many film festival prizes. *Films:* wrote and co-produced The Angry Silence (British Film Acad. Award) 1959; dir Whistle Down the Wind 1961; writer and dir The L-Shaped Room (UN Award) 1962, Seance on a Wet Afternoon (Best Screenplay Award) 1963, King Rat 1964; writer Only Two Can Play (Best Screenplay Award) 1964; producer and dir The Wrong Box 1965; writer, producer and dir The Whisperers 1966, Deadfall 1967, The Madwoman of Chaillot 1968, The Raging Moon (Long Ago Tomorrow in USA) 1970; dir Macbeth 1980, Killing Jessica 1986, Star Quality 1986, The Living Room 1987, One Helluva Life 2002; writer, producer and dir filmed biography of Dame Edith Evans for Yorkshire TV 1973; filmed documentary on lifestyle of Elton John for ATV 1974; wrote and dir The Slipper and the Rose 1975, Jessie (BBC) 1977, Ménage à trois (Better Late than Never in USA) 1981, The Endless Game 1989 (for Channel 4 TV); dir British segment of The Sunday Lovers 1980; dir The King in Yellow (for LWT TV) 1982, The Naked Face 1983; produced, wrote and dir International Velvet 1977. *Publications:* Truth Lies Sleeping (short stories) 1951, The Distant Laughter (novel) 1972, Notes for a Life (autobiography) 1974, The Slipper and the Rose 1976, Ned's Girl (biog. of Dame Edith Evans) 1977, International Velvet (novel) 1978, Familiar Strangers (novel, aka Stranger) 1979, That Despicable Race – A History of the British Acting Tradition 1980, The Rewrite Man (novel) 1983, The Endless Game (novel) 1986, A Song at Twilight (novel) 1989, A Divided Life (autobiography) 1992, The Twisted Playground (novel) 1993, Partly Cloudy (novel) 1995, Quicksand (novel) 1996, The Memory of All That 1999. *Leisure interests:* collecting books, landscape gardening, collecting Napoleonic relics, avoiding bores. *Address:* c/o Curtis Brown Ltd, Haymarket House, 28–29 Haymarket, London, SW1Y 4SP, England (office). *Telephone:* (20) 7393-4400 (office). *Fax:* (20) 7393-4401 (office). *E-mail:* info@curtisbrown.co.uk (office). *Website:* www.curtisbrown.co.uk (office).

FORBES, Admiral Sir Ian, Kt, KCB, CBE; British naval officer (retd); ed RAF Staff Coll., Bracknell, Royal Coll. of Defense Studies (RCDS); joined Royal Navy 1965, tours in HM Yacht Britannia and on American Exchange with USS WH Standley; qualified as Prin. Warfare Officer 1979; specialised as Anti Air Warfare Officer 1978; fmr Commdr HMS Kingfisher, HMS Diomede, HMS Chatham, HMS Invincible (involved in NATO bombing campaign over Bosnia 1995, Operation Desert Fox in Gulf 1999), HMS Illustrious; engaged in active operations off Iceland, the Falklands, the Gulf and Adriatic; Staff Officer Operations to Comas Wsrikfor 1986–88; participant in Standing Naval Force Atlantic; promoted Rear Admiral 1995; served as Mil. Adviser to High Rep. in Sarajevo and Chief of Staff, Office of the High Rep., Bosnia; Commdr UK maritime contribs to NATO operations in Kosovo 1999; Flag Officer Surface Flotilla, NATO 2000, Deputy Saclant 2001, Admiral Supreme Allied Command Atlantic 2002–04; retd from service 2004; mem. Windsor Leadership Trust; Gov. Portsmouth High School for Girls; Chair. of the Council, Eastbourne Coll. 2005–; NATO Meritorious Service Medal, HRH Queen' Commendation for Valuable Service 1995. *Address:* c/o Eastbourne College, Old Wish Road, Eastbourne, East Sussex, BN21 4JY, England.

FORBES, Malcolm Stevenson (Steve), Jr, LHD; American publishing executive; *President and CEO, Forbes Inc.;* b. 18 July 1947, Morristown, NJ; s.

of Malcolm Forbes and Roberta Laidlaw; m. Sabina Beekman 1971; ed Princeton Univ. and Lycoming Coll. Jacksonville Univ.; with Forbes Inc., New York 1970–, Pres. and COO 1980–90, Deputy Ed.-in-Chief 1982–90, Ed.-in-Chief, Forbes Magazine and Pres. and CEO 1990–; Chair. Forbes Newspapers 1989–; mem. Bd for Int. Broadcasting 1983–93, Chair. 1985–93; mem. Advisory Council, Dept of Econs Princeton Univ. 1985–; several hon. degrees. *Wrote:* Some Call It Greed (film script) 1977. *Publication:* Fact and Comment (ed.) 1974. *Address:* Forbes Inc., 60 Fifth Avenue, New York, NY 10011, USA (office). *Telephone:* (212) 295-0893 (office). *Website:* www.forbesinc.com (office).

FORD, Anna, BA, FRGS; British company director and fmr broadcaster; b. 2 Oct. 1943; d. of John Ford and Jean Beattie Winstanley; m. 1st Alan Holland Bittles (divorced 1976); m. 2nd Charles Mark Edward Boxer (died 1988); two d.; ed Minehead Grammar School, White House Grammar School, Brampton and Manchester Univ.; work for students' interests, Manchester Univ. 1966–69; Lecturer, Rupert Stanley Coll. of Further Educ., Belfast 1970–72; staff tutor, Social Sciences, NI Region, Open Univ. 1972–74, 1974–78; presenter and reporter, Man Alive (Granada TV), Tomorrow's World (BBC); newscaster, ITN 1978–80; with TV-AM 1980–83; freelance broadcasting and writing 1983–86; BBC News and Current Affairs 1989–2006; mem. Bd of Dirs J Sainsbury plc 2006–; Trustee Royal Botanic Gardens, Kew 1995–; Chancellor Univ. of Manchester 2001–; Hon. Fellow, Open Univ. 1998; Hon. Bencher Middle Temple 2002; Hon. BA (Cen. Lancs.) 1998; Hon. LLD (Manchester) 1998; Dr hc (Univ. of St Andrews) 2006. *Publication:* Men: A Documentary 1985. *Leisure interests:* talking, walking, drawing. *Address:* c/o Board of Directors, J Sainsbury plc, 33 Holborn, London, EC1N 2HT, England.

FORD, Hon. Anthony David, LLB; New Zealand judge; *Chief Justice of Tonga;* b. 8 May 1942, Hokitika; s. of Tom Ford and Cath Ford; five d. two s.; ed Auckland Univ.; currently Chief Justice of Tonga. *Address:* PO Box 1309, Nuku'alofa, Tonga (home). *Telephone:* (676) 25-906 (home); (676) 24-771 (office). *Fax:* (676) 25-906 (office). *E-mail:* valda@kalianet.to (office).

FORD, Bruce; American singer (tenor); m. H. Ypma 1982; one s.; ed Texas Tech. Univ., Houston Opera Studio; sings in major opera houses in N America and Europe, specializing in Mozart and bel canto composers; Rossini's Otello (Covent Garden), Ermione (Glyndebourne), Zelmira, Ricciardo e Zoraide (Pesaro) revived for him; concert appearances include La Scala, Edin. Festival, Covent Garden, San Francisco Opera, Düsseldorf Symphonic, Chicago Lyric Opera and Amsterdam Concertgebouw; extensive recording career including many rare 19th century operas; Seal of Tex. Tech. Univ. 1997. *Leisure interests:* scuba diving, sailing. *Address:* Athole Still International Management Ltd, 25–27 Westow Street, London, SE19 3RY, England (office). *Telephone:* (20) 8768-6603 (office). *Fax:* (20) 8771-8172 (office). *E-mail:* simon@atholestill.co.uk (office); hetty.ford@gmail.com (office). *Website:* www.atholestill.co.uk; www.bruce-ford.com.

FORD, David Frank, MA, PhD, STM; Irish professor of divinity; *Regius Professor of Divinity, University of Cambridge;* b. 23 Jan. 1948, Dublin; s. of George Ford and Phyllis Woodman; m. Deborah Hardy 1982; one s. two d. (one d. deceased); ed High School, Dublin, Trinity Coll., Dublin, St John's Coll., Cambridge, Yale Univ., USA, Univ. of Tübingen, Germany; Lecturer in Theology, Univ. of Birmingham 1976–90, Sr Lecturer 1990–91; Regius Prof. of Divinity, Univ. of Cambridge 1991–, Chair. Faculty Bd of Divinity 1993–95, Fellow, Selwyn Coll. Cambridge 1991–, Foundation mem. Trinity Coll. Cambridge 1991–, mem. Syndicate Cambridge University Press 1993–, Chair. Man. Cttee Centre for Advanced Religious and Theological Studies, Univ. of Cambridge 1995–; Chair. Council Westcott House Theological Coll. 1991–2006; mem. Archbishop of Canterbury's Urban Theology Working Group 1991–96; Fellow, Center of Theological Inquiry, Princeton Univ. 1993–; Founding mem. and mem. Man. Cttee Soc. for Scriptural Reasoning 1996–; Pres. Soc. for the Study of Theology 1997–98; mem. Postgraduate Panel in Philosophy and Theology, Humanities Research Bd of The British Acad. 1997–99, Church of England Doctrine Comm. 1998–2003; Founding Dir Cambridge Inter-Faith Programme 2002–; Academic mem. World Econ. Forum Council of 100 Leaders for West-Islamic World Dialogue 2003–; mem. Arts and Humanities Research Council Peer Review Coll. 2005–; mem. Advisory Bd Centre for Christian Studies, Hong Kong 2006–, Advisory Bd of ResponsAbility 2007–; mem. Bd of Advisors, John Templeton Foundation 2008–; Trustee, Golden Web Foundation 2006–, Center of Theological Inquiry, Princeton 2007–, The Murray Cox Foundation 2007–; Lay Canon Theologian of Birmingham Cathedral 2006–; Hon. DD (Birmingham) 2000. *Publications:* Barth and God's Story 1981, Jubilate: Theology in Praise (with D. W. Hardy) 1984, Meaning and Truth in 2 Corinthians (with F. M. Young) 1987, The Modern Theologians 1997, The Shape of Living 1997, Self and Salvation: Being Transformed 1999, Theology: A Very Short Introduction 1999, Jesus (ed. with M. Higton) 2002, Reading Texts, Seeking Wisdom (co-ed. with Graham Stanton) 2003, Fields of Faith: Theology and Religious Studies for the Twenty-First Century (co-ed. with Ben Quash and Janet Martin Soskice 2005, The Promise of Scriptural Reasoning (co-ed. with C. C. Pecknold) 2006, Musics of Belonging: The Poetry of Micheal O'Siadhail (co-ed. with Marc Caball) 2006, Christian Wisdom: Desiring God and Learning in Love 2007, Shaping Theology: Engagements in a Religious and Secular World 2007. *Leisure interests:* literature, walking, ball games, kayaking, family and friends. *Address:* Faculty of Divinity, West Road, Cambridge, CB3 9BS, England (office). *Telephone:* (1223) 763031 (office). *Fax:* (1223) 763003 (office). *E-mail:* dff1000@cam.ac.uk (office). *Website:* www.divinity.cam.ac.uk (office).

FORD, Sir David Robert, KBE, LVO; British government official (retd) and business executive; *Chairman, UK Broadband Ltd;* b. 22 Feb. 1935; s. of William Ewart Ford and Edna Ford; m. 1st Elspeth Anne Muckart 1958 (divorced 1987); two s. two d.; m. 2nd Gillian Petersen (née Monsarrat) 1987;

ed Tauntons School, Royal Coll. of Defence Studies; officer, RA 1955–72, retd from army, rank of Maj.; seconded to Hong Kong Govt 1967; Deputy Dir Hong Kong Govt Information Service 1972–74, Dir 1974–76; Deputy Sec. Hong Kong Govt Secr. 1976; Under-Sec. NI Office 1977–79; Sec. for Information, Hong Kong Govt 1979–80; Hong Kong Commr in London 1980–81, 1994–96; Royal Coll. of Defence Studies 1982; Dir of Housing, Hong Kong Govt 1983–84, Sec. for Housing 1985, for the Civil Service 1985–86; Chief Sec., Hong Kong 1986–93, Hong Kong Commr in London 1994–97; retd from public service June 1997; currently Chair. UK Broadband Ltd; mem. Bd of Dirs PCCW Limited; fmr Chair. Council for the Protection of Rural England. *Leisure interests:* rare breeds of cattle and sheep, fishing, tennis. *Address:* UK Broadband Limited, Lakeside House 1, Furzeground Way, Stockley Park East, Uxbridge UB11 1BD (office); Culverwell Farm, Branscombe, Devon, EX12 3DA, England (home). *Telephone:* (20) 8622-3050 (office). *Fax:* (20) 8622-3244 (office). *Website:* www.ukbroadband.com (office).

FORD, Harrison; American actor; b. 13 July 1942, Chicago; m. 1st Mary Ford; two s.; m. 2nd Melissa Ford (divorced 2004); one s. one d.; ed Ripon Coll.; numerous TV appearances; Cecil B. DeMille Award, Golden Globes 2002, American Film Inst. Lifetime Achievement Award 2000. *Films include:* Dead Heat on a Merry-Go-Round 1966, Luv 1967, A Time for Killing 1967, Journey to Shiloh 1968, The Long Ride Home 1967, Getting Straight 1970, Zabriskie Point 1970, The Conversation 1974, American Graffiti 1974, Star Wars 1977, Heroes 1977, Force 10 from Navarone 1978, Apocalypse Now 1979, Hanover Street 1979, Frisco Kid 1979, The Empire Strikes Back 1980, Raiders of the Lost Ark 1981, Blade Runner 1982, Return of the Jedi 1983, Indiana Jones and the Temple of Doom 1984, Witness 1985, The Mosquito Coast 1986, Working Girl 1988, Frantic 1988, Indiana Jones and the Last Crusade 1989, Presumed Innocent 1990, Regarding Henry 1991, The Fugitive 1992, Patriot Games 1992, Clear and Present Danger 1994, Sabrina 1995, The Devil's Own 1996, Air Force One 1996, Six Days and Seven Nights 1998, Random Hearts 1999, What Lies Beneath 2000, K-19: The Widowmaker (also exec. producer) 2002, Hollywood Homicide 2003, No True Glory: The Battle for Fallujah 2006, Firewall 2006, Indiana Jones and the Kingdom of the Crystal Skull 2008. *Address:* 10279 Century Woods Drive, Los Angeles, CA 90067, USA.

FORD, Sir Hugh, Kt, PhD, DSc, FRS, FREng; British academic, engineer and consultant; *Professor Emeritus, Imperial College London;* b. 16 July 1913, Thornby, Northants.; s. of Arthur Ford and Constance Mary Ford; m. 1st Wynyard Scholfield 1942 (died 1991); two d.; m. 2nd Thelma Alys Jensen (née Morgan) 1993; ed Northampton School and Imperial Coll., Univ. of London; served apprenticeship Great Western Railway 1931–36; Research Engineer Imperial Coll. 1936–39, Imperial Chemical Industries 1939–42; Chief Tech. Officer British Iron and Steel Fed. 1942–47; Tech. Dir Paterson Eng 1947–48; Reader, then Prof., Imperial Coll. 1948–65, Prof. of Mechanical Eng and Head of Dept 1969–80, Pro-Rector 1978–80, Prof. Emer. 1980–, Fellow 1983–; Dir Davy Ashmore, Alfred Herbert Ltd, etc. 1965–78; Chair. Ford and Dain Partners 1972–82 (Dir 1972–93), Sir Hugh Ford and Assocs 1982–; Pres. Inst. of Mechanical Engineers 1976–77, The Welding Inst. 1983–85, Inst. of Metals 1985–87; Dr hc (Belfast, Sheffield, Aston, etc.); Hawkesley Gold Medal 1948, Sir James Ewing Medal, James Watt Int. Gold Medal 1985. *Publications:* Advanced Mechanics of Materials 1962; 100 scientific papers. *Leisure interests:* music, gardening, model engineering. *Address:* 18 Shrewsbury House, Cheyne Walk, London, SW3 5LN; Shamley Cottage, Stroud Lane, Shamley Green, Surrey, GU5 0ST, England (home). *Telephone:* (20) 7352-4948; (1483) 898012 (home). *Fax:* (20) 7352-5320.

FORD, Richard, BA, MFA; American writer and academic; *Professor, Trinity College, Dublin;* b. 16 Feb. 1944, Jackson, Miss.; m. Kristina Hensley Ford 1968; ed Michigan State Univ., Univ. of California, Irvine; Lecturer, Univ. of Michigan, Ann Arbor 1974–76; Asst Prof. of English, Williams Coll., Williamstown, Mass 1978–79; Lecturer, Princeton Univ. 1980–81; Prof., Trinity Coll., Dublin 2008–; Guggenheim Fellowship 1977–78; Nat. Endowment for the Arts Fellowships 1979–80, 1985–86; mem. American Acad. of Arts and Letters, PEN, Writers' Guild, American Acad. of Arts and Sciences; Dr hc (Rennes, France, Michigan); Miss. Acad. of Arts and Letters Literature Award 1987, American Acad. and Inst. of Arts and Letters Award for Literature 1989, American Acad. of Arts and Letters Award in Merit for the Novel 1997, PEN-Malamud Award for Short Fiction 2001; Commdr, Ordre des Arts et des Lettres. *Screenplays:* American Tropical 1983, Bright Angel 1991. *Publications:* A Piece of My Heart (novel) 1976, The Ultimate Good Luck (novel) 1981, The Sportswriter (novel) 1986, Rock Springs (short stories) 1987, My Mother in Memory (ed.) 1988, The Best American Short Stories (ed.) 1990, Wildlife (novel) 1990, The Granta Book of the American Short Story (ed.) 1992, Independence Day (novel, Pulitzer Prize for Fiction 1996, PEN/Faulkner Award for Fiction 1996) 1995, Women with Men (short stories) 1997, The Granta Book of the American Long Story (ed.) 1999, A Multitude of Sins (short stories) 2002, The Lay of the Land (novel) 2006, The New Granta Book of the American Short Story (ed.) 2007, The Bascombe Novels 2009. *Address:* International Creative Management, 825 Eighth Avenue, New York, NY 10019, USA (office). *Telephone:* (212) 556-5764 (office).

FORD, Richard John, BA, DipArch; British business executive; b. 10 April 1949; s. of the late Arthur Ford and of Violet Banbury; m. Janet K. Ford; one s.; ed Portsmouth Polytechnic and Polytechnic of London; Exec. Creative Dir Landor 1984–, with Landor Europe, currently with Landor New York; comms include identity and environmental design for British Airways 1984, Chase Manhattan Bank Europe 1985, Royal Jordanian Airlines and Alfred Dunhill 1986, BAe and Abbey National 1987, Cespa Petroleum Spain, Depasco Convenience Stores Spain and Ballantyne Cashmere 1988, Emlak Bank, Turkey 1989, Deutsche Shell 1990, Egnatia Bank Greece 1991, Seville Expo and Neste Petroleum Finland 1992, Lincoln Mercury USA, Telia (Swedish Telecom) and Cathay Pacific Airline 1993, Royal Mail and Delta Air Lines USA 1994, Montell (Worldwide) and KF (Swedish Co-op) 1995, RIBA 1993, Adtranz (Worldwide) and Air 2000 (UK) 1996, Credit Lyonnais 1997, Shell Int. Petroleum and Compaq Computers (USA) 1998, Hyperion Software and Textron (USA) 1999. *Address:* Landor Associates, Klamath House, 230 Park Avenue South, New York, NY 10003, USA (office). *Telephone:* (212) 614-4449 (office). *Fax:* (212) 614-3966. *Website:* www.landor.com.

FORD, Tom; American fashion designer; *President and CEO, Tom Ford International;* b. 1962, Texas; ed New York Univ., Parsons School of Design; fmrly acted in TV commercials, asst to designer Cathy Hardwick, with Perry Ellis Co.; joined Gucci Group 1990, Design Dir 1992–94, Creative Dir 1994–2004, Vice-Chair. Man. Bd 2002–04; Creative Dir, Yves St Laurent Rive Gauche and YSL Beauté 2000–04; est. Tom Ford Int. 2005, currently Pres. and CEO, launched menswear collection Spring 2007; involved in fundraising in US and Europe; four Council of Fashion Designers of America awards, five VH-1/Vogue Fashion awards, two Fashion Editor's Club of Japan awards, two US Accessory Council awards, Best Fashion Designer, Time Magazine 2001, GQ Designer of the Year 2001, Fashion Design Achievement Award, Cooper Hewitt Museum 2002, Andre Leon Talley Lifetime Achievement Award, Savannah Coll. of Art and Design 2005. *Address:* Tom Ford HQ, 845 Madison Avenue, New York, NY 10022, USA (office). *Telephone:* (212) 359-0300 (office). *Fax:* (212) 359-0301 (office). *Website:* www.tomford.com (office).

FORD, Wendell Hampton; American fmr politician; b. 8 Sept. 1924, Owensboro, Ky; s. of E.M. Ford and Irene (Schenk) Ford; m. Jean Neel 1943; one s. one d.; ed Daviess County High School, Univ. of Kentucky, Maryland School of Insurance; served in US Army, Ky 1944–46, Nat. Guard 1949–62; Chief Asst to Gov. of Kentucky 1959–61; mem. Ky Senate 1966–67; Lt-Gov. Kentucky 1967–71, Gov. 1971–74; US Senator from Kentucky 1974–97; Asst Minority Leader 1995–97; fmr mem. Senate Energy and Natural Resources Cttee, Commerce, Science, Transportation Cttee (Chair. Consumer Sub-Cttee); mem. Democratic Steering Cttee, Chair. Democratic Nat. Campaign Cttee 1976, Head of Democratic Senatorial Campaign Cttee; Majority Whip 1991–97; Chair. Senate Rules Cttee, Jt Cttee on Printing; Chair. Nat. Democratic Govs 1973–74; Chair. Jt Congressional Cttee on Inaugural Ceremonies; fmr mem. Nat. Democratic Party Advisory Council; fmr Chair. Common Law Enforcement, Justice and Public Safety, Southern Govs' Conf.; mem. US Chamber of Commerce, Pres. 1956–57; Int. Vice-Pres. Jaycees, Distinguished Fellow Martin School of Public Policy and Admin., Univ. of Ky 1999–. *Leisure interests:* fishing, hunting. *Address:* 2017 Fieldcrest Drive, Owensboro, KY 42301, USA (home).

FORD, William Clay, BS(Econ); American automotive industry executive; *Chairman, Detroit Lions Inc.;* b. 14 March 1925, Detroit; s. of Edsel Ford and Eleanor Clay Ford; brother of Henry Ford II; m. Martha Firestone 1947; one s., William Clay Ford, Jr. (q.v.) three d.; ed Yale Univ.; Dir Ford Motor Co. 1948–; mem. of Sales and Advertising Staff 1948 and of the Industrial Relations Staff 1949; quality control Man. Lincoln-Mercury Div. Jet Engine Defence Project 1951; Man. Special Product Operations 1952; Vice-Pres. Ford Motor Co. and Gen. Man. Continental Div. 1953, Group Dir Continental Div. 1955, Vice-Pres. Product Design 1956–80, Chair. Exec. Cttee 1978–2005, mem. Bd of Dirs 1948–2005, mem. Company Finance Cttee 1987–2005, Dir Emer. 2005–; Chair. and Owner Detroit Lions Inc. (professional football team) 1964–; Chair. Emer. Edison Inst.; Trustee Eisenhower Medical Center, Thomas A. Edison Foundation; mem. Bd of Dirs Nat. Tennis Hall of Fame, Boys Club of America. *Address:* c/o Detroit Lions Inc., 222 Republic Drive, Allen Park, MI 48101, USA. *Telephone:* (313) 216-4000. *Fax:* (313) 216-4226. *Website:* www.detroitlions.com.

FORD, William Clay, Jr, MBA; American automotive industry executive; *Executive Chairman, Ford Motor Company;* b. 3 May 1957, Detroit, Mich.; s. of William Clay Ford (q.v.) and Martha Firestone; m. Lisa Ford; four c.; ed Princeton Univ., Massachusetts Inst. of Tech.; joined Ford Motor Co. 1979 as product-planning analyst, then various positions in mfg, sales, marketing, product devt and finance; served on Ford's Nat. Bargaining Team in Ford–United Auto Workers talks 1982; Vice-Pres. Comm. for Vehicle Marketing, Ford of Europe 1986–87; Chair., Man. Dir Ford of Switzerland 1987–89; elected to Bd of Dirs, Ford Motor Co. 1988, Chair. Bd's Finance Cttee 1995–99, Bd's Environmental and Public Policy Cttee 1997, Bd's Nominating and Governance Cttee 1999, Chair. of Bd 1999–, Exec. Dir Business Strategy, Ford Automotive Group 1991–92, Gen. Man. Climate Control Div. 1992–94, Head of Commercial Truck Vehicle Centre 1994–95, Vice-Pres. Ford Motor Co. 1994, CEO 2001–06, Exec. Chair. 2006–; mem. World Econ. Forum's Global Leaders for Tomorrow; Co-Chair. Detroit Econ. Club Nat. Summit; Chair. Detroit Renaissance Exec. Cttee; Trustee Henry Ford Health System; Vice-Chair. Detroit Lions Inc. (professional football team); mem. Bd of Dirs e-Bay; Hon. Chair. Southeast Mich. Consortium for Water Quality, Hon. mem. Golden Key Int. Honour Soc.; Dr hc (Koc Univ., Istanbul) 2006; Automotive Exec. of the Year 2006, Boneh Kehillah Award, Jewish Community Center of Detroit 2007. *Leisure interests:* fly-fishing, Tae Kwon Do, ice hockey, tennis, cars. *Address:* Ford Motor Company, World Headquarters, One American Road, Dearborn, MI 48126-2798, USA (office). *Telephone:* (313) 322-3000 (office). *Fax:* (313) 845-6073 (office). *Website:* www.ford.com (office).

FORDE, Sir Henry de Boulay, Kt, PC, QC, LLM, KA; Barbadian politician and lawyer; b. 20 March 1933, Christ Church, Barbados; adopted s. of the late Courtley Ifill and of Elise Ifill; m. Cheryl Wendy Forde; four s.; ed Harrison Coll., Barbados, Christ's Coll., Cambridge, Middle Temple, London; Research Asst, Dept of Criminology, Univ. of Cambridge 1958, Research Student, Int. Law, worked on British Digest of Int. Law, Univ. of Cambridge 1958–59, Supervisor and Tutor in Int. Law, Emmanuel Coll., Cambridge 1958–59;

called to English Bar 1959, to Barbadian Bar 1959; Lecturer, Extra-Mural Programme, Univ. of West Indies 1961–68, Part-time Lecturer, Caribbean Studies 1964–69; mem. House of Ass. for Christ Church West 1971–2003; Minister of External Affairs and Attorney-Gen. 1976–81; Minister of State 1993; Leader of the Opposition 1986–89, 1991–93; mem. Privy Council 1976–92, 1996–; Chair. and Political Leader, Barbados Labour Party 1986–93; Chair. Commonwealth Observer Group to the Seychelles 1991, to Fiji Islands 2001; mem. Commonwealth Cttee on Vulnerability of Small States 1985, Commonwealth Parl. Asscn, Editorial Bds of The Round Table, Int. Comm. of Jurists 1987–92, Barbados Bar Asscn, Hon. Soc. of Middle Temple, Int. Tax Planning Asscn, Interparl. Human Rights Network, Barbados Nat. Trust, Int. Acad. of Estate and Trust Law, Int. Inst. for Democracy and Electoral Assistance, Inter-American Comm. on Human Rights; Kt of St Andrew, Order of Barbados. *Leisure interests:* reading, walking, gardening. *Address:* Juris Chambers, Parker House, Wildey Business Park, Wildey Road, St Michael, Barbados (office); Codrington Court, Society, St John, Barbados, West Indies (home). *Telephone:* 429-5320 (office); 429-2203 (office); 423-3881 (home). *Fax:* 429-2206 (office); 423-3949 (home). *E-mail:* shf@jurischambers.com (office).

FOREHAND, Joe W., MSc; American management consulting executive; m.; two s.; ed Auburn Univ., Purdue Univ.; joined Accenture, Atlanta 1972, pnr 1982, various man. positions including Leader, Global Communications and High Tech. Group, CEO 1999–2004, Chair. 2001–06 (retd); mem. Business Roundtable; Carl S. Sloane Award for Excellence in Man. Consulting 2003, Morgan Stanley Leadership Award 2003. *Address:* c/o Accenture Limited, 5221 North O'Connor Boulevard, Suite 1400, Irving, TX 75039, USA (office).

FOREMAN, Amanda, BA, PhD, FRSA; British historian and writer; b. 1968, London; d. of Carl Foreman; m.; one s. two d.; ed Sarah Lawrence Coll., Bronxville, NY, Columbia Univ., New York and Lady Margaret Hall, Oxford; Henrietta Jex Blake Sr Scholarship, Univ. of Oxford 1998; TV and radio presenter 1998–; freelance contrib. to newspapers in the UK and USA. *Publications:* Georgiana: Duchess of Devonshire (Whitbread Award for Biography of the Year) 1998, Georgiana's World 2001, Our American Cousins 2007. *Address:* The Wylie Agency, 17 Bedford Square, London, WC1B 3JA, England (office). *E-mail:* mail@wylieagency.co.uk (office). *Website:* www.wylieagency.co.uk (office); www.amanda-foreman.com.

FOREMAN, George; American fmr professional boxer; b. 10 Jan. 1949, Marshall, Tex.; s. of J.D. Foreman and Nancy Foreman; m. five times; five s. five d.; Olympic heavyweight champion Mexico 1968; World heavyweight champion 1973–74, 1994–95; lost title to Muhammad Ali (q.v.) (knockout in 8th) in 1974; recaptured it on 5 Nov. 1994 at age 45 with a 10-round knockout of WBC/IBF champion Michael Moorer, becoming oldest man to win heavyweight crown; successfully defended title at age 46 against Axel Schulz; gave up IBF title after refusing rematch with Schulz; now an evangelical minister; f. a youth and community centre; has diverse business interests, has endorsed or sold numerous products such as hamburgers, hot dogs and grilling machines and rotisseries; AP Male Athlete of the Year 1994. *Publication:* By George (autobiog.). *Leisure interests:* raising livestock, breeding horses. *Address:* c/o The Church of Lord Jesus Christ, 2501 Lone Oak, Houston, TX 77093, USA. *E-mail:* george@biggeorge.com. *Website:* www.biggeorge.com (office).

FORGEARD, Noël, LèsScEcon; French business executive and mining engineer; b. 8 Dec. 1946, Ferté-Gaucher; s. of Henri Forgeard and Laurence Duprat; m. Marie-Cécile de Place 1972; one s. three d.; ed Lycée Louis-le-Grand, Ecole Polytechnique, Paris; qualified as mining engineer; entered mining industry in Clermont-Ferrand, industry rep. to Auvergne prefecture 1972–73; Asst Sec.-Gen. Dept of Mining, Ministry for Industry 1973–76, Sec.-Gen. 1976–78; Tech. Adviser to Minister of Transport 1978–80, of Defence 1980; Head of Industrial Affairs and Armaments, Ministry of Defence 1980–81; Deputy Pres., Asst Gen. Man. Compagnie française des aciers spéciaux (CFAS) 1982–84, Prés., Dir-Gen. 1984–86; Man. Dir then Pres., Dir-Gen. Ascometal 1985–86; Chair. Asfor Steel Products 1986–87; Tech Adviser and Head of Industrial Affairs, Office of the Prime Minister 1986–87; Man. Defence and Space Divs. Matra 1987, Pres., Dir-Gen. Matra-défense espace finance co. (Sofimades), Matra Hautes technologies, Matra Bac Dynamics, mem. Exec. and Strategy Cttee and Gen. Man. Lagardère SCA 1993–98; Man. Dir Airbus Industrie 1998–2005, CEO 2000–05, Jt CEO European Aeronautic Defence and Space Co. EADS NV (main shareholder of Airbus) 2005–06; Dir Matra systèmes et information, Snecma, Matra-Marconi Space NV; Vice-Pres. Groupement des industries de l'aéronautique et de l'espace (Gifas); Public Enterprise Foundation Award 1971; Chevalier, Légion d'honneur, Ordre nat. du Mérite. *Leisure interests:* modern art, swimming. *Address:* 85 av. de Wagram, 75017 Paris (home); Le Roc, 35800 St-Briac-sur-Mer (home); c/o European Aeronautic Defence and Space Company EADS NV, 37 blvd de Montmorency, 75781 Paris, France (office).

FORIEL-DESTEZET, Philippe, MBA; French business executive; *Honorary President, Adecco SA;* b. 1936; m.; ed Hautes Etudes Commerciales (HEC); Founder Ecco SA, Lyon 1964; apptd Dir 1996, Jt Chair. 1996–2002, Co-Chair. 2004–05, Hon. Pres. 2005–; Chair. Akila Finance SA, Luxembourg; mem. Bd Dirs Vivendi, Securitas AB, Sweden, Carrefour SA; Chevalier, Légion d'honneur. *Address:* Adecco SA, Sägereistrasse 10, 8152 Glattbrugg, Switzerland (office). *Telephone:* (1) 8788888 (office). *Fax:* (1) 8298888 (office). *Website:* www.adecco.com (office).

FORLANI, Arnaldo; Italian politician; b. 8 Dec. 1925, Pesaro; s. of Luigi Forlani and Caterina Forlani; m. Alma Ioni 1956; three s.; ed Univ. of Urbino; mem. Chamber of Deputies 1958; Deputy Sec. of Christian Democrat Party 1962–69, Political Sec. (Leader) 1969–73, 1989; Minister of State Enterprises 1969–70, of Defence 1974–76, of Foreign Affairs 1976–79; Prime Minister 1980–81, Deputy Prime Minister 1983–87; Pres. Christian Democratic Party 1986–89, Sec. Gen. 1989–92. *Leisure interest:* journalism. *Address:* Piazzale Schumann 15, Rome, Italy. *Telephone:* 6784109.

FORMAN, Sir Denis, Kt, OBE; British business executive; b. 13 Oct. 1917, Beattock, Scotland; s. of the late Rev. Adam Forman and of Flora (née Smith) Forman; m. 1st Helen de Mouilpied 1948 (died 1987); two s.; m. 2nd Moni Cameron 1990; one step-s. one step-d.; ed Loretto and Pembroke Coll., Cambridge; war service with Argyll and Sutherland Highlanders 1940–45 (Commdt Orkney and Shetland Defences Battle School 1942, wounded, Cassino 1944); Chief Production Officer, Cen. Office of Information Films 1947; Dir British Film Inst. 1948–55, Chair. Bd of Govs 1971–73; Jt Man. Dir, Granada TV Ltd 1965–81, Chair. 1974–87; Dir Granada Group 1964–90, Deputy Chair. 1984–90, Consultant 1990–96; Chair. Novello & Co. 1971–78, Chair. Scottish Film Production Dept 1990–93; Dir Royal Opera House, Covent Garden 1981–91, Deputy Chair. 1983–92, Fellow BFI 1993; Dir Harold Holt Ltd 1992–; mem. Council Royal Northern Coll. of Music 1975–84, Hon. mem. 1981; Fellow, BAFTA 1977; Ufficiale dell' ordine al Merito della Repubblica Italiana; Hon. DUniv (Stirling) 1982, (Keele) 1990; Hon. DU (Essex) 1986; Hon. LLD (Manchester) 1983, (Lancaster) 1989. *Publications:* Mozart's Piano Concertos 1971, Son of Adam (autobiog.) 1990 (filmed under the title My Life So Far 1999), To Reason Why (autobiog.) 1991, Persona Granada: Some Memories of Sidney Bernstein and the Early Days of Independent Television (autobiog.) 1997, The Good Wagner Opera Guide 2000. *Leisure interests:* music, shooting. *Address:* Flat 2, 15 Lyndhurst Gardens, London, NW3 5NT, England.

FORMAN, Miloš; American film director; b. 18 Feb. 1932, Čáslav, Czechoslovakia; m. Martina Forman; four s.; ed Film Faculty, Acad. of Music and Dramatic Art, Prague; Dir Film Presentations, Czechoslovak TV 1954–56; of Laterna Magika, Prague 1958–62; mem. Artistic Cttee, Šebor-Bor Film Producing Group; Legion d'Honneur; Klement Gottwald State Prize 1967. *Films include:* Talent Competition, Peter and Pavla 1963 (Czechoslovak Film Critics' Award 1963, Grand Prix 17th Int. Film Festival, Locarno 1964), The Knave of Spades, A Blonde in Love (Cidalc Prize, Venice Festival 1965, Grand Prize French Film Acad. 1966) 1965, Episode in Zruč, Like a House on Fire (A Fireman's Ball) 1968, Taking Off 1971; Co-Dir Visions of Eight 1973, One Flew Over the Cuckoo's Nest 1975 (Acad. Award for Best Dir 1976), Hair 1979, Ragtime 1980, Amadeus 1983 (Acad. Award, César Award 1985), Valmont 1988, The People vs. Larry Flynt (Golden Globe for Best Dir 1996) 1996, Man on the Moon (Silver Bear for Best Dir, Berlin Film Festival 2000) 1999, Goya's Ghosts 2006; appeared in New Year's Day 1989, Keeping the Faith 2000. *Publication:* Turnaround: A Memoir (with Jan Novak) 1993.

FORMIGONI, Roberto, MA; Italian politician; *President, Lombardy Region;* b. 30 March 1947, Lecco; s. of the late Emilio Formigoni and Doralice Baroni; ed Catholic Univ. of Milan, Univ. of Sorbonne, Paris; co-f. Movimento Popolare (political arm of Catholic Movt Comunione e Liberazione), Nat. Pres. 1976–87; MEP (Christian Democratic Party) 1984–94, Vice-Chair. Presidential Office 1989–94; elected Deputy 1987, 1992, 1994 (Christian Democratic Party); Under-Sec. Ministry of Environment 1993–94; Pres. Lombardy Region 1995–1999, 2000–(05); Laurea hc (Libera Univ. di Lingue e Comunicazione, Milan) 2004; award for devt cooperation of Lombardy Region. *Leisure interests:* yachting, jogging. *Address:* Palazzo della Regione Lombardia, Via Fabio Filzi 22, 20124 Milan, Italy. *Telephone:* (02) 67654001 (office). *Fax:* (02) 67655653 (office). *E-mail:* roberto_formigoni@regione.lombardia.it (office). *Website:* www.regione.lombardia.it (office).

FORMUZAL, Mihail; Moldovan politician and government official; *Başkan (Governor), Autonomous Territory of Gagauz-Yeri;* b. 7 Nov. 1959, Beşghioz, Ciadir-Lunga dist; m.; three c.; ed Mil. High School of Artillery 'MVFrunze', Odessa, Ukraine, Public Admin Acad.; mil. service 1977–94, achieved rank of Maj.; Deputy Mayor of Ceadir-Lunga 1995–99, Mayor 1999–2007; Chair. People's Republican Party 2005–; Başkan (Gov.) Autonomous Territory of Gagauz-Yeri 2006–, mem. Govt 2007–. *Address:* Office of the Başkan of the Autonomous Territory of Gagauz-Yeri, 3800 Comrat, Moldova (office).

FORNÉ MOLNÉ, Marc; Andorran politician and lawyer; *Leader, Partit Liberal d'Andorra;* b. 1946; ed Univ. of Barcelona; lawyer; fmr Ed. Andorra 7 magazine; currently Leader Partit Liberal d'Andorra; Head of Govt of Andorra 1994–2004. *Address:* Partit Liberal d'Andorra (PLA), Carrer Babot Camp 13, 2°, Andorra la Vella, AD500, Andorra (office). *Telephone:* 807715 (office). *Fax:* 869728 (office). *E-mail:* pla@pla.ad (office). *Website:* www.partitliberal.ad (office).

FORNÉS, María Irene; Cuban/American playwright; b. 14 May 1930, Havana; Man. Dir New York Theatre Strategy 1973–79; fmr TCG (Theatre Communications Group)/Pew Artist-in-Residence, Women's Project and Productions; contrib. to Performing Arts Journal and numerous anthologies; nine Obie awards; NEA (National Endowment for the Arts) awards, including Distinguished Artists Award; Rockefeller Foundation grants; Guggenheim grant; American Acad. and Inst. of Arts and Letters Award; NY State Governor's Arts Award; PEN/Nabokov Award 2002. *Plays (many unpublished):* The Widow 1961, Tango Palace (aka There! You Died) 1963, The Office 1964, Promenade 1965, The Successful Life of 3 1965, The Annunciation 1967, A Vietnamese Wedding 1967, The Red Burning Light (aka Mission XQ3) 1968, Dr Kheal 1968, Molly's Dream 1968, Baboon!!! 1972, Aurora 1974, Cap-a-Pie 1975, Washing 1976, Fefu and Her Friends 1977, In Service 1978, Evelyn Brown 1979, Eyes on the Harem 1979, A Visit 1981, Sarita 1982, The Danube 1982, The Curse of the Langston House 1983, Mud 1983, Abingdon Square 1984, The Conduct of Life 1985, Drowning 1985, The Trial of Joan of Arc on a Matter of Faith 1986, Lovers and Keepers 1986, The Mothers 1986, Oscar and Bertha 1987, Hunger 1988, And What of the Night? 1989, Terra Incognita

1991, Springtime 1992, Enter the Night 1993, Ibsen and the Actress 1995, Manual for a Desperate Crossing 1996, The Summer in Gossensass 1997, The Audition 1998, Letters from Cuba 2000. *Address:* c/o Morgan Jenness, Abrams Artists Agency, 275 Seventh Avenue, 26th Floor, New York, NY 10001, USA (office). *Telephone:* (646) 486-4600 (office). *E-mail:* morgan.jenness@abramsartny.com (office). *Website:* www.abramsartists.com (office).

FORREST, Andrew (Twiggy); Australian business executive; *CEO, Fortescue Metals Group Ltd;* b. 1961; s. of Donald Forrest and Judith Forrest; m.Nicola Forrest; three c.; early career as investment banker; Founding CEO and Deputy Chair. Anaconda Nickel Ltd (now Minara Resources Ltd) 1994, also Chair. Murrin Murrin Jt Venture; fmr Chair. Moly Mines Ltd, Siberia Mining Corpn Ltd; Founder and CEO Fortescue Metals Group Ltd (co. developing Pilbara Iron Ore and Infrastructure Project) 2003–, Chair. 2003–05; Chair. Poseidon Nickel Ltd., Australian Children's Trust; Fellow, Australian Inst. of Mining and Metallurgy; fmr Chair. Athletics Australia; fmr Dir West Australian Chamber of Minerals and Energy. *Address:* Fortescue Metals Group Ltd, Level 2, 87 Adelaide Terrace, East Perth, WA 6004, Australia (office). *Telephone:* (8) 6218-8888 (office). *Fax:* (8) 6218-8880 (office). *E-mail:* fmgl@fmgl.com.au (office). *Website:* www.fmgl.com.au (office).

FORREST, Sir (Andrew) Patrick McEwen, Kt, MD, ChM, FRCS, FRCPE, FRSE; British surgeon; b. 25 March 1923, Mount Vernon, Scotland; s. of Andrew J. Forrest and Isabella Pearson; m. 1st Margaret B. Hall 1955 (died 1961); m. 2nd Margaret A. Steward 1964; one s. two d.; ed Dundee High School and St Andrew's Univ.; Mayo Foundation Fellow, Rochester, Minn. 1952–53; lecturer and Sr lecturer, Univ. of Glasgow 1954–62; Prof. of Surgery, Welsh Nat. School of Medicine 1962–71; Regius Prof. of Clinical Surgery, Univ. of Edinburgh 1970–88, Prof. Emer. 1989–, Hon. Fellow, Faculty of Medicine 1989–95; Visiting Scientist, NIH 1989–90; Assoc. Dean (Clinical Studies) Int. Medical Coll., Kuala Lumpur 1993–96; mem. Medical Research Council 1975–79; Chief Scientist, Scottish Home and Health Dept (part-time) 1981–87; mem. Advisory Bd for Research Councils 1982–85; Hon. DSc (Wales, Chinese Univ. of Hong Kong); Hon. LLD (Dundee); Hon. FACS; Hon. FRACS; Hon. FRCS (Canada); Hon. FRCR; Hon. FFPH; Gimbernat Prize, Catalonian Surgical Asscn 1996; European Inst. of Oncology Breast Cancer Award 2000; Lister Medal 1987, Gold Medal, Netherlands Surgical Asscn 1988. *Publications:* Prognostic Factors in Breast Cancer (jtly) 1968, Principles and Practice of Surgery (jtly) 1985, Breast Cancer: The Decision to Screen 1990; over 250 publs in scientific and medical journals. *Leisure interests:* golf, sailing. *Address:* 19 St Thomas Road, Edinburgh, EH9 2LR, Scotland (home). *Telephone:* (131) 667 3203 (home). *Fax:* (131) 662 1193 (home). *E-mail:* patforresthome@aol.com (home).

FORSEE, Gary D.; American university administrator and fmr telecommunications industry executive; *President, University of Missouri;* b. 10 April 1950, Kansas City; m. Sherry Forsee; two d.; ed Missouri Univ. of Science and Tech.; with Southwestern Bell Telephone 1972–80; with AT&T 1980–89; Vice-Pres. and Gen. Man. Govt System Div. Sprint Corpn 1989–91, Pres. Govt System Div., Business Services Group 1991–93, Sr Vice-Pres. Staff Operations, Long Distance Div. 1993–95, Interim CEO Sprint PCS 1995, Pres. and COO Sprint Long Distance Div. 1995–98, Pres. and CEO Sprint Corpn (now Sprint Nextel Corpn) 2003–07 (resgnd), Pres. and CEO Global One (subsidiary co.), Brussels, Belgium 1998–2000; Chief Staff Officer and Exec. Vice-Pres. BellSouth Int. 1999–2000, Pres. 2000–01, Vice-Chair., Domestic Operations, BellSouth Corpn 2002–03; Chair. Cingular Wireless 2001–02; Pres. Univ. of Missouri 2007–; mem. Bd of Dirs Goodyear Tire & Rubber Co., Great Plains Energy Inc. 2008–. *Address:* Office of the President, University of Missouri, 321 University Hall, Columbia, MO 65211, USA (office). *Telephone:* (573) 882-2011 (office). *E-mail:* umpresident@umsystem.edu (office). *Website:* www.umsystem.edu/ums/president (office).

FORSÉN, K. Sture, MSc, DTech; Swedish chemist and academic; b. 12 July 1932, Piteå; s. of Helmer Forsén and Signe Forsén; m. Dr Gunilla Isaksson 1973 (divorced 1986); ed Royal Inst. of Tech. Stockholm; Assoc. Prof. of Chemical Physics, Royal Inst. of Tech. 1963–67, Prof. of Physical Chem., Univ. of Lund 1966; mem. Bd of Dirs Swedish Natural Science Research Council 1983–86, Perstorp AB 1986–, Swedish Nat. Chemicals Inspectorate 1989–; Fairchild Scholar, Calif. Inst. of Tech. 1986–87, Fogarty Scholar, NIH, USA 1987–94, Visiting Investigator Scripps Research Inst., La Jolla 1990–; mem. Scientific Advisory Council of Volvo Research Foundation 1987–; mem. Royal Swedish Acad. of Sciences 1973–, Nobel Cttee for Chem. 1982–; mem. Royal Swedish Acad. of Eng Sciences 1986–; Celsius Gold Medal, Royal Soc. of Uppsala 1979. *Publications:* co-author of two books on NMR spectroscopy 1972, 1976; over 300 scientific articles, at present mainly concerning biophysical studies of calcium-binding proteins, in int. journals. *Leisure interests:* music from Frescobaldi to Keith Jarrett, renovating old farmhouses. *Address:* St Laurentiigatan 8 IV, S-222 21 Lund, Sweden (home). *Telephone:* 46-14-48-03 (home). *Fax:* 41-45-14-57.

FORSTER, Carl-Peter, BSc; German automobile executive; *President of General Motors Europe, GM Group Vice President, and Chairman of Opel and Saab;* b. 9 May 1954, London, UK; m.; three c.; ed Bonn Univ. and Munich Tech. Univ.; consultant, McKinsey and Co., Munich 1982–86; Head of Planning and Logistics, Tech. Devt Dept, BMW AG 1986–88, Systems and Project Man. 5-series 1988–90, Head of Dept for Test and Pilot Car Mfg, Tech. Devt Centre 1990–93, Head of 5-series 1993–96, Man. Dir BMW (SA) Pty Ltd 1996–99, mem. Man. Bd BMW AG 1999–2000; Chair. and Man. Dir Opel AG 2001–04, Chair. 2004–, Chair. Supervisory Bd 2004–; mem. Bd Dirs Fiat–General Motors Powertrain 2001–; GM Vice-Pres. and Pres. General Motors Europe 2004–, Chair. Saab 2005–, GM Group Vice Pres. 2006–. *Leisure interests:* skiing, regatta-sailing. *Address:* General Motors Europe AG, Stelzenstrasse 4, 8152 Glattbrugg, Switzerland (office). *Telephone:* (44) 828-28-28 (office). *Fax:* (44) 828-26-75 (office). *Website:* www.gmeurope.com (office).

FORSTER, Margaret, BA, FRSL; British writer; b. 25 May 1938, Carlisle; d. of Arthur Gordon Forster and Lilian Forster (née Hind); m. Edward Hunter Davies 1960; one s. two d.; ed Carlisle Co. High School and Somerville Coll., Oxford; chief non-fiction reviewer, London Evening Standard 1977–80; mem. Arts Council Literary Panel 1978–81; RSL Award 1988, Fawcet Soc. Prize 1993. *Publications:* non-fiction: The Rash Adventurer: The Rise and Fall of Charles Edward Stuart 1973, William Makepeace Thackeray: Memoirs of a Victorian Gentleman 1978, Significant Sisters: Grassroots of Active Feminism 1839–1939 1984, Elizabeth Barrett Browning: A Biography 1988, Elizabeth Barrett Browning: Selected Poems (ed.) 1988, Daphne du Maurier: The Authorised Biography 1993, Hidden Lives: A Family Memoir 1995, Rich Desserts and Captains Thin: A Family and Their Times 1831–1931 1997, Precious Lives (memoir) 1997, Good Wives?: Mary, Fanny, Jennie and Me 1845–2001 2001; novels: Dame's Delight 1964, Georgy Girl (filmscript with Peter Nichols 1966) 1963, The Bogeyman 1965, The Travels of Maudie Tipstaff 1967, The Park 1968, Miss Owen-Owen is at Home 1969, Fenella Phizackerley 1970, Mr Bone's Retreat 1971, The Seduction of Mrs Pendlebury 1974, Mother, Can You Hear Me? 1979, The Bride of Lowther Fell 1980, Marital Rites 1981, Private Papers 1986, Have the Men had Enough? 1989, Lady's Maid 1990, The Battle for Christabel 1991, Mothers' Boys 1994, Shadow Baby 1996, The Memory Box 1999, Diary of an Ordinary Woman 1914–1995 2003, Is There Anything You Want? 2005, Keeping the World Away 2006, Over 2007. *Leisure interests:* walking, reading contemporary fiction. *Address:* The Sayle Literary Agency, Bickerton House, 25–27 Bickerton Road, London, N19 5JT, England (office); 11 Boscastle Road, London, NW5 1EE; Grasmoor House, Loweswater, nr Cockermouth, Cumbria, CA13 0RU, England. *Telephone:* (20) 7263-8681 (office); (20) 7485-3785 (London); (1900) 85303 (Cumbria). *Fax:* (20) 7561-0529 (office).

FORSTMOSER, Peter, LLM, PhD; Swiss lawyer and business executive; *Chairman of the Board, Swiss Reinsurance Company (Swiss Re);* b. 22 Jan. 1943, Zürich; s. of Alois Forstmoser-Locher and Ida Forstmoser-Locher; two s.; ed Zürich Univ. Law School, Harvard Law School, USA; attorney 1971–, Pnr, Niederer, Kraft und Frey 1975–; Lecturer, Faculty of Law and Political Science, Univ. of Zürich 1971–74, Assoc. Prof., Univ. of Zürich Law School 1974–78, Full Prof. of Civil, Corp. and Capital Market Law 1978–2008; mem. Bd of Dirs Swiss Reinsurance Co. (Swiss Re) 1990–, Chair. 2000–; Hon. Prof., Beijing Normal Univ. 2001. *Publications:* Schweizer Aktienrecht 1996, Schweizer Gesellschaftsrecht 2007, Einführung in das Recht 2008 and numerous other publs. on Swiss co. and capital market law. *Leisure interests:* sports, modern art. *Address:* Swiss Reinsurance Co., Mythenquai 50/60, 8022 Zürich, Switzerland (office). *Telephone:* (1) 285-96-15 (office). *Fax:* (1) 282-96-15 (office). *E-mail:* peter_forstmoser@swissre.com (office). *Website:* www.swissre.com (office).

FORSYTH, Elliott Christopher, BA, DipEd, DUniv, FAHA, FACE; Australian professor of French; *Professorial Fellow, University of Melbourne;* b. 1 Feb. 1924, Mount Gambier; s. of Samuel Forsyth and Ida Muriel Forsyth (née Brummitt); m. Rona Lynette Williams 1967; two d.; ed Prince Alfred Coll., Adelaide, Univ. of Adelaide and Univ. of Paris; teacher Friends' School, Hobart, Tasmania 1947–49; Lecturer, Sr Lecturer in French Univ. of Adelaide 1955–66; Visiting Lecturer Univ. of Wisconsin, Madison 1963–65; Foundation Prof. of French La Trobe Univ., Melbourne 1966–87, Prof. Emer. 1988–; Visiting Prof., Univ. of Melbourne 1992, Sr Assoc. 1993–98, Professorial Fellow 1999–; Fellow Australian Acad. of Humanities 1973, Australian Coll. of Educ. 1977; Australian Centenary Medal 2003; Commdr Ordre des Palmes Académiques 1983. *Publications:* La Tragédie française de Jodelle à Corneille (1553–1640): le thème de la vengeance 1962, 1994, Saül le furieux/La Famine (tragédies de Jean de la Taille) (ed.) 1968, Concordance des 'Tragiques' d'Agrippa d'Aubigné 1984, Baudin in Australian Waters (ed. with J. Bonnemains and B. Smith) 1988, La Justice de Dieu: "Les Tragiques" d'Agrippa d'Aubigné et la Réforme protestante en France au XVIième siècle 2005. *Leisure interests:* music, photography, bushwalking and church activities. *Address:* 25 Jacka Street, North Balwyn, Vic. 3104, Australia. *Telephone:* (3) 9857-4050. *E-mail:* linecf2@tpg.com.au (home).

FORSYTH, Frederick, CBE; British writer; b. 25 Aug. 1938, Ashford, Kent; m. 1st Carole Cunningham 1973; two s.; m. 2nd Sandy Molloy; ed Tonbridge School, Univ. of Granada, Spain; with RAF 1956–58; reporter, Eastern Daily Press, Norfolk 1958–61; joined Reuters 1961, reporter, Paris 1962–63, Chief of Bureau, E Berlin 1963–64; radio and TV reporter, BBC 1965–66; Asst Diplomatic Corresp., BBC TV 1967–68; freelance journalist, Nigeria and Biafra 1968–69; MWA Edgar Allan Poe Award 1971. *Television appearances include:* Soldiers (narrator) 1985, Frederick Forsyth Presents 1989. *Film appearance:* I Have Never Forgotten You The Life and Legacy of Simon Wiesenthal 2006. *Publications:* fiction: The Day of the Jackal 1971, The Odessa File 1972, The Dogs of War 1974, The Shepherd 1975, The Devil's Alternative 1979, No Comebacks (short stories) 1982, The Fourth Protocol 1984, The Negotiator 1988, The Deceiver 1991, Great Flying Stories (ed.) 1991, The Fist of God 1993, Icon 1996, The Phantom of Manhattan 1999, Quintet 2000, The Veteran and Other Stories 2001, Avenger 2003, The Afghan 2006; non-fiction: The Biafra Story 1969 (revised edn as The Making of an African Legend: The Biafra Story 1977), Emeka 1982, I Remember: Reflections on Fishing in Childhood 1995. *Leisure interests:* sea angling, reading. *Address:* c/o Bantam Books, 62–63 Uxbridge Road, London, W5 5SA, England.

FORSYTH, William (Bill) David; British film director; b. 29 July 1946, Glasgow; one s. one d.; ed Nat. Film School, Beaconsfield; Hon. DLitt (Glasgow) 1984; Hon. DUniv (Stirling) 1989; BAFTA Award for Best Screenplay 1982, for Best Dir 1983. *Films include:* That Sinking Feeling

1979, Gregory's Girl 1980, Andrina (TV film) 1981, Local Hero 1982, Comfort and Joy 1984, Housekeeping 1987, Breaking In 1988, Being Human 1994, Gregory's Two Girls 1999. *Address:* c/o Anthony Jones, United Agents, 12–26 Lexington Street, London, W1F 0LE, England (office). *Telephone:* (20) 3214-0800 (office). *Fax:* (20) 3214-0801 (office). *E-mail:* info@unitedagents.co.uk (office). *Website:* unitedagents.co.uk (office).

FORSYTH OF DRUMLEAN, Baron (Life Peer), cr. 1999, of Drumlean in Stirling; **Rt Hon. Michael Bruce Forsyth,** Kt, PC, MA; British fmr politician and investment banker; *Deputy Chairman, JP Morgan (UK);* b. 16 Sept. 1954, Montrose, Scotland; s. of John Forsyth and Mary Watson; m. Susan Jane Clough 1977; one s. two d.; ed Arbroath High School, St. Andrews Univ.; Minister of State for Health/Educ. (Scotland) 1981–92, Minister of State, Dept of Employment 1992–94, Home Office 1994–95, Sec. of State for Scotland and Lord Keeper of the Great Seal of Scotland 1995–97; Dir Flemings 1997–2000; Vice-Chair. Investment Banking (Europe), JP Morgan 2000–02, Deputy Chair. JP Morgan (UK) 2002–; Parliamentarian of the Year 1996. *Publications:* Reservicing Britain 1980, The Myths of Privatisation 1983. *Leisure interests:* mountaineering, astronomy, gardening, art, fly fishing, photography. *Address:* JP Morgan, 10 Aldermanbury, London, EC2V 7RF (office); c/o House of Lords, London, SW1A 0PN, England. *Telephone:* (20) 7325-6366 (office). *E-mail:* Michael.Forsyth@jpmorgan.com (office). *Website:* www.jpmorgan.com (office).

FORSYTHE, William; American choreographer; b. 1949, New York; ed Jacksonville Univ., Fla, Joffrey Ballet School, NY; joined Stuttgart Ballet 1973, dancer, then choreographer; choreographed works commissioned by cos. including NY City Ballet, San Francisco Ballet, Nat. Ballet of Canada, Royal Ballet, Covent Garden and Nederlands Dans Theater; founder and Dir Ballett Frankfurt 1984–2004, Ballett Frankfurt and TAT 1999–2004; f. The Forsythe Company 2005; f. Forsythe Foundation; Chevalier des Arts et Métiers 1991, Commdr. des Arts et Lettres 1999; Harlekin Preis, Frankfurt 1986, Bessie Award, NY 1988, Deutscher Kritikerpreis 1988, Olivier Award 1992, Evening Standard Award 1999 and numerous other awards. *Ballets include:* Urlicht 1976, Gänge 1983, Artifact 1984, Impressing the Czar 1988, Limb's Theorem 1991, The Loss of Small Detail 1991, Eidos: Telos 1995, Endless House 1999, Kammar/Kammer 2000 (Paris 2002). *Films include:* Berg Ab 1984, Solo 1995, From a Classic Position 1997. *Address:* The Forsythe Company, Bockenheimer Depot, An der Bockenheimer Warte, Carlo-Schmid-Platz 1, 60325 Frankfurt, Germany (office). *E-mail:* info@theforsythecompany.de (office). *Website:* www.theforsythecompany.de (office).

FORT-BRESCIA, Bernardo, BA, MArch, FAIA; American (b. Peruvian) architect; b. 19 Nov. 1951, Lima, Peru; s. of Paul Fort and Rosa Brescia; m. Laurinda Spear 1976; five s. one d.; ed Princeton Univ., Harvard Univ.; co-f. (with Laurinda Spear q.v.) Arquitectonica Int. Corpn 1977–; projects in USA, Europe, S America, Cen. America, Asia and Caribbean; Prof. Univ. of Miami 1975–77; mem. Bd of Dirs New World Symphony, Wolfsonian-FIU Museum; numerous AIA Awards and Honors for Design Excellence; Founder's Award, Salvadori Center 2000. *Publications:* Arquitectonica 1991, numerous articles in specialist and non-specialist journals. *Address:* Arquitectonica International Corporation, 801 Brickell Avenue, Suite 1100, Miami, FL 33131-2517, USA (office). *Telephone:* (305) 372-1812 (office). *Fax:* (305) 372-1175 (office). *E-mail:* bfort@arquitectonica.com (office). *Website:* www.arquitectonica.com (office).

FORTE, Hon. Sir Rocco John Vincent, Kt, MA, FCA; British business executive; *Chairman and CEO, Rocco Forte Hotels;* b. 18 Jan. 1945; s. of Lord Forte; m. Aliai Ricci 1986; one s. two d.; ed Downside and Pembroke Coll., Oxford; Dir of Personnel, Trusthouse Forte 1973–78, Deputy Chief Exec. 1978–82, Jt Chief Exec. 1982–83; Chief Exec. Trusthouse Forte PLC 1983–92; Chair. Forte PLC 1992–96; Chair. and Chief Exec. Rocco Forte Hotels 1996–; mem. Chairs' Cttee Savoy Group 1994–96; fmr Vice-Pres. Commonwealth Games Council for England. *Leisure interest:* triathlon. *Address:* Savannah House, 11 Charles II Street, London, SW1Y 4QU, England (office). *Telephone:* (20) 7321-2626 (office). *Fax:* (20) 7321-2424 (office). *E-mail:* enquiries@rfhotels.com (office). *Website:* www.roccofortehotels.com (office).

FORTEY, Richard Alan, PhD, ScD, FRS; British palaeontologist and writer; *Research Associate, Natural History Museum, London;* b. 15 Feb. 1946, London; s. of Frank Allen Fortey and Margaret Fortey (née Wilshin); m. 1st Bridget Elizabeth Thomas (divorced); one s.; m. 2nd Jacqueline Francis 1977; one. s. two d.; ed Ealing Grammar School for Boys, King's Coll. Cambridge; Research Fellow, then Sr Scientific Officer, Natural History Museum, London 1970–77, Prin. Scientific Officer 1978–86, Sr Prin. Scientific Officer 1986–98, Merit Researcher 1998, currently Research Assoc.; Howley Visiting Prof. Memorial Univ. of Newfoundland 1977–78; Visiting Prof. of Palaeobiology, Univ. of Oxford 2000–; Collier Chair in Public Understanding of Science and Tech., Univ. of Bristol 2002–03; mem. Geological Soc. of London 1972– (Pres. 2007), British Mycological Soc. 1980–; Dr hc (St Andrews) 2007, (Open Univ.) 2007; Natural World Book of the Year Award 1994, Lyell Medal, Geological Soc. of London 1996, Frink Medal Zoological Soc. of London 2001, Lewis Thomas Prize Rockefeller Univ. 2003, Linnean Medal for Zoology 2006, Michael Faraday Prize Royal Soc. 2006, T.N. George Medal, Glasgow Geological Soc. 2007. *Publications:* The Roderick Masters Book of Money Making Schemes (as Roderick Masters) 1981, Fossils: The Key to the Past 1982, The Hidden Landscape 1993, Life: An Unauthorised Biography 1997, Trilobite! 2000, The Earth: An Intimate History 2004, Dry Store Room No. 1: The Secret Life of the Natural History Museum 2008. *Leisure interests:* mycology, humorous writing, cacti. *Address:* Department of Palaeontology, Natural History Museum, Cromwell Road, London, SW7 5BD, England (office). *Telephone:* (20) 7942-5493 (office). *Fax:* (20) 7942-5546 (office). *E-mail:* r.fortey@nhm.ac.uk (office). *Website:* www.nhm.ac.uk/palaeontology (office).

FORTIER, L. Yves, CC, QC, BCL, BLitt; Canadian diplomatist and lawyer; *Chairman, Alcan Incorporated;* b. 11 Sept. 1935, Québec City; s. of François and Louise (Turgeon) Fortier; m. Cynthia Carol Eaton 1959; one s. two d.; ed Univ. of Montreal, McGill Univ. and Univ. of Oxford, UK; called to Bar of Québec 1960; Chair. and Sr Partner, Ogilvy, Renault (law firm), Montreal; Pres. Jr Bar Asscn Montreal 1965–66, Jr Bar Section, Canadian Bar Asscn 1966–67; mem. Gen. Council, Bar of Québec 1966–67; Councillor, Bar of Montreal 1966–67; Pres. London Court of Int. Arbitration; mem. Council, Canadian Section, 1st Comm. of Jurists 1967–87; mem. Canadian Bar Asscn (Pres. Québec br. 1975–76, Nat. Pres. 1982–83); Founding Dir Canadian Bar Asscn Law for the Future Fund; mem. Perm. Court of Arbitration, The Hague, American Arbitration Asscn Panel of Arbitrators and other arbitration insts; Fellow American Coll. of Trial Lawyers (Regent 1992–96); Hon. mem. American Bar Asscn; Dir Canadian Inst. of Advanced Legal Studies, Canadian Law Inst. of the Pacific Rim 1986–88; mem. Int. Trade Advisory Council (ITAC) Canada; Amb. and Perm. Rep. to UN, New York 1988, Pres. UN Security Council 1989, Vice-Pres. UN Gen. Ass. 1990, Advisor to the Sec.-Gen. on territorial dispute between Gabon and Equatorial Guinea 2003–; Dir . Alcan Inc, Montreal 2002–, currently Chair.; Dir Hudson's Bay Co. (also Gov.), Nortel Networks Corpn, Royal Bank of Canada, Nova Chemicals Corpn, and other cos; Gov. McGill Univ. 1970–85; Rhodes Scholar, Oxford Univ. 1958–60, Dir Canadian Asscn of Rhodes Scholars (Pres. 1975–77), Pres. LCIA (fmrly London Court of Int. Arbitration) 1998–2000. *Leisure interests:* skiing, tennis, golf, reading. *Address:* Alcan Inc., 1188 Sherbrooke Street West, Montreal, PQ H3A 3G2 (office); Suite 1100, 1981 McGill College Avenue, Montreal, PQ H3A 3C1 (office); 19 Rosemount Avenue, Westmount, PQ H3Y 3G6, Canada (home). *Telephone:* (514) 848-8000 (Alcan) (office); (514) 847-4747 (office). *Fax:* (514) 848-8115 (Alcan) (office); (514) 286-5474 (office). *Website:* www.alcan.com (office).

FORTIER, Hon. Michael M., PC; Canadian financier, lawyer and politician; m. Michelle Setlakwe; six c.; joined Ogilvy Renault law firm, Montreal 1985–99, managed office in London, UK 1992–96; joined Credit Suisse First Boston 1999, Man. Dir and Sr Advisor and headed Montreal office –2004; Man. Dir (Quebec) TD Securities (subsidiary of TD Bank Financial Group) 2004–06; Pres. Progressive Conservative Party of Canada 1990s, cand. in leadership election 1998, cand. for party in gen. election 2000, mem. Conservative Party of Canada 2003–, Co-Chair. Stephen Harper's nat. leadership campaign 2004, Co-Chair. Conservative nat. elections campaign 2004, 2006; Minister of Public Works and Govt Services 2006–08, of Int. Trade 2008; mem. Senate 2006–. *Address:* Conservative Party of Canada, 130 Albert Street, Suite 1204, Ottawa, ON K1P 5G4, Canada (office). *Telephone:* (613) 755-2000 (office). *Fax:* (613) 755-2001 (office). *Website:* www.conservative.ca (office).

FORTÍN, Mario; Honduran government official and diplomatist; b. 11 Jan. 1954; m. Rosario Duarte de Fortín; four c.; ed Univ. of Chicago, USA; Dir of External Affairs 1978; fmr Amb. to Germany, Perm. Rep. to UN; fmr Minister of Economy and Commerce; Minister of Foreign Affairs 2005–06; est. Foundation for Investment and Devt of Exports (FIDE); Hon. Pres. Consular Asscn; Commdr Order of Bernardo O'Higgins Riquelme, Grand Cross Order of Merit (Chile). *Address:* c/o Ministry of Foreign Affairs, Centro Cívico Gubernamental, Antigua Casa Presidencial, Blvd Kuwait, Contiguo a la Corte Suprema de Justicia, Tegucigalpa, Honduras (office).

FORTOV, Vladimir Yevgenyevich; Russian physicist; *Head of Division of Energetics, Machinery, Mechanics and Control Systems, Russian Academy of Sciences;* b. 23 Jan. 1946, Noginsk, Moscow Region; m.; one d.; ed Moscow Inst. of Physics and Tech.; researcher, Head of Lab., Inst. of Chemical Physics USSR (now Russian) Acad. of Sciences 1971–86; Head of Div., Inst. of High Temperature Physics, USSR Acad. of Sciences 1986–92; Dir Inst. for High Energy Densities, Russian Acad. of Sciences 1992–; Chair. Russian Foundation for Basic Research 1993–97; Deputy Chair., then Chair. State Cttee on (now Ministry of) Science and Tech. of Russian Fed. 1996–98; Corresp. mem. USSR (now Russian) Acad. of Sciences 1987, mem. 1992, Vice-Pres. 1996–2001, Head, Div. for Energetics, Machinery, Mechanics and Control Systems, Russian Acad. of Sciences 2002–; Chair. Tech. Cttee of Judges for the prize 'Novaya generatsiya' (New Generation) 2004–; mem. Presidium Russian Nat. Prize Russkie sozidateli (Russian Creators) 2005–; Corresp. mem. Int. Asscn on Physics and Tech. of High-Pressures; Fellow, US Nat. Acad. of Eng; mem. American Physics Soc., European Acad. of Arts and Sciences, Int. Acad. of Astronautics, Max Plank Soc., Royal Acad. of Eng of GB, Royal Acad. of Eng, Sweden; State Award of Russian Fed., P. Bridgeman Prize for High Pressure Technology, Max Plank Award, A. Einstein Gold Medal UNESCO, Hannes Alfven Prize, EPS, Shock Compression Science Award, APS, Medal of the Pres. of Chechen Repub. for Personal Contrib. to Peace and Co-operation in the Caucasus 2004. *Publications:* numerous works on thermophysics of extremely high temperatures and pressures, physics of gas dynamics and physics of strong shock waves. *Leisure interests:* skiing, sailing. *Address:* Presidium of the Russian Academy of Sciences, Leninski prospekt 32A, 119991 Moscow (office); Institute for High Energy Densities, Izhorskaya str. 13/19, 127412 Moscow, Russia. *Telephone:* (495) 938-18-14 (Acad.) (office); (495) 485-79-88 (Inst.) (office); (495) 975-70-29 (Inst.) (office). *Fax:* (495) 938-52-34 (office). *E-mail:* fortov@ras.ru (office). *Website:* www.ihed.ras.ru.

FORTUÑO, Luis, BSFS, JD; American lawyer and politician; *Governor of Puerto Rico;* b. 31 Oct. 1960, Santurce, Puerto Rico; s. of Luis Fortuño Moscoso and Shirley Burset; m. Lucé Vela 1984; three c.; ed Georgetown Univ., Univ. of Virginia; Exec. Dir Puerto Rico Tourist Co. and Pres. Hotel Devt Corpn 1993–94; Sec., Puerto Rico Dept of Econ. Devt and Commerce 1994–96; Pnr, Correa, Collazo, Herrero, Jiménez and Fortuño (law firm) 1996–2005; mem. US House of Reps for Puerto Rico 2005–09, Vice-Chair. Congressional Hispanic Conf. 2005–07, Chair. 2007–09; Gov. of Puerto Rico 2009–; mem.

New Progressive Party. *Address:* Office of the Governor, La Fortaleza, POB 9020082, San Juan 00902-0082, Puerto Rico (office). *Telephone:* (787) 721-7000 (office). *Fax:* (787) 724-1472 (office). *E-mail:* secretariomail@fortaleza.gobierno.pr (office). *Website:* www.fortaleza.gobierno.pr (office).

FOSHEE, Douglas L., MBA; American oil industry executive; *President, CEO and Director, El Paso Corporation;* b. 1960; ed Southwest Tex. State Univ., Jesse E. Jones Grad. School, Rice Univ., Southwestern Methodist Univ.; began career in commercial banking; various finance and business venture positions, ARCO Int. Oil and Gas Co. –1993; joined Torch Energy Advisers Inc. 1993, held positions successively as Vice-Pres. Special Projects, Exec. Vice-Pres. Acquisitions and Financial Analysis, Pres., COO, CEO 1993–97; Pres., CEO and Chair. Nuevo Energy Co. 1997–2001; Exec. Vice-Pres. and Chief Financial Officer, Halliburton Co. 2001–03, Exec. Vice-Pres. and COO 2003; Pres., CEO and Dir El Paso Corpn 2003–; mem. Bd Dirs Goodwill Industries, Small Steps Nurturing Center; mem. Ind. Petroleum Asscn of America, Nat. Petroleum Council; mem. Council of Overseers, Jesse E. Jones Grad. School, Rice Univ. *Address:* El Paso Corporation, 1001 Louisiana Street, Houston, TX 77002, USA (office). *Telephone:* (713) 420-2600 (office). *Fax:* (713) 420-4417 (office). *Website:* www.elpaso.com (office).

FOSS, Per-Kristian; Norwegian politician; b. 19 July 1950, Oslo; ed Univ. of Oslo; journalist 1971–73; mem. Høyre (Conservative Party), Chair. Høyre Municipal Council 1973–77, Chair. Unge Høyre (Young Conservatives) 1973–77, Chair. Høyre Cttee on Party Program 1981–85, Chair. Høyre Cttee on Cultural Objectives and Strategies 1983–85, Deputy Chair. Høyre Party Parl. Mems' Group 1993–2001, Leader of Høyre 2002–; mem. Storting (Parl.) for Oslo 1977–, mem. Cttee on Energy and Industry 1981–89 (Second Vice-Chair. 1985–89), mem. Standing Cttee on Finance 1989–2001 (Chair. 1989–93, Vice-Chair. 1993–97), mem. Enlarged Foreign Affairs Cttee 1997–2001; Minister of Finance 2001–2005; Ed. of Kontur (periodical) 1979–80; Consultant Norges Rederforbund (Norwegian Shipowners' Asscn) 1980–81; mem. Lillehammer Olympic Organizing Cttee 1994.

FOSSE, Jon, Cand. philol; Norwegian writer, dramatist and poet; b. 29 Sept. 1959, Haugesund; ed Univ. of Bergen; teacher of creative writing, Acad. of Writing, Bergen 1987–93; professional writer 1993–; mem. Norwegian Soc. of Authors; Chevalier, Ordre Nat. du Mérite, Commdr, St Olavs Orden; hon. mem. Norwegian Actors' Soc., Det Norske Samlaget, Norwegian Dramatists' Soc.; Noregs Mållags Prize for Children's Books 1990, Andersson-Rysst Fondet 1992, Prize for Literature in New Norwegian 1993, 2003, Samlags Prize 1994, Ibsen Prize 1996, Sunnmoers Prize 1996, Melsom Prize 1997, Asshehoug Prize 1997, Dobloug Prize 1999, Gyldendal Prize 2000, Nordic Prize for Dramatists 2000, Nestroy Prize 2001, Scandinavian Nat. Theatre Prize 2002, Norwegian Council of Culture Prize of Honour 2003, Norwegian Theatre Prize of Honour (Hedda) 2003, UBU Prize for best foreign play, Italy 2004, Norwegian Prize for Literature of Honour (Brage) 2005, Anders Jahre Prize for Culture 2006, Nordic Prize of The Swedish Acad. 2007, Deutscher Jugendliteraturpreis 2007. *Plays:* Og aldri skal vi skiljast 1994, Namnet 1995, Nokon kjem til å komme 1996, Barnet, Mor og barn, Sonen: Tre skodespel 1997, Natta syng sine songar, Ein sommars dag: To skodespel 1998, Draum om hausten 1999, Besak, Vinter, Ettermiddag. Tre skodespel 2000, Vakkert 2001, Dadsvariasjonar 2002, Jenta i sofaen 2003, Lilla, Royal Nat. Theatre, Suzannah, Norwegian TV (NRK) 2004, Sa ka la, Aarhus Teater 2004, Varmt, Deutsches Theater 2005, Svevn, Nationaltheatret 2005, Rambuku, Det Norske Teatret 2006, Skuggar, Nationaltheatret 2006, Eg er vinden, Nationaltheatret 2007, Desse auga, Rogaland teater 2008. *Publications:* fiction: Raudt, svart 1983, Stengd gitar 1985, Naustet 1989, Flaskesamlaren 1991, Bly og vatn 1992, Melancholia I 1995, Melancholia II 1996; shorter prose: Blod. Steinen er Forteljing 1987, To forteljingar 1993, Prosa frå ein oppvekst. Kortprosa 1994, Eldre kortare prosa 1997, Morgon og kveld 2000, Det er Ales 2004, Andvake 2007; poetry: Engel med vatn i augene 1986, Hundens bevegelsar 1990, Hund og engel 1992, Nye dikt 1997, Ange i vind 2003; essays: Frå telling via showing til writing 1989, Gnostiske essays 1999; also books for children. *Address:* Samlaget, Boks 4672 Sofienberg, 0506 Oslo, Norway (office); Colombine Teaterförlag, Gaffelgränd 1A, 11130 Stockholm, Sweden (office).

FOSSIER, Robert, DèsSc; French historian, academic and writer; *Professor Emeritus of Medieval History, University of Paris, Sorbonne;* b. 4 Sept. 1927, Le Vésinet; s. of the late René Fossier and Marcelle Brillot; m. Lucie Dupont 1949; three s. two d.; ed Ecole des Chartes; Librarian of City of Paris 1949–53; Prof., Lycée de Fontainebleau and Lycée Carnot, Paris 1953–57; Asst, Sorbonne 1957–62; Dir of Studies, then Prof., Univ. of Nancy 1962–71; Prof. of Medieval History, Sorbonne, Paris 1971–93, Prof. Emer. 1993–; Officier des Palmes académiques. *Publications:* La terre et les hommes en Picardie jusqu'à la fin du XIIIe siècle 1968, Histoire sociale de l'occident médiéval 1971, Chartes de coutume en Picardie 1975, Polyptyques et censiers 1978, Le village et la maison au moyen âge 1980, La Picardie au moyen âge 1981, Enfance de l'Europe (Xe–XIIe) 1982, Le moyen âge 1984, Cartulaire: Chronique de S. Georges d'Hesdin, Paysans d'occident (Xe–XIVe) 1984, La Société mediévale 1992, Villages et villageois au moyen âge 1995, The Family 2000, Rural Economy 900–1024 (Vol. 3) 2000, Sources d'histoire économique du Moyen-âge 2000, Islam–Chrétienté occidentale 2000, Le Travail au Moyen-âge 2001, L'Occident médiéval (V-XIIIe) 2006, Ces gens du Moyen-Âge 2007. *Leisure interests:* gardening, mountain-walking. *Address:* Université de Paris 1, 17 rue de la Sorbonne, 75005 Paris (office); 2 rue du Bel Air, 92190 Meudon (home); Le Serre, 84240 La Tour-d'Aigues, France (home).

FOSTER, Brendan, CBE, MBE, BSc; British sports commentator, business executive and fmr athlete; b. 12 Jan. 1948, Hebburn, Co. Durham; s. of Francis Foster and Margaret Foster; m. Susan Margaret Foster 1972; one s. one d.; ed Sussex Univ., Carnegie Coll., Leeds; competed Olympic Games, Munich 1972,

5th in 1,500m; Montreal 1976, won bronze medal in 10,000m, 5th in 5,000m, Moscow 1980, 11th in 10,000m; competed Commonwealth Games, Edinburgh 1970, won bronze medal at 1,500m; Christchurch 1974, won silver medal at 5,000m; Edmonton 1978, won gold medal at 10,000m and bronze medal 5,000m; European Champion at 5,000m 1974 and bronze medallist at 1,500m 1971; has held world record at 3,000m and 2 miles, European record at 10,000m, Olympic record at 5,000m; Dir Recreation, Gateshead 1982; Man. Dir Nike Int. 1982–86, Vice-Pres. Marketing (Worldwide) and Vice-Pres. (Europe) 1986–87; Chair. and Man. Dir Nova Int.; BBC TV Commentator 1980–; Hon. Master of Educ. (Newcastle Univ.); Hon. Fellow Sunderland Polytechnic; Hon. DLitt (Sussex Univ.) 1982; BBC Sports Personality of the Year 1974. *Publications:* Brendan Foster (with Cliff Temple) 1978, Olympic Heroes 1896–1984 1984. *Leisure interests:* sport and running every day. *Address:* Nova International, Newcastle House, Albany Court, Monarch Road, Newcastle upon Tyne, NE4 7YB, England. *Telephone:* (191) 402-0016 (office). *Website:* www.onrunning.com (office).

FOSTER, Brian, OBE, BSc, MA, DPhil, CPhys, FInstP, FRS; British physicist and academic; *Professor of Experimental Physics, University of Oxford;* b. 4 Jan. 1954, Crook, Co. Durham; s. of John and Annie Foster; m. Sabine Margot Foster 1983; two s.; ed Wolsingham Secondary School, Co. Durham, Queen Elizabeth Coll., London Univ., Oxford Univ.; Research Assoc., Rutherford Appleton Lab., Chilton, Oxon. 1978–82; Research Assoc., Dept of Physics, Imperial Coll., London 1982–84; Lecturer, Dept of Physics, Univ. of Bristol 1984–92, Reader 1992–96, Particle Physics and Astronomy Research Council (PPARC) Advanced Fellow 1991–97, Head of Particle Physics Group 1992–2003, Lecturer Fellow 1999–2000, Prof. of Experimental Physics 1996–2003, Prof. Emer. 2003–; Prof. of Experimental Physics, Univ. of Oxford 2003–, also Head of Particle Physics Dept and Professorial Fellow, Balliol Coll.; European Dir Global Design Effort for Int. Linear Collider 2005–; guest lecturer at numerous int. univs; mem. Scientific Council, Deutsches Elektronen Synchrotron (DESY), Hamburg, Germany 1999– (Group Leader, Bristol group on TASSO 1984–90, Group Leader, Bristol group on ZEUS experiment 1985–2003); Chair. Inst. of Physics Nuclear and Particle Physics Div. 1989–93; mem. CERN Large Hadron Collider Cttee, Geneva, Switzerland 1996–99; Acting Dir John Adams Inst. for Accelerator Science 2004–05; mem. many expert cttees including European Cttee for Future Accelerators 1992–96 (Chair. 2002–05, ex officio CERN Council, CERN Scientific Policy Cttee), PPARC Council 2001–06, many PPARC cttees including Science Cttee; Admin. Dir, Oxford May Music; Consultant Ed. for particle physics, Inst. of Physics Publishing 1991–2005, Taylor & Francis Ltd 2005–; mem. Royal Inst. of GB 1979–, BAAS 1993–; Special European Physical Soc. Prize in Particle Physics 1995, Alexander von Humboldt Foundation Research Prize 1999, Max Born Medal and Prize 2003. *Radio:* Einstein's Fiddle, BBC Radio 4 2008, Private Passions, BBC Radio 3 2008. *Publications include:* Topics in High Energy Physics 1988, 40 Years of Particle Physics 1988, Electron-Positron Annihilation Physics 1990. *Leisure interests:* sport, history and politics, music (violin), collecting first edns of books. *Address:* Denys Wilkinson Building, Department of Physics, University of Oxford, Keble Road, Oxford, OX1 3RH (office); 2 Hillview Cottage, Blackford, nr Wedmore, Somerset, BS28 4NL, England (home). *Telephone:* (1865) 273323 (office); (1934) 712699 (home). *Fax:* (1865) 273417 (office). *E-mail:* b.foster1@physics.ox.ac.uk (office). *Website:* www.physics.ox.ac.uk/users/foster (office).

FOSTER, Sir Christopher David, Kt, MA; British economist; b. 30 Oct. 1930, London; s. of George Cecil Foster and Phyllis Joan Foster (née Mappin); m. Kay Sheridan Bullock 1958; two s. three d.; ed Merchant Taylors School and King's Coll., Cambridge; Fellow and Tutor, Jesus Coll., Cambridge 1964–66; Dir-Gen. of Econ. Planning, Ministry of Transport 1966–70; Head, Unit for Research in Urban Econs, LSE 1970–76, Prof. of Urban Studies and Econs 1976–78, Visiting Prof. 1978–86; Gov. Centre for Environmental Studies 1967–70, Dir 1976–78; Visiting Prof. of Econs MIT 1970; Head of Econ. and Public Policy Div. Coopers & Lybrand (fmrly Coopers & Lybrand Assocs., then Coopers & Lybrand Deloitte) 1978–84; Public Sector Practice Leader and Econ. Adviser 1984–86, Dir and Head Econs Practice Div. 1988–, Partner 1988–94, mem. Man. Cttee 1988–90, Adviser to Chair. 1990–92, 1994–99; Special Adviser to Sec. of Transport on Privatization of British Rail 1992–94; mem. Bd Railtrack 1994–2000; Commercial Adviser to Bd of British Telecommunications PLC 1986–88; Chair. RAC (Royal Automobile Club) Foundation 1999–2003; Hon. Fellow Jesus Coll., Cambridge 1992. *Publications:* The Transport Problem 1963, Politics, Finance and the Role of Economics: The Control of Public Enterprise (jtly) 1972, Local Government Finance 1980, Privatization, Public Ownership and the Regulation of Natural Monopoly 1992, The State Under Stress 1996; papers in various econ. and other journals. *Leisure interests:* theatre, reading. *Address:* c/o RAC Foundation for Motoring, 89–91 Pall Mall, London, SW1Y 5HS (office); 6 Holland Park Avenue, London, W11 3QU, England. *Telephone:* (20) 7727-4757. *Fax:* (20) 7229-6581 (home). *E-mail:* cd@foster46.fsnet.co.uk (home).

FOSTER, David Manning, BSc, PhD; Australian writer; b. 15 May 1944, Katoomba; m. 1st Robin Bowers 1964; one s. two d.; m. 2nd Gerda Busch 1975; one s. two d.; ed Univ. of Sydney, Australian Nat. Univ., Univ. of Pennsylvania; professional fiction writer 1973–; The Age Award 1974, Australian Nat. Book Council Award 1981, NSW Premier's Fellowship 1986, Keating Fellowship 1991–94, James Joyce Foundation Award 1996, Miles Franklin Award 1997, Courier Mail Award 1999. *Publications:* novels: The Pure Land 1974, The Empathy Experiment 1977, Moonlite 1981, Plumbum 1983, Dog Rock: A Postal Pastoral 1985, The Adventures of Christian Rosy Cross 1986, Testostero 1987, The Pale Blue Crochet Coathanger Cover 1988, Mates of Mars 1991, The Glade Within the Grove 1996, The Ballad of Erinungarah 1997, In the New Country 1999, The Land Where Stories End

2001, Sons of the Rumour 2009. *Leisure interests:* gardening, bush-walking. *Address:* PO Box 57, Bundanoon, NSW 2578, Australia.

FOSTER, Ian T., PhD; American computer scientist and academic; *Arthur Holly Compton Distinguished Service Professor of Computer Science and Director, Computation Institute, University of Chicago;* Distinguished Fellow and Assoc. Div. Dir, Math. and Computer Science Div., Argonne Nat. Lab., Head of Distributed Systems Lab.; currently Arthur Holly Compton Distinguished Service Prof. of Computer Science, Univ. of Chicago; Dir Computation Inst. (jt project between Univ. of Chicago and Argonne Nat. Lab.) 2006–; co-f. Globus Project 1995; open source strategist, Open Grid Forum and Globus Alliance; co-f. Univa Corpn, Elmhurst, Ill. 2004 (merged with United Devices to form Univa UD 2007); mem. Advisory Bd for IOCOM Communications; Fellow, AAAS 2003, British Computer Soc.; Lovelace Medal, British Computer Soc., Gordon Bell Prize for high-performance computing 2001, named by Network World magazine as one of "the 50 most powerful people in networking" 2004. *Achievements include:* called "the father of the Grid"; research resulted in devt of techniques, tools and algorithms for high-performance distributed computing and parallel computing; led research and devt of software for I-WAY wide-area distributed computing experiment across N America 1995. *Publications:* numerous influential documents on Grid architecture and principles. *Address:* Computation Institute, University of Chicago, 5640 S Ellis Avenue, RI 405, Chicago, IL 60637 (office); Argonne National Laboratory, 9700 South Cass Avenue, Building 221-D156, Argonne, IL 60439, USA (office). *Telephone:* (773) 834-6812 (Chicago) (office); (630) 252-4619 (Argonne) (office). *Fax:* (773) 834-6818 (Chicago) (office). *E-mail:* foster@mcs.anl.gov (office). *Website:* www-fp.mcs.anl.gov/~foster (office); ianfoster.typepad.com.

FOSTER, Jodie (Alicia Christian), BA; American actress, film director and producer; b. 19 Nov. 1962, Los Angeles; d. of Lucius Foster and Evelyn Foster (née Almond); pnr Cydney Bernard; two s.; ed Yale Univ.; acting début in TV programme Mayberry R.F.D. 1968; owner and Chair. EGG Pictures Production Co. 1990–; Hon. DFA (Yale) 1997. *Films include:* Napoleon and Samantha 1972, Kansas City Bomber 1972, One Little Indian 1973, Tom Sawyer 1973, Alice Doesn't Live Here Any More 1975, Taxi Driver 1976, Echoes of a Summer 1976, Bugsy Malone 1976, Freaky Friday 1976, The Little Girl Who Lives Down the Lane 1977, Candleshoe 1977, Foxes 1980, Carny 1980, Hotel New Hampshire 1984, The Blood of Others 1984, Siesta 1986, Five Corners 1986, The Accused (Acad. Award for Best Actress 1989) 1988, Stealing Home 1988, Catchfire 1990, The Silence of the Lambs (Acad. Award for Best Actress 1992) 1990, Little Man Tate (also dir) 1991, Shadows and Fog 1992, Sommersby 1993, Maverick 1994, Nell 1994, Home for the Holidays (dir, co-producer only) 1996, Contact 1997, The Baby Dance (exec. producer only) 1997, Waking the Dead (exec. producer only) 1998, Anna and the King 1999, Panic Room 2001, The Dangerous Lives of Altar Boys (also producer) 2002, Un long dimanche de fiançailles 2004, Flightplan 2005, Inside Man 2006, The Brave One (also producer) 2007, Nim's Island 2008. *Address:* EGG Pictures Production Co., Jerry Lewis Annex, 5555 Melrose Avenue, Los Angeles, CA 90038-3112, USA.

FOSTER, Kent B., BS, MS; American computer distribution executive; *Chairman, Ingram Micro Incorporated;* ed North Carolina State Univ., Univ. of South Carolina; 29 years with GTE Corpn, becoming Dir 1992–99, Vice-Chair. 1993–99, Pres. 1995–99; CEO and Pres. Ingram Micro Inc. 2000–05, Chair. 2000–; mem. Bd of Dirs Campbell Soup Co. Inc., J. C. Penney Co. Inc., New York Life Insurance Co. *Address:* Ingram Micro Incorporated, 1600 East St Andrew Place, Santa Ana, CA 92705-4931, USA (office). *Telephone:* (714) 566-1000 (office). *Fax:* (714) 566-7900 (office). *Website:* www.ingrammicro.com (office).

FOSTER, Lawrence Thomas; American conductor; *Music Director, Gulbenkian Orchestra;* b. 23 Oct. 1941, Los Angeles, Calif.; m. Angela Foster 1972; one d.; studied with Fritz Zweig and Karl Böhm and at Bayreuth Festival and Tanglewood Master Classes; Music Dir Young Musicians Foundation, Los Angeles 1960–64; Conductor San Francisco Ballet 1960–64; Asst Conductor LA Philharmonic Orchestra 1965–68; Chief Guest Conductor Royal Philharmonic Orchestra, London 1969–74; Music Dir Houston Symphony Orchestra 1971–78; Music Dir Orchestre Philharmonique, Monte Carlo 1978–96; Music Dir Duisburg Orchestra, FRG 1982–86; Music Dir Chamber Orchestra of Lausanne 1985; conductor Jerusalem Symphony Orchestra 1990; Music Dir Aspen Music Festival and School 1990–96; Music Dir Orquestra Ciutat de Barcelona 1995–2002, Prin. Guest Conductor 2002–; Artistic Dir Georg Enescu Festival 1998–2001; Music Dir Gulbenkian Orchestra, Lisbon 2002–; Music Dir Orchestre et Opéra Nat. de Montpellier 2009–; Koussevitsky Memorial Conducting Prize, Tanglewood 1966; Pres.'s decoration for services to Romanian music 2003. *Film appearance:* Belle toujours 2006. *Leisure interests:* reading history and biographies, films. *Address:* Harrison Parrott, 5–6 Albion Court, London, W6 0QT, England (office). *Telephone:* (20) 7229-9166 (office). *Fax:* (20) 7221-5042 (office). *E-mail:* info@harrisonparrott.co.uk (office). *Website:* www.harrisonparrott.com (office).

FOSTER, Murphy (Mike) J., Jr, BSc; American business executive and fmr state official; b. 11 July 1930, Shreveport, La; m.; ed La State Univ.; sugar cane farmer, La; founder Bayou Sale, La; Pres. Sterling Sugars Inc.; Senator St Mary/Assumption Parish Dist, La. State Senate 1987, Chair. Commerce Cttee 1991; Gov. of La 1996–2004. *Leisure interests:* hunting, fishing, tennis.

FOSTER, Robert Fitzroy (Roy), FBA; Irish historian, writer and academic; *Carroll Professor of Irish History, Hertford College, University of Oxford;* b. 16 Jan. 1949, Waterford; ed Trinity Coll. Dublin; Prof. of Modern British History, Birkbeck College, London 1989-91; Carroll Prof. of Irish History and Fellow, Hertford Coll., Oxford 1991–; visiting fellowships include St. Anthony's Coll.,

Oxford, Inst. for Advanced Study, Princeton, NJ, Princeton Univ.; Fellow, British Acad. 1989; Hon. DLitt (Aberdeen) 1997, (Queen's, Belfast) 1998, (Trinity Coll. Dublin) 2003, (Nat. Univ. of Ireland) 2004; Hon. Fellow, Birkbeck Coll., Univ. of London 2005. *Publications:* biogs of Charles Stewart Parnell 1976 and Lord Randolph Churchill 1981, Modern Ireland 1600–1972 1988, The Oxford Illustrated History of Ireland 1989, Paddy and Mr Punch 1997, W. B. Yeats: A Life, Vol. I: The Apprentice Mage 1865–1914 2001, The Irish Story: Telling Tales and Making it Up in Ireland 2001 (Christian Gauss Award from Phi Beta Kappa 2003), W. B. Yeats: A Life, Vol. II: The Arch-Poet 1915–1939 2003, Conquering England: the Irish in Victorian London (with Fintan Cullen) 2005, Luck and the Irish 2007. *Address:* Hertford College, Catte Street, Oxford, OX1 3BW, England (office). *Telephone:* (1865) 279400 (office). *E-mail:* roy.foster@hertford.ox.ac.uk (office). *Website:* www.hertford.ox.ac.uk (office).

FOSTER OF THAMES BANK, Baron (Life Peer), cr. 1999 of Reddish in the County of Greater Manchester; **Norman Robert Foster,** Kt, OM, DipArch, MArch, RA, RWA, RIBA; British architect; *Chairman and Founder, Foster + Partners;* b. 1 June 1935, Manchester; s. of Robert Foster and the late Lilian Foster; m. 3rd Elena Ochoa 1996; ed Manchester Univ. School of Architecture and City Planning, Yale Univ. School of Architecture; Urban Renewal and City Planning Consultants work 1962–63; pvt. practice, as "Team 4 Architects" (with Wendy Cheesman, Georgie Wolton, Lord Rogers of Riverside) London 1963–67, Foster Associates (now Foster + Partners), offices Berlin, Singapore 1967–, Chair. Foster + Partners 1967–; collaboration with Buckminster Fuller 1968–83; Consultant Architect to Univ. of E Anglia 1978–87; fmr External Examiner RIBA Visiting Bd of Educ.; fmr mem. Architectural Asscn Council (Vice-Pres. 1974); fmr teacher Univ. of Pa, Architectural Asscn, London, London Polytechnic, Bath Acad. of Arts; FCSD 1975; IBM Fellow, Aspen Design Conf. 1980; Council mem. RCA 1981–; mem. Int. Acad. of Architecture (IAA), European Acad. of Sciences and Arts, American Acad. of Arts and Sciences; mem. Order of French Architects, Akad. der Kunst, Royal Acad. of Fine Arts, Sweden; Hon. FAIA 1980; Royal West of England Academician; Hon. Fellow Royal Acad., Inst. of Structural Engineers, Royal Coll. of Eng, Kent Inst. of Art and Design; Hon. mem. Bund Deutscher Architekten (BDA); Royal Designer for Industry (RDI); Assoc. Acad. Royale de Belgique; Hon. LittD (Univ. of E Anglia) 1980; Hon. DSc (Bath) 1986, (Humberside) 1992, (Valencia) 1992, (Manchester) 1993; Dr hc (Royal Coll. of Art) 1991, (Tech. Univ. Eindhoven) 1996; Hon. DLitt. (Oxford) 1996, (London) 1997; numerous awards including Architectural Design Projects Awards 1964, 1965, 1966, 1969, Financial Times Industrial Architecture Awards 1967, 1974, 1984, RIBA Awards 1969, 1972, 1977, 1978, 1992, 1993, 1997, 1998, 1999; RSA Business and Industry Award 1976, 1991, Int. Design Awards (Brussels) 1976, 1980, R. S. Reynolds Int. Memorial Awards (USA) 1976, 1979, 1986, Structural Steel Awards 1972, 1978, 1984, 1986, 1992, 1999, 2000, Ambrose Congreve Award 1980, Royal Gold Medal for Architecture 1983, Civic Trust Award 1984, 1992, 1995, 1999, 2000, Constructa-European Award Program for Industrial Architecture 1986, Premio Compasso d'Oro Award 1987, Japan Design Foundation Award 1987, PA Innovations Award 1988, Annual Interiors Award (USA) 1988, 1992, 1993, 1994, Kunstpreis Award, Berlin 1989, British Construction Industry (BCI) Award 1989, 1991, 1992, 1993, 1997, 1998, Mies van der Rohe Award, Barcelona 1991, Gold Medal, Acad. Française 1991, Concrete Soc. Award 1992, 1993, 1999, American Inst. of Architects (AIA) Gold Medal 1994, Queen's Award for Export Achievement 1995, AIA Award 1995, 1997, 'Mipim' Man of the Year 1996, 'Building' Construction Personality of the Year 1996, Silver Medal of Chartered Soc. of Designers 1997, Pritzker Prize for Architecture 1999, Visual Arts Award 2000, Praemium Imperiale 2002, British-German Asscn Medal of Honour for Services to Anglo-German Relations 2006, China Friendship Award from Chinese State Admin of Foreign Experts Affairs 2008; German Federal Order of Merit 1999, Officier, Ordre des Arts et des Lettres (France), Order of N Rhine-Westphalia. *Major works include:* Pilot Head Office for IBM, Hampshire 1970, Tech. Park for IBM, Greenford 1975, Willis, Faber and Dumas, Ipswich 1975, Sainsbury Centre for Visual Arts, Norwich 1977, Renault Centre UK 1983, Hong Kong Bank HQ 1986, Third London Airport Terminal Stansted 1991, Century Tower Tokyo 1991, Barcelona Telecommunications Tower 1992, Sackler Galleries, Royal Acad. 1991, Cranfield Univ. Library 1992, Arts Centre, Nîmes 1993, Lycée, Fréjus 1993, Microelectronics Park, Duisburg 1993, Bilbao Metro System 1995, Univ. of Cambridge Faculty of Law 1996, American Air Museum, Duxford 1997, Commerzbank HQ Frankfurt 1997, Chek Lap Kok Airport, Hong Kong 1998, new German Parl. (Reichstag), Berlin 1999, Great Court, British Museum 2000, Al Faisaliah Complex, Riyadh 2000, Research Facility, Stanford Univ. Calif. 2000, Greater London Authority Bldg, London, Millennium Bridge, London, Swiss Re Tower (RIBA Stirling Prize 2004) 2002–03, Millau Viaduct, France 2005, Supreme Court, Singapore, Petronas Univ. Campus, Malaysia, Hearst Headquarters tower, New York 2006, Museum of Fine Arts, Boston, Opera House, Dallas, Smithsonian Inst. Courtyard, Washington DC 2007, Dolder Grand Hotel, Zürich 2008, Beijing Int. Airport Terminal 3, China 2008; work exhibited in Moscow, Antwerp, Barcelona, Berlin, Bilbao, Bordeaux, London, Lyons, Madrid, Milan, Munich, New York, Paris, Tokyo, Valencia, Venice, and Zürich; work in perm. collection of Museum of Modern Art, New York and Centre Georges Pompidou, Paris. *Publications include:* Norman Foster: Buildings and Projects Vols 1, 2, 3, 4, On Foster . . . Foster On 2000 and numerous contribs to the architectural and tech. press. *Leisure interests:* flying, skiing, running. *Address:* Foster + Partners, Riverside Three, 22 Hester Road, London, SW11 4AN, England (home). *Telephone:* (20) 7738-0455 (home). *Fax:* (20) 7738-1107 (home). *E-mail:* enquiries@fosterandpartners.com (office). *Website:* www.fosterandpartners.com (office).

FOTTRELL, Patrick, DSc, MRIA; Irish university administrator; b. 26 Sept. 1933, Youghal, Co. Cork; s. of Matthew Fottrell and Mary (née O'Sullivan) Fottrell; m. Esther Kennedy 1963; two s. two d.; ed Christian Brothers School, Youghal and North Mon Schools, Univ. Coll., Cork, Univ. of Glasgow, UK, Univ. Coll., Galway; Sr Research Officer, Agric. Inst., Johnstown Castle, Wexford 1963–65; lecturer, later Assoc. Prof., Prof. of Biochemistry, Univ. Coll., Galway 1965–; Visiting Prof., Harvard Univ., USA 1972, 1982; Beit Memorial Fellow; EEC Science Writers Award. *Publications:* Perspectives on Coeliac Disease (co-author); more than 100 scientific publs in int. journals on biochemistry. *Leisure interests:* walking, music, soccer. *Address:* University College, Galway (office); Bunowen, Taylorshill, Galway, Ireland (home). *Telephone:* (91) 24411 (office); (91) 21022 (home).

FOTYGA, Anna; Polish politician; b. 12 Jan. 1957, Lębrok; m.; two c.; ed Univ. of Gdańsk; worked in Int. Dept, Nat. Election Comm., NSZZ Trade Union (Solidarity) 1981, Dir 1989–91; mem. Man. Bd, Modem Co. 1987–89; worked at Przekaz publishing house 1992–94; involved in World Bank projects, GPEC Gdańsk 1994–96, Consultant 1996; Vice-Chair. Supreme Supervisory Bd, Social Insurance Inst. (ZUS) 1998–2002; European Integration Adviser to Pres. of Office of Health Insurance Oversight 1999–2001; Int. Affairs Adviser to Prime Minister 2000; Dir Dept of Int. Affairs, Chancellery of the Prime Minister 2001; mem. City Council of Gdańsk 2002, Council Vice-Pres. (Deputy Mayor) responsible for Econ. Affairs and European Integration 2002–04; mem. European Parl. 2004–05, coordinated Union for Europe of the Nations Group in Cttee on Foreign Affairs; Sec. of State, Ministry of Foreign Affairs 2005–06, Minister of Foreign Affairs 2006–07. *Address:* c/o Law and Justice Party, ul. Nowogrodzka 84/86, 02-018 Warsaw Poland (office). *Telephone:* (22) 6215035 (office). *Fax:* (22) 6216767 (office). *E-mail:* biuro@pis.org.pl (office). *Website:* www.pis.org.pl (office).

FOU, Ts'ong; Chinese pianist; *Visiting Professor, International Foundation for Pianists, Como, Italy, and Shanghai Conservatory, China;* b. 10 March 1934; s. of the late Fu Lei; m. 1st Zamira Menuhin 1960 (divorced 1970); one s.; m. 2nd Hijong Hyun 1973 (divorced 1978); m. 3rd Patsy Toh 1987; one s.; ed studied in China with Mario Paci, Warsaw Conservatory with Zbigniew Drzewiecki; debut with Shanghai Municipal Orchestra, playing Beethoven's Emperor Concerto 1951; gave 500 concerts in E. Europe while studying in Poland 1953–58; moved to UK 1958, London debut 1959; solo appearances in Europe, Scandinavia, the Far East, Australia and New Zealand, North and South America; currently Visiting Prof. Int. Foundation for Pianists, Como, Italy and Shanghai Conservatory, China; Dr hc (Hong Kong Univ.); third prize Bucharest Piano Competition 1953, Int. Chopin Competition, Warsaw 1955. *Solo piano CDs:* Bach, Chopin, Debussy, Handel, Mozart, Scarlatti, Schubert and Schumann. *Piano concerto CDs:* Chopin and Mozart. *Leisure interests:* bridge, sport, oriental art. *Address:* 62 Aberdeen Park, London, N5 2BL, England (home). *Telephone:* (20) 7226-9589 (home). *Fax:* (20) 7704-8896 (home). *E-mail:* foutoh@yahoo.co.uk (home).

FOUDA, Yosri; Egyptian journalist; b. 1964; ed American Univ. in Cairo; producer Arabic-language TV Service, BBC, London, UK –1996; reporter, Al Jazeera London Bureau, UK 1996–, currently Bureau Chief, presenter 'Top Secret' TV programme (interviewed April 2002 Khalid Shaikh Mohammed, Chief of Al-Qaeda Mil. Cttee, believed to have masterminded 9/11 US attacks). *Address:* Al-Jazeera International Ltd., 1 Knightsbridge, London SW1X 7XW, England (office). *Website:* www.aljazeera.com (office).

FOURCADE, Jean-Pierre; French politician; b. 18 Oct. 1929, Marmande; s. of Raymond Fourcade and Germaine Fourcade (née Raynal); m. Odile Mion 1958; one s. two d.; ed Coll. de Sorèze, Bordeaux Univ. Faculté de Droit, Inst. des Etudes politiques; student, Ecole Nat. d'Admin. 1952–54; Insp. des Finances 1954–73; Chargé de Mission to Sec. of State for Finance (later Minister of Finance) 1959–61, Conseiller technique 1962, Dir Adjoint du Cabinet 1964–66; Asst Head of Service, Inspection gén. des Finances 1962; Head of Trade Div., Directorate-Gen. of Internal Trade and Prices 1965, Dir-Gen. 1968–70; Asst Dir-Gen. Crédit industriel et commercial 1970, Dir-Gen. 1972–74, Admin. 1973–74; Admin., later Pres. and Dir-Gen. Soc. d'Epargne mobilière 1972–74; Admin. Banque transatlantique 1971–74, Soc. commerciale d'Affrètement et de Combustibles 1972–74; Minister of Econ. and Finance 1974–76, of Supply 1976–77, of Supply and Regional Devt 1977; Mayor of St-Cloud 1971–92, of Boulogne-billancourt 1995–2007; Conseiller-Gén., canton of St-Cloud 1973–89; Conseiller Régional, Ile de France 1976, Vice-Pres. 1982–86, First Vice-Pres. 1986–95; Senator, Hauts de Seine 1977; Pres. Comité des Finances Locales 1980–2004, Comm. des Affaires Sociales du Sénat 1983–99; Pres. Clubs Perspectives et Réalités 1975–82; Vice-Pres. Union pour la Démocratie française (UDF) 1978–86, mem. 1978–; mem. UMP Parl. group 2002–; mem. Admin. Council of RATP 1984–93, Epad 1985–95, SNCF 1993–98; Pres. Conseil de Surveillance de la Caisse Nat. des Allocations Familiales 2002–04; Vice-Pres. Asscn des Maires des Grandes Villes de France 2002–; Pres. Comm. Consultative d'Evaluation des Charges 2005–; Officier, Ordre nat. du Mérite. *Publications:* Et si nous parlions de demain 1979, la Tentation social-démocrate 1985, Remèdes pour l'assurance maladie 1989. *Address:* Mairie, 26 Ave. André Morizet, 92100 Boulogne-Billancourt; Sénat, Palais du Luxembourg, 75291 Paris, cedex 06; 8 Parc de Béarn, 92210 St-Cloud, France (home).

FOURNIER, Guy, OC; Canadian author, screenwriter, producer and broadcasting executive; b. 23 July 1931, Waterloo, Quebec; has written 400 hours of TV drama as well as films, has also produced dramatic films and documentaries; co-wrote, with Wayne Grigsby, script for Trudeau mini-series as well as prequel Trudeau: A Maverick in the Making; mem. Bd of Dirs and Chair. CBC 2005–06 (resgnd). *Film screenplays include:* Y'a toujours moyen de moyenner! (There's Always a Way to Find a Way) 1973, La mer mi-sel 1974, Maria Chapdelaine 1983, Mon amie Max 1994, Histoire de famille 2006. *Television screenplays include:* Les enquêtes Jobidon (series) 1962, Ti-Jean caribou (series) 1963, Bidule de Tarmacadam (series) 1969, Jo Gaillard (series) 1975, Jamais deux sans toi (series) 1977, Rue de l'anse (series) 1983, Manon (series) 1985, L'or et le papier (series) 1990, Coeur à prendre 1994, Jamais deux sans toi (series) 1996, Les parfaits (series) 2001, Trudeau II: Maverick in the Making (mini-series) 2005. *Publications:* has published poems, humorous essays, novels, cookbooks and children's books. *Address:* c/o Canadian Broadcasting Corporation, 181 Queen Street, Ottawa, ON K1P 1K9, Canada.

FOURNIER, Jacques, LenD; French lawyer; b. 5 May 1929, Épinal; s. of Léon Fournier and Ida Rudmann; m. 1st Jacqueline Tazerout (deceased); three s.; m. 2nd Michèle Dubez 1980 (divorced); m. 3rd Noëlle Fréaud-Lenoir 1989 (divorced); ed Inst. for Political Studies, Paris and Nat. School of Admin; Civil Servant, French State Council 1953, Master of Petitions 1960, State Councillor 1978; Legal Adviser, Embassy in Morocco 1961–64; Head of Dept of Social Affairs, Gen. Planning Office 1969–72; Asst Sec.-Gen. to Pres. of France 1981–82; Sec.-Gen. of the Govt 1982–86; Pres. of Admin. Council of Gaz de France 1986–88; Pres. SNCF 1988–94, Centre européen des entreprises publiques 1988–94, Sceta 1989–94, Ciriec-France 1994–; Chair. Carrefour 1992–98; fmr mem. Council of State, renewed mem. 1994–98; mem. Conseil supérieur de la magistrature 1998–2002; Chevalier, Ordre Nat. du Mérite; Commdr, Légion d'honneur. *Publications:* Politique de l'Education 1971, Traité du social, situations, luttes politiques, institutions 1976, Le Pouvoir du social 1979, Le travail gouvernemental 1987, le Train, l'Europe et le service public 1993. *Address:* 19 rue Montorgueil, 75001 Paris, France (home). *E-mail:* jfrnier@easynet.fr (home).

FOURTOU, Jean-René, MA; French business executive; *Chairman of the Supervisory Board, Vivendi;* b. 20 June 1939, Libourne; ed Ecole Polytechnique, Paris, Massachusetts Inst. of Tech., USA; Eng Consultant, Bossard & Michel 1963, mem. Bd of Dirs Bossard Consultants 1972, Chair. and CEO 1977; apptd Chair. and CEO Rhône-Poulenc SA 1986; Vice-Chair. Supervisory Bd AXA (ADR) 1990–, mem. Exec. AXA Millésimes SAS; Vice-Chair. and CEO Aventis 1999–2002, Hon. Chair. and Vice-Chair. Supervisory Bd 2002–; Chair. and CEO Vivendi Universal (now Vivendi) 2002–05, Chair. Supervisory Bd 2005–; Co-Chair. Franco-Moroccan Impetus Group; Chair. Supervisory Bd Canal+ Group; Vice-Chair. ICC –2003, Chair. 2003–05, Hon. Chair. 2005–; mem. Bd Dirs NBC Universal (USA), Cap Gemini, Sanofi Aventis, Nestlé (Switzerland); mem. Supervisory Bd Maroc Telecom; mem. European Round Table of Industrialists (ERT); Co-Founder Entreprise & Cité; Officier, Légion d'honneur, Commdr, Ordre nat. du Mérite; Int. Leadership Award, US Council for Int. Business 2004. *Publications include:* La Passion d'Entreprendre 1985. *Address:* Vivendi, 42 avenue de Friedland, 75380 Paris Cedex 08 (office); International Chamber of Commerce, 38 cours Albert 1er, 75008 Paris, France (office). *Telephone:* 1-71-71-10-00 (Vivendi) (office); 1-49-53-28-28 (ICC) (office). *Fax:* 1-71-71-11-79 (Vivendi) (office); 1-49-53-29-42 (ICC) (office). *E-mail:* info@vivendi.com (office); info@iccwbo.org (office). *Website:* www.vivendi.com (office); www.iccwbo.org (office).

FOWKE, Philip Francis, FRAM; British concert pianist; b. 28 June 1950, Gerrards Cross, Bucks.; s. of Francis H.V. Fowke and Florence L. (née Clutton) Fowke; ed Downside Abbey School; began piano studies with Marjorie Withers 1957; awarded RAM Scholarship to study with Gordon Green 1967; Wigmore Hall debut 1974; UK concerto debut with Royal Liverpool Philharmonic 1975; Royal Festival Hall debut 1977; BBC Promenade Concert debut 1979; US debut 1982; debuts in Denmark, Bulgaria, France, Switzerland, Hong Kong, Belgium and Italy 1983; Austrian debut at Salzburg Mozart week 1984; German debut 1985; New Zealand debut 1994; now appears regularly with all the leading orchestras in UK and gives regular recitals and concerto performances for BBC Radio; Prof. RAM 1984–91, Welsh Coll. of Music and Drama 1994; Head of Keyboard Dept, Trinity Coll. of Music, London 1995–98, Sr Fellow 1998; recordings of Bliss, Chopin, Delius, Finzi, Rachmaninoff and Tchaikovsky piano concertos; Recitalist and Piano Tutor, Dartington Int. Summer School 1996, 1997, 2000; Concerto appearances with the Hallé Orchestra and in USA 1997; 50th Birthday Recital, Wigmore Hall, London 2000; soloist, BBC Proms 2001; mem. London Piano Quartet; Vice-Chair. European Piano Teachers' Asscn (UK) presenter and contrib. to music programmes on BBC Radio and to nat. press; Countess of Munster Musical Trust Award 1972, Nat. Fed. of Music Socs. Award 1973, BBC Piano Competition 1974, Winston Churchill Fellowship 1976 and numerous other awards and prizes. *Recordings include:* Hoddinott Piano Concerto, CD album of film scores 1998. *Publications:* reviews and obituaries in nat. press. *Leisure interests:* architecture, monasticism. *Address:* Patrick Garvey Management, 40 North Parade, York YO30 7AB, England (office). *Telephone:* (1904) 621222 (office). *Fax:* (1723) 330050 (office). *E-mail:* patrick@patrickgarvey.com (office). *Website:* www.patrickgarvey.com (office).

FOWLER, Sir (Edward) Michael Coulson, Kt, MArch, FNZIA, ARIBA; New Zealand architect; b. 19 Dec. 1929, Marton; s. of William Coulson Fowler and Faith Agnes Fowler (née Netherclift); m. Barbara Hamilton Hall 1953; two s. one d.; ed Christ's Coll., Christchurch, Auckland Univ.; with Ove Arup & Partners, London 1954–55; Partner, Gray Young, Morton Calder & Fowler, Wellington 1959; Sr Partner, Calder, Fowler & Styles 1960–89; travelled abroad to study cen. banking systems' security methods; work includes Overseas Terminal, Wellington, Reserve Bank, Wellington, Dalmuir House, Wellington Club, office bldgs, factories, houses, churches; mem. Wellington City Council 1968–74; Chair. NZIA Educ. Cttee 1967–73; Mayor of Wellington 1974–83; Chair. Queen Elizabeth II Arts Council of New Zealand 1983–86; Pres. New Zealand Youth Hostel Asscn 1983–86; architectural consultant 1983–; regular dealer gallery exhbns and sales of paintings; Award of Honour, New Zealand Inst. of Architects 1983, Alfred O. Glasse Award, New Zealand Planning Inst. 1984. *Publications:* Country Houses of New Zealand 1972,

Wellington Sketches: Folios I, II 1973, The Architecture and Planning of Moscow 1980, Eating Houses in Wellington 1980, Wellington-Wellington 1981, Eating Houses of Canterbury 1982, Wellington Celebration 1983, The New Zealand House 1983, Buildings of New Zealanders 1984, Michael Fowler's University of Auckland 1993. *Leisure interests:* sketching, writing, history, politics. *Address:* 1 May Street, Wellington (office); 30 Goring Street, Thorndon, Wellington, New Zealand (home). *Telephone:* (4) 499-9991 (office); (4) 473-0888 (home). *Fax:* (4) 471-0017 (office). *E-mail:* michael.fowler@xtra.co.nz (home).

FOWLER, Rt Hon. (Peter) Norman, Baron (Life Peer), cr. 2001, of Sutton Coldfield in the Co. of West Midlands, PC, MA; British politician; b. 2 Feb. 1938; s. of the late N. F. Fowler and Katherine Fowler; m. 1st Linda Christmas 1968; m. 2nd Fiona Poole 1979; two d.; ed King Edward VI School, Chelmsford, Trinity Hall, Cambridge; Nat. Service Comm., Essex Regt 1956–58; joined The Times 1961, Special Corresp. 1962–66, Home Affairs Corresp. 1966–70; mem. Council, Bow Group 1967–69, Editorial Bd, Crossbow 1962–69; Vice-Chair. N Kensington Conservative Asscn 1967–68; Chair. E Midlands Area, Conservative Political Centre 1970–73; MP for Nottingham S 1970–74, for Sutton Coldfield 1974–2001, mem. Parl. Select Cttee on Race Relations and Immigration 1970–74; Jt Sec. Conservative Parl. Home Affairs Cttee 1971–72, Vice-Chair. 1974; Parl. Pvt. Sec. NI Office 1972–74; Opposition Spokesman on Home Affairs 1974–75; Chief Opposition Spokesman on Social Services 1975–76, on Transport 1976–79; Minister of Transport 1979–81, Sec. of State for Transport 1981, for Social Services 1981–87, for Employment 1987–90; Chair. Conservative Party 1992–94; Opposition Front Bench Spokesman on Environment, Transport and the Regions 1997–98, on Home Affairs 1998–99; mem. House of Lords 2001–, Chair. Select Cttee on Future of BBC 2005–06, Chair. Select Cttee on Communications 2005–; mem. Lloyds 1989–98; Chair. Nat. House Bldg Council 1992–98, Midland Ind. Newspapers 1992–98, Regional Ind. Media (the Yorkshire Post Group) 1998–2002, Numark Ltd 1998–2005, Aggregate Industries 2000–06; mem. Bd Group 4 Security 1990–93, Advisory Council Electra Europe, Development Capital Fund plc; Dir NFC 1990–97; Dir (non-exec.) Holcim Ltd (Switzerland) 2006–09. *Publications:* The Cost of Crime 1973, The Right Track 1977, After the Riots: The Police in Europe 1979, Ministers Decide: A Memoir of the Thatcher Years 1991, A Political Suicide: The Conservatives' Voyage into the Wilderness 2008. *Address:* House of Lords, London, SW1A 0PN, England. *Telephone:* (20) 7219-3525 (office). *E-mail:* fowlern@parliament.uk (office).

FOX, Edward, OBE; British actor; b. 13 April 1937; s. of Robin Fox and Angela Fox; brother of James Fox (q.v.); m. 1st Tracy Pelissier 1958 (divorced 1961); one d.; one s. one d. by Joanna David; ed Ashfold School, Harrow School and Royal Acad. of Dramatic Art; actor since 1957; started in provincial repertory theatre 1958 and has since worked widely in films, stage plays and TV; recipient of several awards for TV performance as Edward VIII in Edward and Mrs Simpson 1978. *Stage appearances include:* Knuckle 1973, The Family Reunion 1979, Anyone for Denis 1981, Quartermaine's Terms 1981, Hamlet 1982, The Dance of Death 1983, Interpreters 1986, The Admirable Crichton 1988, Another Love Story 1990, The Philanthropist 1991, My Fair Lady, Father 1995, A Letter of Resignation 1997, The Chiltern Hundreds 1999, The Browning Version 2000, The Twelve Pound Look 2000. *Films include:* The Go-Between 1971, The Day of the Jackal, A Doll's House 1973, Galileo 1976, A Bridge Too Far, The Duellists, The Cat and the Canary 1977, Force Ten from Navarone 1978, The Mirror Crack'd 1980, Gandhi 1982, Never Say Never Again 1983, Wild Geese, The Bounty 1984, The Shooting Party, Return from the River Kwai 1989, Circles of Deceit (TV) 1989, Prince of Thieves 1990, They Never Slept 1991, A Month by the Lake 1996, Prince Valiant 1997, Nicholas Nickleby 2003. *Television includes:* Daniel Deronda 2002. *Leisure interest:* playing the piano. *Address:* c/o CDA, 19 Sydney Mews, London, SW3 6HL, England.

FOX, Frederick Donald, LVO; milliner; b. 2 April 1931; s. of the late Lesley James Fox and Ruby Mansfield (née Elliott); ed St Joseph's Convent School, Jerilderie, New South Wales, Australia; started millinery business 1962; designer for the Royal Family, granted Royal Warrant to HM The Queen 1974; now consultant to Philip Treacey, London 2002–; private clients; Pres. Millinery Trades Benevolent Asscn; Freeman City of London 1989, Liveryman Worshipful Co. of Feltmakers 1989. *Leisure interests:* gardening, photography. *Address:* Model Hats, 17 Avery Row, London, W1K 4BF, England (office). *Telephone:* (20) 7629-5705 (office). *Fax:* (20) 7629-3048 (office). *E-mail:* frederick@frederick_fox.freeserve.uk (office).

FOX, James; British actor; b. 19 May 1939, London; s. of Robin Fox and Angela Fox (née Worthington); brother of Edward Fox (q.v.) and Robert Fox; m. Mary Elizabeth Fox 1973; four s. one d.; ed Ashfold Prep. School and Harrow School. *Films include:* Mrs Miniver 1952, The Servant 1963, King Rat 1965, Those Magnificent Men in Their Flying Machines 1965, Thoroughly Modern Millie 1966, Isadora 1967, Performance 1969, A Passage to India 1984, Runners 1984, Farewell to the King 1987, Finding Mawbee (video film as the Mighty Quinn) 1988, She's Been Away 1989, The Russia House 1990, Afraid of the Dark 1991, Patriot Games 1991, As You Like It 1992, The Remains of the Day 1993, Elgar's Tenth Muse 1995, Anna Karenina 1997, Mickey Blue Eyes 1998, Jinnah 1998, Up at the Villa 1998, The Golden Bowl 1999, Sexy Beast 2000, The Mystic Masseur 2001, The Prince and Me 2004, The Freediver 2004, Charlie and the Chocolate Factory 2005, Goodbye Mr Snuggles 2006, Mister Lonely 2006. *Plays:* Uncle Vanya 1995. *Television includes:* A Question of Attribution 1991, Gulliver's Travels 1995, The Lost World 2001, The Falklands Play 2002, Cambridge Spies 2003, Colditz 2005, Celebration 2006. *Publication:* Comeback: An Actor's Direction 1983. *Leisure interests:* Russian language and culture. *Address:* c/o ICM, 4-6 Soho Square, London, W1D 3PZ, England (office). *Telephone:* (20) 7432-0800 (office).

FOX, Kerry; New Zealand actress; b. 30 July 1966; m. Jaime Robertson; ed New Zealand Drama School; fmr lighting designer. *Television appearances include:* Mr Wroe's Virgins, A Village Affair, Saigon Baby, The Affair, 40, Footprints in the Snow 2005, Nostradamus 2006, The Shooting of Thomas Hurndall 2008. *Films include:* The Affair 1973, The Decline of Western Civilization 2: The Metal Years 1988, An Angel at My Table (Elvira Notari Best Performance Award) 1991, The Last Days of Chez Nous 1992, Rainbow Warrior 1993, The Last Tattoo 1994, Friends 1994, Shallow Grave 1995, Country Life 1995, The Affair 1995, Saigon Baby 1995, Welcome to Sarajevo 1997, Hanging Garden 1997, Immortality 1998, The Sound of One Hand Clapping 1998, The Wisdom of Crocodiles 1998, The Darkest Light 1998, Fanny and Elvis 1999, To Walk With Lions 1999, The Point Men 2001, Intimacy 2001, Black and White 2002, The Gathering 2002, So Close to Home 2003, Niceland 2004, Rag Tale 2005, The Ferryman 2007, Intervention 2007, He Said 2007, Inconceivable 2008, Storm 2009.

FOX, Liam, MB, ChB; British politician and physician; *Shadow Secretary of State for Defence;* b. 22 Sept. 1961; s. of William Fox and Catherine Young; ed St Bride's High School, E Kilbride, Univ. of Glasgow; civilian army medical officer Royal Army Educ. Corps 1981–91; gen. practitioner, Beaconsfield 1987–91; Div. Surgeon St John's Ambulance 1987–91; contested Roxburgh and Berwickshire 1987; MP for Woodspring 1992–; Parl. Pvt. Sec. to Home Sec. Michael Howard 1993–94, Asst Govt Whip 1994–95, Lord Commr HM Treasury (Sr Govt Whip) 1995–96, Parl. Under-Sec. of State FCO 1996–97, Opposition Front Bench Spokesman on Constitutional Affairs 1997–98, Shadow Sec. for Constitutional Affairs 1998–99, Shadow Sec. of State for Health 1999–2003, Shadow Foreign Sec. 2005, Shadow Defence Sec. 2005–; Co-Chair. Conservative Party 2003–05; mem. Scottish Select Cttee 1992–93; Sec. Conservative Backbench Health Cttee 1992–93; Pres. Glasgow Univ. Conservative Club 1982–83; Nat. Vice-Chair. Scottish Young Conservatives 1983–84; mem. Conservative Political Centre; Sec. Conservative West Country Mems Group. 1992–93. *Publications include:* Making Unionism Positive 1988, Bearing the Standard (contrib.) 1991, contrib. to House of Commons Magazine. *Leisure interests:* tennis, swimming, cinema, theatre. *Address:* House of Commons, London, SW1A 0AA, England. *Telephone:* (20) 7219-4198 (office). *Fax:* (20) 7219-3968 (office); (1275) 790091 (office). *E-mail:* douglasi@parliament.uk (office). *Website:* www.woodspringconservatives.com (office); www.conservatives.com.

FOX, Marye Anne, BS, MS, PhD; American chemist and university chancellor; *Chancellor, University of California, San Diego;* b. 9 Dec. 1947, Canton, Ohio; m. Prof. James K.Whitesell; three s. two step-s.; ed Notre Dame Coll., Cleveland State Univ., Dartmouth Coll.; Postdoctoral Fellow, Univ. of Maryland 1974-76; Asst Prof. of Organic Chem., Univ. of Texas 1976-81, Assoc. Prof. 1981–85, Prof. 1985–86, Rowland Pettit Centennial Prof. 1986–91, Dir Center for Fast Kinetics Research 1986–91, M. June and J. Virgil Waggoner Regents Chair in Chem. 1991–98, Vice-Pres. for Research, Univ. of Texas 1994–98; Chancellor and Distinguished Univ. Prof. of Chem., N Carolina State Univ. 1998–2004; Chancellor Univ. of California, San Diego 2004–; Visiting Scholar, Harvard Univ. 1989, Univ. of Iowa 1993; Professeur Inviteé, Université Pierre et Marie Curie, Paris VI 1992; Visiting Prof., Chem. Research Promotion Center, Nat. Science Council, Taipei, Taiwan 1993; Morris S. Kharasch Visiting Prof., Univ. of Chicago 1997; consultant, Northeastern Ohio Tuberculosis Asscn 1970–71, ACS 1974–76, Texas Air Control Bd 1976–78, Polaroid Corpn 1982–86, Scopas Technology Co., Inc. 1984–86, Tel-Tech Resources 1985–98, VCH Publrs 1988–97, The Scientist (ICI) 1988–91, Coll. of Eng, Continuing Eng Studies, 3M-Austin 1989, Mirrors Project, Lone Star Girl Scout Council 1992; consultant/contrib., McGraw-Hill Encyclopedia of Science and Technology 1992–94; Invited Contrib., News and Views (Nature) 1992; mem. Bd of Dirs Asscn for Advancement of Tech. in Biomedical Sciences 1989–90, Boston Scientific, Inc. (Audit and Strategic Planning Cttee) 2001–, PPD, Inc. 2002–, Red Hat, Inc. 2002–; mem. Camille and Henry Dreyfus Foundation Bd 1990–2002, Nat. Science Bd (Chair. Cttee on Programs and Plans 1993–96, mem. Exec. Cttee 1993–94) 1991–96, Associated Western Univs 1996–98, Council NAS (Exec. Cttee) 1996–99, Environmental Defense Fund (Texas Bd) 1996–98, Oak Ridge Associated Univs 1996–98, Oak Ridge Foundation Bd 1996–98, Nat. Research Council Governing Bd 1997–99, W.R. Grace Cttees (Audit, Exec. Compensation, Nomination and Corp. Responsibilities (Chair.)) 1996–, Kenan Inst. for Eng, Tech., and Science (Chair.) 1998–, Microelectronic Center of N Carolina (Chair. 2001) 1998–, Raleigh Cooperating Colls 1998–, Research Triangle Inst. Bd Govs 1998–2003, Robert A. Welch Foundation Scientific Advisory Bd 1998–, Wake Educational Partnership 1998–, Univ. of Texas-Battelle Man. Bd of Oak Ridge Nat. Lab. (Chair. Science and Tech. Cttee) 1999–, Nat. Inst. for the Environment 2001–, Pres.'s Council of Advisors on Science and Tech. (Chair. Sub-cttee on Infrastructure for the 21st Century 2003) 2001–, Burroughs-Wellcome Fund 2002–, Camille and Henry Dreyfus Foundation 2002, N Carolina Bd of Science and Tech. 2002–, Nat. Asscn of State Univs and Land Grant Colls 2003–, N Carolina Citizens for Business and Industry 2003–; Scientific Advisor, Interdisciplinary Science Programs, David and Lucile Packard Foundation 1998–; Assoc. Ed. Journal of the American Chemical Society 1986–95; Invited Expert Analyst, Chemtracts 1989–96; mem. Editorial Advisory Bd Journal of Organic Chemistry 1984–89, Molecular Structure and Energetics 1985–88, American Chemical Society Symposium Series and Advances in Chemistry 1986–89, CRC Critical Reviews in Surface Chemistry 1988, New Journal of Chemistry 1995–99, The Chemical Intelligencer 1997–2001, Organic Letters 1999; mem. Advisory Bd Heterogeneous Chemistry Reviews 1993–96, Chemical and Engineering News 1994–99, Chemical Reviews 1994–2002, Advanced Oxidation Technologies 1994, Issues in Science and Technology 1996–2002; mem. Int. Advisory Bd Contemporary Concepts in Chemistry 1994–96; mem. Honorary Editorial Bd

Journal of Porphyrins and Phthalocyanines 1994; mem. numerous advisory and scientific bds and review cttees; mem. ACS, Inter-American Photochemical Soc., NAS 1994, American Philosophical Soc. 1996; Foreign Corresp. mem. Royal Acad. of Science and Arts, Barcelona 1996; Fellow, AAAS 1993, American Acad. of Arts and Sciences 1994, American Women in Science 2001; Trustee Univ. of Notre Dame 2002–; Hon. DSc (Notre Dame Coll.) 1994, (Cleveland State Univ.) 1998; Hon. JD (Sandhills Community Coll.) 2000; Hon. DUniv (Univ. of Ulster) 2002; Hon. DHumLitt (Texas A&M Univ.) 2002; Dr hc (Université Pierre et Marie Curie—Paris VI) 2001, (Universidad Nacional de Educacion a Distancia, Madrid) 2003; Honor Scholarship, Notre Dame Coll. 1965–69, Outstanding Freshman Chemist Award, Chemical Rubber Co. 1965, NSF Undergraduate Research Fellow, Illinois Inst. of Tech. 1968, Medal of Midwest Region, Student Affiliates of ACS 1969, Medal of Excellence, American Inst. of Chemists 1969, NSF Grad. Traineeship, Dartmouth Coll. 1971–72, Dartmouth Fellow 1972–73, Goodyear Tire Fellow 1973–74, Postdoctoral Fellow (NSF and RANN), Univ. of Maryland 1974–76, Alfred P. Sloan Research Fellow 1980, Camille and Henry Dreyfus Teacher-Scholar 1980, Distinguished Alumna Award, Notre Dame Coll. 1981, Agnes Fay Morgan Research Award, Iota Sigma Pi Nat. Women's Chem. Honorary Soc. 1984, Citation, Science and Tech., Esquire Magazine: The Best of the New Generation – Men and Women Under Forty Who are Changing America 1984, Selection, UTmost Magazine, Best of the Univ. of Texas Natural Sciences Faculty 1985, Teaching Excellence Award, Univ. of Texas Coll. of Natural Sciences 1986, Hall of Excellence, Ohio Foundation of Ind. Colls 1987, ACS Garvan Medal 1988, Döbereiner Medal, Friedrich Schiller Univ., Jena, GDR 1988, ACS Arthur C. Cope Scholar Award 1989, Medallion for Contribs to Photographic Sciences, Inst. of Chemical Physics, USSR Acad. of Sciences, Moscow 1990, Havinga Medal, Gorleaus Laboratoria der Rijksuniversiteit, Leiden 1991, Outstanding Alumna, Notre Dame Coll. 1992, ACS Research Award (Southwest Region) 1993, Sigma Xi Monie A. Ferst Award 1996, Women of the Year Award, New York Acad. of Sciences 1999, Paul Harris Fellowship, Raleigh Rotary Club 1999, Women Admins in N Carolina Higher Educ. Leadership Award 1999, Citation as Outstanding Woman in Science by the Women's History Cttee of New York Acad. of Science 1999, Woman of Today Award, Pines of Carolina Girls Scout Council 2000, Distinguished Mem. Nat. Soc. of Collegiate Scholars 2001, Hall of Honor, Coll. of Natural Sciences Foundation Advisory Council, Univ. of Texas at Austin 2001, Star Award, Women's Center of Wake Co. 2001, Distinguished Women of N Carolina Award (Educ.) 2001, Nat. Order of Omega 2001, YWCA of Wake Co. Acad. of Women, Science and Tech. 2001, N Carolina Women of Achievement Award, Gen. Fed. of Women's Clubs of N Carolina 2002, designated a Nat. Assoc. of the Nat. Acads 2002, Triangle Business Journal Women in Business Honoree 2003, Business Leader magazine Business Leader of the Year 2003, designated a Wake Co. Woman of Achievement 2003, designated as Woman Extraordinaire, N Carolina Business Leader Magazine 2004, Gov.'s Old North State Award (NC) 2004, Enshrinee in Industrial Hall Wall of Fame, William McKinley Presidential Museum, Stark Co., OH 2005, ACS Parsons Award for Public Service 2005, designated by Metropolitan Magazine as San Diego Metropolitan Mover for 2005, designated as one of 50 San Diegans to Watch in 2005, San Diego of Govt's Indicators of Sustainable Competitiveness Study 2005; numerous named lecturerships. *Publications:* Orbital Symmetry Concepts in Organic Chemistry 1987, Photoinduced Electron Transfer (four vols, co-ed.) 1988, Organic Chemistry (co-author) 1994, Supplemental Problems for Organic Chemistry (co-author) 1995, Instructor's Resource Manual of Tests and Additional Problems to Accompany Organic Chemistry (co-author) 1995, Organic Chemistry (co-author) 1997, Cultivating Academic Careers (co-author) 1998, Containing the Threat from Illegal Bombings (co-author) 1998, Transforming Undergraduate Education in Science, Mathematics, Engineering, and Technology 1999, Evaluating, Rewarding, and Improving Quality Teaching in Science, Mathematics, Engineering, and Technology (co-author) 2007; nearly 30 book chapters, 49 policy papers, three patents and more than 365 scientific papers, mostly on organic photochemistry and electrochemistry. *Address:* Chancellor's Office, University of California San Diego, 9500 Gilman Drive, MC 0005, La Jolla, CA 92093-0005, USA (office). *Telephone:* (858) 534-3135 (office). *Fax:* (858) 534-6523 (office). *E-mail:* chancellor@ucsd.edu (office). *Website:* www-chancellor.ucsd.edu (office).

FOX, Maurice Sanford, PhD, FAAS; American molecular biologist and academic; *Professor Emeritus of Molecular Biology, Massachusetts Institute of Technology;* b. 11 Oct. 1924, New York City; s. of Albert Fox and Ray Fox; m. Sally Cherniavsky 1955 (died 2006); three s.; ed Stuyvesant High School, Queen's Coll. Univ. of Chicago; Instructor, Univ. of Chicago 1951–53; Asst, Rockefeller Univ. 1953–55, Asst Prof. 1955–58, Assoc. Prof. 1958–62; Assoc. Prof., MIT 1962–66, Prof. 1966–79, Lester Wolfe Prof. of Molecular Biology 1979–96, Head, Dept of Biology 1985–89, now Prof. Emer.; mem. Bd Council for a Liveable World 1962–2006; Breast Cancer Task Force 1977–80; mem. NAS Inst. of Medicine, American Acad. of Arts and Sciences, Radiation Effects Research Foundation, Hiroshima 1994–99, Int. Bioethics Cttee, UNESCO 1994–2004; Nuffield Research Fellow 1957. *Publications:* numerous learned papers. *Leisure interest:* ancient history. *Address:* Department of Biology, Massachusetts Institute of Technology, 77 Massachusetts Avenue, Cambridge, MA 02139 (office); 983 Memorial Drive, Cambridge, MA 02138, USA (home). *Telephone:* (617) 253-4728 (office). *E-mail:* msfox@mit.edu (office). *Website:* web.mit.edu/biology (office).

FOX, Michael J.; American actor; b. (Michael Andrew Fox), 9 June 1961, Edmonton, Alberta, Canada; s. of Bill Fox and Phyllis Fox; m. Tracy Pollan 1988; one s. two d.; ed Burnaby Cen. High School, Vancouver, BC, Canada. *TV appearances include:* Leo and Me 1976, Palmerstown USA 1980, Family Ties 1982–89 (Emmy Awards 1987, 1988), Spin City 1996–2000; also Otherwise Engaged (exec. producer) 2002, Hench at Home (writer) 2003. *TV films include:* Letters from Frank 1979, Poison Ivy 1985, High School USA 1985. *Film appearances include:* Midnight Madness 1980, Class of '84 1981, Back to the Future 1985, Teen Wolf 1985, Light of Day 1986, The Secret of My Success 1987, Bright Lights, Big City 1988, Back to the Future II 1989, Back to the Future III 1989, The Hard Way 1991, Doc Hollywood 1991, The Concierge 1993, Give Me a Break 1994, Greedy 1994, The American President 1995, Mars Attacks! 1996, The Frighteners 1996, Stuart Little (voice) 1999, Atlantis: The Lost Empire (voice) 2001, Interstate 60 2002, Stuart Little 2 (voice) 2002. *Address:* c/o Kevin Huvane, CAA, 9830 Wilshire Blvd., Beverly Hills, CA 90212, USA.

FOX, Sir Paul Leonard, Kt, CBE; British business executive; *Chairman, Stepgrade Consultants;* b. 27 Oct. 1925; m. Betty R. Nathan 1948; two s.; ed Bournemouth Grammar School; Parachute Regt 1943; reporter, Kentish Times 1946, The People 1947; scriptwriter, Pathe News 1947; BBC TV scriptwriter 1950; Ed. Sportsview 1953, Panorama 1961; Head, BBC TV Public Affairs Dept 1963, Current Affairs Group 1965; Controller, BBC 1 1967–73; Dir of Programmes, Yorkshire TV 1973–74, Man. Dir Yorkshire TV 1977–89, Dir of Programmes 1973–84; Dir Independent Television News 1977–86, Chair. 1986–89; Man. Dir BBC TV 1988–91; Chair. BBC Enterprises 1988–91, Stepgrades Consultants 1991–; Chair. ITV Network Programme Cttee 1978–80, Council, Independent Television Cos Asscn Ltd 1982–84; mem. Royal Comm. on Criminal Procedure 1978–80; Pres. Royal TV Soc. 1985–92; Dir Channel Four 1985–88, World TV News 1986–88, Thames TV Ltd 1991–95; Chair. Racecourse Asscn Ltd 1993–97, Racecourse Tech. Services 1994–, Disasters Emergency Cttee 1996–99; Dir British Horse Racing Bd 1993–97, Horserace Betting Levy Bd 1993–97, Barnes TV Trust Ltd 1997–; consultant, Oflot 1994–; mem. Cttee Nat. Museum of Photography, Film and TV 1985–95, Cinema and TV Benevolent Fund 1986–92, Pres. 1992–95; Hon. LLD (Leeds) 1984; Hon. DLitt (Bradford) 1991. *Leisure interests:* television, attending race meetings. *Address:* Stepgrades Consultants, 10 Charterhouse Square, London, EC1M 6LQ, England (office).

FOX, Peter Kendrew, MA; British librarian (retd); *Emeritus University Librarian, University of Cambridge;* b. 23 March 1949, Beverley, Yorks.; s. of Thomas Kendrew Fox and Dorothy Wildbore; m. Isobel McConnell 1983; two d.; ed Baines Grammar School, Poulton-le-Fylde, Lancs., King's Coll. London and Univ. of Sheffield; Asst Library Officer, Univ. of Cambridge Library 1973–77, Asst Under-Librarian 1977–78, Under-Librarian 1978–79, Univ. Librarian 1994–2009, now Emer. Librarian; Deputy Librarian, Trinity Coll., Dublin 1979–84, Librarian 1984–94; Fellow, Selwyn Coll., Cambridge 1994–; mem. British Library Project on Teaching and Learning Skills for Librarians 1978–79, Soc. of Coll., Nat. and Univ. Libraries (SCONUL) Advisory Cttee on Information Services 1979–91 (Chair. 1987–91), An Chomhairle Leabharlanna 1982–94, Cttee on Library Co-operation in Ireland 1983–94 (Chair. 1990–91), Nat. Preservation Advisory Cttee British Library 1984–95 (Man. Cttee 1996–2002, Bd 2002–, Chair. Bd 2002–05), Wellcome Trust Library Advisory Cttee 1996–2005, Chair. 2000–05, Consortium of Univ. Research Libraries (Chair. 1997–2000), Lord Chancellor's Advisory Council on Public Records 2001–06, Legal Deposit Advisory Panel (DCMS) 2005–; Assoc. King's College, Library Asscn. *Publications:* Reader Instruction Methods in Academic Libraries 1974, User Education in the Humanities in US Academic Libraries 1979, Trinity College Library Dublin 1982; Ed.: Library User Education – Are New Approaches Needed? 1980, Second (and Third) Int. Conf. on Library User Educ. Proc. 1982 (and 1984), Treasures of the Library – Trinity College Dublin 1986, Commentary Volume: Book of Kells Facsimile 1990, Cambridge University Library: The Great Collections 1998; co-ed. An Leabharlann: The Irish Library 1982–87; contribs to books and journals. *Address:* Selwyn College, Grange Road, Cambridge, CB3 9DQ, England (office).

FOX QUESADA, Vicente; Mexican fmr head of state and business executive; b. 2 July 1942, Mexico City; s. of the late José Luis Fox and of Mercedes Quesada; m. 1st (divorced); two s. two d.; m. 2nd Marta Sahagún 2001; ed Universidad Iberoamericana, Mexico City, Harvard Univ.; worked for Coca Cola Group, first as route supervisor, becoming Regional Pres. for Mexico and Latin America; also worked as farmer and shoemaker; joined Partido Acción Nacional (Nat. Action Party—PAN); Fed. Deputy 1988–; Gov. of Guanajuato 1995–; Pres. of Mexico 2000–Dec. 2006. *Address:* Partido Acción Nacional (PAN), Avda Coyoacán 1546, Col. del Valle, Del. Benito Juárez, 03100 México, DF, Mexico (office). *Telephone:* (55) 5200-4000 (office). *E-mail:* correo@cen.pan.org.mx (office). *Website:* www.pan.org.mx (office).

FOXLEY RIOSECO, Alejandro, MSc, PhD; Chilean politician and economist; b. 26 May 1939, Viña del Mar; s. of Harold Foxley (Chapman) and Carmen Rioseco; m. Gisela Tapia 1963; two c.; ed Univ. of Wisconsin, Harvard Univ. and Catholic Univ., Valparaíso; Dir Global Planning Div., Nat. Planning Office, Govt of Chile 1967–70; Dir Center for Nat. Planning Studies, Catholic Univ. of Chile 1970–76; mem. Exec. Council, Latin-American Social Science Council (CLACSO) 1975–81; mem. Jt Cttee Latin-American Studies, Social Science Research Council, New York 1975–78; founder and Pres. Corpn for Latin-American Econ. Research (CIEPLAN), Santiago 1976–90; Minister of Finance 1990–94, also Gov. World Bank and Inter-American Devt Bank; Pres. Christian Democratic Party (PDC) 1994–96; Senator 1998–2006; Minister of Foreign Affairs 2006–09; Helen Kellogg Prof. of Econs (part-time) and Int. Devt, Univ. of Notre Dame 1982–; Assoc. Ed. Journal of Development Economics 1977–; Visiting Fellow, Univ. of Sussex 1973, Oxford 1975, MIT 1978; Ford Int. Fellow 1963–64, Daugherty Foundation Fellow 1965–66; Ford Foundation Fellow 1970; Co-Pres. Inter-American Dialogue, Wash. 1994–99, now mem. Exec. Cttee; mem. Int. Advisory Bd Journal Latin American Studies; Dr hc (Univ. of Notre Dame) 1991, (Univ. of Wis.) 1993; Orden al Mérito Civil, Rey de Espana 1991, Gran Cruz Orden Nacional Cruzeiro do Sul

(Brazil) 1993, Gran Insignia de Honor (Austria) 1994. *Publications:* Income Distribution in Latin-America 1976, Redistributive Effects of Government Programmes 1979, Estrategia de Desarrollo y Modelos de Planificación, Legados del Monetarismo: Argentina y Chile, Para una Democracia Estable 1985, Chile y su futuro: Un país posible 1989, Chile puede más 1989, numerous articles and working papers. *Address:* c/o Ministry of Foreign Affairs Catedral 1158, Santiago (office); Golfo de Darién 10236, Santiago (Las Condes), Chile (home).

FOXX, Jamie; American actor, comedian and singer; b. (Eric Bishop), 13 Dec. 1967, Terrell, Tex.; one d.; made TV debut in comedy series In Living Color 1991; writer, performer, dir and producer on The Jamie Foxx Show 1996–2001; writer, performer and producer, two songs on Any Given Sunday film soundtrack 1999; Image Award for Best Musical Artist 2006, BET Award for Best Duet/Collaboration (for Gold Digger, with Kanye West) 2006, American Music Award for Favorite Male Soul/R&B Artist 2006. *Films include:* Toys 1992, The Truth About Cats and Dogs 1996, The Great White Hype 1996, Booty Call 1997, The Players Club 1998, Held Up 1999, Any Given Sunday 1999, Bait 2000, Date from Hell 2001, Ali 2001, Shade 2003, Redemption: The Stan Tookie Williams Story 2004, Breakin' All the Rules 2004, Collateral 2004, Ray (Best Actor in a Musical or Comedy, Golden Globe Awards 2005, Best Actor, Screen Actors Guild Awards 2005, Best Actor in a Leading Role, BAFTA Awards 2005, Best Actor, Acad. Awards 2005) 2004, Stealth 2005, Jarhead 2005, Miami Vice 2006, Dreamgirls 2006, The Kingdom 2007. *Television includes:* In Living Colour 1991–94, C-Bear and Jamal (voice) 1996, The Jamie Foxx Show 1996–2001, Jamie Foxx: I Might Need Security (HBO Comedy Special) 2002. *Recording:* Unpredictable (Soul Train Award for Best R&B/Soul Album by a Male Artist 2007) 2005, Intuition 2008. *Address:* The Gersh Agency, 232 North Canon Drive, Beverly Hills, CA 90210, USA (office). *Telephone:* (310) 274-6611 (office). *Website:* www.gershcomedy.com (office).

FRACKOWIAK, Richard S. J., MA, MB, BChir, MD, DSc, FRCP, FMedSci; British neurologist and professor of clinical neuroscience; *Professor of Neurology, University of Lausanne and Centre Hospitalier Universitaire Vaudois (CHUV);* b. 26 March 1950, London; s. of Jozef Frackowiak and Wanda Frackowiak (née Majewska); m. 1st Christine Frackowiak (divorced 2004); one s. two d.; m. 2nd Laura Spinney; ed Latymer Upper School, Peterhouse Coll., Cambridge, Middx Hosp. Medical School; MRC Clinical Scientist 1989–94; Asst Dir MRC Cyclotron Unit; Prof. of Cognitive Neurology, Univ. Coll., London 1994–, Dean Inst. of Neurology 1998–2002; Dir of Leopold Muller Functional Imaging Lab. 1994–2002; Chair. Wellcome Dept of Cognitive Neurology 1994–2002; Prin. Clinical Research Fellow and programme grant holder, Wellcome Trust 1994–2004; Vice-Provost Univ. Coll., London 2002–09; Prof. of Neurology and Chief of Service, Centre Hospitalier Universitaire Vaudois (CHUV), Univ. of Lausanne, Switzerland 2009–; Dir Departement d'Etudes Cognitives, Ecole Normale Superieure, Paris 2005–09; Adjunct Prof., Cornell Univ. Medical School 1992–; Visiting Prof., Univ. Catholique de Louvain, Yale Medical School, Beth Israel Boston, La Sapienza; Hon. Dir, Neuroimaging Unit, Fondazione Santa Lucia, Rome; Scientific Adviser, Dir-Gen. Inst. Nat. de la Santé et Recherche Médicale, France; fmr MRC Training Fellow; Hon. mem. American Neurological Asscn, Royal Belgian Acad. de Medicine, French Acad. de Medicine, etc.; Hon. MD (Liège); Ipsen Prize, Feldberg Prize, Zulch Prize. *Publications include:* Human Brain Function 1997, Brain Mapping: The Disorders 2000, numerous papers in scientific journals. *Leisure interests:* reading, travel, motorcycling. *Address:* CHUV, Service de neurologie, 46 rue du Bugnon, 1011 Lausanne, WC1N 3AR, Switzerland (office). *Telephone:* (21) 314-1220 (office); (21) 711-1005 (home). *E-mail:* richard.frackowiak@gmail.com (office). *Website:* www.fil.ion.ucl.ac.uk (office).

FRADKOV, Mikhail Yefimovich; Russian politician; *Director, Federal Foreign Intelligence Service;* b. 1 Sept. 1950, Kuibyshev (now Samara) Oblast; m. Yelena; two c.; ed Moscow Inst. of Machines and Tools, USSR Acad. of Foreign Trade; on staff, office of Counsellor on econ. affairs USSR Embassy to India 1973–75; on staff Foreign Trade Agency Tyazhpromeksport, USSR State Cttee on Econ. Relations 1975–84; Deputy, First Deputy Dir of Dept USSR State Cttee on Econ. Relations 1985–91; Deputy Perm. Rep. of Russian Fed. to GATT 1991–92; Sr Adviser Perm. Mission of Russian Fed. to UN; Deputy, First Deputy Minister of External Econ. Relations 1993; Interim Acting Minister of External Econ. Relations 1997; Minister of External Econ. Relations and Trade 1997–98; Chair. Bd of Dirs Ingosstrakh 1998–99, Dir-Gen. 1999; Minister of Trade 1999–2000; First Deputy Sec. Security Council of Russia 2000–01; Head Fed. Service of Tax Police 2001–03; Plenipotentary Rep. to EU 2003–04; apptd Special Rep. of the Pres. of the Russian Fed. on the Devt of Relations with the EU June 2003; Chair. of the Govt (Prime Minister) of Russian Fed. 2004–07 (resgnd); Dir Fed. Foreign Intelligence Service (SVR) of Russian Fed. 2007–. *Address:* Federal Foreign Intelligence Service, 101000 Moscow, Glavpochtamt, a/ya 958, Russia (office). *Telephone:* (499) 245-33-68 (office). *Fax:* (499) 255-25-29 (office). *E-mail:* svr@gov.ru (office). *Website:* svr.gov.ru (office).

FRAGA IRIBARNE, Manuel; Spanish politician, writer and diplomatist; b. 23 Nov. 1922, Villalba, Lugo; m. María del Carmen Estévez 1948 (died 1996); two s. three d.; ed Santiago and Madrid Univs; Attorney of the Spanish Parl. 1945; Diplomatic Service 1947–; Prof. of Political Law, Valencia Univ. 1948; Prof. Theory of State and Constitutional Law, Madrid Univ. 1953; Gen. Sec. Inst. of Hispanic Culture 1951; Gen. Sec. Nat. Educ. Ministry 1955; Dir Inst. of Political Studies 1961; Minister of Information and Tourism 1962–69; also Sec.-Gen. of Cabinet 1967–69; Amb. to UK 1973–75; Minister of the Interior and Deputy Premier for Internal Affairs 1975–76; f. Alianza Popular (now Partido Popular) 1976, Leader 1979–86, 1989–90; mem. European Parl. 1987–89; Pres. Govt of Galicia 1990–; mem. Cttee for Defence of Christian Civilization, Union of Family Orgs; Pres. Delegación Española de Comité de las Regiones 1998, Comisión Arco Atlántico, Grupo Intercomisiones 'America Latina' de la CRFM 1998; Gran Cruz Orden de Isabel La Católica, Gran Cruz del Mérito Civil, Gran Cruz Orden de San Raimundo de Peñafort, Gran Cruz Orden del Mérito Militar, del Mérito Naval; Dr hc from 12 Spanish and foreign univs. *Publications:* More than 90 books on political, constitutional and social subjects. *Leisure interests:* hunting, fishing. *Address:* Xunta de Galicia, Edificio San Caetano, No. 1 Santiago de Compostela; Palacio de Rajoy, Plaza del Obradoiro, Santiago de Compostela, Spain. *Telephone:* (81) 541215 (San Caetano); (81) 544915 (Palacio de Rajoy). *Fax:* (81) 541219. *E-mail:* presid@xunta.es.

FRAGA NETO, Armínio, PhD; Brazilian banker; *Member, International Council, J.P. Morgan Chase & Company;* b. 20 July 1957, Rio de Janeiro; m.; two c.; ed Pontificia Univ. Católica do Rio de Janeiro, Princeton Univ.; trainee, Atlantica-Companhia de Seguros Boavista 1976–77, Banco do Estado do Rio de Janeiro 1979–80, Int. Finance Div., Fed. Reserve Bd, Washington, DC 1984; Chief Economist and Operations Man. Banco de Investimentos Garantia 1985–88; Vice-Pres. Salomon Brothers, New York 1988–91; consultant IBRD 1988–89; Dir responsible for Int. Affairs, Banco Cen. do Brasil 1991–92, Gov. 1999–2002; Founding Pnr, Gavea Investimentos, Rio de Janeiro 2003–; mem. Int. Council, J.P. Morgan Chase & Co. 2004–; Man. Dir Soros Fund Man., New York 1993–99; Prof., Grad. School in Econs, Fundação Getúlio Vargas 1985–88, 1999–; Visiting Asst Prof., Finance Dept, Wharton School, Pa Univ. 1988–89; Adjunct Prof. of Int. Affairs, Columbia Univ., New York 1993–99; mem. Bd Pro-Natura USA 1993–99; mem. Council on Foreign Relations, Princeton Univ. Center for Econ. Policy Studies 1993–; Banco Boavista Award. *Publications:* numerous articles on banking and econs. *Address:* Fundação Getulio Vargas, Praia de Botafogo 190, 10º andar, 22253-900, Rio de Janeiro, RJ, Brazil (office). *Telephone:* (21) 255-95860 (office). *Fax:* (21) 255-24898 (office). *E-mail:* arminio@fgv.br (office). *Website:* gaveainvestimentos@virusbusters.com.br (office); www.fgv.br (office); www.gaveainvestimentos.com.br (office).

FRAKER, Ford M., BA; American business executive and diplomatist; *Ambassador to Saudi Arabia;* ed Harvard Coll.; Asst Rep., Chemical Bank, Beirut 1974, then Vice Pres. and Regional Man., Bahrain; Div. Head Middle East, Saudi Int. Bank (JP Morgan affiliate), London 1979, then Div. Head of Gen. Banking, Credit, and Client Devt and Marketing, also Chair. Credit Policy Cttee and mem. Man. Cttee; f. Fraker & Co., London 1991; Man. Dir MeesPierson Investment Finance Ltd (UK 1993–96; Co-Founder and Chair. Trinity Group Ltd (pvt. investment banking firm), London 1996–2007; consultant to Intercontinental Real Estate Corpn, Boston –2007; Amb. to Saudi Arabia 2007–. *Address:* American Embassy, POB 94309, Riyadh 11693, Saudi Arabia (office). *Telephone:* (1) 488-3800 (office). *Fax:* (1) 488-7360 (office). *E-mail:* usisriyadh@yahoo.com (office). *Website:* riyadh.usembassy.gov (office).

FRAME, Ronald William Sutherland, MA, MLitt; British author; b. 23 May 1953, Glasgow, Scotland; s. of Alexander D. Frame and Isobel D. Frame (née Sutherland); ed The High School of Glasgow, Univ. of Glasgow, Jesus Coll. Oxford; full-time author 1981–; many recent Scottish-set short stories published in UK, N America and Australia; regular weekly 'Carnbeg' short story in The Herald (Scotland) 2008, 'Carnbeg Days' in The Scotsman (Scotland) 2008–09, regular contrib. Scottish Review of Books (Sunday Herald); Betty Trask Prize (jt first recipient) 1984, Samuel Beckett Prize 1986, TV Industries' Panel's Most Promising Writer New to TV Award 1986, Saltire Scottish Book of the Year 2000, American Library Asscn's Barbara Gittings Honor Prize for Fiction 2003. *Publications:* Winter Journey 1984, Watching Mrs. Gordon 1985, A Long Weekend with Marcel Proust 1986, Sandmouth People 1987, Paris (TV play) 1987, A Woman of Judah 1987, Penelope's Hat 1989, Bluette 1990, Underwood and After 1991, Walking My Mistress in Deauville 1992, The Sun on the Wall 1994, The Lantern Bearers 1999, Permanent Violet 2002, Time in Carnbeg 2004. *TV screenplays:* Paris 1985, Out of Time 1987, Ghost City 1994, A Modern Man 1996, M R James: Four Ghost Stories for Christmas (adaptation) 2000, Darien: Disaster in Paradise 2003, Cromwell 2003, The Two Loves of Anthony Trollope (script contrib.) 2004. *Radio scripts include:* Winter Journey 1985, Twister 1986, Rendezvous 1987, Cara 1989, A Woman of Judah 1991, The Lantern Bearers 1997, The Hydro (serial) 1997–99, Havisham 1998, Maestro 1999, Pharos 2000, Don't Look Now (adaptation) 2001, Sunday at Sant' Agata 2001, Greyfriars 2002, The Servant (adaptation) 2005, The Razor's Edge (adaptation) 2005, A Tiger for Malgudi (adaptation) 2006, The Blue Room (adaptation) 2007, The Shell House 2008, Blue Wonder 2008, Monsieur Monde Vanishes (adaptation) 2009. *Leisure interests:* swimming, walking. *Address:* Blake Friedmann Ltd, 122 Arlington Road, London, NW1 7HP, England (office). *Telephone:* (20) 7284-0408 (office). *Fax:* (20) 7284-0442 (office). *E-mail:* info@blakefriedmann.co.uk (office). *Website:* www.blakefriedmann.co.uk (office).

FRAMPTON, Kenneth, A.A.Dip., ARIBA,; British architect and academic; *Ware Professor of Architecture, Graduate School of Architecture, Planning and Preservation, Columbia University;* ed Architectural Asscn, London; Tech. Ed. Architectural Design (magazine) 1962–65; emigrated to USA 1964; Faculty mem., School of Architecture, Princeton Univ. 1964–72; Faculty mem., Dept of Architecture, Columbia Univ. 1972–, Chair. Div. of Architecture 1986–89, Dir Postgraduate Program in History and Theory of Architecture 1993–, also Ware Prof. of Architecture; Faculty mem., RCA, London 1974–77; Visiting Prof. at numerous schools of architecture including Berlage Inst., Amsterdam, ETH, Switzerland, Chinese Univ. of Hong Kong, Univ. della Svizzera Italiana, Mendrisio, Switzerland; mem. jury Alvar Aalto Medal Cttee 1988; Pres. EEC Jury, Mies van der Rohe Foundation, Barcelona;

presented Raoul Wallenberg Lecture 1999; Fellow Graham Foundation 1969–72; Loeb Fellow Harvard Univ. Grad. School of Design 1972; Guggenheim Fellow 1975; Fellow Inst. for Architecture and Urban Studies, New York; Fellow Wissenschaftskolleg, Berlin 1986, American Acad. of Arts and Sciences 1993; Dr hc (Royal Inst. of Tech., Stockholm) 1991, (Univ. of Waterloo) 1995, (Calif. Coll. of Arts and Crafts) 1999; AIA Nat. Honors Award 1985, Acad. d'Architecture Gold Medal 1987, AIA New York Chapter Award of Merit 1988, ASCA Topaz Award 1990, President's Medal, Architectural League of New York 2007, Architectural Award, American Acad. of Arts and Letters 2008. *Design work includes:* Duplex apartment building, London 1962–65, Low-Rise High Density, Brownsville, Brooklyn USA 1972–75. *Publications include:* Modern Architecture: A Critical History 1980, 2008, Modern Architecture and the Critical Present 1993, American Masterworks 1995, Studies in Tectonic Culture 1995, Latin American Architecture: Six Voices (co-author) 2002, Le Corbusier 2002, Labor, Work and Architecture 2002, Evolution of 20th Century Architecture: A Synoptic Account 2007. *Address:* Graduate School of Architecture, Planning and Preservation, Columbia University, 1172 Amsterdam Avenue, New York, NY 10027, USA (office). *Telephone:* (212) 854-3414 (office). *E-mail:* Kf7@columbia.edu (office). *Website:* www.arch.columbia.edu (office).

FRANÇA, José-Augusto, DèsLitt et Sc, DHist; Portuguese writer, art historian and academic; *Professor Emeritus, Department of Art History, University of Lisbon;* b. 16 Nov. 1922, Tomar; s. of José M. França and Carmen R. França; m. 2nd Marie-Thérèse Mandroux; one d. (by previous m.); ed Lisbon Univ., Ecole des Hautes Etudes and Univ. of Paris; travels in Africa, Europe, Americas and Asia 1945–; Ed. Lisbon literary review Unicornio 1951–56, Co-Ed. Cadernos de Poesia 1951–53; Founder-Dir Galeria de Marco, Lisbon 1952–54; art critic 1946–; film critic 1948–; lexicographical publr 1948–58; lived in Paris 1959–63; Ed. Pintura & Não 1969–70; Ed. Colóquio Artes 1970–96; Prof. Cultural History and History of Art, Dir Dept of Art History, New Univ. of Lisbon 1974–92, Prof. Emer. 1992–, Dir elect Faculty of Social Sciences 1982; Dir Fondation C. Gulbenkian, Centre Culturel Portugais, Paris 1983–89; Visiting Prof. Univ. of Paris III 1985–89; Vice-Pres. Int. Asscn of Art Critics 1970–73, Pres. 1985–87, Hon. Pres. 1987–; Vice-Pres. Acad. Européenne de Sciences, Arts et Lettres Paris 1985–2000, Hon. Pres. 2000–; City Councillor, Lisbon 1974–75; mem. of City Ass. Lisbon 1990–93; Pres. Inst. Cultura Portuguesa 1976–80, World Heritage Cttee, UNESCO 1999–2005, J-A F's art collection Museu of Tomar 2004; mem. Int. Asscn of Art Critics, Int. Cttee of Art History, PEN Club, Soc. Européenne de Culture, Soc. de l'Histoire de l'Art français, Acad. Nacional de Belas Artes (Pres. 1977–80), Acad. das Ciencias de Lisboa, Acad. Européenne de Sciences, Arts et Lettres, World Acad. of Arts and Science, Acad. Nat. Sciences, Arts et Lettres de Bordeaux, Ateneo Veneto, Real Acad. Bellas Artes San Fernando (Spain); Officier Ordre nat. du Mérite, Chevalier Ordre des Arts et des Lettres, Commdr Ordem Rio Branco (Brazil), Grand Cross Order of Public Instruction, Grand Cross Ordem Infante Dom Henrique, Officer Ordem Santiago; Medal of Honour (Lisbon). *Publications:* Natureza Morta (novel) 1949, Azazel (play) 1957, Despedida Breve (short stories) 1958; essays: Charles Chaplin—the Self-Made Myth 1952, Amadeo de Souza-Cardoso 1957, Situação da Pintura Ocidental 1959, Da Pintura Portuguesa 1960, Dez Anos de Cinema 1960, Une ville des lumières: La Lisbonne de Pombal 1963, A Arte em Portugal no Século XIX 1967, Oito Ensaios sobre Arte Contemporânea 1967, Le romantisme au Portugal 1972, Almada, o Português sem Mestre 1972, A Arte na Sociedade Portuguesa no Século XX 1972, Antonio Carneiro 1973, A Arte em Portugal no século XX 1974, Zé Povinho 1975, Manolo Millares 1977, Lisboa: Urbanismo e Arquitectura, O Retrato na Arte Portuguesa, Rafael Bordalo Pinheiro, o Português tal e qual 1980, Malhoa & Columbano, Historia da Arte Occidental 1780–1980 1987, Os Anos 20 em Portugal 1992, Bosch ou le visionnaire intégral, Thomar revisited 1994, Lisboa 1898, (In) definições de Cultura 1997, Memorias para o Ano 2000 2000, Monte Olivete, minha aldeia 2001, Buridan (novel) 2002, Regra de Três (novel), Cem Cenas, quadros e contos (short stories) 2003, A Bela Angevina (novel), Historia da Arte em Portugal 1750–2000 2004, José e os outros (novel), Exercícios de Passamento (short stories) 2005, Ricardo Coraçao de Leão (novel) 2007, Lisboa: história física e moral 2008. *Leisure interests:* travel and detective stories. *Address:* Rua Escola Politécnica 49/4 1250-069 Lisbon, Portugal (home); 8 route de Beauvau, 49140 Jarzé, France (home). *Telephone:* (21) 3462028 (Lisbon) (home); (2) 41-95-40-04 (Jarzé) (home). *Fax:* (2) 41-95-40-04 (Jarzé) (home).

FRANCESCHI, Patrice, PhD; French writer, sailor and aviator; *Honorary President, Société des explorateurs Français;* b. 18 Dec. 1954, Toulon; ed Sorbonne, Paris, Aix-Marseille Univ.; explorer and humanitarian activist; sponsored by UNESCO to promote dialogue between different cultures; journeys in Guyana 1974, Congo 1975, the Amazon 1976, Burundi, Tanzania, Uganda, and Egypt 1978, Viet-nam 1979, New Guinea 1989, SE Asia 1999–2000; descended the Nile on foot 1978; first world tour in ultra-light motorized vessel 1984–97; world exploration tour with tall ship "La Boudeuse" 2004–07; founding mem. and Pres. Solidarités aid agency, has engaged in numerous humanitarian missions in Thailand 1980, Romania 1989–90, Kurdistan 1991–92, Sarajevo 1992, Rwanda 1996, Afghanistan 1979–99, Bosnia-Herzegovina 1997; Coordinator French Governmental Aid in Somalia 1992–93; currently Hon. Pres. Société des explorateurs français; Chevalier de la Légion d'honneur; Medal Acad. de la Marine 1980, Lauréat de l'Acad. Française 1981, Gold Medal Acad. des sports 1987. *Television:* 18 documentary films about exploration of New Guinea, Amazon, Nagaland, Pacific, SE Asia etc. *Publications include:* Au Congo jusqu'au cou 1977, Terre farrouche 1977, L'exode vietnamien 1979, Ils ont choisi la liberté 1981, Guerre en Afghanistan 1984, Un capitane sans importance 1987, La folle équipée 1987, Qui a bu l'eau du Nil 1989, Raid papou 1990, Chasseurs d'horizons 1991, Quelque chose qui prend les hommes 1992, Tout l'or du fleuve 1995, De l'esprit d'Aventure (co-writer J-C Guilbert, G. Chaliand) 2003, La Boudeuse en Amazonie (illustrator N. Clérice) 2005, La Grande Aventure de La Boudeuse 2008, Le chemin de la mer 2009. *Leisure interests:* literature, philosophy, science, exploration. *Address:* Société des explorateurs Français, 184 Boulevard Saint-Germain, Paris 75006, France (office). *Telephone:* 1-45-49-03-51 (office). *E-mail:* navire@la-boudeuse.org (office). *Website:* www.la-boudeuse.org (office).

FRANCHET, Yves Georges; French international public servant; b. 4 March 1939, Paris; m. Marie Bernard Robillard; two s.; ed Ecole polytechnique, Paris, Université Paris I, Ecole nationale de la statistique et de l'admin économique de Paris; Dir Statistics Office, UDEAC, Brazzaville, Congo 1964–68; mem. Govt econ. planning staff 1968–69; economist, World Bank, Washington, DC 1969–74; Head of Planning, Co-operation Div., Inst. Nat. de la Statistique et des Etudes Economiques (INSEE) 1974–77; Dir Ecole Nat. de la statistique et de l'admin économique (ENSAE) 1977–80; Deputy Dir European Office of World Bank, Paris 1980–83; Vice-Pres. IDB, Washington, DC 1983–87; Dir-Gen. Statistical Office of the European Communities (EUROSTAT) 1987–2003; Chevalier Légion d'honneur, Commdr Order of Merit (Niger); Dr hc (Bucharest). *Address:* c/o Statistical Office of the European Communities (Eurostat), Bâtiment Jean Monnet, rue Alcide de Gasperi, 2920 Luxembourg, Luxembourg (office); 7 rue J. P. Brasseur, 1258 Luxembourg, Luxembourg (home). *Telephone:* 43-01-33-10-7 (office). *Fax:* 43-01-33-01-5 (office).

FRANCIONI, Reto; Swiss business executive; *CEO, Deutsche Börse AG;* b. 18 Aug. 1955, Zürich; m.; two s.; ed Univ. of Zürich; with UBS 1981–85, Credit Suisse 1985–88; Deputy CEO of Man., Asscn Tripartite Bourses 1988–92; Dir, Corp. Finance Div., Hofmann-La Roche 1992–93; mem. Exec. Bd, Deutsche Börse AG 1993–2000, Deputy CEO 1999–2005, CEO 2005–; Co-CEO and Spokesman, Consors 2000–02; Pres. and Chair. SWX Swiss Exchange 2002–05. *Publications:* Equity Markets in Action (co-author) 2004, The Equity Trader Course (co-author) 2006. *Address:* Deutsche Börse AG, Neue Boersenstrasse 1, 60487 Frankfurt, Germany (office). *Telephone:* (69) 21112000 (office). *Fax:* (69) 21112001 (office). *E-mail:* reto.francioni@deutsche-boerse.com (office). *Website:* deutsche-boerse.com (office).

FRANCIS, Julian W., BSc, MBA; Bahamian central banker; *Co-Chairman and CEO, Grand Bahama Port Authority;* m.; two s.; ed New York Univ., USA; Accounting Officer and Credit Officer, SFE Banking Corpn, Nassau 1969–72, Asst Vice-Pres. Credit Dept 1976–79; worked for Barclays Bank, Nassau and Eleuthera; with Banque de la Soc. Financière Européenne, Paris, France 1980–92, positions include Asst Man. for Business Devt in Latin America, Deputy Man. for Assets Man., Man. of Assets Trading Dept, Cen. Man. for Corp. Finance, Jt Gen. Man. and mem. Man. Cttee; Deputy Gov. and mem. Bd Dirs Cen. Bank of the Bahamas 1993–97, Gov. 1997–2005; Co-Chair. and CEO Grand Bahama Port Authority 2005–; Vice-Chair. Securities Bd; Chair. The Bridge Authority; Bahamian jt negotiator on Competition Policy, Free Trade of the Americas negotiations 1997–; fmr Vice-Chair. Securities Market Task Force. *Leisure interests:* reading, fishing, tennis. *Address:* Grand Bahama Port Authority, POB F-42666, Pioneer's Way & East Mall, Freeport, Grand Bahama, The Bahamas (office). *Telephone:* 352-6611 (office). *Fax:* 352-6184 (office). *Website:* www.gbpa.com (office).

FRANCIS, Richard (Dick) Stanley, CBE, FRSL; British writer; b. 31 Oct. 1920, Tenby, S Wales; s. of George V. Francis and Catherine M. Francis; m. Mary M. Brenchley 1947 (died 2000); two s.; fighter and bomber pilot, RAF 1940–46; amateur steeplechase jockey (Nat. Hunt racing) 1946–48; professional steeplechase jockey 1948–57; champion steeplechase jockey 1953–54; racing columnist, Sunday Express 1957–73; author and novelist 1957–; Hon. DHumLitt (Tufts Univ., Mass., USA) 1991; Cartier Diamond Dagger Award for life's work 1990, named Grand Master by Mystery Writers of America 1996, three Edgar Awards. *Publications:* fiction: Dead Cert 1962, Nerve 1964, For Kicks (CWA Silver Dagger Award 1966) 1965, Odds Against (Sid Halley series) 1965, Flying Finish 1966, Blood Sport 1967, Forfeit (Edgar Allan Poe Award 1970) 1968, Enquiry 1969, Rat Race 1970, Bonecrack 1971, Smokescreen 1972, Slayride 1973, Knockdown 1974, High Stakes 1975, In the Frame 1976, Risk 1977, Trial Run 1978, Whip Hand (Sid Halley series) (Edgar Allan Poe Award 1980, CWA Gold Dagger Award 1980) 1979, Reflex 1980, Twice Shy 1981, Banker 1982, The Danger 1983, Proof 1984, Break In (Kit Fielding series) 1985, Bolt (Kit Fielding series) 1986, Hot Money 1987, The Edge 1988, Straight 1989, Great Racing Stories (co-ed.) 1989, Longshot 1990, Comeback 1991, Driving Force 1992, Decider 1993, Wild Horses 1994, Come to Grief (Sid Halley series) (Edgar Allan Poe Award 1996) 1995, To The Hilt 1996, 10lb Penalty 1997, Field of Thirteen 1998, Second Wind 1999, Shattered 2000, Under Orders 2006, Dead Heat (with Felix Francis) 2007, Silks (with Felix Francis) 2008; non-fiction: The Sport of Queens (autobiog.) 1957, Lester (biog. of Lester Piggott) 1986. *Leisure interests:* attending race meetings world-wide, travel, boating, living in the W Indies. *Address:* c/o John Johnson, Johnson & Alcock Ltd, Clerkenwell House, 45–47 Clerkenwell Green, London, EC1R 0HT, England (office).

FRANCISCI DI BASCHI, Marco, DIur; Italian diplomatist; b. 3 Feb. 1920, Angleur, Belgium; s. of Francesco Francisci and Berthe Berlemont; m. Franca Angelini 1974; three c.; ed Rome Univ.; entered diplomatic service 1948; Sec., Washington Embassy 1950–51; mem. Perm. Del. to UN, New York 1951–55; Consul, Klagenfurt, Austria 1955–58; Dir Int. Orgs Branch, Gen. Econ. Affairs Directorate, Foreign Ministry 1958–75; Amb. to People's Repub. of China 1975–80; Amb. and Perm. Rep. to OECD, Paris 1980–83, Amb. and Perm. Rep. to FAO, Rome 1983–85; Pres. Italy–China Asscn 1985; mem. and Counsellor ISMEO (Inst. for the Middle and Far East) 1985–. *Address:* Via Cesalpino 10, 00161 Rome, Italy. *Telephone:* (06) 44231857.

FRANCK, Edouard; Central African Republic politician; *President, Supreme Court;* fmrly Minister in charge of Cabinet Secr.; Prime Minister of the Cen. African Repub. 1991–93; Pres. Supreme Court 1995–. *Address:* Cour Suprême, BP 926, Bangui, Central African Republic (office). *Telephone:* 61-41-33 (office).

FRANCO, Itamar Augusto Cantiero; Brazilian politician and diplomatist; b. 28 June 1930, Juiz de Fora, Minas Gerais; s. of Augusto Cesar Stiebler Franco and Itália Cautiero Franco; two d.; ed univ. studies in civil and electronic eng, Minas Gerais; Mayor of Juiz de Fora, Minas Gerais 1967–71, 1973–74; Senator of the Repub. 1974, 1982; Pres. Parl. Tech. Cttees on Econ. and Finance 1983–84; Vice-Pres. of Brazil 1989–92; Acting Pres. of Brazil Oct.–Dec. 1992, Pres. Dec. 1992–94; Amb. to Portugal 1995–96; Amb. to OAS 1996–98; Gov. of Minas Gerais (PMDB) 1998–2003; Amb. to Italy 2003–05. *Publications:* books on anthropology, history, nuclear energy and political issues. *Address:* c/o Ministry of Foreign Affairs, Palácio do Hamaraty, Esplanada dos Ministérios, 70170 Brasília, Brazil.

FRANCO ESTADELLA, Antonio; Spanish journalist; *Editor, El Periódico de Catalunya (Grupo Zeta);* b. 21 Jan. 1947, Barcelona; s. of Alfonso Franco and Lolita Estadella; m. Marie-Hélène Bigatá; one s. one d. Ed. Sports Section Diario Barcelona 1970, Ed.-in-Chief 1973, Asst Dir 1975; Dir Siete Días (TV programme) 1977; f. El Periódico de Catalunya 1977, Ed. 1987–, Ed.-in-Chief 1987–2006; Jt Ed. El País 1982; Asst Ed., Grupo Zeta 2006; Ed. Espai Public (TV programme, BTV) 2007; Creu de Sant Jordi (Catalonian order); for journalism: Premio Ortega y Gasset, Premio Godó, Premio Luca de Tena, Premio Ciutat de Barcelona, Premio Antonio Asensio. *Leisure interests:* literature, music, sports. *Address:* El Periódico de Catalunya, Consell de Cent 425–427, 08009 Barcelona (office); Grupo Zeta, Bailen 84, 08009 Barcelona, Spain. *Telephone:* (93) 2655353 (office); (93) 4848208. *Fax:* (93) 4846517 (office). *E-mail:* afranco@elperiodico.com (office). *Website:* www.elperiodico.es (office).

FRANCO GOMEZ, Julio César, PhD; Paraguayan politician and doctor; b. 1952; ed Nat. Univ. of Cordoba, Argentina, Asunción Univ.; Senator 1998; Pres. of the Comm. for Public Health, Social Security and Drug Control 1999; Vice-Pres. of Paraguay 2000–03. *Address:* Congreso Nacional, Asunción, Paraguay (office).

FRANCO GÓMEZ, Luis Federico, DrMed; Paraguayan surgeon and politician; *Vice-President;* b. 23 July 1962, Asunción; m. Emilia Alfaro Patricia de Franco; four c.; ed Nat. Univ. of Asunción; Head of Interns and Residents, 1CCM Univ. Hosp. de Clínicas, Asunción 1990–91, also Chief of Emergency, Instructor in Medicial Semiology 1991–92; Chief of Nat. Guard Hosp. MSP and BS, 1994–96, also Chief Resident of Internal Medicine and Chief of Cardiology; Town Councillor Fernando de la Mora 1991–96, also becoming Pres. of Legislation and Pres. of Health, Hygiene and Social Services, Mayor, Fernando de la Mora 1996–2001; mem. Partido Liberal Radical Auténtico, Dir 2002–; Gov. Cen. Prov. 2003–08; Vice-Pres. of Paraguay 2008–; mem. Paraguayan Soc. of Internal Medicine. *Address:* Partido Liberal Radical Auténtico, Azara y General Santos 2486, Asunción, Paraguay (office). *Telephone:* (21) 20-1337 (office). *Fax:* (21) 20-4869 (office). *E-mail:* plra-prensa@mmail.com.py (office). *Website:* www.presidencia.gov.py/elvicepresidente.htm (office).

FRANÇOIS-PONCET, Jean André, PhD; French diplomatist and politician; b. 8 Dec. 1928, Paris; s. of André François-Poncet and Jacqueline Dilais; m. Marie-Thérèse de Mitry 1959; two s. one d.; ed Wesleyan Univ., Fletcher School of Law and Diplomacy at Tufts Univ., Paris Law School, Nat. School of Public Admin., Paris and Stanford Univ. Grad. School of Business; joined Ministry of Foreign Affairs 1955; worked in office of Sec. of State 1956–58; Sec.-Gen. of Del. to Negotiations for Treaties for EEC and EURATOM 1956–57; Head of European Insts section in Ministry 1958–61; Prof., Institut d'Etudes Politiques de Paris 1960–; Head of Assistance and Co-operation Mission in Morocco 1961–63; in charge of African Affairs in Ministry 1963–68; Counsellor, Embassy in Iran 1968–70; Chair. of Bd, Pres. and CEO, Etablissements J. J. Carnaud & Forges 1971–75; Sec. of State for Foreign Affairs Jan.–July 1976; Sec.-Gen. to Presidency of French Repub. 1976–78; Minister of Foreign Affairs 1978–81; mem. Conseil Général, Lot-et-Garonne 1967–, Pres. 1978–94, 1998–2004; Senator for Lot-et-Garonne 1983–; Dir FMC Corpn 1982–1999; Reporter, Figaro 1984–; Chair. Cttee Senate; Chevalier, Légion d'honneur, Ordre nat. du Mérite. *Publication:* The Economic Policy of Western Germany 1970. *Address:* Senate, Palais du Luxembourg, 75291 Paris Cedex 06 (office); Conseil Général du Lot-et-Garonne, cité Saint-Jacques, 47922 Agen Cedex 09 (office); 53 rue de Varenne, 75007 Paris, France (home). *Telephone:* 1-42-34-20-37 (office). *E-mail:* j.francois-poncet@senat.fr (office). *Website:* www.senat.fr/senfic/francois_poncet_jean83033q.html (office).

FRANCON, Nathalie; French business executive; *CEO, Azzaro;* fmr exec. with Chanel; COO Christian Lacroix –2007; CEO Azzaro 2007–. *Address:* Genex International, 33 avenue Montaigne, Bât. 4 – 4ème étage, 75008 Paris, France (office). *Telephone:* 1-40-70-04-08 (office). *Fax:* 1-40-70-04-18 (office). *E-mail:* info@azzaroparis.com (office). *Website:* www.azzaroparis.com (office); www.azzaronow.com (office).

FRANGIALLI, Francesco; French international organization official; *Secretary-General, World Tourism Organization;* b. 23 Jan. 1947, Paris; m. Leila Niiranen; two s. one d.; ed Université de Paris, Institut d'Études Politiques de Paris, École Nationale d'Admin (ENA); Lecturer, Institut d'Études Politiques de Paris 1972–89; extensive background in public admin; Dir Tourism Industry, Govt ministry responsible for tourism 1986–90; Perm. Rep. to World Tourism Org. 1986–89, Deputy Sec.-Gen. 1990–96, Sec.-Gen. ad interim 1996–97, Sec.-Gen. 1998–, led the org.'s conversion to a specialized agency of the UN 2003. *Publications:* La France dans le tourisme mondial 1991,

Tourisme et loisirs – Une question sociale (co-author), published in Observations on International Tourism 1997–2000, and in International Tourism: The Great Turning Point 2001–2003; numerous articles, speeches and papers. *Address:* World Tourism Organization, Capitán Haya 42, 28020 Madrid, Spain (office). *Telephone:* (91) 567-81-00 (office). *Fax:* (91) 571-37-33 (office). *E-mail:* omt@unwto.org (office). *Website:* www.unwto.org (office).

FRÄNGSMYR, Tore, DPhil; Swedish historian and academic; *Professor of History of Science, Uppsala University;* b. 8 July 1938, Skelleftea; s. of Johan Frängsmyr and Linnea Frängsmyr (née Lindberg); m. Birgitta Thunholm 1970; two s. two d.; ed Uppsala Univ.; Assoc. Prof., Uppsala Univ. 1969, Prof. of History of Science 1982–; Prof. of Tech. and Social Change, Linköping Univ. 1981–82; Dir Center for History of Science, Royal Swedish Acad. of Sciences, Stockholm 1988–; Ed. Les Prix Nobel 1988–; Sec.-Gen. Int. Union of History of Science 1989–93; Fellow, Royal Swedish Acad. of Sciences, Royal Acad. of Eng Sciences, Academia Europaea, American Philosophical Soc. *Publications include:* Linnaeus, the Man and His Work 1984, Science in Sweden; The Royal Swedish Acad. of Sciences 1739–1989 1989, The Quantifying Spirit in the Eighteenth Century (co-ed.) 1990, Solomon's House Revisited: The Organization and Institutionalization of Science 1990, Enlightenment Science in the Romantic Era: The Chemistry of Berzelius and its Cultural Setting (co-ed.) 1992, A la recherche des lumières 1999. *Address:* Avd. för vetenskapshistoria, Uppsala University, Box 629, 751 26 Uppsala, Sweden (office). *Telephone:* (18) 471-15-79 (office). *E-mail:* Tore.Frangsmyr@idehist.uu.se (office). *Website:* www.vethist.idehist.uu.se (office).

FRANGULYAN, Georgy; Russian sculptor; b. 29 May 1945, Tbilisi, Georgia; m. Yelena Maximova; four c.; ed Moscow Stroganov Higher School of the Arts; Grekov medal 1979, Sign of Hon. 1986, Silver Medal of Russian Acad. of Fine Arts 1996, Gold Medal of Russian Acad. of Fine Arts 1996; Diploma of Russian Acad. of Fine Arts 1999; Grand Prix Int. Competition of Plastic Arts, Hungary 1982, Grand Prix Int. Competition of Sculpture, Poznań, Poland 1987, Jury Prize at the Int. Competition of Sculpture, Ravenna, Italy 1988. *Address:* Zemledelchesky per. 9 bldg. 1, Moscow 119121, Russia (home). *Telephone:* (495) 248-24-67 (home).

FRANK, Charles Raphael, Jr, PhD; American banker, economist and business executive; b. 15 May 1937, Pittsburgh., Pa; s. of Charles Raphael Frank and Lucille Frank (née Briscoe); m. 1st Susan Patricia Buckman (divorced 1976); one s. one d.; m. 2nd Eleanor Sebastian 1976; two s.; one step s. one step d.; ed Rensselaer Polytechnic Inst. and Princeton Univ.; Sr Research Fellow, East African Inst. for Social Research, Makerere Univ. Coll., Kampala 1963–65; Asst Prof. of Econs, Yale Univ. 1965–67; Assoc. Prof. of Econs and Int. Affairs, Princeton Univ. 1967–70, Prof. 1970–74; Assoc. Dir Research Programme on Econ. Devt, Woodrow Wilson School 1967–70, Dir 1970–74; Sr Fellow, Brookings Inst. 1972–74; mem. Policy Planning staff and Chief Economist, US Dept of State 1974–77, Deputy Asst Sec. of State for Econ. and Social Affairs 1977–78; Vice-Pres. Salomon Bros, Inc. 1978–87; Pres. Frank & Co., Inc. 1987–88; Vice-Pres. and Man. Dir for Structured Finance GE Capital Corpn, Stamford, Conn. 1988–97; First Vice-Pres. EBRD 1997–2001; currently Adviser Sabre Capital, RAO UES; Chair. Baneasa Investments, SA; mem. Bd of Dirs Central European Media Enterprises Group 2001–, Romanian-American Enterprise Fund; mem. Council on Foreign Relations. *Publications:* The Sugar Industry in East Africa 1965, Production Theory and Indivisible Commodities 1969, Economic Accounting and Development Planning (with Brian Van Arkadie) 1969, Debt and the Terms of Aid 1970, Statistics and Econometrics 1971, American Jobs and Trade with the Developing Countries 1973, Foreign Exchange Regimes and Economic Development: The Case of South Korea 1975, Foreign Trade and Domestic Adjustment 1976, Income Distribution and Economic Growth in the Less Developed Countries (jtly) 1977. *Address:* c/o Board of Directors, Central European Media Enterprises Group, 8th Floor, Aldwych House, 71-91 Aldwych, London, WC2B 4HN (office); Flat 5, 70–72 Cadogan Square, London, SW1X 0EA, England (home).

FRANK, Mary E., MD, FAAFP; American physician and academic; b. New Jersey; ed Fairleigh Dickinson Univ., Teaneck, NJ, Penn State Univ., Hershey, Pa; residency and teaching fellowship, Medical Univ. of S Carolina; joined a family practice, Charleston, Calif. 1977; in full-time practice 1977–; fmr Residency Program Dir, Sutter Hosp., Santa Rosa, Calif.; fmr Clinical Instructor of Family, Community and Preventive Medicine, Stanford Univ., Calif.; fmr Facility Medical Dir, Primary Care Assocs, Rohnert Park; currently Assoc. Clinical Prof. of Ambulatory and Community Medicine, Univ. of Calif., San Francisco; mem. American Acad. of Family Physicians (AAFP) 1973–, served as Chair. Comm. on Legislation and Govt Affairs, Cttee on Women, liaison to Carnegie Foundation Conf. on Healthy Youth for the 21st Century, American Coll. of Obstetricians and Gynaecologists Cttee on Adolescent Health, Rep. to Nat. Quality Forum, Nat. Conf. of State Legislatures, Pres. Calif. Acad. of Family Physicians, mem. Bd of Dirs AAFP 2000–03, Pres. (first woman) 2003–05, Chair. 2005–06; mem. Bd of Dirs Comm. on Office Lab. Accreditation (COLA); Vice-Chair. Council on Scientific Affairs, Calif. Medical Asscn; mem. Sonoma Co. Medical Asscn; volunteer, Special Olympics 1994–; regular speaker, Nat. Youth Leadership Forum; nominated Local Legend, American Medical Women's Asscn. *Leisure interests:* photography, reading mystery novels, hiking. *Address:* c/o American Academy of Family Physicians, 11400 Tomahawk Creek Parkway, Leawood, KS 66211-2672 (office); PO Box 11210, Shawnee Mission, KS 66207-1210, USA (office).

FRANK, Sergey Ottovich; Russian politician; *General Director, Sovkomflot;* b. 13 Aug. 1960, Novosibirsk; m.; one s.; ed Far East Higher Marine School of Eng, Far East State Univ., Higher School of Commerce, Ministry of Foreign Econ. Relations of Russian Fed.; Sec., Comsomol Cttee, later Deputy Head, Far East Higher Marine School; on staff, Far East Marine Navigation Agency

1989–93, Deputy Dir-Gen. 1993–95; Deputy Head, Dept of Marine Transport, Ministry of Transport of Russian Fed. 1995–96; First Deputy Minister of Transport of Russian Fed. 1997–98, Minister 1998–2004, First Deputy Minister of Transport and Communications 2004; Chair. Aeroflot 1999–; Gen. Dir Sovkomflot 2004–. *Address:* Sovcomflot, 6 Gasheka str., 125047 Moscow, Russia (office). *Telephone:* (495) 626-1434 (office). *Fax:* (495) 626-1850 (office). *E-mail:* moscow@sovcomflot.ru (office). *Website:* www.sovcomflot.ru (office).

FRANKEL, Max, MA; American journalist; b. 3 April 1930, Gera, Germany; s. of Jacob A. Frankel and Mary (Katz) Frankel; m. 1st. Tobia Brown 1956 (died 1987); two s. one d.; m. 2nd Joyce Purnick 1988; ed Columbia Univ., New York; mem. staff, The New York Times 1952, Chief Washington Corresp. 1968–72, Sunday Ed. 1973–76, Editorial Pages Ed. 1977–86, Exec. Ed. 1986–94, 1994–95, also columnist New York Times magazine 1995–2000; Pulitzer Prize for Int. Reporting 1973. *Publication:* The Time of My Life and My Life with the Times 1999, High Noon in the Cold War: Kennedy, Khrushchev and the Cuban Missile Crisis 2004. *Address:* c/o The New York Times Co., 15 West 67th Street, New York, NY 10023-6226, USA.

FRANKEN, Alan (Al) Stuart; American comedian, author, radio host and politician; b. 21 May 1951, New York, NY; m. Franni Franken; one s. one d.; ed Harvard Univ.; performed stand-up comedy and stage shows with pnr Tom Davis at Harvard Univ. in early 1970s; Franken and Davis signed by Lorne Michaels for TV show Saturday Night Live, New York 1975–80, 1985–95; wrote several unproduced screenplays; political satirist at Democratic Nat. Convention, Atlanta, Ga 1988; co-anchored Comedy Central's election coverage 1992, 1996; wrote and starred in Lateline (NBC) 1998–99; has given speeches to hundreds of corpns, univs and other orgs and has twice been keynote speaker at White House Correspondents' Dinner for Pres. Clinton, Nat. Press Club, USO tours, DNC dinners and commencement speaker at Harvard Univ. 2002; Host, The Al Franken Show (Air America Radio) 2004–07; Fellow, Harvard Univ. Kennedy School of Govt (Shorenstein Center on the Press, Politics and Public Policy); US Senator from Minn. 2009–; mem. Democratic-Farmer-Labor Party; five Emmy Awards (four writing and one producing). *Films:* Tunnel Vision 1976, Trading Places 1983, One More Saturday Night (also writer) 1986, When a Man Loves a Woman (also writer and exec. producer) 1994, Stuart Saves His Family (also writer) 1995, The Definite Maybe 1997, Harvard Man (as himself) 2000. *Television:* writer: The Paul Simon Special 1977, Saturday Night Live (series) 1975–80, 1985–95, The Coneheads 1983, Franken and Davis at Stockton State 1984, Best of John Belushi 1985, Best of Dan Aykroyd 1986, Saturday Night Live Goes Commercial 1991, Politically Incorrect (series) 1996, The 67th Annual Academy Awards 1995, Lateline (series) 1998, Saturday Night Live: Presidential Bash 2000; producer: Saturday Night Live 1985–95, Saturday Night Live Goes Commercial 1991, Lateline (Exec. Producer series, NBC) 1998, Saturday Night Live: Presidential Bash (Consulting Producer, NBC) 2000. *Publications:* I'm Good Enough, I'm Smart Enough and Doggone It, People Like Me 1992, Rush Limbaugh is a Big Fat Idiot (Grammy Award for audio version) 1996, A Father and Son Learn From Newt's Mistakes 1997, Why Not Me? – The Making and Unmaking of the Al Franken Presidency 1999, Franken Sense 1999, Home-Fried Franken 2000, Block That Rush 2000, Is George W. Bush Dumb? 2000, Oh, The Things I Know: A Guide to Success, Or, Failing That, Happiness 2002, Norm and the Other 1 Percent 2003, Lies and the Lying Liars Who Tell Them: A Fair and Balanced Look at the Right (Grammy Award for audio version) 2003, The Truth (With Jokes) 2005; contributed news commentary to Newsweek, The Nation Rolling Stone and other publications. *Address:* Office of Senator Alan S. Franken, United States Senate, Washington, DC 20510, USA. *Telephone:* (202) 224-3121. *Website:* www.alfranken.com (office).

FRANKEN, Hendrik (Hans), PhD; Dutch professor of jurisprudence and information law; *Member, Senate (Eerste Kamer);* b. 17 Sept. 1936, Haarlem; s. of Albert J. Franken and Catherine G. Weijland; m. 1st Boudewine D. M. Bonebakker 1966 (divorced 1993); two s. one d.; m. 2nd Ingrid L. E. Sanders 1995; ed Univ. of Leiden, Sorbonne, Paris, Univ. of Amsterdam; Sec., Mil. Tribunal 1960; Asst Prosecutor, Dist Court, Rotterdam 1964; mem. Rotterdam Bar 1967; judge 1969; Prof. of Jurisprudence, Erasmus Univ., Rotterdam 1974, of Jurisprudence, Univ. of Leiden 1977–, of Information Law 1987–; Prof. of Information Law, Univ. of Groningen 1989–95; mem. State Council 1982–87, Court of Appeal, The Hague 1977–; Chair. Nat. Cttee of Information Tech. and Law; mem. Social Econ. Council 1988–2004, Sec.-Gen. Royal Acad. of Arts and Sciences 1998–2001; mem. Senate (Eerste Kamer) 2004–; Kt of Netherlands Lion 1995; Modderman Prijs 1973, Wolffert van Borselenpenning 1982. *Publications:* Vervolgingsbeleid: the Policy of Public Prosecutors 1973, Maat en Regel 1975, Jurimetrics and the Rule of Law 1975, The New Law and Economics 1982, Models of Contracts in Information Law 1992, Introduction to the Law (8th edn) 1999, Trusted Third Parties 1996, Law and Computer (5th edn) 2004, Independence and Responsibility of the Judge 1997, Nemo Plus.... 2001. *Address:* Universiteit Leiden, Steenschuur 29, PO Box 9500, 2300 RA Leiden (office); Weipoortseweg 95A, 2381 NJ Zoeterwoude, Netherlands (home). *Telephone:* (71) 5277767 (office); (71) 5804764 (home). *Fax:* (71) 5809794 (home). *E-mail:* h.franken@law.leidenuniv.nl (office); hnsfrnk@cs.com (home). *Website:* www.universityleiden/facultyoflaw.

FRANKENTHALER, Helen, BA; American artist; b. 1928, New York; m. 1st Robert Motherwell 1958 (divorced 1971); m. 2nd Stephen M. DuBrul, Jr 1994; ed Bennington Coll., Vt; Trustee Bennington Coll. 1967; Fellow, Calhoun Coll., Yale Univ. 1968; solo exhbns throughout USA and Europe, particularly at André Emmerich Gallery 1959–, Whitney Museum of American Art and Metropolitan Museum of Art, New York 1951–73, Guggenheim Museum, New York 1975, retrospective 1985 (exhbn travelled USA, Canada 1986), Corcoran Gallery, Washington, DC 1975, Museum of Fine Arts, Houston 1976, Modern Art Museum, Fort Worth, 1989 (painting retrospective, travelled USA), Nat. Gallery of Art, Washington, DC 1993 (graphic retrospective, travelled USA, Japan), USIA (United States Information Agency) Exhbn, Janie C. Lee Gallery, Dallas 1973, 1975, 1976, 1978, 1980, Knoedler Gallery, London 1978, 1981, 1983, 1985, Sterling & Francine Clark Art Inst., Williamstown, Mass. 1980, Knoedler and Co., New York 1992, 1994; mem. American Acad. and Inst. of Arts and Letters 1974, Nat. Endowment for the Arts (NEA) Council on the Arts 1985–92, Corpn of Yaddo 1973–78; Trustee Bennington Coll. 1967–82; mem. American Acad. of Arts and Sciences 1991; numerous hon. degrees; First Prize, Paris Biennale 1959; Joseph E. Temple Gold Medal Award, Pennsylvania Acad. of Fine Arts 1968, Spirit of Achievement Award, Albert Einstein Coll. of Medicine 1970, Gold Medal of the Commune of Catania, Florence 1972, Garrett Award, Art Inst. of Chicago 1972, Creative Arts Award, American Jewish Congress 1974, Art and Humanities Award, Yale Women's Forum 1976, Extraordinary Woman of Achievement Award, Nat. Conf. of Christians and Jews 1978; Mayor's Award of Honor for Art and Culture, New York City 1986, Conn. Arts Award 1989, Lifetime Achievement Award, Coll. Art Assen 1994, Artist of the Year Award 1995, Jerusalem Prize 1999. *Address:* c/o M. Knoedler and Co. Inc., 19 East 70th Street, New York, NY 10021, USA.

FRANKL, Peter; British pianist; b. 2 Oct. 1935, Budapest, Hungary; s. of Tibor and Laura Frankl; m. Annie Feiner 1958; one s. one d.; ed High School, Franz Liszt Acad. of Music, Budapest; began career in late 1950s, London debut 1962, New York debut with Cleveland Orchestra under George Szell 1967; has performed with world's major orchestras, including Berlin Philharmonic, Amsterdam Concertgebouw, Israel Philharmonic, Leipzig Gewandhaus and all the London and major American orchestras, under conductors, including Abbado, Boulez, Colin Davis, Antal Dorati, Haitink, Herbig, Leinsdorf, Maazel, Masur, Muti, Rozhdestvensky, Salonen, Sanderling and Georg Solti; Visiting Prof. of Piano, Yale Univ., USA 1987; won first prize in several int. competitions; Officer's Cross Order of Merit (Hungary) 1972. *Recordings include:* complete works for piano by Schumann and Debussy, a solo Bartók and Chopin album, a Hungarian Anthology, Mozart concertos with mems of the English Chamber Orchestra, Brahms piano concertos nos 1 and 2, the complete four-hand works by Mozart with Tamás Vásáry, the three Brahms violin sonatas with Kyung Wha Chung, Brahms, Schumann, Dvořák and Martinů recordings, quintets with the Lindsay Quartet. *Leisure interests:* football, opera, theatre, tennis. *Address:* 5 Gresham Gardens, London, NW11 8NX, England. *Telephone:* (20) 8455-5228. *Fax:* (20) 8455-2176. *E-mail:* info@peterfrankl.co.uk (home). *Website:* www.peterfrankl.co.uk (home).

FRANKLIN, Aretha; American singer and songwriter; b. 25 March 1942, Memphis, Tenn.; d. of the late Rev. C. L. Franklin; m. 1st Ted White (divorced); m. 2nd Glynn Turman 1978 (divorced); began singing in choir at New Bethel Baptist Church, Detroit, where her father was pastor; numerous Grammy Awards 1967–, American Music Award 1984, NARAS Living Legend Award 1990, Rhythm and Blues Foundation Lifetime Achievement Award 1992, John F. Kennedy Center Award 1994; elected to Rock and Roll Hall of Fame (first woman) 1987, Lady of Soul Lena Horne Award for Outstanding Career Achievements 2005, Presidential Medal of Freedom 2005, Grammy Award for Best Traditional R&B Vocal Performance (for A House is Not a Home) 2006, United Negro Coll. Fund Award of Excellence 2006. *Film appearances:* The Blues Brothers 1980, Blues Brothers 2000 1998. *Recordings include:* albums: The Great Aretha Franklin 1960, Aretha 1961, The Electrifying Aretha Franklin 1962, The Tender, the Moving, the Swinging Aretha Franklin 1962, Unforgettable: A Tribute to Dinah Washington 1964, The Gospel Sound Of Aretha Franklin 1964, Runnin' Out Of Fools 1965, Yeah!!! 1965, Soul Sister 1966, I Never Loved A Man (The Way I Loved You) 1967, Aretha Arrives 1967, Aretha: Lady Soul 1968, Aretha In Paris 1968, Aretha's Gold 1969, This Girl's in Love With You 1969, Spirit In The Dark 1970, Live At Fillmore West 1971, Young, Gifted And Black 1972, Amazing Grace 1972, Hey Now Hey (The Other Side Of The Sky) 1973, The First Twelve Sides 1973, Let Me In Your Life 1974, With Everything I Feel In Me 1974, You 1975, Sweet Passion 1977, Almighty Fire 1978, La Diva 1979, Aretha 1980, Love All The Hurt Away 1981, Jump To It 1982, Get It Right 1983, Who's Zoomin' Who? 1985, The First Lady Of Soul 1986, Aretha 1987, One Lord, One Faith, One Baptism 1988, Through The Storm 1989, What You See Is What You Sweat 1991, Jazz To Soul 1992, Queen Of Soul 1993, Aretha After Hours, Chain Of Fools 1993, Love Songs 1997, The Delta Meets Detroit 1998, A Rose Is Still A Rose 1998, You Grow Closer 1998, So Damn Happy 2003, Jewels in the Crown: All-Star Duets with the Queen 2007, Rare and Unreleased Recordings from the Golden Reign of the Queen of Soul 2007, A Woman Falling Out of Love 2008, This Christmas Aretha 2008. *Publication:* Aretha: From these Roots (with David Rib) 1999. *Address:* c/o Arista Records, 888 7th Avenue, New York, NY 10106, USA (office). *Telephone:* (212) 489-7400 (office). *Website:* www.jrecords.com (office); www.sodamnhappy.com.

FRANKLIN, Barbara Ann Hackman, BA, MBA; American business executive and fmr government official; *President and CEO, Barbara Franklin Enterprises;* b. (Barbara Ann Hackman), 19 March 1940, Lancaster, Pa; d. of Arthur A. Hackman and Mayme M. Hackman (née Haller); m. Wallace Barnes 1986; ed Pennsylvania State Univ., Harvard Business School; with Singer Co., New York 1964–68; Asst Vice-Pres. Citibank, New York 1969–71; White House Staff Asst to the Pres. for Recruiting Women to Govt, Washington, DC 1971–73; Commr and Vice-Chair. US Consumer Product Safety Comm., Washington, DC 1973–79; Sr Fellow and Dir Govt and Business Program, Wharton School, Univ. of Pa 1980–88; Pres. and CEO Franklin Assocs., Washington, DC 1984–92, Pres. and CEO Barbara Franklin Enterprises 1995–; US Sec. of Commerce, Dept of Commerce, Washington, DC 1992–93; mem. Pres.'s Advisory Cttee for Trade Policy and Negotiations 1982–86, 1989–92; mem. US Comptroller Gen.'s Consultant Panel 1984–92; mem. Bd of

Dirs Aetna Inc. 1979–92, 1993–, Dow Chemical Co. 1980–92, 1993–; Chair. Emer. Bd of Trustees Econ. Club of NY; mem. Bd of Dirs Nat. Asscn of Corp. Dirs (NACD), Chair. 2009–; Vice-Chair. US-China Business Council; Chair. Asian Studies Advisory Council, Heritage Foundation; Dir or Trustee of three funds in American Funds Family of Mutual Funds; mem. Council on Foreign Relations, Int. Women's Forum (founding mem.), Nat. Cttee for US–China Relations; mem. Int. Advisory Bd Lafarge Inc.; mem. Advisory Council Public Company Accounting Oversight Bd (PCAOB); several hon. degrees; numerous awards for professional achievement, including John J. McCloy Award, NACD Dir of the Year Award 2000, Bd Alert Outstanding Dir 2003, Woodrow Wilson Award for Public Service 2006, recognized by Directorship as one of the 100 most influential people in corp. governance 2007. *Television:* regular commentator, Nightly Business Report, Public Broadcasting Service 1997–. *Leisure interests:* exercise, hiking, reading, painting. *Address:* Barbara Franklin Enterprises, 2600 Virginia Avenue, NW, Suite 506, Washington, DC 20037, USA (office). *Telephone:* (202) 337-9100 (office). *Fax:* (202) 337-9104 (office). *E-mail:* mnoonan@bhfranklin.com (office); bhfranklin@bhfranklin.com (office). *Website:* www.bhfranklin.com (office).

FRANKLIN, H. Allen, BEE, MEng; American business executive; *President and Chief Executive, Southern Company;* b. Corner, Alabama; ed Univ. of Alabama, Stanford Univ.; joined Southern Co. Services 1970, Sr Vice-Pres. Alabama Power 1981, Exec. Vice-Pres. Southern Co. Services 1983–88, Pres. and CEO 1988, Pres. and CEO Southern Co. 2001–, mem. Bd Dirs; Sr mem. IEEE; Dir United Way of Metropolitan Atlanta, Georgia Chamber of Commerce, Atlanta Chamber of Commerce; Pres. Atlanta Area Council of the Boy Scouts of America; Chair. Nat. Wild Turkey Fed.; mem. Georgia Dept of Industry, Trade and Tourism. *Address:* Office of the President, Southern Company, 270 Peachtree Street, NW, Atlanta, GA 30303, USA (office). *Telephone:* (404) 506-5000 (office). *Fax:* (404) 506-0598 (office). *Website:* www.southernco.com (office).

FRANKLIN, Kirk; American singer, songwriter and record company executive; b. (Kirk Smith), 26 Jan. 1970, Fort Worth, TX; m.; one s.; Choir Dir Greater Strangers Rest Baptist Church, Fort Worth 1988; worked with Dallas-Fort Worth Mass Choir on albums I Will Not Let Nothing Separate Me 1991, Another Chance 1993; f. choir group The Family; f. record company Fo Yo Soul; BET Award for Best Gospel Artist 2006, 2007, American Music Award for Favorite Contemporary Inspirational Artist 2006, Grammy Awards for Best Gospel Song (for Imagine Me) 2007, (for Help Me Believe) 2009. *Film soundtrack contributions include:* My Life is in Your Hands (for Get on the Bus 1996), Joy (for The Preacher' Wife 1996). *Recordings include:* albums: with The Family: Kirk Franklin and The Family 1992, Christmas 1995, Watcha Lookin' 4 (Grammy Award for Best Contemporary Soul Gospel Album 1997) 1996; solo: God's Property from Kirk Franklin's Nu Nation (Grammy Award for Best Gospel Album by a choir or chorus 1998) 1997, The Nu Nation Project (Grammy Award for Best Contemporary Soul Gospel Album 1999) 1998, Kirk Franklin and the Family 2001, The Rebirth of Kirk Franklin 2002, Hero (Grammy Award for Best Contemporary R&B Gospel Album 2007) 2006, Songs from the Storm, Vol. 1 2006, The Fight of My Life (Grammy Award for Best Contemporary R&B Gospel Album 2009) 2007. *Publication:* Church Boy: My Music and My Life (autobiog.) 1998. *Address:* William Morris Agency, 1325 Avenue of the Americas, New York, NY 10019, USA (office). *Telephone:* (212) 903-1100 (office). *Fax:* (212) 246-3583 (office). *Website:* www.wma.com (office); www.kirkfranklin.us.

FRANKLIN, Raoul Norman, CBE, DSc, FREng; British scientist, academic and university administrator; *Visiting Professor, Physical Materials Group, Oxford Research Unit, Open University;* b. 3 June 1935, Hamilton, NZ; s. of N. G. Franklin and T. B. Franklin (née Davis); m. Faith Ivens 1961; two s.; ed Auckland Grammar School, Auckland Univ., Oxford Univ.; Sr Research Fellow, Royal Mil. Coll. of Science 1961–63; Tutorial Fellow, Keble Coll., Oxford 1963–78, Univ. Lecturer, Eng Science, Oxford Univ. 1967–78; Consultant, UKAEA Culham Lab. 1968–; Vice-Chancellor, City Univ. 1978–98, Prof. Plasma Physics and Tech. 1986–98; Visiting Prof. Physical Materials Group Open Univ. Oxford Research Unit 1998–; Chair. City Tech. Ltd 1978–93; Chair. Assoc. Examining Bd 1994–98, Assessment and Qualifications Alliance (AQA) 1998–2003; Vice-Chair. Gen. Bd of the Faculties, Oxford Univ. 1971–74; mem. of Hebdomadal Council, Oxford Univ. 1971–74, 1976–78, of Science Bd, Science and Eng Research Council 1982–85, of London Pensions Fund Authority 1989–95, of Bd Arab-British Chamber of Commerce 1995–2002; mem. Council Gresham Coll. 1980–98; mem. Int. Cttee of ESCAMPIG (Europhysics Conf. on Atomic & Molecular Physics of Ionized Gases) 1993–96; Gov. Ashridge Man. Coll. 1986–99, Council City & Guilds 1996–2000, Council Univ. of Buckingham 2001–; Foundation Master Guild of Educators 2001–02; Master Worshipful Co. of Curriers 2002–03; Hon. DCL Distinguished Alumnus Auckland Univ.; Hon. Fellow, Keble Coll., Coll. of Preceptors; Freeman, City of London. *Publications:* Plasma Phenomena in Gas Discharges 1976, Physical Kinetics, Vol. XII 1981, Interaction of Intense Electromagnetic Fields with Plasmas (ed.) 1981. *Leisure interests:* walking, tennis, gardening. *Address:* Open University Oxford Research Unit, Foxcombe Hall, Boars Hill, Oxford, OX1 5HR (office); 12 Moreton Road, Oxford, OX2 7AX, England (home). *Telephone:* (1865) 558311 (home). *Fax:* (1865) 326322 (office). *E-mail:* r.n.frankin@open.ac.uk (office); raoulnfaith@tiscali.co.uk (home). *Website:* technology.open.ac.uk/materials/oru/orumat.html (office).

FRANKS, Lynne; British public relations executive; b. 16 April 1948; d. of Leslie Samuel Franks and Angela Franks (née Herman); m. Paul Howie (separated 1992); one s. one d.; ed Minchenden Grammar School, London; Sec., Petticoat Magazine 1965–67; est. Lynne Franks Ltd public relations consultants 1970, left agency 1992; est. Globalfusion public relations and cause-related marketing agency, Los Angeles 1998; f. SEED Network (empowerment programmes for women) 2001, est. SEED Coaches Training and SEED Community Peer Circles 2007; Founder Judge and Spokesperson Enterprising Britain Awards; Trustee Save the Rainforest Bd 1990–; Dr hc (Surrey Inst. of Art and Design) 2005. *Publication:* Absolutely Now!: A Futurist's Journey to Her Inner Truth 1997, The SEED Handbook: The Feminine Way to Create Business' 2000, GROW – The Modern Woman's Handbook 2004, 'BLOOM' 2007. *E-mail:* info@lynnefranks.com. *Website:* www.lynnefranks.co.uk.

FRANKS, Gen. Tommy Ray, KBE, MS; American army officer (retd); b. 17 June 1945, Wynnewood, Okla; m. Cathryn Carley 1969; one d.; ed Univ. of Texas, Shippensburg Univ., Pa, Armed Forces Staff Coll., US Army War Coll.; commissioned 2nd Lt 1967; served with 9th Infantry Div., Viet-nam, 2nd Armored Cavalry Regt, FRG; Commdr 2nd Bn 78th Field Artillery, FRG 1981–84; Deputy Asst G3, III Corps, Fort Hood, Tex. 1985–87; Commdr Div. Artillery, 1st Cavalry Div. 1987–88; Chief of Staff 1st Cavalry Div. 1988–89; Asst Div. Commdr (Maneuver), 1st Cavalry Div., Operation Desert Shield/Desert Storm, Saudi Arabia, Iraq 1990–91; Asst Commdt Field Artillery School, Fort Sill, Okla 1991–92; Dir La. Maneuvers Task Force, Office Chief of Staff US Army, Fort Monroe, Va 1992–94; Asst Chief of Staff Combined Forces Command and US Forces Korea 1994; Commdr 2nd Infantry Div., Korea 1995–97, Commdr 3rd US Army, Fort McPherson, Ga 1997–2000; promoted Gen., C-in-C US Cen. Command, MacDill Air Force Base, Fla 2000–03; lead American and Coalition troops in Operation Enduring Freedom in Afghanistan 2001 and Operation Iraqi Freedom in Iraq 2004; f. Franks & Assocs LLC 2003; mem. Bd of Dirs Nat. Park Foundation, Intrepid Fallen Heroes; spokesperson Salute America's Heroes Foundation, Southeastern Guide Dogs Org.; Defense Distinguished Service Medal, Distinguished Service Medal (with oak leaf cluster), Legion of Merit (with 3 oak leaf clusters), Bronze Star Medal (with 'V' device and 3 oak leaf clusters), Purple Heart (with 2 oak leaf clusters), Air Medal (with 'V' device), Presidential Medal of Freedom 2004; Hon. Co-Chair. Flight 93 Nat. Memorial 2005. *Publications:* American Soldier 2004. *Leisure interests:* country music, Mexican food, antiques, golf. *Address:* 4 Star Ranch, Roosevelt, OK 73564, USA (office). *Website:* www.tommyfranks.com.

FRANTZ, Justus; German pianist; b. 18 May 1944, Hohensalza; ed under Prof. Eliza Hansen in Hamburg, Wilhelm Kempf in Positano and Wilhalm Brückner-Rückeberg in Hamburg; prizewinner, Int. Music Competition, Munich 1967; since 1969 has appeared at all major European concert venues and toured USA, Far East and Japan; US debut with Leonard Bernstein and the New York Philharmonic Orchestra 1975; has made many tours and recordings in piano duo with Christoph Eschenbach and received Edison Int. Award for their recording of Schubert marches 1983; Co-Founder and Dir Schleswig-Holstein Music Festival; Prof. Hamburg Musikhochschule 1985–; Founder Schleswig-Holstein Music Festival 1986, Dir 1986–94; performed complete cycle of Mozart concertos in several European cities 1987–88; f. Chief Conductor Philharmonia of the Nations 1995; concert with Philharmonia of the Nations for Pope John Paul II 2001; Special Amb. for UNHCR 1989–; Grosse Bundesverdienstkreuz 1989. *Recordings include:* works by Scarlatti, Beethoven, Mozart and concertos for two, three and four pianos by J. S. Bach. *Address:* Gemeinnützige PN Orchester Verwalfunk GmbH, Tempelhofer Ufer 11, 10963 Berlin, Germany (office). *Telephone:* (30) 6416-730 (office). *Fax:* (30) 6416-7320 (office). *E-mail:* jutta.heitmann@justusfrantz.de (office). *Website:* www.justus-frantz.de (office); www.philharmonie-der-nationen.de (office).

FRANZ, Judy R., BA, MS, PhD; American physicist and academic; *Executive Officer, American Physical Society;* b. Chicago, Ill.; m. Frank A. Franz; one s.; ed Cornell Univ., Univ. of Ill.; Research Scientist, IBM Research Labs, Switzerland 1965–67; Asst Prof. of Physics, Ind. Univ., Bloomington 1968–74, Assoc. Prof. 1974–79, Prof. 1979–87, Assoc. Dean, Coll. of Arts and Sciences 1980–82; Prof. of Physics, Univ. of W Va 1987–94; Prof. of Physics, Univ. of Ala 1994–; Visiting Prof., Cornell Univ. 1985–86, 1988, 1990; Councillor-at-Large, American Physical Soc. 1984–88, Exec. Officer 1994–; Councillor-at-Large, American Asscn of Women in Science (AWIS) 1981–83; mem. Editorial Bd American Journal of Physics 1985–88; mem. Exec. Bd Council of Scientific Soc. Presidents 1990; Pres., American Asscn of Physics Teachers 1990; mem. Council of AAAS 1995–98; Assoc. Sec.-Gen. IUPAP 1999–2002, Sec.-Gen. 2002–; mem. Governing Bd, Exec. Cttee of American Inst. of Physics; Rep. to US Nat. Cttee to UNESCO 2004–; mem. Bd ASTRA; Fellow, American Physical Soc., AAAS, American Asscn of Women in Science; Humboldt Research Fellowship, Munich, Germany 1978–79; Distinguished Teaching Award, Ind. Univ. 1978, Alumni Honor Award for Distinguished Service, Coll. of Eng, Univ. of Illinois, Urbana-Champaign 1997, Melba Newell Phillips Medal, American Asscn of Physics Teachers 2008. *Publications:* Physics in the 20th Century (co-ed.) 1999; numerous contribs to Physics Review, Journal of Physics and other professional journals. *Leisure interests:* hiking, reading, concerts. *Address:* Executive Office, American Physical Society, One Physics Ellipse, College Park, MD 20740-3844, USA (office). *Telephone:* (301) 209-3270 (office). *Fax:* (301) 209-0865 (office). *E-mail:* franz@aps.org (office). *Website:* www.aps.org (office).

FRANZEN, Jonathan, BA; American writer; b. 17 Aug. 1959, Western Springs, IL; ed Swarthmore Coll., Free Univ. of Berlin, Germany; fmrly worked part-time in seismology lab., Harvard Univ. Dept of Earth and Planetary Sciences; currently full-time novelist, essayist, and journalist affiliated with The New Yorker; Hon. DHumLitt (Swarthmore Coll.) 2005; Whiting Award 1988, Guggenheim Fellowship, American Acad. Berlin Prize 2000, Granta Best Young American Novelist. *Publications:* The Twenty-Seventh City (Whiting Award) 1988, Strong Motion 1991, The Corrections (Nat. Book Award for Fiction, New York Times Ed.'s Choice, James Tait Black

Memorial Prize for Fiction 2003) 2001, How to be Alone (essays) 2002, The Discomfort Zone: A Personal History 2006; Spring Awakening (new trans. of Frank Wedekind play) 2007. *Address:* Steven Barclay Agency, 12 Western Avenue, Petaluma, CA 94952, USA (office); c/o Farrar, Straus and Giroux, 19 Union Square W, New York, NY 10003 (office); c/o Susan Golomb Agency, 875 Sixth Avenue #2302, New York, NY 10001, USA (office). *Telephone:* (707) 773-0654 (office). *Fax:* (707) 778-1868 (office). *Website:* www.barclayagency.com (office); www.jonathanfranzen.com (office).

FRANZEN, Ulrich J., BFA, MArch, LHD, FAIA; American architect; b. 15 Jan. 1921, Rhineland, Germany; s. of Erik Franzen and Elizabeth (Hellersberg) Franzen; m. 1st Joan Cummings 1942 (divorced 1962); two s. one d.; m. 2nd Josephine Laura Hughes 1980; ed Williams Coll. and Harvard Univ.; Designer, I. M. Pei & Partners, New York 1950–55; Head of Ulrich Franzen and Assocs, New York 1955–; Visiting Critic, Prof., Washington, St Louis, Yale, Harvard and Columbia Univs, various occasions 1960–84; Chair. Architectural Bd of Review, Rye, NY 1960–62; mem. Cincinnati Architectural Bd Review Bd 1964–65; mem. Architectural League New York (Pres. 1968–70, mem. Bd of Dirs. 1962–); Commr New York City Landmarks Preservation Comm., Century Asscn 1992–96; Bronze Star, Croix de Guerre avec Palme (Belgium); numerous awards including Bruner Memorial Prize, Nat. Inst. of Arts and Letters 1962, Thomas Jefferson Award, AIA 1970, Gold Medal, AIA. *Principal works include:* Alley Theatre 1968 (AIA Honor 1970), Agronomy Bldg 1970 (AIA Honor 1971), Christensen Hall 1970 (AIA Honor 1972), Harlem School of Arts 1982, Hunter Coll. New York 1984, Philip Morris World HQ 1984, Whitney Museum Br. 1984, Champion Int. World HQ with Whitney Museum Br. 1985. *Address:* Ulrich Franzen Architect, 530 East 76th Street, Unit 29D, New York, NY 10021-3561 (office); 27 Lamy Drive, Santa Fe, NM 87506-6907, USA.

FRASER, Lady Antonia, CBE, MA, FRSL; British writer; b. 27 Aug. 1932, London; d. of the late Earl and Countess of Longford; m. 1st Hugh Fraser 1956 (divorced 1977, died 1984); three s. three d.; m. 2nd Harold Pinter 1980 (died 2008); ed Dragon School, Oxford, St Mary's Convent, Ascot and Lady Margaret Hall, Oxford; mem. Cttee English PEN 1979–88 (Pres. 1988–89, Vice-Pres. 1990–), Crimewriters Asscn 1980–86, Writers in Prison Cttee, Chair. 1985–88, 1990; Hon. DLitt (Hull) 1986, (Sussex) 1990, (Nottingham) 1993, (St Andrew's) 1994; Prix Caumont-La Force 1985, Norten Medlicott Medal, Historical Asscn 2000. *TV plays:* Charades 1977, Mister Clay 1985. *Publications:* King Arthur 1954, Robin Hood 1955, Dolls 1963, History of Toys 1966, Mary, Queen of Scots 1969 (James Tait Black Memorial Prize), Cromwell: Our Chief of Men 1973, King James VI of Scotland and I of England 1974, Scottish Love Poems, A Personal Anthology 1974, Kings and Queens of England (ed.) 1975, Love Letters (anthology) 1976, Quiet as a Nun 1977, The Wild Island 1978, King Charles II 1979, Heroes and Heroines (ed.) 1980, A Splash of Red 1981, Cool Repentance 1982, Oxford In Verse (ed.) 1982, The Weaker Vessel 1984 (Wolfson History Prize), Oxford Blood 1985, Jemima Shore's First Case 1986, Your Royal Hostage 1987, Boadicea's Chariot: The Warrior Queens 1988, The Cavalier Case 1990, Jemima Shore at the Sunny Grave 1991, The Six Wives of Henry VIII 1992, Charles II: His Life and Times 1993, Political Death: A Jemima Shore Mystery 1994, The Gunpowder Plot (St Louis Literary Award 1996, CWA Non Fiction Gold Dagger 1996) 1996, The Lives of the Kings and Queens of England 1998, Marie Antoinette: the Journey 2001, Love and Louis XIV 2006; ed. The Pleasure of Reading 1992; television adaptations of Quiet as a Nun 1978, Jemima Shore Investigates 1983. *Leisure interests:* cats, grandchildren. *Address:* Curtis Brown Group Ltd., Haymarket House, 28/29 Haymarket, London, SW1Y 4SP, England (office). *Telephone:* (20) 7396-6600 (office). *Fax:* (20) 7396-0110 (office).

FRASER, Bernard William, BA; Australian bank governor and business executive; b. 26 Feb. 1941, Junee, NSW; s. of K. Fraser; m. Edna Gallogly 1965 (divorced); one s. two d.; ed Junee High School, NSW, Univ. of New England, Armidale, NSW, Australian Nat. Univ., ACT; joined Dept of Nat. Devt 1961; joined Dept of Treasury 1963, Treasury Rep., London, UK 1969–72, First Asst Sec. 1979, Sec. Dept 1984–89; with Dept of Finance 1976; mem. Bd of Dirs Nat. Energy Office 1981–83, Queensland Treasury Corpn; Chair. and Gov. Reserve Bank of Australia 1989–96; Chair. Govt Superannuation Office of Victoria, Members Equity; Trustee and Dir Construction and Bldg Unions Superannuation Trust (C+BUS) 1996–, Superannuation Trust of Australia 1996–, Australian Retirement Fund 1996–. *Leisure interest:* farming. *Address:* Superannuation Trust of Australia (STA), Level 28, 2 Lonsdale Street, Melbourne, Vic. 3000; Construction and Building Unions Superannuation Trust, Level 12, 313 La Trobe Street, Melbourne, Vic. 3000, Australia.

FRASER, Brendan; American actor; b. 3 Dec. 1968, Indianapolis; m. Afton Smith; two s.; ed Cornish Inst., Seattle. *Films include:* My Old School (TV) 1991, Dogfight 1991, Child of Darkness, Child of Light (TV) 1991, Guilty Until Proven Innocent (TV) 1991, Encino Man 1992, School Ties 1992, Twenty Bucks 1993, Younger and Younger 1993, With Honors 1994, Airheads 1994, The Scout 1994, The Passion of Darkly Noon 1995, Mrs Winterbourne 1996, Glory Daze 1996, George of the Jungle 1997, The Twilight of the Golds (TV) 1997, Still Breathing 1997, Gods and Monsters 1998, Blast from the Past 1999, The Mummy 1999, Dudley Do-Right 1999, Sinbad: Beyond the Veil of Mists (voice) 2000, Bedazzled 2000, Monkeybone 2001, The Mummy Returns 2001, The Quiet American 2002, Revenge of the Mummy: The Ride 2004, Crash 2004, Beach Bunny (voice) 2005, Journey to the End of the Night 2006, The Last Time 2006, The Air I Breathe 2007, Journey to the Center of the Earth 2007, The Mummy: Tomb of the Dragon Emperor 2008. *Address:* c/o William Morris Agency Inc., 1 William Morris Place, Beverly Hills, CA 90212, USA (office). *Telephone:* (310) 859-4000 (office). *Fax:* (310) 859-4462 (office). *Website:* www.brendanfraser.com (office).

FRASER, Dawn, AO, MBE, JP; Australian fmr swimmer; b. 4 Sept. 1937, Balmain, near Sydney; m. Gary Ware (divorced); one d.; first female swimmer to win gold medals in three consecutive Olympic Games 1956, 1960, 1964; broke women's 100m freestyle world record nine times 1956–64; first female to break 60 seconds in 100m freestyle; shares record for most Olympic medals won by a woman swimmer (four gold, four silver); set 39 world records; banned for 10 years after Tokyo Games for allegedly stealing an Olympic Flag from Japanese Imperial Hotel, forcing retirement; became involved in coaching, business ventures, politics; attaché to Australian Olympic Team 2000; mem. Int. Swimming Hall of Fame Selection Cttee; dedicates most of her time to her sponsors; also does guest speaking for a wide range of cos; Australian of the Year 1965, Int. Swimming Hall of Fame 1965, Olympic Order Award 1981, honoured as one of the greatest Olympians of all time at Atlanta Olympics 1996, named Nat. Living Treasure by Australian Govt, voted Athlete of the Century 1999. *Publication:* Below the Surface: Australian Title Gold Medal Girl (autobiography, with Harry Gordon) 1965, Dawn: One Hell of a Life (autobiography) 2001. *Leisure interests:* spending time with grandson, jet skiing, cycling, walking the dogs. *Address:* PO Box 118, Balmain, NSW 2041, Australia (office). *Telephone:* (417) 900040 (office). *E-mail:* info@dawnfraser.com.au (office). *Website:* www.dawnfraser.com (office).

FRASER, Donald Hamilton, RA; British artist; b. 30 July 1929, London; s. of Donald Fraser and Dorothy Lang; m. Judith Wentworth Sheilds 1954; one d.; ed Maidenhead Grammar School, St Martin's School of Art, London and in Paris (French Govt Scholarship); has held more than 70 one-man exhbns. in Europe, N America and Japan; work represented in public, corp. and pvt. collections throughout the world; taught at Royal Coll. of Art 1958–83, Fellow 1970; Vice-Pres. Artists' Gen. Benevolent Inst. 1981–, Chair. 1981–86; Vice-Pres. Royal Overseas League 1986–; mem. Royal Fine Art Comm. 1986–99; Hon. Curator, Royal Acad. 1992–99, Trustee 1993–99, Sr Royal Academician 2006. *Publications:* Gauguin's 'Vision After the Sermon' 1969, Dancers 1989. *Address:* c/o Royal Academy of Arts, Burlington House, Piccadilly, London, W1V 0DS (office); Bramham Cottage, Remenham Lane, Henley-on-Thames, Oxon., RG9 2LR, England.

FRASER, Hon. John Allen, PC, OC, OBC, CD, QC; Canadian organization official and fmr politician; b. 15 Dec. 1931, Yokohoma, Japan; m. Catherine Findlay; three d.; ed Univ. of BC; law practice, Vic., Powell River, Vancouver 1955–72; mem. House of Commons 1972–94; Minister of the Environment and Postmaster Gen. 1979–80; Minister of Fisheries and Oceans 1984–85 (resgnd), Speaker of the House of Commons 1986–94; Amb. for the Environment 1994–98; Chair. Pacific Fisheries Resource Conservation Council 1998–2005, now mem. Council; Chair. Nat. Defence Minister's Monitoring Cttee on Change 1996–2003; Chair. Parliamentary Precinct Oversight Advisory Cttee; Chair. BC Pacific Salmon Forum 2004–09; Hon. LLD (St Lawrence Univ.) 1999, (Simon Fraser Univ.) 1999, (Univ. of BC) 2004; Hon. Lt-Col Seaforth Highlanders of Canada 1994–, now Hon. Col.

FRASER, Rt Hon. (John) Malcolm, AC, CH, PC, MA; Australian politician; *Honorary Chairman, InterAction Council of Former Heads of Government;* b. 21 May 1930, Melbourne; s. of the late J. Neville Fraser and of Una Fraser; m. Tamara Beggs 1956; two s. two d.; ed Melbourne Grammar School and Oxford Univ.; mem. Parl. for Wannon 1955–83; mem. Jt Parl. Cttee of Foreign Affairs 1962–66; Chair. Govt Mems' Defence Cttee; Sec. Wool Cttee; mem. Council of ANU, Canberra 1964–66; Minister for the Army 1966–68, for Educ. and Science 1968–69, for Defence 1969–71, for Educ. and Science 1971–72; Parl. Leader of Liberal Party 1975–83; Prime Minister 1975–83; Co-Chair. Commonwealth Eminent Persons Group (EPG) 1985–86; Sr Adjunct Fellow, Center for Strategic and Int. Studies 1983; Fellow for Int. Council of Assocs at Claremont Univ. 1985; Chair. UN Cttee on African Commodity Problems 1989–90; mem. InterAction Council for Fmr Heads of Govt 1983– (Co-Chair. 1997–2006, Hon. Chair. 2006–), ANZ Int. Bd of Advice 1987–93; Chair. CARE Australia 1987–2001; Pres. CARE Int. 1990–95, Vice-Pres. 1995–99; Bd mem. Int.-Crisis Group 1995–2000; Co-Founder Australians All 2006; Hon. Fellow, Magdalen Coll., Oxford 1982; Hon. Vice-Pres. Oxford Soc. 1983; Grand Cordon of the Order of the Rising Sun (Japan); Hon. LLD (S Carolina) 1981, (Univ. of NSW) 2002, (Univ. of Tech., Sydney), (Murdoch Univ., Perth), Hon. DLitt (Deakin Univ.) 1989; B'nai B'rith Gold Medal 1980, Australian Human Rights Medal 2000. *Publications:* Common Ground: Issues That Should Bind and Not Divide Us 2002. *Leisure interests:* fishing, photography, vintage cars, motorcycles, golf. *Address:* Level 32, 101 Collins Street, Melbourne, Vic. 3000, Australia (home). *Telephone:* (3) 9654-1822 (office). *Fax:* (3) 9654-1301 (office). *E-mail:* Malcolm.Fraser@aph.gov.au (office). *Website:* australiansall.com.au (office).

FRASER, Shelly-Ann; Jamaican athlete; b. 27 Dec. 1986, Kingston; ed Wolmer's High School For Girls; first Jamaican woman in history to win an Olympic gold medal in 100m, Beijing Olympics 2008 (personal best time of 10.78 seconds); ran personal best time of 22.15 seconds in 200m in Kingston June 2008. *Address:* c/o Jamaica Amateur Athletic Association Ltd, PO Box 272, Kingston 5, Jamaica. *Telephone:* 929-6623. *Fax:* 920-4801. *E-mail:* athleticsja@jamweb.net. *Website:* www.jaaaltd.com.

FRASER, Sir William Kerr, Kt, GCB, MA, LLD, FRSE; British civil servant and administrator; b. 18 March 1929, Glasgow; s. of the late Alexander M. Fraser and Rachel Fraser; m. Marion Anne Forbes (Lady Marion Fraser) 1956; three s. one d.; ed Eastwood School, Clarkston and Univ. of Glasgow; Flying Officer RAF 1952–55; joined Scottish Office, Edinburgh 1955, Perm. Under-Sec. of State 1978–88; Prin. and Vice-Chancellor Univ. of Glasgow 1988–95, Chancellor 1996–2006; Chair. Royal Comm. on the Ancient and Historical Monuments of Scotland 1995–2000, Scottish Mutual Assurance PLC 1999; Hon. FRCP (Glas.) 1992; Hon. FRSAMD 1995; Hon. LLD (Glasgow) 1982, (Strathclyde) 1991, (Aberdeen) 1993; Dr hc (Edinburgh) 1995. *Leisure* *interests:* reading, meditating on democracy. *Address:* Broadwood, Edinburgh Road, Gifford, East Lothian, EH41 4JE, Scotland (home). *Telephone:* (1620) 810319 (home). *Fax:* (1620) 810319 (home). *E-mail:* wkfraser@tiscali.co.uk (home).

FRASER OF CARMYLLIE, Baron (Life Peer), cr. 1989 in the District of Angus; **Peter Lovat Fraser,** BA, LLB, QC, MP; British politician and lawyer; b. 29 May 1945; s. of Rev. George Robson Fraser and Helen Jean Meiklejohn; m. Fiona Macdonald Mair 1969; one s. two d.; ed St Andrew's Prep. School, Grahamstown, SA, Loretto School, Musselburgh, Gonville and Caius Coll., Cambridge, Edinburgh Univ.; called to Scottish Bar 1969; Lecturer in Constitutional Law, Heriot-Watt Univ. 1972–74; Standing Jr Counsel in Scotland to FCO 1979; Chair. Scottish Conservative Lawyers Law Reform Group 1976; Conservative MP for S Angus 1979–83, for Angus E 1983–87; Parl. Pvt. Sec. to Sec. of State for Scotland 1981–82; Solicitor Gen. for Scotland 1982–89, Lord Advocate 1989–92; Minister of State, Scottish Office 1992–95, Dept of Trade and Industry 1995–97; Deputy Leader of Opposition, House of Lords 1997–98; Chair. JFX Oil and Gas PLC 1997–; Dir Int. Petroleum Exchange 1997–, (Chair. 1999–), London Metal Exchange 1997–, Total Fine Elf Exploration UK 2000–; Chair. Ram Energy 2002–; Patron Queen Margaret Univ. Coll. 1999–, Statutory Cttee, Royal Pharmaceutical Soc. 2000. *Leisure interests:* skiing, golf, wind-surfing. *Address:* Slade House, Carmyllie, by Arbroath, Angus, DD11 2RE, Scotland. *Telephone:* (1241) 860215.

FRASYNIUK, Władysław; Polish politician and trade union official; *Chairman, Freedom Union;* b. 25 Nov. 1954, Wrocław; s. of Stanisław Frasyniuk and Zofia Frasyniuk; m. 1978; one s. three d.; driver, mechanic Municipal Transport, Wrocław, organizer of strike in bus depot, Wrocław Aug. 1980; press spokesman Founding Cttee of Ind. Self-Governing Trade Union; Chair. Solidarity Trade Union, Lower Silesia 1981–90 (resgnd); mem. Nat. Consultative Comm. of Solidarity; active underground under martial law, Jt Founder Provisional Exec. Cttee of Solidarity; arrested 1982, amnestied 1984; arrested again Feb. 1985, sentenced to over 4 years, amnestied 1986; mem. Provisional Council of Solidarity 1986–87, Nat. Exec. Comm. of Solidarity 1987–90; mem. Citizens' Cttee of Solidarity, Chair. 1988–90; took part in Round Table talks, Comm. for Trade Union Pluralism Feb.–April 1989; one of founders and leaders of Citizens' Movt for Democratic Action (ROAD) 1990–91; mem. Social-Liberal faction of Democratic Union 1991–94; Vice-Chair. Democratic Union 1991–94; mem. Freedom Union 1994–, Chair. Silesia Region 1999–, Chair. 2001–; Deputy to Sejm (Parl.) 1991–2001. *Leisure interests:* dogs, individual sports, history of Russia. *Address:* Biuro Krajowe Unii Wolności, ul. Marszałkowska 77–79, 00-683 Warsaw; Biuro Dolnośląskiej Unii Wolności, ul. Zelwerowicza 16, 53-676 Wrocław, Poland (office). *Telephone:* (22) 827-50-47; (71) 3548390 (office). *Fax:* (71) 3548399 (office). *E-mail:* frasyniuk@unia-wolnosci.pl (office). *Website:* www.uw.org.pl (office).

FRATTINI, Franco, LLB; Italian attorney and politician; *Minister for Foreign Affairs;* b. 14 March 1957, Rome; s. of Alberto Frattini and Lea Frattini; ed La Sapienza Univ., Rome; State Attorney 1981, Attorney, State Attorney-Gen.'s Office 1984; Magistrate, Regional Admin. Tribunal, Piedmont 1984–86, Council of State Judge 1986–; Legal Adviser to Minister of the Treasury 1986, to Deputy Prime Minister 1990–91, to Prime Minister 1992; Deputy Sec.-Gen. Office of Prime Minister 1993, Sec.-Gen. 1994; Minister for Civil Service and Regional Affairs 1995–96; mem. Camera dei Deputati (Parl.) (Forza Italia) 1995–96, 2001–04; Pres. Parl. Cttee for Intelligence and Security Services and State Secrets 1996–2004; Minister for Civil Service and for Coordination of Intelligence and Security Services 2001–02, for Foreign Affairs 2002–04, 2008–; Vice-Pres. European Comm., Commr for Justice, Freedom and Security 2004–08; City Councillor, Rome 1997–2000; mem. Exec. Cttee Forza Italia 1998–. *Publications include:* numerous specialist articles on law and public works. *Address:* Ministry of Foreign Affairs, Piazzale della Farnesina 1, 00194 Rome, Italy (office). *Telephone:* (06) 36911 (office). *Fax:* (06) 36918899 (office). *E-mail:* relazioni.pubblico@esteri.it (office). *Website:* www.esteri.it (office).

FRAYLING, Sir Christopher John, Kt, PhD; British historian, organization official and broadcaster; b. 26 Dec. 1946; m. Helen Anne Snowdon; ed Repton School, Churchill Coll. Cambridge; lecturer Univ. of Bath, Univ. of Exeter 1970s; Prof. of Cultural History, RCA 1979–, f. Dept of Cultural History, Rector 1996–; mem. Arts Council England 1987–2000, Chair. 2004–09; Chair. Design Council, Crafts Study Centre, Royal Mint Advisory Cttee; fmr Gov. BFI; mem. Arts & Humanities Research Bd; trustee Victoria & Albert Museum. *Television includes:* The Art of Persuasion (New York Film and Television Festival Gold Medal), The Face of Tutankhamun, Strange Landscape. *Radio includes:* The Rime of the Bounty (Sony Radio Award, Soc. of Authors Award). *Publications include:* Napoleon Wrote Fiction 1973, The Vampyre 1976, Spaghetti Westerns 1980, The Face of Tutankhamun 1992, Clint Eastwood: A Critical Biography 1993, Strange Landscape: A Journey through the Middle Ages 1995, Nightmare: The Birth of Horror 1996, Sergio Leone: Something to do with Death 2000, Ken Adam: The Art of Production Design 2005, Mad, Bad and Dangerous? The Scientist and Cinema 2006. *Address:* c/o Arts Council England, 2 Pear Tree Court, London, EC1R 0DS, England (office). *Website:* www.artscouncil.org.uk (office).

FRAYN, Michael, BA, FRSL; British playwright and author; b. 8 Sept. 1933, London; s. of the late Thomas A. Frayn and Violet A. Lawson; m. 1st Gillian Palmer 1960 (divorced 1989); three d.; m. 2nd Claire Tomalin (q.v.) 1993; ed Kingston Grammar School and Emmanuel Coll., Cambridge; reporter, The Guardian 1957–59, columnist 1959–62; columnist, The Observer 1962–68; Hon. Fellow, Emmanuel Coll., Cambridge, Hon. DLitt (Cambridge) 2001; Order of Merit (Germany) 2004; Heywood Hill Literary Prize 2002, Golden PEN Award 2003, Saint Louis Literary Award 2006, McGovern Award 2006, Companion of Literature 2007. *Stage plays:* The Two of Us 1970, The Sandboy

1971, Alphabetical Order (Evening Standard Best Comedy of the Year 1975) 1975, Donkeys' Years (Laurence Olivier Award for Best Comedy 1976, Society of West End Theatre Comedy of the Year 1976) 1976, Clouds 1976, Balmoral 1978, Liberty Hall (new version of Balmoral) 1980, Make and Break 1980 (Evening Standard Best Comedy of the Year 1980), Noises Off (Evening Standard Best Comedy of the Year 1982, Laurence Olivier Award for Best Comedy 1982, Society of West End Theatre Comedy of the Year 1982) 1982, Benefactors (Laurence Olivier/BBC Award for Best New Play 1984) 1984, Look Look 1990, Here 1993, Now You Know 1995, Copenhagen (Evening Standard Award for Best Play of the Year 1998, West End Critics' Circle Best New Play Award 1998, Prix Molière Best New Play 1999, Tony Award for Best Play 2000) 1998, Alarms and Excursions 1998, Democracy (Evening Standard Theatre Award for Best Play, Critics' Circle Award for Best Play 2003) 2003, Afterlife 2007. *TV includes:* plays: Jamie, on a Flying Visit (BBC) 1968, Birthday (BBC) 1969; documentary series: Second City Reports (with John Bird, Granada) 1964, Beyond a Joke (with John Bird and Eleanor Bron) 1972, Making Faces 1975; documentaries: One Pair of Eyes 1968, Laurence Sterne Lived Here 1973, Imagine a City Called Berlin 1975, Vienna: The Mask of Gold 1977, Three Streets in the Country 1979, The Long Straight (Great Railway Journeys of the World) 1980, Jerusalem 1984, Magic Lantern, Prague 1993, Budapest: Written in Water 1996 (all BBC documentaries); films: First and Last 1989, A Landing on the Sun 1994. *Cinema:* Clockwise 1986, Remember Me? 1997. *Plays translated include:* The Cherry Orchard, Three Sisters, The Seagull, Uncle Vanya, Wild Honey, The Sneeze (Chekhov), The Fruits of Enlightenment (Tolstoy), Exchange (Trifonov), Number One (Anouilh). *Publications:* novels: The Tin Men (Somerset Maugham Award 1966) 1965, The Russian Interpreter (Hawthornden Prize 1967) 1966, Towards the End of the Morning 1967, A Very Private Life 1968, Sweet Dreams 1973, The Trick of It 1989, A Landing on the Sun (Sunday Express Book of the Year) 1991, Now You Know 1992, Headlong 1999, Spies (Whitbread Award for Best Novel) 2002; non-fiction: Constructions (philosophy) 1974, Speak after the Beep 1995, Celia's Secret (with David Burke) 2000, The Human Touch: Our Part in the Creation of the Universe 2006, Stage Directions: Writing on Theatre 1970–2008 2008; several vols of collections of columns, plays and trans. *Address:* c/o Greene & Heaton Ltd, 37A Goldhawk Road, London, W12 8QQ, England.

FRAZIER, Charles, PhD; American writer; b. 4 Nov. 1950, Asheville, NC; m. Catherine Frazier; one d.; ed Univ. of North Carolina, Appalachian State Univ., Univ. of South Carolina; fmr faculty mem., Univ. of Colo and North Carolina State Univ. *Publications:* Adventuring in the Andes: The Sierra Club Travel Guide to Ecuador, Peru, Bolivia, the Amazon Basin, and the Galapagos Islands (with Donald Secreast) 1985, Cold Mountain: Odyssey in North Carolina (novel, Nat. Book Award) 1997, Thirteen Moons (novel) 2006. *Address:* c/o Darhansoff, Verrill & Feldman, 236 West 26th Street, Suite 802, New York, NY 10001, USA; c/o Sceptre, 338 Euston Road, London, NW1 3BH, England.

FRCKOVSKY, Ljubomir; Macedonian politician and academic; *Professor of International Law, Skopje University;* b. 2 Dec. 1957; ed Skopje Univ., Ljubljana Univ.; mem. Inst. Francais des Relations Int., Paris; mem. Int. Law Asscn Skopje, Forum for Human Rights Macedonia; Prof. of Int. Law and Theory of Int. Relations Skopje Univ.; co-author of new Constitution of Repub. of Macedonia 1991; Minister without Portfolio 1990; Minister of Interior 1994; Minister of Foreign Relations 1996–97; Prof., Skopje Univ. 1996–98, currently Prof. of Int. Law; adviser to Pres. Boris Trajkovski 2002–04; Fellow, Schloss Leopoldskron, Salzburg, 21st Century Trust, London. *Address:* SS Cyril and Methodius University of Skopje, PO Box 576, Krste Misirkov bb, 91000 Skopje, Macedonia. *Telephone:* (91) 116323 (office).

FREARS, Stephen Arthur; British film director; b. 20 June 1941, Leicester; s. of Dr Russell E. Frears and Ruth M. Frears; m. Mary K. Wilmers 1968 (divorced 1974); two s.; pnr, Anne Rothenstein; one s. one d.; ed Gresham's School, Holt, Trinity Coll., Cambridge; Asst Dir Morgan, a Suitable Case for Treatment 1966, Charlie Bubbles 1967, If... 1968; worked in TV for 13 years, including several TV films and plays in collaboration with Alan Bennett; Chair. jury Cannes Film Festival 2007; Officier Ordre des Arts et des Lettres; Hon. LittD (East Anglia, Norwich); Santa Fe Film Festival Lifetime Achievement Award 2003. *Films include:* Gumshoe 1971, Bloody Kids 1980, Going Gently 1981, Walter 1982, Saigon 1983, The Hit 1984, My Beautiful Laundrette 1985, Prick Up Your Ears 1986, Sammy and Rosie Get Laid 1987, Dangerous Liaisons 1989, The Grifters 1990, Hero 1992, The Snapper 1992, Mary Reilly 1996, The Van 1996, The Hi-Lo Country 1999, High Fidelity 2000, Liam 2000, Dirty Pretty Things (British Ind. Film Awards Best British Film, Best Dir, Best Screenplay) 2002, Mrs Henderson Presents 2005, The Queen (Best Film and co-winner Best Dir, Toronto Film Critics Asscn 2006, Goya Award for Best European Film 2007, Evening Standard Alexander Walker Special Award 2007, Attenborough Award for British Film of the Year 2007, Best British Dir, London Film Critics' Circle Awards 2007, BAFTA Award for Best Film 2007) 2006, Cheri 2009. *Television includes:* Fail Safe 2000, The Deal 2003. *Address:* c/o Casarotto Co. Ltd, National House, 60–66 Wardour Street, London, W1V 4ND, England. *Telephone:* (20) 7287-4450. *Fax:* (20) 7287-9128.

FRÉCHETTE, Louise, OC, BA; Canadian diplomatist, public servant and international organization official; *Distinguished Fellow, Center for International Governance Innovation;* b. 16 July 1946, Montreal; ed College Basile Moreau, Univ. of Montreal, College of Europe, Bruges, Belgium; with Dept of External Affairs, Govt of Canada from 1970s, mem. del. to UN Gen. Ass. 1972, Second Sec., Embassy in Athens 1972–75, worked in European Affairs Div., Dept of External Affairs 1975–77, First Sec., Canadian Mission to UN in Geneva 1978–82, participated in session of CSCE (now OSCE) in Madrid

1980–81, Amb. to Argentina (also accred to Uruguay and Paraguay) 1985–90; Asst Deputy Minister for Latin America and the Caribbean, Ministry of Foreign Affairs, for Int. Econ. and Trade Policy 1990–92; Perm. Rep. to UN, New York 1992–94; Assoc. Deputy Minister, Dept of Finance 1994–95; Deputy Minister of Nat. Defence 1995–98; Deputy Sec.-Gen. UN 1998–2006; Distinguished Fellow, Center for Int. Governance Innovation, Waterloo, Ont. 2006–; Dr hc (Saint Mary's Univ., Kyung Hee Univ., Univ. of Ottawa, Univ. of Toronto, Laval Univ.); ranked by Forbes magazine amongst 100 Most Powerful Women (87th) 2004, (65th) 2005. *Address:* The Centre for International Governance Innovation, 57 Erb Street West, Waterloo, ON N2L 6C2, Canada (office). *Telephone:* (519) 885-2444 (office). *Fax:* (519) 885-5450 (office). *E-mail:* cigi@cigionline.org (office). *Website:* www.cigionline.org (office).

FREDERIK ANDRÉ HENRIK CHRISTIAN, HRH Crown Prince, MSc; Danish; b. 26 May 1968, Copenhagen; s. of HM Queen Margrethe II and HRH Prince Consort Henrik of Denmark; m. HRH Crown Princess Mary Elizabeth (née Donaldson) 2004; one s. one d.; ed Krebs' Skole, École des Roches, France, Øregaard Gymnasium, Univ. of Aarhus and Harvard Univ., USA; heir to the throne of Denmark; began mil. service with the Royal Life Guard 1986, apptd Lt Reserve Army 1988, Reconnaissance Platoon Commdr Royal Guard Hussars' Regt 1988, First Lt Reserve Army 1989, completed training with the Royal Danish Navy Frogman Corps 1995, First Lt Reserve Navy 1995, Capt., Reserve Army 1997, Lt Commdr, Reserve Navy 1997, Royal Danish Air Force Flying School 2000, Capt., Reserve Air Force 2000, Command and General Staff Course Royal Danish Defence Coll. 2001–02, Maj., Reserve Army and Air Force 2002, Commdr, Reserve Navy 2002, Staff Officer, Defence Command Denmark 2002–03, Sr Lecturer, Inst. of Strategy, Royal Danish Defence Coll. 2003–, Commdr Sr Grade in the Navy, Lt-Col in the Army and Air Force 2004–; served at the Danish UN Mission, New York 1994, First Sec. Embassy in Paris 1998–99; participated in expedition to Mongolia 1986, Expedition Sirius 2000 to Greenland 2000; Pres. The Royal Danish Geographical Soc.; patronages include Danish Red Cross, Deaf Asscn, Royal Acad. of Music, Aarhus, Save the Children Fund, Asscn of Fine Arts, Comm. for Scientific Research in Greenland, Dyslexia Org., Foreign Policy Soc., Georg Jensen Prize, Greenlandic Soc.; mem. Int. Sailing Fed. Events Cttee, Young Global Leaders; hon. memberships include Asscn of Cavalry Officers, Mongolian Soc., Naval Asscn, Ancient Guild of Christian IV, Aalborg, Guards' Asscn, Copenhagen, Royal Danish Yacht Club, Sailors' Soc. of 1856; Knight of the Order of the Elephant, Grand Commdr of the Order of Dannebrog, Silver Cross of the Order of Dannebrog, Commemorative Medal 50th Anniversary of HM Queen Ingrid's arrival in Denmark, Badge of Honour, Officers of the Reserve, Commemorative Medal of HM Queen Margrethe II and HRH Prince Consort Henrik's Silver Wedding, Silver Jubilee Medal of HM Queen Margrethe II, Danish Mil. Athletic Asscn Medal, King Frederik IX Centenary Medal, Royal Medal of Recompense with Crown, Commemorative Medal of Queen Ingrid, Greenland Home Rule Medal, Grand Cross of the Order of Honourable Service, Italy, Adolph of Nassau Civilian and Mil. Service Order, Grand Cross, Luxembourg, Orders of Ojaswi Rajanya, Grand Cross, Nepal, Seraphim, Sweden, Saint Olav Grand Cross, Norway, White Roses Grand Cross, Finland, Terra Mariana Grand Cross, Estonia, Three Stars Grand Cross, Latvia, Leopold Grand Cross, Belgium, Icelandic Falcon Grand Cross, Iceland, Jordanian Renaissance Grand Cross, Jordan, Chrysanthemum, Japan, Southern Cross, Brazil, Rio Branco Grand Cross, Brazil, Chula Chom Klao Grand Cross, Thailand, Stara Planina First Class, Bulgaria, Order of Service for the FRG, Grand Cross, Order of the Star of Romania, Grand Cross. *Address:* Court of TRH The Crown Prince and Crown Princess of Denmark, Christian VIII Palace, Amalienborg Slotsplads 7, 1257 Copenhagen K; POB 2143, 1015 Copenhagen K, Denmark. *Telephone:* 33-40-10-10. *Fax:* 33-40-11-15. *Website:* www.crownprincecouple.dk.

FREDERIKSEN, Claus Hjort, LLM; Danish politician; *Minister of Finance;* b. 4 Sept. 1947; s. of Niels Frederiksen and Elna Frederiksen (née Hjort); Head of Div., Ministry of Food, Agric. and Fisheries 1977–79; Sec.-Gen. Asscn of Industrial Employers 1979–83; Admin Man., Liberal Party 1983–85, Sec.-Gen. 1985–2001; Minister for Employment 2001–09, of Finance 2009–; mem. Folketing (Parl.) for Copenhagen County 2005–07, for North Zealand 2007–. *Address:* Ministry of Finance, Christiansborg Slotspl. 1, 1218 Copenhagen K, Denmark (office). *Telephone:* 33-92-33-33 (office). *Fax:* 33-32-30-80 (office). *E-mail:* fm@fm.dk (office). *Website:* www.fm.dk (office).

FREDRIKSEN, John; Cypriot (b. Norwegian) shipping industry executive; *Chairman, CEO, President and Director, Frontline Ltd;* b. 1944, Oslo, Norway; m.; two c.; began as trainee in shipbrokering co.; owner of world's largest tanker fleet, with more than 70 oil tankers, and major interests in oil rigs and fish farming; was Norway's richest man until he abandoned Norwegian citizenship for Cypriot passport 2006; f. investment cos Hemen Holdings Ltd and Meisha; Chair. and CEO Old Frontline –1997, mem. Bd of Dirs, Chair., CEO, Pres. Frontline Ltd 1997–; mem. Bd of Dirs Seatankers Man. Co. Ltd, Golar LNG Ltd. *Leisure interest:* collecting classic Norwegian art. *Address:* Frontline Management AS, Bryggegata 3, PO Box 1327-VIKA, 0112 Oslo, Norway (office). *Telephone:* 23-11-40-00 (office). *Fax:* 23-11-40-40 (office). *E-mail:* Frontline@front.bm (office). *Website:* www.frontline.bm (office).

FREED, Karl Frederick, BS, AM, PhD; American chemist and academic; *Professor of Chemistry, James Franck Institute, University of Chicago;* b. 25 Sept. 1942, Brooklyn, NY; m. Gina Nicole; one d.; ed Columbia Univ., Harvard Univ.; Asst Prof., James Franck Inst., Univ. of Chicago 1968–73, Assoc. Prof. 1973–76, Prof. 1976–, Henry G. Gale Distinguished Service Prof. 2006–, Dir 1983–86; Visiting Scientist, Centre Nucléaires, Strasbourg, France 1977, Inst. of Physical and Chemical Research, Saitama, Japan 1979; Visiting Prof., Univ. of Minn. 1984, Univ. of Strasbourg 1991; Visiting Scientist, IBM Research Labs 1993; Chair. Gordon Conf. on Polymer Physics 1996; mem. Editorial Bd Journal of Statistical Physics 1976–78, Chemical Physics 1979–82, Journal of Chemical Physics 1982–85, Advances in Chemical Physics 1984–, International Journal of Quantum Chemistry 1995; Fellow, Alfred P. Sloan Foundation 1969–71, John S. Guggenheim Foundation 1972–73, American Physical Soc. 1983–, American Acad. of Arts and Sciences 2007–; Chemical Soc. Marlow Medal 1973, Award in Pure Chem. 1976, Case Centennial Scholar Medal 1980. *Publications:* Renormalization Group Theory of Macromolecules; more than 500 articles in scholarly journals. *Address:* James Franck Institute, University of Chicago, 5640 South Ellis Avenue, Chicago, IL 60637, USA (office). *Telephone:* (773) 702-7202 (office). *Fax:* (773) 702-5863 (office). *E-mail:* freed@uchicago.edu (office). *Website:* home.uchicago.edu/~freed (office).

FREEDBERG, Hugh; British business executive; *Chief Executive Officer, London International Financial Futures and Options Exchange;* b. 18 June 1945, Cape Town, South Africa; ed Univ. of Witwatersrand, Univ. of South Africa, Harvard Univ., Amos Tuck School of Business Admin, Dartmouth Coll., USA; Book Club Assocs, UK 1973–75; Marketing and Sales Dir for UK Card Div. American Express 1975–78, Gen. Man. 1978–86, Head of Divs in the Benelux countries, Southern Europe, the Middle East and Africa, the UK, Ireland, SE Asia; joined Salomon Inc. 1986, CEO The Mortgage Corpn –1990; joined TSB Group 1990, Exec. Dir, CEO Insurance and Investment Services Div., Deputy CEO 1992–96; CEO Hill Samuel Group (bought by TSB Group) 1991–96, now CEO Hill Samuel Bank Ltd (div. of Lloyds TSB Group PLC); Dir Macquarie Bank, Australia; Man. Partner Financial Services Practice, Korn Ferry Int.; CEO London Int. Financial Futures and Options Exchange (LIFFE) 1998–. *Address:* London International Financial Futures and Options Exchange, Cannon Bridge House, 1 Cousin Lane, London, EC4R 3XX (office); Hill Samuel Bank Ltd, 100 Wood Green, London, EC2P 2AJ, England (office). *Telephone:* (20) 7623-0444 (LIFFE) (office); (20) 7600-6000 (office). *Fax:* (20) 7588-3624 (LIFFE) (office); (20) 7920-3900 (office). *Website:* www.liffe.com (office).

FREEDMAN, Eugene M., MS; American business executive; *Chairman, Senior Advisory Board, Kaufman & Company LLC;* b. 1932; ed Wharton School, Univ. of Pennsylvania and Columbia Univ. Grad. School of Business; joined Coopers & Lybrand 1954, Deputy Chair., Vice-Chair. NE region, mem. Int. Exec. Comm., Chair. 1991–93, Chair. CEO Coopers and Lybrand Int., New York 1993; Sr Advisor Monitor Co. Group Ltd Partnership 1995–2003; Co-founder, Man. Dir and Pres. Monitor Clipper Pnrs (pvt. equity firm) 1997–99, Sr Advisor and Dir 1999–2002; currently Chair. Sr Advisory Bd Kaufman & Co. LLC; mem. Bd or Dirs Outcome Services Inc. Epoch Holdings Corpn, Concord Coalition; mem. Advisory Bd Cross Country Group Inc. *Address:* Kaufman & Company LLC, 101 Federal Street, No 1310, Boston, MA 02110, USA (office). *Telephone:* (617) 426-0444 (office). *Fax:* (617) 542-6506 (office). *Website:* www.kcollc.com (office).

FREEDMAN, Sir Lawrence David, Kt, KCMG, CBE, DPhil, FRSA, FRHistS, FBA, FKC; British academic; *Professor of War Studies and Vice-Principal (Research), King's College London;* b. 7 Dec. 1948, Tynemouth; s. of the late Lt-Commdr Julius Freedman and Myra Robinson; m. Judith Hill 1974; one s. one d.; ed Whitley Bay Grammar School and Univs of Manchester, Oxford and York; Research Assoc., IISS 1975–76; Research Fellow, Royal Inst. of Int. Affairs 1976–78, Head of Policy Studies 1978–82; Fellow, Head Dept of War Studies, King's Coll. London 1978–, Prof. 1982–, Head School of Social Science and Public Policy 2001–, Vice-Principal (Research); mem. Council, IISS 1984–92, 1993–, School of Slavonic and E European Studies 1993–97; Chair. Cttee on Int. Peace and Security, Social Science Research Council (USA) 1993–98; occasional newspaper columnist; Trustee Imperial War Museum 2001–; Hon. Dir Centre for Defence Studies 1990–; Silver Medallist, Arthur Ross Prize, Council on Foreign Relations (USA) 2002, RUSI Chesney Gold Medal 2006. *Publications:* US Intelligence and Soviet Strategic Threat 1978, Britain and Nuclear Weapons 1980, The Evolution of Nuclear Strategy 1981, 1989, Nuclear War and Nuclear Peace (co-author) 1983, The Troubled Alliance (ed.) 1983, The Atlas of Global Strategy 1985, The Price of Peace 1986, Britain and the Falklands War 1988, US Nuclear Strategy (co-ed.) 1989, Signals of War (with V. Gamba) 1989, Europe Transformed (ed.) 1990, Military Power in Europe (essays, ed.) 1990, Britain in the World (co-ed.) 1991, Population Change and European Security (co-ed.) 1991, War, Strategy and International Politics (essays, co-ed.) 1992, The Gulf Conflict 1990–91, Diplomacy and War in the New World Order (with E. Karsh) 1993, War: A Reader 1994, Military Intervention in Europe (ed.) 1994, Strategic Coercion (ed.) 1998, The Revolution in Strategic Affairs 1998, The Politics of British Defence Policy 1979–1998 1999, Kennedy's Wars 2000, The Cold War 2001, Superterrorism (ed.) 2002, Deterrence 2004, The Official History of the Falklands Campaign 2005; articles etc. *Leisure interests:* tennis, political cartoons. *Address:* King's College London, Office of the Principal, James Clerk Maxwell Building, 57 Waterloo Road, London, SE1 8WA, England (office). *Telephone:* (20) 7848-3984 (office); (20) 7848-3985 (office). *Fax:* (20) 7848-3668 (office). *E-mail:* lawrence.freedman@kcl.ac.uk (office); LFREED0712@aol.com (home).

FREEDMAN, Michael H., PhD; American mathematician and academic; *Senior Researcher, Theory Group, Microsoft Research;* b. 21 April 1951, Los Angeles, Calif.; ed Univ. of California, Berkeley, Princeton Univ., NJ; Lecturer in Math., Univ. of California, Berkeley 1973–75; mem. staff, Inst. for Advanced Study, Princeton 1975–76, 1980–81; Asst Prof. of Math., Univ. of California, San Diego 1976–79, Assoc. Prof. 1979, Prof. 1982–2004, Charles Lee Powell Prof. of Math. 1985–2004; Sr Researcher, Theory Group, Microsoft Research 2004–; mem. NAS, American Acad. of Arts and Sciences, New York Acad. of Sciences 1984; MacArthur Foundation Fellow 1984; Sloan Fellowship, California Scientist of the Year 1984, Fields Medal, Int. Congress of

Mathematicians, Berkeley 1986, Veblen Prize, American Math. Soc. 1986, Nat. Medal of Science 1987, Humboldt Award 1988, Guggenheim Fellowship 1994. *Publications:* numerous publs in math. journals. *Address:* Microsoft Corporation, One Microsoft Way, Redmond, WA 98052-6399, USA (office). *Telephone:* (425) 882-8080 (office). *Fax:* (425) 936-7329 (office). *Website:* research.microsoft.com (office).

FREEDMAN, Wendy L., PhD; American (b. Canadian) astronomer; *Director, Carnegie Observatories, Carnegie Institution;* b. Toronto, Ont.; m.; one s. one d.; ed Univ. of Toronto; Postdoctoral Fellow, Carnegie Observatories, Pasadena, Calif. 1984, mem. Scientific Staff 1987, Dir 2003–, mem. Astronomy and Astrophysics Advisory Cttee; mem. NAS 2003–, American Astronomical Soc., Astronomical Soc. of the Pacific, American Physical Soc.; Fellow, American Acad. of Arts and Sciences 2000, American Philosophical Soc. 2007; Marc Aaronson Prize 1994, Cosmos Club Award, Helen Sawyer Hogg Award 2000, John P. McGovern Award 2000, American Philosophical Soc. Magellanic Prize 2002. *Address:* Carnegie Observatories, 813 Santa Barbara Street, Pasadena, CA 91101, USA (office). *Telephone:* (626) 304-0204 (office). *Fax:* (626) 304-0266 (office). *E-mail:* wendy@ociw.edu (office). *Website:* www.ociw.edu/research/freedman.html (office).

FREEH, Louis J., JD, LLM; American lawyer, judge and fmr government official; b. 6 Jan. 1950, Jersey City, New Jersey; m. Marilyn Freeh; six s.; ed Rutgers Coll., Rutgers Law School and New York Univ. Law School; agent, FBI 1974–80, Dir 1993–2001; Asst Attorney, New York 1980–90, Fed. Judge 1990–92; Adjunct Assoc. Prof. of Law, Fordham Law School 1988–92; Vice-Chair. MBNA America Bank, N.A.2001–06, also Gen. Counsel for MBNA America Bank and MBNA Corpn; mem. Bd of Dirs Bristol-Myers Squibb Co.; mem. Bd of Consultants, Gavel Consulting Group, Washington, DC; Presidential Award for Distinguished Service 1987, 1991, Law Enforcement Officers Award 1989, John Marshall Award. *Publications:* My FBI 2005. *Address:* c/o Board of Directors, Bristol-Myers Squibb Company, 345 Park Avenue, New York, NY 10154-0037, USA. *Telephone:* (202) 390-5959 (Gavel). *E-mail:* JudgeSullivan@West-Point.org.

FREEMAN, Catherine (Cathy) Astrid; Australian fmr athlete; b. 16 Feb. 1973, Mackay; d. of Norman Freeman and Cecilia Barber; m. (Sandy) Alexander Bodecker; works as public relations adviser; winner Australian 200m 1990–91, 1994, 1996, Australian 100m 1996, Amateur Athletics Fed. 400m 1992, 200m 1993; Gold Medallist 4×100m Commonwealth Games 1990; Gold Medallist 200m, 400m, Silver Medallist 4×100m Commonwealth Games 1994; Silver Medallist 400m, Olympic Games, Atlanta 1996; winner World Championships 400m, Athens 1997 (first Aboriginal winner at World Championships); Gold Medallist 400m, Olympic Games, Sydney 2000; set 2 Australian 200m records, 5 Australian 400m records 1994–96; took break from athletics in 2001; returned to int. competition Commonwealth Games Manchester 2002, winning a gold medal in the 4×400m relay; retd from athletics 2003; f. Catherine Freeman Foundation; Media and Communications Officer, Australia Post; Hans Christian Andersen Amb. 2003–; numerous nat. awards including Young Australian of the Year 1990, Australian of the Year 1998 (only person to have been awarded both honours). *Leisure interests:* family, pets, children, movies. *Address:* c/o Carolyn Schuwlow, Point 1 Pty Ltd, PO Box 9271 South Yarra, Vic. 3141, Australia. *Telephone:* (3) 9866-1679. *Fax:* (3) 8648-5773. *E-mail:* enquiries@cathyfreeman.com.au. *Website:* www.cathyfreeman.com.au.

FREEMAN, Charles (Chas) Wellman, Jr, BA, JD; American fmr diplomatist and fmr government official; *President, Middle East Policy Council;* b. 2 March 1943, Washington, DC; s. of Charles W. Freeman and Carla Park; m. 1st Patricia Trenery 1962 (divorced 1993); three s. (one deceased) one d.; m. 2nd Margaret Van Wagenen Carpenter 1993; ed Milton Acad., Milton, Mass., Nat. Autonomous Univ. of Mexico, México, Yale Univ., Harvard Law School, Harvard Univ., Foreign Service Inst. School of Chinese Language and Area Studies; entered US Foreign Service 1965, Vice-Consul, Madras, India 1966–68, Taiwan 1969–71, State Dept, China Desk 1971–74, Visiting Fellow, E Asian Legal Research, Harvard Univ. 1974–75, Deputy Dir, Taiwan Affairs, US Dept of State 1975–76, Dir Public Programs, Dept of State 1976–77, Plans and Man. 1977–78, Dir US Information Agency programs 1978–79, Acting US Co-ordinator for Refugee Programs 1979, Dir, Chinese Affairs, Dept of State 1979–81, Minister, US Embassy, Beijing 1981–84, US Embassy, Bangkok 1984–86, Prin. Deputy Asst Sec. of State for African Affairs 1986–89, Amb. to Saudi Arabia 1989–92; Asst Sec. of Defense (Int. Security Affairs) 1993–94; Chair. Bd Projects Int. Inc. 1995–; Vice-Chair. Atlantic Council of USA 1996; Co-Chair. US-China Policy Foundation 1996; Pres. Middle East Policy Council 1997–; Distinguished Fellow, Inst. for Nat. Strategic Studies, Nat. Defense Univ. 1992–93; US Inst. of Peace, Wash. 1994–95; mem. American Acad. of Diplomacy 1995, mem. Bd 2001; mem. Bd Waashington World Affairs Council 1998–, Pacific Pension Inst. 2001–, Asscn for Diplomatic Studies and Training 2001–, Inst. for Defense Analyses; Overseer, Roger Williams Univ.; Order of King Abd Al-Aziz (First Class) 1992; Forrest Prize, Yale Univ., Superior Honor Awards 1978, 1982, Presidential Meritorious Service Awards 1984, 1987, 1989, Group Distinguished Honor Award 1988, Sec. of Defense Award for Meritorious Civilian Service 1991, Distinguished Honor Award 1991, Sec. of Defense Awards for Distinguished Public Service 1994. *Publications:* Cooking Western in China 1987, The Diplomat's Dictionary 1994, Arts of Power: Statecraft and Diplomacy 1997. *Leisure interests:* swimming, sailing, tennis, reading, computers, cookery. *Address:* Middle East Policy Council, 1730 M Street, NW, Suite 512, Washington, DC 20036, USA (office). *Telephone:* (202) 296-6767 (office). *Fax:* (202) 296-5791 (office). *E-mail:* info@mepc.org (home). *Website:* www.mepc.org (office).

FREEMAN, Rt Hon. Maj. John, PC, MBE; British politician, diplomatist, journalist and business executive (retd); b. 19 Feb. 1915; s. of Horace Freeman; m. 1st Elizabeth Johnston 1938 (divorced 1948); m. 2nd Margaret Kerr 1948 (died 1957); m. 3rd Catherine Dove 1962 (divorced 1976); m. 4th Judith Mitchell 1976; two s. three d. and one adopted d.; ed Westminster School and Brasenose Coll., Oxford; advertising consultant 1937–40; active service in N Africa, Italy and NW Europe 1940–45; MP (Lab.) for Watford 1945–55; Financial Sec. to the War Office 1946–47; Under-Sec. of State for War 1947–48; Parl. Sec. to the Ministry of Supply 1948–51 (resgnd); retd from politics 1955; Deputy Ed. New Statesman 1958–61, Ed. 1961–65; British High Commr in India 1965–68; Amb. to USA 1969–71; Chair. London Weekend TV 1971–84, CEO 1971–76; Chair. and CEO LWT (Holdings) 1977–84; Visiting Prof. of Int. Relations, Univ. of California, Davis 1985–90; mem. Bd ITN (Ind. Television News) 1971–76, Chair. 1976–81; mem. Bd, Ind. Television Publs 1971–76; Chair. Bd Govs BFI 1976–77; Vice-Pres. Royal TV Soc. 1975–84; Chair. Communications and Marketing Foundation 1977–79; Chair. Page and Moy (Holdings) Ltd 1979–84, Thomson-CSF Racal PLC (later Thales PLC); mem. (fmr Chair.) Hutchinson Ltd 1978–84; Trustee Reuters 1984–88; Hon. Fellow, Brasenose Coll. Oxford; Hon. LLD (Univ. of S Carolina); Gold Medal (Royal TV Soc.) 1981.

FREEMAN, Michael Alexander Reykers, BA, MB, BCh, MD, FRCS; British orthopaedic surgeon; b. 17 Nov. 1931, Surrey; s. of Donald G. Freeman and Florence J. Elms; m. 1st Elisabeth Jean Freeman 1951; one s. one d.; m. 2nd Janet Edith Freeman 1959; one s. one d.; m. 3rd Patricia Gill 1968; (one s. deceased) one d.; ed Corpus Christi Coll. Cambridge and London Hosp. Medical Coll.; Intern, London Hosp.; Resident in Orthopaedic Surgery, Westminster Hosp. and Middx Hosp. 1962–68; Consultant, London Hosp. 1968–96; European Ed.-in-Chief Journal of Arthroplasty 1997–; co-founder and Dir Biomechanics Unit, Imperial Coll. London 1956–75; currently Visiting Prof. Dept of Biomechanical Eng, Univ. Coll. London; fmr mem. Bd MRC; inventor of prostheses and surgical procedures for replacement of hip, knee, ankle and joints of the foot; past-Pres. British Hip Soc.;, British Orthopaedic Soc., European Fed. of Nat. Asscns. of Orthopaedics and Traumatology (EFORT) 1994–95; mem. numerous professional socs; Hon. Consultant Royal Hosps NHS Trust 1996–; Robert Jones Medal (British Orthopaedic Asscn) 1964 and numerous other awards. *Publications:* The Scientific Basis of Joint Replacement 1977, Arthritis of the Knee 1980; Ed. Adult Articular Cartilage 1973–79; and 200 papers on hip and knee surgery. *Leisure interests:* gardening, reading. *Address:* Department of Biomechanical Engineering, University College, London, NW1 7LX (office); 79 Albert Street, London, NW1 7LX, England (home). *Telephone:* (20) 7387-0817 (home). *Fax:* (20) 7388-5731 (home).

FREEMAN, Morgan; American actor and director; b. 1 June 1937, Memphis, Tenn.; s. of Grafton Freeman and Mayme Revere; m. 1st Jeanette Bradshaw 1967 (divorced 1979); m. 2nd Myrna Colley-Lee 1984; four c.; ed Los Angeles City Coll.; stage debut in Niggerlover 1967; other stage appearances include: Hello Dolly, Broadway 1967, Jungle of Cities 1969, The Recruiting Officer 1969, Purlie, ANTA Theatre, New York 1970, Black Visions 1972, Mighty Gents 1978 (Clarence Derwent Award, Drama Desk Award) 1978, White Pelicans 1978, Coriolanus, New York Shakespeare Festival 1979, Mother Courage and Her Children 1980, Othello Dallas Shakespeare Festival, 1982, Medea and the Doll 1984, The Gospel at Colonus (Obie Award), Driving Miss Daisy 1987, The Taming of the Shrew; co-founder Revelations Entertainment (production co.) 1996; co-founder ClickStar (broadband entertainment co.) 2006; Spencer Tracy Award, UCLA 2006, Kennedy Center Honor 2008. *Films include:* Who Says I Can't Ride a Rainbow? 1971, Brubaker 1980, Eyewitness 1980, Harry and Son 1983, Teachers 1984, Street Smart 1987, Clean and Sober 1988, Lean On Me 1989, Johnny Handsome 1989, Driving Miss Daisy (Golden Globe Award) 1989, Glory 1989, Robin Hood 1991, Unforgiven 1992, The Power of Ore 1992, Chain Reaction 1993, The Shawshank Redemption 1994, Outbreak 1995, Se7en 1996, Moll Flanders, Amistad (NAACP Image Award) 1997, Kiss the Girls 1998, Hard Rain 1998, Water Damage 1999, Mutiny 1999, Under Suspicion 2000, Nurse Betty 2000, Along Came a Spider 2000, Dreamcatcher 2003, Bruce Almighty 2003, Guilty by Association 2003, The Big Bounce 2004, Million Dollar Baby (Best Supporting Actor, Screen Actors Guild Awards 2005, Acad. Awards 2005) 2004, Batman Begins 2005, Danny the Dog 2005, An Unfinished Life 2005, Edison 2005, Unleashed 2005, Lucky Number Slevin 2006, 10 Items or Less 2006, The Contract 2006, Evan Almighty 2007, Gone Baby Gone 2007, Feast of Love 2007, The Bucket List 2007, Wanted 2008, The Dark Knight 2008; dir: Bopha! 1993. *Address:* Revelations Entertainment, 301 Arizona Avenue, Suite 303, Santa Monica, CA 90401 fax; Clickstar Inc., 520 Broadway, #100, Santa Monica, CA 90401; William Morris Agency, One William Morris Place, Beverly Hills, CA 90212, USA. *Telephone:* (310) 394-3131 (Revelations); (310) 859-4000. *Fax:* (310) 394-3133 (Revelations); (310) 883-6402 (Clickstar); (310) 859-4462. *Website:* www.wma.com.

FREEMAN, Raymond (Ray), MA, DPhil, DSc, FRS; British chemist and academic; *Professor Emeritus, Department of Chemistry, University of Cambridge;* b. 6 Jan. 1932, Long Eaton; s. of the late Albert Freeman and Hilda F. Freeman; m. Anne-Marie Périnet-Marquet 1958; two s. three d.; ed Nottingham High School and Lincoln Coll., Oxford; Engineer, French Atomic Energy Comm., Centre d'Etudes Nucléaires de Saclay 1957–59; Sr Scientific Officer, Nat. Physical Lab. 1959–63; Research Scientist, Instrument Div., Varian Assocs, Palo Alto, Calif. 1963–73; Univ. Lecturer in Physical Chem. and Fellow, Magdalen Coll., Oxford 1973–87, Aldrichian Praelector in Chem. 1982–87; John Humphrey Plummer Prof. of Magnetic Resonance, Univ. of Cambridge 1987–99, Prof. Emer. 1999–, Fellow, Jesus Coll., Cambridge 1987–99, Fellow Emer. 1999–; Hon. DSc (Durham) 1998; Leverhulme Medal, Royal Soc. 1990, RSC Longstaff Medal 1999, Queen's Medal, Royal Soc. 2002, Laukien Prize Experimental NMR Conf. 2005. *Publications:* A Handbook of Nuclear Magnetic Resonance 1987, Spin Choreography: Basic Steps in High

Resolution NMR 1997, Magnetic Resonance in Chemistry and Medicine 2003; several scientific papers on nuclear magnetic resonance spectroscopy in various journals. *Leisure interests:* swimming, traditional jazz. *Address:* Department of Chemistry, Lensfield Road, Cambridge, CB2 1EW (office); Jesus College, Cambridge, CB5 8BL (office); 29 Bentley Road, Cambridge, CB2 8AW, England (home). *Telephone:* (1223) 339403 (office); (1223) 323958 (home). *Fax:* (1223) 336362 (office). *E-mail:* rf110@hermes.cam.ac.uk (office). *Website:* www.ch.cam.ac.uk (office).

FREEMAN, Richard B., PhD; American economist and academic; *Senior Professorial Research Fellow, London School of Economics;* b. 29 June 1953, Newburgh, NY; m. Alida Castillo; one s. one d.; ed Dartmouth and Harvard Univs; fmr Program Dir, Labour Studies, Nat. Bureau of Econ. Research (NBER); fmr Sr Research Fellow Centre for Econ. Performance, LSE, London; Pres. Soc. of Labour Economists 1997; Vice-Pres. American Econ Asscn 1997; AEA Rep. to AAAS Section on Social, Econ. and Political Sciences 2004–07; mem. COSEPUP Cttee on Science, Eng and Public Policy, Nat. Acads 2004–05; Adviser Sigma Xi Postdoc Survey Project; affil. Scholar Nat. Acad. of Eng (CASEE); mem. External Advisory Cttee BECON-NIH Bioengineering Consortium, Scientific Advisory Bd Kiel Inst. for the World Economy, Initiative for Science and Tech., Cttee for Study of Alternative Models of Fed. Funding of Science 2007–; mem. AAAS 2004 (Fellow 2007), American Acad. of Arts and Sciences. *Lectures:* Clarendon Lecturer, Univ. of Oxford 1994, Lionel Robins Lecturer, LSE 1999, Luigi Einauidi Lecturer, Cornell Univ. 2002, Okun Lecturer, Yale Univ. 2003, World Econ. Annual Lecturer, Univ. of Nottingham 2003, Dr Heinz Kienzl Lecturer, OeNB, Vienna 2003, Roco C. Siciliano Lecturer, Univ. of Utah 2004. *Publications:* The Over-Educated American 1976, What Do Unions Do? 1984, Labor Markets in Action 1989, Working Under Different Rules 1994, What Workers Want 1999 (revised edn with Joel Rogers 2006), Can Labor Standards Improve Under Globalization? (with Kimberly Ann Elliott) 2003, America Works: The Exceptional Labor Market 2007. *Leisure interest:* professional wrestling. *Address:* National Bureau of Economic Research, 1050 Massachusetts Avenue, Cambridge, MA 02138, USA (office); Centre for Economic Performance, London School of Economics, Houghton Street, London, WC2A 2AE, England (office). *Telephone:* (617) 588-0303 (USA) (office); (20) 7955-7041 (UK) (office). *Fax:* (617) 868-2742 (USA) (office); (20) 7955-7595 (UK) (office). *E-mail:* freeman@nber.org (office); a.freeman@lse.ac.uk (office). *Website:* (office).

FREETH, Peter, RA, RE; British artist and printmaker; b. 15 April 1938, Birmingham; s. of Alfred William Freeth and Olive Freeth (née Walker); m. Mariolina Meliadò 1967; two s.; ed King Edward's Grammar School, Aston, Birmingham, Slade School, London, British School, Rome; tutor, Etching Royal Acad. Schools 1966–; works on display in British Museum, Victoria & Albert Museum, Arts Council of England, Fitzwilliam Museum, Cambridge, Ashmolean Museum, Oxford, Nat. Gallery, Washington, DC, USA, Metropolitan Museum, New York, Hunterian Gallery, Glasgow; Prix de Rome (engraving) 1960, Best Print, Royal Acad. 1986, Drawing/Print Prize 2002, Hunting Art Prizes, Royal Coll. of Art 2004, 2005. *Publication:* Printmakers' Secrets (contrib.) 2009. *Leisure interests:* books, music, grandchildren. *Address:* 83 Muswell Hill Road, London, N10 3HT, England (home).

FREI RUIZ-TAGLE, Eduardo; Chilean fmr head of state; b. 24 June 1942, Santiago; s. of the late Eduardo Frei Montalva (fmr Pres. of Chile) and María Ruiz-Tagle; m. María Larraechea; ed Univ. of Chile; joined Christian Democrat (CD) Party 1958, fmr Pres.; CD presidential cand., Dec. 1993, Pres. of Chile 1994–2000; C-in-C of Armed Forces 1998–2000; elected to Senate 1989; Pres. Fundación Eduardo Frei Montalva 1982–93. *Address:* c/o Partido Demócrata Cristiano, Almeda B. O'Higgins 1460, 2°, Santiago, Chile.

FRÉMAUX, Louis Joseph Félix; French orchestral conductor; b. 13 Aug. 1921, Aire-sur-la-Lys; m. 1st Nicole Petitbon 11948; four s. one d.; 2nd Cecily Hake 1999; ed Conservatoire Nat. Supérieur de Musique, Paris; Musical Dir and Perm. Conductor of Orchestre Nat. de l'Opéra de Monte-Carlo, Monaco 1955–66; Prin. Conductor, Rhône-Alpes Philharmonic Orchestra, Lyons 1968–71; Prin. Conductor and Musical Dir, City of Birmingham Symphony Orchestra 1969–78; Chief Conductor, Sydney Symphony Orchestra 1979–81, Prin. Guest Conductor 1982–85; guest appearances in Austria, Belgium, Holland, France, Italy, New Zealand, Norway, Switzerland, South America and Germany; Hon. mem. RAM 1978; Chevalier Légion d'honneur; Croix de Guerre (twice); Hon. DMus (Birmingham Univ.) 1978; 8 Grand Prix du Disque Awards; Koussevitsky Award. *Address:* 21 Rue De La Place, 41500 Avaray, France. *Telephone:* (2) 54-81-73-42.

FRENCH, Dawn; British actress and comedienne; b. 11 Oct. 1957, Holyhead, Wales; m. Lenny Henry (q.v.) 1984; one d. (adopted); ed Manchester Univ., London Cen. School of Speech and Drama; stage shows and TV series with Jennifer Saunders (q.v.); co–founder and Man. Sixteen 47 Ltd (fashion business); Hon. Rose, Montreux 2002. *Stage appearances include:* Silly Cow, When We are Married 1996, My Brilliant Divorce 2003, Smaller (Lyric Theatre, London and UK tour) 2006. *Radio:* guest appearances on numerous talk shows. *TV appearances include:* The Comic Strip (Strike, Consuela, Five Go Mad in Dorset, Supergrass, Ken, The Yob, Susie), French and Saunders, The Vicar of Dibley, Tender Loving Care 1993, Sex and Chocolate 1997; presenter: Swank 1987, Scoff 1988 (UK Channel 4). *Films include:* The Supergrass 1985, Eat the Rich 1987, The Adventures of Pinocchio 1996, Maybe Baby 2000, Harry Potter and the Prisoner of Azkaban 2004, The Chronicles of Narnia: The Lion, the Witch and the Wardrobe (voice) 2005. *Publication:* Dear Fatty (auto-biog.) 2008. *Address:* c/o Sixteen 47 Ltd, French and Teague, 719 High Road, Leytonstone, London, E11 4RD, England. *Website:* www.sixteen47.com.

FRENDO, Michael, LLM; Maltese politician and lawyer; b. 29 July 1955; s. of the late Joseph Frendo and of Josephine Frendo (née Felice); m. Irene Brincat 1984; one s. two d.; ed Univ. of Malta and Univ. of Exeter, UK; admitted to the Bar 1977; Lecturer, Faculty of Law, Univ. of Malta 1987–; Nat. Chair. for Malta, World Jurist Ass. 1975–; Dir Press and Media Relations and Editorial Dir (newspapers) of Nationalist Party (Christian Democrat) 1982–85; MP 1987–; mem. of Parl. Ass., Council of Europe 1987–92; mem. Malta Parl. Del. to European Parl. 1987–90, 1996– (Chair. 1990–92); Parl. Sec. for Youth, Culture and Consumer Protection 1990–92; Minister for Youth and the Arts 1992–94, for Transport, Communications and Tech. 1994–96; fmr Parl. Sec., Ministry of Foreign Affairs and Investment Promotion; Minister of Foreign Affairs 2004–08; lawyer in pvt. practice 1996–; First Vice-Chair. Jt Parl. Cttee, European Parl. and Malta Parl. 1999–; Nationalist Party (Christian Democrat); mem. European Convention (EU) 2002–04. *Publications:* books and articles in local and int. magazines and journals. *Leisure interests:* reading, 'talking books'. *Address:* Nationalist Party, Herbert Ganado Street, Pietà PTA 1541, Malta (office). *Telephone:* 21243641 (office). *Fax:* 21243640 (office). *E-mail:* admin@pn.org.mt (office). *Website:* www.pn.org.mt (office).

FRENI, Mirella; Italian singer; b. (Mirella Fregni), 27 Feb. 1935, Modena; d. of Ennio Fregni and Gianna (née Arcelli) Fregni; m. 1st Leone Magiera 1955; one d.; m. 2nd Nicolai Ghiaurov (died 2004); debut 1955 as Micaëla in Carmen, debut at La Scala, Milan 1962, Glyndebourne Festival 1961, Royal Opera House, Covent Garden 1961, Metropolitan Opera, NY 1965; has sung at Vienna State Opera, Rome Opera, Barcelona Gran Teatro del Liceo, Boston Opera, La Scala and at Salzburg Festival and leading opera houses throughout the world; retd from the stage 2005. *Recordings include:* Carmen, Falstaff, La Bohème, Madame Butterfly, Tosca, Verdi Requiem, Aïda, Don Giovanni. *Major roles include:* Nanetta in Falstaff, Mimi in La Bohème, Zerlina in Don Giovanni, Susanna, Adina in L'Elisir d'amore, Violetta in La Traviata, Desdemona in Otello. *Address:* c/o Jack Mastroianni, IMG Artists, Carnegie Hall Tower, 152 West 57th Street, 5th Floor, New York, NY 10019, USA (office). *Telephone:* (212) 994-3525 (office). *E-mail:* jmastroianni@imgartists.com (office). *Website:* www.imgartists.com (office).

FRENK, Alfons Hubert; German accountant and retail executive; b. 1950; m.; three c.; Man. Dir Edeka Minden-Hannover 1991–2002, also acted as spokesman for Minden-Hannover regional office, Man. Dir Edeka Zentrale AG & Co. KG 2002–03, CEO 2003–08, Chair. Supervisory Bd Edeka Group –2008. *Address:* c/o Edeka Zentrale AG & Co. KG, New-York-Ring 6, 22297 Hamburg, Germany. *Telephone:* (40) 63-77-0.

FRENK MORA, Julio José, MA, PhD, MD; Mexican physician, public health administrator and fmr government official; b. 20 Dec. 1953, Mexico City; m. Dr Felicia Knaul; three c.; ed National Autonomojus Univ. of Mexico, Univ. of Mich., USA; Founding Dir Centre of Public Health Research, Ministry of Health 1984–87; Founding Dir Gen. Nat. Inst. of Public Health of Mexico 1987–92; Visiting Prof., Harvard Center for Population and Devt Studies 1992–93; Exec. Vice Pres. and Dir, Centre for Health and Economy, Mexican Health Foundation 1995–98; Exec. Dir Evidence and Information for Policy, WHO, Geneva 1998–2000; Sec. of Health 2000–06; Vice Pres. for Latin Ameica, American Public Health Asscn; fmr Pres. Mexican Soc. for Quality in Health Care; Nat. Researcher, Mexican Research System 1984–98; mem. Nat. Acad. of Medicine of Mexico; US Inst. of Medicine and numerous other professional orgs; mem. editorial bds of 10 journals; Int. Fellow in Health, W.K. Kellogg Foundation 1986–89; Fellow, Mich. Soc. of Fellows, Univ. of Mich. 1982–84; Cecilio A. Robelo Award for Scientific Research (State of Morelos) 1993. *Publications:* author of 28 books and monographs and 103 articles in cultural magazines and newspapers. *Address:* c/o Secretariat of State for Health, Lieja 7, 1°, Col. Juárez, Del. Cuauhtémoc, 06600 México, DF, Mexico (office).

FRENKEL, Jacob A., PhD; Israeli economist, academic and business executive; *Senior Vice-President and Chairman, Merrill Lynch International;* b. 8 Feb. 1943, Tel-Aviv; m. Niza Frenkel 1968; two d.; ed Univ. of Chicago, USA, Hebrew Univ. of Jerusalem; on staff Chicago Univ. 1973–87, various positions including Ed. Journal of Political Economy, David Rockefeller Prof. of Int. Econs; Econ. Counsellor, Dir of Research, IMF 1987–91; joined Tel-Aviv Univ. 1991, Weisfeld Prof. of Econs of Peace and Int. Relations 1994–; Gov. Bank of Israel 1991–2000; Sr Vice-Pres. and Vice-Chair. Merrill Lynch International 2000–, Chair. Sovereign Advisory Group and Global Financial Insts Group 2000–, Chair. Merrill Lynch International 2001–; Co-Chair. of Israeli del. to multilateral peace talks on Regional Econ. Devts 1991; Chair. Bd Govs Inter-American Devt Bank 1995–96; Research Assoc., Nat. Bureau of Econ. Research; distinguished mem. Advisory Cttee Inst. for Global Econs, Korea; mem. G-7 Council, Advisory Cttee for Int. Econs, G-30, Exec. Cttee Int. Econs Asscn; Fellow Econometric Soc.; Foreign Hon. mem. American Acad. of Arts and Science, Japan Soc. of Monetary Econs; Gran Cruz, Orden de Mayo al Mérito (Argentina); Karel Englis Prize in Econs (Czech Repub.). *Publications:* numerous books and articles on int. econs and macro-econs. *Address:* Merrill Lynch & Co., Inc. Global Headquarters, 4 World Financial Center, 250 Vesey Street, New York, NY 10080, USA (office). *Telephone:* (212) 449-1000 (office). *Website:* www.ml.com (office).

FRENZEL, Michael, Dr iur.; German business executive; *Chairman of the Executive Board, TUI AG;* b. 2 March 1947, Leipzig; ed Ruhr Univ., Bochum; joined Westdeutsche Landesbank (WestLB), Düsseldorf 1981, Man. Industrial Holdings Dept 1983–85, Man. Equity Holdings Div. 1985–88; mem. Bd of Dirs Preussag AG (renamed TUI AG 2002) 1988–, Vice-Chair. 1992–93, Chair. Exec. Bd 1994–, also Chair. TUI Travel PLC 2007–; Chair. Creditanstalt AG, Vienna; Chair. Supervisory Bd PreussenElektra AG, Hanover, Deutsche Bahn AG. *Address:* TUI AG, Postfach 610209, 30602 Hanover (office); TUI AG, Karl-Wiechert-Allee 4, 30625 Hanover, Germany (office). *Telephone:* (511)

56600 (office). *Fax:* (511) 5661901 (office). *E-mail:* info@tui-group.com (office). *Website:* www.tui-group.com (office).

FRERE, Baron; **Albert Pol Oscar Ghislain;** Belgian business executive; *Chairman of the Board, Groupe Bruxelles Lambert;* b. 4 Feb. 1926, Fontaine-L'Evêque; s. of Oscar Frère and Madeleine Bourgeois; m. Christine Hennuy; three c.; ed Athénée Provincial du Centre, Morlanwelz; Chair. Frère Bourgeois SA 1970; Vice-Chair. Benelux Paribas Cobepa SA 1973–2000; Chair. Financière de la Sambre 1973–, Erbe SA 1975, Fingen SA 1999, Stichting Administratie Kantoor de Frère-Bourgeois (Pays-Bas) 1982; Vice-Chair., Man. Dir and mem. Exec. Cttee Pargesa Holding SA, Geneva, Switzerland 1981; Chair. Electrafina SA 1982–2001; Man. Dir Groupe Bruxelles Lambert SA 1982–, Chair. 1987–; Chair. PetroFina 1990–2003; Vice-Chair. and mem. Bd Dirs TotalFinaElf 1999–2001; mem. Bd Dirs LVMH (Louis Vuitton Moët Hennessy) (France) 1997, Raspail Investissements (France) 2006), Société Civile Du Château Cheval Blanc (France) 1998, Gruppo Banca Leonardo 2006; mem. Bd Dirs Métropole Télévision M6 2000–, Chair. Supervisory Bd 2003–; Vice-Chair. Suez 2001–08, Vice-Chair. GDF SUEZ 2008–; mem. Int. Advisory Cttee Power Corpn, Montréal 1985–2005, Assicurazioni Generali SpA, Trieste 1992; Perm. Rep. of Belholding Belgium SA; mem. Bd Dirs Groupe Arnault SA (France); Perm. Rep. of Frère-Bourgeois SA; Man. GBL Verwaltung SARL (Luxembourg); Régent honoraire Banque nat. de Belgique 1980; Grand Croix, Légion d'honneur; Grand Officier, Ordre de Léopold; Dr hc (Univ. of Laval). *Leisure interests:* golf, skiing, hunting. *Address:* Groupe Bruxelles Lambert, 24 avenue Marnix, 1000 Brussels, Belgium (office); 33 avenue Foch, 75008 Paris, France (home); La Peupleraie, allée des Peupliers 17, 6280 Gerpinnes, Belgium. *Telephone:* (71) 60-60-15 (office). *Fax:* (71) 60-60-16 (office). *E-mail:* adimillo@cnp.be (office). *Website:* www.gbl.be (office).

FRÈRE, Gérald; Belgian business executive; *Chairman, Compagnie Nationale à Portefeuille (CNP);* b. 17 May 1951, Charleroi; s. of Baron Albert Frère; began career as Man. Dir Frère-Bourgeois Group (family co.); currently Chair. Compagnie Nationale à Portefeuille (CNP); also Chair. Diane SA, Filux SA, Gesecalux SA, Stichting Administratie Kantoor Bierlaire, TVI SA; Vice-Chair. Pargesa Holding SA; Chair. and Man. Dir Haras de la Bierlaire SA, Groupe Bruxelles Lambert SA 1993–; Man. Dir Financière de la Sambre SA; Dir Power Financial Corpn, Erbe SA, Fingen SA, Fonds Charles-Albert Frère asbl, GBL Finance SA, Stichting Administratie Kantoor Frère-Bourgeois, Suez-Tractebel SA; Man. Agriger SPRL; mem. Bd of Regency Nationale Bank van België; mem. Supervisory Bd, Financial Services Authority, Brussels; mem. Bd of Trustees Belgian Governance Inst. *Address:* Compagnie Nationale à Portefeuille, Rue de la Blanche Borne 12, 6280 Gerpinnes (Loverval), Belgium (office). *Telephone:* (71) 60-60-60 (office). *Fax:* (71) 60-60-70 (office). *Website:* www.cnp.be (office).

FRÈRE, Jean; Belgian diplomatist and banker (retd); b. 15 Nov. 1919, Chatou, Seine-et-Oise, France; s. of Maurice Frère and Germaine Schimp; m. Marie-Rose Vanlangenhove 1949; one s. three d.; ed Germany, Austria, Brussels Univs; with Solvay & Cie (Chemical Industries), Brussels 1941–46; entered diplomatic service 1946, Attaché (Commercial and Econ.), Belgian Legation, Prague 1948–51; Political Div., Ministry of Foreign Affairs 1951–52; First Sec. (Econ.), Belgian Embassy, Rome 1952–58; Gen. Sec. EIB 1958–; Conseiller Banque Lambert 1962–, Man. Partner 1967–; Conseiller Général Banque Bruxelles Lambert SA 1975–81, Conseiller Général Honoraire 1981–; fmr Chair. BBL-Australia; fmr mem. of Bd and Exec. Cttee Banco di Roma Belgio; nuerous Belgian and foreign decorations. *Leisure interests:* violin, painting, photography, electronics. *Address:* 3315 San Marco, 30124 Venice, Italy. *Telephone:* (041) 5222647. *Fax:* (041) 5222647.

FRESCO, Paolo; Italian business executive; *Senior Advisor, Credit Suisse First Boston;* b. 12 July 1933, Milan; m. Marlene Fresco; ed Istituto Andrea Doria, Genoa, Univ. of Genoa; law grad., pupillage at Studio Lefebre, Genoa; practised law in Rome; set up legal dept, CGE (Compagnia Generale Elettricità, a Gen. Electric investee co.) 1962, apptd CEO CGE 1972; responsible for Italy, the Middle East and Africa, Int. Activities, Gen. Electric 1976, Head of Int. Activities 1987; restructured Nuovo Pignone (following takeover by CGE) 1992; Exec. Vice-Pres. and Gen. Man. Gen. Electric, Fairfield, Conn., USA 1992–98; mem. Bd Fiat Group 1996–2003, Chair. 1998–2003; mem. Bd Istituto Finanziario Industriale SpA 1999–2003, Giovanni Agnelli & C. SpA 2001–03; Sr Advisor Credit Suisse First Boston 2004–; fmr Vice-Chair. Assonime (Associazione Italiana fra le Società per Azioni); Chair. Organizing Cttee, Chess Olympiads 2006. *Leisure interests:* art, chess, deep-sea fishing, mountain-climbing. *Address:* Credit Suisse First Boston, One Cabot Square, London, E14 4QJ, England (office). *Telephone:* (20) 7888-8888 (office). *Fax:* (20) 7888-1600 (office). *Website:* www.csfb.com (office).

FRESTON, Thomas E., BA, MBA; American media executive; b. 22 Nov. 1945, New York, NY; s. of Thomas E. Freston and Winifred Geng; m. Margaret Badali 1980; one s.; Dir of Marketing MTV, MTV Networks, New York 1980–81; Dir of Marketing, The Movie Channel 1982–83; Vice-Pres. Marketing MTV, MTV Networks 1983–84, Vice-Pres. Marketing 1984–85, Sr Vice-Pres. and Gen. Man. Affiliate Sales, Marketing 1985, Sr Vice-Pres. and Gen. Man. MTV, VH-1 1985–86, Pres. Entertainment 1986–87, Pres. and CEO 1987–89, Chair. and CEO MTV Networks 1989–2004; Co-Pres. and Co-COO Viacom Inc. 2004–05, CEO Viacom (after split of Viacom Inc.) 2005–06; mem. Bd of Dirs Cable Advertising Bureau 1987–, Museum of Natural History, Rock and Roll Hall of Fame 1986–; mem. Smithsonian Comm. Music in America 1987–, Cable TV Admin. and Marketing Asscn, Nat. Acad. of Cable Programming;; Gov.'s Award from Nat. Acad. of Cable Programming, Personality of the Year from MIPCOM, Pres. Award from Cable TV Public Affairs Asscn, Humanitarian of the Year Award from T.J. Martell Foundation; inducted Cable Television Hall of Fame 2005. *Leisure interests:* photography, travel, antique rugs.

FRETTON, Anthony (Tony); British architect; *Professor of Architectural and Interior Design, Technical University of Delft;* b. 17 Jan. 1945, London; s. of Thomas C. Fretton and May Frances Diamond; m. Susan Pearce 1963 (divorced 1988); one s. one d.; ed Architectural Asscn School of Architecture; architect, Arup Assocs, then Neylan and Ungless 1972–81; f. own architectural practice Tony Fretton Architects 1982; Unit Master, AA School of Architecture 1989–91; Visiting Prof., Berlage Inst., Amsterdam, Netherlands, Ecole Polytechnique de Lausanne, Switzerland 1994–96; Prof. of Architectural and Interior Design, Tech. Univ. of Delft, Netherlands 1999–; Visiting Lecturer, Harvard Design School, USA 2005; Corp. mem. RIBA; Dr hc (Oxford Brookes) 2006. *Major projects include:* Lisson Gallery, London 1992, Artsway Centre for Visual Arts, Sway, Hampshire 1996, Quay Arts Centre, Newport, Isle of Wight 1998, house for an art collector, Tite Street, Chelsea, London 2001, apartment bldg in Lutkenieuwstraat, Groningen, Netherlands 2001, The Red House, Chelsea, London (Stone Fed. of GB Natural Stone Award 2002, RIBA Award 2003, Chicago Athenaeum Int. Architecture Award 2006), Faith House, Holton Lee Centre for Disability in the Arts, Poole, Dorset 2002 (ACE/RIBA Awards for Religious Architecture 2003, Guardian Best British Building of the Year Award), Stroud Valley Arts Space 2002–07, Arts Council Sculpture Gallery, Yorkshire Sculpture Park 2003, Camden Arts Centre, London 2004, New British Embassy and Residence, Warsaw, Poland 2003–08, de Prinsendam, Amsterdam 2004–08, House for Anish Kapoor 2004–08, Constantijn Huygenstraat, Amsterdam 2004–08, Vassall Road Housing, London 2004–08, Tietgens Grund, Copenhagen 2004–09, Cultural Centre, House for Two Artists, Clerkenwell, London 2005, Fuglsang, Denmark 2005–07, Fuglsang Kunstmuseum, Lolland, Denmark 2005–08, Andreas Ensemble, Amsterdam 2005–10, Gershwin IV, Zuidas Amsterdam 2006–09. *Publications:* Tony Fretton 1995, Tony Fretton Architects: Abstraction and Familiarity 2001. *Leisure interests:* travel, film, visual arts, poetry. *Address:* 109–123 Clifton Street, London, EC2A 4LD, England (office). *Telephone:* (20) 7729-2030 (office). *Fax:* (20) 7729-2050 (office). *E-mail:* mail@tonyfretton.com (office). *Website:* www.tonyfretton.com (office).

FRETWELL, Sir John Emsley, Kt, GCMG, MA; British diplomatist (retd); b. 15 June 1930, Chesterfield; s. of F. T. Fretwell; m. Mary Ellen Eugenie Dubois 1959; one s. one d.; ed Chesterfield Grammar School, Lausanne Univ., King's Coll., Cambridge; HM Forces 1948–50; entered diplomatic service 1953, Third Sec., Hong Kong 1954–55, Second Sec., Embassy in Beijing 1955–57, Foreign Office 1957–59, 1962–67, First Sec., Moscow 1959–62, First Sec. (Commercial), Washington, DC 1967–70, Commercial Counsellor, Warsaw 1971–73, Head of European Integration Dept (Internal), FCO 1973–76, Asst Under-Sec. of State 1976–79, Minister, Washington, DC 1980–81; Amb. to France 1982–87; Political Dir and Deputy to Perm. Under-Sec. of State, FCO 1987–90; mem. Council of Lloyd's 1991–92; Specialist Adviser, House of Lords 1992–93; Chair. Franco-British Soc. 1995–2005, mem. Council 2005–; currently freelance adviser in int. affairs; Commdr Legion d'honneur, Grand Officier, Ordre nat. du Mérite. *Leisure interests:* walking, history. *Address:* c/o Brooks's, St James's Street, London, SW1A 1LN, England.

FREUD, Anthony Peter, OBE, LLB; British opera administrator and barrister; *General Director and CEO, Houston Grand Opera;* b. 30 Oct. 1957, London; s. of the late Joseph Freud and Katalin Freud (née Löwi); ed King's Coll. School, Wimbledon and King's Coll., London; trained as barrister before becoming theatre manager at Sadler's Wells Theatre Co. 1980–84; Co. Sec., Welsh Nat. Opera 1984, Head of Planning 1989–92, Gen. Dir 1994–2005; Chair. Opera Europe 2001–05; Gen. Dir and CEO Houston Grand Opera 2006–; Exec. Producer, Opera, Philips Classics 1992–94; elected Chair. OPERA America 2008–(10); Chair. Jury, BBC Cardiff Singer of the World Competition 1995–2005; Trustee Nat. Endowment for Science, Tech. and the Arts 2004–05; Hon. Fellow, Univ. of Cardiff 2002, Royal Welsh Coll. of Music and Drama 2005. *Leisure interests:* music, theatre, cinema, visual arts, travel, cookery. *Address:* Houston Grand Opera, 510 Preston Street, Houston, TX 77002 (office); 2814 Ferndale, Houston, TX 77098, USA (home). *Telephone:* (713) 546-0260 (office); (713) 546-0266 (office). *Fax:* (713) 247-0906 (office). *E-mail:* anthony_freud@houstongrandopera.org (office). *Website:* www.houstongrandopera.org.

FREUD, Lucian, OM, CH; British painter; b. 8 Dec. 1922, Berlin; s. of the late Ernst Freud and Lucie Freud; grands. of Sigmund Freud; m. 1st Kathleen Epstein 1948 (divorced 1952); two d.; m. 2nd Lady Caroline Maureen Blackwood 1953 (divorced 1957, died 1996); ed Cen. School of Art, E Anglian School of Painting and Drawing; Teacher at Slade School of Art, London 1948–58; first one-man exhbn 1944, subsequently 1946, 1950, 1952, 1958, 1963, 1968, 1972, 1978, 1979, 1982, 1983, 1988, 1990–96, 1997, 1998, 2000, 2004; retrospectives: Hayward Gallery 1974, 1988, 1989, Tate Gallery, Liverpool 1992, Tate Britain 2002, then transferred to Fundacion la Caixa, Barcelona, Museum of Contemporary Art, Los Angeles; works included in public collections: Tate Gallery, Nat. Portrait Gallery, Victoria and Albert Museum, Arts Council of Great Britain, British Council, British Museum, Fitzwilliam Museum, Cambridge, Nat. Museum of Wales, Cardiff, Scottish Nat. Gallery of Modern Art, Edinburgh, Walker Art Gallery, Liverpool, Ashmolean Museum of Art, Oxford, etc.; in Australia at Brisbane, Adelaide, Perth; in France at Musée Nat. d'Art Moderne, Centre Georges Pompidou, Paris; in USA at The Art Inst. of Chicago, Museum of Modern Art, New York, Cleveland Museum of Art, Ohio, Museum of Art, Carnegie Inst., Pittsburgh, Achenbaach Foundation for Graphic Arts and Fine Arts, San Francisco, The St Louis Art Museum, Hirshhorn Museum and Sculpture Garden, Smithsonian Inst., Washington, DC, Yale Center for British Art, Beaverbrook Art Gallery, Fredericton, Canada; Hon. DLitt (Glasgow) 2003; Rubenspreis, City of Siegen 1997, Serg Ratgeb Prize, Reutlingen 2002. *Publication:* subject of numerous books including Lucian Freud by Lawrence Gowing 1982, Lucian Freud, Paintings by Robert Hughes 1987, Lucian Freud, Works on Paper by

Nicholas Penney and Robert Flynn Johnson 1988, The Etchings of Lucian Freud, a catalogue raisonne by Craig Hartley 1995, Lucian Freud introduction by Bruce Bernard 1996, Lucian Freud 1996-2005 introduction by Sebastian Smee 2005, Freud at Work by Bruce Bernard and David Dawson 2006, Lucian Freud introduction by William Feaver 2007. *Address:* c/o Diana Rawstron, Goodman Derrick, 90 Fetter Lane, London, EC4A 1PT, England (office). *Telephone:* (20) 7404-0606 (office). *Fax:* (20) 7831-6407 (office). *E-mail:* drawstron@gdlaw.co.uk (office). *Website:* gdlaw.co.uk (office).

FREUDENTHAL, Dave; American state official and lawyer; *Governor of Wyoming;* b. 12 Oct. 1950, Thermpolis, Wyo.; m. Nancy Freudenthal; four c.; ed Amhurst Coll., Mass, Univ. of Wyoming Coll. of Law; economist, Wyo. Dept of Econ. Planning and Devt 1973–75, apptd State Planning Co-ordinator 1975–80; f. law office, Cheyenne 1980; US Attorney, Wyo. 1994–2001; Gov. of Wyo. 2003–; fmr. Chair. Greater Cheyenne Chamber of Commerce; Founder-Dir Wyo. Student Loans Corpn; mem. Bd Wyo. Community Foundation, Wyo. State Econ. and Devt Stabilization Dept, Laramie Co. Community Action; Democrat. *Leisure interest:* layreader and vestryperson in local church. *Address:* Office of the Governor, State Capitol Building, Room 124, 200 West 24th Street, Cheyenne, WY 82002, USA (office). *Telephone:* (307) 777-7434 (office). *Website:* wyoming.gov.governor/governor_home.asp (office).

FREY, Bruno S., FRSE; Swiss economist and academic; *Professor of Economics, University of Zürich;* b. 4 May 1941, Basel; s. of Leo Frey and Julie Frey (née Bach); ed Univs of Basel and Cambridge; Assoc. Prof., Univ. of Basel 1969–; Prof. of Econs, Univ. of Konstanz 1970–77, Univ. of Zürich 1977–; Visiting Fellow, All Souls Coll., Oxford 1983; Fellow, Coll. of Science, Berlin 1984–85; Visiting Research Prof., Univ. of Chicago, Ill. 1990; Visiting Prof., Univ. of Rome 1996–97, Antwerp Univ. 1999, Univs of Gothenburg, Stockholm, Linz, Klagenfurt, Siena, Kiel, Valencia, Groningen, Research School of Social Sciences, ANU, Queensland Univ. of Tech., ETH-Zürich 2007–; Research Dir Centre for Research in Econs, Man. and the Arts, Zürich 2000–; Fellow, Collegium Budapest 2002, European Econ. Asscn 2004, Public Choice Soc.; First Jelle Zijlstra Professorial Fellow, Inst. of Advanced Study, Wassenaar 2003; Distinguished Fellow, CESifo Research Network 2005; Man. Ed. Kyklos 1969–; Hon. DUniv (St Gallen) 1998, (Gothenburg) 1998; Vernon Prize, Asscn for Public Policy and Man., Stolper Prize of Verein für Socialpolitik. *Publications include:* Economics as a Science of Human Behaviour 1992, Not Just for the Money: An Economic Theory of Personal Motivation 1997, The New Democratic Federalism for Europe 1999, Arts and Economics: Analysis and Cultural Policy 2000, Managing Motivation: Wie Sie die neue Motivationsforschung für Ihr Unternehmen nutzen können (co-author) 2000, Inspiring Economics: Human Motivation in Political Economy 2001, Successful Management by Motivation – Balancing Intrinsic and Extrinsic Incentives 2002, Happiness and Economics: How the Economy and Institutions Affect Human Well-Being 2002, Dealing with Terrorism: Stick or Carrot? 2004, Economics and Psychology 2007, Happiness: A Revolution in Economics 2008. *Leisure interest:* travel.

FREYNDLIKH, Alisa Brunovna; Russian actress; b. 8 Dec. 1934; d. of Bruno Arturovich Freyndlikh; ed Leningrad Theatre Inst.; worked with Komissarzhevskaya Theatre, Leningrad 1957–61; then with Lensoviet Theatre, Leningrad 1961–83, Gorky Theatre 1983–; worked in films 1958–; RSFSR State Prize 1976, USSR People's Artist 1981, State Prize 1995. *Films include:* Family Happiness 1970, My Life 1973, The Princess and the Pea 1977, An Everyday Novel 1977, Always With Me 1977, The Business Love Affair 1977, Stalker 1980, An Old-Fashioned Comedy 1980, Agony 1981, The Canary Cage 1984, Success 1985, The Hunt 1994, Secrets Shared with a Stranger 1994, Katya Ismailova 1994, On Upper Maslovka Street 2005, Vozvrashenie mushketerov, ili sokrovischa kardinala Mazarini 2009. *Stage roles include:* Lady Milford in Schiller's Perfidy and Love 1990, Autumn Violins 1997 and many others. *Address:* 191002 St Petersburg, Rubinstein str. 11, Apt 7, Russia. *Telephone:* (812) 314-88-40.

FRICK, Aurelia, Lic.iur., DrIur; Liechtenstein lawyer and politician; *Minister of Foreign Affairs, Justice and Cultural Affairs;* b. 19 Sept. 1975; ed Univ. of Fribourg, Univ. of Basel; admitted to Zurich Bar 2004; attorney, Haymann & Baldi, Zurich 2004–05; Assoc., Bjørn Johansson Assocs AG, Zurich 2006–07; man. consultant 2008–09; Minister of Foreign Affairs, Justice and Cultural Affairs 2009–; mem. Progressive Citizens' Party. *Leisure interests:* music, sport, culture. *Address:* Regierungsgebäude, Postfach 684, 9490 Vaduz, Liechtenstein (office). *Telephone:* 2366111 (office). *Fax:* 2366022 (office). *E-mail:* office@liechtenstein.li (office). *Website:* www.liechtenstein.li (office).

FRICK, Mario, DrIur; Liechtenstein politician and civil servant; b. 8 May 1965, Balzers; s. of Kuno Frick-Kaufmann and Melita Frick-Kaufmann; m. Andrea Haberlander 1992; one s. one d.; ed St Gall University, Switzerland; State Admin. Legal Service 1991–93; mem. Municipal Council of Balzers 1991–93; Deputy Head of Govt May–Dec. 1993, Head of Govt 1993–99, also Minister of Finance and Construction. *Leisure interests:* football, tennis, biking. *Address:* c/o Office of Prime Minister, Government Building, 9490 Vaduz, Liechtenstein.

FRICKE, Manfred; German academic and university administrator; *Professor, Technische Universität Berlin;* b. 24 June 1936, Hainichen; m. Edith (née Feldhahn) Fricke; two s.; ed Tech. Univ. Berlin; Univ. Lecturer, Tech. Univ. Berlin 1970, Dean Faculty of Transport and Communications 1970–75, Prof. 1978–, Vice-Pres. 1978–82, Pres. 1985–93; Bundesverdienstkrenz (1st Class) 1994. *Leisure interests:* surfing, tennis, cycling. *Address:* Technische Universität Berlin, Institut für Luft-und Raumfahrt Sekr. F3, Marchstrasse 14, 10587 Berlin (office); Temmeweg 6A, 14089 Berlin, Germany. *Telephone:* (30) 31422362 (office). *Fax:* (30) 31424459 (office). *E-mail:* Manfred.Fricke@ilr.tu-Berlin.de (office).

FRIDAY, William Clyde, BS, LLD, DCL; American university administrator; b. 13 July 1920, Raphine, Va; s. of David Latham and Mary Elizabeth Rowan Friday; m. Ida Willa Howell 1942; three d.; ed Wake Forest Coll., N Carolina State Coll. and Univ. of N Carolina Law School; Asst Dean of Students, Univ. of N Carolina at Chapel Hill 1948–51, Acting Dean of Students 1950–51, Admin. Asst to Pres. 1951–54, Sec. of Univ. 1954–55, Acting Pres. 1956, Pres. 1956–86; Pres. The William R. Kenan, Jr Fund 1986–99; Chair. Center for Creative Leadership 1981–96, Regional Literacy Center Comm. 1989–90; fmr Chair. Southern Growth Policies Bd 1989, LEAF Foundation 1999; Hon. LLD (Wake Forest Coll., Belmont Abbey, Duke Univ., Princeton Univ., Elon Coll., Davidson Coll. Kentucky and Mercer Univs.); Hon. DCL (Univ. of the South) 1976, (St Augustine's Coll.) 1986; Hon. Diploma in Professional Studies (DPS) (Univ. of NC at Charlotte) 1986; Hon. DFA (N Carolina School of Arts) 1987; Hon. LHD (Univ. of North Carolina at Greensboro) 1988; Nat. Humanities Medal 1997. *Leisure interests:* gardening, golf, reading. *Address:* c/o The William R. Kenan, Jr Fund, University of North Carolina, P.O. Box 3858, Bowles Drive, Chapel Hill, NC 27515, USA.

FRIDERICHS, Hans, Dr rer. pol; German politician and business executive; b. 16 Oct. 1931, Wittlich; s. of Dr Paul Friderichs and Klara Neuwinger; m. Erika Wilhelm; two d.; Man., Rhineland-Hesse Chamber of Industry and Trade 1959–63; Deputy Business Man. FDP 1963–64, Business Man. 1964–69; mem. Bundestag 1965–69, 1976–77; Sec. of State, Ministry of Agric., Viniculture and Protection of the Environment for Rhineland Palatinate 1969–72; Fed. Minister of Econs 1972–77; Dir Dresdner Bank 1977–85, Chair. Bd Man. Dirs 1978–85; Deputy Chair. FDP 1974–77; mem. Supervisory Bd AEG Telefunken 1979, Chair. 1980–84, now Pres.; Chair. Supervisory Bd allit AG Kunststofftechnik, Bad Kreuznach, Germany, Goldman Sachs Investment Management GmbH, Frankfurt, Germany, Leica Camera AG, Solms, Germany, Racke-Dujardin GmbH & Co. KG, Bingen, Germany, C.A. Kupferberg & Cie. KGaA, Mainz, Germany; Deputy Chair. Supervisory Bd IIC The New German Länder Industrial Investment Council GmbH, Berlin, Germany, adidas-Salomon AG, Herzogenaurach, Germany; mem. Supervisory Bd Schneider Electric S.A., Paris, France. *Leisure interests:* art, sport. *Address:* c/o Supervisory Board, adidas-Salomon AG, World of Sports, Adi-Dassler-Straße 1, 91074 Herzogenaurach; Kappelhofgasse 2, 55116 Mainz, Germany.

FRIDJONSSON, Thordur, MA (Econs); Icelandic economist; *CEO, NASDAQ OMX Iceland;* b. 2 Jan. 1952, Reykjavík; s. of Fridjon Thordarson and Kristin Sigurdardottir; m. Thrudur Haraldsdottir 1971 (divorced); two s. two d.; ed Univ. of Iceland and Queen's Univ., Ont., Canada; Chief Economist, Fed. of Icelandic Industries 1978–80; Econ. Adviser to Prime Minister of Iceland 1980–86; part-time lecturer Dept of Econs, Univ. of Iceland 1979–87; Man. Dir Nat. Econ. Inst. 1987–2002; Sec.-Gen. Ministry of Industry and Commerce 1998–99; Pres. and CEO Iceland Stock Exchange 2002–06, CEO NASDAQ OMX Iceland 2006–; mem. Bd Dirs Nordic Project Fund 1982–96; Chair. Asscn of Icelandic Economists 1982–85, Icelandic Man. Asscn 1986–87, Econ. Research. Inst. for Agric. 1991–2002, Co-ordinating Cttee Iceland-Norsk Hydro 1998–2001; Alt. Gov. EBRD 1998–99, IMF 1998–99; Rep. for Iceland EDRC and OECD 1987–2002; mem. Econ. Policy Cttee OECD 1987–2002; mem. Bd Dirs NOREX Alliance 2002–06, OMX Nordic Exchanges; John Hicks Fellowship Queen's Univ. 1978. *Publications:* Icelandic Economy 1984; numerous articles in journals and books. *Leisure interests:* outdoor activities and sport. *Address:* NASDAQ OMX Iceland, Laugavegur 182, 105 Reykjavík (office); Kolbeinsmyri 11, 170 Seltjarnarnes, Iceland (home). *Telephone:* 5252800 (office); 5626854 (home). *Fax:* 5252888 (office). *E-mail:* ingibjorg.gudjonsdottir@nasdaqomx.com (office); thordur.fridjonsson@nasdaqomx.com (home). *Website:* www.nasdaqomx.com (office).

FRIDMAN, Mikhail Maratovich; Russian business executive; *Chairman, Alfa-Group, Consortium and Commercial Bank;* b. 21 April 1964, Lvov, Ukraine; m.; two c.; ed Moscow Inst. of Steel and Alloys; with Electrostal, Moscow region 1986–88; Founder Alfa-Foto, Alfa-Eco, Alfa-Capital 1988, Chair. Alfa-Bank (later Alfa-Group) 1991–, Alfa-Consortium 1996–, Alfa Commercial Bank 1998–; mem. Bd of Dirs Russian Public TV (ORTV) 1995–98, Oil Co. SIDANKO 1996–2000, Perekrestok Trade House 1998–; Founder, Vice-Pres. Russian Jewish Congress 1996–, Head Cttee on Culture 1996–; mem. Council on Banking Activity, Fed. Govt 1996–, Council on Business, Council of Ministers 2001–; elected to Russia's Public Chamber 2005; mem. Int. Advisory Bd Council of Foreign Relations; Golden Plate Award, Int. Board of Achievement 2003, included in Financial Times Leaders of the New Europe list 2004. *Address:* Alfa-Bank, 27 Kalanchevskaya str. 9, 107078 Moscow, Russia (office). *Telephone:* (495) 929-91-91 (office). *Fax:* (495) 788-69-81 (office). *E-mail:* mail@alfabank.ru (office). *Website:* www.alfabank.com (office).

FRIDRIKSSON, Fridrik Thor; Icelandic film director; b. 12 May 1954; s. of Fridrik Gudmundson and Gudridur Hjaltested; m. (divorced); one s. one d.; founder Reykjavik Film Festival; est. Icelandic Film Corp. (production co.) 1984. *Films:* Eldsmiðurinn (The Blacksmith) 1981, Rokk í Reykjavik (Rock in Reykjavik) 1982, Kúreakr norðursins (Icelandic Cowboys) 1984, Hringurinn (The Circle) 1985, Skytturnar (White Whales) 1987, Flugprá (Sky Without Limit) 1989, Englakroppar (Pretty Angels) 1990, Börn náttúrunnar (Children of Nature) 1991, Bíódagar (Movie Days) 1994, Á köldum klaka (Cold Fever) 1995, Djöflaeyjan (Devil's Island) 1996, Englar alheimsins (Angels of the Universe) 2000, Fálkar 2002, Næsland 2004, The Boss of It All 2006. *Address:* Icelandic Film Corporation, Hverfisgata 46, 101 Reykjavik (office); Bjarkargata 8, 101 Reykjavik, Iceland (home). *Telephone:* 5512260 (office); 5528566 (home). *Fax:* 5525154 (office). *E-mail:* icecorp@vortex.is (office); f.thor@vortex.is (home). *Website:* www.icecorp.is.

FRIED, Charles, LLB, MA; American lawyer and academic; *Beneficial Professor of Law, Harvard Law School;* b. 15 April 1935, Prague, Czechoslovakia; s. of Anthony Fried and Marta Fried (née Wintersteinova); m. Anne Sumerscale 1959; one s. one d.; ed Princeton and Columbia Univs, Univ. of Oxford, UK; law clerk to Assoc. Justice John M. Harlan, US Supreme Court 1960; mem. Faculty, Harvard Law School 1961–, Prof. of Law 1965–85, Carter Prof. of Gen. Jurisprudence 1981–85, 1989–95, Prof. Emer., Distinguished Lecturer 1995–, Beneficial Prof. of Law 1999–; Deputy Solicitor-Gen. and Counsellor to Solicitor-Gen. 1985, Solicitor-Gen. of USA 1985–89; Assoc. Justice Supreme Judiciary Court of Mass, Boston 1995–99; Fellow, American Acad. of Arts and Sciences. *Publications:* An Anatomy of Values 1970, Medical Experimentation: Personal Integrity and Social Policy 1974, Right and Wrong 1978, Contract as Promise: A Theory of Contractual Obligation 1981, Order and Law: Arguing the Reagan Revolution 1991, Making Tort Law 2003, Saying What the Law Is: The Constitution in the Supreme Court 2004, Modern Liberty 2006, Making Tort Law (with David Rosenberg) 2003; contribs to legal and philosophical journals. *Address:* Harvard Law School, 1545 Massachusetts Avenue, Cambridge, MA 02138, USA (office). *Telephone:* (617) 495-4636 (office); (617) 864-4172 (home). *Fax:* (617) 496-4865 (office). *E-mail:* fried@law.harvard.edu (office). *Website:* www.law.harvard.edu (office).

FRIED, Linda Phyllis, BA, MD, MPh; American physician, academic and university administrator; *DeLamar Professor of Public Health and Dean, Mailman School of Public Health, Columbia University, Columbia University;* b. 1949, New York City; ed Hunter Coll. High School, New York, Rush Medical Coll., Chicago, Johns Hopkins Univ., Colgate Univ.; intern, Rush Presbyterian St Luke's Medical Center, Chicago 1979–80, resident in internal medicine 1980–82; Fellow in Gen. Internal Medicine, Johns Hopkins Medical Inst., Baltimore 1982–85, Fellow in Epidemiology 1983–85, Fellow in Geriatrics 1985–1986, Prof. of Medicine, Epidemiology and Health Policy 2003–08, Mason F. Lord Prof. of Geriatric Medicine 2003-08, Dir Div. of Geriatric Medicine and Gerontology 2003–08, Medical Insts' Center of Excellence for Aging Research –2008, Center on Aging and Health –2008, Dir Program Epidemiology of Aging, Bloomberg School of Public Health –2008; Dean, Mailman School of Public Health, Columbia Univ. 2008–, DeLamar Prof. of Public Health 2008–, Prof. of Epidemiology 2008–, Sr Vice-Pres. Columbia Univ. Medical Center 2008–; Co-founder Experience Corps, Baltimore 2002; mem. Nat. Advisory Council on Aging 2003–; mem. Inst. of Medicine, NAS; mem. World Econ. Forum Council on Challenges of Gerontology; Herbert DeVries Distinguished Research Award, Council on Aging and Adult Devt 2000, Mary Betty Stevens Award, ACP 2007, Archstone Award, American Public Health Asscn, Maxwell Pollack Award, Gerontological Soc. of America, American Geriatrics Soc.'s Henderson Award, Merit Award from Nat. Inst. on Aging. *Address:* Office of the Dean, Mailman School of Public Health, Columbia Univ., 722 West 168th Street, R1408, New York, NY 10032, USA (office). *Telephone:* (212) 305-9300 (office). *Fax:* (212) 305-9342 (office). *E-mail:* lpfried@columbia.edu (office). *Website:* www.mailmanschool.org (office).

FRIEDBERG, Aaron L., PhD; American academic; *Professor of Politics and International Affairs, Woodrow Wilson School, Princeton University;* b. Pittsburgh; ed Harvard Univ.; currently Prof. of Politics and Int. Affairs, Woodrow Wilson School, Princeton Univ.; Henry A. Kissinger Chair in Foreign Policy and Int. Relations, John W. Kluge Center, Library of Congress 2001–02; fmr Fellow Woodrow Wilson Int. Center for Scholars, Smithsonian Inst., Norwegian Nobel Inst. 1998, Harvard Univ. Center for Int. Affairs; consultant to several agencies in US Govt; Deputy Asst for Nat. Security Affairs, Office of the Vice-Pres. 2003–05; Helen Dwight Reid Award 1986, Edgar S. Furniss National Security Book Award 1988. *Publications include:* The Weary Titan: Britain and the Experience of Relative Decline 1895–1905 (Edgar Furniss Nat. Security Book Award), In the Shadow of the Garrison State: America's Anti-Statism and Its Cold War Grand Strategy 2000, Strategic Asia 2001–02: Power and Purpose (co-editor) 2001. *Address:* Woodrow Wilson School, Bendheim 013, Princeton University, Princeton, NJ 08544-1013, USA (office). *Telephone:* (609) 258-9891 (office). *E-mail:* alf@princeton.edu (office). *Website:* www.princeton.edu (office).

FRIEDEL, Jacques, PhD, DèsSc; French physicist; b. 11 Feb. 1921, Paris; s. of Edmond Friedel and Jeanne Friedel (née Bersier); m. Mary Winifred Horder 1952; two s.; ed Ecole Polytechnique, Ecole des Mines de Paris, Univ. of Bristol, Paris Univ.; mining engineer, Ecole des Mines de Paris 1948–56; Maître de Conférences, Univ. de Paris 1956–59; Prof. of Solid State Physics, Univ. de Paris (later Paris Sud) 1959–89; Pres. Section 21, Consultative Cttee on Univs 1975–80; Pres. Consultative Comm. of Scientific and Tech. Research 1978–80; mem. Acad. of Sciences 1977–, Vice-Pres. 1991–92, Pres. 1992–94; Pres. Observatoire nat. de la lecture 1994–2001; Hon. mem. Royal Soc., London, NAS, American Acad. of Sciences and Letters, Swedish Acad. of Sciences, Leopoldina, Belgian Royal Acad. of Sciences, Brazilian Acad. of Sciences, American Physical Soc., Inst. of Physics, Max Planck Gesellschaft; Grand Officier, Légion d'honneur, Commdr Ordre nat. du Mérite, Commdr Order of Scientific Merit (Brazil); Hon. DSc (Bristol) 1977, (Lausanne) 1979, (Geneva) 1992, (Cambridge) 1995, (Zagreb) 1995; Gold Medal, Conseil Nat. de la Recherche Scientifique, Soc. Française de Metallurgie, Acta Metallurgica (USA); several int. scientific awards and prizes. *Publications:* Dislocations 1956, Graine de Mandarin 1994. *Leisure interest:* gardening. *Address:* 2 rue Jean-François Gerbillon, 75006 Paris, France (home). *Telephone:* 1-42-22-25-85 (home).

FRIEDEN, Luc; Luxembourg politician; *Minister of Justice and of the Treasury and Budget;* b. 16 Sept. 1963, Esch-sur-Alzette; m.; two c.; ed Lycée de garçons, Esch-sur-Alzette, Athénée de Luxembourg, Centre universitaire de Luxembourg, Université de Paris I (Panthéon Sorbonne), France, Univ. of Cambridge, UK, Harvard Law School, USA; commentator RTL, Luxembourg Radio 1981–94; attorney-at-law 1989–98; fmr teacher Centre Universitaire de Luxembourg; mem. Parl. 1994–, Chair. Finance and Budget Cttee, Cttee on Constitutional Affairs 1994–98; Minister of Justice, of the Budget and for Relations with Parl. 1998–99; Minister of Justice and of the Treasury and Budget 1999–, also Minister of Defence 2004–05; Gov. World Bank 1998–, Asian Devt Bank 2003–04; mem. moral sciences and politics section, Institut Grand-Ducal. *Address:* Ministry of Justice, 13 rue Erasme, centre administratif Pierre Werner, 1468 Luxembourg (office). *Telephone:* 478-27-01 (office). *Fax:* 22-19-80 (office). *Website:* www.gouvernement.lu (office).

FRIEDERICI, Gonthier Jean-Claude; French government official; *Prefect of Finistère;* b. 23 Aug. 1945, Lille; ed Lycée de Pontoise, Lycée Clémenceau, Reims, Lycée Lakanl, Sceaux, Univ. de Paris VIII; teacher 1970–77; numerous positions in departmental prefectures 1977–84; Deputy Chief of Staff to Prime Minister Laurent Fabius 1984–86; Chief of Mission to Sec.-Gen. of Centre nat. d'études spatiales 1986–88; Sub-Prefect, Alès 1989–90; Sec.-Gen. of Prefecture, Saône-et-Loire 1991–92; Sub-Prefect Saint-Germain-en-Laye Dist 1993–97; Prefect Belfort Territory 1997–2000, Pyrénées-Orientales 2000–01, region and Dept of Réunion 2001–04, Finistère 2004–; Chevalier Légion d'Honneur, Ordre du Mérite Maritime, Ordre nat. du Mérite, Ordre du Mérite agricole. *Address:* Préfecture du Finistère, 42 boulevard Dupleix, 29320 Quimper Cedex, France (office). *Telephone:* 2-98-76-29-29 (office). *Fax:* 2-98-52-09-47 (office). *E-mail:* courrier@finistere.pref.gouv.fr (office). *Website:* www.finistere.pref.gouv.fr (office).

FRIEDKIN, William; American film director; b. 29 Aug. 1939, Chicago; s. of Louis Friedkin and Rae Green; m. 1st Lesley-Anne Down (divorced); one s.; m. 2nd Sherry Lansing (q.v.). *Films directed include:* Good Times 1967, The Night They Raided Minsky's 1968, The Birthday Party 1968, The Boys in the Band 1970, The French Connection 1971 (Acad. Award for Best Picture, 1971), The Exorcist 1973, Sorcerer 1977, The Brinks Job 1979, Cruising 1980, Deal of the Century 1983, To Live and Die in LA 1985, C.A.T. Squad 1986, The Guardian 1990, Rampage 1992, Blue Chip 1993, Jade 1995, Twelve Angry Men 1997, Rules of Engagement 2000, Night Train 2000, The Hunted 2003, Bug 2006; several TV films. *Address:* c/o ICM, 8942 Wilshire Boulevard, Los Angeles, CA 90211-1934, USA (office). *Telephone:* (310) 550-4000 (office).

FRIEDMAN, Jane, BA; American publishing executive; b. Sept. 1945, Brooklyn, NY; ed New York Univ.; dictaphone typist, publicity dept Alfred A. Knopf, subsidiary co of Random House 1968, later Assoc. Publr Alfred A. Knopf; Pres. Random House Audio 1985; Publr Vintage Books 1990; Exec. Vice-Pres. Knopf Publishing Group, Random House Inc. 1992; fmr mem. Random House Exec. Cttee; Pres., HarperCollins Worldwide 1997–2007, CEO 1997–2008 (resgnd). *Address:* c/o HarperCollins, 10 East 53rd Street, New York, NY 10022-5299, USA (office).

FRIEDMAN, Jerome Isaac, PhD; American physicist and academic; *Institute Professor and Professor of Physics, Massachuesetts Institute of Technology;* b. 28 March 1930, Chicago; s. of Selig Friedman and Lillian Warsaw; m. 1st 1956; two s. two d.; m. 2nd Tania Baranovsky 1972; ed Univ. of Chicago; Research Assoc. Univ. of Chicago 1956–57, Stanford Univ. 1957–60; Asst Prof., Assoc. Prof. Mass. Inst. of Tech. 1960–67, Prof. of Physics 1967–, Dir Lab. of Nuclear Science 1980–83, Head, Dept of Physics 1983–88, William A. Coolidge Prof. 1988–90, Inst. Prof. 1990–; mem. NAS; Fellow, American Acad. of Arts and Sciences, American Physical Soc.; Hon. DSc (Trinity Coll.); W. K. H. Panofsky Prize (American Physical Soc.) (jt recipient) 1989, Nobel Prize in Physics (jt recipient) 1990. *Leisure interests:* painting, Asian ceramics, African Art. *Address:* Department of Physics, Room 24-512, Massachusetts Institute of Technology, Cambridge, MA 02139-4307 (office); 75 Greenough Street, Brookline, MA 02146, USA (home). *Telephone:* (617) 253-7585 (office). *Fax:* (617) 253-1755 (office). *E-mail:* jif@mit.edu (office). *Website:* web.mit.edu/physics (office).

FRIEDMAN, Stephen, BA, LLB; American financial services executive, lawyer and fmr government official; b. 1938; m. Barbara Benioff Friedman; ed Cornell Univ., Columbia Univ. Law School, New York; fmr law clerk to Fed. Dist Court judge; attorney, New York City 1963–66; joined Goldman Sachs & Co. 1966, Partner 1973, Man. Cttee 1982, Vice-Chair. and Co-COO 1987–90, Co-Chair. 1990–92, Chair. and Sr Partner 1992–94, Dir 2002, 2005–; Sr Prin., Marsh & McLennan Capital Inc. 1998–2002; Asst to Pres. for Econ. Policy and Dir Nat. Econ. Council, White House 2002–04; Dir Fannie Mae, Wal-Mart Stores Inc., Nat. Bureau of Econ. Research, In-Q-Tel; mem. Pres.'s Foreign Advisory Council; fmr mem. Council on Foreign Relations; Chair. Emer. Bd of Trustees, Columbia Univ.; Chair. Finance Cttee, Memorial Sloan-Kettering Cancer Center; Chair. Emer. Exec. Cttee, The Brookings Inst.; Eastern Collegiate Wrestling Champion 1959, AAU Nat. Wrestling Champion 1961, Maccabiah Games Gold Medal 1961, NCAA Silver Anniversary Medal for outstanding athletic and career achivements 1984. *Address:* c/o Board of Directors, Goldman Sachs Group, Inc., 85 Broad Street, New York, NY 10004, USA (office). *Website:* www.goldmansachs.com.

FRIEDMAN, Thomas Lauren, OBE, BA, MPhil; American journalist and writer; *Foreign Affairs Columnist, New York Times;* b. 20 July 1953, St Louis Park, Minneapolis, Minn.; m. Ann Bucksbaum; two d.; ed St Louis Park High School, Brandeis Univ., St Antony's Coll. Oxford, UK; joined London bureau of United Press International, dispatched a year later to Beirut –1981; joined The New York Times 1981, Beirut Bureau Chief 1982–84, Israel Bureau Chief 1984–88, Washington Chief Diplomatic Corresp., Chief White House Corresp., Chief Econs Corresp., Foreign Affairs Columnist 1995–; fmr Visiting Prof., Harvard Univ.; hon. degrees from several US univs; Pulitzer Prize for Int. Reporting 1983, 1988, for Distinguished Commentary 2002, Overseas Press Club Award for Lifetime Achievement 2004. *Television:* documentaries: The Roots of 9/11 (New York Times TV), Straddling the Fence (Discovery Channel). *Publications include:* From Beirut to Jerusalem (Nat. Book Award for Non-Fiction, Overseas Press Club Award) 1989 (revised edn 1990), The Lexus and the Olive Tree: Understanding Globalization (Overseas Press Club Award for Best Non-Fiction Book on Foreign Policy 2000) 1999 (revised edn 2000), Longitudes and Latitudes: Exploring the World After September 11 2002 (reprinted as Longitudes and Attitudes: The World in the Age of Terrorism 2003), The World is Flat: A Brief History of The Twenty-first Century (Financial Times/Goldman Sachs Business Book Award) 2005 (expanded edn 2006, revised edn 2007), Hot, Flat and Crowded: Why We Need a Green Revolution – And How It Can Renew America 2008. *Address:* The New York Times, 1627 Eye Street, NW, Suite 700, Washington, DC 20006, USA (office). *Telephone:* (202) 862-0300 (office). *Fax:* (202) 862-0340 (office). *E-mail:* fsg.publicity@fsgbooks.com. *Website:* www.nytimes.com (office); www.thomaslfriedman.com.

FRIEL, Brian, FRSL; Irish writer; b. 9 Jan. 1929, Omagh, Co. Tyrone; s. of Patrick Friel and Christina MacLoone; m. Anne Morrison 1954; one s. four d.; ed St Columb's Coll., Derry, St Patrick's Coll., Maynooth, St Joseph's Training Coll., Belfast; taught in various schools 1950–60; full-time writer 1960–; mem. Irish Acad. of Letters, Aosdána 1983–, American Acad. of Arts and Letters, RSL; Hon. Fellow, Univ. Coll. Dublin; Hon. DLitt (Nat. Univ. of Ireland) 1983, (Queen's Univ., Belfast) 1992, (Georgetown Univ., Washington, DC, Dominican Coll., Chicago), (Trinity Coll., Dublin) 2004. *Plays:* Philadelphia, Here I Come! 1965, The Loves of Cass McGuire 1967, Lovers 1968, The Mundy Scheme 1969, Crystal and Fox 1970, The Gentle Island 1971, The Freedom of the City 1973, Volunteers 1975, Living Quarters 1976, Aristocrats 1979, Faith Healer 1979, Translations (Ewart-Biggs Memorial Prize, British Theatre Asscn Award) 1981, Three Sisters (trans.) 1981, The Communication Cord 1983, Fathers and Sons 1987, Making History (Best Foreign Play, New York Drama Critics Circle 1989) 1988, A Month in the Country 1990, Dancing at Lughnasa 1990, The London Vertigo 1991, Wonderful Tennessee 1993, Selected Stories 1994, Molly Sweeney 1995, Give Me Your Answer, Do! 1997, Uncle Vanya (after Chekov) 1998, The Yalta Game 2001, The Bear (trans.) 2002, Afterplay 2002, Performances 2003, The Home Place (Evening Standard Award for Best Play 2005) 2005, Hedda Gabler (trans.) 2008. *Publications:* The Last of the Name (ed.) 1988; collected stories: The Saucer of Larks 1962, The Gold in the Sea 1966. *Address:* Drumaweir House, Greencastle, Co. Donegal, Ireland (home). *Telephone:* (74) 9381119 (home). *Fax:* (74) 9381408 (home).

FRIEND, Cynthia M., BS, PhD; American chemist and academic; *Professor of Materials Science and Chair, Department of Chemistry and Chemical Biology, Harvard University;* ed Univ. of California, Davis, Univ. of California, Berkeley, Stanford Univ.; Post-Doctoral Research Fellow, Stanford Univ. 1981–82; Asst Prof., Harvard Univ. 1982–86, Assoc. Prof. 1986–88, Morris Kahn Assoc. Prof. 1988–89, Prof. of Chem. 1989–98, Theodore William Richards Prof. of Chem. 1998–, Prof. of Materials Science 2002–, Assoc. Dir, Harvard Materials Research Science and Eng Center 2001–, Assoc. Dean, Faculty of Arts and Sciences 2002–05, Chair., Dept of Chem. and Chemical Biology 2004–; Visiting Prof. in Chemical Eng, Stanford Univ. 2001; Trustee, Radcliffe Coll. 1990–93; mem. Faculty Arts and Sciences Resources Cttee Harvard 1999–; mem. numerous professional cttees, panels and bds including NATO Advisory Panel on Organic Chemistry 1987, NSF Chem. Advisory Panel 1989–92, Advanced Light Source Users' Exec. Cttee 1990–93, Bd on Chemical Science and Tech., Nat. Research Council 1992, 56th Annual Conf. on Physical Electronics Cttee 1995–96, Chemical and Eng (C&EN) Advisory Bd 2001–02, Claire Booth Luce Fellowship Selection Bd 2000–, Council of Gordon Research Confs 2002–05, US Dept of Energy Cttee of Visitors, Office of Basic Energy Sciences 2005; Gen. and Program Chair., Biennial Inorganic Chem. Symposium, Molecular Deisgn of Materials 1987, Program Chair., New England Catalysis Soc. 1987–89, Chair., Richards Medal Award Cttee 1994–96; Chair., Canvassing Cttee, ACS Award for Creative Research in Catalysis 1999–2000; US rep., Int. Union of Pure and Applied Chem. 2000–03; Co-Chair., Opportunities in Nanocatalysis Workshop 2005; chair. of numerous academic bds including Harvard Faculty of Arts and Sciences Standing Cttee on Women 1991–94, Elected Docket Cttee, Harvard Univ. 1998–2000; consultant to Lord Corpn, Cary, NC 1987–90, Advanced Tech. Materials, Danbury, Conn. 1988–92, Texaco Lubricants Div. 1995–98, Ryoka Systems, Tokyo, Japan 1995–2003, Kaelow and Assocs LLP 1998–99, Pennie and Edmonds LLP 2002–03, Paul Hastings LLP 2004, Mitsubishi Chemical Co. 2005–07; mem. ACS, American Vacuum Soc., AAAS, American Physical Soc., Iota Sigma Pi; mem. of several editorial bds including Journal of Cluster Science 1990–94, Langmuir 1991–2001, The Chemical Intelligencer 1997–, Surface Science 2000–, Chemical Eng News 1999-2001, e-Journal of Surface Science and Nano tech. (EJSSNT) 2005–; IBM Faculty Devt Award 1983–85, Presidential Young Investigator Award 1985–90, Union Carbide Innovation Recognition Program 1988-89, Distinguished Young Alumni Award, Univ. of Calif.-Davis 1990, Garvan Medal of ACS 1991, Iota Sigma Pi Agnes Fay Morgan Research Award 1991, Smithsonian Inst. Chosen Scientist for Perm. Exhibit "Science and American Life" 1992–. *Publications:* numerous articles in professional journals. *Address:* Harvard University Department of Chemistry and Chemical Biology, 12 Oxford Street, Cambridge, MA 02138, USA (office). *Telephone:* (617) 495-4052 (office). *Fax:* (617) 496-8410 (office). *E-mail:* friend@chemistry.harvard.edu (office). *Website:* www.chem.harvard.edu (office).

FRIEND, Lionel; British conductor; *Conductor-in-Residence, Birmingham Conservatoire;* b. 13 March 1945, London; s. of Norman A. C. Friend and Moya L. Dicks; m. Jane Hyland 1969; one s. two d.; ed Royal Grammar School, High Wycombe, Royal Coll. of Music (RCM), London, London Opera Centre; with Welsh Nat. Opera 1969–72, Glyndebourne Festival/Touring Opera 1969–72; 2nd Kapellmeister, Staatstheater, Kassel, FRG 1972–75; Conductor ENO 1976–89; Musical Dir New Sussex Opera 1989–96; Conductor-in-Residence, Birmingham Conservatoire 1996–; Guest Conductor BBC Symphony, Philharmonia, Nash Ensemble, Scottish Chamber, Royal Ballet and in Australia, Brazil, Denmark, France, Hungary, Norway, Spain, Germany, Netherlands, Belgium, Sweden, USA. *Leisure interests:* reading, theatre, cooking. *Address:* c/o Robert Gilder & Company, 91 Great Russell Street, London, WC1B 3PS, England (office); 136 Rosendale Road, London, SE21 8LG, England (home). *Telephone:* (20) 7580-7758 (office); (20) 8761-7845 (home). *Fax:* (20) 7580-7739 (office). *E-mail:* rgilder@robert-gilder.com (office); lionelfriend@hotmail.com (home). *Website:* www.robert-gilder.com (office).

FRIEND, Sir Richard, Kt, PhD, FRS, FREng; British physicist and academic; *Cavendish Professor of Physics, University of Cambridge;* b. 18 Jan. 1953; ed Trinity Coll., St. John's Coll., Cavendish Lab., Univ. of Cambridge; Research Assoc., Laboratoire de Physique des Solides, Université Paris-Sud 1977–78; Research Fellow, St John's Coll., Cambridge 1977–80, Demonstrator in Physics 1980–85, Dir of Studies in Physics 1984–86, Lecturer in Physics 1985–93, Tutor in Physics 1987–91, Reader in Experimental Physics 1993–95, Cavendish Prof. of Physics 1995–; Visiting Prof., Univ. of California, Santa Barbara 1986–87; Assoc. Chair, Centre de Recherche sur les Très Basses Temperatures, CNRS 1987; Chief Scientist, Cambridge Display Technology Ltd 1996–; Consultant, Epson Cambridge Lab. 1998–; Chief Scientist and Dir Plastic Logic Ltd 2000–; Mary Shepard B. Upson Visiting Prof., Cornell Univ. 2003; mem. Tech. Advisory Council, British Petroleum PLC 1998–2003; Nuffield Foundation Science Research Fellowship 1992–93; Hon. Fellow, Royal Soc. of Chem. 2004; Dr hc (Univ. of Linkoping, Sweden) 2000, (Univ. of Mons-Hainault, Belgium) 2002; Charles Vernon Boys Prize, Inst. of Physics 1988, Royal Soc. of Chem. Interdisciplinary Award 1991, Hewlett-Packard Prize, European Physical Soc. 1996, Rumford Medal, Royal Soc. of London 1998, Italgas Prize 2001, Silver Medal, Royal Acad. of Eng 2002, McRobert Prize, Royal Acad. of Eng 2002, Faraday Medal, Inst. of Electrical Engineers 2003, Gold Medal, European Materials Research Soc. 2003, Descartes Prize, European Comm. 2003. *Publications:* over 600 papers in scientific journals. *Address:* Cavendish Laboratory, University of Cambridge, Madingley Road, Cambridge, CB3 0HE, England (office). *Telephone:* (1223) 337218 (office). *Fax:* (1223) 353397 (office). *E-mail:* rhf10@cam.ac.uk (office). *Website:* www.phys.cam.ac.uk (office).

FRIGGIERI, Oliver, BA, MA, PhD; Maltese academic, writer, poet and literary critic; *Professor of Maltese Literature, University of Malta;* b. 27 March 1947, Furjana, Malta; s. of Charles Friggieri and Mary Galea; m. Eileen Cassar; one d.; ed Univ. of Malta, Catholic Univ. of Milan; Prof. of Maltese Literature, Univ. of Malta 1987–, Head of Dept of Maltese 1987–2004; Founder mem. Academia Internationale Mihai Eminescu, Craiova 1995; mem. Asscn Int. des Critiques Litteraires, Paris; participant and guest speaker at 70 int. congresses throughout Europe; guest poet at numerous poetry recitals in maj. European cities; Co-founder Saghtar (nat. student magazine) 1971; Literary Ed. In-Nazzjon 1971–82; Nat. Order of Merit 1999; First Prize for Literary Criticism XIV Concorso Silarus 1982, Premio Internazionale Mediterraneo, Palermo 1988, Malta Govt Literary Award 1988, 1996, 1997, 1999, Premio Sampieri per la Poesia 1995, Premio Internazionale Trieste Poesia 2002, Gold Medal Award Malta Soc. of Arts, Manufactures and Commerce 2003, Premio Faber (Italy) 2004. *Achievements:* author of first oratorio in Maltese: Pawlu ta' Malta 1985, first poetry album recording in Maltese 1997, various cantatas and religious hymns. *Radio:* weekly cultural programme presenter (Radio Malta). *Television:* regular appearances on Maltese and other networks. *Publications:* novels: Il-Gidba 1977, L-Istramb 1980, Fil-Parlament ma Jikbrux Fjuri 1986, Gizimin li Qatt ma Jiftah 1998, It-Tfal Jigu bil-Vapuri 2000, The Lie 2007; short stories: Stejjer ghal Qabel Jidlam Vol. I 1979, Vol. II 1983 (combined, enhanced edn) 1986, Fil-Gżira Taparsi jikbru I-Fjuri 1991, Koranta and Other Short Stories from Malta 1994, A Malte, histoires du crépuscule 2004; poetry: Mal-Fanal Hemm Harstek Tixghel 1988, Rewwixta (play-poem) 1990, Poeziji 1998, Il-Kliem li Tghidlek Qalbek 2001, Il-Poeziji Migbura 2002, A Poet's Creed 2006; literary criticism: Kittieba ta' Zmienna 1970, Ir-Ruh fil-Kelma 1973, Il-Kultura Taljana f'Dun Karm 1976, Fl-Gharbiel 1976, Storja tal-Letteratura Maltija 1979, Saggi Kritici 1979, Ellul Mercer f'Leli ta' Haz-Zghir Mir-Realta' ghall-Kuxjenza 1983, Gwann Mamo Il'Kittieb tar-Riforma Socjali 1984, Dizzjunarju ta' Termini Letterarji 1986, L'Idea tal'Letteratura 1986, Mekkanizmi Metaforici f'Dun Karm 1988, Dun Karm 'Il-Jien u Lil hinn Minnu' 1988, Il-Kuxjenza Nazzjonali Maltija 1995, L-Istudji Kritici Migbura 1995, L'Istorja tal-Poezija Maltija 2001; numerous works translated into various languages, poems in anthologies and articles in academic journals and newspapers. *Leisure interest:* gardening. *Address:* Faculty of Arts, University of Malta, Msida, Malta (office).

FRIMPONG-ANSAH, Jonathan Herbert, PhD; Ghanaian banker; b. 22 Oct. 1930, Mampong, Ashanti; s. of Hammond Owusu-Ansah and Elizabeth Achiaa; m. Selina Agyemang 1954; three s. one d.; ed Univ. of Ghana, London School of Econs and Univ. of Salford, UK; Statistician, Ghana Govt 1954–59; Bank of Ghana, Dir of Research 1961–65, Deputy Gov. 1965–68, Gov. 1968–73; Chair. Ghana Diamond Marketing Bd 1969–72; Dir Volta River Authority 1972–; Chair. Ashanti Goldfields Corpn Ltd 1973–96; Vice-Chair. Deputies of the Cttee of the Bd of Govs on Reform of the Int. Monetary System and Related Issues, IMF, Wash. 1973–74; Consultant World Bank 1975; Chair. Standard Bank Ghana, Ltd, Accra 1975–81, Akosombo Textiles Ltd 1975–; Chair. UN Experts Group on Establishment of African-Caribbean-Pacific Investment and Trade Bank 1978–79 Dir Soc. Financière pour les Investissements et le Développement en Afrique (SIFIDA), Geneva 1981; Fellow Center for Int. Affairs, Harvard 1978–, Ghana Acad. of Arts and Sciences 1979–; Hon. Prof. of Finance, Univ. of Ghana 1979–. *Publications:* Trade and Development in Africa, 1991, Saving for Africa's Economic Recovery 1991, The Vampire State in Africa – Political Economy of Decline in Ghana 1991; articles in Economic Bulletin (Ghana), Bulletin of the Inter Credit Bank (Geneva), Univ. of Ghana journals; contribs. in International Monetary Reform – Documents of the Committee of Twenty 1974. *Leisure interest:* art. *Address:* 3 Eleventh Road, Ridge, P.O. Box C1582, Accra, Ghana. *Telephone:* (21) 227711.

FRISELL, Bill; American jazz musician (guitar) and composer; b. 18 March 1951, Baltimore, MD; one d.; ed Univ. of Northern Colorado, Berklee Coll. of Music, Boston; played with artists, including Eberhard Weber, Mike Gibbs, Jan Garbarek, Charlie Haden, Carla Bley, John Scofield; David Sylvian, Bono, Marianne Faithfull, Robin Holcomb, Gavin Bryars, Brian Eno, Daniel Lanois, Paul Simon, Van Dyke Parks, Vic Chesnutt, Elvis Costello, Suzanne Vega, Loudon Wainwright III, Ron Carter, Dave Douglas, Rinde Eckart, Wayne Horvitz, Ginger Baker, Rickie Lee Jones, Laurie Anderson, Vernon Reid, Ron Sexsmith, Caetano Veloso, Vinicius Cantuaria, Mark Ribot, Ron Carter, T-Bone Burnett, The Campbell Brothers, Chip Taylor & Carrie Rodriquez, Buddy Miller and Renée Fleming; fmr mem., Power Tools, John Zorn's Naked City, The Paul Bley Quintet, Paul Motian Trio; Music Dir, Century of Song Ruhr Triennale Arts Festival 2003–05; Harris Stanton Guitar Award, Downbeat Critics' Poll Guitarist of the Year 1998, Deutsche Schallplatten Preis 1998, 2005, Critics' Award for Best Guitarist, Industry Award for Best Guitarist 1998. *Compositions include:* Tales from the Far Side (music to TV series). *Recordings include:* albums: In Line 1983, Theoretically (with Tim Berne) 1984, Rambler 1985, News For Lulu (with John Zorn, George Lewis) 1987, Strange Meeting (with Power Tools) 1987, Lookout For Hope 1988, Before We Were Born 1989, Is This You? 1990, Where In The World? 1991, More News For Lulu (with John Zorn, George Lewis) 1992, Grace Under Pressure (with John Scofield) 1992, Have A Little Faith 1993, Music From The Films of Buster Keaton 1995, Going Home Again (with Ginger Baker Trio) 1995, Deep Dead Blue: Live At Meltdown (with Elvis Costello) 1995, Quartet 1996, Nashville 1997, Gone, Just Like a Train 1998, Songs We Know 1998, The Sweetest Punch (with Elvis Costello) 1999, Good Dog, Happy Man 1999, Ghost Town 2000, Blues Dream 2001, Bill Frisell With Dave Holland and Elvin Jones 2001, Selected Recordings 2002, The Willies 2002, The Intercontinentals 2003, Unspeakable 2004, Petra Haden's Bill 2004, Richter 858 2005, East/West 2005, Bill Frisell, Ron Carter, Paul Motian 2005, Floratone 2007, History, Mystery 2007, All Hat 2008, Hemispheres (with Jim Hall) 2008. *Publication:* Bill Frisell – An Anthology. *Address:* c/o Phyllis Oyama, Songline/Tone Field Productions, 1649 Hopkins Street, Berkeley, CA 94707, USA (office). *Telephone:* (510) 528-1191 (office). *Fax:* (510) 528-1193 (office). *Website:* www.songtone.com (office); www.billfrisell.com.

FRISINGER, Haakan H. J., MEng; Swedish business executive; b. 8 Dec. 1928, Skoevde; s. of Anders Johansson and Anna Johansson; m. Annakarin Lindholm 1953; two s. one d.; ed Chalmers Univ. of Tech., Gothenburg and Harvard Business School, USA; Head, Man. Unit Product and Production Coordination, AB Volvo 1966; Head, Volvo Köping Plant 1971; Head of Volvo Car Production and mem. Corporate Exec. AB Volvo 1975; Head, Volvo Car Industry Div. and Exec. Vice-Pres. AB Volvo 1977; Pres. Volvo Car Corpn 1978; Pres. and COO, AB Volvo 1983–87, Dir 1994–99, Chair. 1997–99. *Leisure interests:* music, art, golf, sport, hunting. *Address:* c/o AB Volvo, 405 08 Gothenburg, Sweden.

FRIST, William (Bill) Harrison, MD; American transplant surgeon, business executive and fmr politician; *Frederick H. Schultz Class of 1951 Professor of International Economic Policy, Princeton University;* b. 22 Feb. 1952, Nashville, Tenn.; m. Karyn McLaughlin; three s.; ed Montgomery Bell Acad., Nashville, Princeton Univ., Harvard Medical School; worked in Powell lab., Mass Gen. Hosp. 1977–78, Resident in Surgery 1978–83, Chief Resident and Fellow in Cardiothoracic Surgery 1984–85; worked at Southampton Gen. Hosp., Southampton, England 1983; Sr Fellow and Chief Resident in Cardiac Transplant Service and Cardiothoracic Surgery, Stanford Univ. School of Medicine 1985–86; mem. Faculty, Vanderbilt Univ. Medical Center 1986–89, est. center for new therapies of heart and lung transplantation, also served as Staff Surgeon, Nashville Veterans Admin Hospital; f. Vanderbilt Transplant Center 1989; Senator from Tennessee 1995–2007 (retd), Senate Majority Leader 2002–2007, fmr Chair. Nat. Representative Senatorial Cttee; Frederick H. Schultz Class of 1951 Prof. of Int. Econ. Policy, Princeton Univ. 2007–; Chair. Volunteer Political Action Cttee (VOLPAC) 2007–; Republican. *Publications:* Tennessee Senators, 1911-2001: Portraits of Leadership in a Century of Change 1999, When Every Moment Counts: What You Need To Know About Bioterrorism From the Senate's Only Doctor 2002, Good People Beget Good People: A Genealogy of the Frist Family (co-author) 2003. *Address:* Woodrow Wilson School of Public and International Affairs, Princeton University, Robertson Hall, Princeton, NJ 08544-1013, USA (office). *Telephone:* (609) 258-2943 (office). *E-mail:* whfrist@princeton.edu (office). *Website:* www.wws.princeton.edu (office).

FRISVOLD, Gen. Sigurd; Norwegian army officer (retd); b. 5 July 1947, Kristiansund; ed Befalsskolen for Infanteriet, S. Norway; with Infantry Bn No. 2, N Norwegian Brigade 1970–73; Instructor, Befalsskolen for Infanteriet, Trøndelag 1973–77; rank of Capt. 1975; Co. Chief, Infantry 1979–81, Operations Officer 1981, rank of Major 1982; Force Commdr's Asst, Multi-National Observers' Corps, Sinai 1983; Operations Officer, Trondheim 1983–86; US Marine Corps Command and Staff Coll. 1985–86; with Infantry Bn, N. Norway 1987–89; Chief of Staff, Sixth Div., Harstad 1989-90; US Army War Coll., Int. Fellows Program 1991–92; Commdr, N Europe Allied Forces, Stavanger 1996; Chief of Defence 1999–2005 (retd); Forsvarsmedaljen with laurel wreath 1996, Commdr, Order of St Olav with Star 2000, Commdr Grand Cross Order of the Lion of Finland 2000, Commdr's Cross of the Order of Merit of the Repub. of Poland 2001, Grand Officier de l'Ordre Nat. du Mérite 2002, 1st Class Order of the Cross of the Eagle (Estonia) 2004.

FRITSCHE, Claudia; Liechtenstein diplomatist; *Ambassador to USA;* b. 26 July 1952; m. Manfred Fritsche 1980; ed business and language schools in Schaan and St Gall; personal sec. to Prime Minister 1970–74, to Deputy Prime Minister March–Aug. 1974; joined Office for Foreign Affairs 1978, Diplomatic Officer 1980–87, Sec. to Liechtenstein Parl. del. to Council of Europe and EFTA, First Sec., Embassy in Berne 1987–90, Vienna 1989–90, mem. Liechtenstein Organizing Cttee for the Council of Europe's North-South Campaign 1988, Rep. in EFTA/EC Working Group on Flanking Policies 1989–90, Perm. Rep. of Liechtenstein to UN 1990–2002, Vice-Pres. and mem. Gen. Cttee of UN Gen. Ass. during its 48th Session, Amb. to USA (non-resident) 2000–02 (resident) 2002–; Pres. Int. Asscn of Perm. Reps to the UN 1999–2002; Certificate and Medal of Recognition Foreign Policy Asscn 2002. *Address:* 888 17th Street, NW, Suite 1250, Washington, DC 20006, USA (office). *Telephone:* (202) 331-0590 (office). *Fax:* (202) 331-3221 (office). *E-mail:* tamara.brunhart@was.rep.llv.li (office). *Website:* www.washington.liechtenstein.li (office).

FRITZ, Johann P.; Austrian journalist and broadcasting executive; *Director, International Press Institute;* b. 15 April 1940, Ober-Eggendorf; s. of Johann Fritz and Amalia Piringer; m. Brigitte Weick 1964; one d.; ed Univ. of Vienna, Western Reserve Univ., Cleveland, Ohio and Hochschule für Welthandel, Vienna; Sec.-Gen. Österreichische Jungarbeiterbewegung 1964–67, Exec. Vice-Pres. 1967–70; Ed. Der Jungarbeiter 1964–70, MC Report 1970–75; Deputy Sec.-Gen. Österreichischer Wirtschaftsbund 1970–75; Man. Dir Die Presse 1975–91; Man. Dir Kabel TV Wien 1975–83; founder and Co-Man. Radio Adria 1977–84, Consultant 1984–90; co-founder, Sec. Gen. and Report Ed. Man.-Club 1970–75; founder and Chair., Cable TV Asscn, Austrian Chamber of Commerce 1980–90; mem. Supervisory Bd Telekabel Wien GmbH 1983–98; mem. Bd Austrian Press Agency (APA) 1982–91; Dir Int. Press Inst. (IPI) 1992–; Publr Jazz Information (monthly) 1967–70, Cable TV: Project Study for Austria 1975, iPi Report 1992–97; mem. numerous professional asscns; life-time title 'Senator' conferred by Int. Asscn for Newspaper and Media Tech. 1980; life-time Kommerzialrat Award 1991; life-time title 'Professor' conferred by Austrian Federal Ministry of Science and Research 2000; Gold Medal for Meritorious Service to Province of Vienna 2003; Special Award, Austrian Press Club Concordia 2003. *Television:* scripts for jazz productions 1968–73. *Publications:* Little Jazzbook of Vienna. *Leisure interests:* skiing, ice-skating, jazz, art deco, jugendstil. *Address:* International Press Institute, Speigelgasse 2, 1010 Vienna (office); Hasenauerstrasse 37, 1180 Vienna, Austria. *Telephone:* (1) 5129011 (office). *Fax:* (1) 5129014 (office). *E-mail:* ipi@freemedia.at (office). *Website:* www.freemedia.at (office).

FRITZ, Walter Helmut; German writer; b. 26 Aug. 1929, Karlsruhe; s. of Karl T. Fritz and Hedwig Fritz; ed Univ. of Heidelberg; poetry teacher, Univ. of Mainz; has lectured in Europe, America and Africa; mem. Akad. der Wissenschaften und der Literatur, Mainz, Bayerische Akad. der Schönen Künste, Munich, Deutschen Akad. für Sprache und Dichtung, Darmstadt, PEN; City of Karlsruhe Literature Prize 1960, Grosser Literaturpreis Bayerische Akad. der Schönen Künste Prize 1962, 1995, Heine-Taler Lyric Prize 1966, Fed. of German Industry Culture Circle Prize 1971, Stuttgarter Literaturpreis 1986, Villa Massimo-Stipendium, Georg-Trakl-Preis 1992. *Publications:* poetry and prose, including: Achtsam sein 1956, Veranderte Jahre 1963, Umwege 1964, Zwischenbemerkungen 1965, Abweichung 1965, Die Verwechslung 1970, Aus der Nahe 1972, Die Beschaffenheit solcher Tage 1972, Bevor uns Horen und Sehen Vergeht 1975, Schwierige Uberfahrt 1976, Auch jetzt und morgen 1979, Gesammelte Gedichte 1979, Wunschtraum Alptraum (poems) 1981, Werkzeuge der Freiheit (poems) 1983, Cornelias Traum, Aufzeichnungen 1985, Immer einfacher immer schwieriger (poems) 1987, Zeit des Sehens (prose) 1989, Mit einer Feder aus den Flügen des Ikarus, Ausgewählte Gedichte, Mit einem Nachwort von Harald Hartung 1989, Die Schlüssel sind vertauscht (poems) 1992, Gesammelte Gedichte 1979–1994 1994, Das offene Fenster 1997, Zugelassen im Leben (poems) 1999, Maskenzug (poems) 2003; contrib. to journals and peiodicals. *Address:* Kolbergerstrasse 2A, 76139 Karlsruhe, Germany. *Telephone:* (721) 683346.

FRODSHAM, John David, MA, PhD, FAHA; British/Australian academic and consultant; *Foundation Professor of English and Comparative Literature, Murdoch University;* b. 5 Jan. 1930, Cheshire, UK; s. of J. K. Frodsham and W. E. Frodsham; m. Tan Beng-choo 1964; three s. two d.; ed Emmanuel Coll., Cambridge, Australian Nat. Univ.; Lecturer in English, Univ. of Baghdad 1956–58, in Oriental Studies, Univ. of Sydney 1960–61, in Far Eastern History, Univ. of Malaya 1961–65, Sr Lecturer in Far Eastern History, Univ. of Adelaide 1965–67; Reader in Chinese, ANU 1967–71; Prof. of Comparative Literature, Univ. of Dar es Salaam 1971–73, Foundation Prof. English and Comparative Literature, Murdoch Univ. 1972–; Visiting Prof. Cornell 1965, Hawaii 1968, American Coll. of Greece 1985, Tamkang Univ. of Taiwan 1985; Visiting Fellow, Inst. of E Asian Philosophies, Univ. of Singapore 1989; Sr Teaching Fellow, NTU, Singapore 1990–92; Consultant Ausean Int. Ltd 1987–89; Fellow and Pres. Professors' World Peace Acad. 1983; Pres. Australasian Soc. of Physical Research 1979–; mem. Australia–China Council 1979–83; Current Affairs Commentator for ABC 1958–. *Publications:* An Anthology of Chinese Verse, Vol. 1 1967, The Murmuring Stream (2 vols) 1967, The Poems of Li Ho 1970, New Perspectives in Chinese Literature 1971, The First Chinese Embassy to the West 1973, Foundations of Modernism: Modern Poetry 1980, Goddesses, Ghosts and Demons: The Collected Poems of Li He 1983, Classicism and Romanticism: A Comparative Period Study (4 vols) 1986, Turning Point 1988, Education for What? 1990, The Crisis of the Modern World and Traditional Wisdom 1990, The Decline of Sensate Culture 1990, Structure, Thought and Reality: A Reader (2 vols) 2000. *Leisure interests:* psychical research, sailing, swimming. *Address:* School of Arts, Room E/H 3.78, Murdoch University, Murdoch, Western Australia 6150 (office); 24 Riversea View, Buckland Hill, Mosman Park, Western Australia

6107, Australia (home). *Telephone:* (8) 9360-6203 (office); (8) 9284-3451 (home). *Fax:* (8) 9284-3451 (home). *E-mail:* J.Frodsham@murdoch.edu.au (office). *Website:* www.ssh.murdoch.edu.au (office).

FROGGATT, Sir Leslie (Trevor), Kt; Australian business executive; b. 8 April 1920; s. of Leslie Froggatt and Mary H. Brassey; m. Elizabeth Grant 1945; three s.; ed Birkenhead Park School, Cheshire; joined Asiatic Petroleum Co., Ltd 1937; Shell Singapore, Shell Thailand, Shell Malaya 1947–54, Shell Egypt 1955–56; Dir of Finance, Gen. Man. Kalimantan, Borneo and Deputy Chief Rep. PT Shell Indonesia 1958–62; Area Co-ordinator, S Asia and Australasia, Shell Int. Petroleum Co., Ltd 1962–63, various assignments in Europe 1964–66; Shell Oil Co. Atlanta, Ga 1967–69; Chair. and CEO Shell Group Australia 1969–80, Dir 1980–87; Chair. Ashton Mining Ltd 1981–94, BRL Hardy Ltd 1992–95, Tandem Computers Pty Ltd 1992–98, Cooperative Research Centre for Cochlear Implant, Speech and Hearing Inst. 1993–2001; Dir Pacific Dunlop Ltd 1978–90, Chair. 1986–90; Dir Australian Industry Devt Corpn 1978–90; Dir Australian Inst. of Petroleum Ltd 1976–80, 1982–84, Chair. 1977–79; Dir CARE Australia 1989–2004 (Vice-Chair. 1995–2001), now mem. Advisory Council; mem. Australian Nat. Airlines Comm. 1981–87, Vice-Chair. 1984–87; Committeeman Moonee Valley Racing Club 1977–92, Life Mem. 1992–. *Leisure interests:* reading, music, racing, golf. *Address:* 20 Albany Road, Toorak, Vic. 3142, Australia. *Telephone:* (3) 9822-1357 (home). *Fax:* (3) 9822-1357.

FROGIER, Pierre Edouard Nahéa; New Caledonian politician; b. 16 Nov. 1950, Nouméa; m. Annick Morault; three c.; ed Lycée Lapérouse, Nouméa and Faculty of Law, Dijon, France; elected mem. Ass. Territoriale 1977–, Congress 1977–; Mayor of Mont-Dore 1987–2001; Sec.-Gen. Rassemblement pour la Calédonie dans la République (RPCR) 1989–; Territorial Sec. Rassemblement pour la République (RPR) 1995–; Deputy for New Caledonia in French Nat. Ass. 1996–; Pres. of New Caledonia 2001–04; Chevalier, Ordre nat. du Mérite. *Address:* c/o Présidence du Gouvernement, 19 avenue Maréchal Foch, B.P. M2, 98849 Nouméa Cédex, New Caledonia (office).

FROHNMAYER, John Edward, MA, JD; American civil servant, lawyer and author; b. 1 June 1942, Medford, Ore.; s. of Otto Frohnmayer and Marabel Frohnmayer; m. Leah Thorpe 1967; two s.; ed Stanford Univ., Univs of Chicago and Oregon; pnr Tonkon, Torp, Galen, Marmaduke & Booth 1975–89; Chair. Ore. Arts Comm. 1980–84; mem. Art Selection Cttee Ore. State Capitol Bldg; Chair. Nat. Endowment for the Arts 1989–92; Visiting Professional Scholar, The Freedom Forum, 1st Amendment Center, Vanderbilt Univ. 1993; trial lawyer in pvt. practice, Bozeman, Mont. 1995–; Republican; People for the American Way, 1st Amendment Award 1992, Oregon Gov.'s Award for the Arts 1993; Intellectual Freedom Award, Montana Library Assen 1998. *Publication:* Leaving Town Alive 1993, Out of Tune: Listening to the First Amendment 1994. *Leisure interests:* skiing, rowing, reading, music. *Address:* 14080 Lone Bear Road, Bozeman, MT 59715, USA. *Telephone:* (406) 585-5918. *Fax:* (406) 582-4997. *E-mail:* frohn@wtp.net (office).

FROMENT-MEURICE, Henri, LèsL; French diplomatist; *President (France), Action Committee for European Union;* b. 5 June 1923, Paris; m. Gabrielle Drouilh 1948 (deceased); three s. one d.; ed Ecole libre des Sciences Politiques, Ecole Nat. d'Admin; Sec., Ministry of Foreign Affairs 1950–52, Sec. for Far East, Tokyo 1952–53, Chief of Diplomatic Staff, Commissariat Gén. de France en Indochine 1953–54, Asst Pvt. Sec. to Sec. of State for Foreign Affairs 1954–56, First Sec. Embassy, Moscow 1956–59, with Cen. Admin. (Europe) 1959–63, Chargé d'Affaires, Embassy, United Arab Repub. (now Egypt) 1963–64, First Counsellor, Cairo Embassy, 1964–65, Chief of Cultural Exchange Service, Cen. Admin. 1965–68, Minister Plenipotentiary 1968, Advisory Minister, Moscow 1968–69, Dir Cen. Admin., Asia and Pacific Ocean 1969–75, Econ. Affairs 1975–79, Amb. to USSR 1979–81, to FRG 1982–83; Ambassadeur de France 1984; Adviser to Chair. Banque Paribas 1985–91; Adviser Jeantet et Associés 1991–98; Admin. Phillips France 1984–96, Robert Bosch (France) 1984–97; Pres. (France) Action Cttee for EU 1995–; Pres. du Beirat, Inst. Berlin-Brandebourg 1997–2004; Commdr, Légion d'honneur, Officier, Ordre nat. du Mérite. *Publications:* Une puissance nommée Europe 1984 (Adolphe Bentinck Prize), Une éducation politique 1987, Europe 1992 1988, Vu du quai: Mémories 1945–83 1998, Journal d'Asie 1969–75 2005; several articles in Preuves, Commentaire and Revue des Deux Mondes, Le Monde, Le Figaro, Ouest France. *Leisure interests:* music, piano. *Address:* 23 rue de Civry, 75016 Paris, France (home). *Telephone:* 1-47-43-96-41 (home). *Fax:* 1-47-43-96-41 (home). *E-mail:* henri.froment_meurice@wanadoo.fr.

FROMHERZ, Peter, Dr rer. nat; German biophysicist; *Director, Max Planck Institute for Biochemistry;* b. 1942, Ludwigshafen; ed Technische Hochschule, Karlsruhe, Univ. Marburg; postdoctoral fellow, Max Planck Inst. for Biophysical Chem., Göttingen 1970–81; Chair. of Experimental Physics, Univ. of Ulm 1978–94, Full Prof. of Experimental Physics 1981–; Scientific Mem., Max Planck Soc. 1994–, Dir Max Planck Inst. for Biochemistry, Martinsried 1994–; Hon. Prof. of Physics, Technische Universität Munich 1994–; Pres. German Biophysical Soc.; mem. Heidelberg Acad. of Sciences 1992–; Julius Springer Prize for Applied Physics 1998, Philip Morris Research Award 2004. *Publications:* 150 research papers. *Address:* Max-Planck-Institut für Biochemie, Abteilung Membran- und Neurophysik, Am Klopferspitz 18a, 82152 Martinsried, Germany (office). *Telephone:* (89) 8578-2820 (office). *Fax:* (89) 8578-2822 (office). *E-mail:* fromherz@biochem.mpg.de (office). *Website:* www.biochem.mpg.del (office).

FROMM, Hans Walther Herbert, DPhil; Finnish/German professor of philology; *Professor Emeritus, University of Munich;* b. 26 May 1919, Berlin; s. of Rudolf Fromm and Luise (née Hennig) Fromm; m. 1st Lore Sprenger 1950 (divorced 1974); one d.; m. 2nd Beatrice Müller-Hansen 1974; ed Berlin Univ.; Lecturer and Prof. of Germanic Philology, Univ. of Turku 1952–58; Prof. of German Philology and Finno-Ugric Languages, Univ. of Munich 1960–87, Prof. Emer. 1987–; mem. Bayerische Akad. der Wissenschaften 1971, Finnish Acad. of Sciences 1979, Acad. of Finland 1990–, Akad. der Wissenschaften, Göttingen 1992; Chair. Scientific Reviewers' Cttee, Deutsche Forschungsgemeinschaft, Bonn 1972–76, Comm. for Medieval German Literature, Bayerische Akad., Munich 1978–; Bundesverdienstkreuz (1st Class); Commdr Order of Kts of the Finnish Lion (1st Class) 1985; Hon. DPhil (Turku) 1969; Brüder-Grimm-Preis 1987. *Publications:* Bibliographie deutscher Übersetzungen aus dem Französischen (6 vols) 1950–53, Germanistische Bibliographie seit 1945, Theorie u. Kritik 1960, Der deutsche Minnesang (2 vols) 1961, 1985, Kalevala (2 vols) 1967, Konrad von Fussesbrunnen (ed.) 1973, Finnische Grammatik (1982), Esseitä Kalevalasta 1987, Arbeiten z. deutschen Literatur d. Mittelalters 1989, Heinrich von Veldeke 1992. *Address:* Roseggerstrasse 35A, 85521 Ottobrunn, Germany. *Telephone:* (89) 605882.

FROMME, Friedrich Karl, DPhil; German journalist; b. 10 June 1930, Dresden; s. of Prof. Dr Albert Fromme and Dr Lenka Fromme; m. 1st Traute Kirsten 1961 (died 1992); m. 2nd Brigitte Burkert 1997; ed studies in science, politics and public law; teaching Asst, Univ. of Tübingen 1957–62; Ed. Süddeutscher Rundfunk 1962–64, Frankfurter Allgemeine Zeitung (FAZ) 1964–68; Bonn corresp. FAZ 1968–73; Ed. responsible for internal politics and co-ordination, FAZ 1974–97; freelance writer; Grosses Bundesverdienstkreuz 1995, Theodor Wolff Prize 1997. *Publications:* Von der Weimarer Verfassung zum Bonner Grundgesetz 1962, Der Parlamentarier–ein Freier Beruf? 1978, Gesetzgebung im Widerstreit 1980. *Address:* Welt am Sonntag, 20350, Hamburg (office); Mohrengarten 60, 40822 Mettmann, Germany. *Telephone:* (2104) 958768.

FROMSTEIN, Mitchell S.; American business executive; *Chairman Emeritus, Manpower Inc.;* b. 1928; ed Univ. of Wis.; Krueger Homes Inc. 1948–49; Account Exec. Maultner Advertising Agency 1949–53; fmr Pres. TV Parts Inc.; Pnr Fromstein Assocs.; mem. Bd of Dirs Manpower Inc., Milwaukee 1972–99, Pres., Chair. and CEO 1976–99, Chair. Emer. 1999–; Pres., CEO and Dir The Parker Pen Co., Janesville, Wis. 1985–86 (Parker acquired by Manpower 1976); mem. Bd of Dirs Adelman Travel Group, Public/Private Ventures; co-owner and mem. Bd of Dirs Milwaukee Brewers baseball club –2004. *Address:* c/o Board of Directors, Adelman Travel Group, 6980 North Port Washington Road, Milwaukee, WI 53217, USA.

FROST, Sir David Paradine, Kt, OBE, MA; British broadcast journalist and writer; b. 7 April 1939, Tenterden, Kent; s. of Rev. W. J. Paradine Frost; m. 1st Lynne Frederick 1981 (divorced 1982); m. 2nd Lady Carina Fitzalan Howard 1983; three s.; ed Gillingham and Wellingborough Grammar Schools, Gonville and Caius Coll., Cambridge; appeared in BBC TV satire series That Was The Week That Was 1962–63, That Was The Year That Was 1962–63; other programmes with BBC included A Degree of Frost 1963, 1973, Not So Much A Programme More A Way Of Life 1964–65, The Frost Report 1966–67, Frost Over England 1967; appeared in The Frost Programme, ITA 1966–67, 1967–68, 1972; Chair. and CEO David Paradine Ltd 1966–; Jt Founder London Weekend Television 1967; Jt Deputy Chair. Equity Enterprises 1973–76 (Chair. 1972–73); Jt Founder and Dir TV-AM 1981–93, host of numerous programmes, including That Was The Week That Was (USA) 1964–65, Frost On Friday, Frost On Saturday, Frost On Sunday etc., David Frost Show (USA) 1969–72, David Frost Revue (USA) 1971–73, Frost Over Australia 1972–77, Frost Over New Zealand 1973–74, The Frost Interview 1974, We British 1975, The Sir Harold Wilson Interviews 1967–77, The Nixon Interviews 1976–77, The Crossroads of Civilisation 1977–78; David Frost Presents the Int. Guinness Book of World Records 1981–86, Frost over Canada 1982–83, The Spectacular World of Guinness Records 1987–88, Talking with David Frost 1991–; Presenter Sunday Breakfast with Frost 1993–2005; The Frost Programme 1993–; joined Al-Jazeera International 2005–, Host Frost Over the World; Pres. Lord's Taverners 1985, 1986; Companion TV and Radio Industries Club 1992; Hon. Prof. Thames Valley Univ. 1994; Hon. DCL (Univ. of East Anglia) 2004; Golden Rose, Montreux (for Frost over England) 1967, Royal TV Soc.'s Award 1967, Richard Dimbleby Award 1967, Emmy Award 1970, 1971, Religious Heritage of America Award 1970, Albert Einstein Award (Communication Arts) 1971, BAFTA Fellowship 2005. *Films produced:* The Rise and Rise of Michael Rimmer 1970, Charley One-Eye 1972, Leadbelly 1974, The Slipper and the Rose 1975, Dynasty 1975, The Ordeal of Patty Hearst 1978, The Remarkable Mrs Sanger 1979. *Publications:* That Was The Week That Was 1963, How to Live Under Labour 1964, Talking With Frost 1967, To England With Love (with Antony Jay) 1967, The Americans 1970, Whitlam and Frost 1974, I Gave Them a Sword 1978, I Could Have Kicked Myself 1982, Who Wants to Be a Millionaire? 1983, The Mid-Atlantic Companion (jtly) 1986, The Rich Tide (jtly) 1986, The World's Shortest Books 1987, David Frost An Autobiography: Part One 1993. *Address:* David Paradine Ltd, 5 St Mary Abbots Place, Kensington, London, W8 6LS, England. *Telephone:* (20) 7371-1111. *Fax:* (20) 7602-0411.

FROTSCHER, Michael, PhD; German anatomist and academic; *Professor and Head of Department, Institute of Anatomy and Cell Biology, Albert-Ludwigs-Universität;* b. Dresden; ed East-Berlin Humboldt Univ.; started scientific career at Inst. of Anatomy, East-Berlin Humboldt Univ., GDR; fled to FRG 1979, started new career at Max Planck Inst. of Brain Research, Frankfurt; currently Prof. and Head of Dept, Inst. of Anatomy and Cell Biology, Albert-Ludwigs-Universität, Freiburg; German Research Foundation Leibniz Prize 1993, Max Planck Research Award for Biosciences and Medicine 2000, Ernst Jung Prize for Medicine 2002. *Publications:* numerous publs in medical and scientific journals. *Address:* Institut für Anatomie und Zellbiologie, Albert-Ludwigs-Universität, Albertstrasse 17, 79104 Freiburg i.Br., Germany (office). *Telephone:* (761) 203-5056 (office). *Fax:* (761) 203-5054 (office). *E-mail:* Michael.Frotscher@anat.uni-freiburg.de (office). *Website:* www.anatomie.uni-freiburg.de (office).

FROWEIN, Jochen Abraham, DJur, MCL; German professor of law; *Director Emeritus, Max-Planck-Institut für ausländisches öffentliches Recht und Völkerrecht;* b. 8 June 1934, Berlin; s. of Dr Abraham Frowein and Hilde Frowein (née Matthis); m. Lore Flume 1962; one s. two d.; ed Univs of Kiel, Berlin, Bonn and Univ. of Michigan Law School, Ann Arbor, USA; Research Fellow, Max-Planck-Inst. for Comparative Public and Int. Law 1962–66; Prof., Univ. of Bochum 1967–69, Univ. of Bielefeld 1969–81; Dir Max-Planck-Inst. and Prof., Univ. of Heidelberg 1981–2002, now Dir Emer.; Visiting Prof., Univ. of Michigan Law School 1978, Georgetown Law Faculty, Washington, DC 2003; Expert of European Parl. for Beneš-Decrees 2002; mem. European Comm. on Human Rights 1973–93, Arbitration Tribunal for BIS 2001; Vice-Pres. 1981–93; Vice-Pres. German Research Foundation 1977–80; Pres. Vereinigung Deutscher Staatsrechtslehrer (German Public Law Teachers Asscn) 1999–2001; Vice-Pres. Max Planck Soc. 1999–2002, Int. Comm. for Jurists, Geneva; Grosses Bundesverdienstkreuz 1994; Dr hc (Seville) 1984, (Louvain) 1997, (Szeged) 1998, (Bielefeld) 1999, (University Panthéon-Assas Paris II) 2000. *Publications:* Das de facto-Regime im Völkerrecht 1968, EMRK-Kommentar (with W. Peukert) 1985; and many articles and contributions. *Address:* Max-Planck-Institut für ausländisches öffentliches Recht und Völkerrecht, Im Neuenheimer Feld 535, 69120 Heidelberg, Germany (office). *Telephone:* (6221) 482258 (office). *Fax:* (6221) 482677 (office). *E-mail:* sekrefro@mpil.de (office). *Website:* www.mpil.de (office).

FRÜHBECK DE BURGOS, Rafael; Spanish conductor; *Chief Conductor, Dresdner Philharmonic Orchestra;* b. 15 Sept. 1933, Burgos; s. of Wilhelm Frühbeck and Stephanie Frühbeck (née Ochs); m. María Carmen Martínez 1959; one s. one d.; ed music acads in Bilbao, Madrid and Munich, Univ. of Madrid; Chief Conductor, Municipal Orchestra, Bilbao 1958–62; Music Dir and Chief Conductor, Spanish Nat. Orchestra, Madrid 1962–78, Hon. Conductor 1998; Music Dir of Düsseldorf and Chief Conductor Düsseldorf Symphoniker 1966–71; Music Dir Montreal Symphony Orchestra 1974–76; Prin. Guest Conductor Yomiuri Nippon Symphony Orchestra 1980–90, Hon. Conductor 1991; Prin. Guest Conductor Nat. Symphony Orchestra, Washington, DC 1980–90; Music Dir Vienna Symphony Orchestra 1991–96; Gen. Music Dir Deutsche Oper Berlin 1992–97; Gen. Musik Dir Rundfunk Symphony Orchestra, Berlin 1994–2000; Chief Conductor RAI Nat. Symphony Orchestra, Turin 2001–07; Prin. Guest Conductor, Dresdner Philharmonic Orchestra 2003–04, Chief Conductor 2004–; mem. Real Academia de Bellas Artes, Madrid 1975; Gran Cruz al Mérito Civil Orden de Alfonso X 1966, Orden de Isabel la Católica 1966, Grand Cross of Civil Merit (Germany) 2001, Gold Medal Labour Merit (Spain) 2004; Dr hc (Univ. of Navarra) 1994, (Univ. of Burgos) 1998; Prize for Musical Interpretation, Larios Foundation, Confed. Española de Orgs Empresariales, Madrid 1992, Fundación Guerrero Prize for Spanish Music, Madrid 1996, Gold Medal City of Vienna 1995, Medal of Civil Merit (Austria) 1996, Gold Medal Int. Gustav Mahler Soc., Vienna 1996, Gold Medal State of Vienna 2000, hon. mem. Israel Philharmonic Orchestra 1999. *Orchestrations:* Suite Española (Albéniz) 1965, Tema y Variaciones (Turina) 1985. *Address:* c/o Askonas Holt, Lincoln House, 300 High Holborn, London, WC1V 7JH, England (office); Avenida del Mediterráneo 21, Madrid, 28007, Spain (home). *Telephone:* (20) 7400-1700 (office); (341) 5016933 (home). *Fax:* (20) 7400-1799 (office); (341) 5016933 (home). *E-mail:* info@askonasholt.co.uk (office). *Website:* www.askonasholt.co.uk (office); www.dresdnerphilharmonie.de (office).

FRUNZĂVERDE, Sorin, PhD; Romanian engineer and politician; b. 23 Sept. 1962, Bocsa, Caras-Severin Co.; m.; one c.; ed Faculty of Metallurgy, Polytechnic Inst., Bucharest, Western Univ., Timişoara, Nat. Defence Univ., Bucharest; Chief of Workshop, Resita Siderurgical Works 1985–88, Head Dept for Quality Control-Labs 1988–90; Pres. and Gen. Man. Chamber for Trade and Industry of Caraş-Severin 1991–96; County Counsellor, Sec., Comm. for Budget and Finances Cttee 1992–96; Chair. Caras-Severin Co. Council 1996–97, 2004–06; Minister of Environment, Waters Man. and Forests 1997–98, of Tourism 1998; Chair. Nat. Authority for Tourism 1999–2000; Minister of Nat. Defense 2000, 2006–07; mem. Chamber of Deputies for Caras-Severin Electoral Ward 2000–04; mem. Partidul Democrat (PD), currently Vice-Pres. *Address:* c/o Ministry of National Defence, 050561 Bucharest 5, Str. Izvor 13–15, Sector 5, Romania (office).

FRUTON, Joseph Stewart, PhD; American biochemist and academic; *Professor Emeritus, Yale University;* b. 14 May 1912, Czestochowa, Poland; s. of Charles Fruton and Ella Eisenstadt; m. Sofia Simmonds 1936; ed Columbia Univ.; Assoc., Rockefeller Inst. for Medical Research 1934–45; Assoc. Prof. of Physiological Chem., Yale Univ. 1945–50, Prof. of Biochemistry 1950–57, Chair. Dept of Biochemistry 1951–67, Eugene Higgins Prof. of Biochemistry 1957–82, Emer. 1982–, Dir Div. of Science 1959–62, Prof. History of Medicine 1980–82, Emer. 1982–; Exec. Sec. Yale Corpn Presidential Search Cttee 1985–86; Assoc. Ed. Journal of Biological Chemistry, Journal of Biochemistry; Visiting Prof., Rockefeller Univ. 1968–69; Benjamin Franklin Fellow, Royal Soc. of Arts; mem. American Philosophical Soc., NAS, American Acad. of Arts and Sciences, Harvey Soc., ACS, American Soc. of Biological Chemists, Biochemical Soc., History of Science Soc.; Fellow, Guggenheim Foundation 1983–84; Hon. ScD (Rockefeller Univ.) 1976; Eli Lilly Award in Biological Chem. 1944, Harvey Lecturer 1955, Dakin Lecturer 1962, Pfizer Award in History of Science 1973, Sarton Lecturer 1976, Xerox Lecturer 1977, John Frederick Lewis Award, American Philosophical Soc. 1990, Dexter Award in History of Chem. 1993. *Publications:* General Biochemistry (with S. Simmonds) 1953, Molecules and Life 1972, Selected Bibliography of Biographical Data for the History of Biochemistry since 1800 1974, a Bio-bibliography for the History of the Biochemical Sciences Since 1800 1982,

Contrasts in Scientific Style 1990, A Skeptical Biochemist 1992, Eighty Years 1994, Proteins, Enzymes, Genes 1999, Methods and Styles in the Development of Chemistry 2002, Fermentation 2006; numerous scientific articles in Journal of Biological Chemistry, Biochemistry, Journal of American Chemical Soc., Proceedings of NAS and other journals. *Leisure interests:* history of science, music. *Address:* L134 Sterling Hall of Medicine, Yale University, 333 Cedar Street, New Haven, CT 06520 (office); 123 York Street, New Haven, CT 06511, USA (home). *Telephone:* (203) 785-4340 (office); (203) 624-3735 (home). *Fax:* (203) 737-4130 (office).

FRY, Hedy, PC; Canadian physician and politician; b. 6 Aug. 1941, Trinidad; three s.; ed Coll. of Physicians and Surgeons, Dublin, Ireland; fmr family physician, Vancouver Centre, BC; MP for Vancouver Centre 1993–; Parl. Sec. to Minister of Health 1993–96; Sec. of State (Multiculturalism, Status of Women) 1996–2002; Parl. Sec. to Minister of Citizenship and Immigration with special emphasis on Foreign Credentials 2003–04; Parl. Sec. to Minister of Citizenship and Immigration and Minister of Human Resources and Skills Devt with special emphasis on the Internationally Trained Workers Initiative 2004–06; Critic for Sport Canada in Liberal shadow cabinet 2006–; Vice-Chair. Task Force on Canada–US Relations 2002; Chair. BC Caucus 2002–, Standing Cttee on Health 2002–03, Special Cttee on non-medical use of drugs 2002; fmr Pres. BC Medical Asscn. *Leisure interests:* drama, racquetball, reading, swimming. *Address:* House of Commons, Ottawa, Ont. K1A 0A9; Confederation Building, Room 583, House of Commons, Ottawa, ON K1A 0A6, Canada (office). *Telephone:* (613) 992-3213 (office). *Fax:* (613) 995-0056 (office). *E-mail:* contact@hedyfry.com; fryh0@parl.gc.ca (office). *Website:* www.hedyfry.com (office).

FRY, Jonathan Michael, MA; British business executive; *Chairman, Control Risks Group Holdings Ltd.;* b. 9 Aug. 1937, Jerusalem; s. of the late Stephen Fry and of Gladys Yvonne Blunt; m. Caroline Mary Dunkerly 1970 (divorced 1997); four d.; m. 2nd Marilyn Russell 1999; ed Repton School, Trinity College, Oxford Univ.; Account Exec., Pritchard Wood Ltd 1961–65; Account Supervisor, Norman Craig & Kummel Inc. 1965–66; Consultant, McKinsey & Co. 1966–73; Devt./Marketing Dir Unigate Foods Div. 1973, Man. Dir 1973, Chair. 1976–78; Group Planning Dir Burmah Oil Trading Ltd 1978–81, Chief Exec. Burmah Speciality Chemicals Ltd 1981–87; Chair. Burmah Castrol PLC 1998–2000 (Man. Dir 1990–93, Chief Exec. 1993–98); Chief Exec. Burmah Castrol Trading Ltd 1993–98, Chair. 1998–2000 (Man. Dir 1990–93); Chair. Castrol Int. (fmrly Castrol Ltd) 1993–96 (Chief Exec. 1987–93); Deputy Chair. Northern Foods PLC 1996–2002 (non-exec. Dir 1991–2002); Chair. Christian Salvesen PLC 1997–2003 (non-exec. Dir 1995–2003); Chair. Elementis PLC (fmrly Harrisons & Crosfield PLC) 1997–; Chair. Control Risks Group Holdings Ltd 2000–. *Leisure interests:* cricket, skiing, archaeology. *Address:* Beechingstoke Manor, Pewsey, Wilts., SN9 6HQ, England (home). *Telephone:* (167285) 1669 (home).

FRY, Stephen John, MA; British actor, writer and director; b. 24 Aug. 1957; s. of Alan John Fry and Marianne Eve Fry (née Newman); ed Uppingham School, Queens' Coll. Cambridge; Columnist The Listener 1988–89, Daily Telegraph 1990–; wrote first play Latin, performed at Edin. Festival 1980 and at Lyric Theatre, Hammersmith 1983; appeared with Cambridge Footlights in revue The Cellar Tapes, Edinburgh Festival 1981; re-wrote script Me and My Girl, London, Broadway, Sydney 1984; mem. Amnesty Int., Comic Relief; Pres. Friends for Life Terrence Higgins Trust; Hon. LLD (Dundee) 1995, (East Anglia) 1999, Hon. DLit, Dr hc (Anglia Ruskin) 2005. *Plays:* Forty Years On, Chichester Festival and London 1984, The Common Pursuit, London 1988 (TV 1992). *Radio:* Loose Ends 1986–87, Whose Line Is It Anyway? 1987, Saturday Night Fry 1987, 1998. *TV series:* There's Nothing to Worry About 1982, Alfresco 1983–84, The Young Ones 1984, Happy Families 1985, Blackadder II 1985, Saturday Live 1986–87, A Bit of Fry and Laurie 1987–95, Blackadder's Christmas Carol 1988, Blackadder Goes Forth 1989, Jeeves and Wooster 1990–93, Stalag Luft 1993, Laughter and Loathing 1995, Gormenghast 2000, Absolute Power 2003, QI 2003–, Stephen Fry in America 2008. *Films:* The Good Father, A Fish Called Wanda, A Handful of Dust, Peter's Friends 1992, IQ 1995, Wind in the Willows, Wilde 1997, Cold Comfort Farm 1997, A Civil Action 1997, Whatever Happened to Harold Smith? 2000, Relative Values 2000, Discovery of Heaven 2001, Gosford Park 2002, Bright Young Things (writer, dir, exec. producer) 2003, Mirrormask 2004, A Cock and Bull Story 2005, V for Vendetta 2006, Stormbreaker 2006, St Trinian's 2007. *Publications:* Paperweight (collected essays) 1992, Stephen Fry Mixed Shrinkwrap 1993, X10 Hippopotamus Shrinkwrap 1993, The Liar (novel) 1993, The Hippopotamus 1994, A Bit of Fry and Laurie (with Hugh Laurie) 1994, 3 Bits of Fry and Laurie (with Hugh Laurie) 1994, Fry and Laurie 4 (with Hugh Laurie) 1994, Paperweight Vol. II (collected essays) 1995, Making History 1996, Moab is my Washpot (autobiog.) 1997, The Stars' Tennis Balls (novel) 2000, The Salmon of Doubt by Douglas Adams (ed.) 2002, Revenge (novel) 2002, Rescuing the Spectacled Bear (novel) 2002, Incomplete & Utter History of Classical Music (with Tim Lihoreau) 2005, The Ode Less Travelled: Unlocking the Poet Within 2005, Stephen Fry in America 2008. *Leisure interests:* smoking, drinking, swearing, pressing wild flowers. *Address:* Hamilton Hodell Ltd, Fifth Floor, 66-68 Margaret Street, London, W1W 8SR, England (office); c/o Toni Howard, ICM, 8942 Wilshire Blvd, Beverly Hills, CA 90211, USA (office). *Telephone:* (20) 7636-1221 (office). *Fax:* (20) 7636-1226 (office). *Website:* www.stephenfry.com (office).

FRYE, Richard Nelson, PhD; American orientalist and academic; *Emeritus Professor of Iranian, Harvard University;* b. 10 Jan. 1920, Birmingham, Ala; s. of Nels Frye and Lillie Hagman; m. 1st Barbara York 1948 (divorced 1973); two s. one d.; m. 2nd Eden Naby 1975; one s.; ed Univ. of Illinois, Harvard Univ. and School of Oriental and African Studies, London; Jr Fellow, Harvard Univ. 1946–49, Founder Middle East Centre 1949; Visiting Scholar, Univ. of

Tehran 1951–52; Co-Founder Nat. Asscn of Armenian Studies 1955; Aga Khan Prof. of Iranian Studies, Harvard Univ. 1957–99, now Emer.; Visiting Prof., Oriental Seminary, Frankfurt Univ. 1958–59; Visiting Prof., Hamburg Univ. 1968–69; Dir Asia Inst., Pahlavi Univ., Shiraz 1969–75; Assoc. Ed. Cen. Asian Journal, Bulletin of the Asia Inst.; Corresp. Fellow, German Archaeological Inst. 1966–; Hon. DLitt (Oxford Univ.) 1987; Hon. PhD (Univ. of Tajikistan) 1991. *Publications:* Notes on the Early Coinage of Transoxiana 1949, History of the Nation of the Archers 1952, Narshakhi, The History of Bukhara 1954, Iran 1956, Heritage of Persia 1962, Bukhara, The Medieval Achievement 1965, The Histories of Nishapur 1965, Persia 1968, Inscriptions from Dura Europos 1969, Excavations at Qasr-i-Abu-Nasr 1973, The Golden Age of Persia 1975; Ed. Vol. 4 Cambridge History of Iran 1975, The Ancient History of Iran 1983, The Heritage of Central Asia 1996, Greater Iran 2005, Ibn Fadlan's Voyage to Russia 2005. *Address:* Tower Hill Road, Brimfield, MA 01010 (home); Harvard University, 6 Divinity Avenue, Cambridge, MA 02138, USA (office). *Telephone:* (617) 495-2684 (office); (413) 245-3630 (home). *E-mail:* frye@tas.harvard.edu (office); frye_richard@yahoo.com (home).

FRYER, Geoffrey, PhD, DSc, FRS; British biologist; b. 6 Aug. 1927, Huddersfield; s. of W. Fryer and M. Fryer; m. Vivien G. Hodgson 1953; one s. one d.; ed Huddersfield Coll. and Univ. of London; colonial research student 1952–53; HM Overseas Research Service, Malawi 1953–55, Zambia 1955–57, Uganda 1957–60; Sr, then Prin., then Sr Prin. Scientific Officer, Freshwater Biological Asscn 1960–81; Deputy Chief Scientific Officer, Windermere Lab., Freshwater Biological Asscn 1981–88; H. R. Macmillan Lecturer, Univ. of BC 1963; Distinguished Visiting Scholar, Univ. of Adelaide 1985; Distinguished Lecturer, Dept of Fisheries and Oceans, Canada 1987; Frink Medal, Zoological Soc. of London 1983, Linnean Medal for Zoology, Linnean Soc. of London 1987, Elsdon-Dew Medal, Parasitological Soc. of Southern Africa 1998; Hon. Prof., Univ. of Lancaster 1988–. *Publications:* The Cichlid Fishes of the Great Lakes of Africa: Their Biology and Evolution (with T. D. Iles) 1972, A Natural History of the Lakes, Tarns and Streams of the English Lake District 1991, The Freshwater Crustacea of Yorkshire: A Faunistic and Ecological Survey 1993; numerous articles in scientific journals. *Leisure interests:* natural history, walking, church architecture, photography. *Address:* Elleray Cottage, Windermere, Cumbria, LA23 1AW, England.

FU, Chengyu, MSc; Chinese oil industry executive; *Chairman, President and CEO, China National Offshore Oil Corporation (CNOOC) Ltd;* b. 1951; ed Northeast Petroleum Inst., Univ. of Southern California, USA; fmr oil engineer; joined China Nat. Offshore Oil Corpn (CNOOC) 1982, chair. several jt ventures, Vice-Pres. CNOOC Nanhai East Corpn 1994–95; Vice-Pres. Phillips China Inc. 1995; Gen. Man. Xijiang Devt Project 1995; Pres. CNOOC Nanhai East Corpn 1999, Exec. Dir, Exec. Vice-Pres. and COO CNOOC Ltd 1999, Vice-Pres. CNOOC 2000, Pres. CNOOC Ltd 2000, Chair. and CEO China Oilfield Services Ltd 2002–, Chair., Pres. and CEO CNOOC Ltd 2003–; mem. 17th CCP Cen. Cttee Cen. Comm. for Discipline Inspection 2007–. *Address:* China National Offshore Oil Corpn, Box 4705, 25 Chao Yangmen North Street, Dongcheng District, Beijing 100010, People's Republic of China (office). *Telephone:* (10) 84521010 (office). *Fax:* (10) 64602600 (office). *E-mail:* webmaster@cnooc.com.cn (office). *Website:* www.cnooc.com.cn (office).

FU, Hao; Chinese diplomatist; b. 13 April 1916, Li Quan Co., Xian Yang City, Shaanxi Prov.; m. Jiao Ling 1945; two s., one d.; ed NW China Teachers Coll.; served in PLA during the civil war; CPC rep. (Col) Group of Beiping Exec. HQ of CPC, Kuomintang and USA in Dezhou, Shandong Prov. 1946; Counsellor, Embassy in Mongolia 1950–53; Attaché, Deputy Dir-Gen. Asian Affairs Dept, Ministry of Foreign Affairs 1952–55; Counsellor, frequently Chargé d'affaires, Embassy in India 1955–62; Deputy Dir-Gen., Personnel Dept, Ministry of Foreign Affairs 1963–69, Head Gen. Office 1970–72; Rep. to 26th Session UN Gen. Ass. 1971; Vice-Minister of Foreign Affairs 1972–74; Amb. to Democratic Repub. of Viet Nam 1974–77, to Japan 1977–82; Vice Minister, Adviser Ministry of Foreign Affairs 1982–94; Deputy 6th NPC, mem. Standing Cttee, Vice-Chair. Foreign Affairs Cttee 1983–88; Chinese mem. 21st Century Cttee for Sino-Japanese Friendship 1984–95, Chinese Chair. 1996–98; Chair. NPC China-Japan Friendship Group 1985–93; Deputy 7th NPC, mem. Standing Cttee, Vice-Chair. Foreign Affairs Cttee 1988–93; mem. Exec. Cttee IPU 1989–91; Chair. China-Vietnamese Friendship Asscn 1992–96; Pres. Asscn of fmr Diplomats of China 1994–99, Hon. Pres. 2000; Chair. Inst. for Diplomatic History of People's Repub. of China 1994, Ed.'s Cttee of China Classical Stratagems 1995; Grand Cordon of the Sacred Treasure (Japan). *Publications:* Tian Nan Di Bei (poems) 1992, My Life: Stormy but Memorable 2001, Feng Yu Cang Sang (essay) 2001. *Leisure interests:* poems and literature. *Address:* Retired Personel Bureau, Ministry of Foreign Affairs, 2 Chao Wai Avenue, Chao Yang Meng District, Beijing 100701 (office); 69 Bao Fang Lane, East District, Beijing 100010, People's Republic of China (home). *Telephone:* (10) 65965242 (office); (10) 65252010 (home). *Fax:* (10) 65965241 (office). *E-mail:* lgj4@mfa.gov.cn (office).

FU, Lt-Gen. Kuiqing; Chinese army officer; b. 1920, Yingshan Co., Anhui Prov.; Sec. CCP Prov. Cttee, Heilongjiang 1971–74; Vice-Gov., Heilongjiang 1972–74; Deputy Political Commissar, Shenyang Mil. Region, PLA 1977; Political Commissar, Fuzhou Mil. Region, PLA 1981–85; mem. 12th CCP Cen. Cttee 1982–87; Political Commissar Nanjing Mil. Region, PLA 1985–90, rank of Lt-Gen. PLA 1988; mem. Standing Cttee of 7th NPC; 3rd Class Order of Independence and Freedom, 2nd Class Order of Liberation. *Address:* Nanjing Military Region Headquarters, Nanjing, Jiangsu, People's Republic of China.

FU, Mingxia; Chinese diver; b. Aug. 1978, Wuhan, Hubei Prov.; m. Antony Leung 2002; two s. one d.; ed Qinghua Univ., Beijing; youngest ever 10m platform diving world champion at the age of 12; first woman to win five Olympic diving medals; 10m platform diving gold medallist at Olympics, Barcelona 1992, Olympics, Atlanta 1996 (also won 3m platform gold medal), 3m springboard gold medallist at Sydney Olympics 2000; Nation's Best 10 Athletes Award. *Address:* c/o State General Bureau for Physical Culture and Sports, 9 Tiyuguan Road, Chongwen District, Beijing, People's Republic of China.

FU, Qifeng; Chinese writer and former acrobat; b. 15 March 1941, Chengdu, Sichuan; d. of Fu Tianzheng and Ceng Qingpu; m. Xu Zhuang 1961; one s. one d.; performer, acrobatics troupe, Beijing 1960–70; Founder and Deputy Chief Ed. Acrobatics and Magic (journal); mem. Research Dept, Asscn of Chinese Acrobats 1987–, Council mem. 1991–; mem. Editorial Cttee Acrobatics, in series Contemporary China 1991–; mem. China Magic Cttee 1993–. *Publications:* Chinese Acrobatics Through the Ages 1986, The Art of Chinese Acrobatics 1988; (with brother) Acrobatics in China 1983, History of Chinese Acrobatics 1989, History of Chinese Artistic Skills (in Japanese) 1993; (co-author) Literature and Art volume of China Concise Encyclopedia 1994, Secret of Spiritualist Activities 1995, Illusions and Superstitions 1997. *Address:* 5-2-501 Hongmiao Beili, Jintai Road, Beijing 100025, People's Republic of China. *Telephone:* 65002547.

FU, Gen. Quanyou; Chinese army officer; b. 1930, Yuanping Co., Shanxi Prov.; ed Mil. Acad. of the Chinese PLA; joined PLA 1946, took part in Yanqing Campaign; joined CCP 1947; Deputy Co. Commdr Northwest Field Army, PLA Services and Arms 1948–50, Co. Commdr and Bn Chief-of-Staff 1950–52; soldier, Korean War 1953, Bn Commdr Chinese People's Volunteers 1953–58; Regt Chief-of-Staff, Chengdu Mil. Region, PLA 1961–64, Div. Chief-of-Staff 1968–69, Div. Commdr 1978–80, Army Chief-of-Staff 1981–83, Army Commdr 1983–85, Commdr 1985–88, Lt-Gen. 1988–93, Commdr Lanzhou Mil. Region 1990–92, Dir Gen. Logistics Dept 1992–95, Gen. 1993–, Chief of Gen. Staff 1995–99; Vice-Chair. Nat. Afforestation Cttee; Deputy Dir Nat. Cttee for the Patriotic Public Health Campaign 1994–98; mem. 12th CCP Cen. Cttee 1983–87, 13th CCP Cen. Cttee 1987–92, 14th CCP Cen. Cttee (mem. Cen. Mil. Comm.) 1992–97, 15th CCP Cen. Cttee 1997–2002; mem. Cen. Mil. Comm. of People's Repub. of China 1993–. *Address:* c/o Chinese Communist Party Central Committee, Zhongnanhai, Beijing, People's Republic of China.

FU, Tianlin; Chinese poet; b. 24 Jan. 1946, Zizhong Co., Sichuan Prov.; ed Chongqing Middle School, Electronic Tech. School; worked in orchard Chongqing 1962–79; clerk, Beibei Cultural Centre 1980–82; Ed. Chongqing Publishing House 1982–; First Prize of Chinese Poetry 1983. *Publications:* Green Musical Notes 1981, Between Children and the World 1983, Island of Music 1985, Red Strawberry 1986, Selected Poems of Seven Chinese Poets 1993. *Address:* Chongqing Publishing House, 205 Changjiang 2 Road, Chongqing City 630050, Sichuan, People's Republic of China.

FU, Xishou; Chinese government official and engineer; b. 1931, Beijing; ed Tsinghua Univ.; joined CCP 1959; Chief Designer, Panzhihua Iron and Steel Project, Sichuan Prov. 1959; Deputy Chief Engineer, Chongqing Iron and Steel Designing Inst. 1966–78, Deputy Dir 1978–82; Dir Ma'anshan Iron and Steel Design and Research Inst., Anhui Prov. 1982–84; Man. Ma'anshan Iron and Steel Group Co. Ltd 1984–87 (Sec. CCP Party Cttee 1984–87); Deputy Sec. CCP Ma'anshan City Cttee 1984–87; Deputy Sec. Anhui Prov. CCP Cttee 1987–88; Deputy Gov. of Anhui Prov. 1988–89, Gov. 1989–94; Alt. mem. 14th CCP Cen. Cttee 1987–92, mem. 14th CCP Cen. Cttee 1992–97; mem. Standing Cttee 8th CPPCC Nat. Cttee 1993–98, 9th CPPCC Nat. Cttee 1998–2003; NPC Deputy to Anhui Prov.; Deputy Sec. CCP 5th Anhui Prov. Cttee 1988; Gov. Anhui Prov. People's Govt 1989–94; Chair. Anhui Prov. Disabled Persons' Fed. *Address:* c/o Office of Provincial Governor, Hefei City, Anhui Province, People's Republic of China.

FU, Zhihuan; Chinese politician; *Chairman, Financial and Economic Committee, National People's Congress;* b. March 1938, Haicheng Co., Liaoning Prov.; ed Moscow Railways Inst., USSR; technician, later Deputy Chief, later Chief, later Deputy Dir Zhuzhou Electric Eng Research Inst., Ministry of Railways 1961; joined CCP 1966; Chief Engineer, Science and Tech. Bureau, Ministry of Railways 1983, Dir 1985; Dir Harbin Railway Bureau 1989; Vice-Minister of Railways 1990–97, Minister 2002–03; Chair. Financial and Econ. Cttee, NPC 2003–; mem. CCP Cen. Comm. for Discipline Inspection 1997–2002; mem. 15th CCP Cen. Cttee 1997–2002. *Address:* c/o Zhongguo Gongchan Dang (Chinese Communist Party), Beijing, People's Republic of China (office).

FUCHS, Anke, LLM; German lawyer and politician; *Chairman, Friedrich-Ebert-Stiftung;* b. (Anke Nevermann), 5 July 1937, Hamburg; d. of Paul Nevermann; m.; two c.; ed Hamburg, Innsbruck and School of Public Admin., Speyer; mem. Regional Exec., Young Socialist Org. 1954; joined Social Democratic Party (SPD) 1956; trainee, regional org. of German Fed. of Trade Unions, Nordmark (Hamburg) 1964–68; Regional Sec. Metal Workers' Union (IG Metall), mem. Reform Comm. on Training for Legal Profession, mem. SPD Regional Exec., mem. Hamburg Judge Selection Cttee 1968–70; mem. Hamburg Citizens' Ass. 1970–77; Exec. Sec. IG Metall 1971–77; mem. SPD Party Council 1970, fmr Deputy Chair., Party Man. 1987–91, Chair. SPD Party Council 1993; State Sec. Fed. Ministry of Labour and Social Affairs 1977–80; mem. Bundestag 1980–2002, Vice-Pres. 1998–2002; Parl. State Sec. 1980–82; Pres. des Deutschen Mieterbundes 1995–; Fed. Minister for Youth, Family Affairs and Health April–Oct. 1982; Chair. Friedrich Ebert-Stiftung 2003–; Patron Nat. Coalition; Dr hc 2000. *Address:* Friedrich-Ebert-Stiftung, Berliner Haus, Hiroshimastraße 17, 10785 Berlin, Germany (office). *Telephone:* (30) 269356 (office). *Website:* www.fes.de (office).

FUCHS, Victor Robert, MA, PhD; American economist and academic; *Henry J. Kaiser, Jr Professor Emeritus of Economics, Stanford University;* b. 31 Jan. 1924, New York; s. of Alfred Fuchs and Frances S. Fuchs (née Scheiber); m. Beverly Beck 1948; two s. two d.; ed New York and Columbia Univs; Assoc. Prof. of Econs, New York Univ. 1959–60; Program Assoc. Econs Ford

Foundation 1960–62; Research Assoc., Nat. Bureau of Econ. Research 1962–; Prof. of Community Medicine, Mount Sinai School of Medicine 1968–74; Prof. of Econs, CUNY Grad. Center 1968–74; Prof. of Econs (in Depts. of Econs and Health Research and Policy), Stanford Univ. 1974–95, Henry J. Kaiser, Jr Prof. 1988–95, Prof. Emer. 1995–; Pres. American Econ. Asscn 1995; mem. Inst. of Medicine, American Philosophical Soc.; Fellow, American Acad. of Arts and Sciences; Distinguished Fellow, American Econ. Asscn 1990; Madden Memorial Award 1982, John R. Commons Award 2002 and other awards. *Publications:* The Economics of the Fur Industry 1957, Changes in the Location of Manufacturing in the US since 1929 1962, The Service Economy 1968, Production and Productivity in the Service Industries 1969, Who Shall Live? Health, Economics and Social Choice 1974 (expanded edn 1998), Economic Aspects of Health (ed.) 1982, How We Live 1983, The Health Economy 1986, Women's Quest for Economic Equality 1988, The Future of Health Policy 1993, Individual and Social Responsibility: Child Care, Education, Medical Care and Long Term Care in America (ed.) 1996. *Address:* National Bureau of Economic Research, 30 Alta Road, Stanford, CA 94305 (office); 796 Cedro Way, Stanford, CA 94305, USA (home). *Telephone:* (650) 326-7639 (office); (650) 858-1527 (home). *Fax:* (650) 328-4163 (office); (650) 858-0411 (home). *E-mail:* fuchs@newage3.stanford.edu (office). *Website:* www-econ.stanford.edu (office).

FUDGE, Ann Marie, BA, MBA; American advertising executive (retd); b. 23 April 1951, Washington, DC; m. Richard E. Fudge 1971; two s.; ed Simmons Coll. and Harvard Univ. Grad. School of Business; began career as marketing asst with General Mills, Inc., later Marketing Dir; Pres. Beverage, Desserts and Post Div., Kraft Foods –2003; Chair. and CEO Young & Rubicam Brands and Y&R Advertising 2003–05, Chair. and CEO Y&R Brands 2003–06; mem. Bd Dirs General Electric, Marriott International, Catalyst; mem. Bd of Govs Boys and Girls Club of America; fmr mem. Bd of Dirs The Advertising Council, Advertising Educational Foundation; mem. Harvard Bd of Overseers, Committee of 200, Council on Foreign Relations; Trustee Brookings Inst.; Matrix Award for Advertising, New York Women in Communication, Leadership Awards, Minneapolis and New York City YWCA, Alumni Achievement Award, Harvard Business School 1998, Achievement Award, Executive Leadership Council 2000, Candace Award from Nat Coalition of 100 Black Women, named by Fortune magazine for several years as one of 50 Most Powerful Women in Business in the US, ranked 89th by Forbes magazine amongst 100 Most Powerful Women 2004, named as one of Time Magazine's Global Business Influentials 2004. *Address:* 2400 Beacon Street, PH1, Chestnut Hill, MA 02467, USA.

FUENTES, Carlos; Mexican writer and diplomatist; b. 11 Nov. 1928, Mexico City; s. of Rafael Fuentes Boettiger and Berta Macías Rivas; m. 1st Rita Macedo 1957; one d.; m. 2nd Sylvia Lemus 1973; one s. one d.; ed Univ. of Mexico, Inst. des Hautes Etudes Internationales, Geneva; mem. Mexican Del. to ILO, Geneva 1950–51; Asst Head, Press Section, Ministry of Foreign Affairs, Mexico 1954; Asst Dir Cultural Dissemination, Univ. de Mexico 1955–56; Head, Dept of Cultural Relations, Ministry of Foreign Affairs 1957–59; Ed. Revista Mexicana de Literatura 1954–58, Co-Ed. El Espectador 1959–61, Ed. Siempre and Politica 1960–; Amb. to France 1974–77; Prof. of English and Romance Languages, Univ. of Pennsylvania 1978–83; fmr Prof. of Spanish and Comparative Literature, Columbia Univ., New York; Prof. of Comparative Literature, Harvard Univ. 1984–86, Robert F. Kennedy Prof. of Latin American Studies 1987–89; Simon Bolivar Prof., Univ. of Cambridge 1986–87; Prof.-at-Large, Brown Univ. 1995–; Pres. Modern Humanities Research Asscn 1989–; fmr Adjunct Prof. of English and Romance Languages, Univ. of Pennsylvania; Fellow, Woodrow Wilson Int. Center for Scholars, Washington, DC 1974; Fellow of the Humanities, Princeton Univ.; Virginia Gildersleeve Visiting Prof., Barnard Coll., New York; Edward Leroc Visiting Prof., School of Int. Affairs, Columbia Univ., New York; Founder (with Gabriel García Marquez), Julio Cortozar Chair, Univ. of Guadalajara, Mexico 1994; Founder and Co-Pres. Ibero-American Forum 2000; mem. American Acad. and Inst. of Arts and Letters, El Colegio Nacional, Mexico, Mexican Nat. Comm. on Human Rights; Hon. Citizen of Santiago de Chile 1993, Buenos Aires 1993, Veracruz 1993; Order of Merit (Chile 1992); Légion d'honneur 1992; Order of the South Cross, Brazil 1997; French Order of Merit 1998; Dr hc (Harvard, Wesleyan, Essex, Cambridge, Salamanca, Ghent, Madrid); Biblioteca Breve Prize, Barcelona 1967, Rómulo Gallegos Prize, Caracas 1975, Mexican Nat. Award for Literature 1984, Ruben Dario Prize 1988, Premio Principe de Asturias 1992, UNESCO Picasso Medal 1994, Grinzane-Cavour Award 1994, French and Brazilian Acads Latin Civilization Prize 1999, Mexican Senate Medal 2000, Los Angeles Public Library Award 2001, Commonwealth Award Delaware 2002, Giuseppe Acerbi literature prize, Italy 2004, Galileo Prize, Florence, Italy 2005, Blue Metropolis Award, Montreal 2005, Franklin Delano Roosevelt Freedom of Speech Award 2006. *Film and TV screenplays:* Pedro Paramo 1966, Tiempo de morir 1966, Los caifanes 1967, El espejo enterrado (The Buried Mirror, TV series) 1992. *Publications:* Los días enmascarados 1954, La región más transparente 1958, Las buenas conciencias 1959, La muerte de Artemio Cruz 1962, Aura 1962, The Argument of Latin America 1963, Cantar de ciegos 1964, Zona sagrada 1967, Cambio de piel (Biblioteca Breve Prize) 1967, Paris: la revolución de mayo 1968, Cumpleaños 1969, El mundo de José Luis Cuevas 1969, La nueva novela hispanoamericana 1969, Casa con dos puertas 1970, Todos los gatos son pardos (play) 1970, El tuerto es rey (play) 1970, Tiempo mexicano 1971, Poemas de amor 1971, Los signos en rotación y otros ensayos (ed.) 1971, Los reinos originarios 1971, Cuerpos y ofreadas 1972, Chac Mool y otros cuentos 1973, Cervantes o La crítica de la lectura 1974, Terra Nostra (Javier Villaurrutia Prize 1975, Rómulo Gallegos Prize 1977) 1975, La cabeza de la hidra 1978, Una familia lejana 1980, Agua quemada 1981, Orquídeas a la luz de la luna (play) 1982, High Noon in Latin America 1983, Juan Soriano y su obra 1984, On Human Rights: A Speech 1984, El gringo viejo (IUA Prize 1989) 1985, Latin America: At War with the Past 1985, Gabriel García Marquez and the Invention of America 1987, Cristóbal nonato (novel) (Miguel de Cervantes Prize) 1987, Myself with Others (essays) 1988, Valiante mundo nuevo 1990, La campaña (novel) 1990, Constancia y otras novelas para vírgenes 1990, El espejo enterrado 1992, Geografía de la novela (essays) 1993, Tres discursos para dos aldeas 1993, El naranjo (novellas) 1993, Nuevo tiempo mexicano 1994, Frontera de cristal 1995, Diana o la cazadora solitaria 1995, Por un progreso incluyente 1997, Retratos en el tiempo 1998, Los años con Laura Díaz 1999, Instinto de Inez 2000, Los cinco soles de México 2000, En esto creo 2002, La silla del águila 2003, This I Believe: An A–Z of a Writer's Life 2004, Contra Bush 2004, The Eagle's Throne 2006, Todas las Familias Felices 2007, La Voluntad y La Fortuna 2008. *Address:* c/o Brandt & Brandt, 1501 Broadway, New York, NY 10036, USA; c/o Balcells, Diagonal 580, Barcelona 08021, Spain. *Telephone:* (212) 840-5760 (USA); (93) 200-8933 (Spain). *Fax:* (212) 840-5776 (USA); (93) 200-7041 (Spain).

FUENTES KNIGHT, Juan Alberto, MA, PhD; Guatemalan economist and politician; *Minister of Public Finance;* ed McGill Univ. and Univ. of Toronto, Canada, Univ. of Geneva, Switzerland, Univ. of Sussex, UK; served for 20 years as economist with UN, becoming Co-ordinator Guatemalan Human Devt Report, UNDP; Exec. Dir and Research Co-ordinator Instituto Centroamericano de Estudios Fiscales (Cen. American Inst. for Fiscal Studies) –2007; Minister of Public Finance 2007–. *Publications:* numerous articles in econ. journals. *Address:* Ministry of Public Finance, Centro Cívico, 8a Avda y 21 Calle, Zona 1, Guatemala City, Guatemala (office). *Telephone:* 2248-5005 (office). *Fax:* 2248-5054 (office). *E-mail:* info@minfin.gob.gt (office). *Website:* www.minfin.gob.gt (office).

FUGARD, Athol; South African actor and playwright; b. 11 June 1932; s. of Harold David Fugard and Elizabeth Magdelene Potgiefer; m. Sheila Fugard 1956; one d.; leading role in Meetings with Remarkable Men (film) 1977, The Guest (BBC production) 1977; acted in and wrote script for Marigolds in August (film); Hon. DLit (Natal and Rhodes Univs); Dr hc (Univ. of Cape Town, Georgetown Univ., Washington, DC, New York, Pennsylvania, City Univ. of New York); Hon. DFA (Yale Univ.) 1973; winner Silver Bear Award, Berlin Film Festival 1980, New York Critics Award for A Lesson From Aloes 1981, London Evening Standard Award for Master Harold and the Boys 1983, Commonwealth Award for Contrib. to American Theatre 1984. *Plays:* The Blood Knot, Hello and Goodbye, People are Living Here, Boesman and Lena 1970, Sizwe Banzi is Dead 1973, The Island 1973, Statements After an Arrest Under the Immorality Act 1974, No Good Friday 1974, Nongogo 1974, Dimetos 1976, The Road to Mecca 1984, My Children, My Africa, The Guest (film script) 1977, A Lesson from Aloes 1979 (author and dir Broadway production 1980), Master Harold and the Boys 1981, A Place with the Pigs (actor and dir) 1988, Playland 1992, Sign of Hope 1992, Valley Song (actor and dir) 1996, The Captain's Tiger 1999, Sorrows and Rejoicings 2001, Exits and Entrances 2004, Victory 2007. *Films include:* Marigolds in August 1981, The Guest 1984; acted in films Gandhi 1982, Road to Mecca 1991 (also co-dir). *Publications:* Notebooks 1960–77, Playland 1992; novel: Tsotsi 1980; plays: Road to Mecca 1985, A Place with the Pigs 1988, Cousins: A Memoir 1994. *Address:* P.O. Box 5090, Walmer, Port Elizabeth 6065, South Africa.

FUHRMAN, Robert Alexander, MSE, FRAeS; American business executive and aerospace engineer; b. 23 Feb. 1925, Detroit, Mich.; s. of Alexander A. Fuhrman and Elva Brown Fuhrman; m. 1st Nan E. McCormick 1949 (died 1988); two s. one d.; m. 2nd Nancy Ferguson Richards 1989; ed Univs of Michigan and Maryland, Stanford Univ. Grad. School of Business; Vice-Pres. and Gen. Man. Missiles Systems Div., Lockheed Corpn 1966–70, Pres. Georgia Co. 1970–71, Pres. California Co. 1971–74, Pres. Missiles & Space Co. 1976–83, Group Pres. Missiles Space & Electronics 1983–85, Pres. and COO Lockheed Corpn 1985–88, Vice-Chair. and COO 1988–90, Sr Adviser 1990–; fmr Chair. Bd Bank of the West 1990, USAF Science and Tech. Bd 1996; mem. Bd Charles Stark Draper Lab. 1986–, Burdeshaw Assoc. Ltd 1994–; mem. Defense Science Bd; mem. Nat. Acad. of Eng; Hon. Fellow, AIAA, Pres. 1992–93; Mich. Aviation Hall of Fame 1991. *Publications:* The Fleet Ballistic Weapon System: Polaris to Trident (AIAA Von Karman Lecture) 1976, Defense Science Bd Task Force Report: The Defense Industrial Base (Chair.) 1988, The C-17 Review (Chair.) 1993. *Leisure interest:* golf. *Address:* P.O. Box 9, 1543 Riata Road, Pebble Beach, CA 93953, USA. *Telephone:* (408) 625-2525. *Fax:* (408) 625-2393. *E-mail:* robertfuhrman@sbcglobal.net (office).

FUHRMANN, Horst, DPhil; German historian; b. 22 June 1926, Kreuzburg; s. of Karl Fuhrmann and Susanna Fuhrmann; m. Dr Ingrid Winkler-Lippoldt 1954; one s. one d.; collaborator, Monumenta Germaniae Historica 1954–56; Asst, Rome 1957; Asst and Lecturer 1957–62; Prof. Univ. of Tübingen 1962–71; Pres. Monumenta Germaniae Historica, Munich and Prof. Univ. of Regensburg 1971–94; Pres. Bavarian Acad. of Humanities and Science 1992–97; Orden Pour le Mérite; Grosses Bundesverdienstkreuz mit Stern, Bayerischer Verdienstorden, Maximiliansorden 1998; Hon. DrIur (Tübingen); Hon. DPhil (Bologna, Columbia, New York); Premio Spoleto 1962, Cultore di Roma 1981, Upper Silesian Culture Prize 1989, Premio Ascoli Piceno 1990. *Publications:* The Donation of Constantine 1968, Influence and Circulation of the Pseudoisidorian Forgeries (3 vols) 1972–74, Germany in the High Middle Ages 1978, From Petrus to John Paul II: The Papacy 1980, Invitation to the Middle Ages 1987, Far from Cultured People: An Upper Silesian Town Around 1870 1989, Pour le Mérite: On Making Merit Visible 1992, Scholarly Lives 1996, Überall ist Mittelalter 1996. *Address:* Sonnenwinkel 10, 82237 Wörthsee, Germany (home). *Telephone:* (89) 23031135 (office). *Fax:* (89) 23031100.

FUJIMORI, Alberto Kenyo; Peruvian/Japanese fmr head of state and academic; b. 28 July 1939, Lima; s. of the late Nagochi Minami and Matsue

Inomoto; m. 1st Susana Higushi (divorced 1996); two s. two d.; m. 2nd Satomi Kataoka 2006; ed Nat. School of Agric., Univ. of Wisconsin; fmr Rector, Nat. Agrarian Univ.; Pres. Nat. Ass. of Rectors 1984–89; Founder-mem. Cambio '90 (political party); Pres. of Peru 1990–2000; in exile in Japan Nov. 2000–05; arrested and charged in connection with state-sponsored murders, torture of a journalist, and embezzlement of public funds and dereliction of duty Sept. 2001, Peruvian Govt submitted 700-page document to back its charges 2003, Japanese Govt seeking further evidence in connection with Peruvian Govt's extradition request 2004; returned to Chile and arrested Nov. 2005; sentenced to six years in prison for abuse of power Dec. 2007; sentenced to 25 years in prison for ordering crimes against humanity during his presidency April 2009; Dr hc (Glebloux, Belgium, San Martín de Porres, Lima).

FUJIMOTO, Takao; Japanese politician; b. 1931, Kagawa Pref.; m.; one s.; ed Tokyo Univ.; joined Nomura Securities Co. Ltd 1944; joined Nippon Telegraph and Telephone Public Corpn 1957; elected House of Reps for 1st constituency Kagawa Pref. 1963; Parl. Vice-Minister of Science and Tech. Agency 1970; Chair. Liberal Democratic Party (LDP) Science and Tech. Sub-Cttee of the Policy Research Cttee 1972; Parl. Vice-Minister of the Environment Agency 1973; Chair. Standing Cttee on Foreign Affairs 1976, LDP Standing Cttee on Public Information 1983; Minister of State, Dir-Gen. Okinawa Devt Agency 1985; Deputy Sec.-Gen. LDP 1985–86; Minister of Health and Welfare 1987–88, of Agric., Forestry and Fisheries 1996–98. *Leisure interests:* sports (baseball), reading, golf, karaoke singing. *Address:* c/o Liberal-Democratic Party, 1-11-23 Nagata-cho, Chiyoda-ku, Tokyo 100, Japan.

FUJISHIMA, Akira, PhD; Japanese chemist and academic; *Chairman, Kanagawa Academy of Science and Technology;* b. 10 March 1942; ed Yokohama Nat. Univ., Univ. of Tokyo; Lecturer, Kanagawa Univ. 1971, Asst Prof. 1973; Lecturer, Univ. of Tokyo 1975; Postdoctoral Fellow, Univ. of Texas 1976–77; Assoc. Prof., Univ. of Tokyo 1978, Prof. 1986, Prof. Grad. School 1994–2003, Prof. Emer. 2003–; Chair. Kanagawa Acad. of Science and Tech. 2003–; Pres. Electrochemical Soc. of Japan; advisory mem. Japanese Photochemistry Asscn; Pres. Chemical Soc. of Japan; Asahi Prize 1983, Inoue Harunari Prize 1998, Chemical Soc. of Japan Prize 2000, Japan Prize (jtly) 2004, The Japan Academy Prize 2004. *Address:* KSP West 614, 3-2-1 Sakado, Takatsu-ku, Kawasaki-shi, Kanagawa 213-0012, Japan. *Telephone:* (44) 819-2020. *Fax:* (44) 819-2038.

FUJITA, Hiromichi; Japanese business executive; *Chairman and Representative Director, Toppan Printing Company Ltd;* b. 21 March 1928; ed Dept of Econs, Tokyo Univ.; joined Toppan Printing Company Ltd 1953, apptd Dir 1980, Man.-Dir 1985–87, Exec. Man.-Dir 1987–89, Exec. Vice-Pres. 1989–91, Pres. 1991–2000, Chair. and Rep. Dir 2000–; Chair. Comprint Int.; mem. Bd Japan Productivity Center for Socio-Econ. Devt (JPC-SED) 2004–. *Address:* Toppan Printing Company Ltd, 1 Kanda Izumi-cho, Chiyoda-ku, Tokyo 101-0024, Japan (office). *Telephone:* (3) 3835-5111 (office). *Fax:* (3) 3835-0674 (office). *Website:* www.toppan.co.jp (office).

FUJITA, Hiroyuki, PhD; Japanese scientist and academic; *Professor, Fujita Laboratory;* b. 13 Dec. 1952, Tokyo; s. of Shigeru Fujita and Tokiko Fujita; m. Yumiko Kato 1982; ed Univ. of Tokyo; Lecturer, Inst. of Industrial Science, Univ. of Tokyo 1980–81, Assoc. Prof. 1981–93, Prof. 1993–; Visiting Scientist, Francis Bitter Nat. Magnet Lab., MIT, USA 1983–85; M. Hetényi Award for Experimental Mechanics 1987. *Publications:* contribs to books and numerous scientific papers in professional journals. *Leisure interests:* reading, skiing, tennis. *Address:* Fujita Laboratory, 4-6-1 Komaba, Meguro-ku, Tokyo 153-8505 (office); Institute of Industrial Science, 7-22-1 Roppongi, Minato-ku, Tokyo 106 (office); 1-9-14 Senkawa, Toshima-ku, Tokyo 171, Japan (home). *Telephone:* (3) 3402-6231 ext. 2353 (office); (3) 5452-6249 (office). *E-mail:* fujita@iis.u-tokyo.ac.jp (office). *Website:* www.fujita3.iis.u-tokyo.ac.jp (office).

FUJITA, Yoshio, DrSc; Japanese astronomer; b. 28 Sept. 1908, Fukui City; s. of Teizo Fujita; m. Kazuko Nezu 1941; two s. one d.; ed Tokyo Univ.; Asst Prof. Univ. of Tokyo 1931, Prof. 1951–69, Prof. Emer. 1969–; Visiting Prof. Pa State Univ. 1971; Guest Investigator Dominion Astrophysical Observatory 1960, Mount Wilson and Palomar Observatories 1972, 1974; mem. Japan Acad. 1965–, Pres. 1994–2000; Foreign mem. Royal Soc. of Sciences, Liège 1969–; Imperial Prize, Japan Acad. 1955, Cultural Merit Award, Fukui City 1971, Hon. Citizen, Fukui City 1979, Cultural Merit Award 1996, Fukui Prefecture Award 2002. *Publications:* Interpretation of Spectra and Atmospheric Structure in Cool Stars 1970, Spectrocopic Study of Cool Stars 1977, Collected Papers on the Spectroscopic Behaviour of Cool Stars 1997. *Address:* 6-21-7 Renkoji, Tama-shi, Tokyo 206-0021, Japan. *Telephone:* (42) 374-4186.

FUJITA, Yuzuru; Japanese insurance executive; *President, Asahi Mutual Life Insurance Company* Pres. Asahi Mutual Life Insurance Company. *Address:* Asahi Mutual Life Insurance Company, 1-7-3 Nishi-Shinjuku, Shinjuku-ku, Tokyo 163-8611, Japan (office). *Telephone:* (3) 3342-3111 (office). *Fax:* (3) 3346-9397 (office). *Website:* www.asahi-life.co.jp (office).

FUKAYA, Koichi; Japanese automotive parts executive; *Vice-Chairman, Denso Corporation;* joined Denso Corpn 1966, becoming Gen. Man., Production Eng and Research and Devt Depts, later Pres. Denso Manufacturing Michigan Inc., Man. Dir Thermal Systems Product Group, Dir Denso Corpn March 1995–, Sr Man. Dir, Production Promotion Center 2002–03, Pres. and CEO Denso Corpn 2003–08, Vice-Chair. 2008–. *Address:* Denso Corpn, 1-1 Showa-cho, Kariya, Aichi 448-8661, Japan (office). *Telephone:* (556) 25-5511 (office). *Fax:* (566) 25-4509 (office). *E-mail:* info@globaldenso.com (office). *Website:* www.globaldenso.com (office).

FUKAYA, Takashi; Japanese politician; fmr Minister of Posts and Telecommunications; fmr Parl. Vice-Minister of Labour; mem. House of Reps, fmr Chair. Cttee on Communications; Minister of Home Affairs 1995–96; mem. Horasis Visions Council. *Address:* c/o Horasis: The Global Visions Community, 47, rue du 31-Décembre, 1211 Geneva 6, Switzerland.

FUKSAS, Massimiliano; Italian architect; b. 9 Jan. 1944, Rome; ed Univ. 'La Sapienza', Rome; teaching and research activities, Inst. of History of Architecture, Faculty of Architecture, Univ. 'La Sapienza', Rome; est. architecture practice, Rome 1967, Paris, France 1989, Vienna, Austria 1993; Consultant Architect, Town Planning Advisory Council, Berlin, Germany 1994–97, Planning Council, Salzburg, Austria 1994–97; Adviser, Admin Bd, Institut Français d'Architecture 1997–; writes architecture column of weekly publ. L'Espresso 2000–; Visiting Prof., Staatliche Akad. der Bildenden Kunste, Stuttgart, Germany 1988, Ecole Spéciale d'Architecture, Paris 1990, Columbia Univ., New York, USA 1990–91, Institut für Entwerten und Architektur, Hanover, Germany 1993, Akad. der Bildenden Kunste, Vienna 1995–97; mem. Accademico Nazionale di San Luca 2000; Hon. Fellow, American Inst. of Architects 2002; Hon. mem. RIBA 2006; Commandeur, Ordre des Arts et Lettres (France) 2000; numerous awards including Vitruvio a la Trayectoria, Buenos Aires 1998, Grand Prix d'Architecture Française 1999, Golden Cube Architecture Prize, Naples 2007. *Projects include:* Chamber of Commerce and Industry of Nîmes-Uzès-Le Vigan, Nîmes, France 1991, redevt of areas along bank of Seine, Clichy-la-Garenne, France 1991, renovation of Luth area, Gennevilliers, France 1991, Ecole Nat. Superieure de Mecanique et Aeronautique Futuroscope, Poitiers, France 1991, renovation of Allones town centre, France 1991, urban renovation, Port-de-Bouc, Marseille, France 1991, A tower on 11 towers, Frankfurt, Germany 1991, Ecole Nat. d'Ingenieurs and Institut Scientifique, Brest, France 1991–92, Saint-Exupéry Coll., Noisy-le-Grand, France 1991–93, renovation of old harbour area, Nagasaki, Japan 1993, European Inst. of Interior Design and Architecture, students' housing, Rouen, France 1991–93, Lu Jiazui, Int. Trade Centre, Pudong, China 1991, RIVP devt, Paris 1991–96, Faculty of Law and Econs, Limoges, France 1991–96, restoration and extension of Hotel Dieu, Chartres, France 1991–96, redevt of Domaine Bâti du Petit Arbois, Europole Méditerranéenne Programme, Aix-Les-Milles, France 1992, ZAC Berges-de-Seine, new quarter 'Cables de Lyon', Clichy, France 1992, renovation of Town Hall area, Limoges 1992, Centre Ville Univ., Brest 1992–94, renovation of Cité des Aigues Douces, Marseille 1992–95, residential complex, Clichy-la-Garenne 1992–96, Maison des Arts, exhbn centre, Bordeaux Univ., France 1992–95, masterplan of Tremblay in airport section of Roissy-Charles de Gaulle, Paris 1993–2001, Europark shopping centre, Salzburg 1994–97, Place des Nations, Geneva, Switzerland 1995, Maximilien Perret Coll., Alfortville, Paris 1995–98, Twin Tower, HQ for Wienerberger, Vienna 1995–2001, students and professors' housing, Alfortville, Paris (jtly with D. Mandrelli) 1997–98, Ilot Cantagrel, Paris XIII 1997–2000, harbour and urban rearrangement, Castellammare di Stabia, Italy 1998, Tuscolo Museum, Frascati, Rome 1998–2000, office bldg Hanse-Forum, Axel Springer Platz, Hamburg, Germany 1998–2002, residential and office complex, Alsterfleet, Hamburg 1998–2002, new commercial pavilion, Porta Palazzo, Turin 1998–2004, Peres Peace Centre, Jaffa, Israel 1998–2004, Piazza Mall complex, Eindhoven, Netherlands 1999–2004, Italia Congress and exhbn centre, Roma-Eur, Rome 1999–2003, residential centre, Brachmule, Vienna 2000, houses and commercial area, Rimini 2000–02, HQ Italian Space Agency (ASI), Rome 2000–07, devt of integrated cultural dist at West Kowloon Reclamation, Hong Kong 2001, Queensland Gallery of Modern Art, Brisbane, Australia 2001, devt of Water Front, Hong Kong West 2001, new HQ for Piedmont Region, Turin 2001–05, Emporio Armani Showroom, Hong Kong 2001–02, Europark Insein, Salzburg 2001–05, new HQ for Ferrari SpA, Maranello, Italy 2001–04, new Trade Fair Centre, Pero-Rho Milan 2002–05, inner city devt, Prague, Czech Repub. 2002, Canal+, Louveciennes, Paris 2002, new HQ for Bortolo Nardini Co., Bassano del Grappa, Vicenza, Italy 2002–04, MAB Zeil, Frankfurt, Germany 2002–06, exhbn centre, Rho-Pero, Milan 2002–05, new HQ for Miroglio-Vestebene, Alba, Italy 2003, Concert Hall Zenith, Amiens, France 2003–05, concept store for Palmers, Austria 2003, opera house, Astana, Kazakhstan 2003, Emporio Armani Showroom, Shanghai, China 2004, Sankei Bldg, Osaka, Japan 2004, exhbn complex for new capital of Kazakhstan, Astana 2004–06, tourist port, Marina di Stabia 2004, new HQ for FATER SpA, Pescara, Italy 2004, regeneration of Salford, UK 2005, tourist port at Margonara, Albissola, Savona, Italy 2005, African Inst. of Science and Tech., Abuja, Nigeria 2006, Montecatini Thermal Spa Devt, Italy 2007, Fujeirah Islands Masterplan, UAE 2007, New Silk Road Park, Xi'an, China 2007, Shenzhen Int. Airport, China 2008. *Address:* Massimiliano Fuksas architetto, Piazza del Monte di Pietà 30, 00186 Rome, Italy (office). *Telephone:* 68807871 (office). *Fax:* 68807872 (office). *E-mail:* office@fuksas.it (office). *Website:* www.fuksas.it (office).

FUKUDA, Yasuo; Japanese politician; b. 16 July 1936, Tokyo; s. of the late Takeo Fukuda (fmr Prime Minister of Japan); m. Kiyoko Fukuda; two s. one d.; ed Waseda Univ.; with Maruzen Oil (now Cosmo Oil) petroleum refining and marketing co. 1959–76; Chief Sec. to Prime Minister Takeo Fukuda (father) 1977–78, Pvt. Sec. 1979–89; Dir Kinzai Inst. for Financial Affairs 1978–89; mem. Liberal-Democratic Party (LDP), Pres. 2007–; mem. House of Reps for Gunma 4th Dist 1990–; Parl. Vice-Minister of Foreign Affairs 1995–96; Minister of State, Chief Cabinet Sec., Dir-Gen. Okinawa Devt Agency 2000–01; Chief Cabinet Sec. (Gender Equality) and Minister of State 2001–04 (resgnd); Deputy Sec.-Gen. LDP 1997–98, Chair. Finance Cttee 1998, Dir-Gen. Treasury Bureau 1999–2000, Deputy Chair. Policy Research Council 2000–, Prime Minister 2007–08 (resgnd). *Address:* Liberal-Democratic Party—LDP (Jiyu-Minshuto), 1-11-23, Nagata-cho, Chiyoda-ku, Tokyo 100-8910, Japan (office). *Telephone:* (3) 3581-6211 (office). *Fax:* (3) 3581-1910 (office). *E-mail:* koho@ldp.jimin.or.jp (office). *Website:* www.jimin.jp (office).

FUKUDA, Yoshitaka; Japanese business executive; *President, CEO and Representative Director, Aiful Corporation;* est. sole proprietorship as consumer finance co. 1967; est. Marutaka Inc. 1978, absorbed three related cos and changed name to Aiful Corpn 1982, currently Pres., CEO and Rep. Dir. *Address:* Aiful Corporation, Zip 600-8420, 381-1 Takasago-cho, Gojo-agaru, Karasuma-Dori, Shimogyo-kyu, Kyoto, Japan (office). *Telephone:* (75) 201-2000 (office).

FUKUI, Takeo, BS; Japanese automotive industry executive; *Adviser, Honda Motor Company;* b. 1945, Tokyo; ed Waseda Univ.; joined Honda Motor Co. 1969, engineer 1969–79, Dir 1988–90, Gen. Man. Motorcycle Devt 1991–92, Gen. Man. Motorcycle Operations, Hamamatsu Factory 1992–94, Man. Dir 1996–98, Sr Man. and Rep. Dir 1999–2003, Pres. and CEO 2003–09, Adviser 2009–, Chief Engineer, Honda R&D Co. 1979–82, Man. Dir 1987–88, Sr Man. Dir 1990–91, Pres. 1998–2003, Chief Engineer, Honda Racing Corpn 1982–83, Dir 1983–85, Exec. Vice-Pres. 1985–87, Pres. 1987–88, Exec. Vice-Pres. and Dir Honda of America Manufacturing Inc., OH, USA 1994–96, Pres. and Dir 1996–98. *Address:* Honda Motor Company, 2-1-1 Minami-Aoyama, Minato-ku, Tokyo 107-8556, Japan (office). *Telephone:* (3) 3423-1111 (office). *Fax:* (3) 5412-1515 (office). *E-mail:* info@honda.com (office). *Website:* www.honda.co.jp (office); world.honda.com (office).

FUKUI, Toshihiko; Japanese central banker (retd); b. 7 Sept. 1935; ed Univ. of Tokyo; joined Bank of Japan 1958, Rep. in Paris 1970–77, Dir, Head of Planning Div., Coordination and Planning Dept 1977–80, Gen. Man. Takamatsu Br. 1980–81, Deputy Gen. Man. Osaka Br. 1981–83, First Deputy Dir-Gen. Personnel Dept 1984–85, Dir-Gen. Research and Statistics Dept 1985–86, Dir-Gen. Banking Dept 1986–89, Dir-Gen. Policy Planning Dept 1989, Exec. Dir 1989–94, Deputy Gov. 1994–98, Gov. 2003–08 (retd); Chair. Fujitso Research Inst. 1998–2002; Vice-Chair. Japan Asscn of Corp. Execs (Keizai Doyukai) 2001–03. *Address:* c/o Nippon Ginko (Bank of Japan), 2-1-1, Hongoku-cho, Nihonbashi, Chuo-ku, Tokyo 100-8630, Japan (office).

FUKUKAWA, Shinji; Japanese business executive; b. 8 March 1932, Tokyo; s. of Tokushiro Fukukawa and Maki Fukukawa; m. Yoriko Kawada 1961; two d.; ed Univ. of Tokyo; served at Ministry of Int. Trade and Industry (MITI) 1955–88, Deputy Vice-Minister 1983–84, Dir-Gen. Industrial Policy Bureau 1984–86, Vice-Minister 1986–88; Pvt. Sec. to fmr Prime Minister Ohira 1978–80; Sr Adviser to MITI 1988–90, to Japan Industrial Policy Research Inst. 1988–90, to Global Industrial and Social Progress Research Inst. 1988–, to Nomura Research Inst. 1989–90; Exec. Vice-Pres. Kobe Steel Ltd 1990–94; CEO, Dentsu Inst. for Human Studies 1994–2002, Exec. Adviser, Dentsu Inc. 2002–04; Chair. TEPIA (Machine Industry Memorial Foundation). *Publications:* Japan's Role in the 21st Century: Three Newisms 1990, Industrial Policy 1998, The Thinking of Successful Businessmen in the IT Age 2000, A Warning to Japan 2003. *Leisure interests:* tennis, golf, classical music, reading. *Address:* TEPIA, Machine Industry Memorial Foundation, 2-8-44 Kita-Aoyama, Minato-ku, Tokyo 107-0061 (office); 7-11, Okusawa 8-chome, Setagaya-ku, Tokyo 158-0083, Japan (home). *Telephone:* (3) 5474-6110 (office); (3) 3701-4956 (home). *Fax:* (3) 5474-6114 (office); (3) 3701-4956 (home). *E-mail:* fukukawa@tepia.jp (office). *Website:* www.tepia.jp (office).

FUKUYAMA, Francis, PhD; American writer and academic; *Bernard L. Schwartz Professor of International Political Economy, Paul H. Nitze School of Advanced International Studies, Johns Hopkins University;* b. New York; ed Cornell and Harvard Univs; fmrly a sr social scientist, RAND Corpn, Washington, DC and Deputy Dir State Dept's Policy Planning Staff; Hirst Prof. of Public Policy, George Mason Univ., Fairfax, Va; Dean of Faculty, Paul H. Nitze School of Advanced Int. Studies, Johns Hopkins Univ. 2002–04, now Bernard L. Schwartz Prof. of Int. Political Economy; mem. Pres.'s Council on Bioethics; mem. advisory Bd National Endowment for Democracy, The National Interest, Journal of Democracy, The New America Foundation; fmr mem. US delegation Egyptian-Israeli talks on Palestinian autonomy. *Publications:* The End of History and the Last Man 1992, Trust: The Social Virtues And the Creation of Prosperity 1996, The Great Disruption: Human Nature and the Reconstitution of the Social Order 1999, Our Posthuman Future 2002, State-Building: Governance and World Order in the 21st Century 2004, After the Neocons 2006, America at the Crossroads: Democracy, Power, and the Neoconservative Legacy 2006. *Address:* Paul H. Nitze School of Advanced International Studies, The Rome Building, Room 507, 1619 Massachusetts Avenue, NW, Washington, DC 20036, USA (office). *Telephone:* (202) 663-5765 (office). *Fax:* (202) 663-5769 (office). *E-mail:* fukuyama@jhu.edu (office). *Website:* www.francisfukuyama.com (office).

FULCI, Francesco Paolo, LLD, MCL; Italian diplomatist; b. 19 March 1931, Messina; s. of Sebastiano Fulci and Enza Sciascia; m. Claris Glathar 1965; three c.; ed Messina Univ., Columbia Univ., New York, Coll. of Europe, Bruges and Acad. Int. Law, The Hague; entered Italian Foreign Service 1956; First Vice-Consul of Italy, New York 1958–61; Second Sec. Italian Embassy, Moscow 1961–63; Foreign Ministry, Rome 1963–68; Counsellor Italian Embassy, Paris 1968–74, Minister Italian Embassy, Tokyo 1974–76; Chief of Cabinet Pres. of Senate, Rome 1976–80; Amb. to Canada 1980–85; Amb. and Perm. Rep. to NATO, Brussels 1985–91; Sec.-Gen. Exec. Comm. of Information and Security Services, Rome 1991–93; Amb. and Perm. Rep. to UN, New York 1993–99; Vice-Pres. Ferrero International, Rome 2000–; First Vice-Pres. ECOSOC 1998–99, Pres. 1999–2000; Ed. La Stampa, Turin 2000; Cross of Merit (FRG); Officier, Légion d'honneur (France); Commdr Imperial Order of the Sun (Japan), Great Cross, Order of Merit (Italy), Kt Order of Malta; Hon. LLD (Windsor Univ., Ont.). *Leisure interest:* swimming. *Address:* c/o La Stampa, Via Marenco 32, 10126 Turin, Italy (office). *Telephone:* (011) 656811 (office). *Fax:* (011) 655306 (office). *E-mail:* lettere@lastampa.it (office). *Website:* www.lastampa.it (office).

FULD, Richard (Dick) S., Jr, BA, MBA; American investment banking executive; b. 1946; ed Univ. of Colorado, New York Univ. Stern School of Business; joined Lehman Brothers 1969, various man. positions, including Dir Lehman Brothers Inc. 1984–2008, Vice-Chair. Shearson Lehman Brothers Inc. 1984–90, Pres. and Co-CEO 1990–93, Dir Lehman Brothers Holdings Inc. 1990–2008 (after Chapter 11 filing by Lehman Brothers and acquisition by Barclays Capital); Pres. and COO 1993–94, CEO 1993–2008, Chair. 1994–2008, also Chair. Lehman Brothers Inc. 1994–2008; fmr mem. The Business Council, Exec. Cttee NY City Partnership, Univ. of Colorado Business Advisory Council; Trustee, Middlebury Coll., NewYork-Presbyterian Hosp. *Address:* c/o Lehman Brothers Holdings Inc., 745 Seventh Avenue, New York, NY 10019, USA (office).

FULFORD, Sir Adrian; British judge; *Judge, International Criminal Court;* b. 8 Jan. 1948; called to the Bar, Middle Temple, London 1978; apptd QC 1994; Recorder (Judge in Crown Court) 1996–; Judge, Int. Criminal Court (ICC) 2003–; Lecturer in Advocacy, Middle Temple 1994–; Lecturer to the Bar and Judiciary 1999–2001; mem. Cttee of Criminal Bar Asscn 1997–99, 2001–; Chair. Disciplinary Procedures for Bar Council 1997–; Housing Adviser, Shelter Housing Aid Centre 1975–77; Legal Adviser N Lambeth Law Centre 1979–80; fmr Contrib. Ed. Archbold Criminal Pleading, Practice and Evidence, Atkins Court Forms. *Publications:* A Criminal Practitioners Guide to Judicial Review and Case Stated (co-author) 1999, United Kingdom Human Rights Reports (jt ed.) 2000–, Judicial Review: A Practical Guide (co-author) 2004; articles in professional journals and papers for Criminal Bar Asscn. *Address:* International Criminal Court, Maanweg 174, 2516 AB The Hague, The Netherlands. *Telephone:* (70) 5158515. *Fax:* (70) 5158555. *E-mail:* pio@icc-cpi.int. *Website:* www.icc-cpi.int.

FULLANI, Ardian; Albanian central banker; *Governor, Bank of Albania;* ed Univ. of Tirana; with State Bank of Albania 1985–87, Deputy Dir Foreign Dept 1987–90; Dir Foreign Dept, Albanian Commercial Bank 1990–92; Deputy Dir Gov. Bank of Albania 1992–93, Dir Foreign Dept 1993–96, Gov. 2004–; Deputy Gen. Man. and Head, Financial Dept, Italian-Albanian Bank 1997–2000, Gen. Man. 2000–04; currently Pres. Albanian Asscn of Banks, Chair. Inst. of Banking Studies and Assistance, Commr Albanian Securities Comm. *Address:* Office of the Governor, Bank of Albania, Sheshi Skënderbej 1, Tirana, Albania (office). *Telephone:* (4) 222152 (office). *Fax:* (4) 223558 (office). *E-mail:* public@bankofalbania.org (office). *Website:* www.bankofalbania.org (office).

FULLER, H. Larry, BS; American business executive; ed Cornell Univ.; Dir Amoco Corpn 1981–2000, Chair. and CEO 1991–2000, co-Chair. BP Amoco 2000 (retd); mem. Bd of Dirs Cabot Microelectronics Corpn, Motorola Inc., Abbott Labs, JP Morgan Chase & Co.; fmr mem. Bd Catalyst, American Petroleum Inst., Rehabilitation Inst. of Chicago; Trustee Orchestral Asscn. *Address:* c/o Board of Directors, Cabot Microelectronics Corporation, 870 North Commons Drive, Aurora, IL 60504, USA (office).

FULLER, Kathryn S., BA, MS, JD; American international organization executive, environmentalist and attorney; *Chairman, Board of Directors, Ford Foundation;* b. 8 July 1946, New York, NY; m. Stephen Paul Doyle 1977; two s. one d.; ed Brown Univ., Univs of Maryland and Texas; law clerk, New York, Houston and Austin, Tex. 1974–76, to Chief Justice John V. Singleton, Jr, US Dist Court, Southern Dist of Tex. 1976–77; called to Bar, DC and Tex.; attorney and adviser, Office of Legal Counsel, Dept of Justice, Washington, DC 1977–79, attorney, Wildlife and Marine Resources Section 1979–80, Chief Wildlife and Marine Resources Section 1981–82; Exec. Vice-Pres. and Dir TRAFFIC USA 1982–89; Pres. and CEO World Wildlife Fund US 1989–2005, now mem. Advisory Council; Public Policy Scholar, Woodrow Wilson Int. Center for Scholars 2005–06; mem. Council on Foreign Relations, Int. Council of Environmental Law, Overseas Devt Council; Chair. Ford Foundation 2004–; mem. Bd of Dirs Alcoa Inc. (Compensation and Benefits Cttee, Governance and Nominating Cttee, Public Issues Cttee) 2002–, Resources for the Future, Nicholas School of the Environment and Earth Sciences at Duke Univ.; Trustee, Brown Univ. Corpn, Fondo Mexicano para la Conservacion de la Naturaleza, Resources for the Future; Hon. DSc (Wheaton Coll.) 1990; Hon. LLD (Knox Coll.) 1992; Hon. DHumLitt (Brown Univ.) 1992; William Rogers Outstanding Grad. Award, Brown Univ. 1990, UNEP Global 500 Award 1990. *Publications include:* numerous articles in journals. *Address:* Ford Foundation, 320 East 43rd Street, New York, NY 10017, USA (office). *Telephone:* (212) 573-5000 (office). *Fax:* (212) 351-3677 (office). *E-mail:* office-of-communications@fordfound.org (office). *Website:* www.fordfound.org (office).

FULLER, Lawrence Robert, BJ; American newspaper publisher; b. 9 Sept. 1941, Toledo; s. of Kenneth Fuller and Marjory Rairdon; m. Suzanne Hovik 1967; one s. one d.; ed Univ. of Missouri; reporter, Globe Gazette, Mason City, Ia 1963–67; reporter, later City Ed. Minneapolis Star 1967–75; Exec. Ed. Messenger-Inquirer, Owensborough, Ky 1975–77; Exec. Ed. Argus Leader, Sioux Falls, South Dakota 1977–78, Pres., Publr 1974–84, 1986–99; Pres. Gannett News Media, Washington, DC 1984–85; Dir Corp. Communications, Gannett Co. Inc. Washington 1985–86; Vice-Pres. Gannett/West Regional Newspaper Group 1986–97, The Honolulu Advertisers 1986–97; mem. American Newspaper Publishers' Asscn, American Soc. of Newspaper Eds etc. *Address:* 605 Kapiolani Boulevard, Honolulu, HI 96813, USA.

FULLER, Simon; British music promoter, business executive and artist manager; m. Natalie Swanston 2008; Founder and Dir 19 Group 1985–2005 (comprising 19 Brands, 19 Entertainment, 19 International Sports Management, 19 Management, 19 Merchandising, 19 Productions, 19 Recordings, 19 Songs, 19 Touring, 19 TV, Brilliant 19), sold to CFX 2005 (mem. Bd Dirs 2005–); current or fmr man. of numerous artists, including Annie Lennox, Emma Bunton, Will Young, Gareth Gates, Kelly Clarkson, Paul Hardcastle

(1985), Madonna, Cathy Dennis, Spice Girls (–1997), 21st Century Girls and S Club 7 (later S Club, including TV series and S Club Juniors); dir numerous other cos. *Television:* creator of Popstars (ITV 1), Pop Idol (ITV 1), American Idol – The Search for a Superstar (Fox TV), Popstars – The Rivals (ITV 1). *Address:* 19 Management, Unit 32, Ransomes Dock, 35–37 Parkgate Road, London, SW11 4NP, England (office). *Website:* www.19.co.uk (office).

FULLERTON, R. Donald, BA; Canadian banker; b. 7 June 1931, Vancouver, BC; s. of the late C. G. Fullerton and Muriel E. Fullerton; m.; ed Univ. of Toronto; joined Canadian Bank of Commerce (now CIBC), Vancouver 1953, Agent, New York 1964, Exec. Vice-Pres. 1973, Dir 1974–2004, Pres. and CEO 1976–84, Chair. and CEO 1984–92, Chair. Exec. Cttee 1992–99; Dir Husky Energy Inc., 3 Italia SpA; mem. and fmr mem. numerous bds of Canadian and int. cos and medical, cultural and educational insts. *Address:* c/o CIBC, Head Office, Commerce Court N, Toronto, ON M5L 1A2, Canada.

FULTON, Daniel S., BA, MBA; American business executive; *President and CEO, Weyerhaeuser Company;* b. 1948; ed Miami Univ., Univ. of Washington, Stanford Univ.; fmr Officer, USN Supply Corps; mem. Investment Evaluation Dept, Weyerhaeuser Co. 1976–78, Planning Man. Weyerhaeuser Real Estate Co. 1978–79, Investment Man. Weyerhaeuser Venture Co. 1978–87, Chief Investment Officer Weyerhaeuser Realty Investors Inc. 1994–95, COO 1996–97, Pres. and CEO 1998–2000, Weyerhaeuser Real Estate Co. 2001–08, Pres. Weyerhaeuser Co. Jan. 2008–, mem. Bd Dirs and CEO April 2008–; mem. Bd of Dirs United Way of King Co.; mem. Advisory Bd Univ. of Washington Business School, Policy Advisory Bd Jt Center of Housing with Harvard Univ.; mem. Bd of Govs. Lambda Alpha Int. Land Econs Soc., Nat. Asscn of Homebuilders. *Address:* Weyerhaeuser Company, 33663 Weyerhaeuser Way South, Federal Way, WA 98063-9777, USA (office). *Telephone:* (253) 924-2345 (office). *Fax:* (253) 924-2685 (office). *E-mail:* info@weyerhaeuser.com (office). *Website:* www.weyerhaeuser.com (office).

FUMAROLI, Marc, DèsL; French professor of rhetoric; *Honorary Chairman, Rhetoric and European Society of the 16th and 17th Centuries, Collège de France;* b. 10 June 1932, Marseille; ed Lycée Thiers Marseille, Univ. Aix-en-Provence, Univ. Sorbonne; Prof. Sorbonne, Paris 1976; Titular Prof. Chair. of Rhetoric and European Soc. of 16th and 17th Centuries, Collège de France 1986–2002, now Hon. Chair.; Prof. Univ. of Chicago 1996–; Chair. Instituit européen d'histoire de la Republique de Lettres, Socieété d'Histoire litterature de la France; Dir XVIIe siècle (journal) 1981–88; mem. Advisory Council, Bibliothèque Nationale 1988–92; fmr Pres. Soc. Int. d'Histoire de la Rhétorique; Pres. Soc. of Friends of the Louvre 1996–; mem. Acad. Française 1995–, High Cttee of Nat. Celebrations 1998–; Corresp. mem. British Acad., mem. US Acad. of Sciences, Letters and Arts, Accad. dei Lincei; other appointments; Officier, Légion d'honneur, Commdr, Ordre des Palmes académiques, Officier Ordre nat. du Mérite, Cmmdr des Arts et des Lettres; Dr hc (Naples 1996, Bologna 1999, Madrid 2004); numerous academic prizes. *Publications include:* L'Age de l'éloquence 1980, Héros et Orateurs 1990, L'Etat Culturel: Une Religion Moderne 1991, La Diplomatie de l'esprit 1994, L'école du silence 1994, Trois institutions littéraires 1994, la Période 1600–1630 1994, Fables de Jean de la Fontaine (ed., Vol. I 1985, Vol. II 1995), Le Poète et le roi, Jean de La Fontaine et son siècle 1997, Poussin: Sainte Françoise Romaine 2001, Quand l'Europe parlait français 2001, Chateaubriand: Poésie et Terreur 2003, Exercises de lecture: De Rabelais à Valery 2006; numerous articles in professional journals; numerous pamphlets, essays and articles. *Leisure interest:* photography. *Address:* Collège de France, 11 place Marcelin Berthelot, 75231 Paris cedex 05 (office); 11 rue de l'Université, 75007 Paris, France (home). *Telephone:* 1-44-27-10-17 (office). *Fax:* 1-44-27-17-91 (office). *Website:* www.college-de-france.fr (office).

FUNADA, Hajime; Japanese politician; b. 22 Nov. 1953, Utsunomiya City, Tochigi Pref.; s. of Yuzuru Funada and Masako Funada; m. Rumi Funada 1978; one s. two d.; ed Keio Univ.; mem. House of Reps from Tochigi 1979–; Head, Youth Section of Nat. Organizing Cttee, LDP 1985–86; State Sec. for Man. and Co-ordination Agency 1986–87, for Ministry of Educ. 1987–88; Dir Educ. Div. of Policy Research Council, LDP 1988–89; Dir Foreign Affairs Div. 1990–92; Chair. Sub-Cttee of Counselling Japan Overseas Co-operation Volunteers 1989–90; Minister of State for Econ. Planning 1992–93; Co-Founder of Japan Renewal Party (Shinseito) 1993, Deputy Sec. Gen. for Organizational Affairs 1993–94, Deputy Sec. Gen. for Political Affairs 1994; Vice-Chair. Diet Man. Cttee, 'Reform' In-House Grouping (Kaikaku) 1994; Co-Founder New Frontier Party (Shinshinto) 1994, Vice-Chair. Org. Cttee 1994–95, Deputy Sec. Gen. 1995, Assoc. Chair. Gen. Council 1995–96, resgnd from Party 1996; Head of '21st Century' In-House Grouping (21seiki) 1996; rejoined Liberal Democratic Party 1997, Chair. Sub-Cttee on Asia and the Pacific, mem. Policy Deliberation Comm., mem. Gen. Council 1997–; mem. Ruling Parties Consultative Cttee on Guidelines for Japan–US Defence Co-operation 1997–; Dir Cttee on Health and Welfare, House of Reps 1998–. *Leisure interests:* astronomy, driving. *Address:* Shugiin Daini Giinkaikan, Room 412, 2-1-2 Nagata-cho, Chiyoda-ku, Tokyo 100, Japan. *Telephone:* (3) 3508-7412. *Fax:* (3) 3500-5612.

FUNAI, Tetsuro; Japanese electronics industry executive; *President and CEO, Funai Electric Company Limited;* b. 24 Jan. 1927, Kobe, Hyogo; ed Murano Technical High School; est. Funai Mishin Shokai 1951 (co. name changed to Funai Keiki Kogyo 1959); est. Funai Electric Co. Ltd 1961, Pres. and CEO 1961–. *Address:* Funai Electric Company Limited, 7-7-1 Nakagaito, Daito City, Osaka 574-0013, Japan (office). *Telephone:* (72) 870-4303 (office). *Fax:* (72) 871-1112 (office). *Website:* www.funai.jp (office).

FUNAR, Gheorghe, PhD; Romanian politician; *Secretary-General, Greater Romanian Party;* b. 29 Sept. 1949; m.; one s.; ed Faculty of Econ. Science, Univ. of Cluj-Napoca; began career as agronomist, specialising in collective arm system; joined Party of Romanian Nat. Unity (PRNU) 1990, Leader 1992–97; Mayor of Cluj-Napoca 1992–2004; cand. in presidential elections 1992; Sec.-Gen. Greater Romanian Party (PRM–Partidul România Mare) 2000–. *Address:* Greater Romanian Party (PRM–Partidul România Mare), 70101 Bucharest, Str. G. Clemenceau 8–10, Romania (office). *Telephone:* (21) 6130967 (office). *Fax:* (21) 3126182 (office). *E-mail:* prm@prm.org.ro (office). *Website:* www.prm.org.ro (office).

FUNCKE, Liselotte; German politician; b. 20 July 1918, Hagen; d. of Oscar Funcke and Bertha Funcke (née Osthaus); ed commercial studies in Berlin; fmrly in industry and commerce, Hagen and Wuppertal; mem. Diet of North Rhine-Westphalia 1950–61; mem. Bundestag 1961–79, Vice-Pres. Bundestag 1969–79; Chair. Bundestag Finance Cttee 1972–79; mem. Presidium, FDP 1968–82, Deputy Chair. FDP 1977–82; Minister of Economy and Transport, North Rhine-Westphalia 1979–80; govt rep. responsible for integration of overseas workers and their families 1981–91; Ehrenbürgerin von Hagen; Bundesverdienstkreuz 1973 and other medals; Dr hc. *Publications:* Hagener Strassen erzählen Geschichte, Tuche, Sensen, Federn, Stahl: Hagener Industriebetriebe. *Address:* Ruhrstr. 15, 58097 Hagen, Germany (home). *Telephone:* (2331) 182034.

FUNDANGA, Caleb M., BA, MA, PhD; Zambian economist, international organization official and central banker; *Governor and Chairman, Bank of Zambia;* ed Univ. of Zambia, Univ. of Manchester, UK, Konstanz Univ., Germany; Lecturer in Econs, Univ. of Zambia 1985–87; served as Perm. Sec. wth Zambian Ministry of Econs and Finance; Exec. Dir ADB, Abidjan, Côte d'Ivoire, representing Lesotho, Malawi, Mauritius, South Africa, Swaziland and Zambia 1995–98, Sr Adviser to Pres. of ADB 1998–2002; Gov. and Chair. Bank of Zambia 2002–; fmr mem. Bd of Dirs Zambia Revenue Authority, Afreximbank; fmr Alt. Gov. IMF; fmr Chair. COMESA Cttee of Cen. Bank Govs; mem. Advisory Comm. African Econ. Research Consortium 2002, Chair. Programme Cttee 2005–; fmr Pres. World Univ. Service Int.; Central Banker of the Year (Global and Africa), The Banker 2007. *Address:* Bank of Zambia, Bank Square, Cairo Rd, POB 30080, 10101 Lusaka, Zambia (office). *Telephone:* (1) 228888 (office). *Fax:* (1) 221722 (office). *Website:* www.boz.zm (office).

FUNG, Victor K., BS, MS, CBE; Chinese business executive; *Group Chairman, Li & Fung Group;* b. Hong Kong; m.; three c.; ed Massachusetts Inst. of Tech., Harvard Univ., USA; joined Li & Fung 1973, Man. Dir 1981–89, Chair. 1989, currently Group Chair. Li & Fung Group; Chair. Prudential Asia Investments Ltd; Chair. Hong Kong Trade Devt Council 1991–2000, Hong Kong Airport Authority 1999–2008, Greater Pearl River Delta Business Council 2004–, Hong Kong Univ. Council, Hong Kong-Japan Business Co-operation Cttee; Co-Chair. Evian Group; Vice-Chair. Int. Chamber of Commerce; mem. Hong Kong Judicial Officers Recommendation Cttee, Asian Business Advisory Council, CPPCC, Exec. Cttee of Hong Kong Govt Comm. on Strategic Devt; Hong Kong Rep. on APEC Business Advisory Council 1996–2003; Prof., Harvard Business School 1972–76; Gold Bauhinia Star 2003. *Address:* Li & Fung Group, Li Fung Tower, 888 Cheung Sha Wan Road, Kowloon, Hong Kong Special Administrative Region, People's Republic of China (office). *Telephone:* 23002300 (office). *Fax:* 23002000 (office). *Website:* www.lifunggroup.com (office).

FUNKE, Cornelia Caroline; German children's writer; b. 1958, Dorsten, Westphalia; m. Rolf Funke; one s. one d.; ed Hamburg Univ., Hamburg State Coll. of Design; worked as designer of board games, illustrator of children's books; began writing/illustrating full-time aged 28; also works for ZDF state TV channel. *Publications:* Monstergeschichten 1993, Die Wilden Hühner 1993, Rittergeschichten 1994, Zwei wilde kleine Hexen 1994, Kein Keks für Kobolde 1994, Greta und Eule, Hundesitter 1995, Der Mondscheindrache 1996, Die Gespensterjäger auf eisiger Spur 1996, Die Wilden Hühner auf Klassenfahrt 1996, Hände weg von Mississippi 1997, Drachenreiter (trans. as Dragon Rider) 1997, Prinzessin Isabella (trans. as The Princess Knight) 1997, Tiergeschichten 1997, Das verzauberte Klassenzimmer 1997, Die Wilden Hühner Fuchsalarm 1998, Dachbodengeschichten 1998, Potilla und der Mützendieb 1998, Dicke Freundinnen 1998, Igraine Ohnefurcht (trans. as Igraine the Brave) 1998, Strandgeschichten 1999, Das Piratenschwein (trans. as Pirate Girl) 1999, Herr der Diebe (trans. as The Thief Lord) (Swiss Youth Literature Award, Zurich Children's Book Award, Venice House of Literature Book Award, Mildred L. Batchelder Award for the best trans. children's book of the year) 2000, Lilli und Flosse 2000, Mick und Mo im Wilden Westen (trans. as Mick and Mo in the Wild West) 2000, Die Wilden Hühner und das Glück der Erde 2000, Kleiner Werwolf 2001, Als der Weihnachtsmann vom Himmel fiel 2001, Dicke Freundinnen und der Pferdedieb 2001, Die Gespensterjäger im Feuerspuk 2001, Die Gespensterjäger in der Gruselburg 2001, Die Gespensterjäger in grosser Gefahr 2001, Der geheimnisvolle Ritter Namenlos 2001, Die Wilden Hühner Bandenbuch 2001, Emma und der blaue Dschinn 2002, Die schönsten Erstlesegeschichten 2002, Die Glücksfee 2003, Hinter verzauberten Fenstern 2003, Käpten Knitterbart 2003, Tintenherz (trans. as Inkheart) 2003, Kribbel Krabbel Käferwetter 2003, Der wildeste Bruder der Welt 2003, Der verlorene Wackelzahn 2003, Die Wilden Hühner und die Liebe 2003, Die Wilden Hühner Tagebuch 2004, Tintenblut (trans. as Inkspell) 2005, When Santa Fell to Earth 2006, Tintentod (trans. as Inkdeath) 2008. *Address:* c/o Oliver Latsch Literary Agency & Translations, Dudelsackstraße 36, 67227 Frankenthal, Rheinland-Pfalz, Germany (office). *Telephone:* (6233) 549419 (office). *Fax:* (6233) 62518 (office). *E-mail:* info@oliverlatsch.com (office). *Website:* www.oliverlatsch.com (office); www.cornelia-funke.com.

FUNKE, Karl-Heinz; German politician; b. 29 April 1946, Dangast; m. Petra Timm 1982; three c.; ed Hamburg Univ.; apprenticeship in admin 1960–63; joined SPD 1966; mil. service 1966–68; Dist Councillor, Friesland 1972–, also

City Councillor, Varel; worked at Varel vocational school and on family farm 1974, took over family farm 1983; mem. Lower Saxony Landtag 1978–; Mayor of Varel 1981–96; Minister of Food, Agric. and Forestry Lower Saxony 1990–98; Fed. Minister of Food, Agric. and Forestry 1998–2001. *Leisure interests:* literature, history, hunting. *Address:* c/o Ministry of Food, Agriculture and Forestry, Rochusstrasse 1, 53123 Bonn (office); Calenberger Strasse 2, 30169 Hannover, Germany.

FURCHGOTT, Robert Francis, PhD; American professor of pharmacology; *Distinguished Professor Emeritus, SUNY Downstate Medical Center;* b. 4 June 1916, Charleston, SC; m. 1941; three c.; ed Univ. of N Carolina, Northwestern Univ.; Research Fellow in Medicine, Medical Coll., Cornell Univ. 1940–43, Research Assoc. 1943–47, Instructor in Physiology 1943–48, Asst Prof. of Medical Biochemistry 1947–49; Asst Prof., later Assoc. Prof. of Pharmacology, Medical School, Wash. Univ. 1949–56; Chair. of Dept, State Univ. of New York (SUNY) Health Sciences Center, Brooklyn (also known as SUNY Downstate Medical Center) 1956–83; Prof. of Health Sciences Center, Brooklyn State Univ. (now SUNY) 1956–88, Univ. Distinguished Prof. 1988–, Prof. Emer. of Pharmacology 1990–; Visiting Prof. Univ. of Geneva 1962–63, Univ of Calif., San Diego 1971–72, Medical Univ. of SC 1980, Univ. of Calif. 1980; Adjunct Prof. of Pharmacology, School of Medicine, Univ. of Miami 1989–2001; Distinguished Visiting Prof. Medical Univ. of SC 2001–; mem. AAAS, NAS, ACS, American Soc. Biochem., American Soc. of Pharmacology and Experimental Therapeutics (ASPET) (Pres. 1971–72); Hon. DM (Madrid) 1984, (Lund) 1984; Hon. DSc (NC) 1989, (Ghent) 1995; Goodman and Gilman Award 1984, Research Achievement Award, American Heart Asscn 1990, Bristol-Myers Squibb Award for achievement in cardiovascular research 1991, Gairdner Fund Int. Award 1991, Medal of NY Acad. of Medicine 1992, Roussel Uclaf Prize for research in cell communication and signalling 1994, Wellcome Gold Medal, British Pharmacology Soc. 1995, ASPET Award for Experimental Therapeutics 1996, jt winner Nobel Prize in Physiology or Medicine 1998. *Address:* State University of New York Health Sciences Center, Department of Pharmacology, 450 Clarkson Avenue, Brooklyn, NY 11203-2056, USA. *Website:* www.downstate.edu/Nobel%20Prize/dr._furchgott.htm (office).

FURCHTGOTT-ROTH, Harold W., PhD; American economist and fmr government official; *President, Furchtgott-Roth Economic Enterprises;* b. 13 Dec. 1956, Knoxville, Tenn.; s. of Ernest Furchtgott and Mary A. Wilkes Furchtgott; m. Diana E. Roth; five s. one d.; ed Massachusetts Inst. of Tech., Stanford Univ.; Research Analyst, Center for Naval Analyses, Alexandria, Va 1984–88; Sr Economist, Economists Inc., Washington, DC 1988–95; Chief Economist, US House Cttee on Commerce 1995–97; Commr Fed. Communications Comm. 1997–2001; Visiting Fellow, American Enterprise Inst. 2001–03; Founder and Pres. Furchtgott-Roth Economic Enterprises 2003–. *Publications:* International Trade in Computer Software (co-author) 1993, Economics of a Disaster: The Exxon Valdez Oil Spill (co-author) 1995, Cable TV: Regulations or Competition (co-author) 1996, A Tough Act to Follow 2003, Telecommunications Act of 1996 2006. *Address:* Furchtgott-Roth Economic Enterprises, 1200 New Hampshire Avenue, NW, Suite 800, Washington, DC 20036 (office); 2705 Daniel Road, Chevy Chase, MD 20815, USA (home). *Telephone:* (202) 776-2032 (office); (301) 229-3593 (home). *E-mail:* hfr@furchtgott-roth.com (office). *Website:* www.furchtgott-roth.com (office).

FURLAN, Luiz Fernando, BEng; Brazilian business executive and government official; b. 1945; m. Ana Maria Gonçalves Furlan 1973; one s. one d.; ed São Paulo Univ., INSEAD, France, Georgetown Univ., USA; joined Sadia SA 1976, mem. Bd 1978–2002, Exec. Vice-Pres. and Dir, Investor Relations 1978–83, Chair. 1993–2002; Minister of Devt, Industry and Trade 2002–07; Second Vice-Pres. and Dir of Foreign Trade, Industries Fed. of São Paulo State (FIESP/CIESP); Vice-Pres. Brazilian Foreign Trade Asscn; Pres. Entrepreneurial Leaders Forum 2000–02; Pres., Brazilian Asscn of Open Cos (ABRASCA) 1991–94, Brazilian Asscn of Producers and Exporters of Chicken (ABEF) 1997–2001; fmr Pres. Mercosul European Business Forum (MEBF); fmr mem. Bd Pan American Beverages Inc. (PANAMCO) (USA), Telefónica SA (Spain); mem. Advisory Bd Brasmotor SA, ABN-Amro Bank Brazil; mem. Global Corporate Governance Forum; mem. Nat. Council of Human Rights, Int. Council INSEAD, France; fmr mem. Brazil–USA Business Devt Council. *Address:* c/o Ministry of Development, Industry and Trade, Esplanada dos Ministérios, Bloco J, 7 andar, Sala 700, 70053-900 Brasília, DF, Brazil (office).

FURNO, HE Cardinal Carlo, PhD; Italian ecclesiastic; b. 2 Dec. 1921, Bairo Canavese; Sec. to Nunciature to Colombia 1953–57, to Ecuador 1957–60; Sec. Apostolic Del. to Jerusalem 1960–62; Sec. of State 1962–73; Apostolic Nuncio to Peru 1973–78, to Lebanon 1978–82, to Brazil 1982–92, to Italy 1992–94; Cardinal-Deacon of S. Cuore di Cristo Re (elevated to Cardinal) 1994, Cardinal-Priest of S. Cuore di Cristo Re 2005; mem. Pontifical Comm. for Vatican City State; Grand Master Equestrian Order of the Holy Sepulchre of Jerusalem 1995–2007 (retd); Pres. Admin. Council, Lumsa Univ.; Archpriest St Mary Major Basilica 1997. *Address:* Sacro Cuore di Cristo Re, Viale Mazzini 32, 00195 Rome, Italy. *Telephone:* (06) 3223383. *E-mail:* SacroCuorediCristoRe@VicariatusUrbis.org.

FURSE, Dame Clara Hedwig Frances, DBE, BSc, CIMgt; British/Canadian business executive; *Chief Executive, London Stock Exchange;* b. 16 Sept. 1957; born to Dutch parents in Canada; m. Richard Furse 1981; two s. one d.; ed schools in Colombia, Denmark and St James's School, West Malvern, London School of Econs; began career as broker, Heinold Commodities Ltd 1979; commodity broker, Philips & Drew 1983, Dir 1988, Exec. Dir 1992, Man. Dir UBS Philips & Drew (formed from merger with Union Bank of Switzerland; named changed to UBS following merger with Swiss Bank 1998) 1995–98, Global Head of Futures 1996–98; Deputy Chair. London Int. Financial Futures and Options Exchange (LIFFE) 1992–99 (mem. Bd 1992–99, Chair. Strategy Working Group 1994–95, Membership and Rules Cttee 1995–97, Finance Cttee 1998–99); Group Chief Exec. Crédit Lyonnais Rouse 1998–2000; Chief Exec. London Stock Exchange PLC 2001–; mem. Bd Euroclear PLC, Fortis 2006–; mem. CBI Pres.'s Cttee, Financial Services Practitioner Forum 2001–, Advisory Council Prince's Trust; Trustee RICS Foundation 2002–05; ranked by Fortune magazine amongst 50 Most Powerful Women in Business outside the US (34th) 2003, (17th) 2004, (19th) 2005, (26th) 2006, (17th) 2007, ranked sixth in survey of Europe's most successful female execs 2003, ranked by Forbes magazine amongst 100 Most Powerful Women (97th) 2004, (50th) 2006, (54th) 2007, (85th) 2008, ranked by the Financial Times amongst Top 25 Businesswomen in Europe (tenth) 2005, (sixth) 2006, (fifth) 2007. *Address:* London Stock Exchange, 10 Paternoster Square, London, EC4M 7LS, England (office). *Telephone:* (20) 7797-1000 (office). *Fax:* (20) 7334-8916 (office). *Website:* www.londonstockexchange.com (office).

FURSENKO, Andrei Aleksandrovich, DrPhys; Russian scientist and politician; *Minister of Education and Science;* b. 17 July 1949, Leningrad; ed Leningrad State Univ.; Head of Lab., Deputy Dir for Scientific Research, Chief Scientific Researcher Moscow Ioffe Physico-Tech. Inst. 1971–91; Vice-Pres. Centre of Prospective Techs and Elaborations, St Petersburg 1991–93; Gen. Dir Regional Fund for Scientific Tech. Devt 1994–2001; Deputy Minister of Science, Industry and Technology 2001, First Deputy Minister 2002, Acting Minister 2003; Minister of Educ. and Science 2004–. *Address:* Ministry of Education, ul. Lyusinovskaya 51, 113833 Moscow, Russia (office). *Telephone:* (495) 237-61-55 (office). *Fax:* (495) 237-83-81 (office). *E-mail:* mail@ministry.ru (office). *Website:* www.ed.gov.ru (office).

FURSTENBERG, Hillel (Harry), BA, MSc, PhD; Israeli mathematician and academic; *Professor of Mathematics, Hebrew University;* b. 1935, Berlin; m. Rochelle Furstenberg; three s. two d.; ed Yeshiva and Princeton univs, USA; emigrated to USA as a child; began academic career at Univ. of Minn.; moved to Israel 1965; Prof. of Math., Hebrew Univ. 1965–; mem. Israel Acad. of Sciences and Humanities, NAS; Rothschild Prize 1978, Technion Harvey Prize 1993, Israel Prize 1993, Wolf Foundation Prize in Math. 2007. *Publications include:* Stationary Processes and Prediction Theory, Recurrence in Ergodic Theory and Combinatorial Number Theory. *Address:* Einstein Institute of Mathematics, Edmond J. Safra Campus, Givat Ram, The Hebrew University of Jerusalem, Jerusalem 91904 (office); 7 Alfasi Street, Jerusalem 92302, Israel (home). *Telephone:* 2-6584142 (office); 2-5617641 (home). *Fax:* 2-5630702 (office). *E-mail:* harry@math.huji.ac.il (office). *Website:* www.ma.huji.ac.il (office).

FURTH, Warren Wolfgang, AB, JD; American fmr international official, consultant and lawyer; b. 1 Aug. 1928, Vienna, Austria; s. of John W. Furth and Hedwig von Ferstel; m. Margaretha F. de la Court 1959; one s. one d.; ed Harvard Coll., Harvard Law School and Sloan School of Management, Massachusetts Inst. of Tech.; law clerk, Palmer, Dodge, Gardner, Bickford & Bradford, Boston, Mass 1951; admitted to New York Bar 1952; law clerk to Hon. H. M. Stephens, Chief Judge, US Court of Appeals, DC Circuit 1952–53; served in US Army 1953–57; Assoc. Cravath, Swaine & Moore (law firm) 1957–58; with ILO, Geneva 1959–70, Exec. Asst to Dir-Gen. 1964–66, Chief of Tech. Co-operation Branch and Deputy Chief, Field Dept 1966–68, Deputy Chief, later Chief, Personnel and Admin. Services Dept 1968–70; Asst Dir-Gen. WHO (Admin. Services; Co-ordinator, Special Programme for Research and Training in Tropical Diseases and responsibility for Special Programme for Research, Devt and Research Training in Human Reproduction) 1971–89; int. health consultant to US Govt, World Bank and pharmaceutical industry 1989–94; Assoc. Exec. Dir American Citizens Abroad 1994–2000; Chair. American Democrats Abroad, Switzerland 2001–03. *Address:* 13 route de Presinge, 1241 Puplinge (Geneva), Switzerland (home). *Telephone:* (22) 3497267 (home). *Fax:* (22) 3493826 (home). *E-mail:* wfurth@bluewin.ch (home).

FURUKAWA, Masaaki; Japanese business executive; *President, Toyota Tsusho Corporation;* Pres. Toyota Tsusho Corpn. *Address:* Toyota Tsusho Corporation, 9–8 Meieki 4–chome, Nakamura-ku, Nagoya 450–8575, Japan (office). *Telephone:* (52) 584–5000 (office). *Fax:* (52) 584–5636 (office). *Website:* www.toyotsu.co.jp (office).

FUSSELL, Paul, MA, PhD; American writer and academic; *Professor Emeritus of English Literature, University of Pennsylvania;* b. 22 March 1924, Pasadena, Calif.; s. of Paul Fussell and Wilhma Wilson Sill; m. 1st Betty Harper 1949 (divorced 1987); one s. one d.; m. 2nd Harriette Rhawn Behringer 1987; ed Pomona Coll., Harvard Univ.; Instructor in English, Conn. Coll. 1951–54; Asst Prof. then Prof. of English, Rutgers Univ. 1955–76, John DeWitt Prof. of English Literature 1976–83; Donald T. Regan Prof. of English Literature, Univ. of Pa 1983–94, Emer. Prof. 1994–; Visiting Prof. King's Coll., London 1990–92; Consultant Ed. Random House 1963–64; Contributing Ed. Harper's 1979–83, The New Republic 1979–85; Hon. LittD (Pomona Coll.) 1980, (Monmouth Coll., NJ) 1985; James D. Phelan Award 1964, Lindback Foundation Award 1971, Sr Fellow Nat. Endowment for the Humanities 1973–74, Guggenheim Fellowship 1977–78, Rockefeller Foundation Fellow 1983–84, Nat. Book Award, Nat. Book Critics Circle Award, Emerson Award. *Publications:* Theory of Prosody in 18th Century England 1954, Poetic Meter and Poetic Form 1965, The Rhetorical World of Augustan Humanism 1965, Samuel Johnson and the Life of Writing 1971, The Great War and Modern Memory 1975, Abroad: British Literary Travelling between the Wars 1980, The Boy Scout Handbook and Other Observations 1982, Class: A Guide through the American Status System 1983, Sassoon's Long Journey (ed.) 1983, The Norton Book of Travel (ed.) 1987, Thank God for the Atom Bomb and Other Essays 1988, Wartime: Understanding and Behaviour in the Second World War 1989, Killing in Verse and Prose and other essays 1990, The Norton Book of Modern War (ed.) 1991, BAD: or, The Dumbing of America

1991, The Bloody Game: An Anthology of Modern War 1992, The Anti-Egotist: Kingsley Amis, Man of Letters 1994, Doing Battle: The Making of a Skeptic 1996, Uniforms 2002, The Boys' Crusade 2004. *Leisure interest:* reading. *Address:* Apt 4-H, 2020 Walnut Street, Philadelphia, PA 19103-5636, USA (home). *Telephone:* (215) 557-0144 (home).

FUTA, Pierre André; Democratic Republic of the Congo politician; Minister of Finance 2004–07. *Address:* c/o Ministry of Finance, blvd du 30 juin, BP 12998 KIN 1, Kinshasa-Gombe, Democratic Republic of the Congo (office).

FUWA, Tetsuzo; Japanese politician; *President, Social Sciences Institute, Japanese Communist Party;* b. 26 Jan. 1930, Tokyo; ed Tokyo Univ.; mem. Secr. Fed. of Iron and Steel Workers' Union 1953; mem. Cen. Cttee, Japanese Community Party 1966–, Secr. Head 1970, Chair. Exec. Cttee 1982, Chair. Cen. Cttee 2000–06, Pres. Social Sciences Inst. *Publications:* Stalin and the Great Power Chauvinism 1994, Interference and Betrayal 1994, Remaking Japan 1998, Nuclear Deception: Japan–USA Secret Agreements 2000, On Marx's Scientific View 2001, Re-reading Critique of the Gotha Programme: Marx and Engel's View of a Future Society 2003, Lenin's State and Revolution: A Critical Approach 2003, Asia, Africa and Latin America in the Present-Day World 2005, Seven Days in Tunisia 2005, Breaking Japan's Diplomatic Stalemate 2005, The 21st Century World and Socialism 2006, Japan's War: History of Expansionism 2006. *Address:* Central Committee of the Japanese Communist Party, 4-36-7 Sendagaya, Shibuya-ku, Tokyo 151-8586, Japan (office). *Telephone:* (3) 3403-6111 (office). *E-mail:* info@jcp.or.jp (office). *Website:* www.jcp.or.jp (office).

FUYUSHIBA, Tetsuzo; Japanese lawyer and politician; b. 29 June 1936, Shenyang (then Hōten), NE China; ed Faculty of Law, Kansai Univ.; lawyer 1964; mem. House of Reps for Hyogo Prefecture, 8th Dist 1986–; Parl. Vice-Minister for Home Affairs 1993–94; Chair. Standing Cttee on Audit 1997; Sec.-Gen. New Peace Party 1998; Sec.-Gen. New Komeito 1998–2006, currently Standing Adviser; Minister of Land, Infrastructure and Transport 2006–08, for Tourism and Ocean Policy 2007–08. *Address:* New Komeito, 17, Minami-Motomachi, Shinjuku-ku, Tokyo 160-0012, Japan (office). *Telephone:* (3) 3353-0111 (office). *Website:* www.komei.or.jp (office); fuyusiba.net/pc.

FYFE, William Sefton, CC, PhD, FRS, FRSC, FRSNZ; Canadian chemist and academic; *Professor Emeritus, Department of Earth Sciences, University of Western Ontario;* b. 4 June 1927, New Zealand; s. of Colin Fyfe and Isabella Fyfe; m. Patricia Walker 1981; two s. one d.; ed Univ. of Otago, New Zealand; Lecturer in Chem., Univ. of Otago 1955–58; Prof. of Geology, Univ. of Calif., Berkeley 1958–66; Royal Soc. Prof. Manchester Univ. 1966–72; Chair. Dept of Geology, Univ. of Western Ont. 1972–84, Prof. of Geology 1984–92, Prof. Emer. 1992–, Dean Faculty of Science 1986–90; Pres. Int. Union of Geological Sciences 1992–96; Hon. mem. Brazilian, Russian and Indian Acad. of Sciences; Hon. DSc (Memorial Univ.) 1989, (Lisbon) 1990, (Lakehead) 1990, (Guelph) 1992, (St Mary's) 1994, (Otago) 1995, (Univ. of Western Ont.) 1995; awards include Guggenheim Fellowships, Logan Medal, Holmes Medal, European Union of Geosciences 1989, Day Medal, Geological Soc. of America 1990, NZ Commemorative Medal 1991, Canada Gold Medal 1992, Roebling Medal 1995, Nat. Order of Scientific Merit, Brazil 1996, Wollaston Medal, Geological Soc., London 2000. *Publications:* 5 books, 800 scientific papers. *Leisure interests:* wildlife, swimming, travel. *Address:* Department of Earth Sciences, Room 107 Biology and Building, University of Western Ontario, London, Ont., N6A 5B7 (office); 1197 Richmond Street, London, Ont., N6A 3L3, Canada (home). *Telephone:* (519) 661-3180 (office). *Fax:* (519) 661-3198 (office). *E-mail:* mrice@uwo.ca (office); pjfyfe@uwo.ca (office). *Website:* www.uwo.ca/earth/es4.html (office).

FYODOROV, Nikolai Vasilievich, DrSci; Russian/Chuvash politician and lawyer; *President of Chuvash Republic;* b. 9 May 1958, Chuvash Repub.; m.; one s. one d.; ed Kazan State Univ., Inst. of State and Law, USSR Acad. of Sciences; worked in legal bodies since 1983; teacher Chuvash State Univ. 1980–82, 1985–89; USSR People's Deputy 1989–91; Deputy Chair. Legis. Comm. Supreme Soviet 1989–90; Minister of Justice of RSFSR (later Russia) 1990–93; Pres. Chuvash Repub. 1994–; mem. Council of Fed. 1996–2002; Order for Merits to Fatherland 1998, 2003; State Prize of Russia 1999. *Publications:* more than 100 articles and several books on problems of democratic and federative structure of the state, freedom of mass media, independent judicial power and economic policy. *Leisure interests:* karate, swimming, skiing, water-skiing, chess. *Address:* Office of the President, Republic Square 1, 428004 Cheboxary, Chuvash Republic, Russia (office). *Telephone:* (8352) 62-46-87 (Cheboxary) (office). *Fax:* (8352) 62-17-99 (office). *E-mail:* president@chuvashia.com (office). *Website:* www.cap.ru (office).

G

GABAGLIO, Emilio, BA (Econs); Italian trade union official; b. 1 July 1937, Como; m.; two d.; ed Catholic Univ., Milan; fmr high school teacher; mem. Italian Workers Christian Asscn, Nat. Pres. 1969–72; Officer, Italian Workers Unions Confed. (CISL) 1974–, elected to Nat. Secr. 1983–, represented CISL in ILO and in Exec. Cttees of European Trade Union Confed. (ETUC) and ICFTU; Gen. Sec. ETUC 1991–2003; mem. European Convention 2002–03; Int. Dir'Culture of Work' Section, World Forum of Cultures, Barcelona 2004; Chair. EU Employment Cttee 2007–09; mem. Notre Europe Steering Cttee 2006–; Order of Merit (Poland) 1997, Légion d'Honneur (France) 2000. *Address:* Movimento Cristiano Sociali, Lungotevere dei Mellini, 00193 Rome, Italy (office). *Telephone:* (6) 3210694 (office). *E-mail:* egabagli@etuc.org (office).

GABALLA, Ali Gaballa, PhD; Egyptian archaeologist and Egyptologist; b. (El Menoufiah), m.; three c.; ed Cairo Univ., Liverpool Univ.; Asst Lecturer, Cairo Univ. 1962–63, Lecturer –1974, Assoc. Prof. of Egyptology –1979, Chair. of Dept then Vice-Dean of Faculty of Archaeology, then Dean; f. archaeology section, Faculty of Arts, Kuwait Univ.; now Sec.-Gen. Supreme Council of Antiquities; State Award for History and Archaeology 1979, Order of Merit for Sciences and Arts. *Publications:* Glimpses of Ancient Egypt 1979, The Third Intermediate Period in Egypt 1996, The History and Culture of Nubia 1997, Encyclopaedia of the Egyptian Civilization (co-ed.) and numerous other books.

GABBANA, Stefano; Italian fashion designer; *President, Dolce & Gabbana;* b. 14 Nov. 1962, Milan; studied graphic design; Asst in a Milan atelier; with Domenico Dolce opened fashion consulting studio 1982, selected to take part in New Talents show, Milano Collezioni 1985; f. Dolce & Gabbana 1985, first maj. women's collection 1985, knitwear 1987, beachwear, underwear 1989, men's wear 1990, women's fragrance 1992, D&G line men's fragrance 1994, eyewear 1995; est. Dolce & Gabbana Industria production units 1999–2000; acquired and renovated Cinema Metropol in Milan for fashion shows and exhibitions 2005; opened boutiques in major cities in Europe, America and Asia; with Domenico Dolce, Woolmark Award 1991, Perfume Acad. Int. Prize for Best Feminine Fragrance of Year 1993, Best Masculine Fragrance of Year 1995, French "Oscar des Parfums", FHM magazine Designers of the Year 1996, Footwear News Designers of the Year 1997, Harper's Bizarre Russia Style Award 1999, T de Telva Award for Best Designers of the Year, U.S. GQ magazine Best Designers of the Year 2003, U.K. Elle Magazine Best Int. designers 2004, Premio Risultati 2004, Russian GQ Best Int. Designers 2005. *Publications:* with Domenico Dolce, 10 Years Dolce and Gabbana 1996, Wildness 1997, Dolce and Gabbana Mémoires de la Mode 1998, Hollywood 2003, Calcio 2004, Music 2004, 20 Years Dolce & Gabanna 2005. *leisure interests:* boxing, gym, taking vacations. *Address:* Dolce & Gabbana, Via San Damiano 7, 20122 Milan, Italy (office). *Telephone:* (02) 774271 (office). *Fax:* (02) 76020600 (office). *Website:* www.dolcegabbana.it (office).

GABRE-SELLASSIE, Zewde, PhD; Ethiopian diplomatist; b. 12 Oct. 1926, Metcha, Shoa; ed Haile Sellassie I Secondary School, Coll. des Frères and St George School, Jerusalem, Coll. des Frères and American Mission, Cairo, Egypt, Univs of Exeter and Oxford and Lincoln's Inn, London, UK; Econ. Attaché, later Head of Press, Information and Admin. Div., Ministry of Foreign Affairs 1951–53; Dir-Gen. Maritime Affairs 1953–55; Deputy Minister, Ministry of Public Works, Transport and Civil Aviation 1955–57; Mayor and Gov. of Addis Ababa 1957–59; Amb. to Somalia 1959–60; Minister of Justice 1961–63; Sr mem. St Antony's Coll., Oxford 1963–71; Perm. Rep. to the UN 1972–74; Minister of Interior March–May 1974, of Foreign Affairs May–Dec. 1974; Deputy Prime Minister July–Sept. 1974; Visiting Lecturer, Univ. of Calif. 1965; Vice-Pres. ECOSOC 1974; Officer of Menelik II, Grand Cross of Phoenix (Greece), of Istiqlal (Jordan), Grand Officer Flag of Yugoslavia, Order of Merit (FRG). *Address:* 421 North Broadway, #12, Yonkers NY 10701, USA.

GABRIADZE, Revaz (Rezo) Levanovich; Georgian scriptwriter, film director, sculptor and artist; b. 29 June 1936, Kutaisi; m. 2nd Yelena Zakharyevna Dzhaparidze; one s. one d.; ed Tbilisi State Univ., Higher Courses of Scriptwriters and Film Directors in Moscow; worked as corresp. Molodezh Gruzii; works for Gruzia Film Studio 1970–; wrote scripts for over 35 films including Do Not Grieve 1969, Serenade (after M. Zoshchenko) 1969, Jug (after L. Pirandello) 1970, Unusual Show 1970, White Stone 1973, Cranks 1974, Road, Mimino 1978, Kin-dza-dza; founder and Artistic Dir Tbilisi Puppet Theatre 1981, wrote and produced plays Traviata, Diamond of Marshal Fantier, Fall of Our Spring (USSR State Prize), Daughter of the Emperor of Trapezund; puppet productions in Switzerland and France 1991–94 including Ree Triste la Fin de l'Allee (Lausanne), Kutaisi (Rennes); Artistic Dir Cen. Puppet Theatre, Moscow 1994–95; Dir St Petersburg Satire Theatre 1996; productions include Song of the Volga 1996, Battle of Stalingrad, Forbidden Christmas or The Doctor and the Patient; numerous monumental and miniature sculptures including Chizhik-Pyzhik, Nose (after N. Gogol) ceramics exhibited in St Petersburg, Rabinovich (Odessa); graphic and painting shows in Moscow, St Petersburg, Paris, Rennes, Berlin, Lausanne; in Dijon and St Petersburg; illustrated works of A. Pushkin. *Address:* Pyryeva str. 26. korp. 1, Apt. 14, 119285 Moscow, Russia. *Telephone:* (095) 147-45-94 (home).

GABRIEL, Edward M., BS; American diplomatist and business executive; *Visiting Fellow, Middle East Program, Center for Strategic and International Studies;* ed Gannon Univ., Pa; fmr owner and Pres. Gabriel Group; fmr Sr Vice-Pres. in charge of Corp. Public Affairs, CONCORD Corpn; fmr Pres. and CEO Madison Public Affairs Group; Amb. to Morocco 1997–2001; Advisor on Middle East policy for General Wesley Clark's presidential campaign 2004; currently Visiting Fellow, Middle East Program, Center for Strategic and Int. Studies (CSIS); Sr Counsellor, Middle Eastern and Russian Issues, Center for Democracy; Founding mem. Exec. Cttee and Bd of Dirs, American Task Force on Lebanon; Dir Keystone Center. *Address:* Middle East Program, Center for Strategic and International Studies (CSIS), 1800 K Street, NW, Washington, DC 20006, USA (office). *Telephone:* (202) 775-3213 (office). *Fax:* (202) 775-3199 (office). *Website:* www.csis.org/mideast (office).

GABRIEL, Michal; Czech sculptor; b. 25 Feb. 1960, Prague; s. of František Gabriel and Jarmila Gabrielová; m. Milada Dočekalová 1987; two s. one d.; ed Secondary School of Applied Arts, Acad. of Fine Arts, Prague; apprenticed in timber industry; worked as skilled joiner 1975–78; graduated as woodcarver 1982, as sculptor 1987; Founding mem. creative group Tvrdohlaví ('The Stubborn' group) 1987; First Prize for statue Pegasus, Prague 1988 (work subsequently completed), for gates for Nat. Gallery Bldg 1989 (completed 1992); Angel Sculpture (bronze), Bank in Opava 1995, 'The Winged Leopard', gilded bronze sculpture, entrance Pres.'s Office, Prague Castle 1996; City Hall windows, České Budějovice 2000; Fountain (metal), Hradec Králové 2001; 'Trunk' sculpture, Philosophy Faculty Brno 2002; Lecturer Faculty of Performing Arts, Czech Univ. of Tech., Brno 1999–; co-f. new Exhbn hall, Palace Lucerne, Prague 2000; Jindřich Chalupecký Prize 1994. *Publication:* Tvrdohlaví 2000. *Address:* Dlouhá 32, 110 00 Prague 1, Czech Republic (home). *Telephone:* (2) 22314644 (home). *Fax:* (2) 22314644 (home). *E-mail:* michalgabriel@hotmail.com (office). *Website:* www.ffa.vutbr.cz/gabriel (office).

GABRIEL, Peter; British rock singer and songwriter; b. 13 Feb. 1950, Woking, Surrey; m. 1st Jill Gabriel; two d.; m. 2nd Meabh Flynn 2002; two s.; ed Charterhouse School; f. mem., rock band Genesis 1966–75; solo artist 1975–; f. World of Music, Arts and Dance (WOMAD) featuring music from around the world 1982; f. Real World Group to develop interactive projects in arts and tech. 1985, Real World Studios 1986, Real World Records (world music record label) 1989, Real World Multimedia 1994; launched 'Witness' Human Rights Programme 1992; co-f. Europe digital music wholesaler OD2; co-f., with Brian Eno, the Magnificent Union of Digitally Downloading Artists (MUDDA) 2004; co-f., with Richard Branson, the Elders.org 2000, launched by Nelson Mandela 2007; Dr hc (City Univ.) 1991; Hon. MA (Univ. Coll., Salford) 1994; Hon. DMus (Bath) 1996; Ivor Novello Award for Outstanding Contribution to British Music 1983, Ivor Novello Award for Best Song (for Sledgehammer) 1987, BRIT Award for Best British Music Video (for Sledgehammer) 1987, for Best British Male Artist 1987, for Best Producer 1993, Grammy Awards for Best New Age Performance 1990, Best Short Form Video 1993, for Best Song Written for Motion Picture (for Down to Earth from Wall-E) 2009, for Best Instrumental Arrangement (for Define Dancing from Wall-E) 2009, Q Award for Lifetime Achievement 2006, Ivor Novello Lifetime Achievement Award 2007, BMI Icon 2007, Amb. of Conscience, Amnesty International 2008, Quadriga Award 2008, Time 100 Most Influential People Award 2008, Polar Music Prize 2009. *Film scores:* Birdy 1985, Last Temptation of Christ 1989, Long Walk Home (from Rabbit-Proof Fence) 2002, Wall-E (two Grammy Awards 2009) 2008. *Recordings include:* albums: with Genesis: From Genesis To Revelation 1969, Foxtrot 1972, Genesis Live 1973, Selling England By The Pound 1973, Nursery Crime 1974, The Lamb Lies Down On Broadway 1974; solo: Peter Gabriel I 1977, II 1979, III 1980, IV 1982, Peter Gabriel Plays Live 1983, So 1986, Passion 1989, Shaking The Tree 1990, Us 1992, Revisited 1992, Secret World 1995, Come Home to Me Snow 1998, Ovo 2000, Up 2002, Big Blue Ball 2008. *Publication:* Genesis: Chapter and Verse (with other band mems) 2007. *Address:* Real World, Box Mill, Mill Lane, Box, Wilts., SN13 8PL, England (office). *Telephone:* (1225) 740600 (office). *Website:* www.petergabriel.com.

GABRIEL, Sigmar; German politician; *Federal Minister of the Environment, Nature Conservation and Nuclear Safety;* b. 12 Sept. 1959, Goslar; m.; one d.; ed Göttingen Univ.; children and youth work in Sozialistische Jugend Deutschlands – die Falken 1976–89; joined SPD 1977; adult educ. lecturer 1983–88; teacher, Saxony Adult Educ. Inst. 1989–90; Dist Councillor for Goslar 1987–98, City Councillor 1991–99, Chair. Environmental Cttee 1991–96, Econ. Affairs and Tourism Cttee 1996; mem. Lower Saxony Parl. 1990–2005, mem. Environment Cttee 1990–94, Deputy Chair. SPD Parl. Group 1997–98, Chair. 1998–99, 2003–05; SPD Speaker for Home Affairs 1994–97; mem. Exec. Cttee SPD 1999–2005; Minister-Pres. of Lower Saxony 1999–2003; mem. Bundestag for constituency 49 (Salzgitter-Wolfenbüttel) 2005–; Fed. Minister of the Environment, Nature Conservation and Nuclear Safety 2005–. *Leisure interests:* cycling, sailing. *Address:* Ministry of the Environment, Nature Conservation and Nuclear Safety, Alexanderstr. 3, 10178 Berlin, Germany (office). *Telephone:* (30) 18305-0 (office). *Fax:* (30) 183052046 (office). *E-mail:* sigmar.gabriel@wk.bundestag.de (office). *Website:* www.bmu.de (office); www.sigmargabriel.de (office).

GABRIELLI DE AZEVEDO, José Sergio, PhD; Brazilian economist, academic and business executive; *President and CEO, Petróleo Brasileiro SA (Petrobras);* ed Fed. Univ. of Bahia, Boston Univ., USA; fmr Deputy Dir of Research and Postgraduate Studies, Fed. Univ. of Bahia, fmr Dir Faculty of Econ. Sciences, currently Prof. on leave; fmr Superintendent Foundation for Research and Extension Support; Visiting Research Scholar LSE 2000–01; Chief Financial Officer and Investor Relations Dir Petróleo Brasileiro SA (Petrobras) 2003–05, Pres. and CEO 2005–, mem. Bd of Dirs Petrobras Participaciones SA (PEPSA), Petrobras Energia SA (PESA); Brazilian Inst. of Finance Execs Equilibrist Award 2004, Nat. Asscn of Execs in Finance, Admin and Accounting Professional of the Year 2004, Int. Stevie Business Awards Best Finance Exec. in Latin America 2005. *Publications:* numerous books and articles. *Address:* Petróleo Brasileiro SA, Avenida República do Chile 65, sala 401 E, 20035-900 Rio de Janeiro, Brazil (office). *Telephone:* (21) 2534-1510 (office). *Fax:* (21) 2534-6055 (office). *E-mail:* info@petrobras.com.br (office). *Website:* www.petrobras.com.br (office).

GABRIELSE, Gerald, MS, PhD; American physicist and academic; *George Vasmer Leverett Professor of Physics, Harvard University;* ed Calvin Coll., Grand Rapids, Mich., Univ. of Chicago; teaching asst, Calvin Coll., Grand Rapids, Mich. 1971–72, research asst 1972–73; grad. student, Univ. of Chicago 1973–78; Research Assoc., Univ. of Washington, Seattle 1978–82, Research Asst Prof. 1985–86, Assoc. Prof. 1986–87; George Vasmer Leverett Prof. of Physics, Harvard Univ. 1987– (Chair. Physics Dept 2000–03); Physicist, CERN, leader of ATRAP antimatter physics research project, Geneva, Switzerland; Consultant, Intermagnetics General Corpn 1995, PolyChip Inc. 1999; Scientist in Residence, Lexington Christian Acad. 1995–96; mem. numerous cttees; Levenson Prize, Harvard Univ. 2000, Davisson-Germer Prize, American Physical Soc. 2002. *Lectures include:* around 200 lectures at scientific confs and univs. *Publications include:* more than 100 scientific publs. *Address:* Department of Physics, Harvard University, 17 Oxford Street, Cambridge, MA 02138, USA (office). *Telephone:* (617) 495-4381 (office). *E-mail:* gabrielse@physics.harvard.edu (office). *Website:* physics.harvard .edu/gabrielse.htm (office); hussle.harvard.edu/~gabrielse (office); hussle .harvard.edu/~atrap (office).

GACHECHILADZE, Levan; Georgian business executive and politician; b. 20 Aug. 1964, Tbilisi; m.; three c.; ed Tbilisi Ivane Javakhishvili State Univ.; f. Georgian Wine and Spirits Co. 1994; joined New Right Party 1999; Founding mem. New Faction Group 2000; Chair. Axali Memarjveneebi (New Conservative Party) 2001; currently mem. Sakartvelos Parlamenti (Parl.) for Vake-Saburtalo Dist; presidential cand. of Tavisupleba (Freedom Party) 2008; Businessman of the Year 1999. *Address:* Sakartvelos Parlamenti, Rustaveli 8, 0108 Tbilisi (office); Georgian Wine and Spirits Company, Archinebuli, 2200 Telavi, Georgia (office). *Telephone:* (32) 28-15-39 (Parl.) (office); (35) 07-60-51 (GWS) (office). *Fax:* (35) 05-00-65 (GWS) (office). *Website:* www.gws.ge (office).

GADDAFI, Col Mu'ammar Muhammad al-; Libyan head of state and army officer; *Revolutionary Leader/Chairman of the Revolutionary Command Council;* b. 1942, Serte; s. of Mohamed Abdulsalam Abuminiar and Aisha Ben Niran; m. 1970; four s. one d.; ed Univ. of Libya, Benghazi; served with Libyan Army 1965–; Chair. Revolutionary Command Council 1969– (Head of State); C-in-C of Armed Forces Sept. 1969; Prime Minister 1970–72; Minister of Defence 1970–72; Sec.-Gen. of Gen. Secr. of Gen. People's Congress 1977–79; Chair. OAU 1982–83; mem. Presidential Council, Fed. of Arab Republics 1972; rank of Maj.-Gen. Jan. 1976, retaining title of Col. *Publications:* The Green Book (3 vols), Military Strategy and Mobilization, The Story of the Revolution. *Address:* Office of the President, Tripoli, Libya (office).

GADDAFI, Seif al-Islam, BSc; Libyan charity organization official; *President, Gaddafi Development Foundation;* b. 25 June 1972, Tripoli; s. of Col Mu'ammar Muhammad al-Gaddafi by his second wife; ed Al-Fateh Univ., Tripoli, IMADEC Univ., Vienna, Austria, London School of Econs, UK; involved in assisting Muslims in Mindanao, southern Philippines 1999, later helped negotiate release of western hostages held by Islamic rebels there; mediated with US and British intelligence in negotiations that led to Libya's abandonment of its weapons programmes 2004; co-owner Nat. Eng Service and Supplies Co.; Pres. Gaddafi Devt Foundation which paid $2.7 billion compensation to families of the 270 victims of Lockerbie bombing; Pres. Libyan Nat. Asscn for Drugs and Narcotics Control. *Leisure interests:* four pet tigers, falconry, painting. *Address:* Gaddafi Development Foundation, El Fatah Tower, 5th Floor, No. 57, PO Box 1101, Tripoli, Libya (office). *Telephone:* (21) 3351370 (office). *Fax:* (21) 3351373 (office). *E-mail:* info@ gaddaficharity.org (office). *Website:* www.gdf.org.ly (office).

GADDAFI, Wanis; Libyan politician; Head of Exec. Council in Cyrenaican Prov. Govt 1952–62; Fed. Minister of Foreign Affairs 1962–63, of Interior 1963–64, of Labour 1964; Amb. to FRG 1964–65; Minister of Planning and Devt 1966–68, of Foreign Affairs 1968; Prime Minister 1968–69; imprisoned for two years 1971–73.

GADE JENSEN, Søren, MSc, CandEcon; Danish politician; *Minister of Defence;* b. 27 Jan. 1963, Holstebro; s. of Poul Jørgensen and Anna Gade Jørgensen; ed Århus Univ.; served as Officer, Jutland Regiment of Dragoons 1983–85, Reserve Officer, rank of Maj. 1985–; UN Observer in Middle East, UNTSO 1990–01; Int. Market Analyst, Cheminova Agro A/S 1991–93; Man., Bilka 1993–95; teacher, Holstebro Business Coll. 1997–98; Chief Operating Finance Officer, Færch Plast A/S 1995–2001; Head of Centre, RAR Regnskabscenter 2001–03; cand. for Holstebro Constituency (Liberal Party) 1995; mem. (temp.) Folketing for Ringkøbing County Constituency Oct.–Nov. 1999, mem. 2001–, Deputy Chair. Defence Cttee 2001; Minister of Defence 2004–; Commdr of the Order of Danneborg. *Address:* Ministry of Defence, Holmens Kanal 42, 1060 Copenhagen K, Denmark (office). *Telephone:* 33-92-33-20 (office). *Fax:* 33-32-06-55 (office). *E-mail:* fmn@fmn.dk (office). *Website:* www.fmn.dk (office).

GADGIL, Madhav, MSc, PhD; Indian ecologist, conservationist and academic; b. 1942; ed Univ. of Poona, Bombay Univ., Harvard Univ., USA; main contrib. to establishment of India's first biosphere reserve in the Western Ghats;-worked at Indian Nat. Science Acad. from 1973; fmr IBM Fellow and Lecturer in Biology, Harvard Univ.; Visiting Prof., Stanford Univ., USA; fmr Distinguished Lecturer, Univ. of California, Berkeley, USA; Founder and Prof., Centre for Ecological Sciences, Bangalore, Indian Inst. of Science 1973–2004; mem. Science Advisory Council to Prime Minister 1986–90, Karnataka State

Planning Bd; Vice-Pres. Scientific Advisory Bd to Convention on Biological Diversity 1995; Chair. Scientific and Tech. Advisory Panel of Global Environment Facility; represents Govt of India on Subsidiary Body on Scientific, Tech. and Technological Advice to Int. Convention on Biological Diversity; fmr Chair. Fuel and Fodder Study Group of Planning Comm., Biodiversity Task Force of Dept of Biotechnology, Expert Group on Eastern and Western Ghats, Ministry of Environment and Forests; fmr mem. Steering Cttee Project Tiger, Steering Cttee Indian Bd for Wild Life, Silent Valley Cttee, Bastar Pine Plantation Cttee; broadcasts extensively in Indian languages on environmental issues; Fellow, Indian Acad. of Sciences, Indian Nat. Science Acad., Third World Acad. of Sciences; Foreign Assoc., NAS; Hon. mem. British Ecological Soc., Ecological Soc. of America; Padmashri and Padma Bhushan, Pres. of India; Shanti Swarup Bhatnagar Award, Vikram Sarabhai Award, Iswarchandra Vidyasagar Award, Rajyotsava Award, Centennial Medal, Harvard Univ. 2002, Govt of Karnataka, Volvo Environment Prize 2003. *Publications:* This Fissured Land, Ecology and Equity, Diversity: The Cornerstone of Life, Nurturing Biodiversity: An Indian Agenda, Ecological Journeys, People's Biodiversity Registers: A Methodology Manual; more than 215 research papers (two of them recognized as Citation Classics) on population biology, conservation biology, human ecology and ecological history; writes regularly for popular media in English and Indian languages. *Address:* c/o Centre for Ecological Sciences, Indian Institute of Science, Bangalore 560 012, India (office). *Telephone:* (80) 23600985 (office). *Fax:* (80) 23601428 (office). *E-mail:* madhav@ces.iisc.ernet.in (office). *Website:* ces.iisc.ernet.in (office); ces.iisc .ernet.in/hpg/cesmg.

GADIESH, Orit, MBA; Israeli business executive; *Chairperson, Bain & Company;* ed Hebrew Univ., Jerusalem, Harvard Business School, USA; joined the Israeli army age 17, worked as Aide to Deputy Chief of Staff; joined Bain & Co. (consultancy firm), Boston 1977, worked in steel industry and automotive industry sectors, Chair. 1993–; mem. Bd Harvard Business School, Haute Ecole Commerciale, Paris, Peres Inst. for Peace, Fed. Reserve Bank of New England, WPP Group; mem. Harvard Medical School Advisory Council for Cell Biology and Pathology, Harvard Business School Visiting Cttee, Metropolitan Museum of Art Cttee, New York; mem. Bd of Trustees Eisenhower Fellowships; Del. to World Econ. Forum, Davos, Switzerland; Baker Scholar, Harvard Business School; Brown Award for Outstanding Marketing Student, Harvard Business School 1977, Harvard Business School Alumni Achievement Award 2000, IDC Univ. Distinguished Leadership Award 2000, 25th Annual Golden Door Award, Int. Inst. of Boston 2002, Lifetime Achievement Award from Consulting magazine 2007; ranked by Forbes magazine amongst 100 Most Powerful Women (91st) 2004, (95th) 2005, (99th) 2006, (98th) 2007. *Publications:* series of articles for Harvard Business Review. *Leisure interests:* reading. *Address:* Bain & Company Inc., 131 Dartmouth Street, Boston, MA 02116, USA (office). *Telephone:* (617) 572-2000 (office). *Fax:* (617) 572-2427 (office). *Website:* www.bain.com (office).

GADIO, Cheikh Tidiane, BA, PhD; Senegalese politician; *Minister of State, Minister of Foreign Affairs, African Unity and Senegalese Abroad;* b. 16 Sept. 1956, Saint-Louis; ed Ohio State Univ., USA, Univ. of Montreal, Canada, Univ. of Paris, France; Ed.-in-Chief, Tribune Africaine, Paris 1980–84; Head of Audiovisual section, Festival Panafricain des Arts et de la Culture (FESPAC) 1987–88; various econ. and telecommunications devt advisory posts, World Bank Inst.; Advisor, UN Office for Project Services 1998–; Regional Dir for Africa, School for International Training, Vt, USA 1998–99; Co-ordinator for Africa, World Bank Institute Jan.–April 2000; Minister of State, of Foreign Affairs, African Unity and Senegalese Abroad 2000–. *Address:* Ministry of Foreign Affairs, African Unity and Senegalese Abroad, 1 Place de l'Indépendance, BP 4044, Dakar, Senegal (office). *Telephone:* 889-13-00 (office). *E-mail:* cheikhgadio@senegal.diplomatie.sn (office). *Website:* www .diplomatie.gouv.sn (office).

GADJIYEV, Gadis Abdullayevich, DJur; Russian/Dagestani lawyer and judge; *Justice, Constitutional Court of Russian Federation;* b. 27 Aug. 1957, Shovkra; m.; four s.; ed Moscow State Univ. 1975; teacher Dagestan State Univ. 1975–79; legal consultant Supreme Soviet Dagestan ASSR 1979–80, Head Legal Dept Admin. 1980–90, Chair. Comm. on Law and Local Self-Man. 1990–91; Justice Constitutional Court of Russian Fed. 1991–. *Publications:* over 80 scientific publs including 4 monographs on constitutional law. *Leisure interest:* pigeon raising. *Address:* Constitutional Court of Russian Federation, Ilyinka 21, 103132 Moscow, Russia (office). *Telephone:* (095) 206-17-62 (office). *Fax:* (095) 206-19-78 (office).

GADONNEIX, Pierre, DEcon; French energy industry executive; *Chairman and CEO, Électricité de France;* b. 1943, New York, NY, USA; m.; three c.; ed École Polytechnique, Paris, Ecole Nationale Supérieure du Pétrole et des Moteurs, Harvard Business School, USA; began career as engineer, Groupe Elf Aquitaine 1966–69; f. SEFI 1969, Dir 1970–72; Dir Inst. de Développement Industriel (IDI) 1972–76; Tech. Adviser, Ministry of Industry 1976–78, Dir Mechanical and Metallurgical Industries Div. 1978–87; Pres. and Man. Dir Groupe Gaz de France 1987–96, Chair. and CEO 1996–2004; Chair. and CEO Électricité de France 2004–; Chair. World Energy Council 2007–; mem. Bd Dirs Elf-Erap 1988–95, Renault 1978–86, SNCF 1983–87, France Télécom 1998–; Pres. Eurogas (trade asscn) 2000–, Fondation Gaz de France, Conseil Français de l'Energie 1993–99 (later Vice-Pres.); Lecturer, École Polytechnique 1983–92; mem. Conseil Economique et Social, Bd of Fondation Nationale des Sciences Politiques; Commdr, Légion d'honneur, Ordre nat. du Mérite, Ordre des Arts et des Lettres. *Address:* Électricité de France, 22–30 avenue de Wagram, 75382 Paris Cedex 8, France (office). *Telephone:* 1-40-42-22-22 (office). *Fax:* 1-40-42-79-40 (office). *E-mail:* info@edf.fr (office). *Website:* www .edf.fr (office).

GAEHTGENS, Thomas Wolfgang, DPhil; German art historian and academic; *Professor of Art History, Freien Universität Berlin;* b. 24 June 1940, Leipzig; m. Barbara Feiler 1969; two s.; ed Univs of Bonn and Freiburg and Univ. of Paris, France; teacher, Univ. of Göttingen 1973, Prof. of Art History 1974–79, Technische Hochschule, Aachen 1979, Freie Univ. Berlin 1979–; awarded bursary for the J. Paul Getty Center for the History of Art and the Humanities, Santa Monica, Calif. 1985–86; Dir Centre allemand d'histoire de l'art, Paris; mem. Akad. der Wissenschaften, Göttingen; Chevalier, Légion d'honneur; Dr. hc (Courtauld Institute of Art, UK) 2004. *Publications:* Napoleon's Arc de Triomphe 1974, Versailles als Nationaldenkmal 1984, Joseph-Marie Vien 1988, Anton von Werner 1990, Die Berliner Museuminsel im Deutschen Kaiserreich 1992. *Leisure interests:* art, history. *Address:* Kunsthistorisches Institut der Freien Universität Berlin, Koserstr. 20, 14195 Berlin (office); Peter-Lenne-Strasse 20, 14195 Berlin, Germany. *Telephone:* (30) 83853843 (office); (30) 8311439 (home). *Fax:* (30) 83853842 (office); (30) 8325519 (home). *E-mail:* thogae@zedat.furberlin.de (office).

GAFT, Valentin Iosifovich; Russian actor; b. 2 Sept. 1935, Moscow; m. Olga Mikhailovna Ostroumova; ed Studio-School of Moscow Art Theatre; worked in Mossoviet Theatre, Na Maloy Bronnoy, Lenkom, Satire Theatre 1959–69; leading actor Sovremennik Theatre 1969–; dozens of roles in classical and contemporary plays; in cinema since 1956; People's Artist of Russia 1984, Order of Friendship 1995, Laureate, Theatrical Prize I. Smoktunovskii 1995. *Theatre roles include:* Glumov (Balalaikin and Co.), Lopatin (From the Notes of Lopatin), George (Who's Afraid of Virginia Woolf?), Governor (Inspector), Vershinin (Three Sisters), Bridegroom (Something Like a Comedy), Husband, Wife and Lover (Trusotsii), The Government Inspector (Gorodnichii). *Film roles include:* Murder on Dante Street 1956, First Courier 1968, Crazy Gold 1977, Centaurs 1979, Parade 1980, Fuette 1986, Thieves by Law 1988, Blessed Heavens 1991, Khochu v Ameriku 1993, Tayna Marchello 1997, Nebo v almazakh 1999, Staryye klyachi 2000, Nezhnyy vozrast 2001, roles in TV productions and TV films including Buddenbrooks, The Mystery of Edwin Drood, Archipelago Lenoire, Kings and Cabbage, Po tu storonu volkov (miniseries) 2002, Master i Margarita (miniseries) 2005, 12 2007. *Publications:* Poetry and Epigrams 1989, Life is Theatre (with Leonid Alekseevich Filatov) 1998, Garden of Forgotten Memories 1999, Poems. Epigrams 2003. *Leisure interests:* writing verses and epigrams. *Address:* T. Shchevchenko nab. 1/2, Apt 62, 121059 Moscow, Russia (home). *Telephone:* (495) 243-76-67 (home).

GAGE, Fred H., BS, PhD; American geneticist and academic; *Professor and Vi and John Adler Chair for Research on Age-Related Neurodegenerative Diseases, Salk Institute for Biological Studies;* ed Univ. of Florida, Johns Hopkins Univ.; Nat. Inst. of Mental Health Predoctoral Fellow, Johns Hopkins Univ., Baltimore 1974–76; Asst, later Assoc. Prof., Texas Christian Univ. 1976–80; Assoc. Prof., Dept of Histology, Univ. of Lund, Sweden 1981–85; Assoc. Prof., Dept of Neurosciences, Univ. of California, San Diego 1985–88, Prof. 1988–; Prof. and Vi and John Adler Chair for Research on Age-Related Neurodegenerative Diseases, Lab. of Genetics, Salk Inst. for Biological Studies 1995–; co-f. StemCells Inc. 1988; Fellow, NAS, Inst. of Medicine, American Acad. of Arts and Sciences; mem. Soc. for Neuroscience (Pres. 2001); mem. Science Advisory Bd, Genetics Policy Inst.; numerous awards including Bristol-Myers Squibb Neuroscience Research Award 1987, IPSEN Prize in Neuronal Plasticity 1990, Christopher Reeve Research Medal 1997, Max Planck Research Prize 1999, MetLife Award for Medical Research 2002, Max Planck Soc. Klaus Joachim Zulch-Preis 2003, Keio Medical Science Prize 2008. *Address:* Salk Institute for Biological Studies, 10010 North Torrey Pines Road, La Jolla, CA 92037, USA (office). *Telephone:* (858) 453-4100 (office). *E-mail:* gage@salk.edu (office). *Website:* www.salk.edu (office).

GAGE, Peter William, MB, ChB, PhD, DSc; Australian physiologist; *Professor of Physiology, John Curtin School of Medical Research, Australian National University;* b. 21 Oct. 1937, Auckland, New Zealand; s. of John and Kathleen (née Burke) Gage; m. Jillian Shewan 1960 (divorced 1991); two s. two d.; ed Univ. of Otago; house surgeon, Auckland Hosp. 1961; research asst Green Lane Hosp., Auckland 1962; research scholar, ANU, Canberra 1963–65; NIH Int. Postdoctoral Fellow, Dept of Physiology and Pharmacology, Duke Univ., Durham, NC 1965–67, Asst Prof. 1967–68; Sr Lecturer, School of Physiology and Pharmacology, Univ. of NSW 1968–70, Assoc. Prof. 1971–76, Prof. 1976–84, Dir Nerve-Muscle Research Centre 1982–84; Prof. of Physiology, John Curtin School of Medical Research, ANU 1984–; Fellow, Australian Acad. of Science. *Leisure interests:* horse-riding, agriculture. *Address:* John Curtin School of Medical Research, Australia National University, G.P.O. Box 334, Canberra, ACT 2601; RMB 22, Powell Drive, Greenacres Estate, Queanbeyan, NSW 2620, Australia.

GAGNÈRE, Olivier; French designer; b. 1952, Boulogne; mem. Memphis design group, Milan 1980, worked in Murano, Italy 1989, Arita, Japan 1989–92; collaborated with Bernardaud Porcelain 1992, Cristalleries St Louis 1995; designs include lighting, furniture, china, glassware, accessories; Designer of the Year 1998. *Exhibitions and commissions include:* Galerie Maeght, Paris, Café Marly, Louvre, Paris 1994, Lido workshop, Paris 2003, Galerie Cat'Berro, Paris 2007. *Address:* 47, Boulevard St Jacques, 75014 Paris, France (office). *Telephone:* 1-45-80-79-67 (office). *Fax:* 1-45-80-79-67 (office). *E-mail:* olivier@gagnere.net (office). *Website:* www.gagnere.net (office).

GAGNON, Jean-Marie, MBA, PhD, FRSC; Canadian academic; *Professor Emeritus of Finance, Laval University;* b. 7 July 1933, Fabre; s. of Pierre Gagnon and Yvette Langlois; m. Rachel Bonin 1959; three s.; ed Univ. of Chicago and Laval Univ.; chartered accountant, Clarkson, Gordon, Cie 1957–59; Prof. of Finance, Laval Univ. 1959–2000, Prof. Emer. 2004–; Visiting Prof., Faculté Universitaire Catholique, Mons, Belgium 1972–74, Univ. of Nankai, People's Repub. of China 1985. *Publications:* Income Smoothing Hypothesis 1970, Belgian Experience with Mergers 1982, Taux de rendement et risque 1982, Traité de gestion financière (with N. Khoury) 1987, Taxes and Financial Decisions 1988, Taxes and Dividends 1991, Corporate Governance Mechanisms and Board Composition 1995, Distribution of Voting Rights and Takeover Resistance 1995. *Address:* Département de finance et assurance, Faculté des sciences de l'administration, Pavillon Palasis-Prince, bureau 3646, Université Laval, Québec, PQ G1K 7P4 (office); 1340 Corrigan, Ste-Foy, PQ G1W 3E9, Canada (home). *Telephone:* (418) 656-5535 (office). *Fax:* (418) 656-2164 (office). *E-mail:* jean-marie.gagnon@fas.ulaval.ca (office). *Website:* www.fsa.ulaval.ca/html/jeanmariegagnon.html (office).

GĄGOR, Lt-Gen. Franciszek, PhD; Polish army officer; *Chief of General Staff;* b. 8 Sept. 1951, Koniuszowa, Nowy Sącz; m.; one s. one d.; ed Adam Mickiewicz Univ., Poznań, Univ. of Wrocław, Acad. of Nat. Defence, Warsaw, NATO Defence Coll., Rome, Italy, Nat. War Coll., Washington, DC, USA; began career in Polish Armed Forces 1973; various command and staff posts in mil. units 1973–78; Operations Officer, UNEF II, Egypt 1976–77; Chief of Staff of Pollog to UN Disengagement Observer Force (UNDOF) 1977; Sr Lecturer, Higher Office School of Mechanized Infantry 1978–88; Chief Operations Officer of Polish Battalion, UNDOF, Syria 1980, 1985–86; Sr Staff Officer, Combat Training Inspectorate 1988–90; Deputy Chief Logistics Officer, UNDOF, Syria 1989–90; Head, Peacekeeping Operations Div., Ministry of Defence 1991–92, 1992–94; Deputy Commdr Polish Contingent of Multinational Forces in the Gulf 1991; Deputy Sector Commdr UN Iraq Kuwait Observer Mission (UNIKOM), Kuwait 1991–92; Deputy Dir Mil. Foreign Affairs Dept, Ministry of Defence 1994–96, Dir 1996–99; Chief of Operations Directorate J-3, Gen. Staff 1999–2002; Force Commdr, UNIKOM, Kuwait 2003, UNDOF, Camp Faour 2003–04; Mil. Rep. to NATO and EU, Brussels 2004–05; promoted to Lt-Gen. 2006, Chief of Gen. Staff, Polish Armed Forces 2006–; Officer's and Cavalier's Cross, Order of Polonia Restituta, Golden Cross of Merit. *Address:* Ministry of National Defence, 00-909 Warsaw, ul. Klonowa 1, Poland (office). *Telephone:* (22) 6280031 (office). *Fax:* (22) 8455378 (office). *E-mail:* bpimon@wp.mil.pl (office). *Website:* www.wp.mil.pl (office).

GAGOSIAN, Lawrence (Larry) Gilbert; American art collector and gallery owner; b. 19 April 1945, Los Angeles; s. of Ara Gagosian and Ann Louise Tonkin; ed UCLA; fmr literary agent, William Morris agency; began career in art by selling posters, Santa Monica 1970s; founder and owner of Gagosian Galleries in New York City, Chelsea, NY, Beverly Hills, CA, London, UK and Rome, Italy; est. King's Cross Gallery, Britannia Street, London 2004; clients include Si Newhouse, David Geffen and Charles Saatchi; represents the estate of Andy Warhol; ranked first in ArtReview magazine's Power 100 list 2004, ranked second 2005, 2006, 2007. *Address:* Gagosian Gallery, 980 Madison Avenue, New York, NY 10021, USA; Gagosian Gallery, 6–24 Britannia Street, London, WC1X 9JD, England (office). *Telephone:* (212) 744-2313 (NY); (20) 7841-9960 (office). *Fax:* (212) 772-7962 (NY); (20) 7841-9961 (office). *E-mail:* info@gagosian.com (office). *Website:* www.gagosian.com (office).

GAHMBERG, Carl G., MD, DMedSc; Finnish biochemist and academic; *Professor of Biochemistry, University of Helsinki;* b. 1 Dec. 1942, Helsinki; s. of Gustaf-Adolf Gahmberg and Marie-Louise Gahmberg; m. Marianne Gripenberg-Gahmberg; one s. one d.; ed Univ. of Helsinki; Post-doctoral Fellow, Univ. of Washington 1972–74; Docent of Cell Biology, Univ. of Helsinki 1974; Prof. of Biochemistry, Åbo Akad. 1979–81, Univ. of Helsinki 1981–; Research Prof., Acad. of Finland 1986–91; Visiting Prof., La Jolla Cancer Research Foundation 1988–89; Vice-Chair. Finnish Medical Asscn 1998–99, Chair. 2000–01; Exec. Ed. Biochimica et Biophysica Acta 2000–08; mem. Finnish Acad. of Science, Finnish Soc. of Sciences and Letters (Perm. Sec.), European Molecular Biology Org., Academia Europaea, World Cultural Council; foreign mem. Royal Swedish Acad. of Science, Royal Soc. of Arts and Sciences, Göteborg; Kt of the Finnish White Rose (First Class), Commdr, Order of the Finnish Lion; Komppa Prize 1971, Scandinavian Jahre Prize 1981, 150th Anniversary Prize, Finnish Medical Asscn 1985, Prof. of the Year in Finland 1995, Finnish Äyräpää Prize for Medicine 1997. *Publications:* 270 int. publs on cell membrane, glycoproteins, cell adhesion, cancer research. *Leisure interests:* nature, classical music, gardening. *Address:* University of Helsinki, Department of Biosciences, Division of Biochemistry, PO Box 56, Viikinkaari 5, 00014 Helsinki, Finland. *Telephone:* (9) 1915-9028 (office). *Fax:* (9) 1915-9068 (office). *E-mail:* carl.gahmberg@helsinki.fi (office).

GAICIUC, Brig.-Gen. Victor; Moldovan politician and army officer; *Ambassador to Belgium and Permanent Representative, NATO;* served in Moldovan Armed Forces, rank of Brig.-Gen.; Minister of Defence –2004; Amb. to Belgium 2004–; Perm. Rep. to NATO 2004–. *Address:* Embassy of Moldova, Tenboschstraat 54, 1050 Brussels, Belgium (office). *Telephone:* (2) 732-96-59 (office). *Fax:* (2) 732-96-60 (office). *E-mail:* bruxelles@mfa.md (office).

GAIDAR, Yegor (see Gaydar, Yegor).

GAILIS, Maris; Latvian politician and business executive; *Director, Linstow Varner Company;* b. 1951, Riga; ed Riga Polytech. Inst., Latvian State Univ.; started work in furniture factory; worked in trade unions, co-operatives; author of book Furniture for Young People; f. Riga Videocentre and Cinema Forum Arsenal; responsible for foreign econ. relations in various state insts 1990–; State Sec. Ministry of Foreign Affairs 1992–93; elected to Saeima (Parl.) 1993; Minister for Economy and Economy Reform 1993–94; Minister of Internal Affairs 1994; Deputy Prime Minister 1993–94; Prime Minister 1994–95; Acting Minister of Defence 1995; business exec. 1995–; Dir Linstow Varner Co. 1997–. *Address:* c/o Ms Dina Locmele, Stacijas laukums 4, Riga 1050, Latvia. *Telephone:* 6701-8188 (office). *Fax:* 6701-8195 (office). *E-mail:* linstow@linstow.lv (office). *Website:* www.linstow.lv (office).

GAINES, Ernest James, BA; American writer and academic; *Professor of English, University of Louisiana, Lafayette;* b. 15 Jan. 1933, River Lake Plantation, Pointe Coupee Parish, La; m. Dianne Saulney; ed San Francisco State Univ., Stanford Univ.; writer-in-residence, Denison Univ. 1971, Stanford Univ. 1981; Visiting Prof. 1983, writer-in-residence 1986, Whittier Coll.; Prof. of English and writer-in-residence, Univ. of La Lafayette (fmrly Univ. of Southwestern La) 1983–; Fellow American Acad. of Arts and Letters; Fellow Stanford Univ. Creative Writing Program 1958, Nat. Endowment for the Arts grant 1967, Rockefeller Grant 1970, Guggenheim Fellowship 1971, John D. and Catherine T. MacArthur Foundation Fellowship 1993; Dr hc (Bard Coll.), (Brown Univ.), (Denison Univ.), (La State Univ.), (Loyola Univ.), (Savannah Coll. of Art and Design), (Tulane Univ.), (Univ. of Miami), (Univ. of the South, Sewanee), (Whittier Coll.); Black Acad. of Arts and Letters Award 1972, Commonwealth Club of Calif. Fiction gold medals 1972, 1984, American Acad. and Inst. of Arts and Letters Award 1987, La Humanist of the Year 1989, La Center for the Book Award 2000, Nat. Govs' Asscn Award for Distinguished Service in the Arts 2000, La Govs' Award for Lifetime Achievement 2000, La Writers' Award 2000, Nat. Humanities Medal 2000; Chevalier, Ordre des Arts et des Lettres 1996. *Publications:* Catherine Carmier 1964, Of Love and Dust 1967, Bloodline (short stories) 1968, The Autobiography of Miss Jane Pittman 1971, A Long Day in November 1971, In My Father's House 1978, A Gathering of Old Men 1983, A Lesson Before Dying (Nat. Book Critics Circle Award 1994, Southern Writers Conference Award 1994, La Library Asscn Award 1994) 1993. *Address:* Tanya Bickley Enterprises Inc., PO Box 1656, New Canaan, CT 06840, USA (office); c/o Department of English, University of Louisiana Lafayette, Griffin Hall, Room 221, Lafayette, LA 70504, USA.

GAINUTDIN, Ravil Ibn Ismail, PhD; Russian (Tartar) religious leader; *Chairman, Council of Muftis of Russia;* b. 25 Aug. 1959, Tatarstan; m.; two d.; ed Islam Medrese Mir-Arab Bukhara, Russian Acad. of State Service, Moscow; First Imam-Khatyb Kazan Mosque Nur Islam; Exec. Sec. Ecclesiastical Dept of Moslems, European Section of USSR and Siberia, Ufa 1985–87; Imam-Khatyb Moscow Mosque 1987–88; Chief Imam-Khatyb 1988–; Pres. Islam Cen. of Moscow and Moscow Region 1991–; Chair. Council of Muftis of Russia; Chair. Religious Bd of Muslims of European Part of Russia; Prof., Moscow Higher Islam Coll.; mem. Public Chamber, Russian Fed.; mem. Int. Acad. of Sciences of Eurasia, Int. Slavic Acad., Int. Acad. of Information; mem. Council on Co-operation with Religious Unions, Russian Presidency, Public Chamber of the Russian Fed.; Order of Friendship 1987, 1997, Order of Honour 2004, Public Recognition 2006. *Publications include:* Islam in Russia, Elections in Russia: The Muslims' Choice; books on Moslem dogma and rituals. *Address:* Religious Board of European Region of Russia, Council of Mufties of Russia, Vypolzov per. 7, 129090 Moscow, Russia (office). *Telephone:* (495) 681-49-04 (office); (495) 207-53-07 (home). *Fax:* (495) 681-49-04 (office). *E-mail:* info@muslim.ru (office). *Website:* www.muslim.ru (office).

GÁL, Zoltán, DJur; Hungarian politician and lawyer; m. Krisztina Pölz; one s.; ed Eötvös Loránd Univ.; with Trade Union HQ 1964–74; worked at Exec. and Admin. Dept of Cen. Cttee of HSWP 1974–86; Lecturer, Political Coll. 1987–89; Deputy Minister of Interior, then State Sec. and Minister of Interior 1987–90; mem. Parl. 1990–, mem. Cttee on Constitution, Legislation and Justice 1990–94, Chair. Cttee for Constitutional Reform 1994–, Speaker of Nat. Ass. 1994–98, Vice-Chair. Cttee on Constitution, Legislation and Justice 1998–, Chair. Cttee on Law Enforcement; Govt Spokesman 2002–; Leader, faction of Hungarian Socialist Party 1990–94. *Leisure interests:* tennis, swimming and reading. *Address:* Kossuth Lajos tér 1–3, 1357 Budapest, Hungary. *Telephone:* 4415000 (office); (1) 200-67-35 (home). *Fax:* 4415957 (office). *E-mail:* zoltan.gal@parlament.hu (office); gal.zoltan@nextraimail.hu (home). *Website:* www.mrszp.hu (office); www.drgalzoltan.hu (home).

GALA, Antonio, LicenDer, LicenFilyLetras, LicenCienciasPoliticasyEcon; Spanish writer; b. 2 Oct. 1930, Córdoba; s. of Luis Gala and Adoración Velasco; ed Univs. of Seville and Madrid; f. and Pres., Fundación Antonio Gala; Dr hc (Córdoba); Nat. Prize for Literature, Hidalgo Prize, Planeta Prize; many other literary and theatre awards. *Publications include:* plays: Los Verdes Campos del Edén, El caracol en el espejo 1964, El sol en el hormiguero 1966, Noviembre y un poco de hierba 1967, Canatr del Santiago para todos 1971, Los buenos días perdidos 1972, Suerte, campeón 1973, Anillos para una Dama 1973, Las cítaras colgadas de los árboles 1974, Por qué corres Ulises? 1975, Petra regalada 1980, Le vieja señorita del paraíso 1980, El Cementerio de los Pájaros 1982, Trilogia de la libertad 1983, Samarkanda 1985, El hotelito 1985, Séneca o el beneficio de la duda 1987, Carmen Carmen 1988, La Truhana 1992, Los Bellos Durmientes 1994, Café Cantante 1997, Las manzanas del viernes 2000; novels: El Manuscrito Carmesí 1990, La Pasión Turca 1993, Más Allá del Jardín 1995, La Regla de Tres 1996, El Corazón Tardío 1998, Las Afuneras de Dios 1999, El imposible olvido 2001, Los invitados al jardin 2002, El dueño de la herida 2003, El pedestal de las estatuas 2007; poetry: Enemigo Intimo 1959, 11 Sonetos de la Zubia 1981, Poemas Cordobeses 1994, Testamento andaluz 1994, Poemas de amor 1997, El poema de Tobías desangelado 2005; essays: Charlas con Troylo, La Soledad Sonora. *Address:* Fundación Antonio Gala, Calle Ambrosio de Morales, 20, 14003 Córdoba, Spain (office). *Telephone:* (957) 487395 (office). *Fax:* (957) 487423 (office). *E-mail:* info@fundacionantoniogala.org (office). *Website:* www.fundacionantoniogala.org (office).

GALADARI, Abdel-Wahab; United Arab Emirates business executive; b. 1938, Dubai; ed American Univ., Beirut; clerk with British Bank of Middle East, then admin. post with Dubai Electrical Co.; f. re-export business with brothers Abdel-Rahim and Abdel-Latif 1960, real estate co. cr. 1962; Dir Nat. Bank of Dubai 1965–69; left family business 1976; formed Union Bank of the Middle East 1977, Chair. –1983; Chair. A. W. Galadari Holdings and over 20 associated cos; Propr Hyatt Regency and Galadari Galleria hotels; sponsored 1980 Dubai Grand Prix motor race. *Address:* A. W. Galadari Group of Companies, P.O. Box 22, Dubai, United Arab Emirates.

GALAL, Mohamed Noman, BA, MA, PhD; Egyptian diplomatist and academic; *Advisor for Strategic International Studies and the Dialogue of Civilizations, Bahrain Center for Studies and Research;* b. 10 April 1943, Assiut; m. Kawther Elsherif 1969; two s.; ed Univ. of Cairo; joined Ministry of Foreign Affairs 1965; Third Sec., Embassy in Amman 1969–72; Vice-Consul, Kuwait 1972; Consul, Abu Dhabi 1972–73; Second Sec. Oslo 1975–79; Lecturer, Diplomatic Inst. 1979–80; First Sec. New Delhi 1980, Counsellor 1981–85; Counsellor, Cabinet of Deputy Prime Minister and Minister of Foreign Affairs 1985–87; Counsellor, Egyptian Mission at UN 1987–90, Minister and Deputy Perm. Rep. 1990–92; Perm. Rep. to League of Arab States, Cairo 1992–95; Amb. to Pakistan 1995–98, to People's Repub. of China 1998–2001; Visiting Lecturer, Farleigh Dickinson Univ., NJ, USA 1989–91, Univ. of Cairo 1994–95; fmr Deputy Dir Centre for Int. Studies, Univ. of Bahrain; currently Adviser for Strategic Int. Studies and Dialogue of Civilizations, Bahrain Center for Studies and Research; mem. Nat. Council on Human Rights, Egypt 2004–(10); St Olav Medal (Norway) 1972, Nat. Medal for Merit (Egypt) 1982. *Publications:* more than 40 publs in Arabic and English on Arab and int. affairs, foreign policy, human rights, Egypt, Middle East, Pakistan, China, non-alignment, Islam in a changing world, human rights and Islam, etc. *Leisure interests:* travelling, swimming. *Address:* Bahrain Centre for Studies and Research, POB 496, Manama, Bahrain (office). *Telephone:* (17) 756270 (office); (17) 625072 (home). *Fax:* (17) 754835 (office); (17) 623492 (home). *E-mail:* mjalal@bcsr.gov.bh (office); galal_m@hotmail.com (home). *Website:* www.bcsr.gov.bh (office); mohamed-n-galal.com (home).

GALANOS, James; American fashion designer (retd); b. 20 Sept. 1924, Philadelphia, Pa; s. of Gregory Galanos and Helen Galanos (née Gorgoliatos); ed Traphagen School of Fashion, New York 1943; began career selling sketches to New York clothing mfrs; worked for Hattie Carnegie 1944; asst to Jean Louis, head designer, Columbia Studios, Hollywood 1946–47; apprentice, Robert Piguet, Paris 1947–48; designer, Davidow, New York 1949–50; est. own business, Galanos Originals, Beverly Hills, Calif. 1951–63, LA 1963–; produced collection of couture-quality furs in collaboration with Neustadter Furs 1968; designed costumes for Rosalind Russell in films Never Wave at a WAC, 1952 and Oh Dad, Poor Dad, Mama's Hung You in the Closet and I'm Feeling So Sad 1967; retrospective exhbns LA Co. Museum of Art 1974, 1997, Inst. of Tech., New York 1976, Western Reserve Historical Soc. 1996, LA Co. Museum of Art 1997; designed Inaugural Gown worn by Nancy Reagan 1981; work represented in perm. collections including Metropolitan Museum of Art, New York, Smithsonian Inst. Washington and Art Inst. of Chicago; Council of Fashion Designers of America Lifetime Achievement Award 1985 and numerous fashion awards. *Leisure interests:* collecting art books, music, reading, architecture. *Address:* 1316 Sunset Plaza Drive, Los Angeles, CA 90069-1235 (office); 2254 South Sepulveda Blvd., Los Angeles, CA 90064, USA. *Telephone:* (213) 272-1445. *Fax:* (310) 473-6725.

GALANTE, Edward G., BSc; American oil industy executive; *Senior Vice-President, Exxon Mobil Corporation;* b. Inwood, NY; ed Northeastern Univ.; joined Exxon Co. 1972, Man. Baton Rouge Refinery, LA 1988, CEO and Gen. Man. Esso Caribbean and Central America 1992, Exec. Asst to Chair. Exxon Corpn 1995, Chair. and Man. Dir Esso (Thailand) Public Co. Ltd, Bangkok 1997, Exec. Vice Pres. Exxon Mobil Chemical Co., Houston, TX 1999, Sr Vice Pres. Exxon Mobil Corpn 2001–; Vice Chair. US Council for Int. Business (USCIB) 2004–; Dir Nat. Council, Northeastern Univ., Council for the US and Italy, Council of the Americas, Jr Achievement Int., US–China Business Council. *Address:* Exxon Mobil Corpn, 5959 Las Colinas Boulevard, Irving, TX 75039-2298, USA (office). *Telephone:* (972) 444-1000 (office). *Fax:* (972) 444-1350 (office). *Website:* www.exxonmobil.com (office).

GALASSI, Jonathan White, MA; American publishing executive; *President, Farrar, Straus & Giroux Inc.;* b. 4 Nov. 1949, Seattle, Wash.; s. of Gerard Goodwin Galassi and Dorothea Johnston Galassi (née White); m. Susan Grace Galassi 1975; two d.; ed Harvard Univ. and Univ. of Cambridge, UK; Ed. Houghton Mifflin Co., Boston, New York 1973–81; Sr Ed. Random House, Inc., New York 1981–86; Exec. Ed. and Vice-Pres. Farrar, Straus & Giroux Inc., New York 1986–87, Ed.-in-Chief and Sr Vice-Pres. 1988–93, Exec. Vice-Pres. 1993–99, Publr 1999–, Pres. 2002–; Poetry Ed. Paris Review 1978–88; Guggenheim Fellow 1989; mem. Acad. of American Poets (Dir 1990–2002, Pres. 1994–99, Chair. 1999–2002, Hon. Chair. 2002–); Fellow, American Acad. of Arts and Sciences 2002; Roger Klein Award for Editing, PEN 1984, Award in Literature, American Acad. of Arts and Letters 2000. *Publications:* Morning Run (poetry) 1988, The Second Life of Art: Selected Essays of Eugenio Montale (ed., trans.) 1982, Otherwise: Last and First Poems of Eugenio Montale (ed., trans.) 1986, Eugenio Montale, Collected Poems 1916–56 (ed., trans.) 1998, North Street (poetry) 2000, Eugenio Montale, Postumous Diary 2001. *Address:* Farrar, Straus & Giroux Inc., 18 W 18th Street, New York, NY 10011, USA (office). *Telephone:* (212) 741-6900 (office). *Website:* www.fsgbooks.com (office).

GALATERI DI GENOLA, Count Gabriele, DIur, MBA; Italian business executive; *Chairman, Telecom Italia SpA;* b. 11 Jan. 1947, Rome; s. of Gen. Angelo Galateri di Genola and Carla Fontana; m. Evelina Christillin; one d.; ed Liceo Ennio Quirino Visconti, Rome, Univ. of Rome, Columbia Univ., New York; Asst Lecturer in Econ. Science, Univ. of Rome 1969–70; Head Financial Analysis Dept, later Int. Financing Dept, Banco di Roma 1971–74; Financial Dir Saint Gobain, Italy, then Asst to Financial Group Dir, Paris 1974–77; Head of Foreign Finance Div., Fiat SpA 1977–83, Financial Dir 1983–86, CEO 2002–03; CEO Ifil SpA 1986–93; CEO and Gen. Man. IFI 1993–2002; Chair.

Mediobanca SpA 2003–07; Chair. Telecom Italia SpA 2007–; Vice-Chair. Assicurazioni Generali SpA, RCS MediaGroup SpA; Dir (non-exec.) Banca Esperia SpA, Banca CRS SpA, Italmobiliare SpA, Fiera di Genova SpA, European Inst. of Oncology SpA, Accor SA; Cavaliere del Lavoro. *Leisure interests:* arts, music, tennis, skiing, gym. *Address:* Telecom Italia SpA, Piazza degli Affari 2, 20123 Milan, Italy (office). *Telephone:* (02) 85951 (office). *Fax:* (02) 85954018 (office). *E-mail:* info@telecomitalia.it (office). *Website:* www .telecomitalia.it (office).

GALAYR, Ali Khalif; Somali politician; fmr business exec.; Prime Minister of Somalia 2000–01. *Address:* c/o Office of the Prime Minister, c/o People's Palace, Mogadishu, Somalia (office).

GALE, Gwendoline Fay, AO, PhD, DUniv; Australian geographer and fmr university vice-chancellor; b. (Gwendoline Fay Gilding), 13 June 1932, Balaklava, S Australia; d. of George Jasper Gilding and Kathleen Gertrude Pengelley; one s. one d.; ed Methodist Ladies' Coll., Univ. of Adelaide, S Australia; Lecturer, then Sr Lecturer, Univ. of Adelaide 1966–74, Reader 1975–77, Prof. of Geography 1978–89, Pro-Vice-Chancellor 1988–89, Prof. Emer. 1989–; Australian Heritage Commr 1989–95; Vice-Chancellor Univ. of Western Australia 1990–97; Pres. Inst. of Australian Geographers 1989–90; Chair. Social Justice Advisory Cttee 1989; Chair. Festival of Perth 1992–97; Chair. West Australian Symphony Orchestra 1995–97; Pres. Australian Vice-Chancellors Cttee 1996–97; Pres. Acad. of Social Sciences in Australia 1998–2000; Pres. Asscn Asian Social Science Councils 2001–03; Elin Wagner Fellowship 1971, Catherine Helen Spence Fellowship 1972, Fellow, Acad. of Social Sciences of Australia 1978; mem. Nat. Comm. of UNESCO, Australia 1999–, Australian Research Council 1999–2001; Hon. Life mem. Inst. of Australian Geographers 1994, Hon. Fellow, Acad. of Social Sciences of Australia 2001–, Hon. Fellow, Asscn for Tertiary Educ. Man. 2003; Hon. DLitt (Western Australia) 1998; British Council Award 1972, John Lewis Gold Medal 2000, Griffith Taylor Medal 2001. *Publications:* Women's Role in Aboriginal Society (ed.) 1970, Urban Aborigines 1972, Race Relations in Australia: the Aboriginal situation 1975, Poverty Among Aboriginal Families in Adelaide 1975, We are Bosses Ourselves: the Status and Role of Aboriginal Women Today (ed.) 1983, Tourists and the National Estate: Procedures to protect Australia's Heritage 1987, Aboriginal Youth and the Criminal Justice System: the Injustice of Justice 1990, Inventing Places: Studies in Cultural Geography 1991, Changing Australia 1991, Boyer Lectures 1991, Juvenile Justice: Debating the Issues 1993, Tourism and the Protection of Aboriginal Sites 1994, Cultural Geographies 1999, Making Space: Women and Education at St Aloysius College Adelaide 1880–2000 (ed.) 2000, Youth in Transition: The Challenges of Generational Change in Asia (ed.) 2005. *Leisure interests:* music, theatre, reading. *Address:* c/o Office of the Vice-Chancellor, The University of Adelaide, Adelaide, S Australia 5005, Australia.

GALE, Michael Denis, PhD, FRS; British plant research scientist and academic; *John Innes Foundation Emeritus Fellow, John Innes Centre;* b. 25 Aug. 1943, Wolverhampton; s. of Sydney Ralph Gale and Helen Mary Gale (née Johnston); m. Susan Heathcote Rosbotham 1979; two d.; ed West Buckland School, Barnstaple, Univ. of Birmingham, Univ. Coll. Wales, Aberystwyth; Researcher, Plant Breeding Inst. (subsequently Agric. and Food Research Council, Inst. of Plant Science Research), Cambridge 1968–86, Head Cereals Research Dept and Individual Merit Sr Prin. Scientific Officer, Cambridge Lab. 1986–92, Head Cambridge Lab., Norwich 1992–94; Research Dir John Innes Centre, Norwich 1994–98, Acting Dir Sept.–Dec. 1998, Dir 1999, Assoc. Research Dir 1999–2003, John Innes Foundation Emer. Fellow 2003–; John Innes Prof., Univ. of E Anglia 1999–2003, Professorial Fellow in the School of Biological Sciences 2003–; mem. CGIAR Science Council, Rome 2004–; Chair. Int. Advisory Bd to the Chinese Acad. of Agricultural Science 2007–; Farrer Memorial Bicentennial Fellow, NSW Dept of Agric. 1989; Adviser, Inst. of Genetics, Beijing 1992; Foreign Fellow, Chinese Acad. of Eng 1998; Hon. Research Prof., Inst. of Crop Germplasm Resources, Academia Sinica 1992; Dr hc (Norwegian Univ. of Life Sciences) 2005; Hon. DSc (Birmingham); Research Medal, Royal Agric. Soc. of England 1994, Rank Prize for Nutrition 1997, Darwin Medal 1998. *Publications:* 300 scientific papers and articles on plant genetics and cytogenetics, especially dwarfism, quality and comparative genome research in wheat. *Leisure interest:* golf. *Address:* John Innes Centre, Norwich Research Park, Colney, Norwich, NR4 7UH (office); 9 Mount Pleasant, Norwich, NR2 2DG, England (home). *Telephone:* (1603) 450599 (office). *Fax:* (1603) 450024 (office). *E-mail:* mike .gale@bbsrc.ac.uk (office).

GALEA, Censu; Maltese politician and architect; *Minister for Competitiveness and Communications;* b. 28 Aug. 1956; s. of Joseph Galea; m. Grace Sammut; two s. two d.; ed Lyceum and Univ. of Malta; practising architect 1982; Sec.-Gen. then Pres. of Nationalist Party Youth Section 1978–81; MP (Nationalist Party) 1987–; Parl. Sec. Ministry for Social Security 1992–94; Minister for Food, Agric. and Fisheries 1994–96, for Transport and Communications 1998–2004, for Competitiveness and Communications 2004–; Shadow Minister and Opposition Spokesman for Transport and Ports 1996–98, Sec. and Whip Nationalist Party Parl. Group 1997–98. *Address:* Ministry for Competitiveness and Communications, Casa Leoni, St Joseph High Road, St Venera, CMR 02, Malta. *Telephone:* 21485100 (office). *Fax:* 21493744 (office). *E-mail:* info.mtc@gov.mt (home). *Website:* www.mtc.gov.mt (office).

GALEA, Louis, LLD; Maltese politician and lawyer; *Minister of Education;* b. 2 Jan. 1948, Mqabba; s. of Joseph Galea and Joan Galea (née Farrugia); m. Vincienne Zammit 1977; one s. three d.; mem. Gen. Council and Exec. Cttee Nationalist Party 1972–; Gen. Sec. 1977–87; mem. Parl. 1976–; Minister for Social Policy including Health 1987–92, for Home Affairs and Social Development including Health 1992–95, Minister for Social Devt 1995–96; Shadow

Minister for Educ. 1996–98; Minister of Educ. 1998–. *Leisure interests:* reading, music, tennis. *Address:* Ministry of Education, Floriana CMR02, Malta. *Telephone:* (21) 231374. *Fax:* (21) 230451.

GALEYEV, Albert Abubakirovich, DR.PHYS.MATH.SC.; Russian/Bashkir physicist; *Director, Institute of Space Research, Russian Academcy of Sciences;* b. 19 Oct. 1940, Ufa; m.; two c.; ed Univ. of Novosibirsk; worked at USSR Acad. of Sciences Inst. of Nuclear Physics 1961–70; Sr researcher at Acad. of Sciences Inst. of High Temperatures 1970–73; mem. CPSU 1976–91; Corresp. mem. USSR (now Russian) Acad. of Sciences 1987–92, mem. 1992; Head of Section at Acad. of Sciences Inst. of Space Research 1973–88, Dir 1988–; Ed.-in-Chief Earth Research from Space; Lenin Prize 1984, Order the Badge of Honour 2002. *Publications:* works on physics of plasma and cosmic physics. *Address:* Institute of Space Research, Profsoyuznaya 84/32, 117810 Moscow, Russia (office). *Telephone:* (095) 333-25-88 (office); (095) 135-10-94 (home). *Fax:* (095) 333-33-11 (office). *E-mail:* agaleyev@iki.rssi.ru (office).

GALGUT, Damon; South African playwright and novelist; b. 1963, Pretoria; ed Univ. of Cape Town; CNA Award 1992. *Plays:* Echoes of Anger, Party for Mother, Alive and Kicking, The Green's Keeper. *Publications:* novels: Echoes of Anger: And No.1 Utopia Lane 1983, A Sinless Season 1984, Small Circle of Beings 1988, The Beautiful Screaming of Pigs 1991, The Quarry 1995, The Good Doctor (Commonwealth Writers Prize Africa Region Best Book Award 2004) 2003, The Impostor 2008. *Address:* Peake Associates, 14 Grafton Crescent, London, NW1 8SL, England (office). *Telephone:* (20) 7267-8033 (office). *Fax:* (20) 7267-8033 (office). *E-mail:* tony@tonypeake.com (office). *Website:* www.tonypeake.com (office).

GALIBIN, Aleksander Vladimirovich; Russian actor and theatre director; b. 28 Sept. 1955, Leningrad; m.; three d.; ed Leningrad State Inst. of Theatre, Music and Cinematography, A. Vasilyev Drama School, Moscow; actor, Komissarzhevskaya Drama Theatre 1977–79; Stage Dir Aleksandrinsky Theatre 1995–; worked as stage dir in various St Petersburg theatres 1990–; Meritorious Artist of the RSFSR 1991. *Films include:* acted in more than 35 films 1976–, including Pyatnitskaya Street, Courage, Silver Strings, Letters from the Front, Red Crown, Ragin 2004, Master and Margarita 2005, The First Rule of the Queen 2005, Him, Her and Me 2007, Revenge 2007, 40 2007. *Theatre includes:* (stage dir) Three Sisters, Harp of Greeting, City Romance, Pupil, Tsar Piotr and His Dead Son Aleksey. *Address:* Griboyedova Canal 115, Apt 9, 190088 St Petersburg, Russia. *Telephone:* (812) 114-16-80.

GALIL, Zvi, BSc, MSc, PhD; Israeli computer scientist, academic and university administrator; *President, Tel-Aviv University;* b. 26 June 1947, Tel-Aviv; m. Bella Gorenstein Galil; one s.; ed Tel-Aviv Univ., Cornell Univ., USA; conducted postdoctoral research at IBM Thomas J. Watson Research Center, Yorktown Heights, NY 1975; faculty mem. Computer Science Dept, Tel-Aviv Univ. 1976–81, Full Prof. 1981–95, Dept Chair. 1979–82; Prof., Dept of Computer Science, Columbia Univ., New York City 1982–2006, Chair. Dept of Computer Science 1989–94, Julian Clarence Levi Prof. of Math. Methods and Computer Science, School of Eng and Applied Sciences 1987–2006, Dean Fu Foundation School of Engineering and Applied Sciences, Columbia Univ. 1995–2006; Pres. Tel-Aviv Univ. 2007–; Area Ed. Journal of the ACM (Asscn for Computing Machinery) 1984–2004; Ed. in Chief Journal of Algorithms 1988–2004; Man. Ed. SIAM (Soc. for Industrial and Applied Math.) Journal on Computing 1991–97; Chief Computer Science Adviser in the US to Oxford Univ. Press 1992–2003; mem. Nat. Acad. of Eng 2004–; Fellow, American Acad. of Arts and Sciences 2005–, Asscn for Computing Machinery 1995; Dir Guglielmo Marconi Int. Fellowship Foundation 1997–; Guarantor, Italian Acad. for Advance Studies in America 1997–; Pupin Medal 2005. *Publications:* Combinatorial Algorithms on Words (co-ed.) 1985, SIAM Journal of Computing Special Issue on Cryptography (ed.) 1988, Theory of Computing and Systems, Lecture Notes in Computer Science 601 (co-ed.) 1992, Combinatorial Pattern Matching III, Lecture Notes in Computer Science 644 (co-ed.) 1992, Pattern Matching Algorithms (co-ed.) 1997; has written more than 200 scientific papers. *Leisure interests:* . *Address:* Office of the President, Tel-Aviv University, Ramat-Aviv, 69978 Tel-Aviv, Israel (office). *Telephone:* (3) 6407777 (office). *Fax:* (3) 6408601 (office). *Website:* www.tau.ac.il (office).

GALIMOV, Erik Mikhailovich, PhD, DSc; Russian geochemist; *Director, V. I. Vernadsky Institute of Geochemistry and Analytical Chemistry, Russian Academy of Sciences;* b. 29 July 1936, Vladivostok; s. of Mikhail Piskunov and Zeya Galimova; m. 1st; one d.; m. 2nd Galina Andriukhina; two d.; ed Moscow Inst. of Oil and Gas; operational engineer 1959–60; head of geophysics expeditions 1960–63; sr researcher 1965–73; Dir V. I. Vernadsky Inst. of Geochemistry and Analytical Chem. 1992– (Head of Lab. 1973–92); Prof., Moscow State Univ.; Chair. Geochemistry Council of Russian Acad. of Sciences, Int. Lunar Exploration Working Group; Vice-Pres. Int. Asscn of Geochemical Cosmochemistry 1996–2000, Pres. 2000–04; Ed.-in-Chief International Geochemistry; mem. Editorial Bd Chemical Geology, Astrobiology; Corresp. mem. USSR (now Russian) Acad. of Sciences 1991, mem. 1994–, mem. Presidium 2002–, Chair. Meteorite Cttee; Foreign mem. German Acad. of Sciences and Literature 1998; Geochemical Fellow 1998; research in geochemistry of stable isotopes, organic geochemistry and oil and gas geology, lunar and planetary research, origin of life; Order of Honour 1988, 1996; Vernadsky Prize 1984, Alfred Treibs Medal 2004. *Achievement:* developed theory of ordered isotope distribution in biological systems, devt of isotope thermodynamics, cavitational synthesis of diamond, isotope identification of oil and gas sources, new concept of sustaining ordering as a mechanism of life emerging and evolution, new model of Earth and the Moon formation as a twin system. *Publications:* more than 400 scientific works including Geochemistry of Stable Carbon Isotopes 1968, Carbon Isotopes in Oil and Gas Geology 1973, Biological Isotope Fractionation 1985, Sources and Mechanism of Formation of Natural Gases 1988, Kimberlite Magmatism and Diamond Formation 1991,

Evolution of the Biosphere 1995, Origin of the Moon 1996. *Address:* V. I. Vernadsky Institute of Geochemistry and Analytical Chemistry, Kosygin Street 19, 119991 Moscow (office); Nikitski Blvd 5–5, 119019 Moscow, Russia (home). *Telephone:* (495) 137-41-27 (office); (495) 291-48-60 (home). *Fax:* (495) 938-20-54 (home). *E-mail:* galimov@geokhi.ru (office). *Website:* www.geokhi.ru/eng (office).

GALIN, Alexander; Russian playwright, actor and film and theatre director; b. (Aleksandr Mikhailovich Pourer), 10 Sept. 1947, Rostovskya oblast (USSR); s. of Mikhail Pourer and Lubov Pourer; m. Galina Alekseyevna Pourer 1970; one s.; ed Inst. of Culture, Leningrad; factory worker, later actor in puppet theatre; freelance writer 1978–; Amb. of the Arts, Fla 1989. *Plays include:* The Wall 1971, Here Fly the Birds 1974, The Hole 1975, The Roof 1976, Retro 1979, The Eastern Tribune 1980, Stars in the Morning Sky 1982, The Toastmaster 1983, Jeanne 1986, Sorry 1990, The Title 1991, The Czech Photo 1993, The Clown and the Bandit 1996, The Anomaly 1996, Sirena and Victoria 1997, The Competition 1998; plays translated into several languages include Stars in the Morning Sky (selected plays translated into English) 1989, The Group 1995, Rendez-Vous in the Sea of Rain 2002, New Logic 2005, The Companions 2008, Dzinrikisya 2009. *Film:* Casanova's Coat (The Delegation) (scriptwriter and dir), Photo (scriptwriter, actor and dir) 2003, My Last Will (screenplay) 2004, The Heathen (screenplay) 2005, The Casualty (scriptwriter and dir) 2008. *Publication:* Selected Plays 1989. *Address:* Gorohowsky pereulok 15, Apt 11, 103064 Moscow, Russia (home). *Telephone:* (499) 267-70-21 (home). *Fax:* (499) 267-70-21 (home). *E-mail:* agalin@online.ru (home). *Website:* www.webcenter.ru/~agalin (home).

GALJAARD, Hans, MD, PhD; Dutch professor of cell biology (retd); b. 8 April 1935, Leiden; m. Henriette H. van Boven 1960; two s. one d.; ed State Univ. Leiden; radiobiology training at Medical Biology Lab. Nat. Defence Org. Rijswijk 1962–65 and Atomic Energy Research Establishment, Harwell, England 1965; Prof. of Cell Biology, Erasmus Univ. Rotterdam 1966; Chair. Dept of Clinical Genetics, Univ. Hosp. 1980; Dir Rotterdam Foundation of Clinical Genetics 1980; mem. Nat. Health Council, Nat. Council for Science Policy, Advisory Council on Tech.; consultant for WHO and UNFPA; mem. Royal Dutch Acad. of Sciences 1984–, Acad. Europaea; Hon. mem. Dutch Soc. for Human Genetics, Indian Soc. for Prenatal Diagnosis and Therapy; Carter Memorial Medal, British Clincial Genetics Soc. *Publications:* The Life of the Dutchman 1981; some 400 articles in scientific journals, book chapters and monographs. *Leisure interests:* writing, filming, sailing. *Address:* c/o Department of Cell Biology and Genetics, Erasmus University, P.O. Box 1738, 3000 DR Rotterdam, Netherlands.

GALL, Hugues R.; French opera house director; b. 18 March 1940, Honfleur; s. of Max Gall and Geneviève Carel; ed Inst. des Sciences Politiques, Sorbonne; fmr official, Ministries of Agric., Educ. and Culture; Sec.-Gen. Réunion des Théâtres Lyriques 1969–73; Deputy Dir-Gen. Paris Opéra 1973–80; Dir-Gen. Grand Theatre, Geneva 1980–94; Dir-Gen. Paris Opéra 1995–2004; Chair. Bd of Dirs Institut pour le Financement du Cinéma et des Industries Culturelles 2004–; Conseiller d'État 2004–; Dir École du Louvre 2004–, Fondation Noureev 2004–, Fondation d'entreprisede Veolia Environnement 2004–, Théâtre de l'Opéra-Comique 2004–; Pres. Orchestre Français des Jeunes 2007–; elected mem. Acad. des Beaux-Arts, Inst. de France 2002; Officier des Palmes académiques, Chevalier du Mérite agricole, Commdr des Arts et des Lettres, Légion d'honneur, Ordre nat. du Mérite, Bourgeois d'honneur de Genève, Switzerland; Prix Montaigne 1996, Prix Grand Siècle-Laurent Perrier 1999, Médaille Beaumarchais de la SACD 2004.

GALL, Joseph Grafton, BS, PhD; American biologist and academic; *Professor, Department of Embryology, Carnegie Institution;* b. 14 April 1928, Washington, DC; s. of the late John C. Gall and Elsie Gall (née Rosenberger); m. 1st Dolores M. Hogge 1955; one s. one d.; m. 2nd Diane M. Dwyer 1982; ed Yale Univ.; Instructor, Asst Prof., Assoc. Prof., Prof., Dept of Zoology, Univ. of Minnesota 1952–64; Prof. of Biology and Molecular Biophysics and Biochem., Yale Univ. 1964–83; mem. staff Dept of Embryology, Carnegie Inst. 1983–, American Cancer Soc. Prof. of Developmental Genetics 1984 (lifetime appointment); mem. Cell Biology Study Section, NIH 1963–67, Chair. 1972–74; Pres. American Soc. for Cell Biology 1968, Soc. for Developmental Biology 1984–85; mem. Bd of Scientific Counsellors, Nat. Inst. of Child Health and Human Devt, NIH 1986–90; mem. Bd of Scientific Advisers, Jane Coffin Childs Memorial Fund for Medical Research 1986–94; Visiting Prof., St Andrews Univ., UK 1960, 1968, Univ. of Leicester 1971; Visiting Scientist, Max Planck Inst., Tübingen, Germany 1960; mem. NAS, AAAS, American Acad. of Arts and Sciences, American Philosophical Soc., Accad. Naz. dei Lincei (Rome) 1988; Fellow, Yale Corpn 1989–95; Hon. DrMed (Charles Univ., Prague) 2002; E. B. Wilson Medal, American Soc. for Cell Biology 1983, Wilbur Cross Medal of Yale Univ. 1988, AAAS Mentor Award for Lifetime Achievement 1996, Jan E. Purkyne Medal, Czech Acad. of Science 1999, Lifetime Achievement Award, Soc. for Developmental Biology 2004, Albert Lasker Special Achievement in Medical Science Award 2006, Louisa Gross Horwitz Prize (co-recipient) 2007. *Publications:* scientific articles on chromosome structure, nucleic acid biochemistry, cell fine structure, organelles of the cell. *Leisure interest:* collecting books on the history of biology. *Address:* Department of Embryology, Carnegie Institution, 3520 San Martin Drive, Baltimore, MD 21218 (office); 107 Bellemore Road, Baltimore, MD 21210, USA (home). *Telephone:* (410) 246-3017 (office). *Fax:* (410) 243-6311 (office). *E-mail:* gall@ciwemb.edu (office). *Website:* www.ciwemb.edu (office).

GALLAGHER, Conrad; Irish chef and restaurateur; *Group Executive Chef, Sun International Group;* b. Letterkenny, Donegal; m. Domini Kemp; one c.; began career working in Great Northern Hotel, Bundoran and Renvale House, Connemara; moved to New York aged 17, chef at Queen's Restaurant, Blue Street, then the Plaza Hotel, then Waldorf Astoria Hotel; chef at Hotel de Paris, Monte Carlo; founder and fmr owner Peacock Alley restaurant and Lloyd's Brasserie, Dublin, Conrad Gallagher, London; arrested on four counts for theft of three paintings from Fitzwilliam Hotel, Dublin, found not guilty 2003; currently Group Exec. Chef, Sun Int. Group; Best Irish Chef 1994, Michelin Star 1998. *Television:* Conrad's Kitchen, BBC Food Channel. *Publications:* New Irish Cooking, One Pot Wonders, Take 6 Ingredients: Simple Ideas Make Delicious Meals 2003. *Address:* Cape Town, POB 157, Green Point, Cape Town 8051, South Africa. *Telephone:* (21) 4346100. *Fax:* (21) 4346106. *E-mail:* conrad@conradgallagherfood.com. *Website:* www.conradgallagherfood.com.

GALLAGHER, Liam (William John Paul); British singer, musician (guitar, keyboards) and producer; b. 21 Sept. 1972, Burnage, Manchester; s. of Peggy Gallagher; brother of Noel Gallagher (q.v.); m. 1st Patsy Kensit 1997 (divorced 2000); one s.; one d. (with Lisa Moorish); m. 2nd Nicole Appleton; one s.; ed St Mark's High School, Didsbury, Manchester; founder mem., Oasis 1991–; f. and recorded for Big Brother Records 2000–; numerous concert and festival appearances; regular tours UK, Europe and USA; Q Awards for Best New Act 1994, Best Live Act 1995, BRIT Awards for Best Newcomers 1995, Best Single, Best Video, Best British Group 1996, NME Awards for Best UK Band, Artist of the Year 2003, Q Award for Best Act in the World Today 2006, BRIT Award for Outstanding Contribution to Music 2007. *Recordings include:* albums: Definitely Maybe 1994, (What's The Story) Morning Glory? (BRIT Award for Best Album 1996) 1995, Be Here Now 1997, The Masterplan 1998, Standing On The Shoulder of Giants 2000, Familiar To Millions (live) 2001, Heathen Chemistry 2002, Don't Believe The Truth (Q Award for Best Album) 2005, Stop the Clocks 2006, Dig Out Your Soul 2008. *Address:* Ignition Management, 54 Linhope Street, London, NW1 6HL, England (office). *Telephone:* (20) 7298-6000 (office). *Fax:* (20) 7258-0962 (office). *E-mail:* mail@ignition-man.co.uk (office). *Website:* www.oasisinet.com.

GALLAGHER, Noel David Thomas; British singer, songwriter and musician (guitar); b. 29 May 1967, Burnage, Manchester; s. of Peggy Gallagher; brother of Liam Gallagher (q.v.); m. Meg Matthews 1997 (divorced 2001); one d.; pnr Sara MacDonald; one s.; fmrly worked as guitar technician for Inspiral Carpets 1990–93; mem., Oasis 1991–; f. and recorded for Big Brother Records 2000–; numerous concert and festival appearances; regular tours UK, Europe and USA; founder Sour Mash Records 2001–; mem. Tailgunner; Q Awards for Best New Act 1994, Best Live Act 1995, BRIT Awards for Best Newcomers 1995, Best Single, Best Video, Best British Group 1996, Ivor Novello Award 1995, Music Week Award for Top Songwriter 1996, Grammy Award for Best Song (Wonderwall) 1997, NME Awards for Best UK Band, Artist of the Year 2003, Q Award for Best Act in the World Today 2006, BRIT Award for Outstanding Contribution to Music 2007. *Recordings include:* albums: Definitely Maybe 1994, (What's The Story) Morning Glory? (BRIT Award for Best Album 1996) 1995, Be Here Now 1997, The Masterplan 1998, Standing On The Shoulder of Giants 2000, Familiar To Millions (live) 2001, Heathen Chemistry 2002, Don't Believe The Truth (Q Award for Best Album) 2005, Stop the Clocks 2006, Dig Out Your Soul 2008. *Leisure interest:* supporting Manchester City. *Address:* Ignition Management, 54 Linhope Street, London, NW1 6HL, England (office). *Telephone:* (20) 7298-6000 (office). *Fax:* (20) 7258-0962 (office). *E-mail:* mail@ignition-man.co.uk (office). *Website:* www.oasisinet.com.

GALLAND, Yves; French politician and business executive; *President, Boeing France;* b. 8 March 1941; s. of Jean Galland and Suzanne Vershave; m. Anne Marie Chauvin 1967; one s. two d.; pres. of publishing and publicity cos 1969; mem. European Parl. 1979–, Vice-Pres. 1989–91; Deputy Mayor of Paris in charge of housing 1983–95, of architecture 1995–1998; Minister of Local Affairs and Decentralization 1986–88, of Industry 1995, of Finance and Foreign Trade 1995–97; Pres. Valoise Radical Party 1988–94; mem. nat. council Union pour la démocratie française (UDF), del. to Paris 1979, mem. Nat. Political Bureau 1984–, Pres. Liberal Group, European Parl. 1991–94; Pres. UDF Group 1998–; Chair. European Assistance Group 2000–; Vice-Pres. Int. Relations Boeing Corpn 2003–, Pres. Boeing France 2003–. *Address:* 6 rue des Haudriettes, 75003 Paris; European Assistance, 1 Promenade de la Bonnette, 92230 Gennevilliers, France (office).

GALLEGOS, Carlos M., BS (Econs), MA; Peruvian economist and international organization executive; *Executive Secretary, Inter-American Committee on Ports (Comisión Interamericana de Puertos—CIP);* m.; two c.; ed Universidad La Molina, Lima, Univ. of East Anglia, UK; was involved with Peru's regional econ. integration process, served in govt agencies as Country Economist, Dir of Econ. Studies, Trade Sr Advisor and Financial Advisor to Andean Financial Corpn (CAF), among others; joined OAS in 1980, has served in high-level positions in int. trade, customs and other trade facilitation areas, Exec. Sec. Inter-American Cttee on Ports (Comisión Interamericana de Puertos—CIP), OAS, Washington, DC 1993–, OAS Rep. to IMO, Int. Asscn of Ports and Harbors, American Asscn of Port Authorities and other int. maritime port orgs; lectures at univs and grad. academic centres in Latin America and Spain. *Publications:* numerous papers, studies and articles in professional journals. *Address:* Inter-American Committee on Ports, 1889 F Street, NW, Suite 695, Washington, DC 20006, USA (office). *Telephone:* (202) 458-3871 (office). *Fax:* (202) 458-3517 (office). *E-mail:* cgallegos@oas.org (office). *Website:* www.oas.org/cip (office).

GALLEY, Robert; French politician and engineer; b. 11 Jan. 1921, Paris; s. of Léon and André (neé Habrial) Galley; m. Jeanne Leclerc de Hauteclocque 1960; two s.; ed Lycée Louis-le-Grand, Paris, Lycée Hoche, Versailles, Ecole centrale des arts et manufactures and Ecole Nat. Supérieure du pétrole et des moteurs; engineer, Soc. chérifienne des pétroles 1950–54; in Commissariat à l'Energie atomique 1955–66; Adviser on information tech. to Prime Minister 1966–68; Pres. Institut de recherche d'informatique (IRIA) 1967; mem. Nat.

Ass. (representing L'Aube) 1968–78, 1981, RPR Deputy to Nat. Ass. for L'Aube 1981–; Treasurer RPR 1984–90; fmr Minister holding various portfolios, including Infrastructure and Housing, Scientific Research, Posts and Tele-communications, Transport, the Armed Forces and Devt Co-operation; Mayor of Troyes 1972–95; Chair. Comité de bassin Seine-Normandie 1987–; Pres. l'Office parlementaire d'évaluation des choix scientifiques et technologique-s(Parl. Office for Scientific and Tech. Evaluation) 1996–; Bd Dir Caisse Nationale de l'Industrie 1988–; mem. Comm. de la production et des échanges; mem. French del. to Council of Europe Consultative Ass. 1988; Commdr, Légion d'honneur, Compagnon de la Libération, Croix de guerre (1939–45). *Address:* L'Office Parlementaire d'Evaluation des Choix Scientifiques et Technologiques, Assemblée nationale, 75355 Paris; 18 boulevard Victor Hugo, 10000 Troyes, France.

GALLIANO, John Charles, CBE; British fashion designer; b. 28 Nov. 1960, Gilbraltar; s. of John J. Galliano and Anita Guillen; ed Wilsons Grammar School and St Martin's School of Art; moved to London 1966; designer collections 1985–; worked on Courtelle project 1985; first British designer ever to show collection in Paris at the Louvre during Paris Fashion Week 1990; moved to Paris and introduced Galliano's Girl 1991; designer of costumes for Ballet Rambert 1990, Kylie Minogue's UK tour 1991; Chief Designer Givenchy 1995–96, Christian Dior 1996–; launched 'galliano' womenswear collection 2007; Designer of Year Award (British Council) 1987, 1994, 1995, 1997 (jt winner), Int. Womenswear Designer of the Year, CFDA 1997, VH1 Women-swear Designer of the Year 1997, Int. Designer Award, Council of Fashion Designers of America 1998 and other awards. *Address:* John Galliano, 384-386 rue St. Honoré, 75001, Paris; 60 rue d'Avron, 75020 Paris; Christian Dior, 90 Avenue Montaigne, 75008 Paris, France (office). *Telephone:* 1-55-35-40-40. *Website:* www.johngalliano.com.

GALLINGER, Yuri Yiosifovich, DrMed; German surgeon; *Head, Department of Endoscopic Surgery, B. V. Petrovsky National Research Center for Surgery;* b. 3 Sept. 1939, Krasnaarmejsk, Saratov Region, Russian Feder-ation; s. of Joseph Gallinger and Yekaterina Roor; m.; one s.; ed Kishinev Inst. of Medicine; gen. practitioner in polyclinics, then in 59th Clinic Hosp., Moscow 1962–67; researcher Moscow Medical Univ., Head Dept of Endoscopic Surgery, B. V. Petrovsky Nat. Research Center for Surgery 1986–; Pres. Russian Scientific Soc. of Endoscopic Surgery; mem. European Asscn of Endoscopic Surgery, Pirogov Asscn of Surgeons, New York Acad. of Sciences; State Prize of Russian Fed. 1990. *Publications:* over 200 scientific publs. *Leisure interests:* detective films and literature. *Address:* National Research Center of Surgery, Abrikosovski per. 2, 1199924 Moscow, Russia (office). *Telephone:* (495) 248-13-75 (office). *Fax:* (495) 246-89-88 (office).

GALLO, Max Louis, DenH, DèsSc; French politician, writer and university teacher; b. 7 Jan. 1932, Nice; s. of Joseph Gallo and Mafalda Galeotti; ed Univ. de Paris and Inst. d'Etudes Politiques; teacher Lycée de Nice 1960–65; Sr Lecturer Univ. of Nice 1965–70; Gen. Ed. book series Ce Jour-là, l'Histoire que nous vivons, la Vie selon…, le Temps des révélations; contrib. to various newspapers; devised TV programme Destins du Siècle 1973; Deputy (Social-ist) for Alpes-Maritimes 1981–83; jr minister and Govt spokesman 1983–84; Ed. Matin de Paris newspaper 1985–86; MEP 1984–94; Nat. Sec. (Culture) Parti Socialiste 1988–90. *Publications:* L'Italie de Mussolini 1964, La Grande Peur de 1989 (as Max Laugham) 1966, L'Affaire d'Ethiopie 1967, Maximilien Robespierre, Histoire d'une solitude 1968, Gauchisme, réformisme et révolu-tion 1968, Histoire de l'Espagne franquiste 1969, Cinquième Colonne 1930–1940 1970, la Nuit des longs couteaux 1970, Tombeau pour la Commune, Histoire de l'Espagne franquiste 1971, Le Cortège des vainqueurs 1972, La Mafia, un pas vers la mer 1973, L'Affiche, miroir de l'Histoire (illustrated) 1973, L'Oiseau des origines 1974: La Baie des anges (vol. I) 1975, Le Palais des fêtes (vol. II) 1976, La Promenade des Anglais (vol. III) 1976, Le Pouvoir à vif, Despotisme, démocratie et révolution, Que sont les siècles pour la mer 1977, Les hommes naissent tous le même jour: Aurore (vol. I) 1978, Crépuscule (vol. II) 1979, Une affaire intime 1979, L'Homme Robespierre: histoire d'une solitude 1978, Un crime très ordinaire 1982, Garibaldi 1982, La Demeure des puissants 1983, La Troisième alliance, pour un nouvel individualisme, Le Grand Jaurès 1984, Le Beau Rivage 1985, Lettre ouverte à Maximilien Robespierre sur les nouveaux Muscadins, Belle Epoque 1986, Que passe la justice du roi, la Route Napoléon 1987, Jules Vallès 1988, Une Affaire publique 1989, Les Clés de l'histoire contemporaine 1989, Manifeste pour une fin de siècle obscure 1989, La Gauche est morte, vive la gauche! 1990, Le Regard des femmes 1991, La Fontaine des innocents (Prix Carlton 1992), Une femme rebelle: Vie et mort de Rosa Luxembourg 1992, L'Amour au temps des solitudes 1993, Les Rois sans visage 1994, Le Condottiere 1994, Le Fils de Klara H. 1995, L'Ambitieuse 1995, La Part de Dieu 1996, Le Faiseur d'or 1996, La Femme derrière le miroir, Napoléon, le chant du départ (biog., vol. I) 1997, L'Immortel de Saint-Hélène (vol. IV) 1997, De Gaulle: L'Appel du destin (vol. I) 1998, La Solitude du combattant (vol. II) 1998, Le Premier des Français (vol. III) 1998, La Statue du Commandeur (vol. IV) 1998, L'Amour de la France expliqué a mon fils, le Jardin des oliviers 1999, Bleu, blanc, rouge (three vols) 2000, Les Patriotes (four vols) 2000–01, Victor Hugo: Je suis une force qui va (vol. I) 2001, Je serai celui-là (vol. II) 2001, Les Chrétiens (three vols) 2002, Morts pour la France (three vols) 2003, César Imperator 2003, L'Empire (three vols) 2004, La croix de l'Occident (two vols) 2005, Les Romains (five vols) 2006, Louis XIV: Le Roi-Soleil (vol. I) 2007, L'Hiver du grand roi (vol. II) 2007. *Address:* Editions Robert Laffont, 24 avenue Marceau, 75008 Paris, France. *E-mail:* maxmail@editions-fayard.fr (office). *Website:* www.maxgallo.com.

GALLO, Robert C., MD; American biomedical scientist and academic; *Professor and Director, Institute of Human Virology, University of Maryland;* b. 23 March 1937, Waterbury, Conn.; m. Mary Jane Hayes 1961; two s. one d.;

ed Providence Coll., Jefferson Medical Univ., Philadelphia, Yale Univ., Univ. of Chicago; Intern and Resident in Medicine, Univ. of Chicago 1963–65; Clinical Assoc. Nat. Cancer Inst. Bethesda, Md 1965–68, Sr Investigator 1968–69, Head, Section on Cellular Control Mechanisms 1969–72, Chief, Lab. of Tumor Cell Biology, Div. of Cancer Etiology 1972–93; Prof. and Dir Inst. of Human Virology, Univ. of Md, Baltimore 1993–; Rep. World Conf. Int. Comparative Leukemia and Lymphoma Asscn 1981–; mem. Bd of Govs Franco American AIDS Foundation, World AIDS Foundation 1987; jt discoverer of AIDS virus and first human retroviruses; Hon. Prof., Johns Hopkins Univ. 1985–, Karolinska Inst., Stockholm 1998–; 20 hon. doctorates for 10 countries; numerous honours and awards including Lasker Award for Basic Medical Research 1982, Gen. Motors Cancer Research Award 1984, Armand Hammer Cancer Research Award 1985, Lasker Award for Clinical Medical Research 1986, Gairdner Foundation Int. Award 1987 and other awards for cancer research; 1st Dale McFarlin Award for Research, Int. Retrovirology Asscn. 1994, Promesa Award 1997, Nomura Prize for AIDS and Cancer Research (Japan) 1998, Warren Alpert Prize, Harvard Univ. 1998, Paul Erlich Award (Germany) 1999, Príncipe de Asturias Award (Spain) 2000, Frank Annunzio Award in Science 2000, World Health Award 2001. *Publications:* over 1,100 scientific publs. *Leisure interests:* swimming, reading historical novels, tennis, theatre, biking. *Address:* University of Maryland, Baltimore, Institute of Human Virology, 725 West Lombard Street, Suite S307, Baltimore, MD 21201, USA (office). *Telephone:* (410) 706-8614 (office). *Fax:* (410) 706-1952 (office). *E-mail:* gallo@umbi.umd.edu (office). *Website:* ihv.org (office).

GALLOIS, Louis; French business executive; *CEO, European Aeronautic Defence and Space Company EADS NV;* b. 26 Jan. 1944, Montauban, Tarn-et-Garonne; s. of Jean Gallois and Marie Prax; m. Marie-Edmée Amaudric du Chaffaut 1974; one s. two d.; ed Ecole Nat. d'Admin; Head of Bureau, Treasury 1972; Dir of Cabinet of M. Chevènement, Ministry of Research and Tech. 1981–82, Ministry of Research and Industry 1982; Dir-Gen. for Industry, Ministry of Research and Industry 1983; Civil Admin., Ministry of Econ. and Finance 1986; Dir of Civil and Mil. Cabinet, Minister of Defence 1988–89; Pres.-Dir-Gen. Soc. Nationale d'Etude et de Construction de Moteurs d'Aviation (SNECMA) 1989–92; Pres. (Econ. Interest Group) Avion de Combat européen-Rafale 1989; Pres., Dir-Gen. of Aérospatiale 1992–96; Chair. Société Nationale des Chemins de Fer Français (SNCF) 1996–2006; Co-CEO Euro-pean Aeronautic Defence and Space Company EADS NV 2006–07, CEO 2007–, CEO Airbus div. 2006–; Pres. Société Gestion de Participations Aéronautiques (SOGEPA) 1993–96; Vice-Pres. Supervisory Council Airbus-Industrie 1992–96; Pres. Communauté des chemins de fer européens 1999–; mem. Dassault aviation 1992–, European Aeronautic Defence and Space Co. 1999–; Chevalier, Ordre nat. du Mérite, Légion d'honneur.

GALLOWAY, David A., BA, MBA; Canadian financial services industry executive; *Chairman, Bank of Montreal (BMO) Financial Group;* m.; two c.; ed Univ. of Toronto, Harvard Business School, USA; founding pnr Canada Consulting Group; joined Torstar Corpn 1981, Pres. and CEO Harlequin Worldwide 1982, Group Pres. and CEO 1988–2002; mem. Bd of Dirs Bank of Montreal (BMO) Financial Group 1998–, mem. Risk Oversight Cttee, Man. Compensation Cttee, Chair. BMO Financial Group 2004–; mem. Bd of Dirs Corel Corpn 2001–03, E.W. Scripps Co. 2002–, Toromont Industries Ltd 2002–, Hudson's Bay Co. 2003–06, Abitibi Consolidated Inc. 2006–07, Shell Canada Ltd 2006–07, Cognos Inc. 2007–; fmr Dir Clearnet Communications Inc., Visible Genetics, Westburne Inc., Harris Bankmont; Chair. Bd of Trustees, Hosp. for Sick Children, Toronto. *Address:* Bank of Montreal, 1 First Canadian Place, 100 King Street, West Toronto, ON M5X 1A1, Canada (office). *Telephone:* (416) 867-5000 (office). *Fax:* (416) 867-6793 (office). *E-mail:* info@bmo.com (office). *Website:* www.bmo.com (office).

GALLOWAY, James N., BS, PhD; American chemist, environmental scientist and academic; *Sidman P. Poole Professor in Environmental Science and Professor, Department of Environmental Sciences, University of Virginia;* ed Whittier Coll., Calif.; Univ. of California, San Diego; Postdoctoral appoint-ment, Cornell Univ.; apptd Asst Prof., Univ. of Virginia, Charlottesville 1976, currently Sidman P. Poole Prof. in Environmental Science and Prof., Dept of Environmental Sciences, Pres. Bermuda Biological Station for Research 1988–95, Chair. Dept of Environmental Sciences 1996–2001; currently Chair. Int. Nitrogen Initiative (sponsored by Scientific Cttee on Problems of the Environment and the Int. Geosphere-Biosphere Programme); mem. US Environmental Protection Agency's Science Advisory Bd; currently research-ing acidification of streams in Shenandoah Nat. Park, Va, composition of precipitation in remote regions, air-sea interactions and Asia's impact on global biogeochemistry; Fellow, AAAS 2002–, American Geophysical Union 2008–; Tyler Prize for Environmental Achievement (co-recipient) 2008. *Publications:* Asian Change in the Context of Global Climate Change: Impact of Natural and Anthropogenic Changes in Asia on Global Biogeochemical Cycles (co-ed.) 1998, Biogeochemical Cycling of Sulfur and Nitrogen in the Remote Atmosphere (co-ed.) 2002; numerous scientific papers in professional journals on biogeochemistry and chem. of natural waters at the watershed, regional and global scales, effects of nitrogen in the environment. *Address:* PO Box 400123, Clark Hall, Department of Environmental Sciences, University of Virginia, Charlottesville, VA 22903, USA (office). *Telephone:* (434) 924-1303 (office); (434) 924-0569 (office). *Fax:* (434) 982-2137 (office); (434) 982-2300 (office). *E-mail:* jng@virginia.edu (office). *Website:* www.virginia.edu (office).

GALMOT, Yves; French judge; b. 5 Jan. 1931, Paris; s. of Jean-Jacques Galmot and Marie Germaine Len, gauer; m. Katrine-Marie Nicholson 1958; two s.; ed Lycée Louis le Grand, Paris, Inst. d'Etudes Politiques de Paris, Faculté de Droit de Paris, Ecole Nat. d'Admin; auditor, Council of State 1956; Tech. Adviser, Office of High Commr for Youth and Sport 1958; Maître des Requêtes, Council of State 1962–; Govt Commr Legal Section, Council of State

1964–68; Sec.-Gen. Entreprise Minière et Chimique 1970–74; Councillor of State 1981–94; Judge, Court of Justice of European Communities 1982–88; Chair. Financial Section, Council of State 1994–96; mem. Court of Budget and Finance 1996–99; Chair. Comm. Interministérielle des Installations Nucléaires de Base 1996–2006, Comm. of Appeal, Agence Intergouvernmentale de la Francophonie 1999–. *Leisure interest:* golf. *Address:* Conseil d'Etat, 75100 Paris RP (office); 95 rue de la Santé, 75013 Paris, France (home).

GALSWORTHY, Sir Anthony Charles, KCMG, MA; British organization official and fmr diplomatist; b. 20 Dec. 1944, London; s. of Sir Arthur Galsworthy and Lady Galsworthy; m. Jan Dawson-Grove 1970; one s. one d.; ed St Paul's School, Corpus Christi Coll., Cambridge; Foreign Office, London 1966, Third Sec., Hong Kong 1967, Third, later Second Sec., Beijing 1970, Second, later First Sec., FCO, London 1972, First Sec., Rome 1977, First Sec., later Counsellor, Beijing 1981, Counsellor and Head Hong Kong Dept, FCO 1984, Prin. Pvt. Sec. to Sec. of State for Foreign and Commonwealth Affairs 1986, with Royal Inst. of Int. Affairs, London 1988, British Sr Rep., Jt Liaison Group, Hong Kong 1989, Cabinet Office 1993, Deputy Under-Sec. of State, FCO 1995, Amb. to People's Repub. of China 1997–2002; Adviser on China, Standard Chartered Bank 2002–; Dir Earthwatch, Europe 2002–06; Dir Bekaert SA 2004–; Scientific Assoc. Nat. History Museum, London 2001–; Hon. Fellow, Royal Botanic Gardens, Edin. 2002; Trustee, Wildfowl and Wetland Trust 2002–, British Trust for Ornithology 2002–06. *Leisure interests:* wildlife, entomology. *Address:* c/o Standard Chartered Bank, 1 Aldermanbury Square, London, EC2V 7SB, England (office).

GALTUNG, Johan, PhD; Norwegian academic; *Professor of Peace Studies, Transcend Peace University;* b. 24 Oct. 1930, Oslo; s. of August Galtung and Helga Holmboe; m. 1st Ingrid Eide 1956 (divorced 1968); two s.; m. 2nd Fumiko Nishimura 1969; one s. one d.; ed Univ. of Oslo; Prof. of Sociology, Columbia Univ., New York, USA 1957–60; Founder and Dir Int. Peace Research Inst., Oslo 1959–69; Prof. of Peace Research, Univ. of Oslo 1969–77; Prof., Princeton Univ., USA 1985–89; Prof. of Peace Studies, Univ. of Hawaii 1985–2004; Prof. of Peace and Co-operation Studies, Univ. of Witten-Herdecke, Germany; Olof Palme Prof. of Peace, Stockholm, Sweden 1990–91; Prof. of Peace Studies, Univ. of Alicante 2005–; Founder and Dir TRANSCEND (peace and devt network) 1993–, Rector Transcend Peace Univ., also Prof. of Peace Studies; Hon. Prof., Berlin, Alicante, Sichuan, Witten/Herdecke; Dr hc (Finland, Romania, Uppsala, Tokyo, Hagen, Alicante, Osnabrück, Turin, Puebla); Alternative Nobel Peace Prize (Right Livelihood Award), Bajaj Int. Gandhi Prize. *Publications:* Theory and Methods of Social Research (four vols) 1967, 1977, 1980, 1988, There are Alternatives 1983, Hitlerism, Stalinism, Reaganism 1984; Essays in Peace Research Vols I–VI 1974–88, Human Rights in Another Key, Peace by Peaceful Means: Peace, Conflict, Development, Civilization, Conflict Transformation by Peaceful Means 2000, Johan uten land: På fredsveien gjennom verden (Norwegian Brage Literary Prize) 2000, 50 Years: 100 Peace & Conflict Perspectives 2008, 50 Years: 2 Intellectual Landscapes Explored 2008, The Fall of the US Empire - And Then What? 2009. *Leisure interests:* travel, writing. *Address:* Casa 227, Urb. Escandinavia, ALFAZ Del Pi, Alicante, Spain (home); 11009 Kinship Court, Apt 302, Manassas, VA 20109, USA (home); APA, Garden Court, Apt 912, Kawaramachi/Shomen, Kyoto 600, Japan (home); 51 Bois Chatton, 01210 Versonnex, France (home). *Telephone:* (4) 50-42-73-06 (France) (home); (96) 5889919 (Spain) (home). *Fax:* (4) 50-42-73-06 (France) (home); (96) 5889919 (Spain) (home). *E-mail:* galtung@transcend.org (office). *Website:* www.transcend.org (office).

GALUN, (Amiel) Esra, PhD; Israeli biologist and academic; *Professor Emeritus of Biology, Department of Plant Sciences, Weizmann Institute of Science;* b. 7 April 1927, Leipzig, Germany; s. of David Mendel Galun and Erna Esther Markus; m. Margalith Katz 1953; two s.; ed Hebrew Univ. Jerusalem, California Inst. of Tech., USA; Sr Scientist, Plant Genetics, Weizmann Inst. of Science 1963–67, Assoc. Prof. of Plant Genetics 1968–72, Head, Dept of Plant Genetics 1970–88, Prof. of Biology 1972–, now Prof. Emer., Dean Feinberg Grad. School 1974–75, Dean Faculty of Biology 1988–91; Maria Moors Cabot Research Fellow, Biological Labs, Harvard Univ., USA 1967–68; Chair. Israeli Nat. Council for Research and Devt 1982–84; Distinguished Visiting Scientist, The Roche Inst. of Molecular Biology, Nutley, NY 1985; Armando Kaminitz Award for Achievements in Agric. Research. *Publications:* Pollination Mechanisms, Reproduction and Plant Breeding (co-author) 1977, Transgenic Plants (with Adina Breiman) 1997, Manufacture of Medical and Health Products by Transgenic Plants (with Eithan Galun) 2001, Transposable Elements 2003, RNA Silencing 2005; more than 180 publs in learned journals. *Leisure interests:* music, archaeology, philosophy. *Address:* Department of Plant Sciences, The Weizmann Institute of Science, Rehovot 76100 (office); 54 Hanassi, Harishon Street, Rehovot 76302, Israel (home). *Telephone:* (8) 9342637 (office); (8) 9468103 (home). *Fax:* (8) 9344181 (office); (8) 9464016 (home). *E-mail:* esra.galun@weizmann.ac.il (office). *Website:* www.weizmann.ac.il/Plant_Sciences (office).

GALUŠKA, Vladimír, JD; Czech diplomatist and lawyer; *Ambassador to Slovakia;* b. 2 Oct. 1952, Prague; s. of Miroslav Galuška and Milena Galušková (née Králová); m. Marcela Wintrová 1975; two s.; ed Charles Univ., Prague; corp. lawyer, Škoda Co., Prague 1975–90; Consul, Deputy Chief of Mission, Czech Embassy, Washington, DC 1990–94; Dir Personnel Dept, Ministry of Foreign Affairs 1994–97, Head of Int. Relations 2002–04; Perm. Rep. of Czech Repub. to UN 1997–2001; Amb. to Slovakia 2004–; Pres. ECOSOC 1997, Exec. Bd UNDP/UNFPA 2000; Chair. 3rd Cttee 54th UN Gen. Ass. 1999. *Address:* Embassy of the Czech Republic, Hviezdoslavovo nám. 8, PO Box 208, 810 00 Bratislava, Slovakia (office). *Telephone:* (2) 59203303 (office). *Fax:* (2) 59203330 (office). *E-mail:* bratislava@embassy.mzv.cz (office). *Website:* www.mzv.cz/bratislava (office).

GALVÁN GALVÁN, Gen. Guillermo; Mexican military officer and government official; *Secretary of National Defense;* b. 19 Jan. 1943, Mexico City; ed Colegio Militar, Colegio de Defensa; has been Commdr in numerous mil. zones; fmr Mil. Attaché Embassy in Madrid; fmr Rector Universidad del Ejército y Fuerza Aérea Mexicanos; Under-Sec. of Nat. Defence 2004–06, Sec. of Nat. Defence 2006–. *Address:* Secretariat of State for National Defence, Blvd Manuel Avila Camacho, esq. Avda Industria Militar, 3°, Col. Lomas de Sotelo, Del. Miguel Hidalgo, 11640 México, DF, Mexico (office). *Telephone:* (55) 5557-5571 (office). *Fax:* (55) 5395-2935 (office). *E-mail:* ggalvang@mail.sedena.gob.mx (office). *Website:* www.sedena.gob.mx (office).

GALVÊAS, Ernane; Brazilian politician, economist and banker; b. 1 Oct. 1922, Cachoeiro do Itapemirim; s. of José Galvêas and Maria de Oliveira; m. Odaléa dos Santos 1948; one s. one d.; ed Coll. of Economics and Finance, Rio de Janeiro Univ., Centro de Estudios Monetarios Latino-Americanos, Mexico and Yale Univ.; fmrly Prof. of Banking and Finance, Coll. of Econs and Finance, Rio de Janeiro, subsequently Prof. of Int. Trade, of Monetary Policy and of Int. Monetary Policy; Assoc. Chief, Econs Dept, Supervisory Council for Finance and Credit (SUMOC) 1953–61; Econ. Consultant to Minister of Finance 1961–63; Financial Dir Merchant Marine Comm. 1963–65; Dir Foreign Trade Dept, Banco do Brasil 1966–68; Pres. Banco Central do Brasil 1968–74, 1979; Minister of Finance 1980–84; Exec. Vice-Pres. Aracruz Celulose SA 1974–79, Gen. Man. GB-Repres. Negócios Ltda 1987–; Econ. Consultant Nat. Conf. on Commerce 1987–; Pres. Asscn to Promote Econ. Studies (APEC) 1985–; Dir Lorentzen Empreendimentos, Cia Paraibuna de Metais, Quimio Ind. Farmacêutica, Banco Santista, SANBRA SA; mem. Acad. of Int. Law and Econs (São Paulo). *Publications:* Brazil – Frontier of Development 1974, Development and Inflation 1976, Brazil – Open or Closed Economy? 1978, Apprentice of Entrepreneur 1983, Financial System and Capital Market 1985, The Saga of the Crisis 1985, The Oil Crisis 1985, The Two Faces of Cruzado 1987, Inflation, Deficit and Monetary Policy 1995; numerous articles on economic and financial topics. *Address:* Avenida Atlântica, 2492 Apt. 301, Rio de Janeiro, RJ, Brazil. *Fax:* (21) 2406920.

GALVIN, Gen. John Rogers; American army officer (retd) and academic; *Dean Emeritus, Fletcher School of Law and Diplomacy, Tufts University;* b. 13 May 1929, Wakefield, Mass.; s. of John James Galvin and Mary Josephine Rogers; m. Virginia Lee Brennan 1961; four d.; ed US Military Acad., Columbia Univ., Univ. of Pennsylvania, Command and Gen. Staff Coll. and Fletcher School of Law and Diplomacy; commissioned 2nd Lt US Army 1954; Military Asst and ADC to Sec. of US Army 1968–69; Commdr 1st Bn 8th Cavalry 1970; Mil. Asst to Supreme Allied Commdr, Europe (SACEUR) 1974–75; Commdr Div. Support Command 3rd Infantry Div. 1975–77, Chief of Staff 1977–78; Commanding Gen. 24th Infantry Div. 1981–83; VII (US) Corps 1983–85; C-in-C US Southern Command 1985–87; Supreme Allied Commdr Europe and C-in-C U.S. European Command 1987–92; Olin Distinguished Prof. of Nat. Security, US Military Acad., West Point 1992–93; Distinguished Visiting Policy Analyst Mershon Center, Ohio State Univ. 1994–95; Dean, Fletcher School of Law and Diplomacy, Tufts Univ., Boston 1995–2000, Dean Emer. 2000–; mem. Bd of Dirs J. & W. Seligman & Co. Inc; fmr Dir Raytheon Co.; 20 foreign decorations; Defense Distinguished Service Medal, Army, Navy and Air Force Distinguished Service Medal, Silver Star, Legion of Merit (with 2 oak leaf clusters), Soldier's Medal, Bronze Star with 2 oak leaf clusters, Air Medal (Valor), Combat Infantryman Badge, Ranger Tab. *Publications:* The Minute Men 1967, Air Assault 1969, Three Men of Boston 1974 and 80 articles on leadership, tactics and training. *Leisure interests:* reading, writing and walking. *Address:* 2714 Lake Jodeco Circle, Jonesboro, GA 30236, USA (home). *Telephone:* (770) 210-4110 (home). *Fax:* (770) 210-9488 (home). *E-mail:* johngalvin@comcast.net (home).

GALVIN, Robert W.; American business executive; *Chairman Emeritus, Motorola Inc.;* b. 9 Oct. 1922, Marshfield, Wis.; s. of Paul Galvin, founder of Motorola; m. Mary Barnes 1944; two s. two d.; ed Univs of Notre Dame and Chicago; Motorola Inc., Chicago 1940–, Pres. 1956, Chair. of Bd 1964–90, CEO 1984–86, Chair. Exec. Cttee 1990–2001, now Chair. Emer.; Trustee Santa Fe Institute; Vice-Chair. Bd of Trustees Univs Research Asscn Inc.; fmr Dir Harris Trust and Savings Bank, Chicago; fmr Trustee Illinois Inst. of Tech.; Fellow, Univ. of Notre Dame; Dir Jr Achievement of Chicago; mem. Pres.'s Comm. on Int. Trade and Investment; Dr hc (Ariz. State Univ.), (DePaul Univ.), (Midwest Coll. of Eng), (Quincy Coll.), (St. Ambrose Coll.), (St. Xavier Coll.), (Univ. of Ariz.), (Univ. of Edin.), (Univ. of Limrick), (L'Universite de Technologie de Compiegne) Hon. Adviser Beijing Univ. numerous awards including Electronic Industries Asscn Medal of Honour 1970, Golden Omega Award 1981, Alexis de Tocqueville Award from Independent Inst. 2004. *Publications:* America's Founding Secret: What the Scottish Enlightenment Taught Our Founding Fathers 2004. *Leisure interests:* skiing, water-skiing, tennis, horse-riding. *Address:* c/o Motorola Inc., 1303 East Algonquin Road, Schaumburg, IL 60196, USA (office).

GALWAY, Sir James, Kt, KBE, FRCM, FRCO, FGSM; British flautist and conductor; b. 8 Dec. 1939, Belfast; s. of James Galway and Ethel Stewart Galway (née Clarke); m. 1st 1965; one s.; m. 2nd 1972; one s. two d. (twins); m. 3rd Jeanne Cinnante 1984; ed Mountcollyer Secondary School, Royal Coll. of Music, Guildhall School of Music, Conservatoire National Supérieur de Musique, Paris; first post in Wind Band of Royal Shakespeare Theatre, Stratford-on-Avon; later worked with Sadler's Wells Orchestra, Royal Opera House Orchestra, BBC Symphony Orchestra; Prin. Flute, London Symphony Orchestra and Royal Philharmonic Orchestra; Prin. Solo Flute, Berlin Philharmonic Orchestra 1969–75; int. soloist 1975–; soloist/conductor 1984–; Prin. Guest Conductor, London Mozart Players 1997–; performances worldwide include appearances in The Wall, Berlin, and at the Nobel Peace Prize Ceremony, 1998; as conductor, toured Germany with Wurttembergisches

Kammerorchester and Asia with Polish Chamber Orchestra, 2000–01; has premiered many contemporary flute works commissioned by and for him; numerous recordings; James Galway Rose named after him by David Austin; Hon. MA (Open Univ.) 1979, Hon. DMus (Queen's Univ., Belfast) 1979, (New England Conservatory of Music) 1980, (St Andrew's Univ.); Officier, Ordre des Arts et des Lettres 1987; Grand Prix du Disque 1976, 1989, Nat. Acad. Recording, Arts & Sciences Pres. Merit Award 2004, Classical BRIT Award for Outstanding Contribution to Music 2005. *Recordings include:* Vivaldi The Four Seasons, Sometimes When We Touch, Mozart Concerto No. 1, Andante and Concerto for Flute and Harp, Song Of The Seashore 1979, Annie's Song 1981, Man With The Golden Flute 1982, The Wayward Wind 1982, Nocturne 1983, James Galway Plays Mozart 1984, In The Pink 1984, In Ireland 1986, Christmas Carol 1986, J.S. Bach Suite No. 2 Concerto - Trio Sonatas 1987, Mercadante Concertos 1987, James Galway Plays Beethoven 1988, The Enchanted Forest 1988, James Galway Plays Giuliani 1988, Quantz 4 Concertos 1989, C.P.E. Bach 3 Concertos 1989, The Concerto Collection 1990, Over The Sea To Skye 1990, J.S. Bach Suite No. 2 Concerto for Flute, Violin and Harpsichord 1991, Italian Flute Concertos 1991, In Dulci Jubilo 1991, The Wind Beneath My Wings 1991, Mozart Flute Quartets 1991, Mozart Concerto for Flute and Harp and Sonatas for Flute and Piano 1992, At The Movies 1992, The Magic Flute 1992, Danzi 1993, Dances For Flute 1993, Seasons 1993, The Classical James Galway 1993, Bach Sonatas 1993, Pachelbel Canon 1994, Wind Of Change 1994, The Lark In The Clear Air 1994, The French Recital 1994, Mozart Concerto for Flute and Harp, Concerto No. 1 and Concerto No. 2 1995, Bach Vol. 2 Trio Sonatas 1995, The Celtic Minstrel 1996, James Galway plays the music of Sir Malcolm Arnold 1996, Music for my Friends 1997, James Galway plays Lowell Liebermann 1997, Legends 1997, Flute Sonatas 1997, Meditations 1998, Serenade 1998, Tango del Fuego 1998, Winter's Crossng 1998, Unbreak My Heart 1999, Sixty Years-Sixty Flute Masterpieces Collection 1999, Love Song 2001, Hommage a Rampal 2001, A Song of Home: An American Musical Journey 2002, The Very Best of James Galway 2002, Music for my Little Friends 2002, Wings of Song 2004, My Magic Flute 2006, Ich war ein Berliner 2006, The Essential James Galway 2006. *Film music:* flute soloist, soundtrack of Lord of the Rings – Return of the King. *Publications:* James Galway: An Autobiography 1978, Flute (Menuhin Music Guide) 1982, James Galway's Music in Time 1983, Flute Studies – Boehm 12 Grand Studies 2003. *Leisure interests:* music, walking, swimming, films, theatre, TV, computing, chess, backgammon, talking to people. *Address:* c/o Elixabeth Sobol Gomez, IMG Artists, Carnegie Hall Tower, 152 West 57th Street, 5th Floor, New York, NY 10019, USA (office). *Telephone:* (212) 994-3541 (office). *Fax:* (212) 994-3550 (office). *E-mail:* esobol-gomez@imgartists.com (office). *Website:* www.imgartists.com (office); www.thegalwaynetwork.com.

GAMA, Jaime José Matos Da; Portuguese politician; *President, Assembleia da República;* b. 8 June 1947, Azores; Founding mem. Partido Socialista 1977, unsuccessful cand. for leadership 1986, 1988; Pres. Parl. Comm. for Int. Business 1976–78, of Parl. Comm. for Nat. Defence 1985–91, of Parl. Comm. for European Affairs and Foreign Politics 2002–05; Minister of Home Affairs 1978, Minister of Foreign Affairs 1983–85, 1995–2002; Minister of Nat. Defence 1999; Minister of State 1999–2002; Pres. Assembleia da República (Parl.) 2005–. *Address:* Assembleia da República, Palácio de San Bento, 1249-068 Lisbon, Portugal (office). *Telephone:* (213) 919000 (office). *Fax:* (213) 917440 (office). *E-mail:* gabpar@ar.parlament.pt (office). *Website:* www.parlamento.pt (office).

GAMBARI, Ibrahim Agboola, CFR, BSc, MA, PhD; Nigerian diplomatist, academic and UN official; *Under-Secretary General for Political Affairs and Special Adviser on the Iraq Compact and Other Political Issues, United Nations;* b. 24 Nov. 1944, Ilorin, Kwara State; m. Fatima Oniyangi 1969; three s. one d.; ed Kings Coll., Lagos, LSE, UK, Columbia Univ., New York, USA; Lecturer, Queen's Coll., CUNY 1969–74; Asst Prof., State Univ. of New York (Albany) 1974–77; Sr Lecturer, Ahmadu Bello Univ., Zaria 1977–80, Assoc. Prof. 1980–83, Prof. 1983–89, fmr Chair. Dept of Political Science and Founder, Undergraduate Programme in Int. Studies (first in Nigeria); Dir-Gen. Nigerian Inst. of Int. Affairs 1983–84; Minister for Foreign Affairs 1984–85; Visiting Prof., Johns Hopkins Univ. School of Advanced Int. Studies, Howard Univ., Georgetown Univ. and Brookings Inst. 1986–89; Resident Scholar, Rockefeller Foundation Bellagio Study and Conf. Centre, Italy Nov.–Dec. 1989; Perm. Rep. to UN, New York 1990–99, Chair. Special Cttee against Apartheid; UN Under-Sec.-Gen. and Special Adviser on Africa 1999–2005, Special Rep. of the Sec.-Gen. and Head UN Mission to Angola 2002–03, Under-Sec.-Gen. for Political Affairs 2005–07, Special Adviser on the Int. Compact with Iraq and Other Political Issues 2007–; fmr Guest Scholar, Wilson Center for Int. Scholars, Smithsonian Inst., USA; Chair. Nat. Seminar to Commemorate 25th Anniversary of OAU, Lagos 1988; mem. Soc. of Scholars, Johns Hopkins Univ. 2002–; Hon. Prof., Chugsan Univ., Guangzhou, People's Repub. of China 1985; Commdr Fed. Repub. of Nigeria 2002; Hon. DHumLitt (Univ. of Bridgeport) 2002, (Fairleigh Dickinson Univ.) 2006; Dr hc (Chatham Univ.) 2008; Special Recognition for Int. Devt and Diplomacy award, Africa-America Inst. 2007, Distinguished Service Award 2008. *Publications:* Party Politics and Foreign Policy in Nigeria During the First Republic 1981, Theory and Reality in Foreign Policy Making: Nigeria After the Second Republic 1989, Political and Comparative Dimensions of Regional Integration: The Case of ECOWAS 1991. *Address:* Room 5.933A, United Nations, New York, NY 10017, USA (office). *Telephone:* (917) 367-3671 (office). *Fax:* (917) 367-0150 (office).

GAMBI, Gen. Antoine; Central African Republic army officer and government official; *Minister of Foreign and Francophone Affairs and Regional Integration;* Chief of Gen. Staff, Armed Forces 2002–06; Coordinator, Nat. Comm. Against the Proliferation of Small Arms and Light Weapons to the Disarmament and Reintegration (CNPDR) 2006–09; Pres. Nat. SSR Cttee (security reform preparatory group) 2007–08; Minister of Foreign and Francophone Affairs and Regional Integration 2009–. *Address:* Ministry of Foreign and Francophone Affairs and Regional Integration, Bangui, Central African Republic (office).

GAMBIER, Dominique, DèsSc Econ; French university teacher; b. 14 Aug. 1947, Rouen; s. of Michel Morel and Yvette Morel; two d.; ed Lycée Corneille, Rouen and Ecole Centrale de Paris; Asst Univ. of Rouen 1972–81; Prof. Ecole Centrale de Paris 1981–83; special assignment, Commissariat Général au Plan 1983–84; Maître de conférences and Dir Inst. of Research and Documentation in Social Sciences (IRED), Univ. of Rouen 1984–87; expert adviser, EEC, Brussels 1980–81; scientific adviser, Observatoire français des conjonctures économiques (OFCE) 1981–83; Regional Councillor, Haute-Normandie 1986–, Vice-Pres. of Regional Council 1998–; Pres. Univ. of Rouen 1987–88; Deputy for Seine Maritime 1988–93; Mayor of Déville-les-Rouen 1995–; Officier des Palmes académiques. *Publications:* Analyse conjoncturelle du chômage, Théorie de la politique économique en situation d'incertitude 1980, Le marché du travail 1991, L'emploi en France 1997; numerous articles on economy of work and labour etc. *Leisure interests:* football, tennis, skiing. *Address:* Mairie de Déville, 1 Place François Mitterrand, 76250 Déville; 5 allée du Houssel, 76130 Mont-St-Aignan, France (home). *Telephone:* 35-76-88-18. *Fax:* 35-74-30-73. *E-mail:* dominiquegambin@free.fr (home).

GAMBLE, Christine Elizabeth, PhD; British consultant on culture and sport and fmr cultural administrator; *Consultant to the Commission for Racial Equality;* b. 1 March 1950, Rotherham; d. of the late Albert Edward Gamble and of the late Kathleen Laura Wallis; m. Edward Barry Antony Craxton; ed Royal Holloway Coll., Univ. of London; worked in Anglo-French cultural org. 1974–75; Office of the Cultural Attaché, British Embassy, Moscow 1975–76; joined British Council, New Delhi 1977, UK 1979, then Harare 1980–82, Regional Officer for the Soviet Union and Mongolia 1982–85, Deputy Dir Athens 1985–87, Corp. Planning Dept 1988–90, Head, Project Pursuit Dept and Dir Chancellor's Financial Sector Scheme 1990–92, Dir Visitor's Dept 1992–93, Gen. Man. Country Services Group and Head European Services 1993–96; Cultural Councillor, British Embassy, Paris and Dir British Council, France 1996–98; Dir Royal Inst. of Int. Affairs, London 1998–2002; Co. Sec., Ind. Football Comm. 2002–05; Consultant to Comm. for Racial Equality 2005–; Order of Rio Branco, Brazil 2000. *Leisure interests:* literature, art, music, theatre, sport. *Address:* Syke Fold House, Dent, Sedbergh, LA10 5RE, England (home). *E-mail:* cgamble@cre.gov.uk (office). *Website:* www.cre.gov.uk (office).

GAMBLIN, Jacques; French actor; b. 16 Nov. 1957, Granville, Manche; ed Centre dramatique de Caen; wrote the theatre play Quincaillerie. *Films:* Train d'enfer (Hell Train, USA) 1985, Périgord noir 1988, Il y a des jours... et des lunes (There Were Days... and Moons) 1990, Pont et soupirs 1992, La belle histoire (The Beautiful Story) 1992, Adeus Princesa (Goodbye Princess) 1992, Tout ça... pour ça! (All That... for This?!) 1993, La femme à abattre 1993, Fausto (aka À la mode (USA), aka In Fashion) 1993, Naissances 1994, Les braqueuses (Girls with Guns) 1994, Sans souci 1995, Les misérables (aka Les misérables du vingtième siècle) 1995, À la vie, à la mort! (Til Death Do Us Part) 1995, Au petit Marguery 1995, Mon homme (My Man) 1996, Pédale douce 1996, Une histoire d'amour à la con 1996, Tenue correcte exigée 1997, Mauvais genre 1997, Kanzo sensei (Dr. Akagi, USA) 1998, Au coeur du mensonge (The Color of Lies, USA) 1999, Les enfants du marais (The Children of the Marshland) (Best Actor Award, Cabourg Romantic Film Festival 1999) 1999, Mademoiselle 2001, Bella ciao 2001, Laissez-passer (Safe Conduct) (Silver Berlin Bear for Best Actor, Berlin Int. Film Festival 2002) 2002, Carnages (Carnage) 2002, À la petite semaine (Nickel and Dime) 2003, Dissonances 2003, 25 degrés en hiver (25 Degrees in Winter) 2004, Holy Lola 2004, L'enfer (Hell) 2005, Les brigades du Tigre (The Tiger Brigades) 2006, Serko 2006, Les irréductibles 2006, Fragile(s) 2007, Nos retrouvailles (aka In Your Wake) 2007, Enfin veuve (A Widow at Last) 2008. *Television:* La double inconstance 1984, L'Été 36 1986, Le vagabond des mers (mini-series) 1990, Années de plumes, années de plomb 1991, C'est mon histoire: Présumé coupable 1992, Un cercueil pour deux 1993, Les brouches 1994, Couchettes express 1994, La bougeotte 1996, Les clients d'Avrenos 1996, Le voyageur sans bagage 2004, Les oubliées (mini-series) 2007.

GAMBLING, William Alexander, BSc, PhD, DSc, FRS, FREng; British electrical engineer and industrial consultant; *Consultant in Optoelectronics, LTK Industries Ltd;* b. 11 Oct. 1926, Port Talbot, Glamorgan, Wales; s. of George Alexander Gambling and Muriel Clara Gambling; m. 1st Margaret Pooley 1952 (separated 1987); one s. two d.; m. 2nd Barbara Colleen O'Neil 1994; ed Univs of Bristol and Liverpool; Lecturer in Electric Power Eng, Univ. of Liverpool 1950–55; Fellow, Nat. Research Council, Univ. of BC 1955–57; Lecturer, Sr Lecturer and Reader, Univ. of Southampton 1957–64, Prof. of Electronics 1964–80, Dean of Eng and Applied Science 1972–75, Head of Dept 1974–79, British Telecom Prof. of Optical Communication 1980–95, Dir UK Nat. Optoelectronics Research Centre 1989–95; Royal Soc. Visiting Prof. and Dir, Optoelectronics Research Centre, City Univ. of Hong Kong 1996–2001; Dir of Optoelectronics Research and Devt, LTK Industries Ltd 2002–05, Consultant 2005–; Consultant in Optoelectronics, COTCO Holdings Ltd; Visiting Prof., Univ. of Colo 1966–67, Bhabha Atomic Research Centre, India 1970, Osaka Univ., Japan 1977; Pres. I.E.R.E. 1977–78; Chair. Comm.D, Int. Union of Radio Science 1981–84, Eng Council 1983–88; mem. Bd, Council of Eng Insts 1974–79, Electronics Research Council 1977–80, Nat. Electronics Council 1977–78 and 1984–89; Dir York Ltd 1980–97; mem. British Nat. Cttee for Radio Science 1978–87, Educational Advisory Council, IBA 1980–82, Eng Industries Training Bd 1985–88; mem. Council, Royal Acad. of Eng 1989–92; Selby Fellow, Australian Acad. of Science 1982; Foreign mem. Polish Acad. of

Sciences 1985; Liveryman, Worshipful Co. of Engineers 1988; Fellow Hong Kong Acad. of Eng Sciences (Vice-Pres. 2004–); Hon. FIEE; Hon. Prof. Huazhong Univ. of Science and Tech., Wuhan, 1986–, Beijing Univ. of Posts and Telecommunications, Shanghai Univ. 1991–, Shandong Univ. 1999–; Hon. Dir Beijing Optical Fibres Lab., People's Repub. of China 1987–; Freeman, City of London 1988; Dr hc (Madrid) 1994, (Aston) 1995, (Bristol) 1999, (Southampton) 2005; Academic Enterprise Award 1982, IEE J.J. Thomson Medal 1982, IEE Faraday Medal 1983, Churchill Medal, Soc. of Engineers 1985, Simms Medal, Soc. of Engineers 1988, Micro-optics Award (Japan) 1989, Dennis Gabor Award (USA) 1990, Rank Prize for Optoelectronics 1991, C & C Medal (Japan) 1993, Mountbatten Medal 1993, Royal Soc./Inst. of Civil Engineers James Alfred Ewing Medal 2002; six awards for outstanding research publs, 11 int. prizes and medals for research in optical fibre communications tech. *Publications:* some 400 research papers on electrical discharges, microwave devices, quantum electronics, optical fibre communication and education. *Leisure interests:* reading, music, the Bible, Christian literature. *Address:* LTK Industries, 6/F Photonics Centre, Hong Kong Science Park, Sha Tin, Hong Kong Special Administrative Region, People's Republic of China (office). *Telephone:* 2410-3009 (office). *Fax:* 2943-1709 (office). *E-mail:* wag@ltkcable.com (office); wagconl@yahoo.com (office). *Website:* www.ltkcable.com (office).

GAMBON, Sir Michael John, Kt, CBE; British actor; b. 19 Oct. 1940, Dublin; s. of Edward Gambon and Mary Gambon; m. Anne Miller 1962; one s.; ed St Aloysius School for Boys, London; fmr mechanical engineer; Trustee Royal Armouries 1995–98; Hon. DLitt 2003. *Television:* numerous appearances including: Ghosts, Oscar Wilde, The Holy Experiment, Absurd Person Singular, The Borderers, The Singing Detective (BAFTA for Best Actor 1987), The Heat of the Day, Maigret 1992, The Entertainer, Truth, Wives and Daughters (BAFTA for Best Actor 2000), Longitude 2000 (BAFTA for Best Actor 2001), Perfect Strangers (BAFTA Best Actor 2002). *Films:* The Beast Must Die 1975, Turtle Diary 1985, Paris by Night 1988, The Cook, The Thief, His Wife and Her Lover 1989, A Dry White Season 1989, The Rachel Papers 1989, State of Grace 1989, The Heat of the Day 1989, Mobsters 1992, Toys 1992, Clean Slate 1993, Indian Warrior 1993, The Browning Version 1993, Mary Reilly 1994, Midnight in Moscow 1994, A Man of No Importance 1995, The Innocent Sleep 1995, All Our Fault 1995, Two Deaths 1996, Nothing Personal 1996, The Gambler 1996, Dancing at Lughnasa 1997, Plunket and McClean 1997, The Last September 1998, Sleepy Hollow 1999, Dead On Time 1999, The Insider, End Game 1999, High Heels and Low Lifes 2001, Gosford Park 2001, Charlotte Gray 2001, Ali G Indahouse 2001, Path to War 2001, Christmas Carol: The Movie (voice) 2001, The Actors 2003, Open Range 2003, Sylvia 2003, Standing Room Only 2004, Harry Potter and the Prisoner of Azkaban 2004, Being Julia 2004, Sky Captain and the World of Tomorrow 2004, Layer Cake 2004, The Life Aquatic with Steve Zissou 2004, Harry Potter and the Goblet of Fire 2005, My Boy 2005, Elizabeth Rex 2005, The Good Sheperd 2006, Amazing Grace 2006, John Duffy's Brother 2006, The Good Night 2007, The Baker 2007, The Alps (voice) 2007, Harry Potter and the Order of the Phoenix 2007, Brideshead Revisited 2008. *Theatre:* first stage appearance with Edwards/Mácliammoir Co., Dublin 1962; Nat. Theatre, Old Vic 1963–67; Birmingham Repertory and other provincial theatres 1967–69, title roles including Othello, Macbeth, Coriolanus; RSC Aldwych 1970–71; The Norman Conquests 1974, Otherwise Engaged 1976, Just Between Ourselves 1977, Alice's Boys 1978, The Caretaker 2000; with Nat. Theatre 1980, appearing in Galileo (London Theatre Critics' Award for Best Actor), Betrayal, Tales from Hollywood; with RSC, Stratford and London 1982–83, title roles in King Lear, Antony and Cleopatra, Old Times 1985, A Chorus of Disapproval, Nat. Theatre 1985 (Olivier Award for Best Comedy Performance), A Small Family Business 1987, Uncle Vanya 1988, Mountain Language 1988, Othello 1990, Taking Steps 1990, Skylight (play) 1995, Volpone (Evening Standard Drama Award) 1995, Tom and Clem 1997, The Unexpected Man 1998, Cressida 2000 (Variety Club Award for Best Actor), A Number, Jerwood Theatre, Royal Court, London 2002, End Game 2004, Henry IV parts I and II, Nat. Theatre 2005. *Leisure interests:* flying, gun collecting, clock making. *Address:* c/o ICM, Oxford House, 76 Oxford Street, London, W1N 0AX, England (office).

GAMEDZE, Chief Mgwagwa; Swazi government official; Minister of Home Affairs 2008–. *Address:* Ministry of Home Affairs, POB 432, Mbabane, Swaziland (office). *Telephone:* 4042941 (office). *Fax:* 4044303 (office).

GAMES, David Edgar, PhD, DSc, CChem, FRSC; British scientist and academic; *Professor Emeritus, Mass Spectrometry Research Unit, University of Wales, Swansea;* b. 7 April 1938, Ynysddu; s. of Alfred William Games and Frances Elizabeth Bell Games (née Evans); m. Marguerite Patricia Lee 1961; two s.; ed Lewis School, Pengam, King's Coll., Univ. of London; Lecturer, Sr Lecturer, Reader and Personal Chair., Univ. Coll., Cardiff 1965–89; Prof. of Mass Spectrometry and Dir of Mass Spectrometry Research Unit, Univ. of Wales at Swansea 1989–2003, now Emer., Head Dept of Chem. 1996–2001; fmr Chair. British Mass Spectrometry Soc.; Royal Soc. of Chem. Award in Analytical Separation Methods 1987, The Chromatographic Soc. Martin Medal 1991, Royal Soc. of Chem. SAC Gold Medal 1993, J. J. Thomson Gold Medal, Int. Mass Spectrometry Cttee 1997, Aston Medal, British Mass Spectrometry Soc. 1999. *Leisure interests:* swimming, walking. *Address:* c/o Mass Spectrometry Research Unit, University of Wales Swansea, Singleton Park, Swansea, SA2 8PP (office); 9 Heneage Drive, West Cross, Swansea, SA3 5BR, Wales, UK (home). *Telephone:* (1792) 405192 (home). *E-mail:* d.e.games@swansea.ac.uk (office). *Website:* www.swan.ac.uk/msru (office).

GAMKRELIDZE, Thomas V.; Georgian linguist and cultural historian; *President, Georgian National Academy of Sciences;* b. 23 Oct. 1929, Kutaisi, Georgia; s. of Valerian Gamkrelidze and Olimpiada Gamkrelidze; m. Nino Djavakhishvili 1968; one s. one d.; ed Tbilisi Univ.; post-grad. work 1952–55; Lecturer, Georgian Acad. of Sciences, Inst. of Linguistics 1956–60, Head of Dept 1960–73, Dir The Oriental Inst. 1973–; Head of Dept, Tbilisi State Univ. 1966–72; main work in area of theoretical linguistics, Kartvelian, Semitic and Indo-European linguistics and semiology; People's Deputy of the USSR 1989–91; mem. Parl., Repub. of Georgia 1992–; Ed.-in-Chief Voprosy Jazykoznanija (Russian Acad. of Sciences) 1988–94; mem. Georgian Nat. Acad. of Sciences 1974 (Pres. 2005–), USSR (now Russian) Acad. of Sciences 1984, Austrian Acad. of Sciences, Academia Europaea 2006; Corresp. FBA; Foreign Assoc., NAS 2006; Foreign mem. Sächsische Akad. der Wissenschaften, Latvian Acad. of Sciences 2007; mem. World Acad. of Art and Science 2007; Foreign Hon. Mem. American Acad. of Arts and Sciences; Hon. Mem. Indogermanische Gesellschaft, Linguistic Soc. of America, Societas Linguistica Europaea (Pres. 1986); Dr hc (Bonn, Chicago); Lenin Prize 1988, Humboldt Prize (FRG) 1989, Djavakhishvili Prize, Tbilisi Univ. 1992. *Publications:* Indo-European and the Indo-Europeans (two vols) (with V. V. Ivanov) 1984, Alphabetic Writing and the Old Georgian Script – Typology and Provenance of Alphabetic Writing Systems 1989. *Leisure interests:* music, tennis. *Address:* Georgian National Academy of Sciences, Rustaveli Avenue 52, Tbilisi 0108 (office); Jac. Nikoladze Street 6, 380009 Tbilisi, Georgia (home). *Telephone:* (32) 99-88-91 (office); (32) 22-64-92 (home). *Fax:* (32) 99-88-23 (office). *E-mail:* t.gamkrelidze@science.org.ge (office). *Website:* www.science.org.ge (office).

GAN, Ziyu; Chinese government official and engineer; b. 15 Oct. 1929, Xinyi, Guangdong Prov.; two s.; ed Zhongshan Univ.; engineer and Div. Chief, First Ministry of Machine-Building Industry 1952–56, Ministry of Heavy Industry 1952–56; joined CCP 1953; Sec. Chair.'s Office, State Science and Tech. Comm. 1956–58; apptd Deputy Chief of Planning Group, State Devt and Reform Comm. 1975, Vice-Minister 1978; Deputy Dir State Planning Comm. 1978–, State Admin. Comm. on Import and Export Affairs 1981–82, State Foreign Investment Comm. 1981–82; Vice-Chair. Drafting Cttee for Nat. Defence Law of People's Repub. of China 1993–; Deputy Chair. Nat. Leading Group for Work Concerning Foreign Capital 1994–; mem. Cen. Comm. for Discipline Inspection, CCP Cen. Committee 1992; mem. Preliminary Working Cttee of the Preparatory Cttee of the Hong Kong Special Admin. Region 1993–97, Chinese Govt Del., Hong Kong Handover Ceremony 1997; Chair. Overseas Chinese Affairs Cttee, 9th NPC 1998–2003; mem. Standing Cttee, 9th NPC 1998–2003; Pres. China Asscn for the Peaceful Use of Mil. Industrial Tech.; Prof., Man. Science Centre, Beijing Univ. *Address:* c/o Standing Committee of the National People's Congress, Beijing, People's Republic of China.

GANBAATAR, Adiya; Mongolian politician and academic; *Chairman, Standing Committee on the Budget;* b. 8 Feb. 1959, Ulan Bator; s. of Adiya Ganbaatar and Ichinkhorlo Ganbaatar; m.; three d.; ed Łódź Univ., Poland; Lecturer, Mongolian State Univ. 1983–90; Chair. Democratic Socialist Movt 1990; mem. State Great Hural (Parl.) 1992–2000, Chair. Standing Cttee on the Budget 1997–; Vice-Chair. Cen. Asia Devt Foundation 1992–; Pres. Mongolian Tennis Asscn 1997–; Distinguished Officer, Banking and Finance 1999, Distinguished Officer, Educ. 2000. *Publications:* three books on mathematics. *Leisure interests:* chess, tennis. *Address:* Parliament, State House, Ulan Bator 12, Mongolia. *Telephone:* (1) 372980 (office); (1) 321648 (home). *Fax:* (1) 372980. *E-mail:* ganbaatar@mail.parl.gov.mn (office).

GANBOLD, Davaadorjiin, MSc (Econs), PhD; Mongolian politician; *National Security Adviser to the President;* b. 26 June 1957, Ulan Bator; s. of Tsedevsuren Davaadorj and Lodongiin Oyun; m. M. Tserengav Oyun; two d.; ed Moscow State Univ., USSR; Asst to Prof. of Political Econ., Mongolian State Univ. 1979–84; Prof. of Political Econ., State and Social Studies Acad. 1988–90; Founder-mem. Nat. Progress Party, Chair. Party Council; First Deputy Prime Minister 1990; mem. Great Hural (legislature) 1992–2000; Chair. Standing Cttee on Budget, Finance and Econs; Chair. Mongolian Nat. Democratic Party (merger of four opposition parties) 1992–96, Deputy Leader 1998; fmr Economic Policy Adviser to Prime Minister, currently Nat. Security Adviser to the Pres. and mem. Nat. Security Council; Chair. Railway Authority of Mongolia. *Leisure interests:* fishing, cycling, collecting stamps and model cars. *Address:* Room 258, Government House, Ulan Bator, Mongolia (office). *Telephone:* 942860 (office); 354045 (home). *Fax:* 942864 (office); 354060 (home).

GANDEL, John, AO; Australian business executive; *Chairman, Gandel Group of Companies;* b. 1935; m. Pauline Gandel; four c.; ed Melbourne Univ.; inherited retailer Sussan from parents, sold co. to brother-in-law 1985, used proceeds to build business in shopping malls, currently Chair. Gandel Group of Cos; fmr Chair. Gandel Retail Trust, Gandel Retail Man.; f. Gandel Charitable Trust 1978; Chair. Jewish Museum of Australia 1983–93, currently Chair. Bd of Govs; fmr mem. Bd of Dirs Australian CSIRO; Fellow, Australian Inst. of Man., Australian Inst. of Co. Dirs; Dr hc (Tel-Aviv Univ.) 2006; Nat. Defense Medal 1994, Nat. Service Commemorative Medal 2002, Centenary Medal 2003. *Address:* Gandel Group of Companies, Level 3, 1341 Dandenong Road, Chadstone Shopping Centre, Melbourne, Vic. 3148, Australia (office). *Telephone:* (3) 8564-1222 (office). *Fax:* (3) 8564-1333 (office). *Website:* www.gandel.com.au (office).

GANDHI, Gopalkrishna, MA; Indian diplomatist and government official; *Governor of West Bengal;* b. 22 April 1945, New Delhi; s. of Devdas Gandhi and Laxmiben Gandhi; youngest grand s. of Mahatma Gandhi; m. Tara Gandhi; two d.; ed St Stephen's Coll., Delhi Univ.; joined Indian Admin. Service (IAS) 1968, served in different capacities in Tamil Nadu 1968–85, Sec. to Vice-Pres. of India 1985–87, Jt Sec. to Pres. of India 1987–92, took voluntary retirement from IAS 1992, Sec. to Pres. of India 1997–2000; Minister (Culture) in High Comm. of India, London and Dir The Nehru Centre, London 1992–96; High

Commr in SA, also accred in Lesotho 1996; High Commr in Sri Lanka 2000–02; Amb. to Norway, also accred to Iceland 2002–04; Gov. of West Bengal 2004–, of Bihar (Additional Charge) Jan.–June 2006. *Publications:* one novel and one play. *Address:* Raj Bhavan, Kolkata 700 062, West Bengal, India (office). *Telephone:* (33) 2200-1641 (office). *Fax:* (33) 2200-2444 (office); (33) 2200-1649 (office). *E-mail:* governor@wb.nic.in (office); govsec@wb.nic.in (office). *Website:* rajbhavankolkata.gov.in (office).

GANDHI, Maneka; Indian politician; b. 26 Aug. 1956, New Delhi; d. of the late Col T. S. Anand and of Amteshwar Anand; m. Sanjay Gandhi 1974 (died 1980); one s.; ed Jawaharlal Nehru Univ., New Delhi; Ed. Surya (Sun) magazine 1977–80; Founder and Leader of political party Rashtriya Sanjay Manch (merged with Janata Party 1988) 1983; Minister of State for the Environment and Forests 1989–91; MP 1996–; Minister for Social Justice and Empowerment 1999–2001; Minister of State for Statistics and Programme Implementation 2002–04; Chair. People for Animals Trust, Cttee on Control and Supervision of Experiments on Animals, Soc. for Prevention of Cruelty to Animals; Founder Greenline Trees; Special Adviser to Voice (consumer action forum); cr. environmental film series New Horizons; writer and anchorwoman nat. TV programmes on animals, Heads and Tails, Maneka's Ark, Jeene ki Raah; Pres. Ruth Cowell Trust, Sanjay Gandhi Animal Care Centre; Lord Erskine Award, Royal Soc. for the Prevention of Cruelty to Animals 1991, Vegetarian of the Year, Vegetarian Soc. 1995, Prani Mitra Award, Nat. Animal Welfare Bd 1997, Marchig Prize, Marchig Animal Welfare Trust (GB) 1997, Venu Menon Lifetime Achievement Award 1999, Bhagwan Mahavir Award 1999, Diwaliben Award 1999, Aadishakti Puruskar 2001, Woman of the Year 2001. *Publications:* Sanjay Gandhi 1980, Mythology of Indian Plants, Animal Quiz, Penguin Book of Hindu Names, The Complete Book of Muslim and Parsi Names, First Aid for Animals, Animal Laws of India, Rainbow and Other Stories, Natural Health for Your Dog, Heads and Tails, Wise and Wonderful Animal Alphabet Quiz Book. *Leisure interests:* reading, working with animals. *Address:* 14, Ashoka Road New Delhi 110 001, India. *Telephone:* (11) 23357088. *Fax:* (11) 23354321. *E-mail:* gandhim@nic.in.

GANDHI, Rahul, BA; Indian politician; *General-Secretary, Indian National Congress;* b. 19 June 1970; s. of the late Rajiv Gandhi and of Sonia Gandhi; brother of Priyanka Gandhi-Vadra; ed St Stephen's Coll., New Delhi, Harvard Univ., USA; descendant of Nehru-Gandhi political dynasty; worked in London with strategy consultancy firm Monitor Group; returned to India in 2002 to start software co.; canvassed for Congress Party on behalf of his mother in Amethi constituency, UP 1999; election campaign in parl. elections supervised by his sister Priyanka Gandhi 2004; MP (Lok Sabha) for Amethi constituency 2004–; mem. Indian Nat. Congress, Gen.-Sec. 2007–, mem. Congress Working Cttee 2007–. *Address:* Indian National Congress, 24 Akbar Road, New Delhi 110 011, India (office). *Telephone:* (11) 23019080 (office). *Fax:* (11) 23017047 (office). *Website:* www.congress.org.in (office).

GANDHI, Sonia; Indian (b. Italian) politician; *President, Indian National Congress;* b. 9 Dec. 1946, Italy; d. of Stefano Maino and Paola Maino; m. Rajiv Gandhi 1968 (fmr Prime Minister of India) (died 1991); one s. one d.; ed Univ. of Cambridge, UK, Nat. Gallery of Modern Art, Delhi; Pres. Rajiv Gandhi Foundation; mem. Indian Nat. Congress Cttee, Pres. 1998–2006 (resgnd), reappointed 2007–; mem. Nat. Advisory Council –2006 (resgnd); Leader of Opposition in Parl. (Lok Sabha) –2004; ranked by Forbes magazine amongst 100 Most Powerful Women (third) 2004, (13th) 2006, (sixth) 2007, (21st) 2008. *Publications:* Rajiv 1992, Rajiv's World 1994. *Address:* Indian National Congress, 24 Akbar Road, New Delhi 110011 (office); Rajiv Gandhi Foundation, Jawahar Bhawan, Dr Rajendra Prasad Road, New Delhi 110001; 10 Janpath, New Delhi 110011, India (home). *Telephone:* (11) 23019080 (office); (11) 23014161 (home); (11) 23755117. *Fax:* (11) 23017047 (office). *E-mail:* aicc@congress.org.in (office). *Website:* www.congress.org.in (office); www.soniagandhi.org (home).

GANDOIS, Jean Guy Alphonse; French business executive; b. 7 May 1930, Nieul; s. of Eugène and Marguerite Gandois (née Teillet); m. Monique Testard 1953; two s.; ed École Polytechnique, Paris; Civil Engineer, Ministry of Public Works, French Guinea 1954–58; mem. of tech. co-operation missions to Brazil and Peru 1959–60; Asst to Commercial Dir Wendel & Cie 1961, Econ. Dir 1966; Econ. and Commercial Dir Wendel-Sidelor 1968; Gen. Man. Sacilor 1973; Pres., Dir-Gen. Sollac 1975; Dir-Gen. Rhône-Poulenc SA 1976, Vice-Pres. 1977–79, Chair. and CEO 1979–82 (resgnd); Chair. and CEO Pechiney 1986–94; Chair. Cockerill-Sambre (Belgium) 1987–99; Pres. CNPF (Nat. Council of French Employers) 1994, Hon. Pres. 2000–01; Chair. Supervisory Bd Suez-Lyonnaise des Eaux 2000–01, Vice-Chair. 2001–05; mem. Bd of Dirs, Eurazéo (fmrly Eurafrance); Hon. mem. Order of Australia, Commdr, Légion d'honneur, Grand Cordon, Ordre de Léopold, Grand Croix, Ordre de la Couronne (Belgium), Grand Officier, Couronne du Chêne (Luxembourg); Dr hc (Liège, Louvain). *Address:* c/o Board of Directors, Eurazéo, 32 rue de Monceau, 75008 Paris (office); 55 quai des Grands Augustins, 75006 Paris, France (home). *Telephone:* 1-42-96-29-85 (home). *E-mail:* jeangandois@aol.com (home).

GANDOLFINI, James; American actor; b. 18 Sept. 1961, Westwood, N.J.; m. 1st Marcy Wudarski 1999 (divorced 2002); m. 2nd Deborah Lin 2008; ed Rutgers Univ., Actors Studio; began acting career in NY Theatre; Broadway debut in A Streetcar Named Desire 1982; Golden Globe Best Actor in a Drama Series 2000 (for The Sopranos), Emmy for Outstanding Lead Actor in a Drama Series 2000, 2001, 2003 (for The Sopranos), Outstanding Performance by a Male Actor in a Drama Series, Screen Actors Guild 2003, 2008 (for The Sopranos). *Films include:* A Stranger Among Us 1992, True Romance 1993, Mr Wonderful 1993, Money for Nothing 1993, Italian Movie 1993, Angie 1994, Terminal Velocity 1994, The New World 1995, Crimson Tide 1995, Get Shorty 1995, The Juror 1996, She's So Lovely 1997, Night Falls on Manhattan 1997, Perdita Durango 1997, Gun 1997, Dance with the Devil 1997, The Mighty 1998, A Civil Action 1998, Fallen 1998, 8MM 1999, A Whole New Day 1999, The Mexican 2001, The Man Who Wasn't There 2001, The Last Castle 2001, Surviving Christmas 2004, Romance and Cigarettes 2005, All the King's Men 2006, Club Soda 2006, Lonely Hearts 2006, In the Loop 2009. *Television:* Gun (series) 1997, 12 Angry Men 1997, The Sopranos (Emmy Award, Outstanding Lead Actor in a Drama Series 2003) 1999–2007. *Address:* c/o Creative Artists Agency, 9830 Wilshire Boulevard, Beverly Hills, CA 90212, USA (office).

GANELIUS, Tord Hjalmar, D.PHIL; Swedish mathematician; b. 23 May 1925, Stockholm; s. of Hjalmar Ganelius and Ebba Bejbom; m. Aggie Hemberg 1951; three s. one d.; ed Stockholm Univ.; Asst Prof. Lund Univ. 1953–57; Prof. of Math., Univ. of Göteborg 1957–80, Dean, Faculty of Science 1963–65, 1977–80; Scientific Sec.-Gen. Swedish Royal Acad. of Sciences 1981–91; mem. Bd of Dirs, Nobel Foundation 1981–89, V. and E. Hasselblad Foundation 1983–95; Guest Prof. Univ. of Washington, Seattle 1962, Cornell Univ. 1967–68, Madras Inst. of Math. Sciences 1969, Univ. of Calif., San Diego 1972–73; Fellow, Swedish Royal Acad., Finnish Acad., Royal Soc. of Göteborg, European Acad. of Arts and Sciences; King's Medal 1987. *Publications:* Tauberian Remainder Theorems 1971, Lectures on Approximation, etc. 1982. *Address:* Bergianska trädgården, 104 05 Stockholm, Sweden (home). *Telephone:* (8) 158548 (home). *E-mail:* tord.ganelius@telia.com (home).

GANELLIN, Charon Robin, PhD, DSc, FRS, FRSC; British scientist and academic; *Smith Kline & French Professor Emeritus of Medicinal Chemistry, University College London;* b. 25 Jan. 1934, London; s. of Leon Ganellin and Beila Cluer; m. 1st Tamara Greene 1956 (died 1998); one s. one d.; m. 2nd Monique Garbarg 2003; ed Harrow County Grammar School for Boys and Queen Mary Coll., Univ. of London; Research Assoc., MIT 1960; Research Chemist in Medicinal Chem., Smith Kline & French Labs Ltd (UK) 1958–59, Head of Dept 1961–75, Dir of Histamine Research, Smith Kline & French Research Ltd 1975–80, Vice-Pres. Research 1980–84, Vice-Pres. Chemical Research 1984–86; Hon. Lecturer, Dept of Pharmacology, Univ. Coll., London 1975–86, Smith Kline & French Prof. of Medicinal Chem. 1986–2003, Prof. Emer. 2003–; Fellow, Queen Mary and Westfield Coll., Univ. of London 1992; Corresp. Academician, Académia Nacional Farmacia, Spain 2006; Hon. Prof. of Medicinal Chem., Univ. of Kent 1979–; Hon. mem. Sociedad Española de Química Terapéutica 1982–; Hon. DSc (Aston) 1995; UK Chemical Soc. Medallion in Medicinal Chem. 1977, Prix Charles Mentzer, Soc. de Chimie Thérapeutique (France) 1978, ACS (Div. of Medicinal Chem.) Award 1980, Royal Soc. of Chem. Tilden Medal 1982, Soc. for Chemical Industry Messel Medal 1988, Soc. for Drug Research Award 1989, Nat. Inventors Hall of Fame (USA) 1990, Royal Soc. of Chem. Adrien Albert Medal 1999, European Fed. for Medicinal Chem. Nauta Award in Pharmacochemistry 2004, Societa Chimica Italiana Pratesi Gold Medal 2006. *Achievements include:* co-inventor of Cimetidine (Tagamet®) 1970s. *Publications:* Pharmacology of Histamine Receptors 1982, Frontiers in Histamine Research 1985, Dictionary of Drugs 1990, Medicinal Chemistry 1993, Dictionary of Pharmacological Agents 1997, Analogue-based Drug Discovery 2006, Practical Studies for Medicinal Chemistry (web edn) 2007; research papers and reviews in various journals. *Address:* Department of Chemistry, University College London, 20 Gordon Street, London, WC1H 0AJ, England (office). *Telephone:* (20) 7679-4624 (office). *Fax:* (20) 7679-7463 (office). *E-mail:* c.r.ganellin@ucl.ac.uk (office). *Website:* www.chem.ucl.ac.uk/people/ganellin/index.html (office).

GANEV, Stoyan, PhD; Bulgarian politician and lawyer; b. 23 July 1955, Pazardjik; ed Sofia Univ.; specialises in constitutional law; Leader United Christian Democratic Centre 1990–93; Minister of Foreign Affairs 1991–92; a Deputy Prime Minister of Bulgaria 1991–92; Pres. 47th UN Gen. Ass. 1992–93; Founding Dir New England Center for International and Regional Studies and Distinguished Prof. of Int. Studies, Bridgeport Univ., USA 1996–2001; Chair. of co-ordinating body on Bulgaria's accession to Council on Europe; Chief Envoy of Bulgarian Govt in negotiations for assn with EU; fmr Lecturer, Sofia Univ., Konrad Adenauer Foundation, Germany; mem. Union of Democratic Forces. *Address:* c/o Ministry of Foreign Affairs, bul. E. Georgiyev 117, 1504 Sofia, Bulgaria. *Telephone:* (2) 946-30-79.

GANGOTENA-RIVADENEIRA, Raúl, BSc, MBA; Ecuadorean business executive and diplomatist; b. 1945, Quito; m. Anne Patteet; one s. three d.; ed Nat. Polytechnic School, Quito, Univ. of New Mexico, USA; Sales Man. La Internacional textile mill, Quito 1974–80; Prof., Nat. Polytechnic School 1976–94; CEO Nat. Pre-Investment Fund (FONAPRE) 1980–84; CEO COFIANDINA consultants 1984–87; Finance Man. Palmoriente agro industries 1987–89; Chair. Chicos de la Calle Foundation 1989–92; Chair. QUIMASOC SA 1990–98, Nuevas Fronteras (travel agency) 1990–98; Consultant, UNDP-GTZ Urban Man. Program 1993; Presidential Del. to Monetary Reserve Bd 1994–96; Prof., San Francisco de Quito Univ. 1994–97; Chief of Staff of Pres. Sixto Durán-Ballén 1996; Exec. Dir Nat. Modernization Council (CONAM) 1997–98; Chair. Universidad de Las Américas, Quito 1998–2000; CEO Metrozona (free trade zone) Quito 2000–01; mem. Presidential Comm. for Heavy Crude Oil Pipeline 2000–02; Exec. Dir Quito Chamber of Commerce 2001–03; Amb. to USA 2003–05; columnist, El Universo (daily newspaper), Guayaquil, 1989–97; columnist and mem. Editorial Bd El Comercio (daily newspaper) 1998–2001, columnist, Hoy (daily newspaper) 2001–03; mem. Ecuadorean Fulbright Comm. Chapter Bd 2000–; mem. Bd Ecuadorean Fed. of Exporters 1978–80. *Address:* c/o Ministry of Foreign Affairs, Avda 10 de Agosto y Carrión, Quito, Ecuador.

GANGULY, Ashok, MS, PhD, FRSC; Indian business executive; *Chairman, Firstsource Solutions Limited;* ed Univ. of Illinois, USA, Mumbai Univ.; fmr Chair. Hindustan Lever Ltd; fmr Chief Tech. Officer and Dir Unilever; Chair. Imperial Chemical Industries (ICI) India Ltd 1996–2003, ICICI OneSource Ltd (I-OneSource, later Firstsource Solutions Ltd); Dir Cen. Bd Reserve Bank of India; Dir British Airways plc 1996–2005, Wipro Corpn 1999–, ICICI Knowledge Park Ltd, Mahindra & Mahindra Ltd, Tata AIG Life Insurance Co. Ltd; mem. Advisory Bd Microsoft Corpn (I) Pvt. Ltd, Prime Minister's Council on Trade and Industry, Investment Comm., Nat. Knowledge Comm.; Padma Bhushan 1987, Hon. CBE 2006; Business Man of the Year, India 1996, Madhuri and Jagdish N. Sheth Int. Alumni Award for Exceptional Achievement 2003. *Address:* Firstsource Solutions Ltd, 6th Floor Peninsula Chambers, Ganpatrao Kadam Marg, Lower Parel, Mumbai 400 013, India (office). *Telephone:* (22) 6666-0805 (office). *Fax:* (22) 6666-0807 (office). *Website:* (office).

GANGULY, Sourav Chandidas; Indian cricketer; b. 8 July 1972, Kolkata, Bengal; left-handed middle-order batsman, right-arm medium-pace bowler; teams: Bengal 1989–, Lancashire, India 1992– (test debut versus England at Lords; one-day international debut versus West Indies at Brisbane, Australia 1992); 79 tests (44 as Capt.) for India, scored 4,901 runs (average 42.25, highest score 173 versus Sri Lanka at Mumbai 1997) with 11 hundreds and took 25 wickets; scored 10,888 runs (average 43.55, highest score 200 not out versus Tripura 1993) with 20 hundreds and took 122 wickets in first-class cricket (best bowling 6-46); 266 one-day internationals, scored 9,914 runs (average 41.83, highest score 183 vs Sri Lanka at Taunton, England) with 22 hundreds and took 93 wickets; Capt. Indian Nat. Cricket Team in one-day internationals 1999–2003; Capt. Indian Nat. Cricket Team in tests 2000–05, dropped from team 2006, recalled 2007; led India to 2nd place at World Cup 2003; Arjuna Award 1997, Padma Shri 2004. *Address:* c/o Board of Control for Cricket in India, 'Kairali', GHS Lane, Manacaud, Trivandrum 695 009, India (office). *Website:* www.dd.now.com (office).

GANIĆ, Ejup, DSc; Bosnia and Herzegovina politician and scientist; *Professor, University of Sarajevo;* b. 3 March 1946, Novi Pazar; m. Fahrija Ganić; one s. one d.; ed Univ. of Belgrade, Massachusetts Inst. of Tech.; researcher, consultant, Prof. of Mechanical Eng, Univ. of Illinois, Chicago 1975–82; returned to Bosnia and Herzegovina 1982; Prof., Univ. of Sarajevo 1982–; worked as Exec. Dir UNIS Co.; mem. Presidency of Bosnia and Herzegovina 1990–96, Vice-Pres. 1992–96; Vice-Pres. Fed. of Bosnia and Herzegovina 1994–96, Co-Pres. 1996–2002; Pres. MET Foundation. *Publications:* Handbook of Heat Transfer Applications 1985, Handbook of Heat Transfer Fundamentals 1985, Handbook of Essential Engineering Information and Data 1991, Engineering Companion 2003; more than 100 scientific papers. *Address:* Faculty of Mechanical Engineering, Chair for Process Technique, University of Sarajevo, West Building, Floor IV, Room 407, Vilsonovo šetalište 9, 71000 Sarajevo, Bosnia and Herzegovina (office). *Telephone:* (33) 617205 (office). *Fax:* (33) 617205 (office). *E-mail:* ejup_ganic@hotmail.com; ganic@mef.unsa.ba.

GANIEV, Elyor Majidovich; Uzbekistan politician; *Minister of Foreign Economic Relations, Investment and Trade;* b. 1 Jan. 1960, Syrdarya Prov.; m.; three c.; ed Tashkent Polytechnic Inst.; asst, Tashkent Polytechnic Inst. 1981–84; with Armed Forces 1985–90; Sr Specialist, Man. of State Cttee for Foreign Econ. and Trade Relations 1990–92; Head of Dept, Ministry of Foreign Econ. Relations 1992–93; Head of Dept, Inst. for Strategic and Regional Studies 1993–94; Deputy Minister for Foreign Econ. Relations 1994–95, First Deputy Minister 1995–97, Minister 1997–2002; Deputy Prime Minister and Chair. Agency for Foreign Econ. Relations 2002–05; Deputy Prime Minister and Minister of Foreign Affairs 2005–06; Minister of Foreign Econ. Relations, Investment and Trade 2006–; Pres. Volleyball Fed. of Uzbekistan. *Address:* Ministry of Foreign Economic Relations, Investment and Trade, 100029 Tashkent, Shevchenko 1, Uzbekistan (office). *Telephone:* (71) 138-50-00 (office). *Fax:* (71) 138-52-00 (home). *E-mail:* secretary@mfer.uz (office). *Website:* www.mfer.uz (office).

GANIEV, Rivner Fazilovich; Russian mechanical engineer; *Director, Non-linear Wave Mechanics and Technology Centre, Russian Academy of Sciences;* b. 1 April 1937, Bashkiriya; m. Galina Mikhailovna Antonovskaya; two s.; ed Ufa Aviation Inst.; engineer constructor, jr, sr researcher, Head of Dept, Inst. of Mechanics Ukrainian Acad. of Sciences 1959–78; Head of Lab., Research Inst. of Machine Devt 1978–89, Deputy Dir 1989–95; Dir of Non-linear Wave Mechanics and Tech. Centre, Russian Acad. of Sciences 1995–; Head, Applied Physics Faculty, Moscow Aviation Inst.; Chair. Council of Dirs, United Inst. of Automobile Mechanics and Tech. in Oil Extraction of the Russian Acad. of Sciences and the Acad. of Sciences of the Repub. of Bashkortostan; mem. Scientific Council on Problem Reliability of Machines; Corresp. mem. USSR (now Russian) Acad. of Sciences 1987, mem. 1994; specialist in applied math., theoretical and applied mechanics, mechanical eng; more than 100 inventions and patents; research in theory of resonance phenomena at nonlinear spatial oscillations of solid and deformable matter, theory of nonlinear oscillations of multiphase systems, vibration and wave processes and tech. *Publications include:* Dynamics of Particles under Influence of Vibrations 1975, Solid Matter Oscillations 1976, Oscillatory Phenomena in Multiphase Media and their Applications to Technology 1980; more than 300 other published works, including 15 monographs and numerous articles in scientific journals. *Leisure interests:* sport, skiing. *Address:* Non-linear Wave Mechanics and Technology Centre, Russian Academy of Sciences, 4 Bardin Street, 117334 Moscow, Russia (office). *Telephone:* (495) 135-55-93 (office). *Fax:* (495) 135-61-26 (office). *E-mail:* wavete@ccas.ru (office). *Website:* www.nwmtc.ac.ru (office).

GANSER, Gérard Roger Gaston; French civil servant; b. 6 Jan. 1949, Montreuil-Sous-Bois; s. of Pierre Ganser and Simone Braillon; m. Aimée Fontaine (divorced); one s.; ed Lycées Paul Valéry and Louis le Grand, Ecole polytechnique, Ecole nat. d'admin; auditor, Court of Revenue 1976–80, public auditor 1980, chief adviser 1993–98, Sec.-Gen. 1998–; with Interministerial Mission of the Sea 1979–80; commercial adviser Mexico 1981–82; with Ministry of Agric. 1983, Jt Dir Ministry of Trade and Tourism 1983–84, with Ministry of Industrial Redeployment and Trade 1984, Ministry for Communications 1988, Dir 1989–91; Jt Dir-Gen. Commercial Affairs Télédiffusion de France 1984–86; reporter to Constitutional Council 1987–88; Pres., Chair. Soc. financière de radiodiffusion (Sofirad) 1991–94; Vice-Pres. Radio Monte Carlo 1991–94; auditor European Examinations Office 1995; auditor Inst. des hautes études de la défense nat. 1996; Sec.-Gen. Cour des comptes 1998–99 (Chief Adviser 1993–); Chevalier Ordre nat. du Mérite. *Address:* Cour des Comptes, 13 rue Cambon, 75001 Paris (office); 11 rue de Verneuil, 75007 Paris, France (home). *Telephone:* 1-42-97-59-66 (home). *E-mail:* gganser@ccomptes.fr (office).

GANTAR, Pavel, MA, PhD; Slovenian sociologist and politician; *Chairman, Državni zbor (National Assembly);* b. 26 Oct. 1949, Gorenja vas, nr Škofja Loka, Upper Carniola, Yugoslavia; ed professional school for carpentry, Faculty of Political Sciences, Univ. of Ljubljana, Univ. of Essex, UK, Univ. of Zagreb, Croatia; as student, co-founder of student group 'November 13th' 1971; Asst Prof., Faculty of Social Sciences, Univ. of Ljubljana 1974–94; mem. Urban Planning Council of Ljubljana 1970s; mem. Editorial Bd Journal for the Critique of Science (Časopis za kritiko znanosti, ČKZ) 1976; columnist, Mladina magazine 1980s; Pres. ŠKUC-Forum (org. for alternative culture) 1980s; studied in UK 1984; apptd Chair. CP cell, Faculty of Social Sciences, Univ. of Ljubljana 1984, expelled from CP of Slovenia for using his position to defend essayist Spomenka Hribar accused of denigration of Yugoslav People's Liberation War 1985; among first scholars of contemporary underground social movts in Slovenia and Yugoslavia late 1980s, actively involved in 'Slovenian Spring'; Founding mem. Cttee for the Protection of Human Rights 1988–90; joined Liberal Democratic Party 1990; elected to Državni zbor (Nat. Ass.) 1990– (re-elected 2004, 2008), Chair. 2008–; Minister of the Environment and Spatial Planning 1994–2000, of Information Society 2001–04; mem. social liberal Zares party 2007–. *Publications include:* several articles on civil society under the socialist regime. *Address:* Office of the Chairman, Državni zbor (National Assembly), Šubičeva ulica 4, 1000 Ljubljana, Slovenia (office). *Telephone:* (1) 478-9400 (office). *Fax:* (1) 478-9845 (office). *E-mail:* gpdz-rs.si (office). *Website:* www.dz-rs.si (office).

GANTNER, Carrillo Baillieu, AO, MFA; Australian theatre manager, director, actor and business executive; *Chairman, AsiaLink Centre, University of Melbourne;* b. 17 June 1944, San Francisco, Calif.; s. of Vallejo Gantner and Neilma Gantner; m. 1st Nancy Black 1971 (divorced 1982); two s. one d. (deceased); m. 2nd Dr. Jennifer Webb; two s.; ed Melbourne Grammar School and Melbourne, Stanford and Harvard Univs; Fellow, Stanford Univ. 1968–69; Asst, Admin. Adelaide Festival of Arts 1969–70; Drama Officer, Australian Council for the Arts 1970–73; Gen. Man. Melbourne Theatre Co. 1973–75; Exec. Dir Playbox Theatre Co. Ltd 1976–84, The CUB Malthouse; Cultural Counsellor, Australian Embassy, Beijing 1985–87; Artistic Dir Playbox Theatre Centre 1988–93, Chair. Playbox Malthouse Ltd 1994–96; Councillor, City of Melbourne 1996–99 (Chair. Planning and Devt Cttee 1996–98, Docklands Cttee 1998–99, Deputy Chair. Finance and Service Cttee and Audit Cttee 1998–99); Chair. Performing Arts Bd Australia Council 1990–93, Nat. Circus Summit 1990, Nat. Dance Summit 1991, Nat. Advisory Council, Musica Viva 1993–, Melbourne Int. Comedy Festival 1995–; Pres. Melbourne Chapter of URASENKE 1995–; Dir Myer Foundation 1984–92 (Vice-Pres. 1992–), Asialink 1990–92 (Chair. 1992–), Mayfair Hanoi Ltd (Hong Kong) 1996–98, Deputy Chair. 1999–; mem. Australia–China Council 1989–94, Australia Abroad Council 1991–95, Exec. Cttee Asia Pacific Philanthropy Consortium 1994–, Nat. Advisory Council, Adelaide Festival 1996–; Corresp. mem. The Hague Club 1994–; Trustee Sidney Myer Fund 1991–; Gov. Fed. for Asian Cultural Promotion 1994–; Japan Foundation Visitors Program 1991; mem. Working Group to establish an Asian Business Council for the Arts 1997–98; Chair. Arts Man. Course Advisory Cttee, Victorian Coll. of the Arts 1996–98; Chair. Barclay Investment Pty Ltd, Myer Investment Pty Ltd 1998–. *Publications:* articles in professional journals. *Leisure interests:* viticulture, tennis. *Address:* AsiaLink Centre, Level 4, Sidney Myer Asia Centre, University of Melbourne, Melbourne, Vic. 3010, Australia (office). *Telephone:* (3) 8344-4800 (office). *Fax:* (3) 9347-1768 (office). *Website:* www.asialink.unimelb.edu.au (office).

GANZ, Bruno; Swiss film actor; b. 22 March 1941, Zürich-Seebach; unsuccessful film debut 1960; theatre debut 1961; Co-founder, with Peter Stein, Schaubühne theatre co., Berlin 1970; leading man of the New German Wave of films. *Films include:* Der Herr mit der schwarzen Melone (The Man in the Black Derby) 1960, Es dach überem Chopf (A Roof Over Your Head) 1961, Chikita 1961, Der Sanfte Lauf 1967, Sommergäste (Summer Guests) 1976, Lumière 1976, Die Marquise von O… 1976, Die Wildente (The Wild Duck) 1976, Der amerikanische Freund (The American Friend) 1977, Messer im Kopf (Knife in the Head) 1978, Die Linkshandige Frau (The Left-Handed Woman) 1978, The Boys from Brazil 1978, Nosferatu: Phantom der Nacht 1979, Retour à la bien-aimée (Reurn to the Beloved) 1979, Oggetti smarriti (aka Lost and Found) 1980, Der Erfinder (The Inventor) 1980, 5% de risques 1980, La dame aux camelias (Lady of the Camelias) 1980, Rece do góry (aka Hands Up!) 1981, La provinciale (aka The Girl from Lorraine) 1981, Die Falschung (False Witness) 1981, Logik des Gefühls 1982, Polenta 1982, System ohne Schatten (aka Closed Circuit, USA) 1983, Killer aus Forida 1983, Dans la ville blanche (In the White City) 1983, De IJssalon (aka Private Resistance, USA) 1985, Der Pendler 1986, El Río de oro 1986, Der Himmel über Berlin (The Sky Over Berlin) 1987, The Legendary Life of Ernest Hemingway 1988, Un amore di donna (Love of a Woman) 1988, Nosferatu a Venezia 1988, Bankomatt 1989, Strapless 1989, Schrödingers kat 1990, Erfolg (Success) 1991, Börn náttúrunnar (Children of Nature) 1991, La domenica specialmente (Especially on Sunday) 1992, Prague 1992, The Last Days of Chez Nous 1992, Le quator des possibles (The Quartet of the Possibles) (voice) 1993, L'absence 1993, In weiter Ferne, so nah! (Faraway, So Close! 1993,

Brandnacht (Night on Fire) 1993, Heller Tag 1994, You Can't Go Home Again (voice) 1998, Mia aioniotita kai mia mera (Eternity and a Day) 1998, Pane e tulipani (aka Bread and Tulips) 2000, WerAngstWolf (WhoAfraidWolf) 2000, Epsteins Nacht (Epstein's Night) 2002, La Forza del passato (The Power of the Past) 2002, Luther 2003, The Manchurian Candidate 2004, Der Untergang 2004 (The Downfall: Hitler and the End of the Third Reich) 2004, Vitus 2006, Baruto no gakuen 2006, Youth Without Youth 2007. *Television includes:* Der Spaßvogel 1964, Frühlings Erwachen 1966, Die Unberatenen 1966, Die Schlacht bei Lobositz 1968, Maß für Maß 1968, Im Dickicht der Städte 1968, Torquato Tasso 1969, Eine Große Familie 1970, Die Mutter 1971, Peer Gynt (mini-series) 1971, Der Ignorant und der Wahnsinnige 1972, Prinz Friedrich von Homburg 1973, Die Bakchen 1974, Geschichte einer Liebe 1978, Schwarz und weiß wie Tage und Nächte (Black and White Like Day and Night) 1978, Fermata Etna 1981, Der Park 1985, Väter und Söhne – Eine deutsche Tragödie" (Fathers and Sons) (mini-series) 1986, Die Wette (Journey's End) 1990, Tassilo – Ein Fall für sich (series) 1991, Il grande Fausto (aka The Price of Victory) (mini-series) 1995, Diario senza date 1995, Todliches Schweigen 1996, Anwalt Abel – Ein Richter in Angst 1996, Tatort – Schattenwelt 1996, Gegen Ende der Nacht (Daybreak) 1998, Johann Wolfgang von Goethe: Faust 2001, Have No Fear: The Life of Pope John Paul II 2005, Copacabana 2007.

GAO, Bo; Chinese architect, photographer and curator; *Photographer, Agence VU;* b. 1954, Chongqing, Sichuan Prov.; ed Sichuan Fine Arts Inst., Beijing Acad. of Arts and Crafts, Catholic Inst. of Paris, France; architect, Beijing 1996–; Dir Beijing Boart Culture Devt Co. Ltd; f. China Heritage Soc.; mem. Agence VU (photographic agency), Paris; mem. Chinese Photographers' Inst.; Winner, People's Daily Photography Competition 1986. *Works include:* Portraits and Masks Duality Series 1964, Faint Memory 2006, Unlimited Scenery 2007, Searching 2007. *Exhibitions include:* Int. Festival of Photography, Pingyao, Sichuan 2002, Arles Festival, France 2003, Museum of New Art, Pontiac, Michigan 2004, Three Shadows Photography Art Center, Beijing 2007, 2008. *Publications include:* volumes of photographs on rural China, Tibet and Tiananmen Square. *Address:* Agence Vu, 17 boulevard Henri IV, 75004 Paris, France (office). *Website:* www.agencevu.com (office).

GAO, Changli; Chinese politician; b. July 1937, Yutai, Shandong Prov.; ed Chinese People's Univ.; joined CCP 1956; cadre Yutai Co. People's Govt, cadre Office of CCP Jining Pref. Cttee; Vice-Sec. CCP Yishui Co. Cttee, Sec. CCP Rizhao Co. Cttee, Vice-Chief Sec. then Chief Sec. CCP Shandong Prov. Cttee 1976–87; Vice-Gov. Shandong Prov. and Sec. Political and Legal Cttee of CCP Shandong Prov. Cttee; mem. Trial Cttee of Supreme People's Court; Vice-Chair. Supreme People's Court 1993–98; Minister of Justice 1998–2000; Alt. mem. 14th CCP Cen. Cttee 1992–97, 15th CCP Cen. Cttee 1997–2002. *Address:* c/o Ministry of Justice, 11 Xiaguangli, Sanyuanqiao, Chao Yang Qu, Beijing 100016, People's Republic of China.

GAO, Dezhan; Chinese state official and engineer; b. 6 Aug. 1932, Qixia, Shandong Prov.; ed Dalian Eng Inst., Liaoning Prov.; joined CCP 1950; engineer and Dir China Sugar Refinery, Jilin Prov. 1954–58; Deputy Chief Engineer and Deputy Dir Petrochemical Bureau, Jilin Prov. 1961–76; Dir Jilin Prov. Econ. Comm. 1980–81; Vice-Gov. Jilin Prov. 1983–85, Gov. 1985–87; Deputy Sec. CCP Jilin Prov. Cttee 1985–87; Minister of Forestry 1987–93; Vice-Chair. All-China Greening Cttee 1988–93, Deputy Head Cen. Forest Fire Prevention 1988–93; Deputy Head State Leading Group for Comprehensive Agricultural Devt 1990–; Deputy Head Cen. Forest Fire Prevention 1988–93; Alt. mem. 12th CCP Cen. Cttee 1982–87, 13th CCP Cen. Cttee 1987–92, mem. 14th CCP Cen. Cttee 1992–97; Sec. Tianjin City CCP Cttee 1993–97; Deputy, 8th NPC 1993–98, mem. 9th Standing Cttee of NPC 1998–2003, Chair. Agric. and Rural Affairs Cttee of NPC 1998–2003; Special Gold Prize for Chinese Greening Science and Tech. 1993. *Address:* c/o Standing Committee of the National People's Congress, Beijing, People's Republic of China.

GAO, Hongbo (Xiang Chuan); Chinese poet; b. 1951, Kailu, Nei Monggol; ed Peking Univ.; joined the PLA 1969; Vice-Chief News Section, Literature and Art Gazette; Vice-Dir Gen. Office of Chinese Writers' Asscn; Assoc. Ed. Chinese Writers'; Ed. Journal of Poetry; Sec. Secr. of Chinese Writers' Asscn. *Publications:* Elephant Judge, Geese, Geese, Geese, The Crocodile that Eats Stones, The Secret of the Shouting Spring, I Love You, Fox, The Fox that Grows Grapes, The Maid and the Bubble Gum, Flying Dragon and Magic Pigeon, I Wonder, Whisper (Nat. Award for Best Children's Literature). *Address:* Chinese Writers' Association, Beijing, People's Republic of China (office).

GAO, Shangquan; Chinese government official and professor of economics; b. 1929, Jia Ding Co., Shanghai; s. of Gao Ruyu and Xiang Shi; m. Cha Peijun 1958; one s.; ed St John's Univ., Shanghai; worked as researcher, Deputy Div. Chief, Div. Chief, Bureau for Machine-Bldg Industry of Ministry of Industry of local North-Eastern People's Govt; Policy Research Dept, First Ministry of Machine-Bldg Industry; Research Dept, Ministry of Agricultural Machine-Bldg Industry; Office of Agricultural Mechanization, State Council; Policy Research Dept, State Comm. of Machine-Bldg Industry; Research Fellow, Research Centre for Agricultural Devt and Sr Economist, State Comm. of Machine-Bldg Industry; State Comm. for Restructuring Econ. System 1982, then Deputy Dir and Head, Research Inst. of Restructuring the Econ. System 1985–93; Vice-Minister in charge of State Comm. for Restructuring the Econ. System 1985–93; mem. preliminary working Cttee of preparatory Cttee of the Hong Kong Special Admin. Region and Head of Econ. Panel 1993–97, 9th Nat. Cttee of CPPCC 1998–2003; mem. Sino-Japanese Econ. Exchange Comm.; Vice-Group-Leader, Leading Group for Restructuring Housing System, under State Council; Pres. China Research Soc. for Restructuring the Econ. Systems, China Soc. of Enterprise Reform and Devt, China Reform & Devt Inst., China Reform Foundation, China Soc. of Urban Housing System Reform, Asscn of Future Market of China; Vice-Pres. Asscn of China's Urban Economy, Asscn of China's Industrial Economy, Asscn for Study of China's Specific Condition, Asscn of Social and Economics Publs; Chair. Research Group for Rural and Urban Housing Reform 1995–; mem. UN Cttee for Devt Policy; Doctorate Supervisor, Prof., Beijing Univ. and Shanghai Jiaotong Univ.; Dean Man. School, Zhejiang Univ.; Prof. Nankai Univ., Chinese People's Univ., Shanghai Univ. of Finance and Econs; MBA programme adviser of Nat. Univ. of Australia; Outstanding Scholar Award Hong Kong Polytechnic. *Publications:* Enterprises Should Enjoy Certain Autonomy 1956, Follow A Road of Our Own in Agricultural Modernization 1982, Nine Years of Reform in China's Economic System 1987, A Road To Success 1987, Selected Works of Gao Shangquan 1989, China: A Decade of Economic Reform 1989, The Reform of China's Economic System 1991, Lead to a Powerful Country 1991, On Planning and Market in China 1992, From Planned Economy to the Socialist Market Economy 1993, An Introduction to Socialist Market Economy 1994, China: The Second Revolution 1995, China's Economic Reform 1996, Extensive Talk About China's Market Economy 1998, The Second Revolution 1998, Market Economy and China's Reform 1999, Two Decades of Reform in China 1999; also ed. of numerous publications. *Address:* State Commission for Restructuring the Economic System, 22 Xianmen Street, Beijing 100017, People's Republic of China. *Telephone:* (10) 63096649. *Fax:* (10) 66014562. *E-mail:* sqgao@bj.col.com.cn (office).

GAO, Xingjian, BA; French (b. Chinese) writer and dramatist; b. 4 Jan. 1940, Ganzhou, Jiangxi Prov., People's Republic of China; ed Dept of Foreign Languages, Beijing; translator China Reconstructs (magazine), later for Chinese Writers Asscn.; spent five years in 're-education' during Cultural Revolution; Artistic Dir People's Art Theatre, Beijing 1981; left China 1987 after work banned in 1985, living in Paris 1988–, became French citizen 1998; Chevalier des Arts et des Lettres 1992; Prix Communauté française de Belgium 1994, Prix du Nouvel An Chinois 1997, Nobel Prize for Literature 2000; Légion d'honneur 2000. *Publications include:* plays: Absolute Signal 1982, Bus Stop 1983, Wild Man 1990, The Other Shore 1999, Fugitives 1993, Tales of Mountains and Seas 1993, The Man Who Questions Death 2003; novels: Soul Mountain 1999, Return to Painting 2001, One Man's Bible 2002; other: Snow in August (opera) 2002, Buying a Fishing Rod for my Grandfather (short stories) 2004. *Address:* c/o HarperCollins, 77-85 Fulham Palace Road, London, W6 8JB, England.

GAO, Yan; Chinese government official and engineer; *General Manager, State Electrical Power Corporation;* b. 1942, Yushu Co., Jilin Prov.; joined CCP 1965; Deputy Dir Jilin Thermal Power Plant 1965–74 (also Sec. CCP and Communist Youth League); Sr Engineer and Deputy Dir, later Dir Electricity Bureau 1975; Head Org. Dept, CCP Jilin Prov. Cttee 1988–95, Deputy Sec. Jilin CCP Jilin Prov. Cttee 1988–95; Vice-Gov. of Jilin Prov. 1988–92, Gov. 1992–95; Sec. CCP Cttee, Yunan Prov. 1995–97; Dir Political Dept, Chinese People's Armed Police Force; Sec. CCP 6th Yunnan Prov. Cttee; mem. 14th CCP Cen. Cttee 1992–97, 15th CCP Cen. Cttee 1997–2002; Deputy Gen. Man. State Electrical Power Corpn 1997–98, Gen. Man. 1998–; Vice Minister of Power Industry 1997–98. *Address:* c/o State Council, Beijing, People's Republic of China.

GAO, Yaojie, MD; Chinese physician and activist; b. 1927, cen. Henan Prov.; m.; several c.; ed Henan Univ.; retd gynaecologist from Henan Coll. of Traditional Chinese Medicine who discovered wide-scale HIV infection amongst citizens of Henan Prov. in early 1990s, alerted Govt authorities 1996 but no action taken; spent much of her pension printing pamphlets to educate rural residents and to buy medicine for the sick; currently active in giving AIDS educ. lectures; placed under house arrest 2007; Jonathan Mann Award for Global Health and Human Rights, Global Health Council 2001, Ramon Magsaysay Award for Public Service 2003, named one of 10 People Who Moved China in 2003, Touching China Award from China Central TV 2004, Vital Voices Global Partnership Global Leadership Award, Women Changing Our World 2007, New York Acad. of Sciences Heinz R. Pagels Human Rights of Scientists Award 2007. *Publications:* Ten Thousand Letters (First Chinese Publications and Media Award 2005) 2004. *Address:* c/o China AIDS Orphan Fund, The Minneapolis Foundation, 800 IDS Center, 80 South Eighth Street, Minneapolis, MN 55402, USA. *Website:* www.chinaaidsorphanfund.org.

GAO, Ying; Chinese author and poet; b. 25 Dec. 1929, Jiaozuo, Henan; s. of Gao Weiya and Sha Peifen; m. Duan Chuanchen 1954; one s. two d.; Vice-Chair. Sichuan Br. and mem. Council, Chinese Writers' Asscn; Deputy Dir Ed. Bd, Sichuan Prov. Broadcasting Station 1983–; mem. Sichuan Political Consultative Conf. *Publications:* The Song of Ding Youjun, Lamplights around the Three Gorges, High Mountains and Distant Rivers, Cloudy Cliff (novel), Da Ji and her Fathers (novel and film script), The Orchid (novel), Loving-Kindness of the Bamboo Storey (collection of prose), Mother in my Heart (autobiographical novel), Songs of Da Liang Mountains (poems), Frozen Snowflakes (poems), Reminiscences, Xue Ma (novel), Gao Ying (short stories). *Leisure interests:* painting, music. *Address:* Sichuan Branch of Chinese Association of Literary and Art Workers, Bu-hou-jie Street, Chengdu, Sichuan, People's Republic of China. *Telephone:* 66782836.

GAO, Yisheng, PhD; Chinese scientist; ed Univ. of Oxford, UK; fmr Dir Shanghai Inst. of Materia Medica; Nat. Prize of Science 1990. *Address:* c/o Shanghai Institute of Materia Medica, 294 Tai-Yuan Road, Shanghai 20031, People's Republic of China.

GAO, Youxi; Chinese physicist; *Director, Plateau Atmospheric Physics Institute;* b. 1920; Dir Plateau Atmospheric Physics Inst. 1981–; mem. Dept of Earth Sciences, Academia Sinica, 1985–; Nat. Science Award 1989. *Address:*

c/o Institute of Atmospheric Physics, Chinese Academy of Sciences, Beijing 100029, People's Republic of China.

GAO, Zhanxiang; Chinese party official; b. 1935, Tongxian Co., Hebei Prov.; joined CCP 1953; mem. Communist Youth League Cen. Cttee 1964, Sec. 1978–83; Vice-Chair. All-China Youth Fed. 1978–83; Deputy Sec. CCP Cttee, Hebei Prov. 1983–86; Dir State Ethnic Affairs Comm. 1986–89; Vice-Minister of Culture 1986–96; Sec. Secr. China Fed. of Literary and Art Circles 1990–, Vice-Chair. 1990–; Pres. Soc. of Mass Culture 1990–93; Vice-Chair. Chinese Asscn for Promotion of Popular Culture 1993–; Adviser, China Int. Tea Cultures Soc. 1993–; Chair. Soc. of Photographic Arts 1994; Vice-Chair. China Soc. of Tourism Culture 1994–; Dir, Ed.-in-Chief Chinese Arts 1994–; Alt. mem. 12th CCP Cen. Cttee 1982–87; Del., 13th CCP Nat. Congress 1987–92, 14th CCP Nat. Congress 1992–97, 15th CCP Nat. Congress 1997–2002; mem. 7th CPPCC Nat. Cttee 1988–93, Standing Cttee of 8th CPPCC Nat. Cttee 1993–98 (mem. Educ. and Culture Sub-cttee), Standing Cttee of 9th CPPCC Nat. Cttee 1998–2003; Hon. Chair. Soc. for the Promotion of Chinese Culture 1996–. *Publications:* author of several literary anthologies. *Address:* c/o Ministry of Culture, A83 Beiheyan, Dongamen, Beijing 100722, People's Republic of China.

GAOLATHE, Baledzi, MSc; Botswana politician; *Minister of Finance and Development Planning;* ed UBLS, Univ. of London, UK; fmr Perm. Sec., Ministries of Finance and Devt Planning, of Mineral Resource and Water Affairs; fmr Man. Dir Debswana Diamond Co.; fmr Gov. Bank of Botswana; fmr Chair. Barclays Bank of Botswana Ltd; currently Minister of Finance and Devt Planning; mem. Bd Bank of Botswana, Sefelana Holding Co., Botswana Inst. for Devt Policy Analysis; mem. Bd of Dirs, Botswana Devt Corpn, Botswana Vaccine Inst., Southern Africa Enterprise Devt Fund; mem. Council, Univ. of Botswana. *Address:* Ministry of Finance and Development Planning, Private Bag 008, Gaborone, Botswana (office). *Telephone:* 3950201 (office). *Fax:* 3956086 (office). *E-mail:* kbaleseng@gov.bw (office); gsethebe@gov.bw (office). *Website:* www.finance.gov.bw (office).

GAOMBALET, Célestin-Leroy; Central African Republic politician; b. 1942; Prime Minister of Central African Repub. 2003–05. *Address:* c/o Office of the Prime Minister, Bangui, Central African Republic (office).

GAPONOV-GREKHOV, Andrey Viktorovich; Russian physicist and academic; *Scientific Chief Supervisor, Institute of Applied Physics, Russian Academy of Sciences;* b. 7 June 1926, Moscow; m.; one d.; ed Gorky State Univ.; Instructor, Gorky Polytech. Inst. 1952–55; Sr Scientific Assoc., Gorky (now Nizhny Novgorod) State Univ. 1955–, Head of Dept of Radio Physics, Inst. of Applied Physics 1977–2003, Scientific Chief Supervisor 2003–; Corresp. mem. USSR (now Russian) Acad. of Sciences 1964–68, mem. 1968–; USSR People's Deputy 1989–91; Hero of Socialist Labour 1986; State Prize 1967, 1983, 2003. *Publications:* numerous theoretical and experimental works in the field of electrodynamics and electronics of inducted cyclotronic radiation, which led to development of a new class of electronic instruments – masers with cyclotronic resonance. *Address:* Institute of Applied Physics, Ulyanova str. 46, Nizhny Novgorod 603950, Russia (office). *Telephone:* (831) 436-66-69 (office); (831) 436-36-67 (home). *Fax:* (831) 436-20-61 (office). *E-mail:* gapgr@appl.sci-nnov.ru (office). *Website:* www.ipfran.ru (office).

GARABEDIAN, Paul R., PhD; American professor of mathematics; *Director, Division of Computational Fluid Dynamics, New York University;* b. 2 Aug. 1927, Cincinnati, Ohio; s. of Carl A. Garabedian and Margaret R. Garabedian; m. 1st Gladys Rappaport 1949 (divorced 1963); m. 2nd Lynnel Marg 1966; two d.; ed Brown and Harvard Univs; Nat. Research Council Fellow 1948–49; Asst Prof. of Math., Univ. of Calif. 1949–50; Asst Prof. of Math., Stanford Univ. 1950–52, Assoc. Prof. 1952–56, Prof. 1956–59; Scientific Liaison Officer, ONR-London 1957–58; Prof., Courant Inst. of Math. Sciences, New York Univ. 1959–, Dir Courant Math. and Computing Lab. of US Dept of Energy 1972–73, Dir Div. of Computational Fluid Dynamics 1978–; Sloan Foundation Fellowship 1961–63; Guggenheim Fellowship 1966, 1981–82; Fairchild Distinguished Scholar, Calif. Inst. of Tech. 1975; mem. NAS, American Acad. of Arts & Sciences, American Math. Soc., American Physical Soc. (Fellow 2004), Soc. Industrial and Applied Math., Editorial Bd Applicable Analysis, International Journal of Computational Fluid Dynamics; NASA Public Service Group Achievement Award 1976, NASA Certificate of Recognition 1980, Boris Pregal Award, New York Acad. of Sciences 1980, Birkhoff Prize in Applied Math. 1983, von Karman Prize, SIAM 1989, Applied Mathematics and Numerical Analysis Prize, NAS 1998. *Publications:* numerous books and papers in learned journals. *Leisure interest:* piano. *Address:* Courant Institute of Mathematical Sciences, New York University, 251 Mercer Street, New York, NY 10012 (office); 60 East 8th Street, Apt 9K, New York, NY 10003, USA (home). *Telephone:* (212) 998-3237 (office). *Fax:* (212) 995-4121 (office). *E-mail:* garabedi@cims.nyu.edu (office). *Website:* www.math.nyu.edu (office).

GARAIKOETXEA URRIZA, Carlos, LicenDer; Spanish (Basque) fmr politician, lawyer and economist; b. 2 June 1939, Pamplona; s. of Juan Garaikoetxea and Dolores Urriza; m. Sagrario Mina Apat 1966; three s.; mem. Inst. Príncipe de Viana, org. to protect and promote Basque culture, Navarra Dist Council 1971; Chair. Navarra Chamber of Commerce and Industry 1971; Chair. Nat. Council PNV 1977, re-elected 1978; mem. Navarra Dist Parl. 1979; Pres. Gen. Council of the Basque Country 1979; elected to Basque Parl. as PNV cand. for Guipúzcoa March 1980; Pres. of Basque Govt 1980–86; European Deputy 1987; Pres. Eusko Alkartaruna Party 1987–99; Hon. Pres. and gold medals from many orgs and asscns. *Publications:* Euskadi: la transición inacabada, Memorias Políticas. *Leisure interests:* music (especially classical), skiing, Basque pelota, reading (especially political essays and history). *Address:* Nafarroa Behereko 43, 31002 Pamplona/Iruña, Spain. *Telephone:* (948) 203656.

GARAS, Klára, PhD; Hungarian art historian; b. 19 June 1919, Rákosszentmihály; d. of Pál Garas and Irén Strasser; ed Budapest Univ. of Sciences; joined staff Budapest Museum of Fine Arts 1945, subsequent posts to Gen. Dir 1964–84; Ordinary mem. Hungarian Acad. of Sciences 1972, mem. 1985–; Labour Order of Merit (golden degree) 1974, 1979. *Publications:* Magyarországi festészet a XVII. században (Hungarian Painting in the 17th century) 1953, Magyarországi festészet a XVIII. században (Hungarian Painting in the 18th century) 1955, Franz Anton Maulbertsch 1724–1796, with preface by Oskar Kokoschka 1960, Olasz reneszánsz portrék a Szépmüvészeti Muzeumban (Italian Renaissance Portraits in the Museum of Fine Arts) 1965, 1973, Carlo Innocenzo Carloni (co-author) Milano 1966, Franz Anton Maulbertsch. Leben und Werk 1974, A velencei settecento festészete (Venetian Paintings of the 18th Century) 1977, A 17. század német és osztrák rajzmüvészete (Deutsche und Österreichische Zeichnungen des 18. Jahrhunderts) 1980; several publs on the Budapest Museum of Fine Arts, including Treasures of Venice: Paintings from the Museum of Fine Arts, Budapest (co-author) 1995. *Leisure interests:* 15th- to 18th-century European and Hungarian painting. *Address:* Kiss János altábornagy utca 48/c, 1126 Budapest, Hungary.

GARAUDY, Roger Jean Charles, DèsSc; French writer and academic; b. 17 July 1913, Marseilles; s. of Charles Garaudy and Marie Garaudy; m. 1st Henriette Vialatte 1937 (divorced 1937); m. 2nd Paulette Gayraud; two s. one d.; ed Sorbonne, Paris; POW 1940–43; Deputy to Nat. Ass. 1945–58, Vice-Pres. 1956–58; Senator 1959–62; Dir Inst. Int. pour le Dialogue des Cultures, Geneva 1974–; Prof. of Philosophy, Univ. of Paris (Sorbonne); f. Univ. des Mutants, Dakar, Senegal; f. Fondation Roger Garaudy, Cordoba, Spain; tried to reconcile Marxism with Catholicism 1970s, abandoned both doctrines in favour of Sunni Islam 1982, took the name Ragaa; found guilty in French court of violating a law prohibiting questioning of crimes against humanity 1998; Croix de Guerre; Prix Méditerranée; Dr hc (Konya, Turkey); Prix Faycal, Prix Brennam (Barcelona). *Publications:* 53 books translated into 29 languages including: Hegel 1962, Karl Marx 1965, De l'anathème au dialogue 1965, Appel aux vivants 1979, A contre-Nuit (poem) 1987, Mon Tour du siècle en solitaire (memoirs) 1989, Vers une guerre de religion 1995, Les Etats-Unis, avant-garde de la décadence 1996, L'Avenir, Mode d'emploi 1997, The Founding Myths of Israeli Politics 1998, Le Procès du sionisme israélien 1998. *Address:* 69 rue de Sucy, 94430 Chennevières-sur-Marne, France. *Telephone:* (1) 45-76-90-38. *Fax:* (1) 49-62-77-94.

GARAVANI, Valentino; Italian fashion designer; b. 11 May 1932, Voghera, nr Milan; pnr Giancarlo Giammetti; ed Ecole des Beaux-Arts, Paris, Ecole de la Chambre Syndicale de la Couture, Paris; asst designer at Paris fashion houses of Jean Dessès 1950–55, Guy Laroche 1956–58; est. Valentino fashion house with Giancarlo Giammetti in Rome 1960, debut collection 1962, opened boutiques in Rome, Milan, Paris, New York, Tokyo and other cities; launched first Valentino perfume 1978; designed kit for Italian Olympic team 1984; designed costumes for opera The Dream of Valentino, J. F. Kennedy Center, USA 1994; sold Valentino fashion house to HdP 1998; announced decision to retire 2008; f. Valentino Acad. 1990; f. L.I.F.E for AIDS research and assistance to victims of the disease 1990; retrospective exhbn of creations in Rome 1991, at Columbus Festivities, New York 1992; Grande Ufficiale dell'Ordine al Merito della Repubblica Italiana 1985, Cavaliere del Lavoro 1996, Légion d'honneur, France 2005; Neiman Marcus Prize 1967, Premio speciale dell'arte nella moda, Florence 1995, CFDA Lifetime Achievement Award 2000, Medaille de Vermeil 2008. *Address:* c/o Li.ter Ltd, 26 Upper Brook Street, London W1K 7QE, Italy (office). *Telephone:* (20) 7409-1606 (office). *Fax:* (20) 7409-3110 (office). *E-mail:* ronaldfeijen@btconnect.com. *Website:* www.valentino.com.

GARAYEV, Tamerlan; Azerbaijani politician and fmr diplomatist; b. 1952, Gasimly, Agdam Region; s. of Yelmar Garayev and Khalida Garayeva; m. Farida Garayeva 1976; two s.; ed Azerbaijan Univ.; public prosecutor 1973–78; Lecturer, Azerbaijan Univ. 1978–91; became involved in opposition politics late 1980s; leader, moderate wing Popular Front, elected Deputy to Supreme Soviet 1990, Deputy Chair., First Deputy Chair. 1991–93; Amb. to China 1993–2000; mem. Org. for the Liberation of Karabakh. *Leisure interest:* golf. *E-mail:* safirprc@public.fhnet.cn.net.

GARBERS, Christoph Friedrich, DPhil; South African scientist; b. 21 Aug. 1929, Piet Retief, Transvaal; s. of Andris Wilhelm Friedrich and Lucy Sophia Carolina (née Wolhuter) Garbers; m. Barbara Z. G. Viljoen 1957; three s. one d.; ed Pretoria Univ., Zürich Univ.; Research Officer Klipfontein Organic Products 1951; Research Officer Council for Scientific and Industrial Research (CSIR) 1954–58; Sr Lecturer, Stellenbosch Univ. 1958–65, Prof. Organic Chem. 1966–78; Vice-Pres. CSIR 1979, Deputy Pres. 1980, Pres. 1980–90; Chair. S African Acad. for Science and Arts 1983–85; Chair. S African Inventions Devt Corpn 1980–90; Dir Tech. Finance Corpn (Pty) Ltd 1988–90; Chair. Certification Bd for Technikons 1989–95; Chancellor Univ. of SA 1990; Chair. Foundation for Research Devt 1990–91; mem. Scientific Advisory Council 1980–87 (Chair. 1991–94), Water Research Comm. 1980–89, Advisory Council for Tech. 1987–89; Council mem. Univ. of SA 1980–90; Trustee Hans Merensky Foundation 1980–97 (Vice-Pres. 1992–97), Trust for Health Systems Planning and Devt 1992–95; Dir (non-exec.) Allied Technologies Ltd 1991–96, Power Technologies Ltd 1992–96; mem. Nat. Comm. for Higher Educ. 1995–96, IUPAC/UNESCO Int. Council for Chemistry; Rep. at ICSU 1980–90; Hon. DSc (UNISA) 1989, (Cape Town) 1990, (Stellenbosch) 1991, (Pretoria) 1994; Havenga Prize for Chem. 1977, Gold Medal, SA Chem. Inst. 1980, State Pres. Order for Meritorious Service (Gold) 1989, M.T. Steyn Gold Medal 1990, SA Medal (Gold) 1990, H. J. van Eck Medal 1991. *Address:* POB 36716, Menlo Park 0102; 5 Domein, 443 Sussex Street, Lynnwood, Pretoria. *Fax:* 475114.

GARCIA, Andy; Cuban-American film actor, producer and director; b. (Andres Arturo Garcia Menendez), 12 April 1956, Havana; s. of Rene Garcia and Amelie Garcia; m. Marivi Lorido Garcia; one s., three d.; ed Florida Int. Univ.; moved to USA 1961; several years acting with regional theatres Fla; Hon. DFA (St John's Univ. NY) 2000; numerous awards including Harvard Univ. Foundation Award 1994, Lifetime Achievement Award, American Cancer Soc. 1996, Spirit of Hope Award 2001, Desert Palm Award, Palm Springs Film Festival 2002, Imagen Foundation Creative Achievement Award 2002. *Films include:* The Mean Season 1985, 8 Million Ways to Die 1986, The Untouchables 1987, Stand and Deliver 1987, American Roulette 1988, Black Rain 1989, Internal Affairs 1990, The Godfather III 1990, Dead Again 1991, Jennifer Eight 1992, When A Man Loves A Woman 1994, Steal Big Steal Little (also producer) 1995, Things to Do in Denver When You're Dead 1995, Night Falls on Manhattan 1997, The Disappearance of García Lorca 1997, Hoodlum 1997, Desperate Measures 1998, Just the Ticket (also producer) 1999, The Unsaid (also producer) 2000, The Man from Elysian Fields (also producer) 2000, Oceans Eleven 2001, Confidence 2003, Blackout 2003, Twisted 2004, The Lazarus Child 2004, Ocean's Twelve 2004, The Lost City 2005, Smokin' Aces 2006, The Air I Breathe 2007, Ocean's Thirteen 2007; dir: Cachao, Like His Rhythm There Is No Other 1993. *Albums produced include:* Cachao Master Sessions, Vol. I 1993 (Grammy Award 1994), Vol. II 1994 (Down Beat Critics Poll Winner 1996), Just the Ticket (soundtrack) 1999, Cachao-Cuba Linda 2000, For Love Or Country: The Arturo Sandoval Story (soundtrack) 2000, Score (Emmy Award) 2001. *Television appearances include:* Hill Street Blues, Brothers, Foley Square, Clinton and Nadine, Swing Vote (also producer)1999, For Love Or Country: The Arturo Sandoval Story (also producer) 2000. *Leisure interests:* golf, fishing. *Address:* Paradigm, attn. Clifford Stevens, 200 West 57th Street, New York, NY 10019, USA. *Telephone:* (212) 246-1030 (office). *Fax:* (212) 246-1521 (office). *E-mail:* cineson@cineson.com (office). *Website:* www.cineson.com (office).

GARCIA, Marco Aurelio; Brazilian political adviser; *President's Special Adviser for International Affairs;* b. Porto Alegre, Rio Grande do Sul; ed Fed. Univ. of Rio Grande do Sul, École des Hautes Études en Sciences Sociales, Paris; elected town councillor, Porto Alegre 1967; exiled in France and Chile, teacher Univs of Chile, Paris VIII, Paris X 1968–79; Int. Affairs Sec. and mem. Nat. Exec. Cttee Partido dos Trabalhadores (Workers' Party) 1980–; Municipal Sec. of Culture, Campinas 1989–90; co-f. Foro de São Paulo, pan-Latin American think-tank 1990; Municipal Sec. of Culture, São Paulo 2001–02; Pres.'s Special Adviser for Int. Affairs 2006–; Pres., Partido dos Trabalhadores 2006–07. *Address:* Partido dos Trabalhadores (PT) Rua Silveira Martins 132, Centro, 01019-000 São Paulo SP, Brazil (office). *Telephone:* (11) 3243-1313 (office). *Fax:* (11) 3243-1345 (office). *Website:* www.pt.org.br (office).

GARCÍA BELAÚNDE, José Antonio; Peruvian diplomatist and academic; b. 1948, Lima; ed Pontificia Universidad Católica de Perú, Academia Diplomática, Univ. of Oxford, UK; joined foreign service 1973, posts included First Sec., embassies in Washington, DC, Madrid, Paris, Mexico City, First Sec., Perm. Mission to UN, New York; fmr Dir Econ. Affairs, Ministry of Foreign Affairs; Amb. to Asociación Latinoamericana de Libre Comercio 1986–88; Dir-Sec. Bd Cartegena Agreement 1990–97; Adviser to Sec.-Gen., CAN 1997–2001, Dir-Gen. 2002–06; convenor and tutor Int. Relations Masters Programme, San Martín de Porres Univ.; Minister for Foreign Affairs 2006–08 (resgnd). *Address:* c/o Ministry of Foreign Affairs, Jirón Lampa 535, Lima 1, Peru (office).

GARCÍA BERNAL, Gael; Mexican actor; b. 30 Nov. 1978, Guadalajara, Jalisco; s. of José Angel García; one s.; ed Cen. School of Speech and Drama, London; founding mem. Canana production Co. *Films:* De tripas, corazón 1996, Cerebro 2000, Amores perros (Best Actor, Ariel Awards, Best Actor, Chicago Int. Film Festival) 2000, Y tu mamá también (Marcello Mastroianni Award, Venice Int. Film Festival) 2001, El Ojo en la nuca 2001, Vidas privadas 2001, Sin noticas de Dios 2001, The Last Post 2001, El Crimen del padre Amaro (The Crime of Father Amaro) 2002, I'm With Lucy 2002, Dot the I 2003, Dreaming of Julia 2003, Diarios de motocicleta (The Motorcycle Diaries) 2004, La Mala educación (Bad Education) 2004, Babel 2006, La Science des Rêves (The Science of Sleep) 2006, Déficit (also Dir) 2007. *Television includes:* Teresa 1989, El Abuelo y yo 1992, Fidel 2002. *Plays:* Blood Wedding (Almeida Theatre, London) 2005. *Address:* c/o Endeavor, 9701 Wilshire Blvd, 10th Floor, Beverly Hills, CA 90212, USA.

GARCÍA CARNEIRO, Gen. Jorge Luis; Venezuelan politician and army officer (retd); b. 8 Feb. 1952; m. María del Valle de García; three s.; two d.; ed Mil. Acad. Venezuela; fmr Commdt Pelotón, Batallion; Commdt and teacher, Mil. Acad. Venezuela; Commdt and teacher, Army Tech. Coll.; Commdt First Co. Ricaurte Infantry Battalion; Second in Command, Carabobo Battalion Edo. Táchira; First Commdt GB José Ignacio Pulido, San Juan de Colon, Edo. Táchira; Commdt Barinas, Mérida, Caracas and Táchira garrisons; Chief of Staff, Acquisition of War Materials USA; First Commdt, Ministry of Defence HQ; Dir, Mil. Acad. Venezuela; Minister of Nat. Defence –2005; numerous decorations including Order Francisco de Miranda, Order Rafael Urdaneta, Order Nat. Defence, Order Estrella de Carabobo, Order of Merit Army, Civil Defence, Order José de Cruz Carrillo, Order Tulio Febres Cordero, Order García d'Hevia, Order Bicentenaria de la Ilustre Universidad de Los Andes, Order Rómulo Gallegos. *Address:* c/o Ministry of National Defence, Edif. 17 de Diciembre, planta baja, Base Aérea Francisco de Miranda, La Carlota, Caracas, Venezuela (office).

GARCÍA DE ALBA ZEPEDA, Sergio Alejandro, BA, MA; Mexican government official and business executive; ed Instituto Tecnológico y de Estudios Superiores de Occidente (ITESO), Guadalajara, IPADE, Mexico City; Prof. of Finance ITESO 1980–84; Pres. Regional Chamber of Manufacturing Industry of Jalisco (CAREINTRA) 1993–94; Vice-Pres. Confed. of Industrial Chambers of Mexico (CONCAMIN) 1993–95; founding mem. and Dir-Gen. Fibrart –1995; Sec. of Econ. Promotion, Jalisco state 1995–2001; Regional Vice-Pres. Axtel 2001; Under-Sec. for Small and Medium-Sized Businesses, Secr. of the Economy 2003–05, Sec. of the Economy 2005–06; CAREINTRA Outstanding Businessman Award 1989, Asscn of Sales and Marketing Execs of Guadalajara Exec. of 1993, Ocho Columnas newspaper Columna de Oro 1999, COPARMEX Jalisco Efraín González Luna Prize for Political Merit 2005. *Address:* c/o Secretariat of State for the Economy, Alfonso Reyes 30, Col. Hipódromo Condesa, 06170 México, Mexico (office).

GARCÍA FRANCO, Marco Tulio; Guatemalan politician; Minister of Nat. Defence 2008–. *Address:* Ministry of National Defence, Antigua Escuela Politécnica, Avda La Reforma 1–45, Zona 10, Guatemala City, Guatemala (office). *Telephone:* 2360-9890 (office). *Fax:* 2360-9909 (office). *Website:* www.mindef.mil.gt (office).

GARCÍA-GASCO Y VICENTE, HE Cardinal Agustín; Spanish ecclesiastic; *Archbishop of Valencia;* b. 12 Feb. 1931, Corral de Almaguer; ordained priest 1956; Auxiliary Bishop of Madrid and Titular Bishop of Nona 1985–92; Archbishop of Valencia 1992–; cr. Cardinal (Cardinal-Priest of S. Marcello) 2007; served as Sec.-Gen. Spanish Bishops' Conf. and Bishop-Del. of Caritas (Catholic Church's aid org.); f. distance-learning inst. of theology. *Address:* Archdiocese of Valencia, Palau 2, 46003 Valencia, Spain (office). *Telephone:* (963) 829700 (office). *Fax:* (963) 918120 (office). *E-mail:* info@archivalencia.org (office). *Website:* www.archivalencia.org (office).

GARCÍA LINERA, Álvaro Marcelo; Bolivian politician, mathematician and sociologist; *Vice-President;* b. 19 Oct. 1962, Cochabamba; ed Colegio San Agustin, Nat. Autonomous Univ. of Mexico; fmr Prof. of Sociology, Universidad Mayor de San Andrés, La Paz; mem. Tupaj Katari guerilla group, served five years in prison 1992–97; fmr political commentator; mem. Movt Toward Socialism party; Vice-Pres. of Bolivia 2006–. *Publications:* several books and articles. *Address:* Ministry of the Presidency, Palacio de Gobierno, Plaza Murillo, La Paz, Bolivia (office). *Telephone:* (2) 237-1082 (office). *Fax:* (2) 237-1388 (office). *E-mail:* webmaster@presidencia.gov.bo (office). *Website:* www.presidencia.gov.bo (office).

GARCÍA LUNA, Genaro, BSc; Mexican police officer and politician; *Secretary of Public Security;* b. 10 July 1968, Mexico City; ed Autonomous Metropolitan Univ.; researcher, Sub-Dept of Foreign Affairs, Center for Research and Nat. Security (CISEN) 1988–98; Gen. Intelligence Coordinator for Prevention, Fed. Preventive Police Force 1998–2000; Dir-Gen. of Planning and Operations, Fed. Judicial Police (now Fed. Investigations Agency) 2000–03, Co-ordinator Tech. Cttee 2003–04; Chair. Strategic Information Sub-cttee, Interpol 2004–05; Sec. of Public Security 2006–. *Address:* Secretariat of State for Public Security, Londres 102, 7°, Col. Juaréz, 06600 México DF, Mexico (office). *E-mail:* enlace@ssp.gob.mx (office). *Website:* www.ssp.gob.mx (office).

GARCÍA MACAL, José Carlos; Guatemalan economist and politician; *Minister of the Economy;* fmr Adviser, Secr. for Cen. American Econ. Integration (SIECA); fmr Vice-Minister of the Economy; Minister of the Economy 2008–. *Address:* Ministry of the Economy, 8a Avda 10-43, Zona 1, Guatemala City, Guatemala (office). *Telephone:* 2238-3330 (office). *Fax:* 2238-2413 (office). *E-mail:* einteriano@mineco.gob.gt (office). *Website:* www.mineco.gob.gt (office).

GARCÍA MÁRQUEZ, Gabriel (Gabo) José; Colombian writer; b. 6 March 1928, Aracataca; s. of Gabriel Eligio García and Luisa Santiaga Márquez; m. Mercedes Barch March 1958; two s.; ed secondary school and Universidad Nacional de Colombia, Universidad de Cartagena; began writing books 1946; lived in Baranquilla; corresp. El Espectador in Rome, Paris; first novel published while living in Caracas, Venezuela 1957; est. bureau of Prensa Latina (Cuban press agency) in Bogotá; worked for Prensa Latina in Havana, Cuba, then as Deputy Head of New York Office 1961; lived in Spain, contributing to magazines Mundo Nuevo, Casa de las Américas; went to Mexico; founder-Pres., Fundación Habeas 1979–; invited back to Colombia by Pres. 1982; Hon. Fellow, American Acad. of Arts and Letters; Hon. Pres. Latin America Solidarity Action Foundation (Alas) 2006–; Hon. LLD (Columbia Univ., New York) 1971; Colombian Asscn of Writers and Artists Award 1954, Premio Literario Esso (Colombia) 1961, Chianciano Award (Italy) 1969, Prix de Meilleur Livre Étranger (France) 1969, Books Abroad/Neustadt International Prize for Literature 1972, Rómulo Gallegos Prize (Venezuela) 1972, Nobel Prize for Literature 1982, Los Angeles Times Book Prize for Fiction 1988, Serfin Prize 1989, Premio Príncipe de Asturias 1999. *Publications:* fiction: La hojarasca (trans. as Leaf Storm and Other Stories) 1955, El coronel no tiene quien le escriba (trans. as No One Writes to the Colonel and Other Stories) 1961, La mala hora (trans. as In Evil Hour) 1962, Los funerales de la Mamá Grande (trans. as Funerals of the Great Matriarch) 1962, Cien años de soledad (trans. as One Hundred Years of Solitude) 1967, Isabel viendo llover en Macondo 1967, La incredíble y triste historia de la cándida Eréndira y su abuela desalmada (trans. as Innocent Erendira and Other Stories) 1972, El negro que hizo esperar a los angeles 1972, Ojos de perro azul 1972, El otoño del patriarca (trans. as The Autumn of the Patriarch) 1975, Todos los cuentos de Gabriel García Márquez: 1947–1972 1975, Crónica de una muerte anunciada (trans. as Chronicle of a Death Foretold) 1981, El rastro de tu sangre en la nieve: El verano feliz de la señora Forbes 1982, María de mi corazón (screenplay, with J. H. Hermosillo) 1983, Collected Stories 1984, El amor en los tiempos del cólera (trans. as Love in the Time of Cholera) 1984, El General en su laberinto (trans. as The General in his Labyrinth) 1989, Amores difíciles 1989, Doce cuentos peregrinos (trans. as Strange Pilgrims: Twelve Stories) 1992, Del amor y otros demonios (trans. as Of Love and Other Demons) 1994, La bendita manía de contar 1998, Memoria de mis putas tristes (trans. as

Memories of my Melancholy Whores) 2004, Telling Tales (contrib. to charity anthology) 2004; non-fiction: La novela en América Latina: Diálogo (with Mario Vargas Llosa) 1968, Relato de un náufrago (trans. as The Story of a Shipwrecked Sailor) 1970, Cuando era feliz e indocumentado 1973, Crónicas y reportajes 1978, Periodismo militante 1978, De viaje por los países socialistas: 90 días en la 'cortina de hierro' 1978, Obra periodistica (four vols) 1981–83, El olor de la guayaba: Conversaciones con Plinio Apuleyo Mendoza (trans. as The Fragrance of Guava) 1982, Persecución y muerte de minorías: Dos perspectivas 1984, La aventura de Miguel Littín, clandestino en Chile: Un reportaje (trans. as Clandestine in Chile: The Adventures of Miguel Littín) 1986, Primeros reportajes 1990, Notas de prensa 1980–1984 1991, Elogio de la utopia: una entrevista de Nahuel Maciel 1992, Noticia de un secuestro (trans. as News of a Kidnapping) 1996, Vivir para contarla (memoir, vol. one, trans. as Living to Tell the Tale) 2002. *Address:* Agencia Literaria Carmen Balcells, Avenida Diagonal 580, 08021 Barcelona, Spain (office). *Telephone:* (93) 2008933 (office). *Fax:* (93) 2007041 (office). *E-mail:* ag-balcells@ag-balcells.com (office).

GARCÍA MEDINA, Amalia; Mexican politician; *Governor, Zacatecas State;* b. 6 Oct. 1951, Zacatecas; d. of Francisco García and Conceptión Medina; one d.; ed Autonomous University of Zacatecas, National Autonomous University of Mexico (UNAM), Benemerita Universidad Autónoma de Puebla; Fed. Deputy 1988–91; mem. Rep. Ass. for Fed. Dist 1991–94; Senator 1997–2002; Gov. Zacatecas State 2004–; Founding mem. Partido de la Revolución Democrática, Nat. Pres. 1999–2002; mem. Consultative Council of Women, Human Rights Comm. *Leisure interests:* reading, films. *Address:* c/o General Secretariat of Government, Avenida Hidalgo 604, Centro Histórico, CP 98000, Zacatecas, Zac., Mexico. *E-mail:* agarcia@mail.zacatecas.gob.mx. *Website:* www.zacatecas.gob.mx/Gobernadora.asp.

GARCÍA PELÁEZ, Raúl, LLD; Cuban politician, diplomatist and lawyer; b. 15 Jan. 1922; ed Univ. of Havana; fmr mem. July 26th Revolutionary Cttee; later Prosecutor at Camagüey Court of Appeal, then Chair. Camagüey Municipal Council for Co-ordination and Inspection; then Gen. Treas. Revolutionary Forces in Camagüey Prov., Rep. of Nat. Inst. of Agrarian Reform in Nuevitas and Gen. Sec. Matanzas Prov. Cttee of United Party of Cuban Socialist Revolution; mem. Cen. Cttee of Cuban CP 1965–80, Head of Revolutionary Orientation Comm. of Cent. Cttee of Cuban CP –1967; Amb. to USSR 1967–74. *Address:* c/o Partido Comunista, Plaza de la Revolución, Havana, Cuba.

GARCÍA PÉREZ, Alan Gabriel Ludwig; Peruvian politician and head of state; *President;* b. 23 May 1949, Lima; s. of Carlos García Ronceros and Nyta Pérez de García; m. Pilar Nores; four d.; ed José María Eguren Nat. Coll., Universidad Católica, Lima, Universidad Nacional Mayor de San Marcos (graduated as lawyer), Universidad Complutense, Madrid, Spain, Sorbonne and Inst. of Higher Latin American Studies, Paris, France; mem. of Partido Aprista Peruano since his teens; returned to Peru and elected mem. of Constituent Ass. 1978; subsequently apptd Org. Sec. and Chair. Ideology of Aprista Party (now Alianza Popular Revolucionaria Americana), Parl. Deputy 1980–85, Sec.-Gen. of Party 1982, later Pres.; Senator for Life 1990–; nominated Presidential cand. 1984, obtained largest number of votes, nat. presidential elections April 1985; on withdrawal of Izquierda Unida cand., Alfonso Barrantes Lingán, proclaimed Pres.-elect June 1985, assuming powers 1985–89; granted political asylum in Colombia June 1992; returned from exile Jan. 2001; Pres. of Peru 2006–. *Address:* c/o Ministry of the Presidency, Avda Paseo de la República 4297, Lima 1 (office); Alianza Popular Revolucionaria Americana, Avda Alfonso Ugarte 1012, Lima 5, Peru. *Telephone:* (1) 4465886 (office). *Fax:* (1) 4470379 (office). *Website:* www.peru.gob.pe (office).

GARCÍA RAMÍREZ, Sergio, PhD; Mexican politician, lawyer and judge; b. 1 Feb. 1938, Guadalajara; ed Nat. Univ. of Mexico; Research Fellow and teacher of penal law, Inst. of Juridical Research, Nat. Univ. of Mexico 1966–76; Dir Correction Centre, State of Mexico and Judge, Juvenile Courts; Asst Dir of Govt Ministry of Interior; Attorney-Gen. of Fed. Dist; Under-Sec. Ministries of Nat. Resources, Interior, Educ., Industrial Devt; Dir Prevention Centre of Mexico City; fmr Minister of Labour; Attorney-Gen. 1982–88; Pres. Inter-American Court of Human Rights (IACHR) (Corte Interamericana de Derechos Humanos), OAS, San José, Costa Rica 2004–07; mem. Mexican Acad. of Penal Sciences, Mexican Inst. of Penal Law, Nat. Inst. of Public Admin., Ibero-American Inst. of Penal Law etc. *Publications:* Teseo Alucinado 1966, Asistencia a Reos Liberados 1966, El Artículo 18 Constitucional 1967, La Imputabilidad en el Derecho Penal Mexicano, El Código Tutelar para Menores del Estado Michoacán 1969, La Ciudadanía de la Juventud 1970, La Prisión 1975, Los Derechos Humanos y el Derecho Penal 1976, Legislación Penitenciaria y Correccional Comentada 1978, Otros Minotauros 1979, Cuestiones Criminológicas y Penales Contemporáneas 1981, Justicia Penal 1982. *Address:* Circuito Maestro Mario de la Cueva s/n, Cd. Universitaria, CP 04510, Mexico City, Mexico (office). *Telephone:* (55) 5622-7474 (office). *Fax:* (55) 5665-2193 (office). *E-mail:* sgr@servidor.unam.mx (office). *Website:* www.juridicas.unam.mx (office).

GARCÍA SAYAN LARABURRE, Diego, LLB; Peruvian politician and lawyer; b. 1950; ed Univ. of Lima, Univ. of Texas, USA; constitutional lawyer; Head Andean Comm. of Jurists; Rep. of Peru Inter-American Comm. on Human Rights; fmr Minister of Justice; Minister of Foreign Affairs 2001–02; Chair. UN Working Group on Enforced or Involuntary Disappearances 2002. *Address:* c/o Ministry of Foreign Affairs, Palacio de Torre Tagle, Jirón Ucayali 363, Lima 1, Peru (office).

GARCÍA-VALDECASAS Y FERNÁNDEZ, Rafael, DJur; Spanish judge; *Judge, Court of First Instance of the European Communities;* b. 9 Jan. 1946, Granada; m. Rosario Castaño Parraga 1975; ed Univ. of Granada; lawyer, Office of Attorney-Gen. 1976; mem. Office of Attorney-Gen. Tax and Judicial Affairs Office, Jaén 1976–85; mem. Office of Attorney-Gen. Econ. and Admin. Court of Jaén 1979–85; mem. Jaén Bar 1979–89, Granada Bar 1981–89; mem. Office of Attorney-Gen. Econ. and Admin. Court of Córdoba 1983–85, Tax and Judicial Affairs Office of Granada 1986–87; Head, Spanish State Legal Service for cases before EC Court of Justice (Ministry of Foreign Affairs) 1987–89; Judge, Court of First Instance of the European Communities 1989–; Encomienda de la Orden Civil del Mérito Agrícola 1982, Encomienda de la Orden de Isabel la Católica 1990, Gran Cruz de la Orden del Mérito Civil 1999. *Publications:* Comentarios al Tratado de Adhesión de España a la C.E.: La Agricultura 1985, El 'acquis' comunitario 1986, El medio ambiente: conservación de espacios protegidos en la legislación de la CE 1992, La Jurisprudencia del Tribunal de Justicia CE sobre la libertad de establecimiento y libre prestación de servicios por los abogados 1993, El Tribunal de Primera Instancia de las Comunidades Europeas 1993, El respeto del derecho de defensa en materia de competencia 1997, El desarollo normativo de los reglamentos comunitarios 1999; also papers in books and learned journals. *Leisure interests:* swimming, cycling, fishing. *Address:* European Court of First Instance of the European Communities, Erasmus 2036, Rue du Fort Niedergrünewald, 2925 Luxembourg, Luxembourg (office).

GARDAM, Jane Mary, OBE, BA, FRSL; British novelist; b. 11 July 1928, Coatham; d. of William Pearson and Kathleen Pearson (née Helm); m. David Hill Gardam 1954; two s. one d.; ed Saltburn High School for Girls, Bedford Coll. for Women, Univ. of London; oo-ordinator UK Hosp. Libraries British Red Cross 1951–53; Literary Ed. Time and Tide 1952–54; mem. PEN; Hon. DLitt. *Radio play:* The Tribute. *Publications:* juvenile fiction: A Long Way from Verona 1971, A Few Fair Days 1971, The Summer After the Funeral 1973, Bilgewater 1977; novels: God on the Rocks (Prix Baudelaire) 1978, The Hollow Land (Whitbread Literary Award 1983) 1981, Bridget and William 1981, Horse 1982, Kit 1983, Crusoe's Daughter 1985, Kit in Boots 1986, Swan 1987, Through the Doll's House Door 1987, The Queen of the Tambourine (Whitbread Novel Award) 1991, Faith Fox 1996, Tufty Bear 1996, The Green Man 1998, The Flight of the Maidens 2000, Old Filth 2004, The People of Privilege Hill 2007; short stories: Black Faces, White Faces (David Higham Award 1978, Winifred Holtby Award 1978) 1975, The Sidmouth Letters 1980, The Pangs of Love (Katherine Mansfield Award 1984) 1983, Showing the Flag 1989, Going into a Dark House 1994, Missing the Midnight 1997; non-fiction: The Iron Coast 1994. *Leisure interests:* agriculture. *Address:* Haven House, Sandwich, Kent CT13 9ES; Throstlenest Farm, Crackpot, N Yorks; 34 Denmark Road, London, SW19, England. *Telephone:* (14304) 612680.

GARDE DUE, Ulrik, BBA; Danish business executive; *CEO, Georg Jensen;* b. 14 Jan. 1963, Copenhagen; ed Koebmandskolen, Copenhagen, Schiller Int. Univ., Paris/London, CESDIP (CPA), Paris, Corp. Finance Programme, London Business School; Commercial Asst and Ship Broker, Holm & Wonsild ApS (EAC), Copenhagen 1981–83; Oil Broker, Fretoil (Hunting Group), Paris and London 1984–86; Commercial Counsellor and Export Consultant for the Danish Ministry of Foreign Affairs, Danish Embassy, Paris 1986–89; Commercial Officer in charge of launch/real-estate promotion of the WTC, CNIT (SARI), La Défense, Paris 1989–90; Commercial Officer, Europe Distribution, Wholesale, Licensees and DFS, Celine SA (LVMH), Paris 1990; Commercial Dir of SE Asia, Celine SA (LVMH), Tokyo, Vice-Pres. Celine Inc. (LVMH) N America, New York 1993–97; Int. Dir of Marketing and Sales, Cerruti 1881 GmbH (Escada Group), Paris, global responsibility for Marketing and Sales in SE Asia, the Middle East and USA 1997–98; Sr Vice-Pres., Int. Sales, Burberry Ltd, London 1998, Gen. Man. role in brand turn-around 2002; Dir (non-exec.) Royal Copenhagen (Axcel), Copenhagen 2004–; CEO Georg Jensen 2007–. *Address:* Georg Jensen A/S, 7 Soendre Fasanvej, 2000 Frederiksberg, Denmark (office). *Telephone:* 38-14-98-98 (office). *Fax:* 38-14-99-70 (office). *E-mail:* info@georgjensen.com (office). *Website:* www.georgjensen.com (office).

GARDEL, Louis; French publishing editor, novelist and screenwriter; b. 8 Sept. 1939, Algiers, Algeria; s. of Jacques Gardel and Janine Blasselle; m. 1st Béatrice Herr (deceased) 1963; m. 2nd Hélène Millerand 1990; two s. two d.; ed Lycée Bugeaud, Algiers, Lycée Louis-le-Grand, Paris and Institut d'Etudes Politiques, Paris; Head of Dept Inst. des Hautes Etudes d'Outre-Mer 1962–64; Man. Soc. Rhône-Progil 1964–74; Head of Dept Conseil Nat. du Patronat 1974–80; Literary Consultant, Editions du Seuil 1980, Literary Ed. 1980–; mem. juries Prix Renaudot, Conseil Supérieur de la Langue Française; Chevalier, Légion d'honneur. *Film screenplays:* Fort Saganne, Nocturne Indien, Indochine, La Marche de Radetzky 1996, Est.Ouest, Himalaya 1999, Princesse Marie 2005. *Publications:* L'Eté Fracassé 1973, Couteau de chaleur 1976, Fort Saganne 1980 (Grand Prix du Roman de l'Acad. française), Notre Homme 1986, Le Beau Rôle 1989, Darbaroud 1993. L'Aurore des Bien-Aimés 1997, Grand-Seigneur 1999, La Gare d'Alger 2007. *Leisure interest:* horses. *Address:* 25 rue de la Cerisaie, 75004, Paris (home); Editions du Seuil, 27 rue Jacob, 75006 Paris, France (office). *Telephone:* 1-40-46-50-50 (office). *E-mail:* froumens@seuil.com (office).

GÄRDENFORS, Peter, PhD; Swedish academic; *Professor of Cognitive Science, Lund University;* b. 21 Sept. 1949, Degeberga; s. of Torsten Gärdenfors and Ingemor Gärdenfors (née Jonsson); m. Annette Wald 1975 (divorced 2002); three s. one d.; ed Lund Univ., Princeton Univ., USA; Lecturer in Philosophy, Lund Univ. 1974–80, Reader in Philosophy of Science 1975–77, Reader in Philosophy 1980–88, Prof. of Cognitive Science, 1988–; Visiting Fellow, Princeton Univ., USA 1973–74, ANU 1986–87; Visiting Scholar, Stanford Univ., USA 1983–84; Visiting Prof., Univ. of Buenos Aires 1990; Ed. Theoria 1978–86, Journal of Logic, Language and Information 1991–96; mem. Royal Swedish Acad. of Letters, Academia Europaea, Deutsche Akad. für Naturforscher Leopoldina; Rausing Prize 1986. *Publica-*

tions: Generalized Quantifiers (ed.) 1986, Knowledge in Flux 1988, Decision, Probability and Utility (with N.-E. Sahlin) 1988, Belief Revision (ed.) 1992, Blotta Tanken 1992, Fangslande Information 1996, Cognitive Semantics (with J. Allwood) 1998, Conceptual Spaces 2000, How Homo Became Sapiens 2003. *Leisure interests:* botany, walking, judo, climbing. *Address:* Department of Philosophy, Kungshuset, Lundagard, 222 22 Lund, Sweden (office). *Telephone:* (46) 2224817 (office). *Fax:* (46) 2224424 (office). *E-mail:* peter.gardenfors@lucs.lu.se (office). *Website:* www.lucs.lu.se/people/Peter.Gardenfors (office).

GARDENT, Paul; French mining executive and state councillor; b. 10 July 1921, Grenoble; s. of Louis Gardent and Edith Gardent (née Rocher); m. Janine Robert 1958; one s.; ed Ecole Polytechnique, Ecole Nat. des Mines; Mining Engineer, Valenciennes 1944–48; Asst Chief Mining Engineer, Lille 1948–49, Chief Mining Engineer 1950; Tech. Adviser to J. M. Louvel (Minister of Industry and Commerce) 1950–52; Dir of Gen. Studies, Charbonnages de France 1952–58; Dir of Gen. Studies and Financial Services, Houillères du bassin de Lorraine 1958–63; Asst Dir, then Dir-Gen. Houillères du bassin du Nord et du Pas-de-Calais 1963–68; Dir-Gen. Charbonnages de France 1968–80; Conseiller d'Etat 1980–86; Pres. Coll. de la Prévention des Risques Technologiques 1989–91; Pres. Comm. Interministérielle des Radioéléments artificiels 1981–2002, Comm. d'Aide aux Riverains des Aéroports 1985–97; Hon. Conseiller d'Etat; Commdr Légion d'honneur, Commdr Ordre nat. du Mérite, Officier de l'Ouissam Alaouite. *Publications:* Le Charbon, Panorama Economique 1960. *Address:* 5 rue de la Chaise, Paris 75007, France (home). *Telephone:* 1-45-44-03-43 (home). *Fax:* 1-45-48-64-21 (home). *E-mail:* japa.gardent@wanadoo.fr (home).

GARDINER, Sir John Eliot, Kt, CBE, MA, FRSA; British conductor and music director; b. 20 April 1943, Fontmell Magna, Dorset; s. of the late Rolf Gardiner and of Marabel Gardiner (née Hodgkin); m. 1st Cherryl Anne Ffoulkes 1971 (divorced 1981); m. 2nd Elizabeth Suzanne Wilcock 1981 (divorced 1997); three d.; m. 3rd Isabella de Sabata 2001; ed Bryanston School, King's Coll., Cambridge, King's Coll., London, and in Paris and Fontainebleau with Nadia Boulanger; Founder and Artistic Dir Monteverdi Choir, 1964, Monteverdi Orchestra 1968, the English Baroque Soloists 1978, Orchestre Révolutionnaire et Romantique 1990; concert debut Wigmore Hall, London 1966; youngest conductor Henry Wood Promenade Concerts, Royal Albert Hall 1968; operatic debut Sadler's Wells Opera, London Coliseum 1969; Prin. Conductor CBC Vancouver Orchestra 1980–83; Musical Dir Lyon Opera 1982–88, Chef fondateur 1988–; Artistic Dir Göttingen Handel Festival 1981–90, Veneto Music Festival 1986; Prin. Conductor NDR Symphony Orchestra, Hamburg 1991–94; residency at the Théâtre du Châtelet, Paris Oct. 1999–2003; Bach Cantata Pilgrimage, with performances throughout Europe 2000; Guest Conductor at the Royal Opera House, Covent Garden: Iphigénie en Tauride 1982, Chérubin 1994, The Cunning Little Vixen 2003, La Finta Giardiniera 2006, Simon Boccanegra 2008; regular guest conductor with the London Symphony Orchestra, the Czech Philharmonic and other major orchestras in Amsterdam, Paris, Dresden, Vienna, Berlin, Chicago; Domaine privé, Cité de la musique, Paris 2007; appearances at European music festivals, including Aix-en-Provence, Aldeburgh, Bath, Berlin, Edinburgh, Flanders, Netherlands, London, Salzburg, BBC Proms; Visiting Fellow, Peterhouse Coll., Cambridge 2007–08; Hon. Fellow, King's Coll., London 1992, Royal Acad. of Music 1992; Commdr, Ordre des Arts et des Lettres 1997, City of Leipzig and Bach Archiv Bach Medal for lifetime achievement in the performance of music by J. S. Bach 2005, Officer's Cross of the Order of Merit (Germany) 2005; Dr hc (Univ. Lumière de Lyon) 1987, (Complutense Univ. of Madrid) 2001, (New England Conservatoire) 2005, (Cremona) 2006; 17 Gramophone awards, including Record of the Year 1991, 2005, Artist of the Year 1994, eight Edison Awards, four Grands Prix du Disque, three Prix Caecilia, two Arturo Toscanini Music Critics' awards, three Deutscher Schallplattenpreis, Buxtehude Prize Lübeck 1994, Robert Schumann Preis Zwickau 2001, Halle Handel Prize 2001, Classic FM Gramophone Award 2005, Leonie Sonning Music Prize 2005, Royal Academy of Music/Kohn Foundation Bach Prize 2008. *Leisure interests:* forestry, organic farming.

GARDNER, David Pierpont, BSc, MA, PhD; American university president, professor of education and foundation executive; *President Emeritus, University of California;* b. 24 March 1933, Berkeley, Calif.; s. of Reed S. Gardner and Margaret Pierpont Gardner; m. 1st Elizabeth Fuhriman 1958 (died 1991); four d.; m. 2nd Sheila Sprague Gardner 1995; ed Brigham Young Univ. and Univ. of Calif., Berkeley; Admin. Asst, Personnel Man. and Prin. Asst to Chief Admin. Officer, Calif. Farm Bureau Fed., Berkeley 1958–60; Field and Scholarship Dir Calif. Alumni Asscn, Univ. of Calif., Berkeley 1960–62, Dir Calif. Alumni Foundation 1962–64; Asst to Chancellor Univ. of Calif., Santa Barbara 1964–67, Asst Chancellor and Asst Prof. of Higher Educ. 1967–69, Vice-Chancellor, Exec. Asst and Assoc. Prof. of Higher Educ. 1969–70; Vice-Pres. Univ. of Calif. and Prof. of Higher Educ. (on leave from Univ. of Calif., Santa Barbara) 1971–73; Pres. Univ. of Utah and Prof. of Higher Educ. 1973–83, Pres. Emer. 1985; Pres. Univ. of Calif. 1983–92 (Pres. Emer. 1992–), Prof. of Higher Educ., Univ. of Calif., Berkeley 1983–92, Chair. Nat. Comm. on Excellence in Educ. 1981–83; Pres. William and Flora Hewlett Foundation, Menlo Park Calif. 1993–99; Chair. Bd of Trustees, J. Paul Getty Trust, LA 2000–2004; Visiting Fellow, Clare Hall, Cambridge Univ. 1979, Life Mem. 1979–, Hon. Fellow 2002; numerous professional appointments, directorships, trusteeships etc.; Fellow, American Acad. of Arts and Sciences, Nat. Acad. of Public Admin.; mem. Nat. Acad. of Educ., American Philosophical Soc.; Fulbright Fellow, Japan 1987; mem. Bd of Dirs Fluor Corpn 1988–2006; Chevalier Légion d'honneur 1985, Kt Commdr's Cross Order of Merit (Germany) 1992; 12 hon. degrees; numerous awards and distinctions including James Bryant Conant Award, Educ. Comm. of USA 1985. *Publications:* The California Oath Controversy 1967, Earning My Degree: Memoirs of an American University President 2005; numerous articles in professional journals. *Leisure interests:* fly fishing, travel. *Address:* 2989 American Saddler Drive, Park City, UT 84060 (home); c/o Center for Studies in Higher Education, Evans Hall, University of California, Berkeley, CA 94720, USA (office). *Telephone:* (510) 642-5040 (office); (435) 604-0904 (home). *Fax:* (435) 604-0905 (home).

GARDNER, Edward; British conductor; *Music Director, English National Opera;* b. Gloucester; ed King's Coll., Cambridge and Royal Acad. of Music; fmr Asst Conductor Hallé Orchestra; Music Dir Glyndebourne Touring Opera 2004–06, with productions including La Bohème 2004, La Cenerentola 2005, The Turn of the Screw 2006, Fidelio 2006; has conducted Camerata Salzburg, London Philharmonic, Melbourne Symphony, Belgrade Philharmonic, Royal Scottish Nat. Orchestra, BBC Symphony Orchestra, Philharmonia, Alabama Symphony, Orchestre de Bretagne; season 2005–06 appearances included BBC Scottish Symphony Orchestra, BBC Nat. Orchestra of Wales, Vancouver Symphony, Orquestra Nacional do Porto, MDR Leipzig, Orchestre Philharmonique de Liège; opera highlights include Tchaikovsky's Eugene Onegin with Glyndebourne Touring Opera 2002, Meyerbeer's L'Africaine with Strasbourg Opera 2004, Mozart's Cosí fan Tutte with ENO 2005, Adams' The Death of Klinghoffer with Scottish Opera 2005, Weill's Seven Deadly Sins with Paris Opéra 2005, Royal Opera debut Il re pastore 2006, Donizetti's L'Elisir d'Amore, Paris Opéra 2006, Stravinsky's The Rake's Progress, Paris 2007–08; Music Dir, ENO 2006–; Royal Philharmonic Soc. Award for Best Young Artist 2005, for Best Conductor 2008, Olivier Award for Outstanding Achievement in Opera 2009. *Address:* c/o IMG Artists, The Light Box, 111 Power Road, London, W4 5PY, England (office); English National Opera, London Coliseum, St Martin's Lane, London, WC2N 4ES (office). *Telephone:* (20) 7957-5800 (office). *Fax:* (20) 7957-5801 (office). *E-mail:* labrahams@imgartists.com (office). *Website:* www.imgartists.com (office); www.eno.org.

GARDNER, Sir Richard Lavenham, Kt, PhD, FRS; British scientist and academic; *Royal Society Edward Penley Abraham Research Professor, Department of Zoology, University of Oxford;* b. 10 June 1943, Dorking; s. of the late Allan Constant and Eileen May Gardner; m. Wendy Joy Cresswell 1968; one s.; ed St John's School, Leatherhead, NE Surrey Coll. of Tech., St Catharine's Coll. Cambridge; Research Asst, Physiological Lab., Cambridge 1970–73; Lecturer in Devt and Reproductive Biology, Dept of Zoology, Oxford 1973–77, Research Student Christ Church 1974–77, Ordinary Students 1978–, Royal Soc. Henry Dale Research Prof. 1978–, Royal Soc. Edward Penley Abraham Research Prof. 2003–; Hon. Dir Imperial Cancer Research Fund Developmental Biology Unit 1986–96; ind. mem. Advisory Bd for the Research Councils 1990–93; Pres. Inst. of Biology 2006–08; Scientific Medal, Zoological Soc. 1977, March of Dimes Prize in Developmental Biology 1999, Royal Medal, Royal Soc. 2001, Albert Brachet Prize, Belgian Royal Acad. of Sciences, Letters and Fine Arts. *Publications:* various scientific papers. *Leisure interests:* ornithology, music, sailing, gardening, painting. *Address:* Christ Church, Oxford, OX1 1DP, England (office). *Telephone:* (1865) 281319 (office). *Fax:* (1865) 281310 (office). *E-mail:* richard.gardner@zoo.ox.ac.uk (office). *Website:* www.zoo.ox.ac.uk (office).

GARDNER, Richard Newton, DPhil; American diplomatist, lawyer and academic; *Professor of Law and International Organization, Columbia University;* b. 9 July 1927, New York; s. of Samuel I. Gardner and Ethel E. Gardner; m. Danielle Almeida Luzzatto 1956; one s. one d.; ed Harvard Univ., Yale Law School, Univ. of Oxford, UK; Rhodes Scholar to Oxford Univ. 1951–54; Prof. of Law and Int. Org., Columbia Univ. 1957–61, 1965–76, 1981–; Deputy Asst Sec. of State for Int. Org. Affairs, US State Dept 1961–65; Amb. to Italy 1977–81; Lawyer, Coudert Bros 1981–93; Consultant to Sec.-Gen., UN Conf. on Environment and Devt 1992; Amb. to Spain 1993–97; Counsel, Morgan, Lewis and Bockius 1997–; mem. US Advisory Cttee on Law of the Sea 1971–76, Vice-Pres.'s Advisory Cttee for Foreign Trade Policy and Negotiations 1998–; Del. to UN Gen. Ass. 2000; mem. Trilateral Comm., Council on Foreign Relations; mem. American Philosophical Soc.; Arthur S. Flemming Award 1963, Thomas Jefferson Award 1998. *Publications:* Sterling-Dollar Diplomacy 1956, In Pursuit of World Order 1964, Blueprint for Peace 1966, The Global Partnership: International Agencies and Economic Development 1968, Negotiating Survival: Four Priorities after Rio 1992. *Leisure interests:* tennis, classical music, reading. *Address:* Columbia University School of Law, 435 West 116th Street, New York, NY 10027, USA. *Telephone:* (212) 854-4635 (office). *Fax:* (212) 854-7946 (office). *E-mail:* rgardn@law.columbia.edu (office). *Website:* www.law.columbia.edu (office).

GARDNER, Sir Roy Alan, Kt, FCCA; British business executive; *Chairman, Compass Group PLC;* b. 20 Aug. 1945, Chiswick, London; s. of Thomas Gardner and Iris Gardner; m. Carol Gardner 1969; one s. two d.; ed Strodes School, Egham; Finance Dir, Marconi Space and Defence Systems 1975–84, Marconi 1984–85; Finance Dir STC PLC, Man. Dir STC Communications Ltd 1986–91, mem. Bd Dirs STC PLC 1986–91; COO Northern Telecom Europe Ltd 1991–92; Man. Dir GEC-Marconi Ltd 1992–94; Dir GEC PLC 1994; Finance Dir British Gas PLC 1994–95, Exec. Dir 1995–96; CEO Centrica 1997–2005; Sr Dir (non-exec.) Compass Group 2005–06, Chair. 2006–, Chair. Nomination and Corp. Responsibility Cttees; Dir (non-exec.) Manchester United PLC, Chair. (non-exec.) 2002–05, Willis Group Holdings Ltd, Mainstream Renewable Power Ltd; fmr Dir (non-exec.) Laporte plc; Sr Adviser, Credit Suisse; Pres. Energy Inst., Carers UK; Chair. Advisory Bd of Energy Futures Lab., Imperial Coll. London; Chair. British Olympics Appeal Cttee for the Beijing Games, Apprenticeship Ambassadors Network; mem. Int. Advisory Bd IESE Business School at Univ. of Navarra. *Leisure interests:* golf, running family. *Address:* Compass Group PLC, Compass House, Guildford Street, Chertsey, Surrey KT16 9BQ, England (office). *Telephone:* (1932) 573-

000 (office). *Fax:* (1932) 569-956 (office). *E-mail:* info@compass-group.com (office). *Website:* www.compass-group.com (office).

GARDNER, W. Booth, MBA; American fmr state governor; b. 21 Aug. 1936, Tacoma; m. Jean Gardner; one s. one d.; ed Univ. of Wash. and Harvard Univ.; Asst to Dean, School of Business Admin. Harvard Univ. 1966; Dir School of Business and Econs Univ. of Puget Sound, Tacoma 1967–72; Pres. Laird Norton Co. 1972–80; mem. Wash. state senate 1970–73; County Exec. Pierce Co., Tacoma 1981–84; Gov. State of Wash. 1985–93; US Amb. to WTO Geneva, Switzerland 1994–98; Chair. Emer. Total Living Choices; Chair. Municipal Golf Club of Seattle, Northwest Parkinson's Foundation; Dir Central Area Youth Asscn; mem. Advisory Council of Casey Foundation; fmr mem. Bd of Dirs Weyerhaeuser Corpn, Wash. Mutual, Puget Sound Nat. Bank (now Key Bank), Univ. of Puget Sound, Laird Norton Trust Co.; Democrat. *Address:* c/o Total Living Choices, 1633 Westlake Avenue North, Suite 170, Seattle, WA 98109, USA.

GARDOCKI, Lech; Polish judge and professor of law; *First President, Supreme Court;* b. 13 April 1944, Rydzewo; s. of Józef Gardocki and Filomena Gardocki; one s. two d.; ed Univ. of Warsaw; Deputy Head, Inst. of Criminal Law, Warsaw Univ. 1977–81, 1981–84, Asst Prof. of Law 1980–91, held Chair, Dept of Comparative Studies in Criminal Law 1985–95, Prof. Extraordinary 1991–, Prof. in Legal Art 1992–, holds Chair, Dept of Material Criminal Law 1996–; Justice of the Supreme Court 1996–, First Pres. 1998–; mem. Int. Advisory Cttee on Zeitschrift für die gesamte Strafrechtswissenschaft magazine; First Degree Award in competition organized by State and Law magazine 1979. *Publications:* more than 80 publs including An Outline of International Criminal Law (Second Degree Award of Ministry of Educ.) 1985, Problems of Theory of Criminalization 1990, Criminal Law (Award of Minister of Educ.) 1994. *Leisure interest:* film. *Address:* Office of the First President, Supreme Court, pl. Krasińskich 2/4/6, 00-951 Warsaw 41, Poland (office). *Telephone:* (22) 530-82-03 (office). *Fax:* (22) 530-91-00 (office). *E-mail:* pp@sn.pl (office). *Website:* www.sn.pl (office).

GARDONS, S. S. (see Snodgrass, W. D.).

GAREYEV, Gen. Makhmud Akhmedovich; Russian army officer and historian; *President, Russian Academy of Military Science;* b. 23 July 1923; m.; two c.; ed Tashkent Infantry School, M. Frunze Mil. Acad., Gen. Staff Acad.; involved in mil. operations on Western Front, officer Operative Div., Gen. Staff of Far E Army at end of Second World War; Commdr of Regt, Tank Div. Belarus Mil. Command, Head of Gen. Staff Urals Mil. Command, then officer Gen. Staff; Head Mil. Scientific Dept, then Deputy Head of Chief Operative Dept, apptd Deputy Head of Gen. Staff 1974; Chief Mil. Counsellor, Afghanistan, then Commdr 1989–; mem. Russian Acad. of Mil. Sciences (later Pres.), Council on Interaction with Orgs of War Veterans; Order of Lenin and numerous other decorations and medals. *Publications:* Frunze – Military Theoretician, General Army Exercises, Marshal G. Zhukov and more than 60 scientific works. *Leisure interest:* athletics. *Address:* Academy of Military Sciences, Myasnitskaya str. 37, 103175 Moscow, Russia (office). *Telephone:* (495) 293-33-55 (office).

GARFUNKEL, Arthur (Art), MA; American singer and actor; b. 5 Nov. 1941, Forest Hills, NY; m. Kim Cermak 1988; one s.; ed Columbia Univ.; mem. singing duo Simon & Garfunkel (with Paul Simon) 1964–71; solo artist 1972–; Britannia Award 1977. *Films:* Catch 22 1970, Carnal Knowledge 1971, Bad Timing 1980, Good To Go 1986, Boxing Helena 1993, 54 1998. *Recordings include:* albums: as Simon & Garfunkel: Wednesday Morning 3am 1964, Sounds of Silence 1966, Parsley, Sage, Rosemary and Thyme 1966, The Graduate (film soundtrack) (two Grammy Awards) 1968, Bookends 1968, Bridge Over Troubled Water (six Grammy Awards 1971) 1970, Concert in Central Park (live) 1982, Early Simon & Garfunkel 1993, Old Friends 1997; solo: Angel Clare 1973, Breakaway 1975, Watermark 1977, Fate for Breakfast (Doubt for Dessert) 1979, Art Garfunkel 1979, Scissors Cut 1981, The Animals' Christmas 1986, Lefty 1988, Garfunkel 1989, Up Till Now 1993, Across America 1997, Songs from a Parent to a Child 1997, Everything Waits to be Noticed 2002, Some Enchanted Evening 2007. *Address:* William Morris Agency, 1325 Avenue of the Americas, New York, NY 10019, USA (office). *Telephone:* (212) 586-5100 (office). *Fax:* (212) 246-3583 (office). *Website:* www.artgarfunkel.com.

GARGANAS, Nikos C., MSc (Econ), PhD; Greek central banker; *Governor, Bank of Greece;* m. Maria L. Kokka; one d.; ed Athens School of Econs and Business Studies, London School of Econs and Univ. Coll., London, UK; Head, Research Unit, Agricultural Bank of Greece 1964–66; Research Officer, Nat. Inst. of Econ. and Social Research, London 1968–75; Lecturer, Brunel Univ., Uxbridge, UK 1970–71; Sr Economist, Bank of Greece 1975–84, Dir/Adviser, Econ. Research Dept 1984–93, Econ. Counsellor 1993–96, Deputy Gov. Bank of Greece 1996–2002, mem. Monetary Policy Cttee 1998–, Gov. 2002–; Chief Econ. Adviser, Ministry of Nat. Economy and mem. Council of Econ. Advisers 1985–87; mem. Governing Bd Centre of Econ. Planning and Research (KEPE) 1985–87; mem. ad hoc Prime Minister's Cttee for the Examination of Long Term Econ. Policy 1996–97; Chair. Deposit Guarantee Fund in Greece 1996–2002; Greek Rep. to OECD Econ. Policy Cttee of the European Communities 1975–88, Econ. Policy Cttee of the European Communities 1982–85, European Communities Monetary Cttee 1985–87, 1994–98, EU Economic and Financial Cttee 1998–2002; mem. European Cen. Banks' Governing Council, European Cen. Banks' Gen. Council; Gov. for Greece, IMF; Hon. Fellow, LSE. *Publications:* Greece's Economic Performance and Prospects (co-ed. and contrib.) 2001; books and articles on macro-economics, economic modelling, European economic and monetary union, monetary policy. *Address:* Bank of Greece, Leoforos E. Venizelos 21, 102 50 Athens, Greece (office). *Telephone:* (210) 3201111 (office). *Fax:* (210) 3232239 (office). *E-mail:* secretariat@bankofgreece.gr (office). *Website:* www.bankofgreece.gr (office).

GARGANO, Reinaldo; Uruguayan politician; *President, Partido Socialista del Uruguay (PS);* b. 26 July 1934, Paysandú; m. Judith Grauert; two c.; joined Partido Socialista del Uruguay (PS) 1956, Sec.-Gen. Socialist Youth 1958–59, mem. PS Exec. Cttee 1959–74; mem. Mesa Representativa de la Convención Nacional de Trabajadores del Uruguay (CNT) 1968–70; went into exile Barcelona, Spain after initiation of mil. dictatorship 1974; mem. Partido Socialista Obrero Español (PSOE) 1976–84; returned to Uruguay 1984, apptd Sec.-Gen. of PS, Pres. 2001–; elected Senator 1989–, Pres. of Senate 2000; fmr Sec.-Gen. Federación de Estudiantes Universitarios (FEUU); Minister of Foreign Affairs 2005–08. *Address:* Partido Socialista del Uruguay (PS), Casa del Pueblo, Soriano 1218, 11100 Montevideo, Uruguay (office). *Telephone:* (2) 9013344 (office). *Fax:* (2) 9082548 (office). *E-mail:* info@ps.org.uy (office). *Website:* www.ps.org.uy (office).

GARLAND, George David, PhD, FRSC; Canadian geophysicist; b. 29 June 1926, Toronto, Ont.; s. of N. L. Garland and Jean McPherson; m. Elizabeth MacMillan 1949; two s. one d.; ed Univ. of Toronto and St Louis Univ.; Geophysicist, Dominion Observatory, Ottawa 1950–54; Prof. of Geophysics, Univ. of Alberta, Edmonton 1954–63; Prof. of Geophysics, Univ. of Toronto 1963; Deputy Gen. Sec. Int. Union of Geodesy and Geophysics 1960–63, Gen. Sec. 1963–73, Pres. 1979–; Vice-Pres. Acad. of Science, Royal Soc. of Canada 1980–. *Publications:* The Earth's Shape and Gravity 1965 and papers in scientific journals dealing with gravity, terrestrial magnetism, structure of the earth's crust, electrical conductivity of the crust, heat flow from the earth. *Leisure interests:* canoeing, history of Canadian exploration, early maps. *Address:* 5 Mawhiney Court, Huntsville, Ont., P0A 1K0, Canada.

GARLAND, Patrick, MA; British theatre and television director and writer; b. 10 April 1935, London; s. of the late Ewart Garland and Rosalind Fell; m. Alexandra Bastedo 1980; ed St Mary's Coll., Southampton, St Edmund Hall, Oxford; actor, Bristol Old Vic 1959, Age of Kings, BBC TV 1961; lived Paris 1961–62; wrote two plays for ITV 1962; Research Asst, Monitor, BBC TV 1963; Dir and Producer, BBC Arts Dept 1962–74; Artistic Dir, Festival Theatre, Chichester; Hon. Fellow, St Edmund Hall, Oxford 1997; Hon. DLitt (Southampton) 1994. *Plays directed:* Forty Years On 1968, 1984, Brief Lives 1968, Getting On 1970, Cyrano 1971, Hair (Israel) 1972, The Doll's House (New York and London) 1975, Under the Greenwood Tree 1978, Look After Lulu 1978, Beecham 1980, York Mystery Plays 1980, My Fair Lady (USA) 1980, Kipling (London and New York) 1984, Canaries Sometimes Sing 1987, The Secret of Sherlock Holmes 1988, Victory 1989, A Room of One's Own 1989, 2001, Song in the Night 1989, The Dressmaker 1990, Tovarich 1991, Pickwick! 1993–96, The Tempest 1996, The Importance of Being Oscar 1997, Talking Heads 1998, Chimes at Midnight (Chichester Festival) 1998, The Mystery of Charles Dickens 2000, (NY) 2002, Woman in Black 2001; wrote and directed Brief Lives (on tour and West End) 1998; Co-Author of Underneath the Arches 1982–83; Artistic Dir Chichester Festival Theatre (The Cherry Orchard, The Mitford Girls, On the Rocks, Cavell, Goodbye, Mr Chips, As You Like It, Forty Years On, Merchant of Venice) 1980–84, 1991–94, Mystery of Charles Dickens 2002, Full Circle 2004, Brief Lives (touring revival) 2008, Visiting Mr. Green (on tour) 2008. *Films:* The Snow Goose 1974, The Doll's House 1976; produced: Fanfare for Elizabeth (Queen's 60th birthday gala) 1986, Celebration of a Broadcaster (for Richard Dimbleby Cancer Fund) 1986. *TV work includes:* writer and creative consultant Christmas Glory from St Paul's Cathedral 1997, St George's Chapel, Windsor 1998, Westminster Abbey 1998; Talking Heads – Miss Fozzard Finds Her Feet 1998, Telling Tales – Alan Bennett monologues 2001. *Publications:* Brief Lives 1967, The Wings of the Morning 1989, Oswald the Owl 1990, Angels in the Sussex Air: an Anthology of Sussex Poets 1995, Sussex Seams (Vol. I) 1995, (Vol. II) 1999, The Incomparable Rex 1996; poetry in London Magazine, New Poems, Poetry West, Encounter; short stories in Transatlantic Review; England Erzählt, Gemini, Light Blue, Dark Blue. *Leisure interests:* Victorian novels, walking in Corsica. *Address:* Farthings, Southlands Lane, W Chiltington, Nr. Pulborough, West Sussex, RH20 2JU, England.

GARN, Edwin Jacob (Jake), BS; American fmr politician and business executive; *Managing Director, Summit Ventures LLC;* b. 12 Oct. 1932, Richfield, Utah; s. of Jacob E. Garn and Fern Christensen; m. 1st Hazel R. Thompson 1957 (died 1976); two s. two d.; m. 2nd Kathleen Brewerton 1977; two s. one d.; ed Univ. of Utah; private pilot then USN pilot on active duty for four years; Special Agent, John Hancock Mutual Life Insurance Co., Salt Lake City 1960–61; Asst Man. Home Life Insurance Co. New York, Salt Lake City 1961–66; Gen. Agent, Mutual Trust Life Insurance Co., Salt Lake City 1966–68; City Commr Salt Lake City 1968–72, Mayor 1972–74; Dir Metropolitan Water Dist 1968–72; Senator from Utah 1974–93; Congressional observer and payload specialist space shuttle Discovery Mission STS-51-D 1985; Vice-Chair. Huntsman Chemical Corpn, Salt Lake City 1993–99; Man. Dir Summit Ventures LLC, Salt Lake City 1999–; mem. Bd of Dirs United Space Alliance; Republican; Wright Brothers Memorial Trophy. *Publication:* Night Launch 1989. *Address:* Summit Ventures LLC, One Utah Center, 201 South Main Street, Suite 600, Salt Lake City, UT 84111, USA (office). *Telephone:* (801) 321-0532 (office). *Fax:* (801) 364-0661 (office). *Website:* summit-ventures.com (office).

GARNAUT, Ross Gregory, AO, BA, PhD; Australian economist, government official and fmr diplomatist; *Vice Chancellor's Fellow, University of Melbourne;* b. 28 July 1946, Perth, WA; s. of the late L. Garnaut and P. W. Garnaut; m. Jayne Potter 1974; two s.; ed Perth Modern School, WA and Australian Nat. Univ., Canberra; Research Fellow, Sr Research Fellow and Sr Fellow, Econs Dept, Research School of Pacific Studies, ANU 1972–75, 1977–83; First Asst Sec.-Gen., Financial and Econ. Policy, Papua New Guinea

Dept of Finance 1975, 1976; Research Dir ASEAN-Australia Econ. Relations Research Project 1980–83; Sr Econ. Adviser to Prime Minister Bob Hawke 1983–85; Amb. to People's Repub. of China 1985–88; Prof. of Econs, Head of Dept, Research School of Pacific Studies, ANU 1989–, Dir Asia Pacific School of Econs and Man. 1998–; Vice Chancellor's Fellow, Univ. of Melbourne 2008–; econs adviser to Prime Minister Kevin Rudd 2007–; Chair. Aluminium Smelters of Victoria 1988–89, Rural and Industries Bank of Western Australia 1988–95, Primary Industry Bank of Australia 1988–94, Lihir Gold 1995–, Australian Centre for Int. Agric. Research 1994–. *Publications:* Irian Jaya: The Transformation of a Melanesian Economy 1974, ASEAN in a Changing Pacific and World Economy 1980, Indonesia: Australian Perspectives 1980, Taxation and Mineral Rents 1983, Exchange Range and Macro-Economic Policy in Independent Papua New Guinea 1984, The Political Economy of Manufacturing Protection: Experiences of ASEAN and Australia 1986, Australian Protectionism: Extent, Causes and Effects 1987, Australia and the Northeast Asian Ascendancy (report to Prime Minister) 1989, Economic Reform and Internationalization 1992, Grain in China 1992, Structuring for Global Realities (report on Wool Industry to Commonwealth Governments) 1993, The Third Revolution in the Chinese Countryside 1996, Open Regionalism: An Asian Pacific Contribution to the World Trading System 1996, East Asia in Crisis 1998, Private Enterprise in China (co-author) 2001, Social Democracy in Australia's Asian Future (co-author) 2001, Resource Management in Asia Pacific Developing Countries (ed.) 2002, China 2002: WTO Entry and World Recession (co-ed.) 2002, China: New Engine of World Growth (co-ed.) 2003, China: Is Rapid Growth Sustainable? (co-ed.) 2004, China's Third Economic Transformation (co-ed.) 2004, China's Ownership Transformation (co-author) 2005, The China Boom and its Discontents (co-ed.) 2005, The Turning Point in China's Economic Development (co-ed.) 2006, China: Linking Markets for Growth (co-ed.) 2007. *Leisure interests:* cricket, tennis, Australian football, the history of humanity. *Address:* Arndt-Corden Divison of Economics, RSPAS, Coombs Building, Australian National University, Canberra, ACT 0200, Australia (office). *Telephone:* (2) 6125-3100 (office). *Fax:* (2) 6249-8057 (office). *E-mail:* Ross.Garnaut@anu.edu.au (office). *Website:* rspas.anu.edu.au (office).

GARNEAU, Marc, OC, BSc, DEng; Canadian astronaut and fmr naval engineer; *President, Canadian Space Agency;* b. Feb. 1949, Quebec City; ed Royal Mil. Coll., Kingston, Imperial Coll. of Science and Tech., London, UK, Canadian Forces Command and Staff Coll., Toronto; Combat Systems Engineer, HMCS Algonquin 1974–76; Instructor in Naval Weapon Systems, Canadian Forces Fleet School, Halifax 1976–77, with Naval Eng Unit 1980–82; Project Engineer in Naval Weapon Systems, Ottawa 1977–80; promoted Commdr 1982; Design Authority for Naval Communications and Electronic Warfare Equipment and Systems, Ottawa 1983–86; promoted Capt. 1986; retd from Navy 1989; selected to be Canadian astronaut 1983; seconded to Canadian Astronaut Program from Dept of Nat. Defence 1984; first Canadian to fly in space as Payload Specialist on Shuttle Mission 41-G, Oct. 1984; Deputy Dir Canadian Astronaut Program 1989; selected to be Mission Specialist 1992; trained at NASA's Johnson Space Center 1992–93, worked on tech. issues, Astronaut Office Robotics Integration Team, Capsule Communicator (CAPCOM) in Mission Control during Shuttle flights; served as Mission Specialist on flight STS-41G 1984, STS-77 1996 and STS-97 2000; has logged 677 hours in space; Exec. Vice-Pres., then Pres. Canadian Space Agency 2001–; Chancellor Carleton Univ. 2003; Pres. Bd McGill Univ. Chamber Orchestra; mem. Asscn of Professional Engineers of Nova Scotia, Navy League of Canada, Int. Acad. of Astronauts 2002; Hon. Fellow Canadian Aeronautics and Space Inst., Nat. Hon. Patron of Hope Air and Project N Star, Hon. mem. Canadian Soc. of Aviation Medicine 1998; Canadian Mil. Decoration 1980, Companion of Order of Canada (Officer 1984) 2003; Hon. PhD (Univ. of Laval, Tech. Univ. of Nova Scotia, Royal Mil. Coll. of Kingston) 1985, (Royal Mil. Coll. of St-Jean) 1990, (Univ. of Ottawa) 1997, Hon. DSci (Univ. of Lethbridge) 2001, (York Univ.) 2002; Athlone Fellowship 1970, NASA Space Flight Medals 1984, 1996, 2000, F.W. Baldwin Award, Canadian Aeronautics and Space Journal 1985, NASA Exceptional Service Medal 1997, Golden Jubilee Medal of HM Queen Elizabeth II 2002, Prix Montfort en sciences 2003. *Address:* John H. Chapman Space Centre, 6767 Route de l'Aéroport, Longueil, PQ J3Y 8Y9, Canada (office). *Telephone:* (450) 926-4800 (office). *Fax:* (450) 926-4352 (office). *Website:* www.space.gc.ca (office).

GARNER, Alan, OBE; British writer; b. 17 Oct. 1934, Cheshire, England; s. of Colin Garner and Marjorie Garner (née Greenwood Stuart); m. 1st Ann Cook 1956 (divorced); one s. two d.; m. 2nd Griselda Greaves 1972; one s. one d.; ed Manchester Grammar School, Magdalen Coll., Oxford; mil. service with rank of Lt, RA; mem. Editorial Bd Detskaya Literatura Publrs, Moscow; Lewis Carroll Shelf Award, USA 1970, Chicago Int. Film Festival Gold Plaque 1981. *Plays:* Holly from the Bongs 1965, Lamaload 1978, Lurga Lom 1980, To Kill a King 1980, Sally Water 1982, The Keeper 1983, Pentecost 1997, The Echoing Waters 2000. *Dance drama:* The Green Mist 1970. *Libretti:* The Bellybag 1971, Potter Thompson 1972, Lord Flame 1996. *Screenplays:* The Owl Service 1969, Red Shift 1978, Places and Things 1978, Images 1981 (First Prize, Chicago Int. Film Festival), Strandloper 1992. *Publications:* The Weirdstone of Brisingamen 1960, The Moon of Gomrath 1963, Elidor 1965, Holly from the Bongs 1966, The Old Man of Mow 1967, The Owl Service (Library Asscn Carnegie Medal 1967, Guardian Award 1968) 1967, The Book of Goblins (Ed.) 1969, Red Shift 1973, The Breadhorse 1975, The Guizer 1975, The Stone Book Quartet (Children's Book Asscn of USA Phoenix Award 1996) 1976–78, Tom Fobble's Day 1977, Granny Reardun 1977, The Aimer Gate 1978, Fairy Tales of Gold 1979, The Lad of the Gad 1980, A Book of British Fairy Tales (Ed.) 1984, A Bag of Moonshine 1986, Jack and the Beanstalk 1992, Once Upon a Time 1993, Strandloper 1996, The Little Red Hen 1997, The Voice That Thunders 1997, The Well of the Wind 1998, Thursbitch 2003. *Leisure interest:* work. *Address:* c/o Kate Jones, ICM Books, 4–6 Soho Square, London, W1D 3PZ, England (office).

GARNER, James; American actor; b. (James Baumgardner), 7 April 1928, Norman, Okla; m. Lois Clarke 1956; one s. two d.; ed New York Berghof School; worked as travelling salesman, oil field worker, carpet layer, bathing suit model; Purple Heart; Emmy Award, Life Achievement Award, Screen Actors Guild Awards 2005. *Television appearances include:* Cheyenne, Maverick 1957–62, Nichols 1971–72, The Rockford Files 1974–79, Space 1985, The New Maverick, The Long Summer of George Adams, The Glitter Dome, Heartsounds, Promise (also exec. producer) 1986, My Name is Bill W. (also exec. producer), 1989, Decoration Day 1990, Barbarians at the Gate 1993, God, the Devil and Bob (voice) 2000, First Monday (series) 2002, Roughing It 2002, 8 Simple Rules for Dating My Teenage Daughter (series) 2003–05. *Films include:* Toward the Unknown 1956, Shoot-out at Medicine Bend 1957, Darby's Rangers 1958, Sayonara, Up Periscope 1959, Cash McCall 1960, The Great Escape 1963, The Americanization of Emily 1964, 36 Hours 1964, The Art of Love 1965, A Man Could Get Killed 1966, Duel at Diablo 1966, Mister Buddwing 1966, Grand Prix 1966, Hour of the Gun 1967, Marlowe 1969, Support Your Local Sheriff 1971, Support Your Local Gunfighter 1971, Skin Game 1971, They Only Kill Their Masters 1972, One Little Indian 1973, Health 1979, The Fan 1980, Victor/Victoria 1982, Murphy's Romance 1985, Sunset 1987, Fire in the Sky 1993, My Fellow Americans 1996, Twilight 1998, Space Cowboys 2000, Atlantis: The Lost Empire 2001, Divine Secrets of the Ya-Ya Sisterhood 2002, The Notebook 2004, Al Roach: Private Insectigator 2004, The Ultimate Gift 2006. *Address:* United Talent Agency, 9560 Wilshire Blvd, Beverly Hills, CA 90212, USA.

GARNER, Lt-Gen. Jay, BA, MPA; American business executive, fmr army general and fmr government official; *President, SYColeman;* b. 15 April 1938; m. Connie Garner; one d.; ed Florida State Univ., Shippensburg Univ., Pennsylvania; joined US Army 1960, served in Viet Nam; commanded Patriot missile batteries in first Gulf War, supervised resettlement of Kurdish refugees in immediate post-war period; later Commdr of Space and Strategic Defense Command; Asst Chief of Staff –1997 (retd); Pres. SY Tech. (defence contractor specializing in missile systems) 1997–2003, then Pres. SYColeman (after merger with Coleman Research Corpn) 2003–; mem. Presidential Panel on Space and Missile Threats; Dir Office of Reconstruction and Humanitarian Assistance for Iraq (interim Gov. of Iraq) March–April 2003. *Address:* SYColeman, 241 18th Street South, Suite 900, Arlington, VA 22202, USA (office). *Telephone:* (703) 413-8282. *Website:* www.sycoleman.com.

GARNER, Wendell Richard, PhD; American psychologist and academic (retd); *Professor Emeritus of Psychology, Yale University;* b. 21 Jan. 1921, Buffalo, NY; s. of Richard Charles and Lena Cole Garner; m. Barbara Chipman Ward 1944; one s. two d.; ed Franklin and Marshall Coll. and Harvard Univ.; Instructor, rising to Prof., Johns Hopkins Univ. 1946–67, Chair. Dept of Psychology 1954–64; James Rowland Angell Prof. of Psychology, Yale Univ. 1967–89, Prof. Emer. 1989–, Dir of Social Sciences 1972–73, 1981–88, Chair. Dept of Psychology 1974–77, Dean Grad. School 1978–79; mem. NAS; Hon. DSc (Franklin and Marshall Coll.) 1979; Hon. DHumLitt (Johns Hopkins Univ.) 1983; Distinguished Scientific Contrib. Award, American Psychological Asscn 1964, Warren Medal, Soc. of Experimental Psychologists 1976, Gold Medal, American Psychological Foundation 1999. *Publications:* Applied Experimental Psychology (with A. Chapanis and C. T. Morgan) 1949, Uncertainty and Structure as Psychological Concepts 1962, The Processing of Information and Structure 1974, Ability Testing (ed. with A. Wigdor) 1982. *Leisure interests:* gardening, hiking. *Address:* 1122 Meadow Ridge, Redding, CT 06896, USA (home). *Telephone:* (203) 544-7133 (home). *E-mail:* wendellgarner@sbcglobal.net (home).

GARNETT, Tony; British television producer; b. 3 April 1936, Birmingham; ed Central Grammar School, Univ. Coll., London; began career as television actor; producer of numerous TV programmes and films; worked in USA 1980–90; Co-Founder World Productions 1990; Visiting Prof. of Media Arts, Royal Holloway Coll., Univ. of London 2000–. *TV appearances include:* Dixon of Dock Green 1960s. *TV productions include:* Up the Junction 1965, Cathy Come Home 1966, The Resistable Rise of Arturo Ui 1972, Hard Labour 1973, The Enemy Within 1974, Days of Hope 1975, Law and Order 1978, Between the Lines 1992, Cardiac Arrest 1994, Ballykissangel 1996, This Life 1996, The Cops 1998, Attachments 2000. *Films produced include:* Kes 1969, Handgun 1983, Earth Girls are Easy 1989, Shadow Makers 1989. *Address:* c/o World Productions, Eagle House, 50 Marshall Street, London, W1F 9BQ, England (office). *Telephone:* (20) 7734-3536 (office). *Fax:* (20) 7758-7000 (office). *Website:* www.world-productions.com (office).

GARNIER, Jean-Pierre (JP), PhD, MBA; French business executive; b. 31 Oct. 1947, Le Mans; m.; three d.; ed Univ. of Louis Pasteur, Stanford Univ., USA; joined Schering-Plough 1975, numerous man. positions including Gen. Man. of numerous overseas subsidiaries, then Vice-Pres. of Marketing, US Pharmaceutical Products Div. 1983, then Sr Vice-Pres. and Gen. Man. with responsibility for sales and marketing for US prescription business, then Pres. US business; Pres. pharmaceutical business in N America, SmithKline Beecham 1990, mem. Bd Dirs 1992, Chair. Pharmaceuticals 1994–95, COO 1995–2000, CEO GlaxoSmithKline plc 2000–08; mem. Bd Dirs United Technologies Corpn, Eisenhower Exchange Fellowships Inc., INSEAD, Global Business Coalition on HIV/AIDS, John Hopkins Univ., Hole in the Wall Foundation, Cttee to Encourage Corp. Philanthropy; mem. Quaker BioVentures Int. Business Advisory Council for UK; Chevalier, Légion d'honneur, Officier 2007; Oliver R. Grace Award for distinguished service in advancing cancer research 1997, named a Star of Europe, Business Week 2001, Marco Polo Award 2001, Corporate Citizenship Award, Henry H. Kessler Foundation, Sabin Vaccine Inst. Humanitarian Award 2002, CNBC Leadership

Award 2007. *Leisure interests:* competitive tennis and paddle playing, squash, golf, windsurfing. *Address:* c/o GlaxoSmithKline plc, 980 Great West Road, Brentford, London, TW8 9GS, England (office).

GAROFANO, Giuseppe; Italian engineer and business executive; *Chairman, Reno de Medici SpA;* b. 25 Jan. 1944, Nereto, Teramo; ed Milan Polytechnic Inst., Bocconi Univ. Business School; Man. Dir Cotonificio Cantoni 1981–84; Vice-Chair. and Man. Dir Iniziativa META SpA 1984–88, Chair. and CEO 1988; Man. Dir Ferruzzi Finanziaria SpA 1988–92, Vice-Chair. 1989–; Vice-Chair. Milano Assicurazioni SpA 1987–, Fondiaria SpA 1989–, La Previdente Assicurazioni SpA 1991–; Vice-Chair. Montedison SpA 1989–90, Chair. 1990–92; Chair. Reno de Medici SpA 2003–. *Address:* Reno de Medici SpA, Via G. De Medici 17, Pontenuovo di Magenta, 20013 Milan, Italy. *Website:* www.renodemedici.it.

GAROUSTE, Gérard; French painter and sculptor; b. 10 March 1946, Paris; s. of Henri Garouste and Edmée Sauvagnac; m. Elizabeth Rochline 1970; two s.; ed Académie Charpentier, Beaux-Arts de Paris; Chevalier des Arts et des Lettres, Chevalier Légion d'honneur, Officier Ordre du Mérite. *Address:* La Mésangère, 27810 Marcilly-sur-Eure, France (home). *Telephone:* (2) 37-48-47-18 (home). *Fax:* (2) 37-48-45-39 (office).

GARRÉ, Nilda, BA; Argentine lawyer and politician; *Minister of Defence;* b. 3 Nov. 1945, Buenos Aires; m. Juan Manuel (divorced); three c.; ed Universidad del Salvador; active in Juventud Peronista in 1970s; elected to prov. ass. Buenos Aires as rep. of Frente Justicialista de Liberación 1973–76; lawyer and human rights activist 1976–82; participated in Renovación Peronista of Partido Justicialista 1983; joined Frente del País Solidario; elected to Cámara de Diputados 1995–2000; Deputy Interior Minister 2000–01; elected to Senado 2001–05; Amb. to Venezuela June 2005; Minister of Defence Nov. 2005–; Rep. of Nat. Chamber of Deputies to UN on Penal Legislation 1997; Vice-Pres. Fundación Carlos Auyero 1997–2002, Pres. 2004–05; mem. Advisory Cttee on Penal Reform 2003–04; Gen. Coordinator Centre for Research and Public Policy Advice (CEAPP). *Address:* Ministry of Defence, Azopardo 250, 1328 Buenos Aires, Argentina (office). *Telephone:* (11) 4346–8800 (office). *E-mail:* nildagarre@mindef.gov.ar (office); mindef@mindef.gov.ar (office). *Website:* www.mindef.gov.ar (office).

GARRETT, Lesley, CBE, FRAM; British singer (soprano); b. 10 April 1955; d. of Derek Arthur Garrett and Margaret Wall; m. 1991; one s. one d.; ed Thorne Grammar School, Royal Acad. of Music, Nat. Opera Studio; performed with Welsh Nat. Opera, Opera North, at Wexford and Buxton Festivals and at Glyndebourne; joined ENO (Prin. Soprano) 1984; Hon. DArts (Plymouth) 1995; winner Kathleen Ferrier Memorial Competition 1979, Gramophone Award for Best Selling Classical Artist 1996. *Television:* appeared in BBC TV series Lesley Garrett... Tonight, The Lesley Garret Show. *Major roles include:* Susanna in The Marriage of Figaro, Despina in Così Fan Tutte, Musetta in La Bohème, Jenny in The Rise and Fall of The City of Mahagonny, Atalanta in Xerxes, Zerlinda in Don Giovanni, Yum-Yum in The Mikado, Adèle in Die Fledermaus, Oscar in A Masked Ball, Dalinda in Ariodante, Rose in Street Scene, Bella in A Midsummer Marriage, Eurydice in Orpheus and Eurydice and title roles in The Cunning Little Vixen and La Belle Vivette; numerous concert hall performances in UK and abroad (including Last Night of the Proms); TV and radio appearances. *Recordings:* albums: Diva! A Soprano at the Movies 1991, Prima Donna 1992, Simple Gifts 1994, Soprano in Red 1995, Soprano in Hollywood 1996, A Soprano Inspired 1997, Lesley Garrett 1998, I Will Wait for You 2000, Travelling Light 2001, The Singer 2002, So Deep is the Night 2003, When I Fall in Love 2007, Amazing Grace 2008. *Publication:* Notes From a Small Soprano (autobiog.) 2001. *Leisure interest:* watching cricket. *Address:* The Music Partnership Ltd, New Broad Street House, New Broad Street, London, EC2M 1NH, England. *Telephone:* (20) 7840-9592. *Website:* www.musicpartnership.co.uk; www.lesleygarrett.co.uk.

GARRETT, Malcolm, BA (Hons); British graphic designer; *Creative Director, Applied Information Group;* b. 2 June 1956, Northwich, Cheshire; ed Univ., of Reading, Manchester Polytechnic; f. Assorted Images Design Co. 1978, renamed Assorted Images Ltd 1983, Design Dir 1978–94; designed for artists such as Buzzcocks, Duran Duran, Culture Club and Simple Minds, and pioneered digital and interactive work with Peter Gabriel; f. AMX Digital Ltd 1994, joined Havas Advertising (re-named AMX Studios, then AMX) 1998, Chair. 1999–2001; Visiting Prof. Univ. of the Arts, London (fmrly London Inst.); Visiting Prof. in Interactive Communication, RCA 2001–04; currently Creative Dir Applied Information Group, London, dynamolondon.org (London's showcase of interactive media); mem. RDI Exec. Cttee 2006–, Eye Magazine Editorial Bd 2007–, FontShop Type Bd 2007–08; External Examiner, Manchester Metropolitan Univ. 2008–; designed record sleeves, posters, merchandise for Duran Duran; Royal Designer for Industry; Hon. MA (Salford Univ.) 1999; Hon. Dr of Design (Robert Gordon Univ.) 2005. *Publications:* Duran Duran: Their Story (with Kasper de Graaf) 1982, When Cameras go Crazy: Culture Club (with Kasper de Graaf) 1983, Duran Duran Unseen: Photographs by Paul Edmond (with Kasper de Graaf) 2005. *Address:* Applied Information Group, 26–27 Great Sutton Street, London, EC1V 0DS, England (office). *Telephone:* (20) 7017-8488 (office). *Fax:* (20) 7017-8489 (office). *E-mail:* mx@aiglondon.com (office). *Website:* www.aiglondon.com (office).

GARRETT, Peter Robert, AM, BA, LLB; Australian environmentalist, musician and politician; *Minister for the Environment, Heritage and the Arts;* b. 16 April 1953, Wahroonga, NSW; s. of the late Peter Maxwell Garrett and Betty Garrett; m.; three d.; ed Barker Coll., Hornsby, Australian Nat. Univ., Univ. of New South Wales; mem. Rock Island Line; lead singer, Midnight Oil –2002; benefit concerts for Aboriginal Rights Asscn, Tibet Council, Rainforest Action Network etc.; Exxon Valdez oil spill protest concert 1990; ran for Australian Senate, Nuclear Disarmament Party 1984; Pres. Australian Conservation Foundation 1989–91, 1998–2004; mem. Bd Greenpeace International 1991–93; mem. Australian Labor Party 2004–; MP for Kingsford Smith 2004–; Minister for the Environment, Heritage and the Arts 2007–; Hon. DLitt (Univ. of NSW); four Australian Record Industry Asscn Awards 1991, Sony Music Crystal Globe Award 1991, Australia's Living Treasures Award, Nat. Trust of Australia 1999. *Recordings:* albums with Midnight Oil: Midnight Oil 1978, Head Injuries 1979, Bird Noises 1980, Place Without A Postcard 1981, Red Sails In The Sunset 1982, 10 9 8 7 6 5 4 3 2 1 1983, Diesel and Dust 1987, Blue Sky Mining 1990, Scream In Blue – Live 1992, Earth, Sun and Moon 1993, Breathe 1996, 20,000 Watt RSL – The Midnight Oil Collection 1997, Redneck Wonderland 1998, The Real Thing (live) 2000, Capricornia 2002, Best of Both Worlds 2004. *Publication:* Political Blues 1987. *Leisure interests:* surfing, Australian literature. *Address:* Locked Bag 18/172, Newtown, NSW 2042, Australia (office); Department of the Environment, GPO Box 787, Canberra, ACT 2601 (office); Electorate Office, PO Box 249, Maroubra, NSW 2035 (office). *Telephone:* (2) 6274-1111 (Canberra) (office). *Fax:* (2) 6274-1666 (Canberra) (office). *E-mail:* oils@ozemail.com.au (office). *Website:* www.environment.gov.au (office); www.petergarrett.com.au.

GARRICK, Sir Ronald (Ron), Kt, CBE; British business executive; *Deputy Chairman, HBOS plc;* b. 1940; joined Weir Group 1962, CEO 1982–99, Chair. 1999–2002; Deputy Chair. Scottish Enterprise 1992–96; fmr Dir Shell UK, Scottish Power plc; Dir (Non-Exec.) HBOS plc 2001–, Deputy Chair. 2003–, Sr Ind. Dir 2004–, Chair. Nomination Cttee; Fellow Royal Acad. of Eng. *Address:* HBOS plc, The Mound, Edinburgh EH1 1YZ, Scotland (office). *Telephone:* (870) 600-5000 (office). *Website:* www.hbosplc.com (office).

GARRISON-JACKSON, Zina; American professional tennis coach and fmr professional tennis player; b. 16 Nov. 1963, Houston, Tex.; m. Willard Jackson Jr 1989; winner WTA Championships 1985; singles semi-finalist, Wimbledon Championships 1985, finalist 1990 (lost to Martina Navratilova q.v.); semi-finalist US Open 1988, 1989; gold medal winner, ladies doubles (with P. Shriver), Seoul Olympic Games 1988; winner mixed doubles (with S. Stewart), Australian Open 1987, Wimbledon Championships 1988, (with Leach) 1990; mem. US Fed. Cup Team 1984–87, 1989–91, 1994, Whiteman Cup Team 1987–88; retd 1992; f. Zina Garrison All Court Tennis Academy 1993; f. Zina Garrison Foundation to support various charities 1988; Head Coach US Nat. team 1999; Coach US Fed. Cup team 1999–2004, Capt. 2004–09; Int. Hall of Fame Educ. Merit Award, Texas Tennis Hall of Fame 1998. *Leisure interests:* jogging, softball, artwork – designs own printed T-shirts. *Address:* Zina Garrison All Court Tennis Academy, 12335 Kingsride #106, Houston, TX 77024, USA. *Telephone:* (713) 857-3167. *Fax:* (713) 467-4769. *Website:* www.zinagarrison.org.

GARTON ASH, Timothy John, CMG, MA, FRSA, FRHistS, FRSL; British writer and academic; *Fellow and Senior Research Fellow in Contemporary European History, University of Oxford;* b. 12 July 1955, London, England; m. Danuta Maria 1982; two s.; ed Exeter Coll., Oxford, St Antony's Coll., Oxford; editorial writer The Times 1984–86; Foreign Ed. The Spectator 1984–90; Fellow Woodrow Wilson Int. Center for Scholars, Washington, DC 1986–87; Sr Assoc. mem., St Antony's Coll., Oxford 1987–89, Fellow and Sr Research Fellow in Contemporary European History 1990–; columnist The Independent 1988–90, The Guardian 2002–; Sr Fellow Hoover Inst., Stanford Univ. 2000–; Fellow Acad. of Sciences, Berlin-Brandenburg, European Acad. of Arts and Sciences; Corresp. Fellow Inst. for Human Sciences, Vienna; mem. PEN, Soc. of Authors; Golden Insignia of the Order of Merit, Poland 1992, Kt's Cross of the Order of Merit, Germany 1995, Order of Merit, Czech Repub. 2000; Hon. DLitt (St Andrew's) 2004; Soc. of Authors Somerset Maugham Award 1984, Veillon Foundation Prix Européen de l'Essai 1989, David Watt Memorial Prize 1989, Granada Award for Commentator of the Year 1989, Friedrich Ebert Stiftung Prize 1991, Imre Nagy Memorial Plaque, Hungary 1995, Premio Napoli 1995, Orwell Prize for Journalism 2006, Ischia Prize for Int. Journalism 2008. *Publications:* 'Und willst du nicht mein Bruder sein...': Die DDR heute 1981, The Polish Revolution: Solidarity 1983, The Uses of Adversity: Essays on the Fate of Central Europe 1989, We the People: The Revolution of '89 Witnessed in Warsaw, Budapest, Berlin and Prague 1990, In Europe's Name: Germany and the Divided Continent 1993, Freedom for Publishing for Freedom: The Central and East European Publishing Project (ed.) 1995, The File: A Personal History 1997, History of the Present 1999, Free World 2004; contribs to books, newspapers and magazines. *Address:* St Antony's College, Oxford, OX2 6JF, England (office). *Telephone:* (1865) 274470 (office). *Fax:* (1865) 274478 (office). *E-mail:* european.studies@sant.ox.ac.uk (office). *Website:* www.sant.ox.ac.uk (office); www.timothygartonash.com.

GARWIN, Richard L., MS, PhD; American physicist; b. 19 April 1928, Cleveland, Ohio; s. of Robert and Leona S. Garwin; m. Lois E. Levy 1947; two s. one d.; ed public schools in Cleveland, Case Western Reserve Univ. and Univ. of Chicago; Instructor and Asst Prof. of Physics, Univ. of Chicago 1949–52; mem. staff, IBM Watson Lab., Columbia Univ. 1952–65, 1966–70; Adjunct Prof. of Physics, Columbia Univ. 1957–; Dir of Applied Research, IBM T. J. Watson Research Center 1965–66, IBM Fellow 1967–93, Fellow Emer. 1993–; mem. Defense Science Bd 1966–69; mem. President's Science Advisory Cttee 1962–66, 1969–72; mem. IBM Corporate Tech. Cttee 1970–71; Adjunct Prof. Col Univ. 1957; Prof. of Public Policy, Kennedy School of Govt, Harvard 1979–81, Adjunct Research Fellow 1982–; Andrew D. White Prof.-at-Large, Cornell Univ. 1982–87; mem. Council on Foreign Relations; mem. NAS 1966–, Inst. of Medicine 1975–81, Nat. Acad. of Eng 1978–, American Philosophical Soc. 1979–; Consultant to Los Alamos 1950–93, to Sandia Nat. Lab. 1994–; Fellow, American Physical Soc. American Acad. of Arts and Sciences; Ford Foundation Fellow, CERN, Geneva 1959–60; Dr hc (Case Western Reserve

Univ.) 1966, (Rensselaer Polytechnic Inst.), (State Univ. of New York); R. V. Jones Intelligence Award (Nat. Foreign Intelligence Community) 1996, Enrico Fermi Award 1997. *Publications:* Nuclear Power Issues and Choices (co-author) 1977, Nuclear Weapons and World Politics 1977, Energy, the Next Twenty Years (co-author) 1979, The Dangers of Nuclear Wars 1979, Unresolved Issues in Arms Control 1988, A Nuclear-Weapon-Free World: Desirable? Feasible? 1993, Managing the Plutonium Surplus: Applications and Technical Options 1994, U.S. Intervention Policy for the Post-Cold War World: New Challenges and New Responses 1994, Feux Follets et Champignons Nucléaires (with G. Charpak) 1997; about 200 published papers and 42 US patents. *Leisure interests:* skiing, military technology, arms control, social use of technology. *Address:* c/o T. J. Watson Research Center, P.O. Box 218, Yorktown Heights, New York, NY 10598, USA.

GARZÓN, Baltasar; Spanish judge; *Investigating Judge, Audiencia Nacional;* b. 1955, Villa de Torres (Jaen); m. Jaen; three c.; prov. judge 1978-87, Audiencia Nacional (Nat. Court) 1987–; mem. Parl. 1993–94; has investigated numerous high profile cases involving drug trafficking, Basque terrorism, govt corruption, Spain's security forces and human rights abuses and Islamic fundamentalism; issued arrest warrant for Gen. Augusto Pinochet Ugarte to face charges of genocide, terrorism and torture 1998; banned Basque politicial party Batasuna Aug. 2002; Hon. DJur (New York Univ.) 2007. *Address:* Audiencia Nacional, García Gutiérrez 1, 28004 Madrid, Spain (office). *Telephone:* (91) 3973339 (office). *Fax:* (91) 3973306 (office).

GARZÓN, Luis Eduardo 'Lucho'; Colombian politician and fmr trade union official; *Mayor of Bogota;* b. 15 Feb. 1951, Bogota; s. of Eloísa Garzón; ed Universidad Libre; early work experience as caddie, carpenter and street trader; fmr messenger, Public Relations Div., Ecopetrol; fmr leader Unión Sindical Obrera (USO), later Vice-Pres.; fmr leader Central Unitaria de Trabajadores (CUT); fmr presidential cand., coalición Polo Democrático; fmr mem. Comité Central del Partido Comunista Colombiano; mem. Polo Democrático Independiente (PDI); Mayor of Bogota, Oct. 2003–; mem. several official cttees including Consejo Nacional de Paz, Comisión de Conciliación Nacional, Comité de Búsqueda de la Paz, Comisión Facilitadora par los diálogos con el Eln; AFL-CIO George Meany-Lane Kirkland Prize 2001. *Address:* Office of the Mayor, Bogota, Colombia (office). *E-mail:* info@luchogarzon.com (office). *Website:* www.luchogarzon.com (office).

GASCOIGNE, Paul John; British fmr professional footballer; b. 27 May 1967, Gateshead; s. of John Gascoigne and Carol Gascoigne (née Harold); m. Sheryl Failes 1996 (divorced 1998); one s.; ed Heathfield Sr School; joined Newcastle United as apprentice 1983; played for Newcastle United 1985–88, for Tottenham Hotspur 1988–92 (FA Cup winners' medal 1991), for Lazio, Italy 1992–95, for Rangers 1995–98, for Middlesbrough 1998–2000, for Everton 2000–02, for Burnley 2002; signed as player-coach for Gansu Tianma (Gansu Sky Horses), Chinese B-League 2003; Wolverhampton Wanderers reserves 2003; player coach Boston United 2004; played for England, 13 Under-21 caps, 57 full caps. *Publication:* Paul Gascoigne (autobiog. with Paul Simpson) 2001, Gazza: My Story (with Hunter Davies) (British Book Award for Sports Book of the Year 2005) 2004. *Leisure interests:* football, fishing, tennis, swimming. *Address:* c/o Robertson Craig & Co., Clairmont Gardens, Glasgow, G3 7LW Scotland. *Telephone:* (141) 332-1205. *Fax:* (141) 332-8035.

GASKILL, William; British theatre and opera director; b. 24 June 1930; s. of Joseph Linnaeus Gaskill and Maggie Simpson; ed Salt High School, Shipley and Hertford Coll., Oxford; Dir, Granada Television 1956–57; Asst Artistic Dir Royal Court Theatre, London 1958–60; Dir Royal Shakespeare Co. 1961–62; Assoc. Dir Nat. Theatre, London 1963–65, 1979; Artistic Dir English Stage Co., Royal Court Theatre 1965–72; Dir Jt Stock Theatre Group 1974–83; returned to direct at Arcola Theatre 2005. *Stage productions include:* (Royal Court Theatre) Epitaph for George Dillon, One Way Pendulum, Saved, Early Morning, Man is Man, Lear, Big Wolf, The Sea, The Gorky Brigade; (Nat. Theatre) The Recruiting Officer, Mother Courage, Philoctetes, Armstrong's Last Goodnight, The Beaux Stratagem, The Madras House, A Fair Quarrel, Man, Beast and Virtue, Black Snow; (Royal Shakespeare Co.) The Caucasian Chalk Circle, Richard III, Cymbeline; (Joint Stock) The Speakers, Fanshen, Yesterday's News, A Mad World, My Masters, The Ragged Trousered Philanthropists; other productions include The Way of the World; opera productions include: The Barber of Seville, La Bohème and Lucia di Lammermoor (Welsh Nat. Opera), Carver. *Publication:* A Sense of Direction: life at the Royal Court (autobiog.) 1988. *Address:* 124A Leighton Road, London, NW5 2RG, England.

GASKÓ, István; Hungarian trade union official; *President, Democratic Confederation of Free Trade Unions (LIGA);* b. 21 July 1951, Sajòszentpèter; m.; one s.; ed Econ. Univ., Budapest; mem. Democratic Trade Union of Scientific Workers 1988; f. Social Democratic Party 1989; f. Free Trade Union of Railway Workers 1989, Pres. 1991–; Pres. Democratic Confed. of Free Trade Unions (LIGA) 1996–. *Leisure interests:* reading, music, film, theatre, travelling. *Address:* Democratic Confederation of Free Trade Unions, FSzDL, Benczùr u. 41, 1068 Budapest, Hungary (office). *Telephone:* (1) 321-5262 (office). *Fax:* (1) 321-5405 (office). *E-mail:* info@liganet.hu (office). *Website:* www.liganet.hu (office).

GASPARI, Mitja, BSc; Slovenian central banker and economist; b. 25 Nov. 1951, Ljubljana; ed Univ. of Ljubljana, Univ. of Belgrade; Research Economist, Nat. Bank of Slovenia 1975–81, Head of Research 1981–87, Deputy Gov. 1987–88; Deputy Gov., Nat. Bank of Yugoslavia 1988–91; Sr Financial Economist Trade and Finance Div., Tech. Dept Europe and USSR, The World Bank 1991–92; Minister of Finance 1992–2000; mem. Parl. 2000–01; Gov. Bank of Slovenia 2001–07. *Publications:* numerous articles on fiscal studies. *Address:* c/o Bank of Slovenia, 1505 Ljubljana, Slovenska 35, Slovenia (office).

GASPARINI, Massimo; Italian business executive; *CEO, Missoni SpA;* has over 20 years of experience working for Italian and multinational cos; has worked in fashion since 2001, overseeing Gucci's watch and jewellery div. –2006; CEO Missoni SpA, Milan 2007–. *Address:* Missoni SpA, Via Salvini 1/A, Milan, Italy (office). *Telephone:* (02) 7600-1479 (office). *E-mail:* press.info@missoni.it (office). *Website:* www.missoni.it (office).

GAŠPAROVIČ, Ivan, LLD; Slovak politician, lawyer and head of state; *President;* b. 27 March 1941, Poltár, Lučenec Dist; s. of Vladimír Gašparovič and Elena Gašparovič; m. Silvia Gašparovičová 1964; one s. one d.; ed Komenský Univ., Bratislava; clerk, Prosecutor's Office, Martin Trenčín 1965–66; Municipal Public Prosecutor, Bratislava 1966–68; teacher, Faculty of Law, Komenský Univ., Bratislava 1968–90, Vice-Rector 1990–; Gen. Prosecutor of CSFR 1990–92; mem. Movt for Democratic Slovakia 1992–2002 (movt became a political party 2000); Deputy to Slovak Nat. Council, mem. of Presidium; Chair. of Slovak Nat. Council 1992–98; Chair. Special Body of Nat. Council of Slovakia for Control of Slovak Intelligence Services 1993–98; Founder and Leader Movt for Democracy 2002–; Pres. of Slovakia 2004–. *Publications:* author and co-author of many univ. textbooks, numerous articles and reviews on criminal law. *Leisure interests:* tennis, hockey, motoring. *Address:* Office of the President, Hodžovo nám. 1, PO Box 128, 810 00 Bratislava, Slovakia (office). *Telephone:* (2) 5249-8945 (office). *Fax:* (2) 5441-7028 (office). *E-mail:* informacie@prezident.sk (office). *Website:* www.prezident.sk (office).

GASSIEV, Nikolai Tengizovich; Russian singer (tenor); b. 2 Feb. 1952, Tskhinvali, Georgia; ed Leningrad State Conservatory; soloist Mariinsky Opera and Ballet Theatre 1990–; debut in Metropolitan Opera as Yurodivy (Boris Godunov) and Agrippina (Fairy Angel) 1992, Dresdner Staatsoper 1993, Brooklyn School of Music 1995, Edinburgh Festival 1995, Albert Hall 1995, La Scala 1996; Prize of Union of Theatre Workers Best Actor of the Year 1994. *Address:* Mariinsky Theatre, Teatralnaya pl. 1, St Petersburg, Russia (office). *Telephone:* (812) 315-57-24 (office).

GAT, Joel R., MSc, PhD; Israeli professor of isotope research; *Professor Emeritus, Weizmann Institute of Science;* b. (Joel R. Gutmann), 17 Feb. 1926, Munich, Germany; m.; two c.; ed Hebrew Univ., Jerusalem; emigrated to Israel 1936; Asst, Dept of Physical Chem., Hebrew Univ. 1949–50; Research Officer, Ministry of Defence Labs, Jerusalem 1950–52; Israel Atomic Energy Comm., Rehovot 1952–59; at Isotope Dept (renamed Dept of Environmental Sciences and Energy Research 1990), Weizmann Inst. of Science, Rehovot 1959–, Acting Prof. 1967–71, Prof. 1971–92, Prof. Emer. 1992–, Head of Dept 1975–86, Dean, Faculty of Chem., Weizmann Inst. 1986–89; Dir Centre for Water Science and Tech., Ben Gurion Univ. of the Negev 1997–2003; Visiting Scientist, Enrico Fermi Inst. for Nuclear Science, Univ. of Chicago 1955–56, Scripps Inst. of Oceanography, Univ. of California 1964–65, Nat. Centre for Atmospheric Research, Boulder, Colo 1972–73, Univ. of Wisconsin 1988–89; mem. Editorial Bd Isotope Geosciences, Earth and Planetary Science Letters; undertook IAEA-sponsored projects in Brazil, Iran, Mexico and Turkey. *Publications:* Physics and Chemistry of Lakes (co-ed.) 1995, The Dead Sea: The Lake and its Setting. Oxford Monograph on Geology and Geophysics (co-ed.) 1997, Environmental Isotopes in The Hydrological Cycle: Vol. II, Atmospheric Waters 2001. *Address:* Department of Environmental Sciences and Energy Research, The Weizmann Institute of Science, Sussman Building, Room 307, PO Box 26, Rehovot, Israel (office). *Telephone:* (8) 9342610 (office). *E-mail:* joel.gat@weizmann.ac.il (office). *Website:* www.weizmann.ac.il/ESER (office).

GATES, Henry Louis, Jr, MA, PhD; American academic, author and editor; *W. E. B. DuBois Professor of the Humanities and Director, W.E.B. DuBois Institute for African and African-American Research, Harvard University;* b. 16 Sept. 1950, Piedmont, W Va; s. of Henry-Louis Gates and Pauline Augusta Gates (née Coleman); m. Sharon Lynn Adams 1979; two d.; ed Yale Univ. and Clare Coll. Cambridge; fmr European corresp. for Time magazine; lecturer in English, Yale Univ. 1976–79, Asst Prof. English and Afro-American Studies 1979–84, Assoc. Prof. 1984–85; Prof. of English, Comparative Literature and Africana Studies, Cornell Univ. 1985–90; John Spencer Bassett Prof. of English, Duke Univ. 1990–91; W. E. B. DuBois Prof. of the Humanities and Chair. Dept of African and African-American Studies, Harvard Univ. 1991–, also Dir W. E. B. DuBois Inst. for African and African-American Research; Pres. Afro-American Acad. 1984–; Co-founder AfricanDNA.com (genealogy website); Host African-American Lives (PBS); ed. African American Women's Writings (Macmillan reprint series), Encyclopedia Africana; columnist, New Yorker, New York Times; mem. Pulitzer Prize Bd; Hon. Citizenship of Benin 2001; numerous hon. degrees; American Book Award for The Signifying Monkey; McArthur Foundation Award, Nat. Humanities Medal 1998, Zora Neale Hurston Society Award for Cultural Scholarship, Tikkun National Ethics Award,. *Publications include:* Figures in Black (literary criticism) 1987, The Signifying Monkey 1988, Loose Canons (literary criticism) 1992, Colored People (short stories) 1994, The Future of the Race (with Cornel West) 1996, Thirteen Ways of Looking at a Black Man, Africana (jtly) (TV documentary), Wonders of the African World 1999, The Curitas Enthology of African – American Slave Narratives, The African-American Century 2000; Co-Ed. Encarta Africana Encycloaedia 1999; Ed. The Bondswoman's Narrative 2002, America Behind the Color Line 2004. *Address:* Department of African and African-American Studies, Barker Center, 2nd Floor, 12 Quincy Street, Cambridge, MA 02138, USA. *Telephone:* (617) 496-5468. *Fax:* (617) 495-9490. *Website:* www.fas.harvard.edu/~afroam; www.fas.harvard.edu/~du_bois.

GATES, Holly G.; American computer engineer; *Senior Hardware Engineer, E Ink Corporation;* ed Weihai Br. of Shandong Univ., China, Massachusetts Inst. of Tech., Massachusetts Coll. of Art, Harvard Univ.; worked for Brown

Innovations Inc., Boston Mass 1995–96; Lecturer, MIT Edgerton Center, Cambridge, Mass 1996–97; worked for Zond Systems Inc., Searsburg, Vt June–Aug. 1997; worked for MIT Media Lab., Cambridge, Mass 1996–98; Hardware Engineer, E Ink Corpn, Cambridge, Mass 1998–2002, Sr Hardware Engineer 2002–; First Prize for robot called 'dog' (built with Leila Hasan), 6.270 LEGO Robotics Competition 1998, Rudenberg Memorial Fund 1998, World Tech. Award in Information Tech. (Hardware), The World Tech. Network 2005. *Publications:* papers in professional journals and several patents. *Leisure interests:* welding, renovating, dancing, mountaineering, electronics, sculpture, clothing design, fashion devices. *Address:* E Ink Corporation, 733 Concord Avenue, Cambridge, MA 02138 (office); 189 Summer Street, Apartment 2, Somerville, MA 02145, USA (home). *Telephone:* (617) 499-6000 (office). *Fax:* (617) 499-6200 (office). *E-mail:* info@eink.com (office). *Website:* www.eink.com (office); www.positron.org/people/hgates (office).

GATES, Melinda, BSc, BEcons, MBA; American foundation executive; *Co-Director, Bill and Melinda Gates Foundation;* b. (Melinda Ann French), 15 Aug. 1964, Dallas, Tex.; m. William (Bill) Henry Gates III 1994; one s. two d.; ed Ursuline Acad., Dallas, Duke Univ. and Duke Univ. Fuqua School of Business; several positions at Microsoft Corpn 1987–96, including Product Unit Man. Microsoft Publisher, Microsoft Bob, Microsoft Encarta and Microsoft Expedia; co-f. Bill and Melinda Gates Foundation 1994; mem. Bd of Dirs Drugstore.com –2006, The Washington Post; attends the Bilderberg Group; Trustee, Duke Univ. 1996–2003; named by TIME magazine amongst Persons of the Year 2005, ranked by Forbes magazine amongst 100 Most Powerful Women (10th) 2005, (12th) 2006, (24th) 2007, (40th) 2008, shared Prince of Asturias Award for Int. Cooperation 2006. *Address:* Bill and Melinda Gates Foundation, PO Box 23350, Seattle, WA 98102, USA (office). *Telephone:* (206) 709-3100 (office). *E-mail:* info@gatesfoundation.org (office). *Website:* www.gatesfoundation.org (office).

GATES, Robert M., PhD; American government official and fmr academic administrator; *Secretary of Defense;* b. 25 Sept. 1943, Wichita, Kan.; m. Becky Gates; two c.; ed Coll. of William and Mary, Indiana Univ., Georgetown Univ.; service with USAF 1966–68; career training program CIA 1968, intelligence analyst 1969–72, staff of Special Asst to the Dir of Central Intelligence for Strategic Arms Limitations 1972–73, Asst Nat. Intelligence Officer for Strategic Programs 1973–74, staff Nat. Security Council The White House 1974–76, staff Center for Policy Support 1976–77, Special Asst to Asst to the Pres. for Nat. Security Affairs 1977–79, Dir Strategic Evaluation Center 1979–80, Exec. Asst to Dir of Cen. Intelligence and Dir of the Exec. Staff, Dir of Office of Policy and Planning and Nat. Intelligence Officer for the Soviet Union and Eastern Europe 1980–81, Deputy Dir for Intelligence 1982–86, Chair. Nat. Intelligence Council 1982–86, Acting Dir of Central Intelligence 1986–87, Deputy Dir of Central Intelligence 1986–89, Asst to the Pres. and Deputy for Nat. Security Affairs The White House 1989–91, Dir CIA 1991–93; Interim Dean, George Bush School of Govt and Public Service, 1999-2001, Pres. Texas A&M Univ. 2002–06; US Sec. of Defense 2006–; fmr mem. Bd of Dirs NACCO Industries Inc., Brinker International Inc., Parker Drilling Co. Inc.; fmr mem. Bd of Trustees The Fidelity Funds; mem. Iraq Study Group, US Inst. for Peace 2006; Nat. Intelligence Distinguished Service Medal, Distinguished Intelligence Medal (twice), Intelligence Medal of Merit, Arthur S. Fleming Award, Nat. Security Medal, Presidential Citizen's Medal. *Publication:* From the Shadows: The Ultimate Insider's Story of Five Presidents and How They Won the Cold War 1996. *Address:* Department of Defense, 1000 Defense Pentagon, Washington, DC 20301, USA (office). *Website:* www.defenselink.mil (office).

GATES, William (Bill) Henry, III; American software industry executive and foundation executive; *Chairman, Microsoft Corporation;* b. 28 Oct. 1955, Seattle, Wash.; s. of William H. Gates and the late Mary M. Gates (neé Maxwell); m. Melinda Gates 1994; one s. two d.; ed Lakeside School, Seattle, Harvard Univ.; while at Harvard developed version of BASIC programming language for MITS 1975; programmer for Honeywell 1975; Co-founder with Paul Allen Microsoft Corpn 1975, Gen. Partner 1975–77, Pres. 1977–82, Chair. Bd 1981– (part-time, non-exec. Chair. since 27 June 2008), Chief Software Architect 1999–2006, CEO –2000; f. Corbis (digital archive of art and photography) 1989; co-f. Bill and Melinda Gates Foundation 1994; f. Gates Library Foundation 1997, name changed to Gates Learning Foundation 1999, merged with Bill and Melinda Gates Foundation 2000; mem. Bd of Dirs ICOS (biotechnology co.) 1990–, Berkshire Hathaway Inc. 2004–; Hon. KBE (UK) 2005; Hon. DJur (Harvard) 2007; Howard Vollum Award, Reed Coll. Portland, Ore. 1984, Nat. Medal for Tech. from US Commerce Dept 1992, CEO of the Year, Chief Executive Magazine 1994, named by Time magazine amongst Persons of the Year 2005, Premio Príncipe de Asturias en Cooperación Internacional (co–recipient) 2006, voted by New Statesman magazine eighth in list of Heroes of Our Time 2006, numerous other awards. *Publications:* The Future 1994, The Road Ahead 1995, Business @ the Speed of Thought 1999. *Leisure interest:* reading, golf, bridge. *Address:* Microsoft Corporation, 1 Microsoft Way, Redmond, WA 98052-8300 (office); Bill and Melinda Gates Foundation, PO Box 23350, Seattle, WA 98102, USA. *Telephone:* (425) 882-8080. *Fax:* (425) 936-7329. *Website:* www.microsoft.com (office); www.microsoft.com/billgates/default.aspx (office); www.gatesfoundation.org.

GATLIN, Justin; American sprinter; b. 10 Feb. 1982, Brooklyn, NY; ed Woodham High School, FL, Univ. of Tenn.; first athlete since 1957 to win consecutive Nat. Collegiate Athletic Asscn (NCAA) titles in both 100m. and 200m.; five NCAA titles in total; US Jr Champion on three occasions; finished second in 60m. (beating Maurice Greene) on professional debut at Verizon Millrose Games 2003; secured US $500,000 by winning Moscow Challenge 100m. 2003; World Indoor Champion and US Champion 60m. 2003; gold medal 100m. (in a personal-best time of 9.85 seconds), bronze medal 200m. Olympic Games, Athens 2004; USA Track and Field Jesse Owens Award 2004. *Address:* c/o USA Track and Field, 1 RCA Dome, Suite 140, Indianapolis, IN 46225, USA. *Telephone:* (317) 261-0500. *Fax:* (317) 261-0514. *Website:* www.usatf.org.

GATSINZI, Gen. Marcel, BSc; Rwandan politician and army officer; *Minister of Defence;* b. 9 Jan. 1948, Kigali; s. of Phocas Mpagazehe and Anastasie Nyirabagahe; ed Ecole de Guerre, Brussels, Belgium, Inst. of World Politics, Washington, DC, USA; served in Rwandan Armed Forces, rank of Gen.; fmr Deputy Chief of Staff, then Chief of Staff, Nat. Gendarmerie; mem. Neutral Mil. Observer Group of fmr OAU (now the African Union) 1992–93; Sec.-Gen., Nat. Security Council 2002; Minister of Defence 2002–; rep. to numerous int. negotiations and meetings including African Union, Easbrig, Golden Spear, East African Community. *Address:* Ministry of Defence, PO Box 23, Kigali, Rwanda (office). *Telephone:* 576032 (office). *Fax:* 573411 (office). *E-mail:* marcel_gatsinzi@gov.rw (office). *Website:* www.mod.gov.rw (office).

GATT, Austin, LLD; Maltese politician and lawyer; *Minister for Information Technology and Investment;* b. 29 July 1953; m. Marisa Zammit Maempel; two s.; ed Lyceum and Univ. of Malta; practised law 1975–82; Nationalist Party org. 1980; Chair. Man. Bd Independence Print Co. Ltd 1982–87; Head, Legal Office of Nationalist Party 1982–87, Sec. Gen. 1988–98; Chair. Euro Tours Co. Ltd; MP 1996–, Opposition Spokesman for Justice, Local Councils and Housing 1996–98; Parl. Sec. Office of Prime Minister 1998–99; Minister for Justice and Local Govt 1999–2003, for Information Technology and Investment 2003–. *Address:* Ministry for Information Technology and Investment, 168 Triq id-Dejqa, Valletta, CMR 02, Malta (home). *Telephone:* 226808 (home). *Fax:* 250700 (home). *E-mail:* info@miti.gov.mt (office). *Website:* www.miti.gov.mt (office).

GATTAZ, Yvon; French business executive; b. 17 June 1925, Bourgoin; s. of Marceau Gattaz and Gabrielle Brotel; m. Geneviève Beurley 1954; two s. one d.; ed Coll. of Bourgoin, Lycée du Parc, Lyon, Ecole Centrale des Arts et Manufactures, Paris; with Aciéries du Nord 1948–50; Automobiles Citroën 1950–54; founder Soc. Radiall 1952, Chair. 1952–93, Pres. Supervisory Council 1994–; Chair. group of commercial and industrial cos, Rosny-sous-Bois 1967–81; Admin. Centre for External Trade 1979–82, Nat. Council for Scientific Research 1979–81; Founder Mouvement des entreprises à taille humaine industrielles et commerciales (ETHIC) 1976, Pres. 1976–81, Hon. Pres. 1981–; Founder Les Quatre Vérités 1974, Co-Ed. 1974–81; mem. Conseil économique et social 1979–89; Pres. Conseil National du Patronat Français 1981–86, Hon. Pres. 1986; Pres. Admin. Council, Fondation jeunesse et entreprise 1986–; Pres. Comité d'expansion de Seine-Saint-Denis 1987 (Hon. Pres. 1998–), asscn Entreprises Télévision Educ. Formation (ETEF) 1994, ASMEP (Asscn des moyennes entreprises patrimoniales) 1994–; Pres. Acad. of Moral and Political Sciences 1999–; mem. Institut de France (Acad. des Sciences morales et politiques) 1989; Commdr, Légion d'honneur; Commdr, Ordre nat. du Mérite; Prix Mondial Cino del Duca 2001. *Publications:* Les hommes en gris 1970, La fin des patrons 1980, Les patrons reviennent 1988, Le modèle français 1993 (prix du Livre de l'entreprise 1995), Mitterrand et les patrons 1981–86 (jtly.) 1999. *Address:* c/o Radiall SA, 101 Rue Philibert Hoffmann, 93116 Rosny-sous-Bois Cedex; 4 rue Léo-Delibes, 75116 Paris, France (office).

GATTI, Daniele; Italian conductor; *Music Director, Orchestre Nationale de France;* b. 6 Nov. 1961, Milan; m. Silvia Chiesa 1990; ed Giuseppe Verdi Conservatory, Milan; conducted Verdi's Giovanna d'Arco 1982; appearances with Maggio Musicale Fiorentino Orchestra, Milan Angelicum, Bologna Municipal Orchestra, regional orchestras of Italian radio; f. Stradivari Chamber Orchestra 1986; debut at La Scala, Milan with Rossini's L'occasione fa il Ladro 1987–88 season; US debut with American Symphony Orchestra, Carnegie Hall, New York 1990; Covent Garden debut with I Puritani 1992; Music Dir Accad. di Santa Cecilia, Rome 1992–97; Prin. Guest Conductor, Royal Opera House, Covent Garden 1994–97; debut at Metropolitan Opera, New York with Madama Butterfly 1994–95 season; debut with Royal Philharmonic Orchestra 1994, Music Dir 1995–2009; debut with New York Philharmonic 1995; Music Dir Teatro Communale, Bologna 1997–2007; Music Dir, Orchestre Nat. de France 2008–; has led many orchestras in Europe and USA, including Bavarian Radio Symphony, London Philharmonic, Cleveland Orchestra, Boston and Chicago Symphonies and Accademia Santa Cecilia, Rome; has conducted at many leading opera houses; conducted RPO at London Proms 1999, 2002. *Recordings:* Tschaikovsky's Fourth and Fifth Symphonies, Pathétique Symphony No. 6 2005. *Address:* Orchestre Nationale de France, c/o Radio France, 116 Président Kennedy, 75786 Paris, France (office). *Telephone:* 1-56-40-29-07 (office). *E-mail:* contact@orchestradeparis.com (office). *Website:* radiofrance.fr/chaines/orchestres/national (office).

GATTI, Gabriele, MA; San Marino politician; *Secretary of State for Finance, the Budget, Post and Relations with the Azienda Autonoma di Stato Filatelica e Numismatica;* b. 1943, Domagnano; m. Gina Fiorini; two d.; mem. Parl. 1978–; Deputy Sec. Christian Democratic Party 1979–85, Sec.-Gen. 1985–87; apptd Sec. of State for Foreign Relations and Political Affairs 1986; Pres. Ministerial Chief, Council of Europe; mem. Gen. Comm. of the Inst. for Social Security, Urban Comm.; Sec. of State for Finance, the Budget, Post and Relations with the Azienda Autonoma di Stato Filatelica e Numismatica 2008–. *Address:* Secretariat of State for Finance, the Budget, Post and Relations with the Azienda Autonoma di Stato Filatelica e Numismatica (AASFN) Palazzo Begni, Contrada Omerelli, 47890 San Marino (office). *Telephone:* 882661 (office). *Fax:* 882244 (office). *Website:* www.finanze.sm (office).

GATTING, Michael (Mike) William, OBE; British professional cricket coach and fmr professional cricketer; b. 6 June 1957, Kingsbury, Middx; m. Elaine

Mabbott 1980; two s.; ed John Kelly High School; right-hand batsman and right-arm medium bowler; played for Middx 1975–99 (Capt. 1983–97); 79 Tests for England 1977–95 (23 as Capt.), scoring 4,409 runs (average 35.5) including 10 hundreds; scored 36,549 first-class runs (94 hundreds); toured Australia 1986–87 (Capt.), 1987–95; Capt. rebel cricket tour to SA 1989–90; 92 limited-overs ints, 37 as Capt.; mem. England Selection Cttee 1997–99; Dir of Coaching, Middx Cricket Club 1999–2000; Dir Ashwell Leisure 2001–; Grand Cru Travel Consultant; Wisden Cricketer of The Year 1984. *Radio:* analyst on Test Match Special. *Publications:* Limited Overs 1986, Triumph in Australia 1987, Leading from the Front (autobiog.) 1988. *Leisure interests:* golf, soccer and sport in general. *Address:* c/o Middlesex County Cricket Club, Lord's Cricket Ground, St John's Wood Road, London, NW8 8QN (office); 8A Villlage Road, Enfield, Middlesex, EN1 2DH, England (home). *Telephone:* (20) 7289-1300 (office); (7768) 541693 (Mobile) (home).

GATTUNG, Theresa, BA, LLB; New Zealand business executive; ed Univ. of Waikato, Victoria Univ. of Wellington; fmr Chief Man. of Marketing, National Mutual; Chief Man. of Marketing, Bank of New Zealand –1994; Gen. Man. Marketing, Telecom Corpn Ltd (largest co. in NZ) 1994–96, Group Gen. Man. Services 1996–99, Chief Exec. and Man. Dir Telecom Corpn of New Zealand Ltd 1999–2007; ranked by Fortune magazine amongst 50 Most Powerful Women in Business outside the US (37th) 2003, (32nd) 2004, (29th) 2005, (23rd) 2006, ranked by Forbes magazine amongst 100 Most Powerful Women (49th) 2006. *Address:* c/o Telecom Corporation of New Zealand Ltd, POB 570, Telecom House, 68 Jervois Quay, Wellington, New Zealand (office).

GATZOULIS, Michael Athanasios, MD, PhD, FESC, FACC; Greek cardiologist; *Academic Head, Adult Congenital Heart Centre and Centre for Pulmonary Hypertension, Royal Brompton Hospital; Professor of Cardiology and Congenital Heart Disease, National Heart and Lung Institute;* b. Drama; s. of Dr Athanasios K. Gatzoulis; m. Julie Kohls-Gatzoulis; two s.; ed Aristotelian Univ., Thessaloniki, Greece, MRCPCH, London, Univ. of London, UK; fmr Staff Cardiologist and Asst Prof., Univ. of Toronto Congenital Cardiac Centre for Adults; currently Prof. of Cardiology, Congenital Heart Disease and Consultant Cardiologist and Academic Head, Adult Congenital Heart Centre and Centre for Pulmonary Hypertension, Royal Brompton Hosp.; Prin. Investigator, Adult Congenital Heart Programme, Nat. Heart and Lung Inst., Imperial Coll. School of Medicine, also Prof. of Cardiology and Congenital Heart Disease 2005–; Visiting Prof., Vanderbilt Univ. 2006, Stanford Univ. 2006, Harvard Univ. 2007, Erasmus Univ. and Thorax Centre, Rotterdam, Netherlands, Japan Heart Inst. and Univ. of Tokyo, King Faisal Specialist Hosp. and Research Center, Jeddah, Leiden Univ., Netherlands; Idriss Distinguished Prof., Northwestern Univ., Chicago, USA; Assoc. Ed., Int. Journal of Cardiology 2003–; mem. Int. Editorial Bd and Guest Ed., European Heart Journal; Section Ed., Congenital Heart Disease, Hellenic Journal of Cardiology 2002–; Journal Reviewer, Heart 1994–, Circulation 1997–, Clinical Science 1998–, European Heart Journal 1999–, Arch Dis Child 2001–, Europace 2002–, Lancet, 2003–, American Heart Journal 2003–, Cardiology Young 1994–, Journal of the American College of Cardiology 1997–, Int. Journal of Cardiology 1999–, Drugs 2000–; Sec. Gen. Int. Soc. of Adult Congenital Cardiac Disease 2000–01, Pres. 2004–05; ESC Nucleus and UK Rep. EuroHeart Survey for Adult Congenital Heart Disease 2001–03. *Publications include:* The Adult with Tetralogy of Fallot 2001, Diagnosis and Management of Adult Congenital Heart Disease 2003, Adult Congenital Heart Disease: A Practical Guide 2004, Heart Disease and Pregnancy 2006; co-ed. 40th Edn of Gray's Anatomy; author of more than 150 peer-reviewed scientific papers, including articles in Nature, New England Journal of Medicine, The Lancet, and Circulation. *Leisure interests:* tennis, skiing, model rail (Marklin). *Address:* Royal Brompton Hospital, Sydney Street, London, SW3 6NP, England (office). *Telephone:* (20) 7352-8602 (PA Mrs Rachel Collumbell) (office); (20) 7351-8227 (direct line) (office). *Fax:* (20) 7351-8629 (office). *E-mail:* m.gatzoulis@imperial.ac.uk (office); m.gatzoulis@rbh.nthames.nhs .uk (office). *Website:* www.rbh.nthames.nhs.uk (office).

GAUDÉ, Laurent; French novelist and playwright; b. 6 July 1972, Paris. *Plays include:* Combats de possédés 1999, Onysos le furieux 2000, Cendres sur les mains 2001, Pluie de cendres 2001, Le Tigre bleu de l'Euphrate 2002, Médée Kali 2003, Salina 2003, Les Sacrifiées 2004. *Publications include:* novels: Cris 2001, La Mort du roi Tsongor (Prix Goncourt, Prix des Libraires 2003) 2002, Le Soleil des Scorta (Prix Goncourt) 2004, Eldorado 2006, Dans la nuit Mozambique 2007. *Address:* c/o Actes Sud, BP 38, 13633 Arles Cédex, France.

GAULTIER, Jean-Paul; French fashion designer; b. 24 April 1952, Arcueil, Paris; s. of Paul Gaultier; launched first collection with his Japanese pnr 1978; since then known on int. scale for his men's and women's collections; first jr collection 1988; costume designs for film The Cook, The Thief, His Wife and Her Lover 1989, for ballet Le Défilé de Régine Chopinot 1985, Madonna's World Tour 1990; released record How to Do That (in collaboration with Tony Mansfield) 1989; launched own perfume 1993; designed costumes for Victoria Abril (q.v.) in Pedro Almodóvar (q.v.) 's film Kika 1994, film La Cité des Enfants Perdus 1995, The Fifth Element 1996, Absolutely Fabulous 2001; launched perfume brands Jean-Paul Gaultier (1993), Le Mâle (1995), Fragile (1999); women's wear design dir, Hermès 2004–; Fashion Oscar 1987, Progetto Leonardo Award for How to Do That 1989; Chevalier des Arts et des Lettres. *Leisure interest:* television. *Address:* Jean-Paul Gaultier SA, 30 rue du Faubourg-Saint-Antoine, 75012 Paris, France. *Website:* www .jeanpaulgaultier.com.

GAUR, Babulal, BA, LLB; Indian politician; b. June 1930; fmr trade union activist; mem. Madhya Pradesh Legis. Ass. 1974–, fmr Leader of the Opposition; fmr Madhya Pradesh State Minister of Local Admin, of Legal Affairs, of Legis. Affairs, of Bhopal Gas Tragedy Relief, of Public Relations, of

Urban Admin and Devt; Chief Minister of Madhya Pradesh 2004–05. *Address:* c/o Office of the Chief Minister, Ballabh Bhavan, Mantralaya, Bhopal 461 004, India (office).

GAUTAM, Bamdev; Nepalese politician; *Deputy Prime Minister and Minister of Home Affairs;* b. 14 June 1948, Puthan; m.; joined Communist Party of Nepal (CPN) 1964, Dist Sec. Rupandehi CPN 1972–79, became W Cttee Sec. 1979–80, mem. CPN Cen. Cttee 1980–97, fmr Deputy Sec.-Gen. CPN, Gen. Sec. Communist Party of Nepal–Unified Marxist Leninist (CPN-UML) 1997–; mem. Parl. for Bardiya Constituency 1991–; Deputy Prime Minister and Minister of Home Affairs 1997–99, 2008–. *Address:* Ministry of Home Affairs, Singha Durbar, Kathmandu, Nepal (office). *Telephone:* (1) 4211224 (office). *E-mail:* moha@wlink.com.np (office).

GAUTRAND, Manuelle; French architect; b. 1961; qualified as architect 1985; worked on several jt projects before setting up practice in Lyons 1991, moved to Paris 1993; participated in int. collaboration for François Pinault Foundation of Contemporary Art 2001, Venice Biennale 2002, 2004; invited to Deutsches Architektur Museum, Frankfurt to present design for Citroën showroom on Champs-Elyées 2005; lecturer, Ecole Spéciale d'Architecture 1999–2000, Paris-Val-de-Seine School of Architecture 2000–03; currently teaches at architectural workshops throughout Europe, particularly in Karlsruhe, Madrid, Oslo, Riga, Vienna and Wrocław; consultant, educ. authority, Grenoble 1993–, Mission interministérielle pour la qualité des constructions publiques (French govt body) 1998–; guest lecturer Building Media Group, Moscow 2008, French Week in Vietnam, Ho Chi Minh City 2008, Architecture World Convention, Munster 2008, Waterloo Univ., Canada 2008, Fine Arts Museum, Ottawa 2008, Architects Convention, Bangkok 2008, Architecture World Convention, Munster 2008; elected Statutory mem. French Architecture Acad. 2005; Albums de la Jeune Architecture Award 1992, Winner, French Architecture et Maîtrise d'Ouvrage Prize (for catering bldg, Nantes Airport) 2000, Delarue Prize (Silver Medal), Paris Architecture Acad. 2002, Construction Prize, Asscn of Construction Journalists 2003, Winner, MIPIM Architectural Review Future Project Award (for Citroën showroom, Paris) 2005, Distinction in MIPIM Architectural Review Future Project Awards (for Admin. City, Saint-Etienne) 2006, AIT Magazine (Germany) Int. Contract World winner 2008 (for Citroën showroom, Paris), Int. Interior Design Asscn Interior Design Award (for Citroën showroom, Paris) 2008. *Major built works include:* footbridge, Lyon 1993, Le Fellini four-screen cinema, Villefontaine 1994, Univ. Inst. of Professional Educ., Annecy-le-Vieux 1996, restructuring admin. unit of Georges Pompidou Centre, Paris 1996, restructuring two-screen cinema, Saint-Priest 1996, Laurent-Mourguet School, Écully 1997, toll plazas, A16 motorway 1998, airport catering bldg, Nantes 1998, Nat. Drama Centre, Béthune 1998, Univ. Inst. of Professional Educ., Lieusaint 1999, La Coupole cultural centre, Saint-Louis 2000, two metro stations for the Val line, Rennes 2002, complex of 104 ecological apartments, Rennes 2006, Citroën showroom, Champs-Élysées, Paris 2007, block of 35 apartments, Boulogne-Billancourt 2007, shopping mall, Bangkok 2008. *Current designs and projects:* luxury home unit, Beijing 2008, block of 93 ecological apartments, Acigné 2008, office bldg, Lyons 2008, confluence urban devt zone, Lyons 2008, Rokin 75: office bldg, Amsterdam 2008, automotive showroom, Cairo 2008, mixed-use complex, Brussels city centre 2008, Lille Modern Art Museum, Villeneuve d'Ascq 2008, Ava Tower, La Defense, Paris 2009, Gaîté Lyrique theatre, Paris 2009, Administrative City, Saint-Etienne 2009. *Publications:* La coupole a Saint-Louis 2003, Unaccustomed – Manuelle Gautrand 2004, Manuelle Gautrand Architectures 2005, Manuelle Gautrand Architect 2006, Manuelle Gautrand 2007, Monography Manuelle Gautrand Architect 2008. *Address:* Manuelle Gautrand Architect, 36 boulevard de la Bastille, 75012 Paris, France (office). *Telephone:* 1-56-95-06-46 (office). *Fax:* 1-56-95-06-47 (office). *E-mail:* contact@manuelle-gautrand.com (office). *Website:* www.manuelle-gautrand.com (office).

GAVAHI, Abdulrahim, MBA, PhD; Iranian diplomatist and international organization official; ed Abadan Inst. of Tech., Iran Center for Man. Studies; with Ministry of Oil, Govt of Iran 1979; Amb. to Sweden (also accred to Denmark, Finland, Iceland and Norway) 1980–82, to Japan 1982–84; with Ministry of Foreign Affairs 1987–89, 2000, Ministry of Int. and Econ. Affairs 1989–; Amb. to Norway 1994; Sec.-Gen. Iran Chamber of Commerce, Industries and Mines 1998; Sec.-Gen. Econ. Co-operation Org. (ECO) 2000–02. *Address:* c/o Economic Co-operation Organization, 1 Golbou Alley, Kamranieh Street, P.O. Box 14155-6176, Tehran, Iran (office).

GAVAI, Ramkrishnan Suryabhan, BA; Indian agriculturist, social activist and government official; *Governor of Kerala;* b. 30 Oct. 1929, Darapur village, Amravati Dist, Maharashtra; s. of Suryabhanji Gavai; m. Kamaltai Gavai 1959; two s. one d.; ed Nagpur Univ., Amravati; mem. Maharashtra Legis. Council 1964–94, Deputy Chair. 1968–78, Chair. 1978–84, Leader of Opposition 1986–88; mem. Lok Sabha 1998–, mem. Cttee on Urban and Rural Devt, Consultative Cttee (Ministry of Agric.) 1998–99; Gov. of Bihar 2006–08, of Kerala 2008–; mem. 15th and 20th Commonwealth Parl. Conf., Trinidad and Tobago 1969, Colombo 1974, Lusaka 1978, Asian Conf. on Family Planning and Women, Child Welfare, Beijing 1980, 13th to 19th Gen. Confs of World Fellowship of Buddhists, Thailand, Sri Lanka, Nepal, USA, S Korea, Taiwan, Thailand, 20th Conf. of World Fellowship of Buddhists, Sydney 1998; Pres. Dr Babasaheb Ambedkar Smarak Samiti, Deeksha Bhoomi, Nagpur, Dr Babasaheb Ambedkar Shiksha Prasarak Mandal, Amravati; Vice-Pres. and mem. Exec. Cttee World Fellowship of Buddhists, Maharashtra Br. of Commonwealth Parl. Asscn; runs various colls (Arts, Commerce, Science, Law, MBA), high schools and hosps; mem. Western India Football Asscn, Mumbai; Nat. Integration Award, Kusta Mitra Award. *Publications:* 5-Year Plan in Relation to the Scheduled Castes and Schedule Tribes, Scheduled Castes and Scheduled Tribes – Their Service Privileges, The Caste War Over

Reservation – A Case Before the People's Bar, Facilities to Buddhists Converted from Scheduled Castes, Dr. Babasaheb Ambedkar – Deserving the Thanks of the Country, Dr. Babasaheb Ambedkar Marathwada Vidyapeeth – Petition Before the People of Marathwada, Report for Eradication of Leprosy, Reports on Employment Guarantee. *Leisure interest:* wrestling, swimming, running, reading. *Address:* Raj Bhavan, Thiruvananthapuram, Kerala (office); 151 MP Flats, North Avenue, New Delhi 110001, India (home). *Telephone:* (471) 2721100 (office); (11) 23094315 (home); (11) 23094409 (home). *Fax:* (471) 2720266 (office) (office). *E-mail:* info@keralacm.gov.in (office). *Website:* keralacm.gov.in/governor.htm (office).

GAVASKAR, Sunil ('Sunny') Manohar, BA; Indian business executive, sports administrator and fmr professional cricketer; *Chairman, Cricket Committee, International Cricket Council;* b. 10 July 1949, Bombay (now Mumbai); s. of Manohar Keshav Gavaskar and Meenal Manohar Gavaskar; m. Marshniel Mehrotra 1974; one s.; ed St Xavier's High School, Bombay and St Xavier's College, Bombay Univ.; right-hand opening batsman; played for Mumbai 1967–87, Somerset 1980; 125 Tests for India 1970–97 (47 as Capt.), scoring 10,122 runs (average 51.1) with 34 hundreds (world record held jtly with Sachin Tendulkar) and holding 108 catches; toured England 1971, 1974, 1975 (World Cup), 1979, 1982, 1983 (World Cup); scored 25,834 first-class runs with 81 hundreds; highest score (236 v. Australia Dec. 1983) by Indian in Test match; first player to score more than 10,000 Test runs 1987; first player to score over 2,000 runs against three countries 1987; only man to play in a hundred successive Tests; nominated to Rajya Sabha 1992; Match Referee Int. Cricket Council (ICC) 1993–94; f. Sunil Gavaskar Foundation for Cricket in Bengal 1996; Chair. ICC Cricket Cttee, Indian Nat. Cricket Acad. 2001–; Arjuna Award 1975, Padma Bhushan 1980, both Govt of India, Wisden Cricketer of The Year 1980. *Publications:* Sunny Days – An Autobiography 1976, Idols (autobiog.) 1982, Runs 'n' Ruins 1984, One-day Wonders. *Address:* Nirlon Synthetic Fibres and Chemicals Ltd, Nirlon House, 254-B, Dr Annie Besant Road, Worli, Mumbai 18, India (office).

GAVIDIA, Yolanda Mayora de; Salvadorean economist, civil servant and international organization official; *Secretary-General, Secretaría de Integración Económica Centroamericana (SIECA);* m.; ed Cen. American Inst. of Business Admin, INCAE; worked with various nat. devt orgs; mem. Panel of Econ. Advisers, Ministry of Social Planning 1990–92; Tech. Sec.-Gen. for Econ. and Social Policy, Ministry of Planning 1993–95; Program Coordinator for Improvement of Competitiveness, Presidential Comm. for Modernization of the Public Sector 1995–97; joined Ministry of the Economy 1996, Minister of the Economy 2004–08; Sec.-Gen. Secretaría de Integración Económica Centroamericana (SIECA), Guatemala City, Guatemala 2009–. *Address:* Secretaría de Integración Económica Centroamericana (SIECA), 4a Avda 10–25, Zona 14, Apdo 1237, 01901 Guatemala City, Guatemala (office). *Telephone:* 2368-2151 (office). *Fax:* 2368-1071 (office). *E-mail:* info@sieca.org .gt (office). *Website:* www.sieca.org.gt (office).

GAVIN, John, BA; American actor and diplomatist; *Partner, Gavin, Dailey & Co.;* b. 8 April 1932, Los Angeles; s. of Herald Ray Gavin and Delia Diana Pablos; m. Constance Mary Towers; one s. three d.; ed Stanford Univ.; actor in feature films 1956–80; Special Adviser to Sec.-Gen. OAS 1961–74; Vice-Pres. Atlantic Richfield Co. (to head Fed. & Int. Relations Unit) 1986–87; Pres. Univisa Satellite Communications 1987–90; Pres. Gamma Services Corpn 1968–; spokesman Bank of America 1973–80; Amb. to Mexico 1981–86; Chair. the Century Council 1990–; Partner, Gavin, Dailey & Co., LA 1990–; consultant to Dept of State; mem. Screen Actors' Guild (Pres. 1971–73). *Films include:* A Time to Live, A Time to Die 1958, Imitation of Life 1959, Psycho 1960, Midnight Lace 1960, Spartacus 1960, A Breath of Scandal 1960, Backstreet 1961, Romanoff and Juliet 1961, Tammy Tell Me True 1961, Thoroughly Modern Millie 1967, Mad Woman of Chaillot 1969, Pussycat Pussycat I Love You 1970, Jennifer 1978, The P.A.C.K. (1997). *Television includes:* Destry (series) 1964, Convoy (series) 1965, Cutter's Trail 1970, The Lives of Jenny Dolan 1975, Doctors' Private Lives 1978, The New Adventures of Heidi 1978, Sophia Loren: Her Own Story 1980. *Address:* 2100 Century Park West, #10263, Los Angeles, CA 90067-6900, USA.

GAVIRIA DÍAZ, Carlos, PhD; Colombian lawyer, magistrate and politician; *President, Polo Democratico Alternativo;* b. 8 May 1937, Sopetrán, Antioquia; ed Univ. of Antioquia, Medellín, Harvard Univ. Law School, USA; Dean Law Faculty, Univ. of Antioquia 1967–69, Dir Dept of Public Law 1974–80, Dir Inst. of Political Sciences 1988, Vice-Rector Univ. of Antioquia 1989–92; Magistrate, Constitutional Court, Bogotá 1993–2001, Pres. Constitutional Court 1996; elected Senator for Frente Social y Politico 2002–06; cand. for Polo Democratico Alternativo (Alternative Democratic Pole—PDA) in presidential election March 2006; Pres. PDA 2006–. *Address:* Polo Democratico Alternativo, Carrera 17A 37-27, Bogotá, Colombia (office). *Telephone:* (1) 2886188 (office). *Website:* www.polodemocratico.net (office).

GAVIRIA TRUJILLO, César; Colombian politician, international organization official and economist; b. 31 March 1947, Pereira; m. Ana Milena Muñoz de Gaviria; ed Univ. of the Andes; mem. town council of Pereira, later Mayor; mem. Chamber of Deputies (Partido Liberal Colombiano—PLC) and Dir Comm. for Econ. Affairs 1974; Vice-Minister for Econ. Devt 1978; Speaker of Parl. 1983; journalist in early 1980s; Minister of Finance and Public Credit 1986–87, of the Interior 1987–89; Pres. of Colombia 1990–94; Sec.-Gen. OAS 1994–2004; mem. Inter-American Dialogue, Club de Madrid, La Conférence de Montréal; Hon. Prof., Universidad ICESI, Colombia, Univ. of Miami, USA, Universidad Libre Colombia 1990, Universidade Estácio de Sá, Rio de Janeiro 1991, Northeastern Univ., USA 2002; Hon. LLB (Univ. Libre de Colombia); Hon. DCL (Northeastern Univ.) 2002; W. Averell Harriman Democracy Award 2002, Nat. Democratic Inst. Democracy Award 2002, Washington Times Int. Courage in Leadership Award 2002. *Publications include:* La Deuda Latinoamericana 1982, Reflexiones para una nueva Constitución 1990, La Revolución Pacífica 1990, Las Bases de la Nueva Colombia: El Revolcón Institucional 1990–1994 1994, Reformas Económicas 1990–1994 1994, Plan de Desarrollo Económico y Social 1990–1994 1994, A New Vision of the OAS 1995, Toward the New Millennium: The Road Travelled 1994–1999 1999; book chapters and articles in journals. *Address:* c/o Organization of American States, 17th Street and Constitution Avenue, NW, Washington, DC 20006, USA (office).

GAVRIISKI, Svetoslav; Bulgarian politician and bank governor; b. 18 Dec. 1948, Svishtov; ed Karl Marx Higher Inst. of Econs, Sofia; economist, Ministry of Finance 1972; Sr Expert, Nat. Balance Sheets Directorate, Ministry of the Economy and Planning 1988; Sr Expert in Int. Financial Relations, Ministry of Finance 1990, Head of Int. Finance Dept 1991–92; Deputy Minister of Finance 1992–97, Minister Feb.–May 1997; Gov. of Bulgaria to IMF 1992–96, 1997–, to IBRD, EBRD and European Investment Bank 1997–, to Black Sea Trade and Devt Bank 1998–; Leader Group Negotiations on Bulgaria's External Debt 1991–94; mem. Man. Bd Bulbank 1991–97; Gov. Bulgarian Nat. Bank 1997–2003; Man. mem. Int. Bank for Econ. Co-operation, Moscow 1992–, Int. Investment Bank, Moscow 1992–; mem. Bd Dirs Bank Consolidation Co. 2001–; mem. Supervisory Bd Municipal Bank 2005–; nominee for mayoral elections in Sofia 2005. *Address:* Municipal Bank AD, 6 Vrabcha Str., 1000 Sofia, Bulgaria (office). *Telephone:* (2) 930-01-11 (office). *Fax:* (2) 981-51-47 (office). *E-mail:* contacts@municipalbank.bg (office). *Website:* www .municipalbank.bg (office).

GAVRILOV, Andrei Vladimirovich; Russian pianist; b. 21 Sept. 1955, Moscow; ed Moscow Conservatory; performs regularly throughout Europe, America and Japan, including recitals at Salzburg, Roque d'Antheron, Schleswig-Holstein, Istanbul and Chichester Festivals; has performed in UK with Philharmonia, London Philharmonic, Royal Philharmonic, BBC Symphony and London Symphony Orchestras, in USA with Baltimore Symphony, Detroit Symphony, New York Philharmonic and Philadelphia Orchestras; recorded works with Sviatoslav Teofilovich Richter; lives in Switzerland; winner of the Tchaikovsky Competition in Moscow 1974; disc awards include French suites of J. S. Bach and Etudes of Chopin; several int. prizes. *Address:* c/o Konzertdirektion Schlote, Danreitergasse 4, 5020 Salzburg, Austria (office).

GAVRIN, Alexander Sergeyevich; Russian politician and engineer; b. 22 July 1953, Orlovo, Zaporozhye Region, Ukraine; ed Tumen Industrial Inst., Tumen State Inst. of Oil and Gas; army service 1972–74; controller, master Zaporozhye plant Radiopribor 1974–79; controlling master Manuylsky Research Inst., Kiev 1979–80; engineer constructor Kiev plant generator 1980–81; technician Kiev production co. 1981–83; electrician Povkhneft Kogalym, Tumen Region 1983–88; engineer head of group Kogalymneftegas Co., Tumen Region 1988–89; Chair. Trade Union LUKOil-Kogalymneftegas 1989–93; Head of Admin. Kogalym. Tumen Region 1993–96; Mayor of Kogalym 1996–2000; Minister of Energy of Russian Fed. 2000–01; fmr Rep. of Tumen Region to Council of Fed., Russian Fed. Ass. *Address:* c/o Council of Federation, B. Dmitrovka Str. 26, 103426 Moscow, Russia (office).

GAY, Peter, PhD; American historian and academic; *Sterling Professor Emeritus of History, Yale University;* b. 20 June 1923, Berlin, Germany; s. of Morris Fröhlich and Helga Fröhlich; m. Ruth Slotkin 1959; three step-d.; ed Univ. of Denver and Columbia Univ.; left Germany 1939; Dept of Public Law and Govt, Columbia Univ. 1947–56, Dept of History 1956–69, Prof. of History 1962–69, William R. Shepherd Prof. 1967–69; Prof. of Comparative European Intellectual History, Yale Univ. 1969–, Durfee Prof. of History 1970–84, Sterling Prof. of History 1984–93, Sterling Prof. Emer. 1993–; Guggenheim Fellow 1967–68; Overseas Fellow, Churchill Coll., Cambridge, UK 1970–71; Visiting Fellow, Inst. for Advanced Study, Berlin 1984; Dir Center for Scholars and Writers, New York Public Library 1997–; mem. American Historical Asscn, French Historical Soc.; Hon. DHumLitt (Denver) 1970, (Maryland) 1979, (Hebrew Univ. Coll., Cincinnati) 1983, (Clark Univ., Worcester) 1985; Nat. Book Award 1967, Melcher Book Award 1967, Gold Medal for Historical Science, Amsterdam 1990, Geschwister Scholl Prize 1999. *Publications:* The Dilemma of Democratic Socialism: Eduard Bernstein's Challenge to Marx 1951, Voltaire's Politics: The Poet as Realist 1959, Philosophical Dictionary 1962, The Party of Humanity: Essays in the French Enlightenment 1964, The Loss of Mastery: Puritan Historians in Colonial America 1966, The Enlightenment: An Interpretation, Vols I, II 1966, 1969, Weimar Culture: The Outsider as Insider 1969, The Bridge of Criticism: Dialogues on the Enlightenment 1970, The Question of Jean-Jacques Rousseau 1974, Modern Europe (with R. K. Webb) 1973, Style in History 1974, Art and Act: On Causes in History – Manet, Gropius, Mondrian 1976, Freud, Jews and Other Germans: Masters and Victims in Modernist Culture 1978, The Bourgeois Experience: Victoria to Freud, Vols I, II, III 1984, 1986, 1993, Freud for Historians 1985, Freud: A Life for Our Time 1988, A Freud Reader 1989, Reading Freud: Explorations and Entertainments 1990, The Cultivation of Hatred 1993, The Naked Heart 1995, Pleasure Wars 1998, My German Question: Growing Up in Nazi Berlin 1998, Mozart 1999, Schnitzler's Century 2001, Savage Reprisals 2002, Modernism 2007; also trans and anthologies. *Leisure interests:* reading, listening to music. *Address:* 760 West End Avenue, Apt 15A, New York, NY 10025, USA (home). *Telephone:* (212) 930-9257 (office); (212) 865-0577 (home). *Fax:* (212) 930-0040 (office). *E-mail:* pgay@nypl.org.

GAYAN, Anil Kumarsingh, LLM; Mauritian politician and lawyer; b. 22 Oct. 1948; m. Sooryakanti Nirsimloo; three c.; ed Royal Coll., Port Louis, London School of Econs, UK; called to the Bar, Inner Temple, London 1972; mem. Mauritius Bar and Seychelles Bar 1972–73, pvt. practice 1973–74, 1982, 1986–90, 1995–2000; Chair. Bar Council 1989–90; joined Chambers of Mauritius Attorney Gen. as Crown Counsel 1974, Sr Counsel 1995; Del. to

UN Conf. on the Law of the Sea 1974–82; mem. Parl. 1982–86, Minister of External Affairs, Tourism and Emigration 1983–86, Foreign Affairs and Regional Co-operation 2000–03; Chair. Council of Univ. of Mauritius 1983; Consultant for Geneva-based Centre for Human Rights, consultancy work in Bhutan, Mongolia, Armenia and Togo 1991; Hon. Minister. *Address:* c/o Ministry of Foreign Affairs and Regional Co-operation, New Government Centre, Level 5, Port Louis, Mauritius (office).

GAYDAMAK, Arcadi Alexandrovich; Russian/Israeli business executive; b. 1952, Moscow; moved from USSR to Israel aged 20, moved to France 1973, to Israel 2000; f. Gaydamak Translations, Paris; Owner, Moskovskie Novosti newspaper 2004–, Beitar Jerusalem FC football team 2005–, Tiv Taam supermarkets 2007–; Pres. Hapoel Jerusalem professional basketball team; organized and paid for emergency accommodation for civilians in northern Israel affected by conflict with Lebanon 2006; Founder and Leader Social Justice (Tzedek Hevrati—Za'am) political party 2007–; announced intention to run for Mayor of Jerusalem in 2008 elections; Pres. Congress of Jewish Religious Communities and Orgs of Russia; warrant issued for his arrest by French authorities in connection with alleged arms dealing with Angola 2000; Hon. Pres. World Betar.

GAYDAR, Yegor Timurovich, DSc (Econ); Russian politician; b. 19 March 1956, Moscow; s. of Timur Gaydar and Ariadna Gaydar (née Bajova); m. 2nd Maria Strugatskaya 1986; three s.; ed Moscow State Univ.; journalist, Kommunist and Pravda 1987–90; Dir Inst. of Econ. Policy, USSR (now Russian) Acad. of Sciences 1990–91; Deputy Chair. Russian Govt (and co-ordinator of the 13 ministries responsible for econ. affairs) 1991–92; Acting Chair. Russian Govt June–Dec. 1992; Dir Inst. for the Economy in Transition 1992–93, 1994–; Adviser to Pres. Yeltsin on Econ. Reform 1992–93; First Deputy Chair. Russian Govt 1993–94, Minister of the Economy 1993–94; Head of Political Bloc, Russian Choice (Vibor Rossii) 1993–94; Founder and Leader Democratic Choice of Russia Party 1994–; mem. State Duma (Parl.) 1993–95, 1999–; joined right-wing coalition Pravoye Delo 1999; mem. faction Union of Right-Wing Forces; Cttee mem. for Co-operation in the Baltic Region (attached to Prime Minister of Sweden); mem. Editorial Bd Vestnik Evropy; mem. Consultative Cttee Acta Oeconomica (Budapest); Hon. Prof., Univ. of California, Berkeley. *Publications:* State and Evolution 1996, Anomalies of Economic Growth 1997, Days of Defeats and Victories 1998, A Long Time. Russia in the World: Notes on Economic History 2005, The Death of Empire: Lessons for Contemporary Russia 2006; more than 100 articles in Russian and foreign scientific journals and newspapers. *Address:* Institute for the Economy in Transition, Gazetny per. 5, 111024 Moscow, Russia (office). *Telephone:* (495) 229-64-13 (office). *Fax:* (495) 229-64-48 (office).

GAYER, Yevdokiya Alexandrovna, CandHistSc; Russian/Nanai ethnographer and public servant; *Secretary-General, International League of Small Nations and Ethnic Groups;* b. 8 March 1934, Podali, Khabarovsk Territory; m. (deceased); two s.; ed in Vladivostok; researcher Inst. of History, Archaeology and Ethnography Far E br. of USSR Acad. of Sciences in Vladivostok 1969–89; USSR People's Deputy, mem. Soviet of Nationalities, mem. Comm. on Problems of Int. Relations and Nat. Policy 1989–92; adviser to Pres. 1992–; Deputy Chair. State Cttee on Social-Econ. Devt of the North 1993–; mem. Council of Fed. of Russia 1993–96; Deputy Chair. Comm. of the North and Indigenous Peoples 1996–2000; Sec.-Gen. Int. League of Small Nations and Ethnic Groups 1996–; Chief Adviser State Cttee on Problems of Devt of North Territories (later Cttee on Northern, Siberian and Far Eastern Affairs, Council of Fed.) 1997–98; Prof., Int. Acad. of Marketing and Man. (Mamarmen); mem. Presidium Russian Acad. of Natural Sciences; mem. Acad. of Information Science, Acad. of Polar Medicine. *Address:* Rublyovskoye Sh. 3, korp. 2, Apt 388, 121609 Moscow, Russia. *Telephone:* (095) 413-76-95.

GAYMARD, Clara; French business executive; *President, General Electric France;* b. 9 Jan. 1960, Paris; d. of Jérôme Lejeune; m. Hervé Gaymard; eight c.; ed Institut d'Études Politiques, Ecole Nationale d'Admin., Paris; served as auditor and counsellor, State Audit Office 1986–90; Commercial Counsel, Econ. and Commercial Section, embassy in Cairo 1991–93; Head, Europe Bureau 1993–95; Dir Office of Minister for Solidarity between Generations Colette Codaccioni 1995–96; Sub-Dir for Regional Action, PME 1996–99, Head PME 1999–2003; Chair. Invest in France Agency 2003–06; Pres. General Electric France 2006–;*Telephone:* 1-43-12-78-27 (office). *Fax:* 1-43-12-78-40 (office). *E-mail:* psala@capitalcom.fr. *Website:* www.ge.com/fr (office).

GAYMARD, Hervé, LenD; French politician; *Chairman, Savoie General Council;* b. 31 May 1960, Bourg-Saint-Maurice (Savoie); m.; eight c.; ed Ecole Nationale d'Admin and Institut d'Etudes Politiques, Paris; worked at Budget Ministry 1986–90; Financial Attaché, Cairo Embassy 1990–92; Deputy for Savoie to Nat. Ass. 1993– (RPR then UMP 2002–), mem. Finance Cttee, Vice-Chair. RPR Group; Minister of State for Finance May–Nov. 1995; Minister of State with responsibility for Health and Social Security 1995–97; Minister for Agric., Food, Fisheries and Rural Affairs 2002–04; Minister of the Economy, Finance and Industry 2004–05 (resgnd); Chair. Savoie Gen. Council 1999–2002, 2008–, Vice-Chair. 2002–08; mem. Cttee RPR 1995–98, Political Bureau 1995–2002 (then UMP 2002–05); regional counsellor Rhône Alpes 2004–07; Pres. Assemblée du Pays de Tarentaise Vanoise 2005–; mem. Bd Centre Georges Pompidou. *Publications:* Pour Malraux 1996. *Address:* Secrétariat Parlementaire, BP 78 - 5, Place Ferdinand Million, 73203 Albertville Cedex (office); Assemblee Nationale, 126 rue de l'Université, 75355 Paris Cedex 07, France (office). *Telephone:* 4-79-32-03-68 (office); 1-40-63-60-00 (office). *Fax:* 4-79-37-82-74 (office); 1-45-55-75-23 (office). *E-mail:* infos@assemblee-nat.fr (office). *Website:* www.gaymard-rolland-savoie.com; www.assemblee-nationale.fr (office).

GAYOOM, Maumoon Abdul, MA; Maldivian politician and fmr head of state; b. 29 Dec. 1937, Malé; m. Nasreena Ibrahim 1969; two s. two d.; ed Al-Azhar Univ., Cairo, Egypt; Research Asst in Islamic History, American Univ. of Cairo 1967–69; Lecturer in Islamic Studies and Philosophy, Abdullahi Bayero Coll., Ahmadu Bello Univ., Nigeria 1969–71; teacher, Aminiya School 1971–72; Man. Govt Shipping Dept 1972–73; writer and trans., Press Office 1972–73, 1974; Under-Sec. Telecommunications Dept 1974; Dir Telephone Dept 1974; Special Under-Sec. Office of the Prime Minister 1974–75; Deputy Amb. to Sri Lanka 1975–76; Under-Sec. Dept of External Affairs 1976; Perm. Rep. to UN 1976–77; Deputy Minister of Transport 1976, Minister 1977–78; Pres. of Repub. of Maldives and C-in-C of the Armed Forces and of the Police 1978–2008; Gov. Maldives Monetary Authority 1981–2004; Minister of Defence and Nat. Security 1982–2004, of Finance 1989–93, of Finance and Treasury 1993–2004; Leader Maldivian People's Party (DRP); mem. Constituent Council of Rabitat Al-Alam Al-Islami; Grand Order of Mugunghawa 1984, Hon. GCMG 1997; Hon. DLitt (Aligarh Muslim Univ. of India) 1983, Hon. DrLit (Jamia Millia Islamia Univ., India) 1990, Hon. DLit (Pondicherry Univ.) 1994; Global 500 Honour Roll (UNEP) 1988, Man of the Sea Award (Lega Navale Italiana) 1991, WHO Health-for-All Gold Medal 1998, DRV Int. Environment Award 1998, Al-Azhar Univ. Shield 2002. *Publication:* The Maldives: A Nation in Peril. *Leisure interests:* astronomy, calligraphy, photography, badminton, cricket. *Address:* Maldivian People's Party, Sinamalé 3 Galolhu, Malé, The Maldives (office). *Telephone:* 3320456 (office). *Fax:* 3344774 (office). *E-mail:* www.drp.org.mv (office).

GAYSSOT, Jean-Claude; French politician and trade union official; b. 6 Sept. 1944, Béziers (Hérault); m. Jacqueline Guiter 1963; three c.; ed Lycée Technique, Béziers; worked as technician, SNCF (French state railways); official in Railworkers' Union, then in Conféd. générale du travail (CGT) 1976–79; mem. Parti Communiste Français 1963–, mem. Nat. Secr. 1985–, head dept for relations with other political parties and trade union and community movt 1994–; elected municipal councillor, Bobigny (Seine-Saint-Denis) 1977; Nat. Ass. Deputy for 5th Seine-Saint-Denis Constituency 1986–97; Minister for Public Works, Transport and Housing 1997–2002; Mayor of Drancy 1997–2002; Trombinoscope Prize for Minister of the Year 2000. *Publications:* Le Parti communiste français 1989, Sur ma route 2000. *Address:* Parti Communiste Français, 2 place du Colonel Fabien, 75940 Paris, France.

GAZIT, Maj.-Gen. Shlomo; Israeli army officer and administrator; *Chairman, Galili Centre for Defence-Hagana Studies;* b. 1926, Turkey; s. of Efrayim and Zippora Gazit; m. Avigayil-Gala Gazit; one s. two d.; ed Tel-Aviv Univ.; joined Palmach 1944, Co. Commdr Harel Brigade 1948; Dir Office of Chief of Staff 1953; Liaison Officer with French Army Del., Sinai Campaign 1956; Instructor Israel Defence Forces (IDF) Staff and Command Coll. 1958–59; Gen. Staff 1960–61; Deputy Commdr Golani Brigade 1961–62; Instructor Nat. Defence Coll. 1962–64; Head IDF Intelligence assessment div. 1964–67; Co-ordinator of Govt Activities in Administered Territories, Ministry of Defence 1967–74; rank of Maj.-Gen. 1973; Head of Mil. Intelligence 1974–79; Fellow at Center for Int. Affairs, Harvard Univ. 1979–80; Pres. Ben Gurion Univ. of the Negev 1981–85; Dir-Gen. Jewish Agency, Jerusalem 1985–88; Sr Research Fellow Jaffee Centre for Strategic Studies, Tel-Aviv Univ. 1988–94; Fellow Woodrow Wilson Center, Washington, DC 1989–90; Distinguished Fellow US Inst. of Peace, Washington, DC 1994–95; Adviser to Israeli Prime Minister on Palestinian Peace Process 1995–96; Chair. Galili Centre for Defence-Hagana Studies 1996–. *Publications:* Estimates and Fortune-Telling in Intelligence Work 1980, Early Attempts at Establishing West Bank Autonomy 1980, Insurgency, Terrorism and Intelligence 1980, On Hostages' Rescue Operations 1981, The Carrot and the Stick – Israel's Military Govt in Judea and Samaria 1985, The Third Way – The Way of No Solution 1987, Policies in the Administered Territories 1988, Intelligence Estimates and the Decision Maker 1988, (ed.) The Middle East Military Balance 1988–89, 1990–91, 1993–94, Trapped Fools: 30 Years of Israeli Policy in Judea, Samaria and Gaza Strip, 2003, The Arab-Israeli Wars: War and Peace in the Middle East 1948–2005 2005. *Address:* 58 Enzo Sireni Street, Kfar-Saba 44285, Israel (home). *Telephone:* (3) 6407719 (office); (9) 7466554 (home). *Fax:* (3) 6422404 (office); (9) 7477322 (home). *E-mail:* jcsssg@post.tau.ac.il (office).

GAZIZULLIN, Farit Rafikovich, CPhilSc, DSc; Russian/Tatar politician; b. 20 Sept. 1946, Zelenodolsk, Tatar ASSR; m.; one s.; ed Gorky (now Nizhny Novgorod) Inst. of Water Transport Eng; engineer Zelenodolsk 1965–67; Comsomol and CP work 1967–87; Head of Dept, First Deputy Chair., State Planning Cttee Tatar Autonomous Repub. 1987–95; Vice-Prime Minister of Tatarstan, Chair. State Cttee on Property 1995–96; First Deputy Chair., Cttee on State Property of Russian Fed. 1996–97; Deputy Chair., Govt of Russian Fed. 1997–98; Minister of State Property (temporarily Ministry of Property Relations) 1997–2004; Prof. 2004–; Chair. Bd of Dirs Gazprom 1998–99, Adviser 1999–. *Address:* c/o Ministry of State Property, Nikolsky per. 9, 102132 Moscow, Russia.

GAZZARA, Ben; American actor; b. (Biagio Anthony Gazzara), 28 Aug. 1930, Manhattan, NY; s. of the late Antonio Gazzara and Angela Gazzara; m. 1st Louise Erickson 1951 (divorced 1957); m. 2nd Janice Rule 1961 (divorced 1979); two c.; m. 3rd Elke Krivat 1982; studied engineering; received acting scholarship under coach Erwin Piscator, New School for Social Research, NY; joined Actor's Studio 1953; theatre debut in End as a Man, Broadway 1953; film debut in The Strange One 1957; TV debut in Philco Playhouse and Playhouse 90; numerous appearances on TV shows and series; received Emmy Award for TV film An Early Frost 1985; directed first film Beyond the Ocean 1990; Lifetime Achievement Award, San Sebastian Film Festival, Spain 2005. *Stage appearances include:* End as a Man (Theatre World Award) 1953, Cat on a Hot Tin Roof 1955, A Hatful of Rain 1955, The Night Circus 1958, Strange

Interlude 1963, Traveller without Luggage 1964, Hughie/Duet 1975, Who's Afraid of Virginia Woolf? 1976, Shimada 1992, Nobody Don't Like Yogi 2004, Awake and Sing! 2006. *Films include:* The Strange One 1957, Anatomy of a Murder 1959, Risate di gioia 1960, The Young Doctors 1961, Conquered City 1962, Convicts 4 1962, A Rage to Live 1965, The Bridge at Remagen 1969, Husbands 1970, The Sicilian Connection 1972, The Neptune Factor 1973, Capone 1975, The Killing of a Chinese Bookie 1976, High Velocity 1976, Voyage of the Damned 1976, Opening Night 1977, Bloodline 1979, Saint Jack 1979, Inchon 1981, They All Laughed 1981, Tales of Ordinary Madness 1981, La Ragazza di Trieste 1983, Uno Scandolo perbene 1984, La Donna delle Meraviglie 1985, Secret Obsession 1986, Figlio mio infitamente caro 1987, Il Giorno Primo 1987, Don Bosco 1988, Quicker than the Eye 1989, Road House 1989, Per sempre 1991, Never Love a Thief 1994, Nerferiti figlia del sole 1994, Banditi 1995, Ladykiller 1996, Una Donna in Fuga 1996, The Zone 1996, Vicious Circles 1997, Farmer & Chase 1997, Shadow Conspiracy 1997, Stag 1997, The Spanish Prisoner 1997, Shark in a Bottle 1998. Poor Liza 1998, Too Tired to Die 1998, Buffalo '66 1998, The Big Lebowski 1998, Happiness 1998, Paradise Cove 1999, Summer of Sam 1999, The Thomas Crown Affair 1999, Blue Moon 2000, Believe 2000, Very Mean Men 2000, Undertaker's Paradise 2000, The List 2000, Nella Terra di Nessuno 2001, Schubert 2002, L'Ospito Segreto 2003, Dogville 2003, Quiet Flows the Don 2004, The Shore 2005, Victor in December 2005, Paris, je t'aime 2006. *Television includes:* Arrest and Trial 1963, Run for Your Life (also dir) 1965, The Name of the Game (dir) 1968, Hysterical Blindness (Emmy Award for Best Supporting Actor) 2002, Donne sbagliate 2007. *Publication:* In the Moment: My Life as an Actor (autobiog.) 2004. *Address:* 1080 Madison Avenue, New York, NY 10028, USA.

GBAGBO, Laurent, MA, PhD; Côte d'Ivoirian head of state; *President;* b. 31 May 1945, Central-Western Prov.; m.; four c.; ed Univ. of Abidjan, Univ. of Lyon, Sorbonne, Paris VII Univ.; taught history and geography at Lycée Classique d'Abidjan 1970–71; imprisoned for unauthorized political activities 1971–73; worked in Dept of Educ. 1973–79; exile in France 1982–88; f. Front populaire Ivoirien (FPI) in secret 1982, FPI Sec.-Gen. 1988–1996; mem. Parl. for Ouragahio 1990–2000; arrested Feb. 1992, sentenced to three years' imprisonment under anti-riot law, granted presidential pardon Aug. 1992; Pres. of Côte d'Ivoire Oct. 2000–. *Address:* Office of the President, 01 BP 1354 Abidjan 01, Côte d'Ivoire (office). *Telephone:* 20-22-02-22 (office). *Fax:* 20-21-14-25 (office). *Website:* www.presidence.ci (office).

GBEZERA-BRIA, Michel, BL; Central African Republic politician and diplomatist; b. 1946, Bossongoa; m.; five c.; ed Brazzaville School of Law, Caen School of Econs and Int. Inst. of Public Admin.; with civil service 1973–, Vice-Minister Sec.-in-charge of diplomatic missions 1975; Deputy Minister of Foreign Affairs 1976; Minister of Public Works, Labour and Social Security 1976–77, of Foreign Affairs 1977–78, of Public Works and Social Security 1978–79; State Comptroller 1979–80, Perm. Rep. to UN, Geneva 1980–83, New York 1983–89; Minister of Justice 1987–88, of Foreign Affairs 1988–90; Prime Minister of Cen. African Repub. 1997–99; Dir Econ. Man. Project 1991–. *Address:* c/o Office of the Prime Minister, Bangui, Central African Republic.

GDLYAN, Telman Khorenovich; Russian/Armenian prosecutor and politician; b. 20 Dec. 1940, Samsar, Georgia; m. Susanna Aramovna Gdlyan; one s. one d.; ed Saratov Inst. of Law; mem. CPSU 1962–90, when expelled; investigator Ulyanovsk Dist 1968–83, investigator for important cases of corruption in Uzbekistan, Office of Public Prosecutor of USSR 1983–90; successfully prosecuted mems of political establishment of Uzbekistan for corruption; USSR People's Deputy 1989–91; mem. Armenian Supreme Soviet 1990–; founder and Chair. People's Party of the Russian Federation (Narodnaya partiya Rossiiskoi Federatsii) (NPRF) 1990; expelled from Prosecutor's Office 1990, reinstated 1991; founder and Pres. All-Russian Fund of Progress, Defence of Human Rights and Charity; mem. State Duma (Parl.) 1995–99. *Publications:* Piramide, Mafia in Times of Lawlessness, Kremlin Case. *Address:* c/o People's Party of the Russian Federation, ul. Nizhnyaya Krasnoselskaya 39/2, 107066 Moscow, Russia.

GE, Wujue; Chinese writer; b. 12 Sept. 1937, Wenzhou, Zhejiang; s. of Ge Luyan and Zhang Wencang; m. Zhao Baoqing 1962 (divorced); one s.; ed Beijing Univ.; worked as journalist for over 20 years; published first book 1961; in political disgrace 1963–77; some works translated into English, French and Japanese; Vice-Chair. Fed. of Art and Literature, Ningxia and Ningxia Branch of Union of Chinese Writers. *Publications:* The Wedding, A Journalist and Her Story, An Experience in the Summer, She and her Girl Friend, The Golden Deer, A View of an Ancient Ferry (short stories), Meditate on the Past (novel), Years and Man (novel), Going to the Ancient Ferry on Today (TV Drama), Four Days in All of Life 1988 (short stories), The Earth. The Moon (novel), The Passport on the Earth, Zhang Daqian in Dunhuan (TV drama) 1991, Quality of Life (reportage) 1995, Tango Rumba (screenplay) 1996. *Leisure interests:* sports, music, drawing, calligraphy. *Address:* 268-9 Bailidong Road, Wenzhou, Zhejiang, People's Republic of China. *Telephone:* (577) 8282374 (office); (577) 8525866 (home).

GE, You; Chinese actor; b. 19 April 1957; joined All-China Fed. of Trade Unions Art Troupe 1979. *Films include:* Farewell My Concubine 1993, To Live 1994 (Cannes Film Festival for Best Actor 1994), The Emperor's Shadow 1996, A World without Thieves 2004, Suffocation 2005, Shanghai Red 2006, The Banquet 2006, Crossed Lines 2007. *Address:* All-China Federation of Trade Unions Art Troupe, Beijing, People's Republic of China.

GEACH, Peter (Thomas), (Piotr Tomasz Geach), MA, FBA; British professor of logic; *Professor Emeritus, University of Leeds;* b. 29 March 1916, London; s. of George Hender Geach and Eleonora Frederyka Adolfina Sgonina; m. Gertrude Elizabeth Margaret Anscombe 1941 (died 2001); three s. four d.; ed Balliol Coll. Oxford; Gladstone Research Student, St Deiniol's Library 1938–39; post grad. studies Cambridge Univ. with Profs Wittgenstein and Von Wright; Asst Lecturer, Lecturer, Sr Lecturer, then Reader in Logic, Univ. of Birmingham 1951–65; Prof. of Logic, Univ. of Leeds 1965–81, Prof. Emer. 1981–; Foreign mem. American Acad. of Arts and Sciences 1987; Alexander von Humboldt Prize 1984, Papal Medal, Aquina Medal 1997, Pro Ecclesia et Pontifice 1999. *Publications:* Mental Acts 1957, Reference and Generality 1962 (Polish trans. 2006), God and the Soul 1969, Reason and Argument 1976, Providence and Evil 1977, The Virtues 1977, Truth, Love and Immortality 1979, Logic Matters 1980, Truth and Hope 2001. *Leisure interests:* reading thrillers, reading and marginally annotating bad old logic books. *Address:* 3 Richmond Road, Cambridge, CB4 3PP, England (home). *Telephone:* (1223) 353950 (home). *Fax:* (1223) 353950 (home). *E-mail:* professorptgeach@aob .com.

GEBRSELASSIE, Haile; Ethiopian professional athlete; b. 18 April 1973, Arssi; m. 1996; two c.; set 14 world records or best times indoors and outdoors 1994–98, including world 5,000m and 10,000m records 1997, 1998; silver medal World Jr Cross Country Championships 1992; gold medals World Jr Championships 5,000m and 10,000m 1992; silver medal World Championships 5,000m 1993; gold medal World Championships 10,000m 1995, 1997; gold medal World Indoor Championships 3,000m 1995, 1999, 2003; gold medal Olympic Games 10,000m 1996, 2000, silver medal 2004; winner IAAF World Half-Marathon Championship, England 2001; bronze medal World Championships 10,000m 2001; silver medal World Championships 10,000m 2003; 5,000m (indoor and outdoor), 10,000m, 10 km road race world record holder, 1 hour running event world record holder 2007; indoor record holder for two miles; IAAF Athlete of the Year 1998. *Leisure interests:* boxing, soccer. *Address:* Waterdelweg 14, 5427 LS Boehel 98007, Monaco.

GEDDA, Nicolai; Swedish singer (tenor); b. 11 July 1925, Stockholm; s. of Michael Ustinov and Olga Ustinov (née Gedda); m. Anastasia Caraviotis 1965; one s. one d.; ed Musical Acad., Stockholm; debut, Stockholm 1952; concert appearances Rome 1952, Paris 1953, 1955, Vienna 1955, Aix-en-Provence 1954, 1955; first operatic performances in Munich, Lucerne, Milan and Rome 1953, Paris, London and Vienna 1954; Salzburg Festival 1957–59, Edin. Festival 1958–59; with Metropolitan Opera, NY 1957–2001, Tokyo Opera 1975–2003; worldwide appearances in opera, concerts and recitals; numerous recordings. *Address:* Valhallavagen 110, 114 41 Stockholm, Sweden.

GEDDES, John M., MA; American newspaper editor; *Managing Editor, The New York Times;* b. 1952; ed Univs. of RI and Wis.; reporter Ansonia Evening Sentinel, Ansonia, Conn. 1976; reporter Associated Press-Dow Jones News Service, NY 1976–78, Bonn, Germany 1978–79; econs corresp. The Times, Bonn 1979–80; joined Wall Street Journal 1980, various positions including Bureau Chief, Bonn, Deputy Man. Ed. then Man. Ed. European Edn, News Ed., Asst Man. Ed., Sr Ed. and Nat. News Ed. –1993; fmr Prin. Friday Holdings; CEO BIS Strategic Decisions (market research co.) 1993–94; Business and Financial Ed. New York Times 1994–97, Deputy Man. Ed. 1997–2003, Man. Ed. for News Operations 2003–. *Address:* The New York Times, 229 West 43rd Street, New York, NY 10036, USA (office). *Website:* www.nytco.com (office).

GEE, Gordon; American lawyer and university administrator; *President, Ohio State University;* b. 2 Feb. 1944; m. 1st Elizabeth D. Gee; one d.; m. 2nd Constance Gee (divorced); ed Columbia Univ.; completed a fed. judicial clerkship; served as Asst Dean for Univ. of Utah Coll. of Law; fmr Judicial Fellow and Sr Staff Asst for US Supreme Court Chief Justice Warren Burger; fmr Assoc. Dean and Prof., J. Reuben Clark Law School, Brigham Young Univ.; Dean Law School, West Virginia Univ. 1979, Pres. West Virginia Univ. 1981–85; Pres. Univ. Colorado at Boulder 1985–90; Pres. Ohio State Univ. 1990–97, 2007–; Pres. Brown Univ. 1997–2000; Chancellor Vanderbilt Univ. 2000–07; mem. Bd of Dirs Freedom Forum Diversity Inst., Inc., Montgomery Bell Acad., Tennessee Coll. Asscn; mem. Advisory Cttee Nashville Alliance for Public Educ., Pres.'s Council for Imagining America: Artists and Scholars in Public Life, Bd Christopher Isherwood Foundation, Business-Higher Educ. Forum, Nat. Cttee to Unite a Divided America; has carried out research on behalf of Ford Foundation, Guy Anderson Foundation, American Bar Foundation, and others; mem. Circle of Hope; currently Dir or Trustee The Jason Foundation, Nat. Hospice Foundation, Historic Black Coll. and Univ. Advisory Cttee Kresge Foundation, Hasbro, The Limited, Dollar General Corpn, Massey Energy Corpn, Gaylord Entertainment Co.; Trustee Harry S. Truman Scholarship Foundation 1995–; Mellon Fellow, Aspen Inst. for Humanistic Studies, W. K. Kellogg Fellow, Distinguished Alumnus Award, Univ. of Utah 1994, Distinguished Alumnus Award, Teachers' Coll., Columbia Univ. 1994, Outstanding Promotion of Diversity Award, Nashville Br., Nat. Asscn for the Advancement of Colored People, Nashville Women's Political Caucus' Good Guy Award 2004, Apollo Award for Communications Leadership, Public Relations Soc. of America (Nashville chapter) 2004. *Publications:* co-author of six books; numerous papers and articles in fields relating to both law and education. *Address:* Office of the President, Ohio State University, 205 Bricker Hall, 190 North Oval Mall, Columbus, OH 43210-1357, USA (office). *Telephone:* (614) 292-2424 (office). *Fax:* (614) 292-1231 (office). *Website:* http://president.osu.edu (office).

GEE, Maurice Gough, MA; New Zealand novelist; b. 22 Aug. 1931, Whakatane; m. Margaretha Garden 1970; one s. two d.; ed Avondale Coll., Auckland, Auckland Univ.; school teacher, librarian, other casual employment 1954–75; Robert Burns Fellow, Univ. of Otago 1964; Writing Fellow, Vic. Univ. of Wellington 1989; Katherine Mansfield Memorial Fellow, Menton, France 1992; Hon. DLitt (Victoria) 1987, (Auckland) 2004; NZ Fiction Award 1976, 1979, 1982, 1991, 1993, NZ Book of the Year Award (Wattle Award) 1979, 1993, James Tait Black Memorial Prize 1979, NZ Children's Book of the

Year Award 1986, 1995, Prime Minister's Prize 2004. *Publications include:* Plumb 1978, Meg 1981, Sole Survivor 1983, Collected Stories 1986, Prowlers 1987, The Burning Boy 1990, Going West 1992, Crime Story 1994, Loving Ways 1996, Live Bodies 1998, Ellie and the Shadow Man 2001, The Scornful Moon 2004, Blindsight (Deutz Medal for Fiction 2006, Montana New Zealand Book Award for Fiction 2006) 2005; juvenile fiction includes: Under the Mountain 1979, The O Trilogy 1982–85, The Fat Man 1994; also scripts for film and TV. *Address:* 41 Chelmsford Street, Ngaio, Wellington, New Zealand.

GEFFEN, David Lawrence; American film, recording and theatre executive; b. 21 Feb. 1943, Brooklyn, New York; s. of Abraham Geffen and Batya (Volovskaya) Geffen; ed New Utrecht High School, Brooklyn, Univ. of Texas, Brooklyn Coll.; joined William Morris talent agency as mail clerk 1964, promoted to jr agent; launched new film studio with Steven Spielberg (q.v.) and Jeffrey Katzenberg (q.v.); f. music publishing co. Tunafish Music, with Laura Nyro; joined Ashley Famous Agency, then apptd Exec. Vice-Pres. Creative Man. (now Int. Creative Man.) 1968; f. Asylum Records and Geffen-Roberts Man. Co. with Elliot Roberts 1970; sold Asylum to Warner Communications, but remained Pres. 1971, merged it with Elektra, signed up Bob Dylan and Joni Mitchell, Vice-Chair. Warner Brothers Pictures 1975–76; taught business studies at Yale Univ.; f. Geffen Records, Pres. 1980, signed up Elton John, John Lennon and Yoko Ono and many others, sold label to Music Corpn of America Inc. 1990; f. Geffen Film Co., produced Little Shop of Horrors, Beetlejuice 1988, Men Don't Leave, Defending Your Life; Co-Producer musical Dreamgirls 1981–85, Little Shop of Horrors, Cats 1982, M. Butterfly 1986, Social Security, Chess 1990, Miss Saigon; f. DGC record label 1995; co-founder and Prin. Dreamworks SKG 1995–2005. *Address:* c/o Dreamworks SKG, 1000 Flower Street, Glendale, CA 91201, USA (office).

GEGHMAN, Yahya Hamoud; Yemeni diplomatist; b. 24 Sept. 1934, Jahanah; s. of Hamoud Geghman and Ezziya Geghman; m. Cathya Geghman 1971; one s. one d.; ed Law Schools, Cairo, Paris, Damascus and Boston and Columbia Univs; Teacher of Arabic Language and Literature, Kuwait 1957–59; Dir-Gen. Yemen Broadcasting System 1962–63; Gov. Yemen Bank for Reconstruction and Devt 1962–63; Sec.-Gen. Supreme Council for Tribal Affairs 1962–63; Special Adviser, Ministry of Foreign Affairs 1962–63; Deputy Perm. Rep. to UN 1963–66, 1967–68; Minister Plenipotentiary, Yemen Arab Repub. Embassy to USA 1963–67; Minister of Foreign Affairs 1968–69; Minister of State, Personal Rep. of the Pres. 1969; Deputy Prime Minister, Pres. Supreme Council for Youth Welfare and Sport 1969–71; Perm. Rep. to UN 1971–73; Amb. to USA 1972–74; Minister for Foreign Affairs 1974–75; Deputy Prime Minister for Econ. and Foreign Affairs 1975–76; Personal Rep. of Pres. of the Repub. 1977–85; Chief, Bureau of South Yemen Affairs and Chair. Yemen Reunification Comms 1980–83; Amb. to Switzerland and Perm. Rep. to UN in Vienna and UNIDO 1985–90; Perm. Rep. to UN European HQ and Int. Orgs, Geneva, 1985–; Gov. and Exec. Dir UN Common Fund for Commodities, Amsterdam 1989–; mem. Governing Council, UN Compensation Comm. 1991; Pres. Diplomatic Cttee on Host Country Relations 1991. *Publications:* articles on politics, economics and literature, poems. *Leisure interests:* reading, horseback riding, swimming, writing, chess, music. *Address:* Permanent Mission of the Republic of Yemen, 19 chemin du Jonc, 1216 Cointrin, Geneva, Switzerland. *Telephone:* 798-53-33.

GEHRIG, Bruno, Dr rer. pol; Swiss economist, academic and insurance industry executive; *Chairman, Swiss Life Holding;* b. 26 Dec. 1946; ed Univ. of Berne, Univ. of Rochester, NY, USA; Asst, then Lecturer on Econs, Univ. of Berne 1970–78, Asst Prof. 1978–80; Head of Econs Section, Union Bank of Switzerland (UBS) 1981–84, with Stock Markets and Securities Sales Div., UBS Group 1986–88, Head of Div. 1988–89; Chair. Exec. Bd, Bank Cantrade, Zürich 1989–91; Prof. of Business Admin and Head of Swiss Inst., Univ. of St Gallen 1992–96; apptd mem. Governing Bd, Swiss Nat. Bank 1996, Head of Dept III 1996–2001, Vice-Chair. Governing Bd 2001–03; Chair. Swiss Life Holding 2003–; Dir Roche Holding AG, Basel (Vice-Chair. 2004–, Ind. Lead Dir –2008); Chair. Econ. Policy Study Group, Swiss Christian Democratic Party (CVP) 1984–91; Chair. Bd of Trustees Swiss Air Transport Foundation; mem. Swiss Fed. Banking Comm. 1992–96; Hon. LLD (Univ. of Rochester, NY) 2006. *Address:* Swiss Life Holding, General Guisan-Quai 40, 8022 Zürich, Switzerland (office). *Telephone:* (4) 32843253 (office). *Fax:* (4) 33383253 (office). *E-mail:* bruno.gehrig@swisslife.ch (office). *Website:* www.swisslife .com (office).

GEHRING, Gillian Anne, OBE, MA, DPhil, FInstP; British physicist and academic; *Professor Emeritus of Physics, University of Sheffield;* b. (Gillian Anne Murray), 19 May 1941, Nottingham; d. of H. L. (Max) Murray and F. Joan Murray; m. Karl A. Gehring 1968; two d.; ed Univs of Manchester and Oxford; Leverhulme Postdoctoral Research Fellowship, St Hugh's Coll., Oxford 1965–67; NATO Fellowship, Univ. of Calif., Berkeley 1967–68; Fellow and Tutor in Physics, St Hugh's Coll., Oxford 1968–70; CUF Lecturer in Theoretical Physics, Univ. of Oxford 1970–89; Prof. of Physics, Univ. of Sheffield 1989–2007, Prof. Emer. 2007–; Leverhulme Emer. Fellow; Hon. DSc (Salford) 1994. *Publications:* research papers on theoretical condensed matter physics. *Leisure interest:* family activities. *Address:* Department of Physics and Astronomy, University of Sheffield, Hicks Building, Hounsfield Road, Sheffield, SR3 7RH (office); 27 Lawson Road, Broomhill, Sheffield, S10 5BU, England (home). *Telephone:* (114) 222-4299 (office); (114) 268-2238 (home). *E-mail:* g.gehring@sheffield.ac.uk (office). *Website:* www.shef.ac.uk/physics/ people/ggehring/index.html (office).

GEHRING, Walter Jakob, PhD; Swiss geneticist and biologist; *Professor of Genetics and Developmental Biology, University of Basel;* b. 20 March 1939, Zurich; s. of late Jakob Gehring and of Marcelle Gehring-Rebmann; m. Elisabeth Lott 1964; two s.; ed Realgymnasium, Zürich, Univ. of Zürich and Yale Univ., USA; Assoc. Prof., Depts. of Anatomy and Molecular Biophysics,

Yale Univ. 1969–72; Prof. of Genetics and Developmental Biology, Dept of Cell Biology, Univ. of Basel 1972–; Foreign mem. Royal Soc. 1997; Otto Naegeli Prize, Prix Charles-Leopold, Warren Triennial Prize, Prix Louis Jeantet de médecine, Gairdner Int. Award, Kyoto Prize 2000. *Publications:* Zoologie (with R. Wehner) 1990, Master Control Genes in Development and Evolution: The Homeobox Story; over 160 publs. *Leisure interests:* bird watching, photography. *Address:* Biozentrum, University of Basel, Department of Cell Biology, Klingelbergstrasse 70, 4056 Basel (office); Hochfeldstrasse 32, 4106 Therwil, Switzerland (home). *Telephone:* (61) 2672051 (office); (61) 7213593 (home). *Fax:* (61) 2672078.

GEHRY, Frank Owen, CC, BArch, FAIA; Canadian/American architect; b. (Ephraim Owen Goldberg), 28 Feb. 1929, Toronto, Canada; s. of Irving Gehry and Thelma Caplan; m. 1st Anita Snyder (divorced); two d.; m. 2nd Berta Aguilera 1975; two s.; ed Univ. of Southern California and Harvard Univ. Grad. School of Design; designer, Victor Gruen Assocs, LA 1953–54, Planning, Design and Project Dir 1958–61; Project Designer and Planner, Pereira & Luckman, LA 1957–58; Design Prin. Frank O. Gehry & Assocs, Santa Monica, Calif. 1962–; f. Gehry Partnership LLP 2002; f. Gehry Technologies Inc. (building industry tech. co.); architect for Temporary Contemporary Museum 1983, Calif. Aerospace Museum 1984, Loyola Law School 1981–84, Frances Howard Goldwyn Regional Br. Library 1986, Information and Computer Science Eng Research Facility, Univ. of Calif. Irvine 1986, Vitra Furniture Mfg Facility and Design Museum, Germany 1989, Chiat/Day HQ, Venice, Calif. 1991, American Center, Paris 1992–94, Weisman Art Museum, Minneapolis 1993, Disney Ice, Anaheim 1995, EMR Communication & Tech. Centre, Bad Oeynhausen, Germany 1995, Team Disneyland Admin., Anaheim 1996, ING Office Bldg, Prague 1996, Guggenheim Museum, Bilbao 1997, Experience Music Project, Seattle 2000, Walt Disney Concert Hall, LA 2003, Maggie's Cancer Care Centre, Dundee 2003, bandshell, Millennium Park, Chicago 2004, IAC HQ 2006; Fellow, American Inst. of Architects, American Acad. of Arts and Letters, American Acad. of Arts and Sciences; Charlotte Davenport Chair. Yale Univ. 1982, 1989; Eliot Noyes Design Chair. Harvard 1984; currently Distinguished Prof., Grad. School of Architecture, Planning and Preservation, Columbia Univ.; Dr hc (Calif. Coll. of Arts and Crafts) 1987, (Rhode Island School of Design) 1987, (Tech. Univ. of Nova Scotia) 1989, (Calif. Inst. of Arts), (Otis Art Inst., Parsons School of Design) 1989, (Occidental Coll.) 1993, (Whittier Coll.) 1995, (Southern Calif. Inst. of Architecture) 1997, (Univ. of Toronto) 1998, (Univ. of Edinburgh) 2000, (Univ. of Southern Calif.) 2000, (Yale Univ.) 2000, (Harvard Univ.) 2000, (School of The Art Inst. of Chicago) 2004; Arnold W. Brunner Memorial Architecture Prize 1983, Pritzker Architecture Prize 1989, shared Wolf Prize 1992, Imperial Prize (Japan) 1992, Lillian Gish Award 1994, National Medal of Arts 1998, Kiesler Prize for Architecture and the Arts 1998, Gold Medal of Inst. of Architects 1999, Gold Medal for Architecture, American Acad. of Arts and Letters 2002, Royal Fine Art Comm. Trust Building of the Year Award 2004, Woodrow Wilson Award for Public Service 2004. *Film appearance:* The Cool School 2007. *Publications:* Individual Imagination and Cultural Conservatism 1995, Gehry Draws 2005. *Address:* Gehry Partners LLP, 12541 Beatrice Street, Los Angeles, CA 90066 (office); Frank O. Gehry & Associates, 1520-B Cloverfield Boulevard, Santa Monica, CA 90404 (office). *Telephone:* (310) 482-3000 (office). *Fax:* (310) 482-3006 (office). *Website:* www .gehrypartners.com (office).

GEIDUSCHEK, E(rnest) Peter, PhD; American biologist and academic; *Research Professor, Division of Biological Sciences, University of California, San Diego;* b. 11 April 1928, Vienna, Austria; s. of Sigmund Geiduschek and Frieda Tauber; m. Joyce B. Brous 1955; two s.; ed Columbia and Harvard Univs; Instructor in Chem., Yale Univ. 1952–53, 1955–57; Asst Prof. of Chem., Univ. of Mich. 1957–59; Asst Prof. of Biophysics and Research Assoc. in Biochemistry, Univ. of Chicago 1959–62, Assoc. Prof. of Biophysics and Research Assoc. in Biochemistry 1962–64, Prof. of Biophysics and Research Assoc. in Biochemistry 1964–70; Prof. of Biology, Univ. of Calif., San Diego 1970–94, Chair. 1981–83, Acting Chair. 1994, Research Prof., Dept of Biological Sciences 1994–; mem. Bd of Scientific Counselors, Nat. Cancer Inst., NIH 1998–2003; European Molecular Biology Org. (EMBO) Lecturer 1977, Hilleman Lecturer, Univ. of Chicago 1978, Paul Doty Lecturer, Harvard Univ. 1993, Adriano Buzzati-Traverso Lecture, Rome 1996; Jean Weigle Lecture, Geneva 2001; Lalor Foundation Faculty Fellow, Yale 1957, Guggenheim Fellow, Inst. de Biologie Moléculaire, Geneva 1964–65; mem. NAS, American Acad. of Arts and Sciences; Fellow, AAAS, Acad. of Microbiology (USA); Grande Ufficiale, Ordine al Merito della Repubblica Italiana 1997; Gregor Mendel Medal, Acad. of Sciences of the Czech Repub. 2004. *Publications:* numerous articles on molecular biology, biochemistry and virology. *Address:* University of California, San Diego, Division of Biological Sciences, Center for Molecular Genetics (0634), 9500 Gilman Drive, La Jolla, CA 92093-0634, USA (office). *Telephone:* (858) 534-3029 (office). *Fax:* (858) 534-7073 (office). *E-mail:* epg@biomail.ucsd.edu (office). *Website:* www.cmg .ucsd.edu (office).

GEIGER, Helmut; German banker and lawyer; b. 12 June 1928, Nuremberg; m.; one s. one d.; ed Univs of Erlangen and Berlin; legal asst, Deutsche Bundestag and asst lawyer, Bonn 1957–59; lawyer in Bonn and man. of office of Öffentliche Bausparkassen 1959–66; Man. Dir Deutsche Sparkassen-und Giroverband 1966–72, Pres. 1972–93; Pres. Int. Inst. der Sparkassen (Int. Savings Bank Inst.), Geneva 1978–84; Pres. EEC Savings Banks Group, Brussels 1985–88; Chair. Sparkassenstiftung für Int. Kooperation 1992–98; mem. Bundestag 1965; mem. Admin. Bd Deutsche Girozentrale Int., Luxembourg, Kreditanstalt für Wiederaufbau, Frankfurt, Landwirtschaftliche Rentenbank, Frankfurt, Rhineland-Westphalian Inst. of Econ. Research, Essen; mem. Cen. Cttee, German Group, ICC; mem. Presidium, German Red Cross; Chair. and mem. of various charitable and professional bodies; Grand Fed. Cross of Merit; Dr hc (Cologne). *Publications:* Herausforderungen für Stabilität und Fortschritt 1974, Bankpolitik 1975, Gespräche über Geld 1986, Die deutsche Sparkassenorganisation 1992 and numerous publs on banking matters. *Address:* Simrockstr. 4, 53113 Bonn, Germany. *Telephone:* (228) 9703610.

GEIMAN, Leonid Mikhailovich, DrTechSci; Russian scientific publisher; b. 12 Aug. 1934, Moscow; ed Moscow Ore Inst.; researcher, ore industry research orgs; Head of Div. Publrs' Sovietskaya Encyclopaedia 1963–88; Prof., Moscow Ore Inst.; researcher, All-Union Inst. of Foreign Geology; f. Ind. Encyclopaedic Ed. House (ETA); Pres. Encyclopaedic Creative Asscn; mem. Russian Acad. of Natural Sciences 1992, Academician-Sec. Dept of Encyclopaedia. *Publications:* Russian Encyclopaedia of Banks 1995, Russian National Electronic Encyclopaedia 1995, Encyclopaedia of Moscow Streets 1996, Encyclopaedia America 1997. *Address:* Russian Academy of Natural Sciences, Varshavskoye shosse 8, 113105 Moscow, Russia (office). *Telephone:* (495) 954-26-11 (office). *Website:* www.raen.ru (office).

GEINGOB, Hage Gottfried, MA; Namibian politician; *Executive Secretary, Global Coalition for Africa;* b. 3 Aug. 1941, Grootfontein Dist; m. Loine Kandume 1993; one s. three d. from previous marriage; ed Augustineum Coll. Okahandja and studies in int. relations in USA; joined South-West Africa People's Org. (SWAPO) 1962; teacher, Tsumeb 1962; exiled for political activities Dec. 1962; became SWAPO Asst Rep. Botswana 1963–64; subsequently moved to USA, studied at Fordham Univ. and New School for Social Research, New York and became SWAPO Rep. at UN –1971; mem. SWAPO Politburo 1975; Dir UN Inst. for Namibia, Lusaka, Zambia 1975–89; returned to Namibia as Election Dir 1989; Chair. Constituent Ass. and Namibia Independence Celebrations Cttee 1989; Prime Minister of Namibia 1990–2003; Exec. Sec. Global Coalition for Africa 2003–; Officier Palmes Académiques 1980, Ongulumbashe Medal for bravery and long service 1987; Hon. LLD (Col Coll., Chicago) 1994. *Leisure interests:* playing tennis, reading, watching soccer and rugby. *Address:* Global Coalition for Africa, 1919 Pennsylvania Avenue, NW, Suite 550, Washington, DC 20006, USA. *Telephone:* (202) 458-4338 (office). *Fax:* (202) 522-3259 (office). *Website:* www.gca-cma.org (office).

GEISS, Johannes, Dr rer. nat; Swiss professor of physics; *Honorary Executive Director, International Space Science Institute;* b. 4 Sept. 1926, Stolp, Pomerania, Poland; s. of Hans Geiss and Irene Wilke; m. Carmen Bach 1955; one d.; ed Univ. of Göttingen, Germany; Research Assoc., Enrico Fermi Inst., Univ. of Chicago, USA 1955–56; Assoc. Prof., Marine Lab., Univ. of Miami, USA 1958–59; Assoc. Prof., Univ. of Berne 1960, Prof. of Physics 1964–91, Dir Inst. of Physics 1966–90; Visiting Scientist, NASA Goddard Inst. for Space Studies, New York 1965, NASA Manned Spacecraft Center, Houston 1968–69; Chair. Launching Programme Advisory Cttee, European Space Agency, Paris 1970–72; Visiting Prof., Univ. of Toulouse 1975; Chair. Space Science Cttee, European Science Foundation 1979–86; Exec. Dir Int. Space Science Inst. 1995–, now Hon. Exec. Dir; Adjunct Prof., Univ. of Michigan; Rector, Univ. of Berne 1982–83; Fellow of the American Geophysical Union; Foreign mem. American Acad. of Arts and Sciences, NAS, Max-Planck-Inst. für Aeronomie, Int. Acad. of Astronautics, Max-Planck-Inst. für Kernphysik, Austrian Acad. of Sciences; mem. Academia Europaea; Dr hc (Univ. of Chicago); NASA Medal for Exceptional Scientific Achievement. *Publications:* over 300 publs on nucleosynthesis, cosmology, the origin of the solar system, geochronology, climatic history of the earth, the age of meteorites and lunar rocks, comets, solar wind, solar terrestrial relations. *Address:* International Space Science Institute, Hallestr. 6, 3012 Berne, Switzerland (office). *Telephone:* (31) 6314892 (office). *Fax:* (31) 6314897 (office). *E-mail:* johannes.geiss@issi.unibe.ch (office). *Website:* www.issi.unibe.ch (office); www.phim.unibe.ch (office).

GEISSLER, Heiner, DJur; German politician; b. 3 March 1930, Oberndorff; s. of Heinrich Geissler and Maria Buck; m. Susanne Thunack 1962; three s.; ed Univs of Tübingen and Munich; Dir Office of Minister of Labour and Social Welfare, Baden-Wurttemberg; mem. Bundestag 1965–67, 1980–2002; Minister for Social Welfare, Health and Sport, Rheinland-Pfalz 1967–77; mem. Parl. of Rheinland-Pfalz 1971–79; Gen. Sec. CDU 1977–89, Deputy Chair. 1989–90, mem. Presiding Bd 1990; Deputy Chair. CDU/CSU Parl. group 1991–98; mem. CDU Parl. Cttee 1994; mem. TV Council, Second German TV 1970–82, 1987–92; Fed. Minister for Youth, Family and Health 1982–85; Chair. Kuratoriums Sport und Natur 1992–; Chair. AktionCourage 2002–; Dir Evangelischen Akademie Tutzing 2003–; Bundesverdienstkreuz 1970, Bergverlagspreis Deutsches Alpenverein 1983. *Publications:* Die neue soziale Frage 1976, Der Weg in die Gewalt 1978, Sicherheit für unsere Freiheit 1978, Verwaltete Bürger-Gesellschaft in Fesseln 1978, Grundwerte in der Politik 1979, Zukunftschancen der Jugend 1979, Sport – Geschäft ohne Illusionen? 1980, Mut zur Alternative 1981, Zugluft-Politik in stürmischer Zeit 1990, Heiner Geissler im Gespräch mit Gunter Hofmann und Werner A. Perger 1993, Gefährlicher Sieg 1995, Der Irrweg der Nationalismus 1995, Bergsteigen 1997, Das nicht gehaltene Versprechen 1997, Zeit, das Visier zu öffnen 1998, Where is God? Discussions with the Next Generation 2000, Intolerance: The Misfortune of Our Time 2002, What Say Jesus Today? The Political Message of the Gospel 2003. *Leisure interest:* mountaineering. *Address:* POB 1167, 66990 Dahn, Germany. *Telephone:* (6391) 924949. *Fax:* (6391) 924950. *E-mail:* heiner_geissler@t-online.de. *Website:* www.heiner-geissler.de.

GEITHNER, Timothy F., MA; American banking executive, economist and government official; *Secretary of the Treasury;* m. Carole Sonnenfeld Geithner; one s. one d.; ed Dartmouth Coll., Hanover, NH, Johns Hopkins School of Advanced Int. Studies, Baltimore, Md; worked for Kissinger Assocs, Inc., Washington, DC 1985–88; joined US Treasury Dept 1988, served in several positions in Int. Affairs Div. including Under-Sec. of the Treasury for Int. Affairs 1999–2001; Sr Fellow in Int. Econs, Council on Foreign Relations, Washington, DC Feb.–Aug. 2001; Dir Policy Devt and Review Dept, IMF, Washington, DC 2001–03; Pres. and CEO Fed. Reserve Bank of New York 2003–09, Vice-Chair. and Perm. mem. Fed. Open Market Cttee 2003–09; US Sec. of the Treasury, Washington, DC 2009–; mem. Council on Foreign Relations; mem. Bd of Dirs Center for Global Devt, Washington, DC, Nat. Acad. Foundation 2007–; mem. Bd of Trustees RAND Corpn 2006–08; Trustee Econ. Club of New York. *Address:* Department of the Treasury, 1500 Pennsylvania Avenue, NW, Washington, DC 10045, USA (office). *Telephone:* (202) 622-2000 (office). *Fax:* (202) 622-6415 (office). *Website:* www.ustreas.gov (office).

GEITONAS, Costas I.; Greek politician; b. Lagadia, Arcadia; ed Nat. Tech. Univ. of Athens; Gen. Sec. Ministry of Public Works 1981–85; Deputy Minister of Environment, Land Use and Public Works 1985–86, Alt. Gen. Dir Pvt. Political Office of Prime Minister 1986–89; an mem. Parl. for Athens 1989–; Deputy Minister of Public Order 1993–94; Alt. Minister of Environment, Land Use and Public Works 1994–96, Minister of Public Order 1996, Minister of Health and Welfare 1996–99; mem. Cen. Cttee PASOK (Panhellenic Socialist Movt). *Address:* c/o Ministry of Health and Welfare, Odos Aristotelous 17, 104 33 Athens, Greece. *Telephone:* (1) 5232820. *Fax:* (1) 5231707.

GELB, Bruce S.; American business executive and administrator; fmr Vice-Chair. Bristol-Myers Co., now Sr Consultant; Dir US Information Agency 1989–91; Amb. to Belgium 1991–93; fmr Commr for the UN, Consular Service and Int. Business, New York; fmr Pres. Wilson Council (pvt. sector advisory group for Woodrow Wilson Int. Center for Scholars), also mem. Wilson Center Bd of Trustees; fmr mem. Pres. Bush's Arts and Humanities Cttee; fmr mem. Bd of Trustees John F. Kennedy Center for the Performing Arts; fmr Trustee Howard Univ.; Vice-Chair. Exec. Cttee Madison Square Boys' and Girls' Club; Life Trustee Choate Rosemary Hall School, CT; mem. Bd of Dirs UN Devt Corpn for New York City. *Address:* Wilson Council, Woodrow Wilson International Center for Scholars, Ronald Reagan Building and International Trade Center, One Woodrow Wilson Plaza, 1300 Pennsylvania Avenue, NW, Washington, DC 20004-3027, USA (office). *Telephone:* (202) 691-4000 (office). *Fax:* (202) 691-4001 (office). *Website:* www.wilsoncenter.org (office).

GELB, Peter; American business executive and film and television producer; *Managing Director, Metropolitan Opera;* b. 1959; s. of Arthur Gelb; m. Keri-Lynn Wilson; two c. (from a previous m.); fmr man., Vladimir Horowitz; Pres. Sony Classical USA 1993–95, Pres. Sony Classical Int. Operations 1995–2005; Man. Dir Metropolitan Opera, New York 2006–; Emmy Awards for Outstanding Classical Program in the Performing Arts 1987, 1990, 1991, Emmy Awards for Outstanding Individual Achievement in Int. Programming 1991, Int. Documentary Asscn Award 1991, Grammy Award 2002. *Address:* The Metropolitan Opera, Lincoln Center, New York, NY 10023, USA (office). *Website:* www.metoperafamily.org.

GELBARD, Robert Sidney, MPA; American diplomatist and consultant; *Chairman, Washington Global Partners LLC;* b. 6 March 1944, New York; s. of Charles Gelbard and Ruth Fisher Gelbard; m. Alene Marie Hanola 1968; one d.; ed Colby Coll., Harvard Univ.; volunteer Peace Corps, Bolivia 1964–66, Assoc. Dir, Philippines 1968–70; joined Foreign Service 1967, Staff Asst Sr Seminar in Foreign Policy 1967–68; Vice-Consul Porto Alegre, Brazil 1970–71, Prin. Officer 1971–72; int. economist Office of Devt Finance 1973–75, Office of Regional Political and Econ. Affairs 1976–78; First Sec. Embassy, Paris 1978–82; Deputy Dir Office of Western European Affairs, Washington, DC 1982–84; Dir Office of S African Affairs, Washington, DC 1984–85; Deputy Asst Sec. Bureau of Inter-American Affairs, Washington, DC 1985–88; Amb. to Bolivia 1988–91; Prin. Deputy Asst Sec. of State for Bureau of Inter-American Affairs 1991–93, Asst Sec. of State for Int. Narcotics and Law Enforcement Affairs 1993–97; Special Rep. for Implementation of the Dayton Peace Accords 1997–99; Amb. to Indonesia 1999–2001; Sr Vice-Pres. for Int. Affairs and Govt Relations, ICN Pharmaceuticals 2002; self-employed consultant 2002–05; Chair. Washington Global Pnrs LLC (business consulting firm) 2005–; mem. Bd of Dirs Viisage Tech. Inc.; mem. Museum of American Folk Art int. advisory council, NY, American Foreign Service Asscn, World Affairs Council of Washington, DC; mem. Bd of Trustees Colby Coll.; Hon. LLD; Distinguished Service Award, US State Dept 2002. *Address:* c/o Board of Directors, Viisage Technology Inc., 1215 South Clark Street, Suite 1105, Arlington, VA 22202 (office); 371 Huntington Street NW, Washington, DC 20015, USA. *Telephone:* (21) 344-2211. *Fax:* (21) 380-5583 (office).

GELBART, Larry; American playwright and scriptwriter; b. 25 Feb. 1928, Chicago, Ill.; s. of Harry Gelbart and Frieda Gelbart; m. Pat Marshall 1956; three s. one d.; prin. writer, sometime dir and co-producer (first four seasons) M*A*S*H*; other television shows including Caesar's Hour, United States, The Bob Hope Show, The Danny Kaye Show; scriptwriter for various radio shows; Dir A Funny Thing Happened on the Way to the Forum, Chichester Festival Theatre, UK 1986; mem. Writers Guild of America, Authors League, Motion Picture Acad. of Arts and Sciences, Directors Guild of America, PEN Int; Hon. DLitt (Union Coll.) 1986, Hon. LHD (Hofstra) 1999; Tony Award for co-authoring A Funny Thing Happened on the Way to the Forum, Writers' Guild of America Awards for Oh, God, Movie Movie, Tootsie, 3 M*A*S*H* episodes, and for And Starring Pancho Villa as Himself 2003, Peabody Awards for M*A*S*H*, The Danny Kaye Show, Emmy Awards for M*A*S*H* and V.I.P., Edgar Allan Poe Award for Oh, God, Los Angeles Film Critics', New York Film Critics' and Nat. Soc. of Film Critics' Awards for Best Screenplay for Tootsie, Golden Rose, Montreux for writing/producing The Marty Feldman Comedy Machine, AMA citation for distinguished services 2001; other awards and distinctions. *Plays:* My LA (revue), The Conquering Hero (musical), A Funny Thing Happened on the Way to the Forum (musical), Jump, Mastergate, Sly Fox, City of Angels (musical), Power Failure. *Films:*

Notorious Landlady 1962, The Thrill of It All 1963, The Wrong Box 1966, Oh, God 1977, Movie Movie 1978, Neighbors 1981, Tootsie 1982, Blame it on Rio 1984, Barbarians at the Gate 1994, Weapons of Mass Distraction 1997, Bedazzled 2000, C-Scam (also dir) 2000. *Television includes:* Your Show of Shows 1950, Caesar's Hour 1954, The Danny Kaye Show 1963, The Marty Feldman Comedy Machine 1971, M*A*S*H (also developer) 1972, United States 1980, Mastergate 1992, Barbarians at the Gate 1993, Weapons of Mass Distraction 1997, And Starring Pancho Villa as Himself 2003. *Publication:* Laughing Matters 1998. *Leisure interests:* travel, grand- and great-grand-children. *Address:* 807 North Alpine Drive, Beverly Hills, CA 90210-2901, USA (home).

GELBER, J. David; American television news producer; b. 1941, New York; s. of the late Isaac Gelber and Florence Gelber; m. Kyoko Inouye 2001; ed Swarthmore Coll.; worked several years with Pacifica Radio in 1970s; fmr TV reporter and producer, Boston, Chicago and NY; fmr Exec. Producer, Peter Jennings Reporting, ABC News; consultant, Soros Foundation 1996; joined CBS News 1976, Exec. Producer, Ed Bradley on Assignment and 60 Minutes; mem. Bd of Mans Swarthmore Coll.; Peabody Award 2000. *Award-winning TV Productions include:* While America Watched: The Bosnia Tragedy (Emmy, DuPont Award), The Peacekeepers: How the UN Failed in Bosnia (Emmy, DuPont Award), Ed Bradley on Assignment: Town Under Siege 1997 (named by Time Magazine Award as one of 10 Best TV shows of the year), CBS News 60 Minutes II: The Church on Trial 2003 (Emmy Award for Outstanding Coverage of a Feature News Story in a News Magazine). *Address:* CBS News, 555 West 57th Street, New York, NY 10019, USA (office). *Telephone:* (212) 975-4114 (office). *Website:* www.cbsnews.com (office).

GELDOF, Bob; Irish rock singer; b. 5 Oct. 1954, Dublin; m. Paula Yates 1986 (divorced 1996, died 2000); three d.; ed Blackrock Coll.; many casual jobs, lorry-driving, busking, teaching English, working in factory, etc., then journalist on pop music paper, Georgia Strait, Vancouver, Canada; later journalist for New Musical Express, Melody Maker; returned to Dublin and f. rock group, Boomtown Rats 1975–84; solo artist 1986–; organized recording of Do They Know It's Christmas? by Band Aid, raising money for African famine relief Nov. 1984, f. Band-Aid Trust (incorporating Live Aid, Band Aid, Sport Aid) to distribute proceeds 1984, Chair.; organized Live Aid concerts in Wembley Stadium, London and JFK Stadium, Philadelphia, USA with int. TV link-up by satellite 13 July 1985, raised £40m for famine relief in Africa; f. Live Aid Foundation, USA; organized publ. of Live Aid book The Greatest Show on Earth 1985; Owner, Planet 24 (TV production co.) 1990–99; Co-founder and Dir (non-exec.) Ten Alps plc 2001–; mem. Africa Comm. 2004–; organized re-recording of Do They Know It's Christmas?, raising money for African famine relief Nov. 2004; organized Live 8 concerts in London, Philadelphia, Paris, Rome and Berlin, with int. TV link-up by satellite, to highlight ongoing problem of global poverty and debt 2 July 2005, The Long Walk to Justice, Edinburgh, Scotland, to present leaders of G8 Summit at Gleneagles with plan to double aid, drop debt and make trade laws fair 6 July 2005; Freeman of Ypres 1986; Hon. KBE 1986, Elder of the Repub. of Tanzania; Dr hc (Ghent) 1986, (Univ. Coll. Dublin) 2005; Hon. DLit (London) 1987; Hon. DCL (Newcastle) 2007; Order of Two Niles (Sudan), Order of Leopold II (Belgium), Irish Peace Prize, UN World Hunger Award, EEC Gold Medal, four Ivor Novello Awards, MTV Video Awards Special Recognition Trophy 1985, American Music Awards Special Award of Appreciation 1986, Third World Prize 1986, BRIT Award for Outstanding Contrib. to Music 2005, Golden Rose Charity Award (Switzerland) 2005, MTV Europe Free Your Mind Award 2005, Man of Peace Award 2005. *Film appearances include:* Pink Floyd – The Wall 1982, Number One 1985, Sketches of Frank Gehry 2006. *Recordings:* albums: with Boomtown Rats: The Boomtown Rats 1977, A Tonic For The Troops 1978, The Fine Art Of Surfacing 1979, Mondo Bongo 1981, V Deep 1982, In the Long Grass 1984; solo: Deep In The Heart Of Nowhere 1986, The Vegetarians Of Love 1990, The Happy Club 1993, Sex Age And Death 2001. *Publication:* Is That It? (autobiog.) 1986, Geldof in Africa 2005. *Address:* c/o Amanda Hon, PO Box 13995, London, W9 2FL, England (office); Ten Alps plc, 9 Savoy Street, London, WC2E 7HR, England. *Telephone:* (20) 7289-7331 (office); (20) 7878-2484. *E-mail:* amanda.hon@dsl.pipex.com (office). *Website:* www.bobgeldof.com.

GELDYMYRADOV, Khojamyrat; Turkmenistani politician; Deputy Minister of Economy and Finance 2005–07, Co-ordinator of Int. Tech. Aid to Turkmenistan 2005–07, Deputy Prime Minister responsible for Econ. Affairs 2007–09. *Address:* c/o Ministry of Finance, 744000 Aşgabat, ul. 2008 4, Turkmenistan. *Telephone:* (12) 51-05-63.

GELFAND, Israel Moiseyevich, DSc; Russian mathematician, biologist and academic; *Distinguished Visiting Professor, Department of Mathematics, Rutgers University;* b. 2 Sept. 1913, Krasnye Okny, Ukraine; s. of Moshe Gelfand and Perl Gelfand; m. 1st Zorya Yakovlevna Shapiro 1942 (divorced); m. 2nd Tanya Alekseevskaya 1979; two s. one d.; ed Moscow State Univ.; Asst Professor, Dept of Math., Moscow State Univ. 1935–40, Prof. 1940–91; Corresp. mem. USSR (now Russian) Acad. of Sciences 1953, mem. 1984, Head of Dept Inst. of Applied Math. 1953–91; Head of Lab. of Math. Methods in Biology, Moscow State Univ.; Founder and Ed. Funktsionalny analiz i yego prilozheniya 1967–91; Assoc. mem. and Distinguished Visiting Prof., Dept of Math., Rutgers Univ. 1991–; f. and Head Gelfand Outreach Programme in Math. 1995–; Prof. and Foreign mem. Royal Soc., NAS, Acad. des Sciences (France), Royal Swedish Acad. of Sciences, Royal Irish Soc., American Acad. of Arts and Sciences; Hon. mem. Moscow Math. Soc., London Math. Soc.; Dr hc (Oxford, Harvard, Uppsala, Milan, Pisa, Paris); State Prize 1951, 1953, Lenin Prize 1961, Wolf Prize in Math. 1978, Kyoto Prize 1989; McArthur Fellowship 1994. *Publications:* more than 400 works, including Unitary Representations of Classical Groups 1950, Generalized Functions Vols I–VI 1958–66, Normed

Rings 1960, Automorphic Functions and the Theory of Representations 1962, Cohomology of Infinite Dimensional Lie Algebras and Some Questions of Integral Homology 1970, Representations of the Group SL 2R, Where R is a Ring of Functions 1973, Mechanisms of Morphogenesis in Cell Structures 1977, Collected Papers (Vols 1–3) 1986–89, Discriminants, Resultants and Multidimensional Determinants 1994, GG Functions and Their Relations to General Hyper-geometric Functions 1999, Selected Problems in Integral Geometry 2000, Lagrangian Matroids and Cohomology 2000. *Leisure interest:* classical music. *Address:* Department of Mathematics, Rutgers University, 110 Frelinghuysen Road, Piscataway, NJ 08854, USA (office). *Telephone:* (732) 445-3489 (office); (732) 445-3477 (home). *E-mail:* igelfand@math.rutgers.edu (office). *Website:* www.math.rutgers.edu (office).

GELL-MANN, Murray, PhD; American physicist and academic; *Professor and Distinguished Fellow, Sante Fe Institute;* b. 15 Sept. 1929, New York City; s. of the late Arthur Gell-Mann and Pauline (Reichstein) Gell-Mann; m. 1st J. Margaret Dow 1955 (died 1981); one s. one d.; m. 2nd Marcia Southwick 1992 (divorced 2005); one step-s.; ed Yale Univ., Massachusetts Inst. of Tech.; mem. Inst. for Advanced Study, Princeton 1951, 1955, 1967–68; Instructor, Asst Prof. and Assoc. Prof., Univ. of Chicago 1952–55; Assoc. Prof., Calif. Inst. of Tech. 1955–56, Prof. 1956–66, R. A. Millikan Prof. of Theoretical Physics 1967–93, R. A. Millikan Prof. Emer. 1993–; Research Assoc. Univ. of Illinois 1951, 1953; Visiting Assoc. Prof. Columbia Univ. 1954; Visiting Prof. Collège de France and Univ. of Paris 1959–60, Mass. Inst. of Tech. 1963, European Council for Nuclear Research 1971–72, 1979–80, Univ. of NM 1995–; Consultant, Inst. for Defense Analyses, Arlington, Va 1961–70, RAND Corpn, Santa Monica, Calif. 1956; Overseas Fellow Churchill Col, Cambridge, England 1966; mem. NASA Physics Panel 1964, President's Science Advisory Cttee 1969–72, Council on Foreign Relations 1975–, President's Council of Advisors on Science and Tech. 1994–2001; Consultant to Los Alamos Scientific Laboratory, Los Alamos, NM 1956–, Laboratory Fellow 1982–; Citizen Regent, Smithsonian Inst. 1974–88; Chair. Western Center, American Acad. of Arts and Sciences 1970–76; Chair. of Bd Aspen Center for Physics 1973–79; Founding Trustee Santa Fe Inst. 1982, Chair. Bd of Trustees 1982–85, Co-Chair. Science Bd 1985–2000, Prof. and Distinguished Fellow 1993–; mem. Bd Calif. Nature Conservancy 1984–93, J. D. and C. T. MacArthur Foundation 1979– (Chair. World Environment and Resource Cttee 1982–97), Lovelace Insts 1993–95; mem. Science and Grants Cttee, Leakey Foundation 1977–88, NAS, American Physical Soc. 1960–, American Acad. of Arts and Sciences 1964–, American Philosophical Soc. 1993–, Science Advisory Cttee, Conservation Inst. 1993, AAAS 1994–, Advisory Bd Network Physics 1999–; Hon. mem. French Physical Soc. 1970; Foreign mem. Royal Soc. 1978–, Pakistan Acad. of Sciences 1985–, Indian Acad. of Sciences 1985–, Russian Acad. of Sciences 1993–; Hon. ScD (Yale) 1959, (Chicago) 1967, (Illinois) 1968, (Wesleyan) 1968, (Utah) 1970, (Columbia) 1977, (Cambridge Univ.) 1980, (Oxford Univ.) 1992, (Southern Illinois Univ.) 1993, (Univ. of Florida) 1994, (Southern Methodist Univ.) 1999; Dr hc (Turin, Italy) 1969; Dannie Heineman Prize, American Physical Soc. 1959; Ernest O. Lawrence Award 1966, Franklin Medal 1967, John J. Carty Medal (NAS) 1968, Nobel Prize in Physics 1969, Research Corpn Award 1969, UNEP Roll of Honor for Environmental Achievement 1988, Erice Prize 1990, Sigma Xi Procter Prize for Scientific Achievement 2004, Ellis Island Family Heritage Award 2005, Albert Einstein Medal 2005. *Major works:* Developed strangeness theory, theory of neutral K mesons, eightfold way theory of approximate symmetry; current algebra, quark scheme; contributed to theory of dispersion relations, theory of weak interaction and formulation of quantum chromodynamics. *Publications:* (with Yuval Ne'eman) The Eightfold Way 1964, The Quark and the Jaguar 1994. *Leisure interests:* historical linguistics, wilderness trips, ornithology, numismatics. *Address:* c/o Santa Fe Institute, 1399 Hyde Park Road, Santa Fe, NM 87501, USA (office). *Telephone:* (505) 984-8800. *Fax:* (505) 982-0565. *E-mail:* mgm@santafe.edu (office). *Website:* www.santafe.edu/sfi/people/mgm (office).

GELLEH, Ismael Omar; Djibouti head of state; *President and Commander-in-Chief of the Armed Forces;* b. 1947, Dire Dawa, Ethiopia; joined gen. security dept, French police force 1968, rank of Police Insp. 1970; fmr Chief of Staff of Pres. Hassan Gouled Aptidon; mem. Rassemblement populaire pour le progrès (RPP), currently Pres.; Pres. of Djibouti and Commdr-in-Chief of the Armed Forces May 1999–. *Address:* Office of the President, Djibouti, Republic of Djibouti.

GELLERT, Jay M., BA; American healthcare industry executive; *President and CEO, Health Net Incorporated;* b. 13 March 1954; ed Stanford Univ.; fmr Advisor Shattuck Hammond Pnrs; Pres. and COO Health Systems Int. Inc. (HIS, later Health Net Inc.) 1996–97, Dir 1996–97, Exec. Vice-Pres. and COO Health Net Inc. April-May 1997, Pres. and CEO 1998–, also COO May-Aug. 1998, Dir Feb. 1999–; Dir Ventas Sept. 2001–; American Asscn of Health Plans, MedUnite Inc., Miavita Inc. *Address:* Health Net Incorporated, 21650 Oxnard Street, Woodland Hills, CA 91367, USA (office). *Telephone:* (818) 676-6000 (office); (800) 291-6911 (tollfree in US) (office). *Fax:* (818) 676-8591 (office). *E-mail:* jay.m.gellert@health.net (office). *Website:* www.healthnet.com (office).

GELMAN, Aleksandr Isaakovich; Russian playwright and scriptwriter; b. 25 Oct. 1933, Moldavia; m. Tatyana Pavlovna Kaletskaya; two s.; ed Kishinev Univ.; mem. CPSU 1956–90; worked in factories 1956–67; corresp. for daily papers 1967–71; wrote scripts for series of documentary films 1971–74; work with Moscow Art Theatre 1975–; People's Deputy of the USSR 1989–91; USSR State Prize 1976. *Film scripts include:* Night Shift 1971, Consider me Grown Up 1974, Xenia, Fyodor's Favourite Wife 1974 (all with T. Kaletskaya), Prize 1975, Feedback (Best Script Writer, All-Union Film Festival 1978) 1977, Clumsy Man 1979, We, The Undersigned 1981, Zinulya 1984, We Met in a

Strange Way 1990, Gorbachev: After the Empire 2001. *Theatre work includes:* A Man with Connections, The Bonus, The Bench, We, the Undersigned, Misha's Party (co-author), Pretender 1999, Zinulya, Back, Connection. *Television documentary:* Gorbachev: After Empire 2001. *Publication:* Book of Plays 1985. *Address:* Tverskoy Blvd 3, Apt 12, 103104 Moscow, Russia (home). *Telephone:* (495) 202-68-59 (home). *E-mail:* idcg@cityline.ru (home).

GEMAYEL, Amin; Lebanese politician; b. 10 Nov. 1942, Bikfayya; s. of the late Pierre Gemayel; brother of the late Bashir Gemayel; ed St Joseph Univ., Beirut; mem. Parl. 1970–82; Pres. of Lebanon 1982–88; moved to USA 1988, to France 1989, back to Lebanon 2000; The House of the Future, The Amin Gemayel Educational Foundation, Le Reveil newspaper; mem. Al-Katae'b Party (Phalanges Libanaises).

GEMEDA, Gen. Abedula; Ethiopian army officer and politician; *Minister of Defence;* career in Ethiopian Armed Forces, rank of Gen.; currently Minister of Defence. *Address:* Minister of Defence, POB 125, Addis Ababa, Ethiopia (office). *Telephone:* (1) 445555 (office).

GENACHOWSKI, Julius, BA, JD; American lawyer, business executive and government official; *Chairman, Federal Communications Commission;* b. 19 Aug. 1962; m. Rachel Goslins; ed Columbia Coll., Columbia Univ., Harvard Law School; Law Clerk to Chief Judge Abner Mikva, US Court of Appeals for DC Circuit 1991–92, to US Supreme Court Justice William J. Brennan Jr 1992, to US Supreme Court Justice David Souter 1993–94; Chief Counsel to Chair. Fed. Communications Comm. (FCC) 1994–97, fmr Sr Official, Chair. FCC 2009–; worked with mems of US Congress 1995–98, including as mem. Congressional Cttee investigating Iran-Contra Affair; Gen. Counsel and Sr Vice-Pres. of Business Devt, USA Broadcasting 1997–2000; Vice-Pres. of Corp. Devt Ticketmaster Online-Citysearch, Inc. 2000; Sr Vice-Pres. and Gen. Counsel USA Networks Inc, InterActiveCorp 2000–02, Exec. Vice-Pres. and Gen. Counsel 2002, Chief of Business Operations and mem. Office of the Chair. IAC/InterActive Corpn 2003–06; Special Adviser, General Atlantic LLC, Greenwich, Conn. 2006–09; mem. Bd of Dirs The Motley Fool, Web.com, Mark Ecko Enterprises, Beliefnet, Common Sense Media; fmr mem. Bd of Dirs Expedia, Hotels.com, Ticketmaster, Truveo, Rapt; mem. of Advisory Bd Environmental Entrepreneurs (E2). *Address:* Federal Communications Commission, 445 12th Street, SW, Washington, DC 20554, USA (office). *Telephone:* (888) 225-5322 (office). *Fax:* (866) 418-0232 (office). *E-mail:* fccinfo@fcc.gov (office). *Website:* www.fcc.gov (office).

GENDREAU-MASSALOUX, Michèle; French public servant and organization official; *Rector, Agence Universitaire de la francophonie (AUF);* b. 28 July 1944, Limoges; d. of François Massaloux and Marie-Adrienne Delalais; m. Pascal Gendreau 1970; ed Ecole Normale Supérieure de Jeunes Filles, Sèvres, Inst. d'Etudes Politiques, Paris; univ. teacher, Sorbonne, Villetaneuse (Paris XIII), then Univ. of Limoges (fmr Vice-Pres.); Rector Acad. d'Orléans-Tours 1981–84; Tech. Adviser to Secr.-Gen. for Nat. Educ. and Univs., Presidency of the Repub., then to Secr.-Gen. for Admin. Reform and Improvement of Relations between Public Services and their Users, Deputy Sec.-Gen. 1985–88, Spokesperson 1986–88, Head of Mission May 1988; Rector, Acad. de Paris 1989–98; Conseiller d'Etat 1998; mem. Comm. Nat. de la Communication et des Libertés 1988–89, French Comm. for UNESCO 1991, Conseil orientation Ecole du Louvre 1991, Council, Coll. Univ. Français de Moscou 1991, Council, Coll. Univ. Français de Saint-Petersbourg 1992, Conseil Scientifique de la Cinquième 1996; mem. Comm. de contrôle des sondages 1999; Rector, Agence Universitaire de la francophonie (AUF), Paris 1999–; Prof. Univ. Paris VIII–Vincennes St-Denis 1999–; Dr hc Univ. of Aberdeen), (Univ. of Chile), (Laval Univ.), (Univ. of Moldova), New York Univ.), (Univ. of Toronto), (Univ. of Sofia), (Univ. of Bucharest), (Univ. of Moncton), (l'Université de Ouagadougou) 2004; Chevalier, Légion d'honneur, Officier, Ordre Nat. du Mérite, Chevalier, Ordre des Palmes Académiques. *Publication:* Recherche sur l'Humanisme de Francisco de Quevedo 1977, works and translations concerning the Spanish Golden Age. *Leisure interest:* music. *Address:* Agence Universitaire de la francophonie (AUF), 4, place de la Sorbonne, 75005, Paris (office); Conseil d'Etat, 75100 Paris 01 SP (office); 34 rue de Penthièvre, 75008 Paris, France (home). *Telephone:* 1-44-41-18-18 (office). *Fax:* 1-44-41-18-19 (office). *E-mail:* recteur@auf.org (office). *Website:* www.auf.org (office).

GENERALOV, Sergey Vladimirovich; Russian politician and business executive; *Chairman, Russian Biotechnologies;* b. 7 Sept. 1963, Simferopol; ed Moscow Inst. of Energy, Higher School of Man. at State Acad. of Man.; Commercial Dir TET 1991–92; Deputy Chair. NIPEBANK 1992–93; Head of Div., Head of Dept, Promradtechbank 1993; Vice-Pres. YUKOS Oil Co., 1993–97, ROSPROM-YUKOS 1997; Deputy Chair. MENATEP 1997–98; Minister of Fuel and Power Eng of Russian Fed. 1998–99; Dir Fuel and Energy Complex Investments Agency 1999–2000; mem. State Duma 1999–, faction Right-Wing Forces; Head State Duma Comm. for Protection of Investors' Rights –2002; Chair. Russian Biotechnologies Co., Investor Protection Asscn 2002–, Industrial Investors. *Address:* CJSC Russian Biotechnologies, 40/4 Bolshaya Ordynka str., 119017 Moscow, Russia (office). *Telephone:* (495) 981-29-22 (home). *Fax:* (495) 981-29-22 (office). *E-mail:* enp@rusbio.com (office). *Website:* www.rusbio.com (office).

GENG, Huichang; Chinese politician; *Minister of State Security;* b. 1951, Hebei Prov.; Deputy Dir Univ. of Int. Relations, American Research Dept, Beijing Municipality 1985–90, Dir 1990–92; Head, China Inst. of Contemporary Int. Relations 1992–98; Vice-Minister of State Security 1998–2007, Minister of State Security 2007–; mem. 17th CCP Cen. Cttee 2007–. *Address:* Ministry of State Security, 14 Dongchangan Jie, Dongcheng Qu, Beijing 100741, People's Republic of China. *Telephone:* (10) 65244702.

GENIEVA, Yekaterina Yuryevna, DLitt, DPhil; Russian librarian and literary scholar; *Director-General, All-Russia State Library of Foreign Literature (VGBIL);* b. 1 April 1946, Moscow; m. Yuri S. Belenky; one d.; ed Moscow State Univ.; nurse, Moscow hosp. 1962–63; Sr Deputy Dir All-Russia State Library of Foreign Literature (VGBIL) 1971–92, Dir-Gen. 1992–; Pres. Inst. Open Soc. (Soros Foundation) 1995–2003, The English-Speaking Union; Vice-Pres. Russian Library Asscn 1994–; mem. Council on Culture, Russian Presidency 1996–2000; mem. Bd First Vice-Pres. Int. Fed. of Library Asscns 1990–99; mem. Editorial Bds journals Biblioteka, Libri, Inostrannaya Literatura, Znamya; Order of Friendship 1999, Order of Gabriela Mistral (Chile) 2002, Cross of Recognition (Latvia) 2005, Order of Merit (Lithuania) 2006, Cross of Merit for Service, First Class (Germany) 2007, Hon. OBE (UK) 2007, Cross Maaryamaa (Estonia) 2008; Hon. DLitt (Univ. of Ill. at Urbana-Champaign) 2001. *Publications include:* monographs, trans. of English authors, numerous articles. *Leisure interests:* books, travelling, Irish culture. *Address:* Office of the Director-General, VGBIL, Nikoloyamskaya str. 1, 109189 Moscow, Russia (office). *Telephone:* (495) 915-36-21 (office). *Fax:* (495) 915-36-37 (office). *E-mail:* genieva@libfl.ru (office). *Website:* www.libfl.ru (office).

GENILLARD, Robert Louis, MA (Econ); Swiss financier; b. 15 June 1929, Lausanne; Gen. Pnr, White, Weld & Co., New York 1958; Chair. and Chief Exec. Credit Suisse White Weld 1960–77; Chief Exec. Thyssen-Bornemisza Group and TBG Holdings NV 1977–83, Deputy Chair. 1971–99; Ind. Corp. Dir 1983–, for American Express, Cabot Int., Clariden Bank (also Chair., now Hon. Chair.), Cie des Machines Bull, Credit Suisse Group (Vice-Chair.), Honeywell Int., Novartis, Said Holdings (Vice-Chair.), Soc. des Bains de Mer, Swiss Aluminium. *Publications:* numerous articles in professional journals. *Address:* 1 quai du Mont-Blanc, 1211 Geneva 1, Switzerland (office).

GENISARETSKY, Oleg Igorevich; Russian sociologist and organization executive; *Deputy Director, Institute of Management, Russian Academy of Sciences;* b. 28 Feb. 1942, Kovrov, Vladimir region; ed Moscow Inst. of Physics and Eng, Moscow State Univ.; researcher, All-Union Inst. of Tech. Aesthetics 1965–93; Deputy Dir Inst. of Man., Russian Acad. of Sciences 1993–; Pres. Open Museum Asscn, Russian Asscn of Visual Anthropology; CEO Inst. of Synergetic Anthropology; Prof., Inst. of Corp. Entrepreneurship, Higher School of Econs; Triumph Prize. *Publications:* numerous publs on theory and methods of system and artistic design, ecology of culture, aesthetic educ., theoretical sociology of culture and psychology of creativity. *Address:* Institute of Management, Russian Academy of Sciences, Volkhonka str. 14, 119842 Moscow (office); Institute of Synergetic Anthropology, 31-120 Festivalnaya str., 125195 Moscow; Open Museum Association, krasnoyarsk p/b 25221, 660049 Moscow, Russia. *Telephone:* (495) 203-01-09 (office). *Fax:* (495) 203-91-69 (office). *E-mail:* olegen@msses.ru. *Website:* www.im.mesi.ru (office); www.aom.ru; www.synergia-isa.ru.

GENOVÉS, Juan; Spanish artist; b. 31 May 1930, Valencia; ed Escuela Superior de Bellas Artes, Valencia; has taken part in numerous group exhbns; one-man exhbns in Spain, Portugal, USA, Italy, Germany, Netherlands, Japan, UK, Cuba, Puerto Rico, Canada, Switzerland, France and S America 1957–; took part in Paris Biennale 1961, Venice Biennale 1962, 1966, São Paulo Biennale 1965; works in collections and museums in Germany, SA, Guinea, Australia, Austria, Belgium, Brazil, Canada, Colombia, Cuba, Spain, Finland, France, Netherlands, England, Israel, Italy, Japan, Mexico, Nicaragua, Poland, Switzerland, USA and Venezuela; Gold Medal, San Marino Biennale 1967, Premio Marzotto Internazionale 1968, Premio Nacional de Artes Plásticas 1984. *Address:* c/o Marlborough Fine Art, 6 Albemarle Street, London, W1S 4BY, England; Arandilla 17, 28023 Aravaca (Madrid), Spain (home).

GENOVESE, Eugene Dominick, BA, MA, PhD; American academic and writer; b. 19 May 1930, New York City; m. Elizabeth Ann Fox 1969; ed Brooklyn Coll., CUNY and Columbia Univ.; Asst Prof., Polytechnical Inst., Brooklyn 1958–63; Assoc. Prof., Rutgers Univ. 1963–67; Prof. of History, Sir George Williams Univ., Montréal 1967–69, Social Science Research Fellow 1968–69; Visiting Prof., Columbia Univ. 1967, Yale Univ. 1969; Prof. of History, Univ. of Rochester 1969–90, Distinguished Prof. of Arts and Sciences 1985–90; Pitt Prof. of American History and Insts, Univ. of Cambridge, England 1976–77; Sunderland Fellow and Visiting Prof. of Law, Univ. of Michigan 1979; Visiting Mellon Prof., Tulane Univ. 1986; Distinguished Scholar-in-Residence, Univ. Center, Ga 1990–95; Richard Watson Gilder Fellow, Columbia Univ. 1959, Center for Advanced Study in the Behavioral Sciences Fellow, Stanford, Calif. 1972–73, Nat. Humanities Center Fellow, Research Triangle Park, North California 1984–85, Mellon Fellow 1987–88, Guggenheim Fellowship 1987–88, Fellow, American Acad. of Arts and Sciences; mem. Historical Soc. (fmr Pres.), Nat. Asscn of Scholars; Bancroft Prize 1994. *Publications:* The Political Economy of Slavery 1965, The World the Slaveholders Made 1969, In Red and Black 1971, Roll, Jordan, Roll 1974, From Rebellion to Revolution 1979, Fruits of Merchant Capital (with Elizabeth Fox-Genovese) 1983, The Slaveholder's Dilemma 1991, The Southern Tradition 1994, The Southern Front 1995, A Consuming Fire 1998, The Mind of the Master Class (with Elizabeth Fox-Genovese) 2005, Slavery in Black and White (co-author) 2008, Miss Betsey: A Memoir of Marriage 2009; contrib. to scholarly journals. *Address:* 1487 Sheridan Walk NE, Atlanta, GA 30324, USA. *Telephone:* (404) 634-0596 (home).

GENSCHER, Hans-Dietrich; German politician; b. 21 March 1927, Reideburg, Saalkreis; s. of Kurt Genscher and the late Hilda Kreime; m. 1st Luise Schweitzer 1958; m. 2nd Barbara Schmidt 1969; one d.; ed Leipzig and Hamburg Univs; Scientific Asst, Parl. Free Democratic Party (FDP) 1956, later Sec., Hon. Chair. 1992–; Fed. Party Man. 1962–64, Vice-Chair. 1968–74, Chair. 1974–85; Deputy in Bundestag 1965–98; Fed. Minister of the Interior

1969–74; Vice-Chancellor, Minister of Foreign Affairs 1974–92; Chair. Bd of Dirs WMP Eurocom AG, Berlin 1998–; Counsel Büsing, Müffelmann & Theye, Berlin 1999–; Man. Partner Hans-Dietrich Genscher Consult GmbH 2000–; Pres. German Council on Foreign Relations 2001–03; Asscn Friends and Patrons State Opera, Berlin; Hon. Prof. Free Univ. of Berlin 1994, Peking 1999; Hon. Citizen of Costa Rica 1988; Freeman of Halle 1993, of Berlin 1997; Bundesverdienstkreuz 1973 and other medals; numerous Dr hc 1977–2002; Onassis Foundation Award 1991. *Publications:* Bundestagsreden 1972, Deutsche Aussenpolitik, Reden und Aufsätze aus 10 Jahren, 1974–84, Nach vorn gedacht... Perspektiven deutscher Aussenpolitik 1986, Erinnerungen (memoirs) 1995. *Leisure interest:* reading. *Address:* Hans-Dietrich Genscher's Personal Office, Postfach 200 655, 53136 Bonn, Germany (office). *Fax:* (228) 264652 (office). *E-mail:* buero@genscher.de (office). *Website:* www.genscher.de (office).

GENSLER, Gary, BS, MBA; American government official; *Chairman, Commodity Futures Trading Commission;* b. Baltimore, Md; m. Francesca Danieli (died 2006); three d.; ed Wharton School, Univ. of Pennsylvania; joined The Goldman Sachs Group, LP (int. investment banking firm) in 1979, worked in Mergers and Acquisition Dept 1979–84, assumed responsibility for firm's efforts advising media cos 1984–88, Pnr 1988–97, joined Fixed Income Div. and directed Goldman's Fixed Income and Currency trading efforts in Tokyo –1995, Co-head of Finance for Goldman Sachs world-wide 1995–97; Asst US Sec. of the Treasury for Financial Markets, Washington, DC 1997–99, also served as a sr mem. Treasury Financing Group and Working Group on Financial Markets, Under-Sec. of the Treasury for Domestic Finance 1999–2001; fmr Sr Adviser to US Senator Paul Sarbanes (one of authors of legislation that eventually became Sarbanes-Oxley Act); sr adviser to Senator Hillary Clinton's presidential campaign and, after Democratic Primary, to Barack Obama presidential campaign 2008; Chair. US Commodity Futures Trading Comm., Washington, DC 2009–. *Publication:* The Great Mutual Fund Trap – An Investment Recovery Plan (with Gregory Arthur Baer) 2002. *Address:* Commodity Futures Trading Commission, Three Lafayette Centre, 1155 21st Street, NW, Washington, DC 20581, USA (office). *Telephone:* (202) 418-5000 (office). *Fax:* (202) 418-5521 (office). *E-mail:* Questions@cftc.gov (office). *Website:* www.cftc.gov (office).

GENTIL DA SILVA MARTINS, Antonio, MD; Portuguese paediatric and plastic surgeon and paediatric oncologist; *Consultant in Surgical Pediatric Oncology, Instituto Português de Oncologia Francisco Gentil, Lisbon;* b. 10 July 1930, Lisbon; s. of António Augusto da Silva Martins and Maria Madalena Gentil da Silva Martins; m. Maria Guilhermina Ivens Ferraz Jardim da Silva Martins 1963; three s. five d.; ed Univ. of Lisbon; Medical Faculty, Univ. of Lisbon 1953–; intern, Hospitais Civis, Lisbon; fmr Registrar, Alder Hey Children's Hosp., Liverpool, UK; Founder and Head, Paediatric Dept, Instituto Português de Oncologia de F. Gentil 1960–87, consultant paediatric surgeon 1987–; paediatric surgeon, Hosp. D. Estefania (Children's Hosp.), Lisbon 1965, Dir of Paediatric Surgery 1987–; Assoc. Prof. of Paediatric Surgery, Faculty of Medical Sciences, Lisbon 1984–2002; Temporary Consultant, Paediatric Cancer, WHO 1977, EEC 1991; Pres. Portuguese Soc. of Plastic and Reconstructive Surgery 1968–74, Ordem dos Médicos (Portuguese Medical Asscn) 1978–86, Portuguese Asscn of Paediatric Surgeons 1975–84, 1991–94, World Medical Asscn 1981–83, Southern Br. Portuguese League Against Cancer 1988–94, Portuguese League Against Cancer 1995–97; Vice-Pres. Nat. Confed. of Portuguese Family Asscns 2004–08, Portuguese Fed. of Badminton 2005–08, Int. Coll. of Surgeons 2006–08 (Pres. Portuguese Section 2005–07); mem. Exec. Council World Fed. of Asscns of Paediatric Surgeons 1983–89, Council Int. Conf. of Childhood Cancer Parent Asscns 1994–95; Pres. Portuguese Olympic Athletes Asscn 2003–(12), CAVITOP (Center for Support of Victims of Torture Portugal); mem. numerous other professional socs; Hon. mem. Portuguese League against Cancer, Int. Soc. of Pediatric Oncology, Int. Soc. of Pediatric Surgical Oncology, AMI (Int. Medical Assistance), Portuguese Cancer League, Confed. of Portuguese Family Asscns, Portuguese Badminton Fed. and other orgs; Grande Oficial da Ordem do Infante D. Henrique 1980; Silva Pereia Award 1972, awarded Silver Plate for film on separation of conjoined twins 1980, Keys of Miami and Dale County 1983, Diploma of Honour, Cuban Medical Asscn in Exile 1983, Gold Medal Ministry of Health 2001, Medal of Honour, Portuguese Medical Asscn 2002, Medal of Our Lady of Vila Viçosa 2007 and numerous other awards. *Achievements include:* separation of six pairs of conjoined twins with nine survivors. *Film:* Separation of Siamese Twins. *Publications:* textbook on Plastic Surgery of the Ibero-Latin-American Foundation of Plastic Surgery (co-author) 1986 (revised edn 2008), textbook on Intersexual States (co-author), Le Médecin et les droits de l'homme (co-author) 1982, Atlas of Pediatric Surgery, Head and Neck Cancer, Elementos de Psiquiatria da Criança e do Adolescente, O Médico e a Eutanásia, Atlas of Paediatric Surgery (co-author), Psychosocial Issues in Pediatric Cancer (co-author), Educação pelo Desporto; paediatric chapter in Textbook of Surgery 2006. *Leisure interests:* target-shooting (pistol, Olympics, Rome 1960; Portuguese rifle champion and record holder), volleyball (Portuguese champion), lawn tennis (Portuguese Jr Champion, men's doubles), table tennis, badminton, collecting stamps and coins, music, photography. *Address:* Rua de Campolide 166G, 1070-037 Lisbon (office); Rua D. Francisco Manuel de Melo 1 3° Dto, 1070-085 Lisbon, Portugal (home). *Telephone:* (21) 384-1860 (office); (21) 385-1436 (home); 93-9555162 (mobile). *Fax:* (21) 385-1436 (home). *E-mail:* agentilmartins@netcabo.pt (home); agentilmartins@gmail.com (home).

GENTILINI, Fernando, LLB; Italian diplomatist; *Senior Civilian Representative in Afghanistan, NATO;* b. 2 March 1962, Subiaco, Rome; ed Univ. of Rome; Second Lt, Italian Army (Artillery) 1987; joined diplomatic service 1990, Second Sec. (Econs and Trade), Embassy in Addis Ababa 1992–95, First Sec. 1995–96; First Sec., Perm. Mission to EU, Brussels 1996–99, Rep. Policy Planning and Early Warning Unit, EU Council Secr. 1999–2000; Head of Unit for Western Balkans, Ministry of Foreign Affairs 2002–04; EU High Rep.'s Personal Rep. to Kosovo 2004; seconded to Policy Unit, Office of Sec.-Gen. and High Rep. for Common Foreign and Security Policy, Brussels 2004–06; Deputy Diplomatic Adviser to Prime Minister 2006–08; Sr Civilian Rep. in Afghanistan, NATO 2008–; Cavaliere Ufficiale dell'Ordine al Merito della Repubblica 2006. *Address:* North Atlantic Treaty Organization (NATO), boulevard Léopold III, 1110 Brussels, Belgium (office). *Telephone:* (02) 707-50-41 (office). *Fax:* (02) 707-50-57 (office). *E-mail:* natodoc@hq.nato.int (office). *Website:* www.nato.int (office).

GENTZ, Manfred, LLB, LLD; German business executive; *Chairman, Zurich Financial Services;* b. 22 Jan. 1942, Riga, Latvia; ed Berlin Free Univ. and Univ. of Lausanne; joined Daimler-Benz AG 1970, mem. Man. Bd 1983–90, CEO Daimler-Benz Interservices 1990–95, Chief Financial Officer Daimler-Benz AG 1995–98, mem. Man. Bd DaimlerChrysler AG (after merger of Daimler-Benz and Chrysler Corpn) 1998–2004; Chair. Zurich Financial Services 2005–; Chair. Supervisory Bd Eurohypo AG 2005–06; mem. Bd of Supervisors Agrippina Versicherung AG 1987–95, Zurich Beteiligungs-Aktiengesellschaft (Deutschland) 1996–2005, Hannoversche Lebensversicherung AG 1985–2005 (Proxy Chair. 1990–2005), Adidas AG, Deutsche Börse AG, DWS Investment GmbH; Chair. ICC, Germany, Curatorship of Technische Universität Berlin; mem. several scientific and cultural insts. *Address:* Zurich Financial Services, 2 Mythenquai, PO Box 8022, Zurich, Switzerland (office). *Telephone:* (44) 6252525 (office); (44) 6252100 (office). *E-mail:* info@zurich.com (office). *Website:* www.zurich.com (office).

GEOANĂ, Mircea Dan, LLB; Romanian politician and international organization official; *President, Social Democratic Party;* b. 14 July 1958; m. Mihaela Geoană; one s. one d.; ed Bucharest Polytechnic Inst., Univ. of Bucharest, Ecole Nat. d'Admin, Paris, France, Harvard Univ., USA, Acad. for Econ. Studies, Bucharest; joined Ministry of Foreign Affairs 1990, Dir European Affairs Dept, Head of Romanian Del. to CSCE Cttee of Sr Officials 1991, Ministry Spokesperson 1993–95, Dir-Gen. for Asia, Latin America, Middle East and Africa 1994, Dir-Gen. for Europe, N America, Asia, Latin America, Middle East and Africa 1995; Amb. to USA 1996–2000; Minister of Foreign Affairs 2000–05; Chair.-in-Office OSCE 2001–; cand. for Mayor of Bucharest 2004; mem. Senate 2004–; Pres., Social Democratic Party (Partidul Social Democrat) 2005–; Prof., Nat. School for Political and Admin Sciences, Nicolae Titulescu Univ., Bucharest; NATO Fellow on Democratic Insts 1994; Commdr of Nat. Order Star of Romania 2000. *Publications:* numerous articles on Euro-Atlantic integration. *Address:* Social Democratic Party (Partidul Social Democrat), 011346 Bucharest, Şos. Kiseleff 10, Romania (office). *Telephone:* (21) 2222958 (office). *Fax:* (21) 2223272 (home). *E-mail:* geoana .mircea@senat.ro (office). *Website:* www.psd.ro (office).

GEOGHEGAN, Michael F., CBE; British banking executive; *Group CEO, HSBC Holdings;* b. 4 Oct. 1953, Windsor; m.; two s.; joined HSBC (Hong Kong and Shanghai Banking Corpn) Group 1973, spent 12 years in N and S America, eight years in Asia, seven years in Middle East, Pres. HSBC Bank Brasil S.A./Banco Múltiplo 1997–2003, responsible for all of HSBC's business throughout S America 2000–03, CEO HSBC PLC 2004–06, Exec. Dir HSBC Holdings 2004–, Group CEO 2006–, Chair. Group Man. Bd, Chair. HSBC Bank USA, N.A., HSBC USA Inc. and HSBC Bank Canada, Deputy Chair. HSBC Bank plc, a Dir of The Hongkong and Shanghai Banking Corpn Ltd, HSBC France, HSBC North America Holdings Inc. and HSBC Nat. Bank USA; Dir (non-exec.) and Chair. Young Enterprise. *Address:* HSBC Holdings, 8 Canada Square, London E14 5HQ, England (office). *Telephone:* (20) 7991-8888 (office). *Fax:* (20) 7992-4880 (office). *E-mail:* pressoffice@hsbc.com (office). *Website:* www.hsbc.com (office).

GEOGHEGAN-QUINN, Máire; Irish EU official, politician and fmr business consultant; *Official, Court of Auditors of the European Communities;* b. 5 Sept. 1950, Carna, Co. Galway; d. of the late John Geoghegan and of Barbara Folan; m. John V. Quinn 1973; two s.; ed Carysfort Teacher Training Coll. Blackrock, Co. Dublin; fmr primary school teacher; mem. Galway City Council 1985–92; mem. Dáil (Parl.) 1975–97; Parl. Sec. to Minister of Industry, Commerce and Energy 1977–78; Minister of State with responsibility for Consumer Affairs, Ministry of Industry, Commerce and Energy 1977–78; Minister for the Gaeltacht 1979–81; Minister of State with responsibility for Youth and Sport, Dept of Educ. March–Dec. 1982; Minister of State for European Affairs 1987, 1991; Minister for Tourism, Transport and Communications 1992, of Justice 1993; columnist Irish Times 1997–2000; consultant to several cos; mem. Audit Devt and Reports Group, Court of Auditors of the EC 2000–; fmr Chair. The Saffron Initiative; fmr Vice-Pres., Fianna Fáil; fmr Dir (non-exec.) The Ryan Hotel Group, Aer Lingus; fmr TV broadcaster. *Publication:* The Green Diamond (novel) 1996. *Leisure interests:* reading, writing and travel. *Address:* European Court of Auditors, 12 Rue Alcide de Gasperi, 1615 Luxembourg, Luxembourg (office). *Telephone:* 4398-45303 (office). *Fax:* 4398-46493 (office). *Website:* www.eca.eu.int (office).

GEORGANAS, Nicolas D., Dipl-Ing, PhD, FRSC, FIEEE, FCAE, FEIC; Greek/Canadian computer engineer and academic; *Distinguished University Professor and Associate Vice-President, Research (External), University of Ottawa;* b. 15 June 1943, Athens, Greece; m.; two c.; ed Nat. Tech. Univ. of Athens; mem. faculty, Dept of Electrical and Computer Eng, Univ. of Ottawa 1970– (Chair. 1981–84), later at School of Tech. Technology and Eng, Univ. of Ottawa, Founding Dean Faculty of Eng 1986–93, Distinguished Univ. Prof. 2001–, Assoc. Vice-Pres. Research (External) 2005–; Canada Research Chair in Information Tech. 2001–05; sabbatical with IBM Centre d'Etudes et Recherche, La Gaude, France 1977–78, BULL-Transac and INRIA, Paris, France 1984–85, BNR (now NORTEL Networks) 1993–94, CRC, Ottawa 1997, Univ. of Castilla-La Mancha, Spain 2004, Univ. of Vienna, Austria 2004; Chair.

Electrical Eng Grants Selection Cttee Natural Sciences and Eng Research Council of Canada 1985–86; Gen. Chair. ACM Multimedia 2001, IEEE Int. Conf. on Multimedia Computing and Systems, Ottawa 1997; Co-Chair. Canadian Conf. of Electrical and Computer Eng, Ottawa 1900; Tech. Program Chair. of MULTIMEDIA '89, Second IEEE COMSOC Int. Multimedia Communications Workshop, Canada 1989, ICCC Multimedia Communications '93 Conf., Banff, Alberta; Co-founder and a project leader at Telecommunications Research Inst. of Ontario (now called CITO); fmr Project Leader, Canadian Inst. for Telecommunications Research, Tele-Learning NCE; Ed.-in-Chief ACM Transactions on Multimedia Computing, Communications and Applications; Founding Ed.-in-Chief ACM Transactions on Multimedia Computing, Communications and Applications 2004–; Guest Ed. IEEE Journal on Selected Areas in Communications, issues on Multimedia Communications April 1990, Synchronization Issues in Multimedia Communications 1995; fmr mem. Editorial Bd ACM Computing Surveys, Performance Evaluation, Computer Networks, Computer Communications, Multimedia Tools and Applications, ACM/Springer Verlag Multimedia Systems Journal, IEEE Multimedia Magazine; Fellow, Eng Inst. of Canada 1994; Order of Ontario; Hon. Dr-Ing (Tech. Univ. Darmstadt) 2004; IEEE INFOCOM '95 Prize Paper Award (co-recipient) 1995, Univ. of Ottawa Researcher of the Year 1998, Univ. 150th Anniversary Medal for Research 1998, RSC Thomas W. Eadie Medal 1999, A. G. L. McNaughton Gold Medal and Award 2000, Julian C. Smith Medal, Eng Inst. of Canada 2000, OCRI Pres.'s Award for the creation of the Nat. Capital Inst. of Telecommunications 2000, Bell Canada Forum Award, Corporate-Higher Educ. Forum 2000, Researcher Achievement Award, TeleLearning Network of Centres of Excellence 2000, Killam Prize for Eng 2002, Queen Elizabeth II Golden Jubilee Medal 2003, recognized by IBM Centre of Advanced Studies as Pioneer of Computing in Canada 2005, Canadian Award in Telecommunications Research 2006. *Publications:* Queueing Networks – Exact Computational Algorithms, A Unified Theory by Decomposition and Aggregation (co-author) 1989; more than 360 papers in professional journalson are collaborative virtual environments, tele-haptics, sensor networks, multimedia communication systems, intelligent Internet appliances and performance evaluation of multimedia applications over broadband networks and the Internet. *Address:* School of Information Technology and Engineering (SITE), University of Ottawa, 161 Louis Pasteur, Ottawa, ON K1N 6N5, Canada (office). *Telephone:* (613) 562-5800 ext. 6225 (office). *Fax:* (613) 562-5175 (office). *E-mail:* georganas@discover.uottawa.ca (office). *Website:* www.discover.uottowa.ca (office).

GEORGE; British artist; b. (George Passmore), 1942, Devon; ed Dartington Hall Adult Educ. Centre, Dartington Hall Coll. of Art, Oxford School of Art, St Martin's School of Art, London; began collaboration with Gilbert Proesch in 1967 as Gilbert and George; est. reputation as performance artists, presenting themselves, identically dressed, as living sculptures; later work includes large composite drawings and vividly coloured photo-pieces often featuring likenesses of the artists; collections in Denver Art Museum, San Francisco Museum of Modern Art. *Publication:* Manifesto: What Our Art Means (jtly), Gilbert and George: The Complete Pictures 2007. *Address:* White Cube, 48 Hoxton Square, London, N1 6PB, England (office). *Telephone:* (20) 7930-5373 (office). *Fax:* (20) 7749-7480 (office). *E-mail:* g-and-g@dircon.co.uk (office). *Website:* www.whitecube.com (office).

GEORGE, Andrew Neil; British diplomatist; b. 9 Oct. 1952, Scotland; m. Watanalak George; one s. one d.; Desk Officer, S American Dept, FCO 1980–81, Second Sec., Chancery, Bangkok 1976–80, Desk Officer, West African Dept 1981–82, 1974–75, Under-Sec./Dir Gen. 1982–84, First Sec., Chancery, Canberra 1984–88, First Sec. and Head of Chancery, Bangkok 1988–92, Asst Head, Repub. of Ireland Dept 1993–94, Asst Head, Eastern Dept 1994–95, Head of Section, Counter Proliferation Dept 1995–98, Amb., Asencion 1998–2001, Commercial Counsellor, Jakarta 2002, Asst Dir with Human Resources Directorate 2003–05, Gov. and C-in-C of Anguilla 2006–09. *Address:* c/o Government House, Old Ta, Anguilla (office).

GEORGE, HE Cardinal Francis Eugene, OMI, PhD, STD; American ecclesiastic; *Archbishop of Chicago;* b. 16 Jan. 1937, Chicago, Ill.; ed Univ. of Ottawa, Canada, Catholic Univ. of America, Tulane Univ., Pontifical Urban Univ., Rome; ordained priest 1963; Bishop of Yakima 1990, of Portland, Ore. 1996–97; Archbishop of Chicago 1997–; cr. Cardinal 1998, cr. Cardinal Priest in Consistory 1998; Vice-Pres., US Conf. of Catholic Bishops 2004–07, Pres. 2007–; mem. Congregation for Evangelization of Peoples 1999–, Congregation for Insts of Consecrated Life and for Socs of Apostolic Life 1998–, Congregation for Oriental Churches 2001–, Pontifical Comm. for the Cultural Heritage of the Church 1999–, Pontifical Council Cor Unum 1998–, Pontifical Council for Culture 2004–, Council for World Synod of Bishops 2001–; Chancellor, Catholic Church Extension Soc., Chicago 1997–, Univ. of St Mary of the Lake, Mundelein, Ill. 1997–; Publisher, Catholic New World and Chicago Catolico 1997–; Papal Appointee to Synod on Consecrated Life, 1994; Trustee Basilica of Nat. Shrine of Immaculate Conception 1997–, Catholic Univ. of America 1993–, Papal Foundation 1997–; mem. Bd of Dirs Nat. Catholic Bio-ethics Center, Boston 1994–; Kt of Malta; Dr hc (Univ. of Portland) 1997, (John Marshall Law School) 1998, (Loyola Univ. of Chicago) 1998, (Franciscan Univ. of Steubenville) 2000, (Barat Coll.) 2000, (Creighton Univ.) 2001, (St Xavier Univ.) 2004; Outstanding Educator of America 1972, 1973. *Publication:* Inculturation and Ecclesi Communion 1990. *Address:* Archdiocese of Chicago, PO Box 1979, Chicago, IL 60690-1979 (office); Archdiocese of Chicago, 835 North Rush Street, Chicago, IL 60611, USA (office). *Telephone:* (312) 751-8230 (office). *Fax:* (312) 534-6379 (office). *E-mail:* archbishop@archchicago.org (office). *Website:* www.archdiocese-chgo.org (office).

GEORGE, Jennie, BA; Australian trade union official and politician; b. 20 Aug. 1947, Italy; ed Sydney Univ.; Gen. Sec. NSW Teachers Fed. 1980–82, Pres. 1986–89; mem. Exec. Australian Council of Trade Unions (ACTU) 1983, Vice-Pres. 1987, Asst Sec. 1991–95, Pres. 1996–2000; Fed. MP for Throsby 2001–; Asst Nat. Dir Trade Union Training Authority 1989–91. *Address:* c/o Australian Labour Party, Centenary House, 19 National Circuit, Barton, ACT 2600, Australia (office). *Telephone:* (2) 6273-3133 (office). *Fax:* (2) 6273-2031. *E-mail:* jennie.george.MP@aph.gov.au (office).

GEORGE, Kenneth Montague, LLM; Guyanese judge; b. 12 March 1930; s. of Stephen N. George and Etheline George; m. Hazel Ester McLean 1965; two s. two d.; ed London and Harvard Univs and Gray's Inn, London; Registrar of Supreme Court 1964–66, Judge 1967–76; Justice of Appeal 1976–81; Chief Justice 1981–88; Chancellor of the Judiciary and Pres. Court of Appeal 1988; drafted Civil Rules of Court for Caribbean Court of Justice 2004; Cacique's Crown of Honour, Order of Roraima. *Leisure interest:* reading. *Address:* 43 Arakaka Place, Bel Air Park, Georgetown (home); c/o Court of Appeal, 60 High Street, Kingston, Georgetown, Guyana (office). *Telephone:* (2) 65906 (home).

GEORGE, Peter J., CM, BA, MA, PhD; Canadian economist, academic and university administrator; *President and Vice Chancellor, McMaster University;* b. 1941; m. Allison Barrett; one s. one d.; ed Univ. of Toronto; Lecturer, McMaster Univ. 1965–67, Asst Prof. 1967–71, Assoc. Prof. 1971–80, Prof. of Econs 1980–, Assoc. Dean of Grad. Studies 1974–79, Dean Faculty of Social Sciences 1980–89, Pres. and Vice Chancellor, McMaster Univ. 1995–; Pres. Council of Ont. Univs 1991–95; fmr Chair. Council of Deans of Arts and Science of Ont.; fmr mem. Ont. Council on Univ. Affairs; mem. Bd of Dirs Royal Botanical Gardens, Hamilton, Inst. for Work and Health, C. D. Howe Inst., Golden Key Int. Honour Soc., Foundation for Educ. Exchange between Canada and USA, Ont. Cancer Research Network; Trustee Univ. Sharjah, UAE; Hon. DUniv, Hon. DLitt, Hon. LLD. *Publications:* Government Subsidies and the Construction of the Canadian Pacific Railway 1981, The Emergence of Industrial America: Strategic Factors in American Economic Growth Since 1870 1982. *Leisure interests:* fishing, golf. *Address:* Office of the President, McMaster University, 1280 Main Street West, Hamilton, ON L8S4L8, Canada (office). *Telephone:* (905) 525-9140 (office). *E-mail:* preswww@mcmaster.ca (office). *Website:* www.mcmaster.ca/pres (office).

GEORGE, Richard Lee, BS, JD; Canadian energy industry executive; *President and CEO, Suncor Energy Inc.;* b. 16 May 1950, Colorado; s. of Albert H. George and Betty Lou McDill; m. Julie G. White 1972; two s. one d.; ed Harvard Business School, Univ. of Houston, Colorado State Univ., USA; Deputy Man. Dir Sun Oil Britain, London, UK 1982–86, District Man., Aberdeen, UK 1986–87; Vice-Pres. Sun Exploration and Production, Dallas, Texas 1987–88; Man. Dir Sun Int. Exploration and Production, London 1988–91, Pres. and COO Suncor Inc. Ontario, Canada Feb.–Oct. 1991, Pres. and CEO 1991–93, Pres., CEO 1993–94 (fmr Chair.); Dir Enbridge Inc., Dofasco Inc.; Chair. Canadian Council of Chief Executives; Dir GlobalSantaFe Corpn; Canada's Outstanding CEO for 1999, Canadian Business Leader Award 2001, Alberta Business Person of the Year 2001. *Leisure interests:* skiing, golf, fitness. *Address:* Suncor Energy Inc., 112 4th Avenue, SW, PO Box 38, Calgary, Alberta, T2P 2V5, Canada. *Telephone:* (403) 269-8100. *Fax:* (403) 269-6221. *Website:* www.suncor.com (office).

GEORGE, Susan; British actress; b. 26 July 1950; d. of Norman Alfred George and Eileen Percival; m. Simon MacCorkindale 1984; began acting career 1954; pnr Georgian Arabians, Somerset, Amy Int. Productions, London; Dir SG Naturally Ltd, Susan George Photography Ltd. *Films include:* Cup Fever, Davey Jones' Locker, Billion Dollar Brain, Twinky 1969, Spring and Port Wine 1970, Eyewitness 1970, Straw Dogs 1971, Dirty Mary and Crazy Larry 1974, Mandingo 1975, Out of Season 1975, A Small Town in Texas 1977, Tomorrow Never Comes 1978, Venom 1980, A Texas Legend 1981, The House Where Evil Dwells 1982, The Jigsaw Man 1984, Czechmate 1985, Lightning, The White Stallion 1986, Stealing Heaven (producer) 1987, That Summer of White Roses (also producer) 1988, The House That Mary Bought (also producer) 1994, Diana and Me 1997. *Television appearances include:* Swallows and Amazons, Human Jungle, The Right Attitude 1968, Dr Jekyll and Mr Hyde 1973, Lamb to the Slaughter 1979, Royal Jelly 1979, The Bob Hope Special 1979, Pajama Tops 1982, Masquerade 1983, Hotel 1985, Blacke's Magic 1986, Jack the Ripper 1988, Castle of Adventure 1990, Cluedo 1992, Stay Lucky 1992, Eastenders 2001. *Theatre:* The Sound of Music 1962, The Country Girl 1984, Rough Crossing 1987. *Publication:* illustrated book of poetry 1987. *Leisure interests:* Arab horse breeding, singing, photography. *Address:* c/o MacCorkindale & Holton, PO Box 2398, London, W1G 9WZ, England. *Telephone:* (20) 7636-1888 (office). *Fax:* (20) 7636-2888 (office). *E-mail:* info@georgianarabians.com. *Website:* www.georgianarabians.com.

GEORGE TUPOU V, HM The King of Tonga; b. (Siaosi Taufa'ahau Manumataongo Tuku'aho Tupou), 4 May 1948; s. of the late HM King Taufa'ahau Tupou IV and Queen Halaevalu Mata'aho; proclaimed Crown Prince Tupouto'a 1966; Minister of Foreign Affairs 1979–98; co-founder and Dir Tonfon/Shoreline Group Ltd and Peau Vavau Airlines; succeeded to throne 10 September 2006 on the death of his father, crowned 23rd King of Tonga 1 Aug. 2008. *Address:* The Palace, PO Box 6, Nuku'alofa, Tonga (office). *Website:* www.pmo.gov.to.

GEORGEL, Pierre, D. EN LETT.; French museum director; *Director, Musée de l'Orangerie;* b. 14 Jan. 1943, Safi, Morocco; s. of Lucien Georgel and Santia Maria Georgel (née Santini); m. Chantal Martinet 1985; ed Univs of Montpellier, Paris and Lille, Ecole du Louvre, Paris; Asst, Musée du Louvre 1966–70; seconded to CNRS, Paris 1970–74; Curator of Graphic Art, Musée Nat. d'Art Moderne 1974–79; Dir Musée des Beaux-Arts, Dijon 1980–86; Dir Musée Picasso, Paris 1986–89; Chief Curator of French Museums (based at Musée Picasso) 1989–93; Dir Musée nat. de l'Orangerie des Tuileries 1993–; Prof. Ecole du Louvre 1980–85, 1995–96; Conservateur-général du Patrimoine

2000. *Publications:* Dessins de Victor Hugo 1971, La Gloire de Victor Hugo 1985, La Peinture dans la peinture 1987, Courbet: le Poème de la nature 1995, Monet: le Cycle Nymphéas 1999. *Address:* Musée de l'Orangerie, Jardin des Tuileries, 75041 Paris, Cedex 01 (office); 41 Boulevard Saint-Germain, 75005 Paris, France (home). *Telephone:* 1-40-20-67-71 (office). *Fax:* 1-42-61-30-82 (office).

GEORGELIN, Gen. Jean-Louis; French military officer; *Chief of Defence Staff;* b. 30 Aug. 1948; ed Mil. Acad. of St Cyr, Command and Gen. Staff Coll., Fort Leavenworth, Kan., Centre for Advanced Mil. Studies, Paris; First Lt, Platoon Leader, 9th Airborne Infantry Battalion 1970–73; Instructor, Infantry School, Montpellier 1973–76; Capt. Co. Cadre, 153rd Infantry Battalion 1976–79; Dept of Mil. Intelligence 1979–80; Aide-de-camp to Army Chief of Staff 1980–82; promoted to Maj. 1982, to Lt Col 1985, to Col 1988; Chief of Financial Planning Office, Army Staff 1988–91; Commdr 153rd Infantry Battalion 1991–93; Army Asst to Chief of Mil. Cabinet of the Prime Minister 1994–97; promoted to Brig. Gen. 1997; Second-in-Command 11th Airborne Div., then Chief J5, Stabilisation Force (SFOR) in fmr Yugoslavia 1997–98; Chief of Plans and Programmes Div., Jt Defence HQ 1998–2001; promoted to Maj. Gen. 2000, to Lt Gen. 2002; Chief of Mil. Staff 2002–06; promoted to Gen. 2003; Chief of Defence Staff 2006–; Officier, Légion d'honneur, Ordre Nat. du Mérite. *Address:* Ministry of Defence, 14 rue Saint Dominique, 75007 Paris, France (office). *Telephone:* 1-42-19-30-11 (office). *Fax:* 1-47-05-40-91 (office). *E-mail:* courrier-ministre@sdbc.defense.gouv.fr (office). *Website:* www .defense.gouv.fr (office).

GEORGES, Michel A. J., MSc; Belgian geneticist and academic; *Professor of Genetics, Faculty of Veterinary Medicine, University of Liège;* b. 1959, Schoten; ed Univ. of Liège, Univ. of Brussels; Asst Prof., Univ. of Liège 1983–88, Prof. of Genetics, Faculty of Veterinary Medicine 1994–; specializes in animal genetics and genomics; Assoc. Prof., Dept of Human Genetics, Univ. of Utah, USA 1991–93; mem. Belgian Royal Acad. of Medicine; Wolf Foundation Prize in Agric. 2007. *Address:* Université de Liège, Faculty of Veterinary Medicine, 9 place du 20 Août, Liège 4000, Belgium (office). *Telephone:* (4) 366-21-11 (office). *E-mail:* michel.georges@ulg.ac.be (office). *Website:* www.ulg.ac.be/fmv (home).

GEORGESCU, Florin, PhD; Romanian politician and economist; b. 25 Nov. 1953, Bucharest; ed Acad. of Econ. Studies, Bucharest; Fulbright Scholar, Kansas City Univ., USA 1991–92; Assoc. Prof., Acad. of Econ. Studies; Sec. of State, Ministry of Finance 1992, Minister of State 1992–96; mem. Chamber of Deputies (Social Democratic Party) for Olt Electoral Constituency 1996–, Pres. Chamber of Deputies Comm. for Budget, Finance and Banks 2000–, mem. Del. to Parl. Ass. of Black Sea Econ. Cooperation, Parl. Group of Friendship with Repub. of Slovenia 2000–, Pres. Parl. Group of Friendship with Repub. of Bulgaria 2000–; First Deputy Gov. and Vice-Chair. Nat. Bank of Romania. *Publications:* author of more than 200 studies and papers. *Address:* Chamber of Deputies, Parliament Buildings, September 13 Avenue 1, Sector 5, 76117 Bucharest, Romania (office).

GEORGESCU, Peter Andrew, MBA; American advertising executive; *Chairman Emeritus, Young & Rubicam Inc.;* b. 9 March 1939, Bucharest, Romania; s. of V. C. Georgescu and Lygia Bocu; m. Barbara A. Armstrong 1965; one s.; ed Princeton and Stanford Univs; joined Young & Rubicam Inc., New York 1963–, Dir of Marketing 1977–79; Exec. Vice-Pres. and Dir Cen. Region, Young & Rubicam Inc., Chicago 1979–82; Pres. Young & Rubicam Int., New York 1982–86, Young & Rubicam Advertising, New York 1986–99, Young & Rubicam Inc. 1990–99 (CEO 1994–99), Chair. Emer. 2000–; mem. Bd of Dirs Briggs & Stratton Inc.; mem. Council on Foreign Relations. *Address:* c/o Young & Rubicam Inc., 285 Madison Avenue, New York, NY 10017, USA.

GEORGIEV, Georgii Pavlovich; Russian biologist; *Director, Institute of Gene Biology, Russian Academy of Sciences;* b. 4 Feb. 1933, Leningrad (now St Petersburg); s. of Pavel K. Georgiev and Anastasia Georgieva; m. Nekrasova Anastasia Georgieva; one s. one d.; ed First Moscow Medical Inst.; researcher, A. Severtsev Inst. of Morphology of Animals, USSR (now Russian) Acad. of Sciences 1956–63, Head of Lab., V. Engelhart Inst. of Molecular Biology 1963–88, Founder and Dir Inst. of Gene Biology 1990–; Corresp. mem. USSR (now Russian) Acad. of Sciences 1970, mem. 1987; mem. Academia Europaea, Royal Acad. of Spain, German Acad. Leopoldina, Scientific Acad. of Norway, European Molecular Biology Org.; research in molecular biology and genetics; author of discoveries of pro-m RNA and study of nuclear RNP particles containing pro-m RNA and investigation of a new type of nucleoprotein complex structure; first description of nuclear skeleton components; discovery of mobile elements in animals; studies of chromosome structure and transcription-active chromatin, tumour metastasis genes and cancer gene therapy; Lenin Prize 1976, USSR State Prize 1983, Russian State Prize 1996. *Publications include:* Genes of Higher Organisms and their Expression 1989; more than 400 scientific articles. *Leisure interest:* mountain climbing. *Address:* Institute of Gene Biology, Russian Academy of Sciences, Vavilov str. 34/5, 117334 Moscow, Russia (office). *Telephone:* (495) 135-60-89 (office); (495) 125-74-54 (home). *Fax:* (495) 135-41-05 (office). *E-mail:* georg@biogen .msk.su (office); dna@biogen.msk.su (office). *Website:* www.igb.ac.ru (office).

GEORGIEVSKI, Ljubiša; Macedonian diplomatist, politician, writer and director; *President, Sobranie (Parliamentary Assembly);* b. 30 May 1937, Bitola; ed Acad. of Theatre, Film, Radio and Television, Belgrade; fmr Visiting Prof. of Theatre Ontology and Phenomenology, Univ. of Southern California and Univ. of Texas, USA; Dir of more than 120 plays performed throughout fmr Yugoslavia, Poland, Italy, Romania, Bulgaria and USA; active in movt for autonomous and independent Macedonia 1990–; Amb. to Bulgaria (also accred to Moldova) 2000–04; Pres. Sobranie (Parl. Ass.) 2006–; unsuccessful cand. in presidential elections 1994; two Jovan Sterija Popovich Awards, six Golden

Wreath Awards, 11 October Award. *Plays directed include:* Joan of Arc, Drama Theatre Co., Kurshumli 2000. *Films directed include:* The Mountain of Anger, Under the Same Sky, Republic in Flames, The Price of the City. *Publications:* Apocalypse 1988, City 1991, Direct Investments and Short Stories (essays) 1994, Holy Dream, Exercises in Acting Mastery, Ontology of the Theatre, The Political Future of Macedonia; over 200 articles in daily Dnevnik newspaper. *Address:* Sobranie, 1000 Skopje, 11 Oktomvri bb, Former Yugoslav Republic of Macedonia (office). *Telephone:* (2) 3112255 (office). *Fax:* (2) 3111675 (office). *E-mail:* sobranie@sobranie.mk (office). *Website:* www .sobranie.mk (home).

GEPHARDT, Richard (Dick) Andrew, BS, JD; American lawyer and fmr politician; *Senior Counsel, DLA Piper Rudnick Gray Cary US LLP;* b. 31 Jan. 1941, St Louis; s. of Louis Andrew Gephardt and Loreen Estelle Cassell; m. Jane Ann Byrnes 1966; one s. two d.; ed Northwestern Univ. and Univ. of Michigan Law School; mem. Mo. Bar 1965; Pnr firm Thompson and Mitchell, St Louis 1965–76; Alderman 14th Ward, St Louis 1971–76, Democratic Committeeman 1968–71; mem. 95th to 105th Congress from Third Mo. Dist 1979–2005, Democratic Leader 1989–2002; mem. Labor Advisory Bd, American Income Life Insurance Co. 2005–; Sr Counsel, DLA Piper Rudnick Gray Cary US LLP, Washington, DC 2005–; cand. for Democratic nomination to US Presidency 1988, 2004; Pres. Children's Hematology Research Asscn, St Louis Children's Hosp. 1973–76; mem. Bar Asscn, St Louis, Mo., American Legion, Young Lawyers' Soc. (Chair. 1972–73). *Address:* DLA Piper Rudnick Gray Cary US LLP, 1200 Nineteenth Street, NW, Washington, DC 20036-2412, US (office). *Telephone:* (202) 861-3900 (office). *Fax:* (202) 223-2085 (office). *E-mail:* info@dlapiper.com (office). *Website:* www.dlapiper.com (office).

GERASHCHENKO, Victor Vladimirovich; Russian banker and politician; b. 21 Dec. 1937, Leningrad (now St. Petersburg); s. of Vladimir Gerashchenko and Anastasia Klinova; m. Nina Drozdkova 1960; one s. one d.; ed Moscow Financial Inst.; Man. Div. of Foreign Exchange Dept, USSR Bank for Foreign Trade (BFT) 1960–65, Man. Dir of Dept 1972–74, Man. Dir Foreign Exchange Dept 1982–83, Deputy Chair. 1983–89; Dir Moscow Narodny Bank Ltd, London 1965–67, Deputy Gen. Man., then Gen. Man. Beirut 1967–71, Gen. Man. Singapore 1977–82; Chair. Bd Ost-West Handelsbank, Frankfurt am Main 1974–77; Chair. Bd State Bank of USSR 1989–91, Head of Dept Fund Reforma 1991–92; Chair. Cen. Bank of Russian Fed. 1992–94, 1998–2002 (resgnd), Adviser 1994–96; Chair. Bd Moscow Int. Bank (MIB) 1996–98; Chair. Supervisory Bd Vneshtorgbank 1998–2003; elected to State Duma (Parl.) 2003; co-Chair. Party of the Russian Regions (Partiya Rossiiskikh Regionov–PRR), now Motherland (Rodina) 2004; mem. Bd of Dirs Yukos 2004; Order of Banner of Labour (twice). *Leisure interest:* literature. *Address:* c/o Motherland (Rodina), 107031 Moscow, ul. B. Dmitrovka 32/1, Russia (home). *Telephone:* (495) 221-15-15.

GERBERDING, Julie Louise, BA, MD, MPH; American professor of medicine (infectious diseases); *Director, Centers for Disease Control and Prevention; Administrator, Agency for Toxic Substances and Disease Registry;* b. 22 Aug. 1955, Estelline, SDak; m. David Rose; one step-d.; ed Case Western Reserve Univ., Cleveland, OH; internship and residency in internal medicine, Univ. of California, San Francisco (UCSF); Fellowship in Clinical Pharmacology and Infectious Diseases, UCSF; Faculty mem. and Dir of Prevention Epicentre, UCSF –1998; Dir Healthcare Quality Promotion Div., Nat. Center for Infectious Diseases (NCID) 1998–2001, Acting Deputy Dir NCID 2001–02; Dir Centers for Disease Control and Prevention (CDC) and Admin. Agency for Toxic Substances and Disease Registry 2002–; currently Assoc. Prof. of Medicine (Infectious Diseases), UCSF and Assoc. Clinical Prof. of Medicine (Infectious Diseases), Emory Univ.; Assoc. Ed. American Journal of Medicine; mem. Editorial Bd Annals of Internal Medicine; fmr mem. Bd of Scientific Counselors, Nat. Center for Infectious Diseases, CDC HIV Advisory Cttee; Scientific Program Cttee, Nat. Conf. on Human Retroviruses; mem. American Soc. for Clinical Investigation, American Coll. of Physicians, Soc. for Healthcare Epidemiology of America, American Epidemiology Soc., Phi Beta Kappa, Alpha Omega Alpha; Fellow, Infectious Diseases Soc. of America, also Chair. Cttee on Professional Devt and Diversity and mem. Nominations Cttee; consultant to Nat. Insts of Health, American Medical Asscn, Occupational Safety and Health Admin, Nat. AIDS Comm., Congressional Office of Tech. Assessment, WHO; ranked by Forbes magazine amongst 100 Most Powerful Women (12th) 2005, (23rd) 2006, (32nd) 2007, (24th) 2008. *Publications:* more than 140 peer-reviewed publs and textbook chapters. *Leisure interests:* scuba diving, reading on the beach, gardening. *Address:* Centers for Disease Control and Prevention, 1600 Clifton Road, Atlanta, GA 30333, USA (office). *Telephone:* (404) 639-3311 (office). *Website:* www.cdc.gov (office).

GERDAU JOHANNPETER, André; Brazilian business executive; *CEO, Metalúrgica Gerdau;* b. 1963; s. of Jorge Gerdau Johannpeter and Erica Johannpeter (neé Bier); s. of Jorge Gerdau Johannpeter (q.v.); m.; three c.; ed Catholic Univ. of Rio Grande do Sul, Univ. of Toronto, Canada, Univ. of Pennsylvania, USA; joined Metalúrgica Gerdau 1981, Asst to Exec. Pres., Gerdau Ameristeel (US operation), Cambridge, Mass 1992–94, Business Devt Dir 2001–02, COO Canada operations 2002–03, COO 2002–03, Vice-Pres. Gerdau Ameristeel 2003–04, Exec. Vice-Pres. Metalúrgica Gerdau 2002–07, Dir of Marketing and Sales, Raw Materials, Procurement, Logistics, Human Resources, and Organizational Devt 2004–07, CEO 2007–; mem. Brazilian Olympic Equestrian Team 1996–2000. *Sporting achievements:* Olympic Bronze Medal for Equestrianism 1996, 2000. *Leisure interests:* horseriding. *Address:* Grupo Gerdau, Avenida Farrapos 1811, Floresta, 90220-005 Porto Alegre, Rio Grande do Sul, Brazil (office). *Website:* www.gerdau.com.br (office).

GERDAU JOHANNPETER, Jorge; Brazilian business executive; *Chairman Metalúrgica Gerdau;* b. 8 Dec. 1936, Rio de Janeiro; s. of Curt

Johannpeter and Helda Gerdau; m. 1st Erica Bier; five s. including Andre Gerdau Johannpeter (q.v.); m. 2nd Cristina Harbich; m. 3rd Maria Helena; ed Fed. Univ. of Rio Grande do Sul; began career at Metalúrgica Gerdau as steelworker 1950, Dir 1973, CEO 1983–2007, Chair. 1983–; Pres. Quality and Productivity Programme, Rio Grande do Sul; Pres. Council for Competitive Brazilian Devt 2001–; Coordinator, Brazilian Business Action; mem. Admin. Council, Petrobras; mem. Council on Econ. and Social Devt; Grand Cross, Nat. Scientific Order of Merit 2002; Willy Korf Steel Vision Award 2001. *Leisure interests:* Race horse training, surfing. *Address:* Presidência Grupo Gerdau, Avenida Farrapos 1811, Floresta, 90220-005 Porto Alegre, Rio Grande do Sul, Brazil (office). *E-mail:* jorge.gerdau@gerdau.com.br (office). *Website:* www .gerdau.com.br (office).

GERE, Richard; American actor and activist; b. 31 Aug. 1949, Phila; m. 1st Cindy Crawford (q.v.) 1991 (divorced 1995); m. 2nd Carey Lowell 2002; one s. one step-d.; ed Univ. of Massachusetts; fmrly played trumpet, piano, guitar and bass and composed music with various groups; stage performances with Provincetown Playhouse and off-Broadway; appeared in London and Broadway productions of The Taming of the Shrew, A Midsummer Night's Dream and Broadway productions of Habeas Corpus and Bent; film debut 1975; Founding Chair. and Pres. Tibet House, New York 1987–91; f. Gere Foundation 1991; mem. Bd of Dirs Int. Campaign for Tibet 1992–, Chair. 1995–; Founder and Dir Healing the Divide Foundation 2001–; Hon. DLit (Leicester) 1992; Eleanor Roosevelt Humanitarian Award 2000, Marian Anderson Award 2007. *Films include:* Report to the Commissioner 1975, Baby Blue Marine 1976, Looking for Mr Goodbar 1977, Days of Heaven 1978, Blood Brothers 1978, Yanks 1979, American Gigolo 1980, An Officer and a Gentleman 1982, Breathless 1983, Beyond the Limit 1983, The Cotton Club 1984, King David 1985, Power 1986, No Mercy 1986, Miles From Home 1989, 3000 1989, Internal Affairs 1990, Pretty Woman 1990, Rhapsody in August 1991, Final Analysis 1991, Sommersby (co-exec. producer) 1993, Mr Jones (co-exec. producer) 1994, Intersection 1994, First Knight 1995, Primal Fear 1996, Red Corner 1997, Burn Hollywood Burn 1998, Runaway Bride 1999, Dr T. and the Women 2000, Autumn in New York 2000, The Mothman Prophecies 2002, Unfaithful 2002, Chicago (Golden Globe for Best Actor in a Musical 2003) 2002, Shall We Dance? 2004, Bee Season 2005, The Hoax 2006, The Flock 2007, The Hunting Party 2007, I'm Not There 2007, Nights in Rodanthe 2008. *Publication:* Pilgrim Photo Collection 1998. *Address:* c/o Andrea Jaffe Inc., 9229 Sunset Boulevard, Suite 414, Los Angeles, CA 90069; c/o Healing the Divide, 341 Lafayette Street, #4416, New York, NY 10012, USA. *Website:* www .healingthedivide.org; www.gerefoundation.org.

GERGAWI, HH Mohammed al-; United Arab Emirates business executive and politician; *Minister of State for Cabinet Affairs, UAE Council of Ministers;* m.; three c.; ed Univ. of Mich., USA; CEO Dubai Holding (which manages cos, including Dubai Properties, Dubai International Properties, Jumeirah International, Dubai International Capital, Dubai Internet City, Dubai Media City, Dubai Knowledge Village, Dubai Industrial City, Dubai Humanitarian City) 2004–; Minister of State for Cabinet Affairs, UAE Council of Ministers 2006–; currently Sec.-Gen. Govt of Dubai Exec. Council; Chair. Dubai Devt & Investment Authority (DDIA); CEO Exec. Office of HH Sheikh Muhammad bin Rashid al-Maktoum, ruler of Dubai; Chair. Arab Strategy Forum; Chair. Young Arab Leaders; bd mem. Dubai Media Inc.; founder, Dubai Autism Center, UAE Disabled Sports Federation; Vice-Chair. Handicapped Club; Royal Order of Merit, Morocco, American Business Council Award. *Address:* Dubai Holding, PO Box 66000, Dubai, United Arab Emirates (office). *Telephone:* 3300300 (office). *Fax:* 3300303 (office). *Website:* www .dubaiholding.com (office).

GERGEN, David Richmond, JD; American fmr government official; *Professor of Public Service and Director, Center for Public Leadership, John F. Kennedy School of Government, Harvard University;* b. 9 May 1942, Durham, NC; s. of Dr John Gergen; m. Anne Gergen; one s. one d.; ed Yale and Harvard Univs; staff asst, Nixon Admin, Washington, DC 1971–72; Special Asst to Pres. and Chief, White House writing/research team 1973–74; Special Counsel to Pres. Ford and Dir White House Office Communications 1975–77; Research Fellow, American Enterprise Inst.; Man. Ed. American Enterprise Inst. Public Opinion magazine 1977–81; Asst to Pres. Reagan, Staff Dir White House 1981; Asst to Pres. Reagan for Communications 1981–83; Research Fellow, Inst. of Politics, John F. Kennedy School of Govt, Harvard Univ. 1983–85, Prof. of Public Service 1999–, Dir Center for Public Leadership 2000–; Man. Ed. US News & World Report, Washington, DC 1985–86, Ed.-at-Large 1986–; Commentator, ABC News Nightline 2000–, Marketplace 2002–; Moderator World @ Large PBS discussion series 2000–02; Adviser to Pres. Clinton 1993–2001, for Foreign Policy 1994–95, to Sec. of State 1994; Visiting Prof., Duke Univ., N Carolina 1995–; Sr Fellow Aspen Inst.; mem. Council on Foreign Relations, Trilateral Comm. *Publications include:* Eyewitness to Power: The Essence of Leadership – Nixon to Clinton 2000. *Address:* J.F. Kennedy School of Government, Harvard University, 79 J.F. Kennedy Street, Cambridge, MA 02138 (office); 31 Ash Street, Cambridge, MA 02138, USA (home). *Website:* www.ksg.harvard.edu/leadership (office); www.usnews.com/ usnews/opinion/dgergen.htm (office); www.davidgergen.com.

GERGIEV, Valery Abesalovich; Russian conductor; *Principal Conductor, London Symphony Orchestra;* b. 2 May 1953, Moscow; m. Natalia Gergieva; one s. one d.; ed Leningrad Conservatory; prize winner at All-Union Conductors' Competition, Moscow (while still a student) and at Karajan Competition, Berlin; Chief Conductor Armenian State Orchestra 1981–84; Asst Conductor to Yuriy Temirkanov) Kirov Opera, Leningrad; Music Dir Kirov (now Mariinsky) Opera Theatre Orchestra 1988–, also Artistic and Gen. Dir 1996–; Prin. Guest Conductor Rotterdam Philharmonic 1989–92, Prin. Conductor 1992–2008, Music Dir 1995–2008; Prin. Guest Conductor New York Metropolitan Opera 1998–2008; Prin. Conductor London Symphony Orchestra 2007–; Artistic Dir St Petersburg Stars of the White Nights Festival, Moscow Easter Festival, Gergiev Festival Rotterdam, Mikkeli Int. Festival, Finland; tours extensively in Europe and the USA; has guest-conducted Berlin Philharmonic, Dresden Philharmonic, Bayerischer Rundfunk, Royal Concertgebouw, London Philharmonic, City of Birmingham Symphony, Royal Philharmonic, London Symphony, Orchestra of Santa Cecilia, Japan Philharmonic; orchestras of Boston, Chicago, Cleveland, New York, San Francisco and Toronto; operas at Covent Garden, Metropolitan and San Francisco; State Prize of Russia 1994, 1999, Musical Life Magazine Musician of the Year 1992, 1993, Classical Music Award 1994, Musical America Yearbook Conductor of the Year 1996, People's Artist of Russia 1996, Triumph Prize 1999, Order of Friendship, Russia 2000, Order of St Mesrop Mashtots, Armenia 2000, Russian Presidential Prize 2002, UNESCO Artist of the World 2003, Nat. Pride of Russia Award 2003, For Work and the Fatherland Award 2003, World Econ. Forum Crystal Prize 2004, People's Artist of Ukraine 2004, Royal Swedish Acad. of Music Polar Music Prize 2005. *Recordings:* Prokofiev Complete Symphonies (Gramophone Award for Best Orchestral Recording 2007) 2006. *Address:* Columbia Artists Management, 1790 Broadway, New York, NY 10019-1412, USA (office); London Symphony Orchestra Administration, 6th Floor, Barbican Centre, Silk Street, London, EC2Y 8DS, England; Mariinsky Theatre, Teatralnaya pl. 1, St Petersburg, 190000, Russia. *Telephone:* (212) 841-9500 (office); (20) 7588-1116 (London); (812) 326-41-41. *Fax:* (212) 841-9744 (office); (20) 7374-0127 (London); (812) 314-17-44. *E-mail:* info@cami.com (office); admin@lso.co.uk; post@mariinsky .ru. *Website:* www.cami.com (office); lso.co.uk; www.mariinsky.ru/en.

GERHARDS, Kaspars; Latvian economist and politician; *Minister of the Economy;* b. 7 Feb. 1969, Jelgava; ed Univ. of Latvia, Goethe Inst. and Westfälische Wilhelms-Universität, Germany; CEO Selga 1991–93; Asst Minister, Ministry of the Economy 1993–95; Programme Ed. Economists Asscn May–Sept. 1995; Project Man. Norway–Latvia Business Devt Fund 1995–96; adviser to the Pres. of Latvia on econ. affairs 1996–99; State Sec., Ministry of the Economy 1999–2007, Minister of the Economy 2007–; mem. For Fatherland and Freedom Union/Latvian Nat. Independence Movt Party; mem. Bd of Dirs Naukšēni 1995–96, Lords 1995–96, Libanons 1995–96. *Address:* Ministry of the Economy, Brīvības iela 55, Rīga 1519, Latvia (office). *Telephone:* 6701-3101 (office). *Fax:* 6728-0882 (office). *E-mail:* pasts@em.gov .lv (office). *Website:* www.em.gov.lv (office).

GERHARDT, Wolfgang; German politician; *Parliamentary Leader, Free Democratic Party;* b. 31 Dec. 1943, Ulrichstein-Helpershain; two c.; Hessian Minister for Science and Art 1970; Party Whip FDP, State Parl., Hesse 1983–87, 1991–94, Rep. and Deputy Prime Minister 1987–91; Chair. FDP 1994–2001; Leader FDP Group in Bundestag (Parl.) 1998–. *Publication:* Es geht – wir haben alle Chancen 1997. *Address:* Liebenaustrasse 8B, 75191 Wiesbaden, Germany (office). *E-mail:* wolfgang.gerhardt@bundestag.de (office). *Website:* www.fdp.de (office); www.wolfgang-gerhardt.de (home).

GERINGER, James E. (Jim), BS; American fmr politician and business executive; *Director of Policy and Enterprise Solutions, ESRI;* b. 24 April 1944, Wheatland, Wyo.; m. Sherri Geringer; five c.; ed Kansas State Univ.; farmer and substitute teacher; officer USAF, Space Devt Programs; fmr Wyo. State Rep. Platte Co.; mem. Wyo. State Senate for Platte Co., Dist 3 until 1995; Gov. of Wyoming 1994–2003; Dir Policy and Enterprise Solutions, ESRI (software firm) 2003–; fmr Chair. Western Govs.' Asscn, Educ. Comm. of States; Republican. *Address:* ESRI, 380 New York Street, Redlands, CA 92373-8100, USA. *Telephone:* (909) 793-2853. *Website:* www.esri.com (office).

GERKAN, Meinhard von, PhD, Dipl-Ing; German architect; *CEO, gmp – von Gerkan, Marg and Partners Architects;* b. 3 Jan. 1935, Riga, USSR (now Latvia); m. Sabine von Gerkan; six c.; freelance architect in collaboration with Volkwin Marg 1965– (six other partners 1974–); with Freie Akad. der Künste Hamburg 1972–74; Prof., Inst. für Baugestaltung A, Technische Univ. Brunswick 1974–; with Kuratorium Jürgen-Ponto-Stiftung Frankfurt 1982; Guest Prof., Nihon Univ., Tokyo 1988, Univ. of Pretoria 1993; Visiting Prof., Dalian Univ. of Tech., Architecture and Art Coll., People's Repub. of China 2007; Founder and CEO gmp Foundation to enhance architectural educ. 2007–; work includes airport bldgs, cultural insts, railway stations, hotels, offices, public bldgs, housing, master plans and interior design and housing throughout Germany and in Italy, Latvia, Turkey, China, Viet Nam, Algeria, Saudi Arabia, South Africa, UAE; mem. Convent Chairmanship of Bundesstiftung Baukultur, Berlin 2003; Pres. Acad. for Architectural Culture 2007; mem. Akad. der Künste; Hon. FAIA 1995, Inst. of Mexican Architects 1995; Hon. mem. Berlin-Brandenburg Acad. of Sciences 2000; Hon. Dr in Protestant Theology (Philipps-Univ., Marburg) 2002; Hon Dr in Design (Christian Univ., Chung li, Taiwan) 2005, (East China Normal Univ. Coll. of Design, Shanghai) 2007; more than 230 first prizes at nat. and int. architectur competitions, including Fritz Schumacher Award 2000, Romanian Nat. Award 2002, Plakette of Freie Akad. der Künste, Hamburg 2004, Grand Award, Asscn of German Architects (BDA) 2005; more than 130 award for outstanding architecture. *Publications:* Architektur 1966–78 1978, Die Verantwortung des Architekten 1982, Architektur 1978–83 1983, Alltagsarchitektur, Gestalt und Ungestalt 1987, Architektur 1983–88 1988, Architektur 1988–91 1992, von Gerkan, Marg and Partners 1993, Idea and Model: 30 years of architectural models 1994, Architektur im Dialog 1994, Culture Bridge 1995, Architecture 1991–95 1995, Architecture for Transportation 1997, Architecture 1995–97 1998, Möbel Furniture 1998, Architecture 1997–99: Vol. 1 Selected Projects 2000, Modell Virtuell 2000, Architecture 1999–2000 2002, Vol. 2 Erlebnisräume – Spaces Design Construction 2002, Geometrie der Stille 2002, Luchao – Born from a Drop: Architecture for China 2003, Architecture 2000–01 2003, Vol. 3 Berliner Bauten und Projekte, 1965–2005 2005, Ideal

City – Real Projects in China 2005, Architecture 2001–03 2005, Vol. 4 Private Houses 2006, Vol. 5 Möbel Furniture 2007, Bauten Buildings 2007. *Address:* Elbchaussee 139, 22763 Hamburg, Germany (office). *Telephone:* (40) 881510 (office). *Fax:* (40) 88151177 (office). *E-mail:* hamburg-e@gmp-architekten.de (office). *Website:* www.gmp-architekten.de (office).

GERLACH, Rolf; German banking executive; *President, Westfaelisch-Lippischer Sparkassen- und Giroverband;* b. 1953, Witten; Pres. Westfälisch-Lippischer Sparkassen und Giroverband (Asscn of Savings and Loan Banks of Westphalia-Lippe) 1990–; Chair. Supervisory Bd WestLB AG 2004–07; Deputy Chair. Admin. Bd, DekaBank Deutsche Girozentrale; mem. Bd of Dirs Witten/Herdecke Univ. *Address:* Westfaelisch-Lippischer Sparkassen- und Giroverband, Regina-Protmann-Strasse 1, 48159 Muenster, Germany (office). *Telephone:* (251) 2104602 (office). *Fax:* (251) 2104603 (office). *Website:* www.wlsgv-muenster.de (office).

GERMAIN, Paul, DèsSc; French professor of theoretical mechanics; *Honorary Permanent Secretary, Académie de Sciences;* b. 28 Aug. 1920, Saint-Malo; s. of Paul Germain and Elisabeth Frangeul; m. Marie-Antoinette Gardent 1942; one s. one d.; ed Ecole Normale Supérieure de Paris and Univ. of Paris; research engineer, Office Nat. d'Etudes et de Recherches Aérospatiales (ONERA) 1946–49, Dir 1962–68; Assoc. Prof., Univ. of Poitiers 1949–54; Prof., Univ. of Lille 1954–58; Prof. of Theoretical Mechanics, Univ. of Paris 1958–77, Ecole Polytechnique 1977–85, Univ. Pierre and Marie Curie 1985–87; Visiting Prof., Brown Univ., USA 1953–54, Stanford Univ., USA 1969–70; mem. Acad. des Sciences 1970–, Perm. Sec. 1975–96, Hon. Perm. Sec. 1996–; mem. Int. Acad. of Astronautics 1966, Nat. Air and Space Acad. 1983, Pontifical Acad. of Sciences 1986; Foreign mem. American Acad. of Arts and Sciences 1963, Accad. Nazionale dei Lincei, Rome 1976, Polish Acad. of Sciences 1978; Foreign Assoc. Nat. Acad. of Eng, Washington 1979; Foreign Assoc. Acad. Royale Belgique des Lettres, des Sciences et des Arts 1984, Acad. of Sciences (USSR) 1988; Emer. mem. Acad. des Technologies 2000–; Hon. Fellow, AIAA 1981; Commdr Légion d'honneur, Grand-Croix Ordre nat. du Mérite, Medaille de l'aéronautique, Commdr des Palmes académiques; Dr hc (Louvain) 1961, (Strathclyde) 1975, (Madrid Univ.) 1980, (Brussels) 1984; Montyon de l'Académie des sciences 1949, Prix Henri de Parville de l'Académie des sciences 1960, Médaille de l'Aéronautique 1963, Prix Modesto Panetti de l'Académie des sciences de Turin 1978. *Publications:* Mécanique des milieux continus 1962, Cours de mécanique des milieux continus 1973, Mécanique 1986 and more than 100 papers on theoretical aerodynamics, magnetohydrodynamics, shock wave theory and mechanics of continua, Introduction à la méchanique des milieux continues (co-author) 1993–95, Mémoire d'un scientifique chrétien 2006. *Leisure interests:* hiking, swimming, skiing. *Address:* Institut de France, 23 quai de Conti, 75006, Paris (office); 3 Avenue de Champaubert, 75015 Paris, France (home). *Telephone:* 1-44-41-43-52 (office); 1-43-06-35-53 (home). *Fax:* 1-44-41-43-74 (home). *E-mail:* paul.germain@academie-technologies.fr (office). *Website:* www.academie-sciences.fr/actualites/nouvelles_gb.htm (office).

GERMAIN, Sylvie, PhD; French writer; b. 1948, Châteauroux; ed Sorbonne, Paris; civil servant, attached to Ministry of Culture 1981–86, taught at L'École française, Prague 1986–93, full-time novelist 1994–. *Publications:* novels: Le Livre des nuits 1985, Nuit d'Ambre 1987, Jours de colère (Prix Femina) 1989, Opéra muet 1989, L'Enfant Méduse 1991, La Pleurante des rues de Prague 1992, Immensités 1993, Eclats de sel 1996, L'Encre du poulpe 1998, Tobie des marais 1998, La Chanson des mal-aimants 2002, Magnus (Prix Goncourt des Lycéens) 2005; essays: Les Echos du silence 1996, Céphalophores 1996, Patience et songe de lumière: Vermeer 1996, Bohuslav Reyneck à Petrov: un nomade en sa demeure 1998, Etty Hillesum 1999, Mourir un peu 2000, La Grande nuit de Toussaint, Le Temps qu'il fait 2000, Cracovie à vol d'oiseau 2000, Célébration de la Paternité 2001, J'ai envie de rompre le silence (with René Vouland and Gérard Vouland) 2001, Les Personnages 2004. *Address:* c/o Dedalus Ltd, Langford Lodge, St Judith's Lane, Sawtry, Cambridgeshire, PE28 5XE, England.

GERMAN, Aleksey Georgievich; Russian film director; b. 20 July 1938, Leningrad; s. of Yuri Pavlovich German and Tatyana Rittenberg; m. Svetlana Karmalina; one s. Aleksey German, Jr; ed Leningrad State Inst. of Theatre, Music and Cinema; dir theatres in Leningrad and Smolensk; has worked with Lenfilm Studios 1964–; Artistic Dir St Petersburg experimental film studio; USSR State Prize 1988, Golden Ram Prize for Person of the Cinematographic Year for the Creation of a Unique Studio, Institution and Persistence 1992, Triumph Prize 1998, Sergei Dovlatov Prize 1998. *Films include:* The Seventh Traveller 1968, Twenty Days Without War (George Sadoul Prize 1977) 1977, My Friend Ivan Lapshin (two prizes, People's Artists 1988) 1984, Trial on the Road (State Prize of Russia 1988) 1986, Khrustalev, My Car! 1997. *Address:* Marsovo Pole 7, Apt 37, 191041 St Petersburg, Russia (home). *Telephone:* (812) 315-17-06 (home).

GERMANOVA, Yevdokiya Alekseyevna; Russian actress; b. 8 Nov. 1959, Moscow; ed State Inst. of Theatre Art; with Oleg Tabakov Theatre Studio 1983–; roles in productions including Mystery by J. B. Priestley (production in Austria), Trust, Love, Hope by O. Horvat (Dir M. Schell); Stanislavski Prize of Russia and numerous prizes for best women's roles at int. and nat. festivals in Kiev, Karlovy Vary, Nizhny Novgorod, Ange, Moscow. *Films include:* Limited Life 1989, Crazy 1989, The Miss 1991, The Inner Circle 1991, Hammer and Sickle 1994, A Moslem 1995, One's Own Shadow 2000, Barbarian 2003, Russkoe 2004, Lilacs 2007, Vanechka 2007. *Address:* Chaplygina Str., 1A, Oleg Tabakov Theatre Studio, Moscow, Russia. *Telephone:* (495) 916-21-21 (office).

GERSON, Allan, MA, JD, LL.M, JSD; American lawyer and academic; *Chairman, Gerson International Law Group;* ed NY Univ. Law School, Hebrew Univ. of Jerusalem, Israel, Yale Univ.; joined US Justice Dept 1977, joined Office of Special Investigations (OSI) 1979 to prosecute Nazi collaborators; apptd Counsel to US Ambs to UN Jeane Kirkpatrick and Gen. Vernon Walters 1981; fmr Deputy Asst Attorney-Gen. for Legal Counsel and Counsellor for Int. Affairs, US Dept of Justice; brought first lawsuit against Libya on behalf of families of victims of 1988 Pan Am Lockerbie bombing, led lawsuit against Saudi Royal family and Govt of Sudan on behalf of families of victims of World Trade Center bombing 2001; Sr Fellow, American Enterprise Inst. 1986–89; Distinguished Prof. of Int. Law and Transactions, George Mason Univ. 1989–95; currently Chair. Gerson Int. Law Group PLLC, Washington, DC; fmr Research Prof. of Int. Relations, George Washington Univ. and Co-Dir Inst. for Peacebuilding and Devt (IPD), Elliott School of Int. Affairs; fmr Exec. Dir Morocco–US Council on Trade and Investment; Sr Fellow for Int. Law and Orgs, Council on Foreign Relations 1998–2000; fmr Resident Scholar, American Enterprise Inst. *Publications:* Israel, the West Bank and International Law 1978, Lawyers' Ethics: Contemporary Dilemmas 1980, The Kirkpatrick Mission: Diplomacy without Apology 1991, The Price of Terror: One Bomb. One Plane. 270 Lives. The History-Making Struggle for Justice After Pan Am 103 (co-author) 2001, Privatizing Peace: From Conflict to Security 2002; articles in professional and popular publs. *Address:* Gerson International Law Group, 2131 S Street, NW, Washington, DC 20008, USA (office). *Telephone:* (202) 234-9717 (office).

GERSON, Mark; British photographer; b. 3 Oct. 1921, London; s. of Bernard Gerson and Esther Gerson; m. Renée Cohen 1949; two d.; ed Cen. Foundation School for Boys, London and Regent Polytechnic, London; served in RAF 1941–46; taught photography under EVT scheme while serving in RAF in Paris 1946; specialist portrait photographer concentrating on literary personalities and industrialists; ran photographic studio 1947–87; now freelance photographer; major exhbns Fox Talbot Museum, Lacock, Wilts. 1981, Shaw Theatre, London 1983, Writers Observed, Nat. Theatre, London 1984, The Poetry Library, Royal Festival Hall 1991, Literati, Nat. Portrait Gallery, London 1996; Fellow, British Inst. of Professional Photography. *Leisure interests:* cinema, theatre. *Address:* 3 Regal Lane, Regent's Park, London, NW1 7TH, England. *Telephone:* (20) 7286-5894; (20) 7267-9246. *Fax:* (20) 7267-9246. *E-mail:* mark.gerson@virgin.com.

GERSTNER, Louis Vincent, Jr, BA, MBA; American business executive; *Chairman, Carlyle Group;* b. 1 March 1942, New York; s. of Louis Vincent Gerstner and Marjorie Rutan Gerstner; m. Elizabeth Robins Link 1968; one s. one d.; ed Dartmouth Coll. and Harvard Univ.; Dir McKinsey & Co., New York 1965–78; Exec. Vice-Pres. American Express Co., New York 1978–81, Vice-Chair. 1981–83, Chair. Exec. Cttee 1983–85, Pres. 1985–89, Chair., CEO RJR Nabisco 1989–93; Chair., CEO IBM 1993–2002; Vice-Chair. New American Schools Devt Corpn Bd 1991–98; Dir The New York Times Co. 1986–97, Bristol-Myers Squibb Co.; mem. Exec. Cttee, Bd of Trustees Jt Council on Econ. Educ. 1975–87, Chair. 1983–85; mem. Bd of Dirs Memorial Sloan Kettering Hosp. 1978–89, 1998–, Vice-Chair. 2000–; Chair. Computer Systems Policy Project 1999–2001; Advisory Bd DaimlerChrysler 2001–, Sony Corpn 2002–; Chair. Carlyle Group 2002–; mem. Policy Cttee, Business Roundtable 1991–98; mem. Bd of Overseers Annenberg Inst. for School Reform, Brown Univ.; mem. Business Council, American China Soc., Council on Foreign Relations, Nat. Security Telecommunications Advisory Cttee 1994–97, Advisory Cttee for Trade Policy and Negotiations 1995–, Nat. Acad. of Eng; Trustee NY Public Library 1991–96, American Museum of Natural History 2004–; Co-Chair. of Achieve 1996–2002; founder and Chair. The Teaching Commission 2003–; Hon. KBE 2001; Hon. DBA (Boston Coll.) 1994; Hon. LLD (Wake Forest, Brown) 1997; Hon. DEng (Rensselaer Polytechnic Inst.) 1999; Washington Univ. Acad. for Excellence in Business, Eng and Technology 1999; numerous awards for work in educ. *Publication:* Reinventing Education (co-author) 1994; Who Says Elephants Can't Dance: Inside IBM's Historic Turnaround 2002. *Address:* The Carlyle Group, 1001 Pennsylvania Avenue, NW, Suite 220 South, Washington, DC 20004-2505 (office); The Teaching Commission, 365 Fifth Avenue, Suite 6200, New York, NY 10016, USA. *Telephone:* (202) 347-2626 (office). *Fax:* (202) 347-1818 (office). *Website:* www.thecarlylegroup.com (office); www.theteachingcommission.org.

GERTH, Donald R., PhD; American academic and university administrator; *President Emeritus, California State University;* b. 4 Dec. 1928, Chicago, Ill.; s. of the late George C. Gerth and Madeleine A. Canavan; m. Beverly J. Hollman 1955; two d.; ed Univ. of Chicago; served in USAF 1952–56; Lecturer in History, Univ. of Philippines 1953–54; Admissions Counsellor, Univ. of Chicago 1956–58; Assoc. Dean of Students, Admissions and Records and mem. Dept of Govt, San Francisco State Univ. 1958–63; Assoc. Dean of Institutional Relations and Student Affairs, Calif. State Univ., Chico 1963–64; Dean of Students 1964–68, Prof. of Political Science 1964–76, Co-Dir Danforth Foundation Research Project 1968–69, Coordinator, Inst. for Local Govt and Public Service and of Public Admin. 1968–70, Assoc. Vice-Pres. for Acad. Affairs and Dir Int. Programs (Dir of Center at Univ. of Skopje, Yugoslavia) 1969–70, Vice-Pres. for Acad. Affairs 1970–76; Pres. and Prof. of Political Science and Public Admin., Calif. State Univ., Dominguez Hills 1976–84; Pres. and Prof. of Public Policy and Public Admin. Calif. State Univ., Sacramento 1984–2003, now Emer.; Pres. Int. Asscn of Univ. Presidents 1996–99; numerous other appointments; hon. prof.; numerous hon. doctorates. *Publications:* The Invisible Giant 1971; numerous articles. *Leisure interest:* international affairs. *Address:* California State University, 2000 State University Drive, Sacramento, CA 95819 (office); 7132 Secret Garden Loop, Roseville, CA 95747-6039, USA (home). *Telephone:* (916) 278-7420 (office); (916) 771-3412 (home). *Fax:* (916) 771-3413 (home). *E-mail:* dongerth@csus.edu (office). *Website:* www.calstate.edu (office).

GERWEL, Gert Johannes (Jakes), DLitt, DPhil; South African university administrator, academic and business executive; *Chairman, South African Airways (Proprietary) Limited;* b. 18 Jan. 1947, Somerset East; s. of John Gerwel and Sarah Becket; m. Phoebe Abrahams 1970; one s. one d.; ed Paterson High School, Port Elizabeth and Univs of Western Cape and Brussels; Educ. Adviser, SA Students' Org. Durban 1972–73; Lecturer, Sr Lecturer, Prof., Dean, Univ. of Western Cape, Rector and Vice-Chancellor 1987–94; Dir-Gen. Office of Pres. and Sec. to Parl. 1994–99; Nelson Mandela Prof. in the Humanities, Univ. of Cape Town and Univ. of the Western Cape 1999–; Chancellor Rhodes Univ. 1999–; mem. Bd of Dirs Naspers, Old Mutual and Goldfields Ltd; Chair. South African Airways Ltd 2004–, Brimstone Investment Corpn, Educor, Nelson Mandela Foundation; Trustee African Centre for the Constructive Resolution of Disputes; Chair. Careers Research and Information Centre, Cape Town, Equal Opportunity Foundation, Johannesburg, Community Agency for Social Enquiry, Johannesburg; Order of the Southern Cross (Gold). *Publication:* Literatuur en Apartheid 1983. *Leisure interest:* cricket. *Address:* South African Airways (Proprietary) Limited, Airway Park, Jones Road, Johannesburg International Airport, Kempton Park, Johannesburg, 1627 (office); Private Bag X1000, Cape Town 8000, South Africa. *Telephone:* (11) 9781111 (office). *Website:* www.flysaa.com (office).

GESANG, Doje; Chinese party official; b. Feb. 1936, Qinghai Prov.; s. of Giamucuo and Sangdang Shiji; m. Zenen Namu 1956; one s. three d.; ed Nat. Middle School, Sining, Qinghai and in Beijing; returned to Sining as a corresp. 1955; Vice-Chair. Qinghai Provincial People's Congress Standing Cttee 1991–; started writing poetry 1956. *Publications:* Legend of Hot Spring, The Childbirth of a New Town at Daybreak, The Name of Maji Snow Mountain, You are an Infant of Daylight, Raindrops from the Clouds 1992. *Leisure interests:* riding, hunting, painting.

GESCHKE, Charles M., AB, MS, PhD; American computer executive; *Co-Chairman, Adobe Systems Inc.;* ed Carnegie-Mellon Univ., Xavier Univ.; fmr Prin. Scientist and Researcher, Xerox Palo Alto Research Center (PARC), f. PARC Imaging Sciences Lab. 1980; co-founder Adobe Systems Inc. 1982–, Pres. 1987–2000, Co-Chair. 2000–; Dir Rambus, Inc.; mem. Nat. Acad. of Eng, Govt-Univ. Industry Research Roundtable, Nat. Acad. of Sciences; mem. Bd of Govs. San Francisco Symphony; mem. Advisory Bd Carnegie-Mellon Univ., Princeton Univ.; mem. Bd of Trustees Univ. of San Francisco; honoured by several orgs. including Asscn for Computing Machinery (ACM), Nat. Computer Graphics Asscn, Rochester Inst. of Tech. *Address:* Adobe Systems Inc., 345 Park Avenue, San José, CA 95110-2704, USA (office). *Telephone:* (408) 536-6000 (office). *Fax:* (408) 537-6000 (home). *Website:* www.adobe.com (office).

GETTY, Donald; Canadian politician; b. 30 Aug. 1933, Westmount, Québec; s. of Charles Ross Getty and Beatrice Lillian Getty; m. Margaret Mitchell 1955; four s.; ed Univ. of Western Ont.; joined Imperial Oil Ltd Edmonton 1955; Lands and Contracts Man. Midwestern Industrial Gas Ltd 1961; Pres. and Man. Dir Baldonnel Oil and Gas Ltd 1964–67; Partner, Doherty, Roadhouse & McCuaig Ltd (investment firm) 1967; mem. Alberta Legis. 1967–79, 1985–; Minister of Fed. and Intergovernmental Affairs, Prov. of Alberta 1971–75, of Energy and Natural Resources 1975–79; Pres. D. Getty Investments Ltd 1979; Chair. of Bd Ipsco 1981–85; Pres., CEO Sunnybank Investments Ltd 1993–94; served as dir of numerous cos; Leader Progressive Conservative Party, Alberta 1985–93; Premier of Alberta 1985–92. *Leisure interests:* golf, horse-racing, hunting. *Address:* 3145 Manulife Place, 10180-101 Street, Edmonton, Alberta, T5J 3S4; Box 300, Erskine, Alberta T0C 1G0, Canada.

GETTY, Mark; American business executive; *Executive Chairman, Getty Images, Inc.;* fmr investment banker, Kidder Peabody NY then Hambros Bank Ltd London 1991; co-founded Getty Investments LLC 1993; co-founded Getty Images Inc. 1995, Exec. Chair. 1995–. *Address:* Getty Images Inc., 601 North 34th Street, Seattle, WA 98103, USA (office). *Telephone:* (206) 925-5000 (office). *Fax:* (206) 925-5001 (office). *Website:* www.gettyimages.com (office).

GEVORGIAN, Armen; Armenian politician; *Deputy Prime Minister and Minister of Territorial Administration;* b. 8 July 1973, Yerevan; m.; two s.; ed Orenburg State Pedagogical Inst., St Petersburg Inst. of State Service, Tventey Univ., Netherlands, St Petersburg Gertsen Russian Pedagogical Inst.; Asst to Prime Minister 1997–98; Asst to Pres. of Armenia and First Deputy Head of Admin 1998–2000, First Asst to Pres. 2000–06; Head of Pres.'s Admin 2006–08; Sec. Nat. Security Council 2007–08; Deputy Prime Minister and Minister of Territorial Admin 2008–; mem. CIS Econ. Council 2008–. *Address:* Ministry of Territorial Administration, 0010 Yerevan, Republic Square, Government Building 2, Armenia (office). *Telephone:* (10) 51-13-02 (office). *Fax:* (10) 51-13-31 (home). *E-mail:* mta@mta.gov.am (office). *Website:* www.mta.gov.am (office).

GHADHBAN, Thamir Abbas al-, BSc, MSc; Iraqi petroleum engineer; b. 1945, Babil; ed Univ. Coll. London, London Univ., UK; worked for Ministry of Oil 1973–2003, first as reservoir engineer, then Head of Petroleum and Reservoir Eng, Dir Gen. of Studies and Planning, Chief Geologist and CEO; Interim Minister of Oil 2003–05. *Address:* c/o Ministry of Oil, POB 19244, Zayouna, Baghdad, Iraq (office).

GHAFFARI, Abolghassem, PhD, DSc; Iranian mathematician and academic; b. 1907, Tehran; s. of Hossein Ghaffari and Massoumeh Shahpouri; m. Mitra Meshkati 1966; two d.; ed Darolfonoun High School, Tehran and Univs of Nancy and Paris, France and Univs of London and Oxford, UK; Assoc. Prof., Tehran Univ. 1937–42, Prof. of Math. 1942–72; Temp. Sr Lecturer in Math., King's Coll. London 1946–48; Sr Research Fellow and Research Assoc. in Math., Harvard Univ., USA 1950–51; Visiting Fellow, Princeton Univ. 1951–52; mem. Inst. for Advanced Study, Princeton 1951–52; Sr Mathematician, Nat. Bureau of Standards, Washington, DC 1956–57; aeronautical research scientist 1957–64; aerospace scientist, NASA Goddard Space Flight Center, Greenbelt, Md 1964–72; Professorial Lecturer in Math. and Statistics, American Univ., Washington, DC 1958–60 and other American univs; mem. American, French (1935–70) and London Math. Socs, UNESCO Nat. Cttee 1948–50, Higher Council of Educ. 1953–56, American Astronomical Soc., Philosophical Soc. of Washington (1958–80); Fellow, New York Acad. of Sciences 1961, Washington Acad. of Sciences 1963, AAAS 1965; Chair. Washington Acad. of Science Awards Cttee for Math., Statistics and Computer Science 1975–90; Hon. mem. Asscn of Profs and Scholars of Iranian Heritage 2005; Orders of Homayoun, Danesh (1st Class) and Sepass (1st Class); US Special Apollo Achievement Award, Apollo 11 Commemorative Certificate. *Publications:* Sur l'équation fonctionnelle de Chapman-Kolmogoroff 1936, The Hodograph Method in Gas Dynamics 1950; about 60 research articles on Differential Equations in the Large, Brownian Motion, Transonic and Supersonic Aerodynamics, Lunar Flight Optimization and Orbit Determination, Astrodynamics, General Relativity and Relativistic Cosmology in Persian, French and English in nat. and int. journals. *Leisure interests:* reading, walking. *Address:* 13129 Chandler Boulevard, Sherman Oaks, CA 91401-6040, USA (home). *Telephone:* (818) 373-1314 (home). *Fax:* (818) 373-1314 (home).

GHAI, Dharam Pal, PhD; Kenyan international civil servant and economist; b. 29 June 1936, Nairobi; s. of Basti Ghai and Widya Wati; m. Neela Korde 1963; one s. two d.; ed Queen's Coll., Oxford, UK and Yale Univ., USA; Lecturer in Econs, Makerere Univ., Uganda 1961–65; Visiting Fellow, Econ. Growth Centre, Yale Univ. 1966–67; Research Prof. and Dir of Econs Research, Inst. of Devt Studies, Univ. of Nairobi 1967–71, Dir Inst. of Devt Studies 1971–74; Sr Economist, Comm. on Int. Devt (Pearson Comm.), Washington, DC 1968–69; Chief, World Employment Programme Research Br., Employment and Devt Dept, ILO, Geneva 1973–74, Chief, Tech. Secr., World Employment Conf. 1975–76, Chief, Rural Employment Policies Br., Employment and Devt Dept 1977–87; Dir UN Research Inst. for Social Devt (UNRISD) 1987–97; Coordinator ILO Transition Team 1998–99; Adviser Int. Inst. of Labour Studies; Fellow, African Acad. of Sciences. *Publications:* Collective Agriculture and Rural Development in Soviet Central Asia (with A. R. Khan) 1979, Planning for Basic Needs in Kenya (co-author) 1979, Agricultural Prices, Policy and Equity in Sub-Saharan Africa (with Lawrence Smith) 1987, Labour and Development in Rural Cuba (co-author) 1987, Social Development and Public Policy (ed.), Renewing Social and Economic Progress in Africa (ed.); co-ed. and contrib. to several other books. *Leisure interests:* photography, gardening, swimming. *Address:* 32 chemin des Voirons, 1296 Coppet, Vaud, Switzerland (home). *Telephone:* (22) 7765281 (home). *Fax:* (22) 7765282 (home). *E-mail:* ghai@bluewin.ch (home).

GHAI, Yash P., BA, LLM, DCL; Kenyan constitutional lawyer, legal scholar and UN official; *Secretary-General's Special Representative for Human Rights in Cambodia, United Nations;* b. 1938; ed Univ. of Oxford, UK, Harvard Univ., USA; barrister, Middle Temple, London, UK 1962; Lecturer, Univ. of Dar-es-Salaam 1963–66, Sr Lecturer 1966–69, Prof. and Dean 1969–70; Sr Fellow and Lecturer, Yale Univ., USA 1971–73; Prof., Univ. of Warwick, UK 1974–89; Sir Y. K. Pau Prof. of Public Law, Univ. of Hong Kong 1989–; involved in drafting constitutions for Papua New Guinea, Fiji, Solomon Islands and others; Chair. Constitution of Kenya Review Comm. 2000–03; UN Sec.-Gen.'s Special Rep. for Human Rights in Cambodia 2005–; Distinguished Researcher Award, Univ. of Hong Kong 2001. *Publications include:* Hong Kong's New Constitutional Order: The Resumption of Chinese Sovereignty and Basic Law 1997, Hong Kong's Constitutional Debate: Conflict over Interpretation (co-author) 1999, Autonomy and Ethnicity: Negotiating Competing Claims in Multi-Ethnic States (ed. and contrib.) 2000, Public Participation and Minorities 2001. *Address:* Department of Law, University of Hong Kong, Pokfulam Road, Hong Kong Special Administrative Region, People's Republic of China (office). *Telephone:* (852) 28592111 (office). *Fax:* (852) 28582549 (office). *E-mail:* hrllgyp@hkucc.hku.hk (office). *Website:* www.hku.hk (office).

GHALIB, Omar Arteh; Somali politician; b. 1930, Hargeisa; s. of the late Arteh Ghalib and Sahra Sheikh Hassan; m. Shakri Jirdeh Hussein 1954; six s. six d.; ed St Paul's Coll., Cheltenham, UK and Univ. of Bristol; teacher 1946–49; Headmaster, various elementary schools 1949–54; Vice-Prin. Intermediate School, Sheikh, Somalia 1954–56; Prin. Intermediate School, Gabileh 1958; Officer in charge of Adult Educ. 1959; District Commr in Public Admin 1960–61; First Sec. Somali Embassy, Moscow 1961–62; Rapporteur, Special Cttee on SW Africa, UN 1962–63; Counsellor, Perm. Mission of Somalia at UN 1964; Amb. to Ethiopia 1965–68; mem. Somali Nat. Ass. 1969; Sec. of State for Foreign Affairs 1969–76; Minister of Culture and Higher Educ. 1976–78, in the President's Office 1978–80; mem. Cttee for Social and Political Thought 1976–; Speaker, People's Ass. 1982–91; Prime Minister of Somalia 1991; attended numerous OAU summit and ministerial confs; numerous awards and decorations. *Publications include:* Back from the Lion of Judah. *Leisure interests:* reciting the Koran, writing, poetry, horse riding, social welfare activities. *Address:* c/o Office of the President, People's Palace, Mogadishu, Somalia.

GHALIBAF, Mohammad Baqer, MA, PhD; Iranian politician and fmr police officer; *Mayor of Tehran;* b. 23 Sept. 1961, Torghabeh; ed Tarbiat Modares Univ., Tehran; Commdr Nasr Forces, Iran–Iraq War 1983; Commdr Army of the Guardians of the Islamic Revolution Air Force –2000; Chief of IRI (Islamic Repub. of Iran) Police Forces 2000–05 (resgnd); unsuccessful cand. in presidential election 2005; Mayor of Tehran 2005–; mem. Exec. Bureau and World Council, United Cities and Local Govts. *Address:* Office of the Mayor, Tehran, Iran (office). *Website:* www.tehran.ir (office); www.ghalibaf.ir.

GHA THE INTERNATIONAL WHO'S WHO 2010 GHE

GHANEM, Shokri Mohammed, MSc, PhD; Libyan politician and government official; *Chairman, National Oil Corporation (Libya);* b. 9 Oct. 1942, Tripoli; m.; one s. three d.; ed Univ. of Benghazi, Fletcher School of Econs, Boston, USA; Head of American and European Affairs, Ministry of Econs 1963–65; Deputy Man. Translation Dept, Jamahiriya News Agency (JANA) 1966–68; Dir of Marketing and mem. Man. Council, Nat. Oil Corpn (NOC) 1968–70, Chair. 2006–; Gen. Man. of Econ. Man., Ministry of Oil 1970–75, Acting Minister of Oil 1975, Adviser 1975–77; Head of Econs, Arab Devt Inst. 1977–82; Visitor, SOAS, London 1982–84; Dir Econ. Studies Centre, Tripoli 1984–87; Lecturer, Dept of Econs, al-Jabel al-Gharbi Univ., Gharayan 1987–93; Research Man. OPEC, Vienna 1993–98, Acting Deputy to OPEC Sec. Gen. 1998–2001; Minister of Econs and Trade 2001–03, Sec. of the Gen. People's Cttee (Prime Minister) 2003–06; Petroleum Exec. of the Year, International Herald Tribune and Oil and Money 2006. *Publications:* The Pricing of Libyan Crude Oil 1975, The Petrochemical Industry in the Arab World 1984, The Rise and Fall of an Exclusive Club 1985. *Address:* National Oil Corporation (NOC), Bashir Saadawi Street, POB 2655, Tripoli, Libya (office). *Telephone:* (21) 3342900 (office). *Fax:* (21) 3339539 (office). *E-mail:* Info@noclibya.com (office). *Website:* www.noclibya.com (office).

GHANI, Ashraf, MPh, PhD; Afghan anthropologist, academic, university administrator and fmr government official; *Chairman, Institute for State Effectiveness;* has taught at Århus Univ., Denmark and Univ. of Calif., Berkeley, USA; fmr Adjunct Prof. of Anthropology, Johns Hopkins Univ., USA; broadcasts on BBC and Voice of America Persian and Pashto services 1982–; anthropologist at World Bank 1991–2001; Special Adviser to UN Sec.-Gen.'s Special Rep. for Afghanistan 2001; Minister of Finance, Transitional Authority 2002–04; Chancellor, Kabul Univ. 2004; Co-founder and Chair. Inst. for State Effectiveness 2005–. *Address:* Institute for State Effectiveness, Kabul, Afghanistan (office). *E-mail:* info@effectivestates.org (office). *Website:* www.effectivestates.org (office).

GHANI, Nasimul; Bangladeshi television industry executive; fmr Dir-Gen. Prime Minister's Office; Dir-Gen. Bangladesh TV (govt controlled) 2006–08; mem. Advisory Council Citigroup Microentrepreneurship Awards 2006. *Address:* c/o Bangladesh Television Bhaban, Rampura, Dhaka 1219, Bangladesh. *Telephone:* (2) 9330131. *E-mail:* info@btv.gov.bd. *Website:* www.btv.gov.bd.

GHANI, Owais Ahmed; Pakistani engineer and government official; *Governor of North-West Frontier Province;* Kakar Pushtun by tribe; fmr Fed. Minister for Labour in Musharraf-led mil. govt and later Minister for Industries in NW Frontier Prov. –2003; Gov. of Balochistan 2003–08, of North-West Frontier Prov. 2008–; Pres. Pakistan Red Crescent Soc. Balochistan Br.; Chancellor Balochistan Univ. of Information Tech. and Man. Sciences. *Address:* Office of the Governor, Peshwar, North West Frontier Province, Pakistan (office). *E-mail:* info@nwfp.gov.pk (office). *Website:* www.nwfp.gov pk (office).

GHANIM, Faraj Said bin; Yemeni politician; Prime Minister of Yemen 1997–98; independent. *Address:* c/o Office of the Prime Minister, San'a, Yemen.

GHANNOUCHI, Muhammad; Tunisian politician; *Prime Minister;* b. 1941; fmr Minister of Finance and the Economy, of Int. Co-operation and Foreign Investment; Prime Minister of Tunisia 1999–. *Address:* Bureau du Premier Ministre, La Kasbah, 1008 Tunis, Tunisia (office). *Telephone:* (71) 565-400 (office). *E-mail:* prm@ministeres.tn (office). *Website:* www.ministeres.tn (office).

GHARBI, El Mostafa, LLB; Moroccan international postal official; b. 9 Feb. 1935, El Jadida; m. Lalla Hafida Regragui 1962; three d.; ed Ecole Nat. Supérieure des Postes, Télégraphes et Téléphones, Paris; various positions, Ministry of Posts, Telegraphs and Telephones, Rabat 1956–65, Dir of Postal and Financial Services 1965–71; Counsellor, Universal Postal Union (UPU), Berne 1971–78, Sr Counsellor 1978–81, Asst Dir-Gen. in charge of postal services and studies 1981–90, in charge of legal and admin. questions 1990–, later Asst Dir-Gen., Int. Bureau; Médaille de Chevalier. *Publications include:* The UPU: Present Situation – Main Policies 1990; other books on postal services and strategies. *Leisure interests:* reading, sport. *Address:* c/o International Bureau Universal Postal Union, CP 3000, Berne 15, Switzerland.

GHAZALA, Lt-Gen. Mohamed Abdel Halim Abu- (see Abdel Halim Abu-Ghazala, Marshal Mohamed).

GHAZZALI, Dato' Sheikh Abdul Khalid, BEcons; Malaysian diplomatist; *Ambassador-at-Large, Ministry of Foreign Affairs;* b. 20 March 1946; m. Datin Faridah Ghazzali; ed Univ. of La Trobe, Australia; fmr Deputy Perm. Rep. to UN and Security Council, New York, fmr Deputy High Commr to UK, fmr High Commr to Zimbabwe, fmr Dir-Gen. Inst. of Diplomacy and Foreign Relations, Malaysia, fmr Deputy Sec.-Gen., Ministry of Foreign Affairs, Amb. to USA 1999–2006, Amb.-at-Large, Ministry of Foreign Affairs 2006–. *Leisure interests:* reading, walking. *Address:* Ministry of Foreign Affairs (Kementerian Luar Negeri), Wisma Putra, 1 Jalan Wisma Putra, Presint 2, 62602 Putrajaya, Malaysia (office). *Telephone:* (3) 88874000 (office). *Fax:* (3) 88891717 (office). *E-mail:* webmaster@kln.gov.my (office). *Website:* www.kln.gov.my (office).

GHEDI, Ali Mohamed; Somali politician and academic; b. Mogadishu; m.; ed Somali Nat. Univ., Univ. of Pisa, Italy; qualified veterinary physician; Lecturer and researcher, Somali Nat. Univ. –1991; fmr special adviser and consultant to regional livestock orgs; served with UN, Nairobi, animal disease programme for Somalia; Founding mem. and Pres. Somalia NGO Consortium; Prime Minister of Somalia 2004–07 (resgnd). *Address:* c/o Office of the Prime Minister, PO Box 623, Sarit, 00606, Somalia (office).

GHEIT, Ahmed Aboul, BSc; Egyptian diplomatist; *Minister of Foreign Affairs;* b. 12 June 1942, Heliopolis; m.; two c.; ed Ainshams Univ., Cairo; joined Ministry of Foreign Affairs 1965; Attaché-Third Sec., Embassy in Cyprus 1968–72; staff mem. of Adviser to Pres. on Nat. Security Affairs 1972–74; Second-First Sec., Perm. Mission to UN, New York 1974–77; Counsellor, Special Aide, Cabinet of Minister of Foreign Affairs 1977–79; Political Counsellor, Embassy in Moscow 1979–82; Political Adviser to Minister of Foreign Affairs 1982–84, 1989–90, to Prime Minister 1984–85; Counsellor, Perm. Mission to UN 1985–87, Deputy Perm. Rep. 1987–89; Chef de Cabinet, Minister of Foreign Affairs 1990–92, Asst Foreign Minister for Cabinet Affairs 1996–99; Amb. to Italy, Macedonia, San Marino and Rep. to FAO, Rome 1992–96; Perm. Rep. to UN 1999–2004; Minister of Foreign Affairs 2004–. *Address:* Ministry of Foreign Affairs, Corniche en-Nil, Cairo (Maspiro), Egypt (office). *Telephone:* (2) 5746871 (office). *Fax:* (2) 5747839 (office). *E-mail:* info@mfa.gov.eg (office). *Website:* www.mfa.gov.eg (office).

GHEORGHIU, Angela; Romanian singer (soprano); b. 7 Sept. 1965, Adjud; m. 1st Andrei Gheorghiu 1988; m. 2nd Roberto Alagna (q.v.) 1996; ed Bucharest Acad.; debut at Bucharest as Solveig in Grieg's Peer Gynt 1983; appearances at Covent Garden from 1992, Met debut 1993, and in Washington, Vienna, Monte Carlo, Berlin, Nat. Opera Cluj; repertoire includes Zerlina, Mimi, Nina (all in Cherubin), Suzel (L'Amico Fritz), Juliette (Roméo et Juliette), Magda (La Rondine), Nedda (Pagliacci), and roles in Don Giovanni, La Bohème, Turandot, Carmen, La Traviata, L'Elisir d'Amore, Falstaff; Belvedere Prize, Vienna, Schatzgraber-Preis, Hamburg State Opera, Gulbenkian Prize. *Recordings include:* La Traviata (as Violetta) 1994, Tosca (solo) 2001, selection of arias. *Address:* IMG Artists, Carnegie Hall Tower, 152 West 57th Street, 5th Floor, New York, NY 10019, USA (office). *Telephone:* (212) 994-3500 (office). *Fax:* (212) 994-3550 (office). *E-mail:* jmastroianni@imgartists.com (office); agerdanovits@gmx.net. *Website:* www.imgartists.com (office); www.angelagheorghiu.com.

GHEORGHIU, Ion (Alin); Romanian painter and sculptor; b. 29 Sept. 1929, Bucharest; s. of Emil Gheorghiu and Chiriachiţa Gheorghiu; m. Anamaria Smigelschi 1970; ed N. Grigorescu Fine Arts Coll.; mem. Fine Arts Union, Sec. 1978–; creator of extensive cycles: Suspended Gardens (paintings), Around Archimboldo (drawings, paintings, sculpture), Chimeras (sculpture); Corresp. mem. Romanian Acad. 1993–; Hon. mem. Fine Arts Union of Bulgaria; Romanian Acad. Award 1966, Yomiuri Shimbun Award, Tokyo 1971, Great Award of the Fine Arts Union 1972, Italian Acad. Award and Gold Medal 1980, Trionfo '81 Prize 1981, Homage to Picasso Prize 1981, Homage to Raphael Prize 1993, Sofia Biennial Great Prize 1985, Ministry of Culture Prize (Chişinău, Moldova) 1996, Bucharest Municipality First Prize for Painting 1996. *Leisure interests:* hunting and fishing. *Address:* 27–29 Emil Pangratti Street, Bucharest (Studio); 6 Aviator Petre Creţu Street, Bucharest, Romania (home). *Telephone:* (1) 6335560 (Studio).

GHEORGHIU, Mihnea, PhD, DLitt; Romanian academic, poet, writer and actor; b. 5 May 1919, Bucharest; s. of Dumitru Gheorghiu and Alexandrina Gheorghiu; m. Anda Boldur 1953; one d.; ed Fratii Buzesti High School, Craiova, Univ. of Bucharest and studies in France, Italy and UK, School of Artillery Officers, Craiova; Chief Ed. Scînteia Tineretului (newspaper) 1944–46; Lecturer and Assoc. Prof. of English Language, Acad. of Econ. Studies, Bucharest 1946–48, Prof. 1948–50; Prof. of Theatralogy and Filmology, Inst. of Theatre and Film Art, Bucharest 1954–69; Founder and Ed.-in-Chief Secolul 20 (monthly int. literary review) 1961–63; Ed.-in-Chief Romanian-American Review; Chair. of Bd Social Future (sociology and political sciences bi-monthly), Studies in the History of Art 1975–; Pres. Nat. Film Council 1963–65; Vice-Pres. Nat. Cttee for Culture and Art 1965–68; Pres. Inst. for Cultural Relations 1968–72, Acad. of Social and Political Sciences 1972–89, Romanian Filmmakers' Union 1990–; Corresp. mem. Romanian Acad. 1974, mem. 1996, Pres. Section for Arts, Architecture and Audiovisual 1992–; Adviser UNESCO European Centre for Higher Educ.; mem. Club of Rome, Soc. Européenne de Culture, Venice, Acad. Mondiale de Prospective Sociale, Geneva, New York Acad. of Sciences, Int. Shakespeare Asscn 1964–2000, Nat. Acad. of History of Caracas, Int. Asscn of Film and TV Authors; Hon. Citizen of New Orleans; Ordre des Arts et des Lettres (France), Italian Order of Merit, Grosse Verdienstkreuz mit Stern (FRG), Order of Orange-Nassau (Netherlands); Nat. State Prize, Special Prize, Int. Film Festivals of Barcelona, Buenos Aires and Cork 1964, 1966, I.L. Caragiale Prize, Romanian Acad. 1972, Prize of Writers' Union of Romania 1975, Erasmus Medal. *Film screenplays and scripts:* Porto Franco 1962, Tudor 1963–64, Zodia Feciorei 1967, Pădurea pierdută 1992, Cantemir & Muşchetarul român (Prize of Cineasts' Union of Romania) 1974, Hyperion 1975, Tănase Scatiu 1976, Burebista 1980. *Plays:* Tudor din Vladimiri (Tudor of Vladimiri), Istorii dramatice (Dramatic Histories), Capul (The Head), Zodia Taurului (Taurus' Sign), Patetica '77 (Pathetica '77), Fierul si aurul (Iron and Gold). *Radio:* has written more than 20 plays. *Publications:* poetry: Anna-Mad 1941, Ultimul peisaj al orasului cenusiu (Last Landscape of the Grey Town 1946, Balade (Ballads) 1956, Ultimul peisaj (The Last Landscape) 1974; other: Orientations in World Literature 1957, Doua ambasade (Two Embassies) 1958, Scenes of Shakespeare's Life 1958, Dionysos 1969, Letters from the Neighbourhood 1971, Scenes of Public Life 1972, Five Worlds as Spectacle (collection of plays) 1980, Tobacco Flowers (essays) 1984, Enigma in Fleet Street (novel) 1988, The Two Roses (collection of tales) 1992; translations from Shakespeare, Walt Whitman, Burns, Gabriel García Márquez, etc. *Leisure interest:* swimming. *Address:* Mendeleev Street 28-30, Sector 1, 70169 Bucharest (office); Dionisie Lupu 74, Bucharest, Romania (home). *Telephone:* 6504969 (home); 6505741 (office). *Fax:* 3111246 (office).

GHEZALI, Salima; Algerian newspaper editor; *Editor-in-Chief, La Nation;* b. 1958; m. (divorced); two c.; fmr schoolteacher, Mitidja Hills; Ed.-in-Chief La

Nation weekly newspaper 1994–96, 2001–, newspaper suspended by Algerian authorities 1996–2001; f. Women of Europe and North Africa Asscn, Asscn for Women's Emancipation 1989; f. Nyssa magazine; Int. Press Club Award 1996, Sakharov Human Rights Prize 1997, Olof Palme Prize 1997. *Address:* La Nation, 33 rue Larbi Ben M'hidi, Algiers, Algeria (office). *Telephone:* (21) 43-21-76 (office).

GHIGO, Enzo; Italian politician; b. 1953, Turin; m. Anna Casale; one s.; fmr Scientific Ed., UTET (publishing co.), Turin; self-employed in tech. components industry –1982; joined Pubblitalia '80 (advertising co.) 1982, Man. 1986–90, Area Man. for Veneto and Marche 1990–; Regional Co-ordinator, Forza Italia 1993–; mem. Parl. for Piedmont 2 1994, Pres. Piedmont 1995–2005, Vice-Pres. Regional Presidential Congress 1997; Pres. Conf. of Presidents of Italian Regions 2000–05; Vice-Pres. Foundation Italia in Japan 2001; Grand'Ufficiale al merito della Repubblica Italiana 1999, Cavaliere di Gran Croce 2002. *Leisure interests:* cinema, reading, cycling. *Address:* c/o Giunta Regionale del Piemonte, Piazza Castello 165, 10122 Turin, Italy (office).

GHIUSELEV, Nicola; Bulgarian singer (bass); b. 17 Aug. 1936, Pavlikeni; s. of Nicolai Ghiuselev and Elisaveta Ghiuseleva; m. 1st Roumiana Ghiuseleva 1960; m. 2nd Annamaria Petrova-Ghiuseleva 1984; two s. one d.; ed Acad. of Fine Arts, Sofia and singing studies under Christo Brumbarov; won vocal competitions in Sofia 1959, Prague 1960, Helsinki 1962; joined State Opera Co., Sofia; debut as Timur in Puccini's Turandot, State Opera, Sofia 1961; has since appeared at most of the major opera houses of the world; major roles include Philip II, Boris Godounov, Don Giovanni, Attila, Wotan and the Mefistofele roles of Gounod, Berlioz and Boito; noted for Russian roles such as Dositheus, Prince Igor, Ivan the Terrible and the bass repertoire of Verdi, Rossini, Bellini, Donizetti, Mozart, Berlioz, Cherubini, Ponchielli, etc. *Recordings include:* Turandot 1961, Les Huguenots 1969, Offenbach: Les contes d'Hoffmann, Mefistofele 1983, Orthodox Chants 1997. *Address:* Villa Elpida, 1616 Sofia, Bulgaria; Via della Pisana 370/B2, 00163 Rome, Italy. *Telephone:* (2) 562929 (Sofia); (06) 66162834 (Rome). *Fax:* (2) 562929 (Sofia); (06) 66162834 (Rome).

GHIZ, Robert, BA; Canadian politician; *Premier, Prince Edward Island;* b. 21 Jan. 1974, Charlottetown; s. of the late fmr Premier of PEI Joseph Ghiz; m. Dr Kate Ellis; ed Bishop's Univ.; Special Asst to Minister of Canadian Heritage 1997–98; lobbyist for Bank of Nova Scotia, Ottawa 1998–2001; Atlantic Canada Advisor, Office of the Prime Minister, Ottawa 2001–03; Leader PEI Liberal Party 2003–; MLA for Charlottetown-Rochford Square 2003–07, for Charlottetown-Brighton 2007–, Leader of the Opposition 2003–07; Premier of PEI 2007–. *Address:* Office of the Premier, Shaw Bldg, 5th Floor South, 95 Rochford Street, POB 2000, Charlottetown, PE C1A 7N8, Canada (office). *Telephone:* (902) 368-4400 (office). *Fax:* (902) 368-4416 (office). *E-mail:* rwghiz@gov.pe.ca (office). *Website:* www.gov.pe.ca/premier (office).

GHONDA MANGALIBI, Antoine; Democratic Republic of the Congo politician; b. 19 Feb. 1965, Leuven, Belgium; Minister of Foreign Affairs and Int. Co-operation, Democratic Repub. of the Congo 2003–04. *Address:* c/o Ministry of Foreign Affairs and International Co-operation, Place de l'Indépendence, BP 7100, Kinshasa-Gombe, Democratic Republic of the Congo (office).

GHOSH, Amitav, BA, MA, DPhil; Indian writer and academic; *Visiting Professor, Department of English and American Literature and Language, Harvard University;* b. 1956, Kolkata; m. Deborah Baker; ed St Stephen's Coll., Delhi Univ., Institut Bourguiba des Langues Vivantes, Tunis and Univ. of Oxford; Visiting Fellow Centre for Social Sciences, Trivandrum, Kerala 1982–83; Research Assoc. Dept of Sociology, Delhi Univ. 1983–87, Lecturer Dept of Sociology 1987; Visiting Prof. Depts of Literature and Anthropology, Univ. of Virginia, Charlottesville 1988; Visiting Prof. South Asia Centre, Columbia Univ. 1989; Visiting Prof. Dept of Anthropology, Univ. of Pennsylvania 1989; Fellow Centre for Studies in Social Science, Kolkata 1990–92; Adjunct Prof. Dept of Anthropology, Columbia Univ. 1993, Visiting Prof. 1994–97; Distinguished Visiting Prof. American Univ. in Cairo 1994; fiction workshop Sarah Lawrence Coll., New York 1996; Distinguished Prof. Dept of Comparative Literature, Queens Coll., CUNY 1999–2003; Visiting Prof., Dept of English and American Literature and Language, Harvard Univ. 2004–; Ananda Puraskar 1990, Best American Essays award 1995, Pushcart Prize 1999. *Publications:* The Circle of Reason (Prix Médicis Étranger 1990) 1986, The Shadow Lines (Sahitya Akademi Award 1990) 1988, In an Antique Land (non-fiction) 1992, The Calcutta Chromosome (Arthur C. Clark Award 1997) 1996, Dancing in Cambodia and At Large in Burma (essays) 1998, Countdown 1999, The Glass Palace (Frankfurt International e-Book Awards Grand Prize for Fiction 2001) 2000, The Hungry Tide (Hutch Crossword Book Prize 2005) 2004, Sea of Poppies 2008; contrib. articles in Ethnology, Granta, The New Republic, New York Times, Public Culture, Subaltern Studies, Letra Internacional, Cultural Anthropology, Observer Magazine, Wilson Quarterly, The New Yorker, Civil Lines, American Journal of Archaeology, Kenyon Review, Desh. *Address:* Department of English and American Literature and Language, Harvard University, Barker Center, 12 Quincy Street, Cambridge, MA 02138, USA (home). *Telephone:* (617) 495-4029 (home). *Fax:* (617) 496-8737 (office). *E-mail:* aghosh@fas.harvard.edu (office); amitav@amitavghosh.com. *Website:* www.fas.harvard.edu/~english (office); www.amitavghosh.com.

GHOSH, Gautam; Indian film director; b. 24 July 1950, Calcutta; s. of Prof. Himangshu Ghosh and Santana Ghosh; m. Neelanjana Ghosh 1978; one s. one d.; ed Cathedral Mission School, Calcutta, City Coll., Calcutta and Calcutta Univ.; mem. Int. Jury (Oberhausen) 1979; official del., Cannes and London Film Festivals 1982, Venice and Tokyo Film Festivals 1984; mem. Nat. Jury 1985; Exec. Dir Nat. Film Inst. 1987; Dir Nat. Film Devt Corpn, West Bengal Film Devt Corpn; Pres. Award (five times), Human Rights Award (France), Silver Medal and UNESCO Award, Grand Prix Award (USSR). *Films include:* Hungry Autumn 1974, Ma Bhoomi 1980, Dakhal 1982, Paar 1984, Antarjali Yatra 1988, Padma Nadir Majhi 1992, Patang 1994, Gudiya, Dekha 2001. *Publications:* numerous articles on the cinema. *Leisure interests:* music, reading, travel. *Address:* Block 5, Flat 50, 28/1A Gariahat Road, Kolkata 700029, India. *Telephone:* (33) 4405630 (home). *Fax:* (33) 4640315 (home).

GHOSN, Carlos, BEng, KBE; Brazilian/French/Lebanese automotive industry executive; *President and CEO, Renault SA and Nissan Motor Co. Ltd;* ,b. 9 March 1954, Porto-Velho, Brazil; m. Rita Ghosn; one s. three d.; ed Collège Notre-Dame de Jamhour, Beirut, Ecole Polytechnique, Ecole des Mines, Paris; moved to Beirut, Lebanon with his mother 1960; trained as mining eng; Man. Dir Michelin Le Puy factory 1981, CEO Michelin Brazil 1985, Michelin North America 1989; Asst Dir-Gen. Renault Group 1996, Dir (non-exec.) 2001–, Pres. and CEO Renault SA 2005–, COO Nissan Motor Co. Ltd 1999–2001, Dir 1999–, Pres. and CEO 2001–, Co-Chair. 2003–, Pres. and CEO Nissan N America –2007; mem. Bd of Dirs Alcoa Inc., Sony Corpn, Renault, IBM Corpn 2004–; voted Man of the Year by Fortune magazine's Asian edn 2003. *Publications:* Renaissance 2001, Shift: Inside Nissan's Historic Revival 2005. *Address:* Renault SA, 13–15 quai Le Gallo, 92513 Boulogne-Billancourt Cedex, France (office); Nissan Motor Co. Ltd, 17-1 Ginza 6-chome, Chuo-ku, Tokyo 104-8023, Japan (office). *Telephone:* 1-76-84-50-50 (Paris) (office); (3) 3543-5523 (Tokyo) (office). *Fax:* 1-41-04-51-49 (Paris) (office); (3) 5565-2228 (Tokyo) (office). *Website:* www.renault.com (office); www.nissan-global.com (office).

GHOZALI, Sid Ahmed; Algerian politician and petroleum executive; *Chairman, Front Démocratique;* b. 31 March 1937, Marnia; ed Ecole des Ponts et Chaussées, Paris; fmr Dir of Energy, Ministry of Industry and Energy; Adviser, Ministry of the Economy 1964; Under-Sec., Ministry of Public Works 1964–65; Pres., Dir-Gen. Soc. nationale pour la recherche, la production, le transport, la transformation et la commercialisation des hydrocarbures (SONATRACH) 1966–84, Chair., Man. Dir; Minister of Hydraulics March–Oct. 1979, of Foreign Affairs 1989–91; Prime Minister of Algeria 1991–92; Amb. to Belgium 1987–89, to France 1992–93; mem. Cen. Cttee Front de Libération Nat.; Chair. Front Démocratique 2000–; mem. Org. technique de mise en valeur des richesses du sous-sol saharien 1962. *Address:* Front Démocratique, Algiers, Algeria (office).

GHUKASSIAN, Arkadii Arshavirovich; Azerbaijani politician and fmr journalist; b. 21 June 1957, Stepanakert; m.; one d.; ed Yerevan State Univ., Armenia; reporter Sovetskii Karabakh newspaper (Russian edn) 1979–81, First Deputy Ed. 1981–88; sr mem. Karabakh Movt 1988–; elected Deputy to Supreme Soviet (Supreme Council) of Nagornyi Karabakh 1992; Minister of Foreign Affairs of 'Repub. of Nagornyi Karabakh' 1993–98; Pres. of 'Repub. of Nagornyi Karabakh' 1997–2007; opposed peace settlement suggested by OSCE on grounds that it obstructed aims of attaining full independence for Nagornyi Karabakh 1997; sustained serious injuries as result of assassination attempt 2000. *Address:* c/o Office of the President of the Republic of Nagornyi Karabakh, 20 February Street 3, Xankandi, Nagornyi Karabakh, Azerbaijan (office).

GHUNAIM, Maha K. al-, BSc; Kuwaiti business executive; *Chairperson and Managing Director, Global Investment House;* m.; ed San Francisco State Univ., USA; Founder, Vice-Chair. and Man. Dir Global Investment House, Kuwait 1998–2006, Chair. and Man. Dir 2006–; Pres. Kuwait Chapter, Young Arab Leaders Org.; mem. Bd of Dirs Nat. Industries Group, BankMuscat International (Bahrain); Chair. Global Bahrain; Vice-Chair. Al-Soor Finance Co., Shurooq Investment Services Co. (Oman); mem. DEPA United Group, UAE; mem. Practitioner Cttee Dubai Int. Financial Exchange; Gulf Excellence Award 2005, Arabian Business magazine Business Women of the Year Award 2005, named by Forbes Arabia Magazine as one of Top 50 Leading Arab Women, named by Forbes International amongst Women to Watch in the Middle East 2005, named by Newsweek Arabia amongst the 43 Most Influential Personalities in the Middle East 2005, ranked by Forbes magazine amongst 100 Most Powerful Women (91st) 2006, (72nd) 2007, (89th) 2008. *Address:* Global Investment House, Souk Al-Safat Bldg, 2nd Floor, PO Box 28807, Safat 13149, Kuwait (office). *Telephone:* 804242 (office). *Fax:* 2400661 (office). *E-mail:* maha@global.com.kw (office). *Website:* www.globalinv.net (office).

GIACCONI, Riccardo, PhD; American astrophysicist and academic; *Research Professor, Department of Physics and Astronomy, Johns Hopkins University;* b. 6 Oct. 1931, Genoa, Italy; s. of Antonio Giacconi and Elsa Giacconi (Canni); m. Mirella Manaira 1957; one s. two d.; ed Univ. of Milan; Asst Prof. of Physics, Univ. of Milan 1954–56; Research Assoc. Indiana Univ. 1956–58, Princeton Univ., 1958–59; joined American Science & Eng Inc. 1959–73, mem. Bd of Dirs. 1966–73 Exec. Vice-Pres. 1969–73; Assoc. Harvard Coll. Observatory 1970–72; Assoc. Dir Harvard-Smithsonian Center for Astrophysics 1973–81; Prof. of Astrophysics, Harvard Univ. 1973–82; Prof. of Astrophysics, Johns Hopkins Univ. 1981–99, Research Prof. 1999–; Dir Space Telescope Science Inst., Baltimore 1981–92; Prof. of Astrophysics, Milan Univ., Italy 1991–99; Dir-Gen. European Southern Observatory, Garching, Germany 1993–99; Pres. Associated Universities, Inc. (operates Nat. Radio Astronomy Observatory 1999–2004; Chair. Task Group on Directions in Space Science 1995–; mem. NASA Space Science Advisory Cttee 1978–79, NASA Advisory Council's Informal Ad Hoc Advisory Subcommittee for the Innovation Study 1979–; mem. NAS (mem. Space Science Bd and High Energy Astrophysics Panel of the Astronomy Survey Cttee 1979–), American Acad. of Arts and Sciences, AAAS, American Astronomical Soc., American Physical Soc. (Fellow 1976), Italian Physical Soc., Int. Astronomical Union; Vice-Chair. COSPAR, I.S.C.E.-1 1980; Astronomy Rep. to Int. Astronomical

Union 1979–81; mem. High Energy Astrophysics Division, American Astronomical Soc., Chair. 1976–77, mem. Fachbeirat, Max-Planck Institut für Physik und Astrophysik, Comitato Scientifico del Centro Internazionale di Storia dello Spazio e del Tempo; Foreign mem. Accademia Nazionale dei Lincei; External mem. Max-Planck Soc.; Fulbright Fellow 1956–58; Laurea hc in Astronomy, Univ. of Padua, 1984; Hon. DSc (Chicago) 1983, (Warsaw) 1996; Laurea hc in Physics (Rome) 1998; Hon. DTech and Science (Uppsala) 2000; Space Science Award, AIAA 1976, NASA Medal for Exceptional Scientific Achievement 1980, Gold Medal, Royal Astronomical Soc. 1982, A. Cressy Morrison Award in Natural Sciences, New York Acad. of Sciences 1982, Wolf Prize 1987, Nobel Prize in Physics 2002 and numerous other awards. *Publications:* X-ray Astronomy (co-editor) 1974, Physics and Astrophysics of Neutron Stars and Black Holes (co-editor) 1978, A Face of Extremes: The X-ray Universe (co-ed.) 1985, also numerous articles in professional journals. *Leisure interest:* painting. *Address:* Department of Physics and Astronomy, Johns Hopkins University, Bloomberg 501, 3400 North Charles Street, Baltimore, MD 21218-2686 (office); 5630 Wisconsin Avenue, Apt. 604, Chevy Chase, MD 20815, USA (home). *Telephone:* (410) 516-0621 (office); (301) 941-0464 (home). *Fax:* (410) 516-7239 (office). *E-mail:* giacconi@pha.jhu.edu (office). *Website:* www.pha.jhu.edu (office); www.aui.edu (office).

GIACOMELLI, Giorgio, MA; Italian international civil servant and diplomatist; b. 25 Jan. 1930, Milan; s. of Gino Giacomelli and Maria Van der Kellen; one s. one d.; ed Padua Univ., Univ. of Cambridge, UK and Geneva Inst. of Higher Int. Studies, Switzerland; joined diplomatic service 1956, Second Sec., Madrid 1958, Second Sec., NATO Del. 1961, First Sec. 1962, Chargé d'affaires, Léopoldville (now Kinshasa) 1964, Counsellor, New Delhi 1966, Ministry of Foreign Affairs, Rome: Personnel 1969, Cultural Dept 1971, Head of Service for Tech. Co-operation 1972, Amb. to Somalia 1973, to Syria 1976; Deputy Dir-Gen., Emigration Dept, with Ministry of Foreign Affairs, Rome 1980, Dir-Gen. 1981, Dir-Gen. Devt Co-operation Dept 1981; Commr-Gen. UNRWA 1985–90; Under-Sec. Gen. UN Vienna Office 1992–97; Exec. Dir UN Int. Drug Control Program; Dir Gen. UN Office, Vienna; Chevalier de la Légion d'honneur; Kt Order of Merit (Italy); Silver Medal for Civil Bravery (Italy). *Leisure interests:* music, literature, mountaineering, hunting and riding. *Address:* c/o United Nations, Vienna International Centre, PO Box 500, 1400 Vienna, Austria.

GIAEVER, Ivar, PhD; American physicist and academic; *CEO, Applied BioPhysics, Inc.;* b. 5 April 1929, Bergen, Norway; s. of John A. Giaever and Gudrun M. Skaarud; m. Inger Skramstad 1952; one s. three d.; ed Norwegian Inst. of Tech., Rensselaer Polytechnical Inst., NY; Norwegian Army 1952–53; Patent Examiner, Norwegian Patent Office 1953–54; Mechanical Engineer, Canadian Gen. Electric Co. 1954–56; Applied Mathematician, Gen. Electric Co. 1956–58; Physicist, Gen. Electric Research and Devt Center 1958–88; Inst. Prof., Physics Dept, Rensselaer Polytechnic, NY 1988–; Prof., Univ. of Oslo 1988–; co-f. Applied Biophysics Inc. 1991, currently CEO; mem. NAS 1974–; eight Hon. PhD degrees; Oliver E. Buckley Prize 1965, Nobel Prize for Physics 1973, Zworkin Award 1974. *Publications in Physics Review Letters:* Energy Gap in Superconductors Measured by Electron Tunneling 1960, Study of Superconductors by Electron Tunneling 1961, Detection of the AC Josephson Effect 1965, Magnetic Coupling Between Two Adjacent Superconductors 1965, The Antibody-Antigen Reaction: A Visual Observation 1973, A Morphological Biosensor for Mammalian Cells 1993, Cell Adhesion Force Microscopy 1999. *Leisure interests:* skiing, sailing, tennis, hiking, camping, playing Go. *Address:* Applied Biophysics, Inc., 175 Jordan Road, Troy, NY 12180 (office); 2080 Van Antwerp Road, Schenectady, NY 12309, USA (home). *Telephone:* (518) 880-6860 (office). *Fax:* (518) 880-6865 (office). *E-mail:* giaever@biophysics.com (office). *Website:* www.biophysics.com (office).

GIAMATTI, Paul, MFA; American actor; b. 6 June 1967; s. of A. Bartlett Giamatti and Toni Smith; ed Yale Univ.; began career in regional theatre before developing a successful film career. *Films include:* Singles 1992, Past Midnight 1992, Mighty Aphrodite 1995, Sabrina 1995, Breathing Room 1996, Ripper 1996, Donnie Brasco 1997, Private Parts 1997, My Best Friend's Wedding 1997, Deconstructing Harry 1997, A Further Gesture 1997, Arresting Gena 1997, The Truman Show 1998, Doctor Dolittle 1998, Saving Private Ryan 1998, The Negotiator 1998, Safe Men 1998, Cradle Will Rock 1999, Man on the Moon 1999, Big Momma's House 2000, Duets 2000, Storytelling 2001, Planet of the Apes 2001, Big Fat Liar 2002, Thunderpants 2002, Confidence 2003, American Splendor 2003, Paycheck 2003, Sideways (Best Male Lead, Ind. Spirit Awards 2005) 2004, The Cinderella Man (Critics' Choice Award for Best Supporting Actor 2006, Screen Actors Guild Award for Best Supporting Actor 2006) 2005, Robots (voice) 2005, The Fan and the Flower (voice) 2005, The Hawk Is Dying 2006, Asterix and the Vikings (voice) 2006, The Illusionist 2006, Lady in the Water 2006, The Ant Bully (voice) 2006, The Nanny Diaries 2007, Shoot 'Em Up 2007, Fred Claus 2007, Pretty Bird 2008, Cold Souls 2009, The Haunted World of El Superbeasto (voice) 2009, Duplicity 2009, The Last Station 2009. *Television includes:* Tourist Trap 1998, Winchell 1998, If These Walls Could Talk 2 2000, The Pentagon Papers 2003, The Amazing Screw-On Head (voice) 2006, John Adams (series, HBO) (Golden Globe Award for Best Actor in a Mini-Series 2009) 2008–. *Address:* c/o Endeavor Talent Agency, 9701 Wilshire Boulevard, 10th Floor, Beverley Hills, CA 90212, USA.

GIAMBASTIANI, Adm. Edmund P. Jr; American naval officer; b. Canastota, New York; ed US Naval Acad.; career in US Armed Forces; assignments included Program Man. Navy Recruiting Command HQ, Washington, DC, Special Asst to Deputy Dir of Intelligence, CIA, Deputy Chief of Staff for Resources, Warfare Requirements and Assessments, US Pacific Fleet, Dir Submarine Warfare Div., Naval Operations, Deputy Chief of Naval Operations for Resources, Requirements and Assessments; fmr Commdr Submarine NR-1 (nuclear-powered deep diving submarine), USS Richard B. Russell (nuclear-powered attack submarine); fmr Leader Submar-

ine Devt Squadron Twelve; fmr First Dir Strategy and Concepts, Naval Doctrine Command; fmr Commdr Atlantic Fleet Submarine Force, Anti-Submarine and Reconnaissance Forces Atlantic; Sr Mil. Asst to Sec. of Defense Donald Rumsfeld (q.v.) –2003; Commdr US Jt Forces Command and Supreme Allied Commdr Transformation (SACT), NATO 2003–05; Vice Chair. Jt Chiefs of Staff, Washington DC 2005–07, also served as Chair. Joint Requirements Oversight Council, Vice Chair. Defense Acquisition Bd, mem. Nat. Security Council Deputies Cttee, Nuclear Weapons Council; numerous awards including Defense Distinguished Service Medal, Joint Meritorious Unit Award, eight Battle Efficiency E's, five Navy Unit Commendations, five Navy Meritorious Unit Commendations. *Address:* c/o Office of the Vice Chairman of the Joint Chiefs of Staff, 9999 Joint Staff, Pentagon, Washington, DC 20318-9999, USA (office).

GIAMPIETRI ROJAS, Adm. (retd) Luis; Peruvian naval officer (retd) and politician; *First Vice-President;* b. 31 Dec. 1940, Bellavista; s. of Luis Giampietri Berenice and Rosa Rojas Lapoint; m. Lida Marcela Ramos Seminario; four c.; ed Peruvian Naval School; joined Peruvian Navy as ensign in 1960, positions included Commdr Gen. Naval Zones, Commdr Gen. Defence Coast, Dir Peruvian Naval School; fmr Deputy Rep. of Perm. Del. to OAS; fmr del. to Inter-American Defence Council, Washington, DC; Chair. Bd of Dirs Peruvian Sea Inst. 1996–2000, Chair. Multi-Sector Cttee in charge of Nat. Study of "El Niño" (ENFEN), mem. Nat. Environment Comm., Perm. Comm. for the Pacific SE, Nat. Comm. for Antarctic Affairs; Councillor for Lima 1998–2002; First Vice-Pres. of Peru 2007–; mem. Mexican Acad. of Sciences, Inst. of Maritime History, Peruvian Centre of Mil. Maritime History. *Address:* Office of the President of the Council of Ministers, Avda 28 de Julio 878, Miraflores, Lima, Peru (office). *Telephone:* (1) 6109800 (office). *Fax:* (1) 4449168 (office). *E-mail:* webmaster@pcm.gob.pe (office). *Website:* www.pcm .gob.pe (office).

GIANVITI, François Paul Frédéric, DenD; French professor of law and international organization official; b. 2 Aug. 1938, Paris; s. of Dominique Gianviti and Suzanne Fournier; m. Barbara Zawadsky 1965; one s. two d.; ed Lycées Henri IV and Louis-le-Grand, Paris, Facultés des Lettres et de Droit, Paris and New York Univ. School of Law; Asst Faculté de Droit, Paris 1963–67; Lecturer, Faculté de Droit, Nancy 1967–68, Caen 1968–69; Maître de conférences, Faculté de Droit, Besançon, on secondment to IMF 1970–74; Maître de conférences, Univ. of Paris XII 1974–75, Prof. of Law 1975–, Dean 1979–85; Dir of Legal Dept, IMF 1986–2004, Gen. Counsel 1987–2004 (retd); mem. Monetary Cttee, Int. Law Asscn; Chevalier, Ordre Nat. du Mérite, Chevalier des Palmes académiques. *Publication:* Les Biens 1984; numerous book chapters and journal articles. *Address:* 11402 Dorchester Lane, Rockville, MD 20852, USA (home).

GIAP, Gen. Vo Nguyen; Vietnamese army officer (retd); b. 1912, Quangbinh Prov.; ed French Lycée in Hué and law studies at Univ. of Hanoi; History Teacher, Thang Long School, Hanoi; joined Viet Nam CP in early 1930s; fled to China 1939, helped organize Vietminh Front, Viet Nam 1941; Minister of Interior 1945, became C-in-C of Vietminh Army 1946; defeated French at Dien Bien Phu 1954; Vice-Chair. Council of Ministers 1976–91, Minister of Defence, C-in-C, Democratic Repub. of Viet Nam to 1976, Socialist Repub. of Viet Nam 1976–80; mem. Politburo Lao-Dong Party –1976, CP of Viet Nam 1976–82. *Publications:* People's War, People's Army, Big Victory, Great Task 1968. *Address:* Dang Cong san Viet Nam, 1C boulevard Hoang Van Thu, Hanoi, Viet Nam.

GIAU, Nguyen Van, DEcon; Vietnamese central banker and politician; *Governor, State Bank of Viet Nam;* b. 8 Dec. 1957, An Giang Prov.; Dir An Giang Br. of Viet Nam Bank for Agriculture and Rural Development (Agribank) 1988–90, Deputy Gen. Dir Agribank 1991–96, Gen. Dir 1996–97; Deputy Gov. State Bank of Viet Nam 1998–2003, Gov. 2007–; mem. Party Cen. Cttee, Deputy Party Sec., Ninh Thuan Prov. 2003–05, Party Sec. 2005–07. *Address:* State Bank of Viet Nam, 49 Ly Thai To Street, Hoankiem District, Hanoi, Viet Nam (office). *Telephone:* (8) 242479 (office). *Fax:* (8) 268765 (office). *E-mail:* nhnn@sbv.gov.vn (office). *Website:* www.sbv.gov.vn (office).

GIBARA, Samir G., MBA; French business executive (retd); b. 23 April 1939, Cairo, Egypt; s. of the late Selim Gibara and Renée Bokhazi; m. Salma Tagher 1968; ed Harvard Business School, USA; Adviser, Inst. for Int. Trade, Paris 1967–70; Pres. and Man. Dir Goodyear France 1983; Pres. and CEO Goodyear Canada 1989; Vice-Pres. and Gen. Man. Goodyear Europe 1990; Vice-Pres. Strategic Planning and Acting Chief Financial Officer, Goodyear Tire & Rubber Co. 1992, Exec. Vice-Pres. N American Operations 1994, Pres. and COO 1995–96, Chair., Pres. and CEO Jan. 1996, Chair. and CEO July 1996–2003 (retd); mem. Bd of Dirs Int. Paper Co. 1999–, Dana Corpn; mem. Advisory Bd Proudfoot Consultants; Chevalier, Ordre nat. du Mérite; Chevalier du Tastevin. *Publications:* articles in Le Monde and business journals. *Leisure interests:* theatre, music, reading, tennis, swimming. *Address:* c/o Board of Directors, International Paper Company, 400 Atlantic Street, Stamford, CT 06921, USA.

GIBB, Barry, CBE; British singer, songwriter and record producer; b. 1 Sept. 1946, Isle of Man; s. of Hughie Gibb and Barbara Gibb; m. Linda Gray; five c.; emigrated to Australia 1958, returned to UK 1967; formed The Bee Gees (with brothers Robin and the late Maurice and Andy) 1958–; started singing in nightclubs, Australia; numerous performances at major venues around the world; hon. degree (Univ. of Manchester) 2004; seven Grammy awards, American Music Award for Int. Achievement 1997, BRIT Award for Outstanding Contribution to Music 1997, World Music Award for Lifetime Achievement 1997, Q Lifetime Achievement Award 2005, Ivor Novello Acad. Fellowship 2006, BMI Icon Award 2007. *Compositions:* writer or co-writer, producer or co-producer of numerous songs for other artists including: Elvis

Presley (Words), Cliff Richard (I Cannot Give You My Love), Sarah Vaughan (Run To Me), Al Green, Janis Joplin, Barbra Streisand (Guilty album), Diana Ross (Chain Reaction), Dionne Warwick (Heartbreaker), Dolly Parton and Kenny Rogers (Islands In The Stream), Ntrance (Staying Alive), Take That (How Deep Is Your Love), Boyzone (Words), Yvonne Elliman (If I Can't Have You). *Recordings include:* albums: with The Bee Gees: Bee Gees Sing and Play 14 Barry Gibb Songs 1965, Monday's Rain 1966, Bee Gees 1st 1967, Horizontal 1968, Idea 1968, Odessa 1969, Cucumber Castle 1970, Marley Purt Drive 1970, Sound of Love 1970, Two Years On 1971, Melody (OST) 1971, Trafalgar 1971, To Whom It May Concern 1972, Life in a Tin Can 1973, Mr Natural 1974, Main Course 1975, Children of the World 1976, Here at Last... Bee Gees Live 1977, Saturday Night Fever (OST) 1977, Spirits Having Flown 1979, SWALK 1979, Living Eyes 1981, Staying Alive (OST) 1983, E.S.P. 1987, One 1989, High Civilization 1991, Size Isn't Everything 1993, Still Waters 1997, One Night Only 1998, This Is Where I Came In 2001, Harmonies Down Under 2002, Alone 2002, In the Beginning 2003, Merchants of Dream 2003, Bee Gees Number Ones 2004; solo: Now Voyager 1984, Hawks 1988. *Address:* c/o Crompton Songs, 5820 North Bay Road, Miami Beach, FL 33140, USA. *Telephone:* (305) 672-2390 (office). *Fax:* (305) 531-8041 (office). *E-mail:* middleear@earthlink.het (office). *Website:* barrygibb.com (office).

GIBB, Sir Frank (Francis Ross), Kt, CBE, FREng, FICE; British engineer and business executive; b. 29 June 1927, London; s. of Robert Gibb and Violet M. Gibb; m. 1st Wendy M. Fowler 1950 (died 1997); one s. two d.; m. 2nd Kirsten Harwood (née Møller) 2000; ed Loughborough Coll.; Joint Man. Dir Taylor Woodrow PLC 1979–85, Jt Deputy Chair. 1983–85, Chair. and Chief Exec. 1985–89; Man. Dir Taylor Woodrow Construction Ltd 1970–78, Chair. 1978–85, Pres. 1985; Dir Taylor Woodrow Int. Ltd 1969–85; Chair. Taywood Santa Fe Ltd 1975–85; Jt Deputy Chair. Seaforth Maritime Ltd 1986–89; Dir Seaforth Maritime Holdings 1978–89, Eurotunnel PLC 1986–87, Babcock Int. Group PLC 1989–97, Nuclear Electric PLC 1990–94, Steetley PLC 1990–92, Energy Saving Trust Ltd 1992–99 (Chair. 1995–99), H. R. Wallingford 1995–; Chair. Nat. Nuclear Corpn Ltd 1981–88; mem. Group of Eight 1979–81; mem. Bd British Nuclear Associates 1980–88; Chair. Agrément Bd 1980–82; Chair. Fed. of Civil Eng Contractors 1979–80, Pres. 1984–87; Vice-Pres. Inst. of Civil Engineers 1988–90; Dir (non-exec.) A.M.C.O. Ltd 1995–99, F.B.E. 1998–2002; Hon. FCGI; Hon. FINucE; Dr hc (Loughborough) 1989; Hon. DTech. *Leisure interests:* ornithology, gardening, walking, music. *Address:* Ross Gibb Consultants, 11 Latchmoor Avenue, Gerrards Cross, Bucks., SL9 8LJ, England (office). *Telephone:* (1753) 882544 (office). *Fax:* (1753) 888823 (office). *E-mail:* rossgibb@aol.com (office).

GIBB, Robin, CBE; British singer and songwriter; b. 22 Dec. 1949, Isle of Man; s. of Hughie Gibb and Barbara Gibb; m. Divina Murphy; one s.; emigrated to Australia 1958, returned to UK 1967; formed The Bee Gees (with brothers Barry, and the late Maurice and Andy) 1958–; started singing in nightclubs, Australia; numerous performances at major venues around the world; Pres., Int. Confederation of Societies of Authors and Composers (CISAC) 2007–; Dr hc (Univ. of Manchester) 2004, Hon. Companionship (Liverpool Inst. of Performing Arts) 2005; seven Grammy awards, Int. Achievement Award American Music Awards 1997, BRIT Award for Outstanding Contribution to Music 1997, World Music Award for Lifetime Achievement 1998, Q Lifetime Achievement Award 2005, Ivor Novello Acad. Fellowship 2006, BMI Icon Award 2007. *Compositions:* as writer or co-writer: Elvis Presley (Words), Sarah Vaughan (Run to Me), Al Green, Janis Joplin, Rod Stewart (To Love Somebody), Tina Turner (I Will Be There), Ntrance (Staying Alive), Take That (How Deep is Your Love), Boyzone (Words), Yvonne Elliman (If I Can't Have You). *Recordings include:* albums: with The Bee Gees: Bee Gees Sing and Play 14 Barry Gibb Songs 1965, Monday's Rain 1966, Bee Gees 1st 1967, Horizontal 1968, Idea 1968, Odessa 1969, Cucumber Castle 1970, Marley Purt Drive 1970, Sound of Love 1970, Two Years On 1971, Melody (OST) 1971, Trafalgar 1971, To Whom It May Concern 1972, Life in a Tin Can 1973, Mr Natural 1974, Main Course 1975, Children of the World 1976, Here at Last... Bee Gees Live 1977, Saturday Night Fever (OST) 1977, Spirits Having Flown 1979, SWALK 1979, Living Eyes 1981, Staying Alive (OST) 1983, E.S.P. 1987, One 1989, High Civilization 1991, Size Isn't Everything 1993, Still Waters 1997, One Night Only 1998, This Is Where I Came In 2001, Harmonies Down Under 2002, Alone 2002, In the Beginning 2003, Merchants of Dream 2003, Number Ones 2004; solo: Robin's Reign 1970, How Old Are You? 1983, Secret Agent 1984, Walls Have Eyes 1985, Magnet 2003. *Address:* Middle Ear, 1801 Bay Road, Miami, FL 33139, USA.

GIBBARD, Allan Fletcher, PhD; American academic; *Richard B. Brandt Distinguished University Professor of Philosophy, University of Michigan;* b. 7 April 1942, Providence, RI; s. of Harold A. Gibbard and Eleanor Reid Gibbard; m. 1st Mary Craig 1972 (died 1990); m. 2nd Beth Genné 1991; two s.; ed Swarthmore Coll., Harvard Univ.; teacher of math. and physics with US Peace Corps, Achimota School, Ghana 1963–65; Asst Prof. then Assoc. Prof. of Philosophy, Univ. of Chicago 1969–74; Assoc. Prof. of Philosophy, Univ. of Pittsburgh 1974–77; Prof. of Philosophy, Univ. of Michigan, Ann Arbor 1977–, Richard B. Brandt Univ. Prof. 1992–; Fellow Econometric Soc. 1984, American Acad. of Arts and Sciences 1990. *Publications:* Wise Choices, Apt Feelings: A Theory of Normative Judgement 1990, Thinking How to Live 2003; articles in journals. *Address:* Department of Philosophy, University of Michigan, Angell Hall, 435 South State Street, Ann Arbor, MI 48109-1003, USA (office). *Telephone:* (313) 764-6285 (office); (313) 769-2628 (home). *Fax:* (313) 763-8071 (office). *E-mail:* gibbard@umich.edu (office). *Website:* www-personal.umich.edu/~gibbard (office).

GIBBON, Gary, BA; British journalist; *Political Editor, Channel 4 News;* b. 15 March 1965; s. of Robert Gibbon and Elizabeth Gibbon; m. Laura Pulay 1993; two s.; ed Balliol Coll., Oxford; fmr journalist, BBC; joined Channel 4 News 1990, Political Producer 1992–94, Political Corresp. 1994–2005, Political Ed. 2005–. *Address:* Channel 4 News, ITN, 200 Gray's Inn Road, London, WC1X 8XZ, England (office). *Telephone:* (20) 7430-4996 (office). *E-mail:* gary.gibbon@itn.co.uk (office). *Website:* www.channel4.com/news (office).

GIBBONS, Ian Read, PhD, FRS; British professor of biophysics; *Research Cell Biologist, University of California, Berkeley;* b. 30 Oct. 1931, Hastings, Sussex; s. of Arthur A. Gibbons and Hilda R. Cake; m. Barbara R. Hollingworth 1961; one s. one d.; ed Faversham Grammar School and King's Coll., Cambridge; Research Fellow, Univ. of Pa 1957, Harvard Univ. 1958; Asst Prof. of Biology, Harvard Univ. 1963; Assoc. Prof. of Biophysics, Univ. of Hawaii 1967, Prof. 1969–97; Research Cell Biologist, Univ. of Calif. at Berkeley 1997–; Visiting Prof., Univ. of Siena 1981–82; Guggenheim Fellowship 1973; International Prize for Biology (Japan) 1995; Fellow, Royal Society. *Publications:* numerous articles in learned journals related to cell motility, especially that of cilia, flagella and other microtubule organelles. *Leisure interests:* gardening, music, computer programming. *Address:* Department of Molecular and Cell Biology, University of California, 335 LSA-3200, Berkeley, CA 94720, USA (office). *Telephone:* (510) 642-2439 (office). *Fax:* (510) 643-6791 (office). *E-mail:* igibbons@socrates.berkeley.edu (office). *Website:* mcb.berkeley.edu/site (office).

GIBBONS, James A. (Jim); American geologist, lawyer, politician and state official; *Governor of Nevada;* b. 16 Dec. 1944, Sparks, Nev.; m. Dawn Gibbons; two s. one d.; ed Univ. of Nevada, Reno, Southwestern Law School, Los Angeles, Univ. of Southern California, graduate of USAF Air Command and Staff Coll. and Air War Coll.; served in USAF 1967–71, joined Nev. Air Guard 1975, served as its Vice-Commdr 1990–96, participated in first Gulf War; has worked as lawyer in pvt. practice, airline pilot for Western Airlines and Delta Air Lines, hydrologist and geologist; served in Nev. State Ass. 1989–93, called to active service in Gulf War as RF-4C Flight Leader; cand. for Gov. of Nev. 1994; mem. US House of Reps for 2nd Congressional Dist of Nev. 1997–2006, Vice-Chair. House Resources Cttee, mem. Armed Services Cttee, Homeland Security Cttee, Permanent Select Cttee on Intelligence; Gov. of Nev. 2007–; Republican; earned 19 service medals, including the Legion of Merit, Distinguished Flying Cross, Air Medal with Two Oak Leaf Clusters, Aerial Achievement Medal and Air Force Commendation Medal with One Oak Leaf Cluster. *Address:* Office of the Governor, Capitol Building, 101 N Carson Street, Carson City, NV 89701, USA (office). *Telephone:* (775) 684-5670 (office). *Fax:* (775) 684-5683 (office). *Website:* gov.state.nv.us (office).

GIBBONS, Hon. Sir (John) David, KBE, BA, JP, CBIM; British business executive and fmr politician; *CEO, Edmund Gibbons Ltd;* s. of the late Edmund G. Gibbons and Winifred G. Gibbons; m. Lully Lorentzen 1958; three s.; one d. by previous marriage; ed Saltus Grammar School, Bermuda, Hotchkiss School, Lakeville, Conn., USA, Harvard Univ., USA; govt service in Bermuda with Social Welfare Bd 1948–58, Bd of Civil Aviation 1958–60, Bd of Educ. 1956–59, Chair. 1973–74; mem. Governing Body and later Chair. Bermuda Tech. Inst. 1956–70; Trade Devt Bd 1960–74; MP 1972–84; Minister of Health and Welfare 1974–75, of Finance 1975–84; Prime Minister 1977–82; Chair. Bermuda Monetary Authority 1984–86, Bank of N.T. Butterfield & Son Ltd 1986–97, Econ. Council 1984–87, Global Asset Man. Ltd 1986–, Colonial Insurance Co. 1986–; currently also CEO Edmund Gibbons Ltd; mem. Law Reform Cttee 1966–72. *Leisure interests:* tennis, golf, skiing, swimming. *Address:* Edmund Gibbons Ltd, 21 Reid Street, Hamilton, HM 11 (office); Leeward, 5 Leeside Drive, Pembroke, HM 05, Bermuda (home). *Telephone:* 295-0022 (office). *Fax:* 295-1040 (office). *E-mail:* jbenevides@harbour-trust.com (office).

GIBBONS, John H., PhD; American physicist and fmr government official; *President, Resource Strategies;* b. 15 Jan. 1929, Harrisonburg, Va; s. of Howard Gibbons and Jesse Conrad; m. Mary Hobart 1955; three c.; ed Randolph-Macon Coll. Va and Duke Univ. NC; Group leader (nuclear geophysics), Oak Ridge Nat. Lab. 1954–69, Environmental Programme Dir 1969–73; Dir of Energy, Environmental and Resources Center and Prof. of Physics, Univ. of Tennessee 1973–79; Dir Office of Energy Conservation, Fed. Energy Admin. 1974; Dir Congressional Office of Tech. Assessment 1979–92; Asst to Pres. Clinton for Science and Tech. and Dir Office of Science and Tech. Policy 1993–98; Pres. Resource Strategies Inc. 1998–; Sr Adviser, US Dept of State 1999–2001; Sr Fellow, Nat. Acad. of Eng 1999–2000; Fellow, AAAS, American Physical Soc., American Philosophical Soc., Nat. Acad. of Eng; numerous professional appointments and affiliations; Commdr Ordre des Palmes Académiques (France), Bundesverdienstkreuz (Germany); Hon. PhD (Mount Sinai Medical School) 1995; Hon. ScD (Duke) 1997, (Maryland) 1997; NASA Distinguished Service Medal 1998, Art Beuche Prize, Nat. Acad. of Eng 1998, Abelson Prize, AAAS 1998, Seymour Cray Award 1998; many other awards and distinctions. *Publications:* This Gifted Age: Science and Technology at the Millennium 1997; numerous books and articles in areas of energy and environmental policy, etc. *Leisure interests:* farming, hiking. *Address:* Resource Strategies, PO Box 379, The Plains, VA 20198, USA. *Telephone:* (540) 253-9843 (office); (540) 253-5409 (home). *Fax:* (540) 253-5076 (office); (540) 253-5076 (home). *E-mail:* jackgibbons@direcway.com (office). *Website:* www.johnhgibbons.org.

GIBBONS, Michael Gordon, MBE, BSc, BEng, MSc, PhD; Canadian academic; *Director of the Science Policy Research Unit, University of Sussex;* b. 15 April 1939, Montreal; s. of Albert Gordon Gibbons and Dorothy Mildred Gibbons; m. Gillian Monks 1968; one s. one d.; ed Concordia Univ., Montreal, McGill Univ., Montreal, Queens Univ., Ont., Univ. of Manchester, UK; lecturer Univ. of Manchester 1967–72, Sr Lecturer 1972–75, Prof. 1975–92, Head Dept 1975–92; Dir Univ. UMIST Pollution Research Unit 1979–86, Chair. and Founding Dir Policy Research in Eng, Science and Tech. 1979–92, Dir Research Exploitation and Devt, Vice-Chancellor's Office 1984–92; Dean

Grad. School and Dir Science Policy Research Unit, Univ. of Sussex 1992–96, Dir Science Policy Research Unit 2004–, mem. Senate, Man. Cttee, Court and Council; Sec.-Gen. Asscn of Commonwealth Univs 1996–2004; Visiting Prof., Univ. of Montreal 1976–81, Univ. of Calif., Berkeley 1992; Special Adviser House of Commons Science and Tech. Cttee 1993; mem. Council, ESRC 1997; mem. Research Priorities Bd 1994, Chair. 1997; Consultant Cttee of Science and Tech. Policy, OECD, Paris; Fellow, Royal Swedish Acad. of Eng Sciences 2000; Hon. LLD (Univ. of Ghana, Legon) 1999, (Concordia Univ., Montreal) 2004; Hon. DUniv (Univ. of Surrey) 2005; Lt-Gov.'s Silver Medal 1959, Government of Canada Commemorative Medal 2002. *Publications:* Wealth from Knowledge (jtly.) 1972, Science as a Commodity 1984, Post-Innovation Performance: Technical Development and Competition 1986, The Evaluation of Research: A Synthesis of Current Practice 1987, The New Production of Knowledge 1994, Re-thinking Science 2000. *Leisure interests:* classical music, American football. *Address:* SPRU, Freeman Building, University of Sussex, Brighton (office); 24 Fletsand Road, Wilmslow, Cheshire SK9 2AB, England (home). *Telephone:* (1273) 678175 (office); (1625) 527924 (home). *E-mail:* michael_gibbons@onetel.net (home).

GIBBS, Anthony Matthews, BA, BLitt, MA, FAHA; Australian academic; *Professor Emeritus of English, Macquarie University;* b. 21 Jan. 1933, Victoria; s. of J. F. L. Gibbs and S. T. Gibbs; m. 1st Jillian Irving Holden 1960; m. 2nd Donna Patricia Lucy 1983; two s. one step d.; ed Ballarat Church of England Grammar School, Univ. of Melbourne and Univ. of Oxford; Lecturer in English, Univ. of Adelaide 1960–66, Univ. of Leeds 1966–69; Prof. of English, Univ. of Newcastle, NSW 1969–75; Prof. of English, Macquarie Univ. 1975–98, Prof. Emer. 1999–; mem. Exec. Cttee Int. Asscn for the Study of Anglo-Irish Literature 1973–78, Exec. Cttee English Asscn (Sydney Br.) 1975–91, Founding Council Int. Shaw Soc. 2004; Rhodes Scholarship 1956; Vice-Pres. Australian Acad. of Humanities 1988–89; Ed. 1989–93; Centenary Medal 2003. *Publications:* Shaw 1969, Sir William Davenant 1972, The Art and Mind of Shaw 1983, Shaw: Interviews and Recollections 1990, Bernard Shaw: Man and Superman and Saint Joan 1992, Heartbreak House: Preludes of Apocalypse 1994, A Bernard Shaw Chronology 2001, Bernard Shaw: A Life 2005. *Leisure interests:* theatre, cooking. *Address:* Department of English, Macquarie University, Sydney, NSW 2109 (office); 4 Acacia Close, Turramurra, NSW 2074, Australia (home). *Telephone:* (2) 9850-8739 (office). *Fax:* (2) 9850-6593 (office). *E-mail:* gibbston@gmail.com (home). *Website:* www.engl.mq.edu.au/staff/tonygibbs.html (office).

GIBBS, Lancelot (Lance) Richard; Guyanese sports organizer and fmr professional cricketer; b. 29 Sept. 1934, Georgetown, British Guiana (now Guyana); s. of Ebenezer and Marjorie Gretna (Archer) Gibbs; cousin of cricketer Clive Lloyd; m. Joy Roslyn Margarete Rogers 1963; one s. one d.; ed St Ambrose Anglican Primary School and Day Commercial Standard High School; right-arm off-spin bowler; played for British Guiana/Guyana 1953–54 to 1974–75, Warwickshire 1967 to 1973, S Australia 1969–70; played in 79 Tests for West Indies 1957–58 to 1975–76, taking then world record 309 wickets (average 29); only bowler to take 100 or more wickets against both England and Australia; toured England 1963, 1966, 1969, 1973, 1975 (World Cup); took 1,024 first-class wickets; Man. 1991 West Indies tour of England; now a sports organizer based in USA, which he represented against Canada 1983; Chair. of Lauderhill, Fla bid to host Cricket World Cup in 2007; man. posts in transportation business including Booker Shipping, Guyana and Kent Line, Canada; Wisden Cricketer of The Year 1972. *Leisure interests:* reading, all sport. *Address:* USA/Broward/Lauderhill World Cup Host Committee 2007, 2100 NW 55 Avenue, Lauderhill, FL 33313, USA (office); 276 Republic Park, Peter's Hall, E.B.D., Guyana. *Telephone:* (954) 730-3008 (office). *Website:* www.cricketusabl.com (office).

GIBBS, Robert L., BA; American political consultant and government official; *White House Press Secretary;* b. 29 March 1971, Auburn, Ala; s. of Robert Gibbs and Nancy Gibbs; m.; one s.; ed North Carolina State Univ.; Press Sec. for US Congressman Bob Etheridge 1997; spokesman for Fritz Hollings' senatorial campaign 1998; Press Sec. for John Kerry's presidential campaign 2004; Communications Dir Democratic Senatorial Campaign Cttee and Barack Obama's senatorial campaign 2004; Communications Dir for Senator Barack Obama, Washington, DC 2004–08; Communications Dir Senator Barack Obama's presidential campaign 2007–08; White House Press Sec. 2009–. *Address:* Office of the Press Secretary, The White House, 1600 Pennsylvania Avenue, NW, Washington, DC 20500, USA (office). *Telephone:* (202) 456-1414 (office). *Fax:* (202) 456-2461 (office). *Website:* www.whitehouse.gov/news/briefings (office).

GIBBS, Sir Roger Geoffrey, Kt; British business executive and administrator; b. 13 Oct. 1934, Herts.; s. of Sir Geoffrey Gibbs, KCMG and Lady Gibbs; ed Eton Coll. and Millfield School; with Jessel Toynbee & Co. Ltd 1954–64, Dir 1960, de Zoete & Gorton (later de Zoete & Bevan) stockbrokers 1964–71; Gov. The Wellcome Trust 1983–99 (Chair. 1989–99); Chair. London Discount Market Asscn 1984–86; Dir Arsenal Football Club 1980–, Gerrard & Nat. Holdings PLC 1989–94 (Chair. 1975–89), Howard De Walden Estates Ltd 1989–2001 (Chair. 1993–98), The Colville Estate Ltd 1989–; Chair. Arundel Castle Cricket Foundation 1986–95, Council for Royal Nat. Pension Fund for Nurses 1975–2000, Court of Advisers, St Paul's Cathedral 1989–2000, Fleming Family & Partners 2000–; mem. Cttee Marylebone Cricket Club 1991–94, St Paul's Cathedral Foundation (Chair. 2000–); Trustee Winston Churchill Memorial Trust 2001–; Liveryman, Merchant Taylor's Co.; Freeman, City of London. *Leisure interests:* sport, travel. *Address:* 23 Tregunter Road, London, SW10 9LS, England. *Telephone:* (20) 7370-3465 (home). *Fax:* (20) 7373-5263.

GIBSON, Charles DeWolf, AB; American newscaster; *Anchor, World News Tonight with Charles Gibson, ABC Television;* s. of Burdett Gibson and

Georgiana Gibson (née Law); m. Arlene Joy Gibson 1968; two d.; ed Princeton Univ.; Washington Producer, RKO Network, Washington, DC 1966; News Dir Station-WLVA-TV, Lynchburg, Va 1967–69; anchorman, reporter Station-WMAL-TV (now WJLA-TV), Washington, DC 1970–73; corresp., TVN, Inc. (TV News, Inc.) 1974–75; joined ABC News 1975, White House Corresp., Washington, DC 1976–77, Corresp., gen. assignment 1977–81, Capitol Hill Corresp. 1981–87; Co-host Good Morning America, ABC TV, New York City 1987–98, 1999–2006, Anchor, World News Tonight with Charles Gibson 2006–; mem. Bd of Dirs Knight-Wallace Fellows at Mich. 1988; Trustee Princeton Univ. 2006–; Nat. Journalism Fellow, Nat. Endowment of the Humanities, Univ. of Mich. 1973–74, John Maclean Fellowship, Princeton Univ. 1992. *Address:* ABC World News with Charles Gibson, 77 West 66th Street, New York, NY 10023, USA (office). *Telephone:* (212) 456-4040 (office). *Fax:* (212) 456-3720 (office). *Website:* abcnews.go.com/WNT (office).

GIBSON, Frank William Ernest, AM, DPhil, DSc, FAA, FRS; Australian biochemist and academic; *Professor Emeritus of Biochemistry, Australian National University;* b. 22 July 1923, Melbourne; s. of John William and Alice Ruby (née Hancock) Gibson; m. 1st Margaret Burvill 1949 (divorced 1979); two d.; m. 2nd Robin Barker (née Rollason) Gibson 1980; one s.; ed Collingwood Tech. Coll., Univs of Queensland, Melbourne and Oxford, UK; Research Asst, Melbourne and Queensland Univs 1938–47, Sr Demonstrator, Melbourne Univ. 1948–49, Sr Lecturer 1953–58, Reader in Chemical Microbiology 1959–65, Prof. 1965–66; ANU Scholar, Univ. of Oxford 1950–52; Research Assoc., Stanford Univ., USA 1959; Dir John Curtin School and Howard Florey Prof. of Medical Research, ANU 1977–80, Prof. of Biochemistry 1967–88, Prof. Emer. 1989–; Visiting Prof. and Fellow, Lincoln Coll., Oxford 1982–83; Fellow, ANU 1989–; Pres. Australian Biochemical Soc. 1978–79; Gowland Hopkins Medallist, Leeuwenhoek Lecturer Royal Soc. 1981, Biochemical Soc. 1982, Burnet Medallist, Australian Acad. of Sciences 1991, Centenary Medallist 2003. *Publications:* numerous scientific papers and reviews on biochemistry and microbial metabolism. *Leisure interests:* tennis, music. *Address:* 7 Waller Crescent, Campbell, ACT 2612, Australia (home). *Telephone:* (2) 6247-0760 (home). *E-mail:* frank.gibson@anu.edu.au.

GIBSON, Sir Ian, Kt, CBE; British business executive; *Chairman, William Morrison Supermarkets PLC;* joined Ford Motor Co., 1968, served several exec. positions in UK and Germany –1984; joined Nissan Motor Manufacturing (UK) Ltd as purchasing and production control dir 1984, Man. Dir and CEO 1989–98, Chair. 1998, Pres. Nissan Europe and Sr Vice-Pres. Nissan Motor Co. Ltd 1999–2001; Deputy Chair. (non-exec.) William Morrison Supermarkets PLC 2007–08, Chair. 2008–; Chair. (non-exec.) Trinity Mirror PLC 2006–; fmr Chair. BPB PLC; fmr Deputy Chair. Asda Group PLC; fmr mem. Bd of Dirs Chelys Ltd; fmr Sr Dir (non-exec.) Northern Rock plc; fmr Dir (non-exec.) GKN plc, Greggs plc; fmr mem. Court of the Bank of England. *Address:* William Morrison Supermarkets PLC, Hilmore House, Gain Lane, Bradford, BD3 7DL (office); Trinity Mirror PLC, One Canada Square, Canary Wharf, London, E14 5AP, England (office). *Telephone:* (845) 611-5000 (Morrison) (office); (20) 7293-3000 (Trinity Mirror) (office). *Fax:* (20) 7510-3000 (Trinity Mirror) (office). *E-mail:* info@morrisons.co.uk (office); info@trinitymirror.com (office). *Website:* www.morrisons.co.uk (office); www.trinitymirror.com (office).

GIBSON, Mel, AO; Australian actor, director and producer; b. 3 Jan. 1956, Peekskill, NY, USA; s. of Hutton Gibson and Anne Gibson; m. Robyn Moore; five s. one d.; ed Nat. Inst. for Dramatic Art, Sydney; f. ICONS Productions; Commdr Ordre des Arts et des Lettres. *Films include:* Summer City, Mad Max 1979, Tim 1979, Attack Force Z, Gallipoli 1981, The Road Warrior (Mad Max II) 1982, The Year of Living Dangerously 1983, The Bounty 1984, The River 1984, Mrs. Soffel 1984, Mad Max Beyond Thunderdome 1985, Lethal Weapon, Tequila Sunrise, Lethal Weapon II, Bird on a Wire 1989, Hamlet 1990, Air America 1990, Lethal Weapon III 1991, Man Without a Face (also dir) 1992, Maverick 1994, Braveheart (also Dir, co-producer, Acad. Award for Best Picture 1996) 1995, Ransom 1996, Conspiracy Theory 1997, Lethal Weapon IV 1998, Payback 1997, The Million Dollar Hotel 1999, The Patriot 2000, What Women Want 2000, We Were Soldiers 2002, Signs 2002, The Singing Detective 2003, The Passion of the Christ (dir, producer; US People's Choice Award for Best Drama 2005) 2004, Apocalypto (dir) 2006. *Plays include:* Romeo and Juliet, Waiting for Godot, No Names No Pack Drill, Death of a Salesman. *Address:* c/o ICONS Productions, 4000 Warner Boulevard, Room 17, Burbank, CA 91522, USA; c/o Shanahan Management, P.O. Box 478, King's Cross, NSW 2011, Australia.

GIBSON, Rt Hon. Sir Peter (Leslie), Rt Hon. Lord Justice Peter Gibson; Kt; British judge; *Lord Justice of Appeal;* b. 10 June 1934; s. of Harold Leslie Gibson and Martha Lucy (née Diercking) Gibson; m. Dr Katharine Mary Beatrice Hadow 1968 (died 2002); two s. one d.; ed Malvern Coll., Worcester Coll., Oxford; Nat. Service 2nd Lt RA 1953–55; called to Bar, Inner Temple 1960; Bencher, Lincoln's Inn 1975; Second Jr Counsel to Inland Revenue (Chancery) 1970–72; Jr Counsel to the Treasury (Chancery) 1972–81; Judge of the High Court of Justice, Chancery Div. 1981–93; Chair. Law Comm. for England and Wales 1990–92; a Judge of the Employment Appeal Tribunal 1984–86; Lord Justice of Appeal 1993–; Treasurer Lincoln's Inn 1996; Hon. Fellow, Worcester Coll., Oxford 1993. *Address:* Royal Courts of Justice, Strand, London, WC2A 2LL, England (office).

GIBSON, Rex; South African journalist; b. 11 Aug. 1931, Salisbury; s. of Arthur David Gibson and Mildred Joyce Adam; three d.; ed King Edward VII School, Johannesburg; articled clerk 1948–52; entered journalism 1952; joined Rand Daily Mail 1959, Chief Sub-Ed. 1962, Arts Ed. 1969, Asst Ed. then Chief Asst Ed. 1969–72, Deputy Ed. 1973–76, Ed. 1982–85; Founding Ed. Mining News 1967; Ed. The Northern Reporter (first local suburban newspaper) 1968–69; Ed. The Sunday Express 1976–82; Deputy Ed. The Star, Johannesburg 1985–93; Deputy Man. Dir Sussens Mann Communications 1993–; Bursar Imperial Relations Trust 1960; Atlas World Review Joint Int. Ed. of the Year Award 1979, Pringle Award for Journalism 1979. *Leisure interests:* reading, tennis, golf.

GIBSON, Robert Dennis, AO, MSc, PhD, DSc, FTS, FAIM; Australian university chancellor; *Chancellor, RMIT University;* b. 13 April 1942, Newcastle, UK; s. of Edward Gibson and Euphemia Gibson; m. 1st. Eileen Hancox 1964; one s. two d.; m. 2nd Catherine Bull 1994; ed Univs of Hull and Newcastle, UK; Prof. and Head, School of Math. and Computing, Newcastle Polytechnic 1977–82; Deputy Dir Queensland Inst. of Tech. 1982–83, Dir 1983–88; Vice-Chancellor Queensland Univ. of Tech. (QUT) 1989–2003; mem. Australian Research Council 1988–93; Chair. Grad. Careers Council of Australia 1999–2005, M&MD Ltd 2003–; Premier of Queensland SMART Awards Panel 2003–; Chancellor RMIT (fmrly Royal Melbourne Inst. of Tech.) 2003–; Fellow, Australian Inst. of Co. Dirs; Hon. DSc (CNAA) 1984, Hon. DUniv (USC) 2000, (QUT) 2003. *Publications:* over 80 publs in mathematical modelling. *Leisure interests:* cricket, running. *Address:* GPO Box 2434, Brisbane 4001 (office); RMIT University, PO Box 2476V, Melbourne 3001, Victoria; 173/350 St Kilda Road, Melbourne 3004, Victoria, Australia (home). *Telephone:* (3) 9925-3635 (office); (3) 9690-5222 (home). *Fax:* (3) 9925-3939 (office). *E-mail:* d.gibson@rmit.edu.au (office). *Website:* www.rmit.edu.au (office).

GIBSON, Robin Warwick, OBE, BA; British art historian and museum curator; b. 3 May 1944, Hereford; s. of the late Walter Edward Gibson and Freda Mary Yates (née Partridge); ed Royal Masonic School, Bushey, Magdalene Coll., Cambridge; Asst Keeper, City Art Gallery, Manchester 1967–68; Asst Keeper, Nat. Portrait Gallery, London 1968–83, Curator, Twentieth Century Collection 1983–94, Chief Curator 1994–2001; mem. Cttee Nat. Trust Foundation for Art 1991–2001. *Publications:* The McDonald Collection 1970, British Portrait Painters (co-author) 1971, Flower Painting 1976, The Clarendon Collection 1977, 20th Century Portraits 1978, Glyn Philpot 1984, John Bellany: New Portraits 1986, John Bratby Portraits 1991, The Portrait Now 1993, The Sitwells (co-author) 1994, Glenys Barton (co-author) 1997, The Face in the Corner 1998, Painting the Century (co-author) 2000, A Little English Mass 2005. *Leisure interests:* music, gardening. *Address:* Maple Cottage, 1 The Bull Ring, Thaxted, Essex, CM6 2PL, England (home). *E-mail:* robline@btinternet.com (home).

GIBSON, Roy; British scientific consultant; b. 4 July 1924, Manchester; s. of Fred Gibson and Jessie Gibson; m. Inga Elgerus 1971; one s. one d. (by previous marriage); ed Chorlton Grammar School, Wadham Coll., Oxford, London School of Econs with Colonial Admin. Service, Malaya 1948–58; UK Atomic Energy Authority, London 1959–67; Deputy Dir Tech. Centre, European Space Research Org. (ESRO) 1967–71, Dir of Admin. ESRO 1971–74, Acting Dir-Gen. 1974–75; Dir-Gen., ESA 1975–81, Aerospace Consultant 1980–; Dir-Gen. British Nat. Space Centre 1985–87; fmr special advisor to Dir-Gen., Int. Maritime Satellite Org. (INMARSAT); Adviser to Dir-Gen. EUMETSAT 1987–. *Publications:* Space 1992; numerous articles in aerospace technical journals. *Leisure interests:* music, languages, bridge, walking. *Address:* Résidence Les Hespérides, 51 Allée J. de Beins, 34000 Montpellier, France; EUMETSAT, Am Kavalleriesandd 31, 64295 Darmstadt Germany (office). *Telephone:* (4) 67-64-81-81. *Fax:* (4) 67-22-34-02. *E-mail:* roy.gibson@wanadoo.fr (office). *Website:* www.eumetsat.int (home).

GIBSON, Toby J., PhD; British biologist/biochemist; *Team Leader, European Molecular Biology Laboratory;* ed Univ. of Cambridge; on staff, Lab. of Molecular Biology, Cambridge 1981–86; Team Leader, European Molecular Biology Lab., Heidelberg, Germany 1986–. *Publications:* numerous publs in scientific journals. *Address:* European Molecular Biology Laboratory, Meyerhofstraße 1, 69117 Heidelberg, Germany (office). *Telephone:* (6221) 387-8398 (office). *Fax:* (6221) 387517 (office). *E-mail:* toby.gibson@embl.de (office). *Website:* www.embl.org/aboutus (office).

GIBSON-SMITH, Chris, BSc, MS, PhD; British business executive; *Chairman, London Stock Exchange;* m.; two c.; ed Univs of Durham and Newcastle and Stanford Business School, USA; with British Petroleum (BP) 1970–2001, positions include COO BP Chemicals, CEO BP Exploration Europe, Group Man. Dir 1997–2001; Chair. Nat. Air Traffic Services 2001–03; Chair. London Stock Exchange 2003–; Dir (non-exec.) Lloyds TSB Group PLC 1999–2005, Powergen UK PLC 2001–02, British Land Co. PLC 2003–; Trustee Arts and Business. *Leisure interests:* skiing, golf, music, the arts. *Address:* London Stock Exchange, 10 Paternoster Square, London, EC4M 7LS, England. *Telephone:* (20) 7797-1318 (office). *E-mail:* enquiries@londonstockexchange.com (office). *Website:* www.londonstockexchange.com (office).

GIDADA, Negaso, MA, PhD; Ethiopian fmr head of state and politician; b. 8 Sept. 1943, Dembi Dollo, Wollega; m. Regina Abelt; one s. two d.; ed Addis Ababa Univ., Johann Wolfgang Goethe-Universität, Frankfurt; Minister of Labour and Social Affairs 1991–92, Minister of Information 1992–95, Pres. of Ethiopia 1995–2001; mem. House of Reps 2005–; Interreligious and Int. Fed. for World Peace Amb. for Peace, Int. Lions Club Melvin Jones Fellow. *Publications:* History of the Sayo Oromo of Southwestern Wollega, Ethiopia 2001. *Leisure Interests:* reading, walking. *Address:* House Number 695, Qabele 22, Bole Kifle Ketama, Addis Ababa (home); House Number 1031, Nefas Silk-Lafto Kifle Ketema, Addis Ababa (home); PO Box 26749, C-1000, Addis Ababa, Ethiopia (office). *Telephone:* (1) 231213 (office); (1) 247625 (office). *E-mail:* nereta2003@yahoo.com (home).

GIDASPOV, Boris Veniaminovich, DSc; Russian scientist; b. 16 April 1933, Kuibyshev; s. of Veniamin Aleksandrovich Gidaspov and Maria Aleksandrovna Smirnova; m. Zinaida Ivanovna Kuznetsova 1961; one s.; ed Kuibyshev Industrial Inst.; mem. CPSU 1962–91; research, Kuibyshev Chemical Inst. 1955–59 and Leningrad Tech. Inst. 1959–77; Dir State Inst. of Applied Chem. 1977–89; Consultant Russian Scientific Center 'Applied Chemistry' 1989–; Dir Technoferm Eng (representation in St Petersburg) 1993–; founder mem. of Tekhnokhim (a commercial assen for research), Leningrad 1985–88, Chair. Tekhnokhim Corpn 1991–; corresp. mem. USSR (now Russian) Acad. of Sciences 1981–; USSR People's Deputy 1989–91; First Sec. Leningrad CPSU City Cttee 1989–91; mem. and Sec. CPSU Cen. Cttee 1990–91; mem. Russian Eng Acad. 1994–; Lenin Prize 1976; USSR State Prize 1981. *Leisure interests:* Russian history, sport. *Address:* Tekhnokhim, Angliyskaya nab. 10, St Petersburg 190000, Russia. *Telephone:* (812) 314-91-18 (office); (812) 316-72-31 (home). *Fax:* (812) 311-47-69.

GIDDENS, Baron (Life Peer), cr. 2004, of Southgate in the London Borough of Enfield; **Anthony Giddens,** PhD; British sociologist; *Chairman and Director, Polity Press Ltd;* b. 18 Jan. 1938; m. Jane Ellwood 1963; two d.; ed Minchenden School, Southgate, Univ. of Hull, LSE, Univ. of Cambridge; Lecturer in Sociology, Univ. of Leicester 1961–70; Visiting Asst Prof., Simon Fraser Univ., Vancouver 1967–68, Univ. of Calif., LA 1968–69; Lecturer in Sociology and Fellow King's Coll., Cambridge 1970–84, Reader in Sociology 1984–86, Prof. of Sociology 1986–96; Dir LSE 1997–2003; Chair. and Dir Polity Press Ltd 1985–; Dir Blackwell-Polity Ltd 1985–; Chair. and Dir Centre for Social Research 1989–; BBC Reith Lecturer 1999; numerous visiting professorships; Founder of 'The Third Way'; Hon. Fellow LSE 2004; mem. Russian Acad. of Sciences; Nat. Order of the Southern Cross (Brazil), Grand Cross, Order of the Infante Dom Henrique (Portugal); Hon. DLitt (Salford), (Hull), (Open Univ.), (South Bank); Dr hc (Vesalius Coll., Vrije Univ. Brussels); Prince of Asturias Award (Spain) 2002. *Publications:* Capitalism and Modern Social Theory 1971, Politics and Sociology in the Thought of Max Weber 1972, Emile Durkheim: selected writings (ed. and trans.) 1972, The Class Structure of the Advanced Societies 1973, New Rules of Sociological Method 1976, Positivism and Sociology (ed.) 1973, Elites and Power in British Society (with P. H. Stanworth) 1974, Studies in Social and Political Theory 1977, Emile Durkheim 1978, Central Problems in Social Theory 1979, A Contemporary Critique of Historical Materialism 1981, Sociology: a brief but critical introduction 1982, Classes, Conflict and Power (with D. Held) 1982, Classes and the Division of Labour (with G. G. N. Mackenzie) 1982, Profiles and Critiques in Social Theory 1983, The Constitution of Society: outline of the theory of structuration 1984, The Nation-State and Violence 1985, Durkheim on Politics and the State 1986, Social Theory and Modern Sociology 1987, Social Theory Today (with Jon Turner) 1988, Sociology 1988, The Consequences of Modernity 1990, Modernity and Self-Identity 1991, Human Societies 1992, The Transformation of Intimacy 1992, Beyond Left and Right 1994, Reflexive Modernisation (with Ulrich Beck and Scott Lash) 1994, Politics, Sociology and Social Theory 1995, In Defence of Sociology 1996, Conversations with Anthony Giddens: making sense of modernity (with Christopher Pierson) 1998, The Third Way: the renewal of social democracy 1998, Runaway World: how globalisation is reshaping our lives 1999, The Third Way and its Critics 2000, On the Edge: living with global capitalism (ed., with Will Hutton) 2000, The Global Third Way Debate 2001, The Progressive Manifesto 2003; contrib. articles, review articles and book reviews to professional journals and newspapers. *Leisure interests:* theatre, tennis, cinema, Tottenham Hotspur. *Address:* House of Lords, London, SW1A 0PW; Polity Press, 65 Bridge Street, Cambridge CB2 1UR, England (office). *Telephone:* (20) 7219-6710.

GIELEN, Michael Andreas; Austrian conductor and composer; b. 20 July 1927, Dresden, Germany; m. Helga Augsten 1957; one s. one d.; ed Univ. of Buenos Aires; studied composition under E. Leuchter and J. Polnauer; pianist in Buenos Aires; on music staff, Teatro Colón 1947–50; with Vienna State Opera 1951–60, Perm. Conductor 1954–60; First Conductor Royal Swedish Opera, Stockholm 1960–65; conductor and composer in Cologne 1965–69; Musical Dir Nat. Orchestra of Belgium 1969–73; Chief Conductor Netherlands Opera 1973–75; Music Dir and Gen. Man. Frankfurt Opera House 1977–87; Music Dir Cincinnati Symphony 1980–86; Prin. Conductor SWF Radio Orchestra, Baden-Baden 1986–99, Hon. Conductor 2002–; Prof. of Conducting, Mozarteum, Salzburg 1987–95, Emer. 1995–; Chief Guest Conductor, BBC Symphony Orchestra 1979–82; Perm. Guest Conductor, Berlin State Opera 1998–, Berlin Symphony Orchestra 1998–; Dr hc (Berlin Hochschule der Künste) 2000; State Prize, Hessen 1985, Adorno Prize, Frankfurt 1986, Vienna Music Prize 1997, Frankfurt Music Prize 1999, MIDEM Prize for Lifetime Achievement 2005, Der Faust Prize for Lifetime Achievement 2007, Echo Klassik Prize 2008. *Publications:* Mahler im Gesprach 2002, Unbedingt Musik (auto-biog.) 2005. *Address:* Niedersee 49, 5311, Innerschwand/ Mondsee, Austria (home). *Telephone:* (6232) 2082 (home).

GIELGUD, Maina Julia Gordon, BEPC; British ballet director and teacher; *Guest Repetiteur and Teacher, English National Ballet;* b. 14 Jan. 1945, London; d. of the late Lewis Gielgud and of Elisabeth Grussner; with Cuevas Co. and Roland Petit Co. –1963; Grand Ballet Classique de France 1963–67; Béjart Co. 1967–71; Berlin 1971; London Festival Ballet 1972–76; ballerina, Sadler's Wells Royal Ballet 1976–78; freelance ballerina and guest artist 1978–82; Rehearsal Dir London City Ballet 1982; Artistic Dir The Australian Ballet 1983–96; Ballet Dir Royal Danish Ballet 1997–99; freelance dir, regular guest repetiteur and teacher, English Nat. Ballet 1999–; Artistic Assoc., Houston Ballet 2003–05; Hon. AO 1991. *Plays:* L'Heure Exquise (Maurice Bejart, after Happy Days by Samuel Beckett). *Film:* L'Age en Fleurs. *Ballets produced:* Steps Notes and Squeaks 1968; for The Australian Ballet: The Sleeping Beauty 1985, Giselle 1987; for Boston Ballet: Giselle 2002, 2007; for Ballet du Rhin: Giselle 2003; for Houston Ballet: Giselle 2005. *Ballets performed:* L'Heure Exquisite. *Address:* 1/9 Stirling Court, 3 Marshall Street, London, W1F 9BD, England (home). *Telephone:* (20) 7734-6612 (home).

E-mail: mainagielgud@gmail.com (home). *Website:* www.mainagielgud.com (home).

GIENOW, Herbert Hans Walter, DIur; German business executive; b. 13 March 1926, Hamburg; s. of Günther and Margarethe Gienow; m. Imina Brons 1954; one s. one d.; ed Hamburg Univ.; Head Clerk Deutsche Warentreuhand AG, mem. Bd of Man. 1959; mem. Hamburg Bar; chartered accountant 1961; mem. Bd of Man. Klöckner-Werke AG 1962, Chair. Exec. Bd 1974–91; Pres. ALSTOM Germany 1991–98; Chair. Supervisory Bd ALSTOM GmbH 1994–99, SteelDex AG; Pres. Academia Baltica; fmr Chair. Consultative Cttee Deutsche Bank AG, Essen; Chevalier, Légion d'honneur 1998; Hon. mem. Iron and Steel Inst. Brussels 1992. *Leisure interests:* books, sailing, model soldiers. *Address:* An der Pont 51, 40885 Ratingen (office); Am Adels 7, 40883 Ratingen, Germany (home). *Telephone:* (2102) 126903 (office); (2102) 60692 (home). *Fax:* (2102) 126909 (office). *E-mail:* woneig@aol.com (office).

GIEROWSKI, Stefan; Polish painter; b. 21 May 1925, Częstochowa; s. of Józef Gierowski and Stefania Gierowska (née Wasilewska); m. Anna Golka 1951; one s. one d.; ed Acad. of Fine Arts, Kraków; Docent, Acad. of Fine Arts, Warsaw, Dean of Painting Dept 1975–80, Extraordinary Prof. 1976–; mem. Union of Polish Artists and Designers, Sec.-Gen. 1957–59, Pres. of Painting Section 1959–61, 1963–66; Kt's and Officer's Cross of Order of Polonia Restituta; Silver Medal, Third Festival of Fine Arts, Warsaw 1978, Prize of Chair. Council of Ministers (1st class) 1979, Jan Cybis Prize 1980. *Address:* ul. Gagarina 15 m. 97, 00-753 Warsaw, Poland. *Telephone:* (22) 8411633.

GIERSCH, Herbert, Dr rer. pol; German economist and academic; *Professor Emeritus, University of Kiel;* b. 11 May 1921, Reichenbach; s. of Hermann and Helene (née Kleinert) Giersch; m. Dr. Friederike Koppelmann 1949; two s. one d.; ed Univs of Breslau, Kiel and Münster; Asst to Prof. Walther Hoffmann, Univ. of Münster 1947–48; British Council Fellow, London School of Econs 1948–49; Admin., Econs Directorate, OEEC 1950–51; Lecturer Univ. of Münster 1951–55; Counsellor and Head of Div., Trade and Finance Directorate, OEEC 1953–54; Prof. of Econs, Saar Univ., Saarbrücken 1955–69; Visiting Prof. of Econs, Yale Univ. 1962–63, Dean Acheson Visiting Prof. 1977–78; Prof. of Econs, Univ. of Kiel and Pres. Inst. of World Econs, Kiel 1969–89, Prof. Emer. 1989–; Chair. Asscn of German Econ. Research Insts 1970–82; Pres. Assoc. of European Business Cycle Research Insts 1974–78; f. Herbert Giersch Stiftung, Frankfurt am Main 1998; mem. Advisory Council, Fed. Ministry of Econs 1960–; founding mem. German Council of Econ. Advisers 1964–70, Council and Exec. Comm. Int. Econ. Asscn 1970–82, Treas. 1974–83, Hon. Pres. 1983–; Corresp. Fellow, British Acad. 1983; Foreign mem. Royal Swedish Acad. of Eng Sciences, Stockholm 1987; Hon. mem. American Econ. Asscn; Hon. Fellow, LSE Grosses Bundesverdienstkreuz, mit Stern und Schulterband 1995, Orden pour le Mérite für Wissenschaften und Künste; Dr hc (Erlangen-Nürnberg) 1977, (Basle) 1984, (Saarbrücken) 1993; Ludwig Erhard Award, Paolo Baffi Int. Prize for Econs 1989, Prognos Preis (Basle) 1993, Joachim Jungius Medal 1998, August-Lösch-Ehrenring 2000. *Publications:* Allgemeine Wirtschaftspolitik, Vol. I Grundlagen 1960, Vol. II Konjunktur- und Wachstumspolitik 1977, Kontroverse Fragen der Wirtschaftspolitik 1971, Economic Policy for the European Community (co-author) 1974, Im Brennpunkt: Wirtschaftspolitik. Kritische Beiträge von 1967–77, 1978, Perspectives on the World Economy 1986, Gegen Europessi-mismus. Kritische Beiträge von 1977–85 1986, Offener Rat. Kolumnen aus der Wirtschaftswoche 1986, The World Economy in Perspective: Essays on International Trade and European Integration 1991, The Fading Miracle: Four Decades of Market Economy in Germany (co-author) 1992, Openness for Prosperity, Essays in World Economics 1993, Marktwirtschaftliche Perspektiven für Europa. Das Licht im Tunnel 1993, Kontrovers im Kontext: Wirtschaftspolitische Anstösse 1996, Abschied von der Nationalökonomie 2002. *Address:* Preusserstrasse 17–19, 24105 Kiel, Germany (home). *Telephone:* (431) 8814313 (office); (431) 561872 (home). *Fax:* (431) 8814500 (office). *E-mail:* giersch@ifw.uni-kiel.de (office).

GIERTYCH, Roman, MA, LLM; Polish politician and lawyer; b. 27 Feb. 1971, Srem; s. of Maciej Giertych and Antonina Giertych; m. Barbara Giertych; two c.; ed Adam Mickiewicz Univ., Poznań; owner of a legal practice, Warsaw; reactivated All-Polish Youth (Młodzież Wszechpolska), Chair. 1989 (now Hon. Chair.); mem. Nat. Democratic Party (Stronnictwo Narodowo-Demokratyczne) and Nat. Party (Stronnictwo Narodowe), Vice-Pres. Bd Nat. Party 1994–, both parties merged with several others orgs to form League of Polish Families 2001, Pres. Congress of League of Polish Families (Liga Polskich Rodzin) 2002–; Deputy to Sejm (Parl.) 2001–; Deputy Prime Minister and Minister for Nat. Educ. 2006–07; mem. Polish Academic Union 1988–; mem. and Vice-Chair. PKN Orlen Investigation Comm. (to investigate biggest corruption scandal in modern Polish political history) 2004–. *Publications include:* Kontrrewolucja mlodych (Counter-Revolution of the Young) 1994, Pod walcem historii. Polityka zagraniczna ruchu narodowego 1938–1945 (Under History's Roller. Foreign Policy of the National Movement 1938–1945) 1995, Lot orla (Flight of the Eagle) 2000, Możemy wygrać Polskę (We Can Win Poland) 2001; numerous articles, including several publs in Nasz Dziennik, Mysl Polska, Rodzina Radia Maryja, Wszechpolak. *Leisure interests:* historical books, chess (Vice-Champion of Poznań Voivodship), tennis. *Address:* League of Polish Families (Liga Polskich Rodzin), 00-528 Warsaw, ul. Hoża 9, Poland (office). *Telephone:* (22) 6223648 (office). *Fax:* (22) 6223138 (office). *E-mail:* roman.giertych@sejm.pl (office). *Website:* www.sejm.gov.pl (office).

GIESBERT, Franz-Olivier; French journalist and writer; *Editor, Le Point;* b. 18 Jan. 1949, Wilmington, Del., USA; s. of Frederick Giesbert and Marie Allain; m. 1st Christine Fontaine (divorced); two s. one d.; m. 2nd Natalie Freund 2000; one s., one d.; ed Centre de Formation des Journalistes; journalist at Le Nouvel Observateur 1971, Sr Corresp. in Washington, DC 1980, Political Ed. 1981, Ed.-in-Chief 1985–88; Ed.-in-Chief Le Figaro

1988–2000, Figaro Magazine 1997–2000, mem. Editorial Bd Le Figaro 1993–2000, Figaro Magazine 1997–2000; Ed. Le Point 2000–; Dir/presenter 'le Gai savoir' TV programme, Paris Première cable channel 1997–2001, Dir Culture et Dépendances France 3 TV channel 2001–; mem. jury Prix Théophraste Renaudot 1998–, Prix Louis Hachette, Prix Aujourd'hui; mem. Conseil Admin Musée du Louvre Paris 2000; Aujourd'hui Best Essay Prize 1975, Prix Gutenberg 1987, Prix Pierre de Monaco 1997, Prix Richelieu 1999, Prix Itheme for Best Talk Show 1999. *Publications:* François Mitterrand ou la tentation de l'Histoire (essay) 1977, Monsieur Adrien (novel) 1982, Jacques Chirac (biog.) 1987, Le Président 1990, L'Affreux (Grand Prix du Roman de l'Acad. Française) 1992, La Fin d'une Époque 1993, La Souille (William the Conqueror and Interallie Prize), Le Vieil homme et la Mort 1996, François Mitterrand, une vie 1996, Le Sieur Dieu (Prix Jean d'Heurs de Nice Baie des Anges) 1998, Mort d'un berger 2002, L'Abatteur 2003, La Tragédie du président: scènes de la vie politique 2006. *Address:* Le Point, 74 avenue du Maine, 75682 Paris Cedex, France. *Telephone:* 1-44-10-10-10 (office). *Fax:* 1-44-10-12-49 (office). *E-mail:* fogiesbert@lepoint.tm.fr (office).

GIESKE, Friedhelm, DJur; German business executive; b. 12 Jan. 1928, Schwege/Osnabrück; began career with RWE AG 1953, Deputy mem. Man. Bd 1968, mem. Man. Bd (Finance) 1972, Bd Spokesman 1988, Chair. Man. Bd 1989–94; fmr mem. Supervisory Bd ALLIANZ AG, Munich, Dresdner Bank AG, Frankfurt, Karstadt AG, Essen, MAN AG, Munich, National-Bank, Essen, RWEAG, Essen, Thyssen AG, Duisburg; vice-président d'honneur Société Electrique de l'Our; Grosses Bundesverdienstkreuz 1995. *Address:* Opernplatz 1, 45128 Essen, Germany. *Telephone:* (201) 1200.

GIEVE, Sir John, Kt, CB, MPhil; British civil servant; b. 20 Feb. 1950; m.; two c.; ed New Coll., Oxford; several positions at HM Treasury 1978–2001, including working in Dept of Employment, Pvt. Sec. to the Chief Sec., Treasury Press Sec., Prin. Pvt. Sec. to the Chancellor; Perm. Sec. Home Office 2001–05; Deputy Gov. and mem. Monetary Policy Cttee, Bank of England 2006–09, with responsibility for Bank's Financial Stability work; mem. Bd Financial Services Authority; Gov. Islington Primary School. *Address:* c/o Bank of England, Threadneedle Street, London, EC2R 8AH, England (office). *E-mail:* enquiries@bankofengland.co.uk (office).

GIFFEN, John A., MBA; Canadian business executive; b. 17 Dec. 1938, Ingersoll, Ont.; s. of John Giffen and Kathleen Marion Giffen (née McQuinn); m. Joan E. Rothwell 1962; one s. two d.; ed Univ. of Windsor; plant foreman, Hiram Walker 1962, Project Engineer 1965, Div. Supt 1972, Inventory Man. 1973, N American Distribution Man. 1977, Asst to Pres. 1979, Vice Pres. Worldwide Production 1980–87, Pres. Hiram Walker & Sons Ltd 1987–88, Chair., CEO Hiram Walker-Allied Vintners (Canada) Ltd 1988–89, Allied-Lyons PLC 1988–93, Man. Dir Hiram Walker-Allied Vintners 1989–91, Chair., CEO The Hiram Walker Group 1991–92, Chair. Corby Distilleries Ltd 1992–2003 (Dir 1980–2003); Regional Chair. The Americas, Allied-Lyons 1992–93; Pres. HW-G & W Ltd 1989–92; Deputy Chair. 1992–93; Dir Hallmark Technologies Inc. 1995–; mem. of Windsor Advisory Bd Royal Trustco, of Canadian-UK Cttee, Canadian Chamber of Commerce 1983–91; Dir and Vice-Pres., Windsor Chamber of Commerce 1979–83; Gov. Metropolitan Gen. Hosp., Windsor 1979–85; Dir Inst. of Canadian-American Studies 1983–86. *Leisure interests:* golf, curling. *Address:* PO Box 2518, Walkerville, Windsor, Ont. N8Y 4S5, Canada.

GIFFIN, Gordon D., BA, JD; American diplomatist and lawyer; *Co-Chair, Public Policy and Regulatory Affairs, McKenna Long & Aldridge LLP;* b. Springfield, Mass; m. Patti Alfred Giffin; one d.; ed Duke and Emory Univs; with law firm Hansell and Post 1979–84; Dir of Legis. Affairs and Chief Counsel to Senator Sam Nunn; Treas. Campaign Cttee of Sam Nunn 1974–94; f. Democratic Leadership Council with Senator Nunn and Gov. Clinton 1984, mem. Bd 1984–96; Gen. Counsel Democratic Nat. Convention 1992, 1996; Chair. Clinton Primary Campaign and Clinton–Gore Gen. Election Campaign 1992; Deputy Dir of Personnel, White House Transition Team 1992; Sr Adviser on the South, Clinton Re-election Campaign and Chair. Democratic Campaign in Ga 1996; Sr Pnr, Long, Aldridge and Norman (law firm), specializing in energy regulatory and govt procurement cases –1997, re-joined firm (McKenna Long & Aldridge LLP) as Co-Chair. Public Policy and Regulatory Affairs practice 2001–; Amb. to Canada 1997–2001; fmr Prof. of Law, Emory Univ.; mem. Atlanta Olympic Games Cttee; mem. Bd of Dirs Overseas Pvt. Investment Corpn 1993–97, Carter Center Bd of Trustees, Bd of Dirs Canadian Imperial Bank of Commerce, Canadian Nat. Railway, Canadian Natural Resources, Transalta Inc., Bowater Inc. *Address:* McKenna Long & Aldridge, 303 Peachtree Street, NE, Suite 5300, Atlanta, GA 30308, USA (office). *Telephone:* (404) 527-4020 (office). *Fax:* (404) 527-4198 (office). *E-mail:* ggiffin@mckennalong.com (office). *Website:* mckennalong.com (office).

GIFFORD, Charles (Chad) K., BA; American banking executive; ed Princeton Univ.; Chair., Pres. and CEO BankBoston 1995–96, CEO 1996–97, Chair. and CEO 1997–99; Pres. and COO FleetBoston Financial Corpn 1999–2001, Pres. and CEO 2001–02, Chair. and CEO 2002–04; Chair. Bank of America Corpn (following acquisition of FleetBoston) 2004 (retd), remains as mem. Bd of Dirs; Dir Mass Mutual Life Insurance Co., NSTAR. *Address:* c/o Board of Directors, Bank of America Corporation, Bank of America Corporate Center, 100 North Tryon Street, Charlotte, NC 28255, USA (office).

GIFFORD, Michael Brian, BSc Econ.; British business executive; b. 9 Jan. 1936; s. of Kenneth Gifford and Maude Palmer; m. Nancy Baytos; (two s. two d. by previous m.); ed London School of Econs; joined Leo Computers (later part of ICL) 1960; Man. Dir ICL (Pacific) 1973–75; Chief Exec. Cadbury Schweppes Australia 1975–78; Finance Dir Cadbury Schweppes PLC 1978–83; Man. Dir and Chief Exec. Rank Org. 1983–96; Dir Fuji Xerox

1984–96, English China Clays PLC 1992–99, The Gillette Co. 1993–, Danka Business Systems PLC 2001–. *Address:* 568 9th Street South, Suite 354, Naples, FL 34102, USA.

GIFT, Knowlson; Trinidad and Tobago politician; mem. People's National Movt (PNM); Minister of Foreign Affairs 1995, 2001–06 (resgnd). *Address:* c/o Ministry of Foreign Affairs, Knowsley Building, 1 Queen's Park West, Port of Spain, Trinidad and Tobago (office).

GIL, Gilberto; Brazilian politician, musician (guitar, accordion) and singer; b. (Gilberto Passos Gil Moreira), 26 June 1942, Salvador, Bahia State; s. of José Gil Moreira and Claudina Passos Gil Moreira; ed Fed. Univ., Bahia; began playing accordion aged eight; composed songs for TV advertisements in early 1960s; appeared in Nós Por Exemplo (show directed by Caetano Veloso) 1964; moved to São Paulo 1965; had first hit when Elis Regina recorded Louvação; participated in Tropicalia movt, sang protest songs that proved controversial with mil. dictatorship; imprisoned 1968; forced to leave Brazil on release and moved to UK; worked with groups such as Pink Floyd, Yes, Incredible String Band and Rod Stewart's band in London clubs; returned to Brazil in 1972; toured with Caetano Veloso, Gal Costa and Maria Bethânia; recorded album Nightingale in USA 1978; appearances at Montreux Jazz Festival; Pres. Fundação Gregorio de Matos, Salvador 1987; mem. Council of City Hall of Salvador 1988–92, Pres. Environmental Defence Cttee 1989; mem. Advisory Council Fundação Mata Virgem and Fundação Alerta Brasil Pantanal; Pres. Negro-Mestizo Reference Centre (CERNE); mem. Green Party 1989, later mem. Nat. Exec. Cttee; mem. Parl. for Salvador; Minister of Culture 2003–08 (resgnd); fmr Pres. Fundação Onda Azul (Blue Wave Foundation); Chevalier, Ordre des Arts et des Lettres, Grand Officier, Légion d'honneur 2005; Shell and Sharp Prize 1990, Cruz da Ordem de Rio Branco, Polar Music Prize 2004. *Recordings include:* albums: Louvação 1967, Gilberto Gil 1968, Tropicália ou Panis et Circensis 1968, Gilberto Gil 1969, Expresso 2222 1972, Barra 69 1972, Temporada de Verão 1974, Gilberto Gil ao Vivo 1974, Gil Jorge Ogum Zangô 1975, Refazenda 1975, Doces Bárbaros 1976, Refavela 1977, Refestança 1978, Antologia do Samba-Choro: Gilberto Gil e Germano Mathias 1978, Gilberto Gil ao Vivo em Montreux 1978, Nightingale 1978, Realce 1979, A Gente Precisa Ver o Luar 1981, Brasil: João Gilberto Gil, Caetano e Bethânia 1981, Um Banda Um 1982, Extra 1983, Quilombo 1984, Vamos Fugir (with The Wailers) 1984, Raça Humana 1984, Dia Dorim Noite Neon 1985, Gilberto Gil em Concerto 1987, Ao Vivo Em Tóquio 1987, Soy Loco por Ti, América 1987, O Eterno Deus Mu Dança 1989, Parabolicamará 1992, Tropicália 2 1993, Gilberto Gil Unplugged 1994, Quanta 1997, O sol de Oslo 1998, Ensaio Geral 1999, Cidade do Salvador 1999, O Viramundo 1999, Gilberto Gil – Satisfação 1999, Gil & Milton 2000, São João Vivo 2001, Kaya N'Gan Daya 2002, Eletracústico (Grammy Award for Best Contemporary World Music Album 2006) 2005, Gil Luminoso 2006, Banda Larga de Cordel 2008. *Address:* Gege Produções, Estrada de Gávea 135, 22451-260 Rio de Janeiro, RJ, Brazil (office). *Telephone:* (21) 3323-1600 (office). *Fax:* (21) 2239-9727 (office). *E-mail:* atendimento@gege.com.br (office). *Website:* www.gege.com.br (office); www.gilbertogil.com.br.

GILLANI, Makhdoom Syed Yousaf Raza, BA, MA; Pakistani politician; *Prime Minister;* b. 9 June 1952, Karachi; s. of Alamdar Hussain Gilani; m. Elahi Gilani; four s. one d.; ed La Salle High School, Multan, Univ. of the Punjab, Lahore; mem. Pakistan People's Party 1988–, Sr Vice-Chair. 1998–; mem. Cen. Leadership Muslim League, Pakistan 1978; cabinet mem. in three-year govt of Prime Minister Muhammad Khan Junejo, Minister of Housing and Works 1985–86, of Railways Jan.–Dec. 1986; Chair. Dist Council, Multan; mem. Nat. Ass. from Multan 1985–, Speaker 1993–97; served in cabinet of fmr Prime Minister, the late Benazir Bhutto, as Minister of Tourism 1989–90, of Housing and Works Jan.–Jan. 1990; tried on charges of abusing his authority by govt anti-corruption agency 1997, accused of putting more than 500 unqualified people from his constituency on govt payroll when he was House Speaker, imprisoned 2001–06; Prime Minister of Pakistan 2008–. *Publication:* Reflections of Yusuf's Well. *Address:* Office the Prime Minister's Secretariat, Constitution Avenue, F-6/5, Cabinet Division, Cabinet Block, Islamabad, Pakistan (office). *Telephone:* (51) 9206111 (office); (51) 925190512 (office). *E-mail:* contact@cabinet.gov.pk (office). *Website:* www.cabinet.gov.pk (office).

GILAURI, Nikoloz (Nika), BA, MA; Georgian economist and politician; *Prime Minister;* b. 1975, Tbilisi; ed Ivane Javakhishvili Tbilisi State Univ., Bournemouth Coll., UK, Limerick Univ., Ireland, Temple Univ., Philadelphia, USA, Univs of Paris and Tokyo; worked at Dublin Int. Finance Centre as an Admin./Man. Invesco assets man. corpn 1999; financial consultant for energy conservation projects at Philadelphia Small Business Devt Center 2000; financial consultant, Georgia Telecom 2001; financial consultant, Spanish corpn Iberdrola (Georgian energy market man. contractor) 2002; worked for SBE (Ireland) as man. contractor and financial controller of Georgian state electricity 2003–04; Minister of Energy 2004–07, of Finance 2007–09; First Vice-Prime Minister Dec. 2008–Feb. 2009; Prime Minister Feb. 2009–. *Address:* Chancellery of the Government, 0105 Tbilisi, P. Ingorovka 7, Georgia (office). *Telephone:* (32) 92-22-43 (office). *Fax:* (32) 92-10-69 (office). *E-mail:* primeminister@geo.gov.ge (office). *Website:* www.government.gov.ge (office).

GILBERT; British artist; b. (Gilbert Proesch), 1943, Dolomites, Italy; ed Wolkenstein School of Art, Hallein School of Art, Munich Acad. of Art, St Martin's School of Art, London; began collaboration with George (Passmore) in 1967 as Gilbert and George; est. reputation as performance artists, presenting themselves, identically dressed, as living sculptures; later work includes large composite drawings and vividly coloured photo-pieces often featuring likenesses of the artists. *Publication:* What Our Art Means (jtly), Gilbert and George: The Complete Pictures 2007. *Address:* White Cube, 48 Hoxton Square, London, N1 6PB, England (office). *Telephone:* (20) 7930-5373 (office). *Fax:* (20) 7749-7480 (office). *E-mail:* g-and-g@dircon.co.uk (office). *Website:* www.whitecube.com (office).

GILBERT, Alan, BA, MA, DPhil, FASSA; Australian historian and university administrator; *President and Vice-Chancellor, University of Manchester;* b. 11 Sept. 1944, Brisbane, Queensland; ed Australian Nat. Univ., Nuffield Coll., Oxford, UK; Lecturer, Univ. of Papua New Guinea 1967; Lecturer, Univ. of NSW 1973–81, Prof. of History, Faculty of Mil. Studies 1981, apptd Chair. Faculty of Mil. Studies 1982, Pro-Vice Chancellor Univ. of NSW 1988–90; Vice-Chancellor and Prin. Univ. of Tasmania (at time of merger of Univ. with Launceston CAE) 1991–96; Vice-Chancellor Univ. of Melbourne 1996–2004, played key role in establishing and subsequently developing Melbourne Univ. Pvt. Ltd, (pvt. univ. est. to work alongside Univ. of Melbourne; closed 2005), est. Universitas (inc. asscn of int. univs) 1996–2000; Pres. and Vice-Chancellor-Elect Univ. of Manchester Feb.–Oct. 2004, Pres. and Vice-Chancellor Univ. of Manchester (following merger of UMIST and Victoria Univ. of Manchester) Oct. 2004–. *Address:* Office of the President, University of Manchester, Oxford Road, Manchester, M13 9PL, England (office). *Telephone:* (161) 306-6010 (office). *E-mail:* president@manchester.ac.uk (office). *Website:* www.manchester.ac.uk (office).

GILBERT, Kenneth Albert, OC, DMus, FRCM, FRSC; Canadian harpsichordist and organist; *Adjunct Professor of Harpsichord and Organ, School of Music, McGill University;* b. 16 Dec. 1931, Montreal; s. of Albert George Gilbert and Reta Mabel (née Welch); ed Conservatoire de Musique, Montreal and Conservatoire de Paris, France; Prof., Conservatoire de Musique, Montreal 1965–72; Assoc. Prof., Laval Univ., Québec 1970–76; Guest Prof., Royal Antwerp Conservatory, Belgium 1971–73; Dir Early Music Dept Conservatoire de Strasbourg, France 1981–85; Prof., Staatliche Hochschule für Musik, Stuttgart, Germany 1981–89, Paris Conservatoire 1988–96; Prof., Hochschule Mozarteum, Salzburg, Austria 1984–2000, Prof. Emer. 2000–; Adjunct Prof. of Harpsichord and Organ, McGill Univ., Montreal 1998–; instructor at other music acads, summer schools etc.; Pres. Editions de l'Oiseau-Lyre Monaco 2001–; Fellow, Canada Council 1968, 1974, Calouste Gulbenkian Foundation 1971; Visiting Prof., RAM; Officier, Ordre des Arts et des Lettres, Cross of Honour 1st Class (Austria); Hon. DMus (McGill, Melbourne); Prix Opus Quebec 2006. *Recordings:* complete harpsichord works of Couperin, Scarlatti and Rameau, suites and partitas of J.S. Bach, The Well-Tempered Clavier and Concertos for 2, 3 and 4 Harpsichords by Bach. *Publications:* editions of complete harpsichord works of Couperin, Scarlatti and Rameau, Bach's Goldberg Variations, Frescobaldi Toccatas, Kapsperger's lute works. *E-mail:* kenneth.gilbert@mcgill.ca (office).

GILBERT, Lewis, CBE; British film director; b. 6 March 1920, London; m. Hylda Henrietta Tafler; two s.; entered films as child actor; joined RAF and became Asst Dir to William Keighley on Target for Today 1939; joined GB Instructional (GBI) 1944, for whom he wrote and directed The Ten Year Plan, Sailors Do Care, Arctic Harvest, etc. 1946–47; wrote and directed The Little Ballerina 1947–48, worked on series of documentaries for GBI; Producer/Dir Int. Realist 1948; numerous awards including Special Evening Standard Film Award 1996, Fellowship, British Film Inst. 2001. *Films include:* The Little Ballerina 1947, Once a Sinner 1950, Scarlet Thread 1951, There is Another Sun 1951, Time Gentlemen Please 1952, Emergency Call 1952, Cosh Boy, Johnny on the Run 1953, Albert RN 1953, The Good Die Young 1954, The Sea Shall Not Have Them 1954, Cast a Dark Shadow 1955, Reach for the Sky 1956, The Admirable Crichton 1957, Carve Her Name With Pride 1957, A Cry From the Streets 1958, Ferry to Hong Kong 1959, Sink the Bismarck 1960, Light Up The Sky 1960, The Greengage Summer 1961, HMS Defiant 1962, The Seventh Dawn 1964, Alfie 1966, You Only Live Twice 1967, Paul and Michelle (also producer) 1973, Seven Men at Daybreak 1975, Seven Nights in Japan 1976, The Spy Who Loved Me 1977, Moonraker 1978, Dubai (also producer), Educating Rita 1982, Shirley Valentine (also producer) 1989, Stepping Out 1991, Haunted 1995, Before You Go 2002; co-produced Spare The Rod 1959–60. *Address:* 19 blvd de Suisse, Monaco.

GILBERT, Sir Martin John, Kt, CBE, MA, DLitt, FRSL; British historian and academic; *Fellow, Merton College, Oxford;* b. 25 Oct. 1936; s. of Peter and Miriam Gilbert; m. 1st Helen Robinson 1963; one d.; m. 2nd Susan Sacher; two s.; m. 3rd Esther Poznansky; ed Highgate School and Magdalen Coll., Oxford; Sr Research Fellow, St Antony's Coll., Oxford 1960–62, Fellow, Merton Coll., Oxford 1962–; Visiting Prof. Univ. of S Carolina 1965, Tel Aviv 1979, Hebrew Univ. of Jerusalem 1980–; official biographer of Sir Winston Churchill 1968–; Gov., Hebrew Univ. of Jerusalem 1978–; Non-Governmental Rep. UN Commn. on Human Rights, Geneva 1987, 1988; mem. Prime Minister's del. to Israel, Gaza and Jordan 1995, to USA 1995; has lectured on historical subjects throughout Europe and USA; adviser to BBC and ITV for various documentaries; script designer and co-author, Genocide (Acad. Award for best documentary feature film) 1981; presenter History Channel 1996–; Recent History Corresp. Sunday Times 1967; Hon. Fellow Univ. of Wales, Lampeter 1997; Hon. DLitt (Westminster Coll., Fulton, Mo.) 1981. *Publications:* The Appeasers (with R. Gott) 1963, Britain and Germany between the Wars 1964, The European Powers 1900–1945 1965, Plough My Own Furrow: The Life of Lord Allen of Hurtwood 1965, Servant of India: A Study of Imperial Rule 1905–1910 1966, The Roots of Appeasement 1966, Recent History Atlas 1860–1960 1966, Winston Churchill 1966, British History Atlas 1968, American History Atlas 1968, Jewish History Atlas 1969, First World War Atlas 1970, Winston S. Churchill, Vol. III, 1914–16 1971, companion vol. 1973, Russian History Atlas 1972, Sir Horace Rumbold: Portrait of a Diplomat 1973, Churchill: a photographic portrait 1974, The Arab-Israeli Conflict: its history in maps 1974, Winston S. Churchill, Vol. IV, 1917–22 1975, companion vol. 1977, The Jews in Arab Lands: their history in maps 1975, Winston S. Churchill, Vol. V, 1922–39, 1976, companion Vols 1980, 1981, 1982, The Jews of Russia: Illustrated History Atlas 1976, Jerusalem Illustrated History Atlas 1977, Exile and Return: The Emergence of Jewish Statehood 1978, Children's Illustrated Bible Atlas 1979, Final Journey, the Fate of the Jews of Nazi Europe 1979, Auschwitz and the Allies 1981, Atlas of the Holocaust 1982, Winston S. Churchill, Vol. VI, 1939–41 1983, The Jews of Hope: A Study of the Crisis of Soviet Jewry 1984, Jerusalem: Rebirth of a City 1985, Shcharansky: Hero of our Time 1986, Winston S. Churchill, Vol. VII, 1941–45 1986, The Holocaust, The Jewish Tragedy 1986, Winston Churchill, Vol. VIII 1945–65 1988, Second World War 1989, Churchill, A Life 1991, The Churchill War Papers: At the Admiralty (ed.), Atlas of British Charities 1993, In Search of Churchill: A Historian's Journey 1994, The First World War: A Complete History 1994, The Churchill War Papers: 'Never Surrender' (ed.) 1995, The Day the War Ended 1995, Jerusalem in the 20th Century 1996, The Boys, Triumph over Adversity 1996, A History of the World in the Twentieth Century (Vol. I 1900–1933) 1997, (Vol. II 1933–1951) 1998, (Vol. III 1952–1999) 1999, Holocaust Journey: Travelling in Search of the Past 1997, Israel, A History 1998, Winston Churchill and Emery Reeves; Correspondence 1998, Never Again: A History of the Holocaust 1999, The Jewish Century 2001, History of the Twentieth Century 2001, The Churchill War Papers: '1941, the Ever-Widening War' (ed.) 2001, Letters to Auntie Fori: 5,000 Years of Jewish History and Faith 2002, The Righteous: the Unsung Heroes of the Holocaust 2002, D-Day 2004, Churchill at War: His "Finest Hour" in Photographs, Churchill and America 2005, Kristallnacht: Prelude to Destruction 2006, Somme: The Heroism and Horror of War 2006, Will of the People: Churchill and Parliamentary Democracy 2006, Churchill and the Jews 2007, Routledge Atlas of the Second World War 2008. *Leisure interest:* travel. *Address:* Merton College, Oxford OX1 4JD, England.

GILBERT, Walter, AB, MA, PhD; American molecular biologist, investment company executive and artist; *Managing Director, BioVentures Investors;* b. 21 March 1932, Boston, Mass; s. of Richard V. Gilbert and Emma Gilbert (née Cohen); m. Celia Stone 1953; one s. one d.; ed Harvard Univ., Univ. of Cambridge, UK; NSF Postdoctoral Fellow, Harvard Univ. 1957–58, Lecturer in Physics 1958–59, Asst Prof. of Physics 1959–64, Assoc. Prof. of Biophysics 1964–68, Prof. of Biochemistry 1968–72; American Cancer Soc. Prof. of Molecular Biology 1972–81, Prof. of Biology 1985–86; H. H. Timken Prof. of Science 1986–87; Carl M. Loeb Univ. Prof. 1987–2002, Prof. Emer. 2002–, Chair. Dept of Cellular and Developmental Biology 1987–93; Chair. Scientific Bd, Biogen NV 1978–83, Co-Chair. Supervisory Bd 1979–81, Chair. Supervisory Bd and CEO 1981–84; Vice-Chair. Bd of Dirs, Myriad Genetics, Inc. 1992–; Chair. Bd of Dirs, Paratek Pharmaceuticals, Inc. 1996–; mem. Bd of Dirs Memory Pharmaceuticals, Inc. 1996–; Man. Dir BioVentures Investors, Cambridge, Mass 2002–; mem. NAS, American Physical Soc., American Soc. of Biological Chemists, American Acad. of Arts and Sciences; Foreign mem. Royal Soc.; V.D. Mattia Lectureship, Roche Inst. of Molecular Biology 1976; Smith, Kline and French Lecturer, Univ. of California, Berkeley 1977; Hon. Fellow, Trinity Coll. Cambridge, UK 1991; Hon. DSc (Univ. of Chicago, Columbia Univ.) 1978, (Univ. of Rochester) 1979, (Yeshiva Univ.) 1981; Guggenheim Fellowship, Paris 1968–69, US Steel Foundation Award in Molecular Biology, NAS 1968, Ledlie Prize, Harvard Univ. (with M. Ptashne) 1969, Warren Triennial Prize, Massachusetts Gen. Hosp. (with S. Benzer) 1977, Louis and Bert Freedman Award, New York Acad. of Sciences 1977, Prix Charles-Léopold Mayer, Acad. des Sciences, Inst. de France (with M. Ptashne and E. Witkin) 1977, Harrison Howe Award of the Rochester br. of ACS 1978, Louisa Gross Horwitz Prize, Columbia Univ. (with F. Sanger) 1979, Gairdner Foundation Annual Award 1979, Albert Lasker Basic Medical Research Award (with F. Sanger 1979), Prize for Biochemical Analysis, German Soc. for Clinical Chem. (with A. M. Maxam, F. Sanger and A. R. Coulsen) 1980, Sober Award, American Soc. of Biological Chemists 1980, Nobel Prize for Chem. 1980 with F. Sanger and P. Berg for work on deoxyribonucleic acid (DNA), New England Entrepreneur of the Year Award 1991, Ninth Nat. Biotechnology Ventures Award 1997. *Address:* BioVentures Investors, 101 Main Street, Suite 1750, Cambridge, MA 02142, USA (office). *Telephone:* (617) 252-3443 (office). *Fax:* (617) 621-7993 (office). *E-mail:* wgilbert@bioventureinvestors.com (office). *Website:* www.bioventuresinvestors.com (office); wallygilbert.artspan.com (home); wallygilbert.30art.com (home).

GILCHRIST, Adam Craig; Australian cricketer; b. 14 Nov. 1971, Bellingen, New South Wales; m. Melanie Gilchrist; one s., one d.; left-handed batsman and wicketkeeper; teams played for include New South Wales 1992–1994, Western Australia 1994– (Capt. since 2001), Australia 1996– (one-day int. debut versus South Africa at Faridabad, Pakistan, 1996; test debut versus Pakistan at Brisbane, 1999; Vice-Capt. since 2000); scored 3,879 runs in 62 tests (average 51.72) with 12 hundreds and 266 dismissals; 6,533 runs in 196 one-day ints (average 35.69) with 324 dismissals; 8,488 runs in 152 first-class matches with 649 dismissals; holds record for most wicketkeeping dismissals in one-day ints; fastest strike-rate in test-cricket history for a batsman scoring over 2,000 runs; captained Australia to first test-series victory in India for 34 years; Wisden Cricketer of the Year 2002, mem. Australia's World Cup winning side 2003; Wisden Australia Cricketer of the Year 2003, awarded a record total of six Carlton & United Beverages Gold Cups as Western Australia's best player; selected in Richie Benaud's Greatest XI. *Publications:* One-Day Cricket: Playing the One-Day Game 2000, Walking to Victory 2003; newspaper columns for Sydney Morning Herald, Melbourne Age and West Australian. *Address:* c/o Western Australian Cricket Association, WACA Ground, POB 6045, East Perth, Western Australia 6892, Australia. *Telephone:* (8) 9265-7222. *Fax:* (8) 9221-1823. *E-mail:* info@waca.com.au. *Website:* www.waca.com.au; www.adamgilchrist.info.

GILDRED, Theodore Edmonds, BA; American diplomatist and business executive; *Chairman, Lomas Santa Fe Group;* b. 18 Oct. 1935, Mexico City; s. of Theodore Gildred and Maxine Edmonds; m. 1st Suzanne Gail Green (divorced 1975); three s. one d.; m. 2nd Stephanie Ann Moscini 1978 (divorced 1992); one s. one d.; ed Stanford Univ., Univ. of Paris (Sorbonne), France and Univ. of Heidelberg, Fed. Repub. of Germany; served with US Army 1955–57, US Air Force 1957–69; Project Supervisor, Investors Marine, Inc., Newport Beach, Calif. 1961; owner, Pres. and CEO Costa Pacifica, Inc., Newport Beach, Calif. 1961–65; Admin. Grupo Lindavista, SA, Mexico City 1965–68; owner, Pres. and CEO The Lomas Santa Fe Group (real estate holding and devt co.), Solana Beach, Calif. 1968–86, Chair. 1989–; Chair. Bd of Dirs., Torrey Pines Bank, Solana Beach 1979–86, Inst. of Americas, La Jolla, Calif. 1984–86; Amb. to Argentina 1986–89; mem. Univ. of Calif. at San Diego Center for US–Mexican Studies; Founder-Chair. Bd of Govs, Inst. of Americas; Trustee and Pres. Gildred Foundation; mem. Bd of Dirs Security Pacific Nat. Bank, Int. Advisory Bd, N American Airlines, numerous other orgs; numerous awards. *Address:* The Lomas Santa Fe Group, 265 Santa Helena, Suite 200, Solana Beach, CA 92075-1508 (office); 16056 El Camino Real Rancho, Santa Fe, CA 92067, USA (home). *Telephone:* (858) 755-5572 (office). *Fax:* (858) 755-6821 (office). *E-mail:* tgildred@lsfg.com (office). *Website:* www.lsfg.com (office).

GILES, Alan James, MA, MS; British business executive; b. 4 June 1954, Dorchester, Dorset; m. Gillian Rosser 1978; two d.; ed Blandford School, Dorset, Merton Coll. Oxford, Stanford Univ., USA; buyer, Boots the Chemists 1975–78, Promotions Man. 1978–80, Asst Merchandise Controller 1980–82; Retail Devt Man., WHSmith 1982–85, Merchandise Controller (Books) 1985–88, Operations & Devt Dir, Do It All 1988–92; Man. Dir Waterstone's Booksellers 1992–99; CEO HMV Group PLC 1998–2006; Chair. (non-exec.) Fat Face 2006–. *Address:* c/o Fat Face, Unit 3 Ridgway, Havant, Hants., PO9 1QJ, England (office).

GILIOMEE, Hermann Buhr, MA, DPhil; South African university professor and political columnist; *Extraordinary Professor of History, University of Stellenbosch;* b. 4 April 1938, Sterkstroom; s. of Gerhardus Adriaan Giliomee and Catherine Geza Giliomee; m. Annette van Coller 1965; two d.; ed Porterville High School and Univ. of Stellenbosch; diplomatic service 1963–64; Lecturer in History, Univ. of Stellenbosch 1967–83, Extraordinary Prof. of History 2002–; Prof. of Political Studies, Univ. of Cape Town 1983–2002; recipient of Fellowships to Yale Univ., USA 1977–78, Univ. of Cambridge, UK 1982–83, Woodrow Wilson Center for Int. Scholars, Washington, DC 1992–93; Pres. South African Inst. of Race Relations 1995–97; f. Die Suid-Afrikaan journal 1984; political columnist for Cape Times, Rand Daily Mail, and other periodicals 1980–97, presently writing political column for Die Burger, Beeld and Volksblad morning newspapers; Stals Prize for Political Sciences 2001, Stals Prize for History 2004. *Publications:* The Shaping of South African Society 1652–1820 1979, Ethnic Power Mobilized: Can South Africa Change? 1979, Afrikaner Political Thought 1750–1850 1983, Up Against the Fences: Poverty, Passes and Privilege 1985, From Apartheid to Nation-building 1990, The Bold Experiment: South Africa's New Democracy 1994, Liberal and Populist Democracy in South Africa 1996, Surrender Without Defeat 1997, The Awkward Embrace: Dominant-Party Rule and Democracy in Semi-Industrialized Countries 1999, Kruispad 2001, The Afrikaners – Biography of a People 2003, Die Afrikaners: in Biografie 2004. *Leisure interest:* tennis. *Address:* 5 Dennerandweg, Stellenbosch 7600, South Africa (home). *Telephone:* (21) 8832964 (home). *Fax:* (21) 8878026 (home). *E-mail:* hgiliome@mweb.co.za (home).

GILL, Sir Anthony (Keith), Kt, BSc (Eng), FREng, FCGI, FIMechE; British business executive (retd); b. 1 April 1930, Colchester; s. of Frederick W. Gill and Ellen Gill; m. Phyllis Cook 1953; one s. two d.; ed Colchester High School and Imperial Coll., London; Nat. Service, REME 1954–56; Production Engineer, Bryce Berger Ltd 1956, Dir 1960, Gen. Man. 1965; Dir Lucas CAV Ltd 1967; Gen. Man. Fuel Injection Equipment 1972–74; Dir Joseph Lucas Ltd 1974, Div. Man. Dir 1978; Dir Lucas Industries PLC 1978, Jt Group Man. Dir 1980, Group Man. Dir 1984–87, Deputy Chair. 1986–87, Chair. 1987–94 and CEO 1987–94; Pres. Inst. of Production Eng 1985–86; Chair. London Docklands Light Railway 1994–99; mem. Council IMechE 1986–91, Advisory Council on Science and Tech. 1985–91; Chair. Educ. and Training Comm. 1988–91, Tarmac PLC 1992–2000; Dir (non-exec.) Post Office 1989–91, Nat. Power PLC 1990–98; mem. Eng Council (Deputy Chair. 1994–96); Chair. Teaching Co. Scheme 1990–96; Pro-Chancellor Cranfield Univ. 1991–2001; mem. Nat. Training Task Force 1991–94; Vice-Pres. Inst. of Man. 1992 (Chair. Council 1996–99), Pres. 1998–99; Hon. Fellow Inst. of Eng and Tech.; Hon. DEng (Univ. of Birmingham) 1990; Hon. DSc (Cranfield Univ.) 1991, (Southampton Univ.) 1992, (Warwick Univ.) 1992; Hon. DTech (Coventry Univ.) 1992; Dr hc (Sheffield Hallam Univ.) 1993. *Leisure interests:* music, boating. *Address:* The Point House, Astra Court, Hythe Marina Village, Hythe, Hants., SO45 6DZ, England (home). *Telephone:* (23) 8084-0165 (home). *E-mail:* anthony.gill@btinternet.com (home).

GILL, Michael; Australian editor and media executive; *CEO, Fairfax Business Media;* presenter, Business Sunday (TV) 1988–90; sr writer, The Australian Financial Review 1990–93, Deputy Ed. 1993–96, Gen. Man. Business Devt, John Fairfax Holdings Ltd 1996–98, Publr and Ed.-in-Chief; Publr and Ed.-in-Chief Fairfax Business Media 1998–2007, CEO 2007–, responsible for business man. and editorial direction of The Australian Financial Review, AFR Access, AFR Magazine, BOSS, afr.com, BRW, The Australian Financial Review Smart Investor, CFO, MIS (Australia, NZ, Asia and UK) and Fairfax Business Research; Chair. Australian Associated Press, Nat. Inst. of Econ. and Industry Research; mem. Bd of Dirs UNICEF Australia; fmr Dir The Ian Potter Museum of Art, Victorian Community Foundation, Blue Mountains Festival, Circus Oz. *Address:* John Fairfax Holdings Ltd, PO Box 506, Sydney, NSW 2001, Australia (office); Fairfax Business Media, PO Box 6813, Wellesley Street, Auckland, New Zealand (office). *Telephone:* (2) 9282-2833 (Sydney) (office); (9) 377-9902 (Auckland) (office). *Fax:* (2) 9282-3133 (Sydney) (office); (9) 377-4604 (Auckland) (office). *E-mail:* rvictor@mail.fairfax.com.au (office). *Website:* www.fxj.com.au (office); fairfaxbm.co.nz (office).

GILLAM, Sir Patrick, Kt, BA; British business executive; b. 15 April 1933, London; s. of the late Cyril B. Gillam and of Mary J. Gillam; m. Diana Echlin 1963; one s. one d.; ed LSE; Foreign Office 1956–57; joined British Petroleum (BP) 1957; Vice-Pres. BP North America Inc. 1971–74; Gen. Man. Supply Dept 1974–78; Dir BP Int. Ltd 1978–82; Chair. BP Shipping Ltd 1981–88, BP Minerals Int. Ltd 1981–88; Man. Dir BP Co. 1981–91, Chair. BP Africa Ltd 1982–88, BP Coal Inc. 1988–90, BP Nutrition 1989–91, BP America 1989–91, BP Oil 1990–91; Chair. Booker Tate Ltd 1991–93, Asda Group PLC 1991–96, Royal and Sun Alliance 1997–2003; Deputy Chair. Standard Chartered Bank Africa PLC 1988–89, Standard Chartered Overseas Holdings Ltd 1988–89, Standard Chartered Bank Aug.–Nov. 1988, Chair. 1993–2003, Standard Chartered PLC 1991–92, Chair. 1993–2003 (Dir 1988–2002); Chair. Asia House 2003–05; currently Consultant, CMi; Dir (non-exec.) Commercial Union PLC 1991–96; Chair. ICC (UK) 1989–98; mem. of Court of Govs., LSE 1989–, Hon. Fellow 2000. *Leisure interest:* gardening. *Address:* c/o CMi, 80 Avenue du Vallon, 1380 Lasne, Belgium.

GILLAN, Michael J., DPhil; British physicist and academic; *Professor of Condensed Matter and Materials Physics, University College London;* ed Univ. of Oxford; Post-doctoral researcher, Univ. of Minn., USA; mem. staff, Harwell 1970–88; Prof. of Theoretical Physics, Univ. of Keele 1988–98; Prof. of Condensed Matter and Materials Physics, Physics and Astronomy Dept, Univ. Coll. London 1998–; mem. Peer Review Coll. of UK Eng and Physical Sciences Research Council; Dirac Prize and Medal, Inst. of Physics 2006. *Publications:* numerous scientific papers in professional journals on theory of condensed matter, with a strong emphasis on computer simulation. *Address:* Department of Physics and Astronomy, University College London, Gower Street, London, WC1E 6BT, England (office). *Telephone:* (20) 7679-7049 (office). *Fax:* (20) 7679-7145 (office). *E-mail:* m.gillan@ucl.ac.uk (office). *Website:* www.phys.ucl .ac.uk (office).

GILLARD, Julia Eileen, BA, LLB; Australian lawyer and politician; *Deputy Prime Minister and Minister for Education, Minister for Employment and Workplace Relations, Minister for Social Inclusion;* b. 29 Sept. 1961, Barry, Wales; d. of John Gillard and Moira Gillard; ed Univ. of Melbourne; Solicitor, Slater & Gordon, Werribee 1987–95, Pnr 1990–95; Del. Australian Labor Party (ALP) State Conf. (Victoria) 1982–, Pres. ALP Carlton Branch 1985–89, Co-Convenor, Affirmative Action Working Party 1993–94, mem. Admin. Cttee 1993–97, Deputy Leader Fed. ALP 2006–07; Chief of Staff to Vic. Leader of Opposition J. Brumby 1995–98; MP (Australian Labor Party) for Lalor, Vic. 1998–; Shadow Minister for Population and Immigration 2001–03, for Reconciliation and Indigenous Affairs 2003, for Health 2003–06, for Employment, Industrial Relations and Social Inclusion 2006–07, Deputy Leader of Opposition 2006–07; Deputy Prime Minister and Minister for Educ., Employment and Workplace Relations, and Social Inclusion 2007–. *Address:* Department of Education, Science and Training, GPO Box 9880, Canberra, ACT 2601, Australia (office). *Telephone:* (2) 6240-8111 (office). *Fax:* (2) 6240-8571 (office). *E-mail:* wwweditor@dest.gov.au (office); Julia.Gillard.MP@aph.gov .au (office). *Website:* www.dest.gov.au (office); www.dest.gov.au (office).

GILLES, Herbert Michael Joseph, CMG, KStJ, DMedSc, DSc, MD, FRCP, FFPH, DTM&H; British professor of tropical medicine; *Professor Emeritus, University of Liverpool;* b. 10 Sept. 1921, Port Said, Egypt; s. of Joseph Gilles; m. 1st Wilhelmina Caruana 1955 (died 1972); three s. one d.; m. 2nd Mejra Kacic-Dimitri 1979; ed St Edward's Coll., Malta, Royal Univ. of Malta, Univ. of Oxford; mem. Scientific Staff MRC 1954–58; Sr Lecturer in Tropical Medicine, Univ. of Ibadan, Nigeria 1959–61, Prof. 1962–65; Sr Lecturer in Tropical Medicine, Univ. of Liverpool, England 1965–70, Prof. 1970–86, Prof. Emer. 1986–; Dean Liverpool School of Tropical Medicine 1978–83, Vice-Pres. 1991–; Visiting Prof. of Public Health, Univ. of Malta 1989–; Visiting Prof. of Int. Health, Royal Coll. of Surgeons in Ireland 1994–, of Tropical Medicine, Mahidol Univ. Bangkok 1994–; Pres. Royal Soc. of Tropical Medicine and Hygiene (RSTMH) 1985–87; Hon. Pres. Malta Asscn of Public Health; Consultant in Malariology, British Army 1972–86, in Tropical Medicine, RAF and DHSS 1972–86; Hon. Mem. Swedish Soc. of Tropical Medicine 1999; Officer, Nat. Order of Merit of Malta 2003; Companion, Exalted Order of the White Elephant (Kingdom of Thailand) 2008; Rhodes Scholar (Malta) 1943, WHO Darling Foundation Medal and Prize 1989, Mary Kingsley Medal 1995, BMA Medical Book Competition, First Prize, Medicine Section 1996, BMA Medical Book Competition, Highly Commended, Public Health Section 2002, RSTMH Manson Medal 2007. *Publications:* Management and Treatment of Tropical Diseases 1971, Pathology in the Tropics 1976, Tropical Medicine for Nurses 1979, Recent Advances in Tropical Medicine 1984, Human Antiparasitic Drugs 1985, Epidemiology and Control of Tropical Diseases 1986, Hookworm Infections 1991, Management of Severe and Complicated Malaria 1991, Atlas of Tropical Medicine and Parasitology 1994, Protozoal Diseases 1999, Essential Malariology 2002, Preventive Medicine for the Tropics 2003, Tropical Medicine: A Clinical Text 2006. *Leisure interests:* swimming, music. *Address:* Liverpool School of Tropical Medicine, Pembroke Place, Liverpool, Merseyside, L3 5QA (office); 3 Conyers Avenue, Birkdale, Southport, PR8 4SZ, Merseyside, England (home). *Telephone:* (151) 705-3236 (office); (1704) 566664 (home). *Fax:* (151) 705-3368 (office). *E-mail:* jhowley@liverpool.ac.uk (office). *Website:* www.liv.ac.uk/lstm (office).

GILLESPIE, Norman, BA, PhD; British arts administrator and business executive; *CEO, Sydney Opera House;* b. 1957, Lurgan, NI; m. Nicole Gillespie; one d.; ed Queen's Univ. Belfast, Univ. of London, Harvard Business School, USA, Chinghua Univ., Beijing, China; grad. trainee UK civil service; joined BP (British Petroleum) 1987, various positions including Tax Control-

ler for North Sea Operations, Glasgow, mem. Group Strategy Team, London, Head of Pvt. Office of CEO and Chair., US Man. of Planning and Reporting, Houston, Tex.; Dir of Group Planning and Financial Control, Cable & Wireless, London 1994–97, Head of Group Strategy 1995–97; Chief Financial Officer Cable & Wireless Optus (following merger of Cable & Wireless and Optus 1997), Sydney, Australia 1997–2002, Deputy CEO –2002; Deputy Chair. Australian Brandenburg Orchestra 1998–; Deputy Chair. NSW Div., Australian Business Arts Foundation 2001–; CEO Sydney Opera House 2002–; Dir Australian Business Arts Foundation 2004–. *Leisure interests:* early music, opera, contemporary dance, mountain trekking. *Address:* Sydney Opera House, GPO Box R239, Royal Exchange, Sydney, NSW 1225, Australia (office). *Telephone:* (2) 9250-7201 (office). *Fax:* (2) 9250-7844 (office). *E-mail:* ngillespie@sydneyoperahouse.com (office). *Website:* www.sydneyoperahouse .com (office).

GILLESPIE, Rhondda Marie, BMus; British concert pianist; b. 3 Aug. 1941, Sydney, Australia; d. of David Gillespie and Marie Gillespie; m. Denby Richards 1972; ed NSW Conservatorium with Alexander Sverjensky and in London with Louis Kentner and Denis Matthews; debut on Australian radio aged eight 1949; first public recital 1953; winner NSW Concerto Competition, Sydney 1959; European debut in London with Tchaikovsky Piano Concerto No. 2 1960; since then has played with major orchestras throughout UK, Netherlands, Germany, Scandinavia, Far East and USA and made many festival appearances. *Leisure interests:* golf, languages, exotic cooking. *Address:* 50 Collinswood Drive, St Leonards-on-Sea, East Sussex, TN38 0NX, England (home). *Telephone:* (1424) 715167 (home). *Fax:* (1424) 712214 (office). *E-mail:* rhonmus@aol.com (home).

GILLESPIE, Ronald James, PhD, DSc, FRS, FRSC, FRSC (UK), FCIC, CM; Canadian/British chemist and academic; *Professor Emeritus of Chemistry, McMaster University;* b. 21 Aug. 1924, London; s. of James A. Gillespie and Miriam Gillespie (née Kirk); m. Madge Ena Garner 1950; two d.; ed Univ. Coll., London; Asst Lecturer, Dept of Chem., Univ. Coll., London 1948–50, Lecturer 1950–58; Commonwealth Fund Fellow, Brown Univ., RI, USA 1953–54; Assoc. Prof., Dept of Chem., McMaster Univ., Hamilton, Ont., Canada 1958–60, Prof. 1960–88, Prof. Emer. 1988–, Chair. Dept of Chem. 1962–65; Assoc. Prof., Univ. des Sciences et Techniques de Languedoc, Montpellier, France 1972–73; Visiting Prof., Univ. of Geneva, Switzerland 1976, of Göttingen, FRG 1978; mem. Chem. Soc., ACS; Hon. LLD (Concordia) 1988, (Dalhousie) 1988; Dr hc (Montpellier) 1991; Hon. DSc (McMaster Univ.) 1993, (Lethbridge) 2007; numerous medals and awards. *Publications:* Molecular Geometry 1972, Chemistry (co-author) 1986, 1989, The VSEPR Model of Molecular Geometry (with I. Hargittai) 1991, Atoms, Molecules and Reactions: An Introduction to Chemistry (co-author) 1994, Chemical Bonding and Molecular Geometry: From Lewis to Electron Densities (co-author) 2001; papers in scientific journals. *Leisure interests:* chess, travel. *Address:* Department of Chemistry, McMaster University, Hamilton, Ont., L8S 4M1 (office); 50 Hatt Street, Dundas, Ont. L9H 0A1, Canada (home). *Telephone:* (905) 525-9140 (office); (905) 628-1502 (home). *Fax:* (905) 522-2509 (office). *E-mail:* ronald.gillespie@sympatico.ca (home). *Website:* www.mcmaster.ca/ faculty/gillespie (office).

GILLETT, Sir Robin Danvers Penrose, Bt, GBE, RD, FRCM, KStJ; British company executive (retd); b. 9 Nov. 1925, London; s. of the late Sir (Sydney) Harold Gillett, Bt, MC (Lord Mayor of London 1958–59) and Audrey Isobel Penrose Gillett (née Wardlaw); m. 1st Elizabeth Marion Grace Findlay 1950 (died 1997); two s.; m. 2nd Alwyne Winifred Cox 2000 (separated); ed Nautical Coll., Pangbourne; served Canadian Pacific Steamships 1943–60, Master Mariner 1951, Staff Commdr 1957; Consultant, Sedgwick Ltd –1986; Underwriting Mem. of Lloyd's; Common Councilman for Ward of Bassishaw, City of London 1965–69, Alderman 1969–96, Sheriff 1973–74, Lord Mayor of London 1976–77; Chancellor, City Univ. 1976–77; Liveryman and past Master of the Hon. Co. of Master Mariners; Chair. local Civil Defence Cttee 1967–68; Pres. Nat. Waterways Transport Asscn 1978–83; UK Pres. Royal Life Saving Soc. 1978–82, Deputy Commonwealth Pres. 1982–96 (Vice-Pres. 1996–); Vice-Pres. City of London Centre, St John Ambulance Asscn; Vice-Chair. Port of London Authority 1979–84; Vice-Pres. City of London Dist. Red Cross; Chair. Govs Pangbourne Coll. 1979–92, St Katharine Haven 1990–93; Chair. Council Maritime Volunteer Service 1998–2001, Gov. 2001–; Founder mem. and Fellow, Nautical Inst.; Fellow, Inst. of Admin. Man., Pres. 1980–84 (Inst.'s Medal 1982); HM Lt for City of London 1975; Elder Brother of Trinity House; Trustee, Nat. Maritime Museum 1982–92; Gentleman Usher of the Purple Rod 1985–2000; Hon. Commdr RNR 1971; RNR Decoration (RD) 1965, Officer, Order of the Leopard (Zaire) 1973, Commdr, Royal Order of Dannebrog (Denmark) 1974, Order of Johan Sedia Makhota (Malaysia) 1974, Grand Cross of Municipal Merit (Lima, Peru) 1977; Hon. DSc (City Univ.) 1976; Admin. Man. Soc. Gold Medal (USA) 1983. *Publication:* A Fish Out of Water 2001, Dogwatch Doggerel and Other Compositions 2004. *Leisure interests:* sailing, public speaking, writing.

GILLIAM, Terry Vance, BA; British (b. American) film director, animator, actor, illustrator and writer; b. 22 Nov. 1940, Minn.; s. of James Hall Gilliam and Beatrice Gilliam (née Vance); m. Margaret Weston 1973; one s. two d.; ed Occidental Coll., Calif.; Assoc. Ed. HELP! magazine 1962–64; freelance illustrator 1964–65, advertising copywriter/art dir 1966–67; Hon. Dr of Arts (Occidental Coll.), (Wimbledon Coll. of Art, London) 2000; Hon. DFA (Royal Coll. of Art, London) 1989; BAFTA Fellowship 2009. *Television:* Do Not Adjust Your Set (series writer) 1967, Marty (series writer) 1968, Broaden Your Mind (series writer) 1968, Monty Python's Flying Circus (series writer, actor) 1969–74, presenter The Last Machine (series) 1995. *Films:* Storytime (dir) 1968, Monty Python's And Now for Something Completely Different (writer, actor, animator) 1971, The Miracle of Flight (dir) 1974, Monty Python and the

Holy Grail (writer, actor, dir) 1975, Jabberwocky (screenplay, actor, dir) 1977, Monty Python's Life of Brian (writer, actor, animator) 1979, Time Bandits (writer, dir) 1981, Monty Python Live at the Hollywood Bowl (writer, actor) 1982, Monty Python's The Meaning of Life (writer, actor, dir) 1983, The Crimson Permanent Assurance (writer, actor, dir) 1983, Brazil (screenplay, actor, dir) 1985, Spies Like Us (actor) 1985, The Adventures of Baron Munchausen (screenplay, actor, dir) 1988, The Fisher King (dir) 1991, Twelve Monkeys (dir) 1995, Fear and Loathing in Las Vegas (screenplay, dir) 1998, Lost in La Mancha (appeared in documentary about film project The Man Who Killed Don Quixote) 2002, Tideland (writer, dir) 2005, The Brothers Grimm (dir) 2005, Enfermés dehors (actor) 2006, The Imaginarium of Doctor Parnassus (co-writer, dir, producer) 2009. *Publications:* Monty Python's Big Red Book, Monty Python's Papperbok 1977, Monty Python's Scrapbook 1979, Animations of Mortality 1979, Monty Python's The Meaning of Life, Monty Python's Flying Circus – Just the Words (co-ed.) 1989, The Adventures of Baron Munchhausen 1989, Not the Screenplay of Fear and Loathing in Las Vegas 1998, Gilliam on Gilliam 1999, Dark Nights and Holly Fools 1999, The Pythons Autobiography (co-author) 2003. *Address:* c/o Jenne Casarotto, National House, 60–66 Wardour Street, London, W1V 4ND, England (office). *Telephone:* (20) 7287-4450 (office). *Fax:* (20) 7287-9128 (office). *E-mail:* jenne@casarotto.co.uk (office). *Website:* www.casarotto.co.uk (office).

GILLIBRAND, Kirsten Elizabeth Rutnik, AB, JD; American attorney and politician; *Senator from New York;* b. 9 Dec. 1966, Albany, NY; d. of Douglas P. Rutnik and Polly Noonan Rutnik; m. Jonathan Gillibrand; two s.; ed Acad. of Holy Names, Emma Willard School, Troy, Dartmouth Coll., Univ. of California, Los Angeles School of Law; fmr intern for Senator Alfonse D'Amato; fmr law clerk for Judge Roger Miner, US Court of Appeals for the Second Circuit 1992–93; Sr Assoc. Davis, Polk & Wardell; fmr Special Counsel, US Sec. of Housing and Urban Devt, Washington, DC 2000–01; Pnr, Boies, Schiller & Flexner LLP, Albany 2001–07; mem. US House of Reps 2007–09, mem. Cttees on House Armed Services, on Agric., Nutrition and Forestry, on Environment and Public Works, Special Cttee on Aging; Senator from NY 2009–. *Address:* 532 Dirksen Senate Office Building, Washington, DC 20510, USA (office). *Telephone:* (202) 224-4451 (office). *Website:* www.senate.gov (office).

GILLIES, Rowan, MBBS; Australian physician and international organization official; *President, Médecins Sans Frontières;* b. 1971, Longueville; fmr Surgical Registrar, Mona Vale Hosp., Sydney; with Médecins Sans Frontières (MSF) 1998–, postings included Liberia, Sudan, Sierra Leone, Afghanistan, Pres. Feb. 2004–. *Address:* Médecins Sans Frontières, Rue de Lausanne 78, CP 116, 1211 Geneva 21, Switzerland (office). *Telephone:* (22) 8498400 (office). *Fax:* (22) 8498404 (office). *Website:* www.msf.org (office).

GILLINSON, Sir Clive Daniel, Kt, CBE, ARAM, FRAM, FRNCM; British cellist and arts administrator; *Executive and Artistic Director, Carnegie Hall;* b. 7 March 1946, Bangalore, India; m. Penny Gillinson; one s. two d.; ed Frensham Heights School, Queen Mary Coll., Univ. of London, Royal Acad. of Music; played in Nat. Youth Orchestra of Great Britain 1963–65, Philharmonia Orchestra –1970, London Symphony Orchestra 1970–84; elected to Bd of Dirs London Symphony Orchestra 1976–79, 1983–, Finance Dir 1979, Man. Dir 1984–2005; Exec. and Artistic Dir Carnegie Hall, New York 2005–; owned an antique shop, Hampstead, London 1978–86; Chair. Assen of British Orchestras 1992–95; Gov. and mem. of Exec. Cttee Nat. Youth Orchestra 1995–2004; Founding Partner Masterprize 1997–; Founding Trustee Nat. Endowment for Science, Tech. and the Arts 1998–2004; mem. Int. Music Council of the Children's Hearing Inst., New York 1998–, Brubeck Inst. Hon. Bd 2007–, Curtis Inst. Bd of Overseers 2007–08; Hon. GSMD 1992, Freeman of the City of London 1993; Dr hc (City Univ.) 1995; Royal Acad. of Music May Mukle Cello Prize, ABSA Garrett Award 1992. *Leisure interests:* reading, theatre, cinema and sport. *Address:* Carnegie Hall, 881 Seventh Avenue, New York, NY 10019-3210, USA (office). *Telephone:* (212) 903-9820 (office). *Fax:* (212) 903-0820 (office). *E-mail:* cgillinson@carnegiehall.org (office). *Website:* www.carnegiehall.org (office).

GILMAN, Alfred Goodman, MD, PhD; American pharmacologist and academic; *Executive Vice President for Academic Affairs and Provost, also Dean, University of Texas Southwestern Medical Center;* b. 1 July 1941, New Haven, Conn.; s. of Alfred Gilman and Mabel Schmidt; m. Kathryn Hedlund 1963; one s. two d.; ed Yale and Case Western Reserve Univs; Research Assoc. NIH, Bethesda, Md 1969–71; Asst Prof., Assoc. Prof. of Pharmacology, Univ. of Virginia, Charlottesville 1971–77, Prof. 1977–81; Prof. of Pharmacology and Chair. Dept of Pharmacology, Univ. of Texas (UT) Southwestern Medical Center, Dallas 1981–, Raymond and Ellen Willie Distinguished Chair. of Molecular Neuropharmacology 1987–, Regental Prof. 1994–, also currently Exec. Vice Pres. for Academic Affairs, Provost and Dean, UT Southwestern Medical School; Dir Regeneron Pharmaceutics 1989–, Eli Lilly and Co. 1995–; mem. numerous scientific advisory socs; mem. NAS, Inst. of Medicine of NAS, American Soc. of Biological Chemists etc.; Fellow, American Acad. of Arts and Sciences; Hon. DSc (Chicago) 1991, (Case Western Reserve) 1995, (Miami) 1999, Hon. DMedSc (Yale) 1997; Gairdner Foundation Int. Award 1984; Albert Lasker Basic Medical Research Award 1989, Nobel Prize in Physiology or Medicine (with Martin Rodbell) 1994, many other awards and distinctions. *Publications:* over 220 peer-reviewed scientific journal articles, numerous invited book chapters and reviews; Ed.-in-Chief, Goodman & Gilman's The Pharmacological Basis of Therapeutics, 6th, 7th and 8th edns. *Leisure interests:* reading, golf. *Address:* Office of the Dean, University of Texas Southwestern Medical Center, 5323 Harry Hines Boulevard, Dallas, TX 75390-9003, USA (office). *Telephone:* (214) 648-2509 (office). *Fax:* (214) 648-8955 (office). *E-mail:* alfred.gilman@utsouthwestern.edu (office). *Website:* www.utsouthwestern.edu (office).

GILMARTIN, Raymond V., MBA; American business executive; b. 6 March 1941, Washington, DC; m. Gladys Higham 1965; one s. two d.; ed Union Coll. and Harvard Univ.; Devt Engineer Eastman Kodak 1963–67; various exec. positions, Becton Dickinson & Co. 1976–92, Chair., Pres. and CEO 1992–94; Chair., Pres. and CEO Merck & Co. Inc. 1994–2005 (resgnd); Dir (non-exec.) Microsoft 2001–. *Address:* c/o Merck and Co., 1 Merck Drive, Whitehouse Station, NJ 08889-0100, USA (office).

GILMORE, James Stuart, III, JD; American fmr politician and lawyer; *Partner, Kelley Drye and Warren LLP;* b. 6 Oct. 1949, Richmond, Va; s. of James Stuart Gilmore, Jr and Margaret Kandle Gilmore; m. Roxane Gatling Gilmore; two s.; ed Univ. of Virginia; US Army 1971–74; Pnr Benedetti, Gilmore, Warthen and Dalton (law firm) 1977–80, 1984–87; fmrly Commonwealth's Attorney, Henrico Co., Va; fmr Attorney Gen. State of Va; Gov. of Virginia 1997–2001; Alt. Del. Repub. Nat. Convention 1976; Chair. Henrico Co. Repub. Cttee 1982–85, now Vice-Chair.; Chair. Repub. Nat. Cttee 2001–02; Chair. Congressional Advisory Panel to Assess Domestic Response Capabilities for Terrorism Involving Weapons of Mass Destruction 1999–2003; Bd of Visitors Air Force Academy 2003, Chair. 2003–; currently Pnr Kelley Drye and Warren (law firm) and Chair. Homeland Security Practice Group; Republican. *Address:* Kelley Drye and Warren LLP, 1200 19th Street, NW, Suite 500, Washington, DC 20036, USA (office). *Telephone:* (202) 955-9660 (office). *Fax:* (202) 955-9792 (office). *E-mail:* jgilmore@kelleydrye.com (office). *Website:* www.kelleydrye.com (office).

GILMORE, Rosalind E. J., CB, MA, FRSA, CIMgt; British business executive; b. 23 March 1937, London; d. of Sir Robert Fraser and Lady (Betty) Fraser; m. Brian Terence Gilmore 1962; ed King Alfred School, N London, Univ. Coll. London and Newnham Coll. Cambridge; entered HM Treasury 1960; Exec. Asst to Econs Dir IBRD 1966–67; Cabinet Office 1974; Asst Sec. HM Treasury 1975, Head Financial Insts. Div. 1977–80; Press Sec. to Chancellor of Exchequer 1980–82; Gen. Man. Corp. Planning, Dunlop Ltd 1982–83; Dir of Marketing, Nat. Girobank 1983–86; Directing Fellow, St George's House, Windsor Castle 1986–89; Dir Mercantile Group PLC 1986–89, Mercantile Credit Co. Ltd 1986–89, London and Manchester Group PLC 1986–89; Marketing Consultant, FI Group PLC (Software) 1986–89; mem. Financial Services Act Tribunal 1986–89; Deputy Chair. and Commr Bldg Socs Comm. 1989–91, Chair. 1991–94; Chief Registrar of Friendly Socs and Industrial Insurance Commr 1991–94; Chair. Homeowners Friendly Society Ltd 1996–98, Arrow Broadcasting 1996–98; Dir Moorfields Eye Hosp. Trust 1994–2000, BAT Industries PLC 1996–98, Zurich Financial Services AG (Zurich) 1998–; mem. Securities and Investment Bd 1993–96; Dir Leadership Foundation 1997– (Pres. 2005–), Trades Union Fund Mans 2000–, Int. Women's Forum 2005–; mem. Court, Cranfield Univ. 1992–; mem. Bd Opera North 1993–96; mem. Lloyd's Regulatory Bd 1994–98 (Dir Regulatory Services, Lloyds 1994–95); mem. Council Royal Coll. of Music 1997–; Fellow, Univ. Coll. London 1988; Hon. Fellow, Newnham Coll. Cambridge 1995. *Achievements include:* mem. Cambridge Univ. Swimming Team (blue 1960), Cambridge Univ. Squash Team. *Publication:* Mutuality for the Twenty-first Century 1998. *Leisure interests:* music, reading, house in Greece, languages (Greek, French and Spanish). *Address:* 3 Clarendon Mews, London, W2 2NR, England (home). *Telephone:* (20) 7402-8554 (home). *Fax:* (20) 7402-8554 (home). *E-mail:* rosalindgilmore@btinternet.com (home).

GILOWSKA, Zyta, PhD; Polish academic and politician; *Professor, Katolicki Uniwersytet Lubelski Jana Pawła II (John Paul II Catholic University of Lublin);* b. 7 July 1949, Nowe Miasto Lubawskie; ed Inst. of Econ. Sciences, Warsaw Univ., Maria Curie-Skłodowska Univ., Lublin; Asst Prof., Maria Curie-Skłodowska Univ. 1972–85, Adjunct Prof. 1985–94, Assoc. Prof. 1995–99; Polish Del. to Council of Congress of Local and Regional Authorities of Europe 1992–98; Deputy Chair. Polish Pres.'s Council for Territorial Self-Govt 1992–95; mem. Joint Govt and Territorial Self-Govt Comm. 1993–95; mem. Nat. Council of Freedom Union 1994–96; Prof., Catholic Univ. of Lublin (now John Paul II Catholic Univ. of Lublin) 2001–; mem. leadership of Civic Platform –2005; Deputy Prime Minister and Minister of Finance Jan.–June 2006, Sept. 2006–07. *Publications:* 20 books and over 200 academic publications on public finance, coauthored drafts of Chapter seven of the Polish constitution, and the law on provincial self-government. *Address:* Department of Economics, Katolicki Uniwersytet Lubelski Jana Pawła II, Al. Racławickie 14, 20-950 Lublin, Poland (office). *Telephone:* (81) 445-41-05 (office). *Fax:* (81) 445-41-91 (office). *E-mail:* dwz@kul.lublin.pl (office). *Website:* www.kul.lublin.pl (office).

GIMBRONE, Michael A., Jr, AB, MD, FAAS; American pathologist and academic; *Elsie T. Friedman Professor of Pathology, Harvard Medical School; Director, Vascular Research Division, Department of Pathology, Brigham and Women's Hospital;* b. 6 Nov. 1943, Buffalo, NY; ed Cornell Univ., Ithaca, NY and Harvard Medical School, Boston, Mass; NSF Summer Fellow, Roswell Park Memorial Inst., Buffalo 1960–63; Summer Research Fellow, Dept of Physiology, New York Univ. Medical School 1964, Depts of Anatomy, Biochemistry and Surgery, Harvard Medical School 1965–67 (ind. study and research 1968–69); Intern in Surgery, Massachusetts Gen. Hosp., Boston 1970–71; Research Fellow, Dept of Surgery, Children's Hosp. Medical Center, Boston 1971–72; Commissioned Officer, NIH US Public Health Service, Bethesda, Md 1972–74, Staff Assoc., Lab. of Pathophysiology, Nat. Cancer Inst., NIH 1972–74; Resident in Pathology, Peter Bent Brigham Hosp., Boston 1974–76; Instructor, Dept of Pathology, Harvard Medical School 1975–76, Asst Prof. 1976–79, Assoc. Prof. 1979–85, Prof. 1985–, Elsie T. Friedman Prof. of Pathology 1987–, Research Assoc. 1995–; Adjunct Faculty, W. Alton Jones Cell Science Center, Lake Placid, NY 1976–78; Assoc. in Pathology, Brigham and Women's Hosp., Boston 1976–79, Head, Vascular Pathophysiology Research Lab. 1976–85, Assoc. Pathologist 1979–80, Pathologist 1980–, Dir

Vascular Research Div. 1985–, Chair. Interdisciplinary Research Cttee 1997–, Dir Center for Excellence in Vascular Biology 1998, mem. Bd Dirs Brigham and Women's Hosp. Pathology Foundation, Inc. 1998–, Vice-Chair. for Research and Academic Affairs, Dept of Pathology 2000–01, Chair. Dept of Pathology 2001–; Special Consultant, Hypertension Task Force, Nat. Heart, Lung and Blood Inst., Bethesda 1977, Consultant, Arteriosclerosis Task Force 1979; Visiting Prof., Cardiovascular Research Div., Cleveland Clinic Foundation 1980, Johns Hopkins Univ. School of Medicine, Baltimore, Md 1988–90, Washington Univ. School of Medicine, St Louis, Mo. 1988–90, 1994, Univ. of Pennsylvania School of Medicine, Philadelphia 1988–90, Univ. of S Carolina School of Medicine, Columbia 1988–90, Medical Coll. of Wisconsin, Milwaukee 1996, Bowman Gray School of Medicine, Wake Forest Univ., Winston-Salem, NC 1998; Johanaoff Visiting Prof., Mario Negri Inst. of Pharmacological Research, Milan, Italy 1982; Visiting Scholar in Pulmonary Medicine, Duke Univ. Medical Center and Univ. of N Carolina School of Medicine Research, Triangle Park, Nat. Inst. of Environmental Health Sciences, NC 1988; Pfizer Visiting Professorship in Cardiovascular Medicine, Univ. of Minnesota-Duluth School of Medicine 1991; First Annual Vascular Visiting Prof., Cornell Univ. Medical Coll., New York Hosp. 1992; Horizons in Biomedical Research Lectureship, Cleveland Clinic Foundation Research Inst. 1993; Distinguished Visiting Prof., Johns Hopkins Univ. School of Medicine 1993, Nat. Cardiovascular Research Inst., Osaka, Japan 1996, Kyoto Univ., Japan 1996, Yamanashi Medical Univ., Japan 1996, Tokyo Medical and Dental Univ., Japan 1996; Woznicki Lecturer and Visiting Prof. in Pathology, Baylor Coll. of Medicine Houston, Tex. 1994; Hans Selye Visiting Prof., Univ. of California, Irvine Medical School 1996; Founding Co-Chair. Vascular Biology Inter soc. Council 1991–94; Co-Founder N American Vascular Biology Org. 1994, Pres. 1994–95, Past Pres. 1995–96; Assoc. Ed. Microvascular Research 1976–86; mem. Editorial Bd Arteriosclerosis, Thrombosis and Vascular Biology 1980–, American Journal of Pathology 1982–, Circulation Research 1986–89, Journal of Experimental Pathology 1986–96, Experimental and Molecular Pathology 1987–95, Journal of Vascular Medicine and Biology 1988–91, Journal of Vascular Research 1991–97, Microcirculation 1993–, Trends in Cardiovascular Medicine 1998–; mem. American Heart Asscn 1975– (Fellow 2001–), NAS (mem. Inst. of Medicine 1999–), American Acad. of Arts and Sciences, American Soc. for Investigative Pathology 1975– (Vice-Pres. 1991–92, Pres. 1992–93), Tissue Culture Asscn 1976–, American Soc. for Cell BIology 1976–, Massachusetts Medical Soc. 1978–, New York Acad. of Sciences 1979–, Int. Soc. on Thrombosis and Haemostasis 1979–, American Soc. of Haematology 1980–, American Fed. for Clinical Research 1981–, American Soc. for Clinical Investigation 1986–, Int. Acad. of Pathology 1987–, European Vascular Biology Asscn 1991–, Asscn of American Physicians 1992–, Microcirculatory Soc. 1996–, New England Soc. of Pathologists, Inc. 2002; mem. Cttee of Profs, Harvard Medical School 1985–; mem. Scientific Advisory Bd Stanley J. Sarnoff Endowment for Cardiovascular Science 1994–97, Lankenau Medical Research Center 1994–, Gladstone Inst. of Cardiovascular Disease 1996; Trustee Karin Grunebaum Cancer Research Foundation 1990–; Harvard Medical School awards: Karen Grunebaum Research Award 1968–69, Soma Weiss Research Prize 1969, Leon Reznick Research Prize 1970, Mellon Faculty Award 1975–77; other awards: Herbert I. Horowitz Memorial Lecturer, New York Univ. Medical Center 1977, Established Investigator Award, American Heart Asscn 1977–82, Warner-Lambert/Parke-Davis Award in Experimental Pathology, American Asscn of Pathologists 1982, John Gore Hawley Lecturer, Coll. of Physicians and Surgeons of Columbia Univ. 1985, Erst Roche Distinguished Lecturer, Hoffman-La Roche Co. 1986, Rufus Cole Lecturer in Medicine, Rockefeller Univ. 1990, Robert M. Berne Lecturer in Cardiovascular Sciences, Univ. of Virginia School of Medicine 1990, Univ. Lecturer, Univ. of Texas Southwestern Medical Center, Dallas 1990, Robert R. Linton Distinguished Lecturer, New England Soc. for Vascular Surgery 1991, Dutkevich Memorial Lecturer, Toronto Acad. of Medicine and Univ. of Toronto 1992, Basic Research Prize, American Heart Asscn 1993, William A. Altemeier Lecturer, Surgical Infection Soc. 1993, MERIT Award, Nat. Heart, Lung and Blood Inst. 1994, Cardiovascular Research Award, Bristol-Myers Squibb Research Inst. 1994, Remold Memorial Lecturer, European Soc. for Clinical Investigation 1995, Simon Dack Plenary Lecturer, American Coll. of Cardiology 1995, Pasarow Foundation Award in Cardiovascular Disease 1996, J. Allyn Taylor Int. Prize in Medicine (jtly) 1999, Bristol-Myers Squibb Award for Distinguished Achievement in Cardiovascular Research 2001. *Publications:* more than 450 publs in medical journals. *Address:* Vascular Research Division, Department of Pathology, Brigham and Women's Hospital, 221 Longwood Avenue, LMRC-401, Boston, MA 02115-5817, USA (office). *Telephone:* (617) 732-5901 (office). *Fax:* (617) 732-5933 (office). *E-mail:* mgimbrone@rics.bwh.harvard.edu (office). *Website:* vrd.bwh.harvard.edu/pis/gimbrone (office).

GIMFERRER, Pere; Spanish writer and literary manager; b. 22 June 1945, Barcelona; s. of the late Pere Gimferrer and Carmen Torrens; m. 1st María Rosa Caminals 1971 (died 2003); m. 2nd Cuca de Cominges 2006; ed Univ. of Barcelona; Head of Literary Dept, Editorial Seix Barral 1970, Literary Consultant 1973, Literary Man. 1981–; Academician, Real Acad. Española 1985–, Acad. Européenne de Poésie, Luxembourg, World Acad. of Poetry, Verona; Nat. Prize for Poetry 1966, 1989, Critic's Prize 1983, 1989, Premio Nacional de las Letras Españolas 1998, Queen Sofía Prize for Iberoamerican Poetry 2000, Int. Octavio Paz Prize for Poetry and Essay 2006. *Publications:* Arde el Mar 1966, L'Espai Desert 1977, Dietari 1981, Fortuny 1983, El Vendaval 1988, La Llum 1991, The Roots of Miró 1993, Complete Catalan Work, Vol. I 1995, Vol. II 1995, Vol. III 1996, Vol. IV 1996, Vol. V 1997, Masquerade (poem) 1996, L'Agent Provocador 1998, Marea Solar, Marea Lunar 2000, El Diamant dins l'Aigua 2001, Interludio azul 2006, Amor en vilo 2006, Tornado 2008. *Leisure interests:* cinema, travel. *Address:* Editorial Seix Barral, Diagonal 662, Barcelona 08034 (office); Rambla de Catalunya 113, Barcelona 08008, Spain (home). *Telephone:* (93) 4967003 (office); (93) 2150242 (home). *Fax:* (93) 4967004 (office).

GINER DE SAN JULIAN, Salvador, MA, PhD; Spanish sociologist and academic; *Professor Emeritus of Sociology, University of Barcelona;* b. 10 Feb. 1934, Barcelona; m. Montserrat Sariola 1966; one s. one d.; ed Int. School Barcelona, Univs of Barcelona, Cologne, Germany and Chicago, USA; Visiting Prof., Univ. of Puerto Rico 1962–63; Lecturer, Univ. of Reading, UK 1965–70; Sr Lecturer, Univ. of Lancaster, UK 1970–76; Reader, then Prof. and Head Dept of Sociology and Social Anthropology, Brunel Univ., West London, UK 1976–87; Prof. and Head, Dept of Sociology, Univ. of Barcelona 1987–90, Prof. Emer. 2005–; Dir Inst. of Advanced Social Studies, Higher Council for Scientific Research 1988–97, Barcelona Metropolitan Region Sociological Survey 2001–02; Pres. Spanish Sociological Asscn 1986–91; Vice-Pres. Inst. of Catalan Studies, Barcelona 2000–05, Pres. 2005–; Ed. Revista Internacional de Sociología 1992–; Asst Ed. European Journal of Social Theory 1988–; mem. Scientific Cttee European Prize for Social Science (Amalfi Prize) 1989–; Pres. Acad. of Sciences and Humanities of Catalonia, Barcelona; Order of Civil Merit (Spain) 1987, St George's Cross, Catalonia 1998. *Publications:* Contemporary Europe (Vol. I) 1971, (Vol. II) 1978, Mass Society 1976, Ensayos Civiles 1985, El Destino de la Libertad 1988, España: Sociedad y Política 1990, La Gobernabilidad 1992, Religión y Sociedad en España 1994, Carta sobre la Democracia 1996, Buen Gobierno y Política Social 1997, La Societat Catalana (Coll. of Economists Prize 1999) 1998, Diccionario de Sociología (ed.) 1998, Sociology (revised edn) 2001, Historia del Pensamiento Social (revised edn) 2002, Teoría Sociológica Clásica 2001, 2006, Carisma y Razón 2003, Teoría Sociológica Moderna 2004. *Address:* Department of Sociology, University of Barcelona, Diagonal 690, 08034 Barcelona, Spain (office). *Telephone:* (93) 2110686 (home); (93) 4035553 (office). *Fax:* (93) 4021894 (office). *E-mail:* sginer@ub.edu (office); sginer@iec.cat (office); sginer@diginter.com (home). *Website:* www.ub.edu/sociologia (office); directori.ub.edu/dir (office); www.iec.cat (office).

GINGRICH, Newton (Newt) Leroy, PhD; American fmr politician; *CEO, Gringrich Group;* b. 17 June 1943, Harrisburg, Pa; s. of Robert Bruce Gingrich and Kathleen Gingrich (née Daugherty); m. 2nd Marianne Ginther 1981; two d. by previous marriage; ed Emory and Tulane Univ; mem. faculty, W Ga Coll., Carrollton 1970–78, Prof. of History –1978; mem. 96–103rd Congresses from 6th Dist of Ga 1979–92; Chair. GOPAC, now Chair. Emer.; House Republican Whip 1989; Speaker House of Reps 1994–98; mem. US Comm. on Nat. Security in 21st Century 1999; Founder and CEO Gringrich Group LLC (communications and consulting firm) 1999–; Founder and Chair. American Solutions for Winning the Future 2007–; Adjunct Prof., Reinhardt Coll., Waleska, Ga 1994–95; co-f. Congressional Mil. Reform Caucus, Congressional Space Caucus; mem. AAAS; Sr Fellow, American Enterprise Inst., Distinguished Visiting Fellow, Hoover Inst.; Founder Center for Health Transformation 2003. *Publications:* Window of Opportunity, 1945 1995, To Renew America 1995, Winning the Future: A 21st Century Contract with America 2005, Pearl Harbor: A Novel of December 8th (with William R. Forstchen) 2007, A Contract with the Earth (jtly) 2007, Real Change: From the World That Fails to the World That Works 2008. *Address:* American Solutions for Winning the Future, Glenridge Highlands One, 5555 Glenridge Connector, Suite 200, Atlanta, GA 30342 (office); Gringrich Group LLC, 1425 K Street, NW, Suite 450, Washington, DC 20005, USA (office). *Telephone:* (202) 375-2001 (office). *Fax:* (202) 375-2036 (office). *Website:* www.gingrichgroup.com (office); www.americansolutions.com (office).

GINKAS, Kama Mironovich; Russian theatre director; *Professor, Swedish Theatre Academy, Helsinki;* b. 7 May 1941, Kaunas, Lithuania; m. Yanovskaya Henrietta Yanovna; one s.; ed Leningrad Inst. of Theatre, Music and Cinema; worked in Krasnoyarsk Theatre of Young Spectators 1971–73; accused of aestheticism and barred from working in theatres; currently Prof., Swedish Theatre Acad., Helsinki; teaches directing at Moscow Art Theatre School. *Theatre includes:* Little Car, Moscow Art Theatre 1981, Hedda Gabler, Moscow Mossoviet Theatre 1984, Performing Crime, Moscow Theatre of Young Spectators 1991, Love is Wonderful, Finland, K.I. from Crime, Moscow Theatre of Young Spectators, Idiot (opera), Germany, Lady with a Lapdog 1995, Macbeth, Finland. *Publications:* Provoking Theater (with John Freedman) 2003. *Address:* Moscow Art Theatre School, Tverskaya str., 6, Bldg 7, 125009 Moscow (office); Tishinsky per. 24, Apt 7, Moscow, Russia (home). *Telephone:* (495) 299-53-60 (office); (495) 253-43-15 (home). *Website:* mhatschool.theatre.ru (office).

GINÓBILI, Emanuel (Manu) David; Argentine professional basketball player; b. 28 July 1977, Bahía Blanca; professional debut with Andino 1995–96; with Estudiantes Bahía Blanca 1996–98, Basket Viola Reggio Calabria 1998–2000, Virtus Bologna 2000–02; titles: Italian League Championship 2001, Italian Cup 2001, 2002, Euroleague 2001, Americas Championship 2001; joined Nat. Basketball Asscn (NBA) San Antonio Spurs 2002–; mem. Gold Medal-winning Nat. Team, FIBA Americas Championships, Neuquén 2001, Silver Medal-winning team, San Juan 2003; mem. Silver Medal-winning All-Tournament Team, World Championships 2002; NBA Championship 2003, 2005, 2007; mem. Argentine Nat. Team 1998–, Gold Medal, Olympic Games, Athens 2004, Bronze Medal, Olympic Games, Beijing 2008; UNICEF Goodwill Amb. 2007–; Italian League All-Star 1999, 2000, 2001, Italian League Most Improved Player 2000, 2001, 2002, Euroleague Finals Most Valuable Player 2001, Italian Cup Most Valuable Player 2002, NBA All-Star 2005, All-Tournament Team, FIBA World Championship 2002, 2006, Ideal Olympics Team 2004, Summer Olympic Games Most Valuable Player 2004, Olimpia de Oro 2003, 2004 (shared with Carlos Tévez), 50 Greatest Euroleague Contributors 2008, NBA Sixth Man of the Year Award 2008, All-NBA Third Team 2008. *Address:* San Antonio Spurs, One SBC

www.worldwhoswho.com 781

Center, San Antonio, TX 78219, USA (office). *Telephone:* (210) 444-5000 (office). *Website:* aol.nba.com/spurs (office); www.manuginobili.com.

GINOLA, David; French fmr professional football player; b. 25 Jan. 1967, Gassin, Var; s. of René Ginola and Mireille Collet; m. Coraline Delphin 1990; two d.; ed Lycée du Parc Impérial, Nice; clubs: first div. Toulon clubs 1986–87, Matraracing, Paris 1987–88, Racing Paris 1 1988–89, Brest-Armorique 1989–90, Paris-Saint-Germain 1991–95 (French nat. champions 1993–94, winners Coupe de France 1993, 1995, winners Coupe de la ligue 1995); with Newcastle United, England, 1995–97, Tottenham Hotspur 1997–2000, Aston Villa 2000–02, Everton 2002; 17 int. caps; anti-landmine campaigner for Red Cross 1998–; f. The Centre (retreat) 2004; Professional Football Asscn Player of the Year 1999, Football Writers' Asscn Player of the Year 1999. *Films include:* Rosbeef 2004, Mr Firecul 2004, The Last Drop 2005, Soccer Aid (TV) 2006. *Publication:* David Ginola: The Autobiography (with Neil Silver) 2000. *Leisure interests:* golf, tennis, skiing, car racing. *Website:* www.ginola14.com (office).

GINSBURG, Ruth Joan Bader, BA, LLB; American judge; *Associate Justice, United States Supreme Court;* b. 15 March 1933, Brooklyn, NY; d. of Nathan Bader and Celia Amster; m. Martin D. Ginsburg 1954; one s. one d.; ed Cornell Univ. and Harvard and Columbia Law Schools; admitted New York Bar 1959, DC Bar 1975, US Supreme Court Bar 1967; Law Sec. to Judge, US Dist Court (southern Dist) New York 1959–61; Research Assoc. Columbia Law School, New York 1961–62, Assoc. Dir project on int. procedure 1962–63; Asst Prof. Rutgers Univ. Law School, Newark 1963–66, Assoc. Prof. 1966–69, Prof. 1969–72; Prof. Columbia Univ. School of Law, New York 1972–80; Fellow, Center for Advanced Study in Behavioral Sciences, Stanford, Calif. 1977–78; Gen. Counsel American Civil Liberties Union 1973–80; US Circuit Judge, US Court of Appeals, DC Circuit, Washington, DC 1980–93; Assoc. Justice, US Supreme Court 1993–; mem. American Bar Asscn, AAAS, American Law Inst., Council on Foreign Relations; numerous hon. degrees; ranked by Forbes magazine amongst 100 Most Powerful Women (seventh) 2004, (23rd) 2005, (32nd) 2006, (20th) 2007, (72nd) 2008. *Publications:* Civil Procedure in Sweden (with A. Bruzelius) 1965, Swedish Code of Judicial Procedure 1968, Sex-Based Discrimination (with others); articles in legal journals. *Address:* United States Supreme Court, One First Street, NE, Washington, DC 20543, USA (office). *Telephone:* (202) 479-3211 (office). *Website:* www .supremecourtus.gov (office).

GINWALA, Frene Noshir, LLB, DPhil; South African journalist and politician; b. 25 April 1932, Johannesburg; ed Univs of Oxford and London, UK; left SA in 1960 to establish external mission of the ANC, fmr ANC Spokeswoman, UK; contrib. to The Guardian, The Economist and the BBC, UK; Ed. Tanzania Standard and Sunday News, Tanzania; lectured at various univs; returned to SA 1991; mem. Secr., Office of the Pres. of the ANC, Head of ANC Research Dept 1991–94; Speaker of Nat. Ass. 1994–2004; apptd to head enquiry into Nat. Dir of Public Prosecutions Vusi Pikoli's fitness to hold office 2007–08; Pres. S African Speakers' Forum; Co-Chair. Global Coalition for Africa (GCA); Chair. Presidential Award for Youth Empowerment; Hon. Fellow, Linacre Coll. Oxford, UK; Grand Officier de l'Ordre nat. (Côte d'Ivoire) 1998, Grand Cordon of the Order of the Rising Sun (Japan) 2008; Hon. LLD (Rhodes) 1996, (Natal) 1996, (Cape Town) 1997; Global Award for Outstanding Contrib. to the Promotion of Human Rights and Democracy, Priyadarshni Acad., India 2000, Black Man. Forum Leadership Award 2000, Woman of the Year Award (Univ. of Pretoria Law Faculty) 2000. *Publications include:* Sanctions in South Africa in Question, Gender and Economic Policy in a Democratic South Africa, Women and the Elephant: Putting Women on the Agenda. *Leisure interest:* reading. *Address:* c/o African National Congress of South Africa, POB 61884, Marshalltown 2107, South Africa (office).

GINZBURG, Vitaly Lazarevich, DrSc; Russian physicist and academic; *Professor, Lebedev Physical Institute;* b. 4 Oct. 1916, Moscow; s. of Lazar and Augusta Ginzburg; m. Nina Ginzburg 1946; one d.; ed Moscow Univ.; at P.N. Lebedev Physical Inst., USSR (now Russian) Acad. of Sciences 1940–; Prof., Gorky Univ. 1945–68, Moscow Inst. of Physics 1968–, Adviser to Dir 1987–; Corresp. mem. USSR (now Russian) Acad. of Sciences 1953–66, mem. 1966–; USSR People's Deputy 1989–91; mem. Int. Acad. of Astronautics 1969; Assoc. Royal Astronomical Soc., London 1970; Foreign mem. Royal Danish Acad. of Sciences and Letters 1977; Foreign Fellow, Indian Nat. Science Acad. 1981; Foreign Assoc., NAS, USA 1981; Foreign mem. Royal Soc., London 1987; mem. Academia Europaea 1990; Foreign Hon. mem. American Acad. of Art and Science 1971; Hon. Fellow, Indian Acad. of Science 1977; Order of Lenin 2003; Hon. DSc (Sussex) 1970; Mandelstam Prize 1947, Lomonosov Prize 1962, USSR State Prize 1953, Lenin Prize 1966, Gold Medal, Royal Astronomical Soc. 1991, Bardeen Prize 1991, Wolf Prize 1994, 1995, Vavilov Gold Medal, Russian Acad. of Sciences 1995, Lomonosov Great Gold Medal, Russian Acad. of Sciences 1995, UNESCO-Nils Bohr Gold Medal 1998, APS Nicholson Medal 1998, IUPAP O'Ceallaigh Medal 2001, Nobel Prize for Physics 2003. *Publications:* The Physics of a Lifetime 2001, works on theoretical physics (superconductivity, etc.), astrophysics and radiophysics. *Address:* P.N. Lebedev Physical Inst., Russian Academy of Sciences, Leninsky Prospect 53, 119991 GSP, Moscow B-333, Russia (office). *Telephone:* (499)135-85-70 (office); (495) 135-10-96 (home). *Fax:* (499)132-61-74 (office). *E-mail:* ginzburg@lpi.ru (office). *Website:* www.lebedev.ru (office).

GIOIA, (Michael) Dana, MA, MBA; American writer and poet; *Director, Harman-Eisner Program in the Arts, Aspen Institute;* b. 24 Dec. 1950, Los Angeles; m. Mary Hiecke 1980; three s. (one deceased); ed Stanford and Harvard Univs; fmr Visiting Writer, Colorado Coll., Johns Hopkins Univ., Wesleyan Univ.; Chair. Nat. Endowment for the Arts 2003–09; Dir Harman-Eisner Program in the Arts, Aspen Inst. 2009–; mem. Bd and Vice-Pres. Poetry Soc. of America; mem. Wesleyan Univ. Writers' Conf.; regular contrib.

to various journals, reviews and periodicals including San Francisco magazine (classical music critic); ten Hon. degrees; Esquire Best of New Generation Award 1984, Frederick Bock Prize for Poetry 1985, American Book Award 2001, Nat. Civilian's Medal 2009. *Opera:* Nosferatu, Tony Caruso's Final Broadcast 2008. *Publications include:* The Ceremony and Other Stories 1984, Daily Horoscope 1986, Mottetti: Poems of Love (trans.) 1990, The Gods of Winter 1991, Can Poetry Matter? 1992, An Introduction to Poetry 1994, The Madness of Hercules (trans.) 1995, Interrogations at Noon (American Book Award 2002) 2001, Nosferatu (opera libretto with Alva Henderson) 2001, The Barrier of a Common Language (essays) 2003, Twentieth-century American Poetry 2004, Twentieth-century American Poetics 2004, 100 Great Poets of the English Language 2005; also ed. of several works of literary criticism. *Address:* The Aspen Institute, 1 Dupont Circle, NW, Washington, DC 20036 (office); 7190 Faught Road, Santa Rosa, CA 95403, USA (office). *Telephone:* (202) 736-2521 (office). *Fax:* (202) 467-0790 (office). *E-mail:* dana.gioia@ aspeninst.org (office). *Website:* www.danagioia.net.

GIOJA, José Luis; Argentine politician and lawyer; *Governor of the Province of San Juan;* b. 4 Dec. 1949, San Juan Prov.; m.; ed Escuela Normal de Jáchal, San Juan and Nat. Univ. of Cuyo; Pres. Agrupación Nacional de Estudiantes Universitarios 1972–73; Pvt. Sec. to Gov. Eloy Camus 1973; Sec.-Gen. Juventud Peronista, Partido Justicialista de San Juan 1975; Congresal Prov. 1975–76; Interventor Instituto Prov. de la Vivienda 1974–75; Pres. Unidad Básica del Barrio Edilco 1983; Cand., Departamento de Rawson 1983; Pres. Junta Departamental de Rawson 1984–85; mem. Consejo Nacional Justicialista 1987–93, Consejo Prov. Justicialista 1987–93; Prov. Deputy and Vice-Pres. Justicialista Bloc, Chamber of Deputies, San Juan Prov. 1987–91, Pres. Comisión de Minería, Obras Públicas y Recursos Hídricos; Deputy in Nat. Ass. 1991–99, Pres. Jt Party Comm. Argentina–Chile 1993; Senator 1995–, Pres. Comisión Bicameral de Minería y de Coparticipación Fed. de Impuestos, Pres. Senate Justicialistas Bloc 2000–02, Pres. (provisional) of Senate 2002; Gov. of Province of San Juan 2003–. *Address:* Office of the Governor, San Juan 5400, Argentina (office). *Website:* www.sanjuan.gov.ar (office).

GIORDANA, Marco Tullio; Italian film director and screenwriter; b. 1 Oct. 1950, Milan. *Films:* Forza Italia! (screenwriter) 1978, Maledetti vi amerò (To Love the Damned) (also screenwriter) 1980, Car Crash (screenwriter) 1980, La caduta degli angeli ribelli (also screenwriter) 1981, Notti e nebbie (TV) (also screenwriter) 1984, Appuntamento a Liverpool (also screenwriter) 1988, La domenica specialmente (Especially on Sunday, USA) 1991, L'unico paese al mondo 1994, Pasolini, un delitto italiano (Pasolini, an Italian Crime) (also screenwriter) 1995, I cento passi (The Hundred Steps) (also screenwriter) 2000, Un altro mondo è possibile (Another World Is Possible, USA) 2001, Il cineasta e il labirinto (as himself) 2002, La meglio gioventù (The Best of Youth) 2003, Quando sei nato non puoi più nasconderti (Once You're Born You Can No Longer Hide, UK) 2004.

GIORDANO, HE Cardinal Michele; Italian ecclesiastic; *Archbishop of Naples;* b. 26 Sept. 1930, S. Arcangelo (Pz); ordained 1953, elected to the titular Church of Lari Castello 1971, consecrated bishop 1972, Archbishop of Matera 1974–77, Archbishop of Matera e Irsina 1977–87, Archbishop of Naples 1987–; cr. Cardinal Priest of S. Gioacchino ai Prati di Castello 1988. *Address:* Arcivescovado di Napoli, Largo Donnaregina 22, 80138 Naples, Italy. *Telephone:* (081) 449118. *Fax:* (081) 292487.

GIORDANO, Richard Vincent, BA, LLB, PhD; American business executive; b. 24 March 1934, New York; s. of Vincent Giordano and Cynthia Giordano (née Cardetta); m. Barbara Claire Beckett 1956 (divorced); one s. two d.; ed Stuyvesant School, New York, Harvard Univ. and Columbia Univ. Law School; admitted New York Bar 1961; Assoc. Shearman and Sterling (law firm), New York 1959–63; Asst Sec. Air Reduction Co. Inc., New York 1963–64, Vice-Pres. Distribution of Products Div. 1964–65, Exec. Vice-Pres. 1965–67, Group Vice-Pres. 1967–71, Pres. and COO 1971–74, CEO 1977–79; Dir BOCI 1974; Man. Dir and CEO BOC Group 1979–84, Chair. 1985–92, CEO 1985–91, Chair. (non-exec.) 1994–96; Dir (non-exec.) Reuters 1991–94; Chair. (non-exec.) British Gas PLC (renamed BG PLC 1997, BG Group PLC 1999) 1994–2003; mem. Bd of Dirs (non-exec.) Cen. Electricity Generating Bd 1982–89, Georgia Pacific Corpn 1984–2006, Grand Metropolitan 1985–97 (Deputy Chair. (non-exec.) 1991–97), RTZ (renamed Rio Tinto PLC), Deputy Chair. (non-exec.) 1992–, Lucas Industries (non-exec.) 1993–94; Hon. Fellow, Royal Coll. of Anaesthetists, London Business School; Hon. KBE; Hon. DCS (St John's Univ., USA); Hon. LLB (Bath) 1998. *Leisure interests:* sailing, opera. *Address:* c/o 20 Villet Drive, East Setauket, NY 11733, USA (office). *Telephone:* (631) 689-8523 (office). *Fax:* (631) 675-6182 (office). *E-mail:* kastwood54@optonline.net (office).

GIOVANNI, Nikki, BA; American poet and academic; *University Distinguished Professor, Virginia Polytechnic Institute and State University;* b. (Yolande Cornelia Giovanni), 7 June 1943, Knoxville, Tenn.; d. of Jones Giovanni and Yolande Watson; one s.; ed Fisk Univ., Univ. of Cincinnati and Univ. of Pennsylvania; Asst Prof. of Black Studies, City Coll. of New York 1968; Assoc. Prof. of English, Rutgers Univ. 1968–72; Prof. of Creative Writing, Coll. Mt. St Joseph on the Ohio 1985; Prof. of English, Va Polytechnic Inst. and State Univ. 1987–, Gloria D. Smith Prof. of Black Studies 1997–99, Univ. Distinguished Prof. 1999–; founder, Nixtom Ltd 1970; Visiting Prof. Ohio State Univ. 1984; recordings and TV appearances; recipient of numerous awards and hon. degrees. *Publications:* Black Feeling, Black Talk 1968, Black Judgement 1968, Re: Creation 1970, Poem of Angela Yvonne Davis 1970, Spin A Soft Black Song 1971, Gemini 1971, My House 1972, A Dialogue: James Baldwin and Nikki Giovanni 1973, Ego Tripping and Other Poems for Young Readers 1973, A Poetic Equation: Conversations Between Nikki Giovanni and Margaret Walker 1974, The Women and the Men 1975, Cotton Candy on a

Rainy Day 1978, Vacationtime 1980, Those Who Ride the Night Winds 1983, Sacred Cows . . . and other Edibles 1988, Conversations with Nikki Giovanni 1992, Racism 101 1994, Grand Mothers 1994, Selected Poems of Nikki Giovanni 1996, Nikki in Philadelphia 1997, Love Poems 1997, Blues: For All the Changes 1999, Quilting the Black-Eyed Pea: Poems and Not-Quite Poems 2002, The Collected Poetry of Nikki Giovanni 2003. *Address:* Department of English, Virginia Polytechnic Institute and State University, 323 Shanks Hall, Blacksburg, VA 24061, USA (office). *Telephone:* (540) 231-9453 (office). *E-mail:* info@nikki-giovanni.com (office). *Website:* www.english.vt.edu (office); www.nikki-giovanni.com.

GIRALDO, Luis Guillermo, LLB; Colombian economist, politician and fmr diplomatist; *Secretary-General, Partido Social de la Unidad Nacional (Partido de la U);* b. Manizales; ed Pontificia Universidad Javeriana, Bogota; Sec.-Gen. of Treasury, Manizales 1967; mem. House of Reps 1970–78; Mayor of Manizales 1978; Senator of the Repub. 1978–98; Pres. of Senate 1989; Amb. to Germany 1990–91, to Venezuela 1998–99; Chief of Presidential Campaign of Alvaro Uribe, then mem. team preparing Govt Plan of Action –2003; Perm. Rep. to UN, New York 2003; Amb. to Mexico 2003–05; Sec.-Gen. Partido Social de la Unidad Nacional (Partido de la U) 2005–; mem. Peace Negotiations 1999. *Publications:* Contrapuntos del Poder y la Fama, Algunas Palabras, De Relojes y de Nostalgias, El Antiheroe. *Address:* Partido Social de la Unidad Nacional (Partido de la U) 32-16 Carrera 7, 21°, Bogotá, DC, Colombia (office). *Telephone:* (1) 340-1394 (office). *Website:* www.partidodelau.com (office).

GIRARD, Jean-François, MD, MSc; French civil servant and professor of medicine; *President, Institut de recherche pour le développement;* b. 20 Nov. 1944, Luçon (Vendée); one s. two d.; ed Univ. of Paris; Prof. of Medicine 1979–97; Dir-Gen. Ministry of Health 1986–97; Chair. Exec. Council WHO 1992, 1993; Conseiller d'Etat 1997–; Pres. Inst. de recherche pour le développement 2001–; Chevalier, Légion d'honneur, Commdr, Ordre nat. du Mérite. *Publications:* Quand la santé devient publique 1998, La maladie d'Alzheimer 2000. *Leisure interest:* sailing. *Address:* Institut de recherche pour le développement, Le Sextant, 44 boulevard de Dunkerque 13002 Marseilles, France (office). *Telephone:* 4-91-99-95-55 (office). *Fax:* 4-91-99-92-20 (office). *E-mail:* president@ird.fr (office). *Website:* www.ird.fr (office).

GIRARD, René Noël, PhD; French/American academic and writer; *Professor Emeritus, Stanford University;* b. 25 Dec. 1923, Avignon; s. of Joseph Girard and Thérèse Fabre; m. Martha Virginia McCullough 1951; two s. one d.; ed Lycée d'Avignon, Ecole des Chartes and Indiana Univ.; Instructor of French, Indiana Univ. 1947–51, Duke Univ. 1952–53; Asst Prof. Bryn Mawr Coll. 1953–57; Assoc. Prof. The Johns Hopkins Univ. 1957–61, Prof. 1961–68, Chair. Romance Languages 1965–68, James M. Beall Prof. of French and Humanities 1976–80; Prof. Inst. d'études françaises Bryn Mawr, Avignon 1961–68, Dir 1969; Distinguished Faculty Prof. of Arts and Letters, State Univ. of New York at Buffalo 1971–76; Andrew B. Hammond Prof. of French Language, Literature and Civilization, Stanford Univ. 1981–95, Courtesy Prof. of Religious Studies and Comparative Literature 1986–95, Dir Program of Interdisciplinary Research, Dept of French and Italian 1987–95, Prof. Emer. 1995–; mem. Center for Int. Security and Arms Control, 1990–95; Fellow American Acad. of Arts and Sciences 1979–, Guggenheim Fellow 1960, 1967; elected mem. Acad. française 2005; mem. Acad. Française 2005; Hon. DLit (Vrije Univ.) 1985, Hon. DTheol (Innsbruck) 1988, (St Mary's Seminary, Baltimore) 2003, (Montreal) 2004, (London) 2005, Hon. DLit (Padua) 2001; Chevalier, Ordre Nat. de la Légion d'honneur 1984, Officier, Ordre des Arts et Lettres 1984; Acad. Française Prize 1973, Grand Prix de Philosophie 1996; Prix Médicis-Essai 1990, Premio Nonino (Percoto, Udine, Italy) 1998, Dr Leopold Lucas Prize, Tübingen 2006. *Publications include:* Mensonge romantique et vérité romanesque 1961, Dostoïevski: du double à l'unité 1963, La violence et le sacré 1972, Des choses cachées depuis la fondation du monde 1978, Le bouc émissaire 1982, La route antique des hommes pervers 1985, The Girard Reader 1996, Shakespeare: Les feux de l'envie 1990, A Theatre of Envy. William Shakespeare 1991, Quand ces choses commenceront 1994, Je vois Satan tomber comme l'éclair 1999, (in English) 2001, Celui par qui le scandale arrive 2001, La voix méconnue du réel 2002, Les Origines de la Culture 2004.

GIRARDET, Herbert, BSc (Econs); German ecologist, consultant, writer and television producer; *Director of Programmes, World Future Council;* b. 25 May 1943, Essen; s. of Herbert Girardet and Ingrid Girardet; m. Barbara Hallifax 1967; two s.; ed Tübingen and Berlin Univs, London School of Econs, UK; consultant to Town and Country Planning Asscn, London 1976–86, Channel 4 TV, London 1987–89, UN Habitat II Conf., Istanbul 1995–96; Visiting Prof. of Environmental Planning, Middlesex Univ. 1995–; Visiting Prof. of Sustainable Urban Devt, Univ. of Northumbria 2003–; Visiting Prof. of Cities and the Environment, Univ. of the West of England 2004–; Thinker-in-Residence, Adelaide 2003; Dir Under the Sky Urban Regeneration Co., Bristol 2004–; Dir of Programmes World Future Council 2004–; Chief Consultant to Shanghai City Govt on design of Dongtan Eco-City on Chongming Island; mem. Balaton Group of int. environment experts 1993–; Chair. The Schumacher Soc., UK 1994–; Trustee, The Sustainable London Trust 1996–; Patron The Soil Asscn, UK 1990–; Hon. FRIBA 2000; UN Global Award for Outstanding Environmental Achievements, prizes for TV documentaries. *Television:* initiator and researcher: Far from Paradise (series) 1983–86; writer and producer: Jungle Pharmacy 1988, Halting the Fires 1989, Metropolis 1994, Urban Best Practices 1996, Deadline (28 three-minute films) 1997–99; series consultant: The People's Planet 1999–2000. *Publications:* Far From Paradise: The Story of Human Impact on the Environment (co-author) 1986, Blueprint for a Green Planet (co-author) 1987, Earthrise 1992, The Gaia Atlas of Cities 1992, Making Cities Work (co-author) 1996, Getting London in Shape for 2000 1997, Creating a Sustainable London (co-author) 1998, Creating Sustainable Cities 1999, Tall Buildings and Sustainable Development (co-author) 2001, Creating a Sustainable Adelaide 2003, Cities, People, Planet 2004, Shanghai Dongtan: An Ecocity (co-author) 2006, Surviving the Century (ed.) 2007. *Leisure interests* gardening, country walking. *Address:* World Future Council, Trafalgar House, 11 Waterloo Place, London, SW1Y 4AU, England (office); Forest Cottage, Trelleck Road, Tintern, Chepstow, Monmouthshire, NP16 6SN, Wales (home). *Telephone:* (20) 7863-8833 (office); (1291) 689392 (home). *Fax:* (20) 7389-5162 (office); (1291) 689392 (home). *E-mail:* herbie@worldfuturecouncil.org (office). *Website:* www.worldfuturecouncil.org (office).

GIRARDOT, Annie Suzanne; French actress; b. 25 Oct. 1931, Paris; m. Renato Salvatori 1962 (deceased); one d.; ed Centre d'art dramatique, Paris, Conservatoire nat. d'art dramatique; with Comédie-Française 1954–57; Suzanne-Bianchetti Prize 1956, Prize for Best Actress, Venice Film Festival (for Trois chambres à Manhattan) 1965, Courteline Prize (for Déclics et des claques) 1965, Prize for Best Actress, Mar del Plata Festival (for Vivre pour vivre) 1968, Best Actress of the Year (for Docteur Françoise Gailland) 1976; Commdr des Arts et des Lettres. *Plays include:* La Tour Eiffel qui tue, La paix chez soi, Le jeu de l'amour et du hasard, La machine à écrire, Les amants magnifiques, Aux innocents les mains pleines, Une femme trop honnête, Deux sur une balançoire, l'Idiote, Après la chute 1965, Le jour de la tortue 1965, Seule dans le noir 1966, Persephone (speaking part, La Scala, Milan) 1966, Madame Marguerite (1974–75), Marguerite et les autres 1983, l'Avare 1986, Première Jeunesse 1987, Le roi se meurt 1988, Helden platz 1991, Les Chutes du Zambèze 1995, Le Sixième ciel 1998. *Films include:* Treize à table 1955, l'Homme aux clefs d'or 1956, Le rouge est mis, Maigret tend un piège, Le désert de Pigalle 1957, La corde raide, Recours en grâce 1959, La française et l'amour, La Proie pour l'ombre, Rocco et ses frères 1960, Le rendez-vous, Les amours célèbres, Le bateau d'Emile 1961, Le vice et la vertu 1962, l'Autre femme 1963, Déclics et des claques, Trois chambres à Manhattan, l'Or du duc 1965, Vivre pour vivre 1967, Les Gauloises bleues, La bande à Bonnot 1968, Il pleut dans mon village, Erotissimo, Un homme qui me plaît 1969, Dillinger est mort, l'Histoire d'une femme, Elle boit pas, elle fume pas, elle drague pas, mais . . . elle cause, Disons un soir à dîner, Les novices, Le clair de terre 1970, Mourir d'aimer, La vieille fille, La mandarine 1971, Les feux de la chandeleur, Elle cause plus . . . elle flingue 1972, Traitement de choc, Jessua 1973, Il n'y a pas de fumée sans feu 1972, Ursule et Grelu 1973, Juliette et Juliette, La gifle 1974, Il faut vivre dangereusement, Le Gitan, Il pleut sur Santiago 1975, Docteur Françoise Gailland, Le soupçon, D'amour et d'eau fraîche, Cours après moi . . . que je t'attrape 1976, A chacun son enfer 1977, Le dernier baiser, Jambon d'Ardenne, Le point de mire 1977, La Zizanie, La clé sur la porte, l'Amour en question 1978, Vas-y maman 1978, Cause toujours . . . tu m'intéresses 1979, Bobo, Jacco, Le grand embouteillage 1979, La vie continue, Une robe noire pour un tueur, La revanche 1981, Partir, revenir 1985, Adieu Blaireau 1985, Prisonnières 1988, Cinq jours en juin 1989, Comédie d'amour 1989, Il y a des jours . . . et des lunes 1990, Merci la vie 1991, Les Misérables 1995 (César award for Best Supporting Actress), Préférence et l'age de braise 1998, T'aime 2000, La pianiste 2001, Ceci est mon corps 2001, Epsteins Nacht 2002, La Prophétie des grenouilles 2003, Je préfère qu'on reste amis 2005, Caché 2005, Le Temps des porte-plumes 2006, C'est beau une ville la nuit 2006, Boxes 2007, Christian 2007. *Television includes:* Le pain de ménage 1966, Bobo, Jaco, Florence ou la vie de château 1987, Le vent des moissons 1989, Un pull par-dessus l'autre 1993, Jeanne 1994, Le dernier voyage 1995, La façon de le dire 1999, Les Fleurs de Maureen 2002, Simon le juste 2003, La Petite Fadette 2004, Allons petits enfants 2005, Vorotily (mini-series) 2007. *Publication:* Vivre d'aimer 1989. *Address:* c/o Artmédia, 20 avenue Rapp, 75007 Paris, France.

GIRAUD, Michel Jean Lucien; French politician and business executive; b. 14 July 1929, Pontoise, Seine-et-Oise; s. of Jean Giraud and Suzanne Le Goaziou; m. Simonne Wietzel 1952; two s. (one deceased) one d.; ed secondary school at Saint-Martin de France-Pontoise, Lycée Louis le Grand and Univ. de Paris; Deputy Dir Société Centrale des Bois 1951–57; Dir Société A. Charles & Fils 1960–72; Pres. Dir-Gen. SONIBAT 1972–93, Société d'Economie Mixte d'Aménagement et de Gestion du Marché d'Intérêt Nat. de Paris-Rungis 1975–77; Senator for Val-de-Marne 1977–88; Conseiller-Gén. Val de Marne 1967–85; Admin., Conseil d'Admin Parisian Regional Dist 1968, Sec. 1969–72, Pres. 1972–73; Pres. Conseil Régional, Ile-de-France 1976–88, 1992–98; RPR Deputy for Val-de-Marne 1988–93, 1995–2002; Mayor of Perreux-sur-Marne 1971–92 (Municipal Councillor 1971–); Pres. Nat. Fed. of Local Councillors 1977–83, Asscn of Mayors of France 1983–92; Minister of Labour, Employment and Professional Training 1993–95; Founder and Pres. World Asscn of Major Metropolises–Metropolis 1985–98; Pres. Fondation de la 2ème Chance 2008–; Chevalier, Légion d'honneur, Ordre Nat. du Mérite, des Palmes Académiques; Médaille d'Argent de la Jeunesse et des Sports. *Publications:* Nous tous la France 1983, Raconte-moi Marianne 1984, Notre Ile-de-France région capitale 1985, le Perreux, 100 ans d'histoire 1987, le Temps des Métropoles 1987, Histoire de l'Ile de France 1996, Histoires de communes 1996, Citadins de l'an 2000 1997, Eclats de vie 2001, Rebondir avec la Fondation de la 2ème Chance 2003, Renaître avec la Fondation de la 2ème Chance 2006. *Leisure interests:* sport, history, music, skiing. *Address:* 4 Grande rue, 91250 Morsang-sur-Seine, France (home).

GIRI, Rt Hon. Kedar Prasad; Nepalese judge; *Chief Justice;* experience with various judicial and quasi-judicial bodies, including Royal Law Reform Comm., Chair. Land Limitation Execution Cttee, Land Reform Ministry and all levels of courts in Nepal, Acting Chief Justice of Nepal Sept.–Oct. 2007, Chief Justice of Nepal Oct. 2007–. *Address:* Supreme Court of Nepal, Ramashah Path, Kathmandu, Nepal (office). *E-mail:* info@supremecourt.gov.np (office). *Website:* www.supremecourt.gov.np (office).

GIRI, Tulsi; Nepalese politician; b. Sept. 1926; Deputy Minister of Foreign Affairs 1959; Minister of Village Devt 1960; Minister without Portfolio 1960; Minister of Foreign Affairs, the Interior, Public Works and Communications 1961; Vice-Chair. Council of Ministers and Minister of Palace Affairs 1962; Chair. Council of Ministers and Minister of Foreign Affairs 1962–65; mem. Royal Advisory Cttee 1969–74; apptd Adviser to the King 1974; Prime Minister, Minister of Palace Affairs and Defence 1975–77; Vice-Chair. Council of Ministers and Minister of Land Reform and Man. and of Water Resources 2005. *Address:* c/o Ministry of Land Reform and Management, Singha Durbar, Kathmandu, Nepal.

GIROLAMI, Sir Paul, Kt, BCom, FCA; British/Italian business executive (retd) and chartered accountant; b. (Paolo Girolami), 25 Jan. 1926, Fanna, Italy; s. of Pietro Girolami and Assunta Bertossi; m. Christabel Mary Gwynne Lewis 1952; two s. one d.; ed London School of Econs; with Chantrey and Button (Chartered Accountants) 1950–54, Cooper Brothers 1954–65; mem. Bd Glaxo 1965–94, Finance Dir 1965–80, Chief Exec. 1980–86, Exec. Chair. 1985–94; Pres. Glaxo Finanziaria SpA Italy; mem. Bd of Dirs Nippon Glaxo Ltd, Japan 1975–94, Glaxo-Sankyo Ltd 1984–94, Credito Italiano Int. 1990–93, Forte PLC 1992–96, UIS France 1994–2000; mem. CBI Council 1986–93; Chair. Senate for Chartered Accountants in Business 1990–; Chair. Council Goldsmith's Coll., Univ. of London 1994–2002; Dir American Chamber of Commerce (UK) 1983; mem. Appeal Cttee of Inst. of Chartered Accountants 1987, Stock Exchange Listed Cos Advisory Cttee 1987–92, Open Univ. Visiting Cttee 1987–89; mem. Worshipful Co. of Apothecaries, Worshipful Co. of Chartered Accountants, Court of Assts of The Worshipful Co. of Goldsmiths (Prime Warden) 1986; Pres. British-Italian Soc.; Freeman, City of London Liveryman 1980, Hon. Fellow, LSE 1989, Goldsmiths Coll., Emmanuel Coll., Cambridge 1994; Grande Ufficiale, Ordine al Merito della Repubblica Italiana 1987, Insignia of the Order of the Rising Sun, Cavaliere del Lavoro 1991, Grand Cross, Order of the Holy Sepulchre; Dr hc (Aston) 1991, (Trieste) 1991, Hon. DSc (Sunderland) 1991, (Bradford) 1993, Hon. LLD (Singapore) 1993, (Warwick) 1996; City and Guilds Insignia Award in Tech. (hc) 1988, Public Service Star, Singapore 2000. *Leisure interests:* reading, music. *Address:* Piazza Conte Nicolo' di Maniago 16, Maniago (PN), Italy (office). *Telephone:* (427) 709005 (office). *E-mail:* pgirol@aol.com (home); paolo.girolami@alice.it (home).

GISCARD D'ESTAING, Valéry, KCB; French politician and civil servant; *Chairman, Convention on the Future of Europe, European Union;* b. 2 Feb. 1926, Koblenz, Germany; s. of the late Edmond Giscard d'Estaing and May Bardoux; m. Anne-Aymone de Brantes 1952; two s. two d.; ed Ecole Polytechnique, Ecole Nat. d'Admin; Official, Inspection des Finances 1952, Insp. 1954; Deputy Dir du Cabinet of Prés. du Conseil June–Dec. 1954; Deputy for Puy de Dôme 1956–58, re-elected for Clermont 1958, for Puy de Dôme 1962, 1967, 1984, 1986, 1988, resgnd 1989; Sec. of State for Finance 1959, Minister for Finance and Econ. Affairs 1962–66, 1969–74; Pres. Comm. des Finances, de l'Economie général et du plan 1967–68; Pres. Cttee des Affaires Etrangères 1987–89; Pres. of the French Repub. 1974–81; Founder-Pres. Fed. Nat. des Républicains Indépendants (from May 1977 Parti Républicain) 1965; Del. to UN Gen. Ass. 1956, 1957, 1958; Chair. OECD Ministerial Council 1960; mem. (ex officio) Conseil Constitutionnel 1981–; Conseiller gen., Puy-de-Dôme 1982–88; Pres. Regional Council of Auvergne 1986–2004; Pres. Union pour la democratie française (UDF) 1988–96; Deputy to European Parl. 1989–93; Pres. European Movt Int. 1989–97; Pres. Council of European Municipalities and Regions 1997–2004; Deputy for Puy-de-Dôme 1993–2002; Pres. Comm. of Foreign Affairs, Nat. Ass. 1993–97; Chair. EU Convention on the Future of Europe 2001–; mem. Royal Acad. of Econ. Science and Finance, Spain 1995–; Académie française 2003–; Grand Croix, Ordre de la Légion d'honneur, Grand Croix, Ordre national du Mérite, Croix de guerre, Bailli Grand-Croix, Chevalier, Ordre de Malte, Gran Cruce, Ordén de Isabel la Católica; Nansen Medal 1979, Onassis Foundation Prize 2000, Trombinoscope Prize for Political Personality of the Year 2000, Jean Monnet Foundation Medal 2001, Trombinoscope European of the Year 2002, Charlemagne Prize 2002. *Publications:* Démocratie française 1976, Deux français sur trois 1984, Le Pouvoir et la vie, Vol. I 1988, Vol. II: L'Affrontement 1991, Vol. III: Choisir 2006, Le Passage 1994, Dans cinq ans, l'an 2000 (essay) 1995, Les Français 2000. *Leisure interests:* shooting, skiing. *Address:* 199 blvd Saint-Germain, 75007 Paris, France (office). *Telephone:* 1-45-44-30-30 (office). *Fax:* 1-45-49-11-16 (office). *E-mail:* vge-cab-international@servpm.org (office).

GISKE, Trond; Norwegian politician; *Minister of Culture and Church Affairs;* b. 7 Nov. 1966; ed Univ. of Oslo, Norwegian Univ. of Science and Tech.; Leader, Labour Youth League, Sør-Trøndelag Co. 1989–90, mem. Cen. Exec. Cttee 1990–96, Leader, Labour Youth League 1992–96, mem. Labour Party Cen. Exec. Cttee 1992–96, mem. Parl. Election Cttee 1997–2001; mem. Storting (Parl.) for Sør-Trøndelag Co. 1997–2005, mem. Standing Cttee on Finance and Econ. Affairs 1997–2001, Standing Cttee on Family, Cultural Affairs and Govt Admin 2001–05, Labour Party Parl. Group 2001–05; Minister of Educ., Research and Church Affairs 2000–01, of Culture and Church Affairs 2005–; del. to UN Gen. Ass. 1999. *Address:* Ministry of Culture and Church Affairs, Akersgt. 59, POB 8030 Dep, 0030 Oslo, Norway (office). *Telephone:* 22-24-78-39 (office). *Fax:* 22-24-90-10 (office). *E-mail:* postmottak@kkd.dep.no (office). *Website:* www.regjeringen.no/kkd (office).

GÍSLADÓTTIR, Ingibjörg Sólrún, BA; Icelandic politician; b. 31 Dec. 1954, Reykjavík; m. Hjörleifur Sveinbjörnsson; two s.; ed Univ. of Iceland, Univ. of Copenhagen, Denmark; began political career in Samtök um kvennalista (Women's Alliance), which she represented in Reykjavík's City Council 1982–88; mem. Althing (Parl.) for Reykjavík 1991–94, for Reykjavík N 2005–, mem. Cttee on Foreign Affairs 1991–93, Cttee on Health and Social Security 1991–94, Cttee on Social Affairs 1991–94 (Vice-Chair. 1993–94), Cttee on Economy and Trade 2005–06, Icelandic Del. to EFTA and European Econ. Area Parl. Cttees 2005–; Founding mem. Samfylkingin (The Alliance) 2000, Deputy Leader 1994–2003, Leader 2003–05, Chair. 2005–; Mayor of Reykjavík 1994–2003 (resgnd); Minister for Foreign Affairs and External Trade 2007–09 (resgnd); fmr Ed. Vera (feminist journal); mem. Exec. Bd Cen. Bank of Iceland 2003–05. *Publication:* Þegar sálin fer á kreik. *Address:* Samfylkingin, Hallveigarstíg 1, 101 Reykjavík, Iceland (office). *Telephone:* 4142200 (office). *Fax:* 4142201 (office); 5622386 (office). *E-mail:* samfylking@samfylking.is (office). *Website:* www.samfylking.is (office).

GITARI, Most Rev. David Mukuba, BA, BD; Kenyan ecclesiastic (retd); b. 16 Sept. 1937; s. of Samuel Mukuba Gituku and Jessie Wanjiku; m. Grace Wanjiro Gatembo 1966; three c.; ed Kangaru School, Embu, Royal Coll., Nairobi, Tyndale Coll., Bristol, UK, Ashland Seminary, Ohio, USA; Gen. Sec. Pan-African Evangelical Fellowship 1966–68, Bible Soc. of Kenya 1971–75; Anglican Bishop of Diocese of Mt Kenya E 1975–90, of Diocese of Kirinyaga 1990–96; Archbishop of Anglican Church of Kenya and Bishop of Diocese of Nairobi 1976–2002; Dir Oxford Centre for Mission Studies 1983–; Chair. Kenya Students Christian Fellowship 1971–74, Kenya Peace 1978–, World Evangelical Fellowship Theological Comm. 1978–88, Nat. Council of Churches of Kenya 1978–80, 1981–83; Deputy Chair. WCC Comm. on Evangelism 1983–91; First Chair. Int. Fellowship of Mission Theologians 1981–94; Hon. DD (Ashland Seminary, Ohio, USA) 1983, (Univ. of Canterbury, UK) 1998; Pres. of Kenya's MBS (Moran of Burning Spear) Award for Outstanding Service to the Nation 2004. *Publications:* Let the Bishop Speak, In Season and Out of Season, We Will Serve the Lord 2004, Responsible Church Leadership 2005. *Leisure interests:* driving, farming (keeping pigs, cows and birds and growing mangoes), reading and writing books, counselling. *Address:* Philadelphia Place, Kirinyaga District, PO Box 607, Embu, Kenya (home). *Telephone:* (68) 30832 (home). *Fax:* (68) 30977 (home). *E-mail:* davidgitari@winnet.co.ke (home).

GITELSON, Yosif Isayevich; Russian biophysicist; *Adviser, Institute of Biophysics, Siberian Branch, Russian Academy of Sciences;* b. 6 July 1928; m.; four d.; ed Krasnoyarsk Inst. of Medicine; worked as practitioner Krasnoyarsk Blood Transfusion Station 1952–53; docent Krasnoyarsk Inst. of Agric. 1953–57; Sr Researcher, Head of Lab., Inst. of Physics, Siberian br. of USSR (now Russian) Acad. of Sciences 1957–82; Head of Lab., Inst. of Biophysics Siberian br. of USSR Acad. of Sciences 1982–86, Dir 1986–96, Adviser 1996–; Corresp. mem. USSR Acad. of Sciences 1979, mem. 1990–; adviser to Russian Acad. of Sciences 1996–. *Publications:* Experimental Ecological Systems Including Man, Problems of Space Biology 1975, Light from the Sea 1986, Distant Studies of Siberia 1988; numerous articles in scientific journals. *Address:* Institute of Biophysics, Akademgorodok, 660036 Krasnoyarsk, Russia (office). *Telephone:* (3912) 43-15-79 (office); (495) 433-63-57 (home). *Fax:* (3912) 43-34-00 (office). *E-mail:* ibp@ibp.ru (office). *Website:* www.ibp.ru (office).

GIULIANI, Rudolph (Rudy) W., KBE, BA, JD; American lawyer, business executive and fmr politician; *Senior Partner, Bracewell & Giuliani LLP;* b. 28 May 1944, Brooklyn, NY; s. of the late Harold Giuliani and Helen Giuliani; m. 1st Regina Peruggi (divorced); m. 2nd Donna Hanover (divorced 2002); one s. one d.; m. 3rd Judith Nathan 2003; ed Manhattan Coll., New York Univ. School of Law; law clerk; judge, US Dist Court, New York City 1968–70; Asst US Attorney Southern Dist, New York; US Attorney 1983–89; with Patterson, Belknap, Webb and Tyler 1977–81; with White & Case 1989–90; with Anderson Kill Olick & Oshinsky 1990–93; Mayor of New York 1994–2001; f. Giuliani Partners LLC (with Ernst & Young) 2002, Chair. and CEO 2002–, f. Giuliani Advisors LLC (investment advisory firm) 2004 (acquired by Macquarie Group 2007); Chair. Bd of Advisors Leeds Weld and Co. 2002–; Sr Pnr, Bracewell & Giuliani LLP (law firm), New York 2005–; unsuccessful cand. for Republican nomination for Pres. of US 2007–08; Time Magazine Person of the Year 2001. *Publications:* Leadership 2002. *Address:* Bracewell & Giuliani LLP, 1177 Avenue of the Americas, 19th Floor, New York, NY 10036-2714, USA (office). *Telephone:* (212) 508-6102 (office). *Fax:* (212) 938-3802 (office). *E-mail:* rudy.giuliani@bgllp.com (office). *Website:* www.bracewellgiuliani.com (office).

GIURANNA, Bruno; Italian violist and conductor; b. 6 April 1933, Milan; ed Coll. S. Giuseppe and Conservatorio di Musica Santa Cecilia, Rome and Conservatorio di Musica S. Pietro a Maiella, Naples; Founder-mem. I Musici 1951–61; Prof., Conservatorio G. Verdi, Milan 1961–65, Conservatorio S. Cecilia, Rome 1965–78, Accad. Chigiana, Siena 1966–83, Nordwest-deutsche Musikakademie, Detmold, Germany 1969–83, Hochschule der Künste, Berlin 1981–98, W. Stauffer Foundation 1985–, RAM, London 1994–96, Accad. S. Cecilia, Rome 1995–97; mem. Int. Music Competition jury, Munich 1961–62, 1967, 1969, Geneva 1968, Budapest 1975; soloist at concerts in festivals including Edinburgh Festival, Holland Festival and with orchestras including Berlin Philharmonic, Amsterdam Concertgebouw and Teatro alla Scala, Milan; Artistic Dir of Orchestra da Camera di Padova 1983–92; Academician of Santa Cecilia 1974; Hon. DLit (Univ. of Limerick) 2003. *Address:* Via Bembo 96, 31011 Asolo, TV, Italy (home). *Telephone:* (423) 55734 (home). *Fax:* (423) 529913 (home). *E-mail:* brgiuranna@gmail.com (home). *Website:* www.giuranna.com (home).

GIURESCU, Dinu C., PhD; American historian and museum curator; *Director, Museum of the Romanian Peasant;* b. 15 Feb. 1927, Bucharest, Romania; s. of Constantin C. Giurescu and Maria S. Giurescu; m. Anca Elena Dinu 1960; two d.; ed Univ. Bucharest; curator Bucharest Art Museum 1956–64; with Ministry of Foreign Affairs 1964–68; Prof. of European Civilization, Acad. of Fine Arts, Bucharest 1968–87; lecturer in Switzerland, France, Bulgaria, Hungary, FRG, Dallas (USA) 1977, Washington 1980, Univs of Columbia, Ind., Ill., Ariz., Calif. (Berkeley), Kan., Colo, Ore., Neb.,

Ohio, Rochester and Huntington Coll. 1982–85; Prof. Faculty of History, Univ. of Bucharest 1990–; Pres. Nat. Comm. of Museums and Collections (Romania) 1991–92, 1996–2000; Gen. Dir Museum of the Romanian Peasant 2001–; Visiting Prof., William Paterson Coll., NJ, USA 1988–89, Texas A. & M. Univ., USA 1989–90, Cen. European Univ., Hungary 1993; mem. Romanian Acad. 1990; Prize of the Romanian Acad. 1973. *Publications:* Ion Vodă cel Viteaz 1966, History of the Romanians from Ancient Times Until Today (in Romanian) 1971 (with C. C. Giurescu), Wallachia in the 14th–15th Centuries (in Romanian) 1971, Istoria Românilor I-II, Din cele mai vechi timpuri pînă la finele sec. XVI (History of the Romanians I–II. From Ancient Times to the end of the XVI century) 1974–76 (with C. C. Giurescu), Illustrated History of the Romanian People (in Romanian, English, French, German, Russian, Spanish) 1981–82, The Razing of Romania's Past 1989, The Communist Takeover in Romania, I 1994, The Radescu Government (in Romanian) 1996, The Fall of the Iron Curtain: Romania (in Romanian) 1997, Romania in World War II (in Romanian) 1999 (in English) 2000, The Impossible Attempt. The Royal Strike (1945) (in Romanian) 1999, The "Elections" of November 1946 (in Romanian) 2001. *Leisure interests:* walking, visiting sites and museums, jazz music. *Address:* Museum of the Romanian Peasant, Soseana Kiseleff 3, Bucharest, 71268, Romania (office); 30–33 32nd Street, apt. 3i, Astoria, NY 11102, USA (office). *Telephone:* (21) 2129661 (Bucharest) (office); (718) 545-7269 (New York) (office). *Fax:* (21) 3129875 (Bucharest). *E-mail:* mtr@digicom.ro (office).

GIURGIU, Tudor, (Todor Giurgiu); Romanian film director and broadcasting executive; b. 1972, Cluj-Napoca; fmr Dir Transylvania Film Festival; Pres. and Dir-Gen. Televiziunea Română (TVR) 2005–07. *Films:* Vecini (Neighbours) (dir) 1993, È pericoloso sporgersi (aka Don't Lean Out the Window) (asst set designer) 1994, Prea târziu (aka Too Late (USA)) (first asst dir) 1996, The Midas Touch (first asst dir) 1997, The Shrunken City (video) (first asst dir) 1998, Train de vie (Train of Life) (casting: Romania) 1998, Clockmaker (video) (uncredited casting dir) 1998, Phantom Town (video) (casting: Romania) 1999, Tuvalu (casting: Bucharest; as Todor Giurgiu) 1999, Popcorn Story (dir and producer) 2001, Marele jaf comunist (aka Great Communist Bank Robbery) (producer) 2004, Legaturi bolnavicioase (aka Love Sick) (dir and producer) 2006, Agentul VIP (as himself, Episode 1.46) 2007. *Address:* c/o Televiziunea Română (TVR), PO Box 63-1200, Calea Dorobanţilor 191, 015089 Bucharest, Romania. *Telephone:* (21) 2312704.

GIVENCHY, Hubert de; French fashion designer; b. 21 Feb. 1927, Beauvais; s. of Lucien Taffin de Givenchy and Béatrice Badin; ed Coll. Félix-Faure, Beauvais, Ecole Nat. Supérieure des Beaux-Arts, Paris and Faculté de Droit, Univ. de Paris; apprentice, Paris fashion houses of Lucien Lelong 1945–46, Robert Piguet 1946–48, Jacques Fath 1948–49, Elsa Schiaparelli 1949–51; est. own fashion house in Parc Monceau, Paris 1952–56, in Avenue George V 1956; 1988, sold business to Moet Hennessy-Louis Vuitton 1988; retd 1995; Pres.-Dir-Gen. Soc. Givenchy-Couture and Soc. des Parfums Givenchy, Paris 1954; Hon. Pres. Admin. Council Givenchy SA 1988–; Pres. Christie's France 1997–; work included in Fashion: An Anthology, Victoria and Albert Museum, London 1971; costume designer for films Breakfast at Tiffany's 1961, Charade 1963, The VIPs 1963, Paris When It Sizzles 1964, How to Steal a Million 1966; Chevalier, Légion d'honneur. *Leisure interests:* tennis, riding, skiing. *Address:* 3 Avenue George V, 75008 Paris, France (office). *Telephone:* 1-44-31-50-00 (office). *Fax:* 1-49-52-03-62 (office).

GIZENGA, Antoine; Democratic Republic of the Congo politician; b. 5 Oct. 1925; m.; one d.; Deputy Prime Minister 1960, 1961–62, Prime Minister 1960–61, 2006–08 (resgnd); Pres. and Head of State, in rebellion, at Stanleyville after death of Patrice Lumumba March–Aug. 1961; imprisoned 1962–1964, Oct. 1964–1965; exiled in the former USSR, France, Angola, Congo-Brazzaville (now Republic of the Congo) 1965–1992; Leader, Parti Lumumbiste Unifié 1992–; unsuccessful cand. in presidential elections 2006. *Address:* Parti Lumumbiste Unifié, 9 rue Cannas, C/Limete, Kinshasa, Democratic Republic of the Congo.

GJEDREM, Svein, MA; Norwegian banker; *Governor, Norges Bank;* b. 25 Jan. 1950; ed Univ. of Oslo; Exec. Officer, Norges Bank (Cen. Bank of Norway) 1975–79, Gov. 1999–; Head, Div. for Banking and Monetary Affairs, Ministry of Finance and Customs 1979–82, Deputy Dir 1982–86, Dir.-Gen. Head of Econ. Policy Dept 1986–95, Sec.-Gen. 1996–98; visiting engagement, EU Comm., Brussels 1994–95. *Address:* Office of the Governor, Norges Bank, Bankplassen 2, P.O. Box 1179, Sentrum, 0107 Oslo, Norway (office). *Telephone:* (22) 31-60-67 (office). *Fax:* (22) 33-20-35 (office). *E-mail:* svein.gjedrem@norges-bank.no (office). *Website:* www.norges-bank.no (office).

GJERDE, Bjartmar; Norwegian politician; b. 6 Nov. 1931, Sande Sunnmøre; s. of Astrid Gjerde and Hjalmar Gjerde; m. Anna Karin Hoel 1954; three s.; journalist Sunnmøre Arbeideravis 1948–53; Ed. Fritt Slag 1953–58; Chair. Labour League of Youth 1958–61; mem. State Youth Council; Sec. Labour Parl. Group 1961–62; Chief. Sec. Workers' Educ. League 1962–71; mem. Council on Broadcasting 1963–74, UNESCO Comm. 1964–66, Norwegian Cultural Council 1965–85, Council on Adult Educ. 1966–71; Minister of Church and Educ. 1971–72, 1973–76, for Industries 1976–78, for Petroleum and Energy 1978–80; mem. Labour Party Nat. Exec. 1973–81; Dir-Gen. Norwegian Broadcasting Corpn (NRK) 1981–89, Dir Gen. Directorate of Labour 1989–94.

GJINUSHI, Skender; Albanian politician; *Chairman, Social Democratic Party of Albania;* b. 24 Dec. 1949, Vlorë; ed Univ. of Tirana; fmr univ. lecturer in science; mem. Kuvendi Popullor (People's Ass.) 1992–; fmr Minister of Educ.; Speaker of Parl. 1997–2001; apptd Deputy Prime Minister and Minister of Labour and Social Affairs 2002; Chair. Social Democratic Party of Albania. *Address:* Social Democratic Party of Albania, Rruga Asim Vokshi 26, Tirana, Albania (office). *Telephone:* (4) 226540 (office). *Fax:* (4) 227485 (office).

GLADILIN, Anatoliy Tikhonovich; Russian writer; b. 21 Aug. 1935, Moscow; s. of Tikhon Illarionovich Gladilin and Polina Moïseevna Dreizer; m. Maria Gladilina 1955; two d.; ed Gorky Literary Inst., Moscow; literary activity started 1956; one of main contribs (with V. Aksyonov q.v., to Katayev's journal Youth 1956–65; one of founders of 'Youth Prose' movt in early 1960s; signed letter of 80 writers in support of Solzhenitsyn's letter on abolition of censorship 1967; left USSR, expelled from Union of Writers 1976 (readmitted 1998); settled in France. *Publications include:* Chronicle of the Times of Viktor Podgursky 1956, The Gospel from Robespierre 1970, Prognosis for Tomorrow 1972, The Dreams of Shlisselburg Fortress 1974, The Making and Unmaking of a Soviet Writer 1979, The Paris Fair 1980, A Big Race Day 1983, F.S.S.R. The French Soviet Socialist Republic Story 1985, As I Was Then: Tales 1986, The Beast Pell Killed Me 1991, 2001, A Rider's Shadow 2000, The Big Racing Day: Novels 2001. *Address:* 11 Château Gaillard, Maisons Alfort, 94700 Paris, France (home). *Telephone:* 1-43-96-21-99 (home).

GLADSTONE, Barbara; American gallery owner, art dealer and film producer; *Owner and Director, Gladstone Gallery;* first opened in SoHo, New York in 1979, Owner and Dir Gladstone Gallery, represents many contemporary artists, including filmmaker Shirin Neshat, photographer and installation artist Sarah Lucas, and sculptor and filmmaker Matthew Barney. *Films include:* producer: Cremaster 1 1996, Cremaster 5 1997, Cremaster 2 1999, Cremaster 3 2002, Drawing Restraint 9 (exec. producer) 2005, De Lama Lamina 2007; appears in Drawing Restraint 13, a later film by Barney. *Address:* Gladstone Gallery, 515 West 24th Street, New York, NY 10011, USA (office). *Telephone:* (212) 206-9300 (office). *Fax:* (212) 206-9301 (office). *E-mail:* info@gladstonegallery.com (office). *Website:* www.gladstonegallery.com (office).

GLADYSZ, John A., BS, PhD; American chemist and academic; *Professor Ordinarius and Chairman, Organic Chemistry, Friedrich-Alexander-Universität Erlangen-Nurnberg;* b. 13 Aug. 1952, Kalamazoo, Mich.; ed W Mich. Univ., Univ. of Mich., Stanford Univ.; Asst Prof., UCLA 1974–82; Consultant and Panel Mem., Gas Research Inst., Chicago 1979–80; Consultant, G. D. Searle & Co., Chicago 1980–81; Assoc. Prof., Univ. of Utah 1982–85, Prof. 1985–88; Prof. Ordinarius and Chair., Organic Chemistry, Friedrich-Alexander-Universität Erlangen-Nurnberg, Germany 1998–; Visiting Assoc. in Chemistry, Calif. Inst. of Tech. 1989; Consultant, Procter & Gamble Co. 1983–85, Monsanto Corpn 1984–86, Union Camp Corpn 1988–89, Exxon Research and Engineering 1993–98, Kimberly Clark Corpn 1997–98, 3M Corpn 1998–99, Rhodia (Rhône-Poulenc) Corpn, Lyons, France 1999–2001, Total/Fina/Elf, Paris, France 2002–; mem. Editorial Bd Organometallics 1990–92, Bulletin de la Société Chimique de France 1992–97, New Journal of Chemistry 2001–; mem. American Chemical Soc. 1970–, The Chemical Soc. 1974–, AAAS 1975–, Gesellschaft Deutsche Chemiker 1997–; Arthur C. Cope Scholar Award 1988, Univ. of Utah Distinguished Research Award 1992, American Chemical Soc. Award in Organometallic Chemistry 1994, Von Humboldt Foundation Research Award for Sr Scholars 1995–96. *Address:* Institut für Organische Chemie, Friedrich-Alexander-Universität Erlangen-Nurnberg, Henkestrasse 42, 91054 Erlangen, Germany (office). *Telephone:* (9131) 85-22540 (office). *Fax:* (9131) 85-26865 (office). *E-mail:* gladysz@organik.uni-erlangen.de (office). *Website:* www.organik.uni-erlangen.de/gladysz (office).

GLAMANN, Kristof, DrPhil; Danish business executive, historian, professor and writer; b. 26 Aug. 1923, Kerteminde; s. of Kai Kristof Glamann and Ebba H. K. Glamann (née Madsen); m. Kirsten Jantzen 1954; two s.; ed Univ. of Copenhagen; Assoc. Prof. of History, Univ. of Copenhagen 1948–60, Prof. of Econ. History 1961–80; Visiting Prof., Univ. of Pennsylvania 1960, Univ. of Wisconsin 1961, Visiting Northern Scholar, LSE 1966, Visiting Overseas Fellow, Churchill Coll., Univ. of Cambridge 1971–72, 1994, Visiting Fellow, Toho Gakkai, Tokyo 1977; Master, 4th May and Hassager Coll., Copenhagen; mem. and Chair. Danish Research Council on Humanities 1968–70; Ed.-in-Chief Scandinavian Econ. History Review 1961–80; mem. Bd Dirs Carlsberg Foundation 1969–93 (Pres. 1976–93), Carlsberg Ltd 1970–94 (Deputy Chair. 1975–77, Chair. 1977–93), Carlsberg Brewery Ltd 1978–94, Royal Copenhagen Ltd 1978–93, Fredericia Brewery 1979–94, Politiken Foundation 1990; Chair. Council, Investor and Reinvest Ltd; Deputy Chair. The Scandinavia-Japan Sasakawa Foundation 1985–2005; mem. Royal Danish Acad. of Science and Letters 1969, Royal Danish History Soc. 1961, Swedish Acad., Lund 1963, History Soc. of Calcutta 1962; Corresp. mem. Royal History Soc. 1972; Corresp. Fellow, Royal Belgian Acad. 1989; Hon. Pres. Int. Econ. History Assen 1974; Hon. FBA 1985; Commdr, Order of Dannebrog (First Class), Commdr, Falcon of Iceland 1987, Das Grosse Verdienstkreuz (Germany) 1989, Order of Gorkha Dakshina Bahu (3rd Class) (Nepal) 1989, Hon. OBE; Hon. DScS (Gothenburg) 1974; Erasmus Medal, Academia Europaea 2000. *Publications:* History of Tobacco Industry in Denmark 1875–1950 1950, Prices and Wages 1500–1800 1958, Dutch-Asiatic Trade 1620–1740 1958, Beer and Brewing 1962, 2005, European Trade 1500–1750 1971, Carlsberg Foundation (in Danish) 1976, contributed to the Cambridge Economic History of Europe (Vol. V) 1977, Mercantilism 1982, Festschrift 1983, 1993, J. C. Jacobsen of Carlsberg: A Biography 1990, Beer and Marble: A Biography of Carl Jacobsen 1995, The Carlsberg Group Since 1970 1997, Time-Out 1998, Memoirs 2002, The Carlsberg Foundation 1876–1976 2003, The Scandinavian Pasteür 2004. *Leisure interests:* walking and drawing. *Address:* Hoeghsmindeparken 10, 2900 Hellerup, Denmark (home). *Telephone:* 39-40-39-77 (home). *E-mail:* k.glamann@mail.dk (home).

GLANVILLE, Brian Lester; British writer and journalist; b. 24 Sept. 1931, London; s. of James A. Glanville and Florence Manches; m. Elizabeth De Boer

1959; two s. two d.; ed Charterhouse; first sports columnist and football corresp., Sunday Times 1958–92; sports columnist, The People 1992–96, football writer, The Times 1996–98, Sunday Times 1998–; literary adviser, Bodley Head 1958–62; Silver Bear Award, Berlin Film Festival, for European Centre Forward (BBC TV documentary) 1963. *Plays for radio:* The Rise of Gerry Logan, The Diary, I Could Have Been King, A Visit to the Villa. *Television:* original writer of That Was The Week That Was 1962; wrote BBC documentary European Centre Forward (winner Berlin Prize) 1963. *Publications:* novels: Along the Arno 1956, The Bankrupts 1958, Diamond 1962, The Rise of Gerry Logan 1963, A Second Home 1965, A Roman Marriage 1966, The Artist Type 1967, The Olympian 1969, A Cry of Crickets 1970, The Comic 1974, The Dying of the Light 1976, The Catacomb 1988, Dictators 2001; sport: Soccer Nemesis 1955, Champions of Europe 1991, Story of the World Cup 1993, The Arsenal Stadium History 2006, England Managers: The Toughest Job in Football 2007, For Club and Country (Obits) 2008; short stories: A Bad Streak 1961, The Director's Wife 1963, The King of Hackney Marshes 1965, The Thing He Loves 1985, Love Is Not Love; plays: A Visit to the Villa 1981, Underneath the Arches (musical, co-author) 1982, The Diary (radio play) 1986; other: Football Memories (autobiog.) 1999. *Address:* 160 Holland Park Avenue, London, W11 4UH, England. *Telephone:* (20) 7603-6908 (home).

GLASER, Donald Arthur, PhD; American scientist and academic; *Professor of the Graduate School, Department of Molecular and Cell Biology, University of California, Berkeley;* b. 21 Sept. 1926, Cleveland, Ohio; s. of William Joseph Glaser and Lena Glaser; one s. one d.; ed Case Inst. of Tech., California Inst. of Tech; teacher and researcher, Physics Dept, Univ. of Michigan 1949–57, Prof. 1957–59; Prof. of Physics, Univ. of California, Berkeley 1959–, Biophysicist 1962–64, Prof. of Physics, Neurobiology and Molecular and Cell Biology 1964–; mem. NAS NSF Fellow 1961; Guggenheim Fellow 1961–62; Hon. ScD; Henry Russell Award 1955, Charles Vernon Boys Prize, The Physical Soc. 1958, Nobel Prize in Physics 1960; several other awards. *Publications:* Some Effects of Ionizing Radiation on the Formation of Bubbles in Liquids 1952, A Possible Bubble Chamber for the Study of Ionizing Events 1953, Bubble Chamber Tracks of Penetrating Cosmic-Ray Particles 1953, Progress Report on the Development of Bubble Chambers 1955, Strange Particle Production by Fast Pions in Propane Bubble Chamber 1957, Weak Interactions: Other Modes, Experimental Results 1958, The Bubble Chamber 1958, Development of Bubble Chamber and Some Recent Bubble Chamber Results in Elementary Particle Physics 1958, Decays of Strange Particles 1959, Computer Identification of Bacteria by Colony Morphology 1972, Effect of Nalidixic Acid on DNA Replication by Toluene-treated E. coli 1973, The Isolation and Partial Characterization of Mutants of E.coli and Cold-sensitive Synthesis of DNA 1974, Rates of Chain Elongation of Ribosomal RNA Molecules in E. coli 1974, Chromosomal Sites of DNA-membrane Attachment in E. coli 1974, Effect of Growth Conditions in DNA-membrane Attachment in *E. coli* 1975, Characteristics of Cold-sensitive Mutants of E. coli K12 Defective in Deoxyribonucleic Acid Replication 1975, A New Anisotrophy in Apparent Motion 1986, Differences betweeen Vertical and Horizontal Apparent Motion 1987, Speed Discrimination using Simple Sampled-Motion Stimuli 1987, Motion Interference in Speed Discrimination 1989, Influence of Remote Objects on Local Depth Perception 1991, Shape Analysis and Stereopsis for Human Depth Perception 1992, Depth Discrimination of a Line is Improved by Adding Other Nearby Lines 1992, Temporal Aspects of Depth Contrast 1993, Comparison of Human Performance with Algorithms for Estimating Fractal Dimension of Fractional Brownian Statistics 1993, Depth Discrimination of a Crowded Line Is Better When It Is More Luminant than the Lines Crowding It 1995, Stereopsis Due to Luminance Difference in the Two Eyes 1995, Multiple Matching of Features in Simple Stereograms 1996; numerous papers co-written with other scientists. *Leisure interests:* skiing, sailing, skin diving, music. *Address:* 41 Hill Road, Berkeley, CA 94708-2131 (home); Department of Molecular and Cell Biology, 337 Stanley Hall, University of California, Berkeley, CA 94720-0001, USA (office). *Telephone:* (510) 642-7231 (office). *E-mail:* glaser@socrates.berkeley.edu (office). *Website:* mcb.berkeley.edu/faculty/NEU/glaserd.html (office); www.foresight.berkeley.edu (office).

GLASER, Robert (Rob) Denis, BA, BS; American software industry executive; *Founding Chairman and CEO, RealNetworks Inc.;* b. 16 Jan. 1962, New York City; ed Yale Univ.; joined Microsoft Corpn 1983, head of multimedia tech. and consumer digital appliances, Vice-Pres. Multimedia and Consumer Systems, –1994; Founding Chair. and CEO RealNetworks Inc. (internet software co.) 1994–, cr. RealAudio 1995, RealVideo and RealPlayer; co-owner Seattle Mariners professional baseball team; Founding Chair. Atrium Group, US Library of Congress; apptd to Advisory Cttee on Public Interest Obligations of Digital TV Broadcaster by Pres. Bill Clinton; mem. Bd of Dirs Electronic Frontier Foundation, Wash. Public Affairs Network, Foundation for Nat. Congress, Target Margin Theater Co. of NY, Dwight Hall (Yale Univ. Student Community Service), TVW 1994–. *Address:* RealNetworks Inc., 2601 Elliott Avenue, Suite 1000, Seattle, WA 98121, USA (office). *Telephone:* (206) 674-2700 (office). *Fax:* (206) 674-2699 (office). *Website:* www.realnetworks.com (office).

GLASER, Robert Joy, SB, MD, FRCP (UK), MACP; American foundation executive, physician and medical consultant; *Professor Emeritus, Stanford University;* b. 11 Sept. 1918, St Louis, Mo.; s. of Joseph and Regina Glaser; m. Helen H. Hofsommer 1949 (died 1999); two s. one d.; ed Harvard Coll. and Medical School; appointments include instructor to Assoc. Prof., Washington Univ. School of Medicine 1949–57, Assoc. Dean 1955–57; Dean and Prof. of Medicine, Univ. of Colo School of Medicine 1957–63, Vice-Pres. for Medical Affairs 1959–63; Prof. of Social Medicine, Harvard Univ. 1963–65; Vice-Pres. for Medical Affairs, Dean of the School of Medicine, Prof. of Medicine, Stanford Univ. 1965–70, Acting Pres. 1968, Visiting Prof. of Medicine 1972–73, Consulting Prof. 1972–99, Prof. Emer. 1999–; Clinical Prof. of Medicine, Columbia Univ. Coll. of Physicians and Surgeons 1971–72; Consultant 1997–; Vice-Pres. The Commonwealth Fund 1970–72; Pres. and CEO The Henry J. Kaiser Family Foundation 1972–83; Dir First Boston Inc. 1982–88; Dir Hewlett-Packard Co. 1971–91, Calif. Water Service Co. 1973–93, The Equitable Life Assurance Soc. of the US 1979–86, Maxygen 1998–; mem. Bd of Dirs Alza Corpn 1993–2001, DCI, Hanger Orthopedic Group 1993–2003; Ed. The Pharos of Alpha Omega Alpha Honor Medical Soc. 1962–97, Ed. Emer. 1997–; charter mem., Inst. of Medicine, Nat. Acad. of Science; mem., Bd of Trustees, Washington Univ., St Louis, Mo.; Lucille P. Markey Charitable Trust Dir for Medical Science 1984–97, Trustee 1989–97; mem. American Philosophical Soc. 2000–; Fellow, American Acad. of Arts and Sciences 1964–; Trustee, David and Lucile Packard Foundation 1985–97 (Trustee Emer. 1997–), Packard Humanities Inst. 1987–, Albert and Mary Lasker Foundation 1997–; mem. Harvard Club of New York, Country Asscn (New York); 10 hon. degrees; Centennial Award for Distinguished Service, Univ. of Colo 1983; Medal for Distinguished Service, Univ. of Calif., San Francisco 1983; Abraham Flexner Award, Asscn of American Medical Colls 1984; Hubert H. Humphrey Cancer Research Center Award 1985, Dean's Medal Harvard Medical School 1995, Special Recognition Award, Asscn of American Medical Colls. 1999, John Stearns Award for Lifetime Achievement in Medicine, NY Acad. of Medicine 2000, Harvard Alumni Asscn Medal for Service to Harvard Univ. 2004. *Publications:* 135 papers on experimental streptococcal infections, antibiotics and other topics concerning medicine and medical educ.; numerous chapters in medical books. *Leisure interests:* travel, reading and music. *Address:* 555 Byron Street, #305, Palo Alto, CA 94301, USA. *Telephone:* (650) 328-5869. *Fax:* (650) 473-9775. *E-mail:* robert.glaser@stanford.edu (office).

GLASHOW, Sheldon Lee, PhD, FAAS; American physicist and academic; *Arthur G. B. Metcalf Professor, Physics Department, Boston University;* b. 5 Dec. 1932, New York; s. of Lewis Glashow and Bella Rubin; m. Joan Shirley Alexander 1972; three s. one d.; ed Bronx High School of Science, Cornell and Harvard Univs; NSF Post-Doctoral Fellow, Univ. of Copenhagen 1958–60; Research Fellow, Calif. Inst. of Tech. 1960–61; Asst Prof., Stanford Univ. 1961–62; Assoc. Prof., Univ. of Calif., Berkeley 1962–66; Prof. of Physics, Harvard Univ. 1967–84, Higgins Prof. 1979–2000, Mellon Prof. of Sciences 1988–93, Prof. Emer. 2000–; Visiting Prof., Boston Univ. 1983–84, Distinguished Visiting Scientist 1984–2000, Arthur G. B. Metcalf Prof. 2000–; Alfred P. Sloan Foundation Fellowship 1962–66; Visiting Scientist, CERN 1968; Visiting Prof., Univ. of Marseille 1970, MIT 1974, 1980–81; Consultant, Brookhaven Lab. 1966–73, 1975–; Affiliated Sr Scientist, Univ. of Houston 1983–96; Univ. Scholar, Texas A&M Univ. 1983–86, Einstein Prof., Chinese Acad. of Science 2003–; Fellow, American Physical Soc.; Pres. Int. Sakharov Cttee 1980–85; mem. American Acad. of Arts and Sciences, NAS, American Philosophical Soc.; Sponsor, Fed. of American Scientists (FAS) and Bulletin of the Atomic Scientists; mem. Advisory Council American Acad. of Achievement 1979–, Science Policy Cttee, CERN 1979–84; Founding Ed. Quantum (magazine) 1989–2000; Hon. Prof., Univ. of Nanjing 1998–; Dr hc (Univ. of Aix-Marseille) 1982; Hon. DSc (Yeshiva Univ.) 1978, (Bar Ilan Univ., Gustavus Adolphus Coll., Adelphi Univ.) 1989, (Case Western Reserve Univ.) 1995, (Bologna) 2005; Oppenheimer Memorial Medal 1977, George Ledlie Award 1978; shared Nobel Prize for Physics with Abdus Salam and Steven Weinberg (q.v.) for work on elementary particles 1979. *Publications:* Interactions (with Ben Bova) 1989, Charm of Physics 1990, From Alchemy to Quarks 1994; over 200 articles on elementary particle physics. *Address:* Department of Physics, Boston University, 590 Commonwealth Avenue, Boston, MA 02215 (office); 30 Prescott Street, Brookline, MA 02446, USA (home). *Telephone:* (617) 353-9099 (office). *E-mail:* slg@bu.edu (office). *Website:* buphy.bu.edu (office).

GLASS, David D., BA; American retail executive; *Chairman of the Executive Committee, Wal-Mart Stores, Inc.;* b. 1935, Liberty, Mo.; m.; ed SW Missouri State Univ.; Gen. Man. Crank Drug Co. 1957–67; Vice-Pres. Consumers Markets Inc. 1967–76; Exec. Vice-Pres. Wal-Mart Stores Inc. –1976, Chief Financial Officer 1976–84, Pres. 1984–2000, COO 1984–88, CEO 1988–2000, Chair. Exec. Comm. 2000–, also Dir; CEO and Chair. Bd of Dirs Kansas City Royals professional baseball team 1993–. *Address:* Wal-Mart Stores Inc., 702 SW 8th Street, Bentonville, AR 72716 (office); Kansas City Royals, PO Box 419969, Kansas City, MO 64141, USA (office). *Telephone:* (479) 273-4000 (office). *Fax:* (479) 273-4053 (office). *Website:* www.walmartstores.com (office); www.kcroyals.com (office).

GLASS, Philip; American composer; b. 31 Jan. 1937, Baltimore, Md; s. of Benjamin Glass and Ida Glass (née Gouline); m. 1st JoAnne Akalaitis (divorced); m. 2nd Luba Burtyk (divorced); one s. one d.; m. 3rd Candy Jernigan (died 1991); m. 4th Holly Critchlow 2001; two s. one d.; ed Peabody Conservatory, Baltimore, Univ. of Chicago and Juilliard School of Music; Composer-in-Residence, Pittsburgh Public Schools 1962–64; studied with Nadia Boulanger, Paris 1964–66; f. Philip Glass Ensemble 1968–, concert tours USA and Europe; f. record co. Chatham Square Productions, New York 1972, Dunvagen Music Publrs, Orange Mountain Music record co. 2002; mem. ASCAP; BMI Award 1960, Lado Prize 1961, Benjamin Award 1961, 1962, Ford Foundation Young Composer's Award 1964–66, Fulbright Award 1966–67, Musical America Magazine Musician of the Year 1985, New York Dance and Performance Award 1995. *Film scores include:* North Star 1977, Koyaanisqatsi 1983, Mishima 1985, Powaqqatsi 1987, The Thin Blue Line 1988, Hamburger Hill 1989, Mindwalk 1990, A Brief History of Time 1991, Anima Mundi 1991, Candyman 1992, The Voyage 1992, Orphée 1993, Candyman II: Farewell to the Flesh 1994, Monsters of Grace 1998, Bent 1998, Kundun 1998, The Hours (BAFTA Anthony Asquith Award 2003, Classical BRIT Award for Contemporary Music 2004) 2002, Cassandra's Dream 2007. *Compositions include:* String Quartets (1–4), Violin Concerto, Low Symphony, The Palace of the Arabian Nights, The Fall of the House of Usher, Einstein on the Beach 1976, Madrigal Opera: The Panther 1980, Satyagraha 1980, The Photographer 1982, The Civil Wars: A Tree Is Best Measured When It Is Down 1983, Akhnaten 1983, The Juniper Tree 1985, A Descent Into The Maelstrom 1986, In The Upper Room 1986, Violin Concerto 1987, The Light for Orchestra 1987, The Making of the Representative for Planet 8 1988, The Fall Of The House Of Usher 1988, 1,000 Airplanes on the Roof (with David Henry Hwang) 1988, Mattogrosso 1989, Hydrogen Jukebox (with Allen Ginsberg) 1989, The White Raven 1991, Orphée, chamber opera after Cocteau 1993, La belle et la bête, after Cocteau 1994, Witches of Venice (ballet) 1995, Les enfants terrible (dance opera) 1996, The Marriages Between Zones Three, Four and Five 1997, Symphony No. 5 1999, Symphony No. 6 (Plutonian Ode) 2000, In the Penal Colony (theatre) 2000, Tirol Concerto, piano and orchestra 2000, Concerto Fantasy for two timpanists and orchestra 2000, Voices for Organ, Didgeridoo and Narrator 2001, Concerto for Cello and Orchestra 2001, Danassimo 2001, The Man in the Bath 2001, Passage 2001, Diaspora 2001, Notes 2001, Galileo Galilei (opera) 2002, Waiting for the Barbarians (opera) 2005, Appomattox (opera) 2007. *Publications:* Music by Philip Glass 1987, Opera on the Beach 1988. *Address:* Dunvagen Music, 632 Broadway, Suite 902, New York, NY 10012, USA (office). *Telephone:* (212) 979-2080 (office). *Fax:* (212) 473-2842 (office). *E-mail:* info@dunvagen.com (office). *Website:* www.philipglass.com (office).

GLASSCOCK, Larry Claborn, BA; American insurance executive; *Chairman, Wellpoint, Inc.;* b. 4 April 1948, Cullman, Ala; m. Lee Ann Roden 1969; one s. one d.; ed Cleveland State Univ., Commercial Bank Man. Program, Columbia Univ., New York, School of Int. Banking, participated in American Bankers Asscn Conf. of Exec. Officers; served in US Marine Corps 1970–76; Vice-Pres. of Personnel, AmeriTrust Corpn, Cleveland, OH 1974–75, Vice-Pres. Nat. Div. 1976–78, Vice-Pres. and Man. Credit Card Center 1978–79, Sr Vice-Pres. Consumer Finance 1980–81, Sr Vice-Pres. Nat. Div. 1981–83, Exec. Vice-Pres. Corp. Banking Admin 1983–87, Group Exec. Vice-Pres. AmeriTrust Corpn and AmeriTrust Co. 1987–92; fmr Pres. and CEO Essex Holdings, Inc.; fmr Pres. and COO First American Bank; Pres. and CEO Blue Cross and Blue Shield, Nat. Capital Area 1993–98; COO CareFirst, Inc. Jan.–April 1998; Sr Exec. Vice-Pres. and COO Anthem Insurance (renamed Wellpoint, Inc. following merger with WellPoint Health Networks 2004) 1998–99, Pres. and CEO 1999–2007, Chair. 2005–; mem. Bd Dirs Zimmer Holdings, Inc., Blue Cross and Blue Shield Asscn, Council for Affordable Quality Healthcare (Chair. 2002–03), Nat. Inst. for Health Care Man., Cen. Indiana Corp. Partnership, United Way of Cen. Indiana, Greater Indianapolis Progress Cttee; fmr Pres. Cleveland State Univ. Alumni Asscn; Indiana Ernst & Young Entrepreneur of the Year Award (jtly) 2003. *Address:* Wellpoint, Inc., 120 Monument Circle, Indianapolis, IN 46204, USA (office). *Telephone:* (317) 488-6000 (office). *Fax:* (317) 488-6028 (office). *E-mail:* info@wellpoint.com (office). *Website:* www.wellpoint.com (office).

GLATZ, Ferenc, PhD; Hungarian historian; *Director, Institute of History, Hungarian Academy of Sciences;* b. 2 April 1941; m. Katalin; one s., one d.; Research Fellow, Inst. of History of Hungarian Acad. of Sciences 1968–, Scientific Deputy Dir 1986–88, Dir of Inst. 1988–; Corresp. mem. Hungarian Acad. of Sciences 1993, full mem. 2000; Pres. 1996–2002; Prof., Eötvös Loránd Univ., Budapest 1974–; Minister for Culture and Educ. 1989–90; Organizer and Dir Europa Inst., Budapest 1990–; Szèchenyì Prize 1995, Herder Prize 1997. *Publications:* numerous studies and books on 19th- and 20th-century history of Hungarian and European culture and historiography, including Hungarians and Their Neighbors in Modern Times, 1867–1950 (ed.) 1995. *Leisure interests:* tennis, gardening. *Address:* Institute of History, Hungarian Academy of Sciences, Uri Utca 53, 1014 Budapest (office); Magyar Tudományos Akadémia, 1051 Budapest, Roosevelt tér. 9, Hungary. *Telephone:* (1) 2246750 (office). *Fax:* (1) 2246756 (office). *E-mail:* magdolna@tti.hu (office).

GLAUBER, Robert, DEcon; American economist and organization executive; *Chairman and CEO, National Association of Securities Dealers (NASD);* b. 1939; ed Harvard Univ.; Lecturer, Dept of Econs, Harvard Univ. 1964–73, Prof. 1973–87, Lecturer, John F. Kennedy School of Govt, Harvard; fmr Visiting Prof., Stanford Univ., Calif.; consultant to Reagan Admin. serving as Exec. Dir Task Force on Market Mechanisms ('Brady Commission') 1987, to Bush Admin. 1989; Under-Sec. to Treasury for Finance 1989–92; mem. Bd Nat. Asscn of Securities Dealers 1996–, CEO and Pres. 2000–, Chair. and CEO 2001–; CEO Bond Market Asscn; mem. Bd of Dirs Moody's Corpn, XL Capital Ltd, American Stock Exchange; mem. Council on Foreign Relations, Boston Cttee on Foreign Relations, Int. Advisory Bd of Korean Financial Supervisory Service; fmr Pres. Boston Econ. Club. *Address:* National Association of Securities Dealers, 33 Whitehall Street, New York, NY 10004-2193, USA (office). *Telephone:* (301) 590-6500 (office). *E-mail:* Robert.Glauber@nasd.com (office). *Website:* www.nasd.com (office).

GLAUBER, Roy J., BS, MA, PhD; American physicist and academic; *Mallinckrodt Professor of Physics, Harvard University;* b. 1 Sept. 1925, New York City; s. of Emanuel Glauber and Felicia Fox; ed Bronx High School of Science, Harvard Univ.; research areas include quantum optics; fmr mem. staff Manhattan Project; Mallinckrodt Prof. of Physics, Harvard Univ. 1976–; Adjunct Prof. of Optical Sciences, Univ. of Ariz.; fmr Visiting Scientist, Visiting Prof., CERN, Univ. of Leiden, NORDITA Copenhagen, Collège de France; mem. Advisory Bd Program for Science and Tech. for Int. Security, MIT; hon. degrees (Essen, Erlangen, Arizona); Franklin Inst. A.A. Michelson Medal 1985, American Optical Soc. Max Born Award 1985, A. von Humboldt Research Award 1989, American Physical Soc. Dannie Heineman Prize 1996, Nobel Prize in Physics (co-recipient) 2005, W.E. Lamb Medal 2006. *Publications:* numerous articles and book chapters. *Leisure interest:* gardening. *Address:* Lyman 331, 17 Oxford Street, Cambridge, MA 02138, USA (office). *Telephone:* (617) 495-2869 (office). *Fax:* (617) 495-0416 (office). *E-mail:* glauber@physics.harvard.edu (office). *Website:* www.physics.harvard.edu/people/facpages/glauber.html (office).

GLAVIN, William F., MBA; American business executive and academic administrator; *President Emeritus, Babson College;* b. 29 March 1932, Albany, New York; s. of John Glavin; m. Cecily McClatchy 1955; three s. four d.; ed Coll. of the Holy Cross, Worcester and Wharton Graduate School Univ. of Pennsylvania; fmr Exec. Int. Business Machines and Vice-Pres. Operations, Service Bureau Corpn (an IBM subsidiary); Exec. Vice-Pres. Xerox Data Systems 1970, Group Vice-Pres. 1972, Man. Dir and COO 1974, Exec. Vice-Pres. Xerox 1980, Exec. Vice-Pres. for Reprographics and Operations 1982, Pres. Business Equipment Group 1983–89, Vice-Chair. Xerox Corpn 1985–89; mem. Bd of Dirs Xerox, Fuji Xerox and Rank Xerox, also the Xerox Foundation; Pres. Babson Coll., Wellesley, Mass. 1989–99, now Pres. Emer.; mem. Bd of Dirs Gould Inc., State Street Boston Corpn, Norton Co.; mem. Bd of Trustees and Pres.'s Council Coll. of the Holy Cross; Dr hc (College of the Holy Cross), (Babson College); Distinguished Alumni Award Univ. of Pennsylvania. *Leisure interests:* golf, reading, art, music. *Address:* c/o Office of the President, Babson College, Babson Park, MA 02457, USA.

GLAZER, Malcolm; American business executive; *President and CEO, First Allied Corporation;* b. 1928, Rochester, NY; m.; six c.; head family watch parts co. 1943; business interests include real estate, broadcasting, food services equipment, health care and banking; Pres. and CEO First Allied Corpn 1984–; Dir Specialty Equipment Cos Inc., Omega Protein Corpn; Dir Zapata 1993, Chair. 1994, Pres. and CEO 1994–95; owner Tampa Bay Buccaneers (Nat. Football League American football team) 1995–; est. Glazer Family Foundation 1999; owner Manchester United football team 2005–. *Address:* Tampa Bay Buccaneers, One Buccaneer Place, Tampa, FL 33607, USA (office); Manchester United PLC, Sir Matt Busby Way, Old Trafford, Manchester M16 0RA, England (office). *Telephone:* (813) 870-2700 (Tampa) (office); (161) 868-8000 (Manchester) (office). *Fax:* (813) 878-0813 (Tampa) (office); (161) 868-8804 (Manchester) (office). *Website:* www.buccaneers.com (office); www.glazerfamilyfoundation.com (office); www.manutd.com (office).

GLAZER, Nathan, PhD; American academic; *Professor Emeritus, Graduate School of Education, Harvard University;* b. 25 Feb. 1923, New York; s. of Louis Glazer and Tillie Glazer (née Zacharevich); m. 1st Ruth Slotkin 1943 (divorced 1958); three d.; m. 2nd Sulochana Raghavan 1962; ed City Coll. of New York, Univ. of Pennsylvania and Columbia Univ; mem. of staff, Commentary Magazine 1944–53; Ed. and Editorial Adviser, Doubleday Anchor Books 1954–57; Visiting Lecturer, Univ. of Calif., Berkeley 1957–58; Instructor, Bennington Coll., Vermont 1958–59; Visiting Lecturer, Smith Coll. 1959–60; lived and studied Japan 1961–62; Prof. of Sociology, Univ. of Calif., Berkeley 1963–69; Prof. of Educ. and Sociology, Harvard Univ. 1969–93, now Prof. Emer.; Fellow, Center for Advanced Study in the Behavioural Sciences, Stanford, Calif. 1971–72; Co-Ed. The Public Interest Magazine 1973–2002, now Sr Editorial Assoc.; Contributing Ed. The New Republic; mem. American Acad. of Arts and Sciences, Library of Congress Council of Scholars; Guggenheim Fellow 1954, 1966; Hon. LLD (Franklin and Marshall Coll.) 1971, (Colby Coll.) 1972; Hon. DHL (Long Island Univ.) 1978, (Hebrew Union Coll.) 1986. *Publications:* American Judaism 1957, 1972, The Social Basis of American Communism 1961, Remembering the Answers 1970, Affirmative Discrimination 1976, Ethnic Dilemmas 1964–1982 1983, The Limits of Social Policy 1989, From as Cause to a Style: Modernist Architecture's Encounter with the American City 2007; co-author: The Lonely Crowd 1950, Faces in the Crowd 1952, Studies in Housing and Minority Groups 1960, Beyond the Melting Pot 1963, Conflicting Images, India and the United States 1990, We Are All Multiculturalists Now 1997, Sovereignty under Challenge: How Governments Respond (co-ed.) 2002. *Address:* Graduate School of Education, Harvard University, Appian Way, Cambridge, MA 02138, USA (office). *Telephone:* (617) 495-4671 (office). *E-mail:* nglazer@fas.harvard.edu (office).

GLAZ'IEV, Sergey Yurievich, DrEcSc; Russian economist and politician; b. 1 Jan. 1961, Zaporozhye; m.; three c.; ed Moscow State Univ.; Head of Lab., Cen. Econ. Math. Inst. 1986–91; First Deputy Chair. Cttee on External Econ. Relations Ministry of Foreign Affairs 1991–92; First Deputy Minister of External Econ. Relations of Russia 1992, Minister 1992–93; mem. State Duma (Parl.) 1993–95 (CP of Russian Fed. faction) 1999–; Chair. Cttee for Econ. Policy of State Duma 1994–95, 2000–; Chair. Nat. Cttee of Democratic Party of Russia 1994–97; Head of Econ. Dept, Security Council 1996; Head, Information-Analytical Bd, Council of Fed. (Parl.) 1996–; Co-Chair. Party of the Russian Regions (Partiya Rossiiskikh Regionov—PRR) –2004; Head of Motherland election bloc, then For a Worthy Life Org.; author of econ. programme for CP of Russian Fed. for Parl. Elections 1999; Corresp. mem. Russian Acad. of Sciences 2000. *Publications:* Economic Theory of Technical Development 1993, Economy and Politics 1994, One and a Half Years in the Duma 1995, Under the Critical Level 1996, Genocide 1997 1998, I'm Just Paying My Debt 2007. *Address:* State Duma, Okhotny Ryad 1, 103265 Moscow, Russia (office). *Telephone:* (495) 292-42-60 (office). *Fax:* (495) 292-43-22 (office). *E-mail:* mailbox@glazev.ru (home). *Website:* www.glazev.ru (home).

GLAZUNOV, Ilya Sergeyevich; Russian painter; *Rector, Russian Academy of Painting, Sculpture and Architecture;* b. 10 June 1930, Leningrad; s. of S. F. Glazunov and O. K. Glazunova (née Flug); m. M. Vinogradova-Benua (deceased); one s. one d.; ed Repin Arts Inst. (pupil of B. Ioganson); first solo exhbn, Moscow 1957; teacher of drawing in Izhevsk, then Ivanovo; moved to Moscow 1960; Prof., Surikov Inst., Moscow 1978–; exhibited in art exhbns in Moscow 1959–99, Warsaw, Rome, Copenhagen, Viet Nam, Laos, Paris, Leningrad, Santiago, Stockholm, Berlin (East and West), Leipzig, FRG 1960–77, London (Barbican) 1987; Founder and Rector Russian Acad. of Painting, Sculpture and Architecture 1991–; projects include designs for the decoration of the interior of the Kremlin, Moscow and the Russian Embassy, Madrid; gallery of works est. in Moscow 1999; Corresp. mem. Russian Acad. of Arts 1997; Hon. mem. Royal Acads of Art, Madrid, Barcelona 1979; Order (First Class) for Services to the Motherland 1996; Order of Sergei Radonezsky 1998; First Prize Int. Art Exhbn, Prague 1956, People's Artist of the USSR 1980, Russian State Prize 1997, Pablo Picasso Gold Medal, UNESCO 1999, Jawaharlal Nehru Award. *Publications:* The Road to You 1965, Russia Crucified 1996. *Leisure interests:* philosophy, history, classical music. *Address:* Russian Academy of Painting, Sculpture and Architecture, Myasnitskaya str. 21, 101000 Moscow (office); Ilya Glazunov Art Gallery, 13 Volkhonka str., Moscow; Kamergerski pr. 2, 103009, Moscow, Russia. *Telephone:* (495) 292-33-74 (office). *E-mail:* ilya-glazunov@ya.ru. *Website:* glazunov.ru.

GLEAN, Carlyle Arnold, BEd, MA; Grenadian educator and government official; *Governor-General;* ed Univ. of Calgary, Canada; began career as teacher, St John's RC School 1950; tutor, Grenada Teachers Coll. 1970–72; fmr Prin. Grenada Teachers Coll.; fmr Lecturer, Univ. of the West Indies, Barbados; fmr Asst Chief Examiner, Caribbean Examinations Council; Minister of Educ. 1990–95 (retd); Gov.-Gen. 2008–. *Publications include:* The Caribbean: The Changing Environment (jtly) 1988. *Address:* Office of the Governor-General, Government House, St George's, Grenada (office). *Telephone:* 440-6639 (home). *Fax:* 440-6688 (office). *E-mail:* patogg@caribsurf.com (office).

GLEESON, Hon. (Murray) Anthony Murray, AC; Australian judge and lawyer; *Chief Justice, High Court;* b. 30 Aug. 1938, Wingham, NSW; s. of L. J. Gleeson; m. Robyn Gleeson 1965; one s. three d.; ed Univ. of Sydney; barrister 1963; tutor in law, St Paul's Coll., Univ. of Sydney 1963–65, Lecturer in Co. Law 1965–74; appointed QC 1974; mem. Council NSW Bar Assn 1979–86, Pres. 1984–86; Chief Justice Supreme Court NSW 1988–98; Pres. Judicial Comm. NSW 1988–98; Lt-Gov. NSW 1989–98; Chief Justice High Court of Australia 1998–; mem. Perm. Court of Arbitration 1999; Hon. Bencher Middle Temple 1989. *Leisure interests:* tennis, skiing. *Address:* High Court of Australia, PO Box 6309, Kingston, ACT 2604, Australia (office). *Telephone:* (2) 6270-6811 (office). *Fax:* (2) 6270-6868 (office). *Website:* www.hcourt.gov.au (office).

GLEMP, HE Cardinal Józef, DrIurUtr; Polish ecclesiastic; *Archbishop Emeritus-Metropolitan of Warsaw and Primate of Poland; Apostolic Administrator of Poland;* b. 18 Dec. 1929, Inowrocław; s. of Kazimierz Glemp and Salomea (née Kośmicka) Glemp; ed Primatial Spiritual Seminary, Gniezno and Poznań and Pontifical Lateran Univ., Rome; ordained priest, Gniezno 1956; educational and catechistic work 1956–58; studied in Rome 1958–64; various posts, Curia, Tribunal and Lecturer, Primatial Spiritual Seminary, Gniezno 1964–67; with Secr., Primate of Poland 1967–79; Roman Law Lecturer, Acad. of Catholic Theology, Warsaw 1967–79; mem. Episcopal Comm. for Revision of Canon Law and Sec. Comm. for Polish Insts Rome 1975–79; Hon. Chaplain to His Holiness the Pope 1972; Gremial Canon of the Primatial Capitular, Gniezno 1976; Bishop and Ordinary, Diocese of Warmia, Olsztyn 1979–81; Archbishop-Metropolitan of Gniezno and Warsaw and Primate of Poland 1981–92, Archbishop-Metropolitan of Warsaw and Primate of Poland 1992–2006; Apostolic Admin. of Warsaw 2007–; cr. Cardinal 1983; Co.-Chair. Working Group for Legis. Affairs, Joint Comm. of Govt and Episcopate Jan.–July 1981; Chair. Chief Council of Polish Episcopate, Chair. Conf. of Polish Episcopate 1981–2004; Pres. Bishop's Cttee for Pastoral Care of Poles Abroad; Pres. Bishop's Cttee for Catholic Univ. of Lublin 1981; Ordinary for the Armenian-rite Communities in Poland 1981–92, for the Greek-Catholic Communities in Poland 1981–89, for believers of Oriental rites 1992; mem. Congregation for the Oriental Churches 1983, Pontifical Council of Culture 1993, Supreme Tribunal of the Apostolic Signatura 2002; High Chancellor Stefan Cardinal Wyszyński Univ. and Pontifical Dept of Theology, Warsaw; Dr hc (Acad. of Catholic Theology, Warsaw) 1982, (Villanova Univ., USA) 1985, (Lublin Catholic Univ.) 1985, (St Thomas Univ., Manila) 1988, (Univ. of Bari) 1990, (Seton Hall Univ., NJ) 1991, (Pontifical Dept of Theology, Warsaw, and Warsaw Agricultural Univ.) 1992, (Loyola Univ. of Chicago) 1998, Stefan Card. Wyszyński Univ. Warsaw 2001; Giorgio La Pina Premio della Pace 2000; Hon. Citizen of numerous towns including, Warsaw, Znin, Inowraclaw, Castel Sant'Elia, Italy, Codroipo, Italy. *Publications:* De conceptu fictionis iuris apud Romanos 1974, Lexiculum iuris romani 1974, Przez sprawiedliwośc ku miłości 1982, Człowiek wielkiej miary 1983, Kościół na drogach Ojczyzny 1985, Chcemy z tego sprawdzianu wyjśc prawdomówni i wiarygodni 1985, Kościół i Polonia 1986, Umocnieni nadzieją 1987, W tęczy Franków orzeł i krzyż 1987, O Eucharystii 1987, Nauczanie pasterskie (5 Vols) 1981–95, Let My Call Come to You 1988, A wołanie moje niech do Ciebie przyjdzie 1988, Boże, coś Polskę posłał nad Tamizę 1988, Nauczanie społeczne 1981–1986, 1989, Na dwóch wybrzeżach 1990, U przyjaciół Belgów 1990, I uwierzyli uczniowie 1990, Zamyślenia Maryjne 1990, Solidarietà. La Polonia che sogniamo 1991, Słowo Boże nad Łyną 1991, Tysiąclecie wiary Świętego Włodzimierza 1991, Gniezno ciągła odnowa 1991, Służyć Ewangelii słowem 1991, Na Skałce – na opoce 1991, Niebo ściągają na ziemię 1991, Między Ewangelią a konstytucją 1992, Na wyspie Świętego Patryka 1992, Idźmy do Betlejem 1992, Wartości chrześcijańskie nabywane pod Kalwarią 1993, W blaskach Zmartwychwstania 1994, Byc znakiem miłości 1994, Rodzina drogą Kościoła 1995, Boskie i cesarskie 1995, Idzie, idzie Bóg prawdziwy 1995, Les chemins des pèlerins 1996, Od Kalwarii na drogi Europy 1997, Piętnaście lat posługi prymasowskiej 1997, Święci idą przez Warszawę 1997, Poles – We Enter Now the Twenty-First Century! 1998, The Preservation of National Identity and Interhuman Solidarity 1998, Z krzyzem przez dzieje wierzącej Stolicy 1998, Modlimy się w kraju Helwetów 1998, Odkrywac drogi Opatrzności Bożej 1999, Listy pasterskie 1999, La speranza a Varsavia si stringe alla Croce 1999, Sławny w męczenników gronie 1999, Chrystus wciąż żyje 2001, Ścile duszpasterskie 2002, Caritati in iustitia 2002, Opatrzność pod krzyżem Chrystusa i naszym 2003, Z Jasnogórskiego Szczytu 2004, Prymas Polski do młodzieży: Katechizm nie tylko dla bierzmowanych 2006. *Address:* Rezydencja Prymasa Polski, ul. Miodowa 17/19, 00-246 Warsaw, Poland. *Telephone:* (22) 531 71 00. *Fax:* (22) 635 87 45. *Website:* www.spp.episkopat.pl.

GLENAMARA, Baron (Life Peer), cr. 1977, of Glenridding, Cumbria; **Edward Watson Short,** PC, CH; British politician; b. 17 Dec. 1912; s. of Charles Short and Mary Short; m. Jennie Sewell 1941; one s. one d.; ed Bede Coll., Durham; served Second World War and became Capt. in Durham Light Infantry; Headmaster, Princess Louise County Secondary School, Blyth, Northumberland 1947; Leader Labour Group, Newcastle City Council 1950; MP for Newcastle-upon-Tyne Central 1951–76; Opposition Whip (N Area) 1955–62; Deputy Chief Opposition Whip 1962–64; Parl. Sec. to Treasury and Govt Chief Whip 1964–66; Postmaster-Gen. 1966–68; Sec. of State for Educ. and Science 1968–70; Deputy Leader of Labour Party 1972–76; Lord Pres. of Council, Leader of House of Commons 1974–76; Chair. Cable and Wireless Co. 1976–80; Pres. Finchdale Abbey Training Coll. for the Disabled, Durham; Chancellor Univ. of Northumbria (fmrly Polytechnic of Newcastle-upon-Tyne) 1984–; Hon. DCL (Durham), (Newcastle) 1998; Hon. DUniv (Open Univ.) 1989; Hon. DLitt (CNAA) 1990. *Publications:* The Story of the Durham Light Infantry 1944, The Infantry Instructor 1946, Education in a Changing World 1971, Birth to Five 1974, I Knew My Place 1983, Whip to Wilson 1989. *Leisure interests:* painting. *Address:* House of Lords, London, SW1A 0PW; 21 Priory Gardens, Corbridge, Northumberland, NE45 5HZ, England. *Telephone:* (143) 463-2880 (Corbridge).

GLENDENING, Parris Nelson, MA, PhD; American fmr state governor; *President, Smart Growth Leadership Institute;* b. 11 June 1942, Bronx, NY; m. 1st Frances A. Hughes 1976; one s.; m. 2nd Jennifer E. Crawford; one d.; ed Florida State Univ. Fort Lauderdale and Tallahassee; Asst Prof., Univ. of Maryland, College Park 1967–72, Assoc. Prof. 1972–95; Co. Exec. Prince George's Co. Council, Upper Marlboro, Md 1982–94; various public appointments at co. level; Dir World Trade Center 1990–97; Gov. of Maryland 1995–2003; Pres. Smart Growth Leadership Inst., Washington DC 2003–; Chair. Bd Dirs Smart Growth Investments 2003–; Chair. Nat. Govs' Assn 2001–03; mem. AAAS, American Political Science Assn; Democrat; Hon. LLD (Bowie State) 1995, (Baltimore) 1996, (Maryland at Baltimore) 1998; Hon. Dr of Public Service (Washington Coll.) 1995, (Carroll Community Coll.) 1997, (Maryland Univ. Coll.) 2000, (Bridgewater State Coll.) 2003; Hon. DHumLitt (Towson) 2000; numerous awards including Public Official of the Year Award Governing magazine 1990, 2000, Donald C. Stone Award American Soc. for Public Admin 1995, American Soc. of Landscape Architects' Olmstead Award, Harward Innovations in American Govt Award 2000, Hubert H. Humphrey Award 2002, Morris H. Blum Humanitarian Award 2006. *Publications:* Controversies of State and Local Political Systems (with M. M. Reeves) 1972, Pragmatic Federalism 1977; articles in professional publs. *Address:* Smart Growth Leadership Institute, 1707 L Street, NW, Suite 1050, Washington, DC 20036, USA (office). *Telephone:* (410) 268-6050 (office). *Fax:* (410) 268-6072 (office). *E-mail:* pglendening@sgli.org (office). *Website:* www.sgli.org (office).

GLENDON, Mary Ann, BA, MCompL, JD; American academic, lawyer, writer and fmr diplomatist; *Learned Hand Professor of Law, Harvard University;* b. 7 Oct. 1938, Pittsfield, Berkshire Co., Mass; m. Edward R. Lev; three d.; ed Univ. of Chicago, Université Libre, Brussels, Belgium; early career included period as volunteer civil rights attorney; practised law with Mayer, Brown and Platt, Chicago 1963–68; teacher, Boston Coll. Law School 1968–86; Prof. of Law, Harvard Law School 1986–93, Learned Hand Prof. of Law 1993–; Amb. to the Holy See (Vatican) 2007–09; fmr Visiting Prof., Univ. of Chicago Law School 1974, Gregorian Univ., Rome; fmr Pres. UNESCO-sponsored Int. Assn of Legal Science 1991; mem. Pontifical Acad. of Social Sciences 1994–, Pres. 2004– (first woman head of a major pontifical acad.); Head of Del. of Holy See to UN Women's Conf., Beijing 1995; mem. Bd of Advisors, Notre Dame Center for Ethics and Culture, Harvard Univ. Human Rights Initiative, Harvard Law School Human Rights Program; mem. Bd of Trustees, Catholic Univ. of America, St John's Seminary; mem. Pres. George W. Bush's Council on Bioethics; mem. Editorial and Advisory Bd First Things; hon. doctorates from Univ. of Chicago, Univ. of Louvain and others; Scribes Book Award, American Soc. of Writers on Legal Subjects 1988, Order of the Coif Triennial Book, Legal Acad. 1993. *Publications:* as author: The New Family and the New Property 1981, Abortion and Divorce in Western Law 1987, The Transformation of Family Law 1989, Rights Talk: The Impoverishment of Political Discourse 1991, Law of Decedent's Estates (co-author) 1991, A Nation Under Lawyers 1994, Seedbeds of Virtue (co-author) 1995, Comparative Legal Traditions (co-author) 1999, A World Made New: Eleanor Roosevelt and the Universal Declaration of Human Rights 2001. *Address:* Harvard Law School, Hauser 504, Cambridge MA 02138, USA (office); Pontifical Academy of Social Sciences, Casina Pio IV, 00120 Vatican City. *Telephone:* (617) 495-4769 (Harvard) (office); (06) 69881441 (Pontifical Acad.). *Fax:* (617) 496-4913 (Harvard); (06) 69885218 (Pontifical Acad.). *E-mail:* social.sciences@acdscience.va. *Website:* www.law.harvard.edu (office); glendonbooks.com.

GLENN, Lt-Col John Herschel, Jr; American astronaut, politician and aviator; *Chairman, John Glenn Institute of Public Service and Public Policy, Ohio State University;* b. 18 July 1921, Cambridge, Ohio; s. of John H. Glenn and Clare Sproat; m. Anna Margaret Castor 1943; one s. one d.; ed Muskingum Coll., Univ. of Maryland; naval aviation cadet 1942; commissioned Marine Corps 1943; Marine Fighter Squadron 155 in Marshall Islands 1944 (59 combat missions); mem. Fighter Squadron 218 North China Patrol; Instructor Corpus Christi, Texas 1948–50; Marine Fighter Squadron Korea (63 missions); Fighter Design Branch, Navy Bureau of Aeronautics, Washington 1956; speed record Los Angeles–New York (3 hr 23 min) 1957;

training for space flight 1960–61; completed 3 orbits of the Earth in Spaceship Friendship VII, 20 Feb. 1962; resigned from US Marine Corps 1965; Dir Royal Crown Cola Co. 1965–74; Consultant to NASA; US Senator from Ohio 1975–99; Chair. Bd of Dirs, John Glenn Inst. of Public Service and Public Policy, Ohio State Univ. 1999–; announced return as astronaut Oct. 1997, on board Discovery shuttle 1998; mem.-at-large Ohio State Democratic Cttee 1999–; DFC (8 times) and Air Medal with 18 clusters; NASA Distinguished Service Medal 1962; US Nat. Space Hall of Fame Award 1969, Centennial Award, Nat. Geographic Soc. 1988. *Publications:* (co-author) We Seven 1962, P.S., I Listened to Your Heart Beat. *Address:* John Glenn Institute, Ohio State University, 350 Page Hall, 1810 College Road, Columbus, OH 43210, USA (office). *Telephone:* (614) 292-4545. *Fax:* (614) 292-4868. *Website:* www.glenninstitute.org.

GLENNIE, Dame Evelyn Elizabeth Ann, DBE, GRSM, FRAM, FRCM, FRNCM; British timpanist, percussionist, composer and teacher; b. 19 July 1965, Aberdeen, Scotland; d. of Isobel Glennie and Herbert Arthur Glennie; ed Ellon Acad., Aberdeenshire, Royal Acad. of Music, London; solo debut at Wigmore Hall, London, 1986; concerto, chamber and solo percussion performances worldwide; gave Promenade concerts' first-ever percussion recital 1989; numerous TV appearances, including three documentaries on her life including Touch the Sound 2004 (BAFTA Award); composer of music for TV and radio; many works written for her by composers, including Bennett, Rouse, Heath, Macmillan, McLeod, Muldowney, Daugherty, Turnage and Musgrave; Munster Trust Scholarship 1986; also runs businesses EG Jewellery, EG Images, EG Merchandise, EG 21st Guidance; Hon. DMus (Aberdeen) 1991, (Bristol, Portsmouth) 1995, (Leicester, Surrey) 1997, (Queen's, Belfast) 1998, (Southampton) 2000, (Williams Coll., USA) 2005, (Binghampton) 2007; Hon. DLitt (Warwick) 1993, (Loughborough) 1995, (Salford) 1999; Hon. LLD (Dundee) 1996; Hon. DUniv (Essex, Durham) 1998, (Open Univ.) 2007; many int. prizes and awards, including Shell/LSO Music Gold Medal 1984, Queen's Commendation Prize at RAM 1985, Grammy Award 1988, Scotswoman of the Decade 1990, Charles Heidsieck Soloist of the Year, Royal Philharmonic Soc. 1991, Personality of the Year, Int. Classical Music Awards 1993, Young Deaf Achievers Special Award 1993, Best Studio Percussionist, Rhythm Magazine 1998, 2000, 2002, 2003, 2004, Best Live Percussionist, Rhythm Magazine 2000, Classic FM Outstanding Contribution to Classical Music 2002, Walpole Medal of Excellence 2002, Musical America 2003, Tartan Clef Award 2005, Scotland with Style Classical Award 2005, Best Orchestral Percussionist, Drummies Readers' Poll Awards 2005, Incorporated Soc. of Musicians Distinguished Musician Award 2006, Sabian Lifetime Achievement Award 2006. *Films:* wrote and played music for The Trench, Touch the Sound (Critics' Prize, Locarno Int. Film Festival). *Play:* Playing from the Heart. *Recordings include:* Rhythm Song, Dancin', Light in Darkness, Rebounds, Veni Veni Emmanuel, Wind in the Bamboo Grove, Drumming, Her Greatest Hits, The Music of Joseph Schwantner, Sonata for Two Pianos and Percussion (Bartók), Last Night of the Proms – 100th Season, Street Songs, Reflected in Brass, Shadow Behind the Iron Sun, African Sunrise, Manhattan Rave, UFO: The Music of Michael Daugherty, Bela Fleck-Perpetual Motion, Oriental Landscapes, Fractured Lines, Michael Daugherty: Philadelphia Stories/UFO, Philip Glass: The Concerto Project 2004, Christopher Rouse 2004, Touch the Sound Soundtrack 2004, Margaret Brouwer: Aurolucent Circles 2006. *Television includes:* music for Trial and Retribution 1–5 (Yorkshire TV), music for Mazda commercial Blind Ambition, Survival Special (Anglia) and others. *Publications:* Good Vibrations (autobiog.) 1990, Great Journeys of the World, Beat It!, African Dances, Marimba Encores, 3 Chorales for Marimba. *Leisure interests:* reading, walking, cycling, antiques, collecting musical instruments, psychology, designing jewellery, pets. *Address:* EG Office, PO Box 6, Sawtry, Huntingdon, Cambs., PE28 5WE, England (office). *Telephone:* (870) 774-1492 (office). *Fax:* (870) 774-1493 (office). *E-mail:* carla@evelyn.co.uk (office); brenda@evelyn.co.uk (office). *Website:* www.evelyn.co.uk.

GLESKE, Leonhard, Dr rer. pol; German banker; b. 18 Sept. 1921, Bydgoszcz (Poland); s. of Gustav Gleske and Lydia Gohl; m. Christa Reimann 1956; one s. three d.; fmr mem. of the Bd and mem. Central Bank Council, Deutsche Bundesbank; mem., Bd of Dirs BDO-Deutsche Warentreuhand Aktiengesellschaft; Hon. Prof. (Mannheim) 1986; Dr hc (Univ. of Münster) 1985. *Address:* Kaiser-Friedrich Promenade 151, 61352 Bad Homburg, Germany. *Telephone:* (6172) 42951 (home). *Fax:* (6172) 923993 (home).

GLICKMAN, Daniel Robert, BA, JD; American fmr politician and association executive; *President and CEO, Motion Picture Association of America;* b. 24 Nov. 1944, Wichita, Kan.; s. of Milton Glickman and Gladys A. Kopelman; m. Rhoda J. Yura 1966; one s. one d.; ed Univ. of Michigan, Ann Arbor and George Washington Univ.; mem. Kan. Bar 1969, Mich. Bar 1970; trial attorney, Securities & Exchange Comm. 1969–70; Assoc. then Partner, Sargent, Klenda & Glickman, Wichita 1971–76; mem. 95th–103rd Congresses from 4th Kansas Dist 1977–95; Sec. of Agric. 1995–2001; Partner Akin, Gump, Strauss, Hauer & Feld LLP 2001–; Dir Inst. of Politics, John F. Kennedy School of Govt, Harvard Univ. 2002–04; Pres. and CEO Motion Picture Assсn of America 2004–; mem. Bd of Dirs Chicago Mercantile Exchange, Hain-Celestial Corpn, Ready Pac Produce Corpn, Communities in Schools, America's Second Harvest, Food Research and Action Center, RFK Memorial Foundation; mem. Int. Advisory Bd of The Coca-Cola Co.; co-Chair. US Consensus Council, The Pew Initiative on Food and Biotechnology. *Address:* Motion Picture Association of America (MPAA), 15503 Ventura Boulevard, Encino, CA 91436, USA (office). *Telephone:* (818) 995-6600 (office). *Website:* www.mpaa.org.

GLIDEWELL, Rt Hon. Sir Iain (Derek Laing), Kt, PC; British judge; b. 8 June 1924; s. of Charles Norman Glidewell and Nora Glidewell; m. Hilary Winant 1950; one s. two d.; ed Bromsgrove School, Worcester Coll., Oxford; served RAFVR (pilot) 1942–46; called to Bar, Gray's Inn 1949, Bencher 1977, Treas. 1995; QC 1969; a Recorder of the Crown Court 1976–80; a Judge of Appeal, Isle of Man 1979–80; a Judge of the High Court of Justice, Queen's Bench Div. 1980–85; Presiding Judge, NE Circuit 1982–85; a Lord Justice of Appeal 1985–95; conducted review of Crown Prosecution Service 1997–98; a Judge of Court of Appeal, Gibraltar 1998–2003, Pres. 2003–04; mem. Senate of Inns of Court and the Bar 1976–79, Pres. 2003–04; mem., Supreme Court Rule Cttee 1980–84; Chair. Judicial Studies Bd 1989–92, Panels for Examination of Structure Plans: Worcs. 1974, W Midlands 1975; conducted Heathrow Fourth Terminal Inquiry 1978; Hon. Fellow, Worcester Coll. Oxford 1986. *Leisure interests:* walking, theatre. *Address:* Rough Heys Farm, Macclesfield, Cheshire, SK11 9PF, England (home).

GLIGOROV, Kiro; Macedonian fmr head of state; b. 3 May 1917, Štip; s. of Blagoje and Katarina Gligorov; m. Nada Gligorov; one s. two d.; ed Faculty of Law, Univ. of Belgrade; mem. Presidium of Antifascist Assembly of People's Liberation of Macedonia and Antifascist Council People's Liberation of Yugoslavia during World War II; Deputy Sec.-Gen. to Govt of Yugoslavia 1946–47; Asst Minister of Finance 1947–52; Prof. of Econs Belgrade Univ. 1948–49; Deputy Dir Exec. Council for Gen. Econ. Affairs 1955–62; Fed. Sec. for Finance 1962–67; Vice-Pres. Fed. Exec. Council 1967–69; mem. League of Communists of Yugoslavia (mem. Exec. Bureau 1969–74); mem. Presidency, Socialist Fed. Repub. of Yugoslavia 1971–72; Pres. Parl. 1974–78; Pres. of Macedonia 1991–99; holder of many Yugoslav and foreign honours. *Publications:* many articles and studies in finance and economics. *Leisure interests:* tennis, hunting. *Address:* c/o Office of the President, Dame Grueva 6, 91000 Skopje, Macedonia.

GLIMCHER, Marc; American art gallery executive; *President, PaceWildenstein Gallery;* s. of Arnold Glimcher and Millie Glimcher; m. Andrea Budonis; Exec. Producer The Paint Job 1992; Pres. PaceWildenstein Gallery (operators of Bellagio Gallery of Fine Art) 2001–, past exhbns include Keith Tyson, Chuck Close, Donald Judd, Bridget Riley, Mark Rothko, Julian Schnabel. *Address:* PaceWildenstein Gallery, 32 East 57th Street, 2nd floor, New York, NY 10022, USA (office). *Telephone:* (212) 421-3292 (office). *Fax:* (212) 421-0835 (office). *Website:* www.pacewildenstein.com (office).

GLITMAN, Maynard Wayne, BA, MA; American diplomatist; *Lecturer in Political Science, University of Vermont;* b. 8 Dec. 1933, Chicago; s. of Ben and Reada (née Kutok Klass) Glitman; m. G. Christine Amundsen 1956; three s. two d.; ed Univ. of Ill., Fletcher School of Law and Diplomacy, Univ. of California; with US army 1957; with Foreign Service Dept of State 1956, 1966–67, Dir Office of Int. Trade 1973–74, Deputy Asst Sec. of State for Internal Trade policy 1974–76; economist 1956–59; Vice-Consul Bahamas 1959–61; Econ. Officer Embassy, Ottawa 1961–65; mem. Del. to UN Gen. Ass. 1967, Nat. Security Council Staff 1968; Political Officer, First Sec. Embassy in Paris 1968–73; Deputy Asst Sec. of Defense for Europe and NATO 1976–77, Deputy Perm. Rep. to NATO 1977–81; Amb. and Deputy Chief US Del. to Intermediate Nuclear Forces Negotiations, Arms Control and Disarmament Agency, Switzerland 1981–84; Amb. and US Rep. Mutual and Balanced Forces Negotiation, Vienna 1985; Amb. and Chief US Negotiator Intermediate Nuclear Forces Negotiation, Geneva 1985–88; Amb. to Belgium 1988–91; Diplomat in Residence, Univ. of Vt 1991–94, Adjunct Prof., now also Lecturer in Political Science, Univ. of Vt 1995–; Public Service Medal (USA Dept of Defense) 1977, 1981, Presidential Distinguished Service Award 1984, 1987. *Address:* Department of Political Science, University of Vermont, PO Box 54110, Burlington, VT 05405-0001 (office); PO Box 438, Jeffersonville, VT 05464-0438, USA (home). *E-mail:* mwglitman@pwshift.com (office). *Website:* www.uvm.edu (office).

GLOAG, Ann Heron, OBE; British business executive; *Director, Stagecoach Group plc;* b. 10 Dec. 1942; d. of Iain Souter and Catherine Souter; m. 1st Robin N. Gloag 1965; one s. (deceased) one d.; m. 2nd David McCleary 1990; ed Perth High School; trainee nurse, Bridge of Earn Hosp., Perth 1960–65, Theatre Sister 1969–80; ward sister, Devonshire Royal Hosp., Buxton 1965–69; Founding Partner, Gloagtrotter (renamed Stagecoach Express Services) 1980–83, Co-Dir Stagecoach Ltd 1983–86, Dir Stagecoach Holdings PLC 1986–, Exec. Dir 1986–2000, Man. Dir 1986–94; Trustee Princess Royal Trust for Carers; mem. Int. Bd Mercy Ships; Dir (non-exec.) OPTOS; Scottish Marketing Woman of the Year, Scottish Univs 1989, UK Businesswoman of the Year, Veuve Clicquot and Inst. of Dirs 1989–90. *Leisure interests:* family, travel, charity support. *Address:* Stagecoach Group plc, 10 Dunkeld Road, Perth, PH1 5TW, Scotland (office). *Website:* www.stagecoachgroup.com.

GLOBUS, Yoram; Israeli film producer; b. 7 Sept. 1943; f. Noah Films with Menahem Golan (q.v.) 1963; bought Cannon Films (USA) with Menahem Golan 1979 and has since produced over 100 motion pictures; Chair., CEO Cannon Entertainments 1989; Officer Cannon Group Inc. 1989; Co-Pres. Pathé Communications Corpn, Chair., CEO Pathé Int. until 1991. *Films produced include:* Over the Top, Barfly, Dancers, Missing in Action I, II & III, Death Wish IV, The Assault (winner of 1986 Acad. Award for Best Foreign Language Film), Surrender, Runaway Train, Hanna's War, Masters of the Universe, King Lear, Tough Guys Don't Dance, Shy People, A Cry In The Dark.

GLOCER, Thomas (Tom) Henry, BA, JD; American lawyer and business executive; *CEO, Thomson-Reuters;* b. 8 Oct. 1959, NY; s. of Walter Glocer and Ursula Glocer (née Goodman); m. Maarit Leso 1988; one s. one d.; ed Columbia Univ., Yale Univ. Law School; mergers and acquisitions lawyer, Davis Polk and Wardwell, New York, Paris and Tokyo 1985–93; joined Reuters 1993, mem. Legal Dept Gen. Counsel, Reuters America Inc., New York 1993–96, Exec. Vice-Pres., Reuters America Inc. and CEO Reuters Latin America

1996–98, CEO Reuters business in the Americas 1998–2001, Reuters Inc. 2000–01, CEO Reuters Group (Thomson-Reuters following merger with Thomson 2007) PLC 2001–; Dir New York City Investment Fund 1999–2003, Instinet Corpn 2000–; mem. Advisory Bd Singapore Monetary Authority 2001–; mem. Corp. Council, Whitney Museum of American Art 2000–; New York Hall of Science Award 2000, John Jay Alumni Award 2001. *Publications include:* author of computer software, including Coney Island: A Game of Discovery (co-author) 1983. *Address:* Thomson-Reuters, Reuters Building, Canary Wharf, London, E14 5EP, England (office). *Telephone:* (20) 7250-1122 (office). *Fax:* (20) 7542-4064 (office). *Website:* www.reuters.com (office).

GLOS, Michael; German politician and banking executive; b. 14 Dec. 1944, Brünnau; m.; three c. (one died 1997); served apprenticeship as miller and passed professional examination 1967; managed family flour mill, Prichsenstadt 1968–70; mem. CSU (Christlich-Soziale Union in Bayern) 1970–, first Chair. CSU-chapter, Prichsenstadt 1972–75, Chair. CSU-Dist of Kitzingen 1975–93, mem. Exec. Bd CSU Lower Franconia 1976–, mem. Presidency of CSU Bavaria 1976–, Chair. CSU Bavaria and Asst Chair. CDU/CSU Parl. Group 1993–; mem. Dist Council of Prichsenstadt 1972–78; mem. Council of Dist (Kreistag) of Kitzingen 1975–93; mem. Bundestag (Parl.) 1976–; Fed. Minister for Econs and Tech. 2005–09 (resgnd); Chair. Bd of Supervisory Dirs and Chair. Exec. Cttee KfW Bankengruppe 2008–. *Address:* KfW Bankengruppe, Palmengarten str. 5–9, 60325 Frankfurt am Main, Germany (office). *Telephone:* (69) 7431-0 (office). *Fax:* (69) 7431-2944 (office). *E-mail:* presse@kfw.de (office). *Website:* www.kfw.de/EN_Home/index.jsp (office); www.glos.de.

GLOUCESTER, HRH The Duke of Richard Alexander Walter George, Earl of Ulster and the Baron Culloden, KG, GCVO; b. 26 Aug. 1944, Northampton; s. of the late Duke of Gloucester (third s. of HM King George V) and the late Lady Alice Montagu-Douglas-Scott (d. of the 7th Duke of Buccleuch); m. Birgitte van Deurs 1972; one s. (Alexander, Earl of Ulster) two d. (the Lady Davina Windsor and the Lady Rose Windsor); ed Wellesley House, Broadstairs, Eton Coll. and Magdalene Coll., Cambridge; Corporate mem. RIBA 1972; Commdr-in-Chief St John Ambulance Brigade 1972–74; Col-in-Chief Gloucestershire Regt 1974–94, Deputy Col-in-Chief Royal Gloucestershire, Berks. and Wilts. Regt 1994–; Deputy Col-in-Chief The Royal Logistic Corps 1993–; Hon. Col Royal Monmouthshire Royal Engineers Light Infantry (Militia) 1977–; Hon. Air Cdre RAF Odiham 1993–; Grand Prior Order of St John 1975–; Royal Trustee, British Museum 1973–2003; Pres. Cancer Research Campaign 1973, Nat. Asscn of Clubs for Young People 1974, Christ's Hosp. 1975, St Bartholomew's Hosp. 1975, Royal Smithfield 1975, British Consultants and Construction Bureau 1978; Patron of Heritage of London Trust 1982; Commr Historic Buildings and Monuments Comm. for England 1983-2001; Pres. The London Soc.; Sr Fellow Royal Coll. of Art 1984; as Rep. of HM The Queen visited Australia 1963, wedding of Crown Prince of Nepal 1963, seventieth birthday celebrations of King Olav V of Norway 1973, Mexico 1973, Nepal 1975, Saudi Arabia and the Philippines 1975, independence celebrations of Seychelles 1976 and of Solomon Islands 1978, Australia and Hawaii 1979, independence celebrations of Vanuatu 1980, Philippines, Indonesia and Burma 1981, India, Cyprus and Belgium 1982, France, Repub. of Korea, Canada, Jordan and UAE 1983, USA, Thailand, Brunei, Bahrain, Kuwait and Qatar 1984, New Zealand, Canary Islands, Egypt, Algeria and Tunis 1985, USSR, FRG, Berlin and Italy 1986, Spain, Sweden, Saudi Arabia, Indonesia, Bangladesh and Hong Kong 1987, USA, Gibraltar, Turkey, Pakistan, Kenya, Bahrain and Qatar 1988, Netherlands, Denmark and Portugal 1989, Canada, USA, France, Laos, Malaysia and Singapore 1990, Poland, Dubai, France, Luxembourg, Germany, Hungary and Czechoslovakia 1991, Egypt, Spain, Belgium and USA 1992, Ukraine 1993, USA, Singapore, Japan and Portugal 1994, France, India, Malaysia and Mexico 1995, USA, Vietnam, Philippines, Indonesia and South Africa 1996, Repub. of Korea, Luxembourg, Yemen, Bahrain, Qatar and UAE 1997, Tunisia, China, Hong Kong, Tokyo, Angola, South Africa 1998, Poland, Barbados, Jamaica, Trinidad 1999, Kazakhstan, Kyryzstan, Nigeria 2000, Argentina, Armenia 2001, Kuala Lumpur and Singapore 2002, Panama 2003. *Publication:* On Public View, The Face of London, Oxford and Cambridge. *Address:* Kensington Palace, London, W8 4PU, England. *Telephone:* (20) 7368-1000 (office). *Fax:* (20) 7368-1019 (office). *Website:* www.royal.gov.uk.

GLOVER, Danny; American actor; b. 22 July 1946, San Francisco, Calif.; m. Asake Bomani; one d.; ed San Francisco State Univ.; researcher, Office of Mayor, San Francisco 1971–75; Head TransAfrica (African-American Lobby) 2002–; mem. American Conservatory Theater's Black Actor Workshop; Broadway debut, Master Harold . . . and the Boys 1982; other stage appearances include: The Blood Knot 1982, The Island, Sizwe Banzi is Dead, Macbeth, Suicide in B Flat, Nevis Mountain Dew, Jukebox; appearances in TV movies and series; f. Carrie Productions (film production co.); with his wife f. Bomani Gallery, San Francisco; Chair.'s Award, Nat. Asscn for the Advancement of Colored People (NAACP) 2003. *Films:* Escape from Alcatraz 1979, Chu Chu and the Philly Flash 1981, Out 1982, Iceman 1984, Places in the Heart 1984, Birdy 1984, The Color Purple 1984, Silverado 1985, Witness 1985, Lethal Weapon 1987, Bat 21 1988, Lethal Weapon II 1989, To Sleep with Anger 1990, Predator 2 1990, Flight of the Intruder 1991, A Rage in Harlem 1991, Pure Luck 1991, Grand Canyon 1992, Lethal Weapon III 1992, The Saint of Fort Washington 1993, Bopha 1993, Angels in the Outfield 1994, Operation Dumbo Drop 1995, America's Dream 1996, The Rainmaker 1997, Wings Against the Wind 1998, Beloved 1998, Lethal Weapon IV 1998, Prince of Egypt (voice) 1998, Antz (voice) 1998, The Monster 1999, Bàttu 2000, Boseman and Lena 2000, Wings Against the Wind 2000, Freedom Song 2000, 3 A.M. 2001, The Royal Tenenbaums 2001, Saw 2004, The Cookout 2004, Missing in America 2005, Manderlay 2005, The Shaggy Dog 2006, The Adventures of Brer Rabbit (voice) 2006, Bamako 2006, Dreamgirls 2006, Barnyard (voice) 2006, Shooter 2007, Honeydripper 2007, Be Kind Rewind 2007, Blindness 2008. *Television includes:* The Henry Lee Project 2003, Legend of Earthsea 2004, The Exonerated 2005. *Address:* Carrie Productions, 4444 Riverside Drive, Suite 110, Burbank, CA 91505, USA. *Telephone:* (818) 567-3292.

GLOVER, Jane Alison, CBE, MA, DPhil, FRCM; British conductor; *Music Director, Music of the Baroque, Chicago;* b. 13 May 1949; d. of the late Robert Finlay Glover and Jean Muir; ed Monmouth School for Girls and St Hugh's Coll., Oxford; Jr Research Fellow St Hugh's Coll. 1973–75, Lecturer in Music 1976–84, Sr Research Fellow 1982–84; Lecturer St Anne's Coll., Oxford 1976–80, Pembroke Coll. 1979–84; mem. Univ. of Oxford Faculty of Music 1979–; professional conducting debut at Wexford Festival 1975; operas and concerts for BBC, Glyndebourne 1982–, Royal Opera House 1988–, Covent Garden, ENO 1989–, London Symphony Orchestra, London Philharmonic Orchestra, Royal Philharmonic Orchestra, Philharmonia, Royal Scottish Orchestra, English Chamber Orchestra, Royal Danish Opera, Glimmerglass Opera, New York 1994–, Australian Opera 1996– and many orchestras in Europe and USA; Prin. Conductor London Choral Soc. 1983–2000; Artistic Dir London Mozart Players 1984–91; Prin. Conductor Huddersfield Choral Soc. 1989–96; Music Dir Music of the Baroque, Chicago 2002–; Artistic Dir of Opera, Royal Acad. of Music 2009–; mem. BBC Cen. Music Advisory Cttee 1981–85, Music Advisory Cttee Arts Council 1986–88; Gov. RAM 1985–90, BBC 1990–95; Hon. DMus (Exeter) 1986, (CNAA) 1991, (London) 1992, (City Univ.) 1995, (Glasgow) 1996; Hon. DLitt (Loughborough) 1988, (Bradford) 1992; Dr hc (Open Univ.) 1988, (Brunel) 1997. *Television:* documentaries and series and presentation, especially Orchestra 1983, Mozart 1985. *Radio:* talks and series including Opera House 1995, Musical Dynasties 2000. *Publications:* Cavalli 1978, Mozart's Women: His Family, His Friends, His Music 2005; contribs to The New Monteverdi Companion 1986, Monteverdi 'Orfeo' Handbook 1986; articles in numerous journals. *Leisure interests:* The Times crossword puzzle, theatre, skiing, walking. *Address:* c/o Kaylor Management, 130 West 57th Street, Suite 8G, New York, NY 10019, USA (office). *Telephone:* (212) 977-6779 (office). *E-mail:* hughkaylor@msn.com (office). *Website:* www.hughkaylor.com (office); www.janeglover.co.uk; www.baroque.org.

GŁOWACKI, Janusz; Polish writer, playwright and screenwriter; b. 13 Sept. 1938, Poznań; m.; one d.; ed Warsaw Univ.; columnist in Kultura weekly 1964–81; lecturer in many colls and univs in USA including Bennington, Yale, Cornell, Columbia; playwright in residence New York Shakespeare Festival 1984 and Mark Taper Forum, LA 1989; Fellow in Writing, Univ. of Iowa 1977, 1982; Hon. mem. Univ. of Iowa 1977, 1982; Nat. Endowment for the Arts Fellowship 1988, Master of Arts Atlantic Center for the Arts 1991; mem. American and Polish PEN Club 1984–, Polish Film Union; Joseph Kesserling Award 1987, Drama League of New York Playwrighting Award 1987, Guggenheim Award 1988, Alfred Jurzykowski Foundation Award 1997. *Publications:* short stories: Nowy taniec la-ba-da 1970, Paradis 1973, Polowanie na muchy 1974, My Sweet Raskolnikov 1977, Opowiadania wybrane 1978, Skrzek. Coraz trudniej kochać 1980, Rose Café 1997; novels: Moc truchleje 1981, Ostani cieć 2001; screenplays: Rejs 1970, Psychodrama (with Marek Piwowski) 1971, Polowanie na muchy 1971, Trzeba zabić tę miłość 1974, No Smoking Section (co-author) 1987, Hairdo (Tony Cox Screenwriting Award, Nantucket Film Festival, USA 1999) 1999; plays: Cudzołóstwo ukarane 1971, Mecz 1977, Obciach 1977, Kopciuch (Cinders) (Premio Molière, Argentina 1986) 1981, Fortinbras Gets Drunk 1986, Hunting Cockroaches (1st Prize, American Theatre Critics Asscn 1986, Joseph Kesselring Award 1987, Hollywood Drama League Critics' Award 1987) 1986, Antigone in New York (Le Balladine Award for the Best Play of 1997 in theatres of up to 250 seats) 1993, Ścieki, Skrzeki, karaluchy (selected works) 1996, Czwarta siostra (Grand Prize, Int. Theatre Festival, Dubrovnik 2001) 2000. *Address:* ul. Bednarska 7 m. 4, 00-310 Warsaw, Poland; 845 West End Avenue Apt 4B, New York, NY 10025, USA. *Website:* www.januszglowacki.com.

GLÜCK, Louise Elisabeth; American poet, writer and academic; *Rosenkranz Writer-in-Residence, Yale University;* b. 22 April 1943, New York City; d. of Daniel Glück and Beatrice Glück (née Grosby); m. 1st Charles Hertz (divorced); one s.; m. 2nd John Dranow 1977 (divorced 1996); ed Sarah Lawrence Coll., Bronxville, New York and Columbia Univ.; Artist-in-Residence, Goddard Coll., Plainfield, Vt 1971–72, faculty mem. 1973–74; Poet-in-Residence, Univ. of North Carolina at Greensboro 1973; Visiting Prof., Univ. of Iowa 1976–77; Elliston Prof. of Poetry, Univ. of Cincinnati 1978; Visiting Prof., Columbia Univ. 1979; Holloway Lecturer, Univ. of California, Berkeley 1982; Faculty mem. and Bd mem. MFA Writing Program at Warren Wilson Coll., Swannoa, NC 1980–84; Visiting Prof., Univ. of California, Davis 1983; Scott Prof. of Poetry, Williams Coll., Mass 1983, part-time Sr Lecturer in English 1984–97, Parish Sr Lecturer in English 1997–; Regents Prof. of Poetry, UCLA 1985–88; Baccalaureate Speaker, Williams Coll. 1993; Poet Laureate of Vt 1994; Visiting Mem. of Faculty, Harvard Univ. 1995; Hurst Prof., Brandeis Univ. 1996; Special Consultant in Poetry at Library of Congress, Washington, DC 1999–2000; Poet Laureate of the USA 2003–04; currently Rosenkranz Writer-in-Residence, Yale Univ.; Fellow, American Acad. of Arts and Sciences; mem. PEN, American Acad. and Inst. of Arts and Letters, Acad. of American Poets (mem. Bd of Chancellors 1999–2006); Rockefeller Foundation Grant 1968–69, Nat. Educ. Asscn grants 1969–70, 1979–80, 1988–89, Nat. Endowment for the Arts Fellowships 1969–70, 1979–80, 1988–89, Vt Council for the Arts Grant 1978–79, Lannan Foundation Grant; Hon. LLD (Williams Coll.) 1993, (Skidmore Coll.) 1995, (Middlebury Coll.) 1996; Acad. of American Poets Prize 1967, Eunice Tietjens Memorial Prize 1971, Guggenheim Foundation Grant 1975–76, 1987–88, American Acad. and Inst. of Arts and Letters Literary Award 1981, Nat. Book

Critics' Circle Award for poetry 1985, Poetry Soc. of America Melville Cane Award 1986, Wellesley Coll. Sara Teasdale Memorial Prize 1986, Bobbitt Natil Prize, Library of Congress 1992, William Carlos Williams Award 1993, PEN/Martha Albrand Award 1995, New Yorker Magazine Award in Poetry 1999, English Speaking Union Ambassador Award 1999, 2001, Bollingen Prize 2001, Wallace Stevens Award 2008. *Publications:* poetry: Firstborn 1968, The House on the Marshland 1975, The Garden 1976, Descending Figure 1980, The Triumph of Achilles 1985, Ararat 1990, The Wild Iris (Pulitzer Prize for Poetry 1993) 1992, Proofs and Theories: Essays on Poetry 1994, The First Four Books of Poems 1995, Meadowlands 1996, Vita Nova 1999, The Seven Ages 2001, October 2004, Averno 2007, A Village Life 2009; contrib. to many anthologies and periodicals. *Address:* Steven Barclay Agency, 12 Western Avenue, Petaluma, CA 94952, USA (office); 14 Ellsworth Park, Cambridge, MA 02139, USA. *Telephone:* (707) 773-0654 (office). *Fax:* (707) 778-1868 (office). *Website:* www.barclayagency.com (office); www.williams.edu/English (office); www.artstomp.com/gluck.

GLUSHCHENKO, Fedor Ivanovich; Russian conductor; b. 29 March 1944, Rostov Region; m. 1st; one s. one d.; m. 2nd Galina Baryshnikova; one d.; ed Moscow and Leningrad State Conservatories, Vienna Acad. of Music; studied under Herbert von Karajan; Chief Conductor, Karelian Radio and TV Symphony Orchestra, Petrozavodsk 1971–73; Chief Conductor and Artistic Dir, Ukrainian State Symphony Orchestra, Kiev 1973–87; British debut in 1989 with BBC Scottish Symphony, also appeared with Royal Liverpool Philharmonic and Scottish Chamber Orchestra; Conductor, Istanbul Opera 1990–91; Chief Conductor and Artistic Dir, J. S. Bach Chamber Orchestra, Yekaterinburg 1996–; Guest Conductor, Moscow Philharmonic Orchestra, Russian State Symphony Orchestra, Moscow Symphony, Ministry of Culture Orchestra and orchestras in Riga, Vilnius, Sverdlovsky, Tbilisi and Tashkent; tours in UK, Sweden, Italy, Denmark, People's Repub. of China, Germany, France and Spain. *Address:* 1st Pryadilnaya str. 11, apt. 5, 105037 Moscow, Russia. *Telephone:* (495) 165-49-46 (home).

GLUSHENKO, Yevgeniya Konstantinovna; Russian actress; b. 4 Sept. 1952; m. Aleksandr Kalyagin; one s. one d.; ed Shchepkin Theatre School; worked with Maly Theatre 1974–97, 2000–; worked with Russian Army Theatre 1997–2000; Order of Friendship 2004; State Prize of Russia 2004. *Films include:* Unfinished Play for Mechanical Piano 1977, Profile and Front-View 1979, Oblomov 1980, First-Time Married 1980, In Love of One's Own Accord (Moscow and West Berlin Film Festival Prizes 1983) 1982, Unikum 1983, Zina-Zinulya 1986, Politseiskiye i vory 1997, Proshchaniye v iyune 2003. *Stage roles:* Liza in Misfortune from Sense 1975, Cordelia in King Lear 1979, Masha in The Savage 1990, Yefrosinya in Infanticide 1991, Matrena in The Hot Heart 1992, Susanna in A Criminal Mother or the Second Tartuffe 1993, Glafira in The Feast of Victors 1995, Vera in The Heart is not a Stone 1997, Vasilisa in The Lower Depths 1998, Emilia in Othello 1999, Kupavina in Sheep and Wolves 2000, Josephine in The Corsican Fury 2001, Zinaida Savishna in Ivanov 2002, Mavra Tarasovna in Truth is Dear, but Happiness is Yet Dearer 2003, Belina in The Imaginary Invalid 2005, Melanya in Children of the Sun 2008. *Television includes:* Zhizn Klima Samgina (series) 1986, Zhenshchiny, kotorym povezlo (miniseries) 1989, Koroleva Margo (series) 1996, Zal ozhidaniya (series) 1998, S novym schastiem! (series) 1999. *Address:* Apt 95, Building 17-2, Lavrushinsky Alley, Moscow, Russia (home). *Telephone:* (495) 959-07-52 (home). *E-mail:* dkaliaguin@hotmail.com (home).

GLYNN, Ian Michael, MD, PhD, FRS, FRCP; British scientist and academic; *Professor Emeritus of Physiology, University of Cambridge;* b. 3 June 1928, London; s. of Hyman Glynn and Charlotte Glynn; m. Jenifer Muriel Franklin 1958; one s. two d.; ed City of London School, Trinity Coll. Cambridge, Univ. Coll. Hosp. London; House Physician, Cen. Middlesex Hosp. 1952–53; Nat. Service, RAF Medical Br. 1956–57; MRC Scholar, Physiological Lab., Cambridge 1956, Fellow, Trinity Coll. 1955–, Demonstrator in Physiology 1958–63, Lecturer 1963–70, Reader 1970–75, Prof. of Membrane Physiology 1975–86, Prof. of Physiology 1986–95, Prof. Emer. 1995–, Vice-Master Trinity Coll. 1980–86; Visiting Prof., Yale Univ. 1969; mem. British MRC 1976–80, Council of Royal Soc. 1979–81, 1991–92, Agric. Research Council 1981–86; Chair. Editorial Bd Journal of Physiology 1968–70; Hon. Foreign Mem. American Acad. of Arts and Sciences 1984, American Physiological Soc.; Hon. MD (Århus) 1988. *Publications:* The Sodium Pump (with J. C. Ellory) 1985; An Anatomy of Thought: the Origin and Machinery of the Mind 1999; The Life and Death of Smallpox (with Jenifer Glynn) 2004; papers in scientific journals. *Address:* Trinity College, Cambridge, CB2 1TQ, England (office). *Telephone:* (1223) 353079 (office). *E-mail:* img10@cam.ac.uk (office). *Website:* www.trin.cam.ac.uk (office).

GLYNN, Robert (Bob) D., Jr, BS, MS; American energy industry executive; *Chairman, Pacific Gas & Electric (PG&E) Corporation;* b. Orange, NJ; ed Manhattan Coll., Long Island Univ.; early career with Long Island Lighting Co. and Woodward-Clyde Consultants; joined Pacific Gas & Electric Co. 1984, Pres. and COO 1995–97, Pres. and CEO Pacific Gas & Electric Corpn 1997–, Chair. 1998–; mem. Business Council, Calif. Comm. for Jobs and Econ. Growth, Bd of Govs San Francisco Symphony. *Address:* Pacific Gas & Electric Corporation, 1 Market Square, Suite 2400, San Francisco, CA 94105, USA (office). *Telephone:* (415) 267-7000 (office). *Fax:* (415) 267-7265 (office). *Website:* www.pgecorp.com (office).

GNAEDINGER, Angelo; Swiss international organization official; *Director-General, International Committee of the Red Cross;* b. 1951; trained as lawyer; examining magistrate, Schaffhausen –1984; joined ICRC 1984, followed field assignments in Middle East and Africa, held various positions in Dept of Operations, Geneva, Head of Detention Div. 1992–94, Del.-Gen. for W Cen. Europe and the Balkans 1994–98, Del.-Gen. for Europe, the Middle East and N. Africa 1998–, Dir-Gen. ICRC 2002–. *Address:* International Committee of the Red Cross, 19 avenue de la Paix, 1202 Geneva, Switzerland (office). *Telephone:* (22) 7346001 (office). *Fax:* (22) 7332057 (office). *E-mail:* press.gva@icrc.org (office). *Website:* www.icrc.org (office).

GNANAM, Arumugham, PhD; Indian scientist; b. 5 Oct. 1932, Veeracholagan, Tamil Nadu; s. of Arumugham Pillai; m. Saratham Gnanam 1953; one s. three d.; ed Cornell Univ., USA; Asst Prof. of Plant Sciences, Cornell Univ. 1967–68; Lecturer, Annamalai Univ. 1968–69; Reader, Madurai Kamaraj Univ. 1969–73, Prof. 1973–85, Dir Centre for Plant Molecular Biology 1990–91; Vice-Chancellor Pondicherry Univ. 1991–99; Vice-Chancellor, Bharathidasan Univ., Trichy 1985–88, Univ. of Madras 1988–90; elected Founder Fellow Tamil Nadu Acad. of Sciences 1976; Nat. Fellow Univ. Grants Comm. 1978, Nat. Lecturer in Botany 1980; Fellow Indian Nat. Science Acad., New Delhi 1984, Nat. Acad. of Sciences, Allahabad 1985; Rafi Ahmed Kidwai Award for best contrib. in plant genetics; Best Teacher Award, Govt of Tamil Nadu. *Publications:* numerous scientific papers. *Leisure interests:* photography, music, pets. *Address:* Office of the Vice-Chancellor, University of Pondicherry, R. Venkataraman Nagar, Kalapet, Pondicherry 605014, India. *Telephone:* 65175.

GNASSINGBÉ, Faure Essozimna, MBA; Togolese politician and head of state; *President;* b. 1966; s. of the late Gnassingbe Eyadéma, fmr Pres. of Togo; ed Paris-Dauphine, France, Georgetown Univ., USA; fmr Deputy, Nat. Ass.; Minister of Public Works, Mines and Telecommunications 2003–05; Pres. of Togo 2005–. *Address:* Office of the President, Palais Présidentiel, ave de la Marina, Lomé, Togo (office). *Telephone:* 221-27-01 (office). *Fax:* 221-18-97 (office). *E-mail:* presidence@republicoftogo.com (office). *Website:* www.republicoftogo.com (office).

GNASSINGBÉ, Kpatcha; Togolese government official; *Minister-delegate at the Presidency of the Republic, responsible for Defence and Veterans;* brother of Faure Essozimna Gnassingbé (q.v.), Pres. of Togo; fmr Dir-Gen. Togo Free Zone Authority; Minister-del. at the Presidency of the Repub., responsible for Defence and Veterans 2005–. *Address:* Ministry of Defence and Veterans, Lomé, Togo (office). *Telephone:* 221-28-12 (office). *Fax:* 221-88-41 (office).

GNEDOVSKY, Yuri Petrovich, PhD; Russian architect; *President, Russian Union of Architects;* b. 3 July 1930, Sverdlovsk (Ekaterinburg); m. Elena Andreyevna Borisova; one s. one d.; ed Moscow Inst. of Architecture, Acad. of Architecture; Sr Researcher Research Inst. of Public Bldgs Acad. of Architecture 1957–63; Head of div., Deputy Dir Cen. Research Inst. of Public Bldg Design 1964–82; Sec. Bd USSR Union of Architects 1982–91; Pres. Russian Union of Architects 1992–, Theatre Architects Partnership 1995–; mem. Council of Int. Union of Architects 1996–2002, currently Vice-Pres.; mem. Presidium, Fellow Russian Acad. of Architecture and Construction Sciences; Fellow Int. Acad. of Architecture Sofia; author of projects of numerous bldgs. including Taganka Theatre, Meyerhold Cen., Russian Cultural Cen. Red Hills in Moscow, Moscow Int. Music House; Pres.'s Prize for Arts and Literature 1999, People's Architect of Russia 2002. *Publications include:* Architecture of Soviet Theatre, Architecture of Public Buildings, World Architecture: A Critical Mosaic 1900–2000 (Vol. 7) 2000, over 60 articles. *Address:* Union of Architects of Russia, Granatny per. 22, 123001 Moscow, Russia (office). *Telephone:* (495) 291-55-78 (office); (495) 203-69-11. *Fax:* (495) 202-81-01 (office). *E-mail:* sarrus@rambler.ru (office). *Website:* www.uar.ru (office).

GNEHM, Edward William, Jr, MA; American diplomatist; *J.B. and Maurice C. Shapiro Visiting Professor of International Affairs and Co-Director, Undergraduate Program in International Affairs, Elliott School of International Affairs, George Washington University;* b. 10 Nov. 1944, Ga; s. of Edward W. Gnehm, Sr and Beverly Thomasson; m. Margaret Scott 1970; one s. one d.; ed George Washington Univ. and American Univ. Cairo; Head, Liaison Office, Riyadh 1976–78; Deputy Chief of Mission, Embassy, Sanaa 1978–81; Dir Jr Officer Div. Personnel, Washington, DC 1982–83, Dir Secr. Staff 1983–84; Deputy Chief of Mission, Amman 1984–87; Deputy Asst Sec. of Defense for Near East and S Asia 1987–89; Deputy Asst Sec. of State, Bureau of Near East and S Asian Affairs 1989–90; Amb. to Kuwait 1990–94, to Australia 2000–01, to Jordan 2001–04; J.B. and Maurice C. Shapiro Visiting Prof. of Int. Affairs, Co-Dir, Undergraduate Program in Int. Affairs, and Elliott School Kuwait Chair for Gulf and Arabian and Peninsula Affairs, Elliott School of Int. Affairs, George Washington Univ. 2004–; Deputy Perm. Rep. to UN 1994–97; Dir-Gen. of Foreign Service, Dir of Personnel US Dept of State, Washington DC 1997–2000; mem. American Acad. of Diplomacy, Washington Inst. of Foreign Affairs, American Foreign Service Asscn, Diplomatic and Consular Officers Retired; Presidential Distinguished Service Award 2000, Dept of Defense Meritorious Service Award 1989 and 1994, Dept of State Superior Honor Award 1991. *Leisure interests:* history, foreign policy, cycling, stamps. *Address:* Elliott School of International Affairs, George Washington University, 1957 E Street, NW, Suite 501, Washington, DC 20052, USA (office). *Telephone:* (202) 994-0155 (office). *Fax:* (202) 994-5477 (office). *E-mail:* ambgnehm@gwu.edu (office); www.gwu.edu/~elliott (office).

GNEUSS, Helmut Walter Georg, DPhil; German academic; *Professor Emeritus of English, University of Munich;* b. 29 Oct. 1927, Berlin; s. of Kurt Gneuss and Margarete Gneuss (née Grimm); m. Mechthild Gretsch 1974; ed Freie Universität Berlin, St John's Coll., Cambridge; Lecturer, German Dept, Univ. of Durham 1955–56, Dept of English, Freie Univ., Berlin 1956–62, Heidelberg Univ. 1962–65; Prof. of English, Univ. of Munich 1965–, now Prof. Emer.; Visiting Professorial Fellow, Emmanuel Coll., Cambridge 1970; Visiting Prof., Univ. of N Carolina, Chapel Hill 1974; mem. Bayerische Akad. der Wissenschaften, British Acad., Österreichische Akad. der Wissenschaften, Medieval Acad. of America; Vice-Pres. Henry Bradshaw Soc. *Publications:* Lehnbildungen und Lehnbedeutungen im Altenglischen 1955, Hymnar und Hymnen im englischen Mittelalter 1968, English Language

Scholarship 1996, Language and History in Early England 1996, Books and Libraries in Early England 1996; Handlist of Anglo-Saxon Manuscripts 2001. *Address:* Institut für Englische Philologie, Universität Munich, Schellingstrasse 3, 80799 Munich, Germany (office). *Telephone:* (89) 21803933 (office). *Fax:* (89) 2180 3399 (office). *E-mail:* department3@anglistik.uni-muenchen.de (office). *Website:* www.anglistik.uni-muenchen.de (office).

GNININVI, Léopold Messan Kokou, DSc; Togolese physicist and politician; *Minister of State for Industry, Crafts, and Technological Innovations;* b. 19 Dec. 1942, Aného; ed Univ. of Dijon, France; Head of Solar Energy Lab., Univ. of Lomé 1978–93, Prof. 1981–97; Dir Nat. Inst. of Educational Science 1979–88, Nat. Dir of Scientific Research 1987–93; three years in exile 1995–98; Sec.-Gen. Convention Démocratique des Peuples Africains, unsuccessful cand. in 1998 presidential election; Minister of State for Mines and Energy 2006–07, for Foreign Affairs and Regional Integration 2007–08, for Industry, Crafts, and Technological Innovations 2008–. *Address:* Ministry of Industry, Crafts, and Technological Innovations, Lomé, Togo (office).

GNUDI, Piero, BEcons; Italian business executive; *Chairman, Enel SpA;* b. 17 May 1938, Bologna; m. Francesca Pagnini; ed Univ. of Bologna; mem. Bd Credito Italiano 1980–83, STET 1984–94, EniChem 1992–93; mem. Bd Istituto per la Ricostruzione Industriale (IRI) (state holding co.) 1994–99, Resp. for Privatization 1997–99, Chair. and CEO 1999–2000, Chair. Bd of Liquidators 2000–, Chair. IRI Foundation 2000–; Chair. Enel SpA (electricity co.) 2002–; mem. Bd ENI (state energy co.) 1995–96; Econ. Counsellor to Ministry of Industry 1995–96; Deputy Chair. Rolo Banca 1473 SpA, Bologna 1994–; Chair. Locat SpA 1995–99, Profingest School of Man. 1995–99; mem. Econ. Policy Comm., Consiglio Nazionale dell'Economia e del Lavoro (CNEL) 2000–; mem. Bd Dirs Unicredito Italiano; mem. Exec. Cttee Confindustria, Steering Cttee Assonime (asscn of Italian corpns), Cttee in charge of strategic devt of the Italian Financial Markets, Exec. Cttee of Aspen Inst., Cttee on corp. governance of listed cos reconstituted on initiative of Borsa Italiana; Pres. Mediterranean Energy Observatory, 'e8' (org. of chairmen of major electricity production cos in the world); Chair. Emittenti Titoli. *Address:* Enel SpA, Viale Regina Margherita 137, 00198 Rome, Italy (office). *Telephone:* (6) 83057610 (office). *Fax:* (6) 83057954 (office). *E-mail:* piero.gnudi@enel.it (office). *Website:* www.enel.it (office).

GNUTTI, Vito; Italian politician, chemical engineer and industrialist; b. 14 Sept. 1939, Lumezzane, Brescia; s. of Basilio Gnutti and Leoni Cenzina; m. Nerina Codini 1965; two d.; Chair. Lombardy Regional Group, Young Industrialists 1975–78, mem. Nat. Council, Confindustria (nat. employers' org.) –1993; mem. Chamber of Deputies 1992–, re-elected as Lega Nord Deputy 1994, elected as Lega Nord Senator April 1996; Minister of Industry 1994–95. *Address:* Via Leno 4, 25010 Isorella, Italy. *Telephone:* (030) 9958130. *Fax:* (030) 9958244. *E-mail:* silexport@inwind.it (office). *Website:* www .silexport.it (office).

GOBA, John; Sierra Leonean artist; b. 1944, Marru Jong; sculptor, based in Freetown. *Website:* caacart.com/goba/goba_frameset.html.

GOBER, Robert; American sculptor; b. 12 Sept. 1954, Wallingford, Conn.; ed Middlebury Coll., Vt, Rome campus of Tyler School of Art (div. of Temple Univ.); arrived in New York 1976, worked as carpenter and handyman; also worked as asst to painter Elizabeth Murray; first solo exhbn at Paula Cooper Gallery, New York, consisting of single work titled Slides of a Changing Painting (1982–83) 1984; began creating three-dimensional works 1980s–90s; in recent years sculptures have become more conceptual, with photography in installations; represented USA at Venice Biennale 2001. *Address:* c/o Marianne Boesky Fine Art, 535 West 22nd Street, New York, NY 10011, USA (office). *Telephone:* (212) 680-9889 (office). *Fax:* (212) 680-9887 (office). *E-mail:* info@marianneboeskygallery.com (office). *Website:* www .marianneboeskygallery.com (office).

GOCKLEY, (Richard) David, BA, MBA; American opera director; *General Director, San Francisco Opera;* b. 13 July 1943, Philadelphia, PA; s. of Warren Gockley and Elizabeth Gockley; m. Adair Lewis; one s. two d.; ed Brown Univ., Columbia Univ., New England Conservatory, Boston; Dir of Music, Newark Acad. 1965–67; Dir of Drama, Buckley School, New York 1967–69; Box Office Man., Santa Fe Opera 1969–70; Asst Man.-Dir Lincoln Center, New York 1970; Business Man., Houston Grand Opera 1970–71, Assoc. Dir 1971–72, Gen. Dir 1972–2006; co-founder Houston Opera Studio 1977; Gen. Dir San Francisco Opera 2006–; mem. Bd of Dirs Texas Inst. of Arts in Educ.; mem. Opera America (pres. 1985–); fmr Chair. Houston Theater Dist; Hon. DHL (Univ. of Houston) 1992, Hon. DFA (Brown Univ.) 1993; League of New York Theaters and Producers Tony Award 1977, Columbia Business School Dean's Award 1982, Nat. Inst. of Music Theater Award 1985, Brown Univ. William Rogers Award 1995. *Operas produced include:* Pasatieri's The Seagull 1974, Porgy and Bess (Grammy Award 1977) 1976, Floyd's Bilby's Doll 1976, Willie Stark 1981, Harvey Milk (by Stewart Wallace and Michael Korie), Philip Glass's Akhnaten 1984, John Adams' Nixon in China (Emmy Award 1988) 1987, Tippett's New Year 1989, The Passion of Jonathan Wade 1991, Meredith Monk's Atlas 1991, Robert Moran's Desert of Roses 1992, Florencia en el Amazonas, Treemonisha, A Quiet Place, Resurrection, Carmen. *Leisure interest:* tennis. *Address:* San Francisco Opera, 301 Van Ness Avenue, San Francisco, CA 94102, USA (office). *Website:* www.sfopera.com (office).

GODAL, Bjørn Tore; Norwegian diplomatist and politician; *Ambassador to Germany;* b. 20 Jan. 1945, Skien; s. of Kari Godal and Aksel Godal; m. Gro Balas 1988; one c.; ed Oslo Univ.; office clerk, Skien 1964–65; Pres. Labour League of Youth 1971–73 (Sec. for org. 1970–71), Fritt Forum (Labour Party's Student Org.) 1967–68; research officer, Labour Party 1973–80, Sec.-Gen. Oslo Labour Party 1980–82, Leader 1982–90 (mem. Cen. Cttee Labour Party 1983–90); Pres. Council of European Nat. Youth Cttees 1973–75; Head of Secr.

Labour Party Group of the Oslo Municipal Council 1986; Deputy Rep. Storting (Parl.), then elected Rep.; Minister of Trade and Shipping 1991–94, of Foreign Affairs 1994–97, of Defence 2000–01; Amb. to Germany 2003–; mem. Council for the Study of Power Distribution in Norway 1972–80, Standing Cttee on Finance 1986–89, on Foreign and Constitutional Affairs 1989–91, on Defence 1997–2000, Storting; Chair. Middle East Cttee 1997–2000, Socialist Int.; mem. North Atlantic Ass. 1997–2000. *Address:* Embassy of Norway, Rauchstr. 1, 10787 Berlin, Germany (office). *Telephone:* (30) 505050 (office). *Fax:* (30) 505055 (office). *E-mail:* emb.berlin@mfa.no (home). *Website:* www.norwegen .org (office).

GODARD, Jean-Luc; French film director; b. 3 Dec. 1930, Paris; s. of Paul Godard and Odile Monad; m. 1st Anna Karina 1961 (divorced); m. 2nd Anne Wiazemsky 1967; ed Lycée Buffon and Faculté des Lettres, Paris; journalist and film critic; film director 1958–; mem. Conseil supérieur de la langue française 1989–; Chevalier, Ordre nat. du Mérite; Prix Jean Vigo for A bout de souffle 1960, Jury's Special Prize and Prix Pasinetti, Venice Festival 1962, Diploma of Merit, Edin. Film Festival 1968 for Weekend, Grand Prix Nat. 1982, Grand Prix Nat. de la culture 1999. *Films:* Opération Béton 1954, Une femme coquette 1955, Tous les garçons s'appellent Patrick 1957, Charlotte et son Jules 1958, Une histoire d'eau 1958, A bout de souffle 1959, Le petit soldat 1960, Une femme est une femme 1961, Les sept péchés capitaux 1961, Vivre sa vie 1962, RoGoPaG 1962, Les carabiniers 1963, Le mépris 1963, Les plus belles escroqueries du monde 1963, Paris vu par ... 1963, Bande à part 1964, Une femme mariée 1964, Alphaville 1965, Pierrot le fou 1965, Masculin-féminin 1966, Made in USA 1966, Deux ou trois choses que je sais d'elle 1966, La chinoise 1967, Loin du Vietnam 1967, Weekend 1967, Le plus vieux métier du monde 1967, Vangelo '70 1967, Le gai savoir (TV) 1968, Un film comme les autres 1968, One Plus One 1968, One American Movie – 1 a.m. 1969, British Sounds 1969, Le vent d'est 1969, Lotte in Italia 1970, Vladimir et Rosa 1971, Tout va bien 1972, Numéro deux 1975, Ici et ailleurs 1976, Bugsy 1979, Sauve qui peut 1980, Passion 1982, Prénom Carmen 1983, Detective 1984, Je vous salue, Marie 1985, Soigne ta droite 1987, Aria (segment) 1987, Nouvelle Vague 1989, Allemagne neuf zero 1991, Hélas pour moi 1993, JLG/JLG 1995, Forever Mozart 1996, De l'origine du XXIᵉsiècle 2000, Eloge de l'amour 2001, Liberté et patrie 2002, Ten Minutes Older: The Cello 2002, Notre musique 2004. *Publication:* Introduction à une véritable histoire du cinéma 1980. *Address:* 26 ave Pierre 1er de Serbie, 75116 Paris, France; 15 rue du Nord, 1180 Roulle, Switzerland (home).

GODBER, John Harry, BEd, MA, PhD, FRSA; British playwright, film and theatre director and actor; *Professor of Contemporary Theatre, Liverpool Hope University;* b. 18 May 1956, Hemsworth, W Yorks.; s. of Harry Godber and Dorothy Godber; m. Jane Thornton; two d.; ed Minsthorpe High, Bretton Hall Coll., Wakefield, Univ. of Leeds; fmr Head of Drama, Minsthorpe High; Artistic Dir Hull Truck Theatre Co. 1984–; currently Prof. of Contemporary Theatre, Liverpool Hope Univ. Coll. and Prof. of Drama, Univ. of Hull; Hon. Lecturer, Bretton Hall Coll.; Hon. DLitt (Hull) 1988, (Lincoln) 1997; Hon. DUniv; Sunday Times Playwright Award 1981, Olivier Award 1984, Joseph Jefferson Award, Chicago 1988, Fringe First Winner (five times), BAFTA Awards for Best Schools Drama and for Best Original Drama 2005. *Plays:* 49 stage plays, including Happy Jack 1982, September in the Rain 1983, Up 'n' Under (Laurence Olivier Comedy of the Year Award 1984) 1984, Bouncers (seven Los Angeles Critics' Awards 1986) 1985, Blood, Sweat and Tears 1986, Shakers, Teechers 1987, Salt of the Earth 1988, On the Piste 1990, Happy Families 1991, April in Paris 1992, The Office Party, Passion Killers 1994, Lucky Sods 1995, Dracula 1995, Gym and Tonic 1996, Weekend Breaks 1997, It Started with a Kiss 1997, Unleashed 1998, Perfect Pitch, Thick as a Brick (music by John Pattison) 1999, Big Trouble in Little Bedroom 1999, Seasons in the Sun 2000, On a Night Like This 2000, This House 2001, Departures, Moby Dick, Men of the World, Reunion, Roast Beef and Yorkshire Pudding; also radio plays and TV programmes. *Film:* Up 'n' Under (writer and dir) 1998. *Television:* The Ritz (BBC 2 series), The Continental (BBC Christmas Special), My Kingdom for a Horse (BBC film) 1991, Chalkface (BBC series) 1991, Bloomin' Marvellous (BBC comedy series) 1997, Thunder Road (BBC 4 film), Oddsquad (BBC); has also written numerous episodes of Brookside, Crown Court and Grange Hill. *Leisure interests:* skiing, sport, literature, reading. *Address:* c/o Alan Brodie, ABR, 6th Floor, Fairgate House, 78 New Oxford Street, London, WC1A 1HB, England (office); St Nicholas Swanland, North Ferriby, HU14 3QY, England (home). *Telephone:* (20) 7079-7990 (office); (1482) 633854 (home). *Fax:* (20) 7079-7991 (office). *Website:* www.alanbrodie .com (office); www.johngodber.co.uk (office). *E-mail:* johnhgodber@hotmail .com (home).

GODDARD, Leonard, MA, BPhil, FAHA; British professor of philosophy; *Professor Emeritus, University of Melbourne;* b. 13 Feb. 1925, Nottingham; s. of Bertram Goddard and Frances Goddard; m. 1st Phyllis Dunsdon 1945 (divorced 1981); m. 2nd Patricia Johnson 1988 (divorced 1997); m. 3rd Dorothy Spencer 2001; two d.; ed Univ. of St Andrews, Univ. of Cambridge; served in RAF 1943–47; Asst Lecturer, Univ. of St Andrews 1952–55; Lecturer and then Sr Lecturer Univ. of New England, Australia 1956–61, Prof. of Philosophy 1961–66, Dean of Arts 1964–66; Prof. of Logic and Metaphysics, Univ. of St Andrews 1966–77, Dean of Arts 1972–74; Boyce Gibson Prof. of Philosophy, Univ. of Melbourne 1977–90, Prof. Emer. 1990–; Visiting Fellow, ANU 1974–76; Australian Centenary Medal 2003. *Publications:* (with R. Routley) The Logic of Significance and Context, Vol. 1 1973, Philosophical Problems 1977, (with B. Judge) The Metaphysics of Wittgenstein's Tractatus 1982. *Leisure interests:* golf, boating. *Address:* Department of Philosophy, University of Melbourne, Parkville, Victoria 3052, Australia (office). *Telephone:* (3) 8344-4000 (office). *Fax:* (3) 8344-4280 (office). *E-mail:* office@philosophy .unimelb.edu.au (office). *Website:* www.philosophy.unimelb.edu.au (office).

GODDARD, William A., III, BS, PhD; American chemist, materials scientist, applied physicist and academic; *Charles and Mary Ferkel Professor of Chemistry, Materials Science and Applied Physics and Director, Materials and Process Simulation Center, Beckman Institute, California Institute of Technology;* b. 29 March 1937, El Centro, Calif.; m. Yvonne Amelia Goddard; one s. three d.; ed UCLA, Calif. Inst. of Tech.; Asst Prof. of Theoretical Chem., Calif. Inst. of Tech. 1965, becoming Assoc. Prof. and Prof. –1978, Prof. of Chem. and Applied Physics 1978–84, Dir NSF Materials Research Group, Calif. Inst. of Tech. 1984–90, Charles and Mary Ferkel Prof. of Chem. and Applied Physics 1984–2001, Charles and Mary Ferkel Prof. of Chem., Materials Science and Applied Physics 2001–, Dir Materials and Process Simulation Center, Beckman Inst. 1990–, Dir NSF Grand Challenges Applications Group 1992–97; Co-founder Molecular Simulations Inc. (now Accelrys) 1984, Dir 1984–95, Chair. 1984–91; Co-founder Schrödinger Inc. 1990, Dir 1990–2000; Co-founder Systine Inc. 2001, Chair. 2003–; Co-founder Allozyne 2004; Co-founder GPC-Rx 2008, mem. Bd Dirs 2008–; mem. SAB 2004–; mem. Materials Research Soc., ACS, NAS 1984–, Int. Acad. of Quantum Molecular Science 1988–; Fellow, American Physical Soc. 1988–, AAAS 1990–; Philosophia Doctorem hc, Chem. (Uppsala) 2004; ACS Buck-Whitney Medal 1978, ACS Award for Computers in Chem. 1988, Calif. Inst. of Tech. Richard M. Badger Teaching Prize in Chem. 1995, Foresight Inst. Feynman Prize 1999, NASA Space Sciences Award 2000, ACS Richard Chase Tolman Prize 2000, ISI most Highly-Cited Chemist 1981–99, Inst. of Molecular Manufacturing Prize in Computational Nanotechnology Design 2002, ACS Award in Theoretical Chem. 2007. *Publications:* more than 780 publs in scientific books and journals. *Address:* Beckman Institute (139–74), California Institute of Technology, 1200 East California Boulevard, Pasadena, CA 91125, USA (office). *Telephone:* (626) 395-2731 (office). *Fax:* (626) 585-0918 (office). *E-mail:* wag@wag.caltech.edu (office). *Website:* www.wag.caltech.edu (office).

GODDIO, Franck, BSc; American archaeologist; b. 1947; ed Ecole Nat. de la Statistique Admin. Economique, Paris; adviser to various int. orgs; gained experience in marine archaeology in late 1970s; founder and Chair. Franck Goddio Soc.; excavated historically important sunken ships and discovered submerged ruins of Alexandria. *Address:* The Franck Goddio Society, 3, Rue Bovy-Lysberg, 1204, Geneva, Switzerland (office). *Fax:* (509) 479-3653 (office). *E-mail:* info@franckgoddio.org (office). *Website:* www.franckgoddio.org (office).

GODEAUX, Jean, Baron, DenD, LicEcon; Belgian central banker; b. 3 July 1922, Jemeppe sur Meuse; s. of Léon Godeaux and Claire de Barsy; m. Thérèse Ceron 1950; two s. three d.; ed Univ. Catholique de Louvain; Bar of Namur 1944–47; Asst, Inst. for Econ. and Social Research 1947; Nat. Bank of Belgium 1947–49; Technical Asst, IMF 1949–50, Alt. Exec. Dir 1950–54, Exec. Dir 1954, Adviser 1992–98; Man. Banque Lambert 1955–59, Man. Partner 1960–72, Pres. 1973–74; Pres. Banking Comm. 1974–82; Gov. Nat. Bank of Belgium 1982–89; Pres. and Chair. BIS 1985–87; Hon. Dir Société Générale de Belgique 1990–; Grand officier de l'Ordre de Léopold, Officier, Légion d'honneur, Commdr, Ordre de St Grégoire le grand, Grand Croix, Ordre du Mérite (Luxembourg), (Austria), Grand Croix, Order of Orange-Nassau (Netherlands), Grand Cordon, Order of Sacred Treasure (Japan), Grand Cordon, Order of Infante Enrique (Portugal). *Leisure interests:* swimming, reading. *Address:* rue du Piroy 2, 5340 Strud-Haltinne, Belgium (home). *Telephone:* (81) 58-82-45 (home). *Fax:* (81) 58-98-43 (home).

GODFREY, Malcolm Paul Weston, CBE, MB, BS, FRCP; British medical practitioner (retd); b. 11 Aug. 1926, London; s. of Harry Godfrey and Rose Godfrey; m. Barbara Goldstein 1955; one s. two d. (one deceased); ed Hertford Grammar School, King's Coll. London and King's Coll. Hosp. Medical School; various appointments in Nat. Health Service 1950–60; Fellow in Medicine and Asst Physician, Johns Hopkins Hosp. Baltimore, Md 1957–58; HQ staff, MRC 1960–74; Dean, Royal Postgrad. Medical School, Hammersmith Hosp. 1974–83; Second Sec. MRC 1983–88; Queen's Hon. Physician 1987–90; Chair. Public Health Lab. Service Bd 1989–96, United Medical and Dental Schools of Guys and St Thomas' Hosps 1996–98; mem. Soc. of Scholars, Johns Hopkins Univ. (USA) 2000; Fellow, Royal Postgraduate Medical School 1985, Imperial Coll. School of Medicine 1999, King's Coll. London 2000; Pres. King's Coll. London Asscn 2002–04; Univ. of London Gold Medal 1950. *Publications:* articles on cardio-respiratory disorders in medical and scientific journals. *Leisure interests:* theatre, reading, current affairs, walking. *Address:* 17 Clifton Hill, St John's Wood, London, NW8 0QE, England (home). *Telephone:* (20) 7624-6335 (home). *Fax:* (20) 7328-9474 (home).

GODINE, David R., MA, EdM; American publisher; b. 4 Sept. 1944, Cambridge, Mass; s. of Morton R. Godine and Bernice Beckwith; m. Sara Sangree Eisenman 1988; one s. one d.; ed Dartmouth Coll., Harvard Univ.; f. David R. Godine Publishers Inc., Publisher and Pres. 1969–; mem. Bds Massachusetts Historical Soc., Massachusetts Horticultural Soc.; Fellow, Pierpoint Morgan Library; Dwiggins Award 1984. *Publication:* Renaissance Books of Science 1970. *Leisure interests:* sailing, skiing. *Address:* David R. Godine Publishers Inc., 9 Hamilton Place, Boston, MA 02108-4715 (office); 196 School Street, Milton, MA 02186, USA (home). *Telephone:* (617) 451-9600 (office). *Fax:* (617) 350-0250 (office). *E-mail:* info@godine.com (office). *Website:* www.godine.com (office).

GODLEE, Fiona N., MB, BChir, FRCP; British editor, writer and publisher; *Editor, British Medical Journal;* m.; two c.; apptd Asst Ed., British Medical Journal (BMJ) 1990, Editorial Dir, establishing open-access online publr BioMed Central, Current Science Group 2000–03, Head of Knowledge Div. BMJ Publishing Group 2003–04, Ed. British Medical Journal 2004–; fmr Pres. World Asscn of Medical Eds; Chair., Cttee on Publication Ethics 2004–05; Harkness Fellow, Harvard Univ. 1994. *Address:* BMJ Publishing Group Ltd, BMA House, Tavistock Square, London, WC1H 9JR, England. *Website:* www.bmjpg.com; www.publicationethics.org.uk.

GODLEY, Wynne Alexander Hugh; British economist; b. 2 Sept. 1926; s. of Hugh John, 2nd Baron Kilbracken and Elizabeth Helen Monteith; m. Kathleen Eleonora Epstein 1955; one d.; ed Rugby School, New Coll., Oxford, Conservatoire de Musique, Paris; professional oboist 1950; joined econ. section, HM Treasury 1956, Deputy Dir 1967–70, Econ. Consultant 1975; Dir Investing in Success Ltd 1970–85, Royal Opera House, Covent Garden 1976–87; Dir Applied Econs Dept, Univ. of Cambridge 1970–85, Prof. 1980–93, Dir (a.i.) 1985–87; Official Adviser Select Cttee on Public Expenditure 1971–73; Visiting Prof., Aalborg Univ. 1987–88; Distinguished Scholar, Jerome Levy Econs Inst., Annandale-on-Hudson, New York 1991–92, 1993–95, 1996–2001; Fellow King's Coll., Cambridge 1970–98, Fellow Emer. 2001–; Dir Kent Opera 1993–; mem. Panel of Economists to advise the Chancellor of the Exchequer 1992–95; Visitor Judge, Inst. of Man., Univ. of Cambridge 2001; Prize for Excellence in Journalism, American Psychoanalytic Asscn, 2003. *Publications:* Pricing in the Trade Cycle (jtly) 1978, Macroeconomics (jtly) 1983; numerous articles in magazines and journals. *Address:* Jasmine House, The Green, Cavendish, Suffolk, CO10 8BB, England. *Telephone:* (1787) 281166.

GODMANIS, Ivars, Dr phys; Latvian scientist and politician; b. 27 Nov. 1951, Rīga; s. of Teodors Godmanis and Ingrida Godmanis; m. Ramora Godmane 1978; two s. one d.; ed Univ. of Latvia; engaged in scientific work since 1973, staff-mem., Inst. of Solid-State Physics, Univ. of Latvia 1973–86, lecturer, Univ. of Latvia 1986–90; active involvement in Movt for Independence of Latvia, Deputy Chair., People's Front; Chair. Council of Ministers of Repub. of Latvia (Prime Minister) 1990–93; with commercial co. Software House 1994–95; Vice-Chair. Asscn of Commercial Banks of Latvia 1995–96; Pres. Latvia Savings Bank (jt stock co.) 1996–97; mem. Saeima (Parl.) 1998–; Minister of Finance 1998–99, of the Interior 2006–07, Prime Minister 2007–09 (resgnd); Programme Man. JSC Radio SWH 2003–; Chair. Latvijas ceļš (Latvia's Way) 2004–07; Co-chair. Latvijas Pirmā Partija/Latvijas ceļš (Latvia's First Party/Latvia's Way) 2007; mem. Bd JSC Latvian Shipping Co. 1997–98, JSC Saliena Real 2002–04; Order of the Three Stars (Second Class); Commemorative medal for participation in the barricades of 1991. *Leisure interest:* tennis. *Address:* Latvia's First Party/Latvia's Way (Latvijas Pirmā Partija/Latvijas ceļš), Elizabetes iela 2, Rīga 1010, Latvia (office). *Telephone:* 6722-6070 (office). *Fax:* 6722-6831 (office). *E-mail:* info@lpplc.lv (office). *Website:* www.lpplc.lv (office).

GODREJ, Adi Burjor, MS; Indian business executive; *Chairman, Godrej Group;* b. 3 April 1942, Bombay (now Mumbai); s. of Dr Burjor Pirojsha Godrej and Jai Burjor Godrej; m. Parmeshwar Mader 1966; one s. two d.; ed St Xavier's High School and Coll., Bombay and Massachusetts Inst. of Tech., USA; Chair. The Godrej Group, Godrej Consumer Products Ltd, Godrej Foods Ltd, Godrej Industries Ltd, Godrej Sara Lee Ltd, Godrej Properties Ltd, Godrej Tea Ltd, Keyline Brands UK; Dir Godrej & Boyce Mfg Co. Ltd, Godrej Agrovet Ltd, Godrej Int. Ltd, Godrej Global MidEast FZE; Chair. Bd Trustees Dadabhai Naoroji Memorial Prize Fund; mem. Tau Beta Pi (The Eng Honour Soc.), Confed. of Indian Industries; mem. Governing Bd Indian School of Business; fmr Chair. and Pres. Indian Soap and Toiletries Makers' Asscn, Cen. Org. for Oil Industry and Trade, Solvent Extractors' Asscn of India, Indo-American Soc., Compound Livestock Feeds Mfrs Asscn, Indo-American Soc., Bd Govs Narsee Monjee Inst. of Man. Studies; Rajiv Gandhi Award 2002, Globoil India Legend 2002, Scodet Lifetime Achievement Award 2003. *Leisure interests:* boating, waterskiing, windsurfing, horse riding, bridge. *Address:* Godrej Industries Ltd, Pirojshanagar, Eastern Express Highway, Vikhroli, Mumbai 400079 (office); Aashraye Godrej House, 67 H Walkeshwar Road, Mumbai 400006, India (home). *Telephone:* (22) 25188060 (office); (22) 25188010 (office); (22) 23642956 (home); (22) 23642955 (home). *Fax:* (22) 25188062 (office); (22) 23645159 (home). *E-mail:* abg@godrej.com (office). *Website:* www.godrejindia.com (office).

GODSELL, Robert (Bobby) Michael, BA, MA; South African business executive; b. 14 Sept. 1952, Boksburg; s. of Cyril H. Godsell and Winnefred (née Stephens) Godsell; m. Gillian Hall 1975; three d.; ed Grosvenor Boys' High School, Univ. of Natal, Univ. of Cape Town; Deputy Prov. Leader Progressive Party, Natal 1969–70, Nat. Youth Chair. 1975–76; Dir Industrial Relations and Public Affairs Anglo-American Corpn 1974–95, CEO Gold Div. 1995–, Deputy Chair. 1995–96, Chair. 1996–; Chair. and CEO AngloGold Ltd 2000–04, CEO AngloGold Ashanti (after Anglo merger with Ashanti Goldfields Co. Ltd) 2004–07; Pres. Chamber of Mines 1992, 1997–98; mem. Nat. Econ. Forum 1994–; fmr mem. Buthelezi Comm. *Publications:* A Future South Africa: Visions, Strategies and Realities 1988 (co-ed.). *Leisure interest:* squash. *Address:* c/o AngloGold Ashanti Ltd, PO Box 62117, Marshalltown 2107, South Africa (office).

GODSOE, Peter C., BSc, MBA, FCA; Canadian business executive; *Chairman, Fairmont Hotels & Resorts Inc.;* b. 2 May 1938, Toronto; s. of Joseph Gerald Godsoe and Margaret Graham Cowperthwaite; m. Shelagh Cathleen Reburn 1963; three c.; ed Univ. of Toronto, Harvard Univ., USA; fmr Deputy Chair. Bd, Pres., CEO and Dir Bank of Nova Scotia, Chair. CEO 1995–2004, also Chair. Bd of Dirs Bank of Nova Scotia Int. 1995–2004; Chair. Sobeys Inc., Fairmont Hotels and Resorts Inc. 2004–; mem. Bd of Dirs Barrick Gold Corpn, Ingersoll-Rand Co. Ltd, Lonmin PLC, Onex Corpn, Rogers Communications Inc., Templeton Emerging Markets Investment Trust PLC, Canadian Council of Christians and Jews, Mount Sinai Hosp.; Vice Chair. Atlantic Inst. for Market Research; fmr Chair. and Dir Scotia Centre Ltd, Scotia Futures Ltd, Scotia Mortgage Corpn; fmr Vice-Chair. and Dir Bank of Nova Scotia Properties Inc., Scotia Properties Québec Inc., Scotia Realty Ltd; fmr Dir various Bank of Nova Scotia subsidiary cos, Alexander & Alexander Services

Inc., Reed Stenhouse Cos Ltd, Nova Scotia Corpn, Scotiabank Jamaica Trust and Merchant Bank Ltd, West India Co. of Merchant Bankers Ltd; fmr Chair. Canadian Bankers' Asscn; Dr hc (Univ. of King's Coll.) 1993, (Concordia Univ.) 1995, (Univ. of Western Ontario) 2001, (Dalhousie Univ.) 2004; Ivey Business Leader Award, Univ. of Western Ontario 2005. *Address:* Fairmont Hotels & Resorts Inc., Canadian Pacific Tower, 100 Wellington Street West, Suite 1600, TD Center, Toronto, Ontario M5K 1B7, Canada (office). *Telephone:* (416) 874-2600 (office). *Fax:* (416) 874-2601 (office). *Website:* www .fairmont.com (office).

GODUNOV, Sergey Konstantinovich; Russian mathematician; b. 17 July 1929, Moscow; m.; two c.; ed Moscow State Univ.; jr, sr researcher, Head of Div., Inst. of Math., USSR (now Russian) Acad. of Sciences 1951–66, Head of Div., Inst. of Applied Math. 1966–69, Head of Div., Computer's Cen. Siberian Br. 1969–80, Head of Lab., Deputy Dir, Exec. Dir Inst. of Math., Siberian Br. 1980–86, Head of Dept, S. Sobolev Inst. of Math., Siberian Br. 1986–; Corresp. mem. USSR (now Russian) Acad. of Sciences 1976, mem. 1994; research in computational math., differential equations, math. physics, mem. Scientific Council Math. Modelling; mem. Ed. Board Siberian Math. Journal; Hon. Prof., Michigan Univ., USA 1997; Lenin Prize, A. Krylov Prize. *Publications:* On the Minkowsky Problem 1948, On the Idea of a Generalized Solution 1960, Numerical Solution of Multidimensional Problems of Gas Dynamics 1976, Elements of Continuum Mechanics (M.A. Lavretev Prize, Russian Acad. of Sciences 1993) 1978, Elliptic Dichotomy of a Matrix Spectrum (with M. Sadkane) 1996, Condition Numbers of the Krylov Bases and Subspaces (with J.-F. Carpraux and S. V. Kuznetsov) 1996, Conceptions of a Group of Rotations and their Spherical Functions (with T. Yu. Mikhailova) 1998, Elements of Continuum Mechanics and Laws of Preservation (with Ye. I. Romenskii) 1998. *Address:* Institute of Mathematics, Siberian Branch of Russian Academy of Sciences, Universitetskyi pr. 4, 630090 Novosibirsk, Russia (office). *Telephone:* (3832) 33-38-87 (office); (3832) 33-25-98 (home). *E-mail:* godunov@ math.nsc.ru (office). *Website:* math.nsc.ru (office).

GODWIN, Gail Kathleen, PhD; American writer; b. 18 June 1937, Birmingham, Ala; d. of Mose Godwin and Kathleen Krahenbuhl; m. 1st Douglas Kennedy 1960 (divorced 1961); m. 2nd Ian Marshall 1965 (divorced 1966); ed Peace Jr Coll. Raleigh, NC and Univs of North Carolina and Iowa; news reporter, Miami Herald 1959–60; reporter and consultant, US Travel Service, London 1961–65; Editorial Asst Saturday Evening Post 1966; Fellow, Center for Advanced Study, Univ. of Illinois, Urbana 1971–72; Lecturer, Iowa Writers' Workshop 1972–73, Vassar Coll. 1977, Columbia Univ. Writing Program 1978, 1981; American specialist, USIS 1976; Guggenheim Fellow 1975–76; librettist for various productions; mem. PEN, Authors' Guild, Authors' League, Nat. Book Critics' Circle; American Acad. and Inst. of Arts and Letters Literature Award 1981. *Publications:* novels including: The Perfectionists 1970, Glass People 1972, The Odd Woman 1974, Violet Clay 1978, A Mother and Two Daughters 1982, The Finishing School 1985, A Southern Family 1987, Father Melancholy's Daughter 1991, The Good Husband 1994, Evensong 1998, Evenings At Five 2003, Queen of the Underworld 2005; non-fiction: Heart 2001; The Making of A Writer: Journals (ed.) 1961–63 2006; also short stories, uncollected stories, novellas and librettos. *Address:* PO Box 946, Woodstock, NY 12498-0946, USA. *E-mail:* gail@gailgodwin.com. *Website:* www.gailgodwin.com.

GOEDGEDRAG, Frits Martinus de los Santos, LLM; Dutch government official; *Governor General of Netherlands Antilles;* b. 1 Nov. 1951, Aruba; m. Dulcie Yvonne Terborg; three s.; ed High School, Colegio Arubano, Catholic Univ. of Nijmegen; legal adviser, Dept of Legal and General Affairs 1977–81; Sec. to the Island Territory of Bonaire 1981–92; Sec. to Council of Govs 1981–92; Gov. of Island Territory of Bonaire 1992–98; Attorney Gen. 1998–2002; Gov.-Gen. of Netherlands Antilles 2002–; Pres. Requisition Cttee Public Prosecutor, Application Comm. for the position of Dir of Dept of Justice; Pres. Judicial Governmental Del. to Netherlands 1998, to Belgium 2000, to Italy 2001; mem. Supervisory Bd Drug Rehabilitation Centre (Brasami), Curaçao, Selection Cttee for Public Servants Judicial Trainees (RAIO), and numerous other govt cttees; mem. Supervisory Bd Antillean Airlines Co., ALM, Cttee of Appeal of Football League of Bonaire, Bd Nat. Parks Foundation (Stinapa), Bonaire, Recompression Tanks Foundation, Zuster Maria Höppner Foundation, Jumpers basketball team, Bonaire; Hon. mem. Rotary Club of Curacao 2004–; Kt, Order of Orange Nassau 1998; Naval Medal 'Almirante Luis Brion' for Distinguished Services Rendered to Venezuelan Navy 1994; Person of the Year, Bonaire Lions Club 1992. *Address:* Office of the Governor, Fort Amsterdam 2, Willemstad, Curaçao, Netherlands Antilles (office). *Telephone:* (9) 461-2000 (office). *Fax:* (9) 461-1412 (office). *E-mail:* kabinet@kgna.an (office). *Website:* www.gouverneur.an (office).

GOEHR, Alexander, MA; British composer; b. 10 Aug. 1932, Berlin; s. of Walter Goehr and Laelia Goehr; m. 1st Audrey Baker 1954; m. 2nd Anthea Felicity Staunton 1972; m. 3rd Amira Katz; one s. three d.; ed Berkhamstead School, Royal Manchester Coll. of Music, Paris Conservatoire (with Olivier Messiaen) and privately with Yvonne Loriod; composer, teacher, conductor 1956–; held classes at Morley Coll., London; part-time post with BBC, being responsible for production of orchestral concerts 1960–; works performed and broadcast world-wide; awarded Churchill Fellowship 1968; Composer-in-Residence, New England Conservatory, Boston, Mass. 1968–69; Assoc. Prof. of Music, Yale Univ. 1969–70; Prof. West Riding Chair of Music Univ. of Leeds 1971–76; Prof. of Music, Univ. of Cambridge 1976–99, Prof. Emer. 1999–, Fellow of Trinity Hall, Cambridge 1976–; Reith Lecturer 1987; Hon. Prof. Beijing Univ. 2001; Hon. mem. American Acad. and Inst. of Arts and Letters; Hon. ARCM 1976; Hon. FRNCM 1980; Hon. FRCM 1981; Hon. DMus (Southampton) 1973, (Manchester), (Nottingham) 1994, (Siena) 1999; Dr hc (Cambridge) 2000. *Works include:* Songs of Babel 1951, Sonata 1952, Fantasias 1954, String Quartet 1956–57, Capriccio 1957, The Deluge 1957–58, La belle dame sans merci 1958, Variations 1959, Four Songs from the Japanese 1959, Sutter's Gold 1959–60, Suite 1961, Hecuba's Lament 1959–61, A Little Cantata of Proverbs 1962, Concerto for Violin and Orchestra 1961–62, Two Choruses 1962, Virtutes 1963, Little Symphony 1963, Little Music for Strings 1963, Five Poems and an Epigram of William Blake 1964, Three Pieces for Piano 1964, Pastorals 1965, Piano Trio 1966, Arden muss sterben (Arden Must Die, opera) 1966, Warngedichte 1967, String Quartet 1967, Romanza 1968, Naboth's Vineyard 1968, Konzertstück 1969, Nonomiya 1969, Paraphrase 1969, Symphony in One Movement 1970, Shadowplay 1970, Sonata about Jerusalem 1970, Concerto for Eleven Instruments 1970, Piano Concerto 1972, Chaconne for Wind 1974, Lyric Pieces 1974, Metamorphosis/ Dance 1974, String Quartet No. 3 1976, Psalm IV 1976, Fugue on the Notes of the Fourth Psalm 1976, Romanza on the Notes of the Fourth Psalm 1977, Prelude and Fugue for Three Clarinets 1978, Chaconne for Organ 1979, Das Gesetz der Quadrille 1979, Babylon the Great is Fallen 1979, Sinfonia 1980, Cello Sonata 1984, Behold the Sun 1984, Two Imitations of Baudelaire 1985, Symphony with Chaconne 1986, Eve Dreams in Paradise 1987, Carol for St Steven 1989, ...in real time 1989, Sing, Ariel 1989, String Quartet No. 4 1990, Still Lands 1990, Bach Variations 1990, The Death of Moses 1991, The Mouse Metamorphosed into a Maid 1991, Colossus or Panic 1992, I Said, I Will Take Heed 1993, Cambridge Hocket 1993, Arianna (opera) 1995, Schlussgesang 1997, Kantan (opera) 2000, Piano Quintet 2001, Second Musical Offering (GFH) 2001. *Address:* Trinity Hall, Trinity Lane, Cambridge, CB2 1TJ (office); Faculty of Music, 11 West Road, Cambridge CB3 9DP, England (office). *Website:* www.mus.cam.ac.uk/external/people/academicstaff/goehr.html (office).

GOEMAERE, Eric, MSc, MD; Belgian physician and international organization executive; ed Leuven Univ., Inst. of Tropical Medicine, Antwerp; fmr Head Mission in S Africa, Médecins Sans Frontières (MSF – Doctors Without Borders); est. training programme for primary health care, Univ. of Cape Town; Co-founder Jt Civil Soc. Monitoring Forum; fmr adviser to WHO; currently Lecturer, Univ. of Witwatersrand; Hon. DrSci (Univ. of Cape Town) 2008. *Address:* School of Public Health, Faculty of Health Sciences, University of Witwatersrand, Johannesburg, South Africa. *Telephone:* (11) 717-2543. *Fax:* (11) 717-2084. *Website:* web.wits.ac.za/Academic/Health/PublicHealth.

GOENKA, Harsh Vardhan, MBA; Indian industrialist; b. 10 Dec. 1957, Calcutta; s. of Rama Prasad Goenka and Sushila Goenka; m. Mala Sanghi 1977; one s. one d.; ed St Xavier's Coll., Calcutta, IMD (Int. Inst. for Managerial Devt), Lausanne, Switzerland; joined family business RPG Enterprises, Vice-Chair. Ceat Ltd, Chair. RPG Enterprises 1988–, RPG Life Science, KEC Int. Ltd, RPG Cables, Bayer (India) Ltd; Zensar Technologies Ltd. *Leisure interests:* sports, art. *Address:* RPG Enterprises Ltd, CEAT Mahal, 463 Dr Annie Besant Road, Mumbai 400 025, India. *Telephone:* (22) 24930621 (office); (22) 23630873 (home). *Fax:* (22) 24938933 (office). *E-mail:* hgoenka@rpgnet.com (office).

GOERENS, Charles; Luxembourg politician; *President, Sahel and West Africa Club, Organisation for Economic Co-operation and Development;* b. 6 Feb. 1952, Ettelbruck; m.; three c.; ed Lycée Technique Agricole; mem. Parl. (Northern Dist constituency) for Parti Démocratique 1979; mem. European Parl. 1982–84, 1994–99; Pres. Ass. of WEU (Interparliamentary European Security and Defence Ass.) 1987–90, 2004; Chair. Parti Démocratique 1989–94; Minister for Co-operation, Humanitarian Action and Defence and for the Environment 1999–2004, of Foreign Affairs 20–31 July 2004; Pres. Sahel and West Africa Club, OECD 2006–; mem. Consultative Ass. of Council of Europe. *Address:* Sahel and West Africa Club/OECD, 2 rue André-Pascal, 75775 Paris Cedex 16, France (office). *Telephone:* 1-45-24-89-87 (office). *Fax:* 1-45-24-90-31 (office). *E-mail:* swac.contact@oecd.org (office). *Website:* www .westafricaclub.org (office).

GOETZ, Hannes, PhD; Swiss business executive; b. 27 March 1934, Schaffhausen; m.; one s.; ed Fed. Inst. of Tech., Zürich; Sika AG, Zürich 1961–62; Sika USA 1962–66; Sika Int. 1966–71; CEO Sika Finance AG 1971–79; Sika Finanz AG 1979–83; Pres. Georg Fischer AG, Schaffhausen 1981–83, CEO 1983–92, mem. Bd 1981–2004; Chair. Bd SAirGroup 1992–2000; mem. Hon. Advisory Bd Flight Safety Foundation. *Address:* c/o Board of Directors, Georg Fischer AG, Amsler-Laffon-Str. 9, 8201 Schaffhausen, Switzerland.

GOFF, Martyn, CBE, FIAL, FRSA, FRSL; British author; *Chairman, Advisory Committee and Administrator, Man Booker Prize;* b. 7 June 1923; s. of Jacob Goff and Janey Goff; ed Clifton Coll.; served in RAF 1941–46; worked in film 1946–48; book seller 1948–70; established Booker Prize (later Man Booker Prize) 1969, Admin. 1970–, Chair. Advisory Cttee Man Booker Prize 2002–; CEO, Book Trust 1970–88, Vice-Pres. 2000– (Deputy Chair. 1991–92, 1996–97, Chair. 1992–96); Fiction Reviewer, Daily Telegraph 1975–88, Non-fiction Reviewer 1988–; Dir and Exec. Chair. Sotheran Ltd antiquarian bookseller 1988–; mem. Arts Council Literature Panel 1973–81, British Nat. Bibliography Research Fund 1976–88, British Library Advisory Council 1977–82, PEN Exec. Cttee 1978–, Exec. Cttee Greater London Arts Council 1982–88, Library and Information Services Council 1984–86; mem. Bd British Theatre Asscn 1983–85; Chair. Paternosters '73 Library Advisory Council 1972–74, New Fiction Soc. 1975–88, School Bookshop Asscn 1977–, Soc. of Bookmen 1982–84 (Pres. 1997–), 1890s Soc. 1990–99, Nat. Life Story Collections 1996–2004, Poetry Book Soc. 1996–99 (mem. Bd 1992–99), Wingate Scholarships 1988–2004, H. H. Wingate Foundation 1998–, Books for Keeps; Vice-Pres. Royal Overseas League 1996–; Dir Nat. Book League, Battersea Arts Centre 1992–97 (Trustee 1981–85); Trustee Cadmean Trust 1981–99, Nat. Literary Trust 1993–2004; Hon. DLitt (Oxford Brookes); The

Bookseller Services to Bookselling Award 2001. *Publications:* fiction: The Plaster Fabric 1957, A Season With Mammon 1958, A Sort of Peace 1960, The Youngest Director 1961, Red on the Door 1962, The Flint Inheritance 1965, Indecent Assault 1967, The Liberation of Rupert Bannister 1978, Tar and Cement 1988; non-fiction: A Short Guide to Long Play 1957, A Further Guide to Long Play 1958, LP Collecting 1960, Why Conform? 1968, Victorian and Edwardian Surrey 1972, Record Choice 1974, Royal Pavilion 1976, Organising Book Exhibitions 1982, Publishing 1988, Prize Writing: An Original Collection of Writings by Past Winners to Celebrate 21 Years of the Booker Prize (ed.) 1989. *Leisure interests:* travel, collecting pictures and books. *Address:* Henry Sotheran Ltd, 2 Sackville Street, London, W1S 3DP (office); 95 Sisters Avenue, London, SW11 5SW, England (home). *Telephone:* (20) 7734-1150 (office); (20) 7228-8164 (home). *Fax:* (20) 7434-2019 (office); (20) 7738-9893 (home).

GOFF, Philip (Phil) Bruce, MA, MP; New Zealand politician; *Leader, Labour Party;* b. 22 June 1953, Auckland; s. of Bruce Charles Goff and Elaine Loyola Goff; m. Mary Ellen Moriarty 1979; two s. one d.; ed Papatoetoe High School, Univ. of Auckland, Nuffield Coll., Univ. of Oxford; Lecturer in Political Science, Auckland Univ.; field officer in Insurance Workers' Union; fmr Chair. Labour Youth Council; MP for Roskill 1981–90, 1993–96, for New Lynn 1996–99, for Mt Roskill 1999–; Minister of Housing, for the Environment, responsible for Government Life Insurance Corpn, in charge of the Public Trust Office 1986–87, of Employment, of Youth Affairs and Assoc. Minister of Educ. 1987–89, Minister of Tourism 1987–88, of Educ. 1989–90, of Foreign Affairs and Trade and of Justice 1999–2005, Minister of Defence 2005–08; Minister of Trade, of Pacific Island Affairs and for Disarmament and Arms Control Oct. 2005–08, of Corrections 2007–08; British Council Scholarship to Nuffield Coll. 1992; mem. Labour Party 1969–, Leader 2008–, Leader of the Opposition 2008–. *Leisure interests:* sports, gardening, squash. *Address:* Executive Wing, Parliament Buildings, Wellington (office); Creightons Road RD 2, Papakura, Auckland, New Zealand (home). *Telephone:* (4) 496-6553 (office); (9) 292-8444 (home). *Fax:* (4) 496-0859 (office). *E-mail:* pgoff@ministers.govt.nz (office). *Website:* www.labour.org.nz (office).

GOFF OF CHIEVELEY, Baron (Life Peer), cr. 1986, of Chieveley in the Royal County of Berkshire; Rt Hon. Lord Goff of Chieveley; **Robert (Lionel Archibald) Goff,** Kt, PC, DCL, FBA; British lawyer (retd); b. 12 Nov. 1926; s. of L. T. Goff; m. Sarah Cousins 1953; two s. (one deceased) two d.; ed Eton Coll., New Coll., Oxford; served in Scots Guards 1945–48 (commissioned 1945); called to the Bar, Inner Temple 1951; Bencher 1975; QC 1967; Fellow and Tutor, Lincoln Coll., Oxford 1951–55; in practice at the Bar 1956–75; a Recorder 1974–75; Judge of the High Court, Queen's Bench Div. 1975–82; Judge in charge of Commercial List and Chair. Commercial Court Cttee 1979–81; Chair. Council of Legal Educ. 1976–82, Vice-Chair. 1972–76, Chair. Bd of Studies 1970–76; Chair. Common Professional Examination Bd 1976–78; Chair. British Inst. of Int. and Comparative Law 1986–2001, Court of Univ. of London 1986–91, Sub-Cttee E (Law) of House of Lords Select Cttee on European Communities 1986–88; Chair. Pegasus Scholarship Trust 1987–2001; Pres. Bentham Club 1986, Chartered Inst. of Arbitrators 1986–91, Holdsworth Club 1988, British Inst. of Int. and Comparative Law 2001–; Hon. Prof. of Legal Ethics, Univ. of Birmingham 1980–81; Maccabean Lecturer 1983; Lionel Cohen Lecturer (Jerusalem) 1987; Cassel Lecturer (Stockholm) 1993; mem. Gen. Council of the Bar 1971–74; mem. Senate of Inns of Court and Bar 1974–82; Chair. Law Reform and Procedure Cttee 1974–76; Lord Justice of Appeal 1982–86; Lord of Appeal in Ordinary 1986–98; Sr Law Lord 1996–98; High Steward Oxford Univ. 1990–2001; Hon. Fellow, Lincoln Coll., Oxford, New Coll., Oxford, Wolfson Coll., Oxford; Hon. Fellow, American Coll. of Trial Lawyers 1997; Grand Cross, Order of Merit (Germany) 1999; Hon. DLitt (City) 1977, (Buckingham) 1989; Hon. LLD (Reading, London) 1990, (Bristol) 1996. *Publication:* The Law of Restitution (with Prof. Gareth Jones) 1966. *Address:* House of Lords, Westminster, London, SW1A 0PW, England (office).

GOGGIN, Brian J., MSc; Irish banking executive; ed Trinity Coll. Dublin; joined Bank of Ireland 1969, various sr man. roles within Bank of Ireland Group in USA, UK and Ireland, CEO Corp. and Treasury 1996, apptd to Court of Bank of Ireland 2000, CEO Wholesale Financial Services 2002–03, CEO Asset Man. Services 2003–04, Group Chief Exec. 2004–09 (resgnd), also Chair. Bristol & West PLC (subsidiary co.) 2005–; Pres. Irish Chapter, Ireland-US Council; Dir Post Office Ltd.

GOGGINS, Colleen A.; American business executive; *Worldwide Chairman, Consumer and Personal Care Group, Johnson & Johnson;* ed Kellogg School of Man., Northwestern Univ.; began working at Johnson & Johnson 1981, has held several sr posts, including Dir of Marketing, Johnson & Johnson GmbH, Germany 1990–92, Pres. Johnson & Johnson Canada 1992–94, Pres. Consumer Products Co. 1995–98, Co. Group Chair. 1998–2001, Worldwide Chair. Consumer and Personal Care Group and mem. Exec. Cttee, Johnson & Johnson 2001–; mem. Exec. Advisory Bd Center for Brand and Product Man., School of Business, Univ. of Wis.-Madison; ranked by Fortune magazine amongst 50 Most Powerful Women in Business in US (37th) 2006, (39th) 2007, (24th) 2008. *Address:* Johnson & Johnson, 1 Johnson & Johnson Plaza, New Brunswick, 08933, NJ USA (office). *Telephone:* (732) 524-0400 (office). *Fax:* (732) 524-3300 (office). *Website:* www.jnj.com (office).

GOGOBERIDZE, Lana, DLitt; Georgian film director, translator, politician and diplomatist; *Deputy Permanent Delegate, United Nations Educational, Scientific and Cultural Organization (UNESCO);* b. 13 Oct. 1928, Tbilisi; d. of Levan Gogoberidze and Ninio Gogoberidze; m. Lado Aleksi-Meskhishvili 1958 (died 1978); two d.; ed Georgia State Univ., Tbilisi, State Inst. of Cinematography (VGIK), Moscow; Lecturer, Tbilisi Univ. 1953–54; mem. CPSU 1965–89; Sec. Georgian Cineasts Union 1968–99; Artistic Dir Kartuli Filmi (Georgian

Film) 1972–99; Dir of studio at Rustaveli Theatre School 1975–; mem. Georgian Parl. 1992–99, Chair. Liberal Democratic Faction 1992–95, Leader of Majority 1995–99, Head, Georgia–France Friendship Group 1997–; mem. Citizens' Union party 1997–99; Head, Perm. Nat. Del. to Council of Europe 1996–99; Amb., Perm. Rep. to Council of Europe 1999–2004, Deputy Perm. Del. to UNESCO 2004–; Minister Plenipotentiary, Georgian Embassy, Paris 2007–; Pres. Int. Asscn of Women Film-Makers 1988; mem. Bd of Union of Georgian Film-Makers; Chevalier, Ordre nat. du Mérite 1997; People's Artist of Georgian SSR 1979. *Films include:* documentary: Gelathi 1957, Tbilisi – 1500 1958, Letters to the Children 1981; fiction: Under the Same Sky 1961, I See the Sun 1965, Boundaries 1970, When the Almond Blossomed (Best Dir Alma Ata Festival) 1973, Turmoil 1974, Interviews on Personal Problems (Grand Prix, San Remo Film Festival 1979, Int. Critics' Prize, Locarno, USSR State Prize 1980, Best Film, Dushanbe Festival) 1978, A Day Longer than Night (Georgia State Prize) 1983, Turnover (Best Dir, Tokyo Film Festival Prize 1987) 1986, Waltz on the Pechora River (Italian Critics' Prize, Navicella Prize, Venice Film Festival Prize 1992, Ecumenical Jury Prize, Berlin Film Festival Prize 1993) 1991. *Publications:* Walt Whitman 1955, Walt Whitman: Leaves of Grass (trans.) 1956, Rabindranath Tagore (trans.) 1957, Foreign Poetry in Georgian (trans.) 1995, What I Remember and How I Remember 2003; also trans of Baudelaire, Verlaine, Eluard, Pasternak. *Leisure interests:* tennis, skiing, painting. *Address:* Embassy of Georgia, 104 avenue Raymond Poincare, 75016 Paris, France (office); UNESCO, 7 Place de Fontenoy, 75352 Paris 07 SP (office); Kazbegi Str. 17, Apt 26, Tbilisi, Georgia (home). *Telephone:* 1-45-68-10-00 (office); (32) 22-76-79 (home). *Fax:* 1-45-67-16-90 (office). *E-mail:* l.gogoberidgze@mfa.gov.ge (office). *Website:* www.unesco.org (office).

GOGOI, Tarun, LLB; Indian lawyer and politician; *Chief Minister of Assam (Asom);* b. 1 April 1936, Rangajan Tea Estate, Jorhat Dist; m. Dolly Gogoi 1972; one s. one d.; ed Gauhati Univ.; mem. Jorhat Municipal Council 1968–71, Leader Assam Youth Community 1971; elected to Lok Sabha 1971–; Jt Sec. All India Congress Cttee 1976, Gen. Sec. 1985; Pres. Assam Pradesh Congress (I) Cttee 1986–1990, 1996–, Vice Pres. 1991; Minister of Food 1991–93; Minister of State for the Food Processing Industry 1993–95; mem. Assam Legis. Ass. 1996–98; Pres. Assam Pradesh Congress Cttee 1996–2001; Chief Minister of Assam (Asom) 2001–; Chair. Assam Small Industrial Devt Corpn; Dir Vayudoot; mem. Bar Council Assam;. *Leisure interests:* travelling, reading, gardening. *Address:* Office of the Chief Minister, Government of Assam, Janata Bhavan, Guwahati 781 006, India (office). *Telephone:* (361) 2266188 (office). *Fax:* (361) 2262069 (office). *E-mail:* asmgovt@asm.nic.in (office). *Website:* assamgovt.nic.in (office).

GOH, Chok Tong, MA; Singaporean politician, lawyer and banker; *Senior Minister and Chairman, Monetary Authority of Singapore;* b. 20 May 1941, Pasir Panjang, Singapore; s. of the late Goh Kah Khoon and of Quah Kwee Hwa; m. Tan Choo Leng 1965; one s. one d. (twins); ed Raffles Inst., Univ. of Singapore and Williams Coll., USA; with Singapore Admin. Service 1964–69, Neptune Orient Lines Ltd 1969–77; MP 1976–; Sr Minister of State, Ministry of Finance 1977–79, Minister for Trade and Industry 1979–81, Minister for Health and Second Minister for Defence 1981–82, Minister for Defence 1982–91, First Deputy Prime Minister 1985–90; Prime Minister of Singapore 1990–2004; Sr Minister in Prime Minister's Office 2004–; Chair. Monetary Authority of Singapore 2004–; mem. Central Exec. Cttee People's Action Party 1979–, Second Asst Sec.-Gen. 1979–84, Asst Sec.-Gen. 1984–89, First Asst Sec.-Gen. 1989–92, Sec.-Gen. 1992–2004; Perm. mem. Pres.'s Council for Minority Rights; Grand Knight Cordon (Special Class) of the Most Exalted Order of the White Elephant (Thailand) 1997; Hon. Companion of the Order of Australia 2005; Medal of Honour, Nat. Trade Union Congress (NTUC) 1987, Distinguished Comrade of Labour Award 2001, Jawaharla Nehru Award for Int. Understanding (India) 2004. *Leisure interests:* tennis, golf. *Address:* Monetary Authority of Singapore (MAS), 10 Shenton Way, MAS Bldg, Singapore 079117; Prime Minister's Office, Orchard Road, Istana, Singapore 238823 (office). *Telephone:* 62255577 (MAS); 62358577 (office). *Fax:* 62299491 (MAS); 67324627 (office). *E-mail:* Goh_Chok_Tong@pmo.gov.sg (office); webmaster@mas.gov.sg. *Website:* www.pmo.gov.sg (office); www.mas.gov.sg.

GOH, Keng Swee, PhD; Singaporean politician; b. 6 Oct. 1918, Malacca; s. of Goh Leng Inn and Tan Swee; m. Alice Woon 1942; one s.; ed Anglo-Chinese School, Singapore and Raffles Coll., Univ. of London, UK; fmrly Vice-Chair. People's Action Party; fmr mem. Legis. Ass. from Kreta Ayer Div. and Minister for Finance 1959–65; initiated Singapore's industrialization plan, the establishment of Econ. Devt Bd; Minister of Defence 1965–67, of Finance 1967–70, of Educ. 1979–81, 1981–84, of Defence 1970–79, concurrently Deputy Prime Minister 1973–80, First Deputy Prime Minister 1980–84 and with responsibility for the Monetary Authority of Singapore 1980–81 (Deputy Chair. –1992); Econ. Adviser to Chinese Govt 1985–; mem. Governing Council, Asian Inst. for Econ. Devt and Planning, Bangkok 1963–66; Ramon Magsaysay Award for Govt Service 1972. *Publications:* Urban Incomes and Housing; a Report on the Social Survey of Singapore, 1953–54 1958, Economics of Modernization and Other Essays 1972, The Practice of Economic Growth 1977. *Address:* Parliament House, 1 Parliament Place, Singapore 178880 (office). *Website:* www.gov.sg/parliament.

GOH, Kun, MS; South Korean politician; b. 2 Jan. 1938, Seoul; m.; three s.; ed Kyung Ki High School, Seoul Nat. Univ.; Pres. Gen. Students' Council, Seoul Nat. Univ. 1959; Asst Jr Official Ministry of Home Affairs 1962–65, Asst Dir Planning Office 1965–68; Dir Interior Dept Jeonbuk Prov. 1968–71; Commr New Village Movt 1971–73; Vice-Gov. Gangwon Prov. 1973; Gov. of S Jeolla Prov. 1975–79; Chief Sec. of Political Affairs to the Pres., Chong Wa Dae (The Blue House) 1979–80; Chief Adviser Korea Research Inst. for Human Settlement 1980; Minister of Transportation 1980–81, of Agric. and Marine

Affairs 1981–82; Visiting Fellow, Harvard Univ. 1983; Visiting Prof. MIT 1984; mem. 12th Nat. Ass. 1985–88; Minister of Home Affairs 1987; Dir Local Admin. Bureau 1973–75; Mayor Seoul Metropolitan Govt 1988–90; Pres. Myong Ji Univ. 1994–97; Co-Pres. Korea Fed. for Environment Movt 1996–97; Prime Minister of Repub. of Korea 1997–98, 2003–04 (resgnd); Mayor of Seoul 1998–2002; Acting Pres. of Repub. of Korea March–May 2004; Pres. Transparency Int. Korea 2002–04 (resgnd); Hon. LLD (Won Kwang Univ.) 1992, (Syracuse Univ.) 2001; Order of Service Merit (Blue Stripes) 1972, (Red Stripes) 1982; Outstanding Policy-Maker Award, Korea Univ. 2000, Transparency Int. Global Integrity Medal 2001, Polestar Order from the Mongolian Pres. 2002. *Address:* c/o Office of the Prime Minister, 77 Sejong-no, Jongno-gu, Seoul, Republic of Korea.

GOIRIGOLZARRI TELLAECHE, José Ignacio, DEcon; Spanish banking executive; *President and Chief Operating Officer, Banco Bilbao Vizcaya Argentaria SA;* b. 1954, Bilbao; m., two c.; ed Universidad de Deusto, Leeds Univ., UK; joined the Banco de Bilbao 1978, worked in Strategic Planning, worked with Banco Bilbao Vizcaya Holdings, apptd Gen. Man. 1992, Man. Dir Retail Banking 1995–2000, Man. Dir Banco Bilbao Vizcaya Argentaria (BBVA), US Div. 2000–01, Pres. and COO BBVA 2001–, mem. Bd of Dirs 2001–; Vice-Pres. Repsol YPF 2002–03; mem. Bd of Dirs Telefonica SA 2000–03. *Address:* Banco Bilbao Vizcaya Argentaria SA, Plaza San Nicolás 4, Bilbao 48005, Vizcaya, Spain (office). *Telephone:* (944) 875555 (office). *Fax:* (944) 876161 (office). *Website:* www.bbv.es (office).

GOLAN, Menahem; Israeli film director and film producer; b. 31 May 1929, Tiberius; ed Old Victoria, London; f. Noah Films with Yoram Globus (q.v.) 1963; Sr Vice-Pres. Cannon Group Inc. 1979–89; founder and Chair., CEO 21st Century Production Corpn 1989–. *Films include:* Over the Top, Delta Force, Over the Brooklyn Bridge, Enter the Ninja, The Magician of Lublin, Barfly, Surrender, Death Wish IV, Superman IV, Street Smart, Dancers, 52 Pickup, Otello, The Assault, Hanoi Hilton, Cannon Movie Tales, Masters of the Universe, Duet for One, Tough Guys Don't Dance, Shy People, Hanna's War, The Rose Garden, Rope Dancing, The Phantom of the Opera, Armstrong; all have Golan and Globus as exec. producers.

GOLANI, Rivka; Canadian violist and painter; b. 22 March 1946, Israel; d. of Jacob and Lisa Gulnik; m. Jeremy Fox 1993; one s.; ed Univ. of Tel-Aviv; studied with Oedon Partos; concerts as soloist world-wide; has inspired many new works including viola concerti by Holloway, Hummel, Fontajn, Colgrass, Holmboe, Yuasa and Turner, solo works by Holliger, Holmboe and others; has collaborated with composers as a visual artist in presenting multimedia performances; art exhbns in Israel, UK, Germany and N America; Grand Prix du Disque 1985. *Recordings include:* three-album set of solo works by J. S. Bach. *Publication:* Birds of Another Feather (book of drawings). *Address:* Michael Brewer Artists Management, 8 Toynbee Close, Osbaston, Monmouth, NP25 3NU, Wales (office); c/o Margaret Barkman, 54 Long Point Drive, Richmond Hill, Ont. L4E 3W8, Canada. *Telephone:* (1600) 711608 (office); (416) 722-6977. *E-mail:* mbam@dsl.pipex.com (office); margaretbarkman@yahoo.com. *Website:* www.mbam.co.uk (office); ca.geocities.com/artistassociatesonline. *Fax:* (905) 773-6261.

GOLANT, Victor Yevgenyevich, PhD; Russian physicist; *Chief Editor, Zhurnal tekhnicheskoi fiziki (Journal of Technical Physics);* b. 14 Jan. 1928; m.; one s. two d.; ed Leningrad Polytech Inst.; engineer, head of lab. factories in Leningrad; Sr Researcher, Head of Lab., Head of Div. Inst. of Physics and Eng; Prof., Head of Chair Leningrad Tech. Univ.; Dir Ioffe Inst. of Physics and Tech.; Chief Ed. Zhurnal tekhnicheskoi fiziki (Journal of Technical Physics); Corresp. mem. USSR (now Russian) Acad. of Sciences 1984, mem. 1990–; research in physics of plasma and thermonuclear synthesis; USSR State Prize 1991. *Publications include:* Fundamentals of Plasma Physics 1977, Super High-Frequency Method of Plasma Diagnostics 1985. *Address:* Ioffe Institute of Physics and Technology, Polytekhnicheskaya 26, 194021 St Petersburg, Russia (office). *Telephone:* (812) 247-41-50, ext. 52 (office); (812) 552-59-08 (home).

GÖLCÜKLÜ, Ahmet Feyyaz; Turkish judge and academic; b. 4 Oct. 1926, Ula; s. of Zeki and Ruhiye Gölcüklü; m. (divorced 1977); two s.; ed Univs of Istanbul and Neuchâtel; Asst Prof. Faculty of Political Sciences, Univ. of Ankara 1954–, Assoc. Prof. 1958–, Prof. 1965–, Dir School of Journalism and Broadcasting 1969–72, Dean, Faculty of Political Sciences 1973–76, now Prof. Emer.; Judge, European Court of Human Rights 1977–98; mem. Turkish Consultative Ass. (Constituent Ass.) 1981–82; Dir of Human Rights Research and Implementation Centre, Ankara Univ. 1988–. *Publications:* Examination of the Accused Person in Penal Matters 1952, Personal Liberty of the Accused in Criminal Procedure 1958, Research on Juvenile Delinquency in Turkey 1963, The Turkish Penal System 1965, Mass Communication Law 1973, The European Convention on Human Rights and its Implementation 1994. *Address:* University of Ankara, Tandoğan, 06100 Ankara, Turkey.

GOLD, Christina A.; Canadian business executive; *President and CEO, Western Union Financial Services, Inc.;* ed Carleton Univ., Ottawa; early career with Avon where she served as Pres. Avon North America; Pres. and CEO Excel Communications –2002; joined Western Union in 2002, Pres. and CEO Western Union Financial Services, Inc. 2006–, mem. First Data Corpn Exec. Cttee; mem. Bd of Dirs ITT Industries, New York Life, Torstar Corpn; Batisseur hon. degree (Professional Business School of Montreal); named by Business Week amongst Top 25 US Managers 1996, ranked by Fortune magazine amongst 50 Most Powerful Women in Business in the US (49th) 2003, (49th) 2006, ranked by Forbes Magazine amongst 100 Most Powerful Women (56th) 2007, (90th) 2008, Award of Distinction, Faculty of Commerce and Admin, Concordia Univ., Montreal. *Address:* Western Union Financial Services, Inc., 13022 Hollenberg Drive, Bridgeton, MO 63044, USA (office). *Website:* www.westernunion.com (office).

GOLD, Jack, BSc (Econ), LLB; British film director; b. 28 June 1930; m. Denyse Macpherson 1957; two s. one d.; ed Univ. of London; Asst Studio Man., BBC radio 1954–55; Ed. Film Dept, BBC 1955–60; Dir TV and film documentaries and fiction 1960–. *Television films include:* Tonight, Death in the Morning (BAFTA Award) 1964, Modern Millionairess, Famine, Dowager in Hot Pants, World of Coppard (BAFTA Award 1967), Mad Jack (Grand Prix, Monte Carlo) 1971, The Resistible Rise of Arturo Ui, Stockers Copper (BAFTA Award 1972), Catholics (Peabody Award) 1974, The Naked Civil Servant (Italia Prize, Int. Emmy, Critics Award, Desmond Davies Award 1976), 1976, Thank You Comrades, A Walk in the Forest, Merchant of Venice, Praying Mantis, Macbeth, L'Elégance 1982, The Red Monarch 1983, The Tenth Man 1988, The Rose and the Jackal 1989, Ball Trap on Côte Sauvage 1989, The Shlemiel, The Shlemazi and The Doppess 1990, The War that Never Ends 1991, She Stood Alone 1991, The Last Romantics 1992, Spring Awakening 1995, Kavanagh QC 1995, Heavy Weather 1996, Mute of Malice 1997, Blood Money 1997, Into the Blue 1997, Care in the Community 1998, Goodnight Mr. Tom (Silver Hugo Award, Chicago 1998, BAFTA Award 1999) 1998, The Remorseful Day (BAFTA Award 2001) 2001, Kavanagh QC 2001, The John Thaw Story 2002, The Brief. *Theatre:* Council of Love, The Devil's Disciple, Danger Memory, This Story of Yours, Three Hotels, Crossing Jerusalem, 12 Angry Men. *Films include:* The Bofors Gun 1968, Mad Jack 1971, The National Health (Evening News Best Comedy Film 1973) 1973, Who? 1974, Man Friday 1975, Aces High (Evening News Best Film Award) 1976, The Medusa Touch 1977, The Sailor's Return (Karoly Jary Award, Martin Luther King Award, Monte Carlo Catholic Award, Monte Carlo Critics Award) 1978, Little Lord Fauntleroy (Christopher Award) 1981, A Lot of Happiness (Int. Emmy Award) 1983, Sakharov (Ace Award) 1984, Me and the Girls 1985, Murrow (Ace Award) 1986, Escape from Sobibor, (Golden Globe Award) 1987, Stones for Ibarra 1988, The Lucona Affair 1993, Return of the Native 1994, Spring Awakening 1994, Into the Blue 1997. *Leisure interests:* music, reading. *Address:* 24 Wood Vale, London, N10 3DP, England (home). *Telephone:* (20) 8883-3491 (home). *Fax:* (20) 8444-3406 (home).

GOLD, Phil, CC, OQ, MDCM, PhD, FRCP(C), MACP, FRSE; Canadian physician and academic; *Douglas G. Cameron Professor of Medicine, McGill University; Professor of Physiology and Oncology, McGill University Heath Centre and Research Institute;* b. 17 Sept. 1936, Montreal; s. of the late Jack and Rose Gold; m. Evelyn Katz; three c.; ed McGill Univ.; postgraduate training and research, The McGill Univ. Medical Clinic of The Montreal Gen. Hosp.; Medical Research Council of Canada Centennial Fellow 1967–68, Assoc. and Career Scientist 1969–80; Lecturer, Teaching Fellow, Asst and Assoc. Prof., Dept of Physiology and Dept of Medicine, McGill Univ. 1965–73, Prof. of Medicine and Clinical Medicine, 1973–, of Physiology 1974–, of Oncology 1989–; Chair. Dept of Medicine 1985–90, Douglas G. Cameron Prof. of Medicine 1987–; Dir McGill Cancer Centre 1978–80; Dir McGill Univ. Medical Clinic (now Centre), The Montreal Gen. Hosp. 1980–, Exec. Dir Clinical Research Centre, RIMUHC 1995–; Sr Physician, The Montreal Gen. Hosp. 1973–, Physician-in-Chief 1980–95, Sr Investigator Hosp. Research Inst.; Hon. Consultant, Royal Victoria Hosp., Montreal 1981–; mem. numerous professional socs, scientific research bds and orgs etc. including Royal Soc. of Canada, American Soc. for Clinical Investigation, Asscn of American Physicians; Hon. DSc (McMaster); numerous honours and awards including Sir Arthur Sims Commonwealth Travelling Professorship 1998, Carl Govesky Memorial Award 1999, 20th Anniversary of L'Actualité Medicale Award for Outstanding Contrib. to Medicine 2000, Montreal Gen. Hosp. Corpn Merit Award 2002, Queen Elizabeth II Golden Jubilee Medal 2002, honoured as Founding Dir of McGill Cancer Centre's 25th Anniversary 2003, Edwin F. Ullman Award, American Asscn of Clinical Chem. 2004, Award of Exception Merit, Canadian Soc. for Immunology 2004, Alpha Omega Achievement Medal, Alpha Omega Int. Dental Fraternity 2006, Isaak Walton Killam Award in Medicine of the Canada Council, Nat. Cancer Inst. of Canada R.M. Taylor Medal, Heath Medal of the MD Anderson Hosp., Inaugural Ernest C. Manning Foundation Award, Johann-Georg-Zimmerman Prize for Cancer Research, Medizinische Hochschule, Germany, Abbott Award (ISOBM), Japan, inauguration of Phil Gold Chair in Medicine, McGill Univ. Health Centre 2006. *Publications:* 146 articles in professional journals since 1988. *Leisure interests:* photography, sailing, cinema, music, literature. *Address:* The Clinical Research Centre, Suite D1 173, Montreal General Hospital, 1650 Cedar Avenue, Montreal, PQ H3G 1A4, Canada (office). *Telephone:* (514) 934-1934 (ext. 43061) (office). *Fax:* (514) 934-8338 (office). *E-mail:* phil.gold@mcgill.ca (office). *Website:* www.mcgill.ca (office).

GOLDBERG, Whoopi; American comedienne and actress; b. (Caryn Johnson), 13 Nov. 1955, New York; d. of Robert Johnson and Emma Harris; m. 2nd Dave Claessen 1986 (divorced 1988); one d.; m. 3rd Lyle Trachtenberg 1994 (divorced 1995); first stage appearance, aged 8, Hudson Guild Theater, New York; worked with Helena Rubinstein Children's Theater; moved to San Diego 1974; co-f. San Diego Repertory Theater, appeared in Mother Courage (Brecht) and Getting Out (Marsha Norman); moved to San Francisco, became mem. Blake St Hawkeyes Theater; toured USA in The Spook Show; co-wrote and appeared in Moms (one-woman show); Broadway debut, Lyceum Theater 1984; f. One Ho Productions (production co.) 1992; Grammy Award for Best Comedy Album 1985, Hans Christian Andersen Award for Outstanding Achievement by a Dyslexic, Mark Twain Prize for American Humor, Kennedy Center for Performing Arts 2001. *Films:* The Color Purple (Acad. Award nomination as Best Actress, Image Award from NAACP, Golden Globe Award, Hollywood Foreign Press Asscn), Jumpin' Jack Flash 1986, Burglar 1987, Fatal Beauty 1987, Ghost 1990, Soapdish 1991, Sarafina 1992, Sister Act 1992, The Player 1992, Made in America 1992, Alice 1993, Sister Act II 1993,

Corrina Corrina 1993, The Lion King (voice) 1994, Boys on the Side 1994, Moonlight and Valentino, Bogus, Eddie, The Associate 1996, The Ghost of Mississippi 1996, How Stella Got Her Groove Back 1998, Deep End of the Ocean 1999, Girl Interrupted 1999, Rat Race 2001, Kingdom Come 2001, Monkeybone 2001, Golden Dreams 2001, Star Trek: Nemesis 2002, Blizzard (voice) 2002, More Dogs Than Bones 2002, Good Fences 2003, Blizzard (voice) 2003, Pinocchio 3000 (voice) 2004, Jiminy Glick in La La Wood 2004, Racing Stripes (voice) 2005. *Plays include:* A Funny Thing Happened on the Way to the Forum, Ma Rainey's Black Bottom 2003. *Television includes:* In the Gloaming 1997, Cinderella 1997, A Knight in Camelot 1998, Alice in Wonderland 1999, Jackie's Back! 1999, The Magical Legend of the Leprechauns 1999, What Makes a Family 2001, Call Me Claus 2001, It's a Very Merry Muppet Christmas Movie 2002, Good Fences 2003, Whoopi (series) 2003, Littleburg (series) 2004, The View 2007–; producer, Hollywood Squares 1998–2002. *Address:* One Ho Productions, 375 Greenwich Street, Tribeca Film Center, New York, NY 10013; c/o Brad Cafarelli, Bragman/Nyman/Cafarelli, 9171 Wilshire Blvd, #300, Beverly Hills, CA 90210, USA.

GOLDBERGER, Marvin Leonard, PhD; American physicist and academic; *Professor Emeritus of Physics, University of California, San Diego;* b. 22 Oct. 1922, Chicago, Ill.; s. of Joseph and Mildred Sedwitz Goldberger; m. Mildred C. Ginsburg 1945; two s.; ed Carnegie Inst. of Technology and Univ. of Chicago; Research Assoc. Radiation Lab., Univ. of Calif. (Berkeley) 1948–49, MIT 1949–50; Asst Prof., Prof., Univ. of Chicago 1950–57; Eugene Higgins Prof. of Physics, Princeton Univ. 1957–77, Chair. Physics Dept 1970–76, Joseph Henry Prof. of Physics 1977–78; Pres. Calif. Inst. of Tech. 1978–87; Dir Inst. for Advanced Study 1987–91; Prof. of Physics, Univ. of Calif., LA 1991–93, Univ. of Calif., San Diego 1993–2000, Prof. Emer. 2000– (Dean Div. of Natural Sciences 1994–2000); Chair. Fed. of American Scientists 1971–72; mem. NAS, American Acad. of Arts and Sciences; Hon. ScD (Carnegie-Mellon Univ. 1979, Univ. of Notre Dame 1979, Brandeis Univ. 1991); Hon. LLD (Occidental Coll. 1980); Hon. DHL (Hebrew Union Coll. 1980, Univ. of Judaism 1982); Dannie Heineman Prize for Mathematical Physics 1961. *Publication:* Collision Theory (with K. M. Watson) 1964. *Leisure interests:* running, tennis, cooking. *Address:* Department of Physics, 0354, University of California, San Diego, 9500 Gilman Drive, La Jolla, CA 92093-0354, USA (office). *E-mail:* mgoldberger@ucsd.edu (office). *Website:* physics.ucsd.edu (office).

GOLDBLUM, Jeff; American actor; b. 22 Oct. 1952, Pittsburgh; m. 1st Patricia Gaul (divorced); m. 2nd Geena Davis (q.v.) (divorced); studied at New York Neighborhood Playhouse. *Plays include:* The Pillowman (Broadway) 2005. *Films include:* California Split 1974, Death Wish 1974, Nashville 1975, Next Stop Greenwich Village 1976, Annie Hall 1977, Between the Lines 1977, The Sentinel 1977, Invasion of the Bodysnatchers 1978, Remember My Name 1978, Thank God it's Friday 1978, Escape from Athena 1979, The Big Chill 1983, The Right Stuff 1983, Threshold 1983, The Adventures of Buckaroo Banzai 1984, Silverado 1985, Into the Night 1985, Transylvania 6-5000 1985, The Fly 1986, Beyond Therapy 1987, The Tall Guy 1989, Earth Girls are Easy 1989, First Born (TV) 1989, The Mad Monkey 1990, Mister Frost 1991, Deep Cover 1992, The Favour, the Watch and the Very Big Fish 1992, Father and Sons 1993, Jurassic Park 1993, Lushlife (TV) 1994, Future Quest (TV) 1994, Hideaway 1995, Nine Months 1995, Independence Day 1996, The Lost World 1997, Holy Man 1998, Popcorn 1999, Chain of Fools 2000, Angie Rose 2000, Cats and Dogs 2001, Igby Goes Down 2002, Dallas 362 2003, Spinning Boris 2003, Incident at Loch Ness 2004, The Life Aquatic with Steve Zissou 2004, Mini's First Time 2006, Fay Grim 2006, Man of the Year 2006; producer Little Surprises 1995, Holy Man 1999. *Address:* The Gersh Agency, 232 North Canyon Drive, Suite 201, Beverly Hills, CA 90210; c/o Keith Addis, Industry Entertainment, 2401 Main Street, Santa Monica, CA 90405, USA. *Telephone:* (301) 274-6611 (Gersh).

GOLDEMBERG, José, BSc, PhD; Brazilian physicist, academic and government official; b. 27 May 1928, Santo Ângelo; ed Universidade de São Paulo, Univ. of Saskatchewan, Canada, Univ. of Illinois, USA; Asst Prof., Universidade de São Paulo 1955, Assoc. Prof. 1955–67, Full Prof. of Physics 1967–, Dir Inst. of Physics 1970–78, Rector Universidade de São Paulo 1986–89; Research Assoc., High Energy Physics Lab., Stanford Univ., USA 1962–63; Assoc. Prof., Univ. of Paris (Orsay) 1964; Prof. of Physics, Univ. of Toronto, Canada 1972–73; Sr Research Assoc., Princeton Univ., USA several periods 1977–82; Visiting Prof., Woodrow Wilson School, Princeton Univ. 1993–94, Int. Acad. of the Environment, Geneva, Switzerland 1995, Center for Latin American Studies, Stanford Univ. 1996–97; Pres. Energy Co. of State of São Paulo 1983–86; Sec. of State for Science and Tech., Fed. Govt 1990–91; Minister of State for Educ., Fed. Govt 1991–92; Acting Sec. of State for Environment, Fed. Govt 1992; Sec. of State for the Environment, State of São Paulo 2002–06; Chair. Bd International Energy Initiative 1995–, World Energy Assessment 1998–; mem. Advisory Bd Alliance for Global Sustainability 1997–, Environmental Advisory Bd Asea Brown Boveri (ABB) 1998–, World Comm. on Dams 1998–, Nat. Council for Energy Policy of Brazil 1999–2001, Sustainable Energy Inst.; Pres. Brazilian Asscn for the Advancement of Science 1979–81; mem. Brazilian Acad. of Sciences, Third World Acad. of Science; Ordem Nacional Do Mérito Científico 1995; Hon. DSc (Technion – Israel Inst. of Tech.) 1991; Mitchell Prize for Sustainable Devt (co-recipient) 1991, José Goldemberg Chair in Atmospheric Physics est. at Tel-Aviv Univ. 1994, Volvo Environment Prize (co-recipient) 2000, Blue Planet Prize, Asahi Glass Foundation 2008. *Publications:* several books and numerous scientific papers on nuclear physics, environment and energy in professional journals. *Address:* Centro Nacional de Referência Em Biomassa, Iee, Av. Professor Luciano Gualberto 1289, Cidade Universitária, 05508-010 Sao Paulo, SP, Brazil (office). *Telephone:* (11) 34836983 (office). *Fax:* (11) 30912649 (office). *E-mail:* goldemb@iee.usp.br (office). *Website:* www.iee.usp.br (office).

GOLDENBERG SCHREIBER, Efrain; Peruvian politician, business executive and lawyer; b. 28 Dec. 1929, Lima; s. of Aron Goldenberg and Charna Schreiber; m. Irene Pravatiner 1952; one s. four d.; ed San Andrés (fmrly Anglo-Peruvian) School, Universidad Nacional Mayor de San Marcos; pvt. entrepreneur 1951–; fmr Dir FOPEX, Sociedad Nacional de Pesquería and other cos; Minister of Foreign Affairs 1993–94, Pres. Council of Ministers (Prime Minister) and Minister of Foreign Affairs 1994–95; work in pvt. sector 1995–99; Minister of Econ. and Finance 1999–2000. *Address:* Av. Javier Prado Oeste 1661, Lima 27, Peru. *Telephone:* (1) 421-2264. *Fax:* (1) 221-6458.

GOLDHABER, Maurice, PhD, FAAS; American physicist and academic; *Distinguished Scientist Emeritus, Brookhaven National Laboratory;* b. 18 April 1911, Lemberg, Austria; s. of Charles Goldhaber and Ethel Frisch Goldhaber; m. Gertrude Scharff 1939 (died 1998); two s.; ed Berlin Univ. and Cambridge Univ., UK; Prof. of Physics, Univ. of Ill. 1938–50; Sr Scientist, Brookhaven Nat. Lab. 1950–60, Chair. Dept of Physics 1960–61, Dir 1961–73, Distinguished Scientist Emer. 1973–; Adjunct Prof. of Physics, State Univ. New York 1965–; mem. NAS, American Philosophical Soc.; Fellow American Acad. of Arts and Sciences; Rabi Scholar Lecturer 1995; Hon. PhD (Tel-Aviv) 1974; Dr hc (Univ. of Louvain-La-Neuve) 1982; Tom W. Bonner Prize in Nuclear Physics of American Physical Soc. 1971, US Atomic Energy Comm. Citation for Meritorious Contribs 1973, J. Robert Oppenheimer Memorial Prize 1982, Wolf Foundation Prize 1991. *Publications:* numerous articles in professional scientific journals on neutron physics, radioactivity, nuclear isomers, nuclear photo-electric effect, nuclear models, fundamental particles. *Leisure interests:* tennis, hiking. *Address:* Brookhaven National Laboratory Building, 510 Upton, NY 11973, USA.

GOLDIN, Daniel S., BSc; American space agency official; *Distinguished Fellow, Council on Competitiveness;* b. 23 July 1940, New York City; m. Judith Kramer; two d.; ed City Coll. of New York; research scientist, NASA Lewis Research Center, Cleveland 1962–67; joined TRW Space & Tech. Group, Redondo, Calif. 1967, Vice-Pres. and Gen. Man. –1992; Admin., NASA 1992–2001; Distinguished Fellow Council on Competitiveness 2001–; Dir Lucent Technologies Inc. 2002–; numerous awards. *Address:* Council on Competitiveness, 1500 K Street, NW, Suite 850, Washington, DC 20005, USA (office). *Telephone:* (202) 682-4292 (office). *Fax:* (202) 682-5150 (office). *E-mail:* DGoldin@compete.org (office). *Website:* www.compete.org (office).

GOLDIN, Nan; American artist; b. 12 Sept. 1953, Washington, DC; ed Satya Community School, Lincoln, Mass, Boston School of Fine Arts; began taking black-and-white photographs of drag queen beauty contests early 1970s; introduced flash and vibrant colours created from Cibachrome photographic process into her work, known as the Goldin look; moved to the Bowery, NY 1978; began showing photographs in slide shows at punk rock clubs such as Tin Pan Alley, NY early 1980s; exhibited work at Edin. Film Festival, Scotland and Berlin Film Festival, Germany 1986; entered detoxification clinic and experimented with self-portraiture 1988; created The Cookie Portfolio following death of friend Cookie Mueller 1989, continued adding portraits of friends suffering from AIDS and exhibited portfolio across USA and around the world 1990s; received DAAD grant to work in Berlin; dubbed as mem. of the Boston School following exhbn at Inst. of Contemporary Art, Boston 1995; worked with film-maker Edmund Coulthard to create film about her life and work I'll Be Your Mirror, BBC-TV 1996; retrospective exhbn I'll Be Your Mirror held at Whitney Museum of American Art 1996; first solo show in London at White Cube Gallery; has toured extensively around Europe, Asia, N America; Hasselblad Foundation Int. Award in Photography 2007. *Artistic Works include:* The Cookie Portfolio 1976–89, The Ballad of Sexual Dependency 1981. *Photographs include:* David at Grove Street, Boston 1972, Kenny Putting on Make-up, Boston, 1973, Self-Portrait in front of clinic 1988, Self-Portrait with Milagro 1988. *Publications:* A Double Life (co-author with David Armstrong) 1994, Tokyo Love: Spring Fever (co-author with Nobuyoshi Araki) 1994. *Address:* c/o Fraenkel Gallery, 49 Geary Street, San Francisco, CA 94108, USA.

GOLDING, (Orrett) Bruce, BSc; Jamaican politician; *Prime Minister;* b. 5 Dec. 1947; s. of Tacius Golding and Enid Golding (née Bent); m. Lorna Golding; three c.; ed Jamaica Coll., Univ. of the W Indies; as a student served as Vice-Chair. Jamaica Labour Party (JLP) Constituency Exec. for West St Catherine and mem. Bd of Dirs, Nat. Lotteries Comm.; selected as JLP parl. cand. for West St Catherine 1969, elected to JLP Cen. Exec. 1969, Co-founder Young Jamaica group 1970, elected as youngest-ever MP 1972, defeated in elections 1976; JLP Gen. Sec. 1974–84, Chair. 1984–95; apptd to Senate 1977, re-apptd 1980, Minister of Construction 1980–83; elected MP for South Central St Catherine 1983, re-elected 1989, 1993; left JLP and f. Nat. Democratic Movt (NDM) 1995, Pres. 1995–2002, left NDM and rejoined JLP 2002, Chair. JLP 2003–05, Leader 2005–; Prime Minister 2007–, also Minister of Planning and Devt and of Defence. *Radio:* host, Disclosure 2002. *Address:* Office of the Prime Minister, Jamaica House, 1 Devon Road, POB 272, Kingston 10, Jamaica (office). *Telephone:* 927-9941 (office). *Fax:* 927-4101 (office). *E-mail:* pmo@opm.gov.jm (office). *Website:* www.jamaicalabourparty.com (office).

GOLDMAN, John Michael, DM, FRCP, FRCPath, FMedSci; British physician; *Professor Emeritus of Haematology, Imperial College London;* b. 30 Nov. 1938, London; s. of Carl Heinz Goldman and Bertha Goldman (née Brandt); m. Jeannine Fuller 1967; one s. two d.; ed Westminster School, Magdalen Coll., Oxford, St Bartholomew's Hosp., London; MRC perm. mem. of staff Leukaemia Unit, Hammersmith Hosp., 1976–93, Dir Leukaemia Research Fund Unit 1988–2004; Prof. of Leukaemia, Biology Royal Postgraduate Medical School (later Imperial Coll. Medical School), London 1987–2004, Chair. Dept of Haematology 1994–2004, Prof. Emer. 2004–; Fogarty Scholar Hematology Br. NHLBI, Bethesda, Md 2005–06; Pres. European Haematology Asscn 1996–98, British Soc. for Blood and Marrow Transplantation 1996–98; fmr Pres. Int. Soc. for Experimental Hematology 1983, European Group for Bone Marrow Transplantation 1990–94; Sec. World Marrow Donor Asscn; Medical Dir Anthony Nolan Bone Marrow Trust 1988–; Hon. MD (Louvain, Poitiers). *Publications:* books, chapters and papers on leukaemia, oncogenes, bone marrow transplantation. *Leisure interests:* reading, riding, skiing, travelling. *Address:* Department of Haematology, Hammersmith Hospital/Imperial College London, Du Cane Road, London, W12 0NN (office); 33 Northumberland Place, London, W2 5AS, England (home). *Telephone:* (20) 8383-3238 (office). *Fax:* (20) 8742-9335 (office). *E-mail:* jgoldman@imperial.ac.uk (office).

GOLDMAN, William, MA; American author and screenwriter; b. 12 Aug. 1931, Chicago, Ill.; s. of M. Clarence Goldman and Marion Weil; m. Ilene Jones 1961; two d.; ed Oberlin Coll. and Columbia Univ.; Acad. Award for best original screenplay for Butch Cassidy and the Sundance Kid 1970, Acad. Award for best screenplay adaptation 1977, Laurel Award for Lifetime Achievement in Screenwriting 1983. *Publications:* novels: The Temple of Gold 1957, Your Turn to Curtsy, My Turn to Bow 1958, Soldier in the Rain 1960, Boys and Girls Together 1964, The Thing of It Is 1967, No Way to Treat a Lady (under pseudonym Harry Longbaugh), Father's Day 1971, The Princess Bride 1973, Marathon Man 1974, Wigger 1974, Magic 1976, Tinsel 1979, Control 1982, The Silent Gondoliers 1983, The Color of Light 1984, Heat 1985, Brothers 1986; play: Blood, Sweat and Stanley Poole 1961 (with James Goldman); musical comedy: A Family Affair (with James Goldman and John Kander) 1962; non-fiction: Adventures in the Screen Trade 1983, Hype and Glory 1990; Four Screenplays 1995, Five Screenplays 1997, Which Lie Did I Tell? 2000; screenplays: Harper 1966, Butch Cassidy and the Sundance Kid 1969, The Princess Bride 1973, Marathon Man 1976, All the President's Men 1976, A Bridge Too Far 1977, Magic 1978, Heat 1985, Brothers 1987, Year of the Comet 1992, Memoirs of an Invisible Man 1992, Chaplin 1992, Indecent Proposal 1993, Maverick 1994, The Ghost and the Darkness 1996, Absolute Power 1997, Hearts in Atlantis 2001, Dreamcatcher 2003. *Address:* Creative Artists Agency, 162 Fifth Avenue, 6th Floor, New York, NY 10010, USA (office). *Telephone:* (212) 277-9000 (office). *Fax:* (212) 277-9099 (office). *Website:* www.caa.com (office).

GOLDMARK, Peter Carl, Jr, BA; American newspaper executive and consultant; *Program Director, Climate and Air Program, Environmental Defense Fund;* b. 2 Dec. 1940, New York; s. of Peter Carl Goldmark and Frances Charlotte Trainer; m. Aliette Marie Misson 1964; three d.; ed Harvard Univ.; worked for US Office of Econ. Opportunity, Washington; fmr teacher of history Putney School, Vt; employed in Budget Office, City of New York for four years, later Asst Budget Dir Program Planning and Analysis then Exec. Asst to the Mayor 1971; Sec. Human Services, Commonwealth of Mass. 1972–75; Dir of Budget, NY State 1975–77; Exec. Dir Port Authority of NY and NJ 1977–85; joined Times Mirror Co., Los Angeles 1985, fmr Sr Vice-Pres. Eastern Newspapers Div.; Pres. Rockefeller Foundation 1988–97; Chair. and CEO Int. Herald Tribune 1998–2003; currently, Program Dir, Climate and Air Program, Environmental Defense Fund; mem. Bd of Dirs Financial Accounting Foundation, Lend Lease Corpn, Whitehead Inst. for Biomedical Research. *Address:* Environmental Defense Fund, 257 Park Avenue South, New York, NY 10010, USA (office). *Telephone:* (212) 505-2100 (office). *Fax:* (212) 505-2375 (office). *E-mail:* www.edf.org (office).

GOLDREICH, Peter, PhD; American scientist and academic; *Lee Du Bridge Professor Emeritus of Astrophysics and Planetary Physics, California Institute of Technology;* b. 14 July 1939, New York; s. of Paul Goldreich and Edith Rosenfield Goldreich; m. Susan Kroll 1960; two s.; ed Cornell Univ.; Post-Doctoral Fellow, Univ. of Cambridge 1963–64; Asst Prof. Astronomy and Physics, UCLA 1964–66, Assoc. Prof. 1966; Assoc. Prof. of Planetary Science and Astronomy, Calif. Inst. Tech. 1966–69, Prof. 1969–, Lee Du Bridge Prof. of Astrophysics and Planetary Physics 1981–, now Prof. Emer.; mem. NAS 1972–; Chapman Medal, Royal Astronomical Soc. 1985, Dirk Brouwer Award, American Astronomical Soc. 1986, Nat. Medal of Science 1995. *Publications:* on planetary dynamics, pulsar theory, radio emission from Jupiter, galactic stability and interstellar masers. *Leisure interest:* competitive athletics. *Address:* California Institute of Technology, 1200 East California Boulevard, Pasadena, CA 91125 (office); 471 S Catalina Avenue, Pasadena, CA 91106, USA (home). *E-mail:* pmg@nicholas.caltech.edu (office). *Website:* www.gps.caltech.edu/faculty/goldreich/goldreich.html (office).

GOLDSMITH, Harvey, CBE; British impresario; b. 4 March 1946, London; s. of Sydney Goldsmith and Minnie Goldsmith; m. Diana Goldsmith 1971; one s.; ed Christ's College and Brighton Coll. of Tech.; joined Big O Posters, Kensington Market 1966; organized open-air free concerts, Parliament Hill Fields 1968; in partnership with Michael Alfandary opened Round House, London 1968; organized 13 Garden Party concerts at Crystal Palace, London 1969; merged with John Smith Entertainment 1970–75; formed Harvey Goldsmith Entertainment promoting rock tours by Elton John, Rolling Stones etc.; in partnership with Ed Simons, rescued Hotel Television Network 1983; formed Allied Entertainment Group as public co. 1984–86, returned to pvt. ownership 1986; subsidiary Harvey Goldsmith Entertainment promotes some 250 concerts per year; formed Classical Productions with Mark McCormack, promoting shows at Earls Court including Pavarotti concert and lavish productions of Aida 1988, Carmen 1989, Tosca 1991; produced Bob Dylan Celebration, New York 1992, Mastercard Masters of Music (Hyde Park), The Eagles (Wembley), Three Tenors (Wembley), Lord of the Dance (world tour) 1996, Music for Montserrat (Royal Albert Hall), Boyzone (tour), Paul Weller (tour), Pavarotti (Manchester), Cirque du Soleil (Royal Albert Hall) 1997, Alegria (Royal Albert Hall), The Bee Gees (Wembley), Ozzfest (Milton Keynes Bowl), Paul Weller (Victoria Park) 1998; Chair. Nat. Music Day; Vice-Chair. Prince's Trust Bd; Vice-Pres. React 1989–; Trustee Gret, Band Aid 1985–, Live Aid Foundation 1985–; Dir Pres.'s Club, London First, London Tourist Bd; Amb. for London Judges Award 1997; Chair. Ignition International 2006–; mem. Advisory Group Red Cross; Music Industry Trust Award 2006. *Leisure interest:* golf. *Address:* Harvey Goldsmith Entertainments Ltd, Greenland Place, 115–123 Bayham Street, London, NW1 0AG, England. *Telephone:* (20) 7482-5522. *Fax:* (20) 7428-9252.

GOLDSMITH, Baron (Life Peer), cr. 1999, of Allerton in the County of Merseyside; **Peter Henry Goldsmith,** PC, MA, LLM, QC; British barrister; b. 5 Jan. 1950, Liverpool; ed Quarry Bank High School, Caius Coll. Cambridge, Univ. Coll. London; called to Bar, Gray's Inn, began practising as barrister 1972; a Jr Counsel to Crown (Common Law) 1985–87, QC 1987, Chair. Bar of England and Wales 1995, Financial Reporting Review Panel 1997–2000; called to Paris Bar 1997; Personal Rep. of Prime Minister to EU Charter of Fundamental Rights 1999–2000; Attorney-Gen. 2001–07; Privy Councillor 2002–; European Chair of Litigation, Debevoise & Plimpton LLP, London 2007–; Fellow, American Law Inst. 1997–, Univ. Coll. London 2002–. *Address:* House of Lords, London, SW1A 0PW; Debevoise & Plimpton LLP, Tower 42, Old Broad Street, London, EC2N 1HQ, England. *Telephone:* (20) 7219-8614 (Lords); (20) 7786-9000. *Fax:* (20) 75880-4180. *E-mail:* arunacres@debevoise.com. *Website:* www.parliament.uk; www.debevoise.com.

GOLDSTEIN, Avram, MD; American professor of pharmacology and neurobiologist; *Avram Goldstein Professor Emeritus, School of Medicine, Stanford University;* b. 3 July 1919, New York; s. of Israel Goldstein and Bertha Markowitz; m. Dora Benedict 1947; three s. one d.; ed Harvard Coll. and Harvard Medical School; Instructor, then Asst Prof. of Pharmacology, Harvard 1948–55; Prof. and Chair., Pharmacology, Stanford Univ. 1955–70, Prof. 1970–89, Prof. Emer. 1989–; Dir Addiction Research Foundation, Palo Alto, Calif. 1974–87; mem. NAS; Franklin Medal, Sollmann Award, Nathan Eddy Award. *Publications:* Biostatistics 1964, Principles of Drug Action 1968, Addiction: From Biology to Drug Policy 2001; over 300 articles in the primary scientific journals. *Leisure interests:* aviation and aviation writing. *Address:* Edwards Building, School of Medicine, Stanford University, 300 Pasteur Drive, Stanford, CA 94305 (office); 735 Dolores Street, Palo Alto, CA 94305, USA (home). *Telephone:* (650) 723-4000 (office). *E-mail:* avram.goldstein@stanford.edu (office). *Website:* med.stanford.edu (office).

GOLDSTEIN, Jeffrey Alan, BA MPh PhD; American international civil servant and economist; *Managing Director, Hellman & Friedman LLC;* b. 2 Dec. 1955, Pennsylvania; m. Nancy Coles; two s. one d.; ed Yale Univ., Vassar Coll., London School of Econs; Research Asst, Brookings Inst., Washington, DC 1977–78; Int. Economist, Office of Int. Monetary Affairs, US Dept of Treasury, Washington, DC 1979; Consultant, Securities Group, New York 1980–81; Vice-Chair. Wolfensohn & Co. Inc., New York, then Co-Chair. BT Wolfensohn, New York 1984–99; Man. Dir and Chief Financial Officer, World Bank, Washington, DC 1999–2004; Man. Dir Hellman & Friedman LLC (private equity firm) 2004–; mem. Bd of Trustees and Investment Cttee, Vassar Coll.; Trustee German Marshall Fund of the US; Dir Int. Center for Research on Women; mem. Council on Foreign Relations; Hons Econs (Vassar Coll.); Virginia Swinburn Brownell Prize in Political Econ. Studies. *Address:* Hellman & Friedman LLC, 375 Park Avenue, 20th Floor, New York, NY 10152, USA (office). *Telephone:* (212) 871-6680 (office). *Fax:* (212) 871-6688 (office). *E-mail:* info@hf.com (office). *Website:* www.hf.com (office).

GOLDSTEIN, Joseph Leonard, MD; American geneticist, physician and academic; *Regental Professor, University of Texas Southwestern Medical Center at Dallas;* b. 18 April 1940, Sumter, SC; s. of Isadore E. Goldstein and Fannie A. Goldstein; ed Washington and Lee Univ., Lexington, Va, Univ. of Texas Southwestern Medical Center; Intern, then Resident in Medicine, Mass. Gen. Hosp., Boston 1966–68; Clinical Assoc., NIH 1968–70; Post-doctoral Fellow, Univ. of Washington, Seattle 1970–72; mem. Faculty, Univ. of Texas Southwestern Medical Center, Dallas 1972–, Paul J. Thomas Prof. of Medicine, Chair. Dept of Molecular Genetics 1977–, Harvey Soc. Lecturer 1977, Regental Prof. 1985–; Chair. Albert Lasker Medical Research Awards Jury 1996–; mem. Advisory Bd Howard Hughes Medical Inst. 1985–90, Chair. 1995–2002, Trustee 2002–; non-resident Fellow, The Salk Inst. 1983–93; mem. Scientific Advisory Bd Welch Foundation 1986–, Bd Dirs Passano Foundation 1985–, Bd Trustees Rockefeller Foundation 1994–, Bd of Scientific Govs, Scripps Research Inst. 1996–; mem. Editorial Bd Cell, Arteriosclerosis and Science; mem. NAS (mem. Council 1991–94), American Acad. of Arts and Sciences, American Philosophical Soc., Inst. of Medicine, Asscn of American Physicians, American Soc. of Clinical Investigation (Pres. 1985–86), American Soc. of Human Genetics, American Soc. of Biological Chemists, American Fed. of Clinical Research; Foreign mem. Royal Soc., London; Hon. DSc (Univ. of Chicago, Rensselaer Polytech. Inst., Washington and Lee Univ., Univ. of Paris-Sud, Univ. of Buenos Aires, Southern Methodist Univ., Univ. of Miami, Rockefeller Univ.); Heinrich-Wieland Prize 1974, ACS Pfizer Award in Enzyme Chem. 1976, Passano Award, Johns Hopkins Univ. 1978, Gairdner Foundation Award 1981, Award in Biological and Medical Sciences, New York Acad. of Sciences 1981, Lita Annenberg Hazen Award 1982, Research Achievement Award, American Heart Asscn 1984, Louisa Gross Horwitz Award 1984, 3M Life Sciences Award 1984, Albert Lasker Award in Basic Medical Research 1985, Nobel Prize in Physiology or Medicine 1985, Trustees' Medal, Mass Gen. Hosp. 1986, US Nat. Medal of Science 1988, Albany Medical Center Prize in Medicine and Biomedical Research 2003, Woodrow Wilson Award for Public Service 2005, Builders Science Award, Research America 2007. *Publication:* The Metabolic Basis of Inherited Disease (co-author) 1983. *Address:* Department of Molecular Genetics, University of Texas Southwestern Medical Center at Dallas, 5323 Harry Hines Boulevard, Dallas, TX 75390 (office); 3831 Turtle Creek Boulevard, Apt 22-B, Dallas, TX 75219, USA (home). *Telephone:* (214) 648-2141 (office). *Fax:* (214) 648-8804 (office). *E-mail:* joe.goldstein@utsouthwestern.edu (office). *Website:* www8.utsouthwestern .edu/utsw/cda/dept14857/files/114532.html (office); www8.utsouthwestern .edu/utsw/home/research/molgen/index.html (office).

GOLDSTONE, David Joseph, LLB; British property executive; *Chairman, Swanbourne Development Services Ltd;* b. 21 Feb. 1929; s. of Solomon Goldstone and Rebecca Goldstone (née Degotts); one s. two d.; ed Dynevor Secondary School, Swansea and London School of Econs; admitted as solicitor 1955; legal practice 1955–66; Chief Exec. Regalian Properties PLC 1970–2001 Chair. 1990–2001; Dir Swansea Sound Commercial Radio 1974–95, London Welsh Rugby Football Club 1997–2001, Wales Millennium Centre; Chair. Coram Family 2001–05, Swanbourne Development Services Ltd; mem. Court of Govs LSE 1985– (Fellow 1996); mem. Football Asscn of Wales 1970–72, Welsh Nat. Opera 1984–89, Univ. of London 1994– (Deputy Chair. 2002–), Royal Albert Hall 1999– (Vice-Pres. 2004–). *Leisure interests:* reading, sport. *Address:* 16A Curzon Street, London, W1J 5HP (office); 22 Grosvenor Hill Court, 15 Bourdon Street, London, W1K 3PX, England (home). *Telephone:* (20) 7659-0413 (office); (20) 7499-4525 (home). *Fax:* (20) 7659-0414 (office); (20) 7491-2388 (home). *E-mail:* djg@davstone.co.uk (office).

GOLDSTONE, Jeffrey, MA, PhD, FRS; British physicist and academic; *Cecil and Ida Green Professor Emeritus of Physics, Massachusetts Institute of Technology;* b. 3 Sept. 1933, Manchester; s. of Hyman Goldstone and Sophia Goldstone; m. Roberta Gordon 1980; one s.; ed Manchester Grammar School and Trinity Coll., Cambridge; Research Fellow, Trinity Coll., Cambridge 1956–60, Staff Fellow 1962–82; Univ. Lecturer, Applied Math. and Theoretical Physics, Univ. of Cambridge 1961–76, Reader in Math. Physics 1976; Prof. of Physics, MIT 1977–83, Dir Center for Theoretical Physics 1983–89, Cecil and Ida Green Prof. of Physics 1983–2004, Cecil and Ida Green Prof. Emer. 2004–; Fellow, American Acad. of Arts and Sciences, American Physical Soc.; Hon. Fellow, Trinity Coll., Cambridge 2000; Heineman Prize, American Physical Soc. 1981, Guthrie Medal, Inst. of Physics 1983, Dirac Medal, Int. Centre for Theoretical Physics 1991. *Publications:* articles in scientific journals. *Address:* Department of Physics, 6–407, Massachusetts Institute of Technology, Cambridge, MA 02139, USA (office). *Telephone:* (617) 253-6263 (office); (617) 876-6027 (home). *Fax:* (617) 253-8674 (office). *E-mail:* goldston@ mit.edu (office). *Website:* web.mit.edu/physics/facultyandstaff/faculty/ jeffrey_goldstone.html (office).

GOLDSTONE, Richard J., LLB; South African judge; b. 26 Oct. 1938, Boksburg; m. Noleen Behrman 1962; two d.; ed King Edward VII School, Johannesburg and Univ. of Witwatersrand; admitted to Johannesburg Bar 1963, Sr Counsel 1976; Judge, Transvaal Supreme Court 1980–89; Judge, Appellate Div. Supreme Court of SA 1989–94; Justice, S African Constitutional Court 1994–2003; Chair. Comm. of Inquiry regarding Public Violence and Intimidation 1991–94; Prosecutor, Int. Criminal Tribunal for Fmr Yugoslavia and Int. Criminal Tribunal for Rwanda 1994–96; Nat. Pres. Nat. Inst. for Crime Prevention and Rehabilitation of Offenders 1982–99; Chair. cttee which drafted Valencia Declaration of Human Duties and Responsibilities 1998; mem. Ind. Int. Comm. on Kosovo 1999–2001, Int. Bar Asscn Task Force on Int. Terrorism 2001–; mem. Council, Univ. of Witwatersrand 1988–94, Chancellor 1996–; Chair. Standing Advisory Cttee on Co. Law (Chair. 1991–), Exec. Cttee World ORT (Pres. 1997–); mem. UN Cttee of Inquiry into Iraq Oil for Food Programme (Volcker Cttee); Chair. Bd Human Rights Inst. of SA; Gov. Hebrew Univ. of Jerusalem 1982–; Chair. Bradlow Foundation 1989–; other professional appts; faculty mem. Salzburg Seminar 1996, 1998, 2001; Foreign mem. American Acad. of Arts and Sciences; Fellow Centre for Int. Affairs, Harvard Univ. 1989; Hon. mem. Bar Asscn of New York; Hon. Bencher Inner Temple, London; Hon. Fellow, St John's Coll. Cambridge; 19 hon. degrees including Hon. LLD (Cape Town) 1993, (Natal, Hebrew Univ. of Jerusalem, Witwatersrand) 1994, (Wilfred Laurier Univ.) 1995, (Tilburg Univ.) 1996, (Univ. of Glasgow, Notre Dame Univ.) 1997, (Univ. of Calgary) 1998, (Emory Univ.) 2001; several awards including Toastmasters Int. Communication and Leadership Award 1994, Int. Human Rights Award (American Bar Asscn) 1994. *Publication:* For Humanity – Reflections of a War Crimes Investigator. *Leisure interests:* reading, walking, wine. *Address:* PO Box 396, Morningside 2057 (home); 22 West Road South, Morningside, South Africa (home). *Fax:* (11) 8035472 (home). *E-mail:* rjgoldstone@iafrica.com (home).

GOLDSTRAW, Peter, MB, ChB, FETCS; British thoracic surgeon; *Professor of Thoracic Surgery, Imperial College London;* m. Denise Mary Bowyer 1968; one s. one d.; ed Univ. of Birmingham; Consultant Thoracic Surgeon, Royal Brompton Hospital 1979–, fmr Dir of Surgery, Head of Thoracic Surgery Section; civilian adviser to Royal Navy, RAF; fmr Hon. Consultant Benenden Chest Hospital; Prof. of Thoracic Surgery, Imperial Coll., London; Chair. Int. Staging Cttee Int. Asscn for the Study of Lung Cancer (IASLC); mem. Man. Bd European Bd of Thoracic and Cardiovascular Surgery; UK Rep. UEMS Section of Cardiothoracic Surgery; Chair. Cardiothoracic SHC; mem. Belgian Asscn for Cardio-Thoracic Surgery, Cardiothoracic Surgery Network, European Asscn for Cardio-Thoracic Surgery, European Soc. of Thoracic Surgeons, Soc. of Cardiothoracic Surgeons of Great Britain and Ireland, American Asscn for Thoracic Surgery, Soc. of Thoracic Surgeons; mem. Editorial Bd Thorax, Annals of Thoracic Surgery, Assoc. Ed. for Lung Cancer; Clement Price-Thomas Award Royal Coll. of Surgeons of England 2004. *Publications:* contrib. to 44 textbooks on thoracic surgery; more than 200 articles in scientific journals. *Leisure interests:* sailing, fishing. *Address:* Royal Brompton Hospital, Sydney Street, London, SW3 6NP, England (office). *Telephone:* (20) 7351-8559 (office). *Fax:* (20) 7351-8560 (office). *E-mail:* p.goldstraw@rbh .nthames.nhs.uk (office). *Website:* www.rbh.nthames.nhs.uk (office).

GOLDSWORTHY, Andrew Charles, OBE, BA; British sculptor; b. 25 July 1956, Cheshire; s. of Fredrick Alan Goldsworthy and Muriel Goldsworthy (née Stanger); m. Judith Elizabeth Gregson 1982; two s. two d.; ed Bradford and Lancaster Art Colls; has exhibited internationally in USA, France, Australia, Germany and Japan; numerous public and pvt. comms since 1984 including pieces for Grizedale Forest, Cumbria 1984, 1985, 1991, Enclosure, Royal Botanic Gardens, Edinburgh 1990, Seven Holes, Greenpeace, London 1991, Steel Cone, Gateshead 1991, Black Spring, Botanical Gardens, Adelaide 1992, Fieldgate, Poundridge, NY 1993, Laumeier Sculpture Park 1994, two pieces for Nat. Museum of Scotland, Edin. 1998; works represented in collections at Michael Hue-Williams Fine Arts Ltd, London, Galerie Lelong, New York and Paris, Haines Gallery, San Francisco, Galerij S65, Belgium, Springer and Winckler Galerie, Berlin; residency Yorks. Sculpture Park 1988; featured on Royal Mail Spring issue stamps 1995; Sr lecturer in Fine Art and Craft Univ. of Herts. 1996; Prof.-at-Large Cornell Univ., USA 2000–; Visiting Prof. Crichton Coll., Univ. of Glasgow 2000–; collaborated with Cirque du Soleil, Montreal 1998; Hon. Fellow Univ. of Cen. Lancs. 1995; Hon. BA (Bradford) 1993; North West Arts Award 1979, Yorks. Arts Award 1980, Northern Arts Award 1981, 1995, Scottish Arts Council Award 1988. *Dance:* Vegetal, with Regine Chopinot 1995, La danse du Temps, with Regine Chopinot and Ballet Atlantique 2000. *Film:* Two Autumns (for Channel 4) 1991, Rivers and Tides 2000. *Publications:* A Collaboration with Nature 1989, Hand to Earth 1991, Touching North 1994, Stone 1994, Wood 1996, Time 2000, Passage 2005. *Leisure interests:* fishing, reading, listening to music. *Address:* c/o Michael Hue-Williams Fine Arts Ltd, 21 Cork Street, London, W1X 1HB, England. *Telephone:* (20) 7434-1318. *Fax:* (20) 7434-1321.

GOLDTHORPE, John Harry, CBE, MA, FBA; British sociologist and academic; *Fellow Emeritus, Nuffield College, Oxford;* b. 27 May 1935, Barnsley; s. of Harry and Lilian Eliza Goldthorpe; m. Rhiannon Esyllt Harry 1963; one s. one d.; ed Wath-upon-Dearne Grammar School, Univ. Coll. London, London School of Econs; Asst Lecturer, Dept of Sociology, Univ. of Leicester 1957–60; Fellow, King's Coll., Cambridge 1960–69; Asst Lecturer, then Lecturer in Faculty of Econs and Politics, Univ. of Cambridge 1962–69; Official Fellow, Nuffield Coll., Oxford 1969–2002, Fellow Emer. 2002–; mem. British Econ. and Social Research Council 1988–91; mem. Academia Europaea 1989; Foreign mem. Royal Swedish Acad. of Sciences 2001; Hon. DPhil (Stockholm Univ.) 1990; Helsinki Univ. Medal 1990. *Publications:* The Affluent Worker series (three vols) (with David Lockwood et al.) 1968–69, The Social Grading of Occupations (with Keith Hope) 1974, The Political Economy of Inflation (with Fred Hirsch, eds) 1978, Social Mobility and Class Structure 1980, Order and Conflict in Contemporary Capitalism (ed. and contrib.) 1984, Die Analyse sozialer Ungleichheit: Kontinuität, Erneuerung, Innovation (with Hermann Strasser; ed. and contrib.) 1985, The Constant Flux: a Study of Class Mobility in Industrial Societies (with Robert Erikson) 1992, The Development of Industrial Society in Ireland (with Christopher T. Whelan; ed. and contrib.) 1992, On Sociology: Numbers, Narratives and the Integration of Research and Class Theory 2000. *Leisure interests:* lawn tennis, bird watching, computer chess, cryptic crosswords. *Address:* Nuffield College, Oxford, OX1 1NF (office); 32 Leckford Road, Oxford, OX2 6HX, England. *Telephone:* (1865) 278559 (office); (1865) 556602 (home). *Fax:* (1865) 278621. *E-mail:* john.goldthorpe@nuf.ox.ac.uk (office).

GOLEMBIOVSKY, Igor Nestorovich; Russian journalist; b. 7 Sept. 1935, Samtredia, Georgia; m.; one s.; ed Tbilisi State Univ.; journalist activities since 1958; with Izvestia 1966–97, Deputy Ed. of Div., Special Corresp., Deputy Exec. Sec., Exec. Sec., First Deputy Ed.-in-Chief 1988–91, Ed.-in-Chief 1991–97; Founder and Ed. Noviye Izvestiya 1997–2003. *Publications:* author of articles on key problems of social and political life. *Leisure interests:* tennis, football. *Address:* c/o Noviye Izvestiya, Dolgorukovskaya str. 19/8, 103006 Moscow, Russia. *Telephone:* (495) 795-31-57. *Fax:* (495) 795-31-38.

GOLIKOVA, Tatyana Alekseyevna; Russian politician; *Minister of Health and Social Development;* m. Viktor Khristenko, Minister of Industry and Energy; ed Russian Econ. Acad. (Plekhanov Inst.); served in Ministry of Finance 1990–2007, worked as Deputy Minister of Finance, then First Deputy Minister of Finance 2004–07; Minister of Health and Social Devt 2007–. *Address:* Rakhmanovskii pereulok 3/25, 127994 Moscow, Russian Federation (office). *Telephone:* (495) 927-28-48 (office). *Fax:* (495) 928-58-15 (office). *E-mail:* info@mzsrrf.ru (office). *Website:* www.mzsrrf.ru (office).

GOLITSYN, Georgy Sergeyevich; Russian physicist; b. 23 Jan. 1935, Moscow; s. of Sergei Golitsyn and Claudia Golitsyna; m. Ludmila Lisitskaya; two d.; ed Moscow State Univ.; Head of Lab., Head of Div., Dir Inst. of Atmospheric Physics, USSR (now Russian) Acad. of Sciences 1958–; Corresp. mem. USSR (now Russian) Acad. of Sciences 1979, mem. 1987, mem. Presidium 1988–2001; Chair. Council, Int. Inst. of Applied Systems Analysis 1992–97; main research on geophysical fluid dynamics, climate theory; A. Friedmann Prize, Demidov Prize, Alfred Wegener Prize. *Publications include:* Introduction to Dynamics of Planet Atmospheres 1973, Study of Convection with Geophysical Applications and Analogies 1980, Global Climate Catastrophes 1986, Convection of Rotating Fluids 1995, Dynamics of Natural Processes 2004. *Leisure interests:* history, art, literature. *Address:* A.M. Obukhov Institute of Atmospheric Physics, Russian Academy of Sciences, Pyzhyevsky per. 3, 119017 Moscow, Russia (office). *Telephone:* (495) 951-55-65 (office). *Fax:* (495) 953-16-52 (office). *E-mail:* mail_adm@ifaran.ru (office). *Website:* www.ifaran.ru (office).

GOLL, Gerhard; German business executive and lawyer; b. 18 June 1942, Stuttgart; Chair. Energie Baden-Württemberg (EnBW) AG 1998–2003; investigated for balance sheet fraud while at EnBW 2004. *Address:* c/o Energie Baden-Württemberg AG, Durlacher Allee 93, 76131 Karlsruhe, Germany (office).

GÖLLNER, Theodor, PhD, DrPhil, Habil; German musicologist; *Professor Emeritus and Director, Commission of Music History, Bavarian Academy of Sciences;* b. 25 Nov. 1929, Bielefeld; s. of Friedrich Göllner and Paula Brinkmann; m. Marie Louise Martinez 1959; one s. one d.; ed Univs of Heidelberg and Munich; Lecturer, Univ. of Munich 1958–62, Asst Prof. 1962–67, Assoc. Prof. 1967; Prof., Univ. of Calif., Santa Barbara 1967–73; Prof. and Chair., Inst. of Musicology, Univ. of Munich 1973–97; Prof. Emer. and Dir, Comm. of Music History, Bavarian Acad. of Sciences 1982–; mem. European Acad. of Sciences and Arts 1991–. *Publications:* Formen früher Mehrstimmigkeit 1961, Die mehrstimmigen liturgischen Lesungen 1969, Die Sieben Worte am Kreuz 1986, Et incarnatus est in Bachs h-moll-Messe und Beethovens Missa solemnis 1996, Die Tactuslehre in den deutschen Orgelquellen des 15. Jahrhunderts 2003, Münchner Veröffentlichungen zur Musikgeschichte (ed.) 1977–2006, Münchner Editionen zur Musikgeschichte 1979–97, Die psalmodische Tradition bei Monteverdi und Schütz 2006. *Address:* Institute of Musicology, University of Munich, Geschwister-Scholl-Platz 1, 80539 Munich (office); Bahnweg 9, 82229 Seefeld, Germany (home). *Telephone:* (1089) 21802364 (office). *E-mail:* TheodorGoellner@aol.com (home).

GOLU, Mihai, MA, PhD; Romanian politician and scientist; *Professor and Head, Department of Psychology, Spiru Haret University;* b. 4 March 1934, Bumbeşti-Pitic, Gorj Co.; s. of Ion Golu and Gheorghita Golu; m. Elena Filip 1957; two s.; ed Psychology Coll., Bucharest and Lomonosov Univs; worked as psychologist, Prof., Bucharest Univ.; Researcher, Carnegie-Mellon Univ., USA 1973–74; Deputy (ind. cand.) 1990–92, Party of Social Democracy 1992–96; Minister of Educ. and Science 1991–92, of Culture 1992–93; Deputy, Parl. Ass. of Council of Europe 1993–96; currently Prof. and Head, Dept of Psychology, Spiru Haret Univ.; Pres. Romanian Asscn of Psychologists 1990–2004, Nat. Soc. for Educ. 1993–; Vice-Pres. Nat. Foundation for Gifted Children and Young People 2004–; Nat. Comm. for UNESCO 1990–95; mem. Acad. of Scientists 1998–, New York Acad. of Science; Romanian Acad. Prize 1981, Pablo Picasso Medal, UNESCO 1991, Jan Amos Komenius Medal, Czech Acad. 1992, Nat. Merit Award 2004. *Publications:* Sensibility 1970, Principles of Cybernetic Psychology 1975, Dynamics of Personality 1993, Neuropsychology 2000, Fundamentals of Psychology 2000, General Psychology 2003; scientific papers and articles. *Leisure interests:* reading biographies of famous people, classical music. *Address:* Bulevardul Libertatii 22, Bloc 102, Scara 5, Apt. 89, Bucharest, Romania (home). *Telephone:* 318-77-91 (home). *E-mail:* mgolu@spiruharet.ro.

GOLUB, Harvey, BS; American business executive; *Chairman, Campbell Soup Company;* b. 16 April 1939, New York; s. of Irving Golub and Pearl Fader; m. Roberta Glunts 1980; one s. and two s. one d. by previous m.; Jr Pnr, McKinsey & Co. Inc., New York 1967–74, Sr Pnr 1977–83; Pres. Shulman Air Freight, New York 1974–77; Sr Officer, American Express Co., New York 1983–84, Vice-Chair. 1990–93, CEO, Chair. 1993–2001; Chair., Pres. IDS Financial Services (now American Express Financial Advisors), Minn. 1984–90, Chair., CEO 1990–2001; Chair. AirClic, Blue Bell 2001–, Campbell Soup Co. *Address:* Campbell Soup Company, 1 Campbell Place, Camden, NJ 08103-1799, USA (office). *Telephone:* (856) 342-4800 (office). *Fax:* (856) 342-3878 (office). *Website:* www.campbellsoupcompany.com (office).

GOLUTVA, Alexander Alekseyevich; Russian cinematographer; b. 18 March 1948, Liepaya, Latvia; m.; one d.; ed Moscow State Univ.; fmr teacher; taught philosophy at Leningrad Ulyanov-Lenin Electro-technical Inst. (LETI) 1973–74; fmr Lecturer, Div. of Propaganda and Agitation, Petrograd Exec. CP Cttee 1974–80, then Instructor, then Head; consultant, House of Political Educ. 1980–83; Head of Sector, Div. of Culture, Leningrad Regional CP Cttee 1983–85; Ed.-in-Chief Lenfilm Film Studio 1985–87, Dir 1987–96; First Deputy Chair. State Cttee on Cinematography 1996–97, State Sec. then First Deputy Chair. 1997–99, Chair. 1999–2000; First Deputy Minister of Culture, Head of Cinema Dept 2000–04; mem. Presidential Council for Culture and Art; ORKF 'Kinotvar' Best Producer of Russia 1995, Badge of Honour of Russian Fed. 1998, Nika Prize of Russian Fed. 1995, 1999, 2000. *Films:* Taxi Blues 1990, Peculiarities of the National Hunt 1995, Khrustalyov, My Car! 1998, His Wife's Diary 2000. *Address:* c/o Cinema Departments, Ministry of Culture of Russian Federation, M. Gnezdnikovsky per. 7, 125009 Moscow, Russia.

GOLYSHEV, Vyacheslav Arkadevich, PhD; Uzbekistan government official; First Deputy Presidential Adviser for Econ. Affairs –2005; Deputy Prime Minister, Head of the Econ. Sector and Foreign Econ. Relations Sector, Minister of the Economy 2005. *Address:* c/o Ministry of the Economy, pr. Uzbekistanii 45a, 100003 Tashkent, Uzbekistan (office). *Telephone:* (71) 139-63-20 (office). *Fax:* (71) 132-63-72 (office). *E-mail:* mineconomy@mmes.gov.uz (office). *Website:* www.mineconomy.cc.uz (office).

GOMA, Col Louis Sylvain; Republic of the Congo politician and army officer; b. 1941; ed Versailles and Saint-Cyr; Asst Dir of Mil. Engineers until 1968; Chief of Staff of Congolese People's Nat. Army 1968, promoted Capt. 1968; mem. Parti Congolais du Travail (PCT) 1969, Cen. Cttee 1970, Special Gen. Staff of Revolution 1974, Political Bureau; Sec. of State for Defence 1969–70; Minister of Public Works and Transport 1970–74; promoted Maj. 1973; Chief of Gen. Staff of Armed Forces 1974; Prime Minister 1975–84, 1991, responsible for Plan 1975–79; mem. Council of State 1975–77; mem. PCT Mil. Cttee (Second Vice-Pres.) 1977–79. *Address:* c/o Office du Premier Ministre, Brazzaville, Republic of the Congo.

GOMAN, Vladimir Vladimirovich; Russian politician; *Deputy Representative of the President, Siberian Okrug;* b. 29 Jan. 1952, Baku, Azerbaijan; ed Troitsk Higher School of Civil Aviation, Tumen Industrial Inst., Tumen State Univ.; technician first civil aviation team 1972–74; fmr mechanic Severgaz-

stroi, Nadym, then head of sector, head of dept 1974–89; Chair. Nadym Municipal Exec. Cttee 1989; Head of Admin, Nadym and Autonomous Territory of Yamal 1991–93; mem. State Duma, Chair. State Duma Cttee on Peoples of the N 1993–98, Cttee on Devt of the N 1998–, Cttee on Problems of the N 1999–; Deputy Minister of Regional Policy State Sec. 1999–2000, Deputy Rep. of the Pres. in Siberian Fed. Dist, Novosibirsk 2000–. *Address:* Office of the Plenipotentiary Representative of the President, Derzhavina str. 18, 630091 Novosibirsk, Russia (office). *Telephone:* (3832) 21-56-22 (office).

GOMARD, Bernhard, DJur; Danish lawyer and academic; *Professor of Law, Copenhagen Business School;* b. 9 Jan. 1926, Karise; s. of C. J. Gomard and Karen Gomard (née Magle); m. 1st 1974; one s.; m. 2nd Marianne Rosen 1994 (died 2000); ed Univ. of Copenhagen; Legal Adviser, Danish Dept of Justice 1950–58, Danish Atomic Comm. 1956–76, Danish Insurance Cos 1958–2002; Prof. of Law, Univ. of Copenhagen 1958–96; Prof. of Law, Copenhagen Business School 1996–; mem. Bd of Dirs Danske Bank 1974–96; mem. and Chair. numerous Govt cttees; mem. Danish Acad. of Sciences 1975, Academia Europaea 1989, Inst. of Int. Business Law and Practice; Hon. Prof., Univ. of Freiburg; Commdr, Order of the Dannebrog; Hon. DrIur (Univ. of Lund); Nordic Jurists Prize 1987, Oersted Medal 1995. *Publications:* articles and treatises on contract and company law, civil procedure, with particular emphasis on Danish law. *Leisure interests:* opera, French art and literature. *Address:* Centre for Financial Law, Copenhagen Business School, Solbjergvej 3, 1, 2000 Frederiksberg C (office); 3 Hammerensgade, 1267 Copenhagen K, Denmark (home). *Telephone:* 38-15-26-42 (office); 33-32-80-20 (home). *Fax:* 38-15-26-60 (office). *E-mail:* bg.ckk@cbs.dk (office).

GOMER, Robert, PhD; American chemist and academic; *Professor Emeritus, The James Franck Institute, University of Chicago;* b. 24 March 1924, Vienna, Austria; s. of Richard Gomer and Mary Gomer; m. Anne Olah 1955; one s. one d.; ed Pomona Coll. and Univ. of Rochester; Instructor, then Assoc. Prof., James Franck Inst. and Dept of Chem., Univ. of Chicago 1950–58, Prof. 1958–96, Dir James Franck Inst. 1977–83, Carl William Eisendrath Distinguished Service Prof. of Chem. 1984–96, Prof. Emer. 1996–; Assoc. Ed. Journal of Chemical Physics 1957–59, Review of Scientific Instruments 1963–65; mem. Editorial Bd Surface Science 1964–70; Consultant, Pres.'s Science Advisory Bd 1961–65; Chair. Editorial Bd Bulletin of the Atomic Scientists 1965–70, mem. Bd of Dirs. 1960–84; Assoc. Ed. Applied Physics 1974–89; Co-Ed. Springer Series in Chemical Physics 1978–; mem. NAS, American Acad. of Arts and Sciences and Leopoldina Akademie der Naturforscher; Bourke Lecturer, Faraday Soc. 1959; Kendall Award in Colloid or Surface Science, American Chemical Soc. 1975; Davisson-Germer Prize, American Physical Soc. 1981, M.W. Welch Award, American Vacuum Soc. 1989, ACS A. Adamson Award 1996. *Publications:* over 240 scientific articles; Field Emission and Field Ionization 1961. *Leisure interests:* skiing, music and literature. *Address:* The University of Chicago, The James Franck Institute, RI 127, 5640 South Ellis Avenue, Chicago, IL 60637-1433 (office); 4824 South Kimbark Avenue, Chicago, IL 60615-1916, USA (home). *Telephone:* (773) 702-7191 (office). *Fax:* (773) 702-5863 (office). *E-mail:* r-gomer@uchicago.edu (office). *Website:* jfi.uchicago.edu (office).

GOMERSALL, Sir Stephen John, Kt, KCMG, MA; British business executive and fmr diplomatist; *Chief Executive for Europe, Hitachi Ltd;* b. 17 Jan. 1948, Doncaster; s. of Harry Raymond Gomersall and Helen Gomersall; m. Lydia Veronica Parry 1975; two s. one d.; ed Queens' Coll., Cambridge, Stanford Univ., USA; entered diplomatic service 1970; in Tokyo 1972–77; Rhodesia Dept, FCO 1977–79; Pvt. Sec. to Lord Privy Seal 1979–82; Washington, DC 1982–85; Econ. Counsellor, Tokyo 1986–90; Head of Security Policy Dept, FCO 1990–94, Dir Int. Security 1998–99; Deputy Perm. Rep., Perm. Mission to the UN 1994–98; Amb. to Japan 1999–2004; Chief Exec. for Europe, Hitachi Ltd 2004–; mem. Advisory Council, London Symphony Orchestra. *Leisure interests:* music, golf. *Address:* 87 Highlands Heath, London, SW15 3TY, England (home). *E-mail:* sjgomersall@hotmail.com (home); stephen.gomersall@hitachi-eu.com (office). *Website:* www.hitachi-eu.com (office).

GOMES, Aristides; Guinea-Bissau politician; b. 8 Nov. 1954; ed Univ. of Paris VIII, France; Dir-Gen. Televisão Experimental da Guiné-Bissau 1990–92; fmr Minister of Planning and Int. Cooperation; Prime Minister 2005–07 (resgnd); fmr mem. African Party for the Independence of Guinea and Cape Verde (PAIGC). *Address:* c/o Office of the Prime Minister, Avda Unidade Africana, CP137, Bissau, Guinea-Bissau (office).

GOMES, Daniel; Guinea-Bissau politician; *Minister of Fisheries and the Maritime Economy;* fmr Spokesman, Partido Africano da Independência da Guiné e Cabo Verde (PAIGC); Minister of Defence 2004–05, Minister of the Presidency of the Council of Ministers, Social Communication and Parliamentary Affairs 2005–07, of Fisheries and the Maritime Economy 2007–. *Address:* Ministry of Fisheries and the Maritime Economy, Avenida Amílcar Cabral, CP 102, Bissau, Guinea-Bissau (office). *Telephone:* 201699 (office). *Fax:* 202580 (office).

GOMES JÚNIOR, Carlos; Guinea-Bissau politician; *Prime Minister;* b. 19 Dec. 1949, Bolama; s. of Carlos Domingos Gomes and Maria Augusta Ramalho; m.; four c.; banker and businessman; elected to Parl. 1994–, First Vice-Pres. 1996; mem. African Party for the Ind. of Guinea-Bissau 1991–, Sec. for Foreign Affairs and Int. Co-operation 1999–2002, Leader 2002–; Prime Minister of Guinea-Bissau May 2004–05, 2009–. *Address:* Office of the Prime Minister, Avda Unidade Africana, CP 137, Bissau, Guinea-Bissau (office). *Telephone:* 211308 (office). *Fax:* 201671 (office).

GOMEZ, Alain Michel, LenD; French business executive; b. 18 Oct. 1938, Paris; s. of Francis Gomez and Simone Blet; m. 1st Francine le Foyer 1967 (divorced); m. 2nd Clémentine Gustin 1986; two d.; ed Univ. of Paris, Ecole nat. d'administration; Inspecteur des Finances 1965–69; Asst Dir of Finance,

Saint-Gobain SA 1970–71, Financial Dir 1971–72, Pres. and Dir-Gen. 1977–; joined Société Générale pour l'Emballage 1972, Dir-Gen. 1972, Pres. 1977–; Pres. and Dir-Gen. Saint-Gobain Desjonquères 1973–, Saint-Gobain Emballage 1974–, Dir Duralex br., Saint-Gobain 1978–, Dir Saint-Gobain Pont à Mousson 1977–; Pres. Thomson SA and Thomson-CSF 1982–96, now Hon. Pres.; Chair. and CEO Thomson CSF 1982–96; Vice-Pres., Dir-Gen. Sefimeg 1996–; Counsellor to Bank Wasserstein Perella 1997–99; mem. Exec. Cttee Fimalac 1996–2000; Pres. Strafor Facom 1999–2002; Chevalier, Légion d'honneur. *Publications:* (co-author under name Jacques Mandrin) L'Enarchie 1967, Socialisme ou Social-médiocratie 1968. *Address:* c/o Facom, 6-8 rue Gustave Eiffel, 91420 Morangis, France.

GOMEZ, Jill, FRAM; British singer (soprano); b. 21 Sept. 1942, New Amsterdam, British Guiana; ed St. Joseph's Convent, Trinidad, St. Maur's Convent, Surrey, Royal Acad. of Music, Guildhall School of Music, studied with Luigi Ricci in Rome; operatic debut as Adina in L'Elisir d'Amore with Glyndebourne Touring Opera 1968 and has since sung leading roles with Glyndebourne Festival Opera incl. Mélisande, Calisto and Ann Truelove in The Rake's Progress; has appeared with The Royal Opera, ENO, English Opera Group, and Scottish Opera in roles including Pamina, Ilia, Fiordiligi, the Countess in Figaro, Elizabeth in Elegy for Young Lovers, Ann Trulove, Tytania, Lauretta in Gianni Schicchi and the Governess in The Turn of the Screw; cr. the role of Flora in Tippett's The Knot Garden, at Covent Garden 1970 and of the Countess in Thea Musgrave's Voice of Ariadne, Aldeburgh 1974; sang title role in Massenet's Thaïs, Wexford 1974 and Jenifer in The Midsummer Marriage with Welsh Nat. Opera 1976; cr. title role in William Alwyn's Miss Julie for radio 1977; performed Tatiana in Eugene Onegin with Kent Opera 1977; Donna Elvira in Don Giovanni, Ludwigsburg Festival 1978; cr. title role in BBC world premiere of Prokofiev's Maddalena 1979; Fiordiligi in Così fan tutte, Bordeaux 1979; sang in première of the Eighth Book of Madrigals in Zürich Monteverdi Festival 1979; Violetta in Kent Opera's production of La Traviata, Edin. Festival 1979; Cinna in Lucio Silla, Zurich 1981; The Governess in The Turn of the Screw, Geneva 1981; Cleopatra in Giulio Cesare, Frankfurt 1981; Teresa in Benvenuto Cellini, Berlioz Festival, Lyon 1982, Leila in Les Pêcheurs de Perles, Scottish Opera 1982–83; Governess in The Turn of the Screw, ENO 1984; Helena in Glyndebourne's production of Britten's A Midsummer Night's Dream; Donna Anna in Don Giovanni, Frankfurt Opera 1985 and with Kent Opera 1988; Rosario in Goyescas by Granados 1988, Helena in Midsummer Night's Dream, London Opera 1990; cr. role of Duchess of Argyll in Thomas Adès's Powder Her Face, Cheltenham Int. Music Festival and London 1995; regular engagements including recitals in France, Austria, Belgium, Netherlands, Germany, Scandinavia, Switzerland, Italy, Spain, USA; festival appearances include Aix-en-Provence, Spoleto, Bergen, Versailles, Flanders, Netherlands, Prague, Edin. and BBC Promenade concerts; master-classes at Pears-Britten School, Aldeburgh, Trinity Coll. of Music, London, Dartington Summer Festival, Meridian TV. *Recordings include:* Vespro della Beata Vergine 1610 (Monteverdi), Ode for St, Cecilia's Day (Handel), Acis and Galatea (Handel), Admeto (Handel), A Child of Our Time (Tippett), three recital discs of French, Spanish and Mozart songs with John Constable, Quatre Chansons Françaises (Britten), Trois Poèmes de Mallarmé (Ravel), Chants d'Auvergne (Canteloube), Les Illuminations (Britten), Bachianas Brasileiras No. 5 (Villa Lobos), Cabaret Classics with John Constable, Knoxville-Summer of 1915 (Barber), South of the Border (Down Mexico Way…) arranged by Christopher Palmer for Jill Gomez, Britten's Blues (songs by Britten and Cole Porter); premiere recordings of Quatre Chansons Françaises (Britten), Cantiga – The Song of Inês de Castro commissioned by her from David Matthews, Seven Early Songs (Mahler), A Spanish Songbook (with John Constable), The Knot Garden (Tippett), Miss Julie (William Alwyn), Powder Her Face (Thomas Adès). *Address:* 16 Milton Park, London, N6 5QA, England (home).

GÓMEZ MONT URUETA, Fernando Francisco, LicenDer; Mexican lawyer and politician; *Secretary of Interior;* b. 1963; s. of Felipe Gómez Mont; ed Escuela Libre de Derecho; mem. Cámara Federal de Diputados 1991–94, Chair. Justice Comm. 1991–94; adviser to Pres. Ernesto Zedillo 1994–2000; mem. Partido Acción Nacional, fmr mem. Nat. Exec. Council and Policy Comm., Rep. in Fed. Electoral Inst. –1995 (resgnd); Pnr, Zínser Esponda y Gómez Mont SC, (law firm), Mexico City 1995–2008; Sec. of Interior 2008–. *Address:* Secretariat of State for the Interior, Bucareli 99, Col. Juárez, 06069 México, DF, Mexico (office). *Telephone:* (55) 5592-1141 (office). *Fax:* (55) 5546-5350 (office). *Website:* www.gobernacion.gob.mx (office).

GOMEZ-PIMIENTA, Bernardo, MArch; Mexican architect and lecturer; b. 18 Aug. 1961, Brussels, Belgium; s. of Jose Luis Gomez-Pimienta and Danielle Magar; m. Loredana Dall'Amico; one d. one s.; ed Universidad Anáhuac, Mexico City, Columbia Univ., New York, USA; draftsman, George Wimpey Contractors Ltd, London, UK 1980–81; Co-Dir Ten Arquitectos 1987–; Dir Furniture Design, Visual Int. 1995–; Prof. of Architecture Universidad Iberoamericana 1987–89, Universidad Anáhuac 1989, Universidad Nacional Autónomia de México 1992–96, 1998–, Federico E. Marcial Chair of Architecture 2002; Visiting Prof., Southern Calif. Inst. of Architecture 1994, Univ. of Illinois at Urbana-Champaign 1996–97; mem. Mexican Coll. of Architects 1990; mem. Editorial Bd and founding mem. Arquine Review 1997–; mem. Bd Architecture Cttee, Colegio de Arquitectos de la Ciudad de Mexico AC 1998–; mem. Editorial Bd Periódico Reforma 2002; mem. Jury AIA Design Honour Awards (New Mexico) 1997, (Iowa) 1999, (San Juan) 1999, Premios Alfher 2000, Fere Ambiente, Frankfurt 2002, II Bienal Nacional de Diseño 2003; mem. Academia Nacional de Arquitectura 2003; over 40 architectural awards from Mexico, USA, Ecuador, UK and Argentina. *Architectural works include:* House 'O' 1992, Televisa Services Bldg 1994, Museum of Natural History, Mexico City 1996, Nat. Centre of the Arts, Mexico City 1996, Casa IA 2001, Hotel Habita 2002, Educare 2002, Arquine 2002, Mesa Lupa 2002, Perchero Ti

2002, Mesa Lobe 2002, Silla IA 2002. *Publications include:* numerous books, monographs, periodicals, catalogues and reviews. *Address:* Ten Arquitectos, 22 West 19th Street, 9th Floor, New York, NY 10011, USA (office); Ten Arquitectos, Cuernavaca 114-PB, Col. Condesa, Mexico City 06 140, Mexico (office). *Telephone:* (212) 620-0794 (NY) (office); (55) 5211-8004 (office). *Fax:* (212) 620-0798 (NY) (office); (55) 5286-1735 (office). *E-mail:* b.gomezpimienta@ten-arquitectos.com (office). *Website:* www.ten-arquitectos .com (office).

GÓMEZ-POMPA, Arturo, DrSc; Mexican biologist, botanist and academic; *University Professor Emeritus and Distinguished Professor Emeritus of Botany, University of California, Riverside;* b. 1934, Mexico City; ed Universidad Nacional Autónoma de México (UNAM— Nat. Autonomous Univ. of Mexico); fmr Prof. of Botany, Univ. of California, Riverside, USA, fmr Univ. Prof. and Distinguished Prof. of Botany, now Univ. Prof. Emer. and Distinguished Prof. Emer. of Botany, fmr Dir Inst. of Univ. of California to Mexico and US (UC MEXUS); Founder and CEO Inst. for Research on Biotic Resources (INIREB), Xalapa, Veracruz; Head of Dept of Botany, UNAM-Inst. of Biology, Prof. of Ecology and Botany, Faculty of Nat. Univ.; Founder and first Pres. Asociación Mexicana de Jardines Botánicos, AC (Mexican Asscn of Botanic Gardens, AC) 1983; Pres. Bd El Edén Ecological Reserve, AC; mem. Bd American Inst. of Biological Sciences, Exec. Council Tyler Prize; mem. Awards Cttee Acad. of Sciences for the Developing World, Int. Scientific Advisory Bd INBio, Costa Rica; fmr Vice-Chair. Species Survival Comm. of Int. Union for Conservation of Nature (IUCN); fmr Pres. Int. Coordinating Council of UNESCO's MAB Programme; fmr mem. Bd of Govs The Nature Conservancy; Founder and Exec. Dir US-Mexico Foundation for Science; fmr mem. Advisory Cttee on Science, Space and Tech. of US House of Reps, Bd Smithsonian Inst., Washington, DC; Founder and mem. Bd Pronatura, AC; mem. acads of Mexico, Latin American, Third World and American Acad. of Arts and Sciences; Dr hc (Autonomous Univ. of Morelos); Medal of Merit, Univ. of Veracruz, Tyler Prize for Environmental Achievement, Chevron Conservation Medal, Luis Elizondo Prize in Science and Tech., Instituto Tecnológico de Estudios Superiores de Monterrey, Arca de Oro Medal (Netherlands) 1984, Alfonso L. Herrera Medal, Mexican Inst. of Renewable Natural Resources, Botanical Merit Medal, Botanical Soc. of Mexico. *Publications:* more than 200 scientific papers in professional journals on tropical ecology, ethnobotany, conservation and man. of tropical forests. *Address:* 3133 Batchelor Hall, University of California, 900 University Avenue, Riverside, CA 92521, USA (office). *Telephone:* (951) 827-4686 (office); (951) 827-4748 (office). *Fax:* (951) 827-4748 (office); (951) 827-4437 (office). *E-mail:* arturo .gomez-pompa@ucr.edu (office); floramex@ucr.edu (office). *Website:* www.ucr .edu (office); maya.ucr.edu/pril/PRIL.html (office).

GOMORY, Ralph Edward, PhD; American foundation executive, mathematician and business executive; *President, Alfred P. Sloan Foundation;* b. 7 May 1929, Brooklyn Heights, NY; s. of Andrew L. Gomory and Marian Schellenberg; m. 1st Laura Secretan Dumper 1954 (divorced 1968); two s. one d.; m. 2nd Lilian Wu; ed Williams Coll., King's Coll., Cambridge and Princeton Univ.; Lt, USN 1954–57; Higgins Lecturer and Asst Prof., Princeton Univ. 1957–59; joined IBM 1959, Fellow 1964, filled various managerial positions including Dir Mathematical Science Dept, Dir of Research 1970–86, Vice-Pres. 1973–84, Sr Vice-Pres. 1985–89, mem. Corporate Man. Bd 1983–89, Sr Vice-Pres. for Science and Tech. 1986–89 (retd); Andrew D. White Prof.-at-Large, Cornell Univ. 1970–76; Pres. Alfred P. Sloan Foundation, New York 1989–; Dir Bank of New York 1986–88, Industrial Research Inst. 1986–91; mem. NAS, Nat. Acad. of Eng, American Acad. of Arts and Sciences, Council on Foreign Relations, White House Science Council (1986–89), Visiting Cttee Harvard Univ. Grad. School of Business 1995–; Fellow, Econometric Soc., American Acad. of Arts and Sciences 1973; Trustee, Hampshire Coll. 1977–86, Princeton Univ. 1985–89; Hon. DSc (Williams Coll.) 1973, (Polytechnic Univ.) 1987, (Syracuse Univ.) 1989, (Carnegie Mellon Univ.) 1989; Hon. LHD (Pace Univ.) 1986; Lanchester Prize, Operations Research Soc. of America 1964, John von Neumann Theory Prize 1984, Harry Goode Memorial Award 1984, IRI Medal 1985, IEEE Eng Leadership Recognition Award 1988, Nat. Medal of Science 1988, Presidential Award (New York Acad. of Sciences) 1992, Arthur M. Bueche Award, Nat. Acad. of Eng 1993. *Address:* Alfred P. Sloan Foundation, 630 Fifth Avenue, Suite 2550, New York, NY 10111 (office); 260 Douglas Road, Chappaqua, NY 10514, USA (home). *Telephone:* (212) 649-1649 (office). *Fax:* (212) 757-5117 (office). *E-mail:* gomory@sloan.org (office). *Website:* www.sloan.org/main.shtml (office).

GOMRINGER, Eugen; Swiss poet and academic; b. 20 Jan. 1925, Cachuela Esperanza, Bolivia; s. of Eugen Gomringer and Delicia Rodriguez; m. 1st Klara Stöckli 1950; m. 2nd Nortrud Ottenhausen; five s. one d.; ed Kantonsschule, Zürich and Univ. of Berne; Sec. and Docent, Hochschule für Gestaltung, Ulm 1954–58; Art Dir Swiss Industrial Abrasives 1959–67; Man. Dir Schweizer Werkbund, Zürich 1961–67; Man. of Cultural Relations, Rosenthal AG, Germany 1967–85; Prof. of Aesthetics, Düsseldorf Art School 1976–90; Man. Int. Forum for Design, Ulm 1988–; f. Inst. für Konstruktive Kunst und Poesie IKKP Rehau 1999; Hon. Prof. Univ. of Zwickau; mem. Akad. der Künste, Berlin, PEN. *Publications:* several books of poetry and monographs in the art field. *Leisure interests:* mountaineering, art collecting, farming, dogs. *Address:* Wurlitz 22, 95111 Rehau, Germany (home).

GOMUŁKA, Stanisław, DEcon; Polish economist and academic; *Reader in Economics, London School of Economics;* b. 11 Sept. 1940, Krężoły; m.; one s.; ed Warsaw Univ.; Researcher, Dept of Econs, Warsaw Univ. 1962–65; Reader in Econs, LSE 1970–; Researcher, Dept of Econs, Netherlands Inst. for Advanced Studies 1980–81, Pennsylvania Univ. 1985–86, Stanford Univ. 1986, Columbia Univ. 1987, Harvard Univ. 1989–90; econ. adviser to Polish govts 1989–, to Chair. Nat. Bank of Poland 1996–97; consultant, IMF, OECD,

EU. *Publications:* Inventive Activity, Diffusion and the Stages of Economic Growth 1971, Growth, Innovation and Reform in Eastern Europe 1986, The Theory of Technological Change and Economic Growth 1990, Emerging from Communism – Lessons from Russia, China, and Eastern Europe (co-ed.) 1998, The Theory of Technological Change and Economic Growth (ebook) 2002. *Address:* London School of Economics, Houghton Street, Room S.576, London, WC2A 2AE (office); 4 Woodfield Way, London, N11 2PH, England (home). *Telephone:* (20) 7955-7510 (office). *E-mail:* s.gomulka@lse.ac.uk (office); gomulka@chrzan.demon.co.uk (office). *Website:* www.lse.ac.uk (office); econ.lse.ac.uk/staff/sgomulka/index_own.html (office).

GONCHAR, Andrei Aleksandrovich; Russian mathematician; b. 21 Nov. 1931, Moscow; m.; two c.; ed Moscow State Univ.; Lecturer, Docent, Moscow State Univ. 1957–63, Scientific Sec. Dept of Math. 1964–65; Sr Researcher, Head of Div., then Deputy Dir V.A. Steklov Math. Inst. 1966–68; main scientific research carried out in complex analysis and approximations theory; Ed.-in-Chief Matematicheskiye Sborniki; Corresp. mem. USSR (now Russian) Acad. of Sciences 1974, mem. 1987, Vice-Pres. 1991–98; mem. Nat. Acad. of Math. *Publications:* numerous scientific publs on complex analysis and approximation theory, theory of analytical functions. *Address:* Russian Academy of Sciences, Department of Mathematics, Leninsky pr. 14, Moscow, Russia (office). *Telephone:* (495) 938-18-12 (office). *Fax:* (495) 135-0555 (office). *Website:* www.mi.ras.ru (office).

GONCHAR, Nikolai Nikolayevich, CEconSc; Russian politician; b. 16 Oct. 1946, Murmansk; m.; one d.; ed Moscow Energy Inst.; engineer, then head of div. Moscow City Council on research activities of students 1972–75; Head of Div. Research Inst. of Complex Devt of Nat. Econs of Moscow 1976–82; Deputy, then First Deputy Chair. Exec. Cttee of Deputies, Soviet of Bauman Region of Moscow 1987–89, Chair. 1990–91; Sec. Regional CPSU Cttee 1989–90; Deputy Chair. Moscow City Soviet of People's Deputies 1990–91, Chair. 1991–93; mem. Council of Fed. 1993–95, Deputy Chair. Cttee on Budget and Financial Regulations 1994–95; mem. State Duma 1995–, mem. Cttee on Budget, Banks, Taxes and Finances 1995–. *Address:* State Duma, Okhotny Ryad 1, 103265 Moscow, Russia (office). *Telephone:* (495) 292-75-08 (office). *E-mail:* gonchar@duma.gov.ru (office). *Website:* www.duma.gov.ru (office).

GONCHIGDORJ, Radnaasümberelyn, PhD, DSc; Mongolian politician and mathematician; *Chairman, Mongolian Social Democratic Party;* b. 1954, Tsakhir Dist, Arkhangai Prov.; s. of Radnaasumberel Gonchigdorj and Namjaa Gonchigdorj; m. Damdinsurengiin Hishigt 1977; two s. two d.; ed Mongolian State Univ.; Lecturer in Math., Mongolian State Univ. 1975–88; Dir Inst. of Math., Mongolian Acad. of Sciences 1988–90; Chair. Exec. Cttee Mongolian Social Democratic Movt 1990; Chair. Mongolian Social Democratic Party 1994–; Deputy to Great People's Hural 1990–92; Vice-Pres. of Mongolia and Chair. State Little Hural 1990–92; mem. State Great Hural 1992–96, Chair. 1996–2000; presidential cand. 2001. *Address:* c/o State Great Hural, Government House, Ulan Bator 12, Mongolian People's Republic. *Telephone:* (1) 326877. *Fax:* (1) 322866.

GÖNCZ, Árpád, LLD; Hungarian fmr head of state and writer; b. 10 Feb. 1922, Budapest; s. of Lajos Göncz and Ilona Heimann; m. Mária Zsuzsanna Göntér 1946; two s. two d.; ed Pázmány Péter University of Arts and Sciences, Budapest; employed as banking clerk with Nat. Land Credit Inst.; joined Ind. Smallholders, Landworkers and Bourgeois Party; leading positions in Ind. Youth Org.; Ed.-in-Chief Generation (weekly); sentenced in 1957 to life imprisonment as defendant in political Bibó trial; released under amnesty 1963; then freelance writer and literary translator, especially of English works; Pres. Hungarian Writers Federation 1989–90, Hon. Pres. 1990–; founding mem. Free Initiatives Network, Free Democratic Fed., Historic Justice Cttee; mem. of Parl. 1990; Acting Pres. of Hungary May–Aug. 1990, Pres. of Hungary 1990–2000; Hon. KCMG 1991; Dr hc (Butler) 1990, (Connecticut) 1991, (Oxford) 1995, (Sorbonne) 1996, (Bologna) 1997; Attila József Prize 1983, Wheatland Prize 1989, Premio Meditteraneo 1991, George Washington Prize 2000, Pro Humanitate Award 2001, Polish Business Oscar Award 2002. *Publications include:* Men of God (novel) 1974, Encounters (short stories) 1980, Homecoming and Other Stories (short stories) 1991, Hungarian Medea (play), Balance (play), Iron Bars (play), A Pessimistic Comedy (play), Persephone (play), political essays; translated more than 100 works, mostly by British and American authors, including James Baldwin, Edgar Lawrence Doctorow, William Faulkner, William Golding, Ernest Hemingway, William Styron, Susan Sontag, John Updike, Edith Wharton and others. *Leisure interests:* reading, walking. *Address:* Office of the Former President, 1055 Budapest, Kossuth tér 4, Hungary (office). *Telephone:* (1) 441-3550 (office). *Fax:* (1) 441-3552 (office).

GÖNCZ, Kinga, MD; Hungarian physician and politician; b. 8 Nov. 1947, Budapest; m.; two c.; ed Semmelweis Univ., Budapest; psychiatrist 1978–86; Sr Asst Prof., Nat. Inst. of Medical Rehabilitation, Budapest 1982–89; Asst Prof., Dept of Social Policy, Inst. of Sociology, Eötvös Loránd Univ., Budapest 1989–2002; Dir, Pnrs Hungary Foundation 1994–2002; teaching appointment at Dept of Human Rights, Cen. European Univ. 1998–2003; Political Sec. of State, Ministry of Health, Social and Family Affairs 2002–04; Minister of Equal Opportunities 2004; Minister of Youth, Family, Social Affairs and Equal Opportunities 2004–06; Minister of Foreign Affairs 2006–09; Visiting Scholar, Univ. of Michigan; Lecturer, Mandel School of Applied Social Sciences, Case Western Univ., Cleveland. *Publications:* several publications on social work, supervision and training. *Address:* c/o Ministry of Foreign Affairs, 1027 Budapest, Bem rkp. 47, Hungary (office).

GONDJOUT, Laure Olga, MA; Gabonese politician; *Minister of Communication, Posts, Telecommunications, and New Information Technologies;* b. 18 Dec. 1953, Paris, France; d. of Paul Gondjout, fmr Pres. of Supreme Court and fmr Pres. of Nat. Ass; ed Catholic Univ. of Paris, Polytechnic of Central London, UK; began career as translator; worked at African Devt Bank, Abidjan, mem. Bd of Dirs for Gabon, African Devt Bank, Libreville 1995–2001 returned to Gabon and served as adviser to Pres. 1984–2002, Secrétaire particulière to Pres. 2003; Minister Del. to Minister of State for Foreign Affairs 2006–07; Minister of Communication, Posts, Telecommunications, and New Information Technologies Dec. 2007–Feb. 2008, Oct. 2008–, of Foreign Affairs, Co-operation, Francophonie and Regional Integration Feb.–Oct. 2008; Gen. Sec. Children of Africa Foundation, Libreville. *Address:* Ministry of Post and Telecommunications and New Technologies, Libreville, Gabon (office).

GONDWE, Goodall; Malawi politician and economist; *Minister of Finance;* Dir of African Div., IMF 1998; fmr Econ. Adviser to Pres. of Malawi; Minister of Finance 2004–. *Address:* Ministry of Finance, POB 30049, Capital City, Lilongwe 3, Malawi (office). *Telephone:* 1789355 (office). *Fax:* 1789173 (office). *Website:* www.finance.malawi.gov.mw.

GONG, Ke; Chinese engineer, academic and university administrator; *President, Tianjin University;* b. 1955, Beijing; ed Beijing Inst. of Tech., Tech. Univ. Graz, Austria; Prof., Tsinghua Univ. 1994, also Chair. Dept of Electronic Eng 1997, Dir Chinese Nat. Lab. on Microwave and Digital Communications 1998, Vice-Pres., Tsinghua Univ. 1999, also Dean, School of Information 2004, Dir Tsinghua Nat. Lab. for Information Science and Tech. 2005; Pres. Tianjin Univ. 2006–; Vice-Pres. Chinese Inst. of Electronics, Chinese Inst. of Communication, China Inst. of Measurement and Instrumentations; Exec. Mem. China Asscn of Science and Tech.; Exec. Mem. Ministry of Information Industry Tech. Cttee; Fellow, Russian Acad. of Aerospace Sciences 2002–; Pan Wen Yuan Foundation Award for Outstanding Research in 2006. *Address:* Office of the President, Tianjin University, 92 Weijin Road, Nankai District, Tianjin 300072, People's Republic of China (office). *Telephone:* (22) 27406147 (office). *Website:* www.tju.edu.cn (office).

GONG, Yuzhi; Chinese politician; *Vice-President, China Anti-Cult Association;* b. 1929, Xiangtan, Hunan Prov.; ed Tsinghua Univ.; joined CCP 1948; researcher, CCP Cen. Cttee Propaganda Dept 1952–66; Deputy Office Dir Cttee for Editing and Publishing Works of Mao Zedong 1977–80; Deputy Dir CCP Cen. Cttee Party Documents Research Office 1982; Deputy Dir CCP Cen. Cttee Propaganda Dept 1988; mem. 5th to 8th CPPCC Nat. Cttee 1978–98 (Vice-Chair. Sub-cttee of Study 1993–98), Standing Cttee 9th CPPCC Nat. Cttee 1998–2003 (Vice-Chair. Sub-cttee of Cultural and Historical Data 1998–2003); Vice-Pres. CCP Cen. Cttee Cen. Party School 1994–96, Soc. of Research on History of CCP (Pres. 1999–), China Soc. of Dialectics of Nature, China Anti-Cult Asscn 2000–; Dir Research Centre for Theory of Building Socialism with Chinese Characteristics; Exec. Deputy Dir Cen. Party History Research Centre; fmr mem. Academic Council, Inst. of Philosophy, Chinese Acad. of Social Sciences; fmr Guest Prof., Beijing and Tsinghua Univs. *Publications:* Some Questions on the Law of Development for Natural Sciences, On Science, Philosophy and Society, From New Democracy to Primary Stage of Socialism. *Address:* c/o Central Committee of the Chinese Communist Party, Beijing, People's Republic of China.

GOÑI CARRASCO, José; Chilean government official and diplomatist; *Ambassador to USA;* fmr Dir European Section, Dept of Int. Econ. Relations, Ministry of Foreign Affairs; Amb. to Sweden 1997–2000, to Italy 2000–04, to Mexico 2006–07, to USA 2009–; Head Chilean Trade Office for Sweden, Norway, Finland, Iceland and Baltic Nations, Estocolmo 1997–2000; Rep. to WFP and FAO, Rome 2000–04; Researcher and Prof. of Latin American Econs, Estocolmo Univ. 2000–04; Adviser, Ministry of Foreign Affairs 2005–06; Dir-Gen. Nat. Environment Comm. 2005–06; Minister of Nat. Defence 2007–09; mem. Partido por la Democracia (PPD). *Publications include:* various books and articles on econs. *Address:* Embassy of Chile, 1732 Massachusetts Avenue, NW, Washington, DC 20036, USA (office). *Telephone:* (202) 785-1746 (office). *Fax:* (202) 887-5579 (office). *E-mail:* embassy@embassyofchile.org (office). *Website:* www.chile-usa.org (office).

GONO, Gideon; Zimbabwean central banker; *Governor, Reserve Bank of Zimbabwe;* b. 29 Nov. 1959; m. Hellin Gono; two d. one s.; began career with ZimBank; worked at Commercial Bank of Zimbabwe (re-named Jewel Bank), fmr CEO Jewel Bank; Gov. Reserve Bank of Zimbabwe 2003–; Head Univ. of Zimbabwe Council; fmr Chair. Zimbabwe Broadcasting Holdings; Dr hc (Univ. of Zimbabwe). *Address:* Reserve Bank of Zimbabwe, POB 1283, Harare, Zimbabwe (office). *Telephone:* (4) 703000 (office). *Fax:* (4) 706450 (office). *E-mail:* rbzmail@rbz.co.zw (office). *Website:* www.rbz.co.zw (office).

GONSALVES, Ralph, PhD; Saint Vincent and the Grenadines politician and lawyer; *Prime Minister and Minister of Finance, Planning, Economic Development, Labour and Information, National Security;* b. 1946; ed Univ. of West Indies, Victoria Univ. of Manchester, UK; called to Bar, Gray's Inn, London; practised law at Eastern Caribbean Supreme Court; fmr Lecturer, Depts of Govt, Political Science and Sociology, Univ. of W Indies; Leader United People's Movt (UPM) 1979–82, Movt for Nat. Unity (MNU) 1994–98; Leader United Labour Party (ULP); Prime Minister of Saint Vincent and the Grenadines and Minister of Finance, Planning, Economic Development, Labour and Information 2001–, Minister of Nat. Security 2005–. *Address:* Office of the Prime Minister, Administrative Building, 4th Floor, Bay Street, Kingstown, Saint Vincent and the Grenadines (office). *Telephone:* 451-2939 (office). *Fax:* 457-2152 (office). *Website:* pmosvg@caribsurf.com (office).

GONUL, Mehmet Vecdi; Turkish politician; *Minister of National Defence;* b. 1939, Erzincan; m.; three c.; ed Faculty of Political Science, Ankara Univ.; participated in state training programme for recruiting dist govs 1967; Dist Gov. in several areas of Turkey 1967–76; Gov. of Kocaeli 1976–77, later of Izmir; Dir-Gen. of Nat. Security (Police) Directorate 1977–79; Gov. of Ankara

1979–88; Under-Sec. Ministry of the Interior 1988–91; apptd Head of State Court of Accounts 1991; elected MP for Kocaeli 1999–2001, Deputy Speaker of Parl. 1999–2001; joined AK Party 2001; currently Minister of Nat. Defence; Del. to EU Parl. Ass. *Address:* Ministry of National Defence, Milli Savunma Bakanlığı, 06100 Ankara, Turkey (office). *Telephone:* (312) 4254596 (office). *Fax:* (312) 4184737 (office). *E-mail:* meb@meb.gov.tr (office). *Website:* www.msb.gov.tr (office).

GONZALES, Alberto (Al) R., LLB; American lawyer and government official; b. 4 Aug. 1955, San Antonio, Tex.; m. Rebecca Gonzales; three s.; ed Rice Univ., Harvard Law School; served in USAF 1973–75, attended USAF Acad. 1975–77; joined Vinson & Elkins LLP, Houston, Tex. 1982, Pnr –1994; Adjunct Prof. of Law, Univ. of Houston –1994; Gen. Counsel to Tex. Gov. George W. Bush 1994–97; Sec. of State for Tex. 1977–99; Justice of Supreme Court of Tex. 1999–2001; Legal Counsel to the White House 2001–04, Attorney Gen. 2004–07; Special Legal Counsel to Houston Host Cttee for Summit of Industrialized Nations 1990; mem. Del. of American Council of Young Political Leaders to People's Repub. of China 1995, Mexico 1996; Pres. Houston Hispanic Bar Asscn 1990–91, Leadership Houston 1993–94; Chair. Comm. for Dist Decentralization, Houston Ind. School Dist 1994; mem. Bd of Dirs United Way of Tex. Gulf Coast 1993–94; mem. Cttee on Undergraduate Admissions, Rice Univ. 1994; mem. Bd State Bar of Tex. 1991–94, Bd of Trustees, Tex. Bar Foundation 1996–99; mem. American Law Inst. 1999–; mem. Republican Party; Hispanic Salute Award, Houston Metro Ford Dealers 1989, Outstanding Young Lawyer of Tex., Tex. Young Lawyers Asscn 1992, Presidential Citation, State Bar of Tex. 1997, Latino Lawyer of the Year, Hispanic Nat. Bar Asscn 1999, Distinguished Alumnus of Rice Univ. 2002, Harvard Law School Asscn Award 2002, Hispanic Scholarship Fund Alumni Hall of Fame 2003, Good Neighbour Award, US–Mexico Chamber of Commerce 2003, Pres.'s Award, US Hispanic Chamber of Commerce 2003, Pres.'s Award, League of United Latin American Citizens 2003. *Address:* c/o US Department of Justice, 950 Pennsylvania Avenue, NW, Washington, DC 20530-0001, USA (office).

GONZALES POSADA, Luis; Peruvian politician and lawyer; b. 30 July 1945, Pisco; fmr Legal Adviser, Banco Industrial, Corporación Financiera de Desarrollo, Electricidad del Perú and of Social Security Dept; mem. Bd of Dirs, Seguro Social Obrero, Seguro Social del Empleado, Empresa Nacional de Turismo del Perú, La Crónica, Futura and Visión Peruana publishing cos; Dir and founder daily Hoy and the weekly Visión; has been on staff of La Tribuna, La Prensa, Correo and La Crónica; mem. Colegio de Abogados de Lima (Pres. Foreign Affairs Comm. 1999) and of Colegio de Periodistas de Lima; Minister of Justice 1985–86; currently mem. Congreso. *Address:* Congreso de la República del Perú, Palacio Legislativo, Plaza Bolívar. Avenue, Abancay s/n, Lima, Peru. *Telephone:* 311-7777. *Website:* www.congreso.gob.pe.

GONZALEZ, Antonio Erman; Argentine politician; b. 16 May 1935, La Rioja Prov.; ed Nat. Univ. of Córdoba; fmr Prof. of Accountancy, La Rioja Univ.; econ., accountancy and taxation adviser to various firms in La Rioja; accountant, Inst. for Social Security and Welfare (IPSAS), La Rioja Prov. 1961–64; Sec. for Finance, Buenos Aires Municipality 1963–64, Econ. Adviser ad honorem 1964–66; Gen. Man. IPSAS 1964–65; auditor, Bank of La Rioja Prov. 1966; Under-Sec. of Finance, Prov. of La Rioja 1967; mem. Bd IPSAS 1967–69; mem. State Exchequer of La Rioja 1971–72, 1974–75; Pres. Bank of La Rioja 1972–74, 1985, econ. consultant 1981–82, Dir 1984, adviser 1987; Minister of Finance and Public Works 1985–87, 1988–89, of Health and Social Welfare 1989, of Economy 1989–91, of Defense 1991–93; Dist deputation 1987–88; elected Deputy 1989; Minister of Labor and Social Security 1997-99 (resgnd); Vice-Pres. Argentine Cen. Bank 1989; charged with illegal arms sales to Ecuador and Croatia July 2001. *Publications:* numerous tech. papers.

GONZALEZ, Salvador Anglada; Spanish business executive; *CEO, Eurotel Praha;* ed Instituto de Empresa, Madrid; with Productos Organicos y Minerales and Dow Jones Markets 1990–97; Dir of Banking Sales, Dell Computer from 1997, becoming Dir, Preferred Accounts Div. and later Dir of Sales and Marketing for S Europe –2002; Dir of Sales, Telefónica de Espana 2002–03, Dir of Sales and Marketing 2003; currently CEO, Eurotel Praha. *Address:* Eurotel Praha spol. s.r.o., Vyskočilova 1442/1b, PO Box 70, 14021 Prague 4, Czech Republic (office). *Telephone:* (2) 67011111 (office). *Website:* www.eurotel.cz (office).

GONZÁLEZ CASANOVA, Pablo; Mexican researcher and professor; b. 11 Feb. 1922, Toluca; s. of Pablo González Casanova and Concepción del Valle; m. Natalia Henríquez Ureña 1947; three s.; ed El Colegio de México, Escuela Nacional de Antropología, Univ. Nacional Autónoma de México and Univ. de Paris, France; Asst Researcher, Inst. de Investigaciones Sociales, Univ. Nacional Autónoma de México (UNAM) 1944–50, Researcher 1950–52, Full-time Researcher 1973–78; Researcher, El Colegio de México 1950–54; Sec. Gen. Asscn of Univs 1953–54; Titular Prof. of Mexican Sociology, Escuela Nacional de Ciencias Políticas y Sociales, UNAM 1952–66, of Gen. Sociology 1954–58; Dir Escuela Nacional de Ciencias Políticas y Sociales 1957–65, Full-time Titular Prof. 1964–65, Titular Prof. of Research Planning 1967–; Dir Inst. Investigaciones Sociales, UNAM 1966–70; Rector UNAM 1970–72; Visiting Prof., Univ. of Cambridge, UK 1981–82; Pres. Admin. Cttee Facultad Latinoamericana de Ciencias Sociales, Santiago and Centro Latinoamericano de Investigaciones Sociales, Rio de Janeiro, UNESCO 1959–65; Consultant UN Univ. 1983–87; Dir Centro de Investigaciones Interdisciplinarias en Humanidades Univ. Nacional Autónoma de Mexico 1986–; mem. Asscn Int. de Sociologues de Langue Française, Comité Int. pour la Documentation des Sciences Sociales, Acad. de la Investigación Científica; Pres. Asociación Latinoamericana de Sociología 1969–72. *Publications:* El Poder al Pueblo 1985, El misoneísmo y la modernidad cristiana 1948, Satira del Siglo XVIII (with José Miranda) 1953, Una utopia de América 1953, La literatura perseguida en la crisis de la Colonia 1958, La ideología norteamericana sobre inversiones extranjeras 1955, Estudio de la técnica social 1958, La Democracia en México 1965, Las categorías del desarrollo económico y la investigación en ciencias sociales 1967, Sociología de la explotación 1969, América Latina: Historia de Medio Siglo 1925–1975 (two vols, ed.) 1977, Historia del Movimiento Obrero en América Latina, Siglo XX 1981, El Estado y los Partidos Políticos en México 1981, América Latina, Hoy 1990, El Estado y la Política en el Sur del Mundo 1994. *Address:* Peña Pobre 28, Tlalpan, México, DF 14050, Mexico. *Telephone:* 5506702.

GONZÁLEZ DEL VALLE, Jorge; Guatemalan international organization official, economist and academic; b. 24 Jan. 1929; ed Univ. of San Carlos, Guatemala, Columbia Univ., New York, Yale Univ., New Haven, Conn., USA; worked in Bank of Guatemala and Cen. American Bank for Econ. Integration; Prof. of Econs at various univs including Universidad de San Carlos de Guatemala, Universidad de Costa Rica, en San José y en la Nacional de Costa Rica, en Heredia, el Centro de Estudios Monetarios Latinoamericanos, en México, DF. 1956–; Exec. Dir IMF for four years; Exec. Sec. Cen. American Monetary Council for nine years; Head Centre for Latin American Monetary Studies (CEMLA) 1978–90.

GONZÁLEZ MACCHI, Luis Angel; Paraguayan fmr head of state and lawyer; b. 13 Dec. 1947, Asunción; s. of Dr Saúl González and the late Julia Macchi; m. Susana Galli; two d.; ed Univ. Nacional de Asunción; fmr Pres. Nat. Congress; Dir-Gen. and Pres. of Exec. Council, Servicio Nacional de Promoción Profesional (SNPP) 1993–98; Pres. of Paraguay March 1999–2003; sentenced to eight years in prison for fraud and embezzlement 2006; mem. Asociación Nacional Republicana—Partido Colorado. *Address:* c/o Asociación Nacional Republicana—Partido Colorado, Casa de los Colorados, 25 de Mayo 842, Asunción, Paraguay (office).

GONZÁLEZ MÁRQUEZ, Felipe; Spanish lawyer and politician; b. 5 March 1942, Seville; m. Carmen Romero; two s. one d.; ed lower and high school, school of law, continued studies at Catholic Univ. of Louvain, Belgium; on graduating from law school, opened first labour law office to deal with workers' problems in Seville 1966; mem. Spanish Socialist Youth 1962; mem. Spanish Socialist Party (Partido Socialista Obrero Español, PSOE) 1964–, mem. Seville Prov. Cttee 1965–69, Nat. Cttee 1969–70, mem. Exec. Bd 1970, First Sec. 1974–79, resgnd; re-elected Sept. 1979, then Sec.-Gen. –1997; mem. for Madrid, Congress of Deputies 1977–2004; Prime Minister of Spain and Pres. Council of Ministers 1982–96; fmr Chair. Socialist Parl. Group; fmr EU Special Rep. for Fed. Repub. of Yugoslavia; mem. Club of Madrid, Circle of Montevideo, InterAcción Council, Shimon Peres Int. Council for Peace, Japanese Bonsai Asscn; Grand Cross of the Order of Mil. Merit 1984; Order of Isabel the Catholic 1996; Golden Cross of Merit (Austria) 1997; Dr hc (Louvain) 1995, Charlemagne Prize 1993, Carlos V Prize, Academia Europaea 2000. *Publications:* What is Socialism? 1976, P.S.O.E. 1977, El futuro no es lo que era (with J. Cebrián) 2001. *Leisure interests:* reading, bonsai plants. *Address:* c/o Partido Socialista Obrero Español (PSOE) (Spanish Socialist Worker's Party), Ferraz 68 y 70, 28008 Madrid (office); Fundación Progreso Global, Gobelas 31, 28023 Madrid, Spain. *Telephone:* (91) 5820444 (office). *Fax:* (91) 5820422 (office). *E-mail:* infopsoe@psoe.es (office). *Website:* www.psoe.es (office).

GONZÁLEZ PASTORA, Marco Antonio del Cármen, DScS, LLD; Nicaraguan international organization executive, academic and attorney; *Executive Secretary, Central American Commission for Environment and Development;* b. 16 July 1948, Jinotega; m. Gina Cuthbert; one d.; ed Nicaragua Nat. Univ., Friendship Univ., Moscow, Russia; fmrly with Rosenstiel School of Marine and Atmospheric Science, Univ. of Miami, Fla, USA; Exec. Sec. Comisión Centroamericana de Ambiente y Desarrollo (Cen. American Comm. for Environment and Devt—CCAD), Dir-Gen. for Environment of the Cen. American Integration System, mem. Tech. Cttee Técnico Asesor AEA and Rep. to World Labour Org.; Sr Adviser to Chair. of UN Gen. Ass.; mem. numerous cttees including IUCN Environmental Law Comm., Steering Cttee of Int. Inst. for Environmental Compliance and Enforcement (INECE); Del. to 10 Climate Change Convention Confs; Dr hc (Paulo Freire Univ.); World League of Environmental Lawyers Medal 2007, Academic Award from Autonomous Univ., Mexico. *Publications:* author of many articles and books on environmental law and policy issues, including Central American Manual of Environmental Law 2007, Nicaraguan Manual of Environmental Law 2009. *Address:* c. Verapaz C-32, Arcos de Santa Elena, Antiguo Cuscatlàn, San Salvador (office); Secretaría Ejecutiva de la Comisión Centroamericana de Ambiente y Desarrollo (SE-CCAD), Blvd Orden de Malta 470, Santa Elena, Antiguo Cuscatlàn, San Salvador, El Salvador (office). *Telephone:* 2248-8842 (office). *Fax:* 7888-9799 (office). *E-mail:* magonzalez@sica.int (office); magonzalezp2003@yahoo.com (home). *Website:* www.ccad.ws (office).

GONZÁLEZ RODRÍGUEZ, Francisco; Spanish banking executive; *Chairman and CEO, Banco Bilbao Vizcaya Argentaria SA;* b. 1944, Chantada, Lugo; m.; ed Universidad Complutense de Madrid; fmr computer programmer; fmrly with FG Inversiones Bursátiles; Chair. Argentaria 1996–99; Chair. and CEO Banco Bilbao Vizcaya Argentaria SA (BBVA) 2000–, Chair. Fundación BBVA; Dir Inst. for Int. Finance; Global Counsellor The Conf. Bd; Gov. Red Cross, Guggenheim Museum Bilbao, Museo de Bellas Artes, Fundación Principe de Asturias, Real Instituto Elcano, Foundation for Terrorism Victims, Foundation for Help Against Drug Addiction; mem. European Financial Services Roundtable, Institut Européen d'Etudes Bancaires, IMF Capital Markets Consultative Group, Int. Monetary Conf. *Address:* Banco Bilbao Vizcaya Argentaria SA, Plaza San Nicolás 4, 48005 Bilbao, Vizcaya, Spain (office). *Telephone:* (944) 875555 (office). *Fax:* (944) 876161 (office). *E-mail:* info@bbva.com (office). *Website:* www.bbva.com (office).

GONZÁLEZ SEGOVIA, Roberto Eudez; Paraguayan politician; *Minister of National Defence;* b. 1959, Piribebuy; m. Miriam Benítez de González; four c.; ed Universidad Nacional de Asunción; practised as lawyer from 1986; Legal Adviser, various nat. pvt. enterprises; participant, various congresses, seminars; mem. Students' Rights Centre UNA; Students' Rep. of Hon. Council Bd Law and Social Sciences UNA; apptd Minister of Home Affairs 2002; Minister of Nat. Defence –2007; Minister for Public Works and Communications 2008–. *Address:* Ministry of Public Works and Communications, Oliva y Alberdi, Asunción, Paraguay (office). *Telephone:* (21) 44-4411 (office). *Fax:* (21) 44-4421 (office). *Website:* www.mopc.gov.py (office).

GONZI, Lawrence, LLD; Maltese politician and lawyer; *Prime Minister;* b. 1 July 1953; s. of Louis Gonzi and Inez Gonzi (née Galea); m. Catherine Gonzi (née Callus); two s. one d.; ed Malta Univ.; practised law 1975–88; Speaker House of Reps. 1988–92, 1992–96; MP (Nationalist Party) 1996–, Whip Parl. Group 1997–99, Sec. Gen. 1997–98; Shadow Minister and Opposition Spokesman for Social Policy 1996–98; Leader of the House and Minister for Social Policy 1998–99, Deputy Prime Minister and Minister for Social Policy 1999–2004, Prime Minister 2004–, Minister of Finance 2004–08; Gen. Pres. Malta Catholic Action 1976–86; Chair. Pharmacy Bd 1987–88, Nat. Comm. for Persons with Disabilities 1987–94 (Pres. 1994–96), Nat. Comm. for Mental Health Reform 1987–96, Electoral System (Revision) Comm. 1994–95, Mizzi Org. Bd of Dirs 1989–97; mem. Prisons Bd 1987–88. *Address:* Office of the Prime Minister, Auberge de Castille, Valletta, CMR 02, Malta (office). *Telephone:* 21242560 (office). *Fax:* 21249888 (office). *E-mail:* lawrence.gonzi@gov.mt (office). *Website:* www.opm.gov.mt (office).

GOOCH, Graham Alan, OBE; British professional cricket coach and fmr professional cricketer; b. 23 July 1953, Leytonstone; s. of late Alfred and of Rose Gooch; m. Brenda Daniels 1976; three d.; ed Norlington Junior High School, Leytonstone, Redbridge Tech. Coll.; right-hand opening batsman, right-arm medium bowler; played for Essex 1973–97 (Capt. 1986–87 and 1989–94), Western Province 1982–83 and 1983–84; played in 118 Tests for England 1975 to 1994–95, 34 as Capt., scoring 8,900 runs (England record) (average 42.5) including 20 hundreds (highest score 333 and record Test match aggregate of 456 v. India, Lord's 1990, becoming only batsman to score a triple century and a century in a first-class match) and holding 103 catches; scored 44,841 runs (128 hundreds) and held 555 catches in first-class cricket; toured Australia 1978–79, 1979–80, 1990–91 (Capt.) and 1994–95; 125 limited-overs internationals, including 50 as Capt. (both England records); mem. England Selection Cttee 1996–99; Man. England Tour to Australia 1998–99; Head Coach Essex 2001–; Wisden Cricketer of the Year 1980, mem. Fed. of Int. Cricketers Asscn Hall of Fame 2000. *Publications:* Testing Times 1991, Gooch: My Autobiography 1995. *Leisure interests:* squash, golf, football. *Address:* c/o Essex County Cricket Club, The County Ground, New Writtle Street, Chelmsford, Essex, CM2 0PG, England. *Telephone:* (1245) 252420. *E-mail:* administration.essex@ecb.co.uk. *Website:* www.essexcricket.org.uk.

GOOD, Anthony Bruton Meyrick, FID; British public relations consultant and marketing consultant; b. 18 April 1933, Sutton, Surrey; s. of Meyrick G. B. Good and Amy M. Trussell; m. (divorced); two d.; ed Felsted School, Essex; man. trainee, Distillers Group; Editorial Asst Temple Press 1952–55; Public Relations Officer, Silver City Airways; Public Relations and Marketing Man., Air Holdings Group 1955–60; f. and Chair. Good Relations Ltd (later Good Relations Group PLC) 1961–89; Dir Cox and Kings Travel Ltd 1971–, Chair. 1975–; Chair. Good Relations (India) Ltd 1988–, Cox and Kings (India) Ltd 1988–, Good Consultancy Ltd 1989–, Flagship Group 1999–, Tranquil Moment 2000–, Sage Organic 2000–; (non-exec.) Dir Gowrings PLC 2003–05, Miller Insurance Group Ltd 2000–04, Neutrahealth PLC 2005–, Indo-British Partnership Network 2005–; Fellow, Inst. of Public Relations. *Leisure interest:* travel. *Address:* Clench House, Wootton Rivers, Marlborough, Wilts., SN8 4NT, England (home). *Telephone:* (1672) 810126 (office); (1672) 810670 (home). *Fax:* (1672) 810869 (office); (1672) 810149 (home). *E-mail:* anthony.good@btinternet.com.

GOOD, Leonard, PhD; Canadian international organization official; ed Univ. of Toronto, Univ. of Western Ontario; taught econs at Univ. of Prince Edward Island; various positions in Canadian Dept of Energy 1979–87; Deputy Minister of Environment 1989–93, 1998–99; Canada's Exec. Dir on Bd of IBRD (World Bank) 1994–98; Pres. Canadian Int. Devt Agency 1999–2003; Chair. and CEO Global Environment Facility 2003–06 (retd). *Address:* c/o Global Environment Facility Secretariat, 1818 H Street, NW, Washington, DC 20433, USA. *Telephone:* (202) 473-0508.

GOODALE, Ralph; Canadian politician; b. Wilcox, Sask.; m. Pamela Goodale; ed Univ. of Regina, Sask. and Univ. of Saskatchewan; MP for fed. constituency of Assiniboia 1974; Leader, Sask. Liberal Party 1980s; mem. Sask. Legis. Ass. 1986; MP for Regina-Wascana (now Wascana) 1993–; Minister of Agric. and Agri-Food 1993–97, of Natural Resources Canada 1997–2002, Minister of State and Leader of the Govt in House of Commons Jan.–May 2002, Minister of Public Works and Govt Services Canada, Minister responsible for the Canadian Wheat Bd, Fed. Interlocutor for Métis and Non-Status Indians, Minister responsible for Indian Residential Schools Resolution Canada, Minister responsible for Communication Canada and with regional responsibilities for Sask. and the North 2002–03, Minister of Finance 2003–06. *Address:* 310 University Park Drive, Regina, Sask. S4V 0Y8, Canada. *Telephone:* (306) 585-2202. *Fax:* (306) 585-2280. *E-mail:* goodale@sasktel.net. *Website:* www.rgoodale.ca.

GOODALL, Sir (Arthur) David (Saunders), Kt, GCMG, MA; British diplomatist (retd); b. 9 Oct. 1931, Blackpool; s. of Arthur William Goodall and Maisie Josephine Byers; m. Morwenna Peecock 1962; two s. one d.; ed Ampleforth Coll., Trinity Coll., Oxford; army service in Kenya, Aden, Cyprus 1954–56; joined Foreign (now Diplomatic) Service 1956, served at Nicosia, Jakarta, Bonn, Nairobi, Vienna 1956–75, Head of Western European Dept, FCO 1975–79, Minister, Bonn 1979–82, Deputy Sec., Cabinet Office 1982–84, Deputy Under-Sec. of State, FCO 1984–87, High Commr in India 1987–92; Jt Chair. Anglo-Irish Encounter 1992–97; Pres. Irish Genealogical Research Soc. 1992–; Chair. Leonard Cheshire Foundation 1995–2000 (Chair. Int. Cttee 1992–95), British-Irish Asscn 1997–2002, Governing Body, Heythrop Coll., Univ. of London 2000–06, Advisory Cttee for Ampleforth Coll. 2004–; Visiting Prof. in Irish Studies, Univ. of Liverpool 1996–; mem. Council Univ. of Durham 1992–2000, Vice-Chair. 1997–2000; Distinguished Friend of the Univ. of Oxford 2001; Hon. Fellow, Trinity Coll. Oxford, Heythrop Coll. 2006; Hon. LLD (Hull) 1994. *Publications:* Remembering India 1997, Ryedale Pilgrimage 2000; contribs to The Tablet, The Ampleforth Journal, The Past, The Irish Genealogist, Parliamentary Brief. *Leisure interests:* painting in watercolours, reading, walking. *Address:* Greystones, Ampleforth, North Yorks., YO62 4DU, England (home).

GOODALL, Dame Jane, DBE, PhD; British primatologist, ethologist and anthropologist; *Founder, Jane Goodall Institute;* b. ((Valerie Jane Morris-Goodall)), 3 April 1934, London; d. of Mortimer Herbert Morris-Goodall and Vanne Morris-Goodall (née Joseph); m. 1st Hugo Van Lawick 1964 (divorced 1974); one s.; m. 2nd M. Derek Bryceson 1975 (died 1980); ed Uplands School, Univ. of Cambridge; Sec. Univ. of Oxford; Asst Ed. Documentary Film Studio; Asst Sec. to Louis Leakey, worked in Olduvai Gorge, then moved to Gombe Stream Game Reserve (now Gombe Nat. Park), Tanzania 1960, camp became Gombe Stream Research Centre 1964, Dir of Research on the behaviour of the Olive Baboon, *Papio anubis,* Gombe Nat. Park 1972–2003; Scientific Dir Gombe Stream Research Centre 1967–2003; studied social behaviour of the Spotted Hyena, *Crocutta crocutta,* Ngorongoro Conservation Area 1968–69; Founder, mem. Bd of Dirs and Trustee, Jane Goodall Inst. for Wildlife Research, Educ. and Conservation, USA 1976–; Scientific Gov. Chicago Acad. of Sciences 1981–; Int. Dir ChimpanZoo (research programme involving zoos and sanctuaries world-wide), USA 1984–; Vice-Pres. Animal Welfare Inst., British Veterinary Asscn, UK 1987–; Dir Humane Soc. of the US 1989–; Vice-Pres. for Conservation, Int. Bd of MediSend 1990–; Founder Whole Child Initiative International, USA 1995–; Pres. Advocates for Animals, UK 1998–; Advisor and Founder Whole Child Initiative USA 2001–; Co-founder EETA/CRABS (Ethologists for Ethical Treatment of Animals/Citizens for Responsible Animal Behavior) 2001–; Leading Founder Great Chapter at Grace Cathedral, San Francisco, Calif. 2007–; mem. Int. Advisory Bd of Teachers Without Borders, USA 2001–; mem. Bd Orangutan Foundation, USA 1994–, Save the Chimps/Center for Captive Chimpanzee Care 2000–, North American Bear Center 2001–; mem. Bd of Govs and Officers, For Grace, USA 2002–; mem. Bd of Trustees NANPA Infinity Foundation, USA 2001–; mem. Hon. Cttee Farm Sanctuary, USA 2001–; mem. Bd of Dirs Cougar Fund 2002–, The Many One Foundation, USA 2002–, Nat. Inst. for Play 2006–; mem. Advisory Panel World Summit on Sustainable Devt 2002, and numerous other advisory bds and cttees; Visiting Prof., Dept of Psychiatry and Program of Human Biology, Stanford Univ., Calif. 1971–75; Adjunct Prof., Dept of Environmental Studies, School of Veterinary Medicine, Tufts Univ. 1987–88; Assoc., Cleveland Natural History Museum 1990; Distinguished Adjunct Prof., Depts of Anthropology and Occupational Therapy, Univ. of Southern California 1990; A.D. White Prof.-at-Large, Cornell Univ., NY 1996–2002; Scientific Fellow, Wildlife Conservation Soc., USA 2002–; Papadopoulos Fellow 2002–03; Fellow, Wings WorldQuest, USA 2007; Trustee, L.S.B. Leakey Foundation, USA 1974–, Jane Goodall Inst., UK 1988–, Jane Goodall Inst., Canada 1993–; mem. Explorer's Club, New York 1981, American Philosophical Soc. 1988, Soc. of Women Geographers, USA 1988, Deutsche Akad. der Naturforscher Leopoldina 1990, Academia Scientiarium et Artium Europaea, Austria 1991; Foreign mem. Research Centre for Human Ethology, Max Planck Inst. for Behavioural Physiology 1984; speaker on conservation issues, appearing on numerous TV shows including: 20/20, Nightline, Good Morning America; Hon. Visiting Prof. in Zoology, Univ. of Dar es Salaam 1973–; Hon. Foreign mem. American Acad. of Arts and Sciences 1972; Hon. Fellow, Royal Anthropological Inst. of GB and Ireland 1991; Hon. Wardenship of Uganda Nat. Parks 1995; Hon. Trustee, The Eric Carle Museum of Picture Book Art, USA 2001; Hon. mem. Ewha Acad. of Arts and Sciences 2006; Ordre nat. de la Légion d'honneur 2006; 22 Hon. degrees; Franklin Burr Award, Nat. Geographic Soc. 1963–64, Conservation Award, New York Zoological Soc. 1974, Order of the Golden Ark, World Wildlife Award for Conservation 1980, J. Paul Getty Wildlife Conservation Prize 1984, Living Legacy Award, Int. Women's League 1985, Award for Humane Excellence, American Soc. for the Prevention of Cruelty to Animals 1985, Ian Biggs' Prize 1987, Albert Schweitzer Award, Int. Women's Inst. 1987, Nat. Geographic Soc. Centennial Award 1988, Encyclopaedia Britannica Award for Excellence on the Dissemination of Learning for the Benefit of Mankind 1989, Anthropologist of the Year Award 1989, AMES Award, American Anthropologist Asscn 1990, Whooping Crane Conservation Award, Conoco, Inc. 1990, Gold Medal, Soc. of Women Geographers 1990, Inamori Foundation Award 1990, Washoe Award 1990, The Kyoto Prize in Basic Science 1990, The Edinburgh Medal 1991, Rainforest Alliance Champion Award 1993, Chester Zoo Diamond Jubilee Medal 1994, Hubbard Medal for Distinction in Exploration, Discovery, and Research, Nat. Geographic Soc. 1995, Lifetime Achievement Award, In Defense of Animals 1995, The Moody Gardens Environmental Award 1995, Silver Medal, Zoological Soc. of London 1996, Tanzanian Kilimanjaro Medal 1996, Conservation Award, Primate Soc. of GB 1996; Caring Inst. Award 1996, Polar Bear Award 1996, William Proctor Prize for Scientific Achievement Kilimanjaro 1996, John & Alice Tyler Prize for Environmental Achievement 1997, David S. Ingells, Jr Award for Excellence 1997, Commonwealth Award for Public Service 1997, Field Museum's Award of Merit 1997, Royal Geographical Soc./Discovery Channel Europe Award for A Lifetime of Discovery 1997, Disney's Animal Kingdom Eco

Hero Award 1998, Public Service Award, Nat. Science Bd 1998, John Hay Award, Orion Soc. 1998, Int. Award of Excellence in Conservation, Botanical Research Inst. of Texas 1999, Community of Christ Int. Peace Award 1999, Graham J. Norton Award for Achievement in Increasing Community Livability 2001, Rungius Award, Nat. Museum of Wildlife Art (National USA) 2001, Roger Tory Peterson Memorial Medal, Harvard Museum of Natural History 2001, Master Peace Award 2001, Gandhi/King Award for Non-Violence 2001, Huxley Memorial Medal, Royal Anthropological Inst. of GB and Ireland 2002, UN Messenger of Peace 2002–, Benjamin Franklin Medal in Life Science 2003, Award of Harvard Medical School' Center for Health and the Global Environment 2003, Prince of Asturias Award for Tech. and Scientific Achievement 2003, Hon. Environmental Leader Award, Chicago Acad. of Sciences 2003, Nierenberg Prize for Science in the Public Interest 2004, Will Rogers Spirit Award, Rotary Club of Will Rogers and Will Rogers Memorial Museums 2004, Life Time Achievement Award, Int. Fund for Animal Welfare 2004, Time magazine European Heroes Award 2004, Discovery and Imagination Award 2005, Pax Natura Award 2005, UNESCO 60th Anniversary Gold Medal 2006, Int. Patron of the Immortal Chaplains Foundation 2006, Lifetime Achievement Award, Jules Verne Adventures 2006, Lifetime Achievement Award, WINGS WorldQuest 2007, Protector of Biodiversity and Apes in Africa, Pres. of France 2007, Hon. Medal of the City of Paris, Mayor of Paris 2007, Roger Tory Peterson Memorial Medal and Citation, Harvard Museum of Natural History 2007. *Films:* Miss Goodall and the Wild Chimpanzees (Nat. Geographic Soc.) 1963, Among the Wild Chimpanzees (Nat. Geographic Special) 1984, People of the Forest (with Hugo van Lawick) 1988, Chimpanzee Alert (Nature Watch Series, Central Television) 1990, Chimps, So Like Us (HBO) 1990, The Life and Legend of Jane Goodall (Nat. Geographic Soc. 1990, The Gombe Chimpanzees (Bavarian TV) 1990, Fifi's Boys (Natural World series, BBC TV) 1995, My Life with the Wild Chimpanzees (Nat. Geographic Soc.) 1995, Chimpanzee Diary (BBC 2 Animal Zone) 1995, Animal Minds (BBC) 1995, Jane Goodall: Reason For Hope (PBS special produced by KTCA) 1999, Chimps R Us (PBS special Scientific Frontiers) 2001, Jane Goodall's Wild Chimpanzees (in collaboration with Science North) 2002, Jane Goodall's Return to Gombe (produced by Tigress Productions for Animal Planet/Discovery) 2004, Jane Goodall's State of the Great Ape (Tigress Productions 2004, Jane Goodall – When Animals Talk (Tigress Productions) 2005, Jane Goodall's Heroes (Creative Differences) 2006. *Publications include:* My Friends the Wild Chimpanzees 1967, Innocent Killers (with H. van Lawick) 1971, In the Shadow of Man 1971, The Chimpanzees of Gombe: Patterns of Behavior (R.R. Hawkins Award for the Outstanding Tech., Scientific or Medical Book of 1986, The Wildlife Soc. (USA) Award for Outstanding Publ. in Wildlife Ecology and Man. 1986) 1986, Through a Window: 30 years Observing the Gombe Chimpanzees 1990, Visions of Caliban (with Dale Peterson) (New York Times Notable Book for 1993, Library Journal Best Sci-Tech Book for 1993) 1993, Brutal Kinship (with Michael Nichols) 1999, Reason for Hope: A Spiritual Journey (with Phillip Berman) 1999, 40 Years at Gombe 2000, Africa in My Blood: An Autobiography in Letters (ed. by Dale Peterson) 2000, Beyond Innocence: An Autobiography in Letters, the Later Years (ed. by Dale Peterson) 2001, Performance and Evolution in the Age of Darwin: Out of the Natural Order 2002, Ten Trusts: What We Must Do to Care for the Animals We Love (with Marc Bekoff) 2002, Harvest for Hope: A Guide to Mindful Eating (with Gary McAvoy and Gail Hudson) 2005; for children: Grub: The Bush Baby 1972, My Life with the Chimpanzees (Reading-Magic Award for Outstanding Book for Children 1989) 1988, The Chimpanzee Family Book (UNICEF Award for the Best Children's Book of 1989, Austrian State Prize for Best Children's Book of 1990) 1989, Jane Goodall's Animal World: Chimps 1989, Animal Family Series: Chimpanzee Family; Lion Family; Elephant Family; Zebra Family; Giraffe Family; Baboon Family; Hyena Family; Wildebeest Family 1989, Jane Goodall: With Love 1994, Dr. White (illustrated by Julie Litty) 1999, The Eagle & the Wren (illustrated by Alexander Reichstein) 2000, Chimpanzees I Love: Saving Their World and Ours 2001, Rickie and Henri: A True Story (with Alan Marks) 2004; numerous book chapters and articles in scientific journals. *Address:* The Jane Goodall Institute for Wildlife Research, Education and Conservation, 4245 North Fairfax Drive, #600, Arlington, VA 22203, USA (office). *Telephone:* (703) 682-9220 (office). *Fax:* (703) 682-9312 (office). *E-mail:* info@janegoodall.org (office). *Website:* www.janegoodall.org (office).

GOODE, Anthony William, MD, FRCS FACS; British surgeon; b. 3 Aug. 1945, Newcastle-upon-Tyne; s. of the late William Henry Goode and of Eileen Veronica Goode; m. Patricia Josephine Flynn 1987; ed Corby School and Univ. of Newcastle-upon-Tyne; clinical surgical posts in Newcastle Hosps Group 1968–76; Univ. of London Teaching Hosps 1976–; Prof. of Endocrine and Metabolic Surgery, Univ. of London, Consultant Surgeon, Royal London Hosp., Whitechapel and St Bartholomew's Hosp., Hon. Prof. Centre for Biological and Medical Systems, Imperial Coll. 1982–; Clinical Dir Helicopter Emergency Medical Service, London 1998–2000; Ed.-in-Chief Medicine, Science and the Law 1996–; Asst Sec. Gen. British Acad. of Forensic Science 1982–87, Pres. 1999–; Hon. Sec. British Asscn of Endocrine Surgeons 1983–96; Fellow Royal Soc. of Medicine 1971–; mem. Int. Soc. of Surgery 1984–, Int. Soc. of Endocrine Surgeons 1984–, New York Acad. of Sciences 1986–, MCC 1982–, Hunterian Soc. 1998 (Orator 1998); Trustee Smith and Nephew Foundation 1990–; Liveryman, Worshipful Soc. of Apothecaries of London; Freeman City of London 1992. *Publications:* numerous papers and articles on nutrition in surgical patients, endocrine diseases, metabolic changes in manned spaceflight and related topics. *Leisure interests:* cricket, music (especially opera). *Address:* The Surgical Unit, The Royal London Hospital, Whitechapel, London, E1 1BB, England. *Telephone:* (20) 7601-7032 (office).

GOODE, Charles B., AC, BCom, MBA; Australian business executive; *Chairman, Australia and New Zealand Banking Group Ltd (ANZ);* ed Melbourne Univ., Columbia Univ., USA; mem. Bd Dirs Australia and New Zealand Banking Group Ltd (ANZ) 1991–, Chair. 1995–; mem. Bd Dirs Woodside Petroleum Ltd 1988– (Chair. 1999–2007), Australian United Investment Co. Ltd (currently Chair.) 1990–, Diversified United Investment Ltd (currently Chair.) 1991–, The Ian Potter Foundation Ltd (currently Chair.) 1998–, Howard Florey Inst. of Experimental Physiology and Medicine (fmr Pres.); mem. Bd Dirs Singapore Airlines 1999–2006; fmr mem. Bd Dirs CSR, Pacific Dunlop, Legal & General Assurance, Oliver J. Nilsen Australia, Queensland Investment Corpn; fmr Pres. Inst. of Public Affairs; fmr mem. Council of Monash Univ., Finance Cttee of Australian Acad. of Science, Investment Cttee of Melbourne Univ. Grad. School of Man. Foundation; fmr Dir Melbourne Business School Foundation; Hon. LLD (Melbourne, Monash); Melbourne Business School Award 2006. *Address:* ANZ, Level 6, 100 Queen Street, Melbourne 3000, Australia (office). *Telephone:* (3) 9273-4736 (office). *Fax:* (3) 9273-6478 (office). *E-mail:* goodec@anz.com (office). *Website:* www.anz.com.au (office).

GOODE, Richard Stephen, DipMus, BSc; American pianist; b. 1 June 1943, New York, NY; m. Marcia Weinfeld 1987; ed Mannes Coll. of Music, Curtis Inst., studied with Nadia Reisenberg and Rudolf Serkin; debut, New York Young Concert Artists 1962; Carnegie Hall recital début 1990; founding mem., Chamber Music Soc. of the Lincoln Center; mem. Piano Faculty, Mannes Coll. of Music 1969–; concerts and recitals in USA, Europe, Japan, South America, Australia, Far East; has played with Baltimore, Boston, Chicago, Cleveland, New York, Philadelphia, Berlin Radio, Finnish Radio and Bamberg Symphony Orchestras, New York, Los Angeles, Baltimore, Orpheus, Philadelphia, ECO and Royal Philharmonic Orchestras; Young Concert Artists Award, First Prize Clara Haskil Competition 1973, Avery Fischer Prize 1980, Grammy Award (with clarinettist Richard Stoltzman), Jean Gimbel Lane Prize Northwestern Univ. School of Music 2006. *Leisure interests:* book collecting, museums. *Address:* c/o Intermusica Artists Management Ltd, 16 Duncan Terrace, London, N1 8BZ, England (office); 12 East 87th Street, Apt 5A, New York, NY 10128, USA (office). *Telephone:* (20) 7278-5455 (office). *Fax:* (20) 7278-8434 (office). *E-mail:* mail@intermusica.co.uk (office). *Website:* www.intermusica.co.uk (office).

GOODE, Sir Royston (Roy) Miles, Kt, CBE, QC, LLD, FBA, FRSA; British fmr professor of law and author; *Emeritus Professor of Law and Fellow of St John's College, University of Oxford;* b. 6 April 1933, London; s. of Samuel Goode and Bloom Goode; m. Catherine A. Rueff 1964; one d.; ed Highgate School and Univ. of London; admitted as solicitor 1955; Partner, Victor Mishcon & Co. (solicitors) 1966–67; called to Bar, Inner Temple 1988, Hon. Bencher 1992–; Prof. of Law, Queen Mary Coll., London 1971–73, Crowther Prof. of Credit and Commercial Law 1973–89, Head of Dept and Dean of Faculty of Laws 1976–80, Dir and Founder, Centre for Commercial Law Studies 1980–89; Norton Rose Prof. of English Law, Univ. of Oxford 1990–98, Prof. Emer. 1998–; mem. Monopolies and Mergers Comm. 1981–86, Council of the Banking Ombudsman 1989–92; Chair. Pension Law Review Cttee 1992–93; mem. Council and Chair. Exec. Cttee JUSTICE 1994–96; Hon. Pres. Centre for Commercial Law Studies 1990–, Oxford Inst. of Legal Practice 1994–; Fellow St John's Coll. Oxford 1990–98 (Fellow Emer. 1998–); Hon. Fellow Queen Mary and Westfield Coll. London 1991–; Hon. DSc (London) 1997; Hon. LLD (Univ. of E Anglia), 2003. *Publications include:* Consumer Credit 1978, Commercial Law 1982 (2nd edn 1995, 3rd edn 2004), Legal Problems of Credit and Security 1982 (2nd edn 1988, 3rd edn 2003), Payment Obligations in Commercial and Financial Transactions 1983, Proprietary Rights and Insolvency in Sales Transactions 1985, Principles of Corporate Insolvency Law 1990 (2nd edn 1997), Consumer Credit Law and Practice (looseleaf); Commercial Law in the Next Millennium; books on hire purchase; contribs. to Halsbury's Laws of England (4th edn). *Leisure interests:* chess, reading, walking, browsing in bookshops. *Address:* 42 St John Street, Oxford, OX1 2LH (home); St John's College, Oxford, OX1 3JP, England. *Telephone:* (1865) 515494 (home). *Fax:* (1865) 514744 (home). *E-mail:* roy.goode@sjc.ox.ac.uk (office).

GOODENOUGH, John B., BA, PhD; American physicist, materials engineer and academic; *Professor of Mechanical and Electrical Engineering, University of Texas;* b. 2 July 1922, Jena, Germany; s. of Erwin R. Goodenough and Helen M. Lewis Goodenough; m. Irene J. Wiseman 1951; ed Yale Univ., Univ. of Chicago; Research Engineer, Westinghouse Electric Corpn 1951–52; Group Leader and Residential Physicist, Lincoln Lab., MIT 1952-76; helped develop computer memories for USAF; conducted ground-breaking research on behaviour of metal oxides; Prof. and Head of Inorganic Chem. Lab., Univ. of Oxford, UK 1976–86; Prof. of Mechanical and Electrical Eng, Univ. of Tex. 1986–, apptd Virginia H. Cockrell Centennial Chair in Eng; conducted research on energy and high-temperature superconductivity; mem. Nat. Acad. of Eng, ACS, AAAS, Acad. des Sciences de l'Inst. de France, Royal Soc. of Chem., Physical Soc. of Japan; Fellow, American Physical Soc.; Foreign Assoc., Indian Acad. of Sciences, Acad. de Ciencias Exactas, Físicas y Naturales, Spain; Centenary Lecturer, Royal Soc. of Chem. 1976; Hon. PhD (Univ. of Bordeaux) 1967, (Univ. of Santiago de Compostela) 2002; Solid State Chem. Prize, Royal Soc. of Chem. 1980, Von Hippel Award, Materials Research Soc. 1989, Sr Research Award, American Soc. for Eng Educ. 1990, Medal for Distinguished Achievement, Univ. of Pennsylvania 1996, John Bordeen Award, Mining, Metallurgy & Materials Soc. 1997, Olin Palladium Award, Electrochemical Soc. 1999, Japan Prize 2001, Hocott Award, Univ. of Tex. 2002. *Publications:* Magnetism and the Chemical Bond 1963, Les Oxydes des métaux de transition 1973; numerous articles in scientific journals. *Leisure interests:* travel, Episcopal Church. *Address:* University of Texas, College of Engineering, 1 University Station C2100, Austin, TX 78712-0284,

USA (office). *Telephone:* (512) 471-1646 (office). *Fax:* (512) 471-7681 (office). *E-mail:* jgoodenough@mail.utexas.edu (office). *Website:* www.engr.utexas.edu (office).

GOODFELLOW, Peter Neville, DPhil, FRS, FMedSci; British geneticist; *Senior Vice-President, Discovery Research, GlaxoSmithKline plc;* b. 4 Aug. 1951; s. of Bernard Clifford Roy Goodfellow and Doreen Olga (née Berry); m. Julia Mary Lansdall 1972; one s. one d.; ed Univs of Bristol and Oxford; MRC Postdoctoral Fellow, Univ. of Oxford 1975–76; Jane Coffin Childs Postdoctoral Fellow, Stanford Univ. 1976–78; Sr Fellow American Cancer Soc. 1978–79; Staff Scientist, Imperial Cancer Research Foundation 1979–83, Sr Scientist 1983–86, Prin. Scientist 1986–92; Arthur Balfour Prof. of Genetics, Univ. of Cambridge 1992–96; Sr Vice-Pres. of Biopharmaceuticals and Neuroscience, later Discovery, Smithkline Beecham Pharmaceuticals 1996–2001, Sr Vice-Pres. Discovery Research, GlaxoSmithKline plc 2001–. *Publications include:* The Mammalian Y Chromosome: Molecular Search for the Sex Determining Gene (co-ed.) 1987, Cystic Fibrosis (ed.) 1989, Molecular Genetics of Muscular Disease (co-ed.) 1989, Sex Determination and the Y Chromosone (co-ed.) 1991, Mammalian Genetics (co-ed.) 1992; numerous reviews and specialist articles in learned journals. *Leisure interests:* science, football. *Address:* GlaxoSmithKline plc, 980 Great West Road., Brentford, London TW8 9GS, England (office). *Telephone:* (20) 8047-5000 (office). *Fax:* (20) 8047-7807 (office). *E-mail:* peter.n.goodfellow@gsk.com (office). *Website:* www.gsk.com (office).

GOODHART, Charles Albert Eric, CBE, PhD, FBA; British economist and academic; *Norman Sosnow Professor Emeritus of Banking and Finance, London School of Economics;* b. 23 Oct. 1936, London; s. of Sir A. L. Goodhart; m. Margaret (Miffy) Smith 1960; one s. three d.; ed Eton Coll., Trinity Coll., Cambridge, Harvard Univ.; Asst Lecturer, Dept of Econs, Univ. of Cambridge and Prize Fellow, Trinity Coll.; Economist, Dept of Econ. Affairs, London 1965–66; Lecturer, LSE 1966–68, Norman Sosnow Prof. of Banking and Finance 1985–2002, Prof. Emer. 2002–, mem. Financial Markets Group 1987– (Deputy Dir 2002–04), Hon. Fellow 2006; Adviser on Monetary Affairs, Bank of England 1968–85, External mem. Monetary Policy Cttee 1997–2000; Adviser to Gov. of Bank of England on Financial Regulation 2002–04; mem. Exchange Fund Advisory Council, Hong Kong 1988–97. *Publications:* Money, Information and Uncertainty 1989, The Evolution of Central Banks 1985, The Central Bank and the Financial System 1995, The Emerging Framework of Financial Regulation (ed.) 1998, The Foreign Exchange Market (with R. Payne) 2000, Financial Crises, Contagion and the Lender of Last Resort (co-ed with G. Illing) 2002, Intervention to Save Hong Kong (with Lu Dai) 2003, Financial Development and Economic Growth (ed) 2004, House Prices and the Macroeconomy (with B. Hofmann) 2006. *Leisure interest:* sheep farming. *Address:* Financial Markets Group, Room R414, London School of Economics, Houghton Street, London, WC2A 2AE (office); 27 Abbotsbury Road, London, W14 8EL, England (home). *Telephone:* (20) 7955-7555 (office); (20) 7603-5817 (home). *Fax:* (20) 7371-3664 (home). *E-mail:* c.a.goodhart@lse.ac.uk (office). *Website:* fmg.lse.ac.uk (office).

GOODING, Cuba, Jr.; American actor; b. 2 Jan. 1968, Bronx, NY; s. of Cuba Gooding Sr and Shirley Gooding; two Nat. Asscn for the Advancement of Colored People (NAACP) Awards. *Television appearances include:* Kill or Be Killed 1990, Murder with Motive: The Edmund Perry Story 1992, Daybreak 1993, The Tuskegee Airmen. *Films include:* Coming to America 1988, Sing 1989, Boyz N the Hood 1991, Gladiator 1992, A Few Good Men 1992, Hitz 1992, Judgement Night 1993, Lightning Jack 1994, Losing Isaiah 1995, Outbreak 1995, Jerry Maguire (Acad. Award, Best Supporting Actor 1997, Chicago Film Critics Award, Screen Actor Guild Award) 1996, The Audition 1996, Old Friends 1997, As Good As It Gets 1997, What Dreams May Come 1998, A Murder of Crows 1999, Instinct 1999, Men of Honor 2000, Pearl Harbor 2001, Rat Race 2001, In the Shadows 2001, Snow Dogs 2002, Boat Trip 2002, The Fighting Temptations 2003, Radio 2003, Home on the Range (voice) 2004, Shadowboxer 2005, Dirty 2005, Lightfield's Home Videos 2006, End Game 2006, Norbit 2007, Daddy Day Camp 2007, American Gangster 2007. *Address:* c/o The Endeavor Agency, 9601 Wilshire Blvd., 10th Floor, Beverly Hills, CA 90212, USA.

GOODING, Valerie Francis (Val), CBE, BA, CIMgt; British business executive; b. 14 May 1950; d. of Frank Gooding and Gladys Gooding; m. Crawford Macdonald 1986; two s.; ed Leiston Grammar School, Suffolk, Univ. of Warwick, Kingston Univ.; Reservations Agent, British Airways PLC 1973–76, Man. Trainer 1977–80, Personnel Trainer 1980–83, Reservations Man. 1983–86, Head of Cabin Services 1987–92, Head of Marketing 1992–93, Dir of Business Units 1993–96, Dir Asia Pacific 1996; Man. Dir UK Operations, BUPA 1996–98, CEO 1998–2008; mem. Bd of Dirs J Sainsbury plc 2007–, Standard Chartered Bank plc 2005–, Compass Group PLC 2000–, BBC 2008–, Lawn Tennis Asscn, Cable & Wireless Communications 1997–2000; Pres. Int. Fed. of Health Plans 2002–04; fmr mem. Bd Asscn of British Insurers; mem. Council Univ. of Warwick, Advisory Bd Warwick Business School, Leadership Team for Opportunity Now; Trustee British Museum; Hon. DBA (Bournemouth) 1999; ranked by Fortune magazine amongst 50 Most Powerful Women in Business outside the US (21st) 2002, (32nd) 2003, (18th) 2004, (16th) 2005, (18th) 2006, (21st) 2007, ranked by the Financial Times amongst Top 25 Businesswomen in Europe (third) 2005, (third) 2006, (sixth) 2007. *Leisure interests:* theatre, travel, tennis, keeping fit, family life. *Address:* c/o Board of Directors, J Sainsbury plc, 33 Holborn, London, EC1N 2HT, England.

GOODISON, Sir Nicholas Proctor, Kt, PhD, FBA, FSA, FRSA; British banker; b. 16 May 1934, Radlett; s. of Edmund Harold Goodison and Eileen Mary Carrington Proctor; m. Judith Abel Smith 1960; one s. two d.; ed Marlborough Coll. and King's Coll., Cambridge; joined H. E. Goodison & Co. (now Quilter & Co. Ltd) 1958–88, partner 1962, Chair. 1975–88; mem. Council The Stock Exchange 1968–88, Chair. 1976–88; Pres. British Bankers Asscn 1991–96; Pres. Int. Fed. of Stock Exchanges 1985–86; Chair. TSB Group PLC 1989–95, TSB Bank PLC 1989–2000, Deputy Chair. Lloyds TSB Group PLC 1995–2000; Dir (non-exec.) Corus Group PLC (fmrly British Steel PLC) 1989–2001 (Deputy Chair. 1993–99); Dir Gen. Accident 1987–95; Trustee, Nat. Heritage Memorial Fund 1988–97; Vice-Chair. Bd of English Nat. Opera 1980–98 (Dir 1977–98); Chair. Nat. Art-Collections Fund 1986–2002, Courtauld Inst. 1982–2002, Crafts Council 1997–, Burlington Magazine Publs 2001–; Nat. Life Story Collection 2003–; Hon. Keeper of Furniture, Fitzwilliam Museum, Cambridge; Pres. Furniture History Soc.; Gov. Marlborough Coll. 1981–97; mem. Royal Comm. on Long-term Care of the Elderly 1997–99; Leader and Author Goodison Review: Securing the Best for our Museums; Private Giving and Govt Support (HM Treasury) 2003; Sr Fellow, RCA 1991; Hon. FRIBA 1992; Hon. Fellow, King's Coll. Cambridge 2001, Courtauld Inst. of Art 2003; Chevalier, Légion d'honneur 1990; Hon. DLitt (City Univ.) 1985; Hon. LLD (Exeter) 1989; Hon. DSc (Aston Univ.) 1994; Hon. DArt (De Montfort Univ.) 1998; Hon. DCL (Univ. of Northumbria) 1999; Hon. DLit (Univ. of London) 2003. *Publications:* English Barometers 1680–1860 1968 (revised 1977), Ormolu: the Work of Matthew Boulton 1974 (revised as Matthew Boulton: Ormolu 2003); many papers and articles on the history of furniture, clocks and barometers. *Leisure interests:* visual arts, history of furniture and decorative arts, opera, walking. *Address:* PO Box 2512, London, W1A 5ZP, England.

GOODLAD, John I., PhD; American academic; *Professor Emeritus and President, Institute for Educational Inquiry, University of Washington;* b. Aug. 1920, N Vancouver, BC, Canada; s. of William Goodlad and Mary Goodlad; m. Evalene M. Pearson 1945; one s. one d.; ed Univs of British Columbia and Chicago; fmr school teacher, school prin. and Dir of Educ. in BC; consultant in curriculum, Atlanta (Ga) Area Teacher Educ. Service 1947–49; Assoc. Prof., Emory Univ. and Agnes Scott Coll. 1949–50; Prof. and Dir, Div. of Teacher Educ., Emory Univ. and Dir Agnes Scott Coll. –Emory Univ. Teacher Educ. Program 1950–56; Prof. and Dir, Center for Teacher Educ. Univ. of Chicago 1956–60; Dir Corinne A. Seeds Univ. Elementary School, UCLA 1960–84; Prof., Grad. School of Educ., UCLA 1960–85, Dean 1967–83; Dir of Research, Inst. for Devt of Educ. Activities Inc. 1966–82; Prof., Coll. of Educ., Univ. of Washington 1985, now Prof. Emer., Founder and Pres. Inst. for Educational Inquiry 1992–; 20 hon. degrees; Harold W. McGraw Prize in Educ. 1999, ECS James Bryant Conant Award 2000, Brock Int. Prize in Educ. 2002, New York Acad. of Public Educ. Medal 2003, American Asscn of School Admin Educ. Award 2004, ATE Distinguished Educator Award 2005, Horace Mann League Outstanding Friend of Public Educ. 2009, John Dewey Soc. Outstanding Achievement Award 2009. *Publications:* numerous books, chapters in books and articles in educational journals. *Leisure interests:* boating, fishing, walking. *Address:* Institute for Educational Inquiry, 124 East Edgar Street, Seattle, WA 98102, USA (office). *Telephone:* (206) 325-3010 (office). *Website:* www.ieiseattle.org (office).

GOODMAN, Elinor Mary; British political broadcaster and journalist; b. 11 Oct. 1946; d. of Edward Weston Goodman and Pamela Longbottom; m. Derek John Scott 1985; ed pvt. schools and secretarial coll.; Consumer Affairs Corresp. Financial Times newspaper 1971–78, Political Corresp. 1978–82; Political Corresp. Channel Four News (TV) 1982–88, Political Ed. 1988–2005; freelance journalist 2006–; Chair., Affordable Rural Housing Commission 2005–06; mem. Bd, Commission for Rural Communities. *Leisure interests:* riding, walking. *Address:* Commission for Rural Communities, John Dower House, Crescent Place, Cheltenham Gloucestershire GL50 3RA (office); Martinscote, Oare, Marlborough, Wilts. SN8 4JA, England (home). *Telephone:* (1242) 521381 (office). *E-mail:* info@ruralcommunities.gov.uk (office). *Website:* www.ruralcommunities.gov.uk (office).

GOODMAN, John, BFA; American film actor; b. 20 June 1952, St Louis; m. Annabeth Hartzog 1989; one d.; ed Meramac Community Coll. and SW Missouri State Univ.; Broadway appearances in Loose Ends 1979, Big River 1985. *Films include:* The Survivors 1983, Eddie Macon's Run 1983, Revenge of the Nerds 1984, C.H.U.D. 1984, Maria's Lovers 1985, Sweet Dreams 1985, True Stories 1986, The Big Easy 1987, Burglar 1987, Raising Arizona 1987, The Wrong Guys 1988, Everybody's All-American 1988, Punchline 1988, Sea of Love 1989, Always 1989, Stella 1990, Arachnophobia 1990, King Ralph 1990, Barton Fink 1991, The Babe 1992, Born Yesterday 1993, The Flintstones 1994, Kingfish: A Story of Huey P. Long 1995, Pie in the Sky, Mother Night 1996, Fallen 1997, Combat! 1997, The Borrowers 1997, The Big Lebowski 1998, Blues Brothers 2000 1998, Dirty Work 1998, The Runner 1999, Bringing Out the Dead 1999, Coyote Ugly 2000, O Brother Where Art Thou 2000, The Adventures of Rocky and Bullwinkle 2000, One Night at McCool's 2000, Emperor's New Groove (voice) 2000, Happy Birthday 2001, My First Mister 2001, Storytelling 2001, Monsters Inc. (voice) 2001, Mike's New Car (voice) 2002, Dirty Deeds 2002, Masked and Anonymous 2003, The Jungle Book 2 (voice) 2003, Home of Phobia 2004, Clifford's Really Big Movie (voice) 2004, Beyond the Sea 2004, Marilyn Hotchkiss' Ballroom Dancing and Charm School 2005, Cars (voice) 2006, Evan Almighty 2007, Death Sentence 2007, Bee Movie (voice) 2007, Speed Racer 2008. *Television includes:* The Mystery of Moro Castle, The Face of Rage, Heart of Steel, Moonlighting, Chiefs (mini-series), The Paper Chase, Murder Ordained, The Equalizer, Roseanne (series) 1988–97, Normal, Ohio 2000, Pigs Next Door 2000, Father of the Pride (voice) 2004–05, Center of the Universe (series) 2004–05, Studio 60 on the Sunset Strip 2006, The Year Without a Santa Claus 2006. *Address:* c/o Fred Specktor, CAA, 9830 Wilshire Boulevard, Beverly Hills, CA 90212, USA.

GOODMAN, Marian; American art gallery owner; *President, Marian Goodman Gallery;* f. Multiples 1965, publisher of prints, multiples and publications by artists including Roy Liechtenstein, Andy Warhol and Joseph Beuys; est. Marian Goodman Gallery, New York, NY 1977, currently Pres., past exhbns include Gabriel Orozco, Rineke Dijkstra, Steve McQueen, Jeff Wall, Gerhard Richter, Tacita Dean, est. exhbn space Paris 1999. *Address:* Marian Goodman Gallery, 24 West 57th Street, New York, NY 10019, USA (office). *Telephone:* (212) 977-7160 (office). *Fax:* (212) 581-5187 (office). *E-mail:* goodman@mariangoodman.com (office). *Website:* www.mariangoodman.com (office).

GOODNIGHT, James (Jim) H., PhD; American software industry executive; *CEO, SAS;* b. 6 Jan. 1943, Wilmington, NC; m. Ann Goodnight; three c.; ed NC State Univ.; mem. faculty, NC State Univ. 1972–76, Adjunct Prof. 1976–; co-founder and co-owner, with John Sall, SAS Inst. Inc. (world's largest privately held software co.) 1976–, currently CEO; co-founder (with wife) Cary Acad. 1996; Fellow American Statistics Asscn. *Address:* SAS Institute Inc., 100 SAS Campus Drive, Cary, NC 27513-2414, USA (office). *Telephone:* (919) 677-8000 (office). *Fax:* (919) 677-4444 (office). *E-mail:* software@sas.com (office). *Website:* www.sas.com (office).

GOODWIN, Sir Frederick (Fred) Anderson, Kt, LLB, DUniv, CA, FCIB, FIB; British chartered accountant and banker; b. 17 Aug. 1958, Paisley; ed Paisley Grammar School, Univ. of Glasgow; with Touche Ross & Co. 1979–95, Partner 1988–95; CEO Clydesdale Bank 1995–98, Yorkshire Bank 1997–98; Deputy CEO The Royal Bank of Scotland Group PLC 1998–2000, Group CEO and Exec. Dir 2000–08 (resgnd); Chair. The Prince's Trust; Dir (non-exec.) Bank of China Ltd; Fellow, Chartered Inst. of Bankers in Scotland 1996– (fmr Pres.). *Leisure interests:* cars, golf. *Address:* c/o Royal Bank of Scotland, 42 St Andrew Square, Edinburgh, EH2 2YE, Scotland.

GOODY, Joan Edelman, BA, MArch; American architect; *Principal, Goody Clancy Architects;* b. 1 Dec. 1935, New York; d. of Sylvia Feldman Edelman and Beril Edelman; m. 1st Marvin E. Goody 1960 (died 1980); m. 2nd Peter H. Davison 1984 (died 2004); ed Harvard Univ. Grad. School of Design, Cornell Univ.; Prin. Goody, Clancy & Assocs. Inc., Architects 1975–; Design Critic and Asst Prof. Harvard Univ. Grad. School of Design 1973–80, Eliot Noyes Visiting Critic 1985; Faculty for Mayors Inst. for City Design 1989–; Chair. Boston Civic Design Comm. 1992–2005; Dir Historic Boston; Honor Award for Design (AIA) 1980, Citation for Excellence in Urban Design (AIA) 1988, FAIA 1991, Award of Honor Boston Soc. of Architects 2005. *Publications:* New Architecture in Boston 1965, Housing (with others) 2004. *Leisure interests:* Tavern Club, Saturday Club. *Address:* Goody, Clancy & Associates, Inc., 420 Boylston Street, Boston, MA 02116, USA (office). *Telephone:* (617) 262-2760 (office). *Website:* www.goodyclancy.com (office).

GOODYEAR, Charles W. (Chip), BSc, MBA, FCPA; American mining and oil executive; b. 18 Jan. 1958; m. Elizabeth Goodyear; one s. one d.; ed Yale Univ., Wharton School of Finance, Univ. of Pennsylvania; fmrly with Kidder Peabody Co.; fmr Exec. Vice-Pres. and Chief Financial Officer Freeport McMoRan Copper & Gold Inc.; fmr Pres. Goodyear Capital Corpn; joined BHP Group (BHP Billiton from 2001) 1998, Chief Financial Officer 1999, Dir BHP Billiton Ltd and BHP Billiton PLC 2001–07, Chief Devt Officer 2001–03, CEO 2003–07; mem. Int. Council on Mining and Metals, Nat. Petroleum Council. *Leisure interests:* cycling, tennis, fishing, skiing. *Address:* c/o BHP Billiton Limited, 180 Lonsdale Street, Melbourne, Vic. 3000, Australia (office).

GOOLSBEE, Austan Dean, PhD; American economist and academic; *Staff Director and Chief Economist, President's Economic Advisory Board;* b. 18 Aug. 1969, Waco, Tex.; s. of Arthur Goolsbee and Linda Goolsbee; m. Robin Winters 1997; two s. one d.; ed Milton Acad., Yale Univ., Massachusetts Inst. of Tech.; mem. Macro econ. Task Force for Polish Econ. Restructuring, Warsaw, Poland 1990; mem. Econ. Staff of Senator David Boren, Washington, DC 1991; Asst Prof. of Econs, Grad. School of Business, Univ. of Chicago 1995–99, Assoc. Prof. of Econs 1999–2001, Robert P. Gwinn Prof. of Econs, Booth School of Business 2001–; Staff Dir and Chief Economist, President's Econ. Recovery Advisory Bd, The White House, Washington, DC 2009–, also mem. Council of Econ. Advisers; Research Assoc., Nat. Bureau of Econ. Research 2001–; fmr columnist, Slate.com; columnist, New York Times 2006–; mem. Panel of Econ. Advisers to Congressional Budget Office 2007–; fmr Research Fellow, American Bar Foundation; Alfred P. Sloan Fellow 2000–02; Fulbright Scholar 2006–07; Peter Lisagor Award for Exemplary Journalism 2006. *Television:* History's Business (History Channel). *Address:* Council of Economic Advisers, Eisenhower Executive Office Bldg, 17th St and Pennsylvania Ave, NW, Washington, DC 20502 (office); Booth School of Business, University of Chicago, 5807 South Woodlawn Avenue, Chicago, IL 60637, USA. *Telephone:* (202) 395-5042 (office); (773) 702-5869. *Fax:* (202) 395-6958 (office); (773) 702-0458. *E-mail:* goolsbee@ChicagoBooth.edu (office). *Website:* www.whitehouse.gov/cea (office); www.chicagogsb.edu (office).

GOONETILLEKE, Albert, MD, FRCPA, FRCPath; pathologist; *Consultant Pathologist, Harold Wood Hospital;* b. 4 Feb. 1936, Colombo; s. of late Arlis Goonetilleke; m. Sunanaseele Wijesinghe 1958; one s. one d.; medical officer Sri Lanka Health Dept 1962–68; lecturer Univ. of Edin. 1968–70, Univ. of Leeds 1970–71; with Charing Cross Medical School, London 1972–80; Consultant Pathologist, Charing Cross & Westminster Medical School 1980–88; Chief Pathologist, King Faisal Hosp., Saudi Arabia 1988–94; Chief Pathologist, Royal Comm. Hosp., Saudi Arabia 1994–96; Consultant Pathologist, Princess Margaret Hosp., Swindon 1996–, Harold Wood Hosp. Romford 1998–; mem. British Asscn for Forensic Medicine; Ananda Coll. Gold Medal Sri Lanka 1954, C. H. Milburn Award, BMA 1982. *Publications:* Injuries Caused By Falls from Heights, Safety at Work, Safety in the Home; various articles on forensic medicine and pathology. *Leisure interests:* still and video filming, water colour painting. *Address:* Department of Pathology, Harold Wood Hospital, Romford, RM3 0BE, Essex (office); Morningside, Long Park, Chesham Bois, Amersham, Bucks. HP6 5LF, England. *Telephone:* (1494) 721524.

GOOSEN, Retief; South African golfer; b. 3 Feb. 1969, Pietersburg; m. Tracy Goosen; two s. one d.; turned professional 1990; sr victories, Iscor Newcastle Classic 1991, Spoornet Classic 1992, Bushveld Classic 1992, Witbank Classic 1992, Mount Edgecombe Trophy 1993, Phillips South African Open 1995, Slaley Hall Northumberland Challenge 1996, Peugeot Open 1997, Dunhill Cup 1997, 1998 (both times with Ernie Els and David Frost), Novotel Perrier Open 1999, Lancome Trophy 2000, 2003, Scottish Open 2001, Telefonica Open 2001, EMC World Cup (with Ernie Els) 2001, WGC World Cup (with Ernie Els) 2001, US Open 2001, Johnnie Walker Classic 2002, Dimension Data Pro-Am 2002, BellSouth Classic 2002, Chrysler Championship 2003, European Open 2004, The Tour Championship 2004, Nedbank Challenge 2004, Linde German Masters 2005, VW Masters 2005, Int. Tournament, South African Airways Open 2005; mem. Dunhill Cup team 1996–2000, World Cup team 1993, 1995, 2000, 2001, Presidents Cup team 2000, 2003; Hon. mem. European Tour 2002–; won Volvo Order of Merit 2001, 2002 (first non-European to retain the title), Harry Vardon Trophy 2001. *Leisure interest:* water skiing. *Address:* c/o The European Tour, Wentworth Drive, Virginia Water, Surrey, GU25 4LX, England. *Telephone:* (1344) 840400. *Fax:* (1344) 840500. *E-mail:* info@europeantour.com. *Website:* www.europeantour.com.

GOPAKUMAR, Rajesh, PhD; Indian physicist and academic; *Professor, Harish-Chandra Research Institute;* b. 1967, Trivandrum; m. Rukmini Dey; ed Indian Inst. of Tech., Kanpur, Princeton Univ., USA; Post-doctoral Fellow, Univ. of Calif., Santa Barbara 1997–98, Harvard Univ. 1998–2001; Visiting mem. Inst. of Advanced Study, Princeton, NJ 2001–05; Invited Lecturer, Strings, TIFR, Mumbai 2001, Collège de France, Paris 2004, Beijing 2006; mem. Organizing Cttee Asia-Pacific School on String Theory, Seoul, S Korea 2001, 2004, 2005; currently Prof., Harish-Chandra Research Inst., Allahabad; mem. Adjunct Faculty, Indian Inst. of Tech., Kanpur, TIFR, Mumbai; Fellow, Indian Acad. of Sciences 2009; Best Graduating Student Award in Physics, Indian Inst. of Tech., Kanpur 1992, B. M. Birla Science Prize 2004, ICTP Prize 2006, Swarnajayanthi Fellowship 2006. *Publications:* numerous scientific papers in professional journals on string theory, particularly AdS/CFT correspondence, topological string theories, large N field theories and noncommutative field theories. *Address:* Harish-Chandra Research Institute, Chhatnag Road, Jhusi, Allahabad 211 019, India (office). *Telephone:* (532) 224-4059 (office); (532) 227-4370 (office). *Fax:* (532) 2567-748 (office). *E-mail:* gopakumr@mri.ernet.in (office). *Website:* www.mri.ernet.in (office).

GOPALAKRISHNAN, Adoor; Indian filmmaker and writer; *Chairman, Public Broadcasting Trust of India;* b. 3 July 1941, Adoor, Kerala; s. of late Madhavan Unnithan and Gouri Kunjamma; m. R. Sunanda 1972; one d.; mem. Working Group on Nat. Film Policy 1979–80; Dir Nat. Film Devt Corpn 1980–83; Faculties of Fine Arts, Univ. of Kerala, Calicut and Mahatma Gandhi Univs 1985–89; Chair. Film & Television Inst. of India 1987–89, 1993–96; Chair. 7th Int. Children's Film Festival of India 1991; currently Chair. Public Broadcasting Trust of India; mem. Advisory Cttee Nat. Film Archive of India 1988–90; Chair. Jury Singapore Int. Film Festival; mem. Jury, Int. Film Festival of India 1983, Venice Int. Film Festival 1988, Bombay Int. Festival 1990, Hawaii Int. Film Festival, Sochi Int. Film Festival, Alexandria Int. Film Festival; awarded title of Padmashri 1984; Commdr des Arts et des Lettres; numerous int. film awards. *Films include:* Swayamvaram 1972, Kodiyettam 1977, Elippathayam 1981 (British Film Inst. Award), Mukhamukham 1984 (Int. Film Critics' Prize, New Delhi, Karlovy Vary), Anantaram 1987, Mathilukal 1989 (Int. Film Critics' Prize, Venice), Vidheyan 1993 (Int. Film Critics' Prize, Singapore), Kathapurushan 1995 (Int. Film Critics' Prize, Mumbai), Nizhalkkuthu 2002 (Int. Film Critics' Prize, Mumbai), more than 24 short and documentary films. *Publications include:* plays: Vaiki vanna velicham 1961, Ninte rajyam varunnu 1963; books: The World of Cinema 1983; Screenplays of Ratwap, Face to Face, Monologue, collections of essays. *Leisure interest:* reading. *Address:* Darsanam, Thiruvananthapuram, 695 017, Kerala, India. *Telephone:* (471) 551144. *Fax:* (471) 446567. *Website:* www.psbt.org (office).

GOPALAKRISHNAN, S. Kris, MSc, MTech; Indian business executive; *Deputy Managing Director and Chief Operating Officer, Infosys Technologies;* ed IIT, Madras; co-founder and Dir Infosys Technologies, Bangalore 1981–, Tech. Dir –1987, Tech. Vice-Pres. KSA/Infosys, USA 1987–94, Head of Tech. Support Services 1994, Head of Client Delivery and Tech. 1996–98, now COO and Deputy Man. Dir; Chair. IIT Madras Growth Fund; Chair. CII Nat. Cttee on E-commerce; IIT Madras Distinguished Alumnus Award 1998. *Address:* Infosys Technologies, Plot No. 44 & 97A, Electronics City, Hosur Road, Bangalore 561 229, India (office). *Telephone:* (80) 8520261 (office). *Fax:* (80) 8520362 (office). *Website:* www.infy.com (office).

GOPALASAMY, V., (Vaiko); Indian politician; *Leader, Marumalarchi Dravida Munnetra Kazhagam;* trained as a lawyer; fmr mem. Dravida Munnetra Kazhagam; Founder-Leader Marumalarchi Dravida Munnetra Kazhagam; jailed on charges of terrorism July 2002, later released. *Address:* Marumalarchi Dravida Munnetra Kazhagam, 'Thayagam', No. 141, Rukmani Lakshmi Pathi Salai, Egmore, Chennai 600008, India.

GOPALASWAMI, N., MSc; Indian government official; *Chief Election Commissioner;* b. 21 April 1944, Needamangalam (then in Thanjavur dist), Tamil Nadu; ed St Joseph's Coll., Tiruchirappalli, Univ. of Delhi, Univ. of London, UK; mem. Indian Admin. Service 1966–, served in state of Gujarat in various capacities 1967–92, including Dist Magistrate in dists of Kutch and Kheda, Municipal Commr, Surat, Dir of Relief, Dir Higher Educ. and Jt Sec. (Home Dept) Govt of Gujarat, Man. Dir Gujarat Communication and Electronics Ltd, Vadodara, mem. (Admin and Purchase) Gujarat Electricity Bd, Sec. to Govt (Science and Tech. in Tech. Educ.) and Sec. Dept of Revenue; served Govt of India 1992–2004, worked as Adviser (Educ.) in Planning Comm., Jt Sec., Dept of Electronics, in charge of Software Devt and Industry Promotion Div. and also Head of Software Tech. Park of India Soc. and SATCOMM India Soc., Sec. Dept of Culture, Sec.-Gen. Nat. Human Rights Comm., Union Home Sec. –2004; Election Commr 2004–06, Chief Election Commr (with rank of Judge of the Supreme Court) 2006–; mem. Delimitation Comm. 2005–; int. observer in USA during presidential election Nov. 2004, gen. elections in Mauritius July 2005; first recipient of Prof. Mitra Gold Medal, Univ. of Delhi 1965. *Leisure interests:* listening to carnatic music (classical music from South India), photography. *Address:* 77 Lodhi Estate, New Delhi 110 003 (home); Election Commission of India, Nirvachan Sadan, Ashoka Road, New Delhi 110 001, India (office). *Telephone:* (11) 23713689 (office); (11) 24652424 (home). *Fax:* (11) 23711023 (office). *E-mail:* gopalaswamin@eci.gov.in (office). *Website:* www.eci.gov.in (office).

GOPEE-SCOON, Paula, BSc, LLB (Hons); Trinidad and Tobago politician and business executive; *Minister of Foreign Affairs;* b. 18 April 1958, Point Fortin; m.; three c.; ed St Joseph's Convent, San Fernando, Univ. of the West Indies, Cave Hill, Barbados, Univ. of London, UK; professional experience includes teaching (Point Fortin Intermediate Roman Catholic School), banking and finance (Republic Bank and Royal Bank of Trinidad and Tobago), along with sales, marketing and customer service (BioChem Trinidad and Tobago Ltd and Sunspots Plastics Ltd); MP (People's Nat. Movt —PNM) for Point Fortin 2007–; Minister of Foreign Affairs 2007–; mem. Dyslexia Asscn Bursary Fund Cttee, St Joseph's Convent (Port of Spain) Support Group. *Leisure interests:* sports, Caribbean art and culture. *Address:* Ministry of Foreign Affairs, Knowsley Bldg, 10–14 Queen's Park West, Port of Spain, Trinidad and Tobago (office). *Telephone:* 623-4116 (office). *Fax:* 624-4220 (office). *E-mail:* press@foreign.gov.tt (office). *Website:* www.foreign.gov.tt (office); www.pnm.org.tt.

GORA, Jo Ann M., MA, PhD; American sociologist, academic and university president; *President, Ball State University;* m. Roy Budd; one s. one step-d.; ed Vassar Coll., Rutgers Univ.; prof. of sociology with specialization in criminology, medical sociology and organizational behaviour; Provost and Vice-Pres. for Academic Affairs, Old Dominion Univ., Norfolk, Va 1992–2001; Chancellor Univ. of Massachusetts, Boston 2001–04; Pres. Ball State Univ., Ind. 2004–; mem. Cttee on Leadership and Institutional Effectiveness, American Council on Educ.; mem. Bd Nat. Asscn of State Univs and Land Grant Colls; mem. Cen. Indiana Corp. Partnership 2004–; mem. Bd of Dirs Ball State Univ. Foundation, First Merchants Corpn, Ball Memorial Hosp., Muncie Innovator Connector, Muncie Symphony Orchestra; Sagamore of the Wabash, Gov. of Ind. 2005, Torchbearer Award, Indiana Comm. for Women 2005, one of Women of Wonder, Indiana Minority Business Magazine 2008. *Publications:* The New Female Criminal: Empirical Reality or Social Myth?, Emergency Squad Volunteers: Professionalism in Unpaid Work; numerous articles in professional journals. *Leisure interests:* photography, tennis, golf, reading. *Address:* Office of the President, Ball State University, AD Building 101, Muncie, IN 47306, USA (office). *Telephone:* (765) 285-5555 (office). *Fax:* (765) 285-1461 (office). *E-mail:* president@bsu.edu (office). *Website:* www.bsu.edu (office).

GÖRANSSON, Bengt; Swedish politician; b. 25 July 1932, Stockholm; ed Univ. of Stockholm; Reso Ltd (travel org.) 1960–71; Chair. Manilla School for the Deaf 1970–78; Head, Community Centre Asscn 1971; Chair. of Bd Nat. Theatre Centre 1974–82; mem. various official cttees; Chair. of Bd Fed. of Workers' Educational Asscn 1980–82; Minister for Cultural Affairs 1982–89, Minister of Educ. and Cultural Affairs 1989–91; Chair. Ansvar Insurance Co. 1991–97, Int. Inst. of Alcohol Policy 1996–99, Center for Biotechnology 1996–98, Parl. Cttee on Democracy 1997–2000; Chair. Dalhalla Festival Stage 1994–2002, Norden Asscn 2000–07; Dr hc (Gothenburg); 10GT Veteran Medal 1997, Illis quorum Govt Medal 2000, Royal Gold Medal 2008. *Leisure interests:* culture, politics, education, sports. *Telephone:* (8) 6616607 (home); (70) 5616608 (home). *E-mail:* bengt.goransson@abfstockholm.se (office); a.b .goransson@telia.com (home).

GORBACH, Hubert; Austrian politician; b. 27 July 1956, Frastanz; m.; one s. one d.; ed secondary school in Feldkirch and commercial Coll.; mil. service 1978, cadre and sergeant's training; Export Man., Elektra Bregenz 1978–79; Head of Dept, Authorized Agent, Co. Sec., mem. Bd Textilwerke Ganahl 1979–87; CEO Kolb GmbH 1987–93; mem. Bd prov. Hosp.-GmbH 1999–2003; mem. OW Cttee 2000–01; mem. Freiheitspartei Österreichs (FPÖ—Freedom Party Austria) 1975–2005; Prov. Sec. Ring freiheitlicher Jugend 1976–82, Gen. Sec. 1980–85, mem. Prov. Party Exec. 1975–, Prov. Party Cttee 1984–, Prov. Deputy Gen. Sec. 1984–92, Local Party Rep., Frastanz 1986–92, Dist Rep., Feldkirch 1988–92, Prov. Party Rep., Vorarlberg 1992–2004, mem. Party Leaders' Group 1980–92, Party Exec. 1980–85, Party Cttee 1992–2005, Deputy Gen. Sec. 2000–02; mem. Frastanz District Council 1985–92, Frastanz Local Council 1990–92; mem. State Parl. of Vorarlberg 1989–93, Vorarlberg Prov. Govt 1993–2003; Deputy Head of Prov. 1999–2003; Fed. Minister of Transport, Innovation and Tech. 2003–07; Vice-Chancellor of Austria 2003–07; Foundation mem. Bündnis Zukunft Österreich (BZÖ—Alliance Future Austria) 2005–, mem. Fed. Party Man. *Leisure interests:* skiing, horseback riding (pres. prov. horseback riding club), tennis, jogging, reading, wine culture, shooting, flying (pvt. pilot's licence). *Address:* Alliance for the Future of Austria (BZÖ), Kärntner Ring 11–13/7/4, 1010 Vienna, Austria (office). *Telephone:* (1) 512-04-04 (office). *Fax:* (1) 512-04-04-21 (office). *Website:* www.bzoe.at (office).

GORBACHEV, Mikhail Sergeyevich; Russian organization official and politician; *Leader, Union of Social Democrats;* b. 2 March 1931, Privolnoye, Krasnogvardeiskii Dist, Stavropol Krai; s. of Sergei Andreevich Gorbachev and Maria Panteleimonovna Gorbachev (née Gopcalo); m. Raisa Titarenko 1953 (died 1999); one d.; ed Faculty of Law, Moscow State Univ. and Stavropol Agricultural Inst.; began work as machine operator 1946; joined CPSU 1952; Deputy Head, Dept of Propaganda, Stavropol Komsomol (V. I. Lenin Young Communist League) Territorial Cttee 1955–56, Second, then First Sec. 1958–62; First Sec., Stavropol Komsomol City Cttee 1956–58; del. to CPSU Congress 1961, 1971, 1976, 1981, 1986, 1990; Party Organizer, Stavropol Territorial Production Bd of Collective and State Farms 1962; Head, Dept of Party Bodies of CPSU Territorial Cttee 1963–66; First Sec., Stavropol City Party Cttee 1966–68; Second Sec., Stavropol Territorial CPSU Cttee 1968–70, First Sec. 1970–78; mem. CPSU Cen. Cttee 1971–91, Sec. for Agric. 1978–85, Alt. mem. Political Bureau CPSU, Cen. Cttee 1979–80, mem. 1980–91, Gen. Sec., CPSU Cen. Cttee 1985–91; Deputy Supreme Soviet of USSR 1970–89 (Chair. Foreign Affairs Comm. of Soviet Union 1984–85), mem. Presidium 1985–88, Chair. 1988–89, Supreme Soviet of RSFSR 1980–90, elected to Congress of People's Deputies of USSR 1989, Chair. 1989–90; Pres. of USSR 1990–91; Head, Int. Foundation for Socio-Economic and Political Studies (Gorbachev Foundation) 1992–; Head Int. Green Cross/Green Crescent 1993–; presidential cand. 1996; Co-founder and Co-Chair. Social Democratic Party of Russia 2000–04 (resgnd); Founder and Leader, Union of Social Democrats 2007–; syndicated columnist for numerous newspapers worldwide 1992–; Hon. Citizen of Berlin 1992, Freeman of Aberdeen 1993; Order of Lenin (three times), Orders of Red Banner of Labour, Badge of Honour; Nobel Peace Prize 1990, Albert Schweitzer Leadership Award (jt recipient) 1992, Ronald Reagan Freedom Award 1992, Urania-Medaille (Berlin) 1996, Augsburg Peace Prize 2005. *Recording:* Peter and the Wolf: Wolf Tracks (Grammy Award, Best Spoken Word Album for Children (jtly) 2004) 2003. *Publications:* A Time for Peace 1985, The Coming Century of Peace 1986, Speeches and Writings 1986–90, Peace Has No Alternative 1986, Moratorium 1986, Perestroika: New Thinking for Our Country and the World 1987, The August Coup (Its Cause and Results) 1991, December 1991: My Stand 1992, The Years of Hard Decisions 1993, Life and Reforms 1995. *Leisure interests:* literature, theatre, music, walking. *Address:* International Foundation for Socio-Economic and Political Studies, 125167 Moscow, Leningradskii pr. 39/14, Russia (office). *Telephone:* (495) 945-74-01 (office). *Fax:* (495) 945-74-01 (office). *E-mail:* gf@gorby.ru (office). *Website:* www.gorby.ru (office); sdorg.ru (office).

GORBULIN, Volodomir Pavlovich, DTech; Ukrainian politician and space scientist; *Head, Supreme Economic Council;* b. 17 Jan. 1939, Zaporozhya; ed Dniepropetrovsk State Univ.; fmr engineer and mechanic Pivdenne construction co., then jr researcher 1962–76; took part in devt of Cosmos space rockets; mem. Cen. Cttee CP 1977–; Head Rocket, Space and Aviation Tech. Sector 1980–; Head of Defence Complex Section, Cabinet of Ministers 1990–92; Dir-Gen. Ukrainian Nat. Space Agency 1992–94; Sec. Council on Nat. Security 1994–96, Council on Nat. Security and Defence 1996–; Head Supreme Econ. Council 1997–; Deputy Chair. Council on Problems of Science and Tech. Policy 1999–; Chair. State Cttee of Defence-Industrial Complex 1999–; Pres. Ukrainian Basketball Fed.; mem. Ukrainian Nat. Acad. of Sciences 1997–; USSR State Prize 1990, Ukrainian Nat. Acad. of Sciences Prize. *Leisure interests:* music, playing cards. *Address:* Office of the President, Bankovskaya str. 11, 252011 Kiev, Ukraine (office). *Telephone:* (44) 291-5152 (office).

GORBUNOVS, Anatolijs; Latvian fmr head of state; *Chairman, Latvian–Russian Intergovernmental Commission;* b. 10 Feb. 1942, Pilda, Riga Co.; s. of Valerians Gorbunovs and Aleksandra Gorbunova (née Mekša); m. Lidija Klavina; one s.; ed Riga Polytech. Inst., Moscow Acad. of Social Sciences; constructor on a state farm; Sr Mechanic Riga Polytech. Inst. 1959–62; served Red Army 1962–65; various posts in the structure of the Latvian CP 1974–88; Chair. Supreme Council of Latvia 1988–93 (Pres. of Latvia); Chair. of Saeima (Parl.) 1993–95; mem. Parl. for Latvijas ceļš (Latvian Way); Chair. Saeima Cttee on European Affairs Feb.–Aug. 1996; Minister of Environmental Protection and Regional Devt and Deputy Prime Minister 1996–98; Minister of Communications 1998, of Transport 1999–2004; Chair. Latvian–Russian Intergovernmental Comm. 1996–. *Leisure interests:* hunting, gardening. *Address:* c/o Ministry of Transport, 3 Gogola Street, 1743 Rīga, Latvia (office). *Telephone:* 6722-69-22 (office).

GORCHAKOVA, Galina Vladimirovna; Russian singer (soprano); *Artistic Director, Mariinsky Academy of Young Singers;* b. 1962, Beltsy, Moldova; m. Nikolai Petrovich Mikhalsky (divorced); one s.; ed Novosibirsk State Conservatory; soloist, Sverdlovsk (now Yekaterinburg) Theatre of Opera and Ballet 1987–91, Kirov (now Mariinsky) Theatre 1990–96; Gen. Dir Rimski-Korsakov competition 1992; leading roles in opera productions Madam Butterfly, Prince Igor, The Invisible City of Kitezh, Queen of Spades, Aida, Don Carlos, Tosca, Cavalleria Rusticana; regularly performs in European and American opera theatre including Covent Garden (debut Renata, The Fiery Angel by Prokofiev 1991), Royal Opera House, La Scala, Metropolitan Opera, Opera Bastille, San Francisco Opera, also in Tokyo; Artistic Dir Mariinsky Acad. of Young Singers 1998–, Summer Acad. at Mikkeli Int. Music Festival; gives masterclasses in Europe, USA, Canada and Japan; more than 15 recordings; Merited Artist of Russia, prizes in more than 30 nat. and int. competitions. *Leisure interest:* travelling by car. *Address:* c/o Robert Gilder and Co., 91 Great Russell Street, London, WC1B 3PS, England (office). *Telephone:* (20) 7580-7758 (office). *Fax:* (20) 7580-7739 (office). *E-mail:* rgilder@robert-gilder.com (office). *Website:* www.robert-gilder.com (office).

GORCHAKOVSKY, Pavel Leonidovich; Russian biologist; *Chief Researcher, Institute of Ecology of Plants and Animals, Russian Academy of Sciences;* b. 3 Jan. 1920, Krasnoyarsk; m.; one s.; ed Siberian Inst. of Wood Tech.; Chair. Urals Inst. of Wood Tech. 1945–58; Head of Lab., Inst. of Ecology of Plants and Animals Urals Br., USSR Acad. of Sciences 1958–88, Chief Researcher 1988–; Corresp. mem. USSR (now Russian) Acad. of Sciences 1990, mem. 1994; research in ecology and geography of plants, genesis of flora, protection of environment; Merited Worker of Science. *Publications include:* Main Problems of Historical Phytogeography of Urals 1969, Flora of High-mountain Urals 1975; numerous articles in scientific journals. *Leisure* *interests:* reading fiction, travel. *Address:* Institute of Ecology of Plants and Animals, Urals Branch of Russian Academy of Sciences, 8 March str. 202, 620219 Yekaterinburg, Russia (office). *Telephone:* (3432) 10-38-58 (office); (3432) 55-23-85 (home). *E-mail:* botanica@ipae.uran.ru (office). *Website:* www.uran.ru (office).

GORDEYEV, Aleksey Vassilyevich, CandEconSci; Russian politician and economist; *Minister of Agriculture;* b. 28 Feb. 1955, Frankfurt an der Oder, Germany; ed Acad. of Nat. Econs, USSR Council of Ministers; Sr Supervisor SU-4 Govt Glavmosstroi 1980–81, Chief Expert, Head of Div., then Deputy Head Dept of Glavagrostroi 1981–86; Deputy Dir-Gen. Moskva (agro-industrial co.), Moscow region 1986–92; Deputy Head of Admin., Lyubertsy Dist, Moscow region 1992–97; Head, Dept of Econs, mem. Exec. Bd Ministry of Agric. and Food 1997–98, First Deputy Minister of Agric. and Food 1998–99, Minister of Agric. 1999–, concurrently Deputy Chair. Govt of Russian Fed. 2000–04; Merited Econ. of Russian Fed. *Address:* Ministry of Agriculture, Orlikov per. 1/11, 107139 Moscow, Russia (office). *Telephone:* (495) 207-83-86 (office). *Fax:* (495) 207-95-80 (office). *E-mail:* info@mcx.ru (office). *Website:* www.mcx.ru (office).

GORDEYEV, Vyacheslav Mikhailovich; Russian ballet dancer and choreographer; *Artistic Director, Russian State Ballet Theatre of Moscow;* b. 3 Aug. 1948, Moscow; s. of Mikhail Gordeyev and Lyubov Gordeyeva; m. 2nd Maya Saidova 1987; one s. one d.; ed Moscow State Univ., State Inst. of Theatrical Arts; Leading Dancer, Bolshoi Theatre 1968–87; mem. CPSU 1977–90; Artistic Dir Russian State Ballet; Founder and Artistic Dir Russian State Ballet Theatre of Moscow 1984–; Head, Ballet Co. of Bolshoi Theatre 1995–97; First Prize, Moscow Int. Ballet Competition 1973, USSR People's Artist 1984, Best Choreographer of the Year 1992–93 (Germany), Maurice Béjart Special Prize for Best Choreography 1992. *Roles include:* Prince, Désiré (Tchaikovsky's Nutcracker, Sleeping Beauty), Romeo (Prokofiev's Romeo and Juliet), Spartacus, Ferhat (Melnikov's Legend of Love), Albert (Giselle), Basile (Minkus's Don Quixote), Prince (Tchaikovsky's Swan Lake). *Choreographic works:* Revived Pictures, Memory, Surprise Manoeuvres, or Wedding with the General and more than 30 choreographic compositions; own versions of classical ballets Paquita, Don Quixote and Walpurgisnacht, Nutcracker 1993, Last Tango (Bolshoi Theatre) 1996, Sleeping Beauty (Russian State Ballet) 1999, Cinderella (Russian State Ballet) 2001. *Leisure interests:* classical music, athletics, tennis. *Address:* Volgogradsky Praspekt 121, Moscow 109443 (office); Tverskaya str. 9, Apt 78, Moscow 103009, Russia (home). *Telephone:* (495) 379-94-82 (office); (495) 379-43-24 (office); (495) 201-31-72 (home). *Fax:* (495) 378-89-01 (office). *E-mail:* dilyarsb@front.ru (office); dilyarsb@yandex.ru. *Website:* www.russballet.ru (office).

GORDILLO, Elba Esther; Mexican union leader and politician; *President, Executive Committee, Sindicato Nacional de Trabajadores de la Educación;* b. 6 Feb. 1945, Comitán, Chiapas; joined Sindicato Nacional de Trabajadores de la Educación—SNTE (Nat. Union of Educ. Workers) 1960, held succession of full-time positions 1971–1989, Pres. SNTE 1989–1995, Head of Finance 1995, Pres. Nat. Exec. Cttee 2004–; elected to Chamber of Deputies 1979, re-elected 1985, 2003, Leader Partido Revolucionario Institucional (PRI) in Lower Chamber 2003; party elected to Senate 1994, Chair. Educ. Cttee; Pres. CNOP (org. that marshals pro-PRI orgs in movt) 1996–2003, Sec. Org. of the Nat. Exec. Council 1986–87, Gen. Sec. Council of Nat. Popular Orgs 1997–2002, Sec.-Gen. PRI 2003–05 (resgnd); co-founder Nueva Alianza party 2005. *Publications:* La construcción de un proyecto sindical 1995, El paseo de las Reformas, la batalla por México 2005. *Address:* Sindicato Nacional de Trabajadores de la Educación, República de Venezuela No. 44, Col. Centro, 5to. Piso., México, DF (office); c/o Nueva Alianza, Durango 199, Col. Roma, Del. Cuauhtémoc, 06700 México, DF, Mexico. *Telephone:* (55) 5704-7000 (office). *E-mail:* info@snte.org.mx (office). *Website:* www.snte.org.mx (office).

GORDIMER, Nadine, FRSL; South African writer; b. 20 Nov. 1923, Springs; d. of Isidore Gordimer and Nan Myers; m. 2nd Reinhold Cassirer 1954 (died); one s. one d.; ed convent school; mem. African Nat. Congress 1990–; Vice-Pres. International PEN; Goodwill Amb. UNDP; mem. Congress of S African Writers; mem. jury Man Booker Int. Prize 2007; Hon. Fellow, American Acad. of Arts and Letters, American Acad. of Arts and Sciences; Hon. mem. American Inst. of Arts and Letters; Commdr, Ordre des Arts et des Lettres 1987; Charles Eliot Norton Lecturer in Literature, Harvard Univ. 1994; Dr hc (Cambridge) 1992, (Oxford) 1994; WHSmith Literary Award 1961, Thomas Pringle Award, English Acad. of SA 1969, James Tait Black Memorial Prize 1971, Booker Prize (co-winner) 1974, Grand Aigle d'Or Prize (France) 1975, CNA Literary Award (S Africa) 1974, 1979, 1981, 1991, Scottish Arts Council Neil M. Gunn Fellowship 1981, Modern Language Asscn Award (USA) 1981, Premio Malaparte (Italy) 1985, Nelly Sachs Prize (Germany) 1985, Bennett Award (USA) 1987, Benson Medal, Royal Soc. of Literature 1990, Nobel Prize for Literature 1991, Primo Levi Award 2002, Mary McCarthy Award 2003, Bavarian State Premier's Hon. Award (part of the Corine Int. Book Prize), Grinzane Cavour Prize 2007. *Publications:* The Soft Voice of the Serpent (stories), The Lying Days (novel) 1953, Six Feet of the Country (stories) 1956, A World of Strangers (novel) 1958, Friday's Footprint (stories) 1960, Occasion for Loving (novel) 1963, Not For Publication (stories) 1965, The Late Bourgeois World (novel) 1966, South African Writing Today (co-ed.) 1967, A Guest of Honour (novel) 1970, Livingstone's Companions (stories) 1972, The Black Interpreters (literary criticism) 1973, The Conservationist (novel) 1974, Selected Stories 1975, Some Monday for Sure (stories) 1976, Burger's Daughter 1979, A Soldier's Embrace (stories) 1980, July's People (novel) 1981, Something Out There (novella) 1984, A Sport of Nature (novel) 1987, The Essential Gesture (essays) 1988, My Son's Story (novel) 1990, Jump (short stories) 1991, Crimes of Conscience (short stories) 1991, None to Accompany Me (novel) 1994, Writing and Being (lectures) 1995, The House Gun 1997,

Living in Hope and History: Notes on our Century (essays) 1999, The Pickup 2001, Loot and Other Stories 2003, Telling Tales (ed. and contrib.) 2004, Get A Life 2005, Beethoven was One-Sixteenth Black (short stories) 2007. *Address:* c/o AP Watt Ltd, 20 John Street, London, WC1N 2DR, England (office). *Telephone:* (20) 7405-6774 (office). *Fax:* (20) 7831-2154 (office). *E-mail:* apw@apwatt.co.uk (office). *Website:* www.apwatt.co.uk (office).

GORDIN, Yakov Arkadyevich; Russian writer and historian; b. 23 Dec. 1935, Leningrad; m.; one s.; ed Moscow Ore Inst.; freelancer specializing in ind. historical research of crisis situations in Russian political history of 18th–20th centuries; Dir and Co-Ed. Zvezda (literary journal), St Petersburg. *Publications:* numerous articles and books, including Space, The Death of Pushkin, The Events and People of 14 December, Between Slavery and Freedom, Duels and Duelists, Coup of the Reformers, etc. *Address:* Mokhovaya str. 36, Apt 24, 191028 St Petersburg, Russia (home). *Telephone:* (812) 273-05-27 (home). *E-mail:* ariev@cityline.spb.ru.

GORDON, Alexander G.; Russian actor and journalist; b. 20 Feb. 1964, Obninsk, Moscow region; m.; ed Shchukin Theatre School; actor, Ruben Simonov Studio Theatre 1987–89; emigrated to USA, worked as waiter, asst cameraman of RTN TV co.; Sr Corresp., WMNB Corpn 1989–93; staff mem. Vostok Entertainment Co. 1993–94; writer and narrator of TV shows New York, New York... (TV-6, Moscow); writer of some 100 TV programmes; returned to Russia 1997; staff mem. radio programme Silver Rain 1997–; Founder-mem. and Sec.-Gen. Party of Public Cynicism 1998–; writer and narrator of publicity programmes on ORT TV channel, including Treasury of Mistakes, Gordon (NTV); actor, Theatre of the Contemporary Play. *Film directed:* Shepherd of his Sheep. *Leisure interest:* football. *Address:* ORT TV channel, Koroleva str. 12, 103473 Moscow, Russia (office). *Telephone:* (495) 725-51-24 (office); (495) 217-94-27 (office). *Website:* www.gordon.ru.

GORDON, Sir Donald, Kt; South African/British business executive; *Honorary Life President, Liberty International PLC;* b. 24 June 1930, Johannesburg; s. of Nathan Gordon and Sheila Gordon; m. Peggy Cowan 1958; two s. one d.; ed King Edward VII School, Johannesburg; Chartered Accountant, Partner Kessel Feinstein 1955–57; founder Liberty Life Asscn of Africa Ltd, Chair. 1957–99; Chair. Liberty Holdings Ltd 1968–99, Liberty Investors Ltd 1971–99, Guardian Nat. Insurance Co. Ltd 1980–99; Deputy Chair. Standard Bank Investment Corpn Ltd 1979–99, Premier Group Holdings Ltd 1983–96; Dir Guardbank Man. Corpn Ltd 1969–99, Guardian Royal Exchange Assurance PLC (UK) 1971–94, Charter Life Insurance Co. Ltd 1985–99, The South African Breweries Ltd 1982–99, Beverage & Consumer Industry Holdings Ltd 1989–99, GFSA Holdings Ltd 1990–94, Sun Life Corpn PLC (UK) 1992–95, Chair. Liberty Int. PLC (fmrly Transatlantic Holdings PLC) 1981–2005, Capital & Counties PLC (UK) 1982–94, Capital Shopping Centres PLC 1994–2005; Hon. Life Pres. Liberty Life; Hon. D.Econ.Sc. (Witwatersrand) 1991; Financial Mail Businessman of the Year 1965; Sunday Times Man of the Year 1969; Achiever of the Century in South Africa Financial Services (Financial Mail 1999); Business Statesman Award (Harvard Business School); London Entrepreneur of the Year 2000, Special Award for Lifetime Achievement 2001. *Leisure interests:* opera, ballet. *Address:* Liberty International PLC, 40 Broadway, London SW1H 0BT, England (office). *Telephone:* (20) 7960-1200 (office). *Fax:* (20) 7960-1333 (office). *Website:* www.liberty-international.co.uk (office).

GORDON, Douglas Lamont, BA, MA; British artist; b. 20 Sept. 1966, Glasgow; s. of James Gordon and Mary Clements Gordon (née McDougall); ed Glasgow School of Art, Slade School of Art; works in video, film, photography and sculpture; solo exhibitions at Tate Liverpool 2000, Museum of Contemporary Art, Los Angeles 2001, Hayward Gallery, London 2002, Van Abbemuseum, Eindhoven 2003; curator "The Vanity of Allegory", Deutsche Guggenheim, Berlin 2005, Palais des Papes, Avignon 2008; Visiting Prof. Fine Art, Glasgow School of Art, Glasgow Univ. 1999–; fmr Visiting Prof. and John Florent Stone Fellow, Edinburgh Coll. of Art; Int. Juror, 65th Venice Film Festival 2008; Turner Prize 1996, Premio 2000 1997, Hugo Bass Prize 1998, Roswitha Haftmann Prize 2008. *Address:* c/o Gagosian Gallery, 17–19 Davies Street, London W1K 3DE, England.

GORDON, Ilene, MSc, BSc; American business executive; *President and CEO, Packaging, Rio Tinto Alcan;* m.; two c.; ed Massachusetts Inst. of Tech.; served as Vice-Pres. of Operations, Tenneco Inc. 1994–97, Vice-Pres. and Gen. Man. Folding Carton Business 1997–99; Pres. Pechiney Plastic Packaging Inc. and Sr Vice-Pres. Pechiney Group 1999–2004; Pres. Food Packaging, Americas, Alcan Inc. 2004–06, Sr Vice-Pres. Alcan Inc. and Pres. and CEO Alcan Global Packaging 2006–07, Pres. and CEO Packaging, Rio Tinto Alcan 2007–, mem. Exec. Cttee 2007–, currently based in Paris, France; named in Fortune Magazine's Global Power 50 list 2007. *Address:* Alcan Packaging, Tour Reflets, 17 Place des Reflets, 92097 Paris La Défense Cedex, France (office). *Telephone:* 1-57-00-20-00 (office). *E-mail:* contactpharma_europe@alcan.com (office). *Website:* www.alcanpackaging.com (office).

GORDON, Jeff; American motor racing driver; b. 4 Aug. 1971, Vallejo, Calif.; m. Brooke Sealy 1994 (divorced 2002); current team: Hendrick Motorsports; United States Auto Club (USAC) Rookie of the Year 1989; youngest USAC National Midget Champion 1990 (aged 19); NASCAR racing driver; winner USAC Silver Crown and Busch Series Rookie of the Year 1991; three Busch Series victories 1992; Winston Cup debut 1992 (Atlanta Speedway); 69 Winston Cup victories including: Brickyard 400 1994, 1998, 2001, 2004, Southern 500 1995, 1996, 1997, 1998, 2002, Daytona 500 1997, 1999; Rookie of the Year 1993; Winston Cup Champion 1995, 1997, 1998, 2001; Winston Million Champion 1997; record seven career victories on road courses; youngest driver to achieve 50 career victories 2000; over US $50 million career winnings; runs the Jeff Gordon Foundation charity for children.

Publication: (with Steve Eubanks) Jeff Gordon: Racing Back to the Front – My Memoir 2003. *Address:* Hendrick Motorsports, 4414 Pappa Joe Hendrick Blvd., POB 9, Harrisburg, NC 28075, USA. *Website:* www.jeffgordon.com (office).

GORDON, Pamela; Bermudian politician; b. 2 Sept. 1955, Hamilton; d. of E. F. Gordon and Mildred Layne Bean; one s. one d.; ed Queen's Univ.; elected to Senate 1990; Minister of Youth Devt 1992–95, of the Environment, Planning and Natural Resources 1995–97; Prime Minister of Bermuda 1997–98; Leader United Bermuda Party 1997–2001; fmr Fellow, Inst. of Politics, Harvard Univ.; Hon. LLD (New Brunswick). *Address:* c/o United Bermuda Party, Central Office, 3rd Floor, Bermudiana Arcade, 27 Queen St, Hamilton, HM 11, Bermuda (office).

GORDON, Robert James, PhD; American economist and academic; *Stanley G. Harris Professor in the Social Sciences, Northwestern University;* b. 3 Sept. 1940, Boston, Mass; s. of Robert A. Gordon and Margaret S. Gordon; m. Julie S. Peyton 1963; ed Harvard Univ., Univ. of Oxford, UK, Massachusetts Inst. of Tech.; Assoc. Prof. of Econs, Harvard Univ. 1967–68, Univ. of Chicago 1968–73; Prof. of Econs, Northwestern Univ. 1973–87, Stanley G. Harris Prof. in the Social Sciences 1987–, Chair. Dept of Econs 1992–96; Fellow, Econometric Soc. 1977, American Acad. of Arts and Sciences 1997; John Simon Guggenheim Memorial Fellowship 1980–81, Lustrum Award, Erasmus Univ., Rotterdam 1999. *Publications:* The American Business Cycle: Continuity and Change 1986, The Measurement of Durable Goods Prices 1990, The Economics of New Goods 1997, Macroeconomics (ninth edn) 2003. *Leisure interests:* photography, gardening, mil. history, airline man. *Address:* Department of Economics, 349 Andersen Hall, Northwestern University, Evanston, IL 60208-0001 (office); 202 Greenwood Street, Evanston, IL 60201, USA (home). *Telephone:* (847) 491-3616 (office); (847) 869-3544 (home). *Fax:* (847) 491-7001 (office). *E-mail:* rjg@northwestern.edu (office). *Website:* faculty-web .at.northwestern.edu/economics/gordon/indexmsie.html (office).

GORDON, William Edwin, PhD; American radio physicist and academic; *Distinguished Professor Emeritus, Department of Space Physics and Astronomy, Rice University;* b. 8 Jan. 1918, Paterson, NJ; s. of William and Mary Scott Gordon; m. Elva Freile 1941; one s. one d.; ed Montclair State Coll., NJ and New York and Cornell Univs; Assoc. Prof. Cornell Univ. 1953–59, Prof. 1959–65, Walter R. Read Prof. of Eng 1965–66; Dir Arecibo Ionospheric Observatory, Puerto Rico 1960–66 (conceived and directed construction of world's largest antenna reflector); Prof. of Electrical Eng and Space Physics and Astronomy, Rice Univ. 1966–86, Dean of Eng and Science 1966–75, Vice-Pres. 1969–72, Dean, School of Natural Sciences 1975–80, Provost and Vice-Pres. 1980–86, Distinguished Prof. Emer. 1986–; Foreign Sec., NAS 1986–90; Chair. Bd of Trustees, Upper Atmosphere Research Corpn 1971–72, 1973–78; Pres. Taping for the Blind, Houston 1993–97; Vice-Pres. Int. Union of Radio Science 1975–78, Senior Vice-Pres. 1978–81, Pres. 1981–85, Hon. Pres. 1990–; Bd of Trustees and Exec. Cttee Univ. Corpn for Atmospheric Research 1975–81, Vice-Chair. Bd of Trustees 1977–78, Chair. 1978–81, Trustee 1975–81, 1986–89, 1991–92; Bd of Trustees, Cornell Univ. 1976–80; mem. Arecibo Observatory Advisory Bd 1977–80, 1990–93; mem. NAS, AAAS, Nat. Acad. of Eng, Foreign Assoc. Acad. of Eng Japan; mem. Int. Council of Scientific Unions 1981, Vice-Pres. 1988–93; Councillor American Meteorological Soc.; Fellow, American Geophysical Union, Inst. of Electrical and Electronic Engineers, Guggenheim Fellow 1972–73; Hon. DS (Austin Coll.) 1978; Balth Van der Pol Gold Medal for distinguished research in radio sciences 1966, 50th Anniversary Medal of American Meteorological Soc. 1970, Arktowski Medal 1984, USSR Medal Geophysics 1985, Milestone in Electrical and Mechanical Engineering 2001;. *Publications:* numerous articles in learned journals. *Leisure interests:* sailing, swimming, music. *Address:* Department of Space Physics, Rice University, PO Box 1892, Houston, TX 77251, USA. *Telephone:* (713) 348-4939. *E-mail:* bgordon@spacsun.rice.edu (office).

GORDY, Berry, Jr; music industry executive and songwriter; b. 28 Nov. 1929, Detroit; m. Grace Eaton 1990; six c.; owner, record store, Detroit, 1955; composer and ind. producer, late 1950s; Founder, Jobete Music, 1958, Tamla Records, 1959, Motown Record Corpn 1961–88; currently Chair. The Gordy Co.; American Music Award, Outstanding Contribution to Music Industry, 1975; inducted into Rock and Roll Hall of Fame, 1990; NARAS Trustees Award 1991. *Film:* Lady Sings The Blues (exec. producer) 1972. *Recordings:* as composer/producer: Reet Petite, Jackie Wilson; Shop Around, The Miracles; Do You Love Me, The Contours; Try It Baby, Marvin Gaye; Shotgun, Junior Walker and The All-Stars; I Want You Back and ABC, The Jackson 5; Compilation: The Music, The Magic, The Memories of Motown, 1995. *Address:* Gordy Company, 9100 Wilshire Blvd, Suite 455, Beverly Hills, CA 90212-3401, USA.

GORE, Albert Arnold (Al), Jr; American financial executive, academic and fmr politician; *Chairman, Generation Investment Management LLP;* b. 31 March 1948, Washington, DC; s. of the late Albert Gore, Sr and Pauline Gore (née LaFon); m. Mary E. Aitcheson 1970; one s. three d.; ed Harvard and Vanderbilt Univs; served with US Army during Vietnam war; investigative reporter, editorial writer, The Tennessean 1971–76; home-builder and land developer, Tanglewood Home Builders Co. 1971–76; livestock and tobacco farmer 1973–; Head Community Enterprise Bd 1993–; mem. House of Reps 1977–79; Senator from Tennessee 1985–93; Vice-Pres. of USA 1993–2001; Democrat cand. in presidential elections 2000; Lecturer, Middle Tennessee State Univ., Columbia Univ. 2001–, Visiting Prof., UCLA, Fisk Univ. 2001–; Vice-Chair. Metropolitan West Financial LLC 2001–; Sr Adviser, Google Inc. 2001–; Co-founder and Chair. Current TV (youth cable TV network) 2004–; Co-founder and Chair. Generation Investment Management LLP (fund man. firm) Washington, DC and London, UK 2004–; Partner, Kleiner, Perkins, Caulfield & Byers 2007–; mem. Bd of Dirs Apple Computer Inc.; Dr hc (Harvard) 1994, (New York) 1998; Webby Award 2005, UNEP Champion of the Earth Laureate 2007, Prince of Asturias Award for Int. Co-operation 2007, Nobel Peace Prize (shared with UN Intergovernmental Panel on Climate Change) 2007, Primetime Emmy Award for Current TV 2007, Dan David Prize 2008. *Film:* An Inconvenient Truth (Best Documentary Los Angeles Film Critics Assen 2006, Nat. Soc. of Film Critics 2007, Acad. Award for Best Documentary Feature 2007) 2006. *Publications:* Earth in the Balance 1992, An Inconvenient Truth (Quill Award for History, Current Affairs or Politics) 2006, The Assault on Reason: How the Politics of Blind Faith Subvert Wise Decision-Making (Quill Award for History/Current Affairs/Politics 2007) 2007. *Address:* Generation Investment Management US LLP, 750 17th Street, 11th Floor, Washington, DC 20006, USA (office). *Telephone:* (202) 785-7400 (office). *Fax:* (202) 785-7401 (office). *Website:* www.generationim.com (office); www.current.tv; www.algore.com.

GORE, Frederick John Pym, CBE, RA; British painter; b. 8 Nov. 1913; s. of Spencer Frederick Gore and Mary Joanna Gore (née Kerr); ed Lancing Coll. and Trinity Coll., Oxford, Ruskin, Westminster and Slade Schools of Art; war service 1939–45; taught at Westminster School of Art 1937, Chelsea and Epsom 1947, St Martin's 1946–79, Head of Painting Dept 1951–79, Vice-Prin. 1961–79; Chair. RA Exhbns Cttee 1976–87; Trustee Imperial War Museum 1967–84, Chair. Artistic Records Cttee 1972-86. *Publications:* Abstract Art 1956, Painting, Some Basic Principles 1965, Piero della Francesca's 'The Baptism' 1969. *Leisure interests:* Russian folk dancing, tap-dancing. *Address:* Flat 3, 35 Elm Park Gardens, London, SW10 9QF, England. *Telephone:* (20) 7352-4940.

GÓRECKI, Henryk Mikołaj; Polish composer; b. 6 Dec. 1933, Czernica, nr Rybnik; s. of Otylia Górecka and Roman Górecki; m. Jadwiga Górecka 1959; one s. one d.; studied composition at State Higher School of Music, Katowice, under Boleslaw Szabelski; Docent, Faculty of Composition, State Higher School of Music, Katowice, Rector 1975–79, Extraordinary Prof. 1977–79; Dr hc (Acad. of Catholic Theology, Warsaw) 1993, (Warsaw Univ.) 1994, (American Catholic Univ., Washington, DC) 1995, (Ann Arbor Univ., Mich.) 1996, (Concordia Univ., Montreal) 1998; First Prize, Young Composers' Competition, Warsaw, for Monologhi 1960, Paris Youth Biennale, for 1st Symphony 1961, Prize, UNESCO Int. Tribune for Composers for Refrain 1967, for Ad Matrem 1973, First Prize, Composers' Competition, Szczecin, for Kantata 1968, Prize of Minister of Culture and Arts 1965, 1969, 1973, Prize of Union of Polish Composers 1970, of Cttee for Polish Radio and TV 1974, of Minister of Culture and Arts 1965, 1969, 1973, State Prize 1st class for Ad Matrem and Nicolaus Copernicus Symphony 1976, Award of the Ministry of Foreign Affairs 1992. *Compositions include:* Four Preludes for piano 1955, Sonata No. 1 for piano, Op. 6 1956–90, 3 Diagrams for flute solo, Op. 15 1959, Diagram No. 4 for flute solo, Op.18 1961, Genesis cycle 1962–63, Scontri for large symphony orchestra 1960, Cantata for organ, Op. 26 1968, Old Polish Music 1969, Canticuum graduum for orchestra, Op. 27 1969, Symphony No. 1 "1959" for string orchestra and percussion, Op. 14 1959, Ad Matrem 1971, Symphony No. 2, Copernican 1972, Symphony No. 3 (Threnodies for soprano and orchestra) 1976 (more than 700,000 records sold), Beatus Vir 1979, Concerto for harpsichord (piano) and string orchestra, Op. 40 1980, Lerchenmusik (trio) 1984, Three Cradle Songs for unaccompanied mixed choir, Op. 49 1984, Totus Tuus for unaccompanied mixed choir, Op. 60 1987, Concerto-Cantata for flute and orchestra, Op. 65 1992, Quasi una Fantasia String Quartet No. 2, Op. 64 1992, Little Requiem for a Polka for piano and 13 instruments, Op. 66 1993, Valentine Piece for flute and little bell 1996, Three Fragments to Words of Stanisław Wyspianski for voice and piano 1996, Little Fantasy for violin and piano, Op. 73 1997, Salve Sidus Polonorum, Cantata of St Adalbert, Opus 72, for large mixed choir, two pianos, organ and percussion ensemble 1997–2000, String Quartet No. 3 1999, Niech nam źyją i śpiewają for vocal ensemble 2000. *Address:* Boosey and Hawkes Music Publishers, Aldwych House, 71–91 Aldwych, London, WC2B 4HN, England (office). *Telephone:* (20) 7054-7258 (office). *Fax:* (20) 7054-7293 (office). *Website:* www .boosey.com (office).

GOREGLYAD, Valery Pavlovich, DrEconSci; Russian economist; *Auditor, Accounts Chamber;* b. 18 June 1958, Gluzk, Mogilev Region, Belarus; m. Yaketarina Goreglyad; two s.; ed Moscow Inst. of Aviation; fmrly with mil. space industry; Head Tourism Co. –1990; Peoples' Deputy, Russian Fed. 1990–93; mem. Council of Feds, Fed. Ass. 1994; Exec. Dir Cttee on Budget, Revenue and Banking Activity 1994–2000, Deputy Head 2001–; elected mem. (for Sakhalin region) Fed Council 2001–02 (resgnd), Leader Parl. Grouping Fed. 2002–03 (resgnd); Auditor, Accounts Chamber 2004–. *Publications:* The Budget as a Financial Regulator of Economic Development 2002; five monographs and various scholarly articles on macro-econ. analysis, problems of regional econ. devt, and innovative economy. *Leisure interests:* reading historical literature, tennis, basketball, football. *Address:* Accounts Chamber, 2 Zubovskaya str., GSP-2, 119992 Moscow, Russia (office). *Telephone:* (495) 986-05-09 (office). *Fax:* (495) 986-09-52 (office). *E-mail:* info@ach.gov.ru (office). *Website:* www.ach.gov.ru/about/gor.php (office).

GORELICK, Jamie Shona, BA, JD; American lawyer and fmr government official; *Partner, WilmerHale;* b. 6 May 1950, New York City; m. Richard Waldhorn 1975; two c.; ed Harvard Coll., Harvard Law School; attorney, Miller, Cassidy, Larroca & Lewin, Washington, DC 1975–79, 1980–83; Asst to US Sec. of Energy and Counselor to Deputy Sec., Washington, DC 1979–80; Gen. Counsel, US Dept of Defense 1993–94, Vice-Chair. Task Force on the Audit, Inspection and Investigation Components; Deputy Attorney Gen., US Dept of Justice 1994–97; Vice-Chair. Fannie Mae 1997–2003; Pnr, Wilmer-Hale (law firm), Washington, DC 2003–, Co-Chair. Nat. Security and Govt Contracts Dept, Co-Chair. Public Policy and Strategy Practice, Pnr, Litigation

Dept; Pres. DC Bar 1992–93, mem. Bd of Govs 1982–88; fmr Lecturer, Harvard Law School, fmr mem. Bd of Overseers, Overseers' Visiting Cttee; Raytheon Lecturer on Business Ethics, Bentley Coll. 2004; has served on numerous govt bds and comms including CIA Nat. Security Advisory Panel 1997–2005, Pres.'s Intelligence Review Panel 2001–02, Nat. Comm. on Terrorist Attacks upon the US 2002–04; mem. ABA, American Law Inst., Women's Bar Asscn, Council on Foreign Relations; mem. Bd of Dirs United Technologies Corpn 2000–, Schlumberger Ltd 2002–, John D. and Catherine T. MacArthur Foundation, Washington Legal Clinic for the Homeless, Carnegie Endowment for Int. Peace; Counsellor American Soc. of Int. Peace; Trustee Urban Inst.; Sec. of Energy Outstanding Service Award 1980, Women's Bar Asscn Woman Lawyer of the Year 1993, Sec. of Defense Distinguished Service Award 1994, Prominent Woman in Int. Law 1994, Equal Justice Works Outstanding Advocate of the Year 1997, Dir of Cen. Intelligence Award 1997, Radcliffe Coll. Alumnae Recognition Award 1997, Dept of Justice Edmund J. Randolph Award 1997, American Bar Asscn Margaret Brent Award 1997, Wickersham Award for Exceptional Public Service and Dedication to the Legal Profession 1998, American Jewish Cttee Judge Learned Hand Award 1999, NOW Legal Defense and Educ. Fund Aiming High Award 2002, DC Chamber of Commerce's Corp. Leadership Award 2003, Women's Bar Asscn Star of the Bar Award 2003. *Publications:* Destruction of Evidence (co-author) 1983. *Address:* Wilmer Hale, 1875 Pennsylvania Ave, NW, Washington, DC 20006, USA (office). *Telephone:* (202) 663-6500 (office). *Fax:* (202) 663-6363 (office). *E-mail:* jamie.gorelick@wilmerhale.com (office). *Website:* www.wilmerhale.com/jamie_gorelick (office).

GORENSTEIN, Mark Borisovich; Russian conductor; *Chief Conductor and Artistic Director, State Academic Symphony Orchestra of Russia;* b. 16 Sept. 1946, Odessa, Ukraine; m. 2nd; one s.; ed Chişinău State Conservatory as violinist, Novosibirsk State Conservatory as conductor; violinist with Bolshoi Theatre Orchestra 1973–75, State Academic Symphony Orchestra 1975–84; Chief Conductor and Artistic Dir MAV Orchestra, Budapest, Hungary 1985–88; Chief Conductor Pusan City Symphony Orchestra, S Korea 1989–91; Founder, Chief Conductor and Artistic Dir New Russia State Symphony Orchestra 1992–2002, State Academic Symphony Orchestra of Russia 2002–; Honoured Art Worker of Russia. *Address:* Rublevskoye shosse 28, Apt 25, 121609 Moscow (home); Bolshaya Nikitskaya 13, 125009 Moscow, Russia. *Telephone:* (495) 202-06-25 (office); (495) 414-52-03 (home). *Fax:* (495) 202-10-06 (office); (495) 414-52-03 (home). *E-mail:* director@gaso.ru (office); gaso@inbox.ru (office). *Website:* www.gaso.ru (office).

GORETTA, Claude; Swiss film director; b. 23 June 1929, Geneva. *Films include:* Le fou 1970, Le jour des noces 1971, L'invitation 1973, The Wonderful Crook 1976, La Dentellière (The Lacemaker) 1977, Bonheur toi-même 1980, The Girl from Lorraine 1981, The Death of Mario Ricci 1983, Orpheus 1985, Si le soleil ne revenait pas 1987, Maigret et la Grande Perche 1991, Visages Suisses 1991, Maigret et les Caves du Majestic 1992, Het Verdriet Van Belgie 1994, Le dernier été 1997. *Address:* 10 rue de la Tour de Boël, 1204 Geneva, Switzerland.

GOR'KOV, Lev Petrovich, PhD, DPhysSc; Russian physicist and academic; *Professor and Program Director, Science, Condensed Matter/Theory, National High Magnetic Field Laboratory, Florida State University;* b. 1929, Moscow; s. of Petr Ivanovich Gorkov and Antonina Grigor'evna Gorkova; m. Donara Chernikova 1965; two s. (one d. from 1st m.); ed Moscow Inst. of Mechanics; jr then sr researcher, Inst. of Physical Problems 1953–64; Head of Sector, Inst. of Chemical Physics 1964–65; Head of Sector, L.D. Landau Inst. of Theoretical Physics 1965–88, Deputy Dir 1988–91; Prof. and Dept Head, Inst. for Physics and Tech. 1965–92; Science, Condensed Matter/Theory Program Dir and Prof., Nat. High Magnetic Field Lab., Florida State Univ. 1992–; mem. Int. Program Cttee 5th Int. Conf. STRIPES 2006, Int. Program Cttee M2S-HTSC VIII 2006; Fellow, Russian Acad. of Sciences, American Physical Soc.; mem. NAS; Foreign Hon. mem. American Acad. of Art and Science; Dr hc (New York Univ., Univ. of Illinois); Lenin Prize, L. D. Landau Prize, Bardeen Prize in Superconductivity, Eugene Feenberg Medal 2004. *Publications:* Gradient-Invariant Formulation of Superconductivity Theory in terms of Bose Condensation of Cooper Pairs and Identification of Superconducting Order Parameter 1958, Methods of Quantum Field Theory in Statistical Physics 1962, Superconducting Properties and Structural Transitions in Compounds with A-15 Lattice 1976, Physical Phenomena in Organic Conductors and Superconductors 1984, Phase Stratification of Liquid in New Superconductors 1987, Superconductivity in Heavy Fermion Systems 1987; articles in scientific journals. *Address:* A-310 NHMFL, Florida State University, 1800 East Paul Dirac Drive, Tallahassee, FL 32310-3706, USA (office). *Telephone:* (850) 644-4187 (office); (495) 137-32-44 (Moscow) (home). *Fax:* (850) 644-5038 (office). *E-mail:* gorkov@magnet.fsu.edu (office). *Website:* www.magnet.fsu.edu (office).

GORMAN, Joseph Tolle, BA, LLB; American business executive; b. 1937, Rising Sun, Ind.; m. Bettyann Gorman; ed Kent State Univ. and Yale Law School; Assoc., Baker, Hostetler & Patterson, Cleveland 1962–67; with Legal Dept TRW Inc., Cleveland 1968–69, Asst Sec. 1969–70, Sec. 1970–72, Vice-Pres. Sr Counsel, Automotive Worldwide Operations 1972–73, Vice-Pres. Asst Gen. Counsel 1973–76, Vice-Pres. Gen. Counsel 1976–80, Exec. Vice-Pres. Industrial and Energy Sector 1980–84, Exec. Vice-Pres., Asst Pres. 1984–85, Chair., Pres. and COO 1985–91, Chair., CEO 1988–2000; mem. Bd of Dirs Alcoa Inc. Procter & Gamble Co., Nat. City Corpn, Imperial Chemical Industries plc, US-China Business Council, The Prince of Wales Int. Business Leaders Forum, United Way Services, The Business Roundtable; fmr Dir Soc. Corpn, Soc. Nat. Bank, Cleveland, Standard Oil Co.; mem. Council on Foreign Relations, Pres.'s Export Council, Pres.'s Advisory Group of the US Chamber of Commerce, The Business Roundtable's Policy and Planning Cttee, Nat. Bureau of Econ. Research, The Business Council, Cleveland Council on World Affairs, In Business-Higher Education Forum, Kent State Univ. Foundation, Yale Alumni Asscn; Trustee New Ohio Inst., Cleveland Clinic Foundation, Musical Arts Asscn, Cleveland Play House; Chair. Civic Vision 2000 and Beyond; fmr Chair. Leadership Cleveland, US-Japan Business Council; founding mem. Ohio Gov.'s Educ. Man. Council; Japan Prime Minister's Trade Award 1994. *Address:* c/o The Cleveland Clinic Foundation, 9500 Euclid Avenue, Cleveland, OH 44195, USA.

GORMLEY, Antony Mark David, OBE, RA, MA, DFA, FRSA; British sculptor; b. 30 Aug. 1950, London; s. of Arthur J. C. Gormley and Elspeth Brauninger; m. Vicken Parsons 1980; two s. one d.; ed Ampleforth Coll., Trinity Coll., Cambridge, Cen. School of Arts and Crafts, London, Goldsmiths' Coll., Univ. of London and Slade School of Fine Arts, London; has participated in numerous group exhbns in Europe, N America, Japan, Brazil, Russia, Australia and NZ; works in collections of Tate Gallery, London, Scottish Nat. Gallery of Modern Art, Moderna Museet, Stockholm, Neue Galerie, Kassel, Victoria and Albert Museum, London, British Council, Arts Council of GB, Art Gallery of NSW, Sydney, Leeds City Art Galleries, Modern Art Museum of Fort Worth, Louisiana Museum of Modern Art, Humblebaek, Denmark, Irish Museum of Modern Art, Dublin, Sapporo Sculpture Park, Japan; sculpture in public places: Out of the Dark, Martinsplatz, Kassel 1987, Sculpture for Derry Walls, Derry, NI 1987–2001, Sound II, Winchester Cathedral 1989, Open Space, Place Jean Monnet, Rennes 1993, Iron:Man, Victoria Square, Birmingham 1994, Havmann, Mo I Rana, Norway 1995, Bearing IV, Tongyoung City, S Korea 1997, Angel of the North, Gateshead (Civic Trust Award 2000) 1998 (Civic Trust Award 2000), Rhizome II, Expo Parque, Lisbon 1998, Quantum Cloud, The Thames, Greenwich, London 1999, Well, Ministry of Health, Welfare and Sport, The Hague 2000, Site of Remembrance, Oslo 2000, Mind-Body Column, Osaka 2000, Dorotheenblocke Haus 6, Berlin 2001, Planets, British Library 2002, Inside Australia, Lake Ballard, WA 2002–03, Broken Column, Stavanger, Norway 2003, Fai Spazio, Prendi Posto, Poggibonsi (part of Arte 'all Arte 9), Italy 2004, Another Place, Crosby Beach, Merseyside 2003, You, The Roundhouse, London 2006, Resolution, Shoe Lane, London 2007, Filter, Manchester Art Gallery 2009; Hon. Fellow, Goldsmith's Coll., Univ. of London 1998, RIBA 2001, Jesus College, Cambridge 2003, Trinity College, Cambridge 2003; Dr hc (Univ. of Cen. England, Birmingham) 1998, (Open Univ.) 2001, (Cambridge) 2003, (Newcastle) 2004; Turner Prize 1994, South Bank Art Award for Visual Art 1999, British Design and Art Direction Silver Award for Illustration 2000. *Publications include:* Antony Gormley 1995, Making an Angel 1998, Total Strangers 1999, Antony Gormley, Asian Field 2004, Material Engagements: Studies in Honour of Colin Renfrew/A Meeting of Minds: Art And Archeology 2004, Making Space 2005, Antony Gormley Inside Australia 2005, Asian Field: Makers & Made 2006, Antony Gormley 2007, Antony Gormley: Blind Light 2007, Antony Gormley: Bodies in Space 2007. *Leisure interests:* walking, talking. *Address:* 15–23 Vale Royal, London, N7 9AP(Studio); 13 South Villas, London, NW1 9BS, England (home). *Telephone:* (20) 7697-2180 (Studio); (20) 7482-7383 (home). *Fax:* (20) 7697-2188 (Studio); (20) 7267-8336 (home). *E-mail:* admin-work@antonygormley.com (office). *Website:* www.antonygormley.com (office).

GORMLY, Allan Graham, CMG, CBE; British business executive and chartered accountant; b. 18 Dec. 1937, Paisley, Scotland; s. of William Gormly and Christina Swinton Flockhart; m. Vera Margaret Grant 1962; one s. one d.; ed Paisley Grammar School; with Peat Marwick Mitchell & Co. 1956–61, Rootes Group 1961–65; joined John Brown PLC, apptd. Chief Exec. 1983, Dir Trafalgar House PLC (when it acquired John Brown PLC) 1986–95, CEO 1992–94; Deputy Chair. Royal Insurance Holdings PLC 1992–93, Chair. 1994–96 (mem. Bd 1990–96), Deputy Chair. Royal and Sun Alliance Insurance Group PLC 1996–98; Chair. BPB PLC 1997–2004 (Dir 1995–2004); Chair. Overseas Projects Bd 1989–91; Deputy Chair. Export Guarantees Advisory Council 1990–92; Dir Brixton PLC 1994–2003 (Chair. 2000–03), European Capital Co. 1996–99, Bank of Scotland 1997–2001; Dir (non-exec.) Nat. Grid. Co. 1994–95; Chair. Q-One Group Ltd 1999–2003; mem. British Overseas Trade Bd 1989–91, Top Salaries Review Body 1990–92; Dir Bd of Man., FCO 2000–04. *Leisure interests:* golf, music. *Address:* 56 North Park, Gerrards Cross, Bucks., SL9 8JR, England (home). *Telephone:* (1753) 885079 (home).

GÖRNE, Matthias; German singer (baritone); b. 1966, Weimar; ed in Leipzig from 1985, then with Dietrich Fischer-Dieskau and Elisabeth Schwarzkopf; performed with the children's choir at Chemnitz Opera; sang in Bach's St Matthew Passion under Kurt Masur, Leipzig 1990; appearances with Hanns Martin Schneidt and Munich Bach Choir and with NDR Symphony Orchestra Hamburg; further engagements under Horst Stein, with Bamberg Symphony Orchestra and in Hindemith's Requiem under Wolfgang Sawallisch; concerts at Leipzig Gewandhaus under Helmuth Rilling and in Amsterdam and Paris; Lieder recitals with pianist Eric Schneider; sang title role in Henze's Prinz von Homburg, Cologne 1992, Marcello in La Bohème at Komische Oper, Berlin 1993, Wolfram in Tannhäuser, Cologne 1996, Die Schöne Müllerin, Bath 1997; engaged for Die Zauberflöte, Salzburg Festival 1997; has appeared with Metropolitan Opera, Royal Opera, London, Zurich Opera, Deutsche Opera, Teatro Real, Madrid, Dresden Semperoper, Salzburg Festival, Saito Kinen Festival; Prof. of Lieder Interpretation, Schumann Hochschule, Dusseldorf 2001–2005. *Recordings include:* Matthäuspassion 1994, Winterreise 1997, Entarte Musik, Arias, J.S. Bach Cantatas, Eisler's Deutsche Sinfonie, The Hollywood Songbook, Mahler's des Knaben Wunderhorn, Mendelssohn's Paulus Oratorio op. 36, Schubert's Schwanengesang, Die Schöne Müllerin, Winterreise, Goethe-Lieder, Messe D950, Liedrekreis, Schumann's Dichterliebe,. *Address:* Michael Kocyan Artists Management, Alt-Moabit 104A, 10559 Berlin, Germany (office). *Telephone:* (30) 31004940 (office). *Fax:* (30) 31004984 (office). *E-mail:* artists@kocyan.de (office); info@matthiasgoerne.de (office). *Website:* www.kocyan.de (office); www.matthiasgoerne.de.

GORTON, Slade, BA, LLB; American politician and lawyer; *Of Counsel, Policy and Public Law, Preston Gates & Ellis LLP;* b. 8 Jan. 1928, Chicago, Ill.; s. of Thomas Slade Gorton and Ruth Israel; m. Sally Clark 1958; one s. two d.; ed Evanston High School, Ill., Dartmouth Univ., Columbia Univ. Law School; US Army 1945–46, USAF 1953–56, presently Col USAF Reserve; admitted to Bar, Wash. State 1953; mem. Wash. State House of Reps 1958–68, Majority Leader 1967–68; Wash. State Attorney Gen. 1968–80; Senator from Washington 1981–87, 1989–2001; Pnr Davis, Wright and Jones, Seattle 1987–89; with Preston, Gates & Ellis 2001–; mem. Wash. State Law and Justice Comm. 1969–80 (Chair. 1969–70), State Criminal Justice Training Comm. 1969–80 (Chair. 1969–76), Pres.'s Consumer Advisory Council 1975–77, Nat. Asscn of Attorneys-Gen. 1969–80 (Pres. 1976–77), Nat. Comm. on Federal Election Reform 2001–2002, Nat. Comm. on Terrorist Attacks 2002–04; mem. Bd of Dirs Fred Hutchinson Cancer Research Center 1987–2002; Republican; Wyman Award (Outstanding Attorney Gen. in the US)1980. *Address:* Preston, Gates & Ellis LLP, 925 Fourth Avenue, Suite 2900, Seattle, WA 98104-1158, USA (office). *Telephone:* (206) 623-7580 (office). *Fax:* (206) 623-7022 (office). *E-mail:* sladeg@prestongates.com (office). *Website:* www.prestongates.com (office).

GOSAIBI, Ghazi al-, PhD; Saudi Arabian diplomatist, politician and writer; *Minister of Labour;* b. 2 March 1940, al-Hasa; s. of Abdul Rahman Algosaibi and Fatma Algosaibi; m. Sigrid Presser 1968; three s. one d.; ed Univs of Cairo, Southern Calif. and London; Asst Prof. King Saud Univ., Riyadh 1965, then Prof. and Head of Political Science and Dean of Faculty of Commerce; Dir Saudi Railways 1974; Minister of Industry and Electricity 1975, of Health 1982; Amb. to Bahrain 1984, to UK (also accred to Ireland) 1992–2002; fmrly Minister of Agric. and Water, Minister of Water and Electricity; currently Minister of Labour. *Publications include:* prose: Yes, (Saudi) Minister! A Life in Administration, Seven, An Apartment Called Freedom, The Dilemma of Development, The Gulf Crisis: An Attempt to Understand, Arabian Essays, Dansko, A Revolution in the Sunnah; 18 collections of poetry. *Leisure interests:* swimming, fishing, table tennis. *Address:* Ministry of Labour, Omar bin al-Khatab St, Riyadh 11157, Saudi Arabia (office). *Telephone:* (1) 477-8888 (office). *Fax:* (1) 478-9175 (office). *Website:* www.mol.gov.sa (office).

GOSDEN, Roger Gordon, PhD, DSC; British professor of medical sciences; *Professor, Director of Reproductive Biology, Weill Medical College, Cornell University;* b. 23 Sept. 1948, Ryde, Isle of Wight; s. of the late Gordon Conrad Jason Gosden and Peggy Gosden (née Butcher); two s.; m. 2nd Lucinda Leigh Veeck 2004; ed Chislehurst and Sidcup Grammar School, Univs of Bristol and Cambridge; MRC Research Fellow, Univ. of Cambridge 1973–76; Population Council Fellow, Duke Univ., USA 1974–75; Lecturer in Physiology, Univ. of Edin. 1976–84, Sr Lecturer 1984–94; Prof. of Reproductive Biology, Univ. of Leeds 1994–99, Visiting Prof. 1999–; Research Dir and Prof., McGill Univ., Canada 1999–2001, Adjunct Prof. 2001–; Howard and Georgeanna Jones Prof. of Reproductive Medicine and Scientific Dir, Eastern Virginia Medical School, USA 2001–04, Adjunct Prof., Old Dominion Univ., Va 2002–; Prof. of Reproductive Medicine and of Reproductive Medicine in Obstetrics and Gynecology, Dir of Research in Reproductive Biology, Weill Medical Coll., Cornell Univ., New York 2004–; pioneer in fertility conservation; scientific adviser to govt bodies (UK, The Netherlands, Canada); numerous radio and TV broadcasts; Distinguished Scientist Lecture, American Soc. of Reproductive Medicine 2001, British Fertility Soc. Steptoe Lecture 2003 and many other awards and lectureships. *Publications:* Biology of Menopause 1985, Cheating Time 1996, Designer Babies 1999, Biology and Pathology of the Oocyte (with A. O. Trounson) 2003, Preservation of Fertility (with T. Tulandi) 2004; numerous articles in academic journals, magazines and newspapers. *Leisure interests:* writing, natural history, walking. *Address:* Center for Reproductive Medicine and Infertility, Weill Medical College, Cornell University, 505 East 70th Street (HT340), New York, NY 10021, USA (office). *Telephone:* (212) 746-1287 (office). *Fax:* (212) 746-2101 (office). *E-mail:* rgg2004@med.cornell.edu (office). *Website:* www.ivf.org/phys.html (office).

GOSEV, Petar, MA; Macedonian politician; b. 5 Sept. 1948, Pirava; m.; two s.; ed Univ. of Skopje; with 11 Oktomvri Bus Co. 1971–73; mem. Council Macedonian Trade Union Fed. 1973–87 (Econ. adviser 1973–84, Chief, Office of the Union Pres. 1977, mem. Presidency 1982–87); mem. Presidency, Cen. Cttee Union of Communists of Macedonia (renamed SKM–PDP 1990, Social Democratic Alliance of Macedonia 1991) 1986–89, Pres. 1989–91; Chief of the Del. of the Nat. Ass. in the Ass. of the fmr Socialist Fed. Repub. of Yugoslavia 1990; mem. Parl. 1990–2002; f. Democratic Party 1993, Pres. 1993–97; Pres. Liberal-Democratic Party–LDP (formed from merger of Liberal Party and Democratic Party) 1997–99; Vice-Pres. Parl. Group of the Nat. Ass. to the Inter-Parl. Union 1998–2002; Vice-Pres. of Fmr Yugoslav Repub. of Macedonia and Minister of Finance 2002–04. *Address:* c/o Ministry of Finance, Dame Gruev 14, Skopje, 1000 Former Yugoslav Republic of Macedonia (office).

GOSIEWSKI, Przemysław; Polish politician; b. 12 May 1964, Słupsk; m. Beata Gosiewska; one s. two d.; ed Univ. of Gdańsk and Polish Nat. Defence Univ.; fmr Leader, Ind. Students Asscn (Niezależny Związek Studentów), Gdańsk; Head of Regional Office, Nat. Comm. of Ind. and Self-Governing Trade Unions (NSZZ Solidarność) 1981–91; Deputy, Sejm (Parl.) 1989–, mem. Justice and Human Rights Cttee 2001–05, Nat. Defense Cttee 2001– (Deputy Chair. 2005–); mem. Law and Justice Party (Prawo i Sprawiedliwość), Leader Parl. Group 2005–; Deputy Prime Minister 2007. *Address:* Law and Justice Party, ul. Nowogrodzka 84/86, 02-018 Warsaw Poland (office). *Telephone:* (22) 6215035 (office). *Fax:* (22) 6216767 (office). *E-mail:* biuro@pis.org.pl (office). *Website:* www.pis.org.pl (office).

GOSLING, Sir Donald, Kt, KCVO; British business executive; b. 2 March 1929; m. Elizabeth Shauna Ingram 1959 (divorced 1988); three s.; joined RN 1944, served on HMS Leander; co-founder and Jt Chair. Nat. Car Parks Ltd 1950–98; Chair. Palmer & Harvey 1967; Chair. Council of Man. White Ensign Asscn Ltd 1978–83, Vice-Pres. 1983–93, Pres. 1993– (mem. 1970–); mem. Exec. Cttee Imperial Soc. of Kts Bachelor 1977–; Chair. Berkeley Square Ball Trust 1982–, Mountbatten Memorial Hall Appeals Cttee 1980; Vice-Pres. King George's Fund for Sailors 1993–; Hon. Capt. RNR 1993–; Trustee Fleet Air Arm Museum, Yeovilton 1974–, Royal Yachting Asscn Seamanship Foundation 1981–; Patron Submarine Memorial Appeal 1978–, HMS Ark Royal Welfare Trust 1986–; Companion Rat, Grand Order of Water Rats. *Leisure interests:* swimming, sailing, shooting. *Address:* c/o Grand Order of Water Rats, 328 Gray's Inn Road, London, WC1X 8BZ, England (office).

GOSS, Porter J., BA; American politician and government official; b. 26 Nov. 1938, Waterbury, Conn.; m. Mariel Goss; four c.; ed Yale Univ.; served US Army 1960–66; Clandestine Services Officer CIA 1962–71; co-founder and publisher Community Newspaper 1971–74; Sanibel, Fla, City Council 1974–82, apptd Mayor of Sanibel 1974–77; mem. Lee Co. Bd of Commr 1983–88; mem. US House of Reps 1989–2004, Chair. House Perm. Select Cttee on Intelligence, mem. House Rules Cttee, Select Cttee for Homeland Security; Dir CIA 2004–06 (resgnd). *Address:* c/o Central Intelligence Agency, Office of Public Affairs, Washington, DC 20505, USA (office).

GOTCHEV, Dimitar Bonev; Bulgarian judge; b. 27 Feb. 1936, Sofia; s. of Maj.-Gen. Boncho Gotchev and Zdravka Gotchev; m. Jova Gotcheva-Cholakova 1976; one d.; ed Univ. of Sofia St Kliment Ochridsky; legal adviser 1959–66; Arbiter, State Court of Arbitration 1966–89; Judge, Supreme Court 1990, Judge, Head of Commercial Div. 1990–, Deputy Chief Justice, Supreme Court 1993; Judge, Constitutional Court 1994–2004; Judge, European Court of Human Rights, Strasbourg 1992–98. *Leisure interests:* music, mountaineering, skiing. *Address:* c/o Constitutional Court of Republic of Bulgaria, Bul. Dondoukov 1, 1202 Sofia; Koslodui Str. N34, 1202 Sofia, Bulgaria (home). *Telephone:* (2) 940-23-31; (2) 31-54-25 (home).

GÖTHE, (Lars) Staffan; Swedish playwright, actor and director; *Professor, University of Lund;* b. 20 Dec. 1944, Luleå; s. of the late Thorsten Göthe and of Margit Grape-Göthe; m. Kristin Byström 1969; one s.; ed Acad. of Performing Arts, Gothenburg; actor and playwright, regional theatre of Växjö 1971, Folkteatern, Gothenburg 1974; Headmaster Acad. of Performing Arts, Malmö 1976; actor, Folkteatern, Gävleborg 1983; Dir The RTC Co. 1986–95; actor and playwright, Royal Dramatic Theatre, Stockholm 1995–2003; Prof. of Theatre Acad., Univ. of Lund 2003–; Royal Medal Litteris et Artibus, Award of Royal Swedish Acad. 2005. *Plays:* En natt i februari 1972, Den gråtande polisen 1980, La strada dell'amore 1986, En uppstoppad hund 1986, Den perfekta Kyssen 1990, Arma Irma 1991, Boogie Woogie 1992, Blått Hus Med Röda Kinder 1995, Ruben Pottas Eländiga Salonger 1996, Ett Lysande Elände 1999, Temperance 2000, Byta Trottoar 2001, Stjärnan Över Lappland 2005. *Publication:* Lysande Eländen (complete works) 2004. *Address:* Vindragarvägen 8, 117 50 Stockholm, Sweden (home). *Telephone:* (8) 668-38-18 (office).

GOTT, Karel; Czech singer; b. 14 July 1939, Plzeň; two d.; ed Prague Conservatory (studied under Prof. Karenin); mem. Semafor Theatre, Prague 1963–65; mem. Apollo Theatre, Prague, 1965–67; freelance artist 1967–; numerous foreign tours; charity concerts with Eva Urbanová 1998; CD Rocky mého mládí (Rocks of my Youth) 1999; exhbn of paintings, Bratislava 1999; f. and Chair. Interpo Foundation 1993–96; concerts in Carnegie Hall, New York, Expo, Hanover, Kremlin Palace, Moscow 2000; charity concerts in Czech Repub. after 2002 floods; Golden Nightingale trophy (annual pop singer poll 1963–66, 1968–81, 1983, 1989–90, 1997–2001), MIDEM Prize, Cannes 1967, MIDEM Gold Record 1969, Polydor Gold Record 1970, Supraphon Gold Record 1972, 1973, 1979, 1980, 1996, Music Week Star of the Year 1974 (UK) 1975, Artist of Merit 1982, Gold Aerial 1983, radio station BRT (Belgium) 1984, Nat. Artist 1985, Polydor Golden Pin (Germany) 1986, Czech Nightingale Trophy 1996, 1997, 1999, 2001, 2002 (28 times in total), Czech TV Prize 1997, 1999, Platinum Record (for duets with Lucia Bílá) 1998 and many other awards. *Radio:* presenter monthly show Radio Impuls 2002–. *Film appearance:* Luck from Hell. *Recordings:* Vánoce ve zlaté Praze 1969, 42 největších hitů 1991, Věci blízké mému srdci 1993, Zázrak vánoční 1995, Belcanto 1996, Duety s Lucií Bílou 1997, Miluj 1997, Svátek svátků 1998, Rocky mého mládí 1999, Originálni nahrávky ze 70.let 2000, Originálni nahrávky ze 80.let 2000, Originálni nahrávky ze 90.let 2000, Pokaždé 2002, Gott & Vondaáčková 2003, Lásko má 2004, Můj strážný anděl 2004, K. Gott zpívá hity K. Svobody 2005, Jsou svátky 2006, Má pouť 2006, Každý má svůj sen 2007, Zlatá Kolekce 2007, Zmírám láskou 2008. *Publication:* Why Painting is Important for Me 2001. *Address:* GOJA spol. s r.o., Pod Prusekem 3, 102 00 Prague 10, Czech Republic (office); Nad Bertramkou 18, 150 00 Prague 5, Czech Republic (home). *Telephone:* (2) 72658337 (office). *Fax:* (2) 72659265 (office). *E-mail:* goja@goja.cz (office). *Website:* www.goja.cz (office); www.karelgott.com; www.karel-gott.de.

GOTTI, Irv; American music company executive and producer; *CEO, The Inc. Records;* b. (Irv Lorenzo), Hollis, Queens, New York; m. Debbie Gotti; began music career as DJ Irv; fmr producer Island Def Jam Records, artistes produced include Ashanti, Charli Baltimore, Toni Braxton, DMX, Ja Rule, Jay-Z; currently CEO Murder Inc. Records, now known as The Inc. Records. *Recordings include:* Irv Gotti Presents... (series of albums). *Address:* c/o The Inc. Records, 2220 Colorado Avenue, Santa Monica, CA 90404, USA (office). *Website:* www.theincrecords.com (office).

GOTTLIEB, Robert Adams, BA; American editor and critic; b. 29 April 1931, New York; s. of Charles Gottlieb and Martha (née Kean) Gottlieb; m. 1st Muriel Higgins 1952; m. 2nd Maria Tucci 1969; two s. one d.; ed Columbia

Coll. and Cambridge Univ.; employee Simon and Schuster 1955–65, Ed.-in-Chief 1965–68; Ed.-in-Chief Alfred A. Knopf 1968–87, Pres. 1973–87; Ed.-in-Chief The New Yorker 1987–92; now dance and book critic for New York Observer, New York Times, The New Yorker and New York Review of Books. *Publications:* Reading Jazz 1996, Reading Lyrics (co-author) 2000, George Balanchine – The Ballet Maker 2004, Reading Dance (ed.) 2008. *Leisure interests:* ballet, movies, reading. *Address:* 237 East 48th Street, New York, NY 10017-1538, USA (home).

GOTTSCHALK, Gerhard, Dr rer. nat; German microbiologist, academic and organization administrator; *President, Union of German Academies of Sciences and Humanities;* b. 27 March 1935, Schwedt/Oder; s. of Gerhard Gottschalk and Irmgard Gottschalk (née Ploetz); m. Ellen-Marie Hrabowski 1960; two s. one d.; ed Humboldt Univ., Berlin and Georg-August-Univ., Göttingen; Research Assoc., Dept of Biochemistry, Univ. of Calif., Berkeley, USA 1964–66, Visiting Prof. 1978–79; Docent, Georg-August-Univ. of Göttingen 1967–70, Prof. of Microbiology 1970–2003, Rector 1975–76, Vice-Pres. 1979–81, Prof. of Genome Research 2003–; Visiting Prof., Dept of Bacteriology, Univ. of California, Davis 1972–73; Vice-Pres. Acad. of Science, Göttingen 1996, Pres. 1998–2000; Pres. ALLEA (All European Acads) 1998–2000; Pres. Union of German Acads of Sciences and Humanities 2003–; Philip Morris Prize 1992. *Publications:* Bacterial Metabolism 1986, Biotechnologie 1986, Göttinger Gelehrte (co-ed. with K. Arndt and R. Smend) 2001. *Address:* Institute of Microbiology and Genetics, University of Göttingen, Grisebachstrasse 8, 37077 Göttingen (office); Union of German Academies of Sciences and Humanities, Geschwister-Scholl-str. 2, Mainz 55131, Germany. *Telephone:* (551) 394041 (office). *Fax:* (551) 394195 (office); (5503) 999128 (home). *E-mail:* ggottsc@gwdg.de (office). *Website:* www.img.bio.uni-goettingen.de (office); wwwuser.gwdg.de/~ggottsc (home).

GÖTZE, Wolfgang; German theoretical physicist and academic; Head, Inst. for Theoretical Physics, Munich Univ. of Tech.; Max-Planck-Medal, German Physical Soc. 2006. *Publications:* numerous scientific papers in professional journals. *Address:* Room 3333, Institute for Theoretical Physics, Munich University of Technology, Garching, Germany (office). *Telephone:* (89) 289-12360 (office). *Fax:* (89) 289-14641 (office). *E-mail:* Wolfgang.Goetze@ph.tum.de (office). *Website:* www.physik.tu-muenchen.de/lehrstuehle/T37_wg/Welcome_e.html (office).

GOU, Terry M.; Taiwanese electronics industry executive; *Chairman and CEO, Hon Hai Precision Industry Co. Ltd;* b. 1950; widowed; two c.; f. Hon Hai Precision Industry Co. Ltd (trading name Foxconn; world's largest contract manufacturer) 1974, now Chair. and CEO. *Address:* Hon Hai Precision Industry Co. Ltd, 2 Zihyou Street, Tucheng City, Taipei County 236, Taiwan (office). *Telephone:* (2) 2268-3466 (office). *Fax:* (2) 2268-6204 (office). *E-mail:* webadmin@foxconn.com (office). *Website:* www.foxconn.com (office).

GOUBET, Cédric; French civil servant; *Principal Private Secretary to the President;* b. 12 May 1971, Cambrai; served as Chief of Staff to prefects Claude Guéant, Franche-Comté 1998–2002, Jean-Marie Rebière and Thierry Klinger, Finistère 2000–02; Chief of Staff to Minister of the Interior, Nicolas Sarkozy 2004, Tech. Adviser 2005–07; Prin. Pvt. Sec. to Pres. Nicolas Sarkozy 2007–. *Address:* Palais de l'Elysée, 55 rue du faubourg Saint-Honoré, 75008 Paris, France (office). *Telephone:* 1-42-92-81-00 (office). *Website:* www.elysee.fr (office).

GOUELI, Ahmed, BSc, MSc, MA, PhD; Egyptian professor of agricultural economics and international organization official; *Secretary-General, Council of Arab Economic Unity;* b. 22 March 1937, Behera; m.; two c.; ed Alexandria Univ., Univ. of California, Berkeley; Agricultural Engineer, Authority of Land Reclamation 1957–58; Research Assoc., Dept of Agricultural Econs, Univ. of California, Berkeley 1964–65; Asst Prof. of Agricultural Econs, Faculty of Agric., Ain Shams Univ., Egypt 1965–71; Assoc. Prof., Zagazig Univ., Egypt 1971–74, Prof. 1974–84, 1999–2000, Chair. Dept of Agricultural Econs, Faculty of Agric. 1971–84; Prof. of Agricultural Econs, Faculty of Agric., Cairo Univ. 2000; Gov. of Damietta 1984–91, of Ismailia 1991–94; mem. People's Ass. (Parl.) 1995–2000; Minister of Supply and Home Trade 1994–96, of Trade and Supply 1996–99; CEO and Chair. Bd of Dirs, Kingdom Agricultural Devt Co. 2000–01; Sec.-Gen. Council of Arab Econ. Unity 2000–; Chair. Egyptian Assn of Agricultural Econs 1990–, Egyptian Water Partnership 2003–; currently Chair. Cttee for Assessment of Nominees for Nat. Awards in Agricultural Disciplines, Acad. of Science and Tech.; mem. Bd of Trustees Int. Maize and Wheat Improvement Centre (CIMMYT) 1986–92, The Formulation of the World Food Security Strategy Expert Team, FAO 1984, Food Reserves Stocks Research Team, FAO 1991, Int. Council for Food and Agricultural Policy 2002–, Foundation Cttee of the Arab Water Council 2005; mem. Acad. of Science and Tech. 1988–92, Egyptian Council of Sciences 1995–2000; currently mem. Soc. for Political Economy, Egyptian Assn for Policy Analysis, Food and Agric. Council, Presidential Council for Econ. and Production Affairs; Nat. Award of Sciences 1991, Sciences and Arts Medal 1995, Haas Int. Award, Univ. of California 1997, Mubarak Award 2007. *Address:* Council of Arab Economic Unity, 1191 Corniche en-Nil, 4th Floor, PO Box 1, Mohammed Fareed, 11518 Cairo, Egypt (office). *Telephone:* (2) 25755045 (office). *Fax:* (2) 25754090 (office). *E-mail:* caeu@ Idsc.net.eg (office). *Website:* www.caeu.org.eg (office).

GOUGH, Barry Morton, MA, PhD, DLit, FRHistS; Canadian historian, academic and consultant; *Adjunct Professor of History, The Royal Military College of Canada;* b. 17 Sept. 1938, Victoria, BC; s. of John Gough and Dorothy Mouncy Morton Gough; m. 1st B. Louise Kerr 1964 (divorced 1977); one s. one d.; m. 2nd Marilyn J. Morris 1981; two s.; ed Vic. public schools, Univs of British Columbia and Montana and King's Coll., London, UK; Prof. of History, Western Washington Univ. and Wilfrid Laurier Univ. 1972–2004, now Emer.; Adjunct Prof. of War Studies, Royal Mil. Coll. of Canada 1994–; Asst Dean of Arts and Sciences, Wilfrid Laurier Univ. 1999–2001; Founding mem. Assn for Canadian Studies in the US and Co-Dir and Archivist Center for Pacific Northwest Studies, Western Washington Univ., Bellingham, Wash. 1968–72; mem. Canadian Historical Assn, Canadian Nautical Research Soc.; Visiting Prof., Duke Univ., Univ. of British Columbia, Otago Univ., Natal Univ., ANU, and others; Fellow, King's Coll. London; Archives Fellow, Churchill Coll. Cambridge, UK; Pres. N American Soc. for Oceanic History, Canadian Nautical Research Soc.; Vice-Pres. Social Sciences Fed. of Canada; Ed. American Neptune: Maritime History and Arts 1995–2001; Queen's Jubilee Medal 2002; Roderick Haig-Brown and other book prizes; Lt Gov. of BC Medal for Historical Writing 1985. *Publications:* Royal Navy and the Northwest Coast 1971, Distant Dominion 1980, Gunboat Frontier 1984, Journal of Alexander Henry the Younger 1988, 1992, The Northwest Coast 1992, Falkland Islands/Malvinas 1992, First Across The Continent: Sir Alexander Mackenzie 1997, Historical Dictionary of Canada 1999, HMCS Haida: Battle Ensign Flying 2001, Fighting Sail on Lake Huron and Georgian Bay 1812 2002, Through Water, Ice and Fire: Schooner Nancy of the War of 1812 2006, Fortune's a River 2007; numerous reviews and articles. *Leisure interests:* golfing, jazz clarinet. *Address:* PO Box 5037, Victoria, BC V8R 6N3, Canada (home); 107 Pall Mall, London, SW1Y 5ER, England (home). *Telephone:* (250) 592-0800 (home). *E-mail:* bgough@wlu.ca (office); barrygough@shaw.ca (office). *Website:* www.wlu.ca (office).

GOUGH, Douglas Owen, MA, PhD, FRS, FInstP; British astrophysicist; *Leverhulme Emeritus Fellow, University of Cambridge;* b. 8 Feb. 1941, Stourport; s. of Owen Albert John Gough and Doris May Gough (née Camera); m. Rosanne Penelope Shaw 1965; two s. two d.; ed Hackney Downs School, London, St John's Coll., Cambridge; Research Assoc., JILA, Univ. of Colorado, USA 1966–67, Fellow Adjoint 1986–; NAS Sr Postdoctoral Research Assoc., New York 1967–69; mem. Grad. Staff, Inst. of Theoretical Astronomy, Univ. of Cambridge 1969–73, Lecturer in Astronomy and Applied Math., Inst. of Astronomy and Dept of Applied Math. and Theoretical Physics 1973–85, Reader in Astrophysics, Inst. of Astronomy 1985–93, Prof. of Theoretical Astrophysics 1993–2008, currently Leverhulme Emer. Fellow, Deputy Dir Inst. of Astronomy 1993–99, Dir 1999–2004; Fellow, Churchill Coll. Cambridge 1972–; Visiting Prof. of Physics, Stanford Univ., USA 1996–; Foreign mem. Royal Danish Acad. of Sciences and Letters 1998; Hon. Prof., Queen Mary and Westfield Coll., London 1986–2006; James Arthur Prize, Harvard Univ. (USA) 1982, William Hopkins Prize, Cambridge Philosophical Soc. 1984, George Ellery Hale Prize, American Astronomical Soc. 1994, Mousquetaire d'Armagnac 2001, Eddington Medal, Royal Astronomical Soc. 2002. *Publications:* Problems in Solar and Stellar Oscillations (ed.) 1983, Seismology of the Sun and the Distant Stars (ed.) 1986, Challenges to Theories of the Structure of Moderate-Mass Stars (co-ed. with J. Toomre) 1991, Equation-of-state and Phase-transition Issues in Models of Ordinary Astrophysical Matter (co-ed. with V. Čelebonović and W. Däppen) 2004, The Scientific Legacy of Fred Hoyle (ed.) 2005; more than 300 papers in the professional scientific literature. *Leisure interest:* cooking. *Address:* Institute of Astronomy, Madingley Road, Cambridge, CB3 0HA, England (office). *Telephone:* (1223) 337516 (office). *Fax:* (1223) 337523 (office). *E-mail:* douglas@ast.cam.ac.uk (office).

GOUGH, Michael; British actor; b. 23 Nov. 1917, Malaya; m. Anneke Wills; one s.; ed Wye Agricultural Coll. and studies at the Old Vic, London; theatrical debut 1936. *Plays include:* on Broadway: Bedroom Farce (Tony Award) 1979. *Films include:* Blanche Fury 1947, Anna Karenina 1948, Saraband for Dead Lovers 1948, The Small Back Room 1949, No Resting Place 1950, Ha'penny Breeze 1950 (uncredited) 1950, Blackmailed 1950, Night Was Our Friend 1951, Twice Upon a Time 1953, The Sword and the Rose 1953, Rob Roy, the Highland Rogue 1954, Richard III 1955, The Last Reunion 1955, Reach for the Sky 1956, Ill Met by Moonlight 1957, The Horse's Mouth 1958, Dracula 1958, Model for Murder 1958, Horrors of the Black Museum 1959, The House in the Woods 1959, Konga 1961, Candidate for Murder 1961, Mr. Topaze 1961, The Phantom of the Opera 1962, What a Carve Up 1962, Tamahine 1963, Black Zoo 1963, Game for Three Losers 1964, The Skull 1965, They Came From Beyond Space 1967, Curse of the Crimson Altar 1968, Berserk! 1968, Un soir, un train 1968, Women in Love 1969, Velvet House, A Walk with Love and Death 1969, Julius Caesar 1970, The Corpse 1970, Trog 1970, The Go-Between 1970, Henry VIII and His Six Wives 1972, Savage Messiah 1972, Horror Hospital 1973, The Legend of Hell House (uncredited) 1973, Galileo 1975, Satan's Slave 1976, The Boys from Brazil 1978, L'amour en question 1978, Venom 1982, The Dresser 1983, Memed My Hawk 1984, Oxford Blues 1984, Top Secret! 1984, Out of Africa 1985, Caravaggio 1986, Maschenka 1987, The Fourth Protocol 1987, Rarg (voice) 1988, The Serpent and the Rainbow 1988, Strapless 1989, Batman 1989, The Garden 1990, The Wanderer 1991, Let Him Have It 1991, Batman Returns 1992, Wittgenstein 1993, Blackeyes, The Age of Innocence 1993, The Hour of the Pig 1993, A Village Affair 1994, Uncovered 1994, Nostradamus 1994, Batman Forever 1995, The Life of Galileo, Batman and Robin 1997, The Whisper 1998, What Rats Won't Do 1998, St. Ives 1998, Sleepy Hollow 1999, The Cherry Orchard 1999, Corpse Bride (voice) 2005. *Television includes:* Albert 1951, The Man in the White Suit 1951, Julius Caesar 1959, Dancers in Mourning (series) 1959, The Poisoned Earth 1961, Count of Monte Cristo 1964, The Girl Who Loved Robots 1965, Alice in Wonderland 1966, Days to Come 1966, Play with a Tiger 1967, Pride and Prejudice 1967, The Search for the Nile (mini-series) 1971, Fall of Eagles (mini-series) 1974, Shoulder to Shoulder (mini-series) 1974, QB VII (mini-series) 1974, Notorious Woman (mini-series) 1974, The Trip to Jerusalem 1975, Suez 1956 1979, Brideshead Revisited (mini-series) 1981, Inside the Third Reich 1982, Smiley's People (mini-series) 1982, Witness for the Prosecution 1982, Another Flip for Dominick 1982, Cymbeline 1982, The Citadel (mini-series) 1983, To the Lighthouse 1983, Mistral's Daughter (mini-series) 1984, The Biko Inquest 1984, A Christmas Carol 1984, Arthur the King 1985, Lace II 1985, The Little Vampire (series) 1986, Cariani and the Courtesans 1987, A Killing On the Exchange (mini-series) 1987, The Mountain and the Molehill 1989, After the War (mini-series) 1989, Blackeyes (mini-series) 1989, The Shell Seekers 1989, Sleepers 1991, Children of the North 1991, The Haunting of Helen Walker 1995, Young Indiana Jones: Travels with Father 1996, Dame Edna Live at the Palace 2003.

GOUGH, Piers William, CBE, RIBA, FRSA, RA; British architect; b. 24 April 1946; s. of Peter Gough and Daphne Mary Unwin Banks; m. Rosemary Elaine Fosbrooke Bates 1991; ed Architectural Asscn School of Architecture; partner, CZWG Architects 1975–; Pres. Architectural Asscn 1995–97 (mem. Council 1970–72, 1991); Commr English Heritage 2000; mem. Bd Stonehenge 2002–, Council of the Royal Acad. 2003–04; Hon. DUniv (Middlesex) 1999, (Queen Mary College). *Television:* presenter, Shock of the Old (6-part series), Channel 4 2000. *Principal works include:* Phillips West 2, Bayswater 1976, Cochrane Square (Phase I), Glasgow 1987, China Wharf, Bermondsey 1988, Craft, Design and Tech. Bldg, Bryanston School 1988, Street-Porter House 1988, The Circle, Bermondsey 1990, Westbourne Grove Public Lavatories 1993, 1–10 Summers Street, Clerkenwell 1994, Leonardo Centre, Uppingham School 1995, Cochrane Square (Phase II), Glasgow 1995, 90 Wardour Street, Soho 1995, 19th and 20th Century Galleries, Nat. Portrait Gallery 1996, Suffolk Wharf, Camden Lock 1996–, Brindleyplace Café, Birmingham 1997, Bankside Lofts, London 1997, The Glass Building, Camden 1999, The Green Bridge, Mile End Park 2000. *Publication:* English Extremists 1988. *Leisure interest:* throwing parties. *Address:* CZWG Architects, 17 Bowling Green Lane, London, EC1R 0QB, England (office). *Telephone:* (20) 7253-2523 (office). *Fax:* (20) 7250-0594 (office). *E-mail:* p.gough@czwgarchitects.co.uk (office).

GOULD, Andrew, BA; British business executive; *Chairman and CEO, Schlumberger Limited;* ed Univ. of Wales; began career with Ernst & Young; joined Internal Audit Dept, Schlumberger Ltd, Paris 1975, various man. roles including Treas., Schlumberger Ltd, Pres. Sedco Forex, Wireline & Testing and Oilfield Services Products, Exec. Vice-Pres. Schlumberger Oilfield Services, later Pres. and CEO, Schlumberger Ltd, Chair. and CEO 2003–; Dir Rio Tinto PLC, Rio Tinto Ltd. *Address:* Schlumberger Ltd, 153 East 53rd Street, 57th Floor, New York NY 10022-4624, USA (office). *Telephone:* (212) 350-9400 (office). *Fax:* (212) 350-9457 (office). *E-mail:* info@slb.com (office). *Website:* www.slb.com (office).

GOULD, Bryan Charles, BCL, LLM, MA, CNZM; British/New Zealand politician; b. 11 Feb. 1939, Hawera, NZ; s. of Charles T. Gould and Elsie M. Gould (née Driller); m. Gillian A. Harrigan 1967; one s. one d.; ed Victoria and Auckland Univs, NZ and Balliol Coll., Oxford, UK; in diplomatic service, British Embassy, Brussels 1964–68; Fellow and Tutor in Law, Worcester Coll., Oxford 1968–74; MP for Southampton Test 1974–79, Dagenham 1983–94; presenter and reporter Thames TV 1977–83; Opposition Spokesman on Trade 1983–86, on Trade and Industry 1987–89, on the Environment 1989–92; mem. of Shadow Cabinet, Labour's Campaign Co-ordinator 1986–89; Shadow Heritage Sec. 1992 (resgnd); Vice-Chancellor Waikato Univ. 1994–2004; mem. various bds including Govt-apptd Dir Television New Zealand 2004–; Visiting Fellow, Nuffield Coll., Oxford 2005–; Chair. Foundation for Research Science and Tech., NZ Nat. Comm. for UNESCO. *Publications:* Monetarism or Prosperity? 1981, Socialism and Freedom 1985, A Future for Socialism 1989, Goodbye to All That (memoirs) 1995, The Democracy Sham 2006, Rescuing the New Zealand Economy 2008. *Leisure interests:* food, wine, gardening. *Address:* 239 Ohiwa Beach Road, RD2, Opotiki 3198, New Zealand (office). *E-mail:* Bgould@paradise.net.nz (office). *Website:* www.Bryangould.net (office).

GOULD, Elliott; American actor; b. 29 Aug. 1938, Brooklyn, New York; s. of Bernard and Lucille (née Gross) Goldstein; m. 1st Barbra Streisand (q.v.) 1963 (divorced 1971); one s.; m. 2nd Jenny Bogart 1973 (divorced 1975, remarried 1978); one s. one d.; made Broadway début in Rumple 1957; other appearances include Say Darling 1958, Irma La Douce 1960, I Can Get It For You Wholesale 1962, Drat! The Cat 1965, Alfred in Little Murders 1967; toured in The Fantastiks with Liza Minnelli; nat. tour Deathtrap, Luv with Shelley Winters; Hon. LLD (Univ. of West Los Angeles). *Films include:* The Confession 1966, The Night They Raided Minsky's 1968, Bob and Carol and Ted and Alice 1969, Getting Straight 1970, M*A*S*H 1970, The Touch 1971, Little Murders 1971, The Long Good-Bye 1972, Nashville 1974, I Will . . . I Will . . . For Now 1976, Harry and Walter Go to New York 1976, A Bridge Too Far 1977, Capricorn One (1978), The Silent Partner 1979, The Lady Vanishes 1979, Escape to Athens 1979, The Muppet Movie 1979, Falling in Love Again 1980, The Devil and Max Devlin 1981, Over the Brooklyn Bridge 1984, The Naked Face 1984, Act of Betrayal 1988, Dead Men Don't Die 1989, Secret Scandal 1990, Bugsy 1991, Wet and Wild Summer! 1992, Beyond Justice 1992, Hoffman's Hunger 1993, Amore! 1993, The Feminine Touch 1994, The Dangerous 1994, The Glass Shield 1994, Bleeding Hearts 1994, P.C.H. 1995, I Want Him Back! 1995, Cover Me 1995, Kicking and Screaming 1995, Let It Be Me 1995, Busted 1996, Amanda's Game 1996, A Boy Called Hate 1996, Johns 1996, Camp Stories 1997, The Big Hit 1998, American History X 1998, Playing Mona Lisa 2000, Picking Up the Pieces 2000, Boys Life 3 2000, Ocean's Eleven 2001, The Experience Box 2001, Puckoon 2002, Ocean's Twelve 2004, Open Window 2006, Ocean's Thirteen 2007, Little Hercules in 3-D 2007, Saving Sarah Cain 2007, The Ten Commandments 2007. *TV appearances include:* Doggin' Around (BBC TV), Once Upon a Mattress (CBC), Friends, Kim Possible. *Address:* c/o William Morris Agency, 1 William Morris Place, Beverly Hills, CA 90212; c/o Cunningham, Escott, Dipene, 10635 Santa Monica Blvd., Suite 130, Los Angeles, CA 90025, USA. *Website:* www.elliottgould.net (office).

GOULD OF BROOKWOOD, Baron (Life Peer), cr. 2004, of Brookwood in the County of Surrey; **Philip Gould,** MA; British political adviser; *Chairman, Philip Gould Associates;* b. 30 March 1950; s. of Wilfred Caleb Gould and Fennigien Anna Gould (née de-Jager); m. Gail Rebuck (q.v.) 1985; two d.; ed Knaphill Secondary Modern School, Woking, East London College, Univ. of Sussex, London School of Econs, London Business School; fmrly worked in advertising; Dir Tinker and Partners 1979–81; Founder Brignull LeBas Gould 1981–83, Philip Gould Assocs 1985 (currently Chair.); adviser to Labour Party 1985–; f. Shadow Communications Agency 1995; Co-owner and Partner, Gould Greenberg Carville Ltd, political strategy and polling 1997–; Visiting Prof., LSE 2002–03; Trustee Policy Network; mem. Labour Party. *Publication:* The Unfinished Revolution: How the Modernisers Saved the Labour Party 1998. *Leisure interest:* QPR Football Club. *Address:* House of Lords, Westminster, London, SW1A 0PW, England (office). *Telephone:* (20) 7233-3491 (office).

GOULDEN, Sir (Peter) John, Kt, GCMG, BA; British diplomatist (retd) and civil servant; b. 21 Feb. 1941; s. of George H. Goulden and Doris Goulden; m. Diana Waite 1962; one s. one d.; ed Queen's Coll., Oxford; joined FCO 1962, Ankara 1963–67, Manila 1969–70, Dublin 1976–79, Head Personnel Services Dept 1980–82, News Dept 1982–84, Asst Under-Sec. of State 1988–92; Counsellor, Head Chancery Office of UK Perm. Rep. to EC 1984–87; Amb. to Turkey 1992–95; Amb., Perm. Rep. to North Atlantic Council and WEU 1995–2001; consultant, Home Office 2001–. *Leisure interests:* music, travel, family. *Address:* c/o Home Office, 2 Marsham Street, London, SW1P 4DF, England. *Telephone:* (20) 7035-4848.

GOULDING, Sir Marrack Irvine, Kt, KCMG, MA; British diplomatist and international civil servant; b. 2 Sept. 1936, Plymouth; s. of Sir Irvine Goulding and Gladys Goulding; m. 1st Susan Rhoda D'Albiac 1961 (divorced 1996); two s. one d.; m. 2nd Catherine Pawlow 1996 (divorced 2004); pnr Amezaga Arregi; one d.; ed St Paul's School and Magdalen Coll. Oxford; joined HM Foreign (later Diplomatic) Service 1959; with Middle East Centre for Arab Studies 1959–61; Kuwait 1961–64; Foreign Office 1964–68; Tripoli, Libya 1968–70; Cairo 1970–72; Private Sec. Minister of State for Foreign and Commonwealth Affairs 1972–75; seconded to Cabinet Office 1975–77; Counsellor, Lisbon 1977–79; Counsellor and Head of Chancery, UK Mission to UN, New York 1979–83; Amb. to Angola and concurrently to São Tomé e Príncipe 1983–85; UN Under-Sec.-Gen. for Special Political Affairs, 1986–91, for Peace-keeping Operations 1992–93, for Political Affairs 1993–97; Warden St Antony's Coll., Oxford 1997–2006 (retd). *Publications:* Peacemonger 2002. *Leisure interests:* travel and birdwatching. *Address:* 11 St Gabriel's Manor, 25 Cormont Road, London, SE5 9RH, England (home). *Telephone:* (20) 7820-0284 (home). *E-mail:* marrack.goulding@sant.ox.ac.uk (home).

GOULIAN, Mehran, AB, MD; American physician and academic; *Professor Emeritus, School of Medicine, University of California, San Diego;* b. 31 Dec. 1929, Weehawken, NJ; s. of Dicran Goulian and Shamiram Mzrakjian; m. Susan Hook 1961; three s.; ed Columbia Coll. and Columbia Coll. of Physicians and Surgeons; Medical Internship, Barnes Hosp. 1954–55; Medical Residency, Mass. Gen. Hosp. 1958–59, 1960; Fellow in Medicine (Hematology), Yale Univ. School of Medicine 1959–60; Research Fellow in Medicine (Hematology), Harvard Univ. July–Dec. 1960, 1962–63, Instructor in Medicine 1963–65; Clinical and Research Fellow in Medicine (Hematology), Mass. Gen. Hosp. July–Dec. 1960, 1962–63, Asst in Medicine, 1963–65; Fellow in Biochemistry, Stanford Univ. School of Medicine 1965–67; Research Assoc. in Biochemistry, Univ. of Chicago and Argonne Cancer Research Hosp. 1967–69, Assoc. Prof. of Medicine 1967–70, Assoc. Prof. of Biochemistry 1969–70; Prof. of Medicine, Univ. of Calif., San Diego 1970–1994, now Prof. Emer. *Leisure interest:* music. *Address:* 8433 Prestwick Drive, La Jolla, CA 92037, USA. *Telephone:* (858) 459-0088. *E-mail:* mgoulian@ussd.edu (home).

GOULLI, Salah Eddine el, DIur; Tunisian business executive and fmr diplomatist; b. 22 June 1919, Sousse; m. M. J. Zeineb Larre 1958; one d.; ed Univ. of Paris (Sorbonne); Consul Gen., Marseilles 1956–57; Minister, Embassy, Washington, DC 1958–61; Alt. Exec. Dir Int. Bank for Reconstruction and Devt 1961; Amb. to Belgium (also accred to Netherlands, Luxembourg, EEC) 1962–69, to UN 1969–70, to USA (also accred to Venezuela and Mexico) 1970–73, to Netherlands 1976–78; Adviser to Minister of Foreign Affairs 1973–75, 1979–81; Pres. Philips Electronics Tunisia 1981–90, World Trade Centre, Tunis 1990–; Grand Cordon of the Repub. of Tunisia 1963, Gold Cross of Leopold 1964, Grand Cross Crown of Belgium 1969, Grand Cross Chêne 1964, Grand Cross Nassau, Luxembourg 1969. *Publications:* lectures on political and econ. matters in USA, Europe and Middle East; numerous articles in European and Tunisian press. *Leisure interests:* golf, reading, swimming. *Address:* World Trade Centre Tunis, 34–36 avenue de la Foire, 2035 Lacharguia, Tunis (office); 2 rue des Roses, 2070 Lamarsa, Tunisia. *Telephone:* (1) 809377 (office); (1) 774307 (home). *Fax:* (1) 807955 (office). *E-mail:* wtct@planet.tn (office).

GOULONGANA, Jean-Robert; Gabonese politician and diplomatist; b. 30 April 1953, Lambarene; m.; three c.; ed Dakar Univ., Senegal, Aix-Marseille III Univ., France; Minister of Waters, Forests and the Environment 1990–91; Amb. to Italy 1992, to Belgium 1996; Head, Gabonese Mission to EU; Sec.-Gen. African, Caribbean and Pacific States (ACP) 2000–05; Officier, Ordre du Mérite Maritime Gabonais. *Address:* c/o African, Caribbean and Pacific States Secretariat, ACP House, 451 avenue Georges Henri, Brussels, Belgium (office).

GOUNARIS, Elias, LLM; Greek diplomatist; *Honorary Ambassador;* b. 7 Sept. 1941, Athens; s. of Panayotis Gounaris and Christine Gounaris; one s.; ed Univ. of Athens; served in Greek Navy 1964–66; Attaché, Ministry of Foreign Affairs, Athens 1966, Consul, New York 1969–73, Head of Section, Turkey-Cyprus Dept, Ministry of Foreign Affairs 1973, Sec., Perm. Mission of Greece to Int. Orgs, Geneva 1975, Counsellor 1976, Deputy Chief Minister,

Embassy in Belgrade 1979–83, Head of the American Desk, Ministry of Foreign Affairs 1983–87, Minister-Counsellor, then Minister, Embassy in Bonn 1987–88, Minister Plenipotentiary 1988, Amb. to USSR 1988 (also accred to Mongolia) 1989–93, to UK (also accred to Iceland) 1993–96, Dir Dept of Eastern and Western Europe and Deputy Dir Gen. for Political Affairs, Ministry of Foreign Affairs 1996–97, Dir Gen. for Political Affairs 1997–99, Perm. Rep. to UN, New York 1999–2002; Chair. Cttee for the Environment and Sustainable Devt, Ministry of Foreign Affairs 2002–04; mem. Bd of Dirs OTE SA (Hellenic Telecommunications Org.), M.I. Maillis, Packaging Materials; Hon. Amb.; decorations from Austria, Finland, Germany, Greece, Italy, Spain, Ukraine and Russian Orthodox Church. *Address:* c/o Ministry of Foreign Affairs, Odos Akadimias 1, 106 71 Athens; Akadimias Street 1, 106 71 Athens, Greece. *Telephone:* (210) 3681000. *E-mail:* mfa@mfa.gr.

GOURAD HAMADOU, Barkad; Djibouti politician; fmr mem. of French Senate; fmr Minister of Health; Prime Minister of Djibouti Sept. 1978–2001, Minister of Ports 1978–87, Minister of Planning and Land Devt 1987, Prime Minister, Minister of Nat. and Regional Devt –2001; mem. Rassemblement Populaire pour le Progrès (RPP). *Address:* c/o Office du Premier Ministre, PO Box 2086, Djibouti, Republic of Djibouti (office).

GOURISSE, Daniel, DèsSc; French administrator and professor of chemical engineering; *Honorary Director, Ecole Centrale des Arts et Manufactures;* b. 13 March 1939, Charleville; s. of Robert Gourisse and Marie-Marguerite Lalle; m. Michèle Maës 1961; three s.; ed Ecole Centrale Paris; Laboratory Head, Commissariat à l'Energie Atomique (Atomic Energy Comm.) 1964–73, Tech. adviser to the Gen. Admin. 1973–76, Head, Chem. Eng Dept 1976–84; Prof. of Chem. Eng, Ecole Centrale Paris 1969–78, Dir Ecole Centrale 1978–2003, Hon. Dir 2003–; Pres. Conf. des Grandes Ecoles 1985–93 (now Hon. Pres.), Office de robotique et de productique du Commissariat à l'énergie atomique 1985–89; Scientific Adviser to Dir du Cycle du Combustible 1990–; Pres. Asscn TIME of European Tech. Univs 1998–2001, Hon. Pres. 2001–; Dr hc (Bauman Inst., Tech. Univ., Moscow); Officier, Légion d'honneur, Ordre nat. du Mérite; Commdr, Palmes académiques, Chevalier, Légion d'honneur. *Publications:* many articles in int. journals. *Address:* Ecole Centrale des Arts et Manufactures, Grande Voie des Vignes, 92295 Chatenay-Malabry Cedex (office); 12 avenue de la Cure d'Air, 91400 Orsay, France (home). *Telephone:* 1-41-13-10-00 (office). *Fax:* 1-41-13-10-10 (office). *E-mail:* webmaster@ecp.fr (office). *Website:* www.ecp.fr (office).

GOURNAY, Patrick P.; British business executive; fmrly with Groupe Danone; CEO The Body Shop 1998–2002; currently Vice-Chair. and CEO ARC Int. *Address:* ARC International 41, Avenue du Général de Gaulle, 62510 Arques, France (office). *Telephone:* 3-21-95-46-47 (office). *Fax:* 3-21-38-06-23 (office). *Website:* www.arc-international.com (office).

GOUTARD, Noël; French business executive; b. 22 Dec. 1931, Casablanca, Morocco; s. of F. Antoine Goutard and M. Edmée (née Lespinasse) Goutard; m. Dominique Jung 1964; one s. one d.; ed Lycée Louis le Grand, Paris, Univ. of Bordeaux and Pace Coll., New York; Vice-Pres. Frenville Co., New York 1954–60; Finance Exec., Warner Lambert Int., Morris Plains, NJ 1960–62; African Area Man. Pfizer Inc., New York 1962–66; Exec. Vice-Pres. Gevelot SA Paris 1966–71; Pres. and COO Compteurs Schlumberger SA, Paris 1971–76; Exec. Vice-Pres. and mem. Bd of Dirs Chargeurs SA, Paris 1976–83; Exec. Vice-Pres. and COO Thomson SA, Paris 1983–84, Dir-Gen. 1983–86; Pres.-Dir Gen. Valéo SA 1987–2000, Hon. Pres. 2000–01; Pres. NG Investments 2000–; mem. Bd Thomson CSF, Banque Thomson, Thomson-Brandt Armements, Imétal 1996–, Alcatel-Alsthom 1997–2001; Officier, Légion d'honneur. *Leisure interests:* tennis, travel, golf. *Address:* NG Investments, 90 avenue des Champs-Elysées, 75008 Paris, France (office). *E-mail:* ng.investments@wanado.fr (office).

GOUVEIA, Maria Teresa Pinto Basto; Portuguese politician; *Executive Director and Member, Board of Trustees, Fundação Calouste Gulbenkian;* b. 18 July 1946, Lisbon; d. of Afonso Patrício Gouveia and Maria Madalena d'Orey Ferreira Pinto Basto; m. Alexandre Manuel Vahia de Castro O'Neill de Bulhões (died 1986); one s.; ed Univ. of Lisbon; Sec. of State for Culture 1985–1990; elected mem. Parl. 1987, 1991, 1995, 2002; Sec. of State for Environment 1991–93, Minister for Environment 1993–95; mem. Bd of Govs and Exec. Cttee, European Cultural Foundation, Amsterdam 1996–2002; Vice-Pres. Foreign Affairs Parl. Cttee 2002–03; Minister of Foreign Affairs and Portuguese Communities Abroad 2003–04; fmr Pres. Cttee for Cultural Cooperation, Council of Europe, Strasbourg; mem. Gen. Council O Público newspaper 1990–91; Pres. Bd of Trustees Serralves Foundation, Oporto 2001–03; Exec. Dir and mem. Bd of Trustees Calouste Gulbenkian Foundation 2004–; Great Cross, Ordem de Cristo, Great Cross, Ordem Infante D. Henrique. *Address:* c/o Board of Trustees, Fundação Calouste Gulbenkian, Avenida da Berna, 45A, 1067-001 Lisbon, Portugal (office). *Telephone:* (217) 823306 (office). *Fax:* (217) 823088 (office). *E-mail:* tpgouveia@gulbenkian.pt (office). *Website:* www.gulbenkian.pt (office).

GOUYOU BEAUCHAMPS, Xavier; French television industry executive; *President and Director-General, Antalis-TV;* b. 25 April 1937, Paris; s. of Charles Gouyou Beauchamps and Anne-Marie Coulombeix; m. 2nd Geneviève Decugis 1986; two s. (from previous marriage); ed Ecole St Joseph à Sarlat, Inst. d'études politiques and Ecole nat. d'admin; Dir of Staff Loiret Pref. 1964–66; Asst Head of Staff, Minister of Agric. 1966–68, Minister of Educ. 1968–69; Official Staff Rep., Minister of Econ. and Finance 1969–74; Press Sec. to the Pres. 1974–76; Prefect of Ardèche 1976–77; Pres. and Dir-Gen. SOFIRAD 1977–81; Pres. Télédiffusion de France 1986–92, Pres. Asscn des organismes français de radiodiffusion et de télévision (OFRT) 1990–92; Pres. French broadcasters' group (GRF) of European Union of Radio and TV (UER) 1990, Vice-Pres. UER 1990; Pres. Admin. Council Nat. Park of Port Cros, Sofipost 1992–94; Dir-Gen. France 3 1994–96, Chair. Bd of Dirs. 1998; Pres., Dir-Gen. France 2 and France 3 cos. 1996–99; founder and Pres., Dir-Gen. Antalis-TV; Pres. Asscn des employeurs du service public de l'audiovisuel 1998; founder XGB Conseil 1900–; Chevalier, Légion d'honneur, Officier, Ordre nat. du Mérite, Chevalier du Mérite agricole, Croix de la Valeur militaire. *Publication:* Le ministère de l'économie et des Finances, un Etat dans l'Etat? 1976. *Address:* Antalis-TV, 5/7 rue de la Gare, 92130 Issy-Les-MOulineaux (office); ; 73 avenue Franklin D. Roosevelt, 75008 Paris, France (home). *Telephone:* 1-58-88-32-20 (office). *Fax:* 1-58-88-32-29 (office). *Website:* www.antalis-tv.com (office).

GOVAN, Michael, BA; American museum curator; *Director and CEO, Los Angeles County Museum of Art;* b. Washington, DC; ed Williams Coll., Mass, Univ. of San Diego, Calif., studied Renaissance art in Italy; Acting Curator and Special Asst, Williams Coll. Museum of Art and organized Picasso and Rembrandt in 1986; Deputy Dir Solomon R. Guggenheim Museum, New York, Venice, Italy, Bilbao, Spain 1986–94; Pres. and Dir Dia Art Foundation, New York 1994–2006; Co-curator touring exhbn 'Dan Flavin: A Retrospective' organized by Dia Art Foundation in asscn with Nat. Gallery of Art, Washington, DC, which opened at Hayward Gallery, London, UK 2006; Dir and CEO Los Angeles Co. Museum of Art 2006–. *Publication:* The Great Utopia: The Russian and Soviet Avant-Garde, 1915–1932. *Address:* Los Angeles County Museum of Art, 5905 Wilshire Blvd, Los Angeles, CA 90036, USA (office). *Telephone:* (323) 857-6000 (office). *Fax:* (323) 857-0098 (office). *E-mail:* publicinfo@lacma.org (office). *Website:* www.lacma.org (office).

GOVORUKHIN, Stanislav Sergeyevich; Russian politician, film director and actor; b. 29 March 1936, Berezniki, Sverdlovsk Region; m.; one s.; ed All-Union Inst. of Cinematography; with Odessa Film Studio 1967–89; Mosfilm Studio 1989–; active participant opposition movt since early 1990s; mem. State Duma (Homeland faction) 1993–, mem. Cttee on Security 1994–95, Chair. Cttee on Culture 1996–99; one of leaders of Democratic Party of Russia, Chair. Deputies of Democratic Party of Russia in State Duma 1995; Leader Bloc of Stanislav Govorukhin in elections to Duma 1995; presidential cand. 2000; elected Deputy to State Duma in by-elections 2005–. *Films include:* Vertical 1967, The Day of the Angel 1969, White Explosion 1970, The Life and Wonderful Adventures of Robinson Crusoe 1973, Smuggle 1975, A Wind of Hope 1978, The Place of Meeting Cannot Be Changed (TV) 1979, Adventures of Tom Sawyer 1981, In Search of Captain Grant, Drops of Champagne; Act in Assa, On First Breath; documentaries: It Is Impossible To Live So 1990 (Nica Prize), The Russia We Have Lost 1992, Aleksander Solzhenitsyn 1992, Great Criminal Revolution 1994, The Voroshilov Shooter 1998, Bless the Woman 2003, Not By Bread Alone 2005. *Publications:* Pirates of the 20th Century, Secrets of Madame Vong, Great Criminal Revolution; articles in periodicals. *Address:* State Duma, Okhotny Ryad 1, 103265 Moscow, Russia (office). *Telephone:* (495) 292-83-10 (office). *Fax:* (495) 292-94-64 (office). *E-mail:* govorukhin@duma.ru (home). *Website:* www.duma.ru (office); www.govoruhin.ru.

GOW, Gen. Sir (James) Michael, GCB, DL; British army officer (retd); b. 3 June 1924; s. of the late J. C. Gow and Mrs Alastair Sanderson; m. Jane Emily Scott 1946; one s. four d.; ed Winchester Coll.; commissioned, Scots Guards 1943; served in NW Europe 1944–45; Malayan Emergency 1949; Equerry to HRH Duke of Gloucester 1952–53; graduated Staff Coll. 1954; Brigade Maj. 1955–57; Regimental Adjutant, Scots Guards 1957–60; Instructor, Army Staff Coll. 1962–64; commanded 2nd Bn Scots Guards, Kenya and England 1964–66; GSO1 HQ, London Dist 1966–67; Commdr 4th Guards Brigade 1968–70; at Imperial Defence Coll. 1970; Brig.-Gen. Staff (Int.) HQ, British Army of the Rhine (BAOR) and Asst Chief of Staff G2 HQ, Northag 1971–73; GOC 4th Armoured Div., BAOR 1973–75; Col Commdt Intelligence Corps 1973–86; Dir Army Training 1975–78; GOC Scotland 1979–80; Gov. Edin. Castle 1979–80; Commdr Northern Army Group and C-in-C BAOR, 1980–83; Commdt, Royal Coll. of Defence Studies 1984–86; ADC Gen. to HM The Queen 1981–83; Commr British Scouts W Europe 1980–83; Capt., Queen's Bodyguard for Scotland (Royal Co. of Archers), to Non-Active List 2006; Vice-Pres. Royal Caledonian Schools, Bushey 1980–96, Royal Patriotic Fund Corpn 1983–88; Pres. Royal British Legion Scotland, Earl Haig Fund Scotland, Officers' Asscn 1986–96 (Vice-Pres. 1996–); Sec.-Gen. The Prince's Youth Business Trust 1986; Chair. Scottish Ex-Service Charitable Orgs (SESCO) 1989–96, Scots at War Trust 1994–, Ludus Baroque 1999–; Pres. Nat. Asscn of Supported Employment 1993–2000; Vice-Pres. Scottish Nat. Inst. for War Blinded 1995–; Patron Disablement Income Group Scotland 1993–; Patron Erskine Hosp. 2003–; Freeman, City of London; Freeman and Liveryman, Painters and Stainers Co. *Publications:* Trooping The Colour – A History of the Sovereign's Birthday Parade 1980, Jottings in a General's Notebook 1989, General Reflections: A Military Man at Large 1991; articles in military and historical journals. *Leisure interests:* sailing, music, travel, reading. *Address:* 18 Ann Street, Edinburgh, EH4 1PJ, Scotland (home). *Telephone:* (131) 332-4752 (home). *Fax:* (131) 332-4752 (home).

GOWAN, James, FRCA, ARIBA; British architect; b. 18 Oct. 1925, Glasgow; s. of James Gowan and Isabella G. MacKenzie; m. Marguerite A. Barry 1947; two d.; ed Hyndland School, Glasgow, Glasgow School of Art and Kingston School of Art; pvt. practice 1956–, in partnership with James Stirling 1956–63, design of new hosp., Milan 1991, Techint Int. co. HQ offices, Milan 1999; tutor, Architectural Asscn, London 1958–60, 1970–72; Visiting Prof., Princeton Univ., USA 1965, Simón Bolívar Univ., Venezuela 1982, Heriot Watt Univ., Edin. 1990; Banister Fletcher Prof., Univ. Coll. London 1975; Sr Tutor, RCA 1983–86; exhbn of drawings at RIBA Heinz Gallery 1994, at Scottish Nat. Gallery of Modern Art 1994; recent projects include hosp. buildings in Italy at Bergamo 2003, Rossano, Milan 2005; Hon. Dr of Design (Kingston Univ.) 1996; Reynolds Memorial Award (with James Stirling) 1965. *Publications:*

Projects: Architectural Association 1946–71, 1972, A Continuing Experiment 1975, James Gowan (monograph) 1978, Style and Configuration 1994, Modernity and Reinvention: The Architecture of James Gowan (by Ellis Woodman) 2008. *Leisure interests:* drawing, reading. *Address:* 2 Linden Gardens, London, W2 4ES, England. *Telephone:* (20) 7229-0642. *Fax:* (20) 7792-9771.

GOWANS, Sir James Learmonth, Kt, CBE, MB, DPhil, FRS, FRCP, FRSA; British medical scientist and administrator (retd); b. 7 May 1924, Sheffield; s. of John Gowans and Selma Josefina Ljung; m. Moyra Leatham 1956; one s. two d.; ed Trinity School, Croydon, King's Coll. Hosp. Medical School, Univ. of Oxford; Fellow, St Catherine's Coll., Oxford 1961–; Sec. Gen. Human Frontiers Science Programme, Strasbourg 1989–93; Consultant, WHO Global Programme on AIDS 1987–88; Henry Dale Research Prof. of Royal Soc. 1962–77; Dir MRC Cellular Immunology Unit 1963–77, mem. MRC 1965–69, Sec. (Chief Exec.) 1977–87, Chair. MRC Biological Research Bd 1967–69; mem. Advisory Bd for the Research Councils 1977–87; mem. Council and a Vice-Pres. Royal Soc. 1973–75; Dir Celltech PLC 1980–87; Chair. European Medical Research Councils 1985–87; mem. Academia Europaea 1991; Foreign Assoc. NAS (USA); Hon. ScD (Yale) 1966; Hon. DSc (Chicago) 1971, (Birmingham) 1978, (Rochester, NY) 1987; Hon. MD (Edinburgh) 1979, (Sheffield) 2000; Hon. LLD (Glasgow) 1988; Hon. DM (Southampton) 1987; Gairdner Award, Ehrlich Prize, Feldberg Award, Royal Medal of Royal Soc., Wolf Foundation Prize in Medicine, 1980, Medawar Prize, Galen Medal. *Publications:* articles in scientific journals. *Leisure interest:* old books. *Address:* 75 Cumnor Hill, Oxford, OX2 9HX, England (home). *Telephone:* (1865) 862304 (home). *E-mail:* jamesgowans@btinternet.com (home).

GOWARIKER, Ashutosh, BSc; Indian actor and film director; *Founding Director, Ashutosh Gowariker Productions Pvt. Ltd;* b. 15 Feb. 1964, Mumbai; s. of Kishori Gowariker and Ashok Gowariker; m. Sunita Gowariker 1988; two c.; ed Mithibai Coll., Mumbai; began career as model for commercials by Govind Mihalani and Jenny Pinto for Lifebuoy soap and Close-Up toothpaste; film acting debut in Holi 1984; directed first film Pehla Nasha 1993; directed 5 commercials for Coca-Cola 2001; Founding Dir Ashutosh Gowariker Productions Pvt. Ltd; mem. Acad. of Motion Picture Arts and Sciences 2004. *Film appearances include:* Naam 1986, West Is West 1987, Salim Langde Pe Mat Ro 1989, Goonj 1989, Gawahi 1989, Indrajeet 1991, Jaanam 1992, Chamatkar 1992, Kabhi Haan Kabhi Naa 1993, Vazir 1994, Sarkarnama 1998. *Films directed include:* Pehla Nasha 1993, Baazi 1995, Lagaan: Once Upon a Time in India (Oscar nomination) 2001, Swades 2004, Jodhaa Akbar 2007. *Television appearances include:* Kachchi Dhoop 1987, Circus 1990, Woh 1998, CID 1999. *Address:* Ashutosh Gowariker Productions Pvt. Ltd, 201, Kum Kum, 16th Road, Bandra, Mumbai 400 050, Maharashtra, India (office). *Telephone:* 2604-4236 (office); 2600-4687 (home). *Fax:* 2648-7164 (office). *E-mail:* info@agppl.com; ashgow@hotmail.com (home). *Website:* www.agppl.com; www.ashutoshgowariker.com.

GOWER, David Ivon, OBE; British journalist, broadcaster and fmr professional cricketer; *Presenter, International Cricket, Sky Sports;* b. 1 April 1957, Tunbridge Wells, Kent; s. of Richard Hallam Gower and Sylvia Mary Gower (née Ford); m. Thorunn Ruth Nash 1992; two d.; ed King's School, Canterbury and Univ. Coll. London; left-hand batsman; played for Leicestershire 1975 to 1989 (Capt. 1984–86), Hampshire 1990 to 1993; played in 117 Tests for England 1978 to 1992, 32 as Capt., scoring then England record 8,231 runs (average 44.2) with 18 hundreds; toured Australia 1978–79, 1979–80, 1982–83, 1986–87 and 1990–91; scored 26,339 first-class runs with 53 hundreds; 114 limited-overs ints; Sunday Express Cricket Corresp. 1993–95; Public Relations Consultant for cricket sponsorship NatWest Bank 1993–2000; columnist, Sunday Telegraph 1995–98, The Sun 2000–02, Sunday Times 2002–; presenter Sky Sports 1999–; Trustee, David Shepherd Conservation Foundation; Hon. MA (Southampton Inst., Nottingham Trent Univ., Univ. of Loughborough); Hon. Blue (Herriott Watt Univ., Edinburgh); Wisden Cricketer of the Year 1979, Int. Cricketer of the Year 1982/83. *Television:* Team Capt., They Think It's All Over 1985–2003; commentator, Sky TV cricket 1993–; commentator and presenter, BBC TV 1994–99. *Publications:* With Time to Spare 1979, Heroes and Contemporaries 1983, A Right Ambition 1986, On the Rack 1990, The Autobiography 1992. *Leisure interests:* Cresta run, skiing, tennis, photography, wildlife conservation. *Address:* c/o Diana van Bunnens, Jon Holmes Media Ltd, 5th Floor, Holborn Gate, 26 Southampton Buildings, London, WC2A 1PQ, England (office). *Telephone:* (20) 7861-2550 (office). *Fax:* (20) 7861-3067 (office). *E-mail:* diana@jonholmesmedia.com (office). *Website:* www.jonholmesmedia.com (office).

GOWERS, Andrew, MA; British journalist and communications executive; *Global Co-head of Corporate Communications, Marketing and Brand Management, Lehman Brothers;* b. 19 Oct. 1957, Reading, Berks.; s. of Michael Gowers and Anne Gowers; m. Finola Gowers (née Clarke); one s. one d.; ed Trinity School, Croydon and Univ. of Cambridge; grad. trainee, Reuters 1980, Brussels Corresp. 1981, Zurich Corresp. 1982, joined Foreign Desk, Financial Times (FT), London 1983, Agric. Corresp. 1984, Commodities Ed. 1985, Middle East Ed. 1987, Foreign Ed. 1992, Deputy Ed. 1994, Acting Ed. 1997, Ed. FT Deutschland (German Language Business Paper) 1999, Ed. FT 2001–05; columnist Evening Standard, Sunday Times 2005–06; Leader Gowers' Review of Intellectual Property for UK Government 2005–06; Head of Corp. Communications (Europe and Asia), Lehman Brothers 2006–07, Global Co-head of Corp. Communications, Marketing and Brand Man. 2007–. *Publication:* Arafat, The Biography (co-author) 1991. *Leisure interests:* film, opera, music, theatre, gastronomy. *Address:* 17 Gilkes Crescent, Dulwich, London, SE21 7BP, England (home). *Telephone:* (20) 8299-6765 (home). *Fax:* (20) 8299-3102 (home). *E-mail:* andrew.gowers@lehman.com (office).

GOWERS, (William) Timothy, PhD, FRS; British mathematician and academic; *Rouse Ball Professor of Mathematics, Department of Pure Mathematics and Mathematical Statistics, University of Cambridge;* b. 20 Nov. 1963, Marlborough; s. of (William) Patrick Gowers and Caroline (Molesworth) Maurice; m. 1st Emily Joanna Thomas 1988, two s. one d. (marriage dissolved 2007); m. 2nd Julie Barrau 2008, one s.; ed Eton Coll., Trinity Coll., Cambridge; lecturer Univ. Coll. London 1991–94, Reader 1994–95; Fellow Trinity Coll., Cambridge 1989–93; lecturer Univ. of Cambridge 1995–98, Rouse Ball Prof. of Mathematics 1998–; Hon. Fellow Univ. Coll. London 1999; Jr Whitehead Prize, London Mathematical Soc. 1995, European Mathematical Soc. Prize 1996; Fields Medal 1998. *Publications:* Mathematics: A Very Short Introduction 2002; mathematical papers in various journals. *Leisure interest:* playing jazz piano. *Address:* Department of Pure Mathematics and Mathematical Statistics, Room C2.04, Centre for Mathematical Sciences, Wilberforce Road, Cambridge, CB3 0WB, England (office). *Telephone:* (1223) 337973 (office). *Fax:* (1223) 337920 (office). *E-mail:* W.T.Gowers@dpmms.cam.ac.uk (office). *Website:* www.dpmms.cam.ac.uk/~wtg10 (office).

GOWON, Gen. Yakubu, PhD; Nigerian army officer, organization official and fmr head of state; *President and Chairman, Board of Directors, Yakubu Gowon Center for National Unity and International Co-operation;* b. 19 Oct. 1934, Garam, Pankshin Div., Plateau State; s. of Yohanna and Saraya Gowon; m. Victoria Hansatu Zakari 1969; one s. two d.; ed St Bartholomew's School, Wusasa, Zaria, Govt Coll., Barewa, Zaria, Royal Mil. Acad., Sandhurst, Staff Coll., Camberley and Jt Services Staff Coll., Latimer, UK; Adjutant, Nigerian Army 1960; with UN Peacekeeping Force, Congo 1960–61, Jan.–June 1963; promoted Lt-Col and apptd Adjutant-Gen. Nigerian Army 1963; Chief of Staff 1966; Maj.-Gen. 1967; promoted Gen. 1971; Head of Fed. Mil. Govt and C-in-C of Armed Forces of Fed. Repub. of Nigeria 1966–75 (deposed in coup); studying at Univ. of Warwick, UK 1975–83, postgraduate 1978–82; Chair. Ass. of Heads of State, OAU 1973–74; Chair. Nigerian Nat. Oil and Chemical Marketing Co. 1996; founder, Pres., Chair. Bd of Dirs Yadubu Gowon Center for Nat. Unity and Int. Co-operation; Assoc. Research Prof., Centre for Devt Studies, Univ. of Jos; fmr Chair. Arewa Consultative Forum (ACF); Chair. Trustees, Commonwealth Human Ecology Foundation 1986; Chair. Bd of Dirs Industrial And Gen. Insurance Co. Ltd (IGI); Hon. LLD; Hon. DSc; Hon. DLitt. *Publication:* Faith in Unity 1970. *Leisure interests:* squash, tennis, photography, pen-drawings. *Address:* Yakubu Gowon Center for National Unity and International Co-operation, POB 3995, Garki, Abuja (office); c/o Board of Directors, IGI, Plot, 741 Adeola Hopewell Street, Victoria Island, Lagos, Nigeria. *Telephone:* (9) 3140613 (office). *E-mail:* ygc@inforweb.abs (office).

GOWRIE, Rt Hon. Alexander Patrick Greysteil Hore-Ruthven (Grey), The Earl of Gowrie, PC, BA, AM, FRSL; British/Irish politician and business executive; b. (Alexander Hore-Ruthven), 26 Nov. 1939; s. of the late Hon. A. H. P. Hore-Ruthven and Pamela Margaret Fletcher; m. 1st Xandra Bingley 1962 (divorced 1973); one s.; m. 2nd Adelheid Gräfin von den Schulenburg 1974; ed Eton Coll., Balliol Coll., Oxford and Harvard Univ., USA; Fellow and Tutor, Lowell House, Harvard Univ. 1965–68; Asst Prof., Emerson Coll., Boston 1967–68; Lecturer in English and American Literature, Univ. Coll. London 1969–72; a UK del. to UN 1971; a Lord-in-Waiting to HM the Queen 1972–74; Govt Whip, House of Lords 1972–74; Consultant, Thomas Gibson Fine Art 1974–79; Opposition Spokesman on Econ. Affairs and Adviser to Margaret Thatcher 1977–79; Minister of State, Dept of Employment 1979–81; Minister of State and Deputy to the Sec. of State, Northern Ireland Office 1981–83; Minister of State, Privy Council Office and Minister for the Arts 1983–84; mem. of Cabinet as Chancellor of the Duchy of Lancaster (retaining portfolio as Minister for the Arts) 1984–85; Chair. The Really Useful Group 1985–90, Sotheby's Europe 1985–94, Arts Council 1994–98, Magdi Yacoub Inst., Fine Art Fund; Dir Sotheby's Holdings Inc. 1985–98; Provost RCA 1986–95; Chair. Devt Securities 1995–99, Dir (non-exec.) 1995–2001; Dir (non-exec.) NXT PLC, ITG PLC 1998–2002. *Publications:* A Postcard from Don Giovanni (poems) 1972, The Genius of British Painting: The Twentieth Century 1975, Derek Hill: An Appreciation 1987, The Domino Hymn: Poems from Harefield 2005, Third Day: New and Selected Poems 2008. *Leisure interests:* the arts. *Address:* The Magdi Yacoub Institute, Science Centre, Harefield, Middx, England (office). *Telephone:* (20) 7828-4777 (office).

GOYAL, Naresh, BCom; Indian airline executive; *Chairman, Jet Airways;* b. 1948, Patiala; s. of Chowdhury Jagdish Rai; ed Bikram Coll. of Commerce, Patiala; began career as ticketing and reservations clerk, Lebanese Int. Airlines 1967, various man. positions 1967–74; f. Jetair (Private) Ltd May 1974, f. Jet Airways (India) Private Ltd 1991, Chair. 1991–; owner, Tailwinds Holding Co.; AIMO Visvesvaraya Entrepreneurship Award 1993, Bharat Sarathi Samman Award 1995, Priyadarshni Acad. Award 2000, Ernst & Young Entrepreneur of the Year for Services Award 2000, ITFT Chandigarh Award of Excellence 2001, Qimpro Gold Standard Award 2001. *Address:* Jet Airways (India) Private Limited, SM Centre, Andheri-Kurla Road, Andheri East, Mumbai 400-059, India (office). *Telephone:* (22) 56986111 (office). *Fax:* (22) 28501313 (office). *Website:* www.jetairways.com (office).

GOYDER, Richard, BCom; Australian business executive; *CEO and Managing Director, Wesfarmers Ltd;* ed Univ. of Western Australia, Advanced Man. Program at Harvard Business School, USA; held several positions with Tubemakers of Australia Ltd; joined Wesfarmers Ltd 1993, Gen. Man., Business Devt 1994–96, Finance Dir Wesfarmers Landmark Ltd 1996–99, Man. Dir Wesfarmers Dalgety Ltd (subsequently became Wesfarmers Landmark Ltd) 1999–2002, mem. Bd of Dirs Wesfarmers Ltd 2002–, Finance Dir Wesfarmers Ltd 2002–04, Deputy Man. Dir and Chief Financial Officer 2004–05, CEO and Man. Dir 2005–, mem. Bd of Dirs Gresham Partners Holdings Ltd and several Wesfarmers group subsidiaries and related cos; mem. Bd of Dirs Fremantle Football Club Ltd; mem. Univ. of Western

Australia Business School Advisory Bd. *Address:* Wesfarmers Ltd, 11th Floor, Wesfarmers House, 40 The Esplanade, Perth, 6000, WA, Australia (office). *Telephone:* (8) 9327-4211 (office). *Fax:* (8) 9327-4216 (office). *E-mail:* info@wesfarmers.com.au (office). *Website:* www.wesfarmers.com.au (office).

GOYTISOLO, Juan; Spanish writer; b. 5 Jan. 1931, Barcelona; m. Monique Lange 1978 (died 1996); ed Univs of Barcelona and Madrid; emigrated to France 1957; reporter, Cuba 1965; assoc. with Gallimard Publishing Co.; Visiting Prof. at various univs in USA; Premio Europalia de la Comunidad Europea 1985, Premio Nelly-Sachs, Dortmund 1993, Premio Octavio Paz de Poesía y Ensayo, Mexico 2002, Premio Juan Rulfo 2004. *Writing for television:* Alquibla (TVE series). *Publications:* fiction: Juegos de manos (trans. as The Young Assassins) 1954, Duelo en el Paraíso (trans. as Children of Chaos) 1955, El circo (El mañana efímero trilogy vol. one) 1957, Fiestas (El mañana efímero trilogy vol. two) 1958, La resaca (El mañana efímero trilogy vol. three) 1958, La isla 1961, La chanca 1962, Señas de identidad (trans. as Marks of Identity) 1966, Reivindicación del conde don Julián (trans. as Count Julian) 1970, Juan sin tierra (trans. as John the Landless) 1975, Colera de Aquines 1979, Makbara 1980, Paisajes después de la batalla (trans. as Landscapes After the Battle) 1982, Las virtudes del pájaro solitario (trans. as The Virtues of the Solitary Bird) 1988, La cuarentena (trans. as Quarantine) 1991, La saga de los Marx (trans. as The Marx Family Saga) 1993, Campos de Níjar 1993, Las semanas del jardín (trans. as The Garden of Secrets) 1997, Carajicomedia (trans. as A Cock-Eyed Comedy) 2000, Telón de boca 2003; non-fiction: Crónicas Sarracinas (essays, trans. as Saracen Chronicles) 1982, Coto vedado (autobiog., trans. as Forbidden Territory) 1985, En los reinos de Taifa (autobiog., trans. as Realms of Strife) 1986, Cuaderno de Sarajevo (Premio francés Méditerranée) 1994, Reconocimiento (Gran Premio Proartes de Narrativa Iberoamericana) 1997, Pájaro que ensucia su propio nido (essays) 2001, Cinema Eden: Essays from the Muslim Mediterranean 2004, El Lucernario. La pasión crítica de Manuel Azaña 2004, La saga de los Marx 2005, Contra las sagradas formas 2007, Ensayos escogidos 2008; short stories, travel narratives, literary criticism, essays. *Address:* c/o Sickle Moon Books, Eland Publishing Ltd, Third Floor, 61 Exmouth Market, London, EC1R 4QL, England. *E-mail:* jgoytiso@sauce.pntic.mec.es.

GOZON, Richard C., BS; American business executive; *Chairman, AmerisourceBergen Corporation;* b. 9 Oct. 1938, Pittsburgh, Pa; m. Fran Gozon (neé Burmeister); three c.; ed Valparaiso Univ., Harvard Univ.; began career in paper industry at Nationwide Papers 1970–72; joined Alco Standard Group as Pres. Rourke-Eno Paper Co. 1972–78, Exec. Vice-Pres. Unisource Corpn 1978–79, Pres. 1979, Pres. and CEO Paper Corpn of America 1979–87, elected mem. Bd of Dirs Alco Standard Group 1984, Exec. Vice-Pres. and COO 1987–88, Pres. and CEO 1988–93; Exec. Vice-Pres. for Pulp, Paper and Packaging, Weyerhaeuser Co. 1994–2002; mem. Bd of Dirs AmeriSource Health Corpn 1994–2001, AmerisourceBergen Corpn 2001–, Chair. 2006–; mem. Bd of Dirs U.G.I. Corpn, The Triumph Group, AmeriGas Partners; mem. Bd of Trustees Thomas Jefferson Univ. *Address:* AmerisourceBergen Corporation, 1300 Morris Drive, Suite 100, Chesterbrook, PA 19087, USA (office). *Telephone:* (800) 829-3132 (office). *E-mail:* info@amerisourcebergen.com (office). *Website:* www.amerisourcebergen.com.

GRAB, Christoph, PhD; Swiss physicist; *Senior Scientist, Institute for Particle Physics, Eidgenössische Technische Hochschule (ETH), Zürich;* Research and Fellowships carried: Univ. of California at Berkeley, USA, Stanford Univ. (SLAC), USA, CERN, Geneva, Switzerland, DESY, Hamburg, Germany, Paul Scherrer Inst., Switzerland; currently Sr Scientist, Inst. for Particle Physics, ETH, Zürich, Switzerland; Swiss Rep., High Energy Physics Computing Coordinating Cttee; mem. Particle Data Group, CMS Experiment, CERN, H1 Experiment, DESY. *Publications:* numerous publs in scientific journals. *Address:* ETH Zürich, Institute for Particle Physics, Hönggerberg HPK/F26, 8093 Zürich, Switzerland (office). *Telephone:* (1) 6332022 (office). *Fax:* (1) 6331233 (office). *E-mail:* christoph.grab@phys.ethz.ch (office). *Website:* www.ipp.phys.ethz.ch (office).

GRABAR-KITAROVIĆ, Kolinda, MA; Croatian diplomatist and politician; *Ambassador to USA;* b. 29 April 1968, Rijeka; m.; two c.; ed Los Alamos High School, NM, USA, Univ. of Zagreb, Diplomatic Acad., Vienna, Austria, George Washington Univ., USA; Asst, then Adviser, Dept for Int. Co-operation, Ministry of Science and Tech. 1992–93; Adviser, then Sr Adviser to Deputy Minister, Ministry of Foreign Affairs 1993–95, Head of Dept for N America 1995–97; Diplomatic Counsellor, Embassy in Ottawa 1997–98, Minister Counsellor 1998–2000; Minister Counsellor, Ministry of Foreign Affairs 2001–03; mem. Parl. 2003–; Minister for European Integration 2003–05; Nat. Aid Co-ordinator 2004; Head Del. for negotiations on accession to EU 2005; Minister of Foreign Affairs and European Integration 2005–08; Amb. to USA 2008–; mem. Croatian Democratic Union (Hrvatska demokratska zajednica), Deputy Campaign Dir, Sec.-Gen. for European Integration, mem. Cen. Cttee, Nat. Council, Presidency; Presidential Medal, George Washington Univ. *Leisure interests:* literature, educ. and protection of children, hiking and walks in nature, film. *Address:* Embassy of Croatia, 2343 Massachusetts Avenue, NW, Washington, DC 20008-2803, USA (office). *Telephone:* (202) 588-5899 (office). *Fax:* (202) 588-8937 (office). *E-mail:* public@croatiaemb.org (office). *Website:* www.croatiaemb.org (office).

GRABINER, Baron (Life Peer), cr. 1999, of Aldwych in the City of Westminster; **Anthony Stephen Grabiner,** QC, LLM; British barrister; b. 21 March 1945, London; s. of the late Ralph Grabiner and Freda Grabiner (née Cohen); m. Jane Aviva Portnoy 1983; three s. one d.; ed Cen. Foundation Boys' Grammar School, London School of Econs; called to the Bar (Lincoln's Inn) 1968; Droop Scholar, Lincoln's Inn 1968; Jr Counsel to Dept of Trade 1976–81; QC 1981; Bencher 1989–; Recorder 1990–; Deputy High Court Judge, Chancery and Queen's Bench Divs 1998–; Vice-Chair. Court of Govs LSE 1993–98, Chair. 1998–; Head of Chambers One Essex Court 1994–; Dir London Court of Int. Arbitration; Leader Inquiry into Black Economy 1999–2000; Chair. (non-exec.) Arcadia Group 2002–; Dir (non-exec.) Wentworth Club 2005–. *Publication:* Sutton and Shannon on Contracts 1970, The Informal Economy 2000. *Leisure interests:* golf, theatre. *Address:* One Essex Court, Temple, London, EC4Y 9AR, England (office). *Telephone:* (20) 7583-2000 (office). *Fax:* (20) 7583-0118 (office). *E-mail:* agrabiner@oeclaw.co.uk (office). *Website:* www.oeclaw.co.uk (office).

GRACH, Eduard Davidovich; Russian violinist; b. 19 Dec. 1930, Odessa; s. of David Grach and Evelina Grach; m. 2nd Valentina Vasilenko 1990; one s. one d.; ed P. Stolyarsky Odessa School of Music, Moscow State Conservatory (pupil of A. Yampolsky); winner of int. competitions in Budapest (First Prize) 1949, J. Thibaud in Paris 1955, P. Tchaikovsky in Moscow 1962; solo performances since 1953 in most countries of Europe; performer of classical and contemporary concertos and sonatas for violin; participant in trio with pianist Y. Malinin and cellist N. Shakhovskaya 1960–70; first performer of a number of works by Russian composers dedicated to him, including concertos by A. Eshpai; Head of Violin Dept, Moscow State Conservatory; Founder and Artistic Dir Moskovia Chamber Orchestra 1994–; People's Artist of USSR 1987, 1990. *Leisure interest:* football. *Address:* Moscow State Conservatory, Bolshaya Nikitskaya str. 13/6, 125009 Moscow (office); 1st Smolensky per. 9, kv. 98, 121099 Moscow, Russia (home). *Telephone:* (495) 629-76-26 (office); (495) 241-21-57 (home). *Fax:* (495) 629-73-18 (office); (495) 241-21-57 (home). *E-mail:* spravka@mosconsv.ru (office). *Website:* www.mosconsv.ru (office).

GRACHEV, Army Gen. Pavel Sergeevich; Russian army officer; *Main Adviser, Leader of Group of Advisers to the General Director, Omsk A.S. Popov Production Association (RELERO);* b. 1 Jan. 1948, Revy, Tula Region; m.; two s.; ed Ryazan Air Landing Force School, Mil. Acad., Gen. Staff Acad.; mem. CPSU 1968–91; Commdr parachute landing platoon, Kaunas, Co. Commdr, Ryazan, Commdr of Bn, Lithuania 1969–81; Deputy Commdr, Commdr 354 Parachute landing Regt, Afghanistan 1981–83, Head of Staff 7th Army, Lithuania 1983–85, Div. Commdr, Afghanistan 1985–88; First Deputy Commdr USSR Air Landing Forces 1990–91, Commdr Jan.–Aug. 1991; First Deputy Minister of Defence of USSR (later CIS) 1991–92, Minister of Defence of Russia 1992–96; took part in neutralization of revolt Oct. 1993; Chief Mil. Expert, Rosvooruzheniye (Rosoboronexport from 2000) co. 1997–2007; Main Adviser, Leader of Group of Advisers to the Gen. Dir of Omsk A.S. Popov Production Asscn (RELERO) 2007–; Hero of Soviet Union and other decorations. *Address:* OMPO A.S. Popov Production Assocation (RELERO), 195 10 let Oktyabrya str., 644009 Omsk, Russia (office). *Telephone:* (3812) 32-95-17 (office). *Fax:* (3812) 32-95-17 (office). *E-mail:* info@relero.ru (office). *Website:* www.relero.ru (office).

GRACHEVA, Nadezhda Aleksandrovna; Russian ballet dancer; b. 21 Dec. 1969, Semipalatinsk, Kasakhstan; d. of Aleksander Aleksandrovich Grachev and Vera Petrovna Gracheva; m. 1st Aleksei Yuryevich Seregin (divorced); m. Yevgeny Kern; ed Alma-Ata Choreography School, Moscow School of Choreography; with Bolshoi Theatre 1987–; leading parts in Bayadera, Swan Lake, Nutcracker, Sleeping Beauty, Les Sylphides, Stone Flower, Romeo and Juliet and others; toured in many European and American countries, Japan, Israel, New Zealand; Benoît Prize 1991; prizes at int. competitions Varna 1984, 1986, Moscow 1987, Osaka 1995; State Prize of Russia 1996; People's Artist of Russia 1996. *Leisure interest:* cooking. *Address:* Bolshoi Theatre, 103009 Moscow, Teatralnaya pl. 1; 119121 Moscow, 1st Truzhennikov per. 17, Apt. 49, Russia (home). *Telephone:* (495) 248-27-53 (home). *Website:* www.bolshoi.ru.

GRACIAS, HE Cardinal Oswald, DCL, DiplJur; Indian ecclesiastic; *Archbishop of Bombay;* b. 24 Dec. 1944, Bombay (now Mumbai); ed Pontifical Urbanian Univ.; ordained priest of Bombay 1970; Chancellor Diocese of Jamshedpur and Sec. to Diocesan Bishop 1970–75; Auxiliary Bishop of Bombay and Titular Bishop of Bladia 1997–2000; Archbishop of Agra 2000–06, of Bombay 2006–; cr. Cardinal (Cardinal-Priest of S. Paulo della Croce a 'Corviale') 2007; served as Sec.-Gen. Catholic Bishops' Conf. of India; mem. Vatican's Vox Clara Cttee (advises the Congregation for Divine Worship and the Sacraments on the trans. of Latin liturgical texts into English); currently Pres. Latin-rite Conf. of Catholic Bishops of India. *Address:* Archbishop's House, 21 Nathalal Parekh Marg, Mumbai 400 001, India (office). *Telephone:* (22) 2202-1093 (office); (22) 2202-1193 (office). *Fax:* (22) 2285-3872 (office). *E-mail:* info@archbom.org (office). *Website:* www.archbom.org (office).

GRADE, Michael Ian, CBE, FRTS; British broadcasting executive; *Chairman, Independent Television (ITV);* b. 8 March 1943, London; s. of the late Leslie Grade; m. 1st Penelope Jane Levinson 1967 (divorced 1981); one s. one d.; m. 2nd Hon. Sarah Lawson 1982 (divorced 1991); m. 3rd Francesca Mary Leahy 1998; one s.; ed St Dunstan's Coll., London; trainee journalist, Daily Mirror 1960, sports columnist 1964–66; theatrical agent, Grade Org. 1966; Jt Man. Dir London Man. and Representation 1969–73; Deputy Controller of Programmes (Entertainment), London Weekend TV 1973–77, Dir of Programmes and mem. Bd 1977–81; Pres. Embassy TV 1981–84; Controller BBC One 1984–86, Dir of Programmes BBC TV 1986–87; CEO Channel 4 1988–97; Chair. VCI PLC 1995–98; Chair., CEO First Leisure Corpn 1997–98 (Dir 1991–2000, Chair. (non-exec.) 1995–97); Chair. Ind. Inquiry into Fear of Crime 1989, Devt Council, Royal Nat. Theatre 1997–; Deputy Chair. Soc. of Stars 1995–; Pres. TV and Radio Industries Club 1987–88, Newspaper Press Fund 1988–89, Entertainment Charities Fund 1994–, Royal TV Soc. 1995–97; Vice-Pres. Children's Film Unit 1993–; mem. Bd of Dirs ITN 1989–93, Open Coll. 1989–97, Delfont Macintosh Theatres Ltd 1994–99, Charlton Athletic Football Club 1997–, Jewish Film Foundation 1997–, New Millennium Experience Co. 1997–99, Camelot Group 2000–04, Digitaloctopus 2000–; Chair. Octopus 2000–04, Pinewood Studio Ltd 2000–, Hemscott.NET

2000–06, BBC 2004–06; Exec. Chair. ITV 2006–09, Chair. (non-exec.) 2009–; Dir (non-exec.) SMG 2003–06; mem. Int. Council Nat. Acad. of TV Arts and Sciences 1991–97, Council, London Acad. of Music and Dramatic Art 1981–93, BAFTA 1981–82, 1986–88, 2004– (Fellow 1994), Gate Theatre, Dublin 1990–2004, Cities in Schools 1991–95, Cinema and TV Benevolent Fund 1993–2004, Royal Acad. of Dramatic Art 1996–2004, Royal Albert Hall 1997–2004, 300 Group, Milton Cttee, British Screen Advisory Council 1986–97, Nat. Comm. of Inquiry into Prevention of Child Abuse 1994–96; mem. Bd of Govs BANFF TV Festival 1997–99; Trustee, Band Aid, Nat. Film and TV School, Virgin Health Care Foundation; Hon. Prof., Thames Valley Univ. 1994; Hon. Treas. Stars Org. for Spastics 1986–92; Hon. LLD (Nottingham) 1997; Royal TV Soc. Gold Medal 1997. *Publication:* It Seemed Like a Good Idea at the Time (autobiography) 1999. *Leisure interest:* entertainment. *Address:* ITV plc, 200 Grays Inn Road, London, WC1X 8HF, England (office). *Telephone:* (844) 8818000 (office). *Website:* www.itvplc.com (office).

GRADIN, Anita; Swedish politician; b. 12 Aug. 1933, Hörnefors, Västerbotten Co.; m. Bertil Kersfelt; one d.; ed Coll. of Social Work and Public Admin., Stockholm and in USA; journalist 1950, 1956–58, 1960–63; with Swedish Union of Forest Workers and Log Drivers 1952; with Social Welfare Planning Cttee and Municipal Exec. Bd Cttee on Women's Issues, Stockholm 1963–67; mem. Exec. Cttee, Nat. Fed. of Social Democratic Women 1964–93, Vice-Chair. 1975–93; mem. Stockholm City Council 1966–68; First Sec. Cabinet Office 1967–82; mem. SDP Exec. Cttee of Stockholm 1968–82; mem. Parl. 1968–92; Chair. Dist Br., Fed. of Social Democratic Women, Stockholm 1968–82; Chair. Swedish Union of Social Workers and Public Admin. 1970–81; Chair. Nat. Bd for Intercountry Adoptions 1973–80; del. Council of Europe 1973–82, Chair. Cttee on Migration, Refugees and Democracy 1978–82; Minister with responsibility for Migration and Equality Affairs 1982–86; Vice-Chair. Socialist Int. Women's Council 1983–86, Chair. Socialist Int. Women 1986–92, Vice-Chair. Socialist Int. 1986–92; Minister with responsibility for Foreign Trade and European Affairs 1986–91; Amb. to Austria, Slovenia and to UN insts including IAEA, UNIDO and UNRWA 1992–94; EC Commr for Migration, Home and Judicial Affairs 1995–99; Chair. Research Council of Social Science and Working Life 2001–04; Chair. of Stockholm Conf. on Viet nam 1974–76, of Swedish Cttee for Viet nam, Laos and Cambodia 1977–82, Sr Club, Foreign Office 2002; mem. Exec. Cttee of RFSU (Nat. Asscn for Sexual Enlightenment) and Otterfonden 1969–92; mem. EFTA del. 1991–92; mem. Bd Stockholm School of Econs, Women's Forum 2001–08, Comm. on Gene Medicine 2002–08; Cavalieri di Gran Croce (Italy) 1991, Das Grosse Goldene Ehrenzeichen am Bande (Austria) 1994, The King's Medal in the 12th Dimension with ribbon of the Royal Order of the Seraphim 1998; Dr hc Umeå Univ. 2002; Marisa Bellizario European Prize (Italy) 1998; Pro Merito Medal, Council of Europe 1982, Wizo Woman of the Year 1986. *Leisure interests:* fishing, reading books, jazz music. *Address:* Fleminggatan 85, 11245 Stockholm, Sweden (home). *Telephone:* (8) 269872 (home). *Fax:* (8) 269872 (home). *E-mail:* gradin.kersfelt@telia.com (home).

GRADY, Monica M., BSc, PhD; British meteoritic scientist and academic; *Professor of Planetary and Space Sciences, Planetary and Space Sciences Research Institute, Open University;* b. Leeds, Yorks.; m. Dr Ian Wright; ed Univs of Durham and Cambridge; Head of Div., Petrology and Meteoritics, Natural History Museum, London, Leader, Meteorites and Micrometeorites Programme, Curator Meteorite Collection, Ed. Catalogue of Meteorites 1991–2005; Prof. of Planetary and Space Sciences, Planetary and Space Sciences Research Inst., Open Univ., Milton Keynes 2005–; mem. UK Astrobiology Panel, UK Planetary Forum; mem. Particle Physics and Astronomy Council's Science Cttee 2005–07; Fellow, Meteoritical Soc., Royal Astronomical Soc., Mineralogical Soc.; Hon. Reader in Geological Sciences, Univ. Coll., London; Asteroid (4731) Monicagrady named after her; Royal Inst. Christmas Lecturer 2003. *Publications:* Meteorites: Flux with Time and Impact Effects 1998, Catalogue of Meteorites 2000, Search for Life 2001, Meteorites (co-author) (2nd edn) 2002. *Address:* Faculty of Science, Planetary and Space Sciences Research Institute, Walton Hall, Milton Keynes, MK7 6AA, England (office). *Telephone:* (1908) 659251 (office). *Fax:* (1908) 858022 (office). *E-mail:* m.m.grady@open.ac.uk (office). *Website:* www.open.ac.uk/science (office).

GRAF, Hans; Austrian conductor and administrator; *Music Director, Houston Symphony Orchestra;* b. 15 Feb. 1949, Linz; m. Margarita Graf; one d.; ed Bruckner Conservatory, Linz, Academy of Music, Graz; Music Dir Iraqi Nat. Symphony Orchestra 1975–76, Mozarteum Orchestra, Salzburg 1984–94, Calgary Philharmonic Orchestra 1995–2003, Music Dir Laureate 2006–, Nat. Orchestre de Bordeaux-Aquitaine 1998–2004, Opéra de Bordeaux 1998–2004, Houston Symphony Orchestra 2001–; guest conductor with several orchestras including Vienna Symphony, Vienna Philharmonic, Orchestre Nat. de France, Leningrad Philharmonic, Pittsburgh Symphony, Boston Symphony; Chevalier, Légion d'Honneur 2002; First Prize, Karl Böhm Conductors Competition, Salzburg 1979. *Address:* Houston Symphony Orchestra, 615 Louisiana Street, Suite 102, Houston, TX 77002, USA (office). *Telephone:* (713) 224-4240 (office). *E-mail:* office@houstonsymphony.org (office). *Website:* www.houstonsymphony.org (office).

GRAF, Stefanie (Steffi) M.; German fmr professional tennis player; b. 14 June 1969, Mannheim; d. of Peter Graf and Heidi Graf; m. Andre Agassi (q.v.); one s. one d.; coached by her father; won Orange Bowl 12s 1981, European 14-and-under and European Circuit Masters 1982, Olympic demonstration event, LA; winner German Open 1986, French Open 1987, 1988, 1993, 1995, 1996, 1999; Australian Open 1988, 1989, 1990, 1994; Wimbledon 1988, 1989, 1991, 1992, 1993, 1995, 1996, US Open 1988, 1989, 1993, 1995, 1996, won ATP Tour World Championship 1996, German Open 1989, numerous women's doubles championships with Gabriela Sabatini, Federation Cup 1992; Olympic Champion 1988; ranked No. 1 Aug. 1987; named Official World Champion 1988; Grand Slam winner 1988, 1989; youngest player to win 500 singles victories as a professional Oct. 1991; 118 tournament wins, 23 Grand Slam titles; announced retirement Aug. 1999; Amb. World Wildlife Fund 1984–; Founder and Chair. Children for Tomorrow; Amb. of EXPO 2000; Olympic Order 1999, German Medal of Honour 2002. *Publication:* Wege Zum Erfolg 1999. *Leisure interests:* music, dogs, photography, art, reading. *Address:* 3960 Howard Hughes Pkwy, #750, Las Vegas, NV 89109, USA; Stefanie Graf Marketing GmbH & Co.KG, Gartenstrasse 1, 68723 Schwetzingen, Germany. *Website:* www.stefanie-graf.com (office).

GRAFFMAN, Gary; American pianist; b. 14 Oct. 1928; s. of Vladimir and Nadia (Margdin) Graffman; m. Naomi Helfman 1952; ed Curtis Inst. of Music, Philadelphia under Mme. Isabelle Vengerova; professional début with Philadelphia Orchestra 1947; concert tours all over the world; appears annually in America with major orchestras; Dir Curtis Inst. 1986–, Pres. 1995–2006; year offstage to correct finger injury 1980–81; gramophone recordings for Columbia Masterworks and RCA Victor including concertos of Tchaikovsky, Rachmaninoff, Brahms, Beethoven, Chopin and Prokofiev; Leventritt Award 1949; several hon. degrees. *Publication:* I Really Should be Practising (autobiog.) 1981. *Leisure interest:* Asian art. *Address:* Opus 3 Artists, 470 Park Avenue South, 9th Floor North, New York, NY 10016, USA (office). *Telephone:* (212) 584-7500 (office). *Fax:* (646) 300-8200 (office). *E-mail:* info@opus3artists.com (office). *Website:* www.opus3artists.com (office).

GRAFTON, Sue, BA; American writer; b. 24 April 1940, Louisville, Ky; d. of C.W. Grafton and Vivian Harnsberger; m. 3rd Steven F. Humphrey; one s. two d. from previous marriages; ed Univ. of Louisville, Ky; worked as admissions clerk, cashier and clinic sec., St John's Hosp., Santa Monica, CA; receptionist, later medical educ. sec., Cottage Hosp., Santa Barbara, CA; Cartier Diamond Dagger Award, Crime Writers' Asscn 2008, named Grand Master, Mystery Writers of America 2009. *Television:* has written numerous films for TV, including Walking Through the Fire (Christopher Award) 1979, Sex and the Single Parent, Mark, I Love You, Nurse; also adaptations of Caribbean Mystery and Sparkling Cyanide by Agatha Christie. *Publications:* Keziah Dane 1967, The Lolly-Madonna War 1969, A is for Alibi 1982, B is for Burglar 1985, C is for Corpse 1986, D is for Deadbeat 1987, E is for Evidence 1988, F is for Fugitive 1989, G is for Gumshoe 1990, H is for Homicide 1991, I is for Innocent 1992, J is for Judgement 1993, K is for Killer 1994, L is for Lawless 1995, M is for Malice 1996, N is for Noose 1998, O is for Outlaw 1999, P is for Peril 2001, Q is for Quarry 2003, R is for Ricochet 2004, S is for Silence (RIO Award of Excellence 2007) 2006, T is for Trespass 2007; Killer in the Family (jt author with S. Humphrey), Love on the Run (jt author with S. Humphrey). *Leisure interests:* cats, gardening, good food. *Address:* PO Box 41447, Santa Barbara, CA 93140, USA (office). *Website:* www.suegrafton.com (office).

GRAHAM, Sir Alexander Michael, KStJ, GBE, JP, DCL, CBIM, FCII, FCIS, FRSA; British chartered insurance broker; b. 27 Sept. 1938, London; s. of Dr Walter Graham and Suzanne Simon; m. Carolyn Stansfeld 1964; three d.; ed St Paul's School; nat. service with Gordon Highlanders 1957–59; broker, Frizzell Group Ltd 1957–67, Dir 1967–73, Man. Dir 1973–90, Deputy Chair. 1990–92; Alderman, City of London 1979–, Sheriff 1986–87, Lord Mayor 1990–91; Chair. Nat. Employers Liaison Cttee for TA and Reserve Forces 1992–97; Chair. First City Insurance Brokers Ltd 1993–98; Chair. Council, Order of St John, Herts. 1993–; Chair. Bd of Trustees, Morden Coll. 1995–; Chair. Folgate Insurance Co. Ltd 1995–2002, Employment Conditions Abroad Ltd 1993–, Euclidian PLC 1994–2001, United Response 1994–2002; Pres. British Insurance Law Asscn 1994–96; Underwriting mem. of Lloyd's; Fellow Chartered Insurance Inst.; Liveryman Mercers' Co. 1971–, Master 1983–84; Vice-Pres. Royal Soc. of St George 1999–; Grand Cross Order of Merit (Chile); Order of Wissam Alouite Class 3 (Morocco). *Leisure interests:* golf, shooting, tennis, swimming, wine, music, calligraphy. *Address:* 13–15 Folgate Street, London, E1 6BX (office); Walden Abbotts, Whitwell, Hitchin, Herts., SG4 8AJ, England (home). *Telephone:* (1438) 871997 (home). *Fax:* (1438) 871997 (home).

GRAHAM, Andrew Winston Mawdsley, MA; British economist and academic; *Master, Balliol College, University of Oxford;* b. 20 June 1942; s. of Winston Mawdsley Graham; m. Peggotty Fawssett 1970; ed Charterhouse, St Edmund Hall, Oxford; Econ. Asst, Nat. Econ. Devt Office 1964, with Dept of Econ. Affairs 1964–66, Asst to Econ. Adviser to Cabinet 1966–68, Econ. Adviser to Prime Minister 1968–69; Fellow and Tutor in Econs, Balliol Coll. Oxford 1969–97, Estates Bursar 1978, Investment Bursar 1979–83, Vice-Master 1988, 1992–94, Acting Master 1997–2001, Master 2001–; Policy Adviser to Prime Minister (leave of absence from Balliol) 1974–76; mem. ILO/JASPA Employment Advisory Mission to Ethiopia 1982; Head of Commonwealth/Food Studies Group assisting Govt of Zambia 1984; Econ. Adviser to Shadow Chancellor of Exchequer 1988–92, to Leader of Opposition 1992–94; Tutor, Oxford Univ. Business Summer School 1971, 1972, 1973, 1976; Visiting Scholar, MIT 1994; Chair. St James Group (Econ. Forecasting) 1982–84, 1985–92; consultant, BBC 1989–92; mem. Bd Channel 4 TV 1998–2005; Founder and Acting Dir Oxford Internet Inst. 2001; mem. Media Advisory Cttee, Inst. for Public Policy Research 1994–97, Council of Man. Templeton Coll. Oxford 1990–96; Founder-mem. Editorial Bd Library of Political Economy 1982–94; Sr Fellow, Gorbachev Foundation of N America 1999–; Trustee, Foundation for Information Policy Research 1998–2001, Esmée Fairbairn Foundation 2003–05, Scott Trust (owners of the Guardian and the Observer) 2005–; Hon. DCL Oxon. 2003. *Publications:* Government and Economies in the Postwar Period (ed.) 1990, Broadcasting, Society and Policy in the Multimedia Age (co-author) 1997; contribs to books on econs and philosophy. *Leisure interest:* windsurfing. *Address:* Balliol College, Oxford,

OX1 3BJ, England (office). *Telephone:* (1865) 277777 (office). *Website:* www .balliol.ox.ac.uk (office).

GRAHAM, Billy (see Graham, William Franklin).

GRAHAM, Christopher Forbes, MA, DPhil, FRS; British biologist and academic; *Professor of Animal Development, Department of Zoology, University of Oxford;* b. 23 Sept. 1940; ed Univ. of Oxford; fmrly Jr Beit Memorial Fellow in Medical Research, Sir William Dunn School of Pathology; Lecturer, Dept of Zoology, Univ. of Oxford 1970–85, Prof. of Animal Devt 1985–; Professorial Fellow, St Catherine's Coll., Oxford 1985–; mem. British Soc. for Cell Biology, British Soc. for Developmental Biology, Soc. for Experimental Biology, Genetical Soc. *Publication:* Developmental Control in Plants and Animals 1984. *Address:* St Catherine's College, Oxford, OX1 3UJ, England. *Website:* www.zoo.ox.ac.uk (office).

GRAHAM, Daniel Robert (Bob), BA, LLD; American politician and academic; *Research Fellow, Belfer Center for Science and International Affairs, John F. Kennedy School of Government, Harvard University;* b. 9 Nov. 1936, Coral Gables, Fla; s. of Ernest R. Graham and Hilda Simmons; m. Adele Khoury 1959; four d.; ed Univ. of Fla and Harvard Law School; Vice-Pres. Sengra Devt Corpn 1963–79; Fla State Rep. from Coral Gables 1966–70; Fla State Senator from Coral Gables 1970–78; Gov. of Fla 1979–87, Senator 1986–2005; currently Research Fellow, Belfer Center for Science and Int. Affairs, John F. Kennedy School of Govt, Harvard Univ.; Audubon Soc. Conservation Award 1974. *Leisure interests:* golf, tennis and reading. *Address:* Belfer Center for Science and International Affairs, John F. Kennedy School of Government, 79 JFK Street, Cambridge, MA 02138, USA (office). *Telephone:* (617) 495-1400 (office). *Fax:* (617) 495-8963 (office). *Website:* bcsia.ksg.harvard .edu (office).

GRAHAM, Donald Edward, BA; American newspaper publisher; *Chairman and CEO, The Washington Post Company;* b. 22 April 1945, Baltimore, Md; s. of late Philip L. Graham and of Katharine Meyer Graham; m. Mary L. Wissler 1967; one s. three d.; ed Harvard Univ.; joined the Washington Post 1971, Asst Man. Ed./Sports 1974–75, Asst Gen. Man. 1975–76, Exec. Vice-Pres. and Gen. Man. 1976–79, Publr 1979–; Pres., CEO The Washington Post Co. 1991–93, Chair., CEO 1993–; fmrly reporter and writer for Newsweek. *Address:* The Washington Post, 1150 15th Street, NW, Washington, DC 20071, USA (office). *Telephone:* (202) 334-6000 (office). *Fax:* (202) 334-4536 (office). *E-mail:* twpcoreply@washpost.com (office). *Website:* www.washpostco.com (office).

GRAHAM, Rt Hon. Sir Douglas Arthur Montrose 'Doug', KNZM, PC, LLB, JP; New Zealand lawyer, fmr politician and company director; b. 12 Jan. 1942, Auckland; m. Beverley Virginia Graham 1966; two s. one d.; ed Southwell School, Auckland Grammar School and Univ. of Auckland; practising lawyer since 1965; est. own practice 1968; barrister and solicitor of High Court of NZ; Lecturer in Legal Ethics, Univ. of Auckland 1973–83; MP (Nat. Party) for Remuera 1984–96 (seat abolished), list MP 1996–99; Minister of Justice 1990–99, of Cultural Affairs and Minister for Disarmament and Arms Control 1990–99, Minister in Charge of Treaty of Waitangi Negotiations on behalf of the Crown 1991–99, Minister of Justice and of Courts 1995–99; Attorney Gen. 1997–99; co. dir and consultant 1999–; Dr hc (Waikato) 1999. *Publication:* Trick or Treaty? 1997. *Leisure interests:* golf, music, rugby football, gardening. *Address:* 3A Martin Avenue, Remuera, Auckland, New Zealand (home). *Telephone:* (9) 524-2921 (home). *Fax:* (9) 524-2923 (home). *E-mail:* douglas .graham@xtra.co.nz (home).

GRAHAM, James (see Patterson, Harry).

GRAHAM, Jorie, BFA, MFA; American poet and academic; *Boylston Professor of Rhetoric and Oratory, Harvard University;* b. 9 May 1951, New York, NY; m. James Galvin; ed New York Univ. and Univ. of Iowa; Poetry Ed. Crazy Horse 1978–81, The Colorado Review 1990–; Contributing Ed., Boston Review, Conjunctions, Denver Quarterly; Asst Prof. Murray State Univ., KY 1978–79, Humboldt State Univ., Arcata, CA 1979–81; Instructor Columbia Univ. 1981–83; staff mem. Writers' Workshop and Prof. of English, Univ. of Iowa 1983–1998; Chancellor Acad. of American Poets 1997–; Boylston Prof. of Rhetoric and Oratory in the Dept of English and American Literature and Language, Harvard Univ. 1998–; mem. American Acad. of Arts and Letters 2009–; American Acad. of Poets Award 1977, Poetry Northwest Young Poets Prize 1980, Pushcart Prizes 1980, 1982, Ingram Merrill Foundation grant 1981, Great Lakes Colleges Asscn Award 1981, American Poetry Review Prize 1982, Bunting Fellow Radcliffe Inst. 1982, Guggenheim Fellowship 1983–84, John D. and Catherine T. MacArthur Foundation Fellowship 1990. *Publications:* Hybrids of Plants and of Ghosts 1980, Erosion 1983, The End of Beauty 1987, The Best American Poetry (ed. with David Lehman) 1990, Region of Unlikeness 1991, Materialism 1993, The Dream of the Unified Field (Pulitzer Prize in Poetry 1996) 1995, Errancy 1997, Swarm 1999, Never 2002, Overlord 2004, Sea Change 2008. *Address:* Department of English, Harvard University, 12 Quincy Street, Cambridge, MA 02138, USA (office). *Telephone:* (617) 495-1189 (office). *Fax:* (617) 496-8737 (office). *E-mail:* engdept@fas.harvard.edu (office). *Website:* www.fas.harvard.edu/~english (office).

GRAHAM, Lindsay O.; American politician; *Senator from South Carolina;* served in armed forces, assignments including Operation Desert Shield and Desert Storm; legal career in USAF; Base Staff Judge Advocate, McEntire Air Nat. Guard Base, Eastover 1989–94; est. pvt. law practice 1988; asst attorney in Oconee Co.; mem. S Carolina House of Reps from 2nd Dist Oconee Co. 1992–94; mem. US Congress from 3rd Dist S Carolina 1994–2003, mem. Cttee on Educ. and the Workforce, on Judiciary, on Armed Services; Senator from S Carolina 2003–; currently Lt-Col Air Force Reserves; mem. Republican Party. *Address:* Office of the Senator from South Carolina, US Senate, Senate

Buildings, Washington, DC 20510, USA (office). *Telephone:* (202) 224-5972 (office). *Website:* lgraham.senate.gov (office).

GRAHAM, Patricia Albjerg, PhD; American academic; *Warren Professor Emerita, Graduate School of Education, Harvard University;* b. (Patricia Parks Albjerg), 9 Feb. 1935, Lafayette, Ind.; d. of Victor L. Albjerg and Marguerite Hall Albjerg; m. Loren R. Graham 1955; one d.; ed Purdue and Columbia Univs; teacher, Deep Creek and Maury High Schools, Norfolk, Va 1955–58; Chair. History Dept, St Hilda's and St Hugh's School, New York 1958–60, part-time Coll. Adviser 1961–63, 1965–67; Lecturer, Indiana Univ., School of Educ., Bloomington 1964–65; Asst Prof., Barnard Coll. and Columbia Teacher's Coll., New York 1965–68, Assoc. Prof. 1968–72, Prof. 1972–74; Prof., Harvard Univ. Grad. School of Educ., Cambridge, Mass 1974–79, Warren Prof. 1979–2006, Prof. Emer. 2006–, Dean, Grad. School of Educ. 1982–91; Dean, Radcliffe Inst. and Vice-Pres., Radcliffe Coll., Cambridge, Mass 1974–76; Dir Nat. Inst. of Educ. 1977–79; mem. Bd of Dirs Josiah Macy Jr Foundation 1976–77, 1979–; Vice-Pres. for Teaching, American Historical Asscn 1985–89; Pres. Nat. Acad. of Educ. 1985–89; Dir Spencer Foundation 1983–2000, Pres. 1991–2000; Dir Johnson Foundation 1983–2001, Hitachi Foundation 1985–2004; mem. AAAS (mem. Council 1993–96, Vice-Pres. 1998–2001), American Philosophical Soc. 1999–; mem. Bd of Dirs Center for Advanced Study in the Behavioral Sciences 2001–07; Dir Northwestern Mutual Life 1980–2005, Apache Corpn 2002–; Trustee Cen. European Univ. 2002–; 14 hon. degrees; John Simon Guggenheim award 1972–73, Woodrow Wilson Center Fellow 1981–82. *Publications:* Progressive Education: From Arcady to Academe, A History of the Progressive Education Association 1967, Community and Class in American Education, 1865–1918 1974, Women in Higher Education (co-ed. with Todd Furniss) 1974, S.O.S. Sustain Our Schools 1992, Accountability (with Richard Lyman and Martin Trow) 1995, Schooling America 2005. *Address:* Harvard University Graduate School of Education, Appian Way, Cambridge, MA 02138, USA (office). *Telephone:* (617) 496-4839 (office). *Fax:* (617) 496-3095 (office). *E-mail:* patricia_graham@harvard.edu (office).

GRAHAM, Shawn; Canadian politician; *Premier, President of the Executive Council, Minister of Wellness, Culture and Sport, Minister of Intergovernmental Affairs, Minister responsible for the Premier's Council on the Status of Disabled Persons;* b. 22 Feb. 1968, Kent Co., NB; s. of Alan Graham; m. Roxanne Reeves; mem. (Riding of Kent) Legis. Ass. of NB 1998–; Caucas Chair. Liberal Party of NB 1998–2002, Leader 2002– (youngest Liberal leader and youngest Leader of the Official Opposition in Canada); Premier of NB, Pres. Exec. Council, Minister of Wellness, Culture and Sport, of Intergovernmental Affairs, Minister responsible for the Premier's Council on the Status of Disabled Persons 2006–. *Address:* Office of the Premier, Centennial Building, 670 King Street, PO Box 6000, Fredericton, NB E3B 5H1, Canada (office). *Telephone:* (506) 453-2144 (office). *Fax:* (506) 453-7407 (office). *Website:* www .gnb.ca/0089/index-e.asp (office).

GRAHAM, Stuart E., BSc; American construction industry executive; *Chairman, Skanska USA Building Inc.;* b. 1946; ed Holy Cross Univ.; Asst Field Supt, Sordoni Construction Co. 1969; Pres. Sordoni Skanska 1990–95, Pres. and CEO Slattery Skanska 1995–97, Pres. Skanska USA Inc. 1997–2001, Pres. and CEO Skanska AB 2002–08 (retd), currently Chair. Skanska USA Building Inc.; mem. Bd of Dirs Securitas AB 2005–, PPL Corpn 2008–; mem. and fmr Dir Construction Industry Round Table. *Address:* Skanska USA Building Inc., 1633 Littleton Road, Parsippany, NJ 07054, USA (office). *Telephone:* (973) 753-3500 (office). *E-mail:* info@skanskausa.com (office). *Website:* www.skanskausa.com (office).

GRAHAM, Susan; American singer (mezzo-soprano); b. 23 July 1960, Roswell, NM; ed Manhattan School of Music, Texas Technical Univ.; sang Massenet's Chérubin while a student; engagements with St Louis Opera as Erika in Vanessa, Charlotte and at Seattle as Stephano in Roméo et Juliette; season 1989–90 included Chicago Lyric Opera debut as Annius in La Clemenza di Tito, Sonia in Argento's Aspern Papers at Washington, Dorabella and the Composer at Santa Fe; Carnegie Hall debut in Des Knaben Wunderhorn and Bernstein concert in New York; season 1990–91 as Octavian with San Francisco Symphony, Minerva in Monteverdi's Ulisse with San Francisco Opera, Berlioz's Beatrice at Lyon, Cherubino at Santa Fe; Mozart's C minor Mass under Edo de Waart and with Philadelphia Orchestra under Neville Marriner; season 1991–92 at Metropolitan as Second Lady, Cherubino, and Tebaldo in Don Carlos; L'Opera de Nice as Cherubino and Les Nuits d'Été in Lyon; Beethoven's 9th in Spain conducted by Marriner; Salzburg Mozart Week 1993, as Cecilio in Lucio Silla, Easter and Summer Festivals as Meg Page in Falstaff; season 1993–94 as Massenet's Chérubin and Dorabella at Covent Garden, Ascanio in Les Troyens at the Met, Annius in Tito at San Francisco and 1994 Salzburg Festival; Octavian for WNO and Vienna State Opera and Marguerite in La Damnation de Faust for L'Opéra de Lyon; season 1995 as Dorabella and as Arianna in the premiere of the opera by Goehr at Covent Garden; season 1997 with Chérubin at Covent Garden and in Lucio Silla at Salzburg; sang Octavian at Covent Garden 2000; created Sister Helen Prejean in Jack Heggie's Dead Man Walking, San Francisco 2000; season 2001 as Mignon at Toulouse and Dorabella at the New York Met; Opera News Award 2005. *Recordings include:* Falstaff conducted by Solti, La Damnation de Faust conducted by Kent Nagano, Béatrice et Bénédict conducted by John Nelson, Stravinsky's Pulcinella, Charles Ives Songs (Grammy Award for Best Classical Vocal Performance 2005) 2004, Poèmes de l'amour 2005. *Address:* IMG Artists, Carnegie Hall Tower, 153 West 57th Street, 5th Floor, New York, NY 10019, USA (office). *Telephone:* (212) 994-3500 (office). *Fax:* (212) 994-3550 (office). *E-mail:* atreuhaft@imgartists.com (office). *Website:* www.imgartists.com (office); www.susangraham.com.

GRAHAM, William, BA, LLB, DJur; Canadian politician, lawyer and academic; *Chancellor, Trinity College, University of Toronto;* b. 1939, Montreal; m. Catherine Graham; one d. one s.; ed Upper Canada Coll., Trinity Coll., Univ. of Toronto, Univ. of Paris, France; practised law with Fasken and Calvin, made Partner 1983; Prof. of Law, Univ. of Toronto, Visiting Prof. Univ. de Montréal, McGill Univ.; Dir Centre of Int. Studies, Univ. of Toronto; fmr Pres. Alliance Française, Toronto; MP 1993–2007, Chair. Standing Cttee on Foreign Affairs and Int. Trade 1995–2002; Minister of Foreign Affairs 2002–04, of Nat. Defence 2004–06; Parl. Opposition Leader 2006; Chancellor, Trinity Coll., Univ. of Toronto 2007–; Chair. Atlantic Council of Canada 2007–; fmr Vice-Pres. and Treas. Parl. Asscn of OSCE; Founding Pres. Inter-Parl. Forum of the Americas; mem. Inter-Parl. Council Against Anti-Semitism, PD Burma; Hon. Life mem. Canadian Council of Int. Law; Hon. Lt Col, Gov. Gen's Horse Guards 2007–; Chevalier, Légion d'honneur, Chevalier Ordre de la Pléiade, Ordre du mérite de l'Asscn des juristes de l'Ontario; Prix Jean-Baptiste Rousseaux, Médaille d'argent de la ville de Paris, Médaille d'or de l'alliance française. *Publications:* The Canadian Law and Practice of International Trade (co-author), International Law: Chiefly as Interpreted and Applied in Canada (co-ed.), New Dimensions in International Trade Law (co-author). *Address:* M4Y 1S2 Can 702, 45 Charles Street East, Toronto, ON Canada (office). *Telephone:* 416-920-2205. *Fax:* 416-920-4150. *E-mail:* dilys.williams@afai.ca (office).

GRAHAM, William Franklin (Billy), BA, BTh; American evangelist; b. 7 Nov. 1918, Charlotte, NC; s. of William Franklin and Morrow Graham; m. Ruth M. Bell 1943 (died 2007); two s. three d.; ed Florida Bible Inst., Tampa and Wheaton Coll.; ordained to Baptist Ministry 1939; Minister First Baptist Church, Western Springs, Ill. 1943–45; First Vice-Pres. Youth for Christ Int. 1945–50; Pres. Northwestern Schools, Minneapolis 1947–52; founder World Wide Pictures, Burbank, Calif.; worldwide evangelistic campaigns 1947–; messages featured on weekly Hour of Decision radio programme 1950–; also periodic crusade telecasts; Founder, Billy Graham Evangelistic Asscn 1950; Hon. Chair. Lausanne Congress on World Evangelization 1974; Hon. KBE 2001; Dr hc (Hungarian Calvinist Church) (Christian Acad. of Theol.) 1981; numerous awards including Bernard Baruch Award 1955, Humane Order of African Redemption 1960, Gold Award, George Washington Carver Memorial Inst. 1964, Horatio Alger Award 1965, Int. Brotherhood Award Nat. Conf. of Christians and Jews 1971, Sylvanus Thayer Award, Asscn of Graduates of US Mil. Acad. 1972, Franciscan Int. Award 1972, Man of South Award 1974, Liberty Bell Award 1975, Templeton Prize 1982, Presidential Medal of Freedom 1983, William Booth Award 1989, Congressional Gold Medal 1996, Ronald Reagan Presidential Foundation Award 2000. *Publications:* Peace with God 1953 (revised edn 1984), The Secret of Happiness 1955, My Answer 1960, World Aflame 1965, The Challenge 1969, The Jesus Generation 1971, Angels – God's Secret Agents 1975, How to be Born Again 1977, The Holy Spirit 1978, Till Armageddon 1981, Approaching Hoofbeats: The Four Horsemen of the Apocalypse 1983, A Biblical Standard for Evangelists 1984, Unto The Hills 1986, Facing Death and the Life After 1987, Answers to Life's Problems 1988, Hope for the Troubled Heart 1991, Storm Warning 1992, Just As I Am (autobiog.) 1997, Hope for Each Day 2002, The Journey: How To Live by Faith in an Uncertain World 2006. *Address:* 1 Billy Graham Parkway, Charlotte, NC 28201-0001, USA (office). *Telephone:* (704) 401-2432 (office). *Fax:* (704) 401-3017 (office). *E-mail:* media@bgea.org (office). *Website:* www.bgea.org (home).

GRAHAM-DIXON, Andrew, MA; British critic, writer and broadcaster; *Chief Art Critic, Sunday Telegraph;* b. 26 Dec. 1960, London; s. of Antony Philip Graham-Dixon and Suzanne Graham-Dixon (née Villar); m. Sabine Marie-Pascale Tilly 1986; one s. two d.; ed Westminster School, Christ Church Coll. Oxford, Courtauld Inst., London; Chief Arts Critic The Independent 1986–98; arts writer and presenter, BBC TV 1992–; Curator Broken English, Serpentine Gallery, London 1992; Chief Arts Writer Sunday Telegraph Magazine and columnist, In the Picture 1999–, Chief Art Critic Sunday Telegraph 2005–; BP Arts Writer of the Year 1988, 1989, 1990; First Prize Reportage, Montreal Film & TV Festival 1992; Hawthornden Prize 1992. *Television includes:* Gericault 1992; TV documentary series: A History of British Art 1994, Renaissance 1999, 1,000 Ways of Getting Drunk in England 2001, Secret Lives of the Artists 2003, The Elgin Marbles 2004, The Secret of Drawing 2005, I, Samurai 2006, The Art of Eternity 2007, The Art of Spain 2008, Travels with Vasari 2009, The Medici: Makers of Modern Art 2009. *Publications:* Howard Hodgkin: A Monograph 1994, A History of British Art 1996, Paper Museum 1996, Renaissance 1999, In the Picture 2002, Michelangelo and the Sistine Chapel 2008. *Leisure interests:* walking, snooker, football, existentialism, golf. *Address:* United Agents, 12–26 Lexington Street, London, W1F 0LE, England (office). *Telephone:* (20) 3214-0800 (office). *Fax:* (20) 3214-0801 (office). *E-mail:* info@unitedagents.co.uk (office). *Website:* www.unitedagents.co.uk (office).

GRAHAM-SMITH, Sir Francis, Kt, PhD, FRS, FRAS; British professor of radio astronomy; *Professor Emeritus of Physics, University of Manchester;* b. 25 April 1923, Roehampton, Surrey; m. Elizabeth Palmer 1946; three s. one d.; ed Rossall School, Epsom Coll., Downing Coll., Cambridge; with Telecommunications Research Establishment 1943–46; Cavendish Lab. 1947–64; 1851 Exhbn 1951–52; Warren Research Fellow, Royal Soc. 1959–64; Prof. of Radio Astronomy, Univ. of Manchester 1964–74, 1981–87, Pro-Vice-Chancellor 1987, Dir Nuffield Radio Astronomy Labs 1981–88, Langworthy Prof. of Physics 1987–90, Prof. Emer. 1990–; Deputy Dir Royal Greenwich Observatory 1974–75, Dir 1976–81; Astronomer Royal 1982–90; Visiting Prof. of Astronomy, Univ. of Sussex 1975–81; Sec. Royal Astronomical Soc. 1964–71, Pres. 1975–77; Sec., Vice-Pres. Royal Soc. 1988–94; Fellow, Downing Coll. 1953–64, Hon. Fellow 1970; Chair. Govs Manchester Grammar School 1987–98; Hon. DSc (Queens Univ., Belfast) 1986, (Keele) 1987, (Birmingham) 1989, (Nottingham) 1990, (Trinity Coll. Dublin) 1990, (Manchester) 1993, (Salford) 2003, (Liverpool) 2003; Royal Medal, Royal Soc. 1987, Glazebrook Medal, Inst. of Physics 1991. *Publications:* Radio Astronomy 1960, Optics (with J.H. Thomson) 1971, Pulsars 1977, Pathways to the Universe (with Sir Bernard Lovell) 1988, Introduction to Radioastronomy (with B.F. Burke) 1997, Pulsar Astronomy (with A.G. Lyne) 1990 (3rd edn 2006), Optics and Photonics (with T.A. King) 2000. *Leisure interests:* gardening, beekeeping. *Address:* Old School House, Henbury, Macclesfield, Cheshire, SK11 9PH, England (home). *Telephone:* (1477) 571321 (office); (1625) 612657 (home). *E-mail:* fgs@jb.man.ac.uk (office); fgsegs@btinternet.com (home).

GRAINGE, Lucian Charles; British music company executive; *Chairman and CEO, Universal Music Group International;* b. 1960, London; m.; three c.; song promoter April Music/CBS, later Head Creative Dept 1979–82; Dir and Gen. Man. RCA Music Publishing 1982–84; Dir of A&R MCA Records 1984–86; est. PolyGram Music Publishing UK office 1986–93; Gen. Man. A&R and business affairs, Polydor 1993–97, Man. Dir 1997–2001, following merger of Polygram and Universal promoted to Deputy Chair. Universal Music UK 2001, Chair. and CEO 2001–05, Chair. and CEO Universal Music Group Int. 2005–; Co-Chair. BRITS Cttee 2003–05; Dir BPI; bd mem. Int. Fed. of the Phonographic Industry; Music Industry Trusts Award 2008. *Address:* Universal Music Group International, 1 Sussex Place, London, W6 9XS, England (office). *Website:* www.umusic.co.uk (office).

GRAINVILLE, Patrick; French novelist; b. 1 June 1947, Villers-sur-mer; s. of Jacques Grainville and Suzanne Grainville (née Laquerre); m. Françoise Lutgen 1971; ed Lycée Deauville, Sorbonne; teacher, Lycée de Sartrouville 1975–96; mem. CNRS literature section 1975; Officier, Ordre nat. du Mérite, Ordre des Arts et des lettres. *Publications:* La toison 1972, La lisière 1973, L'abîme 1974, Les flamboyants (Prix Goncourt) 1976, La Diane rousse 1978, Le dernier viking 1980, Les fortresses noires 1982, La caverne céleste 1984, Le paradis des orages 1986, L'atelier du peintre 1988, L'orgie, La neige (Prix Guillaume le Conquérant) 1990, Colère 1992, Mathieu (jtly.) 1993, Les anges et les faucons 1994, Le lien 1996, Le tyran éternel 1998, Le tour de la fin du monde, Une femme me cache 2000, La joie d'Aurélie 2004, La main blessée 2005. *Leisure interests:* travelling, making collages, sculpture. *Address:* c/o Editions du Seuil, 27 rue Jacob, 75261 Paris cedex 06, France.

GRAMM, (William) Philip, PhD; American investment banker and fmr politician; *Vice-Chairman, UBS Warburg LLC;* b. 8 July 1942, Fort Benning, Ga; s. of Kenneth M. and Florence (Scroggins) Gramm; m. Wendy Lee 1970; two s.; ed Univ. of Georgia; mem. of Faculty, Dept of Econs, Texas A&M Univ. 1967–78, Prof. 1973–78; Pnr, Gramm & Assocs 1971–78; mem. US House of Reps, Washington, DC 1979–85; Senator from Texas 1985–2002, fmr Chair. Senate Steering Cttee, Banking, Housing and Urban Affairs Cttee; Vice-Chair. UBS Warburg LLC, Washington, DC 2003–; Republican. *Publications:* The Economics of Mineral Extraction 1980, Role of Government in a Free Society 1982; articles in professional journals. *Address:* UBS AG, Suite 1100, 1501 K Street, NW, Washington, DC 20005 (office); 2323 Bryan Street, Suite 2150, Dallas, TX 75201, USA (home). *Telephone:* (202) 585-4000 (office). *Website:* www.ubs.com (office).

GRAMS, Rod; American radio industry executive and fmr politician; b. 1948; m. Laurel Grams; one s. three d.; ed Univ. of Minn., Brown Inst. Minneapolis and Carroll Coll. Helena, Mont.; eng consultant, Orr-Schelen Mayeron & Assoc. Minneapolis; anchor, producer KFBB-TV, Great Falls, Mont., WSAU-TV, Wausau, Wis., WIFR-TV, Rockford, Ill., KMSP-TV, Minneapolis; Pres. and CEO Sun Ridge Builders; mem. 103rd Congress from 3rd Minn. Dist 1993–95; Senator from Minn. 1995–2001; owns three radio stations in Little Falls, Minn. (WYRQ/KLTF/KFML); Republican. *Address:* Little Falls Radio Corporation, 16405 Haven Road, Little Falls, MN 56345 USA (office). *Telephone:* (320) 632-2992 (office). *Fax:* (320) 632-2571 (office). *Website:* www.fallsradio.com (office).

GRANBERG, Alexander Grigoryevich, DEconSc; Russian economist; *Chairman, Council for the Study of Productive Forces;* b. 25 June 1936, Moscow; m. Tatyana Baranova 1962; one s.; ed Moscow State Econ. Inst.; Sr Economist, USSR State Planning Cttee 1960–63; Prof., Univ. of Novosibirsk 1965–91; Dir Inst. of Econ. and Org. of Production, Siberian Dept, USSR (now Russian) Acad. of Sciences (IEOPP) 1985–91; Corresp. mem. Acad. of Sciences 1984, mem. 1990; Ed.-in-Chief Journal Economics and Organization of Industrial Production 1987–90, Regional Development and Cooperation 1997–; People's Deputy of Russia 1990–93; Chair. Cttee of the Supreme Soviet for Interrepublican Relations and Regional Policy 1990–92; Counsellor to Russian Pres. 1991–93; Chair. Council for the Study of Productive Forces 1992–; Chair. Nat. Cttee on Pacific Econ. Co-operation 1992–99; Prof., Acad. of Nat. Econ. 1993–; Pres. Int. Acad. of Regional Devt and Co-operation 1996–; mem. Comm. for State Prizes under Pres. of Russian Fed.; mem. Scientific Expert Council of Sea Board under Govt of Russian Fed., Chair. 2002–; mem. Econ. Council under Chair. of Goskomsport of Russia; Corresp. mem. Acad. of Spatial Research and Planning of Lands, Germany 1985–; mem. Presidium Russian Acad. of Sciences 2002–; mem. New York Acad. of Sciences 1993; Order 'The Honour Symbol' 1986, Order 'Friendship' 1999, Rank IV Order For Service to the Fatherland 2006; Dr hc (Oscar Lange Acad. of Econs, Poland) 1990; Hon. Prof. (Acad. of Social Sciences, Heilongjiang Prov., China) 2001, (St Petersburg Acad. of Man. and Economy) 2006, V.S. Nemchinov Prize 1990, 'To Free Russia Defender' Medal 1994, State Prize of Russian Fed. 1997, Russian Govt Prize 1999, Hon. Polar Explorer 2001, Hon. Railwayman 2003, Gold Medal, N.D. Kondrat'eva, Int. Fund Kondrat'eva, Nat. Ecological Prize, V.I. Vernadski Fund 2004, L.V. Kantorovich Prize 2008. *Publications:* The Optimization of Territorial Proportions of National Economy 1973, The Russian Federation in the All–Union Economy 1981, Modeling The Socialist Economy 1988, Optimization of Interregional Intersectoral Models 1989, A

Way to the 21st Century 1999, Fundamentals of Regional Economics 2000, Regional Development in Russia: Past Policies and Future Prospects (co-ed.) 2000, Strategy of Macro-regions of Russia: Methodological Approaches, Priorities and Ways of Realization 2004, Multiregional Systems: Economic-Mathematical Research 2007; more than 550 monographs and articles. *Leisure interests:* theatre, skiing, marathon races, travel. *Address:* Council for the Study of Productive Forces, Vavilova Street 7, 117997 Moscow (office); Koroleva str. 8–2, 491, 129515 Moscow, Russia (home). *Telephone:* (495) 135-61-08 (office); (495) 216-41-71 (home). *Fax:* (495) 135-63-39 (office). *E-mail:* granberg@sops.ru (office); granberg@online.ru (home); a-granberg@narod.ru (home). *Website:* www.sops.ru (office); www.a-granberg.narod.ru (home).

GRANCHAROVA, Gergana Hristova, LLM, PhD; Bulgarian politician; *Minister for European Affairs;* b. 14 June 1973, Plovdiv; ed Univ. of Sofia, Asser Coll. of Europe, Belgium; legal asst, Djingov, Gouginsky, Kiuchukov and Velichkov law firm 1995–97; legal consultant, Arthur Andersen Bulgaria 1998–99, Fides Interconsult 1999–2001; mem. Nat. Movt Simeon II (Natsionalno dvizheniye Simeon Vtori); mem. Narodno Sobraniye (Parl.) 2001–, Chair. Pan-European Union, Bulgaria, USA-Bulgaria Relations Cttee 2001–04, Vice-Chair. Nat. Anti-trafficking Cttee 2005–07, mem. Foreign Policy, Defence and Security Cttee, European Integration Cttee, Jt Parl. Cttee Bulgaria-EU 2001–04, mem. Council for Border Control 2005–07; Spokesperson, Ministry of Foreign Affairs 2004–05; Deputy Minister of Foreign Affairs 2004–07; Minister for European Affairs 2007–. *Address:* Ministry for European Affairs, 1040 Sofia, ul. Al. Zhendov 2, Bulgaria (office). *Telephone:* (2) 948-21-06 (office). *Fax:* (2) 973-36-98 (office). *E-mail:* ggrancharova@mfa.government.bg (office). *Website:* www.evroportal.bg (office).

GRANDAGE, Michael; British theatre director; *Artistic Director, Donmar Warehouse;* b. 2 May 1962; ed Humphry Davy Grammar School Cornwall, Cen. School of Speech and Drama; began theatre career as actor 1981–96; full-time dir 1996–, Assoc. Dir Sheffield Theatres (including Sheffield Crucible) 2000–05; Assoc. Dir Donmar Warehouse, London 2000–02, Artistic Dir 2002–; also Visiting Prof., Univ. of Sheffield; Dr hc (Sheffield Hallam Univ.); Best Dir (for As You Like It and Passion Play), Evening Standard Theatre Awards 2000; Best Dir (for As You Like It, Passion Play and Merrily We Roll Along), Critics Circle Awards; Theatre Award (for As You Like It), South Bank Show Awards; Best Dir (for Caligula), Laurence Olivier Awards 2004, Best Dir (for Don Carlos), Evening Standard Theatre Awards 2005, TMA Awards 2005, German-British Forum Award for promoting relations between England and Germany 2005, Sydney Edwards Award for Best Director 2008. *Plays directed include:* Almeida Theatre: The Jew of Malta (also nat. tour), The Doctor's Dilemma (also nat. tour); Sheffield Theatres: Don Carlos, Suddenly Last Summer (also Albery Theatre, London), A Midsummer Night's Dream, The Tempest (also Old Vic, London), Richard III, Don Juan, Edward II, The Country Wife, As You Like It (also Lyric Hammersmith), Twelfth Night, What the Butler Saw; Donmar Warehouse: The Wild Duck, Grand Hotel, Henry IV, After Miss Julie, Caligula, The Vortex, Privates on Parade, Merrily We Roll Along (Olivier Award for Best Musical), Passion Play, Good, Frost/Nixon, Othello, The Chalk Garden; Wyndham's Theatre: Ivanov. *Address:* Donmar Warehouse, 41 Earlham Street, London, WC2H 9LX, England (office). *Telephone:* (20) 7240-4882 (office). *Fax:* (20) 7240-4878 (office). *Website:* www.donmarwarehouse.com (office).

GRANDMONT, Jean-Michel, LèsL, PhD; French economist and researcher; *Director of Research, Centre de Recherche en Économie et Statistique;* b. 22 Dec. 1939, Toulouse; s. of Jancu Wladimir Grunberg and Paule Cassou; m. 1st Annick Duriez 1967 (divorced 1978); m. 2nd Josselyne Bitan 1979; two d.; ed Ecole Polytechnique, Paris, Ecole Nationale des Ponts et Chaussées, Paris, Université de Paris, Univ. of California at Berkeley, USA; Research Assoc., CNRS, Centre d'Etudes Prospectives d'Economie Mathématique Appliquées à la Planification (CEPREMAP) 1970–75, then Dir various research units, Dir of Research, CNRS and CEPREMAP 1987–96, Dir Research Unit, CNRS 928, 'Recherches Fondamentales en Economie Mathématiques' 1991–96, Dir of Research, CNRS and Centre de Recherche en Économie et Statistique (CREST) 1996–; Assoc. Prof., Ecole Polytechnique, Palaiseau 1977–92, Prof. 1992–2004, Chair. Dept of Econs 1997–2000, 2003–04; Prof. (part-time), Yale Univ., USA 1987, 1989–91, 1994; Pres. Econometric Soc. 1990; mem. Academia Europaea 1989–; Hon. mem. American Econ. Asscn; Foreign Hon. mem. American Acad. of Arts and Sciences 1992–; Chevalier, Légion d'honneur 2004; Officier, Palmes académiques 2004; Dr hc (Lausanne) 1990; Alexander von Humboldt Award 1992. *Publications:* Money and Value 1983, Nonlinear Economic Dynamics (ed.) 1987, Temporary Equilibrium (ed.) 1988; articles in scientific econ. journals. *Leisure interests:* skiing, swimming. *Address:* CREST-CNRS, 15 blvd Gabriel Péri, 92245 Malakoff Cedex (office); 55 boulevard de Charonne, Les Doukas 23, 75011 Paris, France (home). *Telephone:* 1-41-17-78-04 (office); 1-43-70-37-28 (home). *Fax:* 1-41-17-60-46 (office). *E-mail:* grandmon@ensae.fr (office). *Website:* www.crest.fr/pageperso/grandmont/grandmont.htm (office).

GRANGE, Kenneth Henry, CBE; British industrial designer; b. 17 July 1929; s. of Harry Alfred Grange and Hilda Gladys Grange (née Long); ed London; tech. illustrator, Royal Engineers 1948–50; design asst, Arcon Chartered Architects 1948; Bronek Katz & Vaughn 1950–51; Gordon Bowyer & Partners 1951–54; Jack Howe & Partners 1954–58; industrial designer, Kenneth Grange Design Ltd (pvt. practice) 1958–; Founding Partner, Pentagram Design 1972–2000; solo shows Victoria and Albert Museum 1974, Tokyo 1985, 'Those That Got Away', London 2003; Pres. Chartered Soc. of Designers 1987–88; Master of Faculty, RDI 1985–87; mem. Bd of Dirs Shakespeare Globe Centre 1997–2002; Hon. Prof., Heriot-Watt Univ. 1987; Hon. DUniv (Heriot-Watt) 1986; Dr hc (RCA) 1985, (De Montfort Univ.) 1998, (Staffordshire Univ.) 1998; ten Design Council Awards, Duke of Edinburgh Award for Elegant Design 1963, Royal Designer for Industry, Royal Soc. of Arts 1969, Chartered Soc. of Designers Gold Medal 1996, Prince Philip Designers' Prize 2001. *Leisure interests:* building. *Address:* 53 Christchurch Hill, London, NW3 1LG, England (home).

GRANGER, Sir Clive W.J., Kt, BA, PhD; British economist and academic; *Professor Emeritus, University of California, San Diego;* b. 4 Sept. 1934, Swansea; ed Univ. of Nottingham; Commonwealth Fellowship, Harkness Funds, Princeton Univ., NJ, USA 1959–60; fmr Lecturer, Nottingham Univ.; Prof. of Econ., Univ. of California, San Diego 1974–2003, Prof. Emer. 2003–; Chancellor's Assocs Chair in Econ. 1994; Distinguished Prof., Canterbury Univ., NZ; Pres. Western Econ. Asscn 2002–03; Fellow, Econometric Soc. 1972–, American Acad. of Arts and Sciences 1994–, Int. Inst. of Forecasters 1996–; Guggenheim Fellow Jan.–June 1988; Corresp. Fellow, British Acad. 2002–; Distinguished Fellow, American Econ. Asscn 2002–; Foreign mem. Finnish Soc. of Arts and Science 1997–; Hon. Fellow (Swansea) 2005, (Trinity Coll., Cambridge) 2005; Hon. DSc (Nottingham) 1992; Dr hc (Univ. Carlos III, Madrid) 1996, (Stockholm School of Econs) 1998; Hon. DSc (Loughborough) 2002; Nobel Prize in Econs 2003 (jt recipient). *Publications include:* Spectral Analysis of Economic Time Series 1964 (jt author), Forecasting Economic Time Series 1977 (jt author), Modeling Nonlinear Dynamic Relationships 1993 (jt author). *Leisure interests:* walking, body surfing, reading. *Address:* Department of Economics, University of California at San Diego, 9500 Gilman Drive, La Jolla, CA 92093-0508, USA (office). *Telephone:* (858) 534-3383 (office). *Fax:* (858) 534-7040 (office). *E-mail:* cgranger@ucsd.edu (office). *Website:* www.econ.ucsd.edu (office).

GRANHOLM, Jennifer Mulhern, BA, JD; American state official and lawyer; *Governor of Michigan;* b. 5 Feb. 1959, Vancouver, BC, Canada; d. of Civtor Ivar Alfreda and Shirley Alfreda (née Dowden); m. Daniel Granholm Mulhern 1986; one s. two d.; ed Univ. of California, Berkeley, Harvard Univ. Law School; law clerk, Sixth Circuit Court of Appeals, Detroit 1987–88; Exec. Asst Wayne Co. Exec., Detroit 1988–89; Asst US Attorney, Dept of Justice, Detroit 1990–94; Corp. Counsel, Wayne Co. 1994–99, Gen. Counsel Detroit/Wayne Co. Stadium Authority 1996–98; Attorney-Gen. of Michigan 1999–2002; Gov. of Michigan 2003–; Vice-Pres. YWCA Inkster, Mich. 1995–; mem. Detroit Bar Asscn, Leadership Detroit, Womens' Law Asscn, Inc. Soc. of Irish Lawyers; Democrat; Public Servant of the Year, Mich. Asscn of Chiefs of Police, Michigander of the Year, Michigan Jaycees. *Leisure interests:* running, family. *Address:* Office of the Governor, State Capitol Building, POB 30013, Lansing, MI 48909, USA (office). *Telephone:* (517) 373-3400 (office). *Fax:* (517) 335-6863 (office). *Website:* www.michigan.gov/gov (office).

GRANIĆ, Mate, DrSc; Croatian politician and physician; *Chairman and CEO, Magra Ltd;* b. 19 Sept. 1947, Baska Voda; m. Jadranka Granic; one s. two d.; ed Zagreb Univ.; physician, Vuk Vrhovac Inst. for Diabetes Endocrinology and Metabolic Diseases, School of Medicine, Zagreb Univ. 1975–79; Head of Clinical Dept Vuk Vrhovac Inst. 1979–85; Prof., Deputy Dir 1985–89; Vice-Dean, Faculty of Medicine, Zagreb Univ. 1989, Dean 1990; mem. and Vice-Pres. Croatian Democratic Union (HDZ); Deputy Prime Minister 1991–99; concurrently Minister of Foreign Affairs 1993–2000; presidential cand. (HDZ) Jan. 2000; led splinter faction of HDZ to form Democratic Centre Party (Demokratski centar—DC) 2000, Pres. 2000–02, left DC and retd from public life 2003; arrested under corruption charges 2004, charges later dropped; foreign policy adviser to Croatian Party of Rights 2005–; f. MAGRA Ltd consulting co. 2004–. *Publications:* papers and articles on diabetes. *Address:* MAGRA Ltd, Petrinjska 61, Zagreb, Croatia (office). *Telephone:* (1) 4811180 (office); (1) 4810510 (office). *E-mail:* magra@magra-doo.hr (office). *Website:* www.magra-doo.hr (office).

GRANIN, Daniil Aleksandrovich; Russian writer; b. (German Daniil), 1 Jan. 1919, Volya, Kursk; m. R. Mayorova; ed Leningrad Polytechnic Inst.; mem. CPSU 1942–90; engineer 1940–50; first publs 1949; USSR People's Deputy 1989–91; Hon. mem. German Acad. of Arts; Hero of Socialist Labour 1989, Order of Merits for Homeland 1999, Cross of Merit (First Class), Germany 2000. *Publications:* Second Variant 1949, Those Who Seek 1955, The House on Fontanka 1958, After the Wedding 1958, I Challenge the Storm 1962, Selected Works 1978, The Picture 1980, The Blockade Book (with A. Adamovich), 1981, The Leningrad Catalogue 1984, Buffalo 1987, The Clemency 1988, Collected Works (5 Vols) 1989, Our Dear Roman Avdeyevich 1991, The Destroyed Clemency 1993, The Escape to Russia 1995, Fear 1997, Evenings with Peter the Great 2000. *Address:* Brat'yev Vasilyevich Str. 8, Apt. 14, 197046 St Petersburg, Russia (home). *Telephone:* (812) 232-85-53.

GRANN, Phyllis, BA; American publisher and editor; *Senior Editor, Doubleday;* b. 2 Sept. 1937, London, UK; d. of Solomon Grann and Louisa (Bois-Smith) Eitingon; m. Victor Grann 1962; two s. one d.; ed Barnard Coll.; Sec., Doubleday Publrs., New York 1958–60; Ed., William Morrow Inc., New York 1960–62, David McKay Co., New York 1962–70, Simon & Schuster Inc., New York 1970; Vice-Pres. Simon & Schuster Inc. 1976; Pres., Publr G. P. Putnam's & Sons, New York 1976–86; Pres. Putnam Publishing Group Inc. (now Penguin Putnam Inc.), New York 1986–96, CEO 1987–96, Chair. 1997–2001; Vice-Chair. Random House, Inc. 2001–02; Sr Ed., Doubleday 2003–; Dir, Warner Music Group Corpn 2006–. *Address:* Doubleday Books, Random House, Inc., 1745 Broadway, New York, NY 10019, USA (office). *Website:* www.randomhouse.com/doubleday (office).

GRANÖ, Olavi Johannes, PhD; Finnish geographer and academic; *Professor Emeritus of Geography, Turku University;* b. 27 May 1925, Helsinki; s. of Prof. Dr J. Gabriel Granö and Hilma Ekholm; m. Eeva Kaleva 1953; two d.; ed Turku, Helsinki and Copenhagen Univs; Asst Prof. of Geography, Helsinki Univ. and Helsinki School of Econs 1948–57; Assoc. Prof. of Geography, Turku Univ. 1958–61, Prof. 1962–88, Chancellor 1984–94, currently Prof. Emer. of

Geography; Pres. Archipelago Research Inst. 1965–84; Pres. Finnish Nat. Research Council for Sciences 1964–69; Pres. Cen. Bd of Research Councils (Acad. of Finland) 1970–73; mem. Science Policy Council 1964–74; Pres. Advisory Cttee for Research of Nordic Council of Ministers 1976–82; Fellow Acad. of Finland 1980–; mem. Finnish Acad. of Science and Letters 1970; (Chair. 1993–95); mem. Royal Swedish Acad. of Sciences 1985, Academia Europaea 1989; Visiting Fellow, Clare Hall, Cambridge Univ. 1982; Hon. Corresp. mem. Royal Geographical Soc. (London) 1980; Hon. mem. Geographical Soc. of S. Sweden 1981, Geographical Soc. of Turku 1991, Students' Union of Turku Univ. 1992, Geographical Soc. of Finland 2001, Finnish Soc. for the History of Science and Learning 2005; Hon. Pres. Finnish Inst. of Migration 1999; Hon. Fellow Acad. of Finland; Dr hc (Toruń, Poland) 1980, (Tartu, Estonia) 1989, (Åbo Academy, Turku) 1993; Finnish Geographical Soc. Fennia Medal 1988, Hon. award Finnish Acad. of Science and Letters 1993. *Publications:* scientific publications on geography, geology, history of science and science policy. *Address:* Department of Geography, Turku University, 20014 Turku (office); Sirppitie 1A, 20540 Turku, Finland (home). *Telephone:* (2) 3335595 (office); (2) 2370640 (home). *Fax:* (2) 3335896 (office). *E-mail:* olavi .grano@utu.fi (office); olavi.grano@nic.fi (home). *Website:* www.sci.utu.fi/ maantiede (office).

GRANT, B. Rosemary, PhD, FRS; British evolutionary biologist and academic; *Senior Research Scholar and Professor, Department of Ecology and Evolutionary Biology, Princeton University;* b. (Barbara Rosemary Matchett), 8 Oct. 1936, Arnside, England; m. Peter R. Grant; two d.; ed Univ. of Edinburgh, Uppsala Univ., Sweden; Research Assoc., Univ. of British Columbia, Canada 1960–64, Yale Univ. 1964–65, McGill Univ., Montreal, Canada 1973–77, Univ. of Michigan 1977–85; Research Scholar and Lecturer, Princeton Univ. 1985–96, Sr Research Scholar and Prof. 1997–; Visiting Prof., Univ. of Zürich, Switzerland 2002, 2003; Foreign Fellow, RSC 2004; mem. American Acad. of Arts and Sciences 1997–, Gen. Ass. Charles Darwin Foundation 2002; carried out, with Peter R. Grant, extensive research into evolution, ecology and behaviour amongst Darwin's finches of the Galápagos Islands from 1973; Hon. Fellow, Deutsche Ornithologen-Gesellschaft 2003; Dr hc (McGill Univ.) 2000, (Universidad San Francisco, Quito) 2005; (with Peter Grant) Leidy Medal, Acad. of Natural Sciences of Philadelphia 1994, E.O. Wilson Prize, American Soc. of Naturalists 1998, Darwin Medal, Royal Soc. of London 2002, Loye and Alden Miller Award, Cooper Ornithological Soc. 2003, Grinnell Award, Univ. of California, Berkeley 2003, A.I.B.S Outstanding Scientist Award 2005, Balzan Prize in Population Biology 2005, Darwin-Wallace Medal (bestowed every 50 years by the Linnean Soc. of London) 2008. *Publications:* Evolutionary Dynamics of a Natural Population: The Large Cactus Finch of the Galápagos (with Peter R. Grant) (Wildlife Soc.'s Wildlife Publication Award 1991) 1989; more than 70 publs in scientific journals. *Address:* Department of Ecology and Evolutionary Biology, Princeton University, Princeton, NJ 08544-1003, USA (office). *Telephone:* (609) 258-6290 (office). *Fax:* (609) 258-1334 (office). *E-mail:* rgrant@princeton.edu (office). *Website:* www.eeb.princeton.edu (office).

GRANT, Bruce Alexander, BA; Australian writer and diplomatist; b. 4 April 1925, Perth; s. of Leslie John Grant and Myrtle Rapson Williams; ed Perth Modern School, Univ. of Melbourne, Harvard Univ.; served Royal Australian Navy 1943–45; with The Age 1950–65, Film, Theatre Critic and Literary Ed. 1950–53, Foreign Corresp., Europe 1954–57, Asia 1959–63, Wash. 1964–65; Fellow in Political Science Univ. of Melbourne 1965–68, Visiting Fellow 1976; columnist 1968–72; High Comm. to India (also accred to Nepal) 1973–76; Research Assoc. Int. Inst. for Strategic Studies., London 1977; Dir Inst. Political Science 1979; Dir, then Chair. Australian Dance Theatre 1979–82; Writer-in-Residence, Monash Univ. 1981; Adviser on Arts Policy, State Govt of Victoria 1982–86; Visiting Fellow, ANU, Canberra 1983; Pres. Melbourne Spoleto Festival of Three Worlds 1984–87; Chair. Victorian Premier's Literary Awards 1984–86, Victorian Australian Bicentennial Authority 1985–86; Consultant to Minister for Foreign Affairs and Trade 1988–91; Chair. Australia-Indonesia Inst. 1989–92; Prof. of Diplomacy and Statecraft, Dept of Man., Monash Univ. 1994–2001; Hon. DLitt (Monash) 2003. *Publications:* Indonesia 1964, The Crisis of Loyalty 1972, Arthur and Eric 1977, The Boat People 1979, Cherry Bloom 1980, Gods and Politicians 1982, The Australian Dilemma 1983, What Kind of Country? 1988, Australia's Foreign Relations (with Gareth Evans) 1991, The Budd Family 1995, A Furious Hunger: America in the 21st Century 1999, What Kind of World? 2001; The Great Pretender at the Bar of Justice (in Best Australian Essays) 2002; numerous short stories, articles and chapters in books on int. affairs. *Leisure interests:* films, theatre, Asian literature, swimming. *Address:* c/o Curtis Brown (Australia) Pty Ltd, 19 Union Street, Sydney, NSW 2021, Australia (office).

GRANT, Hugh, MSc, MBA; British bioengineering industry executive; *Chairman, President and CEO, Monsanto Company;* ed Univs of Glasgow and Edinburgh, Int. Man. Centre, Buckingham; joined Monsanto as product devt rep. for co.'s agricultural business in 1981, led Monsanto's marketing, sales and tech. orgs in Europe and North America, later Man. Dir all Monsanto business units in SE Asia, Australia and NZ, later Exec. Vice-Pres. and COO Monsanto Co. –2003, Chair., Pres. and CEO 2003–, Chair. Exec. Cttee; mem. Int. Advisory Bd Scottish Enterprise, Civic Progress, Pres.'s Advisory Group of CropLife International, Bd Biotechnology Industry Org., Bd of Trustees Donald Danforth Plant Science Centre. *Address:* Monsanto Company, 800 North Lindbergh Boulevard, St Louis, MO 63167, USA (office). *Telephone:* (314) 694-1000 (office). *Fax:* (314) 694-8394 (office). *Website:* www.monsanto .com (office).

GRANT, Hugh John Mungo, BA; British actor; b. 9 Sept. 1960, London; s. of James Murray Grant and the late Fynvola Susan Grant (née Maclean); ed Latymer Upper School, Hammersmith, New College, Oxford; acting in theatre, TV and films and producer for Simian Films; began career in theatre performing Jockeys of Norfolk (written with Chris Lang and Andy Taylor); Best Actor, Venice Film Festival (jtly with James Wilby q.v.) 1987, Golden Globe Award and BAFTA Award for Best Actor in Four Weddings and a Funeral 1995, Peter Sellers Award for Comedy, Evening Standard British Film Awards for Four Weddings 1995, Notting Hill 2000 and Bridget Jones' Diary 2002, Best British Actor, Empire Film Awards for Notting Hill 2000, About a Boy 2003, London Critics Circle Film Awards Best British Actor for About a Boy 2003, BAFTA/LA Stanley Kubrick Britannia Award 2003. *Films include:* White Mischief 1987, Maurice 1987, Lair of the White Worm 1988, La Nuit Bengali 1988, Impromptu 1989, Bitter Moon 1992, Remains of the Day 1993, Four Weddings and a Funeral 1994, Sirens 1994, The Englishman Who Went up a Hill But Came down a Mountain 1995, Nine Months 1995, An Awfully Big Adventure 1995, Sense and Sensibility 1995, Restoration 1996, Extreme Measures (for Simian Films) 1996, Mickey Blue Eyes (for Simian Films) 1998, Notting Hill 1999, Small Time Crooks 2000, Bridget Jones' Diary 2001, About a Boy 2002, Two Weeks' Notice 2002, Love Actually 2003, Bridget Jones: The Edge of Reason 2004, American Dreamz 2006, Music and Lyrics 2006. *Leisure interest:* golf. *Address:* c/o Simian Films, 3 Cromwell Place, London, SW7 2JE, England (office). *Telephone:* (20) 7589-6822. *Fax:* (20) 7589-9405.

GRANT, Sir John Douglas Kelso, Kt, KCMG, BA; British diplomatist; *Permanent Representative, European Union;* b. 17 Oct. 1954; s. of Douglas Marr Kelso Grant and Audrey Stevenson Grant (née Law); m. Anna Maria Lindvall; one s. two d.; ed Edinburgh Acad., St Catharine's Coll., Cambridge; joined FCO 1976, W African Dept 1976–77, Third Sec. (later Second Sec.), Chancery, British Embassy, Stockholm 1977–80, Russian Language Training 1980–81, First Sec., Commercial, British Embassy, Moscow 1982–84, Desk Officer, Soviet Dept, FCO, London 1984–85, Press Office, FCO 1986–89, Press Spokesman (later First Sec. External Relations), UK Rep. Office, Brussels 1989–93, European Secr., Cabinet Office 1993–94, Counsellor, External Relations, UK Rep. Office, Brussels 1994–97, Prin. Pvt. Sec., Sec. of State's Office, London 1997–99, Amb. to Sweden 1999–2003, Perm. Rep. to EU 2003–; Morgan Grenfell and Co. Ltd 1985–86. *Leisure interests:* walking, cross-country skiing. *Address:* UK Permanent Representation to the EU, 10 ave D'Auderghem, Brussels 1040, Belgium (office). *Telephone:* (2) 287-82-71 (office). *Fax:* (2) 287-83-83 (office). *Website:* ukrep.be (office).

GRANT, Keith Frederick, NDD, ARCA; British landscape painter, muralist and lecturer; b. (Frederick Nall), 10 Aug. 1930, Liverpool; adopted s. of Charles Grant and Gladys Emma Grant; m. 1st Gisèle Barka Djouadi 1964 (divorced 1999); one s. (deceased) one d.; m. 2nd Hilde Ellingsen 2000; one d.; ed Bootle Grammar School, Willesden School of Art and RCA, London; State Scholarship to Norway 1960; Head of Fine Art Dept, Maidstone Coll. of Art, Kent 1968–71; Gulbenkian Award Artist-in-Residence, Bosworth Coll., Leics. 1973–75; mem. Fine Art Bd CNAA 1978–81; Head of Painting Dept, Newcastle Polytechnic 1979–81; Head of Dept of Art, The Roehampton Inst., London 1981–90, Artist-in-Residence 1990–95; Expedition Artist to Guyana 1991; Art Dir Operation Raleigh 1991–95; solo shows in London 1960– and shows in Iceland, Norway, France, Italy and Luxembourg; recorded volcanic eruption, Iceland 1973; painted launch of Ariane Rocket 1982; visited Soviet Union for Anglo-Soviet cultural exchange programme of the British Council 1979; other British Council tours to Cyprus 1976, Hungary, Cuba 1985 and Norway 1987; visited Sarawak 1984 and 1985; designed prints for use in Earthlife Foundation's Rainforest Campaign; designed book covers for 6 Peter Mattheissen works 1988–89; visited Greenland to study icebergs at Ilulissat (Jakobshavn); Guest Artist, Ben Gurion Univ. of the Negev and British Israel Art Foundation 1988; elected mem. Telemark Artists' Asscn, Norway 1996; mem. Royal Cambrian Acad. 2001; selected to inaugurate Artists' and Writers' Programme Antarctica 2001/2002 of the British Antarctic Survey; Silver Medal for Mural Painting, RCA 1958. *Works:* works in many public collections including Arts Council of GB, Nat. Gallery of NZ, Nat. Gallery of S Australia, Hamilton Art Gallery, Ontario, Trondheim Art Gallery, Norway, Contemporary Art Soc., Fitzwilliam Museum, Cambridge, Abbot Hall Gallery, Kendal, British Council, All Souls Coll. Oxford, Imperial Coll. London, Victoria and Albert Museum, Richmond College, London, Univ. of E Anglia, Haugesund Art Gallery, Norway, Nat. Gallery of Iceland; mural/mosaics, stained glass window, Charing Cross Hosp., London, Gateshead Metro Station; painting, Guildhall School of Music and Drama, London, Avaldsnes triptych, Karmøy Kommune, Norway; sculpture, Shaw Theatre, London; commissioned to paint triptych for Church of Kopervik, Karmøy, Norway 2004. *Publications:* journals and sketchbooks 1960s–, archived in Fitzwilliam Museum, Cambridge. *Leisure interests:* walking, music, travel and writing. *Address:* Gamlegata, PO Box 7, 3834 Gvarv, Telemark, Norway (home and studio). *Telephone:* 35959795 (studio).

GRANT, Malcolm, CBE, LLB, LLM, LLD, AcSS; New Zealand university administrator, barrister, environmental lawyer, academic and public servant; *President and Provost, University College London;* b. 29 Nov. 1947, Oamaru; s. of Frank Grant and Vera Grant; m. Christine Grant (née Endersbee) 1974; three c.; ed Univ. of Otago; barrister and solicitor, NZ 1969–; barrister, Middle Temple 1998–, Bencher 2004–; Lecturer in Law, Univ. of Southampton 1982–86; Prof. of Law and Vice-Dean, Univ. Coll. London 1986–91, Pres. and Provost 2003–; Prof. of Land Economy and Fellow, Clare Coll., Cambridge 1991–2003, Head, Dept of Land Economy 1993–2001, Pro-Vice-Chancellor Univ. of Cambridge 2002–03; Specialist Adviser, Parl. Jt Cttee on Pvt. Bill Procedure 1987–88; Chair. Asscn of London Govt's Ind. Panel on Remuneration of Councillors in London 1998–2005, Agric. and Environment Biotechnology Comm. 2000–05, UK Ind. Steering Bd for Public Debate on Genetic Modification 2002–03, The Russell Group of UK Research Univs 2006–, Standards Cttee, Greater London Authority 2004–08 (Ind. mem. 2000–08,

Deputy Chair. 2001–04); mem. Local Govt Comm. for England 1992–2002 (Deputy Chair. 1995–96, Chair. 1996–2002), Advisory Bd Environmental Law Foundation 1993–, The Ditchley Foundation 2003– (Gov. 2002–), Compulsory Purchase Policy Review Advisory Group, Dept of Environment, Transport and the Regions 1999–2000; consultant, Singapore Govt 1992–98, UNESCO 1993–94; Ed. Encyclopedia of Planning Law and Practice (seven vols) 1981–2006; Jt Ed. and subsequently Consultant Ed. Encyclopedia of Environmental Law (eight vols) 1993–; Academician, Acad. of Learned Socs for the Social Sciences 2000; Hon. mem. Royal Town Planning Inst. 1993– (mem. Council 1998–2001), Royal Inst. of Chartered Surveyors 1995– (mem. Governing Council 1997–2001, Int. Governing Council 2001–03); Hon. Life mem. NZ Resource Man. Law Asscn 1999–; Officier, Ordre nat. du Mérite 2004; Dr hc (Otago) 2006. *Publications:* Planning Law Handbook 1981, Urban Planning Law 1982, Rate Capping and the Law 1984, The Local Government Finance Act 1988, Permitted Development 1989, The Concise Lexicon of Environmental Terms (co-author) 1995, Singapore Planning Law 1999, The Environmental Court Project: Final Report 2000; numerous articles on planning and environmental law, regulation of biotechnology, local govt structures, finance and political man., central-local govt relations, human rights, property and participation, and environmental dispute resolution. *Address:* Provost's Office, University College London, Gower Street, London, WC1E 6BT, England (office). *Telephone:* (20) 7679-7234 (office). *Fax:* (20) 7388-5412 (office). *E-mail:* provost@ucl.ac.uk (office). *Website:* www.ucl.ac.uk/provost (office).

GRANT, Peter James, CBE; British business executive; *Deputy Chairman, London Merchant Securities;* b. 5 Dec. 1929; s. of the late Lt-Col P. C. H. Grant and Mrs Grant (née Gooch); m. 1st Ann Pleydell-Bouverie; one s. one d.; m. 2nd Paula Eugster; one s. two d.; ed Winchester Coll. and Magdalen Coll., Oxford; Lt Queen's Own Cameron Highlanders; joined Edward de Stein & Co. 1952, merged with Lazard Brothers & Co., Ltd 1960, Dir 1968–85, deputy Chair. 1985–88; Dir Standard Industrial Group 1966–72, Charrington, Gardner, Lockett & Co. Ltd 1970–74, Walter Runciman PLC 1973–90; Dir Sun Life Assurance Soc. PLC 1973–, Vice-Chair. 1976, Chair. 1983–95; Chair. PaineWebber Int. (UK) Ltd 1988–90, Highlands & Islands Airports Ltd 1993–2001; Deputy Chair. LEP Group PLC 1988; Dir London Merchant Securities 1985– (Deputy Chair. 1994–), Scottish Hydro-Electric PLC 1990–94; mem. Industrial Devt Bd 1985–92, Council and Policy Exec. Cttee, Inst. of Dirs 1989–99, Civil Aviation Authority 1993–95, Cromarty Firth Port Authority 1994–2000, Chair. 2000. *Leisure interests:* shooting, golf, gardening. *Address:* 33 Robert Adam Street, London, W1M 5AH, England (office); Mountgerald, nr Dingwall, Ross-shire, IV15 9TT, Scotland. *Telephone:* (1349) 62244.

GRANT, Peter Raymond, PhD, FRS, FRSC, FLS, FAAS; British biologist and academic; *Class of 1877 Professor, Department of Ecology and Evolutionary Biology, Princeton University;* b. 26 Oct. 1936, London; s. of Frederick Thomas Charles Grant and Mavis Irene Grant; m. Barbara Rosemary Matchett 1962; two d.; ed Univ. of Cambridge and Univ. of British Columbia, Canada; Postdoctoral Fellowship, Yale Univ. 1964–65; Asst Prof. of Biology, McGill Univ., Canada 1965–68, Assoc. Prof. 1968–73, Prof. 1973–78; Prof., Univ. of Michigan 1978–85; Prof. of Biology, Princeton Univ. 1985–89, Class of 1877 Prof., Dept of Ecology and Evolutionary Biology 1989–; Fellow, American Acad. of Arts and Science; mem. American Philosophical Soc. 1991; Dr hc (Uppsala) 1986, Hon. DSc (McGill) 2000, Hon. PhD (San Francisco, Ecuador) 2005, (Zurich) 2008; Royal Soc. Darwin Medal 2002, Darwin-Wallace Medal (co-recipient with B. Rosemary Grant), Linnean Soc. of London 2008. *Publications:* Ecology and Evolution of Darwin's Finches 1986, Evolutionary Dynamics of a Natural Population: The Large Cactus Finch of the Galápagos (with B. Rosemary Grant) 1989, Evolution on Islands (ed.) 1998, How and Why Species Multiply (with B. Rosemary Grant) 2008. *Leisure interests:* camping, hiking, music and reading. *Address:* Department of Ecology and Evolutionary Biology, Princeton University, Princeton, NJ 08544-003, USA (office). *Telephone:* (609) 258-5156 (office). *Fax:* (609) 258-1334 (office). *E-mail:* prgrant@princeton.edu (office).

GRANT, Richard E., BA; British actor; b. 1957; s. of the late Hendrick Grant and of Leonie Grant; m. Joan Washington; one d.; ed S Africa; grew up in Swaziland. *Stage appearances include:* Man of Mode 1988, The Importance of Being Earnest 1993, A Midsummer Night's Dream 1994, Otherwise Engaged 2005. *Films include:* Withnail and I 1986, How to Get Ahead in Advertising 1989, Warlock 1989, Henry and June 1990, Mountains of the Moon 1990, LA Story 1991, Hudson Hawk 1991, Bram Stoker's Dracula 1992, The Player 1993, The Age of Innocence 1993, Prêt à Porter 1995, Jack and Sarah 1995, Portrait of a Lady 1995, Twelfth Night 1995, The Serpent's Kiss 1996, Food of Love 1996, All For Love 1997, Spice World – The Movie 1997, The Match 1998, A Christmas Carol 1999, Trial and Retribution 1999, Little Vampires 1999, Hildegarde 2000, Gosford Park 2001, Monsieur 'N' 2002, Tooth 2002, Bright Young Things 2003, The Story of an African Farm 2003, Colour Me Kubrick: A True. . .ish Story 2004, Wah-Wah (dir and writer) 2005, Corpse Bride (voice) 2005, Bustin' Bonaparte (video) 2005, Garfield: A Tail of Two Kitties (voice) 2006, Penelope 2006, Jackboots on Whitehall (voice) 2007. *TV appearances include:* Honest, Decent, Legal and True 1986, Here is the News 1989, Suddenly Last Summer 1992, Hard Times 1993, Karaoke 1996, A Royal Scandal 1996, The Scarlet Pimpernel 1998, Hound of the Baskervilles 2002, Posh Nosh 2003, Frasier 2004, Patrick Hamilton: Words, Whisky and Women (video) 2005, Home Farm Twins (series) 2005, Above and Beyond (mini-series) 2005, Marple: Nemesis 2006, Dalziell & Pascoe 2006, The Secret Policeman's Ball 2006, Freezing 2007. *Publications:* With Nails: The Film Diaries of Richard E. Grant 1995, Twelfth Night 1996, By Design – A Hollywood Novel 1998, The Wah-Wah Diaries: The Making of a Film 2006. *Leisure interests:* scuba diving, building dolls' houses, photography. *Address:* c/o ICM, Oxford House, 76 Oxford Street, London, W1N 0AX, England. *Telephone:* (20) 7636-6565. *Fax:* (20) 7323-0101. *Website:* www.richard-e-grant.com (office).

GRAPSAS, Gen. Dimitrios; Greek military officer; *Chief of Defence Staff;* b. 1948, Ypati; m.; two c.; ed Hellenic Army War Coll., Hellenic Nat. Defense Coll.; fmr Commdr Armored Reconnaissance Battalion, Chief of Staff of 96th Mil. Command, Asst Chief of Staff of Higher Mil. Command of Interior and Islands, Commdr XXV Armored Brigade, Army Corps Chief of Staff; Dir Training Div., then Training and Doctrine Directorate, Hellenic Army Gen. Staff 2002–03; Commdr XX Mechanized Infantry Div. 2003–04; promoted to Lt Gen. 2004; Commdr Higher Mil. Command of Interior and Islands 2005–06; Chief of Hellenic Army Gen. Staff 2006–07; Chief of Defence Staff 2007–; Golden Cross, Order of Phoenix, Order of Merit, Kt Commdr, Order of Phoenix, Order of Merit, High Cross of the Order of Phoenix, High Cross of the Order of Merit; Medal for Mil. Valor, C Class, Medal for Mil. Valor, B Class, Outstanding Command Commendation Medal, B Class, Staff Officer Service Commendation Medal, B Class, Medal for Mil. Valor, A Class, Formation/Maj. Unit Commendation Medal, C Class, Outstanding Command Commendation Medal, A Class, Staff Officer Service Commendation Medal, A Class, Commendation Medal for Merit and Valor. *Address:* Ministry of National Defence, Odos Mesogeion 227–231, 154 51 Athens, Greece (office). *Telephone:* (210) 6598607 (office). *Fax:* (210) 6443832 (office). *E-mail:* minister@mod.mil.gr (office). *Website:* www.mod.gr (office).

GRASS, Günter Wilhelm; German writer, poet and artist; b. 16 Oct. 1927, Danzig (now Gdańsk, Poland); m. 1st Anna Schwarz 1954 (divorced 1978); three s. one d.; m. 2nd Ute Grunert 1979; ed Conradinum, Danzig, Kunstakademie, Düsseldorf, Höchschule für Bildende Künste, Berlin; served in Luftwaffe 1944–45; adviser to Städtischen Bühnen Frankfurt am Main 1967–70; mem. Akad. der Künste, Berlin (pres. 1983–86), American Acad. of Arts and Sciences; mem. Social Democratic Party (resgnd Dec. 1992); Dr hc (Kenyon Coll.) 1965, (Harvard) 1976; Lyric Prize, Süddeutscher Rundfunk 1955, Group 47 Prize 1959, Literary Prize, Asscn of German Critics 1960, Georg-Büchner Prize 1965, Theodor-Heuss Prize 1969, Int. Feltrinelli Prize 1982, Karel Čapek Prize 1994, Sonning Arts Prize (Denmark) 1996, Thomas Mann Prize 1996, Hermann Kestan Medal 1995, Nobel Prize for Literature 1999, Premio Príncipe de Asturias 1999. *Plays:* Beritten, hin und zurück 1954, Hochwasser 1954, Die bösen Köche 1957, Noch Zehn Minuten bis Buffalo 1957, Onkel, Onkel 1958, Zweiunddreissig Zähne 1959, Die Plebejer proben den Aufstand 1965, Davor 1968, Die Vogelscheuchen (ballet) 1970. *Publications:* Die Vorzüge der Windhühner (poems, prose and drawings) 1955, Die Blechtrommel (novel, trans. as The Tin Drum) (Award for Best Foreign Novel, France 1962) 1959, Gleisdreieck (poems and drawings) 1960, Katz und Maus (novella, trans. as Cat and Mouse) 1961, Hundejahre (novel, trans. as Dog Years) 1963, Ausgefragt (poems and drawings) 1967, Über das Selbstverständliche 1968, Örtlich betäubt (novel) 1969, Aus dem Tagebuch einer Schnecke 1972, Dokumente zur politischen Wirkung 1972, Mariazuehren (poems and drawings) 1973, Die Bürger und seine Stimme 1974, Der Butt (novel, trans. as The Flounder) 1976, Denkzettel 1978, Das Treffen in Telgte (novel, trans. as The Meeting in Telgte) 1979, Kopfgeburten oder Die Deutschen sterben aus (novel, trans. as Headbirths, or the Germans are Dying Out) 1980, Aufsätze zur Literatur 1980, Zeichnen und Schreiben Band I 1982, Widerstand lernen-Politische Gegenreden 1980–83 1984 Band II 1984, On Writing and Politics 1967–83 1985, Die Rättin (novel) 1986, Züngezeigen 1987, Werkansgabe (10 vols) 1987, Die Gedichte 1955–1986 1988, Deutscher Lastenausgleich: Wider das dumpfe Einheitsgebot 1990, Two States—One Nation? 1990, Vier Jahrzehnte: Ein Werkstattbericht (drawings and notes) 1991, Unkenrufe (novel, trans. as The Call of the Toad) 1992, Rede vom Verlust: Über den Niedergang der politischen Kultur im geiinten Deutschland 1992, Der Ruf der Kröte (novel) 1992, Studienausgabe (12 vols) 1994, Ein weites Feld (trans. as Too Far Afield) 1995, Fundsachen für Nichtleser (poems) 1997, Auf ein anderes Blatt 1999, Vom Abenteuer der Aufklärung (jtly) 1999, Mein Jahrhundert (trans. as My Century) 1999, Nie wieder schweigen 2000, Fünf Jahrzehnte 2001, Im Krebsgang (novel, trans. as Crabwalk) 2002, Telling Tales (contrib. to charity anthology) 2004, Letzte Tänze (watercolours and drawings) 2003, Beim Häuten der Zwiebel (trans as Peeling the Onion, autobiog.) 2006. *Leisure interest:* cooking. *Address:* Glockengiesserstrasse 21, 23552 Lübeck, Germany.

GRASSER, Karl-Heinz, MBA; Austrian fmr politician and business executive; b. 2 Jan. 1969, Klagenfurt; m. Fiona Pacifico Griffini 2005; one d.; ed Univ. of Klagenfurt; mem. Freedom Party (FPÖ), Spokesperson for Tourism and European Integration 1992, FPÖ Sec.-Gen. and Man. Dir Party Educational Centre 1993; Second Deputy Gov. Prov. of Carinthia 1994–98; Vice-Pres. for Human Resources and Public Relations, Magna Europe 1998; Man. Dir Sport Management International 1999; Fed. Minister of Finance 2000–07; mem. Karl Popper Foundation (mem. Man. Bd –1999); Dir Meinl Power Management Ltd. *Address:* c/o Meinl Power Management Ltd, PO Box 75, 26 New Street, St Helier, Jersey, JE4 8PP, Channel Islands (office).

GRASSLEY, Charles Ernest, MA; American politician, farmer and teacher; *Senator from Iowa;* b. 17 Sept. 1933, New Hartford, Ia; s. of Louis Arthur Grassley and Ruth Corwin; m. Barbara Ann Speicher; five c.; ed Univs of Northern Iowa and Iowa; farmer; Instructor Political Science, Drake Community Coll. 1962, Charles City Coll. 1967–68; mem. Ia House of Reps 1959–75; mem. US House of Reps from 3rd Dist, Ia 1975–81; Senator from Iowa 1981–; Chair. Senate Finance Cttee 2001–; mem. Nat. Farm Bureau; Republican. *Address:* 135 Hart Senate Office Building, Washington, DC 20510-0001, USA (office). *Telephone:* (202) 224-3744 (office). *Website:* grassley.senate.gov (office).

GRASSO, Richard A., BS; American fmr stock exchange executive; ed Pace and Harvard Univs; New York Stock Exchange 1968–2003, Dir Listing and

Marketing 1973–77, Vice-Pres. Corp. Services 1977–81, Sr Vice-Pres. Corp. Services 1981–83, Exec. Vice-Pres. Marketing Group 1983–86, Exec. Vice-Pres. Capital Markets 1986–88, Pres., COO 1988–93, Exec. Vice-Chair., Pres. 1993–95, Chair. CEO 1994–2003; Pres. World Federation of Exchanges, Paris 2003; Dir Nat. Italian American Foundation, Police Foundation, Washington.

GRATTAN, Michelle, AO, BA; Australian journalist and political commentator; *Political Editor, The Age newspaper;* b. 30 June 1944, Melbourne; ed Melbourne Univ.; Chief Political Corresp., The Age 1976–93, Political Ed. 1995–96, 2004–, Political Commentator 2002–04; Ed. Canberra Times 1993–95; sr writer and columnist, Australian Financial Review 1996–98; Chief Political Corresp. Sydney Morning Herald 1999–2002, columnist 2002–; currently Adjunct Prof., School of Journalism and Communication, Univ. of Queensland; Graham Perkin Australian Journalist of the Year Award 1988, Walkley Award for Journalism Leadership 2006. *Publications:* Australian Prime Ministers (ed.) 2000, Reconciliation (ed.) 2000. *Address:* The Age, 250 Spencer St (cnr Lonsdale St), Melbourne, Vic. 3000 (office); 147 Mugga Way, Red Hill, Canberra, ACT 2603, Australia (home). *Telephone:* (3) 9600-4211 (office); 6295-6554 (home). *Fax:* (3) 9601-2598 (office). *E-mail:* inquiries@ theage.com.au (office). *Website:* www.theage.com.au (office).

GRAUBNER, Most Rev. Jan; Czech ecclesiastic; *Archbishop of Olomouc;* b. 29 Aug. 1948, Brno; s. of Oldrich Graubner and Ludmila Graubner; ed Univ. of Olomouc; ordained priest 1973; ordained Bishop 1990; Auxiliary Bishop of Olomouc 1990–92, Archbishop of Olomouc 1992–; Vice-Chair. Czech Bishops' Conf. 1991–2000, Chair. 2000–. *Address:* Archdiocese of Olomouc, Wurmova 9, p. schr. 193, 77101 Olomouc, Czech Republic (office). *Telephone:* (58) 7405111 (office). *Fax:* (58) 5224840 (office). *E-mail:* arcibol@arcibol.cz (office). *Website:* www.ado.cz (office).

GRAUERT, Johannes (Hans), Dr rer. nat; German mathematician and academic; *Professor Emeritus, University of Göttingen;* b. 8 Feb. 1930, Haren/ Ems; s. of Clemens Grauert; m. Marie-Luise Meyer 1956; one s. one d.; ed Univs of Mainz and Münster and ETH, Zürich; Inst. for Advanced Study, Princeton 1957–59; Inst. des Hautes Etudes, Paris 1959 (mem. Supervisory Bd 1976–82); Prof. Univ. of Göttingen 1959–95, Prof. Emeritus, 1995–; mem. Acad. of Science, Göttingen (Pres. 1994–96, mem. Acad. of Science and of Literature Mainz, Acad. Leopoldina (Halle Saale), Acad. Mediterranea Catania, Academia Europaea, Acad. of Bayern (von Staudt Prize 1991); Hon. Dr rer. nat (Bayreuth) 1989, (Bochum) 1990, (Bonn) 1990. *Publications:* ten books and numerous papers in leading journals. *Leisure interests:* pure mathematics, philosophy.

GRAVEL, Mike, BS; American organization official and fmr politician; *Chairman, The Democracy Foundation;* b. 13 May 1930, Springfield, Mass.; s. of Alphonse and Maria Gravel; m. Rita Martin 1959; one s. one d.; ed Columbia Univ.; enlisted in US Army 1951-54, served as adjutant in Communications Intelligence Services and Special Agent in Counter Intelligence Corps; real estate developer; mem. Alaska House of Reps 1962–66; Speaker, Alaska House of Reps 1965; US Senator from Alaska 1969–81; f. Mike Gravel Resource Analysts, Anchorage, Alaska 1981–; founder and Chair. Philadelphia II and Direct Democracy (non-profit orgs), merged to create Democracy Foundation; Democrat. *Publications:* Jobs and More Jobs, Citizen Power, The Pentagon Papers (ed.) *Address:* The Democracy Foundation, 1600 North Oak Street, Suite 1412, Arlington, VA 22209-2757, USA (office). *Telephone:* (703) 516-4056 (office). *Fax:* (703) 516-4057 (office). *Website:* ni4d.us (office).

GRAVES, Jennifer (Jenny), BSc, MSc, PhD; Australian geneticist and academic; *Professor of Comparative Genomics and Group Leader, Comparative Genomics, Research School of Biological Sciences, Australian National University;* b. 1941, Adelaide; m.; two d.; ed Univ. of Adelaide, Univ. of California, Berkeley, USA; Lecturer in Genetics, La Trobe Univ. 1971–91, Prof. of Genetics 1991–2001; Prof. of Comparative Genomics and Group Leader, Comparative Genomics Research Group and ARC Centre for Kangaroo Genomics, Research School of Biological Sciences, ANU 2001–; Fellow, Australian Acad. of Science 1999–; Fulbright Scholar, L'Oréal-UNESCO Women in Science Award (Laureate for Asia/Pacific) 2006. *Address:* Comparative Genomics Group, Research School of Biological Sciences, GPO Box 475, Canberra, ACT 2601, Australia (office). *Telephone:* (2) 61252492 (office). *Fax:* (2) 61254891 (office). *E-mail:* graves@rsbs.anu.edu.au (office); jenny .graves@anu.edu.au (office). *Website:* www.rsbs.anu.edu.au/ResearchGroups/ CGG/index.php (office).

GRAVES, Rupert; British actor; b. 30 June 1963, Weston-Super-Mare. *Theatre includes:* Killing Mr Toad, Sufficient Carbohydrates, Torch Song Trilogy, The Importance of Being Earnest, A Midsummer Night's Dream, Madhouse in Goa, The Elephant Man 2002. *Films include:* A Room With A View 1986, Maurice 1987, A Handful of Dust 1988, The Children 1990, The Plot To Kill Hitler 1990, Where Angels Fear To Tread 1991, Damage 1992, Royal Celebration 1993, The Madness of King George 1994, Sheltering Desert 1994, The Innocent Sleep 1995, Intimate Relations (Best Actor, Montreal Film Festival 1996) 1996, Different for Girls 1996, The Revengers' Comedies 1997, Mrs Dalloway 1997, Dreaming of Joseph Lees 1998, Room to Rent 2000, The Extremists 2001, Snake 2001, Rag Tale 2005, V for Vendetta 2006, Death at a Funeral 2007, Intervention 2007, The Waiting Room 2007. *TV includes:* Fortunes of War 1987, Open Fire 1994, Doomsday Gun 1994, The Tenant of Wildfell Hall 1996, Blonde Bombshell 1999, Cleopatra 1999, The Forsyte Saga 2002, Charles II: The Power & the Passion 2003, A Waste of Shame: The Mystery of Shakespeare and His Sonnets 2005, Son of the Dragon 2006, To Be First 2007, Clapham Junction 2007, The Dinner Party 2007. *Website:* www .rupert-graves.com (office).

GRAVES, William Preston; American national organization official and fmr politician; *President and CEO, American Trucking Associations Inc.;* b. 9 Jan.

1953, Salina, Kan.; s. of William Graves and Helen Mayo; m. Linda Richey 1990; one d.; ed Kan. Wesleyan Univ., Salina and Univ. of Kan.; Deputy Asst Sec. of State, Kan. 1980–85, Asst Sec. of State 1985–87, Sec. of State 1987–95; Gov. of Kan. 1995–2003; Pres. and CEO American Trucking Asscns Inc. 2003–; Trustee Kan. Wesleyan Univ. 1987–; mem. Bd of Dirs Int. Speedway Corpn; Republican. *Leisure interests:* running, reading, travel. *Address:* American Trucking Associations Inc., 950 North Glebe Road, Suite 210, Arlington, VA 22203, USA (office). *Telephone:* (703) 838-1700 (office). *Fax:* (703) 838-1994 (office). *Website:* www.truckline.com (office).

GRAY, Alasdair James; British writer and painter; b. 28 Dec. 1934, Glasgow; s. of Alexander Gray and Amy Fleming; m. 1st Inge Sørensen (divorced); one s.; m. 2nd Morag McAlpine 1991; ed Glasgow School of Art; art teacher, Glasgow and Lanarkshire 1958–62; scene painter, Pavilion and Citizens' theatres 1962–63; freelance writer and painter 1963–76; artist recorder, People's Palace Local History Museum, Glasgow 1976–77; Writer-in-Residence, Glasgow Univ. 1977–79; freelance writer and painter 1979–2001; Prof. of Creative Writing, Univ. of Glasgow 2001–2003; painter of mural decorations in Oran Mor Leisure Centre, Glasgow, 2003–; works in collections of People's Palace Local History Museum, Glasgow, Collin's Gallery, Strathclyde Univ., Hunterian Museum, Univ. of Glasgow; mural paintings in Palace Rigg Nature Reserve Exhibition Centre, New Cumbernauld, Abbot's House Local History Museum, Dunfermline, The Ubiquitous Chip Restaurant, Glasgow; mem. Soc. of Authors, Scottish Artists Union; Saltire Soc. Award 1981, Times Literary Supplement Award 1983, Whitbread and Guardian Awards 1992. *Radio plays include:* Quiet People 1968, The Trial of Thomas Muir 1970, Dialogue 1971, Homeward Bound 1973, The Loss of the Golden Silence 1973, McGrothy and Ludmilla 1993, Working Legs 1998. *Television plays include:* The Fall of Kelvin Walker 1967, The Man Who Knew about Electricity 1973, The Story of a Recluse 1987. *Works include:* has designed and illustrated several books including Shoestring Gourmet 1986, Songs of Scotland 1997. *Publications include:* The Comedy of the White Dog (short story) 1979, Lanark: A Life in Four Books (novel) 1981, Unlikely Stories Mostly 1982, Janine (novel) 1984, The Fall of Kelvin Walker (novel) 1985, Lean Tales (co-writer) 1985, Five Scottish Artists (catalogue) 1986, Saltire Self-Portrait 4 (autobiographical sketch) 1988, Old Negatives (four verse sequences) 1989, Something Leather (novel) 1990, McGrotty and Ludmilla (novel) 1990, Poor Things (novel) 1992, Why Scots Should Rule Scotland (polemic) 1992, Ten Tales Tall and True (Short Stories) 1993, A History Maker (novel) 1994, Mavis Belfrage (novel) 1996, Working Legs (play) 1997, The Book of Prefaces 2000, Sixteen Occasional Poems 2000, A Study in Classic Scottish Writing 2001, The Ends of Our Tethers: 13 Sorry Stories 2003, How We Should Rule Ourselves (polemic, with Adam Tomkins) 2005, Old Men in Love 2007, A Life in Pictures (auto-biog.) 2008. *Leisure interests:* reading, walking. *Address:* c/o Zoe Waldie, 20 Powis Mews, London, W11 1JN, England (office); 2 Marchmont Terrace, Glasgow, G12 9LT, Scotland. *Telephone:* (141) 339-0093. *Website:* www.alasdairgray.co.uk.

GRAY, C. Boyden, BA, JD; American lawyer; *Special Envoy for European Union Affairs and Special Envoy for Eurasian Energy;* b. Winston-Salem, N Carolina; ed Harvard Univ., Univ. of N Carolina, Chapel Hill; Ed.-in-Chief the Law Review, Univ. of N Carolina, Chapel Hill; service in US Marine Corps; clerk for Earl Warren, Chief Justice of US Supreme Court 1968–69; Partner, Wilmer, Cutler, Pickering, Hale and Dorr (law firm), Washington, DC 1969–81, 1993–2005; Legal Counsel to US Vice-Pres. George Bush 1981–89, Legal Counsel to Pres. George H. W. Bush 1989–93; Chair. Admin. Law and Regulatory Practice, ABA 2000–02; Amb. to EU, Brussels 2006–07, Special Envoy for EU Affairs Jan. 2008–, Special Envoy for Eurasian Energy March 2008–; fmr mem. Cttee to Visit the Coll. and Cttee on Univ. Devt, Harvard Univ.; has served on bds of numerous charitable, educational and professional orgs; Presidential Citizen's Medal, Univ., Distinguished Alumnus Award, Univ. of N Carolina Law School. *Address:* US Mission to the European Union, Zinnerstraat 13 Rue Zinner, 1000 Brussels, Belgium (office). *Telephone:* (2) 508-22-22 (office). *Fax:* (2) 511-32-35 (office). *E-mail:* useupa@state.gov (office). *Website:* useu.usmission.gov (office).

GRAY, Douglas, MA, FBA; British/New Zealand academic; *Professor Emeritus, Lady Margaret Hall;* b. 17 Feb. 1930, Melbourne, Australia; s. of Emmerson Gray and Daisy Gray; m. Judith Claire Campbell 1959; one s.; ed Wellington Coll. NZ, Victoria Univ. of Wellington, Merton Coll., Oxford; Asst Lecturer, Victoria Univ. of Wellington 1952–54, Lecturer in English, Pembroke and Lincoln Colls, Univ. of Oxford 1956–61, Fellow in English, Pembroke Coll. 1961–80, J. R. R. Tolkien Prof. of English Literature and Language and Fellow, Lady Margaret Hall, Oxford 1980–97, Prof. Emer. 1997–, Hon. Fellow, Lady Margaret Hall 1997–; Hon. LittD (Victoria Univ. of Wellington) 1995. *Publications:* Themes and Images in the Medieval English Lyric 1972, A Selection of Religious Lyrics 1974, Robert Henryson 1979, Oxford Book of Late Medieval Verse and Prose (ed.) 1985, J. A. W. Bennett, Middle English Literature (ed.) 1986, From Anglo-Saxon to Early Middle English (jt ed.) 1994, Selected Poems of Robert Henryson and William Dunbar (ed.) 1998, Oxford Companion to Chaucer (ed.) 2003, Later Medieval English Literature 2008. *Leisure interests:* travel, walking. *Address:* 31 Nethercote Road, Tackley, Oxford, OX5 3AW, England (home). *Telephone:* (1869) 331319 (home).

GRAY, Dulcie Winifred Catherine, CBE, FRSA, FLS; British actress, playwright and author; b. (Dulcie Savage-Bailey), 20 Nov. 1920, Kuala Lumpur, Federated Malay States (now Malaysia); d. of the late Arnold Savage-Bailey and Kate Edith Clulow Gray; m. Michael Denison (deceased) 1939; ed England and Malaya; has worked in theatre and films since 1939; repertory includes Aberdeen, Edin., Glasgow, Harrogate; debut as Sorrel in Hay Fever 1939; Queen's Silver Jubilee Medal 1977. *Theatre includes:* The

Little Foxes, Midsummer Night's Dream 1942, Brighton Rock, Landslide 1943, Lady from Edinburgh 1945, Dear Ruth, Wind is 90 1946, Queen Elizabeth Slept Here 1949, Sweet Peril 1952, We Must Kill Toni, The Diary of a Nobody 1954, Love Affair (also writer) 1956, Double Cross 1958, Let Them Eat Cake 1959, Candida 1960, Heartbreak House 1961, Where Angels Fear to Tread 1963, An Ideal Husband 1965, Happy Family 1967, Number 10 1967, Out of the Question 1968, Three 1970, The Wild Duck 1970, Ghosts 1972, At the End of the Day 1973, Time and the Conways (tour) 1977, A Murder is Announced 1977, Lloyd George Knew my Father (tour) 1980, A Coat of Varnish 1982, School for Scandal (British Council 50th Anniversary European Tour) 1983, The Living Room 1987, The Best of Friends (tour) 1990, 1991, The Importance of Being Earnest (tour) 1991, Tartuffe 1991–92, Two of a Kind (tour) 1995, The Ladykillers (tour) 1999, Les Liaisons Dangereuses (tour) 2000, The Lady Vanishes (tour) 2001. *Films include:* They Were Sisters 1944, Wanted for Murder 1945, A Man about the House 1946, Mine Own Executioner 1947, The Glass Mountain 1948, There Was a Young Lady 1953, A Man Could Get Killed 1965, The Black Crow 1994. *Radio includes:* Front Line Family (BBC serial) 1941; numerous plays. *Television includes:* Howards' Way (series) 1985–90, several plays. *Publications:* Murder on the Stairs, Murder in Melbourne, Baby Face, Epitaph for a Dead Actor, Murder on a Saturday, Murder in Mind, The Devil Wore Scarlet, No Quarter for a Star, The Murder of Love, Died in the Red, The Actor and His World (with Michael Denison), Death in Denims, Butterflies on my Mind (Times Educational Supplement Sr Information Book Prize 1978), Dark Calypso, The Glanville Women, Anna Starr, Mirror Image, Looking Forward, Looking Back (autobiog.), J.B. Priestly (biog.). *Leisure interests:* swimming, butterflies. *Address:* Shardeloes, Missenden Road, Amersham, Bucks., HP7 0RL, England (home). *Telephone:* (1494) 725555 (home).

GRAY, George William, CBE, PhD, FRS, CChem, FRSC, FRSE; British chemist and academic; *Visiting Professor, University of Southampton;* b. 4 Sept. 1926, Edinburgh; s. of John William Gray and Jessie Colville (née Hunter); m. Marjorie Mary Canavan; three d.; ed Univs of Glasgow and London; mem. staff, Dept of Chem., Univ. of Hull 1946–, Sr Lecturer 1960, Reader 1964, Prof. of Organic Chem. 1978–84, G. F. Grant Prof. of Chem. 1984–90; Research Co-ordinator E. Merck Ltd 1990–93, Consultant 1993–; Emer. Prof. Univ. of Hull, Visiting Prof., Univ. of Southampton 1990–; Ed. Liquid Crystals 1992–2002; Foreign mem. Japanese Acad. of Eng 1996; Hon. MRIA; Hon. DSc (Hull) 1991, (Nottingham Trent) 1994, (Southampton) 1996, (E Anglia) 1997, (Aberdeen) 2001, (Exeter) 2002; Queen's Award for Technological Achievement 1979, 1992, Rank Prize for Optoelectronics 1980, Leverhulme Medal of Royal Soc. 1987, Royal Soc. of Chemistry Fine Chemicals Award 1992, Kyoto Prize Laureate in Advanced Tech. 1995, Karl Ferdinand Braun Medal of Soc. for Information Display 1996, Freedericksz Medal of Russian Liquid Crystal Soc. 1997. *Publications:* Molecular Structure and the Properties of Liquid Crystals 1962, Liquid Crystals and Plastic Crystals (ed. and jtly with P.A. Winsor) 1974, The Molecular Physics of Liquid Crystals (ed. and jtly with G.R. Luckhurst) 1979, Smectic Liquid Crystals – Textures and Structures (with J.W. Goodby) 1984, Thermotropic Liquid Crystals (ed.) 1987, Handbook of Liquid Crystals (four vols) (jt ed.) 1998; 350 papers on liquid crystals in scientific journals. *Leisure interests:* gardening, philately. *Address:* Juniper House, Furzehill, Wimborne, Dorset, BH21 4HD, England. *Telephone:* (1202) 880164. *Fax:* (1202) 840702. *E-mail:* ggray83828@aol.com.

GRAY, Harry Barkus, PhD; American chemist and academic; *Arnold O. Beckman Professor of Chemistry and Founding Director, Beckman Institute, California Institute of Technology;* b. 14 Nov. 1935, Kentucky; m. Shirley Barnes 1957; two s. one d.; ed Northwestern Univ. and Univ. of Copenhagen; Asst Prof. of Chem., Columbia Univ. 1961–63, Assoc. Prof. 1963–65, Prof. 1965–66; Prof. of Chem., California Inst. of Tech. 1966–, now Arnold O. Beckman Prof. and Founding Dir Beckman Inst.; mem. NAS, American Acad. of Arts and Sciences; Foreign mem. Royal Soc., Royal Danish Soc. of Science and Letters; Franklin Award 1967, Fresenius Award 1970, ACS Award in Pure Chem. 1970, Harrison Howe Award 1972, MCA Award 1972, Guggenheim Fellow 1972–73, ACS Award in Inorganic Chem. 1978, Remsen Award 1979, Tolman Award 1979, Centenary Medal 1985, Nat. Medal of Science 1986, Pauling Medal 1986, Calif. Scientist of the Year 1988, Alfred Bader Award 1990, Gold Medal, American Inst. of Chemists 1990, Waterford Prize 1991, Priestley Medal 1991, Gibbs Medal 1992, Linderstrøm-Lang Prize 1992, Chandler Medal, Columbia Univ. 1999, Harvey Prize, Technion Israel Inst. of Tech. 2000, NAS Award in Chemical Sciences 2003, Wolf Prize 2004. *Publications:* Electrons and Chemical Bonding 1965, Molecular Orbital Theory 1965, Ligand Substitution Processes 1966, Basic Principles of Chemistry 1967, Chemical Dynamics 1968, Chemical Principles 1970, Models in Chemical Science 1971, Chemical Bonds 1973, Electronic Structure and Bonding 1981, Molecular Electronic Structures 1980, Braving the Elements 1995. *Leisure interests:* tennis, music. *Address:* Noyes Laboratory of Chemical Physics, 408 Beckman, California Institute of Technology, Mail Code 127-72, 1200 East California Blvd, Pasadena, CA 91125-0001 (office); 1415 East California Boulevard, Pasadena, CA 91106-4101, USA (home). *Telephone:* (626) 395-6500 (office); (626) 793-1978 (home). *E-mail:* hbgray@caltech.edu (office). *Website:* www.cce.caltech.edu/faculty/gray/index.html (office).

GRAY, Rt Hon. Herb E., CC, PC, QC, BComm, LLD; Canadian politician; *Chairman, Canadian Section, International Joint Commission of Canada and the United States;* b. 25 May 1931, Windsor, Ont.; s. of the late Harry Gray and of Fannie Gray; m. Sharon Sholzberg 1967; one s. one d.; ed Victoria Public School, Kennedy Coll. Inst. Windsor, McGill Univ., Montreal and Osgoode Hall Law School, Toronto; MP 1962–2002; Chair. of House of Commons Standing Cttee on Finance, Trade and Econ. Affairs 1966–68; Parl. Sec. to Minister of Finance 1968–69; Minister without Portfolio (Finance) 1969–70, Minister of Nat. Revenue 1970–72, of Consumer and Corp. Affairs 1972–74, of Industry, Trade and Commerce 1980–82, of Regional Econ. Expansion Jan.–Oct. 1982; Pres. of Treasury Bd 1982–84; Opposition House Leader 1984–90, Deputy Opposition Leader 1989–90, Leader of the Opposition 1990, Opposition Finance Critic 1991–93; Solicitor Gen. and Leader of the Govt in House of Commons 1993–97; Deputy Prime Minister 1997–2002; given responsibility for co-ordinating Govt of Canada's activities to mark new Millennium 1998–2000; Chair. Canadian section Int. Jt Comm. of Canada and the United States 2002–; Govt Observer Inter-American Conf. of Ministers of Labour, Bogotá 1963; Vice-Chair. Del. to NATO Parl. Conf., Paris 1963; mem. Del. to Canada–France Interparliamentary Conf. 1966; mem. Canadian Del. to IMF and IBRD meeting 1967, Canada–US Interparliamentary Conf. 1967–68; Dr hc (Univ. of Windsor), (Assumption Univ., Windsor), (Catholic Univ. of Lublin, Poland), (McGill Univ.), (Univ. of Ottawa); B'nai Brith Award of Merit, Centennial Medal Queen's Silver Jubilee Medal, Canada 125 Medal, Queen's Golden Jubilee Medal, John Fraser Award for Environmental Achievement, Sierra Club of Canada; Ordre de la Pléiade (Officier). *Address:* International Joint Commission of Canada and the United States, 234 Laurier Avenue West, 22nd Floor, Ottawa, Ont., K1P 6K6 (office); 1504–75 Riverside Drive East, Windsor, Ont., N9A 7C4, Canada (home). *Telephone:* (613) 992-2417 (office). *Fax:* (613) 947-9386 (office). *Website:* www.ijc.org (office).

GRAY, Sir John Archibald Browne, Kt, MA, MB, BChir, ScD, FRS, FRCP; British physiologist and administrator (retd); b. 30 March 1918, London; s. of Sir Archibald Gray, KCVO, CBE and Elsie Cooper; m. Vera K. Mares 1946; one s. and d.; ed Cheltenham Coll., Clare Coll., Cambridge and Univ. Coll. Hosp., London; Service Research for MRC 1943–45; Surgeon Lt, RNVR 1945–46; MRC Scientific Staff, Nat. Inst. for Medical Research 1946–52; Reader in Physiology, Univ. Coll. London 1952–58, Prof. of Physiology 1958–66; Dean, Faculty of Science, Univ. of London 1960–65; Second Sec. MRC 1966–68, Sec. 1968–77; Chair. of Council, Int. Agency for Cancer Research 1972–74, of EU Cttee for Medical Research 1973–75; mem. Scientific Staff MRC 1977–83; Pres. Freshwater Biological Asscn 1983–88, Vice-Pres. 1988–; mem. Council, Marine Biological Asscn 1969–88, Vice-Pres. 1989–; Hon. Fellow, Clare Coll. Cambridge 1976; Hon. DSc (Exeter) 1985. *Publications:* numerous papers on sensory receptors and sensory nervous system. *Leisure interest:* painting. *Address:* Seaways, Kingsway, Kingsand, nr Torpoint, Cornwall, PL10 1NG, England (home). *Telephone:* (1752) 822745 (home).

GRAY, Paul Edward, SB, SM, ScD; American electrical engineer and academic; *Professor Emeritus, Department of Electrical Engineering and Computer Science, Massachusetts Institute of Technology;* b. 7 Feb. 1932, Newark, NJ; s. of Kenneth F. Gray and Florence Gilleo; m. Priscilla W. King 1955; one s. three d.; ed Grover Cleveland High School, Caldwell, NJ and Massachusetts Inst. of Tech.; Faculty mem. in Electrical Eng, MIT 1960–71, 1990–2007, Dean, School of Eng 1970–71, Prof., Dept of Electrical Eng and Computer Science –2007, Prof. Emer. 2007–, Chancellor MIT 1971–80, Pres. 1980–90, mem. of Corpn 1990–2007, Chair., Dir 1990–97, Pres. Emer. 1990–; Fellow, American Acad. of Arts and Sciences, AAAS, IEEE, Nat. Acad. of Eng (Treas. 1994–2001); Corresp. mem. Nat. Acad. of Eng in Mexico; various trusteeships and other professional appointments; Grand Cordon, Order of the Sacred Treasure (Japan) 1993; hon. degrees from Wheaton Coll., Mass, Technical Univ., Nova Scotia, Cairo Univ., Northeastern Univ., Rensselaer Polytechnic Inst. *Publications:* The Dynamic Behavior of Thermoelectric Devices 1960, Introduction to Electronics 1967; co-author of six other books. *Address:* Massachusetts Institute of Technology, 77 Massachusetts Avenue, Cambridge, MA 02139 (office). *Telephone:* (617) 253-4665 (office). *Fax:* (617) 258-0529 (office). *E-mail:* pogo@mit.edu (office). *Website:* www.eecs.mit.edu (office).

GRAY, Robert Keith, MBA; American business executive; b. 2 Sept. 1928, Hastings, Neb.; s. of Garold Gray and Marie Burchess; ed Carleton Coll. and Harvard Univ.; service in USN 1943–48; Assoc. Prof. of Finance, Hastings Coll., Neb. 1950–51; Prof., Univ. of Southern Calif., Los Angeles 1952; Special Asst to Sec. of Navy 1954; Special Asst to Pres. Eisenhower, White House, Washington, DC 1955–57, Appointments Sec. 1958; Sec. Eisenhower Cabinet, Washington, DC 1959–60; Vice-Pres. Hill & Knowlton Inc., Washington, DC 1961–64, Sr Vice-Pres. 1965–70, Exec. Vice-Pres. 1971–76, Vice-Chair. 1977–81, CEO and Chair. 1991–; founder, Chair. Gray & Co. Public Communications Int. (merger with Hill & Knowlton Inc.), Washington 1981–86, Chair. and CEO Hill & Knowlton Public Affairs Worldwide 1986–91; Chair. and Pres. Gray & Co. II 1988–; Chair. Gray Investment Properties Inc., 1988–; Chair. and CEO Powerhouse Leasing Corpn 1988–; Dir Forward Air Corpn, Official Kiosk Group, Store 2.com, Credit Cars.com, Advanced Multimedia Group; Co-Chair. Reagan–Bush Presidential Inaugural Cttee 1980; mem. numerous bds, advisory cttees; Hon. Doctorate in Business (Marymount Univ.) 1982; Hon. DLitt (Hastings Coll.) 1984; Hon. DH (Creighton Univ.) 1989; Hon. DL (Barry Univ.) 1998; Légion d'honneur, Grande Ufficiale decoration (Italy). *Publications:* Casebook on Organization and Operation of a Small Business Enterprise 1950, Eighteen Acres Under Glass 1962, Right Time, Right Place 2000, January River 2000. *Leisure interests:* tennis, skiing, philanthropy. *Address:* Gray & Co. II, 4731 Pine Tree Drive, Miami Beach, FL 33140 (office); Gray & Co., 1497 Chain Bridge Road, McLean, VA 22101, USA (office). *Telephone:* (305) 538-1050 (office); (305) 970-8158 (home). *Fax:* (305) 538-7338 (office). *E-mail:* grayandco2@aol.com (office); bob@robertkeithgray.com (home).

GRAY, Robin Trevor, BAgrSc, DDA, CPM, CPAg; Australian politician, company director and agricultural consultant; b. 1 March 1940, Victoria; s. of Rev. W. J. Gray; m. Judith F. Boyd 1965; two s. one d.; ed Box Hill High School, Dookie Agric. Coll. and Univ. of Melbourne; teacher, Victoria Educ. Dept 1961, Middx County Council, UK 1964; agric. consultant Colac, Victoria 1965, Launceston, Tasmania 1965–76; part-time lecturer in Agric. Econs Univ of Tasmania 1970–76; Deputy Leader of Opposition, Tasmania 1979–81, Leader of Opposition 1981–82, 1989–91, Premier 1982–89, Minister for Racing and Gaming 1982–84, for Energy 1982–88, for Forests 1984–86, for State Devt 1984–89, for Primary Industry and Sea Fisheries 1992–95, for Energy 1992–95, for TT-Line 1993–95; Chair. R. T. Gray and Assocs. Pty Ltd 1995–; partner Evers Gray 1996–; Dir Gunns Ltd 1996–; Chair. Botanical Resources Australia Pty Ltd 1996–; Dir AMC Search Ltd 1996–. *Leisure interests:* cricket, golf, reading.

GRAYDON, Air Chief Marshal Sir Michael (James), Kt, GCB, CBE, FRAeS; British air force officer (retd), company director and consultant; *Chairman, Symbiotics Ltd;* b. 24 Oct. 1938, Kew, London; s. of James Graydon and Rita Alkan; m. Margaret Clark 1963; ed Wycliffe Coll. and RAF Coll., Cranwell; qualified flying instructor No. 1, Flight Training School, Linton-on-Ouse 1960–62; No. 56 Squadron 1962–64; No. 226 Operational Conversion Unit (Queen's Commendation) 1965–67; Flight Command, No. 56 Squadron 1967–69; RAF Staff Coll., Bracknell 1970; Personal Staff Officer to Deputy C-in-C Allied Forces Cen. Europe, Brunssum 1971–73; Operations, Jt Warfare, Ministry of Defence 1973–75; Nat. Defence Coll. Latimer 1976; Officer Commdg No. 11 Squadron, Binbrook 1977–79; Mil. Asst to Chief of Defence Staff 1979–81; Officer Commdg RAF Leuchars 1981–83, RAF Stanley, Falkland Islands 1983; Royal Coll. of Defence Studies 1984; Sr Air Staff Officer, 11 Group, Bentley Priory 1985–86; Asst Chief of Staff, Policy, SHAPE 1986–89; Air Officer Commdg-in-Chief, RAF Support Command 1989–91, HQ Strike Command 1991–92; Chief of Air Staff 1992–97; Air ADC to HM The Queen 1992–97; fmr Chair. Royal Aeronautical Soc. Air Power Group; Chair. Symbiotics Ltd 2006–; Dir Thomson-CSF (UK) 1999, Air Tanker 2001–; Dir (non-exec.) Thales UK plc 2006–; Pres. Battle of Britain Memorial Trust 1999–, The Officers' Asscn 2000; Chair. Lincolnshire Br., English Speaking Union; Chair. Sutton's Hosp., Charterhouse 2006–; Gov. Wycliffe Coll. 1986–; Vice-Patron Air Cadet Council 1999–; Deputy Chair. United Church Schools Trust 2006–; Freeman, City of London 1995. *Publications:* contribs to professional journals. *Leisure interests:* golf, birdwatching, reading, flying. *Address:* Thales UK plc, 4 Carlton Gardens, London, SW1Y 5AA, England (office). *Telephone:* (20) 7484-8070 (office). *Fax:* (20) 7484-8071 (office). *Website:* www.thalesgroup.co.uk (office).

GRAYFER, Valery, CandTechSci; Russian oil industry executive; *Chairman, OAO Lukoil;* b. 1929; ed I.M. Gubkin Moscow Oil Inst.; began career with Tatneft State Production Asscn 1952, various positions including Deputy Foreman, Chief Engineer, Deputy Head of Tatneft 1952–72; Head of Econ. Planning Directorate, USSR Ministry of Oil Industry 1972–85; Deputy Minister of Oil Industry and Head of Glavtyumenneftegaz State Production Asscn 1985–92; Gen. Dir OAO Russian Innovation Fuel and Energy Co. (RITEK) 1992–; mem. Bd of Dirs and Chair. OAO Lukoil 2000–; Prof., Gubkin Russian State Oil and Gas Univ.; mem. Acad. of Mining Sciences; Hon. Petroleum Specialist; Order of Lenin, Order of the Red Banner of Labour, Order of Int. Friendship, Order of Service Rendered to the Country IVth Grade, Badge of Honour; Merited Worker of Science and Eng, Merited Worker of the Oil and Gas Industry, Lenin Prize, Russian Govt Prize. *Address:* OAO Lukoil, 11 Sretenski Boulevard, 101000 Moscow, Russia (office). *Telephone:* (495) 627-4444 (office). *Fax:* (495) 625-7016 (office). *E-mail:* pr@lukoil.com (office). *Website:* www.lukoil.com (office).

GRAZER, Brian; American film company executive and film producer; *Principal, Imagine Entertainment;* Co-Chair. Imagine Films Entertainment. *Films produced include:* Night Shift 1982, Splash 1984, Real Genius 1985, Spies Like Us (jtly) 1985, Armed and Dangerous (jtly) 1986, Like Father, Like Son (jtly) 1987, Parenthood 1989, Cry Baby (jtly) 1990, Kindergarten Cop 1990, Closet Land (jtly) 1991, The Doors (jtly) 1991, Backdraft (jtly) 1991, My Girl 1991, Far and Away (jtly) 1992, Housesitter 1992, Boomerang 1992, CB4 (jtly) 1993, For Love Or Money 1993, The Paper (jtly) 1994, My Girl 2 1994, Greedy 1994, The Cowboy Way 1994, Apollo 13 (jtly) 1995, Sergeant Bilko 1996, Ransom 1996, Bowfinger 1999, Curious George 2000, Nutty Professor II: The Klumps 2000, How the Grinch Stole Christmas 2000, A Beautiful Mind 2001, 8 Mile 2002, Intolerable Cruelty 2003, The Cat in the Hat 2003, Friday Night Lights 2004, Inside Deep Throat 2005, Cinderella Man 2005. *Television includes:* Sports Night (series) 1998, Felicity (series) 1998, From the Earth to the Moon (mini series) 1998, Student Affairs 1999, Wonderland (series) 2000, 24 (series) 2001–, The Beast (series) 2001, Miss Match (series) 2003, Arrested Development (series) 2003–, The Big House (series) 2004. *Address:* Imagine Films Entertainment, 9465 Wilshire Boulevard, Floor 7, Beverly Hills, CA 90212, USA (office). *Website:* www.imagine-entertainment.com.

GREAVES, Derrick, ARCA; British artist; b. 5 June 1927, Sheffield; s. of Harry Greaves and Mabel Greaves; m. Mary Margaret Johnson 1951; two s. one d.; ed RCA, London and British School at Rome; part-time teacher St Martins School of Art 1954–64, Maidstone Coll. of Art and Royal Acad. Schools 1960; Head of Printmaking, Norwich Coll. of Art 1983–91; first one-man exhbn, Beaux Arts Gallery 1953; subsequent one-man exhbns at Zwemmer Gallery 1958, 1960, 1962, 1963, Inst. of Contemporary Arts (ICA), London 1969, 1971, Bear Lane Gallery, Oxford 1970, 1973, Belfast 1972, Dublin 1972, Whitechapel Gallery 1973, Monika Kinley 1973, City Gallery, Milton Keynes 1975, Cranfield Inst. of Tech. 1978, Exposición Int. de la Plástica, Chile 1978, Gallerie Daniel Wahrenberger, Zurich, Switzerland 1996, James Hyman Fine Art, London 2003, 2005, 2007, 2008; group exhbns include Contemporary Arts Soc. 1956, Venice Biennale 1956, Pushkin Museum, Moscow 1957, Whitechapel Gallery 1963, Carnegie Int. Exhbn, Pa 1964, Haymarket Gallery 1974, Royal Acad. 1977, Graves Art Gallery, Sheffield 1980, Fischer Fine Art 1980, Mall Galleries, London 1981, Mappin Art Gallery 1986, Leeds Art Gallery 1986, Philadelphia Museum of Art 1986, Walker Art Gallery; Prize John Moore's Exhbn 1957, Belfast Open Painting Exhbn purchase prize 1962. *Publications:* Derrick Greaves. Paintings 1958–80; numerous catalogues; Derrick Greaves – Kitchen Sink to Shangri-La (by James Hyman) 2008. *Address:* c/o James Hyman Fine Art, 5 Savile Row, London, SW1Y 6BU, England.

GREAVES, Robert F.; American health care industry executive; *Chairman, Health Net Inc.;* b. LA; m. Erika Greaves; ed Calif. State Univ., Long Beach; various man. positions Blue Cross of Southern Calif., Allstate Insurance Co. –1982; Pres. Health Systems Int. (renamed Health Net Inc.) 1982, Co-Chair., Pres. and CEO –1995, Chair. 2004–; Founding Chair. The Calif. Wellness Foundation (TCWF) 1992, mem. Bd of Dirs 1992–; mem. Leadership Conf. Advisory Council, Schering Plough Pharmaceuticals, Bd of Dirs Health Net of Calif.; Founding mem. Bd of Govs, Calif. State Univ., Long Beach; fmr mem. Bd of Dirs March of Dimes Birth Defects Foundation. *Address:* Health Net Inc., 21650 Oxford Street, Woodland Hills, CA 91367, USA (office). *Telephone:* (818) 676-6000 (office). *Fax:* (818) 676-8591 (office). *Website:* www.health.net.

GREBENÍČEK, Miroslav, PhDr, CSc; Czech politician; b. 21 March 1947, Staré Město, Uherské Hradiště Dist; m.; one s. two d.; ed Masaryk Univ., Brno; worked as teacher at several schools; specialist with Regional Museum, Mikulov 1973–75; mem. CP of Czechoslovakia 1975; Lecturer, Masaryk Univ., Brno 1975–86, Reader 1986–89, Teaching-Training Coll.; Deputy to House of Nations, Fed. Ass. of ČSFR 1990–92; First Vice-Pres. Aug.–Nov. 1991, Pres. 1991–92, Council of the Fed. of CP of Czechlands and Moravia and Party of the Democratic Left; mem. Presidium, Fed. Ass. of ČSFR 1992; Chair. CP of Czechlands and Moravia 1993–2005; mem. Parl. 1996–, of Organizational Cttee of Parl. 1996–, of Parl. Cttee for Petitions 1996–98, for Culture, Youth and Physical Training 1998–. *Publications:* monographs, articles and reviews focusing on the history of 19th and 20th centuries. *Address:* Komunistická strana Čech a Moravy, Politických vězňů 9, Prague 1 (office); Zlámalova 9, 692 01 Mikulov, Czech Republic (home). *Fax:* (257) 173733 (office). *E-mail:* grebenicekm@psp.cz (office).

GREBENNIKOV, Valery Vassil'yevich; Russian lawyer and politician; *Mayor of Volgograd;* b. 14 Oct. 1946; ed Lumumba Univ. of Peoples' Friendship; elected Deputy Chief State Arbiter, Russian Fed. 1990–91, Chief State Arbiter; mem. State Duma 1995–, mem. Our Home Russia Faction (Motherland – All Russia) 1999–; Vice-Chair., then Chair. Cttee on State Construction; First Deputy Chair. Duma Cttee for Civil, Criminal, Arbitration and Procedural Legislation; Deputy Head of Russian Del. to Parl. Ass. of Council of Europe (PACE); Mayor of Volgograd 2007–; Vice-Pres. OLBI co.; mem. Bd of Dirs Bank of Nat. Credit. *Address:* Office of the Mayor, 5 Volodarskogo str., 400131 Volgograd, Russia (office). *Telephone:* (8442) 33-16-82 (office). *Fax:* (8442) 38-54-66 (office). *E-mail:* kancelyaria@volgadmin.ru (office). *Website:* www.volgadmin.ru (office).

GREBENSHCHIKOV, Boris Borisovich; Russian rock musician and singer; b. 27 Nov. 1953, Leningrad; s. of Boris A. Grebenshchikov and Ludmila Grebenshchikova; m.; one s. two d.; ed Leningrad Univ.; worked as a computer programmer 1977–80; lead singer and guitarist of rock group Akvarium 1975–; recordings include Akvarium (USSR) 1987, Radio Africa 1987, Equinox 1988, Radio Silence 1989, Russian Album 1992, Kostroma Mon Amour 1994, Navigator 1995, Snow Lion 1996, Hyperborea 1997, Lilith 1998, Psi 1999, Sister Chaos 2002, Fisherman's Song 2003, Zoom, Zoom, Zoom 2005, Careless Russian Rover 2006; music for films and sound track albums includes Assa 1988, Black Rose 1990; tours and recordings in USA, Canada, Great Britain, all-Russia tour 1991 (110 concerts in 68 cities); as a painter has taken part in various art exhbns throughout fmr USSR; Medal for Services to the Fatherland 2003; Triumph Prize (for outstanding achievements in Russian culture) 1998. *Radio:* presenter, Aerostat. *Publications:* Ivan and Danilo 1989, poetry and song lyrics, trans. of Indian and Tibetan religious works. *Leisure interests:* music, painting, writing, religions, travelling. *Address:* 2 Marata Street, Apt. 3, 191025 St Petersburg, Russia. *Telephone:* 311-04-58. *Fax:* (812) 272-05-41 (home). *E-mail:* bg@aquarium.ru (office). *Website:* www.aquarium.ru (office).

GRECEANÎI, Zinaida, MA; Moldovan economist and politician; *Prime Minister;* b. 7 Feb. 1956; m.; two c.; ed Moldova State Univ.; various roles within finance and budget inspectorate 1974–91; Economist, then Prin. Economist, Dept of Int. Finance, Ministry of Finance 1995–97, various sr positions including Dir of World Bank Section 1997–2001; Vice-Minister of Finance 2001–02, Minister of Finance 2002–05; First Deputy Prime Minister 2006–08, Prime Minister 2008–; fmr Gov. for Moldova to IMF. *Address:* Government of Moldova, Piaţa Marii Adunări Naţionale 1, 2033 Chişinău, Moldova (office). *Telephone:* (22) 25-01-41 (office). *Fax:* (22) 23-84-44 (office). *E-mail:* zinaida.greceanii@gov.md (office). *Website:* www.gov.md (office).

GRECH, Joe Debono; Maltese politician; b. 17 Sept. 1941, B'Kara; s. of Carmelo Debono and Giovanna Grech; m. Edith Vella; two c.; ed St Aloysius Coll.; mem. Gen. Workers, Union Rep. for Gozo 1971; Sec. Petrol and Chemicals Section 1973–76; fmr Pres. Nat. Exec. Socialist Youth Movt, Gen. Sec. 1967–76; fmr mem. Nat. Exec. Labour Party, Propaganda Sec. 1971–88; Man. Nat. Cargo Handling Co., Interprint; MP 1976–; Minister of Parastatal and People's Investments May–Sept. 1983, of Agric. and Fisheries 1983–87, for Transport and Ports 1996–98; Deputy Leader Labour Party 1988. *Leisure interests:* reading, farming. *Address:* c/o Pamit Laburista, National Labour Centre, Mile End Road, Hamrun, HMR 02 (office); 105 Fleur de Lys Road, B'kara, Malta. *Telephone:* 443712. *Website:* www.mlp.org.mt (office); parliament.gov.mt (office).

GREEHEY, William (Bill) E., CPA; American oil industry executive; *Chairman, Valero Energy Corporation;* b. Fort Dodge, Ia; ed St Mary's Univ., San Antonio, TX; began career as accountant, Price Waterhouse; fmr accountant, Exxon; fmr accountant, Coastal Gas Corpn, becoming Vice-Pres.

and Controller, Pres. and CEO LoVaca (subsidiary co., Valero from 1980) 1973, CEO Valero Energy Corpn 1980–2006, Chair. 1980–; Dr hc St. Mary's Univ. 1998 Distinguished Alumnus, St. Mary's Univ. 1986, Int. Citizen of the Year Award, San Antonio World Affairs Council 1999, Horatio Alger Award 2000, Tex. Business Hall of Fame 2002. *Address:* Valero Corporate Headquarters, One Valero Way, San Antonio, TX 78249-1112, USA (office). *Telephone:* (210) 345-2000 (office). *Fax:* (210) 345-2646 (office). *E-mail:* corporatecommunications@valero.com (office). *Website:* www.valero.com (office).

GREEN, Al; American soul singer and songwriter; b. 13 April 1946, Forrest City, Ark.; founder, The Creations 1964; singer, Al Green and The Soul Mates; f. of his own record label Hot Line Music Journal, 1967; purchased his own church, The Full Gospel Tabernacle in Memphis, Tenn. in late 1970s, became pastor; left secular music 1980, returned 1993; American Music Award, Favourite Soul/R&B Album 1974, Grand Prize, Tokyo Music Festival 1978, Al Green Day, Los Angeles 1978, Soul Train, Best Gospel Recording 1987, numerous Grammy awards include: Best Soul Gospel Performances 1982–85, 1988, 1990, Best Male Soul Performance 1987, Best R&B Performance by a Duo or Group (for Stay With Me with John Legend) 2009, Best Traditional R&B Vocal Performance (for You've Got All the Love I Need) 2009, Grammy Lifetime Achievement Award 2002. *Recordings:* albums: Al Green Gets Next To You 1971, Let's Stay Together 1972, I'm Still In Love With You 1972, Green Is Blues 1973, Call Me 1973, Livin' For You 1974, Al Green Explores Your Mind 1975, Al Green Is Love 1975, Full of Fire 1976, Have A Good Time 1977, Truth 'n' Time 1978, The Belle Album 1978, Cream of Al Green 1980, The Lord Will Make A Way 1980, Higher Plane 1982, Precious Lord 1983, I'll Rise Again 1983, White Christmas 1983, Going Away 1986, Soul Survivor 1987, I Get Joy 1989, Al 1992, Love and Happiness 2001, I Can't Stop 2003, Everything's OK 2005, Lay it Down 2008. *Address:* Full Gospel Tabernacle, 787 Hale Road, Memphis, TN 38116, USA. *Telephone:* (901) 396-9192. *E-mail:* algreenmusic@hotmail.com; reverend@algreenmusic.com. *Website:* www.algreenmusic.com.

GREEN, Anthony Eric Sandall, RA; British artist; b. 30 Sept. 1939, Luton; s. of Frederick Sandall and Marie Madeleine Green (née Dupont); m. Mary Louise Cozens-Walker 1961; two d.; ed Highgate School, Slade School of Fine Art, Univ. Coll. London; Asst Art Master, Highgate School 1961–67; Harkness Fellowship, USA 1967–69; Fellow, Univ. Coll. London 1991; elected mem. New English Art Club 2003; held over 100 solo exhbns; works in public and pvt. collections world-wide; French Govt Scholarship, Paris 1960; Hon. RBA, Hon. ROI Exhibit of the Year RA Summer Exhbn 1977, Featured Artist RA Summer Exhbn 2003. *Publication:* A Green Part of the World (with Martin Bailey) 1984. *Leisure interests:* family, travel. *Address:* Mole End, 40 High Street, Little Eversden, Cambridge, CB23 1HE, England (home). *Telephone:* (1223) 262292 (home). *Fax:* (1223) 265656 (home).

GREEN, Dan, BA; American book publishing executive; *Literary agent, Pom Inc.;* b. 28 Sept. 1935, Passaic, NJ; s. of Harold Green and Bessie Roslow; m. Jane Oliphant 1959; two s.; ed Syracuse Univ., NY; Publicity Dir Dover Press 1957–58; Station WNAC-TV 1958–59; Bobbs-Merrill Co. 1959–62; Simon & Schuster Inc. 1962–85, Assoc. Publr 1976–80, Vice-Pres., Publr 1980–84; Pres. Trade Publishing Group 1984–85; Founder, Publr, Kenan Press 1979–80; CEO Grove Press and Weidenfeld & Nicolson, New York 1985–89; Pres. Kenan Books, New York 1989–, Pom Inc. (Literary Agency) 1989–. *Address:* Pom Inc., 611 Broadway, New York, NY 10012 (office); Kenan Books, 611 Broadway, New York, NY 10012, USA. *Telephone:* (212) 673-3835 (office). *E-mail:* info@pomlit.com (office).

GREEN, Grant S., Jr, BA, MS; American business executive, fmr government official and fmr army officer; ed Univ. of Arkansas, George Washington Univ., Army Command and Gen. Staff Coll., USAF Air War Coll.; served in US Army, various Infantry and Aviation command and staff positions with 82nd Airborne Div., 25th Infantry Div., 1st Cavalry Div. and 101st (Airborne) Airmobile Div. in Viet Nam; Commdr 2nd Aviation Battalion, 2nd Infantry Div.; staff assignments in Army Gen. Staff, Pentagon, and Staff Sec. and Deputy Sec. of Defense; several sr man. positions with Sears World Trade (SWT); fmr Special Asst to Pres. Ronald Reagan for Nat. Security Affairs and fmr Exec. Sec., Nat. Security Council; fmr Asst Sec. of Defense; fmr Exec. Vice-Pres. and COO of a consulting and marketing co.; Chair. and Pres., Global Marketing and Devt Solutions Inc. (GMD Solutions) –2001, 2005–; Under-Sec. of State for Man. 2001–05; mem. US Comm. on Wartime Contracting in Iraq and Afghanistan; Dept of Defense Award for Distinguished Public Service, numerous mil. decorations. *Address:* GMD Solutions, 2121 Eisenhower Avenue, Suite 600, Alexandria, VA 22314, USA. *Telephone:* (703) 299-6649 (office). *Fax:* (703) 299-9213 (office). *E-mail:* gmds@gmdsinc.com (office). *Website:* www.gmdsinc.com (office).

GREEN, Hon. Sir Guy Stephen Montague, Kt, AC, KBE, CVO, LLB; Australian administrator and judge; b. 26 July 1937, Launceston, Tasmania; s. of the late Clement Francis Montague and Beryl Margaret Jenour (née Williams) Green; m. Rosslyn Marshall 1963; two s. two d.; ed Launceston Church Grammar School and Univ. of Tasmania; admitted to Bar 1960; Partner Ritchie & Parker Alfred Green & Co. 1963–71; Pres. Tasmanian Bar Asscn 1968–70; Magistrate 1971–73; Chief Justice of Tasmania 1973–95; Lt-Gov. of Tasmania 1982–95; Gov. of Tasmania 1995–2003; mem. Faculty of Law Univ. of Tasmania 1974–85; Chair. Council of Law Reporting 1978–85; Chair. Tasmanian Cttee, Duke of Edinburgh's Award in Australia 1975–80; Dir Winston Churchill Memorial Trust 1975–85, Deputy Nat. Chair. 1980–85; Chancellor, Univ. of Tasmania 1985–95; Deputy Chair. Australian Inst. of Judicial Admin. 1986–88; Pres. St John Council 1984–92; Priory Exec. Officer, Order of St John in Australia 1984–91, Chancellor 1991–95; Deputy Prior St John Ambulance Australia 1995–; Administrator of the Commonwealth (Acting Gov.-Gen. of Australia) 2003; Hon. LLD (Univ. of Tasmania) 1996; Kt of Grace, Most Venerable Order of the Hosp. of St John of Jerusalem 1985. *Address:* 13 Marine Terrace, Battery Point, Tasmania 7004, Australia.

GREEN, Hamilton; Guyanese politician; *Mayor of Georgetown;* b. 9 Nov. 1934, Georgetown; s. of Wilfred Amelius Green and Edith Ophelia Dorothy Green; m. 1st Shirley Field-Ridley 1970 (died 1982); five s. three d.; m. 2nd Dr. Jennifer Veronica Basdeo 1990; two d.; ed Queen's Coll.; fmrly Gen. Sec., People's Nat. Congress, Minister of Works, Hydraulics and Supply, of Public Affairs, of Co-operatives and Nat. Mobilization, of Health, Housing and Labour; fmrly Vice-Pres. with responsibility for Public Welfare, Vice-Pres. with responsibility for Production; Vice-Pres. and Prime Minister of Guyana 1985–92; expelled from People's Nat. Congress 1992; f. political and environmental group Good And Green Guyana; Mayor of Georgetown 1994, 2004–; presidential cand. 1997. *Publication:* From Pain to Peace – Guyana 1953–1964 (series of lectures at Cyril Potter Coll. of Educ. 1986). *Leisure interest:* reading (history and philosophy), table tennis, boxing and fitness training. *Address:* City Hall, Regent Street, Georgetown (office); Plot 'D' Lodge, Georgetown, Guyana (home). *Telephone:* (2) 57870 (office). *Fax:* (2) 57871.

GREEN, Howard, MD, MSc; American medical school professor and scientist; *George Higginson Professor of Cell Biology, Harvard University Medical School;* b. 10 Sept. 1925, Toronto, Canada; s. of Benjamin Green and Rose M. Green; m. Rosine Kauffmann; ed Univ. of Toronto and Northwestern Univ., USA; Research Asst, Dept of Physiology, Northwestern Univ. 1948–50; Research Assoc. (Instructor), Dept of Biochemistry, Univ. of Chicago 1951–53; Instructor, Dept of Pharmacology, New York Univ. School of Medicine 1954; Capt., MC, US Army Reserve, Immunology Div., Walter Reed Army Inst. of Research 1955–56; Dept of Pathology, New York Univ. School of Medicine 1956–68, Prof. and Chair., Dept of Cell Biology 1968–70; Prof. of Cell Biology, MIT 1970–80; Chair. Dept of Physiology and Biophysics, Harvard Medical School 1980–86, Chair. Dept of Cellular and Molecular Physiology 1988–93, George Higginson Prof. of Cell Biology 1993–; mem. NAS, American Acad. of Arts and Sciences, Institut de France (Acad. des Sciences); Hon. Pres. Scientific Council, Institut Curie, Paris; Hon. Mem. Soc. of Investigative Dermatology, Japanese Soc. for Plastic and Reconstructive Surgery; Hon. Fellow, American Acad. of Microbiology; Chevalier, Légion d'honneur; Hon. DSc (Univ. of Connecticut, State Univ. of NY at Stony Brook); Hon. MD (Göteborg); Mr and Mrs J. N. Taub Int. Memorial Award for Psoriasis Research 1977; Selman A. Waksman Award in Microbiology 1978; Lewis S. Rosenstiel Award in Basic Medical Research 1980, Lila Gruber Research Award, American Acad. of Dermatology 1980, Passano Award 1985, Blaise Pascal Medal for Biology and Life Sciences 2007. *Publications:* numerous articles on cell biology, genetics, growth and differentiation. *Address:* Department of Cell Biology, Harvard Medical School, 240 Longwood Avenue, Boston, MA 02115 (office); 82 Williston Road, Brookline, MA 02146, USA (home). *Telephone:* (617) 432-0851 (office). *Fax:* (617) 432-0109 (office). *E-mail:* hgreen@hms.harvard.edu (office). *Website:* cellbio.med.harvard.edu/faculty/green (office).

GREEN, Malcolm L. H., BSc, DIC, PhD, FRS; British chemist and academic; *Professor Emeritus of Inorganic Chemistry, University of Oxford;* b. 16 April 1936, Eastleigh, Hants.; m. Jennifer C. Green (née Bilham); ed Univ. of London, Imperial Coll. of Science and Tech.; Postdoctoral Research Assoc. Fellow, Imperial Coll. of Science and Tech. 1959–60; Asst Lecturer in Inorganic Chem., Univ. of Cambridge 1960–63; Septcentuary Tutorial Fellow, Balliol Coll. 1963–89; Lecturer, Univ. of Oxford 1965–, Prof. of Inorganic Chem. and Head of Dept 1989–2003, Prof. Emer. 2003–; Visiting Prof., Univ. of Western Ontario, Canada 1971, Ecole de Chimie and Inst. des Substances Naturelles, Paris, France 1972, Harvard Univ., USA (A.P. Sloan Visiting Prof.) 1973, Wuhan Univ., China 1985; Distinguished Visiting Prof., Hong Kong Univ. 2002–(10); Sr Research Fellow, British Gas Royal Soc. 1979–84, 1984–86; Head, Chem. Dept Cttee, Royal Soc. of Chem. 1989–; Chair. Editorial Bd RCS Chemical Communication 1997–99; Co-founder Oxford Catalysts PLC 2006, mem. Bd of Dirs and mem. Scientific Advisory Panel 2006–08; mem. Editorial Bd several journals including Topics in Catalysis, Organometallics, Nouveau Journal de Chimie, Journal of Organometallic Chemistry; mem. Bd Inst. of Applied Catalysis 1995–; Fellow, Corpus Christi Coll., Cambridge 1961, Balliol Coll., Oxford 1962–89, St Catherine's Coll., Oxford 1989; invited to present numerous hon. lectures at int. univs; Dr hc (Univ. of Lisbon) 1997; numerous awards including RSC Corday-Morgan Medal 1974, Tilden Prize 1982, ACS Annual Award for Inorganic Chemistry 1984, RSC Medal in Organometallic Chemistry 1986, Gesellschaft Deutscher Chemiker Karl-Ziegler Prize 1992, Royal Soc. Davy Medal 1995, Univ. of NSW Frank Dyer Medal 1997, NW Univ. Fred Basolo Medal 1998, RSC Sir Geoffrey Wilkinson Medal 2000, Soc. française de Chimie Prix Franco-Britannique 2007. *Publications:* around 700 publications and two books. *Address:* Inorganic Chemistry Laboratory, University of Oxford, South Parks Road, Oxford, OX 1 3QR (office); Oxford Catalysts, 115e Milton Park, Oxford, OX14 4RZ, England (office). *Telephone:* (1856) 272600 (office); (1235) 841700 (Oxford Catalysts) (office). *Fax:* (1865) 272690 (office); (1235) 841701 (Oxford Catalysts) (office). *E-mail:* malcolm.green@chem.ox.ac.uk (office); info@oxfordcatalysts.com (office). *Website:* www.chem.ox.ac/researchguide/mlhgreen.html (office); www.oxfordcatalysts.com (office).

GREEN, Martin Andrew, BE, MEngSc, PhD, FAA, FTS, FIEEE; Australian scientist, academic and business executive; *Executive Research Director, Australian Research Council Photovoltaics Centre of Excellence;* b. 20 July 1948, Brisbane, Queensland; s. of Eric William Green and Gwendolyn Lorraine Green (née Horsfall); m.; two c.; ed Univ. of Queensland, McMaster Univ., Canada; initiated Solar Photovoltaics Group at Univ. of New South Wales 1974–, currently Prof., School of Photovoltaic and Renewable Energy Engineering, Exec. Research Dir Australian Research Council Photovoltaics

Centre of Excellence; Research Dir and mem. Bd Pacific Solar Pty Ltd (now CSG Solar), Sydney; Pawsey Medal, Australian Acad. 1982, Award for Outstanding Achievement in Energy Research 1988, IEEE Cherry Award 1990, CSIRO External Medal 1992, IEEE Ebers Award 1995, Australia Prize 1999, Gold Medal, Spanish Eng Acad. 2000, Medal of Eng Excellence for Distinguished Achievement in the Service of Humanity, World Eng Fed., Hanover 2000, Millennium Award, World Renewable Congress 2000, Right Livelihood Award 2002, Karl Böer Solar Energy Medal of Merit Award, Univ. of Delaware 2003, World Tech. Award in Energy, The World Tech. Network 2004, SolarWorld Einstein Award 2007. *Publications:* five books, nine book chapters, numerous reports, patents and conference papers, and more than 300 papers in int. refereed journals on semiconductors, micro-electronics and solar cells. *Address:* Room 127, School of Photovoltaic and Renewable Energy Engineering, Electrical Engineering Building, University of New South Wales, Sydney, NSW 2052, Australia (office). *Telephone:* (2) 9385-4018 (office). *Fax:* (2) 9662-4240 (office). *E-mail:* m.green@unsw.edu.au (office). *Website:* www.pv.unsw.edu.au (office).

GREEN, Michael Boris, PhD, FRS; British physicist and academic; *John Humphrey Plummer Professor of Theoretical Physics, University of Cambridge;* b. 22 May 1946, London; s. of Absalom Green and Genia Green; m. Joanna Chataway; one d.; ed William Ellis School, London, Univ. of Cambridge; Post-doctoral Fellowship, Inst. for Advanced Study, Princeton, NJ, USA 1970–72, Univ. of Cambridge 1972–77; SERC Advanced Fellowship, Univ. of Oxford 1977–79; Lecturer, Queen Mary and Westfield Coll., London 1979–85, Prof. of Physics 1985–93; SERC Sr Fellowship 1986–91; John Humphrey Plummer Prof. of Theoretical Physics, Univ. of Cambridge 1993–; numerous fellowships at US and European Insts, including Distinguished Fairchild Fellowship, Calif. Inst. of Tech. 1990; Hon. DSc (Queen Mary, Univ. of London) 2004; Maxwell Medal, Inst. of Physics 1987, William Hopkins Prize, Cambridge Philosophical Soc. 1987, Dirac Medal, Int. Center for Theoretical Physics 1989, Dannie Heineman Prize, American Physical Soc. 2002, Dirac Medal and Prize, Inst. of Physics 2004, Naylor Prize, London Math. Soc. 2007. *Publications:* Superstring Theory (two vols, with J. H. Schwarz and E. Witten) 1987; numerous publs in scientific journals. *Leisure interests:* pottery, music. *Address:* Department of Applied Mathematics and Theoretical Physics, University of Cambridge, Cambridge, CB3 0WA, England (office). *Telephone:* (1223) 330884 (office). *E-mail:* mbg15@damtp.cam.ac.uk (office). *Website:* www.damtp.cam.ac.uk (office).

GREEN, Michael Philip; British business executive; b. 2 Dec. 1947; s. of Cyril Green and Irene Green; m. 1st Hon. Janet F. Wolfson 1972 (divorced 1989); two d.; m. 2nd Theresa Buckmaster 1990; three s. one d.; ed Haberdashers' Aske's School; Dir and Co-Founder, Tangent Industries 1968–; Chief Exec. Carlton Communications plc 1983–91, Chair. 1983–2004, Chair. Carlton TV Ltd 1991–94, Chair. ITV plc 2003–04; Chair. ITN 1993–; Founder Tangent Charitable Trust 1984; Dir GMTV Ltd 1992–2004, Reuters Holdings PLC 1992–99, Getty Communications PLC 1997–98; Chair. The Media Trust 1997–; Trustee Sainsbury Centre for Mental Health 2001–; Hon. DLitt (City Univ.) 1999. *Leisure interests:* reading, bridge, television. *Address:* Tangent Industries Ltd, 21 South Street, London, W1K 2XB, England (office). *Telephone:* (20) 7663-6464 (office). *Fax:* (20) 7663-6364 (office). *Website:* www.itvplc.com.

GREEN, Norman Michael, PhD, FRS; British biochemist; b. 6 April 1926; s. of Ernest Green and Hilda Margaret Carter; m. Iro Paulina Moschouti 1953; two s. one d.; ed Dragon School, Oxford, Clifton Coll., Bristol, Magdalen Coll., Oxford and Univ. Coll. Hosp. Medical School, London; Research Student, Univ. of Wash., Seattle 1951–53; Lecturer in Biochemistry, Univ. of Sheffield 1953–55; Research Fellow and Lecturer in Chemical Pathology, St Mary's Hosp. Medical School, London 1956–62; Visiting Scientist, NIH, Md 1962–64; Research Staff, Div. of Biochemistry, Nat. Inst. for Medical Research 1964–91, affiliated to Dept of Math. Biology 1992–. *Publications:* research papers in scientific journals on the structure of proteins and of membranes. *Leisure interests:* mountain climbing, pyrotechnics. *Address:* 57 Hale Lane, Mill Hill, London, NW7 3PS, England.

GREEN, Sir Philip, Kt; British retail executive; b. 15 March 1952, Croydon; m. Tina Green; took over family property co. 1973; bought Jean Jeanie 1985 (sold to Lee Cooper), Owen Owen 1994, Sports Division (sold to JJB Sports), Mark One 1996, Shoe Express 1997, Sears 1999, British Home Stores (Bhs) 2000, Arcadia Group (including Top Shop, Top Man, Miss Selfridge, Dorothy Perkins, Wallis, Evans and Burtons clothing chains) 2002; Chair. and CEO Amber Day (now What Everyone Wants) 1988–92. *Address:* Arcadia Group, Colegrave House, 70 Berners Street, London, W1T 3NL; Bhs Ltd, Marylebone House, 129–137 Marylebone Road, London, NW1 5DQ, England (office). *Telephone:* (20) 7636-8040. *Fax:* (20) 7927-0577. *Website:* www.arcadiagroup.co.uk; www.bhs.co.uk (office).

GREEN, Roger Curtis, PhD, NZOM, FRSNZ; American/New Zealand professor emeritus of prehistory; *Adjunct Professor, Te Whare Wānangao Awanuiārangi;* b. 15 March 1932, Ridgewood, NJ; s. of Robert J. Green and Eleanor Richards; m. 1st Kaye Chandler Smith 1959; m. 2nd Valerie J. Sallen 1984; two c.; ed Univ. of New Mexico and Harvard Univ.; Research Assoc., American Museum of Natural History 1959; Sr Lecturer in Prehistory, Univ. of Auckland 1961–66, Assoc. Prof. 1966–67, Prof. in Prehistory 1973–92, Prof. Emer. 1992–; Adjunct Prof., Te Whare Wānangao Awanuiārangi 2004–, Head, Dept of Anthropology 1980–84; Anthropologist, B.P. Bishop Museum 1967–73, Research Assoc. 1973–; RSNZ Capt. James Cook Fellowship 1970–73; Assoc. Prof. in Anthropology, Univ. of Hawaii 1967–70, James Cook Visiting Prof. 1981–82; Visiting Prof., Miller Inst. for Research in Basic Science, Univ. of Calif., Berkeley; Visiting Summer Scholar, School of American Research, Santa Fe 1999; Visiting Research Fellow, Univ. of Otago 2002; mem. Bd

Foundation for Research Science and Tech. 1993–95; mem. NAS 1984–, and numerous other learned socs; Hon. Fellow, Soc. of Antiquaries, London 2000; NZ Order of Merit; Fulbright Scholar 1958–59, Elsdon Best Medal, Polynesian Soc. 1973, Maharaia Winiata Memorial Prize 1974, Hector Memorial Medal, Royal Soc. of NZ 1992, Marsden Medal, NZ Asscn of Scientists 2003. *Publications:* Hawaiki: Ancestral Polynesia (with P.V. Kirch); numerous articles in historical, anthropological, archaeological journals etc. *Leisure interests:* music, travel. *Address:* Department of Anthropology, University of Auckland, Private Bag 92019, Auckland 1142 (office); PO Box 60054, Titirangi, Waitakere, Auckland 0642, New Zealand (home). *Telephone:* (9) 373-7599, ext. 88567 (office); (9) 817-7608 (home). *Fax:* (9) 373-7441 (office); (9) 817-2015 (home). *E-mail:* r.green@auckland.ac.nz (office); pounamu@ihug.co.nz (home). *Website:* www.arts.auckland.ac.nz/ant (office).

GREEN, Stephen K., MSc; British banking executive; *Group Chairman, HSBC Group;* b. 1948; ed Univ. of Oxford, Massachusetts Inst. of Tech., USA; early career with Ministry of Overseas Devt; consultant, McKinsey & Co. 1977; joined Hongkong and Shanghai Banking Corpn (HSBC) 1982, responsible for Corp. Planning, Group Treasurer HSBC Holdings PLC 1992–98, Dir HSBC Bank PLC 1995–, Exec. Dir Corp., Investment Banking and Markets 1998–2003, responsible for Group Corp. Banking Business 2002–, Group CEO 2003–06, Group Chair. 2006–, also Chair. HSBC Bank plc, HSBC North America Holdings Inc. and HSBC Private Banking Holdings (Suisse) SA, a Dir of HSBC France and Hongkong and Shanghai Banking Corpn Ltd; Chair. British Bankers' Asscn; mem. Bd of Trustees British Museum 2005–. *Publication:* Serving God? Serving Mammon? Christians and the Financial Market 1996. *Address:* HSBC Holdings PLC, 8 Canada Square, London, E14 5HQ, England (office). *Telephone:* (20) 7991-8888 (office). *Fax:* (20) 7992-4880 (office). *E-mail:* pressoffice@hsbc.com (office). *Website:* www.hsbc.com (office).

GREEN, William (Bill) D., BS (Econs), MBA; American management consultancy executive; *Chairman and CEO, Accenture Ltd;* m.; two c.; ed Dean Coll., Babson Coll.; joined Accenture Ltd 1977, various positions including Partner 1986, Head of Mfg Industry Group, Man.-Pnr of New England Operations, Head of Resources Operating Group 1997–99, CEO Communications & High Tech. Group 1999–2003, Country Man.-Dir, USA 2000–03, Dir 2001–, COO Client Services 2003–04, CEO 2004–, Chair. 2006–; mem. Business Roundtable; Trustee, Dean Coll.; Hon. LLD (Babson Coll.). *Address:* Accenture Ltd, 1345 Avenue of the Americas, New York, NY 10105, USA (office). *Telephone:* (917) 452-4400 (office). *Fax:* (917) 527-9915 (office). *E-mail:* info@accenture.com (office). *Website:* www.accenture.com (office).

GREEN MACÍAS, Rosario G.; Mexican diplomatist, academic and politician; ed Universidad Nacional Autónoma de México, El Colegio de México, Columbia Univ., USA; fmr Sub-Sec. Foreign Relations Latin America, Int. Cooperation and Cultural Matters; Mexican Rep. to World Bank; Exec. Sec. Nat. Comm. Human Rights; Sec. Comm. Int. Affairs PRI; Dir Matías Romero Inst. Diplomatic Studies, Sec. of Foreign Relations; Amb. to GDR –1990; Gen. Sub-Sec. and mem. Gen. Sec. Cabinet UN 1994–97; Senator Repub. 1997–2000; Nat. Pres. Colosio Foundation AC 1997–98; Foreign Relations Sec. 1998–2000; Amb. to Argentina –2005; Sec.-Gen. Partido Revolucionario Institucional (PRI) 2005–07; elected to Senate 2006, Pres. Foreign Affairs Comm.; Chair. and Visiting Prof., Kozmetsky Center for Excellence in Global Finance, St Edward's Univ., Austin, Tex.; Dr hc (New Rochelle Univ.) 1996, (Tufts Univ.) 1999. *Publications:* more than ten books and 100 articles. *Address:* Torre del Caballito Piso 16, Oficina 6, Reforma 10, Col. Tabacalera, México, DF, 06030, Mexico (office). *Telephone:* (55) 5345-3000 (office). *Fax:* (55) 5345-5306 (office). *E-mail:* rgreen@senado.gob.mx (office). *Website:* www.senado.gob.mx (office).

GREENAWAY, David, BSc, MCom; British economist, academic and university administrator; *Vice-Chancellor, Nottingham University;* b. Glasgow; ed Liverpool Polytechnic, Univ. of Liverpool; Head of Dept of Econs, Nottingham Univ. 1987, currently Prof. of Econs, Dean Faculty of Law and Social Sciences 1991–94, Univ. Pro-Vice-Chancellor (Vice Pres.) 1994–2001, 2004–08, Vice-Chancellor 2008–; mem. Armed Forces Pay Review Body 1998– (Chair. 2004–); f. Leverhulme Centre for Research on Globalisation and Econ. Policy 1998; Gov. Nat. Inst. of Econ. and Social Research; Chair. Scientific Advisory Council, Institut für Weltwirtschaft, Kiel Univ.; mem. Scientific Cttee European Trade Study Group; Man. Ed. The World Economy (journal). *Publications:* numerous journal articles. *Address:* Vice-Chancellor's Office, University of Nottingham, University Park, Nottingham, NG7 2RD, England (office). *Telephone:* (115) 951-3001 (office). *Fax:* (115) 951-3005 (office). *E-mail:* david.greenaway@nottingham.ac.uk (office). *Website:* www.nottingham.ac.uk/economics/staff/details/david_greenaway.html (office).

GREENAWAY, Peter, CBE; British film director, writer and painter; b. April 1942, Newport, Gwent, Wales; m.; two d.; ed Forest School and Walthamstow Coll. of Art; trained as painter and first exhibited pictures at Lord's Gallery 1964; film ed. Cen. Office of Information 1965–76; began making own films in 1966, numerous curatorial exhbns, one-man shows and group shows in Europe, USA, Australia and Japan 1988–; currently Prof. of Cinema Studies, European Graduate School, Saas-Fee, Switzerland; Officier, Ordre des Arts et Lettres. *Films include:* Train, Tree 1966, Revolution, Five Postcards from Capital Cities 1967, Intervals 1969, Erosion 1971, H is for House 1973, Windows, Water, Water Wrackets 1975, Goole by Numbers 1976, Dear Phone 1977, 1–100, A Walk Through H (Hugo Award, Chicago), Vertical Features Remake 1978, Zandra Rhodes (Hugo Award, Chicago 1981) 1979, The Falls (BFI Award, L'Age d'Or Brussels) 1980, Act of God (Melbourne Short Film Prize, Sydney Short Film Prize) 1981, The Draughtsman's Contract 1982, Four American Composers 1983, Making a Splash 1984, Inside Rooms: 26 Bathrooms 1985, A Zed & Two Noughts 1986, The Belly of An Architect (Best Actor Prize, Chicago) 1987, Drowning by Numbers (Best Artistic Contribution

Prize), Fear of Drowning, Death in the Seine 1988, A TV Dante Cantos 1–8, Hubert Bals Handshake 1989, The Cook, The Thief, His Wife and Her Lover 1989, Prospero's Books, M is for Man, Music, Mozart 1991, Rosa (Dance Screen Prize), Darwin 1992, The Baby of Macon 1993, The Stairs, Geneva 1994, The Pillow Book (La Distinction Gervais, Cannes, Best Film and Best Cinematographer, Sitges, Spain) 1995, Flying over Water 1997, 8½ Women 1999, The Death of a Composer: Rosa, a Horse Drama 1999, The Man in the Bath 2001, The Tulse Luper Suitcases, Part 1: The Moab Story 2003, The Tulse Luper Suitcases, Part 3: From Sark to the Finish 2003, The Tulse Luper Suitcases, Part 2: Vaux to the Sea 2004, A Life in Suitcases 2005, Nightwatching 2007, Rembrandt's J'Accuse (documentary) 2008. *Opera:* Rosa, a Horse Drama 1994, Writing to Vermeer 1999. *Publications:* A Zed and Two Noughts 1986, Belly of an Architect 1987, Drowning By Numbers, Fear of Drowning 1988, The Cook, The Thief, His Wife and Her Lover 1989, Papers 1990, Prospero's Books 1991, Prospero's Subjects (picture book) 1992, Rosa, The Falls, The Baby of Macon 1993, The Draughtsman's Contract 1994, The Pillow Book 1996. *Address:* c/o European Graduate School, Building Steinmatte, 3906 Saas Fee, Switzerland; c/o The Vue, 387B King Street, London, W6 9NJ, England. *Fax:* (20) 8748-3597. *E-mail:* info@petergreenawayevents.com. *Website:* www.petergreenawayevents.com; www.egs.edu/faculty/petergreenaway.html.

GREENBERG, Jack, BSc, JD, CPA; American business executive; b. 1942; s. of Edith S. Scher; m. Donna Greenberg; one s. two d.; ed Depaul Univ., Chicago; with Arthur Young & Co. 1964–82; Chief Finance Officer and Exec. Vice-Pres. McDonald's Corpn 1982, Vice-Chair. 1992, Pres., CEO 1997–99, Chair., CEO 1999–2002 (retd), also Dir; mem. Bd of Dirs Abbott Labs, Allstate, Economic Club of Chicago, Exec.'s Club of Chicago; fmr mem. Bd of Dirs Harcourt Gen.; mem. American Inst. of Certified Public Accountants, ABA, Illinois CPA Soc., Inst. of Int. Educ., Council of the World Econ. Forum, Chicago Commercial Club; Trustee Ronald McDonald House Charities, Field Museum, Chicago Symphony Orchestra, DePaul Univ.; Hon. Dir American-Israel Chamber of Commerce and Industry, Inc. of Metropolitan Chicago; Hon. DHumLitt (DePaul) 1999. *Address:* c/o Economic Club of Chicago, 177 North State Street, Suite 404, Chicago, IL 60601, USA (office).

GREENBERG, Jeffrey W.; American business executive; b. 1952; fmr head property/casualty American Int. Group; joined Marsh & McLennan Risk Capital 1996, CEO Marsh and McLennan Cos 1999–2004, Chair. 2000–2004 (resgnd). *Address:* c/o Marsh & McLennan Companies Inc., 1166 Avenue of the Americas, New York, NY 10036-2774, USA.

GREENBERG, Maurice Raymond (Hank), LLB; American lawyer and insurance executive; *Chairman, The Starr Foundation;* b. 4 May 1925; s. of Jacob Greenberg and Ada (Rheingold) Greenberg; m. Corinne Phyllis Zuckerman 1950; four c.; ed Univ. of Miami, New York Univ. Law School; service with US army in Second World War and Korean War, rising to rank of capt.; admitted to NY Bar 1953; employee Continental Casualty Co. 1952–60; joined American Int. Group (AIG) Inc. 1960, Pres. American Home Assurance Co. 1962–67, CEO AIG Inc. 1967–2005, Chair. 1989–2005; CEO C.V. Starr & Co., Starr Int. Co.; mem. The Business Roundtable, Pres.'s Advisory Cttee for Trade Policy and Negotiations; Chair. US–China Business Council, US–ASEAN Council on Business and Tech., US–Philippine Business Cttee, The Starr Foundation; Vice Chair. Center for Strategic and Int. Studies, Council on Foreign Relations; Chair. Emer. and Gov. Soc. of the NY Hosp.; hon. degrees from New England School of Law, NY Law School, Bryant Coll., Middlebury Coll., Brown Univ., Pace Univ. *Address:* The Starr Foundation, 70 Pine Street, 29th Floor, New York, NY 10270, USA (office).

GREENBERG, Robert R., PhD; American chemist; *Research Chemist and Group Leader, Chemical Science and Technology Laboratory, National Institute of Standards and Technology;* Research Chemist and Group Leader, Chemical Science and Tech. Lab., Nat. Inst. of Standards and Tech. (NIST) 1976–; Fellow, American Nuclear Soc. 1998, mem. Exec. Cttee Biology and Medicine Div. 2009; NIST Judson C. French Award 2003, NIST Bronze Medal 2007, Hevesy Medal, Journal of Radioanalytical and Nuclear Chemistry 2007. *Publications:* numerous scientific papers in professional journals on the devt of high accuracy/high precision nuclear analytical methods and quality assurance procedures, and application of these methods to certification of standard reference materials. *Address:* Analytical Chemistry Division (839), National Institute of Standards and Technology, 100 Bureau Drive, Stop 8395, Gaithersburg, MD 20899-8395, USA (office). *Telephone:* (301) 975-6285 (office). *Fax:* (301) 208-9279 (office). *E-mail:* robert.greenberg@nist.gov (office). *Website:* www.nist.gov (office).

GREENBLATT, Hellen Chaya, PhD; American immunologist and microbiologist; *Chief Science Officer, Legacy for Life;* b. 15 May 1947, Frankfurt am Main, Germany; d. of Gedaljie Greenblatt and Sara Greenblatt; ed City Coll. of New York, Univ. of Oklahoma, State Univ. of NY (SUNY) Downstate Medical Center, Brooklyn; came to USA 1948; microbiologist, Walter Reed Army Inst., Washington, DC 1978–80; Sr Research Immunoparasitologist, Merck Sharpe & Dohme, Rahway, NJ 1980–81; Immunology Assoc. Albert Einstein Coll. of Medicine, Bronx, NY 1981–84; Dir Research and New Business Devt Clinical Sciences Inc., Whippany, NJ 1984–87; Sr Devt Researcher, Devt Virology E.I. DuPont, Wilmington, DE 1988–89; Pres. and Man. Dir M-CAP Technologies Int./DCV 1990–93; Dir Tech. Affairs BTR Separations 1993–94; Vice-Pres. Research and Devt, DCV Biologicals 1994–97; Vice-Pres. Product Devt, Life Sciences Div., DCV Inc. 1997–2000; Vice-Pres. Legacy for Life, Div. of Arkion Life Sciences, Melbourne, Fla 2000–04, Chief Science Officer, Legacy for Life 2004–; patents for gastroprotective, anti-inflammatory and anti-diarrhoeal properties of immune egg; foremost authority on applications of hyperimmune egg in humans and pets; numerous int. and nat. research presentations in field; fmr Fellow, Nat. Research Council; mem. American Acad. of Anti-Aging Medicine, New York Acad. of Sciences, American Soc. for Nutrition, Inflammation Research Asscn; Outstanding Young Woman Award 1978, Competitive Research Council Award, Washington, DC 1978, Nat. Research Council Award 1978–80, Outstanding Scientist of the 20th Century 2001, WHO grants. *Publications include:* book chapters and numerous articles in professional journals. *Leisure interests:* gardening, reading, sailing, watercolour. *Address:* Legacy for Life, PO Box 1593, Millville, NJ 08332, USA (office). *Telephone:* (800) 746-0300 (office). *E-mail:* hgreenblatt@legacyforlife.net (office). *Website:* www.HellenGreenblatt.org (office); www.hyperimmuneegg.org (office).

GREENBLATT, Stephen J., BA, MPhil, PhD; American academic; *Cogan University Professor of the Humanities, Harvard University;* b. 7 Nov. 1943, Cambridge, MA; s. of Harry Greenblatt and Mollie Brown; three s.; m. Ramie Targoff 1998; ed Yale Univ., Pembroke Coll., Cambridge; Asst Prof. of English, Univ. of Calif., Berkeley 1969–74, Assoc. Prof. 1974–79, Prof. of English 1979–97; Prof. of English, Harvard Univ. 1997–, Cogan Univ. Prof. of the Humanities 2000–; numerous visiting professorships; Fellow, American Acad. of Arts and Sciences, Wissenschaftskolleg zu Berlin; mem. Int. Asscn of Univ. Profs of English, MLA, Renaissance Soc. of America; Guggenheim Fellow 1975, 1983; Porter Prize 1969, British Council Prize 1982, James Russell Lowell Prize 1989, Distinguished Teaching Award, Erasmus Inst. Prize 2001, Mellon Distinguished Humanist award 2002. *Publications:* Three Modern Satirists: Waugh, Orwell and Huxley 1965, Sir Walter Raleigh: The Renaissance Man and his Roles 1970, Renaissance Self-Fashioning: From More to Shakespeare 1980, Allegory and Representation (ed.) 1981, Power of Forms 1982, Representing the English Renaissance 1988, Shakespearean Negotiations: The Circulation of Social Energy in Renaissance England 1988, Learning to Curse: Essays in Early Modern Culture 1990, Marvelous Possessions: The Wonder of the New World 1991, Redrawing the Boundaries of Literary Study in English 1992, New World Encounters 1992, The Norton Shakespeare (ed.) 1997, The Norton Anthology of English Literature (ed.) 2000, Practising New Historicism 2000, Hamlet in Purgatory 2001, Will in the World: How Shakespeare Became Shakespeare 2004; contribs to scholarly journals. *Address:* Department of English, Harvard University, Cambridge, MA 02138, USA (office). *Telephone:* (617) 495-2101 (office). *Fax:* (617) 496-8737 (office). *E-mail:* greenbl@fas.harvard.edu (office). *Website:* www.fas.harvard.edu/~english (office).

GREENBURY, Sir Richard, Kt; British retail executive; b. July 1936; m. 1st Sian Eames Hughes (divorced); two s. two d.; m. 2nd Gabrielle Mary McManus 1985 (divorced 1996); remarried Sian Eames Hughes 1996; ed Ealing Co. Grammar School; jr man. trainee, Marks and Spencer 1953, Alt. Dir 1970, Dir 1972, Jt Man. Dir 1978–85, 1985–86; COO Marks and Spencer PLC 1986, CEO 1988–99, Chair. 1991–99; part-time mem. British Gas Corpn 1976–87; Dir (non-exec.) Metal Box PLC 1985–89, ICI 1992–96, Lloyds Bank (now Lloyds TSB Group) 1992–97, Zeneca 1993–99; mem. Supervisory Bd, Philips Electronics NV 1998–; Dir (non-exec.) UNIFI Inc. 1999–2002, Game PLC 2000–03; Dr hc (Ulster) 1993, (Greenwich) 1993, (Nottingham Trent) 1994, (City and Guilds of London Inst.) 1994, (UMIST) 1996, (London Business School) 1996, (Bradford) 1999. *Leisure interests:* playing tennis, music, reading, watching football. *Address:* Ambarrow Wood, Ambarrow Lane, Sandhurst, Berks., GU47 8JE, England (home). *Telephone:* (1344) 776985 (home). *Fax:* (1344) 776913 (home).

GREENE, Brian R., PhD; American physicist and academic; *Professor of Physics and Mathematics, Columbia University;* ed Harvard Univ., Univ. of Oxford; post-doctoral fellow, Harvard Univ. 1987–90; Asst Prof. Cornell Univ. 1990, Assoc. Prof. 1995, later Prof.; currrently Prof. of Physics and Mathematics, Columbia Univ.; Dir Theoretical Advanced Study Inst. 1996; has lectured in more than 20 countries; mem. Editorial Bd Physical Review D, Advance in Theoretical and Mathematical Physics. *Television:* The Theory of Everything 2003. *Publications:* journal papers: Duality in Calabi-Yau Moduli Space (with M. R. Plesser) 1990, Calabi-Yau Moduli Space, Mirror Manifolds and Spacetime Topology Change in String Theory (with P. S. Aspinwall and D. R. Morrison) 1994, Black Hole Condensation and the Unification of String Vacua (with D. R. Morrison and A. Strominger) 1995, Orbifold Resolution by D-Branes (with M. R. Douglas and D. R. Morrison) 1997, D-Brane Topology Changing Transitions 1998; books: The Elegant Universe (Aventis Prize for Science Books 2000) 1999, The Fabric of the Cosmos: Space, Time and the Texture of Reality 2004. *Address:* Faculty of Science, Columbia University, New York, NY 10032, USA (office). *Telephone:* (212) 854-3349 (office). *E-mail:* greene@phys.columbia.edu. *Website:* www.phys.columbia.edu/faculty/greene.htm.

GREENE, Graham Carleton, CBE, MA; British publisher; b. 10 June 1936, Berlin, Germany; s. of Sir Hugh Carleton Greene and Helga Mary Connolly; m. 1st Judith Margaret Gordon Walker 1957 (divorced); m. 2nd Sally Georgina Horton 1976 (divorced); one s.; also one step-s. one step-d.; ed Eton Coll. and Univ. Coll., Oxford; Dir Jonathan Cape Ltd 1962–90, Man. Dir 1966–88; Dir Chatto, Virago, Bodley Head and Jonathan Cape Ltd 1969–88, Chair. 1970–88; Dir Book Reps (NZ) Ltd 1971–88, CVBC Services 1972–88, Australasian Publishing Co. Ltd 1969–88 (Chair. 1978–88), Guinness Peat Group PLC 1973–87, Triad Paperbacks 1975–88, Greene King PLC 1979–, Statesman and Nation Publishing Co. 1980–85 (Chair. 1981–85), Statesman Publishing Co. Ltd 1980–85 (Chair. 1981–85), Random House Inc. 1987–88, Jupiter Int. Investment Trust PLC 1989–2001, Henry Sotheran Ltd 1990–, Ed Victor Ltd 1991–, Rosemary Sandberg Ltd 1991–2002, Libra KFT (Budapest) 1991–, London Merchant Securities PLC 1996–2007 (Chair. 2000–07); Chair. Random House UK Ltd 1988–90, British Museum Devt Trust 1986–93 (Vice-Chair. 1993–2004), British Museum Publications (now British Museum Co.) Ltd 1998–2002, Museums and Galleries Comm. 1991–96, Vice-Pres. 1997–;

Chair. Nation Pty Co. Ltd 1981–87, New Society 1984–86, Great Britain-China Centre 1986–1997; Dir Garsington Opera Ltd 1996–; mem. Bd of British Council 1977–88, Council of Publrs Asscn (Pres. 1977–79) 1969–88; Trustee, British Museum 1978–2002 (Chair. 1996–2002, Trustee Emer. 2002–), Open Coll. of the Arts 1990–97; mem. Int. Cttee of Int. Publrs Asscn 1977–88, Groupe des Editeurs de Livres de la CEE 1977–86 (Pres. 1984–86); Chevalier, Ordre des Arts et des Lettres; Hon. DLitt (Keele Univ.) 2002, Hon. DCL (Univ. E Anglia) 2002, Hon. DLitt (Buckingham) 2004. *Address:* D2 Albany, Piccadilly, London, W1J 0AP, England (home). *Telephone:* (20) 7734-0270 (home). *Fax:* (20) 7437-5251 (home). *E-mail:* grahamc.greene@virgin.net (home).

GREENE, Jack Phillip, PhD; American historian and academic; *Andrew W. Mellon Professor in the Humanities, Emeritus, Johns Hopkins University;* b. 12 Aug. 1931, Lafayette, Ind.; s. of Ralph B. Greene and Nellie A. Greene (née Miller); m. 1st Sue L. Neuenswander 1953 (divorced 1990); one s. one d.; m. 2nd Amy Turner Bushnell 1990; ed Univ. of North Carolina, Indiana Univ. and Duke Univ., Durham, NC; History Instructor, Mich. State Univ., East Lansing 1956–59; Asst Prof. of History, Western Reserve Univ., Cleveland, Ohio 1959–62, Assoc. Prof. 1962–65; Visiting Assoc. Prof. and Visiting Ed., William and Mary Quarterly, Coll. of William and Mary, Williamsburg, Va 1961–62; Assoc. Prof. of History, Univ. of Mich., Ann Arbor 1965–66; Visiting Assoc. Prof. of History, Johns Hopkins Univ., Baltimore, Md 1964–65, Prof. 1966–75, Chair. Dept of History 1970–72, Andrew W. Mellon Prof. in Humanities 1975–, now Prof. Emer.; Distinguished Prof., Univ. of Calif., Irvine 1990–92; Harmsworth Prof. of American History, Univ. of Oxford 1975–76; Visiting Prof., Hebrew Univ. of Jerusalem 1979, Ecole des Hautes Etudes en Science Sociale 1986–87; Freeman Prof., Univ. of Richmond, Va 1996; Sweet Prof., Mich. State Univ. 1997; mem. Inst. for Advanced Study 1970–71, 1985–86, American Philosophical Soc., American Acad. of Arts and Sciences; Corresp. mem. British Acad.; Fellow, Woodrow Wilson Int. Center for Scholars 1974–75, Center for Advanced Study in Behavioral Sciences 1979–80, Churchill Coll., Cambridge 1986–, Nat. Humanities Center 1987–88, Guggenheim Fellow 1964–65; John Carter Brown Library Fellow 1999–2000; several awards including American Historical Asscn Award for Scholarly Distinction 2008. *Publications:* 29 books, including Quest for Power 1963, Diary of Colonel Landon Carter of Sabine Hall (two vols) 1965, Settlements to Society 1966, Colonies to Nation 1967, Reinterpretation of American Revolution 1968, All Men are Created Equal 1976, Colonial British America 1983, Encyclopedia of American Political History 1984, Peripheries and Center 1986, Political Life in Eighteenth Century Virginia 1986, Intellectual Heritage of the Constitutional Era 1986, Magna Carta for America 1986, American Revolution 1987, Pursuits of Happiness 1988, Selling the New World 1988, Encyclopedia of the American Revolution (co-ed.) 1991, Imperatives, Behaviors and Identities 1992, Intellectual Construction of America 1993, Negotiated Authorities 1994, Understanding the American Revolution 1995, Interpreting Early America 1996, Companion to the American Revolution 2000, Atlantic History: A Critical Appraisal 2009, Exclusionary Empire 2009. *Leisure interests:* travel, cinema. *Address:* Department of History, The Johns Hopkins University, Baltimore, MD 21218 (office); 1974 Division Road, East Greenwich, RI 02898, USA (home). *Telephone:* (401) 884-5883 (home). *Fax:* (401) 886-4633 (home). *E-mail:* jpgreene@jhem.jhu.edu (office); jack_greene@brown.edu (home). *Website:* www.jhu.edu/~history (office).

GREENE, Mark I., MD, PhD, FRCP; Canadian pathologist and academic; *John Eckman Professor of Medical Science, University of Pennsylvania;* ed Univ. of Manitoba, Canada; MRC Fellow, Harvard Univ., Mass 1976–78, Asst Prof. of Pathology 1978–80, Assoc. Prof. 1980–85; Clinical Consultant in Medicine, Dana Farber Cancer Inst., Boston 1980–86; Head, Basic Research Unit of Immunology, Univ. of Pennsylvania 1986–, Head of Fundamental Research, Cancer Center 1987–, Vice-Chair. Dept of Pathology 1993–, currently Eckman Prof. of Medical Science; Newton Abraham Prof. of Biological Science, Univ. of Oxford; J. Allyn Taylor Int. Prize in Medicine, Robarts Research Inst. 2006. *Publications:* numerous scientific papers in professional journals on receptors, reoviruses, neu-growth factor receptors and T-cell receptors. *Address:* Immunology Graduate Group, University of Pennsylvania, 410 BRB II/III, Philadelphia, PA 19104-6160, USA (office). *Telephone:* (215) 898-2847 (office). *Fax:* (215) 746-5525 (office). *E-mail:* greene@reo.med.upenn.edu (office). *Website:* www.med.upenn.edu/immun/greene.shtml (office); www.uphs.upenn.edu/abramson/greene.html (office).

GREENE, Maurice; American professional athlete; b. 23 July 1974, Kansas City, Mo.; s. of Ernest Greene and Jackie Greene; ed Schlage High School and Park Coll., Kansas City; world record-holder indoor 50m (shared with Donovan Bailey) and 60m (as at end 2002); coached by John Smith 1996–; silver medal US Championships 60m 1995; gold medal US Indoor Championships 60 m 1997; gold medal US Championships 100m 1997; gold medal World Championships 100m 1997, 100m, 200m and 4×100m relay 1999, 100m 2001; Olympic gold medallist 100m and 4×100m 2000, bronze medal 100m 2004; set world record for 100m in Athens 1999 (9.79 seconds); f. Finish the Race Foundation. *Address:* HS International, 9871 Irvine Center Drive, Irvine, CA 92618, USA (office). *Telephone:* (949) 753-9153 (office). *Fax:* (949) 753-9253 (office). *E-mail:* maurice@hsi.net (office). *Website:* www.hsi.net (office).

GREENE, Sally, MBA; British impresario and producer; *Chief Executive, Old Vic Productions plc;* b. 27 May 1954; d. of Basil Greene and Clare Tully; m. Robert Bourne; one s. one d.; ed St Maur's Convent, Weybridge and Guildhall School of Music and Drama; bought Richmond Theatre, Surrey 1986, programmed then restored theatre 1991; took over Criterion Theatre, Piccadilly 1992, restored theatre, re-opening it 1993; f. Criterion Productions PLC 1994; bought The Old Vic Theatre 1998, est. charitable trust to run it; Founder (with Kevin Spacey q.v.) and CEO Old Vic Productions plc 2000; Club Owner Ronnie Scott's, London 2005–. *Productions include:* Taking Sides, Criterion Theatre 1994, Hot House, Comedy Theatre 1994, Jack 1993, Cyrano de Bergerac, RSC 1995, Car Man, Old Vic 2000, Medea 2001, Life x 3, Old Vic 2001, Vagina Monologues, Ambassador's Theatre 2001–02. *Leisure interests:* piano, skiing, singing. *Address:* Old Vic Productions plc, Park House, 26 North End Road, London, NW11 7PT; The Old Vic, The Cut, London, SE1 8NB (office); Lindsay House, 100 Cheyne Walk, London, SW10 0DQ, England (home). *Telephone:* (20) 7401-3534 (office). *Fax:* (20) 7261-9161 (office). *E-mail:* s.greene@dial.pipex.com (home). *Website:* www.oldvicproductions.com (office).

GREENER, Sir Anthony Armitage, Kt, FCMA; British business executive; *Chairman, The Minton Trust;* b. 26 May 1940, Bowden; s. of William Greener and Diana Greener; m. Min Ogilvie 1974; one s. one d.; ed Marlborough Coll.; Marketing Man. Thames Board Mills 1969; Retail Controller, Alfred Dunhill Ltd (later Dunhill Holdings PLC) 1972, Dir 1974, Man. Dir 1975; Man. Dir United Distillers 1987–92; Dir Guinness PLC 1986–97, Jt Man. Dir 1989–91, Chief Exec. 1992–97, Chair. 1993–97; Co-Chair. Diageo (after merger with Grand Metropolitan PLC) PLC 1997–98, Chair. 1998–2000; Chair. University for Industry Ltd 2000–04, Qualifications and Curriculum Authority 2002–08; Deputy Chair. BT 2001–; Chair. The Minton Trust, St Giles Trust 2009–; Dir Louis Vuitton Moet Hennessy 1989–97, Reed Int. 1990–93, Reed Elsevier 1993–98, Robert Mondavi 2000–04. *Leisure interests:* skiing, sailing, gardening. *Address:* The Minton Trust, 26 Hamilton House, Vicarage Gate, London, W8 4HL, England (office). *Telephone:* (20) 7937-2048 (office). *Fax:* (20) 7937-2048 (office). *E-mail:* greenera@mintontrust.com (office).

GREENFIELD, Jerry; American business executive; *Co-founder, Ben & Jerry's Homemade Inc.;* b. 1951, Brooklyn, NY; m. Elizabeth Greenfield 1987; one s.; ed Calhoun High School, Merrick, NY, Oberlin Coll., OH; employed as lab technician, NY and NC –1976; Co-founder Ben & Jerry's Homemade Inc. (with Ben Cohen, q.v.) 1977, first Ice Cream Parlour opened Burlington, VT 1978, responsible for creation of ice-cream, est. Ben & Jerry's Foundation (to oversee donation of 7.5% of profits to non-profit orgs); Founding mem. Businesses for Social Responsibility (org. which promotes socially responsible business practices). *Leisure interests:* basketball, volleyball, spending time with family and friends. *Address:* Ben & Jerry's Homemade Inc., 30 Community Drive, South Burlington, VT 05403-6828, USA (office). *Telephone:* (802) 846-1500 (office). *Website:* www.benjerry.com (office).

GREENFIELD OF OTMOOR, Baroness (Life Peer), cr. 2001, of Otmoor in the County of Oxfordshire; **Susan Adele Greenfield,** CBE, DPhil; British pharmacologist; *Professor in Synaptic Pharmacology, University of Oxford;* b. 1 Oct. 1950; d. of Reginald Myer Greenfield and Doris Margaret Winifred Greenfield; m. Peter William Atkins 1991; ed Godolphin and Latymer School for Girls, St Hilda's Coll., Oxford; MRC Training Fellow Univ. Lab. of Physiology, Oxford 1977–81; fmrly with Coll. de France, Paris; MRC-INSERM French Exchange Fellow 1979–80; Jr Research Fellow Green Coll., Oxford 1981–84, lecturer in Synaptic Pharmacology 1985–96, Prof. in Synaptic Pharmacology 1996–, Gresham Prof. of Physic Gresham Coll. 1995–; Dir Royal Inst. 1998–; Visiting Fellow Inst. of Neuroscience La Jolla, USA 1995; Sr Research Fellow Lincoln Coll. Oxford; Hon. Fellow St Hilda's Coll. Oxford, Royal Coll. of Physicians 2000; Visiting Distinguished Scholar Queen's Univ., Belfast 1996; Trustee Science Museum 2003; awarded 21 Hon. DSc degrees 1997–2002; Légion d'Honneur 2003; Woman of Distinction, Jewish Care 1998, Michael Faraday Medal, Royal Soc. 1998, 2000. *Radio appearances include:* Start the Week, Any Questions and other discussion programmes; presenter of Turn On, Turn Off series on drugs and the brain, Today Programme. *Television appearances include:* Dimbleby Lecture 1999, author and presenter of Brain Story 'Landmark' (series of programmes on the brain) 2000, Big Ideas in Science, Channel 5 (UK). *Publications include:* numerous articles in learned journals; Mindwaves (co-ed. with C. B. Blakemore) 1987, Journey to the Centres of the Brain (with G. Ferry) 1994, Journey to the Centres of the Mind 1995, The Human Mind Explained (ed.) 1996, The Human Brain: A Guided Tour 1997; Brainpower (ed.) 2000, Brain Story 2000, Private Life of the Brain 2000, Tomorrow's People: How 21st Century Technology is Changing the Way We Think and Feel 2003, ID: The Quest for Identity in the 21st Century 2008. *Leisure interests:* aerobics, travel. *Address:* Department of Pharmacology, Mansfield Road, Oxford, OX1 3QT (office). *Telephone:* (1865) 271628 (office). *Fax:* (1865) 271853 (office). *E-mail:* susan.greenfield@pharm.ox.ac.uk (office).

GREENGARD, Paul, PhD; American neuroscientist, biochemist and academic; *Vincent Astor Professor, Rockefeller University;* b. 11 Dec. 1925, New York; ed Johns Hopkins Univ., Baltimore; post-doctoral studies in biochemistry, Univ. of London, Univ. of Cambridge, UK and NIH, Bethesda, Md 1953–59; Dir Dept of Biochemistry, Geigy Research Lab., Ardsley, NY 1959–67; Visiting Assoc. Prof. and Prof. of Pharmacology, Albert Einstein Coll. of Medicine, NY 1961–70; Prof. of Pharmacology and Psychiatry, Yale Univ. School of Medicine 1968–83; Vincent Astor Prof. and Head, Lab. of Molecular and Cellular Neuroscience, Rockefeller Univ., NY 1983–; mem. NAS, NARSAD Scientific Council; numerous awards and prizes including Dickson Prize and Medal in Medicine, Univ. of Pittsburgh 1977, New York Acad. of Sciences Award in Biological and Medicinal Sciences 1980, 1993, 3M Life Sciences Award, Fed. of American Socs for Experimental Biology 1987, NAS Award in the Neurosciences 1991, Lieber Prize for Outstanding Achievement in Schizophrenia Research 1996, Metropolitan Life Foundation Award for Medical Research 1998, Bristol-Myers Squibb Award for Distinguished Achievement in Neuroscience Research 1989, Nobel Prize for Medicine or Physiology (co-recipient) 2000. *Publications:* numerous publs and articles in journals. *Address:* Laboratory of Molecular and Cellular Neuroscience, The Rockefeller University, 1230 York Avenue, New York, NY 10021, USA (office). *Telephone:* (212) 327-8780 (office). *Fax:* (212) 327-7746 (office). *E-mail:* greengard@rockefeller.edu (office). *Website:* www.rockefeller.edu/research/abstract.php?id=53 (office); www.rockefeller.edu/labheads/greengard/greengard-lab.html (office).

GREENGRASS, Paul; British film and television director; b. 13 Aug. 1955, Cheam, Surrey; began career as an investigative journalist and award-winning documentary filmmaker; Pres. Directors UK 2008–; BAFTA Alan Clarke Award for Outstanding Creative Contrib. to Television 2005. *Films directed include:* Resurrected (Interfilm and OCIC Jury Awards, Berlin Film Festival) 1989, Sophie's World, The Theory of Flight 1998, Bloody Sunday (also writer) (Golden Bear, Berlin Int. Film Festival) 2002, The Bourne Supremacy 2004, United 93 (Best Dir, Los Angeles Film Critics Asscn, Best Film, New York Film Critics' Circle Awards, Best Dir, Best British Producer, Best Film, London Film Critics' Circle Awards, BAFTA Award for Best Dir 2007) 2006, The Bourne Ultimatum 2007. *Television work includes:* World In Action, Food and Trucks and Rock and Roll, U2 – Anthem for the Eighties, Moscow Week, Coppers, What Ever Happened to Woodward and Bernstein, When The Lies Run Out (Chicago Film Festival Silver Medal) 1993, Kavanagh QC 1994, Open Fire (writer) 1994, The One That Got Away (also writer) 1996, The Fix (also writer) 1997, The Murder of Stephen Lawrence (also writer) 1999, Omagh (writer and producer) (BAFTA Award for Best Single Drama 2005) 2004. *Publications include:* Spycatcher (with Peter Wright). *Address:* c/o CAA, 2000 Avenue of the Stars, Los Angeles, CA 90067, USA.

GREENLAND, Prof. Dennis James, DPhil, FRS, FIBiol; British soil scientist and academic; *Visiting Professor, University of Reading;* b. 13 June 1930, Portsmouth, Hants.; s. of James John Greenland and Lily Gardener; m. Edith Mary Johnston 1955; one s. two d.; ed Portsmouth Grammar School, Christ Church, Oxford; lecturer Univ. of Ghana 1955–59; lecturer Waite Inst., Univ. of Adelaide, Australia 1960–63, Reader and Head of Soil Science 1963–70, Hanniford Lecturer 1978; Prof. and Head of Dept of Soil Science, Univ. of Reading 1970–79, Visiting Prof. 1988–; Chair. Scientific Advisory Panel, Commonwealth Devt Corpn 1991–96; Research Dir Int. Inst. of Tropical Agric. (seconded from Univ. of Reading) 1974–76; Deputy Dir-Gen. (Research) Int. Rice Research Inst., Philippines 1979–87; Dir Scientific Services, CAB Int., UK 1987–92, Fellow, World Acad. of Arts and Science 1988; Hon. mem. American Soc. of Agronomy, American Soc. of Soil Science 1993; Hon. DrAgr (Univ. of Ghent) 1982, Hon. DSc (Ohio State Univ.) 2003; Blackman Lecturer, Univ. of Oxford 1988. *Publications:* The Soil Under Shifting Cultivation (co-author) 1960, The Sustainability of Rice Farming 1997; numerous scientific articles in learned journals. *Leisure interests:* golf, walking, watching cricket. *Address:* Low Wood, The Street, South Stoke, Oxon., RG8 0JS, England (home). *Telephone:* (1491) 873259 (home). *Fax:* (1491) 872572 (home). *E-mail:* greenland.dennis@virgin.net (home).

GREENSPAN, Alan, KBE, MA, PhD; American economist and central banker (retd) and business consultant; *President, Greenspan Associates LLC;* b. 6 March 1926, New York; s. of Herbert Greenspan and Rose Goldsmith; m. Andrea Mitchell 1997; ed New York and Columbia Univs; Pres., CEO Townsend-Greenspan & Co. Inc. 1954–74, 1977–87; mem. Nixon for Pres. Cttee 1968–69; mem. Task Force for Econ. Growth 1969, Comm. on an All-Volunteer Armed Force 1969–70, Comm. on Financial Structure and Regulation 1970–71; Consultant to Council of Econ. Advisers 1970–74, to US Treasury 1971–74, to Fed. Reserve Bd 1971–74; Chair. Council of Econ. Advisers 1974–77, Nat. Comm. on Social Security Reform 1981–83; Chair. Bd of Govs Fed. Reserve System 1987–2006; Founder and Pres. Greenspan Assocs (consulting firm), Washington, DC 2006–, advisor to Pimco (for fund man.) 2007–, to Deutsche Bank (for investment banking) 2007–; Adviser Paulson and Co., New York 2008–; mem. Sec. of Commerce's Econ. Comm.'s Cen. Market System Cttee 1972, GNP Review Cttee of Office of Man. and Budget, Time Magazine's Bd of Economists 1971–74, 1977–87, Pres.'s Econ. Policy Advisory Bd 1981–87, Pres.'s Foreign Intelligence Advisory Bd 1983–85, Exec. Cttee Trilateral Comm.; Sr Adviser, Brookings Inst. Panel on Econ. Activity 1970–74, 1977–87; Adjunct Prof., Grad. School of Business Man., New York 1977–87; mem. Bd of Dirs Council on Foreign Relations; Past Pres. and Fellow, Nat. Asscn of Business Economists; mem. Bd of Dirs Trans World Financial Co. 1962–74, Dreyfus Fund 1970–74, Gen. Cable Corpn 1973–74, 1977–78, Sun Chemical Corpn 1973–74, Gen. Foods Corpn 1977–86, J.P. Morgan & Co. 1977–87, Mobil Corpn 1977–87, Aluminum Co. of America (ALCOA) 1978–87; Hon. KBE 2002, Commdr Légion d'honneur; Jefferson Award 1976, William Butler Memorial Award 1977, Presidential Medal of Freedom 2005. *Publication:* The Age of Turbulence: Adventures in a New World (memoirs) 2007. *Leisure interest:* golf. *Address:* Greenspan Associates LLC, 1133 Connecticut Avenue, Suite 810, NW, Washington, DC 20036, USA (office). *Telephone:* (202) 457-8250 (office).

GREENSPON, Edward B., BA, MA; Canadian journalist and editor; *Editor-in-Chief, The Globe and Mail;* b. 26 March 1957, Montreal; s. of Mortimer Greenspon and Rosalie Greenspon; m. Janice Neil 1984; three s.; ed Carleton Univ., Ottawa, London School of Econs, UK (Commonwealth Scholar); fmr paperboy for (now defunct) Montreal Daily Star; moved to London, UK to study; Business Reporter, The Globe and Mail 1986, European Business Corresp., London, returned to Canada 1989, Man. Ed. Report on Business section and Deputy Man. Ed. The Globe and Mail 1989–93, Ottawa Bureau Chief and Assoc. Ed. 1993–99, Exec. News Ed., Political Ed. and columnist for Ottawa region 1999–2002, Founding Ed. www.globeandmail.com, Ed.-in-Chief 2002–; Hyman Soloman Award for Excellence in Public Policy Journalism. *Publications:* Double Vision: The Inside Story of the Liberals in Power (co-author) (Douglas Purvis Award for best public policy book 1996) 1995, Searching for Certainty: Inside the New Canadian Mindset (with Darrell Bricker) 2001. *Address:* The Globe and Mail, 444 Front Street West, Toronto, ON M5V 2S9, Canada (office). *Telephone:* (416) 585-5000 (office). *Fax:* (416) 585-5085 (office). *E-mail:* egreenspon@globeandmail.ca (office). *Website:* www.globeandmail.com (office).

GREENSTOCK, Sir Jeremy (Quentin), GCMG, MA; British diplomatist; *Director, Ditchley Foundation;* b. 27 July 1943, Harrow; s. of the late John Wilfrid Greenstock and Ruth Margaret Logan; m. Anne Derryn Ashford Hodges 1969; one s. two d.; ed Harrow School and Worcester Coll., Oxford; Asst Master, Eton Coll. 1966–69; entered diplomatic service 1969, studied Arabic at MECAS 1970–72, served in Dubai 1972–74, Pvt. Sec. to Amb., Washington, DC 1974–78, with FCO (Planning, Personnel Operations Dept, N East and N African Dept) 1978–83; Commercial Counsellor, Jeddah 1983–85, Riyadh 1985–86; Head of Chancery, Embassy in Paris 1987–90; Asst Under-Sec. of State, FCO 1990–93; Minister, Embassy in Washington, DC 1994–95; Deputy Under-Sec. of State FCO 1995; Political Dir FCO 1996–98; Perm. Rep. to UN, New York 1998–2003, Chair. UN Security Council Counter-Terrorism Cttee 2001–03; UK Special Rep. for Iraq 2003–04; Dir The Ditchley Foundation 2004–; Special Adviser to BP Group 2004–; Non-Exec. Dir De La Rue PLC 2005–; Trustee, Int. Rescue Cttee (UK) 2006–. *Leisure interests:* reading, travel, golf, skiing, listening to music, watching sport. *Address:* The Ditchley Foundation, Ditchley Park, Enstone, Oxon., OX7 4ER, England (office). *E-mail:* info@ditchley.co.uk (office). *Website:* www.ditchley.co.uk (office).

GREENWOOD, Duncan Joseph, CBE, DSc, FRS, FRSC, FIHort; British agronomist and academic; *Associate Fellow, Warwick University at Warwick HRI;* b. 16 Oct. 1932, New Barnet, Herts.; s. of Herbert James Greenwood and Alison Fairgrieve Greenwood; ed Hutton Grammar School, Univs of Liverpool and Aberdeen; Research Fellow, Univ. of Aberdeen 1957–59; Research Leader, Nat. Vegetable Research Station 1959–66; Head of Soil Science, Horticulture Research Int. (HRI— fmrly Nat. Vegetable Research Station) 1966–92, Fellow Emer. 1992–2004, Assoc. Fellow, Univ. of Warwick at Warwick HRI 2004–; Visiting Prof. of Plant Sciences, Univ. of Leeds 1985–93; Hon. Prof. of Agricultural Chem., Univ. of Birmingham 1986–93; Chair. Agricultural Group, Soc. of Chemical Industry 1975–77; Pres. Int. Cttee Plant Nutrition 1978–82, British Soc. of Soil Science 1990–92; Hon. Life Mem. Asscn of Applied Biologists 2004; Sir Gilbert Morgan Medal, Soc. of Chemical Industry 1962, Research Medal of the Royal Agricultural Soc. of England 1979, Grower of the Year Lifetime Achievement Award 2000, Pres.'s Medal, Inst. of Horticulture 2004. *Publications:* more than 170 publs in scientific journals, mostly on soils and plant nutrition. *Address:* 23 Shelley Road, Stratford upon Avon, CV37 7JR (home); Warwick HRI, Wellesbourne, Warwick, CV35 9EF, England (office). *Telephone:* (24) 7657-4455 (office); (1789) 204735 (home). *Fax:* (24) 7652-4500 (office). *E-mail:* d.greenwood@warwick.ac.uk (office); duncangreenwood@compuserve.com (home). *Website:* www2.warwick.ac.uk/fac/sci/hri2/about/staff/dgreenwood (office).

GREENWOOD, Norman Neill, PhD, DSc, ScD, FRS, CChem, FRSC, FRIC, MRI; British chemist and academic; *Professor Emeritus of Chemistry, University of Leeds;* b. 19 Jan. 1925, Melbourne, Australia; s. of the late Prof. J. Neill Greenwood and Gladys Uhland; m. Kirsten M. Rydland 1951; three d.; ed Univs of Melbourne and Cambridge; Resident Tutor and Lecturer, Trinity Coll., Univ. of Melbourne 1946–48; Sr Harwell Research Fellow, AERE 1951–53; Lecturer, then Sr Lecturer in Inorganic Chem., Univ. of Nottingham 1953–61; Prof. and Head, Dept of Inorganic Chem., Univ. of Newcastle-upon-Tyne 1961–71; Prof. and Head, Dept of Inorganic and Structural Chem., Univ. of Leeds 1971–90, Prof. Emer. 1990–, Dean of Faculty of Science 1986–88; Visiting Prof. at univs in Australia, USA, Canada, China, Japan and Denmark since 1966; Pres. Inorganic Chem. Div., IUPAC 1977–81; Pres. Dalton Div., Royal Soc. of Chem. 1979–81; Pres. BAAS, Section B (Chem.) 1990–91; Foreign Assoc. Acad. des Sciences, Institut de France 1992; Hon. DUniv (Nancy) 1977; Hon. DSc (Toho Univ., Tokyo) 2000; Tilden Lectureship and Medal, Chem. Soc. 1966, RSC Medal for Main Group Element Chem. 1974, Gold Medal of City of Nancy (France) 1977, A.W. von Hofmann Lectureship, Gesellschaft Deutscher Chemiker 1983, RSC Liversidge Lectureship and Medal 1984, Egon Wiberg Lectureship, Univ. of Munich 1989, Ludwig Mond Lectureship and Medal 1991, Medal for Tertiary Educ. 1993, Humphry Davy Lecturer, Royal Soc. 2000 and other awards and distinctions. *Publications:* more than 490 original research papers in refereed journals and monographs; books include Ionic Crystals, Lattice Defects and Nonstoichiometry 1968, Mössbauer Spectroscopy (with T. C. Gibb) 1971, Chemistry of the Elements (with A. Earnshaw) 1984. *Leisure interests:* music, travel. *Address:* Department of Chemistry, University of Leeds, Leeds, LS2 9JT, England (office). *Telephone:* (113) 3436406 (office). *Fax:* (113) 3436565 (office). *E-mail:* n.n.greenwood@chem.leeds.ac.uk (office). *Website:* www.chem.leeds.ac.uk (office).

GREER, David Steven, MD; American medical specialist; b. 12 Oct. 1925, Brooklyn, New York; s. of Jacob Greer and Mary (née Zaslawsky) Greer; m. Marion Clarich 1950; one s. one d.; ed Univs. of Notre Dame and Chicago; Intern, Yale-New Haven Medical Center 1953–54; Resident in Medicine, Univ. of Chicago Clinics 1954–57; specialist in internal medicine, Fall River, Mass. 1957–74; Chief of Staff, Dept of Medicine, Fall River Gen. Hosp. 1959–62; Medical Dir Earle E. Hussey Hosp., Fall River 1962–72; Chief of Staff, Dept of Medicine, Truesdale Clinic and Truesdale Hosp., Fall River 1971–74; Faculty mem. Tufts Univ. Coll. of Medicine, Boston, Mass. 1969–78; Faculty mem. Brown Univ. Program in Medicine 1973–75, Prof. of Community Health 1975–93, Prof. Emer. 1993–, Assoc. Dean 1974–81, Dean 1981–92, Dean Emer. 1992–, Acting Dir Generalist Physician Programs, AAMC 1993–94; mem. NAS Inst. of Medicine; academic medical consultant 1993–; various public appts.; Cutting Foundation Medal for Service to Religion and Medicine 1976 and other awards. *Publications:* numerous articles on chronic disease, geriatrics, long-term care and health-care evaluation. *Leisure* *interest:* squash. *Address:* Brown University, Box G, Providence, RI 02912, USA. *Telephone:* (401) 729-3100. *E-mail:* Greer@brown.edu.

GREER, Germaine, PhD; Australian feminist, author and broadcaster; b. 29 Jan. 1939, Melbourne; d. of Eric Reginald Greer and Margaret May Greer (née Lafrank); ed Star of the Sea Convent, Vic., Melbourne, Sydney Univ., Univ. of Cambridge, UK; Sr Tutor in English, Sydney Univ. 1963–64; Asst Lecturer then Lecturer in English, Univ. of Warwick 1967–72, Prof. of English and Comparative Studies 1998–2003; lecturer throughout N America with American Program Bureau 1973–78, to raise funds for Tulsa Bursary and Fellowship Scheme 1980–83; Visiting Prof., Grad. Faculty of Modern Letters, Univ. of Tulsa 1979, Prof. of Modern Letters 1980–83, Founder-Dir of Tulsa Centre for the Study of Women's Literature, Founder-Ed. Tulsa Studies in Women's Literature 1981; Dir Stump Cross Books 1988–; Special Lecturer and Unofficial Fellow, Newnham Coll., Cambridge 1989–98; broadcaster/ journalist/columnist/reviewer 1972–; Jr Govt Scholarship 1952, Diocesan Scholarship 1956, Sr Govt Scholarship 1956, Teacher's Coll. Studentship 1956, Commonwealth Scholarship 1964; numerous television appearances and public talks including discussion with Norman Mailer in The Theatre of Ideas, New York; Dr hc (Univ. of Griffith, Australia) 1996, (Univ. of York, Toronto) 1999, (UMIST) 2000; hon. degrees (Melbourne) 2003, (Essex) 2003, (Anglia Polytechnic) 2003, (Sydney) 2005; Australian Living Treasure Nat. Trust Award Centenary Medal 2003. *Film appearance:* Rabbit Fever 2006. *Television:* The Late Review, Celebrity Big Brother. *Publications:* The Female Eunuch 1969, The Obstacle Race: The Fortunes of Women Painters and Their Work 1979, Sex and Destiny: The Politics of Human Fertility 1984, Shakespeare (co-ed.) 1986, The Madwoman's Underclothes (selected journalism 1964–85) 1986, Kissing the Rod: An Anthology of 17th Century Women's Verse (co-ed.) 1988, Daddy, We Hardly Knew You (J. R. Ackerly Prize and Premio Internazionale Mondello) 1989, The Uncollected Verse of Aphra Behn (ed.) 1989, The Change: Women, Ageing and the Menopause 1991, The Collected Works of Katherine Philips, the Matchless Orinda, Vol. III: The Translations (co-ed.) 1993, Slip-Shod Sybils: Recognition, Rejection and The Woman Poet 1995, The Surviving Works of Anne Wharton (co-ed.) 1997, The Whole Woman 1999, John Wilmot, Earl of Rochester 1999, 101 Poems by 101 Women (ed.) 2001, The Boy 2003, Poems for Gardeners (ed.) 2003, Whitefella Jump Up The Shortest Way to Nationhood 2004, Shakespeare's Wife 2007; articles for Listener, Spectator, Esquire, Harper's Magazine, Playboy, Private Eye and other journals. *Leisure interest:* gardening. *Address:* Aitken Alexander Associates Ltd, 18–21 Cavaye Place, London, SW10 9PT, England (office). *Telephone:* (20) 7373-8672 (office). *Fax:* (20) 7373-6002 (office). *E-mail:* reception@aitkenalexander.co.uk (office). *Website:* www.aitkenalexander.co .uk (office).

GREET, Rev. Kenneth Gerald; British ecclesiastic; b. 17 Nov. 1918, Bristol; s. of Walter Greet and Renée Greet; m. Mary Eileen Edbrooke 1947; one s. two d.; ed Cotham Grammar School, Bristol, Handsworth Coll., Birmingham; Cwm and Kingstone Methodist Church 1940–42; Ogmore Vale Methodist Church 1942–45; Tonypandy Cen. Hall 1947–54; Sec. Dept of Christian Citizenship of Methodist Church and Social Responsibility Div. 1954–71; Sec., Methodist Conf. 1971–84, Pres. 1980–81; mem. British Council of Churches 1955–84 (Chair. Exec. 1977–80), World Methodist Council 1957– (Chair. Exec. Cttee 1976–81); Chair. Exec. Temperance Council of Christian Churches 1961–71; Moderator, Free Church Fed. Council 1982–83; Co-Chair. World Disarmament Campaign 1982–86, Pres. 1989–94, Vice-Pres. 1994–; Rep. to Cen. Cttee, WCC, Addis Ababa 1971, Nairobi 1975; Beckly Lecturer 1962, Willson Lecturer, Kansas City 1966, Cato Lecturer, Sydney 1975; Chair. of Govs, Southlands Coll. 1986–98; Hon. DD (Ohio) 1967; Hon. DUniv (Surrey) 1998. *Publications:* The Mutual Society 1962, Man and Wife Together 1962, Large Petitions 1962, Guide to Loving 1965, The Debate About Drink 1969, The Sunday Question 1969, The Art of Moral Judgement 1970, When the Spirit Moves 1975, A Lion from a Thicket 1978, The Big Sin: Christianity and the Arms Race 1982, Under the Rainbow Arch 1984, What Shall I Cry 1986, Jabez Bunting: a biography 1995, Fully Connected 1997. *Leisure interest:* photography. *Address:* 89 Broadmark Lane, Rustington, Sussex, BN16 2JA, England (home). *Telephone:* (1903) 773326 (home). *E-mail:* greet@surefish.co .uk (home).

GREF, German Oskarovich; Russian politician, jurist and banker; *Chairman and CEO, Sberbank;* b. 8 Feb. 1964, Panfilovo, Pavlodar Region, Kazakh SSR; m. 1st; one s.; m. 2nd 2004; ed Omsk State Univ.; legal adviser, Pavlodar regional agric. co. 1981–82; army service 1982–84; Lecturer in Law, Omsk State Univ. 1990; legal adviser, Cttee on Econ. Devt and Property, Petrodvorets Dist Admin., St Petersburg 1991–92; Chair. Cttee on Property Man., concurrently Deputy Head Petrodvorets Dist Admin. 1992–94; Deputy Chair., Dir Dept of Real Estate, First Deputy Chair. Cttee on Man. of Municipal Property, St Petersburg Admin. 1994–97; Vice-Gov., Chair. Cttee on Man. of Municipal Property, St Petersburg Admin. 1997–98; mem. Exec. Bd Ministry of State Property, Russian Fed. 1998; First Deputy Minister 1998–2000; mem. Exec. Bd Fed. Comm. on Market of Securities 1999–; head of team working on econ. reform plan for Pres. Putin 1999–2000; Minister of Econ. Devt and Trade of Russian Fed. 2000–07; Chair. and CEO Sberbank (Savings Bank of Russian Fed.) 2007–. *Address:* Sberbank, 19 Vavilova Street, 117997 Moscow, Russia (office). *Telephone:* (495) 957-58-62 (office). *Fax:* (495) 957-57-31 (office); (495) 747-37-31 (office). *E-mail:* sbrf@sbrf.ru (office); webmaster@sbrf.ru (office). *Website:* www.sbrf.ru (office).

GREGAN, George, BE; Australian rugby football player (rugby union); *Captain, Australian Rugby Union Team;* b. 19 April 1973, Zambia; m. Erica Gregan; three c.; ed St Edmund's Coll., Canberra, Univ. of Canberra; scrum half; teams played for include Randwick, ACT Under-19s, ACT Under-21s, Australian Under-19s, Australian Under-21s, Australian Sevens, ACT

Brumbies (120 state caps, 103 appearances in Super 12 competition), 106 caps and 89 test points (16 tries, three drop-goals) for Australia since 1994 (debut versus Italy in Brisbane); won World Cup 1999 with Australia; nat. Capt. since 2001 and took Australia to World Cup final in 2003; holds record for most Australian test caps; senior tours to South Africa (for World Cup) 1995, Europe 1996, Argentina and UK 1996, France and England 1997, UK (for World Cup) 1999, UK and Europe 2001, 2002, 2003, 2004; Super 12 Player of the Tournament 1997, Int. Players' Asscn Player of the Year 2001, Australian Super 12 Player of the Year 2001, Wallaby Players' Player 2001, awarded the inaugural Rugby Medal for Excellence in 2001. *Leisure interests:* golf, skiing, good food and wine. *Address:* Australian Rugby Union, POB 188, North Sydney, NSW 2060, Australia. *Telephone:* (2) 9956-3444. *Website:* www .rugby.com.au; www.georgegregan.com.

GREGER, Janet L., BS, MS, PhD; American academic; *Vice-Provost of Strategic Planning, University of Connecticut;* b. 18 Feb. 1948, Illinois; d. of Harold Greger and Marjorie Greger; ed Univ. of Illinois, Urbana-Champaign and Cornell Univ.; Asst Prof., Purdue Univ. 1973–78; Asst Prof., then Assoc. Prof., Univ. of Wisconsin, Madison 1978–83, Prof. of Nutritional Sciences 1983–2003, Prof. Emer. 2003–, Assoc. Dean, Grad. School 1990–96, Assoc. Dean, Medical School 1996–98; Vice-Provost of Research and Grad. Educ. and Dean of Grad. School, Univ. of Connecticut 2002–05, Vice Provost for Strategic Planning 2005–, also Prof., Dept of Nutritional Sciences; AAAS Congressional Sciences Eng Fellow 1984–85; mem. Bd of Man. COGR 1993–99; mem. Bd of Dirs AAALAC 1992–2003, NIH Panel on Regulatory Burden 1999–2002; mem. Council Soc. of Experimental Biology and Medicine 2002–05, NAS/NRC Cttees 1991–94, 1996–2000, 2003–07; AAAS Congressional Science and Eng Fellowship 1984–85; Excellence in Nutrition Educ. Award, American Soc. for Nutrition 2008. *Publications:* Nutrition for Living 1985, 1988, 1991, 1994; over 159 papers in scientific journals and books. *Leisure interests:* travel, reading. *Address:* 925 Desert Willow Court, Bernalillo, NM 87004, USA (home). *Telephone:* (860) 933-8589 (office); (505) 876-4832 (home). *E-mail:* janet.greger@uconn.edu (office).

GREGG, Judd, JD, LLM; American politician; *Senator from New Hampshire;* b. 14 Feb. 1947, Nashua, NH; s. of the late Hugh Gregg and Catherine Warner Gregg; m. Kathleen MacLellan 1973; one s. two d.; ed Columbia and Boston Univs; admitted NH Bar 1972; law practice, Nashua, NH; mem. 97th–100th Congresses from 2nd NH Dist 1981–89; mem. NH Gov.'s Exec. Council 1978–80; Gov. of New Hampshire 1989–93; Senator from New Hampshire 1993–; Republican. *Address:* 393 Russell Senate Building, Washington, DC 20510-0001, USA (office). *Telephone:* (202) 224-3324 (office). *E-mail:* mailbox@ gregg.senate.gov (office). *Website:* gregg.senate.gov (office).

GREGOIRE, Christine O., BA, JuD; American lawyer and state official; *Governor of Washington;* b. Auburn, Wash.; m. Mike Gregoire; two d.; ed Univ. of Washington; began career as law clerk in Spokane Office, Attorney Gen. for State of Washington 1976, became Asst Attorney Gen. working on child abuse and neglect cases 1977–81, Sr Asst Attorney Gen. and Man. Spokane Office 1981–82, Deputy Attorney Gen. (first woman) 1982–92, Attorney Gen. (first woman) 1992–2004; Gov. of Wash. 2005–; Dir Wash. Dept of Ecology 1988–92; Inaugural Chair. Bd of Dirs The Legacy Foundation 1999–2002; Pres. Nat. Asscn of Attorneys Gen. (NAAG) 1999–2000; Hon. DJur (Gonzaga Univ.) 1995; US Supreme Court Best Brief Award, Wash. ACORN Fair Lending Champion Award, Campaign for Tobacco-Free Kids Champion Award, Distinguished Alumna Award, Univ. of Wash. Coll. of Arts and Sciences, Friend of Children Award, Wash. State Parent-Teachers Asscn, Pathfinder Award, Tri-City Chamber of Commerce, Woman of Distinction Award, YWCA's 7th Annual Woman of Achievement Awards, Child Health Advocacy Award, American Acad. of Pediatrics, Distinguished Jurisprudence Award, Pacific Northwest Region of Anti-Defamation League, Excellence in Leadership Award, Nat. Leadership Conf. of Women Execs in State Govt, Woman in Govt Award, Good Housekeeping Magazine, Woman of the Year Award, American Legion Auxiliary, Award of Excellence, Wash. State Asscn of Local Public Health Officials, 2000 Special Recognition Award, Wash. State Nurses Asscn, selected by Working Mother Magazine as one of nation's 25 Most Influential Working Mothers, Myra Bradwell Award, Gonzaga Univ. School of Law, Wash. State Bar Asscn Bd of Govs' Award for Professionalism, NAAG Wyman Award, Gleitsman Award for Leadership in Public Health, Gov.'s Child Abuse Prevention Award. *Address:* Office of the Governor, PO Box 40002, Olympia, WA 98504-0002, USA (office). *Telephone:* (360) 902-4111 (office). *Fax:* (360) 753-4110 (office). *Website:* www.governor.wa.gov (office).

GREGORIAN, Vartan, MA, PhD; American university administrator and professor of history; *President, Carnegie Corporation of New York;* b. 8 April 1934, Tabriz, Iran; s. of Samuel B. Gregorian and Shushanik G. Gregorian (née Mirzaian); m. Clare Russell 1960; three c.; ed Coll. Arménien, Stanford Univ.; Instructor, Asst Prof. and Assoc. Prof. of History, San Francisco State Coll. 1962–68; Assoc. Prof. of History, UCLA 1968, Univ. of Texas, Austin 1968–72 (Dir Special Programs 1970–72); Tarzian Prof. of Armenian and Caucasian History, Univ. of Pennsylvania 1972–80, Dean 1974–79, Provost 1978–80; Prof. of History and Near Eastern Studies, New York Univ. 1984–89; Prof., New School for Social Research, New York 1984–89; Pres. New York Public Library 1981–89; Pres. Brown Univ. 1989–97, mem. Nat. Humanities Faculty 1970–; Pres. Carnegie Corpn of New York 1997–; mem. Acad. of Arts and Letters 1989–, Historical Asscn, Asscn for Advancement of Slavic Studies, American Philosophical Soc.; John Simon Guggenheim Fellow 1971–72; Silver Cultural Medal Italian Ministry of Foreign Affairs 1977, Gold Medal of Honour City and Province of Vienna 1976, Ellis Island Medal of Honor 1986, American Acad. and Inst. of Arts and Letters Gold Medal for Service to the Arts 1989, Nat. Humanities Medal 1998, Eleanor Roosevelt Val-Kill Award 1999, Medal of Freedom 2004. *Publications:* The Emergence of Modern

Afghanistan 1880–1946 1969; Islam: A Mosaic, Not a Monolith 2003, The Road to Home: My Life and Times 2003; numerous articles for professional journals. *Address:* Office of the President, Carnegie Corporation of New York, 437 Madison Avenue, New York, NY 10022, USA. *Telephone:* (212) 371-3200. *Fax:* (212) 223-8831 (office). *Website:* www.carnegie.org (office).

GREGORY, Joseph M., BA; American financial services industry executive; m. Niki Gregory; five c.; ed Hofstra Univ.; joined Lehman Brothers 1974, held various man. positions including in Fixed Income Div., Head, Mortgage Business 1980–91, Co-Head Fixed Income Div. 1991–96, Head Global Equities Div. 1996–2000, Chief Admin. Officer 2000–02, Co-COO 2002–04, Pres. and COO 2004–08, mem. Exec. Cttee 2004–, Chair. Lehman Brothers Foundation; mem. Nat. Advisory Bd The Posse Foundation Inc.; mem. Bd of Trustees Harlem Children's Zone; Trustee and mem. Finance, Endowment and Investment Cttees, Hofstra Univ. *Address:* Lehman Brothers Holdings Inc., 745 7th Avenue, New York, NY 10019, USA (office). *Telephone:* (212) 526-7000 (office). *Fax:* (212) 526-8766 (office). *Website:* www.lehman.com (office).

GREGSON, Sir Peter Lewis, GCB, MA, FRSA; British civil servant; b. 28 June 1936, Yorks.; s. of the late Walter Henry Gregson and Lillian Margaret Gregson; ed Nottingham High School, Balliol Coll., Oxford and London Business School; Nat. Service 1959–61; official Bd of Trade 1961–68; Pvt. Sec. to the Prime Minister 1968–72; Asst Sec., Dept of Trade and Industry, also Sec. Industry, Industrial Devt Bd 1972–74; Under-Sec., Dept of Industry, also Sec., Nat. Enterprise Bd 1975–77; Under-Sec., Dept of Trade 1977–80, Deputy Sec. 1980–81; Deputy Sec., Cabinet Office 1981–85; Perm. Under-Sec. of State, Dept of Energy 1985–89; Perm. Sec., Dept of Trade and Industry 1989–96; Dir Scottish Power PLC 1996–2004, Woolwich PLC 1998–2000 (Chair. Woolwich Pension Fund Trust Co. Ltd 1999–2000). *Leisure interests:* gardening, listening to music. *Address:* 36A Elwill Way, Beckenham, Kent, BR3 6RZ, England. *Telephone:* (20) 8650-5925 (home).

GREGURIĆ, Franjo, DSc; Croatian politician; b. 12 Oct. 1939, Lobor, Zlata Bistrica; m. Jozefina Gregurić (née Abramović); one s. one d.; ed Univ. of Zagreb; worked in chemical factories; tech. Dir Radonia at Sisak; Dir-Gen. Chromos factory, Zagreb; rep. of Foreign Trade Co. Astra in Moscow, Gen. Dir Astra-Int. Trade, Zagreb –1990; Vice-Dir, then Dir Chamber of Econs, Zagreb; mem. Christian Democratic Union (CDU); Deputy Premier of Croatia 1990; Prime Minister 1991–92; mem. Sabor (Croatian Parl.) 1990–; Adviser to Pres. of Croatia 1992–, apptd Special Del. (with rank of Amb.) to Croat-Bosnian Fed. and Bosnia and Herzegovina 1997; Dir INA Co., Zagreb 1992–; fmr Pres. Croatian Firefighting Asscn; numerous nat. and int. awards for econs. *Leisure interests:* oenology, pomology. *Address:* Ilica 49, 41000 Zagreb, Croatia. *Telephone:* (41) 517-230 (office). *Fax:* (41) 650-110.

GREIČIUS, Vytautas, LLM; Lithuanian judge; *President of Supreme Court;* b. 9 May 1949, Tauragė; m. Teresė Greičiuvienė; one d. two s.; ed Faculty of Law, Vilnius Univ.; judge, Ukmergė Dist People's Court 1976–90; Judge, Supreme Court of Lithuania 1990–94, Chair. Div. of Criminal Cases 1995–99, Pres. of Supreme Court 1999–. *Address:* Supreme Court, Gynejų 6, 01109 Vilnius, Lithuania (office). *Telephone:* (5) 2610560 (office). *Fax:* (5) 2627950 (office). *E-mail:* lat@lat.lt (office). *Website:* www.lat.lt (office).

GREIDER, Carol W., BA, PhD; American molecular biologist and academic; *Daniel Nathans Professor and Director, Molecular Biology and Genetics, School of Medicine, Johns Hopkins University;* b. 15 April 1961, San Diego, Calif.; ed Univ. of California, Santa Barbara, Univ. of California, Berkeley; Fellow, Cold Spring Harbor Lab. 1988–90, Asst Investigator 1990–92, Assoc. Investigator 1992–94, Investigator 1994–97; Assoc. Prof. of Molecular Biology and Genetics, Johns Hopkins Univ. School of Medicine 1997–99, Prof. of Molecular Biology and Genetics 1999–2003, Prof. of Oncology 2001–, Acting Dir Dept of Molecular Biology and Genetics 2002–03, Daniel Nathans Prof. and Dir Dept of Molecular Biology and Genetics 2003–; mem. Editorial Bd Cancer Cell 2001–, Molecular Cancer Research 2003–; mem. NAS 2003; Fellow, American Acad. of Arts and Sciences 2003, AAAS 2003, American Acad. of Microbiology 2004; Regents Scholarship, Univ. of California 1981, Pew Scholar in the Biomedical Sciences 1990–94, Allied Signal Outstanding Project Award 1992, Gertrude Elion Cancer Research Award, American Asscn for Cancer Research 1994, Glenn Foundation Award, American Soc. for Cell Biology 1995, Cornelius Rhoads Award, American Asscn for Cancer Research 1996, Schering-Plough Scientific Achievement Award, American Soc. for Biochemistry and Molecular Biology 1997, Ellison Medical Foundation Sr Scholar 1998, Gairdner Foundation Award 1998, Passano Foundation Award 1999, Rosenstiel Award in Basic Medical Research 1999, Harvey Soc. Lecturer 2000, NAS Richard Lounsbery Award 2003, Lila Gruber Cancer Research Award 2006, The Wiley Prize in Biomedical Sciences 2006, Albert Lasker Award for Basic Medical Research (co-recipient) 2006, Louisa Gross Horwitz Prize, Columbia Univ. 2007. *Publications:* more than 90 scientific publs. *Address:* Department of Molecular Biology and Genetics, Johns Hopkins University School of Medicine, 617 Hunterian, 725 North Wolfe Street, Baltimore, MD 21205, USA (office). *Telephone:* (410) 614-6506 (office). *Fax:* (410) 955-0831 (office). *E-mail:* cgreider@jhmi.edu (office). *Website:* www.mbg.jhmi.edu (office); telomerase.bs.jhmi.edu/GreiderLab (office).

GREIFELD, Robert, BA, MBA; American business executive and stock exchange official; *President and CEO, Nasdaq Stock Market Inc.;* b. 18 July 1957, Queens, New York; m. Julia Greifeld; two s. one d.; ed Iona Coll., Stern School of Business, NY Univ.; Pres. and COO, Automated Securities Clearance Inc. (ASC) 1991–99; created BRUT, trading consortium; Exec. Vice-Pres. SunGard Data Systems Inc. 1999, then Corp. Vice-Pres. and Group CEO; Pres. and CEO NASDAQ Stock Market Inc. 2003–; Chair. USA Track and Field Foundation 2004–; Vice Chair. Kennedy Center Corp. Fund Bd; mem. Bd of Dirs Partnership for New York City; Brother Arthur A. Loftus Award for Outstanding Achievement, Iona Coll. 2004. *Leisure interest:* running. *Address:* Nasdaq Stock Market Inc., 1 Liberty Plaza, New York, NY 10006, USA (office). *Telephone:* (212) 401-8700 (office). *Fax:* (212) 401-1024 (office). *Website:* www.nasdaq.com (office).

GREIG, Geordie Carron, MA, FRSA; British journalist; *Editor, London Evening Standard;* b. 16 Dec. 1960, London; s. of Sir Carron Greig and Monica Greig (née Stourton); m. Kathryn Elizabeth Terry 1995; one s. two d.; ed Eton Coll. and St Peter's Coll., Oxford; reporter, South East London and Kentish Mercury 1981–83, Daily Mail 1984–85, Today 1985–87; reporter, The Sunday Times 1987–89, Arts Corresp. 1989–91, New York Corresp. 1991–95, Literary Ed. 1995–99; Ed. of Tatler 1999–2009; Ed., London Evening Standard 2009–. *Publication:* Louis and the Prince 1999. *Address:* London Evening Standard, Northcliffe House, 2 Derry Street, London, W8 5TT, England (office). *Telephone:* (20) 7938-6000 (office). *Fax:* (20) 7937-2648 (office). *E-mail:* geordie.greig@standard.co.uk (office). *Website:* www.standard.co.uk (office).

GREIG, Sir (Henry Louis) Carron, KCVO, CBE, DL; British fmr business executive; b. 21 Feb. 1925, London; s. of Sir Louis Greig and Lady Greig; m. Monica Stourton 1955; three s. one d.; ed Eton Coll. and Royal Military Coll., Sandhurst; Scots Guards 1943–47, attained rank of Capt.; joined Horace Clarkson and Co. Ltd 1948, Dir 1954, Man. Dir 1962, Chair. 1973–85; Chair. Horace Clarkson Holdings PLC 1976–93; Dir James Purdey and Sons Ltd 1972–2000; Baltic Exchange Ltd 1978–82, Vice-Chair. 1982, Chair. 1983–85; Dir Williams and Glyn's Bank 1983–85, Royal Bank of Scotland 1985–95; Gentleman Usher to HM the Queen 1961–95. *Address:* Brook House, Fleet, Hants., England; Binsness, Forres, Moray, Scotland. *Telephone:* (1252) 617596 (home).

GREILSAMER, Laurent, LèsL; French journalist; *Vice-President, Le Monde;* b. 2 Feb. 1953, Neuilly; s. of Marcel Greilsamer and Francine Alice Greilsamer; m. Claire Méheut 1979; three s.; ed Ecole Supérieure de Journalisme, Lille; Le Figaro 1974–76, Quotidien de Paris 1976; ed., Le Monde 1977–84, Sr Reporter 1984–94, 1994–2005, Ed. 2005–07, now Vice Pres.; Prix des lectrices de Elle 1999, Grand Prix de la Critique 2004. *Publications:* Interpol, le siège du soupçon 1986, Un certain Monsieur Paul, L'affaire Touvier 1989, Hubert Beuve-Méry 1990, Enquête sur l'affaire du sang contaminé 1990, Les juges parlent 1992, Interpol, Policiers sans frontières 1997, Le Prince foudroyé, la vie de Nicholas de Staël 1998, Où vont les juges? 2002, L'Eclair au front, la vie de René Char 2004, Le dico de la présidentielle 2007. *Leisure interests:* painting, reading. *Address:* Le Monde, 80 Boulevard Blanqui, 75013 Paris, France (office). *Telephone:* 1-57-28-26-05 (office). *Fax:* 1-57-28-21-22 (office). *E-mail:* greilsamer@lemonde.fr (office). *Website:* www.lemonde.fr (office).

GREINER, Walter Albin Erhard, PhD, FInstP, FRSA; German physicist; *Founding Director, Frankfurt Institute for Advanced Studies;* b. 29 Oct. 1935, Neuenbau/Thür; s. of Albin Greiner and Elsa Greiner (née Fischer); m. Bärbel Chun 1960; two s.; ed Univs of Frankfurt, Darmstadt and Freiburg; Research Asst, Univ. of Freiburg 1961–62; Asst Prof., Univ. of Md, USA 1962–64; Prof. and Dir Inst. of Theoretical Physics, Univ. of Frankfurt am Main 1965–; Guest Prof., numerous univs world-wide; Adjunct Prof., Vanderbilt Univ., Nashville, Tenn., USA and Oak Ridge Nat. Lab., Tenn. 1975–; Founding Dir Frankfurt Inst. for Advanced Studies 2004–; Consultant, Gesellschaft für Schwerionenforschung, Darmstadt 1976–97; Ed. Int. Journal of Modern Physics 1075–89, European Ed. 1991–; Ed. Foundations of Physics, Heavy Ion Physics; é Hon. Ed. Journal of Physics G 1985–90; Hon. Prof., Beijing Univ. 1988, Jilin Univ., People's Repub. of China 2001; Hon. mem. Lorand Eötvös Soc. (Budapest) 1989, Romanian Acad. of Science 1992; Officier, Palmes académiques 1998; Hon. DSc (Witwatersrand) 1982; Dr hc (Tel-Aviv) 1991, (Louis Pasteur Univ., Strasbourg) 1991, (Bucharest) 1992, (Lajos Kossuth Univ., Hungary) 1997, (Nantes) 2001, (Universidad Autonoma de México) 2001, (St Petersburg) 2001, (Jt Inst. of Nuclear Research, Dubna) 2002, (Bogoliubov Inst. of Theoretical Physics, Kiev) 2003; Max Born Prize, Inst. of Physics (UK) 1974, Otto Hahn Prize, Frankfurt 1982, Alex von Humboldt Medal 1998. *Publications:* Nuclear Theory (with Eisenberg) (in English and Russian, three vols) 1972, Lectures on Theoretical Physics (in five languages, 12 vols), Dynamics of Heavy-Ion Collisions (with Cindro and Ricci), Quantum Electrodynamics of Strong Fields (with B. Müller and J. Rafelski) 1985; Experimental Techniques in Nuclear Physics (with D.N. Poenaru), Handbook of Nuclear Properties (with D.N. Poenaru), Heavy Elements and Related Phenomena (with R.K. Gupta), Fundamental Issues in Elementary Matter 2000; more than 700 papers in nat. and int. journals. *Leisure interests:* music, mycology, fishing, walking, swimming. *Address:* Institut für Theoretische Physik and Frankfurt Institute for Advanced Studies, Johann Wolfgang Goethe Universität, Max van Laue Strasse 1, 600438 Frankfurt am Main, Germany (office). *Telephone:* (69) 79847525 (office). *Fax:* (69) 79847527 (office). *E-mail:* greiner@fias.uni-frankfurt.de (office).

GREIS, Michael; German biathlete; b. 18 Aug. 1976, Füssen, Bavaria; first competed at Winter Olympics, Salt Lake City 2002; won Individual category, World Cup 2004/05; mem. winning 4×7.5 km relay team, Biathlon World Championships 2004; silver medal, Individual 20 km, World Championships 2005; ranked first, World Cup 2006; gold medal, 20 km Individual, 4×7.5 km Relay, 15k km Mass Start, Olympic Games, Turin 2006. *Leisure interests:* golf, skiing. *Address:* Von-Lingg-Strasse 22, 87484 Nesselwang, Germany (office). *E-mail:* michael@michael-greis.de (office). *Website:* www.michael-greis.de (office).

GRENFELL, 3rd Baron, cr. 1902, of Kilvey; **Julian Pascoe Francis St Leger Grenfell;** British politician; b. 23 May 1935, London; s. of the late 2nd Baron Grenfell of Kilvey; m. 1st Loretta Reali 1961 (divorced 1970); one d.; m. 2nd Gabrielle Raab 1970 (divorced 1987); two d.; m. 3rd Elizabeth Porter Scott

1987 (divorced 1992); m. 4th Dagmar Langbehn Debreil 1993; ed Eton Coll., King's Coll., Cambridge; Second Lt, Kings Royal Rifle Corps 1954–56; Pres. Cambridge Union 1959; Capt. Queen's Royal Rifles (Territorial Army) 1963; television journalist 1960–64; with World Bank 1965–95, Chief of Information and Public Affairs in Europe 1969–72, Deputy Dir European Office 1973–74, Special Rep. to the UN Orgs 1974–81, Adviser HQ 1983–90, Head External Affairs, European Office 1990–95; mem. UK del. to Council of Europe 1997–99; sat in the House of Lords as Lord Grenfell of Kilvey 1976–99, cr. Life Peer 2000; Chair. House of Lords Sub-Cttee on Econ. and Financial Affairs 1998–, mem. Select Cttee on EU 1999–, Chair. 2002–; Prin. Deputy Chair. of Committees 2002–; A Deputy Speaker; non-affiliated; Chevalier Légion d'honneur 2005. *Publications:* novels: Margot 1984, The Gazelle 2004. *Leisure interests:* 20th century European history, writing fiction. *Address:* 24 rue Chaptal, 75009 Paris, France (home); c/o House of Lords, Westminster, London, SW1A 0PW, England. *Telephone:* (20) 7219-3601. *Fax:* (20) 7219-6715. *E-mail:* grenfellj@parliament.uk (office).

GRENIER, Jean-Marie René, LenD; French business executive; b. 27 June 1926, Paris; s. of Henri Grenier and Germaine Pissavy; m. Marie-Alix Bonnet de Paillerets 1958; three s. one d.; ed Lycée Fustel-de-Coulanges, Strasbourg, Ecole Bossuet, Lycée Louis-le-Grand, Faculté de Droit, Paris and Ecole des Hautes Etudes Commerciales, Paris; Deputy Dir Soc. des Usines Chimiques Rhône-Poulenc 1962, Dir 1970, Commercial Dir 1971; Dir Rhône-Poulenc SA 1977–82; Pres. Syndicat de l'industrie chimique organique de synthèse et biochimie 1975–84, Hon. Pres. 1984–; Chevalier, Ordre nat. du Mérite, Croix de la valeur militaire, Chevalier de la Légion d'honneur. *Leisure interest:* tennis. *Address:* Le Moulin Pocancy (Marne), 51130 Pocancy (home); 74 rue Claude Bernard, 75005 Paris, France (home). *Telephone:* (3) 26-70-93-15 (office); 1-47-07-79-82 (home). *E-mail:* jmrgrenier@wanadoo.fr (home).

GRENS, Elmars; Latvian molecular biologist and academic; *Scientific Director, Biomedical Research and Study Centre, University of Latvia;* b. 9 Oct. 1935, Riga; s. of Janis Grens and Melita Grenė; m. Eva Stankevich 1957; one s. one d.; ed Latvian State Univ.; researcher, Head of Lab., Research Dir Inst. of Organic Synthesis, Latvian Acad. of Sciences 1958–90, Dir Inst. of Molecular Biology 1991–93; Scientific Dir, Biomedical Research and Study Centre, Univ. of Latvia 1993–; mem. Latvian Acad. of Sciences, Academia Europaea. *Publications include:* more than 180 scientific articles on molecular biology of viruses, fine biotechnology and genetic eng. *Leisure interest:* downhill skiing. *Address:* Biomedical Research and Study Centre, University of Latvia, Ratsupites 1, Riga 1067, Latvia (office). *Telephone:* 6780-8003 (office). *Fax:* 6744-2407 (office). *E-mail:* grens@biomed.lu.lv (office).

GRETZKY, Wayne; Canadian fmr professional ice hockey player, sports industry executive and ice hockey coach; *Managing Partner and Coach, Coyotes Hockey, LLC;* b. 26 Jan. 1961, Brantford, Ont.; s. of Walter Gretzky and Phyllis Gretzky; m. Janet Jones 1988; three s. two d.; joined Indianapolis Racers of World Hockey Asscn (WHA) 1978 at age 17, immediately traded to Edmonton Oilers (WHA then Nat. Hockey League (NHL) after merger), played 1979–88, traded to Los Angeles Kings, played 1988–96, traded to St Louis Blues 1996, signed as free agent NY Rangers, played 1996–99 (retd); NHL scoring records include 2,857 points, 894 goals, 1,963 assists; NHL Most Valuable Player (Hart Memorial Trophy) nine times 1980–88; NHL scoring champion (Art Ross Trophy) ten times 1981–87, 1990–91, 1994; Most Valuable Player Stanley Cup playoffs (Conn Smythe Trophy) 1985, 1988; Most Gentlemanly Player (Lady Byng Memorial Trophy) 1980, 1991, 1992, 1994, 1999; winner Stanley Cup with Edmonton (four times); winner Canada Cup 1984, 1987, 1991; mem. Canadian Olympic team 1998; Exec. Dir Team Canada Hockey Team 2002 (Olympics), 2004 (World Cup of Hockey); investor Los Acros Sports LLC, Man. Pnr Phoenix Coyotes, 1999–, Coach 2005–; f. Wayne Gretzky Foundation; Hon. LLD (Univ. of Alberta) 2000 Lester Patrick Trophy for Outstanding Service to Hockey in US 1994, voted Greatest Player in NHL History 1997, elected Hockey Hall of Fame 1999, Olympic Order from Int. Olympic Cttee 2002. *Publication:* Gretzky: An Autobiography (with Rick Reilly). *Address:* Coyotes Hockey LLC, 9375 East Bell Road, Scottsdale, AZ 85260, USA (office). *Telephone:* (480) 473-5600 (office). *Fax:* (480) 473-5699 (office). *Website:* www.waynegretzky.com; www.phoenixcoyotes.com (office).

GREY, Dame Beryl Elizabeth, DBE; British prima ballerina; *Chairman, Royal Ballet Benevolent Fund;* b. 11 June 1927, London; d. of Arthur Ernest Groom and Annie Elizabeth Groom; m. Sven Gustav Svenson 1950; one s.; ed Dame Alice Owens School, London, Madeline Sharp School, Royal Ballet School and de Vos School of Dance; debut at Sadler's Wells Co. 1941; Prima Ballerina with Royal Ballet until 1957; freelance int. prima ballerina since 1957; first full-length ballet Swan Lake on 15th birthday; has appeared since in leading roles of classical and numerous modern ballets including Giselle, Sleeping Beauty, Sylvia, Casse Noisette, Les Sylphides, Checkmate, Donald of the Burthens, Dante Sonata, Three Cornered Hat, Ballet Imperial, Lady and the Fool, Les Rendezvous; American, Continental, African, Far Eastern tours with Royal Ballet since 1945; guest artist European Opera Houses in Norway, Finland, Sweden, Denmark, Belgium, Romania, Germany, Italy, etc.; guest artist, South and Central America, Middle East, Union of South Africa, Rhodesia, Australasia; first foreign guest artist ever to dance with the Bolshoi Ballet in Russia 1957–58 (Moscow, Leningrad, Kiev, Tbilisi) and first to dance with Peking Ballet and Shanghai Ballet 1964; Dir-Gen. of Arts Educational Trust, London 1966–68; Artistic Dir London Festival Ballet 1968–79; produced and staged Giselle, Perth, Australia 1984, 1986, Sleeping Beauty, Royal Swedish Ballet, Stockholm 1985, 2002; Pres. Dance Council for Wales 1981–2004, E Grinstead Operatic Soc. 1986–, Keep-fit Soc. 1992–93; Vice-Pres. Fed. of Music Festivals 1985–, The Music Therapy Charity 1980–, Royal Acad. of Dancing 1981–, E Grinstead Music Arts Festival 1991–; Chair. Imperial Soc. Teachers of Dancing 1962–91, Pres. 1991–2001, Life Pres. 2002–, Fellow; Gov. Royal Ballet 1993, Vice-Chair. 1995–2002; Pres. All England Dance Competitions 2005; a Dir Birmingham Royal Ballet 1995–99, Royal Opera House, Covent Garden 1999–2003; Trustee Royal Ballet Benevolent Fund 1983– (Chair. 1992–), Dance Teachers' Benevolent Fund (Vice-Chair. 1987–2004), Discs 1994–; Vice-Patron British School of Osteopathy 1992–; Patron Dancers Resettlement Trust, Benesh Inst., Language of Dance Centre, Lisa Ullman Travelling Scholarship Fund 1986–, Friends of Sadler's Wells 1991–, Furlong Hip Replacement (renamed Furlong Research Charitable Foundation) 1993– (Trustee 2005–), Osteopathic Centre for Children 1992–, Sussex Opera and Ballet Soc. 2001–, Theatre Design Trust for Dance 1995–, Critics' Circle Dance Awards 2005; Hon. DMus (Leicester) 1970, (London) 1996; Hon. DLit (City of London) 1974, (Buckingham) 1993; Hon. DEd (CNAA), 1989; Queen Elizabeth II Coronation Award, Royal Acad. of Dancing 1996, Critics Circle Service to Dance Award 2002, Lifetime Achievement Award Imperial Soc. of Teachers of Dancing 2004. *Films:* Black Swan 1952 (stereoscopic). *Radio:* Desert Island Discs (three times); numerous programmes and interviews since 1950. *Television:* numerous appearances and interviews since early 1950s. *Publications:* Red Curtain Up 1958, Through the Bamboo Curtain 1965; My Favourite Ballet Stories (ed.) 1981. *Leisure interests:* piano playing, painting, swimming, opera. *Address:* Fernhill, Priory Road, Forest Row, East Sussex, RH18 5JE, England (home). *Telephone:* (1342) 822539 (home). *Fax:* (1342) 822539 (home).

GREY-JOHNSON, Crispin, MA, PGCE; Gambian diplomatist and government official; *Secretary of State for Higher Education;* b. 7 Dec. 1946, Banjul; m.; several c.; ed Methodist Girls High School, Methodist Boys High School, Gambia High School, McGill Univ., Montreal, Canada, Univ. of Oxford, UK, George Washington Univ., USA; Master, Sr Master, Head of Dept, Gambia High School, Banjul 1968–77; Assoc. Econ. Affairs Officer, UN Econ. Comm. for Africa (ECA) 1977–81, Econ. Affairs Officer 1981–90, Sr Regional Adviser 1990–94, Coordinator, Multi-disciplinary Regional Advisory Group, Addis Ababa, Ethiopia 1994–96; Man. Dir Galloryaa Farms Ltd, The Gambia 1996–97; High Commr to Canada and Amb. to USA, Brazil and Venezuela 1997–99; High Commr to Sierra Leonea and Amb. to Côte d'Ivoire and Liberia 1999–2002; Perm. Rep. to UN, New York 2002–07; Sec. of State for Higher Educ., Research, Science and Tech. Feb.–Sept. 2007, 2008–, for Foreign Affairs 2007–08; involved in setting up African Inst. for Higher Tech. Training and Research, Kenya, Return of Skills Programme for Africa 1982–92; served as Vice-Pres. UN Gen. Ass. UN Exec. Bd on Comm. on Population and Devt; Chair Group of Friends of Guinea-Bissau, Group of Friends of Taiwan; served as Gen. Ass. Facilitator in negotiations on the resolution on the Prevention of Armed Conflict; served also on many UN Task Forces; mem. African Asscn for Public Admin and Man., African Adult Educ. Asscn, African Asscn for Training and Devt; Millennium Medal in recognition of Services for Peace and Security (Repub. of The Gambia) 2001, Hon. Diploma (Guinea Bissau) 2004; Govt of Canada Special Commonwealth African Aid Programme Scholarship 1965–58, Govt of UK Overseas Devt Agency Scholarship 1970–71, UN Fellowship for Research at African Inst. for Econ. Devt and Planning, Dakar, Senegal 1973, USAID Agency for Int. Devt Fellowship 1980. *Publications:* The Employment Crisis in Africa: Issues in Human Resources Development Policy 1990; book chapters and articles on human resources devt. *Address:* Department of State for Higher Education and Research, Banjul (office); PO Box 26, Banjul, The Gambia (home). *Telephone:* 496090 (home). *E-mail:* cgreyjohnson@hotmail.com (home).

GREY-THOMPSON, Dame Tanni (Carys Davina), DBE, BA; British athlete; b. (Tanni Carys Davina Grey), 26 July 1969, Cardiff; d. of Peter Alexander Harvey Grey and Sulwen Davina Grey (née Jones); m. Dr Ian Thompson 1999; one d.; ed St Cyres Comprehensive School, Penarth, Loughborough Univ. of Tech.; bronze medal for 400m wheelchair races, Seoul Paralympics 1988; gold medals for 100m, 200m, 400m and 800m wheelchair races, Barcelona Paralympics 1988; gold medal for 800m and silver medals for 100m, 200m, 400m wheelchair races, Atlanta Paralympics 1996; gold medals for 100m, 200m, 400m and 800m wheelchair races, Sydney Paralympics 2000, 100m and 400m wheelchair races, Athens Paralympics 2004; gold medals, women's wheelchair race, London Marathon 1992, 1994, 1996, 1998, 2001, 2002, bronze medal 1993, silver medals 1997, 1999, 2000, 2003; three gold medals and one silver medal at European Championships 2003; broke over 20 world records; Devt Officer UK Athletics 1996–2001; TV and radio presenter, conf. and motivational speaker, also numerous guest appearances; Pres. Welsh Asscn of Cricketers with a Disability; Vice-Pres. Women's Sports Foundation, South Wales Region of Riding for the Disabled, Get Kids Going; Deputy Chair. UK Lottery Awards Panel (Sport); mem. The Sports Council for Wales's Nat. Excellence Panel, Sports Council for Wales Sportlot Panel, Minister of Sport Implementation Group for the Devt of Sport, Welsh Hall of Fame Roll of Honour 1992–, English Sports Council Lottery Awards Panel 1995–99, Sports Council for Wales 1996–2002, for UK Sport 1998–2003, Nat. Disability Council 1997–2000, Manchester Commonwealth Games Organising Council Asscn 2002; mem. Elect Laureus World Sports Acad. 2001, mem. 2002–; Patron British Sports Leaders, British Sport Trust, Durham Sport Millennium Youth Games, Regain, Youth Sport Trust, Nat. Sports Medicine Inst. of UK, Shelter Cymru 2003 London Marathon, Lady Taverners, Nat. Blood Service; Vice-Patron Helen Rollason Cancer Care Appeal, Jubilee Sailing Trust 2002–; Hon. Fellow, Univ. of Wales Coll., Cardiff 1997, Univ. of Wales Inst., Cardiff 2001, Univ. of Swansea 2001, Coll. of Ripon and York St John 2001, Inst. of Leisure and Amenity Man. 2001, Univ. of Wales Coll., Newport 2003; Freeman, City of Cardiff 2003; Hon. DUniv (Staffordshire) 1998, (Southampton) 1998; Hon. LLD (Exeter) 2003; Dr hc (Surrey) 2000, (Leeds Metropolitan) 2001, (Wales) 2002, (Loughborough) 2002, (Heriot-Watt) 2004; Hon. Masters degree (Loughborough) 1994, (Teesside) 2001; Hon. MSc (Manchester Metropolitan) 1998; BBC Wales Sports Personality of the Year (three times), Sunday Times Sportswoman of the Year 1992, 2000, (Third Place) 2004, Royal Mail Best Female Performance of the Paralympic Games 1992, Panasonic Special Award 1992, Variety Club Disabled Sportswoman of the Year 1992, Welsh Sports Hall of Fame 1993, Sports Writers' Asscn Female Disabled Athlete of the Year 1994, Sporting Ambassador 1998, Sportswriters Award 2000, Third Place, BBC Sports Personality of the Year 2000, Helen Rollason Award for Inspiration, BBC Sports Personality of the Year 2000, Helen Rollason Award, Sunday Times Sports Woman of the Year 2000, Welsh Woman of the Year 2001, Welsh Sportswoman of the Year 2001, Pride of Britain Special Award 2001, awarded title of UK Sporting Hero by Sport UK 2001, Chancellor's Medal, Univ. of Glamorgan 2001, one of only four British sportswomen to appear in book, 50 British Sporting Greats 2002, Walpole Best British Sporting Achievement Award 2002, Commonwealth Games Sports Award for Best Female Disabled Athlete 2002, voted Third Greatest Briton of all time, 47th Placing in 100 Greatest Sporting Moments 2002, BBC Ouch disability website 2003, UK Sport Fair Play Award 2004, Sports Journalist UK Sport Award 2004. *Radio:* numerous appearances including as presenter The Rush Hour, BBC Radio Wales 1995–96, Sportfirst, BBC Radio 4, BBC Radio 5 Live 1995–96. *Television:* Presenter, From the Edge (BBC 2) 1998–2000, X-Ray (BBC Wales) 2002, BBC Manchester; guest appearances on BBC Question Time, Breakfast with Frost, The Weakest Link, Grandstand, A Question of Sport, Countryside; It's My Funeral, My Favourite Hymns, CBBC's Blue Peter, They Think It's All Over, and various lifestyle programmes such as Gloria Hunniford and GMTV. *Publication:* Seize the Day: My Autobiography 2001; contrib. to leading newspapers including Daily Mail and the Guardian and various magazines including Disability Now, Now Magazine, Woman's Realm, Hello, Best, Good Housekeeping, Ability Needs. *Leisure interests:* reading, IT . *Address:* c/o Helen Williams, Creating Excellence, Equity House, 1st Floor, Knight Street, South Woodham Ferrers, Chelmsford, Essex, CM3 5ZL, England (office). *Telephone:* (1245) 328303 (office). *Fax:* (1245) 323512 (office). *E-mail:* helen@creatingexcellence.co.uk (office). *Website:* www.creatingexcellence.co.uk (office).

GRI, Françoise; French business executive; *President, Manpower France;* ed ENSI Eng Coll., Grenoble; joined IBM as engineer in 1981, various man. positions both in France and abroad, Dir Sales and Marketing, E-Business Solutions, IBM Middle East and Africa 1996–2000, Dir Logistics Devt 2000–01, Dir Commerical Operations Jan.–Aug. 2001, Pres. and Dir-Gen. IBM France 2001–07; Pres. Manpower France, Paris 2007–; mem. Bd Institut de l'Entreprise, SFIB (French asscn of IT cos, now part of Alliance TICS); Chevalier, Ordre nat. du Mérite 2004; ranked by Fortune magazine amongst 50 Most Powerful Women in Business outside the US (24th) 2003, (33rd) 2004, (36th) 2005, (44th) 2006, (37th) 2007, one of Women in Business: Europe's Top 25 2004. *Address:* Manpower France, 7/9 Rue Jacques Bingen, 75017 Paris, France (office). *Telephone:* 1-56-99-10-40 (office). *Fax:* 1-42-67-76-66 (office). *E-mail:* presse@manpower.fr (office). *Website:* www.manpower.fr/emplois (office).

GRIER, Pam; American actress and writer; b. 26 May 1949, Winston-Salem, NC; d. of Clarence Ransom Grier and Gwendolyn (Sylvia) Samuels; mem. Acad. of Motion Picture Arts and Sciences. *Films:* The Big Doll House 1971, Women in Cages 1971, Big Bird Cage 1972, Black Mama, White Mama 1972, Cool Breeze 1972, Hit Man 1972, Twilight People 1972, Coffy 1973, Scream, Blacula, Scream! 1973, The Arena 1973, Foxy Brown 1974, Bucktown 1975, Friday Foster 1975, Sheba Baby 1975, Drum 1976, Greased Lightning 1977, Fort Apache: The Bronx 1981, Something Wicked This Way Comes 1983, Stand Alone 1985, The Vindicator 1986, On the Edge 1986, The Allnighter 1987, Above The Law 1988, The Package 1989, Class of 1999 1991, Bill and Ted's Bogus Journey 1991, Tough Enough, Posse 1993, Serial Killer 1995, Original Gangstas 1996, Escape from LA 1996, Mars Attacks! 1996, Strip Search 1997, Fakin' Da Funk 1997, Jackie Brown 1997, No Tomorrow 1998, Jawbreaker 1999, Holy Smoke 1999, In Too Deep 1999, Fortress 2 1999, Snow Day 2000, Wilder 2000, 3 A.M. 2001, Love the Hard Way 2001, Bones 2001, John Carpenter's Ghosts of Mars 2001, Undercover Brother 2002, The Adventures of Pluto Nash 2002, Baby of the Family 2002, Back in the Day 2005. *Television includes:* Roots: The Next Generations (mini-series) 1979, Badge of the Assassin 1985, A Mother's Right: The Elizabeth Morgan Story 1992, Feast of All Saints (mini-series) 2001, 1st to Die 2003, The L Word (series) 2004–09. *Stage appearances:* Fool for Love, Frankie and Johnnie, In the Claire De Lune; Best Actress NAACP 1986. *Leisure interests:* skiing, scuba diving, western and English horseback riding, tennis.

GRIESINGER, Christian, BSc, PhD; German chemist and academic; *Director, Max-Planck Institute for Biophysical Chemistry;* b. 5 April 1960, Ulm; s. of Karl and Christa Griesinger; ed Univ. of Frankfurt; Research Fellow, Univ. of Frankfurt 1984–86; Research Fellow, ETH Zürich 1985, Postdoctoral Assoc. 1986–89; Co-Founder MRPHARM GmbH, Frankfurt 1998; Prof., Univ. of Frankfurt 1999–2000; Scientific Mem. and Dir, Max-Planck Inst. for Biophysical Chemistry, Göttingen 1999–; mem. German Chemical Soc. 1983– (mem. Nuclear Magnetic Resonance Group Exec. Cttee 1994–96, Chair. 1997–2000); Assoc. Ed. Journal of Magnetic Resonance 1997–, FEBS Letters 2004–; mem. Council ISMAR (Int. Soc. for Magnetic Resonance) 2001, EUROMAR; mem. Acad. of Sciences, Göttingen, Nat. Acad. of Sciences Leopoldina; Hon. Prof., Univ. of Göttingen 2001–; Fonds der Chemischen Industrie Young Investigator Award 1989, Literature Prize 1996, Bavarian Acad. of Science Sommerfeld Prize 1997, Deutsche Forschungsgemeinschaft Leibniz Prize 1998, Otto Bayer Prize 2003. *Address:* Abteilung 030, Max-Planck Institute for Biophysical Chemistry, Am Fassberg 11, 37077 Göttingen, Germany (office). *Telephone:* (551) 201-2201 (office). *Fax:* (551) 201-2202 (office). *E-mail:* cigr@nmr.mpibpc.mpg.de (office). *Website:* www.medusa .nmr.mpibpc.mpg.de (office).

GRIFFEY, George Kenneth (Ken), Jr; American baseball player; b. 21 Nov. 1969, Donora, Pa; s. of Ken Griffey Sr (fmr professional baseball player); m. Melissa Griffey; one s.; one d.; ed Moeller High School, Cincinnati; outfielder; drafted by Seattle Mariners in first round (1st pick) of 1987 amateur draft, played 1987–2000, traded to Cincinnati Reds 2000–; mem. All Star team 12 times 1990–2004, Most Valuable Player in All-Star Game 1992; American League Gold Glove Award winner nine times 1990–99; American League Most Valuable Player 1997; became 20th player to hit 500 career home runs June 2004; supports actively various charities including Make-a-Wish Foundation; many TV and media appearances including The Simpsons; named to All-Century Team 1999. *Address:* Cincinnati Reds, 100 Main Street, Cincinnati, OH 45202, USA. *Telephone:* (513) 765-7000. *Fax:* (513) 765-7048. *Website:* www.cincinnati.reds.mlb.com.

GRIFFIN, Jasper, MA, FBA; British classical scholar; b. 29 May 1937, London; s. of Frederick William Griffin and Constance Irene Cordwell; m. Miriam Tamara Dressler 1960; three d.; ed Balliol Coll., Oxford; Jackson Fellow, Harvard Univ. 1960–61; Dyson Research Fellow, Balliol Coll., Oxford 1961–63, Fellow and Tutor in Classics 1963–2004, Univ. Reader 1989–2004, Prof. of Classical Literature 1992–2004, Public Orator 1992–2004; T. S. Eliot Memorial Lectures, Univ. of Kent 1984. *Publications:* Homer on Life and Death 1980, Snobs 1982, Latin Poets and Roman Life 1985, The Mirror of Myth 1985, Virgil 1986; Ed. The Oxford History of the Classical World 1986, Homer: The Odyssey 1987, The Iliad: Book Nine 1995; articles and reviews. *Leisure interests:* music, wine. *Address:* c/o Balliol College, Oxford, England (office). *Telephone:* (1865) 277782 (office).

GRIFFIN, Michael, BSc, MSc, PhD; American physicist and engineer; *Administrator, National Aeronautics and Space Administration (NASA);* ed Johns Hopkins Univ., Catholic Univ. of America, Univ. of Maryland, Univ. of Southern Calif., Loyola Coll., George Washington Univ.; fmr Deputy for Tech., Strategic Defense Initiative Org.; Chief Engineer, Assoc. Admin. NASA 1990s; fmr Adjunct Prof. Univ. of Maryland, Johns Hopkins Univ., George Washington Univ.; fmrly with Orbital Sciences Corpn, positions including CEO Magellan Systems, Inc.; Pres. and COO In-Q-Tel –2004; Head Space Dept, Applied Physics Lab., Johns Hopkins Univ. 2004–05; Admin. NASA 2005–; Fellow American Inst. of Aeronautics and Astronautics (AIAA); NASA Exceptional Achievement Medal, AIAA Space Systems Medal, Dept of Defense Distinguished Public Service Medal. *Publications:* Space Vehicle Design, numerous technical papers. *Address:* Public Inquiries Business Center, NASA Headquarters, Suite 1M32, Washington, DC 20546-0001, USA (office). *Telephone:* (202) 358-0001 (office). *Fax:* (202) 358-3469 (office). *E-mail:* public-inquiries@hq.nasa.gov (office). *Website:* www.nasa.gov (office).

GRIFFITH, Alan Richard, MBA; American banker; *Vice-Chairman, The Bank of New York;* b. 17 Dec. 1941, Mineola, NY; s. of Charles E. Griffith and Amalie Guenther; m. Elizabeth Ferguson 1964; one s. one d.; ed Lafayette Coll. and City Univ. of New York; Asst credit officer, The Bank of New York 1968–72, Asst Vice-Pres. 1972–74, Vice-Pres. 1974–82, Sr Vice-Pres. 1982–85, Exec. Vice-Pres. 1985–88, Sr Exec. Vice-Pres. 1988–90, Pres. 1990–94, Vice-Chair. 1994–. *Address:* The Bank of New York, 1 Wall Street, New York, NY 10286, USA (office). *Telephone:* (212) 635-1030 (office). *Fax:* (212) 635-1200 (office).

GRIFFITH, Gavan, AO, QC, LLM, DPhil; Australian barrister and international arbitrator; b. 11 Oct. 1941, Melbourne; s. of F. E. Griffith; one s. three d.; ed Melbourne Univ. and Magdalen Coll. Oxford; barrister 1963; Lincoln's Inn 1969; QC 1981; Solicitor-Gen. of Australia 1984–97; del. to UN Int. Trade Law Comm. (UNCITRAL) 1984–, Vice-Chair. 1987–88, 1994–95; Agent and Counsel for Australia at Int. Court of Justice 1989–95; mem. Perm. Court of Arbitration, The Hague 1987–99; mem. Intelsat Panel of Legal Experts 1988–97, Chair. 1993–94; del. Hague Conf. of Pvt. Int. Law 1992–97; Arbitrator, Int. Comm. for Settlement of Int. Disputes (ISCID) 1994–; Consultant, Office of Legal Counsel, UN, New York 1994–95; Dir Australian Centre for Int. Commercial Arbitration 1997–; mem. Council, Nat. Gallery of Australia 1986–92; Visiting Fellow, Magdalen Coll. Oxford 1973–74, 1976, 1980, 1995; Order of the Repub. of Austria 1997. *Publications:* contribs to various legal journals and books. *Leisure interest:* real tennis. *Address:* Essex Court Chambers, Lincolns Inn Fields, London WC2A 3EG, England (office); 205 William Street, Melbourne 3000, Australia (office). *Telephone:* (3) 9225-7658 (Australia) (office); (20) 7813-8000 (London) (office); (4) 1925-0666 (Australia) (home). *Fax:* (3) 9225-8974 (Australia) (office). *E-mail:* Griffithqc@aol.com (office). *Website:* www.listd.com.au (office); www.essxcourt.net (office).

GRIFFITH, Melanie; American actress; b. 9 Aug. 1957, New York; d. of Tippi Hedren and Peter Griffith; m. 1st Don Johnson 1975 (divorced 1976, remarried 1989, divorced 1993); one d.; m. 2nd Steven Bauer (divorced); m. 3rd Antonio Banderas 1996; one d.; ed Hollywood Professional School; co-founder (with Antonio Banderas) Green Moon Productions. *Films:* Night Moves 1975, Smile 1975, The Drowning Pool 1975, One on One 1977, Underground Aces 1979, Roar, Fear City, Body Double 1984, Something Wild 1986, Stormy Monday 1987, The Milagro Beanfield War 1988, Working Girl 1988, Pacific Heights, Bonfire of the Vanities, Shining Through, Paradise 1991, A Stranger Amongst Us 1992, Close to Eden 1993, Born Yesterday 1993, Milk Money 1994, Nobody's Fool 1994, Now and Then, Two Much, Mulholland Falls 1996, Lolita 1996, Shadow of Doubt 1998, Celebrity 1998, Another Day in Paradise 1998, Crazy in Alabama 1999, Cecil B. Demented 2000, Forever Lulu 2000, Life with Big Cats 2000, Tart 2001, Stuart Little 2 (voice) 2002, The Night We Called It a Day 2003, Shade 2003, Tempo 2003, Have Mercy 2006. *Theatre:* Chicago (Broadway) 2003. *Television:* Once an Eagle (mini-series) 1976, Daddy, I Don't Like It Like This 1978, Steel Cowboy 1978, Carter Country (series) 1978–79, Starmaker 1981, She's in the Army Now 1981, Golden Gate 1981, Buffalo Girls 1995, Me & George (series) 1998, RKO 281

1999, Twins (series) 2005–06. *Address:* 501 Doheny Road, Beverly Hills, CA 90210; Green Moon Productions, 11718 Barrington Court, Los Angeles, CA 90041, USA. *Website:* www.melaniegriffith.com (office).

GRIFFITHS, Alan Gordon, BEcons, LLB; Australian trade union official, politician, entrepreneur and investment banker; b. 4 Sept. 1952, Melbourne; s. of Alan Griffiths and Joy Griffiths; m. Sandra Griffiths 1970; one s.; three d.; ed Traralgon High School, Victoria, Monash Univ.; with Maurice Blackburn and Co. solicitors 1979–82; trade union industrial officer, Federated Rubber and Allied Workers' Union of Australia 1982–83; Labor mem. House of Reps for Maribyrnong, Vic. 1983–96; Jt Parl. Cttee Nat. Crime Authority 1984–87; Chair. House Reps Standing Cttee, Legal and Constitutional Affairs 1987–90; Minister for Resources and Energy 1990–93, for Tourism 1991–93, for Industry, Tech. and Regional Devt 1993–94; Chair. Griffiths Group Int. Pty Ltd 1996–; Founder, Exec. Chair. and Prin., Quantm Ltd 1999–. *Leisure interests:* the arts, sport, politics, travel, sailing. *Address:* Level 4, 333 Flinders Lane, Melbourne, Vic. 3000, Australia (office). *Telephone:* (614) 1951-6775 (office). *E-mail:* alan.griffiths@griffithsgroup.biz (office). *Website:* www.quantm.net (office).

GRIFFITHS, Phillip A., PhD; American mathematician and academic; *Professor, School of Mathematics, Institute for Advanced Study, Princeton;* b. 18 Oct. 1938, Raleigh, NC; s. of Phillip Griffiths and Jeanette Griffiths (née Field); m. 1st Anne Lane Crittenden 1958 (divorced 1967); one s. one d.; m. 2nd Marian Jones; two d.; ed Wake Forest and Princeton Univs; Univ. of Calif., Berkeley, Miller Fellow 1962–64, 1975–76, Faculty mem. 1964–67; Visiting Prof., Princeton Univ. 1967–68, Prof. 1968–72; Prof., Harvard Univ. 1972–83, Dwight Parker Robinson Prof. of Math. 1983; Provost and James B. Duke Prof. of Math., Duke Univ. 1983–91; Guest Prof., Univ. of Beijing 1983; Dir Inst. for Advanced Study, Princeton 1991–2003, now Prof. of Math.; Chair. Science Initiative Group 1999–, NSB 1991–96; mem. Bd of Dirs Bankers Trust NY Corpn 1994–99, Oppenheimer Funds 1999–, GSI Group 2001–; Sec., Int. Math. Union 1999–2006; Foreign Assoc., TWAS (Acad. of Sciences for the Developing World) 2001–; mem. NAS 1979–; hon. degrees from Wake Forest, Angers, Oslo and Beijing Univs; Guggenheim Fellow 1980–82, Wolf Foundation Prize in Math. 2008, Brouwer Prize 2008; other awards and distinctions. *Publications:* some 15 books and monographs and 90 articles in professional journals. *Leisure interest:* sailing. *Address:* Institute for Advanced Study, Einstein Drive, Princeton, NJ 08540, USA (office). *Telephone:* (609) 734-8041 (office). *Fax:* (609) 951-4430 (office). *E-mail:* pg@ias.edu (office). *Website:* www.ias.edu (office).

GRIFFITHS, Rachel; Australian actress; b. 18 Dec. 1968, Melbourne; ed Univ. of Melbourne. *TV includes:* Secrets (series) 1993, The Feds 1993, Jimeoin (series) 1994, Since You've Been Gone 1998, Very Annie Mary 2001, After the Deluge (mini-series) 2003, Plainsong 2004, Six Feet Under (series) 2001–05, Angel 2005, Comanche Moon (mini-series) 2008, Brothers & Sisters (series) 2006–09. *Films include:* Muriel's Wedding 1994, Small Treasures 1995, Cosi 1996, Children of the Revolution 1996, Jude 1996, To Have and to Hold 1996, Welcome to Woop Woop 1997, My Best Friend's Wedding 1997, My Son the Fanatic 1997, Among Giants 1998, Divorcing Jack 1998, Amy 1998, Hilary and Jackie 1998, Me Myself I 1999, Blow Dry 2001, Blow 2001, The Rookie 2002, The Hard Word 2002, Ned Kelly 2003, Step Up 2006. *Address:* c/o William Morris Agency, One William Morris Place, Beverly Hills, CA 90212, USA.

GRIFFITHS, Terence (Terry) Martin, OBE; British snooker coach and fmr professional snooker player; b. 16 Oct. 1947, Llanelli, Wales; s. of Martin Griffiths and the late Ivy Griffiths; m. Annette Jones 1968; two s.; turned professional snooker player 1978; Embassy World Champion 1979, Coral UIT Champion 1982, Benson & Hedges Masters Champion 1980, Benson & Hedges Irish Masters Champion 1981, 1982, Welsh Champion three times; Dir World Snooker 1999–2000; Coach: The Sportsmasters Network 2000–. *Publications:* Championship Snooker, Complete Snooker, Griff. *Leisure interests:* golf, music, playing snooker. *Address:* 110sport Ltd, Spencers Leisure, Kerse Road, Stirling, FK7 7SG, Scotland. *Telephone:* (1786) 462634. *Fax:* (1786) 450068. *Website:* www.tsnsnooker.com.

GRIFFITHS, Trevor, BA; British playwright; b. 4 April 1935, Manchester; s. of Ernest Griffiths and Anne Connor; m. 1st Janice Elaine Stansfield 1961 (died 1977); one s. two d.; m. 2nd Gillian Cliff 1992; ed Manchester Univ.; taught English language and literature 1957–65; Educ. Officer, BBC 1965–72; Dir Saint Oscar 1990, The Gulf Between Us 1992, Who Shall be Happy...? 1995, Food for Ravens 1997; Writer's Award, British Acad. of Film and TV Artists 1981. *Film scripts:* Reds (with Warren Beatty q.v., WGA Award 1981) 1981, Fatherland 1986. *Plays include:* Occupations 1970, Apricots and Thermidor 1970, Sam Sam 1972, The Party 1974, Comedians 1976, The Cherry Orchard 1977, Oi for England 1981, Real Dreams 1984, Piano 1990, The Gulf Between Us 1992, Thatcher's Children 1993, Who Shall Be Happy 1994, Camel Station 2001. *TV includes:* All Good Men 1974, Absolute Beginners 1974, Through the Night 1975, Bill Brand 1976, Country 1981, Sons and Lovers 1982, The Last Place on Earth 1985, Hope in the Year Two 1994, Food for Ravens 1997 (Royal TV Soc. Best Regional Programme 1998, Gwyn A. Williams Special Award, BAFTA Wales 1998). *Radio:* These Are The Times: A Life of Thomas Paine, BBC Radio 2008. *Publications:* Occupations, Sam Sam 1972, The Party 1974, Comedians 1976, All Good Men, Absolute Beginners, Through the Night, Such Impossibilities, Thermidor and Apricots 1977, Deeds (co-author), The Cherry Orchard (trans.) 1978, Country 1981, Oi for England, Sons and Lovers (TV version) 1982, Judgement Over the Dead 1986, Fatherland, Real Dreams 1987, Collected Plays for TV 1988, Piano 1990, The Gulf Between Us 1992, Hope in the Year Two, Thatcher's Children 1994, Plays One (Collected Stage Plays) 1996, Food for Ravens 1998, These Are The Times 2005, Theatre Plays One 2007, Theatre Plays Two 2007. *Address:* c/o United Agents, 12–26 Lexington Street, London W1F 0LE, England (office). *Telephone:* (20) 3214-0800 (office). *Fax:* (20) 3214-0801 (office). *E-mail:* info@unitedagents.co.uk (office). *Website:* www.unitedagents.co.uk (office).

GRIFFITHS, Baron (Life Peer), cr. 1985, of Govilon in the county of Gwent; **William Hugh Griffiths,** Kt, MC, PC, BA, MA; British judge; b. 26 Sept. 1923; s. of late Sir Hugh Griffiths; m. 1st Evelyn Krefting 1949; one s. three d.; m. 2nd Baroness Brigstocke 2000; ed Charterhouse and St John's Coll. Cambridge; called to Bar, Inner Temple 1949, QC 1964; Treas. Bar Council 1968–69; Recorder of Margate 1962–64, Cambridge 1964–70; Judge, Queen's Bench Div., High Court of Justice 1971–80; Pres. Senate of Inns of Court and the Bar 1982–; a Lord Justice of Appeal 1980–85; a Lord of Appeal in Ordinary 1985–93; mem. ADR Chambers UK; Chair. Security Comm. 1985–92; Chair. Advisory Cttee on Legal Educ. and Conduct 1991–93; Judge, Nat. Industrial Relations Court 1973–74; mem. Advisory Council on Penal Reform 1967–70; Vice-Chair. Parole Bd 1976–77; Capt. Royal and Ancient Golf Club, St Andrew's; Pres. MCC (cricket) 1991, Bar Golf Club 1990–; mem. Chancellor's Law Reform Cttee 1976–93; Hon. mem. Canadian Bar Asscn 1981, Hon. Fellow American Inst. of Judicial Admin. 1985, American Coll. of Trial Lawyers 1988; Hon. LLD (Wales) 1987, (De Montfort) 1993. *Leisure interests:* golf, fishing. *Address:* c/o House of Lords, London, SW1A 0PW; ADR Chambers UK & Europe, City Point, 1 Ropemaker Street, London, EC2Y 9HT, England. *Website:* www.adrchambers.co.uk.

GRIFFITHS OF FFORESTFACH, Baron (Life Peer), cr. 1991, of Fforestfach in the County of West Glamorgan; **Brian Griffiths,** MSc; British banker; *Vice-Chairman, Goldman Sachs International;* b. 27 Dec. 1941; s. of Ivor Winston Griffiths and Phyllis Mary Griffiths (née Morgan); m. Rachel Jane Jones 1965; one s. two d.; ed Dynevor Grammar School and London School of Econs; Asst Lecturer in Econs, LSE 1965–68, Lecturer 1968–76; Dir Centre for Banking and Int. Finance, City Univ., London 1977–82, Prof. of Banking and Int. Finance 1977–85, Dean, City Univ. Business School 1982–85; Dir Bank of England 1984–86, mem. Panel of Acad. Consultants 1977–86; Head of Prime Minister's Policy Unit 1985–90; Chair. Centre for Policy Studies 1991–2000; Head School Examinations and Assessment Council 1991–93; Vice-Chair. Goldman Sachs Int. 1991–; Dir Thorn-EMI 1991–96, Herman Miller 1991–, HTV 1991–93, Times Newspapers Ltd 1991–2007, Servicemaster 1992–2007, Telewest 1994–98, English, Welsh and Scottish Railway 1996–; Chair. Trillium 1998–2001, Land Securities Trillium, Westminster Health Care 1999–2002; Fellow, Swansea Inst. of Higher Educ. 2003, Sarum Coll. 2006, Univ. Coll. of Wales, Swansea 2006; Hon. Fellow, Trinity Coll., Carmarthen 1997; Hon. DSc (City Univ.) 1999, (Univ. of Wales) 2004. *Publications:* Is Revolution Change? (ed. and contrib.) 1972, Mexican Monetary Policy and Economic Development 1972, Invisible Barriers to Invisible Trade 1975, Inflation: The Price of Prosperity 1976, Monetary Targets (co-ed. with G. E. Wood) 1980, The Creation of Wealth 1984, Monetarism in the United Kingdom (co-ed. with G. E. Wood) 1984, Morality and the Market Place 1989, Globalization, Poverty and International Development 2007, Fighting Poverty Through Enterprise 2007. *Leisure interests:* the family, reading, ornithology. *Address:* House of Lords, Westminster, London, SW1A 0PW, England.

GRIGORESCU, Dan, MA, PhD; Romanian cultural historian and critic; b. 13 May 1931, Bucharest; s. of Vasile Grigorescu and Ecaterina Grigorescu (née Tomescu); m. Petrovan Valentina; one s. one d.; ed Bucharest Univ.; State Publishing House for Art and Literature 1954–58; museographer, Nat. Museum of Art, Bucharest 1958–63; Chief Ed., Meridiane Publishing House 1963–68; Dir Fine Arts Dept, State Cttee for Culture and Arts 1968; Dir Romanian Library New York 1971–74; Prof. in Comparative Literature Bucharest Univ. 1963–; Dir G. Călinescu 1995; Inst. of Literary History and Theory, Romanian Acad.; Visiting Prof., Univ. of Washington, Seattle 1970–71, UCLA 1970; Vice-Pres. Int. Soc. for the History of Culture 1973–85; mem. Romanian Acad., Romanian Fine Arts Union, Romanian Writers' Union, Int. Asscn of Art Criticism, Int. Asscn of Comparative Literature, Int. Asscn for the History of Culture; R. W. Emerson Award 1973, Prize of the Romanian Acad. 1978. *Works include:* Shelley, a monograph 1962; Three Romanian Painters in the 1848 Revolution 1965, Expressionism 1969, Cubism 1971, Pop Art 1972, American Art – A History 1974, Tendencies in 20th Century Poetry 1975, Shakespeare and Romanian Modern Culture 1975, A Chronological Dictionary of American Literature 1977, The Buffalo's Song, an anthology of Indian American verse and prose 1978, The Adventures of the Image 1979, History of a Lost Generation—The Expressionists 1980, Brancusi 1982, Reality, Myth, Symbol: A Portrait of James Joyce 1984, North of Rio Grande 1986, Primitive and Modern Art 1988, A History of English Art 1989, Sentiment and Idea: Trends in Contemporary Romanian Art 1991, History of Culture and its Anxieties, The Twilight of Postmodernism 1992, Mr Rubens and His Voyages 1994, Columbus and the Flying Islands 1996, Introduction to Comparative Literature 1997, A History of American Art 1998, Brancusi and the World Art of the 20th Century 1999, The American Novel in the 20th Century 1999. *Address:* 7 Edgar Quinet, 70118 Bucharest (office); 3-5 Vasile Conta, 70138 Bucharest, Romania (home). *Telephone:* (1) 4103200 (office); (1) 3148334 (home). *Fax:* (1) 4103200 (office). *E-mail:* grigorescudan@hotmail.com (home).

GRIGOROVICH, Yuriy Nikolayevich; Russian balletmaster; *Artistic Director, Grigorovich Ballet Company;* b. 2 Jan. 1927, Leningrad; s. of K. A. Grigorovich-Rozay and N. E. Grigorovich; m. Natalya Igorevna Bessmertnova; ed Leningrad Choreographic School and Lunarcharski Inst. of Theatrical Art, Moscow; soloist, Kirov (now Mariinsky) Theatre 1946–64, Ballet-Master 1962–64; Chief Ballet Master, Bolshoi Theatre, Moscow 1964–95; Chief Choreographer, Artistic Dir Kremlin Palace of Congresses Ballet 1998; now works in various theatres in Russia and abroad; Ed.-in-Chief Soviet

Ballet Encyclopaedia 1981; Founder and Artistic Dir Bolshoi Ballet Grigorovich Co. (now Grigorovich Ballet Co.) 1990–; Chair. Int. Choreography Asscn; mem. Vienna Music Soc.; Hon. Chair. Int. Theatre Inst., Ukrainian Dance Acad.; Order Merit to Fatherland Third Degree 2004; Lenin Prize 1970, People's Artist of USSR 1973, USSR State Prize 1985, Hero of Socialist Labour 1986, Soul of Dance Prize (magazine Balet) 2001, Golden Mask for Honour and Dignity 2003. *Ballets include:* Stone Flower (Kirov-Mariinsky) 1957, Legend of Love (Kirov-Mariinsky) 1960, Sleeping Beauty (Bolshoi) 1963, Nutcracker (Bolshoi) 1966, Spartacus 1968, Swan Lake 1969, Ivan the Terrible 1975, Angara 1976, Romeo and Juliet (Paris) 1978, Giselle 1979, Golden Age (Bolshoi) 1982, Raymonda 1984, Bayaderka 1991, Elektra (Grigorovich Ballet co-produced with Melanin and Bobrov) 1992, La Fille Mal Gardée (Grigorovich Ballet) 1993, Le Corsaire (Bolshoi) 1994. *Address:* Sretenskii Blvd 6/1, Apt 9, Moscow, Russia (home). *Telephone:* (495) 925-6431 (home).

GRIGORYANTS, Sergey Ivanovich; Russian human rights activist and journalist; *Head, Glasnost-Caucasus Information Agency;* b. 12 May 1941, Kiev; s. of Ivan Arkadievich Grigoryants and Vera Sergeevna Shenberg; m. Tamara Vsevolodovna Grigoryants; one s. (died 1995) one d.; studied Moscow Univ., was expelled by KGB 1968; f. and ed. Information Bulletin on violation of human rights in USSR 1982–83; imprisonment for political activities 1975–80, 1983–87; Founder, Ed. and Publr Glasnost magazine 1987–91, Glasnost Information Agency 1991–; Founder, Chair. Public Fund Glasnost 1990–; organized regular conf. KGB Yesterday, Today, Tomorrow; Head Centre on Information and Analysis, Russian Special Service 1993, Initiator of Int. Non-Governmental Tribunal on the War Crimes and Crimes Against Humanity in Chechnya; Co-Chair. Coalition for Support for Int. Criminal Court; Head Glasnost-Caucasus Information Agency 2000–; Gold Pen of Freedom Award, Medal of Bayern Lantague. *Publications:* contribs to New York Times and Washington Post. *Leisure interests:* collecting paintings, antiques, early medieval artefacts. *Address:* Tsvetnoi Boulevard, Building 2215, Apt 40, 103051 Moscow (office); 1st Naprudnaya str. 3, Apt 121, 129346 Moscow, Russia. *Telephone:* (495) 208-28-53 (office); (495) 474-45-90 (home). *Fax:* (495) 299-85-38 (office); (530) 326-88-17. *E-mail:* fondglas@online.ru. *Website:* www.glasnostonline.org (office).

GRIGORYEV, Anatoly Ivanovich, DrMed; Russian biologist and space scientist; *Vice-President, Institute for Biomedical Problems;* b. 23 March 1943, Zhitomir region, Ukraine; s. of Ivan Grigoryevich Grigoryev and Olga Isakovna Grigoryeva; m. Dorokhova Bella Radikovna; two s.; ed 2nd Moscow Medical Inst.; Researcher, Sr Researcher, Head of Lab., Head of Div., Deputy Dir State Research Centre of Inst. for Biomedical Problems, USSR (now Russian) Acad. of Sciences 1966–, Dir 1988–, Vice-Pres. Inst. for Biomedical Problems 2007–; Chief Medical Commr, Russian Space Agency 1988–, Chief Medical Officer 1996–; Co-Chair. Jt Soviet-American Workgroup on Space Biology and Medicine 1989–92; Chair. Section on Sciences of Life, Int. Acad. of Astronautics 1989–93, Section of Space Medicine, Russian Acad. of Sciences 1991–, Scientific Council on Space Medicine, Russian Acad. of Medicine 1993–; Co-Chair. Int. Space Station (ISS) Multilateral Medical Policy Bd 2000–, Man. of Medical Support in space flights on ISS 2001–; Vice-Pres. Int. Acad. of Astronautics 1993–2003, Int. Astronautical Fed. 2004–, Int. Astronomic Fed. 2006–; mem. Co-ordination Council, Russian Fed. Ministry of Science and Tech. 1998–, Presidential Council on Science and Technologies 2004–; mem. Aerospace Medical Asscn, USA 1991–, Int. Union of Physiological Sciences 1992–, Russian Acad. of Medicine 1993–, New York Acad. of Sciences 1994–, Int. Acad. of Sciences 1995–, Russian Acad. of Natural Sciences 1996–, Russian Acad. of Sciences 1997– (mem. Presidium 2001–, Academician-Sec. Biology Dept 2002–), Russian R. Tsyolkovsky Acad. of Cosmonautics 1997–; Order, Sign of Hon. 1976, Labour Red Banner 1982, Banner of Labour (DDR) 1985, Order For Merits to Motherland (IV Degree) 2003, Officier de la Légion d'honneur 2004; Dr hc (Lyon Univ.) 1989; USSR State Prize 1989, Russian Acad. of Medicine Prize 1996, Bointon Prize, American Astronautics Asscn 1995, 1999, Struckhold Prize, American Aviacosmic Asscn 1996, Françoise Xavier Banier Prize, Michigan Univ., USA 1999, S. Korolev and Yu. Gagarin Medals, USSR Fed. of Cosmonautics, Merited Worker of Science of Russia 1996, State Award of Russian Fed. 2001, Louis H. Bauer Founders Award, AMA 2001, IAA Team Achievement Award 2001, Silver Snoopy Award, NASA 2002, Ikarus Stair Medal, Russian Space Agency 2003, Award of Russian Govt 2003, Triumf Prize for achievements in medicine 2006. *Publications:* more than 400 scientific publs including seven monographs and 22 patents. *Leisure interests:* music, theatre, historical literature. *Address:* Institute for Biomedical Problems, Khoroshovskoye shosse 76A, 123007 Moscow, Russia (office). *Telephone:* (495) 195-23-63 (office). *Fax:* (495) 195-22-53 (office). *E-mail:* grigoriev@imbp.ru (office). *Website:* www.imbp.ru (office).

GRILLI, Enzo, PhD; Italian banker and economist; *Professor of International Economics, Paul H. Nitze School of Advanced International Studies, Johns Hopkins University;* b. 7 Oct. 1943, Casarza Ligure; s. of Agostino Grilli and Dominica Giambruno Grilli; m. Mary A. Jacobs; two d.; ed Univ. of Genoa and Johns Hopkins Univ. USA; Dir Econ. Research, Confed. of Italian Industries, Rome 1978–80; Dir-Gen. Ministry of Budget and Planning 1982–84; Dir Econ. Advisory Staff, IBRD, Washington, DC 1989–92; Exec. Dir for Italy, Greece, Portugal, Albania and Malta, IBRD 1993–95; Exec. Dir for Italy, Greece, Portugal, Albania, Malta and San Marino, IMF, Washington, DC 1995–98; Prof. of Int. Econs, Paul H. Nitze School of Advanced Int. Studies, Johns Hopkins Univ. 1998–; Fulbright Fellow; Editorialist of Corriere della Sera; TV Commentator; Grand Officer of Italian Repub. 1981; St Vincent Prize for Econs 1995. *Publications:* The World Rubber Economy: Structure, Changes, and Prospects (co-author) 1980, Sustaining World Economic Recovery: The Challenges Ahead 1985, The New Protectionist Wave (co-ed.) 1990, The European Community and the Developing Countries 1993, Sustaining Export-oriented Development: Ideas from East Asia (co-ed.) 1995, Inter-

dipendenze Macroeconomiche Nord–Sud 1995, Multilateralism and Regionalism after the Uruguay Round (co-ed.) 1997, Prospettive sullo Sviluppo dei Paesi Emergenti 1999. *Leisure interests:* reading, book collection, tennis. *Address:* The Paul H. Nitze School of Advanced International Studies, Johns Hopkins University, The Nitze Building, 1740 Massachusetts Avenue, NW, Room 408, Washington, DC 20036 (office); 3917 Oliver Street, Chevy Chase, MD 20815, USA (home). *Telephone:* (202) 663-5686 (office). *Fax:* (202) 663-5656 (office). *Website:* apps.sais-jhu.edu (office).

GRIMLEY EVANS, Sir John, Kt, MA, MD, FRCP, FFPHM, FMedSci; British physician and academic; *Professor Emeritus of Clinical Geratology, University of Oxford;* b. 17 Sept. 1936, Birmingham; s. of Harry Walter Grimley Evans and Violet Prenter Walker; m. Corinne Jane Cavender 1966; two s. one d.; ed King Edward's School, Birmingham, St John's Coll., Cambridge, Balliol Coll., Oxford; Visiting Scientist, Univ. of Michigan 1966–67; Research Fellow, Wellington, NZ 1967–70; Lecturer, Univ. of London 1970–71; Prof. of Geriatric Medicine, Univ. of Newcastle-upon-Tyne 1973–84; Prof. of Clinical Geratology, Univ. of Oxford 1985–2002, Emer. 2002–, Fellow, Green Coll., Oxford 1985–; Consultant Physician, Oxford Hosps 1985–; mem. MRC 1993–95, Chair. Health Services Research Bd 1990–95; Vice-Pres. Royal Coll. of Physicians 1993–95; Ed. Age and Ageing 1988–95, Oxford Textbook of Geriatric Medicine; Hon. Fellow, Royal Soc. of Medicine 2000; Harveian Orator, Royal Coll. of Physicians 1997, Ignatius Nascher Prize, City of Vienna 2005. *Publications:* papers on epidemiology and gerontology. *Leisure interests:* literature, fly-fishing. *Address:* Green College, Oxford, OX2 6HG, England (office). *E-mail:* john.grimleyevans@green.ox.ac.uk (office).

GRIMMEISS, Hermann Georg, Dr rer. nat, Dipl.Phys; Swedish physicist and academic; *Professor Emeritus of Solid State Physics, University of Lund;* b. 19 Aug. 1930, Hamburg, Germany; s. of Georg Grimmeiss and Franziska März; m. Hildegard Weizmann 1956; one s. one d.; ed Oberschule Nördlingen and Univ. of Munich; Prof. of Solid State Physics, Head of Dept Univ. of Lund 1965–96, Prof. Emer. 1996–, Dean for Research 1993–96; Chair. Int. Conf. of the Physics of Semiconductors, Stockholm 1986; Chair. Nobel Symposium on Hetrostructures in Semiconductors, Sweden 1996; mem. Programme Cttee for Physics-Math. Swedish Natural Science Research Council 1971–80; mem. Bd Swedish Nat. Cttee for Physics 1971–72, 1981–97; Prof. of Physics, Dir, Univ. of Frankfurt am Main 1973–74; mem. Cttee for Electronics, Swedish Bd for Tech. Devt 1978–80; mem. Bd Swedish-German Research Asscn 1980–; mem. f. Cttee Univ. Frankfurt/Oder (Germany) 1991–93; mem. Cttee for Science and Research, Brandenburg (Germany) 1993–95; Vice-Pres. RIFA (mem. Ericsson Group) 1981–83; Visiting Miller Prof., Univ. of California, Berkeley 1990; Dir Inst. of Semiconductor Physics, Frankfurt (Oder), Germany 1991–93; mem. Bd Einstein Forum, Potsdam, Germany 1993–; mem. Exec. Cttee European Materials Research Soc. 2001–, Pres. 2003–; Vice-Pres. European Materials Forum 2004–; mem. Int. Prize Cttee Global Energy, Moscow 2002–; Chair. Scientific Advisory Bd IHP GmbH Frankfurt/Oder 2003–; ed. and co-ed. several int. journals; mem. Royal Physiographic Soc. Lund, Royal Swedish Acad. of Eng Sciences, Royal Swedish Acad. of Sciences, Societas Scéntarium Sennica; Fellow, American Physical Soc.; Hon. mem. Roland Eötvös Physical Soc. 1983, Ioffe Inst., St Petersburg, Russia 1998; Order of North Star 1969, Bundesverdienstkreuz 1 Klasse 1993; King's Medal of 8th Dimension with Blue Ribbon, Stockholm 1998. *Publications:* more than 250 scientific publs in int. journals and books. *Leisure interests:* tennis, classical music. *Address:* Division of Solid State Physics, University of Lund, Box 118, 221 00 Lund, Sweden (office). *Telephone:* (46) 2227675 (office); (46) 140980 (home). *Fax:* (46) 2227675 (office); (46) 140980 (home). *E-mail:* hermann.grimmeiss@ftf.lth.se (office). *Website:* anders.ftf.lth.se (office).

GRIMSHAW, Sir Nicholas Thomas, Kt, CBE, RA, FCSD, RIBA; British architect; *President, Royal Academy of Arts;* b. 9 Oct. 1939, Hove; s. of Thomas Cecil Grimshaw and Hannah Joan Dearsley; m. Lavinia Russell 1972; two d.; ed Wellington Coll., Edinburgh Coll. of Art, Architectural Asscn School, London; Chair. Nicholas Grimshaw & Partners Ltd 1980–; Pres. Architectural Asscn; mem. Royal Acad. of Arts 1994–, Pres. 2004–; Assessor for British Construction Industry Awards, RIBA, Dept of Environment; Hon. FAIA; Hon. DLitt; Hon. BDA; awards and commendations include 19 RIBA awards 1975–2007; seven Financial Times Awards for Industrial Architecture 1977–95, 14 Structural Steel Design Awards 1969–2007, eight Civic Trust Awards 1978–96, eight British Construction Industry Awards 1988–2001, four Royal Fine Art Comm./Sunday Times Bldg of the Year Awards 1989–2004, five Concrete Soc. Awards 1995–2001, Constructa Preis for Industrial Architecture in Europe 1990, European Award for Steel Structures 1981, Quaternario Foundation Int. Awards for Innovative Tech. in Architecture, Gold Award 1993, Mies Van der Rohe Pavilion Award for European Architecture 1994, RIBA Bldg of the Year Award 1994, Design Innovation Award 1996, British Council for Offices Award 1996, Int. Brunel Award 1996, AIA (UK) Excellence in Design Award 2001, 2005, Leisure Property Award for Best Regeneration Scheme 2001, European Award for Aluminium in Architecture 2001, RIBA Lubetkin Prize for Outstanding Architecture outside the EU 2007. *Major projects include:* Channel Tunnel Terminal, Waterloo, London; British Pavilion for Expo '92, Seville, Berlin Stock Exchange and Communications Centre, British Airways Combined Operations Centre, Heathrow Airport, London, Financial Times Printing Plant, HQ for Igus GmbH, Cologne, Germany, head office and printing press for Western Morning News, Plymouth, BMW HQ, Bracknell, new satellite and piers, Heathrow Airport, Western Region HQ for RAC, Herman Miller Factory, Bath, Oxford Ice Rink, Gillingham Business Park, Research Centre for Rank Xerox, J. Sainsbury Superstore, Camden, London, redevelopment of Terminal One, Manchester Airport, New Teaching and Research Bldg, Univ. of Surrey, Regional HQ for Orange Telecommunications, Darlington, Railway Terminus, Pusan, Korea, redevelopment of Zürich Airport, Restoration of Paddington

Station 1996, Restoration of Spa, new Bldg, Bath & E Somerset Council 1997, Ijburg Bridges, Amsterdam 2002, HQ for Lloyds TSB, Gresham Street, London 2002, Caixa Galicia Foundation, La Coruña, Spain, Exhbn Hall for Frankfurt Fair, Eden Project, Cornwall, Nat. Space Science Centre, Leicester 2002, Rolls Royce Factory, Goodwood 2003, Experimental Media and Performing Arts Center for Rensselaer Polytechnic Inst., Troy, NY, USA, HQ for KPMG, Berlin, Southern Cross Station, Melbourne, Australia 2007, Newport City Footbridge, Wales 2007, Fulton Street Station, New York, Stansted Airport Generation 2, New Acad. Building, 24 Kingsway, for LSE, London Southbank Univ. New Building, New Galleries for Queeen's Museum of Art, New York, Museo del Acero, Monterrey, Mexico, Earthpark, Iowa, USA, ExCel London Phase 2 Devt, Garibaldi Republica Fashion and Events Bldg, Milan, Nirah visitor destination and research centre, Adelaide Univ. Project 2, St Botolph's Office Bldg, London, New York Housing Project, Miami Science Museum, New York Univ. Strategic Planning Initiative, Nyetimber Vineyard, Sussex, The Edge, Pulkovo Airport, St Petersburg. *Publications:* Product and Process 1988, Structure, Space and Skin 1993, Architecture, Industry and Innovation 1995, Equilibium 2000, The Architecture of Eden 2003; articles for RSA Journal and RIBA Journal. *Leisure interests:* sailing, tennis. *Address:* Royal Academy of Arts, Burlington House, Piccadilly, London, W1J 0BD, England (office). *Telephone:* (20) 7300-8000 (office). *E-mail:* press.office@royalacademy.org.uk (office). *Website:* www.royalacademy.org.uk (office).

GRÍMSSON, Ólafur Ragnar, PhD; Icelandic head of state; *President;* b. 14 May 1943, Isafjörður; s. of Grimur Kristgeirsson and Svanhildur Ólafsdóttir; m. 1st Guðrún Katrín Thorbergsdóttir 1974 (died 1999); two d. (twins); m. 2nd Dorrit Moussaieff 2003; ed Reykjavik Higher Secondary Grammar School, Univ. of Manchester, UK; Lecturer in Political Science, Univ. of Iceland 1970–, Prof. 1973; involved in production of political TV and radio programmes 1966–70; mem. Bd Progressive Party Youth Fed. 1966–73, Exec. Bd Progressive Party 1971-73, Alt. mem. Althing representing East Iceland (Liberal and Left Alliance) 1974–75; Chair. Exec. Bd Liberal and Left Alliance 1974–75; mem. Althing for Reykjavik 1978–83, for Reykjanes (People's Alliance) 1991–; mem. People's Alliance, Chair. Parl. Group 1980–83, Leader 1987–95; Minister of Finance 1988–91; Pres. of Iceland 1996–; Chair. Cttee on Relocation of Public Insts 1972–75, Icelandic Social Sciences Asscn 1975, Organizing Cttee Parl. Conf. of Council of Europe: 'North-South: Europe's Role' 1982-84, Parliamentarians for Global Action 1984–90 (also fmr Pres., mem. Bd 1990–); Vice-Chair. Icelandic Security Comm. 1979–90; mem. Bd Icelandic Broadcasting Service 1971–75, Nat. Power Co. 1983–88; mem. Parl. Ass. Council of Europe 1980–84, 1995; fmr adviser to several Icelandic cos. *Address:* Office of the President, Staðastaður, Sóleyjargata 1, 150 Reykjavik, Iceland (office). *Telephone:* 540-4400 (office). *Fax:* 562-4802 (office). *E-mail:* president@president.is (office). *Website:* www.president.is (office).

GRIMSTONE, Gerry, MA, MSc; British banking executive; *Chairman, Standard Life PLC;* b. 1950; ed Merton Coll. and Wolfson Coll., Oxford; held sr positions with Dept of Health and Social Security and HM Treasury –1986; with Schroders Investment Bank 1986–99, London, Hong Kong and New York, becoming Vice-Chair. Schroders' worldwide investment banking activities; mem. Bd of Dirs Standard Life Assurance Co. 2003–, Deputy Chair. Standard Life PLC 2006–07, Chair. 2007–; Chair. (non-exec.) Candover Investments PLC, F&C Global Smaller Cos PLC; Dir (non-exec.) Dairy Crest Group PLC, The Tote 1999–; Chair. Jt Audit Cttee, RAF Strike Command Bd; Trustee, The Queille Trust. *Address:* Standard Life House, 30 Lothian Road, Edinburgh, EH1 2DH, Scotland (office). *Telephone:* (131) 225-2552 (office). *Fax:* (131) 245-7990 (office). *E-mail:* info@standardlife.com (office). *Website:* www.standardlife.com (office).

GRIMWADE, Sir Andrew (Sheppard), Kt, CBE, BSc, MA, FAIM; Australian business executive; b. 26 Nov. 1930, Melbourne; s. of the late Frederick Grimwade and Gwendolen Grimwade; m. Barbara Gaerloch Kater 1959 (died 1990); one s.; ed Melbourne Grammar School, Trinity Coll., Melbourne Univ., Oriel Coll. Oxford, UK; Dir Commonwealth Industrial Gases Ltd 1960–90, Nat. Australia Bank Ltd 1965–85, IBM Australia 1975–82, Sony (Australia) 1975–82, Turoa Holdings Ltd 1975–82; Chair. Australian Consolidated Industries Ltd 1977–82; fmr Vice-Chair. Nat. Mutual Life 1988 (Dir 1970); mem. Australian Govt Remuneration Tribunal 1976–82; mem. First Australian Govt Trade Mission to China 1973; Pres. Walter and Eliza Hall Inst. of Medical Research 1978–92 (Bd mem. 1963–); Deputy Pres. Australiana Fund 1978–82; Trustee Nat. Gallery of Victoria (Pres. 1976–90), Trustee Emer. 1990–; mem. Felton Bequests Cttee 1973–, now Chair.; Trustee Victorian Arts Centre 1980–90; mem. Council for Order of Australia 1975–82. *Publication:* Involvement: The Portraits of Clifton Pugh and Mark Strizic 1969. *Leisure interests:* skiing, Santa Gertrudis cattle breeding, Australian art. *Address:* c/o National Gallery of Victoria, PO Box 7259, Melbourne, Victoria 8004, Australia.

GRINBERG, Ruslan Semyonovich, DrSc; Russian institute director and academic; b. 1946; Deputy Dir Inst. for Int. Econ. and Political Studies, Russian Acad. of Sciences, Moscow –2002, Dir 2002–05; Vice-Chair. ECAAR Russia (Economists Allied for Arms Reduction); mem. Russian-American Econ. Transition Group; Ed.-in-Chief The World of Transformations; Admin. Adviser to Gorbachev Foundation; Chair. Cttee of CIS, Nat. Investment Council, Expertise Council for CIS of Russian Fed. Trade and Industry Chamber; mem. Expertise Council Supreme Certifying Comm., Expertise Bd for Ministry of Economy; mem. Cultural Information and Research Centres Liaison in Europe (CIRCLE); Corresp. mem. Russian Acad. of Sciences. *Publications include:* Economic Sociodynamics (with Alexander Rubinstein) 2000, The New Russia – Transition Gone Awry 2001, Rational Behavior of the State 2003; more than 184 publs on econ. theory, credit and monetary policy in post-Socialist countries, integration and disintegration in post-Soviet states, the role of state in transformation economies. *Address:* c/o Institute for International Economic and Political Studies, Novocheryemushkinskaya 42A, Moscow 117418, Russia. *Telephone:* (495) 128-67-80. *Fax:* (495) 120-83-71. *E-mail:* imepi@transecon.ru. *Website:* www.imepi-eurasia.ru.

GRINDENKO, Tatyana Tikhonovna; Russian violinist; *Artistic Director, Moscow Academy of Ancient Music;* b. 29 March 1946, Kharkov, Ukraine; m. 1st Gidon Kremer (q.v.); m. 2nd Vladimir Martynov; ed Moscow State Conservatory; Prize, World Int. Youth Competition in Bulgaria 1968, Wieniawski Competition in Poland 1972; repertoire includes baroque, avant-garde, jazz, rock, experimental music; Co-founder (with A. Lyubimov) and Artistic Dir Moscow Acad. of Ancient Music; est. OPUS-POST ensemble 1999, participates in multimedia projects; various recordings for CD, radio and TV; People's Artist of Russia 2002, State Prize of the Russian Fed. 2003. *Leisure interest:* driving sports cars. *Address:* Moscow State Philharmonia, Tverskaya str. 31, 103050 Moscow, Russia (office). *Telephone:* (495) 253 7425 (home).

GRININ, Vladimir Mikhailovich; Russian diplomatist; *Ambassador to Poland;* b. 15 Nov. 1947; m.; one d.; ed Moscow State Univ. for Int. Relations, Diplomatic Acad., USSR Ministry of Foreign Affairs; mem. staff Ministry of Foreign Affairs 1971–, took part in Soviet-American disarmament and arms control negotiations, Geneva 1982–86, Embassy of USSR in GDR 1986–1990, in FRG 1990–1992, Dir 4th European Dept 1994–96, Dir Gen. Secr. (mem. Collegium) 2000–03; Amb. to Austria 1996–2000, to Finland 2003–06, to Poland 2006–. *Address:* Embassy of the Russian Federation, 00-761 Warsaw, ul. Belwederska 49, Poland. *Telephone:* (22) 6213453. *Fax:* (22) 6253016. *E-mail:* ambrus@poczta.fm. *Website:* www.poland.mid.ru.

GRINSTEIN, Gerald (Jerry), LLB; American business executive; *Strategic Director, Madrona Venture Group;* b. 1932, Seattle, WA; m.; 4 c.; ed Yale Coll., Harvard Law School; Counsel to merchant marine and transport subcttees., Chief Counsel, US Senate Commerce Cttee 1958–67; Admin. Asst to US Senator Warren Magnuson 1967–69; Pnr, Preston, Thorgrimson, Ellis & Holman 1969–73; Chair. Bd Western Air Lines Inc. LA 1983–84, Pres. and COO 1984–85, CEO 1985–86, Chair. and CEO 1986–87; Vice-Chair. Burlington Northern Inc., Fort Worth 1987–88, Pres., CEO 1989–90, Chair. 1990–96, CEO 1990–95; Pres., CEO Burlington Northern R.R. Co. 1989–90, Chair. 1990–96, CEO 1990–95; Chair. Delta Airlines Inc. 1997–99, CEO 2004–07; Chair. Agilent Techs. 1999–2002;; Co-founder and Strategic Dir Madrona Investment Group, Seattle 1995–; mem. Bd of Dirs Long Live the Kings; fmr mem. Bd of Dirs Seattle First Nat. Bank, Browning Ferris Industries Inc., Sundstrand Corpn, Expedia.com, Imperial Sugar Corpn, PACCAR Inc., The Brink's Co.; Trustee Henry M. Jackson Foundation. *Address:* Madrona Venture Group, 1000 Second Avenue, Suite 3700, Seattle, WA 98104, USA (office). *Telephone:* (206) 674-3000 (office). *Fax:* (206) 674-8703 (office). *E-mail:* jerry@madrona.com (office). *Website:* www.madrona.com (office).

GRINVALD, Amiram; Israeli neuroscientist and academic; *Director, Murray H. & Meyer Grodetsky Center for Research of Higher Brain Functions, Weizmann Institute of Science;* b. Kibbutz Ramat Hashofet; ed Weizmann Inst. of Science, Hebrew Univ., Hadassah School of Medicine, Yale Univ., USA; joined Dept of Neurobiology, Weizmann Inst. of Science 1978, currently Prin. Investigator, Israel, Helen and Norman Asher Professorial Chair in Brain Research and Dir Murray H. & Meyer Grodetsky Center for Research of Higher Brain Functions; Foreign Dir Max Planck Inst. for Medicine, Heidelberg, Germany; Guest Staff mem. Frontier Research Program, RIKEN, Japan; Visiting Prof., Lab. of Neurobiology, Rockefeller Univ. 1985–91; Research Staff mem. IBM Thomas J. Watson Research Center 1986–91; Alice and Joseph Brooks Int. Lecturer in Neurosciences, Harvard Medical School 2002; mem. Israel Acad. of Sciences and Humanities 1998; Koerber's Europe Prize 2000, Dan David Prize (co-recipient) 2004. *Publications:* numerous scientific papers in professional journals on functional optical imaging. *Address:* Department of Neurobiology, Weizmann Institute of Science, PO Box 26, Rehovot 76100, Israel (office). *Telephone:* (8) 9343833 (office). *Fax:* (8) 9342438 (office). *E-mail:* Amiram.Grinvald@weizmann.ac.il (office). *Website:* www.weizmann.ac.il/brain/grinvald (office).

GRISEZ, Germain, MA, PhL, PhD; American academic; *Most Reverend Harry J. Flynn Professor of Christian Ethics, Mount Saint Mary's University;* b. 30 Sept. 1929, University Heights, Ohio; m. Jeannette Selby 1951 (deceased); four c.; m. Mariazinha Rozario 2006; ed John Carroll Univ., Univ. Heights, Ohio, Dominican Coll. of St Thomas Aquinas, River Forest, Ill. and Univ. of Chicago; Asst Prof. to Prof., Georgetown Univ. Washington, DC 1957–72; part-time Lecturer in Medieval Philosophy, Univ. of Virginia, Charlottesville 1961–62; Special Asst to HE Cardinal O'Boyle, Archbishop of Washington 1968–69; consultant (part-time) Archdiocese of Washington 1969–72; Prof. of Philosophy, Campion Coll. Univ. of Regina, Canada 1972–79; Most Rev. Harry J. Flynn Prof. of Christian Ethics, Mount St Mary's Univ., Emmitsburg, Md 1979–; mem. Catholic Theol. Soc. of America, American Catholic Philosophical Asscn; Pro ecclesia et pontifice medal 1972; Cardinal Wright Award for service to the Church 1983 and other awards. *Publications:* Contraception and the Natural Law 1964, Abortion: The Myths, the Realities and the Arguments 1970, Beyond the New Morality (with Russell Shaw) 1974, Free Choice (with others) 1976, Life and Death with Liberty Justice (with Joseph M. Boyle, Jr) 1979, The Way of the Lord Jesus, Vol. I, Christian Moral Principles (with others) 1983, Vol. II, Living a Christian Life (with others) 1993, Vol. III, Difficult Moral Questions (with others) 1997, Nuclear Deterrence, Morality and Realism (with J. Finnis and Joseph M. Boyle) 1987, Fulfilment in Christ (with Russell Shaw) 1991, Personal Vocation: God Calls Everyone by Name (with Russell Shaw) 2003, God: A Philosophical Preface to Faith 2005;

numerous articles in learned journals. *Leisure interests:* travel, photography, hiking. *Address:* Mount Saint Mary's University, 16300 Old Emmitsburg Road, Emmitsburg, MD 21727-7799, USA (office). *Telephone:* (301) 447-5771 (office). *E-mail:* grisez@msmary.edu (office). *Website:* www.msmary.edu (office).

GRISHAM, John, BS, JD; American writer and lawyer; b. 8 Feb. 1955, Jonesboro, AR; m. Renée Jones; one s. one d.; ed Mississippi State Univ., Univ. of Mississippi, law school; called to the Bar, Miss. 1981; attorney in Southaven, Miss. 1981–90; mem. Miss. House of Reps 1984–90; Lifetime Achievement Award, British Book Awards 2007. *Film screenplay:* The Gingerbread Man 1998. *Publications:* A Time to Kill 1989, The Firm 1991, The Pelican Brief 1992, The Client 1993, The Chamber 1994, The Rainmaker 1995, The Runaway Jury 1996, The Partner 1997, The Street Lawyer 1998, The Testament 1999, The Brethren 2000, A Painted House 2001, Skipping Christmas 2001, The Summons 2002, The King of Torts 2003, Bleachers 2003, The Last Juror 2004, The Broker 2005, The Innocent Man (non-fiction) 2006, Playing for Pizza 2007, The Appeal 2008, The Associate 2009. *Address:* c/o Doubleday & Co. Inc., 1540 Broadway, New York, NY 10036, USA. *Website:* www.jgrisham.com.

GRISHKOVETS, Yevgeny B.; Russian actor and stage director; b. 1967, Kemerovo; ed Kemerovo State Univ.; f. and artistic dir Theatre Lozha; Anti-Booker Prize 1999, Golden Mask Prize 2000, Nat. Triumph Prize 2000. *Stage productions include:* Winter, How I Have Eaten a Dog, Simultaneously, Notes of a Russian Traveller.

GROCHOLEWSKI, HE Cardinal Zenon, DCL; Polish ecclesiastic; *Prefect, Congregation for Catholic Education;* b. 11 Oct. 1939, Bródki; s. of Stanisław Grocholewski and Józefa Grocholewski (née Stawińska); ed Archbishop's Seminary, Poznań, Pontifical Gregorian Univ., Rome, Studio Rotale, Rome; ordained priest 1963, worked in Christ the Redeemer Parish, Poznań 1963–66; studies in Rome 1966–72; Official of Supreme Tribunal of Apostolic Signatura 1972–82, Sec. 1982–98, Prefect 1998–99; consecrated Titular Bishop of Agropoli 1982; mem. Pontifical Cttee for Int. Eucharistic Congresses 1989–2001; promoted to Archbishop 1991; Prefect Congregation for Catholic Educ. 1999–; mem. Congregation for Bishops 1999–, Pontifical Council for Interpretation of Legis. Texts 2000–; Congregation for the Doctrine of the Faith 2001–; cr. Cardinal (Diaconate of San Nicola in Carcere) 2001–; Lecturer (later Prof.) in Canon Law, Pontifical Gregorian Univ. 1975–99 (currently Grand Chancellor), Pontifical Lateran Univ. 1980–89 and Studio Rotale 1986–98; Hon. Citizen Trenton, NJ 1988, Princeton, NJ 1992, Agropoli, Italy 1992, Levoča, Slovakia 1997, Hon. mem. Pontifical Acad. of St Thomas Aquinas, Rome 2001; Dr hc (Acad. of Catholic Theology, Warsaw) 1998, (Catholic Univ. of Lublin) 1999, (Passau) 2001, (Glasgow) 2001, (Bratislava) 2002, (Catholic Univ. of Buenos Aires) 2002; Polonia Semper Fidelis Medal 1998, Grand Medal of St Gorazd, Slovakia 2000. *Publications:* De exclusione indissolubilitatis ex consensu matrimoniali eiusque probatione 1973, Documenta recentoria circa rem matrimonialem et processualem, Vol. I (with I. Gordon) 1977, Vol. II 1980; La filosofía del derecho en las enseñanzas de Juan Pablo II y otros escritos 2001; four books in Slovakian, Hungarian and Polish and co-author of many other books. *Leisure interest:* tourism. *Address:* Congregazione per l'Educazione Cattolica, Palazzo delle Congregazioni, Piazza Pio XII 3, 00193 Cittàdel Vaticano, Rome (office); Palazzo della Cancelleria 1, 00186 Rome, Italy (home). *Telephone:* (06) 69884167 (office); (06) 69887546 (home). *Fax:* (06) 69884172 (office). *Website:* www.vatican.va/roman_curia/congregations/ccatheduc (office).

GROENING, Matthew (Matt), BA; American writer and cartoonist; b. 15 Feb. 1954, Portland, Ore.; s. of Homer Philip Groening and Margaret Ruth Wiggum; m. Deborah Lee Caplan; two c.; ed Evergreen State Coll.; cartoonist Life in Hell syndicated weekly comic strip, Sheridan, Ore. 1980–; Pres. Matt Groening Productions, Inc., LA 1988–, Bongo Entertainment, Inc., LA 1993–; creator The Simpsons interludes, The Tracey Ullman Show 1987–89; creator and Exec. Producer The Simpsons TV show 1989–; founder and Publr Bongo Comics Group; Founder and Publr Zongo Comics (including Jimbo 1995, Fleener 1996); cartoonist for TV cartoon Futurama 1999. *Publications:* Love Is Hell 1985, Work Is Hell 1986, School Is Hell 1987, Childhood Is Hell 1988, Akbar and Jeff's Guide to Life 1989, Greetings from Hell 1989, The Postcards That Ate My Brain 1990, The Big Book of Hell 1990, The Simpsons Xmas Book 1990, Greetings from The Simpsons 1990, With Love from Hell 1991, The Simpsons Rainy Day Fun Book 1991, The Simpsons Uncensored Family Album 1991, The Simpsons Student Diary 1991, How to Go to Hell 1991, Maggie Simpson's Alphabet Book 1991, Maggie Simpson's Counting Book 1991, Maggie Simpson's Book of Colors and Shapes 1991, Maggie Simpson's Book of Animals 1991, The Road to Hell 1992, The Simpsons Fun in the Sun Book 1992, Making Faces with the Simpsons 1992, Bart Simpson's Guide to Life 1993, The Simpsons Ultra-Jumbo Rain-Or-Shine Fun Book 1993, Cartooning with the Simpsons 1993, Bongo Comics Group Spectacular 1993, Binky's Guide to Love 1994, Love Is Hell 10th Anniversary Edition 1994, Simpsons Comics Extravaganza 1994, Simpsons Comics Spectacular 1994, Bartman: The Best of the Best 1994, Simpsons Comics Simps-O-Rama 1995, Simpsons Comics Strike Back 1995, Simpsons Comics Wing Ding 1997, The Huge Book of Hell 1997, Bongo Comics, Binky's Guide to Love: A Little Book of Hell 2006, The Simpsons Forever – And Beyond! 2006. *Address:* Matt Groening Productions, 9720 Wilshire Blvd, 3rd Floor, Beverly Hills, CA 90212, USA.

GROENINK, Rijkman W. J., MBS; Dutch banking executive; *Senior Partner, Frontiers Capital Partners;* b. 25 Aug. 1949, Den Helder; m. Irene Verboon; ed Utrecht Univ., Univ. of Manchester; joined Amro Bank 1974, apptd Head of Syndicated Loans 1978, Head. of Int. Corp. Accounts, Int. Div. 1980–82, Man. Dutch Special Credit Dept 1982–86, Exec. Sr Pres. of Corp. Business 1986–90, mem. Man. Bd 1988–90, mem. Man. Bd ABN AMRO (following merger with ABN) 1990–2007, Chair. Man. Bd 2000–07; currently Sr Pnr Frontiers Capital Partners; Hon. MBA (Trieste); European Banker of the Year, Frankfurt 2006; Officer, Order of Orange-Nassau. *Leisure interests:* skiing, horse riding, farming, tennis, golf. *Address:* Generaal Lemanstraat 55, 2018 Antwerp, Belgium (office); Oud Over 4, 3632 VA Loenen aan den Vecht, Netherlands (home). *Telephone:* (294) 230289 (office); 33-29-29-000 (Antwerp) (office). *Fax:* (294) 230276 (office); 32-92-90-10 (Antwerp) (office). *E-mail:* rijkman.groenink@vrederijk.nl (office). *Website:* rg@atlasinvest.eu (office).

GROMOV, Aleksey Alekseyevich; Russian politician; b. 1960; m.; two c.; ed Moscow State Univ.; joined staff USSR Ministry of Foreign Affairs 1982, Attaché, Embassy in Prague 1985–88, Sec., Office of the Deputy Minister 1988–91, First Sec., Gen. Office 1991–92, mem. Council Bratislava consulate of Russian Fed., Slovakia 1992–93, Counsellor 1993–96; Head of Press Service of Russian Pres. 1996–2000, Press Sec. 2000–07, Personal Aide to Pres. and Deputy Chief of Staff of Presidential Office 2008–; mem. Bd of Dirs Pervyi Kanal. *Address:* Office of the President, Staraya pl. 4, 103132 Moscow, Russia (office). *Telephone:* (495) 910-07-38 (office). *Fax:* (495) 206-51-73 (office). *E-mail:* president@gov.ru (office). *Website:* www.kremlin.ru (office).

GROMOV, Col-Gen. Boris Vsevolodovich; Russian army officer and politician; *Governor of Moscow Region;* b. 7 Nov. 1943, Saratov; m. 2nd Faina Gromov; two s. two adopted d.; ed Leningrad Gen. Troops School, Frunze Mil. Acad., Gen. Staff Acad.; mem. CPSU 1966–91; Commdr of platoon, co., Bn, Regt, div. 1965–87, Commdr 40 Army in Afghanistan 1987–89, Commdr of troops Kiev Command 1989–90, First Deputy Minister of Internal Affairs of USSR 1990–91, First Deputy Commdr of Armed Forces of CIS 1991–92, First Deputy Minister of Defence of Russia 1992–95; Chief Mil. Expert and Deputy Minister of Foreign Affairs 1995–97; mem. State Duma 1996–99, Chair. Sub-Cttee on Arms Control and Int. Security; Gov. of Moscow Region 2000– (re-elected 2003); f. war veterans' movt, Fighting Fraternity (later Honour and Homeland) 1997–; Hero of Soviet Union and other decorations; Order in the Name of Russia 2004. *Publication:* Memoirs of the Afghan War 1994. *Leisure interests:* tennis, cycling. *Address:* Administration of Moscow Region, Staraya Pl. 6, 103070 Moscow, Russia (office). *Telephone:* (495) 206-68-62 (office); (495) 206-60-42 (office). *Fax:* (495) 928-98-12 (office). *E-mail:* expo@mvesmo.ru (office).

GROMOV, Mikhael, PhD; Soviet-born (now stateless) mathematician; b. 23 Dec. 1943, Boksitogorsk, USSR; s. of Lea Rabinovitz and Leonid Gromov; m. Margarita Gromov 1967; ed Univ. of Leningrad; Asst Prof., Univ. of Leningrad 1967–74; Prof., Univ. of New York, Stony Brook, USA 1974–81; Prof., Univ. of Paris VI, France 1981–82; Perm. Fellow, Dept of Math., Institut des Hautes Etudes Scientifiques 1982–; Foreign Assoc. mem. NAS (USA); Foreign mem. American Acad. of Arts and Sciences; Foreign Assoc., Académie des Sciences, Institut de France, mem. 1997–; Moscow Math. Soc. Prize 1971, Oswald Veblen Prize for Geometry, American Math. Soc. 1981, Prix Elie Cartan, Académie des Sciences, Paris 1984, Prix Union des Assurances de Paris 1989, Wolf Foundation Prize in Mathematics, 1993, Frederic Esser Nemmers Prize in Math. 2004. *Publications:* Structures métriques pour les variétés riemanniennes 1981, Partial Differential Equations 1986. *Address:* Institut des Hautes Etudes Scientifiques, 35 route de Chartres, 91440 Bures-sur-Yvette (office); 91 rue de la Santé, 75013 Paris, France (home). *Telephone:* 1-69-07-48-53 (office); 1-45-88-14-42 (home).

GROMOV, Vassily Petrovich; Russian diplomatist; b. 10 Jan. 1936, Navesnoye, Orel Region; m.; two d.; ed Timiryazev Acad. of Agric., All-Union Acad. of External Trade; economist on Cuba 1961–68; on staff USSR Embassies in Chile, Mexico, Ecuador, Nicaragua; Div. of Latin America USSR Ministry of Foreign Affairs 1971–92; Amb. to Chile 1992–96; Dir Latin American Dept, Ministry of Foreign Affairs 1996–98; Amb. to Brazil (also accred to Surinam) 1999–2004. *Address:* c/o Ministry of Foreign Affairs, 119200 Moscow, Smolenskaya-Sennaya pl. 32/34, Russia.

GROMYKO, Anatoly Andreyevich, DHistSc; Russian political scientist; *Head, Centre for Political Analysis, Institute of African Studies, Russian Academy of Sciences;* b. 15 April 1932, Borisov; s. of Andrei Gromyko and Lidia Dmitrievna Gromyko; m.; two s. one d.; ed Moscow Inst. of Int. Relations; mem. CPSU 1956–91; First Sec., USSR Embassy in London 1961–65; Head of Int. Relations section, Africa Inst., USSR (now Russian) Acad. of Sciences 1966–68, Head of Section for US Foreign Policy, Inst. of the United States and Canada, USSR Acad. of Sciences 1968–73, Dir Africa Inst. 1976–92, Pres. Centre for Global and Strategic Studies 1992–94; Minister Plenipotentiary, Embassy in Wash., DC 1973–74, in Berlin 1974–76; currently Head, Centre for Political Analysis, Inst. of African Studies, Russian Acad. of Sciences; f. Russian Regional Public Org.'For the Democratic Legal World Order and Support of the United Nations' 2003; Corresp. mem. Russian Acad. of Sciences 1981–; mem. Royal Acad. of Morocco 1990–, Russian Acad. of Political Science 1997, Russian Union of Painters 2007; USSR Order of Peoples' Friendship, Order of Peter the Great, First Rank 2007; Dr hc (Leipzig); USSR State Prize 1980, V.V. Vorovskiy State Prize, Italian Acad. Simba Prize. *Publications:* US Congress: Elections, Organization, Powers 1957, The 1,036 Days of President Kennedy 1968, The Foreign Policy of the USA: Lessons and Reality the 60's and 70's 1978, The Conflict in the South of Africa: International Aspects 1979, Africa: Progress, Problems, Prospects 1981, Masks and Sculpture of Sub-Saharan Africa 1984, New Thinking in the Nuclear Age 1984, Kennedy Brothers 1985, Breakthrough (ed.) 1986, Will We Survive? (with others) 1989, Andrei Gromyko: In the Kremlin's Labyrinth 1997, Metamorphoses 2002. *Leisure interest:* lawn tennis, painting. *Address:* c/o Institute of African Studies, Russian Academy of Sciences, 30/1 Spiridonovka Str., Moscow 103001, Russia (office). *Telephone:* (495) 290-63-85 (office); (495) 436-85-24 (home). *Fax:* (495) 436-85-24 (home). *E-mail:* alexey@gromyko.ru (office). *Website:* www.gromyko.ru (office).

GRÖNEMEYER, Herbert; German actor, singer and composer; b. 12 April 1956, Goettingen; wrote first compositions for Bochum Schauspielhaus Theatre 1974; Musical Dir, actor Schauspielhaus 1975. *Film appearances include:* The Hostage 1975, Daheim unter Fremden 1979, Springtime Symphony 1983, Father and Sons 1988. *Theatre appearances include:* John, Paul, George, Ringo and Bert 1974, Spring Awakening 1976, The Winter's Tale 1978, The Merchant of Venice 1979, Big and Little 1982. *Address:* c/o ZBF Agentur, 80802 Munich, Germany (office). *Telephone:* (30) 89355081 (office). *E-mail:* groenland@groenemeyer.de (office). *Website:* www.groenemeyer.de (office).

GRÖNHOLM, Marcus; Finnish racing driver; b. 5 Feb. 1968, Finland; m.; 3 c.; team: Peugeot 1999–; rally debut Finland 1988, Scandinavia Rally Champion 1989, World Rally Championship (WRC) debut Sweden 1995; 16 WRC victories include Sweden 2000, 2002, 2003, Australia 2000, 2001, 2002, Finland 2000, 2001, 2002, Great Britain 2001, Cyprus 2002, New Zealand 2000, 2002, 2003, Argentina 2003; Finnish junior champion 1988; WRC winner 2000, 2002; total WRC points 259. *Address:* Team MGR Finland, Santapellontie 1, Espoo 02780, Finland (office). *Website:* www.mgr.fi (office).

GRONKIEWICZ-WALTZ, Hanna, LLD, PhD; Polish banker and lawyer; *Mayor of Warsaw;* b. 4 Nov. 1952, Warsaw; m.; one d.; ed Warsaw Univ.; mem. of academic staff, Warsaw Univ. 1975–; mem. Solidarity Trade Union 1980; expert on public and econ. law, Polish Parl. 1989; mem. of academic staff, Univ. of Cardinal Wyszy 1990–; Pres. Nat. Bank of Poland 1992–2000; Chair. Faculty, Solidarity Br. 1989–92; ind. cand. in presidential election 1995; Vice-Pres. EBRD 2001–05; mem. of Sejm (Parl.), Platforma Obywatelska Party 2005–; Mayor of Warsaw (first female) 2006–; Dr hc (Marie Curie-Skłodowska Univ., Lublin) 1999; Global Finance magazine award for Best Chair. of a Cen. Bank 1994, 1997, 1998, 1999, The Central European Award 1995, 1998, Życie Gospodarcze Award 1995, The Warsaw Voice Award 1995. *Publications:* Central Bank from Centrally Controlled Economy to Market Oriented Economy: Legal Aspects 1993, Economic Law (co-author) 1996; over 50 works and articles in econ. and financial journals. *Leisure interests:* American literature, classical music. *Address:* Office of the Mayor, pl. Defilad 1, 00-142 Warsaw, Poland (office). *Telephone:* (22) 6567830 (office). *Fax:* (22) 8270635 (office). *E-mail:* biuroprezydenta@warszawa.um.gov.pl (office).

GROS, Francisco Roberto André, BA; Brazilian banker and economist; *President and CEO, Fosfertil;* b. 21 April 1942, Rio de Janeiro; s. of André Paul Adolphe Gros and Dulce Simões Corrêa Gros; m. 1st Sandra Mattmann 1968; m. 2nd Isabel Teixeira Mendes; two s. one d.; ed Woodrow Wilson School of Public and Int. Affairs, Princeton Univ., USA; Founding mem. Brazilian Securities and Exchange Comm. 1977–81; Exec. Dir in charge of investment banking activities, Unibanco–Banco de Investimento do Brasil 1981–85; Exec. Dir Nat. Devt Bank (BNDES) 1985–87; Pres. Cen. Bank of Brazil Feb.–May 1987, 1991–92; Pres. and CEO Aracruz SA (eucalyptus pulp exporter) 1987–89; Founding Partner and CEO BFC Banco SA, Rio de Janeiro 1989–91, 1993; Man. Dir Morgan, Stanley and Co., New York 1994–2000; Pres. and CEO Nat. Devt Bank (BNDES) 2000–01; Pres. and CEO Petrobras 2002; Pres. and CEO Fosfertil 2003–; several Brazilian decorations; Officier, Légion d'honneur (France). *Leisure interests:* travel, tennis, fishing. *Address:* Avenida Luiz Carlos Berrini 1681, 9th Floor, São Paolo, SP 04571-011 (office). *Telephone:* (11) 5501-1156 (office). *Fax:* (11) 5501-1188 (office). *E-mail:* fgros@fosfertil.com.br (office). *Website:* www.fosfertil.com.br (office).

GROS, François; French biochemist; *Honorary Permanent Secretary, French Academy of Sciences;* b. 24 April 1925, Paris; s. of Alexandre Gros and Yvonne Haguenauer; m. 1st Françoise Chasseigne (divorced 1963); m. 2nd Danièle Charpentier 1964; three s.; ed Lycée Pasteur, Neuilly, Univs of Toulouse and Paris, Rockefeller Inst., Univ. of Illinois, USA; joined CNRS 1947, Researcher, Lab. Prof. J. Monod 1955, Head of Research 1959–62, Scientific Dir 1962–; Head, Dept, Inst. de Biologie Physico-chimique 1963–69; Prof., Faculté des Sciences de Paris 1968, Inst. Pasteur 1972, Collège de France (Chair in Cellular Biochemistry) 1973–1996; Dir Inst. Pasteur 1976–81, Dir of Biochemistry Unit 1981, Hon. Dir 1982–; Adviser to Prime Minister 1981–85; mem. EC's CODEST 1984–90; Pres. Asscn Franco-Israélienne pour la recherche scientifique et tech. 1983, Scientific Council of Asscn Française de lutte contre la myopathie 1987–; Scientific Council of Nat. Agency for Research into AIDS 1989–; Chief Ed. Bulletin de la Société de chimie biologique 1964; Perm. Sec. Science Acad. (France) 1991–; mem. Nat. Consultative Cttee on the Ethics of Life and Health Sciences 1990–94; mem. EU Ass. on Science and Tech. 1994–97; mem. Inst. de France 1979–, Perm. Sec. 1991–2000, Hon. Perm. Sec. 2001–; mem. Institut Français, Acad. des Sciences, NAS, Acad. of Athens, Indian Nat. Acad. Sciences 1990; Assoc. mem. Acad. Royale de Belgique, Russian Acad. of Sciences, Acad. of Medical Science, UK; Commdr, Légion d'honneur, Ordre nat. du Mérite; several foreign decorations; Dr hc (Weizmann Inst., Israel); Gold Medal, Pontifical Acad. of Sciences 1964, Fondation Lacassagne Prize 1968, Charles Léopold Mayer Prize, Acad. des Sciences 1969, Alexander von Humboldt Prize 1990, Jawahalral Nehru Medal, Indian Nat. Science Acad. 1999. *Publications:* Initiation à la biochimie (with others); Sciences de la vie et société (with others) 1979, Les secrets du gène 1986, La civilisation du gène 1989, L'ingénierie du vivant 1990, Regard sur la biologie contemporaine 1992, Memoires scientifiques – un demi-siècle de Biologie 2003. *Leisure interests:* music, drawing. *Address:* Institut de France, 23 quai Conti, 75006 Paris (office); 102 rue de la Tour, 75116 Paris, France (home). *Telephone:* 1-44-41-45-57 (office). *Fax:* 1-44-41-44-40 (office); 1-45-68-89-63 (office); 1-45-04-55-92 (home). *E-mail:* gros-zajdman@academie-sciences.fr (office).

GROSS, David Jonathan, BSc, PhD; American physicist and academic; *Director, Kavli Institute for Theoretical Physics, University of California, Santa Barbara;* b. 19 Feb. 1941, Washington, DC; m. Jacquelyn Savani; three d.; ed Hebrew Univ., Jerusalem, Israel, Univ. of Calif., Berkeley; Visiting Prof., CERN, Geneva, Switzerland 1968–69, 1993; Asst Prof., Princeton Univ. 1969–71, Assoc. Prof. 1971–73, Prof. 1973–86, Eugene Higgins Prof. of Physics 1986–95, Jones Prof. of Physics 1995–97, Jones Prof. of Physics Emer. 1997–; Visiting Prof. Ecole Normale Supérieure, Paris, France 1983, 1988–89, Hebrew Univ., Jerusalem, Israel 1984, Lawrence Radiation Lab., Berkeley, Calif. 1992; Dir Kavli Inst. for Theoretical Physics, Univ. of Calif., Santa Barbara 1997–, also Prof. 1997–, Frederick W. Gluck Prof. of Theoretical Physics 2001–; Rothschild Prof., Univ. of Cambridge, UK 2007; visiting lecturer at numerous int. univs; Dir Jerusalem Winter School 1999–; Assoc. Ed. Nuclear Physics 1972–; mem. Advisory Bd Inst. for Theoretical Physics 1983–87 (Chair. 1986); Chair. Solvay Scientific Cttee for Physics 2006–; mem. numerous review cttees; Fellow, Alfred P. Sloan Foundation 1970–74, American Physical Soc. 1974–, American Acad. of Arts and Sciences 1985–, NAS 1986–, AAAS 1987–, Indian Acad. of Science 2007–, Indian Nat. Science Acad. 2007–, Third World Acad. of Sciences 2007–; Hon. PhD (Univ. of Montpellier) 2000, (Hebrew Univ., Jerusalem) 2001, (São Paulo Univ.) 2006, (Ohio State Univ.) 2007, (Univ. of the Philippines) 2008, (De La Salle Univ., Manila) 2008; American Physical Soc. J. J. Sakurai Prize 1986, MacArthur Foundation Fellowship Prize 1987, Dirac Medal 1988, Technion-Israel Inst. of Tech. Harvey Prize 2000, European Physical Soc. High Energy and Particle Physics Prize 2003, Grande Médaille d'Or (France) 2004, Nobel Prize in Physics (co-recipient) 2004. *Address:* Kavli Institute for Theoretical Physics, University of California, Santa Barbara, Kohn Hall, 1219, Santa Barbara, CA 93106, USA (office). *Telephone:* (805) 893-7337 (office). *Fax:* (805) 893-2431 (office). *E-mail:* gross@kitp.ucsb.edu (office). *Website:* www.physics.ucsb.edu (office); www.kitp.ucsb.edu (office).

GROSS, John Jacob, MA; British writer, editor and publisher; b. 12 March 1935, London; s. of late Abraham and Muriel Gross; m. Miriam May 1965 (divorced 1988); one s. one d.; ed City of London School, Wadham Coll., Oxford and Princeton Univ.; Ed. with Victor Gollancz Ltd 1956–58; lecturer, Queen Mary Coll., Univ. of London 1959–62, Hon. Fellow 1988; Fellow of King's Coll., Cambridge 1962–65; Asst Ed. Encounter 1963–65; Literary Ed. New Statesman 1972–73; Ed. Times Literary Supplement 1974–81; Literary Ed. Spectator 1983; journalist, New York Times 1983–88; theatre critic Sunday Telegraph 1989–2005; Dir Times Newspapers Holdings Ltd (fmrly Times Newspapers Ltd) 1982; editorial consultant The Weidenfeld Publishing Group 1982; a Trustee Nat. Portrait Gallery 1977–84; Fellow Queen Mary Coll. 1987; Hon. DHL (Adelphi Univ.) 1995; Duff Cooper Memorial Prize 1969. *Publications:* Dickens and the Twentieth Century (ed. with Gabriel Pearson) 1962, John P. Marquand 1963, The Rise and Fall of the Man of Letters: Aspects of English Literary Life since 1800 1969, James Joyce 1970, Rudyard Kipling: The Man, His Work and His World (ed.) 1972, The Oxford Book of Aphorisms (ed.) 1983, The Oxford Book of Essays (ed.) 1991, Shylock 1992, The Modern Movement (ed.) 1992, The Oxford Book of Comic Verse (ed.) 1994, The New Oxford Book of English Prose (ed.) 1998, A Double Thread: Growing Up English and Jewish in London 2001, The New Oxford Book of Literary Anecdotes (ed.) 2006. *Address:* 74 Princess Court, Queensway, London, W2 4RE, England (home).

GROSS, Mgr Stanislav, LLM; Czech fmr politician; b. 30 Oct. 1969, Prague; m. 2nd Šárka Gross; two d.; ed secondary vocational transport coll., Prague, Charles Univ., Prague; worked briefly as electrician, then as engine driver trainee at Prague-Vršovice locomotive depot 1988; mil. service in Olomouc 1988–90; mem. Czech Social Democratic Party (Česká strana sociálně demokratická—ČSSD), Chair. Young Social Democrats 1990–94, Presidium Cen. Exec. Cttee ČSSD, Vice-Chair. ČSSD 2001–04, Acting Chair. 2004–05; mem. Parl. in Czech Nat. Council, subsequently in Chamber of Deputies 1992–2004, Chair. ČSSD Parl. Club 1995–96, 1996–2000, Deputy Chair. Chamber of Deputies 1998–2000, Spokesman for Security 1996–2005, Vice-Chair. Cttee for Defence and Security 1994–2005, Vice-Chair. of Parl. 1998–2000; Minister of the Interior 2000–04; Deputy Prime Minister 2002–04; Prime Minister of Czech Repub. 2004–05 (resgnd); Cross of Honour First Class 2002. *Leisure interests:* country music, football, hockey, nature. *Address:* c/o Česká strana sociálně demokratická, Lidovy dum, Hybernska 7, 110 00 Prague 1, Czech Republic.

GROSSART, Sir Angus McFarlane McLeod, Kt, CBE, LLD, D.L., FRSE; British merchant banker, lawyer and company director; *Chairman, Noble Grossart Ltd;* b. 6 April 1937; s. of William John White Grossart and Mary Hay Gardiner; m. Gay Thomson 1978; one d.; ed Glasgow Acad. and Gasgow Univ.; mem. Faculty of Advocates 1963; practised at Scottish Bar 1963–69; Man. Dir Noble Grossart Ltd Merchant Bankers, Edin. 1969–, Chair. 1990–; Chair. Scottish Investment Trust PLC 1975–2003; mem. Bd of Dirs of numerous cos including Royal Bank of Scotland PLC 1982– (Vice-Chair. 1996–), Scottish and Newcastle 1998–, Trinity Mirror PLC 1998–; Chair. Bd of Trustees Nat. Galleries of Scotland 1988–97; Trustee Nat. Heritage Memorial Fund 1999–, and other public and charitable appointments; Hon. LLD (Glasgow) 1985, Hon. DBA (Strathclyde) 1998; Livingstone Captain of Industry Award 1990, Lord Provost of Glasgow Award for public service 1994. *Leisure interests:* golf, the applied and decorative arts, Scottish castle restoration. *Address:* Noble Grossart Ltd, 48 Queen Street, Edinburgh, EH2 3NR, Scotland (office). *Telephone:* (131) 226-7011 (office). *Fax:* (131) 226-6032 (office).

GROSSER, Alfred, DèsSc; French academic, writer and journalist; b. 1 Feb. 1925, Frankfurt; s. of the late Paul Grosser and Lily Grosser (née Rosenthal); m. Anne-Marie Jourcin 1959; four s.; ed Univs of Aix en Provence and Paris; Asst Dir UNESCO Office in Germany 1950–51; Asst Prof., Univ. of Paris

1951–55; Lecturer, later Prof., Inst. d'études politiques 1954, Prof. Emer. 1992–; Dir Studies and Research, Fondation nat. des Sciences politiques 1956–92; with Ecole des hautes études commerciales 1961–66, 1986–88, with Ecole Polytechnique 1974–95; Visiting Prof., Bologna Center, Johns Hopkins Univ. 1955–69, Stanford Univ. 1964–67; political columnist La Croix 1955–65, 1984–, Le Monde 1965–94, Ouest-France 1973–, L'Expansion 1979–89; Pres. Centre d'information et de recherche sur l'Allemagne contemporaine 1982–, Eurocréation 1986–92 (Hon. Pres. 1992–); Vice-Pres. Int. Political Science Asscn 1970–73; mem. Bd L'Express 1998–2003; Grosses Verdienstkreuz mit Stern 1995 und Schulterband 2003; Grand Officier Légion d'honneur 2001; Dr hc (Aston, Birmingham, UK) 2001, (European Univ. of Humanities, Minsk, Belarus) 2001; Peace Prize, Union of German Publrs 1975, Grand Prix, Acad. des Sciences Morales et Politiques 1998. *Publications:* L'Allemagne de l'Occident 1953, La démocratie de Bonn 1958, Hitler, la presse et la naissance d'une dictature 1959, La Quatrième Republique et sa politique extérieure 1961, La politique extérieure de la Ve République 1965, Au nom de quoi? Fondements d'une morale politique 1969, L'Allemagne de notre temps 1970, L'explication politique 1972, les Occidentaux: Les pays d'Europe et les Etats Unis depuis la guerre 1978, Le sel de la terre. Pour l'engagement moral 1981, Affaires extérieures: la politique de la France 1944–84, 1984 (updated 1989), L'Allemagne en Occident 1985, Mit Deutschen streiten 1987, Vernunft und Gewalt. Die französische Revolution und das deutsche Grundgesetz heute 1989, Le crime et la mémoire 1989 (revised 1991), Mein Deutschland 1993, Was ich denke 1995, Les identités difficiles 1996, Une Vie de Français (memoirs) 1997, Deutschland in Europa 1998, Les fruits de leur arbre: regard athée sur les Chrétiens 2001, L'Allemagne de Berlin 2002, La France, semblable et differente 2005, Die Früchte ihres Baumes 2005. *Leisure interest:* music. *Address:* 8 rue Dupleix, 75015 Paris, France (home). *Telephone:* 1-43-06-41-82 (home). *Fax:* 1-40-65-00-76 (home). *E-mail:* grosser.alfred@wanadoo.fr (home).

GROSSMAN, David, BA; Israeli writer; b. 25 Jan. 1954, Jerusalem; m. Michal Grossman; two s. (one deceased) one d.; ed Hebrew Univ., Jerusalem; Chevalier, Ordre des Artes et Lettres; Children's Literature Prize, Ministry of Educ. 1983, Prime Minister's Hebrew Literature Prize 1984, Israeli Publishers' Asscn Prize for Best Novel 1985, Vallombrosa Prize (Italy) 1989, Nelly Sachs Prize (Germany) 1992, Prix Eliette von Karajan (Austria), Premio Grinzane (Italy), Premio Mondelo (Italy), Vittorio de Sica Prize (Italy), Marsh Award for Children's Literature in Translation (UK), Juliet Club Prize (Italy), Buxtehuder Bulle (Germany), Sapir Prize (Israel), Italian Critics Prize (Italy), Nelly Sachs Prize (Germany), Mane Sperber Prize (Austria), Bernstein Prize (Israel), Bialik Prize (Israel), Emet Prize (Israel) 2007. *Publications:* Hiyukh ha-gedi (trans. as The Smile of the Lamb) 1983, 'Ayen 'erekh–ahavah (trans. as See Under: Love) 1986, Ha-Zeman ha-tsahov (non-fiction, trans. as The Yellow Wind) 1987, Gan Riki: Mahazeh bi-shete ma'arakhot (play, trans. as Rikki's Kindergarten) 1988, Sefer hakikduk hapnimi (trans. as The Book of Intimate Grammar) 1991, Hanochachim hanifkadim (non-fiction, trans. as Sleeping on a Wire: Conversations with Palestinians in Israel) 1992, The Zigzag Kid (in trans.) (Premio Mondelo, Premio Grinzane), Duel (in trans.), Be My Knife (in trans.) 2002, Someone to Run With (in trans.) 2003, Death as a Way of Life: Dispatches from Jerusalem (non-fiction, in trans.) 2003, Her Body Knows (novel, in trans.), Lovers and Strangers (novel, in trans.) 2005, Lion's Honey: The Myth of Samson; also short stories, children's books, contribs to periodicals. *Address:* c/o Managing Editor, The Deborah Harris Agency, 9 Yael Street, Jerusalem 93502, Israel (office). *Telephone:* (2) 6722145 (office); (2) 6722143 (office). *Fax:* (2) 6725797 (office). *E-mail:* iaustern@netvision.net.il (office).

GROSSMANN, Jürgen, Dr-Ing, Dr Eh; German steel industry executive; *President and CEO, RWE AG;* b. 4 March 1952, Mülheim an der Ruhr; ed Tech. Univs of Clausthal and Berlin, Göttingen Univ., Purdue Univ., USA; various man. positions at Klöckner-Werke AG Group 1980–93, mem. Exec. Bd 1991–93; Man. Pnr, Georgsmarienhütte GmbH 1993–97, Owner and Man. Dir Georgsmarienhütte Holding GmbH 1997–2006, Owner 2007–; Pres. and CEO RWE AG 2007–. *Address:* RWE AG, Opernplatz 1, 45128 Essen, Germany (office). *Telephone:* (201) 1215025 (office). *Fax:* (201) 1215265 (office). *E-mail:* info@rwe.com (office). *Website:* www.rwe.com (office).

GROTHENDIECK, Alexander, PhD; German mathematician; b. 28 March 1928, Berlin; ed Montpellier Univ. and Ecole Normale Supérieure, Paris, France; moved to France in 1941; worked at Univ. of Nancy 1949–53, Univ. of São Paulo, Brazil 1953–55, Univ. of Kansas, USA 1956; Researcher, CNRS 1956–59, Dir of Research 1984–88 (retd); Prof., Institut des Hautes Études Scientifiques, Paris 1959–70; Visiting Prof., Collège de France 1970–72, Orsay 1972–73; Prof., Montpellier Univ. 1973–84; declined Crafoord Prize on ethical grounds 1988; left home and disappeared 1991; Fields Medal 1966. *Publications:* numerous publs in math. journals on algebraic geometry, homological algebra and functional analysis.

GROTTANELLI DE' SANTI, Giovanni, LLD; Italian lawyer; b. 1928, Livorno; m. Felicity Bennett 1962; three c.; ed Ginnasio Liceo E.S. Piccolomini, Siena, Univ. of Siena, Yale Law School and Coll. of Europe, Bruges, Belgium; admitted to Bar 1952; Univ. Asst 1955; law clerk, Constitutional Court, Rome 1956–62; Asst in Constitutional Law, Univ. of Rome 1956–62; libero docente (constitutional law), Univ. of Siena 1962; also taught at Univ. of Florence; Visiting Fellow, Wolfson Coll., Cambridge, UK 1981–82; Visiting Fellow Commoner, Trinity Coll., Cambridge 1985; Visiting Lecturer, Tulane Law School, Univ. of Ga Law School, Dean Rusk Center of Int. and Comparative Law, Athens, Ga 1991, USA; Chair. Monte dei Paschi di Siena 1992–98, Italian Int. Bank 1993–, Accad. Chigiana di Siena 1993–; Deputy Chair. Monte Paschi Banque 1993–; mem. Bd British Inst. of Florence 1993–, Fondo Interbancario Tutela dei Depositi 1993–, Associazione Bancaria Italiana 1993–, Consorzio Siena Ricerche 1993–, IMI SpA 1995–, IMI Int. 1996–. *Publications:* books, articles and reviews on constitutional and comparative law.

GROVE, Andrew (Andy) S., PhD; American engineer and business executive; *Senior Advisor, Intel Corporation;* b. 1936, Budapest, Hungary; m.; two c.; ed City Coll. of New York and Univ. of Calif., Berkeley; Fairchild Instrument & Camera Co. 1963–67; Pres. and COO Intel Corpn, Santa Clara, Calif. 1967–87, Pres. 1987–98, CEO 1987–98, Chair. 1998–2005, now Sr Advisor; mem. Nat. Acad. of Eng; Fellow IEEE; mem. Bd of Dirs Prostate Cancer Foundation; f. Grove Foundation; Nat. Chair of the Campaign, Univ. of Calif., San Francisco; Hon. DSc (City Coll. of NY) 1985; Hon. D. Eng (Worcester Polytechnic Inst.) 1989, Hon. Dr of Laws, Harvard Univ. 2000; American Inst. of Chemists Award 1960, IEEE Achievement Award 1966, IEEE J.J. Ebers Award 1974, Certificate of Merit, Franklin Inst. 1975, Nat. Acad. of Eng 1979, Townsend Harris Medal, City Coll. of New York 1980, Hall of Fame Award, Information Industries Asscn 1984, Council of 100 Members, Ariz. State Univ. 1984, IEEE Eng Leadership Recognition Award 1987, Enterprise Award, Business and Professional Advertising Asscn 1987, George Washington Award, American-Hungarian Foundation 1990, Citizen of the Year Award, World Forum of Silicon Valley 1993, Exec. of the Year Award, Univ. of Ariz. 1993, American Eng Asscn (AEA) Medal of Achievement Award 1993, Heinz Foundation Tech. Award 1995, John von Neumann Medal, American Hungarian Asscn 1995, Steinman Medal, City Coll. of New York 1995, Statesman of the Year Award, Harvard Business School 1996, Int. Achievement Award, World Trade Club 1996, IEEE 1997 Computer Entrepreneur Award 1997, Cinema Digital Technologies Award, Int. Film Festival 1997, CEO of the Year Award, CEO Magazine 1997, Tech. Leader of the Year Award, Industry Week 1997, Man of the Year, Time Magazine 1997, Distinguished Exec. of the Year, Acad. of Man. 1998, IEEE Medal of Honor 2000, Lifetime Achievement Award, Strategic Man. Soc. 2001, Most Influential Business Person of the Last Twenty-Five Years, Wharton School of Business and Nightly Business Report 2004 Ernest C. Arbuckle Award, Stanford Univ. Graduate School of Business 2004. *Publications:* High Output Management (1983, One-on-One With Andy Grove (1987), Only the Paranoid Survive 1996, Swimming Across (autobiography) 2001, Strategic Dynamics: Concepts and Cases (with Robert A. Burgelman) 2005. *Address:* Intel Corporation, P.O. Box 58119, 2200 Mission College Boulevard, Santa Clara, CA 95052, USA. *Telephone:* (408) 765-1904 (office). *Fax:* (408) 765-1739 (office). *Website:* www.intel.com (office).

GRUBBS, Robert H., PhD; American chemist and academic; *Victor and Elizabeth Atkins Professor of Chemistry, California Institute of Technology;* b. 27 Feb. 1942, nr Possum Trot, Ky; s. of Henry Howard Grubbs and Faye Atwood; ed Univ. of Florida and Columbia Univ., New York; Faculty Fellow, Columbia Univ. 1965–66, NIH Trainee 1966–68; NIH Postdoctoral Fellow, Stanford Univ., Calif. 1968–69; Asst Prof., Michigan State Univ. East Lansing 1969–73, Assoc. Prof. 1973–78; Prof. of Chem., Calif. Inst. of Tech., Pasadena 1978–90, Victor and Elizabeth Atkins Prof. of Chem. 1990–; Christensen Visiting Fellow, St Catherine's Coll., Oxford, UK 1997, Rayson Huany Visiting Lectureship in Chem., Hong Kong 2001; Tarrant Visiting Prof. of Organic Chem., Univ. of Florida, Gainesville 2004; mem. NRC Cttee Basic Scientific Research, US Army 1981–; mem. Advisory Panel, NSF ARI Program 1996–; mem. Alexander von Humbolt Asscn of America 1999–2000; mem. Advisory Bd, Center on Polymer Interfaces and Macromolecular Assemblies 1999–2000, Advanced Synthesis and Catalysis 2000–; Advisory Ed. Journal of Polymer Science, Polymer Chemistry 1999–; mem. Editorial Advisory Bd Catalysis Technology 1996–, Accounts of Chemical Research 2000–; mem. ACS 1964–; Fellow, American Acad. of Arts and Sciences 1994; Hon. MRIA (Science Section) 1999; Hon. Prof., Shanghai Inst. of Organic Chem., Chinese Acad. of Sciences 2001; Alfred P. Sloan Fellow 1974–76, Alexander von Humbolt Fellowship 1975, The Camille and Henry Dreyfus Teacher-Scholar Award 1975–78, ACS Nat. Award in Organometallic Chem. 1988, Arthur C. Cope Scholar Award 1990, George Willard Wheland Award, Univ. of Chicago 1992, ACS Award in Polymer Chem., Mobil Chemical Co. 1995, Nagoya Medal of Organic Chem. 1997, Fluka Prize – Reagent of the Year 1998, Mack Memorial Award, Ohio State Univ. 1999, Benjamin Franklin Medal in Chem., The Franklin Inst. 2000, Herman F. Mark Polymer Chem. Award, ACS POLY-The Dow Chemical Co. Foundation 2000, Cliff S. Hamilton Award, Univ. of Nebraska, Lincoln 2000, Herbert C. Brown Award for Creative Research in Synthetic Methods, ACS-Aldrich Chemical Co. and The Purdue Borane Research Fund 2001, Prelog Lecturer, ETH, Zürich 2001, Werner E. Bachmann Memorial Lecturer, Univ. of Michigan, Ann Arbor 2002, Edward Frankland Prize and Lecturer, Royal Soc. of Chem. 2002, Arthur C. Cope Award, ACS Div. of Organic Chem. 2002, ACS Award for Creative Research in Homogenous or Heterogeneous Catalysis, Shell Oil Foundation 2003, Richard C. Tolman Medal, Southern Calif. Section of ACS 2003, Pauling Award Medal, Oregon, Portland, Puget Sound Sections of ACS 2003, ACS Tetrahedron Prize for Creativity in Organic Chem. 2003, Priestly Lecturer, Pennsylvania State Univ. 2003, Ralph Hirschmann Lecturer, Univ. of Wisconsin, Madison 2003, Linus Pauling Distinguished Lecturer, Oregon State Univ. 2003, Gilman Lecturer, Iowa State Univ. 2003, Karabatsos Lecturer, Michigan State Univ. 2003, Nobel Prize for Chem. (jtly) 2005. *Publications:* more than 350 publs in scientific journals on design, synthesis and mechanistic studies of complexes that catalyse useful organic transformations. *Address:* Division of Chemistry and Chemical Engineering, California Institute of Technology, M/C 127-72, Pasadena, CA 91125, USA (office). *Telephone:* (626) 395-6003 (office). *Fax:* (626) 564-9297 (office). *E-mail:* rhg@caltech.edu (office). *Website:* www.chemistry.caltech.edu (office).

GRUBE, Rüdiger, BEng, DSci; German business executive; *Chairman, EADS NV;* b. 2 Aug. 1951, Hamburg; ed Hamburg Univ.; teaching post, Production and Eng. Dept, Univ. of Hamburg 1981–86; joined MMB (Messerschmitt-Bölkow-Blohm) GmbH (later Daimler-Benz Aerospace, DASA), Munich 1989, Head of Marketing, Sales and Int. Relations, Energy and Industrial Tech. Div. 1989–90, Head of Man. Office, Deutsche Airbus GmbH, Hamburg 1990–92, Head of Munich-Ottobrunn site, Daimler-Benz Aerospace AG, Munich 1992–94, Head of Aviation Staff Unit 1994–95, Dir of Corp. Planning and Tech., Deutsche Aerospace AG, Munich 1995, Sr Vice-Pres. and Head of Corp. Strategy, Daimler-Benz AG (later DaimlerChrysler AG) 1996–2000, mem. Man. Bd 2001–, Sr Vice-Pres. for Corp. Devt 2000–, also Chair. Supervisory Bd DaimlerChrysler Off-Highway GmbH, Chair. DaimlerChrysler China Ltd, Beijing, Vice-Chair. Beijing Benz DaimlerChrysler Automotive (BBDC-A), mem. Advisory Bd DaimlerChrysler Fleetboard, DaimlerChrysler Aviation, mem. Supervisory Bd DaimlerChrysler Financial Services AG; Chair. (non-exec.) European Aeronautic Defence and Space Co. (EADS) NV 2004–, also Chair. EADS Participations BV; Chair. Supervisory Bd MTU Friedrichshafen GmbH; mem. Bd of Dirs McLaren Group Ltd; mem. Supervisory Bd Hamburg Port Authority (HPA GmbH). *Address:* European Aeronautic Defence and Space Company EADS NV, Le Carré, Beechavenue 130–132, 1119 PR Schiphol-Rijk, Netherlands (office). *Telephone:* (20) 6554800 (office). *E-mail:* info@eads.com (office). *Website:* www.eads.com (office).

GRUBISICH, José Carlos, BEng, MBA; Brazilian business executive; *CEO, Braskem SA;* b. 1957; m.; two s.; ed Escola Superior de Química Osvaldo Cruz, INSEAD, France; various man., marketing and advertising roles with Grupo Rhône Poulenc, Brazil and other countries, including Pres. Rhodia Brazil and Latin America 1997–2000, mem. Exec. Cttee and Global Vice Pres. 2000–02; Pres. Grupo Odebrecht 2002–; CEO Exec. Braskem SA (fmrly Copene Petroquímica do Nordeste SA) 2002–. *Address:* Braskem SA, Av. Das Nações Unidas, 4777, Edifício Villa Lobos - Alto de Pinheiros, 05477-000 São Paulo, Brazil (office). *Telephone:* 3443-9999 (office). *Fax:* 3443-9017 (office). *Website:* www.braskem.com.br (office).

GRUDZINSKI, Przemyslaw, PhD; Polish diplomatist and academic; *Professor, College of International and Security Studies, George C. Marshall Center;* b. 30 Oct. 1950, Torun; m.; two d.; ed Univ. of Nicolaus Copernicus, Torun, Inst. of History, Polish Acad. of Sciences, Warsaw; Prof., Inst. of History, Polish Acad. of Sciences 1976–96; Adviser to Deputy Minister of Nat. Defence 1990; Dir Bureau of Research and Dir-Gen. Sejm (Parl.) 1991; Deputy Minister of Nat. Defence 1992–93; Prof., Marshall European Centre for Security Studies, Germany 1994–97, Coll. of Int. and Security Studies 2005–; Under-Sec. of State, Ministry of Foreign Affairs 1997–2000; Amb. to USA 2000–05; mem. Solidarity Movt 1980s; Founder-mem. Euro-Atlantic Asscn 1994, Council on Foreign Policy, Warsaw 1996; Fellow, American Council of Learned Socs 1978–80; Fulbright Fellow, Princeton Univ. 1988, Visiting Fellow 1978–80, 1988; Visiting Fellow, Univ. of Southern California, UCLA 1989. *Publications include:* The Future of Europe in the Ideas of Franklin D. Roosevelt 1933–1945 1987, Scientists and Barbarians: The Nuclear Policy of the United States 1939–45 1987, Theology of the Bomb: The Origins of Nuclear Deterrence Vols 1–3 1988, A Critical Approach to European Security: Identity and Institutions 1999; numerous articles in professional journals. *Leisure interests:* walking, mountains. *Address:* College of International and Security Studies, George C. Marshall Center, Gernackerstrasse 2 82467 Garmisch-Partenkirchen, Germany (office). *Telephone:* (8821) 750-2680 (office). *Fax:* (8821) 750-2688 (office). *E-mail:* cisscontact@marshallcenter.org (office). *Website:* www.marshallcenter.org (office).

GRUENBERG, Erich, OBE, FRCM, FGSM; British violinist and music teacher; b. 12 Oct. 1924, Vienna, Austria; s. of Herman Gruenberg and Kathrine Gruenberg; m. Korshed Madan 1956; two d.; ed in Vienna, Jerusalem and London; Leader, Philomusica of London 1954–56, Stockholm Philharmonic Orchestra 1956–58, London Symphony Orchestra 1962–65, Royal Philharmonic Orchestra 1972–76; Leader. London String Quartet and mem. Rubbra-Gruenberg-Pleeth Piano Trio in 1950s; now appears as soloist with leading orchestras in UK and abroad; taught at Royal Coll. of Music 1960–65, Guildhall School of Music and Drama; Prof., RAM 1988–; int. masterclasses; Chair. of Jury, Fritz Kreisler Int. Violin Competition, Vienna 2005, Yehudi Menuhin Int. Violin Competition; Chair. Bd of Trustees, Mattori Foundation; Hon. RAM, Hon. Pres. Stamford Int. Music Festival 2007; Winner, Carl Flesch Int. Violin Competition. *Leisure interests:* family, garden, sport. *Address:* 22 Spencer Drive, Hampstead Garden Suburb, London, N2 0QX, England (home). *Telephone:* (20) 8455-4360 (home). *Fax:* (20) 8455-6234 (home).

GRUEVSKI, Nikola, BEcons, MSc; Macedonian lawyer, economist and politician; *Prime Minister;* b. 31 Aug. 1970, Skopje; s. of Talo Gruevski and Nadezda Gruevski; m. Borkica Gruevska; one d.; ed Sts Cyril and Methodius Univ., Skopje, St Clement Ohrid Univ., Bitola; with Credit Dept, Foreign Dept, then Currency Dealing, Balkanska Banka Skopje 1994–98, Liquidity, Plan, Analyses and Securities Dept 1995–96; with Metal Bank, Frankfurt 1996–97, MG Finance PLC, London 1997, Flemings Pvt. Asset Man. Ltd, London 1997–98; Minister without Portfolio, then Minister of Trade 1998–99; Minister of Finance 1999–2002; Pres. Econ. Council 2000–02; mem. Macedonian Parl. 2002–06; Adviser, Ministry of Finance, Serbia 2003; Pres., Internal Macedonian Revolutionary Org.-Democratic Party for Macedonian Nat. Unity (IMRO-DPMNU) 2003–; Prime Minister 2006–; Vice-Pres. Euro-Atlantic Council of the Repub. of Macedonia 2005–06; Pres. Broker's Asscn of Macedonia 1998, State Securities and Exchange Comm. 2000–02, Parl. Cttee for Co-operation with European Parl. 2002–04; financial affairs commentator, MTM TV, Skopje 1998–. *Publications:* The Macedonian Economy at a Crossroad: On the Way to a Healthier Economy 1998, The Way Out: Foreign Direct Investment, Economic Development and Employment 2007; numerous articles on econ. and political issues. *Leisure interests:* boxing, basketball, football. *Address:* Office of the Prime Minister, 1000 Skopje, Ilindenska bb, Former Yugoslav Republic of Macedonia (office). *Telephone:* (2) 3115389 (office). *Fax:* (2) 3112561 (office). *E-mail:* primeminister@primeminister.gov.mk (office). *Website:* www.gov.mk (office).

GRUMBACH, Melvin Malcolm, MD, FAAP; American physician and academic; *Edward B. Shaw Professor Emeritus of Pediatrics, School of Medicine, University of California, San Francisco;* b. 21 Dec. 1925, New York; s. of Emanuel Grumbach and Adele Grumbach (née Weil); m. Madeleine F. Butt 1951; three s.; ed Columbia Coll. and Columbia Univ. Coll. of Physicians and Surgeons; Resident in Pediatrics, Babies' Hosp., Presbyterian Hosp., New York 1949–51; Visiting Fellow, Oak Ridge Inst. of Nuclear Studies 1952; Post-doctoral Fellow, Asst in Pediatrics, Johns Hopkins School of Medicine 1953–55; mem. Faculty, Columbia Univ. Coll. of Physicians and Surgeons 1955–65; Asst Attending Pediatrician, subsequently Assoc. Prof. of Pediatrics, Head of Pediatric Endocrine Div. and Postdoctoral Training Programme in Pediatric Endocrinology, Babies' Hosp. and Vanderbilt Clinic, Columbia-Presbyterian Medical Center 1955–65; Prof. of Pediatrics, Chair. Dept, Univ. of Calif. School of Medicine, San Francisco 1966–86, first Edward B. Shaw Prof. of Pediatrics 1983–, now Prof. Emer., Acting Dir Lab. of Molecular Endocrinology 1987–89; Dir Pediatric Service Univ. of Calif. Hosps 1966–86; Pres. Asscn of Pediatric Dept Chairmen 1973–75, Lawson Wilkins Pediatric Endocrine Soc. 1975–76, Western Soc. for Pediatric Research 1978–79, Endocrine Soc. 1981–82, American Pediatric Soc. 1989–90; Exec. Cttee Int. Soc. of Endocrinology 1984–92 (Hon. Pres. 2000–04); mem. Inst. of Medicine of NAS 1983–, NAS 1995–, Johns Hopkins Soc. of Scholars 2002–; Fellow, American Acad. of Pediatrics, AAAS 1985–, American Acad. of Arts and Sciences 1995–; Founding Scientific Patron Sir Graham Liggins Inst., Univ. of Auckland, NZ 2001; Hon. mem. Royal Soc. of Medicine, London, and other socs; Hon. DM (Geneva) 1991, Dr hc (Paris V) 2000, (Athens) 2008; Joseph M. Smith Prize, Columbia Univ. 1962, Career Scientist Award, Health Research Council, New York 1961–66, Silver Medal, Bicentenary Columbia Coll. of Physicians and Surgeons 1967, Borden Award, American Acad. of Pediatrics 1971, Robert H. Williams Distinguished Leadership Award, Endocrine Soc. 1980, Alumni Gold Medal, Columbia Coll. of Physicians and Surgeons 1988, Fred Conrad Koch Award, Endocrine Soc. 1992, Lifetime Achievement Award: Medical Educ., American Acad. of Pediatrics 1996, John Howland Award, American Pediatric Soc. 1997, Van Wyck Prize for Career Achievement, Lawson Wilkins Pediatric Endrocrine Soc. 2006 and many others. *Television:* NOVA: Sex Unknown (WBQH Boston) 2001. *Publications:* numerous scientific and clinical papers and monographs. *Leisure interests:* tennis, gardening, literature. *Address:* Department of Pediatrics (S672), University of California San Francisco School of Medicine, San Francisco, CA 94143-0434, USA (office). *Telephone:* (415) 476-2244 (office). *Fax:* (415) 476-8214 (office). *E-mail:* grumbach@peds.ucsf.edu (office). *Website:* www.medschool.ucsf.edu (office).

GRUNBERG, Arnon; Dutch writer; b. 1971, Amsterdam; ed Vossius Gymnasium. *Publications:* Blauwe Maandagen (novel, trans. as Blue Mondays) (Anton Wachter-prijs) 1994, Figuranten 1997, De troost van de slapstick (essays) 1998, Het veertiende kippetje 1998, Liefde is business 1999, Fantoompijn (novel, trans. as Phantom Pain) (AKO-Literatuurprijs) 2000, Amuse-Bouche (short stories, in trans.) 2008. *Address:* c/o Nijgh & Van Ditmar, Singel 262, Amsterdam, Netherlands. *E-mail:* info@grunberg.nl. *Website:* www.grunberg.nl.

GRÜNBERG, Peter, PhD; German physicist and academic; *Lead Research Scientist, Institut fuer Festkoerperforschung (IFF), Forschungszentrum Jülich;* ed Technische Universität Darmstadt, Universität zu Köln; Post-doctoral Fellow, Carleton Univ., Ottawa, Canada 1969–72; Research Scientist, IFF, Forschungszentrum Jülich 1972–, now Lead Research Scientist; Visiting Prof., Universität zu Köln, IMR, Tohoku Univ., Japan, JRCAT, Tsukuba Research Centre, Japan; mem. Max-Planck-Institut für Mikrostrukturphysik; American Physical Soc. Int. Prize for New Materials (jtly) 1994, Int. Union for Pure and Applied Physics Magnetism Award (jtly) 1994, Technologiepreis des Vereins der Freunde und Foerderer des Forschungszentrums Jülich 1996, Hewlett-Packard Europhysics Prize (jtly) 1997, Pres.'s Prize for Innovation and Advancement of Tech. 1998, Manfred-von-Ardenne Prize for Applied Physics, European Soc. of Thin Films 2004, European Inventor of the Year, Univ. and Research category, European Patent Office 2006, Wolf Foundation Prize for Physics (jtly) 2007, Stern-Gerlach Medal, German Physical Soc. 2007, Nobel Prize for Physics (jtly) 2007. *Address:* Forschungszentrum Jülich GmbH, Institut für Festkörperforschung, Jülich 52425, Germany (office). *Telephone:* (2461) 613286 (office). *Fax:* (2461) 614443 (office). *E-mail:* p.gruenberg@fz-juelich.de (office). *Website:* www.fz-juelich.de (office).

GRUNBERG-MANAGO, Marianne, PhD; French biochemist; b. 6 Jan. 1921, Leningrad (now St Petersburg), Russia; d. of Vladimir Grunberg and Catherine Riasanoff; m. Armand Manago 1948 (deceased); one s. one d.; ed Univ. of Paris; Research Asst, subsequently Researcher then Sr Researcher, CNRS 1946–61, Head of Dept of Biochemistry, Inst. of Physico-Chemical Biology 1959, Dir of Research, CNRS 1961, now Emer. Dir of Research, Head of Dept in Biochemistry, Inst. of Physicochemical Biology (IBPC) 1967; Assoc. Prof., Univ. of Paris VII 1972; Ed.-in-Chief Biochimie; Pres.-elect Int. Union of Biochemistry 1983, Pres. 1985–88; Vice-Pres. Comm. for Sciences and Tech., UNESCO 1985; mem. Acad. des Sciences 1982– (Vice-Pres. 1994, Pres. 1995); mem. Soc. de Chimie Biologique, American Soc. of Biological Chemists, Int. Council of Scientific Unions Gen. Cttee, Acad. des Sciences; Foreign mem. American Acad. of Arts and Sciences, New York Acad. of Sciences, Acad. of Sciences of Russia (Ukraine), American Philosophical Soc.; Fogarty Fellow 1977–82; Foreign Hon. mem. NAS; Officier, Légion d'honneur; Commdr, Ordre nat. du Mérite; Charles-Léopold Mayer Prize 1955, 1966, L'Oréal-UNESCO For Women in Science Award 2002. *Publications:* Polynucleotide phosphorylase, in Journal of American Chemical Soc. (with S. Ochoa) 1955, Biosynthèse des acides nucléiques (with F. Gros) 1974, threonine tRNA ligase gene in *Escherichia coli*, in PNAS (with others) 1986, Escherichia coli and Salmonella typhimurium 1987; more than 300 scientific articles. *Leisure interest:* paintings. *Address:* 80 Boulevard Pasteur, 75015 Paris; c/o Institut de France, 23 quai de Conti, 75006, Paris, France.

GRUNDHOFER, Jerry A.; American banker; *Chairman, President and CEO, US Bancorp;* b. 1944; ed Loyola Marymount Univ., LA; began banking career in S Calif. 1967; Dir, Pres. and CEO Security Pacific Nat. Bank 1992, also Dir Security Pacific Corpn; Vice-Chair. and Dir BankAmerica Corpn –1993; joined Star Banc Corpn 1993, becoming Chair., Pres. and CEO –1998; CEO, Firstar Corpn 1998–2001, Pres. and CEO US Bancorp (following acquisition of Firstar) 2001–, also Chair. 2003–; fmr Dir Bank of America NT&SA; Forbes Magazine Banker of the Year 1998, American Banker Magazine Banker of the Year 2000. *Address:* US Bancorp, 800 Nicollet Mall, Minneapolis, MN 55402 USA (office). *Telephone:* (651) 466-3000 (office). *Website:* www.usbancorp.com (office).

GRUNSFELD, John M., BSc, MSc, PhD; American space scientist and astronaut; *Chief Scientist, National Aeronautics and Space Administration (NASA);* b. Chicago, Ill.; s. of Ernest A. Grunsfeld III; m. Carol E. Schiff; ed MIT, Univ. of Chicago; Visiting Scientist Univ. of Tokyo 1980–81; Graduate Research Asst Univ. of Chicago 1981–85, NASA Graduate Student Fellow 1985–87, W. D. Grainger Postdoctoral Fellow in Experimental Physics 1988–89; Sr Research Fellow Calif. Inst. of Tech. 1989–92; scientist and astronaut NASA 1992–, positions include Chief Computer Support Branch, Instructor and Chief Extravehicular Activity Branch, currently Chief Scientist; veteran of four space flights, having logged over 45 days in space; mem. American Astronomical Soc., American Alpine Club, Experimental Aircraft Asscn, Aircraft Owners and Pilots Asscn; Distinguished Alumni Award, Alumni Service Award, Univ. of Chicago, Komarov Diploma 1995, Korolov Diploma 1999, 2002 NASA Space Flight Medals 1995, 1997, 1999, 2002, Exceptional Service Medals 1997, 1998, 2000, Distinguished Service Medal 2002. *Leisure interests:* mountaineering, flying, sailing, bicycling, music. *Address:* Lyndon B. Johnson Space Center, Houston, TX 77058, USA (office). *Website:* www.nasa.gov (office); www.jsc.nasa.gov (office).

GRUSHKO, Alexander; Russian diplomat and politician; *Deputy Minister of Foreign Affairs;* b. 25 April 1955, Oslo, Norway; son of the late Viktor Fedorovich Grushko, fmr diplomatist, KGB agent and chief; ed Moscow State Inst. of Int. Relations (MGIMO); father served in Oslo as trainee in Soviet embassy, family lived in Oslo 1954–58, returned to Oslo where his father was Second Sec. 1962–72, returned with his family to Moscow 1972; adviser, Soviet embassy in Brussels 1980–90s; Head of Russian del. at disarmament negotiations between USSR and NATO within framework of jt consultative group under Treaty on Conventional Armed Forces in Europe (CFE Treaty); Chief Adviser to Dept of Security and Disarmament Affairs, Ministry of Foreign Affairs mid-1990s, Deputy Dir Dept of European Cooperation 2002–03, Dir 2003–05, mem. Bd Ministry of Foreign Affairs 2003, rank of Amb. 2004, Deputy Minister of Foreign Affairs with responsibility for pan-European and Euro-Atlantic orgs 2005–; Lecturer, MGIMO; Order of Friendship 2004. *Address:* Ministry of Foreign Affairs, Smolenskaya-Sennaya pl. 32/34, 119200 Moscow, Russia (office). *Telephone:* (495) 244-16-06 (office). *Fax:* (495) 230-21-30 (office). *E-mail:* ministry@mid.ru (office). *Website:* www.mid.ru (office).

GRYAZNOVA, Alla Georgiyevna, DEcon; Russian economist and academic; b. 27 Nov. 1937, Moscow; m. Viktor Kononov; one s.; ed Moscow Finance Coll., Moscow Inst. of Finance; served in several teaching positions at Moscow Inst. of Finance (now Acad. of Finance of Russian Govt) including Asst, Lecturer, Sr Lecturer and Docent, Prof. 1964–74, Pro-rector on int. relations and research 1976–85, Rector 1985–2006; Pres. VUZ— Inst. of Higher Educ. 2006–; Ed.-in-Chief Banking System in Russia; mem. New Way Movt 1995; First Vice-Pres. Guild of Financiers; Vice-Pres. Acad. of Man. and Market; mem. Acad. of Econ. Sciences, Int. Acad. of Informatics, Int. Acad. of Eurasia; Pres. Moscow Int. School of Finance and Banking; Hon. Prof., Moscow Int. Higher Business School (MIRBIS); Honoured Worker of Science of Russian Fed. *Publications:* over 200 articles on econ. problems. *Leisure interests:* tennis, ballet, volleyball, poetry. *Address:* c/o Academy of Finance, 125468 Moscow, Leningradsky prosp. 49, Russia (office). *Telephone:* (495) 157-56-61 (office). *Fax:* (495) 157-70-70 (office). *E-mail:* academy@fa.ru (office). *Website:* www.fa.ru (office).

GRYBAUSKAITĖ, Dalia, PhD; Lithuanian politician and diplomatist; *Commissioner for Financial Programming and Budget, European Commission;* b. 1 March 1956, Vilnius; ed Leningrad (now St Petersburg) Univ., USSR, School of Foreign Service, Georgetown Univ., Washington, DC, USA; Head, Dept for Science, Inst. of Econs 1990–91; Programme Dir, Govt of Repub. of Lithuania, Prime Minister's Office 1991; Dir European Dept, Ministry of Int. Econ. Relations 1991–93; Dir Econ. Relations Dept, Ministry of Foreign Affairs 1993–94; Chair. Comm. for Aid Coordination (PHARE and G-24) 1993–94; Chief of Negotiations with EU on Free Trade Agreement 1993–94; Envoy Extraordinary and Minister Plenipotentiary, Mission of Lithuania to EU, Brussels 1994–95, Deputy Chief Negotiator on Europe Agreement with EU; Rep. of Nat. Aid Coordinator, Brussels 1994–95; Minister Plenipotentiary, Embassy in USA 1996–99; Deputy Minister of Finance 1999–2000, Chief Negotiator in Negotiations with IMF and World Bank; Deputy Minister of Foreign Affairs 2000–01; Deputy Head of Negotiations, Del. to EU; Minister of Finance 2001–04: Nat. Aid Co-ordinator; EU Commr for Financial Programming and Budget 2004–; Commdr's Cross, Order of Grand Duke Gediminas 2003. *Address:* European Commission, Rue de la Loi 200, 1049 Brussels, Belgium (office). *Telephone:* (2) 2980191 (office); (2) 2988734 (office). *Fax:* (2) 2988490 (office). *E-mail:* cab-grybauskaite-commissaire@ec.europa.eu (office). *Website:* www.ec.europa.eu/commission_barroso/grybauskaite/index_en.htm (office).

GRYSHCHENKO, Kostyantyn; Ukrainian diplomat and politician; *Vice-Chairman, Republican Party of Ukraine;* b. 28 Oct. 1953, Kiev; m.; one d.; ed Moscow State Inst. of Int. Relations; staff mem. UN Secr., New York 1976–80; staff mem. Ministry of Foreign Affairs, USSR 1981–91, with Directorate of Arms Control and Disarmament, Ukraine 1992–95; Deputy Foreign Minister of Ukraine 1995–98; Amb. to Belgium, Netherlands, Luxembourg, Head of Mission to NATO and Perm. Rep. to OPCW (Org. for the Prohibition of Chemical Weapons) 1998–2000; Amb. to USA 2000–03; Minister of Foreign Affairs 2003–05; co-f. Republican Party of Ukraine 2004, Vice-Chair. 2004–; mem. UN Advisory Bd on Disarmament Matters; fmr mem. Coll. of Commr, UN Monitoring, Verification and Inspection Comm. (UNMOVIC); Order of Merit (Ukraine) 1998. *Address:* Republican Party of Ukraine, Starokyivska Street 14, Kiev 03033, Ukraine (office). *Telephone:* (44) 586-46-87 (office). *E-mail:* info@republicanpartyofukraine.com (office). *Website:* www.republicanpartyofukraine.com (office); www.rpu.org.ua (office).

GRYTSENKO, Anatoliy P., MPA; Ukrainian government official and politician; *Chairman of the Verkhovna Rada, Autonomous Republic of Crimea;* b. 21 Sept. 1958, Kerch (Autonomous Repub. of Crimea); m. Olga A. Grytsenko; one s. one d.; ed Kalinin Crimean Agricultural Inst., Simferopol and Kharkov Regional Inst. of Public Admin; began career 1976; held various positions including Chair. Exec. Cttee Chistopolskiy town council of nat. deputies, Chair. Leninskaya Dist State Admin; Deputy Verkhovna Rada (parl.) of the Autonomous Repub. of Crimea 1994–; first Vice-Chair. Verkhovna Rada of the Autonomous Repub. of Crimea 1987–97, Chair. 1997–98, 2006–; Chair. Verkhovna Rada Comm. on Local Self-Govt 1987–97; Order of Merit (third degree) of Ukraine, Order of Peter the Great (first degree), Russia, Order of St Anthony and Feodosiy Pecherski, Ukrainian Orthodox Church. *Leisure interests:* hunting, sociopolitical journalism. *Address:* 95000 Simferopol, 18 K. Marksa Street, the Autonomous Republic of Crimea, Ukraine (office). *Telephone:* (65) 254-42-55 (office). *Fax:* (65) 227-25-81 (office). *E-mail:* svr@rada.crimea.ua (office). *Website:* www.rada.crimea.ua (office).

GRYZLOV, Boris Vyacheslavovich, PhD; Russian engineer and politician; *Chairman, Gosudarstvennaya Duma (State Duma);* b. 15 Dec. 1950, Vladivostok; s. of Vyacheslav Gryzlov; m. Ada; one s. one d.; ed Leningrad (now St Petersburg) Inst. of Electro-Tech. Communications; radio engineer, Heavy Duty Radio Industry Scientific Research Inst. (Comintern), took part in devt of communications systems –1977; Head of construction, later Dept Dir, Electronpribor Production Co. 1977–96; Dir New Training Tech. Centre, Baltic State Tech. Univ. 1996–99; cand. in St Petersburg city elections; Pres. Interregional Business Co-operation Fund Devt of Regions 1999–; Chief of Staff for Viktor Zubkov 1999; Founder mem. Unity (Yedinstvo) Movt 1999–, Head of St Petersburg Regional Br. 1999, Chair. Unity Political Council 2000, Chair. United Russia (Yedinaya Rossiya) 2004–; mem. Gosudarstvennaya Duma (State Duma) 1999–2001, 2003–, Leader, Unity faction 2000–01, Chair. State Duma Dec. 2003–; Minister of Internal Affairs 2001–03; Chair. Inter-Parl. Ass., Eurasian Econ. Community (Eurasec IPA); Perm. mem., Security Council of Russian Fed. *Leisure interests:* soccer and other sports. *Address:* Office of the Chairman, Gosudarstvennaya Duma, 103265 Moscow, Okhotnyi ryad 1, Russia (office). *Telephone:* (495) 292-83-10 (office). *Fax:* (495) 292-94-64 (office). *E-mail:* stateduma@duma.ru (office). *Website:* www.duma.ru (office); www.gryzlov.ru.

GRYZUNOV, Sergey Petrovich; Russian journalist; b. 23 July 1949, Kuybyshev; m.; one s.; ed Moscow State Univ., Acad. of Public Sciences, Cen. Communist Party Cttee; fmr ed. Novosti, then reviewer, then Deputy Head of Bureau, Yugoslavia; Deputy Chair. Cttee on Press April–Sept. 1994, Chair. 1994–95; mem. Pres. Yeltsin's Election Campaign March 1996; Vice-Pres. ICN Pharmaceutical Corpn 1998–2000; Vice-Pres. Moscow News Publrs 2000–. *Leisure interests:* cooking, fishing, underwater swimming. *Address:* Moscow News, Tverskaya str. 16/2, 103829 Moscow, Russia (office). *Telephone:* (495) 200-20-10 (office).

GRZEŚKOWIAK, Alicja, PhD; Polish lawyer, politician and academic; *Professor of Criminal Law, Catholic University of Lublin;* b. 10 June 1941, Świrz, Lvov Prov., Ukraine; m. (husband deceased); one d.; ed Nicolaus Copernicus Univ., Toruń; research worker, Faculty of Law and Admin of Nicolaus Copernicus Univ., Toruń 1966–96, Prof. 1990; on staff, Catholic Univ. of Lublin (KUL) 1990, Prof. of Criminal Law 1991–, mem. Scientific Council of John Paul II Inst.; Lecturer in Religious Law, Higher Ecclesiastic Seminary, Toruń 1994–2002; mem. Solidarity Trade Union 1980; Senator 1989–2001, Vice-Marshal of Senate 1991–93, Marshal 1997–2001, del. Parl. Ass. of the Council of Europe 1989–97, mem. 1991–97, Vice-Chair. Group of Christian Democrats 1992–97; mem. Social Movt of Solidarity Election Action (RSAWS) 1998–2001; mem. Admin. Council of John Paul II Foundation, Vatican 1992–2002; consultant of Pontifical Council for the Family 1993; mem. Pontificia Academia Pro Vita; Founder Foundation of Assistance to Single Mothers, Toruń; Hon. mem. Asscn of Catholic Families; Dr hc (Acad. of Catholic Theology, Warsaw) 1995, (Holy Family Coll., Phila) 1998, (Int. Ind. Univ. of Moldova) 1999; Pro Ecclesia et Pontifice Medal 1991, Medal of 13th Jan. of Lithuanian Repub.; Dame of the Holy Sepulchre Friars of Jerusalem, Great Cross, Order of Crown (Belgium) 1999, Great Cross, Orden del Merito Civil (Spain). *Publications:* numerous scientific publs on penal law, human rights and family rights. *Leisure interests:* reading, listening to music. *Address:* Katolicki Uniwersytet Lubelski, al. Racławickie 14, 20-950 Lublin, Poland (office). *E-mail:* alicja.grzeskowiak@wp.pl (home). *Website:* www.kul.lublin.pl (office).

GU, Binglin, BEng, PhD; Chinese physicist and university administrator; *President, Tsinghua University;* b. 8 Oct. 1945, Harbin, Heilongjiang; ed Tsinghua Univ., Beijing, Univ. of Århus, Denmark; mem. Faculty, Tsinghua Univ. 1970–, Assoc. Prof. of Physics 1983–88, Prof. of Physics 1988–, Head, Dept of Physics 1994–2000, Dean Grad. School 2000–, Pres. Academic Degree Cttee 2001–, Vice-Pres. Tsinghua Univ. 2001–03, Pres. 2003–; Visiting Prof., Tohoku Univ., Japan 1993–94; Sr Visiting Scholar, Notre Dame Univ., USA 1985–86; Dir Steering Cttee for Physics and Astronomy, Ministry of Educ.; Pres. Chinese Stereology Cttee; Vice-Pres. Chinese Physical Soc.; mem. and Dir of Physics and Astronomy Senate; mem. Academic Degree Cttee of the State Council, Nat. Science and Tech. Reward Cttee, Council of Asscn of Asia Pacific Physical Socs; Academician, Chinese Acad. of Science; Second Prize of Scientific Achievement, Ministry of Educ. 1988, 1990, 1994, 1998, Top Award for Excellent Teacher, Baosteel Educ. Fund 1998, First Prize, Chinese Univ. Nature Science 2000, Second Nat. Prize of Nature Science 2000, Second Prize of Scientific Achievement, City of Beijing 2002, Award for Scientific and Technological Progress, Ho Leung Ho Lee Foundation 2002, First LuXun Award, Tohoku Univ. 2004. *Publications:* more than 200 scientific papers in professional journals on the properties of complex materials and phenomena. *Address:* Office of the President, Tsinghua University, 1 Qinghuayuan, Beijing 100084, People's Republic of China (office). *Telephone:* (10) 62782015 (office). *Fax:* (10) 62770349 (office). *E-mail:* gubl@tsinghua.edu.cn (office). *Website:* www.tsinghua.edu.cn (office).

GU, Chaohao; Chinese mathematician; b. 15 May 1926, Wenzhou City, Zhejiang Prov.; ed Zhejiang Univ., Fudan Univ., Shanghai and Moscow Univ., USSR; Assoc. Prof., Dept of Math., Fudan Univ. 1953–57, Prof. 1960, later Dean, Vice-Pres. Fudan Univ. 1984–88, Deputy Dir Inst. of Math., later Dir; Pres. Chinese Univ. of Science and Tech., Hefei 1988, Deputy Dir Advisory Cttee 1993; fmr mem. Math. Discipline Group, State Science and Tech. Comm.; mem. Chinese Acad. of Sciences, Scientific Council of Academia Sinica 1981; Deputy, 6th NPC 1983–88; mem. Dept of Math. and Physics, Academia Sinica 1985; Vice-Chair. China–Brazil Friendship Group of NPC 1986; Dir Mathematical Research Centre, Shanghai Communications Univ. 1988; Deputy, 3rd NPC 1964–66; mem. 5th CPPCC Nat. Cttee 1978–83, 8th CPPCC Nat. Cttee 1993–98, 9th CPPCC Nat. Cttee 1998–2003; 2nd Class Award, Nat. Natural Science 1982, State Educ. Comm. (1st Class Award) 1985, 1986, Hua Luogeng Math. Award 1995, awarded Advancement in Science and Tech., Ho Leung Ho Lee Foundation 1995. *Address:* c/o Science and Technology University, 59 Tunxi Road, Hefei, Anhui Province 230009, People's Republic of China (office). *Telephone:* 74711 (office).

GU, Jianguo; Chinese steel industry executive; *President, Magang (Group) Holding Co Ltd;* b. 1954; has been at Ma'anshan Iron and Steel Co. Ltd (Masteel) for many years, Chair. Masteel 1993–95, Gen. Man. Magang (Group) Holding and Chair. Masteel 1995–99, Pres. Magang (Group) Holding Co. Ltd, Chair. and Exec. Dir Masteel. *Address:* Magang (Group) Holding, 8 Hong Qi Zhong Road, Maanshan City 243003, People's Republic of China (office). *Telephone:* (555) 2888158 (office). *Fax:* (555) 2887284 (office). *Website:* www.magang.com.cn (office).

GU, Jinchi; Chinese party and government official; *Chairman, Sino-Lithuanian Friendship Association;* b. 1932, Xiongxian Co., Hebei Prov.; joined CCP 1949; Deputy Sec. Beijing No. 1 Machine Tools Plant, CCP Party Cttee 1959–65; Sec. Long March Machine Tools Plant, CCP Party Cttee, Zigong City, Sichuan Prov. 1965–75, Sec. CCP City Cttee 1980–81; Vice-Mayor Zigong City 1980–81; Vice-Gov. Sichuan Prov. 1982–85; mem. 13th CCP Cen. Cttee 1987–92, 14th CCP Cen. Cttee 1992–97; Deputy Sec. Sichuan Prov. Cttee 1987–90; Sec. Gansu Prov. Cttee 1990–93, Sec. CCP Liaoning Prov. Cttee 1995–97; Deputy, 8th NPC 1993–98, mem. 9th Standing Cttee of NPC 1998–2003 (Vice-Chair. Internal Affairs and Judicial Cttee 1998–2003); Del., 15th CCP Nat. Congress 1997–2002; Chair. Sino-Lithuanian Friendship Asscn. *Address:* c/o Standing Committee of National People's Congress, Beijing, People's Republic of China.

GU, Mu; Chinese politician (retd); b. 1914, Roncheng City, Shandong Prov.; joined CCP 1932; Mayor of Jinan 1950–52; Deputy Sec. CCP Shanghai 1953–54; Vice-Chair. State Construction Comm. 1954–56, State Econ. Comm. 1956–65; Chair. State Capital Construction Comm. 1965–67; criticized and removed from office during Cultural Revolution 1967; Minister of State Capital Construction Comm. 1973–81, of Foreign Investment Comm. 1979–82, of Import-Export Comm. 1979–82; Political Commissar, PLA Capital Construction Engineering Corps 1979–; Vice-Premier, State Council 1975–82; mem. 11th Cen. Cttee CCP 1977, Deputy for Shandong, 5th NPC 1978, mem. Secr. 1980–82, 1982–85, State Councillor, State Council 1982–88; mem. 12th Cen. Cttee CCP 1982–87, Exec. Chair. 1988–92; Head Co-ordination Group for Tourist Industry 1986–, for Econ. Devt of Ningbo 1985–; Pres. China Econ. Law Research Soc. 1984–92, China Strategy and Admin. Research Soc.; Vice Chair., 7th CPPCC 1988–93; Chair. Econ. Cttee 7th CPPCC Nat. Cttee 1988–92; Pres. China Population Welfare Foundation 1994; mem. Presidium, 14th CCP Nat. Congress Oct. 1992; Most Hon. Pres. Asscn of Enterprises with Foreign Investment; Hon. Pres. Soc. for Study of Econs of Capital Construction 1980–, Confucius Foundation 1986–, China Asscn for Promotion of Int. Science and Tech. 1988–, China Asscn for Advancement of Int. Friendship; Hon. Chair. China Tourism Asscn 1986–; Hon. Adviser 'Happiness Project' Organization Cttee. *Address:* Chinese People's Political Consultative Conference, Taiping Qiao Road, Beijing, People's Republic of China.

GU, Songfen; Chinese aeronautical engineer; b. 1930, Suzhou, Jiangsu Prov.; ed Jiaotong Univ., Shanghai; engineer, Aeronautical Industry Admin. of Ministry of Heavy Industry; Group Leader Aerodynamic Group of Design Dept, Shenyang Aeroplane Mfg Factory; Vice-Chief Designer, Chief Designer, Vice-Pres. then Pres. Aviation Science and Tech. Research Inst.; mem. 4th Presidium of Depts 2000–; responsible for jet fighter design; Chief Designer Shenyang Aeroplane Mfg Co.; Vice-Chair. Science and Tech. Cttee, China Aviation Industry Corpn; joined CCP 1981; Deputy, 7th NPC 1988–93, mem. 8th Standing Cttee of NPC 1993–98 (mem. Educ., Science, Culture and Health Cttee 1993–98), 9th Standing Cttee of NPC 1998–2003; Fellow, Chinese Acad. of Sciences 1991– (Deputy Dir Div. of Technological Sciences 1996–); mem. Chinese Acad. of Eng 1994–; Nat. Model Worker 1988, Gold Nat. Aeronautical Award 1992, Scientific and Technological Progress Award, Ho Leung Ho Lee Foundation 1995. *Address:* Shenyang Aeroplane Manufacturing Company, Shenyang, Liaoning Province, People's Republic of China (office).

GU, Xiulian; Chinese economist, politician and party and government official; *President, All-China Women's Federation;* b. 1935, Nantong, Jiangsu Prov.; ed public security cadre's school, Shenyang, Liaoning Prov., Public Security Bureau of Benxi City, Liaoning, Secondary Metallurgical School of Shenyang; joined CCP 1956; technician and cadre, Communist Youth League of China Metallurgical Corpn 1961–64; technician, Ministry of Textile Industry 1969; cadre, State Council 1970; Vice-Minister, State Planning Comm., State Council 1973–83; Alt. mem. Cen. Cttee, CCP 1977; Vice-Chair. Cen. Patriotic Sanitation Campaign Cttee, Cen. Cttee 1981–89; mem. 12th Cen. Cttee, CCP 1982–87, 13th Cen. Cttee CCP 1987–92, 14th Cen. Cttee CCP 1992–97, 15th Cen. Cttee CCP 1997–2002; Deputy Sec. CCP Prov. Cttee, Jiangsu 1982–89; Gov. of Jiangsu 1983–89; Minister of Chemical Industry 1989–98 (also Party Cttee Sec. at the Ministry); Deputy, 9th NPC 1998–2003, Vice-Chair. 10th NPC Standing Cttee 2003–; Vice-Pres. 7th, 8th and 9th Exec. Cttee, All-China Women's Fed. 1998–2003, Pres. 9th All-China Women's Fed. 2003–; Vice-Pres. 3rd Council, China Women's Devt Fund 1999, Vice-Pres. China Women's Devt Fund 2001–. *Address:* The All-China Women's Federation, 15 Jian Guo Men Nei Street, Beijing 100730, People's Republic of China (office). *Telephone:* (10) 65211639-222. *Fax:* (10) 65211156. *E-mail:* yzhch@women.org.cn; acwf@women.org.cn. *Website:* www.women.org.cn/english.

GU, Yingqi; Chinese politician; b. 1930, Xinmin, Liaoning; m.; two s. one d.; joined PLA 1948, CCP 1950; Vice-Minister of Public Health 1984–95; Chief Physician; mem. Standing Cttee 8th Nat. Cttee 1993–; Co-ordinator State Co-ordination of Control of Narcotics and Against Drugs 1987–90; Head of Del. to UN Int. Conf. on Drug Abuse and Illicit Trafficking 1987, to Signing of Sino-US Memorandum of Understanding on Co-operation and Control of Narcotic Drugs, Washington 1987, to UN Conf. for Adoption of a Convention Against Illicit Traffic in Narcotic Drugs and Psychotropic Substances 1988, to 17th Special Session of UN Gen. Ass. on Int. Co-operation against Drugs 1990, to 44th Gen. Ass. of WHO 1991, to Int. Conf. for Protection of War Victims, Geneva, Switzerland 1993, to 9th Session of Gen. Ass. of Int. Fed. of Red Cross and Red Crescent Socs, Birmingham, UK 1993; Conf. Chair. 15th Meeting of Nat. Drug Law Enforcement Agencies for Asia and Pacific 1990, 4th Asia and Pacific Red Cross and Red Crescent Conf., Beijing 1993; Head of Chinese Red Cross Del. to 26th Int. Conf. of Red Cross and Red Crescent, Geneva 1995; Pres. China Rural Hygiene Asscn 1986–, Chinese Asscn of Rehabilitation Medicine 1985–, Chinese Asscn of Hosp. Man.; Exec. Vice-Pres. Red Cross Soc. of China 1990–; Vice-Pres. Int. Fed. of Red Cross and Red Crescent Socs 1991–93. *Address:* c/o Red Cross Society of China, 53 Ganmian Hutong, Beijing 100010, People's Republic of China. *Telephone:* (10) 513-5838. *Fax:* (10) 512-4169. *Website:* http://202.108.59.10/english/ (office).

GUAINO, Henri; French civil servant and economist; *Special Adviser to the President;* b. 11 March 1957, Arles; ed Institut d'études politiques de Paris, École nationale d'admin.; economist, Crédit Lyonnais 1982–86; Course Dir, École supérieure de commerce de Paris and École normale supérieure de Saint-Cloud 1984–87; Chief of Staff to Treasury Dir 1987–88; Asst Sec.-Gen. Club de Paris 1987–88; worked on Jacques Chirac's presidential campaign 1988; Head of Lectures, Institut d'études politiques de Paris 1988–2003; Head of Finance Research, Louis Dreyfus Group 1989–90; Chief of Staff to Dir-Gen., Mutuelle d'assurance des artisans 1990–93; Chief of Staff to Pres. of Nat. Ass., Philippe Séguin 1993; adviser to Minister of the Interior, Charles Pasqua 1994–95; Chief of Staff, Gen. Planning Commissariat 1995–98; Planning and Devt Adviser to Charles Pasqua for Hauts-de-Seine, Paris 1999–2000; Scientific Adviser, Agence pour la diffusion de l'information technologique 2002–04; Admin., Agence de l'environnement et de la maîtrise de l'énergie 2003; Chief Adviser, Cour des Comptes 2006–; Special Adviser, Pres. of the Repub., Nicolas Sarkozy 2007–. *Address:* Palais de l'Elysée, 55 rue du faubourg Saint-Honoré, 75008 Paris, France (office). *Telephone:* 1-42-92-81-00 (office). *Website:* www.elysee.fr (office).

GUAN, Guangfu; Chinese politician and banker; b. 1931, Muling Co., Heilongjiang Prov.; ed Hubei Univ.; joined CCP 1948; Vice-Pres. Hubei Br. People's Bank of China 1971–78, Pres., Hubei Br. 1978–82; Sec. Hubei Prov. CCP Cttee 1983–94; Chair. Hubei Prov. 8th People's Congress 1993–2002; mem. 12th CCP Cen. Cttee 1982–87, 13th CCP Cen. Cttee 1987–92, 14th CCP Cen. Cttee 1992–97. *Address:* Shui Guo Hu, Wuhan, Hubei Province, People's Republic of China.

GUAN, Qiao; Chinese engineer; b. 2 July 1935, Taiyuan, Shanxi Prov.; ed Moscow Bauman Eng Inst., USSR; Fellow, Chinese Acad. of Eng 1994–; invented low-stress no-distortion welding method; mem. Council Chinese Acad. of Eng; Research Fellow and Vice-Chair. Science and Tech. Cttee, Beijing Aeronautical Manufacturing Tech. Research Inst.; Nat. Invention Prize (2nd Class), Int. Inst. of Welding Lifetime Achievement Award 1999. *Publications:* more than 50 technical papers published in Chinese, 25 papers in English and Russian. *Address:* Beijing Aeronautical Manufacturing Technology Research Institute, PO Box 863, 100024 Beijing, People's Republic of China (office). *Telephone:* (10) 8570-1243.

GUAN, Weiyan; Chinese physicist; b. 18 Aug. 1928, Rudong Co., Jiangsu Prov.; s. of Guan Deyi and Han Quanzheng; m. Zheng Zongshuang 1960; one s. one d.; ed Harbin Polytechnical Inst., Tsinghua, Beijing, Leningrad, Tbilisi and Moscow Univs; researcher, Inst. of Physics, USSR Acad. of Sciences 1957–60; researcher, Inst. of Physics, Chinese Acad. of Sciences, Beijing 1960–, Deputy Dir 1978–81, Dir 1981–85, mem. Dept of Math. and Physics; Visiting Scholar, Low-temperature Research Centre, Grenoble, France 1980; Pres. Univ. of Science and Tech. of China, Hefei 1984–87, Asscn of Science and Tech., Anhui Prov. 1986; Vice-Pres. Chinese Physics Soc. 1987; Visiting Prof., Univ. Giessen 1987, KFK Karlsruhe, Germany 1988, Univ. of Notre Dame (USA) 1989, Univ. of Houston 1989–90, KFA, Julich, Germany 1990–91, Nat. Tsing Hua Univ. (Taiwan) 1991–, Dan Jiang Univ. (Taiwan) 1995–; mem. bd of various Chinese and int. journals; mem. Int. Cttee, Int. Conf. on Low Temperature Physics 1981–. *Address:* Room 1201, Building 812, Zhong Guan Cun, Beijing 100080, People's Republic of China. *Telephone:* 6255-4965.

GUARD, Mark Perrott, MA, RIBA, MRIAI, MCSD; Irish architect; b. 22 May 1952, Dublin; s. of Wilson Perrott Guard and Ethena Joy Wallace; ed Avoca School, Dublin, Univ. of Toronto, Royal Coll. of Art, London; worked for architectural, film and textile design cos in Ireland and UK 1969–73; emigrated to Canada 1973; architect, Toronto and Vancouver 1973–76; worked for Richard Rogers Partnership, Rick Mather Architects, Eva Jiricna Architects, London 1982–86; started pvt. practice in modernist residential design and devt of transformable spaces 1986; Prin. Mark Guard Design 1986–88, Mark Guard Assocs 1988–93, Mark Guard Architects 1993–; Dir Mark Guard Ltd 1998–; Dir Guard Tillman Pollock Ltd 2002–; RIBA Regional Award for New House, London, W2 1992, for house refurbishment, London, NW6 1995, CSD Commendation for transformable flat, London, EC2 1993, for house refurbishment, London, NW6 1995, RIAI Commendation for new house, Galway 1993, RIBA Award for Houses and Housing for penthouse apartment, Paris 1997. *Address:* 161 Whitfield Street, London, W1T 5ET, England (office). *Telephone:* (20) 7380-1199 (office). *Fax:* (20) 7387-5441 (office). *E-mail:* mga@markguard.com (office). *Website:* www.markguard.com (office).

GUARDADO, Facundo; Salvadorean politician; b. 27 Nov. 1954, Arcatao, Dept of Chalatenengo; s. of Sixto Guardado and Herlinda Guardado; m. Carmen Cristina Alvarez Basso 1993; one s. three d.; ed fellowship to econ. seminars at Cen. American Business Admin. Inst. and Heredia Nat. Univ. of Costa Rica; co-operative movt leader 1972–; Sec.-Gen. Revolutionary Popular Bloc 1977; mem. Cen. Cttee Nat. Liberation Front (FMLN) in 1980s, mem. Political Comm. 1993, Campaign Man. 1997, Gen. Co-ordinator 1997–99; Counselor at San Salvador Majorship 1997–; presidential cand. 1999; Leader, Movimiento Renovador (split from FMLN 2002) 2002–03 (dissolved after elections 2003); mem. peace negotiations del. La Palma 1984, Ayagualo 1984, La Nunciatura 1987, Mexico 1991; Vice-Pres. Perm. Conf. of Political Parties of Latin America and the Caribbean; mem. Initiatives Group for Latin America; Pres. El Salvador XXI Century Foundation. *Publications:* Political and Social Struggles in El Salvador, Participation and Social Change, Evolution of the Democratic Process in El Salvador. *Leisure interests:* agriculture, football. *Address:* Paseo Miralvalle 155, Colonia Miralvalle, San Salvador (home); c/o Motocross #49, Colonia Monteverde, San Salvador, El Salvador (home). *Telephone:* 274-2104 (home).

GUARGUAGLINI, Pier Francesco, PhD; Italian aerospace industry executive; *Chairman and CEO, Finmeccanica SpA;* b. 25 Feb. 1937, Castagneto Carducci, Livorno; m., three c.; ed Univ. of Pisa, Univ. of Pennsylvania, USA; Asst Lecturer in Nuclear Electronics, Univ. of Pisa 1961–63; Asst Lecturer in Radar Systems, Univ. of Rome 1963–78; joined Selenia SpA as Systems Analyst 1963, Dir of Research Devt 1970–74, Dir IT and Telecommunications Div. 1975–79, Dir and Man. Civil Div. 1979–81, Deputy Gen. Man. 1981–82, Co-Gen. Man. 1982; Gen. Man. Officine Galileo 1984–87, Man. Dir 1987–94; Man. Dir Oto Melara SpA and Breda Meccanica Bresciana SpA 1994–96; Head, Defence Sector Businesses, Finmeccanica SpA 1996–99, Chair. Alenia Marconi Systems NV (joint venture between Finmeccanica and BAE) 1998–2000, CEO and Chair. Finmeccanica SpA 2002–; CEO Fincantieri Cantieri Navali Italiani 1999–2002; Lecturer, Univ. of Rome; Pres. AeroSpace and Defence Industries Asscn of Europe; mem. Shareholders' Steering Cttee IJVC Horizon Ltd; mem. IEEE; Aviation Week and Space Technology Person of the Year. *Address:* Finmeccanica SpA, Piazza Monte Grappa 4, Rome 00195, Italy (office). *Telephone:* (06) 324731 (office). *Fax:* (06) 3208621 (office). *E-mail:* info@finmeccanica.it (office). *Website:* www.finmeccanica.it (office).

GUARINI, Kathryn Wilder, BS, PhD; American scientist and academic; ed Yale and Stanford Univs; joined IBM Research Div. as Research Staff mem. and Man. 45nm Front End Integration Group, Silicon Tech. Dept, IBM T.J. Watson Research Center, Yorktown Heights, NY 1999, currently on assignment in IBM Corp. Tech. working on tech. assessments for IBM Tech. Team; mem. IEEE, AAAS, Asscn for Women in Science; named to TR100 list of top 100 young innovators by MIT's Technology Review magazine 2003, World Tech. Award in Information Tech. (Hardware), The World Tech. Network (co-recipient) 2004. *Publications:* Scanning Probe Lithography (Microsystems, Vol. 7; with Hyongsok T. Soh and Calvin F. Quate) 2001; more than 45 tech. publs on CMOS device fabrication, three-dimensional integrated circuits, and novel nanofabrication techniques and applications; more than 15 US patents. *Address:* IBM Corporate Division, 294 Route 100, Somers, NY 10598, USA (office). *E-mail:* kwg@us.ibm.com (office). *Website:* www.watson.ibm.com (office).

GUARINI, Renato; Italian statistician, university rector and academic; *Rector, University of Rome 'La Sapienza';* b. 16 March 1932, Naples; ed Univ. of Naples; did research at Univ. of Cen. Bureau of Statistics 1957–75, held post of Head of Dept for Gen. Methodology and Econ. Statistics; fmr Prof. of Econ. Statistics, Univ. of Cagliari; Prof. of Econ., Univ. of Rome 'La Sapienza' 1976–, Pres. Course of Statistics and Econs 1988–95, Dean of Faculty of Statistics 1995–2004, Pro-Rector La Sapienza Univ. 1997–2004, Rector 2004–; mem. Comm. for the Guarantee of Information Statistics at Presidency of Council of Ministers, Scientific Advisory Cttee of Nat. Research Council, Ministry of Educ., Univ. and Research for 'decrees area', Comm. for the Reform of the Nat. Statistical System which prepared DL 322/89; mem. Accad. Nazionale dei Lincei 2001; Kt Grand Cross, Order of Merit of the Italian Repub. 2006. *Publications:* numerous scientific papers in professional journals. *Address:* Office of the Rector, Università degli Studi di Roma'La Sapienza', Piazzale Aldo Moro 5, 00185 Rome, Italy (office). *Telephone:* (06) 49914180 (office). *E-mail:* info@uniroma1.it (office). *Website:* www.uniroma1.it (office).

GUBAIDULINA, Sofia Asgatovna; Russian (b. Tatar) composer; b. 24 Oct. 1931, Chistopol; d. of Asgat Gubaidulin and Fedossia Gubaidulina; m. Peter Meshchaninov; one d.; ed Kazan and Moscow Conservatories, pvt studies with Nikolai Peiko, Vissarion Shebalin and Grigori Kogan; first noticed abroad, Paris 1979; UK debut playing Symphony in 12 Movements 1987; freelance composer in Moscow 1963–91, in Germany 1991–; Premium Imperiale 1998, Léonie Sonnings Music Prize 1999, Royal Swedish Acad. of Music Polar Prize 2002, Bach Prize, Hamburg 2007. *Compositions:* instrumental: Piano quintet 1957, Allegro rustico for flute and piano 1963, Five Etudes for harp, double bass and percussion 1965, Vivente non vivente for synthesizer 1970, Concordanza for chamber ensemble 1971, String Quartet No. 1 1971, Music for harpsichord and percussion 1971, Fairytale Poem 1971, Stufen (The Steps) 1971, Detto II for cello and ensemble 1972, Rumore e Silenzio for percussion and harpsichord 1974, Ten Preludes for solo cello 1974, Quattro for 2 trumpets and 2 trombones 1974, Concerto for bassoon and low strings 1975, Sonata for double bass and piano 1975, Light and Darkness for solo organ 1976, Dots, Lines and Zigzag for bass clarinet and piano 1976, Trio for 3 trumpets 1976, Revue for orchestra and jazz band 1976, Duo-Sonata for 2 bassoons 1977, Quartet for 4 flutes 1977, Misterioso for 7 percussionists 1977, Te Salutant capriccio for large light orchestra 1978, Introitus concerto for piano and chamber orchestra 1978, Detto I sonata for organ and percussion 1978, De profundis for solo bayan 1978, Sounds of the Forest for flute and piano 1978, In Croce for cello and organ 1979, Jubilatio for 4 percussionists 1979, Offertorium concerto for violin and orchestra 1980, Garten von Freuden und Traurigkeiten for flute, harp and viola (speaker ad lib) 1980, Rejoice sonata for violin and cello 1981, Descensio for ensemble 1981, Seven Words for cello, bayan and strings 1982, In the Beginning there was Rhythm for 7 percussionists 1984, Et exspecto sonata for solo bayan 1985, Quasi Hoquetus for viola, bassoon, cello and piano 1985, Stimmen... vetummen..., symphony in 12 movements 1986, String Quartet No. 2 1987, String Quartet No. 3 1987, Answer without Question collage for 3 orchestras 1988, String Trio 1988, Pro et Contra for large orchestra 1989, Silenzio 5 pieces for bayan, violin and cello 1991, Even and Uneven for 7 percussionists 1991, Tatar dance for 2 double basses and bayan 1992, Dancer on a Tightrope for violin and piano 1993, Meditation on the Bach-Choral Vor deinen Thron tret ich hiermit for harpsichord, 2 violins, viola, cello and double bass 1993, String quartet No. 4 1993, Early in the Morning, Right Before Waking for 7 kotos 1993, The Festivities at Their Height for cello and orchestra 1993, Now Always Snow for chamber ensemble and chamber choir on poems of Gennady Aigi 1993, 2nd cello concerto 1994, In anticipation... for saxophone quartet and 6 percussion 1994, Zeitgestalten symphony in 4 movements 1994, Music for flute, strings and percussion 1994, Viola concerto 1996, Quaternion for 4 cellos 1996, Galgenlieder à 3 15 pieces for mezzo, double bass and percussion 1996, Galgenlieder à 5 1996, Ritorno perpetuo for harpsichord 1997, Canticle of the Sun for cello, chamber chorus and 2 percussionists 1997, Two Paths for 2 violas and orchestra 1998, Im Schatten des Baumes for koto, bass-koto, cheng and orchestra 1998; vocal: Phacelia vocal cycle for soprano and orchestra 1956, Night in Memphis cantata for mezzo-soprano, male chorus and chamber orchestra 1968, Rubaiyat 1969, Roses 5 romances for soprano and piano 1972, Counting Rhymes 5 children's songs 1973, Hour of the Soul for mezzo-soprano and large orchestra 1976, Perception for soprano, baritone and 7 string instruments 1981, Hommage à Marina Tsvetava suite in 5 movements for chorus a cappella 1984, Hommage à T. S. Eliot for soprano and octet 1987, Two Songs on German Folk Poetry for soprano, flute, harpsichord and cello 1988, Witty Waltzing in the style of Johann Strauss for soprano and octet 1987, for piano and string quartet 1989, Jauchzt vor Gott for chorus and organ 1989, Alleluja for chorus, boys soprano, organ and large orchestra 1990, Aus dem Stundenbuch for cello, orchestra, male chorus and female speaker 1991, Johannes Passion 2000, Johannes Ostern 2001, Risonanza for chamber ensemble 2001, Reflections on the theme B-A-C-H 2002, Mirage: the Dancing Sun for eight violoncelli 2002, On the Edge of the Abyss for seven violoncelli and two waterphones 2002, The Rider on the White Horse for large orchestra and organ 2002, The Light of the END for large orchestra 2003, Under the Sign of Scorpio for bayan and large orchestra 2003, Verwandlung für Posaune, Saxophonquartett, violoncello, kontrabasso und tam-tam 2004, The Deceitful Face of Hope and Despair for flute and large orchestra 2005, Feast during a Plague for large orchestra 2006, Die Leier des Orpheus für violine, streichorchester und Schlagzeug 2006, Ravvedimento for cello and guitar quartet 2007, In Tempus Praesens for violin and orchestra 2007. *Address:* Ziegeleiweg 12, 25482 Appen, Germany (home). *Telephone:* (41) 2281875 (home).

GUBBAY, Hon. Mr Justice Anthony Roy, MA, LLM; Zimbabwean judge; b. 26 April 1932, Manchester, England; m. Wilma Sanger 1962 (died 2002); two s.; ed Univ. of Witwatersrand, S Africa, Univ. of Cambridge; admitted to practice 1957; advocate Bulawayo, S Rhodesia 1958, Sr Counsel 1974; Pres. Matabeleland and Midlands Valuations Boards; Nat. Pres. Special Court for Income Tax Appeals, Fiscal Court and Patents Tribunal; Vice-Chair. Bar Asscn; Judge of the High Court, Bulawayo 1977–83, Judge of the Supreme

Court 1983; Chair. Legal Practitioners' Disciplinary Tribunal 1981–87, Law Devt Comm., Judicial Service Comm.; Chief Justice of Zimbabwe 1990–2001, retd 2001; mem. Perm. Court of Arbitration; Pres. Oxford and Cambridge Soc. of Zimbabwe; Patron Commonwealth Magistrates and Judges Asscn; mem. Advisory Bd of Commonwealth Judicial Educ. Inst., Commonwealth Reference Group on the Promotion of the Human Rights of Women and the Girl Child through the Judiciary; Hon. Fellow Jesus Coll. Cambridge; Hon. Bencher of Lincoln's Inn (UK); Hon. mem. The Soc. of Legal Scholars (UK) 2004; Great Cross, Rio Branco Order (Brazil) 1999; Dr hc (Essex) 1994; Hon. LLD (London) 2002, (Witwatersrand) 2005; Peter Gruber Foundation Justice Award 2001. *Leisure interests:* classical music, philately, watching all forms of sport, travel. *Address:* 26 Dacomb Drive, Chisipite, Harare, Zimbabwe (home). *Telephone:* (4) 496882 (home). *E-mail:* supreme-court@gta.gov.zw (office); gubbay@zol.co.zw (home).

GUBBAY, Raymond, CBE, FRSA; British music promoter; b. 2 April 1946, London; s. of David Gubbay and the late Ida Gubbay; m. Johanna Quirke 1972 (divorced 1988); two d.; ed Univ. Coll. School, Hampstead; concert promoter 1966–; Founder and Man. Dir Raymond Gubbay Ltd 1966–; presents regular series of concerts at major London and regional concert halls including Royal Albert Hall, Royal Festival Hall, Barbican Centre, Symphony Hall Birmingham, Bridgewater Hall Manchester, Royal Concert Hall Glasgow and in Ireland, Belgium, Germany, Austria, Switzerland, Netherlands and Scandinavia; has presented productions of: (operas and operettas) The Ratepayer's Iolanthe 1984, Turandot 1991–92, La Bohème (centenary production) 1996, 2004, 2006, Carmen 1997, 2002, 2005, Madam Butterfly 1998, 2000, 2003, The Pirates of Penzance 1998–99, 2000, Tosca 1999, Aida 2001; (ballets) Swan Lake 1997, 1999, 2002, 2004, Romeo and Juliet 1998, The Sleeping Beauty 2000, Cavallaria Rusticana and Pagliacci 2002, Showboat 2006, D'Oyly Carte Opera Co. Seasons 2000, 2001, 2002, 2003, Savoy Opera 2004; Hon. FRAM 1988; Hon. FTCL 2000. *Leisure interests:* living in France, gardening. *Address:* Dickens House, 15 Tooks Court, London, EC4A 1QH, England. *Telephone:* (20) 7025-3750 (office). *E-mail:* info@raymondgubbay.co.uk (office). *Website:* www.raymondgubbay.co.uk (office).

GUBBINS, David, BA, PhD, FRS, FInstP; British geophysicist and academic; *Research Professor of Earth Sciences, School of Earth and Environment, University of Leeds;* b. 31 May 1947, Southampton; s. of the late Albert Edmund Gubbins and of Joyce Lucy Gubbins (née Rayner); m. Margaret Stella McCloy 1972; one s. two d.; ed King Edward VI Grammar School, Trinity Coll., Cambridge; Visiting Research Fellow, Univ. of Colorado 1972–73; instructor, MIT 1973–74; Asst Prof., UCLA 1974–76; Asst Dir of Research, Dept of Geodesy and Geophysics, Univ. of Cambridge 1976–89; Fellow, Churchill Coll., Cambridge 1978–90; Head of Geophysics, Univ. of Leeds 1989–2001, Research Prof. 2001–; Ed. Geophysical Journal of the Royal Astronomical Soc. 1982–90, Physics of the Earth and Planetary Interior 1990–2002; Fellow, American Geophysical Union 1985; Foreign mem. Norwegian Acad. of Arts and Sciences 2005; Murchison Medal of Geological Soc. of London 1998, Gold Medal of Royal Astronomical Soc. 2003, John Adam Fleming Medal of American Geophysical Union 2004, Chree Medal of the Inst. of Physics 2005, Augustus Love Medal of European Geophysical Union 2007, Arthur Holmes Medal of European Geophysical Union 2009. *Publications:* Seismology and Plate Tectonics 1990, Time Series Analysis and Inverse Theory for Geophysicists 2004, Encyclopedia of Geomagnetism and Paleomagnetism 2007; more than 100 articles in scientific journals. *Leisure interests:* sailing, walking. *Address:* School of Earth and Environment, University of Leeds, Leeds, LS2 9JT, England (office). *Telephone:* (113) 343-5255 (office). *Fax:* (113) 343-5259 (office). *E-mail:* d.gubbins@see.leeds.ac.uk (office). *Website:* www.see.leeds.ac .uk/people/d.gubbins (office); homepages.see.leeds.ac.uk/~ear6dg (office).

GUBENKO, Nikolai Nikolayevich; Russian actor and theatrical director; b. 17 Aug. 1941, Odessa; m. Jeanna Bolotova; ed All-Union Inst. of Cinema; mem. CPSU 1987–91, Cen. Cttee 1990–91, CP of Russian Fed. 1992–2002, expelled from party 2002, Ind. 2002–; actor at Taganka Theatre, Moscow 1964–, Artistic Dir 1987–89; Founder and Head of Concord of Taganka actors 1993–; dir several films including The Orphans (Soviet entry Cannes Film Festival 1977), The Life of Holidaymakers (based on story by Ivan Bunin), Life. . .Tears. . .Love, Restricted Area 1988; stage appearances include Boris Godunov; USSR Minister of Culture 1989–91; mem. State Duma (Parl.) 1995–2003; Deputy Chair. Cttee for Culture 1997–1999, Chair. 1999–2003; Pres. Int. Asscn of Help for Culture 1992–; RSFSR People's Artist 1985. *Address:* Franzenskaya nab. 46, Apt. 65, 110270 Moscow, Russia.

GUCCIONE, Robert (Bob) Charles Joseph Edward Sabatini; American publisher; b. 17 Dec. 1930, Brooklyn; s. of Anthony Guccione and Nina Guccione; m. Kathy Keeton 1988; five c. from previous m.; artist 1948–55, 1992–; fmr cartoonist and greetings card designer; Man. London American; founder Penthouse Media Group, Inc and publr Penthouse Magazine, 1965–; also Publr Forum, Variations, Penthouse Letters, Omni, Saturday Review, Four Wheeler, Longevity, Girls of Penthouse, Compute, Open Wheel, Stock Car Racing, Superstock and Drag, Hot Talk; Chair. CEO Gen. Media Inc. (now Penthouse Media Group Inc) 1988–2004; producer of film Caligula 1979; exec. producer, TV show Omni: The New Frontier, Omni: Visions of Tomorrow. *Address:* c/o Penthouse Media Group, Inc, 2 Penn Plaza, New York, NY 10121, USA (office).

GUDANOV, Dmitry Konstantinovich; Russian ballet dancer; b. Moscow; ed Moscow Academic School of Choreography; joined Bolshoi Theatre Ballet Company as a corps-de-ballet dancer 1994, soloist 1997, leading soloist 2000–; took part in Bolshoi Theatre project New Choreography Workshop 2004; 1st Prize and Gold Medal 7th Int. Moscow Ballet Competition 1998, 1st Prize Int. Ballet Competition Paris 1998, Soul of Dance Prize, Ballet Magazine 2000. *Ballet:* leading roles in Sleeping Beauty, Nutcracker, Le Mégère Apprivoisée, La Sylphide, Fantasia on the Theme of Casanova, Giselle, Romeo and Juliet, Symphony C-major (production of G. Balanchine), Heir in Hamlet (production of B. Eifman). *Achievements:* Tours in European countries. *Address:* Bolshoi Theatre, Teatralnaya pl. 1, Moscow, Russia (office). *Website:* www.bolshoi.org; mariinsky.ru/en/ballet/gudanov05.

GUĐFINNSON, Einar Kristinn; Icelandic politician; b. 2 Dec. 1955, Bolungarvík; s. of Guđfinnur Einarsson (deceased) and María K. Haraldsdóttir; m. Sigrún J. Þórisdóttir; three c.; ed Coll. of Isafjorđur, Univ. of Essex, UK; fmr journalist; fmr CEO fisheries co.; mem. Parl. 1991–, fmr Chair. Fisheries Cttee, Econs and Trade Cttee, fmr mem. Finance Cttee, Social Cttee, Agric. Cttee, Parls Cttee for Foreign Affairs; fmr Chair. Icelandic Group, IPU; fmr Group Chair. Independence Party; Minister of Fisheries 2005–09 (resgnd), also of Agriculture 2007–09 (resgnd). *Address:* Independence Party, 105 Reykjavik, Iceland (office). *Telephone:* 5151700 (office). *Fax:* 5151717 (office). *E-mail:* xd@xd.is (office). *Website:* www.xd.is (office).

GUÉANT, Claude Henri; French civil servant and government official; *Secrétaire général de la Présidence de la République;* b. 17 Jan. 1945, Vimy; s. of Robert Guéant and Madeleine Guéant (née Leclercq); m. Rose-Marie Benoist 1969; two c.; ed Faculté de droit de Paris, l'Institut d'études politiques de Paris, l'École nationale d'administration; Cabinet Dir, Prefect of Finistère 1971–74; Sec.-Gen. for Econ. Affairs, Guadeloupe 1974–77; served in Ministry of the Interior 1977–81; apptd sous-préfet hors classe, worked in Centre region prefect 1981, then Sec.-Gen. lHérault Prefect, then Sec.-Gen Hauts-de-Seine Prefect; Préfet Hautes-Alpes 1991–94; Dir-Gen Nat.Police Force 1994–98; Préfet Franche-Comté region and Doubs 1998–2000, of Brittany region, Western defence zone and d'Ille-et-Vilaine 2000–02; Chief of Staff to Minister of the Interior Nicolas Sarkozy 2002–04, 2005–07; with Ministry of Finance 2004; campaign man. for presidential campaign of Nicolas Sarkozy 2007; Secrétaire général de la Présidence de la République 2007–; Chevalier, de l'Ordre nat., de la Légion d'honneur. *Address:* Office of the President, Palais de l'Elysée, 55–57 rue du Faubourg Saint Honoré, 75008 Paris, France (office). *Telephone:* 1-42-92-81-00 (office). *Fax:* 1-47-42-24-65 (office). *Website:* www .elysee.fr (office).

GUEBUZA, Armando Emílio; Mozambican politician and head of state; *President;* b. 20 Jan. 1943, Murrupula, Nampula Prov.; joined Frente de Libertação de Moçambique (Frelimo) 1963; elected to Cen. Cttee 1966–, to Politburo 1977–; guerrilla commdr during war with Portugal, rising to rank of Lt-Gen.; Political Commissar 1970–; Minister of Home Affairs 1974–78, 1983–84, Deputy Minister of Defence 1978–81, Resident Minister 1981–84, Minister in the Office of the Pres. 1984–86, Minister of Transport and Communication 1986–94; Head of Frente de Libertação de Moçambique (Frelimo) Parl. Bench 1994–2002, Frelimo Sec.-Gen. June 2002–; Pres. of Mozambique 2005–; Head of Govt Del. to Rome peace talks 1992; Chair. two Comms for Burundi peace process under Julius Nyerere and Nelson Mandela. *Address:* Office of the President, Avda Julius Nyerere 1780, Maputo (office); Frente de Libertação de Moçambique (Frelimo), Rua Pereira do Lago 229, Maputo, Mozambique (office). *Telephone:* (1) 491121 (office). *Fax:* (1) 492065 (office). *E-mail:* gabimprensa@teldata.mz (office); sg@frelimo.org.mz (office). *Website:* www.presidencia.gov.mz (office); www.frelimo.org.mz (office).

GUÉDIGUIAN, Robert; French filmmaker; b. 3 Dec. 1953, L'Estaque, Marseille; m. Ariane Ascaride; producer associated with AGAT Films & Cie. *Films:* Fernand (writer) 1979, Le souffleur (writer, producer) 1985; writer, dir, producer: Dernier été (Prix Georges Sadoul) 1980, Rouge midi 1983, Ki lo sa? 1985, Dieu vomit les tièdes (TV) 1989, Marie-Jo et ses 2 amours 2002, Mon père est ingénieur 2004, Le Voyage en Arménie 2006; writer, dir: L'argent fait le bonheur (Prix Michel Kuhn, Rencontres européennes de Reims) 1992; producer: Un tour de manège, Montalvo et l'enfant, Variétés 1989, Le cri du cochon 1990, Suzanne Linke, Bali, les couleurs du divin 1992, Marseille, la vieille ville indigne 1993, Baudelaire modernité 1986, Vittel Design 1987 (Grand Prix, Vidéo Festival de Biarritz), Le coupeur d'eau 1989, En direct de l'être humain 1991, C'est trop con (Prix du Jury, Festival européen d'Angers) 1992, Ça se passe en Equateur, Que la vie est belle 1993, A la vie à la mort, Marius et Jeannette, La ville est tranquille 2001, Dernier des fous 2006, Sous les toits de Paris 2007, Romances de terre et d'eau 2002, Les Fautes d'orthographe 2004; producer, dir: Le Promeneur du champ de Mars 2005. *Address:* c/o AGAT Films & Cie., 52 rue Jean-Pierre Timbaud, 75011 Paris, France (office).

GUÉGUINOU, Jean, GCVO; French diplomatist; *Ambassador, United Nations Educational, Scientific and Cultural Organization (UNESCO);* b. 17 Oct. 1941; s. of Louis-Bernard Guéguinon and Jeanne-Rose Le Fur; ed Ecole Nat. d'Admin; with Press and Information Dept, Ministry of Foreign Affairs 1967–69; Second Sec., London 1969–71; Head of Mission, Ministry of State/Ministry of Defence 1971–73; Head of Cabinet and Counsellor 1973–76; Dir of Cabinet of Sec. of State reporting to Prime Minister 1976–77; Asst Dir for Southern Africa and Indian Ocean 1977–82; Consul-Gen., Jerusalem 1982–86; Dir Press and Information Service 1986–90; Amb. to Czechoslovakia 1990–92, to Czech Repub. 1993, to UK 1993–98, to the Holy See 1998–2000, Ambassadeur de France 2000, Amb. to UNESCO 2003–; Chair., Cttee de patronage, Franco-Scottish Asscn 2001–; mem. Admin Council, Agence France-Presse 1986–90, Soc. of Friends of the Louvre 2000–, Arts florissants 2001–; Chevalier, Légion d'honneur, Ordre Nat. du Mérite; Commdr Order of St Gregory the Great. *Address:* Délégation permanente de la République française auprès de l'UNESCO, Maison de l'UNESCO, Bureau M8.14 1, rue Miollis, 75732 Paris Cedex 15 (office); 5 avenue Montespan, 75116 Paris, France (office). *Telephone:* 1-45-68-35-47 (office). *Fax:* 1-53-69-99-49 (office). *E-mail:* dl.france@unesco.org (office). *Website:* erc.unesco.org (office).

GUÉHENNO, Jean-Marie; French diplomatist and fmr UN official; b. 30 Oct. 1949, Boulogne sur Seine; s. of the late Jean Guéhenno; m. 1981; one d.; ed Ecole Normale Supérieure, Inst. d'Etudes Politiques, Ecole Nat. d'Admin, Paris; mem. Court of Auditors 1976–2000, Sr Auditor 1993–2000; Dir Cultural Affairs, French Embassy in Washington, DC 1982–86; Dir Policy Planning Staff, Ministry of Foreign Affairs 1989–93; Amb. to WEU 1993–95; Under-Sec.-Gen. for Peace-keeping Operations, UN, New York 2000–08; Chair. Bd, Inst. for Higher Defence Studies, Paris 1998–2000; Chevalier, Légion d'honneur; Commdr, Order of Merit (Germany). *Publications:* La fin de la démocratie (English trans. The End of the Nation-State) 1993, L'avenir de la liberté – la démocratie dans la mondialisation 1999. *Leisure interests:* sailing, walking, reading, museums. *Address:* c/o Ministry of Foreign and European Affairs, 37 quai d'Orsay, 75351 Paris Cedex 07, France. *Telephone:* 1-43-17-53-53. *Fax:* 1-43-17-52-03. *Website:* www.diplomatie.gouv.fr.

GUEILER TEJADA, Lydia; Bolivian politician and diplomatist; b. 1926, Cochabamba; active role in revolution of 1952; became Pvt. Sec. to Pres. Paz Estenssoro 1952; mem. Chamber of Deputies 1956; left Movimiento Nacional Revolucionario and joined Partido Revolucionario de la Izquierda Nacional (PRIN) 1964; f. PRIN-Gueiler as part of Alianza Democrática de la Revolución Nacional 1979; Pres. Chamber of Deputies July–Nov. 1979; Pres. Congress Aug.–Nov. 1979; Pres. of Bolivia 1979–80 (overthrown in coup); in exile in Paris, France 1980–82; Amb. to Colombia 1983–86, to Venezuela 1992–2001. *Publications:* La Mujer y la Revolución 1956, Mi Pasión de Lidereza 2000. *Address:* Casilla de Correo 12345, San Miguel, La Paz, Bolivia. *Telephone:* (2) 2784806 (home). *Fax:* (2) 777777 (home).

GUELAR, Diego Ramiro; Argentine diplomatist and lawyer; b. 24 Feb. 1950; m. Magdalena D. Custodio; three c.; Prof. Sociology of Law, Univ. of Buenos Aires 1971; outlawed by military for political activities (nat. leader, Peronist Youth) 1972–73; attorney, Justicialist Party of Buenos Aires Province 1973–76; Prof. Faculties of Architecture and Law, Univ. of Buenos Aires 1973–76; outlawed for political activities 1976–78; nat. adviser of coordinator for Justicialist activities 1978–83; Vice-Pres. Comm. for Budget and Finance, Nat. Chamber of Deputies 1984; Sec.-Gen. bloc of Nat. Justicialist Deputies 1985; Ed. and Dir La Razón (newspaper) 1987; Head, Foundation for Growth Arrangement (FUNCRE); Amb. to EC (now EU) 1989–96, to USA 2002–03. *Publications include:* Chronicles of Transition (collection), political and econ. works etc. *Address:* c/o Ministry of Foreign Affairs, International Trade and Worship, Esmeralda 1212, Buenos Aires 1007, Argentina.

GUÉNA, Yves René Henri; French politician; *President, Arab World Institute;* b. 6 July 1922, Brest; m. Oriane de la Bourdonnaye 1945; five s. two d.; ed Ecole Nat. d'Administration; mem. Free French Forces 1940–45; Official in Morocco 1947, Maître des Requêtes, Conseil d'Etat 1957, Dir de Cabinet to M. Debré (Minister of Justice) 1958–59, Deputy Dir de Cabinet to M. Debré (Prime Minister) Jan.–July 1959; High Commr Ivory Coast 1959–60, Envoy Extraordinary (Dean of Diplomatic Corps) 1960–61; elected Deputy for Dordogne, Nat. Ass. 1962, 1967, 1968, 1973, 1974, 1978, lost seat 1981, re-elected 1986, lost seat 1988; elected Senator for Dordogne 1989; Vice-Pres. of Senate 1992–95, 1995–97; mem. Constitutional Council 1997–, Pres. 1999–2004; Minister of Posts and Telecommunications 1967–68, 1968–69, of Information May–July 1968, of Transport 1973–74, of Industrial and Scientific Devt, March–May 1974; Deputy Sec.-Gen. UDR 1974, Sec.-Gen. 1976; Political Adviser and Nat. Treasurer, RPR 1977–79; Mayor of Périgueux (Dordogne) 1971, re-elected 1977, 1983, 1989, 1995–97 (resgnd); Pres. Arab World Inst. 2004–; Conseiller d'Etat 1972; Croix de guerre 1944, Médaille de la Résistance 1946, Grand Croix Légion d'honneur 2005. *Publications:* Historique de la communauté 1962, Maintenir l'état 1970, L'enjeu (in collaboration) 1975, Le temps des certitudes 1940–69 1982, Catilina ou la gloire dérobée 1984, Les cent premiers jours (co-author) 1985, Ecrits et discours (25 années de vie publique) 1987, Moi duc de Lauzun, citoyen Biron 1997, Ecrits et discours (II) 1999, Le Baron Louis 1999, Phèdre 2000 (play) 2000, Les Wendel-Trois siècles d'Histoire 2004, L'Histoire de France racontée à mes petits enfants, Vol. 1 2004, Vol. 2, 2005. *Address:* Institut du Monde Arabe, 1 rue des fossés St-Bernard, Place Mohammed V, 75236 Paris Cedex 05 (office); 13 rue René Bazin, 75016 Paris, France (home). *Telephone:* 1-40-51-38-73 (office). *Fax:* 1-46-34-02-08 (office). *E-mail:* yguena@imarabe.org (office).

GUENÉE, Bernard Marie Albert, DèsSc; French academic; *Professor Emeritus, University of the Sorbonne;* b. 6 Feb. 1927, Rennes; s. of Ernest Guenée and Antoinette Guenée (née Caisso); m. Simonne Lucas 1955; ed Ecole Normale Supérieure, Paris, Fondation Thiers; Prof., Univ. de Strasbourg 1958–65, Sorbonne 1965–95 (Prof. Emer. 1995–); Dir of Studies Ecole Pratique des Hautes Etudes 1980–; mem. of Institut de France (Acad. des Inscriptions et Belles-Lettres) 1981; Officier, Légion d'honneur, Commdr, Ordre nat. du Mérite, des Palmes académiques; Grand Prix nat. d'Histoire 1995. *Publications:* Tribunaux et gens de justice dans le bailliage de Senlis à la fin du Moyen Age (vers 1380–vers 1550) 1963, Les entrées royales françaises de 1328 à 1515, 1968, L'occident aux XIVe et XVe siècles: Les etats 1971, Histoire et culture historique dans l'Occident médiéval 1980, Politique et histoire au Moyen Age: recueil d'articles sur l'histoire politique et l'historiographie médiévales (1956–81) 1981, Entre l'Eglise et l'Etat: quatre vies de prélats français à la fin du Moyen Age 1987, Un meurtre, une société: l'assassinat du duc d'Orléans, 23 novembre 1407 1992, Un roi et son historien. Vingt études sur le règne de Charles VI et la "Chronique du Religieux de Saint-Denis" 1999, L'opinion publique à la fin du Moyen Age 2002, La folie de Charles VI Roi Bienaimé 2004, Du Guesclin et Froissart: La fabrication de la renommée 2008. *Address:* 8 rue Huysmans, 75006 Paris, France. *Telephone:* 1-45-48-44-40.

GUENIN, Marcel André, PhD; Swiss scientist, academic and company director; *Honorary Professor, University of Geneva;* b. 17 July 1937, Geneva; s. of Léandré André and Isabelle Guenin-Bontempo; m. Ingrid Marina Selbach 1962; three s.; ed Eidgenössische Technische Hochschule Zürich, Univ. of Geneva and Harvard Univ., USA; Asst and Master Asst, Univ. of Geneva 1960–64; Research Assoc., Princeton Univ. 1964–66; Lecturer, Grad. Programme, Univs. of Lausanne, Neuchâtel and Geneva 1966–68; Asst Prof., Univ. of Geneva 1968–70, Professeur extraordinaire 1970–73, Professeur ordinaire 1973–2000, Hon. Prof. 2000–, Dir Dept of Theoretical Physics 1974–77, Dir Group of Applied Physics (GAP) 1993–2000, Vice-Rector Univ. of Geneva 1980–83, Rector 1983–87; Pres. PBG Pvt. Bank, Geneva 1987–89; Chair. Bd COGITAS 1988–94, E. & L. Schmidheiny Foundation 1992–2007; mem. Bd BBC Brown Boveri Ltd 1987–96, Brunet 1990–93, Lasarray 1990–93, Soc. d'Instruments de physique (SIP) 1998–2000; Sec.-Gen. European Physical Soc. 1974–79, Fellow 1980; Sec. Swiss Physical Soc. 1975–79; mem. Bd Soc. Financière de Genève 1988–89; Founding mem. Int. Asscn of Math. Physicists; mem. American Physical Soc. *Publications:* three books and about 40 scientific publs. *Leisure interests:* skiing, sailing, music. *Address:* Applied Physics Group, University of Geneva, 20 Ecole de Medicine, 1211 Geneva 4 (office); 2B chemin des Manons, 1218 Grand-Saconnex (GE), Switzerland (home).

GUÉRARD, Michel Etienne; French chef, restaurateur and hotelier; b. 27 March 1933, Vetheuil; s. of Maurice Guérard and Georgine Guérard; m. Christine Barthelemy 1974; two d.; ed Lycée Corneille, Rouen; apprentice patissier, Mantes la Jolie; head patissier, Hotel Crillon, Paris; chef to brothers Clérico, Lido, Paris; created restaurant le Pot au Feu, Asnières (two Michelin stars); undertook complex renovation of hotel and thermal treatment centre Les Prés d'Eugénie (now 3 Michelin stars), Eugénie les Bains; consultant to Nestlé; opened first Comptoir Gourmand Michel Guérard; restored Chai de Bachen and produced a white Tursan, Baron de Bachen; Chevalier, Légion d'honneur 1990, Officier, Ordre nat. du Mérite, Chevalier, Ordre nat. du Mérite agricole, Officier des Arts et des Lettres, Officier, Palmes Académiques; Meilleur Ouvrier de France (MOF Patisserie) 1958. *Publications:* La Grande Cuisine Minceur 1976, La Cuisine Gourmande 1978, Mes Recettes à la TV 1982, Minceur Exquise 1989, Le Sud-Ouest Gourmand de Relais en Châteaux 1993, La Cuisine Gourmande des Juniors 1997, Le Jeu de l'Oie et du Canard 1998, La Cuisine à Vivre 2000. *Leisure interests:* antiques, painting, sketch-books, food and wine. *Address:* Les Prés d'Eugénie, 40320 Eugénie les Bains, Geaune, France. *Telephone:* (5) 58-05-06-07. *Fax:* (5) 58-51-10-10. *E-mail:* direction@michelguerard.com. *Website:* www.michelguerard.com.

GUERIN, Orla, MA; Irish journalist; *Africa Correspondent, BBC Television;* b. May 1966; ed Coll. of Commerce, Dublin, Univ. Coll. Dublin; newscaster, presenter and Foreign Corresp. with Irish State TV, RTE, Dublin 1990–94; joined BBC TV as news corresp. 1995, Southern Europe Corresp. covering the Balkans and conflict in the Basque country, among other stories 1996–2000, Middle East Corresp. 2001–05, Africa Corresp. 2006–; Hon. DUniv (Essex) 2002; The Jacobs Award for Broadcasters (Ireland) 1992, London Press Club Broadcaster of the Year Award 2002, News and Factual Award, Women in Film and Television (UK) 2003. *Address:* BBC Television Centre, Wood Lane, London, W12 7RJ, England (office). *Website:* www.bbc.co.uk (office).

GUERRA PASTORA, José Adán, PhD; Nicaraguan politician; b. 28 Oct. 1952, Managua; trained as lawyer; Acting Minister of Foreign Affairs 2000; Minister of Nat. Defence 2001–05; Pres. of Demining Comm.; mem. Office of Nat. Security; mem. Exec., Nat. Comm. for Disaster Prevention, Nat. Council of the War on Drugs; Simón Bolívar Democracy and Human Rights Award, WHINSEC. *Address:* c/o Ministry of National Defence, Casa de la Presidencia, Managua, Nicaragua (office).

GUERRAOUI, Abdellatif; Moroccan organization official and government official; *President, Société Maroc Emirats Arabes Unis de Développement (SOMED);* b. 10 July 1939, Safi; s. of Abdeslam Guerraoui and Oumhani Benazzouz; m. Laila Iaoufir 1968; one s. two d.; ed ENSEEIHT, Toulouse, France; Chief of Staff, Computer Systems, Cherifien Office of Phosphates (OCP) 1964–70, Chief of Personnel Admin. Div. 1970–71, Sec.-Gen. of OCP 1971–90, mem. Bd of Dirs –2000; Admin., Gen. Man. Moroccan-Saudi Investment Co. (ASMA-INVEST) 1991–93; Minister of Energy and Mines 1993–97, of Social Affairs, Health, Youth and Sports, Nat. Mutual Aid 1997–98; Pres. Bd Tharwa Finance 1999–2001; Wall of the S Region Laayoune Boujdour Sakiat El Hamra 2001–02; Gen. Dir Agency for Promotion of Economic and Social Devt Southern Provinces 2002–03; Pres. Société Maroc Emirats Arabes Unis de Développement (SOMED) 2003–; mem. bd of dirs, several pvt cos 1970–; consultant (econ. adviser); Trustee Al Akhawayn Univ., mem. Bd Three Cultures and Three Religions Foundation; Throne Award from King of Morocco 1985, Commdr Nat. Order of Merit Portugal 2003. *Leisure interests:* classical literature, history, management, economy, futurology. *Address:* 45 rue Ksar El Badii, Hay El Hana, Préfecture Ain Chock–Hay Hassani, Casablanca 20200 (home); 71 avenue des F-A-R, Casablanca, Morocco (office). *Telephone:* (2) 2303041 (home). *Fax:* (2) 2318803 (home). *E-mail:* somed@somed.ma (office).

GUERROUJ, Hicham al-; Moroccan professional athlete; b. 14 Sept. 1974, Berkane; set six world records indoors and outdoors 1997–99 (including 1,500m, 3:26.00, Rome, July 1998, one mile, 3:43.12, Rieti, July 1999, 2,000m, 4:44.79, Berlin, Sept. 1999); bronze medal, World Jr Championships 5,000m 1992; World Champion 1,500m 1997, 1999, 2001, 2003; Indoor World Champion 1500m 2001; silver medallist, 2000 Olympics, gold medalist 1,500m 2004 Olympics; winner IAAF Grand Prix Final 1,500m 2001, 2002; silver medallist World Championships 5,000m 2003; holder of outdoor world record for 1,500m, 2,000m and one mile, of indoor record for 1,500m and one mile; winner of 72 races from 75 starts 1996–2002; IAAF Male Athlete of the Year 2001, 2002, US Track and Field Male Athlete of the Year 2002.

GUESNERIE, Roger Sylvain Maxime Auguste, DèsSc (Econs); French economist; *Professor of Economics, Collège de France;* b. 17 Feb. 1943, Ste Gemmes Le Rt.; s. of Sylvain Guesnerie and Marie Chapelière; ed Lycée de Rennes, Ecole Polytechnique and Ecole Nat. des Ponts et Chaussées, Univ. of Toulouse; Research Assoc., Centre d'Études Prospectives et de Recherches en Economie Mathématique Appliquée à la Planification (CEPREMAP) 1967–81; Research Assoc., CNRS 1976, Research Dir 1978; Dir of Studies, Ecole des Hautes Etudes en Sciences Sociales (EHESS) 1979–; Dir Centre d'Études Quantitatives Comparatives (CEQC) 1981–82, Centre d'Études et de Recherches en Analyse Socio-économiques (CERAS) 1982–84, Asscn pour le Développement de la Recherche en Economie et Statistique (ADRES) 1989–94, Dir Delta (mixed research unit of CNRS-EHESS-ENS) 1988–2000, Fédération Paris Jourdan 2001–; Lecturer, l'École Nationale des Ponts et Chaussées 1970–83, Paris X Nanterre 1972–3, École Polytechnique 1974–86, l'Institut d'Études Politiques de Paris 1975–78, Paris IX-Dauphine 1974–76; Prof., École Nationale de la Statistique et de l'Administration Economique 1978–84, Prof., LSE 1990–94, Prof. of Econs, Coll. de France 2000–; Vice-Pres. European Econ. Asscn 1992, Pres. 1994; Pres. Scientific Cttee CEPREMAP 1992–95, Select Cttee on Econ. and Social Sciences, Brussels 1992–95, Asoc. of Applied Econometrics 1997–2001, Asoc. Française de Science Economique 2002–03; mem. Scientific Council EHESS 1985–91, Nat. Cttee CNRS 1987–91, European Ass. of Science and Tech. 1994–97, Research Council of L'École Polytechnique 2000–02, Nat. Cttee on Social and Scientific Coordination 2001–02, Scientific Cttee Ecole Normale Supérieure 2001–05;; Foreign Fellow, Churchill Coll., Univ. of Cambridge 1978; Fellow, Econometric Soc., Pres. 1996; Foreign mem. American Acad. of Arts and Sciences 2000–; Hon. Foreign mem. American Econ. Asscn 1997; Chevalier, Ordre du Mérite, Legion d'Honneur; Dr hc (Ecole des Hautes Etudes Commerciales) 2001; Silver Medal, CNRS 1994. *Publications:* La documentation Française, 2 vols (co-author), Modèles de l'economie publique 1980, A Contribution to the Pure Theory of Taxation 1995, L'Economie de marché 1996, Assessing Rational Expectations 1 2001, Assessing Rational Expectations 2 2005, L'économie de marché 2006; about 100 articles in econ. journals. *Leisure interests:* cycling, jogging, walking. *Address:* DELTA, 48 boulevard Jourdan, ENS, 75014 Paris, France (office). *Telephone:* 1-43-13-63-15 (office). *Fax:* 1-43-13-63-10 (office). *E-mail:* guesnerie@delta.ens.fr (office); guesnerie@pse.ens.fr (office). *Website:* www.delta.ens.fr (office); www.pse.ens.fr/guesnerie.

GUEST, Christopher; American actor, film director and screenwriter; b. (Christopher Haden-Guest), 5 Feb. 1948, New York City; s. of Peter Haden-Guest, Baron of Saling in the Co. of Essex; m. Jamie Lee Curtis 1984; two c.; ed High School of Arts and Music, New York City, Bard Coll.; theatre debut in Room Service, Broadway 1970; writer and performer, Nat. Lampoon radio series 1970s; appeared as Tufnel on Lenny and the Squigtones (album) 1980; wrote script and music for film This is Spinal Tap (with Rob Reiner, Michael McKean and Harry Shearer) 1984, later toured as band Spinal Tap; writer and dir Morton & Hayes TV series 1991. *Films include:* The Hot Rock 1972, Lemmings 1973, Death Wish 1974, The Fortune 1975, Girlfriends 1978, The Last Word 1980, The Long Riders 1980, Hearbeeps 1981, Million Dollar Infield 1982, Blind Ambition 1982, This is Spinal Tap 1984, Little Shop of Horrors 1986, The Princess Bride 1987, Beyond Therapy 1987, Sticky Fingers 1988, The Big Picture 1989 (writer and dir), The Return of Spinal Tap 1992, Spinal Tap: Break Like the Wind 1992 (writer and dir), A Few Good Men 1992, Attack of the 50 Foot Woman 1993 (writer and dir), Waiting for Guffman (also writer and dir) 1996, Spinal Tap: The Final Tour 1998, Small Soldiers 1998, Almost Heroes (writer and dir) 1998, Catching Up with Marty DiBeri 2000, Best in Show (also writer and dir) 2000, A Mighty Wind (also writer and dir) 2003, Mrs Henderson Presents 2005, For Your Consideration (also writer and dir) 2006. *Address:* c/o Sharon Sheinwold, United Talent Agency Inc., 9560 Wilshire Boulevard, Suite 500, Beverly Hills, CA 90212, USA (office). *Telephone:* (310) 273-6700 (office). *Fax:* (310) 247-1111 (office).

GUEST, John Rodney, DPhil, FRS; British microbiologist and academic; *Professor Emeritus of Microbiology, University of Sheffield;* b. 27 Dec. 1935, Leeds; s. of Sidney R. Guest and Kathleen Guest (née Walker); m. Barbara Dearsley 1962; one s. two d.; ed Campbell Coll., Belfast, Univ. of Leeds and Trinity Coll., Oxford; Guinness Research Fellow, Univ. of Oxford 1960–65; Research Assoc. and Fulbright Scholar, Stanford Univ., USA 1963, 1964; Lecturer in Microbiology, Univ. of Sheffield 1965–68, Sr Lecturer and Reader 1968–81, Prof. of Microbiology 1981–2000, Prof. Emer. 2000–; Science and Eng Research Council Sr Fellowship 1981–86; Royal Soc. Leeuwenhoek Lecturer 1995; cloned and sequenced genes of the Citric Acid Cycle and characterised an Oxygen-responding Gene Regulator in Bacteria; Hon. mem. Soc. for Gen. Microbiology 2000. *Publications:* research papers in scientific journals. *Leisure interests:* hill walking, beekeeping, family history. *Address:* Department of Molecular Biology and Biotechnology, University of Sheffield, Western Bank, Sheffield, S10 2TN, England (office). *Telephone:* (114) 222-4406 (office).

GUEVARA OBREGÓN, Alberto José, MSc; Nicaraguan politician and economist; *Minister of Finance and Public Credit;* b. 1963; m.; three c.; ed Carlos Fonseca Amador Univ., Catholic Univ. of Chile and Nat. Univ. of Nicaragua; various positions at Cen. Bank of Nicaragua 1999–2006; Minister of Finance and Public Credit 2007–. *Address:* Ministry of Finance and Public Credit, Frente a la Asamblea Nacional, Apartado 2170, Managua, Nicaragua (office). *Telephone:* (2) 22-6530 (office). *Fax:* (2) 222-6430 (office). *E-mail:* webmaster@mhcp.gob.ni (office). *Website:* www.hacienda.gob.ni (office).

GUHA, Subhendu, PhD; American (b. Indian) scientist and academic; *Senior Vice-President and Chairman, United Solar Ovonic;* b. Calcutta, India; ed Presidency Coll., Univ. of Calcutta, Univ. of Sheffield, UK; worked on semiconductors at Tata Inst. of Fundamental Research –1982; Sr Vice-Pres., Photovoltaic Tech., Energy Conversion Devices, USA 1982–, Pres. United Solar Ovonic (wholly-owned subsidiary) 2000–03, Pres. and COO 2003–07, Sr Vice-Pres. and Chair. 2007–, Co-founder United Solar Systems (jt venture co. with Canon Inc. of Japan) 1990; mem. Advisory Bd Nat. Center for Photovoltaics; Grand Award (Best of What's New), Popular Science 1996, Discover Magazine's Tech. Innovation Award 1997, R&D Magazine's R&D 100 Award 1998, Bright Light Award, US Dept of Energy, World Tech. Award in Energy, The World Tech. Network 2005. *Achievements include:* noted for pioneering work with amorphous silicon; leading inventor of flexible solar shingles for converting sunlight to electricity. *Publications:* more than 200 publs and 30 US patents on the science and tech. of amorphous silicon alloy solar cells. *Address:* United Solar Ovonic, 3800 Lapeer Road, Auburn Hills, MI 48326, USA (office). *Telephone:* (248) 475-0100 (office). *Fax:* (248) 364-0510 (office). *E-mail:* info@uni-solar.com (office). *Website:* www.uni-solar.com (office).

GUI, Luigi; Italian politician; b. 26 Sept. 1914, Padua; s. of Corinto Gui and Angelina Pinzan; m. Alessandra Volpi 1947; three s.; war service, Italy and Russia 1941–43; Christian Democrat underground movement 1943–45; elected to Constituent Ass. 1946, re-elected 1948, 1953, 1958, 1963, 1968, 1972, 1976, 1979; fmr Sec. of the Parl. Comm. on Agric. and Under-Sec. Ministry of Agric. and Forestry; Minister of Labour 1957–58, of Educ. 1962–68, of Defence 1968–70, of Health 1973–74, of Civil Service Reform March–Nov. 1974, of Interior 1974–76; Pres. Christian Democrat Deputies Parl. Group 1958–62; Senate 1976–79, Chamber of Deputies 1979–83, Pres. 1st Comm. on Constitutional Affairs; mem. European People's Party, Paduan Acad. of Sciences, Letters and Arts, Council of European Soc. of Culture; Pres. Nat. Petrarch Soc., Casa di Dante, Rome; Hon. Pres. Associazione Nazionale Combattenti Reduci; Cavaliere di Gran Croce dell'Ordine al Merito. *Publications:* works on history of philosophy, political history, education and travel. *Address:* Via S. Rosa 38, 35141 Padua, Italy (home). *Telephone:* (49) 656607 (home).

GUI, Shiyong; Chinese politician; b. Feb. 1935, Huzhou City, Zhejiang Prov.; ed Chinese People's Univ.; joined CCP 1956; Dir Econs Inst. of Chinese Acad. of Sciences; Deputy Ed.-in-Chief Renmin Ribao (People's Daily); Alt. mem. 13th CCP Cen. Cttee 1987–92, 14th CCP Cen. Cttee 1992–97; mem. State Planning Comm. and Vice-Dir Research Office of the State Council 1988; Vice-Chair. State Planning Comm. and Dir Econs Research Centre 1989; Vice-Pres. Nat. School of Admin. 1994–2000; mem. 15th CCP Cen. Cttee 1997–2002; mem. 9th NPC Standing Cttee 1998–2003; Chair. CPPCC Sub-Cttee of Cultural and Historical Data 2003–. *Address:* Chinese People's Political Consultative Conference, Beijing, People's Republic of China.

GUIG, Mohamed Lemine Ould, DIur; Mauritanian politician; b. 1 July 1959, Oualata; fmr Dir of Higher Educ.; Prof., Nouakchott Univ. 1987–97, Dean, Faculty of Law and Econs 1990–92; Lecturer and Dir of Studies, Int. Inst. of Human Rights, Strasbourg 1989; chargé de mission to Sec. of State in charge of Civil Affairs 1993–95; Dir of Higher Educ., Ministry of Nat. Educ. 1995–97; Prime Minister of Mauritania 1997–98; Pres. Cour des Comptes 1998–2001; Minister Sec.-Gen. of the Presidency 2001–03; Commr for Food Security 2003–04; mem. Nat. Ass., Chair. Human Resources Cttee; founder mem. Association internationale des enseignants et chercheurs des droits de l'homme, Strasbourg; mem. Institut de Droit d'expression française, Paris. *Address:* c/o Office of the Prime Minister, Nouackchott, Mauritania. *Telephone:* 524-10-14 (office). *Fax:* 529-34-73 (office). *E-mail:* mguig@presidence.mr (office).

GUIGNABODET, Liliane (Lily), LèsL; French writer; b. (Lily Lea Graciani), 26 March 1939, Paris; d. of Moïse Graciani and Olympia N. Graciani; m. Jean Guignabodet 1961; one s. two d.; ed primary school in Sofia, Bulgaria, Lycée Jules Ferry, Paris, Sorbonne and Univ. of London; Prof. of French, San José, USA 1961–62; Prof. of Arts and Culture, Ecole Technique d'IBM France 1966–69; author 1977–; mem. PEN Club Français, Soc. des Gens de Lettres, Acad. Européenne des Sciences, des Arts et des Lettres, Acad. Valentin; fmr mem., Jury du Prix de Journalisme de l'Asscn Franco-Bulgare; Prix George Sand 1977, Grand Prix du Roman, Acad. Française 1983, Grand prix du Roman, Ville de Cannes 1991. *Publications:* L'écume du silence 1977, Le bracelet indien 1980, Natalia 1983, Le livre du vent 1984, Dessislava 1986, Car les hommes sont meilleurs que leur vie 1991, Un sentiment inconnu 1998, Orchid Woman. *Leisure interests:* travel, piano, decorating, swimming. *Address:* 55 rue Caulaincourt, 75018 Paris (home); 16 chemin du Clos d'Agasse, 06650 Le Rouret, France (home). *Telephone:* 1-46-06-09-86 (home). *Fax:* 1-46-06-09-86 (home). *E-mail:* lguignabodet@club-internet.fr (home).

GUIGOU, Elisabeth Alexandrine Marie, LèsL; French politician; b. 6 Aug. 1946, Marrakesh, Morocco; d. of Georges Vallier and Jeanne Flecchia; m. Jean-Louis Guigou 1966; one s.; ed Lycée Victor Hugo, Marrakesh, Lycée Descartes, Rabat, Facultés des Lettres, Rabat and Montpellier, Faculté des Sciences Economiques, Montpellier and Ecole Nat. d'Admin; civil servant, Ministry of Finance 1974, Office of the Treasury 1974–75, Office of Banks 1976–78, Office of Financial Markets 1978–79; Deputy Chair. Finance Cttee VIIth Plan 1975–78; Maître de Conférences, Inst. d'Etudes Politiques, Paris 1976; Financial Attaché, Embassy, London 1979–81; Head, Office for Europe, America and Asia, Treasury 1981; Tech. Counsellor, Office of Minister of Economy and Finance 1982; Tech. Counsellor 1982–88; Office of Pres. of Repub. 1988–90; Sec.-Gen. Interministerial Cttee on European Econ. Cooperation 1985–90; Minister Delegate for European Affairs 1990–93; mem. Regional Council of Provence Alpes Côte-d'Azur 1992–2002, European Parl. 1994–97; elected Deputy to Nat. Ass. for Vaucluse (Socialist Party) 1997; Minister of Justice 1997–2000, of Employment and Solidarity 2000–02. *Publications:* Pour les Européens 1994, Etre femme en politique 1997.

Address: c/o Conseil Régional de Provence Alpes Côte d'Azur, 27 place Jules Guesde, 13481 Marseille Cedex, France.

GUILFOYLE, The Hon. Dame Margaret Georgina Constance, AC, DBE, LLB; Australian politician and accountant; b. 15 May 1926, Belfast, Northern Ireland; d. of William McCartney and Elizabeth Jane Ellis; m. Stanley Martin Leslie Guilfoyle 1952; one s. two d.; ed ANU; chartered sec. and accountant 1947–; Liberal mem. Senate for Victoria 1971–87; Minister for Educ. Nov.–Dec. 1975, for Social Security 1975–80, for Finance 1980–83; Deputy Chair. Mental Health Research Inst. 1988–2000, Infertility Treatment Authority 1996–2002; Chair. Judicial Remuneration Tribunal 1995–2001, Ministerial Advisory Cttee on Women's Health 1996–99, Australian Political Exchange Council 1996–; Dir Australian Children's TV Foundation 1989–2003; mem. Nat. Inquiry Concerning Human Rights of People with Mental Illness 1990–93; Fellow, Australian Soc. of Accountants; Fellow, Chartered Inst. of Secs and Administrators; mem. Review of the Australian Blood Banking and Plasma Product Sector 1999; Silver Jubilee Medal 1977, Centenary Medal 2003. *Leisure interests:* reading, opera. *Address:* 21 Howard Street, Kew, Victoria 3101, Australia (home).

GUILLAUD, Jean Louis; French television industry executive; *President, TV France International;* b. 5 March 1929, Caen; s. of Marcel Guillaud and Suzanne Le Brun; m. 2nd Catherine Chichet 1978; one d.; one s. one d. from previous relationships; ed Inst. d'Etudes Politiques, Paris; political journalist, Soc. Générale de Presse 1953–58, Paris-Jour 1958–60, France-Soir and Nouveau Candide 1961–63; Ed.-in-Chief, ORTF 1963, Dir of TV News 1968–69; special assignment at Secr.-Gen. of Presidency of Repub. 1970–72; Dir of Regional Stations and Third Channel, ORTF 1972–74; Dir-Gen. TFI 1975–78, Pres., Dir-Gen. 1978–81; later TV Dir Hachette Group; Pres., Dir-Gen. Agence France Presse (AFP) 1987–90; Pres. Polycom SA 1988–90; Pres., Dir-Gen. HDSA 1990–95, Media Campus 1990–95; Pres. TV France Int. 1994–; mem. (Admin. Council) Revue de Défense Nationale 1991–; Dir Int. Acad. of TV Arts & Sciences; Officier, Légion d'honneur, Officier, Ordre nat. du Mérite, Chevalier des Arts et des Lettres. *Address:* Office of the President, TV France International, 5 rue Cernuschi, 75017 Paris (office); 13 rue de la Mairie, 27140 Bazincourt-sur-Epte, France (home). *Telephone:* 1-40-53-23-00 (office). *Fax:* 1-40-53-23-01 (office). *E-mail:* info@tvfrance-intl.com (office). *Website:* www.tvfrance-intl.com (office).

GUILLAUME, Gilbert, LenD; French judge; *Judge ad hoc, International Court of Justice;* b. 4 Dec. 1930, Bois-Colombes; s. of Pierre Guillaume and Berthe Guillaume; m. Marie-Anne Hidden 1961; one s. two d.; ed Univ. of Paris, Paris Inst. of Political Studies and Ecole Nat. Admin.; mem. Council of State 1957; Legal Adviser, State Secr. for Civil Aviation 1968–79; French Rep. Legal Cttee of ICAO 1968–69, Chair. of Cttee 1971–75; Chair. Conciliation Comm. OECD 1973–78; Dir of Legal Affairs, OECD 1979; French Rep. Cen.l Comm. for Navigation of the Rhine 1979–87, Chair. 1981–82; Dir of Legal Affairs, Ministry of Foreign Affairs 1979–87; Conseiller d'Etat 1981–96; Judge, Int. Court of Justice 1987–2005, Pres. 2000–03, Judge ad hoc 2006–; First Vice-Pres. Institut de droit int.; Counsel/agent for France in int. arbitration proceedings, numerous cases before European Courts etc.; mem. Perm. Court of Arbitration 1980–; Arbitrator, OSCE, ICSID etc.; del. to numerous int. legal and diplomatic confs; Prof. Inst. of Political Studies, Univ. of Paris and other lecturing appointments; mem. Bd Hon. Eds Chinese Journal of International Law; mem. various legal asscns, insts etc.; Commdr, Légion d'honneur, des Arts et des Lettres; Chevalier, Ordre nat. du Mérite, du Mérite agricole, du Mérite maritime. *Publications:* numerous books and articles on admin. and int. law, including Terrorisme et droit international 1989, Les grandes crises internationales et le droit 1994, La Cour Internationale de Justice à l'aube du XXIème siècle 2003. *Address:* International Court of Justice, Peace Palace, 2517 KJ, The Hague, Netherlands (office); 36 rue Perronet, 92200 Neuilly-sur-Seine, France (home). *Telephone:* (70) 302-24-50 (office); 1-46-24-25-67 (home). *Fax:* (70) 302-24-09 (office); 1-47-45-67-84 (home). *E-mail:* g.guillaume@icj-cij.org (office); g.ma.guillaume@wanadoo.fr (home).

GUILLAUME JEAN JOSEPH MARIE, HRH Prince; Luxembourg; b. 11 Nov. 1981; s. of HRH Grand Duke Henri and HRH Grand Duchess Maria Teresa of Luxembourg; ed Lycée Robert Schuman, RMA Sandhurst, England, Univ. of Durham, England); proclaimed Hereditary Grand Duke 18 Dec. 2000; apptd army Lt by Grand-Ducal Decree 2002, apptd First Lt 2003; Chair. Bd of Dirs Kräizbierg Foundation 2000–; Hon. Pres. Bd of Econ. Devt 2001–. *Address:* Grand Ducal Palace, 2013 Luxembourg, Luxembourg (office). *Website:* www.gouvernement.lu.

GUILLEM, Sylvie; French ballet dancer; b. 23 Feb. 1965, Le Blanc Mesnil; joined Ecole de Danse, Paris Opera 1976; Ballet de l'Opéra as Quadrille 1981, promoted to Coryphée 1982, to Sujet 1983, Première Danseuse, later Etoile 1984; Prin. Guest Artist, Royal Ballet, London 1988–2007; choreographer Giselle, Nat. Ballet of Finland 1999; Assoc. Artist, Sadler's Wells Theatre 2005–; Hon. CBE 2003; Commandeur des Arts et Lettres 1988, Médaille de Vermeil de la ville de Paris 1993, Chevalier, Légion d'honneur 1994, Gente Dame d'Honneur des Hospitaliers de Pomerol 2000. *Leading roles in:* Romeo and Juliet, Don Quixote, Raymonda, Swan Lake, Giselle, Notre Dame de Paris, Manon, Marguerite and Armand. *Created roles include:* Cendrillon, In the Middle, Somewhat Elevated, Magnificat, Le Martyre de Saint-Sébastien. *Created and produced:* Evidentia (TV) 1995; Prize for Excellence and Gold Medal, Varna Int. Dance Competition 1983, Prix Carpeau 1984, Hans Christian Andersen Award 1988, Arpège Prize (Lanvin perfumes) 1989. *Address:* c/o Royal Ballet, Royal Opera House, London, WC2E 9DD, England. *Website:* www.sylvieguillem.com.

GUILLEMIN, Roger Charles Louis, BA, BSc, MD, PhD; American professor of medicine; *Distinguished Professor, The Salk Institute;* b. 11 Jan. 1924, Dijon, France; s. of Raymond Guillemin and Blanche Guillemin; m. Lucienne Jeanne Billard 1951; one s. five d.; ed Univs of Dijon and Lyons, France, Univ. of Montreal, Canada; Prosector of Anatomy, Univ. of Dijon Medical School 1946–47; Research Asst, Inst. of Experimental Medicine and Surgery, Univ. of Montreal 1949–51, Assoc. Dir and Asst Prof. of Experimental Medicine 1951–53; Asst Prof. of Physiology, Coll. of Medicine, Baylor Univ., Houston, Tex. 1953, Assoc. Prof. 1957, Prof. of Physiology and Dir Labs for Neuroendocrinology 1963–70, Adjunct Prof. of Physiology 1970–; Consultant in Physiology, Veterans' Admin. Hosp., Houston 1954–60, 1967–70; Lecturer in Experimental Endocrinology, Dept of Biology, W. M. Rice Univ., Houston 1958–60; Assoc. Dir, Dept of Experimental Endocrinology, Coll. de France, Paris, as jt appointment with Coll. of Medicine, Baylor Univ. 1960–63; Resident Fellow and Research Prof., The Salk Inst. for Biological Studies, San Diego, Calif. 1970–89, Dean 1972–73, 1976–77, Adjunct Prof. 1989–97, Distinguished Prof. 1997–; Distinguished Scientist, Whittier Inst. for Diabetes and Endocrinology, La Jolla 1989–93, Medical and Scientific Dir 1993–94; Adjunct Prof. of Medicine, Univ. of Calif., San Diego 1995–97; mem. NAS 1974–, American Acad. of Arts and Sciences, American Physiological Soc., Soc. for Experimental Biology and Medicine, Int. Brain Research Org., Int. Soc. for Research in Biology and Reproduction, Swedish Soc. of Medical Sciences, Acad. Nat. de Médecine, France, Acad. des Sciences, France, Acad. Royale de Médecine de Belgique, Belgium; Pres. The Endocrine Soc. 1986; Citoyen d'Honneur 1983, Officier, Légion d'honneur 1984; hon. degrees (Univ. of Rochester, NY) 1976, (Univ. of Chicago, Ill.) 1977, (Baylor Coll. of Medicine, Houston, Tex.) 1978, (Univ. of Ulm) 1978, (Univ. of Dijon) 1978, (Univ. Libre de Bruxelles) 1979, (Univ. de Montreal) 1979, (Univ. of Manitoba) 1984, (Univ. of Turin) 1985, (Kung Hee Univ., Seoul) 1986, (Univ. Paris VII) 1986, (Autónoma, Madrid) 1988, (McGill Univ.) 1988, (Barcelona, Spain) 1988, (Sherbrook Univ., Quebec) 1997, (Univ. Franche-Conté) 1999; Bonneau and La Caze Awards in Physiology, Acad. des Sciences 1957, 1960, Ayerst-Squibb Award American Endocrine Soc. 1970, Gairdner Award (Toronto) 1974, Lasker Foundation Award 1975, co-recipient of Nobel Prize in Physiology or Medicine with Andrew V. Schally (q.v.) for discoveries relating to peptide hormones 1977, Dickinson Prize in Medicine 1976, Passano Award in Medical Sciences 1976, Nat. Medal of Science 1977, Barren Gold Medal 1979, Dale Medallist, UK Soc. for Endocrinology 1980; numerous int. awards and lectureships. *Publications:* ed. or co-ed. three books on neuroendocrinology and pharmacology; History of Medicine: Neural Modulation of Immunity (co-author); author or co-author of over 700 tech. publs and reviews in scientific journals in USA, France, UK, Canada, USSR, Japan. *Leisure interests:* computer art, music, fine wines. *Address:* The Salk Institute, 10010 North Torrey Pines Road, La Jolla, CA 92037, USA (office). *Telephone:* (858) 453-4100 (office). *Fax:* (858) 625-0688 (office). *E-mail:* guillemin@salk.edu (office). *Website:* www.salk.edu (office).

GUILLEN, Fernando; Peruvian diplomatist; b. 24 July 1939, Arequipa; m.; one c.; ed Catholic Univ. of Peru, Universidad Nacional Mayor de San Marcos, Lima, Diplomatic Acad. of Peru; joined diplomatic service 1966, fmrly mem. staff Mission to UN, Geneva, Head Dept of Int. Econ. Policy, Head Div. of Econ. Integration, Ministry for Foreign Affairs; Minister, Embassy, France 1981, Colombia 1982–84; Amb. to India 1986–91; Under-Sec.-Gen. for Multilateral Affairs, Ministry for Foreign Affairs and Co-ordinator for Peru, Rio Group 1991; Sec. Consultative Cttee to Minister for Foreign Affairs 1991–92; Perm. Rep. to UN, New York 1992–2001; mem. Peruvian Soc. of Int. Law. *Address:* c/o Ministry of Foreign Affairs, Palacio de Torre Tagle, Jirón Ucayali 363, Lima 1, Peru.

GUILLERMIN, John; British film director; b. 11 Nov. 1925, London. *Films include:* High Jinks in Society 1949, Torment 1950, Smart Alec 1951, Two on the Tiles 1952, Four Days 1951, Bachelor in Paris 1952, Miss Robin Hood 1952, Operation Diplomat 1953, Adventure in the Hopfields 1954, The Crowded Day 1954, Dust and Gold 1955, Tormenta 1955, Thunderstorm 1956, Town on Trial 1957, The Whole Truth 1958, I Was Monty's Double 1958, Tarzan's Greatest Adventure 1959, The Day They Robbed the Bank of England 1960, Never Let Go 1960, Waltz of the Toreadors 1962, Tarzan Goes to India 1962, Guns at Batasi 1964, Rapture 1965, The Blue Max 1966, P.J. 1968, House of Cards 1968, The Bridge at Remagen 1969, El Condor 1970, Skyjacked 1972, Shaft in Africa 1973, The Towering Inferno 1974, King Kong 1976, Death on the Nile 1978, Mr Patman 1980, Sheena 1984, King Kong Lives 1986. *Television includes:* The Adventures of Aggie (series) 1956, The Tracker 1988.

GUILLERY, Rainer W., PhD, FRS; British anatomist, neurobiologist and academic; *Professor Emeritus, Department of Anatomy, University of Wisconsin;* b. 28 Aug. 1929, Greifswald, Germany; s. of Eva Hackel and Hermann Guillery; m. Margot Cunningham Pepper 1954 (divorced 2000); three s. one d.; ed Univ. Coll. London; Asst Lecturer, Anatomy Dept, Univ. Coll. London 1953–56, Lecturer 1956–63, Reader 1963–64; Assoc. Prof., Dept of Anatomy, Univ. of Wisconsin, Madison, USA 1964–68, Prof. 1968–77, Visiting Prof. 1996–2002, Prof. Emer. 2002–; Prof., Dept of Pharmacological and Physiological Sciences and Chair. Cttee on Neurobiology, Univ. of Chicago, USA 1977–84; Dr Lee's Prof. of Anatomy, Univ. of Oxford, UK 1984–96; Pres. Anatomical Soc. of GB and Ireland 1994–96; Ed.-in-Chief European Journal of Neuroscience 1988–92; Fellow, Hertford Coll. Oxford 1984–96 (Fellow Emer. 1996–), Univ. Coll. London 1987; Hon. Prof. of Anatomy, Chinese Univ., Hong Kong. *Publications:* Exploring the Thalamus (with M. S. Sherman) 2001–; contribs to Journal of Comparative Neurology, Journal of Neuroscience, Neuroscience, Brain Research, etc. *Leisure interests:* working with wood, growing fruit and vegetables, needle point embroidery. *Address:* Department of Anatomy, Medical Faculty, Marmara University,

Tibiye Cad, 49, Haydarpasa, Istanbul 34668, Turkey (office). *Telephone:* (216) 414-4734 (office). *Fax:* (216) 414-4734 (office). *E-mail:* rguiller@wisc.edu (office).

GUIMARÃES, Eduardo Augusto, PhD; Brazilian economist, academic and banking executive; ed Pontifícia Universidade Católica do Rio de Janeiro (PUC-RIO); fmr Man.-Dir Banespa; Pres. and CEO Banco do Brasil SA 2001–03; Prof. of Econs, Universidade Fed. do Rio de Janeiro (UFRJ); mem. Advisory Bd Chamber of Arbitration ANDIMA. *Publications:* author of numerous articles on econs in scholarly and professional journals. *Address:* c/o Banco do Brasil SA, SBS Qd. 01 Bloco C - Edifício Sede III, 24th Floor, 70073-901 Brasília, DF, Brazil (office).

GUINDON, Yvan, PhD, CM, FRSC; Canadian scientist and academic; *President, Royal Society of Canada;* ed Université de Montréal; joined Merck Frosst Canada as Sr Research Chemist 1979, Dir Medicinal Chem. 1984–85, Sr Dir 1985–87; joined Bio-Méga as Scientific Dir 1987, Vice-Pres. Bio-Méga/Boehringer Ingelheim Research Inc. 1987–94; apptd CEO and Scientific Dir Institut de Recherches Cliniques de Montréal 1994; Prof., Dept of Chem., Université de Montréal; Adjunct Prof., Dept of Chem., McGill Univ.; Pres. Royal Soc. of Canada 2007–; Fellow, Chemical Inst. of Canada 1988; Lionel-Boulet Award 2006. *Publications:* more than 100 papers in scientific journals. *Address:* Royal Society of Canada, 170 rue Waller Street, Ottawa, ON K1N 9B9, Canada (office). *Telephone:* (613) 991-6990 (office). *Fax:* (613) 991-6996 (office). *E-mail:* theacademies@rsc.ca (office). *Website:* www.rsc.ca (office).

GUINGONA, Teofisto T., Jr; Philippine politician, lawyer and writer; b. 4 July 1928, San Juan, Rizal; s. of Teofisto Guingona, Sr; m. Ruthie de Lara; two s. one d.; ed Ateneo de Manila Univ.; fmr Gov. Devt Bank of the Philippines and Pres. Chamber of Commerce of the Philippines; served as human rights lawyer 1970s; Founder SANDATA and Hon. Chair. of BANDILA; jailed in 1972 and 1978 for his opposition to marital law; fmr Chair. Comm. on Audit; Senator 1980s, Senate Pres. Pro-tempore and Majority Leader, Chair. Blue Ribbon Cttee, Senator 1998, Minority Leader; fmr Dir Mindanao Devt Authority; fmr Chair. Mindanao Labor Man. Advisory Council; fmr Exec. Sec. to Pres.; fmr Justice Sec.; Vice-Pres. of the Philippines 2001–04; Sec. of Foreign Affairs 2001–02; Pres. Lakas-Christian Muslim Democrats (Lakas—CMD) –2003 (resgnd); adviser to Fernando Poe, Jr. *Address:* c/o Office of the Vice-President, PICC, 2nd Floor, CCP Complex, Roxas Boulevard, Pasay City, Metro Manila, The Philippines (office). *Telephone:* (2) 8312658 (office). *Fax:* (2) 8312614 (office). *E-mail:* gma@easy.net.ph (office). *Website:* www.teofistoguingonajr.ph.

GUINHUT, Jean-Pierre; French diplomatist; *Ambassador to Afghanistan;* b. 1946; joined French Foreign Service 1975, posted to French Embassy, Qatar 1975–76, Iran 1980–82, 1988–93, First Counsellor, Libya 1982–85, Middle East Desk, French Mission to UN, New York 1985–88, Head of Middle East Div., Foreign Service, Paris 1993–96; Amb. to Azerbaijan 1996–2002, to Afghanistan 2002–. *Publication:* The Man Who Loved Too Much: The Legend of Leyli and Majnun 1998. *Address:* Embassy of France, POB 62, Avenue de Cherpou, Shar-i-Nau, Kabul, Afghanistan (office). *Telephone:* (763) 0198678 (office). *Fax:* (682) 084817 (office). *E-mail:* jean-pierre.guinhut@diplomatic.gouv.fr (office). *Website:* www.ambafrancekaboul.org (office).

GUINN, Kenny C., EdD; American fmr state official; b. 24 Aug. 1936, Garland, Ark.; m.; two c.; ed Fresno State Univ., Utah State Univ.; planning specialist Clark Co. School Dist 1964–69, Supt 1969–1978; Administrative Vice-Pres. Nev. Savings and Loan Asscn (later PriMerit Bank) Las Vegas 1978–80, Pres., COO 1980–85, CEO 1985–87, Chair. 1987; Pres. South West Gas Corpn 1987–88, Chair., CEO 1988–93; interim Pres. Univ. of Nev.-Las Vegas 1994; Gov. of Nev. 1999–2007; Republican. *Address:* c/o Office of the Governor, 101 North Carson Street, Carson City, NV 89701, USA (office).

GUJRAL, Inder Kumar, MA; Indian politician; b. 4 Dec. 1919, Jhelum (now in Pakistan); s. of the late Avtar Narain Gujral and Pushpa Gujral; m. Sheila Gujral 1945; two s.; ed Forman Christian Coll. and Hailey Coll. of Commerce in Lahore, Punjab Univ.; jailed for participation in freedom movt 1930–31 (and again during Quit India movt 1942); Pres. Lahore Students' Union; Gen.-Sec. Punjab Students' Fed.; migrated to India 1947; helped nat. effort for rehabilitation of displaced persons; Vice-Pres. New Delhi Municipal Cttee 1959–64; MP 1964–76, 1989–91, 1992–98, mem. Lok Sabha Punjab 1998; Leader Rajya Sabha June–Nov. 1996, 1997–98; mem. Council of Ministers, Govt of India 1967–76 holding portfolios for Communications and Parl. Affairs, Information, Broadcasting and Communications, Works, Housing and Urban Devt, Information and Broadcasting and Planning 1975–76; Minister of External Affairs 1989–90, 1996–97; Prime Minister of India 1997–98; Chair. Parl. Cttee on External Affairs 1998; Amb. to USSR (with ministerial rank) 1976–80; Vice-Pres. New Delhi Municipal Cttee 1959–64; helped organize Citizens Cttee, for Civil Defence; leader several Indian dels to UNESCO 1970–77, to UN Special Session on Econ. Devt 1990, to UN Gen. Ass. 1990, 1996, to UN Session on Human Rights, Geneva 1995 and leader or mem. numerous Indian dels to other int. orgs; mem. UN Panel of Eminent Persons to study and report on situation in Algeria 1998; Pres. Inst. of Defence Studies and Analysis; Chair. Indian Council of S Asian Co-operation; Founder-Pres. Delhi Arts Theatre; Treas. Fed. of Film Socs of India; fmr Chancellor Vishva Bharati Univ., Shanti Niketan 1997–2000; First Chancellor Maulalna Azad Nat. Urdu Univ., Hyderabad 1999–2005; Order of Friendship (Russia) 2004, Order of Yugoslav Star First Degree 2005; Hon. DLitt (St Rose Coll., Albani, NY, USA, Soka Univ., Tokyo, Univ. of Punjab (Chandigarh), Hon. PhD (The Jamia Urdu, Aligarh, Guru Nanak Dev Univ., Amritsar); Maharaja Ranjit Singh Award, Punjabi Univ., Patiala 2003, St Andrew Int. Award – Dialogue of Civilisations (Russia) 2004. *Publications:* A Foreign Policy for India 2001, Continuity & Change: India's Foreign Policy 2002, Viewpoint: Democracy, Civilisation & Foreign Policy 2004. *Leisure interests:* theatre, poetry, painting, ecological problems. *Address:* 5 Janpath, New Delhi 110011, India (home). *Telephone:* 23014300/23794433 (home). *Fax:* 23794444 (home). *E-mail:* gujralik@sansad.nic.in (home).

GÜL, Abdullah, BA, PhD; Turkish politician and head of state; *President;* b. 1950, Qaisari Prov.; m.; three c.; ed Istanbul Univ., Univ. of London, UK; participated in the foundation of the Dept of Engineering, Sakarya Univ., Lecturer in Econs 1980–83, Assoc. Prof. of Econs 1991–; economist with Islamic Development Bank, Jeddah 1983–91; mem. Parl. representing Al-Rafah Party (now outlawed) 1991, later Al-Rafah Deputy Head of Foreign Affairs; held numerous ministerial posts including Minister of State for Foreign Affairs 1996–97, Spokesman for Al-Rafah Govt, also mem. European Council; Founder-mem. and Deputy Chair. AK Partisi (Justice and Devt Party) 2001–; Prime Minister of Turkey Nov. 2002–March 2003; Deputy Prime Minister and Minister of Foreign Affairs 2003–07; President of Turkey 2007–; Affairs mem. NATO Parl. Ass. 2001–; Pro-Merito Medal of the Council of Europe 2001. *Address:* President's Office, Cumhurbaşkanlığı Köşkü, Çankaya, Ankara (office). *Telephone:* (312) 4685030 (office). *Fax:* (312) 4271330 (office). *E-mail:* cumhurbaskanligi@tccb.gov.tr (office). *Website:* www.cankaya.gov.tr (office); www.abdullahgul.gen.tr (home).

GULABZOI, Maj.-Gen. Sayed Muhammad; Afghan fmr army officer and politician; fmr Communist gen.; mem. Khalq faction of CP, People's Democratic Party of Afghanistan, took part in overthrow of King Muhammad Zahir Shah 1973; close aide of Communist leader, Nur Muhammad Taraki; served as Interior Minister and Commdr Sarandoy (Defenders of the Revolution—nat. gendarmerie) for many years during Soviet occupation; spent 17 years in exile in Russia, returned to run in parl. elections 2004; mem. (Khost Province) Wolasi Jirga (House of the People—Lower House of Parl.) 2004–. *Address:* Wolasi Jirga, Kabul, Afghanistan (office).

GULAMOV, Kadir Gafurovich, PhD; Uzbekistan nuclear physicist, academic and fmr government official; b. 17 Feb. 1945, Tashkent; m. two c.; Sr Scientific Researcher, Physical Tech. Inst., Tashkent, later Head of Lab. 1983–88; Prof. of Physics 1980–; Prof., Faculty of Physics, Tashkent State Univ.; Deputy Minister of Defence –2000, Minister of Defence 2001–05; Presidential adviser 2005–; currently Dir Gen. Scientific Asscn Physics, Uzbekistan Acad. of Sciences; Fellow, Islamic Acad. of Sciences 1995–; Corresp. mem. Uzbekistan Acad. of Sciences 1989–; Beruni State Prize (Uzbekistan) 1983, Independence Memorial Medal (Uzbekistan) 1992. *Publications:* over 250 publs in fields of high energy and nuclear physics. *Address:* c/o Uzbekistan Academy of Sciences, 70 Acad. Gulyamov str., 700047 Tashkent, Uzbekistan. *E-mail:* yuldashev@iae.tashkent.su. *Website:* www.uzsci.net/academy.

GULBINOWICZ, HE Cardinal Henryk Roman, DTheol; Polish ecclesiastic; *Archbishop Emeritus of Wrocław;* b. 17 Oct. 1923, Szukiszki (now Sukiškes in Lithuania); s. of Antoni Gulbinowicz and Waleria Gajewska; ed Metropolitan Higher Ecclesiastic Seminary, Vilnius and Białystok, Catholic Univ. of Lublin; ordained priest, Vilnius, Lithuania 1950; Titular Bishop of Acci and Apostolic Admin. Archdiocese of Białystok, Vilnius 1970–76, Archbishop of Wrocław 1976–2004, Archbishop Emer. 2004–; mem. Congregation for the Evangelization of Nations, Congregation for Eastern Churches, Congregation Clergy Affairs; mem. Main Council Polish Episcopate and several episcopate cttees; High Chancellor Pontifical Faculty Theology, Wrocław; cr. Cardinal (Cardinal-Priest of Immacolata Concezione di Maria a Grottarossa) 1985–; Hon. Citizen of Wrocław 1996; Commdr's Cross with Star, Order of Polonia Restituta; Dr hc (Pontifical Faculty of Theology, Wrocław) 1995, (Agricultural Acad., Wrocław) 2000. *Publications:* more than 240 works on moral theology, ethics, ecumenism and history of the Polish Eastern Territories. *Address:* Kuria Metropolitakna, ul. Katedralna 13, 50-328 Wrocław, Poland (office). *Telephone:* (71) 327-11-11 (office). *Fax:* (71) 322-82-69 (office). *Website:* www.archidiecezja.wroc.pl (office).

GULEGHINA, Maria; Belarusian/Armenian/Ukrainian singer (soprano); b. Odessa; ed Odessa Conservatory (studied with Yevgeni Ivanov); professional debut, Minsk Opera Theatre 1986; debut at La Scala, Milan in Un Ballo in Maschera opposite Luciano Pavarotti 1987; debut at the Met as Maddalena in Andrea Chénier opposite Luciano Pavarotti 1991; Vienna State Opera debut in Andrea Chénier 1991; ROH debut in title role in Fedora opposite Placido Domingo 1995; debut in Arena di Verona as Abigaille in Nabucco 1996; Paris Opera debut with title role in Tosca 1997; toured Japan with La Scala 1991, 1999; solo recital tours of Japan 1999, 2000; has performed recitals worldwide at venues including La Scala, Gran Teatre del Liceu, Carnegie Hall, Wigmore Hall, Suntory Hall and in Lille, São Paolo, Osaka, Kyoto, Hong Kong, Rome and Moscow; has performed with leading singers including Luciano Pavarotti, Placido Domingo, Leo Nucci, Renato Bruson, José Cura and Samuel Ramey, and conductors Gianandrea Gavazzeni, Riccardo Muti, James Levine, Zubin Mehta, Fabio Luisi, Claudio Abbado and Daniel Oren; recent highlights include Abigaille, Maddalena and Tosca, Vienna State Opera, title role in Norma, Santander and La Coruña Festival, Elena in I Vespri Siciliani, Washington Opera, Macbeth, Norma, Cavalleria Rusticana, Tosca and Il Tabarro, the Met, Nabucco and Tosca with Valery Gegiev, Stars at White Nights Festival, Mariinsky Theatre, series of Verdi concerts with the Gulbenkian Foundation, Lisbon, concert performances of Il Trovatore, Miami; mem. Hon. Bd, Int. Paralympics Cttee, UNICEF Int. Goodwill Amb.; order Holy Olga, from Patriarch Alexis of Russia; First Prize All-Union Glinka Competition 1984, Zanatello Award, Verona 1997, Maria Zamboni Gold Medal, Gold Medal, Osaka Festival 1999, Bellini Prize 2001, Arte e Operosita nel Mondo prize, Milan. *Music:* albums include: Tabarro, Oberto, Francesca di Rimini, Pique Dame, Passion of Verismo (live concert recording), Passion of Rachmaninov; video-audio includes: Tosca, Manon Lescaut, Macbeth (all at

La Scala, Milan), Andrea Chenier, Nabucco (both at Metropolitan Opera, New York), Andrea Chenier (DVD, Teatro Communale di Bologna), Macbeth (DVD, Liceu in Barcelona), Nabucco with James Levine (DVD, Metropolitan Opera). *Radio:* many live broadcasts from the Met, La Scala, Vienna etc. *Television:* Nabucco (Vienna Met), Andrea Chenier, Tosca, Manon Lescaut, Macbeth (all at La Scala), Verdi Arias, Italian Arias (both for NHK), Macbeth and Il Trittico (the MET), Nabucco (Arena di Verona). *Opera roles include:* title roles in Tosca, Aida, Manon Lescaut, Norma, Fedora, Adriana Lecouvreur, Turandot, as well as Lady Macbeth in Macbeth, Abigaille in Nabucco, Leonora in Il Trovatore, Oberto and La Forza del Destino, Elvira in Ernani, Elisabetta in Don Carlo, Amelia in Simon Boccanegra, Un Ballo in Maschera, Lucrezia in I due Foscari, Desdemona in Otello, Santuzza in Cavalleria Rusticana, Maddalena in Andrea Chénier, Lisa in Pique Dame, Odabella in Attila, etc. *Address:* RMG International Classic Ltd, Omega 4, No 116 6 Roach Road, London E3 2PA, England (office). *E-mail:* ng@mariaguleghina.com (office); info@mariaguleghina.com (office). *Website:* www.ngproductions.eu (office); www.mariaguleghina.com (home).

GULIYEV, Fuad Khalil-ogly; Azerbaijani politician; b. 6 July 1941, Baku; m.; two c.; ed Azerbaijani Inst. of Oil Chem.; worked in Belorussia in oil chemical industry; Chief Engineer, later Gen. Dir Air Conditioners Factory, Baku; First Deputy Prime Minister of Azerbaijan 1994–95; Prime Minister of Azerbaijan 1995–96; mem. Milli Majlis (Nat. Ass.) 1991–; mem. New Azerbaijan Party; Honoured Engineer of Azerbaijan 1991, Science & Technology Prize Azerbaijan 1986. *Address:* House of Parliament, Azizbekova Prospecti 1, 370001 Baku (office); 7 Samed Vurgun Street, Baku, 370000, Azerbaijan (home). *Telephone:* (12) 4981541 (home). *Fax:* (12) 4335609 (home). *E-mail:* fkuliev@azintex.com (home).

GULLICHSEN, Johan Erik, MSc; Finnish professor of pulping technology and engineer; *President and Partner, Arhippainen, Gullichsen & Company;* b. 28 June 1936, Pihlava; s. of Harry Gullichsen and Maire Ahlström; m. Anna Ramsay 1958; one s. two d.; ed Abo Akademi, Helsinki Univ. of Tech.; Research Asst, FPPRI 1962–64; Project Engineer, EKONO 1964–70; Pres. and Partner, Arhippainen, Gullichsen & Co. 1970–; Prof. of Pulping Tech., Helsinki Univ. of Tech. 1989–2000; Chair. Bd A. Ahlstrom Corpn 1987–2007; fmr Chair. Bd A. Ahlstrom Oy, Dir Kymmene Oy; Hon. DTech (Abo Akademi) 1988; Engineer of the Year in Finland 1984, Marcus Wallenberg Prize 1986. *Publications:* tech. and scientific papers on pulping tech., econs and environmental control. *Leisure interest:* yachting. *Address:* Arhippainen, Gullichsen & Co., Palikaistentie 167, 31460 Hirsjärvi, Finland (office). *Telephone:* (8) 2721-5100 (office). *E-mail:* Johan.Gullichsen@agco.fi (office). *Website:* www.agco.fi/homepage.htm.

GULLIT, Ruud; Dutch football coach and fmr professional footballer; b. 1 Sept. 1962, Amsterdam; m. 1st Yvonne de Vries; two d.; m. 2nd Christina Pensa; one s., one d.; m. 3rd Estelle Cruyff 2000; two c.; played for Haarlem, Netherlands 1979–82, Feyenoord 1982–84, PSV Eindhoven 1984–86, AC Milan, Italy 1986–93, 1994–95, Sampdoria 1993–94, Chelsea, UK 1995–98; Player/Man., Chelsea 1996–98; Man. Newcastle United 1998-99; Head Coach Feyenoord 2004–05; won 66 caps and scored 17 goals for Netherlands team, including one in European Championship final victory over Russia 1988; currently presenter for Dutch TV and analyst for Sky Sports, UK; European Footballer of the Year 1987, World Footballer of the Year 1987, 1989. *Address:* c/o Sky Sports, British Sky Broadcasting Group plc, Grant Way, Isleworth, London, TW7 5QD, England.

GULOMOV, Khodir Gafurovich; Uzbekistan nuclear scientist and politician; b. 17 Feb. 1945, Tashkent; fmr Dir Scientific Inst.; fmr Head, Armed Forces Acad.; Deputy Minister of Defence –2000, Minister of Defence 2000–05; Presidential adviser 2005–. *Address:* c/o Ministry of Defence, ul. Academician Abdullayev 100, 100000 Tashkent, Uzbekistan (office).

GULOMOVA, Dilbar Mukhammadkhonovna; Uzbekistan politician; ed Tashkent Textile Inst.; Deputy Prime Minister and Chair. Women's Cttee 1995–2004; currently Chair. Asscn Business Women of Uzbekistan. *Address:* , 41 Afrosiyob str., 100008 Tashkent, Uzbekistan (office). *Telephone:* (71) 44-84-11 (office). *E-mail:* womancomitet@mail.ru (office).

GULYAEV, Yury Vasilievich, DPhys-MathSc; Russian physicist; *Director, Institute of Radioengineering and Electronics, Russian Academy of Sciences;* b. 18 Sept. 1935, Moscow; m.; two c.; ed Moscow Inst. of Physics and Tech.; jr researcher, sr researcher, Head of Lab., Vice-Dir Inst. of Radioelectronics and Electro tech., USSR (now Russian) Acad. of Sciences 1960–87, Dir 1988–; Corresp. mem. USSR (now Russian) Acad. of Sciences 1979, mem. 1984–, mem. Presidium 1992–; Chair. Saratov br., Russian Acad. of Sciences 1981–; mem. Russian Acad. of Natural Sciences; USSR People's Deputy 1989–91; USSR State Prize, Prize of European Hewlett-Packard Physical Soc.; mem. Polish Acad. of Sciences; Vice-Pres. World Fed. of Eng Orgs (WFEO); Pres. Russian A.S. Popov Scientific and Technical Soc. of Radioengineering, Electronics and Telecommunications; Pres. Int. Union of Scientific and Technical Socs and Unions of CIS; Sr Mem. IEEE and Chair. IEEE Russian Section; Ed.-in-Chief Radiotekhnica i Electronica, Radio and Communications Technology, Photonics and Optoelectronics, Nonlinear Applied Dynamics; Hewlett-Packard Europhysics Prize of European Physical Soc. 1979, State Prize of the USSR 1974, 1984, Konstantinov Prize of Russian Acad. of Sciences 1992, State Prize of Russian Fed. 1993, A.S. Popov Gold Medal of Russian Acad. of Sciences 1995. *Publications:* more than a hundred articles, mainly on acoustic electronics, acoustic optics and spin-wave electronics. *Address:* Institute of Radiotechnology and Electronics, Mokhovaya ul. 11-7, 125009 Moscow, Russia (office). *Telephone:* (495) 200-52-58 (office). *Fax:* (495) 203-84-14 (office). *E-mail:* gulyaev@cplire.ru (office). *Website:* www.cplire.ru (office).

GULYÁS, Dénes; Hungarian singer (tenor); b. 31 March 1954; s. of Dénes Gulyás and Mária Szitár; m. Judit Szekeres; two s. one d.; ed Liszt Ferenc Acad. of Music, Budapest; joined State Opera, Budapest 1978; debut as Rinuccio in Gianni Schicchi; debut in USA, Carnegie Hall and Avery Fisher Hall, New York: concert performances; numerous tours in the USA; 1st Prize, Parma 1979, won Luciano Pavarotti singing competition, Philadelphia 1981, Holder of Liszt Prize, titled Merited Artist. *Repertoire includes:* Faust, des Grieux (Manon), Werther, Hoffman, Titus (La Clemenza di Tito), Percy (Anne Boleyn), Ernesto (Don Pasquale), Duke of Mantua (Rigoletto), Fenton (Falstaff), Ferrando (Così fan tutte), Don Ottavio, Tamino, Alfredo (La Traviata), Edgardo (Lucia di Lammermoor), Nemorino, Rodolfo (La Bohème), Tom Rakewell (The Rake's Progress). *Recordings include:* Caldara, Albinoni, Sammartini, Vivaldi: Magnificat, Erkel: Hunyadi László 1994. *Leisure interests:* riding, sailing, viticulture. *Address:* 2094 Budapest, Nagykovácsi Pf. 93, Hungary (office). *Telephone:* (1) 131-2550 (office). *E-mail:* denes .gulyas@parlament.hu (office). *Website:* www.gulyasdenes.hu.

GULYAS, Diane H., BS; American chemical engineer and business executive; *Group Vice-President, Performance Materials, E. I. du Pont de Nemours and Company;* b. Chicago, Ill.; ed Univ. of Notre Dame, Advanced Man. Program at Wharton School, Univ. of Pennsylvania; joined DuPont in 1978, held a variety of sales, marketing, tech. and systems devt positions, primarily in DuPont Polymers 1978–88, European Business Man., Geneva, Switzerland, for Engineering Polymers, and Plant Supt, Mechelen, Belgium 1988–92, Exec. Asst to Chair. of Bd 1993–94, Global Business Dir Nylon Fibers New Business Devt and Global Zytel Eng Polymers 1997–2001, Vice-Pres. and Gen. Man. DuPont Advanced Fiber Businesses, Spruance Plant, Richmond, Va 1997–2003, Group Vice-Pres. Electronic and Communication Technologies Platform 2003–04, Chief Marketing and Sales Officer 2004–06, Group Vice-Pres. Performance Materials 2006–; mem. Bd of Dirs Viasystems; mem. Strategic Planning and Advocacy Cttees Delaware Nature Soc.; mem. Bd of Dirs Ministry of Caring; fmr mem. Bd of Dirs United Way of Richmond; fmr mem. Exec. Cttee Virginia Business Council; ranked 48th by Fortune magazine amongst 50 Most Powerful Women in Business in the US 2006. *Address:* DuPont Performance Materials, 1007 Market Street, Wilmington, DE 19898, USA (office). *Telephone:* (302) 774-1000 (office). *Fax:* (302) 999-4399 (office). *Website:* www2.dupont.com (office).

GULZAR; Indian filmmaker, poet and lyricist; b. (Sampooran Singh), 18 Aug. 1936, Deena, Jhelum Dist (now in Pakistan); came to Delhi following partition; started as poet and was associated with Progressive Writers Asscn; joined Bimal Roy Productions in 1961; first break as lyricist came when he wrote Mora Gora Ang Lai Lae for Bimal Roy's Bandini 1963; began writing for films for dirs Hrishikesh Mukherjee and Asit Sen; turned filmmaker with first film Mere Apne 1971; began partnership with Sanjeev Kumar; Padma Bhushan, Govt of India 2004; five Nat. Awards, 17 Filmfare Awards, including seven for Best Lyricist, Filmfare Lifetime Achievement Award 2002. *Films directed:* Shriman Satyawadi (Asst Dir) 1960, Kabuliwala (Chief Asst Dir) 1961, Bandini (Asst Dir) 1963, Mere Apne 1971, Parichay 1972, Koshish 1972, Achanak 1973, Mausam (Nat. Award for Best Dir, Filmfare The Best Dir Award) 1975, Khushboo 1975, Aandhi (Storm) 1975, Kitaab (also Producer) 1977, Kinara (also Producer) 1977, Meera 1979, Sahira 1980, Namkeen 1982, Angoor 1982, Suniye 1984, Aika 1984, Ek Akar 1985, Ijaazat (Guest) 1987, Ghalib (TV) 1988, Libaas 1988, Lekin... (But...) 1990, Ustad Amjad Ali Khan 1990, Pandit Bhimsen Joshi 1992, Maachis 1996, Hu Tu Tu 1999. *Film roles in:* Jallianwalla Bagh 1979, Grihapravesh (The Housewarming) (as himself) 1979, Wajood (guest appearance as himself) 1998, Chachi 420 (uncredited cameo appearance during end credits) 1998. *Film dialogue or scripts:* Sangharsh 1968, Aashirwad (The Blessing) 1968, Khamoshi 1969, Anand 1970, Guddi (Darling Child) 1971, Mere Apne 1971, Koshish (Nat. Award for Best Screenplay) 1972, Bawarchi 1972, Namak Haraam (The Ungrateful) 1973, Achanak 1973, Mausam 1975, Khushboo 1975, Chupke Chupke 1975, Aandhi (Storm) 1975, Palkon Ki Chhaon Mein 1977, Meera 1979, Grihapravesh (The Housewarming) 1979, Khubsoorat (Beautiful) 1980, Basera 1981, Namkeen 1982, Angoor 1982, Masoom (Innocent) 1983, New Delhi Times 1986, Ek Pal (A Moment) 1986, Ijaazat (Guest) 1987, Mirza Ghalib (TV) 1988, Lekin... (But...) 1990, Rudaal (The Mourner) 1993, Maachis 1996, Chachi 420 1998, Hu Tu Tu 1999, Saathiya 2002. *Film song lyrics:* Swami Vivekananda 1955, Shriman Satyawadi 1960, Kabuliwala 1961, Prem Patra (Love Letter) 1962, Bandini 1963, Purnima 1965, Sannata 1966, Biwi Aur Makan 1966, Do Dooni Char 1968, Aashirwad (The Blessing) 1968, Rahgir 1969, Khamoshi 1969, Anand 1970, Guddi (Darling Child) 1971, Anubhav (Experience) 1971, Seema 1971, Mere Apne 1971, Parichay 1972, Koshish 1972, Doosri Seeta 1974, Chor Machaye Shor 1974, Mausam 1975, Khushboo 1975, Aandhi (Storm) 1975, Shaque 1976, Palkon Ki Chhaon Mein 1977, Kinara 1977, Gharaonda (The Nest) 1977, Ghar (Home) 1978, Meetha (Sweet and Sour) 1978, Devata 1978, Gol Maal (Hanky Panky) 1979, Ratnadeep (The Jewelled Lamp) 1979, Grihapravesh (The Housewarming) 1979, Sitara 1980, Thodisi Bewafaii 1980, Swayamvar 1980, Khubsoorat (Beautiful India) 1980, Garam 1981, Basera 1981, Namkeen 1982, Angoor 1982, Sadma 1983, Masoom (Innocent) 1983, Ghulami 1985, Jeeva 1986, Ek Pal (A Moment) 1986, Ijaazat (Guest) (Nat. Award for Best Lyricist) 1987, Libaas 1988, Lekin... (But...) 1990, Maya Memsaab (Maya: The Enchanting Illusion) 1992, Rudaali (The Mourner) 1993, Mammo 1994, Daayraa (The Square Circle, USA) 1996, Maachis 1996, Aastha (Aastha in the Prison of Spring) 1997, Satya 1998, Dil Se... (From the Heart, USA) 1998, Chachi 420 1998, Hu Tu Tu 1999, Khoobsurat 1999, Fiza 2000, Aks 2001, Asoka (Ashoka the Great, USA) 2001, Filhaal... 2002, Leela 2002, Lal Salaam (Red Salute) 2002, Dil Vil Pyar Vyar 2002, Makdee (The Web of the Witch) 2002, Saathiya 2002, Chupke Se 2003, Pinjar (The Cage) 2003, Jaan-E-Mann 2006, Slumdog Millionaire (Jai Ho) (Academy Award for Best Original Song 2009) 2008. *Publications:* poetry:

Jaanam 1962, Kuch Aur Nazme 1980, Chand Pukhraj Ka 1995, Triveni 2001, Raat Pashmine Ki 2002; short stories: Dhuaan (Sahitya Acad. Award 2003); 12 books for children, including Ekta (Nat. Council for Educ. Research and Training Award 1989). *Address:* c/o Rupa and Co., 7/16 Ansari Road, Daryagani, PO Box 7017, New Delhi 110 002, India (office). *E-mail:* info@rupapublications.com (office). *Website:* www.rupapublications.com (office).

GUMBEL, Bryant Charles, BA; American broadcaster; b. 29 Sept. 1948, New Orleans; s. of Richard Gumbel and Rhea LeCesne; m. June C. Baranco 1973; one s. one d.; ed Bates Coll.; writer, Black Sports (magazine), New York 1971, Ed. 1972; sportscaster, KNBC-TV, Burbank, Calif. 1972–76, Sports Dir 1976–81; sports host, NBC Sports 1975–82; co-host, Today Show, NBC 1982–97; host Real Sports with Bryant Gumbel, Home Box Office (HBO) 1995–, Public Eye, CBS 1997, The Early Show 1999–2000, Flashpoints USA with Bryant Gumbel and Gwen Ifill PBS; play-by-play announcer NFL Network 2006–08; mem. Bd of Dirs United Negro Coll. Fund, United Way of New York City, Xavier Univ., Bates Coll.; recipient of three Emmy Awards and two Golden Mike Awards (LA Press Club); Edward R. Murrow Award (Overseas Press Club) 1988, Frederick D. Patterson Award (United Negro Coll. Fund), Martin Luther King Award (Congress of Racial Equality), three NAACP Image Awards, International Journalism Award (TransAfrica), Africa's Future Award (US Cttee for UNICEF); Dr. hc (Bates Coll., Xavier Univ., Holy Cross Univ., Providence Coll., Clark Atlanta Univ.). *Address:* c/o Home Box Office, Inc. 1100 Avenue of the Americas, New York, NY 10036, USA (office). *Website:* www.hbo.com/realsports (office).

GUMBS, Walford Vincent, JP; Saint Christopher and Nevis politician; *Speaker of National Assembly;* b. 21 Dec. 1946; m.; three c.; ed Basseterre Senior School, Ruppin Inst. of Agric., Israel, ILO Int. Training Centre, Turin, Italy; customs clerk, St Kitts Sugar Factory Ltd, Basseterre 1965–70; Accounts Officer and Acting Man. Sun Island Clothes Ltd 1973–77; field officer, St Kitts–Nevis Trades and Labour Union 1970–73, Exec. Officer 1978–, Second Vice-Pres. 1979–89, First Vice-Pres. 1989–2000, Pres. 2000–; Pres. Young Labour 1969–71, Vice-Chair. St Kitts–Nevis Labour Party 1992–96; apptd Senator (Labour Party) in Nat. Ass. 1989, Speaker Nat. Ass. 1995–. *Leisure interests:* sports, jogging, int. affairs. *Address:* Office of the Speaker, National Assembly, Basseterre (office); Suncrest Housing #43, Basseterre, Saint Christopher and Nevis (home). *Telephone:* 465-2229 (office); 465-8320 (home). *Fax:* 466-9866 (office). *E-mail:* sknunion@caribsurf.com (office).

GUMMER, Rt Hon. John Selwyn, PC, MA; British politician; *Chairman, Quality of Life Commission;* b. 26 Nov. 1939, Stockport; s. of the late Canon Selwyn Gummer and Sybille Gummer (née Mason); brother of Peter Selwyn Gummer, now Lord Chadlington (q.v.); m. Penelope J. Gardner 1977; two s. two d.; ed King's School, Rochester and Selwyn Coll., Cambridge; Ed., Business Publs 1962–64; Ed.-in-Chief, Max Parrish and Oldbourne Press 1964–66; Special Asst to Chair. BPC Publishing 1967; Dir Shandwick Publishing Co. 1966–81; Dir Siemssen Hunter Ltd 1973–80, Chair. 1979–80; Man. Dir EP Group of Cos 1975–81; Chair. Selwyn Sancroft Int. 1976–81; MP for Lewisham W 1970–74, Eye, Suffolk (now Suffolk Coastal) 1979–; Parl. Pvt. Sec. to Minister of Agric. 1972; Vice-Chair. Conservative Party 1972–74, Chair. 1983–85; Asst Govt Whip 1981, Lord Commr Treasury (Whip) 1982; Under-Sec. of State for Employment Jan.–Oct. 1983, Minister of State for Employment 1983–84, Paymaster-Gen. 1984–85; Minister of State at Ministry of Agric., Fisheries and Food 1985–88; Minister for Local Govt, Dept of Environment 1988–89; Minister of Agric. 1989–93; Sec. of State for the Environment 1993–97; Chair. Conservative Group for Europe 1997–2000, Marine Stewardship Council 1998–2005, Sancroft Int. Ltd 1997–, Valpak Ltd 1998–, Quality of Life Comm. 2006–; mem. Gen. Synod of Church of England 1979–92 (resgnd); joined Roman Catholic Church 1994; Medal of Honour, Royal Soc. for the Protection of Birds 1998. *Publications:* When the Coloured People Come 1966, To Church with Enthusiasm 1969, The Permissive Society 1970, The Christian Calendar (with L. W. Cowie) 1971, Faith in Politics (with Alan Beith and Eric Heffer) 1987, Christianity and Conservatism 1990. *Leisure interests:* gardening, Victorian buildings. *Address:* House of Commons, Westminster, London, SW1A 0AA, England (office).

GUNA-KASEM, Pracha, PhD; Thai diplomatist; *Adviser to the Minister of Foreign Affairs;* b. 29 Dec. 1934, Bangkok; s. of Jote Guna-Kasem and Rabieb Guna-Kasem; m. Sumanee Chongcharoen 1962; one s.; ed Dhebsirinda School, Bangkok, Marlborough Coll. and Hertford Coll., Oxford, UK and Yale Univ., USA; joined Ministry of Foreign Affairs 1959, Chief of Section, Political Div. of Dept of Int. Org. 1960–61, Second Sec., SEATO Div. 1962–63, Alt. mem. for Thailand, SEATO Perm. Working Group 1962–63, Embassy in Egypt 1964–65, Chief of Foreign News Analysis Div. of Information Dept and concurrently in charge of Press Affairs 1966–69, Chief of Press Div. 1970–71, Consul-Gen. in Hong Kong 1971–73, Dir-Gen. of Information Dept 1973–75; Perm. Rep. to UN 1975–80, UN (Geneva) 1980–82; Dir-Gen. ASEAN-Thailand 1982; Dir-Gen. Dept of Econ. Affairs, Foreign Ministry 1984–85; Amb. to France and Algeria 1985–87; Perm. Del. to UNESCO 1985; Dir-Gen. Dept of Econ. Affairs, Bangkok 1988; Perm. Sec. Ministry of Foreign Affairs 1992–1995, Deputy Minister of Foreign Affairs 1996; elected mem. of parliament from Bangkok 1996; Foreign Affairs Adviser to the Prime Minister 1996–98; Adviser to the Minister of Foreign Affairs 2001–; Special Lecturer, Thammasat Univ., Thai Nat. Defence Coll.; mem. del. to UN Gen. Ass. 1962, 1968, 1970, 1974, to 2nd Afro-Asian Conf., Algeria 1965, to SEATO Council 1966; Chair. Oxford Soc. of Bangkok; Grand Cordon of Order of White Elephant, Grand Cordon (Highest Class) of the Order of the Crown of Thailand, Commdr, Order of Chula Chomklao. *Achievements:* elected Vice-Pres. of the UN Gen. Ass. 1978; elected Chair. of the UN Sixth (Legal) Committee. *Leisure interests:* golf, bridge, tennis, swimming. *Address:* Ministry of Foreign Affairs, Thanon Sri Ayudhya, Bangkok, Thailand. *Telephone:* (2) 6435000; (2) 6435313 (office); (2) 2514565 (home). *Fax:* (2) 6435320 (office); (2) 2551179 (home). *Website:* www.mfa.go.th (office).

GUNATILAKA, Nandana; Sri Lankan politician; *General Secretary, National Freedom Front;* Chair. United People's Freedom Alliance (later People's Alliance) 2004–08; Gen. Sec. Nat. Freedom Front 2008–; fmr mem., politburo mem. and presidential cand. Janatha Vimukthi Peramuna party (resgnd 2006). *Address:* National Freedom Front, 377/4 Ratnarama Rd, Hokandara North, Sri Lanka (office). *Telephone:* (60) 2071340 (office). *E-mail:* info@nffsrilanka.com (office). *Website:* www.nffsrilanka.com (office).

GUNESEKERA, Romesh; Sri Lankan writer and poet; b. 1954, Colombo; m. Helen; two d.; New York Times Notable Book of the Year 1993, Yorkshire Post Best First Work Award 1994, Premio Mondello 1997, Ranjana, Sri Lanka 2005. *Publications:* Monkfish Moon (short stories) 1992, Reef (novel) 1994, The Sandglass (novel) 1998, Heaven's Edge (novel) 2002, The Match (novel) 2006. *Address:* c/o Bill Hamilton, A. M. Heath & Co. Ltd, 79 St Martin's Lane, London, WC2N 4RE, England (office). *Telephone:* (20) 7836-4271 (office). *Fax:* (20) 7497-2561 (office). *Website:* www.romeshgunesekera.com.

GUNGAADORJ, Sharavyn; Mongolian politician; b. 2 May 1935, Ikh Khet soum, Dornogobi Aimak (Prov.); ed Acad. of Agriculture, USSR; Chief Agronomist, Amgalan State farm; agronomist, Dept of State Farms 1959–67; Instructor, Mongolian People's Revolutionary Party (MPRP) Cen. Cttee 1967–68; Deputy Minister for Agric.; head of fodder farm in Zabhan Aimak Prov.; Head of group, Ministry of Agric. 1968–80; First Deputy Minister for State Farms 1980–81; First Sec. Party Cttee of Selenge Aimak Prov. 1981–86; Minister for Agric. 1986–90; Deputy Chair. Council of Ministers 1987–90; Alt. mem. MPRP Cen. Cttee 1981–86, mem. 1986–; Deputy to Great People's Hural (Ass.) 1981–89, Chair. Council of Ministers April–Sept. 1990, Counsellor to the Pres., Chair. of the Civic Council attached to the Pres. 1990–91; Amb. to Democratic People's Repub. of Korea and Kazakhstan 1991–96; Pres. Co-operatives Asscn 1997–. *Address:* c/o Ministry of External Relations, Ulan Bator, Mongolia. *Telephone:* 321870. 245

GUNN, James Edward, BS, PhD; American astrophysicist and academic; *Eugene Higgins Professor of Astrophysics, Princeton University;* b. 21 Oct. 1938, Livingstone, Tex.; s. of James Edward Gunn and Rhea Gunn (née Mason); ed Rice Univ., Calif. Inst. of Tech., Pasadena; served with CE US Army Reserve 1967; Sr Space Scientist, Jet Propulsion Lab. 1966–69; Asst Prof., Princeton Univ., NJ 1969–70, Eugene Higgins Prof. of Astrophysics 1980–; Asst Prof. then Prof. of Astrophysics, Calif. Inst. of Tech. 1970–80; taught at Univ. of Calif., Berkeley, Univ. of Wash., Univ. of Chicago, Rice Univ.; Deputy Prin. Investigator, Space Telescope Wide Field Camera/Planetary Camera, Hubble Space Telescope, NASA 1977; fmr Assoc. Dir Apache Point Observatory; fmr Project Scientist and Tech. Dir Sloan Digital Sky Survey; mem. Astronomical Survey Cttee; mem. NAS, American Astronomical Soc., American Philosophical Soc.; Sloan Foundation Fellow 1972–76, MacArthur Foundation Grantee 1983, Heinemann Prize, American Astronomical Soc. 1988, Gold Medal, Royal Astronomical Soc. London 1994, Distinguished Alumni Award, Calif. Inst. of Tech. 2003, Cosmology Prize, Peter Gruber Foundation 2005, Crafoord Prize, Royal Swedish Acad. of Sciences 2005, Henry Norris Russell Lectureship, American Astronomical Soc. 2005. *Publications:* numerous scientific papers in professional journals. *Address:* Department of Astrophysical Sciences, Princeton University, Room 23, 132 Peyton Hall, Ivy Lane, Princeton, NJ 08544-0001, USA (office). *Telephone:* (609) 258-3801 (office). *Fax:* (609) 258-8226 (office). *E-mail:* jeg@astro.princeton.edu (office). *Website:* www.princeton.edu (office).

GUNN, John Charles, CBE, MD, F.R.C.PSYCH., FMedSci; British psychiatrist; *Professor Emeritus of Forensic Psychiatry, Institute of Psychiatry, King's College, London;* b. 6 June 1937, Hove; s. of Albert Gunn and Lily Hilda Gunn (née Edwards); m. Celia Willis 1959 (divorced 1986, died 1989); one s. one d.; m. 2nd Pamela Taylor 1989; ed Brighton, Hove and Sussex Grammar School, Reigate Grammar School, Birmingham Univ. Medical School; Consultant Psychiatrist, Bethlem Maudsley Hosp. 1971–2002; Dir Special Hosps Research Unit 1975–78; Prof. of Forensic Psychiatry, Inst. of Psychiatry, King's Coll., London 1978–2002, Emer. Prof. 2002–; Chair. Research Cttee, Royal Coll. of Psychiatrists 1976–80, Chair. Faculty of Forensic Psychiatry 2000–; Chair. Academic Bd, Inst. of Psychiatry 1980–85; Chair. Forensic Specialist Cttee, Jt Cttee on Higher Psychiatric Training 1982–85; Consultant European Cttee for Prevention of Torture 1993–; Ed. Criminal Behaviour and Mental Health 1991–; mem. Ont. Govt Enquiry in Oakridge, Ont., Canada 1984–85, Home Sec.'s Advisory Bd on Restricted Patients 1982–91, Bethlem Maudsley Special Health Authority 1986–90, Royal Comm. on Criminal Justice 1991–93, Council, Royal Coll. of Psychiatrists 1997–2004; foundation mem. Acad. of Medical Sciences 1998; Chair. Faculty of Forensic Psychiatry, Royal Coll. of Psychiatry 2000–04; RMPA Bronze Medal 1970, H. B. Williams Travelling Professorship to Australasia 1985, Phillipe Pinel Award 1992. *Publications:* Violence 1973, Epileptics in Prison 1977, Psychiatric Aspects of Imprisonment 1978, Current Research in Forensic Psychiatry and Psychology (Vols 1–3) 1982–85, Forensic Psychiatry: Clinical, Legal and Ethical Issues 1993. *Leisure interests:* theatre, cinema, opera, walking, photography. *Address:* Royal College of Psychiatrists, 17 Belgrave Square, London, SW1 8PG (office); POB 725, Bromley, BR2 7WF, England (home). *Telephone:* (20) 8462-1751 (home). *Fax:* (20) 8462-0490 (home). *E-mail:* j.gunn@iop.kcl.ac.uk (office).

GUNNARSSON, Birgir Ísleifur; Icelandic politician, lawyer and central banker (retd); b. 19 July 1936, Reykjavík; s. of Gunnar Espólín Benediktsson and Jorunn Isleifsdóttir; m. Sonja Backman 1956; one s. three d.; ed Univ. of Iceland; advocate to lower courts 1962, Supreme Court 1967; law practice

1963–72; Leader Heimdallur Youth Soc. 1959–62; Sec.-Gen. Youth Fed. of Independence Party 1959–62; mem. Reykjavík City Council 1962–82; Mayor of Reykjavík 1972–78; mem. Parl. for Reykjavík 1979–91; Second Deputy Speaker of Althing 1983–87; Minister for Culture and Educ. 1987–88; Chair. Cttee on Heavy Industry 1983–87; mem. Bd Nat. Power Co. 1965–91, Civil Aviation Bd 1984–87; Gov. Cen. Bank of Iceland 1991–2005, Chair. Bd of Govs 1994–2005; Commdr, Order of the Falcon, Order of Dannebrog (Denmark), Order of St Olav (Norway), Order of the White Rose (Finland), Grosse Verdienstkreuz (Germany). *Leisure interests:* music, the outdoor life. *Address:* Fjölnisvegur 15, 101 Reykjavík, Iceland (home). *Telephone:* 552-0628 (home). *E-mail:* birgirisl@simnet.is (office).

GUNNELL, Sally, OBE; British sports commentator and fmr professional athlete; b. 29 July 1966, Chigwell, Essex; m. Jon Bigg 1992; three s.; ed Chigwell High School; specialized in hurdles; coached by Bruce Longdon; mem. Essex Ladies Athletic Club; competed 400m hurdles Olympic Games, Seoul 1988; second, 400m hurdles World Championship, Tokyo 1991; bronze medal, 400m relay, Olympic Games, Barcelona 1992; women's team capt., Olympic Games 1992–97; gold medal, 400m hurdles, Barcelona 1992; gold medal, 400m hurdles, World Championships 1993 (world record); gold medal, 400m hurdles European Championships, Helsinki 1994; gold medal, 400m hurdles, Commonwealth Games, Canada 1994; only woman in history to have held four gold medals concurrently – Olympic, World, European and Commonwealth (as at end of 2002); retd 1997; sports commentator BBC 1999–2006. *Publications:* Running Tall (with Christopher Priest) 1994, Be Your Best 2001. *Address:* Old School Cottage, School Lane, Pyecombe, W Sussex, England.

GUNNLAUGSSON, Sverrir Haukur, LLB; Icelandic diplomatist; *Ambassador to UK;* b. 20 Oct. 1942, Copenhagen, Denmark; m. Gudny Adalsteinsdottir; three c.; ed Univ. of Iceland; joined Ministry for Foreign Affairs as First Sec., Int. Div. 1970, First Sec., Paris 1971–74, Deputy Perm. Sec. to OECD, UNESCO 1971–74, Chief of Admin. and Consular Affairs 1974–78, Counsellor, Washington, DC 1978–80, Minister-Counsellor 1980–83, Head of Defence Dept, Reykjavík 1983–85, Rep. to NATO 1984–87, Amb. in Foreign Service 1985–87, Perm. Rep. to EFTA, UN, Geneva, Amb. to Egypt (also accred to Ethiopia, Kenya, Tanzania) 1987–89, Head, Dept for Foreign Trade, Reykjavík 1989–90, Perm. Rep. to N Atlantic Council, Brussels, WEU 1990–94, Amb. to France (also accred to Spain, Portugal, Cape Verde, Italy, Andorra), Perm. Rep. to Council of Europe, OECD, UNESCO, FAO 1994–99, Perm. Sec. of State, Reykjavík 1999–2003, Amb. to UK (also accred to Ireland, Netherlands, Greece, Lebanon) 2003–, Perm. Rep. to IMO 2003–. *Address:* Embassy of Iceland, 2A Hans Street, London, SW1X 0JE, England (office). *Telephone:* (20) 7245-3999 (office). *Fax:* (20) 7245-9649 (office). *E-mail:* icemb .london@utn.stjr.is (office). *Website:* www.iceland.org/uk (office).

GUO, Gen. Boxiong; Chinese army officer; *Executive Deputy Chief, Headquarters of the General Staff, People's Liberation Army;* b. 1942, Liquan Co., Shaanxi Prov.; ed Mil. Acad. of the Chinese PLA; worker, No. 408 Factory, Xingping Co., Shaanxi Prov. 1958–61; joined PLA 1961, CCP 1963; Squad Leader 164th Regt, 55th Div., Army (or Ground Force), PLA Services and Arms 1961–66, Platoon Commdr 8th Co. 1964–65, mem. staff Propaganda Group 1965–66, mem. staff HQ 164th Regt, 55th Div., Combat Training Section 1966–70, Leader HQ 164th Regt, 55th Div., Combat Training Section 1970–71, Staff Officer, Deputy Head, later Head, later Divisional Chief-of-Staff 1971–81; Deputy Dir Combat Dept (HQ), Lanzhou Mil. Area Command 1982–83; Army Chief-of-Staff 1983–85; Deputy Chief-of-Staff Lanzhou Mil. Area Command 1985–90; Army Group Commdr 1990–93; Deputy Commdr Beijing Mil. Area Command 1993–97; rank of Lt Gen. 1995, Gen. 1999; Commdr Lanzhou Mil. Area Command 1997–99; Exec. Deputy Gen., PLA 1999–2001, Chief of Staff 1999–2002, Exec. Deputy Chief, HQ of Gen. Staff 2002–; mem. 15th CCP Cen. Cttee 1997–2002 (mem. Cen. Mil. Comm.), 16th CCP Cen. Cttee 2002–07 (Vice-Chair. Cen. Mil. Comm. 2002–07), 17th CCP Cen. Cttee 2007–; Vice-Chair. Cen. Mil. Comm. 2007–), also mem. Politburo 2007–; Deputy Sec. PLA HQ of Gen. Staff, CCP Party Cttee 1999–. *Address:* Ministry of National Defence, 20 Jingshanqian Jie, Beijing 100009, People's Republic of China (office).

GUO, Dongpo; Chinese politician; *Chairman, Sub-committee for Hong Kong, Macao and Taiwan Compatriots and Overseas Chinese, Chinese People's Political Consultative Conference;* b. Aug. 1937, Jiangdu Co., Jiangsu Prov.; ed Beijing Inst. of Foreign Trade; joined CCP 1960; Deputy Div. Chief, China Council for the Promotion of Int. Trade 1972 (Sec. CCP Party Br.), Deputy Dir Printing House, Vice-Pres. China Council for the Promotion of Int. Trade (Sec. CCP Party Cttee) 1982, Pres. 1992; fmr Vice-Pres. China Chamber of Int. Commerce, Pres. 1995; Dir Macau Bureau of Xinhua News Agency 1990–95; Vice-Dir Drafting Cttee of the Basic Law of Macau Special Admin. Zone 1990; Pres. Econ. and Trade Coordination Cttee for the Two Sides of the Straits 1996; Dir Foreign Econ. and Trade Arbitration Comm. 1996; Dir Office of Overseas Chinese Affairs of the State Council 1997–2003; Vice-Pres. China Overseas Exchanges Asscn 1998–; mem. 7th CPPCC Nat. Cttee 1988–93, Standing Cttee 8th CPPCC Nat. Cttee 1993–98, Chair. Sub-cttee for Hong Kong, Macao and Taiwan Compatriots and Overseas Chinese 2003–; Alt. mem. 14th CCP Cen. Cttee 1992–97; mem. 15th CCP Cen. Cttee 1997–2002. *Address:* Chinese People's Political Consultative Conference, State Council, Beijing, People's Republic of China (office). *Website:* www.cppcc.gov.cn (office).

GUO, Guangchang, BA, MBA; Chinese business executive; *Chairman and CEO, Fosun International;* b. 1967, Zhejiang Prov.; m.; one c.; ed Fudan Univ.; Co-founder Guangxin Consulting Co. 1989 (renamed Fosun Holdings Ltd 1993), currently Chair. and CEO Fosun International, also Chair. Fosun Pharmaceutical and Forte Land; Deputy Chair. Shanghai Chamber of Commerce 2002; policy adviser to Shanghai Municipal Govt 2000; fmr

Standing Commissary of Ninth Exec. Council of Greater China Fed. of Industry and Commerce Cttee; mem. China Democratic League; Deputy, 10th NPC 2003–; several nat. awards, including Outstanding Pvt. Entrepreneur Award, Outstanding Youth Entrepreneurs of Shanghai 1997. *Address:* Fosun Group Head Office, No. 2 East Fuxing Road, Shanghai 200010, People's Republic of China (office). *Telephone:* (21) 63325858 (office). *Fax:* (21) 63325028 (office). *Website:* www.fosun.com (office).

GUO, Jingjing; Chinese diver; b. 15 Oct. 1981, Baoding, Hebei Prov.; ed Univ. of Physical Educ., Beijing; began diving aged eight; silver medal, 3 m. springboard, World Championships, Perth, Australia 1998; silver medals, 3 m. springboard and synchronized 3 m. springboard, Olympic Games, Sydney 2000; gold medals, 3 m. springboard and synchronized 3 m. springboard, World Championships, Fukuoka 2001, Asian Games 2002, FINA Diving Grand Prix (Australia/China) 2003, World Championships, Barcelona 2003, Olympic Games, Athens 2004, World Championships 2005, 2007; two gold medals, women's 3 m. springboard and synchronized diving, Olympic Games, Beijing 2008; has won more than 13 Grand Prix events, three first places at World Cup events 1999, 2000, 2004; synchro partner Wu Minxia; fmr synchro partner Fu Mingxia. *Leisure interests:* music, reading, shopping. *Address:* 9 Tiyuguan Road, Beijing, 100763, People's Republic of China. *Telephone:* (10) 67116669. *Fax:* (10) 67115858. *E-mail:* coc@olympic.cn. *Website:* www.olympic .cn.

GUO, Jinlong; Chinese politician; *Mayor of Beijing;* b. July 1947, Nanjing, Jiangsu Prov.; ed Nanjing Univ.; technician, Hydropower Bureau, Zhongxian Co., Sichuan Prov., 1969–73; coach, Physical Culture and Sports Cttee, Zhongxian Co., Sichuan Prov. 1973–79; joined CCP 1979; teacher, Publicity Dept, CCP Co. Cttee 1979–80; Deputy Sec. then Sec. Cultural Bureau of Zhongxian Co., Sichuan Prov. 1980–83; Deputy Sec. CCP Zhongxian Co. Cttee then Magistrate of Zhongxian 1983–85; Deputy Dir Rural Policy Research Office, CCP Sichuan Prov. Cttee, Deputy Dir Sichuan Prov. Rural Econ. Comm. 1985–87; Deputy Sec. then Sec. CCP Leshan City Cttee 1987–92; Deputy Sec. CCP Sichuan Prov. Cttee 1992–93; Deputy Sec. then Exec. Deputy Sec. CCP Tibetan Autonomous Region Cttee 1993–2000, Sec. 2000–04; Alt. mem. 15th CCP Cen. Cttee 1997–2002, mem. 16th CCP Cen. Cttee 2002–07, 17th CCP Cen. Cttee 2007–; Acting Mayor of Beijing 2007–08, Mayor 2008–, also Deputy Sec., CCP Municipal Cttee, Beijing Municipality 2007–; Deputy 11th NPC. *Address:* Office of the Mayor, 2 Zhengyi Lu, Beijing, People's Republic of China (office). *E-mail:* beijing-eng@beijing.gov.cn (office). *Website:* www.ebeijing.gov.cn/default.htm (office).

GUO, Shuqing, BA, DJur; Chinese banking executive; *Chairman and Executive Director, China Construction Bank;* ed Nankai Univ., Acad. of Social Sciences; Deputy Dir Econ. Research Centre, State Planning Comm. 1988–93; Dir, Gen. Planning and Experiment Dept, State Comm. for Econ. Restructuring 1993–96, Sec.-Gen. State Comm. for Econ. Restructuring 1996–98; Deputy Gov. Guizhou Prov. 1988–2001; Dir State Admin of Foreign Exchange 2001–05; Deputy Gov. People's Bank of China 2001–03; Chair. Huijin 2003–05; Chair. and Exec. Dir China Construction Bank 2005–; mem. 10th CPPCC Nat. Cttee; Alt. mem. 17th CCP Cen. Cttee 2007–; Visiting Fellow, Univ. of Oxford, UK 1986–87. *Address:* China Construction Bank, 25 Finance Street, Beijing 100032, People's Republic of China (office). *Telephone:* (10) 6759-7114 (office). *Fax:* (10) 6360-3194 (office). *E-mail:* info@ccb.cn (office). *Website:* www.ccb.cn/portal/en/home/index.html (office).

GUO, Zhengqian; Chinese party and government official; b. Feb. 1933, Loning Co., Henan Prov.; ed People's Univ. of China, Beijing; joined CCP 1949; Judicial Officer and Investigator, Public Security Bureau, Songxian Co., Henan Prov. 1947–49; fmr Deputy Section Chief, Commercial Dept, Hubei Prov.; Vice-Pres. Hubei Prov. Commercial School 1964–66; Deputy Dir then Dir Political Dept, Financial and Trade Office, Hubei Prov. 1964–66, Deputy Dir Financial and Trade Office 1980–83; Gov. Hubei Br., People's Construction Bank of China 1980–83; Deputy Gov. Hubei Prov. 1983–86, Acting Gov. Jan. 1986, Gov. May–Oct. 1986; Deputy Sec. Hubei Prov. CCP Cttee 1985–90; Gov. Hubei Provincial People's Govt 1986–90; Deputy Gov. People's Bank of China 1990–93; First Deputy Auditor-Gen. of People's Repub. of China 1993–94, Auditor-Gen. 1994–98; Sr Economist, concurrently Prof., People's Univ. of China; Del. 12th CCP Nat. Congress 1982–87, mem. 13th and 14th CCP Cen. Cttees 1987–97, Del. 15th CCP Nat. Congress 1997–2002; Deputy, 6th NPC 1983–88, 7th NPC 1988–93, mem. 9th Standing Cttee of NPC 1998–2003 (Vice-Chair. Financial and Econ. Cttee 1998–2003, Chair. Budgetary Work Cttee 1998–2003). *Leisure interests:* reading, swimming, tennis, table tennis. *Address:* c/o NPC Budgetary Work Committee, Beijing, People's Republic of China (office).

GUO MUSUN, Mooson Kwauk; Chinese scientist and academic; *Director Emeritus, Institute of Process Engineering, Chinese Academy of Sciences;* b. 9 May 1920, Hangyang; s. of Zung-Ung Kwauk and Za-Nan Chow; m. Huichun Kwei Kwauk 1950; two s. one d.; ed Univ. of Shanghai, Princeton Univ., USA; Prof., Inst. of Chemical Metallurgy (now Inst. of Process Eng), Chinese Acad. of Sciences 1956, Dir 1982–86, Dir Emer. 1986–; Visiting Prof., Ohio State Univ. 1989; Vice-Pres. Chemical Industry and Eng Soc. of China 1978–; Visiting Prof. Virginia Polytechnic Inst. and State Univ. 1986–87; mem. Chinese Acad. of Sciences 1981–; Pres. Emer. Chinese Soc. of Particuology 1986–; Corresp. mem. Swiss Acad. of Eng Sciences 1997–; Distinguished Scholar, CSCPRC Program, US Nat. Acad. of Science 1984, Davis-Swindin Memorial Lecturer, Univ. of Loughborough, UK 1985, Danckwerts Memorial Lecturer, Inst. of Dirs, London 1989, Int. Fluidization Award 1989. *Publications:* Fluidization: Idealized and Bubbleless, with Applications 1992, Fast Fluidization 1994, Geometric Mobiles 1998. *Leisure interests:* kites, mobiles. *Address:* Institute of Process Engineering, Chinese Academy of Sciences, Beijing, 100080, People's Republic of China (office). *Telephone:* (10) 6255-4241 (office); (10) 6255-4050 (home). *Fax:* (10) 6255-8065 (office). *E-mail:* mooson@home.ipe.ac.cn (office). *Website:* www.ipe.ac.cn/ipe2003_english/people/mooson.htm (office).

GUPTA, Modadugu V., PhD; Indian food scientist; *Senior Research Fellow, WorldFish Center;* b. 1939; began his career in 1962 researching how to bring benefits of fish production to poor farmers in India and SE Asia and Pacific regions; Coordinator Int. Network on Genetics in Aquaculture; trained more than 1,000 scientists from developing countries in continuing devt of sustainable and effective fish production strategies; retd from WorldFish Center 2004, currently Sr Research Fellow; Chair. Organizing Cttee Int. Workshop on Environmentally Friendly Aquaculture; adviser on agricultural and aquacultural research and fisheries to Govts of Mozambique and India; mem. numerous scientific cttees; Fellow of numerous scientific acads; Hon. DSc; World Food Prize Laureate 2005. *Address:* WorldFish Center Global Headquarters, Jalan Batu Maung, Batu Maung, PO Box 500, GPO 10670, 11960 Bayan Lepas, Penang, Malaysia (office). *Telephone:* (40) 23400229 (India) (office); 98-66508555 (India, mobile) (office). *Fax:* (4) 626-5530 (office). *E-mail:* guptamo2000@yahoo.co.in (office). *Website:* www.worldfishcenter.org (office).

GUPTE, Lalita D., BEcons, MMS; Indian banking executive; *Chairman, ICICI Venture Funds Management Co. Ltd;* b. 1948; m.; two c.; ed Univ. of Delhi, Univ. of of Bombay, Jamnalal Bajaj Inst. of Man. Studies; joined ICICI Bank Ltd 1971, held various leadership positions in Corp. and Retail Banking, Strategy and Resources, and Int. Banking depts, Exec. Dir Bd of Dirs ICICI Ltd 1994–96, Deputy Man. Dir 1996–99, Jt Man. Dir and COO 2001–06, Chair. (non-exec.) ICICI Venture Funds Management Co. Ltd 2006–; mem. Advisory Bd RAND Center for Asia-Pacific Policy; mem. Bd of Dirs Bharat Forge Ltd, Kirloskar Brothers Ltd, FirstSource Solutions Ltd, Godrej Properties Ltd, HPCL-Mittal Energy Ltd, Swadhaar FinServe Pvt Ltd, Nokia 2007–; ranked by Fortune magazine amongst 50 Most Powerful Women in Business outside the US 2001, 2002, (31st) 2003, Int. Women's Assсn Woman of the Year Award 2002, ranked 93rd by Forbes magazine amongst 100 Most Powerful Women 2006. *Leisure interest:* looking after her family. *Address:* ICICI Bank Ltd, ICICI Bank Towers, Bandra Kurla Complex, Mumbai 400 051, India (office). *Telephone:* (22) 26531414 (office). *Fax:* (22) 26531167 (office). *Website:* www.icicibank.com (office).

GUPTE, Shridhar, PhD; Indian university vice-chancellor and professor of geography; b. 4 Feb. 1933, Bombay (now Mumbai); s. of Shri Chandrashekhar Trimbak Gupte; m. 1961; two s.; lecturer in Geography, Univ. of Pune, Maharashtra 1959–77, Reader 1977–79, Prof. 1979–, Vice-Chancellor 1989–95; Best Teacher's Award (Pune Municipal Corpn) 1982. *Leisure interests:* music and reading. *Address:* Department of Geography, University of Pune, Ganeshkhind, Pune -411 007 (Maharashtra), India. *Telephone:* (20) 5650765 (home); (20) 56061/9.

GURASSA, Charles Mark, BEcons, MBA, FRSA, FRAeS; British business executive; *Chairman, Virgin Mobile PLC;* b. 1956, London; m.; c.; ed Christ's Coll., London, Univ. of York, Int. Man. Centre, Buckingham; joined Thomas Cook 1977, posts in New York, London, Hong Kong, Gen. Man. Retail Operations 1988–89; Sr Commercial Dir British Airways 1989–99; CEO Thomson Travel Group plc 1999–2000; Chair. TUI N Europe and Airline Group 2000–03, Exec. Dir TUI AG 2000–03; Chair. (non-exec.) 7days Ltd 2003–, Worldwide Excellerated Leasing Ltd 2004–; Chair. Virgin Mobile PLC 2004–; Dir (non-exec.) Whitbread plc 2000–; Trustee Whizz-Kidz 2003–; Travel Industry Hall of Fame 2003. *Leisure interests:* music, travel, theatre, sports. *Address:* c/o Sarah Fosdike, Virgin Mobile, 5th Floor, The Communications Building, 48 Leicester Square, London, WC2H 7LT, England (office). *Telephone:* (20) 7484-4342 (office). *Fax:* (20) 7484-4351 (office). *Website:* www.virginmobile.com (office).

GURBANMYRADOV, Yolly; Turkmenistani politician and economist; b. 1960, Ashgabat; ed Turkmen State Inst. of Nat. Econ.; worker in construction co. 1977–82; Sr Econ., Deputy Head Ashgabat br. USSR State Bank 1982–87; Head Div. of Banking Automation State Bank (Ashgabat) 1988; Deputy Head Regional Dept USSR Zhilsotsbank 1988–89; man. of div. Agroprombank 1989–90; Br. Man. USSR Vnesheconombank 1990–92; First Deputy Chair., then Chair. Bd of Dirs State Bank of Foreign Trade of Turkmenistan 1992–96; Dir Turkmenistan State Agency on Foreign Investments 1996–97; Deputy Chair. Turkmen Cabinet of Ministers, concurrently Chair. Interbanking Council 1997–99; Deputy Prime Minister of Turkmenistan 1999–2004. *Address:* c/o Cabinet of Ministers, Ashgabat, Turkmenistan (office).

GURBANOV, Fakhraddin; Azerbaijani diplomatist; *Ambassador to UK ;* Amb.-at-large for the Repub. of Azerbaijan; Azerbaijan Initiative Fellow, Sr Mans in Govt Program, Kennedy School of Govt, USA Aug. 2002; Amb. to Canada 2004–07, to UK (also accred to Ireland and Norway) 2007–. *Address:* Embassy of the Republic of Azerbaijan, 4 Kensington Court, London, W8 5DL, England (office). *Telephone:* (20) 7938-5482 (office); (20) 7938-3412 (office). *Fax:* (20) 7937-1783 (office). *E-mail:* london@mission.mfa.gov.az (office); azeconsular@btconnect.com (office). *Website:* www.azembassy.org.uk (office).

GURDON, Sir John Bertrand, Kt, DPhil, FRS; British cell biologist; b. 2 Oct. 1933, Hampshire; s. of the late W. N. Gurdon and E. M. Gurdon (née Byass); m. Jean Elizabeth Margaret Curtis 1964; one s. one d.; ed Edgeborough School, Eton Coll., Univ. of Oxford; Beit Memorial Fellow 1958–61; Gosney Research Fellow, California Inst. of Tech., USA 1961–62; Research Fellow, Christ Church, Oxford 1962–72, Departmental Demonstrator 1963–64, Lecturer, Dept of Zoology 1966–72; Visiting Research Fellow, Carnegie Inst., Baltimore, Md, USA 1965; mem. Scientific Staff, Medical Research Council, Molecular Biology Lab., Univ. of Cambridge 1973–83, Head of Cell Biology Div. 1979–83, John Humphrey Plummer Prof. of Cell Biology 1983–2001; Master Magdalene Coll. Cambridge 1995–2002; Fellow, Churchill Coll., Cambridge 1973–95; Croonian Lecturer, Royal Soc. 1976; Dunham Lecturer, Harvard Medical School 1974; Carter-Wallace Lecturer, Princeton Univ. 1978; Fellow, Eton Coll. 1978–93; Fullerian Prof. of Physiology and Comparative Anatomy, Royal Inst. 1985–91; Pres. Int. Soc. for Developmental Biology 1990–94; Foreign Assoc., NAS 1980, Belgian Royal Acad. of Science, Letters and Fine Arts 1984, French Acad. of Sciences 1990; Foreign mem. American Philosophical Soc. 1983; Foreign mem. Inst. of Medicine, USA 2003; Chair. Wellcome Cancer Campaign Inst., Univ. of Cambridge 1990–2001; Gov. The Wellcome Trust 1995–2000; Chair. Co. of Biologists 2001–; Hon. Foreign mem. American Acad. of Arts and Sciences 1978; Hon. Student, Christ Church, Oxford 1985; Hon. Fellow, Magdalene Coll. Cambridge 2002, Churchill Coll. Cambridge 2007; Hon. DSc (Chicago) 1978, (Oxford) 1988, (Hull) 1998, (Glasgow) 2000, (Cambridge) 2007; Dr hc (Paris) 1982; Albert Brachet Prize, Belgian Royal Acad. 1968, Scientific Medal of Zoological Soc. 1968, Feldberg Foundation Award 1975, Paul Ehrlich Award 1977, Nessim Habif Prize, Univ. of Geneva 1979, CIBA Medal, Biochemical Soc. 1981, Comfort Crookshank Award for Cancer Research 1983, William Bate Hardy Triennial Prize, Cambridge Philosophy Soc. 1983, Charles Léopold Mayer Prize, Acad. des Sciences (France) 1984, Ross Harrison Prize, Int. Soc. for Devt Biology 1985, Royal Medal, Royal Soc. 1985, Emperor Hirohito Int. Biology Prize 1987, Wolf Prize for Medicine (jtly with Edward B. Lewis, 1989, Distinguished Service Award, Miami 1992, Jean Brachet Memorial Prize, Int. Soc. of Diffusion 2000, Conklin Medal, Soc. for Developmental Biology 2001, Copley Medal, Royal Soc. 2003, Rosenstiel Award 2009. *Publication:* Control of Gene Expression in Animal Development 1974. *Leisure interests:* skiing, horticulture, lepidoptera. *Address:* Whittlesford Grove, Whittlesford, Cambridge, CB2 4NZ, England. *Telephone:* (1223) 334090 (office); (1223) 832674 (home).

GURFINKEL, Viktor Semenovich; Russian physiologist; b. 2 April 1922; ed Kyrgyz State Medical Inst.; during World War II head div. of blood transfusion 19th Army 1941–45, chief dr hospital 1946–48; sr researcher, head of lab., Inst. of Orthopaedics 1949–58; head of lab. Inst. of Experimental Biology and Medical Siberian br. USSR Acad. of Sciences 1949–58; head of lab. Inst. of Biophysics USSR Acad. of Sciences 1960–67; head of lab. Inst. for Information Transmission Problems, Russian Acad. of Sciences; corresp. mem. USSR (now Russian) Acad. of Sciences 1987, mem. 1994; research in physiology of movements, space physiology and medicine; resident in USA 1999–; Hon. mem. American Physiological Soc.; USSR State Prize, R. Dow Prize (USA), Humboldt Foundation Award. *Publications:* three books and numerous articles in scientific journals. *Leisure interest:* fishing. *Address:* c/o Neurological Sciences Institute, Oregon Health and Science University, West Campus, 505 NW 185th Avenue, Beaverton, OR 97006, USA.

GURGENIDZE, Vladimer (Lado), MBA; Georgian/British banker and politician; b. 7 Dec. 1970, Tbilisi; m. Larissa Gurgenidze; three c.; ed Tbilisi State Univ., Middlebury Coll., VT, USA, Goizueta School of Business of Emory Univ.; began his investment banking career with CEE corp. finance arm of MeesPierson; Dir ABN AMRO Corp. Finance in Russia and CIS 1997–98, served in various sr capacities at ABN AMRO Corp. Finance, London, including as a Dir and Head of Mergers and Acquisitions in the Emerging European Markets 1998–2000 and as a Man. Dir and Head of Tech. Corp. Finance 2001–03; Man. Dir and Regional Man. for Europe, Putnam Lovell NBF (boutique investment banking firm) 2003–04; CEO Bank of Georgia 2004–06, Chair. Supervisory Bd 2006–; Chair. Supervisory Bd Galt & Taggart Securities, Galt & Taggart Capital; mem. Supervisory Bd Georgian Stock Exchange; Prime Minister of Georgia 2007–08. *Television:* hosted a reality TV show The Candidate on Rustavi 2 (Georgian version of Donald Trump's franchise The Apprentice) 2006. *Address:* c/o Chancellery of the Government, P. Ingorovka 7, 0105 Tbilisi, Georgia (office).

GURGULINO DE SOUZA, Heitor, BSc, Lic Math; Brazilian academic, scientist and international organization official; *Secretary General, International Association of University Presidents (IAUP);* b. 1 Aug. 1928, São Lourenço, Minas Gerais; s. of Arthur Gurgulino de Souza and Catarina Sachser de Souza; m. Lilian Maria Quilici; two s.; ed Mackenzie Univ., São Paulo, Aeronautics Inst. of Tech., Sao Jose dos Campos, Univ. of Kansas, USA, Univ. of São Paulo; Program Specialist, Interamerican Science Program, Pan American Union, Washington, DC 1962–64; Head, Unit of Educ. and Research, Dept of Scientific Affairs, OAS, Washington, DC 1964–69; Rector, Fed. Univ. of São Carlos, State of São Paulo 1970–74; Dir Dept of Univ. Affairs (DAU), Ministry of Educ. and Culture, Brasília 1972–74; Chair. Interamerican Cttee on Science and Tech. (CICYT), Council for Educ., Culture, OAS, Washington, DC 1974–77; Vice-Pres. Fed. Council of Educ. of Brazil (CFE) 1972–87; Dir CNPq (Nat. Council for Scientific and Tech. Devt), Brasília 1975–78, Special Adviser to Pres. 1979–80; Vice-Pres. Int. Assсn of Univ. Pres. (IAUP) 1985–87, 1999–2002, Sec.-Gen. 2005–(11); Pres., Grupo Universitario Latinoamericano (GULERPE), Caracas 1985–87; Rector UN Univ., Tokyo 1987–97; Special Adviser for Higher Educ. to Dir-Gen., UNESCO, Paris 1997–99; Vice-Rector Unilegis-Universidade do Legislativo Brasileiro, Fed. Senate, Brasília, DF 2003–05; Pres. Assсn Virtual Educ. Brasil (AVEB) 2003–; mem. APS, USA 1956–, Club of Rome 1996– (Vice-Pres. 2008–); mem. Brazilian Acad. of Educ. 2004–; mem. Nat. Order of Educational Merit, MEC, Brasília 1973, Commdr Order of Rio Branco, MRE, Brasília 1974, Nat. Order of Scientific Merit, MCT 1996; Dr hc (Guadalajara) 1984, (Espírito Santo) 1986, (Universidade Federal de São Carlos, São Paulo) 2006, (IESB, Brasilia) 2008; Hon. DJur (Calif. State Univ.) 1997. *Television:* producer, Educação Tesouro a Descobrir-Rêde Vida 2004–. *Publications:* Gamma Rays from the Proton Bombardment of Natural Silicon 1957, Computers and Higher Education in Brazil (articles) 1984, Science Policy (co-ed.) 1974; author of chapter on Brazil in International Encyclopedia of Higher Education 1978.

www.worldwhoswho.com

Leisure interests: sailing, swimming, music. *Address:* S.Q.S. 116 Bloco B, Apto 501, Edificio Cap Ferrat, Brasília, DF, CEP 70386-020, Brazil (home). *Telephone:* (61) 3346-1414 (home); (61) 8159-9091 (mobile). *Fax:* (61) 3346-0938 (home). *E-mail:* hgurgulino@aol.com (home); heitorgurgulino@gmail.com (office).

GURIRAB, Theo-Ben, PhD; Namibian politician; *President, Inter-Parliamentary Union (IPU);* b. 23 Jan. 1939, Usakos; m. Joan W. Guriras; two s. one d.; ed Augustineum Training Coll., Okahandja, Temple Univ.; in exile 1962; Chief Rep. in N America for South West Africa People's Org. (SWAPO) 1971; Head of SWAPO's Mission, UN 1972–86; mem. of Senate, UN Inst. for Namibia, Lusaka; Sr Adviser to SWAPO Pres. during Resolution 435 negotiations; Minister of Foreign Affairs 1990–2000, Minister of Foreign Affairs, Information and Broadcasting 2000–02, Prime Minister 2002–05; Speaker, Nat. Ass. 2005–; Pres. Inter-Parliamentary Union (IPU) 2008–. *Address:* National Assembly, Windhoek, Namibia (office). *Telephone:* (61) 2882504 (office). *Fax:* (61) 231626 (office). *E-mail:* w.hanse@parliament.gov.na (office). *Website:* www.parliament.gov.na (office).

GURLEY BROWN, Helen; American writer and editor; *Editor-in-Chief, Cosmopolitan International Editions;* b. 18 Feb. 1922, Green Forest, Ark.; d. of Ira M. Gurley and Cleo Gurley (née Sisco); m. David Brown 1959; ed Texas State Coll. for Women, Woodbury Coll.; Exec. Sec. Music Corpn of America 1942–45, William Morris Agency 1945–47; Copywriter Foote, Cone & Belding advertising agency, Los Angeles 1948–58; advertisement writer and account exec. Kenyon & Eckhard advertising agency, Hollywood 1958–62; Ed.-in-Chief Cosmopolitan magazine 1965–97, Editorial Dir Cosmopolitan Int. Edns 1972–, Ed.-in-Chief 1997–; mem. Authors' League of America, American Soc. of Magazine Eds, AFTRA; est. Helen Gurley Brown Research Professorship at Northwestern Univ. 1986; Hon. LLD (Woodbury) 1987; Hon. DLitt (Long Island) 1993; Francis Holm Achievement Award 1956–59, Univ. of S. Calif. School of Journalism 1971, Special Award for Editorial Leadership of American Newspaper Woman's Club 1972, Distinguished Achievement Award in Journalism, Stanford Univ. 1977, New York Women in Communications Inc. Award 1985, Publrs' Hall of Fame 1988, Henry Johnson Fisher Award, Magazine Publrs of America 1995. *Publications:* Sex and the Single Girl 1962, Sex and the Office 1965, Outrageous Opinions 1967, Helen Gurley Brown's Single Girl's Cook Book 1969, Sex and the New Single Girl 1970, Having It All 1982, The Late Show: A Semiwild but Practical Survival Guide for Women over 50 1993, The Writer's Rules: The Power of Positive Prose 1998, I'm Wild Again: Snippets from My Life and a Few Brazen Thoughts 2000, Dear Pussycat: Personal Correspondence of Helen Gurley Brown 2004. *Address:* Cosmopolitan, 959 8th Avenue, New York, NY 10019 (office); 1 West 81st Street, New York, NY 10024, USA (home). *Telephone:* (212) 649-3555 (office). *Fax:* (212) 649-3529 (office). *Website:* www.cosmopolitan.com (office).

GURNAH, Abdulrazak; Tanzanian novelist, literary critic and editor; *Lecturer in English Literature, University of Kent;* b. 1948, Zanzibar; currently Lecturer in English Literature, Univ. of Kent and Contributing Ed. journal, Wasafiri. *Publications:* Memory of Departure 1987, Pilgrim's Way 1988, Dottie 1990, Essays on African Writing: A Re-Evaluation (ed.) 1993, Paradise 1994, Essays on African Writing: Contemporary Literature (ed.) 1995, Admiring Silence 1996, By the Sea 2001, Desertion 2005; numerous works for radio; contrib. to Wole Soyinka: An Appraisal 1994, Modernism and Empire 1998, Essays and Criticism 2000, New Writing 9. *Address:* c/o School of English, Rutherford College, University of Kent, Canterbury, Kent CT2 7NX, England. *E-mail:* A.S.Gurnah@ukc.ac.uk. *Website:* www.wasafiri.org.

GURNEY, Albert Ramsdell, MFA; American playwright; b. 1 Nov. 1930, Buffalo, NY; s. of Albert R. Gurney and Marion Gurney (née Spaulding); m. Mary F. Goodyear 1957; two s. two d.; ed Williams Coll., Yale School of Drama; joined MIT, Faculty of Humanities 1960–96, Prof. 1970–96; mem. American Acad. of Arts and Letters 2006; Hon. DDL (Buffalo State Univ., Williams Coll.); Drama Desk Award 1971, American Acad. of Arts and Letters Award 1987, Lucille Lortel Award 1992, William Inge Award 2000, Theatre Hall of Fame 2005. *Publications include:* plays: The Dining Room, The Cocktail Hour, Love Letters, Later Life, A Cheever Evening, Sylvia, Overtime; Let's Do It!, The Guest Lecturer, Labor Day, Far East, Ancestral Voices 1999, Human Events 2000, Buffalo Gal 2001, The Fourth Wall 2002, Big Bill 2004, Mrs Farnsworth 2004; novels: The Gospel According to Joe, Entertaining Strangers, The Snow Ball; opera libretto: Stawberry Fields 1999. *Address:* 40 Wellers Bridge Road, P.O 150, Roxbury, CT 06783-1616, USA (home). *Telephone:* (860) 354-3692 (home). *Fax:* (860) 354-3692 (home). *E-mail:* a.r.gurney@charter.net (home).

GUROV, Maj.-Gen. Aleksander Ivanovich, DJur; Russian civil servant and politician; *Chairman, Parliamentary Committee on Security;* b. 17 Nov. 1945, Shushkan-Olshanka, Tambov Dist; m. Yelena Nikolayevna Gurova; one s.; ed Moscow State Univ.; inspector Div. of Criminal Investigation, Vnukovo Airport 1970–74; mem. of staff Dept of Criminal Investigation, USSR Ministry of Internal Affairs 1974–78, Head Dept for Struggle Against Organized Crime, Corruption and Drug Business; USSR People's Deputy 1990–93; First Deputy Head Centre of Public Relations, Ministry of Security; Vice-Pres. Inform-Service; Head Tepko-Bank (security service) 1994–98; Head All-Russian Inst., Ministry of Internal Affairs 1998–99; Co-Founder and Co.-Leader Yedinstvo 1999; mem. State Duma 1999–; Chair. Cttee on Security 2000–. *Publications:* Red Mafia; over 150 scientific articles on struggle against original crime. *Address:* State Duma, Okhotny Ryad 1, 103265 Moscow, Russia (office). *Telephone:* (495) 292-89-32 (office). *Fax:* (495) 292-95-75 (office).

GÜRRAGCHAA, Maj.-Gen. Jügderdemidiin; Mongolian politician and army officer; served in Mongolian Armed Forces, rank of Maj.-Gen.; Minister of Defence –2004. *Address:* c/o Ministry of Defence, Government Building 7, Dandaryn Gudamj, Bayanzürkh District, Ulan Bator 61, Mongolia (office).

GURRÍA TREVIÑO, José Ángel, BA, MA; Mexican economist, diplomatist and international organization official; *Secretary-General, Organisation for Economic Co-operation and Development;* b. 8 May 1950, Tampico, Tamaulipas; Dr Lulu Quintana; three c; ed Universidad Nacional Autónoma de México, Univ. of Leeds, UK, Harvard Univ., USA; Perm. Rep. of Mexico to Int. Coffee Org., London 1976–78; held various financial positions in Fed. Electricity Comm., Nat. Devt Bank (Nafinsa), Rural Devt Fund and the Office of the Mayor of Mexico City; position at Finance Ministry 1978–92; Pres. and CEO Bancomext (export-import bank) 1992–93, Nacional Financiera (nat. devt bank) 1993–94; Minister of Foreign Affairs 1994–98, of Finance and Public Credit 1998–2000; Sec.-Gen. OECD 2006–; Chair. mem. External Advisory Group, IDB. *Address:* OECD, 2 rue André Pascal, 75775 Paris Cedex 16, France (office). *Telephone:* 1-45-24-82-00 (office). *Fax:* 1-45-24-85-00 (office). *E-mail:* secretary.general@oecd.org (office). *Website:* www.oecd.org (office).

GURRY, Francis, LLB, LLM, PhD; Australian lawyer and international organization official; *Director General, World Intellectual Property Organization (WIPO);* b. 17 May 1951; m.; three c.; ed Univ. of Melbourne, Gonville and Caius Coll., Cambridge, UK (Tapp Studentship); articled clerk, then attorney-at-law, Arthur Robinson & Co., Melbourne 1974–76; admitted barrister and solicitor, Supreme Court of Vic. 1975; Sr Lecturer in Law, Univ. of Melbourne 1979–84, Professorial Fellow 2001–; Visiting Prof. of Law, Univ. of Dijon, France 1982–83; attorney-at-law, Freehills, Sydney 1984; joined WIPO as consultant in Devt Cooperation and External Relations Bureau for Asia and the Pacific, Geneva, Switzerland 1985, held various posts, including Head of Industrial Property Law Section 1988–90, Special Asst to Dir Gen. and Dir-Counselor in Office of the Dir Gen. 1990–93, Dir WIPO Arbitration and Mediation Center and Acting Legal Counsel 1993–97, Legal Counsel 1997–99, also in charge of WIPO Arbitration and Mediation Center and electronic commerce, Asst Dir Gen. and Legal Counsel 1999–2003, Deputy Dir Gen. 2003–08, Dir Gen. WIPO 2008–; Vice-Pres. Int. Fed. of Commercial Arbitration 1996–2004; mem. Governing Bd Int. School of Geneva 1996–99; mem. Advisory Bd Centre for Intellectual Property and Information Law, Univ. of Cambridge, Intellectual Property Research Inst. of Australia, Univ. of Melbourne, Indian Journal of Intellectual Property, International Review of Industrial Property and Copyright Law, Munich, SCRIPT-ed – A Journal of Law, Technology & Society, Edinburgh; Yorke Prize, Univ. of Cambridge. *Publications:* Breach of Confidence 1984, International Intellectual Property System: Commentary and Materials (with Frederick Abbott and Thomas Cottier) 1999, Intellectual Property in an Integrated World Economy (with Frederick Abbot and Thomas Cottier) 2007; several book chapters and articles in professional journals. *Address:* WIPO, PO Box 18, 34 chemin des Colombettes, 1211 Geneva 20, Switzerland (office). *Telephone:* (22) 338-91-11 (office). *Fax:* (22) 733-54-28 (office). *E-mail:* info@wipo.int (office). *Website:* www.wipo.int (office).

GURSKY, Andreas; German photographer; b. 1955, Leipzig, GDR; s. of Willy Gursky and Rosemarie Gursky; ed Folkwang School, Univ. of Essen, Düsseldorf Acad. of Art; studied under Hilla and Bernd Becher; known for highly textured feel in enormous photographs, often using a high point of view; holds record for contemporary prints with 'Untitled V', which was auctioned for $560,000; lives and works in Düsseldorf; Citybank Photography Prize 1998. *Address:* c/o Regen Projects, 633 North Almont Drive, Los Angeles, CA 90069, USA.

GUSAROV, Yevgeny Petrovich; Russian diplomatist; b. 30 July 1950, Moscow; m.; one s.; ed Moscow State Inst. of Int. Relations; on staff Ministry of Foreign Affairs 1972–; reviewer USSR Gen. Consulate, Montreal 1972–77; attaché, Third, Second Sec. Second European Dept Ministry of Foreign Affairs 1977–81; Second, First Sec., Counsellor USSR Embassy to Canada 1981–86; Head of Sector, Deputy Head Second European Dept 1986–88; Deputy Head Div. (then Dept) of USA and Canada 1988–90, Deputy Head Dept of Security and Co-operation in Europe, USSR Ministry of Foreign Affairs 1990–92; Head Dept of Europe, Russian Ministry of Foreign Affairs 1992; Amb. to Repub. of S Africa (also accred to Lesotho) 1992–98; Dir Dept of All-European Co-operation, Ministry of Foreign Affairs 1998–99; Deputy Foreign Minister 1999–2002. *Address:* c/o Ministry of Foreign Affairs, Smolenskaya-Sennaya 32/34, 119200 Moscow, Russia (office).

GUSENBAUER, Alfred, PhD; Austrian politician; b. 8 Feb. 1960, Sankt Pölten, Lower Austria; ed High School in Wieselburg, Univ. of Vienna; Fed. Leader Sozialdemokratische Partei Österreichs (Social Democratic Party of Austria—SPÖ) Youth Wing, Socialist Youth (SJ) 1984–90, Chair. SPÖ in Ybbs an der Donau and mem. Lower Austria Party Exec. 1991, Chair. SPÖ 2000–08; Vice-Pres. Socialist Youth Int. (IUSY) 1985–89, Socialist Int. 1989; elected Deputy for Lower Austria to Bundesrat 1991, Chair. Cttee for Devt Co-operation 1996–99, Leader of SPÖ Group in Bundesrat 2000–07; Fed. Chancellor 2007–08; Chair. Advisory Bd Signa Holdings 2009–; mem. Austrian del. to parl. meeting of Council of Europe 1991, Chair. Social Cttee of Council of Europe 1995–98; Sr Research Fellow, Econ. Policy Dept, Lower Austria Chamber of Labour 1990–99. *Address:* Social Democratic Party of Austria, Löwelstrasse 18, 1014 Vienna, Austria (office). *Telephone:* (1) 534-27-0 (office). *Fax:* (1) 535-96-83 (office). *E-mail:* Alfred.Gusenbauer@spoe.at (office). *Website:* www.alfred-gusenbauer.at (office); www.spoe.at (office).

GUSEV, Pavel Nikolayevich; Russian journalist; *Editor-in-Chief, Moskovsky Komsomolets;* b. 4 April 1949, Moscow; s. of Nikolai Gusev and Alla Guseva; m. Eugenia Efimova; two d.; ed Moscow Inst. of Geological Survey, Maxim Gorky Inst. of Literature; Komsomol work 1975–; First Sec. Komsomol

Cttee of Krasnaya Presnya Region of Moscow 1975–80; Exec. Cen. Komsomol Cttee 1980–83; Ed.-in-Chief Moskovsky Komsomolets (newspaper) 1983–; Minister, Govt of Moscow, Head of Dept of Information and Mass Media Jan.–Oct. 1992; press adviser to Mayor of Moscow 1992–95; Chair. Comm. for the Politics of Information and Freedom of the Word of the Public Chamber, Public Council of Fed. Agency of Culture and Cinematography 2007–. *Plays:* I Love You, Constance (Moscow Gogol Theatre) 1993, Cardinal's Coat (Maly Theatre) 2002. *Leisure interests:* golf, books, trophy hunting. *Address:* Moskovsky Komsomolets, 1905 Goda str. 7, 123995 Moscow, Russia (office). *Telephone:* (495) 259-50-36 (office). *Fax:* (495) 259-46-39 (office). *E-mail:* letters@mk.ru (office). *Website:* www.mk.ru (office).

GUSEV, Vladimir A., CandArts; Russian arts administrator; *Director, State Russian Museum;* b. 25 April 1945, Kalinin (now Tver); m. Mukhina Xenia Vladimizovna; one d.; ed U.E. Repin Inst. of Painting, Sculpture and Architecture, Leningrad; Exec. Sec. Leningrad br., Russian Fed. Union of Artists 1974–78; Sr Asst, Head of Dept, Deputy Dir for Science, State Russian Museum 1978–88, Dir 1988–; headed reconstruction of Mikhailovsky Castle, Marble Palace and Inzhenerny Castle in St Petersburg; mem. Comm. on State Prizes; Corresp. Mem. Russian Acad. of Fine Arts; Officier, Légion d'honneur 2004; Medal for Valiant Labour 1971, Honoured Cultural Worker of the Russian Fed. 1996, State Award in Literature and Art 2003, Commemorative medal for tricentenary of St Petersburg 2003. *Publications:* more than 60 contribs to various publs in Russian, English, German, French, Italian, Spanish 1986–2005. *Address:* State Russian Museum, Inzhenernaya 4, 191186 St Petersburg (office); Bolshaya Monetnaya Street, app. 9, 197101 St Petersburg, Russia (home). *Telephone:* (812) 595-42-40 (office). *Fax:* (812) 314-41-53 (office). *E-mail:* info@rusmuseum.ru (office). *Website:* www.rusmuseum.ru (office).

GUSINSKII, Vladimir Aleksandrovich; Russian/Spanish banker; b. 6 Oct. 1952, Moscow; m. Yelena Gusinskaya; three s.; ed Moscow Gubkin Inst. of Oil and Chem., A. Lunacharskii State Inst. of Theatrical Art; Dir cultural programme, Moscow Festival of Youth and Students 1982–85; Dir cultural programme, Goodwill Games in Moscow 1985–86; f. co-operative Infex, later transformed into Holding Most, now comprising more than 40 enterprises in the field of construction, construction materials production, real estate and trade operations, also Most-Bank est. 1991; Owner major non-state TV co. NTV, Segodnya (newspaper) 1992, radio station Ekho Moskvy, Obshcheye Delo weekly, weekly TV programme 7 Days, Russian Television International (RTVi); Dir-Gen. Holding Group Most 1989–97, concurrently Pres. Most-Bank 1992–97, Pres. Media-Most co. 1997–2001; Vice Pres. Asscn of Russian Banks, Chair. Council of Authorized Banks of the Govt of Moscow; Pres. Jewish Congress of Russia 1995–2001; arrested in Spain on Russian prosecutor's request for extradition Jan. 2000–01, released after request rejected; took up residence in Israel April 2001; acquired Spanish citizenship Feb. 2007. *Address:* Russian Television International (RTVi), 110 West 40th Street, New York, NY 10018, USA (office). *Telephone:* (212) 944-9899 (office). *E-mail:* info@rtvi.ru (office). *Website:* www.rtvi.ru (office).

GUS'KOVA, Yelena Yuryevna, DHist; Russian historian and political scientist; *Head, Contemporary Studies, Institute of Slavic and Balkan Studies, Russian Academy of Sciences;* b. 23 Sept. 1949, Moscow; m.; two d.; ed Moscow State Univ.; Head Centre of Contemporary Studies, Inst. of Slavic and Balkan Studies, Russian Acad. of Sciences; leading scientific employee INION Russian Acad. of Sciences; mem. Presidium Russian Asscn of Co-operation with the UN; Political and Policy Analyst UN HQ of Peace-keeping Operations in fmr Yugoslavia; mem. Serbian Acad. of Sciences and Arts; Outstanding Scientist of Russia, Njegosha Award (Bosnia & Herzegovina) 1997, 850th Anniversary Medal, Moscow 1997, NATO Medal for peace-making operations in Kosovo 2002. *Publications:* over 340 works on the history of Yugoslavia and recent crises in the Balkans, including History of Yugoslavian Crisis (1990–2000) 2001 (Moscow), 2003 (Belgrade). *Address:* Institute of Slavic and Balkan Studies, Russian Academy of Sciences, 112334 Moscow, Leninsky prosp. 32A, Russia (office). *Telephone:* (495) 938-58-61 (office). *Fax:* (495) 938-00-96 (office); (495) 420-94-20 (home). *E-mail:* centar@guskova.ru (office); eguskova@com2com.ru (home). *Website:* www.inslav.ru (office); www.guskova.ru (home).

GUSMAN, Mikhail Solomonovich; Russian journalist; *First Deputy Director-General, ITAR-TASS Agency;* b. 23 Jan. 1950, Baku, Azerbaijan; m.; one s.; ed Baku Higher CPSU School, Azerbaijan Inst. of Foreign Languages; Deputy Chair. Cttee of Youth Orgs, Azerbaijan 1973–86; Head of Information Dept, then Head of Press Centre, USSR Cttee of Youth Orgs 1986–91; Head of Gen. Admin. of Information Co-operation INFOMOL 1991–95; Vice-Pres. Int. Analytic Press Agency ANKOM-TASS 1995–98; Head of Chief Dept of Int. Co-operation, Public Contacts and Special Projects ITAR-TASS 1998–99, Deputy Dir-Gen., First Deputy Dir-Gen. 1999–; Co-founder World Congress of Russian Press 1999; Exec. Dir World Asscn of Russian Press; Diploma of the USSR Supreme Soviet, numerous medals; Gold Medal for contrib. to devt of TV and radio, Int. Acad. of Radio and Television (Russia) 2007. *Leisure interests:* travelling, reading newspapers. *Address:* ITAR-TASS Agency, Tverskoy Blvd 10-12, 103009 Moscow, Russia (office). *Telephone:* (495) 290-59-89 (office). *E-mail:* info@itar-tass.com (office). *Website:* www.itar-tass.com (office).

GUSMAN, Yuly S.; Russian film administrator, producer and scriptwriter; b. Baku, Azerbaijan; s. of Solomon M. Gusman and Lola Yu. Barsuk; m.; one d.; ed Baku State Medical Inst.; Artistic Dir Baku Theatre of Musical Comedy 1965–72; Dir Central House of Cinematographers; sec. Union of Cinematographers of Russia; mem. bd of dirs State Cttee on Cinematography; mem. Russian Union of Writers, State Duma of Russian Federation; Merited Worker of the Arts. *Address:* Delegatskaya str. 11, apt 10, 103473 Moscow, Russia (home). *Telephone:* (495) 284-31-45 (home).

GUSMÃO, José Alexandre (Xanana); Timor-Leste politician and fmr head of state; *Prime Minister;* b. (José Alexandre Guzmão), 20 June 1946, Laleia, Manatuto; m. 1st Emilia Batista 1969; one s.; m. 2nd Kirsty Sword 2000; ed Nossa Senhora de Fatima seminary, Dare; fmr poet, teacher and chartered surveyor; joined pro-independence Fretilin (Revolutionary Front of the Independence of Timor Leste) 1974, Commdr 1978, now retd; C-in-C FALINTIL (Nat. Liberation Armed Forces of Timor Leste) 1981; arrested by Indonesian troops and sentenced to life imprisonment (later commuted to 20 years) 1992; released August 1999; Pres. Nat. Council of Timorese Resistance 1999–2001; Chair. Timor Leste Nat. Council 2000–01; Pres. of Timor Leste 2002–07; Founder and Pres. Conselho Nacional de Reconstrução do Timor (Nat. Congress for Timorese Reconstruction, CNRT) 2007–; Prime Minister 2007–, also responsible for defence portfolio; Sakharov Prize for Freedom of Expression 1999. *Address:* Office of the Prime Minister, Palácio do Governo, Av. Presidente Nicolau Lobato, Dili, Timor Leste (office). *Telephone:* 7243559 (office). *Fax:* 3339503 (office). *E-mail:* mail@primeministerandcabinet.gov.tp (home). *Website:* www.pm.gov.tp (office).

GUSTAFSON, Kathryn, RLA, ASLA; American architect; *Director, Gustafson Guthrie Nichol Ltd;* b. Yakima, Wash.; ed Univ. of Washington, Seattle, Fashion Inst. of Tech., New York, Ecole Nat. Supérieure du Paysage, Versailles, France; moved to France 1973; environmental artist and landscape designer 1980–; Co-founder Gustafson Guthrie Nichol Ltd, Seattle 2000, currently Dir; Co-founder Gustafson Porter Ltd 1997; Hon. FRIBA; French Acad. of Architecture Medal, Jane Drew Prize, London, Chrysler Design Award. *Architectural works include:* Arthur Ross Terrace, New York, Human Rights Square, Evry, France, American Museum of Natural History, Great Glass House at Nat. Botanic Gardens, Wales, Cultural Park (with Norman Foster), Amsterdam, Garden of Imagination, Terrasson, France, Diana Princess of Wales Memorial Fountain, Hyde Park, London, Civic Center, Seattle, Shell, Esso and L'Oreal HQ, Paris. *Address:* Gustafson Porter, Linton House, 39-51 Highgate Road, London, NW5 1RS, England (office). *Telephone:* (20) 7267-2005 (office). *Fax:* (20) 7485-9203 (office). *E-mail:* enquiries@gustafson-porter.com (office). *Website:* www.gustafson-porter.com (office); www.ggnltd.com (office).

GUSTAFSSON, Lars Erik Einar, DPhil; Swedish writer, philosopher and academic; *Jamail Distinguished Professor Emeritus in the Plan II Program and Adjunct Professor of Germanic Languages and Philosophy, University of Texas;* b. 17 May 1936, Västerås; s. of Einar Gustafsson and Margaretha Carlsson; m. 1st Madeleine Gustafsson 1962; m. 2nd Dena Alexandra Chasnoff 1982; two s. two d.; m. 3rd Agneta Blomqvist 2005; ed Uppsala Univ.; Editor-in-Chief, Bonniers Litterära Magasin 1966–72; Research Fellow, Bielefeld Inst. of Advanced Studies 1980–81; Adjunct Prof., Univ. of Texas 1983–, Jamail Distinguished Prof. in the Plan II Program 1995, now Prof. Emer.; Aby Warburg Foundation Prof., Hamburg 1997; mem. Akad. der Wissenschaften und der Literatur, Mainz, Akad. der Künste, Berlin, Royal Swedish Acad. of Eng, Bayerische Akad. der schönen Künste, Munich; Fellow Berlin Inst. of Advanced Studies 2004–05; Officier des Arts et des Lettres; Kommendör des Bundesverdienstzeichens, Literis et Artibus; Prix Charles Veillon, Heinrich Steffen Preis, Övralidspriset, Bellman Prize of Swedish Acad.; John Simon Guggenheim Memorial Fellow of Poetry 1993. *Television:* 18th Century Pessimism (Swedish TV2), The Philosophers (syndicated). *Plays:* Celebration at Night, Zürich, Frankfurt, Berlin 1979. *Publications:* The Death of a Beekeeper 1978, Language and Lies 1978, Stories of Happy People 1981, Bernard Foy's Third Castle 1986, The Silence of the World before Bach (poems) 1988, Fyra Poeter 1988, Problemformuleringsprivilegiet 1989, Det sällsamma djuret från norr 1989, The Afternoon of a Tiler 1991, Historien med Hunden 1993, The Tail of the Dog 1997, Windy 1999, A Time in Xanadu 2003. *Leisure interests:* painting, boating, tennis. *Address:* University of Texas, Waggener Hall, Room 413, Department of Philosophy, Austin, TX 78712 (office); PMB 317, 3112 Windsor Road, Austin, TX 78703, USA. *Telephone:* (512) 471-5632 (office). *E-mail:* lars.gustafsson@ownit.nu (office); lars.gustafsson@mail.utexas.edu (office). *Website:* www.utexas.edu/cola/depts/philosophy (office); www.utexas.edu/cola/depts/germanic (office).

GUSTAFSSON, Leif Axel, MSc; Swedish business executive; b. 2 Jan. 1940, Hofors; s. of Axel Gustafsson and Brita Brandström; m. Monica Stellan 1965; one s. one d.; ed Royal Inst. of Tech.; operation engineer, rolling mill, Hagfors (Uddeholm) 1966–69; rolling and steel mill man., SKF Steel, Hofors 1969–77; Man. Dir Smedjebacken AB 1978–82; Man. Dir Smedjebacken-Boxholm Stål AB 1982–87; Pres. and CEO SSAB Swedish Steel AB 1987–98, Chair. Bd of Dirs 1998–2003 (retd); mem. Bd of Dirs Sapa AB –2005. *Leisure interests:* hunting, sports. *Address:* c/o SSAB, Box 7280, 103 89 Stockholm, Sweden (office).

GUSTOV, Vadim Anatolyevich; Russian politician; *Representative of Vladimir Region, Federation Council;* b. 26 Dec. 1948, Kalinino, Vladimir Region; m.; two c.; ed Moscow State Inst. of Geological Prospecting, Leningrad Inst. of Politology; Head of uranium mines, Navoi Metallurgy Factory, Uzbekistan 1971–77; Head of mine, Phosphorite Kingisepp, Leningrad Region 1977–78; instructor, Head of Div., Kingisepp City CP Cttee 1978–86; First Deputy Chair. Kingisepp City Exec. Cttee 1986–87; Second Sec. Kingisepp City CP Cttee 1987–90; Chair. Kingisepp City Soviet 1990–91; Chair. Soviet of People's Deputies Leningrad Region 1991–93; mem. Council of Feds of Russia, Chair. Cttee on CIS Cos 1993–98; Gov. Leningrad Region 1996–98; First Deputy Chair., Govt of Russian Fed. 1998–99; Rep. of Vladimir Region to Federation Council 2001–; Chair. Cttee on CIS 2001–; Order of Honour 1998. *Publications:* Russia-CIS: The Path of Integration is Thorny but Tempting (co-author) 2002, Russia-CIS: Co-operation for Development and Progress 2007.

Leisure interests: hunting, fiction, sports. *Address:* Federation Council, ul B. Dmitrovka 26, 103426 Moscow, Russia (office). *Telephone:* (495) 203-90-74 (office); (495) 692-07-18 (office). *Fax:* (495) 203-46-17 (office). *E-mail:* post_sf@gov.ru (office). *Website:* www.council.gov.ru (office).

GUT, Rainer Emil; Swiss banker and business executive; b. 24 Sept. 1932, Baar; s. of Emil Anton and Rosa (Müller) Gut; m. Josephine Lorenz 1957; two s. two d.; ed Cantonal School of Zug; professional training in Switzerland, France and England; Gen. Pnr Lazard Frères & Co., NY 1968–71; Chair. and CEO, Swiss American Corpn (Credit Suisse's US investment banking affiliate) 1971–73; mem. Exec. Bd Credit Suisse, Zürich 1973–77, Speaker of Exec. Bd 1977–82, Pres. Exec. Bd 1982–83, Chair. 1983–2000, Chair. Credit Suisse Group (fmrly CS Holding) 1986–2000, Chair. Credit Suisse First Boston, New York 1988–97, Chair. Credit Suisse First Boston Zürich 1997–2000, Hon. Chair. Credit Suisse Group 2000–; Chair. Nestlé SA 2000–05 (retd); Chair. and Del. Uprona (Canada) Ltd, Toronto 2000–; Vice-Pres. Gesparal, Paris 2000–; mem. Bd of Dirs L'Oréal, Paris, Pechiney SA, Paris, Sofina SA, Brussels. *Address:* c/o Nestlé SA, Avenue Nestlé 55, 1800 Vevey, Switzerland (office).

GUTERRES, António Manuel de Oliveira; Portuguese politician and UN official; *High Commissioner, United Nations High Commissioner for Refugees;* b. 30 April 1949, Lisbon; m. (wife died 1998); one s. one d.; ed Inst. Superior Técnico; trained as electrical engineer; joined Socialist Party 1974; Chief of Staff to Sec. of State for Industry 1974–75; fmr asst to several cabinet ministers; Pres. Municipal Ass. of Fundão 1979–95; Deputy to Ass. of the Repub. 1976–83, 1985–, Pres. several parl. comms, Pres. Socialist Parl. Group 1988–91; Strategic Devt Dir IPE (State Investment and Participation Agency) 1984–85; mem. Council of State 1991–; Leader of Socialist Party 1992–; Vice-Pres. Socialist Int. 1992–99, Pres. 1999–; Prime Minister of Portugal 1995–2001; High Commr, UN High Comm. for Refugees 2005–; Coordinator Tech. Electoral Comm. 1980–87; Founder and Vice-Pres. Portuguese Asscn for the Defence of the Consumer 1973–74; mem. Asscn for Econ. and Social Devt 1970–96. *Publications:* various books and articles for newspapers and magazines. *Leisure interests:* travel, history (especially Middle Ages), cinema, opera. *Address:* United Nations High Commissioner for Refugees, CP 2500, 1211 Geneva 2 dépôt, Switzerland (office). *Telephone:* (22) 7398254 (office). *Fax:* (22) 7397346 (office). *Website:* www.unhcr.ch (office).

GUTERRES, Jose Luis; Timor-Leste politician and diplomatist; m.; two c.; ed Univ. of Cambridge, UK, Univ. of the Western Cape, S Africa, Malaysia Inst. of Diplomacy and Foreign Relations, Inst. of Strategic and Int. Studies, Portugal; Founding mem. Frente Revolucionária do Timor Leste Independente (FRETILIN—Revolutionary Front for an Independent East Timor), mem. FRETILIN external del. 1974–, Rep. to Angola, also Perm. Rep. to Mozambique and FRETILIN Rep. to UN; Vice-Minister for Foreign Affairs and Co-operation 2002–03, Head of Timor-Leste del., Council of Ministers meeting, Comunidade dos Países de Língua Portuguesa, Brazil and ACP/EU meeting, Dominican Repub. July 2002, Timor-Leste Rep. to Sustainable Devt Summit, S Africa Aug. 2002; Amb. to USA and Perm. Rep. to UN, New York 2003–06; Minister of Foreign Affairs and Co-operation 2006–07. *Address:* c/o Frente Revolucionária do Timor Leste Independente (FRETILIN) (Revolutionary Front for an Independent East Timor), Rua dos Mártires da Pátria, Dili, Timor-Leste (office). *Telephone:* 3321409 (office).

GUTERSON, David, BA, MFA; American author; b. 4 May 1956, Seattle; s. of Murray Guterson and Shirley (née Zak) Guterson; m. Robin Ann Radwick 1979; three s. one d.; ed Univ. of Washington, Brown Univ.; high school English teacher, Bainbridge Island, Washington 1984–94; contrib. sports journalism for Sports Illustrated and Harper's, fmr Contributing Ed. Harper's. *Publications:* The Country Ahead of Us, The Country Behind (short stories) 1989, Family Matters: Why Home Schooling Makes Sense 1992, Snow Falling on Cedars (PEN/Faulkner Award for Ficition, Barnes & Noble Discovery Award, Pacific NW Booksellers Award 1995) 1994, East of the Mountains 1998, Our Lady of the Forest 2003, The Other 2008. *Address:* Georges Borchardt Inc., 136 East 57th Street, New York, NY 10020, USA (office). *E-mail:* georges@gbagency.com (office).

GUTFREUND, Herbert, PhD, FRS; British academic; *Professor Emeritus of Physical Biochemistry, University of Bristol;* b. 21 Oct. 1921, Vienna, Austria; s. of Paul Gutfreund and Clara Gutfreund; m. Mary Kathleen Davies 1958; two s. one d.; ed Univs of Vienna, Austria and Cambridge, UK; Research Fellow, Univ. of Cambridge 1947–57; with Agricultural Research Council, Univ. of Reading 1957–64; Visiting Prof., Univ. of Calif. 1965, Max Planck Inst., Germany 1966, Dir Molecular Enzymology Lab. and Prof. of Physical Biochemistry, Univ. of Bristol 1967–86, Prof. Emer. 1986–; part-time Scholar in Residence, NIH, Bethesda, USA 1986–89; Scientific mem. (external) Max Planck Inst. for Medical Research 1987–; Fogarty Scholar, NIH, Washington, DC 1987–89. *Publications:* An Introduction to the Study of Enzymes 1966, Enzymes: Physical Principles 1972, Molecular Evolution 1981, Biothermodynamics 1983, Kinetics for the Life Sciences: Receptors, Transmitters and Catalysts 1995. *Leisure interests:* hill walking, reading, cooking. *Address:* Somerset House, Upton, Oxon., OX11 9JL, England (home). *Telephone:* (1235) 851468 (home). *E-mail:* h.gutfreund@bristol.ac.uk (home).

GUTH, Alan Harvey, PhD; American physicist and academic; *Victor F. Weisskopf Professor of Physics, Massachusetts Institute of Technology;* b. 27 Feb. 1947, New Brunswick, NJ; s. of Hyman Guth and Elaine Cheiten; m. Susan Tisch 1971; one s. one d.; ed Mass. Inst. of Tech.; Instructor Princeton Univ. 1971–74; Research Assoc. Columbia Univ. New York 1974–77, Cornell Univ. 1977–79, Stanford Linear Accelerator Center, Calif. 1979–80; Assoc. Prof. of Physics, MIT 1980–86, Prof. 1986–89, Jerrold Zacharias Prof. of Physics 1989–91; Victor F. Weisskopf Prof. of Physics 1992–; Physicist, Harvard-Smithsonian Center for Astrophysics 1984–89, Visiting Scientist 1990–91; Alfred P. Sloan Fellow 1981; Fellow, American Physics Soc. (Chair. Astrophysics Div. 1989–90), AAAS, American Acad. of Arts and Sciences; mem. NAS, American Astronomical Soc.; Rennie Taylor Award of the American Tentative Soc. 1991, Julius E. Lilienfeld Prize of the American Physical Soc. 1992; Benjamin Franklin Medal for Physics, Franklin Institute 2001, Cosmology Prize, Peter Gruber Foundation 2004. *Address:* Center for Theoretical Physics, Room 6-209, Massachusetts Institute of Technology, 77 Massachussets Ave, Cambridge, MA 02139-4307, USA (office). *Telephone:* (617) 253-6265 (office). *E-mail:* guth@ctp.mit.edu (office). *Website:* web.mit.edu/physics/facultyandstaff/faculty/alan_guth.html (office).

GUTHRIE, Michelle L., BA, BLL; Australian business executive; *Managing Director, Providence Equity Partners LLC;* ed Univ. of Sydney; fmr lawyer, Allen, Allen and Hemsley, Sydney and Singapore; joined News Corpn 1994, becoming Gen. Counsel, BSkyB and News International, London, later Dir of Legal and Business Affairs, FOXTEL, Sydney; joined Star TV 2000, Sr Vice-Pres. Business Devt 2001–03, Exec. Vice-Pres. Regional Distribution and Business Devt June–Nov. 2003, CEO Nov. 2003–07; Man. Dir Providence Equity Partners LLC, Hong Kong 2007–; fmr mem. Bd of Dirs Phoenix Satellite Television, Hathway, China Network Systems, Balaji Telefilms Ltd. (STAR joint venture cos); fmr mem. Council of Govs Cable and Satellite Broadcasting Asscn of Asia; named Young Global Leader by the World Econ. Forum 2005, Veuve Clicquot Business Woman of the Year Award 2005. *Address:* Providence Equity Partners LLC, York House, 15 Queens Road, 18th Floor, Central Hong Kong Special Administrative Region, People's Republic of China (office). *Telephone:* 36533800 (office). *Fax:* 36533900 (office). *Website:* www.provequity.com (office).

GUTHRIE, Roderick (Rod) I. L., BSc (Eng), ARSM, PhD, DIC, FRSC, FCAE, FCIM; British/Canadian metallurgist, engineer and academic; *Macdonald Professor and Director, McGill Metals Processing Centre, McGill University;* b. Sutton Coldfield, England; s. of Lawrence Carr Guthrie and Norah Smith; ed Royal School of Mines, Imperial Coll., Univ. of London; currently Macdonald Prof. of Metallurgy, Dept of Mining, Metals and Materials Eng and Dir McGill Metals Processing Centre, McGill Univ., Montreal, Canada; Fellow, Canadian Inst. of Mining; research consultant to steel and aluminium industries; Distinguished Mem. Iron and Steel Soc., Asscn for Iron and Steel Technologies; 24 Best Paper Awards, Queen's Golden Jubilee Medal 2002, 77th Howe Memorial Lecturer, Iron and Steel Soc., John Elliott Distinguished Lecturer, Iron and Steel Soc. 2003–04, Killam Prize for Eng in Canada 2006. *Publications:* books: Engineering in Process Metallurgy, The Physical Properties of Liquid Metals, The Science and Practice of Steelmaking, and Steel Processing; more than 200 patents on topics ranging from metal delivery systems for high speed strip casting processes, to improved aerodynamics for batch annealing furnaces and in-situ detection of inclusions in liquid aluminium, steel and magnesium; more than 450 scientific papers in professional journals. *Leisure interests:* long distance kayaking, running. *Address:* McGill Metals Processing Centre, 3610 University Street, M.H. Wong Building, 2M040, Montreal, PQ H3A 2B2, Canada (office). *Telephone:* (514) 398-1555 (office); (514) 398-5556 (office). *Fax:* (514) 398-4168 (office). *E-mail:* rod@mmpc.mcgill.ca (office). *Website:* www.mmpc.mcgill.ca (office).

GUTHRIE, Roy David (Gus), AM, DSc; Australian consultant and fmr vice-chancellor; *Director, Gus Guthrie Consulting;* b. 29 March 1934, England; s. of David Ephraim Guthrie and Ethel (née Kimmins) Guthrie; m. 2nd Lyn Fielding 1982; three s. from first m.; ed King's Coll., London; Research Officer, Shirley Inst. 1958–60; Asst Lecturer then Lecturer, Univ. of Leicester 1963–73; Lecturer then Reader, Univ. of Sussex 1963–73; Foundation Prof., Griffith Univ., Australia 1973–81, Pro-Vice-Chancellor 1980–81, Prof. Emer. 1981; Vice-Chancellor Univ. of Tech., Sydney 1986–96; Provost Insearch Educ. 1996–97; Dir, Gus Guthrie Consulting Pty Ltd 1996–; Sec.-Gen. Royal Soc. of Chem. 1982–85; Chair. Queensland Innovation Council 1999–2002, Buderim Foundation 2003–05; Pres. Coastal Caring Clowns 2001–; mem. Council Univ. of the Sunshine Coast 1999–2005; Centenary Medal. *Publications:* Introduction to Carbohydrate Chemistry (with J. Honeyman); more than 130 research papers in learned chemical journals. *Leisure interests:* theatre, croquet, tai chi, caring clowning. *Address:* PO Box 369, Buderim, Queensland 4556, Australia.

GUTHRIE OF CRAIGIEBANK, Baron (Life Peer), cr. 2001, of Craigiebank in the City of Dundee; **Charles (Ronald Llewelyn) Guthrie,** GCB, LVO, OBE; British army officer and business executive; b. 17 Nov. 1938, London; s. of the late Ronald Guthrie and Nina Llewelyn; m. Catherine Worrall 1971; two s.; ed Harrow School and Royal Mil. Acad. Sandhurst; commissioned Welsh Guards 1959; served in BAOR, Aden; 22 Special Air Service (SAS) Regt 1965–69; Staff Coll. 1972; Mil. Asst (GSO2) to Chief of Gen. Staff, Ministry of Defence 1973–74; Brigade Maj., Household Div. 1976–77; CO, 1st Bn Welsh Guards, Berlin and NI 1977–80; Col, Gen. Staff, Mil. Operations, Ministry of Defence 1980–82; Commdr British Forces, New Hebrides 1980; 4th Armoured Brigade 1982–84; Chief of Staff 1st (British) Corps 1984–86; Gen. Officer Commdg NE Dist and Commdr 2nd Infantry Div. 1986–87; Asst Chief of Gen. Staff, Ministry of Defence 1987–89; Commdr 1st (British) Corps 1989–91; Commdr Northern Army Group 1992–93 and C-in-C BAOR 1992–94; Col Commdt, Intelligence Corps 1986–96; ADC Gen. to HM the Queen 1993–, Gold Stick to HM the Queen 1999–; Chief of Gen. Staff 1994–97, of the Defence Staff 1997–2001; Special Envoy to Pakistan 2001; Dir (non-exec.) N. M. Rothschild & Sons 2001–; Col of the Life Guards 1999–; Col Commdt, SAS 1999–2002; Pres. Army Benevolent Fund, Action Research, London Fed. of Youth Clubs; Freeman, City of London; Kt, Sovereign Mil. Order of Malta 1999; Commdr, Legion of Merit (USA) 2001. *Publication:* Just War: The Just War Tradition:

Ethics in Modern Warfare (co-author) 2007. *Leisure interests:* tennis, opera, travel. *Address:* PO Box 25439, London, SW1P 1AG, England.

GUTIERREZ, Carl T. C.; American politician and computer executive; b. 15 Oct. 1941, Agana Heights, Guam; s. of the late Tomas Taitano Gutierrez and of Rita Benavente Cruz; m. Geraldine Chance Torres; one s. two d.; ed S. San Francisco High School; service with USAF; est. first data processing centre in Guam; f. Carltom Enterprises 1971; Propr Carltom Consulting; elected Senator 1972, Speaker of Legislature; Gov. of Guam 1994–98, 1998–2003, indicted on allegations that he abused his power Dec. 2003, charges dismissed April 2004, indicted again over alleged use of Govt funds and personnel May 2004, acquited July 2004; Pres. Asscn of Pacific Island Legislatures; Chair. Guam Tax Code Comm., Cttee on Ways and Means; Vice-Chair. Cttee on Rules, Cttee on Tourism and Transportation; f. People Helping People 1994; Hon. Citizen (Belau); Hon. DHumLitt (World Acad. of Art and Sciences). *Leisure interests:* tennis, fishing, hunting. *Address:* c/o PO Box 2950, Agana, GU 96932-2950, USA.

GUTIERREZ, Carlos M.; American (b. Cuban) business executive and fmr government official; b. 4 Nov. 1953, Havana, Cuba; m.; three c.; ed Monterrey Inst. of Tech.; joined Kellogg de Mexico as sales rep. 1975, supervisor, Latin America marketing services Kellogg HQ Mich., USA 1982–83, Man. int. marketing services 1983–84, Gen. Man. Kellogg de Mexico 1984–89, Pres. and CEO Kellogg Canada Inc. 1989–90, Corp. Vice-Pres. product devt at Kellogg HQ 1990, Vice-Pres. Kellogg Co. and Exec. Vice-Pres. sales and marketing Kellogg USA 1990–93, Exec. Vice-Pres. Kellogg USA and Gen. Man. Kellogg USA Cereal Div. 1993–94, Exec. Vice-Pres. Kellogg Co. and Pres. Kellogg Asia-Pacific 1994–96, Exec. Vice-Pres. business devt 1996–98, Pres. and COO 1998–99, elected to Bd of Dirs Jan. 1999, apptd CEO April 1999, Chair. 2000–04; US Sec. of Commerce, Washington, DC 2004–09. *Address:* c/o Department of Commerce, 14th Street and Constitution Avenue, NW, Washington, DC 20230-0001, USA.

GUTIÉRREZ, Gustavo, DTheol, OP; Peruvian ecclesiastic and academic; *John Cardinal O'Hara Professor of Theology, Department of Theology, University of Notre Dame;* b. 8 June 1928, Lima; ed Univ. Nacional Mayor de San Marcos, Lima, Univ. Catholique de Louvain, Univ. de Lyon, Univ. Gregoriana and Inst. Catholique de Paris; ordained priest 1959; Adviser, Nat. Union of Catholic Students 1960; Prof. Catholic Univ. of Lima 1960; mem. Pastoral-Theological team, Latin American Conf. of Catholic Bishops (CELAM) 1967–68; currently John Cardinal O'Hara Prof. of Theology, Univ. of Notre Dame, USA; mem. Bd of Dirs Inst. Bartolomé Las Casas-Rímac 1974–; Assoc. Vicar, Rímac, Lima 1980–; fmr Prin. Prof. Pontifical Univ. of Peru; Visiting Prof. and lecturer at univs, colls and seminaries in USA and elsewhere; mem. EATWOT (Ecumenical Asscn of Third World Theologians); Dr hc (Nijmegen) 1979, (Tübingen) 1985, (King's Coll., USA) 1989, (Haverford Coll., USA) 1990, (Fribourg, Germany) 1990, (San Marcos, Lima) 1991, (Montreal) 1993, (Universidad Nacional de Ingeniería, Peru) 1993, (State of NY) 1994, (Holy Cross, MA) 1994, (San Agustín Peru) 1995, (Catholic Theol. Union USA) 1995, (St Norbert Coll., USA) 1996, (St Michael, Canada) 1996, (Simón Bolívar, Peru) 1997, (Freiburg, Suiza) 1998, (Southern Methodist, USA) 2000, (Brown, USA) 2000. *Publications:* A Theology of Liberation 1971, The Power of the Poor in History 1980, We Drink from Our Own Wells: the Spiritual Journey of a People 1983, On Job, God-talk and the Suffering of the Innocent 1986, La Verdad los hará libres 1986, Dios o el Oro en las Indias 1989, El Dios de la Vida 1989, Entre las Calandrias 1990, En Busca de los Pobres de Jesucristo 1992, Compartir la Palabra 1995, Essential Writings (with Nikoloff) 1996, Densidad del Presente 1996. *Leisure interests:* swimming, literature. *Address:* University of Notre Dame, Department of Theology, 331 Malloy Hall, Notre Dame, IN 46556, USA (office); Instituto Bartolomé Las Casas-Rímac, Apartado 3090, Lima 100, Peru. *Telephone:* (574) 631-5366 (office). *Website:* www.nd.edu/~theo (office).

GUTIERREZ BORBÚA, Lucio Edwin; Ecuadorean politician and fmr head of state; *Leader, Partido Sociedad Patriótica 21 de Enero (PSP);* b. 1957; m.; fmr pentathelete; fmr col in army; staged Indian uprising against Pres. Jamil Mahuad 2000, sentenced to six months in a mil. prison; Pres. of Ecuador 2003–05 (resgnd); Leader Partido Sociedad Patriótica 21 de Enero (PSP). *Address:* Partido Sociedad Patriótica 21 de Enero (PSP), Quito, Ecuador (office). *Website:* www.sociedadpatriotica.com (office).

GUTIÉRREZ GIRÓN, Edgar Armando; Guatemalan politician; b. 27 July 1960, Guatemala City; m. María Elena Aiza Meade de Gutiérrez; two s. three d.; political and econ. analyst in Guatemala and Central America 1982–; consultant for various int. agencies in Europe and USA; Co-Founder Asscn for the Advancement of the Social Sciences 1987, Coordinadora de ONG y Cooperativas 1992, Myrna Mack Foundation 1993; Co-ordinator-Gen. Interdiocesan Project 'Recuperación de la Memoria Histórica' 1995–98; Jt Ed. Periódico de Guatemala 1999; Sec. of Strategic Analysis 2000–02; Minister of Foreign Affairs 2002–04. *Publications include:* Centroamérica en el vórtice de la crisis 1986, Modelos heterogéneos en Centroamérica 1987, Guatemala: política exterior y estabilidad del Estado 1988, ¿Quién quiso asaltar el cielo? 1998, Sociedad civil y derechos humanos en la difícil transición guatemalteca 1998, Hacia un paradigma democrático del sistema de inteligencia en Guatemala 1999; poetry: Para conjurar su hechizo 1990, Al final de esta luna 1992, Memoria de la Muerte 1997.

GUTIÉRREZ IRIARTE, Waldo M.; Bolivian government official; public servant; fmr Deputy Minister of the Treasury; Minister of Finance 2005–06. *Address:* c/o Ministry of Finance, Edif. Palacio de Comunicaciones, Avenida Mariscal Santa Cruz, La Paz, Bolivia (office).

GUTIONTOV, Pavel Semenovich; Russian journalist; b. 23 Jan. 1953; ed Moscow State Univ.; mem. of staff Moskovski Komsomolets 1970–75; fmr

corresp. Komsomolskaya Pravda, then Head of Div. 1975–85; special corresp. Sovetskaya Rossiya 1985–87; political observer Izvestia; Co-Chair. Liberal Journalists Club –1997; Chair. Cttee for Defence of Freedom of Speech and Journalists' Rights; Sec. Russian Journalists' Union; winner of numerous professional prizes. *Publications:* Games in the Fresh Air of Stagnation 1990, Fate of Drummers 1997 and numerous articles. *Address:* Russian Journalists' Union, Zubovsky blvd 4, 119021 Moscow, Russia (office). *Telephone:* (495) 201-23-95 (office).

GUTMAN, Lt-Gen. Albin; Slovenian military officer; *Chief of General Staff;* b. 17 Dec. 1947, Novo Mesto; m.; one s. one d.; ed Univ. of Ljubljana; previous posts include Territorial-Defence Municipal Staff, Novo Mesto, Defence Secr., Novo Mesto, Territorial-Defence Regional Staff, Dolenjska, Ministry of Defence; Chief of Armed Forces Gen. Staff 1993–98, 2007–; Chief Defence Insp. 1998–2003; mil. adviser to Minister of Defence 2003–06; Silver Order of Freedom of Repub. of Slovenia, Order of Gen. Maister with Swords, Légion d'honneur; Manoeuvre Structure of Nat. Defence (MSNZ) Badge 1990, Defended Slovenia Badge, Slovenian Armed Forces Gold Medal, Slovenian Armed Forces Gold Plaque. *Address:* Ministry of Defence, 1000 Ljubljana, Vojkova 55, Slovenia (office). *Telephone:* (1) 4712211 (office). *Fax:* (1) 4712978 (office). *E-mail:* info@mors.si (office). *Website:* www.mors.si (office).

GUTMAN, Natalia Grigorievna; Russian cellist; b. 14 Nov. 1942; m. Oleg Kagan (deceased); three c.; ed Gnessin Music School, Moscow (under R. Shposhnikov), Moscow Conservatory (under Prof. Kozolupova and Mstislav Rostropovich); tours include: visits to Europe, USA and Japan, appearing with the Berlin Philharmonic Orchestra, Vienna Philharmonic Orchestra, London Symphony Orchestra, Orchestre Nat. de France and Orchestre de Paris; played chamber music in USSR and Europe with Eliso Virsaladze and Oleg Kagan 1982–; played sonatas, trios and quartets with Sviatoslav Richter; plays sonata and concerto written for her by Alfred Schnittke; solo tours include USA with USSR State Symphony Orchestra and Yevgeny Svetlanov, Italy with BBC Symphony and Yuri Temirkanov, USSR with Sir John Pritchard; performed with Royal Philharmonic Orchestra under Yuri Temirkanov, Royal Festival Hall, London, Concertgebouw, London Philharmonic, Munich Philharmonic, Berlin Philharmonic, Orchestre Nat. de France, LA Philharmonic under André Previn, Chicago Symphony under Claudio Abbado 1988–89; teacher at Moscow Conservatory 1967–77; Prof., Stuttgart Conservatory 1997–; f. Oleg Kagan Memorial Festival, Krems, Moscow; prizes at the Vienna Student Festival Competition, the Tchaikovsky Competition, the Munich Chamber Music Competition and the Dvořák Competition, Prague. *Address:* Künstleragentur Augstein & Hahn, Tal 28, 80331 Munich, Germany (office). *Telephone:* (89) 26024333 (office). *Fax:* (89) 26024344 (office). *E-mail:* mail@augstein.info (office). *Website:* www.augstein.info (office).

GUTMANN, Amy, BA, MSc, PhD; American academic and university president; *President, University of Pennsylvania;* m. Michael W. Doyle; one d.; ed Harvard-Radcliffe Coll., London School of Econs, UK, Harvard Univ.; Asst Prof. of Politics, Princeton Univ. 1976–81, Assoc. Prof. 1981–86, Dir of Grad. Studies 1986–88, Prof. 1987–2004, Andrew W. Mellon Professorship 1987–90, Laurance S. Rockefeller Prof. of Politics 1990–2004, Founding Dir Univ. Center for Human Values 1990–95, Dean of Faculty 1995–97, Academic Adviser to Pres. 1997–98, Provost 2001–04; Pres. Univ. of Pennsylvana and Prof. of Political Science, School of Arts and Sciences and Annenberg School for Communication 2004–; Visitor, Inst. for Advanced Study, Princeton 1981–82; Visiting Rockefeller Faculty Fellow, Center for Philosophy and Public Policy, Univ. of Maryland 1984–85; Visiting Prof., John F. Kennedy School of Govt, Harvard Univ. 1988–89; Pres. American Soc. for Political and Legal Philosophy 2001–04; mem. Bd of Dirs Salzburg Seminar 1987–90, Center for Policy Research in Educ. 1987–95, Exec. Cttee Asscn of Practical and Professional Ethics 1990–, Princeton Univ. Press 1996–, Center for Advanced Study in the Behavioural Sciences, Stanford Univ. 1998–, Academic Advisory Bd Inst. for Human Sciences, Vienna 2001–, Advisory Bd Annenburg Public Policy Center Student Voices Project 2000–05, Bd of Govs Partnership for Public Service 2004–; Ed. Univ. Center for Human Values Series, Princeton Univ. Press 1992–; mem. Editorial Bd Teachers' College Record 1990–95, Cambridge Studies in Philosophy and Public Policy 1991–, Raritan 1995–, Journal of Political Philosophy 1995–, Handbook of Political Theory 1999–, Annual Reviews 2001–05; mem. Int. Advisory Bd Ethnicities 2000–; Chair. Bd of Trustees Whig-Cliosophic Soc. 1985–88; Fellow, American Acad. of Arts and Sciences 1997–, Nat. Acad. of Educ. 1997–; W.E.B. Du Bois Fellow, American Acad. of Political and Social Science 2001–; Hon. DIur (Kalamazoo Coll.) 1992; Nat. Endowment for the Humanities Summer Fellowship 1977, American Council of Learned Socs Fellowship 1978–79, Bicentennial Preceptorship, Princeton 1979–82, N American Soc. for Social Philosophy Book Award 1996–97, American Asscn of Univ. Profs Betram Mott Award 1998, Kenneth Robinson Fellowship, Univ. of Hong Kong 1998–99, Spencer Foundation Sr Scholar Award 1999, Princeton Univ. Distinguished Teaching Award 2000, Harvard Univ. Centennial Award 2003. *Publications:* Democracy and the Welfare State (ed.) 1988, Freedom of Association (ed.) 1998, Ethics and Politics: Cases and Comments (co-author) 1984, Liberal Equality 1980, Democratic Education 1987, Multiculturalism and the Politics of Recognition (ed.) 1992, Democracy and Disagreement (co-author) 1996, Color Conscious: The Political Morality of Race (N American Soc. for Social Philosophy Book Award 1996–97, Gustavus Myers Center for the Study of Human Rights in N American Award 1997, Ralph J. Bunche Award, American Political Science Asscn 1997) 1996, A Matter of Interpretation: Federal Courts and the Law (ed.) 1997, Work and Welfare (ed.) 1998, The Lives of Animals (ed.) 1999, Goodness and Advice (ed.) 2001, Identity in Democracy 2003, Why Deliberative Democracy? 2004; numerous chapters in books and articles in professional journals. *Address:* Office of the President, University of Pennsylvania, 100 College Hall, Philadelphia, PA 19104-6380, USA (office).

Telephone: (215) 898-7221 (office). *Fax:* (215) 898-9659 (office). *E-mail:* presweb@pobox.upenn.edu (office). *Website:* www.upenn.edu/president (office).

GUTMANN, Francis Louis Alphonse Myrtil; French diplomatist; *President of Scientific Council for Defence, Ministry of Defence;* b. 4 Oct. 1930, Paris; s. of Robert Gutmann and Denise (née Coulom) Gutmann; m. Chantal de Gaulle 1964; two s. one d.; ed Lycée Pasteur, Neuilly-sur-Seine; Head of Dept, Ministry of Foreign Affairs 1951–57; Asst Head Office of Sec. of State for Econ. Affairs 1955, mem. French Del. to Econ. and Social Council and to UN Gen. Ass. 1952–55, to Common Market Conf., Brussels 1956–57; Adviser Pechiney Co. 1957–59, Sec.-Gen. 1963, Dir 1970–71; Sec.-Gen. Fria 1960–62; mem. Governing Bd Pechiney-Ugine-Kuhlmann group 1962–78, Pres.-Dir-Gen. Ugine-Kuhlmann 1971–76, in charge of social affairs 1975–78; Pres. Alucam 1968–72; Pres. Frialco and Vice-Pres. Friguia 1977–81; Dir-Gen. French Red Cross 1980–81; Sec.-Gen. Ministry for External Relations 1981–85; Admin. representing the State, Paribas 1982–84, Gaz de France 1984–85, St Gobain 1982–85; Amb. to Spain 1985–88; Pres. Admin. Council Gaz de France 1988–93, Hon. Pres. 1993–; Pres. Fondation Méditerranéenne d'Etudes Stratégiques 1989–2000, Assoc. Eurogas-Union 1990–94, (Admin. Council) Institut Français du Pétrole (IFP) 1993–96; Vice-Pres. Mémoire et espoirs de la Résistance 1994–2000; attached to Ministry of Foreign Affairs 1996–; Pres. Scientific Council for Defence, Ministry of Defence 1998–; Dir French Red Cross 1992–2000; Officier, Légion d'honneur; Commdr, Ordre nat. du Mérite; Grand croix de l'ordre du Merité (Spain); numerous foreign awards. *Publications:* Les chemins de l'effort 1975, Le nouveau décor international 1994. *Address:* c/o Institut Français du Pétrole, 1–4 ave. de Bois-Préau, BP 311, 92506 Rueil-Malmaison Cedex, France (office). *Telephone:* 1-47-52-68-84 (office). *Fax:* 1-47-52-67-54 (office).

GUTZWILLER, Peter Max, LLM, DrIur; Swiss lawyer; *Partner, Lenz & Staehelin;* b. 30 April 1941, Basle; s. of Max and Helly Gutzwiller; m. 1st Vreny Lüscher 1971 (divorced); one s.; m. 2nd Barbara Menzel; ed Univs of Basle and Geneva and Harvard Law School, USA; Assoc., Staehelin Hafter & Pnrs (now Lenz & Staehelin) 1970–76, Pnr 1977–; mem. Bd of Int. Law Asscn (Swiss Br.) 1975–; Sec. Swiss Asscn of Int. Law 1976; Maj., Swiss Army 1979. *Publications:* Swiss International Divorce Law 1968, Von Ziel und Methode des IPR 1968, Arbeitsbewilligungen für Ausländer 1975, 1976, Grundriss des schweizerischen Privat- und Steuerrechtes (co-author) 1976. *Leisure interests:* art collection (cartoons), music, travel. *Address:* Lenz & Staehelin, Bleicherweg 58, 8027 Zurich (home); Sonnenrain 15, 8700 Küsnacht, Switzerland (home). *Telephone:* 2041212 (office). *Fax:* 2041200 (office). *E-mail:* peter-max .gutzwiller@lenzstaehelin.com (office). *Website:* www.lenzstaehelin.com (office).

GUZY, Carol; American photographer; b. 7 March 1956, Bethlehem, Pa; m. Jonathan Utz; ed Northampton Co. Area Community Coll., Art Inst. of Fort Lauderdale; attended nursing school; intern then staff photographer Miami Herald 1980–88; staff photograher, The Washington Post 1988–; notable assignments include coverage of volcanic eruption in Colombia, fall of communism, nomads in Mali, Rwandan exodus, famine in Ethiopia, civil war in Somalia, daily life in Haiti, and plight of Kosovo refugees; Pulitzer Prize 1986, 1995, 2000, Photographer of the Year (Nat. Press Photographers Asscn) 1990, 1993, 1997, Robert F. Kennedy Memorial Prize 1997, eight White House Press Photographers Asscn's Photographer of the Year, Leica Medal of Excellence, Overseas Press Club Citation of Excellence and numerous other awards. *Address:* c/o Discovery Galleries, 4840 Bethesda Avenue, Bethesda, MD 20814; The Washington Post, 1150 15th Street, NW, Washington, DC 20071-0002, USA. *Website:* www.washingtonpost.com/wp-dyn/photo/ bestofthepost/guzycarol.

GUZZANTI, Corrado; Italian actor, director, writer and satirist; b. 17 May 1965, Rome; s. of journalist and Senator Paolo Guzzanti; brother of Sabina and Caterina Guzzanti; began career as writer for his sister Sabina; debut as actor in roles for himself in Avanzi, hosted by Serena Dandini; collaborated with her in TV shows, including Tunnel, Maddecheaò, Pippo Chennedy Show and L'ottavo nano; famous for his satirical imitations of Italian politicians and personalities; also cr. several characters, including the Quelo (comical version of a New Age guru) and the poet Brunello Robertetti (satire of a typical Italian alleged intellectual); debut as film dir with Fascisti su Marte 2006. *Films include:* I Cammelli (The Camels) (voice) 1988, Prima le donne e i bambini 1992, DeGenerazione 1994, Und1c1/8ttavi (also writer and dir) 2000, Fascisti su Marte (Fascists on Mars) (also writer, dir and producer) 2006. *Television includes:* Scusate l'interruzione (series) 1990, Avanzi 1992 (series) 1991. *E-mail:* info@corradoguzzanti.it (office). *Website:* www.corradoguzzanti.it (office).

GVOZDENOVIĆ, Branomir; Montenegrin politician; *Minister of Economic Development;* b. 1961, Bar; ed Univ. of Montenegro, Podgorica; Programmer, Republican Information Cttee 1986–89; Adviser for Devt of Information System, Republican Secr. for Devt 1989–90; Sr Adviser for Informatics 1990–91, Asst Dir 1991–95, Republican Devt Bureau; Asst Sec., Secr. for Devt 1995–99; Dir, Post of Montenegro Ltd 1999–2002; acting Minister of Maritime Affairs 2002; Deputy Prime Minister for Economic Policy and Devt 2002–06; Minister of the Economic Devt 2006–; Pres. of Bar Municipality 2002–03; mem. Democratic Socialist Party of Montenegro. *Address:* Ministry of Economic Development, 81000 Podgorica, Rimski trg 46, Montenegro (office). *Telephone:* (81) 234156 (office). *Fax:* (81) 234131 (office). *Website:* www .minekon.vlada.cg.yu (office).

GWATHMEY, Charles, MArch; American architect; b. 19 June 1938, Charlotte, NC; s. of Robert Gwathmey and Rosalie Dean Hook; m. Bette A. Damson 1974; ed Music and Art High School, New York, Univ. of Pennsylvania School of Arch. and Yale Univ. School of Arch; William Wirt Winchester Travelling Fellowship 1962; Fulbright Fellow in France 1962–63; pvt. practice in New York 1964–66; partner, Gwathmey-Henderson, New York 1966–70, Gwathmey-Henderson-Siegel 1970–71; partner, with Robert Siegel, Gwathmey Siegel & Assocs New York 1971–; Prof. of Architectural Design, Pratt Inst. Brooklyn, New York 1964–66, Yale Univ. 1966, Princeton Univ. 1966–69, 1975–76, Harvard Univ. 1970–72, Cooper Union, New York 1971–72, Univ. of Calif. at LA 1973–74, Columbia Univ. 1976–77; Eliot Noyes Prof. of Architecture Harvard Univ. 1985; works include single houses, housing projects, school and coll. bldgs, libraries, offices, public bldgs, interiors etc. throughout USA and addition to Solomon Guggenheim Museum, New York 1995; mem. American Acad., American Inst. of Arts and Letters; Fellow, American Inst. of Architects; numerous awards and distinctions including Distinguished Architecture Award 1982, 1984, Medal of Honor 1983, Nat. Honor Award 1968, 1976, 1984 and Nat. Firm Award, American Inst. of Architects 1982. *Address:* Gwathmey, Siegel and Associates, Architects, 3rd Floor, 475 Tenth Avenue, New York, NY 10018-1198 (office); 1115 5th Ave, New York, NY 10128, USA.

GWYNN-JONES, Peter Llewellyn, CVO, MA, FSA; British public official; *Garter Principal King of Arms;* b. 12 March 1940; s. of the late Maj. Jack Llewellyn Gwynn-Jones and Mary Muriel Daphne Harrison and step-s. of the late Lt-Col Gavin David Young; ed Wellington Coll., Trinity Coll. Cambridge; Asst to Garter King of Arms 1970; Bluemantle Pursuivant of Arms 1973; House Comptroller Coll. of Arms 1982; Lancaster Herald of Arms 1982–95; Garter Prin. King of Arms 1995–; Genealogist, Order of the Bath, Order of St John; Insp. of Regimental Colours, of RAF Badges; Sec. Harleian Soc. 1981–94; Hon. Genealogist, Order of St Michael and St George; KStJ. *Publications:* Heraldry 1993, The Art of Heraldry 1998. *Leisure interests:* tropical forests, wildlife conservation, fishing. *Address:* The College of Arms, Queen Victoria Street, London, EC4V 4BT (office); 79 Harcourt Terrace, London, SW10 9JP, England (home). *Telephone:* (20) 7248-1188 (office). *Fax:* (20) 7248-6448 (office). *E-mail:* garter@college-of-arms.gov.uk (office). *Website:* www.college-of-arms.gov.uk (office).

GYAMTSHO, Lyonpo Thinley, BA; Bhutanese politician; b. 1952; ed Trashigang High School, St Joseph's Coll., India, Wellington Univ., NZ; Jt Dir Dept of Educ. 1985, Dir Dept of Nat. Budget and Accounts 1986, Dir of Educ. 1987–1990, Dir Gen. 1990–94, Sec. 1994–96; Sec. Royal Civil Service Comm. 1996–98, Deputy Minister 1998; Minister of Home Affairs 1998–2003, of Educ. 2003–08; Red Scarf 1991, Orange Scarf 1998, Coronation Medal 1999. *Address:* c/o Education Division, Ministry of Health and Education, Tashichhodzong, PO Box 726, Thimphu, Bhutan. *Telephone:* 325146. *Fax:* 324823. *E-mail:* lyonpo_tg@hotmail.com. *Website:* www.education.gov.bt.

GYANENDRA BIR BIKRAM SHAH DEV, BA; b. 7 July 1974, Kathmandu; s. of the late King Mahendra Bir Bikram Shah and the late Crown Princess Indra Rajya Laxmi Devi Shah; brother of the late King Birendra Bir Bikram Shah Dev; m. Komal Rajya Laxmi Devi Shah 1970; one s. one d.; ed St Joseph's Coll., Darjeeling, India, Tribhuvan Univ. Kathmandu; King of Nepal 2001–08; Supreme Commdr Royal Nepalese Army –2006; made state visits to India 2002, China 2002; official visits to India 1976, Democratic People's Repub. of Korea 1978, Repub. of Korea 1987; other visits to India, Pakistan, China, Bhutan, Thailand, Myanmar, Singapore, USA, USSR, UK, The Netherlands, Denmark, Germany, France, Italy, Switzerland, Saudi Arabia, Turkey, Yugoslavia, Romania, Hungary, Bulgaria, Czechoslovakia, Australia, New Zealand, Belgium, Spain, UAE, Austria, Canada, Iran; Chair. (currently Patron) Lumbini Devt Trust 1986–1991, King Mahendra Trust for Nature Conservation 1982–2001; Founding mem. 1001–Nature Trust 1986; Patron, Pushupati Area Devt Trust; Chancellor Tribhuvan Univ. and Mahendra Sanskrit Univ.; special interest in conservation and preservation of natural and man-made heritage; declared state of emergency, took over as Chair. of Council of Ministers Feb. 2005, relinquished power April 2006, stripped of most constitutional powers 2006, monarchy abolished May 2008; Hon. mem. Worlwide Fund for Nature; Grand Cross of the House Order of Orange (Netherlands) 1967, Kt Grand Cordon of the Most Exalted Order of the White Elephant (Thailand) 1979, Grand Cross Ordre nat. du Mérite 1983, Kt Grand Cross of the Most Distinguished Order of St Michael and St George 1986, Grand Cross of Order of Isabel la Católica (Spain) 1987, His Holy Majesty, King of the Lands of the Nepalese People and Kt of the Holy and Most Majestic Order of the Rose of Jordan, Sovereign of all Orders of the Kingdom of Nepal. *Leisure interests:* nature, reading, writing poetry.

GYELTSHEN, Dasho Rinzin; Bhutanese civil servant (retd); Chair. Royal Advisory Council (Zhung Kalyon) 1998–2008 (retd). *Address:* c/o Royal Advisory Council, Tashicho Dzong, Thimphu, Bhutan. *Telephone:* 322816. *E-mail:* rinzingyaltshen@hotmail.com.

GYIBUG, Puncog Cedain; Chinese politician; b. 1930, Tibet; Vice-Chair. of People's Govt of Tibet Autonomous Region 1983–; Deputy for Tibet to 7th NPC 1988. *Address:* People's Government of Tibet Autonomous Region, Lhasa, People's Republic of China.

GYLL, John Sören; Swedish business executive; *Chairman, Gyttorp Cartridge Company;* b. 26 Dec. 1940, Skorped; s. of Josef Gyll and Gertrud Gyll; m. Lilly Margareta Hellman 1974; two s. one d.; Marketing Dir and Vice-Pres. Rank Xerox 1963–77; Pres. Uddeholms Sweden AB 1977–79, Exec. Vice-Pres. Uddeholms AB 1979–81, Pres. and CEO 1981–84; Pres. and CEO Procordia AB 1984–92; Pres. and CEO AB Volvo 1992–97, also Dir; fmr Chair. Bd of Dirs. Pharmacia and Upjohn Inc.; currently Chair. Gyttorp Cartridge Co.; mem. Bd of Dirs. Svenska Cellulosa AB 1997–, Fenix Outdoor, SKF, Skanska, Topeja Holding, Scandinavian Touch, Medicover Holding; mem. Bd of Dirs. Junior Achievement and Young Entreprise Europe –2004; mem. European Advisory

Bd, Schroder Salomon Smith Barney 2001; fmr Pres. Confederation of Swedish Enterprise; mem. Royal Acad. of Eng Sciences. *Leisure interests:* hunting, skiing. *Address:* Gyttorp Cartridge Company, Staffan Schullström, Malmgatan 1, 713 00 Nora, Sweden (office). *Telephone:* (58) 71-00-40 (office). *Fax:* (58) 71-32-51 (office). *Website:* www.gyttorp.com (office).

GYLLENHAAL, Jake; American actor; b. 19 Dec. 1980, Los Angeles; s. of Stephen Gyllenhaal and Naomi Foner Gyllenhaal; brother of Maggie Gyllenhaal. *Films include:* City Slickers 1991, A Dangerous Woman 1993, Josh and S.A.M 1993, Homegrown 1998, October Sky 1999, Donnie Darko 2001, Bubble Boy 2001, Lovely and Amazing 2001, The Good Girl 2002, Highway 2002, Moonlight Mile 2002, The Day After Tomorrow 2004, The Man Who Walked Between the Towers 2005, Brokeback Mountain (BAFTA Award for Best Actor in a Supporting Role 2006) 2005, Proof 2004, Jarhead 2005, Zodiac 2007, Rendition 2007. *Plays:* This Is Our Youth (New York and London) (Evening Standard Award). *Address:* Creative Artists Agency, 9830 Wilshire Blvd, Beverly Hills, CA, USA (office). *Telephone:* (310) 288-4545 (office). *Fax:* (310) 288-4800 (office). *Website:* www.caa.com (office); www.jakegyllenhaal .com (office).

GYLLENHAAL, Maggie, BA; American actress; b. 16 Nov. 1977, New York City; d. of Stephen Gyllenhaal and Naomi Foner Gyllenhaal; sister of Jake Gyllenhaal; m. Peter Sarsgaard 2009; ed Columbia Univ., Royal Acad. of Dramatic Arts, London. *Films include:* Waterland 1992, A Dangerous Woman 1993, Homegrown 1998, The Photographer 2000, Cecil B. DeMented 2000, Donnie Darko 2001, Riding in Cars with Boys 2001, Secretary 2002, 40 Days and 40 Nights 2002, Adaptation 2002, Confessions of a Dangerous Mind 2002, Casa de los babys 2003, Mona Lisa Smile 2003, The Pornographer: A Love Story 2004, Criminal 2004, Happy Endings 2005, The Great New Wonderful 2005, Trust the Man 2005, SherryBaby 2006, Paris, je t'aime 2006, Monster House 2006, World Trade Center 2006, Stranger Than Fiction 2006, High Falls 2007, The Dark Knight 2008. *Television includes:* Shattered Mind 1996, Patron Saint of Liars 1998, Resurrection 1999, Shake, Rattle and Roll: An American Love Story 1999, Strip Search 2004. *Address:* c/o 200 Park Avenue South, 8th Floor, New York, NY 10003; c/o Creative Artists Agency, Inc., 9830 Wilshire Blvd., Beverly Hills, CA 90212-1825, USA. *Telephone:* (310) 288-4545. *Fax:* (310) 288-4800. *Website:* www.caa.com.

GYLLENHAMMAR, Pehr Gustaf, BLL; Swedish business executive; *Chairman, Investment AB Kinnevik;* b. 28 April 1935, Gothenburg; s. of Pehr Gustaf Victor Gyllenhammar and Aina Dagny Kaplan; m. Eva Christina Engellau 1959; one s. three d.; ed Univ. of Lund, studied int. law in England, vocational studies in maritime law, USA, Cen. d'Etudes Industrielles, Geneva; employed by Mannheimer & Zetterlöf (solicitors), Gothenburg 1959, Haight, Gardner, Poor & Havens (Admiralty lawyers), New York 1960, Amphion Insurance Co., Gothenburg 1961-64; Asst Admin. Man. Skandia Insurance Co., Stockholm 1965-66, Vice-Pres. Corporate Planning 1966-68, Exec. Vice-Pres. 1968, Pres. and CEO 1970; joined AB Volvo, Gothenburg 1970, Man. Dir and CEO 1971-83, Chair. of Bd and CEO 1983-90, Exec. Chair. Bd of Dirs 1990-93; Chair. Bd MC European Capital SA 1994-96; Chair. Bd of Dirs Swedish Ships' Mortage Bank 1976-, Procordia AB 1990-92; Sr Adviser Lazard Frères & Co. 1996-99, Man. Dir 2000-03; Chair. Cofinec NV 1996-2000, CGU PLC 1998- (Chair. CGNU 2000- after merger of CGU PLC and Norwich Union PLC, co. changed name to Aviva 2000); Vice-Chair. Europe NM Rothschild 2003-; Chair. Investment AB Kinnevik (formed by merger of Industriförvaltnings AB Kinnevik and Invik & Co. AB) 2004-; mem. Bd of Dirs, Skandinaviska Enskilda Banken 1979-94, United Technologies Corpn 1981-99, Kissinger Assocs, Inc. 1982-97, Pearson PLC 1983-97, Reuters Holdings PLC 1984-97, Philips Electronics NV 1990-96, Renault SA 1990-93 and numerous other cos and orgs; Trustee Reuters Founders Share Co. Ltd 1997- (Chair. 2000-); mem. Royal Swedish Acad. of Eng Sciences 1974; Officer (1st Class) Royal Order of Vasa 1973, Commdr Order of the Lion of Finland 1977, Commdr Ordre nat. du Mérite 1980, King's Medal (12th Size) with ribbon of Order of the Seraphim 1981, Commdr St Olav's Order 1984, Commdr Order of the Lion of Finland (1st Class) 1986, Commdr Légion d'honneur 1987, Kt Grand Officer, Order of Merit (Italy) 1987, Commdr Order of Leopold 1989; Hon. DrMed (Gothenburg Univ.) 1981; Hon. DTech (Brunel) 1987; Hon. DEng (Nova Scotia) 1988, Hon. DScS (Helsinki) 1990, Hon. LLD (Vermont) 1993; Golden Award, City of Gothenburg 1981. *Publications:* Mot sekelskiftet på måfå (Towards the Turn of the Century at Random) 1970, Jag tror på Sverige (I Believe in Sweden) 1973, People at Work 1977, En industripolitik för människan (Industrial Policy for Human Beings) 1979, Fortsättning följer...

(To Be Continued...). *Leisure interests:* tennis, sailing, skiing, riding. *Address:* Aviva plc, St Helen's 1, Undershaft, London, EC3P 3DQ, England (office). *Telephone:* (20) 7662-2926 (office). *Fax:* (20) 7283-0067 (office).

GYLYS, Povilas, DSc (Econ); Lithuanian politician; b. 14 Feb. 1948, Didžiokai, Molėtai Region; m. Nijole Rezaitė 1969; two s.; ed Molėtai Secondary School and Vilnius Univ.; Lecturer, later Prof. of Econs 1969-92; Head, Dept of Int. Econ. Relations, Vilnius Univ. 1992, currently Chair. Dept of Econ. Theory; mem. Parl. (Seimas) 1992-2000, mem. Lithuanian Democratic Labour Party Parl. Group 1996-2000, Cttee on Foreign Affairs 1998-2000, Comm. on Econ. Crimes Investigation 1999-2000, Seimas Del. to Parl. Ass. of Council of Europe 1999-2000); Minister of Foreign Affairs 1992-97. *Address:* Department of Economic Theory, Economics Faculty, Vilnius University, Sauletekio 9, 10222 Vilnius, Lithuania (office). *Telephone:* (5) 236-6147 (office). *E-mail:* povilas.gylys@ef.vu.lt (office); pogyly@lrs.lt. *Website:* www.ef.vu.lt (office).

GYMNASTIAR, Abdullah, (Aa Gym); Indonesian religious speaker and business executive; *Director, MQCorp;* b. 1962, Bandung; fmr student military leader; began career selling newspapers, and driving minibus; f. Daarut Tauhiid ('Home of the One God') movt 1990; Dir MQCorp; business interests include 15 media cos.; frequent TV appearances as Islamic preacher. *Publications include:* 32 books. *Address:* c/o MQ Media, Kompleks Pesantren Daarut Tauhiid, Jl. Gegerkalong Girang, Bangdung, 40154, Indonesia (office). *Telephone:* 22 2008844 (office). *Fax:* 22 2014543 (office). *E-mail:* info@ mqmedia.com (office). *Website:* www.mqmedia.com (office).

GYOHTEN, Toyoo; Japanese economist; *President, Institute for International Monetary Affairs;* b. 1931, Yokohama; m.; one s. one d.; ed Univ. of Tokyo, Princeton Univ., USA; joined Ministry of Finance 1955; Japan Desk, Asian Dept IMF 1964-66; Special Asst to Pres. of Asian Devt Bank, Manila, Philippines 1966-69; Dir-Gen. Int. Finance Bureau 1984-86, Vice-Minister of Finance for Int. Affairs 1986-89; Visiting Prof., Business School, Harvard Univ., USA 1990, Woodrow Wilson School, Princeton Univ. 1990-91, Univ. of St Gallen, Switzerland 1991; joined Bank of Tokyo Ltd (merged with Mitsubishi Bank Ltd 1996) 1991, Chair. Bd 1992-96, Sr Adviser The Bank of Tokyo-Mitsubishi Ltd 1996-; Pres. Inst. for Int. Monetary Affairs 1995-; Chair. Working Party III, OECD, Paris 1988-90, Inst. of Int. Finance Inc., USA 1994-97; mem. Bd of Trustees, Princeton in Asia, USA 1989-, Advisory Panel, E African Devt Bank, Kampala, Uganda 1990-, Asia Pacific Advisory Cttee, New York Stock Exchange 1990-, Int. Council, The Asia Soc., New York 1991-, Exec. Cttee of Trilateral Comm., New York, Paris and Tokyo 1991-, Group of Thirty, Washington, DC 1992-, Council of Inst. Aspen France, Banking Advisory Group of IFC, Washington, DC 1992-; Founding mem. Int. Advisory Bd of Council on Foreign Relations, New York 1995-; Fulbright Scholar 1956-58. *Publication:* Changing Fortunes (with Paul Volcker) 1992. *Address:* 3-2, Nihombashi Hongokucho 1-chome, Chuo-ku, Tokyo 103-0021, Japan.

GYSI, Gregor; German politician and lawyer; b. 16 Jan. 1948, Berlin; s. of the late Klaus Gysi; m. 1st (divorced); two s.; m. 2nd; one d.; defence lawyer; elected Leader CP 1989, name changed to PDS, now Parl. Leader; mem. Bundestag 1990-2002; Deputy Mayor of Berlin and Senator for Econs, Labour and Women's Issues 2002. *Publications:* Das Waris: Noch Lange Nicht (biog. notes) 1999, Ein Blick Züruck: Ein Schritt Nachvorn 2001. *Address:* c/o Senate Department for Economics, Labour and Women's Issues, 10820 Berlin, Germany (office).

GYURCSÁNY, Ferenc; Hungarian business executive and politician; b. 4 June 1961, Pápa; m. 2nd Klára Dobrev; three s. one d.; ed Faculty of Economy, Janus Pannonius Univ. of Sciences, Pécs; Sec. Pécs City Cttee, Communist Youth Alliance (KISZ) 1984-88, Pres. Univ. and Coll. Council, Cen. Cttee 1988-89, Vice-Pres. Democratic Youth Alliance (DEMISZ) 1989; Consultant, CREDITUM Financial Consultant Ltd 1990-92; Dir EUROCORP Int. Financial Inc. 1992; CEO ALTUS Investment and Assets Man. Inc. 1992-2002, Chair. 2002-03; Sr Adviser to Prime Minister Medgyessy 2002-03; mem. Nat. Exec. Cttee Hungarian Socialist Party (MSZP) 2003-, Chair. Győr-Moson-Sopron Co. Org. Feb.-Sept. 2004; Minister of Children, Youth and Sports 2003-04 (resgnd); Prime Minister of Hungary 2004-09 (resgnd). *Publication:* Útközben (On the Way; political essay) 2005. *Leisure interests:* running, skiing. *Address:* c/o Hungarian Socialist Party, 1081 Budapest, Köztársaság tér 26, Hungary (office).

H

HAACKE, Hans Christoph Carl, MFA; German artist and professor of art; *Professor Emeritus of Art, Cooper Union for the Advancement of Science and Art;* b. 12 Aug. 1936, Cologne; s. of Dr Carl Haacke and Antonie Haacke; m. Linda Snyder 1965; two s.; ed State Art Acad., Kassel; Asst Prof., Cooper Union for the Advancement of Science and Art, New York 1971–75, Assoc. Prof. 1975–79, Prof. 1979–2002, Prof. Emer. 2002–; Guest Prof., Hochschule für Bildende Künste, Hamburg 1973, 1994, Gesamthochschule, Essen 1979; Hon. DFA (Oberlin Coll.) 1991, (San Francisco Art Inst.) 2008; Dr hc (Bauhaus-Universität, Weimar) 1998; numerous awards including Golden Lion, Venice Biennale 1993. *Works include:* perm. sculptural installation in Reichstag Bldg (German Parl.), Berlin 2000, Denkzeichen Rosa Luxemburg, Berlin 2006. *Publications:* solo exhbn catalogues: Werkmonographie (with Edward F. Fry) 1972, Framing and Being Framed (co-author) 1975, *Nach* allen Regeln der Kunst 1984, Unfinished Business (co-author) 1987, Artfairismes 1989, Bodenlos (co-author) 1993,Obra Social (co–author) 1995, AnsichtsSachen/Viewing Matters 1999, Mia san mia (co-author) 2001, Hans Haacke (monograph, co-author) 2004, Hans Haacke – For Real, Works 1959–2006 2006; Libre-Echange (with Pierre Bourdieu) 1994; numerous articles and interviews in int. art magazines. *Address:* Cooper Union for the Advancement of Science and Art, Cooper Square, New York, NY 10003, USA (office). *Telephone:* (212) 353-4200 (office). *Website:* www.cooper.edu (office).

HAAG, Rudolf, Dr rer. nat; German physicist; *Professor Emeritus in Theoretical Physics, Hamburg University;* b. 17 Aug. 1922, Tubingen; s. of Albert Haag and Anna Haag (née Schaich); m. 1st Kaethe Fues 1948 (died 1991); three s. one d.; m. 2nd Barbara Klie 1992; ed Tech. Univ., Stuttgart and Univ. of Munich; Prof. of Physics, Univ. of Illinois, USA 1960–66; Prof. of Theoretical Physics, Hamburg Univ. 1966–87, Prof. Emer. 1987–; Dr hc (Aix-Marseille) 1979; Max-Planck-Medal 1970, Henri Poincaré Prize 1997. *Publications:* Local Quantum Physics 1992; over 100 articles on fundamental physical theory. *Address:* Waldschmidtstrasse 4B, 83727 Schliersee Neuhaus, Germany (home). *Telephone:* 80267444 (home).

HAAK, Willem E. (Pim), LLM; Dutch fmr chief justice; *President, Court of Appeals for the Central Commission for the Navigation of the Rhine;* b. 19 April 1934, Haarlem; s. of Willem Adriaan Haak and Elisabeth Willemina H. ten Hooven; m. Cornelia Jacoba van Heek 1968; two s.; ed Univ. of Amsterdam; worked as advocate in Amsterdam until 1972; Dist Court Judge 1972–76; Justice, Amsterdam Court of Appeal 1976–79; Advocate Gen. to the Supreme Court 1979–81, Justice, Supreme Court 1981–92, Deputy Pres. 1992–99, Chief Justice 1999–2004; Appointing Authority of the Iran-US Claims Tribunal 2004–; Chair. Advisory Bd Foundation of the Old Church Amsterdam 2004–; Pres. Court of Appeals for the Gen. Comm. for the Navigation of the Rhine, Strasbourg 2004–; mem. Advisory Bd Resolution Group (Effective Negotiation and Dispute Resolution), The Hague 2005–; fmr Sec. Asscn of Dutch Lawyers; fmr Deputy Chair. Int. Law Inst.; fmr Pres. Appeals Tribunal, Dutch Inst. of Psychologists; fmr mem. Insurance Cos Supervisory Bd; fmr Pres. Bd Frits Lugt art collection; fmr Deputy Chair. Supervisory Bd, Institut Néerlandais, Paris; mem. Advisory Cttee on Endowed Chairs, Univ. of Amsterdam; mem. Perm. Appeals Tribunal of the Gen. Meeting of the Remonstrant Church; Kt, Order of the Dutch Lion, Commdr, Order Oranje-Nassau, Officier, Légion d'honneur. *Publications:* several articles and monographs on pvt. int. law, transport law, comparative law and criminal law. *Leisure interest:* mountain hiking. *Address:* Joh. Vermeerstraat 75, 1071 DN Amsterdam, The Netherlands (home). *Telephone:* (20) 6796935 (home). *Fax:* (20) 6701821 (home). *E-mail:* pimhaak@xs4all.nl (home).

HAAKON, HRH Crown Prince (Haakon Magnus), BSc; Norwegian; b. 20 July 1973; s. of HM King Harald V and HM Queen Sonja; m. Mette-Marit Tjessem Høiby 2001; one d. one s. one step-s.; ed Kristelig Gymnasium, Officers' Cand. School/Navy, Horten, Royal Norwegian Naval Acad., Bergen, Univ. of California at Berkeley, USA, LSE, UK; second-in-command, missile torpedo boat 1995–96; numerous official functions. *Leisure interests:* skiing, cycling, paragliding, sailing, theatre. *Address:* Royal Palace, 0010 Oslo, Norway (home). *Telephone:* (47) 2204-8700 (home). *Fax:* (47) 2204-8790 (home). *Website:* www.kongehuset.no (office).

HAAKONSEN, Bent, LLB; Danish diplomatist (retd); b. 10 Jan. 1936; m. Kirsten Haakonsen; one d.; joined Ministry of Foreign Affairs 1961; served Bonn 1964–67, Perm. Rep. to EEC, Brussels 1972–74; Amb. to Czechoslovakia 1978–79; Head, Danish del. to CSCE, Madrid 1980–81; Under-Sec. for Trade Relations 1983–86; Perm. Under-Sec. of State 1986–91; Perm. Rep. to UN, New York 1991–95; Amb. to Germany 1995–2001, to Sweden 2001–04; Pres. Franz Schubert Soc., Denmark. *Address:* Provstevænget 10, 4000 Roskilde, Denmark (home).

HAAN, Pieter de, MA; Dutch academic; *Professor Emeritus of Land Law and Administrative Law, Delft University of Technology and Free University of Amsterdam;* b. 4 Nov. 1927, Augustinusga; s. of Aan de Haan and Klaaske de Beer; m. F.A. Zijlstra 1956; two c.; ed Univ. of Groningen; Asst Sec. Landbouwschap, The Hague 1956; Scientific Asst Univ. of Agriculture Wageningen 1956–61; Prof. of Land Law, Delft Univ. of Tech. 1961–88, Prof. Emer. 1988–; Prof. of Admin. Law and Land Law, Free Univ. Amsterdam 1974–88, Prof. Emer. 1988–; Pres. Inst. of Construction Law 1972–97, Scientific Council Inst. of Agrarian Law 1993–2003, Visiting Cttee Faculties of Law 1990–91; mem. Advisory Council for Physical Planning 1976–90, Royal Netherlands Acad. of Sciences 1979–; Dr hc (Amsterdam) 1990. *Publications:* Land Law (10 vols) 1969, 1973, 1983, 1984, 1988, 1992, 1996, 2000, 2001, 2004; Administrative Law (10 vols) 1978, 1981, 1986, 1996, 1998, 2000, 2001, 2002. *Leisure interests:* travelling, gardening, fishing. *Address:* Berkelaan 1, 9203 LM, Drachten, Netherlands (home). *Telephone:* (512) 510376 (home).

HAARDE, Geir H., MA; Icelandic politician and economist; b. 8 April 1951; m. Inga Jona Thordardottir; five c.; ed Brandeis Univ., Johns Hopkins Univ., Univ. of Minnesota, USA; teaching Asst Univ. of Minn. 1976–77; economist Int. Dept, Cen. Bank of Iceland 1977–83; lecturer Econs Dept, Univ. of Iceland 1979–83; Special Asst to Minister of Finance 1983–87; mem. Althing (Parl.) 1987–; mem. Foreign Affairs Cttee 1991–98, Chair. 1995–98; Minister of Finance 1998–2005; Minister of Foreign Affairs 2005–06; Prime Minister 2006–09 (resgnd); Chair. Youth Org. of Independence Party 1981–85, Chair. Parl. Group 1991–98, Vice-Chair. 1999–; Pres. Icelandic Group Inter-Parl. Union 1988–98, mem. Exec. Cttee 1994–98, Vice-Pres. 1995–97; mem. Control Cttee Nordic Investment Bank 1991–95; mem. Presidium Nordic Council 1991–98, Pres. 1995, Chair. Conservative Party Group 1995–97; Chair. Standing Cttee of Parliamentarians of Arctic Region 1995–98. *Address:* Independence Party, Háaleitisbraut 1, 105 Reykjavík, Iceland (office). *Telephone:* 5151700 (office). *Fax:* 5151717 (office). *E-mail:* xd@xd.is (office). *Website:* www.xd.is (office).

HAAS, Peter E., MBA; American business executive; b. 20 Dec. 1918, San Francisco; s. of Walter A. Haas and Elise Stern; m. 1st Josephine Baum 1945; m. 2nd Miriam (Mimi) Lurie 1981; two s. one d.; ed Deerfield Acad., Univ. of Calif. and Harvard Univ.; joined Levi Strauss & Co., San Francisco 1945, Exec. Vice-Pres. 1958–70, Pres. 1970–81, CEO 1976–81, Chair. 1981–89, now Chair. Emer., Chair. Exec. Cttee 1989–2004, mem. Bd of Dirs 1948–2004, remains mem. of voting trust; Dir AT&T 1966, now Dir Emer.; fmr Pres. Jewish Welfare Fed.; f. Miriam and Peter Haas Fund. *Address:* c/o Levi Strauss & Co., 1155 Battery Street, San Francisco, CA 94111, USA.

HAAS, Richard John, BS, MFA; American artist; b. 29 Aug. 1936, Spring Green, Wis.; s. of Joseph F. Haas and Marie N. Haas; m. 1st Cynthia Dickman 1963 (divorced 1970); m. 2nd Katherine Sokolnikoff 1980; one s.; ed Univ. of Wisconsin-Milwaukee and Univ. of Minnesota; Instructor of Art, Univ. of Minn. 1963–64; Asst Prof. of Art, Mich. State Univ. 1964–68; Instructor in Printmaking, Bennington Coll. 1968–80, Fine Arts Faculty, School of Visual Arts 1977–81; mem. New York City Art Comm. 1976–79; mem. Bd Public Art Fund 1980–84, NY State Preservation League 1983–90; Gov. Skowhegan School of Painting and Sculpture 1980–; mem. Bd of Trustees, Hudson River Museum 1989–; Vice-Pres. Nat. Acad. of Design, New York, Dir Abbey Mural Fund; participant in numerous group exhbns 1962–; more than 120 commissioned outdoor and indoor murals, including New York Public Library Periodical Room, Nashville Public Library, Nashville, Tenn., Bank One Ballpark Stadium, Phoenix, Ariz., US Courthouse and Fed. Centers in Beckley, W Va and Kansas City, KS 1975–; Jury Chair, Int. Trompe L'oeil Festival, Lodi, Italy 2005; Guggenheim Fellowship 1983; Fellowship, Macdowell Colony 2003; AIA Medal of Honor 1977, Municipal Art Soc. Award 1977, Nat. Endowment for the Arts Fellowship 1978, Doris C. Freedman Award 1989, Individual Artist Award, Westchester Arts Council 2003, Yonkers Friends of the Arts Public Art Honoree 2003, Jimmy Ernst Award, American Acad. of Arts and Letters 2005. *Publications:* Richard Haas: An Architecture of Illusion 1981, Richard Haas: The City Is My Canvas 2001, The Prints of Richard Haas: 1970–2004 2005. *Leisure interests:* tennis, film. *Address:* David Findlay Jr Gallery, 41 East 57th Street, #1120, New York, NY 10022, USA (office); 361 West 36th Street, New York, NY 10018, USA (office). *Telephone:* (212) 486-7660 (office); (212) 947-9868 (office). *Website:* www.davidfindlayjr.com (office); www.richardhaas.com (office); www.artnet.com (office). *Fax:* (212) 947-7785 (office). *E-mail:* haasnyc@aol.com (office).

HAAS, Robert Douglas, MBA; American business executive; *Chairman, Levi Strauss & Company;* b. 3 April 1942, San Francisco; s. of the late Walter Haas and of Evelyn Danzig; m. Colleen Gershon 1974; one d.; ed Univ. of Calif., Berkeley and Harvard Univ.; with Peace Corps, Ivory Coast 1964–66; with Levi Strauss & Co., San Francisco 1973–, Sr Vice-Pres. (Corp. Planning and Policy) 1978–80, Pres. New Business Group 1980, Pres. Operating Groups 1980–81, Exec. Vice-Pres. and COO 1981–84, Pres. and CEO 1984–89, CEO and Chair. Bd 1989–99, Chair. Bd of Dirs 1989–; Hon. Dir San Francisco AIDS Foundation; Trustee Ford Foundation; mem. Bd of Dirs Levi Strauss Foundation. *Address:* Levi Strauss & Co., 1155 Battery Street, San Francisco, CA 94111, USA (office). *Telephone:* (415) 501-6000 (office). *Fax:* (415) 501-7112 (office). *Website:* www.levistrauss.com (office).

HAASIS, Heinrich; German banking executive and politician; *President, Deutscher Sparkassen- und Giroverband (German Savings Banks and Giro Association);* b. 21 April 1945, Balingen-Streichen (Baden-Wurttemberg); m.; two c.; ed Balingen Gymnasium, Albstadt-Ebingen Commercial Coll.; Mayor of Bisingen Dist 1971–81; mem. State Parl. (Landtag) for Zollernalb Dist 1976–2001, also Chair. Christian Democratic Union (CDU) Parl. Group and Head CDU Regional Party Group for Baden-Württemberg; mem. State Senate (Zollernalb Dist) 1981–91; Pres. Baden-Württemberg Asscn of Savings Banks 1991–, German Savings Banks and Giro Asscn, Berlin 2006–; Chair. Supervisory Bd Landesbank Baden-Württemberg (LBBW) –2008; Pres. European Savings Bank Group 2006–; Chair. DekaBank 2006–; Chair. Supervisory Bd Deutsche Sparkassen Leasing AG Man. 2006–, Supervisory Bd Foundation Schloss Neuhardenberg GmbH 2006–, Supervisory Bd Landesbank Berlin Holding AG 2007–; Chair. Bd of Trustees Savings Bank Foundation for Int. Cooperation Asscn 2006–; mem. Bd of Dirs Kreditanstalt for Wiederaufbau; mem. Bd of Gov. Fed. Financial Supervisory Authority

(BaFin); Chair. Higher Council of Univ. of the Sparkassen finance group; Dist Chair. German Red Cross; mem. Bd Donors' Asscn for German Science, Bd of Trustees of German Sports Aid Foundation, Bd of Trustees of Cultural Foundation of countries eV, and numerous bds in other social and cultural orgs; Hon. Senator, Albstadt-Ebingen Univ. for Applied Science; Verdienstkreuz am Bande des Verdienstordens der Bundesrepublik Deutschland 1983, Verdienstkreuz 1. Klasse 1988, Großes Verdienstkreuz 1999; AMSEL-Landesverband Prize 2002. *Address:* Deutcher Sparkassen- und Giroverband E.V., Postfach 1429, Simrockstrasse 4, 53004 Bonn, Germany (office). *E-mail:* info@ dsgv.de (office). *Website:* www.dsgv.de (office).

HAASS, Christian, Dr rer. nat; German biochemist and academic; *Professor of Neurobiochemistry, Ludwig Maximilians University of Munich;* ed University of Heidelberg; Postdoctoral Fellow, Center for Neurologic Diseases, Harvard Medical School, Boston, Mass, USA, Asst Prof. 1993–95; Assoc. Prof. of Molecular Biology, Cen. Inst. of Mental Health, Mannheim 1995–99; Prof. of Neurobiochemistry, Dept of Biomedicine I, Ludwig Maximilians Univ. of Munich 1999–; awards from Heidelberg Soc. for Molecular Biology for diploma thesis 1986, doctoral thesis 1989, Organon Research Award, Award of Heidelberg Acad. of Sciences, Award of German Brain League, Int. Alois Alzheimer Award, Family Hansen Award, Ernst Jung Prize for Medicine 2002, Gottfried Wilhelm Leibniz Prize 2002, Potamkin Prize, American Acad. of Neurology 2002. *Publications:* Molecular Biology of Alzheimer's Disease: Genes and Mechanisms Involved in Amyloid Generation 1998; numerous articles in scientific journals. *Address:* Adolf-Butenandt-Institut, Lehrstuhl für Stoffwechselbiochemie, Ludwig-Maximilians-Universität, Schillerstraße 44, 80336 Munich, Germany (office). *Telephone:* (89) 218075-472 (office). *Fax:* (89) 218075-415 (office). *E-mail:* chaass@med.uni-muenchen.de (office). *Website:* www.med.uni-muenchen.de/haass (office).

HAASS, Richard N., BA, DPhil; American fmr government official and fmr diplomatist; *President, Council on Foreign Relations;* m.; two c.; ed Oberlin Coll., Ohio and Univ. of Oxford; fmr legis. aide, US Senate; various posts in Dept of Defense 1979–80, Dept of State 1981–85, Special Asst to Pres. and Sr Dir for Near East and S Asian Affairs, Nat. Security Council 1989–93; Vice-Pres. and Dir of Foreign Policy Studies, Sydney Stein Jr Chair in Int. Security, Brookings Inst. –2001; Dir of Policy Planning, Dept of State 2001–03, US Coordinator for Afghanistan policy; leading US Govt Official in support of NI peace process, fmr Special Envoy of Pres. George W. Bush to NI Peace Process; fmr Sr Fellow and Dir of Nat. Security Programs, Council on Foreign Relations, Pres. Council on Foreign Relations 2003–; mem. IISS (fmr Research Assoc.), Trilateral Comm.; Sr Assoc. Carnegie Endowment for Int. Peace; fmr Sol. M. Linowitz Visiting Prof. of Int. Studies, Hamilton Coll.; fmr Lecturer in Public Policy, Harvard Univ. Kennedy School of Govt; fmr consultant, NBC News; Presidential Citizen's Medal 1991, Dept of State Distinguished Honor Award 2003. *Publications:* The Reluctant Sheriff: The United States after the Cold War 1998, Economic Sanctions and American Diplomacy 1998, The Bureaucratic Entrepreneur: How to Be Effective in Any Unruly Organization 1998, Intervention: The Use of American Military Force in the Post-Cold War World 1999, The Opportunity: America's Moment to Alter History's Course 2005, War of Necessity, War of Choice: A Memoir of Two Iraq Wars 2009; frequent contribs to foreign affairs journals. *Address:* Council on Foreign Relations, 58 East 68th Street, New York, NY 10021, USA (office). *Telephone:* (212) 434-9543 (office). *Fax:* (212) 434-9880 (office). *E-mail:* president@cfr.org (office). *Website:* www.cfr.org (office).

HAAVISTO, Heikki Johannes, MSc, LLM; Finnish politician; b. 20 Aug. 1935, Turku; s. of Johan Haavisto and Alli Svensson; m. Maija Rihko 1964; three s.; Head of Dept, Oy Vehnä Ab 1963–66; Sec.-Gen. Cen. Union of Agricultural Producers and Forest Owners in Finland (MTK) 1966–75, Pres. 1976–94; Vice-Pres. Int. Fed. of Agricultural Producers 1977–80, 1986–90, mem. Bd of Dirs 1984–86; mem. Cen. Council of Nordic Farmer Orgs (NBC), Pres. 1977, 1985–87; Chair. Del. of Finn Cooperative Pellervo (Confed. of Finnish Cooperatives) 1979–2000; mem. Admin. Council, Osuuskunta Metsäliitto, Vice-Chair. 1976–82, Pres. 1982–93; Vice-Chair. Admin. Council, OKO (Cen. Union of Cooperative Credit Banks) 1985–93; mem. Bd of Dirs Metsä-Serla Oy 1986–93; Pres. Admin. Council, Raisio Group 1987–96, Pres. Bd of Dirs 1997–2000; mem. Int. Policy Council on Agric. and Trade 1988–2000; Minister for Foreign Affairs 1993–95, for Devt Co-operation 1994–95; three hon. doctorates. *Address:* Hintsantie 2, 21200 Raisio, Finland. *Telephone:* (2) 4383020. *Fax:* (2) 4383499.

HABARUGIRA, Tharcisse; Democratic Republic of the Congo politician; fmr Deputy Minister of Security and Public Order, of Admin of Goma Territory –2006; Minister of Defence 2006–07. *Address:* c/o Ministry of Defence, Demobilization and War Veterans' Affairs, BP 4111, Kinshasa - Gombe, Democratic Republic of the Congo (office).

HABERER, Jean-Yves; French government official (retd); b. 17 Dec. 1932, Mazagan, Morocco; m. Anne du Crest 1959; two c.; ed Inst. d'Etudes politiques, Ecole Nat. d'Admin.; Insp. des Finances 1959, Insp. Gen. 1980; Tech. Adviser to Finance Ministry 1966–68; an Asst Dir of Treasury 1967–69, in charge of Intervention Service, Treasury 1969, of Financial Activities 1970, of Int. Business 1973; Dir of Treasury 1978–82; Head of Office of Minister of Foreign Affairs 1968, of Minister of Defence 1969, of Minister of Econ. and Finance 1976; Prof. Inst. d'Etudes politiques 1970–82; Chair. Monetary Cttee of the EEC 1980–82; Pres. and Dir-Gen. Bank Paribas and Cie Financière de Paribas 1982–86, Chair. of Supervisory Bd Compagnie Bancaire 1982–88; Chair. Crédit Lyonnais 1988–93, Crédit Nat. 1993–94; Dir Cie Bancaire, Pallas Invest, Fondation Recherche Médicale, Institut Vaisseaux et Sang; convicted of fraud during time with Crédit Lyonnais June 2003 (suspended jail sentence); Officier, Ordre nat. du Mérite 1981, Officier, Légion d'honneur 1989. *Publication:* Cinq ans de Crédit Lyonnais 1988–1993 1999. *Address:* 82

avenue Marceau, 75008 Paris (office); 10 rue Rémusat, 75016 Paris, France (home). *Telephone:* 1-53-57-93-12 (office). *Fax:* 1-53-57-93-16.

HABERMAS, Jürgen, DPhil, Habilitation; German academic and writer; *Professor Emeritus of Philosophy, University of Frankfurt;* b. 18 June 1929, Düsseldorf; m. Ute Habermas-Wesselhoeft 1955; one s. two d.; ed Univs of Bonn and Göttingen; Research Asst, Inst. für Soziale Forschung, Frankfurt 1956; Prof. of Philosophy, Univ. of Heidelberg 1961, of Philosophy and Sociology, Univ. of Frankfurt 1964; Dir Max Planck Inst., Starnberg, Munich 1971; Prof. of Philosophy, Univ. of Frankfurt 1983–94, Prof. Emer. 1994–; mem. Academia Europaea; Foreign mem. American Acad. of Arts and Sciences 1984, British Acad. of Science 1994; Hon. DD (New School for Social Research) 1984; hon. degrees from Hebrew Univ. (Jerusalem), Univs of Hamburg, Buenos Aires, Evanston (Northwestern), Utrecht, Athens, Bologna, Paris, Tel-Aviv, Cambridge, Harvard; Hegel Prize 1972, Sigmund Freud Prize 1976, Adorno Prize 1980, Geschwister Scholl Prize 1985, Leibniz Prize 1986, Sonning Prize 1987, Jaspers Prize 1997, Culture Prize of the State of Hesse 1999, Friedenspreis des deutschen Buchhandels 2001, Prince of Asturias Award for Social Science 2003, Kyoto Prize for Philosophy 2004, Holberg Int. Memorial Prize 2005. *Publications:* Strukturwandel der Öffentlichkeit 1962, Theorie und Praxis 1963, Erkenntnis und Interesse 1968, Legitimationsprobleme im Spätkapitalismus 1973, Theorie des kommunikativen Handelns 1981, Moralbewüsstsein und Kommunikatives Handeln 1983, Der Philosophische Diskurs ober Moderne 1985, Eine Art Schadensabwicklüng 1987, Nachmetaphysisches Denken 1988, Nachholende Revolution 1990, Texte und Kontexte 1991, Erläuterungen zur Diskursetnik 1991, Faktizität und Geltung 1992, Vergangenheit als Zukunft 1993, Die Normalität einer Berliner Republik 1995, Die Einbeziehung des Anderen 1996, Vom sinnlichen Eindruck zum symbolischen Ausdruck 1997, Die postnationale Konstellation 1998, Wahrheit und Rechtfertigung 1999, Zeit und Übergänge 2001, Kommunikatives Handeln und Detranszendentalisierte Vernuft 2001, Die Zukunft der Menschlichen Natur 2001, Zeitdiagnosen 2003, Der gespaltene Westen 2004, Ach Europa 2008. *Address:* Department of Philosophy, University of Frankfurt, Grüneburgplatz 1, 60629 Frankfurt am Main (office); Ringstrasse 8B, 82319 Starnberg, Germany (home). *Telephone:* (8151) 13537 (home). *Fax:* (8151) 13537 (home).

HABGOOD, Baron (Life Peer), cr. 1995, of Calverton in the County of Buckinghamshire; **Rt Rev. and Rt Hon. John Stapylton Habgood,** PC, MA, PhD, DD; British ecclesiastic (retd); b. 23 June 1927, Stony Stratford; s. of Arthur Henry Habgood and Vera Chetwynd-Stapylton; m. Rosalie Mary Anne Boston 1961; two s. two d.; ed Eton Coll., King's Coll. Cambridge Univ. and Cuddesdon Coll., Oxford; Demonstrator in Pharmacology, Univ. of Cambridge 1950–53; Fellow, King's Coll. Cambridge 1952–55, Hon. Fellow 1984; Curate, St Mary Abbott's Church, Kensington 1954–56; Vice-Prin. Westcott House, Cambridge 1956–62; Rector, St John's Church, Jedburgh, Scotland 1962–67; Prin. Queen's Coll., Birmingham 1967–73; Bishop of Durham 1973–83; Archbishop of York 1983–95; Pres. (UK) Council on Christian Approaches to Defence and Disarmament 1976–95; Chair. WCCs' Int. Hearing on Nuclear Weapons 1981; mem. Council for Science and Society 1975–90, Council for Arms Control 1981–95; Moderator of Church and Soc. Sub-Unit, WCC 1983–90; Chair. UK Xenotransplantation Interim Regulatory Authority 1997–2003; Hon. DD (Durham) 1975, (Cambridge) 1984, (Aberdeen) 1988, (Huron) 1990, (Hull) 1991, (Oxford) 1996, (Manchester) 1996, (London) 2005; Hon. DUniv (York) 1996; Hon. DHL (York, Pa) 1995; Bampton Lecturer, Univ. of Oxford 1999, Gifford Lecturer, Univ. of Aberdeen 2000. *Publications:* Religion and Science 1964, A Working Faith 1980, Church and Nation in a Secular Age 1983, Confessions of a Conservative Liberal 1988, Making Sense 1993, Faith and Uncertainty 1997, Being a Person 1998, Varieties of Unbelief 2000, The Concept of Nature 2002. *Leisure interests:* carpentry, painting. *Address:* 18 The Mount, Malton, N Yorks., YO17 7ND, England (home). *E-mail:* js.habgood@btinternet.com (home).

HABIB, Irfan; Indian historian; fmrly Prof. of History and Dir Centre for the Advanced Study of History, Aligarh Muslim Univ.; Jt Ed. Cambridge Economic History of India (journal); fmr Chair. Indian Soc. for Historical Research; Padma Bhushan Award 2005. *Publications:* Confronting Colonialism. Resistance and Modernization Under Haidar Ali and Tipu Sultan 2002, Essays in Indian History. Towards a Marxist Perception 2002. *Address:* c/o Department of History, Aligarh Muslim University, Aligarh, UP 202002, India (office).

HABIB, Randa, MA; Lebanese/French journalist; *Director and Head, Agence France Presse, Jordan;* b. 16 Jan. 1952, Beirut, Lebanon; d. of Farid Habib; m. Adnan Gharaybeh 1973; one s. one d.; ed French Lycée, Rio de Janeiro and Univ. of Beirut; corresp., Agence France Presse (AFP) 1980, Dir and Head of AFP Office, Amman 1987–; corresp., Radio Monte Carlo 1988–2006, columnist in local Jordanian papers, corresp. also for several int. publs and TV; Chair. Foreign Press Club, Jordan; mem. Bd Dirs Jordan Media Inst.; Gov., Agence France Presse Foundation; mem. Bd Jordan Transparency, Center to Protect Journalists; Chevalier, Ordre nat. du Mérite 2001, Chevalier, Légion d'honneur 2008; Médaille du Travail (France) 2000. *Publication:* Hussein père et fils, 30 années qui ont changé le Moyen-Orient 2007. *Leisure interests:* reading, swimming, painting. *Address:* Agence France Presse, Jebel Amman, 2nd Circle, PO Box 3340, Amman 11181, Jordan (office). *Telephone:* (6) 4642976 (office). *Fax:* (6) 4654680 (office). *E-mail:* randa.habib@afp.com (office).

HABIBI, Hassan Ibrahim, PhD; Iranian politician and academic; *Head, Academy of Persian Language and Literature;* ed in France; with the late Ayatollah Ruholla Khomeini, Paris 1978–79; mem. Revolutionary Council and Spokesman, Council of Revolution of Iran 1979, Minister of Justice 1984, First Vice-Pres. 1989–2001; Head, Acad. of Persian Language and Literature

2004–; mem. High Council of Cultural Revolution. *Address:* Academy of Persian Language and Literature, No. 36, 15th East Avenue, Velenjak, Tehran, Iran (office). *Telephone:* (21) 24143938 (office). *Website:* www .persianacademy.ir (office).

HABIBIE, Bacharuddin Jusuf, DEng; Indonesian politician and aviation engineer; b. 25 June 1936, Pare-Pare, South Sulawesi; m. H. Hasri Ainun Besari 1962; two s.; ed Bandung Inst. of Tech., Technische Hochschule, Aachen; Head of Research at Messerschmitt-Boelkow-Blohm, Hamburg 1966; Govt Adviser 1976; Chair., CEO, Pres. Indonesian State Aircraft Industry 1976–98; Minister of State for Research and Tech. 1978–98; Head of Agency for Tech. Evaluation and Application 1978–98; Chair., CEO, Pres. Indonesian Shipbuilding Industry 1978–98; Chair. Batam Industrial Devt 1978–98; Chair. Team for Defence Security Industrial Devt 1980–99; mem. Indonesian Parl. 1982–99; Chair., CEO, Pres. Small Arms and Munitions Industry 1983–98; Chair. Nat. Research Council 1984–; Vice-Chair. Bd of Patrons, Indonesian Strategic Industries 1988–; Chair. Agency for Strategic Industries 1989–98; Head of Indonesian Muslim Intellectuals Asscn 1990–; Vice-Pres. of Indonesia March–May 1998, Pres. 1998–99; Founder and Chair. Indonesian Aeronautics and Astronautics Inst.; mem. Royal Swedish Acad. of Eng Sciences, Acad. Nat. de l'Air et de l'Espace, France; Fellow Royal Aeronautical Soc.; Gran Cruz del Mérito Aeronáutico con Distintivo Blanco (Spain) 1980, Grosses Bundesverdienstkreuz 1980, Dwidya Sistha Medal 1982, Grand Cross of the Order of Orange Nassau 1983, Grand Officier Ordre nat. du Mérite and numerous other awards and decorations. *Publications:* numerous scientific and technical papers. *Address:* c/o House of Representatives, Jakarta, Indonesia (office).

HABICHT, Werner, DPhil; German academic; *Professor Emeritus of English, University of Würzburg;* b. 29 Jan. 1930, Schweinfurt; s. of Wilhelm Habicht and Magda Habicht (née Müller); ed Univ. of Munich, Johns Hopkins Univ., Baltimore, USA, Univ. of Paris, France; Asst, Freie Universität, Berlin 1957–60, Univ. of Munich 1960–65; Prof. of English, Univ. of Heidelberg 1966–70, Univ. of Bonn 1970–78, Univ. of Würzburg 1978–95, Prof. Emer. 1995–; Visiting Prof., Univ. of Tex. at Austin 1981, Univ. of Colo, Boulder 1987, Ohio State Univ., Columbus 1988, Univ. of Cyprus 1995–96; mem. Akad. der Wissenschaften und der Literatur, Mainz, Bayerische Akad. der Wissenschaften; Pres. Deutsche Shakespeare-Gesellschaft West 1976–88, Vice-Pres. 1988–93; Hon. Vice-Pres. Int. Shakespeare Asscn 1996–. *Publications:* Die Gebärde in englischen Dichtungen des Mittelalters 1959, Studien zur Dramenform vor Shakespeare 1968, Shakespeare and the German Imagination 1994, English and American Studies in German (ed.) 1968–82, Jahrbuch, Deutsche Shakespeare-Gesellschaft West (ed.) 1982–95, Literatur Brockhaus (three vols) (co-ed.) 1988; numerous articles on English literature and drama. *Address:* Allerseeweg 14, 97204 Höchberg, Germany (home). *Telephone:* (931) 8885658 (office); (931) 49267 (home). *E-mail:* WHabicht@t -online.de (home).

HABILA, Helon; Nigerian writer and academic; *Faculty Member, Graduate Creative Writing Program, Department of English, George Mason University;* b. 1967, Kaltungo, Gombe State; m.; one d.; ed Univ. of Jos; Lecturer in English and Literature, Fed. Polytechnic, Bauchi 1997–99; fmr contrib. to Hints magazine, Lagos; fmr Arts Ed. Vanguard newspaper, Lagos; African Writing Fellow Univ. of E Anglia, UK 2002–04; Chinua Achebe Fellow of Africana Global Studies, Bard Coll., New York 2005–06; faculty mem. Dept of English, Grad. Creative Writing Program, George Mason Univ. 2007–; Contributing Ed. Virginia Quarterly Review; first prize MUSON Festival Poetry Competition (for poem Another Age) 2000, Caine Prize for African Writing, UK (for short story Love Poems) 2001. *Publications:* Mai Kaltungo (biog.) 1997, Prison Stories (short stories) 2000, Waiting for an Angel 2002 (Commonwealth Prize for Best First Book, African Region, 2003), Measuring Time 2007; co-ed. New Writing 14 (British Council Anthology), Miracles, Dreams, and Jazz; short stories and poems in anthologies. *Address:* 117 Science and Technology Bldg, George Mason University, Fairfax, VA 22030 (office); Graduate Creative Writing Program, 4400 University Drive, MSN 3E4, Fairfax, VA 22030, USA (office). *Telephone:* (703) 993-1180 (office). *E-mail:* hhabila@gmu.edu (office). *Website:* creativewriting.gmu.edu (office).

HABRAKEN, Nicolaas John; Dutch architect; *Professor Emeritus of Architecture, Massachusetts Institute of Technology;* b. 29 Oct. 1928, Bandung, Indonesia; s. of the late J.W.L. Habraken and J.L.S. Heyting; m. E. Marleen van Hall 1958; one s. one d.; ed Delft Tech. Univ.; architect, Lucas & Niemeyer (architects), Voorburg 1961–65; Dir Stichting Architecten Research, Voorburg 1965–66, Eindhoven 1966–75; Prof. and First Chair. Dept of Architecture, Eindhoven Tech. Univ. 1966–70, Prof. of Architecture 1966–75; Head, Dept of Architecture, MIT 1975–81, Prof. of Architecture 1975–89, Prof. Emer. 1989–; Pnr, Infill Systems, Delft 1986–99; Hon. mem. Architectural Inst. of Japan 1994; Kt, Order of the Dutch Lion 2003; Dr hc (Tech. Univ. Eindhoven) 2005; David Roell Prize 1979, King Fahd Award for Design and Research in Islamic Architecture 1985, ACSA Creative Achievement Award 1989, BKVB Nat. Architecture Award 1996, BNA (Dutch Architects' Asscn) Kubus Award of Merit 2003. *Publications:* Supports: An Alternative to Mass Housing 1962, Transformations of the Site 1983, The Appearance of the Form 1985, The Structure of the Ordinary 1998, Palladio's Children 2005; research reports and numerous articles. *Address:* 63 Wildernislaan, 7313 BD Apeldoorn, Netherlands (home). *Telephone:* (55) 3556354 (home). *Fax:* (55) 3554765 (home). *E-mail:* habraken@xs4all.nl (office). *Website:* www.habraken.com (office).

HABRÉ, Hissène; Chadian politician; formerly one of the leaders of the Front de Libération Nationale du Tchad (FROLINAT); head of Northern Armed Forces Command Council –1977; held the French archaeologists M. and Mme Claustre captive 1974–77; Leader of Forces Armées du Nord 1977;

negotiated with Govt of Brig.-Gen. Félix Malloum 1978; Prime Minister 1978–79; resigned after Kano peace agreement with FROLINAT forces led by Goukouni Oueddei March 1979; Minister of State for Defence and War Veterans in Provisional Govt April–May 1979; Minister of Defence 1979 (in conflict with Goukouni Oueddei in civil war, reported in exile 1980); Minister of Nat. Defence, Veterans and War Victims 1986–90; Pres. of Chad June–Oct. 1982, Pres. 1982–90 (ousted in coup); living in Cameroon 1990, in Senegal 1999–; indicted for complicity in torture by Senegalese Court, Feb. 2000 (case later dismissed), then under investigation by a Belgian court Feb. 2002.

HABSBURG-LOTHRINGEN, Otto von, DrPolSc; Austrian/German/Hungarian politician and author; b. 20 Nov. 1912, Reichenau, Austria; s. of the late Archduke Charles, later Emperor of Austria and King of Hungary, and Zita, Princess of Bourbon-Parma; m. Regina, Princess of Sachsen-Meiningen 1951; two s. five d.; ed Univ. of Louvain, Belgium; mem. Pan-European Union 1936–, rep. in Washington 1940–46, Vice-Pres. 1957, Pres. 1973–; renounced claim to Austrian throne 1961; MEP for Bavaria (Christian Social Union) 1979–99; lectures throughout the world on int. affairs and is author of weekly column appearing in 21 daily papers in five languages since 1953; mem. Acad. des Sciences Morales et Politiques, Inst. de France, Paris, Real Acad. de Ciencias Morales y Políticas, Madrid, Acad. da Cultura Portuguesa, Acad. Mejicana de Derecho Internacional, Acad. of Morocco, etc.; Maarjaa Maa Order (Estonia), Grand Cross of Merit (Hungary); Dr hc (Univs of Nancy, Tampa, Cincinnati, Ferrara, Pécs, Budapest, Turku, Veszprém); numerous awards and decorations including Bayerischer Verdienstorden, Order of Gregory the Great (Vatican), Robert Schuman Gold Medal 1977, Gold Medal of City of Paris, Konrad Adenauer Prize 1977, Medal of Europe of Free State of Bavaria 1991. *Publications:* 38 books in seven languages on history, politics, world affairs and especially European politics. *Address:* Hindenburgstrasse 15, 82343 Pöcking, Germany. *Telephone:* (8157) 7015 (office). *Fax:* (8157) 7087 (office). *Website:* otto.twschwarzer.de.

HACHETTE, Jean-Louis, LenD; French publisher; b. 30 June 1925, Paris; s. of Louis and Blanche (née Darbou) Hachette; m. Y. de Bouillé 1954; one s. two d.; ed Collège Stanislas, Paris and Faculté de Droit, Paris; joined Librairie Hachette (f. by great-grandfather in 1826) 1946 (now Hachette Livre); entire career spent with Librairie Hachette, Admin. Dir 1971–; Pres. Librairie Générale Française 1954–. *Leisure interests:* polo, golf, skiing. *Address:* Librairie Générale Française, 43 quai de Grenelle, 75905 Paris, Cédex 15, France. *Website:* www.hachette.com.

HACKETT, Brett, BA, BLL; Australian diplomatist; b. 1963; ed Univ. of Queensland; joined public service 1990; First Sec., High Comm. in Ottawa 1994–98; Deputy Dir India and S Asia Section, Dept of Foreign Affairs and Trade, 1998–2002; Deputy High Commr High Comm. in Islamabad 2002–05; Dir Philippines and E Timor Section 2005–06; Amb. to Afghanistan 2006–08. *Address:* c/o Department of Foreign Affairs and Trade, R. G. Casey Bldg, John McEwan Cres., Barton, ACT 0221, Australia. *Telephone:* (2) 6261-1111. *Fax:* (2) 6261-3111. *Website:* www.dfat.gov.au.

HACKETT, Grant George, BCom, BL; Australian swimmer; b. 9 May 1980, Southport, Queensland; s. of Neville Hackett and Margaret Hackett; m. Candice Alley 2007; ed Merrimac State High School, Bond Univ., Gold Coast; mem. Miami Swim Club; Olympic Games, Sydney 2000: Gold Medal 1500m freestyle, 4×200m freestyle relay (heat swim); World Championships, Fukuoka 2001: Gold Medal 4×200m freestyle relay (world record), 1500m freestyle (world record time of 14:34.56), Silver Medal 400m freestyle, 800m freestyle; Commonwealth Games, Manchester 2002: Gold Medal 1500m freestyle, 4×200m freestyle relay, 4×100m freestyle relay (heat swim), Silver Medal 800m freestyle, 400m freestyle; Pan Pacific Games 2002: Gold Medal 1500m freestyle, 800m freestyle, 4×200m freestyle relay, 4×100m freestyle relay, Silver Medal 400m freestyle, 200m freestyle; World Championships, Barcelona 2003: Gold Medal 1500m freestyle, 800m freestyle, 4×200m freestyle relay, Silver Medal 400m freestyle; Olympic Games, Athens 2004: Gold Medal 1500m freestyle (Olympic record), Silver Medal 400m freestyle, 4×200m freestyle relay; Telstra Australian Swimming Championships 2005: Gold Medal 1500m freestyle, 800m freestyle, 400m freestyle, 200m freestyle; World Championships, Montreal 2005: Gold Medal 1500m freestyle, 800m freestyle (world record time of 7:38.65), 400m freestyle, Silver Medal 200m freestyle; World Championships, Melbourne 2007: Bronze Medal 400m freestyle; Olympic Games, Beijing 2008: Silver Medal 1500m freestyle (Olympic record, heat swim), Bronze Medal 4×200m freestyle relay; unbeaten at 1500m freestyle 1996–2007, first to swim under 15 minutes for the distance; won his first Nat. Championship 10km Open Water race 2007; Order of Australia Medal 2001; Australian Swimming Male Distance Swimmer of the Year 1998, 2002, 2003, 2004, Australian Sports Medal 2000, Centenary Medal 2000, Goodwill Games Ambassador 2001, Swimmer of the Year 2003, Telstra People's Choice Award 2004, Telstra Swimmer of the Year (with Ian Thorpe) 2004, Australian Export Awards Special Achievement Award 2004, World Swimmer of the Year 2005, Pacific Rim Swimmer of the Year 2005, Telstra Swimmer of the Year 2005, Telstra Swimmers' Swimmer of the Year 2005, Telstra Middle and Distance Swimmer of the Year 2005, 'The Don' Award, Sport Australia Hall of Fame 2005, Telstra Dolphins Australian Swim Team Captain 2005. *Leisure interests:* surfing, fast cars, playing drums and guitar. *Address:* c/o Lisa Stallard, International Quarterback Pty Ltd, 24/76 Doggett Street, Newstead, Queensland 4006, Australia (office). *Telephone:* (7) 3252-2311 (office). *Fax:* (7) 3252-3411 (office). *E-mail:* lisa@iqsport.com.au (office). *Website:* www.iqsport.com.au (office).

HACKING, Ian MacDougall, CC, PhD, FRSC, FBA; Canadian academic; *Professor, Chair of Philosophy and History of Scientific Concepts, Collège de France;* b. 18 Feb. 1936, Vancouver; s. of Harold Eldridge Hacking and Margaret Elinore MacDougall; m. 1st Laura Anne Leach 1962; m. 2nd Judith

Polsky Baker 1983; one s. two d.; ed Univ. of British Columbia, Univ. of Cambridge, UK; Asst then Assoc. Prof., Univ. of British Columbia 1964–69; Univ. Lecturer in Philosophy, Univ. of Cambridge and Fellow of Peterhouse 1969–74; Prof., then Henry Waldgrave Stuart Prof. of Philosophy, Stanford Univ. 1975–82; Prof., Univ. of Toronto 1983–2003, Univ. Prof. 1991–2003; Prof., Chair of Philosophy and History of Scientific Concepts Collège de France, Paris 2000–; Fellow American Acad. of Arts and Sciences 1991; Hon. Fellow, Trinity Coll. Cambridge 2000; Hon. LLD (Univ. of British Columbia) 2001; Molson Prize, Canada Council 2001, Killam Prize, Canada Council 2002. *Publications:* Logic of Statistical Inference 1965, Why Does Language Matter to Philosophy? 1975, The Emergence of Probability 1975, Representing and Intervening 1983, The Taming of Chance 1991, Le plus pur nominalisme 1993, Rewriting the Soul: Multiple Personality and the Sciences of Memory 1995, Mad Travelers 1998, The Social Construction of What? 1999, Probability and Inductive Logic 2001, Historical Ontology 2002. *Leisure interests:* walking, canoeing. *Address:* Collège de France, 11 place Marcelin Berthelot, 75000 Paris, France (office). *Telephone:* 1-44-27-16-06 (office). *Fax:* 1-44-27-13-30 (office). *E-mail:* ian.hacking@college-de-france.fr (office). *Website:* www .college-de-france.fr (office).

HACKMAN, Gene; American actor; b. 30 Jan. 1930, San Bernardino, Calif.; s. of Eugene Ezra Hackman; m. Fay Maltese 1956 (divorced 1985); one s. two d.; studied acting at the Pasadena Playhouse; Acad. Award for Best Actor, New York Film Critics' Award, Golden Globe Award, British Acad. Award, The French Connection, British Acad. Award, The Poseidon Adventure, Cannes Film Festival Award, Scarecrow, Nat. Review Bd Award, Mississippi Burning 1988, Berlin Film Award 1989, Acad. Award, The Unforgiven 1993; Cecil B. DeMille Award, Golden Globes 2003. *Films include:* Lilith 1964, Hawaii 1966, Banning 1967, Bonnie and Clyde 1967, The Split 1968, Downhill Racer 1969, I Never Sang For My Father 1969, The Gypsy Moths 1969, Marooned 1970, The Hunting Party 1971, The French Connection 1971, The Poseidon Adventure 1972, The Conversation 1973, Scarecrow 1973, Zandy's Bride 1974, Young Frankenstein 1974, The French Connection II 1975, Lucky Lady 1975, Night Moves 1976, Domino Principle 1977, Superman 1978, Superman II 1980, All Night Long 1980, Target 1985, Twice in a Lifetime 1985, Power 1985, Bat 21, Superman IV 1987, No Way Out 1987, Another Woman 1988, Mississippi Burning 1988, The Package 1989, The Von Metz Incident 1989, Loose Connections 1989, Full Moon in Blue Water 1989, Postcards from the Edge 1989, Class Action 1989, Loose Canons 1990, Narrow Margin 1990, Necessary Roughness 1991, Company Business 1991, The William Munny Killings 1991, The Unforgiven 1992, The Firm 1992, Geronimo, Wyatt Earp 1994, Crimson Tide, The Quick and the Dead 1995, Get Shorty, Birds of a Feather, Extreme Measures 1996, The Chamber 1996, Absolute Power 1996, Twilight 1998, Enemy of the State 1998, Under Suspicion 2000, Heist 2001, The Royal Tenenbaums (Golden Globe for Best Actor in a Musical or Comedy) 2001, Runaway Jury 2003, Welcome to Mooseport 2004. *Stage plays include:* Children From Their Games 1963, Cass Henderson in Any Wednesday 1964, Poor Richard, 1964, Death and the Maiden 1992. *Television includes:* many guest appearances on US series; also My Father, My Mother, CBS Playhouse 1968 and Shadow on the Land 1971, Under Suspicion 1999. *Publication:* Wake of the Perdido Star (with David Lenihan) 2000. *Address:* c/o Fred Specktor, Creative Artists Agency, 9830 Wilshire Boulevard, Beverly Hills, CA 90212; c/o Barry Haldeman, 1900 Avenue of the Stars, Suite 2000, Los Angeles, CA 90067, USA.

HACKNEY, Francis Sheldon, PhD; American historian, academic and university administrator; *David Boies Professor of History, University of Pennsylvania;* b. 5 Dec. 1933, Birmingham, Ala; s. of Cecil Hackney and Elizabeth Morris; m. Lucy Durr 1957; one s. two d.; ed Vanderbilt and Yale Univs; mem. faculty, Princeton Univ. 1965–75, Assoc. Prof. of History 1969–72, Prof. and Provost 1972–75; Pres. Tulane Univ., New Orleans 1975–80; David Boies Prof. of History, Univ. of Pennsylvania 1981–93, 1997–, Pres. 1981–93, Pres. Emer. 1999–; mem. Bd Dirs Carnegie Foundation for Advancement of Teaching 1976–84, 1986–93; Chair. Nat. Endowment for the Humanities 1993–97; mem. American Philosophical Soc., American History Asscn; Southern Historical Asscn Sydnor Prize, American Historical Asscn Beveridge Prize. *Publications:* Populism to Progressivism in Alabama 1969, Populism: The Critical Issues (ed.), Understanding the American Experience (with others) 1973, One America Indivisible 1997, The Politics of Presidential Appointment 2002. *Address:* Department of History, University of Pennsylvania, Philadelphia, PA 19104, USA (office). *Telephone:* (215) 898-5912 (office). *E-mail:* shackney@history.upenn.edu (office).

HACKNEY, Roderick Peter, PhD, RIBA; British architect; *Managing Director, Rod Hackney and Associates Ltd;* b. 3 March 1942, Liverpool; s. of William Hackney and Rose Hackney (née Morris); m. Christine Thornton 1964; one s.; ed John Bright's Grammar School, Llandudno, School of Architecture, Univ. of Manchester; Job Architect, Expo '67, Montreal, for monorail stations 1967; Housing Architect for Libyan Govt, Tripoli 1967–68; Asst to Arne Jacobsen, working on Kuwait Cen. Bank, Copenhagen 1968–71; est. practice of Rod Hackney Architect, Macclesfield 1972, architectural practices in Birmingham, Leicester, Belfast, Cleator Moor, Workington, Carlisle, Millom, Clitheroe, Manchester, Stirling, Burnley, Chesterfield and Stoke on Trent 1975–88, Man. Dir Rod Hackney and Assocs Ltd; Council mem. RIBA, including Vice-Pres. for Public Affairs and Vice-Pres. for Overseas Affairs 1978–84, Pres. 1987–89, mem. of Council 1991–, Vice-Pres. Int. Affairs 1992–94, Hon. Librarian 1998–2001; Council mem. Int. Union of Architects 1981–85, 1991–, Pres. 1987–90; Patron Llandudno Museum and Art Gallery 1988–; Pres. Snowdonia Nat. Park Soc. 1987–2003; Pres. North Wales Centre of The Nat. Trust 1990–; mem. Editorial Bd, UIA Journal of Architectural Theory and Criticism; Jury mem. Cembureau Award for Low Rise Housing in France 1982, for Prix Int. d'Architecture de l'Institut Nat. du Logement 1983;

Chair. Jury for Hérouville Town Centre Competition, France 1982–83; Pres. Young Architects Forum, Sofia 1985, Building Communities (Int. Community Architecture Conf.), London 1986; presentation of case for Int. Year of Shelter for the Homeless to all four party confs 1986; Chair. Times/RIBA Community Enterprise Scheme 1985–89, Trustees of Inner City Trust 1986–97, British Architecture Library Trust 1999–2001; Special Prof. in Architecture, Univ. of Nottingham 1987–91; Int. Adviser, Univ. of Manchester School of Architecture Centre for Int. Architectural Studies 1992–2000; adviser on regeneration and inner city problems in Sweden, Italy and USA 1990–; consultant, World Architecture Review Agency 1992–; Adviser, Centre for Human Settlements Int. 1994–, Habitat Centre News Journal, India 1996; Chair. UN Habitat Award 2004–05, UN Habitat Awards, Dubai 2004; mem. Chartered Inst. of Building 1987–, Asscn of Planning Supervisors 1996–; attained registration for BSI ISO9001 1996; Adviser, World Habitat Awards, Social Housing Foundation, Coalville, UK 2003; Hon. FAIA; Hon. Fellow, Fed. de Colegios de Arquitectos de la República Mexicana, United Architects of the Philippines, Royal Architectural Inst. of Canada, Indian Inst. of Architects, Architectural Soc. of China; Hon. DLitt (Keele) 1989; Dept of Environment Good Design in Housing Award 1975, 1980, First Prize, for St Ann's Hospice, Manchester 1976, Prix Int. d'Architecture de l'Institut Nat. du Logement 1979–80, RICS/ Times Conservation Award 1980, Civic Trust Award of Commendation 1980, 1981, 1984, Sir Robert Matthews Award (Honourable Mention) 1981, Manchester Soc. of Architects Pres.'s Award 1982, Otis Award 1982, Gold Medal, Bulgarian Inst. of Architects 1983, Gold Medal, Young Architect of the Year, Sofia 1983, Grand Medal of Federación de Colegios de Arquitectos (Mexico) 1986, Commendation, Business Enterprise Award for Housing 1993, Citation for World Habitat Awards 1996, Stone Award 1996. *Films:* The Hackney Way. *Musical:* Good Golly Miss Molly. *Radio:* panellist on Any Questions (BBC Radio 4). *Television:* Consultant to Chapman Clarke Films' Forever England, Central TV 1995; TV features: Build Yourself a House 1974, Community Architecture 1977, BBC Omnibus 1987. *Publications:* Highfield Hall, A Community Project 1982, The Good, the Bad and the Ugly 1990, Good Golly Miss Molly (musical play) 1991. *Leisure interests:* outdoor pursuits, walking, Butterfly Society, fossils, geology, travelling, ballooning, looking at buildings, talking at conferences. *Address:* St Peter's House, Windmill Street, Macclesfield, Cheshire, SK11 7HS, England (office). *Telephone:* (1625) 431792 (office). *Fax:* (1625) 616929 (office). *E-mail:* rod@stpeter.demon.co.uk (office).

HACON, Christopher, BA, MS, PhD; American (b. British) mathematician and academic; *Professor of Mathematics, University of Utah;* b. 14 Feb. 1970, Manchester, England; m.; two s. one d.; ed Univ. of Pisa, Italy, Univ. of California, Los Angeles; Research Fellowship, CNR 1998; Math. Instructor, Univ. of Utah 1998–2000, Asst Prof. 2002–05, Assoc. Prof. 2005–08, Prof. 2008–; Asst Prof., Univ. of California, Riverside 2000–02; Sloan Fellowship 2003, American Math. Soc. Centennial Fellowship 2006; Clay Research Award, Clay Math. Inst. 2007, Cole Prize in Algebra (jtly), American Math. Soc. 2009. *Publications:* more than 40 papers in professional journals. *Address:* JWB 325, Department of Mathematics, University of Utah, 155 South 1400 East, Salt Lake City, UT 84112-0090, USA (office). *Telephone:* (801) 581-7429 (office). *Fax:* (801) 581-4148 (office). *E-mail:* hacon@math.utah .edu (office). *Website:* www.math.utah.edu (office).

HADDAD-ADEL, Gholam-Ali, MSc, PhD; Iranian politician; b. 1945, Tehran; m.; one d.; ed Univs of Tehran and Shiraz; physics grad.; Prof. of Literature and Philosophy, Univ. of Tehran; fmr Deputy Minister of Educ. and Training, of Culture and Islamic Guidance; fmr Exec. Dir Islamic Encyclopaedia Foundation; Head, Iranian Acad. of Persian Language and Literature –2004; elected to Majilis-e-Shura-e Islami (Parl.) for Tehran 2004–, Head, Islamic Iran Developers' Council (Etelat-e Abadgaran-e Iran-e Islami) in Parl. 2004–, Speaker, Majilis-e-Shura-e Islami 2004–08; mem. Supreme Cultural Revolutionary Council, Iranian Acad. of Persian Language and Literature, Expediency Discernment Council; helped start nat. scientific olympiads in Iran. *Address:* c/o Majlis-e-Shura-e Islami (Parliament), Tehran, Iran (office). *E-mail:* info@abadgaran.ir (office). *Website:* www.abadgaran.ir (office).

HADDON, Mark, MA; British writer and illustrator; b. 1962, Northampton; m. Sos Eltis; one s.; ed Merton Coll., Oxford, Edinburgh Univ.; positions at Mencap and other charity orgs; illustrator and cartoonist; painter; television work. *Screenwriting:* Microsoap (Royal Television Soc. Best Children's Drama), episodes of Starstreet, Fungus and the Bogeyman (adaptation). *Publications:* fiction: Gilbert's Gobstopper 1988, A Narrow Escape for Princess Sharon 1989, Toni and the Tomato Soup 1989, Agent Z Meets the Masked Crusader 1993, Gridzbi Spudvetch! 1993, In the Garden 1994, On Holiday (aka On Vacation) 1994, At Home 1994, At Playgroup 1994, Titch Johnson 1994, Agent Z Goes Wild 1994, Agent Z and the Penguin from Mars 1995, Real Porky Philips 1995, The Sea of Tranquillity 1996, Secret Agent Handbook 1999, Ocean Star Express 2001, Agent Z and the Killer Bananas 2001, The Ice Bear's Cave 2002, The Curious Incident of the Dog in the Night Time (Booktrust Teenage Prize 2003, Guardian Children's Fiction Prize 2003, South Bank Show Best Book Prize 2004, Whitbread Best Novel and Book of the Year 2004, Commonwealth Writers Prize for best first book 2004, Soc. of Authors McKitterick Prize 2004, WHSmith Children's Book of the Year 2004, Waterstone's Literary Fiction award 2004) 2003, A Spot of Bother 2006; poetry: The Talking Horse and the Sad Girl and the Village Under the Sea 2005. *Address:* c/o Jonathan Cape Ltd, 20 Vauxhall Bridge Road, London, SW1V 2SA, England. *Telephone:* (20) 7840-8400.

HADI, Maj.-Gen. Abd ar-Rabbuh Mansur al-; Yemeni politician and army officer; *Vice-President;* b. 1944, Al-Wadhee'a Region, Governorate of Abyan; m.; three s. two d.; ed Supreme Acad. of Nasser, Egypt, Sandhurst Mil. Acad., UK, Frunze Acad., fmr USSR; mem. staff Armoured Brigades, Mil. Acad.; Dir of Combat Training, of Supply and Provisions; Deputy Chief of Staff, Supply and Provisions; Adviser to Presidential Council 1990–; Minister of Defence 1994; Vice-Pres. of Repub. of Yemen 1994–; rank of Gen. 1994, Lt-Gen. 1997, currently Maj-Gen.; many decorations and awards including Medal of Honour of Mil. Service 1980, Order of the First Grade Badge 1995. *Leisure interests:* reading, current affairs, public folklore, local and classical music, swimming. *Address:* c/o Office of the President, San'a, Yemen (office). *Telephone:* (1) 272283. *Fax:* (1) 252803.

HADI, Hashim al-; Sudanese vice-chancellor and academic; m.; four c.; Research Asst then lecturer, Dept of Physiology and Biochem., Univ. of Khartoum 1964–77, Assoc. Prof. 1977–91, Prof. of Animal Physiology 1991, Dean of Students 1990–92, Dean of Veterinary Science 1992–94, Vice-Chancellor 1994–98; Vice-Chancellor Sudan Int. Univ. 1998–; Assoc. Prof. King Faisal Univ., Saudi Arabia 1979–87, Vice-Dean of Veterinary Medicine 1982–84; Chair. Sudan Veterinary Asscn 1997–; Chair. Asscn of Arab Univs. 1995–97, Sudan Asscn of Univs. 1995–98; mem. Bd Asscn of Int. Univs. 1995–2000; fmr Chair. Sudan Nat. Cttee for Dry Land Husbandry; mem. Sudan Veterinary Council 1997–, World Poultry Science Asscn, Euro-Arab Veterinary Asscn 1997–; mem. Editorial Bd Sudan Journal of Animal Production; Fellow Islamic Acad. of Sciences. *Publications:* contribs. to int. scientific journals. *Address:* Islamic Academy of Sciences, PO Box 830036, Amman, Jordan (office); International University of Africa, PO Box 2469 Khartoum, Sudan. *Telephone:* 5522104 (office). *Fax:* 5511803 (office). *E-mail:* africa@sudanet.net (office).

HADID, Zaha, CBE, FAIA; Iraqi architect; b. 31 Oct. 1950, Baghdad; ed American Univ. Beirut, Architectural Asscn, London; fmr Partner, Office for Metropolitan Architecture; taught at Architectural Asscn, led her own studio –1987; Kenzo Tange Chair, Grad. School of Design, Harvard Univ. 1994; Sullivan Prof., Univ. of Chicago School of Architecture 1997; Guest Prof., Hochschüle für Bildende Künste, Hamburg 1997, Knolton School of Architecture, Ohio, Masters Studio, Columbia Univ., New York; Eero Saarinen Visiting Prof. of Architectural Design, Yale Univ., New Haven, CT 2002; currently Prof., Univ. of Applied Arts, Vienna; won competition for The Peak leisure complex, Hong Kong 1982 (project later cancelled); designed restaurant interior, Sapporo 1991 (first completed work); other winning designs include Kurfurstendamm, Berlin 1986, Dusseldorf Art and Media Centre 1992–93, Cardiff Bay Opera House, Wales 1994, Thames Water/Royal Acad. Habitable Bridge, London 1996, Univ. of North London Holloway Road Bridge 1998, Wolfsburg Science Centre 2000, Maritime Ferry Terminal in Salerno 2000, Placa de les Artes in Barcelona 2001, One-north Masterplan for Singapore's Science Hub 2001, Ordrupgaard Museum Extension, Copenhagen 2001, BMW Cen. Plant Bldg, Leipzig 2002, Price Tower Art Center, Bartlesville, USA 2002, Departement de l'Herault Culture Sport Building, Montpellier, France 2003, High Speed Rail Station Napoli-Afragola, Naples 2003, Guangzhou Opera House, China 2003, masterplan for Beijing's Soho City, China 2003; designed British pavilion at Venice Biennale 2000; works included in perm. collections of MoMA, New York, MoMA, San Francisco, Deutsches Architektur Museum, Frankfurt; current projects include: Contemporary Arts Centre MAXXI, Rome, Guggenheim Museum, Taichung, public square and cinema complex, Barcelona, masterplan for Bilbao's Zorrozaurre dist, housing project in Florence, design for hotel in Madrid, social housing project 'Spittelau Viaduct', Vienna, major bridge structure in Abu Dhabi, the Maggie's Centre, Kirkcaldy, Scotland, Ice and Snow Installation, Lapland; Hon. FAIA 2000; Hon. mem. American Acad. of Arts and Letters 2000, Bund Deutsches Architekten 1998; Architectural Asscn Diploma Prize 1977, Gold Medal for Architectural Design 1982, RIBA Awards for Mind Zone, Millennium Dome 2000, AIA UK Chapter and Red Dot Awards for Terminus Honheim-Nord, Strasbourg 2002, Austrian State Architecture Prize and Tyrolian Architecture Award for Bergisel Ski Jump, Innsbruck 2002, Mies van der Rohe Award for Terminus Honheim-Nord, Strasbourg 2003, Pritzker Architecture Prize 2004, ranked by Forbes magazine amongst 100 Most Powerful Women (68th) 2007, (69th) 2008. *Major works include:* Vitra Fire Station, Germany 1991, LFone pavilion, Weil am Rhein, Germany 1993–99, housing project for IBA-Block 2, Berlin 1993, Mind Zone in Millennium Dome, Greenwich, London 1999, Tram Station and Car Park, Strasbourg 2001, Ski Jump, Innsbruck, Austria 2002, Contemporary Arts Centre, Cincinnati 2003, Guangzhou opera house, People's Repub. of China. *Publications include:* Zaha Hadid: The Complete Buildings and Projects 1998, Zaha Hadid, Opere e progetti 2002, Zaha Hadid Architektur 2003; numerous articles and monographs. *Address:* Studio 9, 10 Bowling Green Lane, London, EC1R 0BD, England. *Telephone:* (20) 7253-5147 (office). *Fax:* (20) 7251-8322 (office). *E-mail:* press@zaha-hadid.com (office). *Website:* www.zaha-hadid.com (office).

HADLEE, Sir Richard John, Kt, KBE; New Zealand fmr professional cricketer; b. 3 July 1951, Christchurch; s. of W. A. Hadlee (New Zealand cricketer); m. Dianne Hadlee; ed Christchurch Boys High School; middle-order left-hand batsman, right-arm fast-medium bowler; played for Canterbury 1971–72 to 1988–89, Nottinghamshire 1978–87, Tasmania 1979–80; played in 86 Tests 1972–73 to 1990, scoring 3,124 runs (average 27.1) and taking then world record 431 wickets (average 22.9); first to take 400 Test wickets (at Christchurch in Feb. 1990 in his 79th Test); took five or more wickets in an innings a record 36 times in Tests; highest test score 151 v Sri Lanka, Colombo 1987; best test bowling performance 9-52 v Australia, Brisbane 1985–86; toured England 1973, 1978, 1983, 1986, 1990; scored 12,052 first-class runs (14 hundreds) and took 1,490 wickets, including five or more in an innings 102 times; achieved Double (1,179 runs and 117 wickets) 1984; now Level III Coach, Christchurch; Public Relations Amb. for Bank of NZ 1990–; Chair. NZ's selectors 2001–04, NZ Cricket Selection Man. 2004–; Wisden Cricketer of the Year 1982, NZ Sportsman of the Year 1980, 1986, NZ Sportsman of the Decade 1987, NZ Sportsman of the last 25 years 1987. *Publications:* Rhythm and Swing (autobiog.) 1989, Cricket: The Essentials of the Game, Howzat: Tales from the Boundary, Caught Out, Soft Deliveries, Hard Knocks, Hadlee, Hadlee on Cricket. *Leisure interests:* movies, golf, gardening. *Address:* Box 29186, Christchurch, New Zealand. *E-mail:* hadleerj@ihug.co.nz (office). *Website:* www.hadlee.co.nz (office).

HADLEY, Stephen John, BA, JD; American lawyer and fmr government official; b. 13 Feb. 1947, Toledo; m. Ann Simon; two c.; ed Cornell Univ., Yale Law School; worked as an analyst for Comptroller, US Dept of Defense 1972–74; mem. Nat. Security Council staff 1974–77; Pnr, Shea and Gardner (law firm), Washington, DC 1977–2001; fmr Prin. The Scowcroft Group Inc. (consulting firm), Washington, DC; Counsel, Tower Comm. Special Review Bd 1986–87; Asst US Sec. of Defense for Int. Security Policy 1989–1993; sr foreign policy and defence policy adviser to George W. Bush during his first presidential campaign; Deputy Nat. Security Advisor 2001–05, Nat. Security Advisor 2005–09. *Address:* c/o National Security Council, Eisenhower Executive Office Building, 17th Street and Pennsylvania Avenue, NW, Washington, DC 20504, USA.

HAEFLIGER, Andreas; Swiss pianist; b. Berlin, Germany; ed Juilliard School, New York; studied with Herbert Stessin, twice won Gina Bachauer Memorial Scholarship; has appeared with many of world's leading orchestras in N America, Europe and Japan; numerous recital appearances including Great Performers Series, Lincoln Center, New York, Wigmore Hall, London and in Germany, Austria, France and Italy; has performed regularly at BBC Proms, London; performs in USA with Takacs String Quartet; performs frequently with baritone Matthias Goerner; Preis der Deutschen Schallplattenkritik (for recording of Schubert's Goethe Lieder). *Recordings include:* Mozart Piano Sonatas, Schumann's Davidsbündlertanze and Fantasiestücke, Schubert's Impromptus, music by Sofia Gubaidulina, Schubert's Goethe Lieder (with Matthias Goerne), Perspectives I (including works by Schubert, Adès, Mozart and Beethoven). *Address:* Intermusica Artists Management Ltd, 16 Duncan Terrace, London, N1 8BZ, England (office). *Telephone:* (20) 7278-5455 (office). *Fax:* (20) 7278-8434 (office). *E-mail:* mail@intermusica.co.uk (office). *Website:* www.intermusica.co.uk (office).

HAEFNER, Walter; Swiss business executive; b. Sept. 1910; two c.; owner Amag Group, Careal Holding; investment in Computer Assocs. *Leisure interest:* racehorses. *Address:* AMAG Group, Utoquai 49, 8008 Zurich, Switzerland (office). *Telephone:* (1) 2695353 (office). *Fax:* (1) 2695363 (office). *Website:* www.amag.ch (office).

HAEKKERUP, Hans; Danish politician; *Research Director of China Studies, Royal Danish Defence College;* b. 3 Dec. 1945, Copenhagen; s. of Per Haekkerup and Grete Haekkerup; m. Susanne Rumohr Haekkerup; five s.; ed Copenhagen Univ.; with Ministry of Social Affairs 1973–76, of Educ. 1976–77, of Labour 1977–79; Prof. Danish School of Admin. 1977–80; mem. Folketing (Parl.) 1979–2000, served on several cttees including Cttee on Danish Security Policy, Cttee on Greenlandic Affairs, Cttee on Foreign Policy; economist with Civil Servants Org. 1981–85; Chair. Defence Cttee 1991–93; Minister of Defence 1993–2000; Special Rep. of UN Sec.-Gen. for Kosovo Jan.–Dec. 2001; Advisor on Security Policy 2002–07; Research Dir of China Studies, Royal Danish Defence Coll. 2007–. *Address:* Groennegade 27, 1107 Copenhagen K, Denmark (office).

HAFEN, Ernst, PhD; Swiss geneticist and academic; *Professor, Institute of Molecular Systems Biology, Eidgenössische Technische Hochschule (ETH) Zürich;* b. 1956, St Gallen; ed Univ. of Basel; Research Asst, Biocenter Basel 1983; Postdoctoral Research Asst, Dept of Biochemistry, Univ. of California, Berkeley, USA 1984–86; Asst Prof. for Developmental Genetics, Univ. of Zurich 1987–94, Assoc. Prof. 1994–97, Full Prof. 1997–2005, Dir Zoological Inst. 2005; Dir ETH Zurich 2005–06; fmr mem. Nat. Research Council; fmr rep. profs at Council of Univ. of Zurich; mem. editorial bds of several major journals, including The EMBO Journal; helped develop jt centres of ETH and Univ. of Zurich, including SystemsX, Life Science Zurich, Life Science Learning Center Zurich; Co-founder and Scientific Advisor, The Genetics Co.; Ernst Jung Prize for Medicine, Jung-Stiftung für Wissenschaft und Forschung (co-recipient) 2005. *Publications:* numerous scientific papers in professional journals on developmental and cell biology. *Address:* Institute for Molecular Systems Biology, ETH Zürich, Wolfgang-Pauli-Strasse 16, 8093 Zürich, Switzerland (office). *Telephone:* (44) 633-36-88 (office). *Fax:* (44) 633-10-51 (office); (44) 633-11-41 (office). *E-mail:* hafen@imsb.biol.ethz.ch (office); ernst.hafen@imsb.biol.ethz.ch (office). *Website:* www.zool.uzh.ch (office).

HAFEZ, Maj.-Gen. Amin El; Syrian politician and army officer; b. 1911; fmr mil. attaché in Argentina; took part in the revolution of March 1963; Deputy Prime Minister, Mil. Gov. of Syria and Minister of Interior March–Aug. 1963; Minister of Defence and Army Chief of Staff July–Aug. 1963; Pres. of Revolutionary Council and C-in-C of Armed Forces 1963–64; Prime Minister Nov. 1963–64, 1964–65; Chair. of Presidency Council 1965–66; sentenced to death in absentia Aug. 1971; living in exile.

HAFEZ, Mahmoud, PhD; Egyptian entomologist and academic; *Professor Emeritus of Entomology, Cairo University;* b. 10 Jan. 1912; ed Cairo Univ.; Research Fellow, Univ. of Cambridge 1946–48; Prof. and Head Dept of Entomology, Cairo Univ. 1953, Vice-Dean 1964, Prof. Emer. 1972–; Under-Sec. of State for Scientific Research 1966; Pres. Nat. Research Council for Basic Sciences, Acad. of Scientific Research and Tech. in Egypt, Entomological Soc. of Egypt, Egyptian Soc. of Parasitology, Egyptian Science Asscn, Egyptian Soc. for the History of Science; Chair. Nat. Cttee for Biological Sciences; mem. Higher Council for Educ. and Scientific Research and Tech. in Egypt; Fellow and fmr Pres. Egyptian Acad. of Sciences; Fellow Islamic Acad. of Sciences, African Acad. of Sciences, Royal Entomological Soc., London, Third World Acad. of Sciences; Emer. mem. Entomological Soc. of America;

Founding mem. African Asscn of Insect Sciences; mem. Network of African Scientific Orgs, Int. Union of Biological Sciences, Int. Org. for Biological Control; State Prize (Egypt) 1977, Gold Medal (Egypt) 1977, Order of Merit, First Class 1978, Order of Science and Art (First Class) 1981. *Publications:* 10 books on zoology and entomology; over 150 scientific papers on insect science. *Address:* Entomology Department, Faculty of Science, Cairo University, Giza, Cairo, Egypt (office). *Telephone:* (2) 5729584 (office). *Fax:* (2) 628884 (office).

HAGAN, Kay Ruthven, BA, JD; American lawyer and politician; *Senator from North Carolina;* b. 26 March 1953, Shelby, N Carolina; m. Charles T. (Chip) Hagan III; one s. two d.; ed Florida State Univ., Wake Forest Univ.; served in pvt. law practice as attorney for N Carolina Nat. Bank (now Bank of America) 1978–88; mem. N Carolina State Senate 1999–2003, Co-Chair. Pensions, Retirement and Aging Cttee, mem. Cttees on Appropriations and Base Budget, on Commerce, Small Business and Entrepreneurship, on Educ., on Finance, on Health Care; Senator from N Carolina 2009–. *Address:* Office of Senator Kay Hagan, US Senate, Washington, DC 20510, USA (office). *Website:* www.senate.gov (office).

HAGEDORN, Jürgen, Dr rer. nat; German academic; *Professor Emeritus of Geography, University of Göttingen;* b. 10 March 1933, Hankensbüttel; s. of Ernst Hagedorn and Dorothea Schulze; m. Ingeborg A. Carl 1965; one d.; ed Hermann-Billung-Gymnasium, Celle, Tech. Hochschule Hanover and Univ. of Göttingen; Asst Lecturer, Univ. of Göttingen 1962–69, Dozent 1969–70, Prof. 1970–72, Prof. of Geography and Dir Inst. of Geography 1972–2001, now Prof. Emer.; mem. Göttingen Acad., Akad. Leopoldina. *Publications:* Geomorphologie des Uelzener Beckens 1964, Geomorphologie griechischer Hochgebirge 1969, Late Quaternary and Present-Day Fluvial Processes in Central Europe (ed.) 1995. *Address:* Jupiterweg 1, 37077 Göttingen, Germany (home). *Telephone:* (551) 21323 (home). *E-mail:* jhagedo@gwdg.de (office); a.j.hagedorn@t-online.de (home).

HAGÈGE, Claude, LèsL, TH; Tunisian linguist and writer; b. Carthage; teacher Lycée Carnot, Tunis 1959–61, Lycées Victor Duruy et Saint-Louis, Paris 1963–66; Prof. of Linguistics Univ. of Poitiers 1963–66; Chief of Confs Univ. of Paris XII Val-de-Marne 1971–74, Univ. of Paris IV 1976–78, Univ. of Paris III 1977–78; Dir of Linguistic Studies Ecole Pratique des Hautes Etudes 1977; teacher Collège de France 1982–; Officier, Ordre des Palmes académiques 1995, Chevalier, Ordre des Arts et des Lettres 1995, Officier, Légion d'honneur 2005; Prix Volney de l'Acad. des Inscriptions et Belles-Lettres 1981, Grand Prix de l'Essai de la Soc. des Gens de Lettres 1986, Grand Prix de l'Acad. Française 1986, CNRS Médaille d'or 1995, Prix du Mot d'or des langues 2003. *Publications:* La Structure des langues 1982, L'Homme de paroles 1985, Le Français et les siècles 1987, Le Souffle de la langue 1992, L'Enfant aux deux langues 1996, Le Français, histoire d'un combat 1996, Halte à la mort des langues 2001, Les Destins du français 2005. *Address:* Collège de France, 11 place Marcelin Berthelot, 75231 Paris Cédex 05, France (office). *Telephone:* 1-44-27-17-03 (office). *Fax:* 1-44-27-13-29 (home). *E-mail:* claude.hagege@college-de-france.fr (office); claude-hagege@wanadoo.fr (home). *Website:* claude.hagege.wanadoo.fr (home).

HAGEL, Charles (Chuck), BA; American fmr politician; b. 4 Oct. 1946, North Platte, Neb.; m. Lilibet Hagel (née Ziller); one s. one d.; ed Brown Inst. of Radio & Television, Minneapolis, Minn., Univ. of Nebraska at Omaha; served in US Army 1967–68; Deputy Admin. Va 1981–82; Pres. and CEO World United Service Org. 1987–90; Pres. McCarthy & Co. 1991–96; Senator from Neb. 1996–2009, mem. numerous Senate cttees including Chair. Senate Subcttee on Int. Econ. Policy, Export and Trade Promotion; Distinguished Prof. in the Practice of Nat. Governance, Edmund A. Walsh School of Foreign Service, Georgetown Univ. 2009; Founder-Dir Vanguard Cellular Systems Inc.; mem. American Legion, Veterans of Foreign Wars; Trustee, Omaha Chamber of Commerce; Republican; numerous awards including Cordell Hull Award 2003, Award for Distinguished Int. Leadership, Atlantic Council 2004, Woodrow Wilson Int. Center for Scholars Public Service Award 2005, Marlin Fitzwater Excellence in Public Communication Award 2005, US Chamber of Commerce 'Spirit of Enterprise' Award 2007, Millard E. Tydings Award for Courage and Leadership in American Politics, Univ. of Maryland 2008, Aspen Strategy Group Leadership Award 2008. *Address:* 9900 Nicholas St., Suite 325, Omaha, NE 68114, USA.

HAGEN, Carl I.; Norwegian politician; *Deputy Speaker, Parliament;* b. 6 May 1944, Oslo; s. of Ragnar Hagen and Gerd Gamborg Hagen; m. 1st Nina Aamodt 1970; m. 2nd Eli Engum Hagen 1983; one s. one d.; ed Inst. of Marketing, London; mem. Stortinget (Norwegian Parl.) 1974–77, 1981–, Deputy Speaker 2005–; Leader of Fremskrittspartiet (Progress Party) and Parl. Group 1978–2005. *Publication:* Aerlighet Varer Lengst (biog.). *Leisure interests:* tennis, family, golf. *Address:* Office of the Deputy Speaker, Stortinget, Karl Johansgt. 22, 0026 Oslo (office); Fremskrittspartiet, PO Box 8903, Youngstorget, 0028 Oslo, Norway. *Telephone:* 23-31-30-03 (office). *Fax:* 23-31-38-28 (office). *E-mail:* postmottak.frp@stortinget.no (office). *Website:* www.frp.no (office).

HAGGIS, Paul; Canadian screenwriter, film director and film producer; b. 10 March 1953, London, Ontario; s. of Ted Haggis and Mary Haggis; m. Deborah Rennard; four c.; ed Fanshawe Coll.; directed and wrote plays for parents' Gallery Theatre, London, Ontario 1970s; co-founder Artists for Peace and Justice; mem. Bd of Dirs Environmental Media Asscn, Pres.'s Council of Defenders of Wildlife; mem. Advisory Bd Centre for the Advancement of Non-Violence; Valentine Davies Award, Writers' Guild of America 2001. *Films include:* as screenwriter: Red Hot 1993, Million Dollar Baby (also producer) 2004, Crash (also dir and producer) (Acad. Award for Best Film 2006, Humanitas Prize 2006) 2005, Last Kiss 2006, Flags of Our Fathers 2006, Casino Royale 2006, Letters from Iwo Jima (story) 2006, In the Valley of Elah 2007. *Television includes:* Due South (exec. producer and writer), creator Walker, Texas Ranger, Family Law (exec. producer and writer), EZ Streets (exec. producer and writer), creator The Black Donnellys 2007; writer numerous episodes in series. *Address:* c/o CAA, 9830 Wilshire Blvd., Beverly Hills, CA 90212-1825, USA.

HÄGGLUND, Gen. Gustav; Finnish army officer; b. 6 Sept. 1938, Wyborg; m. Ritva Ekström; one s. two d.; ed Finnish Mil. Acad., Univ. of Helsinki, Finnish War Coll.; nat. mil. service 1957–58; commanded Finnish Bn UNEF II, Sinai 1978–79, Nyland Brigade, Finland 1984–85, UNDOF, Golan Heights 1985–86, UN Interim Force in Lebanon (UNIFIL), Lebanon 1986–88, South East Mil. Area Finland 1988–90; Chief of Defence Staff 1990–94, Chief of Defence 1994–2001; Chair. EU Mil. Cttee, Brussels 2001–04; US Army Command and Gen. Staff Coll. 1972–73; Fellow Harvard Univ. Center for Int. Affairs 1981–82. *Publications:* Peace-making in the Finnish Winter War 1969, Northern Europe in Strategic Perspective 1974, US Strategy for Europe 1974, Parliamentary Defence Committees in Finland 1981, Modern US Cruise Missiles, an Evaluation 1982, Peace-keeping in a Modern War Zone 1990, Defence of Finland 2001. *Leisure interests:* hunting, shooting, roaming in the wilderness. *Address:* c/o rue de la Loi 175, 1048 Brussels, Belgium (office).

HAGIWARA, Toshitaka, LLM; Japanese business executive; *Chairman, Komatsu Ltd;* b. Tokyo; ed Waseda Univ.; joined Komatsu Ltd 1969, mem. Bd of Dirs 1990–, Man. Dir 1995–97, Exec. Man. Dir 1997–99, Rep. Dir 1999–, Exec. Vice-Pres. 1999–2003, Chair. 2003–; Pres. Financial Accounting Standards Foundation; Chair. Jt Cttee on Econ. Regulation, Nippon Keidanren; Co-Chair. Japan Business Fed.'s Econ. Law Cttee; mem. Legislative Council, Ministry of Justice. *Address:* Komatsu Ltd, 2-3-6 Akasaka, Minato-ku, Tokyo 107-8414, Japan (office). *Telephone:* (3) 5561-2687 (office). *Fax:* (3) 3505-9662 (office). *Website:* www.komatsu.com (office).

HAGUE, Rt Hon. William Jefferson, PC, MA, MBA; British politician and writer; *Shadow Foreign Secretary and Senior Member of the Shadow Cabinet;* b. 26 March 1961; s. of Timothy N. Hague and Stella Hague; m. Ffion Jenkins 1997; ed Wath-upon-Dearne Comprehensive School, Magdalen Coll. Oxford and INSEAD, France; Pres. Oxford Union 1981; man. consultant, McKinsey & Co. 1983–88; political adviser, HM Treasury 1983; MP for Richmond, Yorks. 1989–; Parl. Pvt. Sec. to Chancellor of Exchequer 1990–93; Parl. Under-Sec. of State, Dept of Social Security 1993–94; Minister for Social Security and Disabled People, Dept of Social Security 1994–95; Sec. of State for Wales 1995–97; Leader of Conservative Party and Leader of the Opposition 1997–2001; Chair. Int. Democratic Union 1999–2001, now Deputy Chair.; Shadow Foreign Sec. and Sr Mem. of the Shadow Cabinet.2005–; Econ. and Political Adviser JCB PLC 2001–; Dir (non-exec.) AES Eng PLC 2001–; mem. Political Council of Terra Firma Capital Pnrs 2001–; The Spectator Parliamentarian of the Year 1998, Channel 4 Politician of the Year 2001. *Publications:* William Pitt the Younger (biog.) (British Book Award for History Book of the Year 2005) 2004, William Wilberforce: The Life of the Great Anti-Slave Trade Campaigner 2007. *Leisure interests:* walking, judo, playing the piano. *Address:* House of Commons, London, SW1A 0AA, England (office). *Telephone:* (1609) 772060 (office). *Fax:* (1609) 774339 (office). *E-mail:* haguew@parliament.uk (office). *Website:* www.williamhague.org.uk (office).

HAHN, Carl Horst, Dr rer. pol; Austrian business executive; b. 1 July 1926, Chemnitz; m. Marisa Traina 1960; three s. one d.; Chair. of Bd, Continental Gummi-Werke AG 1973–81; Chair. Man. Bd, Volkswagen AG 1981–92; mem. Supervisory Bd HAWESKO, Hamburg, Perot Systems 1993–, Dallas; mem. Int. Supervisory Bd Indesit Co., Fabriano; mem. Int. Advisory Bd, Textron, Wichity, Inst. de Empresa, Madrid; mem. Int. Advisory Cttee, Salk Inst., Calif.; Chair. Bd of Trustees, Kunstmuseum Wolfsburg; mem. Bd Mayo Clinic, Stiftung, Frankfurt, Lauder-Inst., Wharton School, Pa; several hon. doctorates. *Address:* Hollerplatz 1, 38440 Wolfsburg, Germany (office). *Telephone:* (5361) 26680 (office). *Fax:* (5361) 266815 (office). *E-mail:* carl.hahn@volkswagen.de (office).

HAHN, Erwin Louis, BS, PhD, FRS; American physicist and academic; *Professor Emeritus of Physics, University of California, Berkeley;* b. 9 June 1921, Sharon, Pa; s. of Israel Hahn and Mary Hahn; m. 1st Marian Ethel Failing 1944 (deceased); one s. two d.; m. 2nd Natalie Woodford Hodgson 1980; ed Juniata Coll. and Univ. of Illinois; Asst, Purdue Univ. 1943–44; Research Asst, Univ. of Illinois 1950; Nat. Research Council Fellow, Stanford Univ. 1950–51, Instructor 1951–52; Research Physicist, Watson IBM Lab., New York 1952–55; Assoc., Columbia Univ., New York 1952–55; Assoc., Univ. of Calif., Berkeley 1955, Asst Prof. 1955–56, Assoc. Prof. 1956–61, Assoc. Prof., Miller Inst. for Basic Research 1958–59, Prof. of Physics 1961–91, Prof. Emer. 1991–; Visiting Fellow, Brasenose Coll., Oxford 1960–61, 1981–82 (Hon. Fellow 1981–82); Miller Prof., Univ. of Calif. 1985–86; Eastman (Visiting) Prof., Balliol Coll. Oxford 1988–89; mem. NAS 1972; Assoc. mem. Slovenian Acad. of Sciences 1981; Foreign Assoc. mem. Acad. des Sciences (France) 1992; Fellow, American Acad. of Arts and Sciences, American Physical Soc., Int. Soc. of Electron Paramagnetic Spin Resonance; Foreign Fellow, Royal Soc. (UK) 2001, Physical Soc. (UK) 2001; discoverer of spin echoes; introduced pulsed nuclear magnetic resonance free precession spectroscopy; Hon. DSc (Juniata Coll.) 1966, (Purdue Univ., Indiana) 1975, (Warwick Univ., UK) 2007; Hon. Dr rer. nat (Stuttgart) 2001; Guggenheim Fellow 1961, 1970; Buckley Prize 1971, Int. Soc. of Magnetic Resonance Prize 1971, Alexander von Humboldt Foundation Award (FRG) 1976–77, Co-winner, Wolf Foundation Prize 1983/84, Calif. Inventors Hall of Fame 1984, The Berkeley Citation 1991, Comstock Prize (co-recipient), NAS (for research in radiation and electromagnetism) 1993, Russell Varian NMR Prize 2000, and other prizes and awards. *Publications:* Nuclear Quadruple Resonance Spectroscopy (with T.P. Das) 1958; articles in learned journals. *Leisure interests:* violin, chamber music. *Address:* Department of Physics, University of California, 257 Birge Hall,

Berkeley, CA 94720-0001 (office); 69 Stevenson Avenue, Berkeley, CA 94708-1732, USA (home). *Telephone:* (510) 642-2305 (office); (510) 845-0082 (home). *Fax:* (510) 643-8497 (office); (510) 841-4618 (home). *E-mail:* hahn@physics.berkeley.edu (office). *Website:* physics.berkeley.edu/people/directory.php?id=239 (office).

HAHN, Frank, PhD, FBA; British economist and academic; *Professor Emeritus of Economics, University of Cambridge;* b. 26 April 1925, Berlin, Germany; s. of Arnold Hahn and Maria Hahn; m. Dorothy Salter 1946; ed Bournemouth Grammar School, London School of Econs; Lecturer, then Reader in Math. Econs, Univ. of Birmingham 1948–60; Lecturer in Econs, Univ. of Cambridge 1960–67, Prof. of Econs, 1972–92, Prof. Emer. 1992–; Prof. of Econs, LSE 1967–72; Professore Ordinario, Univ. of Siena, Italy 1989–; Frank W. Taussig Resident Prof., Harvard Univ. 1974; Visiting Prof., MIT 1956–57, 1971–72, 1982, Univ. of Calif., Berkeley 1959–60; Pres. Econometric Soc. 1968–69; Man.-Ed. Review of Economic Studies 1963–66; Pres. Royal Econ. Soc. 1986–89; Pres. Section F, British Asscn 1990; Fellow of Churchill Coll., Cambridge 1960–; Fellow American Acad. of Arts and Sciences, American Acad. 1971; Foreign Assoc. NAS 1988; mem. Academia Europaea 1989; Hon. mem. American Econ. Asscn 1986; Hon. Fellow LSE 1989; Hon. DSocSc (Univ. of Birmingham) 1981; Hon. DLitt (Univ. of East Anglia) 1984, (Leicester) 1993; Dr hc (Univ. Louis Pasteur, Strasbourg) 1984, (York) 1991, (Paris X, Nanterre) 1999; Hon. DSc (Econ) (London) 1985; Hon. PhD (Athens) 1993; Palacky Gold Medal of Czechoslovak Acad. of Sciences 1991. *Publications:* General Competitive Analysis (with K. J. Arrow q.v.) 1971, The Share of Wages in National Income 1972, Money and Inflation 1982, Equilibrium and Macroeconomics 1984, Money, Growth and Stability 1985, The Economics of Missing Markets, Information and Games (ed.) 1989, Handbook of Monetary Economics (co-ed.) 1990, A Critical Essay on Modern Macroeconomic Theory (with Robert Solow) 1995, New Theories in Growth and Development (co-ed.) 1998, General Equilibrium: Problems and Prospects (co-ed. with Fabio Petri) 2003; also more than 80 articles in learned journals. *Leisure interests:* reading, gardening. *Address:* 16 Adams Road, Cambridge, CB3 9AD, England (home). *E-mail:* frank.hahn@econ.cam.ac.uk (office).

HAHN, Heinz W., DEng; German engineering executive; b. 13 Feb. 1929, Rüsselsheim; m. Lisel Hummel 1955; one d.; ed Tech. Univ., Darmstadt, Tech. Univ., Karlsruhe; diesel engine engineer, Motoren-Werke, Mannheim 1958–61; Chief Eng Hanomag-Henschel, Hanover 1961–69; Dir and mem. Bd Klöckner-Humboldt-Deutz AG, Cologne 1970–74; Pres. and CEO Magirus-Deutsch AG, Ulm 1975–81; Exec. Vice-Pres. and Deputy Chair. IVECO, Ulm 1981–85; Vice-Pres. IVECO, Turin 1985–89, Deputy Chair. 1989–, now Chair. Admin. Bd IVECO Motorenforschung AG, Switzerland. *Address:* Ginsterweg 31, 89233 Neu-Ulm, Germany (home).

HAHN, James Kenneth (Jim), BA, JD; American politician, lawyer and business executive; *Mediator, Alternative Resolution Centers;* b. 1951, Los Angeles; s. of Kenneth Hahn and Ramona Hahn (née Fox); divorced; one s. one d.; ed Lutheran High School, South LA, Pepperdine Univ.; Deputy City Prosecutor, LA City Attorney's Office 1975–79, City Controller of LA 1981–85, City Attorney of LA 1985–2001; Mayor of LA 2001–05; Man. Dir Chadwick Saylor and Co. Inc., LA 2005–07; Mediator, Alternative Resolution Centers 2007–; pvt. law practice in Marina del Rey, Calif. 1979–81; Democrat. *Address:* Alternative Resolution Centers, 1875 Century Park East, Suite 450, Los Angeles, CA 90067, USA (office). *Telephone:* (310) 284-8224 (office). *Fax:* (310) 284-8229 (office). *E-mail:* jhahn@arc4adr.com (office). *Website:* www.arc4adr.com (office).

HAI, Musharaf; Pakistani business executive; *Country Business Manager, Citibank NA Pakistan;* ed London School of Econs, UK, Boston Univ., USA; joined Unilever 1983, several man. positions including Marketing Man., Co-ordinator for Detergents in East Asia-Pacific and Africa/Middle East regions, Unilever HQ, London 1993–96, responsible for Unilever Pakistan Ice Cream Div. 1996, later Dir Home & Personal Care Div., Sales Dir –2001, Chair. Unilever Pakistan (first woman head of a major multinational co. in Pakistan) 2001–06; Country Business Man. Citibank NA Pakistan, Karachi 2006–, also Head of Consumer Banking Pakistan; mem. Bd of Govs Lahore Univ. Man. Sciences, LEAD Pakistan 2003–; mem. Bd LEAD Pakistan 2003–; mem. Nat. Council Duke of Edinburgh's Award Programme Pakistan; mem. Man. Cttee Overseas Investors' Chamber of Commerce and Industry, Bd of Investment, Govt of Pakistan 2002–03; ranked by Fortune magazine amongst 50 Most Powerful Women in Business outside the US (46th) 2004. *Address:* Citibank NA Pakistan, State Life Building # 1, 3rd Floor I.I.Chundrigar Road, Karachi, Pakistan (office). *Website:* www.citibank.com/pakistan (office).

HAIDALLA, Lt-Col Mohamed Khouna Ould; Mauritanian politician and army officer; Chair. Mil. Cttee for Nat. Recovery (now Cttee for Nat. Salvation) 1978–84; Chief of Staff of Mauritanian Army 1978–79; Minister of Defence April–May 1979, 1980, Prime Minister 1979–80, Pres. of Mauritania 1980–84 (overthrown in coup); stood as unsuccessful cand. in presidential election Nov. 2003; arrested and charged with treason Nov. 2003, trial suspended Dec. 2003.

HAIDAR, Shoukria, MA, PhD; French/Afghan human rights activist and teacher; *President, NEGAR—Support Women of Afghanistan Association;* b. 11 Nov. 1957, Kabul; m.; ed Univ. of Nice; fmr ping-pong champion, Kabul; worked for IOC 1979–80; exile in France 1980–; various jobs in a bakery, dress-making workshop, Paris; Founding Pres. NEGAR—Support Women of Afghanistan Asscn 1996–; obtained French citizenship 1998; currently Prof. of Physical Educ., Collège d'Aulnay-sous-Bois; organiser and Speaker, Women on the Road to Afghanistan Conf., Dushanbe, Tajikistan 2000. *Address:* Negar—Soutien aux Femmes d'Afghanistan, BP 10, 25770 Franois, France (office). *Telephone:* 1-48-35-07-56 (office). *Fax:* 1-48-35-07-56 (office). *E-mail:* negar@wanadoo.fr (office). *Website:* perso.wanadoo.fr/negar (office).

HAIDER, Syed Zahir, PhD, CChem, FRSC; Bangladeshi chemist and academic; *President, Bangladesh Chemical Society;* b. 1 Sept. 1927, Dhaka; ed Imperial Coll., Univ. of London, UK and Stuttgart Univ., Germany; Lecturer in Chem., Dhaka Univ. 1950, Reader then Prof. 1970–98, Chair. Dept of Chem. 1982–85, Khundkar Chair of Chem. 1985–92; currently Pres, Bangladesh Chemical Society, Dhaka; Head Dept of Chem., Chittagong Univ. 1968–70; fmr Dir Bose Centre for Advanced Studies and Research; mem. Swedish Inst. research programme at Arrhenius Lab., Stockholm; Pres. Bangladesh Chemical Soc., Bangladesh Environmental Soc. 1998–2000; Fellow Islamic Acad. of Sciences, mem. Council 1994–99; Fellow and mem. Council Bangladesh Acad. of Sciences, Fellow Asiatic Soc. of Bangladesh; Founding Ed. Journal of Bangladesh Acad. of Sciences 1977; Chief Ed. Journal of Bangladesh Chemical Soc.; First H. P. Roy Gold Medal for original contributions in chemical research 1961, First Gold Medal in Physical Sciences, Bangladesh Acad. of Sciences 1983. *Publications include:* Science in Arts and Architectures, Enlightenment and Environment; over 250 papers on inorganic, analytical co-ordination, nuclear and bio-inorganic chem. *Leisure interests:* tourism, historical places. *Address:* Bangladesh Chemical Society, 10/11, Eastern Plaza, Sonargaon Road, Hatirpool, Dhaka 1205; Department of Chemistry, Dhaka University, Dhaka 1000 (office); 5/12 Block A, Lalmatia, Dhaka 1207, Bangladesh (home). *Telephone:* (2) 864683 (office); (2) 9115991 (home). *Fax:* (2) 8615583 (office). *E-mail:* dumail@du.bangla.net (office); hshabbir@bdmail.net (home).

HAIDUC, Ionel, MSc, PhD; Romanian chemist and academic; *President, Romanian Academy;* b. 9 May 1937, Cluj; ed Babes-Bolyai Univ., Inst. of Fine Chemicals Tech., Moscow, Iowa State Univ., Univ. of Georgia, USA; Lab. Asst, Dept of Chem., Babes-Bolyai Univ. 1959–62, Asst 1962–64, Lecturer 1964–69, Reader 1969–73, Prof. 1979–, Prorector 1976–84, Rector 1990–93; NSF Visiting Scientist, Dept of Chem., Univ. of Georgia, USA 1992; EC Visiting Scientist, Univ. of Santiago de Compostela, Spain 1993; Visiting Scientist, Nat. Univ. of Singapore 2002; Visiting Prof., Instituto de Quimica, Universidad Nacional Autonoma de Mexico 1993–94, Instituto de Quimica, Universidade Federal de Sao Carlos, Brazil 1994, 2000, Univ. of Santiago de Compostela 1998, Univ. of Texas, El Paso 2000–01, 2004, Göttingen Univ., Germany 1998–99, 2002; Consultant Dept of Chem., Univ. of Texas, El Paso 1997, 2005; Visiting Lecturer, Columbia Univ., New York 2003; UNESCO Expert, Consulting Mission to Moldova 1999; Corresp. mem. Romanian Acad. 1990–, mem. 1991–, Pres. Transylvania Br. 1995–, mem. Grant Cttee 1996–, Vice-Pres. 1998–2000, Pres. 2006–; Bd mem. Nat. Council for Academic Research 1992–, Nat. Council for Academic Titles and Diplomas 1992–, Nat. Council for Academic Reform 1998; Pres. Consultative Coll., Nat. Agency for Research, Devt and Innovation 1998–2003; mem. Bd of Dirs Alliance of Univs for Democracy 1991–93; mem. Int. Council of Main Group Chem. 1993–; Founding mem. Nat. Foundation for Science and Arts; mem. Accad. Europaea 2002–; mem. Editorial Bd Synthesis and Reactivity in Inorganic and Metal-organic Chemistry, Main-Group Metal Chemistry, Metal-Based Drugs, Science and Engineering Ethics, Revue Roumaine de Chimie, Revista de Chimie; Hon. Citizen of Cluj-Napoca 1999, Hon. mem. Moldavian Acad. of Sciences 2002; Star of Romania 2000, Order of Honour (Moldova) 2006; Hon. Diploma (Moldavian Acad. of Sciences) 1999; Dr hc (Gh. Assachi Tech. Univ.) 2002, (Polytechnic Univ. of Timisoara) 2004; Fulbright Fellowship 1966, G. Spacu Prize, Romanian Acad. 1974, Pro Colaboratione Award, Hungarian Acad. of Sciences 1999, Romanian Chemical Soc. Prize 2004. *Publications:* Chemistry of Inorganic Ring Systems 1970, Basic Organometallic Chemistry (with J.J. Zuckerman) 1985, Chemistry of Inorganic Homo and Heterocycles 1987, Organometallics in Cancer Chemotherapy (with C. Silvestru) 1990, Supramolecular Organometallic Chemistry (with F.T. Edelmann) 1999; numerous contribs to academic journals. *Address:* Romanian Academy, 125 Calea Victoriei, sector 1, 010071 Bucharest, Romania (office). *Telephone:* (21) 28640 (office). *Fax:* (21) 16608 (office). *E-mail:* ihaiduc@chem.ubbcluj.ro (office). *Website:* www.academiaromana.ro (office).

HAIG, Gen. Alexander Meigs, Jr, BS, MA; American army officer, politician and business executive; *Chairman, Worldwide Associates Inc.;* b. 2 Dec. 1924, Philadelphia, PA; s. of Alexander M. and Regina Murphy Haig; m. Patricia Fox 1950; two s. one d.; ed US Mil. Acad., Naval War Coll., Georgetown Univ. and Columbia Univ.; joined US Army 1947, rising to Brig.-Gen. 1969, Maj.-Gen. 1972, Gen. 1973; Deputy Special Asst to Sec. and Deputy Sec. of Defence 1964–65; Battalion and Brigade Commdr 1st Infantry Div., Repub. of Viet Nam 1966–67; Regimental Commdr and Deputy Commdt US Mil. Acad. 1967–69; Sr Mil. Adviser to Asst to Pres. for Nat. Security Affairs, the White House 1969–70; Deputy Asst to Pres. for Nat. Security Affairs 1970–73; Vice-Chief of Staff, US Army Jan.–July 1973; special emissary to Viet Nam Jan. 1973; retd from US Army Aug. 1973; Asst to Pres. and White House Chief of Staff Aug. 1973–Oct. 1974; recalled to active duty, US Army Oct. 1974; C-in-C, US European Command 1974–79; Supreme Allied Commdr Europe, NATO 1974–79; Pres., COO and Dir United Technologies Corpn 1980–81; Sec. of State 1981–82; Chair. Atlantic and Pacific Advisory Councils of United Technologies 1982; founder, Chair. and Pres. Worldwide Assocs, Inc. (consulting firm) 1984–; Founding Dir America Online, Inc. 1989; Dir Indevus Pharmaceuticals Inc. 1990, MGM Mirage Inc. 1990, Metro-Goldwyn-Mayer Inc. 1995–2005, CompuServe, Inc. 2001–03, SDC International Inc. 2002–04, Tigris Pharmaceuticals 2005, Transcutaneous Technologies Inc. 2005; Chair. & Dir DOR Biopharma Inc. 2003–05; mem. Presidential Comm. on Strategic Forces 1983–84; Sr Fellow, Hudson Inst. for Policy Research 1982–84, now Trustee Emer.; numerous hon. degrees including Hon. LLD (Utah and Niagara); Gold Medal Nat. Inst. of Social Sciences 1980, Distinguished Grad. Award of West Point 1997, James Doolittle Award of Hudson Inst. 1999; numerous medals, awards and citations, including DSC for heroism. *TV:* host of World Business Review. *Publications:* Caveat: Realism, Reagan and

Foreign Policy 1984, Inner Circles: How America Changed the World, A Memoir 1992. *Leisure interests:* golf, tennis. *Address:* Suite 110, 1005 North Glebe Road, Arlington, VA 22201, USA (office). *Telephone:* (703) 525-3939 (office). *Fax:* (703) 525-3955 (office). *E-mail:* AHaig@aol.com (office).

HAIGNERÉ, Claudie, MD, PhD; French politician, astronaut, physician and rheumatologist; *Senior Adviser to the Director General, European Space Agency;* b. (Claudie Andre), 13 May 1957, Le Creusot; m. Jean-Pierre Haigneré; one d.; ed Faculté de Médecine, Dijon and Paris-Cochin, Faculté des Sciences, Paris-VII; physician, rheumatologist and researcher, Rheumatology Clinic and Rehab Dept, Cochin Hosp., Paris 1984–92; postgraduate researcher, Neurosensory Physiology Lab., CNRS 1985–90; cand. astronaut, French Space Agency (CNES) 1985; Science Coordinator Life Sciences experts aboard Antarés mission 1989–92; responsible for French and int. space physiology and medicine programmes, CNES Life Sciences Div., Paris 1990–92; backup cosmonaut for Altair mission, mem. ground team 1992; Coordinator Science Programme Cassiopée mission 1993–94; Coordinator French experts aboard Euromir mission 1994; Research Cosmonaut Cassiopée mission (first French woman in space) 1994–96; French Rep. Starsem, Moscow 1997; backup astronaut for Perseus mission, Crew Interface Coordinator, Mission Control Centre 1998–99; mem. European Astronaut Corps, ESA, Cologne 1999–; trainee Soyuz flight engineer for Andromède mission to Int. Space Station (first European woman on space station) 2001–; Minister for Research and New Technologies, Ministry of Youth, Nat. Educ. and Research 2002–04; Minister-Del. attached to the Ministry of Foreign Affairs, responsible for European Affairs 2004–05; Sr Adviser to Dir Gen. ESA 2005–; Vice-Pres. Int. Acad. of Astronautics; Perm. mem. French Acad. of Tech., French Sport Acad.; mem. Bd France Telecom, Sanofi, Fondation de France, Fondation L'Oréal, Cité des Sciences et de l'Industrie, Fondation Génial, Fondation Lacoste; mem. Acad. de l'Air et de l'Espace, Académie des Sports, Académie des Technologies; Hon. mem. Asscn Aéronautique et Astronautique de France, Soc. Française de Médecine Aéronautique et Spaciale; Commdr, Légion d'honneur, Chevalier, Ordre nat. du Mérite, Russian Order of Friendship, Russian Medal for Personal Valour, German Commandeur Ordre du Mérite; Dr hc (Univ. Polytechnique de Lausanne, Faculté Polytechnique de Mons). *Leisure interests:* contemporary art, painting, sculpture, reading, golf. *Address:* European Space Agency, 8–10 rue Mario Nikis, 75738 Paris Cedex 15, France (office). *Telephone:* 1-53-69-74-13 (office). *Fax:* 1-53-69-73-69 (office). *E-mail:* Claudie.Haignere@esa.int (office). *Website:* www.esa.int (office).

HAIN, Rt Hon. Peter Gerald, BSc, MPhil, PC; British politician; b. 16 Feb. 1950, Nairobi, Kenya; s. of Walter Hain and Adelaine Hain; m. 1st Patricia Western 1975; two s.; m. 2nd Elizabeth Haywood 2003; ed Queen Mary Coll., Univs of London and Sussex; Head of Research, Communication Workers' Union 1976–91; MP (Labour) for Neath 1991–; Labour Party Foreign Affairs Whip 1995–96; Shadow Employment Minister 1996–97; Parl. Under-Sec. of State, Welsh Office 1997–99; Minister of State, FCO 1999–2001; Minister for Energy and Competitiveness in Europe 2001; Minister of State for Europe, FCO June 2001–02; Sec. of State for Wales 2002–08 (resgnd); Leader of the House of Commons 2003–05; Sec. of State for NI Ireland 2005–07, for Work and Pensions 2007–08 (resgnd); Founding mem. Anti-Nazi League 1970s; Chair. Tribune magazine 1993–97; mem. CND, GMB Union, Friends of the Earth, Fabian Soc. *Publications include:* 13 books including Ayes to the Left: A Future for Socialism, Sing the Beloved Country. *Leisure interests:* soccer, cricket, rugby, motor racing. *Address:* Neath Constituency Office, 39 Windsor Road, Neath SA11 1NB (office); House of Commons London, , England (office). *Telephone:* (20) 7210-3000 (House of Commons) (office); (1639) 630152 (constituency office) (office). *Fax:* (1639) 641196 (constituency office) (office). *E-mail:* hainp@parliament.uk (office). *Website:* www.peterhain.org.

HAIRIKYAN, Paruir Arshavirovich; Armenian nationalist leader; *Chairman, Union for National Self-Determination;* b. 5 July 1949; s. of Arshavir Hairikyan and Zaruhi Hairikyan; one s. five d.; ed Yerevan State Univ.; founder and leader of democracy movts in USSR; leading role in Nat. United Party of Armenia (reformed on principle of independence through referendum and renamed Union for Nat. Self-Determination (UNSD) 1987) 1968–; sentenced to imprisonment for various nationalist activities 1969–73, 1974–87, with latest arrest after mass demonstrations in Yerevan in 1988; deprived of Soviet citizenship 1989, deported from USSR; citizenship restored 1990; elected to Parl. 1990; cand. for Presidency of Armenia Oct. 1991; fmrly Chair. Union for Nat. Self-Determination (also 1991–96), now Pres. UNSD; Adviser to Pres. of Armenia 1998–99; Chair. Comm. on Human Rights in Presidential Admin.; elected Pres. int. org. Democracy and Independence, Paris 1989, Prague 1990; has also written nationalistic, freedom-fighting and lyrical songs; Nat. Council to Support Democracy Movements in the USSR Democracy Award (USA) 1990. *Publications:* 7 books of fiction, non-fiction and political journalism, 2 poetry collections: Freedom Songs 1996, And Like This for Life 1997, Three Annals on the Road to Independence, The Human Rights' Point of View of the Election Committee of the Armenian Republic 2000, The Representative Colleague of the Voters or the True Equality of the Voters 2002, Democracy by Word and Act 2002, The Strategically Victorious National Organization 2002, Formula of States' Democracy 2003, Armenian People on the Border of 2003–2004 2004, Cooperation for the Main Issues of Democracy 2004, On the Quest of Light (autobiog.) 2004, With Faith and Love (filmscript) 2004. *Address:* Union for National Self-Determination, Grigor Lusavorichi Street 15, 375013 Yerevan (office); Tpagrichneri 9, Apt 102, Yerevan, Armenia (home). *Telephone:* (10) 57-38-70 (office); (10) 58-94-85 (home). *Fax:* (10) 57-38-70 (office). *E-mail:* hayrikyan@aimusd.org (office). *Website:* www.aimusd.org (office).

HAITINK, Bernard John Herman, KBE; Dutch conductor; b. 4 March 1929, Amsterdam; Conductor Netherlands Radio Philharmonic Orchestra 1955–61; appeared regularly as Guest Conductor for Concertgebouw Orchestra, Amsterdam 1956–61, Jt Conductor 1961–64, Chief Conductor and Musical Dir 1964–88, Hon. Conductor 1999–; Prin. Conductor London Philharmonic Orchestra 1967–79, Artistic Dir 1970–78, Pres. 1990–; Musical Dir Glyndebourne Festival Opera 1978–88, Royal Opera House, Covent Garden 1987–2002, European Union Youth Orchestra 1994; Prin. Guest Conductor Boston Symphony Orchestra 1995–; Chief Conductor and Music Dir, Sächsische Staatskapelle, Dresden 2002–04; Prin. Conductor Chicago Symphony Orchestra 2006–; tours with Concertgebouw in Europe, N and S America, Japan, with London Philharmonic in Europe, Japan, USA; Guest Conductor Los Angeles Philharmonic, Boston Symphony, Cleveland, Chicago Symphony, New York Philharmonic, Berlin Philharmonic, Vienna Philharmonic, Dresden Staatskapelle, Concertgebouw and other orchestras; Conductor Laureate, Concertgebouw 1999; Hon. mem. RAM, London 1973, Int. Gustav Mahler Soc.; records for Philips, Decca and EMI; Royal Order of Orange-Nassau, Chevalier des Arts et des Lettres, Officer, Order of the Crown (Belgium), CH Concertgebouw 2002–; Hon. DMus (Oxford) 1988, (Leeds) 1988; Medal of Honour, Bruckner Soc. of America 1970, Gold Medal of Int. Gustav Mahler Soc. 1971, Erasmus Prize 1991;. *Address:* Askonas Holt Ltd., Lincoln House, 300 High Holborn, London, WC1V 7JH, England (office). *Telephone:* (20) 7400-1700 (office). *Fax:* (20) 7400-1799 (office). *E-mail:* info@askonasholt.co.uk (office). *Website:* www.askonasholt.co.uk (office).

HAJI-IOANNOU, Sir Stelios, Kt, MSc; Greek entrepreneur; *Founder, easyGroup;* b. 14 Feb. 1967, Athens; s. of Loucas Haji-Ioannou and Nedi Haji-Ioannou; ed Doucas School, Athens, London School of Econs and City of London Business School, UK; joined father's co. Troodos Maritime 1988, CEO –1991; f. Cyprus Marine Environment Protection Asscn (CYMEPA) 1992; Founding Chair. Stelmar Tankers, Athens and London 1992–; Founder easyJet 1995– (Chair. 1995–2002), easyGroup 1998, easyInternetCafe (operations in London, Edinburgh, Amsterdam, Rotterdam, Barcelona, Munich, New York) 1999–, easyCar 2000–, easyValue 2000–, easyMoney 2001–, easyCinema 2003, easyBus 2004, easy4men 2004, easyJobs 2004, easyPizza 2004, easyMusic 2004, easyMobile 2005, easyCruise 2005, easyHotel 2005; Dr hc (Liverpool John Moores Univ., Cass Business School City Univ., Cranfield Univ.). *Leisure interest:* yachting. *Address:* easyGroup Head Office, The Rotunda, 42–43 Gloucester Crescent, London, NW1 7DL, England (office). *Telephone:* (20) 7241-9000 (office). *E-mail:* stelios@easygroup.co.uk (office). *Website:* www.easy.com (office); www.stelios.com (office).

HAJJAJI, Najat al-, BA, MA; Libyan journalist, international organization official and diplomatist; *Permanent Representative, United Nations, Geneva;* b. 26 July 1952, Tripoli; d. of Mehdi al-Hajjaji and Ftitima al-Maghur; one d.; ed Cairo Univ., Egypt; Ed. Gen. Inst. for Journalism, Tripoli 1973–75; corresp., Alfajer Al-Jadid (daily newspaper) 1975–77; Dir of Foreign Relations and Training, Jamahiriya News Agency 1978–91; Minister Plenipotentiary, Perm. Mission to UN, Geneva 1992–98, Chargé d'affaires 1998–2000, Amb. and Perm. Rep. to UN, Geneva 2000–; Vice-Pres. UN Human Rights Comm., Geneva 2001, Pres. 2003–05; Head of Del. to UN Human Rights Comm. and Sub-Comm. on Promotion and Protection of Human Rights 1993–2001; Leader Dels to Human Rights Treaty bodies 1993–2001; rapporteur, Main Cttee, World Conf. Against Racism, Racial Discrimination, Xenophobia and Related Intolerance, Durban 2001; Vice-Chair. Preparatory Cttee, World Summit on the Information Soc. 2002, Diplomatic Conf. on the Third Protocol Additional to the Geneva Conventions; mem. UN Special Committee to select winners of UN prize in field of human rights, Working Group on Mercenaries 2005; Pres. Council of Int. Org. for Migration 2006–07; Chair. Durban II UN Human Rights Council, Geneva 2009; Hon. Rep. Int. Org. for Peace, Care and Relief Geneva 2003; Kuala Lumpur World Peace Conf. Award Malaysia 2003, Geneva Inst. for Human Rights 2004, Hon. Distinction, Arab Labour Org. 2004, Medal, Gen. Head of Dubai Police 2004, Medal, Int. Criminal Court on Rwanda, Arab Women Studies Centre Award, Dubai 2006. *Publications include:* wide range of articles on the promotion and protection of human rights and African affairs. *Leisure interests:* playing the piano, classical music, reading, sports. *Address:* Permanent Mission of Libyan Arab Jamahiriya, 25 rue Richemond, 1202 Geneva (office); 10 chemin du Vent Blanc, 1223 Cologny/Geneva, Switzerland (home). *Telephone:* (22) 9598900 (office); (22) 7521862 (home); (22) 9598922. *Fax:* (22) 9598910 (office); (22) 7521458 (home). *E-mail:* mission.libye@bluewin.ch (office); n.alhajjaji@bluewin.ch (home). *Website:* www.unog.ch (office).

HAJJRI, Abdulwahab Abdulla al-, LLM; Yemeni diplomatist; *Ambassador to USA;* b. 1958; m.; three c.; ed Sana'a Univ., American Univ., Washington DC, USA, Al Azhar Univ., Cairo, Egypt; joined Ministry of Foreign Affairs 1980, Diplomatic Attaché, Political Dept, Sana'a 1980–82, Cultural Attaché, Cairo 1982–87, Washington, DC 1987–92, Counsellor, Cairo 1992–95, Minister Plenipotentiary, Embassy in Washington, DC 1995–97, Amb. to USA (also accred to Mexico and Venezuela) and Perm. Observer of Yemen to OAS 1997–. *Address:* Embassy of Yemen, 2319 Wyoming Avenue, NW, Washington, DC 20008, USA (office). *Telephone:* (202) 965-4760 (office). *Fax:* (202) 337-2017 (office). *E-mail:* ambassador@yemenembassy.org (office). *Website:* www.yemenembassy.org (office).

HÄKÄMIES, Jyri, MScS; Finnish business executive and politician; *Minister of Defence and Minister at the Prime Minister's Office;* b. 30 Aug. 1961, Karhula; s. of Erkki Häkämies and Pirkko Häkämies; m. Tuija Arhosola; two s.; Communications Man. Kymen Viestintä Oy (newspaper publr) 1989–91; Sales Man. Kymen Sanomat (newspaper) 1991–94; Man. Dir Kymenlaakso Chamber of Commerce 1994–99; mem. Suomen Eduskunta (Parl.) (Nat. Coalition Party—NCP) 1999–, mem. NCP Communications Sec., Parl. Group

1987–89, Vice-Chair. (Parl. Group) 2003–06, Chair. 2006–; Minister of Defence 2007–, also Minister at the Prime Minister's Office (ownership steering) 2007–; mem. Kotka City Council 2005–, Regional Council of Kymenlaakso Ass. (Chair. 2005–); mem. Supervisory Bd Port of Kotka Ltd (Chair. 2005–07), Sitra, The Finnish Innovation Fund 2006–07, Kymen Puhelin Oy 1998–2007; Vice-Pres. European People's Party 2003–06; mem. Council, Finland-Russia Soc. 2006–. *Address:* Ministry of Defence, Eteläinen Makasiinikatu 8, PO Box 31, 00131 Helsinki, Finland (office). *Telephone:* (9) 16088103 (office). *Fax:* (9) 16088284 (office). *E-mail:* jyri.hakamies@defmin.fi (office). *Website:* www.defmin.fi (office); www.vnk.fi (office).

HAKEEM, Abdul Rauf; Sri Lankan politician; *Minister of Posts and Telecommunications;* ed Royal Coll. Colombo; fmr First Sec. Sri Lanka Muslim Congress (SLMC) Working Cttee, Deputy Sec.-Gen., then Sec.-Gen., currently Leader SLMC; Minister of Internal and Int. Trade and Commerce, of Shipping Devt and of Muslim Religious Affairs –2001; Minister of Port Devt and Shipping and of Eastern Devt and Muslim Religious Affairs 2001–04, of Posts and Telecommunications 2007–. *Address:* Ministry of Posts and Telecommunications, Level 18, West Tower, World Trade Centre, Colombo 1 (office); Sri Lanka Muslim Congress, Sama Mandiraya, 53 Vauxhall Lane, Colombo 2, Sri Lanka (office). *Telephone:* (11) 22431711 (SLMC) (office); (11) 2422591 (office). *Fax:* (11) 2323465 (office). *E-mail:* spostele@sltnet.lk (office). *Website:* www.slmc.org (office); www.priu.gov.lk/Ministries/Min_Posts_Telecommunication (office).

HAKIM, Nadey S., MD, PhD, FRCS, FACS; British surgeon and fmr international organization official; *Max Thorek Professor, International College of Surgeons;* b. 9 April 1958, Beirut, Lebanon; m. Nicole Hakim; four c.; ed René Descartes Univ., Paris, Mayo Clinic, Univ. of Minnesota, USA; Consultant Surgeon and Surgical Dir Transplant Unit, Hammersmith Hosp., London; Fellow, Int. Coll. of Surgeons 1987–, Max Thorek Prof. 2008–; fmr European Fed. Sec., fmr Sec. UK Section, WHO Rep., Pres. 2004–; Ed.-in-Chief Journal of International Surgery; Fellow, Royal Soc. of Medicine; Registered Sculptor, Royal Soc. of British Sculptors; Hon. Prof. of Surgery, Univ. of São Paolo, Ricardo Palma Peru Univ., Univ. of Bashkent; Hon. Prof., Univ. of Lyon, Hon. Fellow Int. Coll. of Surgeons, Royal Coll. of Surgeons of Ireland; Kt Commdr of Justice of the Order of St John of Jerusalem, Kt of the Order of the Cedars (Lebanon); Makhzoumi Prize of Medical Excellence, Laureate, Faculty of Medicine, Paris, J. Wesley Alexander Prize for Outstanding Research in Transplantation 2007. *Music:* five Music Recordings (clarinet), USA. *Television:* presenter, Insider programme (Channel 4) 2007. *Publications include:* over 150 peer-reviewed papers, author or editor of 18 textbooks; Transplantation Surgery (co-ed.), Introduction to Organ Transplantation (ed.), History of Organ and Cell Transplantation (co-ed.), Pancreas and Islet Transplantation (co-ed.), Haemostasis in Surgery (co-ed.), Composite Tissue Allograft (co-ed.), Atlas of Transplantation, Bariatric Surgery State of the Art, Hernias, Artificial Organs. *Leisure Interests:* music, sculpture. *Address:* 84 Harley Street, London, W1G 7LG, England (office). *Telephone:* 7850-503297 (mobile) (office). *Fax:* (20) 7431-9497 (home). *E-mail:* nadey@globalnet.co.uk (home). *Website:* www.icsglobal.org (office).

HÄKKÄNEN, Matti Klaus Juhani, LLM; Finnish diplomatist (retd); b. 21 July 1936, Helsinki; s. of Klaus Häkkänen and Kaiju Broms; m. Pirkko Hentola 1962; two s.; ed Univ. of Helsinki; served in Finnish Foreign Service Helsinki, Paris, New York, Moscow and Peking 1960–76; Amb. to Romania (also accred to Albania) 1976–80; Under-Sec. of State 1980–83; Amb. to Netherlands (also accred to Ireland) 1983–87, to Argentina (also accred to Chile and Uruguay) 1987–88, to France 1988–93, to Italy (also accred to Malta and San Marino) 1993–97, to Portugal (also accred to Morocco) 1997–2001; mem. Selection and Training Bd Finnish Foreign Ministry 2004–07; mem. Bd French-Finnish Chamber of Commerce, Heinola Del.; First Lt, Finnish Naval Forces; Kt Commdr, Order of Lion of Finland, Grand Cross, Orange Nassau of the Netherlands, Officer, Black Star of France, Grand Cross, Nat. Merit of Italy, Kt Commdr, Ordre nat. du mérite, Mil. Medal of Finland, Grand Cross, Order of Infante Dom Henrique (Portugal). *Leisure interest:* tennis. *Address:* Töölönkatu 9, 00100 Helsinki, Finland (home). *Telephone:* (9) 497515 (home); 50-5497895 (mobile). *E-mail:* matti.hakkanen@welho.com (home).

HÄKKINEN, Mika; Finnish racing driver; b. 28 Sept. 1968, Helsinki; m. Erja Honkanen; one s.; fmrly go-kart driver, Formula Ford 1600 driver, Finnish, Swedish and Nordic Champion 1987; Formula 3 driver, British Champion with West Surrey Racing 1990; Formula 1 driver Lotus 1991–93, McLaren 1993–2001; Grand Prix wins: European 1997, Australia 1998, Brazil 1998, 1999, Spain 1998, 1999, 2000, Monaco 1998, Austria 1998, 2000, Germany 1998, Luxembourg 1998, Japan 1998, 1999, Canada 1999, Malaysia 1999, Hungary 1999, 2000, Belgium 2000; Formula One Driver's Championship Winner 1998, 1999; took sabbatical at end of 2001, then announced retirement from Formula 1; driver for Mercedes in German Touring Car Championship 2004–. *Leisure interests:* playing golf.

HAKOPIAN, Vilen Paruirovich; Armenian university rector and neuro-pharmacologist; *Rector, Yerevan State Medical University;* b. 1 May 1938, Garnahovit, Talin; s. of Paruir Hakopian and Inthizar Hakopian; m. Rosa Hovhannes Gasparian; one s. one d.; ed Yerevan Medical Inst.; Jr research worker, Biochem. Inst., Nat. Acad. of Sciences of Armenia 1961–65; Sr research worker and Asst, Dept of Pharmacology, Yerevan State Medical Univ. (YSMU) 1965–80, Prof. 1980–94, Dean of Foreign Students 1972–79, Dean of Medical Faculty 1979–83, Vice-Rector of Educational Affairs 1986–87, Rector of YSMU 1987–, Head Dept of Pharmacology 1994–; mem. Nat. Acad. of Sciences of Armenia, NAS (USA), Int. Union of Pharmacology (Belgium), Int. Pharmaceutical Fed. (Netherlands), Int. Information Acad., Moscow, Int. Higher Educ. Acad. of Sciences, Moscow, Int. Acad. of Ecology and Life Protection Sciences, St Petersburg, Fellow Scientific Council of Int. Coll. of

Angiology, New York; Ed.-in-Chief Medical Science of Armenia; mem. Editorial Bd Experimental and Clinical Pharmacology (Moscow) 1993–, Int. Asscn of Pathophysiology (Moscow) 1991– and many other scientific bodies. *Publications:* nearly 200 works, including 9 monographs. *Leisure interests:* chess, reading, geology, apiculture. *Address:* Department of Pharmacology, Yerevan State Medical University, 2 Korjun Street, 375025 Yerevan (office); Apt. 33, 28 Orbelli Street, Yerevan 375012, Armenia (home). *Telephone:* (10) 581802 (office). *Fax:* (10) 582532 (office). *E-mail:* rector@ysmu.am. *Website:* www.ysmu.am.

HAKOSHIMA, Shinichi; Japanese newspaper executive; *Special Adviser, The Asahi Shimbun Co.;* joined The Asahi Shimbun Co. (newspaper publr) 1962, posts included Chief of Econ. News section, Man. Ed. Tokyo Head Office, Exec. Man. Dir 1994, Pres. and CEO 1999–2005, Special Adviser 2005–; Dir NSK (Japanese Newspaper Publrs and Eds Asscn) 1999–2005, Chair. 2003–05. *Address:* The Asahi Shimbun Co., 5-3-2 Tsukiyi, Chuo-ku, Tokyo 104-8011, Japan (office). *Telephone:* (3) 3545-0131 (office). *Fax:* (3) 3545-0358 (office). *Website:* www.asahi.com (office).

HALAIQA, Mohammad al-, PhD; Jordanian fmr government official; b. 20 May 1951, Al Shioukh; m.; ed Univ. of Jordan, Univ. of Leeds, UK; Gen. Man. of industrial co., Jordan 1981–87; Dir-Gen. Jordan Chamber of Industry 1990–92; Dir Industry and Mineral Resources Sector, Higher Council for Science and Tech. 1992–93, Asst Sec.-Gen. Higher Council for Science and Tech. 1993–94; Dir-Gen. Jordanian Export Devt and Commercial Centres Corpn (JEDCO) 1994–97; Sec.-Gen. Ministry of Trade and Industry 1997–2000; Deputy Prime Minister and Minister of Industry and Trade 2003–05; Pres. Jordan Chemical Soc. 1983–91, Union of Arab Chemists 1985–86, Jordanian Soc. for Quality 1997–99; led Jordanian del. to Free Trade Agreement negotiations with USA and to negotiations for Jordan's accession to WTO; mem. Bd of Dirs Jordan Valley Authority 1997–2000, Aqaba Region Authority 1997–2000, Social Security Corpn 1997–2000, Jordan Cement Factories Co. 1997–2000, Industrial Estates Corpn 1997–2000; Chair. Bd of Trustees, Al Quds Coll.; mem. Econ. Consultative Council, Hashemite Royal Court; mem. Bd Trustees Princess Sumayya Coll. 1995–99, Faculty of Sciences, Hashemite Univ., Faculty of Sciences, Univ. of Jordan; mem. Higher Advisory Bd Talal Abu Ghazaleh Coll. of Business; Independence Medal of the First Order (Jordan), Al-Kawkab Medal of the Second Order. *Address:* c/o Board of Trustees, Al Quds College, Airport Road, POB 183334, Amman 11118, Jordan (office). *Telephone:* (6) 5799020. *Fax:* (6) 5799030. *E-mail:* info@quds.edu.jo. *Website:* www.alqudscollege.com.

HALBERT, David D., BBA; American business executive; *Chairman, Caris Ltd;* m. Kathryn Ann Halbert; three c.; ed Abilene Christian Univ.; f. Halbert & Assocs Inc.; f. AdvancePCS, Chair., Pres. and CEO 1987–2004 (after merger with Caremark Rx); founder and Chair. Caris, Ltd (investment partnership) 2004–. *Leisure interest:* baseball. *Address:* Caris Ltd, 5215 North O'Connor Blvd, Suite 2650, Irving, TX 75039, USA (office). *Telephone:* (972) 590-2100 (office). *Fax:* (972) 590-2103 (office). *E-mail:* David.Halbert@carisltd.com (office). *Website:* www.carisltd.com (office).

HALBRON, Jean-Pierre; French business executive; *Member of the Executive Committee, Alcatel SA;* b. 31 Aug. 1936; ed Ecole Polytechnique, Paris, Corps des Mines, Inst. Français du Pétrole; various posts with Compagnie Financière 1963–82, including Gen. Man. 1968–74, CEO 1974–82; Finance Dir Rhône-Poulenc SA 1983, Deputy Man. Dir 1984–87; Gen. Man. CdF Chimie (later Orkem) 1987–90; Finance Dir Total SA 1990–92; Man. Dir Wasserstein Perella Corpn and Chair. Wasserstein Perella France 1992–95; Dir of Strategy and Finance, Alcatel SA 1995–97, Co-Dir-Gen. 1997–99, Financial Dir 1997–2001, Dir-Gen. 2000–02, mem. Exec. Cttee 2002–. *Address:* Alcatel SA, 54 rue la Boétie, 75006 Paris, France (office). *Telephone:* 1-40-76-10-10 (office). *E-mail:* execoffice@alcatel-lucent.com (office). *Website:* www.alcatel.com (office).

HALE OF RICHMOND, Baroness (Life Peer), cr. 2004, of Easby in the County of North Yorkshire; **Rt Hon. Brenda Marjorie Hale,** DBE, PC, MA; British judge, lawyer and university chancellor; *Lord of Appeal in Ordinary;* b. 31 Jan. 1945, Leeds, Yorks.; d. of Cecil Frederick Hale and Marjorie Hale (née Godfrey); m. 1st Anthony John Christopher Hoggett 1968 (divorced 1992); one d.; m. 2nd Julian Thomas Farrand 1992; ed Richmond High School for Girls, Yorks., Girton Coll., Cambridge and Gray's Inn, London; Asst Lecturer, Faculty of Law, Univ. of Manchester 1966–68, Lecturer 1968–76, Sr Lecturer 1976–81, Reader 1981–86, Prof. 1986–89; Prof. King's Coll., London 1989–90; practice, Manchester Bar 1969–72; Law Commr 1984–93; Recorder 1989–94; Judge High Court, Family Div. 1994–99; Lord Justice of Appeal 1999–2004, apptd Lord of Appeal in Ordinary (first female Law Lord) 2004–; Visiting Fellow, Nuffield Coll., Oxford 1997–2005; Chancellor Univ. of Bristol 2004–; Visitor, Girton Coll., Cambridge 2004–; Pres. Asscn of Women Barristers 1998–2005; Ed. Journal of Social Welfare Law 1978–84; mem. Mental Health Review Tribunal for the North-West 1979–80, Council on Tribunals 1980–84; Chair. Nat. Family Conciliation Council 1989–93; mem. Judicial Studies Bd Civil and Family Cttee 1990–94, Human Fertilization and Embryology Authority 1990–93; Gov. Centre for Policy on Ageing 1990–93; Pres. Nat. Family Mediation 1994–; Man. Trustee Nuffield Foundation 1987–2002; Hon. Fellow, Girton Coll. Cambridge 1996–2004; Hon. FBA 2004; Hon. LLD (Sheffield) 1989, (London Guildhall) 1996, (Manchester) 1997, (Bristol) 2002, (Cambridge) 2005, (Hull) 2006; Hon. DUniv (Essex) 2005. *Publications:* Women and the Law (jtly) 1984, Parents and Children (4th edn) 1993, Mental Health Law (4th edn) 1996, From the Test Tube to the Coffin: Choice and Regulation in Private Life 1996, The Family Law and Society: Cases and Materials (jtly, 5th edn) 2002. *Leisure interests:* bridge, theatre, home. *Address:* Law Lords' Office, House of Lords, Westminster, London, SW1A 0PW, England (office). *Telephone:* (20) 7219-3352 (office); (20) 7219-

3202 (office). *Fax:* (20) 7219-6156 (office). *E-mail:* derrys@parliament.uk (office).

HALEFOĞLU, Vahit M., KCVO, MA; Turkish diplomatist (retd); b. 19 Nov. 1919, Antakya; s. of Mesrur and Samiye Halefoğlu; m. Zehra Bereket 1951; one s. one d.; ed Antakya Coll. and Univ. of Ankara; joined Turkish Foreign Service 1943, served Vienna, Moscow, Ministry of Foreign Affairs, London 1946–59; Dir-Gen., First Political Dept, Ministry of Foreign Affairs 1959–62; Amb. to Lebanon 1962–65, concurrently accred to Kuwait 1964–65, Amb. to USSR 1965–66, to Netherlands 1966–70; Deputy Sec.-Gen. of Political Affairs, Ministry of Foreign Affairs 1970–72; Amb. to Fed. Repub. of Germany 1972–82, to USSR 1982–83; Minister of Foreign Affairs 1983–87; MP 1986; Dr hc; Légion d'honneur and other French, Finnish, British, Lebanese, Saudi and Italian decorations. *Leisure interests:* classical literature, history, international relations, music, walking, swimming. *Address:* c/o Ministry of Foreign Affairs, Dişişleri Bakanlığı, Yeni Hizmet Binası, 06520 Balgat, Ankara, Turkey.

HALES, Antony John (Tony), BSc, CBE; British business executive; *Chairman, Workspace Group PLC;* b. 25 May 1948, Blackpool; s. of S. A. Hales and M. J. Hales; m. Linda Churchlow 1975; three s. one d.; ed Repton School, Univ. of Bristol; Marketing Man. Cadbury Schweppes 1969–79; joined Allied Domecq 1979, Marketing Dir Joshua Tetley 1979–83, Man. Dir Hall's Oxford SW 1983–85, Man. Dir Taylor Walker 1985–87, Man. Dir Ansells 1987–89, Dir Allied Breweries, Chair. and CEO Allied Domecq Spirits and Wine (fmrly Hiram Walker Group) 1995; CEO J. Lyons 1989–91, Dir Allied Domecq (fmrly Allied-Lyons) PLC 1989–99, CEO 1991–99; Dir Hyder PLC 1994–97, Midland Bank PLC (now HSBC Bank) 1994–2001, Aston Villa PLC 1997–2006, David Halsall International 2000–06, Tempo Holdings Ltd 2000–01, Reliance Security Group 2001–05, Satellite Information Services Holdings 2002–, Provident Financial PLC 2006–; Chair. Naati 2001–08, Workspace Group PLC 2002–, British Waterways 2005–. *Address:* Belvoir House, Edstone Court, Wooton Wawen, Henley in Arden, Warwicks., B95 6DD (home); Workspace Group PLC, Magenta House, 85 Whitechapel Road, London, E1 1DU, England (office). *E-mail:* thales_uk@yahoo.com (office). *Website:* www.workspacegroup.co.uk (office).

HALÍK, Rev. Tomáš, ThD, PhDr; Czech philosopher, academic, ecclesiastic and writer; *Professor, Department of Philosophy of Religion, Charles University;* b. 1 June 1948, Prague; s. of Dr Miroslav Halík and Marie Halík; ed Charles Univ., Prague, Pontifical Lateran Univ., Rome; psychologist, Inst. of Ministry of Industry 1972–89; clandestinely ordained priest, Erfurt, GDR 1978; psychotherapist, U Apolináře Hosp., Prague 1984–90; involved in 'underground' RC Church as close co-worker with Cardinal Tomášek; Gen. Sec. Czech Bishops' Conf. 1990–93; consultant, Pontifical Council for Dialogue with non-believers, Vatican 1990–93); Prof. and Head, Dept of Philosophy of Religion, Faculty of Philosophy, Charles Univ., Rector Univ. Church; Visiting Fellow, St Edmund's Coll., Cambridge, UK 2003; lectures in univs world-wide; Pres. Czech Christian Acad.; adviser to Pres. Havel; mem. European Acad. of Sciences and Arts, Cttee of Wise Persons, COMECE (Commissio Episcopatuum Communitatis Europensis— Comm. of the Bishops' Confs of the EC), Brussels 2006–, and various bds and socs in Czech Repub. and abroad; Konrad Adenauer Silver Medal 1995, Masaryk's Arts Acad. Prize 1997, Andrew Elias SVU Human Tolerance Award 2002, Communio et Progressio Cardinal König Prize (Austria) 2003, Prize for Literature 2006. *Television:* 18 tv films on world's religions 2006–07. *Publications:* books: O přítomnou církev a společnost 1992, Sedm úvah o službě nemocným a trpícím 1993, Du wirst das Angesicht der erde erneuern: Kirche und Gesellschaft an der Schwelle zur Freiheit 1993, Víra a kultura 1995, Un proyecto de renovación espiritual 1996, Ptal jsem se cest 1997, Wyzwoleni, jesze nie wolni 1997, Mistica, anima della filosofia? 1999, Radzilem sie dróg 2001, Co je bez chvění, není pevné 2002, Oslovit Zachea 2003, Co nie jest chwiejne, jest nietrwałe 2004, Vzýván i nevzýván 2004, Noc zpovědník 2005, Prolínání světů 2006, Wzywany czy niewzywany 2006, Premówic do Zacheusza 2006, Zacheuszu! 2006; more than 300 articles (some distributed secretly in Czechoslovakia before 1989). *Address:* Univerzita Karlova, ÚFaR FF UK, nám. Jana Palacha 2, 110 00 Prague 2 (office); Czech Christian Academy, Vyšehradská 49, 120 00 Prague 2; Naprstkova 2, 110 00 Prague 1, Czech Republic (home). *E-mail:* haliktom@cesnet.cz (home). *Website:* www.halik.cz (home).

HALILOVIĆ, Safet; Bosnia and Herzegovina politician; *Minister of Human Rights and Refugees;* Chair. Municipal Bd, Party of Democratic Action (Stranka Demokratske Akcije – SDA), Sarajevo 1994–; Pres. of Fed. of Bosnia and Herzegovina 2002–03, Minister of Civil Affairs 2003–07, of Human Rights and Refugees 2007–. *Address:* Ministry of Human Rights and Refugees, 71000 Sarajevo, trg Bosne i Hercegovine 1, Bosnia and Herzegovina (office). *Telephone:* (33) 206673 (office). *Fax:* (33) 206140 (office). *E-mail:* kabmin@mhrr.gov.ba (office). *Website:* www.mhrr.gov.ba (office).

HALIMI, Gisèle Zeïza, Lic. en Droit et Phil; French lawyer and writer; *President, Choisir la cause des femmes;* b. 27 July 1927, La Goulette, Tunisia; d. of the late Edouard Taïeb and Fortunée Metoudi; m. Claude Faux; three s.; ed Institut d'études politiques, Paris; Counsel, Paris Courts 1956–; Deputy to Nat. Ass. 1981–84; Amb. to UNESCO and Pres. Human Rights Cttee 1985–87; special adviser to French Del. at Gen. Ass. of UN 1989; Founder and Pres. Choisir la cause des femmes 1971–; Hon. mem. Bar Asscn, Mexico 1982–; Officier Légion d'honneur, Grand Officier Ordre de la République (Tunisia), Medal of Achievement of the Greek People; Dr. hc (Mons Hainaut Liège Univ., Belgium) 1997–; Prix Minerva 1985, Médaille du Barreau. *Publications:* Djamila Boupacha 1962, Resistance Against Tyranny 1966, Le procès de Burgos 1971, Choisir: Avortement: une loi en procès – L'affaire de Bobigny 1973, La cause des femmes 1974, Viol: le procès d'Aix-en-Provence 1978, Le programme commun des femmes 1978, Choisir de donner la vie 1979, Quel Président pour les femmes? 1981, Fini le féminisme? 1984, Le lait de l'oranger 1988, Femmes: moitié de la terre, moitié du pouvoir 1994, Une embellie perdue 1996, La nouvelle cause des femmes 1997, Fritna 1999, La parité dans la vie politique 2001, Avocate irrespecteuse 2002, L'étrange Mr. K 2004. *Leisure interests:* classical music, football. *Address:* Choisir la cause des femmes, 102 rue Saint Dominique, 75007 Paris, France (office). *Telephone:* 1-47-05-21-48 (office). *Fax:* 1-45-51-56-10 (office). *E-mail:* scp.gisele.halimi@noos.fr; choisirlacausedesfemmes@noos.fr (office). *Website:* www.choisirlacausedesfemmes.org (office).

HALL, Alan, PhD; British molecular biologist and academic; *Chairman, Cell Biology Program, Sloan-Kettering Cancer Institute;* b. 1952; ed Univ. of Oxford, Harvard Univ., USA; Postdoctoral Fellow, Univ. of Edinburgh 1977–79, Univ. of Zurich, Switzerland 1979; mem. staff, Inst. for Cancer Research 1980; Lecturer, Dept of Biochemistry and Molecular Biology, Univ. Coll., London 1992–2001, Prof. of Molecular Biology and Dir MRC Lab. for Molecular Cell Biology and Cell Biology Unit 2001–06; Chair. Cell Biology Program, Sloan-Kettering Cancer Inst., New York 2006–; Jt Winner Louis Jeantet Prize for Medicine 2005. *Publications:* numerous articles in scientific journals. *Address:* Memorial Sloan-Kettering Cancer Center, 1275 York Avenue, New York, NY 10021, USA (office). *Telephone:* (212) 639-2000 (office). *E-mail:* halla@mskcc.org (office). *Website:* www.mskcc.org (office).

HALL, Aleksander, MA; Polish politician, historian and publicist; b. 20 May 1953, Gdańsk; ed Gdańsk Univ.; history teacher, Secondary School No 6, Gdańsk 1977; active in Acad. Pastoral Cure, Gdańsk in early 1970s; mem. Movt for Defence of Human and Civic Rights (ROPCIO) 1977–79; Ed. Bratniak 1977–81; Co-Founder and Leader, Young Poland Movt 1979; mem. Solidarity Trade Union 1980–; co-f. Cttee for Defence of Persons Imprisoned because of their Opinions, attached to Solidarity Trade Union 1980; mem. Regional Co-ordinative Comm. of Solidarity Trade Union, Gdańsk 1981–84; publicist, Przegląd Katolicki (Catholic Review) 1984–89, Polityka Polska (Polish Politics) 1982–89; mem. Primatial Social Council 1986–; mem. Civic Cttee attached to Lech Wałęsa (q.v.), Chair. Solidarity Trade Union 1988–90, Vice-Pres., Dziekania Political Thought Club 1988–89; participant Round Table debates, mem. group for political reforms Feb.–April 1989; Minister-mem. Council of Ministers (for co-operation with political orgs. and asscns.) 1989–90; Deputy to Sejm (Parl.) 1991–93, 1997–2001; Vice-Chair. Solidarity Election Action Parl. Caucus 1997–2000; leader Democratic Right Forum 1990–92; Co-f. and leader Conservative Party 1992–96; mem. Conservative Peasant Party (SKL) 1996– (Conservative Peasant Party-New Poland Movt, SKL-RNP from 2002), mem. Bd and Political Council. *Publications:* Refleksje i polemiki, Wybór publicystyki politycznej 1989, Spór o Polskę 1993, Zanim bęclzie za późno 1994, Polskie patriotyzmy 1997, Pierwsza taka dekada 2000, Widziane z prawej strony 2000; numerous articles in Polish periodicals. *Leisure interests:* reading, history, politics, political thought and history of ideas, culture and history of France. *Address:* Stronnictwo Konserwatywno Ludowe-Ruch Nowej Polski—SKL-RNP, Pl. Dąbrowskiego 5, 00-065 Warsaw, Poland (office). *Telephone:* (22) 8278442 (office). *Fax:* (22) 8278441 (office). *E-mail:* webmaster@skl.org.pl (office). *Website:* www.skl-rnp.pl (office).

HALL, Alfred Rupert, MA, PhD, LittD, FBA; British science historian and academic; *Professor Emeritus, Imperial College London;* b. 26 July 1920, Stoke-on-Trent; s. of Alfred Dawson Hall and Margaret Catherine Ritchie; m. 1st Annie Shore Hughes; m. 2nd Marie Boas; two d.; ed Alderman Newton's School, Leicester, Christ's Coll., Cambridge; served in Royal Corps of Signals 1940–45; Fellow, Christ's Coll., Cambridge 1949–59, Univ. Lecturer, Cambridge 1950–59; posts at Univs of Calif. and Indiana 1959–63; Prof. of History of Science and Tech., Imperial Coll., London 1963–80, Prof. Emer. 1980–; Consultant, Wellcome Trust 1980–85; Pres. Int. Acad. of the History of Science 1977–81; Hon. PhD (Bologna) 1999; Sarton Medal, History of Science Soc. (jtly) 1981; Allen Scholar, Cambridge 1948, Royal Soc. Wilkins Lecturer 1973, Leeuwenhoek Lecturer 1988. *Publications:* various books and articles on history of science and tech. including Philosophers at War 1980, The Revolution in Science 1500–1750 1983, Physic and Philanthropy: A History of the Wellcome Trust 1986, Henry More: Magic, Religion and Experiment 1990, Isaac Newton: Adventurer in Thought 1992, Newton, His Friends and His Foes 1993, All Was Light: An Introduction to Newton's Opticks 1993, Science and Society (essays) 1994, Isaac Newton: Eighteenth Century Perspectives 1998. *Leisure interests:* walking, gardening. *Address:* 14 Ball Lane, Tackley, Kidlington, Oxon., OX5 3AG, England. *Telephone:* (1869) 331257.

HALL, Anthony (Tony) William, CBE, MA, FRSA; British business executive; *Chief Executive, Royal Opera House, London;* b. 3 March 1951, Birkenhead; s. of Donald William Hall and Mary Joyce Hall; m. Cynthia Lesley Davis 1977; one s. one d.; ed King Edward's School, Birmingham, Birkenhead School, Merseyside, Keble Coll., Oxford; joined BBC 1973, News Ed. 1987–90, Dir News and Current Affairs 1990–93, Man. Dir News and Current Affairs 1993–96, Chief Exec. BBC News 1996–2001; Chief Executive Exec. Royal Opera House 2001–; mem. Council Brunel Univ. 1999–2002; Fellow, Vice-Chair. Royal TV Soc. (Chair. 1998–2000); Dir (non-exec.) Customs and Excise 2002–05, Channel 4 TV; Chair. Section Skills Council for the Creative and Cultural Industries, Theatre Royal Stratford East; Patron Newsworld 1999–2000; Hon. Visiting Fellow, City Univ. 1999–2000. *Publications:* King Coal: A History of the Miners 1981, Nuclear Politics 1984, articles in various periodicals. *Leisure interests:* reading, writing, church architecture, opera, walking in Dorset. *Address:* Royal Opera House, Covent Garden, London, WC2E 9DD, England (office). *Telephone:* (20) 7240-1200 (office). *Fax:* (20) 7212-9502 (office). *Website:* www.royaloperahouse.org (office).

HALL, Brian, BSc, PhD; Australian biologist and academic; *George S. Campbell Professor of Biology, Dalhousie University;* ed Univ. of New

England, Armidale, NSW; Asst Prof., Dalhousie Univ., Halifax, NS, Canada 1968–75, Full Prof. of Biology 1975–96, Chair. of Biology 1978–85, Faculty of Science Killam Prof. of Biology 1996–2001, George S. Campbell Prof. of Biology 2001–, Killam Research Fellow 2003–05; Fellow, Centre for Human Biology, Univ. of WA, Perth 1993–; Royal Soc. of Canada 1985; mem. of several editorial bds including Journal of Craniofacial Genetics and Developmental Biology, International Journal of Developmental Biology, Evolution and Development; Assoc. Ed. Molecular and Developmental Evolution 1998–; Foreign Hon. Mem. American Acad. of Arts and Sciences 2002; Fry Medal, Canadian Soc. of Zoologists 1994, Int. Craniofacial Biology Distinguished Scientist Award 1996, Alexander Kowalevsky Medal. St Petersburg Soc. of Naturalists 2001, Killam Prize for Natural Sciences 2005. *Publications:* has written more than 250 scientific articles and more than 16 books including Evolutionary Development Biology (textbook), Neural Crest in Development and Evolution (1999), Homology: Hierarchical Basis of Comparative Biology 2000. *Address:* Department of Biology, Life Science Center, Dalhousie University, 1355 Oxford Street, Halifax, NS B3H 4J1, Canada (office). *Telephone:* (902) 494-3515 (office). *Fax:* (902) 449-3737 (office). *E-mail:* Biology@Dal.ca (office). *Website:* biology.dal.ca/us/f/hall/hall.html (office).

HALL, Sir David Michael Baldock, Kt, MB, BS, BSc, FRCP, FRCPCH; British paediatrician and academic; *Professor of Community Paediatrics, University of Sheffield;* b. 4 Aug. 1945; s. of Ronald Hall and Ethel Gwen Hall (née Baldock); m. Susan M. Luck 1966; two d.; ed Reigate Grammar School, St George's Hosp., Univ. of London; Sr Medical Officer, Baragwanath Hosp., Johannesburg, South Africa 1973–76; Sr Registrar, Charing Cross Hosp., London 1976–78; Consultant Paediatrician, St George's Hosp. 1978–93; Prof. of Community Paediatrics, Univ. of Sheffield 1993–; Fellow, Royal Coll. of Paediatrics and Child Health 1996–, Pres. 2000–03; Hon. FFPHM 1999; Univ. of London Gold Medal. *Publications include:* Child with a Disability 1996, Health for All Children (fourth edn) 2003; numerous articles in scientific journals. *Leisure interests:* horses, travel. *Address:* Storrs House Farm, Storrs Lane, Stannington, Sheffield, S6 6GY, England (home). *E-mail:* d.hall@sheffield.ac.uk (office).

HALL, Donald Andrew, BA, BLitt, LHD, DLitt; American poet, writer and academic; b. 20 Sept. 1928, New Haven, Conn.; s. of Donald A. Hall and Lucy Hall (née Wells); m. 1st Kirby Thompson 1952 (divorced 1969); one s. one d.; m. 2nd Jane Kenyon 1972 (died 1995); ed Harvard Univ., Univ. of Oxford, Stanford Univ.; Jr Fellow, Harvard Univ. 1954–57; Asst Prof., Univ. of Michigan 1957–61, Assoc. Prof. 1961–66, Prof. of English 1966–75; Poetry Ed. Paris Review 1953–62; Consultant Harper & Row 1964–81; Poet Laureate of the USA 2006–07; Guggenheim Fellow 1963, 1972; mem. Authors' Guild, American Acad. of Arts and Letters; Univ. of Oxford Newdigate Prize for Poetry 1952, Acad. of American Poets Lamont Poetry Selection 1955, Edna St Vincent Millay Memorial Prize 1956, Longview Foundation Award 1960, Sarah Josepha Hale Award 1983, Leonore Marshal Award 1987, Los Angeles Times Book Award 1989, Poetry Soc. of America Robert Frost Silver Medal 1991, New Hampshire Writers and Publishers Project Lifetime Achievement Award 1992, New England Booksellers Asscn Award 1993, Ruth Lilly Prize 1994. *Publications:* poetry: Poems 1952, Exile 1952, To the Loud Wind and Other Poems 1955, Exiles and Marriages 1955, The Dark Houses 1958, A Roof of Tiger Lilies 1964, The Alligator Bride: Poems New and Selected 1969, The Yellow Room: Love Poems 1971, A Blue Wing Tilts at the Edge of the Sea: Selected Poems 1964–1974 1975, The Town of Hill 1975, Kicking the Leaves 1978, The Toy Bone 1979, The Twelve Seasons 1983, Brief Lives 1983, Great Day at the Cows' House 1984, The Happy Man 1986, The One Day: A Poem in Three Parts (Nat. Book Circle Critic's Award 1989) 1988, Old and New Poems 1990, The One Day and Poems (1947–1990) 1991, The Museum of Clear Ideas 1993, The Old Life 1996, Without: Poems 1998, The Painted Bed 2000, White Apples and the Taste of Stone: Selected Poems 1946–2006 2006; children's books: Lucy's Christmas 1994, I Am the Dog, I Am the Cat 1994, Lucy's Summer 1995; short stories: The Ideal Bakery 1987, Willow Temple 2002; prose: Henry Moore: The Life and Work of a Great Sculptor 1966, Marianne Moore: The Cage and the Animal 1970, The Gentleman's Alphabet Book 1972, Writing Well 1973, Goatfoot Milktongue Twinbird: Interviews, Essays and Notes on Poetry 1970–76 1978, The Weather for Poetry: Essays, Reviews and Notes on Poetry 1977–81 1982, Poetry and Ambition: Essays 1982–1988 1988, Here at Eagle Pond 1990, Their Ancient Glittering Eyes 1992, Life Work 1993, Death to Death of Poetry 1994, Principal Products of Portugal 1995, Breakfast Served Any Time All Day 2003, The Best Day The Worst Day (biog.) 2005, Unpacking the Boxes: A Memoir of a Life in Poetry 2008; editor: Harvard Advocate Anthology (with L. Simpson and R. Pack) 1950, The New Poets of England and America (with R. Pack) 1957, Second Selection 1962, A Poetry Sampler 1962, Contemporary American Poetry (with W. Taylor) 1962, Poetry in English 1963, A Concise Encyclopaedia of English and American Poets and Poetry (with S. Spender) 1963, Faber Book of Modern Verse 1966, The Modern Stylists 1968, A Choice of Whitman's Verse 1968, Man and Boy 1968, Anthology of American Poetry 1969, Pleasures of Poetry 1971, A Writer's Reader (with D. Emblen) 1976, Remembering Poets: Reminiscences and Opinions: Dylan Thomas, Robert Frost, T. S. Eliot, Ezra Pound 1978, To Read Literature 1981, To Read Poetry 1982, Oxford Book of American Literary Anecdotes 1981, Claims for Poetry 1982, Oxford Book of Children's Verse in America 1985, To Read Fiction 1987, Anecdotes of Modern Art (with Pat Corrigan Wykes) 1990. *Leisure interest:* baseball.

HALL, Henry Edgar, PhD, FRS; British physicist and academic; *Emeritus Professor of Low Temperature Physics, University of Manchester;* b. 1928; s. of John A. Hall; m. Patricia A. Broadbent 1962; two s. one d.; ed Latymer Upper School, Hammersmith and Emmanuel Coll. Cambridge; Royal Soc. Mond Lab. Cambridge 1952–58; Sr Student, Royal Comm. for Exhbn of 1851, 1955–57; Research Fellow, Emmanuel Coll. Cambridge 1955–58; Lecturer in Physics,

Univ. of Manchester 1958–61, Prof. of Low Temperature Physics 1961–95, Emer. Prof. 1995–; has held visiting professorships in Australia, USA and Japan; Simon Memorial Prize (with W. F. Vinen) 1963, Guthrie Medal and Prize, Inst. of Physics 2004. *Publications:* Solid State Physics 1974; papers in scientific journals. *Leisure interest:* mountain walking. *Address:* Schuster Laboratory, School of Physics and Astronomy, University of Manchester, Oxford Road, Manchester, M13 9PL, England (office). *Telephone:* (161) 275-4070 (office). *Fax:* (161) 275-4056 (office). *E-mail:* henry.hall@man.ac.uk (office). *Website:* www.physics.man.ac.uk (office).

HALL, Jerry; American model and actress; b. 2 July 1956, Gonzales, Tex.; d. of the late John P. Hall and Marjorie Sheffield; m. Mick Jagger (q.v.) 1990 (divorced 1999); two s. two d.; ed The Actors' Studio, New York, Nat. Theatre, London, UK, studying third year of Humanities degree, Open Univ.; moved to Paris aged 16, began modelling career in 1970s; numerous TV appearances, USA; stage debut in William Inge's Bus Stop, Lyric Theatre, London 1990; Contributing Ed. Tatler 1999–; contracts include Yves Saint Laurent, Revlon Cosmetics, L'Oriel Hair, Thierry Mugler; Judge, Whitbread Book Awards and WH Smith Travel Book Awards; mem. Leadership Group for Amnesty International; Amb. for Prince's Trust, Caldicott Foundation, Breast Cancer; Patron Richmond Theatre, Tate Museum, Campaign for Stowe School, Pink Ribbon Foundation, Frontline Homeopathy, WELLBEING, UNICEF, Human Rights Centre for Amnesty International; Patron and Spokesperson for Nat. Soc. for Prevention of Cruelty to Children; Vice-Pres. Kingston Theatre Trust; Trustee, Tate Modern; Hon. Chair. British Red Cross London Ball. *Plays include:* The Graduate, Gielgud Theatre, London 2000 (US tour 2003), Picasso's Women 2001, The Play What I Wrote 2002, The Vagina Monologues 2002 (US tour 2003), Benchmark, New End Theatre, Hampstead 2003, UK tour 2007, Bus Stop. *Films include:* Merci Docteur Rey, Willie and Phil 1980, Urban Cowboy 1980, Topo Galileo 1987, Lets Spend the Night Together, Running Out of Luck 1987, Hysteria! 2 (TV) 1989, The Emperor and the Nightingale, Batman 1989, 25 × 5: The Continuing Adventures of the Rolling Stones 1989, The Wall: Live in Berlin (TV) 1990, Bejewelled (TV) 1991, Freejack 1992, Princess Caraboo 1994, Savage Hearts 1995, Vampire in Brooklyn 1995, Diana and Me 1997, R.P.M. 1997, Being Mick (TV) 2001, Comic Relief: Say Pants to Poverty 2001, Tooth 2004. *Television includes:* Married with Children, Just Shoot Me, Saturday Night Live (host), The Clive James Show, French and Saunders, Jerry Hall's Gurus, Popetown, Art Deco, Annie Proulx, Way Out West, The Holiday Show, Lenny Goes to Town, Cluedo (six-part series) 2004, Kept 2005. *Radio:* The Magic Flute (Classic FM), The Betty Grable Story (BBC Radio 3). *Publications:* Tall Tales 1985, Jerry Hall's Gurus 2004. *Leisure interests:* riding, swimming, reading, playing piano, travelling. *Address:* Elite Model Management Ltd, 3–5 Islington High Street, London, N1 9LQ; 12 Macklin Street, Covent Garden, London, WC2B 5EZ, England.

HALL, John L., PhD; American physicist and academic; *Professor Adjoint, Physics Department, University of Colorado;* b. Aug. 1934, Denver, Colo; s. of John Ernest Hall and Elizabeth Rae Hall (née Long); m. Marilyn Charlene Robinson; two s. one d.; ed Carnegie Inst. of Tech., Pittsburgh, Pa; NRC Postdoctoral Fellow, Nat. Bureau of Standards (now Nat. Inst. of Standards and Tech.) 1961–62, Physicist 1962–71, apptd Sr Scientist 1971, currently Scientist Emer.; Lecturer, Physics Dept, Univ. of Colorado 1961–, Prof. Adjoint 2007–; Fellow, Jt Inst. for Lab. Astrophysics (now JILA) 1964–, American Physical Soc., Optical Soc. of America; mem. Acad. of Science; Légion d'honneur 2004; Dr hc (Université Paris Nord) 1989; Hon. DSc (Carnegie Mellon) 2006, (Glasgow) 2007, (Ohio State) 2008; Dept of Commerce Gold Medal 1969, (group) 1974, 2002, Samuel W. Stratton Award 1971, E. U. Condon Award 1979, Optical Soc. of America Charles Hard Townes Award (co-recipient) 1984, American Physical Soc. Davisson-Germer Prize 1988, Optical Soc. of America Frederic Ives Medal 1991, American Physical Soc. Arthur L. Shawlow Prize 1993, Allen V. Astin Measurement Science Award 2000, Optical Soc. of America Max Born Award 2002, Office of Personnel Man. Presidential Rank Award 2002, IEEE Soc. for Ultrasonic, FerroElectricity and Frequency Control I. I. Rabi Prize 2004, Nobel Prize in Physics (co-recipient) 2005. *Publications:* numerous articles and 11 patents. *Leisure interests:* music, photography, electronic design, travel. *Address:* JILA, University of Colorado, 440 UCB, Boulder, CO 80309-0440, USA (office). *Telephone:* (303) 492-7843 (office); (303) 497-3126 (Lab.) (office). *Fax:* (303) 492-5235 (office). *E-mail:* jhall@jila.colorado.edu (office). *Website:* jilawww.colorado.edu/hall (office); www.Sci-TeksDiscoveryProgramforKids.org (office).

HALL, Most Hon. Sir Kenneth O., Kt, BA, MA, PhD, GCMG, OJ; Jamaican academic, university administrator and government official; b. 24 April 1941, Hanover, Jamaica; m. Rheima Holding; one d.; ed Univ. of the West Indies, Mona, Jamaica, Inst. of Int. Relations, Univ. of the West Indies, St Augustine, Trinidad, Queen's Univ., Canada; Prof. of History, State Univ. of NY (SUNY), Oswego, becoming Adjunct Prof. of Caribbean Studies, SUNY, Albany, also Prof. of American Studies, SUNY, Old Wesbury, Vice-Pres., Academic Affairs; Deputy Sec.-Gen. Caribbean Community (CARICOM) Secr. 1994–96; Pro-Vice-Chancellor and Prin. Univ. of the West Indies, Mona campus 1996–2006; Gov.-Gen. of Jamaica 2006–09; mem. Univ. Council of Jamaica; mem. Bd Dirs Bank of Jamaica; Chair. Caribbean Examinations Council 2003–07; Order of the Nation. *Address:* c/o King's House, Hope Road, Kingston 10, Jamaica (office). *Telephone:* 927-6424 (office). *Fax:* 978-6025 (office). *E-mail:* kingshouse@kingshouse.gov.jm (office). *Website:* www.kingshouse.gov.jm (office).

HALL, Nigel John, MA, RA; British sculptor; b. 30 Aug. 1943, Bristol; s. of Herbert John Hall and Gwendoline Mary Hall (née Olsen); m. Manijeh Yadegar 1986; ed Bristol Grammar School, West of England Coll. of Art, RCA, London; Harkness Fellowship to USA 1967–69; first solo exhbn, Galerie

Givaudan, Paris 1967; represented in the following collections: Tate Gallery, London, Musée Nat. d'Art Moderne, Paris, Nat. Galerie, Berlin, Museum of Modern Art, New York, Australian Nat. Gallery, Canberra, Art Inst. of Chicago, Kunsthaus, Zurich, Tokyo Metropolitan Museum, Musée d'Art Moderne, Brussels, Louisiana Museum, Denmark, Nat. Museum of Art, Osaka, Museum of Contemporary Art, Sydney, Tel-Aviv Museum, others; sculpture commissioned for Thameslink Tunnel, London 1993, Bank of America, London 2003; Said Business School, Univ. of Oxford, 2005, Bank for Int. Settlements, Basel 2006; Jack Goldhill Prize for Sculpture, RA, London 2002. *Address:* 11 Kensington Park Gardens, London, W11 3HD, England. *Telephone:* (20) 8675-5945 (office); (20) 7727-3162 (home). *Fax:* (20) 7229-1852.

HALL, Peter Gavin, DPhil, FRS, FAA; Australian statistician and academic; *Professor of Statistics, University of Melbourne;* b. 20 Nov. 1951, Sydney; s. of William Holmen Hall and Ruby Violet Hall; m. Jeannie Jean Chien; ed Sydney Univ., Australian Nat. Univ., Univ. of Oxford, UK; Lecturer in Statistics, Univ. of Melbourne 1976–78, Prof. of Statistics 2006–; Lecturer in Statistics, ANU 1978–82, Sr Lecturer 1983–95, Reader 1986–88, Prof. 1988–2006; Centennial Professorship, LSE, UK 2000–02; Pres. Bernoulli Soc. for Math. Statistics and Probability 1999–2003; mem. Editorial Bd Annals of Statistics and several other journals; Corresp. Fellow, Royal Soc. of Edinburgh; Fellow, Inst. of Math. Statistics 1984, American Statistical Asscn 1996; Hon. Fellow, Royal Statistical Soc. 1989; Dr hc (Univ. Catholique de Louvain) 1997; Hon. DSc (Glasgow) 2005; Australian Math. Soc. Medal 1986, Rollo Davidson Prize, Univ. of Cambridge 1986, S.S. Wilks Lecture, Princeton Univ. 1988, Lyle Medal, Australian Acad. of Science 1989, Pitman Medal, Statistical Soc. of Australia 1990, Hannan Medal 1995, Kolmogorov Lecture, Vienna 1996, Invited Lecture, Int. Congress of Mathematicians, Berlin 1998, Matthew Flinders Medal and Lecture, Australian Acad. of Science 2006. *Publications:* Rates of Convergence in the Central Limit Theorem 1982, Introduction to the Theory of Coverage Processes 1988, The Bootstrap and Edgeworth Expansion 1992; over 400 papers in journals. *Address:* Centre for Mathematics and its Applications, 1163 JDMS Building, Australian National University, Canberra, ACT 0200 (office); Department of Mathematics and Statistics, University of Melbourne, Parkville, Vic. 3010; 6 Ramsay Place, Wanniassa, ACT 2903, Australia (home). *Telephone:* (2) 6125-3474 (Canberra) (office); (3) 8344-9682 (Melbourne) (office). *Fax:* (2) 6125-5549 (Canberra) (office); (3) 8344-4599 (Melbourne) (office). *E-mail:* Peter.Hall@maths.anu.edu.au (office); pghall@unimelb.edu.au (office). *Website:* wwwmaths.anu.edu.au/CMA (office); www.ms.unimelb.edu.au (office).

HALL, Sir Peter Geoffrey, Kt, MA, PhD, FBA; British geographer and academic; *Bartlett Professor of Planning and Regeneration, Bartlett School of Planning, University College London;* b. 19 March 1932, London; s. of Arthur Vickers and Bertha Hall (née Keefe); m. 1st Carla M. Wartenberg 1962 (divorced 1967); m. 2nd Magdalena Mróz 1967; ed Blackpool Grammar School, St Catharine's Coll., Cambridge; Asst Lecturer, Birkbeck Coll., Univ. of London 1956–60, Lecturer 1960–65; Reader in Geography with special reference to planning, LSE 1966–67; Prof. of Geography, Univ. of Reading 1968–89, Prof. Emer. 1989–; Prof. of City and Regional Planning, Univ. of California, Berkeley 1980–92, Prof. Emer. 1993–, Dir Inst. of Urban and Regional Devt 1989–92; Special Adviser to Sec. of State for the Environment 1991–94; Bartlett Prof. of Planning and Regeneration, Bartlett School of Planning, Univ. Coll., London 1992–; mem. South East Econ. Planning Council 1966–79, Social Science Research Council 1974–80; mem. Academia Europea; Hon. Fellow, St Catherine's Coll., Cambridge 1988; nine hon. degrees; Gill Memorial Prize, Royal Geographical Soc. 1968, Adolphe Bentinck Prize 1979, Founder's Medal, Royal Geographical Soc. 1988, Prix Vautrin Lud 2001, Gold Medal, Royal Town Planning Inst. 2003, Deputy Prime Minister's Lifetime Achievement Award 2005, Balzan Int. Prize 2005. *Publications:* The Industries of London 1962, London 2000 1963, Labour's New Frontiers 1964, Land Values (ed.) 1965, The World Cities 1966, Von Thünen's Isolated State (ed.) 1966, Theory and Practice of Regional Planning 1970, The Containment of Urban England 1973, Planning and Urban Growth 1973, Urban and Regional Planning 1974, Europe 2000 1977, Growth Centres in the European System 1980, Great Planning Disasters 1980, The Inner City in Context (ed.) 1981, Silicon Landscapes (ed.) 1985, Can Rail Save the City? 1985, High-Tech America 1986, Western Sunrise 1987, Cities of Tomorrow 1988, The Carrier Wave 1988, London 2001 1989, The Rise of the Gunbelt 1992, Technopoles of the World 1993, Sociable Cities 1998, Cities in Civilization 1998, Urban Future 21 2000, Working Capital 2002, The Polycentric Metropolis 2006. *Leisure interests:* reading, talking. *Address:* 12 Queens Road, London, W5 2SA (home); Bartlett School of Planning, University College London, Wates House, 22 Gordon Street, London, WC1H 0QB, England. *Telephone:* (20) 8997-3717 (home); (20) 8810-8723 (office). *Fax:* (20) 7679-7502 (office). *E-mail:* p.hall@ucl.ac.uk (office).

HALL, Sir Peter Reginald Frederick, Kt, CBE, MA; British theatre director and film director; b. 22 Nov. 1930, Bury St Edmunds, Suffolk; s. of late Reginald Hall and Grace Hall; m. 1st Leslie Caron 1956 (divorced 1965); one s. one d.; m. 2nd Jacqueline Taylor 1965 (divorced 1981); one s. one d.; m. 3rd Maria Ewing (q.v.) 1982 (divorced 1989); one d.; m. 4th Nicola Frei 1990; one d.; ed Perse School and St Catharine's Coll., Cambridge; produced and acted in over 20 plays at Cambridge; first professional production The Letter, Windsor 1953; produced in repertory at Windsor, Worthing and Oxford Playhouse; two Shakespearean productions for Arts Council; Artistic Dir Elizabethan Theatre Co. 1953; Asst Dir London Arts Theatre 1954, Dir 1955–57; formed own producing co., Int. Playwright's Theatre 1957; Man. Dir Royal Shakespeare Co., Stratford-upon-Avon and Aldwych Theatre, London 1960–68 (resgnd), Assoc. Dir –1973; mem. Arts Council 1969–73; Co-Dir, Nat. Theatre (now Royal Nat. Theatre) with Lord Olivier April-Nov. 1973, Dir 1973–88; f. Peter Hall Co. 1988; Artistic Dir Glyndebourne 1984–90; Artistic Dir The Old Vic

1997; Wortham Chair in Performing Arts, Houston Univ., Tex. 1999; Chancellor Kingston Univ. 2000–; Dir Kingston Theatre 2003–; Assoc. Prof. of Drama, Warwick Univ. 1964–67; mem. Bd Playhouse Theatre 1990–91; acted in The Pedestrian (film) 1973; Hon. Fellow St Catharine's Coll. Cambridge 1964; Chevalier, Ordre des Arts et des Lettres 1965; Dr hc (York) 1966, (Reading) 1973, (Liverpool) 1974, (Leicester) 1977, (Essex) 1993, (Cambridge) 2003; Hon. DSocSc (Birmingham) 1989; Hamburg Univ. Shakespeare Prize 1967, Evening Standard Special Award 1979, Evening Standard Award for Outstanding Achievement in Opera 1981, Evening Standard Best Dir Award for The Oresteia 1981, Evening Standard Best Dir Award for Antony and Cleopatra 1987, South Bank Show Lifetime Achievement Award 1998, Olivier Special Award for Lifetime Achievement 1999, New York Shakespeare Soc. Medal 2003. *Productions:* Blood Wedding, The Immoralist, The Lesson, South, Mourning Becomes Electra, Waiting for Godot, Burnt Flowerbed, Waltz of the Toreadors, Camino Real, Gigi, Wrong Side of the Park, Love's Labours Lost, Cymbeline, Twelfth Night, A Midsummer Night's Dream, Coriolanus, Two Gentlemen of Verona, Troilus and Cressida, Ondine, Romeo and Juliet, The Wars of the Roses (London Theatre Critics' Award for Best Dir 1963), Becket, The Collection, Cat on a Hot Tin Roof, The Rope Dancers (on Broadway), The Moon and Sixpence (opera, Sadler's Wells), Henry VI (parts 1, 2 and 3), Richard III, Richard II, Henry IV (parts 1 and 2), Henry V, Eh?, The Homecoming (London Theatre Critics' Award for Best Dir 1965, Antoinette Perry Award for Best Dir 1966), Moses and Aaron (opera, Covent Garden), Hamlet (London Theatre Critics' Award for Best Dir 1965), The Government Inspector, The Magic Flute (opera), Staircase, Work is a Four Letter Word (film) 1968, Macbeth, Midsummer Night's Dream (film) 1969, Three into Two Won't Go (film) 1969, A Delicate Balance, Dutch Uncle, Landscape and Silence, Perfect Friday (film) 1971, The Battle of Shrivings, La Calisto (opera, Glyndebourne Festival) 1970, The Knot Garden (opera, Covent Garden) 1970, Eugene Onegin (opera, Covent Garden) 1971, Old Times 1971, Tristan and Isolde (opera, Covent Garden) 1971, All Over 1972, Il Ritorno d'Ulisse (opera, Glyndebourne Festival) 1972, Alte Zeiten (Burgtheater, Vienna) 1972, Via Galactica (musical, Broadway) 1972, The Homecoming (film) 1973, Marriage of Figaro (opera, Glyndebourne) 1973, The Tempest 1973, Landscape (film) 1974, Akenfield (film) 1974, Happy Days 1974, John Gabriel Borkman 1974, No Man's Land 1975, Judgement 1975, Hamlet 1975, Tamburlaine the Great 1976, Don Giovanni (opera, Glyndebourne Festival) 1977, Volpone (Nat. Theatre) 1977, Bedroom Farce (Nat. Theatre) 1977, The Country Wife (Nat. Theatre) 1977, The Cherry Orchard (Nat. Theatre) 1978, Macbeth (Nat. Theatre) 1978, Betrayal (Nat. Theatre) 1978, Così Fan Tutte (opera, Glyndebourne) 1978, Fidelio (opera, Glyndebourne) 1979, Amadeus (Nat. Theatre) 1979, Betrayal (New York) 1980, Othello (Nat. Theatre) 1980, Amadeus (New York) (Tony Award for Best Dir 1981) 1980, Family Voices (Nat. Theatre) 1981, The Oresteia (Nat. Theatre) 1981, A Midsummer Night's Dream (opera, Glyndebourne) 1981, The Importance of Being Earnest (Nat. Theatre) 1982, Other Places (Nat. Theatre) 1982, The Ring (operas, Bayreuth Festival) 1983, Jean Seberg (musical, Nat. Theatre) 1983, L'Incoronazione di Poppea (opera, Glyndebourne) 1984, Animal Farm (Nat. Theatre) 1984, Coriolanus (Nat. Theatre) 1984, Yonadab (Nat. Theatre) 1985, Carmen (opera, Glyndebourne) 1985, (Metropolitan Opera) 1986, Albert Herring (opera, Glyndebourne) 1985, The Petition (New York and Nat. Theatre) 1986, Simon Boccanegra (opera, Glyndebourne) 1986, Salome (opera, Los Angeles) 1986, Coming in to Land (Nat. Theatre) 1986, Antony and Cleopatra (Nat. Theatre) 1987, Entertaining Strangers (Nat. Theatre) 1987, La Traviata (Glyndebourne) 1987, Falstaff (Glyndebourne) 1988, Salome (Covent Garden) 1988, Cymbeline (Nat. Theatre) 1988, The Winter's Tale (Nat. Theatre) 1988, The Tempest 1988, Orpheus Descending 1988, Salome (opera, Chicago) 1988, Albert Herring 1989, Merchant of Venice 1989, She's Been Away (TV) 1989, New Year (opera, Houston and Glyndebourne) 1989, The Wild Duck 1990, Born Again (musical) 1990, The Homecoming 1990, Orpheus Descending (film) 1990, Twelfth Night 1991, The Rose Tattoo 1991, Tartuffe 1991, The Camomile Lawn (TV) 1991, The Magic Flute 1992, Four Baboons Adoring the Sun (New York) 1992, Siena Red 1992, All's Well That Ends Well (RSC) 1992, The Gift of the Gorgon (RSC) 1992, The Magic Flute (LA) 1993, Separate Tables 1993, Lysistrata 1993, She Stoops to Conquer 1993, Piaf (musical) 1993, An Absolute Turkey (Le Dindon) 1994, On Approval 1994, Hamlet 1994, Jacob (TV) 1994, Never Talk to Strangers (film) 1995, Julius Caesar (RSC) 1995, The Master Builder 1995, The Final Passage (TV) 1996, Mind Millie for Me 1996, The Oedipus Plays (Nat. Theatre at Epidaurus and Nat. Theatre) 1996, A School for Wives 1995, A Streetcar Named Desire 1997, The Seagull 1997, Waste 1997, Waiting for Godot 1997, 1998, King Lear 1997, The Misanthrope 1998, Major Barbara 1998, Simon Boccanegra (Glyndebourne) 1998, Filumena 1998, Amadeus 1998, Kafka's Dick 1998, Measure for Measure (LA) 1999, A Midsummer Night's Dream (LA) 1999, Lenny (Queens Theatre) 1999, Amadeus (LA, NY) 1999, Cuckoos 2000, Tantalus (Denver, Colo) 2000, Japes 2000, Romeo and Juliet (LA) 2001, Japes 2001, Troilus and Cressida (NY) 2001, Tantalus 2001, A Midsummer Night's Dream (Glyndebourne) 2001, Otello (Glyndebourne) 2001, Japes (Theatre Royal) 2001, The Royal Family (Theatre Royal) 2001, Lady Windermere's Fan (Theatre Royal) 2002, The Bacchai (Olivier Theatre) 2002, Design for Living (Theatre Royal, Bath) 2003, Betrayal (Theatre Royal, Bath) 2003, The Fight for Barbara (Theatre Royal, Bath) 2003, As You Like It (Theatre Royal, Bath) 2003, Cuckoos (Theatre Royal, Bath) 2003, The Marriage of Figaro (Lyric Opera of Chicago) 2003, Happy Days (Arts Theatre, London) 2003, Man and Superman (Theatre Royal, Bath) 2004, Galileo's Daughter (Theatre Royal, Bath) 2004, Amy's View 2006, The Vortex 2007. *Publications:* The Wars of the Roses 1970, Shakespeare's three Henry VI plays and Richard III (adapted with John Barton), John Gabriel Borkman (English version with Inga-Stina Ewbank) 1975, Peter Hall's Diaries: The Story of a Dramatic Battle 1983, Animal Farm: a stage adaptation 1986, The Wild Duck

1990, Making an Exhibition of Myself (autobiog.) 1993, An Absolute Turkey (new trans. of Feydeau's Le Dindon, with Nicki Frei) 1994, The Master Builder (with Inga-Stina Ewbank) 1995, Mind Millie for Me (new trans. of Feydeau's Occupe-toi d'Amélie, with Nicki Frei), The Necessary Theatre 1999, Exposed by the Mask 2000, Shakespeare's Advice to the Players 2003. *Leisure interest:* music. *Address:* 48 Lamont Road, London, SW10 0HX, England. *E-mail:* phpetard@aol.com (office).

HALL, Philip David; British journalist and PR consultant; *Chairman, PHA Media;* b. 8 Jan. 1955; s. of Norman Philip Hall and Olive Jean Hall; m. Marina Thomson 1997; two c.; ed Beal Grammar School, Ilford; reporter, Dagenham Post 1974–77, Ilford Recorder 1977–80; Sub-Ed. Newham Recorder 1980–84, Weekend Magazine 1984–85; reporter, The People 1985–86, Chief Reporter 1986–89, News Ed. 1989–92; News Ed. Sunday Express 1992–93; Asst Ed. (Features) News of the World 1993–94, Deputy Ed. 1994–95, Ed. 1995–2000; with Max Clifford Assocs 2000–01; Ed.-in-Chief Hello! 2001–02; Founder and Chair. Phil Hall Assocs. (public relations) (now PHA Media) 2004–; mem. Press Complaints Comm. 1998–2000, 2002–. *Leisure interests:* golf, cinema, theatre, football. *Address:* PHA Media, 103 Dean Street, London, W1D 3 TH, England (office). *Telephone:* (20) 7025-1350 (office). *Fax:* (20) 7025-1351 (office). *E-mail:* info@pha-media.com (office). *Website:* www.pha-media.com (office).

HALL, Rodney, AM; Australian writer, musician and actor; b. 18 Nov. 1935; s. of D. E. Hall; m. Maureen McPhail 1962; three d.; ed City of Bath School for Boys, UK, Brisbane Boys' Coll., Univ. of Queensland; leader, Baroque Music Group; Creative Arts Fellow, ANU 1968, Literary Bd Fellow 1974–80, tutor, New England Univ. Summer School of Music 1967–71, 1977–80; Lecturer, Dept of Foreign Affairs; Recorder, Canberra School of Music 1979–83; Chair. Australia Council 1991–94; Miles Franklin Award 1982, 1994. *Publications:* published over 500 poems in Australia, UK, USA, USSR, Philippines, France, India, several published books of poetry and novels; poetry: The Climber 1962, Penniless till Doomsday 1962, Forty Beads on a Hangman's Rope 1963, Eyewitness 1967, The Autobiography of a Gorgon 1968, The Law of Karma 1968, Australia 1970, Heaven, in a Way 1970, A Soapbox Omnibus 1973, Selected Poems 1975, Black Bagatelles 1978, The Most Beautiful World 1981; fiction: The Ship on the Coin 1972, A Place Among People 1975, Just Relations 1982, Kisses of the Enemy 1987, Captivity Captive 1988, The Second Bridegroom 1991, The Grisly Wife 1994, The Island in the Mind 1996, The Day We had Hitler Home 2000, The Last Love Story 2004, Love Without Hope 2007, The Lonely Traveller by Night 2009. *Address:* c/o Publicity Department, Pan Macmillan Australia, Level 25, 1 Market Street, Sydney, NSW 2000, Australia (office). *Website:* www.panmacmillan.com.au (office).

HALL, Rev. Wesley Winfield; Barbadian politician, public relations consultant and fmr cricketer; b. 12 Sept. 1937, St Michael; m. (divorced); four c.; ed Combermere School and Industrial Soc. London (personnel man.); right-arm fast bowler and lower-order right-hand batsman; took 192 wickets (average 26.38) in 48 Tests; took 546 first-class wickets (average 26.14); played amateur and professional cricket in England, Australia, NZ, India, Sri Lanka and throughout W Indies including 48 Test matches in which he took 192 wickets and first hat-trick by a West Indian 1961–69; Man. W Indies Cricket Team throughout W Indies and abroad 1983–85; Pres. West Indies Cricket Bd 2001–; trainee telegraphist, Cable and Wireless, Barbados 1955–60; Public Relations Consultant, Esso, Queensland, Australia 1960–63, British American Tobacco Co. Ltd (Trinidad and Tobago) 1968–78; Personnel and Public Relations Man. Banks Barbados Breweries Ltd 1975–85; Independent Senator, Barbados Senate 1971–76, Opposition Senator 1981–86; Minister of Employment, Labour Relations and Community Devt 1986–88, of Tourism and Sports 1988–93, of Industrial Relations, Community Devt and Sports 1993–94; Life mem. MCC; Hon. Life mem. Barbados Football Asscn; Humming Bird Gold Medal 1987. *Publications:* Secrets of Cricket 1962, Pace Like Fire 1965. *Address:* c/o Ministry of Tourism and Sports, Harbour Road, St Michael, Barbados.

HALLBERG, Anders; Swedish chemist and university vice-chancellor; *Vice-Chancellor, Uppsala University;* fmr Head, Chem. Div., Astra (now AstraZeneca), Lund; Prof. of Medicinal Chem. and Dean Faculty of Pharmacy, Uppsala Univ. 1990–, Vice-Chancellor Uppsala Univ. 2006–; Visiting Researcher and Prof. at univs in USA; mem. Swedish Natural Science Research Council, Swedish Research Council; mem. Royal Soc. of Sciences, Uppsala, Royal Acad. of Arts and Sciences, Uppsala, Royal Physiographic Soc., Lund, Royal Acad. of Sciences, Royal Acad. of Eng Sciences; Hon. mem. Smalandensis Student Nation, Uppsala, Uplandensis Student Nation; several prestigious scientific awards, Best Teacher Award, Pharmaceutical Student Union, Uppsala Univ. 2006. *Publications:* more than 240 scientific papers on organic synthesis and the devt of new pharmaceuticals against infectious diseases such as HIV/AIDS, HCV and malaria. *Address:* Universitetsledningens kansli S:t Olofsg. 10B, Box 256, 751 05 Uppsala (office); Institutionen for lakemedelskemi, Uppsala biomedicinska centrum BMC, Husarg. 3, Box 574, 751 23 Uppsala, Sweden. *Telephone:* (18) 471-33-10 (office); (18) 471-43-74. *Fax:* (18) 471-16-40 (office); (18) 471-44-74. *E-mail:* rektor@uu.se (office); Anders.Hallberg@orgfarm.uu.se (office). *Website:* www.uu.se (office); www.farmfak.uu.se/organisk (office).

HALLBERG, Paul Thure, Fil Lic; Swedish library director (retd); b. 10 Dec. 1931, Gothenburg; s. of the late Severin Hallberg and Eva Hallberg (née Theorell); m. Elisabeth Löfgren 1958; one s.; ed Göteborg Univ., Yale Univ., USA; Asst Teacher, Dept of English Language and Literature, Göteborg Univ. 1958–59; Librarian, Göteborg Univ. Library 1960–68, Head of Dept 1968–77, Dir 1977–96; Sec. Main Cttee for Scandia Plan 1964–65; Sec. Scandinavian Fed. of Research Librarians 1966–69, mem. Bd 1979–84; mem. Royal Soc. of Arts and Sciences in Göteborg 1977–99, Librarian and Publications Officer 1977–2005, Hon. mem. 1999–; mem. Nat. Bibliographic Council 1983–96; Chair. Swedish Cataloguing Cttee 1979–85; Chair. Steering Group of Swedish LIBRIS system 1992–96; mem. of Bd NORDINFO (Nordic Council for Scientific Information and Research Libraries) 1986–88; mem. Standing Cttee, Int. Fed. of Library Asscns and Insts, Section on Acquisition and Exchange 1977–85, mem. Standing Cttee, Section of Univ. Libraries and other Gen. Research Libraries 1985–93, Sec. 1985–89; Dr hc (Göteborg) 1997. *Publications:* A Passage to China: Colin Campbell's Diary of the First Swedish East India Company Expedition to Canton 1732–33 (co-ed. with C. Koninckx) 1996; author and ed. of numerous books and articles on bibliography and librarianship. *Leisure interests:* music, gardening. *Address:* Orangerigatan 34, 412 66 Göteborg, Sweden (home). *Telephone:* (31) 40-23-18 (home); 70-661-98-80 (mobile). *Fax:* (31) 16-37-97 (office).

HALLIDAY, Frederick, PhD; Irish academic and journalist; *Professor of International Relations, London School of Economics;* b. 1946, Dublin; ed Queen's Coll., Oxford, SOAS, LSE, UK; Prof. of Int. Relations, LSE 1983–; columnist for Prospect magazine, Middle East Research and Information Project (MERIP); broadcaster with ABC, BBC, CNN and CBC; Editorial Assoc. New Left Review; Fellow Transnational Inst. 1976–, also adviser on Middle Eastern and Cen. Asian matters; fmr Chair. Research Cttee, Royal Inst. of Int. Affairs; mem. Advisory Council, Foreign Policy Inst. *Publications include:* 14 books on int. politics including Dictatorship and Development 1978, Rethinking International Relations 1994, Islam and the Myth of Confrontation 1995, Revolution and World Politics 1999, Two Hours that Shook the World 2002. *Address:* Department of International Relations, London School of Economics, Houghton Street, London, WC2A 2AE, England (office). *Telephone:* (20) 7955-7389 (office). *Fax:* (20) 7242-0392 (office). *E-mail:* f.halliday@lse.ac.uk. *Website:* www.lse.ac.uk (office).

HALLIER, Hans-Joachim, DIur; German diplomatist; b. 25 April 1930, Offenbach; s. of Christian L. Hallier and Sophie Heberer; m. Almuth H. Frantz 1966; two s.; ed Lessing Gymnasium, Frankfurt and Univs of Frankfurt and Heidelberg, Western Reserve Univ., Cleveland, Ohio, USA; attaché, German NATO Del. Paris 1960–61; Second Sec., Djakarta 1962–66; First Sec., Tokyo 1966–69; Dir Cabinet of Foreign Minister, Bonn 1970–74; Amb. to Malaysia 1974–76, to Indonesia 1980–83, to Japan 1986–90, to the Holy See 1990–95; Dir-Gen. Foreign Office, Bonn 1983–86. *Publications:* Völkerrechtliche Schiedsinstanzen für Einzelpersonen und ihr Verhältnis zur innerstaatlichen Gerichtsbarkeit 1962, Zwischen Fernost und Vatikan (memoirs) 1999, Das Dorf – eine mecklenburgische Chronik 2001; books and research papers on int. law. *Address:* Eifelblick 11, 53619 Rheinbreitbach, Germany (home). *Telephone:* (2224) 5931 (home). *Fax:* (2224) 70183 (home). *E-mail:* poreta91@aol.com (home).

HALLIWELL, Geri Estelle; British singer; b. 7 Aug. 1972, Watford, England; one d.; mem. (with Victoria Adams, Melanie Brown, Emma Bunton and Melanie Chisholm) Touch, later renamed The Spice Girls 1993–98, as 'Ginger Spice', reunion tour 2007–08; UN Goodwill Amb. 1998–; Prince's Trust Amb.; Patron Breast Cancer Care; solo artist 1998–; two Ivor Novello songwriting awards 1997, Smash Hits Award for Best British Band 1997, BRIT Award for Best Single (for Wannabe, with The Spice Girls) 1997, BRIT Award for Best Video (for Say You'll Be There, with The Spice Girls) 1997, three American Music Awards 1998, Special BRIT Award for Int. Sales 1998. *Films:* Spiceworld The Movie 1997, Fat Slags 2004. *Television appearances:* judge on Popstars – The Rivals (ITV 1) 2002, appearance in Sex and the City (HBO) 2003. *Recordings include:* albums: with The Spice Girls: Spice 1996, Spiceworld 1997, Greatest Hits 2007; solo: Schizophonic 1999, Scream If You Wanna Go Faster 2001, Passion 2005. *Publications:* If Only (autobiog.) 1999, Just for the Record (autobiog.) 2002; Ugenia Lavender children's series: Ugenia Lavender 2008, Ugenia Lavender and the Terrible Tiger 2008, Ugenia Lavender and the Burning Pants 2008, Ugenia Lavender: Home Alone 2008, Ugenia Lavender and the Temple of Gloom 2008, Ugenia Lavender the One and Only 2008. *Address:* Hackford Jones PR, Third Floor, 16 Manette Street, London, W1D 4AR, England (office); c/o A&R Department, Chrysalis Records, 43 Brook Green, London, W6 7EF, England. *Telephone:* (20) 7287-9788 (office); (20) 7605-5000. *Fax:* (20) 7287-9731 (office). *Website:* www.geri-halliwell.com.

HALLSTRÖM, Lasse; Swedish film director; b. 2 June 1946, Stockholm; m. 1st Malou Hallström, one s.; m. 2nd Lena Olin, one d. *Films include:* A Lover and his Lass 1975, Abba – The Movie 1977, Father-to-be 1979, The Rooster 1981, Happy We 1983, My Life as a Dog 1985 (Film of the Year 1985), The Children of Bullerby Village 1986, More about the Children of Bullerby Village 1987, Once Around 1991, What's Eating Gilbert Grape (also co-exec. producer) 1993, Something to Talk About 1995, Lumière and Company 1995, The Cider House Rules 1999, Chocolat 2000, The Shipping News 2002, An Unfinished Life 2004, Casanova 2005, The Hoax 2006. *Address:* c/o David Nochimson, Ziffren, Brittenham, Branca, Fischer, Gilbert-Lurie, Stiffelman & Cook LLP, 1801 Century Park West, Los Angeles, CA 90067-6406; c/o Creative Arts Agency, 2000 Avenue of the Stars, Los Angeles, CA 90067, USA.

HALLÚ, Rubén Eduardo, BSc; Argentine veterinarian, academic and university administrator; *Rector, University of Buenos Aires;* b. 16 Jan. 1951; ed Univ. of Buenos Aires; fmr Assoc. Teacher and Dir of Basic Science, Faculty of Veterinary Sciences, Nat. Univ. of La Pampa, Santa Rosa; fmr Lecturer in Pharmacology, Nat. Univ. of Rosario; Assoc. Prof., later Prof. of Pharmacology, Univ. of Buenos Aires, also Sec. of Admin Supervision, Vice-Dean, Faculty of Veterinary Sciences 1994–2002, Dean 2002–, mem. Univ. of Buenos Aires Superior Bd 2002–, Rector Univ. of Buenos Aires 2006–. *Publications:* more than 50 research papers. *Address:* Office of the Rector, University of Buenos Aires, 430/444 Viamonte, 1053 Buenos Aires, Argentina (office). *Telephone:* (11) 4510-1100 (office). *Website:* www.uba.ar (office).

HALLYDAY, Johnny; French singer, musician (guitar) and actor; b. (Jean-Philippe Smet), 15 June 1943, Paris; s. of Léon Smet; m. 1st Sylvie Vartan; one s.; m. 2nd Elisabeth Etienne; m. 3rd Adeline Blondiau; m. 4th Laetitia Boudou 1996; one c. with Nathalie Baye; appeared on stage aged five; music hall tours with his cousin and her husband, American dancer Lee Halliday; numerous concerts; Prix Cinématographique Jean-Gabin 2003; Chevalier, Légion d'honneur, Officier, Ordre des Arts et des Lettres, Officier, Ordre de la Couronne (Belgium). *Films:* Les Diaboliques 1955, Les Parisiennes 1961, Un Coup dans l'aile 1963, D'où viens-tu, Johnny? 1964, A Tout casser 1968, Visa de censure 1968, Gli Specialisti 1970, Point de chute 1970, Malpertuis 1971, Pour une pomme 1972, L'Aventure, c'est l'aventure 1972, L'Animal 1977, Le Jour se lève et les conneries commencent 1981, Détective 1985, Conseil de famille 1986, Terminus 1987, The Iron Triangle 1989, La Gamine 1991, Pourquoi pas moi? 1999, Love Me 2000, L'Homme du train 2002, Crime Spree 2003, Les Rivières pourpres 2: Les anges de l'apocalypse 2004, Quartier VIP 2004. *Television:* David Lansky (series) 1989. *Recordings include:* albums: Retiens la nuit 1961, Whole Lotta Shakin' Goin' On 1962, Sings America's Rockin' Hits 1962, Les Bras en croix 1963, Da dou ron ron 1963, L'Idole des jeunes 1963, D'Où viens-tu Johnny? 1963, Le pénitencier 1964, Excuse-moi partenaire 1964, Noir c'est noir 1966, Je suis né dans la rue 1968, Que je t'aime 1969, Fils de personne 1971, Toute la musique que j'aime 1972, J'ai pleuré sur ma guitare 1973, Rock 'n' Roll Man 1974, Flagrant Delit 1975, Gabrielle 1975, Hamlet 1976, Johnny Hallyday Story: Palais des Sports 1976, J'ai oublié de vivre 1977, Le Bon temps du rock 'n' roll 1978, Ma gueule 1979, Pavillon de Paris 1979, Mon Amérique à moi 1981, Je suis victime de l'amour 1982, Signes extérieurs de richesse 1983, Nashville Blues 1984, Rock 'n' Roll Attitude 1985, Gang 1986, Mon p'tit loup 1988, Oh ma jolie Sarah 1988, La Peur 1988, Ses 32 premieres chansons 1988, Johnny à Bercy 1988, Mirador 1989, Ca ne change pas un homme 1991, Dans la chaleur de Bercy 1991, La Nuit Johnny 1993, Parc de Princes 1993, Deux étrangers 1993, Cheveux longs et idées courtes 1993, A tout casser 1993, Paroles d'hommes 1995, Rough Town 1996, Destination Vegas 1996, Aimer vivre 1997, Insolitudes 1997, Vie 1998, Stade de France 1998, Derrière l'amour 1998, Ce que je sais 1998, Sang pour sang 1999, Les rocks les plus terribles 1999, Ballades 1999, Solitude a deux 2000, Salut les copains 2000, Rock 'n' Slow 2000, Rock a Memphis 2000, Riviere ouvre ton lit 2000, Reve et amour 2000, Quelque part un aigle 2000, Pas facile 2000, La Generation perdue 2000, Chant 2000, Johnny 67 2000, Jeune homme 2000, Je t'aime, je t'aime, je t'aime 2000, Hollywood 2000, Halleluyah 2000, Entre Violence et Violon 2000, En V O 2000, En pieces detachees 2000, Country Folk Rock 2000, C'est la vie 2000, A Partir de maintenant 2000, La Terre promise 2000, À la vie, à la mort! 2002. *Publications include:* Johnny raconte Hallyday 1980, Johnny la forme (jtly) 1990, Déraciné (1943–1964) 1996. *Address:* c/o Camus and Camus Productions, 6 rue Daubigny, 75017 Paris, France. *Website:* www.johnnyhallyday.com.

HALONEN, Tarja Kaarina, LLM; Finnish politician, lawyer and head of state; *President;* b. 24 Dec. 1943, Helsinki; d. of Vieno Olavi Halonen and Lyyli Elina Loimola; m. Dr Pentti Arajärvi 2000; one d. from previous relationship with Kari Pekkonen; ed Univ. of Helsinki and Univ. of Kent at Canterbury, UK; lawyer, Lainvalvonta Oy 1967–68; social welfare officer, organizing Sec. Nat. Union of Finnish Students 1969–70; lawyer, Cen. Org. of Finnish Trade Unions 1970–2000; Parl. Sec. to Prime Minister Sorsa 1974–75; mem. Helsinki City Council 1977–96; mem. Parl. 1979–2000; Chair. Parl. Social Affairs Cttee 1984–87; Second Minister, Ministry of Social Affairs and Health 1987–90, for Nordic Co-operation 1989–91, of Justice 1990–91, for Foreign Affairs 1995–2000; Pres. of Finland (first woman) 2000– (re-elected 2006); Chair. Int. Solidarity Foundation 1991–2000 (mem. Bd Dirs), TNL Theatre Org.; mem. Social Democratic Party 1971–2000; Co-Chair. World Comm. on the Social Dimension of Globalization, ILO 2002–04; mem. Rep. Body of the Cooperative Retail Co. Elanto 1975–, mem. Supervisory Bd 1980–96; mem. UNCTAD Panel of Eminent Persons 2005–06; mem. Bd Oslo Centre for Peace and Human Rights 2006–; hon. degrees (Univ. of Helsinki) 2000, (Helsinki School of Econs) 2001, (Ewha Womens Univ., Republic of Korea) 2002, (Univ. of Kent) 2002, (Eötvös Loránd Univ., Budapest) 2002, Chinese Acad. of Forestry) 2002, (Finlandia Univ., USA) 2003, (Univ. of Turku) 2003, (Univ. of Bluefiels, Nicaragua) 2004, (Univ. of Tartu, Estonia) 2004, (State Univ. of Yerevan, Armenia) 2005; ranked by Forbes magazine amongst 100 Most Powerful Women (31st) 2004, (31st) 2005, (44th) 2006, (50th) 2007, (71st) 2008. *Leisure interests:* art history, drawing, painting, the theatre, swimming. *Address:* Office of the President, Mariankatu 2, 00170 Helsinki, Finland (office). *Telephone:* (9) 661133 (office). *Fax:* (9) 638247 (office). *E-mail:* presidentti@tpk.fi (office); kirjaamo@tpk.fi (office). *Website:* www.presidentti.fi (office).

HALPERIN, Bertrand Israel, PhD; American physicist and academic; *Hollis Professor of Mathematics and Natural Philosophy, Harvard University;* b. 6 Dec. 1941, Brooklyn, New York; s. of Morris Halperin and Eva Teplitsky Halperin; m. Helena Stacy French 1962; one s. one d.; ed George Wingate High School, Brooklyn, Harvard Coll. and Univ. of California (Berkeley); NSF Postdoctoral Fellow, Ecole Normale Supérieure, Paris 1965–66; mem. tech. staff, Bell Labs 1966–76; Prof. of Physics, Harvard Univ. 1976–, Chair. Dept of Physics 1988–91, Hollis Prof. of Math. and Natural Philosophy 1992–; Assoc. Ed. Reviews of Modern Physics 1974–80; mem. NAS, American Acad. of Arts and Sciences, American Philosophical Soc.; Fellow, American Physical Soc.; Oliver Buckley Prize for Condensed Matter Physics 1982, Lars Onsager Prize 2001, Wolf Prize in Physics (jt recipient) 2003, Goettingen Akademie der Wissenschaften Dannie Heineman Prize 2007. *Publications:* about 200 articles in scientific journals. *Address:* Lyman Laboratory of Physics, Harvard University, 17 Oxford Street, Cambridge, MA 02138, USA (office). *Telephone:* (617) 495-4294 (office). *E-mail:* halperin@physics.harvard.edu (office). *Website:* physics.harvard.edu/halperin.htm (office); www.physics.harvard.edu/fac_staff/halperin.html (office); cmtw.harvard.edu (office).

HALPERIN, (Donghi) Tulio, DPhil; Argentine historian and academic; *Professor, University of California, Berkeley;* b. 27 Oct. 1926, Buenos Aires; ed Univ. de Buenos Aires, Ecole Pratique des Hautes Etudes, Paris; Prof., Univ. Nac. del Litoral (Rosario, Argentina) 1955–61; Prof. Univ. de Buenos Aires 1959–66, Univ. of Oxford 1970–71, Univ. of Calif. (Berkeley) 1971–; Lecturer, History Dept, Harvard Univ. 1967–. *Publications:* El Pensamiento de Echeverría 1951, Un Conflicto Nacional: Moriscos y Cristianos Viejos en Valencia 1955, El Río de la Plata al Comenzar el Siglo XIX 1960, Tradición Política Española e Ideología Revolucionaria de Mayo 1961, Historia de la Universidad de Buenos Aires 1962, Argentina en el Callejón 1964, Historia contemporánea de América Latina 1969, Hispanoamérica después de la Independencia 1972 (in English The Aftermath of Revolution in Latin America 1973), Revolución y guerra 1972 (in English Politics, Economics and Society in Argentina in the Revolutionary Period 1975), Jose Hernandez y Sus Mundos 1992, Argentina en el callejón 1995, Historia Contemporanea de America Latina (Contemporary History of Latin America) 1999, Historia de La Universidad de Buenos Aires 2002, La Argentina y La Tormenta del Mundo 2003. *Address:* History Department, University of California, Berkeley, CA 94720, USA. *Website:* www.berkeley.edu (office).

HALPERN, Daniel, MFA; American editor and writer; *Editorial Director, The Ecco Press;* b. 11 Sept. 1945, Syracuse, NY; s. of Irving Halpern and Rosemary Halpern; m. Jeanne Carter 1982; one d.; ed California State Univ. and Columbia Univ., New York; Editorial Dir, The Ecco Press (Antaeus) 1970–; Adjunct Prof., Columbia Univ. 1975–; Dir Nat. Poetry Series 1978–; Visiting Prof., Princeton Univ. 1975–76, 1987–88; Nat. Endowment for the Arts Fellowship 1974, 1975, 1987; Robert Frost Fellowship, CAPS, Guggenheim Fellow 1988; numerous awards including Carey Thomas Award for Creative Publishing. *Publications:* poetry: Travelling on Credit 1972, Street Fire 1975, Life Among Others 1978, Seasonal Rights 1982, Tango 1987, Halpern's Guide to the Essential Restaurants of Italy 1990, Foreign Neon 1991, Selected Poems 1994, Antaeus 1970 1996, Something Shining 1998; ed. several anthologies including Dante's Inferno: Translations by Twenty Contemporary Poets 1994. *Leisure interest:* cooking. *Address:* The Ecco Press, 10 East 53rd Street, New York, NY 10022, USA.

HALPERN, Jack, PhD, FRS; American chemist and academic; *Louis Block Distinguished Service Professor, Department of Chemistry, University of Chicago;* b. 19 Jan. 1925, Poland; s. of Philip Halpern and Anna Sass; m. Helen Peritz 1949; two d.; ed McGill Univ., Montreal, Canada; NRC Postdoctoral Overseas Fellow, Univ. of Manchester, UK 1949–50; Prof. of Chem., Univ. of BC, Canada 1950–62; Nuffield Fellow, Univ. of Cambridge, UK 1959–60; Louis Block Distinguished Service Prof., Univ. of Chicago 1962–; External Scientific mem. Max Planck Inst. für Kohlenforschung, Mulheim, Germany 1983–; Visiting Prof. at various univs in USA, UK and Copenhagen; Chair. German-American Council 1993–96, Chair. Bd of Trustees 1996–; numerous other lectureships, professional and editorial appointments; Fellow American Acad. of Arts and Sciences; Dir American Friends of the Royal Soc. 2000–; mem. Advisory Bd Humboldt Foundation Transatlantic Science and Humanities Program 2001–; mem. NAS 1984– (mem. Council 1990–, Chair. Chem. Section 1991–93, Vice-Pres. 1993–); Hon. FRSC 1987; Cross of Merit (Germany) 1996; Hon. DSc (Univ. of BC) 1986, (McGill) 1997; ACS Award in Inorganic Chem. 1968, Royal Soc. of Chem. Award in Catalysis 1977, Humboldt Award 1977, Richard Kokes Award 1978, ACS Award for Distinguished Service in the Advancement of Inorganic Chem. 1985, Willard Gibbs Medal 1986, Bailar Medal 1986, German Chemical Soc. August Wilhelm von Hoffman Medal 1988, American Inst. of Chemists Chemical Pioneer Award 1991, Swiss Chemical Soc. Paracelsus Prize 1992, Basolo Medal 1993, Robert A. Welch Award 1994, ACS Award in Organometallic Chem. 1995, Int. Precious Metals Inst. Henry Alberts Award 1995. *Publications:* more than 250 scientific articles in various scientific journals. *Leisure interests:* art, music, theatre. *Address:* Department of Chemistry, University of Chicago, Chicago, IL 60637 (office); 5801 S Dorchester Avenue, Apartment 4A, Chicago, IL 60637, USA (home). *Telephone:* (773) 702-7095 (office); (773) 643-6837 (home). *Fax:* (773) 702-8809 (office). *E-mail:* jhjh@midway.uchicago.edu (office). *Website:* chemistry.uchicago.edu (office).

HALPERN, Sir Ralph (Mark), Kt, CBIM, FID; British business executive; b. 1938, London; s. of Bernard Halpern and Olga Halpern; m. Joan Halpern (divorced); one s. one d.; ed St Christopher School, Letchworth; fmr trainee Selfridges; joined Burton Group PLC 1961, Chief Exec. and Man. Dir 1978–90, Chair. 1981–90; Co-Founder Top Shop 1970; Chair. Halpern Assocs; Chair. CBI Marketing and Common Affairs Cttee 1984; Chair. Police and Community Partnership Group, E Surrey; fmr Hon. Prof., Univ. of Warwick; mem. CBI City-Industry Task Force 1986; mem. Pres.'s Cttee, Chair. British Fashion Council 1990–94; mem. Advisory Council Prince's Youth Business Trust 1991–92. *Leisure interest:* country pursuits. *Address:* c/o The Reform Club, Pall Mall, London, W1, England.

HALSBAND, Frances, BA, MArch, FAIA; American architect; *Partner, Kliment Halsband Architects;* b. 30 Oct. 1943, New York City; m. Robert Kliment 1971; one s.; ed Swarthmore Coll., Columbia Univ., New York; worked at Mitchell & Giurgola Architects, New York 1968–72; Founding Pnr (with Robert Kliment), Kliment Halsband Architects, New York 1972–; fmr Dean School of Architecture, Pratt Inst.; Guest Lecturer, Ball State Univ., Univ. of California, Berkeley, Univ. of Cincinnati, Columbia Univ., Harvard Univ., Univ. of Illinois, North Carolina State Univ., Univ. of Maryland, Univ. of Pennsylvania, Rice Univ. and Univ. of Virginia; fmr Pres. New York Chapter, AIA, Architectural League of New York; fmr Commr New York City Landmarks Preservation Comm.; Chair. Cttee on Design, AIA 1999; mem.

Architectural Review Bd of Fed. Reserve Bank; Architect Advisor, Corpn at Brown Univ.; fmr mem. Architctural Advisory Bd US Dept of State; AIA NY State Award of Merit, Interfaith Forum on Religion, Art and Architecture Design Award, Gen. Services Admin Design Award Citation, AIA New York Chapter Medal of Honour. *Architectural works include:* Roth Center for Jewish Life, Hanover, New Hampshire, Long Island Railroad Entrance Pavilion to Pennsylvania Station, New York. *Publications include:* articles in professional journals. *Address:* Kliment Halsband Architects, 322 Eighth Avenue, New York, NY 10001, USA (office). *Telephone:* (212) 243-7400 (office). *Fax:* (212) 633-9769 (office). *E-mail:* halsband@kliment-halsband.com (office). *Website:* www.kliment-halsband.com (office).

HALSE, Bengt Gösta, DEng; Swedish business executive; *Chairman, Comhem AB;* b. 2 Feb. 1943, Gothenburg; ed Chalmers Inst. of Tech., Gothenburg; with Ericsson Group 1974–95; Pres., CEO Saab AB 1995–2003; Chair. Comhem AB 2003–, Flexlink AB 2003–; Dir Omhex AB, Teleca AB; mem. Royal Swedish Acad. of Engineering Sciences, Royal Swedish Acad. of War Sciences; DrIng hc (Linköping Univ.) 1999; Hon. mem. Royal Swedish Soc. of Naval Sciences 2002; Hon. Fellow Royal Aeronautical Soc., London 2001; King's Medal of the12th Dimension with Ribbon of the Order of the Seraphim 2004. *Telephone:* (734) 187105. *Fax:* (31) 930926.

HALSEY, Albert Henry, MA, PhD; British academic; *Professor Emeritus, University of Oxford;* b. 13 April 1923, London; s. of William T. Halsey and Ada Draper; m. Gertrude M. Littler 1949; three s. two d.; ed London School of Econs; research worker, Univ. of Liverpool 1952–54; Lecturer, Univ. of Birmingham 1954–62; Fellow, Centre for Advanced Study of Behavioral Sciences, Palo Alto, Calif. 1956–57; Prof. of Sociology, Univ. of Chicago 1959–60; Dir Barnett House and Fellow, Nuffield Coll., Oxford 1962–90; Prof. of Social and Admin. Studies, Univ. of Oxford 1978–90, Prof. Emer. 1990–; Sr Fellow British Acad. 1995; mem. Acad. Europaea 1992; Foreign mem. American Acad. of Arts and Sciences 1988; Hon. Fellow, Goldsmiths Coll. London 1992, LSE 1993, Royal Statistical Soc. 1999; Hon. DSc (Birmingham) 1987; Dr hc (Open Univ.) 1989; Hon. DLit (Warwick, Leicester) 1994, (Glamorgan) 1995. *Radio:* Reith Lecturer, BBC 1978. *Publications:* Origins and Destinations 1980, Change in British Society 1986, English Ethical Socialism (with Norman Dennis) 1988, The Decline of Donnish Dominion 1992, No Discouragement: an Autobiography of A. H. Halsey 1996, Education, Culture, Economy and Society 1997, British Social Trends: The Twentieth Century 2000, A History of Sociology in Britain: Science, Literature and Society 2004. *Leisure interest:* gardening. *Address:* Nuffield College, Oxford, OX1 1NF (office); 28 Upland Park Road, Oxford, OX2 7RU, England (home). *Telephone:* (1865) 278521 (office); (1865) 558625 (home). *E-mail:* Chelly .Halsey@nuf.ox.ac.uk (office).

HALSTEAD, Sir Ronald, Kt, CBE, MA, CBIM, FRSC, FRSA; British business executive; b. 17 May 1927, Lancaster; s. of Richard Halstead and Bessie Harrison Halstead; m. Yvonne Cecile de Monchaux 1968 (deceased); two s.; ed Queens' Coll., Cambridge; Research Chemist H.P. Bulmer & Co. 1948–53; Mfg Man. Macleans Ltd 1954–55; Factory Man. Beecham Products Inc., USA 1955–60, Asst Man. Dir Beecham Research Lab. Ltd 1960–62, Pres. Beecham Research Labs, Inc. (USA) 1962–64, Vice-Pres. Marketing, Beecham Products, Inc. (USA) 1962–64, Chair. Food and Drink Div. Beecham Group 1964–67; Chair. Beecham Products 1967–84, Man. Dir (consumer products) Beecham Group 1973–84, Chair. and Chief Exec. Beecham Group PLC 1984–85; Dir The Otis Elevator Co. Ltd 1978–83, Burmah Oil 1983–89; Dir (non-exec.) American Cyanamid Co. 1986–94, Davy Corpn PLC 1986–91, Gestetner Holdings PLC 1986–95; Dir Laurentian Financial Group PLC 1991–95; Chair. CAB Int. 1995–98; Deputy Chair. Tech. Colls Trust 1993–2006; Vice-Chair. Proprietary Asscn of GB 1968–77; Pres. Nat. Advertising Benevolent Soc. 1978–80; Vice-Pres. Inst. of Packaging 1979–81, Pres. 1981–83; Dir British Steel Corpn 1979–86, Deputy Chair. 1986–94; Gov. Ashridge Man. Coll. 1970–2007, Vice-Chair. 1977–2007; Pres. Inc. Soc. of British Advertisers 1971–73; Chair. British Nutrition Foundation 1970–73, Council mem. 1967–79; Vice-Chair. Advertising Asscn 1973–81; Vice-Chair. Food & Drink Industries Council 1973–76; Pres. Food Mfrs Fed. 1974–76; mem. CBI 1970–86, BIM 1972–77, Cambridge Univ. Appointments Bd 1969–73, Agric. Research Council 1978–84; Dir Nat. Coll. of Food Tech. 1977–78, Chair. of Bd 1978–83; Chair. Knitting Sector Working Group, NEDO 1978–90, Textile and Garment Working Group, 1991–93; Fellow, Inst. of Grocery Distribution 1979–, Marketing Soc. 1981–99; Trustee, Inst. of Econ. Affairs 1980–93; mem. Monopolies and Mergers Comm. Newspaper Panel 1980–92; mem. Industrial Devt Advisory Bd Dept of Trade and Industry 1983–93, Chair. 1984–93; Hon. Treas. and Dir, Centre for Policy Studies 1984–93; mem. Priorities Bd for Research and Devt in Agric. and Food, Ministry of Agric. Fish and Food 1984–87; Chair. Bd of Food Studies Univ. of Reading 1983–86; Pres. Eng Industries Asscn 1991–; mem. Monopolies and Mergers Comm. 1993–99; Council mem. European Policy Forum 1993–; Council mem. Univ. of Buckingham 1973–95, Univ. of Reading 1978–98; Council and Exec. Cttee mem., Imperial Soc. of Kts Bachelor 1985–2003; Chair. Conservative Foreign and Commonwealth Council 1995–; Gov. De Montfort Univ. (fmrly Leicester Polytechnic) 1989–97; Fellow, Inst. of Marketing 1975–, Vice-Pres. 1980–99; mem. Council, Food Mfrs Fed. Inc. 1966–85; Hon. Fellow, Inst. of Food Science and Tech., Inst. of Marketing, Queens' Coll. Cambridge 1985; Hon. DSc (Reading) 1982, (Univ. of Lancaster) 1987. *Leisure interests:* sailing, squash racquets, skiing. *Address:* 37 Edwardes Square, London, W8 6HH, England (home). *Telephone:* (20) 7603-9010 (home). *Fax:* (20) 7371-2595 (home).

HALVORSEN, Kristin; Norwegian politician; *Minister of Finance;* b. 2 Sept. 1960; m.; two c.; mem. Stortinget (Parl.) for Oslo 1989–, mem. Standing Cttee on Finance 1989–97, on Scrutiny and Constitutional Affairs 1997–2001, on Foreign Affairs 2001–05, mem. Parl. Del. in Connection with European Parl.

2001–05; Leader, Socialist Left Party of Norway 1997–; Minister of Finance 2005–; Observer UN Gen. Meeting 1985; deputy mem. Cttee on Ex-Gratia Payment of Compensation 1996; mem. Consulting Agency Regarding EEC Matters 1997–2001. *Address:* Ministry of Finance, Akersgt. 40, POB 8008 Dep., 0030 Oslo, Norway (office). *Telephone:* 22-24-90-90 (office). *Fax:* 22-24-95-10 (office). *E-mail:* postmottak@finans.dep.no (office). *Website:* odin.dep.no/fin (office).

HAMAD, Abdul-Latif Yousef al-, BA; Kuwaiti international organization official, banker and politician; *Chairman, Board of Directors, Arab Fund for Economic and Social Development;* b. 1936; m.; four c.; ed Claremont Coll., Calif., Harvard Univ.; mem. del. to UN 1962; Dir-Gen. Kuwait Fund for Arab Econ. Devt 1963–81; Dir, then Man. Dir Kuwait Investment Co. 1963–71; Man. Dir Kuwait Investment Co. 1965–74; Chair. Kuwait Prefabricated Bldg Co. 1965–78, United Bank of Kuwait Ltd, London 1966–84; Exec. Dir Arab Fund for Econ. and Social Devt 1972–81, Dir-Gen. and Chair. Bd of Dirs 1985–; Chair. Compagnie Arabe et Internationale d'Investissements, Luxembourg 1973–81; mem. Bd of Trustees, Corporate Property Investors, New York 1975–; mem. Governing Body Inst. of Devt Studies, Sussex, UK 1975–87; mem. Ind. Comm. on Int. Devt Issues (Brandt Comm.) 1976–79; mem. Bd Int. Inst. for Environment and Devt, London 1976–80; Minister of Finance and Planning 1981–83; Gov. for Kuwait, World Bank and IMF 1981–83; mem. UN Cttee for Devt Planning 1982–91, Chair. 1987; mem. IFC Banking Advisory Bd Group 1987–, Advisory Group on Financial Flows for Africa (UN) 1987–88, South Comm. 1987–89, Group of Ten (African Devt Bank) 1987–, World Bank's Pvt. Sector Devt Review Group 1988–, UN Panel for Public Hearings on Activities of Transnat. Corpns in S Africa and Namibia 1989–92, Bd Trustees of Stockholm Environment Inst. 1989–92, Comm. on Global Governance 1992–. *Address:* Arab Fund for Economic and Social Development, POB 21923, Safat 13080, Kuwait (office). *Telephone:* 4844500 (office). *Fax:* 4815760 (office). *E-mail:* hq@arabfund.org (office). *Website:* www .arabfund.org (office).

HAMAD, Seif Sharif, BA; Tanzanian politician and political scientist; *Secretary-General, Civic United Front;* b. 22 Oct. 1943, Pemba; s. of the late Sharif Hamad Shehe and Time Seif Haji; m. 1st Furtunah Saleh Mbamba 1971; m. 2nd Aweinah Sanani Massoud 1977; one s. four d.; ed King George VI Secondary School, Zanzibar, Univ. of Dar es Salaam; teacher, Lumumba Coll., Fidel Castro Coll. 1964–72; Asst to Pres. of Zanzibar 1975–77, Minister of Educ., Zanzibar 1977–80; mem. Tanzanian Parl. 1977–80; mem. Zanzibar House of Reps 1980–99; mem. Cen. Cttee Chama Cha Mapinduzi (CCM) Party 1977–88, Head Econ. and Planning Dept of CCM 1982–88; Chief Minister of Zanzibar 1984–88; political prisoner in Zanzibar 1989–91; Nat. Vice-Chair. Civic United Front 1992–, now Sec.-Gen.; presidential cand. Zanzibar elections 2000; Chair. Gen. Ass. Unrepresented Nations and Peoples' Org. (UNPO) 1997–. *Leisure interests:* reading, swimming. *Address:* Civic United Front, Mtendeni Street, Urban District, PO Box 3637, Zanzibar (office); PO Box 10976, Dar es Salaam, Tanzania. *Telephone:* (54) 237446 (office); (51) 861009; (812) 787790; (811) 324886. *Fax:* (54) 237445 (office); (51) 861010. *E-mail:* headquarters@cuftz.org (office). *Website:* www.cuftz.org (office).

HAMADA, Hiroshi; Japanese business executive; *Chairman, Ricoh Company Limited;* Chair. Ricoh Co. Ltd; Chair. Keidanren Cttee on Human Resources Devt 2000–; Vice-Chair. Japan Business Fed.; Pres. Japan Business Machines and Information System Industries Asscn (JBMIA) 1992–93; Dir UFJ Holdings; mem. Council, Japan Productivity Centre for Socio-Econ. Devt (JPC–SED); Counselor, Sasakawa Peace Foundation;. *Address:* Ricoh Company Limited, 15–5 Minami Aoyama 1–chome, Minato-ku, Tokyo 107–8544, Japan (office). *Telephone:* (3) 3479–3111 (office). *Fax:* (3) 3403–1578 (office). *Website:* www.ricoh.com (office).

HAMADI, Hassani; Comoran economist and politician; Minister of Finance and the Economy 2006–07, of the Economy, Planning, Employment and Female Enterprise 2007–. *Address:* Ministry of the Economy, BP 324, Moroni, The Comoros (office). *Telephone:* (74) 4140 (office). *Fax:* (74) 4141 (office).

HAMADOU, Jidda; Niger politician; Minister of Nat. Defence 2007–. *Address:* Ministry of National Defence, BP 626, Niamey, Niger (office). *Telephone:* 20-72-20-76 (office). *Fax:* 20-72-40-78 (office).

HÄMÄLÄINEN, Sirkka Aune-Marjatta, DSc (Econs); Finnish banker and economist; b. 8 May 1939, Riihimäki; d. of Martti Hinkkala and Aune Hinkkala; m. Arvo Hämäläinen 1961; one s. one d.; ed Helsinki School of Econs and Business Admin.; Economist, Econs Dept, Bank of Finland 1961–72, Head of Office, Econs Dept 1972–79, Acting Head of Dept 1979–81, Dir 1982–91, mem. Bd 1991–92, Gov. and Chair. Bd 1992–98; Dir Econs Dept, Ministry of Finance 1981–82; Chair. Bd of Dirs Financial Supervision Authority 1996–97; mem. Exec. Bd European Cen. Bank, Frankfurt 1998–2003; Docent, Adjunct Prof. of Econs Helsinki School of Econs and Business Admin 1991–; mem. of numerous orgs including Trilateral Comm. 1995–, Supervisory Bd Finnish Cultural Foundation 1996–, Cen. Bank Governance Steering Cttee, Bank of Int. Settlements 1996–, Finnish Public Research and Devt Financing Evaluation Group 1998–; Dir Investor AB March 2004–, HKKK Holding, Sanoma WSOY; Chair. Finnish Nat. Opera; Vice-Chair. KONE Corpn; Commdr First Class of Order of the White Rose, Merit Medal, First Class of Order of the White Star (Estonia); Dr hc (Turku School of Econs and Business Admin.) 1995. *Address:* Investor AB, Arsenalsgatan 8C, PO Box 1210, 103 32 Stockholm, Sweden (office).

HAMAMOTO, Manso; Japanese politician; Chair. Social Democratic Party of Japan (SDPJ) Diet Affairs Cttee for House of Councillors; Chair. of SDPJ mem. in House of Councillors; Minister of Labour 1994–96. *Address:* c/o Social Democratic Party of Japan, 1-8-1, Nagata-cho, Chiyoda-ku, Tokyo 100-0014, Japan.

HAMARI, Julia; Hungarian/German singer (mezzo-soprano); b. 21 Nov. 1942, Stuttgart; d. of Sándor Hamari and Erzsébet Dokupil; ed Franz Liszt Music Acad. of Budapest, Hochschule für Musik, Stuttgart; debut as soloist, Bach's St Matthew Passion in Vienna under Karl Richter 1966; specializes in Rossini, Mozart, Bellini; lieder recitalist and oratorio performer; has appeared world-wide with conductors including Herbert von Karajan, Sergiu Celibidache, Rafael Kubelik, Georg Solti, Karl Böhm, Pierre Boulez, Carlo M. Giulini, Nikolaus Harnoncourt, Claudio Abbado, Riccardo Muti and Mariss Jansons; debut in USA as soloist with Chicago Symphony Orchestra 1967; opera debut at Salzburg Festival as Mercedes in Bizet's Carmen 1967 and as Carmen in Stuttgart 1968; has appeared with Deutsche Oper am Rhein in various baroque and classical operas; has appeared at major opera houses including La Scala, Covent Garden, Vienna State Opera, Metropolitan Opera; opera roles include Celia in La fedeltia premiata (J. Haydn), Orpheus (Gluck), Dorabella and Despina (Così fan tutte), Angelina in La Cenerentola (Rossini), Rosina in Il Barbiere di Siviglia (Rossini), Sesto in La clemenza di Tito (Mozart), Cherubino in Nozze di Figaro (Mozart), Sinaide in Mosé in Egitto (Rossini), Romeo in I Capuleti ed I Montecchi (Bellini), Farnace in Mitridate (Mozart); Prof., Staatliche Hochschule für Musik, Stuttgart 1989–; prizewinner, Erkel Iinternational Singing Competition, Budapest 1964, Kodály Prize 1987, Offizierskreuz, Hungary 2002. *Participation in festivals:* performed in festivals of Edinburgh, Glyndebourne, Florence (Maggio Musicale), Netherlands (Schleswig-Holstein Musik, Schwetzingen). *Recordings include:* Bach's St John and St Matthew Passion 2006, Bach's Mass in B Minor, Oratorios, Cantatas, Oberon by Weber, Il matrimonio segreto by Cimarosa, Giulio Cesare by Händel, Roméo et Juliette by Berlioz, Mozart's Requiem, Mass in C major by Beethoven, Ernani by Verdi, Tito Manlio, Cavalleria rusticana, Juditha Triumphans by Vivaldi, I Puritani by Bellini, Beethoven's 9th Symphony, Mahler's Second and Eighth Symphonies, Orpheus by Gluck, Stabat Mater by Haydn and Pergolesi, Don Sanche by F. Liszt, Mosé in Egitto by Rossini, Prima la musica by A. Salieri, Eugen Onegin, Meistersinger, Eugen Onegin (video), Zigeunerlieder 1967, Lieder 1969, Bartók Songs 1973, Nausikaa Lieder Recital 1982, Lieder der Romantik 1982–94, Handel German Arias 1990, Julia Hamari Operatic Recital 1983–2000. *Address:* Max Brod-weg 14, 70437 Stuttgart, Germany (office).

HAMARNEH, Sami K., PhD; American medical historian and university professor (retd); b. 2 Feb. 1925, Madaba, Jordan; s. of Khalaf Odeh Hamarneh and Nora Zumot Hamarneh; m. Nazha T. Ajaj 1948; one s.; ed Syrian Univ., Damascus, Syria, North Dakota State Univ., Fargo and Wisconsin Univ., Madison, Wis.; Curator, US Nat. Museum, Washington, DC 1959–78; Curator, Div. of Medical Sciences, Smithsonian Inst. 1977–; Curator Emer. Museum of History and Tech.; Prof. of History of Medical Sciences, Aleppo Univ., Syria 1978–79, King Abdulaziz Univ., Saudi Arabia 1982–83; Prof. and Researcher, Yarmouk Univ., Jordan 1984–87, Prof. and Researcher (History of Medicine, Nursing and Pharmacy), Univ. of Jordan 1987–90; Prof. of Islamic Medicine, Int. Inst. of Islamic Thought and Civilization (ISTAC), Kuala Lumpur, Malaysia 1993–99; mem. Advisory Bd Hamdard Medicus 1980–; Hon. DLitt (Hamdard Univ., Karachi) 1998; Ed. Kremers Award (USA) 1966, Citation of Merit, Univ. of Wis. 1997; Star of Jordan Medal 1965. *Publications:* Customs and Civilization in Bible Lands 1960, Bibliography on Medicine and Pharmacy in Medieval Islam 1964, Origins of Pharmacy and Therapy in the Near East 1973, The Physician, Therapist and Surgeon, Ibn al-Quff 1974, Catalogue on Medicine and Pharmacy at the British Library 1975, Directory of Historians of Arab-Islamic Science 1980, Health Sciences in Early Islam; collected papers 1983–85, Promises, Heritage and Peace 1986, History of Arabic Medicine and Allied Health Sciences 1986, Introduction to al-Biruni's Book on Precious Stones and Minerals 1988, Ibn al-Quff al-Karaki's Book on the Preservation of Health 1989, Ibn al-Quff al-Karaki's Book on Surgery 1994, Directory of Historians of Islamic Medicine and the Allied Sciences 1995, Arabic-Islamic Medicine and Pharmacy During the Golden Age 1997. *Leisure interests:* reading, jogging, travel. *Address:* 4631 Massachusetts Avenue, NW, Washington, DC 20016-2361, USA. *Telephone:* (202) 966-7196. *E-mail:* fham@erols.com (office).

HAMBAYASHI, Toru; Japanese business executive; *Chairman and Co-CEO, Nissho Iwai-Nichimen Holdings Corporation;* Pres. Nichimen Corpn –2003, Chair. and Co-CEO, Nissho Iwai-Nichimen Holding Corpn (following merger) April 2003–. *Address:* Nissho Iwai-Nichimen Holdings Corporation, 1–23 Shiba 4–chome, Minato-ku, Tokyo 108–8408, Japan (office). *Telephone:* (3) 5446–3600 (office). *Fax:* (3) 5446–1542 (office). *Website:* www.nn-holdings.com (office).

HAMBLING, Maggi, OBE; British artist; b. 23 Oct. 1945, Sudbury, Suffolk; d. of Harry Leonard Hambling and Marjorie Rose Hambling; ed Hadleigh Hall School and Amberfield School, Suffolk, Ipswich School of Art, Camberwell School of Art, London, Slade School of Fine Art, London; studied painting with Lett Haines and Cedric Morris 1960–; tutor, Morley Coll., London; First Artist in Residence, Nat. Gallery, London 1980–81; Oscar Wilde memorial Adelaide St, London 1998; Scallop-Benjamin Britten memorial, Aldeburgh, Suffolk 2003; Boise Travel Award 1969, Arts Council Award 1977, Jerwood Prize (jtly) 1995, Marsh Award for Excellence in Public Sculpture (Scallop) 2005. *Public collections include:* Arts Council, Ashmolean Museum, Oxford, British Council, British Museum, Chelmsford and Essex Museum, Contemporary Art Soc., European Parl. Collection, Imperial War Museum, Ipswich Museum, Leicestershire Educ. Cttee, Minories Colchester, Nat. Gallery, Nat. Portrait Gallery, Royal Army Medical Coll., Rugby Museum, Southampton Art Gallery, Tate Gallery, William Morris School, Birmingham City Art Gallery, Morley Coll. London, Clare Coll. Cambridge, Whitworth Art Gallery, Gulbenkian Foundation, Preston Art Gallery, HTV Bristol, Scottish Nat. Gallery of Modern Art, Scottish Nat. Portrait Gallery, St Thomas' Hosp., London, Univ. Coll., London, Wakefield Art Gallery, Swindon Museum, Art

Gallery, All Souls Coll., Oxford, Nat. Gallery of Australia, Yale Center for British Art, New Hall, Cambridge, Victoria & Albert Museum, London, Norwich Castle Museum, Templeton Coll., Oxford, Jesus Coll. Cambridge, The Prudential, Barclays Bank, Govt Art Collection, Usher Gallery, Lincoln, Fitzwilliam Museum, Cambridge, Reading Museum. *Publications:* Maggi and Henrietta 2001, Father 2001, Maggi Hambling – The Works and Conversations with Andrew Lambirth 2006, George Always 2009. *Leisure interest:* tennis. *Address:* Morley College, 61 Westminster Bridge Road, London, SE1 7HT, England (office). *Telephone:* (20) 7928-8501 (office); (20) 7450-1856 (office). *Fax:* (20) 7928-4074 (office). *Website:* www.morleycollege.ac.uk (office).

HAMBRECHT, Jürgen, DSc; German chemical industry executive; *Chairman, BASF SE;* b. 1946, Reutlingen; m.; four c.; ed Univ. of Tübingen; joined BASF AG Polymer Lab. 1976, Head of Research and Purchasing, Lacke und Farben AG, Münster 1985–90, Pres. Eng Plastics Div. 1990–95, Pres. E Asian Div., Hong Kong 1995, mem. Exec. Bd of Dirs 1997–, Chair. BASF AG (renamed BASF SE Jan. 2008) 2003–; mem. Supervisory Bd Bilfinger Berger AG 2000–, Daimler AG, Lufthansa AG; Pres. German Chemical Industry Asscn 2003–; Vice-Pres. Fed. of German Industries (BDI); Chair. Asia Pacific Cttee of German Business (APA). *Address:* BASF SE, Carl-Bosch Str. 38, 67056 Ludwigshafen, Germany (office). *Telephone:* (621) 60-0 (office). *Fax:* (621) 60-42525 (office). *E-mail:* info@basf.de (office). *Website:* www.basf.de (office).

HAMBRO, Rupert Nicholas, FRSA; British banker; *Chairman, J. O. Hambro Mansford Ltd;* b. 27 June 1943, London; s. of the late Jocelyn Olaf Hambro and Anne Silvia Muir; m. Mary Robinson Boyer 1970; one s. one d.; ed Eton Coll., Aix-en-Provence Univ.; with Peat Marwick Mitchell & Co. 1962–64; joined Hambros Bank 1964, Dir 1969, Deputy Chair. 1980–83, Chair. 1983–86; Chair. Rupert Hambro and Partners Ltd 1986–; Group Man. Dir J.O. Hambro & Co. 1986–94, Chair. 1994–99, Chair. J.O. Hambro Mansford Ltd 1998–; Chair. Asscn of Int. Bond Dealers 1979–82, Wiltons (St James's) Ltd 1987–2003, Mayflower Corpn PLC 1988–2004, CTR Group 1990–97, Fenchurch PLC 1993–97, Longshot PLC 1996–2007, Woburn Golf & Country Club Ltd 1998–2003, Third Space Group Ltd 1999–2007, Longshot Health and Fitness Ltd 1999–, The Walpole Cttee Ltd 2000–06, Jermyn Street Asscn 2000–03, Roland Berger and Partners Ltd 2000–02, Kapital Ventures PLC 2001–, Longshot Hotels Ltd 2001–03, Tanner Krolle Ltd 2002–, Woburn Enterprise 2003–, Cazenove & Loyd 2003–, Groucho Club PLC; mem. Bd of Dirs Telegraph Group Ltd 1983–2003 (Dir Advisory Bd 2002–03), Anglo-American Corpn of SA Ltd 1981–97, Pioneer Concrete Holdings PLC 1982–99, KBC Peel Hunt Ltd 1997–2003, Open Europe Ltd 2006–07, Abel Hadden and Co. Ltd 1998–2001, Goldsmiths' Research Foundation 1998–, Bank Gutmann AG 2000–, Business for Sterling Ltd 2002–07; mem. Int. Council US Information Agency 1988–; Chair. of Trustees, Silver Trust, Chiswick House Trust; Patron British Asscn of Adoption and Fostering 2005–08, Pres. 2008–; Vice-Patron Royal Soc. of British Sculptors 1997; Treas. Nat. Art Collections Fund 1991–2003; Deputy Pres. Anglo-Danish Soc. 1987–; Chair. of Govs Museum of London 1996–, Museum in Docklands; mem. Court of Worshipful Co. of Goldsmiths; Hon. Fellow Univ. of Bath 1998, mem. Court of the Co. of Goldsmiths, Freeman Fishmongers' Co.; Kt of the Falcon (Iceland); Walpole Award of British Excellence 2006. *Leisure interests:* country pursuits. *Address:* J. O. Hambro Mansford Ltd, 118 New Bond Street, London, W15 1EW, England (office). *Telephone:* (20) 7493-7820 (office); (20) 7259-0101 (home). *Fax:* (20) 7292-3778 (office); (20) 7823-4803 (home). *E-mail:* rnhambro@joh.co.uk (office).

HAMDAN, Mohammed, PhD; Jordanian mathematician and politician; *Secretary-General, Higher Council for Science and Technology;* b. 3 Nov. 1934; m.; two c.; ed Cairo Univ., Egypt and Sydney Univ., Australia; Visiting Prof., Virginia Polytechnic Inst. and State Univ. 1969–71; Assoc. Prof. of Math., American Univ. of Beirut 1970–76, Prof. of Math. 1976–77, also at American Univ. of Cairo 1977–78; Prof. of Math., Dean Faculty of Sciences, Univ. of Jordan 1984–86; Pres. Yarmouk Univ. 1986–89; Minister of Educ. and Higher Educ. 1989–91, 1998; Pres. Hashemite Univ. 1991–98; Sec.-Gen. Higher Council for Science and Tech. 1998–; mem. Int. Statistical Inst., American Statistical Asscn, Third World Acad. of Sciences, Jordan Acad. of Arabic Language, Union of Arab Physicists and Mathematicians; mem. Bd Trustees Hitteen, Ibn Khaldoun and Al-Razi Community Coll.; mem. Editorial Bd Int. Statistical Review, Arab Journal of Mathematics, Mu'tah Journal of Research and Studies and Research Journal, Univ. of Jordan; mem. Islamic Acad. of Sciences, mem. Council 1994–99. *Publications:* over 60 tech. papers. *Address:* The Higher Council for Science and Technology, PO Box, 36 Jubaiha, Amman, Jordan (office). *Website:* www.hcst.gov.jo (office).

HAMDANI, Smail; Algerian politician; m.; one c.; fmrly Govt Sec.-Gen., adviser to Presidency, Amb. to Scandinavia, Spain, France, to UNESCO, Sec.-Gen. at Foreign Ministry; mem. Council of the Nation; Prime Minister of Algeria 1998–99; fmr Lecturer, École Nat. d'Admin; consultant and mem. Nat. Inst. for Strategic Studies; Chair. Algerian Asscn for Int. Relations. *Address:* c/o Office of the Prime Minister, rue Docteur Saâdane, Algiers, Algeria.

HAMED FRANCO, Alejandro; Paraguayan academic, diplomatist and government official; *Minister of Foreign Affairs;* b. 26 Feb. 1934, Asunción; ed Universidad de la República, Montevideo, Universidad Nacional de Asunción; fmr Prof., Universidad Católica, Universidad Nacional de Ciudad del Este; Asunción; fmr Docent, Universidad Nacional en Asunción; Amb. to Lebanon (also accred. to Qatar, Syria and Kuwait) –2008; Minister of Foreign Affairs 2008–. *Address:* Ministry of Foreign Affairs, Juan E. O'Leary y Presidente Franco, Asunción, Paraguay (office). *Telephone:* (21) 49-4593 (office). *Fax:* (21) 49-3910 (office). *Website:* www.mre.gov.py (office).

HAMEED, A. C. S.; Sri Lankan politician; b. 10 April 1929; MP for Harispattuwa 1960–; Minister of Foreign Affairs 1977–89, of Educ., Science and Tech. 1989–90, of Justice 1990–93, of Foreign Affairs 1993–94; first to hold separate portfolio of foreign affairs; Chair. United Nat. Party (UNP) 1995. *Publications:* In Pursuit of Peace 1983, Owl and the Lotus 1986, Disarmament – A Multi-lateral Approach 1988, Foreign Policy Perspectives of Sri Lanka 1988. *Address:* c/o United National Party, 400 Kotte Road, Pitakotte, Sri Lanka.

HAMEED, Abdulla; Maldivian politician; Speaker of the People's Majlis (People's Council); Minister of Atolls Admin; Gov. Bank of Maldives PLC Ltd (BML). *Address:* c/o Ministry of Atolls Administration, Faashana Building, Boduthakurufaanu Magu (North), Malé 20-05, Maldives.

HAMELIN, Louis-Edmond, (El E Ache Hamelin), OC, MA, PhD, DèsSc, FRSC; Canadian researcher and consultant in polar affairs; b. 21 March 1923, St Didace; m. Colette Lafay 1951; one s. one d.; ed Laval Univ. and Univs of Grenoble and Paris, France; Prof., Laval Univ. 1951–78, Dir Inst. of Geography 1955–61, Founding Dir Centre for Northern Studies 1962–72; mem. Legis Ass., Yellowknife, Northwest Territories, Canada 1971–75; Rector Université de Québec, Trois-Rivières 1978–83; Gov. Int. Devt Research Centre, Ottawa 1984–88; Corresp., Inst. de France, Paris 1989; Ordre des francophones d'Amérique 1994, Grand Officier, Ordre nat. du Québec 1998; Dr hc (McGill, Ottawa, Waterloo, Sherbrooke, Montreal, Trois-Rivières); Léo-Pariseau Prize 1972, Pierre Chauveau Medal 1972, Gov.-Gen.'s Award 1976, Massey Medal 1976, Grand Prix Geography (Paris) 1977, Gloire de l'Escolle Medal 1982, Molson Foundation Prize (Canada) 1982, Human Sciences Prize (Québec) 1987, Léon-Gérin Prize 1987. *Publications:* Illustrated Glossary of Periglacial Phenomena 1967, Atlas du Monde 1967, Canada: A Geographical Perspective 1973, Canadian Nordicity 1979, The Canadian North 1988, Obiou 1990, Le rang d'habitat 1993, Écho des pays froids 1996, Le Québec par des mots 2000–03 (electronic and printed versions, three vols). *Leisure interests:* writing, walking, sightseeing. *Address:* 1244 Albert-Lozeau, Sillery, PQ G1T 1H4, Canada. *Telephone:* (418) 683-0386. *E-mail:* louis-edmond.hamelin@sittel.ca (home). *Website:* www.lehamelin.sittel.ca.

HAMID, Ahmed Munaysi Abd al-; Libyan banker and government official; *Secretary of the General People's Committee for Finance;* Gov. Cen. Bank of Libya –2006; Sec. of the Gen. People's Cttee for Finance 2006–. *Address:* General People's Committee, Tripoli, Libya.

HAMIED, Yusuf K., PhD; Indian pharmaceuticals industry executive; *Chairman and Managing Director, Cipla Limited;* b. 25 July 1936; m.; ed Univ. of Cambridge, UK; began career as research officer Cipla Ltd, Man. Dir 1976–, Chair. 1989–; Fellow, Christ's Coll., Cambridge; Nat. Award, Dept of Science and Tech., Padma Bhushan 2005. *Address:* Cipla Ltd, Mumbai Central, 289 J.B.B. Marg, Mumbai 400 008, India (office). *Telephone:* (22) 23095521 (office). *Fax:* (22) 23070013 (office). *Website:* www.cipla.com (office).

HAMILTON, Andrew D., FRS, BSc MSc, PhD; British chemist, academic and university administrator; *Vice Chancellor-elect, University of Oxford;* b. 1952, Guildford, Surrey; m. Jennifer Hamilton; three c.; ed Exeter Univ., Univ. of British Columbia, Canada, Univ. of Cambridge; Asst Prof., Dept of Chem., Princeton Univ. 1981–88; Assoc. Prof., Dept of Chem., Univ. of Pittsburgh 1988–92, Prof. 1992–97, Chair. Dept of Chem. 1994–97; Irénée duPont Prof. of Chem., Yale Univ. 1997–2004, Chair. Dept of Chem. 1999–2003, Benjamin Silliman Prof. of Chem. 2004–09, Deputy Provost for Science and Tech., Yale Univ. 2003–04, Provost Yale Univ. 2004–08; Vice Chancellor Univ. of Oxford Oct. 2009–; ACS Arthur C. Cope Scholar Award. *Leisure interest:* football. *Address:* c/o Department of Chemistry, Yale University, 225 Prospect Street, PO Box 208107, New Haven, CT 06520-8107, USA (office). *Telephone:* (203) 432-5570 (office). *Fax:* (203) 432-3221 (office). *E-mail:* andrew.hamilton@yale.edu (office). *Website:* ursula.chem.yale.edu/~hamgrp/index1.html (office); www.ox.ac.uk/about_the_university/oxford_people/key_university_officers/vicechancellor.html.

HAMILTON, Lee H., BA, JD; American research institute director and fmr politician; *Director, Woodrow Wilson International Center for Scholars;* b. Daytona Beach, Fla; m. Nancy Ann Hamilton (née Nelson); two d. one s.; ed DePauw Univ., Goethe Inst., Frankfurt, Germany, Indiana Univ. School of Law; practised law in Chicago and Columbus, Ind. –1965; mem. US House of Reps from Ind. 9th Dist 1965–99, served as Chair., ranking mem. Cttee on Int. Relations, Chair. and Vice-Chair. Jt Econ. Cttee, Chair. Perm. Select Cttee on Intelligence, Chair. Jt Cttee on Org. of Congress, Chair. Oct. Surprise Task Force, Chair. Select Cttee to Investigate Covert Arms Transactions with Iran, Chair. Sub-Cttee on Europe and Middle E 1970–93, mem. House Standards of Official Conduct Cttee; Dir Woodrow Wilson Int. Center for Scholars (WWIC) 1999–; has served on numerous panels and comms including Commr US Comm. on Nat. Security in the 21st Century (Hart-Rudman Comm.), Co-Chair. Baker-Hamilton Comm. to Investigate Certain Security Issues at Los Alamos, Commr Carter-Baker Comm. on Fed. Election Reform, Vice-Chair. Nat. Comm. on Terrorist Attacks Upon the US (9-11 Comm.); He is currently a member of the advisory council for the U.S. Department of Homeland Security; currently mem. US Dept of Homeland Security Advisory Council, Co-Chair. Ind. Task Force on Immigration and America's Future, Pres.'s Foreign Intelligence Advisory Bd; Co-Chair. Iraq Study Group, US Inst. of Peace 2006–07; Dir Center on Congress, Indiana Univ.; Grand Cross Order of Merit (FRG) 1985, Chevalier Légion d'Honneur (France) 1984, Bundesverdienstkreutz (Germany) 1999; Dr hc (DePauw Univ.), (Hanover Coll.), (Detroit Coll. of Law), (Ball State Univ.), (Univ. of Southern Ind.), (Wabash Coll.) (Union Coll.), (Marian Coll.), (American Univ.), (Ind. Univ.), (Suffolk Univ.), (Ind. State Univ.), (Anderson Univ.), (Franklin Coll.), (Shenandoah Univ.); Defense Intelligence Agency Medallion 1987, CIA Medallion 1988, Indiana Univ. Inst. for Advanced Study Distinguished Citizen Fellow 1994, Indiana Univ. Pres.'s Medal for Excellence 1996, Center for Nat. Policy Edmund S. Muskie Distinguished Public Service Award 1997, Paul H. Nitze Award for Distinguished Authority on Nat. Security Affairs 1999, American Political Science Asscn Hubert H. Humphrey Award 1998, American Bar Asscn CEELI Award 1998, Center for Civic Educ. Civitas Award 1998, Dept of Defense Medal for Distinguished Public Service 1998. *Publication:* Without Precedent: The Inside Story of the 9/11 Commission (with Thomas H. Kean) 2006. *Address:* Woodrow Wilson International Center for Scholars (WWIC), One Woodrow Wilson Plaza, 1300 Pennsylvania Avenue, NW, Washington, DC 20004-3027, USA (office). *Telephone:* (202) 691-4000 (office). *Fax:* (202) 691-4001 (office). *E-mail:* director@wwic.si.edu (office). *Website:* www.wilsoncenter.org (office).

HAMILTON, Lewis Carl Davidson, MBE; British racing driver; b. 7 Jan. 1985, Stevenage, Herts.; ed John Henry Newman School; took up Karting 1993, Cadet 1993–97, Super One British Champion 1995, STP Champion 1995, Sky TV Kart Masters Champion 1996, Five Nations Champion 1996, Jr Yamaha 1998, Super One British Champion 1998, Jr Intercontinental A 1999, Italian Industrials Champion 1999, Vice European Champion 1999, winner Trophy de Pomposa 1999, Formula A 2000, European Champion 2000, World Cup Champion 2000, Karting World Number 1, Formula Super A 2001, European Champion 2000; signed to McClaren F1 Driver Devt Program 1998; participated in British Formula Renault Winter Series 2001, Formula Renault 2002–03, Champion 2003, Third 2002; competed for Manor Motorsport in Formula 3 Euroseries Championship 2004, for ASM Formule 3 2005, Drivers' Champion 2005, Fifth 2004; joined ART Grand Prix team and competed in GP2 Series 2006, Drivers' Champion 2006; joined McLaren Mercedes' Formula 1 team 2007, Formula 1 debut, Australian Grand Prix 2007, Formula 1 World Drivers' Champion Runner-up 2007, Champion (youngest Formula 1 Drivers' Champion) 2008; British Club Driver of the Year 2003, Rookie Of The Year 2006–07, Hawthorn Memorial Trophy 2007, 2008, British Competition Driver 2007, Int. Racing Driver Award 2007, German GQ magazine Man of the Year 2007, UK Sportsman of the Year 2007, BRDC Gold Star Award 2007, Walpole Award for British Excellence 2007, Laureus World Breakthrough of the Year 2008. *Address:* c/o McLaren Technology Centre, Chertsey Road, Woking, Surrey, GU21 4YH, England (office). *Website:* www.mclaren.com (office); www.lewishamilton.com.

HAMILTON, Linda; American actress; b. 26 Sept. 1956, Salisbury, Md; m. 1st Bruce Abbott (divorced); m. 2nd James Cameron (q.v.) 1996 (divorced); one d. *Stage appearances:* Looice 1975, Richard III 1977. *Films include:* T.A.G.: The Assassination Game 1982, Children of the Corn 1984, The Stone Boy 1984, The Terminator 1984, Black Moon Rising 1986, King Kong Lives! 1986, Mr Destiny 1990, Terminator 2: Judgment Day 1991, Silent Fall 1994, The Shadow Conspiracy 1997, Dante's Peak 1997, The Secret Life of Girls 1999, Skeletons in the Closet 2000, Wholey Moses 2003, Jonah 2004, Smile 2005, Missing in America 2005, In Your Dreams 2007. *Television includes:* Reunion 1980, Rape and Marriage: The Rideout Case 1980, The Secrets of Midland Heights (series) 1980–81, King's Crossing (series) 1982, Country Gold 1982, Secrets of a Mother and Daughter 1983, Secret Weapons 1985, Club Med 1986, Beauty and the Beast (series) 1987–90, Go Toward the Light 1988, The Way to Dusty Death 1995, A Mother's Prayer 1995, On the Line 1998, Point Last Seen 1998, The Color of Courage 1999, Sex & Mrs X 2000, A Girl Thing (mini-series) 2001, Bailey's Mistake 2001, Silent Night 2002, Take 3 2006, Home by Christmas 2006, The Line (series) 2008. *Address:* United Talent Agency, 5th Floor, 9560 Wilshire Boulevard, Beverly Hills, CA 90212, USA.

HAMILTON, Richard, CH; British artist; b. 24 Feb. 1922; s. of Peter Hamilton and Constance Hamilton; m. 1st Terry O'Reilly 1947 (died 1962); one s. one d.; m. 2nd Rita Donagh 1991; ed elementary school, evening classes, St Martin's School of Art, Royal Acad. Schools and Slade School of Art; jig and tool draughtsman, Design Unit 1941–42, Electrical & Musical Industries (EMI) 1942–45; Exhbn of Reaper engravings, Gimpel Fils 1950; devised Growth and Form Exhbn, Inst. of Contemporary Arts (ICA) 1951; teacher of design, Cen. School of Arts and Crafts 1952–53; mem. Independent Group, ICA 1952–55; Lecturer, Fine Art Dept, King's Coll., Univ. of Durham (later Univ. of Newcastle-upon-Tyne) 1953–66; teacher of Interior Design RCA 1957–61;; organized exhbn of works by Marcel Duchamp, Tate Gallery 1966; exhbn of Guggenheim reliefs and studies, London 1966;; William and Noma Copley Foundation Award for painting 1960, Jt First Prize, John Moores Liverpool Exhbn 1969, Talens Prize, Amsterdam 1970, World Print Award 1983, Nord/LB Prize 1996, Arnold Bode Prize 1997, Gold Medal, Ljubljana 1999. *Publications:* Polaroid Portraits (Vol. I) 1972, (Vol. II) 1977, (Vol. III) 1983, (Vol. IV) 2002, Collected Words 1982, Image and Process 1983, Prints 1939–83 1984. *Address:* c/o Tate Gallery, Millbank, London, SW1P 4RG, England.

HAMLISCH, Marvin, BA; American composer and conductor; b. 2 June 1944, New York; s. of Max and Lilly (née Schachter) Hamlisch; m. Terre Blair 1989; ed Queen's Coll., New Yorkm Juilliard School; on tour with Groucho Marx 1974–75; made his debut as pianist with Minnesota Orchestra 1975; conductor of orchestras throughout USA; Musical Dir and Conductor Barbra Streisand Tour 1994 (Emmy Award 1995); Prin. Pops Conductor Pittsburgh Symphony Orchestra 1994–, Baltimore Symphony Orchestra 1996–; three Academy Awards, Emmy Awards for Outstanding Music Direction 1994, Outstanding Music and Lyrics 1994. *Compositions include:* film scores: The Swimmer 1968, The April Fools 1969, Take the Money and Run 1969, Move 1970, Flap 1970, Bananas 1971, Kotch 1971, Something Big 1971, The War Between Men and Women 1972, The World's Greatest Athlete 1972, Save the Tiger 1973, The Way We Were 1974, The Prisoner of Second Avenue 1975, The Absent-Minded Waiter 1977, The Spy Who Loved Me 1977, Same Time Next Year 1978, Ice

Castles 1978, Starting Over 1979, Chapter Two 1979, Ordinary People 1980, Seems Like Old Times 1980, Pennies From Heaven 1981, I Ought to be in the Pictures 1982, Sophie's Choice 1982, D.A.R.Y.L. 1985, Three Men and a Baby 1987, Little Nikita 1988, The Experts 1989, The January Man 1989, Missing Pieces 1991, Frankie and Johnny 1991, Switched at Birth 1991, Open Season 1995, The Mirror Has Two Faces 1996, Every Little Step 2008; popular songs: Sunshine, Lollipops and Rainbows 1960, Good Morning America 1975, Nobody Does It Better (The Spy Who Loved Me) 1977; theme songs for The January Man 1988, Three Men and a Baby, Little Nikita, The Experts; composed symphonic work in one movement Anatomy of Peace 1991, composed music for global anthem One Song (lyrics by Alan and Marilyn Bergman); int. debut at Barcelona Olympics 1992; Broadway musicals: A Chorus Line (Pulitzer Prize 1976) 1975, They're Playing Our Song 1979, The Goodbye Girl 1993, Sweet Smell of Success 2002. *Publication:* The Way I Was 1992. *E-mail:* hamlischinc@marvinhamlisch.com (office). *Website:* www.marvinhamlisch.com.

HAMM, Mariel Margret (Mia); American fmr professional footballballer; b. 17 March 1972, Selma, Ala; m. 1st Christian Corry (divorced); m. 2nd Nomar Garciaparra 2003; ed Lake Braddock Secondary School, Burke, Va, Notre Dame High School, Wichita Falls, Tex., Univ. of North Carolina; centre forward; teams played for include Washington Freedom, USA 1987– (youngest to represent nat. team 1987 (aged 15) versus China); represented USA at World Cup 1991, 1995, 1999, Olympic Games 1996, 2004; US coll. football's leading scorer (103 goals); 276 international caps (2nd highest total), 158 goals (world record); retd 2004; f. Mia Hamm Foundation 1999, which supports young female athletes and bone marrow research; won four NCAA Championships with Univ. of North Carolina 1989, 1990, 1992, 1993; won World Cup with US 1991, 1999 (3rd 1995, 2003); Most Valuable Player (MVP) at Chiquita Cup 1994; US Soccer Athlete of the Year 1994, 1995, 1996; MVP at World Cup 1995; won Gold Medal with US Olympic Games 1996; Women's Sports Foundation Athlete of the Year 1997; ESPN Outstanding Female Athlete 1998; FIFA Female Player of the Year 2001, 2002; won CONCACAF Cup with US 2002. *Publications:* (with Aaron Heifetz) Go for the Goal: A Champions Guide to Winning in Soccer and Life 1999. *Leisure interests:* golf, basketball, reading, cooking. *Address:* c/o Mia Hamm Foundation, POB 56, Chapel Hill, NC 27514, USA. *Website:* www.miafoundation.org (office).

HAMM, Paul; American gymnast; b. 24 Sept. 1982, Washburn, Wis.; ed Univ. of Wis.; took up gymnastics in 1989, int. debut 1999; fifth place in team event Olympic Games, Sydney 2000; team silver medal World Championships 2001; team silver medal, bronze medal floor exercise World Championships 2002; gold medal horizontal bar World Cup 2002; gold medals floor exercise and individual all-round (first US male gymnast to win all-round gold medal at World Championships), team silver medal World Championships 2003; gold medal floor exercise World Cup 2003; gold medals vault and horizontal bar, silver medal floor exercise, bronze medals parallel bars and pommel horse World Cup 2004; gold medal individual all-round (first US male to win all-round Olympic gold medal), silver medals horizontal bar and team event Olympic Games, Athens 2004; mem. Team Chevron, Columbus OH. *Leisure interests:* playing tennis, cards, chess. *Address:* c/o USA Gymnastics, Pan Am Plaza, Suite 300, 201 South Capitol Avenue, Indianapolis, IN 46225, USA. *Website:* www.usa-gymnastics.org.

HAMMAMI, Hamma; Tunisian politician; *Leader, Parti des ouvriers communistes tunisiens (POCT);* b. 8 Jan. 1952, El Aroussa; m. Radhia Nasraoui 1981; three d.; co-founder and Leader Parti des ouvriers communistes tunisiens (POCT) (banned communist party); Dir El Badil (The Alternative—banned newspaper); imprisoned for participation in students' movt 1972–74, for membership of asscn El Aamel Ettounsi (The Tunisian Worker) 1974–80, exiled in France, sentenced in absentia May 1987, returned to Tunisia, numerous arrests 1989–91, went into hiding Oct. 1992, tried in absentia Dec. 1992, arrested Feb. 1994, imprisoned June 1994–Nov. 1995, went into hiding, sentenced in absentia July 1999, emerged from hiding and imprisoned March–Sept. 2002. *E-mail:* pcot@albadil.org. *Website:* www.albadil.org.

HAMMARSKJÖLD, Knut Olof Hjalmar Akesson, PhM; Swedish fmr diplomatist; b. 16 Jan. 1922, Geneva, Switzerland; s. of Åke Hammarskjöld and the late Britte Hammarskjöld; nephew of the late Dag Hammarskjöld, Sec.-Gen. of the UN; four s.; ed Stockholm Univ.; entered Foreign Service 1946, served Paris, Vienna, Moscow, Bucharest, Kabul, Sofia 1947–55; First Sec. Foreign Office 1955–57; Head of Foreign Relations Dept, Royal Bd of Civil Aviation, Stockholm 1957–59; Deputy Head, Swedish Del. to OEEC, Paris 1959–60; Deputy Sec.-Gen. European Free Trade Asscn (EFTA) 1960–66; Minister Plenipotentiary 1966–; Dir-Gen. of Int. Air Transport Asscn (IATA), Montreal, Geneva 1966–84, Chair. Exec. Cttee 1981–84; Dir Inst. of Air Transport, Paris 1974–, Dir Gen. 1985; Chair, CEO Atwater Inst., Montreal 1985–; Special Adviser to Dir-Gen. UNESCO; mem. Inst. of Transport, London; mem. Alexander S. Onassis Public Benefit Foundation Int. Cttee for Award of Athens and Olympia Prizes 1977–83; Gov. Atlantic Inst. for Int. Affairs 1983–87; Chair. Corp. Bd Sydvenska Dagbladet AB, Newspaper Conglomerate, Malmö 1987–94, (Dir 1948–); Hon. Fellow Canadian Aeronautics and Space Inst.; Commdr Order of the Lion (Finland), Order of the Falcon (1st Class) (Iceland), Commdr Order of Orange-Nassau (Netherlands), Légion d'honneur and Order of the Black Star (France), Grand Officer, Order Al-Istiqlal (Jordan); Commdr (1st Class) Order of the North Star (Sweden), NOR (Sweden), Grand Cross of the Order of Civil Merit (Spain). *Publications:* articles on political, economic and aviation topics. *Address:* Rue St Germain 11, Geneva, Switzerland.

HAMMEL, Eugene Alfred, AB, PhD; American demographer and academic; *Professor Emeritus, Department of Demography, University of California, Berkeley;* b. 18 March 1930, New York; s. of William Hammel and Violet Brookes; m. Joan Marie Swingle 1951; ed Univ. of Calif., Berkeley; field work in archaeology and linguistics, Calif. 1947–51, in ethnography, Peru 1957–58, in archaeology and ethnography in New Mexico 1959–61, in ethnography in Mexico 1963, in Yugoslavia and Greece 1963, 1965–66; Asst Prof., Univ. of New Mexico 1959–61; Asst Prof., Univ. of Calif., Berkeley 1961–63, Assoc. Prof. 1963–66, Prof. 1966–93, Prof. of Anthropology and Demography 1978–93, Prof. Emer. 1993–, Dir Quantitative Anthropology Lab. 1974–90, Chair. Demography 1978–88; archival research in Yugoslavia, Hungary, Austria 1983–; mem. NAS; Guggenheim fellow 1965–66; American Acad. Academy of Arts and Sciences Award 1991. *Publications:* Wealth, Authority and Prestige in the Ica Valley, Peru 1962, Ritual Relations and Alternative Social Structures in the Balkans 1968, The Pink Yoyo: Occupational Mobility in Belgrade c. 1915–65 1969, Statistical Studies of Historical Social Structure (with Wachter and Laslett) 1978; approximately 180 articles. *Leisure interests:* hiking, guitar, carpentry, photography. *Address:* Department of Demography, University of California, 2232 Piedmont Avenue, Berkeley, CA 94720-2120, USA (office). *Telephone:* (415) 642-9800 (office). *E-mail:* gene@demog.berkeley.edu (office). *Website:* www.demog.berkeley.edu/~gene (office); www.demog.berkeley.edu/~gene/vita_bez.html (office).

HAMMER, Hans Jörg; German business executive; Chair. Supervisory Bd Otto GmbH & Co. KG –2007; mem. Cttee, Hamburg Acad. of Econs 2002. *Address:* c/o Otto Group, Wandsbeker Strasse 3–7, 2217 Hamburg, Germany (office).

HAMMERGREN, John H.; American pharmaceuticals industry executive; *Chairman, President and CEO, McKesson Corporation;* b. 1959; Vice-Pres. McKesson Health Systems 1996–97, Group Pres. 1997–99, Exec. Vice-Pres. McKesson Corpn Jan.–July 1999, Dir, Co-Pres. and Co-CEO 1999–2001, Pres. and CEO 2001–, Chair. 2002–, CEO Supply Man. Business Jan.–July 1999; mem. Bd of Dirs Hewlett Packard, Nadro SA (Mexico), Verispan LLC. *Address:* McKesson Corporate Headquarters, One Post Street, San Francisco, CA 94104, USA (office). *Telephone:* (415) 983-8300 (office). *Fax:* (415) 983-7160 (office). *E-mail:* corp.communications@mckesson.com (office). *Website:* www.mckesson.com (office).

HAMMES, Gordon G., PhD; American biochemist, academic and fmr university vice-chancellor; *University Distinguished Service Professor of Biochemistry, Medical Center, Duke University;* b. 10 Aug. 1934, Fond du Lac, Wis.; s. of Jacob Hammes and Betty (Sadoff) Hammes; m. Judith Ellen Frank 1959; one s. two d.; ed Princeton Univ. and Univ. of Wisconsin; Postdoctoral Fellow, Max Planck Inst. für physikalische Chemie, Göttingen, FRG 1959–60; instructor, subsequently Assoc. Prof., MIT, Cambridge, Mass. 1960–65; Prof., Cornell Univ. 1965–88, Chair. Dept of Chem. 1970–75, Horace White Prof. of Chem. and Biochemistry 1975–88, Dir Biotechnology Program 1983–88; Prof., Univ. of Calif., Santa Barbara 1988–91, Vice-Chancellor for Academic Affairs 1988–91; Prof., Duke Univ., Durham, NC 1991–, Vice-Chancellor Duke Univ. Medical Center 1991–98, Univ. Distinguished Service Prof. of Biochemistry 1996–; mem. Physiological Chem. Study Section, Physical Biochemistry Study Section, Training Grant Cttee, NIH; mem. Bd of Counsellors, Nat. Cancer Inst. 1976–80, Advisory Council, Chem. Dept, Princeton 1970–75, Polytechnic Inst., New York 1977–78, Boston Univ. 1977–85; mem. Nat. Research Council, US Nat. Comm. for Biochemistry 1989–95; mem. ACS, American Soc. of Biochemistry and Molecular Biology (Pres. 1994–95), NAS, American Acad. of Arts and Sciences; Ed. Biochemistry 1992–2003; ACS Award in Biological Chem. 1967, William C. Rose Award, American Soc. of Biochemistry and Molecular Biology 2002. *Publications:* Principles of Chemical Kinetics, Enzyme Catalysis and Regulation, Chemical Kinetics: Principles and Selected Topics (with I. Amdur), Thermodynamics and Kinetics for the Biological Sciences 2000, Spectroscopy for the Biological Sciences 2005, Physical Chemistry for the Biological Sciences 2007; numerous learned articles. *Leisure interests:* music, tennis. *Address:* 11 Staley Place, Durham, NC 27705 (home); Department of Biochemistry, Duke University, Box 3711, Medical Center, Durham, NC 27710, USA (office). *Telephone:* (919) 684-8848 (office). *Fax:* (919) 684-9709 (office). *E-mail:* hamme001@mc.duke.edu (office). *Website:* www.mc.duke.edu/index3.htm (office).

HAMMES, Michael Noel, MBA; American business executive; *Chairman and CEO, Sunrise Medical Inc.;* b. 25 Dec. 1941, Evanston, Ill.; s. of Ferdinand Hammes and Winifred Hammes; m. Lenore Lynn Forbes 1964; three s. two d.; ed Georgetown Univ., New York Univ.; Asst Controller, Ford Motor Ass. Div. 1974, Plant Man., Ford Wixom Assembly Plant 1975, Man. Program Planning, Ford Automotive Ass. Div. 1976, Dir Int. Business Planning, Int. Operations, Ford 1977, Man. Dir and Pres., Ford Motor Co. of Mexico 1979, Vice-Pres. Truck Operations, Ford of Europe 1983–86; Vice-Pres., Int. Operations, Chrysler Motors Corpn 1986–90; Chair., CEO Coleman Co. 1993–97; CEO Guide Corpn 1998–2000; Chair. and CEO Sunrise Medical Inc., Carlsbad, Calif. 2000–, Chair. audit comm. 1998–; mem. Bd of Dirs Navistar Int. Corpn; mem. Bd of Visitors, Georgetown Univ. School of Business. *Leisure interests:* skiing, tennis, golf, antique cars. *Address:* Sunrise Medical Inc., 2382 Faraday Avenue, Suite 200, Carlsbad, CA 92008, USA (office). *Website:* www.sunrisemedical.com (office).

HAMMOND, Aleqa; Greenlandic politician; b. 23 Sept. 1965, Narsaq; ed in Ellekilde, Denmark, Arctic Coll., Iqaluit; Regional Co-ordinator for Greenland Tourism, Diskobugten 1993–95; Information Officer, Landsstyre Secr. 1995–96; worked for Nuuk Tourism 1996–99; Commr Inuit Circumpolar Conf. 1999–2003; Culture Co-ordinator Arctic Winter Games 2002; worked in Tourism and Culture, Sulisartut Højskoliat, Qaqortoq 2002–03; Head of Tourism, Qaqortoq 2004–05; mem. Parl. for the Social Democratic Siumut (Forward) party 2005–; Minister for Family Affairs and Justice 2005–07, of Finance and Foreign Affairs 2007–08 (resgnd). *Address:* Siumut (Forward)

Party, POB 357, 3900 Nuuk, Greenland (office). *Telephone:* 322077 (office). *Fax:* 322319 (office). *E-mail:* siumut@greennet.gl (office). *Website:* www.siumut.gl (office).

HAMMOND, Norman David Curle, MA, PhD, ScD, FSA, FBA; British archaeologist; *Professor of Archaeology and Chairman of Department, Boston University;* b. 10 July 1944, Brighton; s. of William Hammond and Kathleen Jessie Howes; m. Jean Wilson 1972; one s. one d.; ed Varndean Grammar School, Peterhouse, Cambridge; Research Fellow, Centre of Latin American Studies, Cambridge 1967–71, Leverhulme Research Fellow 1972–75; Research Fellow, Fitzwilliam Coll., Cambridge 1973–75; Sr Lecturer, Univ. of Bradford 1975–77; Visiting Prof., Univ. of Calif., Berkeley 1977, Rutgers Univ., USA 1977–78, Assoc. Prof. 1978–84, Prof. of Archaeology 1984–88; Prof. of Archaeology, Boston Univ. 1988–, currently also Chair. of Dept; Assoc. in Maya Archaeology, Peabody Museum, Harvard Univ. 1988–; Archaeology Corresp. The Times 1967–; Ed. South Asian Archaeology 1970–73, Afghan Studies 1976–79; Consulting Ed. Library of Congress, USA 1977–89; Archaeological Consultant Scientific American 1979–95; Curl Lecturer, Royal Anthropological Inst. 1985; Bushnell Lecturer, Univ. of Cambridge 1997, Stone Lecturer, Archaeological Inst. of America 1998; Acad. Trustee Archaeological Inst. of America 1990–93; mem. Council, Soc. of Antiquaries of London 1996–; excavations and surveys in Libya and Tunisia 1964, Afghanistan 1966, Belize 1970–2002, Ecuador 1972–84; Sackler Distinguished Lecturer, Metropolitan Museum of Art 2001; Fellow Dumbarton Oaks, Washington, DC; Visiting Fellow, Worcester Coll., Oxford, Peterhouse, Cambridge, All Souls Coll., Oxford 2004, Clare Hall, Cambridge 2004; Hon. DSc (Bradford) 1999; British Archaeological Press Award 1994, 1998, Soc. of Antiquaries Medal, London 2001. *Publications include:* South Asian Archaeology (ed.) 1973, Mesoamerican Archaeology (ed.) 1974, Lubaantun: a Classic Maya Realm 1975, Social Process in Maya Prehistory (ed.) 1977, The Archaeology of Afghanistan (co-ed. with F. R. Allchin) 1978, Ancient Maya Civilisation 1982, Nohmul: excavations 1973–83, 1985, Cuello: an early Maya community in Belize 1991, The Maya 2000; Archaeology Proc. 44th Congress of Americanists (Gen. Ed.) 1982–84; contribs to learned and other journals. *Leisure interests:* heraldry, genealogy, wine. *Address:* Department of Archaeology, Boston University, Boston, MA 02215-1406 (office); 83 Ivy Street, Apt 32, Brookline, MA 02446-4073, USA (home); Wholeway, Harlton, Cambridge, CB3 7ET, England (home). *Telephone:* (617) 358-1651 (USA) (office); (1223) 262376 (UK); (617) 739-9077 (USA). *Website:* www.bu.edu/archaeology (office).

HAMMONDS, Bruce L.; American business executive; *President and CEO, MBNA Corporation;* ed Univ. of Baltimore; fmr Chair. Delaware State Chamber of Commerce, currently Dir; COO MBNA Corpn 1990–2002, CEO 2002–, Chair. 2002–03, Pres. 2003–; Dir Financial Services Roundtable; Dir Delaware Business Roundtable, Chair. Roundtable's Educ. Cttee; mem. Bd of Trustees, Goldey-Beacom Coll. *Address:* MBNA Corporation, 1100 North King Street, Wilmington, DE 19884-0131, USA. *Telephone:* (302) 453-9930 (office). *Fax:* (302) 432-3614 (office). *Website:* www.mbna.com (office).

HAMMOUD, Mahmoud, BA, LLB; Lebanese politician and diplomatist; b. 1935; ed Lebanese Univ.; fmr secondary school teacher; fmr Amb. to UAE, FRG, Russia and Finland; Amb. to UK 1990–99; Dir-Gen. State Econ. and Social Council 2000–; Minister of Foreign Affairs and Emigrants 2001–03, 2004–05, of Defence 2003–04. *Address:* c/o Ministry of Foreign Affairs and Emigrants, rue Sursock, Achrafieh, Beirut, Lebanon (office).

HAMNETT, Katharine Eleanor; British designer; b. 16 Aug. 1947; d. of Group Capt. James Appleton; two s.; ed Cheltenham Ladies' Coll. and St Martin's School of Art; co-f. Tuttabankem (with Anne Buck) 1969–74; designed freelance in New York, Paris, Rome and London 1974–76; f. Katharine Hamnett Ltd 1979; launched Choose Life T-Shirt collection 1983; involved in Fashion Aid 1985; opening of first Katharine Hamnett shop, London 1986, followed by two more shops in 1988; production moved to Italy 1989; Visiting Prof., London Inst. 1997–; Hon. Prof. Cen. St Martin's Coll. of Art Int. Inst. of Cotton Designer of the Year 1982, British Fashion Industry Designer of the Year 1984, Bath Costume Museum Menswear Designer of the Year Award 1984, British Knitting and Clothing Export Council Award for Export 1988. *Publications:* various publs in major fashion magazines and newspapers. *Leisure interests:* travel, photography, gardening, archaeology. *Address:* Katharine E. Hamnett Head Office, Unit 3D, Aberdeen Studios, 22-24 Highbury Grove, London, N5 2EA, England. *E-mail:* info@katharinehamnett.com. *Website:* www.katharinehamnett.com.

HAMPE, Michael, DPhil; German stage and television director, actor and academic; *Professor, Hochschule für Musik, Cologne;* b. 3 June 1935, Heidelberg; s. of Hermann Hampe and Annemarie Hampe; m. Sibylle Hauck 1971; one d.; ed Falckenberg Schule, Munich, Univs of Vienna and Munich, Syracuse Univ., USA; Deputy Dir Schauspielhaus, Zürich 1965–70; Dir Nat. Theatre, Mannheim 1972–75, Cologne Opera 1975–95, Salzburg Festival 1984–90, Dresden Music Festival 1992–2000; directs opera at La Scala, Milan, Covent Garden, London, Paris Opera, Salzburg and Edin. Festivals, Munich, Stockholm, Cologne, Geneva, San Francisco, Sydney, Los Angeles, Buenos Aires, Tokyo; directs drama at Bavarian State Theatre, Munich Schauspielhaus, Zürich, etc.; directs and acts in film and TV; Prof., State Music Acad., Cologne and Cologne Univ.; mem. Bd European Acad. of Music, Vienna; theatre-bldg consultant; Prof., Hochschule für Musik, Cologne; teaches at Vienna Univ., UCLA and Univ. of Southern California, USA, Kunitachi Coll. of Music and Studio, New Nat. Theatre, Tokyo, Universität der Kunste, Berlin; Bundesverdienstkreuz, Commendatore Ordine al Merito (Italy), Goldenes Ehrenabzeichen des Landes Salzburg; Olivier West End Award 1983. *Productions include:* Andrea Chénier for Royal Opera House, Covent Garden 1984, Il Barbiere di Siviglia for Royal Opera House, Covent Garden 1985, La Gazza Ladra for Cologne Opera 1987, L'Italiana in Algeri 1987, Die Meistersinger von Nürnberg 1988, Il Barbiere di Siviglia 1988, La Cenerentola for Royal Opera House, Covent Garden 1990, Così fan tutte 1989, Don Giovanni 1991, Falstaff (at the Schwetzingen Festival) 1996, premiere of Farinelli, oder die Macht des Gesangs at Karlsruhe 1998, Così fan tutte in Santiago and in Genova 2005, Fidelio for San Francisco Opera 2005, Die Zauberflöte at Athens 2005, Die Frau ohne Schatten for Helsinki Opera 2006, Die Zauberflöte in Toyko, Dallas and San Diego 2006, La clemenza di Tito for Washington Opera 2006, Così fan tutte at Teatro Colón, Buenos Aires 2006, Maometto II at Pesaro 2008, Trovatore at Semperoper, Dresden. *Publications:* 20 Jahre Kölner Oper 1995, Alles Theater, Reden und Aufsätze 2000; articles in newspapers and periodicals. *Address:* Carl Spitieler Strasse 105, 8053 Zürich, Switzerland (home).

HAMPEL, Sir Ronald Claus, Kt, MA; British business executive; *Chairman, Templeton Emerging Markets Investment Trust;* b. 31 May 1932, Shrewsbury; s. of Karl Victor Hugo Hampel and Rutgard Emil Klothilde Hauck; m. Jane Bristed Hewson 1957; three s. one d.; ed Canford School, Wimborne, Dorset, Corpus Christi Coll., Cambridge; nat. service 2nd Lt Royal Horse Artillery 1950–51; joined ICI 1955; Vice-Pres. ICI Agrochemicals USA 1973–75, ICI Latin America 1975–77; ICI Gen. Man. Commercial 1977–80; Chair. ICI Paints 1980–83, ICI Agrochemicals 1983–85; Dir ICI 1985–99, COO ICI 1991–93, CEO ICI 1993–95, Chair. 1995–99; Chair. United News and Media (now United Business Media) 1999–2002; Dir (non-exec.) Powell Duffryn 1983–88, Commercial Union 1987–95, British Aerospace 1989–2002, ALCOA 1995–, Teijin 1999–2004; Chair. Templeton Emerging Markets Investment Trust 2003–; Dir American Chamber of Commerce 1985–90; mem. Exec. Cttee British North America Cttee 1989–96, Listed Companies Advisory Cttee, London Stock Exchange 1996–99, Nomination Cttee, NY Stock Exchange 1996–99; mem. European Round Table 1995–99, UK Advisory Bd INSEAD 1994–99, Advisory Cttee Karlpreis Aachen 1997–2001, Exec. Cttee All England Lawn Tennis Club 1994–; Chair. Cttee on Corp. Governance 1995–97; Chair. Bd of Trustees Eden Project 2000–; Hon. Fellow, Corpus Christi Coll. Cambridge 1997. *Leisure interests:* tennis, golf, skiing. *Address:* Franklin Templeton Investments, The Adelphi, 1–11 John Adam Street, London, WC2N 6HT, England. *Telephone:* (20) 7073-8500. *Fax:* (20) 7073-8700. *E-mail:* rch@hampelrc.com (home); enquiries@franklintempleton.co.uk (office). *Website:* www.franklintempleton.co.uk (office).

HAMPSHIRE, Susan, OBE; British actress and writer; b. 12 May 1942; d. of the late George Kenneth Hampshire and June Hampshire; m. 1st Pierre Granier-Deferre 1967 (divorced 1974); one s. (one d. deceased); m. 2nd Sir Eddie Kulukundis (q.v.) 1981; ed Hampshire School, Knightsbridge; Hon. DLitt (City Univ., London) 1984, (St Andrews) 1986, (Exeter) 2001; Hon. DArts (Pine Manor Coll., Boston, USA) 1994; Dr hc (Kingston) 1994; Emmy Award, Best Actress for The Forsyte Saga 1970, for The First Churchills 1971, for Vanity Fair 1973, E. Poe Prize du Film Fantastique, Best Actress for Malpertius 1972. *Stage roles include:* Expresso Bongo 1958, Follow that Girl 1960, Fairy Tales of New York 1961, Marion Dangerfield in Ginger Man 1963, Kate Hardcastle in She Stoops to Conquer 1966, On Approval 1966, Mary in The Sleeping Prince 1968, Nora in A Doll's House 1972, Katharina in The Taming of the Shrew 1974, Peter in Peter Pan 1974, Jeannette in Romeo and Jeannette 1975, Rosalind in As You Like It 1975, Miss Julie 1975, Elizabeth in The Circle 1976, Ann Whitefield in Man and Superman 1977, Siri Von Essen in Tribades 1978, Victorine in An Audience Called Edouard 1978, Irene in The Crucifer of Blood 1979, Ruth Carson in Night and Day 1979, Elizabeth in The Revolt 1980, Stella Drury in House Guest 1981, Elvira in Blithe Spirit 1986, Marie Stopes in Married Love, The Countess in A Little Night Music 1989, Mrs Anna in The King and I 1990, Gertie in Noel and Gertie 1991, The Countess of Marshwood in Relative Values 1993, Suzanna Andler in Suzanna Andler, Alicia Christie in Black Chiffon 1995–96, Sheila Carter in Relatively Speaking 2000–01, Felicity Marshwood in Relative Values 2002, Miss Shepherd in The Lady in the Van 2004–05, The Fairy Godmother in Cinderella, Wimbledon 2005–06, The Bargain 2007. *Television roles:* Andromeda in The Andromeda Breakthrough (series) 1962, Katy (series) 1962, Fleur Forsyte in The Forsyte Saga (mini-series) 1967, Becky Sharp in Vanity Fair (mini-series) 1967, Sarah Churchill, Duchess of Marlborough, in The First Churchills (mini-series) 1969, Baffled! 1973, Dr. Jekyll and Mr. Hyde 1973, Glencora Palliser in The Pallisers 1974, The Story of David 1976, Kill Two Birds 1976, Lady Melford in Dick Turpin 1981, Madeline Neroni in The Barchester Chronicles (mini-series) 1982, Martha in Leaving 1984, Martha in Leaving II 1985, Going to Pot 1985, Don't Tell Father (series) 1992, Esme Harkness in The Grand 1996–98, Miss Catto in Coming Home 1998–99, Miss Catto in Nancherrow 1999, Molly in Monarch of the Glen 1999–2005, Lucilla Drake in Sparkling Cyanide 2003, The Lady in the Van 2004, The Circle 2008, The Royal 2008–09, Bridge Celebrity Grand Slam 2009. *Films include:* The Woman in the Hall 1947, Idle on Parade (uncredited) 1959, Upstairs and Downstairs 1959, Expresso Bongo (uncredited) 1960, The Long Shadow 1961, During One Night 1961, The Three Lives of Thomasina 1964, Night Must Fall 1964, Wonderful Life 1964, Paris in August 1965, The Fighting Prince of Donegal 1966, Monte Carlo or Bust 1969, Malpertuis 1971, A Time for Loving 1971, Rogan, David Copperfield, Living Free 1972, Neither the Sea Nor the Sand 1972, Le fils 1973, Peccato mortale (aka Roses and Green Peppers) 1973, Bang! 1977. *Publications:* Susan's Story (autobiographical account of dyslexia) 1981, The Maternal Instinct, Lucy Jane at the Ballet 1985, Lucy Jane on Television 1989, Trouble Free Gardening 1989, Every Letter Counts 1990, Lucy Jane and the Dancing Competition 1991, Easy Gardening 1991, Lucy Jane and the Russian Ballet 1993, Rosie's First Ballet Lesson 1997. *Leisure interests:* gardening, music. *Address:* c/o Dallas Smith, United Agents, 12–26 Lexington Street, London, W1F 0LE, England.

HAMPSON, Christopher, CBE, BEng; Canadian/British business executive; b. 6 Sept. 1931, Montreal; s. of Harold Ralph Hampson and Geraldine Mary Hampson (née Smith); m. Joan Margaret Cassils Evans 1954; two s. three d.; ed Ashbury Coll. School, Ottawa, McGill Univ.; joined Canadian Industries Ltd (subsidiary of ICI) 1956, Vice-Pres., Dir 1973; seconded to ICI PLC as Gen. Man. Planning 1978, Sr Vice-Pres. Canadian Industries Ltd 1982, fmr CEO, Dir ICI Australia Ltd, Exec. Dir, mem. Bd ICI 1987–94; Chair. Yorks. Electricity Group 1995–97, RMC Group 1996–2002, British Biotech PLC 1998–2002. *Leisure interests:* gardening, tennis, skiing. *Address:* 77 Kensington Court, London, W8 5DT, England. *Telephone:* (20) 7937-0325. *Fax:* (20) 7376-1906.

HAMPSON, Sir Stuart, Kt, MA; British business executive; b. 7 Jan. 1947; s. of Kenneth Hampson and Mary Hampson; m. Angela McLaren 1973; one s. one d.; ed Royal Masonic School, Bushey, St John's Coll., Oxford; with Board of Trade 1969–72; FCO Mission to UN, Geneva 1972–74; Dept of Prices and Consumer Protection 1974–79; Dept of Trade 1979–82; with John Lewis Partnership PLC 1982–, Dir of Research and Expansion 1986, Deputy Chair. 1989–93, Chair. and CEO 1993–07. *Address:* c/o John Lewis Partnership, 171 Victoria Street, London, SW1E 5NN, England (office).

HAMPSON, (Walter) Thomas, BA; American singer (baritone); b. 28 June 1955, Elkhart, Ind.; s. of Walter Hampson and Ruthye Hampson; one d.; ed Eastern Washington Univ., Fort Wright Coll., Music Acad. of West; with Düsseldorf Ensemble 1981–84; title role in Der Prinz von Homburg, Darmstadt 1982; debut in Cologne, Munich, Santa Fé 1982–84, Metropolitan Opera, NY, Vienna Staatsoper, Covent Garden 1986, La Scala, Milan, Deutsche Oper, Berlin 1989, Carnegie Hall, San Francisco Opera 1990; has performed with Wiener Philharmoniker, NY Philharmonic, London Philharmonic and Chicago Symphony orchestras; f. The Hampsong Foundation 2003; Hon. RAM 1996; Chevalier des Artes et des Lettres; Dr hc (Whitworth Coll., Washington, San Francisco Conservatory); Edison Prize, Netherlands 1990, 1992, Grand Prix du Disque 1990, 1996, Cannes Classical Award 1994, Echo Klassik 1995, EMI Artist of the Year 1997, Deutsche Schallplattenkritik Award 1999, Cecilia Award 2000, Diapason D'Or Award 2000; Citation of Merit, Vienna Kammersänger 1999. *Recordings include:* Schubert's Winterreise 1997, Das Lied von der Erde 1997, Belshazzar's Feast 1998, Operetta Album with London Philharmonic 1999, No Tenors Allowed: Opera Duets (with Samuel Ramey) 1999, Verdi Arias with Orchestra of the Age of Enlightenment 2001, Wagner's Tannhäuser 2002, Cole Porter's Kiss Me Kate 2002, Forbidden and Banished 2006, I Hear America Singing 2006, Simon Boccanegra 2006, Don Giovanni 2006, Doktor Faust 2007. *Address:* IMG Artists, The Light Box, 111 Power Road, London W4 5PY, England (office); c/o Leonore Rothwangl, Colloredogasse 31, 1180 Vienna, Austria (office). *Telephone:* (20) 7957-5800 (office); (1) 4791286 (office). *Fax:* (20) 7957-5801 (office); (1) 479128620 (office). *E-mail:* jvanderveen@imgartists.com (office); hampsonoffice@hampsong.com (home). *Website:* www.imgartists.com (office); www.hampsong.com (office); www.thomashampson.com (office).

HAMPTON, Christopher James, CBE, MA, FRSL; British playwright; b. 26 Jan. 1946, Fayal, the Azores, Portugal; s. of Bernard Patrick and Dorothy Patience (née Herrington) Hampton; m. Laura Margaret de Holesch 1971; two d.; ed Lancing Coll., New Coll., Oxford; wrote first play When Did You Last See My Mother? 1964; Resident Dramatist, Royal Court Theatre 1968–70; freelance writer 1970–; Officier, Ordre des Arts et des Lettres 1998; Evening Standard Award for Best Comedy 1970, 1983, for Best Play 1986, Plays and Players London Critics' Award for Best Play 1970, 1973, 1985; Los Angeles Drama Critics' Circle Award 1974, Laurence Olivier Award for Best Play 1986, New York Drama Critics' Circle Award for Best Foreign Play 1987, Prix Italia 1988, Writers' Guild of America Screenplay Award 1989, Academy Award for Best Adapted Screenplay 1989, BAFTA Award for Best Screenplay 1990, Special Jury Award, Cannes Film Festival 1995, Tony Awards for Best Original Score (lyrics) and Best Book of a Musical 1995, Scott Moncrieff Prize 1997. *Plays:* When Did You Last See My Mother? 1967, Total Eclipse 1969, The Philanthropist 1970, Savages 1973, Treats 1976, Able's Will (TV) 1978, Tales from Hollywood 1983, Les Liaisons Dangereuses 1985, The Ginger Tree (adaptation) 1989, The Philanthropist/Total Eclipse/Treats 1991, White Chameleon 1991, Sunset Boulevard 1993, Alice's Adventures Underground (adaptation) 1995, Carrington 1995, The Secret Agent/Nostromo (adaptation) 1996, The Talking Cure 2002. *Translations include:* Marya (Babel) 1967, Uncle Vanya, Hedda Gabler 1970, A Doll's House 1971 (film 1974), Don Juan 1972, Tales from the Vienna Woods 1977 (film 1979), Don Juan Comes Back from the War 1978, The Wild Duck 1980, Ghosts 1983, Tartuffe 1984, Faith, Hope and Charity 1989, Art 1996, An Enemy of the People 1997, The Unexpected Man 1998, Conversations After a Burial 2000, Life × Three 2001, Three Sisters 2005, Embers 2006. *Directed:* (films) Carrington 1995, The Secret Agent 1996, Imagining Argentina 2003. *Opera libretto:* Waiting for the Barbarians (music by Philip Glass) 2005. *Publications:* When Did You Last See My Mother? 1967, Total Eclipse 1969 (film 1995), The Philanthropist 1970, Savages 1973, Treats 1976, Able's Will (TV) 1978, The History Man (TV adaptation of novel by Malcolm Bradbury) 1981, The Portage to San Cristobal of A.H. (play adaptation of novel by George Steiner) 1983, Tales from Hollywood 1983, The Honorary Consul (film adaptation of a novel by Graham Greene) 1983, Les Liaisons Dangereuses (adaptation of a novel by Laclos) 1985, Hotel du Lac (TV adaptation of a novel by Anita Brookner q.v.) 1986, The Good Father (film adaptation of a novel by Peter Prince) 1986, Wolf at the Door (film) 1986, Dangerous Liaisons (film) 1988, The Ginger Tree (adaptation of novel by Oswald Wynd, TV) 1989, White Chameleon 1991, Sunset Boulevard (book and lyrics with Don Black) 1993, Alice's Adventures Underground (with Martha Clarke) 1994, Carrington (film) 1995, Mary Reilly (film) 1996, The Secret Agent (film) 1996, Nostromo (screenplay) 1997, The Quiet American (film) 2002, Collected Screenplays 2002, The Talking Cure 2002. Hampton on

Hampton 2005. *Leisure interests:* travel, cinema. *Address:* Casarotto Ramsay and Associates Ltd., Waverley House, 7–12 Noel Street, London, W1F 8GQ, England (office). *Telephone:* (20) 7287-4450 (office). *Fax:* (20) 7287-9128 (office). *E-mail:* info@casarotto.co.uk (office). *Website:* www.casarotto.co.uk (office).

HAMPTON, Philip, MA, MBA; British business executive; *Chairman, J Sainsbury plc;* ed Lincoln Coll. Oxford, Institut Européen d'Admin des Affaires (INSEAD), Fontainebleau, France; qualified as chartered accountant 1978; began career as Auditor, Coopers & Lybrand, London and W Africa 1975–81; various positions in Mergers and Acquisitions, Business Restructurings and Capital Markets, Lazard Brothers 1981–86; seconded to Lazard Freres, New York and Paris 1986–90; Group Finance Dir British Steel plc 1990–95, British Gas plc 1995–97, BG Group plc 1997–2000, British Telecommunications (BT) plc 2000–02, LloydsTSB plc 2002–04; Chair. J Sainsbury plc 2004–; Dir (non-exec.) RMC Group plc 2002–05, Belgacom (Belgian telecom group); led Treasury review on govt red tape 2004–05; Assoc., Inst. of Chartered Accountants. *Address:* J Sainsbury plc, 33 Holborn, London, EC1N 2HT, England (office). *Telephone:* (20) 7695-6000 (office). *Fax:* (20) 7695-7610 (office). *E-mail:* info@j-sainsbury.co.uk (office). *Website:* www.j-sainsbury.co.uk (office).

HAMRAWI, Habib Chawki; Algerian broadcasting executive and international organization executive; *President of the Executive Council, Arab States Broadcasting Union (ASBU);* Minister of Communication and Culture 1992, 1997–99, also Govt Spokesman 1997–99; journalist with Algerian Television (ENTV) 1997, Dir-Gen. 1999–; Pres. High Coordination Cttee of Arab Satellite Channel 2000–; Chair. Conférence Permanente de l'Audiovisuel Méditerranéen (CoPeAM) 2002–06; Pres. Exec. Council, Arab States Broadcasting Union (ASBU); mem. Bd European Broadcasting Union. *Address:* Arab States Broadcasting Union (ASBU), PO Box 250, Rue 8840, Centre urbain nord, 1080 Tunis Cedex, Tunisia (office). *Telephone:* (71) 849000 (office). *Fax:* (71) 843054 (office). *E-mail:* asbu@asbu.intl.tn (office). *Website:* www.asbu.net (office).

HAMUD, Muhammad Ali; Somali politician; *Minister of Finance and Planning;* Minister for Foreign Affairs and Int. Co-operation 2007–08, of Finance and Planning 2008–. *Address:* Ministry of Finance and Planning, Mogadishu, Somalia (office).

HAMUTENYA, Hidipo; Namibian politician; b. 1939; Minister of Trade and Industry 1990–2002; Minister of Foreign Affairs 2002–04. *Address:* c/o Ministry of Foreign Affairs, Government Buildings, Robert Mugabe Avenue, PMB 13347, Windhoek, Namibia (office).

HAMZA, Ahmed Amin, PhD; Egyptian physicist and academic; *Professor of Physics, Mansoura University;* b. 8 March 1941, Giza; s. of late Amin Hamza and Hanim Abdel Meguid; m. Sahar Khalil 1968; three d.; ed Saaidiya Secondary School, Giza and Ain Shams Univ. Cairo; Head, Printing Dept Cairo Dyeing & Finishing Co. 1962–72; Lecturer in Physics, Mansoura Univ. 1972–76, Assoc. Prof. 1994–99, Prof. of Experimental Physics 1999–, Head, Dept of Physics 1984–86, Vice-Dean, Faculty of Science 1986–92, Vice-Pres. Univ. for Community and Environmental Devt 1992–94; Pres. Univ. of Mansoura 1994–2001; Assoc. Prof. Sana'a Univ., Yemen 1989–91; Assoc. Prof. UAE Univ. 1991–94; mem. Cttee for Promoting Asst Profs of Physics 1985–; mem. Cttee (affiliated to Egyptian Acad. of Science and Tech.) for Researches in Textile Industries 1989–; Fellow, Royal Microscopical Soc. (Oxford), Inst. of Physics (London); mem. Int. Soc. for Optical Eng; Dr hc (Tech. Univ. of Liberec, Czech Repub.) 2000; Egyptian Nat. Award in Physics 1987; Sr Academic Prize and Certificate Distinction of the Univ. of Mansoura in Basic Sciences 1992; First-Class Medal for Distinction 1995; State Prize of Merit in Basic Sciences 1997. *Publications:* Interferometry of Fibrous Materials (co-author) 1990; numerous publs in fields of interferometry, fibre optics, colour measurement and polymer physics. *Leisure interest:* playing football. *Address:* Mansoura University, Faculty of Science, 60 El-Gomhoria Street, Mansoura (office); 6 Korash Street, 6th District, Nasr City, Cairo, Egypt (home). *Telephone:* (50) 2259427 (office); (2) 22462549 (home). *Fax:* (50) 247900. *E-mail:* scimphydept@mum.mans.eun.eg (office); hamzaaa@idsc.net.eg (home). *Website:* www.mans.eun.eg (office).

HAMZAH, Tengku Tan Sri Datuk Razaleigh (see Razaleigh).

HAMŽÍK, Pavol, JUDr; Slovak politician, diplomatist and university lecturer; b. 20 Aug. 1954, Trenčín; s. of Pavol Hamžík and Júlia Hamžíková; m. Dagmar Hamžíková (née Kiššová) 1976; two d.; ed Komensky Univ., Bratislava, Diplomatic Acad., Moscow; lawyer 1978–84; joined Czechoslovak Foreign Ministry 1984; Consul in Copenhagen 1985–89; studied at Diplomatic Acad., Moscow 1989–91; Vice-Chair. del. to int. disarmament negotiations, Vienna 1991; mem. del. to CSCE 1991–92, Pres. CSCE Steering Group on crisis in Yugoslavia 1992, head Slovak del. to CSCE 1993, head Slovak Perm. Mission to CSCE 1993–94; Slovak Amb. to Germany 1994–96; Foreign Minister 1996–97; f. Party of Civic Understanding (SOP) 1998, Chair. 1999–2003; MP 1998–2002, mem. Defence and Security Cttee 2001–02; Vice Prime Minister 1998–2001; Deputy of Slovakia in European Convention; Lecturer, mem. Scientific Bd, Faculty of Political Sciences and Int. Relations, Matej Bell Univ. 1997–; Golden Biatec, Informal Economic Forum 2000. *Leisure interests:* history, skiing, literature, tennis. *Address:* Svätoplukova 1, 82109 Bratislava (office); Žilinská 1, 81105 Bratislava, Slovak Republic (home). *Telephone:* (2) 5564-5893 (office); (2) 9079-09011 (home). *Fax:* (2) 5556-6990 (office). *E-mail:* intercons@stonline.sk (office).

HAN, Duck-soo, PhD; South Korean government official; b. 18 June 1949, Jeonju, N Jeolla Prov.; ed Seoul Nat. Univ., Harvard Univ., USA; Presidential Sec. for Econ. Affairs 1993; Asst Minister for Planning and Man., Ministry of

Trade and Industry 1994; Asst Minister, Int. Trade Affairs Bureau, Ministry of Trade, Industry and Energy (MOTIE) 1995–96, Vice Minister MOTIE 1997–98; Commr Korean Industrial Property Office 1996; Minister for Trade Affairs, Ministry of Foreign Affairs and Trade 1998–2000; Amb. to OECD 2001; Sr Presidential Sec. for Policy and Planning 2001, for Econ. Affairs Jan.–July 2002; Minister, Office for Govt Policy Co-ordination 2004–05; Deputy Prime Minister and Minister of Finance and the Economy 2005–06 (resgnd); Prime Minister 2007–08; Pres. Korea Inst. for Industrial Econs and Trade 2003. *Address:* c/o Office of the Prime Minister, 77, Sejong-no, Jongno-gu, Seoul, Republic of Korea (office).

HAN, Lt-Gen. Huaizhi; Chinese army official; b. 1922, Pingshan Co., Hebei Prov.; Asst to the Chief of the PLA Gen. Staff 1980–85; Deputy, 6th NPC 1983–87, 7th NPC 1988–; Dir of the Mil. Training Dept under the PLA Gen. Staff 1984–85; Deputy Chief of the PLA Gen. Staff 1985; Lt-Gen. PLA 1985–; Chair. Sports Comm. 1990–; mem. Nat. Degrees Cttee 1988–. *Address:* Chinese People's Liberation Army General Staff, Beijing, People's Republic of China.

HAN, Joon-ho, BA, PhD; South Korean energy industry executive; ed Seoul Nat. Univ., Kyunghee Univ.; Asst Minister, Ministry of Trade, Industry and Energy 1997–98; Admin. Korean Small and Medium Business Admin 2000–04; Chair., Pres. and CEO Korea Electric Power Corpn (KEPCO) 2004–06; fmr Chair. Korean Productivity Centre (KPC); Chief of Presidential Comm. on Small & Medium Enterprise 2003; mem. Pacific Basin Econ. Council. *Address:* c/o Korea Electric Power Corpn, 411 Yeongdong-daero, Gangnam-gu, Seoul 135-791, Republic of Korea. *Telephone:* (2) 3456-3114. *Fax:* (2) 556-3694. *Website:* www.kepco.co.kr.

HAN, Myong-sook, BA, MA; South Korean politician; b. 24 March 1944, Pyeongyang; m. Park Sung-jun; ed Ewha Womans Univ., Seoul; mem. staff, Korea Christian Acad. 1974–79; jailed as a prisoner of conscience, Christian Acad. Case 1979–81; Lecturer, Dept of Women's Studies, Ewha Womans Univ. 1986–97, Visiting Researcher, Asian Center for Women's Studies 1996–2003; Lecturer, Dept of Women's Studies, Sungsim Womans Univ. 1988–94; Chair. of Special Cttee on Revision of Family Law, Korea Women's Asscns United Jan.–Dec. 1989, Co-rep. 1993–96; Pres. Korean Womenlink 1990–94; Chief Dir Korea Inst. for Environmental and Social Policies 1992; fmr Head, Presidential Comm. on Women's Affairs; mem. Nat. Ass. 2000–01, 2004–, mem. Unification, Foreign Affairs and Trade Cttee; Minister of Gender Equality 2001–03, of the Environment 2003–04; Prime Minister (first woman) 2006–07 (resgnd); Pres. Korean Parl. League on Children, Population and Environment 2004–06, Korea-Singapore Parliamentarians' Friendship Asscn June 2004; Pres. Exec. Cttee Asia-Pacific Parliamentarians' Conf. on Environment and Devt 2004–06; Vice-Pres. Korea–Japan Parl. League 2006–; mem. Exec. Cttee Seoul and Pyungyang Symposium Peace of Asian and Women's Role 1992–96; Co-rep., Viewers Alliance for Fair Broadcasting Policy Advisor 1993–94, Cttee for Interchange and Cooperation, Ministry of Unification 1993–94, Citizens' Asscn for Broadcasting Reform 1994–95; mem. Environmental Reservation Cttee, Ministry of Environment 1993–95, Anti-Corruption Cttee, Bd of Audit and Inspection 1993–95; fmr mem. Uri Party, mem. Cen. Standing Cttee April–Nov. 2005, Nat. Ass. Environment and Labour Cttee 2006–; currently mem. Democratic Party (fmrly United New Democratic Party—UNDP), unsuccessful campaign to become UNDP cand. for Pres. of South Korea 2007; Civil Merit Medal 1998; Order of Service Merit Medal (Blue Stripes) 2005; ranked 68th by Forbes magazine amongst 100 Most Powerful Women 2006. *Address:* c/o Democratic Party, 15–16 Yeouido-dong, Yeongdeungpo-gu, Seoul 150-701, Republic of Korea. *E-mail:* help@undp.kr. *Website:* minjoo.kr.

HAN, Seung-soo, PhD; South Korean politician, economist, diplomatist and international organization official; *Prime Minister;* b. 28 Dec. 1936, Chunchon, Kangwon Prov.; m. Hong Soja; two c.; ed Yonsei Univ., Seoul Nat. Univ. and Univ. of York, UK; taught econs at Univ. of York, UK 1965–68, Univ. of Cambridge 1968–70; Prof. of Econs, Seoul Nat. Univ. 1970–88; Sr Fulbright Scholar, Dept of Econs, Harvard Univ. 1985–86; Visiting Prof., Univ. of Tokyo 1986–87; fmr Distinguished Visiting Prof., Yonsei Univ.; served as advisor to Bank of Korea, Korea Export–Import Bank, Korea Industrial Bank, Korea Chamber of Commerce and Industry, Fed. of Korea Industries and Korea Int. Trade Asscn; consultant to World Bank and UN Econ. Comm. for Asia and the Pacific (ESCAP), seconded by World Bank as Financial Adviser to Govt of Jordan 1974–76; Pres. Korea Int. Econ. Asscn 1983–84; first Chair. Korea Trade Commr 1987–88; elected mem. of Nat. Ass., Repub. of Korea 1988–2004; Minister of Trade and Industry 1988–90; Amb. to USA 1993–94; Chair. Council of the Repub. of Korea Group of the Inter-Parl. Union (IPU); Chief of Staff to Pres. of Repub. of Korea 1994–95; Deputy Prime Minister and Minister of Finance and Economy 1996–97; Minister of Foreign Affairs and Trade 2001–02; Pres. 56th Session of UN Gen. Ass. 2001–02; Pres. Korean Water Forum 2004; UN Special Envoy for Climate Change 2007–08; Prime Minister of Repub. of Korea 2008–; f. Korean Acad. of Industrial Tech. (KAITEC) 1989; Pres. Korea–Britain Soc., Korea–UK Forum for the Future, Alumni Asscn of the Grad. School of Public Admin of Seoul Nat. Univ.; mem. Royal Econ. Soc., Korean Econ. Asscn, Int. Inst. of Public Finance, Seoul Forum for Int. Affairs, Korean Council on Foreign Relations, Korean Soc. for Future Studies, Korean Asscn of Public Admin, Bretton Woods Club; Hon. Prof., Univ. of York, Hon. DUniv (York) 1997; Order of Public Service Merit (First Class, Blue Stripes), Order of Industrial Merit (Bronze Tower), Order of Nat. Security Merit (Cheonsu Medal); Sixth European Communities Prize 1971, Columbia Law School/Parker School Award for Distinguished Int. Service 1997. *Publications include:* Taxes in Britain and the EEC: The Problem of Harmonization (jtly) 1968, Britain and the Common Market (jtly) 1971, The Growth and Function of the European Budget 1971, The Health of

Nations 1985; numerous articles in learned journals and press commentaries in both Korean and English. *Address:* Office of the Prime Minister, 77, Sejong-no, Jongno-gu, Seoul, South Korea (office). *Telephone:* (2) 737-0094 (office). *Fax:* (2) 739-5830 (office). *E-mail:* m-opm@opm.go.kr (office). *Website:* www.opm.go.kr (office).

HAN, Shao Gong; Chinese writer; b. 1 Jan. 1953, Chang Sha; s. of Han Ke Xian and Zhang Jing Xing; m. Liang Yu Li 1980; one d.; ed Hunan Teacher's Univ.; Council mem. Chinese Writers' Asscn 1984; Vice-Chair. Hunan Youth Union 1985; Chief Ed. of Hainan Review 1988; Pres. Hainan Literature Correspondence Coll. 1988; Chair. Hainan Writers Asscn 1995; mem. Standing Cttee CPPCC Hainan Prov. 1988; Chair. Hainan Artists' Asscn 2000; mem. Council Chinese Artists' Union 2001; Prize for Best Chinese Stories 1980, 1981. *Film:* The Deaf and Mute 1983. *Publications:* Biography of Ren Bi Shi 1979; (collections of short stories): Yue Nan 1981, Flying Across the Blue Sky 1983, New Stories 1986, Fondness for Shoes 1994, Red Apple is an Exception 1994; To Face the Mystical and Wide World (selection of articles) 1985, The Other Shore (selection of prose pieces) 1988, The Murder 1990, Pa Pa Pa and Seduction and Femme Femme Femme 1990–91, Homecoming 1992, The Play and Holy War 1993, Raving of a Pedestrian in the Night 1994, The Thought of the Sea 1994, Dictionary of Ma-Bridge (novel) 1995, Ma Qiao ci Dian 1997, Gui Qu Lai 2008; trans: The Unbearable Lightness of Being (Kundera) 1987, The Book of Disquiet (F. Pessoa) 1999, Collected Works (10 vols) 2001. *Leisure interest:* Chinese calligraphy. *Address:* Room 2-602, Hainan Teachers' University, Haikou 571100, Hainan (home); 1st Building, Hainan Plaza, 69 Guoxing Road, Haikou, People's Republic of China (office). *Telephone:* (898) 5882748 (home); (898) 5336231 (office). *Fax:* (898) 53328034 (office). *E-mail:* hanshaog@public.hk.hi.cn (home).

HAN, Sung-joo, PhD; South Korean academic and fmr politician; *President, Seoul Forum for International Affairs;* b. 1940; ed Seoul Nat. Univ. and Univ. of California, Berkeley; taught at CUNY, New York 1970–78, Columbia Univ., New York 1986–87, Stanford Univ., Calif. 1992; Distinguished Fellow, Rockefeller Brothers Fund 1986–87; fmr Vice-Chair. Int. Political Science Asscn; int. columnist, Newsweek 1984–93; Adviser to Govt on foreign affairs, nat. defence and unification since late 1970s; Minister of Foreign Affairs 1993–95; Prof. of Political Science and Pres. Ilmin Int. Relations Inst., Korea Univ. 1995–, fmr Acting Pres. Korea Univ.; UN Sec.-Gen.'s Special Rep. for Cyprus 1996–97; mem. UN Inquiry Comm. on the 1994 Genocide in Rwanda 1999; Amb. to USA 2003–05; Freeman Foundation Visiting Prof. in Asian Affairs, Claremont McKenna Coll., USA 2006; Pres. Seoul Forum for Int. Affairs; Deputy Chair. for Asia Pacific, Trilateral Comm.; Chair. East Asia Vision Group 2000–01; Co-Chair. Council for Security Co-operation in the Asia-Pacific; mem. Int. Panel on Democracy and Devt, Int. Bd of Govs The Peres Center for Peace; fmr mem. Bd Asia Pacific Foundation of Canada, Hon. Advisers of New Zealand's Asia 2000. *Publications include:* The Failure of Democracy in South Korea 1974, The US-South Korean Alliance 1983, The Division and Unification of Korea 1992, Choice for Korea in a World in Transition 1992, Korean Diplomacy in an Era of Globalization 1995, Korea in a Changing World 1995, Changing Values in Asia: Their Impact on Governance and Development (ed.). *Address:* Ilmin International Research Institute, Korea University, 5th Floor, Inchon Memorial Building, 5-1 Anam-dong, Seongbuk-Gu, Seoul 136-701, Korea (office). *Telephone:* (2) 923-2416/7 (office). *Fax:* (2) 927-5265 (office). *E-mail:* irikor@unitel.co.kr (office). *Website:* www.korea.ac.kr/~ilmin (office).

HAN, Wan-sang; South Korean fmr government official, professor of sociology and university administrator; *President, Hansung University;* b. 18 March 1936; s. of Han Young-Jik; m. 1966; three d.; ed in USA; Asst Prof., Coll. of Eng, Univ. of Tenn.1967–69; Asst Prof, E. Carolina Univ 1969–70; Assoc. Prof. of Sociology, Seoul Nat. Univ. 1970–76, Prof., 1984–93; adviser to Kim Young Sam; Deputy Prime Minister and Minister of Unification 1993; Pres. Korea Nat. Open Univ. 1994–98; Pres. Sangji Univ. 1999–2001; First Deputy Prime Minister and Minister of Educ. and Human Resource Devt 2001–02; Pres. Hansung Univ. 2002–; Hon. Dr. of Humanities Emory Univ., Atlanta, GA, USA 1999. *Leisure interest:* tennis. *Address:* Office of the President, Hansung Unversity, 389 Samsoon–dong, 3–ga, Sungbuk-gu, Seoul, Republic of Korea (office). *Telephone:* (2) 760-4114 (office). *Fax:* (2) 745-8943 (office). *Website:* www.hansung.ac.kr/eng (office).

HAN, Zhaoshan; Chinese business executive; *Chairman and General Manager, Panpan Group Limited;* b. 1949, Yingkou, Liaoning Prov.; Vice-Dir Shuiyuan Township Agric. Machinery Factory, Yingkou 1970–83; founded Yingkou Great Wall Metal Product Factory 1983–92; Chair. and Gen. Man. Panpan Group Ltd 1992–; took part as torchbearer during Olympic flame relay, Shenyang, Liaoning Prov. July 2008. *Address:* Panpan Group Ltd, Yingkou, Liaoning Province, People's Republic of China (office). *Website:* www.panpangroup.com (office).

HAN, Zheng, MA; Chinese economist and politician; *Mayor of Shanghai;* b. April 1954, Cixi Co., Zhejiang Prov.; ed East China Normal Univ.; joined CCP 1979; served successively as Sec. CYLC Shanghai Chemical Industry Bureau Cttee 1982–86, Deputy Party Sec. Shanghai Chemical Eng School 1986–87, Party Sec. and Deputy Dir Shanghai No. 6 Rubber Shoes Factory 1987–88, Party Sec. and Deputy Dir Dazhonghua Rubber Factory 1988–90, Sec. Communist Youth League of China Shanghai Cttee 1991–92, Gov. Shanghai Luwan Dist 1992–93, Deputy Sec.-Gen. Shanghai Municipality 1995–97; Dir Shanghai Devt Planning Comm. –1998; mem. Standing Cttee CCP Shanghai Cttee and Vice-Mayor of Shanghai 1997–2002, Vice-Sec. CCP Shanghai Cttee May 2002, Exec. Vice-Mayor Oct. 2002; mem. 16th CCP Cen. Cttee 2002–07, Deputy Sec. CCP Shanghai Cttee and Mayor of Shanghai 2003–, Acting Sec. CCP Shanghai Cttee 2006–07; mem. 17th CCP Cen. Cttee 2007–. *Leisure interest:* dancing. *Address:* Office of the Mayor, Foreign Affairs Office, 1418

West Nanjing Road, Shanghai 200040, People's Republic of China (office). *Telephone:* (21) 62565900 (office). *Fax:* (21) 6255276 (office); (21) 62552761 (office). *Website:* www.shanghai.gov.cn (office).

HAN, Zhubin; Chinese politician and lawyer; b. Feb. 1932, Harbin, Heilongjiang Prov.; ed Beijing Econs Corresp. Univ.; train captain, Railway Admin, Harbin City 1946–50; joined CCP 1950; Dir Railway Admin, Liuzhou City, Guangxi Zhuang Autonomous Region, Railway Admin, Shanghai 1983–90; fmr Vice-Sec., then Sec. Communist Youth League, Liuzhou Railway Bureau Cttee, Dir 1975–83; Vice-Sec. CCP Group and Sec. CCP Cttee for Discipline Inspection, Ministry of Railways 1990–92; Minister of Railways 1993–98; Deputy Head Leading Group for Beijing-Kowloon Railway Construction 1993–; Procurator-Gen., Supreme People's Procuratorate 1998–2003; Pres. Chinese Asscn of Prosecutors 1998–2003; mem. 14th Cen. Cttee CCP 1992–97, 15th Cen. Cttee CCP 1997–2002 (Deputy Sec. Cen. Comm. for Discipline Inspection 1997–2002); Deputy, 8th NPC 1993–98. *Address:* c/o Chinese Association of Prosecutors, Beijing, People's Republic of China.

HANAFUSA, Hidesaburo, PhD; Japanese biochemist and academic; *Director Emeritus, Osaka Bioscience Institute;* b. 12 Jan. 1929, Nishinomiya; m. Teruko Inoue 1958; one d.; ed Univ. of Osaka; Research Assoc. Research Inst. for Microbial Diseases, Univ. of Osaka 1958–61; Postdoctoral Fellow, Virus Lab. Univ. of Calif., Berkeley 1961–64; Visiting Scientist, Coll. de France, Paris 1964–66; Assoc. mem., Chief, Dept of Viral Oncology, Public Health Research Inst. of New York 1966–68, mem. 1968–73; Prof. Rockefeller Univ. 1973, Leon Hess Prof. 1986; fmr Dir Osaka Bioscience Inst., now Dir Emer.; Foreign Assoc. NAS; mem. Editorial Bd Journal of Virology 1975–, Molecular Cell Biology 1984–; Harvey Lecturer 1980; H. T. Ricketts Award 1981, Albert Lasker Basic Medical Research Award 1982, Clowes Memorial Award 1986, Japan Culture Merit Award 1991, Alfred Sloan Prize 1993, Order of Culture 1995. *Publications:* contrib. on retroviruses and oncogenes to professional journals. *Address:* Osaka Bioscience Institute, 6-2-4 Furuedai, Suita, Osaka, 565-0874, Japan. *Website:* www.obi.or.jp.

HANAWA, Yoshikazu, BA; Japanese business executive; *Advisor and Honorary Chairman, Nissan Motor Company;* b. 14 March 1934, Tokyo; ed Tokyo Univ.; joined Nissan Motor Co. 1957, Pres. Nissan N America 1989, various marketing and planning positions, Exec. Vice-Pres. 1991–96, Pres. 1996–2000, CEO and Chair. 2000–03, Advisor and Hon. Chair. June 2003–. *Address:* Nissan Motor Co., 6-17-1 Ginza chome, Chuo-ku, Tokyo 104-8023, Japan (office). *Telephone:* (3) 3543-5523 (office). *Fax:* (3) 3544-0109 (office). *Website:* www.nissan.co.jp (office).

HANCE, James Henry, Jr, BA, MBA; American business executive; *Chairman, Sprint Nextel Corporation;* b. 16 Sept. 1944, St Joseph, Mo.; ed Westminister Coll., Washington Univ.; Pnr, Price Waterhouse, Charlotte, N Carolina 1968–85; Chair. Consolidated Coin Caterers Corpn 1985–86; Exec. Vice-Pres. and Chief Accounting Officer NCNB Corpn 1987–88; Chief Financial Officer Bank of America Corpn 1988–2004, Vice-Chair. 1993–2005 (retd); mem. Bd of Dirs Sprint Nextel Corpn 2005–, Chair. 2007–; mem. Bd of Dirs Cousins Properties Inc., Duke Energy Corpn, Rayonier Corpn; Sr Advisor, The Carlyle Group 2005–. *Address:* Sprint Nextel Corpn, 6200 Sprint Parkway, Overland Park, KS 66251, USA (office). *Telephone:* (703) 433-4000 (office). *E-mail:* info@sprint.com (office). *Website:* www.sprint.com (office).

HANCHARYK, Uladzimir; Belarusian politician and trade union official; mem. Supreme Council –1996; Co-Founder Consultative and Coordinating Council of Democratic Forces (alliance of opposition parties cr. to contest Presidential elections) 2000; cand. in Presidential Elections 2001; requested the opening of criminal case to investigate malpractice during election, rejected by the Supreme Court 2001; Chair. Fed. of Trade Unions of Belarus –2001; denied registration as candidate in Chamber of Reps election 2004. *Address:* c/o Federation of Trade Unions of Belarus, Prospekt Masherova 21, 220126 Minsk, Belarus (office).

HANCOCK, Herbert (Herbie) Jeffrey, BA; American jazz pianist and composer; b. 12 April 1940, Chicago, Ill.; s. of Wayman Edward Hancock and Winnie Griffin; m. Gudrun Meixner 1968, one d.; ed Grinnell Coll., Iowa, Roosevelt Univ., Chicago, Manhattan School of Music and New School for Social Research; owner and publr Hancock Music Co. 1962–; founder Hancock and Joe Productions 1989–; Pres. Harlem Jazz Music Center, Inc.; performed with Chicago Symphony Orchestra 1952, Coleman Hawkins, Chicago 1960, Donald Byrd 1960–63, Miles Davis Quintet 1963–68; recorded with Chick Corea; composed film music for Blow Up 1966, The Spook Who Sat by the Door 1973, Death Wish 1974, A Soldier's Story 1984, Jo Jo Dancer, Your Life is Calling 1986, Action Jackson 1988, Colors 1988, Harlem Nights 1989, Livin' Large 1991; wrote score and appeared in film Round Midnight 1986 (Acad. Award Best Original Score 1986); TV score for Hey, Hey, Hey, It's Fat Albert (Bill Cosby Special); mem. Nat. Acad. of Recording Arts and Sciences, Jazz Musicians Asscn, Nat. Acad. of TV Arts and Sciences, Broadcast Music; numerous awards including Citation of Achievement, Broadcast Music, Inc. 1963, Jay Award, Jazz Magazine 1964, several awards from Black Music Magazine 1967–71, 5 MTV Awards, Grammy Award for Best Rhythm and Blues Instrumental Performance 1983, 1984, for Best Jazz Instrumental Composition (co-composer) 1987, Best Jazz Instrumental Performance 1995. *Albums include:* Takin' Off 1963, Succotash 1964, Maiden Voyage 1965, Speak Like a Child 1968, Fat Albert Rotunda 1969, Mwandishi 1971, Crossings 1972, Sextant 1972, Headhunters 1973, Thrust 1974, The Best of Herbie Hancock 1974, Man-Child 1975, The Quintet 1977, V.S.O.P. 1977, Sunlight 1978, An Evening with Herbie Hancock and Chick Corea In Concert 1979, Feets Don't Fail Me Now 1979, Monster 1980, Greatest Hits 1980, Lite Me Up 1982, Future Shock 1983, Sound System 1984, Perfect Machine 1988, Jamming 1992, Cantaloupe Island 1994, Tribute to Miles 1994, Dis Is Da Drum 1995, The New Standard 1996, Gershwin's World 1998 (Grammy Award), Night Walker 2000, Future 2 Future 2001, Directions in Music (with others) 2002, River: The Joni Letters (Grammy Awards for Best Album and Best Contemporary Jazz Album 2008) 2007; with Miles Davis Quartet: Miles in the Sky, Nefertiti, Sorcerer, ESP, Miles Davis In Concert (My Funny Valentine), In A Silent Way, Jack Johnson, Seven Steps to Heaven; contrib. to Colour and Light – Jazz Sketches On Sondheim 1995. *Publications:* A Tribute to Miles 1994, Dis is Da Drum 1994, The New Standard 1996, I H with Wayne Shorter 1997, Gershwin's World 1998. *Address:* The Verve Music Group, 1755 Broadway, 3rd Floor, New York, NY 10019, USA (office). *Telephone:* (212) 331-2000 (office). *Fax:* (212) 331-2064 (office). *Website:* www.vervemusicgroup.com (home); www.herbiehancock.com.

HÁNDAL HÁNDAL, William Jacobo; Salvadorean business executive and government official; *Minister of Finance;* b. 31 July 1951; ; ed Southeast Lousiana Univ., Loyola Univ. and Louisiana State Univ., USA; served in several positions at Transportes Aéreos del Continente Americano including Gen. Man. and Vice-Pres. 1975–2006; Pres. Salvadorean Airline Asscn 1978–81; Alt. Dir Latin American Air Transport Asscn 1983–; Vice-Pres. Salvadorean Institute of Tourism 1989–92; Pres. Organizing Cttee, Central American Sporting Games 1994, 2005; Dir Salvadorean Tourism Corpn 2000–06; Minister of Tourism 2000–06, of Finance 2006–. *E-mail:* ijimenez@mh.gob.sv (office); webmaster@mh.gob.sv (office). *Address:* Ministry of Finance, Blvd Los Héreoes, 1231, San Salvador, El Salvador (office). *Telephone:* 2244-3000 (office). *Fax:* 2244-6408 (office). *Website:* www.mh.gob.sv (office).

HANDLEY, Eric Walter, CBE, MA, FBA; British professor of Greek; *Professor of Ancient Literature, Royal Academy of Arts;* b. 12 Nov. 1926, Birmingham; s. of Alfred Walter Handley and A. Doris Cox; m. Carol Margaret Taylor 1952; ed King Edward's School, Birmingham and Trinity Coll., Cambridge; Asst Lecturer in Greek and Latin, Univ. Coll., London 1946–49, Lecturer 1949–61, Reader 1961–67, Prof. 1967–68, Prof. of Greek and Head of Greek Dept 1968–84; Dir of Inst. of Classical Studies, Univ. of London 1967–84; Regius Prof. of Greek, Univ. of Cambridge 1984–94, Fellow of Trinity Coll. 1984–; Prof. of Ancient Literature, Royal Acad. of Arts 1990–; Foreign Sec. British Acad. 1979–88; Pres. Classical Asscn 1984–85, Soc. for the Promotion of Hellenic Studies 1993–96; Hon. Fellow, Univ. Coll., London 1989; Hon. RA; Cromer Greek Prize (jtly) 1958. *Publications:* The Telephus of Euripides (with John Rea) 1958, The Dyskolos of Menander 1965, Relire Ménandre (with A. Hurst) 1990, Aristophane (with J.-M. Bremer) 1993, Images of the Greek Theatre (with Richard Green) 1995; edns of Greek literary papyri, papers in classical journals. *Leisure interests:* walking and travel. *Address:* Trinity College, Cambridge, CB2 1TQ, England (office). *Telephone:* (1223) 338400 (office). *Fax:* (1223) 338564 (office). *Website:* www.trin.cam.ac.uk (office).

HANDLEY, Joseph (Joe); Canadian politician and consultant; *Special Advisor, Pacific & Western Bank of Canada;* b. 9 Aug. 1943, Meadowlake, Sask.; m. Theresa Handley; two c.; Asst Prof., Univ. of BC and Univ. of Manitoba –1985; moved to NWT to assume position of Deputy Minister of Educ. with Govt of NWT 1985; Deputy Minister for Govt of NWT –1999; MLA for Weledeh 1999–, Minister of Finance, Chair. Financial Man. Bd and Minister Responsible for Workers' Compensation Bd 2000, Minister of Transportation and Minister Responsible for NWT Power Corpn 2001, Premier of NWT (retd) 2003–07; Special Advisor, Pacific & Western Bank of Canada 2007–; fmr Official Trustee and Chief Supt Frontier School Div., Manitoba; Queen's Golden Jubilee Medal 2002, Saskatchewan Medal for outstanding achievement 2005, Aboriginal Achievement Award 2008. *Address:* Pacific & Western Bank of Canada, 410 22nd Street E, Suite 950, Saskatoon, Sask. S7K 5T6, Canada (office). *Telephone:* (416) 203-0882 (office). *E-mail:* telm@pwbank.com (office). *Website:* www.pwbank.com (office).

HANDOVER, Richard, CBE; British retail executive; b. 1946; joined W H Smith Group 1964, numerous man. posts within the group including Man. Dir, Our Price Music Ltd 1989, Man. Dir W H Smith News 1995, mem. Bd, W H Smith PLC 1995–2004, CEO 1997–2003, Chair. 2003–04; Chair. Adult Learning Inspectorate; Dir (non-exec.) Nationwide Building Soc., Royal Mail Holdings PLC. *Address:* c/o Royal Mail Group PLC, 148 Old Street, London, EC1V 9HQ, England (office).

HANDS, Terence David (Terry), BA; British theatre director; *Director, Clwyd Theatr Cymru;* b. 9 Jan. 1941, Aldershot; s. of Joseph Ronald and Luise Bertha Hands (née Köhler); m. 1st Josephine Barstow 1964 (divorced 1967); m. 2nd Ludmila Mikael 1975 (divorced 1980); one d.; partner Julia Lintott; two s.; m. 3rd Emma Lucia 2002; ed Woking Grammar School, Birmingham Univ., Royal Acad. of Dramatic Art (RADA), London; Founder-Dir Everyman Theatre, Liverpool 1964–66; Artistic Dir Theatregoround, RSC 1966; Assoc. Dir RSC 1967–77, Jt Artistic Dir 1978–86, Artistic Dir and Chief Exec. 1986–91, Dir Emer. 1991; Dir Clwyd Theatr Cymru 1997–; Consultant Dir Comédie Française 1975–80; Hon. Fellow Shakespeare Inst. 1990, Welsh Coll. of Music and Drama 2002, North East Wales Inst. 2002; Chevalier, Ordre des Arts et Lettres; Hon. DLit (Birmingham) 1988; Hon. LLD (Middx) 1997; Meilleur Spectacle de l'Année for Richard III 1972, for Twelfth Night 1976; Plays and Players Award for Henry VI 1977, Society of West End Theatre Award 1978 and 1984, Pragnell Shakespeare Award 1991, Evening Standard Best Dir Award 1993. *Productions:* over 50 plays with RSC, five with Comédie Française, two with Burgtheater, Vienna, one opera at Paris Opera House, one at Covent Garden, London, one at Bremen, 15 at Clwyd Theatr Cymru; Women Beware Women, Teatro Stabile di Genova, Italy; Arden of Faversham, Schauspielhaus, Zürich; Hamlet, Paris 1994, Merry Wives of Windsor, Oslo 1995, Kongsemnerne 1996, The Seagull 1998; recording: Murder in the Cathedral 1976; trans. (with Barbara Wright): The Balcony (Genet) 1971,

Pleasure and Repentance 1976, Henry V (ed. Sally Beauman) 1976, Cyrano de Bergerac (TV). *Translation:* Hamlet, into French. *Address:* Clwyd Theatr Cymru, Mold, Flintshire, CH7 1YA, N Wales (office). *Telephone:* (1352) 756331 (office). *Fax:* (1352) 701558 (office). *E-mail:* terryhands@clwyd-theatre-cymru.co.uk (office). *Website:* www.clwyd-theatr-cymru.co.uk (office).

HANDY, Nicholas C., PhD, FRS; British professor of chemistry (retd); b. 17 June 1941, Wiltshire; ed St Catherine's Coll., Univ. of Cambridge; Research Fellow, St Catherine's Coll., Univ. of Cambridge 1965–68, Dir of Studies in Math. 1965–95, Fellow, St Catherine's Coll. 1970–, Lecturer in Theoretical Chem. 1977–89, Reader, Quantum Chem., 1989–91, Prof. of Quantum Chem. 1991–2004, Pres. St Catherine's Coll. 1994–97; Visiting Prof. Univ. of Calif., Berkeley, USA 1978–79, 1985, 1994; Visiting Prof., Univ. of Bologna, Italy 1984, Univ. of Sydney, Australia 1986, Univ. of Ga, Athens, GA USA 1988; mem. Int. Acad. of Quantum Molecular Science; Fellow, World Asscn of Theoretically Oriented Chemists (WATOC) 1997–; mem. Editorial Bd numerous journals; Dr hc (Univ. Marne-la-Vallée, France) 2000 Royal Soc. of Chem. Prize in Theoretical Chem. 1987, WATOC Schrödinger Medal 1997, Leverhulme Medal 2002. *Publications:* 320 scientific papers published in journals of physical and theoretical chemistry. *Address:* Department of Chemistry, University of Cambridge, Lensfield Road, Cambridge, CB2 1EW, England (office). *Telephone:* (1223) 336377 (office). *Fax:* (1223) 336362 (office). *E-mail:* nch1@cam.ac.uk (office). *Website:* www.ch.cam.ac.uk/cucl/staff/nch.html (office).

HANEDA, Katsuo; Japanese airline industry executive; *Executive Vice-President, Japan Airlines Corporation;* m. Teiko Haneda; ed Faculty of Econs, Keio Univ.; joined Japan Airlines Co. Ltd 1965, apptd mem. Bd of Dirs 1995, Man. Dir and Sr Vice-Pres., Passenger Marketing 2001–02, Vice-Pres. 2002–03, Pres. 2003–04, Exec. Vice-Pres. Japan Airlines Corpn (holding co. cr. following merger of Japan Airlines and Japan Air Systems 2004) 2004–, Pres. Japan Airlines Int. Co. 2004–, Sr Vice-Pres. Japan Airlines Domestic Co. Ltd 2004–. *Address:* Japan Airlines Corpn, 4-11, Higashi-shinagawa 2-chome, Shinagawa-ku, Tokyo 140-8605, Japan (office). *Telephone:* (3) 5769-6097 (office). *Fax:* (3) 5460-5929 (office). *E-mail:* info@jal.com (office). *Website:* www.jal.com (office).

HANEGBI, Tzahi, BA, LLB; Israeli politician; b. 1957, Jerusalem; m.; three c.; ed Hebrew Univ. of Jerusalem; served in an Israeli Defence Forces paratroopers unit 1974–77; Pres. Hebrew Univ. Student Union 1979–80, Nat. Union of Israeli Students 1980–82; Adviser to Minister of Foreign Affairs 1984–86; Bureau Dir, Prime Minister's Office 1986–88; mem. Likud Party, Knesset (Parl.) 1988–, mem. Knesset Foreign Affairs and Defence Cttee, Cttee on Constitution, Law and Justice, Knesset House Cttee, Cttee on Labour and Social Welfare, Cttee on Educ. and Culture 1988–92; Head (in rotation) Econ. Affairs Cttee; mem. Cttee on Constitution, Law and Justice 1992–96; Minister of Health 1996–97, Minister of Justice 1997–2001, of the Environment 2001–03, of Transport 2002–03, of Public Security 2003–04 (resgnd); left Likud party to join Kadima party Dec. 2005. *Address:* c/o Ministry of Public Security, POB 18182, Jerusalem 91181, Israel (office).

HANEKE, Michael; Austrian (b. German) film director and screenwriter; b. 23 March 1942, Munich, Germany; s. Fritz Haneke and Beatrix von Degenschild; ed Univ. of Vienna; fmr film critic; ed. and dramaturg, Südwestfunk (German TV) 1967–70; directed several stage productions in German, including Strindberg, Goethe and Heinrich von Kleist in Berlin, Munich and Vienna; debut as TV dir in 1973; directed first opera, Mozart's Don Giovanni, Paris 2006; currently Prof. of Directing, Kontaktinformationen Universität für Musik und darstellende Kunst Wien. *Films include:* writer and dir: Der siebente Kontinent (The Seventh Continent) 1989, Benny's Video 1992, 71 Fragmente einer Chronologie des Zufalls (71 Fragments of a Chronology of Chance) 1994, Lumière et compagnie (Lumière and Company, segment 'Michael Haneke/Vienne') 1995, Funny Games 1997 (remade 2007), Das Schloß (The Castle) 1997, Code inconnu: Récit incomplet de divers voyages (Code Unknown: Incomplete Tales of Several Journeys) 2000, La pianiste (The Piano Teacher) (Grand Prize, Best Actor and Actress Awards, Cannes Film Festival 2001) 2001, Le temps du loup (The Time of the Wolf) 2003, Caché (Hidden) 2005; actor: Charms Zwischenfälle (Charm's Incidents) 1996. *Television includes:* writer and dir: After Liverpool 1974, Sperrmüll 1976, Drei Wege zum See 1976, Lemminge, Teil 1 Arkadien 1979, Lemminge, Teil 2 Verletzungen 1979, Variation 1983, Wer war Edgar Allan? 1984, Fraulein 1986, Nachruf für einen Mörder 1991, Die Rebellion 1993. *Address:* Universität für Musik und darstellende Kunst Wien, Anton-von-Webern-Platz 1, 1030 Vienna, Austria. *Website:* www.mdw.ac.at/I111/html/regie_prof3.htm.

HANEKOM, Derek; South African politician; *Member of Parliament;* b. 1953; mem. African Nat. Congress (ANC); fmr ANC Co-ordinator of Land and Agricultural Devt; MP 1994–, Minister of Land Affairs 1994–99, of Agric. 1996–99; arrested 1977 for protesting against detentions, imprisoned for ANC activities 1983–86; in exile in Zimbabwe 1987–90 Chair. Man. Cttee Nat. Rural Devt Forum;; Free Market Award 2002. *Address:* c/o Ministry of Agriculture and Land Affairs, Private Bag X844, Pretoria 0001, South Africa.

HANFT, Ruth, PhD, ScD; American health policy consultant; b. 12 July 1929; d. of Max Samuels and Ethel Schechter; m. Herbert Hanft 1951; one s. one d.; ed School of Industrial and Labor Relations, Cornell Univ., Hunter Coll. and George Washington Univ.; Social Science Analyst, US Social Security Admin., Washington, DC 1964–66; Program Analyst, Office of Econ. Opportunity 1966–68, US Dept of Health, Educ. and Welfare 1968–72; Sr Research Assoc., Inst. of Medicine, NAS 1972–76; Deputy Asst Sec., US Dept of Health and Human Services 1977–81; health policy consultant 1981–88; Visiting Prof., Dartmouth Medical School 1976–; Consultant and Research Prof., Dept of Health Services and Admin., George Washington Univ. 1988–91, Prof. 1991–95, consultant 1995–; mem. Inst. of Medicine, NAS, Nat. Acad. of Social Insurance; Fellow, Hastings Inst., Acad. of Health Research and Policy; Walter Patenge Medal of Public Service. *Publications:* Hospital Cost Containment (with M. Zubkoff and I. Raskin) 1978, Improving Health Care Management in the Workplace (with J. Rossow and R. Zager) 1985, Physicians and Hospitals: Changing Dynamics in The Health Policy Agenda (ed. M. Lewin) 1985; Human In Vitro Fertilization; Political, Legal and Ethical Issues, in Gynecology and Obstetrics Vol. 5 Chapter 98 1984, Technology in American Health Care (with Alan B. Cohen) 2004; articles in professional journals. *Leisure interests:* gardening, needlepoint, travel, painting. *Address:* 606 Rainier Road, Charlottesville, VA 22903-4045, USA. *Telephone:* (434) 295-8674 (home). *Fax:* (434) 295-8675 (home). *E-mail:* hrhanft@embarqmail.com (office); hrhanft@aol.com (home).

HANGST, Jeffrey Scott, SB, SM, PhD; American physicist and academic; *Professor of Physics, University of Århus;* b. Pa; ed Massachusetts Inst. of Tech., Univ. of Chicago; Assoc. Prof., later Prof. Dept of Physics and Astronomy, Univ. of Århus; Physics Co-ordinator ATHENA Experiment, CERN, Geneva, Switzerland, Spokesperson, ALPHA Experiment 2004–; Fellow, American Physical Soc.; European Physical Soc. Accelerator Prize 1996. *Address:* Department of Physics and Astronomy, University of Århus, Ny Munkegade, Århus C 8000, Denmark (office). *Telephone:* 89-42-37-51 (office). *Fax:* 86-12-07-40 (office). *E-mail:* hangst@phys.au.dk (office). *Website:* www.phys.au.dk (office).

HANIEL, Franz Markus; German business executive; *Chairman of the Supervisory Board, Franz Haniel & Cie GmbH;* b. 1955; career in family-owned co. Franz Haniel & Cie GmbH, Chair. Supervisory Bd 2003–04, 2007–; mem. Bd of Dirs Giesecke & Devrient GmbH; mem. Supervisory Bd BMW AG 2004–, Security Networks (Secunet) AG 2004–. *Address:* Franz Haniel & Cie GmbH, Franz-Haniel-Platz 1, 47119 Duisberg, Germany (office). *Telephone:* (203) 8060 (office). *Fax:* (203) 806622 (office). *E-mail:* jstolle@haniel.de (office). *Website:* www.haniel.de (office).

HANIF ATMAR, Mohammed, BA, MA; Afghan politician; *Minister of Interior Affairs;* b. 1968, Laghman Prov.; s. of Mohammad Asef Atmar; ed Univ. of York, UK; adviser to aid agencies in Afghanistan and Pakistan 1992–94; Program Man. Norwegian Cttee for Afghanistan 1994–2000; Deputy Dir-Gen. Int. Rescue Cttee 2000–02; Minister of Rural Rehabilitation and Devt 2002–06, of Educ. 2006–08, of Interior Affairs 2008–. *Publications:* Development of Non-Governmental Organizations in Developing Countries, From Rhetoric to Reality, Humanitarian Aid, War and Peace in Afghanistan: What to Learn?, Politics and Humanitarian Aid in Afghanistan and its Aftermath for the People of Afghanistan, Afghanistan or a Stray War in Afghanistan. *Address:* Ministry of Interior Affairs, Shar-i-Nau, Kabul, Afghanistan (office). *Telephone:* (20) 32441 (office).

HANIN, Roger; French actor and director; b. (Roger Paul Lévy), 23 Oct. 1925, Algiers; s. of Joseph Lévy and Victorine Hanin; m. 2nd Christine Gouze-Renal 1959; one d.; ed Faculté Mixte de Médecine et de Pharmacie, Algiers; Dir Pau Festival; producer, Lucrèce Borgia 1979 (play); author and producer, Argent mon bel amour (play) 1983; numerous stage and TV appearances, including Shakespearean roles; Chevalier, Ordre nat. du Mérite; Dramatic Art Grand Prize, Enghiem 1972, Médaille Achir, Algeria 2000. *Films include:* Le Protecteur (also dir) 1973, Big Guns 1974, L'Intrépide 1975, Le Faux Cul (also dir) 1975, Le coup de Sirocco, Le Sucre 1978, Le Grand Pardon 1981, La Baraka 1982, L'Etincelle 1984, La Galette du Roi 1985, Train d'enfer (also dir) 1985, Dernier été à Tanger 1986, La Rumba (also dir) 1987, L'Orchestre Rouge 1989, Jean Galmot, aventurier 1990, Le Grand Pardon II 1992, Le Nombril du Monde 1993. *Television includes:* Palace (miniseries) 1988, Les Grandes familles (miniseries) 1989, Navarro (series) 1989, L'Éternel mari 1993, Le Misanthrope 1994, Samson le magnifique 1995, Une femme explosive 1996, Maître Da Costa (series) 1997, La Femme du boulanger 1999, Bier: Anschlag auf das Oktoberfest 1999, Trilogie marseillaise: La Marius 2000, Fanny 2000, César 2000, Anibal 2000, L'Étrange monsieur Joseph 2001, Ne meurs pas 2003, Mademoiselle Navarro 2005. *Publications:* plays: Ciel, où sont passées les dattes de tes oasis? 1968, Virgule 1974; books: L'Ours en lambeaux 1981, Le Voyage d'Arsène 1985, Les Gants Blancs 1994, L'hotel de la vieille lune 1998, Dentelles 2000, Lettre à un ami mystérieux 2001. *Leisure interests:* basketball, table-tennis, water-polo, boxing. *Address:* 9 rue du Boccador, 75008 Paris, France.

HANIYA, Ismail Abd as-Salam Ahmad, BA; Palestinian politician; b. 1962, Gaza; m.; 12 c.; ed Islamic Univ. of Gaza; jailed by Israelis for three years, released 1992 and deported to Lebanon; returned to Gaza 1993; Dean, Islamic Univ. of Gaza 1993–97; Head of Office of Sheikh Ahmed Yassin (Hamas spiritual leader) 1997–2004; Prime Minister, Palestinian Nat. Authority (Hamas) 2006–07 (resgnd), March–June 2007 (under unity govt), also Minister of the Interior May–June 2007. *Address:* c/o Islamic Resistance Movement (Hamas: Harakat al-Muqawama al-Islamiyya), Gaza Palestinian Autonomous Areas.

HANKEL, Wilhelm; German economist and professor; b. 10 Jan. 1929, Danzig; s. of Oskar and Jenny (née Schoffmann) Hankel; m. Uta Wömpner; three d.; ed Univ. of Mainz and Univ. of Amsterdam, Netherlands; worked in Cen. Planning Bureau of Netherlands Govt 1951; subsequently joined Deutsche Bundesbank; served in Ministry of Econ. Co-operation and later in Foreign Ministry 1954–57; with Berliner Bank, Berlin and Kreditanstalt für Wiederaufbau, Frankfurt am Main 1957–68; Dir Money and Credit Dept, Fed. Ministry of the Economy and Finance 1968–72; Pres. Hessische Landesbank, Girozentrale, Frankfurt am Main 1972–74; Lecturer, Univ. of Frankfurt 1966–70, Hon. Prof. 1971–; Monetary Adviser EEC, Brussels

1974–76; Visiting Prof., Harvard, Georgetown and Johns Hopkins Univs, USA and Wissenschaftszentrum, Berlin. *Publications:* Die zweite Kapitalverteilung 1961, Währungspolitik 1971, Heldensagen der Wirtschaft oder schöne heile Wirtschaftswelt 1975, Der Ausweg aus der Krise 1976, Weltwirtschaft 1977, Caesar 1978, Gegenkurs, von der Schuldenkrise zur Vollbeschaftigung 1984, Keynes, Die Entschlüsselung des Kapitalismus 1986, Vorsicht, unser Geld 1989, Eine Mark für Deutschland 1990, Dollar und Ecu, Leitwährungen im Wettstreit 1992, Die sieben Todsünden der deutschen Vereinigung 1993, Das grosse Geldtheater 1995, Die Euro-Klage. Warum die Währungsunion scheitern muss (jtly.) 1998; various articles, lectures, etc. *Leisure interests:* literature, music. *Address:* Berghausenerstrasse 190, 53639 Königswinter 21, Germany. *Telephone:* (2244) 7447.

HANKEN, James, AB, PhD; American zoologist and academic; *Alexander Agassiz Professor of Zoology, Curator in Herpetology and Director, Museum of Comparative Zoology, and Professor of Biology, Department of Organismic and Evolutionary Biology, Harvard University;* b. 14 July 1952, New York City; m. Sally Hanken 1984; one s. one d.; ed Univ. of California, Berkeley; Post-doctoral studies at Dalhousie Univ., NS, Canada; then faculty position, Univ. of Colorado, Boulder; Prof. of Biology, Dept of Organismic and Evolutionary Biology and faculty mem. Center for Health and the Global Environment, Harvard Medical School, Harvard Univ. 1999–, currently Alexander Agassiz Prof. of Zoology, Curator in Herpetology and Dir Museum of Comparative Zoology; mem. US Nat. Cttee for the Int. Union of Biological Sciences; Past Pres. Int. Soc. of Vertebrate Morphologists; fmr Chair. Int. Bd of Dirs Declining Amphibian Populations Task Force; fmr Co-Chair. Scientific Advisory Bd Consortium for the Barcode of Life; Fellow, AAAS; mem. Soc. for Study of Evolution, Soc. for Integrative and Comparative Biology, Herpetologists League; von Hofsten Lecturer, Uppsala Univ., Sweden, Gompertz Lecture in Integrative Biology, Univ. of California, Berkeley. *Achievements inlcude:* nature and scientific photographer whose photographs appear in several books, field guides and magazines, including Natural History, Geo, Audubon and National Geographic World;. *Publications:* Skull, Vol. 1: Development 1993, Skull, Vol. 2: Patterns of Structural and Systematic Diversity 1993, Skull, Vol. 3: Functional and Evolutionary Mechanisms 1993; has edited four books and published more than 100 scientific papers in professional journals on the evolutionary morphology, development and systematics of vertebrates, especially amphibians. *Address:* 109C Museum of Comparative Zoology, Herpetology Department, 26 Oxford Street, Cambridge, MA 02138, USA (office). *Telephone:* (617) 495-2496 (office). *Fax:* (617) 495-5667 (office). *E-mail:* hanken@oeb.harvard.edu (office). *Website:* www.oeb.harvard.edu/faculty/hanken/public_html (office); www.eol.org/content/page/bio_jhanken.

HANKES, Sir Claude, KCVO; British strategist and financial adviser; b. 8 March 1949; with Robert Fleming & Co. Ltd 1972–77, Dir 1974–77; Chair. Man. Cttee Price Waterhouse and Partners 1983–89, Action Resource Centre 1986–91; Adviser to the Bd Corange (Boehringer Mannheim) 1988–94; mem. Gov. Council, Business in the Community 1986–91, Pres.'s Cttee 1988–91; Deputy Chair. Leutwiler and Partners Ltd 1992–96; Chair. Shaw & Bradley 1993–; Interim Chair. Roland Berger Strategy Consultants Ltd 2003–05; assisted Dr Fritz Leutwiler in his role as ind. mediator between S African Govt and foreign banks 1985–86; Nobel Ind. Report 1991; Chair. Advisory Cttee to Jordan on Strategic Econ. Policy Matters 1993–94; Adviser to Iraq 2003, to Iraq Governing Council 2003–04, to Iraq (on macro-strategic issues) 2005–06; Sr Advisor to Trade Bank of Iraq 2007–; Trustee, Windsor Leadership Trust 1998–2007 (Chair. 2000–07); Trustee and adviser, St George's House, Windsor Castle 2000–06, Hon. Fellow and Life mem. of the Council 2006–; Hon. Fellow, Corpus Christi Coll., Oxford, Coll. of St George, Windsor Castle 2002–06 (Hon. mem. 2006–). *Publication:* The Dangers of the Banking System: Funding Country Deficits 1975. *Leisure interests:* hiking, surfing, photography. *Address:* 1 Berkeley Street, London, W1J 8JD, England (office). *Telephone:* (20) 7016-9181 (office). *Fax:* (20) 7016-9143 (office).

HANKS, Tom; American actor and film producer; b. 9 July 1956, Oakland, Calif.; m. 1st Samantha Lewes 1978 (divorced 1985); two c.; m. 2nd Rita Wilson 1988; two s.; ed California State Univ.; began acting career with Great Lakes Shakespeare Festival; mem. Acad. of Motion Picture Arts and Sciences, mem. Bd of Govs 2001–, Vice-Pres. 2005–; American Film Inst. Lifetime Achievement Award 2002. *Films include:* Splash 1984, Bachelor Party 1984, The Man with One Red Shoe 1985, Volunteers 1985, The Money Pit 1986, Nothing in Common 1986, Every Time We Say Goodbye 1986, Dragnet 1987, Big 1988, Punch Line 1988, The Burbs 1989, Turner & Hooch 1989, Joe Versus the Volcano 1990, The Bonfire of the Vanities 1990, A League of Their Own 1992, Sleepless in Seattle 1993, Philadelphia (Acad. Award for Best Actor 1994) 1993, Forrest Gump (Acad. Award for Best Actor 1995) 1994, Apollo 13 1995, Toy Story (voice) 1995, That Thing You Do (also dir) 1996, Turner & Hooch 1997, Saving Private Ryan 1998, You've Got Mail 1998, The Green Mile 1999, Toy Story 2 (voice) 1999, Cast Away (also producer) 2000, Road to Perdition 2002, My Big Fat Greek Wedding (producer) 2002, Catch Me If You Can 2003, The Ladykillers 2004, Connie and Carla (producer) 2004, The Terminal 2004, Elvis Has Left the Building 2004, The Polar Express (also exec. producer) 2004, Da Vinci Code 2006, Cars (voice) 2006, Neil Young: Heart of Gold (producer) 2006, The Ant Bully (producer) 2006, Starter for Ten (producer) 2006, Charlie Wilson's War 2007, The Great Buck Howard 2008, Angels & Demons 2009. *Television includes:* Bosom Buddies (series) 1980–81, From the Earth to the Moon (miniseries, also exec. producer) 1999, West Point (series, producer) 2000, We Stand Alone Together (exec. producer) 2001, Band of Brothers (miniseries, also exec. producer) 2001, My Big Fat Greek Life (exec. producer) 2003, Freedom: A History of Us 2003, We're with the Band (producer) 2005, Big Love (exec. producer) 2006–07. *Address:* 8383 Wilshire Blvd, Suite 500, Beverly Hills, CA 90211 (office); Creative Artists Agency, 9830 Wilshire Boulevard, Beverly Hills, CA 90212-1825, USA (office). *Telephone:* (310) 288-4545 (office). *Fax:* (310) 288-4800 (office). *Website:* www.caa.com (office).

HANLEY, Rt Hon. Sir Jeremy James, KCMG, PC, FCA; British business executive, politician and chartered accountant; b. 17 Nov. 1945, Amersham, Bucks.; s. of the late Jimmy Hanley and Dinah Sheridan; m. 1st Helene Mason 1968 (divorced 1973); one s.; m. 2nd Verna, Viscountess Villiers (née Stott) 1973; one s. one step d.; ed Rugby School; with Peat Marwick Mitchell & Co. 1963–66; Dir Anderson Thomas Frankel (ATF) 1969, Man. Dir ATF (Jersey and Ireland) 1970–73; Deputy Chair. The Financial Training Co. Ltd 1973–90; Sec. Park Place PLC 1977–83; Chair. Fraser Green Ltd 1986–90; Parl. Adviser to ICA 1986–90; Conservative MP for Richmond and Barnes 1983–97; Parl. Under-Sec. of State, Northern Ireland Office 1990–93; Minister for Health, Social Security and Agric. 1990–92, for Political Devt, Community Relations and Educ. 1992–93; Minister of State for the Armed Forces, Ministry of Defence 1993–94; Cabinet Minister without Portfolio 1995; Chair. Conservative Party 1994–95; Foreign Office Minister of State for the Middle East and Hong Kong 1995–97; Chair. AdVal Group PLC, Int. Trade and Investment Missions Ltd 1998–2002; Dir ITE Group PLC 1996–, GTECH Corpn, USA 2001–06; currently Chair. UK Corporate Governance Cttee; Consultant to Bd Lottomatica; Dir Arab-British Chamber of Commerce 1998–; Chair. British Iran Chamber of Commerce 2000 (Vice-Pres. 2001–06), Brain Games Network PLC 2000–01; Dir European Advisory Bd 2004–05, Calyon (fmrly Crédit Lyonnais) 2000–05, Nymex Europe Ltd 2005–, Blue Hackle Ltd 2006–, Willis Group Holdings Inc. 2006–; Deputy Chair. Langbar International 2006–; mem. British-American Parl. Group 1983–97, Anglo-French Parl. Group 1983–97, CPA 1983–97, IPU 1983–97, British-Irish Interparl. Body 1990, Advisory Bd Talal Abu-Ghazaleh Int.; Vice-Chair. Nat. Anglo-West Indian Conservative Soc. 1982–83; Chair. Conservative Candidates Asscn 1982–83; mem. Bow Group 1974–, European Movt 1974–, Mensa 1968–; Freeman City of London 1989; Master (2005–06) and mem. Court of Assts Worshipful Co. of Chartered Accountants. *Leisure interests:* cookery, chess, cricket, languages, theatre, cinema, music, golf. *Address:* 6 Butts Mead, Northwood, Middx, HA6 2TL, England (home). *Telephone:* (1923) 826675. *Fax:* (1923) 836447 (home). *E-mail:* jeremy@hanley.com (home).

HANLON, Lt-Gen. Edward, BS, MS; American military officer (retd); *President, Raytheon International, Inc. Europe;* ed Southeastern Okla Univ., Pepperdine Univ., Univ. of Minn., Officer Candidates School, Quantico; commissioned Second Lt 1967; posts have included Exec. Officer and Fire Direction Officer 1st Bn, 13th Marines, Vietnam 1968–69, Asst S-3 Legal Officer and Public Affairs Officer, Marine Corps HQ 1969–72, Bn S-4 2nd Bn, later CO E Battery, 12th Marines 1973–74, Exec. Officer Training Support Co., CO Enlisted Instructor Co. and Exec. Officer Company M, The Basic School, Quantico 1974–77, Marine Officer Instructor and Exec. Officer, Naval Reserve Officers Training Course Unit, Univ. of Minn. 1977–80, Bn S-4 2nd Bn, Exec. Officer 3rd Bn and Div. Staff Sec., 1st Marine Div., Camp Pendleton 1981–84, CO 3rd Bn, 12th Marines 1984–85, Dir of Personal Services Marine Corps Recruit Depot, San Diego 1985–86, Asst Chief of Staff for Plans and Operations, HQ Fleet Marine Force Europe, London 1987–90, Atlantic Fleet Marine Officer 1990–92, CO 10th Marines, 2nd Marine Div. 1992–93, promoted to Brig.-Gen. 1993, Deputy Commdr Naval Striking and Support Forces Southern Europe, Naples, Italy 1993–96, promoted to Maj.-Gen. 1996, Dir Expeditionary Warfare Div. 1996–98, Commanding Gen. Marine Corps Base, Camp Pendleton 1998–2001, promoted to Lt-Gen. 2001, Commanding Gen. Marine Corps Combat Devt Command, Quantico and Deputy Commandant Combat Devt, Marine Corps HQ 2001–04; Mil. Rep. to NATO 2004–06; Pres. Raytheon International Inc. Europe 2007–; Defense Superior Service Medal with oak leaf, Legion of Merit with two gold stars, Defense Meritorious Service Medal, Meritorious Service Medal, Navy and Marine Corps Commendation Medal with Combat "V" and gold star, Combat Action Ribbon. *Address:* Raytheon International, 870 Winter Street, Waltham, MA, 02451, USA (office). *Website:* www.raytheon.com (office).

HANNAH, Daryl; American actress; b. 3 Dec. 1960, Chicago, Ill.; ed Univ. of Calif., Los Angeles; studied with Stella Adler; studied ballet with Marjorie Tallchief; appeared on TV in Paper Dolls. *Films:* The Fury 1978, The Final Terror, Hard Country, Blade Runner, Summer Lovers, Splash, The Pope of Greenwich Village, Reckless, Clan of the Cave Bear, Legal Eagles, Roxanne, Wall Street, High Spirits, Steel Magnolias, Crazy People, At Play in the Fields of the Lord, Memoirs of an Invisible Man, Grumpy Old Men, Attack of the 50 ft Woman, The Tie That Binds, Grumpier Old Men 1995, Two Much 1996, The Last Days of Frankie the Fly 1996, Wild Flowers 1999, My Favorite Martian 1999, Dancing at the Blue Iguana 2000, Cord 2000, Speedway Junky 2001, Jackpot 2001, A Walk to Remember 2002, Hard Cash 2002, Northfork 2002, Kill Bill Vol. I 2003, Kill Bill: Vol. 2 2004, Yo puta 2004, Silver City 2004, Careful What You Wish For 2004, Love is the Drug 2006, Keeping Up with the Steins 2006, Olé 2006, The Poet 2007, The Cycle 2008, Vice (also producer) 2008; Dir, Writer, Producer: The Last Supper (Berlin Int. Film Festival Jury Award for Best Short) 1994; Dir: A Hundred and One Nights 1995. *Play:* The Seven Year Itch 2000. *Address:* dhlovelife, 1112 Montana Ave, #721, Santa Monica, CA 90403; Columbia Plaza Producers, Building 8-153, Burbank, CA 91505, USA. *E-mail:* dhlovelife@yahoo.com.

HANNAH, John; British actor; b. 23 April 1962, Glasgow; s. of John Hannah and Susan Hannah; m. Joanna Roth; two c.; ed Royal Scottish Acad. of Music and Drama; fmrly electrician; worked with Workers' Theatre Co. *Television includes:* Bookie 1987, Brond 1987, Paul Calf's Video Diary 1993, Milner 1994, Faith 1994, Pauline Calf's Wedding Video 1994, McCallum (series) 1995, Out of the Blue (series) 1995, Truth or Dare 1996, Circles of Deceit: Kalon 1996, The Love Bug 1997, Rebus: Black and Blue 2000, Rebus: The Hanging Garden

2000, Rebus: Dead Souls 2001, Dr. Jekyll and Mr. Hyde 2002, MDs (series) 2002, Amnesia 2004, Rebus: Mortal Causes 2004, Marple: 4.50 from Paddington 2004, Cold Blood 2005, Ghost Son 2006, New Street Law 2006–07. *Films include:* Harbour Beat 1990, Four Weddings and a Funeral 1994, The Final Cut 1995, Madagascar Skin 1995, The Innocent Sleep 1996, The James Gang 1997, Sliding Doors 1998, Resurrection Man 1998, So This Is Romance? 1998, The Mummy 1999, The Hurricane 1999, The Intruder 1999, Circus 2000, Pandaemonium 2000, The Mummy Returns 2001, Before You Go 2002, I'm with Lucy 2002, I Accuse 2003, Male Mail 2004, The Last Legion 2007, The Mummy: Tomb of the Dragon Emperor 2008. *Address:* c/o William Morris Agency, Inc., 1 William Morris Place, Beverly Hills, CA 90212, USA.

HANNAY OF CHISWICK, Baron (Life Peer), cr. 2001, of Chiswick, of Bedford Park in the London Borough of Ealing; **David Hugh Alexander Hannay,** GCMG, CH, MA; British diplomatist; b. 28 Sept. 1935, London; s. of Julian Hannay and Eileen Hannay; m. Gillian Rosemary Rex 1961; four s.; ed Craigflower School, Torryburn, Fife, Scotland, Winchester Coll. and New Coll. Oxford; Second Lt, King's Royal Irish Hussars 1954–56; Persian language student, Foreign Office and British Embassy, Tehran 1959–61; Oriental Sec., British Embassy, Kabul 1961–63; Second Sec., Eastern Dept, Foreign Office, London 1963–65; Second, then First Sec., UK Del. to EC, Brussels 1965–70, First Sec. UK Negotiating Team 1970–72; Chef de Cabinet to Sir Christopher Soames, Vice-Pres. of the EC Comm. 1973–77; Counsellor, Head of Energy, Science and Space Dept, FCO, London 1977–79, Counsellor, Head of Middle East Dept 1979, Asst Under-Sec. of State (EC) 1979–84; Minister, Embassy in Washington, DC 1984–85; UK Perm. Rep. to EC 1985–90, to UN 1990–95; British Govt Special Rep. for Cyprus 1996–2003; Prime Minister's Personal Envoy to Turkey and EU Special Rep. for Cyprus 1998; Life Peer (Ind.), House of Lords 2001–; mem. UN Sec. Gen.'s High Level Panel on Threats, Challenges and Change 2003–04, House of Lords EU Select Cttee 2002–06, House of Lords Local Governmental Orgs Cttee 2007–; Chair. Int. Advisory Bd EDHEC 2003–, UN Asscn of the UK 2006–; Vice-Chair. All Party Parl. Group on UN 2005–, on Europe 2006–; Dir (non-exec.) Chime Communications 1996–2006, Aegis 2000–03; mem. Court and Council, Univ. of Birmingham 1998–2006, Pro-Chancellor 2001–06; mem. Council of Britain in Europe 1999–2005, Bd Salzburg Seminar 2002–05, TANGGUH Int. Advisory Panel 2002–, Advisory Bd Judge Business Schools 2004; Gov. Ditchley Foundation 2005–; Hon. Fellow, New Coll. Oxford; Hon. DLitt (Birmingham). *Publication:* Britain's Entry into the European Community: Report on the Negotiations (ed.) 1970–72, Cyprus: The Search for a Solution 2004, A More Secure World: Our Shared Responsibility (UN Panel Report) 2004, New World Disorder: The UN After the Cold War 2008. *Leisure interests:* gardening, travel, photography. *Address:* 3 The Orchard, London, W4 1JZ, England (home). *Telephone:* (20) 8987-9012 (home). *Fax:* (20) 8987-9012 (home).

HANNIBALSSON, Jón Baldvin, MA (Econ); Icelandic politician, diplomatist and academic; *University Lecturer, University of Iceland and University of Bifrost;* b. 21 Feb. 1939, Ísafjörður; s. of Hannibal Valdimarsson and Sólveig Ólafsdóttir; m. Bryndís Schram 1959; one s. three d.; ed Menntaskólinn í Reykjavík, Univ. of Edinburgh, UK, Nationalökonomiska Inst., Stockholm, Sweden, Univ. of Iceland and Harvard Univ., USA; teacher in secondary school, Reykjavík 1964–70; journalist, Frjáls thjóð, Reykjavík 1964–67; Founder and Rector Ísafjörður Coll. 1970–79; Chief Ed. Althýðublaðið, Reykjavík 1979–82; mem. Althingi (Parl.) 1982–98; Chair. SDP 1984–96; Minister of Finance 1987–88, for Foreign Affairs and Foreign Trade 1988–95; Chair. Council of Ministers, EFTA 1989, 1992, 1994; Amb. to USA (also accred to Mexico, Brazil, Chile and Argentina) 1998–2002, to Finland (also accred to Estonia, Latvia, Lithuania and Ukraine) 2002–05; Univ. Lecturer, Univ. of Iceland 2005–, Univ. of Bifrost 2005–; Hon. Citizen of Vilnius, Lithuania 1996; Order of Terra Marina, Estonia 1996, Order of Grand Duke Gediminas, Lithuania 1996, Order of Pres. of Latvia 1996, Order of Prince Trpimir and Croatian Morning Star 2001, Presidential Order of Merit, Slovenia. *Television:* Dialogue with Jón Baldvin (TV-2) 1997. *Publications:* Who Owns Iceland? 1985, Economic Strategy for Social Democrats (co-author) 1986, The Icelandic Tax Reform 1987, Iceland and the Baltic Nations' Struggle for Independence 1998, The Age of Extremes 2000, Iceland in a New Century (co-author) 2000, Expectations and Disappointments of the 20th Century 2001, Contemporary Issues (co-author) 2002, Tilhugalíf (Honeymoon, political memoirs) 2002, The Welfare State and its Enemies 2004, The International Financial Crisis: The Case of Iceland - Are There Lessons to be Learnt?. *Leisure interests:* reading, swimming, travel. *Address:* Krosshóll v/ Engjaveg, 270 Mosó, Iceland (home). *Telephone:* 566-6362 (home); 895-6362 (home). *E-mail:* jon.baldvin@simnet.is (home).

HANRAHAN, Paul T.; American energy industry executive; *President and CEO, AES Corporation;* b. 1957; ed Harvard Business School, US Naval Acad.; active service in USN; various man. roles with AES Corpn in USA, Europe and Asia including Gen. Man. AES Transpower Inc. 1990–93, Exec. Vice-Pres., CEO and Sec. AES China Generating Co. (Chigen) 1993–95, Pres. and CEO 1995–98, Vice-Pres. AES 1994–97, Sr Vice-Pres. 1997, CEO and Exec. Vice-Pres. 1997–2002, Pres. and CEO 2002–. *Address:* AES Headquarters, 1001 North 19th Street, Arlington, VA 22209, USA (office). *Telephone:* (703) 522-1315 (office). *Fax:* (703) 528-4510 (office). *Website:* www.aes.com (office).

HANS-ADAM II, HSH Prince of Liechtenstein (Duke of Troppau and Jägerndorf, Count of Rietberg); b. 14 Feb. 1945, Zürich, Switzerland; s. of the late Prince Franz Josef II and Princess Gina; m. Countess Marie Aglaë Kinsky von Wchinitz und Tettau 1967; three s. (including Hereditary Prince Alois Philipp Maria) one d.; ed Schottengymnasium, Vienna, School of Econs and Social Sciences, St Gallen, Switzerland; Chief Exec. of Prince of Liechtenstein Foundation 1970–84; took over exec. authority of Liechtenstein Aug. 1984; transferred exec. power to Hereditary Prince Alois Aug. 2004. *Address:* Schloss Vaduz, 9490 Vaduz, Principality of Liechtenstein. *E-mail:* office@fuerstenhaus.li (office). *Website:* www.fuerstenhaus.li.

HÄNSCH, Theodor W., PhD; German physicist and academic; *Director, Max-Planck-Institut für Quantenoptik;* b. 1941, Heidelberg; ed Helmholtz-Gymnasium, Heidelberg, Univ. of Heidelberg; Asst Prof. Inst. of Applied Physics, Univ. of Heidelberg 1969–70; NATO Postdoctoral Fellow Stanford Univ. 1970–72, Assoc. Prof. of Physics 1972–75, Prof. of Physics 1975–86; Dir Max-Planck-Institut für Quantenoptik (Exec. Dir 1993–96, 2003–04) 1986–, Prof. Ludwig-Maximilians-Universität München 1986–, Chair. Physics Dept 2001–02; Visiting Prof. College de France 1978, Univ. of Kyoto 1979, Univ. of Florence 1979, 1995, Fudan Univ. 1982, Ecole Normale Superieure, Paris 1992; Fellow American Physical Soc., Optical Soc. of America; mem. Editorial Bd Applied Physics B, Physics in Perspective, Springer Series in Optical Sciences, Laser Physics Review; mem. American Acad. of Arts and Sciences, Bavarian Acad. of Arts and Sciences, Berlin-Brandenburg Acad. of Sciences; Bundesverdienstkreuz 1. Klasse, Bayerischer Maximiliansorden; Calif. Museum of Science and Industry Calif. Scientist of the Year 1973, Alexander von Humboldt Sr US Scientist Award 1977, Freie Universität Berlin Otto Klung Prize 1980, NAS Cyrus B. Comstock Prize 1983, American Physical Soc. Herbert P. Broida Prize 1983, Optical Soc. of America William F. Meggers Award 1985, Franklin Inst. Michelson Medal 1986, Italgas Prize for Research and Innovation 1987, Deutsche Forschungsgemeinschaft Gottfried Wilhelm Leibniz Preis 1988, King Faisal Int. Prize for Science 1989, Einstein Medal for Laser Science 1995, American Physical Soc. Arthur L. Schawlow Prize for Laser Science 1996, Philip Morris Research Prize 1998, 2000, Deutsche Physikalische Gesellschaft Stern-Gerlach Medal 2000, Laser Inst. of America Arthur L. Schawlow Award 2000, European Physical Soc. Quantum Electronics and Optics Prize 2001, Int. Union of Pure and Applied Physics SUNAMCO Medal 2001, Italian Nat. Acad. of Sciences Matteucci-Medal 2002, Alfried Krupp Prize for Science 2002, IEEE I. I. Rabi Award 2005, Optical Soc. of America Frederic Ives Medal 2005, Otto-Hahn-Prize for Chemistry and Physics 2005, Nobel Prize in Physics (jtly) 2005. *Publications:* numerous articles. *Address:* Schellingstr. 4/III, 80799 Munich, Germany (office). *Telephone:* (89) 2180-3212 (office). *Fax:* (89) 285192 (office). *E-mail:* t.w.haensch@physik.uni-muenchen.de (office). *Website:* www.mpq.mpg.de/~haensch (office).

HANSEID, Einar; Norwegian journalist (retd); b. 19 Nov. 1943, Sandefjord; m. Mari Onsrud 1977; two s.; reporter, Sandefjords Blad 1965; News Ed. Dagbladet 1974; Chief Ed. Hjem & Fritid 1982; Man. Ed. Verdens Gang 1984, Chief Ed. 1987–93; Chief Ed. Aftenposten 1994–2003. *Address:* Schibsted Asa, Apotekergaten 10, POB 490 Sentrum, N- 0105 Oslo, Norway.

HANSEN, Barbara C., PhD; American professor of physiology and university administrator; *Professor of Physiology and Director, Obesity and Diabetes Research Center and Director, Obesity, Diabetes and Aging Animal Resource, and Director of Research, Joslin Clinic, University of Maryland;* b. 24 Nov. 1941, Boston, Mass; d. of Reynold Caleen and Dorothy Richardson Caleen; m. Kenneth D. Hansen 1976; one s.; ed Univ. of California, Los Angeles, Univ. of Pennsylvania and Univ. of Washington, Seattle; Research Fellow, Univ. of Pennsylvania Inst. of Neurosciences 1966–68; Asst and Assoc. Prof., Univ. of Washington 1971–76; Prof. and Assoc. Dean, Univ. of Michigan, Ann Arbor 1977–83; Assoc. Vice-Pres. of Academic Affairs and Research and Dean of Grad. School, Southern Illinois Univ., Carbondale 1983–85; Vice-Pres. for Grad. Studies and Research, Univ. of Maryland, Baltimore 1986–90, Prof. of Physiology 1990–, Dir Obesity and Diabetes Research Center 1990–, also Dir Obesity, Diabetes and Aging Animal Resource and Dir of Research, Joslin Clinic; Pres. Int. Asscn for Study of Obesity 1987–90, N American Asscn for Study of Obesity 1984–85, American Soc. of Clinical Nutrition 1995–96; mem. NAS Inst. of Medicine. *Publications:* Controversies in Obesity (ed.) 1983, The Commonsense Guide to Weight Loss for People with Diabetes 1998, The Metabolic Syndrome X 1999; book chapters and articles in learned journals. *Leisure interests:* sailing, scuba diving, golf, reading. *Address:* Obesity and Diabetes Research Center, University of Maryland Baltimore, 10 South Pine Street, Baltimore, MD 21201, USA (office). *Telephone:* (410) 706-3168 (office). *Fax:* (410) 706-7540 (office). *E-mail:* bchansen@aol.com. *Website:* physiology.umaryland.edu/faculty/bhansen (office).

HANSEN, Bent, FilDr; Swedish economist; b. 1 Aug. 1920, Ildved, Denmark; s. of Henrik Poulsen and Anna Louise (Pedersen) Hansen; m. Soad Ibrahim Refaat 1962; two s. four d.; ed Univs. of Copenhagen and Uppsala; civil servant, State Dept, Copenhagen 1946; Lecturer Uppsala Univ. 1947–48 and 1950–51, Gothenburg 1948–50; Reader, Uppsala 1951–55; Prof. and Head of Konjunkturinst. (Nat. Inst. of Econ. Research), Stockholm 1955–64, Consultant, Inst. of Nat. Planning, Cairo 1962–65; Special Consultant for OECD, Paris 1965–67; Prof. of Political Economy, Stockholm Univ. 1967–68; Prof. of Econs Univ. of Calif., Berkeley 1967–87, Prof. Emer. 1987–, Chair. Dept of Econs 1977–85; Consultant ECAFE Bangkok 1970–73, IMF 1973, US Treasury 1974, Morocco 1976–77, Bogadizi Univ., Istanbul 1978, World Bank 1985–89 (Consultant Emer. 1987–); Chief ILO Employment Mission to Egypt 1980–81. *Publications:* A Study in the Theory of Inflation 1951, The Economic Theory of Fiscal Policy 1958, Foreign Trade Credits and Exchange Reserves 1961, Development and Economic Policy in the UAR (Egypt) 1965, Lectures in Economic Theory, I and II 1967, Long and Short Term Planning 1967, Fiscal Policy in Seven Countries, OECD, 1969, A Survey of General Equilibrium Systems 1970, Exchange Controls and Development: Egypt 1975, Employment Opportunities and Equity: Egypt in the 1980s, 1982, Political Economy of Poverty, Equity and Growth, Egypt and Turkey 1990.

HANSEN, James E., BA, MS, PhD; American space scientist, environmental scientist, academic and research institute director; *Director, National Aeronautical and Space Administration (NASA) Goddard Institute for Space*

Studies; b. 29 March 1941, Denison, Ia; ed Univ. of Iowa; NASA Grad. Traineeship 1963–66; NAS-NRC Resident Research Assoc., Goddard Inst. for Space Studies (GISS), New York 1967–69, Staff mem./Space Scientist, GISS, Man. GISS Planetary and Climate Programs 1972–81, Dir NASA Goddard Inst. for Space Studies 1981–; NSF Postdoctoral Fellow, Leiden Observatory, Netherlands 1969; Research Assoc., Columbia Univ., New York 1969–72, Adjunct Assoc. Prof., Dept of Geological Sciences 1978–85, Adjunct Prof. of Earth and Environmental Sciences 1985–; Co-Prin. Investigator, AEROPOL Project (airborne terrestrial infrared polarimeter) 1971–74; Co-Investigator, Voyager Photopolarimeter Experiment 1972–85; Prin. Investigator, Pioneer Venus Orbiter Cloud-Photopolarimeter Experiment 1974–78, Co-Investigator 1974–94; Prin. Investigator, Galileo (Jupiter Orbiter) Photopolarimeter Radiometer Experiment 1977–2000, Earth Observing System Interdisciplinary Investigation: Interannual Variability of Earth's Carbon, Energy and Water Cycles 1989–2000; best known for his research in climatology, his testimony on climate change to congressional cttees in 1980s that helped raise awareness of global warming issue, and his continuing advocacy of action to limit impacts of climate change; mem. NAS 1996; Fellow, American Geophysical Union 1992; Goddard Special Achievement Award (Pioneer Venus) 1977, NASA Group Achievement Award (Voyager, Photopolarimeter) 1978, NASA Exceptional Service Medal (Radiative Transfer) 1984, Nat. Wildlife Fed. Conservation Achievement Award 1989, NASA Presidential Rank Award of Meritorious Exec. 1990, Alumni Achievement Award, Univ. of Iowa 1991, NASA Group Achievement Award (Galileo, Polarimeter/Radiometer) 1993, William Nordberg Achievement Medal, Goddard Space Flight Center 1996, Editor's Citation for Excellence in Refereeing for Geophysical Research Letters 1996, NASA Presidential Rank Award of Meritorious Exec. 1997, Alumni Fellow, Univ. of Iowa 2000, GISS Best Scientific Publication (peer vote): 'Global warming – alternative scenario' 2000, John Heinz Environment Award 2001, Roger Revelle Medal, American Geophysical Union 2002, GISS Best Scientific Publication (peer vote): 'Soot climate forcing' 2004, GISS Best Scientific Publication (peer vote): 'Earth's Energy Imbalance' 2005, Duke of Edinburgh Conservation Medal, World Wildlife Fund (WWF) 2006, Laureate, Dan David Prize 2007, Leo Szilard Lectureship Award, American Physical Soc. 2007. *Publications:* numerous scientific papers in professional journals on radiative transfer in planetary atmospheres and interpretation of remote sounding of atmospheres, devt of global climate models, analysis of climate change, current climate trends, and projections of man's impact on climate. *Address:* NASA Goddard Institute for Space Studies, 2880 Broadway, New York, NY 10025 (office); 750 Armstrong Hall, Columbia University, 2880 Broadway, New York, NY 10025, USA (office). *Telephone:* (212) 678-5500 (office). *Fax:* (212) 678-5622 (office). *E-mail:* jhansen@giss.nasa.gov (office); james.e.hansen@nasa.gov (office). *Website:* www.giss.nasa.gov (office).

HANSEN, John Mark, BA, MPhil, PhD; American political scientist, academic and university dean; *Charles L. Hutchinson Distinguished Service Professor, Department of Political Science and Dean, Social Sciences Division, University of Chicago;* ed Univ. of Kansas, Yale Univ.; Asst Prof. in Political Science, Univ. of Chicago 1986–92, Assoc. Prof. 1992–94, Prof. 1994–, Chair. Dept of Political Science 1995–98, Assoc. Provost for Educ. and Research 1998–, William R. Kenan Jr Prof. in Political Science –2001, currently Charles L. Hutchinson Distinguished Service Prof. and Dean of Social Sciences Div.; Prof. of Govt, Harvard Univ. 2001; Fellow, American Acad. of Arts and Sciences 2003; mem. Bd of Overseers, American Nat. Election Studies; Heinz Eulau Award, American Political Science Asscn for the Best Article Published in the American Political Science Review in 1998, 1999. *Publications:* Mobilization, Participation and Democracy in America (with Steven Rosenstone) (Outstanding Book Award, Nat. Conf. of Black Political Scientists 1995) 1993, Gaining Access: Congress and the Farm Lobby, 1919–1981 1991; numerous papers and articles on interest groups, citizen activism, public opinion, public budgeting and politicians' inferences from the outcomes of elections. *Address:* Office of the Dean, Social Sciences Division, 1126 E 59th Street, SS 110, Chicago, IL 60637, USA (office). *Telephone:* (773) 702-8798 (office). *Fax:* (773) 702-9029 (office). *E-mail:* jhansen@uchicago.edu (office). *Website:* www.uchicago.edu (office).

HANSEN, Kai Aaen, MSc(Econ); Danish central banker and international civil servant; *Director, Danmarks Nationalbank (Central Bank of Denmark);* b. 26 Nov. 1942, Hadsten; s. of Hans Helge Hansen and Kathrine Elisabeth Hansen; m. Ann Marie Skovløv 1970; ed Univ. of Århus; economist, Danmarks Nat. Bank 1972–77, Asst Head of Dept 1980–82, Head of Dept 1985–91, Dir 1992–97, 2000–; economist, OECD, Paris 1977–80; Econ. Adviser, IMF, Washington, DC 1983–85, Exec. Dir 1998–2000; Deputy Chair. Nordic Comm. on Money Transmission 1981–83; mem. UN Informal Group on Money Transmission 1981–83, Govt Comm. on Money Transmission 1982–83, Econ. Ministry Cttee on Econ. Policies 1987–91, on Econ. and Monetary Union Issues 1996–97; Alt. mem. EU Comm. of Cen. Bank Govs 1991–94, European Monetary Comm. 1987–93; alt. Council mem. European Monetary Inst. 1994–97; Chair. Nordic-Baltic Monetary and Financial Alt. Cttee 2000–04, Nordic-Baltic Cttee on IMF Governance 2005–06; mem. Int. Relations Cttee, ECB 2000–, Sub-cttee on Int. Monetary and Finance Insts, EU/EFC 2000–; Asst Prof. (part-time), Copenhagen School of Econs 1974–77, 1980–83; Kt, Order of Dannebrog, First Degree. *Publications:* The International Monetary System, an Essay to Interpretation (with Erik Hoffmeyer) 1991, Pengepolitiske Problemstillinger (with Erik Hoffmeyer) 1993. *Leisure interest:* history. *Address:* Danmarks Nationalbank, Havnegade 5, 1093 Copenhagen, Denmark (office). *Telephone:* 33-63-60-70 (office). *Fax:* 33-63-71-29 (office). *E-mail:* kah@nationalbanken.dk (office). *Website:* www.nationalbanken.dk (office).

HANSEN, Lars Peter, BS, PhD; American economist and academic; *Homer J. Livingston Distinguished Service Professor, Department of Economics, University of Chicago;* b. 26 Oct. 1952; m.; one c.; ed Univ. of Minn., Utah State Univ.; Asst Prof., Carnegie-Mellon Univ. 1978–80, Assoc. Prof., Grad. School of Industrial Admin 1980–81; Visiting Assoc. Prof. Univ. of Chicago 1981–82, Prof. 1984–90, Homer J. Livingston Prof. in Econs 1990–98, Homer J. Livingston Distinguished Service Prof., Dept of Econs 1998–, Dir of Grad. Studies, Dept of Econs 1988–94, Chair. Dept of Econs 1998–2002; Visiting Assoc. Prof., MIT 1983; Visiting Prof., Dept of Econs, Harvard Univ. 1986, Stanford Univ. 1989–90, Univ. of Chicago Grad. School of Business 2003–05; fmr Co-Ed. Econometrics, Journal of Political Economy; Fellow, Econometric Soc. 1985–, First Vice Pres. 2006; mem. American Acad. of Arts and Sciences, NAS; Research Assoc., Econs Research Center, N.O.R.C. 1984–; Sloan Foundation Fellow 1982; Guggenheim Fellow; Frisch Prize (co-winner), Econometric Society 1984, Faculty Award for Excellence in Grad. Teaching, Univ. of Chicago 1997–98, Erwin Plein Nemmers Prize in Econs 2006. *Achievements include:* best known as inventor of statistical technique GMM or Generalized Method of Moments 1982. *Publications:* author or co-author of numerous articles and books, including Robust Control and Economic Model Uncertainty (with Thomas J. Sargent); co-ed. Handbook of Financial Econometrics. *Address:* Department of Economics, University of Chicago, 1126 East 59th Street, Chicago, IL 60637, USA (office). *Telephone:* (773) 702-8170 (office). *Fax:* (773) 702-8490 (office). *E-mail:* l-hansen@uchicago.edu (office). *Website:* home.uchicago.edu/~lhansen (office).

HANSEN, Mogens Herman, DPhil; Danish reader in classical philology; b. 20 Aug. 1940, Copenhagen; s. of Herman Hansen and Gudrun Maria (née Heslet) Hansen; m. Birgitte Holt Larsen; one s.; ed Univ. of Copenhagen; Research Fellow, Inst. of Classics, Univ. of Copenhagen 1967–69, Lecturer in Classical Philology 1969–88, Reader 1988–; Dir The Copenhagen Polis Centre 1993–2005; Visiting Fellow, Wolfson College, Cambridge 1974; Visiting Prof., Melbourne Univ. 1988, Univ. of British Columbia, Vancouver 2001; mem. Inst. for Advanced Study, Princeton 1983; Corresp. mem. British Acad., Deutsches Archaeologisches Institut; Fellow, Royal Danish Acad. of Sciences and Letters; Einar Hansen Stipendium 2000, Fordyce Mitchel Memorial Lecturer 2004. *Publications include:* The Sovereignty of the People's Court in 4th Century Athens 1974, Eisangelia 1975, Aspects of Athenian Society 1975, Apagoge, Endeixis and Ephegesis 1976, The Athenian Ecclesia I 1983, II 1989, Demography and Democracy 1985, The Athenian Assembly 1987, The Athenian Democracy in the Age of Demosthenes 1991, Acts of the Copenhagen Polis Centre I 1993, II 1995, III 1996, IV 1997, V 1998, VI 1999, VII 2005, A Comparative Study of Thirty City-State Cultures 2000, A Comparative Study of Six City-State Cultures 2002, An Inventory of Archaic and Classical Poleis 2004; more than 100 articles in int. journals on Athenian democracy and ancient Greek constitutional history. *Leisure interests:* playing the flute, writing poetry, book binding. *Address:* Wilhelm Marstrandsgade 15, 2100 Copenhagen Ø, Denmark. *Telephone:* 35-32-91-03 (office); 35-26-15-88 (home). *E-mail:* mhh@hum.ku.dk (office).

HANSEN, Peter, Cand.Scient.pol; Danish diplomatist and international organization official; *Diplomat-in-Residence, Institute of International Humanitarian Affairs, Fordham University;* b. 2 June 1941, Aalborg; m.; one s. two d.; ed Århus Univ.; Assoc. Prof. Aarhus Univ. 1966–68, Chair. Dept of Political Science 1968–70, Sr Research Fellow 1970–74; Prof. of Int. Relations, Odense Univ.; Adviser, Ministry of Foreign Affairs; Chair. UN Consultative Cttee on Substantive Questions of the Admin. Cttee on Coordination and of the Appointment and Promotion Bd, mem. UN Programme Budgeting Bd, Asst Sec.-Gen. Programme Planning and Co-ordination 1978–85; Asst Sec.-Gen. and Exec. Dir UN Centre on Transnational Corpns 1985–92; Rep. of UN Sec.-Gen. to Food Aid and Policies Cttee, World Food Programme; Team Leader, UN Operation in Somalia 1992; Exec. Dir Comm. on Global Governance, Geneva, Switzerland 1992–94; Special Rep. of Sec.-Gen. ad hoc Liaison Cttee in support of Middle East peace process 1993–; currently Diplomat-in-Residence, Fordham Univ., New York; Under-Sec.-Gen. for Humanitarian Affairs and UN Emergency Relief Co-ordinator, New York, USA 1994–96; Commr-Gen. UNRWA 1996–2005; King Hussein Humanitarian Leadership Prize, King Hussein Foundation 2001, Order of Independence of First Degree (UAE) 2004, Star of Bethlehem Order (Palestine) 2004. *Publications:* World Politics 1969, International Organization 1975. *Address:* Institute of International Humanitarian Affairs, Fordham University, Lincoln Center, 113 West 60th Street, LL1120A, NY 10023, USA (office). *Telephone:* (212) 636-6294 (office). *Fax:* (212) 636-7060 (office). *E-mail:* peter_hansen1941@hotmail.com (home). *Website:* www.fordham.edu/iiha (office).

HANSENNE, Michel, DenD; Belgian politician; b. 23 March 1940, Rotheux-Rimiere; MP 1974–89; Minister of French Culture 1979–81, of Employment and Labour 1981–88, for Civil Service 1988–89; Dir-Gen. Int. Labour Org., Geneva 1989–98; MEP 1999–. *Publication:* Emploi, les scénarios du possible. *Address:* European Parliament, Plateau du Kirchberg, B.P. 1601, 2929, Luxembourg. *E-mail:* mhansenne@europarl.eu.int.

HANSON, Curtis; American film director and screenwriter; b. 24 March 1945, Los Angeles, Calif.; Ed. Cinema magazine; began film career as screenplay writer; mem. Bd Govs Acad. of Motion Picture Arts and Sciences 2001–. *Films directed:* The Arousers 1970, Sweet Kill (also screenplay) 1972, Little Dragons (also co-producer) 1977, Losin' It 1983, The Bedroom Window (also screenplay) 1988, Bad Influence 1990, The Hand that Rocks the Cradle 1992, The River Wild 1994, LA Confidential 1998, The Children of Times Square (TV film), Wonder Boys 1999, 8 Mile 2002, In Her Shoes (also producer) 2005, Lucky You 2007. *Screenplays:* The Dunwich Horror 1970, The Silent Partner 1978, White Dog 1982, Never Cry Wolf 1983. *Television:* Hitchcock: Shadow of a Genius (actor) 1999. *Address:* United Talent Agency, 9560 Wilshire Boulevard, Floor 5, Beverly Hills, CA 90212, USA.

HANSON, Sir John Gilbert, Kt, KCMG, CBE, MA; British fmr government official; b. 16 Nov. 1938, Sheffield; s. of Gilbert F. Hanson and Gladys Kay; m. Margaret Clark 1962 (died 2003); three s.; ed Manchester Grammar School and Wadham Coll. Oxford; War Office 1961–63; British Council, Madras, India 1963–66; Middle East Centre for Arab Studies, Lebanon 1966–68; British Council, Bahrain 1968–72, London HQ 1972–75, Dir British Council, Iran and Cultural Counsellor, British Embassy, Tehran 1975–79, Controller (Finance), British Council, London 1979–82; Royal Coll. of Defence Studies 1983; Dir British Council, India and Minister (Cultural), British High Comm. New Delhi 1984–88; Deputy Dir-Gen. British Council 1988–92, Dir-Gen. 1992–98; Warden Green Coll., Oxford 1998–2006; Chair. Trustees, British Skin Foundation 1997–, Bahrain-British Foundation 1997–2002; mem. Gov. Council, SOAS 1991–99, Univ. of London 1996–98; Hon. Fellow, Wadham Coll., Oxford 1997, St Edmund's Coll., Cambridge 1998; Pres. UK Council for Overseas Student Affairs 1999–; Patron GAP 1989–98; Trustee Charles Wallace (India) Trust 1998–2000; Hon. DLitt (Oxford Brookes) 1995, (Lincolnshire & Humberside) 1996, (Greenwich) 1996; Great Gold Medal, Comenius Univ. (Slovakia) 1997. *Leisure interests:* books, music, sport, travel. *Address:* c/o Green College, 43 Woodstock Road, Oxford, OX2 6HG, England.

HANSON, Margus, PhD; Estonian politician and university professor; b. 6 Jan. 1958, Tartu; m.; two s. one d.; ed Tartu Secondary School No. 2, Leningrad Inst. of Financial Economy, Tartu State Univ.; Engineer, Lab. of Educational Sociology, Tartu Univ. 1981–84, Asst to Chair of Finance and Credit 1984–87, Sr Lecturer 1990–91, Lecturer and Assoc. Prof. of Public Finance, Inst. of Econ. Policy and Public Economy 1992–94; Chair. Bd Estonian Commercial Bank of Industry and Construction 1995–96; Head of Tartu Br., Tallinn Bank 1996–97; mem. Tartu City Council 1996, 1999, 2002; Deputy Mayor of Tartu 1997–2003; mem. Riigikogu (Parl.) 2003–, mem. Nat. Defence Cttee; Minister of Defence 2003–04 (resgnd after admitting that confidential documents had been stolen from his home); professional training courses with Bank of Finland 1990–91, World Bank and Soros Foundation 1992, Austrian Bankers Club 1995, Estonian Banking Assocn, Barcelona 1996; mem. Eesti Reformierakond (Estonian Reform Party), Tartu Rotary Club. *Address:* Riigikogu, Lossi plats 1A, 15165 Tallinn, Estonia (office). *Telephone:* 631-6572 (office). *Fax:* 631-6334 (office). *E-mail:* margus.hanson@riigikogu.ee (office). *Website:* www.riigikogu.ee (office).

HANUSZKIEWICZ, Adam; Polish actor and theatre director; b. 16 June 1924, Lvov, Ukraine; s. of Włodzimierz Hanuszkiewicz and Stanisława Szydłowska; m. 1st Zofia Ryś; one s. two d.; m. 2nd Zofia Kucówna; m. 3rd Magdalena Cwenówna; ed State High School of Drama, Łódź and State Higher School of Drama, Warsaw; début as actor 1945, acted in Cracow, Poznań and Warsaw; début as Dir 1953, directed in Poznań and Warsaw; Artistic Dir Theatre of Polish TV 1956–63; Dir and Producer, Teatr Powszechny (Popular Theatre), Warsaw 1963–68, visited, with theatre company, Prague 1964, 1966, Moscow 1965, London, Paris 1966, Helsinki 1967, Bucharest 1968, Stockholm, Oslo 1969; Gen. Man. and Artistic Dir Teatr Narodowy, Warsaw 1968–82, visited Helsinki, Leningrad, Moscow 1973, Berlin 1975, Bremen, Budapest, Moscow 1976; Gen. Man. and Artistic Dir Teatr Nowy, Warsaw 1989–; visited Wilno 1989; acted in 50 major roles in theatre; directed over 30 plays in theatre, 100 television plays; Order of Banner of Labour, 1st Class 1974; Dr hc (Opole Univ.) 2001; State Prize (First Class) for TV work, City of Warsaw Award for theatre work, Theatre Critics' Prize 1964, Gold Screen TV Award 1978, Prize of Minister of Foreign Affairs 1979. *Principal roles include:* Hamlet (Hamlet) 1951–59, Tytus (Bérénice) 1962, Prospero (The Tempest) 1963, Raskolnikov (Crime and Punishment) 1964, Don Juan (Don Juan) 1965, Fantazy (Fantazy) 1967, Count Henryk (Un-divine Comedy) 1969, Duncan (Macbeth) 1972, Créon (Antigone) 1973. *Plays directed include:* Wesele (The Wedding, Wyspiański), Crime and Punishment, Coriolanus, Don Juan, The Columbus Boys (Bratny), Kordian (Słowacki), St Joan 1969, Hamlet 1970, Norwid 1970, Beniowski (Słowacki) 1971, Three Sisters 1971, 1983, 1988, Twelfth Night 1971, Macbeth 1973, Antigone 1973, The Inspector General 1973, Balladyna (Słowacki) 1974, A Month in the Country 1974, Wacława dzieje (Garczyński) 1974, The Card Index (Różewicz) 1974, Don Juan 1975, Wesele (Wyspiański) 1976, Mickiewicz 1976, Mąż i żona (Fredro) 1977, Phèdre 1977, Peace 1977, Sen srebrny Salomei (Słowacki) 1977, Wyszedł z domu (Różewicz) 1978, Dziady (Mickiewicz) 1978, Białe małżeństwo (Różewicz) 1978, Treny (Kochanowski) 1979, The Brothers Karamazov, The Decameron 1980, As You Like It, Platonov 1962, 1980, School of Wires, Leśmian 1982, Śpiewnik domowy 1982, 1984, 1989, Wilno, Cyd 1984, 1991, Komedia pasterska 1991, Gombrowicz 1992, Panna Isabela (Prus) 1993, Lilla Weneda (Słowacki) 1995, Dulska-musical (Zapolska), Balladyna 1996, Ballads and Romances 1998. *Opera:* Così fan tutte 1986, Marriage of Figaro 1987, La Traviata 1997, Romeo and Juliet 1997, Don Giovanni 1998, The Dance of Death 1998, Six Figures 1998. *Television:* Fuga 1994, Nim przyjdzie wiosna (Iwaszkiewicz) 1994, Panienka z poczty 1994, Chopin: His Life, His Loves, His Music (also wrote screenplay) 1999, Kordian 2002, W imie ojca strinberga 2001, Telepatrzydto 2000, Faust 2000. *Publications:* Psy, hondy i drabina 1994, Zbuy duża różnica peci 2003. *Address:* Teatr Nowy, ul. Puławska 37/39, 02-508 Warsaw (office); Drzymaly 1C, 02-495 Warsaw, Poland (home). *Telephone:* (22) 8498491 (office); (60) 1944111 (home). *Fax:* (22) 8498491 (office); (22) 6623535 (home). *Website:* www.teatrnowy.waw.pl (office).

HANWAY, H. Edward, BA, MBA, CPA; American insurance executive; *Chairman, President and CEO, CIGNA Corporation;* ed Loyola Coll. of Baltimore, Widener Univ.; joined CIGNA Corpn 1978, Pres. CIGNA Int. 1989–96, mem. Bd of Dirs 1992–, Pres. CIGNA HealthCare 1996–99, Pres. and COO Cigna Corpn 1999–2000, Pres. and CEO Jan. 2000–, Chair. Dec. 2000–; mem. Bd of Dirs Philadelphia Orchestra, Council for Affordable Quality Healthcare 2000– (Treas. 2000–01, Chair. 2001–02); mem. Bd of Advisors March of Dimes Foundation; mem. Pennsylvania and American Insts of Certified Public Accountants; Trustee, Loyola Coll. of Baltimore, Eisenhower Exchange Fellowships. *Address:* CIGNA Corpn, 2 Liberty Place, 1601 Chestnut Street, Philadelphia, PA 19192, USA (office). *Telephone:* (215) 761-1000 (office). *Fax:* (215) 761-5515 (office). *E-mail:* info@cigna.com (office). *Website:* www.cigna.com (office).

HAO, Bailin; Chinese physicist; *Research Professor, Institute of Physics, Academia Sinica;* b. 26 June 1934, Beijing; s. of Hao Kingsheng and Zhao Weimei; m. Zhang Shuyu 1959; one s. one d.; ed Kharkov State Univ., Ukraine; Research Asst, Inst. of Physics, Academia Sinica 1959–63, Research Assoc. 1963–78, Research Prof. 1978– (Dir 1990–94); mem. Chinese Acad. of Sciences 1980–; mem. Third World Acad. of Science 1995–; Sr Int. Fellow, External Faculty, Santa Fe Inst., NM, USA 2002–03, 2005–08; Science and Tech. Progress Award 1987, Nat. Award in Natural Science 1993, Chinese Acad. of Sciences Award 1992, 1999. *Publications:* 10 books, including Applied Symbolic Dynamics and Chaos 1998; 130 scientific papers on theoretical physics, computational physics, nonlinear science and theoretical life science. *Leisure interest:* reading classical Chinese poems. *Address:* c/o Institute of Theoretical Physics, PO Box 2735, Beijing 100080 (office); Apartment 1401, Building 811, Huangzhaung Complex, Academy of Sciences, Haidian District, Beijing 100080, People's Republic of China (home). *Telephone:* (10) 62541807 (office); (10) 62559478 (home). *Fax:* (10) 62562587 (office). *E-mail:* hao@itp.ac.cn (office). *Website:* www.itp.ac.cn/~hao (office).

HAO, Jianxiu; Chinese politician; *Vice-Chairwoman, 10th National Committee, Chinese People's Political Consultative Conference;* b. 1935, Qingdao, Shandong Prov.; ed People's Univ. of China, Beijing; worker, State Operated Cotton Factory No. 6, Qingdao 1949; originated Hao Jianxiu Work Method; mem. Exec. Council, Women's Fed. 1953; mem. Cen. Cttee, Communist Democratic Youth League 1953; joined CCP 1954; Deputy Dir Cotton Factory No. 6, Qingdao 1964; mem. Cen. Cttee Communist Youth League 1964–Cultural Revolution; mem. Qingdao Municipality Revolutionary Cttee 1967; mem. Standing Cttee, Cotton Factory No. 6 Revolutionary Cttee 1968; Vice-Chair. Qingdao Municipality Revolutionary Cttee 1971, Trade Union, Shandong Prov. 1975; Chair. Women's Fed., Shandong 1975; mem. Standing Cttee, Shandong Prov. CCP Cttee 1977; Vice-Minister of Textile Industry 1978–81, Minister 1981–83; Vice-Minister, State Planning Cttee 1987; Vice-Minister, State Devt and Reform Comm. 1998; mem. 11th CCP Cen. Cttee 1977–82, 12th CCP Cen. Cttee 1982–87 (mem. Financial and Econ. Leading Group 1986), 13th CCP Cen. Cttee 1987–92, 14th CCP Cen. Cttee 1992–97, 15th CCP Cen. Cttee 1997–2002; Vice-Chair. 10th CPPCC Nat. Cttee 2003–; Vice-Chair. Exec. Cttee All-China Women's Fed. 1978; Vice-Chair. State Tourism Cttee 1988; Deputy Dir Leading Group for the Placement of Demobilized Army Officers 1993–; Hon. Pres. Factory Dirs' Study Soc., Acad. of Social Sciences 1985; Nat. Model Worker in Industry 1951. *Address:* Zhonggong Zhongyang, A8, Taipingjie Street, Beijing 100050, People's Republic of China.

HAOMAE, William Ni'i; Solomon Islands politician; *Minister of Foreign Affairs, External Trade and Immigration;* b. 26 Nov. 1960, Mou Village, Small Malaita; m. Filistas T. Haomae; two s. two d.; ed East-West Centre, Honolulu; early govt posts include Information Officer, Prime Minister's Office, Press Sec. to the Prime Minister, Foreign Affairs Information Officer, Ministry of Foreign Affairs, Dir of Information Dept, Prime Minister's Office; mem. Parl. from Small Malaita, Malaita Prov. 1993–, mem. Parl. House Cttee July–Dec. 2007, Foreign Relations Cttee 2006–07; Minister for Culture, Tourism and Aviation 1994–97; Minister for Police and Justice 2000–01; Deputy Prime Minister and Caretaker Minister for Nat. Unity, Reconciliation and Peace Aug.–Dec. 2001; Minister for Police and National Security April–May 2006; Minister of Foreign Affairs, External Trade and Immigration 2007–. *Leisure interests:* reading, gardening, fishing, soccer. *Address:* Ministry of Foreign Affairs, External Trade and Tourism, PO Box G26, Honiara, Solomon Islands (office). *Telephone:* 28612 (office). *Fax:* 20352 (office). *E-mail:* psforeign@pmc.gov.sb (office). *Website:* www.parliament.gov.sb (office).

HAQ, Gen. Ehsan-ul-; Pakistani army officer; b. 22 Sept. 1949; ed Command and Staff Coll., Quetta, Nat. Defence Coll., Islamabad; first commissioned Army Air Defence Regt 1969, fmr Head of Mil. Intelligence, promoted to Lt-Gen. 2001, to Gen. 2004, Chair. Jt Chiefs of Staff Cttee 2004–07, Dir-Gen. Inter-Services Intelligence; Hilal-e-Imtiaz (Mil.). *Address:* c/o Joint Staff Headquarters, Chaklala, Rawalpindi, Pakistan. *Telephone:* (51) 8462336.

HARA, Hiroshi, DArch; Japanese architect and academic; *Victor L. Regnier Chair in Architecture, Department of Architecture, Kansas State University;* b. 9 Sept. 1936, Kawasaki, Kanagawa Pref.; ed Univ. of Tokyo; mem. generation of avant-garde New Wave architects; developed unique anthropological approach and theories of design from studies of vernacular architecture and indigenous settlements; conducted research trips in Europe, Asia and Africa; Asst Prof., then Prof., Inst. of Industrial Science, Univ. of Tokyo 1969–; cr. so-called 'reflection houses' in 1970s; began receiving commissions for large public bldgs 1980s; developed style of 'architecture of modality' whereby bldgs became metaphors of 'cities with the city' late 1980s; began designing 'modal spaces of consciousness' inspired by electronic and information technologies 1990s; began designing futuristic spaceship-like urban-scale projects late 1990s; Victor L. Regnier Chair in Architecture, Dept of Architecture, Kan. State Univ., USA 2003–; Murano Togo Prize 1986, Suntory Arts and Science Prize 1988. *Architectural Works include:* Awazu Residence, Kawasaki 1972, Hara Resdidence, Machida 1974, Niramu House, Chiba 1978, Sueda Art Gallery, Ōita 1981, Tasaki Museum of Art, Karuizawa 1986, Tsurukawa Nursery, Naha, Okinawa 1987, Yamato Int. Bldg, Tokyo 1987, Iida City Museum 1988, Shin Umeda City, Umeda Sky Bldg, Ōsaka 1993, Miyagi Prefectural Library, Sendai 1997, Kyōto Station Complex 1997, Sapporo Dome 2001. *Publications:* Hiroshi Hara (co-author) 1993, The Floating World of

Architecture (co-author) 2001; numerous monographs, chapters in books and articles in professional journals. *Address:* College of Architecture, Planning and Design, Kansas State University, 115 Seaton Hall, Manhattan, KS 66506-2902, USA (office). *Telephone:* (785) 532-5950 (office). *Fax:* (785) 532-6722 (office). *Website:* www.arch.ksu.edu (office).

HARA, Kazuo; Japanese film director; b. 8 June 1945, Yamaguchi; leading documentary filmmaker; renowned for creating films that blur the distinction between documentary films and fiction films, so-called 'action documentaries'. *Films directed include:* Sayonara CP (Goodbye, CP) 1972, Gokushiteki erosu: Renka 1974 (Extreme Private Eros: Love Song 1974) 1974, Umi to dokuyaku (The Sea and Poison: Asst Dir) 1986, Yuki Yukite shingun (The Emperor's Naked Army Marches On: KNF Award, Director's Guild of Japan New Director's Award 1986, Caligari Film Award, Berlin Film Festival 1987) 1986, Sen no Rikyu (Death of a Tea Master: Asst Dir) 1989, Shikibu monogatari (Mount Aso's Passions: Chief Asst Dir) 1989, Zenshin shosetsuka (A Dedicated Life) 1994, Fukai kawa (Deep River: Second Unit Dir) 1995, Watashi no Mishima 1999.

HARABIN, Štefan, DJur; Slovak judge and politician; *Deputy Prime Minister and Minister of Justice;* b. 4 May 1957, Ľubica; m.; four c.; ed Univ. of Pavel Jozef Šafárik, Košice; Judge, Dist Court, Poprad 1983–90, Regional Court, Košice 1990–91; Judge of the Supreme Court 1991–98, Pres. 1998–2003, Chair. Criminal Panel 2003–06; Head of Penal Dept, Section of Justice Admin., Ministry of Justice, Slovak Repub. 1991–92; Pres. of Senate and Penal Bd 1996–98; Pres. Judicial Council 2002–03; Deputy Prime Minister and Minister of Justice 2006–. *Address:* Ministry of Justice, Župné nám. 13, 813 11 Bratislava, Slovakia (office). *Telephone:* (2) 5935-3504 (office). *Fax:* (2) 5935-3601 (office). *E-mail:* minister@justice.sk (office). *Website:* www.justice.gov.sk (office).

HARAD, George Jay, BA, MBA; American business executive; *Chairman, Harad Capital Management LLC;* b. 24 April 1944, Newark, NJ; s. of Sidney Harad and Irma Harad; m. Beverly Marcia Harad 1966; one s. one d.; ed Franklin & Marshall Coll., Harvard Business School; Admin. Asst to Sr Vice-Pres. Housing Group, Boise Cascade Corpn 1971–72, Finance Man. Boise Cascade Realty Group 1972–76; Man. Corp. Devt, Boise Cascade Corpn 1976–80, Dir Retirement Funds 1980–82, Vice-Pres. Controller 1982–84, Sr Vice-Pres., Chief Financial Officer 1984–89, Exec. Vice-Pres., Chief Financial Officer 1989–90, Exec. Vice-Pres. Paper 1990–91, Pres., COO 1991–94, Pres., CEO 1994–95, Chair. Bd and CEO 1995–2004, Chair. Harad Capital Management LLC 2004–; Exec. Chair. OfficeMax Inc. 2004–05; George F. Baker Scholar. *Leisure interests:* golf, skiing. *Address:* Harad Capital Management LLC, 877 West Main Street, Suite 606, Boise, ID 83702, USA (office). *Telephone:* (208) 429-0606 (office). *E-mail:* gharad@haradcapital.com (office). *Website:* www.haradcapital.com (office).

HARADA, Minoru; Japanese religious leader; *President, Soka Gakkai;* b. 8 Nov. 1941, Tokyo; s. of Eiji Harada and Yuriko Harada; m. Kimie Harada 1968; two s.; ed Univ. of Tokyo; with Soka Gakkai (Buddhist network), Japan 1953–, Head of Student Div. 1973–76, Head of Youth Div. 1976–77, Vice-Pres. 1977–2001, Sec.-Gen. 1984–2006, Vice Gen. Dir 2001–06, Pres. 2006–, Vice-Pres. Soka Gakkai Int. 2003–07, Deputy Pres. 2007–. *Leisure interests:* reading, watching sports. *Address:* Soka Gakkai Headquarters, 32 Shinanomachi, Shinjuku-ku, Tokyo 160-8683 Japan (office). *Telephone:* (3) 3353-7111 (office). *Website:* www.sgi.org (office).

HARADINAJ, Ramush, MBA; Kosovo fmr guerrilla leader and politician; *President, Aleanca për Ardhmërinë e Kosovës (Alliance for the Future of Kosovo);* b. 3 July 1968, Glođane, nr Dečani, Yugoslavia (now Kosovo); m. Anita Haradinaj; one s. one d.; ed High School, Đakovica, Faculty of Law, Univ. of Pristina, American Univ. of Kosovo (associated with Rochester Inst. of Tech.); nat. mil. service in Yugoslav People's Army 1987; emigrated to Switzerland 1991; returned to Kosovo 1998; Commdr Kosovo Liberation Army 1998–99; Co-founder and Pres. Aleanca për Ardhmërinë e Kosovës (Alliance for the Future of Kosovo) 2000–; Prime Minister of Kosovo Dec. 2004–March 2005 (resgnd); acquitted of war crimes by Int. War Crimes Tribunal, The Hague 3 April 2008; asked by Ugandan Rebel Group 'Allied Democratic Forces' to mediate peace talks with Cen. Govt in Kampala Feb. 2009. *Address:* Aleanca për Ardhmërinë e Kosovës, 10000 Prishtina, Kodra e Trimave, Kosovo (office). *Telephone:* (44) 219080 (office).

HARALD V, HM The King of Norway; b. 21 Feb. 1937, Skaugum; s. of the late King Olav V and Crown Princess Märtha; m. Sonja Haraldsen 1968 (now HM Queen Sonja); one s. (HRH Crown Prince Haakon) one d.; ed Oslo Katedralskole, Cavalry Officers' Cand. School, Mil. Acad. and Balliol Coll. Oxford; lived in Washington, DC 1940–45; has participated in many int. sailing competitions representing Norway at Olympic Games several times; undertook frequent official visits abroad while Crown Prince; succeeded his father, King Olav V 17 Jan. 1991. *Address:* Royal Palace, 0010 Oslo, Norway. *Telephone:* 22-04-87-00. *Website:* www.kongehuset.no.

HARASZTI, Miklós; Hungarian writer, journalist, human rights advocate, international organization executive and academic; *Representative on Freedom of the Media, Organization for Security and Co-operation in Europe;* b. 1945, Jerusalem, Israel; ed Budapest Univ.; co-f. Hungarian Democratic Opposition Movt 1976; Ed. samizdat periodical Beszélo 1980; participated in roundtable negotiations on transition to free elections 1989; mem. Hungarian Parl. 1990–94; lectured on democratization and media politics at numerous univs 1990s; Rep. on Freedom of the Media, OSCE 2004–; Dr hc (Northwestern Univ., USA) 1996. *Publications:* A Worker in a Worker's State, The Velvet Prison (both translated into several languages); several essays have been published in The New York Times and The Washington Post. *Address:* Office of the OSCE Representative on Freedom of the Media, Kärntner Ring 5–7, Top 14, 2. DG, 1010 Vienna, Austria (office). *Telephone:* (1) 512-21-450 (office). *Fax:* (1) 512-21-459 (office). *E-mail:* pm-fom@osce.org (office). *Website:* www.osce.org/fom (office).

HARBERGER, Arnold C., PhD; American economist and academic; *Professor, Department of Economics, University of California at Los Angeles;* b. 27 July 1924, Newark, NJ; s. of Ferdinand C. Harberger and Martha L. Bucher; m. 1958; two s.; ed Univ. of Chicago; Asst Prof., Johns Hopkins Univ., Baltimore, Md 1949–53; Assoc. Prof., Univ. of Chicago 1953–59, Prof. 1959–76, Gustavus F. and Ann M. Swift Distinguished Service Prof. 1976–91, Prof. Emer. 1991–; Prof. of Econs, UCLA 1984–; Pres. Western Econ. Asscn 1988–89, American Econ. Asscn 1997; consultant to numerous econ. govt depts and int. orgs; Fellow, Econometric Soc. 1967, American Acad. of Arts and Sciences 1969; mem. NAS 1989. *Publications:* Project Evaluation 1972, Taxation and Welfare 1974, World Economic Growth 1984. *Address:* 8283 Bunche Hall, University of California at Los Angeles, 405 Hilgard Avenue, Los Angeles, CA 90095 (office); 136 Buckskin Road, Bell Canyon, CA 91307, USA (home). *Telephone:* (310) 825-1011 (office). *Fax:* (310) 825-9528 (office). *E-mail:* harberger@econ.ucla.edu (office). *Website:* econweb.sscnet.ucla.edu (office).

HARBI, Mohammed; Algerian historian; b. 16 June 1933, El-Arrouch; s. of Brahimi Harbi; m. (divorced); c.; ed Sorbonne; joined Parti du people algérien 1948; various posts with Front de Libération Nationale (FLN) 1954–62, including leader, French Div. 1957, Dir FLN cabinet 1959, FLN Rep. in Cairo 1960, Del. Evian Accord negotiations 1961; Adviser to Pres. Ahmed Ben Bella 1963; f. mem. Organisation de la résistance populaire 1965; imprisoned 1964–71, house arrest 1971; fled to France 1973; lecturer in sociology, Univ. de Paris-V, prof. of history, Paris-VII 1974. *Publications include:* Aux origines du Front de libération nationale 1975, FLN: Mirage et réalité 1980, L'Algérie et son destin, La guerre commence en Algérie; Mémoires politiques Tome 1: 1945–1962 (first volume of his political memoirs) 2001.

HARBISON, Peter, MA, DPhil, MRIA, FSA; Irish archaeologist, art historian and editor; *Honorary Academic Editor, Royal Irish Academy;* b. 14 Jan. 1939, Dublin; s. of Dr James Austin Harbison and Sheelagh Harbison (née McSherry); m. Edelgard Soergel 1969; three s.; ed St Gerard's School, Bray, Glenstal, Univ. Coll. Dublin and Univs of Marburg, Kiel and Freiburg; awarded travelling scholarship by German Archaeological Inst. 1965; archaeological officer, Irish Tourist Bd 1966–84, editorial publicity officer 1984–86, Ed. Ireland of the Welcomes (magazine) 1986–95; Sec. Friends of the Nat. Collections of Ireland 1971–76; mem. Council, Royal Irish Acad. 1981–84, 1993–96, 1998–2001, 2004–, Vice-Pres. 1992–93, 2006–07, Hon. Academic Ed. 1997–; Prof. of Archaeology, Royal Hibernian Acad. of Arts; Chair. Nat. Monuments Advisory Council 1986–90, Dublin Cemeteries Cttee 1986–89, 1996–2002, Bunratty Castle Ownership and Furniture Trusts 2004–; Vice-Pres. for Leinster, Royal Soc. of Antiquities of Ireland 2005–07; Guest Prof., Univ. of Vienna summer 2004; Corresp. mem. German Archaeological Inst.; Hon. mem. Royal Hibernian Acad. of Arts 1998, Royal Inst. of Architects of Ireland; Hon. Fellow, Trinity Coll., Dublin 2000. *Publications:* Guide to National Monuments of Ireland 1970, The Archaeology of Ireland 1976, Irish Art and Architecture (co-author) 1978, Pre-Christian Ireland (Archaeological Book of the Year Award 1988) 1988, Pilgrimage in Ireland 1991, Beranger's Views of Ireland 1991, The High Crosses of Ireland 1992, Irish High Crosses 1994, Ancient Ireland (with Jacqueline O'Brien) 1996, Ancient Irish Monuments 1997, Beranger's Antique Buildings of Ireland, L'Art Médiéval en Irlande 1998, Spectacular Ireland 1999, The Golden Age of Irish Art 1999, The Crucifixion in Irish Art 2000, Cooper's Ireland 2000, Our Treasure of Antiquities 2002, Treasures of the Boyne Valley 2003, Ireland's Treasures 2004, Beranger's Rambles in Ireland 2004, A Thousand Years of Church Heritage in East Galway 2005; articles in books and journals. *Leisure interests:* music, travel, wining, dining, cruising. *Address:* 5 St Damian's, Loughshinny, Skerries, Co. Dublin (home); Royal Irish Academy, 19 Dawson Street, Dublin 2, Republic of Ireland (office). *Telephone:* (1) 8490940 (home); (1) 6762570 (office). *Fax:* (1) 6762346 (office). *E-mail:* p.harbison@ria.ie (office). *Website:* www.ria.ie (office).

HARCOURT, Geoffrey Colin, AO, PhD, LittD, FASSA; Australian academic; *Emeritus Fellow, Jesus College and Reader Emeritus in the History of Economic Theory, University of Cambridge;* b. 27 June 1931, Melbourne; s. of Kenneth and Marjorie Harcourt (née Gans); m. Joan Bartrop 1955; two s. two d.; ed Univ. of Melbourne and Univ. of Cambridge, UK; Lecturer in Econs, Univ. of Adelaide 1958–62, Sr Lecturer 1962–65, Reader 1965–67, Prof. (Personal Chair) 1967–85, Prof. Emer. 1988–; Lecturer in Econs and Politics, Univ. of Cambridge 1964–66, 1982–90, Reader in the History of Econ. Theory 1990–98, Reader Emer. 1998–, Dir of Studies in Econs and Fellow, Trinity Hall, Cambridge 1964–66, Fellow and Lecturer in Econs, Jesus Coll., Cambridge 1982–98, Fellow Emer. 1998–, Pres. 1988–92; Leverhulme Exchange Fellow, Keio Univ., Tokyo 1969–70; Visiting Fellow, Clare Hall, Cambridge 1972–73; Visiting Prof., Univ. of Toronto, Canada 1977, 1980, Univ. of Melbourne 2002; Visiting Fellow, ANU 1997; Pres. Econ. Soc. of Australia and New Zealand 1974–77; mem. Council Royal Econ. Soc. 1990–95, Life mem. 1998–; Distinguished Fellow, Econ. Soc. of Australia 1996, History of Econs Soc., USA 2004; Academician Acad. of Learned Socs for the Social Sciences (AcSS) 2003; Fellow, Acad. of the Social Sciences in Australia 1971 (exec. cttee mem. 1974–77); Hon. Fellow, Queen's Coll., Melbourne 1998, Sugden Fellow 2002; Hon. Prof., Univ. of NSW 1997, 1999; Hon. mem. European Soc. for the History of Economic Thought 2004; Hon. LittD (De Montfort Univ.) 1997; Hon. DCom (Melbourne) 2003; Hon. Dr rer. pol (Fribourg) 2003; Wellington Burnham Lecturer, Tufts Univ., Medford, Mass 1975, Edward Shann Memorial Lecturer, Univ. of Western Australia 1975, Newcastle Lecturer in Political Economy, Univ. of Newcastle 1977, Acad.

Lecturer, Acad. of the Social Sciences in Australia 1978, G. L. Wood Memorial Lecturer, Univ. of Melbourne 1982, John Curtin Memorial Lecturer, ANU 1982, Special Lecturer in Econs, Univ. of Manchester 1984, Lecturer, Nobel Conf. XXII, Gustavus Adolphus Coll., Minn. 1986, Laws Lecturer, Univ. of Tennessee at Knoxville 1991, Donald Horne Lecturer 1992, Sir Halford Cook Lecturer, Queen's Coll., Univ. of Melbourne, Kingsley Martin Memorial Lecturer, Cambridge 1996, Colin Clark Memorial Lecturer, Brisbane 1997, Bernard Hesketh Lecturer, Univ. of Minn., Kansas City 2006. *Publications:* Economic Activity (with P. H. Karmel and R. H. Wallace) 1967, Readings in the Concept and Measurement of Income (ed., with R. H. Parker) 1969 (2nd edn with R. H. Parker and G. Whittington) 1986, Capital and Growth, Selected Readings (ed., with N. F. Laing) 1971, Some Cambridge Controversies in the Theory of Capital 1972, The Microeconomic Foundations of Macroeconomics (ed.) 1977, The Social Science Imperialists, Selected Essays (edited by Prue Kerr) 1982, Keynes and his Contemporaries (ed.) 1985, Controversies in Political Economy, Selected Essays of G. C. Harcourt (edited by Omar Hamouda) 1986, International Monetary Problems and Supply-Side Economics: Essays in Honour of Lorie Tarshis (edited with Jon S. Cohen) 1986, On Political Economists and Modern Political Economy, Selected Essays of G. C. Harcourt (ed. by Claudio Sardoni) 1992, Post-Keynesian Essays in Biography: Portraits of Twentieth Century Political Economists 1993, The Dynamics of the Wealth of Nations. Growth, Distribution and Structural Change: Essays in Honour of Luigi Pasinetti (edited with Mauro Baranzini) 1993, Income and Employment in Theory and Practice. Essays in Memory of Athanasios Asimakopulos (ed. with Alessandro Roncaglia and Robin Rowley) 1994, Capitalism, Socialism and Post-Keynesianism. Selected Essays of G. C. Harcourt 1995, A 'Second Edition' of The General Theory (two vols, co-ed. with P. A. Riach) 1997, 50 Years a Keynesian and Other Essays 2001, Selected Essays on Economic Policy 2001, L'Economie rebelle de Joan Robinson (ed.) 2001, Joan Robinson: Critical Assessments of Leading Economists (five vols, ed. with Prue Kerr) 2002, Editing Economics: Essays in Honour of Mark Perlman (co-ed.) 2002, Capital Theory (3 Vols, ed. with Christopher Bliss and Avi Cohen) 2005, The Structure of Post-Keynesian Economics: The Core Contributions of the Pioneers 2006. *Leisure interests:* bike riding, politics, reading, watching cricket. *Address:* 43 New Square, Cambridge, CB1 1EZ (home); Jesus College, Cambridge, CB5 8BL, England (office). *Telephone:* (1223) 760353 (office). *E-mail:* fellows-secretary@jesus.cam.ac.uk (office); GCH3@cam.ac.uk (home).

HARDCASTLE, Jack Donald, CBE, MA, MChir, FRCS, FRCP; British surgeon and academic; *Emeritus Professor of Surgery, University of Nottingham;* b. 3 April 1933, Yorks.; s. of Albert Hardcastle and Bertha Hardcastle (née Ellison); m. Rosemary Hay-Shunker 1965; two c.; ed Emmanuel Coll., Cambridge; House Physician, London Hosp. 1959–60; House Surgeon, Hammersmith Hosp., London 1961–62; Research Asst London Hosp. 1962, Lecturer in Surgery 1963, Registrar in Surgery 1964, Registrar in Surgery, Thoracic Unit 1965, Sr Registrar 1965, Sr Lecturer 1968; Sr Registrar St Mark's Hosp., London 1968; Prof. of Surgery, Univ. of Nottingham 1970–98, Prof. Emer. 1998–; Lead Clinician, Mid-Trent Cancer Network 1998–2005; Sir Arthur Sims Commonwealth Travelling Prof., Royal Coll. of Surgeons 1985; Mayne Visiting Prof., Univ. of Brisbane, Australia 1987, Univ. of Melbourne 2001; Dir of Educ. Royal Coll. of Surgeons 1993–98, mem. Council 1987–99, Vice-Pres. 1995–97, Dir of Overseas Office 1996–99; Pres. Surgical Section Royal Soc. Medicine 1981, Pres. Coloproctology Section, Royal Soc. 1983, Pres. Asscn of Surgical Oncology 1992–93; Pres. Surgical Research Soc. 1995–96; Hon. Fellow, Royal Coll. of Physicians and Surgeons (Glasgow), Asscn of Coloproctology; Huntarian Orator 1998, Royal Coll. of Surgeons (England) Gold Medal 1999. *Publications:* Isolated Organ Perfusion (with H. D. Ritchie) 1973; articles in professional journals. *Leisure interests:* golf, gardening. *Address:* Field House, 32 Marlock Close, Fiskerton, Notts., NG25 0UB, England (home). *Telephone:* (1636) 830316 (home). *Fax:* (1636) 830316 (home).

HARDIE, (Charles) Jeremy (Mawdesley), CBE, BPhil (Econs), ACA; British business executive; b. 9 June 1938; s. of Sir Charles Hardie; m. 1st Susan Chamberlain 1962 (divorced 1976); two s. two d.; m. 2nd Xandra, Countess of Gowrie 1978 (divorced 1994); one d.; m. 3rd Kirsteen Margaret Tait 1994; ed Winchester Coll. and New Coll., Oxford; Nuffield Coll., Oxford 1966–67; Jr Research Fellow, Trinity Coll., Oxford 1967–68; Fellow and Tutor in Econs Keble Coll., Oxford 1968–75; Partner, Dixon Wilson & Co. 1975–82; Dir John Swire and Sons Ltd 1982–; Dir (non-exec.) W. H. Smith Group 1988– (Deputy Chair. 1992–94, Chair. 1994–99); Chair. Nat. Provident Inst. 1980–89, Alexander Syndicate Man. Ltd 1982–95, Radio Broadland Ltd 1983–85, David Mann Underwriting Agency Ltd 1983–, Dir Alexanders Discount Co. Ltd 1978–87, Alexanders Laing & Cruickshank Gilts Ltd 1986–87; Dir Northdor Holdings 1989–93; Chair. Centre for Econ. Policy Research 1984–89; other business and public appointments; parl. cand. (SDP), Norwich South 1983 (SDP/Alliance) 1987. *Leisure interests:* sailing, skiing. *Address:* 13 Ainger Road, London, NW3 3AR, England. *Telephone:* (20) 7722-6916.

HARDIE BOYS, Rt Hon. Sir Michael, GNZM, GCMG, QSO, PC; New Zealand fmr Governor-General and fmr judge; b. 6 Oct. 1931, Wellington; s. of Justice Reginald Hardie Boys and Edith May Hardie Boys (née Bennett); m. Edith Mary Zohrab 1957; two s. two d.; ed Wellington Coll., Victoria Univ. of Wellington; barrister, solicitor with pvt. practice 1950–80; Councillor, then Pres., Wellington Dist Law Soc. 1974–79; Judge, High Court 1980–89, Court of Appeal 1989–95; Gov.-Gen. of NZ 1996–2001; mem. Legal Aid Bd (Chair.); Hon. Bencher of Gray's Inn; Hon. Fellow, Wolfson Coll., Cambridge; Hon. LLD (Victoria Univ., Wellington) 1997. *Leisure interest:* the outdoors. *Address:* 340A Ngarara Road, Waikanae, Kapiti Coast, Wellington, New Zealand (home).

HARDING, David, MBA; British business executive; b. Jan. 1956; ed Warwick Univ.; fmr positions include Sr Consultant PA Consulting Group, Operations Dir Mercury One-to-One, COO Sharelink, Man. Dir Charles Schwab Europe, Prudential Life and Pensions, Deputy CEO Scottish Amicable; CEO William Hill PLC 2000–07, fmr mem. Bd of Dirs Corp. Responsibility Cttee. *Address:* c/o William Hill PLC, Greenside House, 50 Station Road, Wood Green, London N22 7TP, England (office).

HARDING, James; British editor and journalist; *Editor, The Times;* ed St Paul's School, London, Trinity Coll., Cambridge; learnt Japanese and moved to Japan, worked as speechwriter in office of Chief Cabinet Sec. Koichi Kato early 1990s; worked in Japan unit of EC; joined Financial Times (FT) 1994, posted to Shanghai bureau (first European newspaper since 1949 revolution) 1996–99, returned to UK as Media Ed. 1999–2002, Chief of Washington bureau 2002–05, Business and City Ed. The Times 2006–07, Ed. The Times 2007–; est. justdosomething.net jtly with Common Purpose civic action group (online service that links professionals with non-exec. positions in local schools, prisons, hosps and nat. charities). *Publication:* Alpha Dogs: How Spin became a Global Business 2008. *Address:* The Times, 1 Pennington Street, London, E98 1XY, England (office). *Telephone:* (20) 7782-5000 (office). *Fax:* (20) 7782-5046 (office). *E-mail:* editor@timesonline.co.uk (office). *Website:* www.timesonline.co.uk (office).

HARDING, Marshal of the RAF Sir Peter Robin, GCB, DSc, FRAeS, FRSA; British air force officer (retd) and business executive (retd); b. 2 Dec. 1933, London; s. of Peter Harding and Elizabeth Kezia Clear; m. Sheila Rosemary May 1955; three s. one d.; ed Chingford High School; joined RAF 1952; pilot, numerous appointments in fighter, light bomber, strike/attack, reconnaissance and helicopters; Air Officer Commanding Number 11 Group 1981–82; Vice-Chief Air Staff 1982–84, of Defence Staff 1985; Air Officer Commanding-in-Chief, RAF Strike Command and C-in-C UK Air Forces (NATO) 1985–88; Chief of Air Staff 1988–92, Chief of Defence Staff 1993–94; ADC to HM the Queen 1975, Air ADC to HM the Queen 1988–92; Deputy Chair. GEC-Marconi Ltd 1995–98; Chair. Thorlock Int. Ltd 1998–2000, Merlyn Int. Assocs Ltd 1995–2002, Sienna Cancer Diagnostics Ltd 2003–05; Council mem. Winston Churchill Memorial Trust 1990–2008; Cttee mem. Leonard Cheshire Conflict Recovery Centre 1996–05; Vice-Pres. The Guild of Aviation Artists 1994–; Liveryman Guild of Air Pilots and Navigators; Fellow and Hon. Companion Royal Aeronautical Soc. 1989; mem. Pilgrims Soc. of GB; Commdr, Legion of Merit (USA); CB 1980, KCB 1982, GCB 1988; Hon. DSc (Cranfield Inst. of Tech.) 1990. *Leisure interests:* ten grandchildren, swimming, piano, bridge, birdwatching and shooting (normally separately); the Beefsteak and Garrick clubs. *E-mail:* alice_merlyn@btinternet.com (home).

HARDY, Sir David William, Kt, CBIM, FCA, FILT; British business executive; *Chairman, Transport Research Laboratory;* b. 14 July 1930, Wilmslow, Cheshire; s. of the late Brig. John H. Hardy; m. Rosemary Collins 1957; one s. one d.; ed Wellington Coll. and Harvard Business School, USA; with Funch Edye Inc. and Imperial Tobacco, USA 1954–70; HM Govt Coordinator of Industrial Advisers 1970–72; Group Finance Dir Tate & Lyle Ltd 1972–77; Dir Ocean Transport & Trading PLC 1977–83; Dir Globe Investment Trust PLC 1976–90, Exec. Chair. 1983–90; Chair. Ocean Inchcape 1980–83, London Park Hotels 1983–87, Docklands Light Railway 1984–87, Swan Hunter 1986–88, MGM Assurance 1986–99, London Docklands Devt Corpn 1988–92, Europa Minerals 1991–94, Bankers Trust Investment Man. Ltd 1992–94, Burmine 1992–96, James Fisher 1992–93, Y. J. Lovell 1994–99; Dir (non-exec.) Imperial Tobacco Group 1996–2001, Milner Estates 1996–99, Sons of Gwalia 1996–98, Hanson 1991–2001, Ciba Geigy 1991–96, J. Devenish 1991–93; mem. Financial Services Practitioner Forum 2001–; numerous other directorships, professional appointments etc.; Chair. of Trustees Nat. Maritime Museum 1995–2005, Transport Research Lab. 1996–; Fellow, Chartered Inst. of Transport; Hon. LLD (Greenwich) 2003. *Address:* Crow Horne House, Nine Mile Ride, Wokingham, RG40 3GA, England (home). *Telephone:* (1344) 773131 (home). *Fax:* (20) 7584-0086 (home). *E-mail:* seahardy@aol.com (office).

HARDY, Françoise; French singer, writer and astrologer; b. 17 Jan. 1944, Paris; m. Jacques Dutronc 1981; one s.; ed Inst. La Bruyère, Faculté des Lettres de Paris; solo recording artist 1962–; lyricist for musicians, including Diane Tell, Julien Clerc, Khalil Chahine, Guesch Patti and composer-arranger Alain Lubrano; also worked as model and actor; presents Horoscope RTL. *Films include:* Château en suède 1963, I Ragazzi dell'hully-gully 1964, Questo pazzo, pazzo mondo della canzone 1965, What's New, Pussycat 1965, Altissima pressione 1965, Une balle au coeur 1966, Europa canta 1966, Grand Prix 1966, Le Lapin de Noël (TV) 1967, Les Colombes 1972, Émilie Jolie (TV) 1980. *Recordings include:* albums: Françoise Hardy 1965, The Yeh-Yeh Girl from Paris 1965, Ma jeunesse fout le camp 1967, Comment te dire adieu 1968, Françoise Hardy en anglais 1969, Je vous aime 1969, Soleil 1970, La Question 1971, Et si je m'en vais avant toi 1972, Love Songs 1972, Message personnel 1973, Star 1977, J'écoute de la musique saoûle 1978, Gin Tonic 1980, Vingt ans vingt titres 1993, Blues 1995, Le Danger 1996, Maison ou j'ai grandi 1996, Clair obscur 2000, En Resume 2000, If You Listen 2000, Ce petit coeur 2004, Tant de Belle Choses 2005, Parenthèses 2006. *Publications:* Le Grand livre de la vierge (with B. Guenin), Entre les lignes, entre les signes (with Anne-Marie Simond) 1986, Françoise Hardy présente L'Astrologie universelle 1986, Notes secrètes (with E. Dumont) 1991, 35 Succès 1992, Les Rythmes du Zodiaque 2003. *Leisure interest:* reading, especially books dealing with spirituality. *Address:* c/o VMA, 20 avenue Rapp, 75007 Paris (office); 13 rue Hallé, 75014 Paris, France. *Website:* www.francoise-hardy.com.

HARDY, John Philips, MA, DPhil; Australian fmr professor of English; b. 1 Jan. 1933, Brisbane; s. of the late E. A. Hardy and N. A. Hardy (née Philips); m. 1st 1961 (divorced); three s. one d.; m. 2nd 1992; ed Church of England

Grammar School, Brisbane, Univ. of Queensland and Univ. of Oxford, UK; Fellow, Magdalen Coll. Oxford 1962–65; Asst Prof., Univ. of Toronto, Canada 1965–66; Prof. of English, Univ. of New England, Armidale, NSW, Australia 1966–72, ANU 1972–87; Foundation Prof. of Humanities and Social Sciences, Bond Univ. 1988–94; Sec. Australian Acad. of the Humanities 1981–88; Harold White Hon. Fellow, Nat. Library of Australia 1992; Queensland Rhodes Scholar 1957. *Publications:* Reinterpretations: Essays on Poems by Milton, Pope and Johnson 1971, Samuel Johnson 1979, Jane Austen's Heroines 1984, Stories of Australian Migration (ed.) 1988, Terra Australis to Australia (co-ed. with Alan Frost) 1989, European Voyaging towards Australia (co-ed. with Alan Frost) 1990. *Leisure interests:* swimming, fishing. *Address:* 26 Rawson Street, Deakin, Canberra, ACT 2600, Australia (home).

HARDY, Robert, CBE, MA (Oxon.), FSA; British actor and author; b. 29 Oct. 1925; s. of the late Maj. Henry Harrison Hardy and Edith Jocelyn Dugdale; m. 1st Elizabeth Fox 1952 (divorced); one s.; m. 2nd Sally Pearson 1961 (divorced 1986); two d.; ed Rugby School, Magdalen Coll., Oxford; Trustee, Royal Armouries 1984–95; Consultant, Mary Rose Trust 1979–, Trustee 1991–; Master of Worshipful Co. of Bowyers 1988–90; Hon. DLitt (Reading) 1990, (Durham) 1997, (Portsmouth) 2006. *Films include:* How I Won the War, Yellow Dog, Dark Places, Young Winston, Ten Rillington Place, Le Silencieux, Gawain and the Green Knight, The Spy Who Came In From The Cold, La Gifle, Robin Hood, The Shooting Party, Paris by Night, War and Remembrance, Mary Shelley's Frankenstein, Sense and Sensibility, Mrs Dalloway, The Tichborne Claimant 1998, An Ideal Husband 1999, The Gathering 2001, Harry Potter and the Goblet of Fire 2005, Lassie 2005, Goodbye Mr Snuggles 2006, Harry Potter and the Order of the Phoenix 2007. *Theatre:* theatre appearances 1949– include four seasons of Shakespeare at Stratford-on-Avon, two at Old Vic; world tours include Henry V and Hamlet, USA; numerous appearances London and Broadway theatres 1952–; Winston Churchill in Celui Qui a Dit Non, Palais des Congrès, Paris 1999–2000. *Television:* writer and/or presenter of numerous programmes 1952– including The Picardy Affair, The History of the Longbow, Heritage, Horses in our Blood, Gordon of Khartoum etc.; other TV appearances have included Prince Hal and Henry V in Age of Kings, Prince Albert in Edward VII, Malcolm Campbell in Speed King, Winston Churchill in the Wilderness Years, Siegfried Farnon in All Creatures Great and Small, Twiggy Rathbone and Russell Spam in Hot Metal, the Commandant in The Far Pavilions, Sherlock Holmes, Inspector Morse, Middlemarch, Castle Ghosts, Gulliver's Travels, Midsomer Murders, Tenth Kingdom, Justice in Wonderland, Lucky Jim, Shackleton. *Publications:* Longbow 1976, The Great Warbow (with Matthew Strickland) 2005. *Leisure interests:* making and shooting longbows, most country pursuits. *Address:* c/o Chatto & Linnit Ltd, 123A Kings Road, London, SW3 4PL, England (office). *Telephone:* (20) 7352-7722 (office). *Fax:* (20) 7352-3450 (office).

HARE, Sir David, Kt, MA, FRSL; British playwright and theatre director; b. 5 June 1947, Hastings, Sussex; s. of Clifford Theodore Rippon Hare and Agnes Cockburn Gilmour; m. 1st Margaret Matheson 1970 (divorced 1980); two s. one d.; m. 2nd Nicole Farhi 1992; ed Lancing Coll., Jesus Coll., Cambridge; Literary Man. and Resident Dramatist, Royal Court 1969–71; Resident Dramatist, Nottingham Playhouse 1973; f. Portable Theatre 1968, Joint Stock Theatre Group 1975, Greenpoint Films 1983; Assoc. Dir Nat. Theatre 1984–88, 1989–; UK/US Bicentennial Fellowship 1978; Hon. Fellow, Jesus Coll. Cambridge 2001; Officier, Ordre des Arts et des Lettres 1997; Evening Standard Drama Award 1970, John Llewelyn Rhys Prize 1974, BAFTA Best Play of the Year 1978, New York Critics' Circle Awards 1983, 1990, 1997, 1999, Golden Bear Award for Best Film 1985, Evening Standard Drama Award for Best Play 1985, Plays and Players Best Play Awards 1985, 1988, 1990, City Limits Best Play 1985, Drama Magazine Awards Best Play 1988, Laurence Olivier Best Play of the Year 1990, 1996, Time Out Award 1990, Dramalogue Award 1992, Time Out Award for Outstanding Theatrical Achievement 1998, Outer Critics' Circle Award 1999, Drama League Award 1999, Drama Desk Award 1999, Joan Cullman Award 1999. *Plays:* Slag, Hampstead 1970, Royal Court 1971, New York Shakespeare Festival (NYSF) 1971, The Great Exhibition, Hampstead 1972, Brassneck (with Howard Brenton q.v.), Nottingham Playhouse 1973 (also Dir), Knuckle, Comedy Theatre 1974, Fanshen, Inst. of Contemporary Arts 1975, Hampstead 1975, Nat. Theatre 1992, Teeth 'n' Smiles, Royal Court 1975 (also Dir), Wyndhams 1976 (also Dir), Plenty, Nat. Theatre 1978 (also Dir), NYSF and Broadway 1982 (also Dir), Albery 1999, A Map of the World, Nat. Theatre 1983 (also Dir) NYSF 1985 (also Dir), Pravda: A Fleet Street Comedy (with Howard Brenton), Nat. Theatre 1985 (also Dir), The Bay at Nice, Nat. Theatre 1986 (also Dir), The Secret Rapture, Nat. Theatre 1988, NYSF and Broadway 1989 (also Dir), Racing Demon, Nat. Theatre 1990, 1993, Broadway 1995, Murmuring Judges, Nat. Theatre 1992, 1993, The Absence of War, Nat. Theatre 1993, Skylight, Nat. Theatre 1995, Wyndhams and Broadway 1996, Vaudeville 1997, Amy's View, Nat. Theatre 1997, Aldwych 1998, Broadway 1999, The Judas Kiss, Almeida and Broadway 1998 (Dir on radio only), Via Dolorosa, Royal Court 1998 (also acted), Almeida and Broadway 1999 (also acted), My Zinc Bed, Royal Court 2000 (also Dir), The Breath of Life, Theatre Royal, Haymarket 2002, The Permanent Way, Nat. Theatre 2003, Stuff Happens, Nat. Theatre 2004, The Vertical Hour (Music Box Theatre, Broadway) 2006, Gethsemane, Nat. Theatre 2009. *Plays adapted:* The Rules of the Game, Nat. Theatre 1971, Almeida 1992, The Life of Galileo, Almeida 1994, Mother Courage and Her Children, Nat. Theatre 1995, Ivanov, Almeida and Broadway 1997 (Dir on radio only), The Blue Room, Donmar and Broadway 1998, Theatre Royal 2000, Platonov, Almeida 2001, The House of Bernarda Alba, Lorca 2005. *Plays directed:* Christie in Love, Portable Theatre 1969, Fruit, Portable Theatre 1970, Blowjob, Portable Theatre 1971, England's Ireland, Portable Theatre 1972 (Co-Dir), The Provoked Wife, Palace, Watford 1973, The Pleasure Principle, Theatre Upstairs 1973, The Party, Nat. Theatre 1974, Weapons of

Happiness, Nat. Theatre 1976, Devil's Island, Joint Stock 1977, Total Eclipse, Lyric 1981, King Lear, Nat. Theatre 1986, The Designated Mourner, Nat. Theatre 1996, Heartbreak House, Almeida 1997. *TV screenplays:* Man Above Men (BBC) 1973, Licking Hitler (BBC) 1978 (also Dir), Dreams of Leaving (BBC) 1979 (also Dir), Saigon: Year of the Cat (Thames) 1983 (also Assoc. Producer), Heading Home (BBC) 1991 (also Dir), The Absence of War (BBC) 1995. *Film screenplays:* Wetherby 1985 (also Dir), Plenty 1985, Paris by Night 1989 (also Dir), Strapless 1990 (also Dir), Damage 1992, The Secret Rapture 1993 (also assoc. producer), Via Dolorosa 2000 (also actor), The Hours (adaptation of Michael Cunningham's novel) 2001, Lee Miller 2003, The Corrections (adaptation of Jonathan Franzen's novel) 2005. *Film directed:* The Designated Mourner 1996 (also Producer). *Opera libretto:* The Knife, New York Shakespeare Festival 1988 (also Dir). *Publications:* Writing Lefthanded 1991, Asking Around 1993, Acting Up: A Diary 1999, Obedience, Struggle and Revolt (collection of speeches) 2005. *Address:* c/o Casarotto Ramsay & Associates Ltd, Waverley House, 7–12 Noel Street, London, W1F 8GQ, England (office). *Telephone:* (20) 7287-4450 (office). *Fax:* (20) 7287-9128 (office). *E-mail:* info@casarotto.co.uk (office). *Website:* www.casarotto.co.uk (office).

HARE DUKE, Rt Rev. Michael Geoffrey, MA; British fmr ecclesiastic; *Honorary Health Care Chaplain, Perth Royal Infirmary;* b. 28 Nov. 1925, Calcutta, India; s. of the late A. R. A. Hare Duke and Dorothy Holmes; m. Grace Lydia Frances McKean Dodd 1949; one s. three d.; ed Bradfield Coll., Berks., Trinity Coll., Oxford, Westcott House, Cambridge; Sub-Lt RNVR 1944–46; ordained Deacon 1952, Priest 1953; Curate St John's Wood, London 1952–56; Vicar St Mark's, Bury 1956–62; Pastoral Dir Clinical Theology Asscn 1962–64; Vicar St Paul's, Daybrook 1964–69; Bishop of St Andrew's, Dunkeld and Dunblane 1969–94; Chair. Age Concern Scotland 1994–2000, Nat. Forum on Older Volunteers 2000–03; Patron RSVP (Scotland) 2003–; Hon. Health Care Chaplain Perth Royal Infirmary 2002–; Hon. DD (St Andrew's). *Publications:* Understanding the Adolescent 1969, The Break of Glory 1970, Freud 1972, Good News 1976, Stories, Signs and Sacraments in the Emerging Church 1982, Praying for Peace: Reflections on the Gulf Crisis 1991, Hearing the Stranger: Reflections, Poems and Hymns 1994, One Foot in Heaven 2001; contrib. to various newspapers and journals. *Leisure interests:* writing and broadcasting. *Address:* 2 Balhousie Avenue, Perth, PH1 5HN, Scotland (home). *Telephone:* (1738) 622642 (home). *Fax:* (1738) 622642 (home). *E-mail:* bishmick@blueyonder.co.uk (home).

HAREWOOD, 7th Earl of, cr. 1812; **George Henry Hubert Lascelles,** KBE; British music administrator; b. 7 Feb. 1923, London; s. of the late 6th Earl of Harewood and HRH Princess Mary, The Princess Royal (d. of HM King George V); m. 1st Maria Donata Stein 1949 (divorced 1967); three s.; m. 2nd Patricia Tuckwell 1967; one s.; ed Eton Coll. and King's Coll., Cambridge; Capt. Grenadier Guards 1942–46; POW 1944–45; ADC to Earl of Athlone, Gov.-Gen. of Canada 1945–46; Counsellor of State during absence of the Sovereign 1947, 1954, 1956; mem. Bd Dirs Royal Opera House, Covent Garden 1951–53, 1969–72, Admin. Exec. 1953–60; Dir-Gen. Leeds Musical Festival 1958–74; Artistic Dir Edinburgh Int. Festival 1961–65; Chair. British Council Music Advisory Cttee 1956–66, Arts Council Music Panel 1966–72; Artistic Adviser New Philharmonia Orchestra, London 1966–76; Pres. English Football Asscn 1964–71, Leeds United Football Club; Chancellor, York Univ. 1963–67; mem. Gen. Advisory Council of BBC 1969–77, Gov. of BBC 1985–87; Man. Dir ENO 1972–85, Chair. 1986–95, Pres. 1995–; Man. Dir Opera North 1978–81, Vice-Chair. 1981–2006; Pres. British Bd of Film Classification 1985–97; Artistic Dir Adelaide Festival for 1988; Artistic Adviser, Buxton Festival 1993–98; Ed. Opera 1950–53, Kobbé's Complete Opera Book 1954, 1976, 1987, 1997; Austrian Great Silver Medal of Honour 1959, Lebanese Order of the Cedar 1970; Janáček Medal 1978. *Publications:* The Tongs and the Bones (autobiog.) 1981, Kobbé's Illustrated Opera Book 1989, Pocket Kobbé 1994. *Leisure interests:* looking at painting, sculpture, football, cricket. *Address:* Harewood House, Leeds, Yorkshire, LS17 9LG, England (home).

HARGROVE, Basil (Buzz); Canadian trade union official; *President, Canadian Auto Workers (CAW);* b. 8 March 1944, Bath, New Brunswick; s. of Percy Hargrove and Eileen Doucet; mem. Cttee Chrysler Canada 1965–75; Nat. Rep. 1975–78; Asst to Pres. and Dir Canadian Auto Workers (CAW) 1978–92; Nat. Pres. CAW 1992–; Vice Pres., Exec. Cttee, Canadian Labour Congress; Dr hc (Brock Univ.) 1998, (Univ. of Windsor) 2003, 9 Wilfred Laurier Univ.) 2004. *Publication:* Labour of Love 1998. *Address:* CAW, 205 Placer Court, North York, Toronto, Ont., M2H 3H9, Canada (office). *Telephone:* (416) 497-4110 (office). *Fax:* (416) 495-6559 (office). *E-mail:* cawpres@caw.ca (office). *Website:* www.caw.ca (office).

HARGROVE, Roy; American jazz musician (trumpet); b. 16 Oct. 1969, Waco, TX; ed Booker T. Washington School for Visual and Performing Arts, Dallas, Berklee School of Music, Boston, New School Univ., New York; toured Europe and Japan, playing with established jazz artists; formed own quintet and made debut solo record 1989; f. Roy Hargrove's Big Band 1995; formed The RH Factor 2003–. *Recordings include:* albums: Tenors Of Our Time 1994, Family 1995, Damn! 1995, Parker's Mood: Tribute to Charlie Parker 1995, The Main Ingredient 1996, Angel Eyes 1996, Crisol: Habana 1997, Jazz 'Round Midnight 1998, I Remember Miles 1998, Moment to Moment 2000, Directions In Music (Celebrating Miles Davis and John Coltrane) 2002, Hard Groove 2003, Strength 2004, Nothing Serious 2006, Distractions (with The RH Factor) 2006. *Website:* www.vervemusicgroup.com.

HARIHARAN, BSc, LLB; Indian singer; b. 3 April 1955, Bombay; s. of the late Ananthasubramani ('H.A.S. Mani') and Shrimati Alamelu; ed trained in Hindustani music with Ustad Ghulam Mustafa Khan; signed by the late music dir Jaidev to sing for Hindi film Gaman following success in singing competition 1977; toured concert circuit and performed on TV for several serials, e.g. Junoon; recorded several successful ghazal albums for which he wrote the scores; sang in several Hindi movies such as Sahibaan, Lamhe, Raam Nagari, Dard Ke Rishte, Zamana, Sindoor; debut singing in Tamil in film Roja 1993; Padma Shri 2004; All-India Sur Singaar Competition Prize 1977, Uttar Pradesh State Award 1977, Best Male Playback Singer, Tamil Nadu State Govt Film Awards 1995, Nat. Award for Best Male Playback Singer 1998. *Albums include:* Shamakhana, Sukoon 1983, Dil Nasheen 1988, Reflections 1989, The Very Best of Hariharan (compilation) 1989, Hariharan In Concert 1989, Dil Ki Baat 1990, My Favourite Hits (compilation) 1990, Hazir 1992, Abshaar-e-Ghazal (Gold), Gulfam (Double Platinum) (Diva Award for Best Album of the Year 1994) 1994, Saptarishi 1995, Paigham 1995, Qaraar, Visaal 1996, Halka Nasha, Jashn 1996, Colonial Cousins (first Indian act to be featured on MTV Unplugged, also won MTV Indian Viewers' Choice Award and US Billboards Award) 1996, Aathwan Sur – The Other Side of Naushad 1998, Kaash (Screen Videocon Award for Best Non-film Album 2000) 2000, Swar Utsav 2001. *Leisure interests:* film, travel, antique collecting, football. *Address:* c/o Sony Music Entertainment India, Span Centre, South Avenue, Santacruz (w), Mumbai 400 054, India (office). *Telephone:* (22) 25701673 (office). *Fax:* (22) 25704619 (office). *E-mail:* singerhari@gmail.com (office). *Website:* harihasanonline.com (office).

HARIRI, Nazek; Lebanese foundation executive; *President, Hariri Foundation;* b. (Nazek Audeh), widow of Raifk Hariri (fmr Prime Minister of Lebanon); four s. one d. three step-c.; supports Lebanese fashion designers and works for several charitable causes, including Children's Cancer Center of Lebanon, Int. Osteoporosis Foundation, Chronic Care Center, Muslim Inst. for Orphanages; Pres. Hariri Foundation; Amb. of Int. Osteoporosis Foundation 2003–; unanimously chosen to head all social and charitable orgs est. by her husband in Lebanon following his assassination 2005; campaigned for her son Saad in Lebanese elections. *Address:* c/o Hariri Foundation, Beirut, Lebanon (office). *E-mail:* info@rafichariri.org (office); m.i.s@hariri-foundation .org.lb (office). *Website:* www.nazekhariri.net; www.hariri-foundation.org.lb (office).

HARISH, Michael, BA; Israeli politician and economist; b. 28 Nov. 1936, Romania; s. of Joseph Harish and Esther Harish; m. Edith Normand 1963; three s. one d.; ed studies in econs and political science; Sec.-Gen. Labour Party's Student Org. 1961–63; Dir and Chair. Int. Dept Israel Labour Party 1967–82, Sec.-Gen. Israel Labour Party 1989–92; Minister of Industry and Trade 1992–96; mem. Knesset 1974–96; Deputy Chair. Defence and Foreign Affairs Cttee 1984–88; Chair. Finance Cttee 1988–89; Co-Chair. Jt Science and Tech. Cttee (US-Israel); mem. several ministerial cttees including Econ. Affairs, Immigrants' Absorption, Devt Areas, Jerusalem Affairs; mem. Cttee for co-ordinating activities between Govt and the Jewish Agency and the Zionist Org.; Pres. Me Harish Enterprises Ltd 1997–. *Leisure interests:* sport, music. *Address:* 5 Mishmar Hayarden Street, Givatayim, 53582 (home); 3 Achout Ha'avoda Street, Givatayim, 53204, Israel (office). *Telephone:* (3) 752-8012 (office); (3) 571-5233 (home). *Fax:* (3) 752-8011 (office); (3) 571-5233 (home). *E-mail:* meharish@internet-zahav.net.il.

HARKIANAKIS, Stylianos, DD; Australian ecclesiastic; *Primate, Greek Orthodox Church of Australia;* b. 29 Dec. 1935, Rethymnon, Crete, Greece; ed Theological School of Halki, Univ. of Athens; Deacon Constantinople (Istanbul) 1957; priest Rethymnon 1958; Abbot Holy Patriarchal Monastery of Vlatadon, Thessaloniki 1966; Pres. Patriarchal Inst. of Patristic Studies; lecturer, Univ. of Thessaloniki 1969–75, Univ. of Sydney 1975–85; Titular Bishop of Miletoupolis 1970; Exarch of Mount Athos 1970–75; Visiting Prof. Univ. of Regensberg 1973; Archbishop Greek Orthodox Church of Australia 1975, Primate 1975–; Co-Chair. official theological dialogue between Roman Catholic and Orthodox Churches 1980–2003; Dean St Andrew's Greek Orthodox Theological Coll. 1986–; mem. jt official comm. of theological dialogue between Orthodox and Anglicans 1970; Dr hc (Univ. of Lublin) 1985; Gottfried von Herder Prize (Vienna) 1973, Award for Poetry (Acad. of Athens) 1980, Golden Cross of St Andrew (Constantinople), Golden Cross of Holy Sepulchre, Archdiocese of Thyateira; awarded Key to City of Adelaide 1995. *Publications include:* The Infallibility of the Church in Orthodox Theology 1965, The Constitution 'De Ecclesia' of the Second Vatican Council 1969, Orthodoxy and Catholicism, Incarnations of Dogma 1996, For Present and Future 1999, 28 vols of poetry (in Greek), over 70 theological essays in periodicals. *Leisure interests:* poetry, reading, swimming, walking. *Address:* 242 Cleveland Street, Redfern, Sydney 2016, Australia. *Telephone:* (612) 9698-5066. *Fax:* (612) 9698-5368.

HARKIN, Thomas R., JD; American politician; *Senator from Iowa;* b. 19 Nov. 1939, Cumming, Ia; s. of Patrick and Frances Harkin; m. Ruth Raduenz 1968; two d.; ed Iowa State Univ. and Catholic Univ. of America; mem. House of Reps. 1975–85; Senator from Iowa 1985–; Chair. Agric. Cttee 2001–; mem. Small Business Cttee, various sub cttees, Democratic Steering Cttee; Democrat. *Publication:* Five Minutes to Midnight 1990. *Address:* 731 Hart Senate Office Bldg, Washington, DC 20510, USA (office). *Telephone:* (202) 224-3254 (office). *Website:* harkin.senate.gov (office).

HARLEY, Ian; British finance executive; articled clerk Touche Ross & Co. 1972; later with Corp. Planning Dept, Morgan Crucible Ltd; joined Abbey Nat. Building Soc. (later Abbey Nat. PLC) 1977, Financial Analyst then various Sr Man. posts with Finance, Treasury and Retail Divs., Reg. Man. for the SE, Retail Operations Div. 1984–86, Commercial Man. for Business Devt 1986, Group Financial Controller 1986–88, Asst Gen. Man. of Finance 1988–91, Finance Dir of Retail Operations 1991–92, Operations Dir Jan.–Oct. 1992, Group Treas. and Chief Exec. Abbey Nat. Treasury Services PLC 1992–98, Finance Dir and mem. Bd 1993–2002, CEO 1998–2002; mem. Bd of Dirs British Energy Group PLC and British Energy Holdings PLC 2004–, Rentokil Initial plc, Remploy; Gov. Whitgift Foundation; Vice-Pres. Nat. Deaf

Children's Soc.; fmr Chair. Asscn for Payment Clearing Services. *Address:* c/o Board of Directors, British Energy Group PLC, Systems House, Alba Campus Livingston EH54 7EG Livingston, EH54 7EG, England.

HARLIN, Renny; Finnish film director; b. 1958, Helsinki; m. Geena Davis (q.v.) (divorced); ed Univ. of Helsinki Film School; f. Midnight Sun Pictures (production co.). *Films:* Born American (debut) 1986, Prison, A Nightmare on Elm Street IV: The Dream Master, Die Hard 2, The Adventures of Ford Fairlane, Rambling Rose (producer only), Cliffhanger, Speechless (co-producer only), Cutthroat Island (also producer), The Long Kiss Goodnight (also producer) 1996, Deep Blue Sea 1999, Blast from the Past (producer) 1999, Exorcist: The Beginning 2004, Mindhunters (also producer) 2004, The Covenant 2006. *Films for television include:* Freddy's Nightmares 1990, T.R.A.X. 2000. *Address:* c/o Alan Gasmer, William Morris Agency, 1 William Morris Place, Beverly Hills, CA 90212, USA (office). *Fax:* (310) 440-9167 (office). *E-mail:* nikki@midnightsunpictures.com (office); renny@rennyharlin .com. *Website:* www.midnightsunpictures.com (office); www.rennyharlin.com.

HÄRMÄLÄ, Jukka, BSc; Finnish business executive; b. 1946; ed Helsinki School of Econs; joined Enso-Gutzeit Oy 1970, Dir of Finance 1981–83, Vice-Pres. and Gen. Man. Sawmill Div. 1983–84, Pres. and COO Enso Oyj 1988–92, Chair., Pres. and CEO 1992–98, CEO Stora Enso Oyj (following merger) 1999–2007; mem. Bd Finnish Forest Industries Fed.; Vice-Chair. Finnlines; mem. European Round Table of Industrialists. *Address:* c/o Stora Enso Oyj, Kanavaranta 1, PO Box 309, FIN-00101 Helsinki, Finland (office).

HARMAN, Gilbert Helms, BA, PhD; American academic and writer; *Stuart Professor of Philosophy, Princeton University;* b. 26 May 1938, E Orange, NJ; s. of William H. Harman, Jr and Marguerite Page; m. Lucy Newman 1970; two d.; ed Swarthmore Coll. and Harvard Univ.; faculty mem. Dept of Philosophy, Princeton Univ. 1963–, Stuart Prof. of Philosophy 1971–, Co-Dir Cognitive Science Lab. 1986–2000; Fellow, Cognitive Science Soc. 2003; mem. American Philosophical Asscn, Philosophy of Science Asscn, Soc. for Philosophy and Psychology, American Psychological Soc., Linguistic Soc. of America, American Acad. of Arts and Sciences 2005; Jean Nicod Prize 2005. *Publications:* Semantics of Natural Language (co-ed. with Donald Davidson) 1971, Thought 1973, On Noam Chomsky (ed.) 1974, The Logic of Grammar (ed. with Donald Davidson) 1975, The Nature of Morality: An Introduction to Ethics 1977, Change in View: Principles of Reasoning 1986, Skepticism and the Definition of Knowledge 1990, Conceptions of the Human Mind (ed.) 1993, Moral Relativism and Moral Objectivity (with Judith Jarvis Thomson) 1996, Reasoning, Meaning and Mind 1999, Explaining Values and other Essays in Moral Philosophy 2000; contrib. to scholarly journals. *Address:* Department of Philosophy, Princeton University, Princeton, NJ 08544-1006 (office); 106 Broadmead Street, Princeton, NJ 08540, USA (home). *Telephone:* (609) 258-4301 (office). *Fax:* (609) 258-1502 (office). *E-mail:* harman@princeton.edu (office). *Website:* www.princeton.edu/~harman (office).

HARMAN, Rt Hon. Harriet, PC, QC; British politician and solicitor; *Leader of House of Commons, Lord Privy Seal and Minister for Women;* b. 30 July 1950; d. of the late John Harman and of Anna Spicer; m. Jack Dromey 1982; two s. one d.; ed St Paul's Girls' School and Univ. of York; Brent Community Law Centre 1975–78; Legal Officer, Nat. Council for Civil Liberties 1978–82; MP for Peckham 1982–97, for Camberwell and Peckham 1997–; Shadow Chief Sec. to Treasury 1992–94; Shadow Spokesperson on Employment 1994–95, on Health 1995–96, on Social Security 1996–97; Sec. of State for Social Security 1997–98; Solicitor-Gen., Law Officers' Dept 2001–05; Minister of State, Dept of Constitutional Affairs 2005–07; Leader, House of Commons, Lord Privy Seal, Minister for Women and Sec. of State for Equalities 2007–; Chair. and Deputy Leader, Labour Party 2007–. *Publications:* Sex Discrimination in Schools 1977, Justice Deserted: The Subversion of the Jury 1979, The Century Gap 1993. *Address:* House of Commons, Westminster, London, SW1A 0AA, England (office); Labour Party, 39 Victoria Street, London, SW1H 0HA, England (office). *Telephone:* (20) 7219-3000 (office); (8705) 900200 (Labour) (office). *Fax:* (20) 7802-1234 (Labour) (office). *E-mail:* harmanh@parliament .uk (office); info@new.labour.org.uk (office). *Website:* www.harrietharman.org (office); www.labour.org.uk (office); www.parliament.uk (office).

HARMAN, Sir John, Kt, BSc, FRSA; British teacher, lecturer and civil servant; *Chairman, Environment Agency;* b. 30 July 1950, Leeds, Yorks., England; s. of John Edward Harman and Patricia Josephine Harman (née Mullins); m. Susan Harman; one s. three d.; ed St George's Coll., Weybridge, Univ. of Manchester and Huddersfield Coll. of Educ.; teacher and lecturer –1997; elected to W Yorkshire Metropolitan Co. Council 1981–86; elected to Kirklees Metropolitan Co. Council 1986, Leader 1986–99; first Leader Regional Ass. for Yorkshire and Humberside 1999–2000; mem. Bd Environment Agency 1996, later Deputy Chair., currently Chair.; Co-Chair. Sustainable Building Task Group 2004–05; Vice-Chair. Asscn of Metropolitan Authorities 1992–97; Deputy Leader Labour Group and Chair. Local Govt Asscn Urban Comm. 1997–2000; Local Govt Adviser to UK Del. to the Earth Summit, Rio de Janeiro 1992; Founder Chair. UK Local Agenda 21 Steering Group; mem. Mathematical Asscn, Child Poverty Action Group; Chair. Kirklees Stadium Devt Ltd, Advisory Cttee Inst. of Govt and Public Man., Univ. of Warwick; mem. Energy Savings Trust, Bd Nat. School of Govt; Trustee, Nat. Coal Mining Museum for England, Forum for the Future; Hon. Fellow, ICE, Chartered Inst. of Wastes Man., Chartered Inst. of Water and Environmental Mans, Soc. for the Environment; Hon. DCL. *Leisure interests:* music, gardening, Huddersfield Town Football Club. *Address:* Environment Agency, 25th Floor, Millbank Tower, 21–24 Millbank, London, SW1P 4XL, England (office). *Telephone:* (20) 7863-8720 (office). *Fax:* (20) 7863-8722 (office). *E-mail:* enquiries@environment-agency.gov.uk (office). *Website:* www .environment-agency.gov.uk (office).

HARMEL, Count Pierre Charles José Marie, DenD; Belgian politician and university professor; b. 16 March 1911, Uccle, Brussels; s. of Charles Harmel and Eusébie André; m. Marie-Claire van Gehuchten 1946; four s. two d.; Prof., Faculty of Law, Univ. of Liège 1947–81; Prof. Emer.; mem. Chamber of Reps 1946–71; Minister of Public Instruction and Fine Arts 1950–54; Minister of Justice 1958; Minister of Cultural Affairs 1959–60; Minister of Admin 1960–61; Prime Minister 1965–66; Minister of Foreign Affairs 1966–73; co-opted Senator 1971; Minister of State Feb. 1973; Pres. of Senate 1973–77; mem. Acad. Royale de Belgique 1977–; Croix de guerre avec palmes 1940. *Publications:* Principes non bis in idem et les droits d'enregistrement 1942, La famille et l'impôt en Belgique 1944, Culture et profession 1944, Les sources et la nature de la responsabilité civile des notaires, en droit Belge de 1830 à 1962 1964, Organisation et déontologie du notariat 1977, Droit commun de la Vente 1985, Grandes avenues du droit 1988. *Address:* 8 avenue de l'Horizon, 1150 Brussels, Belgium. *Telephone:* (2) 762-46-80.

HARMOKO, Haji; Indonesian politician and journalist; *Co-ordinator of Advisors, Partai Golongan Karya;* b. 7 Feb. 1939, Kertosono, E Java; ed Sr High School, Kediri, E Java and Inst. of Nat. Defence (LEMHANAS), Jakarta; journalist, Merdeka (magazine and daily) 1960–65; Ed. Api (daily); Man. Ed. Merdeka and Chief Ed. Merdiko 1966–68; Chief Ed. Mimbar Kita 1968–69; Gen. Man., Chief Ed. Pos Kota (daily); mem. Bd of Film Censors 1974; mem. Press Council 1975; Chief Ed. Warna Sari 1976–83; mem. House of Reps and People's Consultative Ass. and Head of Information and Mass Media Div. of Functional Group (GOLKAR) 1978, Pres. and Chair., then Co-ordinator of Advisors Partai Golongan Karya 1993–; Head of Advisory Bd of Newspaper Publrs Asscn 1979–84; mem. Exec. Bd Press and Graphics Asscn 1980–84; Minister of Information 1983–97; Speaker People's Consultative Ass. and House of Reps 1997–2001. *Address:* c/o People's Consultative Assembly, Jalan Gatot Subroto 6, Jakarta, Indonesia.

HARNEY, Mary, BA; Irish politician; *Minister for Health and Children;* b. 1953, Ballinasloe, Co. Galway; ed Presentation Convent, Clondalkin, Co. Dublin and Trinity Coll. Dublin; mem. Seanad Éireann (youngest ever Senator) 1977–81; mem. Dublin Co. Council 1979–91; TD 1981–, Co-founder Progressive Democrats 1985, Deputy Leader Progressive Democrats 1993, then Leader and Spokesperson on Justice, Equality and Law Reform; Minister for Environmental Protection 1989–92; Tánaiste (Deputy Prime Minister) and Minister for Enterprise, Trade and Employment 1997–2004; Tánaiste 2004–07, Minister for Health and Children 2004–. *Address:* Department of Health and Children, Hawkins House, Hawkins Street, Dublin 2 (office); Constituency Office, Clondalkin, Dublin 22, Ireland (office). *Telephone:* (1) 6354000 (office). *Fax:* (1) 6354001 (office). *E-mail:* info@health.ie (office). *Website:* www.dohc.ie (office); www.maryharney.ie.

HARNICK, Sheldon Mayer; American lyricist; b. 30 April 1924, Chicago; s. of Harry M. and Esther (née Kanter) Harnick; m. 1st Mary Boatner 1950 (annulled 1957); m. 2nd Elaine May 1962 (divorced 1963); m. 3rd Margery Gray 1965; one s. one d.; ed Northwestern Univ.; wrote songs for univ. musicals; contrib. to revues: New Faces of 1952, Two's Company 1953, John Murray Anderson's Almanac 1954, The Shoestring Revue 1955, The Littlest Revue 1956, Shoestring '57 1957; with composer Jerry Bock (q.v.) wrote shows Body Beautiful 1958, Fiorello 1959 (Pulitzer Prize), Tenderloin 1960, Smiling the Boy Fell Dead (with David Baker) 1961, She Loves Me 1963, Fiddler on the Roof (Tony Award) 1964, The Apple Tree 1966, The Rothschilds 1970, Captain Jinks of the Horse Marines (opera, with Jack Beeson) 1975, Rex (with Richard Rodgers) 1976, Dr. Heidegger's Fountain of Youth (opera, with Jack Beeson) 1978, Gold (cantata, with Joe Raposo) 1980, trans.: The Merry Widow 1977, The Umbrellas of Cherbourg 1979, Carmen 1981, A Christmas Carol 1981 (musical; book and lyrics), Songs of the Auvergne 1982, A Wonderful Life 1986, The Appeasement of Aeolus 1990, Cyrano 1994. *Address:* 54 Egypt Close, East Hampton, NY 11937-2656, USA (home). *Telephone:* (631) 324-1909 (home).

HARNONCOURT, Nikolaus; Austrian cellist and conductor; b. 6 Dec. 1929, Berlin, Germany; s. of Eberhard and Ladislaja Harnoncourt (née Meran); m. Alice Hoffelner 1953; three s. one d.; ed Matura Gymnasium, Graz, Acad. of Music, Vienna; cellist mem. of Vienna Symphony Orchestra 1952–69; solo concerts on viola da gamba; int. debuts 1966; Prof., Mozarteum and Inst. of Musicology, Univ. of Salzburg 1972–93; founder-mem., Concentus Musicus, Ensemble for Ancient Music 1953; as conductor has performed in leading concert halls worldwide, including in Amsterdam, Berlin, Vienna, Zürich and at the Salzburg Festival; Hon. DMus (Edin.) 1987; Erasmus Prize (jtly) 1980, H. G. Nägeli Medal, Zürich 1983, Polar Prize, Stockholm 1994, Ernst V. Siemens Preis 2002, Grammy Award (for recording of Bach's St Matthew Passion) 2002, Kyoto Prize (arts and philosophy category, for life's work) 2005. *Recordings include:* more than 450 recordings with period instruments and music from 1200–1900; many works with Concentus Musicus, notably Handel's Messiah, Mozart's early symphonies, Bach's Brandenburg Concertos and Cantatas, Beethoven symphonies with Chamber Orchestra of Europe, Schubert symphonies with Concertgebouw Orchestra Amsterdam, Mozart symphonies with Amsterdam Baroque Orchestra, recordings with Berlin and Vienna Philharmonic Orchestras, Arnold Schoenberg Choir. *Publications include:* Musik als Klangrede, Wege zu einem neuen Musikverständnis 1982, Der musikalische Dialog 1983. *Leisure interests:* cultural history, woodwork. *Address:* 38 Piaristengasse, 1080 Vienna (home); c/o Styriarte, Steirische Kulturveranstaltungen GmbH, Sackstraße 17, 8010 Graz, Austria (office). *Website:* www.harnoncourt.info.

HARNOY, Ofra, CM; Israeli/Canadian cellist; b. 31 Jan. 1965, Hadera, Israel; d. of Jacob Harnoy and Carmela Harnoy; m. Robert S. Cash; ed studied with her father in Israel, William Pleeth in London, Vladimir Orloff in Toronto and in master-classes with Mstislav Rostropovich, Pierre Fournier and Jacqueline du Pré; professional debut with Boyd Neel Orchestra, Toronto aged 10; solo appearances with many major orchestras in USA, Canada, Japan, Europe, Israel and Venezuela; TV appearances in Canada, UK and other European countries, Japan and Australia; played world premiere performance Offenbach cello concerto, N American premiere Bliss cello concerto, world premiere recording of several Vivaldi cello concertos; many solo recordings; prizes and awards include JUNO Award for Instrumental Artist of the Year (Canada) 1987/88, 1988/89, 1991, 1992, 1993, First Prize, Montreal Symphony Competition 1978, Canadian Music Competition 1979, Concert Artists Guild, New York 1982, Young Musician of the Year, Musical America magazine, USA 1983, Grand Prix du Disque, Critics' Choice, Best Records of the Year, The Gramophone, UK 1986, 1988, 1990. *Address:* c/o Robert S. Cash, Suite 1000, 121 Richmond Street West, Toronto, ON M5H 2K1, Canada (office). *Telephone:* (416) 863-1060 (office). *Fax:* (416) 863-9562 (office). *E-mail:* management@ofraharnoy.com (office). *Website:* www.ofraharnoy.com (office).

HAROUN, Mahamat-Saleh; Chadian film director and former journalist; b. 1961, Abéché; ed Conservatoire Libre du Cinéma, Paris, Institut Technique de Bordeaux. *Films include:* Maral Tanié 1994, Goi Goi 1995, A Tea in the Sahel, Bord'Africa 1995, Soitgui Kouyate 1996, Un griot moderne, Bye Bye Africa 1999 (film prizes in Venice 1999, Zanzibar 2000, M-Net All African Awards 2000), Abouna 2002, Dry Season 2006.

HAROUTUNIAN, Gagik G., DL; Armenian politician and lawyer; *Chairman, Constitutional Court;* b. 1948, Gekhashen; three c.; ed Yerevan State Univ.; Lecturer, Yerevan Inst. of Industry 1975–77; in Yugoslavia 1977–78; on staff Cen. Cttee Armenian CP 1982–88; Head of Dept 1988–90; joined nationalist opposition 1990; Deputy Chair. Armenian Parliament 1990–91; Vice-Pres. of Armenia 1991–95; Acting Chair. Council of Ministers (Prime Minister) 1991–92; Chair. Constitutional Court 1996–; Pres. Int. Conf. of Constitutional Control Organs of Young Democracy States; Council Pres. Centre of Constitutional Law; mem. Int. Asscn of Constitutional Law, Comm. for Democracy through Law, Council of Europe. *Publications:* 16 books including Constitutional Review (with A. Mavčič) 1999, 2002; contrib. over 100 articles to journals and newspapers. *Address:* Constitutional Court, Marshal Baghramian Street 10, 375019 Yerevan (office); Avan, Quchak Quart., Apt 11, Yerevan, Armenia (home). *Telephone:* (10) 58-81-40. *Fax:* (10) 52-99-91 (office). *E-mail:* armlaw@concourt.am (office). *Website:* www.concourt.am (office).

HAROUTUNIAN, Martin; Armenian engineer, metallurgist and trade union official; *President, Confederation of Trade Unions of Armenia;* b. 10 Feb. 1928, Sisian Region; one s. one d.; ed Yerevan Polytechnic Inst., Leningrad (now St Petersburg) Polytechnic Inst.; Chief Metallurgist and Head of Founding Workshop, Armenian Electromachine-Building Plant 1949–72; Head of Charentsavan Founding Plant 'Tzentrolit' 1972–76; Deputy Chief Industry, Transport and Communications Dept, Cen. Cttee of Communist Party of Armenia 1976–77; First Sec. Rasdan Dist Cttee 1977–83; currently Pres. Confed. of Trade Unions in Armenia; Hero of Socialist Labour 1981, Order of Lenin (twice), Badge of Honour; Honoured Engineer of Armenia, Honoured Inventor of Armenia. *Publications include:* 35 published works including Founding Industry in Armenia and Moulding Materials of Armenia. *Leisure interests:* reconstruction and production of the technological process of decorative moulding from cast iron, bronze and other materials. *Address:* Confederation of Trade Unions of Armenia, Nalbandian Street 26, 375010 Yerevan (office); 10/1 Zarubyan Street, Apt 17, Yerevan, Armenia (home). *Telephone:* (10) 58-36-82 (office); (10) 52-70-60 (home). *Fax:* (10) 54-33-82 (office).

HAROUTUNIAN, Michael; Armenian army officer and government official; *Minister of Defence;* b. 10 Feb. 1946, Sagiyan village, Shemakhin; m.; three c.; ed Frunze Mil. Acad. and Mil. Acad. of the Soviet Armed Forces; early career in Soviet Army, posts included CO of reconnaissance unit, Deputy Chief of Staff, Head of Reconnaissance Dept; Sr Instructor of Reconnaissance Unit, Military Acad. of the Soviet Armed Forces 1988–92; enlisted in Armed Forces of Armenia 1992; Head of Operations Dept and Deputy Head, Chief of Staff 1992–93; First Deputy Head, Chief of Staff of Armed Forces 1993–94, Chief of Staff of Armed Forces and First Deputy Minister of Defence 1994–2007, Minister of Defence 2007–; 'Service to the Motherland', Second Degree (USSR), Combat Cross, Second Degree (Armenia), Vardan Mamikonyan (Armenia), Combat Cross, Second Degree (NKR), Legion of Honor (USA), Combat Service, First Degree (Armenia), 'For the Service to the Motherland', First Degree (Armenia), Marshal Baghramyan decoration, Ministry of Defence, 'For Perfect Service', First and Second Degrees, Ministry of Defence, Andranik Ozanyan decoration, Ministry of Defence, 'Coat of Arms', Ministry of Defence, Nominal Weapon, Ministry of Defence, 'For Strengthening Combat Collaboration', Ministry of Defence, Russian Fed. *Address:* Ministry of Defence, G. Shaush Street 60, Yerevan 0088, Armenia (office). *Telephone:* (10) 28-39-22 (office). *Fax:* (10) 28-26-30 (office). *E-mail:* press@mil.am (office). *Website:* www.mil.am (office).

HARPER, Charles Michel, MBA; American business executive; b. 26 Sept. 1927, Lansing, Mich.; s. of Charles F. Harper and Alma Michel; m. Joan F. Bruggema 1950; one s. three d.; ed Purdue Univ. and Univ. of Chicago; Gen. Motors Corpn, Detroit 1950–54; Pillsbury Co., Minneapolis 1954–74, Group Vice-Pres. Poultry, Food Service and Venture Businesses 1970–74; Exec. Vice-Pres., COO, Dir Conagra Inc., Omaha 1974–76, Chair., CEO 1976–81, Chair. 1981–92; CEO 1981–92, CEO RJR Nabisco Holdings Inc. 1993–95, Chair. Bd 1995–96; mem. Bd Dirs Norwest Corpn, Valmont Industries, Inc., Peter Kiewit Sons Inc. and numerous other cos; several hon. degrees. *Address:* 6625 State Street, Omaha, NE 68152, USA. *Telephone:* (402) 571-6612. *Fax:* (402) 571-2151. *E-mail:* 104041.2015@compuserve.com (office).

HARPER, Edward James, BA, BMus, ARCM, LRAM; British composer; b. 17 March 1941, Taunton, Somerset; m. 1st Penelope Teece 1969 (divorced 1984); m. 2nd Dorothy C. Shanks 1984 (died 2000); one s. one d.; m. 3rd Louise J. Paterson 2003; ed King Edward VI Grammar School, Guildford, Royal Coll. of Music and Christ Church, Oxford; Lecturer in Music, Univ. of Edin. 1964, Sr Lecturer 1972–90, Reader 1990–2004; Dir New Music Group of Scotland 1973–91. *Compositions include:* Bartok Games 1972, Fanny Robin (chamber opera) 1975, Ricercari 1975, 7 Poems by E. E. Cummings 1977, Symphony 1979, Clarinet Concerto 1981, Hedda Gabler (opera) 1985, Qui creavit coelum (mass) 1986, The Mellstock Quire (opera) 1987, Homage to Thomas Hardy (orchestra, song cycle) 1990, The Lamb (soprano, chorus and orchestra) 1990, Overture for chamber orchestra 1992, And Winds, Austere and Pure (three songs for choir and piano duet) 1993, Chanson Minimale (for chamber orchestra) 1994, chamber opera based on William Golding's The Spire 1996, Psalm 150 for unaccompanied choir 1996, Scena for solo cello 1996, Trio for clarinet, cello and piano 1997, Souvenir for Two pianos and percussion 1998, Etude for orchestra 1999, Lochinvar Opera for Schools 2000, Music for King Arthur for primary school choirs, brass and percussion 2002, Voice of a City for primary school and adult choirs, organ and chamber orchestra 2004, Symphony No. 2 for Baritone, Choir and Orchestra 2006. *Address:* 7 Morningside Park, Edinburgh, EH10 5HD, Scotland (home).

HARPER, John Lander, CBE, MA, DPhil, FRS; British research biologist, consultant and author; *Professor Emeritus of Botany, University of Wales;* b. 27 May 1925, Rugby, Warwicks.; s. of John H. Harper and Harriet M. Harper (née Archer); m. Borgny Lerø 1954; one s. two d.; ed Magdalen Coll., Oxford; Demonstrator, Dept of Agric., Univ. of Oxford 1951–52, Lecturer 1953–59; Rockefeller Foundation Fellow, Univ. of Calif., Davis 1959–60; Prof., Dept of Agric. Botany, Univ. of Wales, Bangor 1960–67, Prof. of Agric. Botany and Head, School of Plant Biology 1967–78, Prof. of Botany and Head, School of Plant Biology 1978–82, Prof. Emer. 1982–, Dir of Unit. of Plant Population Biology 1982–90; Visiting Prof. Univ. of Exeter 1997–; mem. Nat. Environmental Research Council 1971–81, Agricultural and Food Research Council 1980–90, Jt Nature Conservation Cttee 1991–94; Ed. Proc. of the Royal Soc., B. 1993–99; Foreign Assoc. NAS (1984) and other learned socs; Trustee British Museum of Nat. History 1990–98; Hon. DSc (Sussex) 1984; Dr hc (Nat. Autonomous Univ. of Mexico) 1996; Darwin Medal, Royal Soc. 1990. *Publications:* Population Biology of Plants 1977, Ecology: Individuals, Populations and Communities 1986, 1990, 1996, 2006, Fundamentals of Ecology 2000, 2003; numerous papers in scientific journals. *Leisure interest:* gardening. *Address:* The Lodge, Chapel Road, Brampford Speke, Exeter, EX5 5HG, England (home). *Telephone:* (1392) 841929 (home).

HARPER, Judson Morse, BS, MS, PhD; American academic administrator (retd), consultant and academic; b. 25 Aug. 1936, Lincoln, Neb.; s. of Floyd Harper and Eda Harper; m. Patricia A. Kennedy 1958; three s.; ed Iowa State Univ.; with General Mills 1963–70, latterly Man. for New Business Ventures in Research Div.; Prof. of Chemical and Bioresource Eng, Colorado State Univ. 1970–2002, Prof. Emer. 2004–, Vice-Pres. for Research and Information Tech. 1982–2000, Interim Pres. 1989–90, Special Asst to Pres. 2000–04; consultant 1974–; holder of six US patents; Fellow, Inst. of Food Technologists 1992, AAAS 1995; Fulbright-Hayes Scholar 1978–79; Food Eng Award 1983, Int. Award, Inst. of Food Technologists 1990, Charles A. Lory Public Service Award, Colorado State Univ. 1993, Professional Achievement Award, Iowa State Univ. 1986; named Harper Research Complex, Colorado State Univ. 2000. *Publications include:* Extrusion of Foods 1981, Extrusion Cooking 1989; 91 refereed publs. *Leisure interests:* skiing, gardening, reading. *Address:* 1818 Westview Road, Fort Collins, CO 80524, USA (home). *Telephone:* (970) 222-0357 (office); (970) 493-1191 (office). *Fax:* (970) 493-1191 (office). *E-mail:* judson.harper@colostate.edu (office).

HARPER, Stephen, MA; Canadian politician and economist; *Prime Minister;* b. 20 April 1959, Toronto; m. Laureen Teskey; one s. one d.; ed Richview Collegiate Inst., Univ. of Calgary; Chief Aide to Jim Hawkes MP 1985; Exec. Asst to Deborah Grey MP 1989, Chief Adviser and Speech Writer –1993; founding mem. Reform Party; MP (Calgary West) 1993–97, 2002; Vice-Pres. Nat. Citizens Coalition 1997, later Pres.; Leader Canadian Alliance 2002; Leader of the Opposition 2002–06; Co-founder Conservative Party of Canada 2003, Leader 2004–, Prime Minister of Canada 2006–; mem. Queen's Privy Council for Canada. *Address:* Office of the Prime Minister, Langevin Block, 80 Wellington Street, Ottawa, ON K1A 0A2 (office); Conservative Party of Canada, 130 Albert Street, Suite 1720, Ottawa, ON K1P 5G4, Canada (office). *Telephone:* (613) 941-6888 (PM) (office); (613) 755-2000 (office). *Fax:* (613) 941-6900 (PM) (office); (613) 755-2001 (office). *E-mail:* pm@pm.gc.ca (office); info@conservative.ca (office). *Website:* www.pm.gc.ca (office); www.conservative.ca (office).

HARPPRECHT, Klaus Christoph; German/French author, television producer and journalist; b. 11 April 1927, Stuttgart; s. of Christoph Harpprecht and Dorothea Harpprecht (née Bronisch); m. Renate Lasker 1961; ed Evangelical Theological Seminary, Blaubeuren, Württemberg and Univs of Tübingen, Munich and Stuttgart; jr and Bonn Corresp., Christ und Welt 1948–53; commentator and corresp., RIAS Berlin (Rundfunk im amerikanischen Sektor), Sender Freies Berlin and Westdeutscher Rundfunk, Cologne 1953–61; America Corresp., Zweites Deutsches Fernsehen 1962–65; Publr, S. Fischer Verlag and Ed. Der Monat 1966–71; consultant and chief speech writer to Chancellor Willy Brandt 1972–74; Ed. GEO magazine, Hamburg 1978–79; now ind. writer; Theodore Wolff Award 1965, Drexel Award 1966, Medienpreis der Gesellschaft für Deutsche Sprache 2002. *Radio:* regular contribs to political and cultural programmes. *Television:* about 100 documentary films. *Publications:* The East German Rising 1954, Viele Grüsse an die Freiheit 1964, Beschädigte Paradiese 1966, Willy Brandt: Portrait 1970, Deutsche Themen 1973, L'Evolution Allemande 1978, Der Fremde Freund Amerika: Eine Innere Geschichte 1982, Amerikaner: Freunde, Freunde, Ferne Nachbarn 1984, (with Thomas Hoepker) Amerika die Geschichte seiner Eroberung 1986, Georg Forster – oder die Liebe zur Welt 1987, Das Ende der Gemuetlichkeit 1987, Die Lust der Freiheit. Deutsche Revolutionaere in Paris 1989, Die Leute von Port Madeleine-Dorfge-schichten aus der Provence (with Hans Hillmann) 1989, Welt-Anschauung Reisebilder 1991, Thomas Mann. Eine Biographie 1995, Schreibspiele: Bemerkungen zur Literatur 1996, Mein Frankreich – eine schwierige Liebe 1999, Dieu est-il encore français? 2000, Im Kanzleramt Tagebuch der Jahre mit Willy Brandt 2000, Harald Poelchau – Ein Leben im Widerstand 2004, Die Gräfin - Marion Dönhoff, Biographie 2008. *Leisure interests:* music, literature, history. *Address:* 16 Clos des Palmeraies, 83420 La Croix-Valmer, France (home). *Telephone:* (4) 94-79-60-76 (home). *Fax:* (4) 94-54-20-30 (home). *E-mail:* klausharpprecht@aol.com (office).

HARRACH, Péter; Hungarian politician; *Deputy Speaker, Hungarian National Assembly;* b. 2 Nov. 1947, Budapest; m.; three c.; ed Catholic Univ. of Budapest; joined Christian Democratic People's Party (KDNP) 1989, specialist on church policy, Pres. KDNP Budapest Zugló district 1990–97, Pres. Budapest co-ordinating org. 1993–94, Nat. Vice-Pres. 1995–97 (resgnd), Parl. Group Deputy Leader 2006–; mem. of Parliament 1998–; Vice-Pres. Hungarian Christian Democratic Alliance (MKDSZ) 1997–2000, Co-Pres. 2000–04, Pres. 2004–; pastoral assistant at several parishes –1990; official in charge of secular affairs Secr. of Hungarian Catholic Bishops' Conf. 1990–98; mem. Budapest Zugló (District XIV) Ass. 1990–98; mem. Budapest Municipal Ass. 1994–98; Minister for Social and Family Affairs 1998–2002; Deputy Speaker Nat. Ass. 2002–; mem. (as MKDSZ del.) Exec. of Alliance of Young Democrats (FIDESZ); Pres. Szob constituency FIDESZ-Hungarian Civic Alliance 2004–06. *Address:* Hungarian National Assembly, 1357 Budapest, Kossuth tér 1–3, Hungary (office). *Telephone:* (1) 441-4000 (office); (1) 441-4408 (office). *Fax:* (1) 441-4414 (office). *Website:* www.parlament.hu (office).

HARRELL, Lynn; American cellist; *Professor of Cello, Shepherd School of Music, Rice University;* b. 30 Jan. 1944, New York; s. of Mack Harrell and Marjorie Fulton; m. Linda Blandford 1976; one s. one d.; ed Juilliard School of Music, New York and Curtis Inst. of Music, Philadelphia; principal cellist, Cleveland Orchestra (under George Szell) 1963–71; now appears as soloist with the world's major orchestras; Piatigorsky Prof. of Cello, Univ. of Southern California 1987–93; Prof. of Int. Cello Studies, RAM, London 1988–93, 1993–95; Artistic Dir LA Philharmonic Inst. 1988–92; Music Adviser, San Diego Symphony Orchestra 1988–89; soloist, Memorial Concert for Holocaust Victims, Vatican 1994; Prof. of Cello, Shepherd School of Music, Rice Univ. 2002–; collaborations with Anne-Sophie Mutter, André Previn; two Grammy Awards. *Recordings include:* works by J. S. Bach, Beethoven, Bloch, Boccherini, Brahms, Bruch, Debussy, Dutilleux, Dvořák, Elgar, Fauré, Haydn, Herbert, Hindemith, Lalo, Mendelssohn, Prokofiev, Rachmaninov, Rosza, Saint-Saëns, Schoenberg, Schubert, Schumann, Shostakovich, Strauss, Tchaikovsky, Villa-Lobos, Vivaldi, Walton. *Leisure interests:* chess, fishing, golf, writing. *Address:* Opus 3 Artists, 470 Park Avenue South, 9th Floor North, New York, NY 10016, USA (office); 2271 Alice Pratt Brown Hall, Rice University, Houston, TX 77005-1892, USA (office). *Telephone:* (212) 584-7500 (office); 713-348-4854 (office). *Fax:* (646) 300-8200 (office). *E-mail:* eblackburn@opus3artists.com (office). *Website:* www.opus3artists.com (office); www.ruf.rice.edu/~musi/facultybios/harrell (office).

HARRELSON, Woodrow (Woody) Tracy, BA; American actor; b. 23 July 1961, Midland, Tex.; m. Laura Louie 2008; three d.; ed Hanover Coll.; Founder, Voice Yourself (website). *Theatre includes:* The Boys Next Door, Two on Two (author, producer, actor), The Zoo Story (author, actor), Brooklyn Laundry, Furthest from the Sun (also playwright), On An Average Day, Comedy Theatre, London 2002. *Television includes:* Cheers (series) 1985–93, Bay Coven 1987, Killer Instinct 1988, Mother Goose Rock 'n' Rhyme 1990, Will & Grace (series) 2001. *Films include:* Wildcats 1986, Cool Blue 1988, Doc Hollywood 1991, Ted and Venus 1991, White Men Can't Jump 1992, Indecent Proposal 1993, I'll Do Anything 1994, The Cowboy Way 1994, Natural Born Killers 1994, Money Train 1995, The Sunchaser 1996, Kingpin 1996, The People vs Larry Flynt 1996, Kingpin 1996, Wag the Dog 1997, Welcome to Sarajevo 1997, The Thin Red Line 1998, Palmetto 1998, The Hi-Lo Country 1998, EdTV 1999, Play It to the Bone 1999, American Saint 2001, Scorched 2003, Anger Management 2003, She Hate Me 2004, After the Sunset 2004, The Big White 2005, North Country 2005, The Prize Winner of Defiance, Ohio 2005, A Prairie Home Companion 2006, Free Jimmy (voice) 2006, A Scanner Darkly 2006, The Grand 2007, The Walker 2007, No Country for Old Men 2007, Battle in Seattle 2007, Transsiberian 2008, Sleepwalking 2008, Semi-Pro 2008. *Leisure interests:* sports, juggling, writing, chess. *Address:* c/o Creative Artists Agency, 9830 Wilshire Boulevard, Beverly Hills, CA 90212, USA. *Website:* www.voiceyourself.com.

HARRIES OF PENTREGARTH, Baron (Life Peer), cr. 2006, of Ceinewydd in the County of Dyfed; **Richard Douglas Harries,** DD, FKC, FRSL; British ecclesiastic; *Gresham Professor of Divinity;* b. 2 June 1936, Eltham, London; s. of Brig. W. D. J. Harries and G. M. B. Harries; m. Josephine Bottomley 1963; one s. one d.; ed Wellington Coll., Royal Mil. Acad, Sandhurst, Selwyn Coll, Cambridge, Cuddesdon Coll., Oxford; Lt, Royal Corps of Signals 1955–58; Curate, Hampstead Parish Church 1963–69; Chaplain, Westfield Coll. 1966–69; Lecturer, Wells Theological Coll. 1969–72; Warden, Salisbury and Wells Theological Coll. 1971–72; Vicar, All Saints, Fulham, London 1972–81; Dean, King's Coll., London 1981–87; Bishop of Oxford 1987–2006; Prof. of Divinity, Gresham Coll., London 2008–; Vice-Chair. Council of Christian Action 1979–87, Council for Arms Control 1982–87; Chair. Southwark Ordination Course 1982–87, Shalom, End Loans to South Africa (ELSTA)

1982–87, Christian Evidence Soc.; Chair. Church of England Bd of Social Responsibility 1996–2001; Consultant to the Archbishops on Jewish-Christian Relations 1986–92; Chair. Council of Christians and Jews 1993–2001, House of Lords select Cttee on Stem Cell Research 2001–02; Visiting Prof., Liverpool Hope Coll. 2002; mem. Home Office Advisory Cttee for Reform of Law on Sexual Offences 1981–85, Bd Christian Aid 1994–2001, Royal Comm. on Lords Reform 1999–, Nuffield Council of Bioethics 2002–06, Human Fertilisation and Embryology Authority 2003–; Hon. Fellow, Selwyn Coll., Cambridge, St Anne's Coll., Oxford; Hon. Fellow, Acad. of Medical Sciences 2004; Hon. DD (London) 1996; Hon. DUniv (Oxford Brookes) 2001, (Open Univ.); Sir Sigmund Steinberg Award 1989. *Publications:* Prayers of Hope 1975, Turning to Prayer 1978, Prayers of Grief and Glory 1979, Being a Christian 1981, Should Christians Support Guerrillas? 1982, The Authority of Divine Love 1983, Praying Round the Clock 1983, Seasons of the Spirit (co-ed.) 1984, Prayer and the Pursuit of Happiness 1985, Reinhold Niebuhr and the Issues of Our Time (ed.) 1986, Morning has Broken 1985, Christianity and War in a Nuclear Age 1986, C. S. Lewis: The Man and his God 1987, Christ is Risen 1988, Is There a Gospel for the Rich? 1992, Art and the Beauty of God 1993, The Value of Business and its Values (co-author) 1993, The Real God 1994, Questioning Faith 1995, A Gallery of Reflections 1995, In the Gladness of Today 2000, Christianity: Two Thousand Years (co-ed.) 2000, God Outside the Box: Why Spiritual People Object to Christianity 2002, After the Evil: Christianity and Judaism in the Shadow of the Holocaust 2003, The Passionate Act 2004, Praying the Eucharist 2004, The Passion in Art 2005, The Re-Enchantment of Morality 2008; contrib. to several books; numerous articles. *Leisure interests:* theatre, literature, sport. *Address:* House of Lords, London, SW1A 0PW, England (office). *Telephone:* (20) 7219-2910 (office). *E-mail:* harriesr@parliament.uk (office).

HARRINGTON, Anthony Stephen; American diplomatist, lawyer and government official; *President and CEO, Stonebridge International LLC;* b. 9 March 1941, Taylorsville, NC; s. of Atwell Lee Harrington and Louise (Chapman) Harrington; m. Hope Reynolds 1971; two s.; ed Univ. of North Carolina, Duke Univ.; Sr Partner, Hogan & Hartson; Amb. to Brazil 2000–01; Pres. and CEO Stonebridge Int. LCC 2001–; Chair. of Civitas Group llc (investment and consulting group); mem. Bd of Dirs PRE Holdings, Inc; Chair. Pres.'s Intelligence Oversight Bd; Vice-Chair. Pres.'s Foreign Intelligence Advisory Bd 1994–99; mem. Comm. on the Roles and Capabilities of the US Intelligence Community; Co-Chair. Nat. Alliance to End Homelessness; Dir Center for Democracy; co-founder Telecom USA; founder and Dir Ovation. *Leisure interests:* politics, tennis, gardening, reading. *Address:* Stonebridge International LLC, 555 13th Street, NW, Washington, DC 20004 (office); 701 Pennsylvania Avenue, NW, Washington, DC 20004; Ratcliffe Manor, 7768 Ratcliffe Manor Lane, Easton, MD 21601, USA (home). *Telephone:* (202) 637-8600 (office). *Fax:* (202) 637-8615 (office). *E-mail:* aharrington@stonebridge-international.com (office). *Website:* www.stonebridge-international.com (office).

HARRINGTON, Padraig; Irish professional golfer; b. 31 Aug. 1971, Dublin; m. Caroline Harrington 1997; two s.; turned professional 1995, joined European Tour 1996, PGA Tour 2005; European Tour wins include Spanish Open 1996, Brazil Sao Paulo 500 Years Open 2000, BBVA Turespana Masters de Madrid 2000, Volvo Masters 2001, Dunhill Links Championship 2002, 2006, BMW Asian Open 2003, Deutsche Bank Open 2003, Omega Hong Kong Open 2004, Linde German Masters 2004, Irish Open 2007; major tournament wins include Open Championship 2007, 2008, PGA Championship 2008; PGA Tour wins include Honda Classic 2005, Barclay's Classic 2005; other wins include Irish PGA Championship 1998, 2004, 2005, 2007, 2008, Target World Challenge 2002, Dunlop Phoenix Tournament 2006, Hassan II Trophy, Morocco 2007; represented Europe in Ryder Cup 1999, 2002, 2004, 2006, 2008; f. Padraig Harrington Charitable Foundation 2005; European Order of Merit 2006, European Tour Golfer of the Year 2007, 2008, European Tour Shot of the Year 2008, AGW Trophy 2007, 2008, Hon. Mem. European Tour 2007, PGA of America Player of the Year, US PGA Tour Player of the Year 2008. *Address:* c/o IMG, McCormack House, Burlington Lane, Chiswick, London, W4 2TH, England. *Telephone:* (20) 8233-5300 (office). *Fax:* (20) 8233-5268 (office). *E-mail:* katie.powell@imgworld.com (office). *Website:* www.padraigharrington.com (home).

HARRIS, Edward Allen (Ed), BFA; American actor; b. 28 Nov. 1950, Englewood, NJ; s. of Bob L. Harris and Margaret Harris; m. Amy Madigan; one c.; ed Columbia Univ., Univ. of Oklahoma, Calif. Inst. of Arts. *Stage appearances include:* A Streetcar Named Desire, Sweet Bird of Youth, Julius Caesar, Hamlet, Camelot, Time of Your Life, Grapes of Wrath, Present Laughter, Fool for Love (Obie Award 1983), Prairie Avenue (LA Drama Critics Circle Award 1981), Scar 1985 (San Francisco Critics Award), Precious Sons 1986 (Theater World Award), Simpatico 1994, Taking Sides 1996, Wrecks 2005. *Films include:* Coma 1978, Borderline 1978, Knightriders 1980, Creepshow 1981, The Right Stuff 1982, Swing Shift 1982, Under Fire 1982, A Flash of Green 1983, Places in the Heart 1983, Alamo Bay 1984, Sweet Dreams 1985, Code Name: Emerald 1985, Walker 1987, To Kill a Priest 1988, Jacknife 1989, The Abyss 1989, State of Grace 1990, Paris Trout 1991, Glengarry Glen Ross 1992, Needful Things 1993, The Firm 1993, China Moon 1994, Milk Money 1994, Apollo 13 1995, Just Cause 1995, Eye for an Eye 1995, The Rock 1996, Absolute Power 1997, Stepmom 1998, The Truman Show 1998, The Third Miracle 1999, Waking the Dead 2000, The Prime Gig 2000, Pollock (also Producer and Dir) 2001, Enemy at the Gates 2001, Buffalo Soldiers 2001, A Beautiful Mind 2001, Just a Dream (voice) 2002, The Hours 2002, Masked and Anonymous 2003, The Human Stain 2003, Radio 2003, Dirt Nap 2005, Winter Passing 2005, A History of Violence (Nat. Film Critics Supporting Actor Award) 2005, Copying Beethoven 2006, Gone Baby Gone 2007, Cleaner 2007, National Treasure Book of Secrets 2007, Touching Home

2008, Appaloosa (also Dir) 2008. *Television includes:* Gibbsville – Trapped 1976, The Amazing Howard Hughes 1977, The Seekers 1979, The Aliens are Coming 1980, The Last Innocent Man 1987, Running Mates 1992, The Stand 1994, Riders of the Purple Sage 1996, Empire Falls 2005. *Address:* c/o Rick Kurtzman, CAA, 15260 Ventura Blvd, Suite 940, Sherman Oaks, CA 91403, USA.

HARRIS, Emmylou; American singer; b. 2 April 1947, Birmingham, AL; m. 1st Brian Ahern; m. 2nd Paul Kennerley 1985; two d.; ed Univ. of N Carolina; singer 1967–, toured with Fallen Angels Band in USA and Europe; Pres. Country Music Foundation 1983–; Grammy Awards 1976, 1977, 1980, 1981, 1984, 1987, 1992, 1996, Country Music Asscn Female Vocalist of the Year 1980, Grammy Award for Best Female Country Vocal Performance (for The Connection) 2006. *Recordings include:* albums: Gliding Bird 1969, Pieces of the Sky 1975, Elite Hotel 1976, Luxury Liner 1977, Quarter Moon in a Ten-Cent Town 1978, Blue Kentucky Girl 1979, Light of the Stable 1979, Roses In The Snow 1980, Evangeline 1981, Cimarron 1981, Last Date 1982, White Shoes 1983, The Ballad of Sally Rose 1985, Thirteen 1986, Trio (with Dolly Parton and Linda Ronstadt) (Acad. of Country Music Album of the Year 1988) 1987, Angel Band 1987, Bluebird 1989, Brand New Dance 1990, Duets (with Nash Ramblers) 1990, At The Ryman 1992, Cowgirl's Prayer 1993, Songs of the West 1994, Wrecking Ball 1995, Portraits 1996, Nashville 1996, Spyboy 1998, Red Dirt Girl 2000, Singin' with Emmylou Harris (vol. I) 2000, Anthology 2001, Stumble Into Grace 2003, All the Roadrunning (with Mark Knopfler) 2006, Neil Young Heart of Gold 2006, All I Intended to Be 2008. *Address:* Asgard Promotions Ltd, 125 Parkway, London, NW1 7PS, England (office); c/o WEA Records, Time Warner, 75 Rockefeller Plaza, New York, NY 10019, USA. *Telephone:* (20) 7387-5090 (office). *Fax:* (20) 7387-8740 (office). *E-mail:* info@asgard-uk.com (office).

HARRIS, Sir Henry, Kt, FRS, FRCP, FRCPath; British cell biologist; b. 28 Jan. 1925; s. of Sam Harris and Ann Harris; m. Alexandra Brodsky 1950; one s. two d.; ed Sydney Boys High School, Univ. of Sydney, Lincoln Coll., Oxford; Dir of Research, Cancer Research Campaign, Sir William Dunn School of Pathology, Oxford 1954–59; Visiting Scientist, NIH, USA 1959–60; Head, Dept of Cell Biology, John Innes Inst. 1960–63; Prof. of Pathology, Univ. of Oxford 1963–79, Regius Prof. of Medicine 1979–92; Head of the Sir William Dunn School of Pathology, Oxford 1963–94; Corresp. mem. Australian Acad. of Science; Foreign mem. Max Planck Soc.; Foreign Prof., Coll. de France; Hon. mem. American Asscn of Pathologists, German Soc. of Cell Biology; Foreign Hon. mem. American Acad. of Arts and Sciences; Hon. Fellow, Cambridge Philosophical Soc.; Hon. FRCPath (Australia); Hon. DSc (Edinburgh); Hon. MD (Geneva, Sydney); Feldberg Foundation Award; Ivison Macadam Memorial Prize; Prix de la Fondation Isabelle Decazes de Nöue for cancer research, Madonnina Prize for Medical Research; Katherine Burkan Judd Award of the Memorial-Sloan Kettering Cancer Center; Medal of Honour, Univ. of Pavia, Royal Medal of the Royal Soc., Osler Medal of the Royal Coll. of Physicians. *Publications:* Nucleus and Cytoplasm 1968, Cell Fusion 1970, La fusion cellulaire 1974, The Balance of Improbabilities 1987, The Cells of the Body 1995, The Birth of the Cell 1999, Things Come to Life 2002, Remnants of a Quiet Life 2006; papers on cellular physiology and biochemistry in various scientific books and journals and some fiction. *Leisure interests:* history and literature. *Address:* c/o Sir William Dunn School of Pathology, South Parks Road, Oxford, OX1 3RE, England. *Telephone:* (1865) 275500. *Fax:* (1865) 275501.

HARRIS, Jeff, CA; British pharmaceuticals industry executive; *Chairman, Alliance UniChem PLC;* b. 1948; began career as accountant with two major auditing firms; Chief Accountant, Alliance UniChem PLC 1985, Finance Dir 1986, later becoming Deputy CEO then CEO, Chair. 2001–; Dir Bunzl PLC, Andreae-Noris Zahn (ANZAG), Associated British Foods May 2003–. *Address:* Alliance UniChem PLC, Alliance House, 2 Heath Road, Weybridge KT13 8AP, England (office). *Telephone:* (1932) 780550 (office). *Fax:* (1932) 870555 (office). *Website:* www.alliance-unichem.com (office).

HARRIS, Julie; American actress; b. 2 Dec. 1925, Grosse Pointe Park, Mich.; d. of William Picket and Elsie Harris (née Smith); m. 1st Jay I. Julien 1946 (divorced 1954); 2nd Manning Gurian 1954 (divorced 1967); one s.; 3rd Walter Erwin Carroll 1977 (divorced 1982); ed Yale Drama School; New York Drama Critics' Award for I Am a Camera, Nat. Medal of the Arts 1994, Kennedy Center Honor 2005. *Theatre work includes:* Sundown Beach 1948, The Young and Fair 1948, Magnolia Alley 1949, Montserrat 1949, The Member of the Wedding 1950, Sally Bowles in I Am a Camera 1951, The Lark 1956, A Shot in the Dark 1961, Marathon 33 1964, Ready When You Are, C.B. 1964, And Miss Reardon Drinks a Little 1971, Voices 1972, The Last of Mrs. Lincoln 1973, In Praise of Love 1974, The Belle of Amherst, New York 1976, London 1977, Break a Leg, New York 1979, Mixed Couples, New York 1980, Driving Miss Daisy 1988, Lucifer's Child 1991, Lettice and Lovage, The Fiery Furnace (off-Broadway debut) 1993, The Glass Menagerie 1996, The Gin Game 1997, Ellen Foster 1997, Love is Strange 1999. *Films include:* East of Eden 1955 (Antoinette Perry Award), I Am a Camera 1956, Poacher's Daughter 1960, The Haunting, The Moving Target, Voyage of the Damned 1976, The Bell Jar 1979, Gorillas in the Mist, Housesitter, The Dark Half, Carried Away, Bad Manners 1997, The First of May 1998, Frank Lloyd Wright 1998. *Television:* Little Moon of Alban (TV film) 1960, Knots Landing 1982, Scarlett, The Christmas Tree, Ellen Foster. *Address:* c/o Gail Naehlis, William Morris Agency, One William Morris Place, Beverly Hills, CA 90212, USA.

HARRIS, Sir Martin Best, Kt, CBE, PhD, DL; British administrator and fmr university vice-chancellor; *Chairman, Universities' Superannuation Scheme; Director, Office of Fair Access;* b. 28 June 1944, Ruabon, Wales; s. of William Best Harris and Betty Evelyn Harris (née Martin); m. Barbara Mary Daniels 1966; two s.; ed Devonport High School, Plymouth, Queens' Coll., Cambridge,

School of Oriental and African Studies, Univ. of London; Lecturer in French Linguistics, Univ. of Leicester 1967–72; Sr Lecturer in French Linguistics, Univ. of Salford 1972–76, Prof. of Romance Linguistics 1976–87, Pro-Vice-Chancellor 1981–87; Vice-Chancellor, Univ. of Essex 1987–92, Univ. of Manchester 1992–2004; Chair. Cttee of Vice-Chancellors and Prins 1997–99; mem. Univ. Grants Cttee 1984–87, Chair. Northern Ireland Sub-Cttee 1985–87; Chair. Northern Ireland Cttee, Univs Funding Council 1987–91, Nat. Curriculum Working Group on Modern Languages 1989–90, HEFCE/CVCP Review of Postgraduate Educ. 1995–96, Clinical Standards Advisory Group 1996–99, North West Univs Asscn 1999–2001, Higher Educ. Careers Advisory Services Review 2000–01, Manchester: Knowledge Capital 2003–; Deputy Chair. Northwest Devt Agency 2002–; mem. Bd Universities' Superannuation Scheme 1991–, Deputy Chair. 2004–06, Chair. 2006–; Dir Office of Fair Access 2004–; Chair. of Govs, Centre for Information on Language Teaching 1990–96; Crown Gov. SOAS 1990–93; Gov. Anglia Polytechnic Univ. 1989–93; mem. High Council, European Univ. Inst., Florence 1992–97, Comm. for Health Improvement 1999–2002; DL (Greater Manchester) 1997; Hon. mem. Royal Northern Coll. of Music 1996; Hon. Fellow, Queens' Coll., Cambridge 1992, Bolton Inst. 1996, Univ. of Central Lancashire 1999; Hon. LLD (Queen's Univ., Belfast) 1992; Hon. DUniv (Essex) 1993; Hon. DLitt (Salford) 1995, (Manchester Metropolitan) 2000, (Leicester) 2003, (Lincoln) 2003, (Ulster) 2004, (Manchester) 2004, (UMIST) 2004. *Publications:* The Evolution of French Syntax 1978, The Romance Languages (with N. Vincent) 1988; numerous articles in anthologies and professional journals. *Leisure interests:* gardening, walking. *Address:* Northwest Development Agency, Renaissance House, PO Box 37, Centre Park, Warrington, Cheshire, WA1 1XB, England (office). *Telephone:* (1925) 400532 (office). *Fax:* (1925) 400404 (office). *E-mail:* martin.harris@nwda.co.uk (office). *Website:* www.nwda.co.uk (office).

HARRIS, Michael, BSc, PhD; American mathematician and academic; *Professor of Mathematics, Université de Paris 7 Denis Diderot;* ed Princeton and Harvard Univs; held positions at Brandeis Univ. 1977–94, Prof. 1989–94; Prof., Université de Paris 7 Denis Diderot 1994–; mem. Institut Universitaire de France 2001; Sloan Fellowshiop 1982, Grand Prix Sophie Germain de l'Acad. des Sciences 2006, Clay Research Award, Clay Math. Inst. (co-recipient) 2007. *Publications:* more than 60 publs in professional journals. *Address:* Centre de Mathématiques de Jussieu, Université Paris 7 Denis Diderot, Case Postale 7012, 2 place Jussieu, 75251 Paris Cedex 05, France (office). *Telephone:* 1-44-27-86-78 (office). *E-mail:* harris@math.jussieu.fr (office). *Website:* people.math.jussieu.fr/~harris (office).

HARRIS, Michael (Mike) Deane, ICD.D; Canadian business executive, consultant and fmr politician; *Senior Business Adviser, Goodmans LLP;* b. 23 Jan. 1945, Toronto; s. of Deane Harris and Hope Harris; m. Laura Marie Harris; two s.; ed Inst. of Corp. Dirs; fmr school teacher, School Bd Trustee and School Bd Chair. Nipissing Bd of Educ.; began career in tourism and recreation industry owning ventures including tourist resort and ski centre; first elected to Ont. Prov. Legislature as MPP for Nipissing 1981, Minister of Natural Resources and Energy 1985, Premier of Prov. of Ont. 1995–2002; Leader of Conservative Party 1990–2002; mem. Bd Dirs Magna International Inc. 2003, Canaccord Capital 2004, FirstService Corpn, ENMAX Corpn, Augen Capital Corpn, Tim Horton Childrens' Foundation, Mount Royal Coll. Foundation; Dir Chair. Chartwell Srs Housing REIT 2003, Dir Chair. EnGlobe Corpn 2004; currently Sr Business Adviser Goodmans LLP, Toronto; Sr Fellow, Fraser Inst., Vancouver; Nat. Citizens' Coalition Freedom Medal 1996. *Leisure interests:* golf, skiing, bridge. *Address:* Goodmans LLP, 250 Yonge Street, Suite 2400, Toronto, ON M5B 2M6, Canada (office). *Telephone:* (416) 979-2211 (office); (416) 597-6295 (office). *Fax:* (416) 979-1234 (office). *E-mail:* mharris@goodmans.ca (office). *Website:* www.goodmans.ca (office).

HARRIS, Robert Dennis, FRSL; British journalist and writer; b. 7 March 1957, Nottingham; s. of the late Dennis Harris and Audrey Harris; m. Gill Hornby 1988; two s. two d.; ed Univ. of Cambridge; Pres. Cambridge Union; Dir and reporter, BBC 1978–86; Political Ed. Observer 1987–89; columnist, Sunday Times 1989–92, 1996–97. *Publications:* non-fiction: A Higher Form of Killing (with Jeremy Paxman) 1982, Gotcha! 1983, The Making of Neil Kinnock 1984, Selling Hitler 1987, Good and Faithful Servant 1990; novels: Fatherland 1992, Enigma 1995 (film 2001), Archangel 1998, Pompeii 2003, Imperium 2006, The Ghost 2007. *Leisure interests:* collecting books, walking. *Address:* Old Vicarage, Kintbury, Berks. RG17 9TR, England.

HARRIS, Rolf, CBE, AM; Australian entertainer and painter; b. 30 March 1930, Bassendean, WA; s. of C. G. Harris and A. M. Harris (née Robbins); m. Alwen Hughes 1958; one d.; ed Perth Modern School, Univ. of Western Australia, Claremont Teachers' Coll.; backstroke jr champion of Australia 1946; represented Australia at seven World Fairs 1969–85; Hon. mem. Royal Soc. of British Artists. *Television includes:* The Rolf Harris Show (BBC TV) 1967–71, Rolf on Saturday (BBC TV) 1977–79, Rolf's Cartoon Time (BBC TV) 1981–87, Rolf's Cartoon Club (HTV) 1987–92, Animal Hospital (BBC TV) 1994–, Rolf's Amazing World of Animals (BBC TV) 1997–, Bligh of the Bounty—World Navigator 1998–99, Rolf on Art (BBC TV) 2001–, Rolf's Golden Jubilee, Royal Albert Hall (BBC TV) 2003, Rolf Harris Star Portraits (BBC TV) 2004–. *Singles include:* Tie Me Kangaroo Down Sport 1960, Sun Arise 1962, Two Little Boys 1969, Stairway to Heaven 1993. *Publications:* Rolf Harris Picture Book of Cats 1978, Your Cartoon Time 1986, Win or Die 1989, Your Animation Time 1991, Personality Cats 1992, Me and You and Poems Too 1993, Can You Tell What It Is Yet (autobiog.) 2001, Rolf on Art 2002. *Leisure interests:* painting and portraiture, photography, wood carving, lapidary. *Address:* c/o Billy Marsh and Associates, 174–178 North Gower Street, London, NW1 2NB, England. *Telephone:* (20) 7388-6858. *Fax:* (20) 7388-6848. *Website:* www.rolfharris.com (office).

HARRIS, Stephen E., MS, PhD; American physicist and academic; *Kenneth and Barbara Oshman Professor, Stanford University;* b. 29 Nov. 1936, Brooklyn, New York; s. of Henry Harris and Anne Alpern Harris; m. Frances J. Greene 1959; one s. one d.; ed Rensselaer Polytechnic, Troy, New York and Stanford Univ.; Prof. of Electrical Eng, Stanford Univ. 1963–79, of Electrical Eng and Applied Physics 1979–, Dir Edward L. Ginzton Lab. 1983–88, Kenneth and Barbara Oshman Prof. 1988–, Chair. Dept of Applied Physics 1993–96; Guggenheim Fellowship 1976–77; mem., Nat. Acad. of Eng; A. Noble Prize 1965, McGraw Research Award 1973, Sarnoff Award 1978, Davies Medal 1984, C.H. Townes Award 1985, Einstein Prize 1991, Quantum Electronics Award 1994, Frederic Ives Medal 1999, Arthur L. Schawlow Prize in Laser Science 2002. *Publications:* articles in professional journals. *Leisure interests:* skiing, jogging, hiking. *Address:* Edward L. Ginzton Laboratory, Stanford University, 450 Via Palou, Stanford, CA 94305, USA (office). *Telephone:* (650) 723-0224 (office). *Fax:* (650) 725-4115 (office). *E-mail:* seharris@ee.stanford.edu (office). *Website:* www.-ee.stanford.edu/seharris/ (office).

HARRIS, Thomas; American writer; b. 1940, Jackson, TN; s. of William Thomas Harris, Jr and Polly Harris; m. (divorced); one d.; ed Baylor Univ., TX; worked on newsdesk Waco News-Tribune; mem. staff Associated Press, New York City 1968–74. *Publications:* Black Sunday 1975, Red Dragon 1981, The Silence of the Lambs (Bram Stoker Best Novel Award) 1988, Hannibal 1999, Hannibal Rising 2006. *Address:* c/o Arrow, Random House, 20 Vauxhall Bridge Road, London, SW1V 2SA, England. *Website:* www.thomasharris.com.

HARRIS, Timothy Sylvester, BSc, MSc, PhD; Saint Christopher and Nevis politician; *Minister of Foreign Affairs, International Trade, Industry, Commerce and Consumer Affairs;* b. 1964, Tabernacle; ed Cayon High School, Basseterre Sr High School, Univ. of the West Indies, Cave Hill and Sr Augustine, Concordia Univ., Montreal, Canada; worked at Social Security Office, Wellington Ltd and S.L. Horsford & Co. Ltd; mem. Labour Party, Constituency Sec. and Constituency Rep. on Nat. Exec. Bd, mem. Young Labour Advisory Cttee, and Youth Co-ordinator, currently Chair. St Kitts-Nevis Labour Party; mem. Parl. 1993–; Minister of Agric., Lands and Housing 1995–2000, of Foreign Affairs and Educ. 2000–04, of Foreign Affairs, Int. Trade, Industry, Commerce and Consumer Affairs 2004–; Victor Cooke Prize, Univ. of W Indies, Post Graduate Award, Cen. Bank of Trinidad and Tobago, Concordia/UWI Post Graduate Award. *Publications:* several articles in journals. *Leisure interests:* cricket, tennis, swimming, basketball, dominoes, travel. *Address:* Church Street, Basseterre (office); Tabernacle, St Kitts (home). *Telephone:* (869) 465-9085 (office); (869) 465-7768 (home). *Fax:* (869) 465-2556 (office). *E-mail:* tonskb@yahoo.co.uk (home).

HARRISON, Alistair; British diplomatist and government official; *Governor of Anguilla;* m. Sarah Harrison; one s. two d.; joined Defence Dept, FCO 1977; Third, then Second Sec., Embassy in Warsaw 1979–82; First Sec. Cyprus/Malta Desk, FCO 1982–84, Pvt. Sec. to Parl. Under-Sec. 1984–87; First Sec., Perm. Mission to UN, New York 1987–92; Deputy Head of Middle East Dept, FCO 1992–95; Deputy Head of Mission, Embassy in Warsaw 1995–98; Foreign Policy Adviser, European Comm. 1998–2000; Counsellor and Head of Chancery, Perm. Mission to UN, New York 2000–03; Head of UN Dept, then Head of Int. Orgs Dept 2003–05; High Commr to Lusaka 2005–08; Head of Zimbabwe Unit, FCO 2008; Gov. of Anguilla 2008–. *Address:* Office of the Governor, Government House, POB 60, The Valley, Anguilla (office). *Telephone:* 497-2622 (office). *Fax:* 497-3314 (office). *E-mail:* governorsoffice@gov.ai (office).

HARRISON, Sir David, Kt, CBE, ScD, FREng, FRSC, FIChemE, CCMI, FRSA; British academic; b. 3 May 1930, Clacton-on-Sea; s. of Harold David Harrison and Lavinia Wilson; m. Sheila Rachel Debes 1962; one s. one d. (one s. deceased); ed Bede School, Sunderland, Clacton Co. High School, Selwyn Coll., Univ. of Cambridge; Lecturer in Chemical Eng, Univ. of Cambridge 1956–79, Fellow, Selwyn Coll. 1957–, Sr Tutor 1967–79, Master of Selwyn Coll. 1994–2000, Chair. Faculty of Eng 1994–2001, mem. Council, Univ. of Cambridge 1967–75, 1995–2000, Chair. Faculty Bd of Educ. 1976–78, Deputy Vice-Chancellor 1995–2000, Pro-Vice-Chancellor 1997; Vice-Chancellor Univ. of Keele 1979–84, Univ. of Exeter 1984–94; Visiting Prof. of Chemical Eng, Univ. of Delaware, USA 1967, Univ. of Sydney, Australia 1976; Hon. Ed. Transactions, Inst. of Chemical Engineers 1972–78; Chair. Bd Trustees, Homerton Coll., Cambridge 1979–, Council Ely Cathedral 2001–, Univs' Cen. Council for Admissions 1984–91, Church & Associated Colls Advisory Cttee of the Polytechnics and Colls Funding Council 1989–91, Cttee of Vice-Chancellors and Prins of UK 1991–93, Shrewsbury School 1989–2003, Advisory Cttee on Safety of Nuclear Installations 1993–99, Eastern Arts Bd 1994–98, Arts Council of England 1996–98; Dir Salters' Inst. of Industrial Chem. 1993–; Vice-Pres. Inst. of Chemical Engineers 1989, Pres. 1991–92; Liveryman, Salters' Co. 1998; Hon. DUniv (Keele) 1992, (York) 2008; Hon. DSc (Exeter) 1995; George E. Davis Medal, Inst. of Chemical Engineers 2001. *Publications:* Fluidized Particles (with J.F. Davidson) 1963, Fluidization (with J.F. Davidson) 1971, Fluidization (with J.F. Davidson and R. Clift) 1985. *Leisure interests:* music, tennis, hill walking, good food. *Address:* 7 Gough Way, Cambridge, CB3 9LN, England (home). *Telephone:* (1223) 359315 (home). *Fax:* (1223) 359315 (home). *E-mail:* sirdavidharrison@yahoo.co.uk (home).

HARRISON, James (Jim) Thomas, BA, MA; American writer and poet; b. 11 Dec. 1937, Grayling, Mich.; s. of Winfield Sprague Harrison and Norma Olivia Harrison (née Wahlgren); m. Linda May King 1960; two d.; ed Michigan State Univ.; Asst Prof. of English, SUNY at Stony Brook 1965–66; NEA grant 1967–69, Guggenheim Fellowship 1968–69. *Film screenplays:* Cold Feet (with Tom McGuane) 1989, Revenge (with Jeffrey Fishkin) 1990, Wolf (with Wesley Strick) 1994. *Publications:* fiction: Wolf: A False Memoir 1971, A Good Day to

Die 1973, Farmer 1976, Legends of the Fall 1979, Warlock 1981, Sundog 1984, Dalva 1988, The Woman Lit by Fireflies 1990, Sunset Limited 1990, Julip 1994, The Road Home 1998, The Beast God Forgot to Invent 2000, True North 2004, The Summer He Didn't Die 2005, Returning to Earth 2007, The English Major 2008; poetry: Plain Song 1965, Locations 1968, Walking 1969, Outlyer and Ghazals 1971, Letters to Yesinin 1973, Returning to Earth 1977, New and Selected Poems, 1961–81 1982, The Theory and Practice of Rivers 1986, After Ikkyu and Other Poems 1996, The Shape of the Journey 1998, Braided Creek: A Conversation in Poetry 2003, Livingston Suite 2005, Saving Daylight 2006; non-fiction: Just Before Dark 1991, The Raw and the Cooked: Adventures of a Roving Gourmand 2001.

HARRISON, Patricia De Stacy, BA, MA,; American government official and broadcast executive; *President and CEO, Corporation for Public Broadcasting;* b. Brooklyn, New York; m. Emmett Bruce Harrison; three c.; ed American Univ.; mem. Pres.'s Export Council 1990, fmr mem. Exec. Cttee; mem. US Trade Rep.'s Service Policy Advisory Council 1992; Co-Chair. Republican Nat. Cttee 1997–2001; Asst Sec. for Educ. and Cultural Affairs, US Dept of State, Washington, DC 2001–05, Acting Under-Sec. for Public Diplomacy and Public Affairs 2004; Pres. and CEO Corpn for Public Broadcasting, Washington, DC 2005–; Founding Pnr, E. Bruce Harrison Co. (public relations agency) 1973–96; Founder and Pres. Nat. Women's Econ. Alliance; fmr Pres. Capital Press Women; fmr Chair. Guest Services Inc., Int. Cttee, Small Business Advisory Council, Small Business Admin; Visiting Fellow John F. Kennedy School of Govt 1992, Inst. for Public Service, Annenberg Public Policy Center 2000; est. Partnerships for Learning initiative;; Dr hc (American Univ. of Rome) 2002; Entrepreneur of the Year, Arthur Young Co. and Venture Magazine 1988, Northwood Inst. Distinguished Woman Award 1989, Hispanic Heritage Leadership Award 1998, Global Women's Leadership Award 1999, Woman of the Year Award, New York Black Republican Council 1999, Sec.'s Distinguished Service Award. *Publications:* A Seat at the Table: An Insider's Guide for America's New Women Leaders, America's New Women Entrepreneurs 1986. *Address:* Corporation for Public Broadcasting, 401 Ninth Street, NW, Washington, DC 20004-2129, USA (office). *Telephone:* (202) 879-9600 (office). *Website:* www.cpb.org (office).

HARRISON, Sir Terence, Kt, BSc, DL, FREng, FIMechE, FIMARE; British business executive (retd); b. 7 April 1933; s. of the late Roland Harrison and Doris Wardle; m. June Forster 1956; two s.; ed A. J. Dawson Grammar School, Co. Durham, West Hartlepool and Sunderland Tech. Colls. and Univ. of Durham; marine eng apprenticeship, Richardson's Westgarth, Hartlepool 1949–53; mil. service, Nigeria 1955–57; Clarke Chapman Ltd, Gateshead 1957–77, Man. Dir 1976–77; Northern Eng Industries 1977, Chief Exec. 1983–86, Exec. Chair. 1986–89; Dir Rolls-Royce PLC 1989–96, Chief Exec. 1992–96; Dir (non-exec.) Alfred McAlpine PLC 1995–2002, Chair. 1996–2002; Hon. DEng (Newcastle) 1991; Hon. DTech (Sunderland) 1995; Hon. DSc (Durham) 1996. *Publications:* technical papers. *Leisure interests:* golf, fell walking. *Address:* 2 The Garden Houses, Whalton, Northumberland, NE61 3HB, England (home). *Telephone:* (1670) 775400 (home). *Fax:* (1670) 775291 (home).

HARRISON, Tony; British poet and dramatist; b. 30 April 1937, Leeds; s. of Harry Ashton Harrison and Florence Horner (née Wilkinson); ed Leeds Grammar School and Univ. of Leeds; Cholmondeley Award for Poetry, Geoffrey Faber Memorial Award, European Poetry Translation Prize, Whitbread Poetry Prize 1993, Mental Health Award 1994, Prix Italia 1994, Northern Rock Foundation Writers' Award 2004. *Writing for television and film:* Yan Tan Tethera 1983, The Big H 1984, 'V' 1987, Loving Memory 1987, The Blasphemers' Banquet 1989, Black Daisies for the Bride 1993, A Maybe Day in Kazakhstan 1994, The Shadow of Hiroshima 1995, Prometheus 1998, Crossings 2002. *Plays:* Aikin Mata (with J. Simmons) 1965, The Misanthrope (version of Molière's play) 1973, Phaedra Britannica (version of Racine's Phèdre) 1975, The Passion 1977, Bow Down 1977, The Bartered Bride (libretto) 1978, The Oresteia (trans.) 1981, The Mysteries 1985, The Trackers of Oxyrhynchus 1990, The Common Chorus 1992, Square Rounds 1992, Poetry or Bust 1993, The Kaisers of Carnuntum 1995, The Labourers of Herakles 1995, The Prince's Play 1996, Fire and Poetry 1999, Fram 2008. *Publications include:* poetry: Earthworks 1964, Newcastle is Peru 1969, The Loiners 1970, Poems of Palladas of Alexandria (ed. and trans.) 1973, From the School of Eloquence and Other Poems 1978, Continuous 1981, A Kumquat for John Keats 1981, US Martial 1981, Selected Poems 1984, Fire-Gap 1985, 'V' 1985, Dramatic Verse, 1973–1985 1985, 'V' and Other Poems 1990, A Cold Coming: Gulf War Poems 1991, The Gaze of the Gorgon and other poems 1992, The Shadow of Hiroshima and other film/poems 1995, Permanently Bard 1995, Laureate's Block and other poems 2000, Under the Clock 2005, Collected Poems 2007, Collected Film Poetry 2007; collections of plays: Plays 1 1985, Theatre Works 1973–1985 1986, Plays 2 2002, Plays 3 1996, Plays 4 2002, Plays 5 2004, Hecuba 2005, Fram 2008. *Address:* c/o Gordon Dickerson, 2 Crescent Grove, London, SW4 7AH, England.

HARRISON, Wayne David, BA; Australian theatre director and producer; b. 7 March 1953, Melbourne; s. of Lindsay Graham Harrison and Florence Rosina Cannell; ed Christian Brothers' Coll., Melbourne, Univ. of Melbourne, Univ. of NSW; Dramaturge, Sydney Theatre Co. 1981–86; Asst Dir Northside Theatre Co., NSW 1987–89; Artistic Dir Sydney Theatre Co. 1990–99; Creative Dir Back Row Int., London and Clear Channel Entertainment Europe 1999–2001; Creative Dir New Year's Eve celebration, Sydney 2005, Closing Ceremony 2006 Melbourne Commonwealth Games; directed The Return of Houdini for City Theatre, Reykjavik 2005, Sunset Boulevard for The Production Company, elbourne 2005, End of The Rainbow for Ensemble Theatre, Sydney Opera House and MTC, Melbourne 2005. *Address:* c/o Melbourne 2006 Commonwealth Games Corporation, Locked Bag 2006, South Melbourne, Vic. 3205, Australia.

HARRISON, William Burwell, Jr, AB; American banker; b. 12 Aug. 1943, Rocky Mount, NC; s. of William Burwell and Katherine Spruill; m. Anne MacDonald Stephens 1985; two d.; ed Univ. of N Carolina, Chapel Hill; trainee Chemical Bank, New York 1967–69, Mid-South Corpn and corresp. banking group 1969–74, West Coast corp. and corresp. banking group 1974–76, Dist Head and Western Regional Co-ordinator San Francisco 1976–78, Regional Co-ordinator and Sr Vice-Pres. London 1978–82, Sr Vice-Pres. and Divisional Head, Europe 1982–83, Exec. Vice-Pres. US corp. div. New York 1983–87, Group Exec., banking and corporate finance group 1987–90, Vice-Chair. institutional banking 1990–2000; Vice-Chair. Global Bank 1992–2000; Vice-Chair. Manhattan Corpn (then Chase Manhattan Corpn) New York 1995–2000, Pres. and CEO 1999–2000, Chair. and CEO 2000, Pres. JPMorgan Chase (following merger) 2000–04, CEO 2000–05, Chair. 2001–06; mem. investment advisory cttee, Aurora Capital Partners 2008–. *Leisure interests:* athletics, travel. *Address:* c/o Aurora Capital Partners, 10877 Wilshire Boulevard, Suite 2100, Los Angeles, CA 90024, USA (office).

HARRISS, Gerald Leslie, MA, DPhil, FBA; British historian and university teacher; b. 22 May 1925, London; s. of W. L. Harriss and M. J. O. Harriss; m. Margaret Anne Sidaway 1959; two s. three d.; ed Chigwell School, Essex, Magdalen Coll., Oxford; war service in RNVR 1944–46; Univ. of Oxford 1946–53; Lecturer, Univ. of Durham 1953–65, Reader 1965–67; Fellow and Tutor in History, Magdalen Coll., Oxford 1967–92, Fellow Emer. 1992–, Reader in Modern History, Univ. of Oxford 1990–92. *Publications:* King, Parliament and Public Finance in Medieval England 1975, Henry V: the Practice of Kingship (ed.) 1985, Cardinal Beaufort 1988, K. B. McFarlane, Letters to Friends (ed.) 1997, Shaping the Nation: England 1360–1461 2005. *Address:* Fairings, 2 Queen Street, Yetminster, Sherborne, Dorset, DT9 6LL, England (home).

HARRY, Deborah (Debbie) Ann; American singer and actress; b. 1 July 1945, Miami, Fla; d. of Richard Smith and Catherine Harry (Peters); ed Centenary Coll.; singer and songwriter, rock group Blondie 1975–83, reformed 1997; awarded Gold, Silver and Platinum records. *Singles include:* Heart of Glass, Call Me, Tide is High, Rapture. *Albums include:* Blondie: The Hunter 1976, Plastic Letters 1977, Parallel Lines 1978, Eat to the Beat 1979, Autoamerican 1980, Rockbird, Def, Dumb and Blond 1989, Blonde and Beyond 1993, Rapture 1994, Virtuosity 1995, Rockbird 1996, No Exit 1999, Livid 2000, The Curse of Blondie 2003; solo: Koo Koo 1981, Rockbird 1986, Def, Dumb and Blonde 1989, Debravation 1993, Necessary Evil 2007. *Film appearances:* The Foreigner 1978, Unmade Beds 1980, Union City 1980, New York Beat Movie 1981, Videodrome 1983, Forever, Lulu 1987, Satisfaction 1988, Hairspray 1988, New York Stories 1989, Tales from the Darkside: The Movie 1990, Dead Beat 1994, Drop Dead Rock 1995, Heavy 1995, Cop Land 1997, Six Ways to Sunday 1997, Joe's Day 1998, Zoo 1999, Red Lipstick 2000, Deuces Wild 2000, Spun 2002, Try Seventeen 2002, My Life Without Me 2003, A Good Night to Die 2003, Tulse Luper Suitcases, Part 1: The Moab Story 2003, Patch 2005, I Remember You Now 2005, Elegy 2007. *Television appearances:* Saturday Night Live, The Muppet Show, Tales from the Darkside, Wiseguys. *Theatre:* Teaneck Tanzi, The Venus Flytrap. *Address:* Tenth Street Entertainment, 700 San Vicente Boulevard, Suite G410, West Hollywood, CA 90069, USA (office). *Website:* www.blondie.net; www.deborahharry.com.

HARRYHAUSEN, Ray; American film producer, writer and special effects creator; b. 29 June 1920, Los Angeles, Calif.; s. of Frederick W. Harryhausen and Martha Reske; m. Diana Livingstone 1962; one d.; ed Los Angeles City Coll.; model animator for George Pal's Puppetoons in early 1940s; served US Signal Corps; made series of filmed fairy tales with animated puppets for schools and churches; Asst to Willis O'Brien working on Mighty Joe Young 1946; designed and created special effects for The Beast from 20,000 Fathoms; evolved own model animation system Dynarama used for first time in conjunction with producer Charles H. Schneer in film It Came from Beneath the Sea; subsequently made many films in Dynarama with Schneer; Gordon E. Sawyer Award 1992. *Films with visual effects include:* 20 Million Miles to Earth 1957, The 3 Worlds of Gulliver 1960, Mysterious Island 1961, Jason and the Argonauts 1963, First Men in the Moon 1964, One Million Years B.C. 1966, The Valley of Gwangi 1969, The Golden Voyage of Sinbad 1974, Sinbad and the Eye of the Tiger 1977, Clash of the Titans 1981. *Films produced include:* How to Bridge a Gorge 1942, Mother Goose Stories 1946, The Story of Little Red Riding Hood 1949, Rapunzel 1951, Hansel and Gretel 1951, The Story of King Midas 1953, The 7th Voyage of Sinbad (1958, Jason and the Argonauts 1963, First Men in the Moon 1964, The Valley of Gwangi 1969, The Golden Voyage of Sinbad 1974, Sinbad and the Eye of the Tiger 1977, Clash of the Titans 1981, The Story of the Tortoise and the Hare 2002.

HART, Ann Weaver, MA, PhD; American professor of educational administration and university administrator; *President, Temple University;* b. Salt Lake City, Utah; m. Randy B. Hart; four d.; ed Univ. of Utah; began career teaching math., English and history at Cottonwood High School and Bonneville Jr High, Salt Lake City 1971–74; Prin. Farrer Jr High School, Provo, Utah 1983–84; Asst Prof., Educational Admin Dept, Univ. of Utah 1984, held various positions including Prof. of Educational Leadership, Assoc. Dean, then Dean of Grad. School of Educ., Accreditation Liaison Officer and Special Asst to Pres. –1998; Provost, Vice-Pres. for Academic Affairs and Faculty mem., Claremont Grad. Univ., Calif. 1998–2002; Pres. Univ. of New Hampshire 2002–06; Pres. Temple Univ., Phila 2006–; fmr Pres. Western Asscn of Grad. Schools; fmr Chair. Research Cttee Grad. Record Examination, Educational Testing Service; fmr Ed. Educational Administration Quarterly; mem. Bd of Dirs Citizens Bank of New Hampshire, Bd of Govs New

Hampshire Public TV, Bd of Trustees Univ. System of New Hampshire; fmr mem. Bd Council of Grad. Schools; mem. American Educational Research Asscn; consultant to educational insts, univs and nonprofit orgs; awards from Univ. Council for Educational Admin 1992, Business and Professional Women's Foundation 1995, Utah Women's Forum, Univ. of Utah Distinguished Alumna Humanities 2004, Business New Hampshire Magazine (Ten Most Powerful People in NH) 2006. *Publications:* The Principalship: A Theory of Professional Learning and Practice (co-author) 1996, Designing and Conducting Research (co-author) 1996; over 75 refereed journal articles and book chapters, five books and edited vols and numerous articles in publs. *Leisure interests:* cross-country hiking, camping in Wind River Range, Wyo., kayaking, bicycling. *Address:* Office of the President, Temple University, 1801 North Broad Street, Philadelphia, PA 19122, USA (office). *Telephone:* (215) 204-7405 (office). *Fax:* (215) 204-5600 (office). *E-mail:* president@temple.edu (office). *Website:* www.temple.edu/president (office).

HART, Gary, BA, BD, JD, DPhil, LLB; American politician and lawyer; *Of Counsel, Coudert Brothers LLP;* b. 28 Nov. 1936, Ottawa, Kan.; m. Lee Ludwig 1958; one s. one d.; ed Bethany Coll., Okla, Yale Univ.; assisted in John F. Kennedy Presidential Campaign 1960; called to Bar 1964; Attorney, US Dept of Justice and Special Asst to Sec., US Dept of Interior 1964–67; voluntary organizer, Robert F. Kennedy Presidential Campaign 1968; legal practice, Denver, Colo 1967–70, 1972–74; Nat. Campaign Dir, George McGovern Democratic Presidential Campaign 1970–72; Senator for Colorado 1975–86; with Davis, Graham & Stubbs, (law firm) Denver 1985; Of Counsel, Coudert Brothers LLP 1988–; co-Chair. US Comm. on Nat. Security for the 21st Century (Hart-Rudman Comm.) 1998–2000; fmr mem. Bd of Commrs, Denver Urban Renewal Authority; fmr mem. Park Hill Action Cttee. *Publications:* Right From the Start, A New Democracy 1983, The Double Man (with W. S. Cohen,) 1985, America Can Win 1986, The Strategies of Zeus 1987, Russia Shakes the World 1991, The Minutemen: Restoring an Army of the People 1998, The Fourth Power: An Essay Concerning A Grand Strategy for the United States in the 21st Century 2004. *Address:* Coudert Brothers LLP, One Market Spear Street Tower, Suite 2100, San Francisco, CA 94105-1126, USAPhone: 1 Fax: 1 (office). *Telephone:* (415) 267-6200 (office). *Fax:* (415) 977-6110 (office). *Website:* www.coudert.com (office).

HART, Graeme, MBA; New Zealand business executive; b. 1955; m.; two c.; ed Univ. of Otago; f. Rank Group Australia Pty Ltd (pvt. investment co.), Auckland, has acquired several cos including Burns, Philp & Co. Ltd (food products), Carter Holt Harvey (forest products), Evergreen Packaging Inc. (packaging equipment co.), SIG Holding (drink carton mfr). *Address:* Rank Group Ltd, Level 12, 132 Quay Street, Auckland 1001, New Zealand (office). *Telephone:* (9) 366-6259 (office). *Fax:* (9) 366-6263 (office).

HART, Michael, CBE, PhD, DSc, FRS, FInstP; British academic; *Visiting Professor of Physics, University of Bristol;* b. 4 Nov. 1938, Bristol; s. of Reuben H. V. Hart and Phyllis M. Hart (née White); m. Susan M. Powell 1963; three d.; ed Cotham Grammar School, Bristol and Univ. of Bristol; Research Assoc., Dept of Materials Science and Eng, Cornell Univ. 1963–65; Dept of Physics, Univ. of Bristol 1965–67, Lecturer in Physics 1967–72, Reader 1972–76; Sr Resident Research Assoc., Nat. Research Council, NASA Electronics Research Center, Boston, Mass 1969–70; Special Adviser, Cen. Policy Review Staff 1975–77; Wheatstone Prof. of Physics, King's Coll. London 1976–84; Prof. of Physics, Univ. of Manchester 1984–93, Prof. Emer. of Physics 1993–; Visiting Prof. of Applied Physics, De Montfort Univ. 1993–98, Hon. Prof. in Eng, Univ. of Warwick 1993–1995; Science Programme Co-ordinator (part-time), Daresbury Lab. Science and Eng Research Council 1985–88; Chair. Nat. Synchrotron Light Source, Brookhaven Nat. Lab., USA 1995–2000; Visiting Prof. of Physics, Univ. of Bristol 2000–; Bertram Eugene Warren Award, American Crystallographic Asscn 1970, Charles Vernon Boys Award, Inst. of Physics 1971. *Publications:* contribs to learned journals. *Leisure interests:* flying kites, cookery. *Address:* Department of Physics, University of Bristol, Bristol, BS8 1TL (office); 2 Challoner Court, Merchants Landing, Bristol, BS1 4RG, England (home). *Telephone:* (117) 921-5291 (home). *E-mail:* michael .hart8@btopenworld.com (home).

HART, Oliver D'Arcy, PhD; British economist and academic; *Andrew E. Furer Professor of Economics, Harvard University;* b. 9 Oct. 1948, London; s. of Philip D'Arcy Hart and Ruth Meyer; m. Rita B. Goldberg 1974; two s.; ed Univs of Cambridge and Warwick and Princeton Univ., USA; Lecturer in Econs, Univ. of Essex 1974–75; Asst Lecturer, then Lecturer in Econs, Univ. of Cambridge 1975–81; Prof. of Econs, LSE 1981–85; BP Centennial Visiting Prof. 1992–93, 1997–; Prof. of Econs, MIT 1984–93; Prof. of Econs, Harvard Univ. 1993–97, Andrew E. Furer Prof. of Econs 1997–; Fellow, American Acad. of Arts and Sciences; Corresp. Fellow, British Acad. 2000; Dr hc (Free Univ. of Brussels) 1992; Hon. DPhil (Basle) 1994. *Publications:* Firms, Contracts and Financial Structure 1995; numerous articles in professional journals. *Address:* Department of Economics, Littauer 220, Harvard University, Cambridge, MA 02138, USA (office). *Telephone:* (617) 496-3461 (office). *Fax:* (617) 495-1879 (office). *Website:* economics.harvard.edu/faculty/hart/hart .html (office).

HART, Stanley Robert, BS, MS, PhD; American geochemist and academic; *Senior Scientist Emeritus, Woods Hole Oceanographic Institution;* b. 20 June 1935, Swampscott, Mass; s. of Robert W. Hart and Ruth M. Hart; m. 1st Joanna Smith 1956 (divorced 1976); m. 2nd Pamela Shepherd 1980; one s. two d.; ed Massachusetts Inst. of Tech., California Inst. of Tech.; Fellow, Carnegie Inst. of Washington 1960–61, mem. staff 1961–75; Visiting Prof., Univ. of Calif., San Diego 1967–68; Prof. of Geology and Geochemistry, MIT 1975–89; Sr Scientist, Woods Hole Oceanographic Inst. 1989–2007, Sr Scientist Emer. 2007–; mem. NAS; Fellow, American Geophysical Union, Geological Soc. of America, European Asscn of Geochemistry, Geochemical Soc., European

Union of Geosciences, American Acad. of Arts and Sciences; Dr hc (Paris) 2005; Goldschmidt Medal (Geochemical Soc.) 1992, Hess Medal (American Geophysical Union) 1997, Columbus O'Donnell Iselin Chair for Excellence in Oceanography, NAS Arthur L. Day Prize and Lectureship 2007. *Publications:* more than 225 articles in scientific journals. *Leisure interests:* woodworking, fishing, running. *Address:* Woods Hole Oceanographic Institution, Woods Hole, MA 02543 (office); 53 Quonset Road, Falmouth, MA 02540, USA (home). *Telephone:* (508) 289-2837 (office); (508) 548-1656. *Fax:* (508) 457-2175 (office). *E-mail:* shart@whoi.edu (office). *Website:* www.whoi.edu/science/GG/people/ shart (office).

HART OF CHILTON, Baron (Life Peer), cr. 2004, of Chilton in the County of Suffolk; **Garry Richard Rushby Hart,** LLB, FRSA; British solicitor; *Special Expert Adviser to Secretary of State for Constitutional Affairs and Lord Chancellor;* b. 29 June 1940, London; s. of Dennis George Hart and Evelyn Mary Hart; m. 1st Paula Lesley Shepherd 1966 (dissolved 1986); two s. one d.; m. 2nd Valerie Elen Mary Davies 1986; two d.; ed Northgate Grammar School, Ipswich, Univ. Coll. London; solicitor, Herbert Smith 1966–70, partner 1970–98, Head of Property Dept 1988–97; Special Expert Adviser to Secretary of State for Constitutional Affairs and Lord Chancellor 1998–; Trustee Architecture Foundation 1997–2005 (Deputy Chair. 2000–05), Almeida Theatre 1997–2004 (Chair. 1997–2002), British Architectural Library Trust 2000–; Fellow, Univ. Coll. London 2001; Hon. FRIBA 2000. *Publications:* Blundell & Dobry's Planning Applications Appeals and Procedures (co-ed. 4th and 6th edns) 1990, 1996. *Leisure interests:* travel, conservation, talking. *Address:* Department of Constitutional Affairs and Lord Chancellor's Department, Selborne House, 54–60 Victoria Street, London, SW1E 6QW, England (office). *Telephone:* (20) 7210-8594 (office). *Fax:* (20) 7210-1327 (office). *Website:* www.dca.gov.uk (office).

HARTARTO SASTRO SUNARTO, AO, BE; Indonesian politician and engineer; b. 30 May 1932, Delanggu, Cen. Java; s. of Sastro Sunarto; m. Hartini Hartarto; three s. two d.; ed Univ. of Indonesia Bandung School of Chemical Eng and Univ. of NSW, Australia; Head, Expansion Project, Leces Paper Mill 1960, Dir Leces Paper Co. 1961–64, Pulp & Paper Holding Co. 1964–66; on staff of Dir-Gen. for Basic Chemical Industries, Ministry of Industry 1966, Dir-Gen. 1979; Chair. Gresik Petrochemical Co. 1978–83, Tonasa Cement Co. 1978–93, PT Asean Aceh Fertilizer Co. 1978–83, Rekayasa Eng & Contracting Co. 1981–83; mem. The People's Consultative Ass. 1983; Leader and Chair. Indonesian Ministerial Del., APEC Ministerial Meeting, ASEAN Econ. Ministers Meeting, Indonesia-Malaysia-Singapore Growth Triangle; Minister of Industry 1983–93, Co-ordinating Minister for Industrial and Trade 1993–95, for Production and Distribution 1995–98, 1998–99, for Devt Supervision and State Admin. Reform, also acting as Co-ordinating Minister for Econ., Finance and Industry; currently Chair. Foundation of Indonesian Inst. of Tech.; Life Deputy Gov. American Biographical Inst. Research Asscn; Life Sec. Gen. United Cultural Convention, USA 2004–; Groot Kruis, Order Van Oranje Nassau (Netherlands) 1966; Grosse Verdienstkreuz mit Stern und Schulterband (FRG) 1984; Grand Cordon of Order of Al-Istliqlal (Jordan) 1988; Grand Order of Mugunghwa (South Korea) 1992; Kt Commdr's Cross (Austria) 1996; Bohdan Khmelnitsky Order, First Degree (Ukraine) 1997; Hon. DLitt (Univ. of Nagpur, India) 1992, (Nanyang Technological Univ. of Singapore) 1995; Hon. DSc (NSW) 1993, (Bandung Inst. of Tech.) 1996; Dr hc (Erasmus Univ., Netherlands and Bernard Mandeville Foundation, Rotterdam) 1995; Satya Lancana Pembangunam 1974, Bintang Mahaputera Adipradana 1987, Medal of Veteran Legion 1991, Productivity Award, Int. Productivity Network, Rutgers State Univ. of New Jersey 1992, Bintang Republik Indonesia Utama 1998. *Publication:* Industrialisation and the Development of Agriculture Sector and Services to Achieve the Indonesian Vision 2030 2006. *Leisure interest:* world history. *Address:* 34–36 Tirtayasa, Kebayoran Baru, Jakarta 12160, Indonesia (home). *Telephone:* (21) 7260073 (home); (21) 7203049. *Fax:* (21) 72222206 (home).

HÄRTER, Hans-Georg; German engineer and business executive; *CEO, ZF Group;* b. 2 May 1945, Bensheim; ed Berlin Tech. School, Meersburg Acad.; trained as machine fitter; certified as state-approved mechanical engineer (industrial production); joined ZF Passau GmbH, Passau 1973, Head of Dept, Value Analysis/Methods 1982–87, Head of Specialist Dept, Value Analysis/ Methods 1987–90, Sr Head of Tech. Cost Budgeting 1990, Deputy Group Vice-Pres., ZF Passau GmbH, Passau 1990–91, Group Vice-Pres. 1991–94, mem. Bd of Man. ZF Group Off-Road Driveline Tech. and Axle Systems Div., Marine Propulsion Systems Business Unit and Production Tech. 1994–2002, mem. Bd of Man., ZF Group Powertrain and Suspension Components, Div. Business Unit Aftermarket Trading, Asian Pacific Region and CEO ZF Sachs AG, Schweinfurt 2002–06, Exec. Vice-Pres., ZF Group 2006–07, CEO 2007–. *Address:* ZF Friedrichshafen AG, Graf-von-Soden-Platz 1, 88046 Friedrichshafen, Germany (office). *Telephone:* (7541) 77-0 (office). *Fax:* (7541) 77-908000 (office). *E-mail:* postoffice@zf.com (office). *Website:* www.zf.com (office).

HARTL, Franz-Ulrich, MD, DrMed (Habil.); German biochemist and academic; *Professor of Cellular Biochemistry, Max Planck Institute for Biochemistry;* b. 10 March 1957, Essen; ed Univs of Heidelberg and Munich; Postdoctoral Fellow, Inst. of Physiological Chem., Univ. of Munich 1985–86, Group Leader Inst. of Physiological Chem. 1987–89, 'Akademischer Rat', Inst. of Physiological Chem. 1990–91; Postdoctoral Fellow, UCLA and Fellow, Deutsche Forschungsgemeinschaft (German Research Council) 1989–90; Assoc. mem. Program in Cellular Biochemistry and Biophysics, Sloan-Kettering Inst., New York 1991–92, mem. (with tenure) 1993–97; William E. Snee Chair of Cellular Biochemistry 1995; Assoc. Prof. of Cell Biology and Genetics, Grad. School of Medical Science, Cornell Univ., NY 1991–92, Prof. 1993–97; Assoc. Investigator, Howard Hughes Medical Institute 1994–97; Prof. of Cellular Biochemistry and Dir, Max Planck Inst. for Biochemistry, Martinsried 1997–, Man. Dir

2002; mem. European Molecular Biology Org. 1998, Leopoldina (German Acad. of Sciences) 2002, Bavarian Acad. of Sciences 2004; Foreign mem. Acad. of Science of Nordrhein-Westfalen 1997; Hon. Prof., Univ. of Munich 1997; Foreign Hon. mem. American Acad. of Arts and Sciences 2000; Vinci Award, LVMH Science for Art competition 1996, Lipmann Award, American Soc. of Biochemistry and Molecular Biology 1997, Academy Prize, Acad. of Science of Berlin-Brandenburg 1999, Wilhelm Vaillant Research Prize 2000, Gottfried Wilhelm Leibniz-Prize, Deutsche Forschungsgemeinschaft 2002, Feldberg Prize 2003, Gairdner Foundation Int. Award 2004, Ernst Jung Prize for Medicine, Jung-Stiftung für Wissenschaft und Forschung (co-recipient) 2005, Stein and Moore Award, Protein Soc. 2006, Koerber European Science Award 2006, Wiley Prize in Biomedical Sciences 2007, Lewis S. Rosenstiel Award 2008, Louisa Gross Horwitz Prize 2008. *Publications:* numerous scientific papers in professional journals. *Address:* c/o Andrea Obermayr-Rauter, Max Planck Institute of Biochemistry, Department of Cellular Biochemistry, Am Klopferspitz 18, 82152 Martinsried, Germany (office). *Telephone:* (89) 8578-2244 (office). *Fax:* (89) 8578-2211 (office). *E-mail:* uhartl@biochem.mpg.de (office); obermayr@biochem.mpg.de (office). *Website:* www.biochem.mpg.de/en/rd/hartl (office).

HARTLAND, Michael (see James, Michael Leonard).

HARTLEY, Frank Robinson, DSc, FRSC, CCMI; British chemist; *Vice-Chancellor, Cranfield University;* b. 29 Jan. 1942, Epsom; s. of Sir Frank Hartley and Lydia May England; m. Valerie Peel 1964; three d.; ed Kings Coll. School, Wimbledon, Magdalen Coll., Oxford; Post-doctoral Fellow, Commonwealth Scientific and Industrial Research Org., Div. of Protein Chem., Melbourne, Australia 1966–69; ICI Research Fellow and Tutor in Physical Chem., Univ. Coll., London 1969–70; Lecturer in Inorganic Chem., Univ. of Southampton 1970–75; Prof. of Chem. and Head of Dept of Chem. and Metallurgy, Royal Mil. Coll. of Science, Shrivenham 1975–82, Acting Dean 1982–84, Prin. and Dean 1984–89; Man. Dir CIT Holdings Ltd 1989–; Dir (non-exec.) T&N PLC 1989–98, Nat. Westminster Bank Eastern Region Advisory Bd 1990–92, Kalon PLC 1994–99, Kenwood PLC 1995–99; Vice-Chancellor Cranfield Univ. 2000–; Asscn of Commonwealth Univs Sr Travelling Fellow 1986; Special Adviser on Defence Systems to the Prime Minister 1988–90; Specialist Adviser to House of Lords Select Cttee on Science and Tech. 1993–94; Chair. AWE Academic Council 1998–2001; mem. Int. Advisory Bd Kanazawa Acad. of Science and Tech., Japan 1989–; Dir Shuttleworth Trust 1994–97; Trustee Lorch Foundation 1994–; AWE Corp. Advisory Panel 2002–; DL Beds.; Hon. FRAeS. *Publications:* The Chemistry of Platinum and Palladium (Applied Science) 1973, Elements of Organometallic Chemistry (Chemical Soc.) 1974, Solution Equilibria (with C. Burgess and R. M. Alcock) 1980; The Chemistry of the Metal Carbon Bond (Vols 1–5) 1983–89, Supported Metal Complexes 1985, Brasseys New Battlefield Weapons Systems and Technology series 1988– (Ed.-in-Chief), The Chemistry of Organophosphorus Compounds Vols 1–4 1990–96, Chemistry of the Platinum Group Metals 1991, papers in inorganic, co-ordination and organometallic chem. in major English, American and Australian journals. *Leisure interests:* cliff walking, golf, swimming, gardening. *Address:* Vice-Chancellor's Office, Cranfield University, Cranfield, Beds., MK43 0AL, England (office). *Telephone:* (01234) 754013 (office). *Fax:* (01234) 752583 (office). *E-mail:* a.perkins@cranfield.ac.uk (office). *Website:* www.cranfield.ac.uk (office).

HARTLEY, Hal, (also known as Ned Rifle), BA; American film director, producer and scriptwriter; b. 3 Nov. 1959, Lindenhurst, NY; ed State Univ. of New York-Purchase Film School; film maker True Fiction Pictures 1984–. *Films:* Kid 1984, Home of The Brave 1986, The Cartographer's Girlfriend 1987, Dogs 1988, The Unbelievable Truth 1990, Trust 1991, Simple Men 1992, From a Motel 6 1993, Iris 1993, The Only Living Boy in New York 1993, Flirt 1993, Amateur 1994, Henry Fool 1997, The Girl from Monday 2004, Fay Grim 2006. *Television films:* Surviving Desire 1989, Achievement 1991, Ambition 1991. *Address:* True Fiction Pictures, 39 W. 14th Street, Suite 406, New York, NY 10011, USA.

HÄRTLING, Peter; German writer and journalist; b. 13 Nov. 1933, Chemnitz; s. of Rudolf Härtling and Erika Härtling (née Häntzschel); m. Mechthild Maier 1959; two s. two d.; ed Gymnasium (Nürtingen/Neckar); childhood spent in Saxony, Czechoslovakia and Württemberg; journalist 1953–; Literary Ed. Deutsche Zeitung und Wirtschaftszeitung, Stuttgart and Cologne; Ed. of magazine Der Monat 1962–70, also Co-publisher; Ed. and Man. Dir S. Fischer Verlag, Frankfurt 1968–74, Ed. Die Väter; mem. PEN, Akad. der Wissenschaften und der Literatur Mainz, Akad. der Künste Berlin, Deutsche Akad. für Sprache und Dichtung Darmstadt; Hon. Prof. 1996; Grosses Bundesverdienstkreuz 1996; Hon. DPhil 2001; Dr hc (Giessen) 2002; Literaturpreis des Deutschen Kritikerverbandes 1964, Literaturpreis des Kulturkreises der Deutschen Industrie 1965, Literarischer Förderungspreis des Landes Niedersachsen 1965, Prix du meilleur livre étranger, Paris 1966, Gerhart Hauptmann Preis 1971, Deutscher Jugendbuchpreis 1976, Stadtschreiber von Bergen-Enkheim 1978–79, Hölderlin-Preis 1987, Lion-Feuchtwanger-Preis 1992, Stadtschreiber von Mainz 1995, Leuschner-Medaille des Landes Hessen 1996, Eichendorff-Preis 1999, Deutsche Jugendbuchpreis 2001, Deutscher Bücherpreis 2002. *Publications:* Yamins Stationen (poetry) 1955, In Zeilen zuhaus (essays) 1957, Palmström grüsst Anna Blume (essays) 1961, Spielgeist-Spiegelgeist (poetry) 1962, Niembsch oder Der Stillstand (novel) 1964, Janek (novel) 1966, Das Familienfest (novel) 1969, Gilles (play) 1970, Ein Abend, Eine Nacht, Ein Morgen (novel) 1971, Neue Gedichte 1972, Zwettl – Nachprüfung einer Erinnerung (novel) 1973, Eine Frau (novel) 1974, Hölderlin (novel) 1976, Anreden (poetry) 1977, Hubert oder Die Rückkehr nach Casablanca (novel) 1978, Nachgetragene Liebe (novel) 1980, Die dreifache Maria 1982, Vorwarnung 1983, Sätze von Liebe 1983, Das Windrad (novel) 1983, Ich rufe die Wörter zusammen 1984, Der spanische Soldat oder Finden under Erfinden 1984, Felix Guttmann (novel) 1985, Waiblingers Augen (novel) 1987, Die Mösinger Pappel 1987, Waiblingers Augen 1987, Der Wanderer (novel) 1988, Briefe von drinnen und draußen (poetry) 1989, Herzwand (novel) 1990, Brüder under Schwestern: Tagebuch eines Synodalen 1991, Schubert (novel) 1992, Božena (novel) 1994, Schumanns Schatten (novel) 1996, Grosse, Kleine Schwester (novel) 1998, Hoffmann oder Die vielfältige Liebe (novel) 2001, Leben lernen (autobiog.) 2004, Die Lebenslinie (autobiog.) 2005. *Address:* Finkenweg 1, 64546 Mörfelden-Walldorf, Germany. *Telephone:* (6105) 6109 (office). *Fax:* (6105) 74687 (office). *E-mail:* peter@haertling.de (office). *Website:* www.haertling.de (office).

HARTMAN, Arthur A., AB; American diplomatist (retd) and business executive; *Senior Consultant, APCO Worldwide Inc.;* b. 12 March 1926, New York; m. Donna Van Dyke Ford; three s. two d.; ed Harvard Univ., Harvard Law School; served in US Army Air Corps 1944–46; Econ. Officer, Econ. Co-operation Admin., Paris 1948–52; Econ. Officer of US del. to European Army Conf., Paris 1952–54; Politico-Mil. officer, US Mission to NATO, Paris 1954–55; Econ. Officer, Jt US Embassy/Agency for Int. Devt Mission, Saigon, Repub. of Viet Nam 1956–58; Int. Affairs Officer, Bureau of European Affairs, Dept of State 1958–61; Staff Asst to Under-Sec. of State for Econ. Affairs 1961–62, Special Asst 1962–63; Head of Econ. Section, US Embassy, London 1963–67; Special Asst to Under-Sec. of State 1967–69; Staff Dir of Sr Interdepartmental Group 1967–69; Deputy Dir of Co-ordination to Under-Sec. of State 1969–72; Deputy Chief of Mission and Minister-Counsellor, US Mission to European Communities, Brussels 1972–74; Asst Sec. of State for European Affairs 1974–77; US Amb. to France 1977–81, to USSR 1981–87; Sr Consultant APCO Consulting Group, Wash. 1989–; Chair. Barings' First NIS Regional Investment Fund, New Russia Fund; Chair. Advisory Cttee Baring Vostok Equity Fund; mem. Bd of Dirs Dreyfus Funds, Ford Meter Box Company Inc., Baring Vostok Investment Ltd, French American Foundation, Terra Foundation, American Univ. of Paris, American Hospital of Paris Foundation; fmr mem. Bd of Dirs ITT Hartford Insurance Group, Lawter Int.; mem. Council on Foreign Relations; Chair. Int. Arts and Exhibition Foundation; Vice-Chair. American Acad. of Diplomacy; Chair. Policy Council, Cox Foundation; fmr Pres. Harvard Univ. Bd of Overseers; Hon. degrees (Wheaton Coll., American Coll. in Paris); Presidential Man. Improvement Award 1970, Distinguished Honor Award 1972, Veterans of Foreign Wars Medal of Honor 1981, Sec. of State's Distinguished Service Award 1987, Dept of State Wilbur J. Carr Award 1987, Annual Nat. Conf. on Soviet Jewry Award 1987; Officier Légion d'honneur. *Address:* APCO Worldwide Inc., 700 12th Street, NW, Suite 800, Washington, DC 20005 (office); 2738 McKinley Street, NW, Washington, DC 20015, USA (home). *Telephone:* (202) 778-1000 (office). *Fax:* (202) 466-6002 (office). *Website:* www.apcoworldwide.com (office).

HARTMAN, George Eitel, MFA; American architect; *Partner, Hartman-Cox Architects;* b. 7 May 1936, Fort Hancock, NJ; s. of George E. Hartman and Evelyn Ritchie; m. 1st Ann Burdick 1965 (divorced 2000); one s. one d.; m. 2nd Ian Cigliano 2001; ed Princeton Univ.; with Keyes Lethbridge & Condon Architects 1960–64; own pvt. practice George E. Hartman 1964–65, Hartman-Cox Architects 1965–; mem. US Comm. of Fine Arts 1990–93, Architectural Advisory Bd, Foreign Bldg Office, US Dept of State 1991–, American Inst. of Architects (AIA) Coll. of Fellows; Fellow American Acad. Rome; AIA Nat. Honor Awards 1970, 1971, 1981, 1988, 1989 and numerous other awards. *Buildings include:* US Embassy, Kuala Lumpur 1979, 1001 Pennsylvania Avenue, Washington, DC 1979, HEB HQ, San Antonio, Tex. 1982, Chrysler Museum, Norfolk, NJ 1984, Georgetown Univ. Law Library 1989, Market Square, Washington, DC 1990, 800 N Capital Street, Washington, DC 1990, 1200 K Street and 154 K Street, Washington, DC 1991. *Leisure interest:* sailing. *Address:* Hartman Cox Architects, 1074 Thomas Jefferson Street, NW, Washington, DC 20007 (office); 1657 31st Street, Washington, DC 20007, USA (home). *Telephone:* (202) 333-6446; (202) 333-1657 (home).

HARTMANN, Peter, DPhil; German diplomatist (retd); b. 9 Oct. 1935, Aachen; s. of Leonhard Hartmann and Gertrud Hartmann; m. Lonny Freifrau von Blomberg 1968; two d.; ed Gymnasium, Aachen, Univs of Frankfurt, Rome, Cologne, Fribourg; joined Foreign Service 1965, Consulate, Karachi, Pakistan 1968–71, EC Del. Brussels 1971–74, Foreign Ministry Bonn 1974–77, Embassy, Buenos Aires, Argentina 1977–80, Head of Office for Foreign Relations CDU, Bonn 1981–84, Chancellor's Office, Bonn 1984–93, Head European Policy 1987–91, Foreign and Security Policy 1991–93; Amb. to UK 1993–95, to France 1998–2001 (retd); State Sec. of Foreign Affairs 1995–98; Hon. KBE. *Publication:* Interessenpluralismus und politische Entscheidung 1966. *Leisure interests:* tennis, literature. *Address:* Auf dem Reeg 19, 53343 Wachtberg-Pech, Germany (home). *Telephone:* (228) 2894300 (home). *E-mail:* p007hartmann@aol.com (home).

HARTMANN, Peter C., DPhil; German historian and fmr academic; *Professor of History, University of Mainz;* b. 28 March 1940, Munich; s. of Alfred Hartmann and Manfreda Knote; m. Beate Just 1972; two s. two d.; ed Univs. of Munich and Paris; Research Assoc. Deutsches Historisches Institut, Paris 1970–81; Privatdozent, Munich 1979; Prof. Univ. of Passau 1982; Prof. of History, Univ. of Mainz 1988–; Chevalier des Palmes académiques 2001; Hon. DUniv (Paris); Strasbourg Int. Prize. *Publications:* Pariser Archive, Bibl. u. Dok.zentren 1976, Geld als Instrument europäischer Machtpolitik im Zeitalter des Merkantilismus 1978, Das Steuersystem der europäischen Staaten am Ende der Ancien Regime 1979, Karl Albrecht-Karl VII: Glücklicher Kurfürst, Unglücklicher Kaiser 1985, Französische Geschichte 1914–1945, Französische Verfgeschichte der Neuzeit (1450–1980), Ein Überblick 1985, 2nd edn 2003, Bayerns Weg in die Gegenwart: Vom Stammesherzogtum bis zur Freistaat heute 1989, Der Jesuitenstaat in

Südamerika 1609–1768 1994, Franz. Könige u. Kaiser der Neuzeit 1994, Regionen in der Frühen Neuzeit 1994, Der Mainzer Kurfürst als Reichskanzler 1996, Der Bayerische Reichskreis (1500–1803) 1997, Kurmainz, das Reichskanzleramt und der Reich 1998, Geschichte Frankreichs 1999, 3rd edn 2003, Geschichte aktuell, hg. v.K. Amann 2000, Reichskirche, Kurmainz und Reichserzkanzleramt 2001, Die Jesuiten 2001, Kulturgeschichte des Heiligen Römischen Reiches 1648 bis 1806 Verfassung, Religion und Kultur 2001, Die Mainzer Kurfürsten d. Hauses Schönborn 2002, Religion und Kultur im Europa d.17 u.18 Jahrhunderts 2004, Das Heilige Römische Reich deutscher Nation in der Neuzeit 1485–1806 2005, Kleine Mainzer Stadtgeschichte 2005. *Address:* Böcklinstrasse 4a, 80638 Munich; Saarstrasse 21, 55099 Mainz, Germany. *Telephone:* (89) 15780615 (home). *Fax:* (89) 15780615 (home). *E-mail:* peterclaushartmann@gmx.de (home).

HARTMANN, Ulrich; German business executive; *Chairman, Supervisory Board, E.ON AG;* b. 7 Aug. 1938, Berlin; m.; two c.; legal studies in Munich, Berlin and Bonn; auditor, Treuarbeit AG, Düsseldorf 1967–71; Asst to Man. Bd Deutsche Leasing AG, Frankfurt 1971–72; Corp. Counsel, VEBA Kraftwerke Ruhr AG, Gelsenkirchen 1973–75; Head, Bd Office and Public Relations, VEBA AG, Düsseldorf 1975–80; mem. Man. Bd Nordwestdeutsche Kraftwerke AG, Hamburg 1980–85, PreussenElektra AG, Hanover 1985–89; mem. Man. Bd VEBA AG 1989, Chief Finance Officer 1990–93, CEO and Chair. 1993; Chair. Supervisory Bd E.ON AG 2003–, also Chair. Exec. Cttee and Finance and Investment Cttee; Chair. Supervisory Bd of major group cos and Municher Rückversicherungs-Gesellschaft AG, Munich, RAG Aktiengesellschaft, Essen, Degussa AG 1998; Consul-Gen. of Norway 1993; Dir (non-exec.) Cable and Wireless PLC, London; mem. Supervisory Bd Daimler-Benz AG, Stuttgart, Deutsche Lufthansa AG, Cologne, Hochtief AG, Essen, IKB Deutsche Industriebank AG, Düsseldorf, Municher Rückversicherungs-Gesellschaft AG, Munich. *Address:* E.ON-Platz 1, 40479 Düsseldorf, Germany (office). *Telephone:* (211) 45790 (office). *Fax:* (211) 4579501 (office). *Website:* www.eon.com (office).

HARTSHORN, Michael Philip, DPhil, FRSNZ; British/New Zealand chemist and academic; *Professor Emeritus of Chemistry, University of Canterbury;* b. 10 Sept. 1936, Coventry, England; m. Jacqueline Joll 1963; four s.; ed Imperial Coll. of Science and Tech., London, University Coll., Oxford; Lecturer in Chem., Univ. of Canterbury, NZ 1960–66, Sr Lecturer 1966–68, Reader 1968–72, Prof. 1972–97, Prof. Emer. 1996–; Fulbright Visiting Prof., Cornell Univ., New York 1966–67; Guest Prof., Lund Univ., Sweden 1991–92, 1995, 1997; Fürth Visiting Lecturer, Royal Soc. of Edinburgh 1991; Wilsmore Fellow Melbourne Univ. June–July 1996; Fellowship NZ Inst. of Chem. 1969; Hector Medal, Royal Soc. of NZ 1973. *Publications:* approx. 255 scientific papers; Steroid Reaction Mechanisms (with D. N. Kirk) 1968. *Leisure interests:* reading, music, gardening. *Address:* 29 Clare Road, Merivale, Christchurch 8001, New Zealand (home). *Telephone:* (3) 3556-450 (home). *Fax:* (3) 3558-357 (home). *E-mail:* michael.hartshorn@canterbury.ac.nz (office). *Website:* www.chem.canterbury.ac.nz (office).

HARTUNG, Harald; German poet, academic and critic; *Professor, Technische Universität Berlin;* b. 29 Oct. 1932, Herne; s. of Richard Hartung and Wanda Hartung; m. Freia Schnackenburg 1979; two s.; secondary school teacher 1960–66; Prof., Pädagogische Hochschule Berlin 1971–80, Tech. Univ. Berlin 1980–; mem. Akad. der Künste, Berlin, PEN; Kunstpreis Berlin, Drostepreis 1987, Premio Antico Fattore 1999. *Publications:* Experimentelle Literatur und Konkrete Poesie 1975, Das Gewöhnliche Licht 1976, Augenzeit 1978, Deutsche Lyrik seit 1965 1985, Traum im Deutschen Museum 1986, Luftfracht 1991, Jahre mit Windrad 1996, Masken und Stimmen 1996, Jahrhundertgedächtnis.Deutsche Lyrik im 20.Jahrhundert 1998, Machen oder Entstehenlassen 2001, Langsamer träumen 2002, Aktennotiz meines Engels 2005. *Address:* Technische Universität Berlin, Str. des 17 Juni 135, 10623 Berlin (office); Rüdesheimer Platz 4, 14197 Berlin, Germany. *Telephone:* (30) 314-0 (office). *Fax:* (30) 314-23222 (office). *Website:* www.tu-berlin.de (office).

HARTWELL, Leland H., BS, PhD; American geneticist; *President and Director, Fred Hutchinson Cancer Research Center;* b. 30 Oct. 1939; ed California Inst. of Technology, MIT; Assoc. Prof. Univ. of Calif. 1965–68; Assoc. Prof., then Prof. Univ. of Washington 1968–; Pres. and Dir Fred Hutchinson Cancer Research Center 1997–; mem. NAS 1987–; numerous awards including General Motors Sloan Award 1991, Gairdner Foundation Int. Award 1992, Genetics Soc. of America Medal 1994, Albert Lasker Basic Medical Research Award 1998, Nobel Prize in Medicine (jt recipient) 2001. *Address:* Fred Hutchinson Cancer Research Center, 1100 Fairview Avenue North, D1-060 Seattle, WA 98109-1024, USA (office). *Website:* www.fhcrc.org (office).

HARTZENBERG, Ferdinand, DSc; South African fmr politician; b. 8 Jan. 1936, Lichtenburg; s. of Ferdinand Hartzenberg; m. Magdalena Judith de Wet 1962; two s.; ed Sannieshof, Hoër Volkskool, Potchefstroom and Univ. of Pretoria; mem. Parl. for Lichtenburg; Leader Conservative Party of SA (CPSA) 1993–2004; Deputy Minister of Devt 1976; Minister of Educ. and Training 1979–82.

HARVEY, Anthony; British film editor and film director; b. 3 June 1931, London; s. of Geoffrey Harrison and Dorothy Leon; joined Crown Film Unit 1949. *Films:* films edited include Private's Progress 1956, On Such a Night 1956, Happy Is the Bride 1957, Brothers in Law 1957, I'm All Right Jack 1959, Carlton-Browne of the F.O. 1959, The Millionairess 1960, The Angry Silence 1960, The Angry Silence 1960, Lolita 1962, The L-Shaped Room 1962, Dr. Strangelove 1964, The Spy Who Came In from the Cold 1965, Dutchman 1967, The Whisperers 1967; films directed include Dutchman 1967, The Lion in Winter 1968, They Might Be Giants 1971, The Abdication 1974, Players 1979, Eagle's Wing 1979, Richard's Things 1980, Grace Quigley 1984. *Television includes:* The Glass Menagerie 1973, The Disappearance of Aimee 1976, The Patricia Neal Story 1981, Svengali 1983, This Can't Be Love 1994. *Leisure interest:* gardening. *Address:* c/o Arthur Greene, 101 Park Avenue, 26th Floor, New York, NY 10178, USA (office). *Telephone:* (212) 661-8200 (office).

HARVEY, Cynthia Theresa; American ballet dancer and teacher; b. 17 May 1957, San Rafael, Calif.; d. of Gordon Harvey and Clara Harvey; m. Christopher D. Murphy 1990; ed High School of Professional Children's School, New York; joined American Ballet Theater 1974, Prin. ballerina 1982–86, 1988–97; with Royal Ballet, London 1986–88; guest appearances touring with Mikhail Baryshnikov, Rudolf Nureyev and Alexander Godunov; has performed with Stuttgart Ballet, Birmingham Royal Ballet and Northern Ballet Theatre; teacher of ballet at many leading schools in USA; Visiting Faculty, Broadway Dance Center, NY; currently guest teacher, Royal Ballet School, London, La Scala, Milan, Royal Swedish Ballet, American Ballet Theater. *Publication:* The Physics of Dance and the Pas de Deux (with Ken Laws) 1994. *Leisure interests:* reading, music, theatre, design. *Address:* Thickthorn Hall, Hethersett, NR9 3AT, England (office). *E-mail:* cynfull.norfolkbroad@virgin.net (office).

HARVEY, Jonathan Dean, MA, PhD, DMus, FRCM, FRSCM; British composer and academic; b. 3 May 1939, Sutton Coldfield; s. of Gerald Harvey and Noelle Harvey; m. Rosaleen Marie Barry 1960; one s. one d.; ed St Michael's Coll., Tenbury, Repton, St John's Coll., Cambridge, Univ. of Glasgow, Princeton Univ.; Lecturer, Univ. of Southampton 1964–77; Reader, Univ. of Sussex 1977–80, Prof. of Music 1980–94; Prof. of Music, Stanford Univ. 1995–2000; Visiting Prof., Imperial Coll. 1999–2002; Composer in Asscn, BBC Scottish Symphony Orchestra 2004–09; mem. Arts Council of England's Music Advisory Panel 1995–97, British Council's Music Advisory Panel 1993–95, Academia Europaea 1989, Acad. Cttee of RCM 1990–94; Hon. RAM; Hon. Fellow, St John's Coll. Cambridge; Hon. Research Fellow, Royal Coll. of Music 2001–; Fellow, Wissenschaftskolleg, Berlin 2009; Hon. DMus (Southampton, Bristol, Sussex, Huddersfield, Birmingham City); The Britten Award 1993, Royal Philharmonic Soc. Award for Orchestral work 2005, Giga-Hertz Grand Prize 2007, Gramophone Award for Best Contemporary CD 2008. *Compositions include:* Four Quartets 1977, 1989, 1995, 2003, Mortuos plango, vivos voco (for tape) 1980, Passion and Resurrection 1981, Bhakti 1982, Gong Ring 1984, Song Offerings 1985, Madonna of Winter and Spring 1986, Lightness and Weight 1986, Tendril 1987, Time Pieces 1987, From Silence 1988, Valley of Aosta 1989, Ritual Melodies 1990, Cello Concerto 1990, Inquest of Love (opera) 1991, Serenade in Homage to Mozart 1991, Scena 1992, One Evening 1993, The Riot 1993, Missa Brevis 1995, Percussion Concerto 1996, Ashes Dance Back 1997, Wheel of Emptiness 1997, Death of Light/Light of Death 1998, Calling Across Time 1998, Tranquil Abiding 1998, White as Jasmine 1999, Mothers Shall Not Cry 2000, Bird Concerto with Pianosong 2001, The Summer Cloud's Awakening 2001, Songs of Li Po 2002, Jubilus 2003, String Trio 2004, Towards a Pure Land 2005, Wagner Dream (opera) 2006, Body Mandala 2007, Speakings 2008; about 20 works for choir. *Publications:* The Music of Stockhausen 1975, Music and Inspiration 1999, In Quest of Spirit 1999. *Leisure interests:* tennis, meditation. *Address:* c/o Faber Music, Bloomsbury House, 74-77 Great Russell Street, London, WC1B 3DA, England (office). *Telephone:* (20) 7908-5310 (office). *Fax:* (20) 7908-5339 (office). *E-mail:* lis.lomas@fabermusic.com (office). *Website:* www.fabermusic.com (office).

HARVEY, Richard, FIA; British insurance executive; b. 1951; joined Norwich Union 1992, various sr man. posts in NZ and UK, Dir 1995–, Group CEO 1998–2000, Deputy Group CEO Aviva PLC (following merger) 2000–01, CEO 2001–07; Dir Asscn of British Insurers 2001–. *Address:* c/o Aviva PLC, St Helen's, 1 Undershaft, London EC3P 3DQ, England (office).

HARWIT, Martin Otto, BA, MA, PhD; American (b. Czech) astrophysicist, academic and fmr museum director; *Professor Emeritus of Astronomy, Cornell University;* b. 9 March 1931, Prague; s. of Felix Michael Haurowitz and Regina Hedwig Haurowitz (née Perutz); m. Marianne Mark; three c.; ed Bronx High School of Science, Oberlin Coll., Univ. of Michigan, Massachusetts Inst. of Tech.; moved with family to Istanbul, Turkey aged eight, to USA aged 15; served in US Army 1955–57; carried out postdoctoral research on theoretical astrophysical problems with Fred Hoyle at Univ. of Cambridge, UK 1960–61; post-doctoral researcher, Cornell Univ. 1961, mem. astronomy faculty 1962, visited Naval Research Lab. with Herbert Friedman's group 1963–64, returned to Cornell 1964, worked with Aerobee rockets to conduct infrared astronomy from space, built several rocket payloads with liquid nitrogen, helium-cooled telescopes and infrared detectors, went into airborne infrared astronomy working on NASA's Learjet and Kuiper flying observatories, co-pioneered infrared spectroscopy and made many near- and far-infrared observations, Prof. Emer. of Astronomy 1988–; one of original planners of NASA's Great Observatories programme; Mission Scientist, ESA Infrared Space Observatory 1985, worked on Far-Infrared and Submillimeter Interferometer, ESA Herschel Space Observatory; Science Team mem., NASA Submillimeter Wave Astronomy Satellite Project and Vision Mission Far-Infrared and Submillimeter Interferometer study; Dir Smithsonian Nat. Air and Space Museum, Washington, DC 1987–95; External mem. Max Planck Soc., Germany 1979; NAS/Czechoslovak Acad. of Sciences exchange fellow, Prague 1969–70; Adriaan Blaauw Visiting Prof., Univ. of Groningen, Netherlands, 2002; Distinguished Fellow, Inst. of Advanced Study, Durham Univ. UK, 2007; Bruce Medal, Astronomical Soc. of the Pacific 2007. *Publications:* Astrophysical Concepts 1973, Hadamard Transform Optics (with Neil J. A. Sloane) 1979, Cosmic Discovery: The Search, Scope and Heritage of Astronomy 1981, Treasures of the National Air and Space Museum 1995, An Exhibit Denied — Lobbying the History of Enola Gay (translated into Japanese) 1996, The Extragalactic Background and its

Cosmological Implications (with M. G. Hauser) 2001. *Address:* 511 H Street, SW, Washington, DC, USA (office). *Telephone:* (202) 479-6877 (office). *E-mail:* harwit@verizon.net (office). *Website:* www.astro.cornell.edu/people/facstaff-detail.php?pers_id=640 (office).

HARWOOD, Ronald, CBE, FRSL; British author and playwright; b. (Ronald Horwitz), 9 Nov. 1934, Cape Town, South Africa; s. of the late Isaac Horwitz and Isobel Pepper; m. Natasha Riehle 1959; one s. two d.; ed Sea Point Boys' High School, Cape Town and Royal Acad. of Dramatic Art; actor 1953–60; author 1960–; Artistic Dir Cheltenham Festival of Literature 1975; presenter, Kaleidoscope, BBC Radio 1973, Read All About It, BBC TV 1978–79, All The World's A Stage, BBC TV; Chair. Writers' Guild of GB 1969; Visitor in Theatre, Balliol Coll. Oxford 1986; Pres. PEN (England) 1989–93, Int. PEN 1993–97; Gov. Cen. School of Speech and Drama; author of numerous TV plays and screenplays; mem. Council Royal Soc. of Literature 1998–2001, chair. 2001–04; Trustee Booker Foundation 2002; Chevalier des Arts et Lettres 1996; Hon. DLitt (Keele) 2002; New Standard Drama Award 1981, Drama Critics Award 1981, Molière Award for Best Play, Paris 1993. *TV plays include:* The Barber of Stamford Hill 1960, Private Potter (with Casper Wrede) 1961, The Guests 1972, Breakthrough at Reykjavik 1987, Countdown to War 1989. *Screenplays include:* A High Wind in Jamaica 1965, One Day in the Life of Ivan Denisovich 1971, Evita Perón 1981, The Dresser 1983, Mandela 1987, The Browning Version 1994, Cry, Beloved Country 1995, Taking Sides 2002, The Pianist 2002 (Acad. Award for Best Adapted Screenplay 2003), The Statement 2003, Being Julia 2004, Oliver Twist 2005, Le Scaphandre et le Papillon (BAFTA Award for Best Adapted Screenplay 2008) 2007, Love in the Time of Cholera 2007. *Plays include:* Country Matters 1969, The Good Companions (musical libretto) 1974, The Ordeal of Gilbert Pinfold 1977, A Family 1978, The Dresser 1980, After the Lions 1982, Tramway Road 1984, The Deliberate Death of a Polish Priest 1985, Interpreters 1985, J. J. Farr 1987, Ivanov (from Chekhov) 1989, Another Time 1989, Reflected Glory 1992, Poison Pen 1994, Taking Sides 1995, The Handyman 1996, Equally Divided 1998, Quartet 1999, Mahler's Conversion 2002, An English Tragedy 2007. *Publications include:* fiction: All the Same Shadows 1961, The Guilt Merchants 1963, The Girl in Melanie Klein 1969, Articles of Faith 1973, The Genoa Ferry 1976, César and Augusta 1978, Home 1993; non-fiction: Sir Donald Wolfit, CBE: His Life and Work in the Unfashionable Theatre (biog.) 1971; editor: A Night at the Theatre 1983, The Ages of Gielfud 1984, Dear Alec: Guinness at Seventy-Five 1989, The Faber Book of the Theatre 1994; vols of essays and short stories. *Leisure interest:* cricket. *Address:* Judy Daish Associates, 2 St Charles Place, London, W10 6EG, England (office). *Telephone:* (20) 8964-8811 (office).

HASAN, Abdulkasim Salad; Somali fmr head of state; b. 1942; Minister of Industry, of Trade, of Labour, of Information and of the Interior 1973–1990; Pres. of Somalia 2000–04. *Address:* c/o Office of the President, People's Palace, Mogadishu, Somalia (office).

HASAN, Khandaker Mahmud-ul, MA, LLM; Bangladeshi judge; b. 27 Jan. 1939, s. of the late Khandaker Mohammed Hasan; enrolled as Supreme Court advocate 1963, Judge of the High Court 1991–2002, Appellate Div. 2002, apptd Chief Justice, Supreme Court 2003; Amb. to Iraq 1980–82. *Address:* c/o Supreme Court, Dhaka 2, Bangladesh.

HASANI, Baqir Husain, BSc, LLB; Iraqi/Italian diplomatist (retd); b. 12 Feb. 1915, Baghdad; ed Columbia Univ., New York, USA and Law Coll., Baghdad Univ.; Dir of Commerce and Registrar of Patents, Trade Marks and Companies, Ministry of Econs Iraq 1947–51; Dir-Gen. of Contracts and Econ. Research, Devt Bd 1951–54; Dir-Gen. of Income Tax, Ministry of Finance 1954–55; Dir-Gen. and Chair. Bd of Dirs Tobacco Monopoly Admin. 1955–59; Envoy Extraordinary and later Amb. to Austria 1959–63; Chair. Bd of Govs IAEA 1961–62; Special Adviser to Dir-Gen. IAEA, Vienna 1963–66, 1970–76; Adviser to Saudi Arabian Mission in Vienna 1978–81; consultant on Middle Eastern Affairs 1985–; mem. numerous govt cttees and del. to the UN and to int. confs; Lecturer, Coll. of Business Admin., Coll. of Pharmacy, Mil. Staff Coll.; Rafidain Decoration, Austrian Grand Golden Decoration. *Publications:* numerous articles in newspapers and magazines; book of proverbs and sayings in preparation. *Leisure interests:* collecting stamps and coins, composing poetry. *Address:* Via Civelli 9, 21100 Varese, Italy (home); 7 Ashenden Road, Guildford, Surrey, GU2 7UU, England (home). *Telephone:* (0332) 229633 (Italy) (home); (1483) 838371 (England) (home).

HASANOV, Ramiz Ayvaz oglu; Azerbaijani government official and fmr diplomatist; Amb. to Georgia 2004–05; Dir-Gen. State Agency for Standardization, Metrology and Patents (AZSTAND) 2005–; Co-Chair. EuroAsian Interstate Council for Standardization, Metrology and Certification. *Address:* State Agency on Standardization, Metrology and Patents, Mardanov Gardashlary str., 124, 1147 Baku, Azerbaijan (office). *Telephone:* (12) 449-99-59 (office). *Fax:* (12) 440-52-24 (office). *E-mail:* azs@azstand.gov.az (office). *Website:* www.azstand.gov.az (office).

HASEEB, Khair ad-Din, BA, MSc, PhD; Iraqi economist and statistician; *Director-General, Centre for Arab Unity Studies;* b. 1 Aug. 1929, Mosul; m. 1955; one s. two d.; ed Univ. of Baghdad, London School of Econs and Univ. of Cambridge, UK; civil servant, Ministry of Interior 1947–54; Head of Research and Statistics Dept, Iraqi Oil Co. 1959–60; Full-time Lecturer, Univ. of Baghdad 1960–61, Part-time 1961–63; Dir-Gen. Iraqi Fed. of Industries 1960–63; Gov. and Chair. of Bd, Cen. Bank of Iraq 1963–65; Pres. Gen. Org. for Banks 1964–65; Acting Pres. Econ. Org., Iraq 1964–65; Assoc. Prof., Dept of Econs, Univ. of Baghdad 1965–71, Prof. of Econs 1971–74; mem. Bd Dirs Iraq Nat. Oil Co. 1967–68; Chief, Programme and Co-ordination Unit and Natural Resources, Science and Tech. Div. UN Econ. Comm. for Western Asia, then Lebanon and Iraq 1974–76 and 1976–83; Acting Dir-Gen. Centre for Arab Unity Studies, Lebanon 1978–83, Dir-Gen. 1983–; Chair. Bd of Trustees and Dirs Arab Cultural Foundation, London 1987; Chair. Bd of Trustees Arab Org. for Translation, Lebanon 1999–. *Publications:* The National Income of Iraq 1953–1961, 1964, Workers' Participation in Management in Arab Countries (in Arabic) 1971, Sources of Arab Economic Thought in Iraq 1900–71 (in Arabic) 1972, Arab Monetary Integration (co-ed.) 1982, Arabs and Africa (ed.) 1985, The Future of the Arab Nation 1991, Arab-Iranian Relations (ed.) 2002, The Future of Iraq: Occupation, Resistance, Liberation and Democracy 2004, Planning Iraq's Future: A Detailed Project to Rebuild Post-Liberation Iraq (ed.) 2006, An Overview of Arab Concerns: Arab Nationalism; Arab Unity; The Centre for Arab Unity Studies; The Arab Intellectual and Democracy 2008; numerous articles. *Leisure interests:* swimming, tennis. *Address:* Centre for Arab Unity Studies, Beit Al-Nahda Bldg- Basra Str., PO Box 113-6001, Hamra, Beirut 2034 2407, Lebanon (office). *Telephone:* (1) 750084 (office); (1) 740631 (home). *Fax:* (1) 750088 (office). *E-mail:* info@caus.org.lb (office). *Website:* www.caus.org.lb (office).

HASEGAWA, Itsuku; Japanese architect; *Founder, Itsuku Hasagawa Atelier;* b. 1941, Shizuoka Pref.; ed Kanto Gakuin Univ., Tokyo Inst. of Tech.; worked for Kiyonori Kikutate 1964–69; researcher Dept of Architecture, Tokyo Inst. of Tech. 1969–71, Asst to Prof. Kazuo Shinohara 1971–78; est. Itsuku Hasagawa Atelier 1979; Lecturer, Waseda Univ. 1988, Tokyo Inst. of Tech. 1989, Niigata Univ. 1993, Tokyo Denki Univ. 1995; Visiting Prof., Grad. School of Design, Harvard Univ., USA 1992, Kanto Gakuin Univ. 2001; Hon. FRIBA 1997; Hon. FAIA 2006; hon. degree (Univ. Coll. London) 2001; Japan Inter-Design Forum Award 1986, Japan Cultural Design Award 1986, First Prize, Competition for Sumida Cultural Centre 1990, First Prize, Competition for Shiogama City Town Centre 1995, Int. Young Generation Award 1998, Avon Arts Award. *Architectural works include:* House in Kuwahara, Matsuyama 1980, Aono Bldg, Matsuyama 1982, Bizan Hall (Architectural Inst. of Japan Prize for Design) 1986, Shonandai Cultural Centre, Fujisawa, Kanagawa (BCS Award, Bldg Constructors Soc. 1992) 1987–90, STM House, Shibuya-ku, Tokyo 1991, Sumida Culture Factory 1994, Oshima-Machi Picture Book Museum, Toyama (Public Building Award 2000) 1994, Yamanashi Fruit Garden 1995, Imai Newtown Housing, Nagano (Olympic Village) 1998, Niigata City Performing Arts Centre (Japan Art Acad. Award 2000, BCS Award, Bldg Constructors Soc. 2001, Public Bldg Award 2004) 1998, Fukuroi Workshop Centre, Shizuoka 2001, Centre in Shizuoka 2004, Taisei Jr High and High School, Shizuoka 2004, Ohota Project 2005, Suzu Performing Arts Center, Ishikawa 2006, Shizuoka Univ. of Welfare 2006. *Publications include:* Itsuko Hasegawa 1997, The Equipment of Life 1999, Island Hopping 2000; articles in professional journals. *Address:* Itsuku Hasegawa Atelier, 1-9-7 Yushima, Bunkyo-ku, Tokyo 113-0034, Japan (office). *Telephone:* (3) 3818-5470 (office). *Fax:* (3) 3818-1821 (office). *E-mail:* ihasegawa@ihasegawa.com (office). *Website:* www.ihasegawa.com (office).

HASEGAWA, Kaoru, BEcons; Japanese business executive; *Chairman, Rengo Company Ltd.;* b. 15 April 1924, Hyogo; m. Shizue Hasegawa 1952; one s. one d.; ed Naval Acad. of Japan, Gakushuin Univ.; joined Rengo Co. Ltd 1952, Gen. Man. Corp. Planning Dept 1960, Man. Dir 1962, Sr Man. Dir 1970, Exec. Vice-Pres. 1973, Pres. and CEO 1984, now Chairman; Pres. Japan Corrugated Case Asscn 1986; Vice-Chair. Japan Paper Asscn 1995; consultant on overseas Devt, China Packaging Tech. Asscn 1999. *Publications:* Two Lives: My Personal History, Cultural and Economic Dialogues: Learning from the History and Wisdom of Europe. *Address:* Rengo Co. Ltd, 5-25 Umeda, 2-chome, Kita-ku, Osaka 530 0001, Japan (office). *Telephone:* (6) 6342-0266 (office). *Fax:* (6) 6342-0379 (office). *Website:* www.rengo.co.jp (office).

HASEGAWA, Toru; Japanese automotive industry executive; *Chairman and Director, Yamaha Motor Company Ltd;* joined Yamaha Motor Co. Ltd 1960, various positions including export agent, Dir of Procurement 1970s, Dir of European Operations, Netherlands 1990, Sr Man. Dir –2001, Pres. and Rep. Dir, Yamaha Motor Co. Ltd 2001–04, Chair. and Dir 2004–. *Address:* Yamaha Motor Company Ltd, 2500 Shingai, Iwata, Shizuoka 438-8501, Japan (office). *Telephone:* (5) 3832-1103 (office). *Fax:* (5) 3837-4252 (office). *Website:* www.yamaha-motor.co.jp (office).

HASELTINE, William A., PhD; American scientist; *Chairman and CEO, Human Genome Sciences Inc.;* ed Harvard Univ.; Prof., Dana-Farber Cancer Inst., Harvard Medical School and Harvard School of Public Health 1976–93; f. Human Genome Sciences Inc. (HGS) 1992, Chair. and Chief Exec. 1993–; Scientific Adviser HealthCare Ventures; fmr Ed.-in-Chief Journal of AIDS; Founder and Ed. on-line journal E-Biomed; holder of more than 50 patents for his discoveries; numerous awards and honours for his achievements in science, medicine and business. *Publications:* over 250 scientific publs. *Address:* Human Genome Sciences Inc., 9410 Key West Avenue, Rockville, MD 20850-3338, USA (office). *Telephone:* (301) 309-8504 (office). *Fax:* (301) 309-8512 (office). *Website:* www.hgsi.com (office).

HASENFRATZ, Frank J.; Hungarian/Canadian business executive; *Chairman, Linamar Corporation;* b. 1935, Hungary; emigrated to Canada 1957; Supervisor, Sinterings Ltd 1957-66; f. Linamar 1966, Chair. Linamar Corpn 1966–. *Address:* Linamer Corporation, 287 Speedvale Avenue West, Guelph, Ont., N1H 1C5, Canada (office). *Telephone:* (519) 836-7550 (office). *Fax:* (519) 824-8479 (office). *Website:* www.linamar.com (office).

HASHAMI, Hafizullah; Afghan politician; Gov. of Zabul Prov. 2003–Jan. 2004.

HASHIM, Ali; Maldivian business executive and politician; *Minister of Finance and Treasury;* helped establish Maldives Stock Exchange 2007, Man. Dir 2007–08; Minister of Finance and Treasury 2008–; mem. Maldivian Democratic Party, fmr Vice Chair. *Address:* Ministry of Finance and Treasury, Block 379, Ameenee Magu, Malé 20-379, Maldives (office).

Telephone: 3349200 (office). *Fax:* 3324432 (office). *E-mail:* admin@finance.gov.mv (office). *Website:* www.finance.gov.mv (home).

HASHIM AL-KADER, Fawzia; Eritrean politician; *Minister of Justice;* women's rights campaigner; fought as soldier in Eritrean wars of independence in 1970s; Minister of Justice 1991–. *Address:* Ministry of Justice, POB 241, Asmara, Eritrea (office). *Telephone:* (1) 127739 (office). *Fax:* (1) 126422 (office).

HASHIM PREMJI, Azim, BS; Indian business executive; *Chairman and Managing Director, Wipro Ltd;* b. 24 July 1945, Mumbai; s. of Mohamed Husain and G. M. H. Premji; m. Yasmeen Premji; two s.; ed Stanford Univ., USA; took over father's Western India Vegetable Products Ltd (WIPRO) vegetable oil business upon his death 1966; Chair., CEO and Man. Dir Wipro Ltd (IT and software co.), Bangalore 1983–; mem. Prime Minister's Cttee for Trade and Industry; f. Azim Premji Foundation 2001; Dr hc Indian Inst. of Tech., Manipal Acad. of Higher Educ. 2000; Sir M. Visvesvaraya Memorial Award 2000, Businessman of the Year 2000, Business India magazine, Business Leader of the Year, Econ. Times 2004, Padma Bhushan 2005, Faraday Medal 2005. *Leisure interests:* jogging, spending time at hillside resorts. *Address:* Wipro Ltd, Doddakannelli, Sarjapur Road, Bangalore, Karnataka 560 035 (office); Bakhtawar, 229, Nariman Point, Mumbai 400021, India (home). *Telephone:* (80) 28440011 (office); (80) 5569991 (home). *Fax:* (80) 28440256 (office). *E-mail:* azim.premji@corp.wipro.co.in (office). *Website:* www.wipro.com (office); www.azimpremjifoundation.org.

HASHIMI, Tariq al-, MA; Iraqi politician; *Vice-President of Iraq and Secretary-General, Iraqi Islamic Party;* b. 1942, Baghdad; ed Al-Mustansiriyah Univ.; attended Mil. Acad. 1959–62, pursued mil. career –1975; instructor, Leadership Acad. 1975; Iraq Br. Man., Arab Shipping Co. 1979–81, moved to Kuwait, served as Dir-Gen., Arab Shipping Co. –1990; returned to Iraq 1990; mem. Iraqi Islamic Party, fmr mem. Planning Cttee and Shura Council, currently Sec.-Gen.; Vice-Pres. of Iraq 2005–. *E-mail:* info@alhashimi.org (office); info@iraqigovernment.org (office). *Website:* alhashimi.org (office); www.iraqigovernment.org (office).

HASHMI, (Aurangzeb) Alamgir, MA, DLit; Pakistani academic, poet, writer, editor and broadcaster; b. 15 Nov. 1951, Lahore; ed Univ. of Louisville, Univ. of Punjab; Instructor in English, Govt Coll., Lahore 1971–73; Lecturer, Forman Christian Coll., Lahore 1973–74, Univ. of Berne, Univ. of Basel 1982; Davidson Int. Visiting Scholar, Univ. of N Carolina 1974–75; Lecturer in English, Univ. of Louisville 1975–78, Univ. of Zürich and Volkshochschule, Zürich 1980–85; Asst Prof. of English, Univ. of Bahawalpur, Pakistan 1979–80; Lecturer in English, Univ. of Basel, Univ. of Bern 1982; Prof. of English and Commonwealth Literature, Univ. of Geneva, Univ. of Fribourg 1985; Assoc. Prof. of English, Int. Islamic Univ., Islamabad 1985–86; Foundation Chair Prof. of English and Head, Dept of English, Univ. of Azad Jammu and Kashmir, Muzaffarabad 1986–87; Research Prof. of English, American and Comparative Literature, Quaid-i-Azam Univ., Islamabad 1986–2000; Prof. and Ed., PIDE, Islamabad 1988–; Course Dir, Foreign Service Acad., Islamabad 1988–; Prof. of English and Comparative Literature Pakistan Futuristics Inst., Islamabad 1990, Univ. of Iceland 2000; Founder and Chair. Standing Int. Cttee on English in S Asia; Founder and Chair. Townsend Poetry Prize Cttee; judge, Commonwealth Literature Prize, nat. literature prizes, Pakistan Acad. of Letters 1998–; jury mem., Neustadt Int. Prize for Literature; Ed., Advisory Ed., Editorial Adviser and referee for numerous int. scholarly and literary journals and book series; thesis supervisor and external examiner for many univs world-wide; broadcaster, scriptwriter, ed. Radio Pakistan and Pakistan TV 1968–; adviser, Nat. Book Council of Pakistan 1989–95, Nat. Book Foundation 1993–; Judge, Prime Minister's Award for Literature; Fellow, Int. Centre for Asian Studies, Int. PEN; Rockefeller Foundation Fellow 1994; Life Fellow, Pakistan Acad. of Letters; mem. Council Asscn for Commonwealth Studies; mem. Poetry Soc., Associated Writing Programs, Asscn for Asian Studies, New York Acad. of Sciences, Council on Nat. Literatures, Asscn for Commonwealth Literature and Language Studies, Int. Asscn of Univ. Profs of English, Modern Language Asscn of America; Hon. DLitt (Luxembourg, San Francisco State Univ.); First Prize, All Pakistan Creative Writing Contest 1972, Patras Bokhari Award, Pakistan Acad. of Letters 1985, Roberto Celli Memorial Award 1994, inscribed in Academic Roll of Honour, Govt Coll., Lahore, Pres. of Pakistan's Award for Pride of Performance (Medal for Literature); numerous other academic and literary distinctions, prizes and citations from different countries. *Publications:* poetry: The Oath and Amen: Love Poems 1976, America is a Punjabi Word 1979, An Old Chair 1979, My Second in Kentucky 1981, This Time in Lahore 1983, Neither This Time/Nor That Place 1984, Inland and Other Poems 1988, The Poems of Alamgir Hashmi 1992, Sun and Moon and Other Poems 1992, Others to Sport with Amaryllis in the Shade 1992, A Choice of Hashmi's Verse 1997, The Ramazan Libation: Selected Poems 2003; other: Pakistani Literature (two vols; ed., second edn as Pakistani Literature: The Contemporary English Writers) 1978, Ezra Pound 1983, Commonwealth Literature 1983, The Worlds of Muslim Imagination (ed.) 1986, The Commonwealth, Comparative Literature and the World 1988, Pakistani Short Stories in English (ed.) 1992, Postindependence Voices in South Asian Writings (co-ed.) 2001; contrib. to many books, journals and periodicals. *Leisure interests:* walking, cricket, music, films. *Address:* 1542 Service Road West, G-11/2, Islamabad, Pakistan (home). *E-mail:* alamgirhashmi@yahoo.co.uk (home).

HASHMI, Makhdoom Javed; Pakistani politician; b. Multan; m.; two d.; fmr Fed. Minister for Labour, fmr Minister for Health and Population Welfare; mem. Pakistan Muslim League (Nawaz) apptd Parl. Leader 1999, fmr Acting Pres.; mem. Alliance for the Restoration of Democracy 2003–; arrested Oct. 2003, sentenced April 2004 to 23 years in prison for inciting mutiny in the army, forgery and defamation, released Aug. 2007. *Address:* Pakistan Muslim League (Nawaz), House No. 20–H, Street 10, F-8/3, Islamabad, Pakistan (office). *Telephone:* (51) 2852662 (office). *E-mail:* pmlisb@hotmail.com (office). *Website:* www.pmln.org.pk (office).

HASHMI, Moneeza, MEd, MA; Pakistani television executive; *General Manager, International Relations, HUM TV Eye Television Network;* b. (Moneeza Gul Faiz), 22 Aug. 1946, Simla; d. of Faiz Ahmad Faiz; m. Humair Hashmi; two s.; ed Univ. of Hawaii, USA, Punjab Univ., Lahore; Program Man., Pakistan TV (PTV), Lahore 1974–81, Man. Educational TV 1982–88, Gen. Man. 1988–2003, Director of Programs 2003–04; currently Gen. Man. Int. Relations, HUM TV Eye Television Network, Lahore; Chair. Asia-Pacific Media AIDS Initiative; Co-founder Himmat Soc. (charity); mem. Bd of Govs Omar Asghar Khan Devt Foundation; Grad. Award 2000, 2001, Commonwealth Broadcasting Award Citation 2002, Pres. of Pakistan's Pride of Performance 2002, Fatima Jinnah Award 2004. *Television includes:* Khwateen Time (Exec. Producer). *Leisure interests:* travelling, reading. *Address:* HUM TV, Office #102, 1st Floor, Siddique Centre, Gulberg, Lahore; 102-H Model Town, Lahore, Pakistan (home). *Telephone:* (42) 5884324 (home). *Fax:* (42) 5782007 (office); (42) 5884866 (home). *E-mail:* moneezahashmi@yahoo.co.uk (office).

HASHMI, Syed Haseen; Pakistani advertising executive; b. 1935, Gaya, India; s. of the late Syed Abdul Quddoos Hashmi; Chair. Pakistan Advertising Asscn 1978–87, 1992–93, 1996–99; Pres. Int. Advertising Asscn (IAA), Pakistan Chapter 1996–98; fmr Sec.-Gen. Seerat Cttee, Karachi; Presidential Award, APNS Millennium Award, FPCCI Gold Medal, Best Business Performance 1981–98. *Publications include:* Advertising Scene (Blue Book). *Leisure interests:* reading, social welfare. *Address:* 195-A, S.M.C.H.S., Karachi (office); 73/11 Khavaban-e-Badar, Phase-VI, D.H.A., Karachi, Pakistan (home). *Telephone:* (21) 4550184 (office); (21) 5849841 (home). *Fax:* (21) 4550187 (office). *E-mail:* omek@orientmccann.com (office).

HASHWANI, Sadruddin; Pakistani business executive; *Chairman, Hashoo Group;* m.; two s. three d.; business ventures in cotton, petroleum, hotel industry, real estate, trading, and property devt 1950–; f. Hashwani Hotels Ltd, Net 21; Founder and Chair. Hashoo Group. *Address:* Hashoo Group, PEC Building Ataturk Avenue G-5/2, PO Box 1670, Islamabad, Pakistan. *Telephone:* (51) 2272890 (office). *Fax:* (51) 2274812 (office). *E-mail:* info@hashoogroup.com (office); hashwani@net21pk.com (office). *Website:* www.hashoogroup.biz (home).

HASINA, Sheikh Wajed, BA; Bangladeshi politician; *Prime Minister;* b. 28 Sept. 1947, Tungipara, Gopalganj dist; d. of Bangabandhu Sheikh Mujibur Rahman and Begum Fazilatunnesa; m. M.A. Wazed Miah 1968; one s. one d.; ed Dhaka Univ.; Gen. Sec., Student League, Bodrunnessa Girl's Coll., Dhaka, 1965, Pres. 1966; Sec., Student League, Rokeya Hall br., Dhaka Univ. 1968–69, Founder mem. Abahani Krira Chakra (sports club) 1969; Pres. Bangladesh Awami League 1981–, Leader of Opposition, Bangladesh Jatiya Sangsad (Parl.) 1986–87, 1991–95, 2001–09, Prime Minister 1996–2001, 2009–, also in charge of Defence portfolio 2009–; Chair. Bangabandhu Memorial Trust 1994–; Dr hc (Boston Univ.) 1997, (Waseda Univ., Japan) 1997, (Univ. of Abertay, Dundee, UK) 1997, (Visva-Bharati Univ., Shantiniketan, India) 1999, (ANU) 1999, (Bridgeport Univ., Conn.) 2000, (Catholic Univ. of Brussels) 2000, (Barry Univ., Fla) 2004; Head of State Medal, Int. Asscn of Lions Clubs 1996, 1998, Medal of Distinction, Int. Asscn of Lions Clubs 1997, Netaji Subhas Chandra Bosh Memorial Medal, West Bengal Cttee of All India Congress 1997, Mother Teresa Award, All India Peace Council 1998, UNESCO Houphouet-Boigny Peace Prize 1998, CERES Medal, FAO 1999, Asia Personality of 2000, Afro-Asian Lawyers Fed. for Human Rights 2000, Pearl S. Buck Award, Randolph-Macon Women's Coll. 2000. *Publications include:* Elimination of Poverty: Some Thoughts 1993, Birth of Conspiracy in Bangladesh 1994, My Dream My Revolution (ed.) 1996, Development of the Masses 1999, Brihator Jonogoshtir janna unnayon 1999, People and Democracy 2002, Cannot Tolerate the Insult of Humanity 2003, Democracy in Distress: Demeaned Humanity 2003, Biponno Gonotontro lanchhito manobota 2003, Living in Tears 2004. *Address:* Office of the Prime Minister, Old Sangsad Bhaban, Tejgaon, Dhaka 1215 (office); Sudha Sudan, Road # 5, House # 54, Dhanmondi, Dhaka, Bangladesh. *Telephone:* (2) 8151159 (office). *Fax:* (2) 8113244 (office). *E-mail:* info@pmo.gov.bd (office). *Website:* www.cao.gov.bd (office); www.sheikhhasina.ws.

HASKELL, (Donald) Keith, CMG, CVO, MA; British diplomatist (retd); b. 9 May 1939, Southsea; s. of Donald Eric Haskell and Beatrice Mary Haskell (neé Blair); m. Maria Luisa Soeiro Tito de Morais; two s. two d.; ed Portsmouth Grammar School, St Catharine's Coll., Cambridge; joined FCO 1961, served in Baghdad 1962–66, Libya 1969–72; Chargé d'affaires, Consul-Gen. Santiago, Chile 1975–78; Consul-Gen. Dubai, UAE 1978–81; Head Nuclear Energy Dept FCO 1981–83, Head Middle East Dept 1983–84, Counsellor Bonn, FRG 1985–88, on secondment to industry 1988–89; Amb. to Peru 1990–95, to Brazil 1995–99; freelance consultant and lecturer on int. relations 1999–; Grand Cross, Order of Rio Branco (Brazil) 1997. *Leisure interests:* rifle shooting, skiing, tennis, wine and food. *Address:* Barn Cottage, Brightstone Lane, Farringdon, Alton, Hants., GU34 3DP, England (home). *Telephone:* (1420) 588485 (home). *Fax:* (1420) 588485 (home). *E-mail:* maria.haskell@virgin.net (home).

HASKINS, Baron (Life Peer), cr. 1998; of Skidby in the County of the East Riding of Yorkshire; **Christopher Robin Haskins,** BA; Irish business executive; *Chairman of Council and Pro-Chancellor, Open University;* b. 30 May 1937, Dublin; s. of Robert Brown Haskins and Margaret Elizabeth Haskins (née Mullen); m. Gilda Susan Horsley 1959; three s. two d.; ed St Columba's Coll., Dublin, Trinity Coll., Dublin; with Ford Motor Co. 1960–62;

joined Northern Foods PLC 1962, Chair. 1986–2002 (retd); mem. Culliton Irish Industrial Policy Review Group 1991–92, Ind. Comm. Social Justice 1992–94, UK Round Table on Sustainable Devt 1995–98, CBI's Pres. Cttee 1996–99, Hampel Cttee on Corp. Governance 1996–97; Chair. Better Regulation Task Force 1997–2002, Express Dairies 1998–2002, DEFRA (Dept for Environment, Food and Rural Affairs) Review Group 2002–03; Dir Lawes Agricultural Trust, Yorkshire TV 2002–; Dir Yorkshire and Humber Regional Devt Agency 1998–; mem. New Deal Task Force 1997–2001, Yorkshire Forward 1998–; Co-ordinator Rural Recovery 2001–03; Chair. European Movement 2004–; Chair. of Council and Pro-Chancellor Open Univ. 2005–; hon. degrees (Leeds Metropolitan Univ., Dublin, Essex, Nottingham, Hull, Huddersfield, Lincoln, Cranfield, Bradford). *Leisure interests:* farming, watching cricket, writing, politics. *Address:* Quarryside Farm, Main Street, Skidby, nr Cottingham, East Yorks., HU15 6TG, England (home). *Telephone:* (1482) 842692 (home). *Fax:* (1482) 845249 (home). *E-mail:* gshaskins@aol.com (home). *Website:* www.open.ac.uk (office).

HASKINS, Sam (Samuel Joseph); British photographer, designer and author; b. 11 Nov. 1926, Kroonstad, South Africa; s. of Benjamin G. Haskins and Anna E. Oelofse; m. Alida Elzabé van Heerden 1952; two s.; ed Helpmekaar School and Witwatersrand Tech. Coll., Johannesburg, Bolt Court School of Photography (now London Coll. of Communication), London; Ind. Photographic Studio: Johannesburg 1953–68, London 1968–2002, Sydney 2002–; Sr External Assessor, Photographic Course, London Coll. of Printing 1975–82; 500-image slide show set to music, presented as entertainment and to photographic confs in over 50 cities, 50+ solo exhbns on four continents, 14 int. group exhbns; work featured in perm. collection of V&A Museum, London and Nat. Portrait Gallery, Australia; Prix Nadar (France) for Cowboy Kate and Other Stories 1964, Israel Museum Award, Int. Art Book Contest Award 1969, Gold Medal Award for Haskins Posters, New York 1974, Kodak Book of the Year Prize 1980 for Photo Graphics. *Publications:* Five Girls 1962, Cowboy Kate and Other Stories 1964, African Image 1966, November Girl 1967, Haskins Posters 1972, Photo Graphics 1980, Sam Haskins à Bologna 1984, Fashion Etcetera 2009; portfolios in most major int. photographic magazines. *Leisure interests:* vintage car restoration and rallying, books, music, horticulture, collecting antiques and design icons, carpentry. *Address:* The Sam Haskins Partnership, PO Box 1197, NSW 2576, Australia (office). *Telephone:* (2) 4862-1453 (home). *E-mail:* sam@haskins.com (office). *Website:* www.haskins.com (office); www.samhaskinsblog.com (office).

HASLER, Otmar; Liechtenstein politician; b. 28 Sept. 1953; m. Traudi Hasler-Hilti; two s. two d.; ed secondary school-teaching diploma from Fribourg Univ.; teacher, Realschule, Eschen 1979–2001; Pres. Progressive Citizens' Party of Liechtenstein (FBP) 1993–95, mem. Exec. Cttee 1993–; mem. Parl. 1989–2001, Vice-Pres. 1993–94, 1996–2001, Pres. 1995; Prime Minister of Liechtenstein, also responsible for Govt Affairs, Finance, Construction and Public Works 2001–09 (resgnd); Pres. newly founded Liechtenstein Sr Citizens' Org. 1999–; mem. Historical Soc., Liechtenstein Art Soc., Liechtenstein Senior Educational Asscn. *Leisure interests:* reading, music, hiking. *Address:* c/o Progressive Citizens' Party, Aeulestrasse 56, Postfach 1213, 9490 Vaduz, Liechtenstein (office).

HASLER, William A., BA, MBA; American business executive; *Chairman, Solectron Corporation;* b. 1943; ed Pomona Coll., Harvard Univ.; certified public accountant; Vice-Chair. and Dir KPMG Peat Warwick LLP –1991; Dean Haas School of Business, Univ. of Calif. at Berkeley 1991–98; apptd Co-CEO Aphton Corpn 1998, Vice-Chair. 1998–; Chair. Solectron Corpn 2003–; mem. Bd of Dirs Tech. Olympic USA Inc. (TOUSA) 1997–, Solectron Corpn 1998–, The Schwab Funds, DMC Stratex Networks, DiTech Communications Corpn, Genitope Corpn, Aphton Corpn 2000–; Trustee Pomona Coll. *Address:* Solectron Corporation, 777 Gibraltar Drive, Milpitas, CA 95035, USA (office). *Telephone:* (408) 957-8500 (office). *Fax:* (408) 957-6056 (office). *Website:* www.solectron.com (office).

HASQUIN, Hervé, PhD; Belgian politician and academic; *Minister-President of French-speaking Community of Belgium;* b. 31 Dec. 1942, Charleroi; s. of René-Pierre Hasquin and Andrée Jacquemart; m. Michèle Nahum 1986; one s.; Dean Faculty of Arts and Philosophy, Université Libre de Bruxelles 1979–82, Rector 1982–86, Chair. Bd of Dirs 1986–95, Pres. Inst. for Religious and Secular Studies 1987–; Head French-speaking network Scientific Information and Technological Devt 1986–87; Vice-Pres. Parti Réformateur Libéral (PRL) 1986–89, Gen. Sec. 1990–92, Head PRL Group, Council of Brussels, Capital Region 1991–; Senator 1988–95; Regional Councillor, Brussels 1989–99; Minister of Environmental Planning, Town Planning and Transport, Brussels Capital Region 1995–99; Minister-Pres. of French-speaking Community of Belgium responsible for Int. Relations 1999–; Prés. de la Fédération MR du Hainaut 2000–; Royal Acad. of Belgium Prize 1990, Literary Prize of French-speaking Community Council 1981 and other prizes; Chevalier, Légion d'honneur 1989, Commdr, Order of Leopold II 1984, Order of the Lion (Senegal) 1987; Grand Officer, Order of Leopold 1999;sociétaire hc Acad. des Sciences et des Arts 2000, mem. Acad. Royale de Belgique 2002. *Publications:* La Wallonie: Le Pays et les Hommes, Histoire de la Laïcité principalement en Belgique et en France, La Wallonie, son histoire 1999, Dictionnaire d'histoire de Belgique: Vingt siècles d'institutions. Les hommes. Les faits 1988, Dictionnaire d'histoire de Belgique: Les Hommes, les institutions, les faits, le Congo Belge et le Ruanda–Urundi 2000; Les séparatistes wallons et le gouvernement de Vichy (1940–43), Acad. royale de Belgique lecture 2003; about 150 articles and papers in Belgian and foreign learned journals. *Leisure interests:* writing, teaching, football, cycling, cinema. *Address:* Université Libre de Bruxelles, Ave. F. Roosevelt 50, 1050 Brussels ; Cabinet du Ministre-Président de la Communauté Wallonie-Bruxelles, Place Surlet de Chokier 15-17, 1000 Brussels (office); Rue du Long Bois 1, 7830

Graty Silly, Belgium (home). *Telephone:* (2) 227-32-11 (office). *Fax:* (2) 227-33-53 (office). *E-mail:* contact@hasquin.be (office). *Website:* www.hasquin.be (office).

HASSAN, Az-Zobeir Ahmed al-; Sudanese politician; Minister of Finance and Nat. Economy –2008. *Address:* c/o Ministry of Finance and National Economy, POB 735, Khartoum, Sudan (office).

HASSAN, Fred, BSc, MBA; American (b. Pakistani) pharmaceuticals executive; *Chairman and CEO, Schering-Plough Corporation;* b. 12 Nov. 1945, Multan, Pakistan; m. Noreen Hassan; one s. two d.; ed Imperial Coll. of Science and Tech., Univ. of London, UK, Harvard Business School; raised in Lahore where his father was a civil servant and his mother a women's rights activist; joined Sandoz Pharmaceuticals (now Novartis) in 1972, Head, US Pharmaceuticals 1984; Exec. Vice-Pres. Pharmaceutical and Medical Products, Wyeth (fmrly American Home Products), Head, Genetics Inst. (wholly-owned subsidiary), mem. Bd of Dirs 1995–97; CEO and mem. Bd of Dirs Pharmacia & Upjohn 1997–2001, Chair. and CEO Pharmacia Corpn (formed following merger of Monsanto and Pharmacia & Upjohn cos) 2001–03; Chair. and CEO Schering-Plough Corpn 2003–; mem. Bd of Dirs Avon Products, Inc., CIGNA Corpn; fmr Chair. Bd of Dirs Pharmaceutical Research and Manufacturers of America (PhRMA), HealthCare Inst. of New Jersey; CEO-of-the-Year in the Global Pharmaceutical Industry, Financial Times 1999. *Address:* Global Headquarters, Schering-Plough Corporation World Headquarters, 2000 Galloping Hill Road, Kenilworth, NJ 07033-0530, USA (office). *Telephone:* (908) 298-4000 (office). *Fax:* (908) 298-7653 (office). *Website:* www.sch-plough.com (office).

HASSAN, Jean-Claude Gaston; French banker and public servant; b. 11 Nov. 1954, Tunis, Tunisia; s. of Charles Hassan and Yvonne Lellouche; m. Françoise Benhamou 1981; two s. one d.; ed Lycée de Mutuelleville, Tunis, Lycée Louis-le-Grand, Paris, Ecole normale supérieure, Ecole nat. d'admin; mem. Conseil d'Etat, Auditeur 1981, Counsel 1985; Tech. Adviser to Office of Minister of Social Affairs and Nat. Solidarity 1984–85; Deputy Dir-Gen. Banque Stern 1986–89, Dir-Gen. 1989–92; Dir-Gen. Banque Worms 1992–94; rejoined Conseil d'Etat 1994–2000, 2002; Conseiller pour l'euro de Laurent Fabins, Ministry of the Econ., Finance and Industry 2000–02; Conseiller d'État 2005–; mem. Cttee de règlement des différends de la CRE, Comm. de Régulation de l'Energie 2006–. *Address:* Commission de Régulation de l'Energie, 2 rue du Quatre-Septembre, 75084 Paris Cedex 02 (office); Conseil d'Etat, Palais-Royal, 75100 Paris 01 SP, France (office). *E-mail:* wemmestre@cre.fr (office). *Website:* www.cre.fr (office).

HASSAN, M. A.; Bangladeshi pharmaceuticals executive; f. Aristopharma Ltd 1986, currently Chair. and Man. Dir. *Address:* Aristopharma Ltd, 7 Purana Paltan Line, Dhaka 1000, Bangladesh (office). *Telephone:* (2) 93516913 (office). *Fax:* (2) 8317005 (office). *E-mail:* aplhc@bangla.net (office). *Website:* www.aristopharma.com (office).

HASSAN, Ustad Mehdi; Pakistani singer; b. 1927, Luna, Rajasthan, India; s. of Azim Khan; ed studied with his father, Azeem Khan and uncle, Ismail Khan; singer in a range of styles, including Ghazal, Dhrupad, Khayal, Thumri and Dadra; classical singer on Radio Karachi 1952–55; playback singer for films early 1960s–late 1980s; tours worldwide; Pride of Performance medal (Govt of Pakistan) 1985, Pakistan Broadcasting Corpn lifetime achievement award. *Recordings:* numerous albums of classical, popular and film music. *E-mail:* mehdihassan@hotmail.com (office). *Website:* www.mehdihassan.com.

HASSAN, Mohamed Hag Ali, PhD; Sudanese professor of mathematics; *Secretary-General, Third World Network of Scientific Organizations;* b. 21 Nov. 1947; ed Oxford Univ.; Sr Lecturer Dept of Mathematical Sciences, Khartoum Univ. 1977, Assoc. Prof. 1979, Prof. 1986, Dean of Mathematical Sciences 1985; Fulbright Research Fellow 1984; Exec. Dir Third World Acad. of Sciences 1983–; Sec.-Gen. Third World Network of Scientific Orgs 1988–; Fellow African Acad. of Sciences, Pres. 1999–; Fellow Islamic Acad. of Sciences, mem. Council 1999–; Hon. mem. Colombian Acad. of Exact Sciences. *Publications:* over 40 articles on applied mathematics. *Address:* African Academy of Sciences, PO Box 24916, Nairobi, Kenya (office). *Telephone:* (2) 884401 (office). *Fax:* (2) 884406 (office). *E-mail:* aas@africaonline.co.ke (office).

HASSAN, Sabir Muhammad, BSc, MA, PhD; Sudanese banking official; *Governor, Bank of Sudan;* ed Univ. of Khartoum, Syracuse Univ., USA; worked at Bank of Sudan 1968–76, Gov. 1993–96, 1998–; lecturer in various univs 1976–82; Adviser to Exec. Dir, IMF 1983–90; Gen. Man. Bank of Khartoum 1990–93; State Minister of Finance and Economy 1996–98. *Address:* Bank of Sudan, Gamaa Avenue, POB 313, Khartoum, Sudan (office). *Telephone:* (187) 056000 (office). *Fax:* (183) 780273 (office). *E-mail:* sudanbank@sudanmail.net (office). *Website:* www.bankofsudan.org (office).

HASSAN BIN TALAL, HRH Prince, GCVO, MA; *President, Club of Rome;* b. 20 March 1947, Amman; m. Sarvath Khujista Akhter Banu 1968; one s. three d.; ed Harrow School, England, Christ Church, Oxford Univ.; brother of the late Hussein ibn Talal, King of Jordan and heir to the throne until the changes in succession announced by the late King Hussein Jan. 1999; fmrly acted as Regent during absence of King Hussein; Ombudsman for Nat. Devt 1971–; Founder of Royal Scientific Soc. of Jordan 1970, Royal Acad. for Islamic Civilization Research (Al AlBait) 1980, Arab Thought Forum 1981, Forum Humanum (now Arab Youth Forum) 1982; Co-Chair. Independent Comm. on Int. Humanitarian Issues; Pres. Higher Council for Science and Tech., Club of Rome; Moderator World Conf. of Religions for Peace; Co-Patron Islamic Acad. of Sciences; Hon. Gen. of Jordan Armed Forces; Kt of Grand Cross of Order of Merit (Italy) 1983; Hon. PhD (Econ.) (Yarmouk) 1980; Hon. DSc (Bogazici, Turkey) 1982; Hon. Dr Arts and Sciences (Jordan) 1987; Hon. DCL (Durham) 1990; Dr hc (Ulster) 1996; Medal of Pres. of Italian Repub. 1982. *Publications:*

A Study on Jerusalem 1979, Palestinian Self-Determination 1981, Search for Peace 1984, Christianity in the Arab World 1994, Continuity, Innovation and Change 2001, To be a Muslim 2003, In Memory of Faisal I: The Iraqi Question 2003. *Leisure interests:* polo, squash, scuba diving, mountaineering, archaeology, Karate, Taekwondo, helicopter piloting, skiing. *Address:* The Royal Palace, Amman, Jordan. *Telephone:* 64649186 (office). *Fax:* 64634755 (office). *E-mail:* majlis@majliselhassan.org (office). *Website:* www.elhassan.org (office).

HASSAN MARICAN, Tan Sri Dato Sri Mohamed, FCA; Malaysian oil industry executive; *President and CEO, Petroliam Nasional Berhad (PETRONAS);* b. 1952, Sungai Petani, Kedah; m. Puan Sri Datin Sri Noraini Mohd Yusoff; ed Sekoleh Rendah Ibrahim, Malay Coll., Kuala Kangsar; began career as articled clerk, Touche Ross & Co., London 1972, later becoming Audit Man.; Accountant, Tetuan Hanfiah Raslan & Mohamed/Touche Ross & Co., Kuala Lumpur 1980, partner 1981–89; Sr Vice-Pres., Finance, Petroliam Nasional Berhad (PETRONAS) 1989, Pres. and CEO 1995–; Chair. Engen Ltd; Dir Pergaanan Kemajuan Negeri Kedah 1986–94; Dir Malaysia-Thailand Jt Authority; mem. Int. Investment Council for Repub. of SA, Commonwealth Business Council, World Econ. Forum Council of 100 Leaders; fmr mem. council Majlis Amanah Rakyat, Malaysian Accounting Standards Bd, Kumpulan Wang Amanah Pencen Investment Panel;; Darjah Sultan Mahmud Terengganu Yang amat Terpuji 1992, Bintang Darjah Seri Paduka Mahkota Terengganu 1996, Panglima Setia Mahkota 1997, Panglima Negara Bintang Sarawak 2003; Commdr Légion d'Honneur (France) 2000 DEng hc (Univ. Malaya) 2001; Vietnamese Govt Friendship Medal 2001. *Address:* Petroliam Nasional Berhad (PETRONAS), Tower 1, PETRONAS Twin Towers, 50088 Kuala Lumpur, Malaysia (office). *Telephone:* (603) 20265000 (office). *Fax:* (603) 20265050 (office). *Website:* www.petronas.com.my (office).

HASSAN SHARQ, Mohammad; Afghan politician; b. 1925, Farah; Deputy Prime Minister, 1974–77; Prime Minister of Afghanistan 1988–89.

HASSANI, Hajim al-, PhD; Iraqi politician; *Speaker, Transitional National Assembly;* b. 1954, Kirkuk; ed Mosul Univ., Univs of Nebraska and Conn., USA; moved to USA 1979; Researcher, Dept of Agricultural and Resource Econs, Univ. of Conn. 1990; Head of American Investment and Trading Co., Claremont, LA 1991–2003; active mem. of Iraqi Islamic Party (IIP) in exile; returned to Iraq following invasion 2003; worked for Iraqi Interim Governing Council 2003; Leader IIP 2003–04; involved in negotiating unsuccessful ceasefire between US forces and insurgents in Fallujah April 2004; Minister of Industry and Minerals 2004; Speaker Transitional Nat. Ass. 2005–. *Address:* Office of the Speaker, Transitional National Assembly, Green Zone, Baghad, Iraq.

HASSANOV, Hassan Aziz Oglou; Azerbaijani politician; b. 20 Oct. 1940, Tbilisi, Georgia; s. of Aziz Hassanov and Ruhsara Adjalova; m. 1964; one s. one d.; ed Azerbaijan Polytech. Inst., Higher Party School; mem. various student groups 1958–61; with Lenin Young Communists League (Komsomol) Orgs of Yasamal region of Baku 1961–66; with Komsomol Cen. Cttee, Moscow, 1967–; with Construction Section, Cent. Cttee, Azerbaijan CP 1971–; First Sec. CP, Sabail region, then of Communist Party of Sumgayit and Gandja cities 1975–81; mem. Azerbaijan Supreme Soviet (Parliament) 1977–95, USSR Supreme Soviet 1979–84; Sec. Cent. Cttee Communist Party, Azerbaijan (Ideology) 1981, (Construction and Transport) 1983–, (Econ.) 1989; first Prime Minister of the Repub. of Azerbaijan 1990–1992; Perm. Rep. to UN 1992–93; Minister of Foreign Affairs 1993–98; mem. of Mili Mejlis (Parl.) 1995–. *Play:* Letter from Brussels (Azerbaijan State Drama Theatre) 2001. *Publications:* more than 100 articles on Azerbaijani economy, policies, diplomacy and history. *Leisure interests:* art, music, history, politics, chess. *Address:* Gendjler Meydani 3, Baku 370001; Apt. 36, 9 Istiglad Str., Baku 370001 Azerbaijan (home). *Telephone:* (12) 4927744 (home); (12) 4929114. *Fax:* (12) 4651038; (12) 4988480. *E-mail:* Ggassuhov@hotmail.com (home).

HASSELL, Michael Patrick, CBE, MA, PhD, DSc, FRS; British professor of insect ecology; *Honorary Distinguished Research Fellow, Imperial College, London;* b. 2 Aug. 1942, Tel-Aviv; s. of Albert Hassell and Ruth Hassell; m. 1st Glynis M. Everett 1966; m. 2nd Victoria A. Taylor 1982; three s. one d.; ed Whitgift School, Croydon, Clare Coll., Cambridge and Oriel Coll., Oxford; Visiting Lecturer, Univ. of Calif., Berkeley 1967–68; NERC Research Fellowship, Hope Dept of Entomology, Oxford 1968–70; Lecturer, Dept of Zoology and Applied Entomology, Imperial Coll., London 1970–75, Reader 1975–79, Prof. of Insect Ecology, Dept of Biology 1979–, Deputy Head, Dept of Biology 1984–92, Head 1993–2001; Prin. Faculty of Life Sciences 2001–04; Dir Imperial Coll., Silwood Park 1988–2007, Dean 2004–07, Hon. Distinguished Research Fellow 2007–; Storer Life Sciences Lecturer, Univ. of California, Davis 1985; Pres. British Ecological Soc. 1998–99; Assoc. Ed. Researches in Population Ecology; mem. Editorial Bd Journal of Theoretical Biology; mem. Bd of Reviewing Eds Science; mem. Council of Zoological Soc. of London, Chair. Awards Cttee; Fellow, Academia Europea 1998; Trustee, Natural History Museum 1999–2004; Scientific Medal (Zoological Soc.) 1981, Gold Medal (British Ecological Soc.) 1994, Weldon Prize (Univ. of Oxford) 1995. *Publications:* Insect Population Ecology (with G.C. Varley and G.R. Gradwell) 1973, The Dynamics of Competition and Predation 1975, The Dynamics of Arthropod Predator-Prey Systems 1978; The Spatial and Temporal Dynamics of Host-Parasitoid Interactions 2000, numerous publs on population ecology. *Leisure interests:* walking, natural history. *Address:* Biology, Silwood Park, Ascot, Berks., SL5 7PY (office); Barnside, Buckland Brewer, Bideford, Devon, EX39 5NF, England (home). *E-mail:* m.hassell@imperial.ac.uk (office).

HASSELMO, Nils, PhD; American university president and association executive; *President, Association of American Universities;* b. 2 July 1931, Köla, Sweden; s. of Wilner Hasselmo and Anna Backlund; m. 1st Patricia Tillberg 1958 (died 2000); two s. one d.; m. 2nd Ann Die 2003; ed Uppsala Univ., Augustana Coll. Rock Island, Ill. and Harvard Univ.; Asst Prof. of Swedish, Augustana Coll. 1958–59, 1961–63; Visiting Asst Prof. in Scandinavian Studies, Univ. of Wis. 1964–65; Assoc. Prof. of Scandinavian Lang. and Literature, Univ. of Minn. 1965–70, Dir Center for NW European Languages and Area Studies 1970–73, Prof. of Scandinavian Language and Literature 1970–73, Assoc. Dean and Exec. Officer, Coll. of Liberal Arts 1973–78, Vice-Pres. for Admin. and Planning 1980–83; Prof. of English and Linguistics and Sr Vice-Pres. for Academic Affairs and Provost, Univ. of Ariz. 1983–88; Pres. Univ. of Minn. 1988–97, Asscn of American Univs 1998–; mem. Bd of Dirs Swedish Council 1978–, Chair. 1999–2001; mem. Bd of Dirs Nat. Asscn of State Univs and Land-Grant Colls, Chair. 1994–95; mem. Bd Dirs Carnegie Foundation for the Advancement of Teaching; mem. numerous other orgs; Royal Order of North Star (Sweden); Dr hc (Uppsala) 1979, (North Park Univ., Chicago) 1992, (Augustana Coll., Ill.) 1995, elected memberships in the Royal Gustavus Adolphus Acad. and other scholarly socs in Sweden; recipient of many honours and awards including King Carl XVI Gustaf Bicentennial Gold Medal. *Publications:* books and articles and reviews in learned journals. *Leisure interests:* reading, music, hiking, tennis, golf. *Address:* Association of American Universities, 1200 New York Avenue, NW, Suite 550, Washington, DC 20005, USA (office). *Telephone:* (202) 408-7500. *Fax:* (202) 408-8184. *E-mail:* nils_hasselmo_aau@edu (office). *Website:* www.aau.edu (office).

HASSON, Maurice; French/Venezuelan violinist; *Professor of Violin, Royal Academy of Music, London;* b. 6 July 1934, Berck-Plage; m. Jane Hoogesteijn, 1969; one s. three d.; ed Conservatoire Nat. Supérieur de Musique, Paris, further studies with Henryk Szeryng; concert artist in major concert halls throughout world, also in TV and radio performances; Prof., RAM, London 1986–; Hon. Mem. RAM; Orden Andrés Bello, Orden Tulio Febres Cordero (Venezuela), Médaille de Vermeil de la Ville de Paris; First Prize Violin, Prix d'Honneur and First Prize Chamber Music, Conservatoire Nat. Supérieure de Musique, Paris 1950, Int. Prize Long Thibaut 1951, Int. Prize Youth Festival, Warsaw 1955, Grand Prix Musique de Chambre 1957. *Recordings include:* Concerto No. 1 (Paganini), Concerto No. 2 (Prokofiev), Debussy Sonatas, Fauré Sonatas, Concerto No. 1, Scottish Fantasy (Bruch), Concerto for 2 and 4 violins (Vivaldi), Double Concerto (Bach), Concerto (Brahms), Brilliant Showpieces for the Violin, Tzigane (Ravel), Rondo Capriccioso (Saint Saëns), Poème (Chausson), Gypsy Airs (Sarasate), Violin Concerto (Castellanos-Yumar), Sonata (Franck), virtuoso pieces. *Leisure interests:* reading, painting, sport, cars. *Address:* 18 West Heath Court, North End Road, London, NW11 7RE, England (home). *Telephone:* (20) 8458-3647 (home). *E-mail:* jdehasson@btinternet.com (home).

HASTE, Andy; British insurance executive; *Group Chief Executive, Royal & Sun Alliance Insurance Group PLC;* fmrly with National Westminster (NatWest) Bank, Head Consumer Loans Products Div., NatWest US operations 1992–95, Pres. US consumer credit business 1995–99; Pres. and CEO Global Consumer Finance Europe, GE Capital; CEO AXA Sun Life (also Exec. Dir AXA UK) 1999–2003; Group CEO Royal & Sun Alliance Group (also mem. Main Bd Dirs Royal & Sun Alliance) 2003–. *Address:* Royal & Sun Alliance Insurance Group plc, 9th Floor, One Plantation Place, 30 Fenchurch Street, London, EC3M 3BD, England (office). *Telephone:* (20) 7111-7000 (office). *Fax:* (20) 7569-6639 (office). *Website:* www.royalsunalliance.com (office).

HASTERT, (J.) Dennis, BA, MS; American fmr politician; b. 2 Jan. 1942, Aurora, Ill.; m. Jean Kahl 1973; two s.; ed Wheaton Coll., Ill., Northern Illinois Univ.; fmr teacher, Yorkville High School, Ill., also wrestling coach; mem. Ill. House of Reps, Springfield 1980–86; mem. 100th–105th Congresses from 14th Dist Ill. 1987–2007 (resgnd), mem. Commerce Comm., Govt Reform and Oversight Comm.; Speaker of House of Reps 1999–2007; Republican.

HASTINGS, Sir Max Macdonald, Kt, FRSL, FRHistS; British writer and broadcaster; b. 28 Dec. 1945, London; s. of Macdonald Hastings and Anne Scott-James (Lady Lancaster); m. 1st Patricia Edmondson 1972 (divorced 1994); one s. (and one s. deceased) one d.; m. 2nd Penelope Grade 1999; ed Charterhouse and Univ. Coll., Oxford; reporter, London Evening Standard 1965–67, 1968–70; Fellow, US World Press Inst. 1967–68; reporter, current affairs, BBC Television 1970–73; freelance journalist, broadcaster and author 1973–; columnist, Evening Standard 1979–85, Daily Express 1981–83, Sunday Times 1985–86; Ed. Daily Telegraph 1986–95, Dir 1989–95, Ed.-in-Chief 1990–95; Ed. Evening Standard 1996–2002; Dir Evening Standard Ltd 1996–2002; columnist Daily Mail 2002–, Guardian 2004–; book reviewer Sunday Times 2006–; mem. Press Complaints Comm. 1990–92; Trustee Liddell Hart Archive, King's Coll. London 1988–2004, Nat. Portrait Gallery 1995–2004; Pres. Council for the Protection of Rural England 2002–07; Hon. Fellow, King's Coll. London 2004; Hon. DLitt (Leicester) 1992; Journalist of the Year 1982, Reporter of the Year 1982, Somerset Maugham Prize for Non-fiction 1979, Ed. of the Year 1988. *Television:* documentaries: Ping-Pong in Peking 1971, The War About Peace 1983, Alarums and Excursions 1984, Cold Comfort Farm 1985, The War in Korea (series) 1988, We Are All Green Now 1990, Spies (in series Cold War) 1998, Churchill and His Generals (series) 2003. *Publications:* America 1968: The Fire, The Time 1968, Ulster 1969, The Struggle for Civil Rights in Northern Ireland 1970, Montrose: The King's Champion 1977, Yoni: Hero of Entebbe 1979, Bomber Command 1979, The Battle of Britain (with Len Deighton) 1980, Das Reich 1981, Battle for the Falklands (with Simon Jenkins) 1983, Overlord: D-Day and the Battle for Normandy 1984, Victory in Europe 1985, The Oxford Book of Military Anecdotes (ed.) 1985, The Korean War 1987, Outside Days 1989, Scattered Shots 1999, Going to the Wars 2000, Editor (memoir) 2002, Armageddon: The Battle for Germany 1944–45 2004, Warriors: Extraordinary Tales from the Battlefields 2005, Country Fair 2005, Nemesis: The Battle for Japan 1944–45 2007. *Leisure interests:* shooting, fishing. *Address:* c/o PFD, Drury House,

34–43 Russell Street, London, WC2B 5HA, England (office). *Telephone:* (20) 7344-1000 (office). *Fax:* (20) 7836-9539 (office). *E-mail:* info@pfd.co.uk (office). *Website:* www.pfd.co.uk (office).

HASUMI, Shigehiko, MA, PhD; Japanese film critic, academic and fmr university administrator; *Professor Emeritus, University of Tokyo;* b. 29 April 1936, Tokyo; ed Dept of Literature, Univ. of Tokyo, Univ. of Paris, France; began publishing film criticism in Cinema 69 1968; work influenced by Cahiers du Cinéma and post-structuralism; Ed.-in-Chief Lumiére 1985–88; began academic career as Asst Lecturer, Univ. of Tokyo, held positions successively as Asst Prof., Prof. of Pedagogics 1988–, now Prof. Emer., Head of Pedagogics Dept 1993–95, Vice-Chancellor 1995–97, Chancellor 1997–2001; fmr Asst Prof., Rikkyo Univ. *Publications:* Portrait of a Common Artist, The Argument Against Japanese, Statement of Superficial Critique, The Director Yasujirou Ozu; chapters in books. *Address:* c/o Office of the Chancellor, University of Tokyo, 7-3-1 Hongo, Bunkyo-ku, Tokyo 113-8654, Japan (office).

HATA, Tsutomu; Japanese politician; *Special Representative, Democratic Party of Japan;* b. 24 Aug. 1935, Tokyo; ed Seijo Univ.; fmr bus tour operator; elected to House of Reps 1969; fmr Parl. Vice-Minister of Posts and Telecommunications, Agric., Forestry and Fisheries; fmr Minister of Agric., Forestry and Fisheries; Chair. Liberal-Democratic Party (LDP) Research Comm. on the Election System; Minister of Finance 1991–92; left LDP to found Shinseito (New Life Party), Pres. 1993–94, Shinseito dissolved 1994 (merged with eight others to form New Frontier Party); Leader Good Governance Party 1998 (merged with two others to form Democratic Party of Japan—DPJ); currently Special Rep. Standing Officers Council of DPJ; Deputy Prime Minister and Minister of Foreign Affairs 1993–94; Prime Minister of Japan May–June 1994. *Address:* Nagata-cho 2-2-1, Chiyoda-ku, Tokyo 100-8981; House of Representatives, Tokyo, Japan. *Telephone:* (3) 3508-7324 (office). *Fax:* (3) 3508-5080 (office); (3) 3239-3055 (home). *E-mail:* t-hata@nifty.com (office). *Website:* www.t-hata.com (office).

HATAB, Abdul Karim Mahoud al-, (Abu Hattem); Iraqi guerrilla leader; b. 1958, Amara; ed religious school; fmr fighter with peshmerga (Kurdish guerrilla group); imprisoned, Abu Ghraib prison, Baghdad 1980–86; guerrilla leader 1990–, leader Hizbullah of Iraq. *Address:* Hizbullah of Iraq, Amara, Iraq.

HATANO, Yoshio, BA; Japanese university administrator and fmr diplomatist; *Chancellor, Gakushuin Women's College;* b. 3 Jan. 1932, Tokyo; s. of Keizo Hatano and Tatsuko Hatano; m. Sumiko Shimazu 1961; one s. one d.; ed Tokyo Univ., Princeton Univ., USA; joined Foreign Ministry 1953, held various positions including Dir Econ. Affairs, Asian Affairs and Treaties Bureaux, Personnel Div., Gen. Co-ordination Div.; First Sec., Embassy, London 1970; Counsellor, Embassy, Jakarta 1971; Minister, Embassy, Washington, DC 1979, Envoy Extraordinary and Minister Plenipotentiary 1981; Dir-Gen. Middle Eastern and African Affairs Bureau, Dir-Gen. for Public Information and Cultural Affairs, Ministry of Foreign Affairs 1982–87; Perm. Rep. to int. orgs in Geneva 1987–90; Perm. Rep. to UN, New York 1990–94; Pres. Foreign Press Center 1994; Pres. Gakushuin Women's College 2003–06, Chancellor 2006–. *Television:* regular mem. of Wake Up panel, Yomiuri TV. *Leisure interests:* golf, opera. *Address:* 3-20-1 Toyama, Shinjuku-ku, Tokyo (office); 2-14-13 Hiroo, Shibuya-ku, Tokyo, Japan (home). *Telephone:* (3) 3203-1906 (office); (3) 3407-0463 (home). *Fax:* (3) 3203-8373 (office); (3) 3407-0463 (home). *E-mail:* gwc-off@gakushuin.ac.jp (office). *Website:* www2.gwc.gakushuin.ac.jp (office).

HATCH, Marshall Davidson, AM, BSc, PhD, FAA, FRS; Australian research scientist; *Honorary Research Fellow, Division of Plant Industry, Commonwealth Scientific and Industrial Research Organization (CSIRO);* b. 24 Dec. 1932, Perth; s. of Lloyd D. Hatch and Alice Dalziel; m. 2nd Lyndall Langman 1983; two s.; ed Newington Coll., Sydney, Sydney Univ. and Univ. of California; Research Scientist, CSIRO 1955–59; Post-doctoral Fellow, Univ. of California 1959–61; Research Scientist, Colonial Sugar Refining Co., Ltd 1961–70; Chief Research Scientist, Div. of Plant Industry, CSIRO, Canberra 1970–97, Hon. Research Fellow 1998–; Foreign Assoc. NAS 1990; Dr hc (Göttingen) 1993, (Queensland) 1997; Clark Medal, Royal Soc. of NSW 1973, Lemberg Medal, Australian Biochemical Soc. 1974, Charles Kettering Award for Photosynthesis, American Soc. of Plant Physiologists 1980, Rank Award, Rank Foundation 1981, Int. Prize for Biology, Japan Soc. for Promotion of Science 1991. *Publications:* over 165 review articles, chapters in books and research papers in scientific journals relating to the mechanism and function of c-4 photosynthesis. *Leisure interests:* reading, skiing, cycling, hiking. *Address:* Division of Plant Industry, CSIRO, PO Box 1600, Canberra (office); 34 Dugdale Street, Cook, ACT 2614, Australia (home). *Telephone:* 6246-5264 (office); 6251-5159 (home). *Website:* www.csiro.au (office).

HATCH, Orrin Grant, BS, JD; American politician and lawyer; *Senator from Utah;* b. 22 March 1934, Homestead Park Pa; s. of Jesse Hatch and Helen Kamm Hatch; m. Elaine Hansen 1957; three s. three d.; ed Brigham Young Univ., Univ. of Pittsburgh; journeyman metal lather; Partner, Thomson, Rhodes & Grigsby 1962–69; Senior Vice-Pres. and Gen. Counsel, American Minerals Man. and American Minerals Fund Inc., Salt Lake City, Utah 1969–71; Partner, Hatch & Plumb, Salt Lake City 1976; Senator from Utah 1977–; Chair. Senate Labor and Human Resources Cttee 1981, Senate Judiciary Cttee 1995–2001, Jt Cttee on Taxation, Cttee on Indian Affairs, Sub Cttee on Taxation; mem. Senate Cttee on Finance, Senate Cttee on Intelligence 1977–; Dir Holocaust Memorial Museum; Republican; numerous hon. degrees. *Publications:* ERA Myths and Realities 1983, Good Faith under the Uniform Commercial Code, articles in legal journals. *Address:* 104 Hart Senate Building, Washington, DC 20510, USA. *Telephone:* (202) 224-5251 (office). *Fax:* (202) 224-6331 (office). *Website:* hatch.senate.gov (office).

HATFIELD, Mark O.; American politician (retd); *Distinguished Professor, Hatfield School of Government, Portland State University;* b. 12 July 1922, Dallas, Oregon; s. Charles Dolen Hatfield and Dovie Odom; m. Antoinette Kuzmanich 1958; two s. two d.; ed Willamette Univ. and Stanford Univ.; US Navy Second World War; Instructor, Asst Prof., Assoc. Prof. in Political Science, Willamette Univ. 1949–56, Dean of Students 1950–56; State Rep., Marion County 1951–55, State Senator, Marion County 1955–57; Sec. of State, Oregon 1957–59; Gov. of Oregon 1959–67; US Senator from Oregon 1967–97; Chair. Senate Appropriations Cttee 1981–97; fmr mem. Energy and Natural Resources Cttee and Senate Rules and Admin. Cttee; currently Distinguished Prof. Hatfield School of Govt, Portland State Univ.; Republican; numerous awards and over 100 hon. degrees. *Publications:* Not Quite So Simple (autobiog.), Conflict and Conscience (religious speeches), Between a Rock and a Hard Place 1976, The Causes of World Hunger (co-author) 1982, What About the Russians? 1984 (jtly), Vice-Presidents of the United States 1789-1993 (jtly) 1997, Against the Grain: Reflections of a Rebel Republican 2001. *Leisure interests:* gardening, reading. *Address:* POB 2, Marylhurst, OR 97036, USA. *Website:* www.hatfieldschool.pdx.edu.

HATHAWAY, Anne; American actress; b. 12 Nov. 1982, Brooklyn, NY; d. of Gerald Hathaway and Kate McCauley; ed Vassar Coll., New York Univ. *Films include:* The Princess Diaries 2001, The Other Side of Heaven 2001, The Cat Returns 2002, Nicholas Nickleby 2002, Ella Enchanted 2004, The Princess Diaries 2: Royal Engagement 2004, Hoodwinked! 2005, Havoc 2005, Brokeback Mountain 2005, The Devil Wears Prada 2006, Becoming Jane 2007, Get Smart 2008, Passengers 2008, Rachel Getting Married 2008 (Nat. Bd of Review Award for Best Actress, SE Film Critics Award for Best Actress), Bride Wars 2009. *Television:* Get Real (series) 1999–2000. *Address:* Creative Artists Agency (CAA), 2000 Avenue of the Stars, Los Angeles, CA 90067, USA (office). *Telephone:* (424) 288-2000 (office). *Fax:* (424) 288-2900 (office). *Website:* www.caa.com (office).

HATOYAMA, Kunio; Japanese politician; b. 13 Sept. 1948, Tokyo; s. of Iichiro Hatoyama; ed Univ. of Tokyo; mem. House of Reps (Fukuoka Dist 6th) 1976–; fmr Parl. Vice-Minister for Educ., mem. Liberal-Democratic Party (LDP) –1993, 2000–, Dir Educ. Div., Chair. Cttee on Educ., House of Reps, Cttee on Rules and Admin Feb. 2002, Special Cttee on Response to Armed Attacks Oct. 2002, LDP Cttee on Harmony Between Nature and People March 2004; mem. Renaissance Party 1993; Founding mem. Democratic Party of Japan 1996; Minister of Educ. 1991–92, of Labour May–June 1994, of Justice 2007–08; mem. Japan-Korea Parliamentarians' Union. *Address:* Liberal-Democratic Party (LDP), 1-11-23, Nagata-cho, Chiyoda-ku, Tokyo, 100-8910 Japan. *Telephone:* (3) 3581-6211 (office). *E-mail:* koho@ldp.jimin.or.jp (office). *Website:* www.jimin.jp (office); www.hatoyamakunio.org.

HATOYAMA, Yukio, PhD; Japanese politician; *Secretary-General, Democratic Party of Japan (DPJ);* b. 11 Feb. 1947, Tokyo; brother of Kunio Hatoyama; ed Tokyo Univ., Stanford Univ., USA; Asst Prof. Senshyu Univ. 1981; Pvt. Sec. to Iichiro Hatoyama, House of Councillors 1983; elected to House of Reps as mem. Parl. for Hokkaido 9th Dist 1986–, Parl. Vice-Minister, Hokkaido Devt Agency 1990–, Vice Chief Sec. to Hosokawa Cabinet 1993; mem. New Party Sakigake 1993, Chief Sec. New Party Sakigake Perm. Cttee 1994; Jt Leader Democratic Party of Japan (DPJ) 1996–97, Sec.-Gen. 1997, Deputy Sec.-Gen. 1998–99, Pres. of DPJ 1999–2002, currently Sec.-Gen.; Vice-Chair. Japan–Russia Soc.; mem. House of Reps Standing Cttee on Science and Tech.; Chair. Touch Football Asscn of Japan. *Leisure interests:* touch football, tennis, karaoke, computers. *Address:* Democratic Party of Japan, 1-11-1 Nagata-Cho, Chiyoda-ku, Tokyo 100-0014, Japan (office). *Telephone:* (3) 3595-7312 (office); (3) 3595-9960 (office). *Fax:* (3) 3595-7318 (office). *E-mail:* dpjnews@dpj.or.jp (office). *Website:* www.dpj.or.jp (office).

HATTERSLEY, Baron (Life Peer), cr. 1997, of Sparkbrook in the County of West Midlands; **Roy Sydney George Hattersley,** PC, BSc (Econ.), FRSL; British politician, writer and broadcaster; b. 28 Dec. 1932; s. of the late Frederick Roy Hattersley and Enid Hattersley (née Brackenbury); m. Molly Loughran 1956; ed Sheffield City Grammar School, Univ. of Hull; journalist and health service exec. 1956–64; mem. Sheffield City Council 1957–65; MP for Sparkbrook Div. of Birmingham 1964–97; Parl. Pvt. Sec. to Minister of Pensions and Nat. Insurance 1964–67; Dir Campaign for European Political Community 1965; Jt Parl. Sec. Dept of Employment and Productivity 1967–69; Minister of Defence for Admin 1969–70; Opposition Spokesman for Defence 1970–72, for Educ. 1972–74, for the Environment 1979–80, for Home Affairs 1980–83, on Treasury and Econ. Affairs 1983–87, on Home Affairs 1987–92; Minister of State for Foreign and Commonwealth Affairs 1974–76; Sec. of State for Prices and Consumer Protection 1976–79; Deputy Leader of the Labour Party 1983–92; Pres. Local Govt Group for Europe 1998–; Public Affairs Consultant, IBM 1971, 1972; columnist, Punch, The Guardian, The Listener 1979–82; Visiting Fellow, Inst. of Politics, Harvard Univ. 1971, 1972, Nuffield Coll., Oxford 1984–; Labour; Hon. LLD (Hull) 1985; Dr hc (Aston) 1997. *Publications:* Nelson – A Biography 1974, Goodbye to Yorkshire – A Collection of Essays 1976, Politics Apart – A Collection of Essays 1982, Press Gang 1983, A Yorkshire Boyhood 1983, Choose Freedom: The Future for Democratic Socialism 1987, Economic Priorities for a Labour Government 1987, The Maker's Mark (novel) 1990, In That Quiet Earth (novel) 1991, Skylark's Song (novel) 1994, Between Ourselves (novel) 1994, Who Goes Home? 1995, Fifty Years On 1997, Buster's Diaries: As Told to Roy Hattersley 1998, Blood and Fire: The Story of William and Catherine Booth and their Salvation Army 1999, A Brand from the Burning: The Life of John Wesley 2002, The Edwardians 2004, Borrowed Time: The Story of Britain Between the Wars 2007; contrib. to newspapers and journals. *Leisure interests:* watching cricket and football, writing. *Address:* House of Lords, Westminster,

London, SW1A 0PW, England (office). *Telephone:* (20) 7219-3000 (office). *E-mail:* roy@royhattersley.com (office).

HATTIG, Josef; German business executive and politician; *Chairman, Supervisory Board, Deutsche Post AG;* trained as commercial clerk; Dir Thier & Co. Brewery, Dortmund 1965–72; Man.-Dir Beck & Co. Brewery, Bremen 1972–97; Minister for European and Econ. Affairs, German Fed. State of Bremen 1997–99, Minister for the Economy and City Ports 1999–2003; Chair. Supervisory Bd Deutsche Post AG 2003–; fmr Pres. German Brewers' Asscn; fmr Chair. Bremen Chamber of Commerce; mem. Christian Democratic Union (CDU). *Address:* Deutsche Post AG, Charles-de-Gaulle-Strasse 20, 53113 Bonn, Germany (office). *Telephone:* 228-1820 (office). *Fax:* 228-1827099 (office). *Website:* www.dpwn.de (office).

HATTON, Stephen Paul, BComm; Australian politician; b. 28 Jan. 1948, Sydney; s. of Stanley J. and Pauline Hatton (née Taylor); m. 1st Deborah J. Humphreys 1969 (divorced 1993); three s. one d.; m. 2nd Cathy Huyer 1995; one d.; ed Univ. of New South Wales; Personnel Officer, James Hardie & Co. Pty Ltd 1965–70; Industrial Officer Nabalco Pty Ltd 1970–75; Exec. Dir NT Confed. of Industries and Commerce Inc. 1975–83; elected NT Legislative Ass. (Nightcliff) 1984, Minister for Lands, Conservation, Ports and Fisheries, Primary Production 1983–84, for Mines and Energy, Primary Production 1986, for Health and Community Services 1989, for Conservation 1989, for Industries and Devt and for Trade Devt Zone and Liquor Comm. 1990–91, for Lands, Housing and Local Govt and Minister for Aboriginal Devt 1992, for Constitutional Devt 1994, Attorney-Gen., Minister for Educ. for Constitutional Devt 1995–96, for Sport and Recreation 1995–97, for Correctional Services 1996–97, for Parks and Wildlife 1996–97, for Ethnic Affairs 1996–97; Chief Minister for NT 1986–88. *Leisure interest:* sport. *Address:* Shop 5, Nightcliff Shopping Centre, Pavonia Way, Nightcliff, NT 0810, Australia.

HAUB, Christian; American retail executive; *Executive Chairman, Great Atlantic & Pacific Tea Company Incorporated (A&P);* b. 1964; s. of Erivan Haub; joined Great Atlantic & Pacific Tea Co. Inc. 1998, Pres. and CEO 1998–2000, Exec. Chair. 2000–. *Address:* Great Atlantic & Pacific Tea Company Incorporated, 2 Paragon Drive, Montvale, NJ 07645, USA (office). *Telephone:* (201) 573-9700 (office). *Fax:* (201) 571-8719 (office). *Website:* www.aptea.com (office).

HAUB, Erivan Karl; German retail industry executive and political economist; *Chairman of the Board, Tengelmann Warenhandelsgesellschaft;* b. 29 Sept. 1932, Meal; m. Helga Otto; three s.; ed Univ. of Hamburg; with Tengelmannhausebank, Frankfurt 1979; co-owner Kaiser's Kaffee Geschäft AG; fmr CEO Tengelmann Warenhandelsgesellschaft, food retailer with supermarkets and outlets in several countries and majority shareholder in Great Atlantic and Pacific Tea Co. (A&P), currently Chair. Bd; mem. Advisory Bd Arbeitsgemeinschaft der Lebensmittelfilialbetriebe, Bonn; Erivan K. Haub Exec. Conf. Center and Erivan K. Haub School of Business, St Joseph's Univ. are named after him; Distinguished Service Cross First Class, Order of Merit of the Fed. Repub. of Germany; Dr hc (St Joseph's Univ.) 1992; Earth Day Int. Award. *Address:* Tengelmann Warenhandelsgesellschaft KG, Wissollstrasse 5-43, 45478 Mülheim an der Ruhr, Germany (office). *Telephone:* (208) 58067601 (office). *Fax:* (208) 58066401 (office). *Website:* www.tengelmann.de (office).

HAUER, Rutger; Dutch actor; b. 23 Jan. 1944, Amsterdam; m. 2nd Ieneke Hauer 1985; f. Rutger Hauer Starfish Asscn. *Films include:* Turkish Delight 1973, The Wilby Conspiracy 1975, Keetje Tippel 1975, Max Havelaar 1976, Mysteries 1978, Soldier of Orange 1978, Woman Between Dog and Wolf 1979, Spetters 1980, Nighthawks 1981, Chanel Solitaire 1981, Blade Runner 1982, Eureka 1982, Outsider in Amsterdam 1983, The Osterman Weekend 1983, A Breed Apart 1984, Ladyhawke 1984, Flesh and Blood 1985, The Hitcher 1986, Wanted Dead or Alive 1986, The Legend of the Holy Drinker 1989, Salute of the Juggler, Ocean Point, On a Moonlit Night, Split Second, Buffy the Vampire Slayer, Past Midnight, Nostradamus, Surviving the Game, The Beans of Egypt Maine, Angel of Death, New World Disorder 1999, Wilder 2000, Lying in Wait 2000, Partners in Crime 2000, Jungle Juice 2001, Flying Virus 2001, I Banchieri di Dio 2002, Scorcher 2002, Warrior Angels 2002, Confessions of a Dangerous Mind 2002, In the Shadow of the Cobra 2004, Tempesta 2004, Never Enough 2004, Sin City 2005, Batman Begins 2005, Mirror Wars: Reflection One 2005, 7eventy 5ive 2006, Minotaur 2006, Mentor 2006. *TV Films include:* Angel of Death 1994, Menin 1998, The 10th Kingdom 2000. *Publications:* All Those Moments 2007. *Address:* c/o Rutger Hauer Starfish Association, Via Tulipani, 2, 20146 Milan, Italy; c/o William Morris Agency, 151 El Camino Drive, Beverly Hills, CA 90212, USA. *E-mail:* rhinfo1@rutgerhauer.org. *Website:* www.rutgerhauer.org.

HAUFF, Volker, Dr rer. pol; German politician and business consultant; *Chairman, German Council for Sustainable Development;* b. 9 Aug. 1940, Backnang; s. of Richard and Ilse (Dieter) Hauff; m. Ursula Irion 1967; two s.; ed Free Univ. of Berlin; with IBM Deutschland, Stuttgart 1971–72; Sec. of State to Fed. Minister for Research and Tech. 1972–78; Fed. Minister for Research and Tech. 1978–80, of Transport 1980–82; mem. Bundestag 1969; mem. Social Democratic Party (SPD) 1959, Vice-Pres. of Parl. Group 1983; Mayor of Frankfurt 1989–91; Generalbevollmächtigte KPMG Germany 1995–2000, mem. Bd Bearing Point GmbH 2002–, Sr Vice Pres. 2003–; Chair. German Council for Sustainable Devt 2001–; fmr mem. UN World Comm. on Environment and Devt; Bundesverdienstkreuz mit Stern und Schulterband. *Publications:* Programmierfibes—Eine verständliche Einführung in das Programmieren digitaler Automaten 1969, Wörterbuch der Datenverarbeitung 1966, Für ein soziales Bodenrecht 1973, Modernisierung der Volkswirtschaft 1975, Politik als Zukunftsgestaltung 1976, Damit der Fortschritt nicht zum Risiko wird 1978, Sprachlose Politik 1979, Global Denken – Lokal

Handeln 1992. *Leisure interests:* modern art, cooking. *Address:* Hitzeierstrasse 68, 50968 Köln, Germany (home). *Telephone:* (30) 34703841 (office); (172) 2902902. *E-mail:* volker.hauff@bearingpoint.com. *Website:* www.bearingpoint.de.

HAUGHTON, Rosemary Elena Konradin; British/American writer, lecturer, social philosopher and theologian; *Director Emerita, Wellspring House Inc.;* b. 13 April 1927, London; d. of Peter Luling and Sylvia Luling (née Thompson); sister of Dr Virginia Luling; m. Algernon Haughton 1948; seven s. three d.; ed Farnham Girls' Grammar School, Queen's Coll., London, Slade School of Art; had no formal educ. after age of 15; has lectured internationally; Assoc. Dir Wellspring House Inc., providing shelter for homeless families, continuing educ. for low-income women, low-income housing and econ. devt in Mass, USA 1981–, Dir Emer. 2003–; Dr hc (Notre Dame, Nazareth Coll., Georgian Court Coll., St Mary's Coll., Notre Dame); Avila Award. *Publications include:* The Transformation of Man, The Drama of Salvation, Tales from Eternity, Elizabeth's Greeting, The Catholic Thing, The Passionate God, The Re-Creation of Eve, Song in a Strange Land, The Tower that Fell (illustrated), Images for Change: The Transformation of Society, Gifts in the Ruins (illustrated) 2004. *Leisure interests:* wood-carving, embroidery, gardening, reading, country cottage. *Address:* Wellspring House Inc., 302 Essex Avenue, Gloucester, MA 01930, USA (office); 5 Draper Corner, Heptonstall, Hebden Bridge, W Yorkshire, HX7 7EY, England (home). *Telephone:* (978) 281-3221 (USA); (1422) 843199 (home). *E-mail:* rhaughton@wellspringhouse.org (office); rosemary@yorkshire5.plus.net (home).

HĂULICĂ, Dan; Romanian art critic; b. 7 Feb. 1932, Iaşi; s. of Neculai Hăulică and Lucreţia Hăulică; m. Cristina Isbăşescu 1971; one d.; ed Coll. of Philology, Iaşi, N. Grigorescu Fine Arts Inst., Bucharest; Reader, Iaşi Coll. of Philology 1954–56; Ed. Literary Magazine, Bucharest 1956–58; Researcher, Inst. for Literary History and Theory of the Romanian Acad. 1958–63; Deputy Ed.-in-Chief Secolul 20 (journal) 1963–67, Ed.-in-Chief 1967; Prof., N. Grigorescu Coll. of Fine Arts, Bucharest 1965; Pres. Int. Asscn of Art Critics (AICA) 1981–84, Hon. Pres. 1984–; Chair. Conseil audiovisuel mondial pour l'édition et la recherche sur l'art (CAMERA) 1986; UNESCO consultant; Amb. to UNESCO 1990–; mem. European Soc. of Culture 1988, European Acad. of Sciences, Letters and Arts 1987; Chair. Int. Confs on Arts, TV and Problems of the Image: Paris, UNESCO 1981, Biennale di Venezia 1982, Sophia Antipolis, Moscow-Tashkent 1982, Helsinki 1983, Caracas 1983, Delphi 1984, Lisbon, Gulbenkian 1984, Paris 1986, Prague 1987, Alger-Tipasa 1987; Chair. Int. Jury of the Arts Film Festivals, Montreal 1984, Le Carnival et la Fête, Nice 1985, Politiques Culturelles et Télévision, Paris 1986; mem. leading bds Romanian Writers' Union, Romanian Fine Arts Union; Prize of the Romanian Fine Arts Union 1967, Prizes of the Romanian Writers' Union 1974, 1984; Prize of the Romanian Film Studio Al. Sahia, Great Prize of the Romanian Fine Arts Union 1975; Grand Prix Int. de la meilleure revue d'art (Festival Int. d'Art de Beaubourg) Paris 1987. *Works include:* Peintres roumains (UNESCO, Vol. I 1963, Vol. II 1965), Brancusi ou l'anonymat du génie 1967, Critică şi cultură (Criticism and Culture) 1967, Calder, Variations sur le thème Homo Faber 1971, Geografii spirituale (Spiritual Geographies) 1973, Nostalgia sintezei (The Nostalgia for Synthesis) 1984. *Address:* Str. Docenţilor 26, 71311 Bucharest, Romania (home).

HÄUPL, Michael, DPhil; Austrian politician; *Mayor, Vienna City Council;* b. 14 Sept. 1949, Altlengbach; m.; two c.; ed Bundesrealgymnasium, Krems a.d. Donau, Univ. of Vienna; scientific worker, Natural History Museum, Vienna 1975–83; mem. SPÖ (Austrian Socialist Party), Chair. VSSTÖ (Asscn of Austrian Socialist Students) 1975–77, mem. Ottakring Party Cttee 1978–, various appointments in SPÖ Youth Div. (JG) 1978–84, elected Chair. Vienna JG and Vice-Chair. Nat. JG 1982–; mem. Vienna Regional Legislature 1983–88, City Councillor for Environment and Sport 1988–94, Chair. SPÖ Regional Cttee 1993–; Mayor of Vienna Nov. 1994–; Dir Austria Vienna Football Club. *Leisure interest:* football. *Address:* Rathaus, Rathausplatz 1, Stiege 5, 1 Vienna 1010, Austria (office). *Telephone:* (1) 4000-8111 (office). *Fax:* (1) 4000-8111 (office). *E-mail:* buergermeister@magwien.gv.at (office). *Website:* www.wien.gv.at (office).

HAUSER, Claude, MBA; Swiss business executive; *Chairman of the Management Board, Federation of Migros Cooperatives;* ed Collège Calvin, Geneva, Univ. of Geneva, Univ. of Lausanne, Columbia Univ., NY and Stanford Univ., CA, USA; joined Migros Geneva 1967, various positions including Man.-Dir 1976; Chair. Man. Bd, Fed. of Migros Cooperatives, Zürich 2000–; Chair. CIES—The Food Business Forum 2004–. *Address:* Federation of Migros Cooperatives, Limmatstrasse 152, 8005 Zürich, Switzerland (office). *Telephone:* (1) 2772111 (office). *Fax:* (1) 2772525 (office). *Website:* www.migros.ch (office).

HAUSIKU, Marco Mukoso; Namibian politician; *Minister of Foreign Affairs;* b. 25 Nov. 1953, Kapako; m.; ed Bunya Roman Catholic Mission School, Rundu Secondary School, Dobra Training Coll., Augustineum Training Coll.; teacher, Katutura Secondary School 1977–89; mem. SWAPO Windhoek Br. Exec. Cttee 1977–89, mem. Cen. Cttee and Polit-Bureau 1991; Election Dir Kavango and Tsumkwe Area 1989; Minister of Lands, Resettlement and Rehabilitation 1990, of Works, Transport and Communication 1992, of Prisons and Correctional Services 1995, of Labour 2002, of Foreign Affairs 2004–; Founding mem. and Pres. Namibia Nat. Teachers Union 1988. *Leisure interests:* reading, watching television, listening to music. *Address:* Ministry of Foreign Affairs, Government Buildings, Robert Mugabe Avenue, PMB 13347, Windhoek, Namibia (office). *Telephone:* (61) 2829111 (office). *Fax:* (61) 223937 (office). *E-mail:* headquarters@mfa.gov.na (office). *Website:* www.mfa.gov.na (office).

HAUSNER, Jerzy, PhD; Polish politician and economist; *Deputy Prime Minister and Minister of the Economy and Labour;* b. 6 Oct. 1949, Swinovjście; m. Maria Hausner; two d.; ed Kraków Econ. Acad.; began career as Lecturer on Econs, Kraków Econ. Acad. 1972–94; Dir-Gen. Office of the Prime Minister and Adviser to Deputy Prime Minister 1994–96; Commr for Social Security Reform 1997–2001; Minister of Labour and Social Policy 2001–03; Deputy Prime Minister and Minister of the Economy, Labour and Social Policy 2003–04; Deputy Prime Minister and Minister of the Economy and Labour 2004–; Cross of Merit 1996, Kt's Cross of Polonia Restituta Order 1996; Nat. Educ. Comm. Medal 1996, 75th Anniversary Medal of Kraków Econ. Acad. 2001. *Publications:* more than 90 articles in scientific journals. *Leisure interests:* mountain walking, music, soccer. *Address:* Ministry of the Economy and Labour, pl. Trzechkrzyzy 3/5, 00-507 Warsaw, Poland (office). *Telephone:* (22) 6935013 (office). *Fax:* (22) 6934001 (office). *E-mail:* bpi@mpips.gov.pl (office). *Website:* www.mgip.gov.pl (office).

HAUSSLER, David, BA, MS, PhD; American computer scientist and academic; *Distinguished Professor of Biomolecular Engineering and Director, Center for Biomolecular Science and Engineering, University of California, Santa Cruz;* ed Connecticut Coll., New London, Conn., California Polytechnic State Univ. at San Luis Obispo, Univ. of Colorado at Boulder; Asst Prof. of Math. and Computer Science, Univ. of Denver, Colo 1982–86; Asst Prof. of Computer Science, Univ. of California, Santa Cruz (UCSC) 1986–89, Assoc. Prof. 1989–93, Prof. 1993–2004, Dir Center for Biomolecular Science and Eng 1999–, Distinguished Prof. of Biomolecular Eng 2004–, Dir Training Program in the Systems Biology of Stem Cells 2005–, mem. Chancellor's Millennium Cttee 1997–98; Investigator, Howard Hughes Medical Inst. 2000–; Affiliate, Crown Coll.; mem. Univ. of California System-Wide Life Science Informatics Working Group 1998–; Scientific Co-Dir California Inst. for Quantitative Biosciences (QB3) 2000–; Assoc. Ed. Machine Learning 1988–97, Journal of Computational Biology 1996–, Public Library of Science Computational Genomics 2005–; mem. Editorial Bd, Journal of Artificial Intelligence Research 1993–95, Journal of Neurocomputing 1995–2002, Neural Computing Surveys 1996–2002, Drug Discovery Today 2001–; mem. NAS 2006; Fellow, American Asscn of Artificial Intelligence 1992, California Acad. of Sciences 2001, AAAS 2003, American Academy of Arts and Sciences 2006; Julia Bower Math. Award, Connecticut Coll. 1975, Math. Award, California Polytechnic State Univ. at San Luis Obispo 1979, Grad. Student Research Award, Univ. of Colorado at Boulder 1982, Univ. of California Presidential Chair of Computer Science 2000–03, Scientist of the Year, Research and Development Magazine 2001, Featured Scientist, Incyte Genomics 2001, UCSC Faculty Research Lecturer 2001–02, Distinguished Scientist of the Year Award, Boston Biomedical/Clinical Ligand Assay Soc. 2003, Tech Award Laureate, San Jose Tech Museum of Innovation 2003, Allen Newell Award, Asscn for Computing Machinery (ACM) and American Asscn for Artificial Intelligence (AAAI) 2004, Distinguished Eng Alumni Award, Univ. of Colorado, Boulder 2005, AAAI Classic Paper Award, for "Quantifying the inductive bias in concept learning" 1986 2005, World Tech. Award in Information Tech. (Software), The World Tech. Network 2005, Dickson Prize in Science, Carnegie Mellon Univ. 2006, Sr Scientist Accomplishment Award, Int. Soc. for Computational Biology 2008. *Publications:* Proceedings of the First Workshop on Computational Learning Theory (co-ed.) 1988, Proceedings of the Second Workshop on Computational Learning Theory (co-ed.) 1989, Proceedings of the Fifth ACM Workshop on Computational Learning Theory (co-ed.) 1992; numerous scientific papers in professional journals. *Address:* University of California, Santa Cruz, 1156 High Street, MS: CBSE/ITI Engineering 2 Building, Suite 501, Santa Cruz, CA 95064, USA (office). *Telephone:* (831) 459-2105 (office). *Fax:* (831) 459-1809 (office). *E-mail:* haussler@soe.ucsc.edu (office). *Website:* www.cbse.ucsc.edu/staff/haussler.shtml (office).

HAUSSMANN, Helmut, DEcon, Dr rer. pol; German politician; *Honorary Professor of International Management, University of Erlangen-Nürnberg;* b. 18 May 1943, Tübingen; s. of Emil Haussmann and Elisabeth Rau; m. Margot Scheu 1980; business exec. 1968–71; Research and Academic Asst, Univ. of Erlangen-Nuremberg 1971–75; joined FDP 1969; mem. Bad Urach Town Council, FDP Dist Chair., Reutlingen 1975–80; mem. Deutscher Bundestag 1976–2002; Econ. Cttee 1977–88; mem. FDP Fed. Exec. Cttee 1978; Ombudsman FDP Econs Cttee 1980; Econ. Spokesman, FDP Parl. Party 1980–84; Vice-Chair. FDP in Land Baden-Württemberg 1983–88, 1995–; Sec.-Gen. FDP 1984–88; Fed. Minister of Econ. Affairs 1988–91; mem. Foreign Affairs Cttee and Spokesman on EC Policy 1991–2002; Hon. Prof. of Int. Man., Univ. Erlangen-Nürnberg 1996–. *Leisure interests:* tennis and golf. *Address:* Lehrstuhl für Internationales Management, Lange Gasse 20, 90403 Nuremberg, Germany (office). *E-mail:* internationales.management@wiso.uni-erlangen.de.

HAVEL, Jiří, Dr Ing., CSc; Czech politician and academic; b. 20 Aug. 1957, Prague; m. (wife deceased 1994); three s.; ed Univ. of Econs, Prague, Inst. of Econ. Studies, Charles Univ.; worked at Univ. of Econs, Prague 1982–91; Specialist in Econ. Institutions, Capital Markets and Econ. Policy, Inst. of Econ. Studies, Charles Univ. 1991–, also Head, Dept of Macroeconomics and Econometrics, mem. Scientific Bd 2002–; corp. governance consultant 1990–; has served as Bd mem. of various jt stock cos including SPIF, Česká Spořitelna, Paramo, Komerční Banka, Telecom, Unipetrol; Deputy Chair. then Chair. of Exec. Cttee Nat. Property Fund 1999–2001; Deputy Prime Minister Responsible for the Economy 2006; fmr mem. CP, participated in establishment of Ind. Left party, later involved with Convent of Democratic Left, joined Czech Social Democratic Party (ČSSD) 1997; mem. Czech Econ. Soc., Vice-Pres. 2002–04; mem. Academic Bd Inst. of Finance and Admin 2003–, Grant Agency of Czech Repub., Accreditation Comm., Ministry of Educ., Youth and Sports. *Publications:* numerous academic and other publications. *Address:* Institute of Economic Studies, Charles University, 110 00 Prague 1, Opletalova 26, Czech Republic (office). *Telephone:* 222112325 (office). *E-mail:* havel@mbox.fsv.cuni.cz (office). *Website:* ies.fsv.cuni.cz (office).

HAVEL, Richard Joseph, MD, FAAS; American physician and academic; *Professor of Medicine, University of California, San Francisco;* b. 20 Feb. 1925, Seattle, Wash.; s. of Joseph Havel and Anna Fritz; m. Virginia J. Havel 1947; three s. one d.; ed Reed Coll., Portland, Ore., Univ. of Ore. Medical School and Cornell Univ. Medical Coll.; Asst in Biochem. Univ. of Ore. Medical School 1945–49; Asst Resident in Medicine, New York Hospital 1950–51, Chief Resident in Medicine 1952–53; Instructor Cornell Univ. Medical Coll. 1952–53; Clinical Assoc. Nat. Heart Inst. 1953–54, Research Assoc. 1954–56; Asst Prof. of Medicine, Univ. of Calif., San Francisco 1956–59, Assoc. Prof. 1959–64, Prof. of Medicine 1964–, Chief Metabolism Section 1967–97, Dir Cardiovascular Research Inst. 1973–92; Dir Arteriosclerosis Specialized Center of Research 1970–96; Ed. Journal of Lipid Research 1972–75; mem. Editorial Bd, Journal of Arteriosclerosis 1980–; mem. Food and Nutrition Bd, Nat. Research Council 1983, (Chair. 1987–90); mem. NAS, Inst. of Medicine, American Acad. of Arts and Sciences, American Soc. of Clinical Nutrition, Asscn of American Physicians, American Soc. for Clinical Investigation; Fellow American Inst. of Nutrition; Fellow AAAS; T. Smith Award, AAAS 1960, Bristol-Myers Award for nutrition research 1989, McCollum Award 1993, Gold Medal Charles Univ. (Czech Repub.) 1996, Mayo Soley Award 1997. *Publications:* over 300 scientific articles and book chapters. *Address:* University of California, Cardiovascular Research Institute, San Francisco, CA 94143-0130, USA (office). *E-mail:* havelr@itsa.ucsf.edu (office).

HAVEL, Václav; Czech playwright, writer and fmr head of state; b. 5 Oct. 1936, Prague; s. of Václav M. Havel and Božena Havel (née Vavrečková); m. 1st Olga Splíchalová 1964 (died 1996); m. 2nd Dagmar Veškrnová 1997; ed Acad. of Arts, Drama Dept, Prague; worked as freelance; fmr spokesman for Charter 77 human rights movement, received a sentence of 14 months in 1977, suspended for three years, for "subversive" and "antistate" activities, under house arrest 1978–79; mem. Cttee for the Defence of the Unjustly Prosecuted (VONS), convicted and sentenced to 4½ years' imprisonment for sedition 1979, released March 1983, arrested Jan. 1989 and sentenced to nine months' imprisonment for incitement and obstruction Feb. 1989; sentence reduced to eight months and charge changed to misdemeanour March 1989; released May 1989; f. Civic Forum 1989; Pres. of Czechoslovakia 1989–92, Pres. of Czech Repub. 1993–2003; C-in-C of Armed Forces 1989–92; Chair. Prague Heritage Fund 1993–; mem. jury Int. Prize Awarding Body for Human Rights 1994–; mem. Acad. des Sciences Morales et Politiques; Hon. mem. Acad. of Sciences and Arts, Salzburg; Hon. Citizen of Vrtislav 2001; Grand Cross, Order of the Legion of Honour 1990, Order of White Eagle, Poland 1993, Golden Hon. Order of Freedom, Slovenia 1993, Chain of Order of Isabel of Castille, Spain 1995, Hon. KCB, UK 1996, Grand Cross Order with Chain (Lithuania) 1999, Federal Cross for Merit, Berlin 2000; numerous hon. degrees including Dr hc (York Univ., Toronto, Le Mirail Univ., Toulouse) 1982, (Columbia Univ., New York, Hebrew Univ., Jerusalem, Frantisek Palacky Univ., Olomouc, Charles Univ., Prague, Comenius Univ., Bratislava) 1990, (Free Univ. of Brussels, St Gallen Univ.) 1991, (Bar Ilan Univ., Israel, Kiev Univ., Ukraine, Jordan Univ., Oxford) 1997, (Glasgow) 1998, (Manitoba, St Thomas Univ., USA) 1999, (Bilkent Univ., Turkey) 2000; Austrian State Prize for European Literature 1968, Jan Palach Prize 1982, (JAMU, Brno) 2001, Erasmus Prize 1986, Olof Palme Prize 1989, German Book Trade Peace Prize 1989, Simón Bolívar Prize 1990, Malaparte Prize 1990, UNESCO Prize for the Teaching of Human Rights 1990, Chalemagne Prize 1991, Sonning Cultural Prize 1991, Athinai Prize (Onassis Foundation) 1993, Theodor Heuss Prize 1993, Indira Gandhi Prize 1994, European Cultural Soc. Award 1993, Philadelphia Liberty Medal 1994, Premi Internacional Catalunya 1995, TGM Prize (Canada) 1997, Medal of Danish Acad. 1997, European Statesman Prize (USA), 1997, Husajn bin Ali Distinction (Jordan) 1997, J. W. Fulbright Prize for Int. Understanding (USA) 1997, Le Prix Spécial Europe, European Theatre Council 1997, Cino del Duca Prize (France), Prince of Asturias Prize (Spain) 1997, Charles Univ. Medal 1998, Open Soc. Prize, Budapest Univ., Gazeta Wyborcza Prize (Poland), St Vojtěch Prize (Slovakia) 1999, Citizen Prize, Berlin 2000, Evelyn Burkey's Prize, Author's Guild of America 2000, Elie Wiesel Prize 2000. *Plays include:* Garden Party 1963, Memorandum 1965, The Increased Difficulty of Concentration 1968, The Conspirators 1971, The Beggar's Opera 1972, Audience 1975, Vernissage 1975, The Mountain Resort 1976, Protest 1978, The Mistake 1983, Largo Desolato 1984, Temptation 1985, Redevelopment 1987, Tomorrow! 1988, Leaving 2007. *Publications include:* Letters to Olga (in Czech, as Dopisy Olge) 1983, Disturbing the Peace (in Czech, as Dálkový výslech) 1986, (English) 1990, Václav Havel or Living in Truth (essays, in English) 1986, Open Letters: Selected Writings 1965–1990 (in English) 1991, Selected Plays by Václav Havel (in English) 1992, Summer Meditations (in Czech, as Ledric piemidánt) 1991, (English) 1992, Plays (in Czech, as Hry) 1991, Toward a Civil Society 1994, The Art of the Impossible (speeches) 1997, In Various Directions (in Czech, as Do různých stran) 1999, Spisy (seven vols) 1999, The Pizh'duks (in Czech, as Pižďuchové) 2003, To the Castle and Back (memoir; in Czech as Prosím stručně) 2007. *Address:* Voršilská 10, 110 00 Prague 1, Czech Republic (office). *Telephone:* (2) 3409-7830 (office). *Fax:* (2) 3409-7831 (office). *E-mail:* vaclav.havel@volny.cz (office). *Website:* www.vaclavhavel.cz.

HAVELANGE, Jean Marie Faustin Godefroid (João); Brazilian sports administrator; *Honorary President, Fédération Internationale de Football Association (FIFA); Member, International Olympic Committee;* b. 8 May 1916, Rio de Janeiro; m.; one d.; practising lawyer 1936–; Head of Importation and Exportation, Cia Siderúrgica Belgo-Mineira 1937–41; Dir-Pres. Viação

Cometa SA, EMBRADATA, Orwec Química e Metalúrgica Ltda; took part in Olympic Games as swimmer, Berlin 1936, as water polo player, Helsinki 1952, Head of Brazilian Del., Sydney 1956; Pres. Fed. Paulista de Natação, São Paulo 1949–51, Fed. Metropolitana de Natação (GB) 1952–56; mem. Brazilian Olympic Cttee 1955–73; Vice-Pres. Confed. Brasileira de Desportos 1956–58, Pres. 1958–73; Dir, mem. for South America Cttee of Int. Cyclists Union 1958; mem. Int. Olympic Cttee 1963; Pres. Indoor Football Int. Fed. (FIFUSA) 1971; Pres. Fédération Internationale de Football Asscn 1974–98, Hon. Pres. 1998–; decorations from Argentina, Belgium, Brazil, Colombia, France, Italy, Mexico, Paraguay, Peru, Portugal, Saudi Arabia, Spain, Sweden and Uruguay. *Leisure interests:* swimming and water polo. *Address:* Av. Rio Branco 89-B, conj. 602 Centro, 20040-004 Rio de Janeiro, RJ, Brazil. *Telephone:* (21) 2263-3160 (office). *Fax:* (22) 2233-1268 (office); (22) 2233-4709 (office).

HAVIARAS, Stratis, MFA; Greek writer and fmr librarian; b. 28 June 1935, Nea Kios, Argos; s. of Christos Haviaras and Georgia Hadzikyriakos; m. 1st Gail Flynn 1967 (divorced 1973); m. 2nd Heather Cole 1990; one d.; ed Goddard Coll.; fmr construction worker; lived in USA 1959–61; went to USA following colonels' coup in Greece 1967, obtaining position at Harvard Univ. Library; Curator, Poetry Room, Harvard Univ. Library 1974–2000; Founder and Ed. Harvard Review 1992–2000, Founding Ed. Emer. 2000–; Faculty mem., Harvard Univ. Summer School; Admin. and Instructor, writing and translation workshops, Athens; mem. PEN (New England), Signet, Soc. Imaginaire, Hellenic Authors' Soc.; Nat. Book Critics' Circle Awards. *Publications:* four vols of Greek poetry 1963, 1965, 1967, 1972, Crossing the River Twice (poems in English) 1976, Millennial Afterlives 2000; fiction: When the Tree Sings 1979, The Heroic Age 1984; other: The Canon by C. P. Cavafy (trans.) 2004, Seamus Heaney: a Celebration (ed.) 1996; contrib. to newspapers and magazines. *Leisure interest:* wood sculpture. *Address:* 19 Clinton Street, Cambridge, MA 02139, USA; 136 Em. Benaki Street, 11473 Athens, Greece. *Telephone:* (617) 354-4724.

HAVIGHURST, Clark Canfield, JD; American legal scholar; *William Neal Reynolds Professor of Law, Duke University;* b. 25 May 1933, Evanston, Ill.; s. of Harold Canfield and Marion Clay Havighurst (née Perryman); m. Karen Waldron 1965; one s. one d.; ed Princeton and Northwestern Univs; Research Assoc., Duke Univ. School of Law 1960–61; pvt. practice, Debevoise, Plimpton, Lyons & Gates, New York 1958, 1961–64; Assoc. Prof. of Law, Duke Univ. 1964–68, Prof. 1968–86, William Neal Reynolds Prof. 1986–; Interim Dean Duke Univ. School of Law 1999; numerous other professional appointments; mem. Inst. of Medicine, NAS. *Publications:* Deregulating the Health Care Industry 1982, Health Care Law and Policy 1988, Health Care Choices: Private Contracts as Instruments of Health Reform 1995; articles on regulation in the health services industry, the role of competition in the financing and delivery of health care and anti-trust issues arising in the health care field. *Address:* Box 90360, Duke University School of Law, Durham, NC 27708 (office); 3610 Dover Road, Durham, NC 27707, USA (home). *Telephone:* (919) 613-7061 (office); (919) 489-4970 (home). *Fax:* (919) 613-7231 (office). *E-mail:* hav@law.duke.edu (office). *Website:* www.law.duke .edu (office).

HAWASS, Zahi, PhD; Egyptian archaeologist and Egyptologist; *Secretary-General of the Supreme Council of Antiquities;* b. 28 May 1947, Damietta; ed Alexandria Univ., Cairo Univ., Univ. of Pennsylvania, USA; Inspector of Antiquities of Middle Egypt, Tuna El-Gebel and Mallawi 1969, Italian Expedition, Sikh Abada, Minia 1969, Edfu-Esna, Egypt 1969, Pa Yale Expedition at Abydos 1969, Western Delta at Alexandria 1970, Embaba, Giza 1972–74, Abu Simbel 1973–74, Pennsylvania Expedition, Malkata, Luxor 1974, Giza Pyramids (for Boston Museum of Fine Arts) 1974–75; First Inspector of Antiquities, Embaba and Bahariya Oasis 1974–79, Chief Inspector 1980, Gen. Dir 1987–98; Gen. Dir Saqqara and Bahariya Oasis 1987–98; apptd Archaeological Site Man. Memphis 1991; Under-Sec. of State for Giza Monuments 1998–2002; Sec.-Gen. of the Supreme Council of Antiquities 2002–; Dir of numerous excavations, conservation projects and discoveries including tombs of the pyramid builders at Giza and the Valley of the Golden Mummies in Bahariya; numerous consultancy roles; mem. Bd Egyptian Nat. Museum 1996–; Trustee Egyptian Nat. Museum; Sound and Light Co. 1990; mem. German Archaeological Inst. 1991–, Russian Acad. of Natural Sciences 2001–; Explorer-in-Residence Nat. Geographic 2001; mem. of numerous cttees; Hon. PhD (American Univ., Cairo) 2005; Grantee Mellon Fellowship, Univ. of Pennsylvania, Presidential Medal 1988, Golden Plate Award, American Acad. of Achievement 2000, Distinguished Scholar of the Year Asscn of Egyptian-American Scholars 2000, Silver Medal Russian Acad. of Natural Sciences 2001, Achievement Award Mansoura Univ. 2002, named one of Five Distinguished Egyptians Egyptological Soc. of Spain 2002, Paestum Archaeology Award 2006, one of Time magazine's Top 100 Most Influential People of the Year 2005, Emmy Award Nat. Acad. of Television Arts & Sciences 2006. *Television:* numerous appearances in documentaries and features on Egypt including BBC, CNN, Discovery Channel, History Channel, National Geographic, The Learning Channel. *Publications:* Valley of the Golden Mummies 2000, Silent Images: Women in Pharaonic Egypt 2000, Secrets from the Sand 2003, Hidden Treasures of Ancient Egypt 2004, The Curse of the Pharaohs (children's book), Tutankhamun and the Golden Age of the Pharaohs 2005, Mountains of the Pharaohs 2006, The Great Book of Ancient Egypt: In the Realm of the Pharaohs 2006, The Royal Tombs of Egypt 2006; numerous papers on Egyptology and archaeology. *Address:* 3 El Adel Abow Bakr Street, Zamalek, Cairo (office); 42 Aden Street, Mohandiseen, Cairo, Egypt (home). *Telephone:* (202) 736-5645 (office). *Fax:* (202) 735-7239 (office). *E-mail:* pyramiza2004@yahoo.com (office). *Website:* www.guardians .net/hawass (office).

HAWK, Tony; American professional skateboarder; b. 12 May 1968, San Diego, Calif.; s. of Frank Hawk and Nancy Hawk; descendant of Henry Hudson, discoverer of the Hudson River; m. 1st Cindy Dunbar 1990 (divorced 1994); one s.; m. 2nd Erin Lee 1996 (divorced 2004); two s.; ed ; finished in top five in Van's/Offshore Amateur State Finals (Calif.) in boys 11–13 div. 1980; turned professional aged 14, mem. Powell Peralta's Bones Brigade; pioneered modern vertical skateboarding; First, Rusty Harris Series final contest: vert discipline 1982, Del Mar Spring Nationals (Calif.): vert 1983, NSA-Del Mar Skatepark (Calif.): vert 1984, Transworld Skateboard Championships (Vancouver, BC, Canada): vert 1986; Second, Vision Skate Ecape: vert 1988; Third, X Games: vert best trick 2002, First, vert doubles (with Andy MacDonald) 2002; has entered an estimated 103 professional contests, won 73, placed second in 19; est. children's skate clothing co. Hawk Clothing 1998, acquired by Quiksilver 2000; has accomplished numerous historic tricks including ollie 540, kickflip 540, varial 720 and first 900 degree spin (at 1999 X Games after 11 failed attempts, winning the Best Trick competition); retd from competitive skateboarding 1999; launched Boom Boom HuckJam, a 24-city arena tour featuring world's best skateboarders, BMX bike riders and Motocross riders performing choreographed routines 2002; est. Tony Hawk Foundation; voted Best Vert Skater by readers of Transworld Skateboarding magazine. *Film roles in:* Thrashin' 1986, Police Academy 4: Citizens on Patrol 1987, Gleaming the Cube 1989, Destroying America (video) 2001, CKY 3 (video) 2001, Collage (video) (stunts) 2001, xXx 2002, Haggard: The Movie 2003, Lords of Dogtown 2005, . *Television includes:* The Contest 1989, MTV Sports & Music Festival 3: Skate Trick 1999, Reunion X 2004; cameo roles in Cyberchase, Rocket Power, The Simpsons, Max Steel, Sifl and Olly and CSI: Miami, and in films such as Jackass: The Movie, The New Guy, Max Keeble's Big Move, and Dogtown and Z-Boys; hosted documentary, Video Game Invasion. *Publication:* Hawk–Occupation: Skateboarder (autobiog.). *Address:* THI, 1611-A South Melrose Drive, #362, Vista, CA 92081; c/o Terra McGibbon, Tony Hawk Foundation, 1611-A South Melrose Drive, #360, Vista, CA 92081, USA. *Telephone:* (760) 477-2479. *E-mail:* info@tonyhawk.com; questions@ tonyhawkfoundation.org; tony@clubtonyhawk.com. *Website:* www.tonyhawk .com.

HAWKE, Allan, PhD; Australian diplomatist, business executive and university chancellor; *Chancellor, Australian National University;* ed Australian Nat. Univ.; with Australian Public Service 1974–91; Deputy Sec. Dept of Defence 1991–93; Chief of Staff to Prime Minister 1993–94; Deputy Sec. Dept of Prime Minister and Cabinet 1994; Sec. Dept of Veterans' Affairs 1994–96; Sec. Dept of Transport and Regional Services 1996–99; Sec. of Defence 1999–2001; Head of Secr. for Review of Aboriginal and Torres Strait Islander Comm. 2001–03; Amb. to New Zealand 2003–06; Chancellor ANU, Canberra 2006–. *Address:* Australian National University, Canberra, ACT 2600, Australia (office). *Telephone:* (2) 6125-5111 (office). *E-mail:* chancellor@anu .edu.au (office). *Website:* www.anu.edu.au (office).

HAWKE, Ethan; American actor and writer; b. 6 Nov. 1970, Austin, Tex.; m. Uma Thurman (q.v.) 1998 (divorced 2004); one d.; ed New York University; co-f. Malaparte Theatre Co. *Theatre appearances include:* Casanova 1991, A Joke, The Seagull 1992, Sophistry. *Films include:* Explorers 1985, Dead Poets Society 1989, Dad 1989, White Fang 1991, Mystery Date 1991, A Midnight Clear 1992, Waterland 1992, Alive 1993, Rich in Love 1993, Straight to One 1993 (Dir), Reality Bites 1994, Quiz Show 1994, Floundering 1994, Before Sunrise 1995, Great Expectations, Gattaca, Joe the King 1999, Hamlet 2000, Tape 2001, Waking Life 2001, Training Day 2001, The Jimmy Show 2001, Before Sunset 2004, Taking Lives 2004, Assault on Precinct 13 2005, Lord of War 2005, The Hottest State 2006, Fast Food Nation 2006, Before the Devil Knows You're Dead 2007. *Publication:* The Hottest State 1996, Ash Wednesday 2002. *Address:* c/o CAA, 9830 Wilshire Blvd, Beverly Hills, CA 90212; Malaparte Theatre Company, 545 8th Avenue, New York, NY 10018, USA.

HAWKE, Gary Richard, DPhil, FRSNZ; New Zealand economic historian; *Emeritus Professor, Victoria University of Wellington;* b. 1 Aug. 1942, Napier; s. of Vyvyan Nesbitt Hawke and Jean Avis Hawke (née Carver); m. Helena Joyce Powrie 1965; two s.; ed Victoria Univ. of Wellington, Balliol and Nuffield Colls, Oxford; Lecturer, Victoria Univ. of Wellington 1968–70, Reader 1971–73, Prof. of Econ. History 1974–2008, Emer. Prof. 2008–, Head, School of Govt 2003–08; Dir Inst. of Policy Studies 1987–97; Sr Fellow, NZ Inst. of Econ. Research; visiting appointments at Stanford Univ., USA 1972–73, All Souls Coll., Oxford, UK 1977–78, Japan Foundation 1993, Japan Soc. for Promoting Knowledge 1994; Chair. NZ Planning Council 1986–91; Fellow, Inst. of Public Admin of NZ 2008; Distinguished Fellow, New Zealand Asscn of Economists 2005; NZIER-QANTAS Award for Econs 1998. *Publications include:* Railways and Economic Growth 1970, Between Governments and Banks 1973, Economics for Historians 1980, The Making of New Zealand 1985, The Thoroughbred Among Banks (co author) 1997, Innovation and Independence: The Reserve Bank of New Zealand 1973–2002 2006. *Leisure interests:* classical music, armchair criticism. *Address:* School of Government, Victoria University of Wellington, PO Box 600, Wellington (office); 7 Voltaire Street, Karori, Wellington, New Zealand (home). *Telephone:* (4) 463-5794 (office); (4) 476-9109 (home); 27-563-5794 (mobile). *Fax:* (4) 463-5454 (office). *E-mail:* gary.hawke@vuw.ac.nz (office). *Website:* www.vuw.ac.nz (office).

HAWKE, Robert James Lee, AC, BA, LLB, BLitt; Australian politician and fmr trade union official; b. 9 Dec. 1929, Bordertown, S Australia; s. of A. C. Hawke; m. 1st Hazel Masterson 1956 (divorced 1995); one s. two d.; m. 2nd Blanche d'Apulget 1995; ed Univs of Western Australia and Oxford; Rhodes scholar 1953; Research Officer, Australian Council of Trade Unions 1958–70, Pres. 1970–80; Sr Vice-Pres. Australian Labor Party 1971–73, Pres. 1973–78, Leader 1983–91; MP for Wills, Melbourne 1980–92; Prime Minister 1983–91, mem. Nat. Exec. 1971–91; reporter 1992; Business Consultant 1992; Adjunct

Prof. Research School of Pacific Studies and Social Sciences, ANU 1992–95; Hon. Visiting Prof. in Industrial Relations Sydney Univ.; mem. Advisory Council of Inst. for Int. Studies, Stanford Univ., Calif.; Chair. Cttee of Experts on mem. of Educ. Int. 1993–, Sydney City Mission Fundraising Task Force; Dir Quantum Resources Ltd 1996–; mem. Bd Reserve Bank of Australia 1973–83, Governing Body ILO 1972–80; mem. Australian Council for Union Training, Australian Population and Immigration Council; mem. Australian Manufacturing Council 1977, Nat. Labour Consultative Council 1977–92, Australian Refugee Advisory Council; Patron Australia-China Sports Friendship Cttee 2000; Hon. Fellow, Univ. Coll., Oxford 1984; Dr hc (Nanjing) 1986; Hon. DPhil (Hebrew Univ. of Jerusalem) 1987; Hon. LLD (Univ. of NSW) 1987; UN Media Peace Prize 1980. *Publication:* The Hawke Memoirs 1994. *Leisure interests:* tennis, golf, cricket, reading. *Address:* Suite 1, Level 13, 100 Williams Street, Sydney, NSW 2001, Australia.

HAWKEN, Paul; American environmental activist, entrepreneur, journalist and author; *Executive Director, Natural Capital Institute;* b. 8 Feb. 1946; f. or co-f. cos or software cos specializing in proprietary content man. tools, including Smith & Hawken (garden and catalogue retailer) and several first natural food cos in USA relying solely on sustainable agricultural methods; Head of PaxIT, PaxTurbine, PaxFan (three cos associated with Pax Scientific, a research and devt co. focused on energy-saving technologies that apply biomimicry to fluid dynamics); Founder and Exec. Dir Natural Capital Inst., Sausalito, Calif.;; fmr mem. Bd numerous environmental orgs, including Point Foundation (publr of Whole Earth Catalogs), Center for Plant Conservation, Trust for Public Land, Friends of the Earth, Nat. Audubon Soc.; five hon. doctorates; Esquire Magazine Award for the Best 100 People of a Generation 1984, California Inst. of Integral Studies Award "For Ongoing Humanitarian Contributions to the Bay Area Communities", Cine Golden Eagle Award in video for the PBS program "Marketing" from Growing a Business, Metropolitan Home Design 100 Editorial Award for the 100 best people, products and ideas that shape our lives, American Horticultural Soc. Award for commitment to excellence in commercial horticulture, Corp. Conscience Award, Council on Econ. Priorities 1990, Small Business Admin Entrepreneur of the Year 1990,Design in Business Award for environmental responsibility, American Center for Design, Creative Visionary Award, Int. Soc. of Industrial Design, Utne "One Hundred Visionaries Who Could Change Our Lives" 1995, Western Publications Asscn 'Maggie' Award for "Natural Capitalism" as the best Signed Editorial/Essay in 1997, World Council for Corp. Governance 2002, Green Cross Millennium Award for Individual Environmental Leadership 2003. *Achievements include:* has given keynote addresses to Liberal Party of Canada, King of Sweden at his inaugural Environmental Seminar, American Booksellers' Asscn, Urban Land Inst., SRI International, Harvard Univ., Stanford Univ., Wharton School, Cornell Univ., Prime Minister of NZ's Conf. on Natural Capitalism, US Dept of Commerce, Australian Business Council, Yale Univ. and Yale Univ. Commencement, Univ. of California, Berkeley Commencement, French Ministry of Agric., AAAS, Prince of Wales Conf. on Business and the Environment at Univ. of Cambridge, Commonwealth Club, Herman Miller, Nat. Wildlife Fed., State of Washington, American Soc. of Landscape Architects, AIA, American Inst. of Graphic Arts, American Solar Energy Asscn, Apple Computer, World Business Council for Sustainable Devt, Cleveland City Club, Conf. Bd, US Forest Service, Ontario Hydro, Environment Canada, Environmental Protection Agency, and several hundred others. *Television:* host and producer of 17-part PBS series based on his book Growing a Business, shown in 115 countries. *Publications:* author or co-author of numerous articles, op-eds, papers, as well as seven books, including The Next Economy 1983, Growing a Business 1987, The Ecology of Commerce (voted No. 1 coll. text on business and the environment by profs in 67 business schools 1998) 1993, Natural Capitalism: Creating the Next Industrial Revolution (with Amory Lovins) 1999, Blessed Unrest: How the Largest Movement in the World Came Into Being, and Why No One Saw it Coming 2007; writings have appeared in Harvard Business Review, Resurgence, New Statesman, Inc., Boston Globe, Christian Science Monitor, Mother Jones, Utne Reader, Orion, and more than 100 other publs. *Address:* Natural Capital Institute, 3 Gate Five Road, Suite B, Sausalito, CA 94965, USA (office). *Telephone:* (415) 332-2860 (office). *Fax:* (415) 331-6242 (office). *E-mail:* info@paulhawken.com (office). *Website:* www.naturalcapital.org (office); www.paulhawken.com.

HAWKER, Graham Alfred, CBE, CIMgt, FCCA, FRSA; British business executive; *Chief Executive, Welsh Development Agency;* b. 12 May 1947; s. of Alfred Hawker and Sarah Rebecca Bowen; m. Sandra Ann Evans 1967; one s. one d.; ed Bedwelty Grammar School; trainee accountant Caerphilly Dist Council 1964–66; accountant Abercarn Dist Council 1966–67, Chief Accountant 1967–68, Deputy Treas. 1968–70; Chief Auditor Taf Fechan Water Bd 1970–74; Audit Man. Welsh Water Authority 1974–78, Div. Finance Man. 1978–84, Chief Accountant 1984–86, Dir Planning and Devt 1986–87, Finance 1987–89; Dir Finance Welsh Water PLC 1989–91, Group Man. Dir 1991–93, Chief Exec. Hyder (fmrly Welsh Water) PLC 1993–2000; Chair. Dwr Cymru Ltd 1993–2000, Hyder Consulting (fmrly Acer) 1993–2000, Swalec 1996–2000; Dir (non-exec.) Bank of England 1998–2000; Chair. BITC (Wales) 1994–2000; Dir Welsh Devt Agency 1995–, Deputy Chair. 1998–2000, CEO 2000–; Chair. New Deal Task Force Advisory Cttee (Wales) 1997–98; mem. New Deal Advisory Cttee (UK) 1997–98; mem. CBI Council, Wales 1994–97, Prince of Wales Review Cttee on Queen's Awards 1999; Fellow Inst. of Certified Accountants; Hon. DL (Gwent) 1998; Prince of Wales Ambassador's Award for Corporate Social Responsibility 1999. *Leisure interests:* family, walking, wine, career. *Address:* Welsh Development Agency, Principality House, The Friary, Cardiff, CF10 3FE, Wales (office). *Telephone:* (29) 2082-8669 (office). *Fax:* (1874) 624167 (office).

HAWKING, Stephen William, CH, CBE, BA, PhD, FRS; British academic and writer; b. 8 Jan. 1942, Oxford; s. of Dr F. Hawking and Mrs E. I. Hawking; m. 1st Jane Wilde 1965 (divorced); two s. one d.; m. 2nd Elaine Mason 1995 (divorced 2007); ed St Albans School, Univ. Coll., Oxford, Trinity Hall, Cambridge; Research Fellow, Gonville and Caius Coll., Cambridge 1965–69, Fellow for Distinction in Science 1969–; Research Asst, Inst. of Astronomy, Cambridge 1972–73; Research Asst, Dept of Applied Math. and Theoretical Physics, Univ. of Cambridge 1973–75, Reader in Gravitational Physics 1975–77, Prof. 1977–79, Lucasian Prof. of Applied Math. 1979–2009; Distinguished Research Chair, Perimeter Inst. for Theoretical Physics, Waterloo, Ont., Canada 2009–; mem. Inst. of Theoretical Astronomy, Cambridge 1968–72; mem. Papal Acad. of Science 1986; Foreign mem. American Acad. Arts and Sciences 1984; several hon. degrees; Hon. Fellow, Univ. Coll., Oxford 1977, Trinity Hall, Cambridge 1984; Eddington Medal 1975, Pontifical Acad. of Sciences Pius XI Gold Medal 1975, Cambridge Philosophical Soc. William Hopkins Prize 1976, Wolf Foundation Prize for Physics 1988, Inst. of Physics Maxwell Medal 1976, Royal Soc. Hughes Medal 1976, Albert Einstein Award 1978, Royal Astronomical Soc. Gold Medal 1985, Inst. of Physics Paul Dirac Medal and Prize 1987, Sunday Times Special Award for Literature 1989, Britannica Award 1989, RSA Albert Medal 1999, Royal Soc. Copley Medal 2006, Fonseca Prize 2008. *Publications:* The Large Scale Structure of Spacetime (with G. F. R. Ellis) 1973, General Relativity: An Einstein Centenary Survey (ed. with W. Israel) 1979, Is the End in Sight for Theoretical Physics?: An Inaugural Lecture 1980, Superspace and Supergravity: Proceedings of the Nuffield Workshop (ed. with M. Rocek) 1981, The Very Early Universe: Proceedings of the Nuffield Workshop (co-ed.) 1983, 300 Years of Gravitation (with W. Israel) 1987, A Brief History of Time: From the Big Bang to Black Holes 1988, Hawking on the Big Bang and Black Holes 1992, Black Holes and Baby Universes and Other Essays 1993, The Cambridge Lectures: Life Works 1995, The Nature of Space and Time (with Roger Penrose) 1996, The Universe in a Nutshell (Aventis Prize 2002) 2001, The Theory of Everything: The Origin and Fate of the Universe 2002, The Future of Spacetime (co-ed.) 2002, On the Shoulders of Giants 2002, A Briefer History of Time (with Leonard Mlodinow) 2005, George's Secret Key to the Universe (children's fiction; with Lucy Hawking) 2007; also individual lectures, contrib. to scholarly books and journals. *Address:* Department of Applied Mathematics and Theoretical Physics, University of Cambridge, Centre for Mathematical Sciences, Wilberforce Road, Cambridge, CB3 0WA, England (office). *Telephone:* (1223) 337843 (office). *Website:* www.damtp.cam.ac.uk (office); www.hawking.org.uk.

HAWKINS, Jeff, BS; American business executive, computer scientist and inventor; *Chief Technology Officer, Palm Inc.;* b. 1 June 1957, Long Island, Huntingdon, New York; s. of Robert Hawkins; m.; two d.; ed Cornell Univ.; various key tech. positions with Intel Corpn 1979–82; Vice-Pres. of Research, GriD Systems Corpn 1982–92; f. Palm Computing 1994, invented PalmPilot (hand held computer) 1994; co-founder, Chair. and Chief Product Officer, Handspring Inc. 1998–, now Chief Tech. Officer Palm Inc (after Handspring merger with Palm Inc.) 2003–; founder, fmr Exec. Dir and Chair. Redwood Neuroscience Inst. (now Redwood Center for Theoretical Neuroscience) 2002, now mem. Advisory Bd; f. Numenta (medical tech. firm) 2005; mem. Scientific Bd of Dirs Cold Spring Harbor Lab., New York; mem. Nat. Acad. of Eng 2003–; PC Magazine Lifetime Achievement Award for Tech. Excellence 2000, Cornell Univ. Entrepreneur of the Year 2000. *Publications:* On Intelligence: How a New Understanding of the Brain will Lead to the Creation of Truly Intelligent Machines 2004. *Leisure interests:* sailing, music, family. *Address:* Palm Inc., 950 West Maude Avenue, Sunnyvale, CA 94085 (office); Numenta, Inc., 1010 El Camino Real, Suite 380, Menlo Park, CA 94025, USA. *Telephone:* (408) 617-7000 (office). *Fax:* (408) 617-0100 (office). *Website:* www.palm.com (office); www.numenta.com.

HAWKINS, Paula; American business executive and fmr politician; *President, Paula Hawkins and Associates;* b. Salt Lake City, Utah; d. of Paul B. Fickes and Leoan Fickes (née Staley); m. Walter Eugene Hawkins 1947; one s. two d.; ed Utah State Univ.; mem. Republican Precinct Cttee, Orange Co., Fla 1965–74, Rep. Nat. Comm. for Fla 1968–87; Speakers Chair. Fla Republican Exec. Cttee 1967–69, mem. Fla Republican Nat. Convention 1972, S Regional Rep., Republican Nat. Cttee 1972–; Public Service Commr State of Fla, Tallahassee 1972–80; Senator from Fla 1980–87; Pres. Paula Hawkins and Assocs (man. consulting firm) 1988–; mem. Maitland Civic Cen. 1965–76; Charter mem. Bd of Dirs Fla Americans Constitutional Action Cttee of 100 1966–68, Sec.-Treas. 1966–68; mem. Gov. of Fla Comm. on Status of Women 1968–71; mem. Perm. Sub-Cttee on Narcotics Control and Terrorism OAS 1981; US Del. to UN Narcotics Convention, Vienna 1987, US Del. to UN Convention, New York 1994; Chair. Nat. Cttee on Responsibilities for Financing Postsecondary Educ. 1990–92; mem. Bd of Dirs Freedom Foundation 1981, Nu Skin Enterprises 1997–; fmr Chair. Legis. Comm. Orange Co. Drug Abuse Council, fmr Co-Chair. Orange Co. March of Dimes; fmr mem. Cen. Fla Museum Speakers Bureau; Dr hc (Nova Univ.), (St Thomas Villa Nova), (Rollino Coll.); Citation for Service, Fla Republican Party; Above and Beyond Award, Outstanding Woman in Fla Politics. *Address:* PO Box 193, Winter Park, FL 32790-0193; 1214 North Park Avenue, Winter Park, FL 32789, USA.

HAWLEY, Christine, CBE, AADipl, RIBA, FRSA; British architect; *Dean, The Bartlett School;* began career with Dept of the Environment, UK Govt; worked for Pearson Int. Architects, London; fmr Pnr Yorke Rosen Cook & Hawley Architects; f. Christine Hawley Architects, London 1998; fmrly Lecturer, Architectural Asscn and Head School of Architecture, Univ. of E London; currently Dean The Bartlett School, Head Faculty of the Built Environment and Prof. of Architectural Studies, Univ. Coll. London; Visiting Chair. of Design, Tech. Univ. of Vienna and Oslo Univ.; currently Adviser UK Govt

Comm. for Architecture and the Built Environment; lectured extensively throughout USA, Europe and Far Eeast; RIBA Teaching Award. *Architectural works include:* Social Housing for Int. Bau Austellung, Berlin, Canteen, Städel Acad., Frankfurt, Osaka Folly, Japan, Exhbn Pavilions at Osaka and Nagoya Expo, Hix Sac Loqvvntvr Pfaffenberg Museum Ext., Bad Deutch-Altenberg, Austria, Kitagata Housing Reconstruction, Gifu, Japan, Museum for Roman Remains, Carnuntum, Austria. *Publications include:* chapters in books The Architect: Reconstructing Her Practice 1996, The Architect: Women in Contemporary Architecture 2001; numerous articles in professional journals. *Address:* The Bartlett School, Wares House, 22 Gordon Street, London, WC1H 0QB, England (office). *Telephone:* (20) 7679-7505 (office). *Fax:* (20) 7679-7453 (office). *E-mail:* c.hawley@ucl.ac.uk (office). *Website:* www.bartlett.ucl.ac.uk (office).

HAWLEY, Robert, CBE, PhD, DSc, CEng, CPhys, FRSE, FREng, FInstP, FIMechE, FIEE; British business executive and engineer; b. 23 July 1936, Wallasey, The Wirral; s. of William Hawley and Eva Hawley; m. 1st Valerie Clarke 1961 (divorced); one s. one d.; m. 2nd Pamela Swan; ed Wallasey Grammar School, Wallasey Tech. Coll., Birkenhead Tech. Coll. and King's Coll., Univ. of Durham; joined C.A. Parsons 1961, Electrical Designer, Generator Dept 1964, Chief Electrical Eng 1970, Dir of Production and Eng 1973–74; Dir of Production and Eng NEI Parsons 1974, Man. Dir 1976; Man. Dir Power Eng Group, NEI PLC 1984–88, Man. Dir Operations 1989–92; Main Bd Dir Rolls Royce PLC 1989–92; Chief Exec. Nuclear Electric PLC 1992–95, British Energy PLC 1995–97; Chair. Taylor Woodrow PLC 1999–2003; mem. Bd of Dirs Colt Telecom 1998–; Chair. Eng Council 1999–2002, Particle Physics and Astronomy Research Council 1999–2002, Rocktron 2001; Pres. IEE 1996–97; Advisor HSBC Investment Bank PLC; Chair. Council Univ. of Durham; Master Worshipful Co. of Engineers 2005–06; Order of Diplomatic Service Gwanghwa Medal 1999, IEE Honorary Fellowship 2003. *Publications:* Dielectric Solids (co-author) 1970, Conduction and Breakdown in Mineral Oil 1973, Fundamentals of Electromagnetic Field Theory 1974, Vacuum as an Insulator. *Leisure interests:* philately, gardening. *Address:* Summerfield, Rendcomb, nr Cirencester, Glos., GL7 7HB (home); 823 Whitehouse Apartments, 9 Belvedere Road, London, E1 9AT, England (home). *Telephone:* (20) 7265-2340 (office); (1285) 831610 (Glos.) (home); (20) 7620-3145 (London) (home). *Fax:* (20) 7265-2341 (office); (1285) 831801 (Glos.) (home); (20) 7620-3144 (London) (home). *E-mail:* robert.hawley@btinternet.com (home).

HAWN, Goldie; American actress and film producer; b. 21 Nov. 1945, Washington, DC; d. of Edward Rutledge Hawn and Laura Hawn; m. 1st Gus Trikonio 1969 (divorced); m. 2nd Bill Hudson (divorced); two s. one d. (Kate Hudson); pnr, Kurt Russell; ed American Univ., Washington, DC; began career as chorus-line dancer, World's Fair, New York 1964; Pnr, Hawn/Sylbert Movie Co. with Anthea Sylbert 1984–95; Co-founder Cosmic Entertainment (production co., fmrly Cherry Alley Productions) 2003; f. Goldie Hawn Inst. *Stage appearances include:* Romeo and Juliet (Williamsburg), Kiss Me Kate, Guys and Dolls (New York). *Television series include:* Good Morning World (series) 1967, Rowan and Martin's Laugh-In 1968–70, Goldie and Kids—Listen to Us. *Films include:* Cactus Flower 1969, There's a Girl in My Soup 1970, $ 1971, Butterflies are Free 1972, The Girl from Petrovka 1974, The Sugarland Express 1974, Shampoo 1975, The Duchess and the Dirtwater Fox 1976, Foul Play 1978, Viaggio con Anita 1979, Private Benjamin (also producer) 1980, Seems Like Old Times 1980, Best Friends 1982, Swing Shift 1984, Protocol (also producer) 1984, Wildcats (also producer) 1986, Overboard 1987, Bird On A Wire 1990, Deceived 1991, CrissCross 1992, Housesitter 1992, Death Becomes Her 1992, The First Wives Club 1996, Everybody Says I Love You 1996, The Out Of Towners 1999, Town and Country 2001, The Banger Sisters 2003. *Publication:* A Lotus Grows in the Mud (with Wendy Holden) 2005. *Address:* Cosmic Entertainment, 9255 West Sunset Blvd, West Hollywood, CA 90069, USA.

HAWTHORNE, M. Frederick, BA, PhD; American chemist and academic; *University Professor of Chemistry, UCLA;* b. Fort Scott, Kan.; ed Mo. School of Mines and Metallurgy, Pomona Coll., Claremont, CA, UCLA; began career as Postdoctoral Assoc. in Physical-Organic Chemistry, Iowa State Univ.; Sr Research Chemist, Rohm & Haas Co., Huntsville, AL, later Head of Lab. –1962; Prof., Univ. of Calif., Riverside 1962–69; Prof., UCLA 1969–98, Univ. Prof. of Chem. 1998–; Visiting Lecturer at several int. univs including Distinguished Visiting Prof., Ohio State Univ. 1990; Assoc. Ed. Inorganic Chemistry 1966–69, Ed.-in-Chief 1969–; mem. Editorial Advisory Bd Bioconjugate Chemistry; mem. NAS 1973–, American Acad. of Arts and Sciences 1975–, The Cosmos Club, Washington, DC 1976–; Fellow, AAAS 1980–, Japan Soc. for the Promotion of Science 1986–; Alfred P. Sloan Research Fellow 1963; Hon. DSc (Pomona Coll.) 1974; numerous awards including Univ. of California, Riverside Chancellor's Award for Research 1968, UCLA McCoy Award for Contribs to Chem. 1972, ACS Award in Inorganic Chem. 1973, USAF Meritorious Civilian Service Medal 1986, ACS Richard C. Tolman Medal 1986, Boron USA Award 1988, Alexander von Humboldt Foundation Award for Sr US Scientists 1990, Bailar Medal 1991, Chemical Pioneer Award 1994, Willard Gibbs Medal 1994, Seabord Medal 1997, Basolo Medal 2001, King Faisal Int. Prize for Science (co-recipient) 2003, Monie A. Ferst Award 2003. *Achievements:* holder of 30 patents. *Publications:* more than 500 research papers, 10 book chapters. *Address:* Department of Chemistry and Biochemistry, UCLA, Los Angeles, CA 90095, USA (office). *Telephone:* (310) 825-7378 (office). *Fax:* (310) 825-5490 (office). *E-mail:* mfh@chem.ucla.edu (office). *Website:* www.chem.ucla.edu/dept/facutly/hawthorne (office).

HAWTHORNE, Sir William (Rede), Kt, CBE, MA, ScD, FRS, FREng, FIMechE; British professor of thermodynamics; b. 22 May 1913, Benton, Newcastle-on-Tyne; s. of William Hawthorne and Elizabeth Curle Hawthorne; m. Barbara Runkle 1939 (died 1992); one s. two d.; ed Westminster School, London, Trinity Coll., Cambridge and Massachusetts Inst. of Tech., USA; Devt Engineer, Babcock & Wilcox Ltd 1937–39; Scientific Officer, Royal Aircraft Establishment 1940–44, seconded to Sir Frank Whittle 1940–41; British Air Comm., Washington, DC 1944–45; Deputy Dir of Engine Research, Ministry of Supply (UK) 1945–46; Assoc. Prof. of Mechanical Eng, MIT 1946–48, George Westinghouse Prof. of Mechanical Eng 1948–51, Hunsaker Prof. of Aeronautical Eng 1955–56, Visiting Inst. Prof. 1962–68, 1973–78, Sr Lecturer 1978–, mem. Corpn of MIT 1969–73; Hopkinson and ICI Prof. of Thermodynamics, Univ. of Cambridge 1951–80, Head of Eng Dept 1968–73; Fellow, Trinity Coll., Cambridge 1951–68; Master of Churchill Coll., Cambridge 1968–83; Chair. Home Office Scientific Advisory Council 1967–76, Advisory Council on Energy Conservation 1974–79; Dir Cummins Engine Co., Inc. 1974–86, Dracone Developments Ltd 1957–87; Foreign Assoc. NAS, US Nat. Acad. of Eng; Vice-Pres. Royal Soc. 1969–70, 1979–81; mem. Electricity Supply Research Council 1953–83, Comm. on Energy and the Environment 1978–81; Fellow, Fellowship of Eng 1976; Fellow, Imperial Coll. London 1983; Hon. FRAeS, FRSE 1983; Hon. Fellow, AIAA; Hon. Fellow, Trinity Coll. Cambridge 1995; Hon. mem. ASME 1982; Hon. DEng (Sheffield) 1976, (Liverpool) 1982; Hon. DSc (Salford) 1980, (Strathclyde, Bath) 1981, (Oxford) 1982, (Sussex) 1984; Medal of Freedom (USA) 1947, Royal Medal, Royal Soc. 1982, Dudley Wright Prize, Harvey Mudd Coll., Calif. 1985, ASME Tom Sawyer Award 1992. *Publications:* Aerodynamics of Compressors and Turbines, Vol. X (ed.), Design and Performance of Gas Turbine Power Plants, Vol. XI (co-ed.), High Speed Aerodynamics and Jet Propulsion; numerous papers in scientific and tech. journals. *Address:* Churchill College, Cambridge, CB3 0DS, England (home); 19 Chauncy Street, Cambridge, MA 02138, USA (home).

HAY, John, AC, PhD; Australian university administrator; *Vice-Chancellor and President, University of Queensland;* m. Barbara Hay; three s. one d.; ed Univ. of Western Australia, Univ. of Cambridge, UK; fmr Chair of English, Head of Dept, Deputy Chair. Academic Bd, Univ. of Western Australia; fmr Dean of Arts, Chair. Nat. Key Centre, Sr Deputy Vice-Chancellor Monash Univ.; Vice-Chancellor and Pres. Deakin Univ. 1992, Univ. of Queensland 1996–; Chair. Group of Eight 2002–03, Universitas 21 2003–, Carrick Inst. for Learning and Teaching in Higher Educ.; mem. Higher Educ. Review Reference Group 2002; Fellow Australian Coll. of Educators, Australian Inst. of Man.; Hon. DLitt (Deakin, UWA); Centenary Medal 2003. *Address:* Office of the Vice-Chancellor and President, University of Queensland, Brisbane, Qld 4072, Australia (office). *Telephone:* (7) 3365-1300 (office). *Fax:* (7) 3365-1266 (office). *E-mail:* j.hay@uq.edu.au (office). *Website:* www.uq.edu.au (office).

HAY, Lewis, III, MS; American business executive; *Chairman and CEO, Florida Power & Light Company (FPL) Group Inc.;* b. 1955, Pennsylvania; m. Sherry Hay; three c.; ed Lehigh Univ., Carnegie Mellon Univ.; Man. Trainee US Steel Corpn, Pittsburgh 1977–80; Pnr Strategic Planning Assocs (later Mercer Man. Consulting) 1982–91; Chief Financial Officer US Foodservice Inc. 1991–99; Chief Financial Officer Florida Power & Light Co. (FPL) Inc. 1999–2000, Pres. FPL Energy 2000–01, Pres. FPL Group 2001–06, Chair. and CEO 2002–; mem. Bd of Dirs Harris Corpn 2002–. *Address:* Florida Power & Light Company Group Inc., 700 Universe Blvd, Juno Beach, FL 33408 USA (office). *Telephone:* (561) 694-4000 (office). *Fax:* (561) 694-4620 (office). *Website:* www.fplgroup.com (office).

HAYAISHI, Osamu, MD, PhD; Japanese fmr institute director, medical scientist and academic; *Chairman of the Board of Trustees, Osaka Bioscience Institute;* b. 8 Jan. 1920, Stockton, Calif., USA; s. of Jitsuzo Hayaishi and Mitsu Hayaishi; m. Takiko Satani 1946; one d.; ed Osaka High School, Osaka Univ.; Asst Prof., Dept of Microbiology, Washington Univ. School of Medicine, St Louis, Mo., USA, 1952–54; Chief, Toxicology, Nat. Inst. of Arthritis and Metabolic Diseases, NIH, Bethesda, Md, USA 1954–58; Prof., Dept of Medical Chem. 1958–83, Prof., Dept of Molecular Biology, Inst. for Chemical Research, Kyoto Univ. 1959–76; Prof. Dept of Physiological Chem. and Nutrition, Univ. of Tokyo 1970–74; Prof. Inst. of Scientific and Industrial Research, Osaka Univ. 1975–76; Dean Faculty of Medicine, Kyoto Univ. 1979–81; Prof. Emer. Kyoto Univ. 1983–; Pres. Osaka Medical Coll. 1983–89; Dir Osaka Bioscience Inst. 1987–98, Dir Emer. 1998–, now Chair. Bd of Trustees; mem. Scientific Council Int. Inst. of Cellular and Molecular Pathology (Belgium) 1979–; Foreign Assoc. NAS 1972; Dunham Lecture (Harvard) 1980, Pfeizer Lecture, Albert Einstein School of Medicine 1980; mem. Japan Acad. 1974, New York Acad. of Sciences 1975; Foreign Hon. mem. of American Acad. of Arts and Sciences 1969; Hon. mem. American Soc. of Biological Chemists 1974, Int. Soc. on Clinical Entymology 1988, Soc. for Free Radical Research 1988; Hon. Citizen of Kyoto 1984; Int. Hon. Citizen of New Orleans, USA 1990; 1st Order of Merit, Grand Cordon of Sacred Treasure; Hon. DSc (Michigan) 1980; Hon. MD (Karolinska Institutet, Sweden) 1985; Dr hc (Padua) 1988; Award of Japan Soc. of Vitaminology 1964, Award of Matsunaga Science Foundation 1964, Asahi Award for Science and Culture 1965, Award of Japan Acad. 1967, Order of Culture 1972, Award of Fujiwara Science Foundation 1975, Médaille de Bronze de la Ville de Paris 1975, CIBA Foundation Gold Medal 1976, Louis and Bert Freedman Foundation Award for Research in Biochemistry 1976, Deutsche Akad. der Naturforscher Leopoldina (FRG) 1978, Jiménez Díaz Memorial Award (Spain) 1979, Wolf Foundation Prize in Medicine, Israel 1986, Jaroslav Heyrovský Gold Medal, Czechoslovak Acad. of Sciences 1988, Special Achievement Award, Miami Biotech. Winter Symposium 1989, Distinguished Lecturer in Neuroscience Awards, La State Univ. Medical Center, USA 1990, Distinguished Visitor Awards, Univ. of New Orleans, USA 1990; 4th Vaajasalo Lecture, 5th Nordic Neuroscience Meeting, Finland 1991, Invited Lecture, Founding Congress of World Fed. of Sleep Research Socs, France 1991, Luigi Musajo Award, Italy 1995, Distinguished Scientist Award, World Fed. of Sleep Research Socs, 3rd Int. Congress, Germany 1999.

Publications: Oxygenases 1962, Molecular Mechanisms of Oxygen Activation 1974, Molecular Oxygen in Biology 1974 and 510 scientific reviews and articles. *Leisure interest:* golf. *Address:* Osaka Bioscience Institute, 6-2-4 Furuedai Suita, Osaka 565-0874 (office); 159-505 Kageyukoji-cho, Shimotachiuri-agaru, Muromachi-dori, Kamigyo-ku, Kyoto 602-8014, Japan (home). *Telephone:* (6) 6872-4833 (office); (75) 417-2751 (home). *Fax:* (6) 6872-4818 (office); (75) 417-2752 (home). *E-mail:* hayaishi@obi.or.jp (office). *Website:* www.obi.or.jp/index2.html (office).

HAYAMA, Kanji; Japanese construction industry executive; *Chairman and Representative Director, Taisei Corporation;* ed Univ. of Tokyo; joined Taisei Corpn 1960, Vice-Pres. 1997–2001, Pres., CEO and Rep. Dir 2001–07, Chair. and Rep. Dir 2007–; mem. Bd Japan Productivity Center for Socio-Econ. Devt. *Address:* Taisei Corporation, 25–1 Nishi-Shinjuku-ku, Tokyo 163-0606, Japan (office). *Telephone:* (3) 3348-1111 (office). *Fax:* (3) 3345-1386 (office). *Website:* www.taisei.co.jp (office).

HAYAMI, Masaru; Japanese banker and economist; b. 24 March 1925; ed Hitotsubashi Univ.; joined Bank of Japan 1947, Man. Ooita Br. 1967, Chief Rep. Europe 1971, Dir Foreign Dept 1975, Man. Nagoya Br. 1976, Exec. Dir 1978, Gov. Bank of Japan 1998–2003, Alt. Gov. IMF and World Bank for Japan 1998–2003; Sr Man. Dir Nissho Iwai Corpn 1981, Exec. Vice-Pres. 1982, Pres. 1984, Pres. and Chair. 1987, Chair. 1990–94; Chair. Keizai Doyukai (Japan Asscn of Corp. Execs) 1991–95; Chair. Bd of Trustees, Tokyo Woman's Christian Univ. 1992–98. *Publication:* The Day the Yen will be Respected, Integrity of Money, Navigation through Uncharted Water, Honesty (Calling). *Address:* c/o Bank of Japan, 2-1-1, Nihonbashi-Hongokucho, Chuo-ku, Tokyo 103-8660, Japan (office).

HAYAMI, Yujiro, PhD; Japanese economist and academic; *Chairman, Graduate Faculty, Foundation for Advanced Studies in International Development;* b. 26 Nov. 1932, Tokyo; s. of Kannosuke Hayami and Chiyoko Hayami; m. Takako Suzuki 1962; one s. two d.; ed Univ. of Tokyo and Iowa State Univ.; economist, Japan Nat. Research Inst. of Agricultural Econs 1956–66; Assoc. Prof. of Econs Tokyo Metropolitan Univ. 1966–72, Prof. 1972–86; economist, Int. Rice Research Inst. 1974–76; Prof. of Int. Econs Aoyama-Gakuin Univ. 1986–2000; Dir Grad. Program, Foundation for Advanced Studies in Int. Devt 2000–04, Chair. 2004–; Purple Ribbon and Medal for Contribs to Arts and Sciences (Japan). *Publications:* Development Economics: From the Poverty to the Wealth of Nations 1997, 3rd edn 2005, A Rice Village Saga: Three Decades of Green Revolution in the Philippines 2000. *Leisure interest:* tennis. *Address:* GRIPS/FASID Joint Graduate Programme, 7-22-1, Roppongi, Minato-ku, Tokyo 106-8677 (office); 6-8-14 Okusawa, Setagaya-ku, Tokyo 158, Japan (home). *Telephone:* (3) 5413-6033 (office); (3) 3701-1345 (home). *Fax:* (3) 5413-0016 (office); (3) 3701-1345 (home). *E-mail:* hayami@grip.ac.jp (office).

HAYASHI, Fumiko; Japanese business executive; *President, Tokyo Nissan Auto Sales Company Ltd;* ed Aoyama High School, Tokyo; began career working for Toray and Matsushita Electric; salesperson, Honda 1977–87; joined BMW Japan as Br. Man. 1987, Sales Man. –1999, Pres. BMW Tokyo 2003–05; Pres. Fahren Tokyo, Volkswagen Group Japan 1999–2003; CEO Daiei Inc. 2005–07 Chair. 2005–07, Vice-Chair. 2007, Adviser 2005–07; Chair. Tonichi Carlife Group Inc. and Pres. Tokyo Nissan Auto Sales Co. Ltd 2008–; ranked by Fortune magazine amongst 50 Most Powerful Women in Business outside the US (tenth) 2005, (29th) 2006, ranked by Forbes magazine amongst 100 Most Powerful Women (66th) 2005, (39th) 2006. *Address:* Tonichi Carlife Group Inc., 4-32-1, Nishigotanda 141-0031 Shinagawa-Ku, Tokyo, Japan (office). *Website:* www.tn-carlife.co.jp (office).

HAYASHI, Motoo; Japanese politician; *Minister of State, Chairman of the National Public Safety Commission, and Minister of State in charge of Okinawa and Northern Territories and Disaster Management;* b. 3 Jan. 1947, Chiba Pref.; m.; one s. one d.; ed Univ. of Nihon; elected to Chiba Prefectural Ass. 1983; mem. House of Reps (10th Electoral Dist of Chiba Pref.) 1989–; Parl. Sec. Vice-Minister of Transport 1998–2003; Vice-Minister of Land 2003–05, Chair. Ministry of Land, Infrastructure and Transport 2005–08; Minister of State, Chair. Nat. Public Safety Comm., and Minister of State in charge of Okinawa and Northern Territories and Disaster Man. 2008–; First Deputy Sec.-Gen. LDP 2007–. *Publication:* Pursuing Dreams – The Near Future of a Metropolitan Area Airport. *Leisure interests:* walking, reading. *Address:* National Public Safety Commission, 2-1-2, Kasumigaseki, Chiyoda-ku, Tokyo 100-8974, Japan (office). *Telephone:* (3) 3581-0141 (office). *E-mail:* info@npsc.go.jp (office). *Website:* www.npsc.go.jp (office).

HAYASHI, Yoshimasa, LLB, MPA; Japanese lawyer and politician; *Minister of Defence;* b. 19 Jan. 1961; m.; one d.; ed Univ. of Tokyo, Kennedy School of Govt, Harvard Univ., USA; Asst to US Congressman Steve Neal,. Washington, DC 1991, also Int. Affairs Intern at Office of US Senator William Roth; worked in pvt. for Mitui & Co Ltd., Tokyo, Sanden Koutsu Co., Yamaguchi, Yamaguchi Godo Gas Co., Keefe Co., Washington, DC; mem. House of Councillors (LDP) for Yamaguchi Prefecture 1995–, Leader Pro-Whaling League; Sec., Ministry of Finance 1999–2000; Deputy Minister, Cabinet Office 2006–07; Minister of Defence 2008–. *Address:* Ministry of Defence, 5-1, Ichigaya, Honmura-cho, Shinjuku-ku, Tokyo 162-8801, Japan (office). *Telephone:* (3) 3268-3111. *E-mail:* infomod@mod.go.jp (office). *Website:* www.mod.go.jp (office).

HAYASHI, Yujiro, PhD, DEng; Japanese university administrator and academic; *President, Kanazawa University;* Prof. of Mechanical Systems Eng, Kanazawa Univ., currently Pres. Kanazawa Univ. *Address:* Office of the President, Kanazawa University, Kakuma-machi, Kanazawa-shi 920-1192, Japan (office). *Telephone:* (76) 264-5111 (office). *Fax:* (76) 234-4010 (office). *E-mail:* now@kanazawa-u.ac.jp (office). *Website:* www.kanazawa-u.ac.jp (office).

HAYAT, Sardar Sikander; Pakistani politician; b. 1 June 1934, Karela Majhan; s. of Sardar Fateh Mohammad Khan Karelvi; ed Gordon Coll., Rawalpindi, Univ. Law Coll., Lahore; practised law in Kotli 1958; mem. Kolti local council for eight years; elected to first Azad Jammu and Kashmir Legis. Ass. 1970; Minister of Revenue, Forests and Finance 1972–74; Pres. All Pakistan Jammu and Kashmir Conf. 1976–88; Prime Minister Azad Jammu and Kashmir 1985–89, 2001–05; Pres. Azad Jammu and Kashmir 1991–96; fmr Pres. Bar Asscn Kotli.

HAYAT, Makhdoom Syed Faisal Saleh, MA; Pakistani politician; m.; one s. one d.; ed Aitchison Coll., FC Govt Coll., Lahore, King's Coll. London, UK; elected to Nat. Ass. 1977–; Sr mem. Cen. Exec. Cttee, Pakistan People's Party 1987–; fmr Sr Minister for Home and Services and Gen. Admin., Punjab Cabinet; Minister of Commerce, Industries and Local Govt –2002, of the Interior, Narcotics Div., Control and Capital Admin. and Devt Divs 2002–04, Minister of the Environment 2006–07; mem. Nat. Security Council; Pres. Pakistan Football Fed. *Leisure interests:* squash, cricket, riding. *Address:* c/o Ministry of the Environment, Local Government and Rural Development, Block 4, Old Naval Headquarters, Civic Centre, G-6, Islamabad, Pakistan. *Telephone:* (51) 9224578.

HAYDEN, Matthew Lawrence; Australian cricketer; b. 29 Oct. 1971, Kingaroy, Queensland; m. Kellie Hayden; left-hand opening batsman; teams: Queensland 1991–, Hampshire 1997, Northamptonshire 1999–2000 (as Capt., Australia A 2000–01, Australia 1993–2009 (test debut versus South Africa at Johannesburg; one-day int. debut versus England at Manchester 1993); 94 tests for Australia, scored 8,242 runs (average 53.51) with 30 hundreds, highest score 380 (fmr world record versus Zimbabwe, Perth, Australia 9–10 Oct. 2003); scored 20,750 runs (average 54.17) with 68 hundreds in first-class cricket; 153 one-day ints, scored 5,385 runs (average 44.20) with ten hundreds; highest one-day int. score by an Australian of 181; 1st Australian to score 1,000 runs in debut season 1991/92; six centuries in seven consecutive innings in 1993/94; shared in Queensland record 2nd wicket partnership (with Martin Love) versus Tasmania 1995/96; second highest run-scorer for Australia in a calendar year 2001 (1,391 runs); ranked world number one batsman 2003; four consecutive double century 1st wicket partnerships (with Justin Langer) for Australia (world record); Queensland's most prolific century-maker (24); Mercantile Mutual Cup Player of the Year 1998/99, 1999/2000; Allan Border Medal 2002; mem. Australia's World Cup winning side 2003, Wisden Cricketer of the Year 2003, ODI Player of the Year 2007, QLD Sportsman of the Year 2007. *Address:* International Quarterback Pty Ltd, 12 Ross Street, Newstead, Queensland 4006, Australia (office). *Telephone:* (7) 3852-7400 (office). *Fax:* (7) 3252-3411 (office). *E-mail:* charmaine@internationalquarterback.com.au (office). *Website:* www.internationalquarterback.com.au (office).

HAYDEN, Gen. Michael Vincent, BA, MA; American air force officer and fmr government official; b. 17 March 1945, Pittsburgh; s. of Harry Hayden Sr and Sadie Hayden; ed N Catholic High School, Duquesne Univ., Pittsburgh, Academic Instructor School, Squadron Officer School, Air Command and Staff Coll., Air War Coll., Maxwell AF Base, Ala, Defense Intelligence Agency, Bolling AF Base, Washington DC, Armed Forces Staff Coll., Norfolk, Va; rank of Second Lt 1967–70; Analyst and Briefer, Strategic Air Command HQ, Offnut AF Base, Neb. 1970–72; promoted to First Lt 1970, to Capt. 1971; Chief Current Intelligence Div., 8th AF HQ, Andersen AF Base, Guam 1972–75; Academic Instructor and Commdt of Cadets, ROTC Program, St Michael's Coll., Winooski, Vt 1975–79; promoted to Maj. 1980; Chief of Intelligence, 51st Tactical Fighter Wing, Osan Air Base, S Korea 1980–82; Air Attaché, Embassy in Sofia, Bulgaria 1984–86; promoted to Lt–Col 1985; Politico-Mil. Affairs Officer, Strategy Div., USAF HQ, Washington, DC 1986–89, Chief, Sec. of AF Staff Group 1991–93; Dir for Defense Policy and Arms Control, Nat. Security Council 1989–91; promoted to Col 1990; Dir Intelligence Directorate, US European Command HQ, Stuttgart, Germany 1993–95; promoted to Brig. Gen. 1993; Special Asst to Commdr, Air Intelligence Agency HQ, Kelly AF Base Oct.–Dec. 1995, Commdr 1996–97, Dir Jt Command and Control Warfare Center 1996–97; Deputy Chief of Staff, UN Command and US Forces Korea, Yongsan Army Garrison, S Korea 1997–99; promoted to Lt Gen. 1999; Dir Nat. Security Agency 1999–2005, Chief, Cen. Security Service, Fort George G. Meade, Md 1999–2005; promoted to Gen. 2005; Prin. Deputy Dir, Nat. Intelligence, Washington, DC 2005–06; Dir CIA 2006–09; Defense Distinguished Service Medal, Defense Superior Service Medal with oak leaf cluster, Legion of Merit, Bronze Star Medal, Meritorious Service Medal with two oak leaf clusters, AF Commendation Medal, AF Achievement Medal. *Address:* c/o Central Intelligence Agency, Office of Public Affairs, Washington, DC 20505, USA.

HAYDEN, Hon. William (Bill) George, AC, BEcons; Australian fmr politician and farmer; b. 23 Jan. 1933, Brisbane, Queensland; m. Dallas Broadfoot 1960; one s. two d.; ed Brisbane State High School, Queensland Secondary Correspondence School, Univ. of Queensland; Queensland State Public Service 1950–52; mem. Queensland Police Force 1953–61; mem. Fed. Parl. for Oxley 1961–88; Parl. Spokesman on Health and Welfare 1969–72; Treasurer 1975; Minister for Social Security 1972–75, for Foreign Affairs 1983–88, for Foreign Affairs and Trade 1987–88; Gov.-Gen. 1989–96 (retd); Leader Parl. Labor Party (Opposition) 1977–83; Adjunct Prof., Queensland Univ. of Tech. 1996; Chair. Editorial Cttee Quadrant Journal 1998–2004; Resident Visiting Fellow, Jane Franklin Hall, Univ. of Tasmania 2000; mem. The Gen. Sir John Monash Foundation Asscn of Fmr Mems of the Parl. of Australia, Queensland Retd Police Asscn Inc.; Patron Australian Inst. of Int. Affairs (Queensland Br.), Australian Fabian Soc. (Queensland Br.); Hon.

FRACP 1995; KStJ; Commdr Order of the Three Stars, Latvia; Hon. DUniv (Griffith) 1990, (Cen. Queensland) 1992; Hon. LLD (Queensland) 1990; Hon. DLitt (S Queensland) 1997; Gwanghwa Medal (Korean Order of Diplomatic Merit), Australian Humanist of the Year 1996. *Publication:* Hayden: An Autobiography 1996. *Address:* Level 13, Waterfront Place, 1 Eagle Street, Brisbane, Queensland (office); GPO Box 7829, Waterfront Place, Brisbane, Queensland 4001, Australia. *Telephone:* (7) 3229-3500 (office). *Fax:* (7) 3229-3499 (office). *E-mail:* wdhayden@bigpond.net.au (office).

HAYEK, Nicolas G.; Swiss business executive; b. 19 Feb. 1928, Beirut; m.; one s. one d.; of American-Lebanese parentage; f. consultancy firm Hayek Eng 1963; firm acts as adviser to govts and business concerns in Europe, USA, China and notably to Swiss watch and high precision industry; Co-Founder, Chair. and CEO, SMH (high-tech. co.) 1986; alt. Chair. Bd of Dirs MCC Micro Compact Car Ltd (Biel), SMH/Swatch and Chair. Swatch-Telecom (Biel); Chair., CEO Swatch Group Ltd 1986–2002; Pres. French Govt Reflection Group on Econ. Strategy 1996–; mem. Council for Research, Tech. and Innovation (Germany) 1995–; Dr hc Neuchâtel Univ. (Switzerland) 1996. *Leisure interests:* swimming, tennis. *Address:* c/o SMH, Seevorstadt 6, 2502 Biel, Switzerland.

HAYEK, Salma; Mexican actress; b. 2 Sept. 1966, Coatzacoalcos, Veracruz; m. François-Henri Pinault 2009; one d.; Pres. and Chief Exec. Ventanazul (production co.) 2007–. *Films:* Mi vida loca 1993, Desperado 1995, Four Rooms 1995, Fair Game 1995, From Dusk Till Dawn 1996, Fled 1996, Fools Rush In 1997, Breaking Up 1997, Follow Me Home 1997, The Velocity of Gary 1998, 54 1998, Wild Wild West 1999, Dogma 1999, Frida 2002 (also producer), Death to Smoochy 2002, Once Upon a Time in Mexico 2003, Hotel 2003, After the Sunset 2004, Ask the Dust 2006, Lonely Hearts 2006, Across the Universe 2007. *Television appearances include:* NYPD Blue, Dream On, Nurses, Action, Ugly Betty (also Exec. Producer) 2006–07. *Address:* c/o William Morris Agency, 1325 Avenue of the Americas, New York, NY 10019-4701, USA (office).

HAYES, Sir Brian David, Kt, GCB; British civil servant; *Lloyd's Members' Ombudsman;* b. 5 May 1929, Norwich; s. of the late Charles Hayes and Flora Hayes; m. Audrey Jenkins 1958; one s. one d.; ed Norwich School, Corpus Christi Coll., Cambridge; joined Ministry of Agric., Fisheries and Food 1956, Deputy Sec. for Agricultural Commodity Policy 1973–78, Perm. Sec. 1979–83; Jt Perm. Sec., Dept of Trade and Industry 1983–85, Perm. Sec. 1985–89; Advisory Dir Unilever 1990–99; Dir Tate and Lyle PLC 1989–98, Guardian Royal Exchange PLC 1989–99, SANE 1990–; Lloyd's Mems' Ombudsman 1994–. *Leisure interests:* reading, opera, ballet. *Address:* Office of the Lloyd's Members' Ombudsman, G5/86, 1 Lime Street, London, EC3M 7HA, England (office).

HAYES, Francis Mahon, BA, DPA, BL; Irish lawyer, consultant and fmr diplomatist; *Member, Permanent Court of Arbitration;* b. 2 March 1930, Cork; s. of Francis Mahon Hayes and Aileen Hayes (née Walsh); m. Kathleen O'Donoghue 1958; one s. three d.; ed Univ. Coll., Dublin and King's Inns, Dublin; Asst Legal Adviser, Dept of Justice 1957–65; Asst Legal Adviser, First Sec. Dept of Foreign Affairs 1965–70, Legal Adviser, Counsellor 1970–74, Legal Adviser, Asst Sec. 1974–77; Amb. to Denmark, Norway and Iceland 1977–81; Perm. Rep. to UN Office at Geneva 1981–87; Deputy Sec. Dept of Foreign Affairs 1987–89; Perm. Rep. to UN, New York 1989–95; mem. Int. Law Comm. 1986–91, The (Irish) Constitution Review Group 1995–96, Advisory Task Force on Immigrants 2001–02, Perm. Court of Arbitration, The Hague 2005–; Prime Minister's Alt. Rep. on EU Charter of Human Rights Convention 1999–2000; freelance consultant on int. and legal affairs. *Leisure interests:* reading, theatre, music, films, watching sport, golf. *Address:* Tara, 28 Knocknashee, Goatstown, Dublin 14, Ireland (home). *Telephone:* (1) 2983787 (home). *Fax:* (1) 2983787 (home).

HAYES, Roger Peter, BSc (Econ), MA; British public relations executive and company director; *International Director, Perception Management, Perception International;* b. 15 Feb. 1945, Hampton; s. of Peter Hall and Patricia Hall; m. Margaret Jean Eales 1974; one s.; ed Isleworth Grammar School, London Univ., Univ. of Southern Calif., USA; Reuters Corresp., Paris and London 1967–72; Vice-Pres. and Dir Buson-Marsteller 1972–79; Man. P.A. Consulting Group 1979–83; Dir Corp. Communications, Thorn-EMI PLC 1983–87; Chair. Hayes-MacLeod; Sec.-Gen. Int. Public Relations Asscns (Bd mem. 1984–88); Dir (non-exec.) IT World 1985–; Int. Dir Perception Man., Perception International; Chair. Int. Foundation for Public Affairs Studies 1986–89; Dir-Gen. British Nuclear Industry Forum 1993–97; Vice-Pres. (Public Affairs and Govt Relations) Ford of Europe 1991–93; Pres. Int. Public Relations Asscn 1997; Dir Int. Inst. of Communications 1997–; Dir (non-exec.) Echo Communications Research Group 1999–, Communications Ethics Ltd; Group CEO British Amusements Catering Trades Asscn (BACTA) 2004–, Amusements Trades Exhbns Ltd 2004–; Fellow, Inst. of Public Relations (UK). *Publications:* (co-author) Corporate Revolution 1986, Experts in Action 1988, Systematic Networking 1996. *Leisure interests:* books, music, cinema, int. politics, tennis, travel. *Address:* 75 Ellerby Street, London, SW6 6EU, England (home). *Telephone:* (20) 7720-2916 (office); (20) 7731-1255 (home). *Fax:* (20) 7323-9623 (office). *E-mail:* roger_p_hayes@yahoo.co.uk (home).

HAYES, William, MA, PhD, DPhil; Irish physicist and university administrator (retd); b. 12 Nov. 1930, Killorglin, Co. Kerry; s. of Robert Hayes and Eileen Tobin; m. Joan Ferriss 1962 (died 1996); two s. one d.; ed Univ. Coll. Dublin and St John's Coll., Oxford; Official Fellow, St John's Coll. Oxford 1960–87, Prin. Bursar 1977–87, Pres. 1987–2001; Univ. Lecturer in Physics, Univ. of Oxford 1962–87; Dir Clarendon Lab. Oxford 1985–87; Pro-Vice-Chancellor, Univ. of Oxford 1990–2001; Chair. Curators of Oxford Univ. Chest 1992–2000; Sr Foreign Fellow NSF, Purdue Univ. 1963–64; Visiting Prof., Univ. of Ill.

1971; mem. Tech. Staff, Bell Labs, NJ 1974; Hon. MRIA 1998; Hon. Fellow, St John's Coll. Oxford 2001–; Hon. DSc (Nat. Univ. of Ireland) 1988, (Purdue Univ.) 1996. *Publications:* Scattering of Light by Crystals (with R. Loudon) 1978, Defects and Defect Processes in Non-Metallic Solids (with A.M. Stoneham) 1985; research papers in professional journals. *Leisure interests:* walking, reading, listening to music. *Address:* 91 Woodstock Road, Oxford, OX2 6HL, England (home). *E-mail:* w.hayes1@physics.ox.ac.uk (office).

HAYMAN, Baroness (Life Peer), cr. 1996, of Dartmouth Park in the London Borough of Camden; **Rt Hon. Hélène Valerie Hayman,** PC; British politician; *Lord Speaker of the House of Lords;* b. 26 March 1949, Wolverhampton; d. of the late Maurice Middleweek and Maude Middleweek; m. Martin Heathcote Hayman 1974; four s.; ed Wolverhampton Girls' High School, Newnham Coll., Cambridge; Pres. Union, Newnham Coll. Cambridge 1969; with Shelter: Nat. Campaign for the Homeless 1969–71; mem. staff, Social Services Dept, London Borough of Camden 1971–74; MP for Welwyn and Hatfield 1974–79 (Baby of the House 1974–79); Deputy Dir Nat. Council for One Parent Families 1974; Jr Minister, Dept for Environment, Transport and the Regions and Dept of Health 1997–99; Minister of State in the House of Lords for Agric., Fisheries and Food 1999–2001; elected first ever Lord Speaker of the House of Lords 2006–; mem. Royal Coll. of Gynaecologists Ethics Cttee 1982–97, Univ. Coll. London/Univ. Coll. Hosp. Cttee on Ethics of Clinical Investigation 1987–97 (Vice-Chair. 1990–97), Univ. Coll. London 1992–97, Human Fertilisation and Embryology Authority; Chair. Whittington Hosp. NHS Trust 1992–97, Cancer Research UK 2001–04, Specialised Health Care Alliance 2004–, Human Tissue Authority 2005; mem. Bd Roadsafe 2001–05 (Patron 2006–), Review Cttee of Privy Counsellors of the Anti-terrorism, Crime and Security Act 2002–04; Trustee, Royal Botanical Gardens, Health and Educ. Trust; two hon. fellowships; Dr hc. *Address:* Office of the Lord Speaker, House of Lords, Westminster, London, SW1A 0PW, England (office). *Telephone:* (20) 7219-5083 (office). *Fax:* (20) 7219-2075 (office). *E-mail:* lordspeaker@parliament.uk (office). *Website:* www.parliament .uk/about/how/principal/lord_speaker/lordspeaker.cfm (office).

HAYMAN, Walter Kurt, MA, ScD, FRS; British mathematician and academic; *Professor Emeritus and Senior Research Fellow, Department of Mathematics, Imperial College London;* b. 6 Jan. 1926, Cologne, Germany; s. of Franz Samuel Haymann and Ruth Therese Hensel; m. 1st Margaret Riley Crann 1947 (died 1994); three d.; m. 2nd Waficka Katifi 1995 (died 2001); m. 3rd Marie Jennings 2007; ed Gordonstoun School and Univ. of Cambridge; Lecturer, King's Coll., Newcastle and Fellow, St John's Coll., Cambridge 1947; Lecturer 1947–53 and Reader, Univ. of Exeter 1953–56; Visiting Lecturer, Brown Univ., USA 1949–50, Stanford Univ. summer 1950, 1955, American Math. Soc. 1961; Prof. of Pure Math., Imperial Coll. of Science and Tech., London 1956–85, Dean Royal Coll. of Science 1978–81, Prof. Emer. 1985–, Sr Research Fellow 1995–; Prof. Univ. of York 1985–93, Prof. Emer. 1993–; mem. London Math. Soc.; mem. Cambridge Philosophical Soc.; Fellow, Imperial Coll. 1989; Foreign mem. Finnish Acad. of Science and Letters, Accad. dei Lincei; Corresp. mem. Bavarian Acad. of Science; first organizer of British Math. Olympiad 1964–68; Hon. DSc (Exeter) 1981, (Birmingham) 1985, (Giessen) 1992, (Uppsala) 1992, (Nat. Univ. of Ireland) 1997; First Smiths Prize 1948, shared Adams Prize, Univ. of Cambridge 1949, Junior Berwick Prize 1955, Sr Berwick Prize 1964, de Morgan Medal, London Math. Soc. 1995. *Publications:* Multivalent Functions 1958, 1994, Meromorphic Functions 1964, Research Problems in Function Theory 1967, Subharmonic Functions I 1976, II 1989; and over 200 articles in various scientific journals. *Leisure interests:* music, travel, television. *Address:* Department of Mathematics, Room 6M43, Imperial College, London, SW7 2AZ (office); Cadogan Grange, Bisley, Stroud, Glos., GL6 7AT, England (home). *Telephone:* (20) 7594-8535 (office); (1452) 770545 (home). *Fax:* (20) 7594-8517 (office). *Website:* www.ma .ic.ac.uk (office).

HAYMET, A. D. J. (Tony), BSc, PhD, DSc; Australian/American chemist, environmental scientist, academic and research institute director; *Director, Scripps Institution of Oceanography;* ed Sydney Grammar School, Univ. of Sydney, Univ. of Chicago, USA; Postdoctoral Research Fellow, Lyman Lab. of Physics, Harvard Univ. 1981–83; Asst Prof. of Chem., Univ. of California, Berkeley 1983–88; Assoc. Prof. of Chem., Univ. of Utah 1988–91, Prof. of Chem. 1991, Adjunct Prof. of Chem. 1991–95; Deputy Dir for Physical Sciences, UniServe*Science, CAUT Center for Educational Software in Science, Univ. of Sydney, Australia 1994–97, Prof. of Chem. (Established Chair of Theoretical Chem.), Univ. of Sydney 1991–98, Visiting Prof. in School of Chem. 1998–99; Affiliated Faculty mem. W.M. Keck Center for Computational Biology 1998–2002; Affiliate Staff Scientist, Pacific Northwest Nat. Lab., PASS 1996–2002; Chair. Physical Chem. Div., Univ. of Houston, Tex. 1998–2001, Founder Univ. of Houston Environmental Modeling Inst. 2000–02, Distinguished Univ. Prof. of Chem. 1998–2002; mem. Advisory Bd Environmental Inst. of Houston 2001–02; mem. Founding Group, WA Marine Science Inst. 2005–06; mem. Bd of Dirs CRC for Antarctic Climate and Ecosystems 2003–06, Western Australian Marine Science Inst.; seconded as CSIRO Dir of Science and Policy 2005–06, Chief of CSIRO Marine Research, then Marine & Atmospheric Research 2006; Dir Scripps Inst. of Oceanography, Univ. of California, San Diego 2006–, Vice-Chancellor for Marine Sciences and Dean of Grad. School of Marine Sciences, Univ. of California, San Diego 2006–; Visiting Research Fellow, ANU Research School of Chem. 1993; Australian Acad. of Science Fellowship to Japan 1994; Visiting Prof. of Chemical Eng and Petroleum Refining, Colorado School of Mines, Golden, Colo, USA 1997; Chair. Partnership for the Observation of Global Oceans (POGO); mem. Chemical Educ. Sub-cttee Australian Acad. of Science 1997–98, Advisory Editorial Bd PhysChemComm 1998–2001; Fellow, Royal Australian Chemical Inst. 1992; Hon. Research Prof. of Chem., Univ. of Tasmania 2002–06; Sr Knox Prize, Sydney Grammar School 1973, Levey

Scholarship for Chem. I and Physics I and Iredale Prize for Chem. II 1974–75, C.S.R. Chemicals Prize for Chem. and Union Carbide Prize for Chem. 3 1976–77, Univ. Medal and First Class Honours in Theoretical Chem. 1977, Masson Medal, Royal Australian Chemical Inst. 1977, NSF Presidential Young Investigator 1985–90, Alfred P. Sloan Research Fellow 1986–89, Rennie Medal, Royal Australian Chemical Inst. 1988, Student Distinguished Service Award, Univ. of Utah 1990, Antarctic Service Medal, US Dept of Navy and NSF 1994, Distinguished Young Chemist Award, Fed. of Asian Chemical Socs 1997, Woolmers Lecturer in Chemical Educ., Univ. of Tasmania 1997. *Publications:* more than 160 scientific papers in professional journals. *Address:* Director's Office, Scripps Institution of Oceanography, University of California, San Diego, MC 0210, 9500 Gilman Drive, La Jolla, CA 92093, USA (office). *Telephone:* (858) 534-2827 (office). *E-mail:* thaymet@ucsd.edu (office). *Website:* sio.ucsd.edu/director.php (office).

HAYNES, Desmond Leo; Barbadian politician and fmr professional cricketer; *Senator, Barbados Parliament;* b. 15 Feb. 1956, Holders Hill, Barbados; m. Dawn Haynes 1991; ed Fed. High School, Barbados; right-hand opening batsman, teams: Barbados 1976–95 (Capt. 1990–91), Scotland (Benson & Hedges Cup) 1983, Middx 1989–94, W Prov. 1994–97; 116 Tests for W Indies 1977–94 (four as Capt.), scoring 7,487 runs (average 42.2) including 18 hundreds; scored 26,030 first-class runs (61 hundreds); toured England 1979 (World Cup), 1980, 1983 (World Cup), 1984, 1988, 1991; 238 limited-overs ints., scoring record 8,648 runs including record 17 hundreds; Chair. Barbados Cricket Assn Sr Selection Panel 1999–2001; elected Senator in Parl. Sept. 2001–. *Address:* The Senate, Parliament Buildings, Bridgetown, Barbados (office). *Telephone:* (246) 426-5331 (office). *Fax:* (246) 436-4143 (office). *E-mail:* parliamentbarbados@caribsurf.com (office). *Website:* www.parliamentbarbados.gov.bb (office).

HAYS, Hon. Daniel (Dan), BA, LLB; Canadian politician; *Leader of the Opposition in the Senate;* m. Kathy Hays; three d.; ed Univ. of Alberta and Univ. of Toronto; lawyer, farmer and rancher; Senator for Alberta, Parl. of Canada 1984–, Deputy Leader of the Govt in the Senate 1999–2001, Speaker of the Senate 2001–06, Leader of the Opposition 2006–; mem. Liberal Party of Canada, Pres. 1994–98; Chair. Agric. and Forestry Cttee 1986–88, 1994–95, Energy, the Environment and Natural Resources Cttee 1989–93; Chair. Canada-Japan Inter-Parl. Group 1994–99, Asia-Pacific Parl. Forum 1994–99; mem. Law Soc. of Alberta, Bar Assn, Canadian Tax Foundation, Canadian Hays Converter Assn; Trustee Rotary Challenger Park Soc.; mem. Rotary Club; Hon. Col King's Own Calgary Regt; Grand Cordon, Order of the Sacred Treasure, Japan, Ordre de la Pléiade. *Address:* c/o Liberal Party of Canada, 81 Metcalfe Street, Suite 400, Ottawa, Ont., K1P 6M8, Canada (office). *Telephone:* (613) 237-0740 (office). *Fax:* (613) 235-7208 (office). *E-mail:* haysd@sen.parl.gc.ca (office). *Website:* www.sen.parl.gc.ca/dhays (office).

HAYS, Adm. Ronald Jackson, BS; American naval officer (retd); b. 19 Aug. 1928, Urania, La.; s. of George H. Hays and Fannie E. (née McCartney) Hays; m. Jane M. Hughes 1951; two s. one d.; ed Northwestern State Univ., US Naval Acad.; Commdt Ensign US Navy 1950, Destroyer Officer Atlantic Fleet 1950–51, Attack Pilot Pacific Fleet 1953–56; Test Pilot 1956–59, Squadron Leader 1961–63; Air Warfare Officer 7th Fleet Staff 1967–68; Tactical Aircraft Planning Officer, Office Chief Naval Operations 1969–71; C-in-C US Naval Force Europe, London 1980–83; Vice-Chief Naval Operations Dept, Washington 1983–85; C-in-C US Pacific Command 1985–88; rank of Adm. 1983; Pres. and CEO The Pacific Int-Center for High Tech. Research 1988–92, Tech. Consultant 1992–; currently working with Parsons Corpn, Honolulu; Sr Advisory Council mem. Japan-America Soc. of Hawaii; co-founder and head Pacific Aerospace Museum, Honolulu Int. Airport; Dr hc (Northwestern State Univ.) 1988; DSM with three gold stars, Silver Star with two gold stars, DFC with gold and silver star; Legion of Merit and numerous other awards and medals; US Naval Acad. Distinguished Graduate 2005. *Leisure interest:* golf. *Address:* Parsons Corporation, 1132 Bishop Street, Suite 2102, Honolulu, HI 96813; c/o Pacific Aerospace Museum, Honolulu International Airport, Terminal Box 7, Honolulu, HI 96819; 869 Kamoi Place, Honolulu, HI 96825, USA (home). *E-mail:* rjhayshawaii@msn.com (office).

HAYTHORNTHWAITE, Richard (Rick), SM, MA; British business executive; *CEO, Invensys PLC;* b. Dec. 1956; m.; one s. one d.; ed Colston's School, Bristol, Queen's Coll., Oxford; joined 1978, exploration geologist, then Man. Magnus Oilfield, Pres. Venezuela and other group posts until 1995; Corp. and Commercial Dir Premier Oil PLC 1995–97; joined Blue Circle Industries PLC 1997, CEO Heavy Bldg Materials Asia and Europe, CEO 1999–2001; CEO Invensys PLC 2001–; Chair. Centre for Creative Communications, Almeida Theatre; Trustee Nat. Museum of Science & Industry; Sloan Fellow MIT. *Leisure interests:* travel, tennis, skiing, theatre, visual arts. *Address:* Invensys PLC, Carlisle Place, London, SW1P 1BX, England (office). *Website:* www.invensys.com (office).

HAYWARD, Anthony (Tony) Bryan, BSc, PhD; British oil industry executive; *Group Chief Executive, BP PLC;* b. 1957, Slough; m. Maureen Hayward; one s. one d.; ed Univs of Edinburgh and Birmingham; joined BP PLC 1982, various tech. and commercial posts with BP Exploration, London, Aberdeen, France, China and Glasgow, later Exploration Man., Colombia, Pres. BP Exploration Venezuela 1995–97, Dir BP Exploration, London 1997–99, Group Vice-Pres. and mem. Upstream Exec. Cttee 1999–2000, Group Treasurer 2000–02, Exec. Vice-Pres. and CEO Exploration and Production 2003–07, Exec. Dir BP 2003–07, Group Chief Exec. 2007–; Dir (sr ind. non-exec.) Corus Group plc; Dir (non-exec.) Tata Steel; mem. Advisory Bd Tsinghua; mem. Business Council of Britain; Chair. GLOBE CEO Forum for Climate Change. *Leisure interests:* sailing, skiing, triathlons, watching sport. *Address:* BP PLC, International Headquarters, 1 St James's Square, London, SW1Y 4PD, England (office). *Telephone:* (20) 7496-4000 (office). *Fax:* (20) 7496-4630 (office). *Website:* www.bp.com (office).

HAYWARD, Sir Jack (Arnold), Kt, OBE, FRGS; British business executive; b. 14 June 1923, Wolverhampton; s. of the late Sir Charles Hayward and Hilda Arnold; m. Jean Mary Forder 1948; two s. one d.; ed Northaw Preparatory School, Stowe School, Buckingham; joined RAF 1941, active service as pilot officer in SE Asia Command, demobilized with rank of Flight-Lt 1946; joined Rotary Hoes Ltd 1947, with S Africa br. –1950; f. US arm Firth Cleveland Group of Cos. 1951; joined Grand Bahama Port Authority 1956, Chair. Grand Bahama Devt Co. Ltd and Freeport Commercial and Industrial Ltd 1976–; Pres. Lundy Field Soc., Wolverhampton Wanderers FC; Vice-Pres. SS Great Britain Project; Paul Harris Fellow (Rotary) 1983; Hon. Life Vice-Pres. Maritime Trust 1971; Hon. LLD (Exeter) 1971; Hon. DBA (Wolverhampton) 1994; William Booth Award, Salvation Army 1987. *Leisure interests:* sport, watching cricket, amateur dramatics. *Address:* Seashell Lane, PO Box F-40099, Freeport, Grand Bahama Island, Bahamas. *Telephone:* (242) 3525165.

HAZ, Hamzah, BA; Indonesian politician; b. 15 Feb. 1940, Ketapang, W Kalimantan; m. (two wives); twelve c.; ed Sr Econ. High School, Ketapang, Tanjungpura Univ.; newspaper journalist, Pontianak; teacher of econs, Tanjungpura Univ.; mem. W Kalimantan Prov. Legis. Council 1968–71; mem. Nahdlatul Ulama (NU; later amalgamated into United Devt Party – PPP), Leader PPP 1999–; mem. House of Reps 1971–; fmr State Minister of Investment, Co-ordinating Minister for People's Welfare and Eradication of Poverty; Vice-Pres. of Indonesia 2001–04. *Leisure interest:* music. *Address:* Jalan Tegalan No. 27, Matraman, Jakarta Timur, Indonesia (home). *Telephone:* (21) 8581327 (home).

HAZELHOFF, Robertus, LLM; Dutch banker; b. 21 Oct. 1930, Delft; s. of Hendricus Hazelhoff and Rinske van Terwisga; m. G.M. van Huet 1960; ed Univ. of Leiden; Man. Banco Tornquist, Buenos Aires 1965; Man. Algemene Bank Nederland, New York Office 1968, mem. Man. Bd Algemene Bank Nederland NV 1971–, Chair. 1985–90, Vice-Chair. 1990; Vice-Chair. Man. Bd ABN AMRO Holding NV 1991–92, Chair. 1992; Vice-Chair. Amsterdam-Rotterdam Bank NV 1990–; Vice-Chair. ABN AMRO Bank NV 1991–92, Chair. 1992–94; Chair. Supervisory Bd Heineken NV, NV Koninklijke Bijenkorf Beheer KBB, Stork NV, ABN, AMRO Bank NV; mem. Supervisory Bd Nedlloyd NV, Corus Group PLC. *Leisure interest:* playing golf. *Address:* Nw. Bussummerweg 208, 1272 CN Huizen, Netherlands (home).

HAZELTINE, Richard Deimel, MS, PhD; American physicist and academic; *Professor of Physics, University of Texas;* b. 12 June 1942, Jersey City, NJ; s. of the late Alan Hazeltine and of Elizabeth Barrett Hazeltine; m. Cheryl Pickett 1964; one s. one d.; ed Harvard Coll. and Univ. of Michigan; mem. Inst. for Advanced Study 1969–71; research scientist, Univ. of Texas, Austin 1971–82, Prof. of Physics 1986–, Asst Dir Inst. for Fusion Studies 1982–86, Acting Dir 1987–88, 1991, Dir 1991–2002; Assoc. Ed. Reviews of Modern Physics 1990–; Fellow, American Physical Soc., AAAS. *Publications:* Plasma Confinement (with J. D. Meiss) 1992, Framework of Plasma Physics (with F. Waelbroeck) 1998; more than 130 articles in scientific journals. *Address:* University of Texas at Austin, Inst. for Fusion Studies, 1 University Station, CI500, Austin, TX 78712-0262, USA (office). *Telephone:* (512) 471-4307 (office). *Fax:* (512) 471-6715 (office). *E-mail:* rdh@physics.utexas.edu (office).

HAZEN, Paul Mandeville, MBA; American banker; *Chairman, Accel-KKR;* b. 1941, Lansing, Mich.; m.; ed Univ. of Ariz. and Univ. of Calif., Berkeley; Asst Man. Security Pacific Bank 1964–66; Vice-Pres. Union Bank 1966–70; Chair. Wells Fargo Realty Advisors 1970–76; with Wells Fargo Bank, San Francisco 1979–, Exec. Vice-Pres. and Man. Real Estate Industries Group 1979–80, mem. Exec. Office 1980, Vice-Chair. 1980–84, Pres. and COO 1984–94, Chair. 1995–, also Dir; Pres. and Treas. Wells Fargo Mortgage & Equity Trust 1977–84; with Wells Fargo & Co. (parent), San Francisco 1978–2001, Exec. Vice-Pres., then Vice-Chair., Pres., COO and Dir 1978–95, CEO 1995–98, Chair. 1998–2001; currently Chair. Accel-KKR, KKR Financial Corpn; Deputy Chair. and Lead Ind. Dir Vodafone Group plc; Trustee, Wells Fargo Mortgage and Equity Trust; mem. Bd of Dirs Pacific Telesis Group, Alias Systems, Safeway Inc., Xstrada AG, Willis Group Ltd. *Address:* 2500 Sand Hill Road, Suite 100, Menlo Park, CA 94025, USA. *Telephone:* (650) 289-2460 (office). *Fax:* (650) 289-2461 (office). *E-mail:* inquiries@accel-kkr.com (office). *Website:* www.accel-kkr.com (office).

HAZIM, His Beatitude Ignatius IV; Lebanese ecclesiastic; *Greek Orthodox Patriarch of Antioch and All the East;* b. 1920, Mharde; ed Beirut Univ. and Institut Saint-Serge, Paris; Dir of a secondary Theological Inst., Beirut, Lebanon; Rector of Theological Inst. Balamand Monastery then elected Bishop of Lattakia, Syria 1966, took up post 1970; Greek Orthodox Patriarch of Antioch and All the East (with jurisdiction over Syria, Lebanon, Iran and Iraq) 1979–; several times Pres. Middle East Council of Churches, Geneva; Founder Univ. of Balamand, Lebanon 1987, Pres. Bd of Trustees; lectures in European and Middle-Eastern univs. *Publications:* La résurrection et l'homme d'aujourd'hui and in Arabic: I Believe, The Telling of Your Word Enlightens, Words on Pastoral Matters, The Church in the Middle East (trans. of the work by Père Corbon), God's Design (trans. of the work by Suzanne de Dietrich). *Address:* Patriarcat Grec-Orthodoxe, PO Box 9, Damascus, Syria. *Telephone:* (11) 5424400 (office). *Fax:* (11) 5424404 (office). *E-mail:* info@antiochpat.org (office). *Website:* www.antiochpat.org (office).

HAZZARD, Shirley, FRSL; Australian/American writer; b. 30 Jan. 1931, Sydney, Australia; d. of Reginald Hazzard and Catherine Hazzard; m. Francis Steegmuller 1963 (died 1994); ed Queenwood School, Sydney; Special Operations Intelligence, Hong Kong 1947–48; UK High Commr's Office, Wellington, NZ 1949–50; UN, New York (Gen. Service Category) 1952–61; novelist and writer of short stories and contrib. to The New Yorker 1960–;

Guggenheim Fellow 1974; mem. American Acad. of Arts and Letters, American Acad. of Arts and Sciences; Hon. Citizen of Capri 2000; American Acad. of Arts and Letters Award in Literature 1966, First Prize, O. Henry Short Story Awards 1976, Nat. Book Critics Award for Fiction, USA 1981, Boyer Lecturer, Australia 1984, 1988, Clifton Fadiman Medal for Literature 2001, Nat. Book Award for Fiction 2003, William Dean Howells Medal, American Acad. of Arts and Letters 2005. *Publications:* short stories: Cliffs of Fall 1963; novels: The Evening of the Holiday 1966, People in Glass Houses 1967, The Bay of Noon 1970, The Transit of Venus (Nat. Critics Circle Award for Fiction 1981) 1980, The Great Fire (Nat. Book Award for Fiction) 2003, Australia (Miles Franklin Prize 2004) 2004; non-fiction: Defeat of an Ideal: A Study of the Self-destruction of the United Nations 1973, Countenance of Truth: The United Nations and the Waldheim Case 1990, Greene on Capri (memoir) 2000, Ancient Shore: Dispatches from Naples (with Francis Steegmuller) 2009. *Leisure interest:* parthenophile.

HE, Chunlin; Chinese politician; *Chairman, Internal and Judicial Affairs Committee, 10th National People's Congress;* b. Aug. 1933, Wuxi City, Jiangsu Prov.; ed Northeast China Agricultural Coll.; joined CCP 1951; technician, engineer, then Deputy Section Chief and Section Chief, Chinese Acad. of Agricultural Mechanization Sciences 1962–66; clerk, Org. Dept, CCP Hebei Prov. Cttee 1966–67; Deputy Chief, Science and Tech. Div., Agricultural Machinery Research Inst., First Ministry of Machine-Building Industry 1972–78; Chief, Comprehensive Div., Survey and Research Section, Ministry of Agricultural Machinery 1979–80, Dir, Gen. Office and of Survey and Research Section 1980–82; Dir Special Econ. Zones Office of State Council 1984–93; Deputy Sec.-Gen. State Council 1988–98 (Deputy Sec. CCP Leading Party Group 1988–91); Head, Nat. Leading Group for Suppressing Smuggling 1993; mem. State Leading Group for Science and Tech. 1996; mem. Hong Kong Special Admin. Region Preparatory Cttee, Govt Del. at Hong Kong Hand-Over Ceremony 1997; Sec.-Gen. 9th Standing Cttee of NPC 1998–2003, Chair. Internal and Judicial Affairs Cttee of 10th NPC 2003–, Chair. Credentials Cttee 2003–; mem. 14th CCP Cen. Cttee 1992–97, 15th CCP Cen. Cttee 1997–2002. *Address:* State Council, Beijing, People's Republic of China.

HE, Guangwei; Chinese civil servant; *Director, China National Tourism Administration;* Deputy Dir China Nat. Tourism Admin. 1986–95, Dir 1995–. *Address:* China National Tourism Administration, 9A Jian Guo Men Nei Dajie, Beijing 100740, People's Republic of China. *Telephone:* (10) 65138866. *Fax:* (10) 65122096.

HE, Guangyuan; Chinese state official; b. 1930, Anxin Co., Hebei Prov.; ed No. 9 Middle School, Hebei Mil. Dist, PLA Beijing Mil. Region; joined CCP 1945, PLA 194; Deputy Dir Forging Sub-Plant, Changchun No. 1 Motor Vehicle Plant, Changchun City, Jilin Prov. 1956–66, Dir 1966; criticized and denounced in Cultural Revolution 1966–70; Vice-Mayor of Changchun City 1980–82; Vice-Minister of Agricultural Machinery 1980 (Deputy Sec. CCP Leading Party Group); Vice-Minister of Machinery and Electronics Industry 1982–88, Minister 1988–93, of Machine-Building Industry 1993–96; Alt. mem. 12th CCP Cen. Cttee 1982–87, 13th Cen. Cttee 1987–92; mem. 14th CCP Cen. Cttee 1992–97; mem. Standing Cttee, 8th CPPCC 1993–98, 9th CPPCC 1998–2003, Chair. Motions Cttee 9th CPPCC Nat. Cttee 1998–2003. *Address:* c/o National Committee of Chinese People's Political Consultative Conference, 23 Taipingqiao Street, Beijing, People's Republic of China.

HE, Guoqiang; Chinese politician; *Secretary, Central Commission for Discipline Inspection, Chinese Communist Party Central Committee;* b. Oct. 1943, Xiangxiang Co., Hunan Prov.; ed Beijing Chemical Eng Inst.; joined CCP 1966; fmr technician, later Dir Synthesizing Workshop, Lunan Chemical Fertilizer Plant, Shandong Prov. (Sec. CCP Party Br. 1967–78), later Deputy Dir Lunan Chemical Fertilizer Plant, Deputy Chief Engineer 1978–80; Dir Control Office, People's Govt, Shandong Prov. 1980–82; Deputy Dir-Gen. and CCP Sec. Shandong Petro-Chemical Dept 1982–84, Dir-Gen. 1984–86; mem. of the Standing Cttee of CCP Shandong Provincial Cttee, Vice-Sec., Sec. CCP Ji'nan City Cttee 1986; Vice-Minister of Chemical Industry 1991–96; Vice-Sec. CCP Fujian Provincial Cttee, Acting Gov. Fujian Prov. 1996–97, Gov. 1997–99; Sec. CCP Chongqing Municipal Cttee 1999–2002; mem. 12th CCP Cen. Cttee 1982–87, 13th CCP Cen. Cttee 1987–92, 14th CCP Cen. Cttee 1992–97, 15th CCP Cen. Cttee 1997–2002, 16th CCP Cen. Cttee 2002–07 (Head of Org. Dept and mem. Secr. of Politburo 2002–07), Standing Cttee Politburo 17th CCP Cen. Cttee 2007– (Sec. Cen. Comm. for Discipline Inspection 2007–). *Address:* Central Commission for Discipline Inspection, Central Committee of the Chinese Communist Party, Beijing, People's Republic of China (office).

HE, Kang, BSc; Chinese politician; b. 26 Feb. 1923, Hebei Prov.; m. Miao Shixia 1945; two s.; m. 2nd Yu Junmin 1993; ed Agric. Coll. of Guangxi Univ.; Chief Dir of Agric. and Forestry under Shanghai Mil. Control Cttee 1949–50; Deputy Head Dept of Agric. and Forestry under E China Mil. and Political Cttee 1950–52; Dir Dept of Special Forestry of Ministry of Forestry 1952–54; Dir Dept of Tropical Plants, Ministry of Agric. 1955–57; Dir S China Tropical Crop Science Research Inst. and Tropical Crop Coll. 1957–72; Deputy to 3rd NPC 1965–75; Deputy Dir Gen. Bureau of Land Reclamation, Guangdong Prov. 1972–77; Vice-Minister of Agric., Deputy Dir Nat. Planning Comm., Deputy Dir Nat. Comm. on Agric. 1978–82; mem. 12th CCP Cen. Cttee 1982–87, 13th Cen. Cttee 1987–93; mem. 8th NPC Standing Cttee 1993–98; Minister of Agric. 1983–90; Vice-Chair. Nat. Cttee, China Asscn for Science and Tech. 1986–96; Vice-Chair. Nat. Agric. Regional Planning Cttee 1979–90; Pres. Chinese Village & Township Enterprises Asscn 1990–2000, Chair. China-Bangladesh Friendship Asscn 1993–; Vice-Chair. Zhongkai Inst. of Agric. Tech.; Hon. DUniv (Maryland, USA) 1986; World Food Prize 1993. *Publications:* Agricultural Reform and Development in China, Rubber Culture in Northern Tropical Area (ed. and writer). *Leisure interests:* photography, listening to music, reading. *Address:* c/o Ministry of Agriculture, 11 Nongzhanguan Nanli, Chaoyang Qu, Beijing 100026, People's Republic of China (office). *Telephone:* (10) 64192406 (office). *Fax:* (10) 64192468 (office). *E-mail:* heyu@agri.gov.cn (office).

HE, Luli; Chinese politician and paediatrician; *Vice-Chairman, 10th Standing Committee, National People's Congress;* b. 7 June 1934, Jinan, Shandong Prov.; d. of the late He Siyuan and He Yiwen; m. Rong Guohuang 1958 (died 1989); two s.; ed Beijing Coll. of Medicine; paediatrician, Beijing Children's Hosp. 1957–, Beijing No. 2 Hosp. 1988–96; Deputy Head, People's Govt, Xicheng Dist, Beijing 1984–88; Vice-Mayor Beijing Municipality 1988–96; Vice-Chair. Cen. Cttee, 7th Revolutionary Cttee of the Chinese Kuomintang (RCCK) 1988–92, Vice-Chair. Women and Youth Cttee, RCCK 1988–96, Chair. Beijing Municipal Cttee 1988–93, Chair. Cen. Cttee of 8th RCCK 1992–97, Chair. Cen. Cttee of 9th RCCK 1997–2002; Pres. Cen. Acad. of Socialism 1999–; mem. CPPCC 8th Nat. Cttee 1993–98, Vice-Chair. 1996–98; Vice-Chair. Standing Cttee of 9th NPC 1998–2003, of 10th NPC 2003–; Vice-Pres. Exec. Cttee of All China Women's Fed. 1993–; Pres. China Population Welfare Foundation 2000–; mem. Govt Del. at Macao Hand-Over Ceremony, Macao Special Admin. Region Preparatory Cttee 1999; Hon. Vice-Pres. Red Cross Soc. of China 1999; honoured as Nat. March 8 Red-Banner Bearer 1994. *Address:* Central Academy of Socialism, Beijing 100081, People's Republic of China.

HE, Ping; Chinese news agency executive; *Editor-in-Chief, Xinhua News Agency;* b. 1957; ed Beijing Univ.; Deputy Ed.-in-Chief, Xinhua News Agency 1982–2007, Vice-Pres. 1993–2007, Ed.-in-Chief 2007–. *Address:* Xinhua, 20F Dacheng Plaza, 127 Xhuanwumen Street West, Beijing 100031, People's Republic of China (office). *E-mail:* xxp69@xinhuanet.com (office). *Website:* www.xinhuanet.com (office).

HE, Maj.-Gen. Qizong; Chinese army officer; b. 1943, Yingshan Co., Sichuan Prov.; joined PLA 1961; joined CCP 1965; Deputy Commdr Kunming Mil. Region 1979–85; Chief of Staff of Div. 1982–83, Div. Commdr 1983, Deputy Commdr of Army 1983–84, Commdr 1984–85, Deputy Chief of Gen. Staff, PLA 1985; Alt. mem. 13th CCP Cen. Cttee 1987–92; Alt. mem. 14th Cen. Cttee 1992–97; Deputy Commdr Nanjing Mil. Region 1993–; rank of Maj.-Gen. 1988. *Address:* People's Liberation Army General Staff Headquarters, Beijing, People's Republic of China.

HE, Xiangjian; Chinese business executive; *Chairman and CEO, Guangdong Midea Electric Appliances Co. Ltd (Midea Group);* b. 1941, Guangdong Prov.; m.; one s.; co-founded with 23 neighbours (fmr rice-farmers and fishermen) Beijiao Neighbourhood Plastic Production Team 1968 (renamed Midea 1981), currently Chair. and CEO Guangdong Midea Electric Appliances Co. Ltd. *Address:* Guangdong Midea Electric Appliances Co. Ltd, Midea Industrial City, Shunde District, Foshan 528311, Guangdong, People's Republic of China (office). *Telephone:* (757) 26338823 (office). *Fax:* (757) 26651991 (office). *E-mail:* inquiry@midea.com.cn (office). *Website:* www.midea.com.cn (office).

HE, Yong; Chinese politician; *Deputy Secretary, Standing Committee, Central Commission for Discipline Inspection, 17th Chinese Communist Party Central Committee;* b. Oct. 1940, Qianxi Co., Hebei Prov.; ed Tianjin Univ.; joined CCP 1958; technician, Metering Office, No. 238 Factory 1968–70, Production Sec., Head Office 1970–75, Dir Political Dept 1975–78 (mem. Standing Cttee of CCP Party Cttee 1975–78), Dir No. 238 Factory 1978–83 (Deputy Sec. CCP Party Cttee 1978–83); Deputy Dir Office of Science, Tech. and Industry for Nat. Defence, Hubei Prov. 1983–85; Dir-Gen. Personnel Dept, Ministry of Ordinance Industry 1985–86; Deputy Head, Org. Dept of CCP Cen. Cttee 1986–87, Dir Bureau of Party and Govt Personnel Engaged in Foreign Affairs 1986–87; Vice-Minister of Supervision 1987–98, Minister 1998–2002; mem. Standing Cttee of 14th CCP Cen. Comm. for Discipline Inspection 1992–97, mem. 15th CCP Cen. Cttee 1997–2002 (Deputy Sec. Cen. Comm. for Discipline Inspection 1997–2002), 16th CCP Cen. Cttee 2002–07 (mem. Politburo Secr. 2002–07, Deputy Sec. Standing Cttee of Cen. Comm. for Discipline Inspection 2002–07); mem. 17th CCP Cen. Cttee 2007–, Deputy Sec. Cen. Comm. for Discipline Inspection 2007–. *Address:* c/o Zhongguo Gongchan Dang (Chinese Communist Party), Beijing, People's Republic of China.

HE, Zehui, EngD; Chinese physicist; b. 5 March 1914, Suzhou City, Jiangsu Prov.; m. Qian Sanqiang (deceased); three d.; ed Qinghua Univ., Berlin Univ., Germany; first woman nuclear scientist in China; researcher, Curie Inst., France 1941–48; researcher, Modern Physics Inst., Academia Sinica 1953–; Vice-Dir Inst. of Atomic Energy, Academia Sinica 1964–66; in disgrace during Cultural Revolution 1966–76; rehabilitated 1977; Deputy Dir Inst. of High Energy Physics, Academia Sinica 1978–; mem., Dept of Math. and Physics, Academia Sinica 1985–; mem. Chinese Acad. of Sciences 1980–; won Third Prize of Academia Sinica Science Awards for paper Research into the Process of Preparing Nuclear Emulsoid 1957; Ho Leung Ho Lee Foundation Physics Prize 2006. *Address:* Room 203, Building 14, Zhong Guan Cun, Beijing 100080, People's Republic of China (office). *Telephone:* 284314 (office).

HE, Zhenliang; Chinese government official (retd); b. 29 Dec. 1929, Zhejiang Prov.; m. 1953; one s. one d.; ed Aurora Univ., Shanghai; Sec.-Gen. Chinese Olympic Cttee 1982–86, Vice-Pres. 1986–89, Pres. 1989–94, Hon. Pres. 1994–; Dir Int. Liaison Dept, State Comm. of Physical Culture and Sports 1982–85, Vice Minister 1985–94; Vice-Pres. Int. Ass. for the Nat. Org. of Sports 1984; mem. IOC 1981–, Exec. Bd 1985–89, 1994–98, 1999–, Vice-Pres. 1989–93, Pres. Cultural Comm. 1995–99, Pres. Cultural and Olympic Education Comm. 2000–; Vice-Chair. All-China Sports Fed. 1986, Councillor 1997–; mem. CPPCC 1988–92, Standing Cttee of CPPCC 1993–98; Pres. Athletic Asscn of People's Repub. of China 1992–96, Rowing Asscn of People's Repub. of China

1986–, Rowing Fed. of Asia 1990–94. *Address:* 9 Tiyuguan Road, Beijing, People's Republic of China.

HE, Zhiqiang; Chinese government official and engineer; b. 1934, Lijiang Co., Yunnan Prov.; ed Chongqing Univ.; joined CCP 1956; Deputy Chief Engineer, Yunnan Prov. Geological Bureau 1979–83, Deputy Dir 1985; Vice-Gov. of Yunnan Prov. 1983–85, Gov. 1985–98; Deputy Sec., CCP 6th Yunnan Prov. Cttee 1995–; NPC Deputy for Yunnan Prov.; Alt. mem. 13th CCP Cen. Cttee 1987–92, mem. 14th CCP Cen. Cttee 1992–97; Del., 15th CCP Nat. Congress 1997–2002; mem. Standing Committee of 9th CPPCC 1998–2003; Chinese Population Prize 1996. *Address:* Yunnan Provincial Government, 5 Wuchua Shan Road, Kunming City, Yunnan Province, People's Republic of China.

HE, Zuoxiu; Chinese physicist; *Deputy Director of Theoretical Physics Institute, Academia Sinica;* b. 27 July 1927, Shanghai; m. Qing Chengrui 1962; one s.; ed Shanghai Jiaotong Univ., Qinghua Univ.; researcher, Beijing Modern Physics Inst. and Atomic Energy Inst., Academia Sinica 1951–80; Deputy Dir Theoretical Physics Inst., Academia Sinica 1980–, mem. Dept of Math. and Physics, Academia Sinica 1980–; fmr mem. Standing Cttee CPPCC. *Publications:* A New Possible Quantum Field Theory of Composite Particles, (with Falung Gong), From Theory of Elementary Chi to Particle Physics, Wind Power – the most realistic and best choice for sustainable devt of China 2004. *Address:* Theoretical Physics Institute, PO Box 2735, Beijing 100080, People's Republic of China (office). *Telephone:* (10) 62569352 (office). *Fax:* (10) 62562587 (office). *E-mail:* qcr@itp.ac.cn (office); lijing@itp.ac.cn. *Website:* itp.ac.cn.

HEAD, Alan Kenneth, AO, DSc, FAA, FRS; Australian physicist and mathematician; *Honorary Research Fellow, Division of Manufacturing Science, Commonwealth Scientific and Industrial Research Organisation (CISRO);* b. 10 Aug. 1925, Melbourne; s. of Rowland H. J. and Elsie M. (née Burrell) Head; m. Gwenneth N Barlow 1951; ed Univ. of Melbourne and Univ. of Bristol; Research Scientist, CSIRO Div. of Aeronautics 1947–50, Aeronautical Research Labs 1953–57, Div. of Tribophysics 1957–81, Div. of Chemical Physics 1981–86, Div. of Materials Science 1987–1990, Hon. Research Fellow 1990–; Visiting Prof., Brown Univ. 1961–62, Univ. of Florida 1971; Christensen Fellow, St Catherine's Coll., Oxford 1986; Syme Research Medal 1965. *Publications:* Computed Electron Micrographs and Defect Identification 1973. *Address:* CSIRO, Division of Manufacturing Science, Private Bag 33, Clayton South MDC, Vic. 3169 (office); 10 Ellesmore Court, Kew, Vic. 3101, Australia (home). *Telephone:* (3) 9545-2861 (office); (3) 9853-0673 (home). *Fax:* (3) 9544-1128 (office). *E-mail:* alan.head@csiro.au (office). *Website:* www.csiro.au (office).

HEAD, Tim David, BA; British artist; b. 22 Oct. 1946, London; s. of Percy Head and Muriel Head; m. Vivian Katz 1973; two d.; ed Dept of Fine Art, Univ. of Newcastle-upon-Tyne, St Martin's School of Art, London; Lecturer, Goldsmith's Coll. School of Art, London 1971–79; Lecturer, Slade School of Fine Art, Univ. Coll. London 1976–; Fellowship at Clare Hall and Kettle's Yard, Cambridge 1977–78; Gulbenkian Foundation Visual Arts Award 1975, First Prize, John Moores Liverpool Exhbn 15, Walker Art Gallery, Liverpool 1987, Wellcome Trust Artist's Residency, Dept of Biochemistry, Oxford Univ. 2006–07. *Commissions:* Sculpture, Nat. Museum of Photography, Film and TV, Bradford, Yorks. 1985, Floor Design, Science Museum, London 1995 Installation, Chatham Historic Dockyard, Rochester, Kent, Sculpture, Dance Performance with Laurie Booth Co. 1997–98, Light Rain, Artezium Arts and Media Centre, Luton 1998, A Hard Day's Night (CD ROM) 2000 www.eyes-torm.com; Artistic Dir Eurythmics Peace Tour 1999. *Address:* c/o The Slade School of Fine Art UCL, Gower Street, London WC1E 6BT, England. *E-mail:* info@timhead.net (home). *Website:* www.timhead.net (home).

HEAL, (Barbara) Jane, PhD, FBA; British academic; *Professor of Philosophy, University of Cambridge;* b. 21 Oct. 1946, Oxford; d. of William Calvert Kneale and Martha Kneale (née Hurst); m. John Gauntlett Benedict Heal 1968 (divorced 1987); one s. one d.; ed Oxford High School for Girls, New Hall, Cambridge; Research Fellow, Newnham Coll., Cambridge 1971–74; Harkness Fellow of the Commonwealth Fund, Visiting Fellow, Princeton Univ. and Univ. of California, Berkeley, USA 1974–76; Lecturer in Philosophy, Univ. of Newcastle upon Tyne 1976–86, Univ. of Cambridge 1986–96, Reader in Philosophy 1996–99, Prof. 1999–; Pres. St John's Coll. 1999–2003. *Publications:* Fact and Meaning 1989, Mind, Reason and Imagination 2003. *Address:* St John's College, Cambridge, CB2 1TP, England (office). *Telephone:* (1223) 338668 (office); (1223) 314317 (home). *E-mail:* jane.heal@phil.cam.ac.uk (office). *Website:* www.phil.cam.ac.uk (office).

HEALEY, Baron (Life Peer), cr. 1992, of Riddlesden in the County of West Yorkshire; **Denis Winston Healey,** PC, CH, MBE, FRSL, MA, DPhil; British politician; b. 30 Aug. 1917, Mottingham; s. of William Healey; m. Edna May Edmunds 1945; one s. two d.; ed Bradford Grammar School and Balliol Coll., Oxford; Maj., Royal Engineers 1945; Sec. Labour Party Int. Dept 1945–52; MP 1952–92; Sec. of State for Defence 1964–70; Chancellor of the Exchequer 1974–79; Opposition Spokesman for Treasury and Econ. Affairs 1979–80, for Foreign and Commonwealth Affairs 1980–87; Chair. Interim Ministerial Cttee of IMF 1977–79; Deputy Leader of Labour Party 1980–83; Pres. Birkbeck Coll. London 1993–99; Hon. Fellow, Balliol Coll. Oxford 1980; Freeman of Leeds 1991; Grand Cross of Order of Merit (FRG) 1979; Hon. DLitt (Bradford) 1983; Hon. LLD, (Sussex) 1989, (Leeds) 1991. *Publications:* The Curtain Falls 1951, New Fabian Essays 1952, Neutralism 1955, Fabian International Essays 1956, A Neutral Belt in Europe 1958, NATO and American Security 1959, The Race Against the H Bomb 1960, Labour Britain and the World 1963, Healey's Eye (photographs) 1980, Labour and a World Society 1985, Beyond Nuclear Deterrence 1986, The Time of My Life (autobiog.) 1989, When Shrimps Learn to Whistle (collection of essays) 1990, My Secret Planet 1992, Denis Healey's Yorkshire Dales 1995, Healey's World (photographs) 2002. *Leisure interests:* music, painting, literature, photography. *Address:* House of Lords, Westminster, London, SW1A 0PW (office). *Telephone:* (20) 7219-3546 (office).

HEALY, Thomas William, AO, MSc, PhD, FAA; Australian chemist and academic; *Professor Emeritus and Deputy Director, Particulate Fluids Processing Centre, University of Melbourne;* b. 1 June 1937; s. of W. T. Healy and C. M. Healy; m. Beverley M. L. Fay 1960; four s.; ed St Kilda, Univ. of Melbourne and Columbia Univ., New York, USA; Lecturer in Materials Science, Univ. of California, Berkeley 1963–65, Visiting Assoc. Prof. 1970; Queen Elizabeth II Fellow, Univ. of Melbourne 1965–67, Sr Lecturer in Physical Chem. 1967–75, Reader 1976–77, Prof. 1977–98, Prof. Emer. 1998–, Professorial Fellow 1999–, Deputy Chair. School of Chem. 1979–81, Assoc. Dean (Research and Grad. Studies), Faculty of Science 1983–84, Dean 1985–90, mem. Council Univ. of Melbourne 1985–88, Dir Advanced Mineral Products Special Research Centre 1991–99, Vice-Pres. Academic Bd 1994–96, Pres. and Pro-Vice-Chancellor 1997–98, Deputy Dir Particulate Fluids Processing Centre (ARC), Dept of Chemical and Biomolecular Eng 2000–04 (Chair. Scientific Bd 2005), mem. Bd Ian Potter Museum of Art 2004; Sr Visiting Research Fellow, Univ. of Bristol, UK 1975; Visiting Sr Research Scientist, ICI Corp. Colloid Group, Runcorn, Cheshire, UK 1981; Fulbright Sr Scholar, Inst. of Colloid and Surface Science, Clarkson Univ., Potsdam, NY, USA 1981; Visiting Prof., Columbia Univ., New York 2001; mem. Council Australian Research Council (ARC) 1993–, Chair. Institutional Grants Cttee 1995–96, mem. Planning and Review Cttee ARC-ANU Review of the Inst. of Advanced Studies 1994–95, Research Grants Appeals Cttee 1998–2004; Vice-Pres. Victorian Br. Royal Australian Chemical Inst. (RACI) 1983, Pres. 1984, mem. Cttee 1972–74, 1976, 1982–85, mem. Exec. Council RACI 1984; Deputy Chair. Victorian Univs and Schools Examination Bd Science Standing Cttee 1977–79, Course Advisory Cttee, Bendigo, Victorian Inst. of Colls of Advanced Educ.; mem. numerous review bds; Dir UniMelb Ltd 1990–92; part-time consultant to Geopeko Pty Ltd, Australia Mt Morgan Mines Pty Ltd, Australia Peko Wallsend Pty Ltd, BHP Co. Ltd Australia, Monier Ltd, ICI (Australia) Ltd, Tioxide (Australia) Pty Ltd, Burnie, Tasmania and Tioxide International Ltd, Teeside, UK, ICI UK Ltd, ICI Glidden Paints USA, Orica Pty Ltd, Lachlan Resources Pty Ltd NSW, Davies Ryan & De Boos, Corr Pavey Whiting & Byrne, Kitchener Mines Pty Ltd, Supreme Court of NSW, Mallesons, Brisbane, Sienna, NSW; Gov. Ian Potter Foundation 1990–; Chair. Australian Landscape Trust 1995–; mem. Australasian Inst. of Mining and Metallurgy, Royal Soc. of Chem. (Faraday Div.), Soc. of Sigma XI, Council Victorian Inst. of Marine Sciences 1986; mem. and Founding Cttee mem. Int. Asscn of Colloid and Interface Scientists 1979–, Div. of Colloid and Surface Chem., Chemical Soc. of Japan; mem. Editorial Advisory Bd Journal of Colloid and Interface Science 1969–74, Advances in Colloid and Interface Science 1975–; Founding Ed. and Regional Ed. Colloids and Surfaces 1979–83, mem. Editorial Advisory Bd 1979–; mem. Editorial Bd Langmuir 1987–96, Current Opinion in Colloid and Interface Science 1995–; Fellow, RACI, Australian Acad. of Technological Sciences and Eng 1991 (Asst Sec. 2001–03, Asst Hon. Treas. 2004–05); Hon. DSc (Melbourne) 1999; ACS Certificate of Merit 1967, RACI Rennie Medal 1968, Grimwade Prize, Univ. of Melbourne 1974, RACI Hartung Youth Lecturer 1979, Chemical Soc. (London) Lecturer 1980, Freundlich Centennial Lecturer, ACS 55th Colloid Symposium 1981, Liversidge Lecturer, Australia and NZ Asscn for the Advancement of Science Festival of Science 1985, RACI-ICI (Australia) Inaugural Bicentennial Lectureship 1988, Plenary Lecturer, Papua New Guinea Inst. of Chem., Fifth Congress 1988, Plenary Lecturer IACIS Conf., Hakone, Japan 1989, Plenary Lecturer, R. K. Her Symposium, ACS, Washington DC 1990, A. E. Alexander Lectureship, RACI and Univ. of Sydney 1991, Royal Soc. of Vic. Medallist 1992, Plenary Lecturer XVIth Int. Minerals Processing Congress, Sydney 1993, Plenary and Foreign Guest Lecturer, 46th Nat. Colloid Symposium, Japanese Chemical Soc., Tokyo, Japan 1993, Plenary and Foreign Guest Lecturer, Mineral Processing: Recent Advances and Future Trends, Kanpur, India 1995, Plenary and Foreign Guest Lecturer, NEPTIS-5 Conf., Kyoto, Japan 1996, Plenary and Foreign Guest Lecturer, 5 Australian Japan Symposia on Colloid and Surface Chem., Fukuoka, Japan 1998, Ian Wark Medal and Lecture, Australian Acad. of Science 1999, T. G. H. Jones Memorial Lecturer, Univ. of Queensland 2001, T. H. Healy Award est. by School of Chem., Univ. of Melbourne to commemorate his distinguished career 2002, Impact Faraday Partnership Annual Lecture, Royal Chemical Inst. of GB 2003, Australian Centenary Medal 2003, RACI 40 Year Membership Award 2003, Sr Australian of the Year (Victorian Finalist) 2004, Australasian Inst. of Mining and Metallurgy 40 Year Membership Award 2005. *Publications:* more than 200 research papers in physical chem., colloid and surface science, process eng and mineral processing. *Leisure interests:* sailing, photography, reading. *Address:* Particulate Fluids Processing Centre, Department of Chemical and Biomolecular Engineering, University of Melbourne, Melbourne, Vic. 3010 (office); 98 Barkly Street, Carlton, Vic. 3052, Australia (home). *Telephone:* (3) 83446481 (office); (3) 93474741 (home). *Fax:* (3) 83446233 (office). *E-mail:* tomhealy@unimelb.edu.au (office). *Website:* www.pfpc.unimelb.edu.au (office).

HEALY, Tom; Irish stock exchange executive; *CEO, Abu Dhabi Securities Exchange;* ed Trinity Coll., Dublin; early career with Export Board and Industrial Devt Agency; Chief Exec. Irish Stock Exchange 1987–2007 (retd), oversaw Irish Stock Exchange's demerger from London Stock Exchange 1995; CEO Abu Dhabi Securities Exchange 2007–; int. consultancy and advisory assignments included IBRD, EU, USAID; active involvement with World Fed. of Exchanges and Fed. of European Securities Exchanges; mem. Securities Inst., UK. *Address:* Abu Dhabi Securities Exchange, Al Ghaith Tower, Hamdan Street, POB 54500, Abu Dhabi, United Arab Emirates (office).

Telephone: (2) 627-7777 (office). *Fax:* (2) 627-0300 (office). *E-mail:* thealy@adsm.ae (office). *Website:* www.adsm.ae (office).

HEANEY, Seamus, CLit; Irish poet and author; *Ralph Waldo Emerson Poet in Residence, Harvard University;* b. 13 April 1939, Northern Ireland; s. of Patrick Heaney and Margaret Heaney (née McCann); m. Marie Devlin 1965; two s. one d.; ed St Columb's Coll., Londonderry, Queen's Univ., Belfast; Lecturer, St Joseph's Coll. of Educ., Belfast 1963–66, Queen's Univ., Belfast 1966–72; freelance writer 1972–75, Lecturer, Carysfort Coll. 1975–81, Sr Visiting Lecturer, Harvard Univ. 1982–84, Boylston Prof. of Rhetoric and Oratory 1985–97, Ralph Waldo Emerson Poet in Residence 1998–; Prof. of Poetry, Univ. of Oxford 1989–94; Hon. DLitt (Oxford) 1997, (Birmingham) 2000; Commdr des Arts et Lettres; WH Smith Prize 1975, Bennet Award 1982, Sunday Times Award for Excellence in Writing 1988, Lannan Literary Award 1990, Nobel Prize for Literature 1996, Cunningham Medal, Royal Irish Acad. 2008, Lifetime Achievement Award, Queen's Univ., Belfast 2008, David Cohen Prize for Literature 2009. *Poems:* Eleven Poems 1965, Death of a Naturalist 1966, Door into the Dark 1969, Wintering Out 1972, North 1975, Field Work 1979, Selected Poems 1965–1975 1980, Station Island 1984, The Haw Lantern 1987, New Selected Poems 1966–1987 1990, Seeing Things 1991, The Spirit Level 1996 (Whitbread Book of the Year Award 1997), Opened Ground: Poems 1966–96 1998 (Irish Times Literary Award 1999), Beowulf: A New Verse Translation 1999, Electric Light 2001, The Testament of Cresseid (a retelling of Robert Henryson's poem) 2005, District and Circle (T.S. Eliot Prize for Poetry) 2006. *Prose:* Preoccupations: Selected Prose 1968–1978 1980, The Government of the Tongue 1988, The Place of Writing 1990, The Redress of Poetry (lectures) 1995, Finders Keepers: Selected Prose 1971–2001 2002, The Midnight Verdict 2002. *Anthology:* The School Bag 1997 (co-ed. with Ted Hughes). *Plays:* The Cure at Troy 1991, The Burial at Thebes (Abbey Theatre, Dublin) 2004. *Translations:* Sweeney Astray 1984, Sweeney's Flight 1992, Laments, by Jan Kochanowski (with Stanislaw Baranczak); Beowulf: a New Verse Translation (Whitbread Book of the Year 1999) 1999. *Address:* Steven Barclay Agency, 12 Western Avenue, Petaluma, CA 94952, USA (office); c/o Faber and Faber, Bloomsbury House, 74–77 Great Russell Street, London, WC1B 3DA, England (office). *Telephone:* (707) 773-0654 (office). *Fax:* (707) 778-1868 (office). *Website:* www.barclayagency.com (office); www.faber.co.uk (office).

HEAP, Sir Robert Brian, Kt, KBE, CBE, MA, PhD, ScD, FRS, CChem, FRSC, FIBiol; British research scientist and academic; *Vice-President, European Academies Science Advisory Council;* b. 27 Feb. 1935, Derbyshire; s. of the late Bertram Heap and Eva M. Melling; m. Marion P. Grant 1961; two s. one d.; ed New Mills Grammar School, Univ. of Nottingham and King's Coll., Cambridge; Univ. Demonstrator, Cambridge 1960; Lalor Research Fellow, ARC Babraham, Cambridge, staff mem. 1964, Head, Dept of Physiology 1976, Head Cambridge Research Station 1986; Dir of Research, Agricultural and Food Research Council (AFRC) Inst. of Animal Physiology and Genetics Research, Cambridge and Edinburgh 1989–93, Dir of Science, Biotechnology and Biological Sciences Research Council 1991–94, Dir of Research, Babraham Inst. 1993–94; UK Rep., NATO Science Cttee, Brussels 1997–2005; Visiting Prof., Univ. of Nairobi 1974; Visiting Research Fellow, Murdoch Univ. 1976; Special Prof., Univ. of Nottingham 1988–; Visiting Prof., Univ. of Guelph, Canada 1990; Visiting Sr Fellow, School of Clinical Medicine, Univ. of Cambridge 1994–2002, Babraham Inst. 1995; Master St Edmund's Coll., Cambridge 1996–2004; fmr Ed. Philosophical Transactions of the Royal Society, Series B; Pres. Inst. of Biology 1996–98, Int. Soc. of Science and Religion 2006–08; Vice-Pres. European Acads Science Advisory Council; Chair. Trustees Academia Europaea; mem. Council Royal Soc. 1994–2001 (Foreign Sec. and Vice-Pres. 1996–2001), Nuffield Council on Bioethics 1997–2001; other professional appointments and distinctions; Hon. Fellow, Royal Agricultural Soc. of England 1995, Zoological Soc. of London, Green Coll. Oxford, St Edmund's Coll. Cambridge, Korean Acad. of Science; Hon. DSc (Nottingham) 1994; Hon. DUniv (York) 2001, (St Andrews) 2007. *Publications:* papers on reproductive biology, endocrinology, growth, lactation, science policy and biotechnology in biological and medical journals. *Leisure interests:* music, walking, travel. *Address:* St Edmund's College, Cambridge, CB3 0BN (office); Lincoln House, 8 Fendon Road, Cambridge, CB1 7RT, England (home). *Telephone:* (1223) 248509 (home). *E-mail:* rbh22@cam.ac.uk (office).

HEARN, Loyola; Canadian politician; b. Renews, Newfoundland; m. Maureen Hearn; one s. one d.; ed Memorial Univ., Univ. of New Brunswick; elected mem. Newfoundland House of Ass. for St Mary's the Capes, Newfoundland 1982–93; Minister of Educ. for Newfoundland and Labrador 1985–89; left politics and returned to teaching in Renews 1993–2000; MP 2000– (re-elected for new riding of St John's South-Mount Pearl 2004), House Leader for Progressive Conservative Party (later first House Leader for new Conservative Party of Canada following merger with Canadian Alliance parties), also held several critic roles, including lead critic for Fisheries and Oceans; Minister of Fisheries and Oceans and Regional Minister for Newfoundland and Labrador 2006–08. *Address:* Conservative Party of Canada, 130 Albert Street, Suite 1204, Ottawa, ON K1P 5G4, Canada (office). *Telephone:* (613) 755-2000 (office). *Fax:* (613) 755-2001 (office). *Website:* www.conservative.ca (office); www.loyolahearnmp.ca.

HEARNE, Sir Graham James, Kt, CBE; British business executive and solicitor; *Deputy Chairman, Gallaher Group PLC;* b. 23 Nov. 1937, Birmingham; s. of Frank Hearne and Emily (née Shakespeare) Hearne; m. Carol Jean Brown 1961; one s. three d.; ed George Dixon Grammar School, Birmingham; admitted solicitor 1959; with Pinsent & Co. Solicitors 1959–63, Fried, Frank, Harris, Shriver & Jacobson Attorneys, New York 1963–66, Herbert Smith & Co., Solicitors 1966–67, Industrial Reorganization Corpn 1967–68, N.M. Rothschild & Sons Ltd 1968–77; Finance Dir Courtaulds Ltd 1977–81; Chief Exec. Tricentrol 1981–83; Group Man. Dir Carless, Capel & Leonard 1983–84; Dir (non-exec.) N. M. Rothschild & Sons Ltd 1977–, Courtaulds PLC 1991–98, Gallaher Group PLC 1997–, now Deputy Chair., Invensys (fmrly BTR) PLC 1998–2003, Seascope PLC 1999–; Chief Exec. Enterprise Oil PLC 1984–91, Chair. 1991–2002; Dir Novar (fmrly Caradon) PLC 1999–2005, Rowan Companies Inc. 2004–, Stratic Energy Corpn 2005–; High Sheriff of Greater London 1995–96. *Address:* Gallaher Group PLC, Members Hill, Brooklands Road, Weybridge, Surrey, KT13 0QU, England (office). *Telephone:* (1932) 859777 (office). *Fax:* (1932) 832532 (office). *E-mail:* info@gallaherltd.com (office). *Website:* www.gallaher-group.com (office).

HEARNS, Thomas; American fmr professional boxer; b. 18 Oct. 1958, Grand Junction, Tenn.; as amateur won 147 of 155 fights, Amateur Athletic Union (AAU) national and Golden Gloves 147–pound championships 1977; turned professional Nov. 1977 winning 28 straight fights before winning World Boxing Asscn (WBA) welterweight championship knocking out Pepino Cuevas 1980; lost title on technical knockout to Sugar Ray Leonard 1981; won World Boxing Council (WBC) super welterweight championship beating Wilfred Benitez 1982, beat Roberto Duran to win WBA version 1984; as middleweight lost to Marvelous Marvin Hagler for world middleweight championship 1985; won WBC world light-heavyweight championship from Dennis Andries and WBC middleweight championship beating Juan Roldan 1987; won World Boxing Org. (WBO) super-middleweight championship by beating James Kinchen 1988; rematch with Leonard ending in draw 1989; won WBA light-heavyweight championship 1991, lost it to Ivan Barkley 1992; won North American Boxing Fed. (NABF) cruiserweight title 1995, won Int. Boxing Org. (IBO) version 1999, lost IBO title to Uriah Grant 2000; in professional career won 59 of 64 fights (46 by knockout) with one draw. *Address:* 19244 Bretton Drive, Detroit, MI 48223, USA.

HEARST, George Randolph, Jr; American communications industry executive; *Chairman, The Hearst Corporation;* b. 13 July 1927, San Francisco; s. of George Randolph Hearst and Blanche Wilbur; m. 1st Mary Thompson 1951 (died 1969); two s. two d.; m. 2nd Patricia Ann Bell 1969 (divorced 1985); Staff Los Angeles Examiner 1948–50, San Francisco Examiner 1954–56, Los Angeles Evening Herald-Express 1956– (Business Man. 1957, Publr 1960–); Publr Los Angeles Herald-Examiner 1962; Vice-Pres. The Hearst Corpn 1977–96, Chair. 1996–; Pres. The Hearst Foundation, Dir William Randolph Hearst Foundation. *Address:* The Hearst Corporation, 959 8th Avenue, New York, NY 10019, USA (office). *Telephone:* (212) 649-2148 (office). *Fax:* (212) 649-2108 (office). *Website:* www.hearstcorp.com (office).

HEATHER-LATU, Brenda Patricia, LLB, BA; Samoan/New Zealand barrister and solicitor; *Partner, Latu Ey & Clarke, Solicitors;* b. 23 Dec. 1961, Wellington, New Zealand; d. of Cuthbert Stanley Heather and Winnie Anesi Heather; m. George Latu; one d.; ed Wellington Girls Coll., Victoria Univ. of Wellington; solicitor, Educ. Dept Legal Div. 1987–88; Asst Crown Counsel, Crown Law Office, Wellington 1988–91, Crown Counse 1991–96; Prin. State Solicitor, Office of the Attorney-Gen., Apia, Samoa 1996–97; Attorney-Gen. of Samoa 1997–2006; Partner, Latu Ey & Clarke, Solicitors. *Publications:* Pacific Islands AIDS Trust Education Prevention Programme 1993. *Leisure interests:* family, cuisine, genealogy, Samoan culture and traditions. *Address:* Latu Ey & Clarke, Solicitors, First Floor, Post Office Bldg, PO Box 6335, Apia, Samoa (office). *Telephone:* 30363 (office). *Fax:* 30365 (office). *E-mail:* heather-latu@latueylaw.com (office).

HEATON, Brian Thomas, DPhil, DSc, CChem, FRSC; British chemist and academic; *Professor Emeritus, University of Liverpool;* b. 16 Feb. 1940, Broughton-in-Furness; s. of William Edwin Heaton and Mabel Heaton (née Benson); m. Wendy Janet Durrant 1964; three d.; ed Ulverston Grammar School, Hatfield Polytechnic, Univ. of Sussex; Lecturer in Chem., Univ. of Kent at Canterbury 1968–81, Sr Lecturer 1981–84, Reader 1984, Prof. 1984–85; Grant Prof. of Inorganic Chem., Univ. of Liverpool 1985–2004, Prof. Emer. 2005–, Head of Dept of Chem. 1988–97; Chair. SERC Inorganic Cttee 1990–93; Sec. and Treas. Dalton Div., Royal Soc. of Chem. (RSC) 1990–93; Leverhulme Foundation Research Fellowship 1997; Visiting Prof., Univ. Louis Pasteur, Strasbourg 2001, Univ. of Hiedelberg, Germany 2003, Inst. of Chemical and Eng Sciences, Singapore 2007–(10), Nat. Univ. of Singapore 2008; Nuffield Foundation Research Fellowship 1981–82, RSC Tilden Lectureship and Prize 1986, Japanese Soc. for Promotion of Science Fellowship 1989, First Prize, Dept of Trade and Industry 1996, Leverhulme Foundation Research Fellowship 1997–98, RSC Award for research on platinum metals 2002. *Publications:* several books, including Mechanisms in Homogeneous Catalysis (ed.) 2005; numerous articles in professional journals. *Leisure interests:* rugby, walking, listening to and playing music, eating and drinking (especially wine). *Address:* Department of Chemistry, University of Liverpool, PO Box 147, Liverpool, L69 7ZD (office); 44 Graham Road, West Kirby, CH48 5DW, England (home). *Telephone:* (151) 794-3524 (office); (151) 632-3206 (home). *Fax:* (151) 794-3540 (office). *E-mail:* bth@liv.ac.uk (office). *Website:* www.liv.ac.uk/chemistry (office).

HEATON, Frances Anne, BA, LLB; British financial services industry executive; b. 11 Aug. 1944, Winchester, Hants.; d. of John Ferris Whidborne and Marjorie Annie Maltby; m. Martin Heaton 1969; two s.; ed Trinity Coll., Dublin; with Dept of Econ. Affairs 1967–70; joined HM Treasury 1970, Asst Sec. 1979–80; seconded to S. G. Warburg & Co. Ltd 1977–79; with Corp. Finance Div., Lazard Bros & Co. Ltd 1980, Exec. Dir 1987–2001, currently Chair. Lazard London Dirs' Pension Scheme; Dir (non-exec.) W.S. Atkins PLC 1990–2003, Deputy Chair. (non-exec.) 1996–2003; mem. Bd of Dirs (non-exec.) Bank of England (first woman) 1993–2001; Dir Gen. Take-overs and Mergers Panel 1992–94; mem. Bd of Dirs (non-exec.) Legal & General Group PLC 2001–, AWG PLC 2002–07, BMT Limited 2007–, BUPA 1998–2001, World Pay

Group PLC 2000, Fountain GB Ltd 2001; mem. Cttee on Standards in Public Life 1997–2005. *Leisure interests:* bridge, gardening, riding. *Address:* c/o Board of Directors, Legal and General Group plc, I Coleman Street, London EC2R 5AA, England.

HEBEISH, Ali Ali, DSc, PhD; Egyptian chemist and academic; *Professor Emeritus, National Research Centre, Cairo;* b. 21 Dec. 1936, Mehalla El-Kubra, Gharbia; m.; two c.; ed Cairo Univ., Gujarat Univ.; Research Fellow Nat. Research Centre, Cairo 1960–61, other research positions 1962–74, Assoc. Prof. 1974–79, Prof. 1979–84, Prof. Emer. 1996–; Under-Sec. of State Office of the Pres., Acad. of Scientific Research and Tech. (ASRT), Cairo 1985–88, Vice-Pres. 1988–91, Pres. 1992–96; Pres. Egyptian Asscn for Scientific Culture 1993–, Egyptian Textile Soc. 1993–; mem. Council IFSTAD 1992–96; Fellow Alexander von Humboldt Foundation 1973–75; Chair. Egyptian Syndicate for Science Profs 1994–; mem. Research and Devt Council; Vice-Pres. Egyptian Science Union; mem. Bd Egyptian Acad. of Science; Fellow, African Acad. of Sciences, Third World Acad. of Sciences, Islamic Acad. of Sciences; Order of Science and Art, First Class 1974, Order of the Repub. Second Class 1983; Dr hc (Leberec) 1995; State Prize for Chemistry 1972, Production Prize 1985, 1990, TWNSO First Prize in Tech. 1990, State Merit Prize 1995, Mubarak Prize 2004. *Publications:* over 440 publs. *Address:* 26 El-Basra Street, Mohandseen, Dokki, Cairo (home); c/o National Research Centre, Tahrir Street, Dokki, Giza, Egypt. *Telephone:* 3357807 (office); 7499125 (home). *Fax:* 3363261 (office). *E-mail:* hebeish@hotmail.com (office).

HECHE, Anne; American actress; b. 25 May 1969, Aurora, Ohio; d. of Donald Heche and Nancy Heche; m. Coleman Laffoon 2001; one s. *Films:* An Ambush of Ghosts 1993, The Adventures of Huck Finn 1993, A Simple Twist of Fate 1994, Milk Money 1994, I'll Do Anything 1994, The Wild Side 1995, Pie in the Sky 1995, The Juror 1996, Walking and Talking 1996, Donnie Brasco 1997, Volcano 1997, Subway Stories, Wag the Dog 1997, Six Days Seven Nights 1998, A Cool Dry Place 1998, Psycho 1998, The Third Miracle 1999, Auggie Rose 2001, John Q 2002, Prozac Nation 2003, Birth 2004, Sexual Life 2005, Suffering Man's Charity 2006. *Television:* (series) Another World; (films) O Pioneers! 1992, Against the Wall 1994, Girls in Prison 1994, Kingfish: A Story of Huey P. Long 1995, If These Walls Could Talk 1996, If These Walls Could Talk 2 (dir and screenwriter), One Kill 2000, Gracie's Choice 2004, The Dead Will Tell 2004, True 2005, Everwood (series) 2004–05, Silver Bells 2005, Fatal Desire 2006, Men in Trees (series) 2006–07. *Publication:* Call Me Crazy: A Memoir 2001. *Address:* c/o CAA, 9830 Wilshire Blvd, Beverly Hills, CA 90212, USA.

HECHTER, Daniel; French couturier; b. 30 July 1938, Paris; s. of Raymond Hechter and Rosy Mendelsohn; m. 1st Marika Stengl Diez Deaux (deceased); one d.; m. 2nd Jennifer Chambon 1973; ed Lycées Voltaire and Chaptal, Paris; designer 1954–; designer House of Pierre d'Alby 1959–62; first women's collection 1962, first men's collection 1968, first perfume line 1989; sold label to Miltenberger Otto Aulbach 1999; founder and Dir-Gen. Vêtements Hechter 1962–; Pres. Fed. Française du Pret-à-Porter Féminin 1984–87; Pres. Festival de la Mode 1987; Pres. Strasbourg Racing Club 1987; fmr Vice-Pres. Etoile-Carouge football club; co-founder Paris Saint-Germain football club; inventor of Pret-a-Porter or ready-to-wear fashion. *Publications:* Le Boss 2000. *Leisure interests:* football, tennis, swimming, skiing, curling, golf. *Address:* SMB SA, rue de Maurapans, BP 87504, 25075 Besançon, Cedex 09, France. *Website:* www.daniel-hechter.com.

HECKER, Zvi, BArch; Israeli architect; b. 31 May 1931, Kraków, Poland; m. Deborah Houchman 1957; one s. one d.; ed Kraków Polytechnic School of Architecture, Israel Inst. of Tech., Haifa and Avni Acad., Tel-Aviv; worked in office of Arieh Sharon and Benjamin Idelson, Tel-Aviv 1957–58; in partnership with Eldar Sharon, Tel-Aviv 1959–65, with Alfred Neumann, Tel-Aviv 1960–68; Visiting Prof., Laval Univ., Québec, Canada 1968–69, Adjunct Prof. 1969–72; Visiting Lecturer, McGill Univ., Montreal and Univ. of Pennsylvania 1969–72; pvt. practice, Tel-Aviv 1972–; work includes housing projects, synagogues, public bldgs etc. *Publications:* exhbn catalogues, articles in professional journals. *Address:* Oranienburger Straße 41, 10117 Berlin, Germany; Sloterweg 303 H, 1171 VC, Badhoevedorp, The Netherlands; 19 Elzar Street, 65157 Tel-Aviv, Israel. *Telephone:* (30) 282-69-14 (Berlin); (20) 358-14-47 (Badhoevedorp); (3) 517-22-85 (Tel-Aviv). *Fax:* (30) 282-73-22 (Berlin); (20) 449-31-83 (Badhoevedorp); (3) 510-66-85 (Tel-Aviv). *E-mail:* berlin@zvihecker.com; amsterdam@zvihecker.com; tel-aviv@zvihecker.com. *Website:* zvihecker.com.

HECKMAN, James Joseph, PhD; American economist and academic; *Henry Schultz Distinguished Service Professor of Economics, University of Chicago;* b. 19 April 1944, Chicago, IL; s. of John Heckman and Bernice Heckman; m. Lynne Pettler Heckman; one s. one d.; ed Colorado Coll. and Princeton Univ.; systems engineer, Martin-Marietta Aerospace 1965; Junior Economist, Council of Economic Advisors 1967; Adjunct Assistant Professor, New York Univ 1972; Assistant Professor, Columbia Univ. 1970–73, Assoc. Prof. 1973–74; Assoc. Prof. of Econs, Univ. of Chicago 1973–77, Prof. of Econs 1977–, Henry Schultz Prof. of Econs 1985–95, Henry Schultz Distinguished Service Prof. of Econs 1995–, Prof., Irving Harris School of Public Policy 1990–, Dir Center For Evaluation of Social Programs 1991–; A. Whitney Griswold Prof. of Econs, Yale Univ. 1988–90, Irving Fisher Prof. 1984, Prof. of Statistics 1990–; Lecturer, Yale Law School 1989–90; Research Assoc., Nat. Bureau of Econ. Research 1971–85, 1987–, Harry Scherman Fellow 1972–73; consultant, RAND Corpn 1975–76; Social Science Research Council Training Fellow 1977–78; Guggenheim Fellow 1978–79; Fellow, Center for Advanced Study in the Behavioral Sciences, Stanford Univ. 1978–79; Research Assoc., Nat. Opinion Research Center: Econs Research Center 1979–; Sr Research Fellow, American Bar Foundation 1991–; Pres.-elect Midwest Econs Asscn 1996–97, Pres. 1998; Fellow, Econometric Soc. 1980, American Acad. of Arts and Sciences 1985, American Statistical Asscn 2001; mem. NAS 1992–; Co-Ed. Journal of Political Economy 1981–87; Assoc. Ed. Journal of Econometrics 1977–83, Journal of Labor Economics 1982–, Review of Economic Studies 1982–85, Econometric Reviews 1987–, Journal of Economic Perspectives 1989–96; mem. Editorial Bd Review of Economics and Statistics 1994–; Hon. Prof., Univ. of Tucuman 1998, Huazhong Univ., China 2001; Hon. mem. Latin and Caribbean Econ. Asscn 1999; Hon. MA (Yale) 1989; Hon. PhD (Colo Coll.) 2001; Hon. DUniv (Chile) 2002, (UAEM, Mexico) 2003; John Bates Clark Medal, American Econs Asscn 1983, First Annual Louis T. Benezet Distinguished Alumnus Award, Colo Coll. 1985, Nobel Prize in Econs 2000, Statistician of the Year, Chicago Chapter, American Statistical Asscn 2002. *Publications include:* Longitudinal Analysis of Labor Market Data (co-ed.) 1985, Performance Standards in A Government Bureaucracy (ed collection), Lecture Notes on Longitudinal Data Analysis (co-author) 1997, Inequality in America: What Role for Human Capital Policy? (co-ed.) 2003, Law and Employment: Lessons From Latin America and the Caribbean (co-author) 2003, Evaluating Human Capital Policy (The Gorman Lectures) 2004, Incentives in Government Bureaucracies: Can Incentives in Bureaucracies Emulate Market Efficiency? 2004; more than 200 articles in journals. *Address:* Department of Economics, University of Chicago, 1126 East 59th Street, Chicago, IL 60637 (office); 4807 S Greenwood, Chicago, IL 60615, USA (home). *Telephone:* (773) 702-0634 (office); (773) 268-4547 (home). *Fax:* (773) 702-8490 (office); (773) 268-6844 (home). *E-mail:* j-heckman@uchicago.edu (office). *Website:* lily.src.uchicago.edu (office).

HEDELIUS, Tom Christer, MBA; Swedish banker; b. 3 Oct. 1939, Lund; s. of Curt Hedelius and Brita (Påhlsson) Hedelius; m. Ulla Marianne Ericsson 1964; three s.; ed Univ. of Lund; industrial expert, Svenska Handelsbanken 1967–69, Credit Man. 1969–74, Head, Regional Unit (Stockholm City) 1974–76, Head, Cen. Credit Dept 1976–78, Pres. 1978–, Chair. of Bd 1991–2001; Chair. Bd AB Industrivärden, Bergman & Beving AB, Svenska AB Le Carbone, Anders Sandrews Stiftelse, Addtech. AB 2001–, Lagercrantz Group AB 2001–; mem. Bd Svenska Cellulosa AB, AB Volvo; Hon. Chair. Svenska Handelsbanken; Hon. DEcon (Umeå) 1989. *Address:* AB Industrivärden, Box 5403, 11484 Stockholm (office); Sturegatan 38, 11436 Stockholm, Sweden (home). *Telephone:* (8) 6666400. *Fax:* (8) 6616235.

HEEGER, Alan J., PhD; American physicist and academic; *Professor of Physics and Materials Engineering, University of California, Santa Barbara;* b. 22 Jan. 1936, Sioux City; ed Univ. of California, Berkeley; Prof. of Physics, Univ. of Calif. Santa Barbara 1982–, Dir Inst. for Polymers and Organic Solids 1982–2000, Prof. of Physics and Materials Engineering 1987–; Adjunct Prof. of Physics, Univ. of Utah 1988–; Chief Scientist 1999–; Pres. UNIAX Corpn 1990–94, Chair. Bd 1990–99, Chief Tech. Officer 1999–; Nobel Prize for Chemistry (jt recipient) 2000 for pioneering work on conductive polymers. *Address:* Department of Physics, Broida 4415, University of California, Santa Barbara, CA 93106-9530 (office); UNIAX Corporation, 6780 Cortona Drive, Santa Barbara, CA 93117, USA. *Telephone:* (805) 893-3184 (office). *Fax:* (805) 893-4755 (office). *E-mail:* ajh@physics.ucsb.edu (office). *Website:* www.cpos .ucsb.edu (office).

HEEMSKERK, Hubertus (Bert), BEcons; Dutch banker; *Chairman of the Executive Board, Rabobank Group;* b. 13 April 1943, Noordwijkerhoud; ed High School A, Heemstede, Testimonium Europa Inst., Maastricht, Philosophy-Theology Hochschule, Frankfurt, Eberhard Karls Univ., Tübingen, Univ. Catholique, Paris, Nederlandse Economische Hogeschool, Rotterdam; Merger Mediation/Int. Acquisitions, AMRO Bank 1969–72, Head Account Man. 1972–74, Area Man., Germany, Scandinavia and Far East 1974–75, AMRO Bank Rep., Tokyo, Japan 1975–76, Head Area Man. (Europe), Amsterdam 1976–78, Dir AMRO Bank, Dubai 1978–79, Regional Man., Europe, AMRO Bank, Amsterdam 1979–80, Regional Man., Europe 1980–83, Co. Dir AMRO Bank, London, UK 1983–87, Head of Int. Commercial Banking Div., Head of Int. Group Strategy and Project Group Dir of Gen. Affairs 1988, Head of Merger Secr., AMRO-Generale, Dir Gen. Netherlands, ABN AMRO Netherlands 1988–91; Chair. Exec. Bd, F. van Lanschot Bankiers NV 1991–2002; Chair. Exec. Bd Rabobank Group 2003–; mem. Bd of Liquidators of Stock Exchange Asscn, mem. Governing Bd; mem. Advisory Council Amsterdam, Inst. of Finance; mem. Supervisory Bd VADO Beheer BV; mem. AMREF Trust Fund, London; mem. Recommending Cttee AMREF Flying Doctors Netherlands, Passionata Foundation (literary journal in Rotterdam), Ronald McDonald Children's Fund, Special Olympics Nederland Foundation; Chair. Finance and Banking Museum; mem. Bd of Man. European Asscn for Banking and Financial History eV (EABH). *Address:* Rabobank Group, Postbus 17100, Croeselaan 18, 3500 HG Utrecht, Netherlands (office). *Telephone:* (30) 216-00-00 (office). *Fax:* (30) 216-26-72 (office). *E-mail:* info@rabobank.com (office). *Website:* www.rabobank.com (office).

HEFFER, Simon James, MA; British journalist and writer; *Associate Editor, Daily Telegraph;* b. 18 July 1960, Chelmsford, Essex; s. of the late James Heffer and of Joyce Mary Clements; m. Diana Caroline Clee 1987; two s.; ed King Edward VI School, Chelmsford and Corpus Christi Coll., Cambridge; medical journalist 1983–85; freelance journalist 1985–86; Leader Writer Daily Telegraph 1986–91, Deputy Political Corresp. 1987–88, political sketch writer 1988–91, political columnist 1990–91, Deputy Ed. 1994–96; Deputy Ed. The Spectator 1991–94; columnist, Evening Standard 1991–93, Daily Mail 1993–94, 1995–; Assoc. Ed. Daily Telegraph 2005–; Charles Douglas-Home Prize 1993. *Publications:* A Tory Seer (Co-Ed. with C. Moore) 1989, A Century of County Cricket (Ed.) 1990, Moral Desperado: A Life of Thomas Carlyle 1995, Power and Place: The Political Consequences of King Edward VII 1998, Like the Roman: The Life of Enoch Powell 1998, Nor Shall My Sword; The Reinvention of England 1999, Vaughan Williams 2000, The Great British Speeches 2007. *Leisure interests:* cricket, music, ecclesiology, bibliophily.

Address: The Daily Telegraph, 1 Canada Square, London, E14 5DT, England (office). *Telephone:* (20) 7538-5000 (office). *Fax:* (20) 7538-7610 (office). *E-mail:* simon.heffer@telegraph.co.uk (office). *Website:* www.telegraph.co.uk (office).

HEFNER, Hugh Marston, BS; American publisher; *Chairman Emeritus, Playboy Enterprises, Inc.;* b. 9 April 1926, Chicago, Ill.; s. of Glenn L. Hefner and Grace Hefner (née Swanson); m. 1st Mildred Williams 1949 (divorced 1959); one s. one d.; m. 2nd Kimberley Conrad 1989 (divorced); two s.; ed Univ. of Illinois; Ed.-in-Chief Playboy Magazine 1953–, Oui Magazine 1972–81; Chair. Emer. Playboy Enterprises 1988–; Pres. Playboy Club Int. Inc. 1959–86; Int. Press Directory Int. Publisher Award 1997. *Leisure interests:* cinema, jazz. *Address:* Playboy Enterprises Inc., 680 North Lake Shore Drive, Chicago, IL 60611, USA (office). *Telephone:* (312) 751-8000 (office). *Fax:* (312) 751-2818 (office). *Website:* www.playboyenterprises.com (home).

HEGARTY, Anthony Francis, PhD, DSc, MRIA; Irish chemist and academic; *Professor of Organic Chemistry and Head of Section, University College Dublin;* b. 5 Aug. 1942, Cork; s. of Daniel F. Hegarty and Patricia Doyle; m. Ann M. Fleming 1967; two s. two d.; ed Univ. Coll. Cork (Nat. Univ. of Ireland) and Univs of Paris, France and Calif., USA; Lecturer in Chem., Univ. Coll. Cork 1970–79; Prof. and Chair. of Organic Chem., Univ. Coll. Dublin (UCD) 1980–, Head of Dept 1980–83, 1986–89, 1996–99, Dean of Postgraduate Studies 1989–96, mem. Governing Body of UCD 1990–2005, Chair. Bd for Funded Research and Research and Scholarship Bd 1995–2004, Vice-Pres. for Research at UCD 1998–2004; Visiting Prof., Brandeis Univ. 1975, Kuwait Univ. 1983, Univ. of Paris VII 1987; Chair. Nat. Trust for Ireland 1984–87, Royal Soc. of Chem. in Ireland 1987–90; Deputy Chair. Irish Research Council for Science, Eng and Tech. 2001–; mem. Senate Nat. Univ. of Ireland 1992–; Council mem. Royal Irish Acad. 1982–96, 2003–, Sec. for Science 1986–88, Treas. 1988–96. *Publications:* 184 papers in int. journals in area of organic reaction mechanisms and bioorganic chem. *Leisure interests:* sailing, walking, classical music. *Address:* School of Chemistry and Chemical Biology, University College Dublin, Belfield, Dublin 4, Ireland (office). *Telephone:* (1) 7162304 (office). *Fax:* (1) 7161178 (office). *E-mail:* f.hegarty@ucd.ie (office). *Website:* www.ucd.ie/chem/hegarty (office); (office).

HEGAZY, Abdel Aziz Muhammad, DPhil; Egyptian politician; b. 3 Jan. 1923; ed Fuad Univ., Cairo, Univ. of Birmingham, UK; Dean, Faculty of Commerce, Ain Shams Univ. 1966–68; mem. Nat. Ass. 1969–75; Minister of the Treasury 1968–73; Deputy Prime Minister, Minister of Finance, Econ. and Foreign Trade 1973–74; First Deputy Prime Minister April–Sept. 1974, Prime Minister 1974–75; Chair. Allied Arab Bank 1985; teaching and working as a management consultant and certified accountant in Cairo, Jeddah and Beirut.

HEGDE, Ramakrishna; Indian politician; b. 29 Aug. 1926, Doddamane, Siddapur Taluk, Uttara Kannada Dist; m. Saraswati Hegde; three c.; ed Kashi Vidyapeeta, Benares and Lucknow Univs; active in Quit India Movt, imprisoned twice; organized Ryots' (Tenants') Movt, Uttara Kannada Dist; Pres. Dist Congress Cttee, Uttara Kannada Dist 1954–57; entered State Legis. as Deputy Minister for Planning and Devt 1957; Gen. Sec. Mysore Pradesh Congress 1958–62; Minister in charge of Rural Devt, Panchayatraj and Co-operation, Nijalingappa's Cabinet 1962–65, Minister for Finance, Excise, Prohibition, Information and Publicity 1965–67, for Finance, Excise and Planning 1967–68, for Finance, Planning and Youth Services 1968, 1971, of Commerce 1998–99; Leader of Opposition 1971–77; imprisoned during Emergency; elected Gen. Sec. All India Janata Party 1977; elected to Rajya Sabha from Karnataka Ass. 1978; Leader, Karnataka Janata Legislature Party 1983; first-ever non-Congress Chief Minister in the State; continued as head of caretaker ministry 1984; following State Legislature by-election, Chief Minister of Karnataka 1985–88; Deputy Chair. Planning Comm. 1989–90; Pres. World Fed. UN Asscns. *Address:* 229, Rajmahal Vilas Extension, Bangalore 560080, India (home). *Telephone:* (11) 4604749.

HEGEDÜS, Loránt, DTheol; Hungarian ecclesiastic; *President, Bishop of Laszlo Ravasz Association;* b. 1930, Hajdunánás; s. of Géza Hegedüs and Magdolna Szabó; m. Zsuzsa Illés; two s. two d.; ed Theological Acad., Budapest, Basel, Princeton Univ., USA; Asst Minister, Bicske, Budapest 1956, Komló Nagykörös, Alsónémedi 1954–63, Hidas 1963–65; Minister, Hidas 1965–68, Szabadság tér, Budapest 1983–96, Kálvin tér, Budapest 1996–; Bishop 1990–; Prof. 1993–; Acting Chair. Hungarian Presbyterian Churches Ecumenical Council 1994; mem. Presidium of European Churches Conf. 1992–97, Council of Hundreds 1997–; Pres. Bishop of László Ravasz Asscn 2002–; Hon. Prof., Budapest, Veszprém; Dr hc (Cluj, Kolozsvár, Romania); Bocskai Díj Award 1997. *Publications include:* Aspekte der Gottesfrage 1979, Nyitás a Végtelenre (Opening for Eternity) 1989, The Concept of Transcendence 1991, Testvérek, menjünk bátran! (Brethren, Let Us Go On) 1992, Kálvin teológiája (Calvin's Theology) 1996, Isten szuverenitása és az ember felelössége (The Sovereignty of God and the Responsibility of Man) 1996, Jézus és Europa (Jesus and Europe) 1998, Újkantiánus és értékteologia (Neo-Kantian and Value Theology in Hungary) 1998, Isten kezében a történelem (History in God's Hand) 1998, Házasság (Wedding) 1998, Magyar reformatus millénium (Hungarian Reformed Millennium) 2001, Mózes Huszonkettö 2001, Apokalipszsis 2005, Prédikator Könyve 2005, Apokalipszsisböl megmentö emlekezés (Zakarias) 2006, Püspöki jelentések 1991–2002 2007. *Leisure interests:* reading, listening to music. *Address:* Szabadság tér 2, 1054 Budapest, Hungary. *Telephone:* (1) 311-8695. *Fax:* (1) 311-8695.

HEGEL, Eduard, DPhil, DTheol; German theologian; b. 28 Feb. 1911, Wuppertal-Barmen; s. of Albert and Maria (née Ommer) Hegel; ed Univs Bonn, Münster and Munich; Prof. of Middle and New Church History, Trier 1949, Münster 1953, Bonn 1966–76, Prof. Emer. 1976; mem. Historical Comm. for Westphalia 1958, Rheinisch-Westfälische Akad. der Wissenschaften 1973–; Apostolic Protonotar, Prelate. *Publications include:* Die Kirchenpolitischen Beziehungen Hannovers 1934, Kirchliche Vergangenheit im Bistum Essen 1960, Geschichte der Katholisch-Theologischen Fakultät Münster (two vols) 1966, 1971, Geschichte des Erzbistums Cologne, Vols 4–5 1979, 1987, Ecclesiastica Rhenana 1986, St Kolumba in Cologne. Eine mittelalterliche Grossstadtpfarrei in ihrem Werden und Vergehen 1996. *Address:* Gregor-Mendel-Strasse 29, 53115 Bonn, Germany. *Telephone:* (228) 232273.

HEIDE, Ola Mikal, MSc, DrAgr; Norwegian botanist and academic; *Professor Emeritus of Botany, Norwegian University of Life Sciences;* b. 26 April 1931, Trondenes; s. of Hans Kr. Heide and Marit Heide; m. Gerd Lillebakk 1955; three s. two d.; ed Agricultural Univ. of Norway and Univ. of Wisconsin; Research Fellow, Agric. Univ. of Norway 1961–70; Prof. of Plant Sciences, Makerere Univ. of Kampala, Uganda 1970–72; Prof. of Plant Physiology, Univ. of Tromsö 1972–76; Prof. of Botany, Agric. Univ. of Norway (renamed Norwegian Univ. of Life Sciences 2005) 1976–, Head, Dept of Biology and Nature Conservation 1990–95, Rector 1978–83; Vice-Chair. Agric. Research Council of Norway 1979–84; mem. Norwegian Acad. of Sciences, Royal Soc. of Sciences of Uppsala 1991, Finnish Acad. of Science and Letters 1994; Pres. Scandinavian Soc. of Plant Physiology 1976–82, 1988–94, Fed. of European Socs of Plant Physiology 1988–90; Kellogg Foundation Fellowship 1965; Norsk Varekrigsforsikrings Fund Science Prize 1968. *Publications:* more than 125 primary scientific publs in the fields of plant physiology and ecophysiology. *Leisure interests:* sport, especially cross country skiing and running. *Address:* Norwegian University of Life Sciences, Dept of Ecology and Nature Resource Management, 1432 Ås (office); Skogvegen 34, 1430 Ås, Norway (home). *Telephone:* 64-96-53-86 (office); 64-94-16-01 (home). *Fax:* 64-96-58-01 (office). *E-mail:* ola.heide@umb.no (office). *Website:* www.umb.no (office).

HEIDEN, Eric A., MD; American fmr speed skater, fmr professional cyclist and orthopaedic surgeon; *Assistant Professor, University of California, Davis Medical Group, Sports Medicine;* b. 14 June 1958, Madison, Wis.; m. Karen Drews 1995; ed Univ. of Wis., Stanford Medical School; competed in Winter Olympics, Innsbruck, Austria 1976, Lake Placid, New York 1980 (five gold medals for men's speed skating, became first athlete ever to win five gold medals in a single Winter Olympics); winner, three consecutive World Speed Skating Championships 1977–79 (set new world records for 3,000m 1978, 1,000m 1978); retd from speed skating 1980; became professional cyclist 1981, winner US Professional Cycling Championships 1985; took part in Tour de France 1986; currently Asst Prof. Univ. of Calif., Davis Sports Medicine Clinic, Sacramento, Calif.; US speed skating team physician, Winter Olympics 2002; mem. American Acad. of Orthopedic Surgeons; Sullivan Award for Best US Amateur Athlete 1980, UPI Int. Athlete of the Year 1980, USOC Sportsman of the Year 1980. *Address:* UC Davis Medical Group-Sports Medicine, 2805 J Street, Suite 300, Sacramento, CA 95815, USA (office). *Telephone:* (916) 734-6805 (office). *E-mail:* eric.heiden@ucdmc.ucdavis.edu (office). *Website:* www.ucdmc.ucdavis.edu (office).

HEIGHTON, Steven, MA; Canadian author and academic; b. Toronto; ed Silverthorn Coll. Inst., Queen's Univ.; Ed. Quarry magazine 1988–94; Writer-in-Residence, Concordia Univ. 2002–03; Jack McLelland Writer-in-Residence, Massey Coll., Univ. of Toronto 2004; participating author American Movements II course, Univ. of New Orleans 2006; instructor Summer Literature Seminars, Herzen Univ., Russia 2007; Gerald Lampert Award for Best First Book of Poetry 1990, Air Canada Award 1990, Gold Medal for Fiction, Nat. Magazine Awards 1992, Petra Kenney Award 2002, Gold Medal for Poetry Nat. Magazine Awards 2004. *Publications include:* Stalin's Carnival (poetry) 1989, Foreign Ghosts (travelogue/poetry) 1989, Flight Paths of the Emperor (stories) 1992, Théâtre de revenants (French translation of Flight Paths of the Emperor) 1994, The Ecstasy of Skeptics (poetry) 1994, On earth as it is (stories) 1995, The Admen Move on Lhasa: Writing and Culture in a Virtual World (essays) 1997, La rose de l'érèbe (French translation of On Earth As It Is) 1998, The Shadow Boxer (novel) 2000, The Address Book (poetry) 2004, Afterlands (novel) 2006; poetry, fiction and critical articles in nat. and int. periodicals and anthologies 1984–. *Address:* Anne McDermid Agency, 83 Willcocks Street, Toronto, ON M5S 1C9, Canada (office). *E-mail:* anne@mcdermidagency.com (office); sheighton@kos.net (office). *Website:* www.mcdermidagency.com (office); www.stevenheighton.com (office).

HEIKAL, Mohamed Hassanein; Egyptian journalist; b. 1923; m.; three s.; reporter, The Egyptian Gazette 1943, Akher Sa'a magazine 1945; Ed. Al-Akhbar daily newspaper 1956–57; Ed. Al-Ahram 1957–74, Chair. Bd Dirs 1961–74; mem. Central Cttee Socialist Union 1968; Minister of Information and Foreign Affairs 1970; arrested Sept. 1981, released Nov. 1981. *Publications:* Nahnou wa America 1967, Nasser: The Cairo Documents 1972, The Road to Ramadan 1975, Sphinx and Commissar 1979, The Return of the Ayatollah 1981, Autumn of Fury 1983, Cutting the Lion's Tail 1986, Suez Through Egyptian Eyes 1986, Boiling Point 1988, (The) Explosion 1990, Illusions of Triumph 1992, Arms and Politics 1993, Secret Channels 1996.

HEILBRONNER, François; French government official; b. 17 March 1936, Paris; s. of Paul Heilbronner and Elsie Schwob; m. Nathalie Ducas 1966; two s. two d.; ed Lycée Charlemagne, Paris, Inst. d'Etudes Politiques, Paris and Ecole Nat. d'Admin; Insp. des Finances 1964; apptd to Secr. of Interministerial Cttee on Questions of European Econ. Cooperation 1966, Deputy Sec.-Gen. 1969–72; Adviser to Minister of Foreign Affairs 1968–69; Deputy Dir Office of Minister of Agric. 1972–73, Dir 1973–74; Econ. and Financial Adviser to Prime Minister Jacques Chirac 1974, Deputy Dir of Office of Prime Minister Chirac 1975–76, 1986; Insp.-Gen. des Finances 1983; Pres. Groupe des assurances nationales (Gan) 1986, Banque pour l'industrie française, Phénix Soleil SpA (Italy) (now Gan Italia SpA) 1986–94; consultant, FH Conseil 1995–; Pres. HL Gestion 1997–99; Dir Fondation Médecins sans Frontières, COJYP; Man. Dir REFCO HL Securities 1999–2000; Chair. and CEO Arbel 2001; Chevalier, Légion d'honneur, du Mérite maritime; Officier, Ordre nat.

du Mérite; Commdr du Mérite agricole. *Address:* 12 rue Théodule Ribot, 75017 Paris, France.

HEILMEIER, George Harry, BS, MSE, MA, PhD; American electrical engineer and business executive; *Chairman Emeritus, Telcordia, Inc.;* b. 22 May 1936, Philadelphia, Pa; m. Janet Helimeier; one d.; ed Univ. of Pennsylvania, Philadelphia, Princeton Univ., NJ; pioneering contrib. to liquid crystal displays; joined RCA Laboratories, Princeton 1958, discovered several new electro-optic effects in liquid crystals, which led to first working liquid crystal displays 1964; White House Fellow and Special Asst to Sec. of Defense, US Dept of Defense, Washington, DC 1970–71, Asst Dir for Defense Research and Eng, Electronic and Physical Sciences 1971–75, Dir Defense Advanced Research Projects Agency 1975–77; Vice-Pres., Texas Instruments 1977–83, Sr Vice-Pres. and Chief Tech. Officer 1983; Pres. and CEO Bellcore (now Telcordia) 1991–96 (oversaw co.'s sale to Science Applications Int. Corpn), Chair. and CEO 1996–97, Chair. Emer. 1997–; mem. Nat. Acad. of Eng, Defense Science Bd, Nat. Security Agency Advisory Bd; mem. Bd of Trustees Fidelity Investments, Teletech Holdings; mem. Bd of Overseers School of Eng and Applied Science, Univ. of Pennsylvania; IEEE David Sarnoff Award 1976, NEC C&C Prize 1990, Nat. Medal of Science 1991, Nat. Acad. of Eng Founders Award 1992, Vladimir Karapetoff Eminent Members Award, Eta Kappa Nu 1993, John Scott Award for Scientific Achievements, City of Philadelphia 1996, IEEE Medal of Honor 1997, John Scott Award 1997, John Fritz Medal, American Asscn of Eng Socs 1999, Kyoto Prize in Advanced Tech., The Inamori Foundation 2005. *Publications:* numerous papers in professional journals; holds 15 patents. *Leisure interests:* reading, sports. *Address:* Telcordia Corporate Headquarters, Raritan River Software Systems Center, One Telcordia Drive, Piscataway, NJ 08854-4151, USA (office). *Telephone:* (732) 699-2000 (office); (732) 699-5800 (office). *E-mail:* info@telcordia.com (office). *Website:* www.telcordia.com (office).

HEIN, Christoph; German novelist and playwright; b. 8 April 1944, Heinzendorf, Schlesien; ed Gymnasium Berlin, Univ. of Leipzig, Humboldt Univ., Berlin; dramatist and playwright, Volksbühne Berlin 1971–79; author 1979–; Chevalier, Ordre des Arts et des Lettres; Heinrich Mann-Preis der Akad. der Künste Berlin 1982, (westdeutscher) Kritikerpreis für Literatur Berlin 1983, Literaturpreis Hamburg 1985, Lessing Prize 1989, Stefan Andres Prize, Schweich 1989, Erich Fried Prize, Vienna 1990, Ludwig Mülheims Prize 1992, Berliner Literaturpreis der Stiftung Preussische Seehandlung 1992, Norddt. Literaturpreis 1998, Peter-Weiss-Preis 1998, Solothurner Literaturpreis 2000, Premio Grinzane Cavour Turin 2002, State Prize for European Literature Austria 2002, Schiller-Gedächtnispreis 2004, Ver.di-Literaturpreis 2004. *Plays:* Schlötel oder Was solls 1974, Cromwell 1980, Lassalle fragt Herrn Herbert nach Sonja 1981, Die wahre Geschichte des Ah Q 1983, Passage 1987, Die Ritter der Tafelrunde 1989, Randow 1994, Bruch 1998, Himmel auf Erden 1998, In Acht und Bann 1998, Mutters Tag 2000, Noach (opera) 2001, Zur Geschichte des menschlichen Herzens 2002. *Publications:* fiction: Einladung zum Lever Bourgeois (stories) 1980, Nachfahrt und früher Morgen (juvenile) 1980, Der fremde Freund (novel) 1982, Horns Ende (novel) 1985, Das Wildpferd unterm Kachelofen (juvenile) 1985, Der Tangospieler (novel) 1989, Die Vergewaltigung (stories) 1991, Matzeln 1991, Das Napoleonspiel (novel) 1993, Exekution eines Kalbes und andere Erzählungen 1994, Von allem Anfang an (novel) 1997, Willenbrock (novel) 2000, Mama ist gegangen (juvenile) 2003, Landnahme 2004, In seiner frühen Kindheit ein Garten (novel) 2005, Frau Paula Trosseau 2007; non-fiction: Die wahre Geschichte des Ah Q (plays/essays) 1984, Schlötel oder Was solls (essays) 1986, Öffentlich arbeiten. Essays und Gespräche 1987, Die fünfte Grundrechenart. Aufsätze und Reden 1986–1989 1990, Als Kind habe ich Stalin gesehen (essays/speeches) 1990, Die Mauern von Jerichow 1996. *Address:* c/o Suhrkamp-Verlag, Postfach 10 19 45, 60019 Frankfurt am Main, Germany.

HEINÄLUOMA, Eero Olavi; Finnish politician; *Chairman, Social Democratic Party (Suomen Sosialidemokraattinen Puolue);* b. 4 July 1955, Kokkola; MP for Uusimaa constituency 2003–; mem. Defence Cttee 2003, Foreign Affairs Cttee 2003–, Deputy mem. Cttee for the Future 2003; Vice-Chair. and mem. Parl. Supervisory Council 2003–05; Minister of Finance 2005–07, and Deputy Prime Minister 2006–07; Sec. Social Democratic Party –2005, Chair. 2005–. *Address:* Social Democratic Party (Suomen Sosialidemokraattinen Puolue), Saariniemenkatu 6, 00530 Helsinki, Finland. *Telephone:* (9) 478988 (office). *Fax:* (9) 712752 (office). *E-mail:* palaute@sdp.fi (office). *Website:* www .sdp.fi (office).

HEINDORFF, Michael, MA; German artist; b. 26 June 1949, Braunschweig; s. of Hans Heindorff and Sigrid Bootz (née Hampe); m. Monica Buferd 1983 (died 2002); one s. one d.; ed Art Coll. and Univ. of Braunschweig, Royal Coll. of Art; has been represented in numerous group exhbns internationally 1976–, also numerous solo exhbns 1977–; Sr Tutor in Painting, RCA 1980–99, Hon. Fellow 2001; various comms 1986–; Life mem. Chelsea Arts Club 1988–; John Moore's Liverpool Award 10 1976, Schmidt-Rotluff Prize 1981, Villa Massimo Prize 1981. *Art exhibitions:* Drawn to Seeing, London 1995, Drawn to Seeing II, touring Germany 1999–2001, Guildhall Art Gallery, London 2002, Deutsche Bank, London 2003. *Leisure interests:* gardening, living part-time in Andalucia. *Address:* 2 Shrubland Road, London, E8 4NN, England (home). *Telephone:* (20) 7254-9241 (home). *E-mail:* heindorff@aol.com (home).

HEINE, Volker, MSc, PhD, FRS, FInstP; British professor of theoretical physics (retd); b. 19 Sept. 1930, Germany; m. Daphne Hines 1955; one s. two d.; ed Wanganui Collegiate School, Otago Univ., New Zealand and Univ. of Cambridge; Demonstrator, Lecturer and Reader, Univ. of Cambridge 1958–76, Prof. in Theoretical Physics 1976–97; Visiting Prof., Univ. of Chicago 1965–66; Visiting Scientist Bell Labs, USA 1970–71; Fellow, Clare Coll. Cambridge 1960–; Fellow, American Physical Soc.; Foreign mem. Max

Planck Gesellschaft; Maxwell Medal, Inst. of Physics, Royal Medal, Royal Soc., Dirac Medal, Inst. of Physics, Max Born Medal, Inst. of Physics and German Physical Soc. 2001. *Publications:* Group Theory in Quantum Mechanics 1960, Solid State Physics (Vol. 24) 1970, (Vol. 35) 1980; articles in Journal of Physics, Physical Review, etc. *Address:* Cavendish Laboratory, Madingley Road, Cambridge, CB3 0HE, England (office). *Telephone:* (1223) 337258 (office).

HEINEMAN, David (Dave), BS; American politician; *Governor of Nebraska;* b. 12 May 1948, Falls City, Neb.; s. of Jean Heineman and Irene Heineman; m. Sally Ganem 1977; one s.; ed US Mil. Acad., West Point; fmr Capt. US Army; fmr Chief of Staff for Congressman Hal Daub; fmr Fremont Area Office Man. for Congressman Doug Bereuter; elected Neb. State Treas. 1994, 1998; Lt Gov. of Neb. 2001–05, Dir of Homeland Security for Neb. (mem. Homeland Security Advisory Council 2004), Chair. Neb. Information Comm., Presiding Officer Neb. Legislature; US Sec. of Agric. 2005; Gov. of Neb. 2005–. *Address:* Office of the Governor, PO Box 94848, Lincoln, NE 68509-4848, USA (office). *Telephone:* (402) 471-2244 (office). *Fax:* (402) 471-6031 (office). *Website:* gov .nol.org (office).

HEINONEN, Olavi Ensio, LLD; Finnish judge; b. 12 Sept. 1938, Kuopio; s. of Eino Ensio Heinonen and Aili Vesa; m. Marjatta Rahikainen 1962; two s. two d.; ed Univ. of Helsinki; Asst Prof. of Law, Univ. of Helsinki 1969–70; Justice, Supreme Court of Finland 1970–86; Parl. Ombudsman 1986–89; Chief Justice, Supreme Court of Finland 1989–2001 (retd); Grand Cross, Order of White Rose of Finland; Hon. LLD (Turku). *Publications:* books and articles on criminal justice and criminal policy. *Leisure interests:* cycling, basketball. *Address:* c/o Supreme Court, Pohjoisesplanadi 3, PO Box 301, 00171 Helsinki, Finland.

HEISBOURG, François, FRSA; French academic and business executive; *Special Adviser, Fondation pour la Recherche Stratégique;* b. 24 June 1949, London, England; s. of Georges Heisbourg and Hélène Pinet; m. Elyette Levy 1989; two s.; ed Coll. Stanislas, Paris, Inst. d'Etudes Politiques, Cycle Supérieur d'Aménagement et d'Urbanisme, Ecole Nat. d'Admin; Asst to Dir of Econ. Affairs, Ministry of Foreign Affairs 1977–78; policy planning staff, Ministry of Foreign Affairs 1978–79; First Sec. Perm. Mission of France to UN 1979–81; Int. Security Adviser to Minister of Defence 1981–84; Vice-Pres. Thomson Int. 1984–87; Dir IISS, London 1987–92, Chair. 2001–; Sr Vice-Pres. Matra Défense Espace 1992–98; Head French Interministerial Group on teaching of and research in, strategic and int. affairs; Chair. Geneva Centre for Security Policy 1998–; Dir Fondation pour la Recherche Stratégique, Paris 2001–05, Special Adviser 2005–; mem. Royal Soc. for Encouragement of Arts, Manufacture and Commerce; Chevalier, Légion d'honneur, Ordre nat. du Mérite, Grosses Verdienstkreuz (Germany), Commdr, Ordre de la Couronne de Chêne (Luxembourg), Merito Militar (Spain). *Publications:* La Puce, les Hommes et la Bombe (with P. Boniface) 1986, Les Volontaires de l'an 2000 1995, The Future of Warfare 1997, European Defence: Making it Work 2000, Hyperterrorisme: La Nouvelle Guerre 2001, Le fin d'Occident? – Les Etats Unis, l'Europe et le Moyen Orient 2005; numerous articles in int. media and scholarly journals. *Leisure interests:* hiking, chess, collecting atlases. *Address:* Fondation pour la Recherche Stratégique, 27 rue Damesme, 75013 Paris, France (office). *Telephone:* 1-43-13-77-80 (office). *Fax:* 1-43-13-77-78. *E-mail:* f.heisbourg@frstrategie.org (office); heisbour@noos.fr (home). *Website:* www .frstrategie.org (office).

HEITSCH, Ernst, DPhil; German classicist and academic; *Professor of Classical Linguistics, University of Regensburg;* b. 17 June 1928, Celle; s. of Ernst Heitsch and Luise Meineke; m. Paula Sötemann 1961; two s. one d.; ed Univ. of Göttingen; Univ. Lecturer in Classical Linguistics, Univ. Göttingen 1960–66, Prof. 1966–67; Prof. of Classical Linguistics, Univ. of Regensburg 1967–; mem. Akad. der Wissenschaften und der Literatur zu Mainz, Akad. der Wissenschaften zu Göttingen, Deutsches Archäologisches Institut. *Publications:* Die griechischen Dichterfragmente der römischen Kaiserzeit I und II 1963–65, Epische Kunstsprache und Homer 1968, Parmenides 1974, 1995, Parmenides und die Anfänge der Erkenntniskritik und Logik 1979, Xenophanes 1983, Antiphon aus Rhamnus 1984, Willkür und Problembewusstsein in Platons Kratylos 1984, Platon über die rechte Art zu reden und zu schreiben 1987, Überlegungen Platons im Theaetet 1988, Wege zu Platon 1992, Platon Phaidros 1993, 1997, Geschichte und Situationen bei Thukydides 1996, Gesammelte Schriften I 2001, II 2002, III 2003, Platon Apologie 2002, 2004, Dialoge Platons vor 399? 2002, Platon und die Aufänge seines dialektischen Philosophierens 2004, Geschichte und Personen bei Thukydides 2007; numerous articles in periodicals. *Leisure interest:* sailing. *Address:* Mattinger Strasse 1, 93049 Regensburg, Germany (home). *Telephone:* (941) 31944 (home).

HEKMATYAR, Gulbuddin; Afghan politician and fmr guerrilla leader; *Leader, Gulbuddin Islamic Party;* b. 1947, Imam Saheb, Kunduz Prov.; ed Kabul Univ.; mem. Muslim Youth 1970; imprisoned 1972–73; fled to Pakistan 1973; Leader Hizb-i Islami Mujahidin Movt against Soviet-backed regime; Prime Minister of Afghanistan 1993–94, 1996–97; returned from exile in Iran 1998; currently Leader Hizb-i Islami Gulbuddin (Gulbuddin Islamic Party).

HELD, Heinz Joachim, DrTheol; German theologian and fmr bishop; b. 16 May 1928, Wesseling/Rhein; s. of Heinrich Held and Hildegard Röhrig; m. Anneliese Novak 1959 (died 2002); one s. three d.; m. Barbara Mauritz 2003; ed Wuppertal, Göttingen, Heidelberg, Bonn and Austin, Tex.; Research Asst, Wuppertal Theological Seminary 1952, 1953–56; parish pastor, Friedrichsfeld/Niederrhein 1957-64; Prof. of Theology, Buenos Aires Lutheran Seminary 1964–68; Pres. River Plate Evangelical Church, Buenos Aires 1968–74; mem. Cen. Cttee World Council of Churches 1968–91, Moderator of Cen. Cttee and Exec. Cttee 1983–91; Pres. Dept of Ecumenical Relations and Ministries

Abroad of the Evangelical Church in Germany 1975–93; Bishop 1991; Chair. Council of Christian Churches, FRG 1982–88, 1992–95; Hon. DrTheol (Lutheran Theological Univ., Budapest) 1985; Hon. DD (Acad. of Ecumenical Indian Theology and Church Admin., Chennai) 1988. *Publications:* Matthew as Interpreter of the Miracle Stories 1960 (English trans. 1963), Von Nairobi nach Canberra.EKD und ÖRK im Dialog 1975–1991 1994/1996, Den Reichen wird das Evangelium gepredigt 1997, Ökumene im Kalten Krieg 2000, Der Ökumenische Rat der Kirchen im Visier der Kritik 2001. *Leisure interests:* stamp collecting, amateur music (piano), photography. *Address:* Bussilliatweg 32, 30419 Hanover, Germany (home). *Telephone:* (511) 2714308 (home). *E-mail:* heijo.held@t-online.de (home).

HELD, Richard M., MA, PhD; American neuroscientist, psychologist and academic; *Research Professor of Vision Science, New England College of Optometry;* b. 10 Oct. 1922, New York; s. of Lawrence Walter Held and Tessie Klein Held; m. Doris Bernays 1951; three c.; ed Columbia and Harvard Univs and Swarthmore Coll.; Research Asst Dept of Psychology, Swarthmore Coll. 1946–48; Research Asst, Teaching Fellow and NIH Postdoctoral Fellow, Dept of Psychology, Harvard Univ. 1949–53; Instructor, Asst Prof., Assoc. Prof., Prof. and Chair. Dept of Psychology, Brandeis Univ. 1953–62; mem. Inst. for Advanced Study, Princeton 1955–56; Sr Research Fellow NSF and Visiting Prof., Dept of Psychology, MIT 1962–63, Prof., Dept of Brain and Cognitive Sciences 1963–93, Dept Chair. 1977–86, Prof. Emer. 1994–; Research Prof. of Vision Science, New England Coll. of Optometry 1995–; Fellow, American Acad. of Arts and Sciences; mem. NAS and many other learned socs; numerous other professional appointments; Dr hc (Free Univ. of Brussels) 1984, (New England Coll. of Optometry); Glenn A. Fry Award 1979, H.C. Warren Medal 1983, Kenneth Craik Award 1985, Galileo Award 1996. *Publications:* several hundred. *Leisure interests:* tennis, theatre, visual arts. *Address:* New England College of Optometry, 424 Beacon Street, Boston, MA 02115, USA (office). *Telephone:* (617) 369-0180 (office); (617) 491-7218 (home). *Fax:* (617) 369-0188 (office). *E-mail:* heldd@neco.edu (home); helddr@yahoo.com (home).

HELENIUS, Ari, PhD; Finnish biochemist and academic; *Professor, Institute of Biochemistry, Eidgenössische Technische Hochschule Zürich;* b. 3 Sept. 1944, Oulu; ed Univ. of Helsinki; fmr Staff Scientist, European Lab. for Molecular Biology, Heidelberg, Germany, later Assoc. Prof.; Prof., Dept of Cell Biology, Yale Univ., New Haven, Conn., USA 1983–97 (Chair. Dept 1992–97); Prof., Inst. of Biochemistry, ETH, Zürich, Switzerland 1997–; Komppa Prize 1973, Ernst Prize for Medicine 2003, The Schleiden Medal in Cell Biology 2003. *Publications:* numerous publs in scientific journals on membrane biology, virology and protein chem. *Leisure interests:* literature, hiking. *Address:* Institute of Biochemistry, Building HPM, Room E6.3, ETH Hönggerberg, 8093 Zürich, Switzerland (office). *Telephone:* (44) 6326817 (office). *Fax:* (44) 6321269 (office). *E-mail:* ari.helenius@bc.biol.ethz.ch (office). *Website:* www.bc.biol.ethz.ch (office).

HELFT, Jorge Santiago; Argentine arts foundation director; b. 10 June 1934, France; s. of the late Jacques Helft and Marianne Loevi; m. Mariana Eppinger 1955; three s.; ed New York Univ. and Columbia Univ., USA; lived in Paris until 1940, New York 1940–47, Buenos Aires 1947–; business exec. with Continental Grain Co. 1956–74, Vesuvio SA 1974–82; Trustee and Dir Fundación Antorchas 1985–, Fundación Lampadia, Vaduz, Liechtenstein; Pres. Fundación San Telmo 1980–; Founding mem. and Dir Fundación Teatro Colón 1978–; Oficial, Ordem de Rio Branco (Brazil). *Leisure interests:* arts and music. *Address:* Fundación Antorchas, Chile 300 (1098), Buenos Aires (office); Defensa 1364 (1143), Buenos Aires, Argentina (home).

HELINSKI, Donald Raymond, PhD, FAAS; American biologist and academic; *Research Professor, Department of Biology, University of California, San Diego;* b. 7 July 1933, Baltimore, Md; s. of George L. Helinski and Marie M. Helinski; m. Patricia M. Doherty 1962; one s. one d.; ed Univ. of Maryland, Case Western Reserve Univ., Cleveland, Ohio, Stanford Univ.; US Public Health Service Postdoctoral Fellow, Stanford Univ., Calif. 1960–62; Asst Prof., Princeton Univ., NJ 1962–65; Assoc. Prof., Dept of Biology, Univ. of California, San Diego 1965–70, Prof. 1970–, now Research Prof. and Chair. Dept of Biology 1979–81, Dir Center for Molecular Genetics 1984–95, Assoc. Dean of Natural Sciences 1994–97; mem. NIH Advisory Cttee on DNA Recombinant Research 1975–78; mem. NAS, AAAS; Assoc. mem. EMBO; Fellow, American Soc. of Microbiology; Guggenheim Fellow. *Publications:* more than 180 publs and 50 review articles in the fields of biochemistry, molecular genetics and microbiology. *Address:* Department of Biology, Division of Biological Sciences, University of California, San Diego, 9500 Gilman Drive, La Jolla, CA 92093 (office); 8766 Dunaway Drive, La Jolla, CA 92037, USA (home). *Telephone:* (858) 534-3638 (office); (858) 453-2758 (home). *Fax:* (858) 534-0559 (office). *E-mail:* dhelsinki@ucsd.edu (office); helinski@biomail.ucsd.edu (office). *Website:* biology.ucsd.edu/faculty/helinski.html (office).

HELL, Stefan W., Dr rer. nat; German scientist; *Director, Department of NanoBiophotonics, Max Planck Institute for Biophysical Chemistry;* b. 1962; m. Anna Hell; two s.; ed Univ. of Heidelberg; worked at European Molecular Biology Lab., Heidelberg 1991–93; Sr Researcher, Univ. of Turku, Finland 1993–96; Visiting Scientist, Univ. of Oxford, UK 1994; apptd to Max Planck Inst. for Biophysical Chemistry, Göttingen 1997, Dir Dept of NanoBiophotonics 2002–; Dir High Resolution Optical Microscopy Research Group, German Cancer Research Centre; Prize of the Int. Comm. in Optics 2000, Carl Zeiss Research Award 2002, Innovation Award of the German Fed. Pres. 2006, Julius Springer Award for Applied Physics 2007. *Publications:* more than 100 publs in refereed journals. *Address:* Max Planck Institute for Biophysical Chemistry, Am Faßberg 11, 37077 Göttingen, Germany (office). *Telephone:* (551) 2012501 (office). *Fax:* (551) 2011222 (office). *E-mail:* shell@gwdg.de (office). *Website:* www.gwdg.de (office).

HELLAWELL, Keith, QPM, MSc, LLD; British anti-drugs co-ordinator and police officer; b. 18 May 1942, Yorks.; s. of Douglas Hellawell and Ada Alice Hellawell; m. Brenda Hey 1963; one s. two d.; ed Kirkburton Secondary Modern School, Dewsbury Tech. Coll., Cranfield Inst. of Tech. and London Univ.; worked for five years as a miner before joining Huddersfield Borough Police; progressed through every rank within W Yorks. Police to Asst Chief Constable; Deputy Chief Constable of Humberside 1985–90, Chief Constable of Cleveland Police 1990–93, Chief Constable of W Yorks. Police 1993–98; first UK Anti-Drugs Co-ordinator 1998–2001; Adviser to Home Sec. on Int. Drug Issues 2001; Asscn of Police Officers Spokesman on Drugs; mem. Advisory Council on the Misuse of Drugs, Bd Community Action Trust; Chair. Catapult Presentations Ltd; Dir (non-exec.) Universal Vehicles Group Ltd.; fmr Trustee Nat. Soc. for the Prevention of Cruelty to Children; mem. Editorial Advisory Bd Journal of Forensic Medicine. *Publication:* The Outsider (autobiog.) 2002. *Leisure interests:* gardening, design. *Address:* Catapult Presentations Ltd, Premier House, Huddersfield, HD7 5NF, England.

HELLBERG, Klaus; Finnish politician and business executive; *Chairman, Supervisory Board, Neste Oil Oyj;* b. 1945, Porvoo; mem. Eduskunta (Finnish Parl.) for Uusimaa constituency (Suomen Sosialidemokraatinen Puolue/Finnish Social Democratic Party); Chair. Supervisory Bd Neste Oil Oyj 2007–; mem. Supervisory Bd Fortum Corpn; mem. Finnish Council for Environment and Natural Resources. *Address:* Neste Oil Oyj, Keilaranta 8, PO Box 95, 00095 Espoo, Finland (office). *Telephone:* (10) 45811 (office). *Fax:* (10) 4584442 (office). *Website:* www.nesteoil.com (office).

HELLER, Jeffrey M. (Jeff), BBA; American information technology executive; *President, Electronic Data Systems Corporation;* m. Carol Heller; one s. one d.; ed Univ. of Texas, Austin; served in US Marine Corps as jet pilot 1960–66, attained the rank of Capt.; joined Electronic Data Systems Corpn's Systems Eng Devt Program 1968, worked as systems engineer in medicare field in Pa, Calif., Ia, Ind., New York and Boston, worked on a New York Stock Exchange sales study 1970, man. of a regional data center, Dallas 1972, Regional Man., Healthcare, eastern USA 1973–74, Corporate Vice-Pres. 1974–79, Head, Tech. Services 1979–84, led a project for General Motors, Detroit 1984–87, Sr Vice-Pres. 1987–96, Pres. and COO 1996–2000, Vice Chair. 1996–2002, Pres. 2003–; mem. Bd of Dirs Dallas Symphony Asscn, Mutual of Omaha, Trammell Crow Co., Cotton Bowl Athletic Asscn, Temple-Inland; mem. Chancellor's Council, Eng Foundation Advisory Council, McCombs School of Business Advisory Council, Devt Bd, Men's Athletics Council, Univ. of Tex.; mem. Longhorn Foundation; Trustee Southwestern Medical Foundation. *Address:* Electronic Data Systems Corporation, 5400 Legacy Drive, Plano, TX 75024-3199, USA (office). *Telephone:* (972) 604-6000 (office). *Fax:* (972) 605-6033 (office). *Website:* www.eds.com (office).

HELLER, Michał Kazimierz; Polish professor of philosophy of science and ecclesiastic; b. 12 March 1936, Tarnów; ed Inst. of Theology, Tarnów; ordained priest 1959; Catholic Univ. of Lublin, Pontifical Acad. of Theology, Kraków, Extraordinary Prof. 1985, Ordinary Prof. 1990, currently Prof. of Cosmology and Philosophy of Science; Jt mem. Vatican Astronomical Observatory; Rector Inst. of Theology, Tarnów; Ordinary mem. Pontifical Acad. of Sciences, Rome 1991; mem. Petersburg Acad. of Sciences 1997, Int. Astronomical Union, Int. Soc. for General Relativity and Gravitation, European Physical Soc., Int. Soc. of the Study of Time, Polish Physical Soc., Polish Astronomical Soc., Science Soc. of Catholic Univ. of Lublin; Dr hc (Acad. of Mining and Metallurgy, Kraków) 1996; Templeton Prize 2008. *Publications:* The Singular Universe – An Introduction to the Classical Singularity Theory 1991, Theoretical Foundations of Cosmology – Introduction to the Global Structure of Space-Time 1992, Physics of Space-Time and Motion 1993, The New Physics and a New Theology 1996, To Catch Passing Away 1997, Quantum Cosmology 2001, The Beginning is Everywhere 2002, and over 600 publs on relativistic physics, cosmology, history and philosophy of science and relations between science and theology and articles in journals. *Address:* Papieska Akademia Teologiczna, Wydział Filozoficzny, ul. Franciszkańska 1, 30-004 Kraków, Poland (office). *E-mail:* mheller@wsd.tarnow.pl (office); mheller@alumn.wsd.tarnow.pl (home).

HELLMAN, Peter S., MBA, BEcons; American business executive; *President and Chief Financial and Administrative Officer, Nordson Corporation;* b. 16 Oct. 1949, Cleveland, Ohio; s. of Arthur Cerf Hellman and Joan Alburn; m. Alyson Dulin Ware 1976; one s. one d.; ed Hobart Coll. and Case Western Reserve Univ.; with The Irving Trust Co., New York 1972–79; Financial Planning Assoc., BP America 1979–82, Man. Financial Planning 1982–84, Dir, Operations Analysis 1984–85, Asst Treas. 1985–86, Corp. Treas. 1986–89; Vice-Pres. and Treas. TRW Inc. 1989–91, Exec. Vice-Pres. and Chief Financial Officer 1991–94, Exec. Vice-Pres. and Asst Pres. 1994–95, Pres. and COO 1995–2000; Exec. Vice-Pres. and Chief Financial Officer Nordson Corpn, Ohio 2000–2004, Pres. and Chief Financial and Admin. Officer 2004–; Dir Nordson Corpn, Qwest Communications; mem. Cleveland Clinic Foundation Urological Inst. Advisory Cttee; Trustee Baxter International, Case Western Reserve Univ., Lifebank Lorain Co. Community Coll. Foundation, Western Reserve Acad. *Address:* Nordson Corporation, 28601 Clemens Road, Westlake, OH 44145, USA (office). *Telephone:* (440) 892-1580 (office). *Fax:* (440) 892-9253 (office). *Website:* www.nordson.com (office).

HELLSTRÖM, Mats, MA; Swedish politician and diplomatist; *Governor, Stockholm County;* b. 12 Jan. 1942, Stockholm; m. Elisabeth Hellström; two c.; ed Univ. of Stockholm; Lecturer in Econs, Univ. of Stockholm 1965–69; mem. Parl. 1968, 1969–96, mem. Exec. Cttee Social Democratic Party Youth League 1969–72; mem. Bd Social Democratic Party 1969–96; Special Adviser, Ministry of Labour 1973–76; Minister of Foreign Trade at Ministry of Foreign Affairs 1983–86; Minister of Agric. 1986–91, for Foreign Trade and European Union Affairs 1994–96; Amb. to Germany 1996–2001; Gov. Stockholm Co.

2002–. *Publications:* A Seamless Globe? A Personal Story of the Uruguay Round in GATT 1999. *Address:* Box 22067, Laensstyrelsen i Stockholms Laen, 104 22 Stockholm (office); Slottsbacken 4, 111 30 Stockholm, Sweden (home). *Telephone:* (8) 785-50-02 (office); (8) 20-98-48 (home). *Fax:* (8) 652-24-45 (office); (8) 20-12-22 (home). *E-mail:* mats.hellstrom@fab.lst.se (office).

HELLSVIK, Gun, LLB; Swedish politician and government official; *Director-General, Swedish Patent and Registration Office;* b. (Gun Blongren), 27 Sept. 1942, Ängelholm; m.; one s.; ed Lund Univ.; fmr Lecturer in Commercial Law, Lund Univ.; mem. Bd Lund Inst. of Tech., IDEON Research Park; Municipal Commr and Chair. Municipal Exec. Bd, Lund 1982; mem. Nat. Bd Moderate Party 1985–; leader, municipal opposition group 1988; Minister of Justice 1991–94; mem. Parl. 1994–2001, Chair. Standing Cttee of Legal Affairs 1994–2001; Dir-Gen. Swedish Patent and Registration Office 2001–. *Leisure interest:* cooking. *Address:* Swedish Patent and Registration Office, Box 5055, 10242 Stockholm, Sweden (office). *Telephone:* (8) 782-25-01 (office). *E-mail:* gun.hellsvik@prv.se (office). *Website:* www.prv.se (office).

HELLWIG, Fritz, DPhilHabil; German politician and economist; b. 3 Aug. 1912, Saarbrücken; s. of Friedrich H. Hellwig and Albertine Hellwig (née Christmann); m. Dr Margarete Werners 1939; two s. one d.; ed Marburg, Vienna and Berlin Univs; staff mem. of the Saarbrücken Chamber of Industry and Commerce 1933–39; Dir of the Saarwirtschaftsarchiv 1936–39; Man. of Dist Orgs of Iron and Steel Industry at Düsseldorf and Saarbrücken, 1940–43; war service 1943–47; Econ. Adviser and Dir of Deutsches Industrieinstitut, Cologne 1951–59; Substitute del., Consultative Ass. of Council of Europe 1953–56; mem. of Bundestag 1953–59; Chair. of the Econ. Affairs Cttee of the Bundestag 1956–59; mem. of European Parl. 1959; mem. of High Authority of the European Coal and Steel Community, Luxembourg 1959–67; Vice-Pres. of the Comm. of the European Communities, Brussels 1967–70; Exec. mem. Bd of German Shipowners' Asscn 1971–73; Hon. Prof., Univ. of Trier (for History of Cartography 1990); Grosses Bundesverdienstkreuz mit Stern und Schulterband 1971; Int. Charlemagne Prize, Aachen (with EEC Comm.) 1969. *Publications:* Westeuropas Montanwirtschaft, Kohle und Stahl beim Start der Montan-Union 1953, Saar zwischen Ost und West, Die wirtschaftliche Verflechtung 1954, 10 Jahre Schumanplan 1960, Gemeinsamer Markt und Nationale Wirtschaftspolitik 1961, Montanunion zwischen Bewährung und Belastung 1963, Politische Tragweite der europäischen Wirtschaftsintegration 1966, Das schöne Buch und der Computer 1970, Die Forschungs- und Technologiepolitik der Europäischen Gemeinschaften 1970, Verkehr und Gemeinschaftsrecht: Seeschiffahrt und Europäische Wirtschaftgemeinschaft 1971, Die deutsche Seeschiffahrt: Strukturwandel und künftige Aussichten 1973, Zur älteren Kartographie der Saargegend I 1977, II 1981, Alte Pläne von Stadt und Festung Saarlouis 1980, Die Hogenberg-Geschichtsblätter 1983, Landkarten der Pfalz am Rhein (with W. Reiniger and K. Stopp) 1984, Mittelrhein und Moselland im Bild alter Karten 1985, Überwindung der Grenzen. Robert Schuman zum Gedenken 1986, Caspar Dauthendeys Karte des Herzogtums Braunschweig 1987, Europäische Integration aus historischer Erfahrung (Ein Zeitzeugengespräch mit Michael Gehler) 2004. *Leisure interests:* collecting old maps, views and illustrated books. *Address:* Klosterbergstrasse 117C, 53177 Bonn, Germany (home). *Telephone:* (228) 322017 (home).

HELLYER, Hon. Paul Theodore, PC, BA; Canadian politician; b. 6 Aug. 1923, Waterford, Ont.; s. of Audrey S. Hellyer and Lulla M. Anderson; m. 1st Ellen Jean Ralph (died 2004); two s. one d.; m. 2nd Sandra Bussiere (née Meades) 2005; ed Waterford High School, Curtiss Wright Tech. Inst., California and Univ. of Toronto; Fleet Aircraft Manufacturing Co., Fort Erie 1942–44; RCAF 1944–45; Owner, Mari-Jane Fashions, Toronto 1945–56; Treas. Curran Hall Ltd 1950, Pres. 1951–62; Pres. Trepil Realty Ltd 1951–62; Pres. Hendon Estates Ltd 1959–62; mem. House of Commons 1949–57, 1958–74, Parl. Asst to Minister of Nat. Defence 1956–57, Assoc. Minister April–June 1957, Minister of Nat. Defence 1963–67, of Transport 1967–69, responsible for Central Mortgage and Housing Corpn 1968–69; Chair. Task Force on Housing and Urban Devt 1968; Acting Prime Minister 1968–69; joined Progressive Conservative Party July 1972; rejoined Liberal Party 1982; Leader Canadian Action Party 1997–2004; Opposition Spokesman on Industry, Trade and Commerce 1973; Distinguished Visitor, Faculty of Environmental Studies, York Univ. 1969–70; Founding Chair. Action Canada 1971; Syndicated Columnist, Toronto Sun 1974–84; Exec. Dir Canada UNI Asscn 1991–95; Fellow, Royal Soc. for Encouragement of the Arts. *Publications:* Agenda – A Plan for Action 1971, Exit Inflation 1981, Jobs For All – Capitalism on Trial 1984, Canada at the Crossroads 1990, Damn the Torpedos 1990, Funny Money – A Common Sense Alternative to Mainline Economics 1994, Surviving the Global Financial Crisis – The Economics of Hope for Generation X 1996, Arundel Lodge – A Little Bit of Old Muskoka 1996, The Evil Empire: Globalization's Darker Side 1997, Stop – Think 1999, Goodbye Canada 2001, One Big Party – To Keep Canada Independent 2003. *Leisure interests:* swimming, skin and scuba diving, stamp collecting. *Address:* Suite 506, 65 Harbour Square, Toronto, Ont. M5J 2L4, Canada (home). *Telephone:* (416) 850-1375 (office); (416) 366-4092 (home). *Fax:* (416) 850-1486 (office). *E-mail:* phellyer@sympatico.ca (office).

HELME, Mart; Estonian diplomatist; b. 31 Oct. 1949, Parnu; ed Tartu Univ.; Eesti Raamat Publishing House 1973–75; reporter Harju Elu (newspaper) 1975–77; Sr Ed. Literature section Pioneer magazine 1977–86; farmer 1986–89; publisher 1989–91; Acting Dir Union of Publishers of Estonia, political observer Paeveleht (daily) 1991–93; Head Fourth Bureau (Asia, Africa, S America) Political Dept, Ministry of Foreign Affairs Feb.–May 1994; Head Third Bureau (Russia, CIS, E and Cen. Europe) Political Dept, Ministry of Foreign Affairs 1994–95; Amb. to Russian Fed. 1995–2000; apptd Vice-Chancellor Ministry of Foreign Affairs 1999; Counsellor to Minister of Agric.;

fmr Dir Research Center Free Europe; Chair. Nat. Conservative Party-Farmers' Ass.; cand. for People's Union in elections for European Parl. 2004. *Address:* c/o Ministry of Agriculture, 39/41 Lai Street, 15056 Tallinn, Estonia (office).

HELMFRID, Staffan, PhD; Swedish geographer and academic; *Professor Emeritus of Human Geography, University of Stockholm;* b. 13 Dec. 1927, Stockholm; s. of Hartwig E. W. Helmfrid and Greta Helmfrid (née Kristiansson); m. Antje Teichmann 1954; three d.; ed Stockholm Univ.; Asst, Dept of Geography, Stockholm Univ. 1951, Asst Prof. 1955, Assoc. Prof. 1962, Research Fellow 1967, Prof. of Human Geography 1969–92 now Prof. Emer., Dean of Faculty of Social Sciences 1970, Pro-Rector (Vice-Pres.) Stockholm Univ. 1974, Rector 1978–88; Chair. Bank of Sweden Tercentenary Foundation 1980–86, Fulbright Comm. in Sweden 1984–85; Chair. Standing Conf. on Univ. Problems (CC-PU), Council of Europe 1983–88; Chair. Swedish Nat. Cttee of Geography 1988–94; mem. Royal Acad. of Letters, History and Antiquities (Sec.-Gen. 1993–98), Royal Acad. of Sciences (Vice-Pres. 1988–91), Academia Europaea; Hon. Corresp. mem. Royal Geographical Soc., London 1995; Kt, Royal Order of North Star; Dr hc (Helsinki) 1988; HM Gold Medal, 12th size, Lord in Waiting 1987, Great Gold Medal, Royal Acad. of Letters, History and Antiquities 1999, Höpken Gold Medal, Royal Acad. of Sciences 2000, Vitus Behring Medal, Royal Danish Geographical Soc. 2002. *Publications:* Östergötland Västanstång. Studien über die ältere Agrarlandschaft und ihre Genese 1962; books and articles on agrarian and historical geography; textbooks on geography and social science, National Atlas of Sweden. *Leisure interests:* mountain hiking, local history. *Address:* Stockholm University, Department of Human Geography, 106 91, Stockholm (office); Björkhagsvägen 40, 18635 Vallentuna, Sweden (home). *Telephone:* (8) 51-17-48-33 (home). *E-mail:* staffan.helmfrid@swipnet.se (home). *Website:* (office).

HELØE, Leif Arne; Norwegian dentist and politician; b. 8 Aug. 1932, Harstad; ed Univ. of Oslo; school and Dist dentist, Harstad region 1957; Prof. of Community Dentistry, Univ. of Oslo 1975; mem. Harstad City Council 1960–69, mem. Municipal Exec. Bd 1968–69, Mayor of Harstad 1968–69; proxy mem. Storting (Parl.) 1965–73; Minister of Health and Social Affairs 1981–86; Dir-Gen. Norwegian Research Council for Science and Humanities 1988–91; Co-Gov. of Troms 1991–2000; Prof. Norwegian Inst. for Urban and Regional Research 2000–; Conservative; Hon. Dr of Dentistry (Kupio) 1982, (Lund) 1984; Commdr Order of the Finnish Lion 1996. *Address:* Rosenborggaten 5, 0356 Oslo, Norway. *Telephone:* 22-95-89-64 (office); 23-36-75-99 (home). *Fax:* 22-60-77-74 (office). *E-mail:* leif.heloe@nibr.no (office); arn-helo@ online.no (home).

HELSØ, Gen. Hans Jesper; Danish army officer; *Chief of Defence;* b. 9 July 1948, Copenhagen; m. Pernille Vibeke Helsø; four c.; nat. service 1968, rank of Sergeant 1969, 2nd Lt 1970, 1st Lt 1974; Gun Position Officer, Fire Direction Officer, Battery Exec. Officer, Battery Commdr, Kings Artillery 1974–78; Co. Exec. Officer UNFICYP 1979; Capt. 1979; Staff Officer, Logistic Br. LAND-ZEALAND 1979–82, Procurement Br. CHODDEN 1983–87, NATO Office, Ministry of Defence 1987–90; rank of Maj. 1986, Lt-Col 1990; Bn Commdr, 1st and 2nd ARTY-Bn, Kings Artillery 1990–92; DCOS Plans and Policy, Army Operational Command 1992–94; rank of Col 1994; CO Kings Artillery 1994–96; Commdr Bihac Area, UNPROFOR 1995; CO 1st Zealand Brigade 1996–98; rank of Maj.-Gen. 1998; Commdr Army Operational Command 1998–2000; rank of Lt-Gen. 2000; Deputy Chief of Defence 2000–02, Chief of Defence 2002–08; rank of Gen. 2002; Grand Cross, Order of Dannebrog, Badge of Honour for Good Service in the Army, Badge of Honour, Danish Reserve Officers' Org., Grand Officier, Ordre nat. du Mérite, Order of the Cross of the Eagle, Commdr, Légion d'honneur; UN Medals, UNFICYP and UNPROFOR, Medal for Support to Latvia's membership of NATO. *Address:* Defence Command, PO Box 2153, 1016 Copenhagen K, Denmark (office). *Telephone:* 45-67-30-00 (office). *Fax:* 45-89-07-48 (office). *E-mail:* fko-fc@mil.dk (office). *Website:* www.forsvaret.dk (office).

HELTAU, Michael; Austrian actor and singer; b. 5 July 1933, Ingolstadt; s. of Georg Heltau and Jakobine Heltau; ed gymnasium and Reinhardt Seminar; appeared at Würzburg and Bayerische Staatstheater, Munich 1953, Schillertheater, Berlin and Hamburg Schauspielhaus 1964–68, Theater in der Josefstadt, Vienna 1957–69, Volkstheater, Vienna 1970, Salzburg Festival 1965–75, Théâtre du Châtelet, Paris 1986; Kammerschauspieler, Burgtheater, Vienna 1972–, Doyen of the Burgtheater; noted for appearances in Shakespearean roles including Hamlet, Romeo, Richard II, Henry VI, Schnitzler's Anatol, von Hofmannsthal's Der Schwierige, Schiller's Wallenstein, etc.; second career as singer, especially songs of Jacques Brel (in German) and Viennese songs; numerous one-man shows on stage and TV; Hon. mem. Vienna Burgtheater 2003, Vienna Volksoper 2004; Austrian Cross of Honour (First Class) for Science and Art, Order of Merit (Germany) 2006; Karl Skraup Prize, Kainz Medal/Goldener Rathausmann, Gold Award of City of Vienna Nestroy Life Achievement Award 2005. *Films include:* Verlobung Am Wolfgangsee 1956, Der Letzte Mann 1956, Der Liebe Familie 1957, Lemkes Sel. Witwe 1957, Wiener Luft 1958, Das Weite Land 1970, Reigen 1974. *Leisure interests:* reading, swimming. *Address:* Sulzweg 11, 1190 Vienna, Austria (home).

HELY-HUTCHINSON, Timothy Mark, MA; British publisher; *Group Chief Executive, Hodder Headline Ltd;* b. 26 Oct. 1953, London; s. of Earl of Donoughmore and Countess of Donoughmore (née Parsons); ed Eton Coll. and Univ. of Oxford; Man. Dir Macdonald & Co. (Publrs) Ltd 1982–86, Headline Book Publishing PLC 1986–93; Group Chief Exec. Hodder Headline Ltd 1993–; Dir W. H. Smith PLC 1999–, Chair. W. H. Smith News Ltd 2002–04; Group Chief Exec. Hachette Livre UK Ltd 2004–,; Venturer of the Year (British Venture Capital Asscn) 1990, Publr of the Year (British Book Awards) 1992. *Leisure interests:* opera, racing, bridge. *Address:* Hodder Headline Ltd,

338 Euston Road, London, NW1 3BH (office). *Telephone:* (20) 7873-6011 (office). *Fax:* (20) 7873-6012 (office). *Website:* www.hodderheadline.co.uk (office).

HEMINGFORD, Baron of Watford in the County of Hertford; **(Dennis) Nicholas Hemingford,** (Nicholas Herbert), MA, FRSA; British journalist; b. (Dennis Nicholas Herbert), 25 July 1934, Watford, Herts.; s. of Dennis George Ruddock Herbert, 2nd Baron Hemingford and Elizabeth McClare (née Clark); m. Jennifer Mary Toresen Bailey 1958; one s. three d.; ed Oundle School, Clare Coll., Cambridge; Sports Desk, Reuters 1956–57, Diplomatic Desk 1957–60, Washington Bureau 1960–61; Asst Washington Corresp., The Times 1961–65, Middle East Corresp. 1965–69, Deputy Features Ed. 1969–70; Ed. Cambridge Evening News 1970–74; Editorial Dir Westminster Press 1974–91, Deputy Chief Exec. 1991–95; Pres. Guild of British Newspaper Eds 1980–81, Media Soc. 1982–84; Hon. Sec. Asscn of British Eds 1985–95; mem. E Anglian Regional Cttee, Nat. Trust 1983–2000, Chair. 1990–2000; Gov. Bell Educational Trust 1985–90; mem. Council Europa Nostra 1999–2005, Culture Cttee, UK Comm., UNESCO 1999–2003; Pres. Huntingdonshire Family History Soc.; mem. Council Friends of the British Library 2005–; Hon. mem. Soc. of Eds 1999; Hon. Sr mem. Wolfson Coll., Cambridge; Liveryman, Grocers' Co. *Publications:* Jews and Arabs in Conflict 1969, Press Freedom in Britain (with David Flintham) 1991, Successive Journeys 2008. *Leisure interests:* Egyptian War 1882, family history, computers, sport. *Address:* The Old Rectory, Hemingford Abbots, Huntingdon, Cambs., PE28 9AN, England (home). *Telephone:* (1480) 466234 (home). *Fax:* (1480) 380275 (home).

HEMINGWAY, Wayne, MBE, BSc; British designer; b. 19 Jan. 1961, Morecambe, Lancs.; s. of Billy Two Rivers (Mohawk Indian chief); m. Gerardine Hemingway; two s. two d.; ed Univ. Coll., London; together with wife started in business with market stall in Camden, London; cr. footwear, clothing and accessory label Red or Dead 1992 (now non-exec. Chair.); collection retailed through eight Red or Dead shops in UK and three Red or Dead shops in Japan and wholesaled to int. network of retailers; jt venture with Pentland Group PLC 1996–; f. hemingwaydesign 1999; designed new wing for Inst. of Directors 2001; current design and consultancy projects include an award-winning 800-unit housing estate, carpet design, wall coverings and menswear; Chair. Building for Life; Hon. Prof., Univ. of Northumbria; Hon. MA (Surrey); Dr hc (Wolverhampton); Street Designers of the Year, British Fashion Awards 1996, 1997, 1998, Housing Development of the Year 2005. *Television:* appeared in varous TV programmes including The Art Show for Channel 4. *Publications:* Red or Dead: The Good, the Bad and the Ugly (with Gerardine Hemingway) 1998, Kitsch Icons 1999, Just Above the Mantelpiece 2000, Mass Market Classics The Home 2003; articles in newspapers and journals. *Address:* 15 Wembley Park Drive, Wembley, Middx, HA9 8HD, England. *Telephone:* (20) 8903-1074 (office). *Fax:* (20) 8903-1076 (office). *E-mail:* hemingway@tesco.net (office); wayne@hemingwaydesign.co.uk (office).

HEMMING, John Henry, CMG, MA, DLitt, FSA; British/Canadian writer and publisher; *Chairman, Hemming Group Ltd;* b. 5 Jan. 1935, Vancouver, BC; s. of H. Harold Hemming, OBE, MC and Alice L. Hemming, OBE; m. Sukie Babington-Smith 1979; one s. one d.; ed Eton Coll., UK, McGill Univ. and Univ. of Oxford, UK; Dir and Sec. Royal Geographical Soc. 1975–96; Jt Chair. Hemming Group Ltd 1976–; Chair. Brintex Ltd, Newman Books Ltd; explorations in Peru and Brazil 1960, 1961, 1971, 1972, 1986–88, led Maracá Rainforest Project, Brazil (largest ever Amazon research programme by a European country) 1987–88; Hon. Fellow, Magdalen Coll. Oxford 2004; Commdr, Order of Southern Cross (Brazil) 1998, Gran Cruz, Orden al Mérito (Peru) 2007; Hon. DLitt (Oxford) 1981, Dr hc (Warwick) 1989, (Stirling) 1991; Pitman Literary Prize 1970, Christopher Award (USA) 1971, Founder's Medal, Royal Geographical Soc. 1989, Bradford Washburn Medal, Boston Museum of Science 1989, Mungo Park Medal, Royal Scottish Geographical Soc. 1988, Special Award, Instituto Nacional de Cultura (Peru) 1996, Citation of Merit, Explorers' Club (New York) 1997. *Publications:* The Conquest of the Incas 1970, Tribes of the Amazon Basin in Brazil (with others) 1973, Red Gold: The Conquest of the Brazilian Indians 1978, The Search for El Dorado 1978, Machu Picchu 1982, Monuments of the Incas 1983, Change in the Amazon Basin (two vols) (ed.) 1985, Amazon Frontier: The Defeat of the Brazilian Indians 1987, Maracá 1988, Roraima, Brazil's Northernmost Frontier 1990, The Rainforest Edge (ed.) 1993, Royal Geographical Society Illustrated (ed.) 1997, The Golden Age of Discovery 1998, Die If You Must: Brazilian Indians in the Twentieth Century 2003, Tree of Rivers: The Story of the Amazon 2007. *Leisure interests:* travel, writing. *Address:* 10 Edwardes Square, London, W8 6HE (home); Hemming Group Ltd, 32 Vauxhall Bridge Road, London, SW1V 2SS, England (office). *Telephone:* (20) 7602-6697 (home); (20) 7973-6634 (office). *Fax:* (20) 7233-5049 (office). *E-mail:* j.hemming@hgluk.com (office). *Website:* www.hgluk.com (office); www.johnhemming.net (home).

HEMMINGSEN, Ralf, MD, DrMed; Danish psychiatrist, university rector and academic; *Rector (Vice-Chancellor), University of Copenhagen;* b. 12 Oct. 1949; ed Univ. of Copenhagen; research training and clinical training as consultant in psychiatry 1975–76; Sr Lecturer in Psychiatry, Univ. of Copenhagen 1978–80, 1984–95, Prof. of Psychiatry 1995–, Dean of Faculty of Health Sciences 2002–05, Rector Univ. of Copenhagen 2005–, Chair. Faculty Jt Cttee 2002–05, Faculty Occupational Health Cttee 2002–05, Man. Forum, Copenhagen Univ. Hosp. (KUHL) 2002–05, Copenhagen Tech Transfer Consortium 2003–05, mem. Main Jt Cttee 2002–05, Steering Group for Univ. of Copenhagen's Value Process 2003–05, Human Resources Policy Cttee 2004–05; consultant in psychiatry 1983–; Consultant in Psychiatry, Frederiksberg Hosp. 1986; Medical Dir Bispebjerg Hosp. 1986–2002; Chair. Danish Soc. for Biological Psychiatry 1997–2000; mem. Danish Medicolegal Council 1992–, Bd The Medical Soc. in Copenhagen 1991–97; mem., later Chair. Danish Psychiatric Soc. 1986–90; mem., later Pres. European Soc. for Clinical Investigation 1983–87; Gold Medal, Univ. of Copenhagen. *Publications:* more than 150 papers in scientific journals. *Address:* Rector's Office, University of Copenhagen, Nørregade 10, PO Box 2177, 1017 Copenhagen K, Denmark (office). *Telephone:* 35-32-26-12 (office). *E-mail:* rektor@adm.ku.dk (office). *Website:* www.ku.dk (office).

HEMPEL, Rt Rev. Johannes, CBE, DTheol; German ecclesiastic; b. 23 March 1929, Zittau; s. of Albert Hempel and Gertrud Hempel (née Buchwald); m. Dorothea Schönbach 1956; two s. one d.; ed Univs of Tübingen, Heidelberg, Kirchliche Hochschule, Berlin; Rev. Evangelical Lutheran Church, Saxony 1952–57, Bishop 1972–94; Student Pastor and Teacher of Theology, Leipzig 1957–72; a Pres. of WCC; Bundesverdienstkreuz; three hon. degrees. *Publications:* Kirche wird auch in Zukunft sein 1994, Annehmen und frei bleiben 1996, Erfahrungen und Bewahrungen 2004. *Address:* Hutbergstrasse 78, 01326 Dresden, Germany (home). *Telephone:* (351) 2683142 (home). *Fax:* (351) 2632097 (home). *E-mail:* johanneshempel@t-online.de (home).

HEMSLEY, Stephen J.; American business executive; *President and CEO, UnitedHealth Group;* ed Fordham Univ.; fmr Man. Partner, Chief Financial Officer and Head of Strategy, Tech., and Operating Professional Service Lines, Arthur Andersen and Co.; Sr Exec. Vice-Pres. UnitedHealth Group 1997–98, COO 1998–2006, Pres. 1999–, mem. Bd of Dirs 2000–, CEO 2006–. *Address:* UnitedHealth Group, PO Box 1459, Minneapolis, MN 55440-1459, USA (office). *Telephone:* (800) 328-5979 (office). *E-mail:* info@unitedhealthgroup.com (office). *Website:* www.unitedhealthgroup.com (office).

HEN, Józef, (Korab); Polish writer and playwright; b. 8 Nov. 1923, Warsaw; s. of Roman Cukier and Ewa Cukier; m. Irena Hen 1946; one s. one d.; self-educated; Lecturer, Sorbonne, France 1993 and Univ. of Warsaw 1995–96; mem. Acad. des Sciences, Belles Lettres et des Beaux Arts, Bordeaux, France; mem. Polish PEN Club. *Film screenplays include:* Krzyż walecznych (Cross of Valour) 1959, Kwiecień (April) 1961, Nikt nie woła (Nobody's Calling) 1961, Bokser i śmierć (The Boxer and Death), Prawo i pięść (Law and the Fist) and Don Gabriel. *Screenplays for TV serials:* Życie Kamila Kuranta (The Life of Kamil Kurant) 1983, Crimen and Królewskie Sny (Royal Dreams) 1987. *Theatre plays:* Ja, Michał z Montaigne (I, Michel de Montaigne) 1984, Justyn! Justyn!, Popołudnie kochanków (Lovers' Afternoon) 1994. *Publications include:* Skromny chłopiec w haremie (A Modest Boy in a Harem) 1957, Kwiecień (April) 1960 (Book of the Year 1961), Teatr Heroda (Herod's Theatre) 1966, Twarz pokerzysty (Pokerface) 1970, Oko Dajana (Dayan's Eye, as Korab) 1972, Yokohama 1973, Crimen 1975, Bokser i śmierć (The Boxer and Death) 1975, Ja, Michał z Montaigne (I, Michel de Montaigne) 1978, Milczące między nami (Silent between Us) 1985, Nie boję się bezsennych nocy (I'm Not Afraid of Sleepless Nights), 3 books 1987, 1992, 2001, Królenskie sny (Royal Dreams) 1989, Nikt nie woła (Nobody's Calling) 1990, Nowolipie 1991, Odejście Afrodyty (Aphrodite's Departure) 1995, Najpiękniejsze lata (The Most Beautiful Years) 1996, Niebo naszych ojcow (Sky of Our Fathers) 1997, Błazen – wielki mąż (Jester – The Great Man) (ZAiKS Book of the Year Award 1999) 1998, Mójprzyjaciel Król (My Friend the King) (Booker's Club Book of the Year Award 2005) 2003, Bruliony profesora T. (The Bloch-notes of Professor T.) 2006, Ring-pomgista (The Ping-pongist) 2008. *Leisure interests:* historical and literary monographs, watching sports programmes on television, films. *Address:* Al. Ujazdowskie 8 m. 2, 00-478 Warsaw, Poland (home). *Telephone:* (22) 629-19-03 (home).

HENARE, Tau; New Zealand politician; m.; five c.; fmr Advisory Officer in Maori Devt, Waitakere City Council, Youth Educ. Co-ordinator, Race Relations Conciliator, Advisory Officer, Dept of Internal Affairs; MP for Northern Maori (now Te Tai Tokerau) 1993–; Minister of Maori Affairs 1997–99, for Racing, Assoc. Minister for Sport, Fitness and Leisure; Deputy Leader NZ First Party, Spokesperson on Cultural Affairs and Treaty of Waitangi Negotiations. *Address:* c/o Ministry of Maori Affairs, PO Box 3943, Wellington 6015, New Zealand. *Telephone:* (4) 494-7000. *Fax:* (4) 494-7010.

HENAULT, Gen. Raymond (Ray), CMM, CD, BA; Canadian armed forces officer; b. 1949, Winnipeg, Man.; ed Univ. of Man., Nat. Defence Coll., Kingston, Ont., École Supérieure de Guerre Aérienne, Paris, France; began career in Canadian Armed Forces 1968; training at Canadian Force Base (CFB) Borden, Ont. and Gimili, Man.; CF-101 Voodoo Pilot, 425 Squadron, CFB Bagotville, Québec 1971; Flying Instructor, Musketeer, CFB Portage la Prairie 1972–74; Air Traffic Controller, CFB Bagotville 1974–76; Twin Huey Helicopter Pilot, 408 Squadron, CFB Edmonton, Alberta 1976–80; Staff Officer Aviation, 5 Canadian Brigade Group HQ, CFB Valcartier 1980–81; Twin Huey Flight Commdr, 430e Escardon, CFB Valcartier 1981–85; Head of Doctrine and Int. Programs, Directorate of Land Aviation, Nat. Defence HQ, Ottawa 1985; Project Dir Canadian Forces Light Helicopter Project, Ottawa 1985–87; Commdg Officer 444(CA) Tactical Helicopter Squadron, CFB Lahr, Germany 1987–89; Sr Staff Officer Requirements, Air Command HQ, Winnipeg 1989–90; Base Commdr, CFB Portage la Prairie 1990–92; Deputy Commdr 10 Tactical Air Group, CFB Montreal 1992–93, Commdr 1994–95; Chief of Staff Operations, Air Command HQ 1995–96; Chief of Staff J3 and Dir-Gen. Mil. Plans and Operations, Nat. Defence HQ 1996–97; Acting Deputy Chief of Defence Staff 1997, Asst Chief of Air Staff 1997–98, Deputy Chief 1998–2001, Chief 2001–05; Chair. Mil. Cttee NATO 2005–08; promoted to Brigadier-Gen. 1994, Maj.-Gen. 1997, Lt-Gen. 1998, Gen. 2001; Commdr Order of Mil. Merit, Commdr Légion d'honneur, Most Venerable Order of St John of Jerusalem, US Legion of Merit; Hon. LLD (Univ. of Man.), Hon. PhD (Royal Military Coll. of Canada) 2005. *Address:* c/o Department of National Defence, National Defence Headquarters, Maj.-Gen. George R. Pearkes Bldg, 15 NT, 101 Colonel By Dr., Ottawa, ON K1A 0K2, Canada. *Telephone:* (613) 995-2534. *Fax:* (613) 996-8330. *E-mail:* information@forces.gc.ca. *Website:* www.forces.gc.ca.

HENDERSON, Sir Denys (Hartley), Kt, MA, LLB, FRSA; British business executive and solicitor; b. 11 Oct. 1932, Colombo, Sri Lanka; s. of the late John Hartley Henderson and Nellie Henderson (née Gordon); m. Doreen Mathewson Glashan 1957; two d.; ed Aberdeen Grammar School and Univ. of Aberdeen; Commercial Asst ICI 1957–58, Chair. Paints Div. 1977–80, Main Bd Dir 1980, Deputy Chair. 1986–87, Chair. 1987–95; Chancellor Univ. of Bath 1993–98; Chair. Zeneca Group PLC 1993–95; Dir (non-exec.) Barclays Bank PLC 1983–97, Barclays PLC 1985–97, RTZ Corpn PLC 1990–96, Rank 1994–2001 (Chair. 1995–2001), MORI 1995–, Dalgety PLC 1996–98 (Chair. 1997–98); mem. Law Soc. of Scotland 1955–; Chair. Court of Govs. of Henley Man. Coll. 1989–96; mem. Pres.'s Cttee, CBI 1987–96; First Crown Estate Commr 1995–2002; Trustee, The Natural History Museum 1989–98; Chair. Univ. of Aberdeen Quincentenary Appeal Cttee 1993–96; Pres. and Chair. Bd British Quality Foundation 1993–97; Hon. Fellow City and Guilds of London Inst. 1990, Soc. of Chemical Industry Centenary Medal 1993; Hon. DUniv (Brunel) 1987, (Strathclyde) 1993; Hon. LLD (Aberdeen) 1987, (Nottingham) 1990, (Manchester) 1991, (Bath) 1993; Hon. DSc (Cranfield Inst. of Tech.) 1989, (Teesside) 1993. *Leisure interests:* family life, swimming, reading, travel, gardening and "unskilled but enjoyable" golf. *Address:* c/o The Crown Estate, 16 Carlton House Terrace, London SW1Y, 5AH, England (office).

HENDERSON, Donald Ainslie, MD, MPH; American professor of medicine and public health; *Professor, Center for Biosecurity, University of Pittsburgh Medical Center;* b. 7 Sept. 1928, Cleveland, Ohio; s. of David A. Henderson and Grace E. McMillan; m. Nana I. Bragg 1951; two s. one d.; ed Oberlin Coll., Univ. of Rochester and Johns Hopkins Univ.; Intern, Mary Imogene Bassett Hosp., Cooperstown, NY 1954–55, Resident 1957–59; various posts at Communicable Diseases Center, Dept of Health, Educ. and Welfare 1955–66, Chief Smallpox Eradication Program 1965–66; Chief Medical Officer, WHO Smallpox Eradication 1966–77; Prof. of Epidemiology and Int. Health, Johns Hopkins Univ. Bloomberg School of Public Health 1977–2003, Dean 1977–90, Dir Civilian Biodefense Studies Center 1998–2001, now Univ. Distinguished Service Prof. and Dean Emer.; Prof., Univ. of Pittsburgh Medical Center 2003–, Resident Scholar, Center for Biosecurity 2003–; Assoc. Dir, Office of Science and Tech. Policy, Exec. Office of the Pres. 1991–93; Deputy Asst Sec. Dept of Health and Human Services, Washington, DC 1993–95, Sr Scientific Adviser 1993–95; Dir Office of Public Health Preparedness, Dept of Health and Human Services 2001–03, Sr Scientific Adviser 2003–; mem. numerous professional socs, cttees and advisory panels and recipient of numerous scientific awards and recognitions from orgs in USA, Canada, UK, Japan, Brazil, Uruguay, Switzerland, People's Repub. of China, Ethiopia, Afghanistan, Germany, Australia, India and Pakistan; 16 hon. degrees; Presidential Medal of Freedom 2002, Knight Grand Cross, Govt of Thailand 2006; Nat. Medal of Science 1986, Japan Prize 1988, Edward Jenner Medal, Royal Soc. of Medicine. *Publications:* more than 200 articles dealing primarily with smallpox eradication, epidemiology and immunization. *Address:* Center for Biosecurity, University of Pittsburgh Medical Center, Pier IV Building, Suite 210, 621 East Pratt Street, Baltimore, MD 21202 (office); 3802 Greenway, Baltimore, MD 21218, USA (home). *Telephone:* (443) 573-3323 (office); (410) 889-2880 (home). *Fax:* (443) 573-3305 (office); (410) 889-6514 (home). *E-mail:* dahzero@aol.com (office). *Website:* upmc-biosecurity.org (office).

HENDERSON, Horace Edward; American realtor, military historian and world peace advocate; *Chairman, Coalition for World Union Federation;* b. 30 July 1917, Henderson, NC; s. of Thomas Brantley Henderson and Ethel Maude Duke; m. Vera Schubert 1966; two d.; ed Coll. of William and Mary and Yale Univ.; US Army Capt., World War II; Owner, Henderson Real Estate, Williamsburg, Va 1947–52; Vice-Pres. Jr Chamber Int. 1951–52; Nat. Pres. US Jr Chamber 1952–53; Asscns Co-ordinator, Nat. Auto Dealers' Asscn, Washington, DC 1954–55; Dir Chamber of Commerce of the USA 1954; Exec. Cttee US Comm. for the UN 1954; Trustee, Freedoms Foundation 1955; Vice-Chair. Operation Brotherhood 1954–56; Republican Party cand. for Congress 1956 and for Lt-Gov. of Va 1957; ind. cand. for US Senate 1972; Dir Office of Special Liaison and Special Asst, Deputy Under-Sec. of State 1958; US Del. to ILO 1959–60, WHO 1959–60, UNESCO 1960, FAO 1959, UNHCR 1959, ECOSOC 1959, US Del. to UN 1960; Deputy Asst Sec. of State for Int. Orgs, Dept of State, Washington, DC 1959–60; Chair. Republican Party of Virginia 1962–64; mem. Republican Nat. Cttee 1962–64; Chair. of Bd, Henderson Real Estate Agency, McLean, Va 1962–65; Dir-Gen. World Peace Through Law Center, Geneva 1965–69; Pres. and Chair. Community Methods Inc. 1969–75; Chair. World Peace Treaty Campaign 1997–2004, Coalition for World Union Fed. 2006–; Pres. Int. Domestic Devt Corps 1975, Chair. Asscn for Devt of Educ. 1977–78; Exec. Dir World Asscn of Judges 1968; Chair. Congressional Reform Cttee 1976; Exec. Vice-Pres. American Lawmakers' Asscn 1977; real estate and man. consultant 1978–83; Pres. Williamsburg Vacations Inc. 1983–84, Nat. Asscn for Free Trade 1986; mem. St Andrew's Soc.; Elder, Presbyterian Church; Nat. Citizenship Award, American Heritage Foundation 1953, Outstanding Jaycee of the World Award 1954. *Publications:* The Scots of Virginia – America's Greatest Patriots 2001, The Greatest Blunders of World War II 2002, The Final Word on War and Peace 2004. *Address:* 1925 Burnt Bridge Road, Apt 822, Lynchburg, VA 24503, USA (home). *Telephone:* (434) 384-2338 (home). *E-mail:* hDukeHen@aol.com (home). *Website:* WorldUnionFederation.org (office).

HENDERSON, Richard, PhD, FRS; British molecular biologist; *Research Scientist, Medical Research Council;* b. 19 July 1945, Edinburgh; s. of John W. Henderson and Grace S. Henderson (née Goldie); m. 1st Penelope Fitzgerald 1969 (divorced 1988); one s. one d. (one d. deceased); m. 2nd Jade Li 1995; ed Hawick High School, Boroughmuir Secondary School, Univs of Edinburgh and Cambridge; professional interest in structure and function of protein molecules, especially in biological membranes; Helen Hay Whitney Post-

doctoral Fellow, Yale Univ., USA 1970–73; Fellow, Darwin Coll., Cambridge 1982–; mem. research staff, MRC Lab. of Molecular Biology 1973–, Dir 1996–2006; Foreign Assoc. NAS; Ernst Ruska Prize for Electron Microscopy 1981, Lewis S. Rosenstiel Award, Brandeis Univ. 1991, Louis Jeantet Award 1993, Gregori Aminoff Award 1999. *Publications:* many scientific articles in books and journals. *Leisure interests:* canoeing, wine. *Address:* Medical Research Council Laboratory of Molecular Biology, Hills Road, Cambridge, CB2 0QH, England (office). *Telephone:* (1223) 402215 (office); (1223) 248011 (office). *Fax:* (1223) 213556 (office). *E-mail:* rh15@mrc-lmb.cam.ac.uk (office). *Website:* www2.mrc-lmb.cam.ac.uk/SS/Henderson_R (office); www2.mrc-lmb.cam.ac.uk/groups/rh15 (office).

HENDERSON, Vince; Dominican politician; *Minister of Foreign Affairs;* mem. Parl. (Labour Party of Dominica); fmr Minister for Agric., Fisheries and the Environment, Minister of Educ., Human Resource Devt, Sports and Youth Affairs –2008, of Foreign Affairs 2008–; fmr Chair. Dominica Nat. Comm. for UNESCO. *Address:* c/o Office of the Prime Minister, 6th Floor, Financial Centre, Roseau, Dominica (office). *Telephone:* 2663279 (office). *Fax:* 4485200 (office).

HENDRICKS, Barbara Ann, BSc, BMus; Swedish singer (soprano); b. 20 Nov. 1948, Stephens, Ark.; d. of M. L. Hendricks and Della Hendricks; m. Ulf Englund 1978; one s. one d.; ed Univ. of Neb. and Juilliard School of Music, New York, studying with Jennie Tourel; operatic debut, San Francisco Opera (L'Incoronazione di Poppea) 1976; has appeared with opera companies of Boston, Santa Fe, Glyndebourne, Hamburg, La Scala (Milan), Berlin, Paris, LA, Florence and Royal Opera, Covent Garden (London), Vienna; recitals in most maj. centres in Europe and America; has toured extensively in USSR and Japan; concert performances with all leading European and US orchestras; has appeared at many maj. music festivals including Edin., Osaka, Montreux, Salzburg, Dresden, Prague, Aix-en-Provence, Orange and Vienna; nearly 90 recordings; nominated Goodwill Amb. for Refugees at UNHCR 1987; founder Barbara Hendricks Foundation for Peace and Reconciliation 1998; Hon. mem. Inst. of Humanitarian Law, San Remo, Italy 1990; Commdr des Arts et des Lettres; Hon. DMus (Nebraska Wesleyan Univ.) 1988; Dr hc (Univ. of Louvain, Belgium) 1990, 1993, (Juilliard School, New York) 2000; Prince of Asturias Foundation Award 2000, Lions Club International Award for the Defense of Human Rights 2001, Premio Internacional Xifra Heras (Univ. of Gerona, Spain) 2004, La Medaille D'Or de la ville de Paris 2004. *Film appearance:* La Bohème 1988, The Rake's Progress 1994. *Leisure interest:* reading. *Address:* B H Office, c/o Fondberg Produktion, Dalagatan 48, 11324, Stockholm, Sweden (office). *E-mail:* bh.office@bluewin.ch (office). *Website:* www.barbarahendricks.com (office).

HENDRICKSE, Ralph George, MD, FRCP, FRCPE, FRCPCH; British consultant paediatrician (retd); *Professor Emeritus, Department of Tropical Paediatrics and International Child Health, University of Liverpool;* b. 5 Nov. 1926, Cape Town, S Africa; s. of William G. Hendrickse and Johanna T. Hendrickse (née Dennis); m. Begum Johanahara Abdurahman 1948; one s. four d; ed Livingstone High School, Cape and Univ. of Cape Town Medical School, S Africa; Sr Medical Officer, McCord Zulu Hosp. Durban 1949–54; Sr Registrar, Univ. Coll. Hosp. Ibadan, Nigeria 1956–57; Lecturer, Sr Lecturer, Univ. of Ibadan 1957–62, Prof. and Head, Dept of Paediatrics 1962–69, Dir Inst. of Child Health 1964–69; Sr Lecturer and Dir Diploma in Tropical Child Health Course, Univ. of Liverpool and Liverpool School of Tropical Medicine 1969–75, Prof. of Tropical Paediatrics 1975–91, Dean Liverpool School of Tropical Medicine 1988–91, Prof. and Head of newly created Dept of Tropical Paediatrics and Int. Child Health, Liverpool Univ. 1988–91, Prof. Emer. 1991–; Founder and Ed.-in-Chief, Annals of Tropical Paediatrics 1981–2004; mem. Advisory Expert Panel on Tropical Pediatrics of Int. Pediatric Asscn; mem. Standing Panel of Experts in Public Health Medicine of London Univ. 1990–93, 1993–; Sr Heinz Fellow British Paediatric Asscn 1961; Rockefeller Foundation Fellow 1961–62; Hon. Consultant Paediatrician, Liverpool Health Authority 1969–91; Hon. Foundation Fellow Medical Council of Nigera in Paediatrics 1970; Hon. Foundation Fellow Royal Coll. of Paediatrics and Child Health 1996; Hon. DSc (Cape Town) 1998; Hon. FRCPCH, Hon. FMC (Nigeria); Frederick Murgatroyd Memorial Prize, Royal Coll. of Physicians 1970. *Publications:* Tropical Paediatrics: Update and Current Review 1981, Paediatrics in the Tropics 1991, over 150 articles in scientific journals (1954–2001). *Leisure interests:* swimming, gardening, painting, travel, theatre. *Address:* Beresford House, 25 Riverbank Road, Heswall, Wirral, Merseyside, CH60 4SQ, England (home). *Telephone:* (151) 342-5510 (home). *Fax:* (151) 342-1312 (home). *E-mail:* ralphgh.hendrickse@virgin.net (home).

HENDROPRIYONO, Lt-Gen. (retd) Abdullah Mahmud; Indonesian politician; *Head of National Intelligence Agency;* b. 1945, Jakarta; ed AMN Military Acad.; mil. career with Kopassus Unit, including several tours of combat duty in Kalimantan 1960s and 1970s, in East Timor 1975; sr positions in Bais (Indonesian mil. intelligence agency) 1990s, Jakarta Area Commdr 1993–94; Minister of Transmigration and Resettlement 1998–99; Head of Nat. Intelligence Agency (BIN) 2001–; also owner of a law firm. *Address:* c/o Office of the Co-ordinating Minister for Political Affairs, Security and Social Welfare, Jalan Medan Merdeka Barat 15, Jakarta 10110, Indonesia (office).

HENDRY, Stephen Gordon, MBE; British professional snooker player; b. 13 Jan. 1969, Edin.; s. of Gordon J. Hendry and Irene Anthony; m. Amanda Elizabeth Teresa Tart 1995; one s.; ed Inverkeithing High School; commenced professional career 1985; winner of more than 50 major competitions including Grand Prix 1987, 1990, 1991, 1995, British Open 1988, 1991, 1999, UK Championship 1989, 1990, 1994, 1995, 1996, Embassy World Championship 1990, 1992, 1993 1994, 1995, 1996, 1999; Dr hc (Stirling) 2000; MacRoberts Trophy 2001. *Publication:* Snooker Masterclass 1994. *Leisure interests:* golf, music, Formula 1. *Address:* Stephen Hendry Snooker Ltd,

Kerse Road, Stirling, FK7 7SG, Scotland. *Telephone:* (1786) 462634. *Fax:* (1786) 450068.

HENG, Swee Keat, MA, MPA; Singaporean government official; *Managing Director, Monetary Authority of Singapore;* ed Univ. of Cambridge, UK, Kennedy School of Govt, Harvard Univ., USA; fmr Sr Police Officer; Dir of Higher Educ., Ministry of Educ. –1997; served in Prime Minister's Office as Prin. Pvt. Sec. to then Sr Minister Lee Kuan Yew 1997–2000; Deputy Sec. (Trade), Ministry of Trade and Industry 2000–01, concurrently CEO Trade Devt Bd 2001, Perm. Sec. 2001–05; Man. Dir (Designate) Monetary Authority of Singapore March–June 2005, Man. Dir June 2005–; Overseas Singapore Police Force Scholar, Gold Medal in Public Admin 2001. *Address:* Monetary Authority of Singapore, 10 Shenton Way, MAS Building, Singapore City, 079117, Singapore (office). *Telephone:* 6225-5577 (office). *Fax:* 6229-9491 (office). *E-mail:* webmaster@mas.gov.sg (office). *Website:* www.mas.gov.sg (office).

HENG SAMRIN; Cambodian politician; b. 25 May 1934; Political Commissar and Commdr of Khmer Rouge 4th Infantry Div. 1976–78; led abortive coup against Pol Pot and fled to Viet Nam 1978; Pres. Nat. Front for Nat. Salvation of Kampuchea 1978; Pres. People's Revolutionary Council 1979 (took power after Vietnamese invasion of Kampuchea); Chair. Council of State of Cambodia 1991; Sec. Gen. People's Revolutionary Party of Kampuchea (KPRP) 1981–91; mem. Politburo of Cambodia 1991–. *Address:* Council of State, Phnom Penh, Cambodia.

HENIN, Justine; Belgian professional tennis player; b. 1 June 1982, Liege; d. of José Henin and the late Françoise Henin; m. Pierre-Yves Hardenne 2002; winner French Open Jr Championship 1997; professional tennis player 1999–; semi-finalist French Open 2001, winner 2003, 2007; finalist Wimbledon 2001, semi-finalist 2002, 2003; quarter-finalist Australian Open 2002, semi-finalist 2003; winner US Open 2003, 2007; world ranking of number one 2003, 2007; retd from professional tennis 2008. *Address:* c/o Vincent Stavaux, Place Riva Bella 12/5, 1420 Braine L'Alleud, Belgium (office).

HÉNIN, Pierre-Yves, PhD; French university administrator, academic and economist; *President, Université Paris I (Panthéon Sorbonne);* b. 11 April 1946, St-Aubin, Saône et Loire; m.; four c.; ed Faculté de Droit et de Sciences Economiques de Paris, Université Paris I (Panthéon Sorbonne); Research Dir ISEA, CNRS 1967–71; Prof. Université d'Orléans 1972–75; Founder and Dir Macroéconomie et Analyse des Déséquilibres research centre, Université Paris I (Panthéon Sorbonne) 1974–1990, Prof. Université Paris I (Panthéon Sorbonne) 1975–, Dir UER 1978–82, 1985–90, Vice-Pres. Scientific Council 1982–89, 1993–, currently Pres. Université Paris I (Panthéon Sorbonne); Consultant Ministry of Research and Tech. 1985–86; Dir CEPREMAP 1991–; mem. Scientific Council Ecole Nationale des Statistiques et de l'Admin Economique 1980–86; Vice-Pres. Asscn Française de Sciences Economiques 1994–95, Pres. 1995–97; Chevalier de l'Ordre Nationale du Mérite 1993, Chevalier des Palmes Académiques 1998, Chevalier de la Légion d'Honneur 2002; AFSE Thesis Prize 1970, Le Nouvel Economiste Economist of the Year 1996. *Address:* Université Paris I (Panthéon Sorbonne), 12 place du Panthéon, 75231 Paris Cedex 05, France (office). *Telephone:* 1-44-07-80-00 (office). *Website:* www.univ-paris1.fr (office).

HENKEL, Hans-Olaf; German business executive; *Honorary Professor of International Management, University of Mannheim;* b. 14 March 1940, Hamburg; four c.; joined Int. Business Machines (IBM), Germany 1962, Pres. IBM Germany 1987–89, Vice-Pres. IBM Corpn 1989–95, CEO IBM Europe 1993–95; Pres. Bundesverband der Deutschen Industrie 1995–2000; Pres. Leibniz Gemeinschaft 2001–05; Hon. Prof. of Int. Man., Univ. of Mannheim 2000–; mem. Supervisory Bd Bayer AG, Continental AG, Daimler Luft- und Raumfahrt Holding AG, EPG AG, SMS GmbH, Ringier AG; mem. Amnesty Int.; Co-founder Konvent fuer Deutschland; Dr hc (Tech. Univ. of Dresden) 1991; Commdr, Légion d'honneur; WWF Environmental Manager of the Year 1991, Wirtschaftswoche magazine Innovation Award, Corine Writers' Award, Ludwig-Erhard Award, Cicero 'Best Business Speaker' Award, Deutscher Mittelstandspreis 2006, Hayek Medal 2007. *Publications:* Die Macht der Freiheit, Die Ethik des Erfolgs, Die Kraft des Neubeginns, Der Kampf um die Mitte. *Leisure interests:* sailing, jazz. *Address:* Friedrichstrasse 166, 10117 Berlin, Germany (office). *Telephone:* (30) 200597701 (office). *Fax:* (30) 200597729 (office). *E-mail:* petra.ziemer@bankofamerica.com (office).

HENKIN, Louis, LLD, LHD; American professor of law; *Chairman, Institute for Human Rights, School of Law, Columbia University;* b. 11 Nov. 1917, Russia; s. of Yoseph Henkin and Frieda Kreindel; m. Alice Hartman 1960; three s.; ed Yeshiva Coll. and Harvard Univ.; admitted New York Bar 1941, US Supreme Court Bar 1947; law clerk 1940–41, 1946–47; mil. service 1941–45; with State Dept 1945–46, 1948–57; UN Legal Dept 1947–48; Lecturer in Law, Columbia Univ. 1956–57; Visiting Prof. Univ. of Pa 1957–58, Prof. of Law 1958–62; Prof. Columbia Univ. 1962, mem. Inst. for War and Peace Studies 1962–, Hamilton Fish Prof. of Int. Law and Diplomacy 1963–78, Harlan Fiske Stone Prof. of Constitutional Law 1978–79, Univ. Prof. 1979–88, Univ. Prof. Emer. and Special Service Prof. 1988–; Chair. Directorate, Columbia Univ. Center for Study of Human Rights 1986–, Chair. Human Rights Inst., Columbia Univ. Law School 1999–; Pres. US Inst. of Human Rights 1970–93; mem. Lawyers' Cttee on Human Rights, Immigration and Refugee Services 1994–; mem. Human Rights Cttee (UN) under ICCPR 1999–; numerous professional and public appointments, affiliations and distinctions etc. –2002; Fellow, American Acad. of Arts and Sciences; mem. American Philosophical Soc., Council on Foreign Relations, American Soc. of Int. Law, Int. Law Asscn, Inst. de Droit Int., US Asscn of Constitutional Law etc.; Guggenheim Fellow 1979–80; Hon. JD (Brooklyn Law School) 1997. *Publications:* numerous books and articles on constitutional law, constitutionalism, int. law, Law of the Sea and human rights including: How Nations Behave (2nd edn) 1979, Constitutionalism and Rights: The Influence of the United States Abroad 1989, Foreign Affairs and the US Constitution 1990, International Law: Politics and Values 1995, Foreign Affairs and the US Constitution (2nd edn) 1996, The Age of Rights 1996, Human Rights (with others) 1999, International Law (with others) (4th edn) 2001. *Address:* 460 Riverside Drive, New York, NY 10027, USA (home). *Telephone:* 212-854-2634 (office). *Fax:* (212) 854-7946. *E-mail:* lh8@columbia.edu (office).

HENLE, Christian-Peter; German business executive; b. 9 Nov. 1938, Duisburg; s. of the late Günter Henle and of Anne-Liese Henle (née Küpper); brother of Jörg Alexander Henle (q.v.); m. Dr Susanne Beitz 1967; two s.; ed High School, Duisburg, Institut d'Etudes Politiques, Paris; joined Klöckner Eisenhandel GmbH, Düsseldorf 1963–64; with Klöckner and Co., Duisburg 1964–65, Vice-Pres. Klöckner Inc., New York 1965–67; Pres. Klöckner Industrie-Anlagen GmbH, Duisburg 1967–70; mem. Bd of Dirs responsible for depts for liquid fuels, motor fuels and lubricants, gas, chemicals, industrial plants, Klöckner and Co., Duisburg 1971–, partner 1977–; Chair. Supervisory Bd Klöckner-Humboldt-Deutz AG (KHD), Cologne, Mietfinanz GmbH, Mülheim/Ruhr; mem. Supervisory Bd KHD Humboldt Wedag AG, Cologne, Deutsche Babcock AG, Oberhausen, Gerling-Konzern Welt-Versicherungs-Pool AG, Cologne, Gerling-Konzern Globale Rückversicherungs-AG, Cologne, Knipping-Dorn GmbH, Herne; Chair. Advisory Bd Fisser & v. Doornum, Hamburg, Montan Brennstoffhandel und Schiffahrt GmbH & Co. KG, Munich; mem. Advisory Bd Dresdner Bank AG, Frankfurt, Arnold Knipping GmbH, Gummersbach; mem. of Bd Mineralölwirtschaftsverband e.V., Hamburg; mem. Int. Advisory Bd The American Univ., Washington, DC, USA; Pres. Deutsche Gesellschaft für Auswärtige Politik eV, Bonn; Verdienstkreuz am Bande des Verdienstordens (FRG); Chevalier de l'Ordre du Mérite (Senegal). *Publication:* Auf dem Weg in ein neues Zeitalter (ed. and co-author) 1985. *Leisure interests:* music, sports (tennis, golf), collecting contemporary works of art. *Address:* Klöckner & Co. AG, Klöckner Haus, Neudorfer Strasse 3–5, 47057 Duisburg, Germany. *Telephone:* (203) 182253.

HENLE, Jörg Alexander; German business executive; b. 12 May 1934, Aachen; s. of Dr Günter Henle and Anne-Liese Henle (née Küpper); brother of Christian-Peter Henle (q.v.); one s. three d.; ed Cologne, Munich, Princeton (NJ), Stanford, Geneva and Berlin Univs; joined Klöckner-Werke AG 1962; Man. Establecimientos Klöckner SA, Buenos Aires 1964–65; Deputy mem. Directorate of Klöckner Mannstaedt-Werke, Troisdorf 1965–67; mem. Directorate, Klöckner-Werke AG, Hütte Bremen 1967–68; mem. Man. Bd. Klöckner-Werke AG 1968–71, Chair. Supervisory Bd 1979–92; Chair. Bd of Man. Klöckner & Co. AG 1971–92; Chair. Bd Peter-Klöckner-Stiftung, Duisburg 1992–; mem. Bd Stichting Verenigt Bezit, The Hague, Stichting HORIZON, Naarden, Int. Yehudi Menuhin Foundation, Brussels; fmr mem. Supervisory Bd Allianz Lebensversicherungs-AG, Deutsche Bank AG, Mietfinanz GmbH, AG, Robert Bosch GmbH, Readymix AG; fmr mem. Advisory Bd HERMES Kreditversicherungs-Aktiengesellschaft; fmr Vice-Pres. Niederrheinische Industrie- und Handelskammer Duisburg-Wesel-Kleve zu Duisburg; Bundesverdienstkreuz. *Leisure interests:* plastic arts, theatre, music. *Address:* Karlsbader Strasse 1, 14193 Berlin, Germany. *Fax:* (30) 8265228.

HENLEY, Elizabeth (Beth) Becker, BFA, PhD; American playwright and actress; b. 8 May 1952, Jackson, MS; d. of Charles and Lydy Henley; one s.; ed Southern Methodist Univ., Univ. of Illinois; Pulitzer Prize for Drama 1981, NY Drama Critics Circle Best Play Award 1981, George Oppenheimer/Newsday Playwriting Award 1980–81. *Film screenplays:* Nobody's Fool 1986, Crimes of the Heart 1986, Miss Firecracker 1989, Signatures 1990, Revelers 1994, Impossible Marriage 1998. *Publications:* plays: Crimes of the Heart 1981, The Wake of Jamey Foster 1982, Am I Blue 1982, The Miss Firecracker Contest 1984, The Lucky Spot 1987, The Debutante Ball 1988, Abundance 1990, Signatures 1990, Beth Henley: Monologues for Women 1992, Control Freaks 1993, Revelers 1994, Collected Plays: Volume I, 1980–1989 2000, Collected Plays: Volume II, 1990–1999 2000, Family Week 2000, Ridiculous Fraud 2006.

HENLEY, Jeffrey O., BA, MBA; American computer software industry executive; *Chairman, Oracle Corporation;* ed Univ. of California, Santa Barbara, Univ. of California, Los Angeles; fmr Controller of Int. Operations, Fairchild Camera and Instruments; fmr Dir of Finance, Memorex Corpn; fmr Exec. Vice-Pres., Chief Financial Officer, Saga Corpn, Pacific Holding Co.; Exec. Vice-Pres. and Chief Financial Officer, Oracle Corpn 1991–2004, mem. Bd Dirs 1995–, Chair. 2004–, mem. Exec. Man. Cttee; Chair. Mid-Pacific Region Trustees, Boys & Girls Clubs of America; mem. Bd Dirs CallWave Inc.; mem. Bd Govs Boys and Girls Clubs of America; mem. Chancellor's Advisory Council and Int. Advisory Council, Eng Coll., Univ. of California, Santa Barbara; mem. Advisory Bd InTouch Technologies; UCLA Anderson School's Outstanding Alumnus Award 2004. *Address:* Oracle Corpn, 500 Oracle Parkway, Redwood City, CA 94065-1675, USA (office). *Telephone:* (650) 506-7000 (office). *Fax:* (650) 506-7200 (office). *E-mail:* info@oracle.com (office). *Website:* www.oracle.com (office).

HENN, Walter, BArch, DrIng; German architect; b. 20 Dec. 1912, Reichenberg/Bez. Dresden; m. Dr Hilde Leistner 1938 (died 1995); two s. three d.; ed Technische Hochschule Dresden and Akad. der Bildenden Künste, Dresden; Prof. of Bldg and Industrial Construction, Technische Hochschule, Dresden 1946–53, Technische Hochschule, Braunschweig 1953– (Prof. Emer. 1982–); founder and dir of first inst. for industrial construction in Germany 1957–82; mem. Deutsche Wissenschaftsrat 1969; Foreign mem. Acad. of Eng of the Russian Fed. 1992–; mem. numerous comms., working parties etc; has undertaken bldgs in Germany and elsewhere including industrial, admin. and school bldgs, research centres, electricity and water works; mem. Mainz Acad. of Science and Literature, Braunschweig Scientific Soc.; Hon. Dr tech. (T. U.

Vienna); Hon. Dr-Ing. (T. U. Dresden), (Cracow Univ. of Tech.; Peter-Joseph-Krahe Prize, Braunschweig 1965);. *Publications:* several books (translated in 11 languages) and more than 200 articles in professional journals. *Address:* Ramsachleite 13, 82418 Murnau, Germany. *Telephone:* (8841) 9531. *Fax:* (8841) 628994.

HENNEKENS, Charles H., MD, DrPH, FACC; American epidemiologist; *Co-Director, Cardiovascular Research, Mt Sinai Medical Center-Miami Heart Institute;* ed Cornell Univ. Medical Coll. and Harvard School of Public Health; fmr Eugene Braunwald Prof. of Medicine and Prof. of Ambulatory Care and Prevention, Harvard Medical School; fmr Prof. of Epidemiology, Harvard School of Public Health; fmr Head, Div. of Preventive Medicine, Brigham and Women's Hosp.; fmr Prof. of Medicine & Epidemiology and Public Health, Univ. of Miami School of Medicine, Fla; currently Co-Dir Cardiovascular Research, Mt Sinai Medical Center-Miami Heart Inst., Miami Beach, Fla; fmr Pres. Soc. for Epidemiologic Research; Pres. American Epidemiological Soc.; mem. Asscn of American Physicians, Food and Nutrition Bd; fmr Ed.-in-Chief American Journal of Preventive Medicine; Founding Ed.-in-Chief Annals of Epidemiology; Fellow, American Coll. of Preventive Medicine, American Coll. of Epidemiology; Bruce Award, American Coll. of Physicians, Lilienfeld Award American Coll. of Epidemiology. *Publications:* Epidemiology in Medicine (co-author) 1987, Clinical Trials in Cardiovascular Disease: A Companion to Braunwald's Heart Disease (co-author) 1999. *Address:* Mt Sinai Medical Center-Miami Heart Institute, 4300 Alton Road, Miami Beach, FL 33140, USA (office). *Telephone:* (305) 674-2064 (office). *E-mail:* webmaster@msmc .com (office). *Website:* www.msmc.com (office).

HENNEKINNE, Loïc; French diplomatist; b. 20 Sept. 1940, Caudéran, Gironde; s. of Michel Hennekinne and Elisabeth Declemy; m. 2nd Marie Bozelle 1987; one d.; two s. (by first m.); ed Ecole Nat. d'Admin; First Sec. French embassies in Viet Nam 1969–71, Chile 1971–73; Minister-Counsellor, Japan 1979–81; Del. for External Action, Ministry of Industry 1981–82; Dir of Cabinet of Minister of Research and Industry 1982; Dir of Personnel and Admin Ministry of Foreign Affairs 1983–86; Amb. to Indonesia 1986–88; Gen. Sec. summit conf. of Western industrialized nations, Paris 1989; Diplomatic Adviser to Pres. Mitterrand 1989–91; Amb. to Japan 1991–93; Inspector-Gen. of Foreign Affairs 1993–96; Amb. to Canada 1997–98; Sec.-Gen. Ministry of Foreign Affairs (with rank of Amb. of France) 1998–2002; Amb. to Italy 2002–05; numerous int. decorations including Officier, Ordre nat. du Mérite, Officier, Légion d'honneur, Grand' Ufficiale Ordine Naz. al Merito della Repub. Italiana. *Leisure interest:* tennis. *Address:* c/o Ministry of Foreign Affairs, 37 quai d'Orsay, 75351 Paris Cedex 07, France. *Telephone:* 1-43-17-53-53. *Fax:* 1-43-17-52-03. *Website:* www.diplomatie.gouv.fr.

HENNESSEY, Keith, BAS, MPP; American economist and government official; *Director, National Economic Council;* ed Stanford Univ., Calif., John F. Kennedy School of Govt, Harvard Univ., Mass; Program Designer, Symantec Corpn, Cupertino, Calif. 1990–92; Research Asst, Bipartisan Comm. on Entitlement and Tax Reform 1994–95; Health Economist, Budget Cttee, US Senate 1995–97, Policy Dir for Senate Majority and Senator Trent Lott 1997–2002; Deputy Asst to US Pres. for Econ. Policy and Devt and Deputy Dir Nat. Econ. Council 2002–07, Asst to US Pres. for Econ. Policy and Devt and Dir Nat. Econ. Council 2007–. *Address:* The White House Office, 1600 Pennsylvania Avenue, NW, Washington, DC 20500, USA (office). *Telephone:* (202) 456-1414 (office). *Fax:* (202) 456-2461 (office). *E-mail:* vice_president@ whitehouse.gov (office). *Website:* www.whitehouse.gov/nec (office).

HENNESSY, Edward L., Jr, BS; American business executive (retd); b. 22 March 1928, Boston, Mass; s. of Edward L. Hennessy and Celina Mary Doucette; m. Ruth F. Schilling 1951; one s. one d.; ed Fairleigh Dickinson Univ., Rutherford, NJ and New York Univ. Law School; Asst Controller, Textron 1950–55; Group Controller, Eastern Electronics Group, Lear Siegler Inc. 1956–60; Controller, Int. Electronic Corpn, Int. Telephone & Telegraph Corpn (ITT) 1960–61, Controller, Corporate Staff 1961–62, Controller, ITT Europe 1962–64; Dir of Finance, Europe, Middle East and Africa, Colgate Palmolive Co. 1964–65; Vice-Pres. Finance, Heublein Inc. 1965–68, Sr Vice-Pres. Admin. and Finance 1969–72; Dir United Technologies Corpn 1972–79, Sr Vice-Pres. Finance and Admin. 1972–77, Exec. Vice-Pres., Group Vice-Pres. Systems & Equipment Group and Chief Financial Office 1977–79; Chair. and CEO AlliedSignal Corpn 1979–93 (retd); mem. Bd of Dirs Bank of New York, Wackenhut Corpn, Avanir Pharmaceuticals, Automatic Data Processing, Northeast Utilities, Lockheed Martin Corpn, Coast Guard Foundation, Powertrusion 2000; Trustee, Fairleigh Dickinson Univ. (fmr chair.), Catholic Univ. of America; Officier Légion d'honneur 1991, Kt of Malta (Vatican) 1981, Kt of St Gregory (Vatican) 1984, Hilal-i-Quaid-i-Azam (Pakistan) 1985, Kt of the Holy Sepulchre (Vatican) 1986. *Leisure interests:* sailing, tennis, reading, golf. *Address:* PO Box 3000 R, Morristown, NJ 07960 (office); 500 Island Drive, Palm Beach, FL 33480, USA (home). *Telephone:* (973) 455-4811 (office); (561) 655-0107 (home). *Fax:* (973) 455-2973 (office).

HENNESSY, John Basil, AO, DPhil, DLitt, FSA, FAHA; Australian archaeologist; b. 10 Feb. 1925, Horsham, Vic.; s. of Thomas B. Hennessy and Nellie M. Poultney; m. Ruth M. R. Shannon 1954; one s. two d.; ed Villa Maria & St Patrick's Coll. Ballarat, Univ. of Sydney and Magdalen Coll., Oxford, UK; Lecturer, Near Eastern Archaeology, Univ. of Sydney 1955–61; Asst Dir British School of Archaeology, Jerusalem 1965–66, Dir 1966–70; Edwin Cuthbert Hall Visiting Prof. of Middle Eastern Archaeology, Univ. of Sydney 1970–72, Edwin Cuthbert Hall Prof. 1973–90, Prof. Emer. 1991–, also Hon. Assoc. School of Archaeology, Classics and Ancient History; Dir Australian Foundation for Near Eastern Archaeology 1973–91, Gov. 1992–; Gov. Cyprus Research Centre 1992–; Dir of Excavations Sphagion, Stephania (Cyprus) 1951, Damascus Gate, Jerusalem 1964–66, Amman 1966, Teleilat Ghassul (Jordan) 1967–77, Samaria 1968, Pella (Jordan) 1978–88. *Publications:*

Stephania 1964, The Foreign Relations of Palestine During the Early Bronze Age 1967, World Ceramics, The Ancient Near East 1968, The Arab States in the Modern World 1977–79, Masterpieces of Western Ceramics 1978, Pella in Jordan 1982, Archaeology of Jordan I 1986, Ayia Paraskevi and Vasilia 1988, Archaeology of Jordan II 1989. *Address:* 497 Old Windsor Road, Kellyville, NSW 2155, Australia. *Telephone:* 9629-1514 (home).

HENNESSY, John L., MS, PhD; American computer scientist and university administrator; *President, Stanford University;* ed Villanova Univ., State Univ. of New York at Stony Brook; apptd Asst Prof. of Electrical Eng, Stanford Univ. 1977, Full Prof. 1986–, inaugural Willard R. and Inez Kerr Bell Prof. of Electrical Eng and Computer Science 1987–2004, Dir Computer Systems Lab. 1983–93, Chair. Computer Science 1994–96, Dean School of Eng 1996–99, Provost Stanford Univ. 1999– 2000, Pres. 2000–, inaugural holder of Bing Presidential Professorship; a pioneer in computer architecture, particularly RISC (Reduced Instruction Set Computer); Co-founder MIPS Computer Systems (now MIPS Technologies) 1984; mem. NAS, Nat. Acad. of Eng; Fellow, American Acad. of Arts and Sciences, Asscn for Computing Machinery, IEEE; IEEE John von Neumann Medal 2000, ASEE Benjamin Garver Lamme Award 2000, ACM Eckert-Mauchly Award 2001, Seymour Cray Computer Eng Award 2001, NEC C&C Prize for lifetime achievement in computer science and eng 2004, Founders Award, American Acad. of Arts and Sciences 2005. *Publications:* co-author of two internationally used undergraduate and graduate textbooks on computer architecture design. *Address:* Office of the President, Building 10, Stanford University, Stanford, CA 94305-2061, USA (office). *Telephone:* (650) 723-2481 (office). *Fax:* (650) 725-6847 (office). *E-mail:* president@stanford.edu (office). *Website:* www.stanford.edu (office).

HENRETTA, Deborah (Deb) A., BA, MA; American business executive; *Group President - Asia, The Procter & Gamble Company;* b. 1 May 1961, Rochester, NY; two d. one s.; ed St Bonaventure Univ., Syracuse Univ.; intern, WXXI Channel 21, Rochester, NY 1982, WOKR Channel 13, Rochester, NY 1982–85; brand asst, Procter & Gamble 1985–86, Asst Brand Man. Bold/Dawn 1986–88, Brand Man. Cheer 1988–91, Assoc. Advertising Man. Tide 1991–93, Marketing Dir Laundry Products, Procter & Gamble North America 1993–96, Gen. Man. Fabric Conditioners, Procter & Gamble North America 1996–98, Gen. Man. Fabric Conditioners and Bleach, Procter & Gamble Worldwide 1998–99, Vice-Pres. Global Strategic Planning and Design, Laundry Fabric Conditioners/Bleach 1999, Vice-Pres. North America Baby Care 1999–2001, Pres. Global Baby Care 2001–04, Pres. Global Baby and Adult Care 2004–05, Pres. ASEAN/Australasia/India 2005–07, Group Pres. — Asia 2007–; mem. Bd of Dirs WCET/Channel 48 1997–2001, Chair. Strategic Planning Cttee 1998–2001; mem. Conf. Cincinnati Women 1988–90, Advisory Cttee New-house School, Syracuse Univ. 1998–, Advisory Council for Children's Day Care Center 1999–2002, Oversight Cttee for Children's for Children Day Care Center 1999–, Strategy and Marketing Cttee Childrens' Hosp. of Cincinnati 2000–, Bd of Trustees for Childrens' Hosp. 2001–, YWCA Career Women of Achievement Steering Cttee 2002–, The Committee of 200 2003–, Bd of Trustees St Bonaventure Univ. 2003–; mem. Alexis de Tocqueville Soc. of the United Way 2001–; led P&G's Advancement of Women effort (which won P&G the Catalyst Award 1998) 1994–2000; Univ. Wall of Fame 2000, ranked by Fortune magazine amongst 50 Most Powerful Women in Business in the US (34th), 2002, (34th) 2003, (41st) 2004, and amongst 50 Most Powerful Women in Business outside the US (23rd) 2007, YWCA Career Women of Achievement Award 2002, YWCA Acad. of Career Women 2002, Advertising Age magazine Women to Watch 2003, Advertising Age Top Ten Who Made Their Mark on Marketing 2004. *Address:* The Procter & Gamble Co., 238A Thomson Road, #21- 09/10, Novena Square, Tower A, Singapore City 307684, Singapore (office). *Telephone:* 6824-5800 (office). *Fax:* 6824-6309 (office). *E-mail:* henretta.da@pg.com (office). *Website:* www.pg.com (office).

HENRI ALBERT FÉLIX MARIE GUILLAUME, HRH Grand Duke of Luxembourg, LèsScPol; b. 16 April 1955, Château de Betzdorf; s. of Jean Benoît Guillaume Marie Robert Louis Antoine Adolphe Marc d'Aviano, HRH fmr Grand Duke of Luxembourg and the late Princess Josephine-Charlotte of Belgium; m. Maria Teresa Mestre 1981; four s. (including Prince Guillaume Jean Joseph Marie) one d.; ed Royal Mil. Acad. Sandhurst, Univ. of Geneva; mem. State Council 1980–98; apptd Lt Rep. of Grand Duke March 1988; succeeded father as Grand Duke of Luxembourg Oct. 2000; Chair. Bd of Econ. Devt, Galapagos Darwin Trust Luxembourg; Pres. Organizing Cttee, Int. Trade Fairs of Luxembourg; mem. Mentor Foundation, Int. Olympic Cttee; Hon. Maj. Parachute Regt; Hon. Dr rer. pol (Trier); Hon. DHumLitt (Sacred Heart); Hon. LLD (Miami), Hon. DEcon (Khon Kaen). *Leisure interests:* reading, listening to classical music, skiing, swimming, water skiing, tennis, hunting. *Address:* Grand Ducal Palace, 2013 Luxembourg, Luxembourg (office). *Website:* www.gouvernement.lu.

HENRICH, Dieter, DrPhil; German philosopher and academic; *Professor of Philosophy, University of Munich;* b. 5 Jan. 1927, Marburg; s. of Hans Harry Henrich and Frieda Henrich; m. Dr Bettina von Eckardt 1975; two d.; ed Univ. of Heidelberg; Prof., Freie Univ. Berlin 1960–65, Univ. of Heidelberg 1965–81; now Prof. of Philosophy, Univ. of Munich; Visiting Prof., Columbia Univ. 1968–72, Univ. of Mich. 1969, Harvard Univ. 1973–86, Tokyo Univ. 1979, Yale Univ. 1987; mem. Heidelberg and Bavarian Acads; Hon. Prof., Humboldt Univ., Berlin 1997; Hon. Foreign mem. American Acad. of Arts and Sciences; Hon. DTheol (Münster) 1999, (Marburg) 2002; Hon. DrPhil (Jena) 2005; Hoelderlin Prize 1995, Hegel Prize 2003, Kant Prize 2004. *Publications:* Der ontologische Gottesbeweis 1960, Fichtes ursprüngliche Einsicht, 1967, Hegel im Kontext 1971, Identität und Objektivität 1976, Fluchtlinien 1982, Der Gang des Andenkens 1986, Konzepte 1987, Ethik zum nuklearen Frieden 1990, Konstellationen 1991, Der Grund im Bewusstsein 1992, The Moral

Image of the World 1992, The Unity of Reason 1994, I. C. Diez 1997, Bewusstes Leben 1999, Versuch über Kunst und Leben 2001, Fixpunkte 2003, Between Kant and Hegel 2003, Grundlegang aus dem Jeh 2004. *Address:* Gerlichstrasse 7A, 81245 Munich, Germany. *Telephone:* (89) 8119131. *E-mail:* dieter.henrich@lrz.uni-muenchen.de (home).

HENRIKSON, C. Robert (Rob), BA, JD; American insurance industry executive; *Chairman, President and CEO, MetLife Inc.;* m. Mary Henrikson; two s.; ed Univ. of Pennsylvania, Emory Univ., Wharton School; has worked at MetLife Inc. for over 30 years holding numerous sr man. positions, COO 2004–06, Pres. 2004–, mem. Bd of Dirs 2005–, CEO and Chair. 2006–; mem. Bd of Dirs American Council of Life Insurers, The Ron Brown Award for Corp. Leadership, New York Botanical Garden; Emer. Mem. Bd of Dirs American Benefits Council; mem. Nat. Bd of Advisors, Morehouse School of Medicine; Chair. S. S. Huebner Foundation for Insurance Educ., Emory Univ.; mem. Emory Law School Council, Emory Campaign Steering Cttee; Trustee American Museum of Natural History; fmr mem. Cttee on Econ. Devt's Subcommittee on Social Security Reform; fmr adviser and consultant various Congressional and US Dept of Labor hearings; fmr del. Nat. Summit on Retirement Savings. *Address:* MetLife Inc., 2701 Queens Plaza North, Long Island City, NY 11101-4015, USA (office). *Telephone:* (212) 578-2211 (office). *Fax:* (212) 578-3320 (office). *E-mail:* info@metlife.com (office). *Website:* www .metlife.com (office).

HENRY, André Armand; French teacher, trade union official and politician; b. 15 Oct. 1934, Fontenoy-le-Château; s. of Alice Henry; m. Odile Olivier 1956; one s. one d.; ed Cours Complémentaire de Bains-les-Bains, Ecole normale d'instituteurs, Mirecourt; teacher, Fontenoy-le-Château 1955–56, Thaon-les-Vosges 1956–69; began trade union career with Syndicat Nat. des Instituteurs (SNI), Training Coll. Rep. (Vosges) 1954, mem Exec. Comm. (Vosges) 1955–69, Asst Sec.-Gen. 1960–63, Sec.-Gen. 1963–69, mem. Nat. Council, SNI 1965–74, Perm. Sec. 1969–74; in charge of youth, then gen. admin. section of SNI; mem. Fed. Council, in charge of culture, youth and leisure sections, Fédération de l'education nationale (FEN) 1971, Perm. Sec. and Sec.-Gen. 1974–81; Minister for Free Time 1981–83; Délégué Général à l'économie sociale 1983–; Chair. and Man. Dir Caisse Nat. de l'Energie 1984–87; Inspecteur Général de l'administration de l'education nat. 1989-95; Nat. Vice-Pres. Asscn laïque pour l'éducation, la formation, la prévention et l'autonomie (ALEFPA) 1995–2001, Pres. 2001–06, Hon. Pres. 2006–; Délégué départemental de l'education nationale; Vice-Pres. Mission Laïque française 1997–2002; Commdr, Ordre du Mérite; Chevalier, Légion d'honneur, Chevalier des Palmes académiques. *Publications:* Dame l'école 1977, Serviteurs d'idéal (two vols) 1988, Conquérir l'avenir 1992, Le Ministre qui voulait changer la vie 1996. *Leisure interests:* football, volleyball, photography, flying light aircraft. *Address:* 1 bis rue de l'Espérance, 94000 Créteil, France (home). *Telephone:* 1-48-99-37-79 (office); (6) 11-87-30-51 (home). *E-mail:* andre.h@cegetel.net (home).

HENRY, Brad; American state official and lawyer; *Governor of Oklahoma;* b. 10 June 1963, Shawnee, Okla; m. Kimberley Henry (née Blain); three d.; ed Shawnee High School, Univ. of Okla; est. law firm Henry, Canavan & Hopkins PLLC; mem. Okla State Senate 1992–2002, Chair. Senate Judiciary Cttee; Gov. of Okla 2003–; mem. Pottawatomie Co. Bar Asscn, Okla Bar Asscn, Norman Chamber of Commerce; Dir Shawnee Chamber of Commerce; mem. Bd of Trustees, St Gregories Coll.; Democrat; Letzeiser Gold Medal Award, Outstanding Young Oklahoman 1997. *Address:* Office of the Governor, State Capitol Building, 2300 North Lincoln Blvd., Room 212, Oklahoma City, OK 73105, USA (office). *Telephone:* (405) 521-2342. *Fax:* (405) 521-3353. *Website:* www.governor.state.ok.us.

HENRY, Sir Geoffrey Arama, KBE; Cook Islands politician; b. 16 Nov. 1940, Aitutaki; s. of Arama Henry and Mata Uritaua; m. Louisa Olga Hoff 1965; four s. two d.; ed Wanganui Collegiate School, Victoria Univ., Wellington, NZ; school teacher 1965–67; active in politics 1965–68; public service 1970–72; returned to politics, Cabinet Minister 1972–78; Leader of Opposition 1978–89; Prime Minister 1983, Deputy Prime Minister in Coalition Govt 1984, Prime Minister and Minister of Police, State-owned Enterprises, Tourism and Transport 1989–99; organizer Jt Commercial Comm., USA and Pacific Islands 1990; Chair. Econ. Summit of Small Island States 1992; Chancellor Univ. of S Pacific 1992; Leader of the Opposition 1999; Deputy Prime Minister, Minister of Finance 2002–05, Offshore Financial Services Police, PERCA (Audit Comm.); Chancellor Univ. of the S Pacific 1993–95; Samoan High Chief Title of Afionga Tuisaua 1992, Order of Tahiti 1997; Hon. DUniv (Univ. of the S Pacific) 2000; Silver Jubilee Medal 1977, NZ Commemoration Medal 1990, Int. Religious Liberty Asscn 1993, Diploma Int. Olympic Cttee 2001. *Leisure interests:* golf, rugby and other sports, reading, music. *Address:* c/o Office of the Deputy Prime Minister, PO Box 138, Avarua, Rarotonga, Cook Islands (office).

HENRY, Lenny, CBE; British comedian and actor; b. 29 Aug. 1958; m. Dawn French (q.v.); one d.; numerous tours including Loud! UK and Australia 1994 and 1995, Large! UK, Australia and NZ 1998; Monaco Red Cross Award, The Golden Nymph Award (for Alive and Kicking) 1992, BBC Personality of the Year, Radio and Television Industry Club 1993, Golden Rose of Montreux Award for Lenny in Pieces (Christmas Special) 2000, Lifetime Achievement Award for Ongoing Performance UK Comedy Awards 2003. *Live performances:* Have You Seen This Man tour 2001, So Much Things to Say, Wyndhams Theatre 2003, tour 2004. *Television includes:* New Faces (debut) 1975, Tiswas 1978, 1979, 1980, Three of a Kind 1981–83, Coast to Coast 1990, The Lenny Henry Show 1984, 1985, Alive and Kicking 1991, Bernard and the Genie 1991, In Dreams 1992, The Real McCoy 1992, Chef (title role) (three series), Lenny Hunts the Funk, New Soul Nation, White Goods 1994, Funky Black Shorts 1994, Comic Relief, Lenny Go Home 1996, British Acad. Awards (host) 1997, Lenny's Big Amazon Adventure 1997, Lenny Goes to Town 1998, The Delbert Wilkins Show 1987, 1988, The Man 1999, Hope and Glory 1999, 2000, Lenny's Atlantic Adventure 2000, Lenny in Pieces (Christmas Special) 2000, Lenny in Pieces (Christmas Special) 2001, Lenny Henry – This is My Life 2003, Lenny Henry in Pieces series 2 2003, The Lenny Henry Show 2004, Berry's Way 2006, Lenny's Britain 2007. *Films include:* True Identity 1991, Mirrormask 2004, Harry Potter and the Prisoner of Azkaban 2004, MirrorMask 2005, Penelope 2006. *Videos:* Lenny Henry Live and Unleashed 1989, Lenny Henry Live and Loud 1994. *Publications:* The Quest for the Big Woof (autobiog.) 1991, Charlie and the Big Chill (children's book) 1995. *Leisure interests:* R'n'B, HipHop, Funk, reading, tennis, comics, family. *Address:* c/o PBJ Management Ltd, 7 Soho Street, London, W1D 3DQ, England. *Telephone:* (20) 7287-1112. *Fax:* (20) 7287-1191. *E-mail:* general@ pbjmgt.co.uk (office). *Website:* www.pbjmgt.co.uk (office).

HENRY, Pierre; French composer; b. 9 Dec. 1927, Paris; s. of Georges Henry and Germaine Mazet; m. Isabelle Warnier 1971; one d. and one s. by previous m.; ed Conservatoire Nat. Supérieur de Musique and studies with Nadia Boulanger, Olivier Messiaen and Félix Passerone; head of group researching concrete music, ORTF 1950–58; Founder and Dir Studio Apsome 1959–; Founder Asscn for Electro-acoustic Composition and Research 1972; cr. Son et Recherche Asscn 1982; Commdr, Légion d'honneur, Officier, Ordre nat. du Mérite, Commdr des Arts et des Lettres; Grand Prix, Acad. du Disque 1966, Grand Prix, Acad. Charles Cros 1970, Grand Prix nat. de la Musique 1985, Grand Prix de la Musique Symphonique (Sacem) 1987, Victoires de la Musique 1998, Grand Prix Karl Sczuka 1997, etc. *Works include:* Symphonie pour un homme seul 1950, Messe de Liverpool 1967, Messe pour le temps présent 1970, Deuxième Symphonie 1972, Nijinsky, clown de Dieu (ballet by Maurice Béjart) 1973, Dieu, action de voix, de sons et de gestes (spectacular, Lille 1977, Paris 1978), Hommage à Beethoven 1979, Les noces chymiques, rituel féerique en 12 journées (Opéra comique) 1980, Paradis perdus 1982, Berlin, symphonie d'une grande ville (film, concert) 1987, Livre des morts égyptien 1988, Une maison de sons 1990, Maldoror-Feuilleton 1992, L'homme à la caméra (film/concert) 1993, Une ample comédie à cent actes divers: Hommage à La Fontaine 1995, Intérieur/Extérieur 1996, Schubert 97 (1997), Histoire naturelle 1997, La Xème remix 1998, L'homme au microphone 1999, Tam tam du merveilleux 2000, Concerto sans orchestre 2000, Phrases de Quatuor 2000, Poussière de Soleils 2001, Dracula 2002, Requiem profane 2000, Carnet de Venise 2002, Labyrinthe 2003, Faits divers 2003, Duo 2003, Lumières 2003, Metamorphoses d'Ovide 2004, Voyage initiatique 2004, Comme une symphonie 2005, Grande Toccata 2006 Variance 2006, Utopia 2007, Pulsations 2007, Trajectoire 2007, Pleins jeux 2007, Un Monde lacéré 2008, Miroirs du temps 2008. *Address:* 32 rue Toul, 75012 Paris, France (home). *E-mail:* sonre@wanadoo.fr (home).

HENRY, Thierry Daniel; French professional footballer; b. 17 Aug. 1977, Paris; m. Nicole Merry 2003 (divorced 2007); one d.; signed as schoolboy player, Versailles football club; striker, Ulis (Paris), Monaco 1990–98, Juventus (Italy) 1998–99, Arsenal (England) 1999–2007 (winner FA Cup 2002, 2003, Premiership 2002, 2004, Community Shield 2002, 2004), Barcelona 2007–; mem. French nat. team (winner World Cup 1998, European Championship 2000, Confederations Cup 2003); PFA Player of the Year 2003, 2004, Football Writers' Asscn Footballer of the Year 2003, 2004, 2006, Barclaycard Player of the Season 2004, 2006, Golden Boot Winner 2001/02, 2003/04, 2004/05, 2005/06, French Footballer of the Year 2003; runner-up, European Footballer of the Year 2003, World Footballer of the Year 2003, 2004. *Address:* c/o Futbol Club Barcelona, Avenida Arístides Maillol, 08028 Barcelona, 28, Spain (office). *Website:* www.fcbarcelona.com (office).

HENRY de VILLENEUVE, Xavier, LenD; French banker; b. 8 July 1932, Quintin; s. of Jacques Henry de Villeneuve and Yvonne de la Motte de la Motte Rouge; m. Simone de Vigneral 1963; two s. one d.; ed Ecole des Frères, Quintin, Coll. des Cordeliers, Dinan, Coll. St Charles, St Brieuc and Faculté de Droit, Rennes; joined Banque de Bretagne 1959, Asst Dir-Gen. 1971, Dir-Gen. 1979, Pres. and Man. Dir 1986; Pres. and Man. Dir, Banque de la Cité 1978–82, Pres. 1983–85, Hon. Pres. Admin. 1991; Pres. Comm. des Affaires Sociales of Asscn Française des Banques 1988, Pres. Compagnie Financière de Participation 1988, Ronceray 1991–93, ACLPME 1995–98, ACLPME Finances 1997–98; Vice-Pres. Asscn d'Eloge 1995–96, Résidences ACL 1997–98; Pres. Diocesan Cttee of Catholic Educ., Nanterre (Codiec 92) 1999–; Chevalier, Légion d'honneur, des Arts et Lettres, Ordre du Saint-Sépulcre de Jérusalem. *Publication:* Contes et nouvelles des quatre vents. *Leisure interests:* the arts, reading, old wars, hunting. *Address:* 19 rue de la Convention, 75015 Paris (home); Kerbic, 22200 Pommerit-le-Vicomte, France (home).

HENRYSSON, Haraldur; Icelandic judge; b. 17 Feb. 1938, Reykjavik; m. Elisabet Kristinsdóttir 1972; one s.; ed Reykjavik High School, Univ. of Iceland; Asst Judge 1964–73; Judge, Criminal Court, Reykjavik 1973–89, Supreme Court 1989–, Pres. 1996–97; Chair. Cttee Investigating Accidents at Sea 1973–83; Pres. Nat. Life Saving Asscn 1982–90; Vice-mem. Althing 1967–71; Kt Grand Cross of Icelandic Falcon. *Leisure interests:* outdoor sports. *Address:* Hæstirettur Islands, Domhus v. Arnarhol, 150 Reykjavik, Iceland. *Telephone:* 510-3030. *Fax:* 562-3995. *Website:* www.haestirettur.is.

HENSCHEL, Jane Elizabeth, BA; American singer (mezzo-soprano); b. 2 March 1952, Appleton, Wis.; d. of Lester Haentzschel and Betty Haentzschel (née Lau); ed Univ. of Southern California; debut with the Netherlands Opera as the Nurse in Die Frau ohne Schatten 1992; ensemble mem. Aachen Oper 1977–80; joined Wuppertal Opera, Germany 1980, later with Dortmund and Düsseldorf Operas; appearances at the Glyndebourne, Salzburg and Saito Kinen Festivals and at La Scala, Milan, Deutsche Oper, Berlin, Amsterdam Opera, Paris Opera, Bayerische Staatsoper, Munich, Staatsoper, Berlin, Royal Opera House, Covent Garden, London and the San Francisco Opera;

has performed with numerous conductors including Seiji Ozawa, Sir Colin Davis, Daniel Barenboim, Bernard Haitink, Riccardo Muti, Christian Thielemann, Sir Andrew Davis, Lorin Maazel; Baroque repertoire includes Vivaldi's oratorio Juditha Triumphans (Radio France); Grammy Award 2001, Gramophone Award 2003. *Operatic roles include:* Die Amme (the nurse) in Die Frau ohne Schatten (Netherlands Opera, Royal Opera House, London 1992, Los Angeles, Bavarian State Opera, Munich, Vienna, Paris, Deutsche Oper Berlin, Metropolitan Opera), Fricka in Das Rheingold and Die Walküre (Royal Opera House, London 1996), Ulrica in Un Ballo in Maschera (Royal Opera House, London), Klytemnestra in Elektra (Bavarian State Opera, Munich, Royal Opera House, London), Herodias in Salome (Bavarian State Opera, Munich, La Scala, Milan, San Francisco Opera), Brangäne in Tristan und Isolde (Orange Festival, Los Angeles Music Center Opera, Paris Opera), Queen of Sheba in Königin von Saba (Concertgebouw, Amsterdam), Genevieve in Pelléas et Mélisande (Japan), Cassandre in Les Troyens (La Scala, Milan), Waltraute in Götterdämmerung (Royal Opera House, London), Mrs Grose in The Turn of the Screw (Royal Opera House, London), Judy in Birtwistle's Punch and Judy (Netherlands Opera 1993), Kostelnicka in Jenufa (Japan), Mistress Quickly in Falstaff (Vienna, Munich, with the London Symphony Orchestra), The Witch in Rusalka, Ottavia in L'Incoronazione di Poppea (Aachen Oper), Erda in Ring (Royal Opera House, London) 2004. Auntie in Peter Grimes (Salzburg) 2004, Mistress Quickly (LA Opera) 2004; Amneris, Eboli, Ortrud, Carmen, Azucena, Venus. *Recordings include:* Mahler's 8th Symphony with CBSO and Simon Rattle, The Rake's Progress with Ozawa, Krasa's Die Verlobung im Traum, Die Drei Groschen Oper, Britten's The Turn of the Screw with Daniel Harding, Albeniz' Merlin with Placido Domingo. *Leisure interests:* reading, concerts. *Address:* Askonas Holt, Lincoln House, 300 High Holborn, London, WC1V 7JH, England (office). *Telephone:* (20) 7400-1700 (office). *Fax:* (20) 7400-1799 (office). *E-mail:* peter .bloor@askonasholt.co.uk (office). *Website:* www.askonasholt.co.uk (office).

HENSHER, Philip Michael, BA, PhD, FRSL; British writer; b. 20 Feb. 1965, London, England; ed Lady Margaret Hall, Oxford, Jesus Coll., Cambridge; clerk, House of Commons 1990–96; Chief Book Reviewer, The Spectator 1994–; Art Critic, Mail on Sunday 1996–; columnist, The Independent; mem. RSL (mem. of Council 2000–); Somerset Maugham Award 1996. *Publications:* Other Lulus 1994, Kitchen Venom 1996, Pleasured 1998, The Bedroom of the Mister's Wife (short stories) 1999, The Mulberry Empire 2002, The Fit 2004, The Northern Clemency 2008; other: libretto for opera Powder her Face, by Thomas Adès. *Address:* c/o AP Watt Ltd, 20 John Street, London, WC1N 2DR, England (office); 83A Tennyson Street, London, SW8 3TH, England (home).

HENZE, Hans Werner; German composer and conductor; b. 1 July 1926, Gütersloh; s. of Franz Henze and Margarete Geldmacher; ed Staatsmusikschule, Braunschweig, Kirchenmusikalisches Institut, Heidelberg; musical collaborator, Deutsches Theater in Konstanz 1948; Artistic Dir and Conductor Ballet of the Hessian State Theatre in Wiesbaden 1950; living in Italy as an ind. artist since 1953; Prof. of Composition, Mozarteum, Salzburg 1962–67; Prof. of Composition, Hochschule für Musik, Cologne 1980–91; Artistic Dir Accad. Filarmonica Romana 1982–91; Prof. of Composition, RAM, London 1987–91; Founder and Artistic Dir Munich Biennale for Contemporary Music Theatre 1988–; Composer-in-Residence, Berlin Philharmonic Orchestra 1990; 'Voices' series of concerts to celebrate 75th birthday, London 2001; mem. Akad. der Künste, Berlin 1960–68, Bayerische Akad. der Schönen Künste, Munich, Akad. der Künste, Hamburg; Hon. FRNCM 1998; Hon. DMus (Edin.) 1971, Grosses Bundesverdienstkreuz 1991; Robert Schumann Prize 1951, North-Rhine-Westphalia Art Prize 1957, Prix d'Italia 1954, Sibelius Gold Medal, Harriet Cohen Awards, London 1956, Music Critics Prize, Buenos Aires 1958, Kunstpreis, Berlin, Niedersächsischer Kunstpreis 1962, Ludwig-Spohr-Preis 1976, Heidelberg-Bach-Preis 1983, Siemens-Preis 1990, Apollo d'Oro, Bilbao 1990, Preis des Internationales Theaterinstituts 1991, Kultureller Ehrenpreis, Munich 1996, Hans-von-Bülow Medal of the Berlin Philharmonic Orchestra 1997, Bayerischer Maximiliansorden für Wissenschaft und Kunst 1998, Praemium imperiale, Tokyo 2000, Best Living Composer, Cannes Classical Award 2001, German Dance Prize 2001. *Compositions include:* opera and music theatre: Das Wundertheater 1948, Boulevard Solitude 1951, Ein Landarzt 1951, Das Ende einer Welt 1953, König Hirsch (revised as Il Re Cervo) 1953, Der Prinz von Homburg 1958, Elegy for Young Lovers 1959, Der Junge Lord 1964, Die Bassariden 1964, Das Ende einer Welt 1964, Ein Landarzt 1964, Der langwierige Weg in die Wohnung des Natascha Ungeheuer 1971, La Cubana 1973, We Come to the River 1974, Don Chischiotte della Mancia 1976, Pollicino (for children) 1979, The English Cat 1980, Il ritorno d'Ulisse in Patria 1981, Das verratene Meer 1986, Il re Teodoro in Venezia 1991, Venus and Adonis 1993, L'Upapa – oder der Triumph der Sohnesliebe 2003; ballet: Jack Pudding 1949, Ballet-Variationen 1949, Das Vokaltuch der Kammersängerin Rosa Silber 1950, Die Schlafende Prinzessin 1951, Labyrinth 1951, Der Idiot 1952, Maratona 1956, Undine 1956, Des Kaisers Nachtigall 1959, Tancredi 1964, Orpheus 1978, Le disperazioni del Signor Pulcinella 1992, Le fils de l'air 1995, Labyrinth 1996, Tanzstunden, Ballet Triptych 1997; oratorio: Novae de Infinito Laudes 1962, The Raft of the Medusa 1968; cantata: Being Beauteous 1963, Ariosi 1963, Cantata della Fiaba Estrema 1963, Moralities 1967; vocal music: Whispers from Heavenly Death 1948, Der Vorwurf 1948, Apollo and Hyacinth 1949, 5 Neapolitan Songs 1956, Nachtstücke und Arien 1957, Kammermusik 1958, Novae de Infinito Laudes 1962, Ariosi 1963, Being Beateous 1963, Lieder von einer Insel 1964, Musen Siziliens 1966, Versuch über Schweine 1968, Das Floss der Medusa 1968, El Cimarrón 1969, Voices 1973, Jephte 1976, El Rey de Harlem 1979, Canzoni for Orpheus 1980, Paraphrasen über Dostoiewsky 1990, Richard Wagnersche Klavierlieder 1998, Six Songs from the Arabic 1998; orchestral: Sinfonie 1947, three concertos for violin 1947, 1971, 1997, two concertos for piano 1950, 1967, Symphonic Variation 1950, Ode to the West Wind 1953, Quattro Poemi 1955, Concerto per il Marigny 1956, Jeux des Tritons 1957, Quattro Fantaise 1958, Sonata for Strings 1958, 3 Dithyrambs 1958, Antifone 1960, Los Caprichos 1963, Double Bass Concerto 1966, Telemanniana 1967, Compases para preguntas ensimisadas 1970, Heliogabalus Imperator 1971, Tristan 1973, Ragtimes and Habaneras 1975, In Memoriam: Amicizia 1976, Aria de la Folía española 1977, Il Vitalino raddoppiato 1977, Barcarola 1979, Apollo Trionfante 1979, Le Miracle de la Rose 1981, Canzona 1982, I Sentimenti di Carl P. E. Bach 1982, Sonata for 6 1984, Guitar Concerto 1986, Sieben liebeslieder 1986, Allegro brillante 1989, Requiem 1990, Quintetto 1990, Fünf Nachtstücke 1990, Trumpet Concerto 1992, Sieben Boleros 1998, Trio in drei Sätzen 1998, Fraternité 1999, Tempest 2000, Scorribanda Sinfonica 2001, L'heure bleue 2001, 10th Symphony 2002, L'Upupa und der Triumpg der Sohnesliebe 2003, Fünf Botschaften für die Königin von Saba 2004, Sebastian im Traum 2004, Phaedra 2007. *Publications:* Das Ende einer Welt 1953, Undine, Tagebuch eines Balletts 1959, Essays 1964, El Cimarrón: ein Werkstattbericht 1971, Musik und Politik 1976, Die Englische Katze—Ein Arbeitsbuch 1978–82 1983, Reiselieder mit böhmischen Quinten 1996, Komponieren in der Schule 1998, Bohemian Fifths: An Autobiography (trans. by Stewart Spencer) 1998, L'Upupa, Nachtstücke aus dem Morgenland, Biographische Mitteilungen 2003, Briefe Einer Freundschaft (with Ingeborg Bachmann) 2004, Phaedra, Ein Tagebuch (with Christian Lehnert) 2007. *Leisure interests:* poetry, botany. *Address:* Künstler Sekretariat Christa Pfeffer, Schongauer Straße 22, 81377 Munich, Germany (office); c/o Schott Music, Weihergarten 5, 55116 Mainz, Germany (office); c/o Chester Music, 8–9 Frith Street, London, W1D 3JB, England (office). *Telephone:* (89) 718041 (office). *E-mail:* com@schott-musik.de (office); wiebke.busch@musicsales.co.uk (office). *Website:* www.hanswernerhenze.de.

HEPPELL, (Thomas) Strachan, CB; British public service official; *Chairman, European Institute for Health;* b. 15 Aug. 1935, Teesside; s. of the late Leslie Heppell and Doris Potts; m. Felicity Rice 1963; two s.; ed Acklam Hall Grammar School, Middlesbrough and Queen's Coll. Oxford; Asst Prin. Nat. Assistance Bd (NAB) 1958; Prin. NAB, Cabinet Office, Dept of Health and Social Security (DHSS) 1963; Asst Dir of Social Welfare, Hong Kong 1971–73; Asst Sec. DHSS 1973, Under-Sec. 1979; Deputy Sec. DHSS, Dept of Health 1983–95; Chair. Man. Bd European Medicines Agency (EMEA) 1994–2000 (Chair. Audit Advisory Cttee 2004–); Chair. European Inst. for Health 2007–; consultant, Dept of Health 1995–2000; mem. Broadcasting Standards Comm. 1996–2002; Chair. Family Fund Trust 1997–2003; Visiting Fellow, LSE 1996–2000. *Publications:* contribs to publs on social security, social welfare, health and pharmaceuticals. *Address:* c/o EMEA, 7 Westferry Circus, Canary Wharf, London, E14 4HB, England (office). *Website:* www.eih-eu.org (office).

HERAEUS, Jürgen, MBA; German business executive; *Chair, Supervisory Board, Heraeus Holding GmbH;* b. 1936; ed Univ. of Munich; joined family firm Heraeus Holding GmbH 1964, Dir 1970–, Head of Finance 1970, Vice-Chair. Supervisory Bd 1977–83, Chair. 1983–; Chair. TEUTONIA Zementwerk AG, GEA Group AG, Lafarge Roofing GmbH, Messer Group GmbH 2001–; Chair. and mem. Supervisory Bd MG Technologies AG 2003–; mem. Admin. Bd Argor-Heraeus SA, Switzerland; Special Adviser CVC Capital Pnrs; Sr Adviser to WTO Cttee in Shanghai and Chair. China Group, Asia Pacific Cttee of German Business, Berlin 1998–; mem.Bd of Dirs Buderus AG, EPCOS AG, Heidelberger Druckmaschinen AG, IKB Deutsche Industriebank, Schmalbach-Lubeca AG; mem. Presidium, Bundesverbandes der Deutschen Industrie (Fed. Asscn of German Industries) 1990–; mem. Advisory Bd Technische Universität Darmstadt 2001–, Chair. 2007–. *Address:* Heraeus Holding GmbH, Heraeusstrasse 12-14, 63450 Hanau, Germany (office). *Telephone:* (0) 61 81/35-0 (office). *Fax:* (0) 61 81/35-35 50 (office). *E-mail:* pr@heraeus.com (office). *Website:* www.heraeus.com (office).

HERBEN, Mathieu (Mat); Dutch politician; *Leader, Lijst Pim Fortuyn;* b. 15 July 1952, The Hague; m.; one d.; journalist for internal publications, Ministry of Defence 1977–87, Chief Ed. 1990–2002; Ed.-in-Chief, Manna (catholic newspaper) 1987–90; various roles with Orde van Vrijmetselaren (freemasons' lodge) 1993–97; Leader, Lijst Pim Fortuyn (LPT) May–Aug. 2002, Parl. Leader May 2002–, Leader LPF Advisory Council Aug. 2002–. *Publications:* Vijftig jaar vrijmetselaarij. *Leisure interests:* classical music, reading, nature. *Address:* Tweede Kamer der Staten-Generaal, Fractie Lijst Pim Fortun, Postbus 20018, 2500 EA Den Haag, Netherlands (office). *Telephone:* (70) 318-5846 (office). *Fax:* (70) 318-5847 (office). *E-mail:* m.herben@tk .parlement.nl (office). *Website:* www.lijstpimfortuyn.nl (office).

HERBERT, Adam, BA, MPA, PhD; American university administrator and professor of public administration; *President, Indiana University;* b. Muskogee, Okla; m. Karen Herbert; ed Univs of Southern Calif. and Pittsburgh; White House Fellow in Ford Admin 1974, served as Special Asst to US Sec. of Health, Educ. and Welfare; Special Asst to US Under-Sec. of Housing and Urban Devt 1975; academic positions at Univ. of Southern Calif., Howard Univ., Va Polytechnic Inst. and State Univ., Univ. of Pittsburgh; fmr Dean School of Public Affairs and Services and Vice-Pres. for Academic Affairs, Fla Int. Univ.; fmrly Regents Prof. and Founding Exec. Dir, The Fla Center for Public Policy and Leadership, Univ. of N Fla, also Univ. Pres. 1989–1998; Chancellor of State Univ. System of Fla 1998–2000; Prof. of Public Admin and Political Science, and Pres. Indiana Univ. 2003–; led transition team for Gov.-Elect Jeb Bush 1998; Co-Chair. Gov. Bush's Reading Priority Transition Team 2002; fmr Pres. Nat. Asscn of Schools of Public Affairs and Admin; Chair. Jacksonville Chamber of Commerce 1993; served as Fla Commr, Comm. on Educ.; mem. Nat. Acad. of Public Admin (NAPA), Knight Foundation Comm. on Intercollegiate Athletics, Fla Fed. Judicial Nominating Comm. *Address:* Office of the President, Indiana University, 107 South Indiana Avenue, Bloomington, IN 47405-7000, USA (office). *Website:* www.indiana.edu (office).

HERBERT, Rt Rev. Christopher William, BA, MPhil, PhD, FRSA; British ecclesiastic (retd); b. 7 Jan. 1944, Lydney, Glos.; s. of Walter Herbert and the late Hilda Dibben; m. Janet Turner 1968; two s.; ed Monmouth School, Univ. of Wales, Lampeter, Univ. of Bristol and Wells Theological Coll., Univ. of Leicester; Curate, St Paul's, Tupsley, Hereford 1967–71; Adviser in Religious Educ. Diocese of Hereford 1971–76, Dir of Educ. 1976–81; Vicar, St Thomas on the Bourne, Diocese of Guildford 1981–90; Dir of Post-Ordination Training, Diocese of Guildford 1984–90; Archdeacon of Dorking 1990–95; Bishop of St Albans 1995–2009; Hon. Citizen, Fano, Italy; Hon. DLitt (Hertfordshire); Hon. DArts (Bedfordshire). *Publications include:* Be Thou My Vision 1985, This Most Amazing Day 1986, The Question of Jesus 1987, Alive to God 1987, Ways Into Prayer 1987, Help in Your Bereavement 1988, Prayers for Children 1993, Pocket Prayers 1993, The Prayer Garden 1994, Words of Comfort 1994, A Little Prayer Diary 1996, Pocket Prayers for Children 1999. *Leisure interests:* cycling, reading, writing, walking, art history. *Address:* 1 Beacon Close, Farnham, Surrey, GU10 4PA, England (home). *Telephone:* (1252) 795600 (home). *E-mail:* cherbert@threeabbeys.org.uk (home).

HERBIG, George Howard, PhD; American astronomer and academic; *Astronomer Emeritus, Institute for Astronomy, University of Hawaii;* b. 2 Jan. 1920, Wheeling, W Va; s. of George A. Herbig and Glenna Howard; m. 1st Delia McMullin 1943 (divorced 1968); three s. one d.; m. 2nd Hannelore Tillmann 1968; ed Univ. of California, Los Angeles and Berkeley; Jr Astronomer, Lick Observatory, Mount Hamilton, Calif. 1948–50, Asst Astronomer 1950–55, Assoc. Astronomer 1955–60, Astronomer 1960–87; Asst Dir Lick Observatory 1960–63, Acting Dir 1970–71; Prof. of Astronomy, Univ. of Calif. (Santa Cruz) 1967–87; Astronomer, Inst. for Astronomy, Univ. of Hawaii 1987–2001, Astronomer Emer. 2001–; Visiting Prof. and Lecturer Chicago 1959, Mexico 1961, Observatoire de Paris 1965, Max-Planck-Institut für Astronomie, Heidelberg 1969, Stockholm 1973, Hawaii 1976–77; mem. NAS, astronomy del. to People's Repub. of China 1977; Henry Norris Russell Lecturer, American Astronomical Soc. 1975; lectured in USSR and Poland under exchange agreement, US-USSR Acads of Science 1965, 1987; US NSF Sr Postdoctoral Fellow 1965; mem. NAS, American Acad. of Arts and Sciences; Corresp. mem. Soc. scientifique Royale de Liège; Foreign Scientific mem., Max-Planck-Inst. für Astronomie, Heidelberg; Warner Prize, American Astronomical Soc. 1955, Medaille, Univ. de Liège 1969, Gold Medal, Astronomical Soc. of Pacific 1980, Petrie Prize Canadian Astronomical Soc. 1995. *Publications:* Ed. of and contrib. to Non-Stable Stars 1957, Spectroscopic Astrophysics 1970; approx. 250 scientific papers, articles and reviews. *Address:* Institute for Astronomy, University of Hawaii, 2680 Woodlawn Drive, Honolulu, HI 96822, USA (office). *E-mail:* herbig@galileo.ifa.hawaii .edu (office). *Website:* www.ifa.hawaii.edu/users/herbig/default/herbig.html (office).

HERBISH, Suleiman Jasir al-, BA, MEconSc; Saudi Arabian international organization official; *Director General, OPEC Fund for International Development (OFID);* b. 6 Nov. 1942, Ar-Rass; m.; four c.; ed Trinity Univ., San Antonio, Tex., USA, Univ. of Cairo, Egypt; fmr Dir Saline Water Conversion Corpn, Saudi Co. for Precious Metals; fmr Asst Deputy Minister; fmr Chair. Nat. Shipping Co. of Saudi Arabia, Saudi Arabian Oil Texaco Ltd (later renamed Saudi Arabian Chevron Co.), Arabian Drilling Co.; Gov. for Saudi Arabia, OPEC, Vienna 1990–2003; Dir-Gen. OPEC Fund for Int. Devt (OFID) 2003–; head of numerous Saudi Arabian dels to int. confs and negotiations on energy-related issues; Congressional Medal of Achievement (Philippines) 2005, Prix de la Fondation, Crans Montana Forum 2007. *Address:* OPEC Fund for International Development (OFID), PO Box 995, 1011 Vienna, Austria (office). *Telephone:* (1) 51564/164 (office); (1) 51166/165 (office). *Fax:* (1) 513-92-38 (office). *E-mail:* info@ofid.org (office). *Website:* www.ofid.org (office).

HERBST, John Edward; American diplomatist; *Coordinator, Office for Reconstruction and Stabilization, State Department;* ed School of Foreign Service, Georgetown Univ., Fletcher School of Law and Diplomacy; worked in embassies in Moscow and Saudi Arabia; Dir Office of Ind. States and Commonwealth Affairs; Dir Office of Regional Affairs, Near East Asia Bureau; Political Counsellor, Embassy, Tel-Aviv; Deputy Dir for Econs, Office of Soviet Union Affairs; Dir for Policy, Nat. Security Council; Prin. Deputy to Amb.-at-Large for the New Ind. States; Consul-Gen. Jerusalem 1997–2000; Amb. to Uzbekistan 2000–03, to Ukraine 2003–06; Coordinator, Office for Reconstruction and Stabilization, US State Dept, Washington, DC 2006–. *Address:* Office of the Coordinator for Reconstruction and Stabilization, US State Department, 2201 C Street, NW, Washington, DC 20520; 8355 Thompson Road, Annandale, VA 22003, USA (home). *Telephone:* (202) 663-0323 (office). *Fax:* (202) 663-0327 (office). *E-mail:* scrs_info@state.gov (office). *Website:* www .state.gov/s/crs (office).

HERCUS, Luise Anna, AM, PhD; Australian academic; *Visiting Fellow in Linguistics, School of Language Studies, Australian National University;* b. (Luise Anna Schwarzschild), 16 Jan. 1926, Munich, Germany; d. of Alfred Schwarzschild and Theodora Schwarzschild; m. Graham Robertson Hercus 1954; one s.; ed Univ. of Oxford, UK and Australian Nat. Univ., Canberra; Tutor and Lecturer, St Anne's Coll., Oxford 1946–54; Research Fellow, Univ. of Adelaide 1965–68; Sr Lecturer in Asian Studies, ANU 1969–71; Reader 1972–91, now Visiting Fellow in Linguistics; work conducted recording nearly extinct Aboriginal languages 1963–. *Publications:* The Languages of Victoria: A Late Survey 1969, The Bagandji Language 1982, This is What Happened, Historical Narratives by Aborigines (co-ed.) 1986, Nukunu Dictionary 1992, Wembawemba Dictionary 1992, Paakanyi Dictionary 1993, The Wirangu Language of the West Coast of South Australia 1999; articles on Middle Indo-Aryan and on oral traditions of S Australian Aborigines, The Arabana – WangKangurru Language, The Land is a Map (with F. Hodges, J. Simpson) 2002. *Leisure interest:* raising orphaned marsupials. *Address:* School of

Language Studies, Baldessin Precinct Building 110, Australian National University, Canberra ACT 0200 (office); Kintala via Gundaroo, Dick's Creek Road, NSW 2620, Australia (home). *Telephone:* (2) 6236-8145 (home). *E-mail:* Luise.Hercus@anu.edu.au (office); luiseh@dodo.com.au (home).

HERCUS, Dame (Margaret) Ann, DCMG, BA, LLB; New Zealand politician, diplomatist and international consultant; b. 24 Feb. 1942, Hamilton; d. of Horace Sayers and Mary Sayers (née Ryan); m. John Hercus; two s.; ed Univ. of Auckland, Univ. of Kent, UK; Lawyer and Staff Training Officer, Beath & Co., Christchurch 1969–70; mem. Price Tribunal and Trade Practices Comm. 1973–75; Deputy Chair. Commerce Comm. 1975–78; Chair. Consumer Rights Campaign 1975; MP for Lyttelton 1978–87, Opposition Spokesperson on Social Welfare, Consumer Affairs and Women's Affairs 1978–84; Minister of Social Welfare, Police and Women's Affairs 1984–87; Perm. Rep. to UN, New York 1989–90; int. consultant 1991–98; Chief of Mission, UN Force in Cyprus 1998–99; mem. Bd of Dirs Television New Zealand Ltd. 2002–05 (resgnd); Labour. *Leisure interests:* collecting original New Zealand prints, theatre, reading. *Address:* 82A Park Terrace, Christchurch 8001, New Zealand.

HERCZEGH, Géza Gábor, PhD; Hungarian judge; b. 17 Oct. 1928, Nagykapos; s. of the late Károly Herczegh and Jolán Olchváry; m. Melinda Petnehazy 1961; one s. one d.; ed French Grammar School, Gödöllö, Univ. of Szeged; Research Fellow in Public Int. Law Inst. of Political Science, Budapest 1951–67; Prof. of Law, Head Int. Law Dept, Univ. of Pécs 1967–90; Judge, Vice-Pres. Constitutional Court 1990–93; Judge Int. Court of Justice, The Hague 1993–2003; mem. Hungarian Acad. of Sciences 1985; Dr hc (Marburg) 1990, (Pécs) 2000. *Publications:* The Colonial Question and International Law 1962, General Principles of Law and the International Legal Order 1969, Development of International Humanitarian Law 1984, Foreign Policy of Hungary 1896–1919 1987, From Sarajevo to the Potsdam Conference 1999. *Leisure interests:* history, archaeology. *Address:* Ipoly u.1a III, 1133 Budapest, Hungary. *Telephone:* (1) 339-4581 (home). *Fax:* (1) 412-1009 (home).

HERFKENS, Eveline L.; Dutch diplomat, politician and UN official; *Special Adviser to the Millennium Development Goals Campaign, United Nations;* b. 1952, The Hague; ed Leiden Univ.; Policy Officer for Devt Cooperation, Ministry of Foreign Affairs 1976–81; mem. Lower House of Parl. 1981–90; Treasurer and mem. Cttee of Parliamentarians for Global Action 1985–96; mem. Econ. Cttee, Parliamentary Ass. of Council of Europe 1986–89, also Jt Organiser North-South Campaign; Exec. Dir World Bank, Washington, DC 1990–96; Amb. and Perm. Rep. to UN, Geneva 1996–98; Minister for Devt Co-operation 1998–2002; Exec. Coordinator Millennium Devt Goals Campaign, UN, NY 2002–06, Special Adviser 2006–; fmr Chair. Evert Vermeer Foundation, Dutch Fair Trade Org.; fmr mem. Council of the Labour Party (PvdA), Devt Cttee of Netherlands Council of Churches. *Address:* UN Millennium Development Goals Campaign, United Nations, New York, NY 10017, USA. *Telephone:* (212) 963-1234. *Fax:* (212) 963-4879. *E-mail:* inquiries@un.org. *Website:* www.un.org.

HÉRIARD DUBREUIL, Dominique; French business executive; *Chairman of Management Board, Rémy Cointreau;* b. 6 July 1946, Paris; d. of André Hériard Dubreuil and Anne-Marie Hériard Dubreuil (née Renaud); m. Alain-Pierre Jacquet 1975; one d.; ed Univ. of Paris II (Panthéon-Assas) and Inst. des Relations Publiques; press attaché, Havas Conseil 1969–72; est. public relations dept for Ogilvy & Mather 1972; Programme Head, Hill & Knowlton 1973–75; est. public relations dept for McCann-Erickson France 1975–77; Founder, Chair. and Man. Dir Agence Infoplan 1978–87; Man. Dir E. Rémy Martin & Cie SA 1988–, Chair. 1990–; Pres. Fed. of Wine and Spirit Exporters of France 1992–94; Pres. Comite Colbert 1994–98, Vinexpo 1998; CEO Rémy Cointreau 1998–2004, Chair. of Man. Bd 2001–; Chevalier de la Légion d'honneur; Officier de l'Ordre nat. du Mérite; ranked by Fortune magazine amongst 50 Most Powerful Women in Business outside the US (28th) 2003, (24th) 2004, (30th) 2005, (38th) 2006, (42nd) 2007. *Leisure interest:* visual arts. *Address:* Rémy Cointreau, 152 avenue des Champs-Elysées, 75008 Paris, France (office). *Telephone:* 1-44-13-44-13 (office). *Fax:* 1-44-13-44-66 (office). *E-mail:* dominique.heriard.dubreuil@remy-cointreau.com (office). *Website:* www.remy-cointreau.com (office).

HERINCX, Raimund (Raymond Frederick); British singer (bass-baritone) and voice teacher and therapist; b. 23 Aug. 1927, London; s. of Florent Herincx and Marie Cheal; m. Margaret J. Waugh (known as Astra Blair) 1954; one s. two d.; ed Thames Valley Grammar School and Univ. of London; Educ. Officer, Household Cavalry 1946–48; studied singing in Antwerp, Brussels, Barcelona and London with Giovanni Valli, Samuel Worthington and Harold Williams 1949–53; mem. Royal Opera House chorus; joined Welsh Nat. Opera 1956; Prin. Baritone, Sadler's Wells Opera 1957–67; début Royal Opera House, Covent Garden 1968; joined Metropolitan Opera House, New York 1976, subsequently appearing in most major US opera houses mainly in works of Wagner and Richard Strauss; Prof. of Voice RAM 1970–77; Sr Voice Teacher, North East of Scotland Music School 1979–; voice therapist 1979–; voice teacher Trinity Coll. of Music, London 1993–; lecturer, Univ. Coll., Cardiff 1984–87; Music Critic for Music and Musicians; Hon. RAM 1971; Opera Medal, Int. Music Awards 1968. *Leisure interests:* Artists' Asscn Against Aids, vineyard man., plant breeding (begonias and geraniums), wine and its history, wildfowl. *Address:* North East of Scotland Music School, Dorothy Hately Music Centre, 21 Huntly Street, Aberdeen, AB10 1TJ, Scotland (office). *Telephone:* (1224) 649685 (office). *Website:* www.nesms.org (office).

HERING, Jürgen; German librarian; b. 15 Sept. 1937, Chemnitz; s. of the late Karl Hering and of Margot Hering (née Schubert); m. Inge Rich 1961; one s. two d.; ed Univs of Stuttgart, Munich and Tübingen; Library Asst Stuttgart Univ. Library 1968, Library Adviser 1971, Sr Library Adviser 1972, Librarian

1974, Chief Librarian 1975–96; Chief Librarian Sächsische Landesbibliothek–Staats and Dresden Univ. Library 1997–2003; Chair. Verein Deutscher Bibliothekare 1979–83, First Deputy Chair. 1983–85; Geschäftsführer Max-Kade-Stiftung Stuttgart 1982–, Wissenschaftlicher Beirat Bibliothek für Zeitgeschichte, Stuttgart 1986–99, Kuratorium Deutsches Biblioteksinstitut Berlin 1990–95; mem. Exec. Cttee German Libraries Asscn 1992–95 (Chair. 1989–92); Adviser, Stiftung Preussischer Kulturbesitz 1999–2003; Verdienstorden des Freistaates Sachsen 2003; Dr Josef Bick Ehrenmedaille (Austria) 1992. *Leisure interests:* photography, travel. *Address:* Eichenparkstrasse 34, 70619 Stuttgart, Germany (home). *Telephone:* (711) 473944 (home). *Fax:* (711) 47059770 (home). *E-mail:* juergen.k.hering@web.de (home).

HERKSTRÖTER, Cornelius Antonius Johannes, BSc; Dutch business executive; *Chairman, Supervisory Board, ING Groep N.V.;* b. 21 Aug. 1937, Venlo; m. Regina Maria Haske 1959; two s. one d.; qualified as chartered accountant; joined Billiton as business economist 1967, following acquisition of Billiton by Shell Petroleum, apptd. Head Dept Financial and Econ. Affairs 1971, various sr posts in Billiton cos, Switzerland and Netherlands 1972–80, Area Co-ordinator SE Asia, Shell Int. Petroleum Co. Ltd 1980, Vice-Pres. (Finance) Shell Française SA 1982, Chair. Bd of Man. Deutsche Shell AG 1985, Regional Co-ordinator Europe, Dir Shell Internationale Petroleum Mij. BV 1988, Man. Dir The Shell Petroleum Co. Ltd, Chair. Supervisory Bd Shell Nederland BV, Group Man. Dir 1989, Chair. Supervisory Bd Deutsche Shell AG 1990, Dir Shell UK Ltd, Chair. Bd of Dirs Billiton Int. Metals BV 1991, Pres. NV Koninklijke Nederlandsche Petroleum Maatschappij (Royal Dutch Petroleum Co.) 1992–98; mem. Supervisory Bd ING Groep N.V. 1998–, Chair. 1999–; Verdienstkreuz (First Class) (Germany); Kt Order of Netherlands Lion. *Address:* c/o Supervisory Board, ING Groep N.V., ING House, Amstelveenseweg, 500 1081 KL Amsterdam, Netherlands. *Telephone:* (20) 541-5411. *Fax:* (20 541-5497. *Website:* www.ing.com.

HERMAN, Alexis M.; American politician and administrator; *Chairman and CEO, New Ventures LLC;* b. 16 July 1947, Mobile, Ala; m. Dr Charles Franklin 2000; ed Xavier Univ.; with Recruitment and Training Program Inc., US Dept of Labor, New York City 1971–72, Consulting Supervisor 1973–74; Nat. Dir Minority Women's Employment Program 1974–77; Dir Women's Bureau, US Dept of Labor, Washington, DC 1977–81; Founder A.M. Herman & Assocs, Washington, DC 1981, Pres. and CEO 1985–93; Chief of Staff and Deputy Chair. Democratic Nat. Convention Cttee –1991, CEO 1991–92; Deputy Dir Clinton-Gore Presidential Transition Office 1992–93; Asst to Pres. of USA; Public Liaison Dir White House 1993–96; Sec. of Labor 1997–2000; Chair. and CEO New Ventures LLC (corp. consulting firm) 2001–; mem. Bd of Dirs Coca Cola Co., Chair. Human Resources Task Force 2001–06; mem. Sodexo Advisory Bd, Toyota Advisory Bd on Diversity 2001–; mem. Bd of Dirs Cummins Inc., Presidential Life Insurance Co., ULLICO, MGM/Mirage, Inc., Entergy Corpn, New Orleans, Xavier Univ. (La), Nat. Urban League, Leon H. Sullivan Foundation, Nat. D-Day Museum, George Meany Nat. Labor Coll., USA Football, Elizabeth Glazer Pediatric AIDS Foundation; mem. Nat. Council of Negro Women, Ron Brown Foundation; Sara Lee Front Runner Award 1999. *Address:* 892 Linganore Drive, McLean, VA 22102; 1333 H Street, NW, Washington, DC 20005, USA.

HERMAN, Richard, BA, PhD; American mathematician, academic and university administrator; *Chancellor, University of Illinois at Urbana-Champaign;* m. Susan Herman; three c.; ed Stevens Inst. of Tech., Univ. of Maryland; began teaching career as Lecturer in Math., UCLA; joined Pennsylvania State Univ. 1972, Chair. Dept of Math. 1986–90; Dean, Coll. of Computer, Math. and Physical Sciences, Univ. of Maryland 1990–98; Provost and Vice Chancellor for Academic Affairs, Univ. of Illinois at Urbana-Champaign 1998–2005, Chancellor 2005–; Chair. Council of Pres.'s of Univs Research Asscn Inc.; mem. Pres. Bush's Council of Advisors on Science and Tech.; mem. American Acad. of Arts and Sciences 2008–. *Address:* Office of the Chancellor, University of Illinois at Urbana-Champaign, 317 Swanlund Administration Building, 601 E. John Street, Champaign, IL 61820, USA (office). *Telephone:* (217) 333-1000 (office). *Website:* oc.illinois.edu/index.html (office).

HERMANI MELONI, Gen. (retd) Remigio; Peruvian government official; Head of Nat. Bureau of Criminal Investigation (DIRINCRI) 2001–02; Chief of Security, Office of the Comptroller Gen. 2002–08; Minister of the Interior 2008–09 (resgnd). *Address:* c/o Ministry of the Interior, Plaza 30 de Agosto 150, San Isidro, Lima, Peru (office).

HERMANN, Jacques; Danish judge (retd); b. 10 Nov. 1934; ed Univ. of Copenhagen; civil servant, Ministry of Justice 1959–77, section chief from 1972; Public Prosecutor 1977–80; High Court Judge 1981–83; Permanent Under-Sec. Ministry of Defence 1984–88; Justice, Supreme Court 1988–2004, Chief Justice and Pres. Supreme Court 2001–04. *Address:* c/o Supreme Court, Prins Jørgens Gård 13, 1218 Copenhagen K, Denmark (office).

HERMANNSSON, Steingrímur, MSc; Icelandic fmr central bank governor, engineer and politician; b. 22 June 1928, Reykjavik; s. of the late Hermann Jónasson and Vigdís Steingrímsdóttir; m. 1st Sara Jane Hermannsson 1951; m. 2nd Gudlaug Edda Gudmundsdóttir 1962; four s. two d.; ed Reykjavik Coll., Illinois and California Insts. of Tech.; engineer, City of Reykjavik Electrical Power Works 1952–53; electrical engineer, Fertilizer Plant Inc., Iceland 1953–54; engineer S Calif. Edison Co. 1954–56; Dir Nat. Research Council, Iceland 1957–78; mem. Althingi (Parl.) 1971–94; Sec. Progressive Party 1971–79, Chair. 1979–94; Minister of Justice, Ecclesiastical Affairs and Agric. 1978–79; Minister of Fisheries and Communications 1980–83; Prime Minister of Iceland 1983–87, 1988–91, also Minister of Econ. Planning; Minister of Foreign Affairs and Foreign Trade 1987–88; Gov. Cen. Bank of Iceland 1994–98; Chair. Surtsey Research Soc., USA, Leifur Eirikssen Foundaton; Caltech's Alumni Distinguished Service Award 1986, IIT's Professional Achievement Award 1991, Icelandic Athletics Asscn Gold Medal, Paul Harris Rotary Fellow. *Leisure interests:* outdoor sports, skiing, golf, forestry, carpentry, environment. *Address:* Mavanes 19, 210 Gardabae, Iceland (home). *Telephone:* 5641509 (home). *Fax:* 5542402 (home). *E-mail:* steingrimur@vortex.is (home).

HERMANS, Christopher, MA; Botswana banker; b. 23 Dec. 1936, Cape Town, South Africa; s. of Henry Hodgson Hermans and Marjorie Stanhope Hermans; m. 1st Janet Gallagher 1960 (divorced 1987); one s. two d.; m. 2nd Vonna Deulen 1987; two d.; ed Diocesan Coll., Rondebosch, Cape Town, Trinity Coll., Oxford, Howard Univ., Wash., Vanderbilt Univ., Nashville, Tenn.; Asst Sec. for Devt, Bechuanaland Protectorate Admin. 1961–66; Perm. Sec., Ministry of Devt Planning, Botswana Govt 1966–70, Ministry of Finance and Devt Planning 1970–75; Gov. Bank of Botswana 1975–77, 1987–99; Sr Planning Adviser/Loan Officer, World Bank 1977–82, CEO Thailand and Indonesia Programs Div., 1982–84; CEO of World Bank Regional Mission, Bangkok 1984–87; Presidential Order of Meritorious Service. *Leisure interests:* tennis, wildlife, windsurfing, gardening. *Address:* c/o Bank of Botswana, PO Box 712, Gaborone, Botswana.

HERMASSI, Abdelbaki; Tunisian politician; Minister of Culture, Youth and Leisure –2004; Minister of Foreign Affairs 2004–05. *Address:* c/o Ministry of Foreign Affairs, ave de la Ligue des états Arabes, Tunis, Tunisia (office).

HERMASZEWSKI, Gen. Mirosław; Polish astronaut and air force officer (retd); b. 15 Sept. 1941, Lipniki (now Ukraine); s. of the late Roman Hermaszewski and of Kamila Hermaszewska; m. 1965; one s. one d.; ed Air Force Officers' School, Dęblin 1961–64, Karol Sverchevski Mil. Acad., Gen. Staff Acad., Warsaw, Voroshilov Mil. Acad., Moscow; served in Nat. Air Defence 1964–76; 1st class pilot 1966, supersonic MiG-21 pilot 1967, flight leader 1971–72, Deputy Squadron Leader 1972–75, Regt Commdr 1975–76; master's class pilot; in Cosmonauts' Training Centre, Zvezdnoy Gorodok, nr Moscow 1976–78; space flight on board Soyuz-30 and space-station Salyut-6 June–July (7 days 22 hours 2 minutes and 59 seconds) 1978; service in HQ of Nat. Air Defence 1978–80; Chief of Shkola Orlyat High Aviation School 1982–85; Second-in-Command, Air Forces and Air Defence of Polish Repub. 1990–91; Commdr Air Force Officers' School, Dęblin 1984–90; mem. Space Research Cttee of Polish Acad. of Sciences 1978–, Asscn of Space Explorers 1985–; Pres. Gen. Bd Polish Astronautical Soc. 1983–87; Maj.-Gen. 1988; Gold Cross of Merit 1976, Cross of Grunwald Order (1st Class) 1978, Gold Star of Hero of USSR 1978, Order of Lenin 1978, Mil. Champion Pilot 1978, Cosmonaut of Polish People's Repub. 1978, Int. Order of Smile 1991. *Leisure interests:* science fiction novels, sailing, hunting, sports, dogs. *Address:* ul. Czeczota 25, 02-607 Warsaw, Poland.

HERNÁDI, Zsolt, BEcons; Hungarian business executive; *Chairman and CEO, MOL Rt.;* b. 1960; ed Budapest Univ. of Econ. Sciences; various posts with Kereskedelmi és Hitelbank Rt. 1989–94, becoming Deputy Gen. Man. 1992–94; CEO, Cen. Bank of Hungarian Savings Cooperatives 1994–2001, Dir 1994–2002; Dir, MOL Rt. 1999–, Chair. 2000–01, Chair. and CEO 2001–; Dir Hungarian Banking Asscn 1995–2001; Dir Panrusgas; mem. European Round Table of Industrialists 2001–. *Address:* MOL Rt., Október huszonharmadika u. 18., 1502 Budapest, Hungary (office). *Telephone:* (1) 209–0000 (office). *Website:* www.mol.hu (office).

HERNÁNDEZ ALCERRO, Jorge Ramón; Honduran diplomatist and politician; *Minister of the Interior and Justice;* b. 29 Aug. 1948; m.; two c.; ed Inst. Européen de Hautes Etudes Internationales, France, Univ. of Nice and Universidad Nacional Autónoma de Honduras; fmr attorney and lecturer at Univ. Nacional Autónoma de Honduras; fmr Judge, Inter-American Court of Human Rights; fmr Gen. Sec. Inovación y Unidad Party, Deputy to Nat. Ass. and Deputy to Nat. Congress; fmr Deputy Foreign Minister; fmr Amb. on Special Assignment in Latin America, USA and at UN General Ass.; Perm. Rep. to UN 1987–89; currently Minister of the Interior and Justice. *Address:* Ministry of the Interior and Justice, Palacio de los Ministerios, 2°, Tegucigalpa, Honduras. *Telephone:* 237-1130. *Fax:* 237-1121.

HERNÁNDEZ COLÓN, Rafael, AB, LLB; Puerto Rican politician and lawyer; b. 24 Oct. 1936, Ponce; s. of Rafael Hernández Matos and Dorinda Colón Clavell; m. Lila Mayoral 1959; three s. one d.; ed Valley Forge Mil. Acad., Wayne Pa, Johns Hopkins Univ., Univ. of Puerto Rico Law School; pvt. law practice 1959–69, 1977–84; Assoc. Commr of Public Service 1960–62; Lecturer in Law, Catholic Univ. of Puerto Rico 1961–65; Sec. of Justice 1965–67; Senator at Large, Popular Democratic Party 1968; Pres. of Senate 1969–73; Leader of Popular Democratic Party 1969; Gov. of Puerto Rico 1972–76, 1989–93; Trustee Carnegie Foundation for Int. Peace; mem. Inter-American Bar Asscn; Dr hc (Johns Hopkins Univ., Catholic Univ. of Puerto Rico); Harvard Foundation Award 1987, Great Cross of Isabel la Católica (Spain), Order of El Libertador (Venezuela). *Publications:* Text on Civil Procedure 1968 and many articles on topics of law. *Address:* c/o Popular Democratic Party, 403 Ponce de León Avenue, PO Box 5788, Puerta de Tierra, San Juan 00906, Puerto Rico.

HERRERA, Luis Felipe; Chilean banker, lawyer and economist; b. 17 June 1922, Valparaíso; s. of Joaquín Herrera and Inés Lane; m. Inés Olmo 1961; two s.; ed Colegio Alemán de Santiago, Escuela Militar, Univs. of Chile and London; Legal Dept, Central Bank of Chile 1943–47; Attorney for Cen. Bank of Chile and pvt. law practice 1947–52; Prof. of Econs, Schools of Law and Sociology, Univ. of Chile 1947–58; Under-Sec. for Economy and Commerce 1952; Minister of Finance April–Oct. 1953; Gen. Man. Cen. Bank of Chile 1953–58; Gov. Int. Bank for Reconstruction and Development, IMF 1953–58, Exec. Dir 1958–60; Pres. Inter-American Devt Bank 1960–71; Pres. Soc. for Int. Devt 1970–71; Co-ordinator-Gen. ECIEL Program (Jt Studies for Latin

American Econ. Integration) 1974–, Perm. Consultant 1981–; Pres. Admin. Council, Int. Fund for Promotion of Culture (UNESCO) 1976–; Chair. Bd of Trustees, UN Inst. for Training and Research 1976–; Pres. World Soc. of Ekistics, Inst. for Int. Co-operation 1977–80, Corporación Investigaciones para el Desarrollo (CINDE) 1986, Chilean Chapter of SID 1986; mem. Bd of Govs Int. Devt Research Centre (IDRC) 1980; mem. Bd of Trustees, Third World Foundation; mem. Hon. Bd, Raul Prebisch Foundation 1986; Perm. Consultant Emer. Int. American Devt Bank; Great Cross for Distinguished Service, FRG 1958, Kt Grand Cross, Order of Merit, Italy 1966, Medalla Cívica 'Camilo Torres', Colombia 1968, Grand Cross for Educational Merit, Brazil 1969, Gran Cruz de la Orden del Sol, Peru 1971, Gran Cruz Placa de Plata, Dominican Repub. 1971, Gran Cruz Orden Rubén Darío, Nicaragua 1971, Orden Boyacá, Colombia 1971, do Cruzeiro do Sul, Brazil 1971, de la Orden Manuel Amador Guerrero, Panama 1971, Orden Abdón Calderón, Ecuador 1971, al Mérito Nacional, Paraguay 1971, Orden del Aguila Azteca, Mexico 1972, Antonio José de Irisarri, Guatemala 1975, Orden al Mérito Cultural 'Andrés Bello', Venezuela 1978, Officier de l'Ordre Nat. du Mérite, France 1979, Gran Cruz de Isabel La Católica, Spain 1980; Dr hc (Santiago de Chile) 1993 and numerous other hon. degrees; Bronfman Award, American Public Health Asscn 1969, Condecoración al Mérito, Minas Gerais State, Brazil 1969, Premio 'Diego Portales', Chile 1971, Premio Serfin de Integración Mexico 1987, Premio ONU: Medalla Plata a la Paz, Cepal, Santiago 1988, UN Personnel Peace Prize 1989, Universidad Austral de Chile: Condecoración al Mérito Universitario 1990; numerous other awards and prizes. *Publications:* El Banco Central de Chile 1945, Política económica 1950, Fundamentos de la Política Fiscal 1951, Manual de Política Económica 1952, Elementos de Economía Monetaria 1955, ¿Desarrollo Económico o Estabilidad Monetaria? 1958, América Latina Integrada 1964, El Desarrollo Latinoamericano y su Financiamiento 1967, Nacionalismo Latinoamericano 1968, Chile en América Latina 1969, Internacionalismo, Regionalismo, Nacionalismo 1970, América Latina: Experiencias y Desafíos 1974, América Latina: Viejas y Nuevas Fronteras 1978, El Escenario Latinoamericano y el Desafío Cultural 1981, Despertar de un Continente: América Latina 1960–1980 1983, Comunidad Latinoamericana de Naciones: Presencia de Chile 1983, Visión de América Latina: 1974–1984, 1985, América Latina: Desarrollo e Integración 1986. *Address:* Calle El Cerro 1991, Santiago 9, Chile (home). *Telephone:* 232-8097 (home).

HERRERA, Paloma; Argentine ballet dancer; b. 21 Dec. 1975, Buenos Aires; d. of Alberto Herrera and Marisa Herrera; ed Teatro Colón, Buenos Aires, Minsk Ballet School, School of American Ballet; joined American Ballet Theater (ABT) corps de ballet; roles in Sleeping Beauty, Don Quixote and La Bayadère; soloist, ABT 1992, prin. dancer 1995–; leading role in How Near Heaven (cr. for her by Twyla Tharp q.v., 1994; other notable roles include Clara in The Nutcracker, Medora in Le Corsaire, Kitri in Don Quixote, Juliet in Romeo and Juliet 1995; Int. Prize Gino Tani 1997, Top Ten Dancers of the Twentieth Century, Dance Magazine 1999, Leader of the Millennium, Time Magazine and CNN 1999, Konex Platinum Prize, Ballerina of the Decade 1989-1999, Buenos Aires, Argentina 1999, Maria Ruanova Award 2000, NY Immigrant Achievement Award 2001. *Address:* American Ballet Theater, 890 Broadway, New York, NY 10003, (office); One Lincoln Plaza, 20 West 64th Street, Apt F, New York, NY 10023, USA (home); Billinghurst 2553, 10 Piso Dto, CP 1425 Buenos Aires, Argentina. *Website:* www.palomaherrera.com; www.abt.org.

HERRERA ARAYA, Marvin; Costa Rican politician and international organization executive; *Secretary-General, Coordinación Educativa y Cultural Centroamericana;* Deputy Minister of Public Educ. 1978–81; mem. Inter-American Cttee on Educ., OAS 1980–82; Deputy to Legis. Ass. 1982–86; Minister of Public Educ. 1990–94; mem. Higher Council of Educ. 1999–2003; Sec.-Gen. Coordinación Educativa y Cultural Centroamericana 2003–. *Address:* Coordinación Educativa y Cultural Centroamericana, 100m norte de la Nunciatura, Casa 8815, Rohrmoser, San José, Costa Rica (office). *Telephone:* 232-2891 (office). *Fax:* 232-2891 (office). *E-mail:* sgcecc@racsa.co.cr (office). *Website:* www.sica.int/cecc (office).

HERRERA NIETO, Gen. Nelson; Ecuadorean government official, diplomatist and army officer; fmr Dir of Educ. for the Army; fmr Dir Instituto de Altos Estudios Nacionales; fmr Commdr Aerial Brigade of the Army; fmr Amb. to Mexico; fmr Pres. INVEREC; Minister of Nat. Defence 2004–05; mem. Instituto Panamericano de Geografía e Historia. *Address:* c/o Ministry of National Defence, Exposición 208, Quito, Ecuador (office).

HERRERO RODRIGUEZ DE MIÑON, Miguel, LPh, PhD; Spanish politician and barrister; *Magistrate, Constitutional Court of Andorra;* b. 18 June 1940; s. of Miguel Herrero and Carmen Rodríguez de Miñon; m. Cristina de Jáuregui; one s. two d.; ed Univs of Madrid, Oxford, Luxembourg, Geneva, Paris and Louvain; Lecturer in Int. Law, Univ. of Madrid 1963–65; Sr Legal Adviser to Spanish Admin 1966; Gen. Sec. Ministry of Justice 1976; mem. Parl. 1977–93; Leader, Parl. Group of Unión de Centro Democrático in Govt 1980–81; Deputy Leader of Parl. Group of AP, major opposition group in Parl. 1982–87; Magistrate, Constitutional Court, Andorra 2001–; mem. Trilateral Comm. 1982–2004, State Council of Spain; mem. Real Academia de Ciencias Morales y Políticas 1991; Gran Cruz de Isabel la Católica, Gran Cruz de San Raimundo de Peñafort, Orden Mérito Constitucional, Creu San Jordi, G. Off. Merito (Italy), Collar Merito Civil; Dr hc (UNED, Leon). *Publications:* several books on constitutional law and int. relations. *Leisure interests:* collecting old books, hunting. *Address:* Calle Mayor 70, bajo, 28013 Madrid, Spain (office). *Telephone:* (1) 5595405 (office). *Fax:* (1) 5417092 (office). *E-mail:* miguel .herreromignon@consejo-stado.es (office).

HERRING, (William) Conyers, PhD; American physicist and academic; *Professor Emeritus in Applied Physics, Stanford University;* b. 15 Nov. 1914, Scotia, NY; s. of Dr W. Conyers Herring and Mary Joy Herring; m. Louise C. Preusch 1946; three s. one d.; ed Univ. of Kansas and Princeton Univ.; Nat. Research Council Fellow, MIT 1937–39; Instructor in Math. and Research Assoc. in Math. Physics, Princeton Univ. 1939–40; Instructor in Physics, Univ. of Missouri 1940–41; mem. Scientific Staff, Columbia Univ. Div. of War Research 1941–45; Prof. of Applied Mathematics, Univ. of Texas 1946; Research Physicist, Bell Telephone Laboratories 1946–78; Prof. of Applied Physics, Stanford Univ. 1978–81, Prof. Emer. 1981–; mem. Inst. for Advanced Study, Princeton 1952–53; mem. NAS; Fellow, American Acad. of Arts and Sciences; Oliver E. Buckley Solid State Physics Prize, American Physical Soc. 1959, Distinguished Service Citation, Univ. of Kansas 1973, James Murray Luck Award for Excellence in Scientific Reviewing, NAS 1980, Von Hippel Award, Materials Research Soc. 1980, Wolf Prize in Physics 1985. *Publication:* Exchange Interactions among Itinerant Electrons (Vol. 4 of series Magnetism) 1966. *Leisure interests:* church and cultural activities. *Address:* Department of Applied Physics, Stanford University, Stanford, CA 94305 (office); 3945 Nelson Drive, Palo Alto, CA 94306, USA (home). *Telephone:* (650) 723-0686 (office); (650) 856-9649 (home). *Fax:* (650) 725-2189 (office). *E-mail:* conyers@ loki.stanford.edu (office). *Website:* www.stanford.edu/dept/app-physics (office).

HERRMANN, Wolfgang A., Dipl. Chem. Univ., Dr rer. nat; German chemist, academic and university administrator; *Professor of Chemistry and President, Technische Universität München;* b. 18 April 1948, Kehlheim/Donau, Bavaria; ed Technische Universität München, Univ. Regensburg; Research Fellow, Pa State Univ., USA 1975–76; Assoc. Prof., Univ. Regensburg 1979–81; Prof., Univ. of Frankfurt 1982–85; Prof. of Chemistry, Technische Universität München 1985–, Dean of Science Faculty 1988–90, Univ. Pres. 1995–; Chair. Scientific Council VIAG AG, Bonn 1991–96; fmr visiting Prof. at numerous int. univs including Strasbourg, Bordeaux, Rennes and Toulouse, France, Rijksuniversiteit Utrecht, Netherlands, Texas A & M Univ., USA; mem. Editorial Bd numerous publs including Journal of Cluster Science 1988–, Journal of Molecular Catalysis 1994–, Angewandte Chemie 1999–, Catalyis Letters 1999–; mem. Supervisory Bd DEGUSSA AG 2001–, GenPharmTox AG 2001–; mem. Deutsche Akademie der Naturforscher 1995–; Fellow Japanese Soc. for Promotion of Science 1992–; Bundesverdienstkreuz 1997 DrSc hc (Univ. Claude Bernard, Lyons, France) 1990, (Univ. Veszprém, Hungary) 1995, (Univ. of SC, USA) 1999 Otto-Klung Award for Chemistry 1982, Alexander von Humboldt Award 1989, Otto Bayer Award 1990, Max Planck Research Award (Jt recipient) 1991, Italian Chemical Soc. Pino Medal 1994, Luigi Sacconi Medal 2000, Werner Heisenberg Medal 2000. *Address:* Lehrstuhl für Anorganische Chemie, Technische Universität München, Lichtenbergstrassse 4, Garching bei München 85747, Germany (office). *Telephone:* (89) 28913080 (office). *Fax:* (89) 28913473 (office). *E-mail:* wolfgang.herrmann@ch.tum.de (office); praesident@tum.de (office). *Website:* aci.anorg.chemie.tu-muenchen.de/wah/index/php (office).

HERSCHBACH, Dudley Robert, BS, MS, AM, PhD, FRSC; American chemist and academic; *Frank B. Baird, Jr. Professor of Science, Harvard University;* b. 18 June 1932, San José, Calif.; s. of Robert Dudley Herschbach and Dorothy Edith Beer; m. Georgene Lee Botyos 1964; two d.; ed Stanford and Harvard Univs; Asst Prof. Univ. of Calif., Berkeley 1959–61, Assoc. Prof. 1961–63; Prof. of Chem., Harvard Univ. 1963–76, Frank B. Baird, Jr Prof. of Science 1976–, Chair. Chemical Physics Program 1964–77, Chair. Dept of Chem. 1977–80, mem. Faculty Council 1980–83, Co-Master of Currier House 1981–86; Chair. Bd of Trustees Science Service; Assoc. Ed., Journal of Physical Chem. 1980–88; Fellow American Acad. of Arts and Sciences, NAS, American Philosophical Soc.; Hon. DSc (Toronto) 1977, (Adelphi) 1990; shared Nobel Prize for Chem. 1986; ACS Pure Chem. Prize 1965, ACS Pauling Medal 1978, Polanyi Medal, Royal Soc. of Chem. 1981, Langmuir Prize, American Physical Soc. 1983, Nat. Award of Science 1991, Sierra Nevada Distinguished Chemist Award 1993, Kosolapoff Medal 1994, William Walker Prize 1994. *Publications:* more than 350 research papers. *Leisure interests:* viola, running. *Address:* Department of Chemistry and Chemical Biology, Harvard University, 12 Oxford Street, Cambridge, MA 02138, USA. *Telephone:* (617)-495-3218 (office). *Fax:* (617)-495-4723 (office). *E-mail:* herschbach@chemistry.harvard .edu (office). *Website:* www.chem.harvard.edu/herschbach (office).

HERSH, Seymour Myron, BA; American journalist and writer; b. 8 April 1937, Chicago, IL; m. Elizabeth Sarah Klein 1964; two s. one d.; ed Univ. of Chicago; Chicago City News Bureau 1959; corresp. United Press International 1962–63, Associated Press 1963–67, The New Yorker 1992–; mem. of staff New York Times 1972–79; nat. corresp. Atlantic Monthly 1983–86; Pulitzer Prize for Int. Reporting 1970, George Polk Memorial Awards 1970, 1973, 1974, 1981, Scripps-Howard Public Service Award 1973, Sidney Hillman Award 1974, John Peter Zenger Freedom of the Press Award 1975, Los Angeles Times Book Prize 1983, Nat. Book Critics Circle Award 1983, Investigative Reporters and Editors Prizes 1983, 1992, Nat. Magazine Award 2004. *Publications:* Chemical and Biological Warfare: America's Hidden Arsenal 1968, My Lai 4: A Report on the Massacre and Its Aftermath 1970, Cover-Up: The Army's Secret Investigation of the Massacre at My Lai 1972, The Price of Power: Kissinger in the Nixon White House 1983, The Target is Destroyed: What Really Happened to Flight 007 and What America Knew About It 1986, The Samson Option: Israel's Nuclear Arsenal and America's Foreign Policy 1991, The Dark Side of Camelot 1997, Against All Enemies: Gulf War Syndrome: The War Between America's Ailing Veterans and Their Government 1999, Chain of Command: The Road from 9/11 to Abu Ghraib 2004; contribs to various magazines. *Address:* 3214 Newark Street NW, Washington, DC 20008-3345, USA (home).

HERSHEY, Barbara; American actress; b. 5 Feb. 1948, Hollywood, Calif.; d. of William H. Herzstein; one s.; m. Stephen Douglas 1992 (divorced 1995); ed Hollywood High School; debut in TV series The Monroes. *Films include:* With

Six You Get Eggroll 1968, Heaven with a Gun 1969, The Last Summer 1969, The Liberation of L.B. Jones 1970, The Baby Maker 1970, The Pursuit of Happiness 1971, Dealing: Or the Berkeley-to-Boston Forty-Brick Lost-Bag Blues 1972, Boxcar Bertha 1972, Love Comes Quietly 1973, The Crazy World of Julius Vrooder 1974, You and Me 1975, Diamonds 1975, Trial by Combat 1976, The Last Hard Men 1976, The Stuntman 1980, The Entity 1981, Americana 1981, Take This Job and Shove It 1981, The Right Stuff 1983, The Natural 1984, Hannah and Her Sisters 1988, Hoosiers 1986, Tin Men 1987, Shy People 1987 (Best Actress, Cannes Film Festival), The Last Temptation of Christ 1988, A World Apart 1988 (Best Actress, Cannes Film Festival), Beaches 1988, Tune in Tomorrow 1990, Paris Trout 1990, The Public Eye 1991, Defenseless 1991, Swing Kids 1993, Splitting Heirs, Falling Down 1993, A Dangerous Woman 1994, Last of the Dogmen 1995, Portrait of a Lady 1996, The Pallbearer 1996, A Soldier's Daughter Never Cries 1998, Frogs for Snakes 1999, Drowning on Dry Land 1999, Breakfast of Champions 1999, Lantana 2001, 11:14 2003, Riding the Bullet 2004, The Bird Can't Fly 2007, Love Comes Lately 2007, Childless 2008. *Television includes:* Just a Little Inconvenience, A Killing in a Small Town (Emmy and Golden Globe Awards 1990), The Bible 1993, Return to Lonesome Dove 1993, Portrait of a Lady 1996, A Soldier's Daughter Never Cries 1998, Frogs for Snakes 1998, The Staircase 1998, Breakfast of Champions 1999, Passion 1999, Chicago Hope (series) 1999–2000, Daniel Deronda 2002, Hunger Point 2003, The Stranger Beside Me 2003, Paradise 2004, The Mountain (series) 2004–05, Anne of Green Gables: A New Beginning 2008. *Address:* c/o Suzan Bymel, Bymel O'Neill Management, N Vista, Los Angeles, CA 90046 (office); c/o Jenny Rawlings, CAA, 9830 Wilshire Boulevard, Beverly Hills, CA 90212, USA.

HERSHKO, Avram, MD, PhD; Israeli physician and molecular biologist; *Professor, Faculty of Medicine, Technion–Israel Institute of Technology;* b. 1937, Hungary; ed Hebrew Univ. of Jerusalem; prisoner in Nazi concentration camp; emigrated to Israel with parents 1950; mil. service as doctor in Israeli army; studied molecular biology in San Francisco 1969–72; Prof. Faculty of Medicine, Technion–Israel Inst. of Tech.; studied protein degradation at biochemical level with Aaron Ciechanover (q.v.) 1976–81; Albert Lasker Basic Medical Research Award 2000, shared Wolf Prize with Alexander Varshavsky (q.v.) 2001, Nobel Prize in Chemistry (jtly) 2004. *Address:* Faculty of Medicine, Technion–Israel Institute of Technology, Haifa, Israel (office). *Telephone:* (4) 8292111 (office). *Website:* www.technion.ac.il/~rapinst/hershko.html (office).

HERSOV, Basil Edward, DMS, MA, DL, FRSA; South African business executive (retd); b. 18 Aug. 1926, Johannesburg; s. of Abraham Sundel (Bob) Hersov and Gertrude Hersov (née Aronson); m. Antoinette Herbert 1957; two s. two d.; ed Michaelhouse, Natal and Christ's Coll., Cambridge; pilot in S African Air Force (SAAF) 1944–46; joined Anglovaal Ltd as Learner Official on gold mine 1949, later holding a number of sr positions with Anglovaal Group: Deputy Chair. 1970, Chair. and Man. Dir 1973–98; Chair. Hartebeestfontein Gold Mining Co. Ltd, Anglovaal Industries Ltd, The Associated Manganese Mines of SA Ltd; mem. bd of many other cos within and outside Anglovaal Group; Dir Mutual and Fed. Insurance Co. Ltd; Pres. and Fellow, Inst. of Dirs (SA); Hon. Pres., mem. Council, South Africa Foundation; Gov. Rhodes Univ. Bd of Trustees, Business South Africa, Nat. Business Initiative; Fellow, S African Inst. of Mining and Metallurgy, S African Inst. of Man.; Hon. Col 21 Squadron, Doyen SAAF Hon. Cols; Hon. LLD (Rhodes); Decoration for Meritorious Service; Witwaterstand Univ. Award for Business Excellence 1984, Brig. Stokes Memorial Award, S African Inst. of Mining and Metallurgy 1996. *Leisure interests:* skiing, horse racing, tennis, flying, sailing. *Address:* Springwaters, Box 65097, Benmore 2010 (home); PO Box 846, Saxonwold 2132, South Africa (office). *Telephone:* (11) 2830091 (office). *Fax:* (11) 8834006 (home); (11) 2830038 (office). *E-mail:* basilh@hersov.co.za (home).

HERTELEER, Vice-Adm. Willy Maurits; Belgian military officer; b. 1 Oct. 1941, Assenede; m. Jacqueline Liekens 1962; one s. three d.; ed Royal Cadet School, Brussels, Merchant Navy Acad., Belgian Staff Coll., Brussels, Ecole Supérieure de Guerre Navale, Paris; commissioned Belgian Navy 1962, as ensign served on minesweepers and a supply/command ship 1963-68, became mine warfare specialist 1969–70, Staff Officer Mine Countermeasures, Operational Command 1970–72; Commdr coastal minesweeper 1975, ocean minesweeper/hunter 1978, (instructor Belgian-Dutch School for Mine Warfare, Ostend between these postings); rank of Lt-Commdr 1979; apptd to Planning section, Belgian Naval Staff, also mem. Naval Bd, NATO Mil. Standardization Agency 1979–82; Second-in-Command frigate Westdiep 1982–84, Commdg Officer 1984–85; Asst Chief of Staff Operations, Naval Operations Command 1986, Chief of Staff 1986–87; Head Belgian-Dutch School for Mine Warfare 1987–89; mem. Audit Team, Belgian Naval Staff, Brussels 1989, Staff Officer, Operations 1990, Commdr Naval Operations 1990–92; rank of Rear-Adm. 1992; joined Gen. Staff Headquarters, Brussels 1992, Chief of Naval Staff 1993–95; rank of Vice-Adm. 1995; Chief of the Gen. Staff 1995–2002; Aide to King Albert II; Grand Cross, Order of the Crown. *Address:* Rue d'Evère, 1140 Brussels, Belgium. *Telephone:* (2) 701-31-50. *Fax:* (2) 701-66-25.

HERTRICH, Rainer, BCom; German aerospace industry executive; b. 6 Dec. 1949, Ottengrün; ed Tech. Univ. of Berlin, Univ. of Nuremberg; apprenticeship and business training, Siemens AG 1969–71; Information Processing Supervisor controlling Dept, Mil. Aircraft Div., Messerschmitt-Bölkow-Blohm (MBB) GmbH 1977, Head Controlling Dept MBB Service Div., Ottobrunn 1978–83, Chief Financial Officer 1983–84, Head Controlling and Finance Dept, MBB Dynamics Div. 1984–87, Chief Financial Officer and mem. Div. Man., MBB Marine and Special Products Div. 1987–90; Head Divisional Controlling, Cen. Controlling Section, Deutsche Aerospace AG, Dasa (now European Aeronautic Defence and Space Co. —EADS) 1990–91, Sr Vice-Pres., Corp. Controlling, Dasa 1991–96, Head Aeroengines Business Unit, Dasa, Pres. and CEO Motoren- und Turbinen-Union München (MTU München) GmbH, mem. Exec. Cttee Dasa 1996–2000, Pres. and CEO DaimlerChrysler Aerospace (Dasa) AG 2000, CEO EADS 2000–05 (Head of Aeronautic Div. 2004–05); Pres. BDLI (German aerospace industries asscn) 2001–05; Officier Légion d'honneur. *Address:* c/o EADS Deutschland GmbH, CCICP, 81663 Munich, Germany (office).

HERTZ, Noreena, BA, MBA, PhD; British economist, academic and writer; *Fellow, Judge Business School,, University of Cambridge;* b. 24 Sept. 1967, London; ed Univ. Coll. London, Univ. of Cambridge, UK, Wharton School of the Univ. of Pennsylvania; attended business school in USA; helped establish first Leningrad (now St Petersburg) stock exchange 1991; Int. Finance Corpn adviser to Russian Govt on econ. reforms 1992; fmr head of research team working on prospects for regional econ. co-operation in the Middle East; fmr Distinguished Fellow and Assoc. Dir, Centre for Int. Business and Man., Judge Inst. of Man. Studies, Univ. of Cambridge, currently Fellow, Judge Business School; Belle van Zuylen Chair of Global Political Economy, Utrecht Univ. April–Sept. 2005; attended World Econ. Forum 2002; regular commentator on TV and radio. *Television includes:* documentary film of her book The Silent Takeover (Channel 4) 2001. *Publications include:* Russian Business in the Wake of Reform (doctoral thesis) 1996, The Silent Takeover: Global Capitalism and the Death of Democracy 2001, IOU: The Debt Threat and Why We Must Defuse It 2004; contribs to New Statesman, the Observer, the Guardian and the Washington Post. *Address:* Judge Business School, Trumpington Street, Cambridge, CB2 1AG (office); c/o Fourth Estate Ltd, 77–85 Fulham Palace Road, London, W6 8JB, England. *Telephone:* (20) 7724-0829 (office). *Fax:* (20) 7724-1726 (office). *E-mail:* noreenah@yahoo.com (office). *Website:* www.jbs.cam.ac.uk (office).

HERTZBERGER, Herman; Dutch architect and academic; *Principal, Architectuurstudio HH;* b. 6 July 1932, Amsterdam; m. J. C. Van Seters 1959; one s. two d.; ed Delft Tech. Univ.; pvt. practice, Architectuurstudio HH, Amsterdam 1958–; Co-Ed. (Dutch) Forum 1959–63; teacher, Acad. of Architecture, Amsterdam 1965–69; Prof. of Architectural Design, Tech. Univ. of Delft 1970–99; Prof., Univ. of Geneva 1986–93; Chair. Berlage Inst., Amsterdam 1990–95; guest teacher at univs/architectural insts in Argentina, Austria, Belgium, Brazil, Croatia, Denmark, France, Germany, Greece, Ireland, Israel, Italy, Japan, Mexico, the Netherlands, Slovenia, S Korea, Spain, Switzerland, Taiwan, UK, USA; Hon. mem. Acad. Royale de Belgique 1975, Bund Deutscher Architeckten 1983, Akad. der Künste 1993, Accad. delle Arti del Disegno, Florence 1995, Acad. d'Architecture de France 1997, Bond van Nederlandse Architecten 2002; Hon. FRIBA 1991; Hon. Fellow, Royal Incorporation of Architects in Scotland 1996; Hon. FAIA 2004; Kt, Order of Oranje Nassau 1991, Companion, Order of the Dutch Lion; Hon. DUniv (Geneva) 2001; numerous prizes and awards including Architectural Award of the Town of Amsterdam 1968, Eternit Award 1974, Fritz Schumacher Award 1974, Architecture Award of the City of Amsterdam 1985, Premio Europa 1991, BNA Award 1991, Concrete Award 1991, Prix Rhénan 1993, Architecture Award, City of Breda 1998, Premios Vitruvio 98 Trayectoria Internacional 1998, Dutch School Bldg Award 2000, Leone d'oro (Venice) 2002, Architecture Award, City of Apeldoorn 2004, Oeuvre Award for Architecture of the Netherlands Foundation for Visual Arts, Design and Architecture 2004, Dutch School Building Award 2004, Arie Keppler Award 2005, Architecture Award of the Citizens of Apeldoorn 2006. *Major works include:* 12 primary schools, three extended school complexes, three secondary schools 1966–2000, office bldg, 'Centraal Beheer', Apeldoorn 1972, housing for old and disabled people 'De Drie Hoven', Amsterdam 1974, music centre 'Vredenburg', Utrecht 1978, urban renewal 'Haarlemmer Houttinen', Amsterdam 1982, office bldg Ministry of Social Welfare and Employment, The Hague 1990, Theatre Centre Spui, The Hague 1993, library and art and music centre, Breda 1993, Chassé Theater, Breda 1995, Theater Markant, Uden 1996, residential buildings, Haarlem 1996, Düren, Germany 1996, Berlin 1997, extension to Vanderveen Department Store, Assen 1997, YKK Dormitory Guesthouse, Kurobe City, Japan 1998, Bijlmer Monument (with Georges Descombes) 1998, residential area 'Merwestein Noord', Dordrecht 1999, Montessori Coll. Oost, Amsterdam 1999, Waterhouse, Middelburg 2002, Il Fiore office bldg Maastricht 2002, VMBO School Titaan, Hoorn 2004, MediaPark office bldgs and residential complex, Cologne 2004, CODA museum, library and municipal archives, Apeldoorn 2004, Theatre and Congress Centre ORPHEUS, Apeldoorn 2004, Head Office, Waternet, Amsterdam 2005. *Publications:* Homework for More Hospitable Form (Dutch) Forum XXIV 1973, Herman Hertzberger 1959–86 Bauten und Projekte/Buildings and Projects/Bâtiments et Projets (jtly) 1987, Lessons for Students in Architecture 1991, Herman Hertzberger Projekte/Projects 1990–1995 1995, Chassé Theater 1995, Herman Hertzberger: View of Projects of 1960–1997 (jtly) 1997, Space and the Architect: Lessons for Students in Architecture part II 2000, Articulations 2002, Cultuur onder Dak: Shelter for Culture – Herman Hertzberger and Apeldoorn 2004, De theaters van Herman Hertzberger 2005, Waternet Doubeltower 2006, Hertzberger's Amsterdam 2007, Space and Learning 2008. *Leisure interest:* music. *Address:* Architectuurstudio HH, Gerard Doustraat 220, PO Box 74665, 1070 BR Amsterdam, Netherlands (office). *Telephone:* (20) 6765888 (office). *Fax:* (20) 6735510 (office). *E-mail:* office@hertzberger.nl (office). *Website:* www.hertzberger.nl (office).

HERVÉ, Edmond; French politician; b. 3 Dec. 1942, La Bouillie, Côtes du Nord; s. of Marcel Hervé; m. Jeannine Le Gall 1978; two s. one d.; Prof. of Constitutional Law, Rennes Univ.; Conseiller Général, Ille-et-Vilaine 1973–82; Mayor of Rennes 1977–2008; Pres. regional hosp. centre and univ. hosp. centre, both in Brittany 1977–; fmr Minister of Health; Minister Del. to Minister of Industry for Energy 1981–83; Sec. of State for Health 1983–86; Regional Councillor, Brittany 1986–88; Deputy for Ille-et-Vilaine to Nat. Ass. 1986–2002; Pres. Dist Urbain de l'agglomeration rennaise (Audiar) 1989,

Conf. permanente du tourisme urbain 1989–95, Hon. Pres. 1995–; Chair. Conf. de villes de l'arc atlantique 2000–; mem. Conseil de Surveillance du Crédit local de France 1990, City Scientific Cttee on Science and Industry of La Villette 1990, Nat. Council on Towns and Urban Social Devt 1991, Parti Socialiste. *Address:* c/o Hôtel de Ville, Place de la Mairie, BP 3126, 35031 Rennes, France (office).

HERZ, Robert (Bob) H., BEcons, CPA, CA; American financial executive; *Chairman, Financial Accounting Standards Board (FASB);* ed Univ. of Manchester (UK); accountant Price Waterhouse 1974–1996, Pricewaterhouse Coopers 1998–2002, becoming Sr Pnr 1998 and mem. Global and US Bds; Chair. Financial Accounting Standards Bd (FASB) 2002–; Sr Tech. Pnr Coopers & Lybrand 1996; fmr Chair. AICPA SEC Regulations Cttee, Transnational Auditors Cttee, Int. Fed. of Accountants; fmr mem. Emerging Issues Task Force, American Accounting Asscn Financial Accounting Standards Cttee. *Publications:* The Value Reporting Revolution: Moving Beyond the Earnings Game (jt author). *Address:* Financial Accounting Standards Board, 401 Merritt 7, POB 5116, Norwalk, CT 06856–5116, USA (office). *Telephone:* (203) 847-0700 (office). *Fax:* (203) 849-9714 (office). *E-mail:* rhherz@fasb.org (office). *Website:* www.fasb.org (office).

HERZENBERG, Leonard (Len) Arthur, AB, PhD; American geneticist, immunologist and academic; *Professor of Genetics and The Program in Immunology, Stanford University;* b. 5 Nov. 1931, New York City, NY; m. Leonore Herzenberg; ed Brooklyn Coll., California Inst. of Tech., Pasteur Inst., Paris, France; American Cancer Soc. Postdoctoral Fellow, Pasteur Inst. 1955–57; Officer, US Public Health Service, NIH, Bethesda, Md 1957–59; apptd Asst Prof., Stanford Univ. 1959, later Assoc. Prof., currently Prof., Distinguished Prof. in Immunology 1998; mem. NAS 1982–, American Asscn for Microbiology 1992–, New York Acad. of Sciences 1993–; Guggenheim Fellow 1976, 1986, Hon. Award, Int. Soc. of Analytic Cytology 1998, Lifetime Service Award, American Asscn of Immunologists 1998, Edwin F. Ullman Award, American Asscn of Clinical Chem. 2002, Novartis Prize in Immunology 2004, Abbott Laboratories Award in Clinical and Diagnostic Immunology, American Soc. for Microbiology 2005, Kyoto Prize in Advanced Tech., The Inamori Foundation 2006, Ceppellini Award, Int. Foundation for Research in Experimental Medicine (co-recipient with his wife for "their internationally recognized contributions to medicine") 2007. *Achievements include:* developed the fluorescence-activated cell sorter (FACS) 1970, this revolutionized the study of cancer cells and is the basis for purification of adult stem cells. *Publications:* numerous scientific papers in professional journals. *Address:* The Herzenberg Laboratory Stanford University, School of Medicine, Beckman Center B007, Stanford, CA 94305-5318, USA (office). *Telephone:* (650) 723-5054 (office). *Fax:* (650) 725-8564 (office). *E-mail:* lenherz@stanford .edu (office). *Website:* herzenberg.stanford.edu (office).

HERZOG, Jacques, DipArch; Swiss architect; b. 1950, Basel; ed Swiss Federal Tech. Univ. (ETH), Zurich; Asst to Prof. Dolf Schnebli, ETH, Zurich 1977; f. architectural practice Herzog & De Meuron (with Pierre de Meuron, q.v.) 1978; Prof. of Architecture and Design, ETH 1999–; Visiting Prof. Harvard Univ., Cambridge, Mass 1989, Tulane Univ., New Orleans 1991; (all jtly with Pierre de Meuron q.v.) Architecture Prize, Berlin Acad. of Arts 1987, Andrea Palladio Int. Prize for Architecture, Vicenza, Italy 1988, Pritzker Architecture Prize 2001, RIBA Gold Medal (for work on Tate Modern) 2007. *Principal works include:* Blue House, Oberwil 1979–80, Photostudio Frei, Weil am Rhein 1981–82, Sperrholz Haus, Bottmingen 1984–85, Apartment Bldg, Hebelstr. 11, Basel 1984–88, Wohn- und Geschäftshaus Schwitter, Basel 1985–98, Goetz Art Gallery, Munich 1989–92, Wohn- und Geschäftshaus Schützenmattstr., Basel 1992–93, Dominus Winery, Napa Valley, Yountville, Calif. 1995–97, Tate Gallery Extension (Tate Modern), Bankside, London 1995–99, Cultural Centre and Theatre, Zurich 1996, Ricola Marketing Bldg, Laufen 1998, Laban Center for Dance, London (Stirling Prize) 2003. *Works in progress include:* Prada Headquarters, New York, De Young Museum, San Francisco, Walker Art Center Extension, Minneapolis, as well as projects in UK, France, Germany, Italy, Spain and Japan. *Address:* Herzog & de Meuron Architekten, Rheinschanze 6, 4056 Basel, Switzerland (office). *Telephone:* (61) 3855758 (office). *Fax:* (61) 3855757 (office). *E-mail:* hdemarch@access.ch (office).

HERZOG, Maurice, LèsSc, LLL, HEC; French/Swiss fmr mountaineer, civil servant and business executive; b. 15 Jan. 1919, Lyon (Rhône); s. of the late Robert Herzog and Germaine Beaume; m. 1st Comtesse Marie Pierre de Cossé Brissac 1964 (divorced 1976); one s. one d.; m. 2nd Elisabeth Gamper 1976; two s.; ed Collège Chaptal, Paris, Faculty of Science, Lyon and Faculty of Law, Paris; Leader, French Himalayan Expedition 1950, first person to climb a summit of more than 8,000m, the Annapurna, on 3 June 1950; fmr Dir Kléber-Colombes Soc.; High Commr for Youth and Sport 1958–63, Sec. of State 1963–66; mem. UN Econ. and Social Council 1966–67; mem. IOC 1970, Chief of Protocol 1975; fmr Deputy, Haute Savoie, Mayor of Chamonix; Pres. Financial Comm. Rhône-Alpes Regional Council; Pres. Spie-Batignolles Int., Spie-Loisirs; Dir Spie-Capag, Triton-Europe (London), Tractebel-Finance (Geneva), Tractebel (Belgium), Caixa Bank (Paris); Pres. Triton-France 1984–94; Pres. Int. Project Reseach 1995–2001; Hon. Pres. Soc. du Tunnel du Mont-Blanc 1984; Commdr, Légion d'honneur; Croix de guerre and other French and foreign decorations; Prix du Littérature, Académie française. *Publications:* Annapurna premier 8000, Regards sur L'Annapurna, L'Expédition de l'Annapurna, La Montagne, Les Grandes Aventures de l'Himalaya, L'Autre Annapurna (Prix Vérité 1999). *Leisure interests:* history, literature, science, adventure, sports. *Address:* 21 boulevard Richard Wallace, 92200 Neuilly-sur-Seine (home); La Tournette, 84 chemin de la Tournette, 74400 Chamonix-Mont-Blanc, France (home). *Telephone:* 1-47-47-96-11. *Fax:* 1-58-37-30-69.

HERZOG, Roman, DJur; German politician and fmr head of state; b. 5 April 1934, Landshut; m. Christiane Krauss 1958; ed Univ. of Munich, Freie Univ., Berlin and Hochschule für Verwaltungswissenshaft, Speyer; mem. Bd Evangelische Kirche in Deutschland Chamber for Public Accountability 1971–80; Rep. of Rhineland-Palatinate in Bundestag 1973–78; Chair. Evangelical Working Party, CDU/CSU 1978–83; Minister for Culture and Sport, Baden-Württemberg 1978–80, for Interior 1980–83; mem. Fed. Cttee CDU 1979–83; Vice-Pres. Fed. Constitutional Court 1983–87, Pres. 1987–94; Pres. of Germany 1994–99; Chair. Bd of Trustees Stiftung Brandenburger Tor 1999–; Chair. Bd of Trustees Konrad Adenauer Foundation 2000–; Hon. Prof. Hochschule für Verwaltungswissenshaft, Speyer, Univ. of Tübingen; Hon. DCL (Oxford) 1996; Hon. Citizen of Berlin 1999, of Bonn 1999; Karlspreis 1997, Ludger-Westrick-Preis 1999, Forum-Kiedrich-Preis 2000. *Publications include:* Kommentar zur Grundgesetz (co-author) 1968, Staaten der Frühzeit: Ursprünge und Herrschaftsformen 1988. *Address:* Postfach 860445, 81631 Munich (office); Schloss Bellevue, Spreeweg 1, 10557 Berlin, Germany (home). *Telephone:* (228) 2001 (office).

HERZOG, Werner; German film director; b. 5 Sept. 1942, Munich; f. Werner Herzog Filmproduktion 1963. *Films include:* Signs of Life 1967, Even Dwarfs Started Small 1970, Fata Morgana 1971, The Land of Darkness and Silence 1971, Aguirre Wrath of God 1973, The Enigma of Kaspar Hauser 1974, The Great Ecstasy of Woodcutter Steiner 1974, How Much Wood Would Woodchuck Chuck 1976, Heart of Glass 1976, Stroszek 1976–77, Woyzeck 1979, Nosferatu 1979, Le pays du silence et de l'obscurité 1980, Fitzcarraldo 1982, Where the Green Ants Dream 1984, Cobra Verde 1987, Les Gauloises 1988, Echos aus einem düstern Reich 1990, Scream from Stone 1991, Lektionen in Finsternis 1992, Glocken aus der Tiefe 1993, Little Dieter Needs to Fly 1997, Wings of Hope 1998, Mein liebster Feind - Klaus Kinski 1999, Pilgrimage 2001, Invincible 2001, Ten Minutes Older: The Trumpet 2002, Wheel of Time 2003, The White Diamond 2004, Grizzly Man (Dirs Guild of America Best Dir Documentary 2006) 2005, The Wild Blue Yonder 2005, Rescue Dawn 2006, Mister Lonely 2006, Encounters at the End of the World 2008. *Opera directed:* Lohengrin (Bayreuth) 1987. *Address:* Werner Herzog Filmproduktion, Türkenstrasse 91, 80799 Munich, Germany.

HESBURGH, Rev. Theodore M., STD; American ecclesiastic and fmr university administrator; *President Emeritus, University of Notre Dame;* b. 25 May 1917; s. of Theodore Hesburgh and Anna Hesburgh; ed Univ. of Notre Dame, Gregorian Univ., Rome and Catholic Univ. of America; ordained priest of Congregation of Holy Cross 1943; joined Univ. of Notre Dame 1945, Head of Theology Dept 1948–49, Exec. Vice-Pres. of Univ. 1949–52, Pres. 1952–87, Pres. Emer. 1987–; mem. US Comm. on Civil Rights 1957–72 (Chair. 1969–72), President's Comm. on All-Volunteer Armed Force, Carnegie Comm. on the Future Structure and Financing of Higher Educ., Comm. on the Future of Pvt. and Ind. Higher Educ. in New York State, Presidential Clemency Bd 1974–75; Perm. Rep. of Holy See to Int. Atomic Energy Agency, Vienna 1957; Pres. Int. Fed. of Catholic Univs; Trustee, Rockefeller Foundation, Chair. Bd of Trustees 1977–82, Carnegie Foundation for Advancement of Teaching (Pres. 1963–64); Chair. Acad. Council, Ecumenical Inst. for Advanced Theological Studies in Jerusalem; Chair. with rank of Amb. US Del. to UN Conf. on Science and Tech. for Devt 1977–79; Chair. Select Comm. on Immigration and Refugee Policy 1979–81; Dir US Inst. of Peace 1991; fmr Dir American Council on Educ.; Fellow American Acad. of Arts and Sciences; 138 hon. degrees; USN Distinguished Service Medal, Presidential Medal of Freedom 1964, Jefferson Award 1976, Congregational Gold Medal 2000, NCAA President's Gerald R. Ford Award 2004. *Publications:* God and the World of Man 1950, Patterns for Educational Growth 1958, Thoughts for Our Times 1962, More Thoughts for Our Times 1965, Still More Thoughts for Our Times 1966, Thoughts IV 1968, Thoughts V 1969, The Humane Imperative: A Challenge for the Year 2000 1974, The Hesburgh Papers: Higher Values in Higher Education 1979, God, Country, Notre Dame 1990, Travels with Ted and Ned 1992. *Address:* c/o 1315 Hesburgh Library, University of Notre Dame, Notre Dame, IN 46556, USA. *Telephone:* (219) 631-6882. *Website:* www .nd.edu/aboutnd/about/history/hesburgh_bio.shtml (office).

HESELTINE, Colin S., BEcons; Australian diplomatist and international organization official; b. 1947; m.; two d.; ed Monash Univ.; joined Dept of External Affairs, Canberra 1969, served in Embassy in Santiago, Chile 1970–75, in Madrid 1975–80, Chinese language training 1981–82, Minister and Deputy Head of Mission, Embassy in Beijing 1982–85, Dir, China Investment Project, Dept of Industry, Tech. and Resources, Victorian Govt 1985–87, Minister and Deputy Head of Mission, Embassy in Beijing 1988–92, Rep. (Head of Mission), Australian Commerce and Industry Office, Taipei 1992–97; Asst Sec., Maritime South East Asia Br. (covering Indonesia, Malaysia, Singapore, Philippines), Dept of Foreign Affairs and Trade 1997–98, First Asst Sec., North Asia Div. 1998–2001; Amb. to South Korea 2001–05; Deputy Exec. Dir APEC Secr. 2006, Exec. Dir 2007–08. *Address:* c/o Department of Foreign Affairs and Trade, R. G. Casey Bldg, John McEwen Cres., Barton, ACT 0221, Australia. *Telephone:* (2) 6261-1111. *Fax:* (2) 6261-3111. *Website:* www.dfat.gov.au.

HESELTINE, Baron (Life Peer), cr. 2001, of Thenford in the County of Northamptonshire; **Rt Hon. Michael Ray Dibdin Heseltine,** PC, CH; British politician; b. 21 March 1933, Swansea, Wales; s. of the late Col Rupert Heseltine and of Eileen Ray Heseltine; m. Anne Edna Harding Williams 1962; one s. two d.; ed Shrewsbury School, Pembroke Coll., Oxford; Pres. Oxford Union 1954; Chair. Haymarket Press 1965–70, 1999–; MP for Tavistock 1966–74, for Henley 1974–2001; Parl. Sec. Ministry of Transport 1970; Parl. Under-Sec. of State, Dept of the Environment 1970–72; Minister of Aerospace and Shipping 1972–74; Opposition Spokesman for Industry 1974–76, for the Environment 1976–79; Sec. of State for the Environment 1979–83, 1990–92, for Defence 1983–86, Sec. of State for Industry and Pres. of the Bd of Trade 1992–95; Deputy Prime Minister and First Sec. of State 1995–97; Dir Haymarket Publishing Group 1997–, Chair. 2001–; Gardening Corresp., Country Life (magazine) 2007–; Pres. Asscn of Conservative Clubs 1982–83, Chair. Conservative Mainstream 1998–2006; Pres. Quoted Companies Alliance Int. Advisory Council 2000–, Fed. of Korean Industries, Anglo-China Forum 1998–; Pres. Conservative Group for Europe 2001–; Hon. Fellow, Pembroke Coll. Oxford 1986, Univ. of Wales (Swansea); Hon. Fellow, Chartered Inst. of Man. 1998; Hon. FRIBA; Hon. LLD (Liverpool) 1990; Hon. DBA (Luton) 2003. Publications: Reviving the Inner Cities 1983, Where There's a Will 1987, The Challenge of Europe: Can Britain Win? 1988 (Bentinck Prize 1989), Life in the Jungle (memoirs) 2000. Address: House of Lords, Westminster, London, SW1A 0PW (office); Thenford House, nr Banbury, Oxon., England (home).

HESS, John B., BA, MBA; American energy industry executive; Chairman and CEO, Hess Corporation; b. 5 April 1954; s. of Leon Hess and Norma Hess; m. Susan Elizabeth Kessler; ed Harvard Univ.; joined Amerada Hess Corpn (now Hess Corpn) 1977, Sr Vice-Pres. –1986, Sr Exec. Vice-Pres. 1986–95, Chair. and CEO 1995–; mem. US Sec. of Energy's Advisory Bd; mem. J.P. Morgan Nat. Advisory Bd, Council on Foreign Relations. Address: Hess Corporation, 1185 Avenue of the Americas, New York, NY 10036, USA (office). Telephone: (212) 997-8500 (office). Fax: (212) 536-8390 (office). E-mail: info@hess.com (office). Website: www.hess.com (office).

HESSE, Daniel Ryan, BA, MS, MBA; American telecommunications executive; President and CEO, Sprint Nextel Corporation; b. 18 Oct. 1953, Fort Belvoir, Va; s. of Richard Joseph Hesse and Ellen Louise Hesse (née Seidell); m. Diane Yvette Canaday 1990; ed Univ. of Notre Dame, Cornell Univ., Massachusetts Inst. of Tech.; worked for 23 years with AT&T Corpn, becoming Sales Vice-Pres. 1990–91, Pres. and CEO AT&T Network Systems International 1991–95, Sr Vice-Pres. Online Services Group 1996, Exec. Vice-Pres. 1997–2000, Pres. and CEO AT&T Wireless Services Inc. 1997–2000; Chair., Pres. and CEO Terabeam Corpn 2000–04; CEO Local Telecommunications Div., Sprint Nextel Corpn 2005–06, Pres. and CEO Sprint Nextel Corpn 2007–; Chair., Pres. and CEO Embarq Corpn 2006–07; mem. Bd Dirs Nokia Inc. 2005–, VF Corpn 2001–, Better Business Bureau Online, CTIA (Wireless Asscn); Gov. Boys & Girls Club of America; mem. Business Advisory Council, Mendoza Coll. of Business, Univ. Notre Dame; mem. MIT's Soc. of Sloan Fellows, Univ. of Notre Dame's E.F. Sorin Soc., Cornell Univ. Dean's Soc.; Brooks Thesis Prize, MIT 1990, Ellis Island Medal of Honor, RCR Magazine Wireless Industry Person of the Year, Wireless Business and Tech. Magazine Exec. of the Year. Address: Sprint Nextel Corporation, 6200 Sprint Parkway, Overland Park, KS 66251, USA (office). Telephone: (703) 433-4000 (office). E-mail: info@sprint.com (office). Website: www.sprint.com (office).

HESSEL, Stephane F.; French diplomatist (retd); b. 20 Oct. 1917, Berlin; s. of Franz Hessel and Helen Hessel (née Grund); m. 1st Vitia Mirkine-Guetzevitch 1939 (died 1986); two s. one d.; m. 2nd Christiane Chabry 1987; ed Ecole Normale Supérieure; war service 1941–45; Admin. Dir Secr. Gen., UN 1946–50; served in Foreign Ministry 1950–54; Asst to the Pres. 1954–55; Adviser to High Commr, Saigon 1955–57, Foreign Affairs Adviser, Algiers 1964–69; Asst Admin. UNDP 1970–72; Perm. Rep. to UN Office, Geneva 1977–81; mem. High Authority for Audiovisual Communication 1982–85; Chair. Asscn France-Algérie 1985; mem. Haut Conseil à l'intégration 1990–94, Haut Conseil à la Coopération Int. 1999–2001; Commdr, Légion d'honneur 1982, Grand Officier 2006, Grand Croix, Ordre nat. du Mérite, Croix de guerre 1939–45, Médaille des Evadés, Commdr des Palmes académiques; Hon. MBE. Publications: Danse avec le siècle (memoirs) 1996, Dix pas dans le nouveau siècle 2002, Ô ma mimoize (poetry) 2006. Leisure interest: Greek mythology, poetry. Address: 6 rue Antoine Chantin, 75014 Paris, France (home). Telephone: 1-45-42-81-97 (home). Fax: 1-45-42-81-97 (home).

HESTER, James McNaughton, DPhil; American academic administrator; b. 19 April 1924, Chester, Pa; s. of James Montgomery Hester and Margaret (McNaughton) Hester; m. Janet Rodes 1953; three d.; ed Princeton and Oxford Univs; Capt., US Marine Corps 1943–46, 1951–52; Civil Information Officer, Fukuoka Mil. Govt Team, Japan 1946–47; Rhodes Scholar, Oxford Univ. 1947–50; Asst to American Sec. to Rhodes Trustees Princeton 1950; Asst to Pres., Handy Assocs. Inc. (Management Consultants) NY 1953–54; Account Supervisor, Gallup & Robinson Inc. 1954–57; Provost, Brooklyn Center, LI Univ. 1957–60, Vice-Pres., Trustee LI Univ.; Prof. of History, Exec. Dean Arts and Sciences, Dean Grad. School of Arts and Sciences, NY Univ. 1960–61, Trustee 1962, Pres. 1962–75; Rector, UN Univ., Tokyo 1975–80; Pres. New York Botanical Garden 1980–89; Dir Union Carbide Corpn 1963–96, Alliance Fund and related funds 1983; Chair. Pres. Nixon's Task Force on Priorities in Higher Educ. 1969; mem. Asscn of American Rhodes Scholars 1962; Pres. Harry Frank Guggenheim Foundation 1989–2004; Trustee Lehman Foundation 1973; Hon. LLD (Princeton, Moorehouse Coll., Hofstra Univ., Lafayette Coll., Hahnemann Medical Coll., Fordham); Hon. LHD (Hartwick Coll., Pace Univ., Colgate, Pittsburgh, New York); Hon. DCL (Alfred Univ.); Chevalier, Légion d'honneur, First Class Order of the Sacred Treasure. Portraits: of Mary Bunting at Harvard Club, NY and of James Evans at Center Coll., Danville, Ky. Leisure interest: painting. Address: 25 Cleveland Lane, Princeton, NJ 08540, USA (home). Telephone: (609) 921-6727.

HESTER, Ronald Ernest, PhD, DSc, FRSC; British chemist and academic; Professor Emeritus of Chemistry, University of York; b. 8 March 1936, Slough, Bucks.; s. of Ernest Hester and Rhoda Lennox; m. Bridget Maddin 1958; two s. two d.; ed Royal Grammar School, High Wycombe, Univs of London and Cambridge and Cornell Univ., USA; Asst Prof., Cornell Univ. 1962–65; Lecturer, Sr Lecturer, Reader, Univ. of York 1965–85, Prof. of Chem.

1985–2001, Prof. Emer. 2001–; European Ed. Biospectroscopy 1994–2005; mem. Council and various bds, Science and Eng Research Council. Publications: Physical Inorganic Chemistry 1964, Understanding Our Environment 1986, Advances in Spectroscopy (26 vols) 1975–98, Spectroscopy of Biological Molecules 1991, Issues in Environmental Science and Technology 1994–; more than 300 research papers in int. journals. Leisure interests: skiing, tennis, golf, travel. Address: Department of Chemistry, University of York, York, YO10 5DD, England (office). Website: www.york.ac.uk/depts/chem/staff/rehe.html (office).

HESTER, Stephen, BA; British banking executive; Group CEO and Executive Director, Royal Bank of Scotland Group PLC; worked for Credit Suisse First Boston, holding various Investment Banking roles until becoming Chief Financial Officer 1996, then Global Head of Fixed Income Div. –2002; Finance Dir, later COO Abbey National plc 2002–04; mem. Bd of Dirs and Chief Exec. The British Land Company PLC 2004–08; Group CEO and Exec. Dir Royal Bank of Scotland Group PLC 2008–; Trustee, Royal Botanic Gardens, Kew Foundation. Address: Royal Bank of Scotland Group PLC, 42 St Andrew Square, Edinburgh, EH2 2YE, Scotland (office). Telephone: (131) 523-2033 (office). Fax: (131) 556-7468 (office). E-mail: info@rbs.com (office). Website: www.rbs.com (office).

HETFIELD, James Alan; American singer and musician (guitar); b. 3 Aug. 1963, Downey City, CA; s. of Virgil Hetfield and Cynthia Hetfield; fmr mem. Obsession, Leather Charm; mem. and lead singer heavy rock group, Metallica 1981–; world-wide tours and concert appearances; American Music Award for Favorite Heavy Metal Artist (with Metallica) 1993, Grammy Award for Best Metal Performance (for My Apocalypse) 2009. Film: Some Kind Of Monster (Independent Spirit Award for Best Documentary 2005) 2004. Recordings: albums: Kill 'Em All 1983, Ride The Lightning 1984, Master Of Puppets 1986, ...And Justice For All 1988, The Good, The Bad And The Live 1990, Metallica 1991, Load 1996, Reload 1997, Early Days 1997, S&M (live) 1999, St Anger 2003, Death Magnetic 2008; singles: Whiplash 1985, Garage Days Revisited 1987, Creeping Death 1990, Harvester Of Sorrow 1988, One (Grammy Award for Best Heavy Metal Performance) 1989, Stone Cold Crazy (Grammy Award for Best Heavy Metal Performance) 1991, Jump In The Fire 1991, The Unforgiven (Grammy Award for Best Heavy Metal Performance 1992) 1991, Enter Sandman 1991, Nothing Else Matters 1992, Wherever I May Roam 1992, Sad But True 1992, Until It Sleeps 1996, Hero Of The Day 1996, Mama Said 1996, King Nothing 1997, The Memory Remains 1997, Fuel 1998, Turn The Page 1998, Whisky In The Jar (Grammy Award for Best Hard Rock Performance 2000) 1999, Die Die My Darling 1999, No Leaf Clover 2000, I Disappear 2000, Call Of The Ktulu (Grammy Award for Best Rock Instrumental Performance) 2001, St Anger 2003, Frantic 2003, Unnamed Feeling 2003. Address: Q-Prime Inc., 729 Seventh Avenue, 16th Floor, New York, NY 10019, USA (office). Telephone: (212) 302-9790 (office). Fax: (212) 302-9589 (office). Website: www.metallica.com

HEWISH, Antony, PhD, FRS, FRAS; British radio astronomer; Professor Emeritus of Radio Astronomy, University of Cambridge; b. 11 May 1924, Fowey, Cornwall; s. of the late Ernest W. Hewish and Grace F. L. Hewish (née Pinch); m. Marjorie E. C. Richards 1950; one s. one d.; ed King's Coll., Taunton and Gonville and Caius Coll., Cambridge; war service 1943–46; Research Fellow, Gonville and Caius Coll., Cambridge 1951–54, Supernumerary Fellow 1956–61; Univ. Asst Dir of Research 1953–61, lecturer 1961–69; Fellow, Churchill Coll. Cambridge 1962–; Reader in Radio Astronomy, Univ. of Cambridge 1969–71, Prof. 1971–89, Prof. Emer. 1989–; Prof. Royal Inst. 1977; Dir Mullard Radio Astronomy Observatory, Cambridge 1982–88; Vikram Sarabhai Prof., Ahmedabad 1988; Foreign Hon. mem. American Acad. of Arts and Sciences 1970; mem. Belgian Royal Acad. of Arts and Sciences 1989; mem. Emer. Academia Europaea 1996; Foreign Fellow Indian Nat. Science Acad.; Hon. ScD (Leicester) 1976, (Exeter) 1977, (Manchester) 1989, (Santa Maria, Brazil) 1989, (Cambridge) 1996, (Univ. Teknologi Malaysia) 1997; Hamilton Prize (Cambridge) 1951, Eddington Medal, Royal Astronomical Soc. 1968, Boys Prize, Inst. of Physics 1970, Dellinger Medal, Int. Union of Radio Science, Hopkins Prize, Cambridge Philosophical Soc. 1972, Michelson Medal, Franklin Inst. 1973, Holweck Medal and Prize, Soc. Française de Physique 1974, Nobel Prize for Physics (jtly with Sir Martin Ryle) 1974, Hughes Medal, Royal Soc. 1977, Vainu Bappu Prize, Indian Nat. Science Acad. 1998; Hon. Citizen of Kwangju, S Korea 1995. Achievements: discovery of pulsars, first ground-based measurements of the solar wind, and discovery of enhanced speed from the solar pole. Publications: Seeing Beyond the Invisible, Pulsars as Physics Laboratories (ed.), numerous papers in scientific journals. Leisure interests: listening to good music, gardening, cliff walking. Address: Cavendish Laboratory, Madingley Road, Cambridge, CB3 0HE (office); Pryor's Cottage, Kingston, Cambridge, CB3 7NQ, England (home). Telephone: (1223) 337299 (office); (1223) 262657 (home). Fax: (1223) 354599 (office). E-mail: ah120@mrao.cam.ac.uk (office). Website: www.mrao.cam.ac.uk (office).

HEWITT, Lleyton; Australian professional tennis player; b. 24 Feb. 1981, Adelaide; s. of Glynn Hewitt and Cherilyn Rumball; m. Bec Cartwright 2005; turned professional 1998; became youngest-ever season-ending world number one following Masters Cup victory over Pete Sampras (q.v.) 2001; winner Davis Cup 1999, 2003, 2004, finalist 2000, 2001; winner 26 singles titles (including US Open 2001, Wimbledon 2002), two doubles titles. Leisure interests: Australian Rules football, golf. Address: Lleyton Hewitt Marketing, Suite 35, 209 Toorak Road, South Yarra, Vic. 3141, Australia. Website: www.lleytonhewitt.biz.

HEWITT, Patricia Hope, MA, FRSA; British politician; b. 2 Dec. 1948; d. of Sir (Cyrus) Lenox (Simson) Hewitt and Alison Hope Hewitt; m. William Birtles 1981; one s. one d.; ed Church of England Girls' Grammar School, Canberra, Australia, Australian Nat. Univ., Newnham Coll. Cambridge;

Public Relations Officer, Age Concern 1971–73; Women's Rights Officer, Nat. Council for Civil Liberties (now Liberty) 1973–74, Gen. Sec. 1974–83; Labour Party cand. Leicester E, gen. elections 1983; Press and Broadcasting Sec. to Leader of Opposition 1983–88, Policy Co-ordinator 1988–89; Sr Research Fellow, Inst. for Public Policy Research 1989, Deputy Dir 1989–94; Visiting Fellow, Nuffield Coll. Oxford 1992–; Head, then Dir of Research, Andersen Consulting (now Accenture) 1994–97; Labour MP for Leicester W 1997–, mem. Select Cttee on Social Security 1997–98; Econ. Sec. to the Treasury 1998–99, Minister of State, Dept of Trade and Industry 1999–2001, Sec. of State for Trade and Industry 2001–05; Minister for Women 2001–05; Sec. of State for Health 2005–07; mem. Bd of Dirs BT Group plc 2008–; mem. Sec. of State's Advisory Cttee on Employment of Women 1977–84, Nat. Labour Women's Cttee 1979–83, Labour Party Inquiry into Security Services 1980–81, Editorial Advisory Panel, New Socialist 1980–90, Council, Campaign for Freedom of Information 1983–89, Bd, Int. League for Human Rights 1984–97, Exec. Cttee Fabian Soc. 1988–93, Council, Inst. for Fiscal Studies 1996–98; Co-Chair. Human Rights Network 1979–81; Deputy Chair. Comm. on Social Justice 1993–95; Vice-Chair. Healthcare 2000 1995–96, British Council 1997–98; Assoc., Newnham Coll. Cambridge 1984–97; Hon. Fellow, London Business School 2004. *Publications:* Civil Liberties, the NCCL Guide (co-ed.) 1977, The Privacy Report 1977, Your Rights at Work 1981, The Abuse of Power 1981, Your Second Baby (co-author) 1990, About Time: The Revolution in Work and Family Life 1993. *Leisure interests:* reading, theatre, music, gardening. *Address:* Ground Floor Front, 5 Frog Island, Leicester, LE3 5AG (office); House of Commons, London, SW1A 0AA, England (office). *Telephone:* (20) 7219-4180 (office). *Fax:* (20) 7219-2705 (home); (116) 251-0482 (office). *E-mail:* hewittph@parliament.uk (office). *Website:* www.patriciahewitt.org.uk (home).

HEWSON, John Robert, AO, BEcons, MA, PhD; Australian politician, professor of economics and business executive; *Chairman, The John Hewson Group;* b. 28 Oct. 1946, Sydney, NSW; s. of Donald Hewson and of the late Eileen Isabella Hewson (née Tippett); m. 1st Margaret Hewson; two s. one d.; m. 2nd Carolyn Judith Hewson 1988; one d.; ed Univ. of Sydney, Univ. of Saskatchewan, Canada and Johns Hopkins Univ. USA; Research Officer, Bureau of Census and Statistics, Treasury 1967–68; Teaching Fellow, Dept of Econs, Univ. of Saskatchewan 1968–69; Teaching Asst, Dept of Political Economy, Johns Hopkins Univ. 1969–71; Consultant and Economist IMF 1969–74; Research Economist Reserve Bank of Australia 1975–76; Econ. Adviser to Fed. Treas. 1976–77, 1978–81, Chief of Staff 1981–82; Prof. of Econs, Univ. of NSW 1978–87, Head School of Econs 1983–87; MP for Wentworth, Fed. Parl. 1987–95; Shadow Minister for Finance 1988–89, Shadow Treas. 1989–90; Leader of the Liberal Party and Leader of the Opposition 1990–94; Shadow Minister for Industry, Commerce, Infrastrucuture and Customs 1994–95; Dean, Grad. School of Man., Macquarie Univ. 2002–04; Consultant Hill Samuel Australia 1982–85; mem. Advisory Council ABN AMRO Australia Ltd 1998–2004 (Chair. 1995–98); Chair. The John Hewson Goup Pty Ltd 1995–, Network Entertainment Ltd 1996–97, Chair. Churchill Funds Man. 1996–99, subsequently GRD 2000–04, Australian Bus Mfg Co. Ltd (now Universal Bus Co. Pty Ltd) 1999–, Global Renewables Ltd 2000–04, Strategic Capital Man. Pty Ltd 2000–04, Belle Property Pty Ltd 2000–03, Investment Advisory Cttee Australian Olympic Foundation 2001, RepuTex Advisory Cttee 2003–04, X Capital Health 2004–, The Freehand Group 2004–; Foundation Dir Macquarie Bank Ltd 1985–87; Dir and Vice-Chair. TV Shopping Network Ltd 1996–98; Dir Moran Health Care Group 1998–2001; Deputy Chair. Miniproc Ltd 1998–2000; Pres. Arthritis Foundation of Australia 1997–2002; Dir Positive Ageing Foundation 1999–2003; weekly columnist, Australian Financial Review 1998–; Chair. Osteoporosis Australia Council 1997–, Arthritis Research Taskforce 2003–, Business Leaders Forum on Sustainable Devt 2003–; Fellow, Australian Inst. of Co. Dirs, Hong Kong Man. Asscn; Centenary Medal. *Publications:* Liquidity Creation and Distribution in the Eurocurrency Market 1975, The Eurocurrency Markets and their Implications: A New View of International Monetary Problems and Monetary Reform (jtly) 1975, Offshore Banking in Australia 1981; innumerable articles in professional journals. *Leisure interests:* gardening, jazz, theatre, sport, cars, motor sports. *Address:* Level 10, 1 Market Street, Sydney, NSW 2000, Australia (office). *Telephone:* (2) 9372-9764 (office). *Fax:* (2) 9372-0364 (office). *E-mail:* john.hewson@horwath.com (office).

HEWSON, Paul (see Bono).

HEY, John Denis, MA, MSc; British economist, statistician and academic; *Professor of Economics and Statistics, University of York;* b. 26 Sept. 1944; s. of G. B. Hey and E. H. Hey; m. Marlene Bissett 1968 (divorced 1997); one s. two d.; ed Univs of Cambridge and Edinburgh; econometrician, Hoare & Co. London 1968–69; Lecturer in Econs, Univ. of Durham 1969–74, Univ. of St Andrew's 1974–75; Lecturer in Economic Statistics, Univ. of York 1975, Sr Lecturer, Prof. of Econs and Statistics 1984– (part-time 1998–), Co-Dir Centre for Experimental Econs 1986–2005; Prof. Ordinario, Univ. of Bari 1998–2005, LUISS, Rome, Italy 2005–; Hon. Prof. of Econs and Econometrics, Univ. of Vienna. *Publications:* Statistics in Economics 1974, Uncertainty in Microeconomics 1979, Economics in Disequilibrium 1981, Data in Doubt 1984, Experiments in Economics 1991, Experimental Economics (ed.) 1995, Economics of Uncertainty 1997, Intermediate Microeconomics 2003. *Leisure interests:* walking, opera, music. *Address:* Department of Economics and Related Studies, University of York, Heslington, York, YO1 5DD, England; Dipartimento di Scienze Economiche e Aziendale, Libera Universita Internazionale degli Studi Sociali (LUISS), Via Oreste Tommasini 1, 00162 Rome, Italy. *Telephone:* (1904) 433786 (York) (office); (06) 85225747 (Rome) (office). *Fax:* (1904) 433759 (York) (office); (06) 86506506 (Rome) (office). *E-mail:* jdh1@york.ac.uk (office); j.hey@dse.uniba.it (office). *Website:* www.york.ac.uk/users/~jdh1 (office).

HEYDE, Christopher Charles, AM, PhD, DSc, FASSA, FAA; Australian statistician and academic; *Professor of Statistics, Centre for Mathematics and its Applications, Mathematical Sciences Institute, Australian National University;* b. 20 April 1939, Sydney; s. of G. C. Heyde and A. D. Wessing; m. Elizabeth James 1965; two s.; ed Barker Coll., Hornsby, Sydney Univ. and Australian Nat. Univ.; Asst Prof., Mich. State Univ. 1964–65; Lecturer, Univ. of Sheffield, UK 1965–67; Special Lecturer, Univ. of Manchester, UK 1967–68; Reader, ANU 1968–75; Chief Research Scientist, CSIRO 1975–83; Prof. and Chair. Dept of Statistics, Univ. of Melbourne 1983–86; Prof. and Head Dept of Statistics, Inst. of Advanced Studies 1986–88, Dean School of Math. Sciences 1989–91; Prof. of Statistics, Centre for Math. and its Applications, Math. Sciences Inst., ANU 1992–; Prof. of Statistics, Columbia Univ., New York 1993–; Dir Columbia Center for Applied Probability 1993–; Visiting Prof., Stanford Univ., Calif. 1972–73; Ed. Australian Journal of Statistics 1973–78, Stochastic Processes and Their Applications 1983–89, Journal of Advances in Applied Probability 1990–; Fellow, Inst. of Math. Statistics 1973; Pres. Statistical Soc. of Australia 1979–80, also Hon. Life mem.; mem. Int. Statistical Inst. (Vice-Pres. 1985–87, 1993–95), Australian Acad. of Science (Vice-Pres. 1988–89, Treas. 1989–93); Hon. DSc (Sydney) 1998; Pitman Medallist, Statistical Soc. of Australia 1988, Thomas Ranken Lyle Medal, Australian Acad. of Sciences 1994, Inaugural Hannan Medal Australian Acad. of Sciences 1995. *Publications:* I. J. Bienaymé: Statistical Theory Anticipated (with E. Seneta) 1977, Martingale Limit Theory and Its Application (with P. Hall) 1980, Quasi-Likelihood and Its Application 1997, Statisticians of the Centuries (co-ed. with E. Seneta) 2001; plus 200 articles on probability theory and mathematical statistics. *Address:* Mathematical Sciences Institute, Australian National University, Canberra, ACT 0200; 22 Nungara Place, Aranda, ACT 2614, Australia (home). *Telephone:* (2) 6125-2962 (office). *Fax:* (2) 6125-3918 (office). *E-mail:* Chris.Heyde@maths.anu.edu.au (office). *Website:* wwwmaths.anu.edu.au/~chris (office).

HEYMAN, David; British film producer; b. 26 July 1961; ed Hill House London, Westminster School, London, Harvard Univ., USA; began career as production runner for film producers Milos Forman and David Lean; Creative Exec. Warner Bros, Los Angeles 1986–89, Vice-Pres. United Artists 1989; now working as ind. producer; returned to UK 1997, f. Heyday Films 1997; Showest Producer of the Year 2003. *Films produced include:* Juice, The Daytrippers, Harry Potter and the Philosopher's Stone 2001, Harry Potter and the Chamber of Secrets 2002, Harry Potter and the Prisoner of Azkaban 2004, Harry Potter and the Goblet of Fire 2005. *Address:* Heyday Films, 5 Denmark Street, London, WC2H 8LP, England (office). *Telephone:* (20) 7836-6333 (office). *Fax:* (20) 7836-6444 (office). *E-mail:* office@heydayfilms.com (office).

HEYMAN, Ira Michael, JD; American legal scholar, university administrator and academic; *Herman F. Selvin Professor of Law Emeritus and Chancellor Emeritus, University of California, Berkeley;* b. 30 May 1930, New York City; s. of Harold A. Heyman and Judith Sobel; m. Therese Thau 1950; two s. (one deceased); ed Dartmouth Coll. and Yale Law School; Legislative Asst to Senator Irving M. Ives, Washington, DC 1950–51; mem. State Bar of NY 1956; Assoc. Carter, Ledyard & Milburn, New York 1956–57; law clerk, Court of Appeals for Second Circuit, New Haven, Conn. 1957–58; Chief Law Clerk, US Supreme Court 1958–59; Acting Assoc. Prof. of Law, Univ. of Calif., Berkeley 1959–61, Prof. 1961–94, Prof. of Law and City and Regional Planning 1966–93, Prof. Emer. 1993–, Vice-Chancellor 1974–80, Chancellor 1980–90, Chancellor Emer. 1990–; Sec. Smithsonian Inst. 1994–99, Sec. Emer. 2000–; mem. State Bar. of Calif. 1961–; Visiting Prof., Yale Law School 1963–64, Stanford Law School 1971–72; Trustee, Lawyers' Comm. for Civil Rights Under Law 1977, Chair. 1991; Chair. Dartmouth Coll. 1991; Chair. San Francisco Museum and Historical Society (SFMHS) Advisory Cttee; mem. Bd Dirs, Pacific Gas & Electric Co. 1985–, Presidio Trust 2000–; Trustee, Smith Coll. 2004–; other professional appointments and consultancies; Chevalier, Légion d'honneur; Hon. LLD (Univ. of Pacific) 1981, (Md) 1986; Hon. DHumLitt (Hebrew Union Coll.) 1984; Award of Merit, San Francisco Museum and Historical Society 1994. *Publications:* numerous articles in journals, papers and legal documents in areas of civil rights, constitutional law, land planning, metropolitan govt, housing, environmental law and man. *Leisure interests:* tennis, opera. *Address:* School of Law, 453 Boalt Hall, University of California, Berkeley, CA 94720-7200, USA (office). *Telephone:* (510) 642-1731 (office). *Fax:* (510) 643-2673 (office). *E-mail:* mheyman@law.berkeley.edu (office). *Website:* www.law.berkeley.edu/faculty/heymanm (office).

HEYMANN, Daniel, PhD; Argentine economist; *Senior Economist, ECLAC Buenos Aires, and Professor of Economics, University of Buenos Aires;* b. 30 Dec. 1949, Buenos Aires; s. of Gunther Heymann and Marta Weil; m. Cristina Bramuglia 1976; two s.; ed Coll. Français de Buenos Aires, Univ. of Buenos Aires and Univ. of Calif. Los Angeles; Asst Prof. Univ. of Buenos Aires 1973–75, Prof. of Econs 1987–; Research Asst ECLAC, Buenos Aires 1974–78, Sr Economist 1982–; Prof. of Econs, Instituto Torcuato Di Tella, Buenos Aires 1982–2003; Prof. of Econs, Univ. of La Plata 2004–. *Publications:* Fluctuations of the Argentine Manufacturing Industry 1980, Three Essays on Inflation and Stabilization 1986, The Austral Plan 1987, Distributive Conflict and the Fiscal Deficit: Some Inflationary Games (jtly) 1991, Fiscal Inconsistencies and High Inflation (jtly) 1994, On the Interpretation of the Current Account 1994, High Inflation (jtly) 1995, Business Cycles from Misperceived Trends (jtly) 1998, Price Setting in a Schematic Model of Inductive Learning (jtly) 1999, Learning about Trends: Spending and Business Fluctuations in Open Economies (jtly) 2001, Inconsistent Behavior and Macroeconomic Disturbances 2002, Great Expectations and Hard Times: the Argentine Convertibility (jtly) 2003, Land-Rich Economies, Education and Economic Development (jtly) 2006. *Address:*

ECLAC Buenos Aires: Paraguay 1178, Piso 2, 1057 Buenos Aires, Argentina (office). *Telephone:* (11) 4815-7810 (office). *Fax:* (11) 4815-2534 (office).

HEYMANN, Klaus; German business executive; *Chief Executive Officer, Naxos;* m. Takako Nishizaki; one s.; Export Advertising and Promotion Man., Max Braun AG 1961–62; with The Overseas Weekly, Frankfurt 1962–67, ran Hong Kong Office 1967–69; f. Pacific Mail-Order System 1969; organized classical concerts in Hong Kong; mem. Bd Hong Kong Philharmonic Orchestra, later Chair. of Fund-Raising Cttee and Hon. Gen. Man.; f. CEO Naxos. *Address:* HNH International Ltd, 6/F, Sino Industrial Plaza, 9 Kai Cheung Road, Kowloon Bay, Hong Kong Special Administrative Region, People's Republic of China (office).

HEYZER, Noeleen, PhD; Singaporean international organization official; *Executive Secretary, Economic and Social Commission for Asia and the Pacific (ESCAP);* m.; two d.; ed Univ. of Singapore, Univ. of Cambridge, UK; Fellow and Research Officer, Inst. of Devt Studies, Univ. of Sussex, UK 1979–81; with Social Devt Div., ESCAP, Bangkok, Thailand early 1980s; Dir Gender and Devt Programme, Asian and Pacific Devt Centre, Kuala Lumpur, Malaysia 1984–94; Co-ordinator for the Asia-Pacific NGO Working Group for the UN Fourth World Conf. on Women, Beijing, People's Repub. of China; Exec. Dir UN Devt Fund for Women (UNIFEM) 1994–2007; Exec. Sec. ESCAP 2007–; Convener Int. Women's Comm. for a Just and Sustainable Palestinian-Israeli Peace; mem. Bd Pres. Ahtisaari's Crisis Man. Initiative; mem. High-Level Commonwealth Comm. on Respect and Understanding; New Millennium Distinguished Visiting Scholar, Columbia Univ.; Chair. Consortium Advisory Group, Research Programme on Women's Empowerment in Muslim Contexts; has served on bds of several humanitarian orgs including Devt Alternatives with Women for a New Era, the Global South, ISIS, Oxfam, Panos and Soc. for Int. Devt; Global Tolerance Award for Humanitarian Service, Friends of the UN 2000, Lifetime Achievement Award, Inst. for Leadership Devt 2000, Woman of Distinction Award, UN NGO Cttee 2003, Leadership Award, Mount Sinai Hosp., New York 2004, Leadership Award, UN Asscn Greater Boston 2004, Dag Hammarskjöld Medal 2004, NCRW Women Who Make a Difference Award 2005. *Publications include:* Gender, Economic Growth and Poverty, The Trade in Domestic Workers, Working Women in South-East Asia. *Address:* Economic and Social Commission for Asia and the Pacific (ESCAP), United Nations Building, Rajadamnern Nok Avenue, Bangkok 10200, Thailand (office). *Telephone:* (2) 288-1234 (office). *Fax:* (2) 288-1000 (office). *E-mail:* unisbkk.unescap@un.org (office). *Website:* www.unescap.org (office).

HIATT, Fred, BA; American journalist; *Editorial Page Editor, The Washington Post;* b. 30 April 1955, Washington, DC; m. Margaret Shapiro; three c.; ed Harvard Univ.; City Hall reporter, Atlanta Journal-Constitution 1979–80; reporter, The Washington Star 1981; Va Reporter, The Washington Post 1981–83, Pentagon Reporter 1983–86, NE Asia Co-Bureau Chief 1987–90, Moscow Co-Bureau Chief 1991–95, Ed. editorial page 1996–. *Publications:* The Secret Sun 1992 (novel), If I Were Queen of the World 1997 (children's book), Baby Talk 1999. *Address:* The Washington Post, 1150 15th Street, NW, Washington, DC 20071, USA (office). *Telephone:* (202) 334-6000 (office). *E-mail:* twpcoreply@washpost.com (office). *Website:* www.washingtonpost .com (office).

HIBEL, Edna; American artist; b. 1917, Boston, Mass; d. of Abraham Bert Hibel and Lena Hibel (née Rubin); m. Theodore Plotkin; three s.; ed studied under Gregory Michaels and Eliot O'Hara; later under Alexander Yakovlev and Karl Zerbe at Boston Museum School of Fine Arts; leading authority on oil painting, watercolour and expressions in porcelain; exhbns in galleries, museums, govt bldgs and royal residences in more than 20 countries on four continents, including nat. museums in Brazil, China, Costa Rica, Russia and USA, also under patronage of Count and Countess Bernadotte of Germany, Count Thor Bonde of Sweden, the late Prince and Princess Rainier of Monaco, Queen Elizabeth II of UK; first foreign woman to have an exhbn in People's Repub. of China, fmr Soviet Union and fmr Yugoslavia; Founder Boston Art Festival; commissioned by Foundation of the US Nat. Archives to commemorate 75 years of women receiving the universal right to vote 1995; commissioned to commemorate Florida Gov.'s Reading Initiative 2009; curator, Hibel Museum of Art, Jupiter, Fla; six hon. doctorate degrees, including Eureka Coll.; title of Lady Edna from Kts of Malta; Sturtevant Travelling Fellowship to Mexico, Medal of Honour and Citation from Pope Paul II, Medal of Honour, King of Belgium; first person other than US pres to receive a Presidential Award, 'Leonardo da Vinci' World Award of Arts, World Cultural Council 2001, US Nat. Women's History Month Honoree 2008, Honoree of Florida Gov.'s Literacy Initiative 2009. *Television:* Hibel's Russian Palette (documentary broadcast on PBS stations across USA). *Films:* six films, including Hibel's Russian Palette, winner of American Asscn of Museums Cultural Award. *Publications:* several books including Edna Hibel: An Artist's Story of Love and Compassion, The Life and Art of Edna Hibel, The Black Block Battle (children's book). *Leisure interests:* gardening, museums, art books, travel. *Address:* Hibel Studio, Inc., 1910 Seventh Avenue North, Lake Worth, FL 33461, USA (office). *Telephone:* (561) 848-9633 (office). *Fax:* (561) 848-9640 (office). *Website:* www.hibel.com (office).

HICK, Graeme Ashley; Zimbabwean professional cricketer; b. 23 May 1966, Salisbury (now Harare); s. of John and Eve Hick; ed Banket Primary School, Prince Edward Boys' High School; right-hand batsman, off-break bowler, slip fielder; teams: Zimbabwe 1983–86, Worcs. 1984–, Northern Dists 1987–89, Queensland 1990–91; scored his first hundred when aged six (for Banket primary school); youngest player (aged 17) to appear in 1983 World Cup and youngest to rep. Zimbabwe; 65 Tests for England 1991–2001, scoring 3,383 runs (average 31.32), including six hundreds; youngest to score 2,000 first-class runs in a season (1986); scored 1,019 runs before June 1988, including a record 410 runs in April; fewest innings for 10,000 runs in county cricket

(179); youngest (24) to score 50 first-class hundreds; toured Australia 1994–95; mem. England World Cup Squad 1996, 1999; 120 limited-overs ints for 3,846 runs (average 37.33); scored 315 not out vs Durham June 2002 – highest championship innings of the season; Wisden Cricketer of the Year 1987. *Publication:* My Early Life (autobiog.) 1992. *Leisure interests:* golf, tennis, squash, indoor hockey, cinema, television, listening to music. *Address:* c/o Worcestershire County Cricket Club, New Road, Worcester, WR2 4QQ, England. *Telephone:* (1905) 748474.

HICK, John Harwood, MA, PhD, DPhil, DLitt; British academic; *Fellow, Institute for Advanced Research in Arts and Social Sciences, University of Birmingham;* b. 20 Jan. 1922, Scarborough, Yorks.; s. of Mark Day Hick and Mary Aileen Hirst; m. Joan Hazel Bowers 1953 (died 1996); three s. (one deceased) one d.; ed Bootham School, York, Univs of Edinburgh and Oxford, Westminster Theological Coll., Cambridge; Minister, Belford Presbyterian Church, Northumberland 1953–56; Asst Prof. of Philosophy, Cornell Univ., USA 1956–59; Stuart Prof. of Christian Philosophy, Princeton Theological Seminary, USA 1959–64; Lecturer in Divinity, Univ. of Cambridge 1964–67; H.G. Wood Prof. of Theology, Univ. of Birmingham 1967–80, now Prof. Emer., Fellow, Inst. for Advanced Research in Arts and Social Sciences; Danforth Prof. of Philosophy of Religion, Claremont Grad. Univ., Calif., USA 1980–92, now Prof. Emer., Chair., Dept of Religion, Dir Blaisdell Programs in World Religions and Cultures 1983–92; Gifford Lecturer, Univ. of Edinburgh 1986–87; Guggenheim Fellow 1963–64, 1986–87; SA Cook Bye-Fellow, Gonville and Caius Coll., Cambridge 1963–64; Vice-Pres. World Congress of Faiths, British Soc. for the Philosophy of Religion; Hon. TheolDr (Uppsala) 1977; Hon. DD (Glasgow) 2002; Grawemeyer Award in Religion 1991. *Publications include:* Faith and Knowledge, Evil and the God of Love, God and the Universe of Faiths, Death and Eternal Life, Arguments for the Existence of God, Problems of Religious Pluralism, God Has Many Names, Philosophy of Religion, The Second Christianity, An Interpretation of Religion, Disputed Questions in Theology and the Philosophy of Religion, The Metaphor of God Incarnate, The Rainbow of Faiths, The Fifth Dimension, John Hick: An Autobiography, The New Frontier of Religion and Science; Ed.: The Myth of God Incarnate, The Many-Faced Argument, The Myth of Christian Uniqueness, The Existence of God, Truth and Dialogue, Christianity and Other Religions, Faith and the Philosophers. *Leisure interests:* reading, sitting in the garden, discussing. *Address:* 144 Oak Tree Lane, Selly Oak, Birmingham, B29 6HU, England (home). *Telephone:* (121) 689-4803 (home). *E-mail:* j.h.hick@bham.ac.uk (office). *Website:* (home).

HICKEL, Walter Joseph; American business executive, fmr government official and fmr politician; *Chairman, Institute of the North, Alaska Pacific University;* b. 18 Aug. 1919, nr Claflin, Kan.; s. of Robert A. Hickel and Emma Zecha; m. 1st Janice Cannon 1941 (died 1943); one s.; m. 2nd Ermalee Strutz 1945; five s.; ed public schools in Claflin; mem. Republican Nat. Cttee 1954–64; Gov. of Alaska 1966–68, 1990–94; US Sec. of the Interior 1969–70; Co-founder Commonwealth North Alaskan forum 1979; Co-founder and Sec.-Gen. The Northern Forum (24 Arctic and sub-Arctic regional govts) 1994–; Founder and Chair. Inst. of the North, Alaska Pacific Univ. 1995–; Founder and Chair. Hickel Investment Co., Anchorage 1947–2007; Distinguished Prof. of Public Policy, Univ. of Alaska Anchorage 2005; builder/Owner Hotel Captain Cook, Anchorage; fmr builder/Owner Univ. Shopping Center, Northern Lights Shopping Center, Valley River Shopping Center; Founder and fmr Chair. Yukon Pacific Corpn; fmr mem. Bd of Dirs Rowan Cos; mem. Bd of Dirs Salk Inst. 1972–79; mem. NASA Advisory Council Exploration Task Force 1989–91; several hon. degrees; Grand Cordon of the Order of the Sacred Treasure from the Emperor of Japan 1988; several other awards. *Publications:* Who Owns America? 1971, Crisis in the Commons: The Alaska Solution 2002. *Leisure interests:* walking, travelling, writing. *Address:* Hickel Investment Company, 939 West Fifth Avenue, Suite 388 Anchorage, AK 99501-2019 (office); PO Box 101700, Anchorage, AK 99510; 1905 Loussac Drive, Anchorage, AK 99517, USA (home). *Telephone:* (907) 343-2400 (office); (907) 248-0013 (home). *Fax:* (907) 343-2211 (office). *E-mail:* wjhickel@gci.net (office). *Website:* www.institutenorth.org (office).

HICKEY, John; Papua New Guinea politician; *Minister of Agriculture and Livestock;* mem. Parl. (Nat. Alliance Party) 2002–, Chair. Public Accounts Cttee 2003–05; Minister of Finance and Nat. Planning and Monitoring 2005–07, of Agriculture and Livestock 2007–. *Address:* Department of Agriculture and Livestock, PO Box 2033, Port Moresby 121, NCD, Papua New Guinea (office). *Telephone:* 3202884 (office). *Fax:* 3202883 (office). *E-mail:* dalit@daltron.com.pg (office). *Website:* www.agriculture.gov.pg (office).

HICKS, Kenneth C., MBA; American retail executive; *President and Chief Merchandising Officer, J.C. Penney Company, Inc.;* ed US Mil. Acad., Harvard Business School; worked for McKinsey and Co. (man. consultancy firm); fmr Sr Vice-Pres. and Gen. Merchandise Man. May Department Stores; fmr Exec. Vice-Pres. and Gen. Merchandise Man. Home Shopping Network; fmr Pres. Payless Shoes Inc.; Pres. and COO Stores and Merchandise Operations, J.C. Penney Co. Inc. 2002–05, Pres. and Chief Merchandising Officer 2005–. *Address:* J.C. Penney Co. Inc., 6501 Legacy Drive, Plano, TX 75024-3698, USA (office). *Telephone:* (972) 431-1000 (office). *Fax:* (972) 431-9140 (office). *E-mail:* info@jcpenney.net (office). *Website:* www.jcpenney.net (office).

HIDAKA, Masahiro; Japanese music promoter and event manager; *President, Smash Corporation;* Pres. and Co-founder Smash Corpn 1983; runs the annual Fuji Rock Festival 1997–, and the Asagiri Jam (on Mount Fuji); Hon. OBE (UK). *E-mail:* mail@smash-jpn.com (office). *Website:* www .smash-jpn.com (office).

HIDAYAT, Bambang, PhD; Indonesian astronomer and academic; *Professor, Bandung Institute of Technology (ITB);* b. 18 Sept. 1934, Kundus, Cen. Java;

m. (wife deceased); two c.; ed Case Inst. of Tech., Cleveland; Dir Bosscha Observatory 1968–83; Asst Prof. of Astronomy, Bandung Inst. of Tech. (ITB) 1968, Assoc. Prof. 1974, Prof. 1976–; Chair. Indonesian–Dutch Astronomy Programme 1982–, Indonesian–Japan Astronomy Programme 1980–94; Vice-Pres. Int. Astronomical Union 1994–2000; f. Indonesian Astronomical Soc. 1978, co-f. Indonesian Physics Soc.; mem. American Astronomical Soc., Royal Astronomical Soc., Indonesian Inst. of Sciences 1991; mem. Royal Comm. Al Albait Univ., Jordan 1993; Fellow Islamic Acad. of Sciences. *Publications:* several astronomy textbooks and more than 40 scientific papers. *Address:* Institut Teknologi Bandung (ITB), Jalan Tamansari 64, Bandung 40116 (office); Indonesian Institute of Sciences, Jl. Jendral Gatot Subroto no. 10, PO Box 250, Jakarta, Indonesia (office). *Telephone:* (22) 2500935 (office); (21) 5251542 (office). *Fax:* (21) 5207226 (office). *E-mail:* info-center@itb.ac.id (office); bhidayat@as.itb.ac.id. *Website:* www.itb.ac.id (office).

HIDAYAT, Taufik; Indonesian badminton player; b. 10 Aug. 1981, Bandung, West Java; s. of Aries Harris and Enok Dartilah; m. Armidianti Gumelar; one d.; winner Djarum Indonesia Open 1999, 2000, 2002, 2003, 2004, Singapore Open 2005; Gold Medal Athens Olympics 2004, XIV World Championships, Anaheim 2005; Bintang Jasa Utama (First Class Merit Star). *Leisure interests:* travelling, football. *Address:* Taufik Hidayat Management (THForce), Rasuna Office Park Blok MO-03, Jl. HR. Rasuna Said, Kuningan, Jakarta, 12960, Indonesia (office). *Telephone:* (81) 116-8909 (office). *E-mail:* info@taufik-hidayat.com (office); melatikarina@th-force.com (office). *Website:* www.taufik-hidayat.com (office).

HIDE, Raymond, CBE, MA, ScD, CPhys, FRS, FInstP; British research geophysicist and academic; *Senior Research Investigator, Imperial College London;* b. 17 May 1929, Bentley, nr Doncaster, S Yorks.; s. of the late Stephen Hide and Rose Edna Hide (née Cartlidge, later Mrs T. Leonard); m. Phyllis Ann Licence 1958; one s. two d.; ed Percy Jackson Grammar School, Doncaster, Univs of Manchester and Cambridge; Research Assoc. in Astrophysics, Yerkes Observatory, Univ. of Chicago 1953–54; Sr Research Fellow, Gen. Physics Div. AERE, Harwell 1954–57; Lecturer in Physics, King's Coll. Univ. of Durham 1957–61; Prof. of Geophysics and Physics at MIT 1961–67; Head of the Geophysical Fluid Dynamics Lab., Chief Scientific Officer (Individual Merit), Meteorological Office, Bracknell 1967–90; Gresham Prof. of Astronomy, Gresham Coll., City of London 1985–90; Dir Robert Hooke Inst. 1990–92 and Visiting Prof. of Physics, Univ. of Oxford 1990–92, Research Prof., Dept of Physics 1992–94, Prof. Emer. of Physics, Univ. of Oxford 1994–; Sr Research Investigator, Imperial Coll., London 2000–; Visiting Prof., Dept of Math., Univ. Coll., London 1969–84; Adrian Visiting Fellow, Univ. of Leicester 1981–83; Fellow, Jesus Coll. Oxford 1983–97, Hon. Fellow 1997–; mem. Council, Royal Soc. of London 1988–90; mem. Pontifical Acad. of Sciences, American Acad. of Arts and Sciences, Academia Europaea, Royal Astronomical Soc. (Pres. 1983–85), Royal Meteorological Soc. (Pres. 1974–76, Hon. mem. 1989), European Geophysical Soc. (Pres. 1982–84, Hon. mem. 1988), American Geophysical Union, Inst. of Physics, Int. Astronomical Union and numerous other socs and cttees; Chair. British Nat. Cttee for Geodesy and Geophysics, UK Chief Del. to Int. Union of Geodesy and Geophysics 1979–85; Hon. Fellow, Gonville and Caius Coll., Cambridge 2001, Jesus Coll., Oxford 1997; Hon. DSc (Leicester) 1985, (UMIST) 1994, (Paris) 1995; Charles Chree Medal and Prize of Inst. of Physics 1975, Holweck Medal and Prize, Société Française de Physique and Inst. of Physics 1982, Gold Medal, Royal Astronomical Soc. 1989, William Bowie Medal, American Geophysical Union 1997, Hughes Medal, Royal Soc. 1998, L.F. Richardson Medal, European Geophysical Soc. 1999, Symons Gold Medal, Royal Meteorological Soc. 2003. *Publications:* numerous scientific articles and papers. *Address:* Room 6M33, Department of Mathematics, Imperial College, London, SW7 2BZ, England (office). *Telephone:* (20) 7594-8488 (office); (20) 8873-3366 (home). *E-mail:* r.hide@ic.ac.uk (office); r.hide@imperial.ac.uk (office); arhide@ntlworld.com (home). *Website:* www2.imperial.ac.uk/mathematics (office); www3.imperial.ac.uk/people/r.hide (office).

HIDE, Rodney, MSc; New Zealand politician; *Minister of Local Government;* b. 1956, Oxford, North Canterbury; ed Univs of Canterbury and Lincoln, Montana State Univ., USA; fmrly rig worker on North Sea oil rig, truck driver; fmr Lecturer, Centre for Resource Man. and Dept of Econs, Univ. of Lincoln; Founding Chair. Asscn of Consumers and Taxpayers 1993; Founding Chair. and first Pres. ACT New Zealand 1994, Vice-Pres. 2000–04, Leader 2004–; elected MP for Auckland Cen. 1996, ACT Spokesman for Finance 1996–, ACT Rep., Finance and Expenditure Select Cttee 1996–; ACT cand. for Epsom 1998, 2002, 2005; Minister of Local Govt 2008–; 'Backbencher of the Year' New Zealand Herald 2001, 'Opposition MP of the Year' Dominion 2001, 'Leader of the Opposition' North and South 2002, 'Politician of the Year' Dominion 2003. *Publications:* The Power to Destroy 1999; HideSight column for Nat. Business Review 1989–99; HideSight email newsletter published by rodneyhide.com 2003–, My Year of Living Dangerously 2007. *Address:* PO Box 9209, Newmarket 1149, Auckland, New Zealand (office). *Telephone:* (4) 470-6630 (office). *Fax:* (4) 473-3532 (office). *E-mail:* rodney.hide@parliament.govt.nz (office). *Website:* rodneyhide.com (office); www.act.org.nz (office).

HIEBERT, Erwin Nick, BA, MA, MSc, PhD; American academic; *Professor Emeritus of the History of Science, Harvard University;* b. 27 May 1919, Saskatchewan, Canada; s. of Cornelius N. Hiebert and Tina Harms; m. Elfrieda Franz 1943; one s. two d.; ed Bethel Coll., N Newton, Kan., Univs of Kansas, Chicago and Wisconsin-Madison; Research Chemist, Standard Oil Co. of Indiana and the Manhattan Project 1943–46; Research Chemist, Inst. for Study of Metals, Univ. of Chicago 1947–50; Asst Prof. of Chem., San Francisco State Coll. 1952–55; Instructor in History of Science, Harvard 1955–57; Asst Prof., Assoc. Prof., Prof. of History of Science, Univ. of Wisconsin-Madison 1957–70; Prof. of History of Science, Harvard 1970–90,

Chair. 1977–84, Prof. Emer. 1990–; Pres. Midwest History of Science Society 1967–68, History of Science Soc. (US Nat. Soc.; Vice-Pres. 1971, 1972), Div. of History of Science, Int. Union of History and Philosophy of Science 1982–86 (Vice-Pres. 1974–81); Fulbright Lecturer, Max-Planck-Institut für Physik, Göttingen 1954–55; Visiting Prof., History of Science, Harvard Univ. 1965–66; Visiting Scholar, School of Historical Studies, Inst. for Advanced Study, Princeton 1961–62, 1968–69; Visiting Scholar, Zentrum fur interdisziplinäre Forschung der Universität Bielefeld 1978–79, 1979; Visiting Lecturer, Hebrew Univ. and the Van Leer Foundation, Jerusalem 1973, 1981; Visiting Research Scholar, Churchill Coll. Cambridge 1980, 1981, 1982, Overseas Fellow 1984, Fellow-in-Residence 1984–85; Visiting Lecturer, Inst. for the History of Natural Science, Chinese Acad. of Sciences, and China Asscn for Science and Tech., Beijing 1985; Hill Prof. in the History and Philosophy of Science, Dept of Physics, Univ. of Minnesota and Minnesota Center for the Philosophy of Science 1987; Visiting Prof., Institut für Wissenschaftsgeschichte, Univ. of Göttingen 1991–92; Visiting Scholar, Max-Planck-Institut für Wissenschaftsgeschichte zu Berlin 1998, 2002, 2007; mem. Editorial Bd Dictionary of Scientific Biography (18 vols) 1970–; Fellow, American Acad. of Arts and Sciences 1975, AAAS (Chair.-elect Section L (History and Philosophy of Science) 1981, Chair. 1982), Acad. Int. d'Histoire des Sciences 1971, Dunster House, Harvard Univ. 1980, Wissenschaftskolleg zu Berlin (Inst. for Advanced Study, Berlin) 1987–88, American Physical Soc. 1989; Foreign Fellow, Sächsische Akad. der Wissenschaften, Leipzig 1988; mem. Asscn of Mems of the Inst. for Advanced Study, Princeton 1962; Honorabilis Sodalis, Czechoslovak Soc. for the History of Science and Tech. 1985. *Publications:* Impact of Atomic Energy 1961, Historical Roots of the Principle of Conservation of Energy 1962, The Conception of Thermodynamics in the Scientific Thought of Mach and Planck 1967; and papers on history and philosophy of physics and chem. since 1800, science and religion, common frontiers between the exact sciences and the humanities, history of musical acoustics since 1850, science and music in the culture of late 19th century physicists. *Leisure interests:* music, gardening. *Address:* Department of History of Science, Harvard University Science Center 371, Cambridge, MA 02138 (office); Harvard University, Widener Library 172, Cambridge, MA 02138 (office); 40 Payson Road, Belmont, MA 02178, USA (home). *Telephone:* (617) 495-0325 (office); (617) 489-1741 (home). *Fax:* (617) 495-3344 (office). *E-mail:* ehiebert@fas.harvard.edu (office). *Website:* www.fas.harvard.edu/~hsdept (office).

HIERRO LÓPEZ, Luis; Uruguayan politician, teacher and journalist; b. 6 Jan. 1947, Montevideo; s. of Luis Hierro Gambardella and Celia Lopez; m. Ligia Armitran; four c.; journalist 1965–84; history teacher 1968–73; researcher, Museo Histórico Nacional 1974–84; mem. Nat. Exec. Cttee Colorado Party and Nat. Convention 1982–98, Chamber of Deputies (Pres. 1989) 1985–94; Chair. Cttees on the Constitution, Gen. Legislation and Admin and Human Rights, Special Cttee dealing with proposed anti-corruption legislation, Uruguayan Section of Jt Parl. Cttee of MERCOSUR; Senator, Colorado Party 1995–97; Vice-Pres. of Uruguay 2001–05. *Publications:* Diario del Uruguay (co-author) 1975, Battle y la Reforma del Estado 1978. *Address:* c/o Office of the Vice-President, Casa de Gobierno, Edif. Libertad, Avda Luis Alberto de Herrera 3350, esq. Avda José Pedro Varela, Montevideo, Uruguay (office).

HIGGINS, Chester, Jr, BS; American photographer; *Staff photographer, New York Times;* b. Nov. 1946, Lexington, Ky; s. of Varidee Loretta Young Higgins Smith and step-s. of Johnny Frank Smith; m. 1st Renalda Walker (divorced); one s. one d.; m. 2nd Betsy Kissam; ed Tuskegee Inst., Ala (now Tuskegee Univ.); became photographer 1967; photographer for Look magazine 1970; part-time photography instructor, New York Univ. School of Fine Arts 1975–78; staff photographer, New York Times 1975–; photographs have appeared in Art News, Look, New York Times Magazine, Life, Newsweek, Fortune, Ebony, Essence, Archaeology; Fellow Int. Center for Photography, Ford Foundation, Nat. Endowment for the Arts, Rockefeller Foundation, Andy Warhol Foundation; UN Award, American Graphic Design Award, Art Dirs of New York Award. *Publications include:* Student Unrest at Tuskagee Institute 1968, Black Woman 1970, Drums of Life 1974, Some Time Ago: A Historical Portrait of Black Americans 1850–1950 1980, Feeling the Spirit: Searching the World for the People of Africa 1994, Elder Grace: The Nobility of Aging 2000, Echo of the Spirit: A Visual Journey 2004; numerous reviews and articles in journals. *Address:* 57 South Portland Avenue, Brooklyn, New York, NY 11217–1301, USA (office). *Telephone:* (718) 625-2474. *Fax:* (718) 625-2830. *Website:* www.chesterhiggins.com.

HIGGINS, Christopher, BSc, PhD, FRSE, FRSA, FMedSci; British academic and university administrator; *Vice-Chancellor and Warden, University of Durham;* b. 1955, Cambridge; s. of Philip Higgins; pnr; five d.; ed Raynes Park Comprehensive, London, Royal College of Music, Univ. of Durham and University of California, Berkeley, USA; Lecturer, then Reader in Molecular Genetics, Dundee Univ. 1981–88, Prof. 1988–89; Dir of Research Labs, Imperial Cancer Research Fund (now Cancer Research UK), Inst. of Molecular Medicine 1989–94, Nuffield Prof. and Head, Dept of Clinical Biochemistry 1994–98; Dir Clinical Science Centre, Medical Research Council 1998–2007; Head of Div., Faculty of Medicine, Imperial Coll., London 1998–2007; Scientific Adviser, House of Lords Select Cttee on stem cells 2001–02; Vice-Chancellor and Warden, Univ. of Durham 2007–; Chair. Spongiform Encephalopathy Advisory Cttee; fmr Bd mem. Acad. of Medical Sciences, Biotechnology and Biological Sciences Research Council; mem. Human Genetics Comm.; CIBA Medal, British Biochemical Society, Fleming Award, Soc. for General Microbiology. *Publications:* numerous articles in academic journals. *Address:* Office of the Vice-Chancellor, University of Durham, University Office, Durham, DH1 3HP, England (office). *Telephone:* (191) 334-

6214 (office). *E-mail:* vice.chancellor@durham.ac.uk (office). *Website:* www .dur.ac.uk (office).

HIGGINS, Desmond G., PhD; Irish biologist/biochemist and academic; *Professor of Bioinformatics and Conway Investigator, Conway Institute of Biomolecular and Biomedical Research, University College Dublin;* ed Trinity Coll. Dublin; Postdoctoral Researcher, Sharp Lab., Dept of Genetics, Trinity Coll. Dublin 1985–90; Staff Scientist, European Molecular Biology Lab. (EMBL), Heidelberg, Germany 1990–94; Staff Scientist and Group Leader, EMBL/EBI, Hinxton, UK 1994–96; Statutory Lecturer, Dept of Biochemistry, Univ. Coll. Cork 1997–2003; Prof. of Bioinformatics and Conway Investigator, Conway Inst. of Biomolecular and Biomedical Research, Univ. Coll. Dublin 2003–. *Publications:* numerous articles in scientific journals. *Address:* Bioinformatics Department, Conway Institute of Biomolecular and Biomedical Research, University College Dublin, Belfield, Dublin 4, Ireland (office). *Telephone:* (1) 7166833 (office). *Fax:* (1) 7166701 (office). *E-mail:* des.higgins@ucd.ie (office). *Website:* www.ucd.ie/conway (office); bioinf.ucd.ie (home).

HIGGINS, Jack (see Patterson, Harry).

HIGGINS, Dame Julia Stretton, DBE, BA, DPhil, FRS, FREng; British polymer scientist and academic; *Professor of Polymer Science and Senior Research Investigator, Department of Chemical Engineering and Chemical Technology, Imperial College London;* b. 1 July 1942, London; d. of George Stretton Downes and Sheilah Stretton Downes; ed Ursuline Convent School, Wimbledon, Somerville Coll., Oxford; physics teacher, Mexborough Grammar School 1966–68; Research Assoc. Manchester Univ. 1968–72, Centre de Recherche sur les Macromolécules, Strasbourg, France 1972–73; physicist, Institut Laue-Langevin, Grenoble, France 1973–76; Lecturer, Chemical Eng Dept, Imperial Coll., London 1976–85, Reader in Polymer Science 1985–89, Prof. of Polymer Science and Sr Research Investigator 1989–, Dir Grad. School in Eng and Physical Sciences 2002–06, Prin. Faculty of Eng 2006–; Dean City and Guilds Coll. 1993–97; Chair. UK Engineering and Physical Sciences Research Council 2003–07; Pres. BAAS; Foreign Sec. and Vice-Pres. Royal Soc. 2001–; Foreign mem. Nat. Acad. of Eng, USA. *Publications:* more than 200 articles in scientific journals. *Leisure interests:* theatre, opera, travel. *Address:* Department of Chemical Engineering and Chemical Technology, ACE Building, Room 510, Imperial College, London, SW7 2BY, England (office). *Telephone:* (20) 7594-5565 (office). *Fax:* (20) 7594-5638 (office). *E-mail:* j.higgins@imperial.ac.uk (office); j.higgins@ic.ac.uk (office). *Website:* www3 .imperial.ac.uk/people/j.higgins (office).

HIGGINS, Michael D., BComm, MA; Irish politician and writer; *President, Irish Labour Party;* b. April 1941, Limerick; m. Sabina Coyne; three s. one d.; ed Univ. Coll. Galway, Indiana Univ., USA and Univ. of Manchester, UK; fmr Lecturer in Sociology and Politics, Univ. Coll. Galway; Senator 1973–77; mem. Galway Co. Council 1974–85; Alderman, Galway Borough Council 1974–85, Mayor of Galway 1982–83; mem. Galway City Council 1985–93; many other public appointments; TD 1981–82, 1987–; Chair. The Labour Party 1978–87, Pres. 2003–; Minister for Arts, Culture and the Gaeltacht 1993–97; Pres. European Council of Culture Ministers 1996; Pres. Council of Broadcasting Ministers 1996; mem. Sociological Asscn of Ireland, American Sociological Asscn, PEN, Irish Writers' Union; Hon. Adjunct Prof., Univ. Coll. Galway; Sean McBride Peace Prize, Int. Peace Bureau, Helsinki 1992, Robert Adams Medal 1993, Kilkenny Award for Contrib. to Arts 1997. *Publications:* Poetry: Betrayal 1990, The Season of Fire 1993, An Arid Season 2004; numerous papers on cultural and political issues. *Address:* Dail Eireann, Kildare Street, Dublin 2 (office); Letteragh, Rahoon, Galway, Ireland (home). *Telephone:* (1) 6183268 (office); (1) 528500 (home). *Fax:* (1) 6184586 (office); (1) 528501 (home). *E-mail:* michaeld.higgins@oireachtas.ie (office). *Website:* www.labour .ie (office); www.michaeldhiggins.ie (home).

HIGGINS, Dame Rosalyn, DBE, JSD, QC, FBA; British judge and fmr professor of international law; *President, International Court of Justice;* b. 2 June 1937; d. of the late Lewis Cohen and Fay Inberg; m. Rt Hon. Sir Terence L. (now Lord) Higgins 1961; one s. one d.; ed Burlington Grammar School, London, Girton Coll. Cambridge and Yale Law School, USA; UK Intern, Office of Legal Affairs, UN 1958; Commonwealth Fund Fellow 1959; Visiting Fellow, Brookings Inst. Washington, DC 1960; Jr Fellow in Int. Studies, LSE 1961–63; staff specialist in int. law, Royal Inst. of Int. Affairs 1963–74; Visiting Fellow, LSE 1974–78; Prof. of Int. Law, Univ. of Kent at Canterbury 1978–81; Prof. of Int. Law, LSE 1981–95; Judge, Int. Court of Justice 1995–, Pres. 2006–; mem. UN Cttee on Human Rights 1985–95; Visiting Prof., Stanford Univ. 1975, Yale Univ. 1977; Vice-Pres. American Soc. of Int. Law 1972–74, British Inst. of Int. and Comparative Law 2002–; Ordre des Palmes académiques 1988; Dr hc (Paris XI); Hon. DCL (Dundee) 1992, (Durham, LSE) 1995, (Cambridge, Sussex, Kent, City Univ., Greenwich, Essex) 1996, (Birmingham, Leicester, Glasgow) 1997, (Nottingham) 1999, (Bath, Paris II, Sorbonne) 2001, (Oxford) 2002, (Reading) 2003; Yale Law School Medal of Merit 1997, Manley Hudson Medal (ASIC) 1998, Harold Weig Medal, New York Univ. 1995, Prize of Int. Balzan Foundation 2007. *Publications include:* The Development of International Law Through the Political Organs of the United Nations 1963, Conflict of Interests 1965, The Administration of the United Kingdom Foreign Policy Through the United Nations 1966, Law in Movement – Essays in Memory of John McMahon (co-ed., with James Fawcett) 1974, UN Peace-keeping: Documents and Commentary: (Vol. I) Middle East 1969, (Vol. II) Asia 1971, (Vol. III) Africa 1980, (Vol. IV) Europe 1981, Problems and Process – International Law and How We Use It 1994; articles in law journals and journals of int. relations. *Leisure interests:* sport, cooking, eating. *Address:* International Court of Justice, Peace Palace, 2517 KJ The Hague, Netherlands (office). *Telephone:* (70) 302-2415 (office). *Fax:* (70) 302-2409 (office). *E-mail:* r.higgins@icj-cij.org (office). *Website:* www.icj-cij.org (office).

HIGGINS, Stuart; British journalist; b. 26 April 1956; m. Jenny Higgins; one s. one d.; ed Chase School for Boys, Filton Tech. Coll., Arblaster's of Bristol, Cardiff Coll. of Food, Tech. and Commerce; Dist reporter, The Sun, Bristol 1979, fmr NY corresp., Royal reporter, Features Ed., Exec. News Ed., Deputy Ed. 1991–93, Ed. 1994–98; public relations consultant 1998–; Acting Ed. News of the World 1993–94.

HIGGS, Peter Ware, PhD, FRS, FRSE; British professor of theoretical physics; b. 29 May 1929, Newcastle-upon-Tyne; s. of Thomas W. Higgs and Gertrude M. Higgs (née Coghill); m. Jo Ann Williamson 1963; two s.; ed Cotham Grammar School, Bristol and King's Coll. London; Sr Research Fellow, Univ. of Edinburgh 1955–56; ICI Research Fellow, Univ. Coll. London 1956–57, Imperial Coll. London 1957–58; Lecturer in Math., Univ. Coll. London 1958–60; Lecturer in Math. Physics, Univ. of Edinburgh 1960–70, Reader 1970–80, Prof. of Theoretical Physics 1980–96; Fellow, King's Coll. London 1998; Hon. FInstP 1998; Hon. Fellow, Univ. of Swansea 2008; Hon. DSc (Bristol) 1997, (Edin.) 1998, (Glasgow) 2002, (King's Coll., London) 2009; Hughes Medal, Royal Soc. 1981, Rutherford Medal, Inst. of Physics 1984, James Scott Prize, Royal Soc. of Edin. 1994, Paul Dirac Medal and Prize, Inst. of Physics 1997, High Energy and Particle Physics Prize, European Physical Soc. 1997, Royal Medal, Royal Soc. of Edin. 2000, Wolf Prize in Physics 2004, Oskar Klein Medal, Swedish Royal Acad. of Sciences 2009. *Publications:* numerous papers in scientific journals. *Leisure interests:* walking, swimming, listening to music. *Address:* 2 Darnaway Street, Edinburgh, EH3 6BG, Scotland (home). *Telephone:* (131) 225-7060 (home).

HIGHTOWER, John B., BA; American museum director; *President and Chief Executive, The Mariners' Museum;* b. 23 May 1933, Atlanta, Georgia; s. of Edward A. Hightower and Margaret K. Hightower; m. 2nd Martha Ruhl 1984; one s. one d. (from 1st marriage); ed Yale Univ.; Gen. Asst to Pres. and Publisher, American Heritage Publishing Co. 1961–63; Exec. Dir New York State Council on the Arts 1964–70; Dir Museum of Modern Art, New York 1970–72; Pres. Assoc. Councils of Arts, New York 1972–74; Pres. South Street Seaport 1977–84; Exec. Dir Richard Tucker Music Foundation 1977–89, The Maritime Center, Norwalk 1984–89; Cultural Adviser to Presidential Latin American Comm. 1969; Founder and Chair., Advocates for the Arts 1974–77; Instructor, Arts Man., Wharton School 1976–77, New School 1976–77; Chair. Planning Corpn for the Arts; Dir Planning and Devt of the Arts, Univ. of Va 1989–93; Interim Dir Bayly Museum, Univ. of Va 1990–91; Pres., CEO The Mariners' Museum, Va 1993–; Vice-Chair. Newport News Public Arts Foundation 2002–; Dir Downing Gross Cultural Center 2004–; NY State Award 1970. *Leisure interests:* gardening, cooking, travel. *Address:* 101 Museum Parkway, Newport News, VA 23606, USA (home). *E-mail:* jhightower@mariner.org (office). *Website:* www.mariner.org (office).

HIGUCHI, Takeo; Japanese business executive; *Chairman and CEO, Daiwa House Industry Company Ltd;* Pres. Daiwa House Industry Co. Ltd –2004, Chair. and CEO 2004–; mem. Bd of Dirs Kansai Int. Public Relations Promotion Office (KIPPO) 2004–. *Address:* Daiwa House Industry Company Ltd, 3-3-5 Umeda, Kita-ku, Osaka 530-8241, Japan (office). *Telephone:* (6) 6346-2111 (office). *Fax:* (6) 6342-1419 (office). *Website:* www.daiwahouse.co.jp (office).

HIGUCHI, Tomio; Japanese insurance executive; *Chairman, Millea Holdings Inc.;* joined Nichido Fire & Marine Insurance Co. Ltd 1965, various sr positions include Dir 1993–95, Man.-Dir 1995–98, Sr Man.-Dir 1998–2000, Vice-Pres. 2000–01, Pres. and Sr Gen. Man. of Marketing and Sales Promotion HQ 2001–02, Chair. and Pres. 2002–04; Chair. Millea Holdings Inc. (following merger between Nichido Fire & Marine Insurance Co. and Tokio Marine 2004) 2004–; mem. Bd of Dirs Transatlantic Holdings Inc. 2003–. *Address:* Millea Holdings Inc., Otemachi First Square, West Tower, 1-5-1 Otemachi, Chiyoda-ku, Tokyo 100-0004, Japan (office). *Telephone:* (3) 6212-3341 (office). *Fax:* (3) 6212-3343 (office). *Website:* www.millea.co.jp (office).

HIJIKATA, Takeshi; Japanese business executive; b. 18 March 1915, Ena City, Gifu Prefecture; s. of Kikusaburo and Sue Hijikata; m. Michiko Kumakura; two s. one d.; ed Tokyo Imperial Univ.; joined Sumitomo Chemical Co. Ltd 1941, Dir 1971, Man. Dir 1973, Exec. Vice-Pres. 1977, Pres. 1977, Chair. 1985–93, Counsellor 1993–; Chair. Japan Tobacco Inc.; Dir Fuji Oil Co. Ltd, Sumitomo Seika Chemicals Co. Ltd, Japan Cttee for Econ. Devt; Dir and Counsellor Sumitomo Pharmaceuticals Co. Ltd; Dir Sumitomo Bakelite Co. Ltd, Inabata and Co. Ltd; Adviser and Hon. mem. Fed. of Econ. Orgs (Keidanren); Adviser Japan Chemical Industry Asscn; Standing Dir Japan Fed. of Employees' Asscn, Kansai Econ. Fed.; mem. Trade Conf., Prime Minister's Office, Atomic Energy Comm., Science and Tech. Agency, Japan Singapore Asscn. *Leisure interests:* golf, reading. *Address:* Sumitomo Chemical Co. Ltd, 5-33 Kitahama, 4-chome, Chuo-ku, Osaka 541; 27-1, Shinkawa, 2-chome, Chuo-ku, Tokyo 104, Japan.

HILBE, Alfred J., DEcon; Liechtenstein politician; b. 22 July 1928, Gmunden, Austria; s. of Franz and Elisabeth (née Glatz) Hilbe; m. Virginia Joseph 1951; one d.; ed classical secondary schools in Vaduz and Zürich, Ecole Nationale des Sciences Politiques, Paris and Univ. of Innsbruck; several posts in pvt. business 1951–54; in Foreign Service 1954–65, Counsellor, Liechtenstein Embassy, Berne –1965; Deputy Head of Govt of Liechtenstein 1965–70, Head of Govt 1970–74; Financial Consultant 1974–; Grosskreuz of Liechtenstein Order of Merit, Grosses Silbernes Ehrenzeichen am Bande (Austria) 1975, Order of St Gregory (Vatican); Fatherland Union Party. *Leisure interests:* skiing, tennis, photography. *Address:* 9494 Schaan, Garsill 11, Principality of Liechtenstein. *Telephone:* 2322002 (home); 2328320 (office).

HILBORN, Raymond, BA, PhD, FRSC; Canadian marine biologist and academic; *Professor, School of Aquatic and Fishery Sciences, University of Washington, Seattle;* b. 31 Dec. 1947; ed Grinnell Coll., Ia, Univ. of British

Columbia; Research Scholar, Int. Inst. for Applied Systems Analysis, Laxenburg, Austria 1974–75; Policy Analyst, Depts of Environment and Fisheries, Govt of Canada 1975–80; Hon. Lecturer, Inst. of Animal Resource Ecology, Univ. of British Columbia 1975–80, Adjunct Assoc. Prof. 1980–85; Sr Fisheries Scientist, Tuna and Billfish Program, South Pacific Comm., Noumea, New Caledonia 1985–87, Prof., School of Aquatic and Fishery Sciences, Univ. of Washington, Seattle 1987–, H. Mason Keeler Prof. of Recreational Fisheries Man. 1988–91, Dir Fisheries Research Inst. 1996–98, Richard C. and Lois M. Worthington Prof. of Fisheries Man. 2001–06; Chair. NAS/Nat. Research Council Cttee on Cooperative Research in the Nat. Marine Fisheries Service 2002–03; American Co-Chair. Pacific Salmon Comm. working group on mark-recovery statistics 1989–94; mem. NAS Panel on Fisheries Stock Assessment Methods 1996–97, NMFS panel to review fisheries closures to protect Steller's Sea Lions 1997–99, NAS Panel on status of New England groundfish stocks 1997–98, Int. Cttee for recovery of the vaquita (*Phocoena sinus*) 1996–2000, Ocean Studies Bd, Nat. Research Council 1999–2001, Scientific Advisory Bd for Pres.'s Comm. on Ocean Policy 2002–04; Ind. Science Advisor, Comm. for Conservation of Southern Bluefin Tuna 1999–; Ed. for Fisheries, Marine Policy Reports 1988–90; mem. Editorial Bd, Natural Resource Modeling 1993–, Reviews in Fish Biology and Fisheries 1993–, Fish and Fisheries 1999–, New Zealand Journal of Marine and Freshwater Research 2003–, Canadian Journal of Fisheries and Aquatic Sciences 2002–; mem. Bd of Reviewing Eds, Sciences 2006–; Nat. Research Council Canada Grad. Fellowship 1972–74, Wildlife Soc. (USA) Award for Best Paper in Fisheries Science 1976, Stevenson Memorial Lecture, Canadian Conf. for Fisheries Research 1985, Coll. of Ocean and Fisheries Sciences Distinguished Research Award, Univ. of Washington, Seattle 1997, Award of Excellence, American Fisheries Soc. (Western Div.) 2005, Nat. Award of Excellence, American Fisheries Soc. 2005, Volvo Environment Prize, Volvo Environment Foundation (co-recipient) 2006. *Publications:* Adaptive Environmental Assessment and Management (co-author) 1978, Quantitative Fisheries Stock Assessment: Choice, Dynamics and Uncertainty (co-author) 1992 (also translated into Russian), Biomass Dynamics Models. FAO Computerized Information Series (Fisheries). No. 10 (co-author) 1996, The Ecological Detective: Confronting Models with Data (co-author) 1997, Bayesian Stock Assessment Methods in Fisheries. FAO Computerized Information Series (Fisheries) No. 12 (co-author) 2002; numerous scientific papers in professional journals. *Address:* School of Aquatic and Fishery Sciences, University of Washington, Box 355020, Seattle, WA 98195-5020, USA (office). *Telephone:* (206) 543-3587 (office). *Fax:* (206) 685-7471 (office). *E-mail:* rayh@u.washington.edu (office). *Website:* www.fish.washington.edu (office).

HILDENBERG, Humphrey; Suriname economist and government official; *Minister of Finance;* ed Univ. of Groningen, The Netherlands; with Nationale Ontwikkelings Bank (NOB) 1981–92, 1996–2000; Minister of Finance 1992–96, 2000–. *Address:* Ministry of Finance, Tamarindelaan 3, Paramaribo, Suriname (office). *Telephone:* 472610 (office). *Fax:* 476314 (office). *E-mail:* financien@sr.net (office). *Website:* www.minfin.sr (office).

HILDENBRAND, Werner; German economist and academic; *Professor of Economics, University of Bonn;* b. 25 May 1936, Göttingen; Lecturer, Univ. of Heidelberg 1964–66; Visiting Asst Prof., Univ. of Calif., Berkeley 1966–67, Visiting Assoc. Prof. 1967–68; Research Prof., Univ. of Louvain, Belgium 1968–76; Prof. of Econs, Univ. of Bonn 1969–; Visiting Prof. of Econs, Univ. of Calif., Berkeley and Stanford Univ. 1970, Univ. of Calif., Berkeley 1973–74, Visiting Ford Prof., Univ. of Calif., Berkeley 1985–86, European Univ. Inst., Florence 1989–, Univ. of Calif., San Diego 1986–91; European Chair., Coll. de France 1993–94; Fellow, Econometric Soc. 1972; mem. Rhein-West Akad. der Wissenschaften 1981–, Academia Europaea 1985–, Berlin-Brandenburgischen Akad. der Wissenschaften 1993–; Foreign Hon. mem. American Acad. of Arts and Sciences 2005–; Dr hc (Univ. Louis Pasteur Strasbourg) 1988, (Bern) 2002, (Manchester) 2007; Leibniz-Preis Deutsche Forschungsgemeinschaft 1987, Max-Planck-Forsch-Preis 1995, Alexander-von-Humboldt-Preis 1997, Gay-Lussac-Preis 1997. *Publications:* Core and Equilibria of a Large Economy 1974, Lineare ökonomische Modelle (with K. Hildenbrand) 1975, Introduction to Equilibrium Analysis (with A. Kirman) 1976, Equilibrium Analysis (with A. Kirman) 1988, Market Demand: Theory and Empirical Evidence 1994; numerous papers. *Address:* University of Bonn, Wirtschaftstheorie II, Lennestr. 37, 53113 Bonn (office); Buchbitze 21, 53797 Lohmar, Germany (home). *Telephone:* (228) 739242 (office); (2246) 4339 (home). *Fax:* (228) 737940 (office); (2246) 16610 (home). *E-mail:* with2@uni-bonn.de (office). *Website:* www.wiwi.uni-bonn.de/fgh/ (office).

HILDRETH, Eugene A., BS, MD, FRSM, FRCP; American physician and academic; *Professor Emeritus of Clinical Medicine, University of Pennsylvania;* b. 11 March 1924, St Paul, Minn.; s. of Eugene A. Hildreth and Lila K. Hildreth; m. Dorothy Ann Meyers 1946; two s. two d.; ed Washington and Jefferson Coll., Univ. of Virginia School of Medicine, Johns Hopkins Hosp., Baltimore, Md, Univ. of Pennsylvania; Research in Dept of Research Medicine, Univ. of Pa, Philadelphia 1957–60, Markle Scholar in Academic Medicine 1958–63, Assoc. Dean, Univ. of Pa 1964–67, Prof. of Clinical Medicine 1971–90, Prof. Emer. 1990–; Dir Dept of Medicine, The Reading Hosp. and Medical Center, Reading, Pa; Chair. Allergy and Immunology Subspeciality Bd 1966–72, American Bd of Allergy and Immunology 1971–72, American Bd of Internal Medicine 1975–82, Federated Council of Internal Medicine 1981–82, American Coll. of Physicians (ACP) Cttee on Developing Criteria and Standards for Delineation of Clinical Privileges 1986–90, Regent ACP 1985–92, Chair. Bd of Regents 1989–91, Pres. ACP 1991–92, Master 1992–, mem. nominating Cttee 1997–; mem. Federated Council of Internal Medicine, Fed. of the American Socs. for Experimental Biology, AAAS, ACP Cttee on Ethics, ACP Cttee on Int. Medicine, Inst. of Medicine (IOM), NAS, Council of IOM, Nominations Cttee of IOM, Bower Award Cttee of Franklin Inst. 1994, working group on disability of US Presidents 1994–2000. *Publications:* 150 scientific papers, 6 chapters in books, 1 book, reviews etc. *Leisure interests:* reading, white water kayaking, backpacking, museums. *Address:* 5285 Sweitzer Road, Mohnton, PA 19540, USA (home). *Telephone:* (610) 775-3421 (home).

HILDREW, Bryan, CBE, MSc, DIC, FCGI, FREng; British fmr engineer; b. 19 March 1920, Sunderland, Co. Durham; s. of Alexander William Hildrew and Sarah Jane Hildrew; m. Megan Kathleen Lewis; two s. one d.; ed Bede Collegiate School, Sunderland, Sunderland Tech. Coll., City and Guilds Coll., Univ. of London; Prin. Surveyor, Eng Investigations, Lloyds Register of Shipping 1961–65, Deputy Chief Engineer Surveyor 1965–67, Chief Engineer Surveyor 1967–70, Tech. Dir 1970–77, Man. Dir 1977–85; Pres. IMechE 1980–81; Chair. Council of Eng Insts 1981–82; Pres. Inst. of Marine Engineers 1983–85; Chair. Abbeyfield Orpington Soc. 1985–2004; Hon. DEng (Newcastle-upon-Tyne) 1987; Hon. DUniv (Surrey) 1994. *Leisure interests:* walking, orienteering. *Address:* 8 Westholme, Orpington, Kent, BR6 0AN, England (home).

HILFIGER, Tommy; American fashion designer; b. 24 March 1951, Elmira, NY; m. Susie Hilfiger; four c.; opened first store, People's Place, Elmira, NY 1969; owned ten clothes shops throughout NY by 1978; moved to NY City to became full-time designer 1979; launched own sportswear label 1984; acquired fashion business from Mohan Muranji, cr. Tommy Hilfiger Inc. 1989, now Hon. Chair. and Prin. Designer; mem. Bd Fresh Air Fund, Race to Erase Multiple Sclerosis; f. Tommy Hilfiger Corporate Foundation 1995; winner From the Catwalk to the Sidewalk Award, VH-1 Fashion and Music Awards 1995, Menswear Designer of the Year, Council of Fashion Designers of America 1995, Parsons School of Design, Designer of the Year Award 1998. *Publication:* Iconic America: A Roller-Coaster Ride through the Eye-Popping Panorama of American Pop Culture (with George Lois) 2007. *Leisure interests:* fishing, scuba diving, skiing. *Address:* Tommy Hilfiger USA Inc., 601 West 26th Street, New York, NY 10001, USA (office). *Telephone:* (212) 549-6000 (office). *Website:* www.tommy.com (office).

HILL, Anita F., BS, JD; American legal scholar and academic; *Professor of Social Policy, Law and Women's Studies, Heller School for Social Policy and Management, Brandeis University;* b. 30 July 1956, Lone Tee, Okla; d. of Albert Hill and Emma Hill; ed Oklahoma State Univ., Yale Univ. Law School; admitted to DC Bar 1980; Assoc., Wald, Harkrader & Ross, Washington, DC 1980–81; Special Counsel to Asst Sec., Office for Civil Rights, US Dept of Educ. 1981–82; Adviser to Chair. of Equal Employment Opportunity Comm. 1982–83; Asst Prof., Oral Roberts Univ. 1983–86; Prof., Coll. of Law, Univ. of Oklahoma 1986–97; Visiting Prof., Univ. of California Inst. for the Study of Social Change 1997; Prof. of Social Policy, Law and Women's Studies, Heller Grad. School, Brandeis Univ. 1997–; Visiting Scholar, Wellesley Coll., Newhouse Center for the Humanities and Wellesley Centers for Women 2007; Dr hc (Simmons Coll.) 2001, (Dillard Univ.) 2001; Ford Hall Forum First Amendment Award 2008. *Publications include:* Race, Gender and Power in America: The Legacy of the Hill-Thomas Hearings 1995, Speaking Truth to Power (on her testimony of sexual harassment during US Senate confirmation hearings of Supreme Court nominee Clarence Thomas 1991) 1997; articles on int. commercial law, bankruptcy and civil rights. *Address:* Heller 374, Heller School for Social Policy and Management, Brandeis University, 415 South Street, Waltham, MA 02454-9110, USA (office). *Telephone:* (781) 736-3896 (office). *E-mail:* ahill@brandeis.edu (office). *Website:* heller.brandeis.edu (office).

HILL, Anthony, (Achill Redo); British artist; b. 23 April 1930, London; s. of Adrian Hill and Dorothy Whitley; m. Yuriko Kaetsu 1978; ed Bryanston School, St Martin's School of Art, Cen. School of Arts and Crafts; works in nat. collections in UK, USA, France, Israel, Denmark; Leverhulme Fellowship 1971–72, Hon. Research Fellow, Dept of Math., Univ. Coll. 1971–72, Hon. Research Assoc. 1972–; mem. The London Math. Soc. 1979–; First Prize, Norwegian Print Biennale 1999. *Publications:* Data: Directions in Art, Theory and Aesthetics (ed.) 1968, Duchamp: Passim 1994; numerous articles in art and math. journals. *Leisure interest:* erotology. *Address:* 24 Charlotte Street, London, W1, England. *Telephone:* (20) 7636-5332 (office); (20) 7636-5332 (home). *E-mail:* achillredo@tiscali.co.uk.

HILL, Bonnie Guiton, BA, MS, EdD; American business executive; *President, B. Hill Enterprises LLC;* b. 30 Oct. 1941, Springfield, Ill.; d. of Henry Frank Brazelton and Zola Elizabeth Brazelton (née Newman); m. Walter Hill, Jr; one d.; ed Mills Coll., California State Univ., Hayward, Univ. of California, Berkeley; Admin. Asst to Presidential Special Asst, Mills Coll., Oakland, Calif. 1970–71, Admin. Asst to Asst Vice-Pres. 1972–73, Student Services Counsellor, Adviser to Resuming Students 1973–74, Asst Dean of Students, Interim Dir Ethnic Studies, Lecturer 1975–76; Exec. Dir Marcus A. Foster Educational Inst. 1976–79; Admin. Man. Kaiser Aluminium & Chemical Corpn 1979–80; Vice-Pres. and Gen. Man. Kaiser CTR, Inc. 1980–84; Vice-Chair. Postal Rate Comm., Washington, DC 1985–87; Asst Sec. for Vocational and Adult Educ., US Dept of Educ. 1987–89; Special Adviser to Pres. Bush for Consumer Affairs 1989–90; Pres. and CEO Earth Conservation Corps, Washington, DC 1990–91; Sec., State and Consumer Services Industry, State of Calif. 1991–92; Dean McIntire School of Commerce, Univ. of Virginia, Charlottesville 1992–97; Vice-Pres. The Times Mirror Co. Ltd 1997–2000; Co-founder and COO Icon Blue, Inc. (marketing consultancy) 2001–; Sr Vice-Pres. Communications and Public Affairs, LA Times newspaper 1998–2001, Pres. and CEO The Times Mirror Foundation 1997–2001; Pres. B. Hill Enterprises LLC (consulting firm) 2001–; mem. Bd of Dirs The Home Depot Co., Hershey Foods Corpn, AK Steel Holding Corpn, Choice Point, Inc., The Nat. Grid Group PLC 2001–, Albertsons, Inc., Yum! Brands 2003–; mem. Nat. Advisory

Panel, Inst. for Research on Women and Gender, Stanford Univ.; mem. LA Urban League, United Way of Greater LA, Goodwill Industries of Southern Calif.; Nat. Women's Econ. Alliance Foundation Dirs' Choice Award, YWCA Tribute to Women in Int. Industry Award, Angeles Girl Scouts Council Grace Award, Anti-Defamation League Deborah Award. *Address:* Icon Blue, 5670 Wilshire Boulevard, Suite 600, Los Angeles, CA 90036, USA (office). *Telephone:* (323) 634-5301 (office). *Fax:* (323) 634-5314 (office). *E-mail:* info@iconblue.com (office). *Website:* www.iconblue.com (office).

HILL, Rt Rev. Christopher John, BD, MTh; British ecclesiastic; b. 10 Oct. 1945; s. of Leonard Hill and Frances Hill; m. Hilary Ann Whitehouse 1976; three s. one d.; ed Sebright School, Worcs. and King's Coll., London; ordained (Diocese of Lichfield) 1969; Asst Chaplain to Archbishop of Canterbury for Foreign Relations 1974–81, Sec. for Ecumenical Affairs 1981–89; Anglican Sec. Anglican-Roman Catholic Int. Comm. I and II 1974–91; Anglican-Lutheran European Comm. 1981–82; Hon. Canon Canterbury Cathedral 1982–89; Chaplain to Queen 1987–96; Canon Residentiary of St Paul's Cathedral, London 1989–96; Area Bishop of Stafford, Diocese of Lichfield 1996–, Hon. Canon Lichfield Cathedral 1996–; mem. Gen. Synod 1999–, House of Bishops 1999–; mem. Church of England-German Churches Conversations 1987–89, Church of England-Nordic-Baltic Conversations 1989–93, Church of England Legal Advisory Comm. 1991–, Faith and Order Advisory Group of Gen. Synod 1997– (Vice-Chair. 1998–); mem. Council for Christian Unity 1992–97; Co-Chair. London Soc. of Jews and Christians 1991–96, Church of England-French Protestant Conversations 1993–98; Vice-Chair. Ecclesiastical Law Soc. 1993–2002, Chair. 2002–; Chair. Cathedrals' Precentors Conf. 1994–96; Anglican Co-Chair. Meissen Theological Conf. 1999–2001; mem. London Soc. for the Study of Religion 1990–2000, Working Party on Women in the Episcopate 2001–, Liturgical Comm. 2003–, Clery Discipline Comm. 2004–; Assoc. King's Coll., London. *Publications:* Anglicans and Roman Catholics: the search for Unity (co-ed.), The Documents in the Debate. A Retrospect on the Papal Decision on Anglican Orders 1896 (co-ed.) 1996; ecumenical articles. *Leisure interests:* music, walking, reading. *Address:* Ash Garth, 6 Broughton Crescent, Barlaston, Stoke On Trent, ST12 9DD, England. *Telephone:* (1782) 373308. *Fax:* (1782) 373705. *E-mail:* bishop.stafford@lichfield.anglican.org (office).

HILL, Christopher R., MA; American diplomatist; *Ambassador to Iraq;* b. Little Compton, RI; m.; three c.; ed Bowdoin Coll., Maine, Naval War Coll.; with Peace Corps in Cameroon; joined Foreign Service, overseas assignments in Yugoslavia, Albania, S Korea and Poland; Sr Country Officer for Polish Affairs, Dept of State; Amb. to Macedonia 1996–99, to Poland 2000–04, to S Korea 2004–05; Asst Sec. Bureau of E Asian and Pacific Affairs 2005–09; Amb. to Iraq 2009–; Head of US del. to Six-Party Talks on N Korean nuclear issue 2005; Special Envoy to Kosovo 1998–99; fmr Sr Dir Southeast European Affairs, Nat. Security Council; several State Dept awards including Robert S. Frasure Award and Distinguished Service Award. *Address:* Embassy of the United States, APO AE 09316, Baghdad, Iraq (office). *E-mail:* BaghdadPressOffice@state.gov (office). *Website:* iraq.usembassy.gov (office).

HILL, Damon Graham Devereux, OBE; British fmr racing driver and company director; *President, British Racing Drivers' Club;* b. 17 Sept. 1960, Hampstead, London; s. of the late Graham Hill (fmr Formula One world champion) and of Bette Hill; m. Georgie Hill 1988; two s. two d.; ed Haberdashers' Aske's School, London; first drove a car aged five years; first drove in motorcycle racing 1979; driver with Canon Williams team 1993, Rothmans Williams Renault team 1994–96, Arrows Yamaha team 1997, Benson and Hedges Jordan team 1998–99; first motor racing victory in Formula Ford 1600, Brands Hatch 1984; first Formula One Grand Prix, Silverstone 1992; winner, Italian Grand Prix 1993, 1994, Belgian Grand Prix 1993, 1994, 1998, Hungarian Grand Prix 1993, 1995, Spanish Grand Prix 1994, British Grand Prix 1994, Portuguese Grand Prix 1994, Japanese Grand Prix 1994, 1996, Argentine Grand Prix 1995, 1996, San Marino Grand Prix 1995, 1996, Australian Grand Prix 1995, 1996, French Grand Prix 1996, Brazilian Grand Prix 1996, German Grand Prix 1996, Canadian Grand Prix 1996; third place, Drivers' World Championship 1993, second place 1994, 1995, Formula One World Champion 1996; 84 Grand Prix starts, 22 wins, 20 pole positions, 19 fastest laps, 42 podium finishes; retd end of 1999 season; Co-founder and Chair. P1 Int. 2000–; Pres. British Racing Drivers' Club 2006–; British Competition Driver of the Year Autosport Awards 1995; BBC Sports Personality Award 1994, 1996; numerous racing awards. *Publications:* Damon Hill Grand Prix Year 1994, Damon Hill: My Championship Year 1996, F1 Through the Eyes of Damon Hill. *Leisure interests:* family, reading. *Address:* British Racing Drivers' Club, Silverstone Circuit, Towcester, Northants. NN12 8TN, England (office). *E-mail:* enquiries@brdc.co.uk. *Website:* www.brdc.co.uk (office).

HILL, David Rowland; British government adviser; *Director of Communications, Prime Minister's Office;* b. 1948, Birmingham; partner Hilary Coffman; ed King Edward's School, Birmingham, Brasenose Coll., Oxford; began career as industrial relations officer, Unigate Dairies, Birmingham; fmr press aide to Labour MP Roy Hattersley; Dir of Communications and Chief Media Spokesperson, Labour Party 1991–98; Labour cand. for Burton-on-Trent (unsuccessful), Sr Labour Party Press Spokesman during 2001 election campaign; Dir of Communications, Prime Minister's Office 2003–; Dir Good Relations (public relations co.) 1998–2003. *Leisure interest:* football. *Address:* Prime Minister's Office, 10 Downing Street, London, SW1A 2AA, England (office). *Telephone:* (20) 7930-4433 (office). *Website:* www.number-10.gov.uk (office).

HILL, Geoffrey William, MA, FRSL; British poet and academic; *University Professor Emeritus of Literature and Religion, Boston University;* b. 18 June 1932; s. of William George Hill and Hilda Beatrice Hill (née Hands); m. 1st

Nancy Whittaker 1956 (divorced 1983); three s. one d.; m. 2nd Alice Goodman 1987; one d.; ed County High School, Bromsgrove and Keble Coll., Oxford; mem. academic staff, Univ. of Leeds 1954–80, Prof. of English Literature 1976–80; Univ. Lecturer in English and Fellow, Emmanuel Coll., Cambridge 1981–88; Univ. Prof. of Literature and Religion, Boston Univ. 1988–2006, Emer. 2006–; Co-Dir Editorial Inst., Boston Univ. 1998–2004; Churchill Fellow, Univ. of Bristol 1980; Clark Lecturer, Trinity Coll., Cambridge 1986; Tanner Lecturer, Brasenose Coll., Oxford 2000; Assoc. Fellow, Centre for Research in Philosophy and Literature, Univ. of Warwick 2003; Empson Lecturer, Univ. of Cambridge 2005; Fellow, American Acad. of Arts and Sciences 1996; Hon. Fellow, Keble Coll., Oxford 1981, Emmanuel Coll., Cambridge 1990; Hon. DLitt (Leeds) 1988; Whitbread Award 1971, RSL Award (W. H. Heinemann Bequest) 1971, Loines Award, American Acad. and Inst. of Arts and Letters 1983, Ingram Merrill Foundation Award in Literature 1985, Kahn Award 1998, T. S. Eliot Prize, Ingersoll Foundation 2000. *Publications:* poetry: Poems 1952, For the Unfallen (Gregory Award 1961) 1959, Preghiere 1964, King Log (Hawthornden Prize 1969, Geoffrey Faber Memorial Prize 1970) 1968, Mercian Hymns (Alice Hunt Bartlett Award) 1971, Somewhere is Such a Kingdom: Poems 1952–71 1975, Tenebrae (Duff Cooper Memorial Prize 1979) 1978, The Mystery of the Charity of Charles Péguy 1983, Collected Poems 1985, New and Collected Poems 1952–1992 1994, Canaan 1996, The Triumph of Love 1998, Speech! Speech! 2000, The Orchards of Syon 2002, Scenes from Comus 2005, Without Title 2006, Selected Poems 2006, A Treatise of Civil Power 2007; poetic drama: Henrik Ibsen's Brand: a version for the English stage 1978 (produced at Nat. Theatre, London 1978); criticism: The Lords of Limit: essays on literature and ideas 1984, The Enemy's Country 1991, Style and Faith 2003.

HILL, Jay, PC; Canadian politician; *Leader of the Government in the House of Commons;* b. 27 Dec. 1952, British Colombia; fmr Pres. BC Grain Producers Asscn and Dir for Grain, BC Fed. of Agric.; mem. Parl. for Prince George–Peace River 1993–; mem. Reform Party of Canada 1993–2000, Canadian Alliance 2000–03, Conservative Party of Canada 2003–; Chief Govt Whip 2006–08; Leader of the Govt in the House of Commons 2008–. *Address:* Office of the Leader of the Government in the House of Commons, 4th Floor, 14 Metcalfe Street, Ottawa, ON K1A 0A3, Canada (office). *Telephone:* (613) 952-4930 (office). *Website:* www.pco-bcp.gc.ca/lgc (office); www.jayhillmp.com.

HILL, Lynn, BS; American rock climber; b. (Carolynn Marie Hill), 1961, Detroit, Mich.; one s.; ed Staffs. State Univ. of NY, New Paltz, NY; began climbing aged 14; won over 30 int. climbing titles during 1980s; f. Lynn Hill Rock Climbing Camps; first person to free climb Nose route on El Capitan, Yosemite Valley, Calif. 1993, later free climbed the route in 23 hours in 1994, feat not repeated by any other climber until 2005; winner Survival of the Fittest TV competition (for times). *Main achievements:* competition winner, Troubat 1987, 1988, 1989, Worldwide indoor competition, Grenoble 1987, Arco Rock Master 1987, 1990, 1992, Bercy 1988, 1990, World Cup (jt winner) 1991, Stopped Competition 1993. *Film appearances include:* Extreme, Free Climbing the Nose, La Maitresse du Vide (French version). *Publications:* Climbing Free: My Life in the Vertical World (autobiography) 2002. *Address:* Lynn Hill Rock Climbing Camps, PO Box 383, Eldorado Springs, CO 80025, USA (office). *Telephone:* (303) 919-3223. *E-mail:* lynn@lynnhillblogs.com. *Website:* www.lynnhillclimbs.com; lynnhillblogs.com.

HILL, Michael William, MA, MSc, MRSC, FIInfSc, FCILIP; British information consultant, research chemist and library director; b. 27 July 1928, Ross-on-Wye; s. of Geoffrey Hill and Dorothy Hill; m. 1st Elma Jack Forrest (died 1967); one s. one d.; m. 2nd Barbara Joy Youngman; ed King Henry VIIIth School, Coventry, Nottingham High School, Lincoln Coll., Oxford; Research Chemist, Laporte Chemicals Ltd 1953–56; Tech. and Production Man., Morgan Crucible Group 1956–64; Asst Keeper, British Museum 1964–68, Deputy Librarian Nat. Reference Library of Science and Invention (NRLSI) 1965–68, Keeper 1968–73; Dir, Science Reference Library, British Library 1973–86; Assoc. Dir Science, Tech. and Industry, British Library 1986–88; Hon. Pres. Fed. Int. d'Information et de Documentation 1985–90; fmr Chair. Circle of State Librarians; fmr Vice-Pres. Int. Asscn of Tech. Univ. Librarians; Co-founder European Council of Information Asscns; Hon. Fellow Fed. Int. d'Information et de Documentation 1992–, European Council of Information Asscns 1996–. *Publications:* Patent Documentation (with Wittmann and Schiffels) 1979, Michael Hill on Science, Technology and Information 1988, National Surveys of Library and Information Services: 2: Yugoslavia (with Tudor Silovic), National Information Policies and Strategies 1994, The Impact of Information on Society 1998; Jt Series Ed. Saur Guides to Information Sources. *Leisure interests:* golf, theatre, music, Scottish dancing. *Address:* Jesters, 137 Burdon Lane, Cheam, Surrey, SM2 7DB, England. *Telephone:* (20) 8642-2418.

HILL, Robert Lee, PhD; American academic; *James B. Duke Professor of Biochemistry, Duke University;* b. 8 June 1928, Kansas City, Mo.; s. of William Alfred Hill and Geneva Eunice Sculock Hill; m. 1st Helen Root Hill 1948 (divorced); m. 2nd Deborah Anderson Hill 1982; one s. three d. (from previous marriage); ed Kansas Univ.; Research Instructor, Univ. of Utah, Salt Lake City 1956–57, Asst Research Prof. 1957–60, Assoc. Research Prof. 1960–61; Assoc. Prof., Duke Univ., Durham, NC 1961–65, Prof. 1965–74, Chair. Dept of Biochemistry 1969–93, James B. Duke Prof. 1974–; Fellow, American Acad. of Arts and Sciences 1974–; mem. NAS 1975–; Pres. American Soc. of Biological Chemists 1976–77; Pres. Asscn of Medical Depts of Biochemistry 1982–83; Gen. Sec. Int. Union of Biochemistry 1985–91. *Publications:* Principles of Biochemistry (co-author) 1978, The Proteins (co-ed.) (Vol. I 1975, Vol. V 1982). *Address:* Department of Biochemistry, Nanaline H. Duke Building, Box 3711, DUMC, Durham, NC 27710, USA (office). *Telephone:* (919) 681-8805 (office).

Fax: (919) 684-8885 (office). *E-mail:* hill@biochem.duke.edu (office). *Website:* www.biochem.duke.edu/Hill/hill (office).

HILL, Robert Murray, BA, BLL, LLM; Australian politician and diplomatist; *Permanent Representative, United Nations;* b. 1946, Adelaide, S Australia; m.; four c.; ed Scotch Coll., Univ. of Adelaide, Univ. of London; barrister and solicitor 1970–; Liberal Party Campaign Chair. 1975–77, Chair., Constitutional Cttee 1977–81; Vice-Pres. Liberal Party, S. Australian Div. 1977–79, State Pres. of S Australia Div. 1985–87; mem. Fed. Exec. of Liberal Party 1985–87, 1990–2006; Senator for S Australia 1981–2006; shadow portfolios in opposition include Foreign Affairs –1993, Defence 1993–94, Public Admin 1993–94, Educ., Science, Tech. 1994–96, Leader of Opposition in Senate 1993–96, Leader of Govt in Senate 1996–2006; Fed. Minister for Environment 1996–98, for Environment and Heritage 1998–2001, of Defence 2001–06; Perm. Rep. to UN, New York 2006–; mem. Law Soc. of S Australia. *Leisure interests:* law reform, Australian and Asian history, legal and environmental educ., the arts. *Address:* Office of the Permanent Representative of Australia to the United Nations, 150 East 42nd Street, 33rd Floor, New York, NY 10017, USA (office). *Telephone:* (212) 351-6600 (office). *Fax:* (212) 351-6610 (office). *E-mail:* australia@un.int (office). *Website:* www.australiaun.org (office).

HILL, Rodney, MA, PhD, ScD, FRS; British professor of mechanics of solids (retd); b. 11 June 1921, Leeds; s. of Harold H. Hill; m. Jeanne K. Wickens 1946 (died 2003); one d.; ed Leeds Grammar School and Pembroke Coll., Cambridge; Armament Research Dept 1943–46; Cavendish Lab. Cambridge 1946–48; British Iron and Steel Research Asscn 1948–50; Research Fellow, Univ. of Bristol 1950–53, Reader 1953; Prof. of Applied Math., Univ. of Nottingham 1953–62; Professorial Research Fellow 1962–63; Berkeley Bye-Fellow, Gonville and Caius Coll. Cambridge 1963–69, Fellow 1972–88, Life Fellow 1988–; Reader, Univ. of Cambridge 1969–72, Prof. of Mechanics of Solids 1972–79; Hon. DSc (Manchester) 1976, (Bath) 1978; Von Karman Medal, American Soc. of Civil Engineers 1978, Gold Medal and Int. Modesto Panetti Prize, Turin Acad. of Sciences 1988, Royal Medal, The Royal Soc., London 1993. *Publications:* Principles of Dynamics 1964, Mathematical Theory of Plasticity 1950. *Leisure interests:* field botany and mycology, pianoforte, chess, rockery gardening. *Address:* Gonville and Caius College, Cambridge, CB2 1TA, England.

HILL, Susan Elizabeth, BA, FRSL; British writer and playwright; b. 5 Feb. 1942; d. of the late R. H. Hill and Doris Hill; m. Prof. Stanley W. Wells 1975; two d. (and one d. deceased); ed grammar schools in Scarborough and Coventry and King's Coll. London; literary critic, various journals 1963–; numerous plays for BBC 1970–; Fellow, King's Coll. London 1978; presenter, Bookshelf, BBC Radio 1986–87; Founder and Publr Long Barn Books 1996–. *Publications:* The Enclosure 1961, Do Me a Favour 1963, Gentleman and Ladies 1969, A Change for the Better 1969, I'm the King of the Castle 1970, The Albatross 1971, Strange Meeting 1971, The Bird of the Night 1972, A Bit of Singing and Dancing 1973, In the Springtime of the Year 1974, The Cold Country and Other Plays for Radio 1975, The Ramshackle Company (play) 1981, The Magic Apple Tree 1982, The Woman in Black 1983 (stage version 1989), One Night at a Time (for children) 1984, Through the Kitchen Window 1984, Through the Garden Gate 1986, Mother's Magic (for children) 1986, The Lighting of the Lamps 1987, Lanterns Across the Snow 1987, Shakespeare Country 1987, The Spirit of the Cotswolds 1988, Can it be True? (for children) 1988, Family (autobiog.) 1989, Susie's Shoes (for children) 1989, Stories from Codling Village (for children) 1990, I've Forgotten Edward (for children) 1990, I Won't Go There Again (for children) 1990, Pirate Poll (for children) 1991, The Glass Angels 1991, Beware! Beware! 1993, King of Kings 1993, Reflections from a Garden (with Rory Stuart) 1995, Contemporary Women's Short Stories 1995 (Ed., with Rory Stuart), Listening to the Orchestra (short stories) 1996, The Second Penguin Book of Women's Short Stories 1997, The Service of Clouds 1998, The Boy Who Taught the Beekeeper to Read and Other Stories 2003, The Various Haunts of Men 2004, The Pure in Heart 2005, The Risk of Darkness 2006, The Man in the Picture 2007, Desperate Diary of a Country Housewife (non-fiction) 2007, The Battle for Gullywith (for children) 2008, The Beacon 2008, The Man in the Picture 2008, The Vows of Silence 2008. *Leisure interests:* walking in the English countryside, friends, reading, broadcasting. *Address:* Longmoor Farmhouse, Ebrington, Chipping Campden, Glos., GL55 6NW, England (home). *Telephone:* (1386) 593352 (home). *Fax:* (1386) 593443 (home). *E-mail:* susan@susan-hill.com (home). *Website:* www.susan-hill.com.

HILL, Terrell Leslie, PhD; American biophysicist, chemist and academic; *Professor Emeritus, University of California, Santa Cruz;* b. 19 Dec. 1917, Oakland, Calif.; s. of George Leslie Hill and Ollie Moreland Hill; m. Laura Etta Gano 1942; one s. two d.; ed Univ. of California, Berkeley and Harvard Univ.; Instructor in Chem., Western Reserve Univ. 1942–44; Research Assoc., Radiation Lab., Univ. of Calif., Berkeley 1944–45; Research Assoc. in Chem., then Asst Prof. of Chem., Univ. of Rochester 1945–49; Chemist, US Naval Medical Research Inst. 1949–57; Prof. of Chem., Univ. of Oregon 1957–67; Prof. of Chem., Univ. of Calif., Santa Cruz 1967–71, Vice-Chancellor, Sciences 1968–69, Adjunct Prof. of Chem. 1977–89, Prof. Emer. 1989–; Sr Research Chemist, NIH 1971–88, Scientist Emer. 1988–; mem. NAS, ACS, Biophysical Soc., American Civil Liberties Union, Nat. Asscn for Advancement of Colored People, etc.; Guggenheim Fellow, Yale 1952–53; Sloan Foundation Fellow 1958–62; Arthur S. Flemming Award, US Govt 1954, Distinguished Civilian Service Award, USN 1955, Award of Washington Acad. of Sciences 1956, ACS Kendall Award 1969, Superior Service Award, US Public Health Service 1981, Distinguished Service Award, Univ. of Oregon 1983. *Publications:* Statistical Mechanics 1956, Statistical Thermodynamics 1960, Thermodynamics of Small Systems Vol. I 1963, Vol. II 1964, Matter and Equilibrium 1965, Thermodynamics for Chemists and Biologists 1968, Free Energy Transduction in Biology 1977, Cooperativity Theory in Biochemistry 1985, Linear Aggregation Theory in Cell Biology 1987, Free Energy Transduction and Biochemical Cycle Kinetics 1989; also 260 research papers. *Leisure interests:* reading, walking, music. *Address:* 3400 Paul Sweet Road, Apt C220, Santa Cruz, CA 95065, USA (home).

HILLE, Bertil, PhD; American physiologist, neurobiologist and academic; *Professor of Physiology and Biophysics, School of Medicine, University of Washington;* ed Yale Univ. and The Rockefeller Univ.; Asst Prof., Dept of Physiology and Biophysics, Univ. of Washington School of Medicine 1968–71, Assoc. Prof. 1971–74, Prof. 1974–, Head of Section for Neuronal Signalling Mechanisms 2001–; mem. NAS 1986–, American Asscn for the Advancement of Science, Biophysical Soc., Physiological Soc., Soc. for Neuroscience; Fellow, American Acad. of Arts and Sciences 1998–, Acad. of Medicine 2002–; Louisa Gross Horwitz Prize for Biology or Biochemistry, Columbia Univ. (jtly) 1996, Albert Lasker Award for Basic Medical Research (jtly) 1999, Gairdner Int. Award, Gairdner Foundation (Canada) (jtly) 2001. *Publications:* Ionic Channels of Excitable Membranes 2001; more than 50 publs in scientific journals on cell signalling by ion channels, neurotransmitters and hormones acting through G-protein coupled receptors and intracellular calcium. *Address:* Department of Physiology and Biophysics, University of Washington School of Medicine, G-424 HSB, Box 357290, Seattle, WA 98195-7290, USA (office). *Telephone:* (206) 543-8639 (office). *Fax:* (206)-685-0619 (office). *E-mail:* hille@u.washington.edu (office). *Website:* depts.washington.edu/mcb (office).

HILLEL, Shlomo; Israeli politician; *President, The Society for the Preservation of Heritage Sites in Israel;* b. (Selim Hillel), 1923, Baghdad, Iraq; s. of Aharom Hillel and Hanini Hillel; m. Tmima Rosner 1952; one s. one d.; ed Herzliah High School, Tel-Aviv and Hebrew Univ., Jerusalem; mem. Ma'agan Michael Kibbutz 1942–58; Jewish Agency for Palestine—mission to countries in Middle East 1946–48, 1949–51; Israel Defence Forces 1948–49; Prime Minister's Office 1952–53; mem. of Knesset 1953–59, 1974–; Amb. to Guinea 1959–61, to Ivory Coast, Dahomey, Upper Volta and Niger 1961–63; mem. Perm. Mission to UN with rank of Minister 1964–67; Asst Dir-Gen. Ministry of Foreign Affairs 1967–69; Minister of Police 1969–77; Co-ordinator of political contacts with Arab leadership in administered territories 1970–77; Minister of the Interior June–Oct. 1974, 1996–97; Chair. Ministerial Cttee for Social Welfare 1974–77, Cttee of the Interior and Environment 1977–81, of Foreign Affairs and Defence 1981–84; Perm. Observer to Council of Europe 1977–84; Speaker of the Knesset 1984–88; Chair. Sephardi Fed. 1976–; World Chair. Keren Hayesod United Israel Appeal 1989–98; Pres. Soc. for Preservation of Historical Sites in Israel 1996–; Chair. Zalman Shazar Center, Jerusalem; Commdr Nat. Order of Repubs of Ivory Coast, Upper Volta and Dahomey; Dr hc (Hebrew Univ.) 1995, (Ben-Gurion Univ.) 1997, (Tel-Aviv) 1998; Israel Prize for Life Achievement 1998. *Publication:* Operation Babylon 1988. *Leisure interests:* tennis, gardening. *Address:* 4 Shalom Aleichem str., Ra'anana 43368, Israel (home). *Telephone:* 3-5057179 (office); 9-7741789 (home). *Fax:* 3-5034828 (office); 9-7741788 (home). *E-mail:* s-t-h@zahav.net.il (home).

HILLER, István, PhD; Hungarian academic and politician; *Minister of Education and Culture;* b. 7 May 1964, Sopron; m. Julianna Hillerné Farkas; two c.; ed Eötvös Loránd Univ., Karls-Ruprecht Univ., Germany; Asst Lecturer, Eötvös Loránd Univ. 1989–94, Sr Lecturer 1994–2001, Prof. 2001–02; Founding mem. Hungarian Socialist Party (MSZP) 1989, Deputy Pres. MSZP Nat. Bd 1998–, Vice-Pres. MSZP 2003–04, Pres. 2005–; mem. Parl. 2002–; Parl. State Sec., Ministry of Educ. 2002–03; Minister of Cultural Heritage 2003–05, of Educ. and Culture 2006–; Researcher, Historical Inst., Univ. of Vienna 1995, 1997; Chevalier, Ordre des Arts et des Lettres, Cavaliere di Gran Croce (Italy), Große Verdienstkreuz (Germany); Professor of the Year, Eötvös Loránd Univ. 1999. *Address:* Ministry of Education and Culture, 1055 Budapest, Szalay u. 10–14, Hungary (office). *Telephone:* (1) 302-0600 (office). *Fax:* (1) 302-2002 (office). *E-mail:* info@okm.gov.hu (office). *Website:* www.okm.gov.hu (office).

HILLER, Susan, MA; American/British artist; b. 7 March 1940, New York City; d. of Paul Hiller and Florence Ehrich; m. David Coxhead 1962; one s.; ed Smith Coll. and Tulane Univ.; Residency, Karolyi Foundation, Vence, France 1968, Ministère des Beaux Arts, Morocco 1969; moved to UK 1969; Lecturer, Slade School of Art, London 1982–91; Artist-in-Residence, Univ. of Sussex 1975; Distinguished Visiting Prof. of Fine Art, California State Univ., Long Beach 1988; Visiting Arts Council Chair., UCLA 1991, 1992; Prof. of Art, Dept of Fine and Applied Arts, Univ. of Ulster, Belfast 1986–91; Baltic Prof. of Fine Art, Univ. of Newcastle 1999–2002; Residency, Couvent des Recollets, Paris 2005; works in public collections, including Tate Gallery, London, Ludwig Museum, Cologne, Israel Museum, Jerusalem, Arts Council of GB, Henie-Onstad Kunstsenter, Oslo, Tokyo Metropolitan Museum of Photography, Victoria & Albert Museum, London, Seibu Saison Corpn, Japan, Nat. Gallery of Art of S Australia, Adelaide, Henry Moore Sculpture Collection, Leeds City Museum and Art Gallery, Imperial War Museum, London, Contemporary Art Soc., London, Museum of London, MAG Collection, Ferens Museum and Art Gallery, Hull, John Creasy Collection, Salisbury, UK; Hon. Fellow, Dartington Coll. of Arts 1998; Gulbenkian Foundation Visual Artist's Award 1976, 1977, Greater London Arts Asscn Bursary 1981, Nat. Foundation for the Arts Fellowship (USA) 1982, Visual Arts Board Travelling Fellowship (Australia) 1982, Guggenheim Fellowship 1998, DAAD Fellowship, Berlin 2002, Kulturstiftung des Bundes, Halle, Germany 2003. *Art works include:* Hand Grenades 1969–72, Dedicated to the Unknown Artists 1972–76, Measure by Measure 1973–, Sisters of Menon 1972, Dream Mapping 1974, Monument 1980–81, Midnight Self Portraits 1980–89, Inside a Cave Home 1983, Belshazzar's Feast 1983–84, Magic Lantern 1987, The Secrets of Sunset Beach 1987, An Entertainment 1990–91, From the Freud Museum 1991–97, Wild Talents

1997, Split Hairs: The Art of Alfie West 1998, Psi Girls 1999, Witness 2000, What every gardener knows 2003, Clinic 2004, The J Street Project: Film Index 2002–05, Psychic Archaeology 2005. *Publications include:* The Myth of Primitivism (ed.) 1991, After the Freud Museum 1995, Dreams – Visions of the Night (co-author) 1996, Thinking about Art: Conversations wth Susan Hiller 1996, Dream Machines 1999, Witness 2000, Split Hairs: The Art of Alfie West (with David Coxhead) 2004. *Address:* 83 Loudoun Road, London, NW8 0DQ, England (office). *Telephone:* (20) 7372-0438 (office). *E-mail:* studioassist@aol .com (office); Aceposible@aol.com (home). *Website:* www.susanhiller.org (office).

HILLIER, Bevis, FRSA; British writer and editor; b. 28 March 1940; s. of the late Jack Ronald Hillier and of Mary Louise Palmer; ed Reigate Grammar School and Magdalen Coll., Oxford; Editorial Staff, The Times 1963–68, Antiques Corresp. 1970–84, Deputy Literary Ed. 1981–84; Ed. British Museum Soc. Bulletin 1968–70; Guest Curator, Minn. Inst. of Arts 1971; Ed. The Connoisseur 1973–76; Assoc. Ed., Los Angeles Times 1984–88; Ed. Sotheby's Preview 1990–93. *Publications:* Master Potters of the Industrial Revolution: The Turners of Lane End 1965, Pottery and Porcelain 1700–1914 1968, Art Deco of the 1920s and the 1930s 1968, Posters 1969, Cartoons and Caricatures 1970, The World of Art Deco 1971, 100 Years of Posters 1972, Austerity-Binge 1975, The New Antiques 1977, Greetings from Christmas Past 1982, The Style of the Century 1900–1980 1983, John Betjeman: A Life in Pictures 1984, Young Betjeman 1988, Early English Porcelain 1992, Art Deco Style, A Tonic to the Nation: The Festival of Britain (co-ed.) 1951 1976, Betjeman: The Bonus of Laughter 2004. *Leisure interests:* piano, collecting, awarding marks out of ten for suburban front gardens. *Address:* The Maggie Noach Literary Agency, Unit 4, 246 Acklam Road, London, W10 5YG, England (office). *Telephone:* (20) 8748-2926 (office). *E-mail:* info@mnla.co.uk (office). *Website:* www.mnla.co.uk (office).

HILLIER, Gen. Rick J., BSc; Canadian army officer; *Chief of Defence Staff;* b. Newfoundland and Labrador; m.; two s.; ed Memorial Univ. of Newfoundland; posted to 8th Canadian Hussars 1976, Royal Canadian Dragoons 1979; staff officer, Army Headquarters, Montreal, Nat. Defence Headquarters, Ottawa; Canadian Deputy Commdg Gen. 1998–2000; Commdr Multinational Div. (Southwest), Bosnia-Herzegovina; Asst Chief of the Land Staff –2003, Chief of the Land Staff 2003–05, Chief of Defence Staff 2005–; Commdr Int. Security Assistance Force, Kabul, Afghanistan Feb.–Aug. 2004. *Address:* National Defence Headquarters, Major-General George R. Pearkes Building, 101 Colonel By Drive, Ottawa, ON K1A 0K2, Canada (office). *Telephone:* (613) 996-3100 (office). *Fax:* (613) 995-8189 (office). *Website:* www.forces.gc.ca (office).

HILLS, Carla Anderson, AB, LLD; American lawyer and fmr government official; *Chairman and CEO, Hills and Company;* b. 3 Jan. 1934, Los Angeles; d. of Carl Anderson and Edith Anderson (née Hume); m. Roderick Maltman Hills 1958; one s. three d.; ed Stanford Univ., Calif., St Hilda's Coll., Oxford, UK, Yale Law School; Asst US Attorney, Civil Div., LA, Calif. 1958–61; Pnr, Munger, Tolles, Hills & Rickershauser (law firm) 1962–74; Adjunct Prof., School of Law, UCLA 1972; Asst Attorney-Gen. Civil Div., US Dept of Justice 1974–75; Sec. of Housing and Urban Devt 1975–77; Pnr, Latham, Watkins & Hills (law firm) 1978–86, Weil, Gotshal and Manges, Washington 1986–88, Mudge Rose Gutherie Alexander & Ferdon 1994; Chair., CEO Hills & Co. (consulting firm) 1993–; US Trade Rep., Exec. Office of the Pres. 1989–93; Co-Chair. Alliance to Save Energy 1977–89; Vice-Chair. Bar of Supreme Court of the US, Calif. State and DC Bars, Council Section of Anti-trust Law, ABA 1974, American Law Inst. 1974–, Fed. Bar Asscn (LA Chapter, Pres. 1963), Women Lawyers Asscn (Pres. 1964), LA Co. Bar Asscn, Chair. of various cttees including Standing Cttee on Discipline, Calif. 1970–74; mem. Bd Dirs American Int. Group (AIG), Lucent Technologies Inc., Bechtel Enterprises, Trust Co. of the West Group Inc., AOL Time-Warner Inc. 1993–2006, Chevron Corp. 1993–; mem. Carnegie Comm. on the Future of Public Broadcasting 1977–78, Sloan Comm. on Govt and Higher Educ. 1977–79, Advisory Cttee Woodrow Wilson School of Public and Int. Affairs 1977–80, Yale Univ. Council 1977–80, Fed. Accounting Standards Advisory Council 1978–80, Trilateral Comm. 1977–82, 1993–, American Cttee on East–West Accord 1977–79, Int. Foundation for Cultural Cooperation and Devt 1977, Editorial Bd, Nat. Law Journal 1978, Calif. Gov.'s Council of Econ. Policy Advisers 1993–, Council on Foreign Relations 1993–; Co-Chair. Int. Advisory Bd, Center for Strategic and Int. Studies; Chair. Nat. Cttee on US-China Relations 1993–; Contributing Ed., Legal Times 1978–88; Fellow, American Bar Foundation 1975; Trustee, Pomona Coll. 1974–79, Norton Simon Museum of Art 1976–80, Brookings Inst. 1977, Univ. of Southern Calif. 1977–79; Advisor, Annenberg School of Communications, Univ. of Southern Calif. 1977–78; Chair. Urban Inst. 1983; Dir Time Warner 1993–2006, AIG –2006; Vice-Chair. Interamerican Dialogue 1997–; mem. Bd Trustees Asia Soc., Inst. for Int. Econs, Americas Soc.; Dr hc (Pepperdine Univ.) 1975, (Washington Univ., St Louis, Mo.) 1977, (Mills Coll., Calif.) 1977, (Lake Forest Coll.) 1978, (Williams Coll.), (Notre Dame Univ.), (Wabash Coll.). *Publications:* Federal Civil Practice (co-author) 1961, Antitrust Adviser (ed. and co-author) 1971. *Leisure interest:* tennis. *Address:* Hills & Company, 1120 20th Street, NW, Suite 200 North, Washington, DC 20036 (office); 3125 Chain Bridge Road, NW, Washington, DC 20016, USA (home). *Telephone:* (202) 822-4700 (office). *Fax:* (202) 822-4710 (office). *E-mail:* CAHills@hillsandco.com (office). *Website:* www.hillsandco.com (office).

HILLY, Francis Billy; Solomon Islands politician; b. 1947; ed Univ. of S Pacific; joined pre-independence govt working under Solomon Mamaloni; later worked for a pvt. co. in Gizo; mem. Parl. 1976–84, 1993–; fmr Premier of Western Prov.; Prime Minister of the Solomon Islands 1993–94. *Address:* c/o Office of the Prime Minister, Legakiki Ridge, Honiara, Solomon Islands.

HILMER, Frederick G., AO, LLB, LLM, MBA; Australian university administrator and academic; *Vice-Chancellor and President, University of New South Wales;* ed Sydney Univ., Univ. of Pennsylvania, Wharton School of Finance, USA; mem. Higher Educ. Council 1987–93; Dean and Prof. of Man., Australian Grad. School of Man., Univ. of New South Wales 1989–98; CEO John Fairfax Holdings Ltd 1998–2005; Vice-Chancellor and Pres. Univ. of New South Wales 2006–; fmr Chair. Commonwealth Higher Educ. Council; Chair. Nat. Competition Policy Review Cttee 1992–93; fmr Joseph Wharton Fellow, Wharton School of Finance; John Storey Medal, Australian Inst. of Man. 1991. *Publications:* numerous books and articles in the fields of gen. man., industrial relations, and competition law and policy. *Address:* Office of the Vice-Chancellor and President, University of New South Wales, Sydney, NSW 2052, Australia (office). *Telephone:* (2) 9385-2885 (office). *Fax:* (2) 9385-1949 (office). *Website:* www.unsw.edu.au (office).

HILSKÝ, Martin, PhD; Czech translator and academic; *Professor of English Literature, Charles University;* b. 8 April 1943, Prague; s. of Václav Hilský and Vlasta Hilská; m. Kateřina Hilská; two s. one d.; ed Charles Univ., Prague; Asst Prof., Charles Univ., Prague 1965, Prof. of English Literature 1993–, Dir Inst. of English 1988–98; Jr Research Fellow, Univ. of Oxford 1968–69; Hon. OBE; IREX grant, USA 1985, Jungmann's Translation Prize 1997, Tom Stoppard Award 2003. *Achievements:* Shakespeare translations performed throughout the Czech Repub. *Publications:* Contemporary English Novel (Rector's Prize) 1992, Modernists 1995; over 80 papers on English and American literature; translations of works by J. M. Synge, D. H. Lawrence, T. S. Eliot, J. Goldman and Shakespeare, 23 plays (including the Sonnets). *Leisure interests:* literature, theatre, arts, good wine, skiing, jogging, gardening. *Address:* Room 105, Department of English and American Studies, Faculty of Philosophy and Arts, Charles University, Jana Palacha 2, 116 38 Prague (office); Tychonova 10, 160 00 Prague 6, Czech Republic (home). *Telephone:* (2) 21619341 (office); (2) 24315722 (home). *E-mail:* martin.hilsky@ ff.cuni.cz (office); hilsky@volny.cz (home).

HILSUM, Cyril, CBE, PhD, FRS, FREng, FIEE, FIEEE; British research scientist and academic; *Visiting Professor, University College London;* b. 17 May 1925, London; s. of Ben Hilsum and Ada Hilsum; m. Betty Hilsum 1947 (died 1987); one d. (one d. deceased); ed Raines School, London and Univ. Coll., London; HQ Admiralty 1945–47; Admiralty Research Lab., Teddington 1947–50; Services Electronics Research Lab., Baldock 1950–64; Royal Signals and Radar Establishments, Malvern 1964–83; Visiting Prof., Univ. Coll., London 1988–; Chief Scientist, Gen. Electric Co. (GEC) Research Labs 1983–85; Dir of Research, GEC PLC 1985–92, Corp. Research Adviser 1992–; Pres. Inst. of Physics 1988–90; mem. Science and Eng Research Council 1984–88; Hon. FInstP; Hon. DEng (Sheffield) 1992, (Nottingham Trent) 1998; recipient of several awards. *Publications:* Semiconducting III-V Compounds 1961; over 100 scientific and tech. papers. *Leisure interests:* tennis, chess, ballroom dancing. *Address:* 12 Eastglade, Moss Lane, Pinner, Middx, HA5 3AN, England (home). *Telephone:* (20) 8866-8323 (home). *E-mail:* cyrilhilsum@aol .com (home).

HILSUM, Lindsey, BA; British journalist; *International Editor, Channel 4 News (UK);* b. 3 Aug. 1958; d. of Cyril Hilsum and Betty Hilsum; ed Univ. of Exeter; joined Oxfam working in Guatemala and Haiti 1979; began journalism career freelance reporting from Mexico and the Caribbean 1980; worked for three years as Information Officer for UNICEF, Nairobi; covered events in E Africa for BBC and The Guardian newspaper 1986–89; Sr Producer, BBC World Service 1990–93, reported from Rwanda, Middle East, Mexico, S Africa, S Pacific; Diplomatic Corresp., Channel 4 News 1996–2003, Int. Ed. 2003–; China Corresp. 2006–08; regular contrib. to New Statesman, Granta, Observer; Amnesty Int. Press Award 1997, TV News Award 2004, Royal Television Soc. Specialist Journalist of the Year 2003, Emmy Award for coverage of fall of Saddam Hussein (jtly) 2004, Royal Television Soc. TV Journalist of the Year Award 2005, James Cameron Award 2005, Women in Film and Television Award 2005. *Leisure interest:* bird watching, horse riding. *Address:* Channel 4 News, ITN, 200 Grays Inn Road, London, WC1X 8XZ, England (office). *Telephone:* (20) 7430-4606 (office). *Fax:* (20) 7430-4607 (office). *E-mail:* c4foreign@itn.co.uk (office). *Website:* www.channel4.com/ news (office).

HILTON, Janet, ARMCM, FRCM; British clarinettist; *Head of Woodwind, Royal College of Music;* b. 1 Jan. 1945, Liverpool; d. of H. Hilton and E. Hilton; m. David Richardson 1968; two s. (one deceased) one d.; ed Belvedere School, Liverpool, Royal Northern Coll. of Music, Vienna Konservatorium; BBC concerto debut 1963; appearances as clarinet soloist with major British orchestras including Royal Liverpool Philharmonic, Scottish Nat., Scottish Chamber, City of Birmingham Symphony Orchestra (CBSO), Bournemouth Symphony, Bournemouth Sinfonietta, City of London Sinfonia, BBC Scottish and Welsh Symphony, BBC Philharmonic; guest at Edinburgh, Aldeburgh, Bath, Cheltenham, City of London Festivals, Henry Wood Promenade concerts; appearances throughout Europe and N America; Prin. Clarinet Scottish Chamber Orchestra 1974–80, Kent Opera 1984–88; teacher Royal Scottish Acad. of Music and Drama 1974–80, Royal Northern Coll. of Music 1983–87; Head of Woodwind, Birmingham Conservatoire 1992–; Head of Woodwind, RCM, London 1998–; Prof., Univ. of Cen. England 1993; Dir Camerata Wind Soloists; several recordings for Chandos, including all Weber's music for clarinet with the CBSO, Lindsay Quartet and Keith Swallow, the Neilsen and Copland Concertos with the Scottish Nat. Orchestra, Stanford Clarinet Concerto with Ulster Orchestra, Mozart Clarinet Quintet with the Lindsay Quartet 1998; dedicatee of works by Iain Hamilton, John McCabe, Edward Harper, Elizabeth Maconchy, Alun Hoddinott, Malcolm Arnold. *Recordings:* works by McCabe, Harper, Maconchy and Hoddinott concertos with BBC Scottish Symphony Orchestra on Clarinet

Classics 2001. *Leisure interests:* cookery, reading. *Address:* Royal College of Music, Prince Consort Road, London, SW7 2BS (office); 56B Belsize Park Gardens, London, NW3 4ND, England (home). *Telephone:* (20) 7589-3643 (office); (20) 7586-7374 (home). *E-mail:* jhilton@rcm.ac.uk (office). *Website:* www.impulse-music.co.uk/hilton.htm (home).

HIMMELFARB, Gertrude, PhD, FBA, FRHistS; American historian, academic and writer; *Professor Emerita, City University of New York;* b. 8 Aug. 1922, New York, NY; d. of Max Himmelfarb and Bertha Himmelfarb (née Lerner); m. Irving Kristol 1942; one s. one d.; ed Brooklyn Coll., CUNY, Univ. of Chicago, Girton Coll., Cambridge; Distinguished Prof. of History, Graduate School, CUNY 1965–88, Prof. Emer. 1988–; Fellow, American Philosophical Soc., American Acad. of Arts and Sciences, Royal Historical Soc., etc.; many public and professional appts.; Guggenheim Fellow 1955–56, 1957–58; Nat. Endowment for the Humanities Fellowship 1968–69, American Council of Learned Socs. Fellowship 1972–73, Woodrow Wilson Int. Center Fellowship 1976–77, Rockefeller Foundation, Humanities Fellowship 1980–81, and other fellowships; numerous hon. degrees including Hon. DHumLitt (Boston) 1987, (Yale) 1990; Hon. DLitt (Smith Coll.) 1977; Rockefeller Foundation Award 1962–63, Nat. Humanities Medal 2004. *Publications:* Lord Acton: A Study in Conscience and Politics 1952, Darwin and the Darwinian Revolution 1959, Victorian Minds 1968, On Liberty and Liberalism: The Case of John Stuart Mill 1975, The Idea of Poverty 1984, Marriage and Morals Among the Victorians 1986, The New History and the Old 1987, Poverty and Compassion: The Moral Imagination of the Late Victorians 1991, On Looking Into the Abyss: Untimely Thoughts on Culture and Society 1994, The De-Moralization of Society from Victorian Virtues to Modern Values 1995, One Nation, Two Cultures 1999, The Road to Modernity: The British, French and American Enlightenments 2004, The Moral Imagination 2006. *Address:* 2510 Virginia Avenue, NW, Washington, DC 20037-1902, USA (home).

HINAULT, Bernard; French fmr professional cyclist; b. 14 Nov. 1954, Yffiniac, Côtes du Nord; s. of Joseph and Lucie (Guernion) Hinault; m. Martine Lessard 1974; two s.; competitive cycling début 1971; French jr champion 1972; French champion 1978; world champion 1980, third 1981; winner, Tour de France 1978, 1979, 1981, 1982, 1985, Tour d'Italie 1980, 1982, 1985, Tour d'Espagne 1978, 1983, Grand Prix des Nations 1978, 1982, 1984, Luis Puig Trophy 1986, Coors Classic, USA 1986 and many other int. racing events; retd from racing 1986; Technical Adviser, External Relations Dir Tour de France 1986–; Sports Dir French team 1988–; Dir-Gen. Ouest Levure 1992–; Chevalier, Légion d'honneur, Ordre Nat. du Mérite. *Publications:* Moi, Bernard Hinault (with others) 1979, Le Pentolou des souvenirs, Cyclisme sur route, technique, tactique, entraînement, Vélo tout terrain, découverte, technique et entraînement. *Address:* c/o Fédération française de cyclisme, Bâtiment Jean Monet, 5 rue de Rome, 93561 Rosny-sous-Bois, cedex (office); Ouest Levure, 7 rue de la Sauvaie, 21 Sud-est, 35000 Rennes, France.

HINCH, Edward John, PhD, FRS; British academic; *Professor of Fluid Mechanics, University of Cambridge;* b. 4 March 1947, Peterborough; s. of Joseph Edward Hinch and Mary Grace Hinch (née Chandler); m. Christine Bridges 1969; one s. one d.; ed Univ. of Cambridge; Fellow, Trinity Coll., Cambridge 1971–; Asst Lecturer, Univ. of Cambridge 1972–75, Lecturer 1975–94, Reader in Fluid Mechanics 1994–98, Prof. 1998–; Chevalier, Ordre nat. du Mérite 1997. *Publications:* Perturbation Methods 1991; various papers in learned journals on fluid mechanics and its application. *Address:* Trinity College, Cambridge, CB2 1TQ, England. *Telephone:* (1223) 338427. *Fax:* (1223) 338564. *E-mail:* e.j.hinch@damtp.cam.ac.uk (office).

HINCHCLIFFE, Peter Robert Mossom, CVO, CMG, MA; British diplomatist (retd) and academic; *Honorary Fellow, University of Edinburgh;* b. 9 April 1937, Mahableshwar, India; s. of Peter Hinchcliffe and Jeannie Hinchcliffe; m. Archbold Harriet Siddall 1965; three d.; ed Radley Coll., Trinity Coll., Dublin; British Army 1955–57; HMOCS, Aden Protectorate 1961–67; First Sec., FCO 1969–71; mem. UK Mission to UN 1971–74; Head of Chancery, British Embassy, Kuwait 1974–76, FCO 1976–78, Deputy High Commr, Dar es Salaam 1978–81, Consul Gen., Dubai 1981–85; Head of Information Dept, FCO 1985–87, Amb. to Kuwait 1987–90; High Commr in Zambia 1990–93; Amb. to Jordan 1993–97; Chair. Hutton and Paxton Community Council 2001–07; Adjunct Fellow, Curtin Univ., Perth, WA 2001–04; Sr Reseach Fellow, Queens Univ. Belfast 1997–2002; Hon. Fellow, Univ. of Edinburgh 1997–. *Publications:* Time to Kill Sparrows (anthology of diplomatic verse) 1999, History of Conflicts in the Middle East Since 1945, (2nd edn) 2003, Without Glory in Arabia: End of British Rule in Aden 1960–67 2006, Jordan: A Hashemite Legacy (2nd edn) 2009. *Leisure interests:* golf, tennis, cricket, hill walking, writing poetry, blogging. *Address:* Old Bakery, Willis Wynd, Duns, TD113AD, England (home). *Telephone:* (1361) 883315 (home). *E-mail:* phinchcliffe1@aol.com (home). *Website:* www.huttonian.blogspot.com (office).

HINCK, Walter, DPhil; German academic; *Professor of Modern German Language and Literature, University of Cologne;* b. 8 March 1922, Selsingen; s. of Johann Hinck and Anna Hinck (née Steffens); m. Sigrid Graupe 1957; one d.; ed Univ. of Göttingen; Prof. of Modern German Language and Literature, Literary Criticism, Univ. of Cologne 1964–; mem. Rheinisch-Westfälischen Akad. der Wissenschaften 1974– (Vice-Pres. 1986–87), Sektion Bundesrepublik Deutschland des Internationalen PEN-Clubs 1986–; Kasseler Literaturpreis 1992, Preis der Frankfurter Anthologie 2003. *Publications:* Die Dramaturgie des späten Brecht 1959, Das deutsche Lustspiel des 17. und 18. Jahrhunderts und die italienische Komödie 1965, Die deutsche Ballade von Bürger bis Brecht 1968, Das moderne Drama in Deutschland 1973, Von Heine zu Brecht—Lyrik im Geschichtsprozess 1978, Goethe—Mann des Theaters 1982, Germanistik als Literaturkritik 1983, Heinrich Böll: Ausgewählte Erzählungen 1984, Das Gedicht als Spiegel der Dichter 1985, Theater der Hoffnung, Von der Aufklärung bis zur Gegenwart 1988, Die Wunde Deutschland, Heinrich Heines Dichtung 1990, Walter Jens. Un homme de lettres 1993, Magie und Tagtraum. Das Selbstbild des Dichters in der deutschen Lyrik 1994, Geschichtsdichtung 1995, Im Wechsel der Zeiten: Leben und Literatur (autobiog.) 1998, Jahrhundertchronik, Deutsche Erzählungen des 20. Jahrhunderts 2000, Stationen der deutschen Lyrik von Luther bis in die Gegenwart. 100 Gedichte mit Interpretation 2000, Literatur als Gegenspiel. Essays zur deutschen Literatur von Luther bis Böll 2001, Selbstannäherungen. Autobiographien im 20. Jahrhundert von Elias Canetti bis Marcel Reich-Ranicki 2004, Romanchronik des 20. Jahrhunderts 2006, Wahmehmung des Lebens: Vom Schreiben im Nebenberuf 2008. *Address:* Am Hammergraben 13/15, 51503 Rösrath, (Hoffnungsthal) bei, Cologne, Germany. *Telephone:* (1) 22055147.

HINDE, Robert Aubrey, CBE, BSc, MA, DPhil, ScD, FRS; British biologist, psychologist and academic; *Fellow, St John's College, University of Cambridge;* b. 26 Oct. 1923, Norwich; s. of Ernest B. Hinde and Isabella Hinde; m. 1st Hester Cecily Coutts (divorced); two s. two d.; m. 2nd Joan Stevenson 1971; two d.; ed Oundle School, St John's Coll., Cambridge, Balliol Coll., Oxford; pilot, RAF Coastal Command 1940–45; Curator, Ornithological Field Station, Dept of Zoology, Univ. of Cambridge 1950–64, Fellow, St John's Coll., Cambridge 1951–54, 1958–89, 1994–, Master 1989–94; Royal Soc. Research Prof. 1963–89; Hon. Dir MRC Unit of Devt and Integration of Behaviour 1970–89; Hitchcock Prof., Univ. of California 1979; mem. Academia Europaea 1990; Foreign Hon. mem. AAAS 1974; Hon. Fellow, American Ornithologists' Union 1976; Hon. Foreign Assoc. NAS 1978; Hon. Fellow, Royal Coll. of Psychiatry 1988, British Psychological Soc. 1981, Balliol Coll. Oxford 1986, Trinity Coll., Dublin 1990; Hon. FBA 2002; Hon. ScD (Univ. Libre, Brussels) 1974, (Nanterre) 1978, (Gothenburg) 1991; Dr hc (Stirling) 1991, (Edin.) 1992, (Western Ont.) 1996, (Oxford) 1998; Croonian Lecturer, Royal Soc. 1990, Frink Medal, Zoological Soc. of London 1992, Royal Medal, Royal Soc. 1996, Soc.'s Medal, Asscn for the Study of Animal Behaviour 1997, and numerous other awards. *Publications:* Animal Behaviour: A Synthesis of Ethology and Comparative Psychology 1966, Social Behaviour and its Development in Subhuman Primates 1972, Biological Bases of Human Social Behaviour 1974, Towards Understanding Relationships 1979, Ethology 1982, Individuals, Relationships and Culture 1987, Relationships: A Dialectical Perspective 1997, Why Gods Persist 1999, Why Good is Good 2002, War No More (jtly) 2003; Bird Vocalizations (co-ed.) 1969, Primate Social Behaviour 1983; Short-term Changes in Neural Activity and Behaviour (co-ed.) 1970, Constraints on Learning (co-ed.) 1973, Growing Points in Ethology (co-ed.) 1976, Social Relationships and Cognitive Development (co-ed.) 1985, Relationships Within Families (co-ed.) 1988, Aggression and War: Their Biological and Social Bases (co-ed.) 1988, Education for Peace (co-ed.), Co-operation and Prosocial Behaviour (co-ed.) 1991; The Institution of War (ed.) 1991, War: A Cruel Necessity? (co-ed.) 1994; numerous articles in learned journals. *Leisure interests:* ornithology, reading, walking. *Address:* St John's College, Cambridge, CB2 1TP, England (office). *Telephone:* (1223) 339356 (office). *Fax:* (1223) 337720 (office). *E-mail:* rah15@cam.ac.uk (office). *Website:* www.joh.cam.ac.uk/contact/fellows (office).

HINDE, Thomas (see Chitty, Sir Thomas Wiles).

HINDERY, Leo Joseph, Jr, MBA; American business executive; *Executive-in-Residence, Business School, Columbia University;* b. 31 Oct. 1947, Springfield, Ill.; s. of Leo Joseph Hindery and E. Marie Whitener; m. Deborah Diane Sale 1980; one s.; ed Seattle Univ. and Stanford Business School; U.S. Army 1968–70; Asst Treasurer Utah Int., San Francisco 1971–80; Treas. Natomas Co., San Francisco 1980–82; Exec. Vice-Pres. Finance Jefferies and Co., LA 1982–83; Chief Finance Officer AG Becker Paribas, New York 1983–85; Chief Officer Planning and Finance Chronicle Publishing Co., San Francisco 1985–88; Man. Gen. Pnr Intermedia Partners, San Francisco 1988–97; Pres. TCI Cable Vision 1998–2000; Chair. and CEO Global Crossing Ltd 2000; Chair. The YES Network 2001-04; Chair. InterMedia Advisors, LLP (investment firm); currently Exec.-in-Residence Columbia Business School; fmr Chair. Nat. Cable TV Asscn; mem. Bd of Dirs DMX Inc., NETCOM On-Line Comm. Services Inc., Cable Telecommunications Asscn, C-Span. *Leisure interest:* golf. *Address:* Columbia Business School, 221 Uris, Columbia University, 3022 Broadway, New York, NY 10027, USA (office). *Telephone:* (212) 854-6100 (office). *Fax:* (212) 932-8614 (office). *E-mail:* ml503@columbia.edu (office). *Website:* www0.gsb.columbia.edu (office).

HINDLIP, 6th Baron (cr. 1886); **Charles Henry Allsopp;** British business executive; b. 5 April 1940; s. of the late Baron Hindlip and Cecily Valentine Jane Borwick; m. Fiona Victoria Jean Atherley McGowan 1968; one s. three d.; ed Eton Coll.; served in Coldstream Guards 1959–62; joined Christie's 1962, Gen. Man. New York 1965–70, Chair. 1996–; Dir Christie Manson & Wood 1970–, Deputy Chair. 1985–86, Chair. 1986–96; fmr Chair. Christie's Int. *Leisure interests:* painting, shooting, skiing. *Address:* 32 Maida Avenue, London, W2 1ST; Lydden House, King's Stag, Sturminster Newton, Dorset, DT10 2AU, England.

HINDS, Samuel Archibald Anthony, BSc; Guyanese politician; *Prime Minister;* b. 27 Dec. 1943, Mahaicony, E Coast, Demerara; m. Yvonne Zereder Burnett 1967; three c.; ed Queen's Coll. Georgetown and Univ. of New Brunswick; various positions with Bauxite Co., Linden, Guyana 1967–92; mem. Science and Industry Cttee Nat. Science Research Council 1973–76; fmr Chair. Guyanese Action for Reform and Democracy (GUARD); Prime Minister of Guyana 1992–97, 1997–99, 2001–; also Minister of Public Works and Communication; leader CIVIC (special political movt of business people and execs). *Address:* Office of the Prime Minister, Oranapai Towers, Wights Lane, Georgetown (office); CIVIC, New Garden Street, Georgetown, Guyana. *Telephone:* 227-3101 (office). *Fax:* 226-7573 (office). *E-mail:* pmoffice@sdnp.org.gov.gy (office).

HINDUJA, Gopichand Parmanand; British (b. Indian) business executive; b. 29 Feb. 1940; s. of Parmanand Deepchand Hinduja and Jamuna Parmanand Hinduja; brother of Srichand Hinduja (q.v.); m. Sunita Hinduja; two s. one d.; ed Jai Hind Coll., Mumbai; joined family business 1958; Pres. Hinduja Foundation and Hinduja Group of Cos. 1962–; Head of Hinduja Group Operations in Iran –1978; Chair. of Gurnanank Trust, Tehran; mem. Advisory Council, Hinduja Cambridge Trust 1991, Advisory Cttee Prince's Trust, Duke of Edin.'s Fellowship; patron Balaji Temple, Swaminaryan Hindu Mission, London; charged in connection with an arms bribery case in India Nov. 2002; Hon. LLD (Univ. of Westminster) 1996; Hon. DEcon (Richmond Coll.). *Leisure interests:* Indian music, travel, sailing, yoga. *Address:* Hinduja Group of Companies, New Zealand House, 80 Haymarket, London, SW1Y 4TE, England (office). *Telephone:* (20) 7839-4661 (office). *Fax:* (20) 7839-5992 (office). *E-mail:* gph@hindujagroup.com (office). *Website:* www.hindujagroup.com (office).

HINDUJA, Srichand Parmanand; Indian business executive; b. 28 Nov. 1935; s. of Parmanand Deepchand Hinduja and Jamuna Parmanand Hinduja; brother of Gopichand Hinduja (q.v.); m. Madhu Srichand Hinduja; two d.; ed Nat. Coll., Mumbai, Davar Coll. of Commerce, Mumbai; joined family business; Chair. Hinduja Foundation and Hinduja Group of Cos. 1962–; Global Co-ordinator IndusInd 1962; Pres. IndusInd Int. Fed. 1996; mem. Advisory Council, Dharam Hinduja Indic Research Centres in Columbia, USA and UK, Advisory Council, Hinduja Cambridge Trust, Corpn of Mass. Gen. Hosp., Duke of Edin.'s Award Fellowship; patron Centre of India–US Educ., Asia Soc.; charged in connection with an arms bribery case in India Nov. 2002; Hon. LLD (Univ. of Westminster) 1996; Hon. DEcon (Richmond Coll.) 1997. *Publications:* Indic Research and Contemporary Crisis 1995, Conceptualiser of Series of Paintings Theorama 1995, The Essence of Vedic Marriage For Success and Happiness 1996. *Leisure interests:* tennis, volleyball, cricket, Indian classical music. *Address:* Hinduja Group of Companies, New Zealand House, 80 Haymarket, London, SW1Y 4TE, England (office). *Telephone:* (20) 7839-4661 (office). *Fax:* (20) 7839-5992 (office).

HINE, Air Chief Marshal Sir Patrick, Kt, GCB, GBE, FRAeS, CBIM; British air force officer; b. 14 July 1932, Chandlers Ford, Hants.; s. of Eric Graham Hine and Cecile Grace Hine (née Philippe); m. Jill Adèle Gardner 1956; three s.; ed Sherborne House Preparatory School 1937–41, Peter Symonds School, Winchester 1942–49; fighter pilot and mem. RAF 'Black Arrows' and 'Blue Diamonds' Formation Aerobatic Teams 1957–62; Commdr No. 92 Squadron 1962–64 and 17 Squadron 1970–71, RAF Germany Harrier Force 1974–75; Dir RAF Public Relations 1975–77; Asst Chief of Air Staff for Policy 1979–83; C-in-C RAF Germany and Commdr NATO's 2nd Allied Tactical Air Force 1983–85; Vice-Chief of the Defence Staff 1985–87; Air mem. for Supply and Organization, Air Force Bd 1987–88; Air Officer Commanding-in-Chief, Strike Command, C-in-C UK Air Forces 1988–91; Jt Commdr British Forces in Gulf Conflict, Aug. 1990–April 1991; with reserve force, rank of Flying Officer 1991–; Mil. Adviser to British Aerospace 1992–99; King of Arms, Order of the British Empire 1997–. *Leisure interests:* golf, mountain walking, skiing, photography, caravanning, travel.

HINGIS, Martina; Swiss professional tennis player; b. 30 Sept. 1980, Košice, Czechoslovakia; d. of Karol Hingis and Mélanie Molitor; competed in first tennis tournament 1985; family moved to Switzerland at age eight; winner French Open Jr championship 1993, Wimbledon Jr Championship 1994; turned professional and won first professional tournament Filderstadt (Germany) 1996; winner Australian Open 1997 (youngest winner of a Grand Slam title), 1998, 1999 (singles and doubles), beaten finalist 2000, 2001, 2002; won US Open 1997, beaten finalist 1998, 1999; Wimbledon singles champion 1997; Swiss Fed. Cup Team 1996–98; semi-finalist US Open 2001; won 76 tournament titles including five Grand Slam singles and nine doubles titles; elected to WTA Tour Players' Council 2002; retd 2002, returned to WTA Tour 2006; won Italian Open 2006; retd 2007; WTA Tour Most Impressive Newcomer 1995, Most Improved Player 1996, Player of the Year 1997. *Leisure interests:* horse-riding, roller-blading, skiing, swimming, going to musicals. *Address:* c/o AM Seidenbaum 17, 9377 Truebbach, Switzerland.

HINGORANI, Narain G., PhD, DSc; Indian/American engineer and consultant; b. 15 June 1931, Pakistan; m. Joyce Hingorani; ed Baroda Univ., Univ. of Manchester Inst. of Science and Tech.; worked for Bombay Electricity Bd 1953–55; moved to UK to study 1955; Lecturer, Univs of Loughborough and Salford, UK 1960s; Sr Scientist, Bonneville Power Admin 1968–74; mem., later Vice-Pres. Electrical Systems Div., Electric Power Research Inst., Palo Alto, Calif. 1974–94; f. consulting business, Hingorani Power Electronics; mem. Nat. Acad. of Eng; Life Fellow, IEEE; considered father of flexible alternating current transmission systems (FACTS) and custom power innovations; IEEE Lamme Medal, Uno Lamm Award, IEEE Power Eng Soc., IEEE Power Eng Soc. renamed its FACTS and Custom Power Awards as the Nari Hingorani FACTS Award and the Nari Hingorani Custom Power Award 2004, Benjamin Franklin Inst. Bower Award and Prize for Achievement in Science 2006, Franklin Inst. Laureate 2006. *Publications:* HVDC Transmission (co-author) 1960, Understanding FACTS Flexible AC Transmission (co-author) 2000. *Address:* 26480 Weston Drive, Los Altos Hills, CA 94022, USA (office). *Telephone:* (650) 941-5240 (home). *E-mail:* nhingorani@aol.com (home).

HINSHAW, Virginia S., BS, MS, PhD; American medical researcher, academic and university administrator; *Chancellor, University of Hawai'i-Manoa;* m. Bill Hinshaw; two s.; ed Auburn Univ.; Clinical and Research Microbiologist, Medical Coll. of Virginia 1967–68; Research Virologist, Univ. of California, Berkeley 1974; Research Assoc., Div. of Virology, St Jude Children's Research Hosp., Memphis, Tenn. 1974–83, 1984–85; one year sabbatical, Harvard Medical School 1983–84; Assoc. Prof. of Virology, Dept of Pathobiological Sciences, School of Veterinary Medicine, Univ. of Wisconsin 1985–88, Prof. 1988–92, Interim Assoc. Dean, Research and Grad. Studies 1992–93, Assoc. Vice-Chancellor 1994–95, Vice-Chancellor, Research, Dean of Grad. School 1995–2001; Provost and Exec. Vice-Chancellor, Univ. of California, Davis 2001–07, also Prof. of Virology, Dept Internal Medicine, School of Medicine 2001–07, Prof. of Virology, Dept of Pathology, Microbiology, Immunology, School of Veterinary Medicine 2001–07; Chancellor, Univ. of Hawai'i-Manoa 2007–. *Address:* Office of the Chancellor, Haw 202, University of Hawaii at Manoa, 2500 Campus Road, Honolulu, HI 96822, USA (office). *Telephone:* (808) 956-7651 (office). *Fax:* (808) 956-4153 (office). *E-mail:* vhinshaw@hawaii.edu (office); virginia.hinshaw@hawaii.edu (office). *Website:* www.hawaii.edu (office).

HINSON, David R.; American airline executive; b. 2 March 1933; m. Ursula Hinson; three c.; fighter pilot, USN 1956–60, airline and eng pilot 1960–72; founder, Dir Midway Airlines Inc. 1979–91, Chair., CEO 1985–91; Admin. US Fed. Aviation Admin (FAA) 1993–96; mem. Bd Nat. Air and Space Museum, Washington, DC; Chair. Bd of Visitors, Air Safety Foundation, Aircraft Owners and Pilots Asscn (AOPA); Operations Award, Aviation Week and Space Tech. 1997. *Leisure interests:* aviation history, collecting aviation art. *Address:* c/o Board of Visitors, Air Safety Foundation, AOPA, 421 Aviation Way, Frederick, MD 21701; c/o Board of Directors, National Air and Space Museum, 6th and Independence Avenue, SW, Washington, DC 20560, USA.

HINTIKKA, Jaakko, PhD; Finnish/American philosopher and academic; *Professor of Philosophy, Boston University;* b. 2 Jan. 1929, Vantaa; ed Univ. of Helsinki; Jr Fellow, Harvard Univ. 1956–59; held professorial appointments at Univ. of Helsinki, Acad. of Finland and Fla State Univ.; mem. staff, Stanford Univ. 1965–82; Prof. of Philosophy, Boston Univ. 1990–; known as main architect of game-theoretical semantics and of interrogative approach to inquiry; Dr hc (Liège) 1984, (Jagiellonian Univ. of Kraków) 1995, (Uppsala) 2000, (Oulu) 2002, (Turku) 2003; John Locke Lectureship, Univ. of Oxford 1964, Hägerström Lectureship, Uppsala Univ. 1983, Immanuel Kant Lectureship, Stanford Univ. 1985, Wihuri Int. Prize 1976, Guggenheim Fellowship 1979–80, Rolf Schock Prize in Logic and Philosophy 2005. *Publications:* author or co-author of more than 30 books and monographs in nine languages; five vols of selected papers appeared 1996–2003; ed. or co-ed. 17 vols; more than 300 scholarly papers. *Address:* Department of Philosophy, Boston University, Office STH 502, 745 Commonwealth Avenue, Boston, MA 02215, USA (office). *Telephone:* (617) 353-2571 (office). *Fax:* (617) 353-6805 (office). *E-mail:* hintikka@bu.edu (office). *Website:* www.bu.edu/philo/faculty/hintikka.html (office).

HIQUILY, Philippe; French sculptor; b. 27 March 1925, Paris; s. of Jules Hiquily and Madeleine Velvet; m. Meei-Yen Wo 1985; two s.; ed secondary school and Ecole Nat. Supérieure des Beaux-Arts Paris; mil. service in Indochina 1943–47; since 1951 has concentrated on sculpture in metal, influenced by primitive art; Chevalier des Arts et Lettres; Ordre Royal de Louang-Brabang (Laos). *Leisure interests:* fishing, agriculture, viticulture. *Address:* 21 rue Olivier-Noyer, Paris, France. *Telephone:* 1-45-39-30-25.

HIRAMATSU, Morihiko, LLB; Japanese civil servant; b. 12 March 1924, Oita; s. of the late Oriji Hiramatsu and Kun Hiramatsu; m. 1st Chizuko Ueda 1949; m. 2nd Teruko Mihara 1976; two d.; ed Kumamoto No. V. High School and Tokyo Univ.; employee Ministry of Commerce and Industry 1949–64; Dir Industrial Pollution Div. Enterprises Bureau, Ministry of Int. Trade and Industry 1964–65, Petroleum Planning Div. Mining Bureau 1965–67, Export Insurance Div. Trade Promotion Bureau 1967–69, Electronics Policy Div. Heavy Industries Bureau 1969–73, Co-ordination Office Basic Industries Bureau 1973–74; Counsellor Secr. Land Agency 1974–75; Vice-Gov. Oita Pref. 1975–79, Gov. 1979–2003; Chair. Kyushu G Govs' Asscn 1991–, Nat. Expressway Construction Promotion Council 1995–, Nat. Port Devt & Promotion Council 1998–; Pres. Fed. of Japan Port Promotion Orgs 2003–, Oita OVOP Int. Exchange Promotion Cttee 2005–; Special Advisor, Nat. Highway Construction Cttee 2003–; Hon. Consul-Gen. Repub. of Tunisia 2003–; Gran Cruz da Legião de Honra Giuseppe Garibaldi (Brazil) 1987, Commdr, Ordem do Infante D. Enrique (Portugal) 2001, Kt, Order of Orange Nassau (Netherlands) 2001, Grand Cordon Order of the Rising Sun 2004, Kt Grand Cross (First Class) Most Noble Order of the Crown of Thailand 2004; Ramon Magsaysay Award for Govt Service (Philippines) 1995; Friendship Award (People's Repub. of China) 2002. *Publications:* Talks on Software, Exhortations to One Village One Product, Challenging Technopolis, Age of Decentralised Management, Let's Try What's Impossible in Tokyo, Think Globally and Act Locally, Locally Generated Ideas, The Road to the 'United States of Japan', My Views on the 'United States of Japan', A Better Tomorrow for Rural Regions, Hot Disputes over the 'United States of Japan'. *Leisure interests:* reading, golf, early morning walks. *Address:* 1-6-10 Funai-machi, Oita City, Oita Prefecture 870-0021 (office); NPO Oita OVOP International Exchange Promotion Committee, 3F Oita Mitsui Building, 1-4-35, Maizuru-machi, Oita 870-0044; 2-2-38 Nakashima-chuo, Oita City, Oita Prefecture 870-0049, Japan (home). *Telephone:* (97) 537-2296 (office); (97) 540-5243 (NPO office) (office); (97) 537-6321 (home). *Fax:* (97) 538-2269 (office); (97) 540-5253 (NPO office) (office); (97) 538-0312 (home). *E-mail:* hiramatsu@fat.coara.or.jp (office); hiramatsu@ovop.jp (office). *Website:* www.coara.or.jp/hiramatsu (office).

HIRANO, Hiroshi; Japanese insurance industry executive; Pres. Yasuda Fire and Marine Insurance Co. Ltd –2003, Pres. and CEO Sompo Japan Insurance Inc. (following merger) 2002–06; Pres. Sompo Japan Environment Foundation; Vice-Chair. Gen. Insurance Asscn of Japan; Dir Japan Telework Asscn. *Address:* c/o Sompo Japan Insurance Inc., 26-1 Nishi-Shinjuku 1-chome, Shinjuku-ku, Tokyo 160-8338, Japan (office).

HIRANO, Shin-ichi, BEng, MEng, DEng; Japanese university administrator; *President, Nagoya University;* b. 7 Aug. 1942, Aichi Pref.; ed Nagoya Univ.; Research Assoc., Research Lab. of Eng Materials, Tokyo Inst. of Tech. 1970–76, Assoc. Prof. 1976–78; Assoc. Prof., School of Eng, Nagoya Univ. 1978–83, Prof. 1983–97, Prof., Grad. School of Eng 1997–2004, Dir Research Center for Advanced Energy Conversion 1999–2002, Dir Center for Cooperative Research in Advanced Science and Tech. 2002–03, Dean Grad. School of Eng and School of Eng 2003–04, Pres. Nagoya Univ. 2004–; fmr Adjunct Prof. of Materials Science and Eng, Pennsylvania State Univ.; mem. Man. Council Nat. Insts of Natural Sciences; mem. World Acad. of Ceramics; ACerS Fellow affiliated with Basic Science and Electronics Divs; Pres. Int. Ceramic Fed. 1997–99, Asia-Oceania Ceramic Fed. 2003–; fmr Pres. Ceramic Soc. of Japan; Trustee Japan Univ. Accreditation Asscn; Fellow, American Ceramic Soc. 1989; Soc. Award, Tokai Chemical Industry Soc. 1982, Soc. Award, Powder and Powder Metallurgy Soc. of Japan 1984, Academic Award, Ceramic Soc. of Japan 1986, Academic Award, Chemical Soc. of Japan 1989, Richard M. Fulrath Award, American Ceramic Soc. 1989, Memorial Award, Ceramic Soc. of Japan 1991, Int. Prize, Japanese Fine Ceramic Asscn 2000. *Publications:* numerous scientific papers in professional journals on inorganic materials chem. *Address:* Office of the President, Nagoya University, Furo-cho, Chikusa-ku, Nagoya 464-8601, Japan (office). *Telephone:* (52) 789-2044 (office). *Fax:* (52) 789-2045 (office). *E-mail:* intl@post.jimu.nagoya-u.ac.jp (office). *Website:* www.nagoya-u.ac.jp (office).

HIRANUMA, Takeo; Japanese politician; fmr Parl. Vice-Minister of Finance; Deputy Chair. LDP Policy Research Council, Chair. LDP Nat. Org. Cttee; mem. House of Reps; Minister of Transport 1995–96; Minister of Int. Trade and Industry 2000–01, of Economy, Trade and Industry 2001–03. *E-mail:* info@hiranuma.org. *Website:* www.hiranuma.org.

HIRASHIMA, Osamu; Japanese construction industry executive; *Senior Advisor and Representative Director, Taisei Corporation;* Pres. and CEO Taisei Corpn 2000, Chair. –2007, Sr Advisor and Rep. Dir 2007–; Chair. Japan Fed. of Construction Contractors 2004; Vice-Chair. Bd of Councillors, Japan Fed. of Econ. Orgs (KEIDANREN) 2004–; mem. Bd Dirs Japan Productivity Center for Socio-Econ. Devt (JPC-SED), Japan Accreditation Bd for Conformity Assessment (JAB) 2004–. *Address:* Taisei Corporation, 25-1 Nishi-Shinjuku, Shinjuku-ku, Tokyo 163-0606, Japan (office). *Telephone:* (3) 3348-1111 (office). *Fax:* (3) 3345-1386 (office). *Website:* www.taisei.co.jp (office).

HIRCHSON, Abraham; Israeli politician; b. 11 Feb. 1941, Tel Mond; m. (deceased); three c.; Staff Sergeant, Israeli Army; mem. Knesset 1981–, Deputy Speaker 16th Knesset, also Chair. Finance Cttee; Minister of Tourism 2005–06, of Communications Jan.–May 2006, of Finance 2006–07; fmr mem. Likud, joined Kadima 2005; Sec. Gen., Hanoar Haleumi Haoved Vehalomed 1970–92; Gen. Sec. Nat. Labourers' Youth Org. Israel 1981–84; Founder Jewish Heroism Quiz Project 1987; Founder and Pres. March of the Living Project 1988–; Chair., Nat. Labour Union 1995–, Nat. Health Fund 1996–; mem. Bd Special Swiss Cttee for Needy Holocaust Survivors. *Address:* The Knesset, HaKiryah, Jerusalem, 91950, Israel (office). *Telephone:* 2-6753382 (office). *Fax:* 2-6753764 (office). *E-mail:* ahirshson@knesset.gov.il (office). *Website:* www.knesset.gov.il (office).

HIRONAKA, Heisuke, PhD; Japanese mathematician and academic; *Professor Emeritus, Department of Mathematics, Harvard University;* b. 9 April 1931, Yamaguchi-ken; ed Kyoto Univ. and Harvard Univ., USA; mem. staff, Harvard Univ. following graduation, later Prof. of Math., now Prof. Emer.; Visiting Scholar, Research Inst. for the Math. Sciences, Kyoto Univ. 1991–92; fmr Pres. Yamaguchi Univ.; Foreign Assoc. Acad. des sciences 1981–; currently lives in Japan; active in fund-raising for math. educ.; Order of Culture (Japan) 1975; Fields Medal, Int. Congress of Mathematicians, Nice, France 1970. *Publications:* numerous articles in math. journals on complex analysis and singularity theory. *Address:* Department of Mathematics, Office 325, Harvard University, One Oxford Street, Cambridge, MA 02138, USA (office). *Telephone:* (617) 495-2171 (office). *Fax:* (617) 495-5132 (office). *E-mail:* hironaka@math.harvard.edu (office). *Website:* www.math.harvard.edu (office).

HIRSCH, Georges-François; French opera administrator; *General Director, Orchestre de Paris;* b. 5 Oct. 1944, Paris; s. of Georges Hirsch; stage-hand, Théâtre des Capucines 1960; later stage man. Théâtre de la Culture de l'Ile de France; Dir Théâtre de Limoges 1969–74; directed various productions especially in USA 1974–79; Dance Admin. Paris Opéra 1979–82; mem. directing team, RTLN 1982–83; Dir Théâtre des Champs-Elysées 1983–89; Gen. Admin. Opéra Bastille 1989–92, Opéra de Paris (Garnier Bastille) 1991–92; mem. council CSA 1993–96; Dir-Gen. Orchestre de Paris 1996–; Chair. Syndicat nat. des orchestres et théâtres lyriques subventionnés de droit privé 1999–; Vice-Chair. French Asscn of Orchestras 2000–; Officier, Légion d'honneur, Chevalier, Ordre nat. du Mérite, Commdr des Arts et Lettres. *Address:* Orchestre de Paris, Salle Pleyel, 252 rue du Faubourg St-Honoré, 75008 Paris, France. *Telephone:* 1-56-35-12-01. *Fax:* 1-56-35-12-25. *Website:* www.orchestredeparis.com.

HIRSCH, Judd, BS; American actor; b. 15 March 1935, New York; s. of Joseph S. Hirsch and Sally Kitzis; ed City Coll. of New York; has appeared in numerous TV plays, series, films etc.; mem. Screen Actors Guild, AEA, AFTRA. *Stage appearances include:* Barefoot in the Park 1966, Knock Knock 1976 (Drama Desk Award), Scuba Duba 1967–69, King of the United States 1972, Mystery Play 1972, Hot L Baltimore 1972–73, Prodigal 1973, Chapter Two 1977–78, Talley's Folly 1979 (Obie Award), The Seagull 1983, I'm Not Rappaport 1985–86 (Tony Award), Conversations with My Father (Tony Award) 1992, A Thousand Clowns 1996, Below the Belt 1996, Death of a Salesman 1997, Art 1998, I'm Not Rappaport (revival) 2002, Sixteen Wounded 2004. *Films include:* King of the Gypsies 1978, Ordinary People 1980, Without a Trace 1983, Teachers 1984, The Goodbye People 1984, Running on Empty 1988, Independence Day 1996, Man on the Moon 1999, A Beautiful Mind 2002, Zeyda and the Hitman 2004, Brother's Shadow 2006. *Television appearances include:* Delvecchio (series) 1976–77, Taxi (series) 1978–83 (Emmy Award), Dear John (series) 1988–92 (Golden Globe Award), George and Leo (series) 1997, Regular Joe (series) 2003, Numbers (series) 2005–07, numerous appearances in TV episodes and movies. *Address:* c/o J. Wolfe Provident Financial Management, 2850 Ocean Park Blvd, Santa Monica, CA 90405, USA. *Telephone:* (310) 789-5223. *Fax:* (310) 282-5199.

HIRSCH, Leon; American business executive; *Chairman, Jarvik Heart, Inc;* b. 20 July 1927, Bronx, New York; s. of the late Roslyn Hirsch and Isidor Hirsch; m. 2nd Turi Josefsen 1969; two s. one d. from 1st m.; ed Bronx School of Science; Chair. and CEO US Surgical Corpn 1964–2000; founder JHK Investments, LLC, invested in Jarvik Heart, Inc., now Chair. 2001–; f. inventor and developer of Auto Suture surgical staplers; Chair. Advisory Bd American Soc. of Colon and Rectal Surgeons Research Foundation; mem. American Business Conf.; Dir Americans for Medical Progress; mem. Bd of Trustees, Boston Univ.; Gordon Grand Fellow, Yale Univ.; Surgery Award Nessim Habif, Univ. of Geneva. *Leisure interests:* fishing, horseback riding, skiing, tennis. *Address:* Jarvik Heart, Inc., 333 West 52nd Street, New York, NY 10019, USA (office). *Telephone:* (212) 397-3911 (office). *Fax:* (212) 397-3919 (office). *Website:* www.jarvikheart.com (office).

HIRSCH, Sir Peter Bernhard, Kt, PhD, FRS; British scientist and academic; *Professor Emeritus of Metallurgy, University of Oxford;* b. 16 Jan. 1925, Berlin; s. of Ismar Hirsch and Regina Meyersohn; m. Mabel A. Kellar (née Stephens) 1959; one step-s. one step-d.; ed Univ. of Cambridge; Lecturer in Physics, Univ. of Cambridge 1959–64, Reader 1964–66; Fellow, Christ's Coll., Cambridge 1960–66, Hon. Fellow 1978; Isaac Wolfson Prof. of Metallurgy, Univ. of Oxford 1966–92, Prof. Emer. 1992–, Fellow, St Edmund Hall 1966–92, Fellow Emer. 1992–; Chair. Metallurgy and Materials Cttee, SRC 1970–73; mem. Council, Inst. of Physics 1968–72, Inst. of Metals 1968–73, Electricity Supply Research Council 1969–82, Council for Scientific Policy 1970–72, Metals Soc. Council 1978–82, Council Royal Soc. 1977–79; Royal Soc. UK-Canada Lecture 1992; mem. Bd (part-time) UKAEA 1982–94, Chair. 1982–84; mem. Tech. Advisory Cttee Advent 1982–89; Dir Cogent 1985–89, Rolls-Royce Assocs. 1994–98; Dir (non-exec.) OMIA 2000–01; mem. Tech. Advisory Cttee Monsanto Electronic Materials 1985–88; Chair. Isis Innovation Ltd 1988–96, Tech. Advisory Group on Structural Integrity 1993–2002, Materials and Processes Advisory Bd Rolls-Royce PLC 1996–2000; Fellow, Imperial Coll., London 1988; Assoc. mem. Royal Acad. of Sciences, Letters and Fine Arts of Belgium 1996; Foreign Assoc. Nat. Acad. of Eng, USA 2001; Hon. Fellow, St Catharine's Coll., Cambridge 1982, Royal Microscopical Soc. 1977, Japan Soc. of Electron Microscopy 1979, Japan Inst. of Metals 1989, Inst. of Materials 2002; Hon. mem. Spanish Electron Microscopy Soc., Materials Research Soc., India 1990, Chinese Electron Microscopy Soc. 1992; Foreign Hon. mem. American Acad. of Arts and Sciences 2005; Hon. DSc (Newcastle Univ.) 1979, (City Univ.) 1979, (Northwestern Univ.) 1982, (East Anglia Univ.) 1983, Hon. DEng (Liverpool) 1991, (Birmingham) 1993; Rosenhain Medal, Inst. of Metals 1961, Boyes' Prize, Inst. of Physics and Physical Soc. 1962, Clamer Medal, Franklin Inst. 1970, Wihuri Int. Prize 1971, Hughes Medal of the Royal Soc. 1973, Platinum Medal of the Metals Soc. 1976, Royal Medal of Royal Soc. 1977, A. A. Griffith Medal, Inst. of Materials 1979, Arthur Von Hippel Award, Materials Research Soc. 1983, Wolf Prize in Physics (jtly) 1984, Distinguished Scientist Award, Electron Microscopy Soc. of America 1986, Holweck Prize, Inst. of Physics and French Physical Soc. 1988, Gold Medal, Japan Inst. of Metals 1989, Acta Metallurgica Gold Medal 1997, Heyn Medal of German Soc. for Materials Science 2002, Lomonosov Gold Medal, Russian Acad. of Sciences 2006. *Publications:* Electron Microscopy of Thin Crystals (co-author) 1965, The Physics of Metals, 2, Defects (ed.) 1975, Progress in Materials Science, Vol. 36 (co-ed.) 1992, Topics in Electron Diffraction and Microscopy of Materials (ed.) 1999, Fracture, Plastic Flow and Structural Integrity (co-ed.) 2000, Methods for the Assessment of the Structural Integrity of Components and Structures (co-ed.) 2003; and numerous articles in learned journals. *Leisure interest:* walking. *Address:* Department of Materials, University of Oxford, Room 10.06, 21 Banbury Road, Oxford, OX1 3PH (office); 104A Lonsdale Road, Oxford, OX2 7ET, England (home). *Telephone:* (1865) 273700 (office); (1865) 559523 (home). *Fax:* (1865) 273789 (office). *E-mail:* peter.hirsch@materials.ox.ac.uk (office). *Website:* www.materials.ox.ac.uk/peoplepages/hirsch.html (office).

HIRSCH, Robert Paul; French actor; b. 26 July 1925; s. of Joachim Hirsch and Germaine Anne Raybois; mem. Comédie Française 1952–74; Brig. d'honneur 1992; Officier des Arts et des Lettres; Prix Jean-Jacques Gautier 1987. *Stage appearances include:* La belle aventure, Le prince travesti, Monsieur de Pourceaugnac, Les temps difficiles, La double inconstance, Le dindon, Amphitryon, Britannicus, Crime et Châtiment, La faim et la soif, Monsieur Amilcar, L'abîme et la visite, Le Piège, Deburau, Chacun sa vérité, Les dégourdis de la 11e 1986, Mon Faust 1987, Moi, Feuerbach 1989, Le Misanthrope 1992, Une Folie 1993, Le bel air de Londres 1998. *Films include:* les Intrigantes 1954, Votre dévoué Blake 1954, En effeuillant la marguerite 1956, Notre Dame de Paris 1956, La Bigorne 1958, Mimi Pinson 1958, Maigret et l'affaire Saint-Fiacre 1959, 125 rue Montmartre 1959, Adieu Philippine 1962, Pas question le samedi 1965, Monnaie de singe 1966, Martin Soldat 1966, Toutes folles de lui 1967, Les Cracks 1968, Appelez-moi Mathilde 1969, Traitement de choc 1973, Chobizenesse 1975, La Crime 1983, Hiver 54, l'abbé Pierre 1989, Mon homme 1996, Mortel transfert 2001, Une affaire privée 2002. *Television includes:* La Nuit des rois 1962, Georges Dandin 1973, Tartuffe 1975, Trente ans ou La vie d'un joueur 1975, Les Papas naissent dans les armoires 1979, Deburau 1982, Sarah 2003, Volpone 2003. *Leisure interests:*

painting, dancing. *Address:* Agence JFPM, 11 rue Chanez, 75016 Paris; 1 place du Palais Bourbon, 75007 Paris, France.

HIRSCH BALLIN, Ernst, LLD; Dutch lawyer and judge; *Minister of Justice;* b. 15 Dec. 1950, Amsterdam; s. of Ernst D. Hirsch Ballin and Maria Koppe; m. Pauline van de Grift 1974; two c.; ed Univ. of Amsterdam; mem. Faculty of Law, Amsterdam Univ. 1974–77; Legal Expert, Ministry of Justice 1977–81; Prof. of Constitutional and Admin. Law, Tilburg Univ. 1981–89, Prof. of Int. Law 1994–; Minister of Justice and Netherlands Antillean and Aruban Affairs 1989–94, Minister of Justice 2006–; mem. Parl. (Christian Democrat; Lower House) 1994–95, (Upper House) 1995–2000; Councillor of State 2000–; Pres. Admin. Jurisdiction Div. Council of State 2003–06; mem. Royal Netherlands Acad. of Science 2005; Kt, Order of the Dutch Lion; Grand Cross, Order of the Chest Crown (Luxembourg); Grand Cross, Orden del Libertador (Venezuela); Chevalier de la Légion d'honneur; Kt Order of Holy Sepulchre of Jerusalem; G.A. van Poelje Prize 1980. *Publications:* Publiekrecht en beleid 1979, Rechtsstaat en beleid 1992; 300 other publs on int. and comparative law, legal theory, constitutional and admin. law. *Leisure interests:* Brazilian music, philosophy, tennis. *Address:* Ministry of Justice, Schedelhoekshaven 100, POB 20301, 2500 EH, The Hague, Netherlands (office); Council of State, PO Box 20019, 2500 EA The Hague (office); Bruggenrijt 12, 5032 BH Tilburg, Netherlands (home). *Telephone:* (70) 3707911 (office); (70) 4264657 (office). *Fax:* (70) 3707900 (office); (13) 5920687 (home). *E-mail:* ballin@uvt.nl (office). *Website:* www.justie.nl (office).

HIRSCHFIELD, Alan J., BS, MBA; American business executive; b. 10 Oct. 1935, Oklahoma City; ed Univ. of Okla and Harvard Univ.; Vice-Pres. Allen and Co. 1959–67; Vice-Pres. (Finance) and Dir Warner Bros Seven Arts Inc. 1967–68; Vice-Pres. and Dir American Diversified Enterprises Inc. 1968–73; Pres. and CEO, Columbia Pictures Industries Inc. 1973–79; Consultant, Warner Communications Inc. 1979; Vice-Chair. and COO, 20th Century-Fox Film Corpn 1979–81, Chair., CEO and COO 1981–84; CEO Data Broadcasting Corpn 1990–2000, Dir 2000; Pres. Jackson Hole Land Trust, Cantel, Inc., CPP Belwin, Conservation Int., Trout Unlimited; mem. Bd of Dirs Cantel Medical Corpn, Carmike Cinemas, Inc., Peregrine Systems, Inc., Leucadia Nat. Corpn, Interactive Data Corpn (co-Chair. 1992–2000, co-CEO 1992–99); fmr mem. Bd of Dirs Straight Arrow Publishing Co., John B. Coleman Co., Motion Picture Asscn of America, New York State Motion Picture and TV Advisory Bd, Film Soc. of Lincoln Cen., Will Rogers Memorial Fund, George Gustav Heye Center, Nat. Museum of the American Indian 1997, CBSmarket.com, Jackpot Inc. 1998–; Vice-Chair. JNet Enterprises 2000; Trustee, Cancer Research Inst. (Sloan-Kettering). *Address:* c/o Board of Directors, Interactive Data Corporation, 22 Crosby Drive, Bedford, MA 01730; PO Box 7443, Jackson, WY 83002, USA.

HIRSCHHORN, Thomas; Swiss artist; b. 1957, Bern; ed Schule für Gestaltung, Zürich; moved to France and joined Grapus, Parisian collective of communist graphic designers 1984; first solo exhbn at Bar Floréal, Paris 1986; influenced by Kurt Schwitters and Andy Warhol; translates leftist ideals into sculptural displays combining everyday materials such as aluminum foil, tape, board, plastic, and paper with wide array of cultural references; lives and works in Paris; Preis für Junge Schweizer Kunst 1999, Marcel Duchamp Prize 2000, Rolandpreis für Kunst im öffentlichen Raum 2003, Joseph Beuys Prize 2004, Beaux-Arts magazine Art Award 2005, Prix Aica 2006. *Major works include:* FlugplatzWelt/World Airport, Venice Biennale 1999, Battle Monument, Documenta XI, Kassel 2002; works on display in Kunstsammlung Nordrhein-Westfalen, Dusseldorf, S.M.A.K. (Stedelijk Museum voor Actuele Kunst), Ghent, Tate Modern, London, Walker Art Center, Minn., Art Inst. of Chicago, La Caixa, Barcelona, Centre Pompidou, Paris, Musée Précaire Albinet Aubervilliers 2004; and in major contemporary art museums in LA, Miami, New York, Philadelphia, Boston, Amsterdam, Porto, Basel, Munich, Marseille, Bordeaux, Paris, Santiago de Compostela, Zürich. *Publications:* Parkett #57 (co-author) 2000, Material: Public Works – The Bridge 2000 2001, Bataille Maschine (with M. Steinweg) 2003. *Address:* c/o Stephen Friedman Gallery, 25-28 Old Burlington Street, London, W1S 3AN, England.

HIRSCHMAN, Albert Otto, DEconSc; American political economist and academic; *Professor Emeritus, Institute for Advanced Study;* b. 7 April 1915, Berlin, Germany; s. of Carl Hirschmann and Hedwig Marcuse; m. Sarah Chapiro 1941; one d. (one d. deceased); ed Lycée Français, Berlin, Ecole des Hautes Etudes Commerciales, Paris, London School of Econs, Univ. of Trieste, Italy; Research Fellow in Int. Econs, Univ. of Calif., Berkeley USA 1941–43; Economist, Fed. Reserve Bd, Washington, DC 1946–52; Econ. Adviser and Consultant, Bogotá, Colombia 1952–56; Prof. of Econs, Yale Univ. 1956–58, Columbia Univ. 1958–64, Harvard Univ. 1964–74; Prof. of Social Science, Inst. for Advanced Study, Princeton 1974–85, Prof. Emer. 1985–, Albert O. Hirschman Chair in Econs 2000; mem. NAS; Distinguished Fellow, American Econ. Asscn; Corresp. Fellow, British Acad.; Foreign mem. Accad. Nazionale dei Lincei, Italy; 19 hon. degrees; several prizes and awards, including Toynbee Prize 1998, Thomas Jefferson Medal 1998. *Publications include:* National Power and the Structure of Foreign Trade 1945, The Strategy of Economic Development 1958, Journeys Towards Progress: Studies of Economic Policy-Making in Latin America 1963, Development Projects Observed 1967, Exit, Voice and Loyalty 1970, A Bias for Hope: Essays on Development and Latin America 1971, The Passions and the Interests: Political Arguments for Capitalism Before its Triumph 1977, Essays in Trespassing 1981, Shifting Involvements: Private Interest and Public Action 1982, Getting Ahead Collectively: Grassroots Experiences in Latin America 1984, Rival Views of Market Society and Other Recent Essays 1986, The Rhetoric of Reaction: Perversity, Futility, Jeopardy 1991, A Propensity to Self-Subversion 1995, Crossing Boundaries: Selected Writings and an Interview 1998. *Leisure interests:* art and art history. *Address:* School of Social Science, Institute for

Advanced Study, Einstein Drive, Princeton, NJ 08540 (office); 16 Newlin Road, Princeton, NJ, USA (home). *Fax:* (609) 951-4457 (office). *E-mail:* aoh@ias.edu (office). *Website:* www.sss.ias.edu (office).

HIRSCHMANN, Ralph F., AB, PhD; American chemist and academic; *Rao Makineni Term Professor of Bioorganic Chemistry, University of Pennsylvania;* b. 1922; ed Oberlin Coll., Univ. of Wis.; Chemist, Devt Research, Merck & Co., Inc., Rahway, NJ 1950, Dir of Protein Research 1968, Sr Dir, Medicinal Chemistry 1972, Vice-Pres., later Sr Vice-Pres., Merck & Co., Inc. 1976–87; Research Prof. of Chemistry, Univ. of Pennsylvania 1987–, Rao Makineni Term Prof. of Bioorganic Chemistry 2003–; Prof. of Biomedical Research, Medical Univ. of SC 1987–99; mem. Pimentel Cttee 1982–86; mem. Acad. of Arts and Sciences 1981–, Nat. Acad. of Sciences 1999–; Sr Fellow, Inst. of Medicine 2001–; DSc hc (Oberlin Coll.) 1969, (Univ. of Wis.) 1996, (Medical Univ. of SC) 1997 numerous awards including Alfred Burger Award 1994, Edward E. Smissman Bristol-Myers Squibb Award 1998, Nichols Medal 1988, Nat. Acad. of Sciences Award for Industrial Application of Science 1999, American Chemical Soc. Arthur C. Cope Medal 1999, Nat. Medal of Science 2000, Willard Gibbs Medal 2002, American Inst. of Chemists Gold Medal 2003, E.B. Hershberg Award, Villanova Univ. Mendel Medal 2004. *Achievements:* holder of 100 patents. *Publications:* more than 160 papers. *Address:* Department of Chemistry, University of Pennsylvania, 231 South 34th Street, Room 453N, Philadelphia, PA 19104–6323, USA (office). *Telephone:* (215) 898–7398 (office). *E-mail:* rfh@sas.upenn.edu (office). *Website:* www.sas .upenn.edu/chem/faculty/hirschmann/hirschmann.html (office).

HIRST, Damien; British artist; b. 1965, Bristol; m. Maia Norman; three s.; ed Goldsmiths Coll., London; winner Turner Prize 1995; ranked first in ArtReview magazine's Power 100 list 2005, ranked 11th 2006; various other awards. *Television:* Channel 4 documentary about Damien Hirst and Exhbn at Gagosian Gallery, directed by Roger Pomphrey 2000. *Publication:* I Want to Spend the Rest of My Life Everywhere, One to One, Always, Forever 1997, Theories, Models, Methods, Approaches, Assumptions, Results and Findings 2000. *Leisure interests:* losing myself, pub lunches. *Address:* c/o White Cube, Hoxton Square, London, N1 6PB, England. *Telephone:* (20) 7930-5373. *E-mail:* enquiries@science.ltd.uk (office).

HIRST, Paul Heywood, MA; British academic; *Emeritus Professor of Education, University of Cambridge;* b. 10 Nov. 1927, Huddersfield; s. of Herbert Hirst and Winifred Hirst; ed Huddersfield Coll., Trinity Coll., Cambridge and Univ. of London; school teacher of math. 1948–55; Lecturer and Tutor, Dept of Educ., Univ. of Oxford 1955–59; Lecturer in Philosophy of Educ., Inst. of Educ., Univ. of London 1959–65; Prof. of Educ., King's Coll., Univ. of London 1965–71; Prof. of Educ. and Head Dept of Educ., Univ. of Cambridge 1971–88, Emer. Prof. 1988–; Fellow, Wolfson Coll., Cambridge 1971–88, Fellow Emer. 1988–; Visiting Prof., Univs of British Columbia, Alberta, Malawi, Otago, Melbourne, Sydney, Puerto Rico, London 1988–; Vice-Chair. Cttee for Educ., CNAA 1975–81, Chair. Cttee for Research 1988–92; Chair. Univs Council for Educ. of Teachers 1985–88; mem. Swann Cttee on Educ. of Children of Ethnic Minorities 1981–85; Hon. Vice-Pres. Philosophy of Educ. Soc. 1979–; Hon. DEd (CNAA) 1992; Hon. DPhil (Cheltenham and Gloucester Coll. of Higher Educ.) 2000; Hon. DLitt (Huddersfield) 2002. *Publications:* Logic of Education (with R. S. Peters) 1970, Knowledge and the Curriculum 1974, Moral Education in a Secular Society 1974, Educational Theory and its Foundation Disciplines (ed.) 1983, Initial Teacher Training and the Role of the School (with others) 1988, Philosophy of Education: Major Themes in the Analytic Tradition (four vols) (co-ed.) 1998; numerous articles in educational and philosophical journals. *Leisure interest:* music (especially opera). *Address:* Flat 3, 6 Royal Crescent, Brighton, BN2 1AL, England (home). *Telephone:* (1273) 684118 (home).

HIRZEBRUCH, Friedrich Ernst Peter, Dr rer. nat; German mathematician and academic; *Retired Scientific Member, Max-Planck-Institut für Mathematik;* b. 17 Oct. 1927, Hamm, Westfalia; s. of Dr Fritz Hirzebruch and Martha Hirzebruch (née Holtschmit); m. Ingeborg Spitzley 1952; one s. two d.; ed Westfälische Wilhelms-Univ., Münster and Technische Hochschule, Zürich; Scientific Asst Univ. of Erlangen 1950–52; mem. Inst. for Advanced Study, Princeton, NJ, USA 1952–54; Dozent, Univ. of Münster 1954–55; Asst Prof., Princeton Univ., NJ 1955–56; Full Prof., Bonn Univ. 1956–93, Dean, Faculty of Math. and Natural Sciences 1962–64; Dir Max-Planck-Inst. für Mathematik, Bonn 1981–95, now Retd Scientific Mem.; Pres. German Math. Soc. 1961–62, 1990, European Math. Soc. 1990–94; mem. Leopoldina, Heidelberg, Mainz, Netherlands and Nordrheinwestfalen Acads, NAS, Bayerische Akad. der Wissenschaften, Finnish Acad. of Sciences, Russian (fmrly USSR) Acad. of Sciences, Acad. des Sciences (Paris), Akad. der Wissenschaften, Göttingen, American Acad. of Arts and Sciences, Ukrainian Acad., Sächsische Akad., Berlin-Brandenburgische Akad., Royal Soc., Royal Irish Acad., Polish Acad. of Sciences, Academia Europaea, European Acad. of Arts and Sciences, Austrian Acad. of Sciences; Orden pour le Mérite 1991, Grosses Verdienstkreuz mit Stern 1993, Order of the Holy Treasure, Gold and Silver (Japan) 1996; Dr hc (Univs of Warwick, Göttingen, Oxford, Wuppertal, Notre Dame, Dublin, Athens, Potsdam, Konstanz, Humboldt-Berlin, Bar-Ilan, Oslo, UIC Chicago); Hon. DSc (Oxford) 1984; Silver Medal, Swiss Fed. Inst. of Technology 1950, Wolf Prize in Mathematics 1988, Lobachevskii Prize, USSR Acad. of Sciences 1989, Seki Prize, Japanese Mathematical Soc. 1996, Cothenius Gold Medal Leopoldina 1997, Lomonosov Gold Medal, Russian Acad. of Sciences 1997, Albert Einstein Medal 1999, Stefan Banach Medal, Polish Acad. of Sciences, Krupp-Wissenschaftspreis 2000, Helmholtz Medal Berlin-Brandenburg Acad. of Sciences 2002, Georg Cantor Medal German Math. Soc. 2004. *Publications:* Neue topologische Methoden in der algebraischen Geometrie 1956, Collected Papers (two vols) 1987. *Address:* Max-Planck-Institut für Mathematik, Vivatsgasse 7, 53111 Bonn (office); Thüringer Allee 127, 53757 St Augustin,

Germany (home). *Telephone:* (228) 4020 (office); (2241) 332377 (home). *Fax:* (228) 402277 (office). *E-mail:* hirzebruch@mpim-bonn.mpg.de (office). *Website:* www.mpim-bonn.mpg.de (office).

HISLOP, Ian David, BA (Hons); British editor, writer and broadcaster; *Editor, Private Eye magazine;* b. 13 July 1960; s. of the late David Atholl Hislop and of Helen Hislop; m. Victoria Hamson 1988; one s. one d.; ed Ardingly Coll. and Magdalen Coll., Oxford; joined Private Eye (satirical magazine) 1981, Deputy Ed. 1985–86, Ed. 1986–; columnist, The Listener magazine 1985–89, The Sunday Telegraph 1996–2003; TV critic, The Spectator 1994–96; Underhill Exhbn; Violet Vaughan Morgan Scholarship; BAFTA Award for Have I Got News for You 1991, Editors' Editor, British Soc. of Magazine Eds 1991, Magazine of the Year, What the Papers Say 1991, Editor of the Year, British Soc. of Magazine Eds 1998, Award for Political Satire, Channel 4 Political Awards 2004, Award for Political Comedy, Channel 4 Political Awards 2006. *Radio:* The News Quiz (BBC Radio 4) 1985–90, Fourth Column 1992–96, Lent Talk 1994, Gush (scriptwriter, with Nick Newman) 1994, Words on Words 1999, The Hislop Vote (BBC Radio 2) 2000, A Revolution in 5 Acts (BBC Radio 4) 2001, The Real Patron Saints (BBC Radio 4) 2002, The Choir Invisible 2003, A Brief History of Tax (BBC Radio 4) 2003, Blue Birds over the White Cliffs of Dover (BBC Radio 4) 2004, Are We Being Offensive Enough? (BBC Radio 4) 2004, Looking for Middle England (BBC Radio 4) 2006. *TV scriptwriting:* Spitting Image (with Nick Newman; ITV) 1984–89, The Stone Age (with Nick Newman) 1989, Briefcase Encounter (with Nick Newman) 1990, The Programme (with Nick Newman) 1990–92, Harry Enfield and Chums (with Nick Newman) 1994–98, Mangez Merveillac (with Nick Newman) 1994, Dead on Time (with Nick Newman) 1995, Gobble (with Nick Newman; BBC 1) 1996, Sermon from St Albions (ITV Granada) 1998, Songs and Praise from St Albions (with Nick Newman) (ITV Granada) 1999, Confessions of a Murderer (with Nick Newman) 1999, My Dad's the Prime Minister (with Nick Newman; BBC) 2003, 2004. *TV performer:* Have I Got News for You (BBC 2) 1990–2000, (BBC 1) 2000–. *TV presenter:* Canterbury Tales (Channel 4) 1996, School Rules (Channel 4) 1997, Pennies from Bevan (Channel 4) 1998, Great Railway Journeys East to West (BBC) 1999, Who Do You Think You Are? (BBC 2) 2004, Not Forgotten (Channel 4) 2005, Not Forgotten: Shot at Dawn (Channel 4) 2007, Scouting for Boys (BBC 4) 2007. *Publications:* various Private Eye collections 1985–, contribs to newspapers and magazines on books, current affairs, arts and entertainment. *Address:* Private Eye, 6 Carlisle Street, London, W1D 3BN, England (office). *Telephone:* (20) 7437-4017 (office). *Website:* www.private-eye.co.uk (office).

HITAM, Tan Sri Dato' Musa bin; Malaysian politician (retd); b. 18 April 1934, Johor; ed English Coll., Johor Baharu Univ. of Malaya and Univ. of Sussex, UK; Assoc. Sec. Int. Student Conf. Secr. (COSEC), Leiden 1957–59; civil servant 1959–64; political sec. to Minister of Transport 1964; mem. Parl. 1968–90; Asst Minister to Deputy Prime Minister 1969; studied in UK 1970, subsequently lectured at Univ. of Malaya; Chair. Fed. Land Devt Authority 1971; Deputy Minister of Trade and Industry 1972–74; Minister of Primary Industries 1974–78, of Educ. 1978–81; Deputy Prime Minister and Minister of Home Affairs 1981–86; Deputy Pres. UMNO 1981–86; Special Envoy to UN 1990–91; Malaysia's Chief Rep. to UN Comm. on Human Rights 1994–; Special Envoy of the Prime Minister to Commonwealth Ministerial Action Group. *Address:* No. 12, Selekoh Tunku, Bukit Tunku, 50480 Kuala Lumpur, Malaysia.

HITCHCOCK, Karen R., BS, PhD; American university administrator, biologist and academic; *Principal and Vice-Chancellor, Queen's University;* ed St Lawrence Univ., Univ. of Rochester; fmr Postdoctoral Fellow Webb-Waring Inst. for Medical Research, Univ. of Colo Medical Centre; fmr George A. Bates Prof. of Histology and Chair Dept of Anatomy and Cellular Biology, Tufts Univ.; Assoc. Dean for Basic Sciences, Research and Grad. Studies, School of Medicine, Tex. Tech Health Sciences Center 1985–87; fmr Vice-Chancellor for Research, Dean Grad. Coll., Prof. of Anatomy and Cell Biology, of Biological Sciences, Univ. of Ill. at Chicago; Vice-Pres. of Academic Affairs, Univ. of Albany, State Univ. of NY 1991–95, Interim Pres., Pres. 1996–2004; Prin. and Vice-Chancellor Queen's Univ., Kingston, Ont., Canada 2004–; Nat. Science Foundation Professorship for Women in Science and Eng 1983–84; fmr Pres. American Asscn of Anatomists; fmr mem. Nat. Bd of Medical Examiners; Dr hc (Albany Medical Coll., St Lawrence Univ.); Marketer of Excellence Award, New York Capital Region Chapter, American Marketing Asscn 2002, Capital Region Business Hall of Fame 2004, Woman in the Media Award, Women's Press Club of New York State 2004. *Publications:* numerous works on cell and developmental biology. *Address:* Office of the Principal, Queen's University, 74 University Avenue, 140 Dunning Hall, Kingston, ON, K7L 3N6, Canada (office). *Telephone:* (613) 533-2200 (office). *Fax:* (613) 533-6838 (office). *E-mail:* khitchcock@queensu.ca (office). *Website:* www.queensu.ca/principal (office).

HITCHENS, Christopher Eric, BA; British/American journalist and writer; b. 13 April 1949, Portsmouth, England; m. 1st Eleni Meleagrou 1981; one s. one d.; m. 2nd Carol Blue 1991; one d.; ed Balliol Coll., Oxford; social science correspondent, THES 1971–73; writer and Asst Ed. 1973–81, columnist and Washington correspondent 1982–, New Statesman; columnist, The Nation 1982–2002, Vanity Fair 1982–, also columnist Slate; contributor, London Review of Books 1989–; Mellon Prof. of English, Univ. of Pittsburgh 1997. *Publications:* Karl Marx and the Paris Commune 1971, James Callaghan 1976, Hostage to History: Cyprus From the Ottomans to Kissinger 1984, Imperial Spoils: The Curious Case of the Elgin Marbles 1986, Prepared for the Worst: Selected Essays 1989, Blood, Class and Nostalgia: Anglo-American Ironies 1990, For the Sake of Argument: Selected Essays 1993, When the Borders Bleed: The Struggle of the Kurds 1994, The Missionary Position: Mother Teresa in Theory and Practice 1995, No One Left to Lie to 1999,

Letters to a Young Contrarian 2001, Orwell's Victory 2001, Love, Poverty and War: Journeys and Essays 2005, Thomas Paine's Rights of Man: A Biography 2006, God is Not Great: How Religion Poisons Everything 2007, The Parthenon Marbles: The Case for Reunification 2008. *Address:* c/o Slate, 1800 M Street, NW, Suite 330, Washington, DC 20036, USA. *Telephone:* (202) 261-1310. *E-mail:* dcoffice@slate.com. *Website:* www.slate.com.

HITE, Shere D., MA, PhD; American/German cultural historian, writer and researcher; *Director, Hite Research International;* b. 1942, St Joseph, Mo.; m. Friedrich Hoericke 1985; ed Univ. of Florida, Columbia Univ., Nihon Univ., Japan; Dir feminist sexuality project NOW, New York 1972–78; Dir Hite Research Int., New York 1978–; Researcher, The Hite Reports, 1976, 1981, 1987, 1996, 2006; fmr instructor in female sexuality, New York Univ.; lecturer Harvard Univ., McGill Univ., Columbia Univ., also numerous women's groups, int. lecturer 1977–89, currently Visiting Prof., Nihon Univ., Japan; mem. Advisory Bd Foundation of Gender and Genital Medicine, Johns Hopkins Univ.; Consultant Ed. Journal of Sex Education and Therapy, Journal of Sexuality and Disability; mem. NOW, American Historical Asscn, American Sociological Asscn, AAAS, Acad. of Political Science, Women's History Asscn, Soc. for Scientific Study of Sex, Women's Health Network; Prof., Maimonides Univ. 2003; f. Nike Prize for Women's Non-Fiction Writing, Frankfurt 1997; Hon. Prof. Chongqing Medical Univ., China 2004; Award for Distinguished Contribs, American Asscn of Sex Educators, Counsellors and Therapists 1988. *Publications:* Sexual Honesty: By Women For Women 1974, The Hite Report: A Nationwide Study of Female Sexuality 1976, The Hite Report on Male Sexuality 1981, Hite Report on Women and Love: A Cultural Revolution in Progress 1987, Good Guys, Bad Guys (with Kate Colleran) 1989, Women as Revolutionary Agents of Change: The Hite Reports and Beyond 1993, The Hite Report on the Family: Growing Up Under Patriarchy 1994, The Divine Comedy of Ariadne and Jupiter 1994, The Hite Report on Hite: A Sexual and Political Autobiography 1996, How Women See Other Women 1998, Sex and Business 2000, Shere Hite Reader 2004, Oedipus Revisited: Sexual Behaviour in the Human Male Today 2005, Shere Hite Reader: Sex, Globalisation and Private Life 2006. *Leisure interests:* answering e-mails, writing weekly columns for int. newspapers. *Address:* c/o Seven Stories Press, 140 Watts Street, New York, NY 10013, USA (office). *Telephone:* (7703) 538-796 (UK). *Fax:* (20) 7928-9809 (UK) (office). *E-mail:* info@hite-research.com; hite2000@hotmail.com. *Website:* www.hite-research.com.

HITOTO, Yo; Japanese singer; b. 20 Sept. 1976, Taipei, Taiwan; ed Keio Univ.; J-pop style singer and songwriter; released debut single 2002; made her film acting debut 2004. *Recordings include:* albums: Tsukitenshin 2002, Hito-omoi 2004, & 2005, Bestyo 2006, Key 2008; singles: Morai naki (Sympathy Tears), Da-jia, Kingyo Sukui, Edo Polka, Hanamizuki. *Films:* Café Lumière 2004. *Address:* c/o Nippon Columbia Company Limited, 4-14-14 Akasaka, Minato-ku, Tokyo 107-8011, Japan (office). *Website:* www.hitotoyo.ne.jp.

HJELM-WALLÉN, Lena, MA; Swedish politician; *Chairman, International Institute for Democracy and Electoral Assistance;* b. 14 Jan. 1943, Sala; d. of Gustaf Hjelm and Elly Hjelm-Wallén; m. Ingvar Wallén 1965; one d.; ed Univ. of Uppsala; teacher in Sala 1966–69; active in Social Democratic Youth League; elected to 2nd Chamber of Parl. 1968; mem. Exec. Cttee Västmanland br. of Socialdemokratiska Arbetarepartiet (Social Democratic Labour Party—SDLP) 1968, mem. SDLP Parl. Exec. 1976–82, SDLP Spokeswoman on Schools, mem. Bd SDLP 1978–87, SDLP Spokeswoman on Educ. 1991–94; Minister without Portfolio, with responsibility for schools 1974–76; Minister of Educ. and Cultural Affairs 1982–85, of Int. Devt Co-operation 1985–91, for Foreign Affairs 1994–98; Deputy Prime Minister of Sweden 1998–2002; Govt Rep. to the EU Convention on the Future of Europe; Chair. Bd Int. Inst. for Democracy and Electoral Assistance (IDEA) 2003–. *Leisure interests:* nature, books, gardening, family. *Address:* International IDEA, Strömsborg, 103 34 Stockholm, Sweden (office). *Telephone:* (8) 698-37-00 (office). *Fax:* (8) 20-24-22 (office). *E-mail:* info@idea.int (office). *Website:* www.idea.int (office).

HJÖRNE, Lars Goran; Swedish newspaper editor and publisher; b. 20 Oct. 1929, Gothenburg; s. of the late Harry Hjörne; m. Lena Hjörne (née Smith); one s. one d.; Chief Ed. Göteborgs-Posten 1969–89, Chair. 1969–95, Hon. Chair. 1995–; Hon. British Consul-Gen. in Gothenburg 1991–98; Hon. OBE. *Address:* Polhemsplatsen 5, 405 02 Gothenburg (office); Stora Vägen 43, 260 43 Arild, Sweden (home). *Telephone:* (31) 62-40-00 (office); (42) 34-68-03 (home).

HJÖRNE, Peter Lars; Swedish newspaper editor and publisher; *Editor-in-Chief, Göteborgs-Posten;* b. 7 Sept. 1952, Gothenburg; s. of Lars Hjörne and Anne Gyllenhammar; m. 2nd Karin Linnea Tufvesson Hjörne 1995; five d.; ed Göteborgs Högre Samskola and Univ. of Gothenburg; Man. Trainee John Deere Co., USA 1978–79; Exec. Asst Göteborgs-Posten 1979–82, Deputy Man. Dir 1983–85, Man. Dir 1985–93, Owner, Publr and Ed.-in-Chief 1993–. *Leisure interests:* sailing, literature, music, art. *Address:* Göteborgs-Posten, Polhemsplatsen 5, 405 02 Gothenburg, Sweden (office). *Telephone:* 31-62-40-00 (office). *Fax:* 31-15-76-92 (office). *E-mail:* peter.hjorne@gp.se (office). *Website:* www.gp.se (office).

HLA, Maj.-Gen. Tun; Myanma politician; *Minister of Finance and Revenue;* b. 11 July 1951, Yangon; s. of U Tin Ngwe and Daw Khin Kyi; m. Daw Khin Than Win; two c.; ed Defence Services Acad., Pyin-Oo-Lwin; fmr Deputy Dir.-Gen. Myanmar Police Force; fmr Gov. Bank of Myanmar; Minister of Finance and Revenue 2003–; General Service Medal, People's War Medal, State Peace and Tranquility Medal, Maing Yan/Me Tha Waw Battle Star, Distinguished Service Medal, Service Medal. *Leisure interests:* golf, painting. *Address:* Ministry of Finance and Revenue, 26(A) Setmu Road, Yankin Township, Yangon, Myanmar (office); No. 28, Pan Wah Street, Kamayut Tsp., Yangon,

Myanmar (home). *Telephone:* (1) 274894 (office). *Fax:* (1) 543632 (office). *Website:* www.myanmar.com/Ministry/finance (office).

HLAWITSCHKA, Eduard, Dr Habil.; German academic; *Professor, University of Munich;* b. 8 Nov. 1928, Dubkowitz; s. of Ernst Hlawitschka and Emilie Tschwatschal; m. Eva-Marie Schuldt 1958; one s. one d.; ed Univs of Rostock, Leipzig, Freiburg and Saarbrücken; Prof., Univ. of Düsseldorf 1969, Univ. of Munich 1975–; Pres. Sudetendeutsche Akad. der Wissenschaften und Künste 1991–94; Sudetendeutscher Kulturpreis für Wissenschaft 1987, Prix de Liechtenstein, Conf. Int. de Généalogie et d'Héraldique 1991. *Publications:* Franken, Alemannen, Bayern und Burgunder in Oberitalien 1960, Studien zur Äbtissinnenreihe von Remiremont 1963, Lotharingien und das Reich an der Schwelle der deutschen Geschichte 1968, Die Anfänge des Hauses Habsburg-Lothringen 1969, Libri memoriales I 1970, Vom Frankenreich zur Formierung der europäischen Staaten- und Völkergemeinschaft 840–1046 (1986), Untersuchungen zu den Thronwechseln der ersten Hälfte des 11. Jahrhunderts und zur Adelsgeschichte Süddeutschlands 1987, Stirps Regia 1988, Dübkowitz im Böhmischen Mittelgebirge 1997, Andechser Anfänge 2000, Konradiner-Genealogie, unstatthafte Verwandtenehen und spätottonisch-frühsalische Thronbesetzungspraxis 2003, Die Ahnen der hochmittelalterlichen deutschen Könige, Kaiser und ihrer Gemahlinnen Bd I (Vols 1 & 2) 2006. *Address:* Panoramastrasse 25, 82211 Herrsching/Ammersee, Germany. *Telephone:* (70) 81524991.

HO, Chih-Chin, BA, PhD; Taiwanese economist, academic and government official; b. 16 June 1952; ed Nat. Taiwan Univ., Univ. of Michigan; Economist, Okla State Resources Planning Bd, USA; Sr Researcher, Sentencing Comm., US Dept of Justice 1988–90; Sr Economist, US Internal Revenue Service 1990–98, Prin. Economist 1998–2003; Prof., Dept of Econs, Nat. Taiwan Univ. 2003–06, Dir 2004–06; mem. Kuomintang (KMT) Party; Minister of Finance 2006–08 (resgnd). *Address:* c/o Kuomintang (KMT) Party, 11 Jongshan South Road, Taipei 100, Taiwan (office). *Telephone:* (2) 23121472 (office). *Fax:* (2) 23434561 (office). *Website:* www.kmt.org.tw (office).

HO, Ching, BSc, MS; Singaporean business executive; *Executive Director and CEO, Temasek Holdings;* b. 1953, d.-in-law of Lee Kuan Yew (Minister Mentor); m. Brig.-Gen. (retd) Lee Hsien Loong (Prime Minister of Singapore and Minister of Finance) 1985; four c.; ed Nat. Univ. of Singapore, Stanford Univ., USA; began career as engineer at Ministry of Defence with System Integration Man. Team –1986; Deputy Chair., later Chair. Singapore Technologies (state-controlled defence contractor) 1987–2002; Exec. Dir Temasek Holdings (controls 40 cos including Singapore Airlines, SingTel, DBS Bank, SMRT Corpn, Neptune Orient Lines, Keppel Corpn, SembCorp Industries, Singapore Technologies, PSA Corpn, Singapore Power) 2002–, currently also CEO; Hon. Fellow, Inst. of Engineers, Singapore; Distinguished Engineering Alumnus Award, Nat. Univ. of Singapore 1995; ranked by Fortune magazine as one of 50 Most Powerful Women in Business outside the US (tenth) 2003, (fifth) 2004, (11th) 2005, (12th) 2006, (12th) 2007, ranked by Forbes magazine amongst 100 Most Powerful Women (24th) 2004, (30th) 2005, (36th) 2006, (third) 2007, (eighth) 2008. *Address:* Temasek Holdings (Pte) Ltd, 60B Orchard Road, 06–18, Tower 2, The Atrium, Singapore 238891, Singapore (office). *Telephone:* (65) 6828-6828 (office). *Fax:* (65) 6821-1188 (office). *E-mail:* enquire@temasek.com (office). *Website:* www.temasek.com.sg (office).

HO, Edmund H. W., BA; Chinese business executive and politician; *Chief Executive of Macao Special Administrative Region;* b. 13 March 1955; s. of Ho Yin and Chan Keng; m.; one s. one d.; ed York Univ., Canada; chartered accountant and certified auditor 1981–; worked for accounting firm in Toronto, Ont. 1981–82; Gen. Man. Tai Fung Bank 1983, CEO 1999; mem. CPPCC 1986–; elected Deputy to NPC 1988, elected to 8th and 9th Standing Cttees; mem. Legis. Ass. of Macao 1988–, Vice-Pres. 1988–99; Vice-Pres. Macao Chamber of Commerce; Chair. Macao Asscn of Banks 1985–; Chief Exec. Macao Special Admin. Region (MSAR) May 1999–; Vice-Chair. All-China Fed. of Industry and Commerce, Econ. Council of the Macao Govt, Kiang Wu Hosp. Bd of Charity, Tung Sin Tong Charitable Inst.; Vice-Pres. Drafting Cttee of the Basic Law of the MSAR 1988, Consultative Cttee of the Basic Law of the MSAR 1989, Preparatory Cttee of the MSAR 1998; Convenor of Land Fund Investment Comm. of the MSAR; Chair. Bd of Dirs Univ. of Macao; Vice-Chair. Bd of Dirs Jinan Univ., Guangzhou; Pres. Exec. Cttee Macao Olympic Cttee; Pres. Macao Golf Asscn. *Address:* Headquarters of the Government of the Macao Special Administrative Region, Av. da Praia Grande, Macao Special Administrative Region, People's Republic of China (office). *Telephone:* 726886 (office). *Fax:* 726665 (office). *Website:* www.gov.mo (office).

HO, Pansy, BA; Hong Kong business executive; *Managing Director, Shun Tak Holdings;* b. 1962; d. of Dr Stanley Ho; ed Univ. of Santa Clara, USA; fmrly with high soc. events promotion co.; joined Shun Tak Group (cr. by father Stanley Ho in 1972) 1995, Exec. Dir 1995–99, Man. Dir (oversaw establishment of Macau Tower Convention and Entertainment Centre 2001) 1999–, also CEO Shun Tak-China Travel Shipping Investments Ltd (oversaw merger between shipping operations of Shun Tak and China Travel Services 1999) 1999–; CEO and Dir Melco Int. Devt Ltd; Dir Air Macau Corpn, Asia TV Ltd, Sociedade de Turismo e Diversões de Macau; entered into jt venture with MGM MIRAGE of Las Vegas, Nev. to build and operate MGM Grand Macau hotel and casino resorts 2005–; mem. Cttee CPPCC of Guangdong Prov.; Founding Hon. Adviser and Bd Dir Univ. of Hong Kong Foundation for Educational Devt and Research; mem. Advisory Council The Better Hong Kong Foundation; ranked by Fortune magazine amongst 50 Most Powerful Women in Business outside the US (31st) 2002, (46th) 2003, (49th) 2004, (39th) 2005, (42nd) 2006, (36th) 2007. *Address:* Shun Tak Holdings Ltd, Penthouse 39/F, West Tower, Shun Tak Centre, 200 Connaught Road Central, Hong Kong Special Administrative Region, People's Republic of China (office). *Telephone:* (852) 2859-3111 (office). *Fax:* (852) 2857-7181 (office). *E-mail:* enquiry@shuntakgroup.com (office). *Website:* www.shuntakgroup.com (office).

HO, Peng-Yoke, PhD, DSc, CPhys, FInstP, FAHA; Australian professor of Chinese; *Director Emeritus, Needham Research Institute, Cambridge;* b. 4 April 1926, Malaysia; s. of the late Tih-Aun Ho and Yeen-Kwai Ng; m. Lucy Mei-Yiu Fung 1955; one s. four d.; ed Raffles Coll., Singapore and Univ. of Malaya, Singapore; Asst Lecturer in Physics, Univ. of Malaya, Singapore 1951–54, Lecturer in Physics 1954–60, Reader Dept of Physics 1960–64; Prof. of Chinese Studies, Univ. of Malaya, Kuala Lumpur 1964–73, Dean of Arts 1967–68; Foundation Prof. Griffith Univ., Queensland 1973–89, Foundation Chair. School of Modern Asian Studies 1973–78, Prof. Emer. 1989–; Prof. of Chinese, Univ. of Hong Kong 1981–87, Master Robert Black Coll. 1984–87; mem. Academica Sinica; Dir Needham Research Inst., Cambridge 1990–, now Dir Emer.; Professorial Research Assoc., SOAS, Univ. of London; Hon. Prof., Chinese Acad. of Science, Beijing, Univ. of Science and Tech., Beijing, North-West Univ., Xian, China; Hon. DLitt (Edinburgh) 1995. *Publications:* The Astronomical Chapters of the Chin Shu 1966, Li, Qi and Shu: An Introduction to Chinese Science and Civilization 1985, Science and Civilization in China (with Joseph Needham), Vol. 5, Part 3 1976, Part 4 1980, Part 7 1986, Chinese Mathematical Astrology 2003. *Leisure interest:* chess. *Address:* Needham Research Institute, 8 Sylvester Road, Cambridge, CB3 9AF, England (office); 8 Holdway Street, Kenmore, Queensland 4069, Australia (home). *Telephone:* (7) 3378-0131 (home). *Fax:* (1223) 362703 (office); (7) 3378-4724 (home). *E-mail:* admin@nri.org.uk (office). *Website:* www.nri.org.uk (office).

HO, Stanley Hung Sun, OBE; Chinese business executive; *Group Executive Chairman, Shun Tak Holdings Ltd;* b. 25 Nov. 1921, Hong Kong; m.; 17 c.; ed Univ. of Hong Kong; Group Exec. Chair. Shun Tak Holdings Ltd (operator of world's largest jetfoil fleet); Founder and Man. Dir Sociedade de Turismo e Diversões de Macao, (SARL—tourism and entertainment, banking, property, airport and airline); Man. Dir Sociedade de Jogos de Macao, SA; Pres. Real Estate Developers' Asscn 1984–; Chair. Univ. of Hong Kong Foundation for Educational Devt and Research 1995–; mem. Court of Univ. of Hong Kong 1982–, Council 1984–; Vice-Patron Community Chest 1986–; Vice-Chair. Basic Law Drafting Cttee, Macao Special Admin. Region (MSAR) 1988–93, Vice-Chair. Preparatory Cttee, MSAR 1988–99; mem. Selection Cttee for First Govt of Hong Kong Special Admin. Region 1996–97; mem. Standing Cttee 9th CPPCC Nat. Cttee 1998–2003; Co-Chair. Int. Cttee Franklin Delano Roosevelt Memorial Comm. 1994–97; mem. Econ. Council of Macao SAR 2000–; Hon. Citizen of Beijing 2001; Comendador da Ordem de Benemerência (Portugal) 1970; Comendador da Ordem de Infante Dom Henrique (Portugal) 1981; CStJ 1983; Chevalier, Légion d'honneur 1983, Grande-Oficial da Ordem do Infante Dom Henrique (Portugal) 1985, Order of the Sacred Treasure (Japan) 1987, Equitem Commendatorem Ordinis Sancti Gregorii Magni 1989, Darjah Dato Seri Paduka Mahkota Perak (Malaysia) 1990, Grã-Cruz, Ordem do Mérito (Portugal) 1990, Medalha Naval de Vasco da Gama (Portugal)1991, Cruz de Plata de la Medalla de la Solidaridad (Spain) 1993, Grã-Cruz, Ordem do Infante Dom Henrique (Portugal) 1995, Hon. Order of the Crown of Terengganu Darjah Seri' Paduka Mahkota Terengganu (Malaysia) 1997, Nuno Gonçalo Vieira Matias (Portugal) 1999; Hon. DScS (Univ. of Macao) 1984, (Univ. of Hong Kong) 1987; Global Award for Outstanding Contrib. for the Devt of Int. Trade and Relations, Priyadashni Acad. (India) 2000, Gold Medal of Merit in Tourism (Portugal) 2001. *Leisure interests:* ballroom dancing, swimming, playing tennis. *Address:* Shun Tak Holdings Ltd, 39/F, West Tower, Shun Tak Centre, 200 Connaught Road Central, Hong Kong Special Administrative Region, People's Republic of China (office). *Telephone:* (852) 28593111 (Hong Kong) (office); (853) 566065 (Macao) (office). *Fax:* (852) 28581014 (Hong Kong) (office); (853) 371981 (Macao) (office).

HO, Tao, BA, MArch, LHD; Chinese architect, urban planner and artist; b. 17 July 1936, Shanghai; s. of Ping-Yin Ho and Chin-Hwa Chiu; m. 1st Chi-Ping Lu 1960, one s. two d.; m. 2nd Irene Lo 1978, one d.; ed Pui Ching Middle High School, Hong Kong 1950–56, Williams Coll., Williamstown, Mass. and Harvard Univ., USA; Research Asst, Albright-Knox Art Gallery, Buffalo, NY 1959; Architectural Asst to Walter Gropius 1963–64; Visiting Lecturer, Fine Arts Dept, Chinese Univ., Hong Kong 1965–67; f. own practice, Taoho Design Architects, Hong Kong 1968–; Co-founder, Hong Kong Arts Centre 1969, Chair. Visual Arts Cttee, Hong Kong Arts Centre 1972–77; Visiting Critic, Harvard Univ. Grad. School of Design 1975; External Examiner of Art, Chinese Univ., Hong Kong 1975–79; Visiting Critic, Design Dept, Hong Kong Polytechnic 1979–; Hon. Lecturer, School of Architecture, Hong Kong Univ. 1979–; Chair. Hong Kong Designers Asscn 1981; Hon. Adviser, City Hall Museum, Hong Kong 1981–; Chinese Govt Adviser for Hong Kong Affairs 1995; mem. Bd of Architects, Singapore 1981–; Assoc. mem. Chartered Inst. of Arbitrators 1979–; Core mem. Asian Planning and Architectural Consultants Ltd 1975–; Founder and Dir Vision Press Ltd, Hong Kong 1982–; Fellow, Hong Kong Inst. of Architects 1971–; mem. Singapore Inst. of Architects 1988, Ordre des Architectes, France, 1992; Founding mem. Hong Kong Artists' Guild 1987; f. Philharmonic Soc. of Hong Kong Professionals 1991; has organized more than 20 exhbns for Hong Kong Arts Centre 1972–; Arthur Lehman Fellow, Harvard Univ. 1960–63; Forum Fellow of World Econ. Forum at Davos 1997–2001; Justice of Peace of Hong Kong 1997–; mem. Political Consultative Cttee of Pudong, Shanghai 2001; Hon. FAIA 1988–; Hon. Fellow, Philippines Inst. of Architects 1993–; Hon. DHumLitt (Williams Coll., Mass., USA) 1979; Design Merit Award (Chinese Manufacturers' Asscn), Silver Medal (Hong Kong Inst. of Architects), Bicentennial Medal (Williams Coll., USA). *Radio:* 17-programme weekly radio series 'Tao Ho on Music' for RTHK 1987; regular panellist on 'Free as the Wind' (RTHK) 1997–. *Major works include:* Hong Kong Govt Pavilion, CMA Exhbn, Hong Kong 1969; Hong Kong Int. Elementary School 1975, Hong Kong Arts Centre 1977, residential devt,

Shouson Hill, Hong Kong (with K. C. Lye) 1979, planning and rban design of Chinese cities Xiamen, Qingdao and Harigzhou 1985–86, 6A Bowen Road Apt 1983 (HKIA Silver Medal), Bayview Residential Devt 1988, (HKIA Design Award), Hong Kong Baptist Coll. Redevelopment 1988–89; revitalization of Western Market, Hong Kong 1992; Eng Bldg, Chinese Univ. of Hong Kong 1993; renovation of Hong Kong Govt House 1993; designed commemorative stamps for Hong Kong Govt 1975; commissioned by SWATCH to design art clock tower to represent Hong Kong at 1996 Olympic Games, Atlanta; solo painting exhbns at China Art Gallery, Beijing 1993, La Maison de Verre, Paris 1993, Hong Kong Univ. Museum 1995, Villa Turque, La Chaux-de-Fonds, Switzerland; China Construction Bank Headquarters, Beijing 1998, Giant Panda Habitat, Hong Kong 1999, Pentecostal Holiness Wing Kwong Church (including stained glass design), Hong Kong 2000, Industrial and Commercial Bank Data Centre, Beijing 2002; light sculpture 'BIG BANG' created for new HQ of World Econ. Forum, Geneva. *Publications:* Taoho Building Dreams 2000; numerous papers on theory and practice of art and architecture. *Leisure interests:* collecting art, writing about art, listening to music, painting, reading in cosmology and philosophy of science, sculpture. *Address:* 8/B, 499 King's Road, North Point, Hong Kong Special Administrative Region, People's Republic of China. *Telephone:* (852) 28118780. *Fax:* (852) 28110337. *Website:* www.taoho.com (office).

HOA, Truong My; Vietnamese politician; joined People's Army aged 15; captured aged 19 and imprisoned for 11 years; Pres. Nat. Cttee for the Advancement of Women 1995; Pres. The Women's Union 1995; Vice-Chair. 10th Nat. Ass.; Vice-Pres. of Socialist Repub. of Viet Nam 2002–06; currently Vice-Chair. Nat. Cttee for Population and Family Planning; mem. Party Cen. Cttee (PPP). *Address:* c/o National Committee for Population and Family Planning, 12 Ago Tat To, Dong Da, Hanoi, Viet Nam (office).

HOAGLAND, Edward, AB; American author; b. 21 Dec. 1932, New York; s. of Warren Eugene Hoagland and Helen Kelley Morley; m. 1st Amy J. Ferrara 1960 (divorced 1964); m. 2nd Marion Magid 1968 (died 1993); one d.; ed Harvard Univ.; faculty mem. New School for Social Research, New York 1963–64, Rutgers Univ. 1966, Sarah Lawrence Coll., Bronxville, New York 1967, 1971, City Univ. 1967, 1968, Univ. of Iowa 1978, 1982, Columbia Univ. 1980, 1981, Brown Univ. 1988, Bennington Coll., Bennington, Vt 1987–2005, Univ. of Calif. at Davis 1990, 1992, Beloit Coll., Wis. 1995; Gen. Ed. Penguin Nature Library 1985–2004; Houghton Mifflin Literary Fellow 1954; American Acad. of Arts and Letters Travelling Fellow 1964; Guggenheim Fellow 1964, 1975; mem. American Acad. of Arts and Letters; Longview Foundation Award 1961, O. Henry Award 1971, Brandeis Univ. Citation in Literature 1972, New York State Council on Arts Award 1972, American Acad. of Arts and Letters Harold D. Vursell Memorial Award 1981, Nat. Endowment for the Arts Award 1982, NY Public Library Literary Lion Award 1988, Nat. Magazine Award 1989, Lannan Foundation Literary Award 1993, Boston Public Library Literary Lights Award 1995. *Publications:* Cat Man 1956, The Circle Home 1960, The Peacock's Tail 1965, Notes from the Century Before: A Journal from British Columbia 1969, The Courage of Turtles 1971, Walking the Dead Diamond River 1973, The Moose on the Wall: Field Notes from the Vermont Wilderness 1974, Red Wolves and Black Bears 1976, African Calliope: A Journey to the Sudan 1979, The Edward Hoagland Reader 1979, The Tugman's Passage 1982, City Tales 1986, Seven Rivers West 1986, Heart's Desire 1988, The Final Fate of the Alligators 1992, Balancing Acts 1992, Tigers and Ice 1999, Compass Points 2001, Hoagland on Nature 2003; numerous essays and short stories. *Address:* PO Box 51, Barton, VT 05822, USA (home).

HOAGLAND, Richard E.; American diplomatist; *Ambassador to Kazakhstan;* b. Fort Wayne, Ind.; ed Univ. of Va and Univ. of Grenoble, France; taught English as a foreign language in Zaïre 1974–76, and African literature at Carter-Woodson Inst. of African and Afro-American Studies, Univ. of Va; joined Foreign Service 1985, now career mem. Sr Foreign Service with rank of Minister-Counselor, foreign assignments have included Russia (Press Spokesman for the Embassy), Uzbekistan, Pakistan (twice), has also served in State Dept's Bureau of Intelligence and Research (Lead Analyst for Afghanistan 1989–91), US Deputy Special Envoy for Afghanistan 1991–92, Dir Office of Public Diplomacy, Bureau of S Asian Affairs and Special Adviser to Nat. Security Council for public diplomacy on Afghanistan 1999–2001, Dir Office of Caucasus and Cen. Asian Affairs, Bureau of Europe and Eurasian Affairs 2001–03, Amb. to Tajikistan 2003–06, to Kazakhstan 2008–; Chargé d'affaires a.i. in Turkmenistan 2006–08; Meritorious Honor Award, two Superior Honor Awards, several Group Honor Awards, Presidential Performance Awards. *Address:* US Embassy, 010010 Astana, Ak Bulak 4/23-22/3, Kazakhstan (office). *Telephone:* (7172) 70-21-00 (office). *Fax:* (7172) 34-08-90 (office). *E-mail:* info@usembassy.kz (office). *Website:* kazakhstan.usembassy.gov (office).

HOAR, Gen. Joseph P., MA; American marine corps officer (retd) and business consultant; *President, J.P. Hoar and Associates Inc.;* b. 30 Dec. 1934, Boston, Mass.; s. of the late Joseph J. Hoar and of Marion J. Hoar; m. Charlene Hoar 1956; one s. four d.; ed Tufts Univ., George Washington Univ.; 2nd Lt Marine Corps 1957, rifle platoon Commdr 5th Marines, battalion staff officer 1st Bn 1st Marines, platoon Commdr, later guard company Commdr Marine Barracks Yorktown, VA., Asst G-1 Marine Corps Base, Camp Lejeune, NC, Bn operations officer 2nd Marine Div., Bn and brigade adviser Vietnamese Marines 1966–68, special Asst to Asst Commdt Marine Corps, Exec. Officer 1st Battalion 9th Marines 1968–71, instructor Marine Corps Command and Staff Coll. 1972–76, served Personnel Man. Div. HQ US Marine Corps 1976–77; Commdr 3rd Battalion 1st Marines 1977–79, promoted Col Regimental Commdr 1st Marines 1979–81; commanded 31st Marine Amphibious Unit on board USS Belleau Wood 1981–84; Asst Chief-of-Staff G-1 Marine Corps Recruit Depot, San Diego 1984–85; rank of Brig.-Gen. 1984; Asst Div. Commdr 2nd Marine Div., Dir Facilities and Services Div. Installations and Logistics Dept HQ Marine Corps Washington 1985–87; commanding Gen. Marine Corps Recruit Depot and Eastern Recruiting Region Parris Island 1987–88; promoted Maj.-Gen. 1987, Chief-of-Staff US Cen. Command 1988–90; Deputy Chief-of-Staff Plans, Policies and Operations 1990–91; rank of Lt-Gen. 1990, rank of Gen. 1991; C-in-C US Cen. Command 1991–94; Pres. J. P. Hoar and Assoc. Inc. 1994–; Co-Chair. Middle East Panel, Council on Foreign Relations 1994–; Fellow World Econ. Forum; Trustee CNA Corpn, Suffolk Univ., Center for Naval Analyses; mem. Bd of Dirs Hawaiian Airlines; three Defense Distinguished Service Medals, Bronze Star Medal with Combat 'V' and Gold Star, Meritorious Service Medal with Gold Star and other decorations; awards from nine foreign govts. *Leisure interest:* tennis. *Address:* c/o Board of Trustees, CNA Corporation, 4825 Mark Center Drive, Alexandria, VA 22311 (office); 386 13th Street, Del Mar, CA 92014, USA. *Telephone:* (858) 794-0546. *Fax:* (858) 794-0531.

HOARE, Sir Charles Antony Richard, Kt, FRS, FREng; British computer scientist; *Principal Researcher, Microsoft Research Ltd;* b. 11 Jan. 1934, Colombo, Ceylon (now Sri Lanka); s. of the late Henry S. M. Hoare and Marjorie F. Hoare; m. Jill Pym 1962; one s. one d.; ed Dragon School, Oxford, King's School, Canterbury, Merton Coll., Oxford, Unit of Biometry, Oxford and Moscow State Univ.; with Elliott Brothers (London) Ltd 1960–68; Prof. of Computing Science, Queen's Univ., Belfast 1968–77; Prof. of Computation, Univ. of Oxford 1977–93; James Martin Prof. of Computing 1993–99, Prof. Emer. 1999–; Sr Researcher, Microsoft Research Ltd 1999–, now Prin. Researcher; Fellow, Wolfson Coll. 1977–99; mem. Academia Europea; Foreign mem. Accad. dei Lincei, Italy; Corresp. mem. Bavarian Acad. of Sciences; Assoc. mem. US Nat. Acad. of Eng; Distinguished Fellow, British Computer Soc.; Hon. Fellow, Kellogg Coll. Oxford 1998, Darwin Coll. Cambridge 2001, Merton Coll. Oxford; Hon. DSc (Univ. of Southern Calif., Warwick, Pennsylvania, Queen's, Belfast); Hon. DUniv (York) 1989, (Essex) 1991, (Bath) 1993, (Oxford Brookes) 2000, (QMWC, London) 2005, (Heriot Watt) 2007, (Athens) 2007; A.M. Turing Award 1980, Harry Goode Memorial Award, Faraday Medal 1985, Kyoto Prize 2000. *Publications:* Structured Programming (co-author) 1972, Communicating Sequential Processes 1985, Essays in Computing Science 1989, Unifying Theories of Programming (co-author) 1998. *Leisure interests:* walking, music, reading, travel, gardening. *Address:* Microsoft Research Ltd, 7 J. J. Thomson Avenue, Cambridge, CB3 0FB, England (office). *Telephone:* (1223) 479800 (office). *Fax:* (1223) 479999 (office). *E-mail:* thoare@microsoft.com (office). *Website:* www.research.microsoft.com (office).

HOBAN, Russell Conwell, FRSL; American writer; b. 4 Feb. 1925, Lansdale, PA; s. of Abram Hoban and Jenny Hoban (née Dimmerman); m. 1st Lillian Aberman 1944 (divorced 1975, died 1998); one s. three d.; m. 2nd Gundula Ahl 1975; three s.; ed Lansdale High School and Philadelphia Museum School of Industrial Art; served US Infantry, Italy 1943–45; gen. illustrator Wexton co., New York 1950–51; TV Art Dir Batten, Barton, Durstine & Osborne (BBDO) Advertising, New York 1951–56; freelance illustrator 1956–65; copywriter, Doyle Dane Bernbach, New York 1965–67; novelist and author of children's books 1967–; mem. PEN, Soc. of Authors; Ditmar Award 1983. *Writing for theatre:* The Carrier Frequency (Impact Theatre Co-operative) 1984, Riddley Walker (Manchester Royal Exchange Theatre Co.) 1986, The Second Mrs Kong (opera libretto, premiere Glyndebourne) 1994. *Radio play:* Perfect and Endless Circles 1995. *Publications:* adult fiction: The Lion of Boaz-Jachin and Jachin-Boaz 1973, Kleinzeit 1974, Turtle Diary 1975, Riddley Walker (John W. Campbell Memorial Award and Australian Science Fiction Achievement Award 1983) 1980, Pilgermann 1983, The Medusa Frequency 1987, Angelica's Grotto 1991, The Moment under the Moment (stories, essays and libretto) 1992, Fremder 1996, The Trokeville Way 1996, Mr Rinyo-Clacton's Offer 1998, Amaryllis Night and Day 2001, The Bat Tattoo 2002, Her Name Was Lola 2003, Come Dance with Me 2005, Linger Awhile 2006, My Tango with Barbara Strozzi 2007; juvenile fiction includes: Bedtime for Frances 1960, Baby Sister for Frances 1964, The Mouse and his Child 1967, Best Friends for Frances 1969, The Pedalling Man 1970, The Sea-thing Child 1972, How Tom Beat Captain Najork and his Hired Sportsmen (Whitbread Prize for children's book) 1974, Dinner at Alberta's 1975, A Near Thing for Captain Najork 1975, The Twenty-Elephant Restaurant 1978, Ace Dragon 1980, The Marzipan Pig 1986, The Rain Door 1986, Ponders 1988, Bread and Jam for Frances 1993, Birthday for Frances 1994, The Trokeville Way 1996, Trouble on Thunder Mountain 1999, Jim's Lion 2001; poetry: The Last of the Wallendas 1997; contrib. essays and articles to Granta, The Fiction Magazine. *Leisure interest:* writing. *Address:* David Higham Associates Ltd, 5–8 Lower John Street, Golden Square, London, W1R 4HA, England (office). *Telephone:* (20) 7437-7888 (office). *Fax:* (20) 7437-1072 (office). *E-mail:* noctys@globalnet.co.uk (office).

HOBDAY, Sir Gordon (Ivan), Kt, PhD, FRSC, CChem, DL; British business executive (retd); b. 1 Feb. 1916, Derbyshire; s. of the late Alexander Thomas Hobday and Frances Cassandra Hobday (née Meads); m. 1st Margaret Jean Joule 1940 (died 1995); one d.; m. 2nd Patricia Shaw (née Birge) 2002; ed Long Eaton Grammar School, Univ. Coll., Notts.; joined The Boots Co. Ltd 1939, Dir of Research 1952–68, Deputy Man. Dir 1968–70, Man. Dir 1970–72, Chair. 1973–81; Dir The Metal Box Co. Ltd 1976–81, Lloyds Bank 1981–86; Deputy Chair. Price Comm. 1977–78; Chair. Cen. Ind. TV Co. Ltd 1981–85; Chancellor Univ. of Nottingham 1979–91 (Pres. of the Council 1973–82); Pres. Portland Coll. 1990–93; Lord Lt and Keeper of the Rolls for Notts. 1983–91; Hon. LLD. *Leisure interests:* handicrafts, gardening. *Address:* Newstead Abbey Park, Nottingham, NG15 8GD, England.

HOBERMAN, Brent, MA; British business executive; ed Univ. of Oxford; Sr Consultant, Media and Telecoms Spectrum Strategy Consultants, LineOne; Gen. Man., Head of Business Devt and Founder mem. QXL; co-f. with Martha Lane Fox (q.v.) and CEO lastminute.com 1998–2006, Chair. and Chief Strategy Officer 2006–07, Consultant 2007–; Dir (non-exec.) Guardian Media Group 2007–; Chair. (non-exec.) Wayn.com (travel and social networking site) 2007–; Exec. Chair. mydeco.com (home design website) 2007–; Advisor Twitter Partners 2009–; Gov. Univ. of the Arts, London. *Address:* Guardian Media Group PLC, 75 Farringdon Rd, London, EC1M 3JY, England (office). *Telephone:* (20) 7713-4452 (office). *Fax:* (20) 7742-0679 (office). *Website:* www.gmgplc.co.uk (office).

HOBSBAWM, Eric John Ernest, CH, MA, PhD, FBA; British academic (retd) and university administrator; *President, Birkbeck College, London;* b. 9 June 1917, Alexandria; s. of Leopold Percy Hobsbawm and Nelly Gruen; m. Marlene Schwarz 1962; one s. one d.; ed in Vienna, Berlin, London and Univ. of Cambridge; Lecturer, Birkbeck Coll. 1947–59, Reader 1959–70, Prof. of Econ. and Social History 1970–82, Prof. Emer. 1982–, currently Pres.; Fellow, King's Coll., Cambridge 1949–55, Hon. Fellow 1973–; Andrew D. White Prof.-at-Large, Cornell Univ. 1976–82; Prof., New School for Social Research, New York 1984–97; Hon. Foreign mem. American Acad. of Arts and Sciences, Hungarian Acad. of Sciences, Accad. delle Scienze, Turin; Chevalier des Palmes académiques, Order of the Southern Cross (Brazil) 1996; Dr hc (Stockholm) 1970, (Chicago) 1976, (East Anglia) 1982, (New School) 1982, (Bard Coll.) 1985, (York Univ., Canada) 1986, (Pisa) 1987, (London) 1993, (Essex) 1996, (Columbia Univ.) 1997, (Buenos Aires, Univ. of ARCIS, Santiago, Chile) 1998, (Univ. de la República, Montevideo, Uruguay) 1999, (Turin) 2000, (Oxford) 2001, (Pennsylvania) 2002, (Thessaloniki) 2004, (The Japan Acad.). *Publications:* Primitive Rebels 1959, The Age of Revolution 1962, Labouring Men 1964, Industry and Empire 1968, Captain Swing 1969, Bandits 1969, Revolutionaries 1973, The Age of Capital 1975; Ed. Storia del Marxismo (five vols) 1978–82, Worlds of Labour 1984, The Age of Empire 1875–1914 1987, Politics for a Rational Left: Political Writing 1989, Nations and Nationalism since 1780 1990, Echoes of the Marseillaise 1990, The Jazz Scene 1992, The Age of Extremes 1914–1991 1994, On History (essays) 1997, Uncommon People: Resistance, Rebellion and Jazz 1998, On the Edge of the New Century 2000, Interesting Times 2002, Globalisation, Democracy and Terrorism 2007. *Address:* Birkbeck College, University of London, Malet Street, Bloomsbury, London, WC1E 7HX, England (office). *Telephone:* (20) 7631-6000 (office). *Fax:* (20) 7631-6270 (office). *Website:* www.bbk.ac.uk (office).

HOBSON, Mellody, BA; American investment management executive; *President, Ariel Investments LLC;* b. 3 April 1969, Chicago; ed St Ignatius Coll. Prep., Woodrow Wilson School of Int. Relations and Public Policy, Princeton Univ.; joined Ariel Capital Man. LLC (now Ariel Investments) 1991, Pres. 2000–, also Chair. Bd of Trustees Ariel Investment Trust; financial analysis contrib., Good Morning America, ABC; appearances on CNN, WGN-TV; mem. Bd of Dirs Field Museum, Chicago Public Library, Chicago Public Educ. Fund, Sundance Inst., Tellabs Inc., DreamWorks Animation SKG Inc., Estée Lauder Cos Inc., Starbucks Corpn; term mem. New York Council on Foreign Relations; mem. Econ. Club of Chicago, Commercial Club of Chicago, Young Pres.'s Org.; Trustee Princeton Univ.; Global Leader of Tomorrow, World Econ. Forum, Davos 2001. *Address:* Ariel Investments LLC, 200 East Randolph Drive, Suite 2900, Chicago, IL 60601, USA (office). *Telephone:* (312) 726-0140 (office). *Fax:* (312) 726-7473 (office). *E-mail:* email@arielinvestments.com (office). *Website:* www.arielinvestments.com (office).

HOCH, Orion, PhD; American business executive; b. 21 Dec. 1928, Canonsburg, Pa; m. 1st Jane Lee Ogan 1952 (died 1978); one s. two d.; m. 2nd Catherine Nan Richardson 1980; one s.; ed Carnegie Mellon Univ., UCLA and Stanford Univ.; engaged in research and devt Hughes Aircraft 1952–54; various positions, Electron Devices Div. Litton Industries Inc. 1957–68; Vice-Pres. Litton Components Group 1968–70; Corp. Vice-Pres. Litton Industries Inc. 1970, Sr Vice-Pres. 1971, Deputy Head, Business Systems and Equipment Group 1973–74; Pres. Advanced Memory Systems (later Intersil Inc.) 1974–81; Pres. Litton Industries Inc. 1982–88, Dir and COO 1982, CEO 1986–93, Chair. 1988–94, Chair. Emer. 1994–; mem. Bd of Dirs UNOVA Inc. 1982–2001; Chair. Exec. Cttee, Dir Western Atlas Inc. 1994–98.

HOCHHUTH, Rolf; German playwright; b. 1 April 1931; m.; three s.; fmr publisher's reader; Resident Municipal Playwright, Basel 1963; mem. PEN of FRG. *Publications include:* plays: The Representative 1962, The Employer 1965, The Soldiers 1966, Anatomy of Revolution 1969, The Guerillas 1970, The Midwife 1972, Lysistrata and the NATO 1973, A German Love Story (novel) 1980, Judith 1984, The Immaculate Conception 1989. *Address:* Agentur Hegmann, Essener Str. 32, 45529 Hattingen, Germany (office). *Telephone:* (23) 2443157 (office). *E-mail:* ahegmann@web.de (office). *Website:* www.hegmann.de.tt (office); www.rolf-hochhuth.de.

HOCHSCHILD, Eduardo; Peruvian mining industry executive; *Executive Chairman, Hochschild Mining plc;* s. of Luis Hochschild; ed Tufts Univ., Boston, USA; joined Hochschild Mining Group as Safety Asst, Arcata Unit 1987, Head of Group 1998–2006, Exec. Chair. 2006–, oversaw listing of co. on London Stock Exchange 2006; Vice-Chair. Cementos Pacasmayo SAA; mem. Bd of Dirs COMEX Peru, Banco de Crédito del Perú, Sociedad Nacional de Minería y Petróleo, Asian Pacific Econ. Council Business Advisory Cttee, Conferencia Episcopal Peruana, Pacífico Peruano Suiza, TECSUP, Universidad Nacional de Ingeniería, Universidad de Ciencias Aplicadas. *Address:* Hochschild Mining plc, Pasaje El Carmen, #180, Surco, Lima, 33, Peru (office). *Telephone:* (1) 3172000 (office). *Website:* www.hochschildmining.com (office).

HOCKFIELD, Susan, BA, PhD; American neuroscientist, academic and university administrator; *President and Professor of Neuroscience, Massachusetts Institute of Technology;* m. Thomas N. Byrne; one d.; ed Univ. of Rochester, Georgetown Univ. School of Medicine; Postdoctoral Fellow, Univ. of California, San Francisco 1979–80; Jr Staff Investigator, Cold Spring Harbor Lab. 1980–82, Sr Staff Investigator 1982–85, Dir Summer Neurobiology Program 1985–97; Asst Prof., Section of Neurobiology, Yale Univ. School of Medicine 1985–89, Dir of Grad. Studies, Section of Neurobiology 1986–94, Assoc. Prof. 1989–94, Prof. 1994–2004, Dean Grad. School of Arts and Sciences 1998–2002, William Edward Gilbert Prof. of Neurobiology 2001–04, Provost 2003–04; Pres. and Prof. of Neuroscience, MIT 2004–; mem. Editorial Bd Learning and Memory 1993–, NeuroImage 1994–; mem. Bd of Dirs General Electric Co. 2006–, Lord Foundation of Massachusetts 2005–, Nat. Math and Science Initiative 2007–, World Econ. Forum 2008–; mem. Leadership Council, The Climate Group 2009–; mem. Bd of Overseers Boston Symphony Orchestra 2006–; Trustee Carnagie Corpn of New York 2006–; Corpn mem. Woods Hole Oceanographic Inst. 2006–; Fellow, American Acad. of Arts and Sciences 2004–, AAAS 2005–; mem. Soc. for Neuroscience, NIH Nat. Advisory Neurological Disorders and Stroke Council 2002–04; Trustee Cold Spring Harbour Lab.; Dr hc (Brown Univ.) 2006, (Cold Spring Harbor Lab., Watson School of Biological Sciences) 2006, (Tsinghua Univ.) 2006; Charles Judson Herrick Award, American Asscn of Anatomists 1987, Wilbur Lucius Cross Medal, Yale Univ. 2003, Meliora Citation for Career Achievement, Univ. of Rochester 2003, Sheffield Medal, Yale Univ. 2004, Golden Plate Award, Acad. of Achievement 2005, Amelia Earhart Award, Women's Union 2005. *Address:* Office of the President, Massachusetts Institute of Technology, 77 Massachusetts Avenue, Building 3-208, Cambridge, MA 02139-4307, USA (office). *Telephone:* (617) 253-0148 (office). *Fax:* (617) 253-3124 (office). *Website:* web.mit.edu (office).

HOCKNEY, David, CH, RA; British artist and stage designer; b. 9 July 1937, Bradford; s. of the late Kenneth Hockney and Laura Hockney; ed Bradford Coll. of Art and Royal Coll. of Art; taught at Maidstone Coll. of Art 1962, Univ. of Iowa 1964, Univ. of Colorado 1965, UCLA 1966 (Hon. Chair. of Drawing 1980), Univ. of California, Berkeley 1967; has travelled extensively in Europe and USA; Assoc. mem. Royal Acad. 1985; Hon. PhD (Aberdeen) 1988, (Royal Coll. of Art) 1992: Hon. DLitt (Oxford) 1995, (Cambridge) 2007; Guinness Award 1961, Graphic Prize, Paris Biennale 1963, First Prize 8th Int. Exhbn of Drawings and Engravings, Lugano 1964, prize at 6th Int. Exhbn of Graphic Art, Ljubljana 1965, Cracow 1st Int. Print Biennale 1966, First Prize 6th John Moores Exhbn 1967, Hamburg Foundation Shakespeare Prize 1983, Praemium Imperiale, Japan Art Asscn 1989, Fifth Annual Gov.'s Award for Visual Arts in Calif. 1994. *Film:* A Bigger Splash (autobiographical documentary) 1974. *Stage design:* set: Ubu Roi, Royal Court Theatre, London 1966, Rake's Progress, Glyndebourne 1975, Die Zauberflöte, Glyndebourne 1978, La Scala 1979, Nightingale, Covent Garden 1983, Varii Capricci, Metropolitan Opera House, New York 1983, Tristan and Isolde, LA Music Centre Opera, LA 1987, Turandot, Lyric Opera 1992–, San Francisco 1993, Die Frau Ohne Schatten, Covent Garden, London 1992, LA Music Centre Opera 1993; costume and set: Les Mamelles de Teresias, Metropolitan Opera House, New York 1980, L'Enfant et les sortilèges, Metropolitan Opera House, New York 1980, Parade, Metropolitan Opera House, New York 1980, Oedipus Rex, Metropolitan Opera House, New York 1981, Le Sacre du Printemps, Metropolitan Opera House, New York 1981, Le Rossignol, Metropolitan Opera House, New York 1981. *Publications:* Hockney by Hockney 1976, David Hockney, Travel with Pen, Pencil and Ink 1978 (autobiog.), Paper Pools 1980, Photographs 1982, China Diary (with Stephen Spender), 1982, Hockney Paints the Stage 1983, David Hockney: Cameraworks 1984, Hockney on Photography: Conversations with Paul Joyce 1988, David Hockney: A Retrospective 1988, Hockney's Alphabet (ed. by Stephen Spender) 1991, That's the Way I See It 1993 (autobiog.), Off the Wall: Hockney Posters 1994, David Hockney's Dog Days 1998, Hockney on Art: Photography, Painting and Perspective 1999, Hockney on 'Art': Conversation with Paul Joyce 2000, Secret Knowledge: Rediscovering the Lost Techniques of the Old Masters 2001, Hockney's Pictures 2004; illustrated Six Fairy Tales of the Brothers Grimm 1969, The Blue Guitar 1977, Hockney's Alphabet 1991. *Address:* c/o 7508 Santa Monica Boulevard, Los Angeles, CA 90046-6407, USA.

HOCQ-CHOAY, Nathalie; French business executive; b. 7 Aug. 1951, Neuilly (Hauts-de-Seine); d. of Robert Hocq and Christiane Arnoult; m. Patrick Choay; one d.; ed École Mary Mount, Neuilly, Cours Victor-Hugo, Paris and Univ. of Paris-Dauphine; Publicity Asst, Havas-conseil 1970; in charge of duty-free network, Briquet Cartier 1970; Exec. Cartier SA 1974, Gen. Man. 1977, Man. Dir Devt 1979–81; Vice-Chair. Cartier Int. 1981; acquired Poiray Joailliers Paris 1988, Pres., Dir-Gen. and CEO 1988–2003, René Boivin Joaillier 2000; shareholder, Artamis SA, Geneva; Prix de l'Innovation dans le Commerce (France). *Leisure interests:* riding, tennis, skiing and swimming. *Address:* Artamis SA, 4 rue de Neuchatel, 1201 Geneva, Switzerland.

HODDLE, Glenn; British football manager and fmr professional football player; b. 27 Oct. 1957, London; s. of Derek Hoddle and Teresa Roberts; m. Christine Anne Stirling (divorced 1999); one s. two d.; ed Burnt Mill School, Harlow; player with Tottenham Hotspur 1976–86, AS Monaco, France 1986; (12 Under-21 caps, 53 full caps on England nat. team 1980–88, played in World Cup 1982 and 1986); player/man. Swindon Town 1991–93 (promoted to FA Premier League 1993); player/man. Chelsea 1993–96; coach English nat. team 1996–99; Man. Southampton 2000–2001, Tottenham Hotspur 2001–03, Wolverhampton Wanderers 2004–; FA Cup winners' medal (Tottenham Hotspur) 1981 and 1982, UEFA Cup winners' medal (Tottenham Hotspur) 1984, French Championship winners' medal (Monaco) 1988. *Publications:* Spurred to Success (autobiog.), Glenn Hoddle: The 1998 World Cup Story

1998. *Leisure interests:* tennis, golf, reading. *Address:* Wolverhampton Wanderers Football Club, Molineux Stadium, Waterloo Road, Wolverhampton, WV1 4QR, England. *Telephone:* (0870) 442-0123. *Website:* www.wolves.co.uk.

HODEL, Donald Paul, JD; American lawyer (retd) and fmr government official; b. 23 May 1935, Portland, Ore.; s. of Philip E. Hodel and Theresia R. (Brodt) Hodel; m. Barbara B. Stockman 1956; two s. (one deceased); ed Harvard Coll. and Univ. of Oregon; admitted to Ore. Bar 1960 (retd 2008); Attorney, Davies, Biggs, Strayer, Stoel & Boley 1960–63; Georgia Pacific Corpn 1963–69; Deputy Admin., Bonneville Power Admin. 1969–72, Admin. 1972–77; Pres. Nat. Elec. Reliability Council, Princeton, NJ 1978–80; Pres. Hodel Assocs. Inc. 1978–81; Under-Sec. Dept of Interior 1981–83; Sec. of Energy 1982–85, of the Interior 1985–89; Founder and Chair. Summit Power Group Inc. 1989–; Pres. and CEO Focus on the Family 2003–05; Republican. *Address:* c/o Board of Directors, Focus on the Family, Colorado Springs, CO 80995, USA.

HODGE, Sir James William, KCVO, CMG, MA; British diplomatist; b. 24 Dec. 1943; s. of the late William Hodge and Catherine Hodge (née Carden); m. Frances Margaret Coyne 1970; three d.; ed Holy Cross Acad., Edin., Univ. of Edin.; entered FCO 1966, Rhodesia Political Dept 1966–67, Second Sec. (Information), Tokyo 1967–72, FCO Marine and Transport Dept 1972–73, UN Dept 1973–75, First Sec. (Devt and later Chancery), Lagos 1975–78, FCO Personnel Operations Dept 1978–81, First Sec. (Econ.) and later Counsellor (Commercial), Tokyo 1981–86, Head of Chancery, Copenhagen 1986–90, FCO Security Dept 1990–93, attached to Royal Coll. of Defence Studies 1994; Minister Consular Gen. and Deputy Head of Mission, Beijing 1995–96; Amb. to Thailand 1996–2000; Consul-Gen. to Hong Kong Special Admin. Region, People's Repub. of China (concurrently non-resident Consul-Gen. to Macao) Aug. 2000–03. *Leisure interests:* books, music. *Address:* c/o British Consulate-General, 1 Supreme Court Road, Hong Kong, People's Republic of China (office). *Telephone:* (852) 2901-3000. *Fax:* (852) 2901-3066. *E-mail:* information@britishconsulate.org.hk. *Website:* www.britishconsulate.org.hk.

HODGE, Patricia; British actress; b. 29 Sept. 1946, Grimsby; d. of the late Eric Hodge and Marion Phillips; m. Peter Owen 1976; two s.; ed London Acad. of Music and Dramatic Art; Eveline Evans Award for Best Actress LAMDA, Olivier Award for Best Supporting Actress 1999; Hon. DLitt (Hull) 1996, (Brunel) 2001, (Leicester) 2003; Olivier Award 2000. *Stage appearances include:* No-one Was Saved, All My Sons, Say Who You Are, The Birthday Party, The Anniversary, Popkiss, Two Gentlemen of Verona, Pippin, Maudie, Hair, The Beggar's Opera, Pal Joey, Look Back in Anger, Dick Whittington, Happy Yellow, The Brian Cant Children's Show, Then and Now, The Mitford Girls, As You Like It, Benefactors, Noel and Gertie, Separate Tables, The Prime of Miss Jean Brodie, Boeing Boeing, The Country Wife, A Little Night Music (Royal Nat. Theatre), Heartbreak House 1997, Money (Royal Nat. Theatre) 1999 (Olivier Award 2000), Summer-folk (Royal Nat. Theatre) 1999, Noises Off (Royal Nat. Theatre and tour) 2000–01, His Dark Materials (Royal Nat. Theatre) 2004. *Film appearances:* The Disappearance, Rose Dixon—Night Nurse, The Waterloo Bridge Handicap, The Elephant Man, Heavy Metal, Betrayal, Sunset, Just Ask for Diamond, The Secret Life of Ian Fleming, The Leading Man 1996, Prague Duet 1996, Jilting Joe 1997, Before You Go 2002. *TV appearances:* Valentine, The Girls of Slender Means, Night of the Father, Great Big Groovy Horse, The Naked Civil Servant, Softly, Softly, Jackanory Playhouse, Act of Rape, Crimewriters, Target, Rumpole of the Bailey, The One and Only Mrs Phyllis Dixey, Edward and Mrs Simpson, Disraeli, The Professionals, Holding the Fort, The Other 'Arf, Jemima Shore Investigates, Hayfever, The Death of the Heart, Robin of Sherwood, O.S.S., Sherlock Holmes, Time for Murder, Hotel du Lac, The Life and Loves of a She Devil, Rich Tea and Sympathy 1991, The Cloning of Joanna May 1991, The Legacy of Reginald Perrin 1996, The Moonstone 1996, The Falklands Play 2002, Sweet Medicine 2003, Miss Marple: The Sittaford Mystery 2006. *Address:* c/o I.C.M., Oxford House, 76 Oxford Street, London, W1N 0AX, England. *Telephone:* (20) 7636-6565. *Fax:* (20) 7323-0101.

HODGES, Jim, BA, JD; American fmr state governor and consultant; *CEO and Managing Director, Hodges Consulting Group;* b. 19 Nov. 1956, Lancaster, SC; m. Rachel Gardner; two s.; ed Davidson Coll., Univ. of South Carolina; Lancaster Co. Attorney, Gen. Counsel, Springs Co.; mem. SC House of Reps 1986–97; Gov. of South Carolina 1999–2002; founder, CEO and Man. Dir Hodges Consulting Group 2003–; Legislator of the Year, SC Chamber of Commerce 1993, Compleat Lawyer Silver Medallion 1994, Guardian of Small Business Award, Nat. Fed. of Ind. Businesses 1996, Special Service Award, Common Cause 1998. *Address:* Hodges Consulting Group, 1122 Lady Street, Suite 850, Columbia, SC 29201, USA (office). *Telephone:* (803) 251-2301 (office). *Fax:* (803) 251-2315 (office). *E-mail:* jhodges@hodgesconsulting.com (office). *Website:* www.hodgesconsulting.com (office).

HODGKIN, Sir Howard, Kt, CH, CBE, DLitt; British painter; b. 6 Aug. 1932; m. Julia Lane 1955; two s.; ed Camberwell School of Art and Bath Acad. of Art; Trustee, Tate Gallery 1970–76, Nat. Gallery 1978–85; British rep., Venice Biennale 1984; works in many public collections including Tate Gallery, London, Museum of Modern Art, New York, Nat. Gallery of Washington, Metropolitan Museum of Art, New York, Nat. Gallery of S Australia, Adelaide, Walker Art Center, Minneapolis; mem. Cttee Nat. Art Collections Fund 1989–90; Hon. Fellow, Brasenose Coll., Univ. of Oxford 1988, London Inst. 1999; Hon. DLitt (Birmingham) 1997, (Oxford) 2000; Tate Gallery Turner Prize 1985, Shakespeare Prize, Alfred Toepfer Stiftung FVS, Germany 1997. *Address:* c/o Gagosian Gallery, 6–24 Britannia Street, London, WC1X 9JD, England (office). *Telephone:* (20) 7841-9960 (office). *Fax:* (20) 7841-9961 (office). *Website:* www.gagosian.com (office).

HODGKINSON, Sir Mike, Kt, BA; British business executive; *Chairman, The Post Office (UK);* b. 7 April 1944, Essex; m.; three c.; ed Hornchurch Grammar School, Nottingham Univ.; Ford Grad. Training Programme 1965; Finance and Admin. Dir Leyland Cars (Eng Div.) 1973–77; Man. Dir Land Rover 1978–82; Man. Dir Express Dairy Group 1985; CEO GM Foods Europe, Grand Metropolitan Group 1986–91; Group Airports Dir BAA 1992–99, CEO 1999–2003; Dir Airports Council Int.; Dir (non-exec.) FKI, Transport for London, Royal Mail Holdings PLC 2002–; Chair. The Post Office 2003–; mem. ACI World Gov. Bd, Advisory Bd Essex Econ. Partnership 2001–; Chair. Hayes West Drayton Partnership. *Leisure interests:* golf, theatre. *Address:* The Post Office, Royal Mail Group PLC, 148 Old Street, London, EC1V 9HQ, England (office). *Website:* www.postoffice.co.uk (office).

HODGSON, Pete; New Zealand politician; *Minister for Economic Development, Tertiary Education, and of Research, Science and Technology;* b. 1950, Whangarei; m.; two s.; ed Massey Univ.; fmrly worked as Veterinary Surgeon in New Zealand and UK; mem. New Zealand Labour Party 1976–; MP for Dunedin N 1990–; Minister of Energy, Fisheries, Forestry, Research Science and Tech. 1999–2004, Minister for Crown Research Insts, Assoc. Minister of Econ., Industry and Regional Devt and Assoc. Minister of Foreign Affairs and Trade 1999–2005; Minister of Transport, of Commerce, for Land Information, of Statistics and Assoc. Minister of Health 2004–05; Minister of Health 2005–07, of Econ. Devt, Tertiary Educ. and Minister of Research, Science and Tech. 2007–. *Address:* Ministry of Economic Development, POB 1473, 33 Bowen Street, Wellington, New Zealand (office). *Telephone:* (4) 472-0030 (office). *Fax:* (4) 473-4638 (office). *E-mail:* info@med.govt.nz (office). *Website:* www.med.govt.nz (office).

HODGSON, Thomas R., BS, MS, MBA; American business executive; b. 17 Dec. 1941, Lakewood, Ohio; s. of Thomas J. Hodgson and Dallas L. Hodgson; m. Susan Cawrse 1963; one s. two d.; ed Purdue Univ., Univ. of Mich. and Harvard Univ. Business School; Devt engineer DuPont 1964; Assoc. Booz-Allen & Hamilton 1969–72; with Abbott Labs. 1972–99, Gen. Man. Faultless Div. 1976–78, Vice-Pres. and Gen. Man. Hosp. Div. 1978–80, Pres. Hosp. Div. 1980–83, Group Vice-Pres. and Pres. Abbott Int. Ltd 1983–84, Exec. Vice-Pres. 1985–80, Pres. and COO Abbott Laboratories Oct. 1990–99 (retd); Visiting Prof. Purdue Univ. 1996; mem. Bd of Dirs Idenix Pharmaceuticals Inc., 2002–, The St. Paul Travelers Inc. 1997–, Intermune, Inc. 2003–; fmr mem. Bd of Dirs ARUP Laboratories, Trainseek.com, St. Paul Cos; Dr hc (Purdue Univ.). *Leisure interests:* skiing, scuba, wind-surfing, racquetball, tennis, kayaking. *Address:* c/o Board of Directors, Idenix Pharmaceuticals, Inc., 60 Hampshire Street, Cambridge, MA 02139 (office); 1015 Ashley Road, Lake Forest, IL 60045, USA (home).

HØEG, Peter; Danish writer; b. 1957, Copenhagen; m.; two d.; ed Univ. of Copenhagen; worked as sailor, ballet dancer, athlete and actor before becoming full-time writer; f. Lolwe Foundation 1996. *Publications:* Forestilling om det Tyvende århundrede (trans. as The History of Danish Dreams) 1988, Fortællinger om natten (trans. as Tales of the Night; short stories) 1990, Frk. Smillas fornemmelse for sne (trans. as Miss Smilla's Feeling for Snow) 1992, De måske egnede (trans. as Borderliners) 1994, Kvinden og aben (trans. as The Woman and the Ape) 1996, Den stille pige (trans. as The Quiet Girl) 2006. *Address:* c/o Rosinante, Købmagergade 62, Postbox 2252, 1019 Copenhagen K, Denmark (office). *Telephone:* 33-41-18-00 (office). *E-mail:* rosinante@rosinante.dk (home). *Website:* www.rosinante.dk (office).

HOEVEN, John, MBA; American state official; *Governor of North Dakota;* b. 13 March 1957, Bismarck, ND; m. Mical (Mikey) Hoeven; one s. one d.; ed Dartmouth Coll., Northwestern Univ.; Exec. Vice-Pres. First Western Bank, Minot 1986–93; Pres. and CEO Bank of ND 1993–2000; Gov. of ND 2000–; mem. Souris Valley Humane Soc.; Dir Minot Kiwanis Club; Republican. *Address:* Office of the Governor, State Capitol, 600 East Boulevard Avenue, Department 101, Bismark, ND 58505-0001, USA (office). *Telephone:* (701) 328-2200 (office). *Fax:* (701) 328-2205 (office). *E-mail:* governor@state.nd.us (office). *Website:* governor.state.nd.us (office).

HOFFMAN, Alan Jerome, AB, PhD; American mathematician and educator; *IBM Fellow Emeritus, T.J. Watson Research Center, IBM;* b. 30 May 1924, New York; s. of Jesse Hoffman and Muriel Hoffman; m. 1st Esther Walker 1947 (died 1988); two d.; m. 2nd Elinor Hershaft 1990; ed George Washington High School, Columbia Univ.; mem. US Army Signal Corps 1943–46; mem. Inst. for Advanced Study 1950–51; Mathematician, Nat. Bureau of Standards 1951–56; Scientific Liaison Officer, Office of Naval Research, London 1956–57; Consultant, Gen. Electric Co. 1957–61; Adjunct Prof., CUNY 1965–75; Research Staff mem. T.J. Watson Research Center, IBM 1961–2002, IBM Fellow 1977–2002, IBM Fellow Emer. 2002–; Visiting Prof., Yale Univ. 1975–80, Rutgers Univ. 1990–96, Georgia Inst. of Tech. 1992–93; Consulting Prof., Stanford Univ. 1981–91; mem. NAS; Fellow, New York Acad. of Sciences, American Acad. of Arts and Sciences, INFORMS; Hon. DSc (Technion) 1986; Von Neumann Prize, Operations Research Soc. and Inst. of Man. Science 1992, Founders Award, Math. Programming Soc. 2000. *Publications:* Selected Papers of Alan Hoffman 2003; numerous articles in math. journals. *Address:* T.J. Watson Research Center, IBM, Box 218, Yorktown Heights, NY 10598, USA (office). *E-mail:* ajh@us.ibm.com (office). *Website:* www.research.ibm.com/people/a/ajh (office).

HOFFMAN, Darleane, BS, PhD; American nuclear chemist and academic; *Faculty Senior Scientist, Nuclear Science Division, Lawrence Berkeley National Laboratory;* b. (Darleane Christian), 8 Nov. 1926, Terril, IA; d. of Carl Christian and Elverna Christian; m. Marvin Hoffman 1951; one s. one d.; ed Iowa State Univ., Ames; Researcher, Oak Ridge Nat. Lab. 1952–53; Researcher, Los Alamos Nat. Lab. 1953–84, becoming Assoc. Group Leader and later Leader, Nuclear Chem. Div., Isotope and Nuclear Chem. Div.; Prof.

of Chem., Univ. of California, Berkeley 1984–91, Prof. Emer. 1991–93, Prof., Grad. School 1993–, now Emer.; Faculty Sr Scientist and Group Leader, Heavy Element, Nuclear and Radiochemistry Group, Lawrence Berkeley Lab. 1984–, Faculty Sr Scientist, Nuclear Science Div. 2001–; Dir Seaborg Inst. for Transactinium Science 1991–96; Fellow, Norwegian Acad. of Science and Letters 1990, American Acad. of Arts and Sciences 1998; Hon. Int. mem. Japan Soc. of Nuclear and Radiochemistry 2004; Dr hc (Clark Univ.) 2000, (Univ. of Bern) 2001; Alumni Citation Merit, Iowa State Univ. 1978, Guggenheim Fellow 1978–79, ACS Award for Nuclear Chem. 1983, Distinguished Achievement Award, Iowa State Univ. 1988, ACS Garvan Medal 1991, US Nat. Medal of Science 1997, ACS Priestley Medal 2000, Women in Science and Tech. Hall of Fame 2000, Alpha Chi Sigma Hall of Fame 2002, Sigma Xi Procter Prize 2003, Radiochemistry Soc. Lifetime Achievement Award 2003. *Publications:* The Transuranium People: The Inside Story (co-author) 2000; more than 250 articles in books and scientific journals. *Leisure interests:* swimming, music. *Address:* Nuclear Science Division, MS70R0319, Lawrence Berkeley National Laboratory, One Cyclotron Road, Berkeley, CA 94720, USA (office). *Telephone:* (510) 486-4474 (office). *Fax:* (510) 486-7444 (office). *E-mail:* dchoffman@lbl.gov (office). *Website:* sheiks.lbl.gov/index.htm (office).

HOFFMAN, Dustin Lee; American actor; b. 8 Aug. 1937, Los Angeles, Calif.; s. of Harry Hoffman; m. 1st Anne Byrne 1969 (divorced); two d.; m. 2nd Lisa Gottsegen 1980; two s. two d.; ed Santa Monica City Coll.; worked as an attendant at a psychiatric inst.; demonstrator, Macy's toy dept; first stage role in Yes is for a Very Young Man (Sarah Lawrence Coll., Bronxville, NY); Broadway debut in A Cook for Mr. General 1961; Founder Punch Productions; Officier, Ordre des Arts et des Lettres; Britannia Award (BAFTA) 1997, Golden Globe Lifetime Achievement Award 1997, American Film Inst. Lifetime Achievement Award 1999. *Other stage appearances in:* Harry, Noon and Night 1964, Journey of the Fifth Horse (Obie Award) 1966, Star Wagon 1966, Fragments 1966, Eh? (Drama Desk, Theatre World, Vernon Rice Awards) 1967, Jimmy Shine 1968, Death of a Salesman 1984, The Merchant of Venice 1989; Asst Dir A View from the Bridge; Dir All Over Town 1974. *Films include:* The Tiger Makes Out 1966, Madigan's Millions 1966, The Graduate 1967, Midnight Cowboy 1969, John and Mary 1969, Little Big Man 1970, Who is Harry Kellerman...? 1971, Straw Dogs 1971, Alfredo Alfredo, Papillon 1973, Lenny 1974, All the President's Men 1975, Marathon Man 1976, Straight Time 1978, Agatha 1979, Kramer vs. Kramer (Acad. Award 1980, New York Film Critics Award) 1979, Tootsie (New York Film Critics Award, Nat. Soc. of Film Critics Award) 1982, Ishtar 1987, Rain Man (Acad. and Golden Globe Awards) 1988, Family Business 1989, Dick Tracy 1990, Hook 1991, Billy Bathgate 1991, Hero 1992, Outbreak 1995, American Buffalo, Sleeper 1996, Wag the Dog 1997, Mad City 1997, Sphere 1997, The Messenger: the Story of Joan of Arc 1999, Being John Malkovich 1999, Moonlight Mile 2002, Confidence 2003, Runaway Jury 2003, Finding Neverland 2004, I Heart Huckabees 2004, Meet the Fockers 2004, Racing Stripes (voice) 2005, The Lost City 2005, Perfume: The Story of a Murderer 2006, Stranger Than Fiction 2006, Mr. Magorium's Wonder Emporium 2007, Kung Fu Panda (voice) 2008. *TV appearance in:* Death of a Salesman 1985. *Leisure interests:* tennis, piano, photography, reading. *Address:* Punch Productions, 1926 Broadway, Suite 305, New York, NY 10023; PO Box 492359, Los Angeles, CA 90049-8359; c/o The Endeavor Agency, 9601 Wilshire Blvd., 10th Floor, Beverly Hills, CA 90212, USA. *Telephone:* (212) 595-8800 (Punch Productions).

HOFFMAN, Jerzy; Polish film director; b. 15 March 1932, Kraków; m. (deceased); one d.; ed All-Union State Inst. of Cinematography, Moscow; has directed 27 documentaries with Edward Skórzewski including Remembrance of Kalwaria (Oberhausen and Florence Film Festival awards), Two Aspects of God, and others 1955–62; mem. Acad. of Fine Arts, Ukraine; Great Cross with Star, Order of Polonia Restituta; numerous Polish and int. film prizes including Minister of Culture and Arts Prize (four times). *Films include:* Gangsters and Philanthropists (feature film debut with Edward Skórzewski) 1962, Colonel Wolodyjowski (also wrote screenplay) 1969, Mazowsze 1971, The Deluge 1973, Leper 1976, The Quack 1981, Medicine Man, Beautiful Stranger 1993, With Fire and Sword (also wrote screenplay) (Polish Eagles for Best Film Producer 2000) 1999, Sienkiewicz Trilogy 2004; documentary: Ukraine 2005. *Leisure interests:* historical books, bridge, cooking, swimming. *Address:* Zodiak Jerzy Hoffman Production, ul. Puławska 61, 02-595 Warsaw, Poland (office). *Telephone:* (22) 845-20-47 (office).

HOFFMAN, Mat; American professional BMX rider; b. 9 Jan. 1972, Edmond, Okla; entered Freestyle BMX circuit as amateur aged 13, quickly rose to top of amateur class and turned professional aged 16; considered the greatest vert-ramp rider in history of BMX; nicknamed 'The Condor'; founder and owner Hoffman Bikes, Hoffman Sports Asscn/Hoffman Promotions and Hoffman Enterprises, Inc.; first rider to perform 900 degree spin in competition and take backflip to vert; came out of retirement to compete in Summer X-Games 2002 and won Bronze Medal, also landed no-handed 900 for first time in competition resulting in Silver Medal; set record for highest air jump 26 feet 6 inches (8.07m) on 24-foot (7.31m) ramp (jump listed in 2004 Guinness Book of World Records as High Air World Record holder for BMX bike) 2002; creator of Mat Hoffman's Crazy Freakin Stunt Show for Universal Studios, Orlando, Fla 2003, 2005; involved in several film projects, including Keep Your Eyes Open, IMAX film Ultimate X, xXx, Jackass – The Movie; host of series of behind-the-scenes segments for Tomb Raider 2 2003; appeared in video games such as Mat Hoffman BMX, Mat Hoffman BMX 2, and Tony Hawk Pro Skater 4; participated in Tony Hawk's (q.v.) Boom Boom Huck Jam 2002, 2003, 2005; Vice-Pres. Int. BMX Freestyle Fed., US BMX Freestyle Fed.; mem. Olympic Sub-cttee working to get Vert into 2008 Olympics in Beijing; Lifetime Achievement Award, ESPN Action Sports and Music Awards 2002. *Television:* has produced, directed and hosted several TV series for ESPN including Kids in the Way, HBtv, Mat's World, a nine-episode segment on X-2day and the CFB Series; mem. cast of MTV's Trippin' 2005. *Publications:* The Ride of My Life (autobiog.) 2002. *Address:* c/o Brian Dubin, William Morris Agency, 1325 Avenue of Americas New York, NY 10019, USA. *Telephone:* (212) 903-1184. *E-mail:* bd@wma.com. *Website:* www.mathoffman.com.

HOFFMAN, Philip Seymour; American actor; b. 23 July 1967, Fairport, New York; ed New York Univ. Tisch School of Drama; Co-Artistic Dir and mem. Bd of Dirs LAByrinth Theater Company, New York. *Films include:* Scent of a Woman 1992, My New Gun 1993, When a Man Loves a Woman 1994, Nobody's Fool 1994, The Getaway 1994, Twister 1996, Montana 1997, Boogie Nights 1997, Hard Eight 1997, The Big Lebowski 1998, Patch Adams 1998, The Talented Mr Ripley 1999, Magnolia 1999, Flawless 1999, Almost Famous 2000, State and Main 2000, Red Dragon 2002, Love Liza 2002, 25th Hour 2002, Owning Mahowny 2003, Cold Mountain 2003, Along Came Polly 2004, Strangers with Candy 2005, Capote (Best Actor Critics' Choice Awards 2006, Golden Globe Award for Best Actor in a Drama, Screen Actors Guild Award for Best Actor 2006, BAFTA Award for Best Actor in a Leading Role 2006, Acad. Award for Best Actor 2006) 2005, Mission: Impossible III 2006, The Savages 2007, Before the Devil Knows You're Dead 2007, Charlie Wilson's War 2007, Synecdoche, New York 2008. *Television includes:* Empire Falls (mini-series) 2005. *Address:* c/o Paradigm Talent and Literary Agency, 360 North Crescent Drive, North Building, Beverly Hills, CA 90210 (office); LAByrinth Theater Company, 16 West 32nd Street, Suite 10J, New York, NY 10001, USA. *Telephone:* (212) 513-1080 (LAByrinth). *Website:* www .labtheater.org.

HOFFMANN, Claus Dieter; German business executive; *Chairman of the Supervisory Board, Energie Baden-Württemberg AG;* b. 1942; fmrly with Robert Bosch GmbH, becoming Chief Financial Officer –2002; Man. Pnr, H + H Senior Advisors GmbH; Chair. Supervisory Bd Energie Baden-Württemberg AG 2006–; mem. Supervisory Bd ING Group 2003–, Bauerfeind AG, Jowat AG, De Boer Group; Chair. Charlottenklinik Foundation; Chair. Bd of Trustees (Vereinigung der Freunde), Stuttgart Univ.; mem. Foundation Council Japanisch-Deutsches Zentrum Berlin. *Leisure interest:* golf. *Address:* Energie Baden-Württemberg AG, Durlacher Allee 93, 76131 Karlsruhe, Germany (office). *Telephone:* (7) 21-63-00 (office). *Fax:* (7) 21-63-126-72 (office). *E-mail:* info@enbw.com (office). *Website:* www.enbw.com (office).

HOFFMANN, Baron (Life Peer), cr. 1995, of Chedworth in the County of Gloucestershire; **Rt Hon. Leonard Hubert Hoffmann,** Kt, MA, PC; British judge; b. 8 May 1934; s. of B.W. Hoffmann and G. Hoffmann; m. Gillian Sterner 1957; two d.; ed South African Coll. School, Cape Town, Univ. of Cape Town and Queen's Coll. Oxford; Advocate, Supreme Court of S Africa 1958–60; called to Bar, Gray's Inn, London 1964, Bencher 1984; QC 1977; Judge, Courts of Appeal of Jersey and Guernsey 1980–85; Judge, High Court of Justice, Chancery Div. 1985–92; Lord Justice of Appeal 1992–95; a Lord of Appeal in Ordinary 1995–; Judge Court of Final Appeal, Hong Kong Special Admin. Region 1997–; Dir ENO 1985–90, 1991–94; Stowell Civil Law Fellow, Univ. Coll. Oxford 1961–73; Pres. British-German Jurists Asscn 1991–; Hon. Fellow, Queen's Coll. Oxford 1992; Hon DCL (City) 1992, (Univ. of West of England) 1995. *Publication:* The South African Law of Evidence 1963. *Address:* c/o House of Lords, London, SW1A 0PW (office); Surrey Lodge, 23 Keats Grove, London, NW3 2RS, England.

HOFFMANN, Luc, DPhil; Swiss biologist; b. 23 Jan. 1923, Basel; s. of Dr Emanuel Hoffmann and Marie-Anne Hoffmann (née Stehlin); m. Daria Razumovsky 1953 (died 2003); one s. three d.; ed Gymnasium Basel and Flim, Grisons, Univ. of Basel; f. Station Biologique de la Tour du Valat 1954, Man. Dir 1954–84, Chair. of Bd Fondation Tour du Valat 1974–2003, Hon. Pres. 2004–; f. World Wildlife Fund (WWF) (later World Wide Fund for Nature) 1961, Vice-Pres. of Bd 1961–88 (Exec. Vice-Pres. 1971–78, Vice-Pres. Emer. 1989); Vice-Pres. of Bd Int. Union for Conservation of Nature (IUCN) 1966–69; Dir Int. Wildfowl Research Bureau (IWRB) 1962–69; Hon. Dir Wetlands Int. (fmrly IWRB); Vice-Pres. Wildfowl Trust 1979, Hon. Life Fellow 1983; mem. Exec. Cttee Int. Council for Bird Preservation (ICBP) 1984–90; f. Fondation Int. du Banc d'Arguin (FIBA) 1985, Pres. 1985–2000, Hon. Pres. 2000–; Vice-Pres. Bd of Dirs Hoffmann-La Roche and Co., Basel 1990–96; Pres. WWF France 1996–2000, Hon. Pres. 2001–; Founder and Pres. MAVA Foundation for Nature Conservation 1997–; Fellow, American Ornithologists Union 2004; Commdr Order of the Golden Ark (Netherlands) 1989, Croix du Mérite pour les Sciences et les Arts (Austria), Chevalier, Légion d'honneur 1989; Officier, Ordre du Mérite Nat. de la République Islamique de Mauritanie 1998, Officier, Ordre de l'Honneur (Greece) 1998; Dr hc (Basel) 1990, (Thessaloniki) 1992; Kaj Curry-Lindhal Award, Waterbird Soc. 1994, Duke of Edin. Conservation Medal 1999, Intecol Int. Wetland Award 2004, European Prize for Culture, European Foundation for Culture 2004, John C. Philipps Memorial Medal, IUCN 2004, Byron Antipas Medal, Hellenic Soc. for the Protection of Nature 2005. *Publications:* Camargue (with K. Weber) 1968; 60 publs in the fields of ornithology, wetland ecology and conservation. *Leisure interests:* contemporary art, bird watching. *Address:* La Tour du Valat, Le Sambuc, 13200 Arles, France (office); Le Petit Essert, 1147 Montricher, Switzerland (home). *Telephone:* (4) 90-97-20-13 (office); (21) 8645977 (home). *Fax:* (4) 90-97-20-19 (office); (21) 8644230 (home). *E-mail:* l.hoffmann@tourduvalat.org (office). *Website:* www.tourduvalat.org (office).

HOFFMANN, Roald, PhD; American chemist and academic; *Frank H.T. Rhodes Professor Emeritus of Humane Letters, Cornell University;* b. (Roald Safran), 18 July 1937, Złoczów, Poland; s. of Hillel Safran and Clara Rosen, step-s. of Paul Hoffmann; m. Eva Börjesson 1960; one s. one d.; ed Columbia and Harvard Univs; Jr Fellow, Soc. of Fellows, Harvard Univ. 1962–65; Assoc. Prof. of Chem., Cornell Univ. 1965–68, Prof. 1968–74, John A. Newman Prof. of Physical Science 1974–96, Frank M. Rhodes Prof. of Humane Letters 1996–;

mem. American Acad. of Arts and Sciences, NAS, American Philosophical Soc.; Foreign mem. Royal Soc., Indian Nat. Acad. of Sciences, Royal Swedish Acad. of Sciences; mem. USSR (now Russian) Acad. of Sciences, Societas Scientarum Fennica 1986; Hon. DTech (Royal Inst. of Technology, Stockholm) 1977; Hon. DSc (Yale) 1980, (Columbia) 1982, (Hartford) 1982, (City Univ. of New York) 1983, (Puerto Rico) 1983, (Uruguay) 1984, (La Plata) 1984, (Colgate) 1985, (State Univ. of New York at Binghamton) 1985, (Ben Gurion Univ. of Negev) 1989, (Lehigh) 1989, (Carleton) 1989, (Md) 1990, (Ariz.) 1991, (Bar-Ilan Univ.) 1991, (Central Fla) 1991, (Athens) 1991, (Thessaloniki) 1991, (St Petersburg) 1991, (Barcelona) 1992, (Northwestern Univ.) 1996, (The Technion) 1996, (Durham) 2000 and others; ACS Award 1969, Fresenius Award 1969, Harrison Howe Award 1969, Annual Award of Int. Acad. of Quantum Molecular Sciences 1970, Arthur C. Cope Award, ACS 1973, Linus Pauling Award 1974, Nichols Medal 1980, shared Nobel Prize for Chemistry 1981, Inorganic Chemistry Award, ACS 1982, Nat. Medal of Science 1984, Nat. Acad. of Sciences Award, in Chemical Sciences 1986, Priestley Medal 1990 and others. *Plays:* Oxygen (with Carl Djerassi), Should've. *Publications:* Conservation of Orbital Symmetry 1969, The Metamict State 1987, Solids and Surfaces 1988, Gaps and Verges 1990, Chemistry Imagined (co-author) 1993, The Same and Not the Same 1995, Old Wine, New Flasks (co-author) 1997, Memory Effects 1999, Soliton 2002, Catalísta (Spanish) 2002. *Address:* Department of Chemistry and Chemical Biology, 222A Baker Laboratory, Cornell University, Ithaca, NY 14853-1301, USA (office). *Telephone:* (607) 255-3419 (office). *Fax:* (607) 255-5707 (office). *E-mail:* rh34@cornell.edu (office). *Website:* www.chem.cornell.edu (office); www.roaldhoffmann.com.

HOFFMANN JACOBY, Adriana E.; Chilean biologist, botanist, environmentalist and author; b. 1940, Santiago de Chile; d. of Franz Hoffmann; leading environmentalist in various pressure groups such as Lahuen, Defensores del Bosque Chileno (Defenders of the Chilean Forests, which she founded) and Protege; plays leading role in the Chilean Science Soc., Biology Soc. of Chile, Earth Foundation, Asscn of Chilean Female Leaders, Int. Union for Conservation of Nature (IUCN); Exec. Dir Nat. Environmental Comm. (CONAMA) 2000–01; recognized by UN as one of the 25 leading ambientalistas of the decade 1990s 1997, Nat. Prize for the Environment (category of Environmental Educ. Award) 1999, Conservation Merit Award, Worldwide Fund for Nature 2001. *Achievement:* the abbreviation AEHoffm. is used to indicate Adriana Hoffmann Jacoby as the authority in the description and scientific classification of plants; had identified and classified 106 new species of Cactaceae by April 2008. *Publications include:* Flora silvestre de Chile 1983, El árbol urbano en Chile 1989, Cactáceas en la flora silvestre de Chile 1990, De cómo Margarita Flores puede cuidar su salud y ayudar a salvar el planeta (with Marcelo Mendoza) 1992. *Address:* c/o Defensores del Bosque Chileno, Álvaro Casanova 613, Peñalolén, Santiago; c/o Obispo Donoso 6, Castilla 520 via Correo 21, Providencia, Santiago, Chile. *Telephone:* (2) 278-0237. *Fax:* (2) 278-0237. *E-mail:* bosquech@gmail.com. *Website:* www.elbosquechileno.cl.

HOFMANN, Peter; German singer (tenor); b. 22 Aug. 1944, Marienbad; ed Hochschule für Musik, Karlsruhe; operatic début as Tamino, Lübeck 1972; mem. Stuttgart Opera 1973–; sang Siegmund, centenary production of The Ring, Bayreuth 1976, Covent Garden London 1976; US début as Siegmund, San Francisco Opera 1977; début Metropolitan New York (Lohengrin) 1980; pop artist 1984–; seven week tour across Germany performing Phantom of the Opera 1999. *Address:* c/o Marita Türschmann, Music and More, Postfach 1325, 64334 Seeheim-Jugenheim, Germany (office). *E-mail:* office@peterhofmann.com (office); PH@peterhofmann.com (office). *Website:* www.peterhofmann.com.

HOFMANN, Werner, DPhil; Austrian museum administrator (retd) and author; b. 8 Aug. 1928, Vienna; s. of Leopold Hofmann and Anna Hofmann (née Visvader); m. Jacqueline Hofmann (née Buron) 1950; ed Univ. of Vienna; Asst Albertina, Vienna 1950–55; Dir Museum of the 20th Century, Vienna 1962–69, Hamburger Kunsthalle 1969–90; Guest Lecturer, Barnard Coll., New York 1957; Guest Prof., Berkeley, Calif. 1961, Harvard Univ. 1981, 1982, Columbia Univ. 1984, New York Univ. 1991, Vienna Univ. 1991; Commdr des Arts et des Lettres; Gold Ehren-Medaille City of Vienna 1988, Sigmund-Freud-Preis 1991, Aby M. Warburg Preis der Stadt Hamburg 2008. *Publications:* Die Karikatur von Leonardo bis Picasso 1956, Die Plastik des 20. Jahrhunderts 1958, Das irdische Paradies-Kunst im 19. Jahrhundert 1960, Grundlagen der modernen Kunst 1966, Turning Points in 20th Century Art 1969, Gustav Klimt und die Wiener Jahrhundertwende 1970, Nana, Mythos und Wirklichkeit 1973, Kataloge der Ausstellungsreihe "Kunst um 1800" 1974–80, Edouard Manet: Das Frühstück im Atelier 1985, Ausstellungskatalog 'Zauber der Medusa' 1987, Une Époque en rupture 1750–1830 1995, Die Moderne im Rück-Spiegel. Hauptwege der Kunstgeschichte 1998, Caspar David Friedrich 2000, Goya 2003, Die gespaltene Moderne 2004, Degas und sein Jahrhundert 2007 (also in French and English), Ruptures et Dialogues 2008. *Address:* Sierichstr. 154, 22299 Hamburg, Germany (home). *Telephone:* 464711 (home). *Fax:* 464711 (home).

HOFMEKLER, Ori, BFA; Israeli artist; b. 12 March 1952, Israel; s. of Daniel Hofmekler and Rina Kune; m. Ilana Wellisch 1977; one s. one d.; ed Bezalel Acad., Jerusalem and Jerusalem Univ.; Herman Struck Prize for Graphic Art 1975. *Publications:* Hofmekler's People 1983; contribs. to Penthouse Magazine since 1983 and to magazines in France, Germany and USA. *Leisure interests:* reading, sports and travel. *Website:* www.orihofmekler.com.

HOGAN, Joseph M., BS, MBA; American business executive; *CEO, ABB Ltd;* b. 7 May 1957; m. Lisa Hogan; three c.; ed Geneva Coll., Robert Morris Univ.; Sales, Marketing and Product Devt roles with GE Plastics, USA 1985–90, Business Leader, Lexan Europe, GE Plastics, Netherlands 1990–93, Gen. Man. Americas Marketing, GE Plastics, USA 1994–96, Staff Exec., GE Corp., USA 1996–98, Pres. and CEO, GE Fanuc Automation N America 1998–2000,

Exec. Vice-Pres. and COO GE Medical Systems, USA 2000, Pres. and CEO GE Healthcare, USA and UK 2000–08; CEO ABB Group worldwide and ABB Ltd, Switzerland 2008–. *Address:* ABB Ltd, Affolternstrasse 44, 8050 Zurich, Switzerland (office). *Telephone:* (43) 317-71-11 (office). *Fax:* (43) 317-44-20 (office). *E-mail:* info@abb.com (office). *Website:* www.abb.com (office).

HOGAN, Mark T., BSc, MBA; American automobile industry executive; *President, Magna International Inc.;* b. 15 May 1951, Chicago; ed Univ. of Ill., Harvard Univ.; joined General Motors (GM) 1973, Factory Analyst, Electro-Motive Div., Chicago 1973–77, several analytical and supervisory positions, GM Financial Staff 1977–81, Sr Admin. for Forward Business Planning, Fisher Body Div. 1981–82, Dir of Material, Labour and Forecast Section, Comptroller's Staff 1982–83, Dir Treasurer's Office, Detroit 1983–84, Group Dir Public Affairs Staff, Chevrolet-Pontiac-Canada Group 1984–86, Gen. Man. and Comptroller, New United Motor Mfg Inc. 1986–88, Group Dir of Business Planning, Truck and Bus Group 1988–92, Exec. Dir of Planning, N American Operations (NAO) 1992–94, Exec. Dir NAO Planning and Corp. Information Man. 1994, Pres. and Man.-Dir GM do Brasil, Group Vice-Pres. e-GM 1999–2004, Group Vice-Pres. for Advanced Vehicle Devt 2001–04; Pres. Magna Int. Inc. 2004–. *Address:* Magna International Inc., 337 Magna Drive, Aurora, Ont. L4G 7K1, Canada (office). *Telephone:* (905) 726-2462 (office). *Fax:* (905) 726-7164 (office). *Website:* www.magnaint.com (office).

HOGAN, Paul, AO; Australian film actor; b. 8 Oct. 1940, Lightening Ridge; m. 1st Noelene Hogan (divorced 1989); five c.; m. 2nd Linda Kozlowski 1990; one s.; ed Parramatta High School; fmr rigger on Sydney Harbour Bridge; filmed TV specials on location in England 1983; commercials for Australian Tourist Comm., Fosters Lager; Australian of the Year 1985. *Films:* Crocodile Dundee (Golden Globe Award) 1986, Crocodile Dundee II 1989, Almost An Angel 1993, Lightning Jack 1994, Flipper 1996, Sorrow Floats 1997, Crocodile Dundee in Los Angeles 2001, Strange Bedfellows 2004. *TV:* The Paul Hogan Show 1973, Hogan in London 1975, Anzacs (miniseries) 1985. *Address:* c/o Silverstream Management, Level 4 350 Kent Street, Sydney, NSW 2001, Australia (office).

HOGE, James F., Jr, BA, MA; American academic and editor; *Peter G. Peterson Chair and Editor, Foreign Affairs, Council on Foreign Relations;* ed Yale Univ., Univ. of Chicago, Harvard Univ.; fmr Ed.-in-Chief Chicago Sun-Times newspaper, then Publr and Pres. NY Daily News; fmr Dir Council on Foreign Relations, now Peter G. Peterson Chair and Ed., Foreign Affairs (journal) 1992–; Congressional Fellow, American Political Science Asscn 1962; Fellow John F. Kennedy School of Govt Harvard Univ. 1991; Sr Fellow Freedom Forum Media Studies Columbia Univ. 1992; Dir Foundation for Civil Society, Human Rights Watch; mem. Bd of Dirs Int. Center for Journalists (ICFJ) 1992–; mem. American Council on Germany; Chair. Program Cttee American Ditchley Foundation; Hon. degree (Columbia Coll.) 1985; Public Service Award, Univ. of Chicago 1973, Award for Contributions to Journalism The Better Govt Asscn of Chicago 1975, Public Service Award The Citizens Cttee for NY City 1985, 6 Pulitzer Prizes (to Chicago Sun Times while Ed. and Publr), Pulitzer Prize (to New York Daily News while Publr). *Television:* The Threat of Terrorism (documentary writer and narrator). *Publications include:* The American Encounter: The United States and the Making of the Modern World (co-ed.) 1997, How Did This Happen? Terrorism and the New War (co-ed.) 2001; numerous articles, reviews and chapters in journals, newspapers and books. *Address:* Foreign Affairs, 58 East 68th Street, New York, NY 10021-5987, USA (office). *Telephone:* (212) 434-9504 (office). *Fax:* (212) 434-9849 (office). *E-mail:* jhoge@cfr.org (office). *Website:* www.foreignaffairs.org (office).

HOGG, Sir Christopher Anthony, Kt, MA, MBA; British business executive; *Chairman, Financial Reporting Council;* b. 2 Aug. 1936, London, England; s. of Anthony Wentworth Hogg and Monica Mary Gladwell; m. 1st Anne Patricia Cathie 1961 (divorced 1997); two d.; m. 2nd Dr Miriam Stoppard 1997; ed Marlborough Coll., Trinity Coll., Oxford and Harvard Business School, USA; Nat. Service, Parachute Regt 1955–57; Research Assoc. Institut pour l'Etude des Méthodes de Direction de l'Entreprise (business school), Lausanne, Switzerland 1962–63; with Philip Hill, Higginson, Erlangers Ltd (later Hill Samuel & Co. Ltd) 1963–66; staff mem. Industrial Reorganisation Corpn 1966–68; joined Courtaulds Group 1968, Man. Dir 1971, Dir (non-exec.) British Celanese Ltd 1971–72, Chair. 1972–75, Dir Courtaulds Ltd 1973–96, a Deputy Chair. 1978–80, Chief Exec. 1979–91, Chair. Courtaulds PLC 1980–96, Courtaulds Textiles PLC 1990–95; Deputy Chair. Allied Domecq 1995–96, Chair. 1996–2002; Dir (non-exec.) Reuters Group PLC 1984–2004 (Chair. 1985–2004), SmithKline Beecham PLC 1993–2000, GlaxoSmithKline 2000–04 (Chair. 2002–04); Air Liquide SA 2000–05; Chair. Financial Reporting Council 2006–; Chair. (non-exec.) Royal Nat. Theatre 1995–2004; Trustee Ford Foundation 1987–99; mem. Dept of Industry Industrial Devt Advisory Bd 1976–81, Cttee of Award for Harkness Fellowships 1980–86, Int. Council J.P. Morgan 1988–, Court, Bank of England 1992–96; Hon. Fellow, Trinity Coll. Oxford 1982, London Business School 1992, City and Guilds of London Inst. 1992; Hon. FCSD 1987; Foreign Hon. mem. American Acad. of Arts and Services 1991; Hon. DSc (Cranfield Inst. of Tech.) 1986, (Aston) 1988; BIM Gold Medal 1986, Centenary Medal, Soc. of Chemical Industry 1989, Hambro Businessman of the Year 1993. *Publication:* Masers and Lasers 1962. *Leisure interests:* theatre, reading, walking. *Address:* Financial Reporting Council, 5th floor, Aldwych House, 71-91 Aldwych, London, WC2B 4HN, England (office). *Telephone:* (20) 7492-2388 (office). *Fax:* (20) 7492-2399 (office). *E-mail:* c.hogg@frc.org.uk (office). *Website:* www.frc.org.uk (office).

HOGG, Baroness (Life Peer), cr. 1995, of Kettlethorpe in the County of Lincolnshire; **Sarah Elizabeth Mary Hogg;** British economist; *Chairman, 3i Group PLC;* b. 14 May 1946; d. of Lord Boyd-Carpenter; m. Rt Hon. Douglas M. Hogg QC, MP 1968; one s. one d.; ed St Mary's Convent, Ascot and Lady Margaret Hall, Oxford Univ.; staff writer, The Economist 1967, Literary Ed.

1970, Econs Ed. 1977; Econs Ed. Sunday Times 1981; Presenter, Channel 4 News 1982–83; Econs Ed. and Deputy Exec. Ed. Finance and Industry, The Times 1984–86; Asst Ed. and Business and City Ed. The Independent 1986–89; Econs Ed. The Daily Telegraph 1989–90; Head Policy Unit, 10 Downing Street (rank Second Perm. Sec.) 1990–95; Chair. London Econs 1997–99 (Dir 1995–97), Frontier Econs 1999–; mem. Int. Advisory Bd, Nat. Westminster Bank 1995–97, Advisory Bd, Bankinter 1995–98, House of Lords Select Cttee on Science and Tech. 1995–98, House of Lords Select Cttee on Monetary Policy 2000, Council, Royal Econ. Soc. 1996–, Council, Hansard Soc. 1995–99; Dir London Broadcasting Co. 1982–90, Royal Nat. Theatre 1988–91, Foreign & Colonial Smaller Cos Investment Trust 1995–2002 (Chair. 1997–2002), Nat. Provident Inst. 1996–99, GKN 1996– (Deputy Chair. 2003–), 3i Group 1997– (Deputy Chair. 2000, Chair. 2002–), P&O 1999–2000, P&O Princess Cruises 2000–03, Carnival Corpn & Carnival PLC 2003–, Martin Currie Portfolio Investment Trust 1999–02; Gov. BBC 2000–04, Centre for Econ. Policy Research 1985–92, London Business School 2004–, Financial Reporting Council 2004–; Fellow, Eton Coll. 1996–; Hon. Fellow, Lady Margaret Hall, Oxford 1994; Hon. MA (Open Univ.) 1987; Hon. DPhil (Loughborough Univ.) 1992; Hon. DL (Lincoln) 2001; Hon. DSc (City Univ.) 2002; Wincott Foundation Financial Journalist of the Year 1985. *Publication:* Too Close to Call (with Jonathan Hill) 1995. *Address:* 3i Group PLC, 91 Waterloo Road, London, SE1 8XP (office); House of Lords, Westminster, London, SW1A 0PW, England. *Website:* www.3igroup.com (office).

HOGGART, Richard, MA, DLitt; British sociologist, writer and academic (retd); b. 24 Sept. 1918, Leeds; s. of Tom Longfellow Hoggart and Adeline Emma Hoggart (née Long); m. Mary Holt France 1942; two s. one d.; ed Cockburn Grammar School and Univ. of Leeds; RA 1940–46; Staff Tutor and Sr Staff Tutor, Univ. Coll. of Hull and Univ. of Hull 1946–59; Sr Lecturer in English, Univ. of Leicester 1959–62; Visiting Prof., Univ. of Rochester, NY 1956–57; Prof. of English, Univ. of Birmingham 1962–73; Pres. British Asscn of fmr UN Civil Servants 1978–86; Chair. European Museum of the Year Award Cttee 1977–, Broadcasting Research Unit 1980–90; mem. Albemarle Cttee on Youth Services 1958–60, Youth Service Devt Council 1960–62, Pilkington Cttee on Broadcasting 1960–62; Gov. Birmingham Repertory Theatre 1963–70; Dir Centre for Contemporary Cultural Studies 1964–73; mem. BBC Gen. Advisory Council 1959–60, 1964–70, Arts Council of GB 1976–81, Culture Advisory Cttee of UK Nat. Comm. to UNESCO 1966–70, Communications Advisory Cttee of UK Nat. Comm. to UNESCO 1977–79, Wilton Park Academic Council 1983–; Chair. Arts Council Drama Panel 1977–80, Vice-Chair. Arts Council 1980–81, Chair. Advisory Council for Adult and Continuing Educ. 1977–83, The Statesman and Nation Publishing Co. Ltd 1978–81; Gov. Royal Shakespeare Theatre 1966–88; Asst Dir-Gen. for Social Sciences, Humanities and Culture UNESCO 1970–75; Warden of Goldsmiths' Coll., London 1976–84; Chair. Book Trust 1995–97; Pres. Nat. Book Cttee 1997–; Hon. Visiting Prof., Univ. of E Anglia 1985–, Univ. of Surrey 1985–; Hon. Fellow, Sheffield City Polytechnic 1983, Goldsmiths' Coll. 1987, Ruskin Coll. Oxford 1994; Hon. DUniv (Open Univ.) 1972, (Surrey) 1981; Hon. DèsSc (Bordeaux) 1974, (Paris) 1987; Hon. LLD (CNAA) 1982, (York Univ., Toronto) 1988; Hon. LittD (E Anglia) 1986, (Metropolitan Univ. of London) 2003; Hon. DLitt (Leicester), (Hull) 1988, (Keele) 1995, (Metropolitan Univ. of Leeds) 1995, (Westminster) 1996, (Sheffield) 1999, (London) 2000; Hon. EdD (E London) 1998; BBC Reith Lecturer 1971. *Publications:* Auden 1951, The Uses of Literacy 1957, W. H. Auden – A Selection 1961, Teaching Literature 1963, The Critical Moment 1964, How and Why Do We Learn 1965, Technology and Society 1966, Essays in Literature and Culture 1969, Speaking to Each Other 1970, Only Connect (Reith Lectures) 1972, An Idea and Its Servants 1978, An English Temper 1982, The Future of Broadcasting (ed. with Janet Morgan) 1978, An Idea of Europe (with Douglas Johnson) 1987, A Local Habitation (autobiog.) 1988, Liberty and Legislation (ed.) 1989, A Sort of Clowning 1990, An Imagined Life 1992, Townscape with Figures 1994, The Way We Live Now 1995, First and Last Things 1999, Hoggart en France 1999, Between Two Worlds 2001, Everyday Language and Everyday Life 2003, Mass Media in a Mass Society: Myth and Reality 2004, Promises to Keep: Thoughts in Old Age 2005. *Leisure interests:* family, reading, writing. *Address:* Curtis Brown Ltd, Haymarket House, 28–29 Haymarket, London, SW1Y 4SP, England (office). *Telephone:* (20) 7393-4400 (office). *Fax:* (20) 7393-4401 (office). *E-mail:* info@curtisbrown.co.uk (office). *Website:* www.curtisbrown.co.uk (office).

HOGNESS, David Swenson, PhD; American geneticist and academic; *Rudy J. and Daphne Donohue Munzer Professor Emeritus in the School of Medicine, Stanford University;* b. 1925; ed California Inst. of Tech.; Post-doctoral fellowship at Institut Pasteur, France 1952; joined faculty of Washington Univ.; held various chairs at Stanford Univ. 1955–59, currently Rudy J. and Daphne Donohue Munzer Prof. Emer. in the School of Medicine; 23rd Int. Prize for Biology, Japan Soc. for the Promotion of Science 2007. *Publications:* numerous scientific papers in professional journals on the study of gene structure in higher eukaryotes, the developmental genetics of the fruit fly *Drosophila melanogaster* and how the hormone ecdysone acts to regulate metamorphosis in *Drosophila*. *Address:* Stanford University School of Medicine, 300 Pasteur Drive, Stanford, CA 94305, USA (office). *Telephone:* (650) 723-6166 (office). *E-mail:* tran@cmgm.stanford.edu (office). *Website:* med.stanford.edu (office).

HOGWOOD, Christopher Jarvis Haley, CBE, MA, FRSA; British musician, conductor, musicologist and keyboard player, writer, editor and broadcaster; b. 10 Sept. 1941, Nottingham; s. of Haley Evelyn and Marion Constance Hogwood (née Higgott); ed Univ. of Cambridge, Charles Univ., Prague, Czechoslovakia; keyboard continuo, Acad. of St Martin-in-the-Fields 1965–76, keyboard soloist 1970–76, consultant Musicologist 1971–76; Founder-mem. Early Music Consort of London 1965–76; writer and presenter, The Young Idea (BBC Radio) 1972–82; Founder and Dir Acad. of Ancient Music 1973–2006, Dir Emer. 2006–; mem. Faculty of Music, Univ. of Cambridge 1975–; Artistic Dir King's Lynn Festival 1976–80; Dir Handel and Haydn Soc., Boston, USA 1986–2001, Conductor Laureate 2001–; Dir of Music, St Paul Chamber Orchestra, Minn., USA 1987–92, Prin. Guest Conductor 1992–98; Visiting Artist, Harvard Univ. 1988–89, Tutor, Mather House 1991–93; Artistic Adviser, Australian Chamber Orchestra 1989–93; Artistic Dir Summer Mozart Festival, Nat. Symphony Orchestra, USA 1993–2001; Assoc. Dir Beethoven Acad., Antwerp 1998–2002; Prin. Guest Conductor, Kammerorchester Basel, Switzerland 2000–07; Kayden Visiting Artist, Learning from Performers Programme, Harvard Univ. 2001; Prin. Guest Conductor, Orquesta Ciudad de Granada 2001–04, Orchestra Sinfonica di Milano Giuseppe Verdi 2003–06; Int. Prof. of Early Music Performance, RAM, London 1992–; Visiting Prof., Dept of Music, King's Coll., London 1992–96; Series Ed. Music for London Entertainment 1983–97; mem. Editorial Cttee C.P.E. Bach Edn (Md) 1986–98, Chair. Advisory Bd C.P.E. Bach Complete Works 1999–; mem. Editorial Bd Early Music (Oxford Univ. Press) 1993–97, Early Music Performers, Peacock Press 2002, Bd Eds Bohuslav Martinu Foundation 2003–, Advisory Panel, Eighteenth-Century Music, Cambridge Univ. Press 2003; Pres. Early Music Wales 1996–, Nat. Early Music Asscn (NEMA) 2000, The Handel Inst. 2000–; Hon. Prof. of Music, Univ. of Keele 1986–90, Univ. of Cambridge 2002–; Hon. Fellow, Jesus Coll., Cambridge 1989, Pembroke Coll., Cambridge 1992; Hon. mem. RAM 1995; Freeman Worshipful Co. of Musicians 1989; Hon. DMus (Keele) 1991; Winner, Yorkshire Post Music Book Award 1984, Walter Willson Cobbett Medal, Worshipful Co. of Musicians 1986, UCLA Award for Artistic Excellence 1996, Scotland on Sunday Music Prize, Edin. Int. Festival 1996, Distinguished Musician Award, Inc. Soc. of Musicians 1997, Martinu Medal, Bohuslav Martinu Foundation, Prague 1999; Handel & Haydn Soc. Fellowship named 'The Christopher Hogwood Historically Informed Performance Fellowship' 2001, Regione Liguria per il suo contributo all'arte e alla filogia della musica 2003, Halle Hon. Handel Prize 2008. *Publications:* Music at Court 1977, The Trio Sonata 1979, Haydn's Visits to England 1980, Music in Eighteenth Century England (co-author) 1983, Handel 1984, Holmes' Life of Mozart (ed.) 1991, The Keyboard in Baroque Europe (ed.) 2003; many edns of musical scores; contribs to The New Grove Dictionary of Music and Musicians 1980 and 2001; numerous recordings. *Address:* 10 Brookside, Cambridge, CB2 1JE, England. *Telephone:* (1223) 363975. *Fax:* (1223) 327377. *E-mail:* office@hogwood.org (office). *Website:* www.hogwood.org (office).

HOHLER, Erla Bergendahl, DPhil, FSA; Norwegian archaeologist, art historian and academic; *Professor, Institute of Archaeology, Art History and Numismatics, Oslo University;* b. 20 Nov. 1937, Oslo; m. Christopher Hohler 1961; three c.; ed Univ. of Oslo, Courtauld Inst., London; Asst Prof. Inst. of Art History, Univ. of Oslo 1975; Keeper Medieval Dept, Univ. Museum of Nat. Antiquities, Oslo 1987; Prof. Inst. of Archaeology, Art History and Numismatics, Oslo Univ. 1993–; Prof. of Art History Univ. of Tromsø 1994; mem. Soc. of Antiquaries of London 1986, Det Norske Videnskapsakademi 1994. *Publications:* The Capitals of Urnes Church 1975, Stavkirkene 1981, Stilentwicklung in der Holzkirchen Architektur 1981, Norwegian Stave Church Carving 1989, Norwegian Stave Church Sculpture I-II 1999, Catalogue Raisonné 1999, Painted Altar Frontals of Norway I-III 2004. *Address:* Lyder Sagens Gt. 23, 0358 Oslo (home); Universitetets Kulturhistoriske Museer, Frederiks Gt. 3, 0164 Oslo, Norway (office). *Telephone:* 22-46-57-32 (home); 22-85-95-36 (office). *E-mail:* erla.hohler@ukm.uio.no (office). *Website:* www.khm.uio.no (office).

HOHOFF, Curt, DPhil; German writer; b. 18 March 1913, Emden; s. of Caspar Hohoff and Elisabeth (née Waterman) Hohoff; m. Elfriede Federhen 1949; four s. one ; ed Univs of Münster, Munich, Berlin and Univ. of Cambridge, UK; journalist, Rheinischer Merkur, Koblenz 1948–49, Süddeutsche Zeitung, Munich 1949–50, freelance 1950–; mem. Akad. der Künste, Berlin 1956, Bayerische Akad. der Künste, Munich 1958; Bundesverdienstkreuz 1992. *Publications:* Woina-Woina, Russisches Tagebuch 1951, Geist und Ursprung (essays) 1954, Heinrich von Kleist (biog.) 1957, Schnittpunkte (essays) 1963, Die Märzhasen (novel) 1966, Munich 1970, Jakob M. R. Lenz (biog.) 1977, Grimmelshausen (biog.) 1978, Unter den Fischen (memoirs) 1982, Die verbotene Stadt (novel) 1986, Besuch bei Kalypso, Landschaften und Bildnisse 1988, J. W. von Goethe, Dichtung und Leben (biog.) 1989, Scheda – im Flug vorbei (novel) 1993, Veritas christiana (essays) 1994, Glanz der Wirklichkeit, Gelehrte Prosa als Kunst (essays) 1998. *Address:* Adalbert-Stifter-Strasse 27, 81925 Munich, Germany. *Telephone:* (89) 9828980.

HOJAMUHAMMEDOV, Baymyrat; Turkmenistani hydrogeologist and government official; *Minister of Petroleum, Natural Gas and Mineral Resources;* b. 15 Nov. 1961, Aşgabat; s. of Geldymyrat Hojamuhammedov and Aynagozel Hojamuhammedov; m.; two s. two d.; ed Ordxhonikidze Moscow Geology Inst.; Hydrogeologist, Turkmen Research Inst. 1984–86; Sr Scientist, Turkmenistan Geology Scientific Research Inst. 1991–93; Sr Hydrogeologist, Turkmengeologiya 1993–97; Head of Gas Export Dept, Turkmenneftgas State Trade Corpn 1997, later Deputy Chair. Nat. Clearing Center; Head of Gas Export Dept, Turkmengas 2006–07; Head of Investments and Mineral Resources, Ministry of Petroleum 2007, Minister of Petroleum, Natural Gas and Mineral Resources 2007–. *Address:* Ministry of Petroleum, Natural Gas and Mineral Resources, Archabil sh. 56, 744036 Aşgabat, ul. 2002 28, Turkmenistan (office). *Telephone:* (12) 40-30-01 (office). *Fax:* (12) 40-30-44 (office). *E-mail:* ministryoilgas@online.tm (office).

HOLBOROW, Leslie Charles, BPhil, MA; New Zealand fmr university vice-chancellor; b. 28 Jan. 1941, Auckland; s. of George Holborow and Ivah V. Holborow; m. Patricia L. Walsh 1965; one s. two d.; ed Henderson High School,

Auckland Grammar School, Univ. of Auckland and Univ. of Oxford, UK; Jr Lecturer, Univ. of Auckland 1963; Lecturer, Sr Lecturer, Univ. of Dundee (until 1967 Queen's Coll. Univ. of St Andrew's) 1965–74; Prof. of Philosophy, Univ. of Queensland, Brisbane 1974–85, Pres. Professorial Bd 1980–81, Pro-Vice-Chancellor (Humanities) 1983–85; Vice-Chancellor, Victoria Univ. of Wellington 1985–98, now Prof. Emer.; Chair. NZ Vice-Chancellors' Cttee 1990, 1996; Council mem. Asscn of Commonwealth Univs 1990–91, 1996; Pres. Australasian Asscn of Philosophy 1977; Nat. Pres. NZ Inst. of Int. Affairs 1987–90, Standing Cttee 2002–; Chair. Bd NZ Univs Acad. Audit Unit 2003–, Itburn Residence Trust; mem. NZ Cttee for Pacific Econ. Co-operation 1986–94, Educ. Sub-cttee of NZ Nat. Comm. for UNESCO 1996–99; Trustee, NZ String Quartet 1990–; Hon. LLD (Victoria Univ. of Wellington) 1998. *Publications:* articles in philosophical journals. *Leisure interests:* golf, tramping, listening to music. *Address:* 29 Upoko Road, Hataitai, Wellington, New Zealand (home). *Telephone:* (4) 972-8867 (home); (4) 905-8867 (home). *Fax:* (4) 972-8867 (home). *E-mail:* leshol@paradise.net.nz (home).

HOLBROOK, Karen A., BS, MS, PhD; American biologist, university administrator and academic; *Vice-President for Research and Innovation, University of South Florida;* ed Univ. of Wisconsin, Madison, Univ. of Washington, Seattle; Teaching Asst, Zoology, Univ. of Wisconsin 1963–66; Instructor of Biology, Ripon Coll. 1966–69, Instructor, Upward Bound Program 1967; Instructor, NSF Summer Inst. 1969; Teaching Asst, Biological Structure, Univ. of Washington 1969–72, Instructor, Biological Structure, School of Medicine 1972–75, Asst Prof., Biological Structure, Adjunct Asst Prof., Dermatology 1975–79, Assoc. Prof., Biological Structure, Adjunct Assoc. Prof., Dermatology 1979–84, Assoc. Chair. Biological Structure 1981–85, Prof., Biological Structure, Adjunct Assoc. Prof., Dermatology 1984–93, Assoc. Dean, Scientific Affairs 1985–94; Prof. of Anatomy and Dermatology, Vice-Pres. for Research and Dean Grad. School, Univ. of Florida 1993–98; Prof. of Cell Biology, Sr Vice-Pres. for Academic Affairs and Provost Univ. of Georgia 1998–2002, Medical Coll. of Georgia Adjunct Prof. of Anatomy, Cell Biology and Medicine 1998–2002; Prof. of Internal Medicine—Dermatology, Ohio State Univ. 2002–07, Prof. of Physiology and Cell Biology 2002–07, Pres. Ohio State Univ. 2002–07; Vice-Pres. for Research and Innovation, Univ. of South Florida 2007–; Sr Fellow, Dermatology, Univ. of Wash. 1976–79; Assoc. Ed. Journal of Investigative Dermatology 1987–92, Journal of Investigative Dermatology 1997–; mem. Editorial Bd Journal of Investigative Dermatology 1978–82, Journal of Pediatric Dermatology 1982–89, American Journal of Anatomy 1983–92, Medicine Northwest 1985–87, Journal of Investigative Dermatology 1992–97, The Anatomical Record 1993–96; mem. Editorial Advisory Bd University Business magazine 2003–; mem. AAAS, American Soc. for Cell Biology, American Asscn of Anatomists, Soc. for Investigative Dermatology, Soc. for Pediatric Dermatology, American Civilization Seminar, Univ. of Florida; Hon. Mem. Epsilon Lambda Chi Alpha Engineering Leadership Circle, Nat. Bd Medical Coll. of Pennsylvania; Distinguished Mem. Nat. Soc. for Collegiate Scholars; Hon. DSc (Punjab Agricultural Univ.) 2006; Kung Sun Oh Memorial Prize, Yonsei Medical College, Seoul, S Korea 1994, 34th Annual Marion Spencer Fay Nat. Bd Award to a Distinguished Woman Physician/Scientist, Medical Coll. of Pennsylvania 1996, Pinkus Award, American Soc. of Dermatopathology 1997, Distinguished Contrib. to Research Admin Award, Soc. of Research Admins Int. 2002, Director's Award, Ohio Dept of Alcohol and Drug Addiction Services 2003, The Women's Center Leadership Award 2004, Acad. for Leadership Award, Harding-Evans Foundation 2004, Pres.'s Leadership Group Award, US Dept of Educ., Higher Educ. Center for Alcohol and Other Drug Abuse and Violence Prevention 2004, Women in Higher Educ. Award, Nat. Panhellenic Conf. Foundation, Inc. 2005, YWCA Women of Achievement Award 2006, Sixth Annual Empowered Woman Award, Columbus Women Pres.'s Org. 2006. *Films:* Prenatal Diagnosis of Inherited Skin Disease, Video Journal of Dermatology 1990, Fetal Skin Sampling, Dialogs in Dermatology 1994. *Publications:* more than 30 book chapters and more than 150 scientific papers in professional journals. *Address:* University of South Florida Office of Research, 3702 Spectrum Boulevard, Suite 175, Tampa, FL 33612-9444, USA. *Telephone:* (813) 974-5481 (office). *Fax:* (813) 974-3348 (office). *E-mail:* kholbrook@research.usf.edu (office). *Website:* www.research.usf.edu (office).

HOLBROOKE, Richard C.; American business executive and diplomatist; *Special US Representative for Afghanistan and Pakistan;* b. 24 April 1941, New York City; s. of Dan Holbrooke and Trudi Moos Kearl; two s.; m. 2nd Kati Marton 1995; ed Brown Univ. and Woodrow Wilson School, Princeton Univ.; Foreign Service Officer in Viet Nam and related posts 1962–66; White House Viet Nam staff 1966–67; Special Asst to Under-Secs of State Katzenbach and Richardson and mem. US del. to Paris peace talks on Viet Nam 1967–69; Fellow, Woodrow Wilson School, Princeton Univ. 1969–70; Dir Peace Corps, Morocco 1970–72; Man. Ed. Foreign Policy (quarterly magazine) 1972–76; consultant, Pres.'s Comm. on Org. of Govt for Conduct of Foreign Policy and contributing Ed. Newsweek 1974–75; coordinator of nat. security affairs, Carter-Mondale campaign 1976; Asst Sec. of State for E Asian and Pacific Affairs 1977–81; Vice-Pres. Public Strategies (consulting firm) 1981–85; Man. Dir Lehman Brothers 1985–93; Amb. to Germany 1993–94; Asst Sec. of State for European and Canadian Affairs 1994–96; Chief Negotiator for Dayton Peace Accord in Bosnia 1995; Vice-Chair. Credit Suisse First Boston Corpn 1996–99; Adviser, Baltic Sea Council 1996–98; Special Presidential Envoy for Cyprus 1997–98, to Yugoslavia; Perm. Rep. to UN, New York 1999–2000, Amb. to UN 1999–2001; Vice-Chair. Persius LLC (pvt. equity fund man. co.) 2001–; Special US Rep. for Afghanistan and Pakistan 2009–; mem. Bd of Dirs Council on Foreign Relations, American Int. Group –2008, Quebecor World, American Museum of Natural History, Nat. Endowment for Democracy, The Africa-America Inst., Citizens Cttee for New York City, Refugees Int.; Chair. Bipartisan Comm. on Reorganizing Govt for Foreign Policy 1992; Founding Chair. American Acad. in Berlin; Chair. Refugees Int., American Acad. in Berlin, Nat. Advisory Council of Harriman Inst., Asia Soc. 2002–; Pres. and CEO Global Business Coalition (business alliance against HIV/AIDS) 2001–; Fellow, American Acad. of Arts and Sciences; 20 hon. degrees; numerous awards including Distinguished Public Service Award, Dept of Defense 1994, 1996, Humanitarian of the Year Award, American Jewish Congress 1998, Dr Bernard Heller Prize, Hebrew Union Coll. 1999. *Publications include:* Counsel to the President (co-author) 1991, To End a War 1998; articles and essays on foreign policy. *Leisure interest:* tennis. *Address:* Department of State, 2201 C St, NW, Washington, DC 20520 (office); Perseus LLC, 2099 Pennsylvania Avenue, NW, 9th Floor, Washington, DC 20006, USA (office). *Telephone:* (202) 647-4000 (office); (202) 452-0101 (Perseus) (office). *Fax:* (202) 647-6738 (office); (202) 429-0588 (Perseus) (office). *Website:* www.state.gov (office); www.perseusllc.com (office).

HOLDEN, Bob, BS; American fmr state official; *Vice-Chairman, Midwest US China Association;* m. Lori Hauser; two s.; ed Southwest Mo. State Univ., Harvard Univ.; fmr Admin. Asst to Congressman Richard Gephardt (q.v.), St. Louis; mem. Mo. House of Reps. 1983–89; State Treas. of Mo. 1993, Gov. of Mo. 2001–04; mem. Bd Fund Commrs., Mo. State Employees Retirement System, Mo. Rural Opportunities Council, Holden Scholarship Fund, Leadership St. Louis, Council of State Govts., Nat Asscn State Treas.; Vice-Chair. Mo. Cultural Trust; Vice-Chair. Midwest US China Association 2005–. *Address:* Midwest US China Association, 20 North Clark Street, Suite 750, Chicago, IL 60602, USA (office). *Telephone:* (773) 909-2168 (office). *Fax:* (773) 281-4812 (office). *Website:* www.midwestuschina.org (office).

HOLDER, Eric H., Jr., BA, JD; American lawyer, judge and government official; *Attorney-General;* b. 21 Jan. 1951, New York; s. of Eric Holder and Miriam R. Yearwood; m. Dr Sharon Malone; three c.; ed Columbia Coll., Columbia Law School; Trial Attorney, Public Integrity Section, US Dept of Justice 1976–88, US Attorney 1993–97, US Deputy Attorney-Gen. 1997–2001, Attorney-Gen. 2009–; Pnr, Covington & Burling (law firm), Washington, DC 2001–; Assoc. Judge Superior Court, Washington, DC 1988–93. *Address:* Department of Justice, 950 Pennsylvania Avenue, NW, Washington, DC 20530-0001, USA (office). *Telephone:* (202) 514-2000 (office). *Fax:* (202) 307-6777 (office). *E-mail:* askdoj@usdoj.gov (office). *Website:* www.usdoj.gov (office).

HOLDER, Rt Rev. John Walder Dunlop, BA, STM, PhD; Barbadian ecclesiastic; *Bishop of Barbados;* b. 16 Feb. 1948, Barbados; m. Betty Lucas-Holder; one s.; ed Codrington Coll., Barbados, Univ. of the West Indies, The School of Theology (Univ. of the South), King's Coll., London; ordained priest 1975; tutor in Biblical Studies, Codrington Coll. 1977–81, Lecturer 1984–93, Acting Prin. Sept.–Dec. 1988, Sr Lecturer 1993–99, Deputy Prin. 1999–; Visiting Lecturer in Religious Studies, Erdiston Teacher Training Coll., Barbados; Lecturer in Biblical Studies, Lay Training Programme, Diocese of Barbados 1984–90; Visiting Lecturer at Barbados Community Coll. 1985; Visiting Sabbatical Prof. Gen. Theological Seminary, New York March–May 1988; Chair. Ministry of Educ. Cttee on Religious and Moral Educ. Syllabus for the primary schools of Barbados 1992–94; Visiting Lecturer Bucknell Univ. Summer Programme 1996–98; Curate St George's Cathedral, St Vincent, West Indies 1975–77; Asst Priest, St John's Parish Church, Barbados 1977–81, Priest-in-Charge 1990–92; Hon. Chaplain, Univ. Church of Christ the King, London 1981–84; Asst Priest, St Michael's Cathedral, Barbados 1984–86, St Augustine 1986–89, Priest-in-Charge 1989–90; Priest-in-Charge, St Mark and St Catherine, Barbados 1992–93, St Mark 1993–94, Holy Trinity 1994–95, Holy Cross 1995–; Hon. Canon Diocese of Barbados 1996; Bishop of Barbados 2000–; Long and Dedicated Service Award, Codrington Coll. 1994. *Television:* Religion in Barbados During the First Twenty-Five Years of Independence 1966–91 CBC 1990, CBC presentation on professions 1994. *Publications:* Christian Commitment 1985, Set the Captives Free: The Challenge of the Biblical Jubilee 1987, A Layman's Guide to the Bible (Vols I & II) 1989, The Intertestamental Period 1994, Biblical Reflections on the Book of Hosea 1999. *Address:* Diocesan Office, Mandeville House, Henry's Lane, St Michael (office); Leland, Philip Drive, Pine Gardens, St Michael, Barbados (home). *Telephone:* 426-2761 (office); 435-0466 (home). *Fax:* 426-0871 (office). *E-mail:* bishop_holder@sunbeach.net (office).

HOLDGATE, Sir Martin Wyatt, Kt, CB, MA, PhD, FIBiol; British biologist; b. 14 Jan. 1931, Horsham; s. of the late Francis W. Holdgate and Lois M. Holdgate (née Bebbington); m. Elizabeth M. Weil (née Dickason) 1963; two s.; ed Arnold School, Blackpool and Queens' Coll. Cambridge; Research Fellow, Queens' Coll. Cambridge 1953–56; Jt Leader Gough Island Scientific Survey 1955–56; Lecturer in Zoology, Univ. of Manchester 1956–57, Univ. of Durham 1957–60; Leader, Royal Soc. Expedition to Southern Chile 1958–59; Asst Dir of Research, Scott Polar Research Inst., Cambridge 1960–63; Chief Biologist, British Antarctic Survey 1963–66; Deputy Dir (Research), The Nature Conservancy (UK) 1966–70; Dir Central Unit on Environmental Pollution, Dept of Environment 1970–74; Dir Inst. of Terrestrial Ecology 1974–76; Dir-Gen. of Research, Dept of Environment 1976–81; Chief Scientist and Deputy Sec. (Environment Protection), Dept of Environment and Chief Scientific Adviser, Dept of Transport 1981–88; Dir-Gen. Int. Union for Conservation of Nature and Natural Resources (renamed World Conservation Union) 1988–94; Pres. Zoological Soc. of London 1994–2004; Co-Chair. Intergovernmental Panel on Forests, UN Comm. on Sustainable Devt 1995–97; mem. Royal Comm. on Environmental Pollution 1994–2002; Chair. Int. Inst. for Environment and Devt 1994–2000, Governing Council, Arnold School 1997–2004; Pres. Freshwater Biological Asscn 2002–; Hon. mem. British Ecological Soc. 1996, Int. Union for the Conservation of Nature and Natural Resources 2000; Commdr Order of the Golden Ark 1991; Hon. DSc (Durham) 1991, (Sussex) 1993, (Lancaster) 1995, (Queen Mary, London) 2006; Bruce

Medal, Royal Soc. of Edinburgh and Royal Scottish Geog. Soc. 1964, Silver Medal, UNEP 1983, UNEP Global 500 1988, Patrons Medal, Royal Geographical Soc. 1992, Livingstone Medal, Royal Scottish Geographical Soc. 1993, Int. Conservationist of the Year Award, Nat. Wildlife Fed. (USA) 1993. *Publications include:* Mountains in the Sea: The Story of the Gough Island Expedition 1958, A Perspective of Environmental Pollution 1979, From Care to Action: Making a Sustainable World 1996, The Green Web: A Union for World Conservation 1999, Penguins and Mandarins 2003, The Story of Appleby in Westmoreland 2006. *Leisure interests:* natural history, local history. *Address:* Fell Beck, Hartley, Kirkby Stephen, Cumbria, CA17 4JH, England (home). *Telephone:* (1768) 372316 (home). *E-mail:* martin@holdgate.org (home).

HOLDING, Clyde, LLB; Australian politician; b. 27 April 1931, Melbourne; m. 1st Margaret Sheer (divorced); two s. one d.; m. 2nd Judith Crump; one d.; ed Melbourne Univ.; solicitor; mem. Victorian Parl. for Richmond 1962–77; Leader State Parl. Labor Party and Leader of Opposition 1967–77; mem. Fed. Parl. for Melbourne Ports 1977–; Minister for Aboriginal Affairs 1983–86, for Arts and Territories 1988–89, of Employment Services and Youth Affairs and Minister Assisting the Treasurer 1987–88, Minister, assisting the Minister for Immigration, Local Govt and Ethnic Affairs 1988–89, assisting the Prime Minister 1988–89; Minister for Arts, Tourism and Territories 1989–90; Pres. Victorian Labor Party 1977–79. *Leisure interests:* swimming, surfing, films, reading. *Address:* 58 Milton Street, Elwood, Vic. 3184; 117 Fitzroy Street, St Kilda, Vic. 3183, Australia. *Telephone:* (3) 9534-8126. *Fax:* (3) 9534-1575.

HOLDREN, John Paul, SB, SM, PhD; American environmental scientist and academic; *Teresa and John Heinz Professor of Environmental Policy and Director, Science, Technology and Public Policy Program, Belfer Center for Science and International Affairs, Kennedy School of Government, Harvard University;* b. 1 March 1944, Sewickley, Pa; m. Cheryl Edgar 1966; one s. one d.; ed Massachusetts Inst. of Tech., Stanford Univ.; Assoc. Engineer, Performance Analysis, Lockheed Missiles and Space Co., Sunnyvale, Calif. Summer 1965, Sr Assoc. Engineer, Re-Entry Aerodynamics Summer 1966, Consultant in Re-Entry Physics 1966–67; Research Asst, Inst. for Plasma Research, Stanford Univ. 1969–70; Physicist, Theory Group, Magnetic Fusion Energy Div., Lawrence Livermore Nat. Lab. 1970–73 (on leave 1972–73); Sr Research Fellow, Div. of Humanities and Social Sciences and Environmental Quality Lab., California Inst. of Tech. 1972–73; Asst Prof. of Energy and Resources, Univ. of California, Berkeley 1973–75, Assoc. Prof. 1975–78, Acting Chair. Energy and Resources Group 1982–83, Fall 1990, Vice-Chair. 1983–96 (on leave 1987–88), Chair. of Grad. Advisors, Energy and Resources Group 1988–96, Prof. of Energy and Resources 1978–96, Class of 1935 Prof. of Energy 1991–96, Prof. Emer. of Energy and Resources 1996–; Teresa and John Heinz Prof. of Environmental Policy and Dir Science, Tech. and Public Policy Program, Belfer Center for Science and Int. Affairs, Kennedy School of Govt, Harvard Univ. 1996–, also Prof. of Environmental Science and Policy, Dept of Earth and Planetary Sciences, mem. Bd of Tutors; Visiting Scholar, Woods Hole Research Center 1992–94, Distinguished Visiting Scientist and Vice-Chair Bd of Trustees 1994–2005, Dir-Designate 2004–05, Dir 2005–; Guest Prof., Tsinghua Univ., Beijing, People's Republic of China 2008–; Pres.-elect AAAS 2005, Pres. 2006, Chair. Bd of Dirs 2007; Chair. Exec. Cttee Pugwash Conf. on Science and World Affairs 1987–97, NAS Cttee on Int. Security and Arms Control 1993–2004; mem. Pres. Clinton's Cttee of Advisors on Science and Tech. 1994–2001; Co-Chair. Nat. Comm. on Energy Policy 2002–; Asst to Pres. Obama for Science and Tech. 2009–; mem. NAS, Nat. Acad. of Eng, American Acad. of Arts and Sciences, Council on Foreign Relations; MacArthur Prize Fellowship 1981–86, Volvo Environment Prize 1993, Tyler Prize for Environment 2000, John Heinz Prize for Public Policy 2001, gave acceptance speech for Nobel Peace Prize on behalf of Pugwash Conf. on Science and World Affairs 1995. *Publications:* numerous scientific papers in professional journals on global environmental change, energy technologies and policies, nuclear proliferation, and science and technology policy. *Address:* Littauer-370, John F. Kennedy School of Government, Mailbox 53, 79 JFK Street, Cambridge, MA 02138 (office); Woods Hole Research Center, The Gilman Ordway Campus, 149 Woods Hole Road, Falmouth, MA 02540-1644, USA (office). *Telephone:* (617) 495-1464 (Cambridge) (office); (508) 540-9900 (Falmouth) (office). *Fax:* (617) 495-8963 (Cambridge) (office); (508) 540-9700 (Falmouth) (office). *E-mail:* john_holdren@harvard.edu (office); info@whrc.org (office). *Website:* www.hks .harvard.edu (office); www.whrc.org (office).

HOLDSWORTH, Sir (George) Trevor, Kt, CVO, FCA; British business executive and accountant; b. 29 May 1927, Bradford; m. 1st Patricia June Ridler 1951 (died 1993); three s.; m. 2nd Jenny Watson 1995; ed Hanson Grammar School, Bradford, Keighley Grammar School; with Rawlinson, Greaves and Mitchell (accountants), Bradford 1944–51; with Bowater Corpn 1952–63, becoming Dir and Controller of UK paper-making subsidiaries; Deputy Chief Accountant, Guest Keen and Nettlefolds Ltd 1963–64, Group Chief Accountant 1965–67, Gen. Man. Dir, GKN Screws and Fasteners Ltd 1968–70, Dir and Group Controller 1970–72, Group Exec. Vice-Chair., Corpn Controls and Services 1973–74, Deputy Chair. 1974, Man. Dir and Deputy Chair. 1977, Chair. 1980–88; Chair. British Satellite Broadcasting 1987–90; Dir Thorn EMI PLC 1977–86, Equity Capital for Industry Ltd 1976–83, Midland Bank PLC 1979–88, Prudential Corpn 1986–96 (Deputy Chair. 1988–92); Chair. Allied Colloids Group PLC 1983–96; Dir Opera Now Enterprises Ltd 1988; Dir (non-exec.) Owens-Corning 1994–98; mem. Council, British Inst. of Man. 1974–84, Vice-Chair. 1978–80, Chair. 1980, Vice-Pres. 1982; mem. Council CBI 1974–90, Econ. and Financial Policy Cttee CBI 1976–80, Pres. CBI 1988–90; Chair. (part-time) Nat. Power 1990–95, Beauford PLC 1991–99; Chancellor Bradford Univ. 1992–97; Council, Inst. of Dirs 1978–80, Steering Group on Unemployment 1982, Programmes Unit 1982, Bd of Govs Ashridge Man. Coll. 1978–92; Chair. Tax Reform Working Party 1984–86 (Deputy Pres. 1987–88), Lambert Howarth Group PLC 1993–98; Chair. Wigmore Hall Trust 1992–99; Vice-Pres. Eng Employers' Fed. 1980; mem. Exec. Cttee Soc. of Motor Mfrs and Traders 1980–83; mem. Eng Industries Council 1980; mem. Advisory Bd LEK Partnerships 1992–99; Trustee, Anglo-German Foundation for the Study of Industrial Soc. 1980–92; mem. British North American Cttee 1981–85, European Advisory Council AMF Inc. 1982–85, Council Royal Inst. of Int. Affairs 1983–88; Vice-Pres. Ironbridge Gorge Museum Devt Trust 1981–; Trustee, Royal Opera House Trust 1981–84; mem. Duke of Edinburgh's Award (Business and Commercial Enterprises Group) 1980, Int. Trustee 1987–94, UK Trustee 1988–96; mem. Council Foundation for Mfg and Industry; Liveryman, Worshipful Co. of Chartered Accountants in England and Wales; Freeman, City of London; Hon. D. Tech. (Loughborough) 1981; Hon. DSc (Aston) 1982, (Sussex) 1988; Hon. DBA (Inst. Man. Centre from Buckingham) 1986; Hon. DEng (Bradford) 1983, (Birmingham) 1992; British Inst. Man. Gold Medal 1987, City and Guilds Insignia Award in Tech. (hc) 1989, Chartered Accountants Founding Socs' Centenary Award 1983. *Leisure interests:* music, theatre. *Address:* c/o The Athenaeum, Pall Mall, London, SW1, England.

HOLENDER, Ioan; Romanian opera house director; *Intendant, Vienna Staatsoper;* b. 18 July 1935, Timisoara; m.; two s. one d.; ed Timisoara Polytechnic Inst., Vienna Conservatory; expelled from Romanian higher educ. system on political grounds 1956; worked as tennis trainer and stage dir's asst 1956–59; moved to Vienna and began singing studies 1960; opera singer, Vienna and Klagenfurt 1962–66; joined Starka Theater Agency 1966, later took control of agency and renamed it Holender Opera Agency; Gen. Sec. Vienna Staatsoper and Vienna Volksoper 1988–92, Dir Vienna Volksoper 1992–96, Intendant Vienna Staatsoper 1992–; Guest Lecturer, Univ. of Vienna; Artistic Adviser, Teatro Massimo Bellini, Catania 2008–; hon. mem. Romanian Acad., Hon. Citizen of Timisoara; Vienna Municipality Golden Medal of Merit, Golden Medal for Services to Vienna Community, Grand Golden Hon. Medal of Austrian Repub., Austrian Hon. Cross for Science and Art, First Class, Officier, Ordre des Artes et des Lettres; Dr hc (Gheorge Dima Music Acad.); Vienna Philharmonic Franz Schalk Gold Medal. *Publications:* Ioan Holender: Der Lebensweg des Wiener Staatsoperndirektors (autobiog.) 2001. *Address:* Wiener Staatsoper, Opernring 2, Vienna 1010, Austria (office). *Telephone:* (1) 51444-2250 (office). *Website:* www.staatsoper.at (office).

HOLKERI, Harri Hermanni, KBE, MPolSc; Finnish politician and UN official; b. 6 Jan. 1937, Oripää; s. of Antti Edvard Holkeri and Maire Kyllikki Ahlgren; m. Marja-Liisa Lepisto 1960; one s. one d.; Sec. Nat. Coalition Party Youth League 1959–60, Information Sec. 1960–62; Information Sec. Nat. Coalition Party 1962–64, Research Sec. 1964–65, Party Sec. 1965–71, Chair. 1971–79; mem. Helsinki City Council 1969–88, Chair. 1981–87; mem. Parl. 1970–78; mem. Bd Bank of Finland 1978–97; Chair. of Standing Finnish-Soviet Intergovernmental Comm. for Econ. Co-operation 1989–91; Prime Minister of Finland 1987–91; mem. Int. Body addressing the decommissioning of illegal weapons in NI 1995–98; Pres. 55th Session of the UN Gen. Ass. (Millennium Ass.) 2000–01; Head of UN Interim Admin. Mission in Kosovo (UNMIK) 2003–04. *Address:* c/o United Nations, United Nations Plaza, New York, NY 10017, USA (office).

HOLLAMBY, David James; British diplomatist; *Governor and Commander-in-Chief, St Helena and Dependencies;* b. 19 May 1945; s. of Reginald William Hollamby and Eva May Hollamby (née Ponman); m. Maria Helena Guzmán 1971; two step-s.; ed Albury Manor School, Surrey; joined Foreign Office 1964; Beirut 1967–69; Latin American Floater 1970–72; Third Sec. and Vice Consul Asunción 1972–75; Second Sec. FCO 1975–78; Vice Consul (Commercial) New York 1978–82; Consul (Commercial) Dallas 1982–86; First Sec. FCO 1986–90, Rome 1990–94; Asst Head, Western European Dept, FCO 1994–96, Deputy Head, W Indian and Atlantic Dept 1996–98, Dept Head, Overseas Territories Dept 1998–99; Gov. and C-in-C, St Helena and Dependencies 1999–. *Leisure interests:* music, skiing, travel, reading. *Address:* c/o Foreign and Commonwealth Office, King Charles Street, London, SW1A 2AH, England (office).

HOLLÁN, R. Susan, MD; Hungarian professor of haematology; *Consultant, National Institute of Haematology and Blood Transfusion;* b. 26 Oct. 1920, Budapest; d. of Dr Henrik Hollán and Dr. Malvin Hornik; m. Dr György Révész; one s. one d.; ed Univ. Medical School, Budapest; intern, Rokus Hosp., Budapest 1945–50; Research Fellow, Univ. Medical School, Budapest 1950–54; Science Adviser, Inst. for Experimental Medical Research 1954–91; Dir Nat. Inst. of Haematology and Blood Transfusion 1959–85, Dir-Gen. 1985–90, Consultant 1990–; Prof. of Haematology, Postgraduate Medical School 1970–90; Corresp. mem. Hungarian Acad. of Sciences 1973, mem. 1982– (mem. of Presidium 1976–84); fmr Pres. Int. Soc. of Haematology and Vice-Pres. Int. Soc. of Blood Transfusion; mem. WHO Global AIDS Research Steering Cttee; mem. WHO Expert Cttee on Biological Standardization; mem. Clinical and Immunological Work Cttee of Hungarian Acad. of Sciences; Pres. Bd of Special Cttee for Clinical Sciences; Exec. mem. Hungarian Medical Research Council; Ed.-in-Chief Hungarian Medical Encyclopaedia and Haematologia (quarterly); mem. HSWP Cen. Cttee 1975–89; Foreign Corresp. mem. Soc. de Biologie, Collège de France, Paris; Vice-Pres. Nobel Prize Award, Int. Physicians Prevention of Nuclear War 1983–89; Hon. mem. American Soc. of Hematology, Polish Soc. of Haematology, German Soc. of Haematology (FRG), Purkinje Soc. (Czechoslovakia), Turkish Soc. of Haematology, All-Union Scientific Soc. of Haematology and Blood Transfusion (USSR); Hon. Pres. Hungarian Soc. of Human Genetics; Hungarian Academic Award 1970, State Prize 1974, Socialist Hungary Medal, Nobel Peace Prize 1986. *Publications:* Basic Problems of Transfusion 1965, Haemoglobins and Haemoglobinopathies 1972, Genetics, Structure and Function of Blood Cells 1980, Management of Blood Transfusion Services

1990; over 300 papers in Hungarian and int. medical journals. *Leisure interest:* fine arts, sport. *Address:* Daróczi ut 24, 1113 Budapest (office); Palánta u. 12, 1025 Budapest, Hungary (home). *Telephone:* (1) 372-4210 (office); (1) 326-0619 (home). *Fax:* (1) 372-4352. *E-mail:* hollan@ella.hu (office).

HOLLAND, Agnieszka; Polish film director and screenwriter; b. 28 Nov. 1948, Warsaw; m. Laco Adamik; one d.; ed FAMU film school, Prague; Asst to Krzysztof Zanussi in filming of Illumination 1973; mem. production group 'X' led by Andrzej Wajda in Warsaw 1972–81; Dir first TV film 1973; subsequently worked in theatre in Kraków; Co-Dir (with Jerzy Domaradzki and Paweł Kędzierski) film Screen Test 1977; co-scripted Wajda's film Rough Treatment 1978; also worked with Wajda on A Love in Germany, Man of Marble, Man of Iron, The Orchestra Conductor, Korczak, Danton 1982; wrote screenplay for Yurke Bocayevicz's Anna; has also made documentaries for French TV; directs plays for TV theatre (with Laco Aolamik); mem. Polish Film Asscn, European and American Acad. Award; Robert L. Hess Scholar in Residence, Brooklyn Coll. 2005; Officer's Cross, Order of Polonia Restituta 2001; Las Vegas Film Festival Award 1999. *Achievements include:* retrospective of films held at Museum of Modern Art, New York 2008–09. *Films directed include:* Provincial Actors (Critics' Award, Cannes 1980) 1979, The Fever (Gdańsk Golden Lions 1981) 1980, The Lonely Woman 1981, Angry Harvest (Germany) 1985, To Kill a Priest (France) 1987, Europa, Europa (Germany, France) 1990, (Golden Globe 1991), Olivier, Olivier (France) 1992, The Secret Garden (USA) 1993, Red Wind (USA) 1994, Total Eclipse (England, France) 1995, Washington Square (USA) 1996, The Third Miracle (USA) 1999, Golden Dreams 2001, Shot in the Heart (TV, USA) 2001, The Wire (three TV series episodes) 2002–08, Julie Walking Home (Poland–Canada–Germany) 2002, Cold Case (four TV series episodes) 2004–09, Veronica Mars (TV series) 2004, Prawdziwa historia Janosika i Uhorcika (co-dir) 2005, Copying Beethoven 2006. *Play:* Dybuk (Polish TV) 1999. *Publications:* Magia i pieniadze (Magic & Money) – Conversations with Maria Komatowska, ZNAK Poland 2002. *Address:* Agence Nicole Cann, 1 rue Alfred de Vigny, 75008 Paris, France (office). *Telephone:* 1-44-15-14-21 (office).

HOLLAND, Julian (Jools) Miles, OBE; British musician (piano, keyboard) and broadcaster; b. 24 Jan. 1958, London, England; s. of Derek Holland and June Rose Lane; one s. two d.; m. Christabel McEwen 2005; ed Invicta Sherington School, Shooters' Hill School; pianist 1975–78; Founder-mem. Squeeze 1974–81, 1985–90; regular tours and concerts; formed The Jools Holland Big Band 1987, later renamed The Rhythm and Blues Orchestra 1991–; BBC Radio 2 Jazz Artist of the Year 2006. *Films:* Spiceworld: The Movie 1997, Milk (wrote score) 1999. *Radio:* presenter BBC Radio 2 1997–. *Television:* The Tube (presenter) 1981–86, Walking to New Orleans (writer, producer and presenter, documentary) 1985, The Groovy Fellas (actor and writer) 1988, Juke Box Jury (presenter) 1989–90, Saturday Night (co-presenter New York NBC music show with David Sanborn) 1989, The Happening 1990, Mr Roadrunner (writer and producer, film) 1991, Later with Jools Holland (presenter) 1993–, Hootenanny (presenter for 13th time, New Year's Eve 2005), Name That Tune, Don't Forget Your Toothbrush, Beat Route (writer and producer, film) 1998, Jools Meets The Saint (writer and producer) 1999, Jools' History of the Piano 2002. *Recordings include:* albums: with Squeeze: Squeeze 1978, Cool for Cats 1979, Argy Bargy 1980, East Side Story 1981, Cosi Fan Tutti Frutti 1985, Babylon and On 1987, Frank 1989, Tom Jones and Jools Holland 2004, Swinging the Blues, Dancing the Ska 2005; solo: A World of his Own 1990, Full Complement 1991, A–Z of the Piano 1992, Live Performance 1994, Solo Piano 1994, Sex and Jazz and Rock and Roll 1996, Lift the Lid 1997, Sunset Over London 1999, Hop the Wag 2000, Small World, Big Band – Friends 2001, Small World, Big Band Vol. 2 – More Friends 2002, Small World, Big Band Vol. 3 2003, Moving Out to the Country (with Rhythm & Blues Orchestra) 2006, The Informer 2008. *Publications:* Beat Route 1998, The Hand That Changed Its Mind 2004, Barefaced Lies and Boogie-Woogie Boasts (autobiog.) 2007. *Leisure interests:* sketching, giving advice. *Address:* One-Fifteen, 1 Prince of Orange Lane, Greenwich, London, SE10 8JQ, England (office); Helicon Mountain Ltd, Helicon Mountain, Station Terrace Mews, London, SE3 7LP, England (office). *Telephone:* (20) 8293-0999 (office); (20) 8858-0984 (office). *Fax:* (20) 8293-4555 (office). *Website:* www .joolsholland.com.

HOLLANDE, François; French politician; b. 12 Aug. 1954, Rouen (Seine-Maritime); fmr pnr, Ségolène Royal; four c.; ed HEC, Paris, Institut d'Études Politiques de Paris, École Nat. d'Admin; fmr Councillor, Cour des comptes; mem. Ussel City Council 1983–89; Deputy for Corrèze (1ère) in Nat. Ass. 1988–93, 1997–, mem. Defence Comm.; Deputy Mayor of Tulle 1989–95, mem. Tulle City Council 1995–2001, Mayor of Tulle 2001–08; mem. Limousin Regional Council March 1992, 1998–2001; Pres. Conseil Gen. Corrèze 2008–; First Sec. Parti Socialiste 1997–2008; mem. European Parl. July–Dec. 1999. *Address:* Parti Socialiste, 10 rue de Solférino, 75333 Paris Cedex 07 (office); La Mairie, 36 avenue Victor Hugo, 19000 Tulle, France. *Telephone:* 1-45-56-77-00 (office); 5-55-20-48-48. *Fax:* 1-47-05-15-78 (office). *E-mail:* infops@parti -socialiste.fr (office). *Website:* www.parti-socialiste.fr (office).

HOLLANDER, John, PhD; American poet and academic; *Sterling Professor Emeritus of English, Yale University;* b. 28 Oct. 1929, New York; s. of Franklin Hollander and Muriel Hollander (née Kornfeld); m. 1st Anne Loesser 1953 (divorced 1977); two d.; 2nd Natalie Charkow 1981; ed Columbia, Harvard and Indiana Univs; Lecturer in English, Connecticut Coll. 1957–59; Instructor in English, Yale Univ. 1959–61; Asst Prof. of English 1961–64, Assoc. Prof. 1964–66, Prof. 1977–85, A. Bartlett Giamatti Prof. 1986–95, Sterling Prof. of English 1995–2002, Sterling Prof. Emer. 2002–; Prof. of English, Hunter Coll., New York 1966–77; Christian Gauss Seminarian, Princeton Univ. 1962; Visiting Prof., School of Letters and Linguistic Inst., Indiana Univ. 1964; Visiting Prof., Seminar in American Studies, Salzburg, Austria 1965; Clark

Lecturer, Trinity Coll., Cambridge 2000; editorial assoc. for Poetry Partisan Review 1959–65; mem. Poetry Bd Wesleyan Univ. Press 1959–62; mem. Editorial Bd Raritan 1981–; Chancellor Acad. of American Poets 1981–, MacArthur Fellow 1990–95; Fellow, American Acad. of Arts and Sciences, Ezra Stiles Coll., Yale Univ. 1961–64, Nat. Endowment for Humanities 1973–, Silliman Coll. 1977–; Overseas Fellow, Churchill Coll., Univ. of Cambridge 1967–68; mem. American Acad. of Arts and Letters (Sec. 2000–03), Asscn of Literary Scholars and Critics (Pres. 2000); Hon. DLitt (Marietta Coll.) 1982; Hon. DHL (Indiana) 1990, (CUNY Grad. Center) 2001, (New School Univ.) 2003; Hon. DFA (Maine Coll. of Art) 1993; Nat. Inst. of Arts and Letters Award 1963, Levinson Prize 1964, Washington Monthly Prize 1976, Guggenheim Fellow 1979–80, Bollingen Prize 1983, Ambassador Book Award English Speaking Union 1994, Governor's Arts Award for Poetry, State of Connecticut 1997, Robert Penn Warren–Cleanth Brooks Award 1998, Poet Laureate State of Connecticut 2006–, Frost Medal, Poetry Soc. of America 2007. *Publications include:* A Crackling of Thorns 1958, The Untuning of the Sky 1961, Movie-Going and Other Poems 1962, Visions from the Ramble 1965, Types of Shape 1969 (enlarged edn) 1991, The Night Mirror 1971, Town and Country Matters 1972, Selected Poems 1972, The Head of the Bed 1974, Tales Told of the Fathers 1975, Vision and Resonance 1975, Reflections on Espionage 1976, 1999, Spectral Emanations 1978, In Place 1978, Blue Wine 1979, The Figure of Echo 1981, Rhyme's Reason 1981 (enlarged edn) 1989, Powers of Thirteen 1983, In Time and Place 1986, Harp Lake 1988, Some Fugitives Take Cover 1988, Melodious Guile 1988, William Bailey 1991, Tesserae 1993, Selected Poetry 1993, The Gazer's Spirit 1995, The Work of Poetry 1997, The Poetry of Everyday Life 1998, Figurehead and Other Poems 1999, Picture Window 2003; contributor of numerous poems and articles to journals; ed. and contributing ed. of numerous books including: Poems of Ben Jonson 1961, The Wind and the Rain 1961, Jiggery-Pokery 1966, Poems of Our Moment 1968, Modern Poetry: Essays in Criticism 1968, American Short Stories Since 1945 1968, The Oxford Anthology of English Literature (with Frank Kermode q.v.), 1973, For I. A. Richards: Essays in his Honor 1973, Literature as Experience (with Irving Howe and David Bromwich) 1979, The Essential Rossetti 1990, American Poetry: the Nineteenth Century 1993, Animal Poems (ed.) 1994, Garden Poems (ed.) 1996, Marriage Poems (ed.) 1997, Frost (ed.) 1997, Committed to Memory (ed.) 1999, Figurehead and Other Poems 1999, War Poems (ed.) 1999, Selected Poetry 1999, Sonnets (ed.) 2000, A Gallery of Poems 2001, American Wits (ed.) 2003, Selected Poems of Emma Lazarus 2005, Poems Haunted and Bewitched 2005; contributing ed. Harper's magazine 1969–71. *Address:* Department of English, Yale University, PO Box 208302, New Haven, CT 06520, USA (office). *Telephone:* (203) 432-4566 (office). *Fax:* (203) 387-3497 (office). *E-mail:* john.hollander@yale.edu (office). *Website:* www.yale.edu/english (office).

HOLLANDER, Samuel, OC, PhD, FRSC; British/Canadian/Israeli economist and academic; *Professor of Economics, Ben Gurion University;* b. 6 April 1937, London, England; s. of Jacob Hollander and Lily Bernstein; m. Perlette Kéroub 1959; one s. one d.; ed Gateshead Talmudical Acad., Hendon Tech. Coll., Kilburn Polytechnic, London School of Econs, Princeton Univ., NJ; emigrated to Canada 1963; Asst Prof., Univ. of Toronto 1963–67, Assoc. Prof. 1967–70, Prof. 1970–84, Univ. Prof. 1984–98, Univ. Prof. Emer. 1998–; Research Dir, Univ. of Nice (CNRS) 1999–2000; Visiting Prof., Florence Univ., Italy 1973–74, Univ. of London 1974–75, Hebrew Univ., Jerusalem 1979–80, 1988, La Trobe Univ., Melbourne, Australia 1985, Auckland Univ., NZ 1985, 1988, Sorbonne, Paris 1997, Nice Univ. 2001; several guest lectureships; emigrated to Israel 2000; currently Prof. of Econs, Ben Gurion Univ.; Hon. LLD (McMaster) 1999; Fulbright Fellowship 1959; Guggenheim Fellowship 1968–69; Social Science Fed. of Canada 50th Anniversary Book Award 1990. *Publications:* The Sources of Increased Efficiency 1965, The Economics of Adam Smith 1973, The Economics of David Ricardo 1979, The Economics of J. S. Mill 1985, Classical Economics 1987, Ricardo – The New View: Collected Essays I 1995, The Economics of T. R. Malthus 1997, The Literature of Political Economy: Collected Essays II 1998, John Stuart Mill on Economic Theory and Method: Collected Essays III 2000, Jean-Baptiste Say and the Classical Canon in Economics 2005. *Address:* Department of Economics, Ben Gurion University of the Negev, 84105, Beer Sheva (office); 2 Rehov Sapir, 89066 Arad, Israel (home). *Telephone:* (8) 6472305 (office); (8) 9771664 (home). *Fax:* (7) 6472941 (office). *E-mail:* sholland@bgumail.bgu.ac.il (office). *Website:* econ.bgu.ac.il (office).

HOLLEIN, Hans, MArch; Austrian architect; b. 30 March 1934, Vienna; ed Acad. of Graphic Arts, Vienna, Ill. Inst. of Tech., Univ. of Calif., Berkeley; Visiting Prof., Univ. of Washington, USA 1963–64, 1966; worked in architectural offices in Australia, S America, Sweden and Germany; work as ind. architect in Vienna 1964–; Prof., Acad. of Fine Arts, Düsseldorf, Germany 1967–82; Dir Inst. of Design, Vienna 1976–; Visiting Prof., Yale Univ. 1979; Austrian Rep., Venice Biennale, Visual Arts 1978–90, Architecture 1991, 1996, Dir Architecture Sector 1994–; mem. Austrian Art Senate, AIA 1980; Hon. mem. Royal Swedish Acad., Koninklijke Acad. van Beeldende Kunsten, Netherlands, RIBA 1995, Bund Deutscher Architekten 1996; Reynolds Memorial Award, USA 1966, 1984, Vienna City Prize 1974, Deutscher Architekturpreis 1983, Pritzker Architecture Prize 1985, Chicago Architecture Award 1990. *Buildings designed include:* Rettl Kerzenladen, Vienna 1965, Headquarters, Siemens AG, Monaco 1972, Museum of Glass and Ceramics, Tehran 1977–88, Haas Haus, Vienna 1985–90, Headquarters, Banco Santander, Madrid 1988–93, Donau-City, Vienna 1993, Lichtforum Zumtobel, Vienna 1995–96. *Address:* La Biennale di Venezia, Settore Architettura, Ca Giustinian San Marco 1364, 30124 Venice, Italy (office). *Telephone:* (41) 5218860 (office). *Fax:* (41) 5200569 (office). *E-mail:* pressoffice@labiennale.com (office).

HOLLEIN, Max; Austrian fine arts administrator, curator and director; *Director, Schirn Kunsthalle Frankfurt, Städel Museum and Liebieghaus Sculpture Collection;* b. 1969, Vienna; ed Wirtschaftsuniversität Wien, Universität Wien; Project Dir for Exhbns, Solomon R. Guggenheim Museum, New York 1995, Exec. Asst to the Dir 1996–98, Chief of Staff and Man. of European Relations 1998–2000; Commr and Curator American Pavilion, Seventh Biennale of Architecture, Venice 2000; Dir Schirn Kunsthalle Frankfurt 2001–, Städel Museum, Frankfurt 2006, Liebieghaus-Museum alter Plastile, Frankfurt 2006; Commr Austrian Pavilion, Biennale of Visual Art, Venice 2005; mem. Bd Dirs Kulturveranstaltungen des Bundes in Berlin GmbH; mem. Bd of Trustees Neue Galerie, New York. *Publications:* Zeitgenössische Kunst und der Kunstmarktboom (Contemporary Art and the Boom on the Art Market) 1999, Unternehmen Kunst: Entwicklungen und Verwicklungen (The Business of Art) 2006. *Address:* Schirn Kunsthalle Frankfurt, Römerberg, 60311 Frankfurt (office); Städel Museum, Dürerstrasse 2, 60596 Frankfurt, Germany (office). *Telephone:* (69) 299882-111 (office); (69) 605098-100 (office). *Fax:* (69) 299882-240 (office); (69) 605098-198 (office). *E-mail:* welcome@schirn.de (office). *Website:* www.schirn.de (office); www.staedelmuseum.de (office).

HÖLLER, Carsten, DHabil; Belgian artist; b. 1961, Brussels; ed Univ. of Kiel, Germany; began his artistic career in 1988; uses his training as a scientist in his work as an artist, concentrating particularly on the nature of human relationships and demanding viewer participation; rejected any specific artistic identity, creating works that range from films, drawings, architectural plans and photographs to performances, sculptures and installations; works are most frequently devoted to chemically analysing the nature of human emotions; has collaborated with many other artists, notably with German artist Rosemarie Trockel, with whom, for Documenta X, they together A House for Pigs and People 1997, in which people and pigs share the same physical space; works include: Addina 1997, Valerio I and II 1998, The Forest, Light Wall 2000, Solandra Greenhouse (garden filled with the Solandra maxima vine); lives and works in Fasta, Sweden. *Address:* c/o Casey Kaplan Gallery, 525 West 21st Street, New York, NY 10011, USA.

HOLLICK, Baron (Life Peer), cr. 1991, of Notting Hill in the Royal Borough of Kensington and Chelsea; **Clive Richard Hollick,** BA; British business executive; *Managing Director, Kohlberg Kravis Roberts;* b. 20 May 1945, Southampton; s. of Leslie George Hollick and Olive Mary Hollick (née Scruton); m. Susan Mary Woodford 1977; three d.; ed Univ. of Nottingham; joined Hambros Bank 1968, Dir 1973; CEO MAI PLC (fmrly Mills & Allen Int. PLC) 1974–96, Shepperton Studios 1976–84, Garban Ltd (USA) 1983–97, United Business Media PLC 1996–2005; Man. Dir Kohlberg Kravis Roberts UK 2005–; CEO; mem. Bd of Dirs Logica PLC 1987–91, Meridian Broadcasting 1991–96, British Aerospace 1992–97, Anglia TV Ltd 1994–97, TRW Inc. 2000, Diageo PLC 2001–, Honeywell Int.; mem. Nat. Bus Co. 1984–91, Applied Econs Dept Advisory Cttee Univ. of Cambridge 1989–97, Financial Law Panel 1993–97; Special Adviser to Dept of Trade and Industry 1997–98; Chair. South Bank Centre, London 2002–; Founder and Trustee, Inst. for Public Policy Research 1988–; Hon. LLD (Nottingham) 1993. *Leisure interests:* cinema, countryside, reading, tennis, theatre. *Address:* Kohlberg Kravis Roberts, Stirling Square, 7 Carlton Gardens, London, SW1Y 5AD (office); House of Lords, Westminster, London, SW1A 0PW, England. *Telephone:* (20) 7839-9800 (office). *Fax:* (20) 7839-9807 (office). *Website:* www.kkr.com (office).

HOLLIDAY, Charles O. (Chad), Jr, BS; American engineer and business executive; *Chairman and CEO, E.I. du Pont de Nemours & Co.;* b. 9 March 1948, Nashville, Tenn.; s. of Charles O. Holliday, Sr and Ann Hunter; m. Ann Holliday; two s.; ed Univ. of Tennessee; joined DuPont Fibers Dept as engineer, Old Hickory, Tenn. 1970, Business Analyst, Wilmington, Del. 1974, later product planner, Asst Plant Man., Seaford, Del. 1978, joined DuPont Corp. Planning Dept 1984, Global Business Man. for Nomex 1986, Global Business Dir for Kevlar 1987, Dir of Marketing DuPont Chemicals and Pigments Dept 1988, Vice-Pres., then Pres. DuPont Asia-Pacific 1990, Chair. 1995, Sr Vice-Pres. DuPont 1992, Exec. Vice-Pres. and mem. Office of Chief Exec., E.I. du Pont de Nemours & Co. 1995, Dir 1997–, Pres. Oct. 1997–, CEO 1998–, Chair. 1999–; Chair. Catalyst; mem. Bd Dirs DuPont Photomasks Inc., Deere & Co.; Chair. US Council on Competitiveness; fmr Chair. Business Roundtable's Task Force for Environment, Tech. and Economy, World Business Council for Sustainable Devt, The Business Council, Soc. of Chemical Industry (American Section); Founding mem. Int. Business Council; mem. Chancellor's Advisory Council for Enhancement Univ. of Tennessee, Knoxville; Sr mem. Inst. of Industrial Engineers; mem. Nat. Acad. of Eng. *Publication:* Walking the Talk (co-author). *Address:* E.I. DuPont de Nemours & Co., 1007 Market Street, Wilmington, DE 19898, USA (office). *Telephone:* (302) 774-1000 (office). *Fax:* (302) 999-4399 (office). *E-mail:* info@dupont.com (office). *Website:* www.dupont.com (office).

HOLLIDAY, Sir Frederick (George Thomas), Kt, CBE, FIBiol, FRSE; British fmr university vice-chancellor, zoologist and business executive; *Chairman, Northumbrian Water Group plc;* b. 22 Sept. 1935; s. of the late Alfred Holliday and Margaret Holliday; m. Philippa Davidson 1957; one s. one d.; ed Bromsgrove County High School and Univ. of Sheffield; Fisheries Research Training Grant (Devt Comm.), Marine Lab. Aberdeen 1956–58, Scientific Officer 1958–61; Lecturer in Zoology, Univ. of Aberdeen 1961–66; Prof. of Biology, Univ. of Stirling 1967–75, Deputy Prin. 1972, Acting Prin. 1973–75; Prof. of Zoology, Univ. of Aberdeen 1975–79; Vice-Chancellor and Warden, Univ. of Durham 1980–90; Dir Shell UK 1980–99; mem. Bd Northern Investors Ltd 1984–90, BRB 1990–94 (Chair. BR (Eastern) 1986–90), Union Railways 1992–97, Lyonnaise des Eaux 1996–97, Suez Lyonnaise des Eaux 1997–, Wise Speke PLC 1997–98, Brewin Dolphin PLC 1998–; mem. Northern Regional Bd Lloyd's Bank 1985–91, Chair. 1986–89, Deputy Chair. 1989–91; Independent Chair. Jt Nature Conservation Cttee 1991; mem. numerous cttees; Chair. Northumbrian Water Group plc 1993–, Ondeo Services UK Ltd 2001–, Council, Water Aid 1995–97, Northern Venture Trust plc 1996–, Go-Ahead Group PLC 1997–2002; mem. Bd of Dirs Northern 2 VCT plc; Pres. British Trust for Ornithology 1996–2001; Vice-Pres. Freshwater Biological Asscn, Marine Biological Asscn; Chair. South Bank Centre 2002–; Hon. DUniv (Stirling) 1984; Hon. DSc (Sheffield) 1987, (Cranfield) 1991; Hon. DCL (Durham) 2002. *Publications:* Wildlife of Scotland (ed. and contrib.) 1979; numerous publs on fish biology and wildlife conservation in Advanced Marine Biology, Fish Physiology, Oceanography and Marine Biology etc. *Leisure interests:* walking, gardening, ornithology. *Address:* Northumbrian Water Group plc, Abbey Road, Pity Me, Durham, DH1 5FJ, England. *Telephone:* (191) 301-6462 (office). *Fax:* (191) 301-6272 (office). *Website:* www.nwg.co.uk (office).

HOLLIDAY, Robin, PhD, FRS, FAA; British geneticist and cell biologist; b. 6 Nov. 1932, Palestine; s. of Clifford Holliday and Eunice Holliday; m. 1st Diana Collet Parsons 1957 (divorced 1983); one s. three d.; m. 2nd Lily I. Huschtscha 1986; one d.; ed Hitchin Grammar School and Univ. of Cambridge; mem. scientific staff, Dept of Genetics, John Innes Inst., Bayfordbury, Herts. 1958–65; mem. scientific staff, Div. of Microbiology, Nat. Inst. for Medical Research 1965–70, Head, Div. of Genetics 1970–88; Chief Research Scientist CSIRO 1988–97; proposed DNA 'Holliday Structure' 1964; mem. European Molecular Biology Org.; Foreign Fellow, Indian Nat. Science Acad. 1995; Fulbright Scholar 1962; Lord Simon Prize 1987. *Publications:* The Science of Human Progress 1981, Genes, Proteins and Cellular Ageing 1986, Understanding Ageing 1995, Slaves and Saviours 2000, Aging: The Paradox of Life; about 250 research publs. *Leisure interests:* sculpture, writing. *Address:* 12 Roma Court, West Pennant Hills, NSW 2125, Australia (home). *Telephone:* (2) 9873-3476 (home). *Fax:* (2) 9871-2159 (home). *E-mail:* randl.holliday@bigpond.com (home).

HOLLIDAY, Steven, BSc; British business executive; *CEO, National Grid PLC;* b. 1957; m.; three c.; ed Univ. of Nottingham; 19 years with Exxon Group; fmrly Exec. Dir British Borneo Oil & Gas PLC; Group Dir, UK and Europe, Nat. Grid PLC 2001–02, Head of Electricity and Gas Transmission Businesses 2002–03, Group Dir responsible for UK Gas Distribution and Business Services 2003–06, Deputy CEO April–Dec. 2006, CEO 2007–; mem. Bd of Dirs Marks & Spencer Group PLC 2004–. *Address:* National Grid PLC, 1–3 Strand, London, WC2N 5EH, England (office). *Telephone:* (20) 7004-3000 (office). *Fax:* (20) 7004-3004 (office). *E-mail:* corpcomms@ngrid.com (office). *Website:* www.nationalgrid.com (office).

HOLLIGER, Heinz; Swiss oboist and composer; b. 21 May 1939, Langenthal; m. Ursula Holliger; ed in Berne, Paris and Basel under Emile Cassagnaud (oboe) and Pierre Boulez (composition); Prof. of Oboe, Freiberg Music Acad. 1965–; has appeared at all the major European music festivals and in Japan, USA, Australia, Israel, etc.; conducted Chamber Orchestra of Europe, London 1992, London Sinfonietta 1997; Composer-in-Residence, Lucerne Festival 1998; recorded over 80 works, mainly for Philips and Deutsche Grammophon; recipient of several int. prizes. *Compositions include:* Der magische Tänzer, Trio, Siebengesang, Wind Quintet, Dona nobis pacem, Pneuma, Psalm, Cardiophonie, Kreis, String Quartet, Atembogen, Die Jahreszeiten, Come and Go, Not I. *Recording:* Koechlin's Vocal works with orchestra (Midem Classical Award for Vocal Recitals 2006). *Address:* Konzertgesellschaft, Hochstrasse 51/Postfach, 4002 Basel, Switzerland (office).

HOLLINGHURST, Alan James, BA, MLitt, FRSL; British writer; b. 26 May 1954, Stroud, Gloucestershire; s. of the late James Kenneth Hollinghurst and of Elizabeth Lilian Hollinghurst (née Keevil); ed Canford School, Dorset and Magdalen Coll., Oxford; Asst Ed. Times Literary Supplement 1982–84, Deputy Ed. 1985–90, Poetry Ed. 1991–95; Visiting Prof. Univ. of Houston 1998; Old Dominion Fellow Princeton Univ. 2004. *Publications:* Confidential Chats with Boys (poems) 1982, The Swimming-Pool Library (novel) (Somerset Maugham Award 1989, American Acad. of Arts and Letters E. M. Forster Award 1989) 1988, Bajazet, by Racine (trans.) 1991, The Folding Star (novel) (James Tait Black Memorial Prize) 1994, New Writing 4 (ed. with A. S. Byatt) 1995, The Spell (novel) 1998, Three Novels, by Ronald Firbank (ed.) 2000, A. E. Housman: Poems Selected by Alan Hollinghurst (ed.) 2001, The Line of Beauty (novel) (Man Booker Prize for Fiction) 2004. *Leisure interests:* music, architecture. *Address:* Antony Harwood Ltd, 103 Walton Street, Oxford, OX2 6EB, England (office).

HOLLINGS, Ernest F(ritz), BA, LLB; American fmr politician and lawyer; b. 1 Jan. 1922, Charleston, SC; s. of Adolph G. Hollings and Wilhelmine D. Meyer; m. 2nd Rita Liddy 1971; two s. two d. (by previous m.); ed Charleston Public Schools, The Citadel and Univ. of South Carolina; served in US Army 1942–45; admitted to S Carolina Bar 1947; mem. S Carolina House of Reps 1948–54, Speaker *pro tem.* 1951–53; Lt-Gov. of S Carolina 1955–59, Gov. of S Carolina 1959–63; law practice, Charleston 1963–66; Senator from S Carolina 1966–2005 (retd); Chair. Democratic Senatorial Campaign Cttee 1971–73; mem. Hoover Comm. on Intelligence Activities 1954–55, Pres.'s Advisory Comm. on Intergovernmental Relations 1959–63, on Federalism 1981; mem. Senate Cttees on Appropriations, Commerce, Budget, Chair. Budget Cttee 1980, Commerce Cttee 1982; fmr mem. Democratic Policy Cttee, Office of Tech. Assessment, Nat. Ocean Policy Study; mem. Advisory Bd Hollings Cancer Center, Medical Univ. of South Carolina; Democrat; numerous awards. *Publication:* The Case against Hunger: A Demand for a National Policy 1970. *Address:* Advisory Board, Medical University of South Carolina, Hollings Cancer Center, 86 Jonathan Lucas Street, PO Box 250955, Charleston, SC 29425, USA (office).

HOLLINGWORTH, Clare, OBE; British journalist; b. 10 Oct. 1911; d. of John Albert Hollingworth and Daisy Gertrude Hollingworth; m. 1st Vyvyan Derring Vandeleur Robinson 1936 (divorced 1951); m. 2nd Geoffrey Spence Hoare 1952 (died 1966); ed Girls' Collegiate School, Leicester, Grammar School, Ashby-de-la-Zouch, School of Slavonic Studies, Univ. of London; mem. staff League of Nations Union 1935–38; worked in Poland for Lord Mayor's Fund for Refugees from Czechoslovakia 1939; Corresp. for Daily Telegraph Poland, Turkey, Cairo (covered Desert Campaigns, troubles in Persia and Iraq, Civil War in Greece and events in Palestine) 1941–50, for Manchester Guardian (covered Algerian War and trouble spots including Egypt, Aden and Viet Nam), based in Paris 1950–63; Guardian Defence Corresp. 1963–67; foreign trouble-shooter for Daily Telegraph (covering war in Viet Nam) 1967–73, Corresp. in China 1973–76, Defence Corresp. 1976–81; Far Eastern Corresp. in Hong Kong for Sunday Telegraph 1981–; Research Assoc. (fmrly Visiting Scholar), Centre for Asian Studies, Univ. of Hong Kong 1981–; Hon. DLitt (Leicester) 1993; Granada Journalist of the Year Award and Hannan Swaffer Award 1963; James Cameron Award for Journalism 1994. *Publications:* Poland's Three Weeks War 1940, There's A German Just Behind Me 1945, The Arabs and the West 1951, Mao and the Men against Him 1984, Front Line 1990. *Leisure interests:* visiting second-hand furniture and bookshops, collecting modern pictures and Chinese porcelain, music. *Address:* 302 Ridley House, 2 Upper Albert Road, Hong Kong Special Administrative Region, People's Republic of China (home). *Telephone:* 2868-1838 (home).

HOLLINGWORTH, Rt Rev. Peter, AC, OBE, MA, DipSocialStudies, ThL, FAIM; Australian ecclesiastic; b. 10 April 1935, Adelaide; m. Kathleen Ann Turner 1960; three d.; ed Trinity Coll. Univ. of Melbourne; Deacon-in-Charge then Priest-in-Charge, St Mary's, N Melbourne 1960–64; Chaplain to the Brotherhood of St Laurence 1964–90, Assoc. Dir 1970, later Dir of Social Services, Exec. Dir 1980–90; Hon. Curate, St Silas's, North Balwyn, later Hon. Curate at St Faith's, Burwood and Priest-in-Charge, St Mark's, Fitzroy; recipient of travelling bursary 1967; elected Canon, St Paul's Cathedral 1980; Bishop of the Inner City 1985–90, Archbishop of Brisbane 1990–2001; Gov.-Gen. of the Commonwealth of Australia 2001–03; Prior to Order of St John of Jerusalem; Chair. Int. Year of Shelter for the Homeless, Nat. Cttee of Non-Governmental Orgs 1986–88, Anglican Social Responsibilities Comm. of Gen. Synod 1990–98, Anglicare in diocese of Brisbane; Pres. Victorian Council of Social Services 1969; mem., Hon. Chair. Centenary of Fed. Council, Constitutional Convention (as non-parl. Rep.); Fellow, Trinity Coll. Melbourne; Hon. LLD (Monash Univ.) 1986, (Melbourne) 1990; Hon. DUniv (Griffith Univ.) 1993, (Queensland Univ. of Tech.) 1994, (Cen. Queensland) 1995; Hon. DLitt (Univ. of Southern Queensland) 1999; Victorian Rostrum Award of Merit 1985, Advance Australia Award 1988, Paul Harris Fellowship, Rotary Club 1989, Australian of the Year 1992, Nat. Living Treasure of Australia (Nat. Trust) 1997. *Publications:* The Powerless Poor 1972, The Poor: Victims of Affluence? 1974, Australians in Poverty 1979, Kingdom Come 1991, Public Thoughts of an Archbishop 1996. *Leisure interests:* swimming, Australian Rules football, theatre, reading, music. *Address:* POB 18081, Collins Street East, Melbourne, Victoria, 8003, Australia (office). *Telephone:* (3) 8633-3990 (office). *Fax:* (3) 9671-3954 (office). *E-mail:* amanda.dinsdale@pmc.gov.au (office).

HOLLÓ, Janos; Hungarian chemical engineer and academic; *Professor of Research, Central Research Institute of Chemistry, Hungarian Academy of Sciences;* b. 20 Aug. 1919, Szentes; s. of Gyula Holló and Margit Mandl; m. 1st Hermina Milch (1944); m. 2nd Vera Novák 1956; two s. one d.; ed Tech. Univ., Budapest; Tech. Dir Budapest Breweries 1948; Prof. of Agricultural and Chemical Tech., Budapest Tech. Univ. 1952–90, Dean Chemical Eng Faculty 1955–57, 1963–72, Prof. Emer. 1991–; Dir Hungarian Acad. of Sciences Cen. Research Inst. of Chemistry 1972–91, Prof. of Research 1991–; Pres. Comm. Int. des Industries Agricoles et Alimentaires (CIIA); Chair. Cereals and Pulses Cttee, Int. Org. for Standardization (ISO) 1960–99, Agricultural and Food Products Cttee 1971–98; Gen. Sec. Scientific Asscn of Hungary Food Industry 1949, Chair., Pres. 1981–91, Hon. Pres. 1991–; Pres. Int. Soc. for Fat Research (ISF) 1964–66, 1982–83, Exec. mem. 1964–; Ed.-in-Chief Acta Alimentaria, Journal of Food Investigation, Biotechnology and Environmental Protection Today and Tomorrow; mem. numerous editorial bds; mem. Hungarian Acad. of Sciences 1967; Foreign mem. Finnish Acad. of Tech. Sciences 1984, German Acad. of Sciences 1984, Polish Acad. of Sciences 1991, New York Acad. of Sciences 1994, Int. Union of Food Science and Tech. 1997–; Hon. mem. Polish Science Asscn of Food Industries 1971, Austrian Soc. for Food and Biochemistry 1983; Commdr Ordre du Mérite pour la recherche et l'invention 1962, Chevalier des Palmes académiques 1967, Labour Order of Merit 1971, 1979; Dr hc (Tech. Univ. of Vienna) 1973, (Berlin, Charlottenburg) 1984, (Tech. Univ. Budapest) 1991, (Univ. of Horticulture and Food Industry, Budapest) 1991; Hon. Dip. (Int. Standards Organization) 1999; Medal of French Starch Syndicate 1963, Saare Medal 1972, Premio d'Oro Interpetrol 1973, Copernicus Medal 1974, State Prize 1975, Prix d'honneur de l'Acad. Int. du Lutèce 1978, Chevreul Medal 1986, Normann Medal 1986, Award for Outstanding Paper Presentation (American Oil Chem. Soc.) 1992. *Publications:* numerous books (with others) including Technology of Malting and Brewing, Biotechnology of Food and Feed Production, Bioconversion of Starch, Aliments non-conventionnels à destination humaine, Automatization in the Food Industry, The Application of Molecular Distillation; co-author of some 600 articles for professional journals. *Address:* Central Research Institute for Chemistry of the Hungarian Academy of Sciences, Pusztaszeri ut 59/67, 1025 Budapest (office); Szt. Gellért tér 4, 1111 Budapest, Hungary (home). *Telephone:* (1) 325-7750 (office); (1) 463-2615 (home). *Fax:* (1) 463-2598 (home). *Website:* www.ch .bme.hu/hun/tanszek/mkt/hollo.html.

HOLLOWAY, Bruce William, AO, PhD, DSc, FAA, FTSE; Australian geneticist and academic; *Honorary Professorial Fellow and Professor Emeritus, Monash University;* b. 9 Jan. 1928, Adelaide; s. of Albert Holloway and Gertrude C. Walkem; m. Brenda D. Gray 1952; one s. one d.; ed Scotch Coll., Adelaide, Univ. of Adelaide, Calif. Inst. of Tech. and Univ. of Melbourne; Lecturer in Plant Pathology, Waite Agric. Research Inst. 1949–50; Research Fellow in Microbial Genetics, John Curtin School of Medicine, ANU 1953–56; Sr Lecturer 1956–60, then Reader in Microbial Genetics, Univ. of Melbourne 1956–67; Foundation Prof. of Genetics, Monash Univ. 1968–93, Head, Dept of Genetics and Developmental Biology 1968–93, Hon. Professorial Fellow and Prof. Emer. 1993–, Chair. Bd CRC for Vertebrate Biological Control 1994–99; Dir, Master Classes, Crawford Fund 1994–; Visiting Lecturer in Microbiology and Fellow, MIT 1962–63; Sec. Biological Sciences, Australian Acad. of Science 1982–86; Visiting Prof., Univ. of Newcastle-upon-Tyne 1977–78; Chair. Nat. Biotechnology Program Research Grants Scheme 1983–86; mem. Industry and Research Devt Bd 1986–89; Kathleen Barton-Wright Lecturer, Soc. for Gen. Microbiology, UK 1998; Hon. Professorial Fellow, Monash Univ. 1994–2001; 50th Anniversary Research Award, Monash Univ. 2008. *Publications:* more than 190 papers on genetics and microbiology in scientific journals and conf. proceedings. *Leisure interests:* music, reading, tennis. *Telephone:* (3) 9836-5515 (home). *Fax:* (3) 9836-6869 (home). *E-mail:* hollowab@ozemail.com .au (home).

HOLLOWAY, Adm. James Lemuel, III; American naval officer (retd); b. 23 Feb. 1922, Charleston, S Carolina; s. of Admiral James L. Holloway, Jr and the late Jean Hagood; m. Dabney Rawlings 1942; one s. (died 1964), two d.; ed US Naval Acad., Md; Commissioned Ensign in US Navy 1942, served on destroyers in Atlantic and Pacific Theatres, World War II; Gunnery Officer USS Bennion, took part in Battle of Surigao Straits; Exec. Officer of Fighter Squadron Fifty-two, USS Boxer, Korean War 1952–54; Commdr Attack Squadron Eighty-three, USS Essex, Sixth Fleet during Lebanon landings 1958; Nat. War Coll. 1961; nuclear training under Admiral Rickover 1963; Commdg Officer USS Enterprise (first nuclear-powered carrier) Viet Nam War 1965–67; promoted to rank of Rear-Adm. 1967; Dir Strike Warfare Div., Program Coordinator Nuclear Attack Carrier Program, Office of Chief of Naval Operations; Commdr Sixth Fleet Carrier Striking Force, directed operations in E Mediterranean during Jordanian crisis 1970; Deputy C-in-C Atlantic and US Atlantic Fleet, Vice-Adm. 1971; Commdr Seventh Fleet during combat operations in Viet Nam 1972–73; Vice-Chief of Naval Operations 1973–74; Chief of Naval Operations 1974–78; mem. Jt Chiefs of Staff 1974–78; Chair. Special Operations Review Group, Iranian Hostage Rescue 1981; Special Envoy of Vice-Pres. of USA to Bahrain 1986; mem. Pres.'s Comm. on Merchant Marine and Defense 1986; Pres. Council of American Flagship Operators 1981–87; Chair. of Bd Asscn of Naval Aviation; Chair. Academic Advisory Bd to US Naval Acad.; Exec. Dir, Vice-Pres.'s Task Force on Combating Terrorism 1985; Pres.'s Blue Ribbon Comm. on Defense Man. 1985–86; Commr, Comm. on Merchant Marine and Defense 1987, Comm. on Integrated Long-Term Strategy 1987; mem. Bd of Dirs US Life Insurance Co. 1985–95, UNC Inc. 1987–98, George Marshall Foundation 1988–98, Atlantic Council 1990–98; mem. Bd of Govs, St John's Coll. 1996–99; Pres. Naval Historical Foundation 1984–98 (Chair. 1998–); Chair. Emer. Bd Historic Annapolis Foundation 1998–; Chair. Emer. Naval Acad. Foundation 1994–2000; Chair. Emer. Bd of Trustees, St James School, Md 2000–; Tech. Adviser for film Top Gun 1985; awarded numerous medals for meritorious service including Defense Distinguished Service Medal (twice), Navy Distinguished Service Medal (four times), Legion of Merit, Distinguished Flying Cross, Bronze Star Medal with Combat "V", Air Medal (four times), Modern Patriot Award 1994, US Navy League Annual Award for Distinguished Civilian Leadership 1997, Sons of the Revolution Distinguished Patriot Award 1999, Distinguished Grad. Award, Naval Acad. 2000, US Nat. Wrestling Hall of Fame 1999; Commdr., Légion d'honneur, Grand Cross of Germany (First Class), Order of The Rising Sun (Japan) (First Class), Italian Grand Cross. *Film:* stunt pilot in Bridges at Toko-Ri 1955. *Publications:* numerous articles on aviation, sealift and defence organization. *Leisure interest:* sailing. *Address:* 1694 Epping Farms Lane, Annapolis, MD 21401, USA. *Telephone:* (410) 849-2115. *Fax:* (410) 849-2115.

HOLLOWAY, Rt Rev. Richard Frederick, BD, STM, FRSE; British ecclesiastic; b. 26 Nov. 1933, Glasgow; s. of Arthur Holloway and Mary Holloway; m. Jean Holloway 1963; one s. two d.; ed Kelham Theological Coll., Edinburgh Theological Coll. and Union Theological Seminary, New York; Curate, St Ninian's, Glasgow 1959–63; Priest-in-Charge, St Margaret's and St Mungo's, Gorbals, Glasgow 1963–68; Rector, Old St Paul's, Edin. 1968–80, Church of the Advent, Boston, Mass. 1980–84; Vicar, St Mary Magdalen's, Oxford 1984–86; Bishop of Edin. 1986–2000; Primus, Scottish Episcopal Church 1992–2000; Prof. of Divinity, Gresham Coll. London 1997–2001; Chair. Jt Bd Scottish Arts Council, Scottish Screen 2006–; mem. Human Fertilisation and Embryology Authority 1991–97, Broadcasting Standards Comm. 2001–04; Hon. DUniv (Strathclyde) 1994, (Open Univ.); Hon. DD (Aberdeen) 1994, (Glasgow) 2001; Hon. DLitt (Napier) 2001. *Radio:* Cover Stories (BBC) 2003, 2004, Divine Comedy (BBC) 2003. *Television:* Holloway's Road (BBC) 2000, The Sword and the Cross (BBC) 2003. *Publications include:* Beyond Belief 1981, The Killing (Winifred M. Stanford Award) 1984, Paradoxes of Christian Faith and Life 1984, The Sidelong Glance 1985, The Way of the Cross 1986, Seven to Flee, Seven to Follow 1986, Crossfire 1988, Another Country, Another King 1991, Who Needs Feminism? 1991, Anger, Sex, Doubt and Death 1992, The Stranger in the Wings 1994, Churches and How To Survive Them 1994, Behold Your King 1995, Limping Towards the Sunrise 1996, Dancing on the Edge 1997, Godless Morality 1999, Doubts and Loves 2001, On Forgiveness 2002, Looking in the Distance 2004, Between the Monster and the Saint: Reflections on the Human Condition 2008. *Leisure interests:* walking, movies, reading, cooking. *Address:* 6 Blantyre Terrace, Edinburgh, EH10 5AE, Scotland (home). *Telephone:* (131) 446-0696 (home). *E-mail:* doc .holloway@virgin.net (home).

HOLLOWAY, Robin Greville, PhD, DMus; British composer, writer and academic; *Professor of Musical Composition, University of Cambridge;* b. 19 Oct. 1943, Leamington Spa; s. of Robert Charles Holloway and Pamela Mary Holloway (née Jacob); ed St Paul's Cathedral Choir School, King's Coll. School, Wimbledon, King's Coll., Cambridge and New Coll., Oxford; Lecturer in Music, Univ. of Cambridge 1975–, Reader in Musical Composition 1999–, Prof. 2001–; Fellow, Gonville and Caius Coll., Cambridge 1969–. *Compositions include:* Garden Music Op. 1 1962, First Concerto for Orchestra 1969, Scenes from Schumann Op. 13 1970, Evening with Angels Op. 17 1972, Domination of Black Op. 23 1973, Clarissa (opera) Op. 30 1976, Second Concerto for Orchestra Op. 40 1979, Brand (dramatic ballad) Op. 48 1981, Women in War Op. 51 1982, Seascape and Harvest Op. 55 1983, Viola Concerto Op. 56 1984, Peer Gynt 1985, Hymn to the Senses for chorus 1990, Serenade for strings 1990, Double Concerto Op. 68, The Spacious Firmament for chorus and orchestra Op. 69, Violin Concerto Op. 70 1990, Boys and Girls Come Out To Play (opera) 1991, Winter Music for sextet 1993, Frost at Midnight Op. 78, Third Concerto for Orchestra Op. 80 1994, Clarinet Concerto Op. 82 1996, Peer Gynt Op. 84 1984–97, Scenes from Antwerp Op. 85 1997, Gilded Goldberg for two pianos 1999, Symphony 1999, Missa Caiensis 2001, Cello Sonata 2001, Spring Music Op. 96 2002, String Quartet No. 1 2003, String Quartet No. 2 2004. *Recordings:* Sea Surface Full of Clouds chamber cantata, Romanza for violin and small orchestra Op. 31, 2nd Concerto for Orchestra Op. 40, Horn Concerto Op. 43, Violin Concerto Op. 70, Third Concerto for orchestra, Fantasy Pieces Op. 16, Serenade in DC Op. 41, Gilded Goldberg Op. 86, Missa Caiensis, Organ Fantasy, Woefully Arrayed. *Publications:* Wagner and Debussy 1978, On Music: Essays and Diversions 1963–2003 2004; numerous articles and reviews. *Leisure interest:* cities, architecture, books. *Address:* Gonville and Caius College, Cambridge, CB2 1TA (office); Finella, Queen's Road, Cambridge, CB3 9AH, England (home). *Telephone:* (1223) 335424. *E-mail:* rgh1000@cam.ac.uk (home). *Website:* www.rhessays.co.uk.

HOLM, Erik, PhD; Danish foundation director and political economist; *Director, Eleni Nakou Foundation;* b. 6 Dec. 1933, Hobro; s. of Carl Holm and Anne Margrethe Holm (née Nielsen); m. Annie Jacoba Kortleven 1960 (died 1984); two s. two d.; ed Univ. of Copenhagen; economist, Cen. Statistical Office, Copenhagen 1961–65; Lecturer in Econs, Univ. of Copenhagen 1962–65, in Political Science 1971–81; economist, IMF, Washington, DC 1965–69; Sr Economist, Ministry of Econ. Affairs, Copenhagen 1969–72; Adviser on European Affairs to Prime Minister 1972–82; Prin. Adviser (econ. and financial affairs), EC Comm., Brussels 1982–87; Visiting Scholar, Inst. of Int. Studies, Univ. of Calif., Berkeley 1987–89; Dir Eleni Nakou Foundation, London 1989–; Kt of the Dannebrog. *Publications:* Stabilitet og Uligevagt 1986, Money and International Politics 1991, Union eller Nation 1992, Europe, a Political Culture? Fundamental Issues for the 1996 IGC 1994, The European Anarchy: Europe's Hard Road into High Politics 2001; articles in Danish and int. publs on European econ. and political affairs. *Address:* Wiedeweltsgade 27, 2100 Copenhagen (home); Xylografensvej 4, 3220 Tisvildeleje, Denmark (Summer) (home). *Telephone:* 48-70-97-15 (Tisvildeleje) (home); 35-42-03-62 (Copenhagen) (home). *E-mail:* erik-holm@mail.dk (home).

HOLM, Sir Ian, Kt, CBE; British actor; b. 12 Sept. 1931, Ilford, Essex; s. of Dr James Harvey Cuthbert and Jean Wilson Cuthbert; m. 1st Lynn Mary Shaw 1955 (divorced 1965); two d.; one s. one d. (with Bee Gilbert); m. 2nd Sophie Baker 1982 (divorced 1986); one s.; m. 3rd Penelope Wilton 1991 (divorced); one step-d.; ed Chigwell Grammar School, Essex, RADA (Royal Acad. of Dramatic Art); joined Shakespeare Memorial Theatre 1954; Worthing Repertory 1956; on tour with Lord Olivier in Titus Andronicus 1957; mem. RSC 1958–67; Laurence Olivier Award 1998, Evening Standard Award for Best Actor 1993 and 1997. *Roles include:* Puck, Ariel, Lorenzo, Henry V, Richard III, The Fool (in King Lear), Lennie (in The Homecoming); appeared in Moonlight 1993, King Lear 1997, Max in The Homecoming 2001. *Films include:* Young Winston, Oh! What a Lovely War, Alien, All Quiet on the Western Front, Chariots of Fire, The Return of the Soldier, Greystoke 1984, Laughterhouse 1984, Brazil 1985, Wetherby 1985, Dance with a Stranger 1985, Dreamchild 1985, Henry V 1989, Another Woman 1989, Hamlet 1990, Kafka 1991, The Hour of the Pig 1992, Blue Ice 1992, The Naked Lunch 1992, Frankenstein 1993, The Madness of King George 1994, Loch Ness 1994, Big Night 1995, Night Falls on Manhattan 1995, A Life Less Ordinary 1996, The Sweet Hereafter 1997, The Fifth Element 1997, eXistenZ 1998, Simon Magus 1998, Esther Kahn 1999, Joe Gould's Secret 1999, Beautiful Joe 1999, From Hell 2000, The Emperor's New Clothes 2000, The Lord of the Rings – The Fellowship of the Ring 2001, The Lord of the Rings – The Return of the King 2003, Garden State 2004, The Day After Tomorrow 2004, The Aviator 2004, Strangers with Candy 2005, Chromophobia 2005, Lord of War 2005, Renaissance (voice) 2006, O Jerusalem 2006, The Treatment 2006, Ratatouille (voice) 2007. *Television appearances include:* The Lost Boys 1979, We, the Accused 1980, The Bell 1981, Strike 1981, Inside the Third Reich 1982, Mr. and Mrs. Edgehill 1985, The Browning Version 1986, Game, Set and Match 1988, The Endless Game 1989, The Last Romantics 1992, The Borrowers 1993, The Deep Blue Sea 1994, Landscape 1995, Little Red Riding Hood 1996, King Lear 1997, Alice Through the Looking Glass 1998, Animal Farm (voice) 1999, The Miracle Maker (voice) 2000, The Last of the Blonde Bombshells 2000, D-Day 6.6.1944 (voice) 2004. *Publication:* Acting My Life (autobiog.) 2004. *Leisure interests:* tennis, walking. *Address:* The Peggy Thompson Office, 296 Sandycombe Road, Kew, Richmond, Surrey, TW9 3NG (office); c/o Markham & Froggatt Ltd, Julian House, 4 Windmill Street, London, NW1T 2HZ, England (office).

HOLM, Richard H., PhD; American academic and chemist; *Higgins Professor of Chemistry, Harvard University;* b. 24 Sept. 1933, Boston, Mass.; m. Florence L. Jacintho 1958; four c.; ed Univ. of Massachusetts and Massachusetts Inst. of Tech.; Asst Prof. of Chem., Harvard Univ. 1960–65; Assoc. Prof. of Chem., Univ. of Wisconsin 1965–67; Prof. of Chem., MIT 1967–75, Stanford Univ. 1975–80; Prof. of Chem., Harvard Univ. 1980–83, Higgins Prof. 1983–, Chair. Dept of Chem. 1983–86; mem. American Acad. of Arts and Sciences, NAS; Hon. AM; Hon. DSc; Chemical Sciences Award 1993, several awards for research in inorganic chem. *Publications:* numerous research papers in professional journals in the fields of inorganic chem. and biochemistry. *Address:* Department of Chemistry, Harvard University, Cambridge, MA 02138 (office); 483 Pleasant Street, #10, Belmont, MA 02418, USA (home). *Telephone:* (617) 495-0853 (office). *Fax:* (617) 496-9289 (office). *E-mail:* holm@chemistry.harvard.edu (office). *Website:* bioinorg.harvard.edu/~rhhgroup (office).

HOLM, Stefan Christian; Swedish high jumper; b. 25 May 1976, Forshaga; s. of Johnny Holm and Elisabeth Holm; m. Anna; one s.; Silver Medal Swedish Championships 1994–96, European Indoor Championships 2002, European Championships 2002, World Championships 2003; Gold Medal Swedish Indoor Championships 1997–2004, Swedish Championships 1998–2005, Goodwill Games 2001, World Indoor Championships 2001, 2003, 2004, Athens Olympics 2004, European Indoor Championships 2005; winner IAAF Grand Prix 2002, World Athletics Final 2004; ranked No. 1, Athletics Ints World Ranking 2002, 2004, Track & Field News World Ranking 2001, 2002, 2004; mem. Kils AIK Friidrottsklubb. *Address:* c/o Swedish Athletics Association (Svenska Friidrottsförbundet), Box 11, 171 18 Solna, Sweden (office). *Telephone:* (8) 587-721-00 (office). *Fax:* (8) 587-721-88 (office). *E-mail:* info@friidrott.se (office). *Website:* www.friidrott.se (office); www.scholm.com.

HOLM-NIELSEN, Lauritz Broder, MSc; Danish botanist, academic and university administrator; *Vice-Chancellor, University of Århus;* b. 8 Nov. 1946, Nordby; m. Helle Holm-Nielsen; two s. one d.; ed Univ. of Århus; Asst Prof. of Botany, Univ. of Århus 1972–75, Assoc. Prof. 1975–86, Dir Botanical Inst. 1983–85, Vice-Chancellor Univ. of Århus 2005–; Prof., Universidad Católica, Quito, Ecuador 1979–81; Rector, Danish Research Acad. 1986–93; Lead Higher Educ. Specialist, The World Bank 1993–2005; Chair. Danish Science Research Council 1985–87, Danish Council for Devt Research 1990–93, Danish Strategic Environment Research Programme 1991–2004, Nordic Univs Asscn 2008–; Pres. Nordic Acad. for Advanced Study 1991–93; Fellow, The Linnean Soc., London, Danish Acad. of Natural Sciences, Acad. of Tech. Sciences; mem. The Learned Soc.; Hon. mem. Instituto Ecuatoriano de Ciencias Naturales; Kt of First Class, Order of Dannebrog, Gran Oficial del Orden Gabriela Mistral (Chile). *Publications:* over 130 research publs. *Address:* Office of the Vice-Chancellor, University of Århus, Administrationen, bygning 1430, Nordre Ringgade 1, 8000 Århus C, Denmark (office). *Telephone:* 89-42-11-41 (office). *E-mail:* rektor@au.dk (office). *Website:* www.au.dk/en/rector (office).

HOLMES, Sir John Eaton, Kt, GCVO, KBE, CMG; British diplomatist and UN official; *Under-Secretary-General for Humanitarian Affairs and Emergency Relief Coordinator, United Nations Office for the Coordination of Humanitarian Affairs;* b. 29 April 1951, Preston; s. of Leslie Holmes and Joyce Holmes; m. Penelope Morris 1976; three d.; ed Preston Grammar School, Balliol Coll., Oxford; joined FCO 1973; with Embassy, Moscow 1976–78; First Sec. FCO 1978–82; Asst Pvt. Sec. to Foreign Sec. 1982–84; First Sec. Embassy, Paris 1984–87; Asst Head Soviet Dept, FCO 1988–89; seconded to Thomas De La Rue & Co. 1989–91; Counsellor, British High Comm., India 1991–95; Prin. Pvt. Sec. to Prime Minister 1996–99; Amb. to Portugal 1999–2001, to France 2001–07; Under-Sec.-Gen. for Humanitarian Affairs and Emergency Relief Coordinator, UN Office for Coordination of Humanitarian Affairs, New York 2007–. *Leisure interests:* reading, music, sport. *Address:* Office for the Coordination of Humanitarian Affairs, United Nations Plaza, New York, NY 10017, USA (office). *Telephone:* (212) 963-2738 (office). *Fax:* (212) 963-0116 (office). *E-mail:* holmes@un.org (office). *Website:* ochaonline.un.org (office).

HOLMES, John T., BA, LLB; Canadian diplomatist; *Ambassador to Indonesia;* m. Carol Bujeau; two c.; ed McGill Univ.; joined Dept of External Affairs 1982, positions in Bridgetown, Accra and Perm. Mission to UN, New York, fmr Dir Legal Advisory Div.; Dir UN Human Rights and Econ. Law Div. 2002–03; Amb. to Jordan 2003–06, concurrently non-resident Amb. to Iraq 2005–06; Amb. to Indonesia, also accred to Timor Leste 2006–. *Address:* Canadian Embassy, World Trade Centre, 6th Floor, Jalan Jenderal Sudirman, Kav. 29–31, POB 8324/JKS.MP, Jakarta 12920, Indonesia (office). *Telephone:* (21) 25507800 (office). *Fax:* (21) 25507811 (office). *E-mail:* canadianembassy.jkrta@international.gc.ca (office). *Website:* www.international.gc.ca/asia/jakarta (office).

HOLMES, Dame Kelly, DBE; British runner; b. 19 April 1970, Pembury, Kent; d. of Constantine Holmes and Pamela Thomson (née Norman); ed Hugh Christie Comprehensive School, Tonbridge, Kent; mem. Ealing, Southall and Middlesex Athletics Club; competes primarily in 800m. and 1,500m. events; won English Schools' titles then Recreation Asst 1986–87, Nursing Asst 1987–88; joined Army as Physical Training Instructor 1988–97; 12 major championship medals include silver medal, 1,500m. European Championships 1994, gold medal, 1,500m. Commonwealth Games 1994, bronze medal, 800m., silver medal, 1,500m. World Championships 1995, silver medal, 1,500m. Commonwealth Games 1998, bronze medal, 800m. Olympic Games, Sydney 2000, bronze medal, 800m. European Championships 2002, gold medal, 1,500m. Commonwealth Games 2002, silver medal, 1,500m. World Indoor Championships 2003, silver medal, 800m. World Championships 2003, gold medal, 800m., gold medal, 1,500m. Olympic Games, Athens 2004; 1,500m., European Cup results include second 1994, first 1995, first 1997; 800m. European Cup results include second 1996, fourth 2002; third 1,500m. World Cup 2003; Amateur Athletics Asscn titles include 800m. 1993, 1995, 1996, 1999, 2000, 2001, indoors 800m. 2001, UK 800m. 1993, 1997, 1,500m. 1994, 1996, 2002; Founder and Dir Double Gold Enterprises Ltd 2004–; Dir

Nat. School Sport Champion 2006–; Chair. Dame Kelly Holmes Legacy Trust 2008–; Dr hc (Kent, Leeds Metropolitan) 2005; European Athlete of the Year 2004, BBC Sports Personality of the Year 2004, winner, Performance of the Year Award, IAAF Gala 2004, Laureus World Sports Woman of the Year Award 2005. *Publications:* My Olympic Ten Days (with Richard Lewis) 2004, Black, White and Gold 2006, Get Your Kids Fit 2007, Katy the Shooting Star 2008. *Address:* Double Gold Enterprises Ltd, PO Box 240, Tonbridge, TN11 9ZF, England. *Telephone:* (1732) 838800. *Website:* www.doublegold.co.uk.

HOLMES, Kenneth Charles, MA, PhD, FRS; British research biophysicist and academic (retd); b. 19 Nov. 1934, London; s. of Sidney C. Holmes and Irene M. Holmes (née Penfold); m. Mary Lesceline Scruby 1957; one s. three d.; ed Chiswick Co. School, St John's Coll., Cambridge and Birkbeck Coll., London; Research Asst, Birkbeck Coll., London 1955–59; Research Assoc., Children's Hosp., Boston 1960–62; scientific staff, MRC Lab. of Molecular Biology, Cambridge 1962–68; Dir Dept of Biophysics, Max-Planck-Inst. for Medical Research, Heidelberg 1968–2003; Prof. of Biophysics, Heidelberg Univ. 1972–99; mem. European Molecular Biology Org. 1968, Heidelberger Akad. der Wissenschaften 1994; Corresp. mem. Nordrhein-Westfälische Akad. der Wissenschaften, Düsseldorf; Gabor Medal, Royal Soc. of London 1997, European Latsis Prize 2000, Gregori Aminoff Prize, Royal Swedish Acad. of Sciences 2001. *Publications:* articles in scientific books and journals. *Leisure interests:* rowing, singing. *Address:* Max-Planck-Institute for Medical Research, Abt. Biophysik, Jahnstrasse 29, 69120 Heidelberg (office); Mühltalstrasse 117B, 6900 Heidelberg, Germany (home). *Telephone:* (6221) 486270 (office); (6221) 471313 (home). *E-mail:* holmes@mpimf-heidelberg.mpg.de (office). *Website:* www.mpimf-heidelberg.mpg.de/~holmes (office).

HOLMES, Larry; American fmr boxer; b. 3 Nov. 1949, Cuthbert, Georgia; s. of John and Flossie Holmes; m. Diana Holmes; one s. four d.; ed Easton, Pa; amateur boxer 1970–73; 22 amateur fights, 19 wins; lost by disqualification to Duane Bobick in finals of American Olympic trials 1972; won World Boxing Council (WBC) version of world heavyweight title from Ken Norton June 1978; made nine defences, all won inside scheduled distance (breaking previous record held by Joe Louis); became first man to stop Muhammad Ali Oct. 1980; stripped of WBCl version 1983; lost Int. Boxing Fed. version to Michael Spinks 1985, beaten again by Spinks 1986; defeated by Mike Tyson (q.v.) in attempts to win World Boxing Asscn, WBC and Int. Boxing Fed. heavyweight titles 1988; beaten by Evander Holyfield (q.v.) for World Boxing Asscn, WBC and Int. Boxing Fed. heavyweight titles 1992, by Oliver McCall for WBC heavyweight title 1995; was undefeated for record 13 years; career record 69 wins, (44 KO s), six defeats; runs an Internet casino business. *Leisure interests:* food, sport and self-education. *Address:* Larry Holmes Enterprises Inc., 91 Larry Holmes Drive, Suite 200, Easton, PA 18042, USA (office). *Telephone:* (610) 253-6905 (office). *E-mail:* larryholmes@larryholmes.com (office). *Website:* www.larryholmes.com (office).

HOLMES, Richard Gordon Heath, OBE, MA, FBA, FRSL; British writer and poet; *Professor of Biographical Studies, University of East Anglia;* b. 5 Nov. 1945, London; s. of Dennis Patrick Holmes and Pamela Mavis Gordon; partner Rose Tremain; ed Downside School, Churchill Coll., Cambridge; literacy features writer, The Times 1967–92; Visiting Fellow, Trinity Coll., Cambridge 2000; Prof. of Biographical Studies, Univ. of E Anglia 2001–; Hon. DLitt (E Anglia) 2000, (Tavistock Inst.) 2001, (Kingston Univ.) 2008; Somerset Maugham Award 1977, James Tait Black Memorial Prize 1994, Whitbread Book of the Year Prize 1989, Duff Cooper Prize 1998. *Radio:* BBC Radio: Inside the Tower 1977, To the Tempest Given 1992, The Nightwalking (Sony Award) 1995, Clouded Hills 1999, Runaway Lives 2000, The Frankenstein Project 2002, A Cloud in a Paper Bag 2007. *Publications:* Thomas Chatterton: The Case Re-Opened 1970, One for Sorrows (poems) 1970, Shelley: The Pursuit 1974, Shelley on Love (ed.) 1980, Coleridge 1982, Nerval: The Chimeras (with Peter Jay) 1985, Footsteps: Adventures of a Romantic Biographer 1985, Mary Wollstonecraft and William Godwin (ed.) 1987, Kipling: Something Myself (ed. with Robert Hampson) 1987, Coleridge: Early Visions 1989, Dr Johnson and Mr Savage 1993, Coleridge: Selected Poems (ed.) 1996, The Romantic Poets and Their Circle 1997, Coleridge: Darker Reflections 1998, Sidetracks: Explorations of a Romantic Biographer 2000, Classic Biographies (series) 2004–, Insights: The Romantic Poets and Their Circle 2005, The Age of Wonder 2008. *Address:* c/o HarperCollins, 77–85 Fulham Palace Road, Hammersmith, London, W6 8JB, England.

HOLMES, Roger; British business executive; *Managing Director, Change Capital Partners;* began career with McKinsey & Co.; joined Kingfisher Group 1994, Finance Dir B&Q (subsidiary co.) 1994, becoming Man. Dir Woolworths and later CEO Kingfisher Electrical Retailing Div. –2000; joined Marks & Spencer Group PLC as Head of UK Retail Sales 2001–02, CEO 2002–2004; Man. Dir Change Capital Pnrs (pvt. equity firm) 2004–. *Address:* Change Capital Partners, 2nd Floor, College House, 272 Kings Road, London, SW3 5AW, England (office). *Telephone:* (20) 7808-9110 (office). *Fax:* (20) 7808-9111 (office). *E-mail:* rholmes@changecapitalpartners.com (office). *Website:* www.changecapitalpartners.com (office).

HOLMES À COURT, Janet Lee, AO, BSc; Australian business executive; b. 1943, Perth; m. Robert Holmes à Court (died 1990); three s. one d.; ed Perth Modern School and Univ. of Western Australia; fmr science teacher; Exec. Chair. Heytesbury Pty Ltd (family-owned co. which includes Heytesbury Beef Ltd, Vasse Felix (Vineyards), Heytesbury Thoroughbreds, John Holland Group and Key Transport) –2005 (retd); Chair. John Holland Group, Australian Children's TV Foundation, Black Swan Theatre Co., Western Australian Symphony Orchestra; Dir Goodman Fielder Ltd. 1998, Koala Corpn Australia Ltd 2001; f. Holmes à Court Gallery 2000; fmr Pro-Chancellor, Univ. of Western Australia; mem. Bd Man. Festival of Perth; British Business Woman of the Year 1996. *Leisure interest:* the arts. *Address:* c/o Heytesbury Holdings Ltd, 11 Brown Street, East Perth, WA 6004, Australia (office).

HOLMES À COURT, Peter, BA; Australian business executive; b. 1969; s. of the late Robert Holmes à Court and of Janet Lee Holmes à Court; m.; two s.; ed Univ. of Oxford, UK and Middlebury Coll., Vt, USA; employed in family business, Heytesbury 1990–92; Financial Analyst James D. Wolfensohn, USA 1992–93; Founder and Man. Dir Back Row Productions 1993–2000; Chief Exec. The Australian Agric. Co. (AACo) 2001–; Dir Stoll Moss Theatres, London –1999; mem. Arts Advisory Bd, Middlebury Coll. *Address:* Level 25, Chifley Tower, 2 Chifley Place, Sydney, NSW 2000, Australia (office). *Telephone:* (2) 9293-2880 (office). *Fax:* (2) 9293-2828 (office).

HOLOMISA, Maj.-Gen. Bantubonke Harrington, (Bantu); South African politician and army officer; *President, United Democratic Movement;* b. 25 July 1955, Mqandull, Transkei; s. of the late Chief B. Holomisa; m. Tunyelwa Dube 1981; one s. one d.; ed Army Coll. of South Africa; joined Transkei Defence Force 1976, Lt Platoon Commdr 1978–79, Capt. Training Wing Commdr 1979–81, Lt-Col Bn Command 1981–83, Col SS01 Operations and Training 1984–85, rank of Brig., Chief of Staff, Transkei Defence Force 1985–87, Commdr 1987–94; Leader of Transkei 1987–94; mem. African Nat. Congress Nat. Exec. Cttee 1994; Deputy Minister of Environmental Affairs, Govt of Nat. Unity 1994–96; Pres. United Democratic Movt 1997–; several mil. medals. *Publications:* Future Plan for South Africa, Comrades in Corruption (booklet). *Leisure interests:* soccer, rugby, cricket, athletics, wildlife gaming resorts. *Address:* PO Box 15, Parliament, Cape Town 8000 (office); PO Box 26290, Arcadia 0007, South Africa (home). *Telephone:* (21) 4033921 (Cape Town) (office); (12) 3210010 (Pretoria) (office); (82) 5524156 (Pretoria) (home). *Fax:* (21) 4032525 (Cape Town) (office); (12) 3210014 (Pretoria) (home). *E-mail:* holomisa@udm.org.za (home); bholomisa@holomisa.org.za (office). *Website:* www.udm.org.za (office).

HOLONYAK, Nick, Jr, MS, PhD; American physicist and academic; *John Bardeen Endowed Chair in Electrical and Computer Engineering and Physics, University of Illinois;* b. 3 Nov. 1928, Zeigler, Ill.; ed Univ. of Ill.; Researcher, Bell Labs 1954; Researcher, US Army Signal Corps; Consulting Scientist, General Electric Co., Syracuse, NY –1963; Prof., Dept of Electrical and Computer Eng, Univ. of Ill. 1963–, John Bardeen Endowed Chair in Electrical and Computer Eng and Physics 2003–; mem. NAS, Nat. Acad. of Eng, IEEE; Nat. Medal of Science 1990, Japan Prize 1995, Optical Soc. of America Frederic Ives Medal 2002, IEEE Medal of Honor 2003, Global Energy Int. Prize 2003, Nat. Medal of Tech. 2003, Lemelson-MIT Prize 2004, MRS Von Hippel Award 2004, Laureate Lincoln Acad. of Sciences 2005, US Consumers Electronics Hall of Fame 2006, US Inventors Hall of Fame 2008. *Achievements:* inventor of the light emitting diode (LED); holder of 36 patents. *Publications:* Semiconductor Controlled Rectifiers 1964, Physical Properties of Semiconductors 1989. *Address:* University of Illinois at Urbana-Champaign, 1406 West Green Street, Urbana, IL 61801-2918, USA (office). *Telephone:* (217) 333-2300 (office). *Fax:* (217) 244-7075 (office). *Website:* www.ece.uiuc.edu (office).

HOLROYD, Sir Michael de Courcy Fraser, Kt, FRHistS, CLit; British writer; *President, Royal Society of Literature;* b. 27 Aug. 1935, London; s. of Basil Holroyd and Ulla Holroyd (née Hall); m. Margaret Drabble 1982; ed Eton Coll.; Chair. Soc. of Authors 1973–74, Nat. Book League 1976–78; Pres. English Centre of PEN 1985–88; Chair. Strachey Trust 1990–95, Public Lending Right Advisory Cttee 1997–2000, Royal Soc. of Literature 1998–2001 (Pres. 2003–); Vice-Pres. Royal Literary Fund 1997–; mem. Arts Council (Chair. Literature Panel) 1992–95; Gov. Shaw Festival Theatre, Niagara-on-the-Lake 1993–; Trustee Laser Foundation 2001–03; Hon. DLitt (Ulster) 1992, (Sheffield, Warwick) 1993, (East Anglia) 1994, (LSE) 1998; Saxton Memorial Fellowship 1964, Bollingen Fellowship 1966, Winston Churchill Fellowship 1971, Irish Life Arts Award 1988, Meilleur Livre Etranger 1995, Heywood Hill Prize 2001, David Cohen Prize for Literature 2005. *Publications:* Hugh Kingsmill: A Critical Biography 1964, Lytton Strachey: A Critical Biography 1967–68 (new edn 1994), A Dog's Life (novel) 1969, The Best of Hugh Kingsmill (ed) 1970, Lytton Strachey by Himself: A Self-Portrait (ed) 1971, Unreceived Opinions (essays) 1973, Augustus John 1974–75 (new edn 1996), The Art of Augustus John (with Malcolm Easton) 1974, The Genius of Shaw (ed) 1979, The Shorter Strachey (ed with Paul Levy) 1980, William Gerhardie's God's Fifth Column (ed with Robert Skidelsky) 1981, Essays by Diverse Hands (ed) Vol. XLII 1982, Peterley Harveset: The Private Diary of David Peterley (ed) 1985, Bernard Shaw: Vol. 1: The Search for Love 1988, Vol. II: The Pursuit of Power 1989, Vol. III: The Lure of Fantasy 1991, Vol. IV: The Last Laugh 1992, Vol. V: The Shaw Companion 1992, Bernard Shaw 1997 (one-vol. biog.), Basil Street Blues 1999, Works on Paper: The Craft of Biography and Autobiography 2002, Mosaic: Portraits in Fragments 2004, A Strange Eventful History: The Dramatic Lives of Two Remarkable Families 2008. *Leisure interests:* music, stories. *Address:* A. P. Watt Ltd, 20 John Street, London, WC1N 2DL, England (office). *Telephone:* (20) 7405-6774 (office); (20) 7405-6774 (home). *Fax:* (20) 7831-2154 (office); (20) 7831-2154 (home). *E-mail:* apw@apwat.co.uk (office). *Website:* www.apwatt.co.uk (office).

HOLST, Per; Danish film producer; b. 28 March 1939, Copenhagen; s. of Rigmor Holst and Svend Holst; m. 1st Anni Møller Kjeldsen 1962–72; m. 2nd Kristina Holst 1976; four s.; joined Nordisk Film 1957; film man. and copywriter, WA Advertising Agency 1962; returned to Nordisk Film 1965; f. Per Holst Filmproduktion ApS 1965; numerous film awards including Palme d'Or, Cannes Film Festival and Acad. Award (Oscar) for Pelle the Conqueror 1988. *Films:* Afskedens Time 1967, Benny's Bathtub 1967, Kaptajn Klyde og Hans Venner vender tilbage 1981, The Tree of Knowledge 1982, Zappa 1983, Beauty and the Beast 1983, The Boy Who Disappeared 1984, Twist and Shout 1984, Element of Crime 1984, Up on Daddy's Hat 1985, Coeurs Flambés 1986,

Pelle the Conqueror 1987, The Redtops 1988, Aarhus by Night 1989, Sirup 1990, War of the Birds 1990, Cassanova 1990, The Hideaway 1991, Pain of Love 1992, Jungle Jack 1993, All Things Fair 1995, Barbara 1998, Let's Get Lost 1998, Bornholms Stemme 2000, I Am Dina 2002, Ondskan 2003. *Leisure interest:* golf. *Address:* Nordisk Film, Mosedalvej 14, 2500 Valby, Denmark. *Website:* www.nordiskfilm.com.

HOLT, Sir James Clarke, Kt, DPhil, FBA, FSA; British historian and academic; b. 26 April 1922, Bradford, Yorks.; s. of the late Herbert Holt and Eunice Holt; m. Alice Catherine Elizabeth Suley 1950 (died 1998); one s.; ed Bradford Grammar School and Queen's Coll., Oxford; served in army 1942–45; Harmsworth Sr Scholar, Merton Coll., Oxford 1947–49; Lecturer, Univ. of Nottingham 1949–62, Prof. of Medieval History 1962–66; Prof. of History, Univ. of Reading 1966–78, Dean of Faculty of Letters and Social Sciences 1972–76; Professorial Fellow, Emmanuel Coll., Cambridge 1978–81, Prof. of Medieval History, Univ. of Cambridge 1978–88, Master of Fitzwilliam Coll., Cambridge 1981–88; Visiting Prof., Univ. of Calif., Santa Barbara, USA 1977; Visiting Hinkley Prof., Johns Hopkins Univ., USA 1983; Raleigh Lecturer, British Acad. 1975; Visiting Prof., Japan 1986; mem. Advisory Council on Public Records 1974–81; Pres. Royal Historical Soc. 1980–84; Vice-Pres. British Acad. 1986–88; Pres. Lincoln Record Soc. 1987–96, Pipe Roll Soc. 1999–; Corresp. Fellow Medieval Acad. of America; Hon. Fellow, Emmanuel Coll. 1985–, Fitzwilliam Coll. 1988–, The Queen's Coll. 1996–, Merton Coll., Oxford 2001–; Hon. DLitt (Reading) 1984, (Nottingham) 1996; Comendador de la Orden del Mérito Civil 1988. *Publications:* The Northerners: A Study in the Reign of King John 1961, Praestia Rolls 14–18 John 1964, Magna Carta 1965, The Making of Magna Carta 1966, Magna Carta and the Idea of Liberty 1972, The University of Reading: The First Fifty Years 1977, Robin Hood 1982, War and Government in the Middle Ages (ed. with John Gillingham), Magna Carta and Medieval Government 1985; Hand-list of Acta Henry II and Richard I surviving in British Repositories (with Richard Mortimer) 1986, Domesday Studies (ed.) 1987, Colonial England 1066–1215 1997, Jersey 1204 (with Judith Everard) 2004; papers in English Historical Review, Past and Present, Economic History Review, trans. Royal Historical Soc. *Leisure interests:* music, mountaineering, cricket, fly-fishing. *Address:* 5 Holben Close, Barton, Cambridge, CB23 7AQ, England. *Telephone:* (1223) 332041 (office); (1223) 264923 (home).

HOLTON, A. Linwood, Jr, BA, LLB; American politician and lawyer; *Partner, McCandlish Holton, PC;* b. 21 Sept. 1923, Big Stone Gap, Va; s. of Abner Linwood Holton and Edith Holton (née Van Gorder); m. Virginia Harrison Rogers 1953; two s. two d.; ed public schools in Big Stone Gap, Washington and Lee Univ. and Harvard Law School; Partner, Eggleston, Holton, Butler and Glenn (law firm); served submarine force during Second World War; fmr Chair. Roanoke City Republican Cttee; Vice-Chair. Virginia Republican State Cen. Cttee 1960–69; del. to Republican Nat. Convention 1960, 1968, 1972; mem. Nat. Nixon for Pres. Cttee 1967; Regional Co-ordinator for Nixon for Pres. Cttee; Gov. of Virginia 1970–74; Asst Sec. of State for Congressional Relations, Dept of State 1974–75; Partner in law firm of Hogan and Hartson 1975–78; Vice-Pres., Gen. Counsel American Council Insurance, Washington 1978–84; Chair. Burket Miller Center for Public Affairs, Univ. of Va 1979–; Pres. Supreme Court Historical Soc. 1980–89; Chair. Metropolitan Washington Airports Authority 1987–93; Pnr McCandlish Holton PC (law firm) 1994–; Pres. Center for Innovative Tech., Herndon, Va 1988–94. *Address:* McCandlish Holton PC, PC, 1111 East Main Street, Suite 1500, PO Box 796, Richmond, VA 23218 (office); 3883 Black Stump Road, Weems, VA 22576, USA (home). *Telephone:* (804) 775-3817 (office); (804) 435-0604. *Website:* www.lawmh.com (office).

HOLTON, Gerald, PhD; American physicist, historian of science and academic; *Mallinckrodt Research Professor of Physics and Research Professor of the History of Science, Harvard University;* b. 23 May 1922, Berlin, Germany; s. of Dr Emanuel Holton and Regina Holton (née Rossmann); m. Nina Rossfort 1947; two s.; ed Wesleyan Univ., Middletown, Conn., Harvard Univ.; Harvard Univ. staff, officers' radar course and Lab. for Research on Electro-Acoustics 1943–45, various faculty posts 1945–, Mallinckrodt Research Prof. of Physics, Research Prof. of History of Science 1975–; Visiting Prof., MIT 1976–94; NSF Faculty Fellow, Paris 1960–61; Exchange Prof., Leningrad Univ. 1962; Founder and Ed.-in-Chief, Daedalus 1958–61; mem. Council, History of Science Soc. 1959–61, Pres. 1982–84; Visiting mem. Inst. for Advanced Study, Princeton 1964, 1967; mem. NAS Cttee on Communication with Scholars in the People's Repub. of China 1969–72, US Nat. Comm. on IUHPS 1982–88 (Chair. 1988); mem. German-American Acad. Council Kuratorium 1997–2000; mem. Bd Govs, American Inst. of Physics 1969–74; Fellow, Center for Advanced Study in Behavioral Sciences, Stanford, Calif. 1975–76; mem. US Nat. Comm. on UNESCO 1975–80, Library of Congress Council of Scholars 1979–98, US Nat. Comm. on Excellence in Educ. 1981–83, Advisory Bd Nat. Humanities Center 1989–93; mem. Editorial Bd Collected Papers of Albert Einstein; Nat. Assoc. NAS; Fellow, American Physical Soc. (Chair. Div. History of Physics 1992–93), American Acad. of Arts and Sciences (mem. Council 1991–95), American Philosophical Soc., American Asscn for the Advancement of Science, Acad. Internationale d'Histoire des Sciences (Vice-Pres. 1982–89), Deutsche Akad. der Naturforscher Leopoldina, Acad. Internationale de Philosophie des Sciences; eight hon. degrees; Robert A. Millikan Medal 1967, Herbert Spencer Lecturer, Univ. of Oxford 1979, Jefferson Lecturer 1981, Oersted Medal 1980, Guggenheim Fellowship 1980–81, Presidential Citation for Service to Educ. 1984, McGovern Medal 1985, Andrew Gemant Award 1989, George Sarton Medal 1989, Bernal Prize 1989, Joseph Priestley Award 1994, Joseph H. Hazen Prize of the History of Science Soc. 1998, Abraham Pais Prize, American Physical Soc. 2008. *Film:* People and Particles (co-producer), The Life of Enrico Fermi (co-producer). *Publications:* Introduction to Concepts and Theories in Physical Science 1952,

Thematic Origins of Scientific Thought 1973, 1988, Scientific Imagination 1978, Limits of Scientific Inquiry (ed.) 1979, Albert Einstein, Historical and Cultural Perspectives (ed.) 1982, The Advancement of Science and its Burdens 1986, Science and Anti-Science 1993, Einstein, History and Other Passions 1995, Gender Differences in Science Careers (co-author) 1995, Who Succeeds in Science? The Gender Dimension (co-author) 1995, Physics, the Human Adventure (co-author) 2001, Ivory Bridges: Connecting Science and Society (co-author) 2002, Understanding Physics (co-author) 2002, Victory and Vexations in Science 2005, What Happened to the Children Who Fled Nazi Persecution (co-author) 2006. *Leisure interests:* music, kayaking. *Address:* 64 Francis Avenue, Cambridge, MA 02138 (home); 358 Jefferson Physical Laboratory, Harvard University, Cambridge, MA 02138, USA (office). *Telephone:* (617) 868-9003 (home); (617) 495-4474 (office). *Fax:* (617) 868-9003 (home); (617) 495-0416 (office). *E-mail:* holton@physics.harvard.edu (office). *Website:* physics.harvard.edu/holton.htm (office); www.fas.harvard.edu/~hsdept/faculty/holton (office).

HOLTZMAN, Wayne Harold, MS, PhD; American psychologist and academic; *Hogg Professor Emeritus in Psychology and Education, University of Texas;* b. 16 Jan. 1923, Chicago, Ill.; s. of Harold H. Holtzman and Lillian Manny; m. Joan King 1947; four s.; ed Northwestern and Stanford Univs; Asst Prof., Univ. of Texas at Austin 1949–53, Assoc. Prof. 1954–59, Prof. of Psychology 1959–, Dean Coll. of Educ. 1964–70, Hogg Prof. of Psychology and Educ. 1964–93, Prof. Emer. 1993–; Assoc. Dir Hogg Foundation for Mental Health 1955–64, Pres. 1970–93, Special Counsel 1993–2003; Dir Science Research Assocs 1974–89, Population Resource Center 1980–; Pres. Int. Union of Psychological Science 1984–88; other professional affiliations; Faculty Research Fellow, Social Science Research Council 1953–54, Center for Advanced Study in Behavioral Sciences 1962–63; Hon. LHD (Southwestern) 1980. *Publications:* Tomorrow's Parents (with B. Moore) 1964, Computer Assisted Instruction, Testing and Guidance 1971, Personality Development in Two Cultures (with others) 1975, Introduction to Psychology 1978, School of the Future (with others) 1992, History of the International Union of Psychological Science (with others) 2000. *Leisure interests:* travel, photography, gardening. *Address:* 3300 Foothill Drive, Austin, TX 78731, USA (home). *Telephone:* (512) 471-5041 (office); (512) 452-8296 (home). *E-mail:* wayne.holtzmann@mail.utexas.edu. *Website:* www.psy.utexas.edu (office).

HOLUM, John D., BS, JD; American fmr government official; b. 4 Dec. 1940, Highmore, S Dak; m. Barbara P. Pedersen; one d.; ed Northern State Teachers' Coll. and George Washington Univ.; professional staff mem. Foreign Relations Cttee US Senate (on staff of Senator George McGovern) 1965–79; mem. Policy and Planning Staff, US State Dept 1979–81; attorney O'Melveny & Myers 1981–93; defence and foreign policy adviser to Gov. Bill Clinton during 1992 Presidential Campaign; Exec. Dir 1992 Democratic Nat. Convention; Dir Arms Control and Disarmament Agency (ACDA) 1993–98, Sr Advisor for Arms Control and Int. Security Affairs 1998–2000; Undersecretary of State for Arms Control and Int. Security 2000; Vice Pres., Int. and Govt Affairs, Atlas Air Inc. 2000–03; mem. Center for Nonproliferation Studies Int. Advisory Bd. *Leisure interests:* flying, scuba diving, playing bluegrass and country music. *Address:* c/o International Advisory Board, Center for Nonproliferation Studies, Monterey Institute of International Studies, 460 Pierce Street, Monterey, CA 93940, USA.

HOLYFIELD, Evander; American professional boxer; b. 19 Oct. 1962, Atlanta, Ga; s. of Anna Laura Holyfield; Bronze Medal, 1984 Olympic Games; World Boxing Asscn (WBA) cruiserweight title 1986; Int. Boxing Fed. cruiserweight title 1987; World Boxing Council (WBC) cruiserweight title 1988; world heavyweight champion 1990–92, 1993–94, 1996–99 (following defeat of Mike Tyson q.v. Nov. 1996), defended title against Tyson 1997 (Tyson disqualified for biting off part of Holyfield's ear); defended IBF heavyweight title against Michael Moorer 1997; defended WBA and IBF titles and contested WBC title, against Lennox Lewis (q.v.) March 1999, bout declared a draw; lost to Lennox Lewis Nov. 1999; 2000–01 WBA heavyweight champion; career record 38 wins, eight defeats, two draws; suspended by NY State Boxing Comm. after defeat by Larry Donald Nov. 2004 f. Real Deal Record Label 1999; f. Holyfield Foundation to help inner-city youth; Espy Boxer of the Decade 1990–2000. *Leisure interests:* all kinds of music, American football. *Address:* Holyfield Management, 794 Evander Holyfield Highway, Fairburn, GA 30213, USA (office). *Telephone:* (770) 460-6807 (office). *Website:* www.evanderholyfield.com (office).

HOLZER, Jenny, BFA, MFA; American artist; b. 29 July 1950, Gallipolis, Ohio; d. of Richard Vornholt Holzer and Virginia Beasley Holzer; m. Michael Andrew Glier 1984; one d.; ed Ohio Univ., Rhode Island School of Design, Whitney Museum of American Art Ind. Study Program; became working artist in New York 1977; special projects and comms since 1978 include Green Table, Univ. of Calif., San Diego 1993, Lustmord, Süddeutsche Zeitung Magazin, No. 46, Germany, Black Garden, Nordhorn, Germany 1994, Allentown Benches, Allentown, Pa 1995, Erlauf Peace Monument, Erlauf, Austria 1995, installation at Schiphol Airport, Amsterdam, Netherlands 1995, Biennale di Firenze, Florence, Italy 1996, installation for Hamburger Kunsthalle, Hamburg, Germany 1996, perm. installation at Guggenheim Museum, Bilbao, Literaturhaus Munich, Germany, Oskar Maria Graf Memorial 1997, Kunsthalle Zürich, Switzerland, Telenor HQ, Norway 2002, Univ. of Pennsylvania 2003, Paula Hodersohn—Becker Museum 2005, Lawrence Convention Center, Pittsburgh 2005, SDtora Torget, Karlstad 2005; Fellow American Acad., Berlin 2000; Resident, American Acad. Rome 2003; Hon. DArts (Ohio Univ.) 1994, (Williams Coll.) 2000, (Rhode Island School of Design) 2003, (New School Univ.) 2005; Golden Lion Award for Best Pavilion, 44th Venice Biennale, Italy 1990, Gold Medals for Title and Design,

Art Directors' Club of Europe 1993, Skowhegan Medal for Installation, New York 1994, Crystal Award, for outstanding contrib. to cross-cultural understanding, World Econ. Forum, Switzerland 1996, Kaiserring, City of Goslar 2002, Urban Visionaries Award, The Copper Union 2006; Chevalier de L'Ordre des Arts et Lettres 2002. *Publications:* A Little Knowledge 1979, Black Book 1980, Eating Through Living 1981, Truisms and Essays 1983. *Leisure interests:* reading, riding. *Address:* c/o Cheim and Read Gallery, 547 West 25th Street, New York, NY 10001; 80 Hewitts Road, Hoosick Falls, NY 12090, USA. *Telephone:* (518) 686-9323. *Fax:* (518) 686-9019. *E-mail:* jh@jennyholzer.com. *Website:* www.jennyholzer.com.

HOMBACH, Bodo; German politician and business executive; *Managing Director, Westdeutsche Allgemeine Zeitung Media Group;* b. 19 Aug. 1952, Mülheim; m. 1977; ed Düsseldorf Polytechnic, Duisberg Comprehensive Univ., Hagen Correspondence Univ.; fmrly trainee telecommunications worker, youth affairs spokesman and youth worker; Personal Asst to Chair. of German TU Confed. (DGB) North Rhine Westphalia 1974; Educ. Policy Sec. Educ. and Science TU North Rhine Westphalia 1976, Regional Dir 1977; Deputy Regional Dir German Social Democratic Party (SPD) North Rhine Westphalia 1979, Regional Dir 1981–91, Sr Election Campaign Man., 1979–91; Deputy Chair. Mülheim Dist 1993, Deputy Chair. Niederrhein Dist 1998; Fed. Minister Without Portfolio and Head Fed. Chancellery 1998–99; mem. North Rhine Westphalia Landtag 1990–98, Chair. Parl. Inquiry Comm. 1992–94, Parl. Econ. Affairs Spokesman 1994–98, State Minister for Econ. SMEs, Tech. and Transport 1998; Dir Marketing, Org. and Corp. Strategy Preussag Handel GmbH (fmrly Salzgitter Stahl AG) 1991, Man. Dir Preussag Trade Ltd 1992–98, mem. Bd Preussag Int. GmbH 1995–98; Special Co-ordinator of the Stability Pact for S Eastern Europe 1999–2001; Man. Dir Westdeutsche Allgemeine Zeitung Media group 2002–. *Publications include:* Der SPD von innen, Die Zukunft der Arbeit, Aufruf für eine Geschichte des Volkes in Nordrhein-Westfalia, Die Lokomotive in voller Fahrt der Räder wechseln, Anders Leben, Sozialstaat 2000, Die Kraft der Region: Nordrhein-Westfalia in Europa, The Politics of the New Centre 2002. *Address:* Zeitungsverlagsgesellschaft E. Brost und J. Funke GmbH & Co., Friedrichstr. 34-38, 45123 Essen, Germany. *Telephone:* (201) 804-0. *Fax:* (201) 804-2841. *Website:* www2.waz.de.

HOME, 15th Earl of, cr. 1605; **David Alexander Cospatrick Douglas-Home,** CVO, CBE, MA; British banker; *Chairman, Coutts & Company;* b. 20 Nov. 1943, Coldstream, Scotland; s. of the late Rt Hon. Alexander Frederick, Lord Home of the Hirsel and Elizabeth Hester Alington; m. Jane Margaret Williams-Wynne; one s. two d.; ed Eton Coll., Christ Church, Oxford; Dir Morgan Grenfell & Co. Ltd 1974–99; Chair. Coutts & Co. 1999–, Chair. Coutts Bank (Switzerland) Ltd 2000–; Chair. MAN Ltd 2000–; Trustee The Grosvenor Estate 1993–. *Leisure interest:* outdoor activities. *Address:* Coutts & Co., 440 Strand, London, WC2R 0QS (office); 99 Dovehouse Street, London, SW3 6JZ, England (home). *Telephone:* (20) 7753-1000 (office); (20) 7352-9060 (home). *Fax:* (20) 7753-1066 (office).

HOMER-DIXON, Thomas F., BA, PhD; Canadian political scientist, academic and writer; *Centre for International Governance Innovation Chair of Global Systems, Balsillie School of International Affairs, University of Waterloo;* b. 1956, Victoria, BC; m. Sarah Wolfe; one s.; ed Carleton Univ., Ottawa, Massachusetts Inst. of Tech., USA; jobs in construction, forestry and petroleum industries in western Canada and as leader of nat. student org. based in Ottawa 1975–83; research position with Project Athena, MIT, Cambridge, Mass 1983–89; consultant, World Resources Inst., Washington, DC 1983–89; Prin. Investigator, Univ. of Toronto 1990–93, Dir Peace and Conflict Studies Program, Univ. Coll. 1990–2001, Asst Prof. of Political Science, Univ. of Toronto 1993–98, Assoc. Prof. 1998–2006, Prof. 2006–08, George Ignatieff Chair of Peace and Conflict Studies 2007–08, Dir Trudeau Centre for Peace and Conflict Studies 2001–07; Prof., Faculty of Arts, and Centre for Environment and Business, Faculty of Environment, Univ. of Waterloo, Ont. 2008–, Centre for Int. Governance Innovation Chair of Global Systems, Balsillie School of Int. Affairs 2008–; Dir Centre for Int. Governance Innovation, Waterloo; Adjunct Research Fellow, Center of Science and Int. Affairs, Kennedy School of Govt, Harvard Univ. 1986–88; SSRC/MacArthur Foundation Dissertation Fellowship in Int. Peace and Security 1986–88; Social Sciences and Humanities Research Council of Canada, Postdoctoral Fellow 1989–90; Visiting Scholar, Aspen Inst. 1994; Assoc. Fellow, Canadian Inst. for Advanced Research 1995–. *Publications:* Science in Society: Its Freedom and Regulation (co-ed.) 1982, Ecoviolence: Links Among Environment, Population, and Security (co-ed.) 1998, Environment, Scarcity, and Violence (American Political Science Asscn Caldwell Prize) 1999, The Ingenuity Gap (Gov.-Gen.'s Non-fiction Award 2001) 2000, The Upside of Down: Catastrophe, Creativity, and the Renewal of Civilization (Nat. Business Book Award 2006) 2006, Carbon Shift: How the Twin Crises of Oil Depletion and Climate Change Will Define the Future (co-ed.) 2009; numerous book chapters, and articles in learned journals and newspapers. *Address:* Balsillie School of International Affairs, c/o Centre for International Governance Innovation, 57 Erb Street West, Waterloo, ON N2L 6C2, Canada (office). *Telephone:* (519) 888-4567 (ext. 38750) (office). *E-mail:* tad@homerdixon.com (office). *Website:* www.trudeaucentre.ca/faculty-profthomerdixon.html (office); www.balsillieschool.ca; www.homerdixon.com.

HOMMELHOFF, Peter, DrIur; German lawyer and university rector; *Rector, Ruprect-Karls University of Heidelberg;* b. 1942, Hamburg; ed law studies in Berlin, Tübingen and Freiburg Univs, Univ. of Bochum; in-house legal adviser, Preußen Elektrizitäts AG, Hanover 1972; Academic Research Asst, Univ. of Bochum (Chair for German and European Commercial and Econ. Law) 1974; Chair of Civil Law, Commercial and Econ. Law, Univ. of Bielefeld 1981; part-time judge, Higher Regional Court (Oberlandesgericht), mem. Special Div. for Commercial and Co. Law 1983, Hamm –1990, Karlsruhe 1993–98; Dean Faculty of Law, Univ. of Heidelberg 1993–95, Partnership Commr Exchange Relations between Univ. of Heidelberg and Jagellonian Univ. of Kraków –2002, Chair. Company Law Asscn (Gesellschaftsrechtliche Vereinigung) 1998–2001, mem. and Deputy Chair. Heidelberg Univ. Council 2000–01, Rector Ruprecht-Karls Univ. of Heidelberg 2001–; mem. Bd of Examiners for Chartered Accountants, Ministry of Econ. Affairs, North Rhine-Westphalia –2001, Ministry of Econ. Affairs, Baden-Württemberg 1986, Extended Bd in Asscn of Profs of Civil Law 1995; Expert for Civil, Econ. and Labour Law, German Research Asscn (Deutsche Forschungsgemeinschaft) 1996–2001; Deputy Chair. Professional Bd of Advisors, Max Planck Inst. for Intellectual Property, Competition and Tax Law, Munich; Vice-Pres. Council of Acad. Pres (Hochschulrektorenkonferenz); Speaker for the Univs 2002–; mem. Scholarly Bd of Advisors, German Railway Corpn (Deutsche Bahn AG) and of its Strategic Council 1999–, Speaker of Legal Bd of Advisors 2006–; mem. Professional Bd of Advisors, Max Planck Inst. for Foreign and Int. Pvt. Law, Hamburg; mem. Editorial Bd Journal for Business and Corporate Law (Zeitschrift für Unternehmens- und Gesellschaftsrecht, ZGR), Man. Ed. 1997–; Max Planck Research Prize for Int. Cooperation 1997, Medal of Honour, Jagellonian Univ. of Kraków 1999, Leo Baeck Prize, Cen. Council of Jews in Germany 2005; Hon. DrIur (Jagiellonian Univ. of Kraków) 2002, (Univ. of Montpellier I) 2005. *Publications:* more than 300 publs in professional journals. *Address:* Office of the Rector, Grabengasse 1, 69117 Heidelberg, Germany (office). *Telephone:* (6221) 542315/6 (office). *Fax:* (6221) 542147 (office). *E-mail:* rektor@rektorat.uni-heidelberg.de (office). *Website:* www.rektorat.uni-heidelberg.de/rector.html (office).

HOMMEN, Jan H. M.; Dutch business executive; *Chairman of the Executive Board, ING Groep NV;* b. 29 April 1943, Hertogenbosch; Controller, Alcoa Nederland BV, Drunen 1970–74, Financial Dir 1974–78, Corp. Finance Man. Aluminum Co. of America (Alcoa), Pittsburgh 1978–79, Asst Treas. 1979–86, Vice Pres. and Treas. 1986–91, Exec. Vice Pres. and Chief Financial Officer 1991–97; Vice Chair., Chief Finance Officer and mem. Bd of Man. Koninklijke Philips Electronics NV 1997–2005; mem. Supervisory Bd ING Groep NV 2005–09, Chair. 2008–09, Chair. Exec. Bd 2009–; mem. Supervisory Bd TNT NV 1998–2009, Chair. 2005–09; Chair. Supervisory Bd Reed Elsevier 2005–09, Academisch Ziekenhuis Maastricht, TiasNimbas Business School; Chair. MedQuist, USA –2006; mem. Bd of Dirs Campina BV. *Address:* ING Groep NV, ING House, Amstelveenseweg 500, 1081 KL Amsterdam, The Netherlands (office). *Telephone:* (20) 5415411 (office). *Fax:* (20) 5415497 (office). *Website:* www.ing.com (office).

HONDA, Katsuhiko, LLB; Japanese tobacco industry executive; b. 12 March 1942, Kagoshima Pref.; ed Univ. of Tokyo; joined Japan Tobacco and Salt Public Corpn 1965, Vice-Pres. Corp. Planning Div. 1989–92, Man. Dir Human Resources Div. 1992–94, Exec. Dir Personnel and Labor Relations 1994–95, Exec. Dir Tobacco Business 1995–96, Exec. Vice-Pres. Tobacco Business 1996–98, Sr Exec. Vice-Pres., Japan Tobacco Inc. 1998–2000, Pres., Rep. Dir and CEO 2000–06, mem. Bd of Dirs 2006–. *Address:* c/o 2–1 Toranomon 2-chome, Minato-ku, Tokyo 105-8422, Japan (office). *Website:* www.jti.co.jp (office).

HONDROS, Ernest Demetrios, CMG, DSc, FRS; British scientist and academic; *Visiting Professor, Department of Materials, Imperial College London;* b. 18 Feb. 1930, Kastellorizo, Dodecanese, Greece; s. of Demetrios Hondros and Athanasia Paleologos; m. Sissel Kristine Garder-Olsen 1968; two s.; ed Univ. of Melbourne, Australia, Univ. of Paris; CSIRO Tribophysics Lab., Melbourne 1955–59; Research Fellow, Laboratoire de Chimie Minérale, Univ. of Paris 1959–62; Sr Research Fellow, Nat. Physical Lab. 1962, Prin. Research Fellow 1965, Sr Prin. Research Fellow 1974, Supt Materials Div. 1979–85; Dir Petten Establishment, EC (now EU) Jt Research Centre, Netherlands 1985–95, Dir Inst. for Advanced Materials 1989–95; Visiting Prof., Imperial Coll. of Science, Tech. and Medicine 1988–; Hon. mem. Soc. Française de Metallurgie; Hon. DSc (Univ. of London) 1997; Rosenhain Medal, Howe Medal, Griffiths Medal, Hatfield Memorial Lecturer, Univ. of Sheffield 1986. *Publications:* Energetics of Solid-Solid Interfaces 1969, Grain Boundary Segregation (with M.P. Seah) 1973. *Leisure interest:* reading, writing. *Address:* 37 Ullswater Crescent, London, SW15 3RG, England (home). *Telephone:* (20) 8549-9526 (home). *Fax:* (20) 8549-9526 (home). *Website:* www.mt.ic.ac.uk (office).

HONEGGER, Eric; Swiss business executive and politician; b. 29 April 1946, Zürich; m.; ed Univ. of Zürich; Sec. for City and Canton of Zürich, Free Democratic Party (FDP) 1975–79; with Gesellschaft zur Förderung der Schweizerischen Wirtschaft (Soc. for the Promotion of Swiss Trade and Industry) 1980–81; Dir Swiss printing industry employers' asscn 1982–87; rep. of Zürich Canton on Bd of Dirs SAirGroup 1993, mem. Bd Exec. Cttee 1995, Chair. 2000–01; mem. Bd of Dirs UBS 1999–2001; municipal councillor, Rüschlikon 1974–78; Zürich Cantonal Councillor (FDP) 1979–87; Cantonal Govt Councillor 1987–99, Minister of Public Works 1987–91, of Finance 1991; Prime Minister of Zürich Cantonal Govt 1993–94, 1998–99; Pres. Cantonal Govts' Conf. 1993–95; Col Transport Corps 1994–.

HONEYCUTT, Van B., BS; American business executive; *Chairman and CEO, Computer Sciences Corporation;* ed Franklin Univ., OH, Stanford Univ.; joined Computer Sciences Corpn 1975, various man. positions, including Regional Marketing Man. 1975, Vice-Pres. and Gen. Man. Business Services Div., Pres. CSC Credit Services 1983–87, Group Vice-Pres. and Pres. Industry Services Group 1987–93, Pres. and COO 1993–95, Chair., Pres. and CEO 1995–2001, Chair. and CEO 2001–; mem. Bd of Dirs Beckman Coulter, Inc., Tenet Healthcare Corpn; Chair. US Pres.'s Nat. Security Telecommunications Advisory Cttee 1998–. *Address:* Computer Sciences Corporation, 2100 East

Grand Avenue, El Segundo, CA 90245, USA (office). *Telephone:* (310) 615-0311 (office). *Fax:* (310) 322-9768 (office). *Website:* www.csc.com (office).

HONG, Guofan; Chinese molecular biochemist; b. Dec. 1939, Ningbo, Zhejiang Prov.; ed Fudan Univ., Shanghai; researcher, Biochemical Research Inst., Chinese Acad. of Sciences 1964–; researcher, MRC Molecular Biological Lab., UK 1979–83; Research Prof., Shanghai Inst. of Biochemistry; coordinated Chinese Rice Genome Program 1992–98; Fellow, Chinese Acad. of Sciences 1997–; Dir Nat. Genetics Research Centre 1993–; now Prof., Coll. of Pharmaceuticals and Biotechnology, Tianjin Univ.; Fellow, Acad. of Sciences for the Developing World 1993–; Ho Leung Ho Lee Foundation Life Sciences Award 2006. *Address:* Department of Molecular and Cellular Pharmacology, College of Pharmaceuticals and Biotechnology, Tianjin University, 92 Weijin Road, Tianjin 300072; Chinese Academy of Sciences, 17 Zhongguacun Lu, Beijing 100864, People's Republic of China (office). *Telephone:* (22) 27906148. *Fax:* (22) 23358706. *Website:* www.tj.edu.cn.

HONG, Hu; Chinese politician; b. June 1940, Jinzhai Co., Anhui Prov.; ed Beijing Eng Inst.; joined CCP 1965; fmr technician, later Deputy Chief, Dye Plant, Jilin Chemical Industry Co.; fmr Workshop Chief, Liming Chemical Industry Factory, Qinghai Prov. (Vice-Chair. CCP Revolutionary Cttee); fmr Head, Comprehensive Planning Div., 2nd Bureau, Ministry of Chemical Industry; fmr Div. Chief, Planning Bureau, State Machine-Building Industry Comm.; Deputy Sec.-Gen., Sec.-Gen. State Comm. for Econ. Restructuring 1982–91; Vice-Minister, State Comm. for Econ. Restructuring 1991–98; Vice-Gov. Jilin Prov. (also Acting Gov.) 1998–99, Gov. 1999–2004; mem. Comm. of Securities of the State Council 1992–98; mem. CCP Cen. Cttee for Discipline Inspection 1992; mem. 15th CCP Cen. Cttee 1997–2002, 16th CCP Cen. Cttee 2002–07; Del., 10th NPC 2002–, Vice-Chair. 10th NPC Law Cttee 2005–; holds title of Outstanding CCP Mem. at State Organs Level 2002–. *Address:* National People's Congress Law Committee, Beijing, People's Republic of China (office).

HONG, Jae-hyong; South Korean politician; b. Cheongju City, N Chungcheong Prov.; ed Seoul Nat. Univ.; joined Foreign Exchange Bureau, Ministry of Finance 1963; later worked at IBRD, Washington, DC; Admin., Korean Customs Admin.; Pres. Export-Import Bank of Korea, Korea Exchange Bank; Minister of Finance 1993; Deputy Prime Minister, Minister of Finance and Econs 1994–96. *Address:* c/o Ministry of Finance, 1 Jungang-dong, Gwacheon City, Gyeouggi Province, Republic of Korea.

HONG, Song-nam; North Korean politician; b. 1924, Kangwon Prov.; ed Kimilsung Univ.; Chief of a Korean Workers' Party Cen. Cttee Dept 1970; Deputy Premier and Chair. State Planning Comm. 1973, 1986; Assoc. mem., Politburo 1982, Sec. of Party chapter, S. Pyongan Prov. 1982, Full mem. of Politburo and First Deputy Premier 1986, Assoc. mem. 1989; Acting Premier of the Democratic People's Repub. of Korea Feb. 1997–Sept. 1998, Premier Sept. 1998–2003. *Address:* c/o Office of the Premier, Pyongyang, Democratic People's Republic of Korea (office).

HONIG, Edwin, MA; American academic and poet; *Professor Emeritus, Brown University;* b. 3 Sept. 1919, New York; s. of Abraham David Honig and Jane Freundlich; m. 1st Charlotte Gilchrist 1940 (died 1963); m. 2nd Margot S. Dennes 1963 (divorced 1978); two s.; ed Univ. of Wisconsin; Instructor in English, Purdue Univ. 1942–43, New York Univ. and Ill. Inst. of Tech. 1946–47, Univ. of NM 1947–48, Claremont Coll. 1949, Harvard Univ. 1949–52, Briggs-Copeland Asst Prof. of English, Harvard Univ. 1952–57; mem. Faculty, Brown Univ. 1957, Prof. of English 1960–82, Prof. of Comparative Literature 1962–82, Chair. Dept of English 1967, Prof. Emer. 1983–; Visiting Prof., Univ. of Calif., Davis 1964–65; Mellon Prof., Boston Univ. 1977; Dir Copper Beech Press; Guggenheim Fellow 1948, 1962; Amy Lowell Travelling Poetry Fellow 1968; Kt of St James of the Sword, Portugal 1987, Kt of Queen Isabel, Spain 1996; Golden Rose Award New England Poetry Club 1961, Poetry Prize, Saturday Review 1956, Nat. Inst. of Arts and Letters Award 1966, NEA Award (in poetry) 1980, (in trans.) 1983, Columbia Univ. Trans. Center Nat. Award 1985. *Publications:* poems: The Moral Circus 1955, The Gazebos 1960, Survivals 1964, Spring Journal 1968, Four Springs 1972, Shake a Spear With Me, John Berryman 1974, At Sixes 1974, The Affinities of Orpheus 1976, Selected Poems (1955–1976) 1979, Interrupted Praise 1983, Gifts of Light 1983, God Talk 1992, The Imminence of Love: Poems 1962–92 1993, Time and Again: Selected Poems 1970–97 2000; plays: The Widow 1953, The Phantom Lady 1964, Life is a Dream, Calisto and Melibea (play/libretto) 1972, Ends of the World and Other Plays 1983, Calderón: Six Plays 1993; (selected prose of Fernando Pessoa) Always Astonished 1988; criticism: García Lorca 1944, Dark Conceit: The Making of Allegory 1959, Calderón and the Seizures of Honor 1972, The Poet's Other Voice 1985; fiction: Foibles and Fables of an Abstract Man 1979; anthologies with Oscar Williams: The Mentor Book of Major American Poets 1961, The Major Metaphysical Poets 1968; Spenser 1968; also trans. of works by García Lorca, Calderón de la Barca, Fernando Pessoa, Miguel Hernández and Lope de Vega; produced opera Calisto and Melibea 1979, play Life is a Dream 1988, The Phantom Lady; A Glass of Green Tea With Honig 1993. *Leisure interests:* trees, ponds, woods, travel abroad: Spain, Portugal, China. *Address:* Brown University, Box 1852, Providence, RI 02912 (office); 229 Medway Street, Apt. 305, Providence, RI 02906, USA (home). *Telephone:* (401) 831-1027. *Website:* www.brown.edu/Departments/English/Writing (office).

HONJO, Tasuku, MD, PhD; Japanese immunologist; *Professor, Department of Immunology and Genomic Medicine, Graduate School of Medicine, Kyoto University;* b. 27 Jan. 1942, Kyoto; s. of Shoichi Honjo and Ryu Honjo; m. Shigeko Kotani 1969; one s. one d.; ed Ube High School and Kyoto Univ.; Fellow, Carnegie Inst. of Washington, Baltimore, Md, USA 1971–73; Visiting Fellow and Assoc. Lab. of Molecular Genetics, NIH 1973–74; Asst Prof., Dept of Physiological Chem. and Nutrition, Faculty of Medicine, Univ. of Tokyo 1974–79; Prof. Dept of Genetics, Osaka Univ. School of Medicine 1979–84; Prof. Dept of Immunology and Genomic Medicine, Grad. School of Medicine, Kyoto Univ. 1984–, Dir Center for Molecular Biology and Genetics 1988–97, Dean, Faculty of Medicine, Kyoto Univ. 1996–2000, 2002–04; Science Adviser, Ministry of Educ., Culture, Sports, Science and Tech. (MEXT) 1999–2003; Dir Japan Soc. for the Promotion of Science, Research Centre for Science Systems 2004–06; Exec. mem. Council for Science and Tech. Policy, Cabinet Office 2006–; mem. Leopoldina German Acad. of Natural Scientists 2003, Japan Acad. 2006; Foreign Assoc., NAS 2001; Hon. mem. American Asscn of Immunologists; Noguchi Hideyo Memorial Award for Medicine 1981, Asahi Award 1981, Erwin von Baelz Prize 1985, Takeda Medical Prize 1988, Behring-Kitasato Prize 1992, Imperial Prize and Japan Acad. Prize 1996, Person of Cultural Merit Award by Japanese Govt 2000. *Publications:* Molecular Biology of B Cell 2003. *Leisure interest:* golf. *Address:* Department of Immunology and Genomic Medicine, Graduate School of Medicine, Kyoto University, Yoshida, Sakyo-ku, Kyoto 606-8501, Japan (office). *Telephone:* (75) 753-4371 (office). *Fax:* (75) 753-4388 (office). *E-mail:* honjo@mfour.med.kyoto-u.ac.jp (office). *Website:* www2.mfour.med.kyoto-u.ac.jp/E_Home.htm (office).

HONKAPOHJA, Seppo Mikko Sakari, DSocSc; Finnish economist, banker and fmr academic; *Member of the Board, Bank of Finland;* b. 7 March 1951, Helsinki; m. Sirkku Anna-Maija Honkapohja 1973; one s. one d.; ed United World Coll. of the Atlantic, UK, Univ. of Helsinki; Scientific Dir Yrjö Jahnsson Foundation 1975–87; Prof. of Econs, Turku School of Econs and Business Admin 1987–91, Prof.-at-Large (Docent) 1992–; Prof.-at-Large (Docent) of Econs, Univ. of Helsinki 1981–91, Acting Prof. of Econs (Econometrics) 1985–87, Prof. of Econs 1992–; Visiting Lecturer and Scholar, Harvard Univ., USA 1978–79; Visiting Assoc. Prof. of Econs, Stanford Univ., USA 1982–83; Sr Fellow Acad. of Finland 1982–83, Acad. Prof. 1989–95, 2000–04; Prof. of Int. Macroeconomics, Univ. of Cambridge, UK 2004–08, Professorial Fellow, Clare Coll. 2004–08; mem. Bd Bank of Finland 2008–; Man. Ed. Scandinavian Journal of Economics 1984–88; Ed. European Economic Review 1993–98; mem. Bd Finnish Econ. Asscn 1989–91, Finnish Soc. for European Studies 1994–2000; mem. Council, European Econ. Asscn 1985–86, 1999–2003, mem. Exec. Cttee 2004–06; Vice-Chair. Kansallis Foundation for Financial Research 1989–96; mem. Governing Body, The Finnish Cultural Foundation 1994–, Chair. 1997–2001, mem. Supervisory Bd 2003–; mem. Supervisory Bd, Okopankki Ltd 1996–, Chair 1997–2007; mem. Finnish Acad. of Science and Letters, Academia Europaea; Fellow, Econometric Soc., European Econ. Asscn; Jaakko Honko Medal, Helsinki School of Econs and Business Admin 1998, Yrjo Jahnsson Foundation Anniversary Prize 2004. *Publications:* Limits and Problems of Taxation 1985; ed. several books including The State of Macroeconomics 1990, Macroeconomic Modelling and Policy Implications 1993, Learning and Expectations in Macroeconomics 2001; numerous articles in journals. *Leisure interest:* fishing. *Address:* Bank of Finland, PO Box 160, 00101, Helsinki, Finland (office). *Telephone:* (10) 8312015 (office). *Website:* www.bof.fi (office).

HONORÉ, HE Cardinal Jean, DTheol; French ecclesiastic; *Bishop of Evreux;* b. 13 Aug. 1920, Saint Brice en Coglès; ed Collège de St Mâlo, Grand Séminaire de Rennes, Inst. Catholique de Paris, Ecole Pratique des Hautes Etudes, Paris; fmr Archbishop of Tours, Archbishop Emer. 1997–; cr. Cardinal 2001; Prof. of Letters and Theology, Rector, Université Catholique d'Angers; Bishop of Evreux; Commdr Légion d'honneur 2001, Commdr des Arts et Lettres 2007; Dr hc (Louvain la Neuve). *Publications:* Itinéraire spirituel de Newman 1964, La fidélité d'une conscience 1987, La pensée christologique de Newman 1996, Fais paraître ton jour 2000, Newman, un homme de Dieu 2003, La Grâce d'être né (memoirs) 2006, Les Aphorismes de Newman 2007. *Address:* 1 Allée de la Rocaille, 37390 La Membrolle sur Ch., France (home). *Fax:* (2) 47-41-15-83 (home).

HONSCHEID, Klaus, PhD; German particle physicist and academic; *Professor, Department of Physics, Ohio State University;* ed Univ. of Bonn; fmr Asst Prof., Ohio State Univ., USA, now Prof.; Alfred P. Sloan Foundation Fellowship 1995–96, Alumni Award for Distinguished Teaching, Ohio State Univ. 2004. *Publications:* numerous publs in scientific journals on particle and high-energy physics. *Address:* Department of Physics, Ohio State University, 174 W 18th Avenue, Columbus, OH 43210, USA (office). *Telephone:* (614) 292-3287 (office). *Fax:* (614) 292-8261 (office). *E-mail:* kh@mps.ohio-state.edu (office). *Website:* www.physics.ohio-state.edu (office).

HOOD, John, BE, MPhil PhD; New Zealand engineer, academic and university administrator; *Vice-Chancellor, University of Oxford;* ed Univ. of Auckland, Univ. of Oxford, UK; held various sr positions with Fletcher Challenge Ltd, including Head of Paper, Bldg and Construction Divs 1980–98; Vice-Chancellor Univ. of Auckland 1998–2004, Univ. of Oxford 2004–(09); fmr Visiting Lecturer, Dept of Civil Eng, Univ. of Auckland; Chair. NZ Vice-Chancellors' Cttee, The Knowledge Wave Trust, Universitas 21 Ltd 2002–04; fmr Chair. Tonkin & Taylor Ltd; fmr Dir Universitas 21 Global, ASB Bank Ltd, ASB Group, Fonterra Cooperative Group Ltd; fmr mem. Prime Minister's Growth and Innovation Advisory Bd, Prime Minister's Enterprise Council; Chair. Prime Minister's Think Tank on High Performance Sport 1996; fmr Gov. and mem. Exec. Bd, NZ Sports Foundation; fmr NZ Sec., The Rhodes Trust; fmr Trustee Asia 2000 Foundation, King's School (also Gov.); Rhodes Scholarship. *Address:* University Offices, Welllington Square, Oxford, OX1 2JD, England (office). *Telephone:* (1865) 270243 (office). *Fax:* (1865) 270085 (office). *E-mail:* vice-chancellor@admin.ox.ac.uk (office). *Website:* www.ox.ac.uk (office).

HOOD, Leroy Edward, MD, PhD; American biologist, academic and entrepreneur; *President, Institute for Systems Biology;* b. 10 Oct. 1938, Missoula,

Mon.; s. of Thomas Edward Hood and Myrtle Evylan Wadsworth; m. Valerie A. Logan 1963; one s. one d.; ed California Inst. of Tech. and Johns Hopkins School of Medicine; NIH Predoctoral Fellowship, California Inst. of Tech. 1963–64, NIH Postdoctoral Fellowship 1964–67; Sr Investigator, Immunology Branch, GL&C, NCI, NIH, Bethesda, Md 1967–70; Asst Prof. of Biology, California Inst. of Tech. 1970–73, Assoc. Prof. 1973–75, Prof. 1975–77, Bowles Prof. of Biology 1977–92, Chair. Div. of Biology 1980–89, Dir Cancer Center 1981; Gates Prof. and Chair. of Molecular Biotech. Univ. of Washington 1992–99; Dir NSF Science and Tech. Center for Molecular Biotechnology 1989–2000; Founder and Pres. Inst. for Systems Biology 1999–; mem. IOM, NAS, Nat. Acad. of Eng, American Acad. of Arts and Sciences, AAAS, American Asscn of Immunologists, American Philosophical Soc., American Soc. for Clinical Investigation, American Soc. of Biological Chemists, Asscn of American Physicians, Int. Soc. of Molecular Evolution, Sigma Xi, Soc. for Integrative and Comparative Biology; Fellow, American Acad. of Microbiology; Hon. DSc (Montana State) 1986, (Mount Sinai School of Medicine, CUNY) 1987, (Univ. of British Columbia) 1988, (Univ. of S California) 1989, (Wesleyan) 1992, (Whitman Coll.) 1995, (Bates Coll.) 1999, (Penn State) 2001, (Zhejiang Univ., Tsinghua Univ., China) 2004, (Medical Coll. of Wisconsin) 2005, (Coll. of Wooster) 2007; Hon. DHumLitt (Johns Hopkins) 1990, (Loyola) 2005; Albert Lasker Basic Medical Research Award 1987, Commonwealth Award of Distinguished Service 1989, Cetus Award for Biotechnology 1989, American Coll. of Physicians Award 1990, Ciba-Geigy/Drew Award 1993, Lynen Medal 1994, Distinguished Alumnus Award, Johns Hopkins Univ. 1994, Beckman Lecturer Award 1998, Distinguished Service Award, American Asscn for Clinical Chem. 1998, Koyoto Prize in Advanced Technologies 2002, Economists Award for Innovation in Biosciences 2002, Lemelson-MIT Prize 2003, World Tech. Award for Biotechnology 2003, American Asscn for Pathology Award for Excellence in Clinical Diagnosis 2004, Heinz Award for Tech. and Econ. Devt 2006, Inventors Hall of Fame 2007. *Publications:* co-author of six books on immunology, biochemistry, molecular biology, genetics and the human genome project and of more than 650 papers in learned journals. *Leisure interests:* mountaineering, running, exercise, photography, reading. *Address:* Institute for Systems Biology, 1441 N34 Street, Seattle, WA 98103, USA (office). *Telephone:* (206) 732-1201 (office). *Fax:* (206) 732-1254 (office). *E-mail:* lhood@systemsbiology.org (office). *Website:* www.systemsbiology.org (office).

HOODA, Bhupinder Singh, BA, LLB; Indian politician, agriculturist and lawyer; *Chief Minister of Haryana;* b. 15 Sept. 1947, Sanghi, Rohtak Dist; s. of Choudhary Ranbir Singh; m. Asha Hooda 1976; one s. one d.; ed Punjab Univ., Chandigarh, Univ. of Delhi; Pres. Block Congress Cttee, Kiloi, Haryana 1972–77; Sr Vice-Pres. Haryana Pradesh Youth Congress 1982–83, Pres. 1982–83; Chair. Panchayat Samiti, Rohtak 1983–87, Panchayat Parishad, Haryana 1984–87; mem. Lok Sabha 1991–, mem. Cttee on Agric. 1996–97, 1998–99, on Subordinate Legislation 1998–99; mem. All India Congress Cttee 1992–; mem. Exec. Congress Parl. Party 1994–; Convenor Haryana Congress Parl. Group 1994–96; Pres. Haryana Pradesh Congress Cttee 1997–2002; mem. Consultative Cttee Ministry of Communication 1998–99, Cttee on Subordinate Legislation; mem. Haryana Vidhan Sabha 2000–, Leader of the Opposition 2002–04; Leader Haryana Legislature Party 2005–; Chief Minister of Haryana 2005–; Pres. All India Young Farmers' Asscn, Haryana; Founder-mem. and Working Pres. All India Freedom Fighters' Successors' Org.; Working Pres. Nat. Fed. of Railway Porters, Vendors and Bearers; Sec. Jat Educ. Soc., Rohtak, Farmers' Parl. Forum 1991–; mem. Man. Cttee, D.A.V. Educational Soc., Hasangarh, Haryana. *Leisure interests:* reading, sports. *Address:* Kothi No. 1, Sector 3, Chandigarh (office); Matu Ram Bhawan, Model Town, Delhi Road, Rohtak, Haryana, India (home). *Telephone:* (172) 2749394 (office); (1262) 42283 (home). *Fax:* (1262) 212030 (home). *E-mail:* cm@hry.nic.in (office); hoodabhupindersingh@hry.nic.in (office). *Website:* haryana.nic.in/government/cmbio (office).

HOOGENDOORN, Piet; Dutch business executive; b. 1946; ed Netherlands Inst. of Registeraccountants; worked as public auditor; Man. Partner Deloitte & Touche Netherlands 1990–2001; Vice-Chair. Deloitte Touche Tohmatsu Global Bd 1999–2000, Chair. July 2000–07; Pres. Royal NIvRAm (professional org. of Dutch accountants); mem. Supervisory Bd ING Groep NV 2007–, Nyenrode Univ.; mem. Bd Netherlands Foundation for Annual Reporting. *Address:* ING House, Amstelveenseweg 500, 1081 Amsterdam, Netherlands (office).

HOOGLANDT, Jan Daniel, DSc; Dutch steel industry executive; b. 15 Feb. 1926, Tangier, Morocco; m.; four c.; ed Hilversum Gymnasium, Municipal Univ. of Amsterdam; joined Koninklijke Nederlandsche Hoogovens en Staalfabrieken NV 1954 as Asst in Econ. Dept 1954; retd 1988 as Chair. Bd Hoogovens Groep BV; Chair. Supervisory Bd ABN/AMRO –1996, Ned. Participatie Maatschappij NV; mem. Supervisory Bd Koninklijke Nederlandsche Hoogovens en Staalfabrieken NV –1996, NV Koninklijke Nederlandse Petroleum Maatschappij –1996, Heineken NV; Order of the Netherlands Lion 1976; Commdr Order Oranje Nassau 1988. *Address:* Zwartweg 16, 2111 AJ Aerdenhout, Netherlands.

HOOKER, Charlie (Charles Raymond); British artist; b. 1 June 1953, London; s. of Raymond C. Hooker and Daphne Hooker; m. Stephanie J. Burden 1980; one s.; ed Purley Grammar School, Croydon Coll. of Art and Brighton Polytechnic; founder mem. The Artistics (music ensemble) 1972–75, 2B Butlers Wharf (art space) 1974–75; Visiting Lecturer, Chelsea, Croydon, Winchester, Trent, Cardiff, Central, Brighton, Newport, Newcastle, Camberwell Schools of Art/Polytechnics 1977–; part-time Lecturer, Brighton Polytechnic 1990–92; External Examiner, Chelsea School of Art 1995–; Sr Lecturer, Camberwell Coll. 1990–92; Sr Lecturer/Area Leader—Sculpture, Univ. of Brighton 1992–; Artist in Residence, Amherst Jr and Hatcham Wood Secondary Schools 1985; Co-ordinator, Artists' Open Week, Camberwell School of Art 1989; several one-man and group shows of maquettes and drawings and numerous installations and performances in UK, Europe, America and Australia 1975–; works in Arts Council collection and pvt. collections and perm. public outdoor work in UK; Art/Science projects with Science Museum, London and Herstmonceux Science Centre 1995; Subject Leader for Sculpture and Critical Fine Art Practice, Univ. of Brighton. *Radio interviews:* BBC Radio Nottingham 1981, BBC Radio Cambridge 1986, Warsaw Radio 1988. *TV interviews:* BBC Look North 1983, Anglia TV 1985, Western Australia TV News 1985; published video recording 'Charlie Hooker Talks to Mike Archer' (Havering Educational) 1988. *Audio recordings:* Restricted Movement 1982, Transitions 1984, Charlie Hooker and Performers 1987, Wave-Wall/Dust and a Shadow 1991 for Audio Arts, Separate Elements 1992. *Leisure interest:* walking. *Address:* 28 Whippingham Road, Brighton, Sussex, BN2 3PG, England. *Telephone:* (1273) 600048. *Fax:* (1273) 643128.

HOOKER, Morna Dorothy, MA, PhD, DD; British theologian and academic; *Lady Margaret's Professor Emerita of Divinity, University of Cambridge;* b. 19 May 1931, Surrey; d. of P. F. Hooker and L. Hooker (née Riley); m. Rev. Dr W. D. Stacey 1978 (died 1993); one step-s. two step-d.; ed Univ. of Bristol, Univ. of Manchester; Research Fellow, Univ. of Durham 1959–61; Lecturer in New Testament, King's Coll. London 1961–70, Fellow 1979–; Lecturer in Theology, Univ. of Oxford 1970–76, Keble Coll. Oxford 1972–76; Fellow, Linacre Coll. Oxford 1970–76, Hon. Fellow 1980–; Visiting Fellow, Clare Hall, Cambridge 1974; Lady Margaret Prof. of Divinity, Univ. of Cambridge 1976–98, Prof. Emer. 1998–; Fellow, Robinson Coll. Cambridge 1977–; Visiting Prof. York St John Univ.; Jt Ed. Journal of Theological Studies 1985–2005; Visiting Prof., McGill Univ. 1968, Duke Univ. NC 1987, 1989; Pres. Studiorum Novi Testamenti Societas 1988–89; Hon. DLitt (Bristol) 1994; Hon. DD (Edinburgh) 1997; Burkitt Medal 2004. *Publications:* Jesus and the Servant 1959, The Son of Man in Mark 1967, Pauline Pieces 1979, Studying the New Testament 1979, The Message of Mark 1983, Continuity and Discontinuity 1986, From Adam to Christ 1990, A Commentary on the Gospel According to St Mark 1991, Not Ashamed of the Gospel 1994, The Signs of a Prophet 1997, Beginnings: Keys that Open the Gospels 1997, Paul: A Short Introduction 2003, Endings 2003. *Leisure interests:* molinology, music, walking. *Address:* Robinson College, Cambridge, CB3 9AN, England (office). *Telephone:* (1223) 339100 (office). *Fax:* (1223) 351794 (office). *E-mail:* mdh1000@cam.ac.uk (office).

HOOKER, Steven; Australian athlete; b. 16 July 1982, Melbourne, Vic.; s. of Bill Hooker (represented Australia in 800m and 4×400m at 1974 Commonwealth Games) and Erica Hooker (1972 Olympian and Commonwealth Games long jump silver medallist 1978); pole vaulter; finished fourth at World Jr Championships, Santiago, Chile 2000; Gold Medal, Commonwealth Games, Melbourne 2006; finished fifth at World Athletics Final, Stuttgart 2006; finished first at World Cup, Athens 2006; Bronze Medal, World Athletics Final, Stuttgart 2007, World Indoor Championships, Valencia 2008; set personal best of 6.00m in Perth, WA Jan. 2008; Gold Medal, Olympic Games, Beijing 2008 (set new Olympic record of 5.96m), first Australian male track and field gold medallist since 1968. *Address:* c/o Australian Athletics Federation, Suite 22, Fawkner Towers, 431 St Kilda Road, Melbourne, Vic. 3004, Australia. *Telephone:* (3) 98203511. *Fax:* (3) 98203544. *E-mail:* info@athletics.org.au. *Website:* www.athletics.org.au.

HOOKWAY, Sir Harry Thurston, Kt, PhD; British administrator and librarian; b. 23 July 1921, London; s. of William Hookway and Bertha Hookway; m. Barbara Butler 1956; one s. one d.; ed Trinity School of John Whitgift and Univ. of London; Asst Dir Nat. Chem. Lab. 1959; Dir UK Scientific Mission (N America), Scientific Attaché, Embassy in Washington, DC, Scientific Adviser, High Comm., Ottawa, Canada 1960–64; Head, Information Div. Dept of Scientific and Industrial Research 1964–65; Chief Scientific Officer, Dept of Educ. and Science 1966–69, Asst Under-Sec. of State 1969–73; Deputy Chair. and Chief Exec. British Library Bd 1973–84; Pro-Chancellor Loughborough Univ. of Tech. 1987–93; mem. Royal Comm. on Historical Monuments (England) 1981–88; Chair. Publrs Data Bases Ltd 1984–87, LA Publishing Ltd 1986–89; Pres. The Library Asscn 1985; Dir Arundel Castle Trustees 1976–89; Hon. Fellow, Inst. of Information Scientists, Hon. FLA; Hon. LLD; Hon. DLitt; Gold Medal Int. Asscn of Library Asscns 1985. *Publications:* papers in learned and professional journals. *Leisure interests:* music, travel. *Address:* 3 St James Green, Thirsk, North Yorks., YO7 1AF, England.

HOOLEY, Christopher, PhD, FRS; British academic; b. 7 Aug. 1928, Edinburgh; s. of Leonard Joseph Hooley and Barbara Hooley; m. Birgitta Kniep 1954; two s.; ed Abbotsholme School and Corpus Christi Coll. Cambridge; Capt., Royal Army Educational Corps 1948–49; Fellow, Corpus Christi Coll. 1955–58; Lecturer in Math., Univ. of Bristol 1958–65; Prof. of Pure Math., Univ. of Durham 1965–67; Prof. of Pure Math. 1967–95, Distinguished Research Prof. 1995–, Head of Dept of Math. Wales Univ., Coll. of Cardiff (fmrly Univ. Coll. Cardiff) 1988–96, Dean of Faculty of Science 1973–76, Deputy Prin. Univ. Coll. Cardiff 1979–81, Wales Univ. Coll. of Cardiff 1991–94; Visiting mem., Inst. for Advanced Study, Princeton, USA on several occasions since 1970, Institut des Hautes Etudes Scientifiques, Paris 1984; Adam's Prize, Cambridge 1973, Sr Berwick Prize, London Math. Soc. 1980. *Publications:* Applications of Sieve Methods to the Theory of Numbers 1976, Recent Progress in Analytic Number Theory (ed. with H. Halberstam) 1981. *Leisure interests:* antiquities and classic cars. *Address:* Rushmoor Grange, Backwell, Bristol, BS19 3BN, England. *Telephone:* (1275) 462363.

HOON, Rt Hon. Geoffrey William, PC, MA; British politician and lawyer; *Secretary of State for Transport;* b. 6 Dec. 1953; s. of Ernest Hoon and June Hoon; m. Elaine Ann Dumelow 1981; one s. two d.; ed Jesus Coll., Cambridge; labourer at furniture factory 1972–73; Lecturer in Law, Leeds Univ. 1976–82;

Visiting Prof. of Law, Univ. of Louisville 1979–80; called to the Bar, Gray's Inn 1978; in practice in Nottingham 1982–84; MEP for Derbyshire 1984–94, mem. Legal Affairs Cttee 1984–94; MP for Ashfield 1992–; Opposition Whip 1994–95; Opposition Spokesman on Information Tech. 1995–97; Parl. Sec., Lord Chancellor's Dept 1997–98, Minister of State 1998–99, Sec. of State for Defence 1999–2005, for Transport 2008–; Leader of the House of Commons 2005–06; Minister for Europe, FCO 2006–07; Parl. Sec. to the Treasury and Chief Whip 2007–08; Vice-Chair. and Gov. Westminster Foundation 1994–97; mem. Labour Party; US Dept of Defense Distinguished Public Service Award 2004. *Leisure interests:* cinema, cricket, football, music. *Address:* Department for Transport, Great Minster House, 76 Marsham Street, London SW1P 4DR (office); 8 Station Street, Kirby-in-Ashfield, Notts., NG17 7AR, England (home). *Telephone:* (20) 7944-8300 (office); (1623) 720399 (home). *Fax:* (20) 7944-9643 (office); (1623) 720398 (home). *E-mail:* fax9643@dft.gsi.gov.uk (office); contact@geoffhoonmp.co.uk (office). *Website:* www.dft.gov.uk (office); www.geoffhoonmp.co.uk (office).

HOPE, Christopher David Tully, MA, FRSL; South African writer; b. 26 Feb. 1944, Johannesburg; s. of Dudley Mitford Hope and Kathleen Mary Hope; m. Eleanor Marilyn Margaret Klein; two s.; ed Natal Univ., Univ. of the Witwatersrand; Founder and Dir Franschhoek Literary Festival 2007–; mem. Soc. of Authors; Cholmondeley Award 1972, David Higham Award 1981, Int. PEN Award 1983, Whitbread Award 1986, CNA Literary Award (S Africa) 1989, Travelex Travel Writer of the Year 1997. *Publications:* A Separate Development 1981, Private Parts 1982, The King, the Cat and the Fiddle (with Yehudi Menuhin) 1983, Kruger's Alp (Whitbread Prize for Fiction 1985) 1984, The Dragon Wore Pink 1985, The Hottentot Room 1986, Black Swan 1987, White Boy Running 1988, My Chocolate Redeemer 1989, Moscow! Moscow! 1990, Serenity House 1992, The Love Songs of Nathan J. Swirsky 1993, Darkest England 1996; poetry: Cape Drives 1974, In the Country of the Black Pig 1981, Englishman 1985, Me, the Moon and Elvis Presley 1997, Signs of the Heart 1999, Heaven Forbid 2002, Brothers Under the Skin 2003, My Mother's Lovers 2006, The Garden of Bad Dreams 2008; contrib. to TLS, London Magazine, Les Temps Modernes. *Leisure interest:* getting lost. *Address:* Rogers, Coleridge & White Ltd, 20 Powis Mews, London, W11 1JN, England (office). *Telephone:* (20) 7221-3717 (office). *Fax:* (20) 7229-9084 (office).

HOPE, Maurice; British fmr professional boxer; b. 6 Dec. 1951, Antigua, West Indies; s. of Norris Hope and Sarah Andrew Hope; m. Patricia Hope; one s. two d.; ed Hackney Secondary Modern School, London; came to Britain 1961; rep. England and Great Britain as amateur boxer with Repton Amateur Boxing Club; quarter-finalist at Olympic Games, Munich 1972; professional boxer June 1973–1982; won British light-middleweight title from Larry Paul Nov. 1974, retained it v. Paul (Sept. 1975) and Tony Poole (April 1976); won Lonsdale Belt outright and became Commonwealth champion by beating Poole; lost to Bunny Sterling for vacant British middleweight title, June 1975; won European light-middleweight title from Vito Antuofermo, Rome Oct. 1976; drew with Eckhard Dagge for World Boxing Council (WBC) version of world light-middleweight title, Berlin March 1977; retained European title v. Frank Wissenbach, Hamburg (May 1977) and Joel Bonnetaz, Wembley (Nov. 1977); relinquished European title Sept. 1978; won WBC version of world light-middleweight title from Rocky Mattioli, San Remo March 1979; retained it v. Mike Baker (Sept. 1979), Mattioli (July 1980) and Carlos Herrera (Nov. 1980), lost title to Wilfredo Benitez (May 1981); 35 fights, 30 wins, one draw; now a trainer; flag carrier at 2002 Commonwealth Games opening ceremony. *Leisure interests:* table tennis, snooker, pool.

HOPE-CROSBY, Polly, FRSA; British artist, designer, writer and photographer; b. 21 June 1933, Colchester; d. of Gen. Sir Hugh Stockwell and Lady Stockwell; m. 1st John Hope 1953; one s.; m. 2nd Theo Crosby 1990; ed Heatherley, Chelsea and Slade Schools of Art; trained as a classical ballet dancer; has completed various comms including pointillist mural for Barbican Centre, London, four life-size terracotta figures for Shakespeare's Globe Theatre; collaborated on bldg Shakespeare's Globe Theatre, vestments for Wakefield Cathedral 1999–2000 and many other public works; works with several composers writing librettos; has composed Greek song cycles; has written film scripts, made videos, films and animated films. *Animated film:* Memories, Memories 1995. *Productions include:* Il Giardino degli Uccelli (one act opera, music by Quentin Thomas) 1999, Death of Lord Byron (one act opera, music by Quentin Thomas) 2000, Bran's Singing Head (music by Geoffrey Alvarez) 1996, The Bird Garden, Oper-am-Rhein, Düsseldorf (sets, libretto and book), design for Kiss Me Kate for Deutsch Oper-am-Rhein 2000, SW by NE, Pam King's Olridia 2005. *Plays include:* Freedom and Death 1992, General Hughie 1993. *Artistic works:* many embroideries for Church of England, chasubles, altar frontals, tapestries. *Publications include:* Here Away From it All 1969, Us Lot 1970, The Immaculate Misconception 1972, A Baker's Dozen of Greek Folk Songs 1994, Songs My Parrot Taught Me 1994, Egyptian Love Songs and Songs for Aphrodite 1998, Il Giardino degli Uccelli 1999. *Leisure interests:* music, sitting in the sun and sleeping. *Address:* 5B Heneage Street, Spitalfields, London, E1 5LJ, England (home). *Telephone:* (20) 7247-3450 (home). *Fax:* (20) 7247-3450 (home). *E-mail:* polly@doxy.demon.co.uk (office). *Website:* www.hopeart.com (office).

HOPE OF CRAIGHEAD, Baron (Life Peer), cr. 1995, of Bamff in the District of Perth and Kinross; **Rt Hon. James Arthur David Hope,** PC, LLB, MA, FRSE; British judge; b. 22 June 1938, Edinburgh, Scotland; s. of Arthur Henry Cecil Hope and Muriel Ann Neilson Hope; m. Katharine Mary Kerr 1966; two s. one d.; ed The Edinburgh Acad., Rugby School, St John's Coll. Cambridge; nat. service, Seaforth Highlanders 1957–59; admitted to Faculty of Advocates, to practise at Scottish Bar 1965; Standing Jr Counsel to Bd of Inland Revenue in Scotland 1974–78; apptd. QC in Scotland 1978; Advocate-Depute, Crown Office, Edinburgh 1978–82; Chair. and Legal Chair. Medical Appeal Tribunals 1985–86; Dean Faculty of Advocates 1986–89; Lord Justice Gen. of Scotland and Lord Pres. of Court of Session 1989–96; a Lord of Appeal in Ordinary 1996–; Chair. Sub-cttee E (Law and Insts), House of Lords Select Cttee on the EU 1998–2001; Pres. Stair Soc. 1993–, Int. Criminal Lawyers Asscn 2000, Commonwealth Magistrates' and Judges' Asscn 2003–06; Chancellor Univ. of Strathclyde 1998–; Hon. Prof. of Law, Univ. of Aberdeen 1994–; Hon. Fellow, St John's Coll., Cambridge 1995, American Coll. of Trial Lawyers 2000; Hon. LLD (Aberdeen) 1991, (Strathclyde) 1993, (Edin.) 1995. *Publications:* Gloag & Henderson's Introduction to the Laws of Scotland (co-ed.) 1968, (asst ed.) 1980, 1987, 2001, Armour on Valuation for Rating (co-ed.) 1971, 1985, The Rent (Scotland) Act (jtly) 1984, 1986, Stair Memorial Encyclopedia of Scots Law (contrib.). *Leisure interests:* walking, ornithology, music. *Address:* House of Lords, Westminster, London, SW1A 0PW, England (office); 34 India Street, Edinburgh, EH3 6HB, Scotland (home). *Telephone:* (20) 7219-3202; (131) 225-8245. *E-mail:* hopejad@parliament.uk (office).

HOPE OF THORNES, Baron (Life Peer), cr. 2005, of Thornes in the County of West Yorkshire; **Rt Rev. and Rt Hon. David Michael Hope,** KCVO, PC, DPhil; British ecclesiastic (retd); b. 14 April 1940; ed Wakefield Grammar School, Nottingham Univ., Linacre Coll. Oxford; Curate, St John's, Tuebrook, Liverpool 1965–70; Chaplain, Church of Resurrection, Bucharest 1967–68; Vicar, St Andrew's, Warrington 1970–74; Prin. St Stephen's House, Oxford 1974–82; Warden, Community of St Mary the Virgin, Wantage 1980–87; Vicar, All Saints', Margaret Street, London 1982–85; Bishop of Wakefield 1985–91, of London 1991–95; Archbishop of York 1995–2005; Vicar of St Margaret's, Ilkley, W Yorks. 2005–06 (retd); Prelate of the Order of the British Empire 1991–95; Dean of the Chapels Royal 1991–95; mem. Court of Ecclesiastical Causes Reserved 2006–; Hon. Asst Bishop, Diocese of Bradford 2006, Diocese of Gibraltar in Europe 2007. *Publications:* The Leonine Sacramentary 1971, Living the Gospel 1993. *Address:* 2 Aspinall Rise, Hellifield, Skipton, BD23 4JT, England. *Telephone:* (1904) 707021. *Fax:* (1904) 709204.

HOPFIELD, John Joseph, AB, PhD; American scientist and academic; *Howard A. Prior Professor Emeritus of Molecular Biology, Princeton University;* b. 15 July 1933, Chicago; s. of John Joseph Hopfield and Helen Hopfield; m. Mary Waltham; three c.; ed Swarthmore Coll., Cornell Univ.; mem. tech. staff, Bell Labs 1958–60, 1973–89; Research Physicist, École Normale Supérieure, Paris 1960-61; Asst/Assoc. Prof. of Physics, Univ. of California, Berkeley 1961–64; Prof. of Physics, Princeton Univ. 1964–80, Eugene Higgins Prof. of Physics 1979–80, Prof., Dept of Molecular Biology 1997–, Howard A. Prior Prof. of Molecular Biology 2001–08, now Emer.; Roscoe Gilkey Dickinson Prof. and Prof. of Chem. and Biology, Calif. Inst. of Tech. 1980–97; Chair. NAS Cttee on Publication 1995–98, Selection Cttee, Burroughs-Wellcome Fund Interfaces Program 1997–99; mem. NASA Tycho Study Group on the nature of the lunar surface 1965–67, Strategic Mil. Panel of PSAC 1971–73, American Physical Soc. (APS) Study on Solar Photoelectricity 1977–78, Neurosciences Research Program 1978–89, Solar Photovoltaic Energy Advisory Cttee 1980–82, Advisory Council, Keck Grad. Inst. of Applied Life Sciences 1997–2001, NAS Cttee Bio 2010: Undergraduate Biology Educ. for Future Scientists 2000–02; Pres. APS 2006; mem. American Acad. of Arts and Sciences, NAS, American Philosophical Soc.; Trustee, Battelle Memorial Inst. 1982–2006, Neuroscience Research Inst. 1986–87, Harvey Mudd Coll. 1990–96, Huntington Medical Research Inst. 1991–96; Hon. DSc (Swarthmore Coll.) 1992, (Univ. of Chicago) 2007; Alfred Sloan Fellow 1962–64, Guggenheim Fellow (Univ. of Cambridge, UK) 1969, APS Oliver E. Buckley Prize 1969, John and Catherine T. MacArthur Award 1983–88, APS Prize in Biophysics 1985, Michelson-Morley Award, Case-Western Univ. 1988, The Wright Prize, Harvey Mudd Coll. 1989, California Scientist of the Year, California Museum of Science and Industry 1991, IEEE Neural Network Pioneer Award 1997, Helmholtz Award, Int. Neural Network Soc. 1999, Dirac Medal and Prize, Int. Centre for Theoretical Physics, Trieste 2001, Pender Award, Moore School of Eng, Univ. of Pennsylvania 2002, Albert Einstein World Award of Science, World Cultural Council 2005, among others. *Achievements include:* most widely known for his invention of the associative neural network, the Hopfield Model 1982. *Publications:* more than 190 scientific papers in professional journals. *Address:* Lewis-Sigler Institute for Integrative Genomics, Princeton University, Carl Icahn Laboratory, Princeton, NJ 08544, USA (office). *Telephone:* (609) 258-1239 (office). *Fax:* (609) 258-7599 (office). *E-mail:* hopfield@princeton.edu (office). *Website:* genomics.princeton.edu/hopfield/Biography.html (office).

HOPKINS, Sir Anthony, Kt, CBE; American (b. British) actor; b. 31 Dec. 1937, Port Talbot, Wales; s. of Richard Hopkins and Muriel Hopkins; m. 1st Petronella Barker 1967 (divorced 1972); one d.; m. 2nd Jennifer Lynton 1973 (divorced 2002); m. 3rd Stella Arroyave 2003; ed Cowbridge Grammar School, S Wales, Welsh Coll. of Music and Drama, Cardiff, Royal Acad. of Dramatic Art; mil. training and service: clerk Royal Artillery Unit, Bulford 1958–60; joined Manchester Library Theatre, Asst Stage Man. 1960; then at Nottingham Repertory Co.; joined Phoenix Theatre, Leicester 1963; then Liverpool Playhouse, then Hornchurch Repertory Co.; joined Nat. Theatre Co. 1967; Film debut The Lion in Winter 1967; film, TV, stage actor in UK and USA 1967–, in USA 1974–84; Hon. Fellow St David's Coll., Lampeter 1992; Hon. DLitt (Univ. of Wales) 1988; Commdr, Ordre nat. des Arts et Lettres; BAFTA TV Actor Award 1972, Emmy Awards 1976, 1981, Variety Club Film Actor of the Year (The Bounty) 1984, Stage Actor of the Year (Pravda) 1985, Soc. of West End Theatres. The Observer Award for Pravda 1985, Best Actor, Moscow Film Festival, for 84 Charing Cross Road 1987, BAFTA Award and Acad. Award for Best Actor for The Silence of the Lambs 1992, BAFTA Award for Best Actor in The Remains of the Day 1994, US Film Advisory Bd Special Career Achievement Award for US Work 1994, BAFTA (US) Britannia Award for Outstanding Contrib. to the Int. Film and TV Industry 1995, Golden Globe

Cecil B. DeMille Award 2006, and numerous others worldwide. *Stage appearances include:* title role in Macbeth, Nat. Theatre 1972, Dr Dysart in Equus, Plymouth Theatre, New York 1974, 1975, Huntingdon Hartford Theatre, Los Angeles (also Dir) 1977, Prospero in The Tempest, Los Angeles 1979, Old Times, New York 1983, The Lonely Road, Old Vic Theatre, London 1985, Pravda, Nat. Theatre 1985, King Lear (title role), Nat. Theatre 1986, Antony and Cleopatra (title role), Nat. Theatre 1987, M. Butterfly 1989, August (also Dir) 1994. *Film appearances include:* The Lion in Winter 1967, The Looking Glass War 1967, Claudius in Hamlet 1969, When Eight Bells Toll 1969, Torvald in A Doll's House 1972, The Girl from Petrovka 1973, Juggernaut 1974, A Bridge Too Far 1976, Audrey Rose 1976, International Velvet 1977, Magic 1978, The Elephant Man 1979, A Change of Seasons 1980, Capt. Bligh in The Bounty 1983, The Good Father 1985, 84 Charing Cross Road 1987, The Old Jest 1987, A Chorus of Disapproval 1988, The Tenth Man 1988, Desperate Hours 1989, The Silence of the Lambs 1990, Spotswood 1990, One Man's War 1990, Howard's End 1991, Freejack 1991, Bram Stoker's Dracula 1991, Chaplin 1992, The Trial 1992, The Innocent 1992, The Remains of the Day 1992, Shadowlands 1993, Legends of the Fall 1993, The Road to Wellville 1993, August (also Dir) 1994, Nixon 1995, Surviving Picasso 1995, The Edge 1996, The Mask of Zorro 1997, Meet Joe Black 1998, Amistad 1998, Instinct 1999, Titus 1999, Mission Impossible 2, Hannibal 2001, Hearts in Atlantis 2001, The Devil and Daniel Webster 2001, Bad Company 2002, Red Dragon 2002, Human Stain 2003, Alexander 2004, Proof 2004, The World's Fastest Indian 2005, All the King's Men 2006, Bobby 2006, Slipstream 2007, Fracture 2007, Beowulf (voice) 2007, The City of Your Final Destination 2007, Where I Stand: The Hank Greenspun Story (voice) 2008, Immutable Dream of Snow Lion 2008, Bare Knuckles 2009. *TV appearances include:* A Heritage and its History, A Company of Five 1968, The Three Sisters, The Peasants Revolt 1969, title roles in Dickens, Danton, Astrov in Uncle Vanya, Hearts and Flowers 1970, Pierre in War and Peace 1971–72, title role in Lloyd George 1972, QB VII 1973, A Childhood Friend, Possessions, All Creatures Great and Small, The Arcata Promise 1974, Dark Victory, The Lindbergh Kidnapping Case (Emmy Award) 1975, Victory at Entebbe 1976, title role in Kean 1978, The Voyage of the Mayflower 1979, The Bunker (Emmy Award), Peter and Paul 1980, title role in Othello, Little Eyolf, The Hunchback of Notre Dame 1981, A Married Man 1982, Strangers and Brothers 1983, Old Times, The Arch of Triumph, Mussolini and I, Hollywood Wives, Guilty Conscience 1984, Blunt (role of Guy Burgess) 1987, Heartland 1989, Across the Lake (Donald Campbell) 1989, Great Expectations (Magwitch) 1989, To Be the Best 1990, A Few Selected Exits (Gwyn Thomas) 1993, Big Cats 1993. *Leisure interests:* music, playing the piano, reading philosophy and European history. *Address:* c/o CAA, 9830 Wilshire Blvd., Beverly Hills, CA 90212-1825, USA; c/o The Peggy Thompson Office, 296 Sandycombe Road, Kew, Surrey TW9 3NG, England.

HOPKINS, Antony, CBE, FRCM; British composer, writer and broadcaster (retd); b. 21 March 1921, London; s. of the late Hugh Reynolds and Marjorie Reynolds; m. Alison Purves 1947 (died 1991); ed Berkhamsted School and Royal Coll. of Music (RCM) with Cyril Smith; fmr Lecturer, RCM for 15 years; Dir Intimate Opera Co. 1952–64; composed incidental music for theatre (Old Vic, Stratford-upon-Avon), radio and cinema; Hon. FRAM; Hon. Fellow, Robinson Coll. Cambridge 1980; Hon. DUniv (Stirling) 1980; Hon. Dr of Arts (Bedford); Italia Prizes for composition 1952, 1957, City of Tokyo Medal for services to music 1973, Royal Coll. of Music Chappell Gold Medal 1943, Royal Coll. of Music Cobbett Prize. *Radio:* presenter of series, Talking About Music (BBC) 1954–92. *Compositions include:* operas: Lady Rohesia, Three's Company, Hands Across the Sky, Dr Musikus, Ten o'clock Call, The Man from Tuscany; ballet music: Etude, Café des Sports; others: Psalm 42, Magnificat and Nunc Dimittis for girls' choir), A Time for Growing, Early One Morning, Partita for solo violin, John and the Magic Music Man for narrator and orchestra (Grand Prix Besançon Film Festival) 1976, songs, recorder pieces, three piano sonatas; incidental music, including Oedipus, The Love of Four Colonels, Cast a Dark Shadow, Pickwick Papers, Billy Budd, Decameron Nights. *Publications:* Talking about Symphonies 1961, Talking about Concertos 1964, Music All Around Me 1967, Music Face to Face 1971, Talking about Sonatas 1971, Downbeat Guide 1977, Understanding Music 1979, The Nine Symphonies of Beethoven 1980, Songs for Swinging Golfers 1981, Sounds of Music 1982, Beating Time (autobiog.) 1982, Pathway to Music 1983, The Concertgoer's Companion Vol. I 1984, Vol. II 1986, The Seven Concertos of Beethoven 1996; contrib. to numerous books. *Leisure interest:* watching TV. *Address:* Woodyard Cottage, Ashridge, Berkhamsted, Herts., HP4 1PS, England (home). *Telephone:* (1442) 842257 (home).

HOPKINS, Bernard; American professional middleweight boxer; b. 15 Jan. 1965, Philadelphia; ed Germantown High School; 95 victories and four defeats as an amateur; spent four years in jail for armed robbery when 17; turned professional on 11 Oct. 1988 (defeated by Clinton Mitchell); suffered second defeat versus Roy Jones, Jr, in world title bout on 22 May 1993; won Int. Boxing Fed. world title defeating Segundo Mercado on 29 April 1995; added World Boxing Council belt defeating Keith Holmes on 14 April 2001 and World Boxing Asscn title defeating Felix Trinidad on 29 Sept. 2001; undisputed middleweight champion of the world with 19 title defences (middleweight record), defeating Oscar de la Hoya on 19 Sept. 2004 in Las Vegas, NV; light heavyweight champion of the world after defeating Antonio Tarver in Atlantic City on 10 June 2005; won 46 fights, including 32 knock-outs, two defeats, one draw. *Address:* c/o Swanson Communications, 102 Vermont Avenue, NW, Washington, DC 20005, USA (office). *Telephone:* (202) 783-5500 (office). *Fax:* (202) 783-5516 (office). *E-mail:* kswanson@swansonpr.com (office). *Website:* www.swansonpr.com (office).

HOPKINS, Godfrey Thurston; British photojournalist and writer; b. 16 April 1913, London; s. of Sybil Beatrice Bately and Robert Thurston Hopkins; m. Grace Fyfe Robertson 1955; one s. one d.; ed Salesian RC School, Burwash, Sussex, Montpelier Coll., Brighton, Brighton Coll. of Art; trained as magazine illustrator, then as photographer; photographer with RAF Italy and N Africa 1939–45; freelance photographer in Europe 1946–49; mem. staff Picture Post, assignments world-wide 1949–57 and particular interest in aspects of British life; worked for London advertising agencies 1958–68; tutor, Studies in Photojournalism, Guildford School of Photography, W Surrey Coll. of Art and Design 1970–78; work in public collections including Victoria and Albert Museum, Arts Council, Museum of London, Metropolitan Museum of Art, New York, Helmut Gernsheim Collection, Switzerland, J. Paul Getty Museum, USA, Museum of Photographic Arts, San Diego, CA, USA, The Hulton-Getty Archive, London; Encyclopaedia Britannica Award (twice). *Publication:* Thurston Hopkins 1977. *Leisure interests:* painting, writing. *Address:* Wilmington Cottage, Wilmington Road, Seaford, East Sussex, BN25 2EH, England (home). *Telephone:* (1323) 897656 (home). *Fax:* (1323) 897656 (home). *E-mail:* gracerobertson@btinternet.com (home).

HOPKINS, Sir Michael John, Kt, CBE, FRIBA, RA; British architect; b. 7 May 1935, Poole, Dorset; s. of the late Gerald Hopkins and Barbara Hopkins; m. Patricia Wainwright 1962; one s. two d.; ed Sherborne School, Architectural Asscn and RIBA; partnership with Norman Foster 1969–75; f. Michael Hopkins & Partners 1976–; Consultant Architect Victoria & Albert Museum 1985; Vice-Pres. Architectural Asscn 1987–93, Pres. 1997–99; mem. Royal Fine Art Comm. 1986–99; Trustee Thomas Cubitt Trust 1987–, British Museum 1993–; mem. RIBA Council, London Advisory Cttee to English Heritage, Architectural Advisory Group, Arts Council; Hon. mem. Bund Architekten; Hon. FAIA 1996; Hon. Fellow, Royal Incorporation of Architects of Scotland 1996; Hon. DLitt (Nottingham) 1995; Hon. DTech (London Guildhall); RIBA Award 1977, 1980, 1988, 1989, 1994, 1996; Civic Trust Award 1979, 1988, 1990, 1997; Financial Times Award 1980, 1982; Structural Steel Award, 1980, 1988; Royal Acad. Architectural Award 1982, co-winner (with wife Patricia Hopkins) RIBA Gold Medal for Architecture 1994. *Major works include:* Patera Bldg System 1984, Research Centre for Schlumberger, Cambridge 1984, Bicentenary Stand, Lord's Cricket Ground 1987, redevelopment of Bracken House for Ohbayashi Corpn 1987–91, R&D Centre, Solid State Logic 1988, Glyndebourne Opera House 1987–94, Portcullis House, Westminster 1989–2000, Westminster Underground Station 1990–99, The William Younger Centre 1990–99, Inland Revenue Centre, Nottingham 1992–95, Office Bldg for IBM at Bedfont Lakes, The Queen's Bldg, Emmanuel Coll., Cambridge 1993–95, Dynamic Earth, Edinburgh 1990–99, Jubilee Campus, Nottingham 1996–99, Saga Group Headquarters 1994–99, Hampshire Co. Cricket Club 1994–2001, Wildscreen @ Bristol 2,000 1996–99, Goodwood Racecourse 1997–2001, Haberdashers' Hall 1996–2002, The Forum, Norwich 1996–2001, Manchester City Art Gallery 1994–, Nat. Coll. of School Leadership, Nottingham 2000–02. *Works in progress include:* Evelina Children's Hosp., The Wellcome Trust Headquarters. *Leisure interests:* sailing, Catureglio, Blackheath. *Address:* Hopkins Architects, 27 Broadley Terrace, London, NW1 6LG (office); 49A Downshire Hill, London, NW3 1NX, England (home). *Telephone:* (20) 7724-1751 (office); (20) 7435-1109 (home). *Fax:* (20) 7723-0932 (office); (20) 7794-1494 (home). *E-mail:* mail@hopkins.co.uk (office). *Website:* www.hopkins.co.uk (office).

HOPKINS, Patricia Anne, Lady Hopkins; British architect; *Partner, Hopkins Architects;* b. 7 April 1942, Staffs.; d. of Denys Wainwright; m. (now Sir) Michael Hopkins 1962; one s. one d.; ed Wycombe Abbey School, Architectural Asscn, London; Co-Founder and Pnr, Michael Hopkins and Pnrs (now Hopkins Architects) 1976–; Assessor for Civic Trust Award Schemes 1993–2000; Gov. Queen's Coll., Harley St 1998–; mem. Arts Council Nat. Lottery Advisory Bd 1994–99, Architectural Asscn 150 Campaign Bd 1994–99; Trustee Nat. Gallery, London 1998–; Hon. Fellow, Royal Inst. of Architects in Scotland 1996, American Inst. of Architects; Hon. DTech (London Guildhall) 1996. *Architectural works include:* Hopkins House, Hampstead (RIBA Award 1997) 1996, Hopkins Office, Marylebone 1985, Fleet Velmead School, Hants (RIBA Award, Civic Trust Award 1988) 1986, Victoria and Albert Museum (Consultant Architect and Masterplan) 1988, Glyndebourne Opera House (RIBA Award, Royal Fine Art Comm. Award 1994, Civic Trust Award, FT Award 1995) 1994, Queen's Bldg, Emmanuel Coll. Cambridge (RIBA Award, Royal Fine Art Comm. Award 1996) 1995, Jewish Care Home for the Elderly 1996, Preacher's Court, Charterhouse 2000, Wildscreen at Bristol (Civic Trust Award, DTLR Urban Design Award 2001) 2001, Manchester Art Gallery 2002, Haberdasher's Hall 2002. *Leisure interests:* family and friends at Catureglio and Blackheath. *Address:* Hopkins Architects, 27 Broadley Terrace, London, NW1 6LG (office); 49A Downshire Hill, London, NW3 INX, England (home). *Telephone:* (20) 7724-1751 (office); (20) 7794-1494 (home). *Fax:* (20) 7723-0932 (office); (20) 7794-1494 (home). *E-mail:* patty.h@hopkins.co.uk (office). *Website:* www.hopkins.co.uk (office).

HOPKINS, Paul Jeffrey, BA, PhD; American academic; *Emeritus Professor of Tibetan Buddhist Studies, University of Virginia;* b. 30 Sept. 1940, Providence, RI; s. of Charles E. Hopkins and Ora Adams; m. Elizabeth S. Napper 1983 (divorced 1989); ed public school in Barrington, RI, Pomfret School, Conn., Harvard Univ., Univ. of Wisconsin and Lamaist Buddhist Monastery of America; Asst Prof. of Religious Studies, Univ. of Virginia 1973–77, Assoc. Prof. 1977–89, Prof. 1989–2005, Emer. 2005–, Dir Center for South Asian Studies 1979–82, 1985–94; Pres. Inst for Asian Democracy 1994–2000; Visiting Prof., Univ. of BC 1983–84; Yehan Numata Distinguished Visiting Prof. of Buddhist Studies, Univ. of Hawaii 1995; Chief Interpreter to Dalai Lama (q.v.) on overseas tours 1979–89, 1996; Fulbright Scholar, India and Germany 1971–72, India 1982, Taiwan 2002–03; Leverett Poetry Prize 1963. *Achievement:* organized and directed the Nobel Peace Laureates Conf., Univ. of Virginia 1998. *Publications:* Meditation on Emptiness 1973, Emptiness Yoga 1987, Fluent Tibetan 1993, Emptiness in the Mind-Only School of

Buddhism 1999; author or trans. of 36 other books including 14 in collaboration with the Dalai Lama; more than 20 articles. *Leisure interests:* meditation, walking in woods.

HOPP, Dietmar, MS; German software executive; *Member of Supervisory Board, SAP AG;* m.; two c.; ed Univ. of Karlsruhe; fmrly with IBM; co-f. SAP, fmr Bd Spokesman, now mem. Supervisory Bd. *Leisure interests:* beer, golf. *Address:* SAP AG, PO Box 1461, D-69185, Walldorf, Germany (office). *Telephone:* (6227) 747474 (office).

HOPPER, Dennis; American actor, author, photographer and film director; b. 17 May 1936, Dodge City, Kan.; m. 1st Brooke Hayward; one d.; m. 2nd Doria Halprin; one d.; m. 3rd Katherine La Nasa 1989; one s.; m. 4th Victoria Duffy 1996; one d.; ed public schools in San Diego; numerous TV appearances include Loretta Young Show; has held several public exhbns of photographs; Commdr, Légion d'honneur 2008; named Best New Dir, Cannes 1969, Best Film Awards at Venice 1971, Cannes 1980, Lifetime Achievement Award, CineVegas Film Festival 2003, Method Fest 2004. *Film appearances include:* Rebel Without a Cause 1955, I Died a Thousand Times 1955, Giant 1956, Story of Mankind, Gunfight at the O.K. Corral 1957, Night Tide, Key Witness, From Hell to Texas 1958, Glory Stompers 1959, The Trip 1961, The Sons of Katie Elder 1962, Hang 'Em High 1966, Cool Hand Luke 1967, True Grit 1968, The American Dreamer 1971, Kid Blue 1973, The Sky is Falling 1975, James Dean: The First American Teenager 1976, Mad Dog Morgan 1976, Tracks 1979, American Friend 1978, Apocalypse Now 1979, Wild Times 1980, King of the Mountain 1981, Human Highway 1981, Rumble Fish 1983, The Osterman Weekend 1984, Black Widow 1986, Blue Velvet 1986, Hoosiers 1986, River's Edge 1987, Blood Red 1989, Flashback 1989, The American Wars 1989, Chattahoochie 1990, Motion and Emotion 1990, Superstar: The Life and Times of Andy Warhol 1990, Hot Spot 1990, True Romance, Boiling Point, Super Mario Bros 1993, Chasers 1994, Speed 1994, Waterworld 1995, Search and Destroy 1995, Basquiat 1996, Carried Away 1996, Star Truckers 1997, Blackout 1997, Tycus 1998, Sources 1999, Lured Innocence 1999, Justice 1999, EdTV 1999, Straight Shooter 1999, Jesus' Son 1999, Venice Project 1999, Bad City Blues 1999, Prophet's Game 1999, Spreading Ground 2000, Luck of the Draw 2000, Held for Ransom 2000, Choke 2000, Ticker 2001, Knockaround Guys 2001, L.A.P.D.: To Protect and Serve 2001, Unspeakable 2002, Leo 2002, The Night We Called It a Day 2003, Keeper 2003, Out of Season 2004, House of 9 2004, Americano 2005, Land of the Dead 2005, The Crow: Wicked Prayer 2005, Mem-o-re 2005, 10th & Wolf 2006, Tainted Love 2006, Sketches of Frank Gehry 2006, Elegy 2007, The Cool School 2007, Hell Ride 2008, Sleepwalking 2008, Palermo Shooting 2008, Swing Vote 2008, An American Carol 2008; actor, writer, Dir Easy Rider 1969, The Last Movie 1971, Paris Trout 1990, The Indian Runner 1991; actor, Dir Out of the Blue 1980; Dir Colors 1988, The Hot Spot 1990, Catchfire 1991, Nails 1991. *Television includes:* 24 (series) 2002, E-Ring (series) 2005–06, Entourage 2007, Crash (series) 2008–09. *Publication:* Out of the Sixties (photographs) 1988. *Address:* c/o ICM, 8942 Wilshire Boulevard, Beverly Hills, CA 90211, USA.

HOPWOOD, Sir David Alan, Kt, MA, PhD, DSc, FRS, FIBiol; British geneticist and academic; *Fellow Emeritus, John Innes Centre;* b. 19 Aug. 1933, Kinver, Staffs.; s. of Herbert Hopwood and Dora Grant; m. 1962 Joyce Lilian Bloom; two s. one d.; ed Purbrook Park County High School, Hants., Lymm Grammar School, Cheshire, St John's Coll., Cambridge; John Stothert Bye-Fellow, Magdalene Coll., Cambridge 1956–58, Research Fellow, St John's Coll. 1958–61, Univ. Demonstrator 1957–61; Lecturer in Genetics, Univ. of Glasgow 1961–68; Prof. of Genetics, Univ. of E Anglia, Norwich 1968–98; Prof. Emer. 1999–; Head of Genetics Dept, John Innes Centre 1968–98, Fellow Emer. 1999–; fmr Pres. Genetical Soc. of GB; Foreign Fellow, Indian Nat. Science Acad.; Pres. Soc. for Gen. Microbiology 2000–03; Hon. Prof., Chinese Acad. of Medical Science, Inst. of Microbiology and Plant Physiology, Chinese Acad. of Sciences, Huazhong Agricultural Univ., Wuhan, China, Jiaotong Univ., Shanghai, Guangxi Univ., Nanning; Hon. mem. Hungarian Acad. of Sciences, Soc. for Gen. Microbiology, Spanish Soc. of Microbiology; Hon. Fellow, UMIST, Magdalene Coll. Cambridge; Dr hc (ETH, Zürich, Univ. of E Anglia, Norwich); Medal for Research in New Bioactive Compounds, Kitasato Inst. (Japan) 1988, Hoechst Award for Research in Antimicrobial Chemotherapy, American Soc. for Microbiology 1988, Chiron Biotech. Award, American Soc. for Microbiology 1992, Mendel Medal, Czech Acad. of Sciences 1995, Gabor Medal, Royal Soc. 1995, Stuart Mudd Prize Int. Union of Microbiological Sciences 2002, Ernst Chain Medal Imperial Coll., London 2003, Andre Lwoff Prize Fed. of European Microbiology Socs 2003. *Publications:* Genetics of Bacterial Diversity (co-ed. with K. F. Chater) 1989, Streptomyces in Nature and Medicine: The Antibiotic Makers 2007; 270 articles and chapters in scientific journals and books. *Leisure interests:* gardening and cooking. *Address:* John Innes Centre, Norwich Research Park, Colney, Norwich, NR4 7UH (office); 244 Unthank Road, Norwich, NR2 2AH, England (home). *Telephone:* (1603) 450000 (office). *Fax:* (1603) 450778 (office). *E-mail:* david.hopwood@bbsrc.ac.uk (office). *Website:* www.jic.ac.uk/profile/david-hopwood.asp (office); www.micron.ac.uk/people%5Chopwood.html (office).

HORBULIN, Volodymyr Pavlovych, DTech; Ukrainian politician and space scientist; b. 17 Jan. 1939, Zaporozhya; ed Dnipropetrovsk State Univ.; with CB Yuzhnoye (Southern Design Bureau), Dnipropetrovsk 1962–77; mem. admin. staff, Cen. Cttee CP of Ukraine 1977–90, Chief of Missile and Aviation Section 1980; Gen. Dir Nat. Space Agency 1992; Sec. Nat. Security Council, Adviser to Pres. on nat. security issues 1994, Sec. Nat. Security and Defence Council 1996–99; Chair. State Comm. for Defence and Industrial Complex 2000–; Leader, Democratic Union Party, Chair. Party Council 2001–; fmr Head Ukraine-NATO Inter-Agency Comm.; mem. Ukrainian Nat. Acad. of Sciences 1997–; Ukrainian Nat. Acad. of Sciences Prize 1988, USSR State Prize 1990; Order of Red Banner of Labour 1976, 1982, First Class Order of Yaroslav the Wise 1997. *Leisure interests:* music, literature, theatre. *Address:* State Commission for Defence and Industrial Complex of Ukraine, Moskovska Str., 45/1, Kiev, 01011, Ukraine (office). *Telephone:* (44) 254-37-91 (office). *Fax:* (44) 254-48-72 (office).

HORECKER, Bernard L., BS, PhD; American biochemist and academic; *Professor Emeritus of Biochemistry, Cornell University;* b. 31 Oct. 1914, Chicago, Ill.; s. of Paul Horecker and Bessie Horecker; m. Frances Goldstein 1936; three d.; ed Univ. of Chicago; Research Assoc., Dept of Chem., Univ. of Chicago 1939–40; Examiner US Civil Service Comm., Washington, DC 1940–41; biochemist, US Public Health Service, NIH Industrial Hygiene Research Lab. 1941–47, Nat. Inst. of Arthritis and Metabolic Diseases 1947–53, Chief, Section on Enzymes and Cellular Biochemistry, NIH Nat. Inst. of Arthritis and Metabolic Diseases 1953–56; Head Lab. of Biochemistry and Metabolism 1956–59; Prof. and Chair. Dept of Microbiology, New York Univ. School of Medicine 1959–63, Dept of Molecular Biology, Albert Einstein Coll. of Medicine 1962–71, Dir Div. of Biological Sciences 1970–72, Assoc. Dean for Scientific Affairs 1971–72; Vice-Chair. Div. of Biological Chem., ACS 1975–76, Chair. 1976–77; mem. Roche Inst. of Molecular Biology 1972–84, Head Lab. of Molecular Enzymology 1977–84; Professorial Lecturer on Enzymes, George Washington Univ. 1950–57; Visiting Prof., Univ. of California 1954, Univ. of Illinois 1957, Univ. of Paraná, Brazil, 1960, 1963, Cornell Univ. 1964, Univ. of Rotterdam 1970; Visiting Investigator, Pasteur Inst. 1957–58, Indian Inst. of Science, Bangalore 1971; Ciba Lecturer, Rutgers Univ. 1962; Phillips Lecturer, Haverford Coll. 1965; Reilly Lecturer, Notre Dame Univ. 1969; Visiting Prof., Albert Einstein Coll. of Medicine 1972–84; Adjunct Prof., Cornell Univ. Medical Coll. 1972–84, Prof. of Biochemistry 1984–89, Prof. Emer. 1989–, Dean Grad. School of Medical Sciences 1984–92; Ed. Biochemical and Biophysical Research Communications 1959–89; Chair. Editorial Cttee Archives of Biochemistry and Biophysics 1968–84; Ed. Current Topics in Cellular Regulation 1969–89; mem. Scientific Advisory Bd, Roche Inst. of Molecular Biology 1967–70, Chair. 1970–72; Dir Academic Press 1968–73; mem. Comm. on Personnel, American Cancer Soc. 1969–73; Medical Scientist Training Program Study Section NIH 1970–72; mem. Scientific Advisory Comm. for Biochemistry and Chemical Carcinogenesis, American Cancer Soc. 1974–78, Council for Research and Clinical Investigation Awards, American Cancer Soc.; Pres. American Soc. of Biological Chem. 1968–69, Harvey Soc. of New York 1970–71; Vice-Chair. Pan American Asscn of Biochemical Socs 1971, Chair. 1972; Fellow, American Acad. of Arts and Sciences; mem. NAS, Indian Nat. Acad. of Science; Corresp. mem. Argentine Acad. of Science; Hon. Prof. Fed. Univ. of Paraná, Brazil 1981–; Hon. mem. Swiss, Japanese, Spanish Socs, Hellenic Biochemical and Biophysical Soc., Greece, Brazilian Acad. Sciences; Hon. DSc (Univ. of Urbino, Italy); Paul Lewis Labs Award in Enzyme Chem. 1952, Fed. Security Agency's Superior Accomplishment Award 1952, ACS Hillebrand Prize 1954, Washington Acad. of Sciences Award in Biological Sciences 1954, Rockefeller Public Service Award 1957, Fulbright Travel Award 1963, Commonwealth Fund Fellow 1967, Merck Award, American Soc. of Biological Chemists 1981, Carl Neuberg Medal, Virchow-Pirquet Med. Soc. 1981. *Publications:* Reflections: The Pentose Phosphate Pathway 2002. *Leisure interests:* gardening, ornithology. *Address:* 16517 Cypress Villa Lane, Fort Myers, FL 33908, USA (home). *Telephone:* (914) 267-5578 (home). *E-mail:* blhorecker@aol.com (home).

HORI, Kosuke; Japanese politician; mem. House of Reps; fmr Chair. LDP Diet Affairs Cttee; Parl. Vice-Minister for Agric., Forestry and Fisheries; fmr Minister for Educ.; Minister of Home Affairs, Chair. Nat. Public Safety Comm. 1999–2000. *Address:* c/o Ministry of Home Affairs, 2-1-1, Kasumigaseki, Chiyoda-ku, Tokyo 100, Japan (office).

HORINOUCHI, Hisao; Japanese politician; mem. House of Reps; fmr Minister of Agric., Forestry and Fisheries; Minister of Posts and Telecommunications 1996–98. *Address:* c/o Ministry of Posts and Telecommunications, 1-3-2, Kasumigaseki, Chiyoda-ku, Tokyo 100, Japan (office).

HORLOCK, Sir John Harold, Kt, ScD, FREng, FRS; British university administrator and engineer; b. 19 April 1928, Edmonton; s. of Harold E. Horlock and Olive M. Horlock; m. Sheila J. Stutely 1953; one s. two d.; ed Latymer School, Edmonton and St John's Coll., Cambridge; design engineer, Rolls-Royce Ltd 1949–51; Demonstrator, Lecturer in Eng, Univ. of Cambridge 1952–58, Prof. of Eng 1967–74; Harrison Prof. of Mech. Eng, Univ. of Liverpool 1958–67; Vice-Chancellor, Univ. of Salford 1974–80, Open Univ. 1981–90; Fellow, Open Univ. 1991–; Treas. and Vice-Pres. Royal Soc. 1992–97; Pro-Chancellor UMIST 1995–2001; Pres. Asscn for Science Educ. 1999; Hon. Fellow UMIST, St John's Coll. Cambridge, Royal Aeronautical Soc. 2003; Hon. DSc (Heriot Watt, Salford, CNAA, East Asia, De Montfort, Cranfield); Hon. DEng (Liverpool); Hon. DUniv (Open Univ.); IMechE Hawksley Gold Medal, ASME R. T. Sawyer Award 1997, ICE Ewing Medal 2001, Isabe Achievement Award 2003. *Publications:* Axial Flow Compressors 1958, Axial Flow Turbines 1967, Actuator Disc Theory 1978, Thermodynamics and Gas Dynamics of I.C. Engines (ed.) Vol. I 1982, Vol. II 1986, Cogeneration: Combined Heat and Power 1987, Combined Power Plants 1992, Advanced Gas Turbine Cycles 2003. *Leisure interests:* music, sport. *Address:* 2 The Avenue, Ampthill, Bedford, MK45 2NR, England (home). *Telephone:* (1525) 841307.

HÖRMANDER, Lars Valter, PhD; Swedish mathematician and academic; *Professor Emeritus, Centre for Mathematical Sciences, Lund University;* b. 24 Jan. 1931, Mjällby, Blekinge; ed Gymnasium, Lund and Lund Univ.; visited various univs in USA; fmr Prof., Stockholm Univ.; worked at Inst. for Advanced Study, Princeton, NJ and at Stanford Univ., Calif.; Prof., Centre for Math. Sciences, Lund Univ. 1968–95, Prof. Emer. 1996–; Vice-Pres. Int. Math. Union 1987–90; Fields Medal 1962, Wolf Prize 1988, Steele Prize for Mathematical Exposition 2006. *Publications:* Prospects in Mathematics

(Annals of Mathematics Studies) 1971, Seminar on Singularities of Solutions of Linear Partial Differential Equations (Annals of Mathematics Studies) 1979, The Analysis of Linear Partial Differential Operators I–IV 1983–85, Marcel Riesz Collected Papers 1988, An Introduction to Complex Analysis in Several Variables 1966, 1973, 1990, Partial Differential Equations and Mathematical Physics: The Danish-Swedish Analysis Seminar (Progress in Nonlinear Differential Equations and Their Applications, Vol. 21) 1995, Lectures on Nonlinear Hyperbolic Differential Equations 1997. *Address:* Lund University, Matematiska Institutionen, Room 511, Box 118, 221 00 Lund, Sweden (office). *Telephone:* (46) 222 85 56 (office). *E-mail:* Lars.Hormander@math.lu.se (office). *Website:* www.maths.lth.se (office).

HORN, Sir Gabriel, Kt, KB, BSc, MA, MD, ScD, FRS; British neuroscientist and academic; *Professor Emeritus and Senior Research Scientist, Sub-Department of Animal Behaviour, Department of Zoology, University of Cambridge;* b. 9 Dec. 1927, Birmingham; s. of the late Abraham Horn and Anne Horn; m. 1st Ann L. D. Soper 1952 (divorced 1979); two s. two d.; m. 2nd Priscilla Barrett 1980; ed Handsworth Tech. School and Coll., Birmingham Coll. of Tech., Univ. of Birmingham; served in RAF 1947–49; house appointments in Birmingham hosps 1955–56; demonstrator in Anatomy, Univ. of Cambridge 1956–62, Lecturer 1962–72, Reader in Neurobiology 1972–74, Fellow, King's Coll. 1962–74, 1978–92, 1999–; Prof. and Head Dept of Anatomy, Univ. of Bristol 1974–77; Prof. of Zoology, Univ. of Cambridge 1978–95, Head of Dept 1979–94, Prof. Emer. and Sr. Research Scientist Sub-Dept of Animal Behaviour 1995–; Master Sidney Sussex Coll., Cambridge 1992–99, Fellow Emer. 1999–; Deputy Vice-Chancellor, Univ. of Cambridge 1994–98; Chair. Animal Sciences and Psychology Research Cttee Biotech. and Biochemistry Research Council 1994–96; Chair. Univ. of Cambridge Govt Policy Programme 1998–; Sr Research Fellow in Neurophysiology, Montreal Neurological Inst., McGill Univ. 1957–58; Leverhulme Research Fellow Laboratoire de Neurophysiologie Cellulaire, France 1970–71; visiting professorships and lectureships Canada, Hong Kong, USA, UK and Uganda 1963–90; Chair. Cttee on Biology of Spongiform Encephalopathies (BSE) 1991–94, Cttee on Origins of BSE 2001, working group on Brain Sciences, Addiction and Drugs 2005–; mem. Biological Sciences Cttee, Science Research Council 1973–75, Research Cttee Mental Health Foundation 1973–78; Dir Co. of Biologists 1980–93; mem. Agricultural and Food Research Council 1991–94; Leverhulme Emer. Fellowship 2002–04; Foreign mem. Georgian Acad. of Sciences 1996; Hon. mem. Anatomical Soc. 1997, European Brain and Behaviour Soc. 2004; Hon. Fellow, Royal Coll. of Physicians 2007; Hon. DSc (Birmingham) 1999, (Bristol) 2003, (Beritashvili Inst. of Physiology, Georgian Acad. of Sciences) 2004; Kenneth Craik Award 1962, Royal Medal of Royal Soc. 2001. *Publications:* Short-Term Changes in Neural Activity and Behaviour (co-ed. with R. A. Hinde) 1970, Memory, Imprinting and the Brain 1985, Behavioural and Neural Aspects of Learning and Memory (co-ed. with J. R. Krebs) 1991; papers in scientific journals, mainly on neuroscience topics. *Leisure interests:* walking, cycling, music, wine. *Address:* Sub-Department of Animal Behaviour, University of Cambridge, Madingley, Cambridge, CB23 8AA, England (office). *Telephone:* (1223) 741813 (office); (1223) 338815 (home). *Fax:* (1223) 741802 (office); (1223) 330869 (home). *E-mail:* gh105@cam.ac.uk (office). *Website:* www.zoo.cam.ac.uk/zoostaff/horn.htm (office); www.zoo.cam.ac.uk/zoostaff/madingley/member_pages/ghorn.htm (office).

HORN, Gyula, DEcon; Hungarian politician and economist; *Member of Parliament;* b. 5 July 1932, Budapest; s. of Géza Horn and Anna Horn (née Csörnyei); m. Anna Király; one s. one d.; ed Rostov Coll. of Econs (USSR) and Political Acad. of Hungarian Socialist Workers' Party; staff mem., Ministry of Finance 1954–59; Desk Officer, Ministry of Foreign Affairs 1959–61, Perm. Sec. 1985–89, Minister for Foreign Affairs 1989–90; Embassy Sec., Sofia 1961–63, Belgrade 1963–69; staff mem. to Head of Int. Dept, Hungarian Socialist Workers' Party 1969–85; mem. of Parl. 1990–; Chair. Foreign Affairs Standing Cttee of Parl. 1990–93; Prime Minister of Repub. of Hungary 1994–98; Founding mem. of Hungarian Socialist Party 1989, Pres. 1990–98; mem. European Honorary Senate 1991–; Regional Vice-Pres., Socialist Int. (New York) 1996–2003; Grand Decoration of Honour in Gold with Sash for Services to the Repub. of Austria 2005; Gold Medal, Stresemann Soc. (Mainz, Germany) 1990, Karl Prize for work towards European unification (Aachen, Germany) 1991; Golden Order of Labour, Grand Cross of Germany, Sharp Blade Award, Solingen 1991, Humanitarian Award of German Freemasons 1992, Gold Europe Award 1994, Kassel Glass of Understanding Award 1995, Prize of Understanding Between Peoples 2003, Courage Award, Bad Iburg 2005, Freedom Award, Memmingen 2005. *Publications:* Yugoslavia: Our Neighbour, Social and Political Changes in Albania Since World War II, Development of East–West Relations in the 70s, Pikes (autobiog.) 1991, Those Were the '90s... 1999; co-author of over 100 articles published in tech. journals. *Leisure interests:* tennis, swimming, jogging. *Address:* Hungarian Parliament, 1055 Budapest, Kossuth Lajos tér 1/3, Hungary (office). *Telephone:* (1) 441-4059 (office). *Fax:* (1) 441-4888 (office). *E-mail:* gyhorn@mszp.hu (office).

HORN, Heinz, Dr rer. pol; German business executive; b. 17 Sept. 1930, Duisberg; s. of Heinrich and Elisabeth (née Eckernkamp) Horn; m.; two s. two d.; ed Univ. of Frankfurt, Univ. of Munster; fmrly with Mannesmann for six years; Financial Dir, Erschweiler Bergweks-Verein 1965–68, mem. Bd and later Pres. 1974–83; mem. Bd, Krupp 1968–72; Deputy Chair. of the Bd, Ruhrkohle AG, Essen 1983–85, Chair. Man. Bd 1985–95; Chair. Supervisory Bd Rütgerswerke AG, EBV 1989–95.

HORN, Paul M., PhD; American electronics industry executive and physicist; *Senior Vice-President, IBM Corporation;* b. NY; ed Clarkson Coll. of Tech., Univ. of Rochester; trained as solid state physicist; Asst, then Assoc. Prof., Dept of Physics, James Franck Inst., Univ. of Chicago 1973–79; joined IBM Corpn 1979, various positions include Vice-Pres. and Lab. Dir of Almaden Research Centre, San Jose, Sr Vice-Pres. and Dir of Research 1996–; fmr Assoc. Ed. Physical Review Letters; mem. Council on Competitiveness, Govt Univ. Industry Research Roundtable, Univ. of Calif., Berkeley Industrial Advisory Bd, Gallaudet Univ. Advisory Bd; Fellow American Physical Soc., Grad. Fellow Nat. Science Foundation; mem. Bd of Trustees, Clarkson Univ. 1998–, NY Hall of Science, Cttee for Econ. Devt; Alfred P. Sloan Research Fellowship 1974–78, Bertram Eugene Warren Award, American Crystallographic Asscn 1988, Distinguished Leadership Award, NY Hall of Science 2000, Hutchison Medal, Univ. of Rochester 2002, Pake Prize, American Physical Soc. 2002, Golden Kt Award, Clarkson Univ. 2004. *Publications:* over 85 scientific and technical papers. *Address:* Research Headquarters, IBM Research, POB 218, Yorktown Heights, NY 10598, USA (office). *Website:* www.research.ibm.com (office).

HORNBY, Andrew (Andy) H., MBA; British banking executive; b. 1967; m. Cathy Hornby; ed Univ. of Oxford, Harvard Univ.; worked for Boston Consulting Group for three years; held sr line man. posts with Blue Circle; worked at ASDA plc 1996–99, held posts of Dir of Corp. Devt, Retail Man. Dir, Man. Dir of George, ASDA's clothing business; Chief Exec. Halifax Retail 1999–2001, Chief Exec. Retail Div., HBOS plc (after merger between Halifax and Bank of Scotland) 2001–05, COO Retail Div. 2005–06, Chief Exec. HBOS plc 2006–08 (resgnd); Dir (non-exec.) GUS plc, Home Retail Group. *Address:* c/o HBOS plc, PO Box 5, The Mound, Edinburgh, EH1 1YZ, Scotland.

HORNBY, Nick; British journalist and novelist; b. 1957, London, England; William Hill Sports Book of the Year Award 1992, Writers' Guild Best Fiction Book Award 1995, American Acad. of Arts and Letters E. M. Forster Award 1999, WHSmith Fiction Award 2002, London Award 2003. *Publications:* Contemporary American Fiction (essays) 1992, Fever Pitch (memoir) 1992, (screenplay) 1997, My Favourite Year: A Collection of New Football Writing (ed.) 1993, High Fidelity (novel) 1995, Speaking With the Angel (ed.) 2000, About a Boy (novel) 2000, How to be Good (novel) 2001, 31 Songs (non-fiction) 2003, A Long Way Down 2005, The Complete Polysyllabic Spree (collected columns) 2006, Slam (juvenile fiction) 2007; contrib. to Sunday Times, TLS, Literary Review, New York Times, New Yorker, the Believer. *Address:* United Agents, 12–26 Lexington Street, London, W1F 0LE, England (office). *Telephone:* (20) 3214-0800 (office). *Fax:* (20) 3214-0801 (office). *E-mail:* info@unitedagents.co.uk (office). *Website:* unitedagents.co.uk (office).

HORNBY, Sir Simon Michael, Kt; British business executive; b. 29 Dec. 1934; s. of the late Michael Hornby and Nicolette Ward; m. Sheran Cazalet 1968; ed Eton Coll., New Coll. Oxford and Harvard Business School; entered W.H. Smith & Son 1958, Dir 1965; Dir W. H. Smith & Son (Holdings) 1974–1994, Group Chief Exec. 1978–82; Chair. W.H. Smith Group PLC 1982–94; Dir Pearson PLC 1978–97, Lloyds Bank 1988–99; Chair. Lloyds Abbey Life 1992–97; Chair. Nat. Book League 1978–80 (Deputy Chair. 1976–78), Pres. Book Trust 1990–96, Chelsea Soc. 1994–2000; Chair. Design Council 1986–92, Asscn for Business Sponsorship of the Arts 1988–97, Nat. Literacy Trust 1993–2001; mem. Council, Royal Horticultural Soc. 1992–2001 (Pres. 1994–2001); Trustee British Museum 1978–88; Hon. DUniv (Stirling) 1992; Hon. DLitt (Hull) 1994; Hon. LLD (Reading) 1996. *Leisure interests:* gardening, reading, cooking. *Address:* The Ham, Wantage, Oxon., OX12 9JA, England (home). *Telephone:* (1235) 770222 (home). *Fax:* (1235) 768763 (home).

HORNE, Marilyn; American singer (mezzo-soprano); b. 16 Jan. 1934, Bradford, PA; d. of Bentz and Berneice Horne; m. 1st Henry Lewis (divorced); one d.; ed Univ. of Southern California with William Vennard; debut as Hata in The Bartered Bride, Guild Opera Co. 1954; performed with several German opera cos in Europe 1956; has since appeared at Covent Garden, London, San Francisco Opera, Chicago Lyric Opera, La Scala, Milan, Metropolitan Opera, New York; repertoire includes Eboli in Don Carlo, Marie in Wozzeck, Adalgisa in Norma, Jane Seymour in Anna Bolena, Amneris in Aida, Carmen, Rosina in Il Barbiere di Siviglia, Fides in Le Prophète, Mignon, Isabella in L'Italiana in Algeri, Romeo in I Capuletti ed i Montecchi, Tancredi in Tancredi, Orlando in Orlando Furioso, Malcolm in La Donna del Lago, Calbo in Maometto II; retd from singing 1999, with galas in New York and San Francisco 1998; f. Marilyn Horne Foundation to coach and encourage young singers 1993; numerous hon. doctorates, including Hon. DMus (Univ. of Pittsburgh) 2005; Nat. Medal of Arts 1992, Kennedy Center Honor 1995, Musical American Musician of the Year 1995, Classic FM Gramophone Award for Lifetime Achievement 2005, Opera News Award 2008, Nat. Endowment for the Arts Opera Award 2009. *Publication:* My Life (autobiog., with Jane Scovell), The Song Continues (autobiog., with Jane Scovell) 2005. *Leisure interests:* needlepoint, swimming, reading, sightseeing. *Address:* The Marilyn Horne Foundation, Inc., 25 West 57th Street, Suite 603, New York, NY 10107, USA (office). *Telephone:* (212) 582-2000 (office). *Fax:* (212) 582-6934 (office). *E-mail:* mhf@marilynhornefdn.org (office). *Website:* www.marilynhornefdn.org (office).

HORNER, James; American film music composer; b. 14 Aug. 1953, Los Angeles, Calif.; ed Royal Coll. of Music, London, Univ. of S Carolina, Univ. of Calif. at Los Angeles. *Film scores include:* The Lady in Red, Battle Beyond the Stars, Humanoids from the Deep, Deadly Blessing, The Hand, Wolfen, The Pursuit of D.B. Cooper, 48 Hours, Star Trek II: The Wrath of Khan, Something Wicked This Way Comes, Krull, Brainstorm, Testament, Gorky Park, The Dresser, Uncommon Valor, The Stone Boy, Star Trek III: The Search for Spock, Heaven Help Us, Cocoon, Volunteers, Journey of Natty Gann, Commando, Aliens, Where the River Runs Black, The Name of the Rose, An American Tail (Grammy Award for song Somewhere Out There), P.K. and the Kid, Project X, Batteries Not Included, Willow, Red Heat, Vibes, Cocoon: The Return, The Land Before Time, Field of Dreams, Honey I Shrunk the Kids, Dad, Glory (Grammy Award for instrumental composition), I Love You to Death, Another 48 Hours, Once Around, My Heroes Have Always Been Cowboys, Class Action, The Rocketeer, An American Tail: Fievel Goes West,

Thunderheart, Patriot Games, Unlawful Entry, Sneakers, Swing Kids, A Far Off Place, Jack the Bear, Once Upon a Forest, Searching for Bobby Fischer, The Man Without a Face, Bopha!, The Pelican Brief, Clear and Present Danger, Legend of the Fall, Braveheart, Casper, Apollo 13, Jumanji, Courage Under Fire, Ransom, To Gillian on Her 37th Birthday, Titanic (Acad. Award, Grammy Award), Mighty Joe Young, The Mask of Zorro, Deep Impact, Perfect Storm, A Beautiful Mind, The Chumscrubber 2005, House of Sand and Fog, Troy, The Forgotten, All the King's Men 2006, The Boy in the Striped Pyjamas 2008. *Address:* c/o Gorfaine Schwartz Agency, 13245 Riverside Drive, Suite 450, Sherman Oaks, CA 91423, USA.

HORNHUES, Karl-Heinz, Dr rer. pol; German politician; *Chairman of German Delegation to Assembly, Western European Union;* b. 10 June 1939, Stadtlohn; m. Ellen Buss 1965; two s.; ed Univ. of Münster; adviser, Catholic Adult Educ. Center, Ludwig-Windthorst-Hause, Holthausen 1966–71, Dir 1970–71; Educ. and Teaching Dir Hofmann-La Roche AG, Grenzbach 1971; Assoc. Prof. of Social Econs and Political Science 1974, Prof. 1977; mem. Bundestag 1972–; Deputy Chair. of CDU/CSU Parl. Party in Bundestag in charge of foreign policy, defence policy and European affairs 1989–94; Chair. Foreign Affairs Cttee 1994–98; Chair. German Del., Ass. of WEU 2000–; Chair. German African Foundation; mem. Ass., Council of Europe; Kommendeurkreuz 1999. *Address:* Friedrichstr. 83, 10117 Berlin (office); Pius-str. 19, 49134 Wallenhorst, Germany. *Telephone:* (30) 22794348. *Fax:* (30) 22796888 (office).

HÖRNLUND, Börje; Swedish politician; b. 17 June 1935, Nordmaling, Västerbotten; Regional Forestry Man. Forest Owners' Asscn Västerbotten 1963–67, Inspector of Forests; mem. Exec. Cttee Centre Party Youth League 1963, Centre Party Nat. Bd 1977–; Municipal Councillor Skellefteå and mem. Västerbotten Co. Council 1966; mem. Bd Swedish Fed. of Co. Councils 1972–, Chair. 1977–80; MP 1976–; Minister of Labour 1991–94; fmr Chair. Official Cttee on Health and Medical Care, mem. Regional Econ. Cttee; mem. Bd of Govs Bank of Sweden. *Address:* c/o Centre parteit Bergsgt 7B, PO Box 22107, Stockholm 104 22, Sweden.

HORNSBY, Claude (Chip) A. S.; American business executive; *Group Chief Executive, Wolseley PLC;* m. Lynn Hornsby, three c.; ed Virginia Polytechnic and State Univ.; joined Ferguson Enterprises Inc. as man. trainee, worked with Ferguson for 28 years, Pres. and CEO 2001–05; mem. Bd of Dirs Wolseley PLC 2001–, Group Chief Exec. 2006–; Dir (non-exec.) Virginia Co. Bank; mem. Visitors Bd Christopher Newport Univ. 2001–; mem. Nat. Asscn of Wholesalers, Southern Wholesalers Asscn, American Supply Asscn, Virginia Tech. Pamplin Advisory Council. *Address:* Wolseley PLC, Parkview 1220, Arlington Business Park, Theale, West Berks., RG7 46A, England (office). *Telephone:* (118) 929-8700 (office). *Fax:* (118) 929-8701 (office). *E-mail:* info@wolseley.com (office). *Website:* www.wolseley.com (office).

HOROI, Rex Stephen, BEd, MA; Solomon Islands diplomatist and academic; *Executive Director, Foundation for the Peoples of the South Pacific International;* b. 8 Sept. 1952, Makira; m. Kate Watson; three s. one d.; ed Univ. of South Pacific, Univ. of Papua New Guinea, Univ. of Sydney, Australia, Univ. of London and Huddersfield Tech. Educ. Centre, UK; teacher, St Joseph Catholic Secondary School 1978–79, Deputy Prin. 1983–84; consultant, Univ. of Hawaii 1979; Perm. Rep. to UN 1992–2001; Amb. to USA and High Commr to Canada 1992–2000; Exec. Dir Foundation for the Peoples of the South Pacific Int. 2000–. *Publications:* Peace Corps Language Handbook (co-author); handbooks on grammar, communications and culture; articles and papers. *Address:* Foundation for the Peoples of the South Pacific International, Victoria Corner, Level 2, Office 2, GPO Box 18006, Suva, Fiji (office). *Telephone:* 3312250 (office). *Fax:* 3312298 (office). *E-mail:* admin@fspi.org.fj (office). *Website:* www.fspi.org.fj (office).

HOROVITZ, Joseph, MA, BMus, FRCM; British composer and conductor; *Professor of Composition, Royal College of Music;* b. 26 May 1926, Vienna; ed New Coll., Oxford and Royal Coll. of Music (RCM), London and studied with Nadia Boulanger, Paris; resident in UK 1938–; Music Dir Bristol Old Vic 1949–51; Conductor Festival Gardens Orchestra and open-air ballet, London 1951; Co-Conductor Ballets Russes, English season 1951–52; Assoc. Dir Intimate Opera Co. 1952–63; Asst Conductor Glyndebourne Opera 1956; Prof. of Composition, RCM 1961–; mem. Council, Composers' Guild 1970–, Council, Performing Right Soc. 1969–96; Pres. Int. Council of Composers and Lyricists of Int. Fed. of Socs of Authors and Composers 1981–89; Cross of Honour for Science and Art, First Class (Austria) 2007; Commonwealth Medal Composition 1959, Leverhulme Music Research Award 1961, Gold Order of Merit of Vienna 1996, Nino Rota Prize (Italy) 2002, Cobbett Medal for services to chamber music, Worshipful Co. of Musicians 2008. *Compositions:* 12 ballets including Alice in Wonderland, Les Femmes d'Alger, Miss Carter Wore Pink, Concerto for Dancers; opera: Ninotchka; one-act operas: The Dumb Wife, Gentlemen's Island; concertos for violin, trumpet, jazz-piano (harpsichord), oboe, clarinet, bassoon, percussion, tuba; other orchestral works include Horizon Overture, Jubilee Serenade, Sinfonietta for Light Orchestra, Fantasia on a Theme of Couperin, Toy Symphony; brass band music includes a euphonium concerto, Sinfonietta, Ballet for Band, Concertino Classico, Theme and Co-operation, The Dong with a Luminous Nose; music for wind band includes a divertimento Bacchus on Blue Ridge, Windharp, Fête Galante, Commedia dell'Arte, Dance Suite and Ad Astra in commemoration of the Battle of Britain; choral music includes Samson, Captain Noah and his Floating Zoo (Ivor Novello Award for Best British Music for Children 1976), Summer Sunday, Endymion, Sing Unto the Lord a New Song, three choral songs from As You Like It; vocal music includes Lady Macbeth (mezzo-soprano and piano) and works for the King's Singers (e.g. Romance); chamber music includes five string quartets, oboe sonatina, oboe quartet and clarinet sonatina; contribs to Hoffnung Concerts: Metamorphoses on a Bed-Time

Theme and Horrortorio for chorus, orchestra and soloists; numerous scores for theatre productions, films and TV series (Ivor Novello Award for Best TV Theme of 1978 for the series Lillie); productions of Son et Lumière include St Paul's Cathedral, Canterbury Cathedral, Brighton Pavilion, English Harbour, Antigua, Bodiam Castle, Chartwell. *Address:* Royal College of Music, Prince Consort Road, London, SW7 2BS, England (office). *Website:* www.rcm.ac.uk (office).

HOROWITZ, Irving Louis, BSS, MA, PhD; American academic, writer, editor and publisher; *Hannah Arendt Distinguished Professor of Social and Political Theory, Rutgers University;* b. 25 Sept. 1929, New York, NY; m. 1st Ruth Lenore Horowitz 1950 (divorced 1964); two s.; m. 2nd Mary Curtis Horowitz 1979; ed City Coll., CUNY, Columbia Univ. and Univ. of Buenos Aires; Assoc. Prof. Univ. of Buenos Aires 1955–58; Postgraduate Fellow Brandeis Univ. 1958–59; Asst Prof. Bard Coll. 1960; Chair Dept of Sociology, Hobart and William Smith Colls 1960–63; Ed.-in-Chief Transaction Soc. 1962–94; Assoc. Prof. to Prof. of Sociology, Washington Univ., St Louis 1963–69; Pres. Transaction Books 1966–94; Chair Dept of Sociology, Livingston Coll., Rutgers Univ. 1969–73, Prof. of Sociology Grad. Faculty, Rutgers Univ. 1969–, Hannah Arendt Distinguished Prof. of Social and Political Theory 1979–; Bacardi Chair of Cuban Studies Miami Univ., 1992–93; Editorial Chair. and Pres. Emer. Transaction/USA and Transaction/UK; Bd Chair. ILH Foundation for Social Policy 1998–2004; mem. American Acad. of Arts and Sciences, American Asscn of Univ. Profs, American Political Science Asscn (APSA), Authors' Guild, Council on Foreign Relations, Int. Soc. of Political Psychology (founder), Nat. Asscn of Scholars; APSA Harold D. Lasswell Award, Festschrift 1994, Nat. Jewish Book Award in Biography/Autobiography, Inter-Univ. Armed Forces Soc. Lifetime Service Award, Laissez-Faire Soc. Civil Liberties Award. *Publications:* Idea of War and Peace in Contemporary Philosophy 1957, Philosophy, Science and the Sociology of Knowledge 1960, Radicalism and the Revolt Against Reason: The Social Theories of Georges Sorel 1962, The War Game: Studies of the New Civilian Militarists 1963, Professing Sociology: The Life Cycle of a Social Science 1963, Revolution in Brazil: Politics and Society in a Developing Nation 1964, The Rise and Fall of Project Camelot 1967, Three Worlds of Development: The Theory and Practice of International Stratification 1967, Latin American Radicalism: A Documentary Report on Nationalist and Left Movements 1969, Sociological Self-Images 1969, The Knowledge Factory: Masses in Latin America 1970, Cuban Communism 1970, Foundations of Political Sociology 1972, Social Science and Public Policy in the United States 1975, Ideology and Utopia in the United States 1977, Dialogues on American Politics 1979, Taking Lives: Genocide and State Power 1979, Beyond Empire and Revolution 1982, C. Wright Mills: An American Utopian 1983, Winners and Losers 1985, Communicating Ideas 1987, Daydreams and Nightmares: Reflections of a Harlem Childhood 1990, The Decomposition of Sociology 1993, Behemoth: Main Currents in the History and Theory of Political Sociology 1999, Searching for the Soul of American Foreign Policy: The Cuban Embargo and the National Interest 2000, Tributes: An Informal History of Social Science in the Twentieth Century 2004; contribs to professional journals. *Address:* Transaction Publishers, Rutgers University, Piscataway, NJ 08854 (office); 1247 State Road, Route 206, Blanwenberg Road-Rocky Hill Intersection, Princeton, NJ 08540, USA (home). *Telephone:* (732) 445-2280 (office); (609) 921-1479 (home). *Fax:* (732) 445-3138 (office); (609) 921-7225 (home). *E-mail:* ihorowtiz@transactionpub.com (office). *Website:* www.transactionpub.com (office).

HORROCKS, Jane; British actress; b. 18 Jan. 1964, Lancs.; d. of John Horrocks and Barbara Horrocks; pnr Nick Vivian; one s. one d.; ed Royal Acad. of Dramatic Art. *Stage appearances include:* The Rise and Fall of Little Voice, Cabaret, Absurd Person Singular 2007. *Television:* Road 1987, Absolutely Fabulous 1992–2004, Bad Girl 1992, Suffer the Little Children (Royal TV Soc. Award) 1994, Never Mind the Horrocks 1996, Who Do You Think You Are 2005, The Street 2006, The Amazing Mrs Pritchard 2006. *Films:* The Dressmaker 1989, The Witches 1989, Life is Sweet (Best Supporting Actress LA Critics Award) 1991, Little Voice 1998, Chicken Run 2002, Corpse Bride 2005, Garfield 2 (voice) 2006, Brothers of the Head 2006. *Address:* c/o ICM, Oxford House, 76 Oxford Street, London, W1D 1BS, England (office). *Telephone:* (20) 7636-6565 (office).

HORROCKS, Paul John; British editor; *Editor, Manchester Evening News;* b. 19 Dec. 1953; s. of Joe Horrocks and Eunice Horrocks; m. Linda Jean Walton 1976; two s. one d. one step-d.; ed Bolton School; reporter, Daily Mail 1974–75; reporter, Manchester Evening News 1975–80, Crime Corresp. 1980–87, News Ed. 1987–91, Asst Ed. 1991–95, Deputy Ed. 1995–97, Ed. 1997–; Pres. UK Soc. of Editors; mem. Organizing Cttee, Commonwealth Games, Manchester 2002; Vice-Pres. Community Foundation for Greater Manchester; Patron Francis House Children's Hospice; mem. Bd New Children's Hosp.; Trustee Tatton Trust. *Address:* Manchester Evening News, 1 Scott Place, Manchester, M3 3RN, England (office). *Telephone:* (161) 2112465 (office). *Fax:* (161) 2112030 (office). *Website:* www.manchesteronline.co.uk (office).

HORTEFEUX, Brice, LenD; French politician; *Minister Labour, Social Relations, the Family, Solidarity and Urban Affairs;* b. 11 May 1958, Neuilly-sur-Seine; s. of Claude Hortefeux and Marie-Claude Hortefeux (née Schuhler); m. Valérie Dazzan 2000; three c.; ed Inst. of Political Studies, Paris, Univ. Paris X–Nanterre; Territorial Admin. 1986–94; mem. Regional Council, Auvergne 1992–2007; Chief of Cabinet of Minister for Budget and Communications 1993–95; Govt Spokesperson 1993–95; fmr mem. Political Cttee Rassemblement pour la République 1998–2002; currently mem. Union pour un Mouvement Populaire (UMP), mem. Political Cttee 2002–; MEP 1999–2005; Adviser to Minister of Interior and Security, later to Minister of Finance, Economy and Industry 2002–04; Minister-Del. for Territorial

Collectivities 2005–07; Minister of Immigration, Integration, Nat. Identity and Co-Devt 2007–09, of Labour, Social Relations, the Family, Solidarity and Urban Affairs 2009–. *Publication:* Jardin à la française, plaidoyer pour une république de proximité 2003. *Leisure interest:* tennis. *Address:* Ministry of Labour, Social Relations, the Family, Solidarity and Urban Affairs, 127 rue de Grenelle, 75007 Paris, France (office). *Telephone:* 1-44-38-38-38 (office). *Fax:* 1-44-38-20-20 (office). *Website:* www.travail.gouv.fr (office).

HORTON, Donald R.; American real estate executive; *Chairman, D. R. Horton Inc.;* m. Marty Horton; two s.; ed Univ. of Cen. Ark., Univ. of Okla; took over father's Marshall, Ark. real estate business 1971; f. D. R. Horton Inc., Fort Worth, Tex. 1978, Pres. 1991–98, Chair. 1991–; Distinguished Alumni Award, Univ. of Cen. Ark. 2004. *Address:* D.R. Horton, Inc., 301 Commerce Street, Suite 500, Fort Worth, TX 76102, USA (office). *Telephone:* (817) 390-8200 (office). *Fax:* (817) 436-6717 (office). *Website:* www.drhorton.com (office).

HORTON, Frank Elba, MS, PhD; American academic and university administrator; *President Emeritus, University of Toledo;* b. 19 Aug. 1939, Chicago; s. of Elba E. Horton and Mae P. Prohaska; m. Nancy Yocom 1960; four d.; ed Western Illinois and Northwestern Univs; mem. Faculty, Univ. of Iowa 1966–75, Prof. of Geography 1966–75, Dir Inst. of Urban and Regional Research 1968–72, Dean of Advanced Studies 1972–75; Vice-Pres. for Acad. Affairs and Research, Southern Illinois Univ. 1975–80; Chancellor Univ. of Wisconsin, Milwaukee 1980–85; Pres. Univ. of Oklahoma 1985–88; Pres. and Prof. of Geography and Higher Educ., Univ. of Toledo 1988–98, Pres. Emer. 1999–; Prin. Horton and Assocs 1999–; Trustee Toledo Symphony Orchestra 1989–, Toledo Hosp. 1989–, Public Broadcasting Foundation, NW Ohio 1989–93, Soc. Bank and Trust 1990–; Vice-Chair. Toledo Chamber of Commerce 1991–93; mem. Bd Dirs Inter-State Bakeries, GAC Corpn; Interim Pres. Southern Illinois Univ. 2001; Interim Dean School of Biological Sciences, Univ. of Missouri 2002–03, Exec. Consultant to the Provost, Univ. of Missouri, Kansas City 2003–04. *Publications:* Geographic Perspectives on Urban Systems with Integrated Readings (with B. J. L. Berry) 1970, Urban Environmental Management Planning for Pollution Control 1974. *Leisure interests:* hiking, skiing, golf, jogging. *Address:* Horton & Associates, 13171 East Saddlerock Road, Tucson, AZ 85749 (office); 288 River Ranch Circle, Bayfield, CO 81122, USA (home). *Telephone:* (970) 884-2102 (office); (970) 884-2102 (home). *E-mail:* fehorton@attglobal.net (office).

HORTON, Richard C., FRCP; British physician; *Editor, The Lancet;* Visting Prof., London School of Hygiene and Tropical Medicine; Ed., publisher, The Lancet; bd mem. Council of Science Editors 1994–. *Publications:* non-fiction: Preventing Coronary Artery Disease (with Martin Kendall) 1997, How to Publish in Biomedicine 1997, Second Opinion: Doctors and Diseases 2003, Health Wars: On the Global Front Lines of Modern Medicine 2003, MMR: Science and Fiction 2004; contrib. to New York Review of Books, London Review of Books, The Lancet, journals. *Address:* The Lancet, 32 Jamestown Road, London, NW1 7BY, England (office). *Telephone:* (20) 7424-4910 (office). *Fax:* (20) 7424-4911 (office). *E-mail:* richard.horton@lancet.com (office). *Website:* www.lancet.com (office).

HORTON, Sir Robert Baynes, Kt, BSc, SM, FRSA, CBIM; British business executive; *Chairman, Chubb PLC;* b. 18 Aug. 1939, London; s. of the late William H. Horton and of Dorothy Joan Baynes; m. Sally Doreen Wells 1962; one s. one d.; ed King's School, Canterbury, St Andrew's Univ., Massachusetts Inst. of Technology; with British Petroleum Ltd (now BP PLC) 1957–86, 1988–92, Gen. Man. BP Tankers 1975–76, Gen. Man. Corporate Planning 1976–79, Man. Dir and CEO BP Chemicals 1979–83, BP Bd 1983–86, Deputy Chair. 1989–90, Chair. and CEO 1990–92; Chair., CEO Standard Oil Co. 1986–88; Vice-Chair. British Railways Bd 1992–94; Chair. Railtrack PLC 1993–99, Chubb PLC 2002–; Dir (non-exec.) ICL PLC 1982–84, Pilkington Bros. 1985–86, Emerson Electric 1987–, Partner Re 1993–2003, Premier Farnell PLC 1995–, Six Continents; Pres. Chemical Industries Asscn 1982–84, BESO 1993–97; Vice-Chair. BIM 1984–90, Business in the Arts (ABSA) 1988–98; Gov. King's School, Canterbury 1984–; Chair. Sloan School (MIT) Visiting Cttee; mem. MIT Corpn 1987–97; Chancellor, Kent Univ. 1990–95; Chair. Bodleian and Oxford Univ. Libraries Devt 1999–; Chair. Tate Gallery Foundation 1988–92; Hon. FCGI; Hon. FIChemE; Hon. FCIMgT; Hon. LLD (Dundee) 1988; Hon. DCL (Kent) 1990, (Aberdeen) 1992; Hon. DSc (Cranfield Inst. of Tech.) 1992, (Kingston) 1993; Hon. DBA (N London) 1991; Hon. DUniv (Open Univ.) 1993; Corporate Leadership Award, MIT 1987. *Leisure interests:* music, country activities, reading. *Address:* Chubb PLC, Cleveland House, 33 King Street, London, SW1Y 6RJ (office); Stoke Abbas, South Stoke, Oxon., RG8 0JT, England (home). *Telephone:* (20) 7766-4800. *E-mail:* info@chubbplc .com (office). *Website:* www.chubbplc.com (office).

HORVITZ, H. Robert, MA, PhD; American biologist and academic; *David H. Koch Professor of Biology, Massachusetts Institute of Technology;* b. 8 May 1947; ed Harvard Univ.; Asst Prof. of Biology, MIT 1978, Assoc. Prof. 1981, Prof. 1986–, now David H. Koch Prof.; Investigator, Howard Hughes Medical Inst. 1988–; also currently Neurobiologist and Geneticist, Mass Gen. Hosp., Boston; mem. NAS 1991–, Inst. of Medicine; Fellow, American Acad. of Arts and Sciences, American Acad. of Microbiology; numerous awards and honours including Spencer Award in Neurobiology 1986, US Steel Foundation Award in Molecular Biology 1988, Hans Sigrist Award 1994, Gairdner Foundation Int. Award 1999, Segerfalk Award 2000, Bristol-Myers Squibb Award for Distinguished Achievement in Neuroscience 2001, Genetics Soc. of America Award 2001, Nobel Prize in Physiology or Medicine (jtly) 2002. *Address:* Department of Biology, Massachusetts Institute of Technology, 77 Massachusetts Avenue, Cambridge, MA 02139, USA (office). *Telephone:* (617) 253-3162 (office). *Fax:* (617) 253-8126 (office). *E-mail:* horvitz@mit.edu (office). *Website:* web.mit.edu/biology/www/facultyareas/facresearch/horvitz.shtml (office); web .mit.edu/horvitz/www (office); www.hhmi.org/research/investigators/ horvitz_bio.html.

HOSEIN, Mainul, BA; Bangladeshi barrister, newspaper executive and politician; *Chairman, Editorial Board, The Daily Ittefaq;* b. Jan. 1940, Pirojpur (then Barisal) Dist; s. of the late Tafazzal Hossain; ed Dhaka Univ., studied law in London, UK; joined Middle Temple, London; called to Bar 1965; represented The Daily Ittefaq (f. by his father), Ed. 1969–73, Chair. Editorial Bd 1973–; mem. Commonwealth Press Union, London; practised law at Dhaka High Court 1965; mem. official del. to China on occasion of Nat. Day 1969; attended CPU Conf., Zimbabwe 1988; MP for village constituency at Bhandaria, Pirojpur (Barisal) 1973–75, resgnd in protest over changes to electoral system; Pres. Bangladesh Sangbadpatra Parishad (asscn of newspaper owners); mem. Press Council; Deputy Head Press Comm. 1984; Pres. Bangladesh Supreme Court Bar Asscn 2000–01; Hon. Adviser to Caretaker Govt, in charge of Ministry of Law, Justice and Parl. Affairs, of Parl. Secr., of Ministry of Housing and Public Works, of Ministry of Land and of Ministry of Information 2007–08. *Address:* The Daily Ittefaq, 1 Ramkrishna Mission Road, Dhaka, Bangladesh (office). *Telephone:* (2) 7122660 (office). *Fax:* (2) 7122651 (office). *E-mail:* rahat.khan@ittefaq.com (office). *Website:* www .ittefaq.com (office).

HOSKING, Geoffrey Alan, PhD, FBA, FRHistS; British historian and academic; *Professor Emeritus of Russian History, School of Slavonic and East European Studies, University College London;* b. 28 April 1942, Troon, Ayrshire, Scotland; s. of Stuart Hosking and Jean Smillie; m. Anne Lloyd Hirst 1970; two d.; ed Maidstone Grammar School, Moscow State Univ., Kings Coll., Cambridge, St Antony's Coll., Oxford; Lecturer in Govt, Univ. of Essex 1966–71, Lecturer in History 1972–76, Sr Lecturer and Reader in History 1976–84; Prof. of Russian History, School of Slavonic and East European Studies, Univ. Coll. London 1984–99, 2004–07, Prof. Emer. of Russian History 2007–, Leverhulme Research Prof. 1999–2004, Deputy Dir School of Slavonic and East European Studies 1996–98; Visiting Prof. in Political Science, Univ. of Wisconsin-Madison, USA 1971–72, Slavisches Institut, Univ. of Cologne, Germany 1980–81; mem. Inst. for Advanced Studies, Princeton, USA 2006–07; mem. Booker Prize Jury for Russian Fiction 1993; Dr hc (Russian Acad. of Sciences) 2000; LA Times History Book Prize 1986, BBC Reith Lecturer 1988, US Ind. Publrs History Book Prize 2001. *Publications:* The Russian Constitutional Experiment 1973, Beyond Socialist Realism 1980, The First Socialist Society: A History of the Soviet Union from Within 1985, The Awakening of the Soviet Union 1990, The Road to Post-Communism: Independent Political Movements in the Soviet Union 1985–91 (with J. Aves and P. Duncan) 1992, Russia: People and Empire (1552–1917) 1997, Myths and Nationhood (co-ed. with George Schöpflin) 1997, Russian Nationalism Past and Present (co-ed. with Robert Service) 1998, Reinterpreting Russia (co-ed. with Robert Service) 1999, Russia and the Russians: A History from Rus to Russian Federation 2001, Rulers and Victims: The Russians in the Soviet Union 2006. *Leisure interests:* music, walking, chess. *Address:* School of Slavonic and East European Studies, University College London, Gower Street, London, WC1E 6BT (office); 18 Camden Mews, London, NW1 9DA, England (home). *Telephone:* (20) 7267-5543 (office). *E-mail:* geoffreyhosking@ mac.com (office).

HOSKINS, Robert (Bob) William; British actor; b. 26 Oct. 1942; s. of Robert Hoskins and Elsie Lillian Hoskins; m. 1st Jane Livesey 1970; one s. one d.; m. 2nd Linda Banwell 1984; one s. one d.; ed Stroud Green School; several stage roles at Nat. Theatre; numerous awards including Best Actor Award, Cannes Film Festival, Variety Club Best Actor Award 1997, Richard Harris Award for Outstanding Contribution by an Actor to British Film, British Ind. Film Awards 2004. *Films include:* National Health 1973, Royal Flash 1974, Zulu Dawn 1980, The Long Good Friday 1980, The Wall 1982, The Honorary Consul 1983, Lassiter 1984, The Cotton Club 1984, Brazil 1985, The Woman Who Married Clark Gable 1985, Sweet Liberty 1985, Mona Lisa 1986 (New York Critics Award, Golden Globe Award, Best Actor Award, Cannes Festival), A Prayer for the Dying 1987, The Lonely Passion of Judith Hearne 1987, Who Framed Roger Rabbit? 1987, The Raggedy Rawney (dir, acted in and wrote) 1988, Mermaids 1989, Shattered 1990, Heart Condition 1990, The Projectionist 1990, The Favour, The Watch and the Very Big Fish 1990, Hook 1991, The Inner Circle 1992, Super Mario Brothers 1992, Nixon 1995, The Rainbow (also dir) 1996, Michael 1996, Cousin Bette 1996, Twenty-four-seven 1998, The Secret Agent 1998, Felicia's Journey 1999, Parting Shots 1999, Enemy at the Gates 2001, Last Orders 2001, Where Eskimos Live 2002, Maid in Manhattan 2002, Sleeping Dictionary 2003, Den of Lions 2003, Vanity Fair 2004, Beyond the Sea 2004, Unleashed 2005, Son of the Mask 2005, Mrs Henderson Presents 2005, Stay 2005, Paris, je t'aime 2006, Garfield 2 (voice) 2006, Hollywoodland 2006, Sparkle 2007, Ruby Blue 2007, Outlaw 2007, Doomsday 2008, Go Go Tales 2007. *Television appearances include:* Omnibus – It Must be Something in the Water 1971, Villains 1972, Thick as Thieves 1972, Schmoedipus 1974, Shoulder to Shoulder 1974, Pennies from Heaven 1975, Peninsula 1975, Sheppey 1980, Flickers 1980, Othello 1981, The Beggar's Opera 1983, Mussolini and I 1984, The Changeling 1993, World War Two: Then There Were Giants 1993, David Copperfield 1999, The Lost World (film) 2001, The Wind in the Willows 2006, The Englishman's Boy 2007, Pinocchio 2008. *Stage:* Old Wicked Songs 1996. *Leisure interests:* photography, gardening, playgoing. *Address:* c/o Fred Specktor, Creative Artists Agency, 9830 Wilshire Blvd, Beverly Hills, CA 90212-1825, USA.

HOSKYNS, Sir John Austin Hungerford Leigh, Kt; British business executive; b. 23 Aug. 1927, Farnborough, Hants.; s. of the late Lt-Col Chandos Hoskyns and Joyce Hoskyns; m. Miranda Jane Marie Mott 1956; two s. one d.; ed Winchester Coll.; Capt. British Army 1945–57; with IBM UK Ltd 1957–64; Chair. and Man. Dir Hoskyns Group Ltd 1964–75; Part-time Policy Adviser to

Opposition 1975–77, Full-time Adviser to Rt Hon. Margaret Thatcher (q.v.) and Shadow Cabinet 1977–79, Head, Prime Minister's Policy Unit 1979–82; Dir-Gen. Inst. of Dirs 1984–89; Chair. Burton Group 1990–98 (Dir 1990–98), EMAP 1994–98 (Dir 1993–98), Arcadia Group PLC 1998; Dir ICL PLC 1982–84, AGB Research PLC 1983–88, Clerical Medical and Gen. Life Assurance Soc. 1983–98, McKechnie Brothers PLC 1983–93, Ferranti PLC 1986–94; Hon. DSc (Salford) 1986; Dr hc (Essex) 1987. *Publication:* Just In Time 2000. *Leisure interests:* opera, shooting. *Address:* c/o Child & Co., 1 Fleet Street, London, EC4Y 1BD, England.

HOSNI, Naguib, DenD; Egyptian professor of criminal law, politician and university administrator; *Professor, University of Cairo;* b. 5 Nov. 1928, Cairo; m. Fawzia Ali 1957; two s. one d.; ed Cairo Univ. and Univ. of Paris, France; Asst Prof. of Criminal Law, Cairo Univ. 1959, Prof. 1964–, Vice-Dean Faculty of Law 1970–73, Dean 1977–83, Pres. 1987–89; Visiting Prof., Arab Univ. of Beirut, Lebanon, 1967–70, Univ. of UAE 1974–76, Univ. of Paris (12) 1991; Pres. Bd of Legal Studies 1987–, African Univs 1989–; Dir Centre for the Prevention of Crime and Treatment of Offenders, Cairo Univ. 1993–; mem. Int. Soc. of Penal Law, Int. Soc. of Criminology, Int. Soc. of Social Defence; Senator 1989–; State Prize 1961, 1967, Medal of Science 1960, 1979, Medal of the Republic 1976, State Award 1991, Palmes Académiques (France) 1979. *Publications include:* International Criminal Law 1960, Abnormal Criminals 1967, Criminal Participation 1969, Criminal Intent 1988, Treatment of Mentally Ill Offenders 1992, The Constitution and Criminal Law 1992. *Leisure interests:* reading, music. *Address:* 30 Aden Street, Mohandessin, Giza, Egypt. *Telephone:* 3490555; 3490857.

HOSODA, Hiroyuki, LLB; Japanese politician; b. 5 April 1944, Matsue City, Shimane Pref.; ed Faculty of Jurisprudence, Tokyo Univ.; joined Ministry of Int. Trade and Industry (MITI) 1967, Dir Price Policy Div., Industrial Policy Bureau 1985–86; Dir Washington Office, Japan Nat. Oil Corpn, USA 1983–85; elected mem. House of Reps for Shimane Constituency 1990–; Parl. Vice-Minister for Econ. Planning 1994–97; Dir Transport Div., Liberal Democratic Party (LDP) 1997–98, Dir Foreign Affairs Div. 1998–99, Deputy Sec.-Gen. LDP 2001, Dir-Gen. Election Bureau 2001–02; Parl. Sec. for Int. Trade and Industry 1999–2001, currently Exec. Deputy Sec.-Gen.; Minister of State for Okinawa and Northern Territories Affairs, for Science and Tech. Policy, and for Information Tech. Policy 2002–03; Deputy Chief Cabinet Sec. 2003; Minister of State for Gender Equality and Chief Cabinet Sec. 2004–05. *Address:* Liberal-Democratic Party–LDP (Jiyu-Minshuto), 1-11-23, Nagatacho, Chiyoda-ku, Tokyo 100–8910, Japan (office). *Telephone:* (3) 3581-6211 (office). *E-mail:* koho@ldp.jimin.or.jp (office). *Website:* www.jimin.jp (office).

HOSOI, Susumu; Japanese business executive; *Representative Director and President, Isuzu Motors Ltd;* joined Isuzu Motors Ltd 1973, has led operations in USA and Asia, has overseen divs including Corp. Planning, Finance, and Supplier Relations, Dir 2002, Vice-Pres. 2006, Exec. Vice-Pres. 2006–07, Pres. March 2007–. *Address:* Isuzu Motors Ltd, 26-1 Minami 6-chome, Shinagawa-ku, Tokyo 140-8722, Japan (office). *Telephone:* (3) 5471-1141 (office). *Fax:* (3) 5471-1043 (office). *E-mail:* info@isuzu.com (office). *Website:* www.isuzu.com (office).

HOSOKAWA, Morihiro; Japanese politician; b. 14 Jan. 1938, Tokyo; m. Kayoko Hosokawa; one s. two d.; ed Sophia Univ., Tokyo; reporter, The Daily Asahi Shimbun; mem. House of Councillors 1971–83; Gov. of Kumamoto 1983–91; Founder, Chair. Japan New Party 1992; mem. House of Reps 1993; Prime Minister 1993–94; fmr mem. LDP; retd from politics 1998; Chair. Eisei-Bunko Foundation. *Leisure interests:* skiing, golf.

HOSPITAL, Janette Turner, (Alex Juniper), MA; Australian writer and academic; *Professor and Distinguished Writer-in-Residence, University of South Carolina;* b. 12 Nov. 1942, Melbourne; d. of Adrian Charles Turner and Elsie Turner; m. Clifford Hospital 1965; one s. one d.; ed Univ. of Queensland, and Queen's Univ., Canada; high school teacher, Queensland 1963–66; librarian, Harvard Univ. 1967–71; Lecturer in English, St Lawrence Coll., Kingston, Ont., in maximum and medium-security fed. penitentiaries for men 1971–82; professional writer 1982–; Writer-in-Residence and lecturer Writing Program, MIT 1985–86, 1987, 1989, Writer-in-Residence Univ. of Ottawa, Canada 1987, Univ. of Sydney, Australia 1989, Queen's Univ. at Herstmonceux Castle, UK 1994; Adjunct Prof. of English, La Trobe Univ., Melbourne 1990–93; Visiting Fellow and Writer-in-Residence Univ. of E Anglia, UK 1996; O'Connor Chair. in Literature, Colgate Univ., Hamilton, NY 1999; Dickey Prof. and Distinguished Writer-in-Residence, Univ. of S Carolina 1999–; Dr hc Griffith Univ. (Queensland) 1995; Hon. DLitt (Univ. of Queensland) 2003; several awards for novels and short stories; Gold Medal, Nat. Magazine Awards (Canada) 1991 (for travel writing), First Prize, Magazine Fiction, Foundation for the Advancement of Canadian Letters 1982. *Publications:* The Ivory Swing (Seal First Novel Award) 1982, The Tiger in the Tiger Pit 1983, Borderline 1985, Charades 1988, The Last Magician 1992, Oyster 1996, Due Preparations for the Plague 2003; short story collections: Dislocations (Fellowship of Australian Writers Fiction Award 1988) 1986, Isobars 1990, Collected Stories 1995, North of Nowhere, South of Loss 2003; as Alex Juniper: A Very Proper Death 1991; numerous articles. *Leisure interests:* hiking, mountain climbing, music, gardening. *Address:* Department of English, University of South Carolina, Welsh Humanities Office Building, Room 504, Columbia, SC 29208, USA (office); c/o Barbara Mobbs, PO Box 126, Edgeclif, Sydney, NSW 2027, Australia; c/o Mic Cheetham, 11–12 Dover Street, London, W1X 3PH, England. *Telephone:* (803) 777-2186 (office). *E-mail:* hospitjt@mailbox.sc.edu (office). *Website:* www.cla.sc.edu/ENGL (office).

HOSS, Selim al-, MBA, PhD; Lebanese fmr politician and professor of economics; b. 20 Dec. 1929; s. of Ahmad El-Hoss and Wadad Hoss; m. Leila Hoss (died 1990); one d.; ed American Univ. of Beirut, Indiana Univ., USA; teacher, later Prof. of Business, American Univ. of Beirut 1955–69; Financial Adviser, Kuwait Fund for Arab Econ. Devt, Kuwait 1964–66; Pres. Banking Supervision Comm. 1967–73; Chair. of Bd and Gen. Man. Nat. Bank for Industrial Devt 1973–76; Prime Minister 1976–80, remaining as Prime Minister in caretaker capacity July–Oct. 1980, Minister of the Econ. and Trade and Information 1976–79, of Industry and Petroleum 1976–77, of Labour, Fine Arts and Educ. 1984–85 (resgnd); Adviser to Arab Monetary Fund, Abu Dhabi, UAE 1983; Chair. of Bd Banque Arabe et Int. d'Investissement, Paris 1982–85; Head, Arab Dinar Study Group, Arab Monetary Fund 1984–85; Minister of Educ. 1985–87; Head, Arab Experts Team commissioned by Arab League 1986–87; Prime Minister 1987–90, also Minister of Foreign and Expatriate Affairs; elected Deputy to Parl. 1992–2000; Pres. of Council of Ministers (Prime Minister of Lebanon) 1976–80, 1987–90, 1998–2000; mem. Bd of Trustees, American Univ. of Beirut 1991–; mem. Consultative Council, Int. Bank for the Middle East and North Africa 1992–. *Publications:* The Development of Lebanon's Financial Markets 1974, Lebanon: Agony and Peace 1982 and 13 books in Arabic; numerous articles on economics and politics. *Leisure interests:* reading. *Address:* Aisha Bakkar, Beirut, Lebanon. *Telephone:* 736000. *Fax:* 354929.

HOSSAIN, Kemaluddin, LLB; Bangladeshi judge; b. 31 March 1923, Calcutta, India; ed Ballygunge Govt High School, Calcutta, St Xavier's Coll. and Calcutta Univ. Law Coll.; advocate, High Court, Dacca 1950–69; Sr Advocate Supreme Court, Pakistan 1966–69; Deputy Attorney-Gen., Pakistan 1968–69; Judge, High Court, Dacca 1969–72; Judge, High Court, Bangladesh 1972–75, Appellate Div. 1975–78; Chief Justice, Bangladesh 1978–82; Negotiator, Indus Water Treaty 1960; part-time Lecturer in Law, City Law Coll., Dacca 1956–68; Chair. Law Cttee 1978; attended several int. law confs including Commonwealth Chief Justices Conf., Canberra May 1980. *Address:* c/o Chief Justice's House, 19 Hare Road, Dhaka, Bangladesh. *Telephone:* 243585 (office); 404849 (home).

HOSSAIN, Shah Moazzem, MA; Bangladeshi politician; b. 10 Jan. 1939, Munsigonj Dist; m.; one s. one d.; ed Dhaka Univ.; Gen. Sec. East Pakistan Students League 1959–60, Pres. 1960–63; Chair. the All-Party Action Cttee 1962; political prisoner for several years between 1953 and 1978; Chief Whip, Bangladesh Parliament 1972–73; co-f. Democratic League 1976, Gen. Sec. 1977–83; Minister of Land Admin. and Land Revenue 1973–75, in charge of Ministry of Labour and Manpower 1984–85, of Information 1985–86, of Local Govt, Rural Devt and Co-operatives 1986–88, of Labour and Manpower 1988–90, of Food 1990; Deputy Prime Minister 1987–90. *Publication:* Nitta Keragarey 1976.

HOSSEIN, Robert; French actor and director; *Artistic Director, Théâtre Marigny;* b. 30 Dec. 1927, Paris; s. of Amin Hossein and Anna Mincovschi; m. 1st Marina de Poliakoff 1955 (divorced); two s.; m. 2nd Caroline Eliacheff 1962 (divorced); one s.; m. 3rd Candice Patou 1976; one s.; stage actor, dir and playwright, film dir and producer, scriptwriter and actor; Chair. and Man. Dir Sinfonia Films 1963–; founder and Dir Théâtre Populaire de Reims and of Théâtre-Ecole de Reims 1971; Artistic Dir Théâtre de Paris-Théâtre Moderne 1975–, Théâtre Marigny 2000–; Commdr, Ordre nat. du Mérite, Officier, Légion d'honneur, Commdr des Arts et des Lettres; Prix Orange 1963, Médaille de Vermeil de la Ville de Paris, Molière d'honneur 1995, Prix Grand siècle Laurent Perrir 2000. *Plays include:* La neige était sale, Haute surveillance, Les voyous (writer), La P. respectueuse, Huis-Clos, Vous qui nous jugez (writer), Les six hommes en question (co-writer with Frédéric Dard and producer), La moitié du plaisir (producer), Crime et châtiment, Les bas-fonds, Roméo et Juliette, Pour qui sonne le glas, La maison des otages, Hernani (produced for the Comédie Française) 1974, La maison de Bernada (produced at the Odéon) 1975, Le cuirassé Potemkine (dir at Palais des Sports) 1975, Des souris et des hommes, Shéhérazade (ballet) 1975, Procès de Jeanne d'Arc (producer) 1976, Pas d'orchidées pour Miss Blandish (producer and actor) 1977, Notre-Dame de Paris (producer) 1978, Le cauchemar de Bella Manningham (producer) 1978, Danton et Robespierre (producer) 1979, Lorna et Ted 1981, Un grand avocat 1983, Les brumes de Manchester 1986, Liberty or Death and the Heritage of the French Revolution (Dominique Prize for Best Dir) 1988, Dans la nuit la liberté (producer) 1989, Cyrano de Bergerac (producer) 1990, Jésus était son nom 1991, Les bas-fonds 1992, Je m'appelais Marie-Antoinette 1993, La nuit du crime (producer and actor) 1994, Angélique, Marquise des anges (director and actor) 1995, Ouragan sur le Caine 1997, La Vie en bleu 1997, Surtout ne coulez pas (producer) 1997, De Gaulle, celui qui a dit non (producer) 1999, Jésus, la Résurrection 2000, Coupable ou non coupable 2001, Lumières et ténèbres 2002. *Films include:* Quai des blondes, Du rififi chez les hommes, Crime et châtiment, Toi le venin (script-writer and producer), Le jeu de la vérité (writer), Le goût de la violence (script-writer and producer), Le repos du guerrier, Le vice et la vertu, Les yeux cernés, Angélique marquise des anges, Banco à Bangkok, Le vampire de Düsseldorf, Le tonnerre de Dieu, La seconde vérité, J'ai tué Raspoutine (writer and producer), Indomptable Angélique, Don Juan 1973, Prêtres interdits, Le protecteur, Le faux cul 1975, Les uns et les autres, Le professionnel 1981, Les Misérables (producer) 1982, Un homme nommé Jésus (director) 1983, Jules César 1985, Les brumes de Manchester 1986, Un homme et une femme, vingt ans déjà 1986, Les Enfants du désordre 1989, L'Affaire 1994, la Nuit du Crime 1994, L'Homme au masque de cire 1996, Vénus beauté 1999, Gialloparma 1999, San Antonio 2004. *Television includes:* Les Uns et les autres (miniseries) 1983, Le Juge (miniseries) 2005. *Publications:* La sentinelle aveugle 1978, Nomade sans tribu 1981, En désespoir de cause (memoirs) 1987, La Nostalgie (autobiog.) 2001. *Leisure interest:* skiing. *Address:* Théâtre Marigny, Carré Marigny, 75008 Paris (office); c/o Mme Ghislaine de Wing, 10 rue du Docteur Roux, 75015 Paris, France. *Telephone:* 1-53-96-70-30 (office). *Fax:* 1-53-96-70-31 (office). *E-mail:* ehamel@theatre-marigny.fr (office). *Website:* www.theatremarigny.fr (office).

HOSSEINI, Seyed Safdar, BA, PhD; Iranian politician; b. 1954, Khuzestan; ed Shiraz Univ.; Minister of Labour and Social Affairs 2001–04; Minister of Econ. Affairs and Finance 2004–05.

HOSSEINI, Shamseddin; Iranian politician; *Minister of Economic Affairs and Finance;* fmr Dir-Gen. for Econ. Studies, Ministry of Commerce; fmr Deputy Minister of Welfare and Social Security; Sec., Working Group for Econ. Transformation –2008; Minister of Econ. Affairs and Finance 2008–. *Address:* Ministry of Economic Affairs and Finance, Sour Esrafil Avenue, Nasser Khosrou Street, Tehran 11149-43661, Iran (office). *Telephone:* (21) 22553401 (office). *Fax:* (21) 22581933 (office). *E-mail:* info@mefa.gov.ir (office). *Website:* mefa.gov.ir (office).

HOSTETTER, Amos Barr, Jr, BA, MBA; American media executive; *Chairman, Pilot House Associates, LLC;* b. 12 Jan. 1937, New York City; s. of Amos Barr Hostetter and Leola Hostetter (née Conroy); m.; three c.; ed Amherst Coll., Harvard Univ.; Asst to Vice-Pres. of Finance, American and Foreign Power Co., New York 1958–59; investment analyst, Cambridge (Mass.) Capital Corpn 1961–63; Co-founder and Exec. Vice-Pres. Continental Cablevision Inc., Boston, Mass 1963–80, Pres. and CEO 1980–85, Chair. and CEO (co. renamed MediaOne) 1985–96, CEO MediaOne Inc., Boston 1996–2000, returned as Bd mem.; Chair. AT&T Broadband and Internet Services (BIS) 1999–2003; Chair. Pilot House Assocs LLC 1997–; Founder and mem. Bd of Dirs and Exec. Cttee, Cable-Satellite Public Affairs Network (C-SPAN) 1979– (fmr Chair.); Founding Chair. and mem. Exec. Cttee, Cable in the Classroom; mem. Bd of Dirs Commodities Corpn, Princeton, NJ, Corpn for Public Broadcasting, Washington, DC 1975–79, The Walter Kaitz Foundation 1981–; Corporator, Perkins School for the Blind, Watertown, Mass 1982–; mem. Bd Overseers Museum of Fine Arts, Boston 1987–; mem. Nat. Cable TV Asscn (Dir 1965–75, 1982–, Nat. Chair. 1973–74), Amherst Coll. Soc. of Alumni (Pres. 1982–84, Exec. Comm. 1982–, Chair. 1987–), Int. Radio and TV Soc.; Trustee, various mutual funds, Massachusetts Financial Services 1985–, Children's TV Workshop, New York 1980–, New England Medical Center Hosp., Boston 1981–, Nantucket Conservation Foundation 1986–, Amherst Coll. (Chair. –2005), WGBH-TV (currently Chair.), Colonial Williamsburg Foundation 2005–; named Cablevision Magazine Man of the Year 1972, Nat. Cable TV Asscn Larry Boggs Award 1975, named to Broadcasting magazine's Hall of Fame 1991, Cable Television Public Affairs Asscn Beacon Award 1991, Cable Television Admin and Marketing Soc. 'Grand TAM Award' 1993, Walter Kaitz Foundation Award 1993, Harvard Business School Alumni Achievement Award 1994, Mass Telecommunications Council Hall of Fame 2000. *Address:* Pilot House Assocs LLC, The Pilot House, Lewis Wharf, Boston, MA 02110, USA (office).

HOU, Hsiao-hsien; Taiwanese film director; b. 8 April 1947, Meihsien, Canton Prov.; ed Taipei Nat. Acad. of Arts Film and Drama Dept; worked as an electronic calculator salesman; entered film industry in 1973; asst to several directors from 1974; Chair. Asian Film Soc. *Films include:* Chiu shih liu-liu-te t'a (Cute Girl) 1981, Feng-erh t'i-t'a-ts'ai (Cheerful Wind) 1982, Tsai na ho-pan ch'ing-ts'ao-ch'ing (Green Grass of Home) 1982, Erh-tzu-te ta wan-ou (The Sandwich Man) 1983, Feng-kuei-lai-te jen (The Boys from Fengkuei/All the Youthful Days) 1983, Tung-tung-te chia-ch'i (A Summer at Grandpa's) 1984, T'ung-nien wang-shih (The Time to Live and the Time to Die) 1985, Lien-lien feng-ch'en (Dust in the Wind/Rite of Passage) 1986, Ni-lo-ho nü-erh (Daughter of the Nile) 1987, Pei-ch'ing ch'eng-shih (A City of Sadness) 1989 (winner of Golden Lion at the Venice Film Festival), Three Times 2005, Flight of the Red Balloon 2006.

HOU, Jianguo; Chinese chemist, academic and university administrator; *President, University of Science and Technology;* b. 1960; Prof., School of Science, Univ. of Science and Tech., also currently Univ. Pres.; mem. Chinese Acad. of Sciences 2003–; US Overseas Chinese Physics Asscn Achievement in Asia Award 2002–02 (co-winner), Tan Kah Kee Science Prize in Chem. 2008. *Address:* Office of the President, University of Science and Technology, Hefei 230026, People's Republic of China (office). *Telephone:* (10) 82649026 (office). *Fax:* (10) 82649027 (office). *E-mail:* wlxbcp@aphy.iphy.ac.cn (office). *Website:* www.ustc.edu.cn/en (office).

HOU, Runyu; Chinese orchestral conductor; b. 6 Jan. 1945, Kunming; s. of Hou Zhu and Zhu Bangying; m. Su Jia 1971; one s. one d.; ed Music Middle School of Shanghai Conservatory, Shanghai Conservatory, Musikhochschule, Cologne, Germany and Mozarteum, Salzburg, Austria; started playing piano aged seven, debut, Kunming 1954; Prin. Conductor Shanghai Symphony Orchestra 1990; Headmaster, Xiamen Music School 2002–; debut Carnegie Hall, New York 1990; currently conductor, East China Normal Univ. (ECNU) Orchestra and Chair. Music Dept; Hon. mem. Richard Wagner Asscn, Cologne. *Leisure interests* sport, literature. *Address:* 105 Hunan Road, Shanghai (office); RD. 1601 No. 12 Lane 125, Cao Xi Road, Shanghai, People's Republic of China. *Telephone:* (21) 64690942 (office); (21) 315234747 (home). *E-mail:* rhou@gmx.net (home).

HOU, Yunde, DMSc; Chinese virologist; b. 13 July 1929, Changzhou, Jiangsu Prov.; ed Tongji Univ. Medical Coll., Russian Inst. of Medical Sciences; Fellow Chinese Acad. of Eng; Dir Inst. of Virology, Chinese Acad. of Preventive Medicine 1985–; Dir WHO Virus Research Centre, researches on para-influenza and the structure and function of virus gene; Vice-Pres. Chinese Acad. of Eng 1994–98; Dir Nat. Key Research Lab. for Virogenetic Eng 1998–; now Dir Inst. of Virology, Chinese Acad. of Preventive Medicine; Chair. Bd of Tri-Prime Gene 1998–; Assoc. Chief Ed. Chinese Medical Sciences Journal; 21 prizes including one First Prize and two Second Prizes of Nat. Science and Tech. Advancement Award, He Liang & He Li Medical Prize 1994, China Medical Science Award 1996. *Publications:* nine monographs and over 400 scientific treatises. *Address:* Virology Research Institute, Chinese Academy of Preventative Medical Science, 100 Yingxin Street, Xuanwu District, Beijing 100052, People's Republic of China (office). *Telephone:* (10) 63529224 (office). *Fax:* (10) 63532053 (office). *E-mail:* engach@mail.cae.ac.cn (office).

HOU, Zongbin; Chinese administrator; b. 1929, Nanhe Co., Hebei Prov.; one s. one d.; joined CCP 1946; Vice-Gov., Gansu Prov. 1983–88; Deputy Sec. of Gansu Prov. CP 1986–88; Deputy Sec. Shaanxi Prov. CP 1989–90; Gov. Shaanxi Prov. 1989–90; Sec. Henan Prov. CP 1990–92; a Deputy Sec. Cen. Comm. for Discipline Inspection; Chair. Internal Affairs and Judicial Cttee of 9th NPC 1998–2003; mem. 14th CCP Cen. Cttee 1992–97. *Address:* c/o Standing Committee of National People's Congress, Beijing, People's Republic of China.

HOUBEN, Francine M. J., MSc; Dutch architect, director and professor; *Director of Mecanoo Architects and Professor in Architecture and Aesthetics of Mobility, Delft University of Technology;* b. 2 July 1955, Sittard; m.; two d. one s.; ed Delft Univ. of Tech.; f. pnr Döll-Houben-Steenhuis architecten 1980–84; Dir Mecanoo architecten, Delft 1984–; Prof. in Architecture and Aesthetics of Mobility, Delft Univ. of Tech. 2000–; Visiting Prof. Philadelphia Univ., USA 1990, Univ. of Calgary, Canada 1992, Berlage Inst., Amsterdam 1994, Oxford Univ., UK 1994, Università della Svizzera Italiana, Mendrisio, Switzerland 2000–01, Harvard Univ., USA 2007; Dir/curator First Int. Architecture Biennale Rotterdam 1997–2000; columnist Het Financieele Dagblad 2006–; mem. Bd Netherlands Architecture Inst. 1990–92, Int. Design Cttee (London) 1990–92, Fine Art, Design and Architecture Fund 1990–06, Forum for Urban Renewal 2003–, Int. Film Festival, Rotterdam 2005–; mem. supervisory Bd Kröller Museum, Otterlo 2005–; jury mem. for awards in Netherlands, Turkey, Germany, USA, UK, Canada; appeared in TV documentaries; Hon. FRIBA 2001, Hon. Fellow Royal Architectural Inst. of Canada 2007; numerous awards include Rotterdam-Maaskant Prize for Young Architects 1987, Nieuwe Maas Prize for Housing Hillekop, Rotterdam 1990, Berlagevlag Award for Offices for Gravura Lithographers, The Hague 1993, Auszeichnung Guter Bauten and Hugo Häring Prize Bund Deutscher Architekten for Experimental Housing Int. Gartenbau Ausstellung, Stuttgart, Germany 1993/1994, Jhr Victor de Stuerspenning for Herdenkingsplein housing project, Maastricht 1994, Scholenbouwprijs 1996, 2003, Nat. Staalprijs and Corus Construction Award for the Millennium for Library at Delft Tech. Univ. 1996/2000, Bouwkwaliteitsprijs, Rotterdam 2000, TECU Architecture Award and Dutch Building Prize for Nat. Museum of Heritage, Arnhem 2000/2003, Gezichtsbepalend 3 Culture Award Province of South Holland 2005, Building Quality Award for Montevideo Rotterdam 2006. *Publications include:* Mecanoo architecten (with P. Volland and L. Waaijers) 1998, Maliebaan, een huis om in te werken 2000, Composition, Contrast, Complexity 2001, Mobility – A Room with a View 2002. *Address:* Mecanoo architects, Oude Delft 203, 2611 HD Delft, Netherlands (office). *Telephone:* (15) 2798100 (office). *Fax:* (15) 2798111 (office). *E-mail:* francine.houben@mecanoo.nl (office). *Website:* www.mecanoo.nl.

HOUEIZ, Muhammad Ali al-; Libyan economist and politician; *Deputy Prime Minister;* fmr oil economist, responsible for man. overseas investments; Sec. of Finance, Govt of Libya 2004–06; Deputy Prime Minister 2006–. *Address:* General People's Committee, Tripoli, Libya (office).

HOUELLEBECQ, Michel, DipAgr; French novelist and poet; b. 26 Feb. 1958, Réunion; m. 1st 1980 (divorced); one s.; m. 2nd Marie-Pierre Gauthier 1998; first works (poetry) published in Nouvelle Revue de Paris 1985; Grand Prix Nat. des Lettres Jeune Talent 1998. *Publications include:* Contre le monde, contre la vie 1991, Rester vivant 1991, La poursuite de bonheur (Prix Tristan Tzara) 1992, Extension du domaine à la lutte 1994, Le sens du combat (Prix de Flore) 1996, Interventions, Les Particules élémentaires (Prix Novembre), Renaissance 1999, Lanzarote 2000, Plateforme (Int. Impac Dublin Literary Prize) 2002, La Possibilité d'une île (trans. as The Possibility of An Island) 2005, HP Lovecraft: Against the World, Against Life 2006, Ennemis Publics (with Bernard-Henri Lévy) 2008. *Address:* c/o Editions Fayard, 13 rue du Montparnasse, 75006 Paris, France (office).

HOUGH, Stephen Andrew Gill, MMus, FRNCM, GMus, PPRNCM; British pianist, composer and writer; b. 22 Nov. 1961, Heswall, Cheshire; ed Chetham's School of Music, Royal Northern Coll. of Music (RNCM) and Juilliard School, New York; guest performer with London Symphony, New York Philharmonic, Cleveland, Philadelphia, Los Angeles Philharmonic, Chicago Symphony, Berlin Philharmonic, Philharmonia, Royal Philharmonic and London Philharmonic Orchestras; Visiting Prof., RAM; Int. Chair of Piano, RNCM; regular appearances with other orchestras and as recitalist in USA, Europe, Australia, Far East and at int. music festivals including Salzburg, Edinburgh, BBC Proms; Hon. mem. RAM; Dayas Gold Medal, RNCM, Terence Judd Award 1982, Naumburg Int. Piano Competition 1983, Gramophone Record of the Year 1996, 2002, MacArthur Foundation Fellowship 2001, Jean Gimbel Lane Prize 2007. *Recordings include:* complete Beethoven violin sonatas (with Robert Mann), Hummel piano concertos, recitals of Liszt and Schumann, Brahms concerto Nos 1 and 2, The Piano Album Vols I, II, Britten Music for One and Two Pianos, Scharwenka and Sauer concertos, Grieg, Liszt, Rubinstein cello sonatas (with Steven Isserlis), Brahms violin sonatas (with Robert Mann), York Bowen piano music, Franck piano music, Mompou piano music, Liebermann piano concertos, Mendelssohn piano and orchestral works, Schubert sonatas and New York Variations, Brahms clarinet trio, The New Piano Album, Liszt sonata, Mozart piano and wind quintet, Brahms F minor sonata, Saint-Saëns Complete Music for Piano and Orchestra, English Piano Album, Hummel piano sonatas, Chopin ballades and scherzos, Rachmaninov and Franck cello sonatas (with Steven Isserlis), Rachmaninov piano concertos (with Dallas Symphony and A. Litton) (Classical BRIT Critics' Award 2005, Classic FM Gramophone Editor's Choice Award 2005) 2004, Brahms, Dvořák and Suk 2005, Liszt Années de

Pèlegrinage (Suisse), Brahms cello sonatas with Stephen Isserlis, Children's Cello with Steven Isserlis, Beethoven and Mozart piano and wind quintets with the Berlin Philharmonic Wind Quintet, Stephen Hough's Spanish Album, Tsontakis Man of Sorrows, Brahms piano quintet with the Takacs Quartet. *Compositions:* Transcriptions, Suite R-B and Other Enigmas, Piano Album, songs and choral works 2005, Viola Sonata 2000, Piano Pieces, The Loneliest Wilderness: Elegy for Cello and Orchestra 2005, Mass of Innocence and Experience 2006, Missa Mirabilis 2007, The Bible as Prayer 2007, Un Piccolo Sonatina, Threody for Guitar, Three Grave Songs, Was mit den Tranen Geschieht: trio for piccolo, contrabassoon and piano, Herbstlieder for tenor and piano. *Leisure interests:* reading, writing, painting. *Address:* Harrison Parrott, 5–6 Albion Court, London, W6 0QT, England (office). *Telephone:* (20) 7229-9166 (office). *Fax:* (20) 7221-5042 (office). *E-mail:* info@harrisonparrott.co.uk (office). *Website:* www.harrisonparrott.co.uk (office); www.stephenhough.com.

HOUGHTON, James Richardson, AB, MBA; American business executive; *Chairman, Corning Incorporated;* b. 6 April 1936, Corning, NY; s. of the late Amory Houghton and Laura Richardson Houghton; m. May Kinnicutt 1962; one s. one d.; ed St Paul's School, Concord, NH, Harvard Coll. and Harvard Univ. Business School; worked in investment banking, Goldman, Sachs and Co., New York 1959–61; in production and finance, Corning Glass Works, Danville, Ky and Corning, New York 1962–64; Vice-Pres. and Area Man., Corning Glass Int., Zurich and Brussels 1964–68; Vice-Pres. and Gen. Man. Consumer Products Div., Corning Glass Works (Corning Inc. 1989–), Corning, New York 1968–71, Vice-Chair. of Bd 1971–83, Chair. and CEO 1983–96, 2002–05, Chair. 2005–; Dir Exxon Mobil, Corning Inc., Metropolitan Life Insurance Co.; Trustee Corning Glass Works Foundation, Corning Museum of Glass, Metropolitan Museum of Art, Pierpont Morgan Library; mem. Council on Foreign Relations, The Business Council, Harvard Corpn. *Address:* Corning Inc., One Riverfront Plaza, Corning, NY 14831. *Telephone:* (607) 974-8332 (office). *Fax:* (607) 974-8444 (office). *E-mail:* houghtonjr@corning.com (office). *Website:* www.corning.com (office).

HOUGHTON, Sir John, Kt, CBE, MA, DPhil, FRS; British physicist; b. 30 Dec. 1931, Dyserth, Clwyd; s. of Sidney Houghton and Miriam Houghton (née Yarwood); m. 1st Margaret E. Broughton 1962 (died 1986); one s. one d.; m. 2nd Sheila Thompson 1988; ed Rhyl Grammar School and Jesus Coll., Oxford; Research Fellow, Royal Aircraft Establishment. Farnborough 1954–57; Lecturer in Atmospheric Physics, Univ. of Oxford 1958–62, Reader 1962–76, Prof. 1976–83, Fellow, Jesus Coll. 1960–83, Hon. Fellow 1983–; Dir Appleton, Science and Eng Research Council 1979–83; Chair. Earth Observation Advisory Cttee, ESA 1980–93; Chair. Jt Scientific Cttee, World Climate Research Prog. 1981–83; Dir-Gen. Meteorological Office 1983–90, Chief Exec. 1990–91; mem. Exec. Cttee WMO 1983–91, Vice-Pres. 1987–91; Pres. Royal Meteorological Soc. 1976–78; Chair. (or Co-Chair.) Scientific Assessment Working Group, Intergovernmental Panel on Climate Change 1988–2002, Royal Comm. on Environmental Pollution 1992–98, Jt Scientific and Tech. Cttee, Global Climate Observing System 1992–95; mem. UK Govt Panel on Sustainable Devt 1994–2000; Chair. John Ray Initiative 1997–2007, Pres. 2007–; Hon. Scientist Rutherford Appleton Lab. 1992–, Hadley Centre 2002–; Fellow, Optical Soc. of America; mem. Academia Europaea; Trustee, Shell Foundation 2000–; Hon. FRIBA 2001; Hon. mem. Royal Meteorological Soc., American Meteorological Soc.; Hon. DSc (Univ. of Wales) 1991, (Stirling) 1992, (East Anglia) 1993, (Leeds) 1995, (Heriot-Watt) 1997, (Greenwich) 1997, (Glamorgan) 1998, (Reading) 1999, (Birmingham) 2000, (Gloucestershire) 2001, (Hull) 2002, (Oxford) 2006; Charles Chree Medal and Prize (Inst. of Physics) 1979, jt recipient Rank Prize for opto-electronics 1989, Glazebrook Medal (Inst. of Physics) 1990, Symonds Gold Medal, Royal Meteorological Soc. 1991, Bakerian Lecturer, Royal Soc. 1991, Global 500 Award, UNEP 1994, Gold Medal, Royal Astronomical Soc. 1995, Int. Meteorological Org. Prize 1998, Japan Prize 2006. *Publications:* Infra Red Physics (with S. D. Smith) 1966, The Physics of Atmospheres 1977, Remote Sounding of Atmospheres (with F. W. Taylor and C. D. Rodgers) 1984, Does God Play Dice? 1988, The Search for God: Can Science Help? 1995, Global Warming: The Complete Briefing 1997. *Address:* Hadley Centre, Meteorological Office, Exeter, Devon, EX1 3PB, England.

HOUGHTON, Michael, PhD; American virologist; *Vice-President, Hepatitis C Research, Chiron Corporation;* Vice-Pres. Hepatitis C Research, Chiron Corpn, Emeryville, Calif. 1982–, headed research team that discovered Hepatitis C virus in 1987 and cloned it in 1989; Lasker Award for Clinical Medical Research 2000. *Publications:* numerous articles in scientific journals. *Address:* Chiron Corpn, 4560 Horton Street, Emeryville, CA 94608-2916, USA. *Telephone:* (510) 655-8730 (office). *Fax:* (510) 655-9910 (office). *Website:* www.chiron.com (office).

HOUGRON, Jean (Marcel), LenD; French writer; b. 1 July 1923, Caen; s. of Jean Hougron and Denise Grude; m. 1st Noëlle Desgouille (divorced); two s. two d.; m. 2nd Victoria Sanchez 1974; one s.; ed Faculty of Law, Univ. of Paris; schoolmaster 1943–46; commercial employment in export-import firm, Saigon 1946–47; lorry driver 1947–49; trans. in American Consulate 1950; news ed., Radio France Asie 1951; returned to France to write 1952; bookseller in Nice 1953–54; lived in Spain 1958–60; Grand Prix du Roman, Acad. Française 1953, Prix Populiste 1965, Grand Prix de la Science-Fiction for Le Naguen 1982; Chevalier des Arts et Lettres. *Publications:* Tu récolteras la tempête 1950, Rage blanche 1951, Soleil au ventre 1952, Mort en fraude (film) 1953, La nuit indochinoise 1953, Les portes de l'aventure 1954, Les Asiates 1954, Je reviendrai à Kandara (film) 1955, La terre du barbare 1958, Par qui le scandale 1960, Le signe du chien 1961, Histoire de Georges Guersant 1964, Les humiliés 1965, La gueule pleine de dents 1970, L'homme de proie 1974, L'anti-jeu 1977, Le Naguen 1979, La chambre (novel) 1982, Coup de soleil 1984, Beauté chinoise 1987. *Address:* c/o Editions J'ai hu, 84 rue de Grenelle, 75007 Paris (office); 1 rue des Guillemites, 75004 Paris, France (home).

HOUK, Kendall N., AM, PhD; American chemist and academic; *Professor of Chemistry, University of California at Los Angeles;* b. 27 Feb. 1943, Nashville, Tenn.; ed Harvard Univ.; Instructor, Harvard Extension School 1966–68; Asst Prof., Louisiana State Univ. 1968–72, Assoc. Prof. 1972–75, Prof. 1975–80; Visiting Prof., Princeton Univ. 1974–75; Prof., Univ. of Pittsburgh 1980–85; Prof. of Chem., UCLA 1986–, Chair. 1991–94; Dir NSF Chem. Div. 1988–90; Visiting Lecturer at numerous univs, including Lady Davis Fellow and Visiting Prof., Technion (Israel Inst. of Tech.) 2000; mem. Int. Acad. of Quantum Molecular Science 2003–; Sr Ed. Accounts of Chemical Research; mem. Editorial Advisory Bd of several learned journals including Central European Journal of Chemistry, Chinese Journal of Chemistry, Chemical and Engineering News; Fellow, AAAS 1988–, American Acad. of Arts and Sciences 2002–; Hon. Dr rer. nat (Univ. of Essen) 1999; ACS Akron Section Award 1983, Arthur C. Cope Scholar Award 1988, James Flack Norris Award 1991, Schroedinger Medal 1998, Richard C. Tolman Medal 1999, ACS Award for Computers in Chemical and Pharmaceutical Research 2003. *Address:* Department of Chemistry and Biochemistry, UCLA, 405 Hilgard Avenue, Los Angeles, CA 90095-1569, USA (office). *Telephone:* (310) 206-0515 (office). *Fax:* (310) 206-1843 (office). *E-mail:* houk@chem.ucla.edu (office). *Website:* www.chem.ucla.edu (office).

HOUMADI, Halifa; Comoran politician; Prime Minister of Comoros 1994–95; mem. Rassemblement pour la Démocratie et le Renouveau (RDR). *Address:* c/o Office of the Prime Minister, BP 421, Moroni, Comoros.

HOUNGBÉDJI, Adrien; Benin politician and lawyer; *Leader, Parti du renouveau démocratique;* sentenced to death in absentia March 1975 after alleged involvement in attempted coup; Speaker of Nat. Ass. 1991–96; Prime Minister 1996–98; Leader Parti du renouveau démocratique (PRD). *Address:* Parti du renouveau démocratique, BP 281, Cotonou, Benin (office). *Telephone:* 33-94-88 (office). *Fax:* 33-94-89 (office). *Website:* www.prd-by.net (office).

HOUNGBO, Gilbert Fossoun, Maîtrise en Gestion d'Entreprises, BA, DESS (Diplôme d' Etudes Supérieures Specialisées); Togolese UN official and politician; *Prime Minister;* ed Université de Lomé; worked at Price Waterhouse Canada; mem. UNDP Strategic Man. Team and Dir of Finance and Admin, then Chief of Staff UNDP, New York 2003–05; Asst Sec.-Gen., Asst Admin. of UNDP and Dir of UNDP's Regional Bureau for Africa 2005–08; Prime Minister of Togo 2008–; mem. Canadian Inst. of Chartered Accountants. *Address:* Office of the Prime Minister, Palais de la Primature, BP 1161, Lomé, Togo (office). *Telephone:* 221-15-64 (office). *Fax:* 221-37-53 (office). *Website:* www.gouvernement.tg (office).

HOUNSOU, Djimon; Benin actor and fmr fashion model; b. 24 April 1964, Cotonou. *Films include:* Without You I'm Nothing 1990, Unlawful Entry 1992, Stargate 1994, The Small Hours 1997, Amistad 1997, Ill Gotten Gains 1997, Deep Rising 1998, Gladiator 2000, The Middle Passage Narrator 2000, The Tag 2001, Dead Weight 2002, The Four Feathers 2002, In America (Independent Spirit Award) 2002, Heroes 2002, Biker Boyz 2003, Lara Croft Tomb Raider: The Cradle of Life 2003, Blueberry 2004, Constantine 2005, Beauty Shop 2005, The Island 2005, Blood Diamond 2006, Eragon 2006. *Television includes:* ER (series) 1999, Alias (series) 2003–04.

HOUSE, Karen Jo Elliott, BJ; American publishing executive and journalist; *Senior Fellow, Belfer Center for Science and International Affairs, Kennedy School of Government at Harvard University;* b. (Karen Jo Elliott), 7 Dec. 1947, Matador, Tex.; d. of Ted Elliott and Bailey Elliott; m. 1st Arthur House 1975 (divorced 1983); m. 2nd Peter Kann 1984; one s. three d.; ed Univ. of Texas at Austin and Harvard Univ. Inst. of Politics, Cambridge, Mass; Educ. Reporter Dallas Morning News 1970–71, with Washington bureau 1971–74; Regulatory Corresp. Wall Street Journal 1974–75, Energy and Agric. Corresp. 1975–78, Diplomatic Corresp. 1978–83, Asst Foreign Ed. 1984, Foreign Ed. 1984–89; Vice-Pres. Dow Jones Int. Group 1989–95, Pres. 1995–2006, Vice-Pres. and mem. Exec. Cttee Dow Jones & Co. 2002, Sr Vice-Pres. 2002–06, Publr The Wall Street Journal 2002–06; Sr Fellow, Belfer Center for Science and Int. Affairs, Kennedy School of Govt, Harvard Univ. 2006–; Public Del., US Mission to UN 2008; Dir German-American Council 1988–, Council on Foreign Relations 1987–98, Cttee to Protect Journalists; Trustee Boston Univ.; mem. Bd of Trustees RAND; Fellow, American Acad. of Arts and Sciences; Dr hc (Lafayette Coll., Pa) 1992, (Boston Univ.) 2003; Georgetown Univ. Edward Weintal Award 1980, Nat. Press Club Edwin Hood Award 1982, Univ. of Southern California Distinguished Achievement Award 1983, Pulitzer Prize in Int. Reporting for coverage of Middle East 1984, Overseas Press Club Bob Considine Award 1984, 1988, Pulitzer Prize for International Reporting 1984, Univ. of Texas Distinguished Alumnus Award 1992, ranked by Forbes magazine amongst 100 Most Powerful Women (54th) 2004, (73rd) 2005. *Leisure interest:* tennis. *Address:* Belfer Center, Kennedy School of Government, 79 John F. Kennedy Street, Cambridge, MA 02138, USA (office). *Telephone:* (617) 496-4264 (office); (609) 921-8923 (home). *Fax:* (212) 416-2885 (office); (609) 921 2041 (home). *E-mail:* karenehouse@gmail.com (home). *Website:* www.belfercenter.ksg.harvard.edu (office).

HOUSE, Lynda Mary; Australian film producer; b. 30 April 1949, Tasmania; d. of Graeme House and Patricia House; m. Tony Mahood 1993; mem. Bd Film Vic. 1993–96, Australian Film Finance Corpn 1997–2002. *Films produced include:* 100% Wool 1986, Bachelor Girl 1987, Rikky and Pete 1988, Sweethearts 1990, Death in Brunswick 1991, Proof (Australian Film Inst. Best Film 1991), Muriel's Wedding (Australian Film Inst. Best Film 1994), River Street 1996, The Missing 1999, Pozieres 2000, Secret Bridesmaid's Business 2001, Ned Kelly 2003, Kokoda 2006, Kanyini 2006, September 2007. *Leisure interests:* watching films, reading, gardening. *Address:* 117 Rouse

Street, Port Melbourne, Vic. 3121, Australia. *Telephone:* (3) 9646-4025. *Fax:* (3) 9646-6336.

HOUSER, Sam; British computer games industry executive; *President, Rockstar Games;* s. of Geraldine Moffat; started career as in-house music video dir BMG Entertainment; Head int. product devt BMG Interactive Div. –1998; Co-Founder and Pres. Rockstar Games 1998–. *Address:* Rockstar Games, 622 Broadway, New York, NY 10012, USA (office). *Website:* www.rockstargames .com (office).

HOUSHIARY, Shirazeh, BA; British (b. Iranian) sculptor; b. 15 Jan. 1955, Shiraz, Iran; ed Tehran Univ., Chelsea School of Art and Cardiff Coll. of Art; sculptor at the Lisson Gallery, London; Jr Fellow, Cardiff Coll. of Art 1979–80; Prof., London Inst. 1997–; comms include Art for the World with UNICEF 2000; lives and works in London. *Address:* c/o Lisson Gallery London Ltd, 67 Lisson Street, London, NW1 5DA, England; c/o Lehmann Maupin Gallery, 540 West 26th Street, New York, NY 10001, USA. *Telephone:* (20) 7724-2739 (London); (212) 255-2923 (New York). *Fax:* (20) 7724-7124 (London). *E-mail:* info@lehmannmaupin.com. *Website:* www.lehmannmaupin.com.

HOUSLAY, Miles Douglas, PhD, FRSE, FMedSci, CBiol, FIBiol, FRSA; British biochemist and academic; *Gardiner Professor of Biochemistry, University of Glasgow;* b. 25 June 1950, Wolverhampton; s. of Edwin Douglas Houslay and Georgina Marie Houslay (née Jeffs); m. Rhian Mair Gee 1972; two s. one d.; ed The Grammar School, Brewood, Staffs., Univ. Coll., Cardiff, King's Coll., Cambridge; ICI Postdoctoral Research Fellow, Univ. of Cambridge 1974–76, Research Fellow, Queen's Coll. 1975–76; Lecturer in Biochemistry, UMIST 1976–82, Reader 1982–84; Gardiner Prof. of Biochemistry, Univ. of Glasgow 1984–; Hon. Sr Research Fellow, Calif. Metabolic Research Foundation, La Jolla, USA 1980–91; Deputy Chair. Editorial Bd Biochemical Journal; Ed.-in-Chief, Cellular Signalling; mem. Editorial Bd Progress in Growth Factor Research 1988–93; external assessor, Univ. of Malaysia 1991–; mem. Cttee Biochemical Soc. 1982–86; mem. MRC Cell Bd 1989–94, Chair. MRC Cell Bd Research Grant Cttee A 1990–92, British Heart Foundation Research Grant Panel 1996–98; mem. Scottish Home and Health Dept Research Cttee 1991–94, Wellcome Trust Biochemistry Cell Biology Grant Panel 1996–2000; Selby Fellow, Australian Royal Soc. 1984; Trustee, British Heart Foundation 1996–2000; Colworth Medal, Biochemical Soc. 1985. *Publications:* Dynamics of Biological Membranes and over 400 scientific articles. *Leisure interests:* walking, music, driving. *Address:* Molecular Pharmacology Group, Division of Biochemistry and Molecular Biology, IBLS, Wolfson Link Building, University of Glasgow, Glasgow, G12 8QQ, Scotland (office). *Telephone:* (141) 330-4624 (office). *Fax:* (141) 330-4365 (office). *E-mail:* m.houslay@bio.gla .ac.uk (office).

HOUSTON, Whitney; American singer and actress; b. 9 Aug. 1963, East Orange, NJ; d. of the late John Houston and of Cissy Houston; m. Bobby Brown 1992 (divorced 2007); one d.; trained under direction of mother; mem. Hew Hope Baptist Jr Choir 1974; backing vocalist for Chaka Khan and Lou Rawls 1978; appeared in Cissy Houston night club act; recording debut Hold Me (duet with Teddy Pendergrass) 1984; solo artist 1985–; first US and European tours 1986; Montreux Rock Festival 1987; Nelson Mandela Tribute Concert, Wembley, London 1988; US nat. anthem, Super Bowl XXV, Miami 1991; Speaker, HIV/AIDS rally, London 1991; Hon. HHD (Grambling Univ.); Grammy Award for Best Female Pop Performance 1985, 1987, for Best R & B Vocal Performance 2000; seven American Music Awards; Emmy 1986; Songwriter's Hall of Fame 1990. *Albums:* Whitney Houston 1985, Whitney 1986, I'm Your Baby Tonight 1990, My Love is Your Love 1998, Whitney: The Greatest Hits 2000, Love Whitney 2001, Just Whitney 2002. *Film soundtracks:* The Bodyguard 1992, Waiting to Exhale 1995, The Preacher's Wife 1996. *Singles:* You Give Good Love 1985, Saving All My Love For You 1985, How Will I Know 1986, Greatest Love of All 1986, I Wanna Dance With Somebody 1987, Didn't We Almost Have It All 1987, So Emotional 1987, Where Do Broken Hearts Go 1988, Love Will Save The Day 1988, I'm Your Baby Tonight 1990, All The Man That I Need 1991, Miracle 1991, My Name Is Not Susan 1991, I Will Always Love You 1992, I'm Every Woman 1993, I Have Nothing 1993, Run To You 1993, Queen of the Night 1994, Something In Common (with Bobby Brown) 1994, Exhale (Shoop Shoop) 1995, Count On Me (with CeCe Winans) 1996, Why Does It Hurt So Bad 1996, Step By Step 1997, I Believe In You And Me 1997, When You Believe (with Mariah Carey) 1998, It's Not Right But It's Okay 1999, My Love Is Your Love 1999, I Learned From The Best 1999, If I Told You That (with George Michael) 2000, Could I Have This Kiss Forever (with Enrique Iglesias) 2000, Heartbreak Hotel (with Faith Evans and Kelly Price) 2000, Whatchulookinat 2002, One Of Those Days 2002. *Films:* The Bodyguard 1992, Waiting to Exhale 1995, The Preacher's Wife 1996, Scratch the Surface 1997, Anything for You 2000. *Address:* c/o Nancy Seltzer, Nancy Seltzer Associates, 6220 Del Valle Drive, Los Angeles, CA 90048, USA. *Website:* www.whitneyhouston.com.

HOVE, Andrew C., Jr; American finance executive; *Director, Sovereign Bancorp Inc.;* b. 9 Nov. 1934, Minden, Neb.; s. of the late Andrew C. Hove and Rosalie Vopat; m. Ellen Matzke 1956; one s. two d.; ed Univ. of Nebraska and Univ. of Wisconsin Grad. School of Banking; US Navy 1956–60; Neb. Nat. Guard 1960–63; officer, Minden Exchange Bank & Trust Co. 1960–81, Chair. and CEO 1981–90, Vice-Chair. then Acting Chair. 1990–2001; mem. Bd of Dirs Sovereign Bancorp Inc. 2001–, Great Western Bancorporation, Inc. 2002–, Saline State Bank. *Address:* c/o Board of Directors, Sovereign Bancorp Inc., 1500 Market Street, Philadelphia, PA 19102, USA.

HOVE, Chenjerai, BA; Zimbabwean journalist and writer; b. 9 Feb. 1956, Zvishavane; s. of R. Muza Hove and Jessie Muza Hove; m. Thecla Hove 1978; three s. two d.; ed Gweru Teacher's Coll.; high school teacher 1978–81; Ed. Mambo Press, Gweru 1981; Sr Ed. Zimbabwe Publishing house, Harare 1985; Ed. Cultural Features, Interpress Service 1988; Writer-in-Residence, Univ. of Zimbabwe 1991–94; Visiting Prof. Lewis and Clark Coll., Oregon, USA 1995; full-time writer 1999–; in exile in France 2002–; Democracy and Freedom of Speech in Africa Prize, Berlin 2001. *Publications:* Swimming in Floods of Tears (co-author) 1983, Red Hills of Home 1985, Bones (Zimbabwe Book Publishers Literary Award 1988, Noma Award for Publishing in Africa 1989) 1988, Shebeen Tales 1989, Shadows 1991, Guardians of the Soil 1996, Ancestors 1996, Shebeen Tales: Messages from Harare 1997, Rainbows in the Dust 1997, Palaver Finish (essays) 2003, Blind Moon 2004, The Keys of Ramb 2004. *Leisure interests:* gardening, reading, snooker, table tennis. *Address:* c/o Édition Actes Sud, BP 38, 13633 Arles Cedex, France (office).

HOVERS, Joannes Coenradus Maria, PhD; Dutch business executive; *Chairman of the Board, Océ NV;* b. 29 July 1943, Beek; m. Ineke van der Heijde 1971; three s.; ed Michiel Lyceum, Geleen, Tilburg Univ.; with Océ NV 1967–76, Chair. Bd of Exec. Dirs 1998–; Chair. Man. Bd Teewen Group (bldg materials), later Chair. Man. Bd Synres (synthetic resins) 1976–83; mem. Man. Bd Stork NV 1983–88, Exec. Vice-Pres. Man. Bd 1988–89, CEO Man. Bd 1989–98; Chair. Comm. of Int. Econ. Relations; Supervisory Dir De Nederlandsche Bank NV, Hoechst AG, Koninklijke Grolsch NV, Ericsson Telecommunicatie BV, Randstad Holding NV; mem. Supervisory Bd TIAS Training Inst., Gooi-Noord Regional Hosp.; Asscn of European Man. Publrs Award 1973. *Address:* Océ NV, PO Box 101, 5900 MA Venlo, Netherlands. *Telephone:* (77) 3592205. *Fax:* (77) 3595436.

HOVING, Thomas, PhD; American museum director and cultural administrator; *President, Hoving Associates Inc.;* b. 15 Jan. 1931, New York; s. of Walter Hoving and Mary Osgood Field; m. Nancy Bell 1953; one d.; ed The Buckley School, New York, Eaglebrook School, Deerfield, Mass., Exeter Acad., Exeter NH, The Hotchkiss School, Lakeville, Conn. and Princeton Univ.; Curatorial Asst of Medieval Art and The Cloisters, Metropolitan Museum of Art 1959–60, Asst Curator 1960–63, Assoc. Curator 1963–65, Curator of Medieval Art and The Cloisters 1965; Commr of Parks, New York 1966; Admin. of Recreation and Cultural Affairs, New York 1967; Dir Metropolitan Museum of Art 1966–77; Ed.-in.-Chief Connoisseur Magazine 1981–90; Arts and Entertainment Corresp. ABC News 20/20 1978–84; currently Pres. Hoving Associates Inc. (cultural affairs consulting); Fellowship, Nat. Council of Humanities 1955, Kienbusch and Haring Fellowship 1957; Hon. LLD (Pratt Inst.) 1967; Hon. DFA (New York) 1968; Hon. DHum (Princeton) 1968; Hon. DLitt (Middlebury Coll.) 1968; Distinguished Citizen's Award, Citizen's Budget Cttee 1967, Creative Leadership in Educ. Award, New York Univ. 1975, Woodrow Wilson Award, Princeton 1975. *Publications:* Guide to the Cloisters 1962, Tutankhamun, The Untold Story 1978, Two Worlds of Andrew Wyeth 1978, King of the Confessors 1981, Masterpiece 1986, Discovery 1989, Making the Mummies Dance, Inside the Metropolitan Museum of Art 1992, False Impressions: The Hunt for Big-Time Art Fakes 1996, Andrew Wyeth: Autobiography 1996, Greatest Works of Art of Western Civilization 1997, Art for Dummies 1999, The Art of Dan Namingha 2000. *Leisure interests:* sailing, skiing, bicycling, flying. *Address:* Hoving Associates Inc., 150 East 73rd Street, New York, NY 10021, USA. *Telephone:* (212) 734-1480 (office). *Fax:* (212) 570-0348. *E-mail:* tomhoving@earthlink.net (office).

HOWARD, Alan Mackenzie, CBE; British actor; b. 5 Aug. 1937, London; s. of the late Arthur John Howard and of Jean (Compton Mackenzie) Howard; m. 1st Stephanie Hinchcliffe Davies 1965 (divorced 1976); m. 2nd Sally Beauman 2004; one s.; ed Ardingley Coll.; nat. service with RAF in Germany 1956–58; stage hand, Asst Stage Man., actor, Belgrade Theatre Coventry 1958–60; London West End debut, Duke of York's Theatre in Roots 1959; played in London at Royal Court, Arts, Mermaid, Strand, Phoenix theatres, also outside London 1960–65; with RSC 1966–, Assoc. Artist 1967–; Plays and Players London Theatre Critics Most Promising Actor Award 1969, Best Actor Award 1977; Soc. of West End Theatre Managers Best Actor in a Revival Award 1976, 1978; Evening Standard Drama Award for Best Actor 1978, 1981; Variety Club of Great Britain Best Actor Award 1980. *Plays include:* Twelfth Night, Revenger's Tragedy, As You Like It, The Relapse, King Lear, Troilus and Cressida, Much Ado About Nothing, Bartholomew Fair, Dr. Faustus, Hamlet, Midsummer Night's Dream, Enemies, Man of Mode, The Balcony, The Bewitched, Henry IV Parts 1 and 2, Henry V, Wild Oats, Henry VI Parts 1, 2 and 3, Coriolanus, Antony and Cleopatra, Children of the Sun, Richard II, Richard III, The Forest, Good 1981, 1982–83, Breaking the Silence 1985, The Silver King 1990, Scenes from a Marriage 1990, Pygmalion 1992, Macbeth 1993, La Grande Magia 1995, Rosencrantz and Guildenstern Are Dead 1995, Oedipus Plays 1996, Waiting for Godot 1997, King Lear 1997, Khludov in Flight 1998, The Play About the Baby 1998, Sloper in the Heiress 2000, Lulu 2001, Gates of Gold 2002, Keepers of the Flame 2003, The Hollow Crown, The Hollow Crown 2005. *Films include:* Victim / 1961, The Password is Courage / 1962, The V.I.Ps / 1963, The Americanisation of Emily / 1964, The Heroes of Telemark / 1965, Work is a Four Letter Word / 1968, Royal Flash / 1975, Oxford Blues / 1984, The Return of the Musketeers / 1989, The Cook, The Thief, His Wife And Her Lover / 1989, Strapless / 1989, Dakota Road / 1991, The Secret Rapture / 1994, The Lord Of The Rings: The Fellowship of the Ring (voice) 2001, The Lord of the Rings: The Two Towers (voice) 2002, The Lord of the Rings: The Return of the King (voice) 2003. *Television includes:* A Perfect Spy 1987, David Copperfield 2000. *Leisure interests:* reading, music. *Address:* c/o Julian Belfrage Associates, 46 Albemarle Street, London, W1X 4PP, England. *Telephone:* (20) 7491-4400. *Fax:* (20) 7493-5460. *Website:* www .alanhoward.org.uk.

HOWARD, Ann; British singer (mezzo-soprano); b. 22 July 1936, Norwood, London; d. of William A. Swadling and Gladys W. Swadling; m. Keith Giles 1954; one d.; ed with Topliss Green and Rodolfa Lhombino, London and Dominic Modesti, Paris; repertoire includes Carmen, Dalila in Samson et

Dalila, Dulcinée in Don Quichotte, Hélène in La Belle Hélène, Eboli in Don Carlo, Azucena in Il Trovatore, Amneris in Aida, Isabella in L' Italiana in Algeri, Proserpina in Orfeo, Ortrud in Lohengrin, Brangaene in Tristan und Isolde, Fricka in Das Rheingold and Die Walküre, Baba the Turk in The Rake's Progress, Katisha in The Mikado, Czipra in Gipsy Baron, Lilli Vanessi in Kiss Me Kate, Clytemnestra in Electra, La Grande Duchesse de Gerolstein, Stepmother in Into The Woods, Prince Orlofsky in Die Fledermaus, Old Lady in Candide, Auntie in Peter Grimes, Hostess in Boris Godunov, Jezi Baba in Rusalka, Marcellina in Marriage of Figaro, Emma Jones in Street Scene, performed in world premières of Mines of Sulphur (Bennett) 1970, Rebecca (Josephs) 1982, The Tempest (Eaton, USA) 1985, The Plumber's Gift (Blake) 1989, The Doctor of Myddfai (Maxwell Davies) 1996 and in UK première of Le Grand Macabre 1981; series of Gilbert and Sullivan operas Performing Arts Centre, NY State Univ. 1993–98; has appeared in UK, France, Canada, USA, Mexico, Chile, Portugal, Germany, Austria and Italy and on BBC radio and TV; teaches privately; The Worshipful Co. of Musicians Sir Charles Santley Memorial Award 2002. *Leisure interests:* gardening, cooking.

HOWARD, Anthony Michell, CBE, MA; British journalist; b. 12 Feb. 1934, London; s. of the late Canon W. G. Howard and Janet Howard (née Rymer); m. Carol Anne Gaynor 1965; ed Westminster School and Christ Church, Oxford; on editorial staff, Manchester Guardian 1959–61; Political Corresp., New Statesman 1961–64; Whitehall Corresp., Sunday Times 1965; Washington Corresp., Observer 1966–69; Asst Ed. New Statesman 1970–72, Ed. 1972–78; Ed. The Listener 1979–81; Deputy Ed. The Observer 1981–88; presenter Face the Press, Channel 4 1982–85; presenter and reporter BBC TV 1989–92; Obituaries Ed. The Times 1993–99, weekly columnist 1999–2005; Harkness Fellow, USA 1960; mem. Editorial Bd, London Evening Standard 2009–; Hon. Student, Christ Church, Oxford 2003; Hon. LLD (Nottingham) 2001, Hon. DLitt (Leicester) 2003; Gerald Barry Award, What the Papers Say 1998. *Publications:* The Making of the Prime Minister (with Richard West) 1965, The Crossman Diaries (ed.) 1964–70, 1979, Rab: The Life of R. A. Butler 1987, Crossman: The Pursuit of Power 1990, Basil Hume: The Monk Cardinal 2005. *Address:* 11 Campden House Court, 42 Gloucester Walk, London, W8 4HU, England (office). *Telephone:* (20) 7937-7313 (office).

HOWARD, Sir David Howarth Seymour, Bt , MA, DSc; British business executive; *Chairman, Charles Stanley & Company, Stockbrokers;* b. 29 Dec. 1945, Lincoln; s. of Sir Edward Howard, Bt; m. Valerie Picton Crosse 1968; two s. two d.; ed Radley Coll., Worcester Coll., Oxford; Chair. Charles Stanley & Co., Stockbrokers 1971–; Pro-Chancellor and Chair. City Univ. 2003–08; Pres., Chartered Man. Inst. 2008–; mem. Sutton London Borough Council 1974–78; Common Councilman, City of London 1972–86, Alderman 1986–, Sheriff 1997–98, Lord Mayor of London 2000–01; Master, Gardeners' Co. 1990–91; Hon. Fellow, Securities & Investment Inst. *Leisure interest:* gardening. *Address:* Office of the Chairman, Charles Stanley & Co. Ltd, 25 Luke Street, London, EC2A 4AR, England (office). *Telephone:* (20) 7739-8200 (office). *Fax:* (20) 7739-7798 (office).

HOWARD, Elizabeth Jane, CBE, FRSL; British writer; b. 26 March 1923, London, England; d. of David Liddon and Katharine M. Howard; m. 1st Peter M. Scott 1942; one d.; m. 2nd James Douglas-Henry 1959; m. 3rd Kingsley Amis 1965 (divorced 1983, died 1995); ed at home and at London Mask Theatre School; BBC TV modelling 1939–46; Sec. Inland Waterways Asscn 1947; then professional writer, including plays for TV; Hon. Artistic Dir Cheltenham Literary Festival 1962; Artistic Co-Dir Salisbury Festival of Arts 1973; mem. Authors Lending and Copyright Soc.; John Llewellyn Rhys Memorial Prize 1950, Yorkshire Post Prize 1982. *Film scripts:* Getting It Right 1985, The Attachment 1986, The Very Edge. *Television:* Our Glorious Dead, Sight Unseen, Skittles, adaptations of After Julius (three plays for TV), Something in Disguise (six plays) 1982. *Publications:* The Beautiful Visit 1950, The Long View 1956, The Sea Change 1959, After Julius 1965, Something in Disguise 1969, Odd Girl Out 1972, Mr Wrong 1975, A Companion for Lovers (ed.) 1978, Getting It Right (Yorkshire Post Novel of the Year) 1982, Howard and Maschler on Food: Cooking for Occasions (co-author) 1987, The Light Years (The Cazalet Chronicle Vol. One) 1990, Green Shades (gardening anthology) 1991, Marking Time (The Cazalet Chronicle Vol. Two) 1991, Confusion (The Cazalet Chronicle Vol. Three) 1993, Casting Off (The Cazalet Chronicle Vol. Four) 1995, Falling 1999, Slipstream (autobiog.) 2002, Love All 2008; contrib. to The Times, Sunday Times, Telegraph, Encounter, Vogue, Harpers & Queen. *Leisure interests:* music, gardening, enjoying all the arts, travelling, natural history, reading. *Address:* c/o Jonathan Clowes Ltd, 10 Iron Bridge House, Bridge Approach, London, NW1 8BD, England (office); c/o Pan MacMillan Ltd, 20 New Wharf Road, London, N1 9RR, England. *Telephone:* (20) 7722-7674 (office). *Fax:* (20) 7722-7677 (office).

HOWARD, James Kenneth (Ken), RA, RWS, RWA, ARCA, PPNEAC; British painter; *Professor of Perspective, Royal Academy of Arts;* b. 26 Dec. 1932, London; s. of Frank Howard and Elizabeth Howard; m. 1st Ann Popham (divorced 1974); m. 2nd Christa Gaa (née Köhler; died 1992); m. 3rd Dora Bertolutti 2000; ed Kilburn Grammar School, Hornsey School of Art, Royal Coll. of Art; British Council Scholarship to Florence 1958–59; taught in various London art schools 1959–73; Official Artist for Imperial War Museum, NI 1973, 1978; painted for British Army in NI, Germany, Cyprus, Oman, Hong Kong, Brunei, Nepal, Canada, Norway, Belize, Beirut 1973–83; Prof. of Perspective, Royal Acad. of Arts 2004–; works in public collections including Plymouth City Art Gallery, Ulster Museum, Imperial War Museum, Nat. Army Museum, Hove City Art Gallery, Guildhall Art Gallery; comms for UN, BAOR, Stock Exchange, London, States of Jersey, Banque Paribas, Drapers Co., Royal Hosp. Chelsea, Richard Green 2003; Pres. NEAC 1998–2003; Hon. mem. Royal Inst. of Oil Painters, Royal Soc. of British Artists; First Prize Lord Mayor's Art Award 1965, Hunting Group Award 1982, Sparkasse Karlsruhe 1983, Prizewinner John Moores 1978, Annual Critics' Prize, New English Art Club 2000. *Publications:* The Paintings of Ken Howard 1992, Ken Howard: A Personal Viewpoint 1998. *Leisure interests:* opera, cinema. *Address:* St Clements Studio, Paul Lane, Mousehole, Cornwall, TR19 6TR; 8 South Bolton Gardens, London, SW5 0DH, England (home); 6262 Canareggio, Venice, Italy (home). *Telephone:* (1736) 731596 (Cornwall) (office); (20) 7373-2912 (London) (home); (41) 5202277 (Italy) (home). *Fax:* (20) 7244-6246 (home).

HOWARD, Hon. John Winston, LLB; Australian lawyer and fmr politician; b. 26 July 1939, Sydney; s. of Lyall Falconer Howard and Mona Jane Howard; m. Alison Janette Parker 1971; two s. one d.; ed Univ. of Sydney; solicitor to Supreme Court, NSW 1962; Pnr, Sydney solicitors' firm 1968–74; Liberal MP for Bennelong, NSW, Fed. Parl. 1974–2007; Minister for Business and Consumer Affairs 1975–77, Minister Assisting Prime Minister 1977, Fed. Treas. 1977–83; Deputy Leader of Opposition 1983–85, Leader 1985–89; Prime Minister of Australia 1996–2007; Shadow Minister for Industrial Relations, Employment and Training, Shadow Minister Assisting the Leader on the Public Service and Chair. Manpower and Labour Market Reform Group 1990–95; mem. State Exec., NSW Liberal Party 1963–74; Vice-Pres., NSW Div., Liberal Party 1972–74; Fed. Parl. Leader Liberal Party 1985–1989, 1995–2007; US Presidential Medal of Freedom 2009. *Leisure interests:* reading, cricket, tennis. *Address:* c/o Liberal Party of Australia, Federal Secretariat, cnr Blackall and Macquarie Streets, Barton, ACT 2600, Australia.

HOWARD, Rt Hon. Michael, PC, QC; British politician and barrister; b. 7 July 1941; s. of Bernard Howard and Hilda Howard; m. Sandra Clare Paul 1975; one s. one d. one step-s.; ed Llanelli Grammar School, Peterhouse, Cambridge; Pres. Cambridge Union 1962; called to Bar, Inner Temple 1964, Master of the Bench of Inner Temple 1992; Jr Counsel to the Crown (Common Law) 1980–82; a Recorder 1986–; Conservative parl. cand., Liverpool (Edge Hill) 1966, 1970; Chair. Bow Group 1970–71; MP for Folkestone and Hythe 1983–; Parl. Pvt. Sec. to Solicitor-Gen. 1984–85; Under-Sec. of State, Dept of Trade and Industry, Minister for Corp. and Consumer Affairs 1985–87; Minister of State, Dept of the Environment 1987–88, Minister of Water and Planning 1988–90; Sec. of State for Employment 1990–92, for the Environment 1992–93, Home Sec. 1993–97; Opposition Front-Bench Spokesman on Foreign and Commonwealth Affairs 1997–99; Shadow Chancellor of the Exchequer 2001–03; Leader of the Conservative Party and Leader of the Opposition 2003–05; Chair. of Diligence, Europe 2006–. *Leisure interest:* watching football and films, reading, walking. *Address:* House of Commons, Westminster, London, SW1A 0AA, England. *Telephone:* (20) 7219-5493. *Fax:* (20) 7219-5322. *Website:* www.michaelhowardmp.com.

HOWARD, Sir Michael Eliot, Kt, CH, CBE, MC, MA, DLitt, FBA, FRHistS; British historian; *Regius Professor Emeritus of Modern History, University of Oxford;* b. 29 Nov. 1922, London; s. of the late Geoffrey Eliot Howard and of Edith Howard (née Edinger); ed Wellington Coll., Christ Church, Oxford; served in army 1942–45; Asst Lecturer, Lecturer in History, King's Coll., London 1947–53; Lecturer, Reader in War Studies, Univ. of London 1953–63; Prof. of War Studies, Univ. of London 1963–68; Fellow in Higher Defence Studies, All Souls Coll., Oxford 1968–77; Chichele Prof. of the History of War, Univ. of Oxford 1977–80; Regius Prof. of Modern History, Univ. of Oxford 1980–89, Prof. Emer. 1989–; Robert A. Lovett Prof. of Mil. and Naval History, Yale Univ. 1989–93; Leverhulme Lecturer 1996; Lee Kuan Yew Distinguished Visitor, Nat. Univ. of Singapore 1996; Founder and Pres. Emer. Int. Inst. for Strategic Studies; mem. The Literary Soc. (Pres. –2004); Foreign mem. American Acad. of Arts and Sciences; Hon. Fellow, Oriel Coll., Oxford 1990; Hon. Student Christ Church 1990; Order of Merit; Hon. LittD (Leeds) 1979; Hon. DLitt (London) 1988; Duff Cooper Memorial Prize 1961, Wolfson Foundation History Award 1972, NATO Atlantic Award 1989, Chesney Memorial Gold Medal, Royal United Services Inst., Samule Eliot Morrison Prize, Soc. for Mil. History 1992, Paul Nitze Award, Center for Naval Analysis 1994, Political Book Prize, Friedrich Ebert Stiftung 2002. *Publications:* The Coldstream Guards 1920–1946 (with John Sparrow) 1951, Disengagement in Europe 1958, Wellingtonian Studies 1959, The Franco-German War 1961, The Theory and Practice of War 1965, The Mediterranean Strategy in the Second World War 1967, Studies in War and Peace 1970, Grand Strategy, Vol. IV (in UK History of Second World War) 1972, The Continental Commitment 1973, War in European History 1976, Clausewitz on War (trans. with Peter Paret) 1976, War and the Liberal Conscience 1978, Restraints on War (ed.) 1979, The Causes of Wars 1983, Clausewitz 1983, Strategic Deception: British Intelligence in the Second World War 1990, The Lessons of History (essays) 1991, The Oxford History of the Twentieth Century (co-ed. with W. R. Louis) 1998, The Invention of Peace 2000, The First World War 2001. *Leisure interests:* music, gardening. *Address:* The Old Farm, Eastbury, Hungerford, Berks., RG17 7JN, England (home). *Telephone:* (1488) 71387. *Fax:* (1488) 71387.

HOWARD, Ron; American film director, film producer and actor; *Principal, Imagine Entertainment;* b. 1 March 1954, Duncan, Okla; s. of Rance Howard and Jean Howard; m. Cheryl Alley 1975; two s. two d.; ed Univ. of Southern Calif. and Los Angeles Valley Coll.; Co-founder and Prin. Imagine Entertainment 1986–; National Medal of Arts 2003. *Television includes:* (series) The Andy Griffith Show 1960–68, The Smith Family 1971–72, Happy Days 1974–80 and many other TV appearances. *Films directed include:* Night Shift 1982, Splash 1984, Cocoon 1985, Gung Ho 1986, Return to Mayberry 1986, Willow 1988, Parenthood 1989, Backdraft 1991, Far and Away (also co-producer) 1992, The Paper 1994, Apollo 13 1995 (Outstanding Directorial Achievement in Motion Picture Award from Directors' Guild of America (DGA) 1996), How the Grinch Stole Christmas 2000, A Beautiful Mind (Acad. Awards for Best Dir and Best Film (producer) 2002, DGA Best Dir Award 2002) 2001, The Missing 2003, Cinderella Man 2005, Da Vinci Code 2006,

Frost/Nixon 2008, Angels & Demons 2009. *Film appearances include:* The Journey 1959, Five Minutes to Live 1959, Music Man 1962, The Courtship of Eddie's Father 1963, Village of the Giants 1965, Wild County 1971, Mother's Day, American Graffiti 1974, The Spikes Gang, Eat My Dust 1976, The Shootist 1976, More American Graffiti 1979, Leo and Loree (TV), Act of Love 1980, Skyward 1981, Through the Magic Pyramid (Dir, exec. producer) 1981, When Your Lover Leaves (co-exec. producer) 1983, Return to Mayberry 1986, Ransom 1996, Ed TV 1999. *Address:* Imagine Entertainment, 1925 Century Park East, Suite 230, Los Angeles, CA 90067, USA. *Website:* www.imagine-entertainment.com.

HOWARTH, Elgar, ARAM, DMus, FRCM, FRNCM; British musician (trumpet), conductor and composer; b. 4 Nov. 1935, Cannock, Staffs.; s. of Oliver Howarth and Emma Wall; m. Mary Bridget Neary 1958; one s. two d.; ed Eccles Grammar School and Manchester Univ./Royal Northern Coll. of Music (jt course); orchestral player 1958–70; Chair. Royal Philharmonic Orchestra 1968–70; Prin. Guest Conductor Opera North 1985–88; freelance orchestral conductor 1970–; Musical Adviser Grimethorpe Colliery Brass Band 1972–; compositions: Trumpet Concerto 1968, Trombone Concerto 1962, Music for Spielberg 1984, Songs for BL for brass band; Fellow, Welsh Coll. of Music and Drama; Hon. FRNCM 1999; Hon. Fellow Royal Coll. of Music 2001, Univ. Coll. Salford; Hon. DUniv (Cen. England, York); Hon. DMus (Keele) 1996, (York) 2000; Hon. DLitt (Salford) 2003; Eddison Award 1977, Olivier Award for Outstanding Achievement in Opera 1997. *Leisure interests:* hypochondria, cricket, football. *Address:* c/o Andrew Rosner, Allied Artists, 42 Montpelier Square, London, SW7 1JZ, England (office). *Telephone:* (20) 7589-6243 (office). *Fax:* (20) 7581-5269 (office). *E-mail:* info@alliedartists.co.uk (office). *Website:* www.alliedartists.co.uk (office).

HOWARTH, Judith; British singer (soprano); b. 11 Sept. 1962, Ipswich; m. 1986; ed Royal Scottish Acad. of Music and Drama and studies with Patricia Macmahon; recipient of special bursary to join Royal Opera House, Covent Garden as prin. soprano in 1985–86 season; maj. roles with Royal Opera include Musetta, Ännchen in Der Freischütz, Gilda, Adela, Marguerite de Valois in Les Huguenots, Liu, Norina, Marzelline and Morgana in Alcina 1989–96; now freelance; numerous concert and recital engagements in UK, USA, Far East, Australia and NZ; debut at Salzburg Festival in Mozart's Der Schauspieldirektor 1991; has also appeared with Florida Grand Opera, Drottningholm Festival, Opera North and Glyndebourne Touring Opera; debut with Deutsche Staatsoper, Berlin in Cavalli's La Didone 1996. *Leisure interest:* cooking.

HOWATCH, Susan, LLB; British writer; b. 14 July 1940, Leatherhead, Surrey; d. of G. S. Sturt; m. Joseph Howatch 1964 (separated 1975); one d.; ed Sutton High School, King's Coll., London; emigrated to USA 1964, lived in Ireland 1976–80, returned to UK 1980; first book published 1965; Fellow, King's Coll. London 1999–; f. Starbridge Lectureship in Theology and Natural Science Univ. of Cambridge 1992; mem. Soc. of Authors; Winifred Mary Stanford Memorial Prize 1991. *Publications:* novels: The Dark Shore 1965, The Waiting Sands 1966, Call in the Night 1967, The Shrouded Walls 1968, April's Grave 1969, The Devil on Lammas Night 1970, Penmarric 1971, Cashelmara 1974, The Rich are Different 1977, Sins of the Fathers 1980, The Wheel of Fortune 1984, Glittering Images 1987, Glamorous Powers 1988, Ultimate Prizes 1989, Scandalous Risks 1991, Mystical Paths 1992, Absolute Truths 1994, A Question of Integrity (US title: The Wonder Worker) 1997, The High Flyer 1999, The Heartbreaker 2003. *Leisure interest:* theology. *Address:* Aitken Alexander Associates Ltd, 18–21 Cavaye Place, London, SW10 9PT, England (office). *Telephone:* (20) 7373-8672 (office). *Fax:* (20) 7373-6002 (office). *E-mail:* reception@aitkenalexander.co.uk (office). *Website:* www.aitkenalexander.co.uk (office).

HOWDEN, Timothy Simon; British business executive; b. 2 April 1937, London; s. of Phillip Alexander Howden and Rene Howden; m. 1st Penelope Mary Howden 1958 (divorced 1984); two s. one d.; m. 2nd Lois Chesney 1999; ed Tonbridge School; on staff of Reckitt & Colman in France, FRG and UK, ending as Dir Reckitt & Colman Europe 1962–73; Dir RH.M. Flour Mills 1973–75, Man. Dir RH.M. Foods Ltd 1975–80, Chair. and Man. Dir British Bakeries Ltd 1980–85, Planning Dir RH.M. PLC 1985–89, Man. Dir RH.M. PLC 1989–92; Group Chief Exec. for Europe, The Albert Fisher Group 1992–96, CEO for N America 1996–97; Dir (non-exec.) SSL Int. PLC 1994–, 1996–, FMMing Int. Inc. 1998–, Hyperion Insurance Group Ltd 2000–; Chair. Zwetshoot Ltd 2001–, Benchmark Dental Holdings Ltd 2001–; Assoc. Dir Mahendra British Telecom Ltd. *Leisure interests:* skiing, scuba diving, tennis, sailing, opera. *Address:* Flat 72, Berkeley House, Hay Hill, London, W1X 7LH, England. *Telephone:* (1628) 484121. *Fax:* (1628) 478838 (office). *E-mail:* timlwe@email.msn.com (office).

HOWE, Brian Leslie, AM, MA; Australian politician; *Professional Associate, Center for Public Policy, University of Melbourne;* b. 28 Jan. 1936, Melbourne; s. of John Percy Howe and Lilian May Howe; m. Renate Morris 1962; one s. two d.; ed Melbourne Univ., McCormick Theological Seminary, Chicago; worked as Uniting Church Minister, Melbourne and Morwell, Victoria; fmr Sr Lecturer in Sociology and Chair. Dept of Social and Political Studies, Swinburne Inst. of Tech., Melbourne; joined Australian Labor Party 1961; MP for Batman, House of Reps. 1977–96; Minister for Defence Support 1983–84, for Social Security and assisting the Prime Minister for Social Justice 1984–90, for Health, Housing and Community Services and assisting the Prime Minister for Social Justice 1990–93, for Housing, Local Govt and Community (now Human) Services 1993–94, for Housing and Regional Devt 1994–96; Deputy Prime Minister 1991–95; Minister assisting the Prime Minister for Commonwealth Relations 1991–93; Professional Assoc. Centre for Public Policy and Dept of Social Work, Univ. of Melbourne 1996–; Visiting Research Fellow Woodrow Wilson School of Public Policy and Int. Affairs 1997, 1998; fmr Chair. Caucus Econs Cttee; fmr mem. Caucus Resources Cttee, Urban and Regional Affairs Cttee, House of Reps. Standing Cttee on the Environment, Jt House Cttee on Publs; Fellow Queen's Coll., Univ. Melbourne 2000. *Leisure interests:* Australian Rules football, tennis, films, reading. *Address:* Centre for Public Policy, 2/234 Queensberry Street, Carlton, Vic. 3053 (office); 6 Brennand Street, North Fitzroy, Vic. 3068, Australia (home). *Telephone:* (3) 8344-9469 (office); (3) 9489-4787 (home). *Fax:* (3) 9482-3202 (home). *E-mail:* b.howe@arts.unimelb.edu.au (office).

HOWE, Geoffrey Michael Thomas, MA; British solicitor and business executive; *Chairman, Nationwide Building Society;* b. 3 Sept. 1949, Cambridge; s. of Michael Edward Howe and Susan Dorothy Howe (née Allan); m. Karen Mary Webber (née Ford); two d.; ed Manchester Grammar School, St John's Coll., Cambridge; with Stephenson Harwood law firm 1971–75 (qualified as solicitor 1973); joined Clifford Chance 1975, apptd Partner, Corp. Dept 1980, Man. Partner 1989–97; Dir and Gen. Counsel, Robert Fleming Holdings Ltd 1998–2000; Dir J.P. Morgan, Fleming Overseas Investment Trust PLC 1999–; Chair. Railtrack Group PLC March–Oct. 2002; Dir (non-exec.) Jardine Lloyd Thompson Group PLC 2002– (currently Chair.), Investec PLC 2003–; mem. Bd Dirs Nationwide Building Society 2005–, Chair. 2007–; consultant to several financial and professional orgs. *Leisure interests:* opera, wine, tennis, paintings. *Address:* Nationwide Building Society, Pipers Way, Swindon, Wilts., SN38 1NW (office); 11 Highbury Terrace, London, N5 1UP, England (home). *Telephone:* (1793) 656789 (office). *Fax:* (1793) 455341 (office). *E-mail:* info@nationwide.co.uk (office); geoffreymt.howe@lineone.net (home). *Website:* www.nationwide.co.uk (office).

HOWE, Yoon Chong, BA, DSO; Singaporean politician and banker; *Chairman and CEO, Straits Trading Company Ltd.;* b. 1923, China; m.; three c.; ed St Francis' Inst. Malacca, Raffles Coll. and Univ. of Malaya in Singapore; fmr civil servant; Sec. to Public Service Comm.; CEO Housing and Devt Bd 1960; Perm. Sec. Ministries of Finance and Nat. Devt; Deputy Chair. Econ. Devt Bd; Chair. and Pres. Devt Bank of Singapore, concurrently Chair. and Gen. Man. Port of Singapore Authority; Perm. Sec. Prime Minister's Office and Head of Civil Service; mem. Parl. 1979–84; Minister of Defence 1979–82, of Health 1982–84; Chair. and Chief Exec. Devt Bank of Singapore 1985–90, Straits Trading Co., Ltd 1992–; Chair. Great Eastern Life Assurance Co. Ltd 1992–2000; mem. Bd of Trustees, Eisenhower Exchange Fellowships Inc. 1980–90; Hon. DLitt (Singapore) 1971; Malaysia Medal, Meritorious Service Medal 1963. *Address:* Straits Trading Company Ltd, 9 Battery Road, 21-00 Straits Trading Building, Singapore 049910. *Telephone:* 65354722 (office). *Fax:* 65327939 (office). *Website:* www.stc.com.sg (office).

HOWE OF ABERAVON, Baron (Life Peer), cr. 1992, of Tandridge in the County of Surrey; **(Richard Edward) Geoffrey Howe,** CH, PC, QC; British politician and lawyer; b. 20 Dec. 1926, Port Talbot, Glam.; s. of the late B. Edward Howe and of E. F. Howe; m. Elspeth R. M. Shand (cr. Baroness Howe of Idlicote 2001) 1953; one s. two d.; ed Winchester Coll. and Trinity Hall, Cambridge; called to the Bar, Middle Temple 1952, Bencher 1969; Deputy Chair. Glamorgan Quarter Sessions 1966–70; MP for Bebington 1964–66, for Reigate 1970–74, for East Surrey 1974–92; Solicitor-Gen. 1970–72; Minister for Trade and Consumer Affairs 1972–74; Opposition Spokesman for Social Services 1974–75, for Treasury and Econ. Affairs 1975–79; Chancellor of the Exchequer 1979–83; Sec. of State for Foreign and Commonwealth Affairs 1983–89; Lord Pres. of the Council, Leader of House of Commons and Deputy Prime Minister 1989–90; Visitor SOAS Univ. of London 1991–2001; Special Adviser on European and Int. Affairs to int. law firm Jones, Day, Reavis & Pogue 1991–2000; Herman Phleger Visiting Prof. Stanford Law School, USA 1992–93; Pres. GB-China Centre 1992–, Consumers Asscn (renamed Which?) 1992–, Acad. of Experts 1993–2003; Chair. Framlington Russian Investment Fund 1994–2003; a Gov. IMF 1979–83; Chair. Int. Cttee 1983, Steering Cttee Tax Law Rewrite Project 1996–2003, Trustees Thomson Foundation 2004–; fmr Pres. British Overseas Trade Bd; Dir Sun Alliance and London Insurance Group 1974–79, BICC 1991–97, Glaxo 1991–96; Dir EMI Ltd 1974–79, AGB Research Ltd 1974–79; mem. Int. Advisory Councils, J. P. Morgan 1992–2001, Stanford Univ. Inst. for Int. Studies 1991–, Fuji Wolfensohn Int. European Advisory Bd 1996–98, Carlyle European Advisory Bd 1996–2001, Fuji Bank Advisory Council 1999–2003; Conservative; Hon. Fellow, American Bar Foundation 2000; Hon. Fellow, Trinity Hall 1992, SOAS, London 2003; Grand Cross Order of Merit (Portugal) 1987, (Germany) 1992; Order of Ukraine for Public Service 2001; Hon. LLD (Wales) 1988, LSE 2004, (Glamorgan) 2004; Hon. DCL (City Univ.) 1993; Joseph Bech Prize 1993, Paul Harris Fellow, Rotary International 1995. *Publication:* Conflict of Loyalty 1994. *Leisure interest:* photography. *Address:* House of Lords, Westminster, London, SW1A 0PW, England (office). *Telephone:* (20) 7219-6986 (office). *Fax:* (20) 7219-0587 (office). *E-mail:* howeg@parliament.uk (office).

HOWELL OF GUILDFORD, Baron (Life Peer), cr. 1997, of Penton Mewsey in the County of Hampshire; **David Arthur Russell Howell,** PC, BA; British politician, journalist and economist; *Opposition Spokesman on Foreign and Commonwealth Affairs and Deputy Leader of the Opposition, House of Lords;* b. 18 Jan. 1936, London; s. of the late Col Arthur Howell and of Beryl Howell; m. Davina Wallace 1967; one s. two d.; ed Eton Coll., King's Coll., Cambridge; Lt Coldstream Guards 1954–56; Econ. Section, HM Treasury 1959, resgnd 1960; Leader-writer The Daily Telegraph 1960; Chair. Bow Group 1961–62; fmr Crossbow; MP for Guildford 1966–97; a Lord Commr of Treasury 1970–71; with Civil Service Dept 1970–72; Parl. Under-Sec. Dept of Employment 1971–72; Minister of State, Northern Ireland Office 1972–74, Dept of Energy Jan.–Feb. 1974; Sec. of State for Energy 1979–81, for Transport 1981–83; Chair. House of Commons Foreign Affairs Cttee 1987–97, One Nation Group of Conservative MPs 1987–97, European Cttee on Common Foreign and Security Policy 1999–2000; Opposition Spokesman on Foreign and Commonwealth Affairs 2000–; Chair. UK–Japan 2000 Group 1989–2001; Dir Conservative Political Centre 1964–66; Dir Monks Investment Trust 1992–2005, John Laing Investments PLC 1997–2002; Advisory Dir UBS-Warburg 1996–2000; Sr Adviser, Japan Cen. Railway Co. 2001–; European Adviser, Mitsubishi Electric BV; Adviser to Kuwait Investment Office; Pres. British Inst. of Energy Economists; mem. Governing Bd Centre for Global Energy Studies; Visiting Fellow, Nuffield Coll., Oxford 1993–2001; Gov. Sadler's Wells Trust 1995–98; Trustee Shakespeare's Globe Theatre 2000–; Foundation Scholar, King's Coll. Cambridge, Richmond Prize 1959; Grand Cordon of the Order of the Sacred Treasure (Japan) 2001. *Publications:* Principle in Practice (co-author) 1960, The Conservative Opportunity 1965, Freedom and Capital 1981, Blind Victory 1986, The Edge of Now 2000. *Leisure interests:* family life, writing. *Address:* House of Lords, Westminster, London, SW1A 0PW (office). *Telephone:* (20) 7219-5415 (office). *Fax:* (20) 7219-0304 (office). *E-mail:* howelld@parliament.uk (office). *Website:* www.lordhowell.com (office).

HOWELLS, Kim, BA, PhD; British politician; *Minister of State for the Middle East and South Asia;* b. 27 Nov. 1946, Merthyr Tydfil, Wales; m. Eirlys Howells; three c.; ed Mountain Ash Grammar School, Hornsey Coll. of Art, Cambridge Coll. of Art and Tech., Univ. of Warwick; lecturer 1975–79; Official Research Officer, Coalfield History Project, Nat. Union of Miners (NUM) 1979–82, research officer and journal ed., NUM S Wales Area 1982–89; writer and broadcaster 1986–89; Labour MP for Pontypridd 1989–, Opposition Spokesman on Devt and Co-operation 1993–94, for Home Affairs 1994–95, for Foreign and Commonwealth Affairs 1994–95, for Trade and Industry 1995, Parl. Under-Sec. of State for Lifelong Learning, Dept for Educ. and Employment 1997–98; Minister for Consumers and Corp. Affairs, Dept for Trade and Industry 1998–2001; Minister for Tourism, Broadcasting and Media, Dept of Culture, Media and Sport 2001–03; Minister of State for Transport 2003–04, for Further and Higher Educ. and Lifelong Learning 2004–05, for the Middle East and South Asia, FCO 2005–; mem. Welsh Affairs Select Cttee 1989–90, mem. Environmental Select Cttee 1990–92, mem. Public Accounts Cttee 1992–93, 1993–94; Dr hc (Anglia Polytechnic Univ.). *Leisure interests:* painting, mountaineering, cycling, jazz. *Address:* Foreign and Commonwealth Office, King Charles Street, London, SW1A 2AH, England (office); 16 Tyfica Road, Pontypridd, Wales (home). *Telephone:* (20) 7008-2090 (office); (1443) 402551 (home). *Fax:* (20) 7008-2988 (office). *E-mail:* helen.perry@fco.gov.uk (office). *Website:* www.fco.gov.uk (office).

HOWIE, Archibald, CBE, PhD, FRS; British academic and research physicist; *Professor Emeritus of Physics, University of Cambridge;* b. 8 March 1934, Kirkcaldy, Scotland; s. of Robert Howie and Margaret Marshall McDonald; m. Melva Jean Scott 1964; one s. (deceased), one d.; ed Kirkcaldy High School, Univ. of Edinburgh, California Inst. of Tech., USA, Univ. of Cambridge; ICI Research Fellow, Cavendish Lab. and Research Fellow, Churchill Coll., Cambridge 1960–61, Demonstrator in Physics, Cavendish Lab. 1961–65, Teaching Fellow and Dir of Studies in Physics, Churchill Coll. 1961–86, Lecturer 1965–79, Reader 1979–86, Professorial Fellow 1986–2001, Pensioner Fellow 2001–, Head of Dept of Physics 1989–97; part-time consultant, Union Carbide Corpn 1977–78, World Bank China Univ. Devt Programme 1984, Norwegian Research Council 1986; Dir (non-exec.) NPL Man. Ltd 1995–2001; Pres. Royal Microscopical Soc. 1984–86, Int. Fed. of Socs for Electron Microscopy 1999–2002; Hon. FRSE 1995; Hon. Fellow, Royal Microscopical Soc. 1978, Japanese Microscopy Soc. 2003; Hon. mem. Electron Microscopy Soc. of America 1991, Chinese Electron Microscopy Soc. 2000; Hon. Dr of Physics (Univ. of Bologna) 1989, (Univ. of Thessaloniki) 1995; C.V. Boys Prize (jtly), Guthrie Medal, Inst. of Physics 1992, Hughes Medal (jtly), Royal Soc. 1988, Distinguished Scientist Award, Electron Microscopy Soc. of America 1991, Royal Medal, Royal Soc. 1999. *Publications:* Electron Microscopy of Thin Crystals (jt author) 1965 and numerous articles on electron microscopy and related subjects in scientific journals. *Leisure interest:* making wine. *Address:* Cavendish Laboratory, Madingley Road, Cambridge, CB3 0HE (office); 194 Huntingdon Road, Cambridge, CB3 0LB, England (home). *Telephone:* (1223) 337335 (office); (1223) 570977 (home). *Fax:* (1223) 363263 (office). *E-mail:* ah30@cam.ac.uk (office). *Website:* (office).

HOWIE, J. Robert, BA, BCL, QC; Canadian politician and lawyer; b. 29 Oct. 1929, Fredericton, NB; s. of James R. Howie and Mary L. Pond; m. Nancy Goulding 1955; one s. three d.; ed Univ. of New Brunswick; solicitor, Oromocto 1962–72; Clerk of the New Brunswick Legislature 1970–72; mem. House of Commons 1972, 1974; Minister of State (Transport) 1979–80, 1984–88; Presiding mem. Veterans' Appeal Bd 1990–93; lawyer in pvt. practice 1993; mem. Bd of Govs, Univ. of New Brunswick 2003–; Progressive Conservative. *Leisure interests:* curling, hockey, theatre, swimming, writing. *Address:* 678 Churchill Row, Fredericton, NB E3B 1P6, Canada (home). *Telephone:* (506) 455-9320 (home). *Fax:* (506) 455-6256 (office). *E-mail:* jrh@nbnet.nb.ca (office).

HOY, Sir Christopher Andrew (Chris), Kt, MBE, BSc (Hons); British cyclist; b. 23 March 1976, Edinburgh, Scotland; ed George Watson's Coll., Edinburgh, Univ. of St Andrews, Univ. of Edinburgh; track cyclist representing GB team at three Olympic Games 2000, 2004, 2008, World and European Championships 1996–2008, World Cup Team 1997–2008, and Scotland Team at three Commonwealth Games 1998, 2002, 2006; most successful Scottish Olympian ever; multiple World and Olympic Champion; first Briton to win three medals in a single Olympic games since Henry Taylor in 1908; most successful Olympic male cyclist of all time; raced BMX (Scotia BMX 1984–86, GT Factory BMX Team 1986–91) and was ranked 2nd in Britain, 5th in Europe and 9th in the world; sponsored by Slazenger and Kwik-Fit and competed in GB, Europe and USA; also rowed for Scottish jr team, coming second in British Championships with Grant Florence in coxless pairs 1993; also played rugby as part of his school's team; joined his first cycling club, Dunedin Cycling Club 1992–94; joined City of Edinburgh Racing Club and began concentrating on track cycling 1994–2001; set sea-level kilometre record of 1:00.711 seconds by winning gold at Athens Olympics 2004; set second fastest time ever (58.880) in attempt on world record for the kilometre May 2007; set record of 24.758 seconds for 500m flying start; World Championships: Silver Medal, Team sprint, Berlin 1999, Manchester 2000, Bronze Medal, Team sprint, Antwerp 2001, Gold Medals, 1km time trial and Team sprint, Copenhagen 2002, Bronze Medal, Team sprint, Stuttgart 2003, Gold Medal, 1km time trial, Bronze Medal, Team sprint, Melbourne 2004, Gold Medal, Team sprint, Bronze Medal, 1km time trial, Los Angeles 2005, Gold Medal, 1km time trial, Silver Medal, Team sprint, Bordeaux 2006, Gold Medals, Keirin and 1km time trial, Silver Medal, Team sprint 2007, Gold Medals, Sprint and Keirin, Silver Medal, Team sprint, Manchester 2008; Commonwealth Games: Gold Medal, 1km time trial, Bronze Medal, Team sprint (with Craig MacLean and Ross Edgar), Manchester 2002, Bronze Medal, 1km time trial, Gold Medal, Team sprint (with Craig MacLean and Ross Edgar), Melbourne 2006; Olympic Games: Silver Medal, Team sprint (with Craig MacLean and Jason Queally), Sydney 2000, Gold Medal, 1km track time trial, Athens 2004, Gold Medal, Team sprint (with Jason Kenny and Jamie Staff), Gold Medal, Keirin, Gold Medal, Sprint, Beijing 2008; raced for Team Athena 2001–03, Team Persil 2004, Team Wolfson Microelectronics/Miller 2005–07; Amb. for 2012 Summer Olympics in London; Hon. PhD (Edinburgh) 2005, (Heriot-Watt) 2005; BBC Sports Personality Team of the Year 2000, 2008, Glenfiddich Scottish Sports Personality 2002, Edinburgh City Council Civic Reception 2002, 2007, Commonwealth Games Council Scottish Sports Personality 2003, 2004, 2005, 2007, BBC Scottish Sports Personality of the Year 2003, Radio Forth Sports Personality 2004, cyclingnews.com Track Cyclist of the Year 2005, Glasgow Sportsperson of the Year 2007, BBC Sports Personality of the Year 2008. *Address:* c/o British Cycling, Stuart Street, Manchester, M11 4DQ, England. *Telephone:* (161) 274-2000. *Fax:* (161) 274-2001. *E-mail:* info@britishcycling.org.uk; admin@chrishoy.com. *Website:* www.britishcycling.org.uk; www.chrishoy.com.

HØYEM, Tom, MA; Danish politician, teacher, journalist and business executive; *Headmaster, European School, Karlsruhe, Germany;* b. 10 Oct. 1941, Nykøbing, Falster; s. of Ove Charles Høyem and Karen Høyem; m. 1st Inge-Lise Bredelund 1969 (died 2000); one s. one d.; m. 2nd Gerlinde Martin 2002; ed Univ. of Copenhagen, Univ. of Bergen, Norway; schoolteacher 1960–64; teacher, Skt Jørgens Gymnasium 1964–80; Sr Master, Foreningen Norden, Sweden 1967–68; business exec. 1968–; co-founder, Chair. Centre Democratic Party 1973; Asst Prof. of Danish Language and Literature, Univ. of Stockholm 1975–79; Foreign corresp., Berlingske Tidende, Sweden 1975–80; headmaster Høng Gymnasium 1979; Sec. of State for Greenland 1982–87; Headmaster European School, Culham 1987–94, Munich 1994–2000, Karlsruhe 2000–; mem. (Liberal) Karslruhe Town Council 2004–; Co-founder European Folk High School, Møn, Denmark and of similar insts in Sicily, Austria, Ireland and Luxembourg; Leader of European Movt West Zeeland, Denmark 1980–82; election observer in Albania and Bosnia 1996; Goodwill Amb. for Copenhagen; mem. Ausländerbeirat, Munich 1997–2000; OSCE observer of elections in Bosnia, Albania, Montenegro, Ukraine and Palestine; Hon. Pres. European Inst., Luxembourg 1983; Kt of the Dannebrog. *Publications:* Avisens spiseseddel-avisens ansigt 1975, Tabloidetik i Norden 1976, Mulighedernes Samfund (co-author) 1985, Laegaest 1985, Dagens Grønland 1986, There is Something Wonderful in the State of Denmark 1987, Gud, Konge, Faedreland 1987, Nordisk i Europa 1988, From My Office 1999, Danmark 2020 (co-author) 2004. *Leisure interests:* politics, reading, golf, walking. *Address:* European School, Albert-Schweitzer-str. 1, 76139 Karlsruhe, Germany. *Telephone:* (721) 680090 (office). *Fax:* (721) 6800950 (office). *E-mail:* hmtm@eursc.org (office). *Website:* www.eskar.org (office).

HOYER, Steny Hamilton; American politician; *House Majority Leader;* b. 14 June 1939, New York City; s. of Steen Hoyer; m. Judy Pickett (died 1997); three d.; ed Suitland High School, Md, Univ. of Maryland, College Park, Georgetown Univ. Law Center, Washington, DC; intern for Senator Daniel Brewster of Md; elected to Md State Senate for Prince George's Co. 1966–81, Pres. State Senate 1975–81 (youngest in state history); mem. Bd of Higher Educ. 1978–81; mem. US House of Reps for Md 5th Congressional Dist 1981–, Deputy Majority Whip 1987–89, Chair. Democratic Caucus 1989–94, fmr Co-Chair. (and current mem.) Democratic Steering Cttee, Chief Cand. Recruiter for House Democrats 1995–2000, House Democratic Minority Whip 2002–06, Sr mem. House Appropriations Cttee, mem. Transportation, Treasury and Housing Sub-cttee, Labor, Health and Human Services, Educ., and Related Agencies Sub-cttee, House Majority Leader 2007–; mem. Bd of Trustees St Mary's Coll. of Md; Democrat; Congressional Leadership Award, Epilepsy Foundation 2002. *Address:* 1705 Longworth House Office Building, Washington, DC 20515, USA (office). *Telephone:* (202) 225-4131 (office). *Fax:* (202) 225-4300 (office). *Website:* www.hoyer.house.gov (office).

HOYLAND, John, RA; British artist; b. 12 Oct. 1934, Sheffield; s. of John Kenneth Hoyland and Kathleen Hoyland; m. Airi Karkainen 1958 (divorced 1968); one s.; ed Sheffield Coll. of Art and Crafts and Royal Acad. Schools; teacher Hornsey School of Art 1960–61; Chelsea School of Art 1962–70, Prin. Lecturer 1965–69; St Martin's School of Art 1974–77; Slade School of Fine Art 1974–77, 1979–89; Charles A. Dana Prof., Colgate Univ., Hamilton, NY, USA 1972; Artist in Residence, Studio School, New York 1978, Melbourne Univ., Australia 1979; has exhibited all over the world; exhibited ceramic and glass sculptures 1994; Selector, Hayward Annual and Silver Jubilee RA Exhbns 1979; Faculty mem. and Visitor, British School at Rome 1984; Curator, Hans Hofman Exhbn, Tate Gallery, London 1988; Prof. of Painting, Royal Acad. Schools 2000–; foreign painter, Accad. Nat. di San Luca, Italy 2000; Order of the Southern Cross (Brazil) 1986; Dr hc (Sheffield Hallam) 2002, (Sheffield); Young Artist Int. Award, Tokyo 1963, Gulbenkian Foundation Award 1963,

Peter Stuyvesant Travel Award 1964, John Moores Exhbn Prize 1965, First Prize Edin. Open 100 1969, Chichester Nat. Art Award 1975, Arts Council of GB Purchase Award 1979, First Prize John Moores Exhbn 1982, First Prize Athena Award, Barbican Gallery, London 1987, Charles Wollaston Award 1998. *Publications:* John Hoyland, 1989, John Hoyland 2006. *Address:* c/o Royal Academy of Arts, Piccadilly, London, W1V 0DS (office); 41 Charterhouse Square, London, EC1M 6EA, England.

HRŮZA, Jiří, CSc, Ing.Arch; Czech architect and urban planner; *Senior Lecturer, Technical University, Prague;* b. 31 May 1925, Prague; s. of the late Václav Hrůza and of Františka Hrůza; m. 1st Emilie Hrůza (died 1991); one s. (deceased) one d.; m. 2nd Marta Opplová; ed Faculty of Architecture, Tech. Univ., Prague; with City Planning Office 1961–90; Chief Designer Master Plan of Prague 1961–91, Master Plan of Colombo, Sri Lanka 1978; Chief Specialist, Terplan, AS 1990–98; Guest Lecturer, Charles Univ. and Acad. of Graphic and Plastic Arts 1991; currently Sr Lecturer Inst. of Urbanism, Technical Univ., Prague; Founding mem. Int. Soc. of City and Regional Planners 1965; Corresp. mem. German Acad. for Town Planning 1993; Herder's Prize, Univ. of Vienna 1979. *Publications:* Czech Towns 1960, Theory of Towns 1965, International History of City Development (co-author) 1972, The City of Prague 1990, The Development of Urban Planning, Vols 1 and 2 1996, The World of Architecture (2nd edn) 2003. *Leisure interests:* foreign languages, history, classical literature, theory and history of architecture and urban design. *Address:* Institute of Urbanism of Technical University, Thákurova 7, 16000 Prague 6 (office); K Matěji 18, 16000 Prague 6, Czech Republic (home). *Telephone:* (2) 24354986 (office); (2) 33334645 (home). *Fax:* (2) 24310185 (office). *E-mail:* dubna@sa.cvut.cz (office); hruza-praha@volny.cz (home).

HRYSHCHENKO, Kostyantyn I.; Ukrainian politician and diplomatist; *Ambassador to Russia;* b. 28 Oct. 1953, Kyiv; ed Moscow State Institute of Int. Relations, USSR; staff mem., UN Secr., NY, USA 1976–80; various positions in Ministry of Foreign Affairs, USSR 1981–91; various positions in Arms Control and Disarmament Directorate, Ministry of Foreign Affairs of Ukraine, Kiev 1992–95; Deputy Foreign Minister 1995–98; Amb. to Belgium, Netherlands and Luxembourg, Head of Mission to NATO and Perm. Rep. to Org. for Prohibition of Chemical Weapons, The Hague, Netherlands 1998–2000; Amb. to USA 2000–03; Minister of Foreign Affairs 2003–05; Counselor of Prime Minister 2006–07; First Deputy, Nat. Security and Defence Council (RNBO) 2008; Amb. to Russia June 2008–; Chair. UN Advisory Bd on Disarmament Matters 2003; mem. Foundation Council, Geneva Centre for Security Policy 1995–98, Coll. of Commrs of UN Monitoring, Verification and Inspection Comm. (UNMOVIC); Order of Merit 1998. *Address:* Embassy of Ukraine, 103009 Moscow, Leontiyevskii per. 18, Russia (office). *Telephone:* (495) 629-35-42 (office). *Fax:* (495) 629-46-81 (office). *E-mail:* emb_ru@mfa.gov.ua (office). *Website:* www.mfa.gov.ua/russia (office).

HRYTSENKO, Anatoliy Stepanovych, DTechSci; Ukrainian government official and politicial analyst; b. 1957, Cherkasy oblast; ed Kyiv School of Higher Mil. Aviation Eng and Acad. of Armed Forces; Lecturer, Kyiv Higher School of Mil. Aviation Eng; fmr Head, Problem-Analytical Dept, Science-Research Centre, Armed Forces of Ukraine; fmr Head, Dept for Mil. Security and Construction, Nat. Scientific Research Centre for Defence Techs; Head, Analytical Apparatus, Nat. Security and Defence Council 1997–99; Pres. Center for Econ. and Political Studies 1999–2005; Minister of Defence 2005–07; mem. People's Union Our Ukraine party. *Address:* People's Union Our Ukraine, 04070 Kiev, vul. Borychiv Tik 22A, Ukraine (office). *Telephone:* (44) 206-60-95 (office). *E-mail:* tak@ua.org.ua (office). *Website:* www.razom .org.ua (office).

HSIAO, Hsin-Huang Michael, BA, MA, PhD; Taiwanese academic; *Executive Director, Center for Asia-Pacific Area Studies, Academia Sinica;* b. 26 Dec. 1948, Taipei; m. Yu-Hyang Lee Hsiao; two s.; ed Nat. Taiwan Univ., State Univ. of New York at Buffalo; Assoc. Research Fellow, Inst. of Ethnology, Academia Sinica 1979–83, Research Fellow 1983–95, Chair. 1980–82, Deputy Dir 1989–94; Dir Program for SE Asian Area Studies 1996–2001; Dir Asia-Pacific Research Program 2001–02; Exec. Dir Centre for Asia-Pacific Area Studies, Academia Sinica 2003–; Assoc. Prof., Dept of Sociology, Nat. Taiwan Univ. 1980–84, Prof. 1984–; Int. Assoc., Inst. on Culture, Religion and World Affairs, Boston Univ. 1990–; Exec. Dir Foundation for Advancement of Outstanding Scholarship 1994–; Nat. Policy Adviser to Pres. of Taiwan 1996–2005; Hon. Sr Research Fellow, Hong Kong Inst. of Asia-Pacific Studies, Chinese Univ. of Hong Kong 1999–; Chair. Advisory and Monitoring Cttee on the Privatization of Public Enterprise, Exec. Yuan of Taiwan 2004–05; Chair. Foundation for Excellent Journalism 2005–; Pres. Taiwanese Sociological Asscn 1992–93, Taiwan Asscn of Southeast Asian Studies 2004–; mem. Bd of Dirs Public TV Service 1998–2001, Nat. Culture and Art Foundation 1998–2001; mem. Nat. Unification Council 1997–2000; Councillor Nat. Council on Sustainable Devt, Exec. Yuan of Taiwan 1999–; Pres. Inst. of Nat. Devt 2000–02, Adviser 2002–; Councillor, Govt Reform Council, Office of the Pres. of Taiwan 2002–03; Man. Dir Asia Foundation in Taiwan 2003–; standing supervisor, Taiwan Foundation for Democracy 2003–; mem. editorial bd several journals; Fulbright Sr Visiting Scholar, Center for Asian Devt Studies, Boston Univ. and Fairbank Center for East Asian Research, Harvard Univ. 1983–84; Visiting Prof., Dept of Sociology and Center for Int. Studies, Duke Univ. 1988; Adjunct Chair Prof., Coll. of Hakka Studies, Nat. United Univ.; Dr Hu Shi Visting Chair, Prof. Sinological Inst., Leiden Univ., Netherlands 1994; Distinguished Research Award, Nat. Science Council, Exec. Yuan of Taiwan 1990–91, 1992–94, Distinguished Int. Alumni Award, State Univ. of New York at Buffalo 2005. *Publications:* more than 80 books including: Exploration of the Middle Classes in Southeast Asia (ed.) 2003, Chinese Enterprise, Transnationalism and Identity (co-ed.) 2003, Sustainable

Taiwan 2011 (co-ed.) 2003, Taiwan and Southeast Asia: Go-South Policy and Vietnamese Brides (ed.) 2004, Green Blueprint: Toward Local Sustainable Development in Taiwan (in Chinese, co-ed.) 2005, Notebook on Taiwan Observation (in Chinese) 2005, Taiwan's New Paradigms (in Chinese, co-author) 2006, Asian New Democracies: The Philippines, South Korea and Taiwan Compared (ed.) 2006, Capital Cities in Asia-Pacific: Primacy and Diversity (co-ed.) 2007, Frontiers of Southeast Asia and Pacific Studies (ed.) 2007, Deepening Local Sustainable Development: Taiwan's Nine Counties and Cities Examined 2008, NPO: Organization and Practice 2009; 100 book chapters and more than 100 journal articles in the fields of sociology of devt, civil society and democracy, and the middle classes in East and Southeast Asia. *Leisure interests:* gardening, classical music, travel, film. *Address:* Centre for Asia-Pacific Area Studies, Academia Sinica, Nankang, Taipei, Taiwan (office). *Telephone:* (2) 2652-5140 (office); (2) 2782-2191 (office); (2) 2691-3880 (home). *Fax:* (2) 2788-8911 (office); (2) 2782-2199 (office); (2) 2691-3895 (home). *E-mail:* michael@gate.sinica.edu.tw (office). *Website:* www.sinica .edu.tw/~capas (office).

HSIEH, Frank Chang-ting, LLM; Taiwanese politician; b. 18 May 1946, Taipei; ed Nat. Taiwan Univ., Kyoto Univ., Japan; practised as attorney 1969–81; Defence Counsel in Kaohsiung Incident 1990; mem. Taipei City Council 1981–88; mem. Cen. Standing Cttee, Democratic Progressive Party (DPP) 1986–96, Legislator 1989–96, Chair. Cen. Review Cttee 1996–98, DPP Vice-Presidential cand. 1996, Chair. DPP 2000–02, Jan.–March 2008; Mayor of Kaohsiung 1998–2005; Premier of Taiwan 2005–06; cand. for Mayor of Taipei 2006; DPP Presidential cand. 2008 elections. *Address:* Democratic Progressive Party (DPP), 10/F, 30 Beiping East Road, Taipei 10051, Taiwan (office). *Telephone:* (2) 23929989 (home). *Fax:* (2) 23929989 (office). *E-mail:* foreign@dpp.org.tw (office). *Website:* www.dpp.org.tw (office).

HSIEH, Hsiang-chuan, BS, MS, PhD; Taiwanese academic and politician; *Secretary-General, Executive Yuan;* b. 12 Dec. 1944; ed Nat. Taiwan Univ., Univ. of Wisconsin, USA; Post-Doctoral Fellow, Dept of Biochemistry, Florida State Univ. 1974–77; Investigator, Inst. of Dental Research, Univ. of Alabama 1977–82; Visiting Specialist, Nat. Science Council, Exec. Yuan 1982–84, Dir-Gen. Dept of Planning and Evaluation 1984–86, Dept of Life Sciences 1986, Deputy Dir-Gen. Hsinchu Science-based Industrial Park Admin 1989–96, Deputy Minister 1996–2001, Convener, Economy and Tech. Div., Nat. Policy Foundation 2003–08, Sec.-Gen. Exec. Yuan 2008–, concurrently Gov. Fujian Prov. *Address:* Office of the Secretary-General, Executive Yuan, 1, Section 1, Jhongsiao East Road, Jhongjheng District, Taipei 10058, Taiwan (office). *Telephone:* (2) 33566500 (office). *Fax:* (2) 23566920 (office). *Website:* www.ey .gov.tw (office).

HSÜ, Kenneth Jinghwa, MA, PhD; Swiss scientist, inventor and writer; *President, Tarim Associates AG; Professor, Nanjing University; Director, KJH Center, Beijing Institute of Geosciences;* b. (Jinghwa Hsü), 28 June 1929, China; s. of Sin-wu Hsü and Su-lan; m. 1st Ruth Grunder 1958 (deceased); two s. one d.; m. 2nd Christine Eugster 1966; one s.; ed Chinese Nat. Univ., Nanking, Ohio State Univ., Univ. of Calif. at Los Angeles and ETH, Zürich; Research Geologist and Research Assoc. Shell Devt Co., Houston, Tex. 1954–63; Assoc. Prof. State Univ. of New York, Binghamton, NY 1963–64; Assoc. Prof. Univ. of Calif. Riverside 1964–67; Prof. Swiss Fed. Inst. of Tech. (ETH) Zürich 1967–94, Prof. Emer. 1994–; Pres. Tarim Assocs AG 1994–, Fengshui Water Tech. Ltd 1998–; Prof. Nanjing Univ. 2004–; Pres. Int. Asscn of Sedimentologists 1978–82; Chair. Int. Marine Geology Comm. 1980–89; Dir Kenneth Center for ZHC Development, Beijing Inst. of Geosciences 2004–; mem. NAS, Acad. Sinica (Taiwan); Fellow, Inst. of Advanced Studies, Berlin 1995–96; Assoc. Fellow, Third World Acad. of Sciences; Hon. Prof. Chinese Acad. of Sciences; Hon. mem. Int. Asscn of Sedimentologists; Dr hc (Nanjing Univ.) 1994; Wollaston Medal, Geological Soc. of London; Twenhofel Medal, American Sedimentological Soc., Penrose Medal, Geological Soc. of America, President's Award, American Asscn of Petroleum Geologists, Alumnus of the Century, Nanjing Univ., Int. Writer of the Year, IBC 2003. *Publications:* Ein Schiff revolutioniert die Wissenschaft 1982, The Mediterranean was a Desert 1984, The Great Dying 1986, Challenger at Sea 1994, Geology of Switzerland 1995, Tectonic Facies Map of China 1996, Geologic Atlas of China 1998, Klima macht Geschichte 2000, Mozart in Love (in Chinese) 2003, Physics of Ledimen trilogy 2004; other books and more than 400 scientific articles. *Leisure interest:* Chinese aerophilately. *Address:* Tarim Associates AG, 127 Acker-steinerstrasse, 8049 Zürich, Switzerland (office); Oakcombe, Marley Common, Haslemere, GU27 3PT, Surrey, England (home). *Telephone:* (1) 3621462 (office); (1428) 641457 (home). *E-mail:* kenjhsu@aol.com (home).

HSU, Li-Teh, LLM, MPA; Taiwanese politician; b. 6 Aug. 1931, Loshan County, Honan; m.; two s.; ed Taiwan Prov. Coll. of Law and Commerce, Nat. Chengchi Univ. and Harvard Univ.; Dir Fifth Dept Exec. Yuan 1972–76; Admin. Vice-Minister of Finance 1976–78; Commr Dept of Finance, Taiwan Prov. Govt 1978–81; Minister of Finance 1981–84, of Econ. Affairs 1984–85; Chair. Lien-ho Jr Coll. of Tech., Global Investment Holding Co. Ltd 1986–88; Chair. Finance Comm. Cen. Cttee Kuomintang 1988–93; Deputy Sec.-Gen. and Exec. Sec. Policy Coordination Comm. Cen. Cttee Kuomintang 1990–93; Vice-Premier of Taiwan 1993–97. *Address:* c/o National Assembly, Taipei, Taiwan.

HSU, Shui-Teh, MA; Taiwanese politician; b. 1 Aug. 1931, Kaohsiung City; m. Yang Shu-hua; two s.; ed Nat. Taiwan Normal Univ., Nat. Chengchi Univ. and Japan Univ. of Educ.; official, Pingtung County Govt 1968–70, Kaohsiung City Govt 1970–75; Commr Dept of Social Affairs, Taiwan Provincial Govt 1975–79; Dir Dept of Social Affairs, Cen. Cttee, Kuomintang 1979; Sec.-Gen. Kaohsiung City Govt 1979–82; Mayor of Kaohsiung 1982–85, of Taipei 1985–88; Minister of the Interior 1988–91; Rep. Taipei Econ. and Culture Rep. Office in Japan 1991–93; Hon. LLD (Lincoln Univ.) 1985. *Publications:* The

Childhood Education of Emile, My Compliments—Recollections of Those Days Serving as Kaohsiung Mayor, A Thousand Sunrises and Midnights, My Scoopwheel Philosophy, A Study of Welfare Administration for the Aged, several works on psychology and educ. *Address:* c/o Kuomintang, 53 Jen Ai Road, Section 3, Taipei, Taiwan.

HU, Fuguo; Chinese politician and engineer; b. 1937, Changzi Co., Shanxi Prov.; ed Fuxin Mining Coll.; Dir Xishan Coal Mining Admin. of Shanxi Prov., 1978–82, Gov. (a.i.) of Shanxi Prov. 1992–93; Sec. CCP 6th Shanxi Prov. Cttee 1993–99; Chair. CCP 7th Shanxi Prov. Cttee 1994; Vice-Minister of Coal Industry 1982–88; Vice-Minister of Energy 1988; mem. State Econ. Examination Cttee 1983; mem. 14th CCP Cen. Cttee 1992–97, 15th CCP Cen. Cttee 1997–2002. *Address:* c/o Shanxi Provincial Committee of CCP, Taiyuan, People's Republic of China.

HU, Han, PhD; Chinese academic; b. 1924; s. of Hu Yen Bo and Xiao Shi Xun; m. Dong Yu Shen; one d.; ed Central Univ., Zhongqing; Lab. of Genetics and Breeding, Dept of Biology Univ. of Leningrad, USSR; Asst Prof., Inst. of Genetics, Academia Sinica 1964–78, Assoc. Prof. 1977–87, Dir 1978–96, Prof. 1992–; Chair. of Scientific Cttee of State Key Lab. of Plant Cell & Chromosome Eng; Vice-Pres. Genetics Soc. of China 1978–91; Ed. Science in China and Chinese Sciences Bulletin 1978–91, Theoretical Applied Genetics 1978–91, Plant Science 1992–2000; Nat. Science Congress Prize 1978, Major Prize, Academia Sinica 1978, Holeung Ho Lee Foundation Life Sciences Prize 2006. *Publications:* (co-ed.) Haploids of Higher Plants in Vitro 1986, Plant Somatic Genetics and Crop Improvement 1988, Plant Cell Manipulation and Breeding 1990, numerous articles on androgenesis in cereals and chromosome eng of pollen-derived plants in wheat. *Address:* Institute of Genetics, Academia Sinica, Bei Sha Tan Building, Beijing 100101, People's Republic of China.

HU, Jason Chih-chiang, DPhil; Taiwanese politician and academic; *Mayor of Taichung City;* b. 15 May 1948, Yungchi Co., Kirin Prov., China; m. Shirley S. Hu; one s. one d.; ed Nat. Chengchi Univ., Univ. of Southampton, Univ. of Oxford; Exec. Sec. Nat. Union of Students 1966–68; led del. to UN World Youth Asscn 1970; fmr instructor Inst. of Int. Studies, Univ. of SC, USA; taught Oxford Overseas Studies Programme 1982–83, Research Fellow, St Antony's Coll., Oxford 1985; Assoc. Prof. Nat. Sun Yat-sen Univ. 1986–90; Deputy Dir Sun Yat-sen Center for Policy Studies 1986–90; Deputy Dir First Bureau, Office of the Pres. concurrently Presidential Press Sec. 1991; Dir-Gen. Govt Information Office and Govt Spokesman 1991–96; Rep. of Taipei Econ. and Cultural Office, Washington, DC; Minister of Foreign Affairs 1997–99; Presidential Campaign Man., Kuomintang 1999–2000, Dir Cultural and Communication Affairs Central Comm. 2000–01, Deputy Sec.-Gen. 2001; Mayor of Taichung City 2001–; Dr hc (Southampton) 1997; Best Govt Spokesman Award 1993, Top Ten Chinese Award 1994, Outstanding Professional Achievement Award 1996. *Publications include:* Say Yes to Taiwan! 1997, Quiet Revolution (in Chinese) 1996; many other books in Chinese. *Address:* No. 99, Ming Chuan Road, Taichung, Taiwan (office). *Telephone:* (2) 2228-8211 (office). *Fax:* (2) 2229-1136 (office). *E-mail:* 10001@tccg.gov.tw (office). *Website:* www.tccg.gov.tw (office).

HU, Jia; Chinese platform diver; b. 10 Jan. 1983, Wuhan, Hubei Prov.; joined Guangdong prov. team 1994, nat. team 1998; winner 10m. Platform Synchronized, World Championships, Fukuoka 2001, Grand Prix, Southern Cross 2003; winner 10m. Platform, Grand Prix, Bangkok 2000, Grand Prix, USA Diving 2001; Silver Medal 10m. Platform, Platform Synchronized, Sydney Olympics 2000; Gold Medal 10m. Platform, Athens Olympics 2004. *Leisure interests:* music, computers, travelling. *Address:* c/o China Swimming Association, 5 Tiyuguan Road, Chongwen District, Beijing 100763, People's Republic of China (office). *Telephone:* (10) 67020332 (office). *Fax:* (10) 67020320 (office). *Website:* (office).

HU, Jintao; Chinese head of state; *President;* b. 21 Dec. 1942, Jixi, Anhui Prov.; m. Liu Yongqing; ed Tsinghua Univ., Beijing; joined CCP 1964; postgraduate and political instructor, Water Conservancy Eng Dept, Tsinghua Univ. 1964–65, researcher 1965–68; Sec. Gansu Prov. Construction Cttee, Deputy Dir 1974–75, Vice-Chair. 1980–82; Chair. All-China Youth Fed. 1982–84; Sec. Gansu Prov. Br. Communist Youth League 1982; Sec. Communist Youth League 1982–84, First Sec. 1984–85; mem. Standing Cttee, 6th NPC, mem. Presidium and mem. Standing Cttee, CPPCC 6th Nat. Cttee 1983–98; Sec. CCP Prov. Cttee, Guizhou 1985–88, Tibet 1988–92; Vice-Pres. of People's Repub. of China (PRC) 1998–2003, Pres. 2003–; Vice-Chair. Cen. Mil. Comm. of PRC 1999–2002; mem. 12th CCP Cen. Cttee 1982–87, 13th CCP Cen. Cttee 1987–92, 14th CCP Cen. Cttee 1992–97 (mem. Secr. and Standing Cttee of Politburo 1992–97), 15th CCP Cen. Cttee 1997–2002 (mem. Secr. and Standing Cttee of Politburo 1992–97, Vice-Chair. Cen. Mil. Comm. 1997–2002), 16th CCP Cen. Cttee 2002–07, (Gen. Sec. 2002–, Vice-Chair. Cen. Mil. Comm. 2002–05, Chair. 2005–07, mem. Standing Cttee of Politburo 2002–07); Gen. Sec. 17th CCP Cen. Cttee 2007– (mem. Standing Cttee of Politburo 2007–, Chair. Cen. Mil. Comm. 2007–); Pres. Cen. Party School 1993–. *Address:* Office of the President, Great Hall of the People, West Edge, Tiananmen Square, Beijing, People's Republic of China (office). *Website:* www .gov.cn (office).

HU, Kehui; Chinese lawyer; *Deputy Procurator-General, Supreme People's Procuratorate;* b. Feb. 1944, Anshun, Guizhou Prov.; ed Southwest Univ. of Political Science and Law; joined CCP 1971; Chief Procurator of Guizhou Prov. People's Procuratorate 1993–98; Deputy Procurator-Gen., Supreme People's Procuratorate 1998–; Vice-Pres. Chinese Asscn of Public Prosecutors. *Address:* Supreme People's Procuratorate, Beijing, People's Republic of China.

HU, Maoyuan; Chinese automobile industry executive; *Chairman, Shanghai Automotive Industry Corporation (SAIC);* b. 1951, Shanghai; ed Fudan Univ.; began career in automotive industry 1968; mem. CCP 1980–; Man. Dir Shanghai Tractor Plant 1983; Vice-Pres. Shanghai Automotive Industry Corpn (SAIC) 1991–99, Pres. 1999–, currently Chair. SAIC Group and Chair. SAIC Motor Corpn Ltd; Pres. Shanghai Huizhong Automotive Mfg Co. Ltd; Pres. Shanghai Gen. Motors Co. Ltd 1997–99; State Model Worker, State Advanced Individual in Quality Man., Excellent Party Mem. of Shanghai Municipality, Master of Operation and Man. in Machinery Industry, CCTV Award for People of Economy. *Publications:* Dialogue with the World. *Address:* Shanghai Automotive Industry Corporation (SAIC), 487 Wei Hai Road, Shanghai 200041, People's Republic of China (office). *Telephone:* (21) 22011888 (office). *Fax:* (21) 22011777 (office). *E-mail:* info@saicgroup.com (office). *Website:* www.saicgroup.com (office).

HU, Ping; Chinese government official; b. 1930, Jiaxing Co., Zhejiang Prov.; ed Jiangsu Industry Inst.; joined CCP 1950; Vice-Gov. of Fujian 1981–83; Sec. CCP Prov. Cttee Fujian 1982; Deputy Sec. CCP Prov. Cttee, Fujian 1982; Dir Fujian Cttee for Econ. Reconstruction 1983; Alt. mem. 12th CCP Cen. Cttee 1982–87; mem. 13th CCP Cen. Cttee 1987–92; Sec. CCP Prov. Cttee 1982–83; Acting Gov. of Fujian 1983, Gov. 1983–87 (removed from post); Vice-Minister, State Planning Comm. 1987–88; Minister of Commerce 1988–93; Dir Special Econ. Zones Office 1993–96; Chair. Bd of Regents, Overseas Chinese Univ. 1986. *Address:* c/o Ministry of Commerce, 45 Fuxingmen Nei Dajie, Beijing 100801, People's Republic of China.

HU, Qiheng; Chinese scientist and public official; *Chairman, Internet Society of China;* b. 15 June 1934, Beijing; d. of Shu Wei Hu and Wen Yi Fan; m. Yuan Jian Lian 1959; one s. one d.; ed Moscow Inst. of Chemical Machinery, USSR; Dir Inst. of Automation, Academia Sinica 1980–89; Vice-Pres. Chinese Acad. of Sciences 1988–96; mem. Nat. Cttee, 8th and 9th CPPCC 1993–; Vice-Pres., China Asscn for Science and Tech. 1996–; Chair. Internet Soc. of China 2001–; mem. UN Working Group on Internet Governance 2004; Visiting Research Prof., Case Western Reserve Univ., USA 1980–82; mem. Chinese Acad. of Eng; Outstanding Woman of China 1984, Award for contrib. to Nat. Hightech. Programme 863 1996. *Publications:* book chapters in Advances in Information Systems Science 1986; Processing of Pattern-Based Information, Parts I and II (with Yoh Han Pao). *Leisure interests:* reading novels, growing flowers, pets (kittens and guinea-pigs), bicycling, computer drawing. *Address:* Internet Society of China, No.13, West Chang'an Avenue, Beijing 100804, People's Republic of China. *Telephone:* (10) 66068552 (office). *Fax:* (10) 68512458 (office); (10) 66418201 (office). *E-mail:* isc@isc.org.cn (office).

HU, Qili; Chinese politician; *Chairman, Song Qingling Foundation;* b. 1929, Yulin Co., Shaaxi Prov.; m.; one s. one d.; ed Beijing Univ.; joined CCP 1948; Sec. Communist Youth League (CYL) Cttee, Beijing Univ. 1954; Vice-Chair. Students' Fed. 1954; mem. Standing Cttee, Youth Fed. 1958; Sec. CYL 1964, 1978; Vice-Chair. Youth Fed. 1965; purged 1967; Vice-Pres. Tsinghua Univ., Beijing 1976; Sec. CYL 1978; Chair. Youth Fed. 1979–80; mem. Standing Cttee, 5th CPPCC 1979–83; Mayor, Tianjin 1980–82; Sec. CCP Cttee, Tianjin 1980–82; Dir Gen. Office Cen. Cttee CCP 1982–87; Vice-Chair. Cen. Party Consolidation Comm. 1983–89; mem. Presidium, 1st session 7th NPC; Vice-Minister of Electronics Industry and Machine-Building Industry 1991–93; Minister of Electronics Industry 1993–98; Deputy Head, State Leading Group for Information 1996; Chair. Song Qingling Foundation 1998–; mem. 12th CCP Cen. Cttee 1982–87, 13th CCP Cen. Cttee 1987–92 (mem. Politburo 1982–89, Politburo Standing Cttee 1987–89, Sec. Secr. CCP 1982–89), mem. 14th CCP Cen. Cttee 1992–97; Vice-Chair. 9th Nat. Cttee of CPPCC 1998–2003. *Leisure interests:* tennis, cycling. *Address:* Song Qingling Foundation, A12F, Zhejiang Plaza, No. 29 Anzhen Xili, Chaoyang District, Beijing, People's Republic of China (office).

HU TSU TAU, Richard, PhD; Singaporean politician; *Chairman, Government of Singapore Investment Corporation Real Estate Pte Ltd;* b. 30 Oct. 1926; m. Irene Tan Dee Leng; one s. one d.; ed Anglo-Chinese School, Univ. of California, Berkeley, USA, Univ. of Birmingham, UK; Lecturer in Chemical Eng, Univ. of Manchester, UK 1958–60; joined Shell (Singapore and Malaysia) 1960, Dir Marketing and Gen. Man. Shell (KL) 1970, with Shell Int. Petroleum Co., Netherlands 1973, Chief Exec. Shell Cos (Malaysia) 1974, Chair. and Chief Exec. Shell Cos (Singapore) 1977, Chair. 1982; Man. Dir The Monetary Authority of Singapore and Man. Dir Govt of Singapore Investment Corpn Pte. Ltd 1983–84; elected MP (People's Action Party) 1984; Chair. The Monetary Authority of Singapore, Chair. Bd of Commrs of Currency 1985; Minister for Trade and Industry Jan.–May 1985, for Health 1985–87, for Finance 1985–2001, of Nat. Devt 1992; Chair. Govt of Singapore Investment Corpn (GIC) Real Estate Pte Ltd, Mapletree Investments; Chancellor Singapore Man. Univ.; mem. Bd of Dirs Buildfolio. *Leisure interests:* golf, swimming. *Address:* Singapore Management University, Tanglin PO Box 257, 912409, Singapore.

HUA, Jun-Duo; Chinese diplomatist and government official; *Commissioner-General, Shanghai Expo 2010;* Amb. to India –2006; Commr-Gen. World Expo 2010 Shanghai China 2006–. *Address:* c/o Executive Committee, 2010 Shanghai World Leisure Expo, No. 3588, Pudong Rd, Shanghai 200125, People's Republic of China (office).

HUANG, An-Lun, MM, FTCL; Chinese composer; b. 15 March 1949, Guangzhou City, Guangdong Prov.; s. of Huang Fei-Li and Zhao Fang-Xing; m. Ouyang Rui-Li 1974; one s.; ed Central Conservatory of Music, Beijing, Univ. of Toronto, Canada, Trinity Coll. of Music, London and Yale Univ., USA; started piano aged five; studied with Shaw Yuan-Xin and Chen Zi; works have been widely performed in China, Hong Kong, Philippines, northern Africa, Australia, Europe, USA and Canada; Resident Composer, Cen. Opera House of China 1976–; Pres. Canadian Chinese Music Soc., Ont. 1987–96; Fellowship in Composition, Trinity Coll. of Music, London 1983; Yale Alumni Asscn Prize, Yale Univ. 1986; Skills for Change New Pioneer Award, Ontario 2004.

Compositions: operas: Flower Guardian Op. 26 1979, Yeu Fei Op. 37 1986 and 6 others; symphonic, chamber, vocal, choral and film music, including: Symphonic Concert Op. 25, Symphonic Overture, The Consecration of the Spring in 1976 Op. 25a 1977, Piano Concerto in G Op. 25b 1982, Symphony in C Op. 25c 1984, The Sword (symphonic poem) Op. 33 1982, Easter Cantata (text by Semuel Tang) Op. 38 1986; Psalm 22-A Cantata in Baroque Style Op. 43c 1988, Piano Concerto in G; ballets: The Little Match Girl Op. 24 1978, A Dream of Dun Huang Op. 29 1980, The Special Orchestra Album 1997. *Leisure interests:* reading, sport. *Address:* 15 Carlton Road, Markham, Ont., L3R 17E, Canada (office); The Central Opera House of China, Zuojia Zhuang, Out of Dongzhimen Gate, Beijing, People's Republic of China. *Telephone:* (416) 423-6396.

HUANG, Anren; Chinese artist; b. 8 Oct. 1924, Yangjiang County, Guandong; s. of Huang Ting Jin and Lin Fen; m. Tan Su 1941; two s. two d.; fmr Vice-Sec.-Gen. Guangdong Br., Chinese Artists' Asscn; Chair. Guangzhou Hairi Research Inst. of Painting and Calligraphy; Adviser, Guangdong Writers' Asscn of Popular Science. *Publications:* Selected Paintings of Huang Anren, Album of Sketches by Huang Anren, On Arts: Collection of Commentaries by Huang Anren. *Leisure interests:* literature, music. *Address:* Room 602, No. 871-2 Renminbei Road, Guangzhou, People's Republic of China.

HUANG, Chih-Fang, BA; Taiwanese diplomatist and politician; b. 14 Sept. 1958; ed Nat. Taiwan Univ.; Officer, Taipei Rep. Office, UK 1985–86; Officer, Dept of N American Affairs, Ministry of Foreign Affairs (MoFA), Exec. Yuan 1986–91; Sec. Congressional Liaison Div., Taipei Econ. and Cultural Rep. Office in USA 1991–96; Chief, Section 1, Dept of N American Affairs (DNAA), MoFA 1996–99; Sr Specialist, and concurrently Chief of Section 1, DNAA 1999; Sr Specialist, Dept of Policy Planning, Mainland Affairs Council (MAC), Exec. Yuan 1999, Sr Researcher, MAC 1999, Deputy Dir Dept of Information and Liaison, MAC 2001–02; Dir-Gen. Dept of Public Affairs, Office of the Pres. 2002–04, Deputy Sec.-Gen., Office of the Pres. 2004–06; Minister of Foreign Affairs 2006–08; mem. Democratic Progressive Party. *Address:* Democratic Progressive Party, 10/F, 30 Beiping East Road, Taipei 10051, Taiwan (office). *Telephone:* (2) 23929989 (office). *Fax:* (2) 23929989 (office). *E-mail:* foreign@dpp.org.tw (office). *Website:* www.dpp.org.tw (office).

HUANG, Da, MA; Chinese economist and academic; b. 22 Feb. 1925, Tianjin; s. of Shu-ren and Gao Huang; m. Shu-zhen Luo 1952; two s.; ed Northern China United Univ.; Dir Finance Dept Renmin Univ. of China 1978–83, Vice-Pres. 1983–91, Pres. 1991–94; mem. NPC, NPC Cttee on Finance & Econ. 1993–98; mem. and head of econ. group, Academic Degrees Cttee of the State Council 1988–; mem. Monetary Policy Cttee of People's Bank of China 1997–; Dir Expert Advisory Cttee on Humanities and Social Sciences Studies, State Educ. Comm. 1997–; in charge of Eighth 5-Year Plan 1991–95; Vice-Chair. Chinese Soc. for Finance and Banking 1984–95 (Chair. 1995), Chinese Soc. for Public Finance 1983, Chinese Soc. for Prices 1986, Chinese Soc. for Materials Circulation 1990; Vice-Pres. China Enterprise Man. Asscn and the Securities Asscn of China 1987; Council mem., Chinese Asscn for Int. Understanding 1982; Chair. Chinese Cttee on Econs Educ. Exchange with USA 1985. *Publications:* Money and Money Circulation in the Chinese Socialist Economy 1964, Socialist Fiscal and Financial Problems 1981, Introduction to the Overall Balancing of Public Finance and Bank Credit 1984, The Price Scissors on the Price Parities Between Industrial and Agricultural Products 1990, The Economics of Money and Banking 1992, Macro-economic Control and Money Supply 1997. *Leisure interest:* calligraphy. *Address:* c/o Office of the President, Renmin University of China, Beijing 100872, People's Republic of China.

HUANG, Daren; Chinese mathematician, academic and university administrator; *President, Zhongshan University;* b. 1945, Zhejiang Prov.; ed Zhejiang Univ.; Visiting Scholar, Dept of Math., Univ. of South Carolina, USA 1985–86; Vice-Pres., Zhejiang Univ. 1992–98; Vice-Pres. Zhongshan Univ. (Sun Yat-sen Univ.) 1998–99, Pres. 1999–; Progress in Science and Tech. Award, Nat. and Prov. Awards for Excellence in Teaching. *Publications:* over 100 research papers on math. *Address:* Office of the President, Zhongshan University, Guangzhou 510275, Guangdong Province, People's Republic of China (office). *Telephone:* (20) 84112828 (office). *Website:* www.sysu.edu.cn/en/index.html (office).

HUANG, Fanzhang; Chinese economist; *Senior Adviser, China Reform Forum;* b. 8 Feb. 1931, Jiang-Xi; s. of Qi-Kun Huang and Yun-Jin Hua; m. Yue-Fen Xue 1959; two s.; ed Peking Univ.; Researcher, Inst. of Econs, Chinese Acad. of Social Science (CASS) 1954–, Sr Researcher and Prof. 1979–, Deputy Dir 1982–85; Visiting Scholar, Harvard Univ. 1980–82, Stockholm Univ. 1982; Exec. Dir for China, IMF 1985–86; Visiting Research Assoc. Center for Chinese Studies, Univ. of Mich. 1986–87; Consultant to World Bank 1987–88; Dir Dept of Int. Econ. Studies, State Planning Comm. 1988–90; Vice-Pres. Acad. of Macro-Economic Research, State Devt and Reform Comm. 1990–97, Sr Researcher 1997–; Vice-Chair. China Reform Forum 1997–2008, Sr Adviser 2008–; CASS Prize 1985. *Publications include:* Modern Economics in Western Countries (with others) 1963, The Evolution of Socialist Theories of Income Distribution 1979, Swedish Welfare State in Practice and its Theories 1987, The Reform in Banking System and The Role of Monetary Policy in China 1989, China's Exploration of the Theories of Economic Reform in the Last Ten Years (1979–89) 1991, Stock Ownership, Privatization, Socialization and Other Topics 1992, Foreign Direct Investment in China Since 1979 1992, East Asian Economics: Development, Prospects for Co-operation and China's Strategy 1993, China's Transitional Inflation 1994, China's Use of Foreign Direct Investment and Economic Reform 1995, Selected Works of Huang Fan-Zhang (1980–93) 1995, White Paper on East Asian Economies 1996, Economic Globalization and Financial Supervision In Internationalization 1998, Whither Will the East Asian Economies Go? 1999, China's Reform: Opening to the Outside and Its International Environment 2002, China's New Road of Industrialization and its Peaceful Rise 2004, The Blue Book on East Asian Economies 2000–05 2006, 30 Years of Institutional Innovation and Theoretical Innovation: In Memory of 30th Anniversary of Reform & Open Policy 2008. *Leisure interest:* classical music. *Address:* Apartment 801, Building 13, Mu-Xi-Di, Bei-Li, Beijing 100038, People's Republic of China (home). *Telephone:* (10) 63261950 (home). *Fax:* (10) 63908071 (home). *E-mail:* Huangfz@hotmail.com (home). *Website:* www.chinareform.org (office).

HUANG, Guangyu, (Wong Kwong Yu); Chinese business executive; *Chairman, GOME Appliances;* b. 1969, Shantou, Guangdong Prov.; brother of Huang Junqin (q.v.); left high school 1987, moved to Beijing with older brother Huang Junqin, took out small bank loan and began selling household appliances; Founder and Chair. GOME Appliances (fmrly China Eagle Group Co. Ltd, name changed to GOME 1993) 1987–, GOME Electrical Appliances Holdings Ltd 1987–. *Address:* GOME Appliances, 11th Floor, Block B, Eagle Plaza, No. 26 Xiaoyun Road, Chao Yang District, Beijing 100016 (office); GOME Electrical Appliances Holding Ltd, Unit 6101, 61st Floor Queen's Road, The Center, Hong Kong Special Administrative Region, People's Republic of China (office). *Telephone:* (10) 8458 4285 (Beijing) (office); 212-11005 (Hong Kong) (office). *Fax:* (10) 84584073 ext. 8413 (Beijing) (office); 253-02582 (Hong Kong) (office). *E-mail:* yuanling@guomei.cn (office); info@gome.com.hk (office). *Website:* www.gome.com.cn (office); www.gome.com.hk (office).

HUANG, Hua; Chinese fmr diplomatist; b. 1913, Cixian Co., Hebei Prov.; m. He Liliang; two s. one d.; ed Yanqing Univ., Beijing; joined CCP 1936; fmr Dir, Foreign Affairs Bureau of Tianjin, Nanking and Shanghai; later Dir, West European Dept, Ministry of Foreign Affairs; Chief of Chinese Del. at Panmunjom (Korean War political negotiations) 1953; political adviser to Premier Zhou En-lai, Spokesman of Chinese Del. to Geneva Conf. on Indo-China and Korea 1954, First Afro-Asian Conf., Bandung 1955; Adviser, Sino-American negotiations, Warsaw 1958; Amb. to Ghana 1960–66, to Egypt 1966–69, to Canada July–Nov. 1971; Perm. Rep. to UN 1971–76; Minister of Foreign Affairs 1976–83; mem. 10th Cen. Cttee CCP 1974, 11th 1978, 12th 1983–87; a Vice-Premier, State Council 1980–82; State Councillor 1982–83; Vice-Chair. Standing Cttee, 6th NPC 1983–88; mem. Standing Cttee of Cen. Advisory Comm. 1987; mem. Presidium, 14th CCP Nat. Congress 1992; Pres. Exec. Cttee, China Welfare Inst. 1988; Pres. Chinese Asscn for Int. Friendly Contacts 1992–; Hon. Pres. China Int. Public Relations Asscn 1991–, Chinese Environmental Protection Foundation 1993–; Chair. Soong Ching Ling Foundation 1992; Adviser Chinese Asscn for Promotion of the Population Culture; Pres. Smedley, Strong, Snow Soc. of China; mem. Policy Bd Interaction Council; Hon. Pres. Yenching Alumnae Assoc.; Hon. DHumLitt (Missouri). *Leisure interests:* fishing, jogging. *Address:* Standing Committee, National People's Congress, Beijing, People's Republic of China.

HUANG, Huang; Chinese party official; b. 1933, Lianshui Co., Jiangsu Prov.; joined PLA 1946, CCP 1949; Leading Sec. CCP Cttee, Anhui Prov. 1983–86; mem. 12th CCP Cen. Cttee 1985–87; mem. Presidium 6th NPC 1986–88; Deputy Gov. Jianxi Prov. 1987–90; Sec. CCP 7th Ningxia Hui Autonomous Regional Cttee 1990–; Political Commissar 1990–96; mem. 14th CCP Cen. Cttee 1992–97.

HUANG, Jack; Taiwanese editor and newspaper executive; s. of Y. P. Huang and Nancy Huang, co-founders of The China Post; Publr and Ed. The China Post. *Address:* The China Post, 8 Fu Shun Street, Taipei 10452, Taiwan (office). *Telephone:* (2) 2596-9971 (office). *Fax:* (2) 2595-7962 (office). *E-mail:* cpost@msl.hinet.net (office); info@mail.chinapost.com.tw (office). *Website:* www.chinapost.com.tw (office).

HUANG, James C. F., BA; Taiwanese government official; b. 14 Sept. 1958, Tainan City; m. Charlene Ting; one s. two d.; ed Nat. Taiwan Univ.; Officer Dept of N American Affairs, Ministry of Foreign Affairs 1986, Officer Secr. 1989, Section Chief, First Section 1996, Asst Deputy-Gen. and Section Chief, First Section 1999; Sec., Congressional Liaison Div., Taipei Econ. and Cultural Rep. Office, USA 1991; Asst Deputy-Gen. Dept of Policy and Planning, Mainland Affairs Council, Exec. Yuan 1999, Sr Researcher, Mainland Affairs Council 2000, Deputy Dir-Gen. Dept of Information and Liaison, Mainland Affairs Council 2001; Dir-Gen. Dept of Public Affairs, Office of the Pres. 2002, Deputy Sec.-Gen. to the Pres. 2004; Minister of Foreign Affairs 2006–08 (resgnd). *Address:* c/o Ministry of Foreign Affairs, 2 Kaitakeland Boulevard, Taipei 100, Taiwan (office).

HUANG, Jianxin; Chinese film director; b. 1954, Shenxian, Hebei Prov.; ed Northwest Univ., Beijing Motion Picture Acad. *Films include:* As Director: The Black Cannon Incident (Golden Rooster Best Director Award 1986) 1985, Samsara, Lun Hui (Golden Rooster Best Director Award) 1989, Stand Straight, Don't Collapse 1993, Back to Back, Face to Face 1994, Signal Left, Turn Right 1996, Surveillance 1997, Shuibuzhao (Can't Fall Asleep) 1998, Shei Shuo Wo Bu Zaihu (Who Says I Don't Care?) 2001; As Producer: 2 Young 2005. *Address:* Xian Film Studio, Xian, People's Republic of China.

HUANG, Junqin, (Wong Chung-yam); Chinese business executive; *Chairman, Towercrest Group;* b. Shantou, Guangdong Prov.; brother of Huang Guangyu (q.v.); moved to Beijing with younger brother Huang Guangyu, took out small bank loan and began selling household appliances; f. Gome brand for their electronics business 1987; moved into real estate industry, two brothers later separated and Junqin obtained assets of real estate business; f. Towercrest Group, currently Chair.; Chair. Shandong Jintai Group Co. 2002–. *Address:* Towercrest Group, Beijing, People's Republic of China (office). *Website:* www.towercrest.com.cn (office).

HUANG, Pi-twan, BA, MA, PhD; Taiwanese academic and politician; *Minister of the Council for Cultural Affairs;* b. 14 Nov. 1945; ed Nat. Taiwan Univ., Univ. of Wisconsin, USA; Assoc. Prof. and Chair. Dept of Foreign Languages and Literature, Nat. Sun Yat-sen Univ. 1980–92; Deputy Dir Nat. Chiang Kai Shek Cultural Center 1992–95; Chair. Dept of Foreign Languages and Literature, Nat. Chi Nan Univ. 1995–97, Dean, Coll. of Humanities 2000; Dir Dept of Higher Educ., Ministry of Educ., Exec. Yuan 1997–2000; Pres. Tainan Nat. Univ. of the Arts 2000–06; Minister of the Council for Cultural Affairs 2008–; Hon. Fellow, Univ. of Wisconsin 1989–90. *Address:* Council for Cultural Affairs, 30-1 Beiping East Road, Taipei 10051, Taiwan (office). *Telephone:* (2) 23434000 (office). *Fax:* (2) 23222937 (office). *E-mail:* adm@cca.gov.tw (office). *Website:* www.cca.gov.tw (office).

HUANG, Rayson Lisung, CBE, JP, DPhil, DSc, FRCPE; Singaporean chemist and university vice-chancellor (retd); b. 1 Sept. 1920, Shantou, China; s. of Rufus Huang and Roseland Huang; m. Grace Wei Li 1949 (deceased); two s.; ed Munsang Coll., Hong Kong, Univ. of Hong Kong, Univ. of Oxford, UK; Demonstrator in Chem., Nat. Kwangsi Univ., Kweilin, China 1943; Post-Doctoral Fellow and Research Assoc., Univ. of Chicago 1947–50; Lecturer in Chem., Univ. of Malaya, Singapore 1951–54, Reader in Chem. 1955–59; Prof. of Chem., Univ. of Malaya, Kuala Lumpur 1959–69, Dean of Science 1962–65; Vice-Chancellor, Nanyang Univ., Singapore 1969–72, Univ. of Hong Kong 1972–86; Pres. Asscn of Southeast Asian Insts of Higher Learning 1970–72, 1981–83; Chair. Council, Asscn of Commonwealth Univs 1980–81; unofficial mem. Legis. Council of Hong Kong 1977–83; Vice-Chair. Council, Shantou Univ., China 1987–94; mem. Drafting Cttee and Vice-Chair. Consultative Cttee for Basic Law of the Hong Kong Special Admin. Region of the People's Repub. of China 1985–90; Life mem. of Court, Univ. of Hong Kong; Life mem. Bd Trustees Croucher Foundation, Hong Kong, Rayson Huang Foundation, Kuala Lumpur; Dir Ming Pao Enterprise Corpn Ltd, Hong Kong 1990–94; Order of the Rising Sun (Japan) 1986; Hon. DSc (Hong Kong) 1968; Hon. LLD (E Asia, Macao) 1986. *Publications:* The Chemistry of Free Radicals 1974, A Lifetime in Academia (autobiog.) 2000; about 50 research papers on chemistry of free radicals, molecular rearrangements and synthetic oestrogens. *Leisure interests:* opera, ballet, concerts, violin-playing. *Address:* Raycrest II, 10 The Stables, Selly Park, Birmingham, B29 7JW, England (home). *Telephone:* (121) 472-0180 (home).

HUANG, Tiao-kuei, MA; Taiwanese insurance industry executive; ed Nat. Tsing Hua Univ., Swiss Insurance Training Centre, Switzerland; fmrly Exec. Vice-Pres. Cathay Life Insurance Co. Ltd, Pres. –2008, also fmr Pres. Cathay Financial Holdings; fmr Man.-Dir Life Insurance Asscn of Repub. of China, Chair. 2003; mem. Int. Insurance Soc. *Address:* c/o Cathay Life Insurance Company Ltd, 296 Jen Ai Road, Section 4, Taipei 10639, Taiwan. *Telephone:* (22) 755-1399.

HUANG, Weilu, MSc; Chinese engineer; b. 1916, Wuhu City, Anhui Emer. Prov.; ed Cen. Univ. for Nationalities, Beijing, Imperial Coll., Univ. of London, UK; one of the pioneers of rocket science in China and later of Earth satellites; Chief Engineer, Ministry of Astronautics Industry 1982; Sr Tech. Consultant, China Aviation Industry Corpn; Vice-Chair. Science and Tech. Cttee 1982–; Deputy 6th NPC 1983–88, 7th NPC 1988–93; Corresp. mem. Int. Acad. of Astronautics 1986–; mem. Chinese Acad. of Sciences 1991–; Star Meritorious Service Medal 1999. *Address:* Science and Technology Committee, Beijing, People's Republic of China (office).

HUANG, Yongyu; Chinese artist and poet; b. 1924, Fenghuang Co., Hunan Prov.; best known for his satirical picture Maotouying (Owl) of an owl with its left eye closed, produced during the 'Gang of Four' era; Vice-Chair. Chinese Artists' Asscn 1985–; mem. Nationalities Cttee 7th CPPCC; Olympic Art Prize 2008; Commendatore (Italy) 1986. *Works include:* Maotouying (Owl), Ahshima, Spring Tide, Collected Woodcarvings, World Peace (donated to UN), China = MC2 2008. *Publications:* A Can of Worms, An Old Man who is Older than Me 2003. *Leisure interest:* watching sport. *Address:* Central Academy of Fine Arts, Beijing, People's Republic of China.

HUANG, Zhendong; Chinese politician; b. 1941, Dafeng Co., Jiangsu Prov.; ed Nanjing Navigation Eng School, Shanghai Shipping Inst.; Sr Engineer at Research Fellow level, Nanjing Navigation Eng School 1962; entered work-force, Admin. Bureau, Qinhuangdao Harbour, Hebei Prov. 1963, Deputy Chief of Planning Div. and Deputy Dir Admin. Bureau 1963–82, Dir 1982; joined CCP 1981; Vice-Minister of Communications 1985–88, Minister 1991–2003 (Sec. CCP Leading Party Group, Ministry of Communications 1991); Gen. Man. State Communications Investment Co. 1988–91; Chair. China Merchants' Steam Navigation Group Ltd 1991; mem. 14th CCP Cen. Cttee 1992–97, 15th Cen. Cttee 1997–2002, 16th CCP Cen. Cttee 2002–07; Sec. Chongqing CCP Municipal Cttee 2002–05; Chair. Standing Cttee Chongqing Municipal People's Congress 2003–06. *Address:* c/o Zhongguo Gongchan Dang (Chinese Communist Party), 1 Zhong Nan, Beijing, People's Republic of China.

HUANG, Zhiquan; Chinese politician; b. Feb. 1942, Tongxiang, Zhejiang Prov.; ed Zhejiang Agricultural Univ.; joined CCP 1979; Div. Head and Deputy Dir Jiangxi Prov. Planning Comm. 1984–91, Dir 1991–93; Asst Gov. Jiangxi Prov. 1991–93, Vice-Gov. 1993–2001, Gov. 2001–06; Deputy Sec. CCP Jiangxi Prov. Cttee 1995–; mem. 15th CCP Cen. Cttee 1997–2002, 16th CCP Cen. Cttee 2002–07. *Address:* c/o Jiangxi Provincial People's Government, 5 Beijing West Road, Nanchang 330046, People's Republic of China (office).

HUBBARD, Allan (Al) Brooks, BA, MA, JD; American business executive and government official; b. 8 Sept. 1947, Jackson, Tenn.; m. Kathryn Hubbard (née Fortune) 1979; one s.; ed Vanderbilt Univ., Harvard School of Business Admin, Harvard Law School; Co-founder and Pres. E&A Industries Inc., Indianapolis 1983–; Deputy Chief of Staff to Vice-Pres. Dan Quayle 1990–92, fmr Dir Pres.'s Council on Competitiveness; Asst to Pres. for Econ. Policy and Dir Nat. Econ. Council 2005–07. *Address:* c/o National Economic Council, The White House, 1600 Pennsylvania Avenue, NW, Washington, DC 20502, USA (office).

HUBBARD, John, BA; American painter; b. 26 Feb. 1931, Ridgefield, Conn.; s. of G. Evans Hubbard and Dorothea Denys Hubbard; m. Caryl Whineray 1961; one s. one d.; ed Milton Acad., Harvard Univ. and Art Students' League; served US Army in Counter-Intelligence 1953–56; designed décor and costumes for Le Baiser de la Fée, Dutch Nat. Ballet 1968, Midsummer, Royal Ballet, London 1983 and Sylvia Pas de Deux, Royal Ballet, London 1985; mem. Advisory Panel, Tate Gallery, St Ives 1993–2000; Astra Award (Garden Design) 1992, Jerwood Prize 1996. *Television:* The South Bank Show 1981. *Publications:* Second Nature 1984, The Tree of Life 1989. *Leisure interests:* walking, gardening. *Address:* Chilcombe House, Chilcombe, Bridport, Dorset, DT6 4PN, England (home). *Telephone:* (1308) 482234 (home). *E-mail:* john@johnhubbard.com (home).

HUBBARD, Richard (Dick), B Tech; New Zealand business executive and politician; *Mayor of Auckland;* Chairman, Hubbard Foods Ltd; currently Mayor of Auckland; Dir, Outward Bound Inst. of NZ; councillor, Massey Univ.; Trustee, NZ Nat. Parks and Conservation Foundation; Fellow NZ Inst. of Food Science and Tech., NZ Inst. of Man.; Dr hc (Massey Univ.). *Leisure interests:* climbing, motorcycling, photography. *Address:* c/o Auckland City Council, Private Bag 92516, Wellesley Street, Auckland, NZ (office). *Fax:* (9) 307-7579 (office). *E-mail:* mayor@aucklandcity.govt.nz (office). *Website:* www.aucklandcity.govt.nz (office).

HUBBARD, R(obert) Glenn, PhD; American economist, academic and fmr government official; *Russell L. Carson Professor of Finance and Economics and Dean, Graduate School of Business, Columbia University;* b. 4 Sept. 1958, Apopka, Fla; m. Constance Pond Hubbard; two s.; ed Univ. of Cen. Florida, Harvard Univ.; Asst Prof. of Econs, Northwestern Univ. 1983–88; Prof. of Finance and Econs, Grad. School of Business, Columbia Univ. 1988–, Russell L. Carson Prof. of Finance and Econs 1994–, Sr Vice-Dean 1994–97, Co-Dir Entrepreneurship Program 1998–2004, Dean 2004–; Deputy Asst Sec. for Tax Policy, US Treasury Dept, Washington, DC 1991–93; Chair. Pres. Council of Econ. Advisers, White House 2001–03; Visiting Scholar, American Enterprise Inst., Washington, DC; econ. advisor to Mitt Romney campaign for Republican nomination for Pres. 2008; Visiting Prof. of Business Admin, Harvard Business School 1997–98; mem. Bd of Dirs ADP Inc. 2004–, KKR Financial Corpn 2004–, BlackRock Closed-End Funds 2004–, MetLife 2007–; Chair. Econ. Policy Cttee OECD 2001–03, Econ. Club of New York 2008–; Co-Chair. Cttee on Capital Markets Regulation 2006–; Life Mem. Council on Foreign Relations 2007–; mem. Advisory Bd Nat. Center for Addiction and Substance Abuse 2004–; mem. Panel of Econ. Advisors, Fed. Reserve Bank of New York 1993–2001, 2007–, Panel of Academic Advisors, Tax Foundation 2003, American Council for Capital Formation 2003–; Fellow, Nat. Asscn of Business Economists 2005; Nat. Soc. of Professional Engineers Award, Univ. of Cen. Florida, Northwestern Univ. Associated Student Govt Teaching Awards 1985, 1986, 1987, John M. Olin Fellowship, Nat. Bureau of Econ. Research 1987–88, Distinguished Alumnus Award, Univ. of Cen. Florida 1991, Exceptional Service Award, US Treasury Dept 1992, Best Paper Award for Corp. Finance, Western Finance Asscn 1998, Alumni Hall of Fame, Univ. of Cen. Florida 2000, Michelle Akers Award for Distinguished Service, Univ. of Cen. Florida 2001, Exceptional Service Award, The White House 2002,; William F. Butler Memorial Award, New York Asscn of Business Economists 2005. *Television:* commentator, Nightly Business Report (PBS) 2003–. *Radio:* commentator, Marketplace, Nat. Public Radio 2003–. *Publications:* as co-author: Healthy, Wealthy and Wise: Five Steps to a Better Health Care System 2005, Principles of Economics 2006; commentator for press titles including Business Week, Wall Street Journal, New York Times, Financial Times, Washington Post, Nikkei, Daily Yomiuri; books: Money, the Financial System and the Economy 1994; over 100 scholarly articles. *Address:* Graduate School of Business, Columbia University, 3022 Broadway, New York, NY 10027, USA (office). *Telephone:* 212-854-2888 (office). *Fax:* 212-932-0545 (office). *E-mail:* rgh1@columbia.edu (office). *Website:* www.columbia.edu (office).

HUBBARD, Thomas C.; American business executive and fmr diplomatist; *Senior Advisor, Akin Gump Strauss Hauer & Feld LLP;* b. 1943, Ky; m. Joan Magnusson Hubbard; two c.; ed Univ. of Ala; joined Foreign Service 1965; Political/Econ. Officer, US Embassy, Santo Domingo 1966; Econ./Commercial Officer, Fukuoka, Japan; with Political Section, Tokyo 1971; Econ. Officer, Japan Desk, Dept of State 1973–75; Exec. Sec. to Del., then Energy Adviser, US Mission to OECD, Paris 1975–78; with Political Section, Tokyo 1978–81; Dir Training and Liaison Staff, Bureau of Personnel, State Dept, Deputy Dir, Philippine Desk 1984–85, Country Dir 1985–87; Deputy Chief of Mission, Kuala Lumpur 1987; Minister-Counsellor, Sr Foreign Service 1989; Minister and Deputy Chief of Mission, Manila 1990–93; Deputy Asst Sec., East Asian and Pacific Affairs, Dept of State 1993–96; Amb. to Philippines 1996–2000; Prin. Deputy Asst Sec. of State for E Asian and Pacific Affairs 2000–01; Amb. to Repub. of Korea 2001–04; Sr Advisor, Akin Gump Strauss Hauer & Feld LLP 2004–; Dr hc (Univ. of Maryland), (Univ. of Ala). *Address:* Akin Gump Strauss Hauer & Feld LLP, Robert S. Strauss Building, 1333 New Hampshire Avenue, NW, Washington, DC 20036-1564, USA (office). *Telephone:* (202) 887-4305 (office). *Fax:* (202) 887-4288 (office). *E-mail:* thubbard@akingump.com (office). *Website:* www.akingump.com (office).

HUBEL, David Hunter, MD; Canadian neurobiologist and academic; *Emeritus Professor of Neurobiology, School of Medicine, Harvard University;* b. 27 Feb. 1926, Windsor, Ont., Canada; s. of Jesse H. Hubel and Elsie M. Hunter; m. S. Ruth Izzard 1953; three s.; ed McGill Univ; Prof. of

Neurophysiology, Harvard Medical School 1965–67, George Packer Berry Prof. of Physiology and Chair. Dept of Physiology 1967–68, George Packer Berry Prof. of Neurobiology 1968–82, John Franklin Enders Univ. Prof. 1982–2004, now Emer. Prof.; George Eastman Prof., Univ. of Oxford 1991–92; First Annual George A. Miller Lecture, Cognitive Neuroscience Soc. 1995; mem. NAS, Leopoldina Acad., Bd of Syndics, Harvard Univ. Press 1979–83; Foreign mem. Royal Soc., London; Sr Fellow, Harvard Soc. of Fellows 1971–; Fellow American Acad. of Arts and Sciences; Hon. AM (Harvard) 1962; Hon. DSc (McGill) 1978, (Manitoba) 1983, (Oxford), (Univ. of Western Ont.) 1993, (Gustavus Adolphus Coll.) 1994, (Ohio State Univ.) 1995; Hon. DHumLitt (Johns Hopkins Univ.) 1990, (McMaster Univ.) 2005; Lewis S. Rosenstiel Award for Basic Medical Research (Brandeis Univ.) 1972, Friedenwald Award (Asscn for Research in Vision and Ophthalmology) 1975, Karl Spencer Lashley Prize (American Philosophical Soc.) 1977, Louisa Gross Horwitz Prize, (Columbia Univ.) 1978, Dickson Prize in Medicine, Univ. of Pittsburgh 1979, Soc. of Scholars, Johns Hopkins Univ. 1980, Ledlie Prize (Harvard Univ.) 1980, Nobel Prize in Medicine or Physiology 1981, New England Ophthalmological Soc. Award 1983, Paul Kayser Int. Award of Merit in Retina Research 1989, City of Medicine Award 1990, Gerald Award (Soc. for Neuroscience) 1993, Charles F. Prentice Medal (American Acad. of Optometry) 1993, Helen Keller Prize (Helen Keller Eye Research Foundation) 1995. *Publications:* Eye, Brain and Vision 1987; articles in scientific journals. *Leisure interests:* music, photography, astronomy, languages, weaving, amateur radio. *Address:* Department of Neurobiology, Harvard Medical School, 220 Longwood Avenue, Boston, MA 02115; 98 Collins Road, Newton, MA 02168, USA (home). *Telephone:* (617) 527-8774 (home). *Fax:* (617) 432-0210 (office). *Website:* neuro.med.harvard.edu/site/dh (office).

HUBER, Bernd, DHabil; German economist, university rector and academic; *Rector, Ludwig-Maximilians University of Munich;* b. 20 May 1960, Wuppertal; m.; ed Univs of Giessen and Würzburg; Lecturer in Econs, Univ. of Würzburg 1985–89, Akademischer Rat 1989–94, on leave of absence 1993–; Visiting Prof., Univ. of Bochum (Vertretung einer C-3 Professur) 1993–94, Univ. of Dresden April–July 1994, Univ. of Munich (Lehrstuhlvertretung) April–July 1994; currently Prof. of Econs, Ludwig-Maximilians Univ. of Munich, Rector 2002–. *Publications:* Staatsverschuldung und Allokationseffizienz – Schriften zur öffentlichen Verwaltung und öffentlichen Wirtschaft 1990, Optimale Finanzpolitik und zeitliche Inkonsistenz, Studies in Contemporary Economics 1996, Chancen und Grenzen föderalen Wettbewerbs – ifo Beiträge zur Wirtschaftsforschung (co-author) 2000, Die Einwohnergewichtung auf Länderebene im Länderfinanzausgleich – ifo Beiträge zur Wirtschaftsforschung (co-author) 2000; numerous articles on public finance, govt and debt, European fiscal and monetary integration, int. taxation and labour markets. *Address:* Office of the Rector, Ludwig-Maximilians-Universität München, Leopoldstr. 3, 80802 Munich, Germany (office). *Telephone:* (89) 2180-2412 (office). *Fax:* (89) 2180-3656 (office). *E-mail:* rektorat@lmu.de (office). *Website:* www.lmu.de (office).

HUBER, Erwin; German politician; b. 26 July 1946, Reisbach, Lower Bavaria; m.; two c.; ed Univ. of Munich; started career at Bavarian state finance office 1963; joined Bavarian State Ministry of Finance 1970; fmr Borough and Dist Chair., Junge Union (Young Conservative Party); mem. Borough Council and Cttee, Dingolfing-Landau 1972–78; mem. Bavarian Landtag (Parl.) 1978–, Chair. Parl. Cttee on Devt and Environmental Affairs 1986–87; State Minister and Head of State Chancellery 1994–95, 1998–2005, State Minister of Finance 1995–98, Minister of State for Fed. Matters and Admin. Reform 2003–05, for Economy 2005–; Deputy Sec.-Gen. CSU party 1987–88, Sec.-Gen. 1988–94, Dist Chair., Lower Bavaria 1993–2007, Party Leader 2007–08 (resgnd). *Address:* c/o Büro des Vorsitzenden, Nymphenburger Straße 64, 80335 Munich, Germany (office).

HUBER, Robert, Drrer.nat, FRS; German biochemist; *Director Emeritus, Max-Planck-Inst. für Biochemie;* b. 20 Feb. 1937, Munich; s. of Sebastian Huber and Helene Huber; m. Christa Huber 1960; two s. two d.; ed Tech. Univ. Munich; Dir Max-Planck-Inst. für Biochemie 1972–2005, Dir Emer. 2006–; fmr External Prof. then Assoc. Prof. Munich Tech. Univ. 1976–; Visiting Prof. Univs of Barcelona, Singapore, Duisburg-Essen, Cardiff; Ed. Journal of Molecular Biology 1976–; Scientific mem., Max-Planck-Gesellschaft; mem. Bavarian Acad. of Sciences, Acad. Nazionale dei Lincei and numerous socs.; Fellow American Acad. of Microbiology; Assoc. Fellow Third World Acad. of Sciences, Trieste, Italy; Foreign Assoc. NAS; mem. Orden pur le Merite für Wissenschaften und Künste; Dr hc (Louvain) 1987, (Ljubljana) 1989, (Tor Vergata, Rome) 1990, (Lisbon) 2000, (Barcelona) 2000, (Tsinghua Univ., Beijing) 2003; numerous hon. professorships; Grosse Verdienstkreuz mit Stern und Schulterband 1997; E. K. Frey Prize (German Surgical Soc.) 1972, Otto Warburg Medal (Soc. for Biological Chem.) 1977, Emil von Behring Prize (Univ. of Marburg) 1982, Keilin Medal (Biochemical Soc. London), Richard Kuhn Medal (Soc. of German Chemists) 1987, E. K. Frey-E. Werle Medal 1989, Kone Award (Asscn of Clinical Biochemists) 1990, Nobel Prize for Chemistry 1988, Sir Hans Krebs Medal 1992, Bayerischer Maximiliansorden für Wissenschaft und Kunst 1993, Linus Pauling Medal 1993, Distinguished Service Award (Miami Winter Symposia) 1995, Max Tishler Prize (Harvard Univ.) 1997, Max-Bergmann-Medaille (Max-Bergmann-Kreises zur Förderung der peptidchemischen Forschung) 1997, Röntgenplakette der Stadt Remscheid-Lennep 2004, Premio Citta di Firenze sulle Scienze Molecolari 2004. *Leisure interests:* hiking, biking, skiing. *Address:* Max-Planck-Institut für Biochemie, Am Klopferspitz 18, 82152 Martinsried, Germany (office). *Telephone:* (89) 85782678 (office). *Fax:* (89) 85783516 (office). *E-mail:* huber@biochem.mpg.de (office).

HUBER-HOTZ, Annemarie; Swiss politician; b. 16 Aug. 1948, Baar, Canton Zug; m.; three c.; ed Univ. of Geneva, Swiss Fed. Inst. of Tech., Zürich; fmr Head Secr. Dept for German Law, Faculty of Law, Univ. of Geneva; translator, ILO, Geneva 1973–75; mem. staff Regional Planning Office, Canton of Zug 1976–77; Asst to Sec.-Gen. Fed. Ass. 1978–81, Dir Scientific Services 1989–99, Sec.-Gen. 1992–99; Chancellor of the Swiss Confed. 2000–07; mem. Radical Free Democratic Party. *Address:* c/o Federal Chancellery, Bundeshaus-West, 3003 Berne, Switzerland (office).

HUBERT, Jean-Paul, BA, BCL, MIA, DPolSci, PhD; Canadian lawyer, diplomatist, international organization executive and academic; *President, Inter-American Juridical Committee;* b. 16 Dec. 1941, Grand-Mère, QC; s. of Jean-Paul Hubert and Cecile Hubert (née Laperrière); m. 1st Mireya Melgar 1967 (divorced 1995); two s. one d.; m. 2nd Florence Fournier 1995; ed Laval Univ., McGill Univ., Columbia Univ., New York, Univ. of the Sorbonne, Paris, Moncton (New Brunswick) Univ.; with Dept of Foreign Relations and Int. Trade, Canadian Diplomatic Service, Ottawa 1971–72, Second Sec., Vice-Consul for Spain and Morocco, Madrid 1972–74, Legal Affairs Div., Ottawa 1974–76, Personnel Div. 1976–78, First Sec. and Consul, Havana 1978–81, Political Counsellor and Rep., Agency for Cultural and Tech. Co-operation, Paris 1991–95, Econ. and Treaty Law Div., Ottawa 1985–86, Fed. Co-ordinator for La Francophonie 1986–88, Amb. to Senegal, Mauritania, Guinea, Guinea-Bissau, Cape Verde and Senegal 1988–90, High Commr to the Gambia 1988–90, Prime Minister's Personal Rep. for La Francophonie 1988–90, Embassy in Dakar 1988–90, first Amb. and Perm. Rep. of Canada to OAS, Washington, DC 1990–93, Sr Advisor, Commonwealth La Francophonie/Hemispheric Affairs, Ottawa 1993–94, Prime Minister's Personal Rep. for La Francophonie, Ottawa, Brussels 1994–98, Amb. to Belgium and Luxembourg 1994–98, to Argentina and Paraguay 1998–2005; Pres. Inter-American Juridical Cttee, OAS 2005–; Interim Pres. Int. Centre for Human Rights and Democratic Devt (Rights & Democracy) 2007–; currently Visiting Prof., Dept of History and Political Sciences, Univ. of Sherbrooke, QC; Designated Order of la Pleiade, Int. Asscn of French-Speaking Parliamentarians 1989. *Leisure interest:* genealogy. *Address:* Comissão Jurídica Interamericana, Avenida Marechal Floriano 196, 3° andar, Palácio de Itamaraty, Centro 20080-002, Rio de Janeiro, RJ, Brazil (office). *Telephone:* (21) 2206-9903 (office). *Fax:* (21) 2203-2090 (office). *E-mail:* cjioea.trp@terra.com.br (office). *Website:* www.oas.org/cji (office).

HUBERT, Yves; French engineer and banking executive; *Chairman of the Supervisory Board, Caisse Nationale des Caisses d'Epargne;* early career with Rohm and Haas chemical co.; Chair. Supervisory Bd, Caisse d'Epargne de Picardie 1992–2007, Chair. Supervisory Bd, Caisse Nationale des Caisses d'Epargne 2007–, also Chair. Steering and Supervisory Bd Caisse d'Epargne de Picardie. *Address:* Caisse Nationale des Caisses d'Epargne, 50 avenue Pierre Mendès, 75201 Paris Cedex 13, France (office). *Telephone:* 1-58-40-40-02 (office). *Fax:* 1-58-40-50-30 (office). *E-mail:* info@groupe.caisse-epargne.com (office). *Website:* www.groupe.caisse-epargne.com (office).

HÜBNER, Danuta; Polish politician and economist; *Commissioner for Regional Policy, European Commission;* b. 8 March 1948, Nisko; two d.; ed Warsaw School of Econs; researcher, Main School of Planning and Statistics, Warsaw (now Warsaw School of Econs) 1971–, Deputy Dir Research Inst. for Developing Countries, Warsaw School of Econs 1981–87, Deputy Dir Inst. for Devt and Strategic Studies 1991–94; Deputy Ed.-in-Chief Ekonomista (bi-monthly) 1991–97; Ed.-in-Chief Gospodarka Narodowa (monthly) 1994–97; Under-Sec. of State Ministry of Industry and Trade 1994–96; Sec. Cttee for European Integration 1996–97, 2001–04; Sec. of State for European Integration 1996–97; Head, Chancellery of the Pres. of Poland 1997–98; Econ. Adviser to Pres. of Poland 1998–2001; Deputy Exec. Sec. UN Econ. Comm. for Europe 1998–2000, Exec. Sec. 2000–01, UN Under-Sec.-Gen. 2000–01; Sec. of State, Ministry of Foreign Affairs 2001–04; Minister for European Affairs 2003–04; EU Commr without Portfolio 2004, for Regional Policy 2004–; Chair. Council for Social Planning 1996–98; mem. Exec. Cttee European Asscn of Devt Research and Training Insts 1987–96, Nat. Statistics Council 1995–97, Scientific Bd Econ. Sciences Inst., Polish Acad. of Science 1996–98; Hon. LLB (Univ. of Sussex) 2005; Dr hc (Univ. of Nat. and World Economy, Sofia) 2007. *Address:* European Commission, Rue de la Loi 200, 1049 Brussels, Belgium (office). *Telephone:* (2) 298-86-26 (office). *Fax:* (2) 298-86-34 (office). *E-mail:* Cabinet-Huebner@ec.europa.eu (office). *Website:* ec.europa.eu/commission_barroso/hubner (office).

HUCKABEE, Michael Dale, BA; American politician, ecclesiastic and fmr state official; b. 24 Aug. 1955, Hope, Ark.; m. Janet McCain 1974; three s. one d.; ed Ouachita Baptist Univ., Arkadelphia, Ark., Southwestern Baptist Theological Seminary, Fort Worth; ordained to ministry 1974; pastor, various Baptist churches 1974–, Beech St 1st Baptist Church, Texarkana, Ark. 1986–; Lt Gov. State of Ark. 1994–96, Gov. of Arkansas 1996–2007; Founder, Past-Pres. American Christian TV System, Pine Bluff; Pres. Ark. Baptist Convention 1989–91; columnist weekly newspaper Positive Alternatives; unsuccessful cand. for Republican nomination for Pres. of US 2007–08. *Address:* 1800 Center Street, Little Rock, AR 72206, USA (home).

HUCKLE, Alan Edden, MA; British diplomatist; *Governor of Falkland Islands and Commissioner of South Georgia and South Sandwich Islands;* b. 15 June 1948, Penang, Malaya; s. of the late Albert Arthur Huckle and of Ethel Maud Pettifer Huckle (née Edden); m. Helen Myra Gibson 1973; one s. one d.; ed Rugby School, Univ. of Warwick; Personnel Man. Div., Civil Service Dept (CSD) 1971–74; Asst Pvt. Sec. to Sec. of State for Belfast 1974–75, Machinery of Govt Div., CSD 1975–78; Political Affairs Div., NI Office 1978–80; with FCO 1980–83; Exec. Dir British Information Services, New York, USA 1983–87; Head of Chancery, Manila 1987–90; Head, Dept of Arms Control and Disarmament, FCO 1990–92; Counsellor and Head of Del. to CSCE, Vienna 1992–96; Head, Dept Territories Regional Secr., Bridgetown 1996–98; Head, OSCE/Council of Europe Dept, FCO 1998–2001; Head,

Overseas Territories Dept, FCO and Commr (non-resident) British Antarctic Territory and British Indian Ocean Territory 2001–04; Gov. of Anguilla 2004–06; Gov. of Falkland Islands and Commr S Georgia and S Sandwich Islands 2006–; Leverhulme Trust Scholar, British School at Rome 1971. *Leisure interests:* armchair mountaineering, hill-walking. *Address:* Office of the Governor, Government House, Stanley, FIQQ 1ZZ, Falkland Islands (office). *Telephone:* 27433 (office). *Fax:* 27434 (office). *E-mail:* gov.house@horizon.co.fk (office).

HUCKNALL, Michael (Mick) James, BA; British singer and songwriter; b. 8 June 1960, Manchester; pnr Gabriella Wesberry; one d.; ed Manchester Polytechnic; fmrly with own punk band, Frantic Elevators 1979; founder mem. and lead singer, Simply Red 1984–(2009); numerous world tours; co-f. reggae music label, Blood and Fire 1992; mem. Govt Task Force on the Music Industry 1997–; founded record label, Simplyred.com 2003–; Hon. MSc (UMIST) 1997; BRIT Award for Best British Band 1991, 1992, Best Male Solo Artist 1992, Ivor Novello Songwriter of the Year Award 1992, Mobo Award for Outstanding Achievement 1997, Manchester Making it Happen Award 1998. *Recordings include:* albums: with Simply Red: Picture Book 1985, Early Years 1987, Men and Women 1987, A New Flame 1989, Stars 1991, Life 1995, Blue 1997, Love and the Russian Winter 1999, It's Only Love 2000, Home 2003, Simplified 2005, Stay 2007; solo: Tribute to Bobby 2008. *Address:* Creative Artists Agency, 9830 Wilshire Blvd, Beverly Hills, CA 90212-1825, USA (office); simplyred.com, PO Box 6215, Basildon, SS14 0AN, England. *Telephone:* (310) 288-4545 (office); (20) 8969-2498 (office). *Fax:* (310) 288-4800 (office); (20) 8969-2506 (office). *Website:* www.caa.com (office); www.simplyred.com; www.mickhucknall.com. *E-mail:* info@simplyred.com (office).

HUCKSTEP, Ronald Lawrie, CMG, MA, FRCS, FRCSE, FRACS, FAOrthA; British/Australian consultant orthopaedic surgeon, academic, writer and inventor; *Professor Emeritus, University of New South Wales;* b. 22 July 1926, Chefoo (now Yantai), China; s. of Herbert George Huckstep and Agnes Huckstep (née Lawrie-Smith); m. Ann Macbeth 1960; two s. one d.; ed Cathedral School, Shanghai, Queens' Coll., Cambridge, Middlesex, Royal Nat. Orthopaedic and St Bartholomew's Hosps, London; Registrar and Chief Asst, Orthopaedic Dept, St Bartholomew's Hosp. and various surgical appointments, Middx and Royal Nat. Orthopaedic Hosps 1952–60, Hunterian Prof., Royal Coll. of Surgeons 1959–60; Lecturer, Sr Lecturer and Reader in Orthopaedic Surgery, Makerere Univ., Kampala, Uganda 1960–67, Prof. 1967–72; Hon. Consultant Orthopaedic Surgeon, Mulago and Mengo Hosps and Round Table Polio Clinic, Kampala 1960–72; Hon. Orthopaedic Surgeon to all Govt and Mission hosps in Uganda and Adviser on Orthopaedic Surgery to Ministry of Health, Uganda 1960–72; Prof. and Head, Dept of Traumatic and Orthopaedic Surgery, Univ. of NSW 1972–92 and fmr Rotating Chair., School of Surgery; Chair. Dept of Traumatic and Orthopaedic Surgery and Dir of Accident Services, Prince of Wales/Prince Henry Hosps 1972–92, Consultant Orthopaedic Surgeon, Royal S Sydney and Sutherland Hosps, Sydney 1974–92; Prof. Emer. of Traumatic and Orthopaedic Surgery, Univ. of NSW and Consultant Orthopaedic Surgeon, Prince of Wales and Prince Henry Hosps 1993–; Visiting Prof., Univ. of Sydney 1995–; Sr Medical Disaster Commdr, Dept of Health, NSW and Chair. and mem. of various disaster and emergency cttees in Australia 1972–; Vice-Pres. Australian Orthopaedic Asscn 1982; Pres. Coast Medical Asscn, Sydney 1985–86; Corresp. Ed. British and American Journals of Bone and Joint Surgery 1965–72, Injury, British Journal of Accident Surgery 1972; mem. Traffic Authority of NSW 1982–2008; Consultant to Archives of Orthopaedic Surgery 1984; Founder World Orthopaedic Concern 1973; Patron Medical Soc. of Univ. of NSW 1976; numerous orthopaedic inventions including Huckstep nail, hip, femur, knee, shoulder, humerus, staple, circlip, plate, bone screw, caliper, wheelchairs and skelecasts; Hon. Dir Orthopaedic Overseas, USA 1978; Hon. Fellow, Western Pacific Orthopaedic Asscn 1968, Asscn of Surgeons of Uganda 1993; Hon. Adviser, Rotary Int., The Commonwealth Foundation, WHO and UN on starting services for the disabled in developing countries 1970–; Hon. MD (Univ. of NSW) 1988; Irving Geist Award, Int. Soc. for Rehabilitation of the Disabled 1969, Melsome Memorial Prize, Cambridge 1948, Raymond Horton Smith Prize, Cambridge 1957, Betts Memorial Medal, Australian Orthopaedic Asscn 1983, James Cook Medal, Royal Soc. of NSW 1984, K.L. Sutherland Medal, Australian Acad. of Tech. Sciences 1986, Paul Harris Fellow and Medal, Rotary International and Rotary Foundation 1987, Humanitarian Award (Orthopaedics Overseas, USA) 1991, Vocational Service Award, Rotary Club of Sydney 1994, Australian Centenary Medal 2003, Eyre-Brook Medal, World Orthopaedic Concern 2009. *Film:* Polio in Uganda 1966. *Publications:* Typhoid Fever and Other Salmonella Infections 1962, A Simple Guide to Trauma 1970 (fifth edn) 1994, Poliomyelitis: A Guide for Developing Countries, Including Appliances and Rehabilitation 1975, A Simple Guide to Orthopaedics 1993, Picture Tests – Orthopaedics and Trauma 1994; numerous book chapters and papers. *Leisure interests:* photography, designing orthopaedic appliances and implants, swimming and travel. *Address:* 108 Sugarloaf Crescent, Castlecrag, Sydney, NSW 2068, Australia (home). *Telephone:* (612) 9958-1786 (home). *Fax:* (612) 9967-2971 (home). *E-mail:* rlh333@optusnet.com.au (home). *Website:* www.worldortho.com (office).

HUDA, A. T. M. Shamsul, BA, MA, MPA, PhD; Bangladeshi civil servant; *Chief Election Commissioner;* b. 10 July 1943; ed East Pakistan Secondary Educ. Bd, Dhaka Univ., Cen. Public Service Comm., Syracuse Univ., USA; Asst Commr, Cadre of the Civil Service of Pakistan 1966–68; Sub-Div. Officer, in sub-dist in what is now Bangladesh and Pakistan 1968–71; Deputy Dir (Food), Punjab, West Pakistan 1971; Additional Deputy Commr 1971–72; Deputy Sec., Establishment Div. 1972–75, 1979–82; Research Asst, World Bank, Washington, DC, USA 1978–79, Maxwell School, Syracuse Univ. 1978–79; Deputy Sec., Ministry of Agric. and Forests 1981–82, Jt Sec. 1982–84, Project Coordinator, Bangladesh Jute Seed Project 1982–84, Project Dir, Agricultural Man. Devt Programme 1981–84; mem. Directing Staff, Bangladesh Public Admin Training Centre 1984–88; Jt Sec., Ministry of Irrigation, Water Devt and Flood Control 1988–91, Additional Sec. and Chair. Bangladesh Water Devt Bd 1991–92; Man. Dir Bangladesh Agricultural Devt Bank 1992–94; Sec., Banking Div., Ministry of Finance 1994–96; Sec., Ministry of Water Resources 1996–2000 (retd); Chief Election Commr 2007–. *Publications include:* The Small Farmer and the Problem of Access 1983, Co-ordination in Public Administration in Bangladesh 1987, Sustainability of Projects for Higher Agricultural Education: A Case Study of Bangladesh Agricultural University 1988. *Address:* Election Commission Secretariat, Block-5/6, Sher-e-Bangla Nagar, Dhaka 1207, Bangladesh (office). *Telephone:* (2) 8115212 (office). *Fax:* (2) 8117834 (office). *E-mail:* ecs@bol-online.com (office). *Website:* www.ecs.gov.bd (office).

HUDEČEK, Václav; Czech violinist; b. 7 June 1952, Rožmitál pod Třemšínem, Příbram Dist; m. Eva Trejtnarová 1977; ed Faculty of Music, Acad. of Performing Arts, Prague 1968–73; worked with David Oistrakh, Moscow 1970–74; worked as musician 1974–; mem., Union of the Czech Composers and Concert Artists 1977–; individual concerts, 1967–; soloist with Czech Philharmonic Orchestra 1984–90, Royal Philharmonic Orchestra, London, Berlin Philharmonic, Leipzig Gewandhaus Orchestra, NHK Orchestra of Tokyo; freelance musician 1990–; concert tours to Austria, GDR, Norway, Hungary, USSR, Switzerland, Turkey, USA, Yugoslavia, Japan, Italy, Iceland, Finland, Jordan; solo recitals with pianist Petr Adamec and with guitarist Lubomir Brabec; est. School for Talented Young Violinists in Czech Repub.; charity concerts after floods in Czech Repub. 2002; Concertino Praga int. radio competition 1967, Award for Outstanding Labour 1978, Artist of Merit 1981, Supraphon Gold Record Prize 1994. *Recordings include:* Bach: Concertos, Bravo Vivaldi, Czech Christmas – Eva Urbanová, Drdla/Sarasate/Hubay/Lehár/Ravel, Dvořák: Compositions for Violin and Piano, Dvorák: Concerto for Violin and Orchestra in A minor, Op. 53, Guitar: Prague Guitar Concertos, Haydn: Sitkovetsky, Davidovich, Hudeček play Haydn, Mendelssohn-Bartholdy/Sibelius: Violin Concertos, Mozart: The Famous Violin Concertos, Music for Weddings, P. I. Tchaikovsky, J. Sibelius: Violin Concertos, Paganini: Hudeček – Brabec play Paganini, Prokofjev/Tchaikovsky, Souvenir, Václav Hudeček – Violin Recital, Supraphon Stars 2000, Tartini/Paganini/Gragnani/Giuliani, Triny – Gipsy Streams, Trojan: Suites from the Films, Violin: Hudeček Il Giardino di Musica, Vivaldi: Concertos for Various Instruments, Vivaldi: Le Quattro Stagioni. *Television:* Musical Nocturne (TV Prague) 2001. *Address:* Euroconcert, Bellebern 10A, 78234 Engen, Germany (office); Londynska 25, 120 00 Prague 2, Czech Republic (home). *Telephone:* (2) 24254010 (home). *E-mail:* violin@quick.cz.

HUDSON, Hugh; British film director and film producer; b. 25 Aug. 1936; s. of the late Michael Donaldson-Hudson and Jacynth Ellerton; m. 1st Susan Caroline Michie 1977; one s.; 2nd Maryam d'Abo 2003; ed Eton Coll.; numerous awards and prizes. *Films include:* The Tortoise and the Hare 1967, Chariots of Fire 1980 (five BAFTA Awards, four Acad. Awards, other awards), Greystoke: The Legend of Tarzan (also producer) 1984, Revolution 1985 (BFI Anthony Asquith Award for Music), Lost Angels 1989, Lumière et compagnie 1996, A Life So Far 1999, I Dreamed of Africa 2000; numerous documentaries, political films (for Labour Party) and over 600 advertisements. *Address:* Hudson Film Ltd, 24 St Leonard's Terrace, London, SW3 4QG, England (office). *Telephone:* (20) 7730-0002 (office). *Fax:* (20) 7730-8033 (office). *E-mail:* hudsonfilm@aol.com (office).

HUDSON-PHILLIPS, Karl Terrence, QC, MA, LLM; Trinidad and Tobago judge; b. 20 April 1933; ed Selwyn Coll., Univ. of Cambridge, UK; called to the Bar, Gray's Inn, London 1959, Trinidad and Tobago 1959, Jamaica 1974, Antigua and Barbuda 1977, Grenada 1983, St Vincent and the Grenadines 1985, St Kitts and Nevis 1985, Anguilla 1985, Bahamas 1985, St Lucia 1985, Barbados 1985, British Virgin Islands 1985; apptd QC, Bar of Trinidad and Tobago 1970, Sr Counsel of Bar, Cooperative Repub. of Guyana 1971; pvt. practice in Trinidad and Tobago and Commonwealth Caribbean 1959–; mem. Parl. 1966–76; Attorney-Gen. and Minister for Legal Affairs 1969–73; Judge, Int. Criminal Court (ICC), The Hague 2003–08; Founder Nat. Land Tenants and Ratepayers Asscn of Trinidad and Tobago 1974, Org. for Nat. Reconstruction 1980; Chair. Comm. of Inquiry into Operations of St Lucia Police Force 1987; Pres. Law Asscn of Trinidad and Tobago 1999–; mem. Council Commonwealth Law Asscn 1992–, Bd of Dirs Justice Studies Center of the Americas, Santiago, Chile 1999–. *Publications:* articles in professional journals. *Address:* c/o International Criminal Court, Maanweg 174, 2516 AB The Hague, The Netherlands. *Telephone:* (70) 5158515.

HUE, Robert; French politician and nurse; b. 19 Oct. 1946, Cormeilles-en-Parisis; s. of René Hue and Raymonde Gregorius; m. Marie-Edith Solard 1973; one s. one d.; ed Coll. d'Enseignement Technique and Ecole d'Infirmier; mem. Young Communists 1962; mem. French CP 1963–, mem. Secr. Fed. of Val d'Oise 1970–77, mem. Cen. Cttee 1987, mem. Politburo 1990, Nat. Sec. 1994–2001, Pres. 2001, Chair. 2001–03, Senator 2004; cand. of CP in French presidential election 1995, 2002; Mayor of Montigny-les-Cormeilles 1977–; Conseiller-Général Val d'Oise 1988–97; Deputy for Argenteuil-Bezons 1997–; mem. European Parl. 1999–2000; Pres. Nat. Asscn of Communist and Republican elected mems 1991–94, Fondation Gabriel Péri 2003–. *Publications:* Histoire d'un village du Parisis des origines à la Révolution 1981, Du village à la ville 1986, Montigny pendant la Révolution 1989, Communisme: la mutation 1995, Il faut qu'on se parle 1997, Communisme: un nouveau projet 1999, Qui êtes-vous? 2001. *Leisure interests:* reading, painting, cinema, music (jazz and rock), walking, judo. *Address:* SENAT, 15 rue de Vauginard, 75291 Paris Cedex 06, France (office). *E-mail:* fondation@gabrielperi.fr (office).

HUERTA, Dolores C.; American trade union official; *First Vice-President Emerita, United Farm Workers of America;* b. 10 April 1930, New Mexico; d. of

Juan Fernandez and Alicia Chavez; 11 c.; ed Delta Community Coll., Univ. of the Pacific; fmr teacher at grammar school; Founding mem. Stockton Chapter, Community Service Org. (campaigned against segregation and police brutality) 1955–62; Founder Agricultural Workers Asscn 1960; est. (with Cesar Chavez) Nat. Farm Workers Asscn 1962; during Delano Grape Strike 1965–70, merger of Nat. Farm Workers Asscn and Agricultural Workers Organizing Cttee to form United Farm Workers Organizing Cttee (UFWOC) 1966; negotiated UFWOC contract with Schenley Wine Co. (first time a negotiating cttee comprised of farmworkers negotiated collective bargaining agreement with agric. corpn in USA) 1966;; co-f. (with Cesar Chavez) Robert F. Kennedy Medical Plan, Juan De La Cruz Farm Worker Pension Fund, Farm Workers Credit Union, Nat. Workers Service Center, Inc.; currently First Vice-Pres. Emer. United Farm Workers of America (AFL–CIO), Vice-Pres. Coalition for Labor Union of Women, Vice-Pres. AFL–CIO Calif.; mem. Bd Fund for the Feminist Majority, Democratic Socialists of America, Latinas for Choice, Fairness in Media Reporting, Center for Voting and Democracy; Founder and Pres. Dolores Huerta Foundation; Hon. PhD (New Coll. of San Francisco) 1990, (San Francisco State Univ.) 1993, (SUNY New Palz Univ.) 1999; Dr hc (Wayne State) 2004, (California State, Northridge) 2003, (SUNY School of Law) 2004, (North Texas) 2005, (Princeton) 2006; Calif. State Senate Outstanding Labor Leader Award 1984, inducted into Nat. Women s Hall of Fame 1993, American Civil Liberties Union Roger Baldwin Medal of Liberty Award 1993, Eugene V. Debs Foundation Outstanding American Reward 1993, Ellis Island Medal of Freedom Award 1993, Consumers Union Trumpeter's Award, Eleanor Roosevelt Human Rights Award 1998, Community of Christ Int. Peace Award (jtly) 2007. *Achievements include:* instrumental in passage of legislation allowing voters right to vote in Spanish language 1961; lobbied for end to 'captive labour' Bracero Programme 1962; instrumental in securing Aid For Dependent Families for un- and under-employed, and disability insurance for farm workers in Calif. 1963; negotiated contracts to establish first health and benefit plans for farmworkers; led consumer boycotts resulting in enactment of Agricultural Labor Relations Act 1974; lobbied against fed. guest worker programmes resulting in Immigration Act 1985. *Address:* National Headquarters, United Farm Workers of America, PO Box 62, Keene, CA 93531 USA (office). *Website:* www.ufw.org (office).

HUERTA DÍAZ, Vice-Adm. Ismael; Chilean diplomatist (retd) and naval officer; b. 13 Oct. 1916; s. of Rear-Adm. Ismael Huerta Lira and Lucrecia Díaz Vargas; m. Guillermina Wallace Dunsmore Aird 1942; two s. two d.; ed Sacred Heart School, Valparaíso, Naval Acad., Ecole Supérieure d'Electricité, Paris, Naval Polytechnic Acad., Chile; successive posts in Chilean Navy include Dir of Armaments, Dir of Instruction, Dir of Scientific Investigation, Dir of Naval Polytechnic Acad., Dir of Shipyards, Dir-Gen. of Army Services; Prof. of Electronics, Univ. de Concepción 1954, 1955, 1956; Prof. of Radionavigation, Univ. Católica de Valparaíso 1962–67; mem. Org. Cttee, Pacific Conf., Viña del Mar 1970, Pres. Centre of Pacific Studies 1970–72; Dir Compañía de Acero del Pacífico (CAP) 1970, 1971, 1972; Pres. Nat. Transport Cttee 1972; Minister of Public Works 1973, of Foreign Affairs 1973–74; Perm. Rep. to UN 1974–77; Rector Univ. Técnica Federico Santa María 1977–85; Chair. Bd Empresa Marítima del Estado 1978–; mem. Coll. of Chilean Engineers. Inst. of Mechanical Engineers of Chile; Decoration of Pres. of the Repub. (Chile), Grand Officer Order of Léopold II (Belgium), Gran Cruz de la Orden del Libertador San Martín (Argentina), Gran Cruz Extraordinaria de la Orden Nacional al Mérito (Paraguay), Medall Kim-Kank (Repub. of Viet Nam). *Publications:* The Role of the Armed Forces in Today's World 1968, Volvería a ser Marino (memoirs) 1988 and various technical articles.

HUF, Jaroslav, DipEng; Czech business executive; *Chairman and Managing Director, Moravolen Holding a.s.;* b. 24 May 1966, Zábreh; s. of František Huf and Jirina Huf; m. Lenka Huf; one s.; ed Tech. Univ. of Agric., Brno; various engineering positions 1989–95; Dir Finance Moravolen a.s. 1995–96, and and Man. Dir Moravolen Holding a.s. 1996–. *Leisure interest:* sport. *Address:* Moravolen Holding a.s., M.R. Štefánika 1, 78701 Šumperk, Czech Republic (office). *Telephone:* (5) 83387111 (office). *Fax:* (5) 83387187 (office). *E-mail:* hufj@moravolen.cz (office). *Website:* www.moravolen.cz (office).

HUFFINGTON, Arianna, MA; American writer and columnist; b. Greece; two d.; ed Univ. of Cambridge, UK; fmr Pres. Cambridge Union; nationally syndicated columnist and author; provided political coverage of Nat. Elections for Comedy Central 1996; co-f. Americans for Fuel Efficient Cars; spokesperson Detroit Project 2003; f. The Huffington Post (internet blog site) 2005; guest appearances on numerous TV shows including Larry King Live, The O'Reilly Factor, Hannity & Colmes, Oprah, Nightline, Inside Politics, Good Morning America, The Today Show; mem. Bd Points of Light Foundation, A Place Called Home; mem. Bd Trustees Archer School for Girls; mem. Advisory Bd Council on American Politics, George Washington Univ.; mem. Bd Reform Inst. *Publications include:* The Female Woman 1974, After Reason 1978, Maria Callas: The Woman Behind the Legend 1981, The Gods of Greece, Pablo-Picasso: Creator and Destroyer 1988, The Fourth Instinct 1994, Greetings From the Lincoln Bedroom 1998, How to Overthrow the Government 2000, Pigs at the Trough: How Corporate Greed and Political Corruption are Undermining America 2002, Fanatics and Fools 2003, Right is Wrong 2008. *Address:* The Huffington Post, 1158 26th Street, POB 428, Santa Monica, CA 90403, USA (office). *E-mail:* arianna@ariannaonline.com (office). *Website:* www.huffingtonpost.com (office).

HUG, Michel, PhD; French civil engineer; b. 30 May 1930, Courson; s. of René Hug and Marcelle (née Quenee) Hug; m. Danielle Michaud; one s. two d.; ed Ecole Polytechnique, Ecole Nationale des Ponts et Chaussées, Univ. of Iowa; joined Electricité de France 1956, various positions at the Chatou Research and Test Centre 1956–66, Regional Man. (Southern Alps) 1967–68, Research and Devt Man. 1969–72, Planning and Construction Man. 1972–82; Gen. Man. Charbonnages de France (French Coal Bd) 1982–86; Prof. of Fluid Mechanics, Ecole Nationale des Ponts et Chaussées 1963–80; Chair. Bd Ecole Nationale Supérieure d'Electrotechnique, d'Electronique, d'Informatique et d'Hydraulique de Toulouse 1980–90; Chair. Bd CdF Chimie 1985–86; Deputy Admin. Org. des Producteurs d'Energie Nucléaire (OPEN) 1992–2000; mem. Applications Cttee of Acad. des Sciences 1987; Foreign mem. US Nat. Acad. of Eng 1979–; mem. American Nuclear Soc.; Hon. mem. Int. Assoc. of Hydraulics Research; Lauréat de l'Institut (Prix des Laboratoires) 1964; Commdr Ordre nat. du Merite 1980; Officier, Légion d'honneur 1977; Officier des Palmes académiques (Ministry of Educ.) 1986; Chevalier des Arts et Lettres 1981, du Mérite agricole. *Publications:* Mécanique des fluides appliquée aux problèmes d'aménagement et d'énergétique 1975, Organiser le changement dans l'entreprise—une expérience à E.D.F. 1975. *Leisure interests:* tennis, shooting, swimming, flying. *Address:* 57 avenue Franklin Roosevelt, 75008 Paris,; Design Stratégique, BP 14, 78115 Le Vésinet cedex, France (office). *E-mail:* michelhug@imaginet.fr (office).

HUGH SMITH, Sir Andrew Colin, Kt, BA; British business executive; *Chairman, British Smaller Technology Companies VCT 2 plc;* b. 6 Sept. 1931; s. of the late Lt-Commdr Colin Hugh Smith; m. Venetia Flower 1964; two s.; ed Ampleforth Coll. and Trinity Coll., Cambridge; called to Bar (Inner Temple) 1956; with Courtaulds Ltd 1960–68; joined Capel-Cure Carden (subsequently Capel-Cure Myers) 1968, Pnr 1970, Sr Pnr 1979; Deputy Chair. ANZ McCaughan Merchant Bank 1985–90; Chair. Holland & Holland PLC 1987–95; elected to Council, The Stock Exchange 1981; Chair. The Int. Stock Exchange (now London Stock Exchange), London 1988–94; currently Chair. British Smaller Tech. Cos VCT 2 plc; Chair. Penna PLC 1995–, Microtransfer Ltd 1995–, European Advisory Bd Andersen Consulting 1995–; Dir Matheson Lloyds Investment Trust 1994–97, (non-exec.) J. Bibby & Sons (now Barlow Int.) 1995–, Barbour Ltd 1998–; mem., Hon. Treas. Malcolm Sargent Cancer Fund for Children 1992–. *Leisure interests:* gardening, shooting, fishing, reading. *Address:* British Smaller Technology Companies VCT 2 plc, Saint Martins House, 210-212 Chapeltown Road, Leeds, West Yorkshire, LS7 4HZ, England (office).

HUGHES, Anthony Vernon, MA; Solomon Islands banking executive and civil servant; b. 29 Dec. 1936, England; s. of Henry Norman Hughes and Marjorie Hughes; m. 1st Carole Frances Robson 1961 (divorced 1970); one s.; m. 2nd Kuria Vaze Paia 1971; one s. one d. two adopted d.; ed Queen Mary's Grammar School, Walsall, England, Pembroke Coll., Oxford and Bradford Univ.; Commr of Lands, Registrar of Titles, Solomon Islands 1969–70, Head of Planning 1974–76, Perm. Sec. Ministry of Finance 1976–81, Gov. Cen. Bank 1982–93; Devt Sec., Gilbert and Ellice Islands 1971–73; Regional Econ. Adviser UN Econ. and Social Comm. for Asia and the Pacific 1994–99; currently freelance consultant in econ. man.; Cross of Solomon Islands 1981. *Publications:* numerous articles on land tenure, econ. planning, devt admin, foreign investment, expecially jt ventures, with special emphasis on small countries. *Leisure interests:* working outside, sculling, sailing. *Address:* PO Box 486, Honiara, Solomon Islands (home).

HUGHES, Rt Hon. Beverley, PC, MSc; British politician; *Minister for Children and Youth Justice;* b. 30 March 1950; d. of the late Norman Hughes and of Doris Hughes; m. Tom McDonald 1973; one s. two d.; ed Ellesmere Port Girls' Grammar School, Univs of Manchester and Liverpool; probation officer, Merseyside –1976; Research Assoc., Univ. of Manchester 1976–81, Lecturer 1981–93, Sr Lecturer and Head of Dept 1993–97; Councillor, Trafford Metropolitan Borough Council 1986–97, Council Leader 1995; MP (Labour) for Stretford and Urmston 1997–, mem. Select Cttee on Home Affairs 1997–98; Parl. Pvt. Sec. to Hilary Armstrong, Minister for Local Govt and Housing 1998–99, Parl. Under-Sec. of State, Dept of the Environment, Transport and the Regions 2000–02; Minister of State for Immigration, Citizenship and Counter-Terrorism 2002–04, for Children, Young People and Families 2005–07, for Children and Youth Justice 2007–. *Leisure interests:* walking, jazz. *Address:* Department for Children, Schools and Families, Sanctuary Buildings, Great Smith Street, London, SW1P 3BT; House of Commons, Westminster, London, SW1A 0AA, England (office). *Telephone:* (870) 000-2288 (office); (161) 749-9120 (office). *Fax:* (1928) 794248 (office). *Website:* www.dfes.gov.uk (office); www.parliament.uk (office); www.bevhughes.co.uk.

HUGHES, Rev. Gerard Joseph, MA, STL, PhD; British ecclesiastic and academic; *Tutor in Philosophy, Campion Hall, University of Oxford;* b. 6 June 1934, Wallington, Surrey; s. of Henry Hughes and Margaret Hughes; ed St Aloysius Coll. Glasgow, London Inst. of Educ., Campion Hall, Univ. of Oxford, Heythrop Coll., Oxford and Univ. of Mich.; Chair. Dept of Philosophy, Heythrop Coll., Univ. of London 1973–96, Vice-Prin. 1986–98; mem. Senate and Academic Council, Univ. of London 1987–96; Vice-Provincial, British Prov. of SJ 1982–88; Austin Fagothey Prof. of Philosophy, Univ. of Santa Clara, Calif. 1988, 1992; Master Campion Hall, Univ. of Oxford 1998–2005, Tutor in Philosophy 2005–. *Publications:* Authority in Morals 1978, Moral Decisions 1980, The Philosophical Assessment of Theology (ed.) 1987, The Nature of God 1995, Aristotle on Ethics 2001, Is God to Blame? 2007. *Leisure interests:* music, crosswords, walking, gardening. *Address:* Campion Hall, Oxford, OX1 1QS, England (office). *Telephone:* (1865) 286111 (office). *E-mail:* gerard.hughes@campion.ox.ac.uk (office).

HUGHES, H. Richard, AADiploma, FRIBA; British architect; b. 4 July 1926, London; s. of Maj. Henry Hughes and Olive Hughes (née Curtis); m. Anne Hill 1951 (died 2006); one s. two d.; ed Kenton Coll., Nairobi, Kenya, Hilton Coll., Natal, SA, Architectural Asscn School of Architecture, London; Corporal, Kenya Regt, attached to Royal Engineers 1945–46; Asst Architect Kenya and Uganda 1950–51; Architect, Hartford, Conn., USA 1953–55, Nairobi, Kenya 1955–57; Prin. Richard Hughes and Partners 1957–86; Chair. Kenya Branch, Capricorn Africa Soc. 1958–61, Environment Liaison Cen. 1976–78, Lamu

Soc. 1977–79; UNEP Consultant on Human Settlements 1978; UN Cen. for Human Settlements Consultant on bldg materials, construction tech. in developing countries 1979; Ed., Fireball Int. 1986–92; mem. Exec. Cttee, Friends of the Elderly, London 1987–92; mem. Zebra Housing Asscn Bd, London 1988–98, Trustee, Zebra Trust, London 1988 (Vice-Chair. 1994); Guide, Tate Britain & Tate Modern, London 1987; NADFAS Lecturer 1995. *Publications:* Habitat Handbook (co-author with Graham Searle) 1982, In the Frame 1989, Capricorn – David Stirling's Second African Campaign 2003; and contribs to books on architecture and articles in New Commonwealth, Architectural Review, Architects Journal and Modern Painters; Living Paintings Trust Albums of Architecture for the Blind (ed.)1991, 1994. *Leisure interests:* collecting modern art, dinghy sailing. *Address:* 47 Chiswick Quay, London, W4 3UR, England (home).

HUGHES, John Lawrence, BA; American publisher; b. 13 March 1925, New York; s. of John C. Hughes and Margaret Kelly; m. Rose M. Pitman 1947; three s. one d.; ed Yale Univ.; reporter, Nassau Review Star, Rockville Centre, Long Island, NY 1949; Asst Sr Ed., Pocket Books, Inc. New York 1949–59; Vice-Pres. Washington Square Press 1958; Sr Ed., Vice-Pres., Dir William Morrow & Co. 1960–65, Pres. and CEO 1965–85; Pres. The Hearst Trade Book Group 1985–87, Chair., CEO 1988–90, Ed.-at-Large, Group Adviser 1990–; Consultant, Ed.-at-Large HarperCollins Publrs., NY 1999–; Trustee, Yale Univ. Press, Pierpont Morgan Library, Library of America, Acad. of American Poets; mem. Bd Asscn of American Publishers 1986–90 (Chair. 1988–90); mem. Bd Nat. Book Awards 1982–94 (Chair. 1988–89); mem. Publrs Hall of Fame 1989. *Leisure interest:* golf. *Address:* HarperCollins Publishers, 10 East 53rd Street, New York, NY 10022-5299 (office); PO Box 430, Southport, CT 06490, USA (home). *Telephone:* (212) 207-7569 (office); (203) 259-8957 (home). *Fax:* (212) 207-7506 (office); (203) 259-8142 (home). *E-mail:* larry.hughes@harpercollins.com (office). *Website:* www.harpercollins.com (office).

HUGHES, John W.; American film producer, screenwriter and director; b. 18 Feb. 1950, Lansing, Mich.; m. Nancy Ludwig; two s.; ed Univ. of Arizona; copywriter and Creative Dir Leo Burnett Co.; Ed. Nat. Lampoon magazine which led to writing screenplay of Nat. Lampoon's Class Reunion; founder and Pres. Hughes Entertainment 1985–; Commitment to Chicago Award 1990, NATO/ShoWest Producer of the Year 1990. *Films:* National Lampoon's Class Reunion (screenplay) 1982, National Lampoon's Vacation (screenplay) 1983, Mr. Mom (screenplay) 1983, Nate and Hayes (screenplay) 1983, Sixteen Candles (screenplay and dir) 1984, National Lampoon's European Vacation (screenplay) 1985, Weird Science (screenplay and dir) 1985, The Breakfast Club (screenplay, dir and producer) 1985, Ferris Bueller's Day Off (screenplay, dir and producer) 1986, Pretty in Pink (screenplay and producer) 1986, Some Kind of Wonderful (screenplay and producer) 1987, Planes, Trains and Automobiles (screenplay, dir and producer) 1987, The Great Outdoors (screenplay and producer) 1988, She's Having a Baby (screenplay, dir and producer) 1988, National Lampoon's Christmas Vacation (screenplay and producer) 1989, Uncle Buck (screenplay, dir and producer) 1989, Home Alone (screenplay and producer) 1990, Career Opportunities (screenplay and producer) 1990, Dutch (screenplay and producer) 1991, Curly Sue (screenplay, dir and producer) 1991, Only the Lonely (co-producer) 1991, Beethoven (screenplay, as Edmond Dantès) 1992, Home Alone 2: Lost in New York (screenplay and producer) 1992, Dennis the Menace (screenplay and producer) 1993, Baby's Day Out (screenplay and producer) 1994, Miracle on 34th Street (screenplay and producer) 1994, 101 Dalmatians (screenplay) 1996, Home Alone 1997, Reach the Rock 1998, New Port South 1999, 102 Dalmatians 2000, Just Visiting 2001. *Address:* Jacob Bloom, Bloom and Dekom, 150 South Rodeo Drive, Beverly Hills, CA 90212 (office); Hughes Entertainment, 10201 West Pico Boulevard, Los Angeles, CA 90064, USA (office).

HUGHES, Karen, BA, BFA; American communications consultant, fmr political adviser and fmr diplomatist; b. 27 Dec. 1956, Paris, France; d. of Harold Parfitt; m. Jerry Hughes; one s. one step-d.; ed Southern Methodist Univ.; TV news reporter, KXAS-TV, Dallas/Fort Worth, Tex. 1977–84; press coordinator for Reagan-Bush presidential campaign 1984; fmr Exec. Dir Republican Party of Tex.; Communications Dir for George W. Bush (while Gov. of Tex. and US Pres.) 1995–2002, left Bush admin to return to Tex. July 2002, returned to full-time service with Bush campaign Aug. 2004; mem. White House Iraq Group 2002; Sr Advisor to White House 2004–05; Under-Sec. of State for Public Diplomacy and Public Affairs with rank of Amb., US State Dept 2005–07 (resgnd); Global Vice-Chair Burson-Marsteller (communications consultancy), Austin, Tex. 2008–; ranked by Forbes magazine amongst 100 Most Powerful Women (18th) 2004. *Publication:* Ten Minutes from Normal 2004. *Address:* Burson-Marsteller, 701 Brazos Street, Suite 1100, Austin, TX 78701-3232, USA (office). *Telephone:* (512) 372-6363 (office). *Fax:* (512) 372-6360 (office). *Website:* www.burson-marsteller.com (office).

HUGHES, Leslie Ernest, MB, DS, FRCS, FRACS; Australian surgeon and academic; *Professor Emeritus of Surgery, College of Medicine, University of Cardiff, Wales;* b. 12 Aug. 1932, Parramatta; s. of Charles J. Hughes and Vera D. Hughes (née Raines); m. Marian Castle 1955; two s. two d.; ed Parramatta High School and Univ. of Sydney; surgical trainee, Sydney 1955–59; Registrar, Derby and London, UK 1959–61; British Empire Cancer Research Campaign Research Fellow, King's Coll. Hosp., London 1962–63; Reader in Surgery, Univ. of Queensland 1964–71; Eleanor Roosevelt Int. Scholar, Roswell Park Memorial Inst., Buffalo, NY 1969–71; Prof. of Surgery, Univ. of Wales Coll. of Medicine, Cardiff 1971–92, Prof. Emer. 1992–; Visiting Prof., Univs of Queensland, Allahabad, Sydney, Witwatersrand, Cairo, Melbourne, Lund, Albany, New York and NSW; Pres. Welsh Surgical Soc. 1991–93, Surgical Research Soc. 1992–94; Chair. Editorial Cttee, European Journal of Surgical Oncology 1992–97; Pres. History of Medicine Soc. of Wales 1999–2000; Hon. Fellow, Asscn of Coloproctology of GB and Ireland 2000. *Publications:* Benign Disorders and Diseases of the Breast (third edn) 2008; more than 200 papers and book chapters dealing mainly with tumour immunology, disease of the breast, inflammatory bowel disease, surgical oncology, surgical pathology and wound healing. *Leisure interests:* history, gardening, travel. *Address:* 1 Park View Apartments, 74 Lake Road East, Cardiff, CF23 5NN, Wales.

HUGHES, Louis R., MBA; American business executive; *Chairman, Maxager Technology, Inc.;* b. 10 Feb. 1949, Cleveland, OH; m. Candice Ann Hughes 1972; two c.; ed Gen. Motors Inst. Flint, Mich. and Harvard Univ.; began career with Gen. Motors on financial staff in New York; Asst Treas 1982; Vice-Pres. of Finance, Gen. Motors of Canada 1985–86; Vice-Pres. for Finance, Gen. Motors (Europe), Zürich 1987–89; Chair., Man. Dir Adam Opel AG 1989–92; Exec. Vice-Pres. Gen. Motors Corpn (responsible for int. operations) 1992–; Pres. Gen. Motors (Europe) AG 1992–94; Chair. Bd Saab Automobile AB 1992; Pres. Gen. Motors Int. Operations, Inc., Switzerland 1994–98; Exec. Vice-Pres. New Business Strategies, Gen. Motors Corpn, Detroit 1998–2000; Pres. and COO Lockheed Martin 2000; Chair. Maxager Technology Inc. 2001–; mem. Bd of Dirs British Telecom, Electrolux ABB; fmr mem. Supervisory Bd Deutsche Bank; Pres. Swiss-American Chamber of Commerce; Chair. European Council of American Chambers of Commerce; Order of Merit (Germany). *Leisure interests:* skiing, mountain climbing, antiques. *Address:* Maxager Technology, Inc., 2173 East Francisco Blvd., San Rafeal, CA 94901, USA (office). *Telephone:* (415) 454-1000 (office). *Fax:* (415) 454-7460 (office). *E-mail:* info@maxager.com (office). *Website:* www.maxager.com (office).

HUGHES, Mervyn Gregory; Australian fmr professional cricketer; b. 23 Nov. 1961, Euroa, Vic.; s. of Ian Hughes and Freda Hughes; m. Sue Hughes 1991; one d.; right-arm fast bowler and right-hand lower-order batsman; played for Victoria 1981–95, Essex 1983; 53 Test matches for Australia 1985–94, taking 212 wickets (average 28.3) and scoring 1,032 runs (average 16.6), took hat-trick v. W Indies, Perth 1988; toured England 1989, 1993; 33 limited-overs ints.; took 593 wickets (average 29.4) in first-class cricket; Wisden Cricketer of the Year 1994. *Leisure interests:* golf, relaxing at home, going to the beach, Australian Rules, basketball. *Address:* c/o Australian Cricket Board, 90 Jolimont Street, Jolimont, Vic. 3002, Australia.

HUGHES, Sean Patrick Francis, MS, FRCS, FRCSE (Orth.), FRCSI; British surgeon and academic; *Professor Emeritus of Orthopaedic Surgery, Imperial College London;* b. 2 Dec. 1941, Farnham, Surrey; s. of Patrick Hughes and Kathleen E. Hughes; m. Felicity M. Anderson 1971; one s. two d.; ed Downside School and St Mary's Hosp. Medical School, Univ. of London; Asst Lecturer in Anatomy, St Mary's Hosp. Medical School 1969; Research Fellow, Mayo Clinic, USA 1975; Sr Registrar in Orthopaedics, Middlesex Hosp., London 1977; Sr Lecturer in Orthopaedics, Royal Postgraduate Medical School, London 1979, Prof. of Orthopaedic Surgery, Royal Postgraduate Medical School (became part of Imperial Coll. School of Medicine) 1991–96, Prof. of Orthopaedic Surgery Imperial Coll. London 1996–2006, Prof. Emer. of Orthopaedic Surgery Imperial 2006–, Head of Div. Surgery, Anaesthetics and Intensive Care 1996–2004, Hon. Consultant, Imperial Coll. Health Care Trust 2007–; Prof. of Orthopaedic Surgery, Univ. of Edinburgh 1979–91; Hon. Consultant, Orthopaedic Surgeon Hammersmith Hosps 1991–2006; Clinical Dir Surgery and Anaesthetics Hammersmith Hosps NHS Trust 1998–2002; Medical Dir Ravenscourt Park Hosp., Hammersmith Hosps NHS Trust 2002–07; Rahume Darwood Prof., E Africa 1993, Patrick Kelly Prof., May Clinic 1999; Hon. Civilian Consultant to RN; Hon. Consultant, Nat. Hosp. for Nervous Diseases, London 1994–; Aris and Gale Lecturer, Royal Coll. of Surgeons 1976. *Publications:* textbooks and scientific publications on orthopaedics, particularly bone blood flow, musculoskeletal infection, fractures and management of spinal disorders. *Leisure interests:* sailing, golf, walking, skiing, opera, ballet, watching Tottenham Hotspur, running. *Address:* Department of Surgery, Imperial College London Hammersmith Hospital, Du Cane Road, London, W12 0HS (office); The Old Dairy, Maugersbury, Cheltenham, Glos. GL54 1HR, England (home). *Telephone:* (1451) 870234 (home). *E-mail:* s.hughes@imperial.ac.uk (office).

HUGHES, Simon Henry Ward, MA; British politician and barrister; *Liberal Democrat Energy and Climate Change Spokesperson;* b. 17 May 1951; s. of the late James Henry Annesley Hughes and of Sylvia Hughes (née Ward); ed Christ Coll., Brecon, Selwyn Coll., Cambridge, Inns of Court School of Law; called to The Bar, Inner Temple 1974; trainee, EEC, Brussels 1975–76; trainee and mem. Secr., Directorate and Comm. on Human Rights, Council of Europe, Strasbourg 1976–77; practising barrister 1978–; Vice-Chair. Bermondsey Liberal Asscn 1981–83; MP for Southwark and Bermondsey 1983–97 (Liberal 1983–88, Liberal Democrat 1988–97), Southwark N and Bermondsey 1997–; Vice-Chair. Parl. Youth Affairs Lobby 1984–; Vice-Pres. Southwark Chamber of Commerce 1987– (Pres. 1984–87); Liberal Spokesman on the Environment 1983–87, 1987–88; Alliance Spokesman on Health Jan.–June 1987; Liberal Democrat Spokesperson on Educ. and Science 1988–90, on Environment 1988–94, on Natural Resources 1992–94, on Community and Urban Affairs and Young People 1994–95, on Social Welfare 1995–97, on Health 1995–99, on Home Affairs 1999–2003, on Constitutional Affairs and Attorney-Gen. 2006–07, on the House of Commons 2007–08, on Energy and Climate Change 2009–, cand. for London Mayor 2004; Chair. Liberal Party Advisory Panel on Home Affairs 1981–83; mem. Accommodation and Works Select Cttee 1992–97; mem. Southwark Area Youth Cttee, Anti-Apartheid Movt; mem. Liberal Democrat Party, (Pres. 2004–08); Hon. Fellow, South Bank Univ. *Publications:* Across the Divide 1986, Pathways to Power 1992. *Leisure interests:* music, sport, theatre, the outdoors. *Address:* House of Commons, London, SW1A 0AA (office); 6 Lynton Road, Bermondsey, London, SE1 5QR, England (home). *Telephone:* (20) 7219-6256 (office). *Fax:* (20) 7219-

6567 (office). *E-mail:* simon@simonhughes.org.uk (office). *Website:* www.simonhughes.org.uk (office).

HUH, Chang-soo, MBA; South Korean business executive; *Chairman, GS Holdings Corporation;* m.; two c.; ed Korea Univ., St Louis Univ., USA; joined LG Group strategic planning office 1977, worked in LG International and LG Chemical, Man. Dir LG International Hong Kong and Tokyo offices 1982–86, Exec. Vice-Pres. LG Industrial Systems 1992–95, Chair. LG Cable 1995–2001, with LG Engineering and Construction 2002–04, Chair. GS Holdings Corpn (conglomerate of 59 affiliate cos spun off from LG Group in 2004) 2004–, mem. Exec. Bd; f. J.K. Huh Foundation (charity); Dr hc (St Louis Univ.) 2007. *Leisure interest:* football fan. *Address:* GS Holdings Corpn, 23 F, GS Tower, 679 Yoksam Dong, Gangnam Gu, Seoul, South Korea (office). *Telephone:* (2) 2005-1114 (office). *Fax:* (2) 2005-8181 (office). *E-mail:* info@gsholdings.com (office). *Website:* www.gsholdings.com (office).

HUI, Ann; Chinese film director; b. 23 May 1947, Anshan, Liaoning Prov.; ed Hong Kong Univ., London Film School; moved to Hong Kong aged five; fmr asst to Hu Jingquan; joined TVB and began career making TV documentaries and features; joined Ind. Comm. for Anti-Corruption 1977, made seven TV episodes for drama series (two of which were banned); joined RTHK (Govt TV network) 1978, directed three segments of Beneath the Lion Rock (series); acted in The River 1998, 2001. *Films include:* The Secret 1979, The Spooky Bunch 1980, Boy From Vietnam (TV feature), The Story of Woo Viet (TV feature) 1981, The Boat People (TV feature) (Official Selection at Cannes Film Festival, Best Film, Hong Kong Film Awards) 1982, Love in a Fallen City 1984, The Romance of Book and Sword/Princess Fragrance 1987, Starry is the Night 1988, Song of the Exile (Best Film, Asian Pacific Film Festival and Rimini Film Festival) 1990, Zodiac Killers 1991, My American Grandson 1991, A Boy and His Hero 1993, The Day the Sun Turned Cold (exec. producer) (Best Film, Tokyo Int. Film Festival) 1994, Ah Kam 1996, Opium War (assoc. producer) 1997, Ordinary Heroes 1999, Black Mask (screenwriter) 1999, Summer Show (Silver Bear Award, Berlin Film Festival), Ordinary Heroes, Visible Secret 2002, July Rhapsody 2002, Jade Goddess of Mercy 2003, The Postmodern Life of My Aunt 2006, The Way We Are 2008. *Publications:* The Secret 1979, Boat People 1982, Romance of Book and Sword 1987, Yakuza Chase 1991, Summer Snow 1995.

HUI, Liangyu; Chinese politician and economist; *Vice-Premier, State Council;* b. Oct. 1944, Yushu Co., Jilin Prov.; ed Jilin Agricultural School, Party School of CCP Jilin Prov. Cttee; clerk, Agricultural Bureau and Personnel Supervision Bureau, Yushu Co. 1964–68; joined CCP 1966; clerk and Deputy Head, CCP Revolutionary Cttee (Political Dept), Yushu Co. 1969–72; Deputy Dir Org. Dept, CCP Yushu Co. Cttee 1972–74; Deputy Sec. CCP Yushu Co. Cttee 1974–77; Deputy Dir Jilin Prov. Agricultural Bureau, Prov. Agricultural and Animal Husbandry Dept; Deputy Sec. CCP Leading Group 1977–84; Deputy Sec. CCP Baichengzi Prefectural Cttee, Commr Baichengzi Admin. Office 1984–85; elected mem. Standing Cttee CCP Jilin Prov. Cttee 1985; Dir Rural Policy Research Office, Dir Rural Work Dept CCP Jilin Prov. Cttee 1985–87; apptd Vice-Gov. Jilin Prov. 1987; Deputy Dir CCPCC Policy Research Office 1990; Deputy Sec. CCP Hubei Prov. Cttee 1992; Chair. 1993 Hubei Prov. CPPCC Cttee, Deputy Sec. CCP Anhui Prov. Cttee and Acting Gov. Anhui Prov. 1994–95, Gov. 1995–98; Sec. CCP Anhui Prov. Cttee 1998, Sec. CCP Jiangsu Prov. Cttee 1999–2002; Rep. 15th CCP Congress; Alt. mem. 14th CCP Cen. Cttee, mem. 15th CCP Cen. Cttee 1997–2002, 16th CCP Cen. Cttee 2002–07, 17th CCP Cen. Cttee 2007–, also mem. Politburo 2007–; Rep. of 7th, 8th and 9th NPC; Vice-Premier, State Council 2003–. *Address:* State Council, Beijing, People's Republic of China.

HUI SI-YAN, Rafael, MPA; Hong Kong government official; ed Harvard Univ., USA; joined Civil Service 1970, Admin. Officer 1971, with Ind. Comm. Against Corruption 1977–79, Deputy Sec.-Gen. Unofficial Mems of the Exec. and Legis. Councils Office 1985–86, Deputy Sec. for Econ. Services 1986–90, for Works 1990–91, Dir New Airport Projects Co-ordination Office 1991, Commr for Transport 1992–95, Sec. for Financial Services 1995–2000; Man. Dir Mandatory Provident Fund Schemes Authority 2000–03; Dir Kowloon Motor Bus Holdings Ltd 2004–05; Chief Sec. for Admin, Hong Kong Special Admin. Region 2005–07; Vice-Chair. Hong Kong Arts Festival Soc. 2001–05; mem. Exec. Cttee Hong Kong Philharmonic Soc. Ltd 2004–05; Steward Hong Kong Jockey Club 2002; Justice of the Peace 1986, Hon. Sec. Hong Kong Int. Film Festival Soc. Ltd 2004–05; Gold Bauhinia Star 1998. *Address:* c/o Executive Council, Central Government Offices, Lower Albert Road, Central, Hong Kong Special Administrative Region, People's Republic of China (office).

HUILLARD, Xavier; French construction industry executive; *CEO, Vinci;* b. 27 June 1954; ed Ecole Polytechnique, Ecole Nationale des Ponts et Chaussées; served as civil servant in a local Public Works and Planning Dept and in Ministry for Infrastructure's Dept of Int. Business; joined SGE as Dir of Int. Business at SOGEA 1996, Chair. 1997–2000; Chair. Vinci Construction 2000–02, Sr Exec. Vice-Pres. Vinci and Chair. Vinci Energies 2002, CEO Vinci 2006–, also Chair. and CEO VINCI Concessions.

HUISGEN, Rolf, PhD; German chemist and academic; *Professor Emeritus of Organic Chemistry, University of Munich;* b. 13 June 1920, Gerolstein, Eifel; s. of Edmund Huisgen and Maria Flink; m. Trudl Schneiderhan 1945; two d.; ed Univs of Bonn and Munich; Lecturer, Univ. of Munich 1947–49, Full Prof. of Organic Chem. 1952–88, Prof. Emer. 1988–; Assoc. Prof., Univ. of Tübingen 1949–52; Rockefeller Fellow, USA 1955; numerous guest professorships, USA, Israel, Japan, Spain and Switzerland; mem. Bavarian Acad. of Science, Deutsche Akad. der Naturforscher Leopoldina; Foreign Assoc. NAS, Washington; Corresp. mem. Real Acad. de Ciencias Exactas, Madrid, Heidelberg Acad. of Sciences, Polish Acad. of Sciences; Hon. FRSC, London; Hon. mem. American Acad. of Arts and Sciences, Soc. Chimique de France, Pharmaceutical Soc. of Japan, Gesellschaft Deutscher Chemiker, Accad. Nazionale dei Lincei (Italy), Istituto Lombardo, Polish Acad. Sciences; Hon. Prof., Univ. of St Petersburg; Bavarian Order of Merit 1982, Bavarian Maximilian Order for Science and Art 1984; Hon. Dr rer. nat (Freiburg) 1977, (Erlangen-Nuremberg) 1980, (Würzburg) 1984, (Regensburg) 1985, (Tech. Inst., St Petersburg) 1993; Dr hc (Univ. Complutense de Madrid) 1975; Liebig Medal, Gesellschaft Deutscher Chemiker 1961, Médaille Lavoisier, Soc. Chimique de France 1965, ACS Roger Adams Award in Organic Chem. 1975, Otto Hahn Award for Chem. and Physics 1979, Adolfo Quilico Medal, Italian Chemical Soc. 1987 and other awards. *Publications:* The Adventure Playground of Mechanisms and Novel Reactions (autobiog.) 1994; more than 500 research papers on organic reaction mechanisms and cycloadditions. *Leisure interests:* modern art, archaeology. *Address:* Department Chemie, Universität München, Butenandtstr. 5–13, 81377 Munich (office); Kaulbachstr. 10, 80539 Munich, Germany (home). *Telephone:* (89) 218077712 (office); (89) 281645 (home). *E-mail:* rolf.huisgen@cup.uni-muenchen.de (office). *Website:* www.cup.uni-muenchen.de (office).

HUISMANS, Sipko, BA; British business executive; b. 28 Dec. 1940, Ede, Netherlands; s. of Jouko Huismans and Roelofina Huismans; m. Janet Durston 1969; two s. one d.; ed Stellenbosch Univ., S Africa; joined Courtaulds as shift chemist with Ustu Pulp Co., Ltd 1961; Sales Man., later Gen. Man. Springwood Cellulose Co. Ltd 1968; Exec. responsible for Courtaulds trading interests in Eastern Europe and Far East 1974; apptd to Courtaulds Fibres Bd 1980, Man. Dir of Fibres 1982, apptd to Int. Paint Bd 1986, Chair. 1987, Chair. Courtaulds Chemical and Industrial Exec. 1988–96, responsible for films and packaging 1989, mem. Courtaulds Group Exec. 1986–96, Man. Dir Courtaulds PLC 1990–91, Chief Exec. 1991–96, Dir (non-exec.) Vickers PLC 1994–99, Imperial Tobacco Group PLC 1996–2006; Special Adviser to Chair. Texmaco, Indonesia 1996–99; mem. Supervisory Bd Reemtsma Cigarette Fabriken 2003–; mem. Bd Altadis 2008. *Leisure interests:* motor racing, sailing and 'competition'. *Address:* 7 Stella Maris Street, Flat 4, Sliema, Malta (home). *E-mail:* sipko.huismans@gmail.com (office).

HUIZENGA, John R., PhD; American nuclear chemist and academic; *Professor Emeritus, University of Rochester;* b. 21 April 1921, Fulton, Ill.; s. of Harry M. Huizenga and Josie B. Huizenga (née Brands); m. Dorothy J. Koeze 1946; two s. two d.; ed Calvin Coll., Grand Rapids, Mich. and Univ. of Illinois; Lab. Supervisor, Manhattan Wartime Project, Oak Ridge, Tenn. 1944–46; Assoc. Scientist, Argonne Nat. Lab., Chicago 1949–57, Sr Scientist 1958–67; Prof. of Chem. and Physics Univ. of Rochester, New York 1967–78, Tracy H. Harris Prof. of Chem. and Physics 1978–91, Prof. Emer. 1991–, Chair. Dept of Chem. 1983–88; Fulbright Fellow, Netherlands 1954–55; Guggenheim Fellow, Paris 1964–65, Berkeley, Munich and Copenhagen 1973–74; mem. NAS, ACS; Fellow, American Acad. of Arts and Sciences, American Physical Soc., AAAS; E.O. Lawrence Award, Atomic Energy Comm. 1966, Award for Nuclear Application in Chem., ACS 1975, Leroy Grumman Medal 1991. *Publications:* Nuclear Fission (with R. Vandenbosch) 1973, Damped Nuclear Reactions (with W. U. Schröder), Treatise on Heavy-Ion Science, Vol. 2 1984, Cold Fusion: The Scientific Fiasco of the Century 1992; 275 articles in professional journals. *Leisure interests:* tennis, golf. *Address:* 43 McMichael Drive, Pinehurst, NC 28374, USA (home). *Telephone:* (910) 690-5868 (home). *E-mail:* johnrhuizenga@earthlink.net (home).

HUIZENGA, (Harry) Wayne; American business executive; *Chairman, Huizenga Holdings, Inc.;* b. 29 Dec. 1939, Evergreen Park, Ill.; s. of G. Harry Huizenga and Jean Huizenga (née Riddering); m. Martha Jean Pike 1972; three s. one d.; ed Calvin Coll.; Vice-Chair., Pres., COO Waste Man. Inc., Oak Brook, Ill. 1968–84; Prin. and Chair. Huizenga Holdings, Inc., Fort Lauderdale, Fla 1984–; Chair. and CEO Blockbuster Entertainment Corpn, Fort Lauderdale 1987–94; Owner Florida Marlins, Miami 1992–99, Miami Dolphins, Dolphin Stadium; Chair. Boca Resorts Inc. 1996–, Auto Nation Inc. 1995–2002, Extended Stay America Inc.; mem Bd Dirs Republic Services, ANC Rental Corpn; mem. Team Republican Nat. Cttee, Washington, DC 1988–90; Man of Year, Billboard/Time Magazine 1990 and numerous other awards. *Leisure interests:* golf, collecting antique cars. *Address:* Huizenga Holdings, Inc., 450 E. Las Olas Boulevard, Suite 1500, Fort Lauderdale, FL 33301, USA (office). *Telephone:* (954) 627-5000 (office). *Fax:* (954) 627-5050 (office).

HULCE, Thomas (Tom) Edward; American actor and producer; b. 6 Dec. 1953, Detroit, Mich.; ed North Carolina School of Arts. *Plays include:* Broadway: The Rise and Rise of Daniel Rocket 1982, Eastern Standard 1988, A Memory of Two Mondays, Equus, A Few Good Men 1990, Spring Awakening (producer) (Tony Award) 2007; London: The Normal Heart, Hamlet. *Films:* September 30th 1955, National Lampoon's Animal House, Those Lips Those Eyes, Amadeus 1985, Echo Park 1985, Slam Dance 1987, Nicky and Gino 1988, Parenthood 1989, Shadowman, The Inner Circle, Fearless, Mary Shelley's Frankenstein 1994, Wings of Courage 1995, The Hunchback of Notre Dame (voice) 1996, Home at the End of the World (producer) 2004, Stranger Than Fiction 2006. *Television includes:* Emily Emily, St Elsewhere, Murder in Mississippi 1990, Black Rainbow, The Heidi Chronicles (Emmy Award) 1995. *Address:* c/o CAA, 9830 Wilshire Boulevard, Beverly Hills, CA 90212, USA.

HULL, Brett; American (b. Canadian) professional ice hockey player (retd); b. 9 Aug. 1964, Belleville, Ont., Canada; s. of Bobby Hull; ed Univ. of Minn.-Duluth; right-winger; played two seasons for Univ. of Minn.-Duluth; began professional career with Calgary Flames of National Hockey League (NHL) 1986, traded to St Louis Blues, played 1988–1998, signed as free agent Dallas Stars, played 1998–2001 (team won Stanley Cup 1999), signed as free agent Detroit Red Wings, played 2001–04 (team won Stanley Cup 2002), signed as free agent Phoenix Coyotes 2004–05 (retd); All-Star games appearances 1989,

1990, 1991, 1992, 1993, 1994, 1995, 1997, 2001, All-Star First Team 1990, 1991, 1992; led the NHL in goals with 72 1989/90, with 86 1990/91 (2nd highest total, record for a right-winger); 3rd highest goal total in NHL history (741); 3rd fastest to 600 goals (900 games); 494 goals in 1990s (record); record 17 consecutive seasons of 20 goals or more, including 13 seasons of 30 or more; represented USA at Canada Cup 1991–92, World Cup 1996–97, 2004, Winter Olympics 1998, 2002; Exec. Dallas Stars 2006–07, Co-Gen. Man. 2007–; studio analyst NHL on NBC TV 2006; WCHA Freshman of the Year 1984/85, NHL Lady Byng Trophy 1989/90, NHL Most Valuable Player 1990/91, NHL Lester B. Pearson Award 1990/91, Gold Medal at World Cup 1996 (and named in All-Tournament Team), USA Hockey Distinguished Achievement Award 2003. *Address:* Dallas Stars, L.P., 2601 Avenue of the Stars, Frisco, TX 75034, USA (office). *Telephone:* (214) 387-5500 (office). *Fax:* (214) 387-5610 (office). *Website:* www.dallasstars.com (office).

HULME, Keri; New Zealand novelist; b. 9 March 1947, Christchurch, NZ; ed Canterbury Univ., Christchurch; worked as tobacco picker, fish and chip cook, TV dir and woollen mill worker and studied law, before becoming full-time writer 1972; Writer-in-Residence Otago Univ. 1978, Univ. of Canterbury, Christchurch 1985; awarded New Zealand Book of the Year Award 1984, Mobil Pegasus Prize 1984, Booker McConnell Prize for Fiction, UK 1985. *Publications:* The Bone People 1984, Te Kaihau 1987, Homeplaces 1989, Strands (poems) 1992, Bait 1996, Te Whenua Te Iwi 1987, Homeplaces 1989, Stonefish 2004. *Address:* PO Box 1, Whataroa, South Westland, Aotearoa, New Zealand.

HULSE, Russell Alan, PhD; American research physicist; *Principal Research Physicist, Plasma Physics Laboratory, Princeton University;* b. 28 Nov. 1950; s. of Alan Earle Hulse and Betty Joan Wedemeyer; ed The Cooper Union, New York and Univ. of Massachusetts; worked at Nat. Radio Astronomy Observatory 1975–77; researcher at Plasma Physics Lab., Princeton Univ. 1977–80, Prin. Research Physicist 1992–, Head Advanced Modelling Sciences Lab. 1994–; Fellow American Physical Soc. 1993, Distinguished Resident Fellow, Princeton Univ. 1994; Nobel Prize in Physics (jt winner) 1993. *Publications:* papers in professional journals and conf. proceedings in fields of pulsar astronomy, controlled fusion plasma physics and computer modelling. *Leisure interests:* cross-country skiing, canoeing, nature photography, bird watching, other outdoor activities, target shooting, music. *Address:* Princeton University, Plasma Physics Laboratory, James Forrestal Research Campus, PO Box 451, Princeton, NJ 08543, USA. *Telephone:* (609) 243-2621.

HULTQVIST, Bengt Karl Gustaf, DrSci; Swedish space physicist; *Secretary-General, International Association of Geomagnetism and Aeronomy;* b. 21 Aug. 1927, Hemmesjö; s. of Eric Hultqvist and Elsa Hultqvist; m. Gurli Gustafsson 1953; two s. one d.; ed Univ. of Stockholm; Dir Kiruna Geophysical Observatory 1956–73, Kiruna Geophysical Inst. 1973–87, Swedish Inst. of Space Physics 1987–94, Int. Space Science Inst. (ISSI), Berne, Switzerland 1995–99; Sec.-Gen. Int. Asscn of Geomagnetism and Aeronomy 2001–; Chair. Swedish Space Science Cttee 1972–97, Swedish Nat. Cttee for Geodesy and Geophysics 1980–94, EISCAT Council 1987–88, Nordic Soc. for Space Research 1989–92, Space Science Advisory Cttee, European Space Agency 1998–2000, and others; Kt of the Northern Star Award 1965; Royal Swedish Acad. of Science Prize 1968, 1972, Gold Medal, Royal Swedish Acad. of Eng Sciences 1988, King's Medal 1991, Berzelius Medal, Royal Swedish Acad. of Science 1994, Julius Bartels Medal, European Geophysical Soc. 1996, Haunes Alfvén Medal, European Geophysical Soc. 2002, and other awards. *Publications include:* Introduction to Geocosmophysics 1967, High Latitude Space Plasma Physics (ed.) 1983, Space, Science and I 1997, Magnetospheric Plasma Sources and Losses (ed.) 1999; more than 200 scientific papers on radiation and space physics. *Address:* Swedish Institute of Space Physics, Box 812, 981 28 Kiruna (office); Grönstensv. 2, 981 40 Kiruna, Sweden (home). *Telephone:* (980) 790-60 (office); (980) 843-40 (home). *Fax:* (980) 790-50 (office); (980) 843-40 (home). *E-mail:* hultqv@irf.se (office); hultqv@irf.se (home).

HUM, Sir Christopher Owen, Kt, KCMG, MA; British diplomatist (retd) and college principal; *Master, Gonville and Caius College Cambridge;* b. 27 Jan. 1946; s. of the late Norman Charles Hum and Muriel Kathleen Hum (née Hines); m. Julia Mary Park 1970; one s. one d.; ed Pembroke Coll., Cambridge, Hong Kong Univ.; joined British Diplomatic Service 1967; Office of the Chargé d'Affaires, Embassy in Beijing 1971–73; Office of the Perm. Rep. to EEC, Brussels 1973–75; FCO, London 1975–78; First Sec., Embassy in Beijing 1979–81, Embassy in Paris 1981–83; Asst Head of Hong Kong Dept 1983–85, Head 1986–89; Deputy Head of Falkland Islands Dept 1985–86; Political Counsellor and Head of Chancery, Perm. Mission to UN, New York 1989–92; Asst Under-Sec. of State, N Asia and the Pacific 1992–95; Amb. to Poland 1996–98, Deputy Under-Sec. of State and Chief Clerk, FCO 1998–2001; Amb. to China 2002–05 (retd); Master Gonville and Caius Coll., Cambridge 2006–; Hon. Fellow, Pembroke Coll. Cambridge 2004; Hon. LLD (Univ. of Nottingham) 2006, Hon. PhD (London Metropolitan Univ.) 2006. *Leisure interests:* walking, music. *Address:* The Master's Lodge, Gonville and Caius College, Cambridge, CB2 1TA, England (home). *Telephone:* (1223) 332431 (home). *E-mail:* master@cai.cam.ac.uk (office). *Website:* www.cai.cam.ac.uk (office).

HUMAIDHI, Badr Mishari al-, BA; Kuwaiti economist and government official; b. 23 Oct. 1948; ed Kuwait Univ.; Lecturer of Econs, Kuwait Univ. 1972–74; Econ. Expert, Operations Dept, Kuwaiti Fund for Arab Econ. Devt 1974–78, Deputy Dir-Gen. 1981–86, Dir-Gen. 1986–; Minister of Finance 2006–08; Bd mem. Arab Gulf Program for Supporting UN Devt Orgs 1981, Arab Fund for Social and Econ. Devt 1986, Arab Planning Institute; fmr Deputy Gov. World Bank, Int. Fund for Agricultural Devt for Kuwait. *Address:* c/o Ministry of Finance, POB 9, 13001 Safat, al-Morkab Street, Ministries Complex, Kuwait City, Kuwait (office).

HUMALA TASSO, Ollanta Moisés, BA, MA; Peruvian politician; *President, Partido Nacionalista Peruano (PNP);* b. 27 June 1963, Lima; m. Nadine Humala Tasso; c.; ed Colegio Franco Peruano, Universidad Católica; began military career in 1982, officer 1984; formed clandestine group within army called Militares etnocaceristas (MEC) 1989; promoted to Capt. 1991, to Major 1996, to Col 2000; led uprising against then Pres. Alberto Fujimori in Tacna 2000, imprisoned but pardoned; Exec. Dir of mobilisation Ministry of Nat. Defence, Sedena 2001; military attaché to Peruvian embassy in Paris 2003, in Seoul 2004; Leader Partido Nacionalista Peruano (PNP) and unsuccessful presidential cand. Unión por el Perú 2006; Cross of Military Merit, Officer level 1996, Cross of Military Merit, Commander level 2001. *Address:* c/o Unión por el Perú (UPP), Pablo de Olavide 270, San Isidro, Lima, Peru. *Telephone:* (1) 4403227. *E-mail:* pnacionalista@yahoo.com. *Website:* www .partidonacionalistaperuano.com; www.partidoupp.org.

HUME, Cameron R.; American diplomatist; *Ambassador to Indonesia;* m.; four d.; ed Princeton Univ., American Univ. School of Law; joined Foreign Service 1970, early assignments included Vice-Consul in Palermo, Adviser on Human Rights, US Mission to UN, mem. planning staff, Sec. of State, Desk Officer for South Africa; Political Counsellor in Damascas and Beirut; Dir Foreign Service Inst. field school, Tunis –1986; Advisor on Middle East, Mission to UN 1986–90, Sr Advisor 1990–91; Deputy Chief of Mission, Holy See and US Rep. to Mozambique Peace Talks 1991–94; Minister Counsellor for Political Affairs, Mission to UN 1994–97; Amb. to Algeria 1997–2000; Special Advisor to Perm. Rep. to UN 2000–01; Amb. to South Africa 2001–05, to Sudan 2005–07, to Indonesia 2007–; Fellow, Council on Foreign Relations 1975–76, Harvard Univ. Center for Int. Affairs 1989–90; Guest Scholar, US Inst. of Peace 1994. *Publications include:* The United Nations, Iran and Iraq: How Peacemaking Changed 1994, Ending Mozambique's War 1994, Mission to Algiers: Diplomacy by Engagement 2001; numerous articles on diplomacy. *Address:* Embassy of USA, Jalan Merdeka Selatan 4–5, Jakarta, Indonesia (office). *Telephone:* (21) 34359000 (office). *Fax:* (21) 34359922 (office). *E-mail:* jakconsul@state.gov (office). *Website:* jakarta.usembassy.gov (office).

HUME, Gary, RA; British artist; b. 9 May 1962, Tenterden, Kent; ed Goldsmiths Coll., Univ. of London; mem. RA Summer Exhbn Selection Cttee 2002; Jerwood Painting Prize 1997. *Address:* c/o Matthew Marks Gallery, 523 West 24th Street, New York, NY 10011, USA; Royal Academy of Arts, Burlington House, Piccadilly, London, W1J 0BD, England.

HUME, John, MA; British teacher and fmr politician; *Tip O'Neill Chair, University of Ulster;* b. 18 Jan. 1937, Londonderry, N Ireland; s. of Samuel Hume and Anne Hume (née Doherty); m. Patricia Hone 1960; two s. three d.; ed St Colomb's Coll., Londonderry, St Patrick's Coll., Maynooth, Nat. Univ. of Ireland; Research Fellow, Trinity Coll.; Assoc. Fellow, Centre for Int. Affairs, Harvard Univ., USA; Founder mem. Credit Union in NI, Pres. 1964–68; non-violent civil rights leader 1968–69; rep. Londonderry in NI Parl. 1969–72, in NI Ass. 1972–73; Minister of Commerce, Powersharing Exec. 1974; rep. Londonderry in NI Convention 1975–76; MEP 1979–2004; Leader, Social Democratic and Labour Party (SDLP) 1979–2001; mem. NI Ass. 1982–86; MP for Foyle 1983–98; mem. for Foyle, NI Ass. 1998–2005 (Ass. suspended 2002–07); currently Tip O'Neill Chair., Univ. of Ulster; mem. SDLP New Ireland Forum 1983–84, Irish Transport and Gen. Workers Union, Bureau of European Parl. Socialist Group 1979, Regional Policy and Regional Planning Cttee 1979, EEC, Socialist Co-Chair. Intergroup on Minority Cultures and Languages; Co-Leader Int. Democratic Observers for 1986 Philippines Election; mem. Advisory Cttee on Pollution of the Sea (ACOPS) 1989; Sponsor, Irish Anti-Apartheid Movt; Club Pres. Derry City FC; Freedom, City of Cork 2004; Légion d'honneur; Dr hc (Massachusetts) 1985, (Catholic Univ. of America) 1986, (St Joseph's Univ., Phila) 1986, (Univ. of Mass., Catholic Univ. of America, Washington, DC, Tusculum Coll., Tenn.); Hon. LLD (Queen's) 1995, (Wales) 1996; Hon. DLitt (Ulster) 1998; shared Nobel Peace Prize 1998; Martin Luther King Award 1999, Gandhi Peace Prize 2002. *Publication:* Politics, Peace and Reconciliation in Ireland 1996. *Address:* Faculty of Social Sciences, University of Ulster, Magee Campus, Derry, BT48 7JL, Northern Ireland (office). *Telephone:* (28) 71375575 (office). *E-mail:* j.hume@ulster.ac .uk.

HUMER, Franz B., LLD, MBA; Swiss/Austrian pharmaceutical industry executive; *Chairman, Roche Holding Limited;* b. 1 July 1946; ed Univ. of Innsbruck, Institut Européen d'Admin des Affaires (INSEAD), Paris; ICME, Zurich 1971–73; Asst to Vice-Pres., Schering-Plough Corpn 1973–81; Area Man., S Europe, Glaxo Holdings PLC 1981, later becoming Dir of Marketing Devt, Man. Dir Glaxo Pharmaceutical Ltd, UK Dir Glaxo Holdings PLC –1995; joined F. Hoffman-La Roche Ltd 1995, Dir Roche Holding Ltd 1995–, Head of Pharmaceuticals Div. 1995–, COO 1996–98, CEO Roche Holding Ltd 1998–2008, Chair. 2001–; Chair. (non-exec.) Diageo Plc 2008–; mem. Supervisory Bd Allianz AG; mem. Bd Dirs Chugai Pharmaceuticals, Japan (Roche subsidiary); Vice-Chair. Swiss Business Fed., EFPIA (trade asscn); Dir Project Hope (charity); mem. European Round Table of Industrialists (ERT), JPMorgan Int. Council, Int. Business Leaders' Advisory Council for the Mayor of Shanghai, Bd Univ. of Salzburg, Int. Advisory Bd Nat. Centre for Missing and Exploited Children; Chair. Friends of Phelophepa Foundation, Switzerland, Humer Stiftung, INSEAD; Dr hc (Basel). *Address:* Roche Holding Ltd, Grenzacherstrasse 124, 4070 Basel, Switzerland (office). *Telephone:* (61) 688-11-11 (office). *Fax:* (61) 691-93-91 (office). *E-mail:* info@roche .com (office). *Website:* www.roche.com (office).

HUMMES, HE Cardinal Cláudio; Brazilian ecclesiastic; *Prefect for the Congregation of the Clergy;* b. 8 Aug. 1934, Montenegro; s. of Pedro Adão Hummes and Maria Frank Hummes; ordained priest 1958; Bishop 1975; Coadjutor Santo André 1975–96; Archbishop of Fortaleza 1996–98, of São Paulo 1998–2006; cr. Cardinal 2001; apptd Prefect for the Congregation of the

Clergy by Pope Benedict XVI 2006. *Address:* Palazzo delle Congregazioni, Piazza Pio XII, 3, 00193 Rome, Italy (office). *Telephone:* (06) 69884151 (office). *Fax:* (06) 69884845 (office). *Website:* www.clerus.org.

HUMPHREYS, James Charles, BCom, MSc; Australian economist, diplomatist and development banker; *Chief Executive, Global Economics Ltd;* b. 6 Oct. 1934, Melbourne; s. of James Thomas Humphreys and Mary Charlotte Humphreys; m. Diane May Dummett 1962 (divorced 1991); two d.; ed Scotch Coll., Melbourne, Univs of Melbourne and London; with Dept of Trade and Customs 1951–62; Dept of Treasury 1963–71; Counsellor (Financial), Tokyo 1972–74; Dept of Foreign Affairs, Canberra 1974–78; Amb. to Denmark 1978–80, to OECD, Paris 1980–83; First Asst Sec. Dept of Foreign Affairs, Canberra 1984–86, Dept of Foreign Affairs and Trade, Canberra 1987–88; High Commr in Canada, also accred to Bermuda 1989–91; Exec. Dir EBRD, London 1991–94; Consul-Gen. in USA, New York 1994–96; Chief Exec. Global Econs Ltd 1997–. *Leisure interests:* sailing, tennis, golf, reading, music. *Address:* PO Box 4847, Kingston, ACT 2604, Australia.

HUMPHRIES, (John) Barry, AO, CBE; Australian entertainer and author; b. 17 Feb. 1934; s. of J.A.E. Humphries and L.A. Brown; m. 1st Rosalind Tong 1959; two d.; m. 2nd Diane Millstead; two s.; m. 3rd Lizzie Spender 1990; ed Melbourne Grammar and Univ. of Melbourne; repertory seasons at Union Theatre, Melbourne 1953–54, Phillip Street Revue Theatre, Sydney 1956, Demon Barber Lyric, Hammersmith 1959, Oliver, New Theatre 1960; one-man shows (author and performer): A Nice Night's Entertainment 1962, Excuse I 1965, Just a Show 1968, A Load of Olde Stuffe 1971, At Least You Can Say That You've Seen It 1974, Housewife Superstar 1976, Isn't It Pathetic at His Age 1979, A Night with Dame Edna 1979, An Evening's Intercourse with Barry Humphries 1981–82, Tears Before Bedtime 1986, Back with a Vengeance, London 1987–88, Look at Me When I'm Talking to You 1993–94, Edna: The Spectacle 1998, Dame Edna: The Royal Tour, San Francisco 1998, Remember You're Out 1999; numerous plays, films and broadcasts; best-known for his comic characterizations of Dame Edna Everage, Sir Les Patterson and Sandy Stone; Pres. Frans de Boewer Soc. (Belgium); Vice-Pres. Betjeman Soc. 2001–; Dr hc (Melbourne Univ., Griffith Univ.); Hon. LLD (Melbourne) 2003; J.R. Ackerley Prize, Golden Rose of Montreux, Outer Critics Circle Award. *Publications:* Bizarre 1964, Innocent Austral Verse 1968, The Wonderful World of Barry McKenzie (with Nicholas Garland) 1970, Bazza Holds his Own (with Nicholas Garland) 1972, Dame Edna's Coffee Table Book 1976, Les Patterson's Australia 1979, Treasury of Australian Kitsch 1980, A Nice Night's Entertainment 1981, Dame Edna's Bedside Companion 1982, The Traveller's Tool 1985, The Complete Barry McKenzie 1988, My Gorgeous Life: The Autobiography of Dame Edna Everage 1989, The Life and Death of Sandy Stone 1991, More Please: An Autobiography 1992, Women in the Background (novel) 1996, My Life As Me (autobiog.). *Leisure interests:* reading secondhand booksellers' catalogues in bed, inventing Australia. *Address:* c/o Janet Linden, PBJ Management, 7 Soho Street, London, W1D 3DQ, England. *Telephone:* (20) 7287-1112. *Fax:* (20) 7287-1191. *E-mail:* general@pbjmgt.co.uk. *Website:* www.pbjmgt.co.uk.

HUMPHRY, Richard George, AO, FCA, FAIM; Australian administrator and stock exchange official; *Managing Director and CEO, Australian Stock Exchange;* b. 24 Feb. 1939, Perth; s. of Arthur D. Humphry and Enid G. Humphry; m. Rose Friel 1961; one s. one d.; ed Univ. of Western Australia; computer programmer in public service 1967–77; Asst Sec. Supply Computer Systems Br. 1978–79, Accounting Devt Br. 1979–81; Asst Sec. Defence Br. Commonwealth Dept of Finance 1981–82; First Asst Sec. Financial Man. and Accounting Policy Div. 1982–85; Deputy Sec. Commonwealth Dept of Aboriginal Affairs 1985; Auditor-Gen., Victoria 1986–88; Dir Gen. Premier's Dept of NSW 1988–94; Chair. Audit and Compliance Cttee, State Super Financial Services 1992–2001; Dir State Super Financial Services 1992–2001; Chair. NSW Financial Insts Comm. 1994–99; Man. Dir and CEO Australian Stock Exchange 1994–; Chair. Australian Financial Insts Comm. 1996–2000 (Dir 1992–96); Dir Garvan Medical Research Foundation 1997–; Deputy Chair. Zoological Parks Bd, NSW 1998–; Pres. Commonwealth Remuneration Tribunal 1998–; Ind. Reviewer Govt Information Tech. Outsourcing Initiative 2000; mem. Advisory Bd Nat. Office for Information Economy 1997–98, Financial Sector Advisory Cttee Taskforce 1998–, Foreign Affairs Council 2000–; Business Council of Australia 2000–; mem. Australian Computing Soc., Australasian Inst. of Banking and Finance; Fellow Australian Soc. of Certified Practising Accountants, Australian Inst. of Co. Dirs; Int. Fed. of Accountants Award 1988, Accountant of the Year (Public Sector Div.) 1989, Best Financial Services Exec. (Australian Banking and Finance Awards) 2000. *Leisure interests:* bush walking, reading, scuba diving. *Address:* Australian Stock Exchange Ltd, PO Box H224, Australia Square, Sydney, NSW 2000, Australia (office). *Telephone:* (2) 9227-0400 (office). *Fax:* (2) 9227-0007 (office). *Website:* www.asx.com.au (office).

HUMPHRYS, John; British broadcaster; b. 17 Aug. 1943; s. of Edward George Humphrys and Winifred Matthews; m. (divorced); two s. one d.; ed Cardiff High School; Washington Corresp., BBC TV 1971–77, Southern Africa Corresp. 1977–80, Diplomatic Corresp. 1981; presenter, BBC Nine o'Clock News 1981–87; presenter, BBC Radio 4 Today Programme 1987–, On the Record, BBC TV 1993–, John Humphrys Interview Radio 4 1995–, Mastermind (TV) 2003–; Hon. Fellow, Cardiff Univ. 1998; Hon. DLitt (Dundee) 1996; Hon. MA (Univ. of Wales) 1998; Hon. LLD (St Andrews) 1999; Sony Gold for News Journalist of the Year 2007. *Publication:* Devil's Advocate 1999, Lost for Words: The Mangling and Manipulation of the English Language 2004, Beyond Words 2006, In God We Doubt: Confessions of an Angry Agnostic 2007. *Leisure interests:* cello, trees, books, farming, music. *Address:* Today Programme, BBC Radio 4, Room G630, Stage 6, Television Centre, Wood Lane, London, W12 7RJ, England. *Website:* www.bbc.co.uk/radio4/today.

HUN SEN, BA, PhD; Cambodian politician; *Prime Minister;* b. 5 Aug. 1952, Stoeung Trang District, Kompang-Cham Prov.; m. Bun Rany 1975; three s. three d.; ed Lycée Indra Devi, Phnom Penh, Univ. of Phnom Penh, Nat. Political Acad., Hanoi; joined Khmer Rouges 1970, rising to Commdt; in Viet Nam with pro-Vietnamese Kampucheans 1977, returned to Kampuchea (now Cambodia) after Vietnamese-backed take-over; Founding mem. United Front for the Nat. Salvation of Kampuchea 1978; Minister for Foreign Affairs 1979–85; Deputy Prime Minister 1981–85; Chair. Council of Ministers of Cambodia (Prime Minister) 1985–91, Second Prime Minister Royal Govt of Cambodia 1993–98, Prime Minister of Cambodia 1998–; Vice-Pres. Cambodian People's Party (CPP); mem. Russian Acad. of Sciences 2002–, Bar Asscn of Cambodia 2004–; Hon. mem. ASEAN Eng Fed. 2002; Hon. PhD (Southern Calif. Univ.) 1995, (Iowa Wesleyan Coll.) 1996; Dr hc (Dankook Univ., S Korea) 2001, (Ramkhamhaeng, Thailand) 2001, (Irish Int. Univ.) 2004, (Univ. of Cambodia) 2004, (Soon Chun Hyang Univ., S Korea) 2006, (Rajabhat Univ., Thailand) 2006, (Hanoi Nat. Univ. of Educ.) 2007; awarded title Samdech by the King of Cambodia, World Peace Award, Int. Peace Center 'Lifting Up the World with a Oneness-Heart' Award 2001, Irish Int. Univ. Medal of Excellence 2004, U Thant Peace Award 2005. *Address:* Council of Ministers, Russian Federation Blvd, Phnom Penh, Cambodia (office). *Telephone:* (12) 804442 (office). *Fax:* (23) 880624 (office). *E-mail:* ocm@cambodia.gov.kh (office). *Website:* www.ocm.gov.kh (office).

HUNAITI, Abdelrahim A., PhD; Jordanian university administrator, academic and biochemist; *President, University of Jordan;* b. Feb. 1952, Abu Alanda; m.; four c.; ed Univ. of Jordan, Calif. State Univ., Wash. State Univ., USA; Teaching Asst Wash. State Univ. 1980–81, Research Asst 1981–83; Asst Prof. Yarmouk Univ. 1983–87, Assoc. Prof. 1987–92, Chair. Dept of Biological Sciences 1989–91, Prof. 1992–93; Visiting Prof. Gar Younis Univ. 1991–92; Dean of Academic Research and Grad. Studies, Mu'tah Univ. 1993–94, Asst to Univ. Pres. for Admin. Affairs 1993–94, Foundation Dean Faculty of Agric. 1994–95, Vice-Pres. for Admin. Affairs and Projects 1994–96, for Academic Affairs 1996–98, for Faculties of Sciences Affairs 1998–2000; Vice-Pres. for Academic Affairs, Philadelphia Univ. 2000–04; Pres. Univ. of Jordan 2004–; mem. Higher Educ. Accreditation Council 1997–2004, Dir-Gen. Nov.–Dec. 2004; mem. Editorial Bd Yarmouk Applied and Eng Scientific Journal 2000–; mem. Jordanian Biological Sciences Soc., Jordanian Environmental Pollution Soc., Int. Soc. for Free Radical Research in Medicine, Biology and Chemistry, Arab Biophysics Union, New York Acad. of Sciences; Von Humboldt Fellow 1992; Abdel Hamid Shouman Prize for Young Arab Scientists 1990. *Publications:* Laboratory Manual for Experimental Biochemistry 1986, Biochemistry (Arabic) (co-author) 1993, General Science (Arabic) (co-author) 1993, Science and Technology in the Arab World (co-author) 2002. *Address:* Office of the President, University of Jordan, Amman 11942, Jordan (office). *Telephone:* (6) 5355000 ext. 2110 (office). *Fax:* (6) 4161234 (office). *E-mail:* ahunaiti@ju.edu.jo (office). *Website:* www.ju.edu.jo (office).

HÜNER, Tomáš, DipEng; Czech business executive and engineer; *Chairman and CEO, ČEZ Group;* b. 26 June 1959, Ostrava; s. of Julius Hüner and Olga Hüner; m. Katerina Trnková; two d.; ed Brno Univ. of Tech.; engineer 1985–90; Deputy-Dir Severomoravská Energetika a.s. (SME) Energy works 1990–94, CEO and Chair. SME 1994–2004, CEO ČEZ Group distribution cos in Bulgaria (following merger between Severočeská energetika, Severomoravská energetika, Středočeská energetická, Východočeská energetika and Západočeská energetika) 2004–; Chair. Supervisory Bd Aliatel a.s.; Chair. Energetika Vítkovice a.s., ePRIM, a.s.; Vice-Chair. Supervisory Bd Union Group a.s. *Publications include:* Chronicle of Corporate Heads, Historica Prague (Publr); papers in specialist journals. *Leisure interests:* skiing, tennis, surfing. *Address:* ČEZ a.s., Hlavni Sprava, Duhova 2/1444, 140 53 Prague 4 (office); ul. Přátelství 269/15, 73601 Havírov, Czech Republic (home). *Telephone:* (2) 71131111 (office); (6) 96415491 (home). *Fax:* (2) 71132001 (office). *E-mail:* tomas.huner@cez.cz (office). *Website:* www.cez.cz (office).

HUNG, Nguyen Sinh, PhD; Vietnamese economist and government official; b. 18 Jan. 1946, Nam Dan, Nghe An; previous posts include accountant in Finance Ministry, econ. researcher in Bulgaria, Deputy Dir, then Dir Treasury, Vice Minister of Finance; Minister of Finance –2006; mem. Central Standing Cttee Communist Party. *Address:* c/o Ministry of Finance, 8 Phan Huy Chu, Hoan Kiem District, Hanoi, Viet Nam (office).

HUNGERFORD, John Leonard, MA, MB, BChir, FRCS, FRCOphth; British ophthalmologist and ocular oncologist; *Consultant Ophthalmic Surgeon, St Bartholomew's Hospital;* b. 12 Sept. 1944; s. of Leonard Harold Hungerford and Violet Miriam Hungerford (née Bickerstaff); m. Yvonne Carole Rayment 1987; one d.; ed The Glyn School, Epsom, Gonville and Caius Coll. Cambridge, Charing Cross Hosp. Medical School; consultant surgeon, Moorfields Eye Hosp. 1983–; consultant Ophthalmic Surgeon, St Bartholomew's Hosp. 1983–; Vice-Pres. Int. Soc. for Ocular Oncology 2001; Ridley Medal 1998, Gregg Medal 2001. *Publications:* several publs on ocular cancer. *Leisure interests:* travel, reading, music, gardening, architecture. *Address:* 114 Harley Street, London, W1N 1AG, England (office). *Telephone:* (20) 7935-1565 (office). *Fax:* (20) 7224-1752 (office). *E-mail:* john.hungerford@moorfields.nhs.uk (office); john.hungerford@btopenworld.co.uk (home).

HUNKAPILLER, Michael W., PhD; American scientist and business executive; *Partner, Alloy Ventures;* b. 1949; ed Oklahoma Baptist Univ., California Inst. of Tech.; joined Research and Devt Dept of Applied Biosystems Inc. 1983, Exec. Vice-Pres. 1995, Gen. Man. 1995–97; Vice-Pres. PE Corpn 1995–97, Sr Vice-Pres. and Pres. of Applied Biosystems Div. 1997–98, Pres. Appled Biosystems Group 1998–2004 (retd); Pnr, Alloy Ventures (investment capital firm) 2004–; Dir ACLARA Biosciences Inc. 2000; mem. Bd of Dirs Fluidigm Corpn 2005–; mem. of numerous professional socs. *Publications:* more than 100 publs. *Address:* Alloy Ventures, 400 Hamilton Avenue, 4th

Floor, Palo Alto, CA 94301, USA (office). *Telephone:* (650) 687-5000 (office). *Fax:* (650) 687-5010 (office). *E-mail:* info@alloyventures.com (office). *Website:* www.alloyventures.com (office).

HUNKIN, John S.; Canadian banking executive; joined Canadian Imperial Bank of Commerce (CIBC) 1969, various man. positions becoming Pres. Investment and Corp. Banking Div. (known as CIBC World Markets from 1997), Dir 1993–, Pres. and CEO CIBC 1999–2004, CEO 2004–05; Gov. Council for Canadian Unity, York Univ.; mem. Advisory Council, Schulich School of Business, York Univ.; mem. Conf. Bd of Canada; Trustee Montreal Museum of Fine Arts. *Address:* c/o Canadian Imperial Bank of Commerce, Commerce Court, Toronto Ont. M5L 1A2, Canada (office).

HUNLÉDÉ, Ayi Houénou, LenD; Togolese politician; b. 2 Feb. 1925, Anécho; ed Univ. of Montpellier, France; Asst Insp. of Schools, Northern Togo, then teacher at Ecole Normale d'Atakpamé 1953–56; worked for French Overseas Territories Admin 1958; Asst Admin. Mayor, Lomé; Chief, Admin. Subdivision of Tabligbo; Admin. Mayor of Tsévié 1958–60; Amb. to France, UK, EEC 1960–65; High Commr for Planning 1965–67; Minister of Foreign Affairs 1967–76; ordained pastor in Togolese Evangelical Church 1977; Commdr, Légion d'honneur, Great Cross of Merit (FRG), Commdr, Order of Liberia.

HUNT, Caroline Rose, PhD; American business executive; *Honorary Chairman, Rosewood Hotels & Resorts, LLC;* b. 8 Jan. 1923, El Dorado; d. of H. L. Hunt and Lyda Bunker; four s. one d.; ed Mary Baldwin Coll., Univs. of Texas and Charleston; beneficiary of Caroline Hunt Trust Estate which includes Corpn, Rosewood Properties, Rosewood Resources, Rosewood Hotels (Hon. Chair.) with interests in oil and gas properties, luxury hotels and resorts; owner Lady Primrose's Shopping English Countryside, Lady Primrose's Royal Bathing and Luxuries; Hon. Chair. and Chair. numerous socs and cttees; Award for Excellence in Community Service in the Field of Business, Dallas Historical Soc. 1984, Les Femmes du Monde Award 1988, Grande Dame d'Escoffier 1989, Nat. Fragrance Council Award 1994, British American Commerce Award 1994, Texas Business Hall of Fame 1999, Silver Plume Outstanding Citizen 2000, Featured Author, Texas Book Festival 2001 and Dallas Historical Soc. Centennial 2002. *Publications:* The Compleat Pumpkin Eater 1980, Primrose Past, The 1848 Diary of Young Lady Primrose 2001. *Leisure interests:* antiques, writing. *Address:* Rosewood Hotels & Resorts, LLC, 500 Crescent Court, Suite 300, Dallas, TX 75201, USA. *Website:* www.rosewoodhotels.com.

HUNT, Helen Elizabeth; American actress; b. 15 June 1963, LA; d. of Gordon Hunt and Jane Hunt; m. Hank Azaria 1999 (divorced); f. Hunt-Tavel Productions (production co.). *Stage appearances include:* Been Taken, Our Town, The Taming of the Shrew, Methusalem. *Films include:* Rollercoaster 1977, Girls Just Want to Have Fun 1985, Peggy Sue Got Married 1986, Trancers 1985, Waiting to Act 1985, Project X 1987, Stealing Home 1988, Miles from Home 1988, The Frog Prince 1988, Next of Kin 1989, Trancers II 1991, The Waterdance 1992, Only You 1992, Bob Roberts 1992, Mr Saturday Night 1992, Sexual Healing 1993, Kiss of Death 1995, Twister 1996, As Good As It Gets (Acad. Award for Best Actress) 1997, Pay It Forward 2000, Dr. T and the Women 2000, Cast Away 2000, What Women Want 2000, The Curse of the Jade Scorpion 2001, A Good Woman 2004, Bobby 2006, Then She Found Me (also dir) 2007. *Television includes:* Swiss Family Robinson 1975, St. Elsewhere (series) 1984–86, Mad About You (series, Emmy Award 1996, 1997, Golden Globe Award 1997), Empire Falls 2005. *Address:* Hunt-Tavel Productions, 10202 West Washington Blvd., Astaire 2410, Culver City, CA 90232, USA. *Telephone:* (310) 244-3144.

HUNT, James Baxter, Jr, BA, MS, JD; American lawyer and fmr politician; *Attorney, Womble, Carlyle, Sandridge & Rice PLLC;* b. 16 May 1937, Guilford Co., NC; s. of James Baxter and Elsie (Brame) Hunt; m. Carolyn Joyce Leonard 1958; one s. three d.; ed North Carolina State Univ., Univ. of North Carolina; called to Bar of NC 1964; Econ. Adviser to Govt of Nepal for Ford Foundation 1964–66; partner with Kirby, Webb and Hunt 1966–72, Poyner and Spruill, Raleigh, NC 1985–93; mem. Womble, Carlyle, Sandridge & Rice PLLC 2001–; Lt-Gov. N Carolina 1973–77, Gov. of N Carolina 1977–85, 1993–2000; Chair. Nat. Bd for Professional Teaching Standards 1987–; Chair. Nat. Center for Public Policy and Higher Educ.; Democrat; 1st Annual Harry S. Truman Award Nat. Young Democrats 1975, Soil Conservation Honors Award 1986, Outstanding Govt Leader in US Conservation, Nat. Wildlife Fed. 1983 and other awards. *Address:* Womble, Carlyle, Sandridge & Rice PLLC, 150 Fayetteville Street Mall, Suite 2100, PO Box 831, Raleigh, NC 27602, USA (office). *Telephone:* (919) 755-2105 (office). *Fax:* (919) 755-6089 (office). *Website:* www.wcsr.com (office).

HUNT, Jay; Australian broadcasting executive; *Controller, BBC One;* ed Lady Eleanor Holles School, Hampton, Middx, St John's Coll., Cambridge; joined BBC as researcher on Breakfast News 1989, becoming Output Ed., later Producer Newsnight –1998, Sr Producer Panorama 1998, Ed. One O'Clock News and Six O'Clock News 1999, Exec. Producer for Daytime TV 2002–03, BBC Controller Daytime and Early Peak –2007, Controller BBC One 2008–; Dir of Programmes, Channel Five 2007. *Address:* BBC Television Centre, London, W12 7RJ, England (office). *Telephone:* (20) 8743-8000 (office). *Website:* www.bbc.co.uk/bbcone (office).

HUNT, Rt Hon. Jonathan Lucas, ONZ, PC, MA; New Zealand politician and diplomatist; b. 2 Dec. 1938, Lower Hutt; s. of H. Lucas Hunt and A. Z. Hunt; ed Auckland Grammar School, Auckland Univ.; teacher, Kelston Boys' High School 1961–66; tutor, Univ. of Auckland 1964–66; MP for New Lynn 1966–2005; Jr Govt Whip 1972, Chair. of Cttees and Deputy Speaker of House of Reps 1974–75, Acting Speaker 1975; Labour Opposition Spokesman on Health 1976–79, Constitution and Parl. Affairs 1978–81; Sr Opposition Whip 1980–84; Shadow Minister of Broadcasting 1982; Minister of Broad-

casting and Postmaster-Gen. 1984–87, Minister of State 1987–89, Leader of the House 1987–90, Minister of Broadcasting 1988–90, for Tourism 1988–89, of Housing 1989, of Communications Jan.–Oct. 1990; Sr Opposition Whip 1990–96, Shadow Leader of the House 1996–99; Speaker, House of Reps 1999–2005; High Commr to UK and Nigeria and Amb. to Ireland 2005–08. *Leisure interests:* music, int. affairs, cricket, literature. *Address:* Ministry of Foreign Affairs and Trade, Private Bag 18901, Wellington, New Zealand (office). *Telephone:* (4) 439-8000 (office). *Fax:* (4) 472-9596 (office). *E-mail:* enquiries@mfat.govt.nz (office). *Website:* www.mfat.govt.nz (office).

HUNT, Sir Rex Masterman, Kt, CMG, BA; British diplomatist (retd); b. 29 June 1926, Redcar, Yorks.; s. of the late H. W. Hunt and of Ivy Masterman; m. Mavis Buckland 1951; one s. one d.; ed Coatham School, St Peter's Coll., Oxford; service with RAF 1944–48; with Overseas Civil Service 1951; Dist Commr, Uganda 1962; in Commonwealth Relations Office 1963–64; First Sec., Kuching, Malaysia 1964–65, Jesselton (now Kota Kinabalu), Malaysia 1965–67, Brunei 1967; First Sec., (Econ.), Embassy in Ankara 1968–70; First Sec. and Head of Chancery, Embassy in Jakarta 1970–72; Asst, Middle East Dept, FCO 1972–74; Counsellor, Embassy, S Viet Nam 1974–75, Deputy High Commr, Malaysia 1976–79; Gov. and C-in-C Falkland Islands and Dependencies 1980–82; expelled after Argentine seizure of Falkland Islands April 1982, returned as Civil Commr June, after UK recapture of islands; Civil Commr Falkland Islands 1982–Sept. 1985, Gov. Oct. 1985, High Comm. British Antarctic Territory 1980–85; Freeman of the City of London 1978, of Stanley, Falkland Islands 1985. *Publications:* My Falkland Days 1992, Politicos 2002. *Leisure interests:* gardening, golf. *Address:* The Groom's House, Elton, Stockton-on-Tees, TS21 1AG, England (home). *Telephone:* (1642) 589762 (home).

HUNT, Richard Timothy (Tim), PhD, FRS; British biologist; *Principal Scientist, Cancer Research UK;* b. 19 Feb. 1943, Neston, Wirral; s. of Richard William Hunt and Kit Rowland; m. Mary Collins; two d.; ed Dragon School, Oxford, Magdalen Coll. School, Oxford and Univ. of Cambridge; Research Fellow in Biochemistry, Univ. of Cambridge 1970–81, Univ. Lecturer 1982–90; Prin. Scientist, Cancer Research UK 1990–; Officier, Légion d'honneur 2002; Nobel Prize for Physiology or Medicine 2001. *Publications:* Molecular Biology of the Cell – Problems Book (co-author), The Cell Cycle: An Introduction (co-author); papers in cell and molecular biology. *Address:* Rose Cottage, Ridge, Herts., EN6 3LH (home); Cancer Research UK, Clare Hall Laboratories, South Mimms, Herts., EN6 3LD, England (office). *Telephone:* (1707) 646484 (home); (1707) 625981 (office). *Fax:* (20) 7269-3803 (office). *E-mail:* tim.hunt@cancer.org.uk (office). *Website:* www.cancer.org.uk (office).

HUNT, Swanee, MA, PhD; American research institute director and diplomatist; *Director, Women and Public Policy Program, Harvard University;* b. Dallas, Tex.; d. of H. L. Hunt; m. Charles Ansbacher; three c.; civic leader and philanthropist; led community efforts on public educ., mental health services and affordable housing in Denver, Colo; Founder Women's Foundation of Colo; co-dir half-way house for the mentally ill; Founder Hunt Alternatives (pvt. foundation addressing issues of poverty and discrimination), Chair. Inclusive Security: Women Waging Peace; Amb. to Austria 1993–97; hosted negotiations and int. symposia on efforts to secure peace in Balkans; launched Vienna Women's Initiative 1997; Dir Women and Public Policy Program (WAPPP), John F. Kennedy School of Govt, Harvard Univ. 1997–, also Adjunct Lecturer in Public Policy; mem. Council on Foreign Relations; Contrib. Ed. The American Benefactor; syndicated columnist Scripps Howard news service; awards and hons from Anti-Defamation League, Inst. for Int. Educ., American Mental Health Asscn, Nat. Women's Forum, named Woman of Peace, Together for Peace Foundation, Rome, Italy. *Publications:* This Was Not Our War: Bosnian Women Reclaiming the Peace 2004, Half Life of a Zealot 2006; articles in professional journals and US and int. newspapers. *Leisure interests:* photography, music (composed The Witness Cantata, performed in Washington DC), poetry, hiking, running marathons. *Address:* Women and Public Policy Program (WAPPP), John F. Kennedy School of Government, Harvard University, 79 JFK Street, Cambridge, MA 02138 (office); Inclusive Security: Women Waging Peace, 2040 S Street, NW, Washington, DC 20009, USA (office). *Telephone:* (617) 995-1950 (office); (202) 403-2000 (office). *Fax:* (617) 496-6154 (office); (202) 299-9520 (office). *E-mail:* swanee_hunt@huntalternatives.org (office); information@ womenwagingpeace.net (office). *Website:* www.ksg.harvard.edu/wappp (office); www.womenwagingpeace.net (office).

HUNT OF KINGS HEATH, Baron (Life Peer), cr. 1997, of Birmingham in the County of West Midlands; **Philip Alexander Hunt,** OBE, BA; British politician; *Parliamentary Under-Secretary of State, Department for Work and Pensions;* b. 19 May 1949, Birmingham; m.; five c.; ed City of Oxford High School, Oxford School and Univ. of Leeds; joined Oxford Regional Hosp. Bd 1972; with Nuffield Orthopaedic Centre 1974; Sec. Edgware and Hendon Community Health Council 1975–79; joined Nat. Asscn of Health Authorities 1978, Dir 1990; mem. House of Lords 1997–; apptd Govt Whip and Spokesman on Educ. and Employment and Health, House of Lords 1998; Parl. Under-Sec. of State, Dept of Health 1999–2003, Dept for Work and Pensions 2005–; mem. Oxford City Council 1973–79, Birmingham City Council 1980–82; Jt Chair. All Party Care and Public Health Group 1997–98; Vice-Chair. All Party Group on AIDS 1997–98; Dr hc (Birmingham) 2005. *Leisure interests:* swimming, Birmingham City Football Club, music. *Address:* House of Lords, Westminster, London, SW1A 0PW, England (office). *Telephone:* (20) 7238-0681 (office).

HUNTE, Julian Robert; Saint Lucia diplomatist and politician; b. 1940; fmr Mayor of Castries; mem. and fmr Leader L St Lucia abour Party (SLP); fmr Chair. Standing Conf. of Popular Democratic Parties of the Eastern Caribbean (SCOPE); Perm. Rep. of Saint Lucia to UN, New York –2001, 2004–06 (resgnd); Chair. and CEO The Julian R. Hunte Group of Cos; Minister of

Foreign Affairs, Int. Trade and Civil Aviation 2001–04; Pres. of 58th Session, UN Gen. Ass. 2003–04; Vice-Pres. W Indies Cricket Bd; Knight of the Grand Cross Pian Order from Pope John Paul II 2004. *Address:* c/o Saint Lucia Labour Party (SLP), Tom Walcott Bldg, 2nd Floor, Jeremie Street, POB 427, Castries, Saint Lucia (office). *Telephone:* 451-8446 (office). *Fax:* 451-9389 (office). *E-mail:* slp@candw.lc (office). *Website:* www.geocities.com/~slp (office).

HUNTEN, Donald Mount, PhD, FRSC; American astronomer, physicist and academic; *Regents Professor of Planetary Science, University of Arizona;* b. 1 March 1925, Montreal, Canada; s. of Kenneth William Hunten and Winnifred Binnmore Mount; m. 1st Isobel Ann Rubenstein 1949 (divorced 1995); two s.; m. 2nd Ann Louise Sprague; ed Univ. of Western Ontario, McGill Univ.; Research Assoc. to Prof., Univ. of Sask., Saskatoon 1950–63; Physicist Kitt Peak Nat. Observatory 1963–78; Consultant to NASA 1964–, Science Adviser to NASA Assoc. Admin. for Space Science 1977–78; Prof. of Planetary Science, Univ. of Ariz., Tucson 1978–88, Regents Prof. 1988–; mem. NAS; numerous awards including Space Science Award, Cttee on Space Research 2000. *Publications:* Introduction to Electronics 1964, Theory of Planetary Atmospheres (with J. W. Chamberlain) 1987; several NASA publs, numerous papers in scientific journals. *Leisure interest:* music. *Address:* Department of Planetary Sciences, Space Sciences 515, University of Arizona, Tucson, AZ 85721 (office); 3445 W Foxes Den Drive, Tucson, AZ 85745, USA (home). *Telephone:* (602) 621-4002 (office). *Fax:* (602) 621-4933 (office). *E-mail:* dhunten@lpl.arizona.edu (office). *Website:* www.lpl.arizona.edu/people/faculty/hunten.html (office).

HUNTER, Anthony (Tony) Rex, MA, PhD, FRS, FRSA; British molecular biologist and cell biologist; *American Cancer Society Professor, Molecular and Cell Biology Laboratory, The Salk Institute;* b. 23 Aug. 1943, Ashford, Kent; s. of Ranulph Rex Hunter and Nellie Ruby Elsie Hitchcock; m. 1st Philippa Charlotte Marrack 1969 (divorced 1974); m. 2nd Jennifer Ann Maureen Price 1992; two s.; ed Felsted School, Essex and Gonville and Caius Coll., Cambridge; Research Fellow Christ's Coll., Cambridge 1968–71, 1973–75; Research Assoc. Salk Inst., San Diego, Calif. 1971–73, Asst Prof. 1975–78, Assoc. Prof. 1978–82, Prof. 1982–, American Cancer Soc. Prof. 1992–; Adjunct Assoc. Prof., Dept of Biology, Univ. of Calif., San Diego 1979–82, Adjunct Prof. 1982–; mem. Inst of Medicine (USA) 2004, American Philosophical Soc. 2006; Assoc. mem. European Molecular Biology Org. 1992; Foreign Assoc. NAS 1998; Fellow, American Acad. of Arts and Sciences 1992; American Business Foundation for Cancer Research Award 1988, Katharine Berkan Judd Award (Memorial Sloan-Kettering Cancer Center) 1992, Hopkins Medal (Biochemical Soc.) 1994, Gairdner Foundation Int. Award 1994, General Motors Cancer Research Foundation Mott Prize 1994, Feodor Lynen Medal 1999, J. Allyn Taylor Int. Prize in Medicine 2000, Keio Medical Science Prize 2001, Sergio Lombroso Award in Cancer Research 2003, City of Medicine Award 2003, American Cancer Soc. Medal of Honor 2004, Kirk A. Landon Prize for Basic Cancer Research, American Asscn for Cancer Research 2004, Prince of Asturias Award for Scientific and Tech. Research 2004, Louisa Gross Horwitz Prize 2004, Daniel Nathans Memorial Award 2005, Wolf Foundation Prize in Medicine 2005, Pasarow Award in Cancer Research 2006, American Soc. of Biochemistry and Molecular Biology, Herbert Tabor Award 2007, Clifford Prize for Cancer Research 2007. *Publications:* more than 475 papers and journal articles. *Leisure interests:* white-water rafting, desert camping. *Address:* Molecular and Cell Biology Laboratory, The Salk Institute, 10010 North Torrey Pines Road, La Jolla, CA 92037-1099 (office); 4578 Vista de la Patria, Del Mar, CA 92014-4150, USA (home). *Telephone:* (858) 453-4100 (ext. 1385) (office); (858) 792-1492 (home). *Fax:* (858) 457-4765 (office). *E-mail:* hunter@salk.edu (office). *Website:* www.salk.edu/faculty/faculty/details.php?id=27 (office); pingu.salk.edu/~hunter (office).

HUNTER, Holly, BFA; American actress; b. 20 March 1958, Conyers, Ga; d. of Charles Hunter and Opal M. Catledge; m. Janusz Kaminski (q.v.) 1995; two c. (twins) with Gordon MacDonald; ed Carnegie-Mellon Univ.; Dir Calif. Abortion Rights Action League; Emmy Award for TV production Roe vs. Wade 1989; Best Actress Award, American TV Awards, for cable TV production of The Positively True Adventures of the Alleged Texas Cheerleader Murdering Mom 1993; Best Actress Award, Cannes Film Festival Award 1993 and Acad. Award 1994 for role in The Piano. *Theatre:* on Broadway: Crimes of the Heart, The Wake of Jamey Foster, The Miss Firecracker Contest; other: A Weekend Near Madison, The Person I Once Was, Battery (all in New York), A Lie of the Mind (Los Angeles), By the Bog of Cats (Wyndham's Theatre, London) 2004 and regional productions. *Films include:* The Burning 1981, Swing Shift 1984, Broadcast News 1987, Raising Arizona 1987, End of the Line 1988, Miss Firecracker 1989, Always 1989, Animal Behavior 1989, Once Around 1990, The Piano 1993, The Firm 1993, Home for the Holidays 1995, Copycat 1995, Crash 1996, A Life Less Ordinary 1997, Living Out Loud 1998, Jesus' Son 1999, Timecode 2000, Things You Can Tell Just by Looking at Her 2000, Woman Wanted 2000, O Brother, Where Art Thou? 2000, Moonlight Mile 2002, Thirteen 2003, Levity 2003, The Incredibles (voice) 2004, Little Black Book 2004, Nine Lives 2005, The Big White 2005. *Television includes:* Roe vs. Wade 1989, The Positively True Adventures of the Alleged Texas Cheerleader-Murdering Mom 1993, Harlan County War 2000, When Billie Beat Bobby 2001, Saving Grace (series) 2007–09. *Address:* c/o International Creative Management, 8942 Wilshire Blvd, #219, Beverly Hills, CA 90211, USA.

HUNTER, Howard O., AB, JD; American university administrator, academic and lawyer; *President, Singapore Management University;* ed Yale Univ.; admitted to State Bar of Georgia 1971; mem. Faculty of Law, Emory Univ. 1976–2004, Asst Prof. 1976–79, Assoc. Prof. 1979–82, Prof. 1982–2004, Dean School of Law 1989–2001, Interim Provost and Exec. Vice-Pres. for Academic Affairs 2001–03, Prof. of Law and Dean Emer. 2005–; Pres. Singapore Man. Univ. 2004–; Fulbright Sr Scholar Sydney Univ. Law School 1988; Recurring Visiting Prof. of Law Cen. European Univ., Budapest 1999–; Visiting McWilliam Prof. of Commercial Law, Sydney Univ. 2004; mem. Bd of Dirs Georgia Volunteer Lawyers for the Arts Inc. 1975–89, Pres. 1985–87, mem. Bd of Advisers 1997–; mem. Chief Justice's Comm. on Professionalism 1990–2004, Georgia Supreme Court Comm. on Indigent Defense 2000–; mem. Editorial Bd Journal of Contract Law 1988–; mem. American Law Inst., ABA, Asscn of American Law Schools; Hon. Prof. of Law Hong Kong Univ. 1986; Bar and Media Award 1980, Supreme Court of Georgia Amicus Curiae Award 1998. *Publications include:* Recent Reforms in Swedish Higher Education (co-author) 1980, Universities and Community Service: Concepts and Problems 1980, Modern Law of Contracts, Law in Perspective: The Integrative Jurisprudence of Harold J. Berman (ed.) 1996, numerous journal articles. *Address:* Singapore Management University, Tanglin, POB 257, 912409 Singapore (office). *Telephone:* 68220100 (office). *Fax:* 68220101 (office). *E-mail:* enquire@smu.edu.sg (office). *Website:* www.smu.edu.sg (office).

HUNTER, Robert John, AM, PhD, FAA, FRACI, CChem; Australian research chemist and academic; *Honorary Associate Professor, School of Chemistry, University of Sydney;* b. 26 June 1933, Abermain, NSW; s. of Ronald Hunter and Elizabeth Dixon; m. Barbara Robson 1954 (divorced 1995); one s. one d.; ed Cessnock High School, NSW, New England Univ. Coll. and Univ. of Sydney; secondary school teacher 1953–54; Tech. Officer, CSIRO 1954–57, Research Officer 1960–64; Lecturer, Univ. of Sydney 1964, Assoc. Prof. of Physical Chem. 1972–90, Head, School of Chem. 1987–90, Hon. Research Assoc. 1990–94, Hon. Assoc. Prof. 1994–; Dir Colloidal Dynamics Pty Ltd 1988–96; Chair. Nat. Science and Industry Forum 1991–93; Pres. Int. Asscn of Colloid and Interface Scientists 1992–94; Nat. Pres. Scientists for Global Responsibility (fmrly Scientists Against Nuclear Arms) 1986–88, 1990–92, 1996–; Archibald Ollé Prize 1982, 1993, Alexander Memorial Lecturer 1987, Liversidge Lecturer of Royal Soc. of NSW 1988, to Australia and New Zealand Acad. for Advancement of Science 2001. *Publications:* Chemical Science 1976, Zeta Potential in Colloid Science 1981, Foundations of Colloid Science, (Vol. I) 1987, (Vol. 2) 1989, (2nd edn) 2001, Introduction to Modern Colloid Science 1993. *Leisure interests:* music, drama, reading, lawn bowls. *Address:* School of Chemistry, Building F11, University of Sydney, Sydney, NSW 2006 (office); 26/20A Austin Street, Lane Cove, NSW 2066, Australia (home). *Telephone:* (2) 9351-4785 (office); (2) 9427-6261 (home). *Fax:* (2) 9351-3329 (office); (2) 9427-6261 (home). *E-mail:* hunter_r@chem.usyd.edu.au (office); sgr@hotkey.net.au (home). *Website:* www.chem.usyd.edu.au/research/hunter.html (office); www.hotkey.net.au/~sgr (home).

HUNTSMAN, Jon Meade, BA, MBA; American chemical industry executive; *Chairman, Huntsman International LLC;* b. 1937, Blackfoot, Ida; m. Karen Haight 1959; nine c.; ed Univ. of Pa Wharton School, Univ. of Southern Calif.; family moved to Palo Alto, Calif. 1950; salesman for egg-producing co., LA 1961; set up side-business selling repackaged music recordings 1964; Pres. Dolco Packaging (jt venture between egg business and Dow Chemical) 1967–70; Co-founder and CEO Huntsman Container Corpn 1970–80; Assoc. Admin. Dept of Health, Educ. and Welfare and later Special Asst to Pres. Nixon 1970; Founder, Chair. and CEO Huntsman Chemical Corpn, Salt Lake City, UT 1982; est. with Dow Chemical Co. a plastic, glass and aluminium-recycling programme in US Nat. Parks 1990; f. Huntsman Packaging 1992; est. Huntsman Cancer Inst., Univ. of UT, Salt Lake City 1993; Founder and Chair. Huntsman Corpn 1994–, all Huntsman operating entities brought under man. of Huntsman Corpn 1996–; Texas Gov.'s Award for Environmental Excellence 1996. *Address:* Huntsman International LLC, 500 Huntsman Way, Salt Lake City, UT 84108, USA (office). *Telephone:* (801) 584-5700 (office). *Fax:* (801) 584-5781 (office). *Website:* www.huntsman.com (office).

HUNTSMAN, Jon Meade, Jr, BA; American politician; *Governor of Utah;* b. 26 March 1960, Palo Alto, Calif.; s. of Jon Huntsman, Sr; m. Mary Kaye Cooper; six c.; ed Univs of Utah and Pennsylvania; served as missionary for the Church of Jesus Christ of Latter-day Saints (Mormon) in Taiwan; fmr White House Staff Asst to Pres. Ronald Reagan; served as Deputy Asst Sec. of Commerce for Trade Devt, then Deputy Asst Sec. of Commerce for East Asian and Pacific Affairs, then US Amb. to Singapore (youngest amb. in more than a century) under Pres. George H. W. Bush; served as Deputy US Trade Rep./US Trade Amb. for Asia, South Asia and Africa under Pres. George W. Bush; currently Chair. and CEO Huntsman Family Holdings Co. LLC (holding co. for Huntsman Corpn, fmr Chair. Exec. Cttee); Gov. of Utah 2005–; first Pres. and CEO Huntsman Cancer Foundation, responsible for organizing and funding of Huntsman Cancer Inst., Univ. of Utah; mem. Bd of Dirs three Fortune 500 cos; fmr Bd mem. Intermountain Health Care, ARUP Laboratories; fmr Br. Dir San Francisco Fed. Reserve Bank Bd; fmr mem. Int. Advisory Council, Singapore Econ. Devt Bd, Nat. Bd, Juvenile Diabetes Foundation; fmr Chair. KSL's Family Now Campaign, Envision Utah, Utah Opera; fmr Vice-Chair. Coalition for Utah's Future; fmr mem. Advisory Bd, Univ. of Utah School of Business; fmr Trustee Univ. of Pennsylvania. *Address:* Utah State Capitol Complex, East Office Building, Suite E220, PO Box 142220, Salt Lake City, UT 84114-2220, USA (office). *Telephone:* (801) 538-1000 (office); (800) 705-2464 (office). *Fax:* (801) 538-1528 (office). *Website:* www.utah.gov/governor (office).

HUO, Da; Chinese writer; b. 1945, Beijing; ed Beijing Constructional Eng Coll.; translator, Beijing Bureau of Cultural Relics; screenplay writer, Beijing TV Station and Beijing TV Art Centre; Vice-Chair. Chinese Soc. of Writers of Ethnic Minorities. *Screenplay:* Dragon Foal (Best Film Screenplay Award). *Publications:* The Burial Ceremony of Muslims (Mao Dun Prize for Literature), Red Dust (Fourth Nat. Prize), The Worry and Joy of Thousands of Households (Fourth Nat. Prize), Magpie Bridge (Flying Apsaras Award),

Collected Works of Huo Da (six vols). *Address:* Beijing Television Station, Beijing 100089, People's Republic of China (office).

HUPPERT, Herbert Eric, MA, MSc, MS, PhD, ScD, FRS; Australian scientist and academic; *Professor of Theoretical Geophysics and Director, Institute of Theoretical Geophysics, University of Cambridge;* b. 26 Nov. 1943, Sydney; s. of Leo Huppert and Alice Huppert (née Neumann); m. Felicia Ferster 1966; two s.; ed Sydney Boys High School, Univ. of Sydney, Australian Nat. Univ. and Univ. of California, San Diego; ICI Research Fellow, Univ. of Cambridge 1968–69, Asst Dir Research Dept Applied Math. and Theoretical Physics 1970–81, Univ. Lecturer 1981–88, Reader Geophysical Dynamics 1988–89, Prof. of Theoretical Geophysics and Dir Inst. of Theoretical Geophysics 1989–, Fellow, King's Coll., Cambridge 1970–; Prof. of Math., Univ. of NSW 1991–95; BP Venture Unit Sr Research Fellow 1983–89; fmr Visiting Research Scientist, Univ. of Calif., Univ. of Canterbury, Univ. of NSW, ANU, MIT, Univ. of Western Australia, Woods Hole Oceanographic Inst., California Inst. of Tech.; Vice-Chair. Scientists for the Release of Soviet Refuseniks 1985–88, Co-Chair. 1988–92; mem. Council NERC 1993–98, Scientific Council, The Earth Centre 1995–, Council Royal Soc. 2001–03; Ed. Journal of Soviet Jewry 1986–92; Assoc. Ed. Journal of Fluid Mechanics 1971–90; mem. Editorial Bd Philosophical Transactions of the Royal Society A 1994–99, Reports on Progress in Physics 1997–2000; Fellow, American Geophysical Union 2002, American Physical Soc. 2004; Evnin Lecturer, Princeton Univ. 1995, Mid-West Mechanics Lecturer 1996–97, Henry Charnock Distinguished Lecturer 1999, Smith Industries Lecturer, Univ. of Oxford 1999, Nat. Acad. of America's Arthur L Prize and Lectureship 2005, Distinguished Israel Pollak Lecturer of Technion 2005, William Hopkins Prize, Cambridge Philosophical Soc. 2005, Murchison Medal, London Geological Soc. 2007. *Achievement:* played squash for Cambridgeshire 1970–72. *Publications:* more than 200 papers on fluid motions associated with the atmosphere, oceans, volcanoes and the interior of the earth. *Leisure interests:* his children, squash, mountaineering, lawn tennis, music, travel. *Address:* Institute of Theoretical Geophysics, Department of Applied Mathematics and Theoretical Physics, University of Cambridge, Centre for Mathematical Sciences, Wilberforce Road, Cambridge, CB3 0WA (office); 46 De Freville Avenue, Cambridge, CB4 1HT, England (home). *Telephone:* (1223) 337853 (office); (1223) 356071 (home). *Fax:* (1223) 765900 (office). *E-mail:* heh1@esc.cam.ac.uk (office). *Website:* www.itg.cam.ac.uk/people/heh/index.html (office).

HUPPERT, Isabelle Anne; French actress; b. 16 March 1953, Paris; d. of Raymond Huppert and Annick Beau; two s. one d.; ed Lycée de St-Cloud, Ecole nat. des langues orientales vivantes; Pres. Comm. d'avances sur recettes 1994–; several theatre appearances including Mary Stuart (London) 1996, 4.48 Psychose (Paris) 2002; Pres. Cannes Film Festival Jury 2009; Prix Susanne Blanchetti 1976, Prix Bistingo 1976, Prix César 1978 and for Best Actress (for La Cérémonie) 1996, Palme d'Or, Cannes 1978, Prix d'Interpretation, Cannes 1978, Donostia Prize, San Sebastián Film Festival 2003. *Theatre:* 4.48 Psychosis (New York) 2005. *Films include:* Le bar de la Fourche, César et Rosalie, Les valseuses, Aloïse, Dupont la joie, Rosebud, Docteur Françoise Gailland, Le juge et l'assassin, Le petit Marcel 1976, Les indiens sont encore loin 1977, La dentellière, Violette Nozière 1978, Les soeurs Brontë 1978, Loulou 1980, Sauve qui peut (la vie), Les Héritières 1980, Heaven's Gate 1980, Coup de Torchon 1981, Dame aux Camélias 1981, Les Ailes de la Colombe 1981, Eaux Profondes 1981, Passion, travail et amour, La Truite 1982, Entre Nous 1984, My Best Friend's Girl 1984, La Garce 1984, Signé Charlotte, Sac de noeuds 1985, Cactus 1986, Sincerely Charlotte 1986, The Bedroom Window 1986, The Possessed 1988, Story of Women 1989, Milan Noir 1990, Madame Bovary 1991, Malina 1991, Après l'amour 1992, La Séparation 1994, Amateur 1994, L'Inondation 1994, La Cérémonie 1995, Les Affinités électives 1996, Rien ne va plus 1997, Les Palmes de M. Schutz 1997, L'Ecole de la chair 1998, Merci pour le chocolat 2000, Les Destineées sentimentales 2000, La Fausse suivante et Saint-Cyr 2000, La Pianiste (Best Actress, Cannes Film Festival) 2001, 8 Femmes 2002, Deux 2002, La Vie promise 2002, Le Temps du loup 2003, Ma Mère 2004, I Heart Huckabees 2004, Les Soeurs fâchées 2004, Gabrielle (Venice Film Festival Special Lion) 2005, L'Ivresse du pouvoir, Nue Propriété. *Publication:* Madame Deshoulières 2001. *Address:* c/o VMA, 10 avenue George V, 75008 Paris, France.

HÜPPI, Rolf; Swiss financial services executive; b. 1943; joined Zurich Financial Services 1963, Man. India Office 1964–70, Zurich Office 1970–72, Regional Man. US Office, Pittsburgh, PA 1972–74, mem. Group Exec. Bd 1983–, CEO for US Br. 1983–87, Deputy COO 1987–88, COO 1988–91, Pres. and CEO 1991–98; mem. Bd of Dirs Zurich Insurance Co. 1993–2002, Chair. 1995–2002; Chair. and CEO Zurich Financial Services Group (following merger) 1998–2002. *Address:* c/o Zurich Financial Services, Mythenquai 2, 8022 Zurich, Switzerland (office).

HUQOOQMAL, Mahbuba; Afghan politician; *Adviser on Women's Affairs;* b. Kabul; ed Malalai High School, Kabul Univ.; scientific cadre, Faculty of Law and Political Sciences, Kabul Univ. 1965, Lecturer 1965–96; Dir Women Lawyers Asscn 1965–69; mem. Constitutional Comm. –1979; Head of Afghan Women's Rights Asscn 1994; migrated to Peshawar when the Taliban took power in Kabul; Lecturer, Ummahatul Moamenin (Afghan) Univ., Peshawar; Vice-Chair. Special Ind. Comm. for Convening Emergency Loya Jirga 2001; apptd Minister of State for Women's Affairs 2002, currently Adviser on Women's Affairs. *Address:* c/o Ministry of Women's Affairs, Kabul, Afghanistan (office).

HUR, Won-joon, BSc; South Korean business executive; ed Pusan High School, Yonsei Univ., Seoul; joined Hanwha Chemical 1968, Head of Research, Hanwha Group Research Centre, 1982–89, Head of Business Devt Div., Hanwha Chemical Corpn, 1989–92, Head of Tech. Planning Div. 1992–97, Head of New Business Devt Div. 1997–98, Head of Restructuring Team 1998–2001, Chief Planning, Tech. and Information Officer 2001, Pres. and CEO –2008; Order of Industrial Service Merit, Ivory Tower 2000. *Address:* c/o Hanwha Chemical Corpn, Hanwha Building, 1 Changgyo-Dong, Chung-Ku, Seoul 100-797, Republic of Korea. *Telephone:* (2) 729-2700.

HURD, Mark V., BA; American computer industry executive; *Chairman, President and CEO, Hewlett-Packard Company;* ed Baylor Univ.; various positions with NCR 1980–2005, including Vice-Pres. Worldwide Marketing and Americas Professional Services Div., Sr Vice-Pres. Teradata Solutions Group 1998–2000, COO Teradata Div., Pres. NCR 2001–05, COO 2002–03, CEO 2003–05; CEO and Pres. Hewlett-Packard Co. 2005–, Chair. 2006–; mem. Computer Systems Policy Project. *Address:* Hewlett-Packard Company, 3000 Hanover Street, Palo Alto, CA 94304, USA (office). *Telephone:* (650) 857-1501 (office). *Fax:* (650) 857-5518 (office). *Website:* www.hp.com (office).

HURD OF WESTWELL, Baron (Life Peer), cr. 1997, of Westwell in the County of Oxfordshire; **Douglas Richard Hurd,** CH, CBE, PC; British politician, diplomatist, banker and author; *Deputy Chairman, Coutts Bank;* b. 8 March 1930, Marlborough; s. of the late Baron Hurd and Stephanie Corner; m. 1st Tatiana Elizabeth Michelle Eyre 1960 (divorced 1982); three s.; m. 2nd Judy Smart 1982; one s. one d.; ed Eton Coll., Trinity Coll., Cambridge; joined diplomatic service 1952; served in Beijing 1954–56, UK Mission to UN 1956–60, Pvt. Sec. to Perm. Under-Sec. of State, Foreign Office 1960–63, in British Embassy, Rome 1963–66; joined Conservative Research Dept 1966, Head of Foreign Affairs Section 1968; Private Sec. to Leader of the Opposition 1968–70, Political Sec. to the Prime Minister 1970–74; MP for Mid-Oxon 1974–83, for Witney 1983–97; Opposition Spokesman on European Affairs 1976–79, Minister of State, FCO 1979–83, Home Office 1983–84; Sec. of State for NI 1984–85; Home Sec. 1985–89; Sec. of State for Foreign and Commonwealth Affairs 1989–95; mem. Royal Comm. for Lords Reforms 1999–; Deputy Chair. NatWest Markets 1995–98; Dir NatWest Group 1995–99; Chair. British Invisibles 1997–2000; Deputy Chair. Coutts and Co. 1998–; cand. for Conservative Leadership 1990; Chair. Prison Reform Trust 1997–2001; Chair. Booker Prize Cttee 1998; Sr Adviser to Hawkpoint Partners Ltd 1999–; Chair. Council for Effective Dispute Resolution (CEDR) 2001–04; High Steward Westminster Abbey 2000–; Jt Pres. Royal Inst. Int. Affairs 2002–; Spectator Award for Parliamentarian of the Year 1990. *Publications:* The Arrow War 1967, Send Him Victorious (with Andrew Osmond) 1968, The Smile on the Face of the Tiger 1969, Scotch on the Rocks 1971, Truth Game 1972, Vote to Kill 1975, An End to Promises 1979, War Without Frontiers (with Andrew Osmond) 1982, Palace of Enchantments (with Stephen Lamport) 1985, The Last Day of Summer 1992, The Search for Peace 1997, The Shape of Ice 1998, Ten Minutes to Turn the Devil (short stories) 1999, Image in the Water 2001, Memoirs 2003, Robert Peel 2007. *Leisure interests:* writing and broadcasting. *Address:* House of Lords, Westminster, London, SW1A 0PW, England (office). *Telephone:* (20) 7665-4538 (office); (20) 7219-3000. *Fax:* (20) 7665-4694 (office).

HURFORD, Peter John, OBE, MusB, MA, FRCO; British organist; b. 22 Nov. 1930, Minehead, Somerset; s. of Hubert John Hurford and Gladys Winifred James; m. Patricia Mary Matthews 1955; two s. one d.; ed Blundell's School, Royal Coll. of Music (Open Foundation Scholar), Jesus Coll., Cambridge (organ scholar) and pvt. studies with André Marchal, Paris; commissioned, Royal Signals 1954–56; debut, Royal Festival Hall, London 1956; Organist and Choirmaster, Holy Trinity Church, Leamington Spa 1956–57; Dir of Music, Bablake School, Coventry 1956–57; Master of the Music, Cathedral and Abbey Church of St Alban 1958–78; freelance concert and recording organist 1978–98; Visiting Prof., Coll. Conservatory of Music, Cincinnati, USA 1967–68, Univ. of Western Ontario, Canada 1976–77; Acting Organist, St John's Coll. Cambridge 1979–80; Visiting Artist-in-Residence, Sydney Opera House 1980–82; Prof., RAM 1982–88; John Betts Fellow, Univ. of Oxford 1992–93; Decca recording artist 1977–; concerts in USA, Canada, Australia, NZ, Japan, Far East, Eastern and Western Europe 1958–98; f. St Albans Int. Organ Festival 1963, Artistic Dir 1963–78, Hon. Pres. 1978–; Pres. Inc. Asscn of Organists 1995–97; mem. Council Royal Coll. of Organists 1964–2003, Pres. 1980–82; Fellow, Royal School of Church Music 1977; Hon. FRCM 1987; Hon. Fellow in Organ Studies, Univ. of Bristol 1997–98; Hon. Fellow, Jesus Coll. Cambridge 2006; Hon. mem. RAM 1982; Hon. DMus (Baldwin-Wallace Coll., Ohio, USA) 1981, (Bristol) 1992, Hon. DArts. (Univ. of Hertfordshire) 2007; Gramophone Award 1979. *Compositions include:* organ music; Suite – Laudate Dominum, Chorale Preludes; choral music: The Communion Service, Series III, The Holy Eucharist, Rite 2 (for American Episcopal Church), music for the Daily Office, miscellaneous anthems, songs, carols, etc. *Recordings include:* complete organ works of J.S. Bach, Handel, F. Couperin, P. Hindemith, music of Franck, Mendelssohn; numerous recitals for BBC, including 34 commentated programmes of J.S. Bach's complete organ works 1980–82, Bach organ music cycle (Herald Angel Critics Award), 50th Edin. Int. Festival 1997. *Publications:* Making Music on the Organ 1988, numerous forewords, contribs to journals. *Leisure interest:* hill walking, wine, silence. *Address:* Broom House, St Bernard's Road, St Albans, Herts., AL3 5RA, England (home).

HURLEY, Alfred Francis, PhD; American university chancellor, professor of history and fmr air force officer; *Chancellor Emeritus, University of North Texas;* b. 16 Oct. 1928, Brooklyn, NY; s. of Patrick F. Hurley and Margaret C. Hurley; m. Joanna Leahy Hurley 1953; four s. one d.; ed St John's Univ., New York and Princeton Univ.; US Air Force Navigator, Planner and Educator; enlisted as Pvt., retd as Brig.-Gen.; served in Tex., Colo and Germany with brief assignments in Washington, DC and Viet Nam 1950–80; Instructor, Asst Prof. and Research Assoc. USAF Acad. 1958–63; Perm. Prof. of History and Head of History Dept, USAF 1966–80; Chair. Humanities Div. and mem. Acad. Bd USAF Acad. 1977–80; Vice-Pres. for Admin. Affairs, Univ. of N Tex. 1980–82, Prof. of History 1982–, Chancellor and Pres. 1982–2000, Chancellor

2000–2002, Emer. Chancellor 2002–; Guggenheim Fellow 1971–72, Eisenhower Inst. Fellow, Smithsonian Inst. 1976–77; Legion of Merit, USAF 1972; Oak Leaf Cluster 1980; Pres.'s Medal, St John's Univ. 1990. *Publications:* Billy Mitchell: Crusader for Air Power 1964, Air Power and Warfare (ed.) 1979. *Leisure interests:* jogging, reading, international travel. *Address:* c/o Office of the Chancellor, University of North Texas Systems, Denton, TX 76203 (office); 828 Skylark Drive, Denton, TX 76205, USA (home). *Telephone:* (940) 565-2904 (office).

HURLEY, Elizabeth Jane; British actress, film producer and model; b. 10 June 1965; d. of the late Roy Leonard Hurley and of Angela Mary Hurley; m. Arun Nayar 2007; one s. (from previous relationship); producer for Simian Films and producer of Extreme Measures 1996, Mickey Blue Eyes 1999; Spokeswoman and model for Estée Lauder. *Television includes:* title role in Christabel (series), The Orchid House, Act of Will, Rumpole, Inspector Morse, The Young Indiana Jones Chronicles, Sharpe's Enemy. *Films include:* Aria 1987, Rowing With the Wind 1987, The Skipper 1989, The Long Winter of 39, Passenger '57 1992, Mad Dogs and Englishmen 1994, Dangerous Ground 1995, Samson and Delilah 1996, Austin Powers: International Man of Mystery (ShoWest Award for Best Supporting Actress 1997) 1996, Permanent Midnight 1997, My Favourite Martian 1999, Ed TV 1999, Austin Powers: The Spy Who Shagged Me 1999, Bedazzled 2000, Serving Sara 2002, The Weight of Water 2002, Double Whammy 2002, Method 2004, The Last Guy on Earth 2006. *Leisure interest:* gardening. *Address:* c/o DSS, Unit 3b, Farm Lane Trading Estate, 101 Farm Lane, London, SW6 1QJ; Simian Films Ltd, Regent House, 1-2 Pratt Mews, London, NW1 0AD, England. *E-mail:* press@elizabethhurley.com. *Website:* www.elizabethhurley.com.

HURLEY, Rev. Michael Anthony, SJ, STD; Irish ecumenical theologian and priest; b. 10 May 1923, Ardmore, Co. Waterford; s. of Martin Hurley and Johanna Foley; ed Mount Melleray Seminary, Cappoquin, Univ. Coll., Dublin, Jesuit Theological Faculty, Louvain, Pontifical Gregorian Univ., Rome; entered Soc. of Jesus 1940; ordained priest 1954; Lecturer in Dogmatic Theology, Jesuit Theological Faculty, Dublin 1958–70; Dir Irish School of Ecumenics, Dublin 1970–80; mem. Columbanus Community of Reconciliation, Belfast 1983–93 (Leader 1983–91); Hon. LLD (Queen's Univ., Belfast) 1993, (Trinity Coll., Dublin) 1995. *Publications:* Church and Eucharist (ed.) 1966, Ecumenical Studies: Baptism and Marriage (ed.) 1968, Theology of Ecumenism 1969, John Wesley's Letter to a Roman Catholic (ed.) 1968, Irish Anglicanism (ed.) 1970, Beyond Tolerance: The Challenge of Mixed Marriage (ed.) 1975, Reconciliation in Religion and Society (ed.) 1994, Christian Unity: An Ecumenical Second Spring? 1998, Healing and Hope: memories of an Irish Ecumenist 2003; articles in various periodicals. *Leisure interest:* reading. *Address:* Jesuit Community, Milltown Park, Dublin 6, Ireland (home). *Telephone:* 218-0237 (home). *Fax:* 218-0279 (home). *E-mail:* mhurley@jesuit.ie (home).

HURN, David; British photographer and lecturer; b. 21 July 1934, Redhill, Surrey; s. of Stanley Hurn and Joan Maynard; m. Alita Naughton 1964 (divorced 1971); one d.; ed Hardy's School, Dorchester and Royal Mil. Acad., Sandhurst; Asst Photographer to Michael Peto and George Vargas, Reflex Agency, London 1955–57; Freelance Photographer for The Observer, Sunday Times, Look, Life, etc. 1957, working from Wales 1971; mem. Magnum Photos co-operative agency, New York, Paris, London and Tokyo 1967–; Editorial Adviser Album Photographic magazine, London 1971; Head, School of Documentary Photography, Gwent Coll. of Higher Educ., Newport, Gwent 1973–90; Distinguished Visiting Artist and Adjunct Prof., Arizona State Univ., USA 1979–80; mem. Photographic Cttee, Arts Council of GB 1972–77, Arts Panel 1975–77, CNAA 1978–87; works in collections of Welsh Arts Council, Arts Council of GB, British Council, Bibliothèque Nationale, Paris, Int. Center of Photography, New York, San Francisco Museum of Modern Art, Museum of Modern Art, New York and others; Hon. Fellow, Univ. of Wales 1997; Welsh Arts Council Award 1971, Imperial War Museum Arts Award 1987–88; Kodak Photographic Bursary 1975; UK/USA Bicentennial Fellowship 1979–80; Bradford Fellow 1993–94; Arts Council of Wales Bursary 1995. *Publications:* David Hurn: Photographs 1956–1976 1979, On Being a Photographer 1997, Wales: Land of My Father 2000, On Looking at Photographs 2000, Living in Wales 2003. *Leisure interests:* music, looking, meeting people. *Address:* Prospect Cottage, Tintern, Monmouthshire, Wales (home). *Telephone:* (1291) 689358 (home). *Fax:* (1291) 689464 (home).

HURN, Sir (Francis) Roger, Kt; British business executive; b. 9 June 1938; s. of Francis James Hurn and Joyce Elsa (née Bennett) Hurn; m. Rosalind Jackson 1980; one d.; ed Marlborough Coll.; Eng apprentice, Rolls Royce Motors 1956; joined Smiths Industries PLC 1958, Export Dir Motor Accessory Div. 1969–74, Man. Dir Int. Operations 1974–75, Div. Man. Dir 1975–76, Exec. Dir 1976, Man. Dir 1978–91, Chief Exec. 1981–96, Chair. 1991–98; Deputy Chair. Glaxo Wellcome PLC 1997–2000, GlaxoSmithKline 2000–03; Chair. Gen. Electric Co. (now Marconi) PLC 1998–2001, Prudential PLC 2000–02; Dir (non-exec.) Ocean Transport and Trading 1982–88, Pilkington 1984–94, S.G. Warburg Group 1987–95, ICI PLC 1993–2001, Cazenove; Chair. of Govs. Henley Man. Coll. 1996–2004 (Gov. 1986–2004); Liveryman, Coachmakers' and Coach Harness Makers' Co. 1979. *Leisure interests:* outdoor pursuits, travel. *Address:* c/o Henley Management College, Greenlands, Henley-on-Thames, Oxon., RG9 3AU, England.

HURNÍK, Ilja; Czech pianist and composer; b. 25 Nov. 1922, Ostrava-Poruba; m. Jana Hurníková 1966; one s.; ed Conservatoire, Prague; composition; Acad. of Music and Dramatic Arts, Prague 1948–52; self-employed artist 1942–; one-man concerts since 1942, Poland, Switzerland, FRG, Cuba, USA; Dr hc (Univ. of Ostrava) 1992; Czech Musical Fund Prize 1967, Supraphon Prize 1971, Grand Prix, Piano Duo Assn of Japan 1990, Int. Antonín Dvořák Prize 2001. *Compositions:* orchestral works: Things. Divertimento for small orchestra 1977, Overture a la Klicpera 1985, Symphony in C 2001; concertos: Flute Concerto 1952, Concerto for Oboe and Strings 1959, Concerto for wind instruments, piano and timpani 1956, Concerto for piano and chamber orchestra 1972, New Clavecin, version for piano and strings 1975, Concertino for piano and strings (also for 2 violins and strings) 1981, Concerto for viola and strings 1994; chamber compositions: Motifs from Childhood 1934, revised 1944, Partita in A for flute and piano 1950, Sonata for viola and piano 1951, Four Seasons of the Year for 12 instruments 1952, Sonata da Camera for flute, oboe, cello and harpsichord or piano 1953, Moments musicaux for 11 wind instruments 1955, Eserzii for flute, oboe, clarinet and bassoon 1956, Little Faun, for flute and piano 1956, Stories of a Band, for narrator and chamber ensemble to the composer's own text 1968, Chamber music for strings 1962, Musicians – Suite for narrator and 18 soloists to poems by Frantisek Branislav 1963, Concertino for violin and piano 1971, Simfonia Facile, for strings and piano 1975, Wind Quintet No. 2 1985, Sonatina for double bass and piano 1986; piano compositions: The First Melodies 1931, Preludes for piano 1943, Sonatina for piano 1950, Piano Pieces in an easy style, Piano Duets for Homework 1963, Ditties for Keys. Easy pieces for the piano 1969, Waltzes, for piano duet 1971, Piano Duets – Exercises and studies 1972, New Clavecin, version for piano solo 1975, Studies for four hands 1975, Vorsil Alley – A cycle of easy party pieces 1976, Jazz-piccolo – A cycle of easy party pieces 1977, Fantasy for two pianos 1979, Variations on a theme by Pergolesi, as a piano duet 1984, Innocenza 1992; vocal works: Flowers – A song cycle for soprano and piano to lyrics by Frantiçek Vrba 1940, Ditties for the flute, for a higher voice, flute (violin) and piano to folk poetry lyrics 1953, cantata Maryka 1955, Choruses about Mothers for mixed choir 1955, Sun-Warmed Balk – A cycle of children's (girls) choruses with piano accompaniment 1955, Children's Tercets 1956, Noah – Oratorio for tenor solo, mixed choir and orchestra to Biblical texts 1959, Three Daughters – Small cantata for children's (girl's) chorus to folk-poetry lyrics 1960, Solomon, for bass and string quartet or organ to the text of the Song of Songs 1961, Minute-Long Ditties, for soprano, flute and piano 1961, Children's Terzettos, for 3 children's voices, flute, harp and double bass to lyrics by Frantisek Branislav 1962, Sulamit, songs for alto and orchestra 1963, Aesop – Cantata suite for mixed choir and orchestra according to Aesop's Fables 1964, June Night – A cycle of duets for children's (girls) choir to piano accompaniment to folk poetry lyrics 1965, Pastorella for children's chorus and chamber ensemble 1965, Scenes for children's chorus to texts by Vaclav Fischer 1971, Echo – Chamber Cantata for soloists, girl's choir, chamber and string orchestra, oboe and piano to the composer's own text 1982, Conversation Between Mother And Child – Children's choruses to folk and the composer's own texts 1984, Seasonal Madrigals 1984, The Carp, The Flea And So On – Ditties for children's choruses with piano accompaniment to the composer's own texts 1985, Water, Little Water – Children's choruses to lyrics by Vaclav Fischer 1986, Oratorio for children's chorus and orchestra 1990, Missa Vinea Crucis for children's choir and orchestra/organ 1991; ballets: Ondráš 1949, Faux pas de quatre 1987; operas: The Lady and Robbers 1966, Diogenes 1973, Fishermen In Their Own Nets 1981, Oldřich a Boženka 1985, Wisemen and Fools 1986; recorded complete works of Debussy. *Publications:* The Journey with a Butterfly, Marshland, Childhood in Silesia (memoirs), Laurel Leaves 1987; children's books, including Kterak psáti a řečniti (How to Write and Speak) 1997, Final Report 2000. *Address:* Český rozhlas, Vinohradská 12, 120 99 Prague 2; Národní třída 35, 110 00 Prague 1, Czech Republic. *Telephone:* (2) 2421-4226. *E-mail:* jana.hurnikova@volny.cz (office). *Website:* www.hurnik.cz.

HURST, Sir Geoffrey Charles, Kt, MBE; British fmr professional footballer; b. 8 Dec. 1941, Ashton-under-Lyne, England; s. of Charles Hurst and Evelyn Hurst; m. Judith Harries 1964; three d.; player, West Ham United 1957–72, Stoke City 1972–74, West Bromwich Albion 1975–76; player and Man. Telford United 1976–79; Man. Chelsea 1979–81, England nat. team 1966–72; scored hat-trick in victory over W Germany, World Cup 1966 (only player to do so in a World Cup final); Dir Aon Warranty Group 1995–; Patron Ludlow Town Football Club. *Publication:* 1966 and All That 2001, World Champions 2006. *Leisure interests:* sport in general, family. *Address:* c/o Dave Davies, PO Box 99, Hockley, Essex, SS5 4TB, England (office). *Telephone:* (1702) 202036 (office). *Fax:* (871) 871-2065 (office). *E-mail:* dave@football1966.com (office); david@geoffhurst.net (office). *Website:* www.geoffhurst.net.

HURT, John, CBE; British actor; b. 22 Jan. 1940, Chesterfield; s. of Rev. Arnould Herbert and Phyllis Hurt (née Massey); m. 1st Annette Robertson; m. 2nd Donna Peacock 1984 (divorced 1990); m. 3rd Jo Dalton 1990 (divorced 1995); two s.; ed The Lincoln School, Lincoln and Royal Acad. of Dramatic Art; began as painter; stage debut, Arts Theatre, London 1962; Dir United British Artists 1982; Richard Harris Award for Outstanding Contrib. to British Film, British Ind. Film Awards 2003. *Stage appearances include:* Chips With Everything, Vaudeville Theatre 1962, The Dwarfs, Arts 1963, Hamp (title role), Edinburgh Festival 1964, Inadmissible Evidence, Wyndhams 1965, Little Malcolm and his Struggle against the Eunuchs, Garrick 1966, Belcher's Luck (RSC), Aldwych 1966, Man and Superman, Gaiety, Dublin 1969, The Caretaker, Mermaid 1972, The Only Street, Dublin Festival and Islington 1973, Travesties (RSC), Aldwych and The Arrest, Bristol Old Vic 1974, The Shadow of a Gunman, Nottingham Playhouse 1978, The London Vertigo, Dublin 1991, A Month in the Country, Albery 1994, Krapp's Last Tape, New Ambassadors Theatre 2000, Gate Theatre, Dublin 2001, Afterplay, Gielgud Theatre 2002. *Films include:* The Wild and the Willing 1962, A Man for All Seasons 1966, Sinful Davey 1968, Before Winter Comes 1969, In Search of Gregory 1970, Mr. Forbush and the Penguins 1971, 10 Rillington Place, The Ghoul 1974, Little Malcolm 1974, East of Elephant Rock 1977, The Disappearance, The Shout, Spectre, Alien, Midnight Express (British Acad. Best Supporting Actor Award 1978, Golden Globe Best Supporting Actor Award 1978, Variety Club Best Actor Award 1978) 1978, Heaven's Gate 1980,

The Elephant Man (British Acad. Best Actor Award 1980, Variety Club Best Film Actor Award 1980) 1980, Champions (Evening Standard Best Actor Award 1984) 1983, The Hit (Evening Standard Best Actor Award 1984) 1984, Jake Speed 1985, Rocinante 1986, Aria 1987, White Mischief 1987, Scandal 1988, From the Hip 1989, Frankenstein Unbound, The Field 1989, Windprints 1990, King Ralph 1991, Lapse of Memory 1991, Dark at Noon 1992, Monolith 1994, Even Cowgirls Get the Blues 1994, Wild Bill 1994, Rob Roy 1994, Two Nudes Bathing (Cable Ace Award 1995) 1995, Dead Man 1996, Wild Bill 1996, Contact 1997, Love and Death on Long Island 1998, All the Little Animals 1999, You're Dead 1999, The Love Letter 1999, Krapp's Last Tape 1999, Lost Souls 2000, Night Train 2000, Captain Corelli's Mandolin 2001, Harry Potter and the Philosopher's Stone 2001, Tabloid 2001, Bait 2001, Owning Mahony 2001, Crime and Punishment 2002, Miranda 2003, Dogville (voice) 2003, Hellboy 2004, The Proposition 2004, Manderlay 2005, Shooting Dogs 2005, V for Vendetta 2006, Perfume: The Story of a Murderer (voice) 2006, The Oxford Murders 2007, Indiana Jones and the Kingdom of the Crystal Skull 2008, Hellboy II: The Golden Army 2008, Lezione 21 2008, Outlander 2008, An Englishman in New York 2009, No Limits, No Control 2009. *Television appearances include:* The Waste Places 1968, Nijinsky: God of the Dance (Best Television Actor 1975) 1975, The Naked Civil Servant (British Acad. Award 1975, Emmy Award 1978) 1975, Caligula in I, Claudius 1976, Treats 1977, Raskolnikov in Crime and Punishment 1979, Poison Candy 1988, Deadline 1988, Who Bombed Birmingham? 1990, Journey to Knock 1991, Red Fox (Best Actor Monte Carlo TV Awards 1991) 1991, Six Characters in Search of an Author 1992, Prisoner in Time 1995, Saigon Baby 1995, Alan Clark Diaries 2004, Hellboy: Sword of Storms (voice) 2006, Merlin (series) 2008. *Address:* c/o Julian Belfrage Associates, 46 Albemarle Street, London, W1S 4DF, England. *Telephone:* (20) 7491-4400.

HURT, William; American actor; b. 20 March 1950, Washington, DC; m. 1st Mary Beth Hurt (divorced 1982); m. 2nd Heidi Henderson 1989; two s.; ed Tufts Univ., Juilliard School; appeared with Ore. Shakespeare Festival production of Long Day's Journey Into Night; mem. Circle Repertory Co.; recipient of first Spencer Tracy Award 1988, for outstanding screen performances and professional achievement. *Stage appearances include:* Henry V 1976, Mary Stuart, My Life, Ulysses in Traction, Lulu, Fifth of July, Childe Byron, The Runner Stumbles, Hamlet, Hurlyburly, Beside Herself 1989, Ivanov 1991, others. *Films include:* Altered States 1980, Eyewitness 1981, Body Heat 1981, The Big Chill 1983, Gorky Park 1983, Kiss of the Spider Woman (Best Actor Award Cannes Film Festival 1985, Acad. Award for Best Actor 1985) 1985, Children of a Lesser God 1986, Broadcast News 1987, A Time of Destiny 1988, The Accidental Tourist 1989, I Love You to Death 1990, The House of Spirits 1990, Alice 1990, The Doctor 1991, Until the End of the World 1991, Mr. Wonderful 1993, The Plague 1993, Trial by Jury 1994, Second Best 1994, Jane Eyre 1995, Secrets Shared With a Stranger, Smoke 1995, A Couch in New York 1996, Michael 1996, Loved 1997, Lost in Space 1998, One True Thing 1998, The Proposition 1998, Dark City 1998, The 4th Floor 1999, The Big Brass Ring 1999, Sunshine 1999, Do Not Disturb 1999, The Simian Line 2000, The Contaminated Man 2000, AI: Artificial Intelligence 2001, The Flamingo Rising 2001, Rare Birds 2001, Changing Lanes 2002, Au plus pres du paradis 2002, Tuck Everlasting 2002, Tulse Luper Suitcases: The Moab Story 2003, Blue Butterfly 2004, The Village 2004, A History of Violence 2005, Syriana 2005, The King 2005, Neverwas 2005, The Legend of Sasquatch (voice) 2006, Beautiful Ohio 2006, The Good Shepherd 2006, Mr. Brooks 2007, Into the Wild 2007, Vantage Point 2008, The Incredible Hulk 2008, Endgame 2009, The Countess 2009. *Television includes:* The Flamingo Rising 2001, Master Spy: The Robert Hanssen Story 2002, Frankenstein (miniseries) 2004, Hunt for Justice 2005, Damages (series) 2009. *Address:* 88 SW Century Drive, #348, Bend, OR 97702-1047; c/o Creative Artists Agency, 9830 Wilshire Blvd, Beverly Hills, CA 90212-1825, USA. *Telephone:* (310) 288-4545. *Fax:* (310) 288-4800.

HURTADO LARREA, Osvaldo, BrerPol, DIur; Ecuadorean fmr head of state; *President, Corporation for Development Studies (CORDES);* b. 26 June 1939, Chambo, Chimborazo Prov.; s. of José Hurtado and Elina Larrea de Hurtado; m. Margarita Pérez Pallares; three s. two d.; ed Catholic Univ. of Quito; f. Ecuadorian Christian Democratic Party 1964; Pres. of Congress 1966; Prof. of Political Sociology, Catholic Univ., Quito; Dir Instituto Ecuatoriano de Desarrollo Social (INEDES) 1966; Under-Sec. of Labour 1969; Sub-Dean, Faculty of Econs and Dir Inst. of Econ. Research, Catholic Univ., Quito 1973; invited to form part of World Political Council of Christian Democracy 1975; joined with other political groups to form Popular Democracy 1978; Pres. Org. of Christian Democrats of America, Vice-Pres. Int. Christian Democrats; Pres. Comm. to prepare Law of Referendum of Elections and Political Parties 1977; Vice-Pres. of Ecuador and Pres. Consejo Nacional de Desarrollo (Nat. Devt Council) 1979–81; Pres. of Ecuador 1981–84; Pres. Nat. Ass. 1998; Pres. CORDES (org. for study of Latin American Devt problems), Quito; fmr Vice-Pres. Inst. for European Latin-American Relations, Madrid; mem. Council of ex-Pres, Atlanta, Interamerican Dialogue, Washington, DC (Co-Pres, Bd of Dirs), The Carter Center, Atlanta, Club de Madrid, Foro de Biarritz, Emerging Markets Forum, Washington, DC, Foro Iberoamericano; mem. comm. that prepared the environmental reports Nuestra Propia Agenda 1990, Amazonía Sin Mitos 1992 and Amanecer en los Andes 1997 at request of IDB and UNDP; Dr hc (Georgetown); various foreign decorations. *Publications:* numerous essays and several books about Ecuadorian politics, sociology and economy, including El Poder Político en el Ecuador (Political Power in Ecuador) 1977, Las Costumbres de los Ecuatorianos 2005, Los Costos del Populismo 2006; academic work about Latin America gathered in several books published in collaboration with other authors in many countries. *Leisure interests:* tennis, gardening. *Address:* Suecia 277 y Av. Los Shyris, Edificio Suecia Piso 2, PO Box 5087, Quito (office); Tomás Chariove 405 y Agustín Zambrano, Quito, Ecuador (home). *Telephone:* (5932) 2455701 (office). *Fax:* (5932) 2446414 (office). *E-mail:* cordes2@cordes.org (office). *Website:* www.cordes.org (office).

HURVICH, Leo M., PhD; American sensory psychologist and academic; *Professor Emeritus, Department of Psychology, University of Pennsylvania;* b. 11 Sept. 1910, Malden, Mass.; s. of Julius S. Hurvich and Celia Chikinsky; m. Dorothea Jameson 1948 (died 1998); ed Harvard Coll. and Harvard Univ.; Asst, Dept of Psychology, Harvard Univ. 1936–37, Instructor and Tutor 1937–40, Research Asst, Div. of Research, Graduate School of Business Admin. 1941–47; Research Psychologist, Color Tech. Div., Eastman Kodak Co. 1947–57; Prof. of Psychology, New York Univ. 1957–62; Prof. of Psychology, Dept of Psychology, Univ. of Pa 1962–79, now Prof. Emer., mem. Inst. of Neurological Sciences, Dir Vision Training Program 1979–91; Visiting Prof. Columbia Univ. 1971–72, Univ. of Rochester, NY 1974; fmr Chair. Psychology Dept., Washington Square Coll. 1957–62; mem. Research Advisory Cttee, Lighthouse 1993–; mem. NAS, Int. Brain Research Org., Int. Colour Vision Soc., Asscn for Research in Vision and Ophthalmology; Fellow, Center for Advanced Study in the Behavioral Sciences, Stanford 1981–82; Fellow American Acad. of Arts and Sciences, American Psychological Asscn, Soc. of Experimental Psychologists 1958–, Optical Soc. of America, Guggenheim Fellow 1964–65, William James Fellow American Psychological Soc. 1989; Hon. DSc (State Univ. of NY); several awards including Howard Crosby Warren Medal for Outstanding Research, Soc. of Experimental Psychologists 1971, I. H. Godlove Award, Inter-Soc. Color Council, Distinguished Scientific Contrib. Award 1973, American Psychological Asscn 1972, Edgar D. Tillyer Medal, Optical Soc. of America, Deane B. Judd-AIC Award 1982, Asscn Internationale de la Couleur 1985, Helmholtz Prize 1987 (Cognitive Neuroscience Inst.). *Publications:* The Perception of Brightness and Darkness (with D. Jameson) 1966, Outlines of a Theory of the Light Sense (trans., with D. Jameson) 1964, Handbook of Sensory Physiology: Visual Psychophysics VII/4 (ed. with D. Jameson) 1972, Color Vision 1981; contribs to Elsevier Encyclopedia of Neuroscience 1999, American Psychological Asscn Encyclopedia of Psychology 2000. *Leisure interest:* summer vacations. *Address:* Department of Psychology, Room B4, University of Pennsylvania, 3720 Street, Philadelphia, PA 19104 (office); 1 Fifth Avenue 2-J, New York, NY 10003, USA (home). *Telephone:* (215) 898-7173 (office); (212) 673-5646 (home). *Fax:* (215) 898-7301 (office); (212) 674-1586 (home). *E-mail:* hurvich@cattell.psych.upenn.edu (office); lhurvich@aol.com (home); leo@psych.upenn.edu (office). *Website:* www.psych.upenn.edu (office).

HUSA, Karel; American composer and conductor; b. 7 Aug. 1921, Prague, Czech Repub.; s. of the late Karel Husa and Bozena Husova; m. Simone Husa (née Perault); four d.; ed Prague Conservatory of Music, Prague Acad. of Music, Paris Conservatory of Music, Ecole normale de musique de Paris; composer, conductor in Paris, guest conductor with European orchestras, Kappa Alpha Prof. of Music, Cornell Univ. 1954, Asst Prof. 1954, Assoc. Prof. 1957, Prof. 1961; conductor of the univ. orchestras, teacher of composition (retd 1992), guest conductor with American orchestras and lecturer; Prof. Ithaca Coll., School of Music 1967–86; mem. Belgian Royal Acad. of Arts and Sciences 1974–, American Acad. of Arts and Letters 1994–; hon. degrees include Coe Coll. 1976, Cleveland Inst. of Music 1985, Ithaca Coll. 1986, Baldwin-Wallace Coll. 1991, St Vincent Coll. 1995, Hartwick Coll. 1997, New England Conservatory 1998, Masaryk Univ., Brno 2000, Acad. of Musical Arts, Prague 2000; awards include Pulitzer Prize 1969, Sudler Prize 1984, Friedheim Award 1985, Grawemeyer Award 1993, Guggenheim Award 1964, 1965, Sousa Order of Merit 1985, Czech Repub. Medal of Merit (First Class) 1995, Medal of Honor of the City of Prague 1998. *Dance:* Monodrama (ballet) for Butler Ballet, Indiana 1976, The Steadfast Tin Soldier for Boulder Philharmonic, Colorado 1974, The Trojan Women for Louisville Ballet, Kentucky 1980. *Film:* Young Generation 1946, Gen, Prague 2001, Karel Husa Comes Home 2002. *Music:* Music for Prague 1968, Apotheosis of this Earth 1972, four string quartets; concertos for piano, brass quintet, organ, viola, violin, cello, saxophone, percussion, trumpet, orchestra; symphonies (Mosaiques, Fantasies); chamber music includes quintets for wind, brass, works for piano, sonatas for violin, music for band. *Publications:* Music for Prague; Apotheosis of this Earth; Concerto for Orchestra; The Trojan Women; An American Te Deum; Concerto for Sax and Winds; Concerto for Wind Ensemble; Les couleurs fauves, Cayuga Lake; Four Quartets; Twelve Moravian Songs; Sonata a Tre; Symphony No. 1; Evocation de Slovaquie; Serenade. *Leisure interests:* painting, poetry, tennis. *Address:* 4535 S. Atlantic Avenue, Apt. 2106, Daytona Beach, FL 32127 (office); 1 Belwood Lane, Ithaca, NY 14850, USA (home). *Telephone:* (386) 322-0635 (Winter) (office); (607) 257-7018 (Summer) (office). *Fax:* (607) 257-0616 (home).

HUSAIN, Maqbool Fida; Indian painter; b. 17 Sept. 1915, Sholapur, Maharashtra State; s. of Fida Husain and Zainub Husain; m. Fazila Abbasi 1943; four s. two d.; joined Progressive Artists Group, Bombay 1948; first one-man exhbn, Bombay 1950, later at Rome, Frankfurt, London, Zürich, Prague, Tokyo, New York, New Delhi, Calcutta, Kabul and Baghdad; mem. Lalit Kala Akademi, New Delhi 1954, Gen. Council Nat. Akademi of Art, New Delhi 1955; mem. Rajya Sabha 1986; went into voluntary exile 2006, returned to India 2007 to face obscenity charges brought by Hindu fundamentalist groups; First Nat. Award for Painting 1955, Int. Award, Biennale Tokyo 1959, Padmashree 1966, Padma Vibhushan. *Major works:* Murals for Air India Int. at Hong Kong, Bangkok, Zürich and Prague 1957 and WHO Building, New Delhi 1963; Mural in Mosaic for Lever Bros. and Aligarh Univ. 1964; High Ceramic Mural for Indian Govt Building, New Delhi; Exhibitor 'Art Now in India' Exhbn, London 1967; world's largest painting on canvas (240 ft × 12 ft) 1985; India Through the Lens of a Painter (photographic show), USSR 1988. *Film:* Through the Eyes of the Painter 1967 (Golden Bear Award, Berlin 1967), Gajagamini (producer) 2000. *Publications:* Husain's Letters 1962,

Husain 1971, Poetry to be Seen 1972, Triangles 1976, Tata's Book Husain 1988. *Address:* Jolly Maker 3, Cuffe Parade, Mumbai 400 005, India. *Website:* www.mfhussain.com.

HUSAR, Cardinal Lubomyr, MA, DTheol; Ukrainian ecclesiastic; *Major Archbishop, Ukrainian Catholic Church;* b. 26 Feb. 1933, Lviv; ordained priest 1958; consecrated Bishop 1977; Auxiliary Bishop of the Greater Archiepiscopate of Lviv of the Ukrainians 1996–2001, Major Archbishop Jan. 2001–; cr. Cardinal 2001. *Address:* Ploscha Sviatoho Jura 5, 79000 Lviv, Ukraine (office). *Telephone:* (32) 297-11-21 (office). *Fax:* (32) 298-69-18 (office). *Website:* www .ugcc.org.ua (office).

HUSBANDS, Sir Clifford (Straughn), Kt, GCMG, CHB, GCM, QC; Barbadian barrister and fmr judge; *Governor-General;* b. 5 Aug. 1926; s. of Adam Straughn Husbands and Ada Augusta (née Griffith); m. Ruby Parris 1959; one s. two d.; ed Parry School, Harrison Coll., Middle Temple, Inns of Court, London, UK; called to Bar, Middle Temple 1952; in pvt. practice, Barbados 1952–54; Acting Deputy Registrar, Barbados 1954; Legal Asst to Attorney-Gen., Grenada 1954–56; magistrate, Grenada 1956–57, Antigua 1957–58; Crown Attorney, Magistrate and Registrar, Montserrat 1958–60; Acting Crown Attorney, St Kitts-Nevis-Anguilla 1959, Acting Attorney-Gen. 1960; Asst to Attorney-Gen., Barbados 1960–67 (legal draftsman 1960–63); Dir Public Prosecutions, Barbados 1967–76; QC Barbados 1968; Judge, Supreme Court, Barbados 1976–91; Justice of Appeal 1991–96; Gov.-Gen. of Barbados 1996–; Pres. Privy Council for Barbados 1996–; Kt of St Andrew, Order of Barbados 1995; Kt of Grace, Order of St John 2204; Queen's Silver Jubilee Medal 1977, Paul Harris Fellowship Award 2001. *Leisure interests:* music, swimming, photography, cricket. *Address:* c/o Private Secretary to the Governor-General, Government House, St Michael, Barbados (office). *Telephone:* 4292646 (office). *Fax:* 4365910 (office). *E-mail:* ruthnita@sunbeach.net (office). *Website:* www.barbados.gov.bb/gg.htm (office).

HUSÉN, Torsten, PhD; Swedish educationist; b. 1 March 1916, Lund; s. of Johan Husén and Betty Husén (née Prawitz); m. Ingrid Joensson 1940 (died 1991); two s. one d.; ed Univ. of Lund; Research Asst, Inst. of Psychology, Univ. of Lund 1938–43; Sr Psychologist, Swedish Armed Forces 1944–51; Reader in Educational Psychology, Univ. of Stockholm 1947–52, Prof. 1953–56, Prof. of Educ. and Dir Inst. of Educ. Research, Univ. of Stockholm 1956–71, Prof. of Int. Educ. 1971–82; Fellow, Center for Advanced Study in the Behavioral Sciences, Stanford, Calif. 1965–66, 1973–74, Wissenschaftskolleg, Berlin 1984; Expert in Royal Comms. on Swedish School Reform 1957–65; mem. Panel of Scientific Advisers to Swedish Govt 1962–69; Chair. Int. Asscn for the Evaluation of Educ. achievement 1962–78; Consultant to OECD and the World Bank 1968–85, United Nations Univ.; Co-Ed. in Chief, Int. Encyclopedia of Educ.; Chair. Governing Bd, Int. Inst. Educ. Planning, Paris 1970–81; mem. Governing Bd Max Planck Inst., Berlin 1964–82, Int. Council for Educ. Devt 1971–93; Chair. Int. Acad. of Educ. 1986–97; Chair. Int. Jury, Gravemeyer Award in Educ. 1988–90; Chair. Acad. Europaea Task Force on Educ. 1988–91; Visiting Prof., Univs. of Chicago 1959, Hawaii 1968, Ontario Inst. for Studies in Educ. 1971, Stanford Univ. 1981, California 1984; mem. Swedish Royal Acad. of Sciences 1972–, US Nat. Acad. of Educ. 1967–, Advisory Bd Int. Encyclopedia of the Social and Behavioral Sciences; Hon. Prof. (East China Normal Univ.) 1984; Hon. mem. American Acad. of Arts and Sciences, Academia Europaea, USSR (now Russian) Acad. of Pedagogical Sciences; Hon. LLD (Chicago) 1967, (Glasgow) 1974; Hon. DTech (Brunel Univ.) 1974; Hon. LHD (Rhode Island Univ.) 1975; Hon. DEd (Joensuu) 1979, (Amsterdam) 1982, (Ohio State Univ.) 1985; Medal for Distinguished Service in Int. Educ., Teachers Coll., Columbia Univ. 1970, Comenius Medal 1993. *Publications:* Psychological Twin Research 1959, Problems of Differentiation in Swedish Compulsory Schooling 1962, International Study of Achievement in Mathematics I-II 1967, Educational Research and Educational Change 1968, Talent, Opportunity and Career 1969, Talent, Equality and Meritocracy 1974, Social Influences on Educational Attainment 1975, The School in Question 1979, An Incurable Academic (autobiog.) 1983, Educational Research and Policy 1984, Becoming Adult in a Changing Society (with James Coleman) 1985, The Learning Society Revisited 1986, Higher Education and Social Stratification 1987, Educational Research and School Reforms 1988, Education and the Global Concern 1990, Schooling in Modern European Society 1992, The Role of the University 1994, School and University Facing the 21st Century 1995, The Information Society 1999, Research on the Reserve of Ability 2000, Conversations with Torsten Husén 2001. *Leisure interest:* book collecting (old books). *Address:* Institute for International Education, Stockholm University, 10691 Stockholm (office); Armfeltsgatan 10, 11534 Stockholm, Sweden (home). *Telephone:* (8) 16-43-24 (office); (8) 664-19-76 (home). *E-mail:* torsten.husen@interped.su.se (office).

HUSH, Noel S., PhD, AO, FAA, FRS; Australian/British chemist and academic; *Professor Emeritus, University of Sydney;* ed Univ. of Sydney; began career as Lecturer in Physical Chem., Univ. of Manchester, UK 1950; faculty mem., Univ. of Bristol 1955–71; Foundation Prof. of Theoretical Chem., Univ. of Sydney 1971–89, currently Convenor, Molecular Electronics Group and Prof. Emer.; Fellow, Australian Chemical Inst.; mem. American Acad. of Arts and Sciences; Australian Acad. of Science Flinders Medal, Royal Soc. of Chem. Centenary Medal, Australian Acad. of Science David Craig Medal, Royal Australian Chemical Soc. Physical Chem. Medal, Australian Federation Medal, Welch Award in Chem. 2007. *Address:* School of Chemistry, University of Sydney, Building F11, Sydney, NSW 2006, Australia (office). *Telephone:* (2) 9351-4504 (office). *Fax:* (2) 9351-3329 (office). *E-mail:* hush_n@chem.usyd.edu .au (office). *Website:* www.chem.usyd.edu.au (office).

HUSSAIN, Abdul Rasheed; Maldivian politician; Minister of State for Presidential Affairs, Sec. to the Cabinet 1989–1993; Minister of Atolls Admin 1993–96, of Planning, Human Resources and the Environment 1996–98, of Fisheries, Agric. and Marine Resources 1998–2003, of Employment and Labour 2003–04; fmr Deputy Speaker People's Majlis (People's Council). *Address:* c/o Ministry of Human Resources, Employment and Labour, Ghaazee Building, 4th Floor, Ameer Ahmed Magu, Malé 20-05, Maldives.

HUSSAIN, Altaf, BPharm; Pakistani politician; *Leader, Muttahida Qaumi Movement;* b. 17 Sept. 1953, Karachi; s. of Nazir Hussain and Khurshid Begum; m.; ed Karachi Univ.; Founder and Leader Muttahida Qaumi Movt (MQM); in exile in UK since 1992. *Address:* MQM International Secretariat, 54–58, First Floor, Elizabeth House, High Street, Edgware, Middx, HA8 7EJ, England (office). *Telephone:* (20) 8905-7300 (office). *Fax:* (20) 8952-9282 (office). *E-mail:* mqm@mqm.org (office). *Website:* www.mqm.org (office).

HUSSAIN, Chaudhry Amir, BA, BL; Pakistani barrister and politician; b. 22 June 1942, Jammu and Kashmir; s. of Chaudhry Diwan Ali; m.; ed Punjab Univ.; mem. Pakistan Muslim League (QA); mem. Nat. Ass. for NA-111, Sialkot constituency 1985–2002, Chair. Standing Cttee on Law, Justice, Human Rights and Parl. Affairs 1997–99, mem. Standing Cttee on Science and Tech. 1997–99, Speaker of Nat. Ass. 2002–08; Parl. Sec. for Law and Justice 1985–88; Fed. Minister for Law, Justice and Parl. Affairs 1990–91, for Parl. and Youth Affairs 1991–93; signatory of first Asscn of Asian Parls for Peace (AAPP) Conf. held in Dhaka 1999; Leader of Pakistan Parl. Del. Exec. Council Meeting of AAPP, Beijing 2003; Leader and mem. Pakistan Parl. and Official Dels to USA, UK, Saudi Arabia, Dubai, UAE, Egypt, Malta, Canada, Nicaragua, Libya, Sri Lanka, Democratic People's Repub. of Korea, Thailand, Philippines, S Africa, Namibia, Bangladesh, Russian Fed., Turkey, Kuwait, Morocco, Japan, Belgium, Chile, China, India, Algeria, France, Mexico, Switzerland and Malaysia; Pres. AAPP 2004–05. *Leisure interests:* reading, farming. *Address:* National Assembly of Pakistan, Parliament House, Islamabad (office); House No. 22, Ministers' Enclave, Sector F-5, Islamabad, Pakistan (home). *Telephone:* (51) 9221082 (office). *Fax:* (51) 9221106 (office). *E-mail:* assembly@na.gov.pk (office). *Website:* www.na.gov.pk (office).

HUSSAIN, Chaudhry Shujaat; Pakistani politician; *President, Pakistan Muslim League;* b. 27 Jan. 1946; s. of Chaudhry Zahoor Elahi; m.; two s. one d.; ed Forman Christian Coll., Lahore and Univ. of London, UK; mem. Majlis-e-Shoora 1982–85; mem. Nat. Ass. 1985–, Leader of Opposition 1988–90; Fed. Minister for Infomationa and Broadcasting 1986, for Industries and Production 1987–88, of the Interior 1990–93, 1997–99, of Narcotics Control 1997–99; Pres. Pakistan Muslim League 2004–; Prime Minister of Pakistan June–Aug. 2004; Hon. Consul-Gen. to Repub. of Korea 1982–; Order of Diplomatic Service Merit Ueung-in-Metal. *Address:* Pakistan Muslim League, PML House, F-7/3, Islamabad, Pakistan (office). *Telephone:* (11) 1001947 (office). *E-mail:* shujaat_hussain@pakistanmuslimleague.info (office). *Website:* www .pakistanmuslimleague.info (office).

HUSSAIN, Ishrat, MA, PhD; Pakistani economist and central banker (retd); *Chairman, National Commission for Government Reforms;* b. 17 June 1941, Allahabad, India; s. of the late Rahat Husain and Khursheed Rahat Husain; m. Shahnaz Husain; two d.; ed Williams Coll., Boston Univ. and Grad. Exec. Devt Programme (Harvard, Stanford and INSEAD); mem. Staff Sr Managerial, Planning and Devt Dept and Finance Dept, Govt of Sindh; Additional Deputy Commr for Devt, Chittagong, Bangladesh; mem. Govt of Pakistan's Panel of Economists; Adjunct Prof. of Econs, Karachi Univ., Dir Poverty and Social Policy Dept; IBRD Resident Rep. for Nigeria 1986, Chief Economist for Africa, IBRD 1991–94, Chief Economist for E Asia and Pacific Region 1995, also Chief Debt and Int. Finance Div., Dir for Cen. Asian Repubs; Gov. State Bank of Pakistan 1999–2005; Chair. Nat. Comm. for Govt Reforms with rank of Fed. Minister 2005–; Hilal-e-Imtiaz; Central Bank Gov. of the Year in Asia Award, The Banker magazine (first Pakistani Gov. to receive award) 2005. *Publications:* Dollars, Debts, and Deficits, Pakistan: The Economy of an Elitist State, The Political Economy of Reforms: Case Study of Pakistan, Adjustment in Africa: Lessons from Case Studies: Dealing with Debt Crisis, African External Finance in the 1990s, The Economy of Modern Sindh; numerous articles and papers on debt, external finance and adjustment issues. *Leisure interests:* reading and writing economics, poetry. *Address:* National Commission for Government Reforms, Prime Minister's Secretariat, Block B, Second Floor, Benevolent Fund Building, Zero Point, Islamabad, Pakistan (office). *Telephone:* (51) 9203932 (office). *E-mail:* webmaster@ncgr.gov.pk (office). *Website:* www.ncgr.gov.pk (office).

HUSSAIN, Nasser, OBE, BSc; British fmr professional cricketer; b. 28 March 1968, Chennai, India; s. of Joe Hussain; m. Karen Hussain; two s.; ed Forest School, London, Durham Univ.; youngest-ever batsman to represent Essex Under-15 Schools 1980; right-hand batsman, right-hand leg-break bowler; England debut against West Indies, Kingston 1989; Capt. England 'A' team in tour of Pakistan 1996; scored first Test centuries at Edgbaston and Trent Bridge against India 1996 and career-best 207 against Australia at Edgbaston 1997; 96 Tests for 5,764 runs (average 37.18); scored 20,698 first-class runs (average 42.06) including 52 centuries; fmr Capt. of Essex; Capt. of England 1999–2003; retd 2004; cricket commentator, Sky; Cricket Writers' Club Young Cricketer of the Year Award 1989, Wisden Cricketer of the Year 2003. *Publication:* The Autobiography 2004, Playing with Fire (British Sports Book Awards) 2005. *Leisure interests:* golf, football (Leeds United fan), reading. *Address:* c/o England and Wales Cricket Board, Lord's Cricket Ground, London, NW8 8QZ, England (office). *Telephone:* (20) 7289-1611 (office). *Website:* www.ecb.co.uk (office).

HUSSAIN, Prince Sharif Ali bin al-, MA; Iraqi royal; *Leader, Constitutional Monarchy Movement;* b. 1956, Baghdad; s. of Sharif Al Hussain bin Ali and Princess Badia; cousin of the late King Faisal II; m.; ed schools in Lebanon, univ. in UK; royal family in exile following revolution 1958–; childhood spent in Lebanon and UK; began career in investment banking,

London; currently Leader Constitutional Monarchy Movt (a mem. of Iraq Nat. Congress—INC); returned to Iraq to make claim to the throne June 2003. *Leisure interest:* fencing. *Telephone:* (1) 778-2897 (office). *Fax:* (1) 778-0199 (office). *E-mail:* info@iraqcmm.org (office). *Website:* www.iraqcmm.org (office).

HUSSAIN (ALLARAKHA QURESHI), Zakir; Indian musician (tabla), producer, actor and composer; b. 9 March 1951, Mumbai; s. of Ustad Alla Rakha, plays with Ali Akbar Khan, Birju Maharaj, Ravi Shankar, Shivkumar Sharma; formed Shakti with John McLaughlin and L. Shankar 1970s; also formed percussion group, Rhythm Experience, Diga Rhythm Band, Making Music, Planet Drum with Mickey Hart, Tabla Beat Science, Sangam with Charles Lloyd and Eric Harland; founder, Moment! Records 1992–; composed music for opening ceremony, Olympic Games, Atlanta, USA 1996; commissioned by Indian Govt to compose anthem to celebrate 60 years of Indian independence 2007; Prof. of Indian classical music, Princeton Univ. 2005–06, Stanford Univ. 2007; tours and appearances world-wide; Padma Shri 1998, Padma Bhushan 2002; Indo-American Award 1990, Sangeet Natak Akademi Award 1991, Nat. Heritage Fellowship, USA 1999, Kalidas Samman 2006. *Films:* soundtracks: Heat and Dust 1982, Miss Beatty's Children 1992, In Custody 1994, Saaz 1997, Gaach 1998, Zakir and his Friends 1998, Vaanaprastham 1999, Everybody Says I'm Fine 2001, The Mystic Masseur 2001, Mr and Mrs Iyer 2001, One Dollar Curry 2004, Parzania 2005, For Real 2006. *Recordings include:* albums: Making Music 1987, Planet Drum (with Mickey Hart) (Grammy Award for Best World Music Album) 1992, Tabla Duet (with Ustad Alla Rakha) 1988, Zakir Hussain And The Rhythm Experience 1991, Venu 1972 1991, Essence Of Rhythm 1998, Drums of India 2003. *Address:* c/o Kevin Kastrup, IMG Artists, Carnegie Hall Tower, 152 West 57th Street, 5th Floor, New York, NY 10019, USA (office). *Telephone:* (212) 994-3500 (office). *Fax:* (212) 994-3550 (office). *E-mail:* kkastrup@imgartists.com (office). *Website:* www.imgartists.com (office).

HUSSEIN, Maj.-Gen. Abd ar-Rahim Muhammad; Sudanese politician; *Minister of National Defence;* career in Armed Forces; attained rank of Maj.-Gen.; Minister of Interior 1998; Minister of Presidential Affairs –2001; Minister of Internal Affairs 2001–04; Minister of Nat. Defence 2005–. *Address:* Ministry of National Defence, POB 371, Khartoum, Sudan (office). *Telephone:* (183) 774910.

HUSSEIN, Abdul-Aziz; Kuwaiti politician and diplomatist; b. 1921, Kuwait; m. 1948; two s. one d.; ed Teachers Higher Inst., Cairo, Egypt and Univ. of London; fmr Dir 'House of Kuwait', Cairo, Dir-Gen. Dept of Educ., Kuwait; Amb. to the UAR 1961–62; Perm. Rep. to Arab League Council; State Minister in Charge of Cabinet Affairs 1963–64; Minister of State for Cabinet Affairs 1971–85; Counsellor of HM the Amir of Kuwait 1985–. *Publication:* Lectures on Arab Society in Kuwait 1960. *Address:* Amari Diwan, Seif Palace, Kuwait City, Kuwait.

HUSSEIN, Muhammad al-, PhD; Syrian politician; *Minister of Finance;* fmr Chair. Econ. Bureau, Govt Exec.; Minister of Finance 2003–. *Address:* Ministry of Finance, BP 13136, rue Jule Jammal, Damascus, Syria (office). *Telephone:* (11) 2239624 (office). *Fax:* (11) 2224701 (office). *E-mail:* mof@net.sy (office). *Website:* www.syriafinance.org (office).

HUSSEIN, Col Nur Hassan, (Nur Adde); Somali lawyer, police officer and politician; b. 1938, Mogadishu; from Abgal sub-clan of Hawiye clan; ed Mogadishu Nat. Univ., Fiscal Law School, Rome; started his career as customs officer in 1958, rose through ranks to become Interpol Liaison Officer in Somalia and finally Chief Police Officer in charge of planning and training under fmr regime of Mohamed Siad Barre until the latter's ousting in 1991, served as Attorney Gen. –1991; Sec.-Gen. Somali Red Crescent Soc. 1991–2007; Prime Minister 2007–08. *Address:* c/o Office of the Prime Minister, Mogadishu, Somalia (office).

HUSSEINOV, Col Suret Davud ogly; Azerbaijani politician; b. 1959; m.; two s.; ed Gyanja Inst. of Tech.; worker, Asst foreman carpet factory, Gyanja 1982–83, sorter procurement station, Sheki 1984–86; Sr controller, foreman wool processing factory, Yevlakh 1987–, Dir 1989–; Pres. Consortium Azersherstprom 1983; mem. Parl. 1990, Vice-Prime Minister, plenipotentiary of Pres. in Nagorny Karabakh, Comm. of Nat. Army Corps 1992–93; rank of Col 1992; deprived of all his posts by order of the Pres. Feb. 1993; Prime Minister of Azerbaijan 1993–94; dismissed after organizing an abortive coup d'état 1994; lived in exile in Russia 1997; extradited to Azerbaijan 1997, sentenced to life imprisonment on 40 charges for involvement in coup Feb. 1999; Nat. Hero of Azerbaijan 1992.

HUSSON, Philippe Jean Louis Marie, DenD; French fmr diplomatist; b. 22 July 1927, Nouméa, New Caledonia; s. of Jean Husson and Antoinette Leclerc; m. Christiane Marchand 1956; three s. two d.; ed Inst. d'études politiques; Ecole nat. d'admin; Contrôleur Civil, Morocco 1954–56; Moroccan Desk, Foreign Ministry, Paris 1956–58; First Sec., French Embassy, Bucharest 1958–61, Moscow 1961–64, Second Counsellor, Washington, DC 1964–67; Deputy Dir Cultural and Scientific Relations, Foreign Ministry 1967–71; First Counsellor, French Embassy, Ottawa 1971–74, Minister-Counsellor, Moscow 1974–77; Deputy Perm. Rep. to the UN, New York 1977–81; Amb. to Finland 1981–84; Deputy Inspector-Gen., Foreign Ministry 1984–87; Amb. to Canada 1987–89; Dir Archives and Documentation, Foreign Ministry 1990–92; Govt Diplomatic Adviser 1992; mem. Comm. on Publ. of French diplomatic documents 1992–2005, Comm. on archives of Ministry of Foreign Affairs 1995–; Dir-Gen. 3M Santé 2006–; Commdr, Légion d'honneur, Ordre nat. du Mérite, Order of Merit (Malta), Great Cross, Order of the Lion (Finland), Great Cross Ordre Equestre du St Sépulcre de Jérusalem, Officier Ordre du Cèdre (Lebanon). *Address:* Laboratoires 3M Santé, boulevard de l'oise, 95029 Cergy Pontoise Cedex, France (office); 7 promenade Venezia, Grand Siècle,

78000 Versailles, France (home). *Telephone:* 1-30-31-82-82 (office). *Fax:* 1-30-31-83-83 (office). *E-mail:* phhusson@club-internet.fr (home).

HUSTON, Anjelica; American actress; b. 8 July 1951, Los Angeles, Calif.; d. of the late John Huston and Enrica Huston (née Soma); m. Robert Graham 1992 (died 2008). *Films include:* Sinful Davey, A Walk with Love and Death 1969, The Last Tycoon 1976, The Postman Always Rings Twice 1981, Swashbuckler, This is Spinal Tap 1984, The Ice Pirates 1984, Prizzi's Honor (Acad. Award for Best Supporting Actress 1985, New York and Los Angeles Film Critics' Awards 1985), Gardens of Stone, Captain Eo, The Dead, Mr North, A Handful of Dust, The Witches, Enemies, A Love Story, The Grifters, The Addams Family, Addams Family Values, The Player, Manhattan Murder Mystery, The Crossing Guard 1995, The Perez Family 1995, Buffalo '66 1997, Phoenix 1997, Ever After 1998, Breakers 1999, The Golden Bowl 2001, The Royal Tenenbaums 2002, Blood Work 2002, The Man from Elysian Fields 2002, Daddy Day Care 2003, The Life Aquatic with Steve Zissou 2004, These Foolish Things 2006, Art School Confidential 2006, Material Girls 2006, Seraphim Falls 2006, The Darjeeling Limited 2007, Choke 2008, Tinker Bell (voice) 2008, Spirit of the Forest (voice) 2008, The Kreutzer Sonata 2008; films directed: Bastard Out of Carolina 1996, Agnes Browne 1999. *Stage appearances include:* Tamara, Los Angeles 1985. *Television appearances include:* The Cowboy and the Ballerina (NBC-TV film) 1984, Faerie Tale Theatre, A Rose for Miss Emily (PBS film), Lonesome Dove (CBS mini-series), The Mists of Avalon (TNT mini-series) 2001, Iron Jawed Angels (Best Supporting Actress in a Series, Miniseries or TV Movie, Golden Globe Awards 2005) 2004, Riding the Bus with My Sister (dir) 2005, Covert One: The Hades Factor 2006, Medium (series) 2008. *Address:* ICM, 10250 Constellation Boulevard, Beverly Hills, CA 90067, USA.

HUSTVEDT, Siri, PhD; American poet, novelist and essayist; b. 19 Feb. 1955, Northfield, Minn.; d. of the late Lloyd Hustvedt and of Ester Vegan Hustvedt; m. Paul Auster 1981; one d.; ed Columbia Univ.; worked as ed. and trans. *Publications:* Reading to You (poems) 1982, The Blindfold (novel) 1990, The Enchantment of Lily Dahl (novel) 1996, Yonder: Essays 1998, What I Loved (novel, Prix des Libraires de Québec) 2003, Mysteries of the Rectangle (essays) 2005, A Plea for Eros (essays) 2006, The Sorrows of an American (novel) 2008; contrib. to Paris Review. *Address:* c/o ICM International Creative Management, 40 West 57th Street, New York, NY 10019, USA (office); c/o ICM International Creative Management, 4–6 Soho Square, London, W1D 3PZ, England (office). *Telephone:* (212) 556-5764 (New York) (office); (20) 7432-0800 (London) (office). *Fax:* (212) 556-5624 (New York) (office); (20) 7432-0808 (London) (office).

HUTAPEA, Eva Riyanti; Indonesian business executive; *President Director, PT Usaha Kita Makmur Indonesia;* b. 26 Dec. 1952; m. Bunbunan Hutapea; three d.; ed School of Econs, Univ. of Indonesia; trained as accountant; fmr auditor; joined Salim Group 1982, owner of Indofood, worked through Indofood ranks to become CEO and Pres. Dir 1999–2004 (retd); Pres. Dir PT Usaha Kita Makmur Indonesia (UKM Way) 2004–; Deputy Chair. Indonesian Chamber of Commerce and Industry (KADIN) for the field of Small and Medium Enterprises and Cooperatives; mem. Advisory Council Nat. Bd of the Indonesian Employers Asscn (APINDO); Deputy Chair. Exec. Council Indonesian Inst. of Commrs and Dirs; Dir Gen. Instant Ramen Mfrs Asscn 1999–2001. *Address:* PT Usaha Kita Makmur Indonesia, RP Suroso No. 6, Gondangdia Lama, Jakarta 10350, Indonesia (office). *Telephone:* (21) 31909730 (office).

HUTCHEON, Linda Ann Marie, MA, PhD, FRSC; Canadian writer and academic; *Distinguished University Professor, University of Toronto;* b. (Linda Bortolotti), 24 Aug. 1947, Toronto, Ont.; d. of Roy Bortolotti and Elisa Rossi; m. Michael Alexander Hutcheon 1970; ed Univ. of Toronto, Cornell Univ., USA; Asst, Assoc. and Full Prof. of English, McMaster Univ. 1976–88; Prof. of English and Comparative Literature, Univ. of Toronto 1988–96, Distinguished Univ. Prof. 1996–; mem. Modern Language Asscn of America, American Acad. of Arts and Sciences; Hon. LLD 1995, Hon. DLitt 1999, 2000, 2005, 2007, 2008; Killam Prize 2005. *Publications:* Narcissistic Narrative 1980, Formalism and the Freudian Aesthetic 1984, A Theory of Parody 1985, A Poetics of Postmodernism 1988, The Canadian Postmodern 1988, The Politics of Postmodernism 1989, Splitting Images 1991, Irony's Edge 1995, A Theory of Adaptation 2004, Opera: Desire, Disease, Death (with Michael Hutcheon) 1996, Bodily Charm: Living Opera (with Michael Hutcheon), 2000, Opera: The Art of Dying (with Michael Hutcheon), 2004. Ed.: Other Solitudes 1990, Double-Talking 1992, Likely Stories 1992, A Postmodern Reader 1993, Rethinking Literary History: A Forum on Theory 2002; contribs to Diacritics, Textual Practice, Cultural Critique and other journals. *Leisure interests:* piano, cycling. *Address:* Department of English, University of Toronto, Toronto, ON M5R 2M8, Canada (office). *Telephone:* (416) 978-6616 (office). *Fax:* (416) 978-2836 (office). *E-mail:* l.hist@utoronto.ca (office). *Website:* http://individual.utoronto.ca/lindahutcheon/ (office).

HUTCHINSON, (John) Maxwell, AADipl; British architect, broadcaster and writer; *Director, The Hutchinson Studio Architects;* b. 3 Dec. 1948; s. of the late Frank M. Hutchinson and Elizabeth R. M. Wright; ed Oundle, Scott Sutherland School of Architecture, Aberdeen and Architectural Asscn School of Architecture; Founder Hutchinson & Partners (Chartered Architects) 1972, Chair. Hutchinson & Partners Architects Ltd 1987–92; Dir The Hutchinson Studio Architects 1992–, SMC Group PLC; Visiting Prof. of Architecture, Queen's Univ., Belfast 1988–93; Special Prof. of Architectural Design, Univ. of Nottingham 1993–96; Visiting Prof., Univ. of Westminster 1997–2001; Chair. Permarock Products Ltd, Loughborough 1985–96, London Br. Elgar Soc. 1987–93, East Midlands Arts Bd 1991–94, British Architectural Library Trust 1991–99, Schools of Architecture Accreditation Bd 1991–97; Chair. Industrial Bldg Bureau 1988–91; Founder and Life Pres. Architects for Aid 2005–; Vice-

Chair. Construction Industry Council 1990–91; mem. Council RIBA 1978–93, Sr Vice-Pres. 1988–89, Pres. 1989–91; Church Warden Our Most Holy Redeemer, Clerkenwell 2007–; mem. Council Royal School of Church Music 1997–2000; regular broadcaster on TV and radio; freelance writer; Hon. Fellow, Univ. of Greenwich 1990, Royal Soc. of Ulster Architects 1992, Univ. Coll. London 2008 Hon. Dr of Design (Robert Gordon Univ.) 2007. *Television:* presenter of major series including No. 57 – The History of a House (Channel 4), Demolition Detectives (Channel 4), Maxwell's Hidden Treasures (ITV 1), Prefabs and Palaces, Pure Inventions, Mod Cons (Discovery Channel), How to Rescue a House (BBC 2), Songs of Praise (BBC 1). *Compositions:* The Kibbo-Kift 1979, The Ascent of Wilberforce 111 1984, Requiem in a Village Church 1988, Christmas Cantata 1990. *Publications:* The Prince of Wales, Right or Wrong: An Architect Replies 1989, Number 57 – The Story of a House 2003; contrib. to How to Rescue a House 2005. *Leisure interests:* composing, travel, beer, music. *Address:* 26 Exmouth Market, London, EC1R 4QE, England (office). *Telephone:* (20) 7273-9288 (office). *E-mail:* info@hutchinsonstudio.co.uk (office). *Website:* www.hutchinsonstudio.co.uk.

HUTCHISON, Kay Bailey, LLB; American politician; *Senator from Texas;* b. 22 July 1943, Galveston, Tex.; d. of Allan Bailey and Kathryn Bailey; m. Ray Hutchison; two c.; ed Univ. of Texas; TV news reporter, Houston 1969–71; pvt. law practice 1969–74; Press Sec. to Anne Armstrong 1971; Vice-Chair. Nat. Transport Safety Bd 1976–78; Asst Prof., Univ. of Texas, Dallas 1978–79; Sr Vice-Pres., Gen. Counsel, Repub. of Tex. Corpn Dallas 1979–81; counsel, Hutchison, Boyle, Brooks & Fisher, Dallas 1981–91; mem. Tex. House of Reps. 1972–76; elected Treas. of Tex. 1990; Senator from Texas 1993–; Chair. Science and Space Sub-cttee of Commerce Cttee (overseeing NASA and NSF) 2005–; Fellow, American Bar Foundation, Tex. Bar Foundation; mem. ABA, State Bar of Tex.; Republican; Outstanding Alumna, Univ. of Texas 1995, Republican Woman of the Year, Nat. Fed. of Republican Women 1995, Silver Ingot Ward, Coastal Conservation Asscn 1997, inducted into Texas Women's Hall of Fame 1997, Texan of the Year, Texas Legis. Conf. 1997, named by Texas Women's Chamber of Commerce amongst 100 Most Influential Texas Women of the Century 1999, CLEAT Award for Support of Law Enforcement 2000, Nat. Mil. Family Asscn Award for Service to Mil. Families 2001, Nat. Leadership Award, Hispanic Asscn of Colls and Univs 2002, Inaugural Congressional Leadership Award, Women's Foreign Policy Group 2004, Distinguished Public Service Award, Alliance for Aging Research 2004, Adam Smith Fed. Elected Official Medal, Business Industry Political Action Cttee 2004, Wetland Sponsor of the Year Award, Ducks Unlimited 2005, named 'Mr. South Texas' by Washington's Birthday Celebration Asscn 2005, named Legislator of the Year by Deep East Texas Council of Govts 2005, ranked 87th by Forbes magazine amongst 100 Most Powerful Women 2005, American Legion Nat. Commdr's Distinguished Public Service Award 2006. *Publications:* Nine and Counting: The Women of the Senate (co-author) 2000, American Heroines: The Spirited Women Who Shaped Our Country 2004. *Address:* 284 Russell Senate Office Building, Washington, DC 20510, USA (office). *Telephone:* (202) 224-5922 (office). *Website:* hutchison.senate.gov (office).

HUTH, John E., AB, PhD; American physicist and academic; *Professor of Physics, Harvard University;* ed Princeton Univ., Univ. of Calif., Berkeley; Postdoctoral Scientist, Fermi Nat. Accelerator Lab. (Fermilab), Batavia, IL 1985–87, Wilson Fellow 1987–90, Staff Scientist 1990–93, mem. Fermilab Physics Advisory Panel 1993–97; Prof. of Physics, Harvard Univ. 1993–, also Chair., Dept of Physics; Project Man., ATLAS Computing and Physics Project; mem. Steering Cttee, Brookhaven Nat. Lab. Science and Tech. 1998–. *Address:* Department of Physics, 236 Lyman Avenue, Harvard University, Cambridge, MA 02138, USA (office). *Telephone:* (617) 495-8144 (office). *Fax:* (617) 495-0416 (office). *E-mail:* huth@physics.harvad.edu. *Website:* www.physics.harvard.edu/huth.htm (office).

HUTT, Peter Barton, BA, LLB, LLM; American lawyer; *Senior Counsel, Covington & Burling LLP;* b. 16 Nov. 1934, Buffalo, NY; s. of Lester Ralph Hutt and Louise Rich Fraser; ed Phillips Exeter Acad., Yale, Harvard and New York Univs; Assoc., Covington & Burling LLP (law firm) 1960–68, Pnr 1968–71, 1975–2004, Sr Counsel 2004–; Lecturer on Food and Drug Law, Harvard Law School 1994–, Stanford Law School 1998; Chief Counsel, US Food and Drug Admin. 1971–75; Counsel, Soc. for Risk Analysis, American Coll. of Toxicology; Chair. Alcoholic Beverage Medical Research Foundation 1986–92; Vice-Chair. Legal Action Center, New York 1984–2003, Foundation for Biomedical Research 1988–; mem. Inst. of Medicine, NAS 1970–, Advisory Bd, Tufts Center for Study of Drug Devt 1976–99, Univ. of Virginia Center for Advanced Studies 1982–, Nat. Cttee on New Drugs for Cancer and AIDS 1988–90, Inst. of Medicine Round Table on Drugs and Vaccines against AIDS 1988–95, Nat. Acad. of Public Admin's Panel on restructuring NIH 2004–, Nat. Inst. of Allergy and Infections Disease Working Group on Div. of AIDS 2005–; mem. Bd of Dirs numerous cos; mem. Advisory Bd of numerous other scientific, academic and financial orgs; Underwood-Prescott Award, MIT 1977, and numerous other honours and awards. *Publications:* Dealing with Drug Abuse (with Patricia M. Wald) 1972, Food and Drug Law: Cases and Materials (with Richard A. Merrill) 1980, 1991, 2007. *Leisure interests:* research on the history of govt regulation of food and drugs. *Address:* 124 South Fairfax Street, Alexandria, VA 22314 (home); Covington & Burling LLP, 1201 Pennsylvania Avenue, NW, Washington, DC 20004, USA (office). *Telephone:* (202) 662-5522 (office). *Fax:* (202) 778-5522 (office). *E-mail:* phutt@cov.com (office). *Website:* (office).

HUTTON, Baron (Life Peer), cr. 1997, of Bresagh in the County of Down; **Rt Hon. (James) Brian Edward Hutton,** PC; British fmr judge; b. 29 June 1931, Belfast, Northern Ireland; s. of the late James Hutton and Mabel Hutton; m. 1st Mary Gillian Murland 1975 (died 2000); two d.; 2nd Rosalind Ann Nickols 2001; 2 step s. one step d.; ed Shrewsbury School, Balliol Coll. Oxford, Queen's Univ. of Belfast; called to NI Bar 1954, QC (NI) 1970, Bencher, Inn of Court of NI 1974, Sr Crown Counsel 1973–79, Judge of High Court of Justice 1979–88, Lord Chief Justice of NI 1988–97; a Lord of Appeal in Ordinary 1997–2004; mem. Jt Law Enforcement Comm. 1974, Deputy Chair. Boundary Comm. for NI 1985–88; Pres. NI Asscn for Mental Health 1983–1990; Visitor Univ. of Ulster 1999–2004; Chair. of Inquiry into death of Dr David Kelly 2003–04; Hon. LLD Queen's University of Belfast, University of Ulster Hon. Fellow, Balliol Coll.; Hon. Bencher Inner Temple, King's Inns, Dublin. *Address:* House of Lords, Westminster, London, SW1A 0PW, England (office). *Telephone:* (20) 7219-3202 (office).

HUTTON, Rt Hon. John, PC, BCL, MA; British politician; *Secretary of State for Defence;* b. 6 May 1955; m. Heather Rogers 2004; four s. (one deceased) one d.; ed Westcliffe High School, Essex, Magdalen Coll., Oxford; Research Assoc., Templeton Coll. 1980–81; Sr Lecturer in Law, Newcastle Polytechnic (now Univ. of Northumbria) 1981–92; unsuccessful cand. for MP for Penrith and the Border 1987, for MEP for Cumbria and N Lancs. 1989; MP for Barrow and Furness 1992–; Parl. Pvt. Sec. to Margaret Beckett 1997–98; Parl. Under-Sec. of State, Dept of Health 1998–99, Minister of State for Health 1999–2005; Chancellor of the Duchy of Lancaster and Minister for the Cabinet Office 2005; Sec. of State for Work and Pensions 2005–07, for Business, Enterprise and Regulatory Reform 2007–08, for Defence 2008–; mem. Home Affairs Select Cttee 1994–97; Chair. Labour Parl. Cttees for Defence 1992–94, for Home Affairs 1994–97, for Home Affairs, Trade and Industry, for the Treasury 1997–2001; Trustee Furness Animal Refuge; Chair. Welfare and Park Home Owners All-party Subject Group 1995–97; Chair. British Latin American Group 1997. *Leisure interests:* football, cricket, films, music, history. *Address:* Ministry of Defence, Main Building, Whitehall, London SW1A 2HB (office); 22 Hartington Street, Barrow in Furness, Cumbria, LA14 5SL (office); House of Commons, London, SW1A 0AA, England (office). *Telephone:* (20) 7218-9000 (Ministry); (1229) 431204 (constituency) (office); (20) 7238-0800 (office). *Fax:* (1229) 432016 (constituency) (office). *E-mail:* public@ministers.mod.uk (office); huttonj@parliament.uk (office). *Website:* www.mod.uk (office); www.johnhuttonmp.co.uk (office); www.parliament.uk (office).

HUTTON, Timothy; American actor; b. 16 Aug. 1960, Malibu, Calif.; s. of Jim Hutton and Maryline Hutton; m. Debra Winger (q.v.) 1986 (divorced); one s. *Plays:* Prelude to a Kiss, Broadway 1990, Babylon Gardens 1991. *Television appearances include:* Zuma Beach 1978, Best Place to Be, Baby Makes Six, Sultan and the Rock Star, Young Love, First Love, Friendly Fire 1979, Aldrich Ames: Traitor Within 1998, Nero Wolfe Mystery (series) 2001–02, WW3 2001, 5ive Days to Midnight (mini series) 2004, Avenger 2006, Kidnapped 2006–07, Leverage 2008. *Films include:* Ordinary People (Oscar for Best Supporting Actor) 1980, Taps 1981, Daniel 1983, Iceman 1984, Turk 1985, The Falcon and the Snowman 1985, Made in Heaven 1987, A Time of Destiny 1988, Everybody's All-American 1988, Betrayed 1988, Torrents of Spring 1990, Q & A 1990, The Temp 1993, The Dark Half 1993, French Kiss 1995, City of Industry, Scenes From Everyday Life 1995, The Substance of Fire 1996, Mr and Mrs Loving 1996, Beautiful Girls 1996, City of Industry 1997, Playing God 1997, Deterrance 1998, The General's Daughter 1999, Just One Night 2000, Deliberate Intent 2000, Deterrence 2000, Lucky Strike 2000, Sunshine State 2002, Secret Window 2004, Kinsey 2004, Turning Green 2005, Last Holiday 2006, Stephanie Daley 2006, The Kovak Box 2006, Heavens Fall 2006, Falling Objects 2006, Off the Black 2006, The Good Shepherd 2006, The Last Mimzy 2007, The Killing Room 2008, The Alphabet Killer 2008. *Address:* c/o The Endeavor Agency, 9601 Wilshire Boulevard, Beverly Hills, CA 90210, USA.

HUTTON, Will Nicholas, MBA; British writer and broadcaster; *Chief Executive, Work Foundation;* b. 21 May 1950, London; s. of the late William Hutton and Dorothy Haynes; m. Jane Atkinson 1978; one s. two d.; ed Chislehurst and Sidcup Grammar School, Univ. of Bristol and Institut Européen d'Admin des Affaires (INSEAD), Fontainebleau, France; with Phillips & Drew (stockbrokers) 1971–77; Sr Producer Current Affairs, BBC Radio 4 1978–81; Dir and Producer The Money Programme, BBC 2 1981–83; Econs Corresp. Newsnight, BBC 2 1983–88; Ed. European Business Channel 1988–90; Econs Ed. The Guardian 1990–95, Asst Ed. 1995–96; Ed. The Observer 1996–98, Ed.-in-Chief 1998–2000; Chief Exec. The Work Foundation (fmrly The Industrial Soc. –2002) 2000–; Gov. LSE 2000–; Hon. DLitt (Kingston) 1995, (De Montfort) 1996; Political Journalist of the Year, What the Papers Say 1993. *Publications:* The Revolution That Never Was: An Assessment of Keynesian Economics 1986, The State We're In 1994, The State to Come 1997, The Stakeholding Society 1998, The World We're In 2002, The Writing on the Wall: China and the West in the 21st Century 2007. *Leisure interests:* family, reading, squash, tennis, cinema, writing. *Address:* The Work Foundation, Peter Runge House, 3 Carlton Terrace, London, SW1Y 5DG (office); 34 Elms Avenue, London, N10 2JP, England (home). *Telephone:* (20) 7004-7103 (office). *Fax:* (20) 7004-7111 (office). *E-mail:* sholden@theworkfoundation.com (office). *Website:* www.theworkfoundation.com (office).

HUXLEY, Sir Andrew Fielding, Kt, OM, ScD, FRS; British physiologist and academic; *Professor Emeritus of Physiology, University of London;* b. 22 Nov. 1917, London; s. of Leonard Huxley and Rosalind Huxley (née Bruce); m. Jocelyn Richenda Gammell Pease 1947 (died 2003); one s. five d.; ed Univ. Coll. School, Westminster School and Trinity Coll., Cambridge; Operational Research, Anti-Aircraft Command 1940–42, Admiralty 1942–45; Fellow, Trinity Coll., Cambridge 1941–60, 1990–, Dir of Studies 1952–60, Hon. Fellow 1967–90, Master, Trinity Coll. 1984–90; Demonstrator, Dept of Physiology, Univ. of Cambridge 1946–50, Asst Dir of Research 1951–59, Reader in Experimental Biophysics 1959–60; Jodrell Prof. of Physiology, Univ. Coll. London 1960–69; Royal Soc. Research Prof. 1969–83, Prof. Emer. of

Physiology, Univ. of London 1983–; Pres. BAAS 1976–77; Chair. Medical Research Cttee of the Muscular Dystrophy Group 1974–80, Vice-Pres. Muscular Dystrophy Group 1980–; mem. Govt's Scientific Authority for Animals 1976–77, Agric. Research Council 1977–81, Nature Conservancy Council 1985–87, Home Office Animal Procedures Cttee 1987–95; mem. Council, Royal Soc. 1960–62, 1977–79, 1980–85; Pres. Royal Soc. 1980–85, Int. Union of Physiological Sciences 1986–93; mem. Leopoldina Acad. 1964, Royal Danish Acad. of Sciences and Letters 1964, American Philosophical Soc. 1975; mem. Emer. Academia Europaea 1989; Trustee, British Museum (Natural History) 1981–91, Science Museum 1983–88; Fellow, Imperial Coll. of Science and Tech. 1980; Foreign Fellow, Indian Nat. Science Acad. 1985; Assoc. mem. Royal Acad. of Sciences, Letters and Fine Arts, Belgium 1978; Foreign Assoc. NAS 1979; Foreign mem. Dutch Soc. of Sciences 1984; Hon. Fellow, Univ. Coll. London 1980; Hon. MRIA 1986, Japan Acad. 1988; Hon. Foreign mem. American Acad. of Arts and Sciences 1961, Royal Acad. of Medicine, Belgium 1978; Hon. FIBiol 1981; Hon. Fellow, Darwin Coll., Cambridge 1981; Hon. FRSE 1983; Hon. FREng 1986; Hon. Fellow, Queen Mary Coll. 1987; Hon. FRCP 2000; Grand Cordon of Sacred Treasure (Japan) 1995; Hon. MD (Saar) 1964, (Ulm) 1993, (Charles Univ., Prague) 1998; Hon. DSc (Sheffield) 1964, (Leicester) 1967, (London) 1973, (St Andrews) 1974, (Aston) 1977, (Oxford) 1983, (Keele) 1985, (Md) 1987, (Brunel) 1988, (Hyderabad) 1991, (Glasgow) 1993, (Witwatersrand) 1998; Hon. ScD (Cambridge) 1978, (Pennyslvania) 1984, (East Anglia) 1985; Hon. LLD (Birmingham) 1979, (Dundee) 1984; Hon. DHL (New York) 1982; Dr hc (Marseilles) 1979, (York) 1981, (W Australia) 1982, (Harvard Univ.) 1984, (Humboldt Univ.) 1985, (Toyama) 1995; Nobel Prize for Physiology or Medicine (jtly) 1963, Copley Medal, Royal Soc. 1973, Swammerdam Medal, Soc. for Natural Science, Medicine and Surgery, Amsterdam 1997; Croonian Lecturer, Royal Soc. 1967; First Florey Lecturer, Australia 1982, Romanes Lecturer, Oxford 1982–83, Fenn Lecturer, Sydney 1983, Davson Lecturer, American Physiological Soc. 1998. *Publications:* Reflections on Muscle (Sherrington Lectures, Liverpool Univ.) 1977; papers on nerve conduction and muscle contraction, chiefly in Journal of Physiology. *Leisure interests:* walking, design of scientific instruments. *Address:* Manor Field, 1 Vicarage Drive, Grantchester, Cambridge, CB3 9NG, England (home). *Telephone:* (1223) 840207 (home). *Fax:* (1223) 840207 (home).

HUXLEY, George Leonard, MA, FSA, MRIA; British academic; *Honorary Professor, School of Classics, Trinity College, Dublin;* b. 23 Sept. 1932, Leicester; s. of Sir Leonard Huxley and Lady (Molly) Huxley; m. Davina Iris Best 1957; three d.; ed Blundell's, Magdalen Coll., Oxford; commissioned into Royal Engineers 1951; Acting Operating Supt, Longmoor Mil. Railway 1951; Fellow, All Souls Coll., Oxford 1955–61; Prof. of Greek, Queen's Univ., Belfast 1962–83, Prof. Emer. 1988–; Hon. Pres. Classical Asscn of Ireland 1999–2000; Dir Gennadius Library, American School of Classical Studies, Athens 1986–89; mem. Exec. NI Civil Rights Asscn 1971–72; mem. Man. Cttee ASCSA 1991–; mem. Irish Advisory Bd, Int. Irish Studies, Liverpool Univ. 1996–2005; Hon. Prof., Trinity Coll., Dublin 1989–; Adjunct Prof., Nat. Univ. of Ireland; Sr Vice-Pres. Fédération Int. des Sociétés d'Etudes Classiques 1984–89; Irish mem., Humanities Cttee of European Science Foundation 1978–86; Vice-Pres. Royal Irish Acad. 1984–85, 1997–98, Hon. Librarian 1990–94, Special Envoy 1994–99, Sr Vice-Pres. 1999–2000; mem. Acad. Europaea 1990–; mem. Int. Comm. Thesaurus Linguae Latinae, Munich 1999–2000; mem. Editorial Bd Dictionary of Mediaeval Latin from Celtic Sources 2001–; Patron Irish Inst. of Hellenic Studies, Athens 1998–; Keynote Speaker XVI Int. Congress on Classical Archaeology, Boston 2003; Hon. LittD (Dublin) 1984, Hon. DLitt (Belfast) 1996; Cromer Greek Prize 1963. *Publications:* Early Sparta 1962, Achaeans and Hittites 1960, The Early Ionians 1966, Greek Epic Poetry 1969, Kythera (Jt) 1972, Pindar's Vision of the Past 1975, On Aristotle and Greek Society 1979, Homer and the Travellers 1988; articles on Hellenic,Byzantine, and railway subjects. *Leisure interest:* siderodromophilia. *Address:* School of Classics, Trinity College, Dublin 2, Ireland (office); Forge Cottage, Church Enstone, Oxfordshire, OX7 4NN, England (home). *Telephone:* (1608) 677595 (home).

HUXLEY, Hugh Esmor, MBE, PhD, DSc, FRS; British scientist and academic; *Lucille P. Markey Distinguished Professor Emeritus of Biology, Rosenstiel Basic Medical Sciences Research Center, Brandeis University;* b. 25 Feb. 1924, Birkenhead, Cheshire; s. of Thomas Hugh Huxley and Olwen Roberts; m. Frances Fripp 1966; one d. two step-s. one step-d.; ed Park High School, Birkenhead and Christ's Coll., Cambridge; Radar Officer, RAF Bomber Command and Telecommunications Research Establishment, Malvern 1943–47; Research Student, MRC Unit for Molecular Biology, Cavendish Lab., Cambridge 1948–52; Commonwealth Fund Fellow, Biology Dept, MIT 1952–54; Research Fellow, Christ's Coll., Cambridge 1953–56; mem. of External Staff of MRC and Hon. Research Assoc., Biophysics Dept, Univ. Coll. London 1956–61; mem. of Scientific Staff, MRC Lab. of Molecular Biology, Cambridge 1962–87, Jt Head, Structural Studies Div. 1976–87, Deputy Dir 1977–87; mem. Advisory Bd, Rosenstiel Basic Medical Sciences Center, Brandeis Univ., Boston, Mass. 1971–77, Prof. of Biology 1987–97, Dir 1988–94, Lucille P. Markey Distinguished Prof. Emer. 1997–, Ziskind Visiting Prof. of Biology 1971; Fellow, King's Coll., Cambridge 1961–67, Churchill Coll., Cambridge 1967–87; Harvey Soc. Lecturer, New York 1964–65; Sr Visiting Lecturer, Physiology Course, Woods Hole, Mass. 1966–71; Wilson Lecturer, Univ. of Tex. 1968; Dunham Lecturer, Harvard Medical School 1969; Croonian Lecturer, Royal Soc. of London 1970; Penn Lecturer, Univ. of Pa 1971; Mayer Lecturer, MIT 1971; Miller Lecturer, State Univ. of New York 1973; Carter-Wallace Lecturer, Princeton Univ. 1973; Pauling Lecturer, Stanford Univ. 1980; Jesse Beams Lecturer, Univ. of Va 1980; Ida Beam Lecturer, Univ. of Ia 1981; mem. Council of Royal Soc. of London 1973–75, 1984–86; mem. Scientific Advisory Cttee, European Molecular Biology Lab. 1975–81; mem. Bd of Trustees, Associated Univs Inc. 1987–90; mem. German Acad. of Science Leopoldina 1964; Foreign Assoc., NAS 1978, American Asscn of Anatomists 1981, American Physiological Soc. 1981, American Soc. of Zoologists 1986; Foreign Hon. mem. American Acad. of Arts and Sciences 1965, Danish Acad. of Sciences 1971, American Soc. of Biological Chemists 1976; Hon. Fellow, Christ's Coll., Cambridge 1981; Hon. DSc (Harvard) 1969, (Univ. of Chicago) 1974, (Univ. of Pennsylvania) 1976, (Leicester) 1988; Feldberg Award for Experimental Medical Research 1963, William Bate Hardy Prize of the Cambridge Philosophical Soc. 1965, Louisa Gross Horwitz Prize 1971, Int. Feltrinelli Prize for Medicine 1974, Int. Award, Gairdner Foundation 1975, Baly Medal, Royal Coll. of Physicians 1975, Royal Medal, Royal Soc. of London 1977, E.B. Wilson Medal, American Soc. for Cell Biology 1983, Albert Einstein World Award of Science 1987, Franklin Medal 1990, Distinguished Scientist Award, Electron Microscopy Soc. of America 1991, Copley Medal, Royal Soc. of London 1997. *Publications:* articles in scientific journals. *Leisure interests:* skiing, sailing, travel. *Address:* Rosenstiel Basic Medical Sciences Research Center, Brandeis University, Waltham, MA 02454 (office); 349 Nashawtuc Road, Concord, MA 01742, USA (home). *Telephone:* (617) 736-2490 (office). *E-mail:* huxley@brandeis.edu (office).

HUXLEY BARKHAM, Selma de Lotbinière, OC; British historical geographer and writer; b. 8 March 1927, London, UK; d. of Michael Huxley and Ottilie Huxley (née de Lotbinière Mills); m. John Brian Barkham 1954 (died 1964); two s. two d.; Asst, Cttee on Geographical Names, Royal Geographical Soc., UK 1949; Librarian, Arctic Inst. of N America, Montréal 1951–54; Founder African Students Asscn 1960s; prepared and presented brief to Royal Comm. on Bilingualism and Biculturalism which was deemed instrumental in bringing French immersion to Canadian public school system; founding mem., French Section, Citizens' Cttee on Children; helped Edgar Demers start first French Canadian theatre group for children in the Outaouais, 'La compagnie des Trouvères' 1960s; researcher for historic sites (including Louisbourg) 1964–68; teacher, Instituto Anglo-Mexicano, Guadalajara, Mexico until moving to Spain 1969–72; identified earliest ports used by Basques in the Strait of Belle Isle, and found earliest civil documents written in Canada 1972–87; Royal Canadian Geographical Soc. grant to lead first expedition to identify 16th century Basque whaling sites in Labrador including what is now the Red Bay Nat. Historic Site 1977; led teams of underwater and land archaeologists to these sites; worked for Public Archives of Canada in Spain 1973–85; Social Sciences and Humanities Research Council of Canada grant for publ. of documents relating to Basques in Newfoundland and Labrador 1984–86; mem. Historical Cttee, Museo Naval de San Sebastian 1992–, Advisory Cttee For Red Bay, Labrador, Nat. Historic Site 1996–; advocates Basque Nat. Trust for the Preservation of Basque Architecture 1993–; co-founder, Northern Peninsula Heritage Soc. 1997–; elected mem. Réal Sociedad Bascongada de Amigos del País 1981; numerous publs, lectures and confs; Hon. Consul of Bilbao, Bizkaia Chamber of Commerce (first woman nominee) 1992; Dr hc (Memorial Univ. of Newfoundland) 1993, (Univ. of Windsor, Ont.) 1985; Gold Medal, Royal Canadian Geographical Soc. (first woman) 1980, Award for Culture, Fundación Sabino Arana, Bilbao 1999, Queen's Golden Jubilee Medal 2002. *Publications include:* Los Vascos en el Marco Atlántico Norte, Siglos XVI y XVII, Itsasoa (Vol. 3) 1987, The Basque Coast of Newfoundland 1989. *Leisure interest:* languages, bird watching. *Address:* 7 Chapel Street, Chichester, West Sussex, PO19 1BU, England; 23 Des Estacades, Cantley, PQ J8V 3J3, Canada. *E-mail:* alv-bar@cyberus.ca.

HUXTABLE, Ada Louise, AB; American writer and architecture critic; *Architecture Critic, The Wall Street Journal;* b. New York; d. of Michael Louis Landman and Leah Landman (née Rosenthal); m. L. Garth Huxtable 1942; ed Hunter Coll. and Inst. of Fine Arts, New York Univ.; Asst Curator of Architecture and Design, Museum of Modern Art, New York 1946–50; Fulbright Scholarship to study contemporary Italian architecture and design 1950, 1952; contributing ed. Progressive Architecture, Art in America, freelance writer on architecture and design 1952–63; Architecture Critic, New York Times 1963–82, mem. Editorial Bd 1973–82; ind. architectural consultant and critic 1982–96; Architecture Critic, The Wall Street Journal 1996–; mem. Corpn Visiting Cttees on Architecture, Harvard Univ., MIT, Rockefeller Univ. Council, Smithsonian Council; mem. Soc. of Architectural Historians, American Acad. of Arts and Letters, American Philosophical Soc.; Fellow, American Acad. of Arts and Sciences, Center for Scholars and Writers, New York Public Library 2000; Hon. FRIBA, Hon. mem. AIA; Dr hc in letters, law and fine arts (Harvard, Yale, New York, Pennsylvania, Massachusetts, Nottingham, UK, Fordham, Washington, Williams, Hamilton, Colgate, Trinity, Oberline, Smith, Skidmere, Mt Holyoke Coll. and others); numerous prizes and awards, including Guggenheim Fellowship for studies in American architecture 1958, Frank Jewett Mather Award of Coll. Art Asscn for Art Criticism 1967, Pulitzer Prize for Distinguished Criticism 1970, AIA Architectural Criticism Medal 1969, Special Award of Nat. Trust for Historic Preservation 1970, Nat. Arts Club Medal for Literature 1971, Diamond Jubilee Medallion of the City of New York 1973, US Sec. of Interior's Conservation Award 1976, Thomas Jefferson Medal for Architecture 1977, Jean Tschumi Prize for Architectural Criticism, Int. Union of Architects 1987, Medal for Architectural Criticism, Acad. d'Architecture Française 1988, MacArthur Prize Fellowship 1981–86, Henry Allen Moe Prize in the Humanities, American Philosophical Soc. 1992, Medal, Nat. Inst. of Social Sciences 2005. *Publications:* Pier Luigi Nervi 1960, Classical New York 1964, Will They Ever Finish Bruckner Boulevard? 1970, Kicked a Building Lately? 1976, The Tall Building Artistically Reconsidered: The Search for a Skyscraper Style 1985, Architecture, Anyone? 1986, Goodbye History, Hello Hamburger 1986, The Unreal America: Architecture and Illusion 1997, Frank Lloyd Wright 2004, On Architecture: Collected Reflections on a Century of Change 2008. *Address:* c/o Wall Street Journal, 200 Liberty Street, New York,

NY 10281 (office); 969 Park Avenue, New York, NY 10028, USA. *Telephone:* (212) 416-2000 (office). *Website:* www.wsj.com (office).

HUYGENS, Robert Burchard Constantijn, PhD; Dutch professor of medieval Latin (retd); b. 10 Dec. 1931, The Hague; m. Caroline Sprey 1962; one s. two d.; ed Leiden Univ.; army service 1952–54; Lecturer in Medieval Latin, Univ. of Leiden 1964, Prof. 1968–96; Fellow, Dumbarton Oaks, Washington, DC 1982, Inst. for Advanced Study, Jerusalem 1983–84, Inst. for Advanced Study, Princeton, NJ 1986–87, Herzog August Bibliothek, Wolfenbüttel 1987; mem. Royal Netherlands Acad., Soc. des Antiquaires de France, Monumenta Germaniae Historica; Past Pres. Rotary Club, Leiden. *Publications include:* Jacques de Vitry 1960, Accessus ad Auctores 1970, Vézelay 1976, William of Tyre 1986, Berengar of Tours 1988, Guibert of Nogent 1992, Serta mediaevalia 2000, Ars edendi 2001, Christian of Stavelot 2008. *Address:* Witte Singel 28, 2311 BH Leiden, Netherlands (home). *Telephone:* (71) 5143798 (home).

HUYGHE, Pierre; French artist; b. 1962, Paris; ed École Nationale Supérieure des Arts Decoratifs, Paris; Artist in Residency, DAAD (German Academic Exchange Service), Berlin 1999–2000; Special Award, Jury of the Venice Biennial 2001, Hugo Boss Prize 2002, Prix du meilleur artiste français, Beaux-Arts Magazine Art Awards 2005. *Address:* c/o Marian Goodman Gallery, 24 West 57th Street, New York, NY 10019, USA. *Telephone:* (212) 977-7160. *Fax:* (212) 581-5187. *E-mail:* goodman@mariangoodman.com. *Website:* www.pierrehuyghe.com (office).

HUYGHEBAERT, Jan, LLM; Belgian business executive; *Chairman, KBC Group NV;* ed Catholic Univ., Louvain; Attaché, Science Policy Programme 1970–74; Adviser, Cabinet of Prime Minister Leo Tindemans 1974–78; Alderman, Port of Antwerp 1978–85; Pres. Kredietbank NV 1985–91, Chair. Almanij NV 1991–2005, Chair. KBC Group NV (after merger between Almanij and KBC) 2005–; Chair. Kredietbank Luxembourg. *Address:* KBC Group NV, Havenlaan 2, Brussels 1080, Belgium (office). *Telephone:* (2) 429-50-45 (office). *Fax:* (2) 429-63-40 (office). *E-mail:* jan.huyghebaert@kbc.be (office). *Website:* www.kbc.be (office).

HVEDING, Vidkunn; Norwegian engineer, economist and politician; b. 27 March 1921, Orkdal; s. of Johan Hveding and Ida Marie Hveding (née Songlid); m. 1st Ellen Palmstrom 1948 (divorced 1963); m. 2nd Tone Barth 1963 (died 1980); m. 3rd Grete Blydt Quisler 1986; one s. three d.; ed Norwegian Inst. of Tech. (NTH), Univ. of Trondheim; Eng (design and supervision), various hydro-power projects 1946–54; Assoc. Prof. of Hydro-electric Eng, NTH 1954–56, Prof. 1958–61; Adviser, Ethiopian Electric Light and Power Authority 1956–57; Man. Project Dept, Noreno Brasil SA, São Paulo 1957–58; Asst Dir-Gen. Norwegian Water Resources and Elec. Bd 1961–63; Adviser, Kuwait Fund for Arab Econ. Devt 1963–65; Sec.-Gen. Norwegian Ministry of Industry 1967–68; Chair. and Chief Exec., Norwegian Water Resources and Electricity Bd 1968–75; Planning Man. Industrial Bank of Kuwait 1975–77; Dir of various cos. in banking industry, shipping, consulting 1977–81, 1983–; Minister of Petroleum and Energy 1981–83; Commdr, Royal Order of St Olav. *Publications:* Comprehensive Energy Analysis Norway 1969, Hydropower Development in Norway 1992, articles on hydroelectric power tech., energy econs, resource conservation and political philosophy. *Leisure interests:* skiing, sailing, woodwork. *Address:* Voksen-kollv. 23B, 0790 Oslo, Norway (home). *E-mail:* vidkunn@online.no (home).

HVIDT, Gen. Christian, DFC; Danish air force officer; b. 15 July 1942, Copenhagen; m. 1st; three c.; m. 2nd Jane Hvidt; two step-c.; flying service (F-100 Super Sabre) 1962–69; test pilot on F-35 Draken at SAAB factories, Linköping, Sweden 1969–72; Deputy Squadron Commdr (F-35 Draken) 1972–74; Br. Chief Tactical Air Command, Denmark 1975–79; Squadron Commdr First Danish F-16 Squadron, Air Station Skrydstrup 1979–83; staff officer and Br. Chief Plans and Policy Div., HQ Chodden 1983–87; Commdg Officer Air Station Karup 1987–88; Chief of Staff Tactical Air Command, Denmark 1989–90; Deputy Chief of Staff Plans and Policy, Operations, Budget and Finance HQ Chodden 1991–93; Perm. Danish Rep., NATO Mil. Cttee 1994–96; Chief of Staff, HQ Chodden 1996; Chief of Defence 1996–2002; Grand Cross of the Order of Dannebrog, Danish Air Force Badge of Honour, Badge of Honour of the Danish Reserve Officers Asscn., Medal of Merit of the Home Guard, Commdr, Grand Cross, Royal Swedish Order of the Northern Star, Jordanian Military Order of Merit of the First Degree, Commdr, Cross with the Star of Merit of the Repub. of Poland, Commdr, Légion d'honneur, de l'Ordre Nat. du Mérite. *Address:* c/o Defence Command, PO Box 202, 2950 Vedbaek, Denmark (office).

HVOROSTOVSKY, Dmitri Alexandrovich, (Dmitri Khvorostovsky); Russian opera singer (baritone); b. 17 Oct. 1962, Krasnoyarsk; m. Florence Hvorostovskay; ed Krasnoyarsk Inst. of Arts; debut as opera singer 1984; soloist Krasnoyarsk Opera Theatre 1984–90; winner All-Union Glinka Competition 1987; winner int. competitions in Toulouse, Nice, Cardiff; has gained worldwide reputation after his recitals around the world; performances in La Scala, Covent Garden, Metropolitan Opera and Paris Opéra; roles include The Queen of Spades (Opéra de Nice) 1989, (Metropolitan Opera, New York) 1999, Eugene Onegin (La Fenice) 1991, (Châtelet, Paris) 1992, (Covent Garden) 1993, Il Barbiere di Siviglia (San Francisco Opera) 1991, I Puritani (Covent Garden) 1992, La Traviata (Chicago Lyric Opera) 1993, (Metropolitan Opera, New York) 2003, (Cagliari) 2004, (San Francisco Opera) 2004, (La Fenice) 2004, I Masnadieri (Covent Garden) 1998, 2002, Rigoletto (Novaya Opera, Moscow) 2000, (Covent Garden) 2005, Don Giovanni (Metropolitan Opera, New York) 2002, (Hamburg) 2003, Don Carlos (Zurich Oper) 2003, (Vienna) 2005, Don Juan and Leporello in Don Zhuan bez maski (Don Juan with a Mask) 2003 (film), Pikovaya Dama (Metropolitan Opera, New York) 2004, (Teatro Real, Madrid) 2004, (La Scala, Milan) 2005, War and Peace (Salzburg Festival) 2004, Il Trovatore (Bastille Opera, Paris) 2004, Faust (Metropolitan Opera, New York) 2005; First Prize USSR Nat. Glinka Competition 1987, BBC Cardiff Singer of the World Competition 1989, State Prize of Russia 1991, People's Artist of Russia 1995. *Recordings include:* Tchaikovsky and Verdi Arias, Cavalleria Rusticana, Eugene Onegin, Don Carlos. *Address:* c/o Mark Hildrew, Askonas Holt Ltd, Lincoln House, 300 High Holborn, London, WC1V 7JH, England (office). *Telephone:* (20) 7400-1700 (office). *Fax:* (20) 7400-1799 (office). *E-mail:* mark.hildrew@askonasholt .co.uk (office). *Website:* www.askonasholt.co.uk (office); www.hvorostovsky .com.

HWANG, In-sung; South Korean politician; b. 9 Jan. 1926; ed Korea Mil. Acad. and Seoul Nat. Univ.; army officer 1960–68; Asst Minister without Portfolio 1970; Chief Sec. to Prime Minister 1973; Gov. N Cholla Prov. 1973–78; Minister, Ministry of Transport 1978; Pres. KNTC 1980; mem. Nat. Ass. 1981, 1985, 1992; Minister, Ministry of Agric., Forestry and Fisheries 1985–87; Chair. Asiana Air Lines 1988–93; Pres. Kumho Air Lines 1989–93; Chair. Political Cttee Democratic Liberal Party 1992; Prime Minister of Repub. of Korea March–Dec. 1993. *Address:* c/o Office of the Prime Minister, Seoul, Republic of Korea.

HWANG, Yeong Gi, MBA; South Korean banker and financial services industry executive; *Chairman, KB Financial Group Inc.;* ed Univ. of London, UK; Pres. Woora Bank 2004–07; Adviser, Shin & Kim (law firm), Seoul –2008; Chair. KB Financial Group Inc. (fmrly Kookmin Bank) 2008–. *Address:* KB Financial Group Inc., ADR 9-1, 2-ga, Namdaemoon-ro, Jung-gu Seoul 100-703, South Korea (office). *Telephone:* (2) 2073-8354 (office). *Fax:* (2) 2073-8360 (office). *Website:* www.kookmin-bank.com (office).

HYLAND, J. M(artin) E., DPhil; British mathematician and academic; *Professor of Mathematical Logic, King's College, Cambridge;* b. 1949; ed Univ. of Oxford; currently Prof. in Mathematical Logic and Head of Dept of Pure Math. and Math. Statistics, King's Coll., Cambridge; Pres. British Logic Colloquium; Vice-Pres. Cambridge Philosophical Soc.; mem. Bd of Eds Mathematical Proceedings, Cambridge Philosophical Soc.; mem. Man. Cttee Isaac Newton Inst. for Math. Sciences. *Address:* Department of Pure Mathematics and Mathematical Statistics, King's College, University of Cambridge, Cambridge, CB2 1ST, England (office). *Telephone:* (1223) 337986 (office). *Fax:* (1223) 337986 (office). *E-mail:* j.m.e.hyland@dpmms.cam.ac.uk (office). *Website:* www.dpmms.cam.ac.uk (office); www.statslab.cam.ac.uk (office).

HYLTON, G. Anthony, BA, JD, LLM; Jamaican lawyer and politician; b. 27 April 1957, Yallahs, St Thomas; ed Kingston Coll., Morgan State Univ. and Georgetown Univ., USA, Univ. of London, UK; lawyer with Melnicove, Kaufman, Weiner and Smouse, Baltimore, 1983–85, with Curtis, Mallet-Prevost, Colt and Mosle, New York 1986–88, with Dickstein, Shapiro and Morin, Washington DC 1988–89; fmr legal asst to Gen. Counsel Inter-American Foundation; fmr Dir Jamaica Public Service Co.; mem. Parl. for Western St Thomas 1993–2002; Exec. Dir of Legal and Foreign Affairs, Policy Review Unit, Ministry of Foreign Affairs and Trade 1990–93, Minister of State 1993–2001; Minister of Mining and Energy 2001–02; Amb. and Special Prime Ministerial Envoy 2002–06; Minister of Foreign Affairs and Foreign Trade 2006–07, also mem. of Senate; negotiator at WTO, Contonou Agreement, Free Trade Area of the Americas and CARICOM; Chair. Inst. of Law and Econs, People's Nat. Party Policy Comm.; Chair. Commercial Div., Coffee Industry Bd; mem. Md and Jamaica Bar Asscns; Nat. Honours from Govt of Benin. *Leisure interests:* dominos, music, writing, debating, sport. *Address:* People's National Party, 89 Old Hope Road, Kingston 5, Jamaica (office). *Telephone:* 978-1337 (office). *Fax:* 927-4389 (office). *E-mail:* information@pnpjamaica.com (office). *Website:* www.pnpjamaica.com (office).

HYMAN, Timothy; British painter and writer; b. 17 April 1946, Hove; s. of Alan Hyman and Noreen Gypson; m. Judith Ravenscroft 1982; ed Charter-house and Slade School of Fine Art, London; Curator Narrative Paintings at Arnolfini and ICA Galleries, etc. 1979–80; public collections include Arts Council, Bristol City Art Gallery, Museum of London, Contemporary Art Soc., British Museum, Govt Art Collection, Los Angeles Co. Museum; Visiting Prof. at Baroda, India, two British Council lecture tours 1981–83; Artist-in-Residence, Lincoln Cathedral 1983–84, Sandown Racecourse 1992; Purchaser for Arts Council Collection 1985; selector, John Moores Prize 1995; Lead Curator Stanley Spencer retrospective exhbn, Tate Gallery, London 2001–; Co-curator British Vision, Museum of Fine Arts, Ghent 2007; Leverhulme Award 1992, Rootstein Hopkins Foundation Award 1995, Wingate Award 1998, Medaglio Beato Angelico, Florence 2005, Nat. Portrait Gallery/BP Travel Award 2007. *Publications:* Hodgkin 1975, Kitaj 1977, Beckmann 1978, Balthus 1980, Narrative Paintings 1979, English Romanesque 1984, Kiff 1986, Domenico Tiepolo 1987, Bhupen Khakhar (monograph) 1998, Bonnard (monograph) 1998, Carnivalesque (catalogue) 2000, Stanley Spencer (catalogue) 2001, Sienese Painting (monograph) 2003; numerous articles on contemporary figurative painting in London Magazine, Artscribe, Times Literary Supplement 1975–. *Leisure interests:* the novels of John Cowper Powys, reading, travel, cinema, walking London. *Address:* 62 Myddelton Square, London, EC1R, England. *Telephone:* (20) 7837-1933.

HYND, Ronald; British choreographer; b. 22 April 1931, London; s. of William John Hens and Alice Louisa Griffiths; m. Annette Page 1957; one d.; ed Holloway Co. School, numerous wartime emergency schools; trained with Marie Rambert 1946; joined Ballet Rambert 1949, Royal Ballet (then known as Sadler's Wells Ballet) 1952 (Prin. Dancer 1959–70); Ballet Dir Bavarian State Opera 1970–73, 1984–86; freelance choreographer; ballets presented by numerous int. ballet cos, including English Nat. Ballet, Royal Sadler's Wells, La Scala Milan, Deutsche Oper Berlin, Vienna State Opera, Houston Ballet,

Bavarian State Opera, American Ballet Theater, Australian Ballet, Santiago Ballet, Tokyo Ballet, Canadian Nat. Ballet, Grands Ballets Canadiens, Dutch Nat. Ballet, Northern Ballet, Slovenian Nat. Ballet, South African State Theatre Ballet, Tulsa Ballet Theater, Royal Danish Ballet, Ballet Maggio Musicale, Florence and Pacific Northwest Ballet, Ballet West, USA, Cincinnati Ballet, Bonn Opera, Ballet de Nice Opera, New London Ballet, Hong Kong Ballet. *Works choreographed include:* Three Act Ballets: Merry Widow 1975 (11 productions), The Nutcracker 1976, Rosalinda 1978 (ten productions), Papillon 1979, Le Diable à Quatre 1984, Coppelia 1985, Ludwig II 1986, The Hunchback of Notre Dame 1988, The Sleeping Beauty 1993; one act ballets include: The Fairy's Kiss 1967, Dvorak Variations 1970, Wendekreise 1971, Mozartiana 1972, Das Telefon 1972, Marco Polo 1975, Sanguine Fan 1976, La Chatte 1978, Les Valses 1981, Seasons 1982, Scherzo Capriccioso 1982, Fanfare 1985, Liaisons Amoureuses 1989, Ballade 1989. *Choreography for:* Galileo (film) 1974, La Traviata (BBC TV) 1974, Amahl and Night Visitors (BBC TV) 1975, ice ballets for John Curry 1977, The Sound of Music 1981, Camelot 1982, Sylvia for Princess Diana's 30th Birthday Banquet 1992, Merry Widow (TV and video in Canada and Australia), Rosalinda (Slovenian TV), Sanguine Fan (BBC TV), Nutcracker (BBC TV). *Leisure interests:* gardens, music, travel. *Address:* Fern Cottage, Upper Somerton, Bury St Edmunds, Suffolk, IP29 4ND, England (home). *Telephone:* (1284) 789284 (home). *Fax:* (1284) 789284 (home).

HYNDE, Chrissie; American singer, songwriter and musician; b. 7 Sept. 1951, Akron, Ohio; one d. with Ray Davies; m. 1st Jim Kerr (divorced); one d.; m. 2nd Lucho Brieva 1999; contrib. to New Musical Express; Co-Founder Chrissie Hynde and the Pretenders 1978–, singer, songwriter and guitarist, new band formed 1983; tours in Britain, Europe and USA; platinum and gold discs in USA; Ivor Novello Award for Outstanding Contrib. to British Music 1999. *Singles include:* Stop Your Sobbing (debut) 1978, Kid 1979, Brass in Pocket 1979, I Go to Sleep 1982, Back on the Chain Gang 1982, Middle of the Road 1984, Thin Line Between Love and Hate, Don't Get Me Wrong 1986, Hymn to Her 1987, Night in my Veins 1994, I'll Stand By You 1994, Human 1999. *Albums include:* Pretenders (debut) 1980, Pretenders II 1981, Extended Play 1981, Learn to Crawl 1985, Get Close 1986, The Singles 1987, Packed! 1990, Last of the Independents 1994, The Isle of View 1995, Viva El Amor 1999, Loose Screw 2002, Break Up the Concrete 2008. *Address:* c/o Shangri-La Music, 2202 Main Street, Santa Monica, CA 90405, USA. *Website:* www .shangrilamusic.com; www.thepretenders.com.

HYNES, James T., AB, PhD; American chemist and academic; *Professor of Chemistry, University of Colorado;* b. 16 Oct. 1943, Miami Beach, Fla; ed Catholic Univ., Princeton Univ.; Post-Doctoral Fellow, MIT 1969–70; Asst Prof., Univ. of Colo, Boulder 1971–76, Assoc. Prof. 1976–79, Faculty Foundation Fellow 1978–79, Prof. of Chem. 1979–, Faculty Fellow 1986–87, Research Lecturer, Council on Research and Creative Work 1988; Visiting Assoc. Prof., Univ. of Toronto, Canada 1978–79; Visiting Prof., Univ. of Paris VI, France 1985, 1987, Univ. Autonoma de Barcelona, Spain 1995, Univ. Paris Sud, France 1997; Visiting Sr Research Fellow, Univ. of Oxford, England 1985, Visiting Prof. 1987; Visiting Prof., Ecole Normale Supérieure (ENS), Paris 1997, CNRS Dir of Research, ENS 1999–; American Ed. Progress in Reaction Kinetics and Mechanism 1999–2005; Co-Chair. Editorial Bd ChemPhysChem-A European Journal 1999–; mem. Editorial Bd Journal of Physical Chemistry 1990–98, Journal of Molecular Liquids 1991–, International Journal of Quantum Chemistry 1993–97; mem. ACS (Vice Chair. Theoretical Div. 1984, Chair. 1986), French Chemical Soc.; Fellow, American Physical Soc. 2000–, American Acad. of Arts and Sciences 2008–; ACS Nobel Laureate Signature Award 1983, Nat. Science Foundation Creativity Award 1991, Hirschfelder Prize in Theoretical Chemistry 2004, ISI Highly Cited Researcher 2002, ACS Hildebrand Award in Theoretical and Experimental Chem. of Liquids 2005. *Address:* Department of Chemistry and Biochemistry, University of Colorado, Campus Box 215, Boulder, CO 80309, USA (office); Dept de Chimie, Ecole Normale Superieure, 24 rue Lhomond, 75231 Paris, France (office). *Telephone:* (303) 492-6926 (USA) (office); (1) 44-32-32-78 (France) (office). *Fax:* (303) 492-5894 (USA) (office); (1) 44-32-33-25 (France) (office). *E-mail:* james.hynes@colorado.edu (office); hynes@chimie.ens.fr (office). *Website:* www.colorado.edu/chemistry (office); www.chimie.ens.fr/ w3hynes (office).

HYNES, Samuel, DFC, PhD, FRSL; American academic and writer; *Professor Emeritus, Department of English, Princeton University;* b. 29 Aug. 1924, Chicago; s. of Samuel Lynn and Margaret Hynes (née Turner); m. Elizabeth Igleheart 1944; two d.; ed Univ. of Minnesota, Columbia Univ.; served in USMCR 1943–46, 1952–53; mem. Faculty, Swarthmore Coll. 1949–68, Prof. of English Literature 1965–68; Prof. of English, Northwestern Univ., Evanston, Ill. 1968–76; Prof. of English, Princeton Univ. 1976–90, Woodrow Wilson Prof. of Literature 1978–90, Prof. Emer. 1990–; Fulbright Fellow 1953–54; Guggenheim Fellow 1959–60, 1981–82; Bollingen Fellow 1964–65; American Council of Learned Socs Fellow 1969, 1985–86; Nat. Endowment for Humanities Sr Fellow 1973–74, 1977–78; American Acad. of Arts and Letters Award in Literature 2004. *Publications:* The Pattern of Hardy's Poetry (Explicator Award 1962) 1961, William Golding 1964, The Edwardian Turn of Mind 1968, Edwardian Occasions 1972, The Auden Generation 1976, Flights of Passage:

Reflections of a World War Two Aviator 1988, A War Imagined: The First World War and English Culture 1990, The Soldiers' Tale (Robert F. Kennedy Book Award 1998) 1997, The Growing Seasons: An American Boyhood Before the War 2003; Ed.: Further Speculations by T. E. Hulme 1955, The Author's Craft and Other Critical Writings of Arnold Bennett 1968, Romance and Realism 1979, Complete Poetical Works of Thomas Hardy, Vol. I 1982, Vol. II 1984, Vol. III 1985, Vols IV, V 1995, Thomas Hardy 1984, Complete Short Fiction of Joseph Conrad (Vol. I–III) 1992, (Vol. IV) 1993. *Address:* 130 Moore Street, Princeton, NJ 08540 (home); Department of English, 22 McCosh Hall, Princeton University, Princeton, NJ 08544-1006, USA (office). *Website:* web .princeton.edu/sites/english/new_web/index.htm (office).

HYSENI, Skënder; Kosovo politician; *Minister of Foreign Affairs;* b. 17 Feb. 1955, Dobratin; m. Drita Hyseni; two s. two d.; ed Dept of English Language and Literature, Univ. of Priština, Bloomberg State Coll., USA, Aberdeen Univ., UK; early political career with newly est. Democratic League of Kosava 1989, began working with Kosovo Information Center 1992 as journalist and interpreter; Co-founder and Ed. Kosova Daily Report; Adviser to Pres. Ibrahim Rugova 1992–2006, to Pres. Fatmir Sejdiu 2006–; Spokesperson Kosovo negotiating team that took part in UN-sponsored talks with Serbia, launched in 2006; mem. Kuvendi i Kosovës/Skupština Kosova (Kosovo Ass.) (Parl.), Minister of Culture, Youth and Sports Jan.–April 2008, of Foreign Affairs April 2008–; mem. Kosovo Democratic League, mem. of Presidency and Chair. Ctte for External Relations; mem. Constitutional Comm. charged with compiling first draft of Constitution of Kosovo. *Address:* Office of the Government of Kosovo, 10000 Priština; Kuvendi i Kosovës/Skupština Kosova (Kosovo Assembly), 10000 Priština, Rruga Nënë Terezë, Kosovo. *Telephone:* (38) 211186 (Ass.). *Fax:* (38) 211188 (Ass.). *Website:* www.ks-gov.net; www .assembly-kosova.org.

HYTNER, Nicholas Robert, MA; British theatre director; *Artistic Director, Royal National Theatre;* b. 7 May 1956, Manchester; s. of Benet A. Hytner and Joyce Myers; ed Manchester Grammar School and Trinity Hall, Cambridge; staff producer, ENO 1978–80; Assoc. Dir Royal Exchange Theatre, Manchester 1985–89; Assoc. Dir Royal Nat. Theatre 1989–97, Artistic Dir 2003–; Evening Standard Opera Award 1985, Evening Standard Best Dir Award 1989. *Theatre and opera productions include:* Wagner's Rienzi (ENO) 1983, Tippett's King Priam (Kent Opera) 1984, Handel's Xerxes (ENO) (Olivier Award 1985), The Scarlet Pimpernel (Chichester Festival) 1985, As You Like It, Edward II, The Country Wife, Schiller's Don Carlos, (Royal Exchange) 1986, Handel's Giulio Cesare (Paris Opera), Measure for Measure (RSC) 1987, Tippett's The Knot Garden (Royal Opera), The Magic Flute (ENO), The Tempest (RSC) 1988, The Marriage of Figaro (Geneva Opera), Joshua Sobol's Ghetto (Nat. Theatre), Miss Saigon (Theatre Royal, Drury Lane) 1989, King Lear (RSC) 1990, The Wind in the Willows (Nat. Theatre) 1990, Volpone (Almeida) 1990, The Madness of George III (Nat. Theatre) 1991, The Recruiting Officer (Nat. Theatre) 1992, Carousel (Nat. Theatre) (Tony Award for Best Dir of a Musical 1994) 1992, The Importance of Being Earnest, Aldwych 1993, Don Giovanni (Bavarian State Opera) 1994, The Cunning Little Vixen (Paris) 1995, The Cripple of Inishmaan 1997, The Crucible 1997, The Lady in the Van 1999, Cressida 2000, Orpheus Descending 2000, The Winter's Tale (Nat. Theatre) 2001, Mother Clap's Molly House (Nat. Theatre) 2001, Sweet Smell of Success (Broadway) 2002, The History Boys (Nat. Theatre) (Olivier Award for Best Director 2004, Tony Award for Best Director 2006) 2004, Cosí fan Tutte (Glyndebourne) 2006, The Man of Mode (Nat. Theatre) 2007, The Rose Tattoo (Nat. Theatre) 2007, England People Very Nice (Nat. Theatre) 2009. *Films:* The Madness of King George 1994, The Crucible 1996, The Object of My Affection 1998, The History Boys 2006. *Address:* c/o Askonas Holt, Lincoln House, 300 High Holborn, London, WC1V 7JH, England (office); c/o Royal National Theatre, South Bank, London, SE1 9PX, England. *Telephone:* (20) 7400-1700 (office). *Fax:* (20) 7400-1799 (office). *E-mail:* info@askonasholt.co.uk (office). *Website:* www.askonasholt.co.uk (office); www.nationaltheatre.org.uk.

HYUN, Jeong-eun, MA; South Korean business executive; *Chairwoman, Hyundai Merchant Marine Co., Ltd;* m. Chung Mong-hun (died 2003); three c.; ed Ewha Woman's Univ., Fairleigh Dickinson Univ., USA; named Chair. in 2003 following suicide of her husband, Hyundai's Chair. and heir apparent, after he was charged with hiding govt fund transfers to N Korea, currently Chair. Hyundai Group and its affiliate cos Hyundai Asan, Hyundai Elevator, Hyundai Logistics, Hyundai Merchant Marine, Hyundai Research Inst., Hyundai Securities; Chair. Hyundai Merchant Marine Co. Ltd. (holding co. of Hyundai Group and cos 2007–; mem. Bd of Dirs Girl Scouts of Korea; mem. Special Advisory Cttee, Woman Volunteers of Korea Red Cross, Civil Service Comm., Presidential Cttee on GoVea; ranked 36th by The Wall Street Journal amongst Fifty Woman to Watch 2007, ranked by Forbes magazine amongst 100 Most Powerful Women (73rd) 2008; elected mem. Pinnacle Soc., Fairleigh Dickinson Univ. 2006. *Address:* Hyundai Merchant Marine Co., Ltd, 66 Jeokseon-dong, Jongno-gu, 110-052 Seoul, South Korea (office). *Telephone:* (2) 3706-5114 (office). *Fax:* (2) 736-8517 (office). *E-mail:* webmaster@ hyundaigroup.com (office). *Website:* www.hmm.co.kr (office); www .hyundaigroup.com (office).

I

IACOCCA, Lee A.; American business executive; *Chairman, Iacocca Foundation;* b. 15 Oct. 1924, Allentown, Pa; s. of Nicola Iacocca and Antoinette Perrotto; m. 1st Mary McCleary 1956 (died 1983); two d.; m. 2nd Peggy Johnson 1986 (divorced); m. 3rd Darrien Earle 1991; ed Lehigh and Princeton Univs; with Ford Motor Co. 1946; Dist Sales Man., Washington 1956; Ford Div. Truck Marketing Man. 1956; Car Marketing Man. 1957; Vice-Pres. and Gen. Man., Ford Div. 1960–65; Vice-Pres. Car and Truck Group 1965; Exec. Vice-Pres., North American Automotive Operations 1967; Exec. Vice-Pres., Ford Motor Co. and Pres. Ford North American Automotive Operations 1969–70, Pres. Ford Motor Co. 1970–78; Pres., COO, Chrysler Corpn 1978–79, Chair. 1979–93, CEO 1979–93, Dir –1993; Prin. Iacocca Pnrs 1994–; Acting Chair. Kro Koo Roo Inc. 1998; Pres. Iacocca Assocs, LA 1994–; Founding Chair. CEO EV Global Motors Co.; f. Olivio Premium Products 2000; Fellow, Princeton Univ.; mem. Soc. Automotive Engineers; Chair. of Presidential Comm. to restore Statue of Liberty 1982–86; mem. Nat. Acad. of Eng 1986–; Founder and Chair. Iacocca Foundation 1984–; Kt, Order of Labour (Italy) 1989; Dr hc (Muhlenberg Coll., Babson Inst.); Detroit's Man of the Year 1982; Jefferson Award 1985. *Publications:* Iacocca, An Autobiography (with William Novak) 1984, Talking Straight 1988, Where Have All the Leaders Gone? 2007. *Address:* Iacocca Foundation, 17 Arlington Street, Boston, MA 02116, USA (office). *Telephone:* (617) 267-7747 (office). *Website:* www.iacoccafoundation .org; www.olivioproducts.com (office).

IACOVOU, Georgios Kyriakou, MA, MSc; Cypriot politician and diplomatist; b. 19 July 1938, Peristeronopigi, Famagusta Dist; s. of Kyriacos Iacovou and Maria Michalopoulou; m. Jennifer Bradley 1963; one s. three d.; ed Greek Gymnasium for Boys, Famagusta and Univ. of London; Eng, Cyprus Building and Road Construction Corpn Ltd 1960–61; Man. Electron Ltd, Nicosia 1961–63; with Operations Research and Finance Depts, British Railways Bd, London 1964–68; Sr Consultant (Man.), Price Waterhouse Assocs, London 1968–72; Dir Cyprus Productivity Centre, Nicosia 1972–76; Dir Special Service for Care and Rehabilitation of Displaced Persons 1974–76; Chief, E African Region, UNHCR, Geneva 1976–79; Amb. to FRG (also accred to Austria and Switzerland) 1979–83; Dir-Gen. Ministry of Foreign Affairs Jan.–Sept. 1983; Minister of Foreign Affairs 1983–93, 2003–06; High Commr to UK 2006–07; Pres. and CEO Nat. Foundation of Overseas and Repatriated Greeks 1993–97; presidential cand., Cyprus presidential elections 1998; Pres. Cttee of Ministers, Council of Europe 1983; participated in Commonwealth Heads of State and Govt Confs in Delhi 1983, Bahamas 1985, Vancouver 1987, Kuala Lumpur 1989 and non-Aligned Summit, Harare 1986, Belgrade 1989; Chair. Ministerial Conf. of Non-Aligned Movt, Nicosia 1988; Hon. Citizen, Tsalka, Georgia and City of Sappes, Thrace, Greece; Hon. Prof., Donetsk State Univ., Ukraine; Grosses Verdienstkreuz mit Stern und Schulterband (FRG), Grosses Goldenes Ehrenzeichen (Austria), Grand Cross, Order of Phoenix (Greece), Grand Cross of the Order of Isabella the Catholic (Spain), Grand Cross of the Order of Honour (Greece), Order of the Flag with Sash (Yugoslavia), Order of the Repub. First Class (Egypt), Grand Cross of Infante D. Henrique (Portugal), Decoration of the Cross of St Mark of the First Order of the Patriarchate of Alexandria and All Africa, Decoration of St Catherine's Monastery of Sinai; Dr hc (State Univ. of Tbilisi, Georgia), (Panteion Univ. Athens); Meritorious Service Award, Municipality of Peristeri, Athens. *Address:* c/o Ministry of Foreign Affairs, Presidential Palace Avenue, 1447 Nicosia, Cyprus. *Telephone:* (22) 401000. *E-mail:* minforeign1@mfa.gov.cy.

IBARRETXE MARKUARTU, Juan José, BEcons; Spanish politician; b. 15 May 1957, Llodio, Alava; ed Llodio Secondary School, Univ. of the Basque Country; mem. Partido Nacionalista Vaso (PNV); Mayor of Llodio 1983–87; Pres. Alava Prov. Parl. 1986–91; mem. Basque Parl., Chair. Econ. and Budgetary Comm. 1986–90, 1991–94; Vice-Pres. Basque Govt and Minister for Inland Revenue and Public Admin 1995–98, Pres. 1999–2009; fmr mem. Univ. of the Basque Country Social Council. *Address:* Euzko Alderdi Jeltzalea-Partido Nacionalista Vasco, Sabin Etxea, Ibáñez de Bilbao 16, 48001 Bilbao, Spain.

IBBS, Sir (John) Robin, Kt, KBE, MA, DSc, LLD, AM IMechE, FCIB, FRSA, FRSocMed; British business executive; b. 21 April 1926, Birmingham; s. of the late Prof. T. L. Ibbs and of Marjorie Bell; m. Iris Barbara Hall 1952 (died 2005); one d.; ed Gresham's School, Upper Canada Coll., Toronto, Univ. of Toronto, Trinity Coll., Cambridge and Lincoln's Inn; called to Bar 1952; Instructor Lt, RN 1947–49; C. A. Parsons & Co. Ltd 1949–51; joined ICI 1952, held various eng, tech., production, commercial and gen. man. appointments at Head Office, Gen. Chemicals Div. and Metals Div.; Man. Planning Dept, Imperial Metal Industries Ltd 1969–74, Exec. Dir 1972–74, Dir (non-exec.) 1974–76; Gen. Man. Planning, ICI 1974–76, Exec. Dir 1976–80, 1982–88; Dir ICI Americas Inc. 1976–80; Dir ICI Australia Ltd 1982–87; Dir Lloyds Bank PLC 1985–97, Deputy Chair. 1988–93, Chair. 1993–97; Deputy Chair. Lloyds Bank Canada 1989–90; Chair. Lloyds TSB Group PLC 1995–97; Chair. Lloyds Merchant Bank Holdings Ltd 1989–92; mem. Industrial Devt Advisory Bd, Dept of Industry 1978–80, Head, Cen. Policy Review Staff, Cabinet Office 1980–82; mem. Council, Chemical Industries Asscn 1976–80, 1982–88, Vice-Pres. 1983–87, Hon. mem. 1987; mem. Governing Body and Council, British Nat. Cttee, ICC 1976–80, Chair. Finance and Gen. Purposes Cttee 1976–80; mem. Council of CBI 1982–87; mem. Top Salaries Review Body 1983–88; mem. Council, Royal Inst. of Int. Affairs, Chatham House 1983–89; mem. Court, Cranfield Inst. of Tech. 1983–88; Adviser to the Prime Minister on Efficiency and Effectiveness in Govt 1983–88; mem. Advisory Cttee on Business Appointments 1991–98; second mem. Sierra Leone Arms Investigation 1998; Trustee and Deputy Chair. Isaac Newton Trust 1988–99; leader of review of House of Commons services 1990; Chair. Council, Univ. Coll., London 1989–95; Pres. Bankers Club 1994–95; Vice-Pres. Chartered Inst. of Bankers 1993–97; mem. Council Foundation for Science and Tech. 1997–2002; Chair. Salisbury Cathedral Close Preservation Soc.; Hon. Fellow Univ. Coll., London 1993, Hon. Bencher Lincoln's Inn 1999; Hon. DSc (Bradford) 1986; Hon. LLD (Bath) 1993. *Leisure interests:* walking, natural history, gardening, social history, music and arts. *Address:* c/o Lloyds TSB Group, 25 Gresham Street, London, EC2V 7HN, England. *Telephone:* (20) 7626-1500.

IBERS, James Arthur, PhD; American chemist and academic; *Charles E. and Emma H. Morrison Professor of Chemistry, Northwestern University;* b. 9 June 1930, Los Angeles, Calif.; s. of Max Ibers and Esther Ibers (née Imerman); m. Joyce Audrey Henderson 1951; one s. one d.; ed Calif. Inst. of Tech.; NSF Post-doctoral Fellow, Melbourne, Australia 1954–55; chemist, Shell Devt Co. 1955–61, Brookhaven Nat. Lab. 1961–64; mem. Faculty Northwestern Univ. 1964–, Prof. of Chem. 1964–85, Charles E. and Emma H. Morrison Prof. of Chem. 1986–; mem. NAS, American Acad. of Arts and Sciences, ACS, American Crystallographic Asscn; ACS Inorganic Chem. Award 1978, ACS Distinguished Service Award 1992, ACS Pauling Medal 1994, Distinguished Alumni Award, Calif. Inst. of Tech. 1997, American Crystallographic Asscn Buerger Award 2002. *Address:* Department of Chemistry, Tech G147, Northwestern University, Evanston, IL 60208-3113, USA (office). *Telephone:* (847) 491-5449 (office). *Fax:* (847) 491-2976 (office). *E-mail:* ibers@chem.northwestern.edu (office). *Website:* www.chem.northwestern .edu/~ibers (office).

IBOBI SINGH, Okram, BA; Indian politician and social worker; *Chief Minister of Manipur;* b. 19 June 1948, Thoubal Athokpam Makha Leikai; s. of Angoubi Singh; m. Landhoni Devi; one s. two d.; mem. Manipur Legis. Ass. 1984–; Chair. Khadi and Village Industries Board 1985–88; fmr Minister of Municipal Admin, Housing and Urban Devt and of Industries, Manipur; Chief Minister of Manipur 2002–; Pres. Manipur Pradesh Congress Cttee 1999–; Sec. Congress Legislature Party. *Leisure interest:* reading. *Address:* Chief Minister's Secretariat, Imphal 795 001, Manipur, India (office). *Telephone:* (385) 2225206 (office). *E-mail:* cmmani@hub.nic.in (office). *Website:* manipur .nic.in (office).

IBRAGIMBEKOV, Maksud Mamed Ibragim ogli; Azerbaijani/Russian writer, scriptwriter and playwright; b. 1935, Baku; s. of Mamed Ibragim Ibragimbekov and Fatima Alekper-kyzy Meshadibekova; m. Anna Yuryebna Ibragimbekova (née Gerulaitis); one s.; ed Baku Polytech. Inst., High Scenario and Directoral Courses, Moscow; Supt Aztyazhpromstroi 1960–62; freelance scriptwriter, theatre dir 1964–; mem. USSR Union of Writers 1965–; mem. Azerbaijan Parl. 1985–2005; Pres. PEN Club, Azerbaijan 1991–; Chair. Nobility Ass. of Azerbaijan; Order of Labour Red Banner 1981, Order of Glory of Azerbaijan Repub. 1995; State Prize of Azerbaijan Repub. 1975, People's Writer of Azerbaijan 1998. *Films:* Latest Night of Childhood, Djabish-muallim, Who is Going to Travel to Truskavets?, Latest Interview. *Plays:* Mesozoic Story (Moscow Maly Theatre) 1975, Death of All the Good (Leningrad Theatre of Young Spectator) 1978, Men for Young Woman (Dramatic Theatre) 1992, The Oil Boom is Smiling on Everyone 2002. *Television:* Gold Voyage 1993, The History with Happy End 1998. *Publications:* Who is Going to Travel to Truskavets?, There Was Never a Better Brother, Let Him Stay With Us; novels and prose in magazines and separate editions. *Leisure interests:* travelling, gardening. *Address:* 28 Boyuk Qala str., 370004 Baku (office); 38 Kutkashenli str., 370006 Baku, Azerbaijan (home). *Telephone:* (12) 4929843 (office); (12) 4975300 (home). *Fax:* (12) 4928459 (office). *E-mail:* maksud@planet-az.com (office); Maksud@azeurotel.com (home).

IBRAGIMBEKOV, Rustam Mamed Ibragimovich; Azerbaijani/Russian screenwriter and writer; b. 5 Feb. 1939, Baku; s. of Mamed Ibragim Ibragimbekov and Fatima Alekper-kyzy Meshadibekova; m. Shokhrat Soltan-kyzy Ibragimbekova; one s., one d.; ed Azerbaijan State Inst. of Oil and Gas; Chair. Confed. Unions of Cinematographers of CIS and Baltic States; Sec. Union of Cinematographers of Russian Fed.; Chair. Jewish Film Festival in Moscow; Chair. Union of Cinematographers of Azerbaijan, Confederation of Filmmakers' Unions (CFU); Sec., Russian Filmmakers' Union; mem. European Film Acad. Felix, American Acad. of Cinema Oscar; Order for Service to Motherland, Commdr des Arts et des Lettres; USSR State Prize 1981, State Prizes of Russian Fed. 1993, 1998, 1999, 2000, State Prize of Azerbaijan SSR 1980, Comsomol Prize 1979. *Film scripts include:* In This Young Town 1971, White Sun of the Desert 1971, Then I Said No 1974, Heart... Heart 1976, Country House for One Family 1978, Strategy of Risk 1979, Interrogation 1979, Mystery of Vessel Watch 1981, Birthday 1983, In Front of the Closed Door 1985, Save Me, My Talisman 1986, Free Fall, Other Life 1987, Cathedral of Air 1989, Hitchhiking, Taxi-Blues (producer) 1989, Seven Days After Murder, To See Paris and To Die 1990, Duba-Duba (producer) 1990, Urga Territory of Love (producer) 1992, Destroyed Bridges (also producer) 1993, Tired with the Sun 1994, The Man Who Tried (jtly) 1997, Barber of Siberia, Family (also dir and producer) 1998, East–West 1999; Mysteria 2000, Karu süda 2001, Nomad (The Warrior) (also producer) 2005, Proshaj, yuzhny gorod (also producer) 2006. *Plays:* 15 plays produced including A Woman Behind a Closed Door, Funeral in California, A House on the Sand, Like a Lion. *Publications:* 10 books and collections of stories including Ultimatum 1983, Woken Up with a Smile 1985, Country House 1988, Selected Stories 1989, Solar Plexus 1996. *Address:* Russian Filmmakers' Union, 3 Vasilevskaya St,

Moscow 123825, Russia (office); Lermontova str. 3, Apt. 54, 370006 Baku, Azerbaijan (home). *Telephone:* (495) 250-18-41 (office); (12) 4926313 (home).

IBRAHIM, Abdul Latif, PhD; Bangladeshi professor of veterinary physiology; b. 1938; ed Bangladesh Agric. Univ., Univs of Hawaii and California, USA; Lecturer, Faculty of Veterinary Medicine and Animal Science, Univ. of Pertanian, Malaysia 1973, later Prof., Dean 1983–93; known for research on Newcastle Disease; Fellow, Islamic Acad. of Sciences 1988–, Malaysia Acad. of Sciences; Svon Brohult Award, First Int. Science Award (jtly), Malaysia. *Publications:* over 120 publs on animal science. *Address:* c/o Islamic Academy of Sciences, PO Box 830036, Amman, Jordan (office). *Telephone:* 5522104 (office). *Fax:* 5511803 (office). *Website:* www.vet.upm.edu.my (office).

IBRAHIM, Encik Anwar bin, BA; Malaysian politician; *Advisor, Parti Keadilan Rakyat (People's Justice Party);* b. 10 Aug. 1947, Penang; m. Dr. Wan Azizah Wan Ismail; six c.; ed Univ. of Malaya; Pres. UMNO Youth Movt 1982–; Vice-Pres. UMNO 1982–; Head UMNO Permatang Pauh Div. 1982–; Deputy Minister, Prime Minister's Dept 1982; Minister of Sport, Youth and Culture 1983, of Agric. 1984–86, of Educ. 1986–91, of Finance 1991–98; Deputy Prime Minister 1993–98; arrested Sept. 1998; sentenced to six years' imprisonment for corruption April 1999; put on trial for sodomy 1999; sentenced to nine years' imprisonment and banned for five years from running for public office after release; sodomy conviction overturned, released from prison Sept. 2004; Visiting Lecturer Johns Hopkins Univ., Georgetown Univ., USA and Univ. of Oxford, UK 2005–07; Advisor People's Justice Party (Parti Keadilan Rakyat, PKR) 2006–; Chair. Foundation for the Future 2006–; Hon. Pres. AccountAbility 2005. *Address:* People's Justice (Party Parti Keadilan Rakyat, PKR), 110–3 Jalan Tun Sambanthan, 50470 Kuala Lumpur, Malaysia (office). *Telephone:* (3) 22723220 (office). *Fax:* (3) 22721220 (office). *E-mail:* contact@partikeadilanrakyat.org (office). *Website:* www .keadilanrakyat.org (office); www.anwaribrahim.com (home).

IBRAHIM, Fahad Rashid al-; Kuwaiti business executive and international organization executive; currently Dir-Gen. Inter-Arab Investment Guarantee Corpn. *Address:* Inter-Arab Investment Guarantee Corporation, PO Box 23568, Safat 13096, Kuwait City, Kuwait (office). *Telephone:* 4959000 (office). *Fax:* 4841240 (office). *E-mail:* fahad@iai.org.kw (office). *Website:* www.iaigc .org (office).

IBRAHIM, Izzat; Iraqi politician; b. 1942, al-Dour Shire; Ed. Voice of the Peasant 1968, Head Supreme Cttee for People's Work 1968–70; Minister of Agrarian Reform 1970–74; Vice-Pres. Supreme Agric. Council 1970–71, Head 1971–79; Minister of Agriculture 1973–74, of the Interior 1974–79; mem. Revolutionary Command Council, Vice-Pres. 1979–2003; Deputy Sec.-Gen. Regional Command of Arab Baath Socialist Party 1979–2003; mem. Nat. Command Arab Baath Socialist Party –2003, Leader Baath Party 2007–.

IBRAHIM, Mohamed (Mo), BSc, MSc, PhD; British (b. Sudanese) telecommunications industry executive; *Founder, Mo Ibrahim Foundation;* b. 1946; ed Univ. of Alexandria, Egypt, Univs of Bradford and Birmingham, UK; worked for Sudan Telecom; Tech. Dir Cellnet (subsidiary of British Telecom) 1983–89, involved in establishing the UK's first mobile telephone network; f. MSI consultancy and software firm 1989, est. MSI Cellular Investments (later renamed Celtel) 1998, built co. into one of leading mobile telephone networks in Africa, sold Celtel to Kuwaiti MTC 2005; Founder and mem. Bd of Dirs Mo Ibrahim Foundation, foundation's work includes Ibrahim Index of African Governance and Prize for Achievement in African Leadership; mem. Africa Regional Advisory Bd, London Business School. *Address:* Mo Ibrahim Foundation, 3rd Floor North, 35 Portman Square, London W1H 6LR, England (office). *E-mail:* info@moibrahimfoundation.org (office). *Website:* www .moibrahimfoundation.org (office).

IBRAHIM, Mohamed Rasheed; Maldivian judge; Chief Justice, Supreme Court. *Address:* Supreme Court of the Maldives, Malé, Maldives. *Telephone:* 3323092. *Fax:* 3316471.

IBRAHIM, Muhyadin Muhammad Haji; Somali politician; mem. Parl. 2000–05; Minister of Defence 2008 (resgnd). *Address:* c/o Ministry of Defence, Mogadishu, Somalia (office).

IBRAHIM, Qasim, (Buruma Qasim); Maldivian politician and business executive; b. 10 Feb. 1952, Malé; m.; four s. four d.; began career as clerk at Govt Hosp., Malé 1969, accountant 1972–73; Man. M/S Alia Furniture Mart 1973; subsequently worked for Crescent (trading org.) 1973; joined outlet of Maldivian Govt Bodu Store (now known as State Trading Org.) 1974; set up own trading business in 1976, registered business as Villa Shipping and Trading Co. Ltd 1986, Villa Shipping (Singapore) Pte Ltd was incorporated in Singapore 1991, opened offices in Frankfurt, Germany 1996, est. Villa Hotels, Tokyo 2001, Villa Hotels, Hong Kong 2002, currently Chair. and Man. Dir Villa Group of Cos; mem. Parl. 1989; Founding mem. Maldivian Democratic Party 2001; Minister of Finance and Treasury 2005–08, of Home Affairs 2008; Gov. Maldives Monetary Authority –2008; fmr Pres. People's Special Majlis; Pres. South Asian Asscn for Regional Cooperation Chamber of Commerce and Industry; Founder-mem. and Pres. Maldives Nat. Chamber of Commerce and Industry; Founder-mem., Vice-Pres. and mem. Bd Maldives Asscn of Tourism Industry; mem. Bd Maldives Ports Authority; fmr mem. Bd Bank of Maldives. *Address:* Huravee Building, 3rd Floor, Ameer Ahmed Magu, Malé 20-05; M-Maafannu Villa, Malé, Maldives (home). *Telephone:* 3323820 (office). *Fax:* 3324739 (office). *E-mail:* minhah@dhivenhinet.net.mv (office); qasim@villa .com.mv (home). *Website:* www.homeaffairs.gov.mv (office); www.villahotels .com (home).

IBRAHIM, Yusuf Hasan; Somali politician and diplomatist; fmr Amb.; Minister of Foreign Affairs 2002–04. *Address:* c/o Ministry of Foreign Affairs, Mogadishu, Somalia (office).

IBRAHIMI, Bedredin, LLB; Macedonian politician and legal administrator; b. 25 Oct. 1952, Mala Recica, nr Tetovo; ed Pristina Univ.; fmr doctor; Sr Officer for Legal Affairs and Sec. of Poloska Kotlina Co., Tetovo Agric. Complex, Belgrade 1976–81; Officer in charge of Gen. Legal Affairs and Sec. Jelak Tetovo Co., Interpromet Complex 1981–89; with Tekom-Tetovo Trade Co. 1990–96; Sec. of Council, Municipality of Tetovo 1997–98; fmr Gen. Sec. Democratic Party of Albanians (DPA); Deputy Prime Minister of Macedonia 1998–2002, apptd Minister of Labour and Social Welfare 1998. *Address:* c/o Democratic Party of Albanians (DPA) (Partia Demokratike Shqiptare) (PDSh), Maršal Tito 2, Tetovo, Macedonia (office).

IBRAIMOVA, Elmira; Kyrgyzstani diplomatist and economist; *Executive Director, Community Development and Investment Agency (ARIS);* b. 13 April 1962, Frunze (now Bishkek); ed Moscow State Univ.; Perm. Rep. to UN, New York 1999–2002; Exec. Dir Community Devt and Investment Agency, Bishek 2004–; Hon. Freeman of Gulchinskiy ayil kenesh of Alay rayon of Osh oblast 2007. *Address:* Community Development and Investment Agency (ARIS), 102 Bokonbaev Street, Bishkek 720040, Kyrgyzstan (office). *Telephone:* (312) 66-78-79 (office). *Fax:* (312) 62-47-48 (office). *E-mail:* office@aris.kg (office). *Website:* eng.aris.kg/news (office).

IBROW, Salim Aliyow; Somali politician; fmr Sec. of State; Deputy Prime Minister 2004, Minister of Finance 2004–05, of Livestock 2005–07, of Higher Educ. and Culture 2007, and Deputy Prime Minister 2007, Acting Prime Minister Oct.–Nov. 2007; mem. Transitional Fed. Parl. 2004–. *Address:* Transitional Parliament, Mogadishu, Somalia (office).

IBUKI, Bunmei, BA; Japanese politician; *Minister of Finance;* b. 9 Jan. 1938, Kyoto; ed Kyoto Univ.; mem. staff, Ministry of Finance from 1960, Dir Treasury Div. 1980, Sec. to Minister of Finance 1982; Sec., Japanese Embassy, London 1965–69; mem. LDP, Deputy Sec.-Gen. 1996, Chair. Public Relations HQ 1999, Research Comm. on the Pension System 1999, Party Org. HQ 2000, Working Group of the Research Comm. on the Tax System 2004, Sec.-Gen. 2007–08; mem. House of Reps for Kyoto Pref., 1st Dist 1983–, Chair. Standing Cttee on Educ. 1994; Parl. Vice-Minister of Health 1990; Minister of Labour 1997; Minister of State for Disaster Man. 2000, for Nat. Emergency Legislation 2000; Chair. Nat. Public Safety Comm. 2004; Minister of Educ., Culture, Sports, Science and Tech. 2006–08, of Finance 2008–. *Leisure interests:* go (board game), rakugo, dining tours, tennis, kimono. *Address:* Ministry of Finance, 3-1-1, Kasumigaseki, Chiyoda-ku, Tokyo 100-8940, Japan (office). *Telephone:* (3) 3581-4111 (office). *Fax:* (3) 5251-2667 (office). *Website:* info@mof.go.jp (office); www.mof.go.jp.

ICAHN, Carl Celian, BA; American business executive; *Chairman, Starfire Holding Corporation;* b. 16 Feb. 1936, Queens, New York; m. 1st Liba Icahn (divorced 1999); two c.; m. 2nd Gail Golden 1999; ed Princeton Univ. and New York Univ. School of Medicine; apprentice broker, Dreyfus Corpn, New York 1960–63; Options Man. Tessel, Patrick & Co., New York 1963–64, Gruntal & Co. 1964–68; Chair. and Pres. Icahn & Co., Inc 1968–, Chair. and Pres. Icahn Holding Corpn (now Starfire Holding Corpn) New York 1984–, Chair. ACF Industries Inc. (Starfire subsidiary), St. Charles, Mo. 1984–, American Real Estate Pnrs 1990–, American Property Investors Inc. 1990–, American Railcar Industries 1990–; Chair. Lowestfare.com, LLC 1998, GB Holdings 2000–, XO Communications 2003–; Chair. Trans World Airlines Inc. 1986–99, Manpintour Holdings LLC 1998–2002; Pres. Stratosphere Corpn 1998–; mem. Bd of Dirs ImClone 2006–. *Address:* Starfire Holding Corporation, 767 5th Avenue, 47th Floor, New York, NY 10153-0023 (office); Icahn and Company Inc., 100 South Bedford Road, Mount Kisco, NY 10549-3425, USA (office). *Telephone:* (212) 702-4300 (Starfire) (home).

ICE CUBE; American rap artist and actor; b. (O'Shea Jackson), 15 June 1969, Los Angeles; ed Univ. of Phoenix; formed duo (with Sir Jinx), CIA, then leader of group, HBO; founder mem., N.W.A. 1987–89; formed rap group, Da Lench Mob 1989–; simultaneous solo artist 1989–; collaborated with Public Enemy; began own corpn, producing work by protegée YoYo 1989–; numerous tours; founder mem., Westside Connection 1996–; Founder Cube Vision Productions (film production co.). *Films:* Boyz n the Hood (actor) 1991, Trespass (actor) 1992, The Glass Shield (actor) 1994, Higher Learning (actor) 1995, Friday (actor, writer, exec. prod.) 1995, Dangerous Ground (actor, exec. prod.) 1997, Anaconda (actor) 1997, The Player's Club (actor, writer, exec. prod.) 1998, I Got the Hook Up (actor) 1998, Three Kings (actor) 1999, Thicker Than Water (actor) 1999, Next Friday (actor, writer, exec. prod.) 2000, Ghosts of Mars (actor) 2001, All About the Benjamins (actor, writer, exec. prod.) 2001, Barbershop (actor) 2002, Friday After Next (actor, writer, exec. prod.) 2002, Torque (actor) 2004, Barbershop 2: Back in Business (actor, exec. prod.) 2004, Are We There Yet? (actor, prod.) 2005, xXx 2: The Next Level (actor) 2005, Are We Done Yet? (actor) 2007. *Recordings include:* albums: with N.W.A.: N.W.A. And The Posse 1987, Straight Outta Compton 1989; solo: AmeriKKKa's Most Wanted 1990, Death Certificate 1991, The Predator 1992, Lethal Injection 1993, Bootlegs And B Sides 1994, War And Peace 1998, War And Peace 2: The Peace Disc 2000, Greatest Hits 2001, Laugh Now, Cry Later 2006, Raw Footage 2008; with da Lench Mob: Guerillas In Tha Mist 1992, Planet Of Da Apes 1994; with Westside Connection: Bow Down 1996. *Address:* Cube Vision Productions, 2900 West Olympic Blvd., Santa Monica CA 90404 (office); c/o Capitol Records, 1750 N Vine Street, Hollywood, CA 90028, USA (home). *Telephone:* (310) 255-7100 (Cube Vision) (office). *Fax:* (310) 255-7163 (Cube Vision) (office). *Website:* www.icecubemusic.com; www.icecube.com.

ICE-T; American rap artist and actor; b. (Tracey Marrow), 14 Feb. 1959, Newark, NJ; m. Darlene Ortiz; one c.; recording artist 1987–; mem., Body Count 1992–; world-wide tours, numerous television and film appearances; created Rhyme Syndicate Records early 1990s; involved in two youth intervention programmes, Hands Across Watts and South Central Love;

Rolling Stone Readers' Poll Best Male Rapper 1992. *Recordings include:* albums: solo: The Pimp Penal Code, Sex, Money, Guns, Rhyme Pays 1987, Power 1988, The Iceberg 1989, O. G. Original Gangster 1991, Home Invasion 1993, VI: Return Of The Real 1996, Seventh Deadly Sin 1999, Ice-T Presents the Westside 2004; with Body Count: Body Count 1992, Born Dead 1994, Violent Demise, The Last Days 1997. *Films:* Breakin' 1984, Breakin' 2: Electric Boogaloo 1984, New Jack City 1991, Ricochet 1991, Trespass 1992, Why Colors? 1992, Who's the Man? 1993, Surviving the Game 1994, Tank Girl 1995, Johnny Mnemonic 1995, Mean Guns 1997, The Deli 1997, Below Utopia 1997, Crazy Six 1998, Urban Menace 1999, Final Voyage 1999, Jacob Two Two Meets the Hooded Fang 1999, Corrupt 1999, The Wrecking Crew 1999, Sonic Impact 1999, Point Doom 1999, Judgment Day 1999, The Heist 1999, Frezno Smooth 1999, Stealth Fighter 2000, Leprechaun in the Hood 2000, Luck of the Draw 2000, The Alternate 2000, Sanity, Aiken's Artifact 2000, Guardian 2000, Gangland 2000, 3000 Miles to Graceland 2001, Deadly Rhapsody 2001, 'R Xmas 2001, Ticker 2001, Out Kold 2001, Ablaze 2001, Tara 2001, Stranded 2001, Kept 2001, Crime Partners 2000, Air Rage 2001, Tracks 2002, Pimpin' 101 2002, On the Edge 2002, Lexie 2004, Copy That 2006. *Television:* Players (series) 1997, Exiled (film) 1998, Law & Order: Special Victims Unit (series) 2000–, The Disciples (film) 2000, Ice T's Rap School (series) 2006, The Magic 7 (voice) 2007. *Publications:* The Iceberg/Freedom of Speech... Just Watch What You Say 1989, The Ice Opinion 1994. *Address:* c/o Rhyme Syndicate Management, Warner Bros Records, 75 Rockefeller Plaza, New York, NY 10019-6908, USA (office). *Website:* www.icet.com.

ICHIKAWA, Ennosuke III; Japanese actor; *Founder, 21st Century Kabuki Company;* b. (Kinoshi Masahiko), 9 Dec. 1939; s. of Ichikawa Danshiro III (died 1963); grands. of En'o (died 1963); ed Keio Univ.; stage debut age 7; studied under experimentalist Kabuki actor En'o; took official name Ennosuke III 1963; est. ind. experimental group and spearheaded reformation and modernisation of traditional Kabuki theatre; f. 21st Century Kabuki Co.; cr. new style of energetic, fast-paced Kabuki, called Super Kabuki; producer, dir and lead actor in Super Kabuki shows 1986–; teachings, lectures, tours and performances worldwide. *Address:* c/o Kabuki-za, 4-12-15 Ginza, Chuo-ku, Tokyo, Japan (office).

ICHIKAWA, Kon; Japanese film director; b. 20 Nov. 1915, Mie; ed Ichioka Commercial School, Osaka. *Films include:* Musume Dojoji 1946, Toho senichi-ya 1947, Hana hiraku-Machiko yori 1948, Sambyakurokujugo ya-Tokyo-hen 1948, Sambyakurokujugo ya-Osaka-hen 1948, Sambyaku-rokujugo ya 1949, Ningen moyo 1949, Hateshinaki jonetsu 1949, Netsudeichi 1950, Ginza Sanshiro 1950, Akatsuki no tsuiseki 1950, Nusumareta koi 1951, Koibito 1951, Ieraishan 1951, Bungawan soro 1951, Kekkon koshinkyoku 1951, Mukokuseki-sha 1952, Rakki-san 1952, Wakai hito 1952, Ashi ni sawatta onna 1952, Ano te kono te 1952, Pu-san 1953, Aoiro kakumei 1953, Seishun Zenigata Heiji 1953, Aijin 1953, Josei ni kansuru junisho 1954, Watashi no subete o 1954, Okuman choja 1954, Kokoro 1955, Seishun kaidan 1955, Biruma no tategoto 1956, Shokei no heya 1956, Nihonbashi 1956, Manin densha 1957, Tohoku no zunmu-tachi 1957, Ana 1957, Enjo 1958, Anata to watashi no aikotoba: Sayônara, konnichiwa 1959, Kagi 1959, Nobi 1959, Jokyo 1960, Bonchi 1960, Ototo 1960, Kuroi junin no onna 1961, Hakai 1962, Watashi wa nisai 1962, Dokonjo monogatari-zeni no odori 1963, Yukinojo henge 1963, Taiheiyo hitori-botchi 1963, Tokyo orimpikku 1965, Genji monogatari 1966, Toppo Jijo no botan senso 1967, Seishun 1968, Kyoto 1969, Nihon to nihonjin 1970, Ai futatabi 1971, Matatabi 1973, Visions of Eight 1973, Wagahai wa neko de aru 1975, Tsuma to onna no aida 1976, Inugamike no ichizoku 1976, Akuma no temari-uta 1977, Gokumon-to 1977, Gokumon-to 1977, Hi no tori 1978, Byoinzaka no kubikukuri no ie 1979, Koto 1980, Kofuku 1981, Sasame-yuki 1983, Ohan 1984, Biruma no tatekoto 1985, Rokumeikan 1986, Eiga joyu 1987, Taketori monogatari 1987, Tsuru 1988, Tenkawa densetsu satsujin jiken 1991, Fusa 1993, Shinjitsu ichiro (TV) 1993, Kaettekite Kogarashi Monjiro 1993, Shijushichinin no shikaku 1994, Yatsu haka-mura 1996, Shinsengumi 2000, Dora-heita 2000, Kah-chan 2001, Tobo (TV) 2002, Musume no kekkon (TV) 2003, Yume jûya 2006, Inugamike no ichizoku 2006.

IDA, Yoshinori; Japanese automotive industry executive; *Chairman and Representative Director, Isuzu Motors Limited;* b. 1943; joined Izuzu 1966, Man. Dir responsible for domestic sales, eng, Gen. Motors affairs and portfolio integration, Isuzu Motors Ltd –2000, Rep. Dir, Pres. and COO 2000–07, Chair. and Rep. Dir 2007–. *Address:* Isuzu Motors Ltd, 26-1 Minami 6-chome, Shinagawa-ku, Tokyo 140-8722, Japan (office). *Telephone:* (3) 5471-1141 (office). *Fax:* (3) 5471-1043 (office). *E-mail:* info@isuzu.com (office). *Website:* www.isuzu.com (office).

IDEI, Nobuyuki, BA; Japanese business executive; *CEO, Quantum Leaps Corporation;* b. 1937, Tokyo; m. Teruyo Idei; one d.; ed Waseda Univ., Institut des hautes études internationales, Geneva, Switzerland; joined Sony 1960, est. Sony of France 1968, fmrly Head of Corp. Communications and Brand Image, Pres. and Rep. Dir Sony Corpn 1995–99, Pres. and CEO 1999–2000, Chair. and CEO 2000–05, now Chief Corp. Adviser; Founder and currently CEO Quantum Leaps Corpn (consulting firm); Counsellor, Bank of Japan 1999–; mem. Bd of Dirs General Motors 1999–2003, Nestlé SA 2001–, Accenture 2006–, Baidu.com Inc. 2007–; mem. IT Strategy Council (advisory cttee to Japan's Prime Minister) 2000–05, Chair. July–Nov. 2000; Co-Chair. Admin. Reform, Nippon Keidanren (Japanese Business Fed.) 2002–03, Vice-Chair. 2003–. *Leisure interests:* music, cinema, golf, reading. *Address:* Quantum Leaps Corporation, Tokyo Ginko Kyokai Building 16F, 1-3-1 Marunouchi, Chiyoda-ku, Tokyo 100-0005, Japan (office). *Telephone:* (3) 5224-6540 (office). *Fax:* (3) 5224-6541 (office). *Website:* www.qxl.jp (office).

IDEMITSU, Akira, BEcons; Japanese oil industry executive; *Chairman, Idemitsu Kosan Company Limited;* b. 5 May 1932, Tokyo; ed Univ. of Tokyo;

joined Idemitsu Kosan Co. Ltd April 1961, Gen. Man., Yokohama Br. 1977–79, Deputy Gen. Man., Marketing Dept 1979–81, Dir and Gen. Man. Hokkaido Refinery 1981–83, Gen. Man. Overseas Operations 1983–91, also Man. Dir 1988–91, Pres. Idemitsu Oil Devt Co. Ltd 1991–93, Sr Man. Dir Idemitsu 1993–95, Exec. Vice-Pres. 1995–98, Pres. and Rep. Dir 1998–2002, Rep. Dir and Chair. 2002–. *Address:* Idemitsu Kosan Company Limited, 1–1 Marunouchi 3-chome, Chiyoda-ku, Tokyo, Japan (office). *Telephone:* (3) 3213-3115 (office). *Fax:* (3) 3213-9354 (office). *Website:* www.idemitsu.co.jp (office).

IDEMITSU, Yuji; Japanese business executive; b. 1 Jan. 1927, Fukuoka; m. Yoko Idemitsu 1956; two s.; ed Kyushu Teikoku Univ.; joined Idemitsu Kosan Co. 1948, Gen. Man. London Office 1974–77, Man. Dir and Gen. Man. Overseas Operations Dept 1981–83, Sr Man. Dir and Gen. Man. Chiba Refinery 1985–86, Exec. Vice-Pres. 1986–93, Pres. 1993–98, Exec. Adviser 1998–; mem. Petroleum Asscn of Japan (Pres. 1995), Fed. Econ. Orgs (mem. Exec. Bd 1993). *Leisure interests:* reading, golf, calligraphy. *Address:* c/o Idemitsu Kosan Co. Ltd, 1-1, 3 chome, Marunouchi, Chiyoda-ku, Tokyo 100, Japan.

IDJI, Antoine Kolawolé; Benin politician; b. 1946; Minister of Foreign Affairs and African Integration 1998; Pres. Assemblée Nationale 2003–06; cand. in Presidential election 2006; fmr Chair. African Parliamentarians' Forum for New Partnership for Africa's Devt (NePAD). *Address:* c/o Office of the President, Assemblée Nationale, BP 371, Porto-Novo, Benin (office).

IDLE, Eric, BA; British writer, lyricist and actor; b. 29 March 1943, South Shields, Tyne and Wear, England; m. 1st Lynn Ashley (divorced); one s.; m. 2nd Tania Kosevich; one d.; ed Royal School, Wolverhampton and Pembroke Coll., Cambridge. *Films:* Albert Carter, Q.O.S.O. (writer) 1968, And Now for Something Completely Different (actor, writer) 1971, Monty Python and the Holy Grail (actor, writer, exec. prod.) 1975, Life of Brian (actor, writer) 1979, The Meaning of Life (actor, writer) 1983, Yellowbeard (actor) 1983, European Vacation (actor) 1985, The Transformers: The Movie (voice) 1986, The Adventures of Baron Munchausen (actor) 1988, Nuns on the Run (actor) 1990, Missing Pieces (actor) 1991, Too Much Sun (actor) 1991, Mom and Dad Save the World (actor) 1992, Splitting Heirs (actor, writer, exec. prod.) 1993, Casper (actor) 1995, The Wind in the Willows (actor) 1996, Quest for Camelot (voice) 1998, Rudolph the Red-Nosed Reindeer: The Movie (voice) 1998, The Secret of NIMH 2: Timmy to the Rescue (voice) 1998, Pirates: 3D Show (actor, writer) 1999, Journey into Your Imagination (actor) 1999, Hercules: Zero to Hero (voice) 1999, South Park: Bigger Longer & Uncut (voice) 1999, Dudley Do-Right (actor) 1999, Brightness (actor) 2000, 102 Dalmatians (voice) 2000, Pinocchio (voice) 2002, Hollywood Homicide (actor) 2003, Ella Enchanted (actor) 2004, The Nutcracker and the Mouseking (voice) 2004, Delgo (voice) 2007, Shrek the Third (voice) 2007. *Television:* Alice in Wonderland (actor) 1966, The Frost Report (series, writer) 1966, No, That's Me Over Here! (series, writer) 1967, At Last the 1948 Show (series, actor) 1967, Do Not Adjust Your Set (series, actor and writer) 1967–69, Simply Sheila (writer) 1968, According to Dora (series, writer) 1968, We Have Ways of Making You Laugh (series, actor and writer) 1968, Broaden Your Mind (series, writer) 1968, Hark at Barker (series, writer) 1969, Monty Python's Flying Circus (four series, actor and writer) 1969–74, Euroshow 71 (actor) 1971, The Two Ronnies (series, writer) 1971, The Ronnie Barker Yearbook (writer) 1971, Ronnie Corbett in Bed (writer) 1971, Monty Python's Fliegender Zirkus (actor, writer) 1972, Christmas Box (writer) 1974, Commander Badman (writer) 1974, Rutland Weekend Television (series, actor and writer) 1975, The Rutles (actor, writer, dir) 1978, The Mikado (film, actor) 1987, Nearly Departed (series, actor) 1989, Around the World in 80 Days (series, actor) 1989, Mickey Mouse Works (series, voice) 1999, Suddenly Susan (series, actor) 1999–2000, House of Mouse (series, voice) 2001, The Scream Team (film, actor) 2002, Rutles 2: Can't Buy Me Lunch (writer, dir) 2002, Christmas Vacation 2: Cousin Eddie's Island Adventure (film, actor) 2003, The Simpsons (voice) 2003–07, Super Robot Monkey Team Hyperforce Gol (voice) 2004–05. *Stage productions:* I'm Just Wild About Harry (actor, Edinburgh Festival) 1963, Monty Python Live at the Hollywood Bowl (actor, writer) 1982, The Mikado (actor, ENO) 1987, (actor, Houston Opera House) 1989, Monty Python's Spamalot (writer, The Shubert Theatre, Broadway) 2005. *Compositions:* songs for Monty Python's Flying Circus series 1969, Always Look on the Bright Side of Life.. (for Life of Brian film) 1979, Bruces' Philosophers Song (for Monty Python Live at the Hollywood Bowl) 1982, Sit On My Face (for Monty Python Live at the Hollywood Bowl) 1982, songs for The Meaning of Life film 1983, The Adventures of Baron Munchausen (song, for film) 1988, One Foot in the Grave (TV series theme song) 1990, That's Death (song for video game, Discworld II: Missing Presumed...!?) 1996, songs for Monty Python's Spamalot stage production 2005. *Publications include:* Hello Sailor 1975, The Rutland Dirty Weekend Book 1976, Pass the Butler 1982, Monty Python's Flying Circus: Just the Words (co-author, two vols) 1989, The Fairly Incomplete and Rather Badly Illustrated Monty Python Song Book (co-author) 1994, The Quite Remarkable Adventures of the Owl and the Pussycat (co-author) 1996, The Road to Mars 1998, The "Pythons" Autobiography by the "Pythons" (co-author) 2003, The Greedy Bastard Diary: A Comic Tour of America 2005. *Address:* c/o HarperEntertainment, 10 E 53rd Street, New York, NY 10022, USA.

IDRAC, Anne-Marie André, LenD; French politician, civil servant and business executive; b. 27 July 1951, Saint-Brieuc, Côtes-du-Nord; d. of André Colin and Marguerite Médecin (née Laurent); m. Francis Idrac 1974; four d.; ed Univ. of Paris II, Inst. d'Etudes Politiques de Paris and Ecole Nat. d'Admin; civic admin., Dept of Building and Public Works, Ministry of Equipment, Housing and Transport 1974–77; Chargée de Mission to the Prefect of the Midi-Pyrénées 1977–79; Tech. Councillor in the Cabinets of Marcel Cavaillé (Sec. of State for Housing) and Michel d'Ornano (Minister of the Environment)

1979–81; Deputy Dir for Housing Improvement, Ministry of the Quality of Life 1981–83; Deputy Dir for Finance and Judicial Affairs 1983–87; Chief of Service and Deputy Dir, Dept of Construction, Ministry of Supply 1987–90, Dir-Gen. Public Devt in Cergy-Pontoise 1990–93; Dir of Territorial Transport (DTT) 1993–95; Sec. of State for Transport 1995–97; elected Deputy of Yvelines (Union pour la démocratie française—UDF) 1997; Sec.-Gen. Force Démocrate; mem. Regional Council Ile-de-France 1998–2002; Pres. Mouvement Européen France 1999–2002; Vice-Pres., then Sec.-Gen. UDF 2001–02; Pres. and Dir-Gen. Régie Autonome des Transports Parisiens 2002–06; Chair. Soc. Nationale des Chemins de Fer Français 2006–08; mem. Bd of Dirs Institut Français de Relations Internationales; mem. Advisory Bd Dexia 2002–07, Hautes études commerciales; mem. Orientation Council Asscn En Temps Réel; Chevalier, Ordre nat. du Mérite; Nat. Foundation for Public Enterprise Award 1977, ranked by Fortune magazine amongst 50 Most Powerful Women in Business outside the US (third) 2006, (sixth) 2007, ranked by the Financial Times amongst Top 25 Businesswomen in Europe (22nd) 2007. *Address:* c/o Board of Directors, Institut Français de Relations Internationales, 27 rue de la Procession, 75740 Paris, Cedex 15, France (office). *Telephone:* 1-40-61-60-00 (office). *Fax:* 1-40-61-60-60 (office). *Website:* www.ifri.org (office).

IDRIS, Kamil E., LLB, BA, MA, PhD; Sudanese diplomatist and lawyer; *Secretary-General, International Union for the Protection of New Varieties of Plants (UPOV);* b. 1945; ed Univ. of Khartoum, Cairo, Egypt, Ohio, USA, Grad. Inst. of Int. Studies, Geneva, Switzerland, Inst. of Public Admin, Khartoum; part-time journalist, El-Ayam and El-Sahafa newspapers, Sudan 1971–79; Lecturer, Univ. of Cairo 1976–77, Ohio Univ. 1978, Univ. of Khartoum 1986; Asst Dir Arab Dept, Ministry of Foreign Affairs, Khartoum 1977–78, Asst Dir Research Dept Jan.–June 1978, Deputy Dir Legal Dept July–Dec. 1978; mem. Perm. Mission of Sudan to UN Office, Geneva 1979–82; Vice-Consul of Sudan, Switzerland 1979–82; Sr Program Officer, Devt Cooperation and External Relations Bureau for Africa, WIPO 1982–85, Dir Devt Cooperation and External Relations Bureau for Arab and Cen. and Eastern European Countries 1985–94, Deputy Dir-Gen. WIPO 1994–97, Dir-Gen. 1997–2008 (resgnd); Sec.-Gen. Int. Union for the Protection of New Varieties of Plants (UPOV) 1997–; mem. UN Int. Law Comm. (ILC) 1992–96 (Vice-Chair. 45th session 1993), 2000–02; served on numerous cttees of int. orgs including WHO, ILO, ITU, UNHCR, OAU, Group of 77 etc. and Sudanese del. to numerous int. and regional confs; Prof. of Public Int. Law, Univ. of Khartoum; mem. African Jurists Asscn; Hon. Prof. of Laws, Peking Univ., People's Repub. of China 1999; decorations from Sudan 1983, 2002, Egypt 1985, 2000, 2001, Senegal 1998, Russian Fed. 1999, 2000, Saudi Arabia 1999, Slovakia 1999, Syrian Arab Repub. 2000, Portugal 2001, Romania 2001, Mexico 2001, 2005, Repub. of Moldova 2001, Côte d'Ivoire 2002, Poland 2002, Kyrgyzstan 2003, Bulgaria 2003, Italy 2004, Oman 2004; Dr hc (State Univ. of Moldova) 1999), (Franklin Pierce Law Center) 1999, (Fudan Univ., Shanghai) 1999, (Univ. of Nat. and World Economy, Sofia) 2000, (Univ. of Bucharest) 2001, (Hannam Univ., Repub. of Korea) 2001, (Mongolian Univ. of Science and Tech.) 2001), (Matej Bel Univ., Slovakia) 2001, (Nat. Tech. Univ. of Ukraine) 2002, (Al Eman Al Mahdi Univ., Sudan) 2003, (Indira Gandhi Nat. Open Univ.) 2005), (Latvian Acad. of Sciences) 2005, (Univ. of Al Gezira) 2007; Scholars and Researchers State Gold Medal (Sudan) 1983, Scholars and Researchers Gold Medal, Egyptian Acad. of Scientific Research and Tech. 1985. *Publications include:* State Responsibility in International Law 1977, North-South Insurance Relations: The Unequal Exchange 1984, The Law of Non-navigational Uses of International Water Courses; the ILC's draft articles: An Overview 1995, The Theory of Source and Target in Child Psychology 1996 and articles on law, economics, jurisprudence and aesthetics in newspapers and periodicals. *Address:* International Union for the Protection of New Varieties of Plants, 34, chemin des Colombettes, 1211 Geneva 20, Switzerland (office). *E-mail:* upov.mail@upov.int (office). *Website:* www.upov .int (office).

IDRISOV, Yerlan Abilfaizovich; Kazakhstani politician and diplomatist; b. 28 April 1959, Karkalinsk, Karaganda Oblast; m. Nurilla Anarbekovna Idrisova; two s. one d.; ed Moscow Inst. of Int. Relations, Diplomatic Acad., USSR Ministry of Foreign Affairs; rep. for Tyzahpromexport, Pakistan 1981–85; mem. of staff, Ministry of Foreign Affairs, Kazakh SSR 1985–90, trainee USSR Embassy, New Delhi 1991–92, First Sec., Perm. Mission of Kazakhstan to UN, New York 1992–95, Head of American Dept and Amb.-at-Large, Ministry of Foreign Affairs 1995–96, Asst to Pres. on Int. Issues 1996–97, First Deputy Minister of Foreign Affairs 1997–99, 1999–2002, Minister Feb.–Oct. 1999, Amb. to UK (also accred to Ireland, Norway and Sweden) 2002–07, to USA 2007–. *Address:* Embassy of Kazakhstan, 1401 16th Street, NW, Washington, DC 20036, USA (office). *Telephone:* 202-232-5488 (office). *Fax:* 202-232-5845 (office). *E-mail:* kazakh.embusa@verizon.net (office). *Website:* www.kazakhembus.com (office).

IDURI, Shemuel Sam; Solomon Islands teacher and politician; *Minister for National Unity, Reconciliation and Peace;* b. Boboilangi Village, Malaita; ed Solomon Islands Teacher's Coll., Teacher's Coll., Western Australia; fmr educ. officer; fmr secondary school prin.; mem. Parl. for West Kwara'ae, Malaita Prov. 2006–; Minister for Nat. Unity, Reconciliation and Peace 2006–10 Nov. 2007, 22 Dec. 2007–. *Address:* Ministry of Provincial Government, National Reconciliation and Peace, PO Box 1548, Honiara, Solomon Islands (office). *Telephone:* 28616 (office). *Fax:* 21289 (office).

IEHSI, Ieske K., BA, MPA; Micronesian politician and government official; *General Manager, Pohnpei Ports Authority;* b. 4 Jan. 1955, Pingelap Atoll; m. Merihne John; five c.; ed Univ. of Hawaii, Manoa, Harvard Univ., USA; Asst Chief Clerk, Congress of Micronesia 1977–97, Man., Office of the Attorney-Gen. 1980–81; Special Asst to the Pres. 1981–87, Chief of Staff, Exec. Office of

the Pres. 1987–92; Deputy Sec. of the Dept of Foreign Affairs 1997–2001, Sec. of Foreign Affairs 2001–03; Gen. Man. Pohnpei Ports Authority 2003–; mem. Pingelap Council of Traditional Leaders (Benik), holding title of Noahs. *Address:* Pohnpei Ports Authority, PO Box 1150, Kolonia, Pohnpei FM 96941, Federated States of Micronesia (office). *Telephone:* 320-2793 (home). *Fax:* 320-2832 (office). *E-mail:* ieske@mail.fm (office). *Website:* www.ppa.fm (office).

IELEMIA, Apisai, BA; Tuvaluan politician; *Prime Minister and Minister of Foreign Affairs and Labor;* b. 19 Aug. 1955; m.; one d. one s.; ed USP Suva, Fiji; fmr civil servant; Prime Minister and Minister of Foreign Affairs and Labor 2006–. *Address:* Ministry of Foreign Affairs and Labour, Vaiaku, Funafuti, Tuvalu (office). *Telephone:* 20100 (office). *Fax:* 20820 (office). *E-mail:* primeminister@tuvalu.tv (office).

IGARASHI, Mitsuo; Japanese business executive and fmr politician; *Chairman, Okawa Foundation;* Deputy Minister for Policy Coordination, Ministry of Posts and Telecommunications 1990, Dir-Gen. Telecommunications Bureau then Minister of Telecommunications 1995; Exec.Vice Pres. KDDI Corpn (telecommunications co.) 2000–03, Chair. 2003–04; Pres. Okawa Foundation 2005, now Chair.; also currently Adviser Nomura Research Inst. *Publications:* articles in professional journals on econs. *Address:* Okawa Foundation, Riviera Minami Aoyama Building-A, 4th Floor, 3-3-3 Minami-Aoyama, Minato-ku, Tokyo 107-0062, Japan (office). *Telephone:* (3) 6438-4030 (office). *Fax:* (3) 6438-4031 (office). *E-mail:* okawa-foundation.kd@csk.com (office). *Website:* www.okawa-foundation.or.jp (office).

IGEL, Anders, BSc, MSc; Swedish telecommunications executive; b. 1951, Stockholm; m.; three d.; ed Stockholm School of Econs, Stockholm Royal Inst. of Tech.; began career as a radar-system devt engineer Philips Electronics; joined Ericsson 1978, positions included Marketing Exec., Head Ericsson UK 1990–95, Head of Public Networks 1995–97, Head of Infocom Systems 1997–99; Pres. and CEO Esselte 1999–2002; mem. Bd Telia 1999, Pres. and CEO TeliaSonera 2002–07. *Address:* c/o TeliaSonera AB, Sturegatan 1, 10663 Stockholm, Sweden (office).

IGER, Robert (Bob) Allen, BA; American business executive; *President and CEO, The Walt Disney Company;* b. 10 Feb. 1951, New York City; m. Willow Bay 1995; two s. two d.; ed Ithaca Coll.; studio supervisor, ABC-TV 1974–76, various positions, ABC-TV Sports 1976–85, Vice-Pres. Programme Planning and Devt 1985–87, Vice-Pres. Programme Planning and Acquisition 1987–88, Exec. Vice-Pres. ABC TV Network Group 1988–99, Pres. 1992–94, Pres. ABC Entertainment 1989–92, Exec. Vice-Pres. Capital Cities/ABC Inc., New York 1993–94, Pres. and COO 1994–96, Pres. ABC Inc., New York 1996–99, Chair. ABC Group 1999–2000; Pres. Walt Disney Int. 1999–2000, Pres. and COO The Walt Disney Co., Calif. 2000–05, Pres. and CEO 2005–; CEO MarketWatch Inc. 2006–; mem. Bd of Dirs Nat. September 11 Memorial & Museum, Lincoln Center for the Performing Arts, Inc.; Trustee, American Film Inst. Bd; mem. Exec. Advisory Bd Elizabeth Glaser Pediatric AIDS Foundation; fmr Trustee, Ithaca Coll.; Hon. Chair. Campaign for Ithaca Coll.; Trustees Award, Nat. TV Acad. 2005. *Address:* The Walt Disney Co., 500 South Buena Vista Street, Burbank, CA 91521-9722, USA (office). *Telephone:* (818) 560-1000 (office). *Fax:* (818) 560-1930 (office). *E-mail:* TWDC.Corp.Communications@disney.com (office). *Website:* disney.go.com (office); (office).

IGLESIAS, Enrique; Spanish singer and songwriter; b. 8 May 1975, Madrid; s. of Julio Iglesias; sings in English and Spanish; numerous tours; Grammy Award 1997, eight Premios Los Nuestro, Billboard Awards for Artist of the Year, Album of the Year 1997, ASCAP Award for Songwriter of the Year 1998, American Music Award for Favorite Latin Artist 2002, Billboard Latin Music Award for Best Latin Dance Club Play Track (for Not In Love/No Es Amor) 2005. *Recordings include:* albums: Enrique Iglesias 1995, Master Pistas 1997, Vivir 1997, Cosas Del Amor 1998, Enrique 1999, Escape 2001, Quizás 2002, 7 2003; singles: Experienca Religiosa, No Llores Por Mi, Bailamos 1999, Rhythm Divine 1999, Be With You 2000, Solo Me Importas Tu 2000, Sad Eyes 2000, Hero 2001, Escape 2002, Don't Turn Off The Lights 2002, Love To See You Cry 2002, Maybe 2002, Addicted 2003, Not In Love… 2004, Insomniac 2007. *Address:* c/o Interscope Records, 2220 Colorado Avenue, Santa Monica, CA 90404, CA (office). *Website:* www.enriqueiglesias.com (office).

IGLESIAS, Enrique V.; Uruguayan international official; *General Secretary, Iberoamerican General Secretariat;* b. 26 July 1931, Asturias, Spain; s. of Isabel García de Iglesias; ed Univ. de la República, Montevideo; held several positions, including Prof. Agregado, Faculty of Political Economy, Prof. of Econ. Policy and Dir Inst. of Econs, Univ. de la República, Montevideo 1952–67; Man. Dir Unión de Bancos del Uruguay 1954; Tech. Dir Nat. Planning Office of Uruguay 1962–66; Pres. (Gov.) Banco Cent. del Uruguay 1966–68; Chair. Council, Latin American Inst. for Econ. and Social Planning, UN 1967–72, Interim Dir-Gen. 1977–78; Head, Advisory Mission on Planning, Govt of Venezuela 1970; Adviser UN Conf. on Human Environment 1971–72; Exec. Sec. Econ. Comm. for Latin America and the Caribbean 1972–85; Minister of External Affairs 1985–88; Pres. IDB 1988–2005; Gen. Sec. Iberoamerican Gen. Secr., Madrid, Spain 2005–; Pres. Soc. for Int. Devt; Acting Dir-Gen. Latin American Inst. for Econ. and Social Planning 1973–78; Pres. Third World Forum 1973–76; mem. Steering Cttee, Soc. for Int. Devt 1973–92, Pres. 1989, Selection Cttee, Third World Prize 1979–82; Sec.-Gen. UN Conf. on New and Renewable Sources of Energy Feb.–Aug. 1981; Chair. UN Inter-Agency Group on Devt of Renewable Sources of Energy, Energy Advisory Panel, Brundtland Comm. 1984–86; mem. North-South Round Table on Energy, Club of Rome; Order of Rio Branco; Grand Cross (Brazil); Grand Cross Silver Plaque, Nat. Order of Juan Mora Fernandez (Costa Rica); Commdr Légion d'honneur; Commdr des Arts et des Lettres 1999; Grand Cross of Isabel the Catholic (Spain); numerous other foreign decorations; Hon.

LLD (Liverpool) 1987; Hon. PhD (Univ. de Guadalajara, Mexico) 1994, (Candido Mendes Univ., Rio de Janeiro) 1994; Prince of Asturias Award 1982, UNESCO Pablo Picasso Award 1997. *Leisure interests:* music, art. *Address:* Iberoamerican General Secretariat, Paseo de Recoletos 8, 28001 Madrid, Spain (office). *Telephone:* (91) 590-19-80 (office). *E-mail:* info@segib.org (office). *Website:* www.segib.org (office).

IGLESIAS (DE LA CUEVA), Julio José; Spanish singer and songwriter; b. 23 Sept. 1943, Madrid; m. Isabel Preysler 1971 (divorced); one d. two s.; pnr Miranda Rijnsburger 1990; three s. two d.; ed Univ. of Cambridge; goalkeeper Real Madrid junior team; professional singer, songwriter 1968–; English language releases 1981–; concerts and television appearances worldwide; hon. mem. Spanish Foreign Legion; winner Spanish Song Festival, Benidorm 1968, Eurovision Song Contest winner 1970, Guinness Book of Records Diamond Disc Award (most records in most languages) 1983, Medaille de Vermeil de la Ville de Paris 1983, Grammy Award for Best Latin Pop Performance 1987. *Compositions include:* La Vida Sigue Igual, Mi Amor, Yo Canto, Alguien El Alamo Al Camino, No Llores. *Recordings include:* albums: Soy 1973, El Amor 1975, A Mis 33 Años 1977, De Niña A Mujer 1981, 1100 Bel Air Lace 1984, Un Hombre Solo 1987, Starry Night 1990, La Carretera 1995, Tango 1996, Corazón Latino 1998, Noche De Cuatro Lunas 2000, Una Donna Puo Cambiar La Vita 2000, Ao Meu Brasil 2000, Divorcio 2003, Romantic Classics 2006; also appears on: Duets (with Frank Sinatra) 1993. *Publication:* Entre el Cielo y el Infierno (autobiog.) 1981. *Address:* Anchor Marketing, 1885 NE 149th Street, Suite G, North Miami, FL 33181, USA (office). *Website:* www.julioiglesias.com (office).

IGNARRO, Louis J., BS, PhD; American scientist and academic; *Jerome J. Belzer, MD, Distinguished Professor of Pharmacology, Department of Molecular and Medical Pharmacology, School of Medicine, University of California at Los Angeles;* b. 31 May 1941, Brooklyn, NY; m. Sharon E. Ignarro (née Williams); ed Columbia Univ., New York, Univ. of Minnesota; Postdoctoral Fellow, NIH 1966–68; Staff Scientist, Research Dept, Pharmaceutical Div., CIBA-GEIGY Corpn, Ardsley, NY 1968–72; Asst Prof., Dept of Pharmacology, Tulane Univ. School of Medicine, New Orleans 1973, Assoc. Prof. 1973–78, Prof. 1979–85; Prof., Dept of Pharmacology, UCLA School of Medicine 1985–, Prof. and Acting Chair. Dept of Pharmacology 1989–90, Prof. of Pharmacology and Asst Dean for Student Research 1990–93, Jerome J. Belzer, MD, Distinguished Prof. of Pharmacology, Dept of Molecular and Medical Pharmacology 1993–; mem. American Soc. for Pharmacology and Experimental Therapeutics, American Soc. for Biochemistry and Molecular Biology, American Physiological Soc., American Soc. for Cell Biology, American Rheumatism Asscn, American Soc. of Hematology, Soc. for Experimental Biology and Medicine, American Heart Asscn, NAS 1999–, American Acad. of Arts and Sciences 1999–, Inst. of Medicine 2005, American Philosophical Soc. 2007; Founder and Pres. Nitric Oxide Soc. 1996–; Founder and Ed.-in-Chief Nitric Oxide Biology and Chemistry (journal) 1996–; Dr hc (Buenos Aires School of Medicine), 1996, (Napoli School of Medicine) 1999, (Napoli School of Medicine II) 1999, (Univ. of the Republic, Montevideo, Uruguay) 1999, (UniNorte School of Medicine, Paraguay) 2000, (Charles Univ. School of Medicine, Prague) 2000, (Univ. of Bologna School of Medicine) 2000, (Tulane Univ.) 2001, (Univ. of Minnesota) 2002, (Univ. of Athens) 2002, (Univ. of Perugia, Italy) 2004; Roussel UCLA Prize 1994, CIBA Award for Hypertension Research 1995, Nobel Prize for Medicine (jtly) 1998, Basic Research Prize, American Heart Asscn 1998. *Publications:* numerous articles in scientific journals. *Leisure interests:* marathon runner, cyclist. *Address:* Department of Molecular and Medical Pharmacology, David Geffen School of Medicine, UCLA, 23-120 CHS, 650 Charles E. Young Drive, South, Los Angeles, CA 90095-1735, USA (office). *Telephone:* (310) 825-5159 (office); (310) 825-9930 (Lab.) (office). *Fax:* (310) 825-4791 (office). *E-mail:* lignarro@mednet.ucla.edu (office). *Website:* www.nuc.ucla.edu (office); www.ignarro.com (home).

IGNATENKO, Vitaly Nikitich; Russian journalist; *Director-General, ITAR-TASS News Agency;* b. 19 April 1941, Sochi; m. Svetlana Ignatenko; one s.; ed Moscow Univ.; corresp., Deputy Ed.-in-Chief Komsomolskaya Pravda 1963–75; Deputy Dir-Gen. TASS (USSR Telegraph Agency) 1975–78; Deputy Head of Int. Information Section, CPSU Cen. Cttee 1978–86; Ed.-in-Chief Novoe Vremya 1986–90; Asst to fmr Pres. Gorbachev, Head of Press Service 1990–91; Dir-Gen. ITAR-TASS News Agency 1991–; Deputy Chair. Council of Ministers 1995–97; Pres., Chair. of Bd Russian Public TV (ORT) 1998–; Pres. World Asscn of Russian Press; mem. Int. Acad. of Information Science, Russian Fed. Comm. on UNESCO Affairs, Union of Russian Journalists, Union of Russian Cinematographers; Order of the Friendship of Peoples (twice) 1996, Order of Merit to the Fatherland 1999; Lenin Prize 1978, Prize of USSR Journalists' Union 1975. *Publications:* several books and more than 30 film scripts. *Leisure interest:* tennis. *Address:* ITAR-TASS, Tverskoy blvd 10-12, 125993 Moscow, Russia (office). *Telephone:* (495) 629-79-25 (office). *Fax:* (495) 203-31-80 (office). *E-mail:* info@itar-tass.com (office). *Website:* www.itar-tass.com/eng (office).

IGNATIEFF, Michael, BA, MA, PhD; Canadian writer, historian, academic and politician; *Leader, Liberal Party of Canada;* b. 12 May 1947, Toronto, Ont.; m. 1st Susan Barrowclough 1977; one s. one d.; m. 2nd Zsuzsanna Zsohar; ed Univ. of Toronto, Harvard Univ., Univ. of Cambridge; reporter, Globe and Mail newspaper, Toronto 1966–67; Teaching Fellow, Harvard Univ. 1971–74; Asst Prof., Univ. of British Columbia, Vancouver 1976–78; Sr Research Fellow, King's Coll., Cambridge 1978–84; Visiting Prof., École des Hautes Études, Paris 1985; editorial columnist, The Observer, London 1990–93; corresp. for BBC, Observer, New Yorker 1984–2000; mem., Int. Comm. on Sovereignty and Intervention; Carr Prof. of Human Rights Practice, Harvard Univ. 2000–05, Dir Carr Center for Human Rights Policy, John F. Kennedy School of Govt 2001–05; Chancellor Jackman Visiting Prof. in Human Rights Policy, Univ. of Toronto 2005; MP (Liberal) for Etobicoke-Lakeshore 2006–, assoc. critic for Human Resources and Skills Devt in Official Opposition Shadow Cabinet 2006; unsuccessful campaign for leadership of Liberal Party of Canada 2006, Deputy Leader 2006–08, interim Leader of Liberal Party of Canada 2008–09, Leader 2009–; Dr hc (Bishop's Univ.) 1995; Lionel Gelber Award 1994. *Television:* host of Thinking Aloud (BBC) 1986, Voices (Channel Four) 1986, The Late Show (BBC 2) 1989. *Publications:* A Just Measure of Pain: The Penitentiary in the Industrial Revolution 1978, Wealth and Virtue: The Shaping of Classical Political Economy in the Scottish Enlightenment (co-ed. with Istvan Hont) 1983, The Needs of Strangers: An Essay on the Philosophy of Human Needs 1984, The Russian Album: A Family Memoir (RSL W. H. Heinemann Award, UK, Governor-General Award, Canada 1988) 1987, Asya 1991, Scar Tissue (novel) 1993, Blood and Belonging: Journeys into the New Nationalism 1993, Isaiah Berlin: A Life 1998, The Warrior's Honor: Ethnic War and the Modern Conscience 1998, Virtual War: Kosovo and Beyond 2000, The Rights Revolution (Massey Lectures 2000) 2001, Human Rights as Politics and Idolatry (Tanner Lectures) 2001, Charlie Johnson in the Flames 2003, The Lesser Evil: Political Ethics in an Age of Terror 2004, After Paradise 2005; contribs to New York Times, New Yorker, New York Review of Books. *Address:* Room 435-S, Centre Block, House of Commons, Ottawa ON K1A 0A6 (office); Liberal Party of Canada, 81 Metcalfe St, Suite 400, Ottawa, ON K1P 6M8; Etobicoke Constituency Office, 656 The Queensway, Toronto, ON M8Y 1K7, Canada (office). *Telephone:* (613) 995-9364 (office). *Fax:* (613) 992-5880 (office). *E-mail:* ignatm@parl.gc.ca (office). *Website:* www.liberal.ca; www.michaelignatieffmp.ca (office).

IGNATIUS, David; American journalist and editor; *Associate Editor, The Washington Post;* b. 1950, Cambridge, Mass; m. Dr Eve Ignatius; three d.; ed Harvard Univ., King's Coll., Cambridge, UK; Ed. The Washington Monthly magazine 1975; reporter, The Wall Street Journal 1976–86, assignments included Steelworkers Corresp., Pittsburgh, Senate Corresp., Washington, DC, Middle East Corresp., Chief Diplomatic Corresp.; Ed. Sunday Outlook, The Washington Post 1986–90, Foreign Ed. 1990–93, apptd Asst Man. Business Ed. 1993, Assoc. Ed. 2004–; Exec. Ed. International Herald Tribune 2000–03; mem. Washington Post Writer's Group 2003–; Frank Knox Fellow, Harvard–Cambridge Univs 1973–75; Edward Weintal Prize for Diplomatic Reporting 1985, Gerald Loeb Award for Commentary 2000, Edward Weintal Certificate 2006. *Publications include:* Agents of Innocence 1987, SIRO 1991, The Bank of Fear 1994, A Firing Offense 1997, The Sun King 1999, Body of Lies 2007, The Increment 2009; contribs to The New York Times Magazine, The Atlantic Monthly, Foreign Affairs and The New Republic. *Address:* Washington Post Writers Group, 1150 15th Sreet, NW, Washington, DC 20071, USA (office). *Telephone:* (202) 334-6548 (office). *Fax:* (202) 334-5269 (office). *E-mail:* davidignatius@washpost.com (office). *Website:* www.postwritersgroup.com (office).

IGNATIUS ZAKKA I IWAS, His Holiness Patriarch; Iraqi ecclesiastic; *Patriarch of Antioch and All the East (Supreme Head of Universal Syrian Orthodox Church);* b. 21 April 1933, Mosul; ed St Aphrem Syrian Orthodox Theol. Seminary, Mosul, Gen. Theol. Seminary, New York and New York Univ.; ordained 1957; consecrated Metropolitan for Archdiocese of Mosul 1963, transferred to Archdiocese of Baghdad 1969; Patriarch of Antioch and All the East (Supreme Head of Universal Syrian Orthodox Church) 1980–; fmr mem. Iraq Acad. of Science, Arabic Acad. of Jordan; fmr mem. Cen. Cttee WCC; Fellow, Faculty of Syriac Studies, Lutheran School of Theology, Chicago 1981; Hon. DD (Gen. Theol. Seminary, NY). *Publications:* several books and articles. *Address:* Syrian Orthodox Patriarchate, Bab Touma, B.P. 914, Damascus, Syria. *Telephone:* (11) 447036.

IGNATIYEV, Sergey Mikhailovich, CandSci, PhD; Russian economist and central banker; *Chairman, Bank Rossii (Central Bank of the Russian Federation);* b. 10 Jan. 1948, Leningrad (now St Petersburg); m.; ed Moscow M. V. Lomonosov State Univ.; Sr Lecturer, Engels Leningrad Inst. of Soviet Trade 1978–88; Sr Lecturer and Assoc. Prof., Voznesenskii Leningrad Inst. of Finance and Econs 1988–91; Deputy Minister of Econs and Finance 1991–92, of Finance 1992–94, of Econs 1993–96; econ. adviser to Pres. Boris Yeltsin 1996–97; First Deputy Minister of Finance 1997–2002; Deputy Chair. Bank Rossii (Cen. Bank of the Russian Fed.) 1992–93, Chair. 2002–; Hon. Diploma, Russian Govt 1998; 850th Anniversary of Moscow Medal 1997, several govt awards. *Publications:* numerous articles and more than 20 research papers on econs. *Address:* Bank Rossii, 107016 Moscow, ul. Neglinnaya 12, Russia (office). *Telephone:* (495) 771-91-00 (office). *Fax:* (495) 921-64-65 (office). *Website:* www.cbr.ru (office).

IGRUNOV, Vyacheslav Vladimirovich; Russian politician; *Director, International Institute of Humanitarian and Political Studies;* b. 28 Oct. 1948, Cheznitsky, Zhytomer region, Ukraine; m.; four c.; ed Odessa State Inst. of Nat. Econs; detained by KGB due to his protest against invasion of Soviet army into Czechoslovakia 1968, participated in dissident movt 1960s, arrested 1975; released after campaign by Andrei Sakharov and Aleksandr Solzhenitsyn in his defence 1977; f. Samizdat Library; mem. staff 20th Century and World (bulletin) 1987; f. ideological Movt Memorial July 1987; f. Moscow Public Information Exchange Bureau M-BIO, newspaper Panorama 1988; Head of Programme Civil Soc. Foundation of Cultural Initiative 1990–92; Head of Analytical Centre in Goscomnats; Dir Int. Inst. of Humanitarian and Political Studies; mem. State Duma (Parl.) 1993–2003; Deputy Chair. public movt Yabloko 1996–2000, mem. faction Yabloko 1993–2003; mem. Expert Bd of Fed. Council (Parl.) 2005–. *Publications:* Problematics of Social Movements, Informal Political Clubs in Moscow 1989, Economic Reform as One of the Sources of National Clashes 1993, Russia and Ukraine 2001, Common Future 2004, The Shadow Theatre on the Eve of Distemper 2005, Phantoms of

Freedom, Equality, and Fraternity 2005, The East is Rising 2006, Nationalism is Exported from the West 2006, The Year Results. A View from Russia 2007, The End of Multi-Ethnicity 2007, Fundamentalistic Liberalism has Ceased to Exist 2008. *Leisure interests:* reading, talking with friends, writing memoirs and fairy tales for children. *Address:* International Institute of Humanitarian and Political Studies, Gazetny per. 5, 103918 Moscow, Russia (office). *Telephone:* (495) 232-26-43 (office); (495) 940-83-31 (home). *Fax:* (495) 232-26-43 (office). *E-mail:* igrunov@igpi.ru (office). *Website:* www.igrunov.ru (office).

IHAMUOTILA, Jaakko, MSEng; Finnish business executive; *Chairman, Millenium Prize Foundation;* b. 15 Nov. 1939, Helsinki; s. of Veikko Artturi Ihamuotila and Anna-Liisa Ihamuotila (née Kouki); m. Tuula Elina Turja 1965; two s. one d.; ed Univ. of Tech., Helsinki; Asst in Reactor Tech. 1963–66, Acting Asst to Prof. of Physics 1964–66; with Canadian Gen. Electric Co. Ltd, Toronto 1966; Imatran Voima Oy 1966–68; Valmet Oy 1968–70, Asst Dir 1970–72, Dir of Planning 1972–73, Man. Dir 1973–79, mem. Bd 1980–82; Pres. Int. Council of Acads of Eng. and Technological Sciences 2001; mem. Bd Neste Oy 1979–, Chair. and Chief Exec. 1980, now retd; Chair. Asko Oy, Silja Oy Ab, Chemical Industry Fed. of Finland; Chair. Millenium Prize Foundation, Finnish Acads of Tech.; mem. Supervisory Bd Merita Bank Ltd, MTV Finland, Finnish Cultural Foundation a.o.; mem. Bd of Dirs Finnair, Confed. of Finnish Industry and Employers, Pohjola Insurance Co.; mem. Council Econ. Orgs in Finland, Nat. Bd of Econ. Defence, Council of Univ. of Tech.; Hon. DTech. *Leisure interests:* tennis, outdoor pursuits. *Address:* Finnish Academies of Technology (FACTE), Mariankatu 8 B, 00170 Helsinki (office); Millenium Prize Foundation, Fredrikinkatu 25 B 26, 00120358 Helsinki, Finland (office). *Telephone:* (9) 2782400 (FACTE) (office); (9) 6818090 (office). *Fax:* (9) 2782177 (FACTE) (office). *E-mail:* jaakko.ihamuotila@facte.com (office). *Website:* www.facte.com (office); www.technologyawards.org (office).

IHSANOĞLU, Ekmeleddin, BSc, MSc, PhD; Turkish academic and international administrator; *Secretary-General, Organization of the Islamic Conference;* b. 26 Dec. 1943, Cairo, Egypt; m. Füsun Bilgiç 1971; three s.; ed Ankara Univ.; cataloger of printed and manuscript books, Dept of Oriental Studies, Cairo Nat. Library, 1962–66; Lecturer in Turkish Literature and Language, Ain Shams Univ., Cairo 1966–70, Ankara Univ., Turkey 1971–75; Research Fellow, Univ. of Exeter, UK 1975–77; Lecturer and Assoc. Prof., Faculty of Science, Ankara Univ. 1970–80; Assoc. Prof., İnönü Univ., Malatya, Turkey 1978–80; Dir-Gen. Islamic Conf. Research Centre for Islamic History, Art and Culture, Org. of the Islamic Conf. (OIC), Istanbul 1980–2004, Sec.-Gen. OIC, Jeddah, Saudi Arabia 2005–; Sec. Islamic Conf. Org. Int. Comm. for Preservation of Islamic Cultural Heritage, Istanbul 1983–2000 (now defunct); Founder and Chair. first Dept of History of Science in Turkey, Univ. of Istanbul 1984–2000; Chair. Turkish Soc. for History of Science, Istanbul 1989–; Vice-Chair. Al Furqan Islamic Heritage Foundation, London, UK 1998–; Pres. Int. Union of History and Philosophy of Science/Div. of History of Science 2001–; mem. numerous orgs concerned with study of history of science and Islamic civilization, including Acad. Int. d'Histoire des Sciences, Paris, Cultural Centre of the Atatürk Supreme Council for Culture, Language and History, Ankara, Int. Soc. for History of Arabic and Islamic Sciences and Philosophy, Paris, Royal Acad. of Islamic Civilization Research, Jordan, Middle East and the Balkans, Research Foundation, Istanbul, Acad. of Arabic Language (Jordan, Egypt, Syria), Egyptian History Soc., Cairo, Tunisian Acad. of Sciences, Letters and Arts 'Bait al Hikma', Tunis, Int. Soc. for History of Medicine, Paris; apptd Amb.-at-Large by Govt of Bosnia-Herzegovina 1997; Visiting Prof., Ludwig Maximilians Univ., Munich, Germany 2003; Hon. Consul, The Gambia 1990–; Commdr de l'Ordre Nat. du Mérit (Senegal) 2002, Commdr de l'Ordre Nat. du Lion (Senegal) 2006; Dr hc (Mimar Sinan Univ., Istanbul) 1994, (Dowling Coll., New York) 1996, (Azerbaijan Acad. of Sciences) 2000, (Univ. of Sofia) 2001, (Univ. of Sarajevo) 2001, (Univ. of Padova) 2006, (Islamic Univ. of Islamabad) 2007, (Univ. of Exeter) 2007, (Islamic Univ., Uganda) 2008; Distinction of the First Order Medal (Egypt) 1990, Certificate of Honour and Distinction, Org. of the Islamic Conf. 1995, Independence Medal of the First Order (Jordan) 1996, Medal of Distinguished State Service (Turkey) 2000, World Prize for Book of the Year (Iran) 2000, UNESCO Avicenna Medal 2004, Medal of Glory (Russia) 2006, Medal of Glory (Azerbaijan) 2006, Int. Acad. of the History of Science Alexandre Koyre Medal 2008. *Publications:* has written, edited and translated several books on Islamic culture and science; over 70 articles and papers. *Leisure interests:* reading and music, sponsoring and collecting Islamic works of art. *Address:* Organization of the Islamic Conference, POB 178, Jeddah 21411, Saudi Arabia (office); Türk Bostani Sokak, Dostlar Sitesi 35, Yenikoy 34464 Istanbul, Turkey (home). *Fax:* (2) 2751953 (Jeddah) (office). *E-mail:* cabinet@oic-oci.org (office). *Website:* www.oic-oci.org (office).

IIJIMA, Sumio, BEng, PhD; Japanese physicist and academic; *Professor, Meijo University;* b. 2 May 1939; ed Univ. of Electro-Communications, Tokyo, Tohoku Univ., Ariz. State Univ., USA; Research Assoc., Research Inst. for Scientific Measurements, Tohoku Univ. 1968–70; Postdoctoral Research Fellow and Research Scientist, Ariz. State Univ., USA 1970–82; Visiting Scholar, Cambridge Univ., England 1979; Researcher, Research Devt Corpn, Japan 1982–87; Prof., Dept of Materials Science and Eng, Meijo Univ., Nagoya 1999–; Sr Research Fellow, NEC Corpn, Ibaraki 1987–; Research Dir, Nanotubulite Project, Int. Cooperative Research Project (ICORP), Japan Science and Tech. Agency Corpn 1998–2002; Dir Research Center for Advanced Carbon Materials, Nat. Inst. of Advanced Science and Tech. (AIST) 2001–; Project Reader, NEDO Advanced Nanocarbon Application Project 2002–06, Carbon Nanotube Capacitator Devt Project 2006–; Research Dir JST/SORST Iijima Team 2003–08; Dean, Sungkyunkwan Univ. Advanced Inst. of Nanotechnology 2005–; mem. Royal Microscopy Soc., Materials Research Soc., American Crystallographic Asscn, Science Council of Japan, Physical Soc. of Japan, Japanese Soc. of Microscopy, Chemical Society of Japan; Fellow, Japan Soc. for Applied Physics 2007; Foreign Assoc., NAS 2007; Hon. Prof., Xi'an Jiaotong Univ. 2005, Peking Univ. 2005; Hon. Mem. Crystallographic Soc. of Japan; Hon. Fellow, American Physical Society; Dr hc (Univ. of Antwerp) 2002, (ETH) 2003,; Seto Award 1980, Nishina Memorial Award 1985, Ban Memorial Award 1989, Asahi Award 1996, Tsukuba Prize 1998, Ishikawa Carbon Award 2001, Agilent Technologies Europhysics Prize 2001, Benjamin Franklin Medal in Physics 2002, American Physical Soc. McGroddy Materials Prize 2002, Mukai Award 2002, Chunichi Bunka Award 2002, Japan Acad. Award and Imperial Award 2002, Outstanding Achievement Award, Japan Soc. of Applied Physics 2002, Person of Cultural Merits 2003, Honda Frontier Award 2004, Soc. Medal, American Carbon Soc. 2004, Distinguished Scientist Award, Microscopy Soc. of America 2005, John M. Cowley Medal 2006, Gregori Aminoff Prize 2007, Fujiwara Award 2007, Balzan Prize 2007. *Achievements:* discovered carbon nanotubes 1991. *Address:* Meijo University, Faculty of Science and Technology, 1-501, Shiogamaguchi, Tenpaku, Nogoya, Aichi 468-8502, Japan (office). *Telephone:* (52) 834-4001 (office); (298) 50-8501 (office). *Fax:* (52) 834-4001 (office); (298) 56-6136 (office). *E-mail:* iijimas@ccmfs.meijo-u.ac.jp (office).

IKAWA, Motomichi, PhD; Japanese banking and finance executive and academic; *Professor, Graduate School of Business, Nihon University;* b. 10 Feb. 1947, Tokyo; m. Yoshiko Ikawa; ed Tokyo Univ., Univ. of California at Berkeley; economist Balance of Payments Div., OECD, Paris 1976–79; various man. posts Ministry of Finance, Tokyo 1979–85; Asst Regional Commr, C.I.D., Osaka Taxation Bureau 1985–86; Dir Budget, Personnel and Man. Systems Dept, Asian Devt Bank 1986–89; Asst Vice-Minister of Finance, Int. Affairs 1989–90; Dir Int. Org. Div., Int. Finance Bureau, Ministry of Finance 1990–91, Foreign Exchange and Money Market Div. 1991–92, Devt Policy Div. 1992–93, Co-ordination Div. 1993–94; Man. Dir Co-ordination Dept, Overseas Econ. Co-operation Fund 1994-96; Deputy Dir-Gen. Int. Finance Bureau 1996–97, Sr Deputy Dir-Gen. 1997–98; Exec. Vice-Pres. Multilateral Investment Guarantee Agency (MIGA), World Bank Group 1998–2003; Prof., Exec. Man. Course, Nihon Univ. Grad. School of Business, Tokyo 2003–. *Publications:* Exchange Market Interventions during the Yen Depreciation 1980 1982, IMF Handbook 1990, The Role of the Overseas Economic Co-operation Fund Towards 2010 1994. *Leisure interests:* tennis, golf, hiking. *Address:* Nihon University Grad. School of Business, Kudanminami 4-8-24, Chiyoda-ku, Japan, Tokyo, 102-8275, Japan (office). *E-mail:* mikawa@gsb.nihon-u.ac.jp (office). *Website:* www.gsb.nihon-u.ac.jp (office).

IKEDA, Daisaku; Japanese Buddhist philosopher, peace activist and author; *President, Soka Gakkai International;* b. 2 Jan. 1928, Tokyo; s. of Nenokichi Ikeda and Ichi Ikeda; m. Kaneko Shiraki 1952; two s.; ed Fuji Coll.; Pres. Soka Gakkai 1960–79, Hon. Pres. 1979–, Pres. Soka Gakkai Int. 1975–; Founder Soka Univ., Soka Univ. of America, Soka Women's Coll., Tokyo and Kansai Soka Schools, Soka Kindergartens (Japan, Hong Kong, Singapore, Malaysia, Brazil, South Korea), Makiguchi Foundation for Educ., Inst. of Oriental Philosophy, Boston Research Center for the 21st Century, Toda Inst. for Global Peace and Policy Research, Tokyo Fuji Art Museum, Min-On Concert Asscn, Victor Hugo House of Literature and Komeito Party; mem. Advisory Bd World Centers of Compassion for Children Int., Ireland 2004–; Poet Laureate, World Acad. of Arts and Culture, USA 1981–; World People's Poet, World Poetry Soc. Intercontinental, India 2007–; Foreign mem. Brazilian Acad. of Letters 1993–; Hon. Prof., Nat. Univ. of San Marcos 1981, Peking Univ. 1984 and others; Hon. Senator, European Acad. of Sciences and Arts 1997–; Hon. Adviser, World Fed. of UN Asscns (WFUNA) 1999–; Hon. mem., The Club of Rome 1996–, Inst. of Oriental Studies of Russian Acad. of Sciences 1996–, Russian Acad. of Arts 2007–, and others; Order of the Sun of Peru with Grand Cross 1984, Grand Cross, Order of Merit of May (Argentina) 1990, Nat. Order of Southern Cross (Brazil) 1990, Kt Grand Cross of the Most Noble Order of the Crown (Thailand) 1991, Hon. Cross of Science and the Arts (Austria) 1992, Kt Grand Cross of Rizal (Philippines) 1996, Grande Officiale, Ordine al Merito (Italy) 2006, Order of Friendship (Russia) 2008, and others; Dr hc (Moscow State Univ.) 1975, (Sofia) 1981, (Buenos Aires) 1990, (Univ. of the Philippines) 1991, (Ankara) 1992, (Fed. Univ. of Rio de Janeiro) 1993, (Glasgow) 1994, (Hong Kong) 1996, (Havana) 1996, (Univ. of Ghana) 1996, (Cheju Nat. Univ.) 1999, (Delhi) 1999, (Queens Coll. City Univ. of NY) 2000, (Univ. of Sydney) 2000, (Morehouse Coll.) 2002, (Univ. of Guadalajara) 2004, (Tagore Int. Univ.) 2006, (Palermo) 2007, and others; UN Peace Award 1983, Kenya Oral Literature Award 1986, UNHCR Humanitarian Award 1989, Rosa Parks Humanitarian Award (USA) 1993, Simon Wiesenthal Center Int. Tolerance Award (USA) 1993, Tagore Peace Award, The Asiatic Soc. (India) 1997 and others. *Publications:* The Human Revolution Vols I–VI 1972–99, The Living Buddha 1976, Choose Life (with A. Toynbee) 1976, Buddhism: The First Millennium 1977, Songs From My Heart 1978, Glass Children and Other Essays 1979, La Nuit Appelle l'Aurore (with R. Huyghe) 1980, A Lasting Peace Vols I–II 1981, 1987, Life: An Enigma, a Precious Jewel 1982, Before It Is Too Late (with A. Peccei) 1984, Buddhism and the Cosmos 1985, The Flower of Chinese Buddhism 1986, Human Values in a Changing World (with B. Wilson) 1987, Unlocking the Mysteries of Birth and Death 1988, 2003, The Snow Country Prince 1990, A Lifelong Quest for Peace (with L. Pauling) 1992, Choose Peace (with J. Galtung) 1995, A New Humanism: The University Addresses of Daisaku Ikeda 1996, Ikeda-Jin Yong Dialogue (in Japanese) 1998, The New Human Revolution, Vols I–XIX (in Japanese) 1998–2008, The Wisdom of the Lotus Sutra, Vols I–VI 2000–03, The Way of Youth 2000, For the Sake of Peace 2001, Soka Education 2001, Diálogo sobre José Martí (with C. Vitier) 2001, The World is Yours to Change 2002, Choose Hope (with D. Krieger) 2002, Alborada del Pacífico (with P. Aylwin) 2002, On Being Human (with R. Simard and G. Bourgeault) 2002, Global Civilization: A Buddhist–Islamic Dialogue (with M. Tehranian) 2003, Fighting for Peace 2004,

Planetary Citizenship (with H. Henderson) 2004, One by One 2004, Moral Lessons of the Twentieth Century (with M. Gorbachev) 2005, Revolutions: To Green the Environment, To Grow the Human Heart (with M. S. Swaminathan) 2005, A Quest for Global Peace (with J. Rothblat) 2006, A Dialogue between East and West (with R. Díez-Hochleitner) 2008, Embracing the Future 2008, A Passage to Peace (with N. Yalman) 2008, and other writings on Buddhism, civilization, life and peace. *Leisure interests:* poetry, photography. *Address:* 32 Shinano-machi, Shinjuku-ku, Tokyo 160-8583, Japan (office). *Telephone:* (3) 5360-9831 (office). *Fax:* (3) 5360-9885 (office). *E-mail:* sgipr@sgi .gr.jp (office). *Website:* www.sgi.org (office); www.daisakuikeda.org (home).

IKEDA, Yukihiko; Japanese politician; b. 13 May 1937, Kobe City, Hyogo Pref.; ed Univ. of Tokyo; Overall Co-ordination Div. Minister's Secr., Ministry of Finance 1961; seconded to Ministry of Foreign Affairs (served four years as Vice-Consul, New York) 1964; Pvt. Sec. to Minister of Finance 1974; mem. House of Reps 1976–, House of Reps Budget Cttee; Deputy Chief Cabinet Sec. 1981; Chair. Prime Minister's Office Div., Policy Research Council of LDP 1983; Chair. House of Reps Cttee on Finance 1986, Cttee on Basic Policies of the Nation 2002; Dir-Gen. Man. and Co-ordination Agency June–Aug. 1989; Deputy Sec.-Gen. LDP March–Dec. 1990, Chair. Policy Research Council 1998–99, Gen. Council 1999–2000; Dir-Gen. Defence Agency 1990–91; Minister for Foreign Affairs 1996–97. *Address:* c/o Liberal-Democratic Party, 1-11-23, Nagata-cho, Chiyoda-ku, Tokyo 100, Japan.

IKLÉ, Fred Charles, PhD; American social scientist and fmr government official; *Distinguished Scholar, Center for Strategic and International Studies;* b. 21 Aug. 1924, Fex, Switzerland; s. of Frederick A. Iklé and Hedwig Iklé (née Huber); m. Doris Eisemann 1959; two d.; ed Univ. of Chicago; research scholar, Bureau of Applied Social Research, Columbia Univ. 1950–54; mem. Social Science Dept, Rand Corpn 1955–61, Head of Dept 1968–73; Research Assoc. in Int. Relations, Center for Int. Affairs, Harvard Univ. 1962–63; Assoc. Prof., then Prof. of Political Science, MIT 1963–67; Dir US Arms Control and Disarmament Agency 1973–77; Under-Sec. of Defense for Policy 1981–88; Distinguished Scholar, Center for Strategic and Int. Studies 1988–; Dir Defense Forum Foundation 1988–; Dir Nat. Endowment for Democracy 1992–2001; Co-Chair. US Comm. on Integrated Long Term Strategy 1987–88; mem. Bd Int. Peace Acad. 1977–81; Chair. Council on Nat. Security of Republican Nat. Cttee 1977–79; Chair. CMC Energy Services 1978–81, mem. Bd 1988–, Chair. Telos Corpn 1995–2002, mem. Bd 2003–06; Gov. Smith Richardson Foundation 1996–; Chair. US Cttee for Human Rights in N Korea 2001–04, mem. Bd 2004–; US Defense Dept Distinguished Public Service Awards 1975, 1987, 1988. *Publications:* The Social Impact of Bomb Destruction 1958, After Detection...What? 1961, How Nations Negotiate 1964, Every War Must End 1971, Can Nuclear Deterrence Last Out The Century? 1973, Annihilation From Within 2006; numerous contribs to books and articles in journals on int. affairs. *Address:* Center for Strategic and International Studies, 1800 K Street, NW, Washington, DC 20006 (office); 7010 Glenbrook Road, Bethesda, MD 20814, USA (home). *Telephone:* (202) 775-3155 (office). *Fax:* (202) 775-3199 (office). *E-mail:* aditus9@verizon.net (office). *Website:* www.csis.org/experts (office).

IKOUEBE, Basile; Republic of the Congo diplomatist; *Minister of Foreign Affairs;* b. 1 July 1946; m.; six c.; ed Int. Inst. of Public Admin, Paris, Inst. for Political Studies, Bordeaux; apptd Chief Int. Orgs Div., Ministry of Foreign Affairs 1974, Prin. Pvt. Sec. to Minister 1975–77, Sec. to Ministry 1977–79; training assignment in France 1980–82; Diplomatic Adviser to Head of State 1982–92; Minister and Prin. Pvt. Sec. to Head of State 1987–94; Amb.-at-Large 1994–95; Sec. to Ministry of Foreign Affairs and Co-operation 1996–98; Perm. Rep. to UN 1998–2007, Pres. UN Security Council 2006; Minister of Foreign Affairs 2007–. *Address:* Ministry of Foreign Affairs, BP 2070, Brazzaville, Republic of the Congo (office). *Telephone:* 81-10-89 (office). *Fax:* 81-41-61 (office).

IKUTA, Masaharu; Japanese business executive; ed Keio Univ.; joined Mitsui OSK Lines Ltd 1957, mem. Bd of Dirs 1987–2003, Pres. 1994–2000, Chair. 2000–03; Pres. Japan Post (now Japan Post Holdings Co., Ltd) 2003–07; Chair. Business and Industry Advisory Cttee, Japan Fed. of Econ. Orgs (Nippon Keidanren) –2003; fmr Vice-Chair. Japan Asscn of Corp. Execs; mem. Int. Advisory Council, PSA Corpn Ltd 2002; Hon. Consul of the Repub. . of Mauritius 2002–; Blue Ribbon Medal Award 1998. *Address:* c/o Japan Post, 1-3-2 Kasumigaseki, Chiyoda-ku, Tokyo 100-8798, Japan (office).

ILIA II, Catholicos-Patriarch of All Georgia; Georgian ecclesiastic; b. 4 Dec. 1933, Irakli Ghudushauri-Shiolashvili, Vladikavkaz, N Ossetia; ed Moscow Theological Seminary, Moscow Theological Acad.; took monastic vows 1957; Father-Superior 1960; Archimandrite 1961; Bishop of Shemokmedi and Vicar to the Georgian Patriarch Ephrem II Aug. 1963; entrusted with Sukhumi and Abkhazia Diocese 1967; Sukhumi-Abkhaz Mitropolite 1969; Rector Mtskheta Orthodox Theological Seminary 1963–72; awarded Second Panagya 1972; enthroned as Archbishop of Mtskheta-Tbilisi and Catholicos-Patriarch of All Georgia 1977–; Co-Pres. World Council of Churches 1978–83; Dr of Theology, American St-Vladimir Theological Acad.; Hon. Academician, Georgian Acad. of Sciences 2003, Int. Acad. for the Promotion of Scientific Research 2007; Order of Friendship of Peoples; Hon. DTheol (St Vladimir's Orthodox Theological Seminary, New York, USA) 1986, (Acad. of Sciences, Crete) 1997, (St Tikhon's Orthodox Theological Seminary, Pa, USA) 1998; holder of highest awards of churches of Georgia, Constantinople, Alexandria, Antioch, Jerusalem, Russia, Czechoslovakia and Poland; David Guramishvili Prize 2008. *Address:* Patriarchate of the Georgian Orthodox Church, 0105, Tbilisi, King Erekle II Sq. 1, Georgia. *Telephone:* (32) 99-03-78. *Fax:* (32) 98-71-14. *E-mail:* orthodox@patriarchate.ge. *Website:* www.patriarchate.ge.

ILIĆ, Venceslav; Bosnia and Herzegovina judge; *President of Appellate Division, Supreme Court of the Federation of Bosnia and Herzegovina;* b. 10 Sept. 1937, Sarajevo; s. of Anto Ilić and Ema Ilić (née Uršić); m. Bogdanka Ilić (née Mioković); two d.; Dist Court Judge 1972–78; Public Prosecutor 1978–84; Supreme Court Judge 1984–87, 1992–96; Pres. Dist Court 1987–92; apptd Pres. Supreme Court, Fed. of Bosnia and Herzegovina 1996, currently Pres. Appellate Div.; Medallion of the City of Sarajevo. *Publications:* work on educ. of juridical personnel. *Leisure interests:* work for sports orgs, walking in the countryside. *Address:* Appellate Division, Supreme Court of the Federation of Bosnia and Herzegovina, 71000 Sarajevo, Valtera Perića 15, Federation of Bosnia and Herzegovina (office). *Telephone:* (33) 664754 (office).

ILIESCU, Ion; Romanian fmr head of state and engineer; *Senator;* b. 3 March 1930, Oltenița, Ilfov Dist; s. of Alexandru Iliescu; m. Elena (Nina) Șerbănescu 1951; ed Bucharest Polytechnic Inst. and Energy Inst., Moscow, USSR; researcher, Energy Eng Inst., Bucharest 1955; Pres. Union of Student Asscns 1957–60; Alt. mem. Cen. Cttee of RCP 1965–68, mem. 1968–84; First Sec. Cen. Cttee of Union of Communist Youth and Minister for Youth 1967–71; Sec. RCP Cen. Cttee 1971; Vice-Chair. Timiș Co. Council 1971–74; Chair Iași Co. Council 1974–79; accused of "intellectual deviationism" and kept under surveillance; Chair. Nat. Water Council 1979–84; Dir Tech. Publishing House, Bucharest 1984–89; Pres. Nat. Salvation Front 1989–90, Provisional Council for Nat. Unity Feb.–May 1990; Pres. of Romania 1990–96, 2000–04; Senator 1996–2000, 2004–; fmr Pres. Party of Social Democracy of Romania (merged with SDP to become Social Democratic Party 2001); Chevalier de la Légion d'honneur and other state decorations; hon. doctorates from numerous univs. *Publications:* Global Problems and Creativity, Revolution and Reform, Romania in Europe and in the World, Where is Romanian Society Going?, Romanian Revolution, Hope Reborn, Integration and Globalisation – A Romanian Vision, Romanian Culture and European Identity, For Sustainable Development, The Great Shock at the End of a Short Century; studies on water man. and ecology, political power and social relations. *Leisure interests:* global problems, political and econ. sciences. *Address:* c/o Office of the Former President, Athena str. 11, Bucharest; Senate of Romania, Bucharest, Romania.

ILIOPOULOS, John, PhD; Greek physicist and academic; *Director, Theoretical Physics Laboratory, École Normale Supérieure;* b. 1940, Kalamata; m.; one s.; ed École Normale Supérieure, Paris, France; currently Dir Theoretical Physics Lab., École Normale Supérieure, Paris; J.J. Sakurai Prize for Theoretical Particle Physics (co-recipient) 1987, Aristeio Prize (first recipient) 2002, Dirac Medal, Abdus Salam Int. Centre for Theoretical Physics 2007. *Achievements include:* first person to present the Standard Model of particle physics in a single report 1974; also first, along with colleagues Glashow and Maiani, to recognize the critical importance of a fourth quark, later known as the 'Charm quark'. *Publications:* numerous scientific papers in professional journals. *Address:* Laboratoire de Physique Théorique, Ecole Normale Supérieure, École normale supérieure, 45 rue d'Ulm, 75230 Paris Cedex 05, France (office). *Telephone:* 1-44-32-34-22 (office). *Fax:* 1-44-32-20-99 (office). *E-mail:* info@lpt.ens.fr (office). *Website:* www.lpt.ens.fr (office).

ILLARIONOV, Andrei (Nikolayevich), PhD; Russian economist; *Senior Fellow, Center for Global Liberty and Prosperity, Cato Institute;* b. 16 Sept. 1961, Leningrad (now St Petersburg); ed Leningrad Univ., Univ. of Birmingham, UK, Georgetown Univ., USA; Asst Researcher, Leningrad State Univ. 1983–90; Head of Sector, St Petersburg Financial and Econ. Inst. 1990–92; Deputy Dir Centre for Econ. Reforms, Russian Govt 1992–93; Adviser to the Prime Minister 1993–94; Dir Inst. of Econ. Analysis 1994–2000, Pres. 2000–; Adviser to Pres. Putin on Econ. Problems 2000–05 (resgnd); Russian Sherpa to G8 2000–05 (resgnd); Sr Fellow, Center for Global Liberty and Prosperity, Cato Inst., Washington, DC 2006–. *Publications:* Russian Economic Reforms: Lost Year 1994, Financial Stabilization in Russia 1995, Russia in a Changing World 1997, Economic Freedom of the World (co-author and co-ed.) 2000; more than 300 articles on Russian econ. and social policy. *Address:* Cato Institute, 1000 Massachusetts Avenue, NW, Washington, DC 20001-5403, USA (office). *Telephone:* (202) 842-0200 (office). *Fax:* (202) 842-3490 (office). *E-mail:* aIllarionov@cato.org (office). *Website:* (office).

ILLNEROVÁ, Helena, RNDr, DSc; Czech physiologist and academic; *Senior Scientist, Institute of Physiology, Academy of Sciences of the Czech Republic;* b. 28 Dec. 1937, Prague; d. of the late Karel Lagus and Libuše Lagusova; m. Michal Illner; one s. one d.; ed Charles Univ., Prague; researcher, Inst. of Physiology Acad. of Sciences, Prague 1961–, Vice-Pres. Acad. of Sciences, Prague 1993–2001, Pres. 2001–05, now Sr Scientist, Inst. of Physiology; Sr Lecturer, Charles Univ., Prague 1995–; Pres. Czech Comm. for UNESCO 2006–09; mem. European Research Advisory Bd 2001–07, Ethics Panel of Czech TV 2005–, Learned Soc. of the Czech Repub., Cttee of Club of Melatonin and numerous other academic and scientific orgs; unsuccessful cand. for Senate 2008; J.E. Purkyně Prize 1987, Medal of the Slovak Acad. of Sciences 2004, Univ. Gold Medal 2005, Votočkova Medal, Inst. of Chemical Tech. 2005, Medal of the Learned Society of the Czech Repub. 2007, ASCR Medal of Merit for Science and Humanity 2007. *Publications:* over 100 scientific publs. *Leisure interests:* literature, hiking, academic activities. *Address:* Bronzová 2021, 155 00 Prague 5 (home); Institute of Physiology, Academy of Sciences, Vídeňská 1083, 142 20 Prague 4, Czech Republic (office). *Telephone:* (2) 24229610 (office); (2) 41062437 (office); (2) 35512182 (home); (2) 41062485 (office). *E-mail:* illner@biomed.cas.cz (office). *Website:* www.cas.cz (office); www.helenaillnerova.cz.

ILLUECA SIBAUSTE, Jorge Enrique, LLD; Panamanian politician and diplomatist; b. 17 Dec. 1918, Panama City; m.; four c.; ed Univ. de Panamá, Harvard Law School, Univ. of Chicago, USA; Prof., Univ. de Panamá 1962–63, 1966–68; Pres. Nat. Bar Asscn 1963–64, 1966–68; Dir El Panamá América (newspaper) 1963–64, 1967–68; Special Amb. to USA to begin negotiations for new Panama Canal Treaty 1964, Special Envoy for negotiations on the treaty 1972; mem. dels to UN Gen. Ass. 1957, 1961, 1975, also to 3rd Special Emergency Session; Head of Del. to 1st Session of 3rd UN Conf. on Law of the Sea 1974, mem. Del. to 4th Session 1976; Deputy Perm. Rep. to UN 1957, Perm. Rep. 1960, 1976–81, 1994–97, Pres. 38th Session of UN Gen. Ass. Sept.–Dec. 1983; mem. Perm. Court of Arbitration, The Hague, Netherlands 1974–76; Foreign Minister 1983–84; Vice-Pres. of Panama 1982–83, Pres. Feb.–Oct. 1984; U Thant Award 1983. *Address:* c/o Ministry of Foreign Affairs, Panamá 4, Panama.

ILOILOVATU ULUIVUDA, Ratu Josefa, CF, MBE, JP; Fijian head of state; *President;* b. 29 Dec. 1920, Vuda, Ba Prov.; m. Adi Salaseini Kavunono; fmr teacher, civil admin., prov. admin.; Vice-Pres. Methodist Church of Fiji and Rotuma 1997–98; fmr MP and Pres. of Senate; Vice-Pres. –2000, Acting Pres. Dec. 2000–01, Pres. of Fiji 2001– (presidential powers seized by Cdre Frank Bainimarama Dec. 2006, reinstated to interim govt Jan. 2007); Pres. Bd Trustees Native Land Trust Bd 2001–. *Address:* Office of the President, Government House, Berkley Crescent, PO Box 2513, Government Buildings, Suva, Fiji (office). *Telephone:* 3314244 (office). *Fax:* 3301645 (office). *Website:* www.fiji.gov.fj/publish/president.shtml.

ILVES, Toomas Hendrik, MA; Estonian politician, diplomatist, scientist and head of state; *President;* b. 26 Dec. 1953, Stockholm, Sweden; m. 1st Merry Bullock (divorced); one s. one d.; m. 2nd Evelin Ilves; one d.; ed Columbia Univ., New York, Univ. of Pennsylvania, USA; Research Asst, Dept of Psychology, Columbia Univ. 1974–76, 1979; Asst to Dir and English Teacher, Center for Open Educ., Englewood, NJ 1979–81; Arts Admin. and Dir Vancouver Literary Centre, Canada 1981–82; Lecturer in Estonian Literature and Linguistics, Dept of Interdisciplinary Studies, Simon Fraser Univ., Vancouver 1983–84; Research Analyst, Radio Free Europe, Munich, Germany 1984–88, Dir Estonian Service 1988–93; Amb. to USA (also accred to Canada and Mexico) 1993–96; Minister of Foreign Affairs 1996–98, 1999–2002; Chair. Bd Estonian N Atlantic Trust 1998; mem. Riigikogu (Estonian State Ass.) 1999–; Deputy Chair. Moodukad Party, Chair. 1999; mem. European Parl. (Sotsiaaldemokraatlik Erakond) 1999–2006, Vice-Chair. Cttee on Foreign Affairs, mem. Del. for Relations with the USA, Substitute mem. Cttee on Budgets, Sub-cttee on Security and Defence, Del. to EU-Russia Parl. Cooperation Cttee; Pres. of Estonia 2006–; Pres. Estonian Special Olympics 1997–2004; Bd mem. Tartu Univ. 1996–2003, European Movt Estonia (EME) 1999–2004, Estonian Acad. of Arts 2004–06, Trilateral Comm. 2004–06, Friends of Europe (think-tank) 2005, Viljandi Co. Municipal Fund; Grand Commdr, Légion d'honneur 2001, Third Class, Order of the Seal (Estonia) 2004, Three Star Order of the Repub. (Latvia) 2004, Collar of the Order of the Cross of Terra Mariana (Estonia) 2006, Hon. GCB (UK) 2006, Order of the White Rose of Finland 2007, Golden Fleece, Order of Georgia 2007, Grand Cordon of the Supreme Order of the Chrysanthemum of Japan 2007, Order of Isabel the Catholic with collar (Spain) 2007, Collar of the Order of the Nat. Coat of Arms (Estonia) 2008, Order of Vytautas the Great with Golden Chain (Lithuania) 2008, Grand Cross, Order of the Netherlands Lion 2008, Grand Cordon, Leopold of Belgium 2008. *Leisure interests:* reading, cooking, farming. *Address:* Office of the President, A. Weizenbergi 39, Tallinn 15050, Estonia (office). *Telephone:* 631-6202 (office). *Fax:* 631-6250 (office). *E-mail:* vpinfo@vpk.ee (office). *Website:* www.president.ee (office).

ILYASOV, Stanislav; Russian politician; b. 24 July 1953, Kizlyar, Repub. of Dagestan; m.; four c.; ed Leningrad Electricity Inst.; fmr nat. champion in free-style wrestling; served in armed forces 1972–75; supervisor Kizlyar power grid; deputy dir electrical equipment plant, Zaterechny; elected Deputy Chair. Kizlyar Municipal Exec. Cttee 1987, later Chair.; Gen. Dir Spetsenergoremont (repairs and construction co.), Makhachkala 1990–93; Gen. Dir Southern Grid, Unified Energy Systems (UES) 1993–94, Deputy CEO of a UES subsidiary, N Caucasus 1994, later CEO, Vice-Pres. of UES May–Aug. 1997; CEO Energoperetok Inc. 1997; apptd First Vice-Prime Minister of Stavropol 1997, Premier of Stavropol 1997–99; First Vice-Pres. Yediny Elektroenergeticheski Kompleks Rossiiskoi Federatsii Corpn 1999–2001; Prime Minister of Govt of Chechnya 2001–02; Fed. Minister for Chechen Affairs 2002–04; Dir Fed. Agency for Fisheries 2004–07. *Address:* c/o Office of the Government, Krasnopresnenskaya nab. 2, 103274 Moscow, Russia (office).

ILYENKO, Yuriy Gerasimovich; Ukrainian cinematographer, director, writer, producer and actor; b. 18 July 1936, Ukraine; s. of Gerasim Ilyenko and Maria Ilyenko; m. Liudmyla Yefymenko 1977; two s.; ed VGIK, Moscow; Head Sub-Faculty of Directing and Dramatic Composition, State Inst. of Theatrical Arts, Kiev; founder mem. Ukrainian Acad. of Arts 1996–; T. Sherchenko Prize 1991, People's Artist of Ukraine 1987. *Films include:* 1 Newton Str. (as actor) 1963, Shadows of Our Forgotten Ancestors (by Paradzhyanov) 1964 (16 int. prizes); (as director), A Spring for the Thirsty 1965, On the Eve of Ivan Kupalo Day 1968, A White Bird with a Black Mark 1971, In Defiance of All 1972, To Dream and to Live 1974, Baked Potato Festival 1977, The Forest Song 1981, Strip of Wild Flowers 1982, Legend of Queen Olga 1983, Straw Bells 1985, Swan Lake – The Zone 1990 (2 prizes, Cannes Film Festival), A Score of Christ 1991, A Prayer for Hetman Mazepa 2002. *Publications:* The Paradigm of Film (Theory of Film) 1999. *Leisure interest:* painting (exhibited in Kiev, Munich and Vienna). *Address:* 9 Michail Kotzybinksy Str., Apt. 22, Kiev 252030, Ukraine (home). *Telephone:* (44) 234-75-40 (home). *Fax:* (44) 234-75-40 (home).

IL'YIN, Leonid Andreyevich, DMed; Russian toxicologist and academic; *Professor Emeritus, State Research Center of Russia, Institute of Biophysics;* b. 15 March 1928; ed First Leningrad Medical Inst.; worked as doctor in the navy, Head of Lab. of Irradiation Protection, Deputy Dir Leningrad Inst. of Irradiation Protection, USSR Ministry of Public Health 1961–67; Dir, Prof., State Research Center of Russia, Inst. of Biophysics, Ministry of Public Health 1968–89, Prof. Emer. 1989–; Dir Inst. of Radiation Medicine 1989–; Pres. Sectiya Radiazionnoy Gigieny of Russia, Int. Radiation Protection Asscn; mem. Russian Acad. of Medical Sciences 1982, Vice-Pres. 1984–90; Deputy Chair. Soviet Cttee Doctors Against the Nuclear Threat 1984–90; Hero of Socialist Labour; USSR State Prize, Pirogov Prize. *Publications:* more than 100 works on problems of toxicology and radiation medicine, including A Threat of Nuclear War (with E. Chazov). *Address:* State Research Center of Russia, Institute of Biophysics, Ministry of Public Health, Zhivopisnaya Street 46, 123182 Moscow, Russia (office). *Telephone:* (495) 190-94-11 (office). *Fax:* (495) 190-35-90 (office). *E-mail:* clinic@rcibph.dol.ru (office).

ILYUMZHINOV, Kirsan; Russian politician, business executive and international organization official; *President of the Republic of Kalmykiya; President, Fédération Internationale des Échecs, FIDE (World Chess Federation);* b. 5 April 1962, Elista; m.; one s.; ed Moscow State Inst. of Int. Relations; Pres. Repub. of Kalmykiya, S Russia 1993–, re-elected 2000 (youngest leader of any fed. subject of Russian Fed. when first elected); Pres. Fédération Internationale des Échecs (FIDE) 1995–; Honoured Citizen of Elista; Order of Friendship, Order of Nicholas the Wondermaker, Order of Merit – George with a Sword; Gold Medal of Peace for Humanitarian Activity. *Publications include:* The President's Crown of Thorns 1998. *Leisure interest:* chess (chess champion of Kalmykiya as schoolboy). *Address:* Dom Pravitelstva, pl. Lenina, 358000 Elista, Republic of Kalmykia, Russian Federation (office). *Telephone:* (84722) 330-88 (office). *Fax:* (84722) 338-57 (office). *E-mail:* ki@kalm.ru (office). *Website:* www.fide.com (office); glava.kalm.ru.

ILYUSHIN, Viktor Vasilyevich; Russian politician and business executive; *Head, Corporate Interrelations with Regional Authorities of the Russian Federation, Gazprom;* b. 4 June 1947, Nizhny Tagil, Sverdlovsk Oblast; m.; one s. one d.; ed Urals Polytech. Inst., Acad. of Social Science; metalworker Nizhny Tagil metallurgy plant; First Sec. Nizhny Tagil City Komsomol Cttee, then First Sec. Sverdlovsk Regional Komsomol Cttee, Asst to First Sec. Sverdlovsk Regional CPSU Cttee; First Sec. Leninsky Dist CPSU Cttee (Sverdlovsk); counsellor Cen. Cttee Afghanistan People's Democractic Party; Asst to Chair. Russian Supreme Soviet 1990–91; Head, Pres. Yeltsin's Secr. 1991–92; First Asst Pres. of Russian Fed. 1991–96; First Deputy Prime Minister 1996–97; Head, Public Relations and Corp. Interrelations with Regional Authorities of Russian Fed. Admin, Gazprom 1997–98, Head, Corp. Interrelations with Regional Authorities of Russian Fed. Admin 1998–, mem. Man. Cttee; Badge of Honour. *Leisure interests:* tennis, mountain skiing, riding, jazz, cars, computers. *Address:* Gazprom, Nametkina str. 16, 117997 Moscow, Russia (office). *Telephone:* (495) 719-30-01 (office). *Fax:* (495) 719-83-33 (office). *Website:* www.gazprom.ru (office).

IM, Kwon-taek; South Korean film director; b. 2 May 1936, Changsong, Cheollanam-do; ed Sr High School, Kwangju; began career as labourer, Pusan; Production Asst with film Dir Chung Chang-Hwa, Seoul 1956–61; made first feature film 1962, subsequently directed over 100 films; prof. Coll. of Arts, Dongguk Univ. (Seoul) 1998–; mem. Nat. Acad. of Arts Republic of Korea 2002; Hon. DLit (Catholic Univ. of Korea); UNESCO Fellini Gold Medal 2002 for his work as a whole, Hon. Golden Bear Berlin Film Festival 2005; numerous other Korean and int. film festival awards. *Films include:* Dumanganga jal itgeola (Farewell to the Duman River) 1962, Danjang lok (The Prince's Revolt) 1963, Mangbuseog (A Wife Turned to Stone) 1963, Shibjamae seonsaeng (Father of Ten Daughters) 1964, Bisog e Jida (Death of an Informer) 1965, Pungunui gomgaek (Swordsmen) 1967, Cheongsa cholong (The Feudal Tenant) 1967, Tola-on oensonjabi (Return from the Sea) 1968, Mongnyeo (The Waking Woman) 1968, Sibo Ya (Full Moon Night) 1969, Roe Gom (Thunder Sword) 1969, Weolha ui geom (Swords under the Moon) 1970, Bigeom (The Flying Sword) 1970, Yogeom (Swordswoman) 1971, Tuljjae omoni (A Stepmother's Heartache) 1971, Myeongdong janhoksa (Cruelty on the Streets of Myongdong) 1972, Jung eon (The Testimony) 1973, Jabcho (The Deserted Widow) 1973, Yeonhwa (The Hidden Princess) 1974, Wae geulaessteunga (Who and Why?) 1975, Anae (The Industrious Wife) 1976, Sangnok su (The Evergreen Tree) 1978, Chopko (Genealogy) 1978, Tchak Ko (Pursuit of Death) 1980, Mandala 1981, Angae Maul (Village in the Mist) 1982, Gilsottum 1985, Sibaji (The Surrogate Woman) 1986, Yonsan Ilgi (Diary of King Yongsan) 1987, Adada 1988, Janggunui adeul (Son of the General) 1990, Kae Byok (Fly High Run Far) 1992, Sopyonje 1993 (most honoured Korean film ever: 27 domestic and three international prizes), Taebek sanmaek (Taebak Mountains) 1994, Ch'ukje 1986, Chunhyang 2000, Chihwaseon (Strokes of Fire) (Best Director Award at 2002 Cannes International Film Festival) 2002, Haryu insaeng 2004, Chun nyun hack 2007.

IMAI, Nobuko; Japanese violist; b. 18 March 1943, Tokyo; m. Aart van Bochove 1981; one s. one d.; ed Toho School of Music, Tokyo, Juilliard School and Yale Univ., USA; mem. Vermeer Quartet 1974–79; soloist with Berlin Philharmonic, London Symphony Orchestra, Royal Philharmonic, the BBC orchestras, Detroit Symphony, Chicago Symphony, Concertgebouw, Montréal Symphony, Boston Symphony, Vienna Symphony, Orchestre de Paris, Stockholm Philharmonic; festival performances include Marlborough, Salzburg, Lockenhaus, Casals, South Bank, Summer Music, Aldeburgh, BBC Proms, Int. Viola Congress (Houston), New York "Y", Festival d'Automne, Paris; conceived Int. Hindemith Viola Festival (London, New York, Tokyo) 1995; Prof. High School of Music, Detmold, Germany 1985–2003; Artistic Adviser, Casals Hall, Tokyo; over 20 recordings; First Prize Munich, Second Prize Geneva Int. Viola Competitions; Avon Arts Award 1993, Japanese Educ. Minister's Art Prize for Music 1993, Mobil Japan Art Prize 1995, Suntory Hall Prize 1996. *Leisure interest:* cooking. *Address:* c/o Sue Lubbock Artist Management, 25 Courthope Road, London NW3 2LE, England (office).

Telephone: (20) 7485-5932 (office). *Fax:* (20) 7900-1727 (office). *E-mail:* lubbockartist@clara.co.uk (office).

IMAI, Takashi; Japanese business executive; *Senior Vice-President, Chairman Emeritus and Executive Counselor, Nippon Steel Corporation;* b. 23 Dec. 1929, Kamakura; ed Univ. of Tokyo; joined Fuji Iron & Steel 1952, Man. Raw Materials 1963; Deputy Gen. Man. Fuel and Ferrous Metals, Nippon Steel (formed by merger of Fuji Iron & Steel and Yawata Steel) 1970, Gen. Man. Iron Ore 1973, Man. Dir 1983, Exec. Vice-Pres. 1989, Pres. Nippon Steel Corpn 1992–98, Chair. 1998–2003, Sr Vice-Pres, Chair. Emer. and Exec. Counselor 2003–; mem. Bd of Dirs Nippon Telegraph and Telephone 1999–. *Address:* Nippon Steel Corporation, 2-6-3 Otemachi, Chiyoda-ku, Tokyo 100-8071, Japan. *Telephone:* (3) 3242-4111. *Fax:* (3) 3275-5641. *E-mail:* www-info@www.nsc.co.jp (office). *Website:* www.nsc.co.jp (office).

IMAKI, Hisakazu, BS; Japanese automobile industry executive; *Chairman, President, CEO and Representative Director, Mazda Motor Corporation;* b. 5 Dec. 1942; m.; one s. one d.; ed Himeji Inst. of Tech.; joined Toyo Kogyo Co. Ltd (later renamed Mazda Motor Corpn) 1965, Gen. Man. Admin Group and Advanced Production Eng Group 1988–89, Gen. Man. Painting, Trim and Final Ass. Eng Dept 1989–92, Deputy Gen. Man. Production Eng Div. and Gen. Man. Production Planning Dept 1992–93, Dir, Gen. Man. Production Eng Div. and Gen. Man. Production Planning Dept 1993–96, Dir and Gen. Man. Hiroshima Plant 1996–97, Man.-Dir in charge of Production Eng, Mfg and Business Logistics 1997–99, Sr Man.-Dir 1999–2002, Rep. Dir, Exec. Vice-Pres. and Chief Eng and Mfg Officer in charge of Research & Devt, Production, Quality Assurance and Business Logistics 2002–03, CEO, Pres. and Rep. Dir 2003–06, Chair., Pres., CEO and Rep. Dir 2006–; Person of the Year in Japan, Automotive Researchers and Journalists Conference 2006. *Leisure interests:* basketball, photography, driving. *Address:* Mazda Motor Corpn, 3-1 Shinchi, Fuchu-cho, Aki-gun, Hiroshima 730-8670, Japan (office). *Telephone:* (82) 282-1111 (office). *Fax:* (82) 287-5190 (office). *E-mail:* info@mazda.com (office). *Website:* www.mazda.com (office).

IMAM, Adel; Egyptian actor; *Goodwill Ambassador, United Nations High Commissioner for Refugees;* b. 17 May 1940, Cairo; m. Hala Al Shalaqani; three c.; ed Cairo Univ.; has appeared in over 100 films and nine plays; early success as a comic actor on stage and film, subsequently famous for topical roles, often depicting victims of poverty and injustice, one of most successful actors in Arab world; his play Al -Zaeem (The Leader) has been performed worldwide; apptd UNHCR Goodwill Amb. 2001. *Films include:* Ana Wa Hua Wa Hia (I, He and She) 1964, El Ragol da hai Ganini 1967, Khouroug min el Guana 1967, Karamet Zawgaty 1967, Kayfa Tesrak Millionaire 1968, Helwa wa Shakia 1968, Ana al-Doctor 1968, Afrit Merati 1968, Al-Bahth an Fadiha 1973, Katel ma Katelsh had 1979, Athkiya' Laken Aghbiya' 1980, Ala Bab e l'Wazir 1982, El Harrif (The Street Player) 1983, Al Avokato 1984, Al-Irhabi wal Kabab (Terrorism and Bar-B-Q) 1993, Al-Irhabi (The Terrorist) 1994, Tuyoor Al-Zalam (Birds of Darkness) 1995, Al-Wad Mahrous Beta' Al-Wazir (Mahrous, The Minister's Boy) 1999, Amir El Zalam 2002, Tag Rubah el Danemarkiyyah 2003, Aris Min Geha Amneya 2004, Amarit Ya'koubian 2005, The Yacoubian Building (in trans.) 2006. *Plays include:* Al -Zaeem (The Leader), Shahid ma Shafesh Haga, Bodyguard. *Address:* c/o United Nations High Commissioner for Refugees (UNHCR), CP 2500, 1211 Geneva 2 dépôt, Switzerland.

IMAMURA, Harusuke; Japanese business executive; *Adviser, Shimizu Corporation;* Chair. and Rep. Dir Shimizu Corpn –2007, now Adviser; Vice-Chair. Bd of Councillors, Japan Fed. of Econ. Orgs (KEIRANDEN) 2000, also Chair. Cttee on Land & Housing Policies; Vice-Chair. Japan Business Fed. (JBF) 2002; Chair. Jusoken Housing Research Foundation 2003–. *Address:* Shimizu Corporation, Seavans South, 1-2-3 Shibaura, Minato-ku, Tokyo 105-8007, Japan (office). *Telephone:* (3) 5441-1111 (office). *Fax:* (3) 5441-0526 (office). *Website:* www.shimz.co.jp (office).

IMAN; American (b. Somali) model and actress; b. (Iman Abdul Majid), 25 July 1955, Mogadishu; m. 1st Spencer Haywood (divorced 1987); one d.; m. 2nd David Bowie 1992; one d.; ed Nairobi Univ.; fashion model 1976–90, has modelled for Claude Montana and Thierry Mugler; signed Revlon Polish Ambers contract (first black model to be signed by int. cosmetics co.) 1979; Founder and CEO IMAN Cosmetics, Skincare and Fragrances 1994–. *Films include:* The Human Factor 1979, Jane Austen in Manhattan 1980, Exposed 1983, Out of Africa 1985, No Way Out 1987, Surrender 1987, L.A. Story 1991, House Party 2 199, The Linguini Incident 1991, Star Trek VI: The Undiscovered Country 1991, Exit to Eden 1994, The Deli 1997, Omikron: The Nomad Soul 1999. *Television appearances include:* Miami Vice, The Cosby Show, In the Heat of the Night, Lies of the Twins 1991, Heart of Darkness 1994. *Publications:* I Am Iman 2001, The Beauty of Color 2005. *Address:* c/o Independent, 2nd Floor, 2 Henrietta Street, Covent Garden, London WC2E 8PS, England. *Telephone:* (20) 7557-7100. *E-mail:* info@indtalent.com; info@i-iman.com. *Website:* www.imancosmetics.com.

IMANAKA, Hiroshi, LLD; Japanese academic; *Professor Emeritus, Faculty of Law, Hiroshima University;* b. 2 Dec. 1930, Fukuoka City; s. of the late Tsugumaro Imanaka; ed Univs of Hiroshima and Nagoya; Lecturer, Faculty of Educ., Miyazaki Univ. 1960–65; Lecturer, Dept of Gen. Educ., Hiroshima Univ. 1965–67, Assoc. Prof. 1967–78, Prof. of Political Science, Faculty of Integrated Arts and Sciences 1978–81, Faculty of Law 1981–91, Prof. Emer. 1991–; Dean and Prof., Kinjogakuin Univ. 1991–2001; Prof. Emer. 2001–. *Publications:* Constitutional Law (co-author) 1971, George Lawson's Political Theory of Civil Government 1976, A Study of the History of English Political Thought 1977, Parliamentarism and its Origin in the Era of English Revolution, The English Revolution and the Modern Political Theory of George Lawson 2000. *Address:* 2-6-10 Yoshijima-Higashi, Naka-ku, Hir-

oshima Shi, Japan (home). *Telephone:* (82) 244-4756 (home). *Fax:* (82) 244-4756 (home). *E-mail:* hiro-imanaka@go7.enjoy.ne.jp (home).

IMBALI, Faustino Fudut; Guinea-Bissau politician; *Leader, Manifesto do Povo;* cand. presidential election 1999; Minister of Foreign Affairs Jan.–March 2001, Prime Minister of Guinea-Bissau March–Dec. 2001; unsuccessful cand. for Pres. 1999, 2005; currently Leader, Manifesto do Povo party. *Address:* Manifesto do Povo, Bissau, Guinea-Bissau (office).

IMBERT, Baron (Life Peer), cr. 1999, of New Romney in the County of Kent; **Peter Michael Imbert,** CVO, QPM; British police officer and business executive; b. 27 April 1933, Folkestone, Kent; s. of the late William Henry Imbert and of Frances May Hodge; m. Iris Rosina Dove 1956; one s. two d.; ed Harvey Grammar School; Metropolitan Police 1953–93, Asst Chief Constable, Surrey Constabulary 1976–77, Deputy Chief Constable 1977–79, Chief Constable, Thames Valley Police 1979–85, Deputy Commr Metropolitan Police 1985–87, Commr 1987–93; Metropolitan Police Anti-Terrorist Squad 1973–75; Police negotiator in Balcombe Street (London) IRA Siege Dec. 1975; Sec. Nat. Crime Cttee, ACPO Council 1980–83, Chair. 1983–85; Chair. Vehicle Security Installation Bd 1994–96; Chair. Capital Eye Security Ltd 1997–; Dir (non-exec.) Securicor 1993–2000, Camelot Group 1994–2000, Retainagroup 1995–; consultant, CDR Int. 1997–2000; mem. Gen. Advisory Council, BBC 1980–87, Criminal Justice Consultative Cttee 1992–93; Chair. Surrey Co. Cricket Club Youth Trust 1993–96; mem. Ministerial Advisory Bd on Royal Parks 1993–2000, Public Policy Cttee of Royal Automobile Club 1993–2000; Trustee Help the Aged 1993–95, St Catherine's Foundation Cumberland Lodge; DL Greater London 1994–98, Lord Lt of Greater London 1998–2008; Hon. DLitt (Reading); Hon. MBA (Int. Man. Centre). *Leisure interests:* golf, bad bridge, watching good cricket, talking about his grandchildren. *Address:* House of Lords, Westminster, London, SW1A 0PW, England (office).

IMBUSCH, George Francis, DSc, PhD, FInstP, FAIP, FIEE; Irish physicist, academic and university administrator; *Professor Emeritus of Experimental Physics, National University of Ireland, Galway;* b. 7 Oct. 1935, Limerick; s. of George Imbusch and Alice Neville; m. Mary Rita O'Donnell 1961; one s. one d.; ed Christian Brothers' School, Limerick, Univ. Coll., Galway and Stanford Univ., USA; mem. tech. staff, Bell Labs, USA 1964–67; Lecturer in Physics, Univ. Coll. Galway (now Nat. Univ. of Ireland Galway) 1967–74, Prof. of Experimental Physics 1974–2002, Prof. Emer. 2002–, Head, Dept of Physics 1986–89, Vice-Pres. 1992–98; Science Sec. Royal Irish Acad. 1989–93, Sr Vice-Pres. 2005–, Hon. Academic Research Officer 2005–; Visiting Prof., Univ. of Wisconsin 1978, Regensburg 1981, Utrecht 1988, Canterbury, NZ 1995, Georgia 1998;. *Publications:* Optical Spectroscopy of Inorganic Solids (co-author) 1989; more than 100 scientific papers in journals. *Leisure interests:* painting, reading. *Address:* Department of Physics, National University of Ireland, Galway, University Road, Galway (office); Forramoyle West, Barna, Co. Galway, Ireland (home). *Telephone:* (91) 524411 ext. 2510 (office); (91) 592159 (home). *Fax:* (91) 750584 (office); (91) 525700 (office). *E-mail:* gfimbusch@eircom.net (home); g.f.imbusch@physics.nuigalway.ie (office). *Website:* www.nuigalway.ie/physics/research_top.html (office).

IMMELT, Jeffrey R., BA, MBA; American business executive; *Chairman and CEO, General Electric Company;* b. 19 Feb. 1956, Cincinnati, Ohio; s. of Joseph Immelt and Donna Immelt; m. Andrea Immelt (née Allen) 1986; one d.; ed Finneytown High School, Dartmouth Coll., Harvard Univ.; joined Gen. Electric Co. 1982, Corp. Marketing Dept 1982, various positions with GE Plastics 1982–89, Vice-Pres. 1992–93, Vice-Pres. GE Appliances 1989–91, Vice-Pres. Worldwide Marketing and Product Man. 1991, Vice-Pres. and Gen. Man. GE Plastics Americas 1993–97, Pres. and CEO GE Medical Systems 1997–2001, Chair. and CEO Gen. Electric Co. 2001–; mem. Bd of Dirs Catalyst, Robin Hood, New York City, New York Fed. Reserve Bank; mem. The Business Council; named three times by Barron's as one of the 'World's Best CEOs', Man of the Year, Financial Times 2003. *Leisure interest:* golf. *Address:* General Electric Company, 3135 Easton Turnpike, Fairfield, CT 06828-0001, USA (office). *Telephone:* (203) 373-2211 (office). *Fax:* (203) 373-3131 (office). *Website:* www.ge.com (office).

IMRAN IBNI TUANKU JAAFAR, Tan Sri Tunku, LLB; Malaysian business executive; *Executive Chairman, Petra Group;* b. 21 March 1948, Seremban, Negeri Sembilan; s. of HM Tuanku Ja'afar the fmr 10th King of Malaysia and HM Tuanku Najihah; m. HH Che Engku Mahirah; two s.; ed The King's School, Canterbury and Univ. of Nottingham; called to the Bar at Gray's Inn, London 1971; joined Malaysian Nat. Corp. (PERNAS) 1971, Rep. in Indonesia, later Group Co. Sec.; joined Haw Par Group, 1973, Man. Dir Haw Par Malaysia until 1976; CEO Anttah Group of Cos. 1977–2001; Exec. Chair. Petra Group 2001–; mem. Bd of Dirs of several other publicly listed cos. in Malaysia and abroad; Dir Inst. of Strategic and Int. Studies (ISIS) Malaysia; mem. Malaysian Business Council and Malaysian-British Business Council (MBBC); Past Pres. Badan Warisan (Heritage of Malaysia Trust); Pres. Olympic Council of Malaysia; mem. Nat. Sports Council of Malaysia; Pres. Malaysian Cricket Asscn; Founding Chair. Foundation for Malaysian Sporting Excellence (SportExcel); Pres. Emer. World Squash Fed. (Pres. 1989–96); Exec. Bd mem. Int. Cricket Council (ICC); Vice-Pres. Commonwealth Games Fed.; Malaysia's first nat. squash champion 1973; Chef-de-Mission, Seoul Olympic Games 1988; Nat. Sports' Leadership Award 1991, Panglima Setia Mahkota, conferring the title Tan Sri 1992, Darjah Seri Urama Negeri Sembilan, conferring the title Dato' Seri Utama 1999. *Address:* 9th Floor, Wisma Antah, Off Jalan Semantan, Damansaia Heights, 50490 Kuala Lumpur (office); No. 33, Jalan Semantan Dua, Damansaia Heights, 50490, Kuala Lumpur, Malaysia (home). *Telephone:* (603) 2545144 (office); (603) 2556031 (home). *Fax:* (603) 2561044 (office); (603) 2533641 (home). *E-mail:* tunku-imran@antah.com.my (office).

IMRAN KHAN NIAZI (see KHAN NIAZI, Imran).

IMRAY, Sir Colin Henry, Kt, KBE, CMG, KStJ, MA; British diplomatist; *Chairman, Royal Overseas League;* b. 21 Sept. 1933, Newport, Mon.; s. of Henry Gibbon Imray and Frances Olive Badman; m. Shirley Margaret Matthews 1957; one s. three d.; ed Highgate School, London, Hotchkiss School, Conn., USA and Balliol Coll., Oxford; Second Lt Seaforth Highlanders, Royal W African Frontier Force 1952–54; Asst Prin. Commonwealth Relations Office 1957–58, 1961–63; Third then Second Sec. British High Comm., Canberra 1958–61; First Sec., Nairobi 1963–66; Asst Head Personnel Dept FCO 1966–70; British Trade Commr, Montreal 1970–73; Counsellor, Consul Gen. and Head of Chancery, Islamabad 1973–77; Royal Coll. of Defence Studies 1977–; Commercial Counsellor British Embassy, Tel-Aviv 1977–80; Deputy High Commr, Bombay 1980–84; Asst Under-Sec. of State (Chief Inspector and Deputy Chief Clerk) 1984–85; High Commr in Tanzania 1986–89, in Bangladesh 1989–93; Sec. Gen. OStJ 1993–97, Dir Overseas Relations 1997–98; mem. Cen. Council Royal Over-Seas League 1998–, Exec. Cttee 1999–, Chair. 2000–; High Steward of Wallingford 2001–; Freeman City of London 1994. *Leisure interests:* travel, walking, gardening. *Address:* Over-Seas House, Park Place, St James's Street, London, SW1A 1LR (office); Holbrook House, Reading Road, Wallingford, Oxon., OX10 9DT, England (home). *Telephone:* (20) 7408-0214 (office); (1491) 833044 (home). *Fax:* (20) 7499-6738 (office). *E-mail:* imray@rosl.org.uk (office). *Website:* www.rosl.org.uk (office).

INAGAKI, Masao; Japanese advertising industry executive; b. 27 Oct. 1922, Aichi Pref.; s. of Gonpachi Inagaki and Katsu Inagaki; m. Teruko Inagaki 1949; one d.; ed Training Inst., Ministry of Foreign Affairs; with Civil Property Bureau, Ministry of Foreign Affairs 1948–50; joined Sekai-Sha, apptd Gen. Man., Advertising Div. 1950; Founder and Dir Daiichi-Tsushinsya; f. Asatsu Inc. (changed to Asatsu-DK after acquisition by WPP 1998), CEO and Pres. 1992–2004, mem. Bd of Dirs WPP 1998–2004 (retd). *Leisure interest:* writing poems. *Address:* 2-32-7 Matusgaoka, Nakano-ku, Tokyo 165, Japan (home). *Telephone:* (3) 3951-8644 (home).

IÑÁRRITU, Alejandro González; Mexican film director and screenwriter; b. 15 Aug. 1963, Mexico City; early career as radio DJ in Mexico City; fmr Head, Televisa (TV production co.); f. Zeta Films (advertising agency and film production co.). *Films include:* El Timbre (also writer) 1996, Amores perros (also producer) 2000, Powder Keg (also writer) 2001, 11'09''01: September 11 (Mexico segment, also writer and producer) 2002, 21 Grams (also producer) 2003, Nine Lives (exec. producer) 2005, Toro negro (exec. producer) 2005, Babel (Best Dir Cannes Film Festival 2006, Palm Springs Int. Film Festival 2007) (also producer) 2006. *Address:* c/o Endeavor Agency, 9601 Wilshire Blvd., 10th Floor, Beverly Hills, CA 90212, USA. *Telephone:* (310) 248-2000. *Fax:* (310) 248-2020.

INBAL, Eliahu; British/Israeli conductor; *Music Director, Teatro La Fenice;* b. 16 Feb. 1936, Jerusalem; s. of Jehuda Joseph Inbal and Leah Museri Inbal; m. Helga Fritzsche 1968; two s. one d.; ed Acad. of Music, Jerusalem, Conservatoire Nat. Supérieur, Paris, courses with Franco Ferrara, Hilversum and Sergiu Celebidache, Siena; from 1963 guest conductor with numerous orchestras including Milan, Rome, Berlin, Munich, Hamburg, Stockholm, Copenhagen, Vienna, Budapest, Amsterdam, London, Paris, Tel Aviv, New York, Chicago, Toronto and Tokyo; Chief Conductor, Radio Symphony Orchestra, Frankfurt 1974–90, Hon. Conductor 1995–; Guest Conductor, Teatro La Fenice 1984–87, Music Dir. 2007–; Chief Conductor Berlin Symphony Orchestra 2001–05; Prin. Conductor, Tokyo Metropolitan Symphony Orchestra 2008–; Chief Conductor, Czech Philharmonic Orchestra 2009–; Hon. Conductor, Nat. Symphony Orchestra, RAI Torino 1996–; has made numerous recordings, particularly of Mahler, Bruckner, Berlioz and Shostakovich; First Prize, Int. Conductors' Competition 'G. Cantelli' 1963; Officier des Arts des Lettres 1995; Goldenes Ehrenzeichen, Vienna 2001. *Leisure interests:* music reproduction, photography. *Address:* Teatro La Fenice, Campo San Fantin 1965, 30124, Venice, Italy (office). *Telephone:* (041) 786511 (office). *E-mail:* direzione.artistica@teatrolafenice.org (office). *Website:* www.teatrolafenice.it (office).

INDIANA, Robert, BFA; American artist; b. 13 Sept. 1928, New Castle, Ind.; ed John Herron School of Art, Indianapolis, Munson-Williams-Proctor Inst., Utica, New York, Art Inst. of Chicago, Skowhegan School of Painting and Sculpture, Univ. of Edinburgh and Edinburgh Coll. of Art, UK; served USAAF 1946–49; Artist-in-Residence, Center of Contemporary Art, Aspen, Colo 1968; Hon. DFA (Franklin and Marshall Coll., Lancaster, Pa) 1970. *Address:* c/o Simon Salama-Caro, 45 East 80th Street, New York, NY 10021, USA. *Telephone:* (212) 585-3624. *Fax:* (212) 585-3623.

INDRAWATI, HE Sri Mulyani, PhD; Indonesian economist, academic and government official; *Minister of Finance and State Enterprises Development and Acting Co-ordinating Minister for Economic Affairs;* b. 26 Aug. 1962, Tanjungkarang, Lampung; ed Univ. of Indonesia, Jakarta, Univ. of Illinois Urbana-Champaign, USA; several positions at Inst. for Econ. and Social Research, Faculty of Econs, Univ. Indonesia (LPEM-FEUI) 1992–2004 including Assoc. Dir Research 1992–93, Assoc. Dir Educ. and Training 1993–95, Dir Program Magister, Planning and Public Policy, Grad. Program Econs 1996–99, Dir 1998–2004; Staff Expert in Policy Analysis, Overseas Training Office (OTO) 1994–95; adviser, Nat. Econ. Council 1999–2001, currently Sec.-Gen.; consultant to USAID 2001; Visiting Faculty mem. Andrew Young School of Policy Studies, Ga State Univ. 2001–02; Exec. Dir IMF 2002–; Minister of State, Nat. Devt Planning 2004–05; Minister of Finance and State Enterprises Devt and Acting Co-ordinating Minister for Econ. Affairs 2005–; ranked by Forbes magazine amongst 100 Most Powerful Women (23rd) 2008. *Publications include:* Potential and Student Savings in

DKI Jakarta 1995, Domestic Industry Preparedness for the Free Trade Era 1997, Forget CBS, Get Serious About Reform 1998. *Address:* Ministry of Finance and State Enterprises Development, Jalan Lapangan Banteng Timur 2–4, Jakarta, 10710, Indonesia (office). *Telephone:* (21) 3814324 (office). *Fax:* (21) 353710 (office). *Website:* www.depkeu.go.id (office).

INDURÁIN, Miguel; Spanish fmr professional cyclist; b. 16 July 1964, Villava, Navarre; m. Marisa Induráin; one d.; mem. Reynolds team 1984–89, Banesto team 1989–96; five successive wins, Tour de France 1991–95, 1995 winning time, 92 hrs. 44 min. 59 sec.; Gold Medal, Atlanta Olympics 1996; ranked No. 1 cyclist 1992, 1993; announced retirement Jan. 1997. *Address:* Villava, Pamplona, Spain.

INDYK, Martin S., BEcons, PhD; American diplomatist and academic; *Senior Fellow, Foreign Policy Studies and Director, Saban Center for Middle East Policy, Brookings Institution;* b. 1 July 1951, London, England; m. Jill Indyk; two c.; ed Sydney Univ., Australian Nat. Univ.; worked as Deputy Dir of current intelligence for Middle East, Austalia intelligence service 1978; Adjunct Prof. Johns Hopkins School of Advanced Int. Studies; Exec. Dir Washington Inst. for Near East Policy 1985; sworn in as US citizen 1993; Special Asst to the Pres. and Sr Dir for Near East and S Asian Affairs, Nat. Security Council; Prin. Adviser to the Pres. and Nat. Security Adviser on Arab–Israeli Issues, Iraq, Iran and S Asia; Sr mem. Warren Christopher's Middle East peace team; Amb. to Israel 1995–97, 2000–01; Asst Sec. for Near Eastern Affairs 1997–2000; Sr Fellow and Dir Saban Center for Middle East Policy, The Brookings Institution 2002–; mem. Int. Inst. for Strategic Studies, Middle East Inst. *Publications:* Innocent Abroad: An Intimate Account of American Peace Diplomacy in the Middle East 2009; numerous articles and contribs to foreign policy journals. *Address:* Saban Center for Middle East Policy, The Brookings Institution, 1775 Massachusetts Avenue, NW, Washington, DC 20036, USA (office). *Telephone:* (202) 797-6462 (office). *Fax:* (202) 797-2481 (office). *E-mail:* SabanCenter@brookings.edu (office). *Website:* www.brookings.edu (office).

ING, Nita; Taiwanese business executive; *Chairman, Taiwan High Speed Rail Corporation;* d. of the late Glyn T. H. Ing; two d.; ed Taipei American School, boarding schools in Mass and New Jersey, UCLA, USA; joined family business Continental Engineering Corpn as personal asst to her father, apptd Pres. 1987, later Chair., currently CEO; Chair. Taiwan Hi-Speed Railway Corpn 1998–; mem. Bd of Dirs Taiwan Mobile; ranked by Fortune magazine amongst 50 Most Powerful Women in Business outside the US (23rd) 2002, (35th) 2003. *Address:* 2190 Broadway Street, Apt 6W, San Francisco, CA 94115, USA; Continental Engineering Corpn, 5, Tun Hua South Road, Sec 2, Taipei, Taiwan (office). *Telephone:* (2) 3701-1000 (office). *Fax:* (2) 8712-8888 (office). *E-mail:* webadmin@mail.cec.com.tw (office). *Website:* www.cec.com.tw (office); www.thsrc.com.tw (office).

INGAMELLS, John, BA; British museum director and art historian; *Senior Fellow, Paul Mellon Centre for Studies in British Art;* b. 12 Nov. 1934, Northampton; s. of the late George H. Ingamells and Gladys L. Ingamells (née Rollett); m. Hazel Wilson 1964; two d.; ed Hastings and Eastbourne Grammar Schools and Fitzwilliam House, Cambridge; Art Asst, York Art Gallery 1959–62; Asst Keeper of Art, Nat. Museum of Wales 1963–67; Curator, York Art Gallery 1967–77; Asst to Dir Wallace Collection 1977–78, Dir 1978–92; currently Sr Fellow, Paul Mellon Centre for Studies in British Art; mem. Exec. Cttee Nat. Art Collections Fund 1992–97. *Publications:* The Davies Collection of French Art 1967, The English Episcopal Portrait 1981, Wallace Collection, Catalogue of Pictures (Vol. I) 1985, (Vol. II) 1986, (Vol. III) 1989, (Vol. IV) 1992, A Dictionary of British and Irish Travellers in Italy 1701–1800 (ed.) 1998, Allan Ramsay, A Complete Catalogue by A. Smart (ed.) 1999, The Letters of Sir Joshua Reynolds (ed.) 2000, Nat. Portrait Gallery Mid-Georgian Portraits 2004; numerous museum catalogues, exhbn catalogues and articles in learned journals. *Address:* Paul Mellon Centre for Studies in British Art, 16 Bedford Square, London, WC1B 3JA (office); 39 Benson Road, London, SE23 3RL, England (home). *Telephone:* (20) 7580-0311 (office). *Website:* www.paul-mellon-centre.ac.uk (office).

INGARDEN, Roman Stanisław, MA, DrSc; Polish physicist and academic; *Professor Emeritus of Physics, Nicolaus Copernicus University;* b. 1 Oct. 1920, Zakopane; m. Regina Urbanowicz; two s.; ed Jagiellonian Univ., Kraków, Warsaw Univ.; researcher, Wrocław Univ., Sr Asst 1945–49, Asst Prof. 1949–54, Prof. 1954–66; Prof., Nicolaus Copernicus Univ., Toruń 1966–91, Prof. Emer. 1991–; Visiting Prof. univs in USA, Germany, France, Belgium, Canada, Japan; fmr Dir Research Centres of Geometrical Optics and Low Temperature Physics, Wrocław, then Centre of Math. Physics, Toruń; mem. Polish Socialist Party (PPS) 1936–44, Polish United Workers' Party (PZPR) 1954–90; Ed.-in-Chief Reports on Mathematical Physics 1970–91, Open Systems and Information Dynamics 1992–2004; Gold Cross of Merit, Order of Polonia Restituta 1964, Officer's Cross 1972, Order of Saint Treasury with Ribbon (Japan) 1994; Dr hc (Nicolaus Copernicus Univ.) 1996; Maria Skłodowska-Curie Award, Polish Acad. of Sciences 1972. *Publications include:* The Theory of Sprays and Finsler Spaces with Applications in Physics and Biology 1993, Information Dynamics and Open Systems (co-author) 1997, Physics and Physicists, Historical and Philosophical Studies (in Polish) 1994, Roman Witold Ingarden, Philosopher in Toruń (in Polish) 2000; numerous scientific papers. *Leisure interests:* Japanese language and culture, philosophy, history of physics. *Address:* Institute of Physics, Nicolaus Copernicus University, ul. Grudziądzka 5–7, 87-100 Toruń (office); ul. Kraszewskiego 22B m. 28, 87-100 Toruń, Poland (home). *Telephone:* (56) 6226370 (office); (56) 6223835 (home). *Fax:* (56) 6225397 (office). *E-mail:* romp@fizyka.umk.pl (office). *Website:* www.fizyka.umk.pl/en (office).

INGE, Baron (Life Peer), cr. 1997, of Richmond in the County of North Yorkshire; **Field Marshal Peter Anthony Inge,** KG, GCB; British army officer; b. 5 Aug. 1935; s. of Raymond Albert Inge and the late Grace Maud Caroline Inge; m. Letitia Marion Beryl Thornton-Berry 1960; two d.; ed Summer Fields, Wrekin Coll., Royal Mil. Acad., Sandhurst; commissioned, Green Howards 1956, ADC to GOC 4 Div. 1960–61, Adjutant, 1st Green Howards 1963–64, student, Staff Coll. 1966, Ministry of Defence 1967–69, Co. Commdr 1st Green Howards 1969–70, student, Jt Service Staff Coll. 1971, Brigade Maj., 11th Armoured Brigade 1972, Instructor, Staff Coll. 1973–74, CO 1st Green Howards 1974–76, Commdt, Jr Div. Staff Coll. 1977–79, Commdr 4th Armoured Brigade 1980–81, Chief of Staff HQ 1st (BR) Corps 1982–83, GOC NEDIST and Commdr 2nd Infantry Div. 1984–86, Dir-Gen. Logistic Policy (Army) 1986–87, Commdr 1st (BR) Corps 1987–89, Commdr NORTHAG and C-in-C British Army of the Rhine 1989–92, Chief of Gen. Staff 1992–94, of the Defence Staff 1994–97, Constable of HM's Fortress and Palace, The Tower of London 1996–2001; ADC Gen. to the Queen 1991–94, Deputy Lt of N Yorks. 1994; Deputy Chair. Historic Royal Palaces 1997–2007; Chair. King Edward VII Sister Agnes' Hosp. 2004–; mem. Council Marlborough Coll. 1997–2006; Commr Royal Hosp. Chelsea 1998–2004; Pres. The Pilgrims 2002–; Col The Green Howards 1982–94, Col Commdt Royal Mil. Police 1987–92, Col Commdt Army Physical Training Corps 1988–97; Freeman City of London 1994. *Leisure interests:* cricket, walking, music, reading, military history. *Address:* House of Lords, Westminster, London, SW1A 0PW, England.

INGHAM, Sir Bernard, Kt; British fmr civil servant; *Chairman, Bernard Ingham Communications;* b. 21 June 1932, Halifax, Yorkshire; s. of Garnet Ingham and Alice Ingham; m. Nancy Hilda Hoyle 1956; one s.; ed Hebden Bridge Grammar School, Tech. Colls of Todmorden, Halifax and Bradford; reporter, Hebden Bridge Times 1948–52, The Yorkshire Post and Yorkshire Evening Post, Halifax 1952–59; with The Yorkshire Post, Leeds 1959–61, Northern Industrial Corresp. 1961; with The Guardian 1962–67, Labour Staff, London 1965–67; Press and Public Relations Adviser Nat. Bd for Prices and Incomes 1967–68; Chief Information Officer, Dept of Employment and Productivity 1968–72; Dir of Information Dept of Employment 1973; with Dept of Energy 1974–79, Dir of Information 1974-77, Under-Sec. and Head of Energy Conservation Div. 1978–79; Chief Press Sec. to the Prime Minister 1979–90, Head, Govt Information Service 1989–90; columnist, Daily Express 1991–98; Chair. Bernard Ingham Communications 1990–; Pres. British Franchise Asscn 1994–; Vice-Pres. Country Guardian 1991–; Dir (non-exec.) McDonald's Restaurants Ltd 1991–2005 (mem. Advisory Bd 2005–), Hill and Knowlton 1991–2002; Visiting Fellow and Hon. Dir Applied Policy Science Unit, Univ. of Newcastle-upon-Tyne 1991–2003; mem. Council Univ. of Huddersfield 1994–2000; Visiting Prof., Univ. of Middlesex Business School 1997–, Univ. of Surrey 2005–; mem. Cttee, Supporters of Nuclear Energy (Sec. 1998–2008); Dr hc (Buckingham) 1997, (Middx) 1999, (Bradford) 2004. *Publications:* Kill the Messenger 1991, Yorkshire Millennium 1999, Yorkshire Castles 2001, Yorkshire Villages 2001, The Wages of Spin 2003, Yorkshire Greats 2005. *Leisure interests:* walking, reading, gardening, visiting Yorkshire. *Address:* 9 Monahan Avenue, Purley, Surrey, CR8 3BB, England (home). *Telephone:* (20) 8660-8970 (home). *E-mail:* bernardinghamcom@aol.com (office).

INGLIS, Kenneth Stanley, AO, MA, DPhil; Australian historian, academic and university administrator; *Professor Emeritus of History, Research School of Social Sciences, Australian National University;* b. 7 Oct. 1929, Melbourne; s. of Stanley W. Inglis and Irene Inglis (née Winning); m. 1st Judy Betheras 1952 (deceased 1962); one s. two d.; m. 2nd Amirah Gust 1965; ed Univ. of Melbourne and Univ. of Oxford, UK; Sr Lecturer, Univ. of Adelaide 1956–60, Reader 1960–62; Reader, ANU 1963–65, Prof. 1965–66, Professorial Fellow 1975–76, Prof. of History, Research School of Social Sciences 1977–94, Prof. Emer. 1994–; Prof., Univ. of Papua New Guinea 1967–72, Vice-Chancellor 1972–75; Overseas Visiting Fellow, St John's Coll., Cambridge 1990–91; Hon. DLitt (Melbourne) 1996; Ernest Scott Prize for History 1983–84, 1999, Fellowship of Australian Writers Prize for Literature 1999, NSW Premier's Prize for Australian History 1999; Nat. Centre for Cultural Studies Award 1999. *Publications:* Churches and the Working Classes in Victorian England 1963, The Australian Colonists 1974, This is the ABC: The Australian Broadcasting Comm. 1932–1983, 1983, The Rehearsal 1985, Australians: A Historical Library (11 vols, Gen. Ed.) 1987–88, Nation: The Life of an Independent Journal of Opinion 1958–72 (ed.) 1989, Observing Australia 1959–99 1999, The Stuart Case (revised edn) 2002, Sacred Places: War Memorials in the Australian Landscape (revised edn) 2008. *Address:* Dundas Lane, Albert Park 3206, Australia.

INGOLD, Keith Usherwood, OC, PhD, FRS, FRSC, FCIC; Canadian research chemist and academic; *Distinguished Research Scientist, National Research Council Canada;* b. 31 May 1929, Leeds, England; s. of Sir Christopher Kelk Ingold and Lady Edith Hilda Usherwood; m. Carmen Cairine Hodgkin 1956; one s. one d.; ed Univ. Coll., Univ. of London, Oxford Univ.; Postdoctoral Fellow, Nat. Research Council of Canada 1951–53, Research Officer, Div. of Chem. 1955–90, Head, Hydrocarbon Chem. Section 1965–90, Assoc. Dir 1977–90; Postdoctoral Fellow, Univ. of BC 1953–55; Distinguished Research Scientist, Steacie Inst. for Molecular Sciences 1990–2000, Nat. Research Council 2000–; Adjunct Prof., Dept of Biochem., Brunel Univ., UK 1983–94; Adjunct Prof., Dept of Chem. and Biochem. Univ. of Guelph, Ont. 1985–89; Adjunct Research Prof., Carleton Univ., Ottawa 1991–; Adjunct Prof., Dept of Chem., Univ. of St Andrews, Scotland 1997–; visiting scientist to numerous univs, numerous lectureships; Sr Carnegie Fellowship, Univ. of St Andrews, Scotland 1977; Fellow, Univ. Coll. London 1987; mem. ACS; Vice-Pres. Canadian Soc. for Chem. 1985–87, Pres. 1987–88; Hon. mem. Sociedad Argentina de Investigaciones en Química Orgánica; Dr. hc (Univ. degli Studi di Ancona) 1999; Hon. DSc (Guelph, Ontario) 1985, (St Andrews) 1989, (Carleton Univ.) 1992, (McMaster Univ., Ontario) 1995, (Dalhousie Univ., NS) 1996; Hon. LLD (Mount Allison) 1987; numerous awards including Chem. Inst. of Canada Medal 1981, Syntex Award in Physical Organic Chem. 1983, Royal Soc. of Canada Centennial Medal 1982, Henry Marshall Tory Medal, Royal Soc. of Canada 1985, ACS Pauling Award 1988, Alfred Bader Award in Organic Chem., Canadian Soc. for Chem. 1989, Humboldt Research Award 1989, Davy Medal, Royal Soc. 1990, ACS Arthur C. Cope Scholar Award 1992, Izaak Walton Killam Memorial Prize, Canada Council 1992, ACS James Flack Norris Award in Physical Organic Chem. 1993, Angelo Mangini Medal, Italian Chemical Soc. 1997, Canada Gold Medal for Science and Eng, Natural Science and Eng Research Council 1998, Royal Medal A, Royal Soc. 2000. *Publications:* Free-Radical Substitution Reactions (with B. P. Roberts) 1971, Nitrogen-centered Radicals, Aminoxyl and Related Radicals (with J. C. Walton) 1994; over 480 publs in the open scientific literature. *Leisure interests:* skiing, water skiing. *Address:* National Research Council of Canada, 100 Sussex Drive, Ottawa, ON K1A 0R6, Canada (office). *Telephone:* (613) 822-1123 (home); (613) 990-0938 (office). *Fax:* (613) 941-8447 (office). *E-mail:* keith.ingold@nrc.ca (office). *Website:* www.nrc-cnrc.gc.ca/main_e.html (office).

INGÓLFSSON, Thorsteinn; Icelandic diplomatist and banker; *Permanent Representative, NATO;* b. 9 Dec. 1944, Reykjavik; s. of Ingólfur Thorsteinsson and Helga Gudmundsdóttir; m. 1st Gudrún Valdís Ragnarsdóttir (divorced 1986); one s. one d.; m. 2nd Hólmfrídur Kofoed-Hansen 1994; ed Commercial Coll. of Iceland, Univ. of Iceland; First Sec. and Deputy Chief of Mission, Washington, DC 1973–78; Chief of Div., Ministry of Foreign Affairs 1978–85; Minister Counsellor 1981; Deputy Perm. Rep. to Int. Orgs, Geneva 1985–87, Acting Perm. Rep. Feb.–June 1987; rank of Amb. 1987; Dir Defence Dept Ministry for Foreign Affairs, 1987–90; Chair. Icelandic-American Defence Council 1987–90; Perm. Under-Sec. for Foreign Affairs 1990–94; Perm. Rep. to N Atlantic Council and WEU 1994–99, to UN, New York 1999–2003; Amb. to Cuba 2001, to Barbados 2002, to Jamaica (with residence in New York) 2003; Exec. Dir for Nordic and Baltic Countries, World Bank Group, New York 2003–06; Special Envoy of Foreign Minister 2006–08; Perm. Rep. to NATO, Brussels 2008–; Grande Croix, Légion d'honneur, Hon. GCMG, numerous decorations. *Address:* Office of the Permanent Representative of Iceland, blvd Léopold III, 1110 Brussels, Belgium (office). *Telephone:* (2) 707-41-11 (office). *Fax:* (2) 707-45-79 (office). *E-mail:* natodoc@hq.nato.int (office). *Website:* www.nato.int (office).

INGRAHAM, Rt Hon Hubert Alexander, PC; Bahamian lawyer and politician; *Prime Minister and Minister of Finance;* b. 4 Aug. 1947, Pine Ridge, Grand Bahama; m. Delores Velma Miller; five c.; ed Cooper's Town Public School, Southern Sr School and Govt High School Evening Inst. Nassau; called to the Bar, Bahamas 1972; Sr Pnr, Christie, Ingraham & Co. (law firm); fmr mem. Air Transport Licensing Authority; fmr Chair. Real Property Tax Tribunal; mem. Nat. Gen. Council Progressive Liberal Party (PLP) 1975; Nat. Chair. and mem. Nat. Exec. Cttee PLP 1976; elected to House of Ass. as PLP mem. 1977, 1982, fmr Speaker; Minister of Housing, Nat. Insurance and Social Services 1982–84; Chair. Bahamas Mortgage Corpn 1982; Alt. Del. Conf. of IDB, Uruguay 1983, IMF/IBRD 1979–84; expelled from PLP 1986; elected to Nat. Ass. as ind. 1987; Parl. Leader, Official Opposition 1990–92; Leader, Opposition Free Nat. Movt and of Official Opposition 1990–92, 2002–07; Prime Minister of the Bahamas 1992–2002, 2007–, also Minister of Finance and Planning 1992–97, of Housing and Local Govt 1995–97 and Trade and Industry 1995–97, of Housing and Social Devt 2001–02, of Finance 2007–; mem. Privy Council; Dr hc (Buckingham) 2000. *Leisure interests:* reading, swimming, fishing. *Address:* Office of the Prime Minister, Sir Cecil Wallace-Whitfield Centre, West Bay St, PO Box N 3217, Nassau, N.P. Bahamas (office). *Telephone:* 327-1530 (office). *Fax:* 327-1618 (office). *E-mail:* primeminister@bahamas.gov.bs (office); hai@coralwave.com (home). *Website:* www.bahamas.gov.bs (office).

INGRAM, Christopher (Chris) John; British advertising and marketing executive; *Founding Partner, Ingram;* b. 9 June 1943; s. of Thomas Frank Ingram and Gladys Agnes Ingram (née Louttid); m. Janet Elizabeth Rye; one s. one d.; ed Woking Grammar School, Surrey; Media Dir KMP Partnership 1969–71; Man. Dir TMD Advertising 1972–75; founder and Chair. CIA Group/Tempus Group PLC 1976–2002; f. Genesis Investments 2002; Chair. Woking Football Club Holdings 2002–; Founding Pnr Ingram 2003–; Chair. Bd of Dirs Centre for Creative Business, London Business School 2005–; Ernst & Young London Entrepreneur of the Year 2000, Ernst & Young UK Business-to-Business Entrepreneur of the Year 2000. *Leisure interests:* art, theatre, wildlife, travel in cold climates, entrepreneurship, the voluntary sector, Woking Football Club. *Address:* Ingram, 7–10 Beaumont Mews, London W1G 6EB, England. *Telephone:* (20) 7317-2904 (office). *Fax:* (20) 7317-2996 (office). *E-mail:* chrisingram@theingrampartnership.com (office). *Website:* www.theingrampartnership.com (office).

INGRAM, James Charles, AO, BA (Econs); Australian diplomatist and international civil servant; b. 27 Feb. 1928, Warragul, Vic.; s. of James Edward Ingram and Gladys May (née Johnson); m. Odette Koven 1950; one s. two d.; ed De la Salle Coll., Melbourne Univ.; joined Dept of External Affairs 1946; Third Sec., Tel-Aviv 1950; First Sec., Washington, DC 1956; Chargé d'Affaires, Brussels 1959; Counsellor, Djakarta 1962, Australian Mission to UN, New York 1964; Asst Sec. External Affairs, Canberra 1967; Amb. to Philippines 1970–73; High Commr in Canada, Jamaica, Barbados, Guyana, Trinidad and Tobago 1973–74; First Asst Sec., Australian Devt Assistance Agency 1975–76; Dir-Gen. Australian Devt Assistance Bureau, Dept of Foreign Affairs 1977–82; Exec. Dir UN World Food Programme 1982–92; Dir Australian Inst. of Int. Affairs 1992–93; Visiting Fellow, Centre for Int. and Public Law, ANU, Canberra 1993–94; Chair. Australian Govt Advisory

Cttee on Non-Govt Devt Orgs 1995; mem. Bd of Trustees, Int. Food Policy Research Inst. 1991–98, Crawford Fund for Int. Agric. Research, Melbourne 1994–99 (Chair. 1996–99), Int. Crisis Group, Brussels 1995–99, Chair. Crawford Fund Expert Advisory Panel on Global Food Security 2008; mem. Governing Council Soc. for Int. Devt 1988–94, Commonwealth Intergovernmental Group on the Emergence of a Global Humanitarian Order, London 1994–95; Chair. UN Asscn of Australia (ACT Div.) 1998–99; mem. Bd Trustees Asia-Pacific Coll. of Diplomacy, ANU 2005–; Alan Shawn Feinstein World Hunger Award, Brown Univ. 1991, Inaugural Food for Life Award, UN World Food Programme 2000. *Publication:* Bread and Stones: Leadership and the Struggle to Reform the United Nations World Food Programme 2006; contrib. numerous articles to journals and chapters to books. *Leisure interests:* music, reading, gardening, cycling. *Address:* 4 Stokes Street, Manuka, ACT 2603, Australia (home). *Telephone:* (2) 6295-0446 (home). *E-mail:* jingram@homemail.com.au (home).

INGRAM, Tamara, BA; British advertising executive; *Chairman Visit London Ltd;* b. 1961; m.; two c.; began career in film production; joined Saatchi & Saatchi 1985, Bd Account Dir 1989–93, Exec. Account Dir 1993–95, Jt CEO 1995–2001, Exec. Chair. 2001–02; Chair. and CEO McCann-Erickson 2002–03; Pres. Added Value, Fusion 5 and Henley Centre (marketing consulting firms of Kantar Div. of WWP Group PLC) 2003–05, CEO Grey London (div. of WPP) 2005–07, also CEO Grey Group UK (comprising Grey London, Joshua, GCI and MDS Global Consulting), Pres. Team P&G (WPP Group's team for Proctor & Gamble Co.) 2007–; Chair. Visit London Ltd 2002–; mem. Bd of Dirs Sage Group plc 2004–, London Devt Agency (LDA), Council Inst. of Practitioners in Advertising (IPA), Marketing Soc., Marketing Group of GB, Women in Advertising and Communications London (WACL); Chair. Devt Bd, Royal Court Theatre; Trustee, The Bacon Fellowship. *Address:* Visit London, 2 More London Riverside, London, SE1 2RR, England (office). *Telephone:* (20) 7234-5800 (office).

INGRAMS, Richard Reid; British journalist; *Editor, The Oldie;* b. 19 Aug. 1937, London; s. of Leonard St Clair and Victoria Ingrams (née Reid); m. Mary Morgan 1962 (divorced 1993); two s. (one deceased) one d.; ed Shrewsbury School, Univ. Coll., Oxford; co-founder Private Eye 1962, Ed. 1963–86, Chair. 1974–; founder and Ed. The Oldie 1992–; TV critic The Spectator 1976–84; columnist The Observer 1988–90, 1992–. *Publications:* Private Eye on London (with Christopher Booker and William Rushton) 1962, Private Eye's Romantic England 1963, Mrs Wilson's Diary (with John Wells) 1965, Mrs Wilson's Second Diary 1966, The Tale of Driver Grope 1968, The Bible for Motorists (with Barry Fantoni) 1970, The Life and Times of Private Eye (ed.) 1971, Harris in Wonderland (as Philip Reid with Andrew Osmond) 1973, Cobbett's Country Book (ed.) 1974, Beachcomber: the works of J. B. Morton (ed.) 1974, The Best of Private Eye 1974, God's Apology 1977, Goldenballs 1979, Romney Marsh (with Fay Godwin) 1980, Dear Bill: The Collected Letters of Denis Thatcher (with John Wells) 1980, The Other Half 1981, Piper's Places (with John Piper) 1983, Dr Johnson by Mrs Thrale (ed.) 1984, Down the Hatch (with John Wells) 1985, Just the One (with John Wells) 1986, John Stewart Collis: A Memoir 1986, The Best of Dear Bill (with John Wells) 1986, Mud in Your Eye (with John Wells) 1987, The Eye Spy Look-alike Book (ed.) 1988, The Ridgeway 1988, You Might As Well Be Dead 1988, England: An Anthology 1989, No. 10 1989, On and On... Further Letters of Denis Thatcher (with John Wells) 1990, The Oldie Annual (ed.) 1993, The Oldie Annual II (ed.) 1994, Malcolm Muggeridge (ed.) 1995, I Once Met (ed.) 1996, The Oldie Annual III (ed.) 1997, Jesus: Authors Take Sides (anthology) 1999, The Oldie Annual IV (ed.) 1999, The Life and Adventures of William Cobbett (biog.) 2005. *Leisure interests:* music, book selling. *Address:* The Oldie, 65 Newman Street, London, W1T 3EG, England. *Telephone:* (20) 7436-8801. *Fax:* (20) 7436-8804. *E-mail:* editorial@theoldie.co.uk. *Website:* www.theoldie.co.uk.

INGRAO, Pietro; Italian politician and journalist; b. 30 March 1915, Lenola, Latina; m. Laura Lombardo Radice 1944; one s. four d.; ed Univ. of Rome; began career as a journalist; active in anti-fascist student groups at Univ. of Rome 1939; joined Italian Communist Party (PCI) 1940; joined editorial staff of l'Unità (PCI newspaper) 1943; took part in resistance movement in Rome and Milan 1943–45; Ed. l'Unità 1947–57; mem. Nat. Exec. and Sec. of PCI 1956; mem. Chamber of Deputies (lower house of Parl.) for Rome, Latino, Frosinone, Viterbo 1948–58, for Perugia, Terni, Rieti 1958–63, 1968–, for Ancona and Perugia 1963–68; Pres. of PCI Parl. Group 1972–76; Pres. of Chamber of Deputies 1976–79; Pres. of Centre of Studies and Activities for the Reform of the State 1979; joined Partito della Rifondazione Comunista (Communist Refoundation Party) 2004. *Publications:* essays on political and social subjects in periodicals, including Rinascita, Critica Marxista 1945–, Masse e Potere 1977, Crisi e Terzavia 1978, Tradizione e Progetto 1982, Il Dubbio dei Vincitori (poetry) 1987. *Address:* Partito della Rifondazione Comunista (PRC) (Party of Communist Refoundation), Viale del Policlinico 131, 00161 Rome, Italy.

INGVES, Stefan, MSc, PhD; Swedish banking official; *Governor, Sveriges Riksbank;* ed Stockholm School of Econs; Lecturer, Stockholm School of Econs 1976–84; Asst Vice-Pres., Cen. Finance and Fund Man. Div., Svenska Handelsbanken 1984–86; Pres. Sweden Options and Futures Exchange 1987; Under-Sec. for Financial Markets and Insts, Ministry of Finance 1988–92; Dir-Gen. Swedish Bank Support Authority 1993–94; Deputy Gov. Sveriges Riksbank (Swedish Cen. Bank) 1994–98, Gov. 2006–, also Chair. Exec. Bd; Dir Monetary and Financial Systems Dept, IMF 1999–2005, currently Gov. for Sweden; mem. Bd of Dirs BIS; mem. European Cen. Bank Gen. Council; fmr mem. Toronto Int. Leadership Centre for Financial Sector Supervision. *Address:* Sveriges Riksbank, Brunkebergstorg 11, 103 37 Stockholm, Sweden (office). *Telephone:* (8) 787-00-00 (office). *Fax:* (8) 21-05-31 (office). *E-mail:* registratorn@riksbank.se (office). *Website:* www.riksbank.se (office).

INHOFE, James Mountain, BA; American politician; *Senator from Oklahoma;* b. 17 Nov. 1934, Des Moines, Ia; s. of Perry Inhofe and Blanche Mountain; m. Kay Kirkpatrick 1958; two s. two d.; ed Univ. of Tulsa; mem. Okla House of Reps 1966–68; mem. Okla State Senate 1968–76, Minority Leader 1970–76; Mayor of Tulsa 1978–84; mem. US House of Reps., 1st Dist Okla 1987–94; Senator from Oklahoma Jan. 1995–, mem. Environment and Public Works Cttee (fmr Chair.); Pres. Fly Riverside Inc. 1978, Quaker Life Insurance Co.; Republican. *Address:* 453 Russell Senate Building, Washington, DC 20510-0001, USA (office). *Telephone:* (202) 224-4721 (office). *E-mail:* jim-inhofe@inhofe.senate.gov (office). *Website:* inhofe.senate.gov (office).

INK, Claude; French business executive; b. 17 March 1928, Hussigny; s. of Gilbert Ink and Paule Rollin; m. Annie Beaurain-Verdollin 1952; two s. one d.; ed Ecole Polytechnique; engineer, Sollac 1952, Asst Dir-Gen. 1966, Vice-Pres., Dir-Gen. Sollac 1978; Dir-Gen. SCAC 1969; Pres. Bd of Dirs, Solmer 1980, Dir-Gen. 1985; Pres. and Dir-Gen. Solnetal, Vice-Pres. Sollac; Dir-Gen. Sacilor; Pres. Chambre syndicale Fer blanc 1986; Del. Gen. Fondation l'Ecole Polytechnique 1987–95, Conseilleur 1996; Pres. Asscn Professionnelle des Producteurs Européens de l'Acier pour l'Emballage Léger (APEAL) 1988–90; Pres. Comité Int. du titre de l'ingénieur 1996–99; Officier, Légion d'honneur, Chevalier des Palmes académiques. *Address:* 65 bis avenue du Belloy, 78110 Le Vesinet, France (home). *Telephone:* 39-52-45-03 (home). *E-mail:* claude.ink2@wanadoo.fr (home).

INKELES, Alex, PhD; American sociologist and academic; *Professor Emeritus, Stanford University;* b. 4 March 1920, Brooklyn, New York; s. of Meyer Inkeles and Ray Gewer Inkeles; m. Bernadette Mary Kane 1942; one d.; ed Cornell and Columbia Univs, Washington School of Psychiatry; Social Science Research Analyst, Dept of State 1942–46, Int. Broadcasting Div. 1949–51; Instructor in Social Relations, Harvard Univ. 1948–49, Lecturer in Sociology 1948–57, Prof. 1957–71, Dir Russian Research Center Studies in Social Relations 1963–71, Dir Center of Int. Affairs Studies on Social Aspects of Econ. Devt 1963–71; Margaret Jacks Prof. of Educ., Stanford Univ. 1971–78, Prof. of Sociology and, by courtesy, Educ. 1978–90, Prof. Emer. of Sociology 1995–; Sr Fellow, Hoover Inst. on War, Revolution and Peace 1978–, Prof. Emer. 1990–; numerous fellowships including Inst. for Advanced Study, Princeton, Guggenheim, Fulbright, Rockefeller Foundation, Bellagio, Italy, NAS Exchange Program with People's Repub. of China, Nankai Univ. 1983; mem. American Acad. of Arts and Sciences, NAS, AAAS, American Philosophical Soc., American Psychology Asscn; Hon. PhD (Faculdade Candido Mendes, Brazil); numerous awards. *Publications:* Public Opinion in Soviet Russia 1950, How the Soviet System Works 1956, The Soviet Citizen: Daily Life in a Totalitarian Society 1959, What is Sociology? 1964, Social Change in Soviet Russia 1968, Becoming Modern: Individual Change in Six Developing Countries 1974, Exploring Individual Modernity 1983, On Measuring Democracy: Its Consequences and Concomitants 1991, National Character: A Psycho-Social Perspective 1996, One World Emerging? Convergence and Divergence in Industrial Societies 1998, Social Capital as a Policy Resource (co-ed.) 2001. *Leisure interests:* travel, East Asian art collection, biking, swimming. *Address:* Hoover Institution, LHH-239, Stanford University, Stanford, CA 94305 (office); 1001 Hamilton Avenue, Palo Alto, CA 94301, USA (home). *Telephone:* (415) 723-4856 (office); (415) 327-4197 (home). *Fax:* (415) 723-0576 (office). *E-mail:* inkeles@hoover.stanford.edu (office). *Website:* (office).

INNANI, Brij Gopal; Nepalese business executive; *Group President, Mahalaxmi Garment Industries Group;* Group Pres. Mahalaxmi Garment Industries Group; fmr Pres. Garment Asscn of Nepal; Chair. Asian Textiles and Garments Council 2001–03; Chair. Shri Laxmi Narsingh Dibyadham, Maheswari Soc. of Kathmandu; mem. Fed. of Nepalese Chambers of Commerce and Industry, London Chamber of Commerce and Industry, Nepal-India Chamber of Commerce and Industry, Nepal-Britain Chamber of Commerce and Industry, Red Cross Soc.; King Birendra Coronation Silver Jubilee Gold Medal, Golden Jubilee Gold Medal. *Address:* Mahalaxmi Garment Industries Group, V. Narsing Kunj, New Plaza, Putali Sadak, POB 4206, Kathmandu, Nepal (office). *Telephone:* (1) 4421048 (office). *Fax:* (1) 4421258 (office). *E-mail:* mgigroup@inani.com.np (office).

INNES OF EDINGIGHT, Sir Malcolm Rognvald, Kt, KCVO, KStJ; b. 25 May 1938; s. of the late Sir Thomas Innes of Learney and of Lady Lucy Buchan; m. Joan Hay 1963; three s.; ed Edinburgh Acad., Univ. of Edinburgh; Falkland Pursuivant Extraordinary 1957; Carrick Pursuivant 1958; Lyon Clerk and Keeper of the Records 1966; Marchmont Herald 1971, Lord Lyon King of Arms 1981–2001; Sec. to Order of the Thistle 1981–2001; Orkney Herald Extraordinary 2001–; mem. Queen's Body Guard for Scotland (Royal Company of Archers) 1971–; Grand Officer of Merit, Sovereign Mil. Order, Malta. *Leisure interest:* visiting places of historical interest. *Address:* Castleton of Kinnairdy, Bridge of Marnoch, Aberdeenshire, AB54 7RT, Scotland (home). *Telephone:* (1466) 780866.

INNIS, Roy Emile Alfredo; American human rights organization executive and chemist; *Chairman, Congress of Racial Equality (CORE);* b. 6 June 1934, St Croix, Virgin Islands; s. of Alexander Innis and Georgianna Innis; m. Doris Funnye 1965; six s. (two deceased) two d.; ed City Coll., New York; joined US Army 1950, Sergeant 1951, discharged 1952; pharmaceutical research work, Vick Chemical Co., then medical research Montefiore Hosp. until 1967; active in Harlem Chapter of Congress of Racial Equality (CORE) 1963–, Chair. Harlem Educ. Cttee 1964, Chair. Harlem CORE 1965–67, Second Nat. Vice-Chair. 1967–68, Assoc. Nat. Dir CORE Jan–Sept. 1968, Nat. Dir 1968–70, Nat. Chair. 1982–; Founder Harlem Commonwealth Council, First Exec. Dir

1967–68, now mem. of Bd; Res. Fellow, Metropolitan Applied Research Center 1967–; Co-Publisher The Manhattan Tribune 1968–71; mem. Bd and Steering Cttee Nat. Urban Coalition; mem. of Bd New York Coalition, Haryou Inc., Bd of Dirs New Era Health Educ. and Welfare, Bd of Advisers Pan-African Journal; mem. Editorial Staff Social Policy Magazine; Publr The Correspondent; Co-Chair. Econ. Devt Task Force, New York Urban Coalition; Founder CORE Community School, South Bronx 1977. *Publications:* The Little Black Book 1971; chapters in: The Endless Crisis, Black Economic Development 1970, Integrating America's Heritage: A Congressional Hearing to Establish A National Commission on Negro History and Culture 1970, Profiles in Black 1976; articles and editorials in Manhattan Tribune, CORE Magazine, Business Weekly, etc. *Leisure interests:* reading, sports, music. *Address:* Congress of Racial Equality, 817 Broadway, New York, NY 10003, USA (office). *Telephone:* (212) 598-4000 (office). *Fax:* (212) 529-3568 (office). *E-mail:* corenyc@aol.com (office). *Website:* www.core-online.org (office).

INOGUCHI, Kuniko, BA, MA, PhD; Japanese academic and politician; b. 3 May 1952, Chiba Pref.; m.; two d.; ed Sophia Univ., Yale Univ., USA; Assoc. Prof. of Political Science, Faculty of Law, Sophia Univ. 1981–90, Prof. 1990–2006; Visiting Fellow, Center for Int. Affairs, Harvard Univ. 1983–84; Visiting Prof., ANU 1985; Amb. to Conf. on Disarmament, Geneva 2002–04, Head of Japanese Del. 2003–04, Pres. of Conf. 2003, Western Group Co-ordinator 2004; elected mem. House of Reps 2005, Minister of State for Gender Equality and Social Affairs 2005–06; Foreign Policy Adviser to Sec.-Gen. LDP 2006–07, Acting Sec.-Gen., LDP Int. Bureau 2006–; mem. UN Advisory Bd on Disarmament Issues, New York 2003–06; Co-Chair. Standing Cttee on Mine Clearance, Mine Risk Educ. and Mine Action Technologies, Meeting of States Parties to Convention on Prohibition of Use of Anti-Personnel Mines 2004; mem. Prime Minister's Defence Policy Review Council 1994–95, Prime Minister's Admin. Reform Council 1996–98, Prime Minister's Gender Equity Council 2001–02; mem. Bd Inst. for Democracy and Electoral Assistance (IDEA), Stockholm, Sweden; Exec. mem. Japan Asscn of Gaming and Simulation 1999, Japan Asscn for Int. Relations 2004–, Exec. mem. Science Council of Japan 2005–; Educ. Minister Award 1972, AVON Awards to Women 2003. *Publications include:* An Emerging Post-Hegemonic System: Choices for Japan 1987, War and Peace (Yoshino Sakuzo Prize) 1989, Invitation to Political Science 1989; articles in newspapers, periodicals and professional journals on disarmament matters. *Address:* Office of Kuniko Inoguchi, 2-2-1 Nagata-cho, Chiyoda-ku, 1st Office Building of the House of Representatives, Room 541, Tokyo 100-8981, Japan (office). *Telephone:* (3) 3508-7271 (office). *Fax:* (3) 3508-3130 (office). *Website:* www.kunikoinoguchi .jp (office).

INOKUCHI, Takeo; Japanese insurance industry executive; b. 9 April 1942; joined Taisho Marine & Fire Insurance Co. Ltd (renamed Mitsui Marine & Fire Insurance Co. Ltd 1993) 1965, Gen. Man. of Non-Marine Underwriting Dept 1990–94, apptd Dir 1993, Man.-Dir 1994–96, Pres. 1996–2000, Chair., Pres. and CEO 2000–01; Chair. and CEO Mitsui Sumitomo Insurance Co. Ltd (cr. following merger of Mitsui Marine & Fire Insurance Co. Ltd and Sumitomo Marine & Fire Insurance Co. Ltd 2001) 2001–04; Vice-Chair. Radio Regulatory Council, Ministry of Public Man., Home Affairs, Posts and Telecommunications 2002–; Corp. Auditor, Sanki Engineering Co. Ltd 2003–, Kikkoman Corpn; Deputy Chair. Ind. Admin. Inst. Evaluation Cttee (IAIEC) and Chair. IAIEC Sub-cttee for Japan Int. Cooperation Agency, Ministry of Foreign Affairs 2003–; Vice-Chair. Japan Asscn of Corp. Execs (Keizai Doyukai) 2003–, Chair. Cttee on Fiscal and Admin. Reforms 2003–; Exec. Dir Japan Business Federation (Nippon Keidanren) 1997–, Co-Chair. Cttee on Econ. Policy 2002–; Exec. Councillor Tokyo Chamber of Commerce 1997–; Dir Int. Insurance Soc. Inc. 2002–; Personality of the Year Award, Asia Insurance Industry 2003, inducted into Insurance Hall of Fame, Insurance Soc. 2004. *Address:* c/o Mitsui Sumitomo Insurance Co. Ltd, 27-2 Shinkawa 2-chome, Chuo-ku, Tokyo 104-8252, Japan. *Telephone:* (3) 3297-1111.

INONI, Ephraim, MBA; Cameroonian politician; *Prime Minister;* b. 16 Aug. 1947, Bakingili; s. of Sarah Enjema Elonge; m.; five c.; ed Catholic Teachers' Training Coll., Bonjongo, Higher Elementary Teachers' Training Coll., Mutengene, South Eastern Univ., USA; Head Teacher, Catholic Primary School, Mabanda, Kumba, then Teacher, Sasse Coll.; Asst Prov. Chief of Accounts in the NW, then Asst Prov. Treas., Financial Controller, Douala; Financial Attaché, Embassy in Washington, DC, USA; Dir, Gen. Admin. Ministry of Finance, then Sec. of State; Asst Sec.-Gen. to the Presidency 1992–2004; Prime Minister of Cameroon 2004–; mem. Bakweri ethnic group. *Address:* Office of the Prime Minister, Yaoundé, Cameroon. *Telephone:* 2223-8005 (office). *Fax:* 2223-5735 (office). *E-mail:* spm@spm.gov.cm (office). *Website:* www.spm.gov.cm (office).

INOUE, Akihisa, PhD; Japanese engineer, academic and university administrator; *President, Tohoku University;* b. 13 Sept. 1947; ed Grad. School of Eng, Tohoku Univ.; Research Assoc., Inst. for Materials Research, Tohoku Univ. 1976–85, Assoc. Prof. 1985–90, Prof. 1990–, also Prof. of Precision and Intelligence Lab., Tokyo Inst. of Tech. 1997–, Dir Inst. for Materials Research 2000–, Deputy Pres. Tohoku Univ. 2002–08, Pres. 2008–; Visiting Scientist, AT&T Bell Labs, USA 1982–83, 1984, 1986; Visiting Scientist, Swedish Inst. of Metals Research 1985, 1987; Science Adviser to Ministry of Educ., Culture, Sports, Science and Tech. 2001–; over 50 awards including Japan Acad. Prize, Houkou Prize, CONA Award. *Address:* Office of the President, Tohoku University, 1-1 Katahira, 2-chome, Aoba-ku, Sendai 980-8577, Japan (office). *Telephone:* (22) 217-4807 (office). *Website:* www.eng.tohoku.ac.jp (office).

INOUE, Hisashi; Japanese playwright and novelist; *President, Japan P.E.N. Club;* b. 1934, Yamagata Pref.; ed Sofia Univ.; during univ. studies worked part-time for a theatre in Asakusa; began writing radio and TV scripts, including educational programmes and children's drama late 1950s; writer Hyokkori hyōtan-jima (The Floating Island Gourd), NHK TV 1964–69; est. name as playwright and novelist early 1970s; played important role in so-called parody boom of 1970s; writer of lectures, essays and commentaries on the production of rice; Pres. Japan P.E.N. Club 2003–; several major theatre and literary prizes including Naoki Prize, People of Cultural Merit Award, Govt of Japan 2004. *Publications include:* Tegusari Shinju (The Love Suicide in Manacles) 1972, Kirikirijin (The Kirikirians) 1981, The Face of Jizo, The Great Doctor Yabuhara 1990. *Website:* www.japanpen.or.jp.

INOUE, Shinya, PhD; American (b. Japanese) biologist and academic; *Distinguished Scientist and Director, Architectural Dynamics in Living Cells Program, Marine Biological Laboratory;* b. 5 Jan. 1921; ed Univ. of Tokyo, Princeton Univ., NJ; Lecturer in Anatomy, Univ. of Washington, Seattle 1951–53; Asst Prof. of Biology, Tokyo Metropolitan Univ. 1953–54; Research Assoc. then Assoc. Prof. in Biology and Instructor in Optics, Univ. of Rochester, NY 1954–59; Prof. and Chair. Dept of Cytology, Dartmouth Medical School, Hanover, NH 1959–66; Prof. of Biology and Dir Program in Biophysical Cytology, Univ. of Pennsylvania 1966–82; Instructor in Chief, Analytical and Quantitative Microscopy, Marine Biological Lab. (MBL), Woods Hole, Mass 1979–87, Distinguished Scientist and Dir, Architectural Dynamics in Living Cells Program 1986–; Fellow, John Simon Guggenheim Foundation 1971–72; Fellow, AAAS 1971; mem. NAS 1993; Hon. Fellow, Royal Microscopical Soc., UK 1988; NIH Merit Award 1982–86; E. B. Wilson Award, American Soc. for Cell Biology 1992, Distinguished Scientist Award, Microscopy Soc. of America 1995, Ernst Abbe Award, New York Microscopical Soc. 1997, Int. Prize for Biology, Japan Soc. for the Promotion of Science 2003. *Publications:* Video Microscopy 1986 (2nd edn with K.R. Spring 1997); numerous papers in specialist journals. *Address:* Marine Biological Laboratory, 7 MBL Street, Woods Hole, MA 02543, USA (office). *Telephone:* (508) 289-7382 (office). *E-mail:* jmacneil@mbl.edu (office). *Website:* www.mbl.edu/research/resident/lab_arch_dyn.html (office); www.mbl.edu/research/resident/lab_inoue.html (office).

INOUE, Yuko, BA, PPRNCM; Japanese violist; b. Hamamatsu; ed Royal Northern Coll. of Music, Manchester, UK; fmr Prin. Viola, Netherlands Chamber Orchestra; now soloist and chamber musician; Prof., RAM, London; performed as soloist with Hungarian State Philharmonic Orchestra, Hallé Orchestra, Netherlands Chamber Orchestra; performed as prin. with Philharmonia Orchestra, London Sinfonietta; has appeared at Lockenhaus, Kuhmo, Cheltenham, Bath and Aldeburgh Festivals; mem. Fibonacci Sequence; Hon. ARAM; winner, 17th Budapest Int. Viola Competition. *Address:* c/o Upbeat Classical Management, PO Box 479, Uxbridge, UB8 2ZH, England (office). *Telephone:* (1895) 259441 (office). *Fax:* (1895) 259341 (office). *E-mail:* info@upbeatclassical.co.uk (office). *Website:* www.upbeatclassical.co.uk (office).

INOUE, Yutaka, DMedSc; Japanese politician; b. 17 Nov. 1927, Chiba; m.; three d.; ed Tokyo Dental Coll.; mem. Chiba Prefectural Ass. 1963–72; mem. House of Reps. 1976–79; mem. House of Councillors 1980–, Pres. 2000–02; State Sec. for Finance 1983–84; Minister of Educ. 1990–91; Chair. Cttee on the Budget 1995–96; Chair. Research Cttee on Int. Affairs 1999–2000; Grand Cordon, Order of the Rising Sun. *Publication:* Major Airports in the World. *Leisure interests:* golf, comic story telling, Sumo. *Address:* c/o Secretariat of the House of Councillors, Kokkai, Nagata-cho, Chiyoda-ku, Tokyo, Japan (office).

INOUYE, Daniel Ken, AB, JD; American lawyer and politician; *Senator from Hawaii;* b. 7 Sept. 1924, Honolulu, Hawaii; s. of Hyotaro Inouye and Kame Imanaga Inouye; m. Margaret Shinobu Awamura 1949; one s.; ed Univ. of Hawaii and George Washington Univ. Law School; served in US Army 1943–47; Majority Leader, Territorial House of Reps 1954–58, mem. Territorial Senate 1958–59; mem. US Congress 1959–62; Senator from Hawaii (Democrat) 1962–, mem. Senate Cttee on Appropriations, Commerce Cttee, Asst Majority Whip 1964–76, mem. Senate Watergate Cttee 1973, Democratic Senatorial Campaign Cttee, mem. Defence Appropriations Sub-Cttee, Chair. Senate Appropriations Sub-Cttee on Foreign Operations, Chair. Senate Commerce Sub-Cttee on Merchant Marine and Tourism, Chair. Senate Select Cttee on Intelligence 1976–77, Chair. Senate Sub-Cttee on Budget Authorizations 1979–84, Head Special Cttee on Iran Affairs 1986, Co-Chair. Senate Cttee on Commerce, Science and Transportation; mem. and fmr Chair. Senate Cttee on Indian Affairs; Temp. Chair. and Keynoter 1968 Democratic Nat. Convention; Sec. Dem. Conf. 1977; Purple Heart with Cluster, Distinguished Service Cross, Bronze Star; Horatio Alger Award 1989, Medal of Honour with Blue Ribbon, (Japan) 1989, Medal of Honor 2000. *Address:* 722 Hart Senate Office Building, Washington, DC 20510-0001 (office); 300 ALa Moana Boulevard, Honolulu, HI 96850-4975, USA (office). *Telephone:* (202) 224-3934 (office); (808) 541-2542 (HI) (office). *Fax:* (202) 224-6747 (office). *Website:* inouye.senate.gov (office).

INOUYE, Minoru, BL; Japanese banker; *Advisor, Bank of Tokyo-Mitsubishi UFJ Ltd;* b. 1924, Tokyo; m.; one s.; ed Univ. of Tokyo; joined Bank of Tokyo 1947, Deputy Agent, New York 1964–66, Deputy Gen. Man. Int. Funds and Foreign Exchange Div. 1966–67, Deputy Gen. Man. Planning and Co-ordination Div. 1967–70, Gen. Man. 1970–72, Dir and Gen. Man. London Office 1972–75, Resident Man. Dir for Europe 1975, Man. Dir 1975–79, Sr Man. Dir 1979–80, Deputy Pres. 1980–85, Pres. 1985–90, Advisor 1990, Advisor, Bank of Tokyo-Mitsubishi Ltd 1996–2005, Advisor, Bank of Tokyo-Mitsubishi UFJ Ltd 2006–; Orden Mexicana del Aguila Azteca, Mexico 1986; Medal of Honour, with Blue Ribbon, Japan 1989; Ordem Nacional de Cruzeiro do Sul, Brazil 1989; Chevalier, Légion d'honneur 1990; Order of the Rising Sun, Gold and Silver Star, Japan 1994. *Leisure interests:* golf, travel. *Address:* The Bank of Tokyo-Mitsubishi UFJ Ltd, 3-2 Nihombashi Hongokucho 1-

chome, Chuo-ku, Tokyo 103-0021, Japan (office). *Telephone:* (3) 240-1111 (office). *Fax:* (3) 245-9117 (office).

INSANALLY, Samuel R. (Rudy), BA; Guyanese diplomatist; *Permanent Representative, United Nations;* b. 23 June 1936, Georgetown; ed Univ. of London, UK and Univ. of Paris, France; teacher of modern languages, Kingston Coll., Jamaica, Queen's Coll., Guyana and Univ. of Guyana 1959–66; Counsellor, Embassy in Washington, DC 1966–69; Chargé d'affaires, Embassy in Venezuela 1970, Amb. 1972–78; Deputy Perm. Rep. to UN, New York 1970–72, Perm. Rep. 1987–; Perm. Rep. to EEC 1978–81; Amb. to Belgium (also accred to Sweden, Norway and Austria) 1978–81, to Colombia 1982–86; Head of Political Div. Ministry of Foreign Affairs 1982–86; High Commr to Barbados, Trinidad and Tobago and the Eastern Caribbean 1982–86; Minister of Foreign Affairs 2001–08; mem. Bd of Govs Inst. of Int. Relations, Trinidad and Tobago 1982–86; Gran Cordon, Order of the Liberator (Venezuela) 1973, Cacuque Crown of Hon.1980; Golden Arrow of Achievement 1986. *Publications include:* several articles and works on int. relations and diplomacy. *Address:* Permanent Mission to the United Nations, 866 United Nations Plaza, Suite 555, New York, NY 10017, USA (office). *Telephone:* (212) 527-3232 (office). *Fax:* (212) 935-7548 (office). *E-mail:* guyana@un.int (office).

INSULZA SALINAS, José Miguel, MA; Chilean politician, lawyer and international organization official; *Secretary-General, Organization of American States;* b. 2 June 1943; m. Georgina Núñez Reyes; three c.; ed St George's Coll., Santiago, Law School, Universidad de Chile, Facultad Latinoamericana de Ciencias Sociales and Univ. of Michigan, USA; Prof. of Political Theory, Universidad de Chile, of Political Sciences, Pontificia Universidad Católica de Chile –1973; Political Adviser to Ministry of Foreign Relations, Dir Diplomatic Acad. –1973; researcher, then Dir Instituto de Estudios de Estados Unidos, Centro de Investigación y Docencia Económicas, Mexico 1981–88; Prof., Universidad Autónoma de México 1981–88; Head, Multilateral Econ. Affairs Dept, Ministry of Foreign Relations, Deputy Chair. Int. Co-operation Agency 1990–94; Under-Sec. for Foreign Affairs 1994, Minister 1994–99, Minister Sec.-Gen. Office of the Pres. 1999; Minister of the Interior (Vice-Pres. of the Repub.) 2000–; Sec.-Gen. OAS 2005–; mem. Bd of Dirs Instituto de Fomento de Desarrollo Científico y Tecnológico; mem. Consejo Chileno de Relaciones Internacionales, Consejo de Redacción, Nexos Magazine, Mexico, Corporación de Desarrollo Tecnológico Empresarial, Chilean Asscn of Political Science, Bar Asscn. *Address:* Organization of American States, 17th Street and Constitution Avenue, NW, Washington, DC 20006, USA (office); Ministry of the Interior, Palacio de la Moneda, Santiago, Chile (office). *Telephone:* (2) 690-4000 (Santiago) (office); (202) 458-3000 (Washington) (office). *Fax:* (2) 699-2165 (Santiago) (office). *E-mail:* pi@oas.org (office). *Website:* www.oas.org (office).

INTRILIGATOR, Michael David, SB, MA, PhD; American economist and academic; *Professor Emeritus of Economics, Political Science, and Public Policy, University of California, Los Angeles;* b. 5 Feb. 1938, New York, NY; s. of Allan Intriligator and Sally Intriligator; m. Devrie Shapiro 1963; four s.; ed Massachusetts Inst. of Tech., Yale Univ.; Asst Prof., Dept of Econs, UCLA 1963–66, Assoc. Prof. 1966–72, Prof. 1972–, now Prof. Emer. of Econs, Political Science, and Public Policy, Dir UCLA Inst. of Contemporary Econs 1967, 1969, Prof., Dept of Political Science, UCLA 1981–, mem. Steering Cttee Center for Arms Control and Int. Security 1975–78, Steering Cttee Center for Int. and Strategic Affairs 1978–92, Steering Cttee Summer Inst. for the Study of Conflict Theory and Int. Security 1980–84, Assoc. Dir Center for Int. and Strategic Affairs 1979–82, Dir Center for Int. and Strategic Affairs 1982–92, Vice-Chair. 1991–94, Dir Burkle Center for Int. Relations 2000–02, Prof., Dept of Policy Studies, School of Public Policy and Social Research 1994–, Vice-Chair. 1995–99, Prof., Dept of Public Policy, School of Public Affairs 2004–, Consultant Research Assoc., UCLA Security Studies Project 1967–68; Research Assoc., Human Resources Research Center, Univ. of Southern California 1969–81; Lecturer, Div. of Humanities and Social Sciences, California Inst. of Tech. 1969–71; Sr Economist and Consultant, Analytical Assessments Corpn, Marina del Rey, Calif. 1977–81; Co-Dir Center for Int. Studies: Int. Security at UCLA and Univ. of Southern California 1985–86, Dir 1986–91; Co-Dir (with Anatoly A. Gromyko), Project on 'Soviet-US Cooperation for Africa' 1987–; mem. Bd Dirs California-Russia Trade Asscn, Los Angeles 1989–93, California-Russia Trade Asscn 1992–, Los Angeles-St Petersburg Sister City Cttee 1999–2000; mem. Bd of Advisers, California Council on Europe 1991–94; mem. Panel of Experts, Study on Econ. Aspects of Disarmament, UN Inst. for Disarmament Research (UNIDIR), Geneva 1990–92; mem. Int. Advisory Bd Russian Science Foundation, Moscow 1994–; mem. Center for Econ. Design, Bogazici Univ., Istanbul 1997–2003; reviewer (math. econs) for Mathematical Reviews 1975–79; Assoc. Ed. numerous journals; expert witness before admin. agencies and courts, testifying for govt agencies, corpns and asscns 1976–; Pres. Peace Science Soc. (Int.) 1993; Vice-Chair. Economists Allied for Arms Reduction (ECAAR) 1998–2005 (mem. Bd Dirs 1989–2005), Economists for Peace and Security 2005–; Vice-Pres. Western Econ. Asscn Int. 2006–07, Pres. 2008–09; mem. American Econ. Asscn, American Political Science Asscn, Council on Foreign Relations, New York 1984, Econometric Soc., Economists Allied for Arms Reduction, IISS, London 1983, Int. Political Science Asscn, Int. Studies Asscn, Peace Science Soc. (Int.), Western Econ. Asscn Int.; Founding mem. Pacific Council on Int. Policy 1995–; Foreign mem. Russian Acad. of Sciences 1999; Fellow, Econometric Soc. 1982, AAAS 2001; Sr Fellow, The Gorbachev Foundation of N America, Boston 1998–, The Milken Inst., Santa Monica 1999–; Woodrow Wilson Fellow, Yale Univ. 1959–60; MIT Fellow 1960–61; Ford Faculty Research Fellow, Stanford Univ. and LSE 1967–68; Distinguished Teaching Award, Grad. Student Asscn, UCLA 1966, Warren C. Scoville Distinguished Teaching Award, Dept of Econs, UCLA 1976, 1979, 1982, 1984, invited by Swedish Econ. Asscn and Stockholm Int. Peace Research Inst. to present lecture on 'Non-Armageddon Solutions to the Arms Race' to dels to Conf. on Confidence- and Security-Building Measures and Disarmament in Europe, Stockholm 1984. *Publications include:* Strategy in a Missile War: Targets and Rates of Fire (monograph) 1967, Mathematical Optimization and Economic Theory 1971 (translated into several languages), co-ed. book series Advanced Textbooks in Economics 1972–78, co-ed. book series Handbooks in Economics 1980, co-ed. Handbook of Econometrics, Vol. I 1983, Vol. II 1984, Vol. III 1986, co-ed. Handbook of Mathematical Economics Vol. I 1981, Vol. II 1982, Vol. III 1985, National Security and International Stability (co-ed.) 1983, Strategies for Managing Nuclear Proliferation – Economic and Political Issues (co-ed.) 1983, Non-Armageddon Solutions to the Arms Race (lecture and monograph), Stockholm 1984, Arms Control: Problems and Prospects 1987, Arms Control: The Changing Strategic Environment and the Long-Term Future (monograph) 1989, Accidental Nuclear War (co-ed.) 1990, Economic Aspects of Disarmament: Disarmament as an Investment Process (monograph) 1992, Implications of the Dissolution of the Soviet Union for Accidental/Inadvertent Use of Weapons of Mass Destruction (co-ed.) 1992, Cooperative Models in International Relations Research (co-ed.) 1994, Statistical Sampling in the Medicare Program: Challenging its Use 2001, Eurasia: A New Peace Agenda (co-ed.) 2005, Countering Terrorism and WMD: Creating a Global Anti-Terrorism Network (co-ed.) 2006. *Leisure interests:* travel and art collecting, classical music. *Address:* 140 Foxtail Drive, Santa Monica, CA 90402 (home); Department of Economics, University of California, Los Angeles, CA 90095-1477, USA (office). *Telephone:* (310) 825-4144 (office); (310) 395-7909 (home). *Fax:* (310) 825-9528 (office); (310) 394-8007 (home). *E-mail:* intriligator@econ.ucla.edu (office). *Website:* econweb.sscnet.ucla.edu (office).

INUBUSHI, Yasuo; Japanese metal industry executive; *President, CEO and Representative Director, Kobe Steel Ltd (KOBELCO);* b. 10 Feb. 1944, Tokushima; ed Osaka Univ.; joined Kobe Steel (KOBELCO) 1967, worked in Sales Planning and Admin Dept 1969–74, posted to Titan Steel & Wire Co., Canada 1974, also served at Kobe Steel offices New York and Los Angeles, Man. Cold Rolled Sheet Sales Section 1981–90, Gen. Man. Int. Operations Dept, Iron and Steel Div. 1990–99, mem. Bd of Dirs 1996–, Sr Officer 1999–2001, Exec. Officer and Gen. Man. Steel Sales Div. 2001–02, Rep. Dir 2002–, Exec. Vice-Pres. 2002–04, Pres. and CEO 2004–. *Address:* Kobe Steel Ltd, Shinko Building, 10-26 Wakinohamacho 2-chome, Kobe 651-8585, Japan (office). *Telephone:* (78) 261-5111 (office). *Fax:* (78) 261-4123 (office). *E-mail:* info@kobelco.co.jp (office). *Website:* www.kobelco.co.jp (office).

INZAMAM-UL-HAQ; Pakistani cricketer; b. 3 March 1970, Multan, Punjab; right-handed middle order batsman; teams played for Multan, Faisalabad, Rawalpindi, United Bank Ltd, Nat. Bank of Pakistan, Pakistan (test debut versus England at Birmingham, 1992; one-day int. debut versus West Indies at Lahore, 1991); scored 8,813 runs in 119 tests (highest score 329 versus New Zealand at Lahore, 2002) with 25 hundreds; scored 11,739 runs in 378 one-day ints (average 39.33) with 10 centuries; scored 16,679 runs in 241 first-class matches with 45 hundreds; Pakistan's second highest-ever run-scorer in tests (behind Javed Miandad Khan); Pakistan Capt. 2003–07; retd from one-day cricket 2007. *Address:* c/o Pakistan Cricket Board, Gaddafi Stadium, Ferozepur Road, Lahore 54600, Pakistan. *Telephone:* (42) 571-7231.

INZKO, Valentin, Jr, DIur; Austrian diplomatist; *High Representative of the International Community and Special Representative of the European Union in Bosnia and Herzegovina;* b. 22 May 1949, Klagenfurt am Wörthersee, Carinthia; s. of the late Valentin Inzko, Sr; m. Bernarda Fink; one s. one d.; ed attended a Slovene-German bilingual school in Suetschach, Feistritz im Rosental, Univ. of Graz, Diplomatic Acad., Vienna; entered Austrian diplomatic service 1974, UNDP Deputy Dir, Ulan Bator, Mongolia 1974–78, Colombo, Sri Lanka 1978–80, Political Section, Dept of Cen., Eastern and Southern Europe, Cen. Asia and Southern Caucasus, Ministry of Foreign Affairs 1981, Press and Culture Attaché, Embassy in Belgrade 1982–86, Counsellor, Del. to First Mission and Deputy Dir UN Disarmament Mission, Austrian Mission to UN, New York, USA 1986–89, Deputy Head of Press and Information Dept, Ministry of Foreign Affairs 1989–90, Cultural Council, Embassy in Prague 1990–96, Founding Dir Austrian Cultural Inst., Prague 1993–96, Founding Head of OSCE Observer Mission in Novi Pazar, Sandzhak, Serbia Oct.–Dec. 1992, Amb. to Bosnia and Herzegovina 1996–99, Head of Dept for Middle, E and S Europe, Cen. Asia and S Caucasus, Ministry of Foreign Affairs 1999–2005, Observer of Montenegrin Parl. Elections 2002, Amb. to Slovenia 2005–09, High Rep. of Int. Community and Special Rep. of EU, Mission in Bosnia and Herzegovina 2009–; Hon. Citizen of the City of Sarajevo, Bosnia and Herzegovina 2000. *Publications:* translated essays of Václav Havel, Living in Truth and Power of the Powerless, into Slovene. *Address:* Office of the High Representative and EU Special Representative, Emerika Bluma 1, 71 000 Sarajevo, Bosnia and Herzegovina (office); Office of the EU Special Representative for BiH, Council of the European Union, 133 Rue Froissart, 1040 Brussels, Belgium (office). *Telephone:* (33) 283500 (Sarajevo) (office); (2) 281-76-49 (Brussels) (office). *Fax:* (33) 283501 (Sarajevo) (office); (2) 281-69-47 (Brussels) (office). *E-mail:* info@ohr.int (office). *Website:* www.ohr.int (office).

IOFFE, Boris Lazarevich, MS; Russian theoretical physicist; *Head of Laboratory, A.I. Alikhanov Institute of Theoretical and Experimental Physics;* b. 6 July 1926, Moscow; s. of Lazar Iof and Pesia Ioffe; m. 1st Svetlana Mikhailova 1957 (divorced 1974); one s.; m. 2nd Nina Libova 1990; ed Moscow Univ.; Jr Scientist, A.I. Alikhanov Inst. of Theoretical and Experimental Physics (ITEP), Moscow 1950–55, Sr Scientist 1955–77, Head of Lab. 1977–, Prof. 1977–, Chair. ITEP Scientific Council 1990–97; Deputy Ed. Moscow Physics Soc. Journal 1991–98; mem. High Energy Physics Scientific Policy Cttee (Russia) 1992–98, Russian Nuclear Soc. –1990; Corresp. mem. USSR (now Russian) Acad. of Sciences 1990; mem. Exec. Cttee United Physical Soc. of Russian Fed. 1998; Fellow, American Physical Soc. 1995; Order of Honour of USSR 1954, 1974; Veteran of Labour Medal 1985, USSR Award for Discovery 1986, 1989, Alexander von Humboldt Award (Germany) 1994, 850 Years of Moscow Medal 1997, Novy Mir Magazine Prize 1999, Acad. of Sciences I.E. Tamm Prize 2008. *Publications:* Hard Processes 1984, The Top Secret Assignment 1999, 2001, Without Retouching 2004; 280 articles. *Leisure interests:* mountaineering (especially in Cen. Asia and Far East), skiing. *Address:* A.I. Alikhanov Institute of Theoretical and Experimental Physics, Bolshaya Cheremushkinskaya 25, 117218 Moscow (office); Bolotnikovskaya Street 40, Korp 4, Apt 16, 117209 Moscow, Russia (home). *Telephone:* (499) 123-31-93 (office); (499) 123-31-93 (home). *Fax:* (495) 127-05-43 (office). *E-mail:* ioffe@itep.ru (office). *Website:* www.itep.ru (office).

IOSIFESCU, Marius Vicenţiu Viorel, PhD, DSc; Romanian mathematician and academic; *Director, Institute of Mathematical Statistics and Applied Mathematics and Vice-President, Casa Academiei Romane (Romanian Academy);* b. 12 Aug. 1936, Piteşti; s. of the late Victor Iosifescu and Ecaterina Iosifescu; m. Ştefania Eugenia Zamfirescu 1973; one s.; ed Bucharest Univ.; consultant, Cen. Statistical Bd 1959–62; Asst Prof., Bucharest Polytechnical Inst. 1961–63; Research Mathematician, Inst. of Math. and Centre for Math. Statistics, Romanian Acad., Bucharest 1963–76, Dir 1976–2002, Dir Inst. of Math. Statistics and Applied Math. 2002–, Vice-Pres. Romanian Acad. 2002–; Visiting Prof., Univs of Paris 1974, 1991, 1996, 1998, Mainz 1977–78, Frankfurt am Main 1979–80, Bonn 1981–82, Melbourne 1991, Lille 1997, Bordeaux 1998, 1999; Overseas Fellow, Churchill Coll., Cambridge 1971; mem. Editorial Bds Journal of the Mathematical European Soc., Bulletin Mathématique de la Soc. des Sciences Mathématiques de Roumanie, Mathematica, Revue d'Analyse Numérique et de Théorie de l'Approximation; Deputy Chief Ed. Revue Roumaine de Mathématiques Pures et Appliquées; mem. Int. Statistical Inst., Bernoulli Soc. for Math. Statistics and Probability (mem. council 1975–79), American Math. Soc., Société de Mathématiques Appliquées et Industrielles; Corresp. mem. Romanian Acad. 1991, Titular mem. 2000; Chevalier, Ordre des Palmes académiques 1993; Romanian Acad. Prize 1965, 1972, Bronze Medal Helsinki Univ. 1975. *Publications:* Random Processes and Learning (with R. Theodorescu) 1969, Stochastic Processes and Applications in Biology and Medicine, Vol. I Theory, Vol. II Models (with P. Tăutu) 1973, Finite Markov Processes and Their Applications 1980, 2007; Proceedings of Braşov Conference on Probability Theory (ed.) 1971, 1974, 1979, 1982, Dependence with Complete Connections and its Applications (with Ş. Grigorescu) 1982, 1990; Studies in Probability and Related Topics (ed.) 1983, Elements of Stochastic Modelling (with Ş. Grigorescu, G. Oprişan and G. Popescu) 1984, From Real Analysis to Probability: Autobiographical Notes 1986, Metrical Theory of Continued Fractions (with C. Kraaikamp) 2002, Modèles Stochastiques (with N. Limnios and G. Oprisan) 2007. *Leisure interests:* music, playing violin. *Address:* Institute of Mathematical Statistics and Applied Mathematics, Casa Academiei Romane, Calea 13 Septembrie nr 13, 050711 Bucharest 5 (office); Str. Dr N. Manolescu 9–11, 050583 Bucharest 35, Romania (home). *Telephone:* (21) 3182433 (office); (21) 4103523 (home). *Fax:* (21) 2116608 (office). *E-mail:* miosifes@acad.ro (office). *Website:* www.csm .ro (office).

IOVINE, Jimmy; American record company executive, record producer and film producer; *Chairman, Interscope Records;* b. 11 March 1953, Brooklyn, New York; early career as recording engineer at Record Plant, New York 1973; worked as producer 1977–90, produced first album for Flame 1977, produced Patti Smith's Easter 1978; Co-founder Interscope Records 1989, Co-Chair. Interscope Geffen A&M Records, Chair. 2001–; Co-founder (with Doug Morris), Chair. and CEO Jimmy and Doug's Farm Club (project comprising a record label, website and cable TV show) 1999–; has worked with Dr Dre, Marilyn Manson, Stevie Nicks, Nine Inch Nails, No Doubt, 2Pac, Tom Petty, The Pretenders, Brian Setzer Orchestra, Patti Smith and U2; Producer of the Year, Rolling Stone Magazine (twice). *Films produced include:* 8 Mile 2002, Get Rich or Die Tryin' 2005. *Address:* Interscope Records, 2220 Colorado Avenue, Santa Monica, CA 90404, USA (office). *Website:* www.interscope.com (office); www.farmclub.com (office).

IOVV, Vasile, PhD; Moldovan economist and politician; b. 29 Dec. 1942, Corjova, Dubasari dist.; ed Technologic Inst. of Kiev, Social Science Acad., Moscow; Vice-Pres. then Pres. Balti town exec., fmr inspector, CP of Moldova, First Sec. of Balti Party Cttee then Sec.; fmr Sr Counsellor CP of USSR; fmr Dir Scientific Research and Production, Sugar Industrial Asscn of Moldova; fmr Chief Commercial-Econ. Office, Embassy of Moldova in Moscow; fmr Minister of Transport and Roads, then First Deputy Prime Minister of Moldova 2002–05, 2005–. *Address:* Office of the Council of Ministers, Piaţa Marii Adunări Naţionale 1, 2033 Chişinău, Moldova. *Telephone:* (2) 23-30-92. *E-mail:* info@parlament.md. *Website:* parlament.moldova.md.

IOZZO, Alfonso; Italian banking executive; *Managing Director, Grupp Sanpaolo IMI SpA;* ed Turin Univ.; joined Sanpaolo IMI SpA, Turin 1961, fmr Head, Research Dept, then Foreign Dept and subsequently Deputy Gen. Man., Jt Gen. Man. 1992–95, Gen. Man. holding Gruppo Bancario Sanpaolo (holding co.) 1995, Gen. Sec. Compagnia di San Paolo 1995–2001, Jt CEO Gruppo Sanpaolo IMI 2001–04, Man. Dir 2004–; Chair. Cassa Depositi e Prestiti SpA, Associazione Prometeia; Pres. Movimento Federalista Europeo; Pres. A. Spinelli Inst.; Dir NHS Mezzogiorno SGR SpA, CDC Finance–CDC Ixis SpA. *Address:* Sanpaolo IMI SpA, Piazza San Carlo 156, Turin 10121, Italy (office). *Telephone:* (11) 55 51 (office). *Fax:* (11) 54 84 69 (office). *Website:* www.sanpaoloimi.com (office).

IP, Nancy Yuk-Yu, BSc, PhD; Hong Kong neurobiologist and academic; *Chair, Professor and Head of Biochemistry and Director, Molecular Neuroscience Center, Hong Kong University of Science and Technology;* ed Simmons Coll.,

Boston, USA, Harvard Univ.; Post-doctoral Fellow, Harvard Univ. 1983–84, Sloan-Kettering Inst., New York 1984–85; Lab. Head, Lifecodes Corpn, New York 1987–89, Regeneron Pharmaceuticals Inc., New York 1989–96; mem. staff, Hong Kong Univ. of Science and Tech. 1993–, currently Chair., Prof. and Head of Biochemistry, also Dir Molecular Neuroscience Center; Founding-mem. and Council mem. Asia-Pacific Int. Molecular Biology Network (A-IMBN); Ed.-in-Chief NeuroSignals; mem. Editorial Bd Journal of Neuroscience, Cell Research, Developmental Neurobiochemistry; mem. Chinese Acad. of Sciences 2001–; mem. Bd Hong Kong Science and Tech. Parks Corpn 2005–; Fellow, Acad. of Sciences for the Developing World 2004–; Dr hc (Simmons Coll.) 2007; HK Govt Medal of Honour 2008; Croucher Foundation Sr Research Fellowship 1998, Nat. Natural Science Award 2003, L'Oréal-UNESCO Women in Science Award 2004, Outstanding Women Professionals Award 2005, Ho Leung Ho Lee Foundation Prize for Scientific and Technological Progress 2008. *Publications:* over 180 articles in scientific journals with more than 13,000 SCI citations, holder of 18 patents. *Address:* Department of Biochemistry, Hong Kong University of Science and Technology, Clear Water Bay, Kowloon, Hong Kong Special Administrative Region, People's Republic of China (office). *Telephone:* 2358-7304 (office). *Fax:* 2358-2765 (office). *E-mail:* boip@ust.hk (office). *Website:* www.ust.hk/bich/en/mnl/index.html (office).

IP, Regina, (Lau Suk-yee), MA, MSc; Hong Kong politician; b. 24 Aug. 1950; m. (husband deceased); one d.; ed Hong Kong Univ., Univ. of Glasgow, UK, Stanford Univ., USA; joined Hong Kong Admin. Service 1975, service in Civil Service Br., Home Affairs Dept, New Territories Admin, City and New Territories Admin, Security Br., Trade Dept, Office of the Chief Sec., Trade and Industry Br.; Dir-Gen. of Industry 1995–96; Dir of Immigration (first woman apptd to head a disciplined service) 1996–98; Dir of Immigration of Hong Kong Special Admin. Region (HKSAR) 1997–98; Sec. for Security (first woman in position) 1998–2002, 2002–03 (resgnd); attended Stanford Univ. 2003–06, then returned to Hong Kong; est. Savantas Policy Inst. (think tank) 2006; apptd mem. Comm. on Strategic Devt 2007; mem. Legis. Council 2008–; Vice-Chair. China Reform Council 2008–; Outstanding Person for Chinese Entrepreneurial Innovation 2008. *Address:* Legislative Council, Room 306, West Wing, Central Government Offices, 11 Ice House Street, Central (office); G/F, Sun Shing Building, 6C, Belcher's Street, Kennedy Town, Hong Kong Special Administrative Region, People's Republic of China. *Telephone:* 25373265 (office). *Fax:* 28100358 (office). *Website:* www.reginaip.hk/ en_index.php.

IPPEN, Erich P., SB, MS, PhD; American physicist and academic; *Elihu Thompson Professor of Electrical Engineering, Massachusetts Institute of Technology;* ed Massachusetts Inst. of Tech., Univ. of California, Berkeley; mem. tech. staff, Bell Labs 1968–80; joined MIT faculty 1980, currently Prin. Investigator, Research Lab. of Electronics (RLE), Elihu Thomson Prof. of Electrical Eng, Dept of Electrical Eng and Computer Science and Prof. of Physics, one of leaders of RLE's Optics and Quantum Electronics Group; mem. NAS, Nat. Acad. of Eng; Fellow, American Acad. of Arts and Sciences; MIT James R. Killian, Jr Faculty Achievement Award 2001–02, Frederic Ives Medal, Optical Soc. of America 2006. *Achievements include:* a founder of field of femtosecond optics. *Publications:* numerous scientific papers in professional journals on femtosecond science and ultra-highspeed devices to probe ultrafast phenomena in materials. *Address:* Room 36-319, Research Laboratory of Electronics, Massachusetts Institute of Technology, 77 Massachusetts Avenue, Cambridge, MA 02139, USA (office). *Telephone:* (617) 253-8504 (office). *Fax:* (617) 253-9611 (office). *E-mail:* ippen@mit.edu (office). *Website:* www.rle.mit.edu/rleonline/People/ErichP.Ippen.html (office).

IRAN, fmr Empress of (see Pahlavi, Farah Diba).

IRANI, Jamshed Jiji, PhD, DMet; Indian business executive; *Director, Tata Sons Limited;* b. 2 June 1936, Nagpur; s. of Jiji D. Irani and Khorshed Irani; m. Daisy Irani 1971; one s. two d.; ed Univ. of Sheffield, UK; worked for British Iron and Steel Research Asscn 1963–67; Tata Iron and Steel Co. Ltd (now Tata Sons Ltd) 1968–, Gen. Man. 1979–81, Deputy Man. Dir 1981–83, Vice-Pres. (Operations) 1983–85, Pres. 1985–88, Jt Man. Dir 1988–92, Man. Dir 1992–97, Dir 1997–; dir of numerous cos; Hon. KBE 1997; Padma Bhushan 2007; DSc hc (Banaras Hindu Univ.); Nat. Metallurgist Award 1974, Platinum medal of IIM 1988, Steel Vision Award. *Publications:* numerous tech. papers. *Leisure interests:* philately, photography. *Address:* 7 Beldih Lake, Jamshedpur, 831001 Jharkhand, India. *Telephone:* (657) 2431024 (office); (22) 66657565 (office); (22) 66352000 (home); (657) 2431025 (home). *Fax:* (657) 2431818 (office); (22) 66658030 (office); (22) 66352001 (home). *E-mail:* jjirani@ tata.com (office). *Website:* www.tata.com (office).

IRANI, Ray R., DSc; American business executive; *Chairman and CEO, Occidental Petroleum Corporation;* b. 15 Jan. 1935, Beirut, Lebanon; s. of Rida Irani and Naz Irani; m. Ghada Irani; two s. one d.; ed Univ. of Southern California; Sr Research Leader, Monsanto Co. 1957–67; Assoc. Dir New Products, later Dir of Research, Diamond Shamrock Corpn 1967–73; joined Olin Corpn 1973, Pres. Chemicals Group 1978–80, Dir and Corp. Pres. 1980–83; Exec. Vice-Pres. Occidental Petroleum Corpn, Los Angeles 1983–84, Dir 1984–, COO 1984–90, Pres. 1984–96, Chair. and CEO 1990–, Chair. Exec. Cttee; CEO Occidental Chemical Corpn 1983–91, Chair. 1983–94; Chair. Canadian Occidental Petroleum Ltd (now Nexen Inc.), Calgary 1987–99, Hon. Chair. 1999–2000; mem. Bd of Dirs American Petroleum Inst., KB Home 1992–, Lyondell Chemical Co. 2002–, Cedars Bank, Wynn Resorts Ltd, TCW Group; mem. ACS, Scientific Research Soc., American Industrial Research Inst., Council on Foreign Relations, Conf. Bd, US-Saudi Arabian Business Council, World Affairs Council; Trustee, Univ. of Southern Calif.; Vice-Chair. Bd American Univ. of Beirut; Hon. Fellow, American Inst. of Chemists. *Publications:* Particle Size; numerous papers in field of particle physics. *Address:* Occidental Petroleum Corpn, 10889 Wilshire Blvd ., Los Angeles, CA

90024-4201, USA (office). *Telephone:* (310) 208-8800 (office). *Fax:* (310) 443-6690 (office). *E-mail:* info@oxy.com (office). *Website:* www.oxy.com (office).

IRELAND, Norman Charles, CA, FCMA; British business executive; b. 28 May 1927, Aden; s. of Charles Ireland and Winifred A. Ireland; m. Gillian M. Harrison 1953; one s. one d.; ed in UK, USA and India; Chartered Man. Accountant with Richard Brown & Co. 1944–50, Brown Fleming & Murray 1950–54, Avon Rubber Co. 1955–64; Chief Accountant, United Glass 1964–66; Finance Dir BTR PLC (now part of Invensys) 1967–87, Chair. 1993–96; Chair. Bowater PLC 1987–93, The Housing Finance Corpn 1988–93, Intermediate Capital Group 1989–93, Meggitt 1987–93. *Leisure interests:* gardening, ballet, opera, music.

IRINEOS I, His Holiness Patriarch; Greek ecclesiastic; b. 1939, Samos; rep. of church of Jerusalem in Athens 1972–81; Bishop and mem. Holy Synod in Jerusalem 1981, elected Greek Orthodox Patriarch of Jerusalem 2001, dismissed 2005, demoted to rank of monk. *Address:* c/o PO Box 19632-633, Greek Orthodox Patriarchate Street, Old City, Jerusalem, Israel (office).

IROBE, Yoshiaki; Japanese banker; *Adviser and Honorary Chairman, Asahi Bank;* b. 18 July 1911, Tokyo; s. of Tsuneo Irobe and Tsuneko Irobe (née Hirohata); m. Kiyoko Kodama 1939; three s. one d.; ed Tokyo Imperial Univ.; Man., Matsuyama Branch, The Bank of Japan 1954, Deputy Chief, Personnel Dept 1956, Chief Sec. and Chief, Foreign Relations Dept 1959, Chief, Personnel Dept 1962, Man. Nagoya Branch 1963; Sr Man. Dir, The Kyowa Bank Ltd (now Asahi Bank) 1966, Deputy Pres. 1968, Pres. 1971–80; Chair. 1980–86, Adviser and Hon. Chair. 1986–. *Leisure interests:* 'Go', travel, reading. *Address:* 26-6, Saginomiya 6-chome, Nakano-ku, Tokyo, Japan (home). *Telephone:* 999-0321 (home).

IRONS, Andy; American professional surfer; b. 24 July 1978, Hanalei, Kauai; s. of Phil Irons and Danielle Irons; winner HIC Pipeline Pro 1996, Black Pearl Horue Pro 1997, Op Pro, USA 1998, Billabong Pro, USA 2000, Tahiti 2002, Spain 2002, South Africa 2004, Rip Curl Pro, Australia 2001, 2003, Hawaii 2005, Mexico 2006, Hawaii 2006, Chile 2007, Xbox Pipeline Masters Hawaii 2002, 2003, Quiksilver Pro, Tavarua 2003, France 2004, Niijima Quicksliver Pro 2003, O'Neill World Cup of Surfing 2004; Vans Triple Crown Champion 2002, 2003, Asscn of Surfing Professionals (ASP) World Champion 2002, 2003, 2004; Australian Surfing Life Peer Poll Award 2002, Surfer Magazine Surfer of the Year 2002, 2003, Surfing Hall of Fame 2003. *Address:* c/o Association of Surfing Professionals, 2385 Halekoa Drive, Honolulu, HI 96821, USA (office). *Telephone:* (808) 739-3965 (office). *Fax:* (808) 734-0355 (office). *Website:* www.aspworldtour.com (office).

IRONS, Jeremy; British actor; b. 19 Sept. 1948, Cowes, Isle of Wight; s. of the late Paul Dugan Irons and Barbara Ann Brereton Sharpe; m. 1st (divorced); 2nd Sinead Cusack (q.v.) 1978; two s.; ed Sherborne School, Dorset, Bristol Old Vic Theatre School; TV debut 1968; mem. Gaia Foundation, European Film Acad.; Patron, Prison Phoenix Trust, Archway Foundation; Officier, Ordre des arts et Lettres; European Film Acad. Special Achievement Award 1998. *Stage appearances:* The Real Thing, Broadway (Tony Award) 1984, Rover 1986, The Winter's Tale 1986, Richard II, Stratford 1986, Embers (Duke of York Theatre, London) 2006. *Films include:* Nijinsky 1980, The French Lieutenant's Woman 1981, Moonlighting 1982, Betrayal 1983, The Wild Duck 1983, Swann in Love 1984, The Mission 1986, A Chorus of Disapproval 1988, Dead Ringers (New York Critics Best Actor Award 1988) 1988, Australia 1989, Danny, The Champion of the World 1989, Reversal of Fortune (Acad. Award 1991, Golden Globe Award for Best Actor 1991) 1990, Zebracka opera 1991, Kafka 1991, Damage 1992, Waterland 1992, M. Butterfly 1993, The House of the Spirits 1993, The Lion King (voice) 1994, Die Hard with a Vengeance 1995, Stealing Beauty 1996, Chinese Box 1997, Lolita 1997, The Man in the Iron Mask 1998, Dungeons and Dragons 2000, The Fourth Angel 2001, The Time Machine 2002, And Now... Ladies and Gentlemen... 2002, Callas Forever 2002, The Merchant of Venice 2004, Being Julia 2004, Kingdom of Heaven 2005, Casanova 2005, Inland Empire 2006, Eragon 2006, Appaloosa 2008. *Television includes:* The Pallisers (series) 1974, Notorious Woman (mini-series) 1974, Love for Lydia (mini-series) 1977, Langrishe Go Down 1978, The Voysey Inheritance 1979, Brideshead Revisited 1981, The Captain's Doll 1983, Saturday Night Live (episode 16.16, host) 1991, Tales from Hollywood 1992, Mirad (also dir) 1997, The Great War and the Shaping of the 20th Century (Primetime Emmy Award for Outstanding Voice-Over Performance 1997), Ohio Impromptu 2000, Longitude 2000, Last Call 2002, RSC Meets USA: Working Shakespeare (video) 2002, Comic Relief 2003, Dame Edna Live at the Palace 2003, Elizabeth I (Primetime Emmy Award 2005, Golden Globe Award for Best Supporting Actor in a mini-series 2005, Screen Actors' Guild Award for Outstanding Performance by a Male Actor in a Television Movie 2006) 2005, The Colour of Magic 2008. *Leisure interests:* skiing, riding, sailing. *Address:* c/o Hutton Management, 4 Old Manor Close, Askett, Bucks., HP27 9NA (office); c/o CAA, 2 Queen Caroline Street, Hammersmith, London, W6 9DX, England (office).

IRVINE, Ian Alexander Noble, FCA, CBIM, FRGS, FRSA; British media executive; *Chairman, Van Tulleken Company;* b. 2 July 1936, Derby; m. Noelle Irvine; ed Surbiton County Grammar School and London School of Econs; joined Touche Ross & Co. 1961, Partner 1965; Man. Dir Fleet Holdings PLC 1982–85, also Dir Express Newspapers PLC and Morgan-Grampian PLC (subsidiaries); consultant to United Newspapers PLC –1985; Dir (non-exec.) Capital Radio 1982–2002, Chair. 1992–2002; Dir TV-AM PLC 1983, Chair. 1988–90; Chief Exec. Octopus Publishing Group 1986, with responsibility for Butterworths 1989; Chair. British Sky Broadcasting 1990–91; Chief Exec. Reed Int. Books 1990–94; Dir Reed Int. PLC 1987, Chair. 1994–97; mem. Exec. Cttee Reed Elsevier 1993–96, Chair. 1994–96; Chair. (non-exec.) Video Networks 1997–2003, Dawson Int. PLC 1998–2003, Van Tulleken Co. 2003–; Freeman of the City of London. *Address:* Van Tulleken Company, 33 Lowndes Street, London, SW1X 9HX, England (office). *Telephone:* (20) 7235-1099 (office). *Fax:* (20) 7235-7956 (office). *E-mail:* london@vantulleken.com (office). *Website:* www.vantulleken.com (office).

IRVINE, John Maxwell, PhD, CPhys, FInstP, FRAS, FRSA, FRSE, CIMgt, DL; British theoretical physicist and consultant; *Professor of Physics, University of Manchester;* b. 28 Feb. 1939, Edinburgh; s. of John MacDonald Irvine and Joan Paterson Irvine; m. Grace Ritchie 1962; one s.; ed George Heriot's School, Edinburgh, Univs of Edinburgh, Manchester, Michigan; Asst Lecturer in Theoretical Physics, Univ. of Manchester 1964–66, Lecturer 1968–73, Sr Lecturer 1973–76, Reader 1976–83, Prof. 1983–91, Dean of Science 1989–91; Prin. and Vice-Chancellor Univ. of Aberdeen 1991–96; Prin. and Vice-Chancellor Univ. of Birmingham 1996–2001; Prof. of Physics, Univ. of Manchester 2001–; Chair. Scottish Advisory Group on the Academic Year 1993–96, Cttee of Scottish Univ. Prins 1994–96; Research Assoc., LNS, Cornell Univ., USA 1966–68; Head of Nuclear Theory, Science and Eng Research Council (SERC) Daresbury Lab. 1974–78; Dir Rowett Research Inst. 1992–96, Cobuild Ltd 1996–2001, Barber Trust 1996–2001; mem. Bd Scottish Council Devt and Industry 1991–96, Grampian Enterprise Ltd 1992–96; Council mem. Inst. of Physics 1981–87, 1988–92 (Vice-Pres. 1982–87), European Physical Soc. 1989–92; mem. Nuclear Physics Bd and Chair. Nuclear Structure Cttee SERC 1984–88; mem. Scottish Econ. Council 1993–96, Council Asscn of Commonwealth Univs 1993–2004 (Chair. 1994–95, Treas. 1998–2004), BT Scottish Advisory Forum 1993–96, British Council (Scotland) 1993–96, Council Cttee of Vice-Chancellors and Prins (now Universities UK) 1995–98, Bd Higher Educ. Quality Cttee 1994–97, Univ. Council for Educational Admin 1995–2001, Univs and Colls Admissions Service (UCAS) 1995–2001, Birmingham Chamber of Commerce and Industry 1996–2001, Public Health Labs Service 1997–2005, Commonwealth Scholarships Comm. 2002–, Educ. Consultancy Service of the British Council 2002–03; Nursing and Midwifery Council 2005–; Oxford Round Table 2002–; Chair. West Midlands Regional Innovation Strategy Group 1996–2001, Jt Information Structure Cttee 1998–2003, Royal Soc. of Edinburgh Inquiry 'Energy Issues for Scotland' 2005–; Specialist Advisor, Cttee on Radioactive Waste Man. 2005; mem. Energy Steering Group, European Acads Science Advisory Council 2005–; Gov. English Speaking Union 1998–2004; Hon. FRCSE 1995; Hon. DSc (William and Mary) 1995, (Aston) 2001; Hon. DEd (RGU) 1995; Hon. DUniv (Edin.) 1995, (Birmingham) 2002; Hon. LLD (Aberdeen) 1997. *Publications:* The Basis of Modern Physics 1967, Nuclear Structure Theory 1972, Heavy Nuclei, Superheavy Nuclei and Neutron Stars 1975, Neutron Stars 1978; more than 100 research publs on physics. *Leisure interests:* hill walking, tennis. *Address:* 27 Belfield Road, Manchester, M20 6BJ, England (home). *Telephone:* (161) 445-1434 (home). *E-mail:* j.m.irvine@manchester.ac.uk (office). *Website:* www.irvinereports.man.ac.uk.

IRVINE OF LAIRG, Baron (Life Peer), cr. 1987, of Lairg in the District of Sutherland; **Alexander (Derry) Andrew Mackay Irvine,** QC, MA, LLB; British lawyer; b. 23 June 1940; s. of Alexander Irvine and Margaret Christina Irvine; m. 1st Margaret Veitch (divorced 1973); m. 2nd Alison Mary McNair 1974; two s.; ed Inverness Acad., Hutcheson's Boys' Grammar School, Univ. of Glasgow, Christ's Coll., Cambridge; Lecturer, LSE 1965–69; called to the Bar, Inner Temple 1967, Bencher 1985; a Recorder 1985–88; Deputy High Court Judge 1987–97; Shadow Spokesman on Legal Affairs and Home Affairs 1987–92; Shadow Lord Chancellor 1992–97, Lord High Chancellor of GB 1997–2003, Hon. Pres. Legal and Constitutional Affairs Group 2007–; Pres. Magistrates' Asscn; Jt Pres. House of Lords British-American Parl. Group, Commonwealth Parl. Asscn, Inter-Parl. Union; Pres. NI Youth and Family Courts Asscn 1999; Hon. Bencher, Inn of Court of NI 1998; Vice-Patron World Fed. of Mental Health; Trustee Whitechapel Art Gallery 1990–, Hunterian Collection 1997–; Hon. Fellow, LSE; Hon. LLD (Glasgow) 1997, Laurea hc (Siena) 2000. *Leisure interests:* cinema, theatre, art, travel. *Address:* House of Lords, Westminster, London, SW1A 0PW, England. *Telephone:* (20) 7219-1446.

IRVING, Amy; American actress; b. 10 Sept. 1953, Palo Alto, Calif.; m. Steven Spielberg (q.v.) 1985 (divorced); one s.; pnr Bruno Barreto; one s.; ed American Conservatory Theater and London Acad. of Dramatic Art; frequent TV appearances. *Stage appearances include:* Juliet in Romeo and Juliet, Seattle Repertory Theater 1982–83, on Broadway in Amadeus 1981–82, Heartbreak House 1983–84, off Broadway in The Road to Mecca 1988. *Films include:* Carrie, The Fury, Voices, Honeysuckle Road, The Competition, Yentl, Mickey and Maude, Rumpelstiltskin, Crossing Delancey, A Show of Force, Benefit of the Doubt, Kleptomania, Acts of Love (also co-exec. producer), I'm Not Rappaport, Carried Away, Deconstructing Harry, One Tough Cop 1998, Blue Ridge Fall 1999, The Confession, The Rage: Carrie 2 1999, Traffic 2000, Bossa Nova 2000, Thirteen Conversations About One Thing 2002, Tuck Everlasting 2002, Hide and Seek 2005, Adam 2009. *Television includes:* Alias (series) 2002–05.

IRVING, Edward (Ted), CM, ScD, FRS, FRSC; Canadian (b. British) scientist and academic; *Research Scientist Emeritus, Pacific Geoscience Centre;* b. 27 May 1927, Colne, Lancs.; s. of George E. Irving and Nellie Irving; m. Sheila A. Irwin 1957; two s. two d.; ed Colne Grammar School and Univ. of Cambridge; army service 1945–48; Research Fellow, Fellow and Sr Fellow, ANU 1954–64; Dominion Observatory, Canada 1964–66; Prof. of Geophysics, Univ. of Leeds 1966–67; Research Scientist, Dominion Observatory, later Earth Physics Br. Dept of Energy, Mines and Resources, Ottawa 1967–81; Research Scientist, Pacific Geoscience Centre, North Saanich, BC 1981–92, Research Scientist Emer. 1992–; Adjunct Prof., Carleton Univ., Ottawa 1975–81, Univ. of Vic. 1985–95; Fellow, American Geophysical Union; Fellow, Foreign Assoc. NAS; Distinguished Fellow, Geological Asscn of Canada; Hon. FGS; mem. Order of

Canada; Hon. DSc (Carleton Univ.) 1979, (Memorial Univ.) 1986, (Victoria Univ.) 1999; Queen's Golden Jubilee Medal 2002. *Publications:* Palaeomagnetism 1964; contribs to learned journals. *Leisure interests:* gardening, carpentry, choral singing. *Address:* Pacific Geoscience Centre, 9860 West Saanich Road, PO Box 6000, North Saanich, BC, V8L 4B2 (office); 9363 Carnoustie Crescent, North Saanich, BC, V8L 5G7, Canada (home). *Telephone:* (250) 656-9645 (home). *Fax:* (250) 363-6565 (office). *E-mail:* tirving@pgc-gsc.nrcan.gc.ca (office). *Website:* www.pgc.nrcan.gc.ca (office).

IRVING, John Winslow, BA, MFA; American writer; b. 2 March 1942, Exeter, NH; s. of Colin F.N. Irving and Frances Winslow; m. 1st Shyla Leary 1964 (divorced 1981); two s.; m. 2nd Janet Turnbull 1987; one s.; ed Univs of Pittsburgh, Vienna, New Hampshire and Iowa; Asst Prof. of English, Mt. Holyoke Coll. 1967–72, 1975–78; writer-in-residence, Univ. of Iowa 1972–75; with Bread Loaf Writers' Conf. 1976; Rockefeller Foundation grantee 1971–72; Nat. Endowment for Arts Fellow 1974–75, Guggenheim Fellow 1976–77; mem. American Acad. of Arts and Letters 2001; Nat. Book Award 1980, O. Henry Award 1981. *Publications:* novels: Setting Free the Bears 1969, The Water-Method Man 1972, The 158-Pound Marriage 1974, The World According to Garp 1978, The Hotel New Hampshire 1981, The Cider House Rules 1985, screenplay (Acad. Award for the best adapted screenplay 2000) 1999, A Prayer for Owen Meany 1989, A Son of the Circus 1994, A Widow for One Year 1998, The Fourth Hand 2001, Until I Find You 2005; non-fiction: An Introduction to Great Expectations 1986, Trying to Save Piggy Sneed (memoirs, short stories and essays) 1996, An Introduction to A Christmas Carol 1996, My Movie Business (memoir) 1999; contrib. to New York Times Book Review, New Yorker, Rolling Stone, Esquire, Playboy. *Address:* Turnbull Agency, PO Box 757, Dorset, VT 05251, USA (office).

IRWIN, Flavia, Lady de Grey, RA; British artist; b. 15 Dec. 1916, London; d. of Clinton Irwin and Everilda Irwin; m. Sir Roger de Grey 1942; two s. one d.; ed Hawnes School, Ampthill, Beds. and Chelsea School of Art; taught gen. design at Medway Coll. of Art 1970–75; Sr tutor, Decorative Arts Course, City & Guilds of London Art School, Kennington, London 1975–; work in collections including Westminster Conf. Centre, London, Midland Montague Morgan Grenfell, Carlisle City Art Gallery, Dept of the Environment, Govt Art Collection; Hon. Academician, Royal West of England Acad., Bristol. *Leisure interests:* swimming, reading. *Address:* 5 Camer Street, Meopham, Kent, DA13 0XR, England. *Telephone:* (1474) 812327.

IRYANI, Abd al-Karim al-, PhD; Yemeni politician and economist; *Secretary-General, General People's Congress Party;* b. 12 Oct. 1934, Eryan; m.; three s. three d.; ed Univ. of Georgia, Yale Univ., USA; worked in an agricultural project in Yemen 1968–72; Chair. Cen. Planning Org. 1972–76; Minister of Devt 1974–76, of Educ. and Rector San'a Univ. 1976–78; Adviser, Kuwait Fund for Arab Econ. Devt 1978–80; Prime Minister 1980–83; Deputy Prime Minister and Minister of Foreign Affairs 1984–90, 1994–98; Minister of Foreign Affairs 1990–93, of Planning and Devt 1993–94; Prime Minister of Yemen 1998–2001; Sec.-Gen. Gen. People's Congress Party; Chair. Council for the Reconstruction of Earthquake Areas 1983–84. *Address:* General People's Congress, San'a, Republic of Yemen (office). *E-mail:* gpc@y.net.ye (office). *Website:* www.gpc.org.ye.

ISA, Dato' Haji Pehin; Brunei politician; b. 1935; trained as barrister in UK; fmrly Gen. Adviser to Sultan of Brunei, now Special Adviser, with ministerial rank in Prime Minister's Office; Minister of Home Affairs 1988–95, Special Adviser to the Prime Minister –1995; currently with Ahmad Isa and Pnrs (law firm). *Address:* Ahmad Isa and Partners, Unit 405A/410A, 4th Floor Wisma Jaya, Jalan Pemanca, Bandar Seri Begawan, BS8811, Brunei (office). *E-mail:* ahmisa@brunet.bn (office).

ISAACS, Sir Jeremy Israel, Kt, MA; British television executive and arts administrator; *Director, Jeremy Isaacs Productions Ltd;* b. 28 Sept. 1932; s. of Isidore Isaacs and Sara Jacobs; m. 1st Tamara (née Weinreich) 1958 (died 1986); one s. one d.; m. 2nd Gillian Widdicombe 1988; ed Glasgow Acad., Merton Coll., Oxford; TV Producer, Granada TV (What the Papers Say, All Our Yesterdays) 1958, Associated Rediffusion (This Week) 1963, BBC TV (Panorama) 1965; Controller of Features, Associated Rediffusion 1967; with Thames TV 1968–78, Producer, The World at War 1974, Cold War 1998; Dir of Programmes 1974–78; special ind. consultant TV series Hollywood, ITV, A Sense of Freedom, ITV, Ireland, a Television Documentary, BBC, Battle for Crete, NZ TV, Cold War, Turner Broadcasting; CEO, Channel Four TV Co. 1981–88; Gen. Dir Royal Opera House 1988–96 (Dir 1985–97); Chief Exec. Jeremy Isaacs Productions 1998–; Gov. BFI 1979–84; Chair. BFI Production Bd 1979–81, Artsworld Channels Ltd 2000–; Chair. judging panel, European City of Culture competition 2008; James MacTaggart Memorial Lecturer, Edinburgh TV Festival 1979; Fellow Royal Television Soc. 1978, BAFTA 1985, BFI 1986; Hon. DLitt (Strathclyde) 1983, (Bristol) 1988; Dr hc (CNAA) 1987, (RCA) 1988; Hon. LLD (Manchester) 1998; Desmond Davis Award for Outstanding Creative Contrib. to TV 1972; George Polk Memorial Award 1973; Cyril Bennett Award 1982; Lord Willis Award for Distinguished Service to TV 1985. *Publications:* Storm Over Four: A Personal Account 1989, Cold War (co-author) 1999, Never Mind the Moon 1999, Look Me in the Eye: a Life in Television (autobiog.) 2006. *Leisure interests:* books, walks, sleep. *E-mail:* jip@jip.co.uk (office).

ISAACSON, Walter Seff, MA; American journalist and international organization official; *President and CEO, Aspen Institute;* b. 20 May 1952, New Orleans, La; s. of Irwin Isaacson and Betsy Isaacson; m. Cathy Wright 1984; one d.; ed Harvard Univ., Pembroke Coll., Univ. of Oxford; reporter Sunday Times, London 1976–77, States-Item, New Orleans 1977–78; staff writer Time magazine, New York 1978–79, political corresp. 1979–81, Assoc. Ed. 1981–84, Sr Ed. 1985–91, Asst Man. Ed. 1991–93, Man. Ed. 1995–2000; Editorial Dir Time Inc. 2000–01; Chair. and CEO CNN Newsgroup 2001–03; Ed. New Media Time, Inc. 1993–96; Pres. and CEO Aspen Inst. 2003–; mem. Council on Foreign Relations, Century Asscn; Overseas Press Club Award, New York 1981, 1984, 1987, Harry Truman Book Prize 1987. *Publications:* Pro and Con 1983, Kissinger: A Biography 1992, The Wise Men (jtly) 1986, Benjamin Franklin: An American Life 2003, Einstein: His Life and Universe (Quill Award for Biography 2007) 2007. *Address:* The Aspen Institute, Suite 700, One Dupont Circle, NW, Washington, DC 20036-1133, USA (office). *Telephone:* (202) 736-5800 (office). *Fax:* (202) 467-0790 (office). *Website:* www.aspeninstitute.org (office).

ISAAKOV, Yuri Fedorovich, DM; Russian surgeon; *Vice-President, Russian Academy of Medical Sciences;* b. 28 June 1923, Kovrov, Vladimir Region; s. of Fedor Fedorovich Isaakov and Kladvia Fedorovna Isaakov; m. Tamara Gennadievna Isaakov; one s.; ed Russian State Medical Univ.; Asst, Docent, Prof., Russian State Medical Univ. 1953–65, Head, Pediatric Surgery Chair 1966–; Vice-Pres. Russian Acad. of Medical Sciences; Chair. Russian Asscn of Children Surgeons; mem. Int. Soc. of Surgeons, Presidium of Russian Soc. of Surgeons; expert for WHO on scientific directions in public health. *Publications:* more than 300 scientific works, including 13 monographs on plastic and reconstructive surgery, surgery of intestine and lungs. *Leisure interest:* sports. *Address:* Russian Academy of Medical Sciences, Solyanka str. 14, 103001 Moscow (office); Frunzenskaya nab. 50, Apt 89, 119270 Moscow, Russia (home). *Telephone:* (495) 254-10-77 (office); (495) 242-46-15 (home). *Website:* www.mcramn.ru (office).

ISABEKOV, Azim Beishembayevich; Kyrgyzstani economist and politician; b. 4 April 1960, Arashan, Chui Oblast; ed Kyrgyz State Univ.; Chief of Staff, Office of Gov. of Chui Oblast Kurmanbek Bakiyev 1997–2000; Head of Admin. Dept, Office of Prime Minister 2001–02; Dir State Fund for Econ. Devt 2002–04; Deputy Chief of Staff, Office of Pres. Kurmanbek Bakiyev 2005–06; Minister of Agric., Water Resources and Mfg Industry June–Dec. 2006; Prime Minister Jan.–March 2007. *Address:* c/o Office of the Prime Minister, Dom Pravitelstva, 720003 Bishkek, Kyrgyzstan.

ISAKOV, Gen. Ismail Isakovich; Kyrgyzstani army officer and government official; *Minister of Defence;* b. 1950, Spou-Korgon, Alai Dist., Osh Duban; ed Tashkent Higher Mil. Acad., Frunze Mil. Acad., Moscow, Gen. Staff Mil. Acad., Moscow; Platoon Commdr, then Co. Commdr in southern group of troops, Hungary 1973–78; Deputy Bn Commdr, then Bn Commdr in Ukraine 1978–81; Regimental Chief of Staff, Regimental Commdr, Div. Chief of Staff, Combat Training Deputy Chief of the State Cttee for Defence 1984–94; Chief of the Main Staff 1994–95; First Deputy Minister of Defence 1994–99; Deputy in Legis. Ass. of the Jogorku Kenesh (Parl.) from Alai Dist 2000–05, Chair. Cttee on Nat. Security Issues 2000–05, Dir of Coordinating Cttee For the Resignation of Askar Akaev and For Reforms for the People (political movt) 2003–04; Acting Minister of Defence March–Sept. 2005, Minister of Defence 2005–06 (resgnd), reappointed 2007–; rank of Gen. (two stars); Medal of 3 Degrees For Irreproachable Service, Medal for Combat Merits, Medal For Strengthening of Mil. Cooperation. *Leisure interests:* chess, reading. *Address:* Ministry of Defence, 720001 Bishkek, Logvinenko 26, Kyrgyzstan (office). *Telephone:* (312) 66-38-28 (office). *Fax:* (312) 66-16-02 (office). *E-mail:* ud@bishkek.gov.kg (office). *Website:* www.mil.kg (office).

ISAKOV, Army-Gen. Vladimir Ilyich; Russian military officer; *Chief of Logistics and Deputy Minister of Defence;* b. 21 July 1950, Voskresenskoye, Kaluga region; ed Moscow Mil. School of Civil Defence, Mil. Acad. of Home Front Transport, Mil. Acad. of Gen. Staff; Platoon Commdr of Civil Defence Forces; served in Group of Soviet Armed Forces in Germany; Deputy Regt Commdr, then Deputy Army Commdr of Home Front.; Deputy Commdr Div. of Home Front, Siberian Mil. Command 1982–84, 40th Army in Afghanistan 1984–86; Deputy Army Commdr, then Head of Home Front, Kiev Mil. Command 1988–89; Head of Gen. Staff of Home Front, W Group of Armed Forces 1989–94; Head of Chair. Mil. Acad. of Gen. Staff 1994; Head of Gen. Staff Armed Forces of Russian Fed. 1996, First Deputy Head of Home Front 1996–97, Head 1997; Chief of Logistics and Deputy Minister of Defence 1997–. *Address:* Ministry of Defence, ul. Myasnitskaya 37, 105175 Moscow, Russia (office). *Telephone:* (495) 293-38-54 (office). *Fax:* (495) 296-84-36 (office). *Website:* www.mil.ru (office).

ISAKSON, Johnny, BBA; American politician and business executive; *Senator from Georgia;* m. Dianne Isakson; three c.; ed Univ. of Ga; served in Ga Air Nat. Guard 1966–72; began business career with Northside Reality (family-owned real estate Co.) 1967, est. Cobb County Office, apptd Pres. 1979; elected to State of Ga House of Reps 1976, Republican Leader in State House 1983–90; Republican nominee for Gov. of Ga 1989; elected to State of Ga Senate 1993, Republican Chair. of Ga Bd of Educ. 1996–99; Ga Chair. for Bob Dole for Pres. Campaign 1996; elected to US Congress 1999, served as mem. House Transportation Cttee, Educ. Cttee, Co-Chair. Sub-Cttee on 21st Century Competitiveness, Deputy Major Whip to House Republican Leadership; Senator from Ga 2005–; fmr Pres. Realty Alliance; fmr mem. Exec. Cttee, Nat. Asscn of Realtors, Bd of Dirs Ga Chamber of Commerce, Riverside Bank, Advisory Bd SunTrust; teacher Sunday School, Mount Zion United Mehtodist Church 1978–; Best Legislator in America Award, Republican Nat. Cttee 1989. *Address:* 120 Russell Senate Office Building, Washington, DC 20510, USA (office). *Telephone:* (202) 224-3643 (office). *Fax:* (202) 228-0724 (office). *Website:* isakson.senate.gov (office).

ISAMUDDIN, Riduan, (Hambali); Indonesian religious leader; *Leader, Jemaah Islamiah;* b. (Encep Nurjaman), 4 April 1966, Sukamanah, W Java; m. Noral Wizaah Lee; active in opposition to Suharto regime 1970s and 1980s; sought exile in Malaysia 1985; fought as mujahideen guerilla against Soviet occupation, Afghanistan 1988; recruited Muslim supporters to join a jihad (holy war) in order to est. a Pan-Asian Islamic State, Malaysia 1990; believed to have co-f. Jemaah Islamiah (JI—Islamic Community) network with Abu Bakar Bashir with operations throughout SE Asia 1990; returned to Indonesia to recruit supporters 2000; mem. consultative council al-Qaeda; alleged liaison officer between al-Qaeda and radical Islamic groups in SE Asia; allegedly funded numerous mil. terrorist groups fighting jihad, in particular in Maluko Islands 1999; wanted by Govts of Indonesia, Malaysia, Singapore and The Philippines as key suspect for involvement in series of bomb attacks on World Trade Center 1993, Philippine airliner 1994, USS Cole, Yemen 2000, Christian church bombings, Indonesia 2000, Manila bombings 2000, Sept. 11 attacks in USA 2001, Operation Jabril (attempted mass terrorist attacks on US targets in Malaysia, Singapore and Philippines) 2001, Bali nightclub 2002; captured in Thailand by US forces 11 August 2003 and currently in custody.

ISARANGURA, Gen. Thammarak, BSc; Thai government official and military officer; b. 22 July 1938, Roiet Prov.; m. Waneda Isarangura; ed Chulachomklao Royal Mil. Acad.; Commdr Training Directorate of Jt Communications 1964–66, with Radio Station Directorate 1967–72, Asst Chief, Intelligence Section, Seconded to Second Army Area Command Sakon Nakhon 1973–76, Chief, Intelligence Section, Fourth Army Area Command, Nakhonsrithammarat 1982–83, Chief, Intelligence Section, Directorate of Intelligence, Army Operation Centre 1984–88, Commdr of Army Mil. Intelligence 1989–90, Chief of Staff to Deputy Supreme Commdr, Supreme Command Headquarters 1991–95, Commanding Gen. of Armed Forces Security Centre, Supreme Command 1996–97, Special Adviser, Supreme Command Headquarters 1998; Deputy Prime Minister of Thailand 2004; Minister of Defence 2005–06; banned from politics by Constitutional Tribunal 2007; Kt Grand Cordon (Special Class) of the Most Exalted Order of the White Elephant, of the Most Noble Order of the Crown of Thailand. *Address:* c/o Ministry of Defence, Thanon Sanamchai, Bangkok 10200, Thailand (office).

ISARD, Walter, PhD, FAAS, FRSA; American economist and academic; *Professor Emeritus of Economics, Cornell University;* b. 19 April 1919, Philadelphia, Pa; s. of Lazar Isard and Anna (Podolin) Isard; m. Caroline Berliner 1943; four s. four d.; ed Temple, Harvard and Chicago Univs; Instructor, Wesleyan Univ. 1945, MIT 1947; Visiting Lecturer, Tufts Coll. 1947; Assoc. Prof. of Econs, Assoc. Dir of Teaching, Inst. of Econs, American Univ. 1948–49; Research Fellow and Lecturer, Harvard Univ. 1949–53; Assoc. Prof. of Regional Econs, Dir Urban and Regional Studies, MIT 1953–56; Prof. of Econs, Chair. Dept of Regional Science, Univ. of Pa 1956–75, Head Dept of Peace Science 1975–77; Visiting Prof. of Regional Science, Yale Univ. 1960–61, of Landscape Architecture and Regional Science, Harvard Univ. 1966–71; Chair. Graduate Group in Peace Research and Peace Science Unit 1970–78; Sr Research Assoc., Visiting Prof. of Econs, Regional Science and Policy Planning, Cornell Univ. 1971–79, Prof. 1979, now Prof. Emer.; Distinguished Visiting Prof., Inst. für Regionalwissenschaft, Karlsruhe 1972; Consultant, Tenn. Valley Authority 1951–52, Resources for the Future Inc. 1954–58, Ford Foundation 1955–56; Founder Regional Science Asscn 1954, Ed., Co-Ed. Papers 1954–58, Pres. 1959, Hon. Chair. 1960–; Ford Foundation Fellow in Econs and Business Admin 1959–60; Ed., Co-Ed., Journal of Regional Science 1960–; Chair. OEEC Econ. Productivity Agency Conf. on Regional Econs and Planning, Bellagio, Italy 1960; Co-Chair. AIXPS Forum; Founder Peace Science Soc. (Int.) 1963, Co-Ed. Papers 1963–, Exec. Sec. 1964–, Pres. 1968; Pres. World Acad. of Art and Science 1977–81; Dir ECAAR 1989–, (Trustee 2001); Assoc. Ed. Quarterly Journal of Econs 1968–71, Peace Economics, Peace Science and Public Policy 1994–; mem. Editorial Bd Journal of Conflict Resolution 1972–; mem. NAS; Hon. Prof. (Peking Univ., Northwest Univ.) 1993; Dr hc (Poznan Acad. of Econ.) 1976, (Erasmus Univ.) 1978, (Karlsruhe) 1979, (Umeå) 1980, (Univ. of Ill.) 1982, (Binghamton Univ.) 1997, (Geneva) 2002; August Lösch Ring 1988. *Publications:* Atomic Power: An Economic and Social Analysis 1952, Location Factors in the Petrochemical Industry 1955, Location and Space Economy 1956, Municipal Costs and Revenues Resulting from Community Growth 1957, Industrial Complex Analysis and Regional Development 1959, Methods of Regional Analysis 1960, Regional Economic Development 1961, General Theory: Social, Political, Economic and Regional 1969, Regional Input-Output Study 1971, Ecologic-Economic Analysis for Regional Planning 1971, Spatial Dynamics and Optimal Space-Time Development 1979, Conflict Analysis and Practical Conflict Management Procedures 1982, Arms Races, Arms Control and Conflict Analysis 1988, Practical Methods of Regional Science and Empirical Applications 1990, Location Analysis and General Theory 1990, Economics of Arms Production and the Peace Process 1992, The Science of Peace 1992, Commonalities in Art, Science and Religion 1997, Methods of Interregional and Regional Analysis 1998. *Leisure interests:* music, dancing. *Address:* Department of Economics, 476 Uris Hall, Cornell University, Ithaca, NY 14853 (office); 3218 Garrett Road, Drexel Hill, PA 19026, USA (home). *Telephone:* (607) 255-3306 (office); (610) 259-6080 (home). *Fax:* (607) 255-2818 (office). *E-mail:* wi11@cornell.edu (office). *Website:* www.arts.cornell.edu/econ/mainwindow.shtml (office).

ISĂRESCU, Mugur Constantin, PhD; Romanian economist and central banker; *Governor, National Bank of Romania;* b. 1 Aug. 1949, Drăgăşani, Vâlcea Co.; s. of Constantin Isărescu and Aritina Isărescu; m. Elena Isărescu; one s. one d.; ed Acad. of Econs; Research Fellow, Inst. for World Econ. 1971–90; Asst Lecturer, Acad. of Econs, Bucharest 1975–89, Prof. 1996–; Prof. Timişoara West Univ. 1994–96; fmrly Prof. of Banking, Coll. of Romanian Banking Inst.; First Sec. Embassy, Washington, DC 1990; Gov. Nat. Bank of Romania 1990–99, 2001–; Prime Minister of Romania 1999–2000; Chair. Romanian Chess Fed.; Chair. for Romania, Club of Rome; Vice-Pres. Cen. Banks' Govs' Club; mem. Romanian Acad.; mem. Bd Romanian American Enterprise Fund; Honour Medal (Architects' World Forum). *Publications:* Financial Crisis 1979, Gold, Myth and Reality 1981, Stock Exchange 1982,

Recent Developments in Romania 1990, Monetary Policy, Macroeconomic Stability and Banking Reform in Romania 1995, Banking System in Romania: Recent Developments and Prospects 1996, Reform of Financial System in Romania and European Integration 1996, Monetary Policy After 1989 1997. *Leisure interests:* literature, history. *Address:* National Bank of Romania (Banca Naţională a României), 030031 Bucharest 3, Str. Lipscani 25, Romania (office). *Telephone:* (21) 3130410 (office). *Fax:* (21) 3123831 (office). *E-mail:* Info@bnro.ro (office). *Website:* www.bnro.ro (office).

ISAYEV, Alexander Sergeyevich; Russian biologist and forester; *Professor and Scientific Head of Centre for Ecological Problems and Productivity of Forests, Russian Academy of Sciences;* b. 26 Oct. 1931, Moscow; m. Lidia Pokrovskaya 1953; two d.; ed Leningrad Forestry Acad.; mem. CPSU 1965–91; Deputy Chair. Council for Protection of the Environment and Rational Exploitation of Resources in USSR Supreme Soviet 1979–89; mem. USSR (now Russian) Acad. of Sciences 1984–; Dir V.N. Sukachev Forestry Inst., Krasnoyarsk, Chair. Krasnoyarsk Div., Siberian Dept of USSR Acad. of Sciences 1977–88; Pres. GOSKOMLES (State Comm. on Forestry) 1988–91; Chair. Higher Ecological Council at Russian Fed. Supreme Soviet 1992–93; Prof. and Scientific Head of Centre for Ecological Problems and Productivity of Forests 1991–; Dir Int. Forestry Inst. 1991–; Hon. Diploma (UNEP Programme) 1989; Gold Medal (Int. Union of Forestry Research Orgs.) 1976, Gold Medal (Russian Acad. of Sciences) 1992. *Publications:* eight books, over 310 articles. *Leisure interests:* fishing, hunting. *Address:* Centre for Ecological Problems and Productivity of Forests, Russian Academy of Sciences (CEPL RAS), Profsoyuznaya str. 84/32, 117810 Moscow (office); Novocheremushkinskaya str. 69, 117418 Moscow, Russia. *Telephone:* (495) 332-2617 (office). *Fax:* (495) 332-2617 (office). *E-mail:* isaev@cepl.rssi.ru (office). *Website:* www.cepl.rssi.ru (office).

ISCHINGER, Wolfgang Friedrich; German diplomatist; *Ambassador to UK;* b. 6 April 1946, Beuren, Stuttgart; m. Jutta Falke-Ischinger; three c.; ed Univs of Bonn and Geneva, Fletcher School of Law and Diplomacy, Harvard Univ. Law School, USA; mem. cabinet staff of UN Sec.-Gen., New York 1973–75; joined Foreign Service 1975, mem. Policy Planning Staff 1977–79; posted to Washington, DC 1979–82; mem. cabinet staff, Minister of Foreign Affairs, Bonn 1982–90, Pvt. Sec. to Minister 1985–87, Dir Cabinet and Parl. Affairs 1987–90; Minister-Counsellor, Head Political Section, German Embassy, Paris 1990–93; Dir Policy Planning Staff, Bonn 1993–95, Dir-Gen. for Political Affairs 1995–98, State Sec. 1998–2001, 2000–01; Amb. to USA 2001–06, to UK 2006–; apptd to represent EU in negotiations on status of Kosovo 2007; mem. High Level German-Russian Strategy Group; mem. Bd of Overseers, Fletcher School of Law and Diplomacy, Alfred Herrhausen Gesellschaft, Frankfurt, Council on Public Policy, AFS Germany (American Field Service), Bd East-West Inst., New York; fmr Chair. Ambs' Advisory Bd, Exec. Council on Diplomacy, Washington, DC. *Publications:* numerous articles on foreign policy, security and arms control policy, European policy issues. *Leisure interests:* skiing, mountaineering, flying. *Address:* German Embassy, 23 Belgrave Square, London, SW1X 8PZ, England (office). *Telephone:* (20) 7824-1300 (office). *Fax:* (20) 7824-1435 (office). *E-mail:* mail@german-embassy.org.uk (office). *Website:* www.german-embassy.org.uk (office).

ISDELL, E(dward) Neville, BS; Irish beverage industry executive; b. 8 June 1943, Downpatrick, Co. Down, NI; m. Pamela Anne Gill 1970; one d.; ed Univ. of Cape Town, S Africa, Harvard Business School, USA; joined Coca-Cola Zambia 1966, held positions in S Africa, Australia, The Philippines, Pres. Cen. European Div. 1985–89, Group Pres. for NE Europe, the Middle East and Africa 1989–98, Pres. Greater Europe Group 1995, Chair. Coca-Cola Beverages 1998–2000, CEO Coca-Cola HBC 2000–01, Sr Int. Consultant to CEO, The Coca-Cola Co. 2001–04, Chair. The Coca-Cola Co. 2004–09, CEO 2004–08; mem. Bd Dirs Global Water Challenge, General Motors Corpn; Chair. US-Russia Business Council, Bd of Trustees Int. Business Leaders Forum, Atlanta Cttee for Progress; mem. US-Brazil CEO Forum; Hon. DSc (Univ. of Ulster) 2007. *Address:* c/o The Coca-Cola Co., 1 Coca-Cola Plaza, Atlanta, GA 30313-2499, USA (office).

ISHI, Hiroyuki; Japanese environmental scientist and academic; *Professor, Public Policy School, Hokkaido University;* ed Univ. of Tokyo; with Asahi Shimbun newspaper 1965–94, positions including Science Writer, New York Bureau Corresp., Science Ed., Sr Staff Writer; undertook field research in 125 countries; apptd Prof., Grad. School of Frontier Sciences, Univ. of Tokyo 1994; fmr Visiting Prof., Int. Research Center for Japanese Studies; Amb. to Zambia 2002; currently Prof., Public Policy School, Hokkaido Univ.; fmr Special Adviser to Exec. Dirs of UNEP and UNDP, to Pres. Japan Int. Co-operation Agency; fmr Chair. Japan Council of Sustainable Devt; fmr mem. Bd Regional Environmental Centre for Cen. and Eastern Europe, Hungary; mem. Selection Cttee, UNEP Sasakawa Environment Prize; FAO A.H. Boerma Award 1986–87. *Publications include:* Crisis of the Global Environment, Acid Rain, The Destruction of the Earth, Undermined Forests. *Address:* Public Policy School, Hokkaido University, Kita 9, Nishi 7, Kita-ku, Sapporo, Japan (office). *Telephone:* (11) 706-3074 (office). *Fax:* (11) 706-4947 (office). *E-mail:* shomu@juris.hokudai.ac.jp (office). *Website:* www.hops.hokudai.ac.jp (office).

ISHIBA, Shigeru; Japanese politician; b. 4 Feb. 1957; s. of Jiro Ishiba; ed Keio Univ.; began career with Bank of Mitsui 1979; mem. Liberal Democratic Party; first elected to House of Reps 1986, Parl. Vice-Minister for Agric., Forestry and Fisheries 1992, Chair. Special Cttee on Deregulation 1996, Cttee on Transport 1998; Sr State Sec. for Minister of Agric., Forestry and Fisheries 2000; Sr State Sec. of Defence 2000–01, Sr Vice-Minister for Defence 2001–02, Minister of Defence 2002–04, 2007–08. *Address:* Liberal-Democratic Party, 1-11-23, Nagata-cho, Chiyoda-ku, Tokyo 100-8910, Japan (office). *Telephone:* (3)

3581-6211 (office). *E-mail:* koho@ldp.jimin.or.jp (office). *Website:* www.jimin .jp (office).

ISHIBASHI, Kanichiro; Japanese business executive; *Honorary Chairman, Bridgestone Corporation;* b. 1 March 1920, Kurume-shi, Fukuoka-ken; s. of Shojiro and Masako Ishibashi; m. Saeko Ishibashi 1944; one s. two d.; ed Faculty of Law, Univ. of Tokyo; naval service 1943–45; joined Bridgestone Tire Co. Ltd (now called Bridgestone Corpn) 1945, Dir 1949–, Vice-Pres. 1950–63, Pres. 1963–73, Chair. 1973–85, Hon. Chair. 1985–; Exec. Dir Fed. of Econ. Orgs, Japan Fed. of Employers' Asscns; fmr Pres. Japan Rubber Mfrs Asscn. *Leisure interests:* pictures, photography, music, golf. *Address:* 1 Nagasaka-cho, Azabu, Minato-ku, Tokyo, Japan (home). *Telephone:* (3) 583-0150 (home).

ISHIGURO, Kazuo, OBE, MA, DLitt, FRSL; British writer; b. 8 Nov. 1954, Nagasaki, Japan; s. of Shizuo Ishiguro and Shizuko Ishiguro; m. Lorna Anne Macdougall 1986; one d.; ed Woking Grammar School, Univs of Kent and East Anglia; fmr community worker, Renfrew; writer 1980–; Hon. DLit (Kent) 1990, (East Anglia) 1995, (St Andrews) 2003; Chevalier, Ordre des Arts et des Lettres 1998; Premio Scanno 1995, Premio Mantova 1998. *Publications include:* A Pale View of Hills (RSL Winifred Holtby Prize 1983) 1982, A Profile of Arthur J. Mason (TV play) 1985, An Artist of the Floating World (Whitbread Book of the Year, Fiction Prize 1986) 1986, The Gourmet (TV play) 1987, The Remains of the Day (Booker Prize 1989) 1989, The Unconsoled (Cheltenham Prize 1995) 1995, When We Were Orphans (novel) 2000, The Saddest Music in the World (screenplay, co-author) 2003, Never Let Me Go (novel) (Premio Serono 2006, Corine Int. Book Prize 2006, Casino de Santiago European Novel Prize 2007) 2005, White Countess (screenplay) 2005, Nocturnes: Five Stories of Music and Nightfall 2009. *Address:* c/o Rogers, Coleridge & White Literary Agency, 20 Powis Mews, London, W11 1JN, England (office). *Telephone:* (20) 7221-3717 (office). *Fax:* (20) 7229-9084 (office). *E-mail:* info@rcwlitagency.co .uk (office). *Website:* www.rcwlitagency.co.uk (office).

ISHIHARA, Kunio, LLB; Japanese insurance executive; *Chairman, Millea Holdings Incorporated;* ed Tokyo Univ.; joined Tokio Marine and Fire Insurance Co. Ltd 1966 as underwriter, Non-Marine Dept, various man. positions including Gen. Man. Information Systems Devt Dept, later Dir and Gen. Man. Hokkaido Regional Headquarters, Man. Dir and Sr Man. Dir and Pres. 2001–07, Chair. 2007–; Pres. Millea Holdings Inc. 2002–07, Chair. 2007–; Chair. Marine and Fire Insurance Asscn of Japan 2002–03; Gov. Japan Broadcasting Corpn 2002–; mem. Financial System Council of Experts 2003–; mem. Strategic HQ for the Promotion of an Advanced Information and Telecommunications Network Soc. 2003–. *Address:* Millea Holdings Incorporated, West Tower, Otemachi First Square, 5–1 Otemachi 1–chome, Chiyoda-ku, Tokyo 100–0004, Japan (office). *Telephone:* (3) 6212–3341 (office). *Fax:* (3) 6212–3343 (office). *Website:* www.millea.co.jp (office).

ISHIHARA, Nobuteru; Japanese politician; b. 1957; s. of Shintaro Ishihara; mem. Parl. (Liberal Democratic Party); Minister of State (Admin. Reform, Regulatory Reform) 2001–02; Minister of Land, Infrastructure and Transport 2003–06; Deputy Sec.-Gen. LDP 2006–07, Acting Sec.-Gen. 2007–. *Address:* Liberal-Democratic Party—LDP (Jiyu-Minshuto), 1-11-23, Nagata-cho, Chiyoda-ku, Tokyo 100-8910, Japan (office). *Telephone:* (3) 3581-6211 (office). *E-mail:* koho@ldp.jimin.or.jp (office). *Website:* www.jimin.jp (office).

ISHIHARA, Shintaro; Japanese politician and author; *Governor of Tokyo;* b. 30 Sept. 1932, Kobe; brother of the late Yujiro Ishihara; m.; four s.; ed Hitotsubashi Univ.; mem. House of Councillors 1968; mem. House of Reps 1972–95; Minister of State, Dir-Gen. Environment Agency 1976–77; Minister of Transport 1987–88; mem. LDP, cand. in LDP presidential election 1988; left nat. politics 1995; Gov. of Tokyo 1999– (re-elected 2003, 2007); mem. Selection Cttee for Akutagawa Prize 1995–. *Publications include:* Season of the Sun (Akutagawa Prize for Literature 1956) 1955, The Tree of the Young Man 1959, The Forest of Fossils 1970, The Japan that Can Say No 1989, Undercurrents – Episodes from a Life on the Edge 1990, The State Becomes an Illusion 1999, Victorious Japan (with Soichiro Tahara) 2000. *Leisure interests:* yachting, tennis, scuba diving. *Address:* Tokyo Metropolitan Government, 8-1, Nishi-Shinjuku 2-Chome, Shinjuku-ku, Tokyo 163-8001, Japan (office). *Telephone:* (3) 5388-2226 (office). *Fax:* (3) 5388-1215 (office). *E-mail:* s0000573@section .metro.tokyo.jp (office). *Website:* www.metro.tokyo.jp (office); www .sensenfukoku.net (home).

ISHII, Hajime, MA; Japanese politician; b. 17 Aug. 1934, Kobe; m. Tomoko Sugiguchi 1961; one s.; ed Konan Univ., Stanford Univ. Grad. School, USA; mem. House of Reps 1969–; fmr Parl. Vice-Minister of Transport; Minister of State, Dir-Gen. Nat. Land Agency 1989; Minister of Home Affairs 1994; fmr Chair. LDP Nat. Org. Cttee; fmr Chair. LDP Research Comm. on Foreign Affairs; Chair. Special Cttee on Political Reform (House of Reps); fmr Vice-Pres. Democratic Party of Japan (DPJ). *Publications:* The Dream of Young Power, Dacca Hijacking, The Future of Kobe, A Distant Country Getting Closer. *Leisure interests:* golf, saxophone, scuba diving. *Address:* c/o Democratic Party of Japan (DPJ), 1-11-1, Nagata-cho, Chiyoda-ku, Tokyo 100-0014, Japan. *Telephone:* (03) 3580-1777. *Fax:* (03) 3580-1788. *E-mail:* pin@ hajimeishii.net. *Website:* www.hajimeishii.net (office).

ISHII, Kazuhiro; Japanese architect; b. 1 Feb. 1944, Tokyo; s. of Toshio Ishii and Kyoko Ishii; m. Noriko Nagahama 1988; two d.; ed Univ. of Tokyo and Yale Univ., USA; est. Kazuhiro Ishii and Assocs 1976; Lecturer, Waseda Univ. 1991–, Univ. of Tokyo 1992–; Japan Inst. of Architecture Prize 1989. *Major works include:* Noshima Educational Zone 1970–82, Tanabe Agency Bldg 1983, Gyro-Roof 1987, Sukiya Mura 1989, Kitakyu-shu City Hall 1991. *Publications:* Rebirth of Japanese-style Architecture 1985, Thought on Sukiya 1985, My Architectural Dictionary 1988. *Leisure interests:* golf, music (playing saxophone). *Address:* 4-14-27 Akasaka, Minato-ku, Tokyo 107 (office); 7-5-1-303 Akasaka, Minato-ku, Tokyo 107, Japan (home). *Telephone:* (3) 3505-0765

(office); (3) 3584-0779 (home). *Fax:* (3) 3505-0766 (office). *E-mail:* ishiiarc@ ishiiarc.com (office); ishiiarc@blue.ocn.ne.jp (office). *Website:* www.ishiiarc .com (office).

ISHIKAWA, Hirokazu, BA; Japanese banking and insurance executive; *Chairman, Mitsui Life Insurance Company Ltd;* b. 1942; ed Faculty of Econs, Keio Univ.; joined The Mistui Bank Ltd 1966, Sr Deputy Gen. Man. Europe Div. HQ and Man.-Dir Mitsui Finance Int. Ltd 1989–90, Man.-Dir and Chief Rep. Mitsui Taiyo Kobe Int. Ltd 1990–92, Man.-Dir and Chief Rep. Sakura Finance Int. Ltd 1992, Gen. Man. Europe, Middle E and Africa Div. 1992–94, Gen. Man. Planning Div. 1994–97, apptd Dir 1994, Man.-Dir 1997–99, Man.-Dir and Sr Exec. Officer 1999–2000, Deputy Pres. Sakura Bank Ltd 2000–01; currently Chair. Mitsui Life Insurance Company Ltd; Trustee Hasegawa Int. Scholarship Foundation. *Address:* Mitsui Life Insurance Company Ltd, 1-2-3 Otemachi, Chiyoda-ku, Toyko 100-8123, Japan (office). *Telephone:* (3) 3211-6111 (office). *Fax:* (3) 3215-1580 (office). *Website:* www.mitsui-semei.co.jp (office).

ISHIKAWA, Shigeru, DEcon; Japanese economist and academic; *Professor Emeritus, Hitotsubashi University;* b. 7 April 1918; m. Michiko Ishikawa; ed Tokyo Univ. of Commerce (now Hitotsubashi Univ.); attached to Jiji Press News Agency 1945–56, Hong Kong Corresp. 1951–53; Asst Prof., Inst. of Econ. Research, Hitotsubashi Univ. 1956–63, Prof. 1963–82, Dir 1972–74, Prof. Emer. 1982–; Far Eastern Fellow, East Asian Research Center, Harvard Univ. 1957–58; Visiting Prof., SOAS, Univ. of London 1980, Hon. Fellow 1991; Prof., School of Int. Politics, Econs and Business, Aoyama Gakuin Univ. 1982–94, Prof. Emer. 1994–, Dir Univ. Library 1996–98, mem. Japan Acad. 1998–, Visiting Prof., Josai Univ. 1994–2003; Order of Friendship (Viet Nam) 1997–. *Publications:* National Income and Capital Formation in Mainland China 1965, Economic Development in Asian Perspective 1967, Agricultural Development Strategies of Asia 1970, Labor Absorption in Asian Agriculture 1978, Essays on Technology, Employment and Institutions in Economic Development: Comparative Asian Experience 1981, Basic Issues in Development Economics (in Japanese) 1990, Treatise on International Development Policy (in Japanese) 2006. *Address:* 19-8, 4 chome Kugayama, Suginami-ku, Tokyo 168-0082, Japan. *Telephone:* (3) 3332-8376 (home). *Fax:* (3) 3332-0877 (home).

ISHIKAWA, Tadashi; Japanese business executive; *Chairman, Toyota Industries Corporation;* joined Toyoda Automatic Loom Works (later Toyota Industries Corpn) 1968, various man. roles including Corp. Auditor 2003, Exec. Vice-Pres., later Pres., currently Chair. *Address:* Toyota Industries Corpn, 2-1, Toyota-cho, Kariya-shi, Aichi 448-8671, Japan (office). *Telephone:* (566) 222511 (office). *Fax:* (566) 275650 (office). *E-mail:* info@toyota-industries .com (office). *Website:* www.toyota-industries.com (office).

ISHIMARU, Akira, PhD, FIEEE, FInstP; American electrical engineer and academic; *Professor Emeritus, University of Washington, Seattle;* b. 16 March 1928, Fukuoka, Japan; s. of Shigezo Ishimaru and Yumi Ishimaru (née Yamada); m. Yuko Kaneda 1956; two s. two d.; ed Univ. of Tokyo, Univ. of Washington, USA; Asst Prof., Univ. of Washington 1958–61, Assoc. Prof. 1961–65, Prof. of Electrical Eng 1965– Boeing Martin Prof. 1993–, also Adjunct Prof. of Applied Math., now Prof. Emer.; Visiting Assoc. Prof. Univ. of Calif. at Berkeley 1963–64; Ed. Radio Science 1978–82; mem. Editorial Bd Proc. IEEE 1973–83; mem. Nat. Acad. of Eng 1996–; Founding Ed. Waves in Random and Complex Media 1990–; Fellow, Optical Soc. of America 1982, Acoustical Soc. of America 1997; IEEE Centennial Medal 1984, Distinguished Achievement Award 1995, 1998, IEEE Heinrich Hertz Medal 1999, URSI John Dellinger Gold Medal 1999, IEEE Third Millennium Medal 2000. *Publications:* Wave Propagation and Scattering in Random Media, Vols 1 and 2 1978, Electromagnetic Wave Propagation, Radiation and Scattering 1991. *Address:* Electrical Engineering Department, Box 352500, University of Washington, Seattle, WA 98195 (office); 2913 165th Place, NE, Bellevue, WA 98008, USA (home). *Telephone:* (206) 543-2169 (office); (425) 885-0018 (home). *Fax:* (206) 543-3842 (office); (425) 881-1622 (home). *E-mail:* ishimaru@ee .washington.edu (office). *Website:* www.ee.washington.edu (office).

ISHIOKA, Eiko; Japanese designer; b. 12 July 1939, Tokyo; ed Nat. Univ. of Fine Arts, Tokyo; fmr Art Dir Shiseido cosmetics co.; designer of advertising posters, television commercials and stage sets; designed official poster for Expo 1970 in Japan; designed cover for Miles Davis album Tutu (Grammy Award best Album Package Design) 1987; elected mem. Art Dirs Club Hall of Fame 1992. *Plays include:* M. Butterfly (scenic design and costume design, Outer Critics Circle Award, American Theater Wing Design Award for Outstanding Theater Design) 1988; opera includes The Ring of the Nibelung, De Nederlandse Opera, Amsterdam (costume design); also David Copperfield: Dreams and Nightmares (Visual Artistic Dir) 1996. *Films (as costume designer):* Mishima: A Life in Four Chapters (also production designer) 1985, Closet Land (also production designer) 1991, Bram Stoker's Dracula (Academy Award for Costume Design 1992) 1991, The Cell 2000, The Fall 2006, Teresa, el cuerpo de Cristo 2007. *Publication:* Eiko by Eiko: Eiko Ishioka, Japan's Ultimate Designer 1990.

ISHIZAKA, Kimishige, MD, PhD; Japanese biomedical research scientist and academic; *President Emeritus, La Jolla Institute for Allergy and Immunology;* b. 12 March 1925, Tokyo; m. Teruko Ishizaka 1949; one s.; ed Univ. of Tokyo; Chief, Dept of Serology, Div. of Immunoserology, Tokyo 1953–62; Prof., Dept of Microbiology, Univ. of Colo Medical School and Chief, Dept of Immunology, Children's Asthma Research Inst. and Hosp., Denver, Colo, USA 1962–70; Assoc. Prof. of Medicine and Microbiology, Johns Hopkins Univ., Baltimore, Md 1970–81; Dir Subdept. of Immunology 1981–88, O'Neill Prof. of Immunology and Medicine 1981–89; Scientific Dir and Head, Div. of Immunobiology, La Jolla Inst. of Allergy and Immunology (LIAI), La Jolla, Calif. 1989–91,

Pres. 1991–96, Pres. Emer. 1996–, also LIAI Bd of Dirs as Dir Emer.; Pres. American Asscn of Immunologists 1984–85; mem. NAS 1983–; Emperor's Award 1974, Pioneer of Modern Allergy Award 1982, American Coll. of Physicians Award for Achievement in Medical Science 1985, Distinguished Scientist Award, Japanese Medical Soc. of America 1989, Japan Prize, Science and Tech. Foundation of Japan 2000, and numerous other awards. *Publications:* numerous contribs to scientific journals. *Address:* La Jolla Institute for Allergy and Immunology, 10355 Science Center Drive, San Diego, CA 92121, USA (office). *Telephone:* (858) 558-3500 (office). *Website:* www.liai.org (office).

ISHIZAKA, Koji; Japanese actor; b. 20 June 1941, Ginza, Tokyo; ed Keio Univ.; TV debut in Taikouki (drama series), NHK 1965; film debut in Wakai Musame ga Ippai 1966; achieved fame playing role of Kosuke Kindaichi in a series of five detective movies directed by Kon Ichikawa 1976–79; directed and performed in film Chushin-Gura: 47 Assassins 1994; lead actor in Genroku Ryoran (drama series), NHK 1999; currently Co-Host Nademo Kantei Dan (We'll Appraise Anything, TV antique show); regular appearances on TV show Sekai Ururun Taizaiki. *Film appearances include:* Wakai Musame ga Ippai (Young Girls are Everywhere) 1966, Hi mo tsuki mo 1969, Kaze no bojo 1970, The Inaugami Family 1976, Devil's Bouncing Ball Song 1977, Island of Horror 1977, Jo-oh-bachi (Queen Bee) 1978, Death on Hospital Hill 1979, Sasameyuki (The Makioka Sisters) 1983, Ohan 1984, The Return of Godzilla 1984, The Harp of Burma 1985, Rokumeikan 1986, Eiga jouu (Film Actress) 1987, Taketori Monogatari 1987, Tsuru 1988, Yushun 1988, Tenkawa Densetsu Satsujin Jiken (The Noh Mask Murders) 1991, Last Song 1993, Fusa 1993, Shijushichinin no shikaku (47 Ronin) 1994, Shinsengumi 1999, Urutoraman Kosumosu: First Contact 2001, Kenchô no hoshi 2006, Nihon chinbotsu 2006, Yume jûya 2006, Inugamike no ichizoku 2006. *Leisure interests:* collecting antiques.

ISHIZU, Shinya, LLB; Japanese business executive; *Chairman, Asahi Glass Company Limited;* b. 23 Aug. 1938, Tokyo; ed Hitotsubashi Univ.; joined Asahi Glass Co. Ltd April 1962, Gen. Man. Fine Ceramics Div. 1988–90, Fukuoka Sales Office 1990–93, Osaka Sales Office 1993–95, Dir March 1994–, Gen. Man. Corp. Planning Div. 1995–96, Man. Dir 1996–97, Exec. Vice-Pres. 1997–98 Pres. 1998–2003, Chair. 2003–; Dir Asahi Glass Foundation. *Address:* Asahi Glass Company Limited, 1–12–1 Yurakucho, Chiyoda-ku, Tokyo 100–8405, Japan (office). *Telephone:* (3) 321 85519 (office). *Website:* www.agc.co.jp (office).

ISHMAEL, Mohammed Ali Odeen; Guyanese diplomatist; *Ambassador to Venezuela;* m.; two c.; fmr teacher; served in Ministry of Foreign Affairs 1970s; Amb. to USA 1993–2003, to Venezuela 2003–; Perm. Rep. to OAS 1993–2003, Vice-Chair. Perm. Council 1993, Chair. 1994, 2003; mem. Del. of Guyana to UN Gen. Ass. 1993–; Chief Negotiator Summit of the Americas 1994, 1998; Head Del. of Guyana to CARICOM 1997–, to Org. of Islamic Conf., Tehran 1999; mem. Cen. Cttee Progressive Youth Org., People's Progressive Party; Cacique Crown of Honour 1997; Gandhi Centenary Medal, Univ. of Guyana 1974, King Legacy Award for Int. Service 2002. *Publications include:* Problems of Transition of Education in the Third World, Towards Education Reform in Guyana, Amerindian Legends of Guyana, The Trail of Diplomacy; numerous articles on educ., Guyanese history and int. political issues. *Address:* Embassy of Guyana, Quinta 'Roraima', Avenida El Paseo, Prados del Este, Apdo 51054, Caracas 1050, Venezuela (office). *Telephone:* (212) 977-1158 (office). *Fax:* (212) 976-3765 (office). *E-mail:* embaguy@caracas.org.ve (office).

ISINBAYEVA, Yelena; Russian pole vaulter; b. 3 June 1982, Volgograd; d. of Gadzhi Gadzhiyevich Isinbayev; ed Volgograd State Acad. of Physical Culture; Sr Lt, Russian Army; gold medal, pole vault, World Youth Games 1999, European Jr Championships 2001, European Under 23 Championships 2003, Olympic Games, Athens 2004, World Indoor Championships 2004, 2006, World Athletics Championships 2005, 2007, European Indoor Championships 2005, European Championship 2006, Olympic Games, Beijing 2008; set women's pole vault world record of 5.05m at Olympic Games, Beijing 18 Aug. 2008; Distinguished Citizen of Donetsk 2006; IAAF Female Athlete of the Year 2004, 2005, Laureus Sportswoman of the Year 2007. *Address:* Yelena Isinbaeva, 3 av. de Grande Bretagne, Monaco 98000 (office). *Website:* www.yelenaisinbaeva.com (office).

ISKANDER, Fazil Abdulovich; Russian/Abkhaz writer; b. 6 March 1929, Sukhumi, Georgian SSR; m.; one s. one d.; ed Maxim Gorky Inst. of Literature, Moscow; first works Publ 1952; USSR People's Deputy 1989–91; Pres. Asscn of Authors and Publrs against Piracy; Head, World of Culture Asscn; Vice-Pres. Russian Acad. of Arts; Academician of RAN, Natural Sciences Dept, Bayerische Akad. der Khönen Künste; Dr hc (Norwich Univ., USA); Malaparti Prize (Italy) 1985, USSR State Prize 1989, State Prize of Russia 1993, A. Sakharov Prize, A. Pushkin Prize (Germany) 1994, Moscow-Penne Prize (Italy) 1996, Triumph Prize (Russia) 1998. *Films include:* Time of Lucky Finds, Crime Kings 1986, A Little Giant of Big Sex, A Night with Stalin. *Plays:* Djamchuch: A Son of a Deer 1986, A Greeting from Zürüpa (The One Who Thinks About Russia) 1999. *Publications include:* Green Rain 1960, Youth of the Sea 1964, Goatibex Constellation 1966, Forbidden Fruit 1966 (English trans. 1972), Summer Forest 1969, Time of Lucky Finds 1970, Tree of Childhood and Other Stories 1970, Sandro from Chegem 1978, Metropol (co-ed.) 1979, Small Giant of the Big Sex 1979, Rabbits and Boa Constrictors 198, The Path (poems) 1987, School Waltz or the Energy of Shame 1990, Poets and Tsars 1991, Man and His Surroundings 1992, Pshada 1993, Sofichka 1996, The One Who Thinks About Russia and the American 1997, Poet 1998, The Swallow's Nest 2000 and other stories. *Leisure interest:* reading fiction. *Address:* Leningradski prosp. 26, korp. 2, Apt. 67, 125040 Moscow, Russia. *Telephone:* (495) 973-94-53 (office); (495) 212-73-60. *Fax:* (495) 973-94-53 (office).

ISKENDERIAN, Mary Ellen, BS, MBA; American banking executive; *President and CEO, Women's World Banking;* d. of Mr and Mrs Ara Iskenderian; m. Gregory Owen Lipscomb 1991; ed Yale School of Org. and Man., Georgetown Univ. School of Foreign Service; numerous leadership positions at Int. Finance Corpn (pvt. sector arm of World Bank) including Dir Partnership Devt, Dir Global Financial Markets Portfolio and Dir S Asia Regional Dept –2006; Pres. and CEO Women's World Banking 2006–; mem. Bd of Dirs ASA Foundation, Nat. Bank of Commerce, Tanzania, ShoreCap International; fmr Corp. Dir Banco Caja Social, Confisura SA, Infrastructure Devt Finance Corpn; mem. Advisory Bd Dignity Fund, Kiva; mem. Women's Leadership Bd of Harvard Univ., Council on Foreign Relations. *Address:* Women's World Banking, 8 West 40th Street, 9th Floor, New York, NY 10018, USA (office). *Telephone:* (212) 768-8513 (office). *Fax:* (212) 768-8519 (office). *E-mail:* wwb@swwb.org (office). *Website:* www.swwb.org (office).

ISKROV, Ivan, MSc; Bulgarian central banker; *Governor, Bulgarian National Bank;* b. 26 March 1967, Pirdop; m.; one c.; ed Univ. of Nat. and World Economy, Sofia; began career as Visiting Lecturer, Univ. of Nat. and World Economy, Sofia 1992–93; expert and examiner, Bulgarska Narodna Banka (Bulgarian Nat. Bank) 1993–97, Gov. 2003–; Exec. Dir and mem. Man. Bd DSK Bank 1997–99; Exec. Dir and mem. Man. Bd Rosseximbank 1999–2001; mem. Parl. 2001–03, held various parl. positions including Chair. Budget and Finance Comm., mem. Bulgaria-EU Jt Parl. Comm. *Address:* Bulgarska Narodna Banka (Bulgarian National Bank), Sofia 1000, 1 pl. Knyaz Alexander I 1, Bulgaria (office). *Telephone:* (2) 914-59 (office). *Fax:* (2) 980-24-25 (office). *E-mail:* press_office@bnbank.org (office). *Website:* www.bnb.bg (office).

ISLAM, A. B. Mirza Azizul, BA, MA, PhD; Bangladeshi economist and politician; b. 23 Feb. 1941, Sujanagar, Pabna; m. Nilufar Aziz; one s.; ed Dhaka Univ., Williams Coll. and Boston Univ., USA; Lecturer, Dhaka Univ. 1962–64; joined Civil Service of Pakistan 1964; worked in different capacities in admin. service 1967–82; Econ. Affairs/Sr Econ. Affairs Officer, UN-ESCAP, Bangkok 1982–86, Dir Research and Policy Analysis Div. 1993–2001; Chief of Developing Econs Section, UN Centre on Transnational Corpns, New York 1987–92; consultant to UNCTAD, World Bank and Centre for Policy Dialogue 2002–03; Chair. Bangladesh Securities & Exchange Comm. 2003–06; Chair. Sonali Bank April–Nov. 2006; Hon. Adviser to Caretaker Govt, in charge of Ministry of Finance, of Planning, of Commerce and of Posts and Telecommunications 2007–08, in charge of Ministry of Finance, Ministry of Planning 2008–09. *Address:* c/o Ministry of Finance, Bangladesh Secretariat, Building 7, 3rd Floor, Dhaka 1000, Bangladesh (office).

ISLAM, Ahmad Shamsul, MSc, PhD; Bangladeshi plant geneticist and academic; *Professor, Brac University;* b. 1 Jan. 1926; ed Presidency Coll., Calcutta, Manchester Univ.; research in genetics, plant breeding and tissue-culture 1955–; postdoctoral research work at Cornell Univ., Univ. of Calif., Davis, USA and Nottingham Univ.,UK; Lecturer, Univ. of Texas, Austin; Prof. of Botany, Dhaka Univ. –1990 (retd); Consultant and Prof., Brac Univ., Dhaka 2003–; Founder Ed. Sind Univ. Research Journal, Pakistan Journal of Botany, Dar-es-Salaam Univ. Scientific Research Journal, Bangladesh Journal of Botany; fmr Pres. Bangladesh Asscn for Plant Tissue Culture; fmr Sec.-Gen. Bangladesh Asscn for the Advancement of Science; mem. Indian and Japanese Socs of Genetic and Plant Breeding; Fellow, Islamic Acad. of Sciences; Ekushey Padak for promoting education 1985-86, President's Gold Medal, Bangladesh Acad of Science 1987. *Publication:* Fundamentals of Genetics (Bongshogati bidyar Moolkatha). *Address:* Brac University, 66 Mohakhali, Dhaka, 1212, Bangladesh (office). *Website:* www.bracu.ac.bd (office).

ISLAM, Atharul; Bangladeshi government official and business executive; Additional Sec., Govt of Bangladesh and Chair. Bangladesh Jute Mills Corpn. *Address:* Bangladesh Jute Mills Corporation, Adamjee Court (Annexe-1), 115-120, Motijheel Commercial Area, Dhaka 1000, Bangladesh (office). *Telephone:* (2) 9553364 (office). *Fax:* (2) 9564740 (office). *E-mail:* bjmc@bttb.net.bd (office); info@bjmc.gov.bd (office). *Website:* www.bjmc.gov.bd (office).

ISLAM, Nurul, PhD; Bangladeshi economist and academic; *Research Fellow Emeritus, International Food Policy Research Institute;* b. 1 April 1929, Chittagong; s. of Abdur Rahman and Mohsena Begum; m. Rowshan Ara 1957; one s. one d.; ed Univ. of Dhaka and Harvard Univ., USA; Reader in Econs, Dhaka Univ. 1955–60, Prof. 1960–64; Dir Pakistan Inst. of Devt Econs, Karachi 1964–72; Visiting Prof., Econ. Devt Inst., World Bank 1967–68; Professorial Research Assoc., Yale Econ. Growth Cen. 1968 and 1971; Deputy Chair. Bangladesh Planning Comm. (with ministerial status) 1972–75; Chair. Bangladesh Inst. of Devt Studies, Dhaka 1975–77; mem. Bd of Trustees Int. Rice Research Inst., Manila 1973–77, Exec. Cttee Third World Forum 1974–, Bd of Govs. Int. Food Policy Research Inst. 1975–87 (Research Fellow Emer. 1987–), UN Cttee on Devt Planning 1975–77; Asst Dir-Gen. Econ. and Social Policy Dept, Food and Agric. Org. of UN 1977–; mem. Editorial Bd The World Economy, London, Research Advisory Cttee, World Bank 1980, Advisory Group, Asian Devt Bank, Manila 1981–82, Advisory Cttee, Inst. of Int. Econ., Washington, DC; consultant for various UN cttees, ESCAP, UNESCO, UNCTAD; Nuffield Foundation Fellow at Univs of London and Cambridge 1958–59; Rockefeller Fellow, Netherlands School of Economics 1959. *Publications:* A Short-Term Model of Pakistan's Economy: An Econometric Analysis 1964, Studies in Foreign Capital and Economic Development 1960, Studies in Consumer Demand 1965, Studies in Commercial Policy and Economic Growth 1970, Development Planning in Bangladesh – A Study in Political Economy 1977, Development Strategy of Bangladesh 1978, Interdependence of Developed and Developing Countries 1978, Foreign Trade and Economic Controls in Development: The Case of United Pakistan 1980, Aid and Influence: The Case of Bangladesh (co-author) 1981; Agriculture Towards 2000 (co-author) 1981, The Fifth World Food Survey 1985, Agriculture Price

Policies 1985. *Leisure interests:* reading political and historical books, movies. *Address:* International Food Policy Research Institute, 2033 K Street, NW, Washington, DC 20006-1002, USA (office). *Telephone:* (202) 862-5600 (office). *Fax:* (202) 467-4439 (office). *E-mail:* N.Islam@cgiar.org (office). *Website:* www .ifpri.org (home).

ISLAM, Yusuf, (Cat Stevens); British singer, songwriter and producer; b. (Steven Demetre Georgiou), 21 July 1948, London, England; m. Fawzia Mubarik Ali 1979; two s. (one deceased) four d.; solo artist as Cat Stevens –1978, then as Yusuf Islam; extensive tours worldwide, numerous television appearances; mem. Musicians' Union; Founder and Chair. Small Kindness (charity); Founder and Chair. Islamia Schools Trust, f. Islamia Primary School, Islamia Girls' Secondary School, Brondesbury Coll. for Boys, London; World Social Award 2003, Gorbachev Foundation Man for Peace Award 2004, ASCAP Award for Songwriter of the Year 2006, Mediterranean Prize for Peace 2007. *Recordings include:* albums: (as Cat Stevens) Matthew And Son 1967, New Masters 1967, World Of Cat Stevens 1970, Mona Bone Jakon 1970, Tea For The Tillerman 1970, Teaser And The Firecat 1971, Very Young and Early Songs 1971, Catch Bull At Four 1972, Foreigner 1973, Buddha And The Chocolate Box 1974, Saturnight (Live in Tokyo) 1974, View From The Top 1974, Numbers 1975, Greatest Hits 1975, Izitso 1977, Back To Earth 1978, Cat's Cradle 1978, Footsteps In The Dark 1984, Classics Vol. 24 – Cat Stevens 1989, Very Best of Cat Stevens 1990, (as Yusuf Islam) The Life Of The Last Prophet 1995, Prayers Of The Last Prophet 1999, I Have No Cannons That Roar 2000, A Is For Allah 2000, Majikat: Earth Tour 1976 2004, An Other Cup (Ivor Novello Award for Outstanding Song Collection 2007) 2006, Roadsinger 2009. *E-mail:* office@yusufislam.com (office). *Website:* www.yusufislam.com.

ISLAMI, Kastriot, MA, DSc; Albanian politician and physicist; b. 18 Feb. 1952, Tirana; s. of Selman Islami; m.; one s. one d.; ed Univ. of Tirana, Univ. of Paris XI, Orsay, France; Vice-Dean, Faculty of Natural Sciences, Univ. of Tirana 1987–91; Minister of Educ. 1991; Deputy Speaker (Chair.) of Albanian Parl. 1991–92, Head, Parl. Comm. for Preparation of Draft of Albanian Constitution 1991–96; Minister of State to Prime Minister of Albania 1997–98; Deputy Prime Minister 1998–2002; Minister of Finance 2002–03; Minister of Foreign Affairs 2003–05; Deputy Kuvendi Popullor (People's Ass.) 2006–; mem. Parl. Ass., Council of Europe, mem. Cttee on Legal Affairs and Human Rights, Cttee on the Honouring of Obligations and Commitments by Member States of the Council of Europe (Monitoring Cttee) 2006–. *Publications include:* The Basis of Quantum Mechanics Vol. I 1989, Vol. II 1990; publs in nat. and int. media. *Address:* Kuvendi Popullor (People's Assembly), Bulevardi Deshmoret e Kombit nr. 4, Tirana (office); Rruga: Dora D'Istria, Pallati R 8-Katesh, Tirana, Albania (home). *Telephone:* (5) 4237413 (office); (5) 4240669 (home). *Fax:* (5) 4227949 (office). *E-mail:* marlind@parlament.al (office); dshtypi@abissnet.com.al; kislami@icc-al.org. *Website:* www .parlament.al (home).

ISMAIL, Abdullahi Sheikh; Somali politician; Minister of Foreign Affairs 2004–07, of Constitutional and Federal Affairs 2007–; fmr Chair. Southern Somali Nat. Movt (SSNM). *Address:* Ministry of Constitutional and Federal Affairs, Mogadishu, Somalia (office).

ISMAIL, Amat; Chinese politician; *Vice-Chairman, 10th Standing Committee, National People's Congress;* b. 1935, Qira, Xinjiang Uygur Autonomous Region; ed CCP Cen. Cttee Cen. Party School (Xinjiang Class); joined CCP 1953; active in People's Commune Movt –1960; Magistrate, Qira Co. (Dist) People's Court 1954–62; Deputy Sec. CCP Cttee, a country admin., Xinjiang 1960; Deputy Head, Publicity Dept, CCP Autonomous Prefectural Cttee, Hotan, Xinjiang Uygur Autonomous Region 1963–65; Deputy Dir Cultural, Educ. and Political Work Dept, CCP Xinjiang Uygur Autonomous Regional Cttee 1966–67, mem. Standing Cttee, CCP Revolutionary Cttee and Head, Group for Regional Cultural, Educational and Health Work 1969–72; Sec. and Head, Org. Dept, CCP Xinjiang Uygur Autonomous Regional Cttee 1972–85; Vice-Chair. CCP Revolutionary Cttee, Xinjiang Uygur Autonomous Region 1972–85; Chair. Xinjiang Uygur Autonomous Regional People's Govt 1972–85; Sec. CCP Cttee, Xinjiang 1974–79; Vice-Chair. Aubnavan Regional Revolutionary Cttee, Xinjiang 1974–79; Political Commissar, Xinjiang Mil. Region 1976–85; First Deputy Dir Party School, Xinjiang 1977–85; Chair. People's Govt, Xinjiang 1979–85; Minister of State Nationalities Affairs Comm. 1985–98; Minister in Charge of State Nat. Ethnic Affairs Comm. 1993–98; State Councillor 1993–2003; Dir China Comm. of Int. Decade for Disaster Reduction 1998–2000, China Comm. for Int. Disaster Reduction 2000–; mem. 10th CCP Cen. Cttee 1972–77, 11th CCP Cen. Cttee 1977–82, 12th CCP Cen. Cttee 1982–87, 13th CCP Cen. Cttee 1987–92, 14th CCP Cen. Cttee 1992–97, 15th CCP Cen. Cttee 1997–2002, 16th CCP Cen. Cttee 2002–07; Vice-Chair. 7th CPPCC Nat. Cttee 1988–93; mem. Standing Cttee of NPC 1978–83, Vice-Chair. 10th Standing Cttee of NPC 2003–; Pres. China-Turkey Friendship Asscn; Hon. Pres. Chinese Asscn of Ethnic Minorities for External Exchanges. *Address:* The State Council, Zhongnanhai, Beijing, People's Republic of China (office).

ISMAIL, Mustafa Osman, PhD; Sudanese politician; b. 1955, Dongola; Minister of External Relations 1998–2005; currently Presidential Adviser; mem. Nat. Congress Party. *Address:* c/o National Congress Party, Khartoum, Sudan (office).

ISMAIL, Tan Sri Razali, BA; Malaysian diplomatist and foundation executive; *Chairman, Force of Nature Aid Foundation;* b. 1939, Kedah; m.; three c.; joined Ministry of Foreign Affairs 1962; served in Delhi 1963–64; Asst High. Commr in Madras 1964–66; Second Sec. Paris 1966–68; Prin. Asst Sec. Ministry of Foreign Affairs 1968–70; Counsellor, London 1970–72; various posts at Ministry of Foreign Affairs and Chargé d'affaires, Vientiane 1972–78; Amb. to Poland 1978–82; High Commr in India 1982; Deputy Sec.-Gen.

Ministry of Foreign Affairs 1985–88; Perm. Rep. to UN 1988, Pres. UN Gen. Ass. 1996–97; apptd Special Adviser to Prime Minister 1998; UN Special Envoy to Myanmar 1998–2006; currently Chair. Force of Nature Aid Foundation. *Address:* Force of Nature Aid Foundation, 23, Lorong Tanjung 5/4D, 46000 Petaling Jaya, Selangor Darul Ehsan, Malaysia (office). *Telephone:* (3) 79600366 (office). *Fax:* (3) 79601366 (office). *E-mail:* contact@ forceofnature.org (office). *Website:* www.forceofnature.org (office).

ISOKALLIO, Kaarlo, MSc; Finnish business executive; b. 13 May 1948, Helsinki; m. Ammi Kristiina; one d.; ed Univ. of Tech., Helsinki; Project Engineer Wärtsilä Corpn 1972–74; Marketing Dir IBM (Finland) 1974–81; Man. Dir Kabmatik AB, Sweden 1981–83; with Nokia Corpn 1983–, Dept Man. Cables Dept, Machinery Div., 1983–85, Pres. Electronics, Information Systems 1985–86, Pres. Information Systems 1986–88, Exec. Pres. Nokia Data Group 1988–90, Pres. and COO Nokia Corpn 1990–91, Deputy to CEO, Vice-Chair. Group Exec. Bd 1990; mem. Bd of Dirs Oy Lindell Ab 1987–, Taloudellinen Tiedotustoimisto 1991–; mem. Supervisory Bd Mecrastor Oy 1987–, Oy Rastor Ab 1987–, Helsinki Univ. Cen. Hosp. Foundation 1991–; mem. Bd Econ. Information Bureau 1991–, ICL PLC 1991–; mem. Tech. Del., Ministry of Trade and Industry 1990; Chair. Bd MTV (Finnish commercial TV) 1991; mem. Acad. for Tech. Sciences 1991.

ISOZAKI, Arata; Japanese architect; b. 23 July 1931, Oita City; s. of Soji Isozaki and Tetsu Isozaki; m. Aiko Miyawaki 1974; two s.; ed Univ. of Tokyo; with Kenzo Tange's team 1954–63; Pres. Arata Isozaki and Assocs 1963–; juror, Pritzker Architecture Prize 1979–84, Concours Int. de Parc de la Villette 1982, The Peak Int. Architectural Competition 1983, R. S. Reynolds Memorial Award 1985, The Architectural Competition for the New Nat. Theatre of Japan 1986, competitions for Passenger Terminal Bldg, Kansai Int. Airport 1988, Triangle de la Folie, Paris 1989, Int. Architects' competition, Vienna EXPO '95 1991, Kyoto Station Bldg Renovation Design competition 1991; visiting prof. at numerous univs including Harvard, Yale and Columbia; Hon. Fellow, Acad. Tiberina, AIA, RIBA 1994–; Hon. Academician Royal Acad. of Arts 1994; Hon. mem. Bund Deutscher Architekten (BDA), American Acad. of Arts and Letters 1998; Chevalier Ordre des Arts et des Lettres (France), Grande Ufficiale, Ordine al Merito (Italy) 2007; numerous prizes including RIBA Gold Medal 1983–86, Chicago Architecture Prize 1990, Leon d'Oro, La Biennale di Venezia VI Int. Exhbn of Architecture 1996. *Works include:* Expo '70, Osaka 1966–70, Oita Medical Hall 1959–69, Annex 1970–72, Oita Prefectural Library 1962–66, head office of Fukuoka Mutual Bank 1968–71, Museum of Modern Art, Gunma 1971–74, Kitakyushu City Museum of Art 1972–74, Shuko-sha Bldg, Fukuoka 1974–75, Kamioka Town Hall 1976–78, Gymnasium and Dining Hall, Nippon Electric Glass Co., Otsu 1978–80, Los Angeles Museum of Contemporary Art 1981–86, Tsukuba Centre Bldg 1979–83, Palladium Club, New York 1983–85, Sant Jordi Sports Hall, Barcelona 1983–90, Brooklyn Museum 1986–92, Art Tower, Mito 1986–90, Bond Univ., Australia 1987–89, Hara Museum—ARC 1987–88, Kitakyushu Int. Conf. Center 1987–90, Team Disney Bldg 1987–91, Tokyo Univ. of Art and Design 1986–92, Guggenheim Museum, New York 1991–92, Centre for Advanced Science and Tech., Hyogo 1994–98, Japanese Art and Tech. Centre, Kraków 1990–94, Nagi Museum of Contemporary Art 1991–94, B-Con Plaza (int. conf. centre), Oita 1991–95, Toyonokuni Libraries for Cultural Resources, Oita 1991–95, Kyoto Concert Hall 1991–95, Domus: la casa del hombre, La Coruña, Spain 1993–95, Akiyoshidai Int. Art Village, Yamaguchi 1995–98, Nara Centennial Hall 1992–98, Center of Science and Industry, Columbus, OH 1994–99, Ceramics Park MINO 1996–2002, Yamaguchi Center for Arts and Media 1997–2003, Turin Ice Hockey Stadium 2002–06, Shenzhen Cultural Centre, China 1998–2008, China Cen. Acad. of Fine Arts, Beijing 2003–08. *Publications include:* Kukane 1971, Kenchiku no Kaitai 1975, Shuhō ga 1979, Kenchiku no Shūji 1979, Kenchiku no Seijigaku 1989, Image Game 1990, Arata Isozaki 1960–90, Architecture 1991, Kenchiku to iu Keishiki 1991, GA Architect 6 – Arata Isozaki (Vol. 1) 1991, Arata Isozaki – Works 30 1992, Arata Isozaki – Four Decades of Architecture 1998, GA Architect 15 – Arata Isozaki 2000, UNBUILT 2001, GA Document 77—Arata Isozaki 2004. *Address:* Arata Isozaki and Associates, 6-17 Akasaka 9-chome, Minato-ku, Tokyo 107-0052, Japan (office). *Telephone:* (3) 3405-1526 (office). *Fax:* (3) 3475-5265 (office). *E-mail:* info@isozaki.co.jp (office). *Website:* www.isozaki.co.jp (office).

ISRAEL, Werner, OC, PhD, FRSC, FRS, FInstP; Canadian physicist and academic; *Adjunct Professor of Physics, University of Victoria;* b. 4 Oct. 1931, Berlin, Germany; s. of Arthur Israel and Marie Kappauf; m. Inge Margulies 1958; one s. one d.; ed Univ. of Cape Town, SA and Trinity Coll., Dublin, Ireland; Asst Prof., then Full Prof. of Math., Univ. of Alberta 1958–71, Prof. of Physics 1971–96, Univ. Prof. 1986–; Adjunct Prof. of Physics, Univ. of Victoria, BC 1997–; Pres. Int. Soc. of General Relativity and Gravitation 1997–2001; Research Scholar, Dublin Inst. for Advanced Studies 1956–58; Sherman Fairchild Scholar, Calif. Inst. of Tech. 1974–75; Fellow, Canadian Inst. for Advanced Research 1986–; Hon. DSc (Queen's Univ.) 1987, (Univ. of Victoria) 1999; Dr hc (Univ. de Tours) 1994; Izaak Walton Killam Prize 1983, Tomalla Prize (Tomalla Foundation for Gravitational Research, Switzerland) 1996. *Publications:* Relativity, Astrophysics and Cosmology (Ed.) 1973, (Co-Ed. with S. W. Hawking), General Relativity, an Einstein Centenary Survey 1979, 300 Years of Gravitation 1987; numerous papers on black hole theory, general relativity, statistical mechanics. *Leisure interest:* music. *Address:* Department of Physics and Astronomy, University of Victoria, PO Box 3055, Victoria, BC V8W 3P6 (office); Suite 401, 2323 Hamiota Street, Victoria, BC V8R 2N1, Canada (home). *Telephone:* (250) 721-7708 (office). *E-mail:* israel@ uvic.ca (office). *Website:* www.phys.uvic.ca (office).

ISRAELACHVILI, Jacob Nissim, BS, PhD, FRS, FAA; Australian/Israeli/American scientist and academic; *Professor of Chemical Engineering and*

Materials Science and Associate Director, Materials Research Laboratory (MRL), University of California, Santa Barbara; b. 19 Aug. 1944, Tel-Aviv; s. of Haim Israelachvili and Hela Israelachvili; m. Karin Haglund 1971; two d.; ed Christ's Coll., Univ. of Cambridge; Postdoctoral Research Fellow, Cavendish Lab., Univ. of Cambridge, UK 1971–72; European Molecular Biology Org. Research Fellow, Univ. of Stockholm 1972–74; Professorial Fellow, Inst. of Advanced Studies, ANU, Canberra 1974–86; Prof. of Chemical Eng and Materials Science, Univ. of Calif., Santa Barbara 1986–, also Assoc. Dir Materials Research Lab.; Debye Lecturer, Cornell Univ. 1987; Foreign Assoc. Nat. Acad. of Eng (USA) 1999; Fellow, American Physical Soc. in Biological Physics 2004; mem. NAS 2004–; Pawsey Medal, Australian Acad. of Science 1977, Alpha Chi Sigma Award for Chemical Eng Research, AICHE 1997, Adhesion Soc. Award for Excellence in Adhesion Science 2003, MRS Medal 2004. *Publications:* Intermolecular and Surface Forces 1985; numerous scientific publs on surface forces in liquids and biological membrane structure and interactions. *Leisure interest:* history of science. *Address:* Room 1200–Bldg 570, Department of Chemical Engineering, University of California, Santa Barbara, CA 93106-5080 (office); UCSB, Department of Chemical Engineering, 3357 Engineering II, Santa Barbara, CA 93106-5080; 2233 Foothill Lane, Santa Barbara, CA 93105, USA (home). *Telephone:* (805) 893-8407 (office); (805) 893-8353 (Lab.) (office); (805) 252-5568; (805) 963-9545 (home). *Fax:* (805) 893-7870 (office). *E-mail:* jacob@engineering.ucsb.edu (office). *Website:* www.chemengr.ucsb.edu/people/faculty/israelachvili (office). (office).

ISSAD, Mohand; Algerian lawyer and academic; b. 1939; ed Univ. de Rennes; lawyer specializing in commercial law, Algiers 1965–; Lecturer, Faculty of Law, Ben-Aknoun Univ. 1965–99; currently Prof. of Int. Law, Univ. of Algiers; apptd by Pres. as Chair. Nat. Comm. for Judicial Reform 2000, Comm. investigating disturbances in Kabylia 2001, Comm. on conditions in Algerian prisons and judicial reform 2002. *Address:* School of Law, University of Algiers, Ben Aknoun II Campus, Ben Aknoun, Algiers (office); 9 Place des Martyrs, Algiers, Algeria. *Telephone:* (21) 91-46-21 (office). *Fax:* (21) 71-37-74 (office).

ISSELBACHER, Kurt Julius, MD; American medical scientist, academic and university administrator; *Director Emeritus, Massachusetts General Hospital Cancer Center and Mallinckrodt Distinguished Professor of Medicine, Harvard University;* b. 12 Sept. 1925, Wirges, Germany; s. of Albert Isselbacher and Flori Isselbacher; m. Rhoda Solin 1950; one s. three d.; ed Harvard Univ. and Harvard Medical School; Chief. Gastrointestinal Unit, Mass Gen. Hosp. 1957–88, Chair. Research Cttee 1967, Dir Cancer Center 1987–, now Dir Emer.; Prof. of Medicine, Harvard Medical School 1966–, Mallinckrodt Prof. of Medicine 1972–97, Distinguished Mallinckrodt Prof. 1998–, Chair. Exec. Cttee Medicine Depts 1968–, Chair. Univ. Cancer Cttee 1972–87; mem. Governing Bd Nat. Research Council 1987–90; Ed.-in-Chief Harrison's Principles of Internal Medicine 1991–; mem. NAS (Chair. Food and Nutrition Bd 1983–88, Exec. Cttee and Council 1987–90); Hon. DSc (Northwestern Univ.) 2001; Distinguished Achievement Award, American Gastroenterological Asscn (AGA) 1983, Friedenwald Medal, AGA 1985, John Phillips Memorial Award, American Coll. of Physicians 1989, Bristol-Myers Squibb Award for Distinguished Achievement in Nutrition Research 1991, Kober Medal, Asscn of American Physicians 2001, Jewish Nat. Fund Tree of Life Award 2001. *Leisure interest:* tennis. *Address:* Massachusetts General Hospital, Building 149, 13th Street, Charlestown, MA 02129 (office); 20 Nobscot Road, Newton, MA 02114, USA (home). *Telephone:* (617) 726-5610 (office). *Fax:* (617) 726-5637 (office). *E-mail:* isselbacher@helix.mgh.harvard.edu (office). *Website:* www.massgeneral.org/cancer/research/basic/ccr/faculty/shioda.asp (office).

ISSERLIS, Steven John, CBE; British cellist; b. 19 Dec. 1958, London; s. of George Isserlis and the late Cynthia Isserlis; m. Pauline Mara; one s.; ed City of London School, Int. Cello Centre, Scotland, Oberlin Coll., Ohio, USA; concerts and recitals world-wide 1977–; exponent of contemporary music as well as authentic period performance; 2007/2008 season includes: residency at Frankfurt's Alte Oper, performances with Orchestre de Paris under Christoph Eschenbach, Enescu Festival, Bucharest, Philadelphia Orchestra under Charles Dutoit, Philharmonia Orchestra, tours with City of Birmingham Symphony and Australian Chamber orchestras, Gala Concert with Israel Philharmonic and Zubin Mehta marking 50th anniversary of the Mann Auditorium; chamber concerts include own Russian series at Wigmore Hall, London 2008, series at NZ Int. Arts Festival; gives regular children's concerts, 92nd Street Y, New York; Artistic Dir Saint-Saëns Festival London 2004; Artistic Dir IMS Prussia Cove, Cornwall; writer of children's books about the lives of great composers; Hon. mem. RAM; Piatigorsky Award 1993, Royal Philharmonic Soc. Award 1993, Schumann Prize, Zwickau 2000, Time Out Classical Musician of the Year 2002. *Recordings:* Brahms Sonatas 2005, Bach Solo Cello Suites (Gramophone Award for Best Instrumental Recording) 2007, Schumann Music for Cello and Piano 2009. *Publications:* transcription of Beethoven Variations in D arranged for violin or cello and piano or harpsichord, Edn of Saint-Saëns pieces for cello and piano, Steven Isserlis's Cello World, Unbeaten Tracks, Why Beethoven Threw the Stew 2001, Why Handel Waggled His Wig 2006. *Leisure interests:* books, films, gossip, e-mail, eating too much, avoiding exercise, wishing I was fitter, wondering why I have so few worthwhile hobbies. *Address:* c/o Bridget Canniere, IMG Artists, The Light Box, 111 Power Road, London, W4 5PY, England (office). *Telephone:* (20) 7957-5832 (office). *Fax:* (20) 7957-5801 (office). *E-mail:* bcanniere@imgartists.com (office). *Website:* www.imgartists.com (office); www.stevenisserlis.com.

ISSING, Otmar, PhDr; German economist and central banker; *President, Centre for Financial Studies;* b. 27 March 1936, Würzburg; ed Humanistisches Gymnasium, Würzburg, Univ. of Würzburg; Prof. of Econs, Univ. of Erlangen-Nuremberg 1967–73, Univ. of Würzburg 1973–90; mem. Council of Experts for Assessment of Overall Econ. Trends at Fed. Ministry of Econs 1988–90; mem. Directorate Deutsche Bundesbank 1990–98; mem. Exec. Bd European Cen. Bank 1998–2006; Pres. Centre for Financial Studies 2006–; mem. Acad. of Sciences and Literature, Mainz, Acad. Europaea, Salzburg; Co-founder and Co-ed. of the scientific journal WiSt; mem. Verein für Socialpolitik, American Econ. Asscn, List Gesellschaft, Arbeitskreis Europäische Integration, European Acad. of Arts and Sciences, Acad. of Sciences and Literature, Walter Eucken Inst.; Hon. Prof., Univ. of Würzburg 1991–, Univ. of Frankfurt 2007–; Grosses Verdienskreuz des Verdienstordens der Bundesrepublik Deutschland; Dr hc (Bayreuth) 1996, (Konstanz) 1998, (Frankfurt am Main) 1999; Int. Prize, Friedrich-August-Hayek Foundation 2003. *Publications:* Introduction to Monetary Policy (sixth edn) 1996, Introduction to Monetary Theory 1998 (14th edn 2007), Monetary Policy in the Euro Arena (co-author) 2001, Imperfect Knowledge and Monetary Policy (co-author) 2005, The Birth of the Euro 2008. *Address:* Georg-Sittig-Str. 8, 97074 Würzburg, Germany (office).

ISSOIBEKA, Pacifique; Republic of the Congo politician; *Minister of Finance, the Economy and the Budget;* Vice-Gov. Banque des États de l'Afrique Centrale (BEAC) 2003–; Minister of Finance, the Economy and the Budget 2005–; Alt. Gov. of Repub. of the Congo to World Bank 2005–. *Address:* Ministry of Finance, the Economy and the Budget, ave de l'Indépendance, croisement ave Foch, BP 2083, Brazzaville, Republic of the Congo (office). *Telephone:* 81-45-24 (office). *Fax:* 81-43-69 (office). *Website:* www.mefb-cg.or (office).

ISSOUFOU, Mahamadou; Niger mining engineer and politician; *Secretary-General, Parti nigérien pour la démocratie et le socialisme—Tarayya (PNDS);* b. 1952, Illéla; Nat. Dir of Mines 1980–85; Sec.-Gen. Mining Co. of Niger (SOMAIR) 1985; Sec.-Gen. Parti nigérien pour la démocratie et le socialisme—Tarayya (PNDS); Prime Minister of Niger 1993–94 (resgnd); Chief Economist 1999; presidential cand. 1993, 1996, 1999, 2004. *Address:* Parti nigérien pour la démocratie et le socialisme—Tarayya (PNDS), pl. Toumo, Niamey, Niger. *Telephone:* 20-74-48-78.

ITO, Masao, MD, PhD; Japanese neuroscientist and academic; *Head of Laboratory for Memory and Learning, RIKEN Brain Science Institute;* b. 1928, Nagoya; ed Univ. of Tokyo; Asst Prof., Kumamoto Univ. 1954–57; Asst Prof., Univ. of Tokyo 1957–62, Assoc. Prof. 1963–70, Prof. 1970–90, Dean 1986–89, Prof. Emer. 1990–; Research Scholar and Research Fellow, Sir John Eccles' Lab., ANU 1959–62; Team Leader, Frontier Research Program, Inst. of Physical and Chemical Research (RIKEN) 1989–, Dir-Gen. 1993–, Head of Lab. for Memory and Learning, Brain Science Inst.; Pres. Int. Brain Research Org. 1980–86 (Hon. Pres. 1987–), Int. Union of Physiological Sciences 1994–, Fed. of Asian and Oceanian Physiological Societies 1990–; mem. Gen. Cttee and Exec. Bd Int. Council for Science (ICSU) 1984–; mem. Science Council of Japan 1988–, (Pres. 1994–), Prime Minister's Council for Science and Tech. 1994–, Japan Neuroscience Soc. (Pres. 1983–); mem. Japan Acad.; Foreign mem. Royal Swedish Acad. of Science, Royal Soc., Armenian Acad. of Science, Russian Acad. of Science; Order of Culture 1996; hon. science degree (Univ. of Southern California) 1995, (Torino Univ.) 1996; Fujiwara Prize 1981, Academy Prize and Imperial Prize 1986, Robert Dow Neuroscience Award 1993, IPSEN Foundation Award 1993, Person of Cultural Merit 1994, Japan Prize 1996, Gruber Neuroscience Prize, The Peter and Patricia Gruber Foundation (co-recipient) 2006. *Achievements include:* discovered inhibitory action of cerebellar Purkinje cells and characteristic synaptic plasticity, long-term depression in these cells; developed theory that cerebellum is a general learning machine for acquiring not only motor skills but also implicit memory in thought. *Publications:* The Cerebellum as a Neuronal Machine (with J. C. Eccles and J. Szenthgothai) 1967, The Cerebellum and Neural Control 1984; more than 90 scientific papers in professional journals on brain chemistry. *Address:* RIKEN Brain Science Institute, 2-1 Hirosawa, Wako City, Saitama 351-0198, Japan (office). *Telephone:* (48) 462-1111 (office). *Fax:* (48) 462-4914 (office). *E-mail:* ito-BSI@brain.riken.jp (office). *Website:* www.brain.riken.jp/en/m_ito.html (office).

ITO, Masatoshi; Japanese retail executive; *Founder and Honorary Chairman, Ito-Yokado Group;* m.; three c.; ed Yokohama City Univ.; Founder and Hon. Chair. Ito-Yokado Co. Ltd (now Ito-Yokado Group) with Seven-Eleven Japan and Denny's Japan brands. *Address:* Ito-Yokado Co. Ltd, 1-4, Shibakoen 4-chome, Minato-ku, Tokyo 105-8571, Japan (office). *Telephone:* (3) 3459-2111 (office). *Fax:* (3) 3459-6873 (office). *Website:* www.itoyokado.iyg.co.jp (office).

ITO, Takanobu; Japanese automotive industry executive; *President, CEO and Representative Director, Honda Motor Company;* joined Honda Motor Co. in 1978, began career as engineer designing chassis, was in charge of developing frame structure for NSX sports car (went on sale 1990), Exec. Vice-Pres. Honda R&D Americas, Inc. 1998–2000, helped develop first sport-utility vehicle under Acura brand 1998–2000, Dir Honda R&D Co. Ltd 2000–, Sr Man. Dir 2001–03, Man. Dir 2003–04, Pres. and Dir Honda R&D Co. Ltd 2003–04, Motor Sports 2003–04, Gen. Supervisor, Motor Sports 2004–05, Gen. Man. Suzuka Factory of Production Operations 2005–07, Man. Officer 2005–07, COO for Automobile Operations 2007–09, Sr Man. Dir and Head of Core Automaking Operations, Honda Motor Co. 2007–09, Rep. Dir 2007–, Pres. and CEO 2009–. *Address:* Honda Motor Company, 2-1-1 Minami-Aoyama, Minato-ku, Tokyo 107-8556, Japan (office). *Telephone:* (3) 3423-1111 (office). *Fax:* (3) 5412-1515 (office). *E-mail:* info@honda.com (office). *Website:* www.honda.co.jp (office); world.honda.com (office).

ITO, Tatsuya, LLB; Japanese politician; b. 6 July 1961, Tokyo; ed Faculty of Law, Keio-Gijuku Univ.; Researcher, Matsushita Inst. of Govt and Man. 1984–87; Visiting Researcher, Grad. School of Public Policy and Admin, Calif.

State Univ., USA 1987–88; Sec.-Gen. Japan–US Tech. Exchange Programme 1988–93; elected to House of Reps 1993–, Dir Cttee on Commerce and Industry 1993–96, Parl. Under-Sec. for Int. Trade and Industry 2000, Dir Cttee on the Environment 2000–01, Dir Cttee on Economy, Trade and Industry 2001–02, Sr Dir Cttee on Economy, Trade and Industry 2002; Acting Dir Science and Tech. Div., Liberal Democratic Party (LDP) 1999–2000, Dir of Economy, Trade and Industry Div. 2000–01, Sec. Admin Reform Promotion HQ 2000–01, Sec.-Gen. Select Comm. on e-Japan Priority Programme 2001–02; Sr Vice Minister for Financial Services 2002–03, Sr Vice Minister for Financial Services and for Econ. and Fiscal Policy 2003–04, Minister of State for Financial Services 2004–05. *Address:* c/o Liberal-Democratic Party–LDP (Jiyu-Minshuto), 1-11-23, Nagata-cho, Chiyoda-ku, Tokyo 100-8910, Japan (office).

ITO, Toyo; Japanese architect; *Owner, Toyo Ito & Associates;* b. 1941; ed Tokyo Univ.; began career with Kiyonori Kikutake Architects and Assocs 1965; est. studio Urban Robot (Urbot), Tokyo 1971 (renamed Toyo Ito and Assocs 1979); fmr Guest Prof., Columbia Univ., New York, USA; Hon. Prof., Univ. of N London, UK, Hon. Diploma of the Architectural Asscn 2003; AA Interarch '97' Grand Prix Gold Medal, Union of Bulgarian Architects 1997; Art Encouragement Prize, Ministry of Educ. 1998; Arnold W. Brunner Memorial Prize, American Acad. of Arts and Letters 2000; Gold Prize, Japanese Good Design Award 2001; Golden Lion for Lifetime Achievement Award, Venice Biennale 2002, XX AOI Compasso d'Ore Award 2004. *Architectural works include:* White U 1976, Silver Hut (Architecture Inst. of Japan Award 1986) 1984, A Dwelling for the Tokyo Nomad Woman 1985, Tower of Winds 1986, Egg of Winds 1991, Yatsushiro Municipal Museum (33rd Mainrich Art Award 1992) 1991, Old People's Home, Yatsushiro 1994, Sendai Mediatheque (multi-resource public cultural centre), Sendai 2001, Brugge 2002 Summer Pavilion, Serpentine Gallery, London 2002, Codan Shinonome Canal Court (Block 2) 2003, Matsumoto Performing Arts Centre 2004. *Publication:* Toyo Ito Architetto 2001. *Address:* Toyo Ito & Associates, Architects, Fujiya Building, 1-19-4, Shibuya, Shibuya-ku, Tokyo, 150-0002, Japan (office).

ITZIK, Dalia, BA; Israeli teacher and politician; b. 20 Oct. 1952, Jerusalem; m.; three c.; ed Hebrew Univ. of Jerusalem, Interdisciplinary Centre, Herzliya, Efrata Teachers Seminary, Jerusalem; Vice-Prin. Katznelson School, Jerusalem 1974–82; Acting Chair. Jerusalem Teachers Union 1982–88; fmr Deputy Mayor of Jerusalem in charge of Educ.; mem. Bd of Govs Israel Broadcasting Authority 1988–91, Bd of Jerusalem Theatre, Gerard Behar Centre 1990–91; mem. Cen. Cttee of the Labour Party 1985–91; mem. Knesset 1992–, served in Finance Cttee 1992–96, Educ. and Culture Cttee 1992–99 (Chair. 1995–96), Cttee on Status of Women 1992–99; Chair. Special Cttee for Research and Scientific Technological Devt 1997–99; Minister of the Environment 1999–2001, of Industry and Trade 2001–02, of Communications 2005; Speaker of the Knesset 2006–09, Acting Pres. (while Israeli prosecutors decide whether to bring charges of rape and sexual assaults against Pres. Mishe Katsav) 2007–09; mem. Kadima party 2006–. *Address:* The Knesset, HaKiryah, Jerusalem, 91950, Israel (office). *Telephone:* 2-6753444 (office). *Fax:* 2-6496193 (office). *E-mail:* dizik@knesset.gov.il (office). *Website:* www.knesset.gov.il (office).

IUE, Satoshi, BEng; Japanese electronics industry executive; *Adviser, Sanyo Electric Company Ltd;* b. 28 Feb. 1932; s. of the late Toshio Iue; ed Doshisha Univ.; joined Sanyo Electric Co. Ltd 1956, Dir 1961–, Man. Dir 1968–72, Exec. Man. Dir 1972–85, Exec. Vice-Pres. 1985–86, Pres. and CEO 1986–92, Chair. and CEO 1992–2005, Exec. Dir and Chair. 2006, now Adviser; Chair. Osaka Symphonic Asscn 1991–, Ashiya Cosmopolitan Asscn 1993–, Kansai New Business Conf. 1996; Vice-Chair. Japan-China Asscn on Economy and Trade 1995–, Osaka Chamber of Commerce and Industry 1995–; Dir Fed. of Econ. Orgs, Kansai Econ. Fed.; Hon. Citizen of Dalian, China 1995, Tarlac, Philippines 1996, Hefei, China 1997; Darjah Dato' Paduka Mahkota Perak, Malaysia; Hon. LLD (Boston Univ. School of Man.) 1990, Hon. DSc (Dalian Univ.) 1995; numerous awards and honours including Nat. Medal of Honor for Philanthropy 1970, Nat. Medal of Honor for Contrib. to Devt of Industry 1992. *Address:* Sanyo Electric Company Limited, 5-5 Keihan-Hondori, 2-chome, Moriguchi City, Osaka 570-8677, Japan (office). *Telephone:* (6) 6991-1181 (office). *Fax:* (6) 6991-6566 (office). *Website:* www.sanyo.co.jp (office).

IUE, Toshimasa, MBA; Japanese electronics industry executive; s. of Satoshi Iue, grands of the late Toshio Iue; ed Konan Univ., Boston Univ., USA; joined Sanyo Electric Co. 1989, Exec. Vice Pres., also Div. Man. of Group Marketing and CEO Sanyo Consumer Group, Commercial Group, Int. Group, and Components Group 2002-05, Chief Marketing Officer 2003–05, Exec. Dir, Pres. and COO Sanyo Electric Co. 2005–07 (resgnd); mem. Boston Univ. Bd of Trustees 2004–; Boston Univ. Alumni Award for Distinguished Service 2003. *Address:* c/o Sanyo Electric Company, 2-5-5 Keihan-Hondori, Moriguchi 570-8677, Japan (office).

IURES, Marcel; Romanian actor; *Founder and Artistic Director, Theatre ACT;* b. 2 Aug. 1951, Bailesti; ed Inst. of Theatrical Arts and Cinematography; film debut in Vis de ianuarie (January Dream) 1978; comedian Bulandra and Odeon Theatres, Bucharest 1980–94; performed title role in Richard III, Bucharest and London, UK 1994; Founder and Artistic Dir Theatre ACT (ind. theatre), Bucharest 1998–. *Films include:* Vis de ianuarie (January Dream) 1978, Sa mori ranit din dragoste de viata (To Die from Love of Life) 1983, Domnisoara Aurica 1985, Vacanta cea mare (The Great Vacation) 1988, Cei care platesc cu viata (Those Who Pay with Their Lives) 1991, Balanta (The Oak) 1992, Un été inoubliable (An Unforgettable Summer) 1994, Interview with the Vampire 1994, Somnul insulei (Sleep of the Island) 1994, Mission Impossible 1996, The Peacemaker 1997, Faimosul paparazzo (The Famous Paparazzo) 1999, Elite 2000, I Hope 2001, Amen 2002, Hart's War 2002, Dracula the Impaler (voice) 2002, 3 pazeste 2003, Cambridge Spies (TV) 2003, The Tulse Luper Suitcases, Part 2: Vaux to the Sea 2004, The Cave 2005, Isolation 2005, Project W 2005, Goal! 2005, Isolation 2005, Logodnicii din America 2007, Pirates of the Caribbean: At World's End 2007, Youth Without Youth 2007. *Address:* Theatre ACT, Calea Victoriei 126, sector 1, Bucharest, Romania (office). *Telephone:* (1) 3103103 (office). *Fax:* (1) 3103103 (office). *E-mail:* act@teatrulact.ro (office); info@teatrulact.ro (office). *Website:* www.teatrulact.ro (office).

IVANCHENKO, Aleksander Vladimirovich, DJur; Russian lawyer and politician; *Head, Russian Centre for the Studies of Voting Technologies, Central Electoral Commission;* b. 8 Jan. 1954, Krasnodar; m.; one d.; ed Higher School of Ministry of Internal Affairs; worked in Moscow militia forces; Lecturer, Higher School of Ministry of Internal Affairs 1983–88; on staff Supreme Soviet Russian Fed. 1988–93; Deputy Chair. Cen. Electoral Comm. of Russian Fed. 1993–96, Chair. 1996–99, Head, Russian Centre for the Studies of Voting Technologies; Founder and Dir Inst. of Election Tech. Studies 1999–; mem. State Duma/JCP faction 1999–; Chair. Cttee on Fed. Affairs 2000–07. *Publications:* papers and articles on problems of political rights and freedom, on election law. *Leisure interests:* tennis, walks in the countryside. *Address:* Russian Centre for the Studies of Voting Technologies, Central Electoral Commission, 9 B. Cherkasskii per., 109012 Moscow (office); State Duma, Okhotny Ryka 1, 103265 Moscow, Russia. *Telephone:* (495) 606-79-57 (office); (495) 292-97-75. *Fax:* (495) 292-51-40. *Website:* www.cikrf.ru (office).

IVANENKO, Sergei Victorovich, CandEcon; Russian politician and economist; *Deputy Chairman, Yabloko Russian Democratic Party (Rossiisskaya demokraticheskaya partiya 'Yabloko');* b. 12 Jan. 1959, Zestafoni, Georgia; ed Lomonosov Moscow State Univ.; researcher and Asst Prof., Moscow State Univ. 1985–90; Chief Expert State Comm. on Econ. Reform RSFSR Council of Ministers 1994–96; Researcher, Cen. of Econ. and Political Studies 1991–92; mem. State Duma 1993–, Chair. Cttee on Property, Privatisation and Econs 1993–95, mem. Cttee on Ecology 1995–99; currently Deputy Chair. Yabloko Russian Democratic Party (Rossiisskaya demokraticheskaya partiya 'Yabloko'), Chair. Moscow Yabloko; Vice-Pres. Russian Chess Fed. 2003–. *Address:* Yabloko Russian Democratic Party (Rossiisskaya demokraticheskaya partiya 'Yabloko'), 119034 Moscow, per. M. Levshinskii 7/3, Russia (office). *Telephone:* (495) 201-43-79 (office). *Fax:* (495) 292-34-50 (office). *E-mail:* admin@yabloko.ru (office). *Website:* www.yabloko.ru (office).

IVANENKO, Maj.-Gen. Victor Valentinovich; Russian intelligence officer (retd) and business executive; *Chairman, Arctic Trade and Transport Company;* b. 19 Sept. 1947, Koltsovka, Tyumen region; m.; three c.; ed Tyumen State Industrial Inst., Higher KGB Courses; mem. staff KGB, Tyumen region 1970-86, Sr Inspector, Head of Div., Deputy Head of Dept USSR KGB 1986-91, Chair. RSFSR KGB 1991; Dir-Gen., with rank of Minister, Russian Agency of Fed. Security 1991-1992; Vice-Pres., then First Vice-Pres. YUKOS Jt Stock Oil Co. 1993–98; adviser Ministry of Taxation and Revenues 1998-99; mem. Bd of Dirs. ROSPROM Jt Stock Co. 1996; Vice-Pres. Foundation for Devt of Parliamentarianism in Russia 2000–03; Chair. Arctic Trade and Transportation Co. (ATTC Joint Stock Co.) 2003–; mem. Supervisory Bd Russia-ASEAN Collaboration Fund; Presidium Mem. Nat. Cttee on cooperation with law-enforcement, legislative and law authorities, Independents Civil Society; mem. Foreign and Defence Policy Council; mem. Otechestvo Movt; mem. Moscow English Club; Order Red Star, 6 medals. *Address:* Arctic Trade and Transport Company, 21A Obrazcova str., 127018 Moscow, Russia (office). *Telephone:* (495) 737-31-41 (office). *E-mail:* attk@mail.ru (office). *Website:* www.attk.ru (office).

IVANIĆ, Mladen, MA, PhD; Bosnia and Herzegovina politician, economist and academic; *Chairman, Party of Democratic Progress of Republika Srpska;* b. 16 Sept. 1958, Sanski Most, Bosnia; m.; two c.; ed Faculties of Econs, Banja Luka and Belgrade, Univ. of Meinheim, Germany and Univ. of Glasgow, UK; journalist Radio Banja Luka 1981–85; Asst Prof. of Political Economy, Faculty of Econs, Banja Luka 1985–88, Docent 1988–, Head of Post-Grad. Study of Reconstruction and Transition (held in conjunction with Univs of Bologna, Sussex and LSE); Teacher Faculty of Econs, Sarajevo 1990–92; Teacher Faculty of Econs, Srpsko Sarajevo 1992–98; Lecturer Univ. of Glasgow, UK 1998; mem. Presidency of Yugoslav Repub. of Bosnia and Herzegovina 1988–91; Founder and Chair. Party of Democratic Progress 1999–; mem. Govt Econ. Council 1999; Prime Minister of Serb Repub. of Bosnia and Herzegovina Jan. 2001–03; Minister of Foreign Affairs, Council of Ministers of Bosnia and Herzegovina 2003–05 (resgnd); Head Deloitte & Touche Consultancy Office –2001; mem. Editorial Bd Ideje magazine, Belgrade 1988–91, Aktuelnosti magazine, Banja Luka 1998–99; Del. to OSCE sessions 1991; participant World Forum, Davos, Switzerland 1999, 2000; Pres. Serb Intellectual Forum. *Publications include:* Political Economy, Principles of Political Economy; numerous contribs to newspapers and magazines including Savremenost (Modernity), Pregled (Overview), Ideje (Ideas), Opredjeljenja (Determinations), Lica (Faces), Aktuelnosti (Updates); author or co-author of several programmes for World Bank, UNDP and other int. orgs. *Address:* Party of Democratic Progress of Republika Srpska (PDP), 78000 Banja Luka, ul. Prvog Krajiškog Korpusa 130, Bosnia and Herzegovina (office). *Telephone:* (51) 346210 (office). *Fax:* (51) 300956 (office). *E-mail:* pdp@blic.net (office). *Website:* www.pdp-rs.org (office).

IVANIŠEVIĆ, Goran; Croatian fmr professional tennis player; b. 13 Sept. 1971, Split; s. of Srdjan Ivanišević and Gorana Ivanišević; one d.; won US Open Jr doubles with Nargiso 1987; turned professional 1988; joined Yugoslav Davis Cup squad 1988; semi-finalist, ATP World Championship 1992; bronze medal, men's doubles, Barcelona Olympic Games 1992; runner-up, Wimbledon Championship 1992, 1994, 1998; winner Wimbledon Championship 2001; winner of numerous ATP tournaments, including Kremlin Cup, Moscow 1996;

winner of 22 tours singles and nine doubles titles, and over US $19 million prize money; once ranked No. 2 in the world, behind Pete Sampras; retd 2004; now playing on Masters Tennis (sr) tour; Founder and Pres. Children in Need Foundation 1995–; BBC Overseas Sports Personality of the Year Award 2001. *Leisure interests:* football, basketball, reading, music, cinema.

IVANOV, Gjorge; Macedonian political scientist, academic, politician and head of state; *President-Elect;* b. 2 May 1960, Valandovo; m. Maja Ivanova; two c.; ed secondary school in Valandovo; activist in League of Socialist Youth of Yugoslavia –1990; Pres.-Elect of Macedonia April 2009–, Pres. and Supreme Commdr of the Army 12 May 2009–; fmr Visiting Prof. in Greece. *Publications:* (in Macedonian): Civil Society, Democracy in the Divided Societies: The Macedonian Model, Current Political Theories, Political Theories – Antiquity. *Address:* Office of the President, 1000 Skopje, 11 Oktomvri bb, Former Yugoslav Republic of Macedonia (office). *Telephone:* (2) 3113318 (office). *Fax:* (2) 3112147 (office). *E-mail:* n.rakidziev@president.gov.mk (office). *Website:* www.president.gov.mk (office); www.ivanov.com.mk.

IVANOV, Igor Sergeyevich; Russian diplomatist and politician; b. 23 Sept. 1945, Moscow; m.; one d.; ed Moscow Pedagogical Inst. of Foreign Languages; Jr researcher Inst. of World Econs and Int. Relations, USSR Acad. of Sciences 1969–73; diplomatic service 1973–; Second, then First Sec., Counsellor, Counsellor-Envoy USSR Embassy, Spain 1973–83; expert First European Dept, Ministry of Foreign Affairs 1983–84; Counsellor of Minister 1984–85; Asst Minister 1985–86; Deputy Chief, then Chief of Dept 1987–92; Chief Gen. Sec., mem. of Bd 1989–91; Russian Amb. to Spain 1991–93; First Deputy Minister of Foreign Affairs 1994–98, Minister of Foreign Affairs 1998–2004; Perm. mem. Security Council of Russia 1998–, Sec. 2004–07; Lecturer, Moscow State Inst. of Int. Relations 2007–; Co-Chair. EU-Russia Co-operation Council 1998–; Orders For Services to the Fatherland (2nd, 3rd and 4th Degrees); Order of Honour; Hon. Dr of Historical Science. *Publications:* New Russian Diplomacy 2001, External Russian Policy in the Epoch of Globalization 2002, Global Security in the Epoch of Globalization: Russia in Global Policy 2003, Russia in the Contemporary World: Responses for the Challenges of the 21st Century 2004; numerous papers and articles. *Address:* Moscow State Institute of International Relations, 119454 Moscow, pr. Vernadskogo, 76, Russia (office). *Telephone:* (495) 434-00-89 (office). *Fax:* (495) 434-90-66 (office). *E-mail:* inf@mgimo.ru (office). *Website:* www.mgimo.ru (office).

IVANOV, Ivan Dmitriyevich, DEcon; Russian diplomatist, politician and economist; *Deputy Director, Institute of Europe, Russian Academy of Sciences;* b. 1934, Moscow; m.; two c.; ed Moscow Inst. of Foreign Trade; Head of Div., Inst. of USA and Canada, USSR (now Russian) Acad. of Sciences 1971–76, Deputy Dir, Prof., Inst. of World Econs and Int. Relations 1977–86, Deputy Dir Inst. of Europe, Russian Acad. of Sciences 2001–; Deputy Chair. State Cttee for Foreign Econ. Relations, USSR Ministry of Foreign Affairs, also Chair. USSR State Comm. on Foreign Econ. Orgs 1986–91; Deputy Dir Inst. of Foreign Econ. Research 1991–94; Russian Trade Rep. to Belgium 1994–96, Deputy Perm. Rep. to EU, Brussels 1996–99; Deputy Minister of Foreign Affairs 1999–2001. *Address:* Institute of Europe, Russian Academy of Sciences, 11-3B, Mokhovaya Street, 125993 Moscow, Russia (office). *Telephone:* (495) 203-41-87 (home). *Fax:* (495) 609-92-98 (office). *E-mail:* europe@ieras.ru (office). *Website:* www.ieras.ru (office).

IVANOV, Mikhail Vladimirovich; Russian microbiologist; *Director, Department of Microbial Biogeochemistry and Biogeotechnology, Institute of Microbiology, Russian Academy of Sciences;* b. 6 Dec. 1930; m.; ed Moscow State Univ.; researcher, Inst. of Microbiology, USSR (now Russian) Acad. of Sciences, later Head of Lab. and Deputy Dir Inst. of Biochemistry and Physiology of Plants and Micro-organisms, later Dir Dept of Microbial Biogeochemistry and Biogeotechnology, Inst. of Microbiology 1984–; Ed.-in-Chief Microbiology journal; Corresp. mem. USSR (now Russian) Acad. of Sciences 1981, mem. 1987; research in geochemistry activities of microorganisms and biotechnology, marine microbiology, global ecology and biogeochemistry; S. Vernadsky Prize. *Leisure interest:* coin collecting. *Address:* Department of Microbial Biogeochemistry and Biogeotechnology, Institute of Microbiology, Russian Academy of Sciences, 60-letiya Oktyabrya pr., 7 kor. 2, 117811 Moscow, Russia (office). *Telephone:* (495) 135-11-71 (office); (495) 299-65-30 (home). *E-mail:* ivanov@inmi.host.ru (office). *Website:* www.inmi.ru (office).

IVANOV, Lt-Gen. Sergei Borisovich; Russian politician; *Deputy Chairman of the Government;* b. 31 Jan. 1953, Leningrad (now St Petersburg); m.; two s.; ed Leningrad State Univ., Yu V. Andropov Inst. at KGB; various posts in KGB including missions abroad 1976–97; Deputy Dir Fed. Service of Security, 1998–2001; Head, Dept of Analysis, Prognosis and Strategic Planning 1998–99; Sec. Security Council of Russian Fed. 1999–2001; Minister of Defence 2001–07, Deputy Chair. of the Govt 2005–07, 2008–, First Deputy Chair. 2007–08; Order for Services to the Fatherland (2nd Class) 2003. *Leisure interests:* fishing, reading detective stories in English and Swedish. *Address:* Office of the Government, Krasnopresnenskaya nab. 2, 103274 Moscow, Russian Federation (office). *Telephone:* (495) 205-57-35 (office). *Fax:* (495) 205-42-19 (office). *Website:* www.government.ru (office).

IVANOV, Vadim Tikhonovich; Russian biochemist; b. 18 Sept. 1937; s. of Tikhon Timofeevitch Ivanov and Lidia Ivanovna Ivanova; m. Raisa Alexandrovna Ivanova (née Osadchaya); one s. one d.; ed Moscow State Univ.; Jr, Sr Researcher, Head of Lab., Deputy Dir, Dir Shemyakin-Ovchinnikov Inst. of Bioorganic Chem., Russian Acad. of Sciences; Corresp. mem. USSR (now Russian) Acad. of Sciences 1976, mem. 1987–, mem. Presidium; research in chem. of proteins and peptides, structure and functions of neuropeptides, synthetic vaccines; Lenin Prize, USSR State Prize, Russian Govt Prize. *Publications include:* Membrane Active Complexones 1974, The Way to

Protein Synthesis 1982. *Leisure interests:* chess, nature. *Address:* Institute of Bioorganic Chemistry, Russian Academy of Sciences, Miklukho-Maklay str. 16/10, 117997 Moscow, Russia (office). *Telephone:* (495) 330-56-38 (office). *Fax:* (495) 330-56-92 (office). *E-mail:* ivavt@mail.ibch.ru (office). *Website:* www.ibch.ru (office).

IVANOV, Col Viktor Petrovich; Russian administrator; *Adviser to the President;* b. 12 May 1950, Novgorod; m.; one s. one d.; ed Leningrad Bonch-Bruyevich Electrical Inst. of Communications; engineer, Scientific-Production co. Vektor 1971–77; employee in nat. security orgs rising to Head of Div., Dept of Fed. Service of Security of St Petersburg and Leningrad region 1977–94, Head of Dept 1998, Deputy Dir, concurrently Head of Dept of Econ. Security 1999–2000; Head of Admin, Office of Mayor of St Petersburg 1994–98; Deputy Head of Admin, Office of the Pres. 2000–04; Adviser to the Pres. 2004–; participated in mil. operations in Afghanistan 1987–94; Medal for Mil. Service. *Address:* Administration of President of Russian Federation, Staraya pl. 4, 103132 Moscow, Russia (office). *Telephone:* (495) 206-34-17 (office).

IVANOV, Vladimir; Bulgarian physician; b. 6 June 1923, Simeonovgrad; s. of Boris Ivanov and Maria Ivanova; m. Liliana Kirova 1948; one s.; ed Univ. of Sofia, Acad. of Medical Sciences, Moscow, USSR and Univ. of London, UK; Deputy Dir Scientific Psychoneurological Inst., Sofia 1956–63; Asst Prof. and Head Dept of Psychiatry and Medical Psychology, Varna 1963–67, Prof. 1967–85; Deputy Rector Higher Medical Inst., Varna 1964–66, Rector 1966–72; Dir Scientific Inst. of Neurology, Psychiatry and Neurosurgery, Medical Acad. Sofia and Head, First Psychiatric Clinic 1985–88; Ed.-in-Chief Neurology, Psychiatry and Neurosurgery 1987–91; Adviser, Medical Univ., Sofia 1988–; Pres. Bulgarian Scientific Soc. of Psychosomatic Medicine 1989; mem. Admin. Bd Union of Scientific Medical Socs of Bulgaria 1991–95; mem. Council, Neurosciences and Behaviour Foundation 1991–; Ed.-in-Chief Psychosomatic Medicine 1993–; mem. Bulgarian Nat. Acad. of Medicine 1995–; several awards and medals. *Publications:* some 16 monographs and numerous articles in professional journals. *Leisure interests:* philosophy, poetry. *Address:* Medical University, 1 Psychiatric Clinic, Sofia 1431 (office); Praga 26, Sofia 1606, Bulgaria (home). *Telephone:* (2) 52-03-33 (office); (2) 52-42-68 (home).

IVANOV, Vyacheslav Vsevolodovich, DPhil; Russian philologist, translator and academic; *Professor, Slavic Languages and Literatures and Professor, Indo-European Studies Program, Department of Slavic Languages and Literature, University of California at Los Angeles;* b. 21 Aug. 1929, Moscow; s. of Vsevolod Vyacheslavovich Ivanov; m.; one s.; ed Moscow State Univ., Univ. of Vilnius; Dir Library of Foreign Literature, Moscow 1991–94; People's Deputy of the USSR 1989–91; Dir Inst. of World Culture 1990–94; Prof., Dept of Slavic Languages and Literatures, UCLA 1994–; Ed.-in-Chief Baltic and Slavic Studies 1980–, Elementa: Journal of Slavic Studies and Comparative Cultural Semiotics 1992–; mem. Int. Editorial Bd Interdisciplinary Journal of Germanic Linguistics and Semiotic Analysis 1996–; mem. Advisory Bd Eisenstein Center of Cinema Cultural Studies 1993–; mem. Council of Scholars, Library of Congress 1990–, Russian Acad. of Natural Sciences 1991–, Russian PEN Club 1992–, American Acad. of Arts and Sciences 1993–, Russian Acad. of Sciences 2000–; Fellow, Latvian Acad. of Arts and Sciences 1993–, American Philosophical Soc. 1994–; Foreign Fellow, British Acad. 1977–; Hon. mem. American Linguistics Soc. 1968; Lenin Prize 1988, Best Zvezda Publication, St Petersburg 1995. *Publications:* works on Indo-European linguistics, Slavic and general linguistics, semiotics, including: Indo-European, Praslavic and Anatolian Linguistic Systems 1965, Slavic Linguistic Modelling Systems (with V. Toporov) 1965, Studies in the Field of Slavic Antiquities (with V. Toporov) 1974, Indo-European Language and Indo-Europeans Vols 1-2 (with T. Gamrekelidze) 1984, Balkan Peninsula in the Mediterranean Context 1986, The Ethnolinguistics of the Text 1988, The Category of Passivity in Slavic and Balkan Languages 1989, Novelties in Linguistics 1990, The Hittite Language 2001; ed. works on Balto-slavic spiritual culture. *Address:* Department of Slavic Languages and Literatures and Indo-European Studies Program, UCLA, 2514 Hershey Hall, Box 951502, Los Angeles, CA 90095-1502, USA (office). *Telephone:* (310) 825-6397 (office). *Fax:* (310) 206-5263 (office). *E-mail:* ivanov@ucla.edu (office). *Website:* www.humnet.ucla.edu/humnet/slavic (office).

IVANOVA, Ludmila Nikolayevna, MD; Russian physiologist; *Head of Laboratory, Institute of Cytology and Genetics, Siberian Branch, Russian Academy of Sciences;* b. 10 Feb. 1929, Novosibirsk; ed Novosibirsk Inst. of Medicine; Head of Lab., Inst. of Cytology and Genetics, Siberian br., Russian Acad. of Sciences 1971–; Corresp. mem. Russian Acad. of Sciences 1991, mem. 1997–; main research in the hormonal regulation of water–salt metabolism and kidney function; L.A. Orbeli Award, Russian Acad. of Sciences. *Publications:* contribs to journals include (with N. N. Melidi) Effects of vasopressin on hyaluronate hydrolase activities and water permeability in the frog urinary bladder, in Pflugers-Archiv European Journal of Physiology, Vol. 443, No. 1, 2001; (with others) Brain serotonin metabolism during water deprivation and hydration in rats, in Neuroscience and Behavioural Physiology, Vol. 31, No. 3, 2001. *Leisure interests:* music, cookery. *Address:* Institute of Cytology and Genetics, Akademika Lavretyeva prosp. 10, 630090 Novosibirsk 90, Russia (office). *Telephone:* (3833) 30-74-74 (office); (3833) 30-79-02 (home). *Fax:* (3833) 33-12-78 (office). *E-mail:* ludiv@bionet.nsc.ru (office). *Website:* www.bionet.nsc.ru/ICIG (office).

IVANOVIĆ, Predrag, DOec.; Montenegrin politician and academic; b. 10 Oct. 1954, Danilovgrad; m.; three c.; ed Univ. of Montenegro, Podgorica; Research Fellow, Inst. for Social and Econ. Research 1978–; Asst, then Assoc., then full Prof., Univ. of Montenegro Faculty of Econs 1993–, fmr Vice-Dean for Scientific Research and Head of Business Econs Dept, twice elected as Dean of Faculty of Econs, twice elected as Vice-Pres. of the Univ. of Montenegro;

Minister of Educ. and Science, Govt of Repub. of Montenegro 2001–03, of Int. Econ. Relations 2003–06. *Publications:* several books and research papers. *Address:* c/o Ministry of International Economic Relations, 11070 Belgrade, Bulevar Mihaila Pupina 2, Serbia (office).

ĪVĀNS, Dainis; Latvian politician; *Chairman, Latvian Social Democratic Workers' Party;* b. 25 Sept. 1955, Madona; s. of Evalds Ivans and Ilga Ivans; m. Elvira Chrschenovitch 1979; two s. two d.; ed Latvian Univ.; school teacher and journalist; Reporter Latvian TV 1980–85; organized opposition to hydro-electric scheme nr Daugavpils 1986; Ed. School and Family magazine 1986–88; Pres. of Latvian People's Front 1988–90; USSR People's Deputy 1989–90; mem. Latvian Supreme Soviet 1990–, Vice-Chair. 1990–91; currently Chair. Latvian Social Democratic Workers' Party; Gen. Sec. Latvian Comm. of UNESCO 1992–; Sec. Writers Union 1994–; Chair. Riga Council Culture, Art and Religion Cttee 2001–; Deputy Head, Latvian Literature Museum; Best Journalist of the Year, Latvian Journalistic Union 1987. *Publications:* six books. *Leisure interests:* Oriental philosophy, literature, fishing. *Address:* Bruninieku Str. 89, Apt 6, Riga, Latvia. *Telephone:* (2) 323142 (office); (2) 274644 (home).

IVANTER, Ernest Viktorovich; Russian biologist and academic; *Professor and Chairman, Department of Zoology and Ecology, Petrozavodsk University;* b. 15 Nov. 1935, Moscow; s. of Victor S. Ivanter and Irina F. Riss; m. Tatyana Matusevich 1960; one s. one d.; ed Moscow K. Timiryazev Acad. of Agric.; jr researcher, Kivach Karelian Br. USSR Acad. of Sciences 1958–60; jr researcher, Inst. of Biology, Karelian Br. of USSR Acad. of Sciences 1960–63; Asst, Docent, Prof., Dean Petrozavodsk Univ. 1965–; Chair. Dept of Zoology and Ecology, Petrozavodsk Univ. 1987–; Corresp. mem. USSR (now Russian) Acad. of Sciences 1991; mem. Scientific Council for Biological Fundamentals of Protection and Rational Use of Fauna; mem. US Zoological Soc.; Hon. mem. Finnish Soc. of Teriologues. *Publications include:* Population Ecology of Small Mammals 1975, Adaptive Peculiarities of Mammals 1985, Fauna of Karelia 1988, Statistical Methods for Biologists 1992, Zoogeography 1993, Territorial Ecology of Shrews 2002; numerous articles in scientific journals on ecology, biocenology, morphophysiology and evolutional ecology of animals. *Leisure interests:* books, sport, tourism. *Address:* Room #327, Petrozavodsk University, Krasnoarmeiskaya str. 31, 185910 Petrozavodsk (office); ul. Anohina la Kv. 5, 185035 Petrozavodsk, Russia (home). *Telephone:* (8142) 78-17-41 (office); (8142) 78-21-08 (home). *Fax:* (8142) 76-38-64 (office). *E-mail:* ivanter@psu.karelia.ru (office). *Website:* www.karelia.ru/psu/Chairs/zool_e.html (office).

IVANY, J. W. George, MA, PhD; Canadian academic and fmr university president; *President Emeritus, University of Saskatchewan;* b. 26 May 1938, Grand Falls, Newfoundland; s. of Gordon Ivany and Stella Skinner; m. Marsha Gregory 1983; one s. three d.; ed Memorial Univ. of Newfoundland, Columbia Univ., New York and Univ. of Alberta; Head of Science Dept, Prince of Wales Coll., St John's, Newfoundland 1960–63; Grad. Teaching Fellow, Univ. of Alberta 1963–64, Asst Prof. of Elementary Educ. 1965–66; Asst Prof. of Natural Science, Teachers Coll., Columbia Univ. 1966–68, Assoc. Prof. 1968–74, Head, Dept of Science Educ. 1972–74; Visiting Fellow, Inst. of Educ., Univ. of London, UK 1972–73; Dean and Prof., Faculty of Educ., Memorial Univ. of Newfoundland 1974–77; Dean and Prof., Faculty of Educ., Simon Fraser Univ. 1977–84, Vice-Pres. (Academic) 1984–89; Pres. and Vice-Chancellor, Univ. of Sask. 1989–99, Pres. Emer. 1999–; Chair. Bd Nat. Inst. of Nutrition 1995–98; mem. Bd of Dirs Cameco Corpn 1999–, Western Garnet Int., Canada West Foundation; Chair. Bd of Govs Okanagan Univ. Coll., Kelowna, BC 2001–04; Chair. Ivany Comm., Grenfell Coll., Memorial Univ. 2005; Hon. LLD (Memorial Univ. Newfoundland) 1991, (Univ. of Chernivtsi, Ukraine). *Publications include:* High School Teaching: A Report on Current Practices 1972, Today's Science: A Professional Approach to Teaching Elementary School Science 1975, Who's Afraid of Spiders: Teaching Science in the Elementary School 1988; textbooks; articles in professional journals. *Address:* c/o Board of Directors, Cameco Corporation, 2121 11th Street West, Saskatoon, Sask., S7M 1J3, Canada.

IVANYAN, Eduard Aleksandrovich, DHist; Russian journalist and political scientist; *Editor-in-Chief, USA and Canada: Economics, Politics and Culture, Institute for USA and Canadian Studies, Russian Academy of Sciences;* b. 4 June 1931, Tbilisi, Georgia; two d.; ed Moscow State Inst. of Int. Relations; mem. staff, Ministry of Culture 1955–60, UN Secr., Geneva and New York 1961–71; Head of Sector, Prof., Inst. for USA and Canadian Studies, USSR (now Russian) Acad. of Sciences 1971–, Ed.-in-Chief USA and Canada: Economics, Politics and Culture (monthly journal) 1998–; Prof., State Univ. for Humanitarian Sciences 2000–; Order of the Friendship of Nations; Distinguished Scholar of the Russian Fed. 1999. *Publications:* more than 100 scientific publs, including 25 books on the history of USA, presidential power in USA, Russian (Soviet)-American relations, Russian-American cultural relations, including 'Istoriya SShA.' Uchebnoye posobiye. 2 e izdaniye, pererabotannoye (The History of the USA: A Study Aid, 2nd edn, revised) 2006, U istokov sovetsko-amerikanskikh otnoshenii, fevral 1917 g.-yanvar 1924 g. (Among the Sources of Soviet-American Relations, February 1917 to January 1924) 2006, Reader on US History (ed.) 2005, Inaugural Speeches of US Presidents (ed.) 2001), John F. Kennedy's 'Profiles in Courage' (trans. and ed.) 2005, David Rockefeller's 'Memoirs' (ed. of Russian trans.) 2003, When Muses Speak – History of Russian-American Cultural Relations 2007. *Address:* USA–Canada Journal, Khlebny per. 2/3, 121814 Moscow, Russia (office). *Telephone:* (495) 690-46-80 (office). *Fax:* (495) 609-95-07 (office). *E-mail:* edivanian@yahoo.com (office). *Website:* www.iskran.ru (office).

IVASHOV, Col-Gen. Leonid Grigoryevich, CandHistSc; Russian business executive and security officer; b. 1943, m.; ed Tashkent Commdr School, M. Frunze Mil. Acad.; army service 1964, various positions 1964–76; with cen. staff, Ministry of Defence 1976–, Head Admin. Dept 1987–92; Sec. Council of Defence Ministers, CIS Countries 1992–96; Head of Dept, Int. Mil. Co-operation 1996–2001, Head of Staff, Co-ordination of Mil. Co-operation, CIS Countries 1999–2001; Adviser to Minister of Defence 2001–03; mem. Leadership, Great Russia–Eurasian Union electoral bloc, State Duma elections 2003; Chair. Soyuz russkogo naroda (Russian People's Union) 2006–; Vice-Pres. Acad. of Geopolitics 2002–; Order Red Star; six medals. *Address:* Ministry of Defence, ul. Myasnitskaya 37, 105175 Moscow, Russia (office). *Telephone:* (495) 293-38-54 (office). *Fax:* (495) 296-84-36 (office). *Website:* www.mil.ru (office); www.ivashov.ru.

IVE, Jonathan, CBE, BA; British designer; *Senior Vice-President of Industrial Design, Apple Inc.;* b. 1967, London; ed Newcastle Polytechnic; Co-founder and Pnr, Tangerine (design consultancy), London 1989; Designer, Apple Inc., Cupertino, Calif. 1992, Dir of Design 1996, then Vice-Pres. of Industrial Design, now Sr Vice-Pres.; Dr hc (Northumbria Univ.) 2000; winner of design influence polls by Creative Review, the BBC and Q magazine; RSA student design awards 1988, 1989, RSA Medal for Design Achievement 1999, apptd RSA Designer for Industry 2003, Design Museum Designer of the Year 2003, RSA Benjamin Franklin Medal 2005, Royal Acad. of Eng. Pres.'s Medal 2005, Design and Art Direction (D&AD) Pres.'s Award 2005. *Designs include:* bathroom fittings, electrical appliances, computers (including iMac 1998, iPod 2001). *Address:* Apple, 1 Infinite Loop, Cupertino, CA 95014, USA (office). *Telephone:* (408) 996-1010 (office). *Website:* www.apple.com (office).

IVERSEN, Leslie Lars, BA, PhD, FRS; British pharmacologist, academic and business executive; *Chairman, ACADIA Pharmaceuticals, Inc.;* b. 31 Oct. 1937; s. of Svend Iversen and Anna Caia Iversen; m. Susan Diana Iversen (née Kibble) 1961; one s. one d. (one d. deceased); ed Cambridge, Harkness Fellow, USA; with Nat. Inst. of Mental Health and Dept of Neurobiology, Harvard Medical School 1964–66; Locke Research Fellow of Royal Soc., Dept of Pharmacology, Cambridge 1967–71, Dir MRC Neurochemical Pharmacology Unit 1971–82; Exec. Dir Merck, Sharp and Dohme Neuroscience Research Centre 1982–95; Visiting Prof., Dept of Pharmacology, Univ. of Oxford 1995–96, Visiting Prof. of Pharmacology 1996–99; Visiting Prof. of Pharmacology, Univ. of Oxford 1995–, Imperial Coll. School of Medicine 1997–; Prof. of Pharmacology and Dir Wolfson Centre for Age-Related Diseases, King's Coll., London 1999–2004; Founder and Dir Panos Therapeutics Ltd (pharmaceutical co.); mem. Bd of Dirs ACADIA Pharmaceuticals, Inc. 1998– (Chair. 2000–), NsGene A/S; mem. Scientific Advisory Bd Lectus Therapeutics Ltd, NeuroTargets Ltd., Neurome, Inc.; Fellow, Trinity Coll., Cambridge 1964–84; Foreign Assoc., NAS 1986. *Publications:* The Uptake and Storage of Noradrenaline in Sympathetic Nerves (with S. D. Iversen) 1967, Behavioural Pharmacology 1975, The Science of Marijuana 2000, A Very Short Introduction to Drugs 2001. *Leisure interests:* reading, gardening. *Address:* ACADIA Pharmaceuticals, Inc., 3911 Sorrento Valley Blvd., San Diego, CA 92121, USA (office). *Telephone:* (858) 558-2871 (office). *Fax:* (858) 558-2872 (office). *E-mail:* info@acadia-pharm.com (office). *Website:* www.acadia-pharm.com (office).

IVERSON, Allen; American professional basketball player; b. 7 June 1975, Hampton, Va; m. Tawanna; two s. two d.; ed Bethel High School, Hampton Univ., Georgetown Univ., Washington, DC; shooting guard; played at Georgetown Univ. 1994–96; selected by Philadelphia 76ers with first overall pick in 1996 Nat. Basketball Asscn (NBA) draft, traded to Denver Nuggets 2006–08, to Detroit Pistons 2008–; career scoring average of nearly 28 points per game is third best in NBA history; one of only 30 players to score more than 20,000 career points; scored 40 points in a game for 50th time versus Seattle 19 Feb. 2004; served as a Co-Capt. for Team USA Olympic Games, Athens, Greece 2004, won bronze medal and led team in scoring (13.8 points per game); named to All-Star Team ten times, named Most Valuable Player (MVP) of All-Star Game 2001, 2005; NBA MVP 2001; f. Cross-Over Foundation 2000. *Leisure interest:* drawing. *Address:* c/o Detroit Pistons Basketball Company, 5 Championship Drive, Auburn Hills, MI 48326, USA. *Telephone:* (248) 377-0100. *Fax:* 9248) 377-3260. *Website:* www.nba.com/pistons; www.crossoverfoundation.org.

IVERSON, Ann; American retail executive and consultant; *President and CEO, International Link, Inc.;* b. 1944; d. of John Earl Van Eenenaam and Dorothy Ann Knight; m. 4th (divorced); one s. one d.; ed Arizona State Univ.; with Bullock's Dept Store, LA, Harzfield's, Kansas City, T.H. Mandy, Va; Operating Vice-Pres. Bloomingdale's (two main brs) 1984; Sr Vice-Pres. of Stores, Regional Vice-Pres. Bonwit Teller, New York 1989–90; joined Storehouse (UK retailer group) 1989, Stores Dir British Home Stores (BHS), Chief Exec. Mothercare; Pres. and CEO Kay-Bee Toys; Group CEO Laura Ashley 1995–97; Founder, Pres. and CEO International Link, Inc., Scottsdale, Ariz. (consulting firm) 1998–; Chair. Brooks Sports 2000–04; consultant, Financo Global Consulting Group, New York; mem. Bd of Dirs Owens Corning Inc. 1996–, Candie's, Inc. 2001–; mem. Bd of Trustes Thunderbird School of Int. Man.; mem. Whitney & Co. Advisory Bd; Ellis Island Medal of Honor, Retailer of the Year (UK). *Address:* International Link, Inc., 8100 Camelback Road, #170, Scottsdale, AZ 85251, USA. *Telephone:* (480) 874-0186.

IVEY, Susan M., BS, MBA; American tobacco industry executive; *Chairman, President and CEO, Reynolds American Inc.;* ed Univ. of Florida and Bellarmine Univ., Louisville, Ky; sales rep., Brown & Williamson Tobacco Corpn (subsidiary of British American Tobacco—BAT) 1981, held various trade and brand positions, including Div. Man. and Brand Dir, Marketing Dir for BAT in China 1994–96, returned to Brown & Williamson in 1999, later Sr Vice-Pres. Marketing and mem. Exec. Cttee, Pres. and CEO Brown & Williamson Tobacco Corpn 2001–04, Pres. and CEO Reynolds American Inc. (following merger with R.J. Reynolds Tobacco Holdings Inc.) 2004–, Chair. 2006–, Chair. and CEO R.J. Reynolds Tobacco Co. 2004–08; mem. Exec. Cttee

Bellarmine Univ. and Greater Louisville Inc.; Campaign Chair. Greater Metro United Way of Louisville 2003; mem. The Committee of 200 (int. org. of women CEOs, entrepreneurs and business leaders), Women's Leadership Initiative for the United Way of America; mem. Bd Winston-Salem YWCA, Bd Bellarmine Univ., Wake Forest Univ., Univ. of Florida Foundation; mem. Advisory Bd of Dirs Wachovia Forsyth Co., Bd of Advisors for Center for Women in Business and Econs at Salem Coll.; ranked by Fortune magazine amongst 50 Most Powerful Women in Business in the US (36th) 2004, (24th) 2005, (20th) 2006, (24th) 2007, ranked by Forbes magazine amongst 100 Most Powerful Women (61st) 2006, (42nd) 2007, (81st) 2008. *Address:* Reynolds American Inc., 401 N Main Street, PO Box 2990, Winston-Salem, NC 27102-2990, USA (office). *Telephone:* (336) 741-5500 (office). *Fax:* (336) 741-4238 (office). *Website:* www.reynoldsamerican.com (office).

IVORY, James Francis, MFA; American film director; b. 7 June 1928, Berkeley, Calif.; s. of the late Edward Patrick Ivory and Hallie Millicent De Loney; ed Univs of Oregon and Southern California; began to work independently as a film maker 1952; dir, writer and cameraman in first films; co-f. (with the late Ismail Merchant) Merchant Ivory Productions 1962; has collaborated on screenplay of numerous films with author Ruth Prawer Jhabvala (q.v.); Guggenheim Fellow 1974; BAFTA Fellowship 2002; Commdr des Arts et des Lettres 1995; D. W. Griffith Award (Dirs Guild of America) 1995. *Films:* documentaries: Venice, Theme and Variations 1957, The Sword and the Flute 1959, The Delhi Way 1964; feature films: The Householder 1963, Shakespeare Wallah 1965, The Guru 1969, Bombay Talkie 1970, Savages 1972, The Wild Party 1975, Roseland 1977, The Europeans 1979, Quartet 1981, Heat and Dust 1983, The Bostonians 1984, A Room with a View 1986, Maurice 1987, Slaves of New York 1989, Mr and Mrs Bridge 1990, Howards End 1992, The Remains of the Day 1993, Jefferson in Paris 1995, Surviving Picasso 1996, A Soldier's Daughter Never Cries 1998, The Golden Bowl 2000, Le Divorce 2003, The White Countess 2005, City of Your Final Destination 2008; TV films: Adventures of a Brown Man in Search of Civilisation 1971, Autobiography of a Princess 1975 (also published as a book 1975), Hullabaloo over Georgie and Bonnie's Pictures 1978, The Five Forty-Eight 1979, Jane Austen in Manhattan 1980. *Leisure interest:* looking at pictures. *Address:* Merchant Ivory Productions, 250 West 57th Street, New York, NY 10107 (office); 18 Patroon Street, Claverack, NY 12513, USA. *Telephone:* (212) 582-8049 (office); (518) 851-7808 (home). *E-mail:* assistant@merchantivory.com (office).

IVRY, David, BS; Israeli business executive and diplomatist; *President, Boeing Israel;* b. 20 Sept. 1934, Tel-Aviv; m. Ofra Ivry; three s.; ed Technion-Israel Inst. of Tech., Haifa; Chief Rep. US–Israel Strategic Dialogue 1986–89; Dir-Gen. Ministry of Defence 1986–96, Prin. Asst Minister of Defence for Strategic Affairs 1996–99; Head, Nat. Security Council 1999, Nat. Security Adviser to Head of Nat. Security Council 1999–2000; Amb. to USA 2000–02; Pres. Boeing Israel 2003–; Chair. Elul Asia and Global Outsourcing Services 2002–03; Head of Inter-Ministerial Steering Cttee on Arms Control and Regional Security of the Middle East Peace Process 1992–99; Head of Israeli Del. to Multilateral Working Group on Arms Control and Regional Security 1992–99; mem. Bd of Dirs El-Al 1978–82, Israel Aircraft Industries 1982–92 (Chair. 1983, 1985–86); mem. Bd of Govs Technion, Haifa 1987–; Maj.-Gen., Commdr Israel Air Force 1977–82, Israeli Defence Forces Deputy Chief of Staff 1983–85; Legion of Merit (USAF), Distinguished Service Order (Singapore); Kt Commdr's Cross, Order of Merit (FRG); Dr hc (Bar-Ilan), (Technion, Haifa); Amitai Distinction Award for Ethical Admin and Conduct, Israel. *Address:* 6 Hazamir Street, Ramat Hasharon 47226 (home); The Boeing Company, The Museum Tower, 4 Berkowitz Street, Tel-Aviv 64238, Israel (office). *Telephone:* (3) 5406085 (home); (3) 7776100 (office). *Fax:* (3) 5499183 (home); (3) 7776101 (office). *E-mail:* david.e.ivry@boeing.com (office). *Website:* www.boeing.com (office).

IWAN, Dafydd, BArch; British politician, singer-composer and record company director; *President, Plaid Cymru;* b. (Dafydd Iwan Jones), 24 Aug. 1943, Brynaman, Wales; s. of Rev. Gerallt Jones and Elizabeth Jane Jones; m. 1st Marion Thomas 1968 (divorced 1986); two s. one d.; m. 2nd Bethan Jones 1988; two s.; ed Aman Valley Grammar School, Ysgol Ty Tan Domen, Y Bala, Univ. Coll. of Wales, Aberystwyth and Welsh School of Architecture, Cardiff; f. Sain (Recordiau) Cyf (now Wales' leading record co.) 1969; Man. Dir 1984–; f. Tai Gwynedd Housing Asscn 1971; Founder-Trustee, Nant Gwrtheyrn Language Centre 1975; Chair. Welsh Language Soc. 1968–71; parl. cand. 1974, 1983, 1984; Chair. Plaid Cymru (Nationalist Party of Wales) 1982–84, Vice-Pres. 1984–95, Pres. 2003–; Plaid Cymru mem. of Gwynedd Unitary Authority 1995–; Chair. Planning and Economic Devt Cttee, Cyngor Gwynedd Council 1995–, mem. Exec. Cttee responsible for Planning, Highways and Environment 1999–; Trustee, Portmeirion Foundation; nonconformist lay preacher; has promoted the Welsh language and culture for four decades; Hon. mem. Gorsedd of Bards for services to Welsh language; Hon. Fellow Univ. of Wales, Bangor and Aberystwyth 1998; Hon. LLD (Univ. of Wales) 2004; Gold Disc for services to Welsh music. *Music:* composed, sung and recorded about 250 songs; over 40 records, cassettes, CDs and video of live concert 1965–; numerous concert tours abroad. *Television:* Yma Mae Ngân, S4C (three series introducing own songs), documentaries on various countries. *Publications:* Dafydd Iwan (autobiog.) 1982, 100 O Ganeuon (collection of songs) 1983, Caneuon Dafydd Iwan (2nd collection of songs) 1991, Cân Dros Gymru (new autobiog.) 2002. *Leisure interests:* composing songs, sketching, reading. *Address:* Plaid Cymru—Party of Wales, Tŷ Gwynfor, 18 Park Grove, Cardiff, CF10 3BN, Wales (office); Sain, Canolfan Sain, Llandwrog, Caernarfon, Gwynedd, LL54 5TG (office); Carrog, Rhos-Bach, Caeathro, Caernarfon, Gwynedd, LL55 2TF, Wales (home). *Telephone:* (29) 2064-6000 (office); (1286) 676004 (home); 7961-098311 (Mobile). *Fax:* (29) 2064-6001 (office); (1286) 676004 (home). *E-mail:* post@plaidcymru.org (office); dafydd@sain.wales.com

(office); dafyddiwan@cymru1.net (home). *Website:* www.plaidcymru.org (office); www.sain.wales.com (office); www.dafyddiwan.com (home).

IWASAKI, Yoichi, BS, MS, PhD; Japanese theoretical physicist, university administrator and academic; *President, University of Tsukuba;* b. 12 Sept. 1941; ed Univ. of Tokyo; Asst, Research Inst. for Fundamental Physics, Kyoto Univ. 1969–72; Postdoctoral Fellow, Dept of Physics, CUNY, USA 1972–75; Asst Prof., Inst. of Physics, Univ. of Tsukuba 1975–76, Assoc. Prof. 1976–77, Prof. 1984–, Vice-Pres. (Research), Univ. of Tsukuba 1998–2004, Pres. Univ. of Tsukuba 2004–; mem. Inst. for Advanced Study, Princeton, USA 1977; mem. Physical Soc. of Japan; Nishina Memorial Prize, Nishina Memorial Foundation 1994. *Publications:* numerous publs on high-energy physics, in particular large-scale numerical study of quantum chromodynamics and the devt of massively parallel computers for computational physics. *Address:* Office of the President, University of Tsukuba, 1-1-1 Tennodai, Tsukuba-shi, Ibaraki -ken 305-8577, Japan (office). *Telephone:* (29) 853-2111 (office). *Fax:* (29) 853-2059 (office). *E-mail:* koryuka@sakura.cc.tsukuba.ac.jp (office). *Website:* www.tsukuba.ac.jp (office).

IYENGAR, B(ellur) K(rishnamachar) S(undara Raja), FRCP; Indian yoga teacher; *Founder, Ramamani Iyengar Memorial Yoga Institute;* b. 14 Dec. 1918, Bellur, Kolar Dist, Karnataka; s. of Sri Krishnamachar; m. Shrimati Ramamani Iyengar 1943 (died 1973); one s. five d.; introduced to yoga by his brother-in-law Guru Sri T. Krishnamacharya in Mysore 1934; gave several demonstrations of yoga and successfully completed a yoga teaching assignment at Dharwar for faculty mems of Karnataka Coll. 1936; yoga instructor, Deccan Gymkhana 1937–40; taught yoga to Shri J. Krishnamurthi 1948–68; introduced by violinist Yehudi Menuhin to the West and made numerous visits world-wide to promote yoga 1954–; developed his own system of yoga which has gained a worldwide following; laid foundation stone for Yoga Inst. in Pune 1973 (renamed the Ramamani Iyengar Memorial Yoga Inst. after his wife who died three days after the dedication), Hon. Pres. Iyengar Yoga Asscns world-wide; gave lecture-demonstration at Harvard Coll., Philadelphia which inspired creation of monumental sculpture 'After Iyengar' 1976; invited by UK Dept for Educ. to participate in Festival of India, London 1982; inaugurated Iyengar Yoga Inst., London 1984; first Int. Iyengar Yoga Convention held in San Francisco 1984; invited by Jacques Chirac, Mayor of Paris, to Festival of India in France 1985; conducted Mega Classes for his 75th birthday in USA (750 students), Canada (250 students), Bombay (300 students), Bangalore (300 students) 1993, more than 1,050 dels representing 33 countries were present in Mega Glass taught at Crystal Palace, London 1993; also conducted yoga classes organized by Govt UP at Rishikesh 1994, 1995, 1996; has given more than 15,000 demonstrations of yoga and numerous lectures and radio and TV interviews; hundreds of Iyengar Yoga Centres give training in his method of yoga world-wide, including his native India (with centres in Bangalore, Bombay, Delhi, Madras, Dehra Dun, Rishikesh, etc.), Argentina, Australia, Austria, Belgium, Canada, Czech Repub., Chile, Denmark, France, Germany, Ireland, Israel, Italy, Japan, Kenya, Korea, Lestho, Malaysia, Mauritius, Mexico, Morocco, the Netherlands, New Zealand, Poland, Slovenia, Russia, S Africa, Sri Lanka, Swaziland, UK, USA, Ukraine, Uzbekistan, Zimbabwe; involved in social, cultural, educational and health-promotion projects for the poor of India; Fellow, Int. Council of Ayurveda 1991; Padmasri, Govt of India 1991, Priyadarshani 2000, Swasthya Seva Ratna 2000, Padmabhushan 2002; Hon. DSc (Medicina Alternativa Inst., affiliated to Open Int. Univ. for Complementary Medicine, Colombo, Sri Lanka) 1991, (Mysore) 1997; Hon. DLitt (Tilak Maharashtra Vidyapeeth, Pune) 2002; Dr hc (Medicina Alternativa Inst.) 2003; earned title of Yogi Raja from Swami Shivananda of Rishikesh 1952, Yoganga Shikshaka Chakravati 1962, Yogi Ratna Award 1981, 2002, Rajyotsava Award 1988, Patanjali Award, Govt of Karnataka 1990, All India Vasistha Award 1991, Purna Swasthya Award, World Fed. of Socs of Holistic Medicine 1991, Gold Medal for Outstanding Contrib. in the Field of Yoga Educ., All India Bd of Alternative Medicine 1991, felicitated by Pune Municipal Corpn and presented with a Scroll of Honours 1991, Puma Swasthya Award, 4th Congress of World Fed. of Socs of Holistic Medicine (Italy) 1991, honoured with Shri Krishnanugraha Prashasti Patra by Jagadguru Shri Madhya Mula Matha Mahasamstanam 1992, Pune Pride Gold Medal, Residency Club 1992, Punya Bhushan Award, Tridal, Pune and Gem of Alternative Medicine, All India Bd of Alternative Medicine 1995, Health Care for 1996 Award, Top Management Club (India) Pune Chapter 1996, Vipra Ratna, Karnataka Brahman Mahasabha 1997, title of Arsa-Kula-Sresthah conferred upon him by Arsa Vidya Gurukulam for his achievements in introducing yoga all over the world 1998, Jeevan Sadhana Gaurav, Pune Univ. for his lifetime achievement in the field of yoga, Cyan Kalyan Charitable Award, Sri Murli Manohar Joshi HRD & S&T Minister, Govt of India 1999, conferred with title Abhinava Patanjali Maharsh by Sri Chaitanya Vaishnava Vardhini Sabha 1999, Rotary Excellence Award, Rotary Club of Kothrud 1999, Swami Vivekanand Puruskar Award, Acharya Kishore Vyas 1999, Best Citizen of India Award, International Publishing House, New Delhi 1999, 2000, Eminent Personalities of India, Int. Biographical Research Foundation of India 1999, Yoga Dron Award offered to Guruji as a Millennium Honour for being the Greatest Yoga Exponent, World Yoga Soc. 31st Dec. 1999, Hall of Fame Award, Int. Publishing Centre 2000, 2000 Millennium Medal of Achiever, Int. Inst. of Success of Awareness 2001, Priyadarshni Acad. Award for Lifetime Achievement in the field of Yoga 2000, Swasthya Seva Ratna, Int. Inst. of Health Sciences, Calcutta 2000, honoured by Sharada Jnana Pitam as one of ten eminent people who have crossed 80 and with the Rishi Award 2001, Yoga Ratna Award, Mumbai Citizens 2002, Yoga Panchajanya Pithamaha Award, village people of Bellur (his birthplace) 2002, awarded Guru Mahatama Puruskar and a cash award of As 5000/- from Kai. Sri. Laxmibai Smt. Laxmibhai Daghaduseth Halwai Shri. Sansthan Dutt Mandir Trust

2002, Rising Personalities of India Award and Gold Medal, Int. Penguin Publishing House 2002, Yoga Bhaskara Award, Samskrita Acad., Chennai 2002, Jewel of India Award, Int. Inst. of Educ. and Man., Delhi 2003, Life Time Achievement Award, Nat. and Int. Compendium 2003, Vidya Vyas Award, Vidya Sahakari Bank, Pune 2003, included in list of most powerful and influential people in the world, compiled by Time Magazine (category of Heroes & Icons) 2004, Industrial Tech. Foundation Award for extraordinary achievement in his chosen field of activity 2004, felicitated by Karnataka Legislature Council 2004, felicitated by Ajit Kumar Memorial Yoga Research Centre Students of Yoga Center for his outstanding contrib. 2004, felicitated by Maharashtriya Mandal, Pune and awarded As 10,000/- for outstanding achievement 2004, Indira Gandhi Excellence Award, Indian Solidarity Council, New Delhi 2005, Rajdhani Rattan Gold Medal Award, Int. Inst. of Educ. and Man. 2005, Suryadatta Life Time Achievement Award, Suryadatta Group of Insts, Pune 2005, Yoga Shikshana Puraskar Award, Shri. Raghavendra Anugraha and cash prize of Rs 5000/- from HH Sri. Sri. Sri. Sushvendra Swamiji 2005, Bharati Jeevan Sadhana Gaurav Puraskar, Bharati Vidyapeeth, Pune 2005, Golden Life Time Achievement Award, Industrial Tech. Foundation, Delhi 2005, Kasba Ganapati Award and a shawl from Sri. Sri. Ravi Shankar 2006, Puruskar Medal, Pune 2006, Yogiraj of the Millennium Award, Inst. of Educ. Research and Devt in asscn with the 'Global Institutes' 2007, Rising Personalities of India Award and Gold Medal, Int. Penguin publishing House 2007. *Achievements:* Ministry of Fed. Star Registration (USA) announced that a star in the northern hemisphere had been named after Yogacharya B.K.S. Iyengar Aug. 1988; 'Iyengar' now officially recognized by the Oxford English Dictionary 2003 (defines Iyengar: noun (mass noun) a type of Hatha Yoga focusing on the correct alignment of the body, making use of straps, wooden blocks, and other objects as aids to achieving the correct postures; ORIGIN: named after B.K.S. Iyengar (born 1918), the India yoga teacher who devised this method). *Publications include:* Light on Yoga (hailed as the "Bible of Yoga" and has been translated into 14 Indian and foreign languages; more than a million copies sold) 1966, Light on Pranayama (translated into 12 languages) (winner first cash prize of Rs 5000/- at 16th Nat. Prize Competition for published literature on Physical Educ., Sports, Yoga and Health as the Best Book in Hindi 1991) 1981, The Art of Yoga 1985, The Tree of Yoga 1988, Light on the Yoga Sutras of Patanjali 1993, Light on Astanga Yoga 1999, Astadala Yogamala Vols 1–6 2000–06, Yoga: The Path to Holistic Health 2001, Yog Sarvansathi (in Marathi) 2001, Light on Life 2005. *Leisure interests:* listening to music, drama. *Address:* Ramamani Iyengar Memorial Yoga Institute, 1107 B/1 Hare Krishna Mandir Road, Model Colony, Shivaj Nagar, Pune 411 016, Maharashtra, India (office). *Telephone:* (20) 25656134 (office). *E-mail:* info@bksiyengar.com (office). *Website:* www.bksiyengar.com (office).

IZMEROV, Nikolay Fedotovich, MD, CandMedSci, PhD; Russian medical official and physician; *Director, Institute of Occupational Health, Russian Academy of Medical Sciences;* b. 19 Dec. 1927, Frunze, Kyrgyzstan; ed Tashkent Medical School and Moscow Cen. Inst. for Advanced Medical Training; worked as doctor in Khavast rural areas, Tashkent Dist; Postgraduate training, Moscow 1952–53; Sr Insp. USSR Ministry of Health 1953–55; Postgraduate training (Municipal Hygiene) 1955–58; doctor in Moscow City Sanitary Epidemiological Station 1956–59; Deputy Dir (Int. Health), Dept of External Relations, USSR Ministry of Health 1960–62; Vice-Minister of Health of RSFSR and Chief Sanitary Insp. 1962–64; Asst Dir-Gen. WHO 1964–71; Dir Inst. of Occupational Health of the USSR (now Russian) Acad. of Medical Sciences 1971–; Corresp. mem. Russian Acad. of Medical Sciences 1980, mem. 1986, Acad.-Sec. Dept of Preventive Medicine 1990–; Order of the Red Banner of Labour (twice), Order of October Revolution, Order for Merit to Home Country (4th Degree) 1997, (3rd Degree) 2002; Merited Scientist of Russia. *Publications:* author or co-author of 20 reference books, monographs, manuals and more than 350 scientific papers in the field of occupational hygiene and industrial ecology etc.; Chief Ed. Russian Encyclopaedia of Occupational Health 2005. *Leisure interest:* theatre, music, art. *Address:* Research Institute of Occupational Health, Russian Academy of Medical Sciences, 31 Prospekt Budennogo, 105275 Moscow, Russia (office). *Telephone:* (495) 365-02-09 (office). *Fax:* (495) 366-05-83 (office). *E-mail:* izmerov@rinet.ru (office). *Website:* www.niimt.ru (office).

IZRAEL, Yury Antonievich, DPhys-MathSc; Russian geophysicist, ecologist and meteorologist; *Director, Institute of Global Climate and Ecology, Russian Academy of Sciences;* b. 15 May 1930, Tashkent; s. of Antony I. Izrael and Antonina S. Shatalina; m. Elena Sidorova 1958; one s. one d.; ed Tashkent State Univ.; engineer, Research Assoc., Geophysics Inst. of USSR Acad. of Sciences 1953–63; Deputy Dir, Dir of Inst. of Applied Geophysics 1963–70; First Deputy Head of Main Admin. of Hydrometeorological Service of USSR 1970–74, Head 1974–78; Corresp. mem. USSR (now Russian) Acad. of Sciences 1974, mem. 1994, Acad.-Sec., Dept of Oceanography, Atmospheric Physics and Geography 1996–2002; mem. Russian Acad. of Ecology 1994–, Pres. 2000–; Chair. USSR State Cttee for Hydrometeorology and Environmental Control 1978–88; Chair. USSR State Cttee for Hydrometeorology 1988–91, Dir Research Inst. of Global Climate and Ecology 1990–; Deputy to Supreme Soviet 1979–89; Sec. and First Vice-Pres. WMO 1975–87; Vice-Chair. Intergovernmental Panel on Climate Change 1992–; mem. Int. Acad. of Astronautics 1990; Hon. mem. Int. Radiological Union 1999; State Prize in the field of Environment 1981, Gold Medal of USSR Acad. of Sciences in the field of Ecology 1983, Fedorov's Environmental Prizes 1984, 1991, 1997, Gold Medal (per Chernobyl) of Int. Centre 'Ettore Majorana' (Italy) 1990, Gold Medal of Soviet State Exhbn 1991, UN-UNEP Sasakawa Environmental Prize 1992, Gold Medal and Prize of Int. Meteorological Org. 1992, Renowned Scientist of the Russian Fed. 1996, mem. of team sharing Nobel Peace Prize with Al Gore 2007; seven state orders. *Publications:* Peaceful Nuclear Explosions and Environment 1974, Ecology and Control of Environment 1979, Global Climatic Catastrophes 1986, Anthropogenic Climate Change 1987, Anthropogenic Ecology of the Ocean 1989, Chernobyl: Radioactive Contamination of the Environment 1990, Earth's Ozone Shield and its Changes (co-author) 1992, Radioactive Fallout after Nuclear Explosions and Accidents 1996; and numerous other scientific books and articles. *Leisure interests:* organ music, mountaineering, philately. *Address:* Institute of Global Climate and Ecology (IGCE), Glebovskaya str. 20B, 107258 Moscow (office); Department of Earth Sciences, Russian Academy of Sciences, Leninsky pr. 32A, 117993 Moscow (office); Apt 84, Romanov per. 3, 84, Moscow, Russia (home). *Telephone:* (495) 169-24-30 (IGCE) (office); (495) 938-14-63 (office). *Fax:* (495) 160-08-31 (IGCE) (office); (495) 938-18-59 (office). *E-mail:* yu.izrael@g23.relcom.ru (office). *Website:* www.igce.comcor.ru (office).

IZRAELEWICZ, Erik, DEcon; French journalist; *Editor-in-Chief, La Tribune;* b. 6 Feb. 1954, Strasbourg; ed Haute Ecole de Commerce, Centre de Formation des Journalistes and Univ. de Paris I; journalist, L'Expansion 1981–85; Banking Finance Ed. Le Monde 1986–88, Head of Econ. Service 1989–92, Deputy Ed.-in-Chief 1992–94, New York Corresp. 1993–94, Econs Reporter, Europe 1994–95, leader writer 1994, Ed.-in-Chief 1996–2000; Ed.-in-Chief Les Echos 2000–08, La Tribune 2008–. *Address:* La Tribune, 51 rue Vivienne, 75095 Paris, Cedex 02, France. *Telephone:* 1-44-82-16-16 (office). *E-mail:* directiondelaredaction@latribune.fr (office). *Website:* www.latribune.fr (office).

IZUMI, Shinya; Japanese politician; b. 1 Aug. 1937, Yoshii, Fukuoka; ed Kyushu Univ.; previously worked as official at transport ministry; mem. House of Councillors (Upper House) 1992–, has held numerous govt posts including Sr State Sec. of Transport, Sr Vice-Minister of Economy, Trade and Industry, Sr Vice-Minister of Land, Infrastructure and Transport; Chair. Nat. Public Safety Comm. and Minister of State for Disaster Man. and Food Safety 2007–08 (resgnd); mem. LDP (Liberal Democratic Party), left party 1993, rejoined 2003. *Address:* Liberal-Democratic Party (LDP), 1-11-23, Nagata-cho, Chiyoda-ku, Tokyo 100-8910, Japan (office). *Telephone:* (3) 3581-6211. *E-mail:* koho@ldp.jimin.or.jp (office). *Website:* www.jimin.jp (office).

IZZO, Lucio; Italian economist, academic and financial executive; b. 5 April 1932, Rome; m. Marga Berg; two d.; ed Univ. of Oxford, UK and Massachusetts Inst. of Tech., USA; Econ. Research Dept, Bank of Italy 1958–60, 1962–63; Rockefeller Fellow, Dept of Econs, MIT 1960–62; Asst Prof. of Econs, Univ. of Rome 1963–66; Assoc. Prof., then Prof. of Econs, Univ. of Siena 1966–74; Visiting Prof. of Econs, LSE 1971–72; Prof. of Econs, Univ. of Rome 1974–94; Econ. Adviser to Minister of the Budget 1974–78, to Minister of the Treasury 1980–82; Vice-Pres. and Vice-Chair. Bd of Dirs EIB 1982–94; mem. Bd of Dirs Efibanca Spa 1995–99, Società Interbancaria di Gestione 1996–98, Stet SpA 1997, Telecom Italia SpA; Italian Rep. OECD Working Party 3, Econ. Policy Cttee 1976–81; mem. American Econ. Asscn, American Finance Asscn, Econometric Soc.; Pres. of Italy's Gold Medal for studies in field of public finance 1978.

J

JAAFAR ALBAR, Datuk Seri Syed Hamid bin Syed; Malaysian lawyer and politician; *Minister of Home Affairs and Internal Security;* b. 15 Jan. 1944, Kampong Melayu Air Hitam, Penang; m. Datin Seri Sharifah Aziah bte Syed Zainal Abidin; three s. three d.; ed Monash Univ., Melbourne, Australia; Magistrate and Pres. of Sessions Court, Kuala Lumpur 1970–72; Head of Legal Dept, Bank Bumiputra Malaysia Bhd (BBMB) 1972, Legal Adviser and later Sr Man. 1972–78, Asst Sec. and Sec. to Man. 1974–79, first Gen. Man. of Bahrain Br. 1979–80, Gen. Man. of London Br., transferred to Kuala Lumpur as Head of Int. Banking Div. (Credit Supervision) 1980–82, Chief Gen. Man. and Sec. of the Bank 1985–86; Sec. Kewangan Bumiputra and Bank Pembangunan Malaysia Bhd 1976–79, Inst. of Bankers 1978–79; Dir and CEO Bumiputra Merchant Bankers 1982–85; Dir Koperasi Usaha Bersatu 1983–88, Kewangan Bumiputra Malaysia Bhd, Bumiputra Lloyds Leasing Bhd, Bumiputra Merchant Bankers, Syarikat Nominee Sdn Bhd, BBMB Properties 1985–86; Advocate and Solicitor-Gen. Pnr, Albar Zulkifly and Yap 1986–90; Chair. Shamelin Holdings 1989–90, Koperasi Shamelin Bhd 1989–90; MP for Kota Tinggi (Johor) 1990; Minister of Justice in Prime Minister's Dept (in charge of oil and gas affairs) 1990–92; Minister of Law and Minister in Prime Minister's Dept 1992–95; Minister of Defence 1995–99, of Foreign Affairs 1999–2008, of Home Affairs and Internal Security 2008–. *Address:* Ministry of Home Affairs (Kementerian Hal Ehwal Dalam Negeri), Blok D2, Parcel D, Pusat Pentadbiran Kerajaan Persekutuan, 62546 Putrajaya, Malaysia (office). *Telephone:* (3) 88863000 (office). *Fax:* (3) 88891613 (office). *E-mail:* azmi@mofa.gov.my (office). *Website:* www.moha .gov.my (office).

JA'AFARI, Bashar, BA, PhD; Syrian diplomatist; *Permanent Representative, United Nations;* b. 14 April 1956; m.; three c.; ed Damascus Univ., Univ. of Paris V-La Sorbonne, Univ. of Sharif Hedayatuallah, Jakarta; joined Ministry of Foreign Affairs 1980, Attaché and Third Sec., Embassy in Paris 1983–88; First Sec. and Counsellor, Perm. Mission to UN, New York 1991–94; Charge d'Affaires, Embassy in Jakarta 1998–2002; Dir Dept of Int. Orgs and Conferences 2002–04; Perm. Rep. to UN, Geneva 2004–06, to UN, New York 2006–. *Address:* Permanent Mission of Syria, 820 Second Avenue, 15th Floor, New York, NY 10017, USA (office). *Telephone:* (212) 661-1313 (office). *Fax:* (212) 867-3985 (office). *E-mail:* syria@un.int (office). *Website:* www.syria-un .org (office).

JAAFARI, Ibrahim al-, MD; Iraqi politician and physician; b. 1947, Karbala; ed Mosul Univ.; after medical school joined Islamic Dawa Party (Hizb ad-Da'wa al-Islamiya), Chief Spokesman 1966, remains leader; moved to Iran when Dawa party in Iraq was outlawed 1980, then to London 1989; fmr mem. Iraq Governing Council; Interim Vice-Pres. of Iraq 2004–05; Prime Minister of Iraq 2005–April 2006. *Address:* Islamic Dawa Party (Hizb ad-Da'wa al-Islamiya), Baghdad, Iraq (office). *E-mail:* info@islamicdawaparty.org (office). *Website:* www.islamicdawaparty.org (office).

JÄÄTTEENMÄKI, Anneli Tuulikki, LLM; Finnish politician; b. 11 Feb. 1955, Lapua; m. Jorma Melleri 1994; ed Univ. of Helsinki; acting lawyer, Office of the Local Authorities Negotiating Del. 1981–82; Temporary Asst, Ministry for Foreign Affairs 1982, Ministerial Political Adviser 1983–84; Legis. Sec. to Finnish Centre Party Parl. Faction 1986, mem. 1987–, Deputy Party Parl. Faction 1991–94, 1999–2000; mem. Parl. for Vaasa 1987–2003, for Helsinki 2003–; mem. Finnish Del. to the Nordic Council 1987–94; mem. Parl. Cttee for Constitutional Law 1987–99, Legal Affairs Cttee 1987–91, Electors Cttee 1987–91, Parl. Salary Del. 1987–92, Foreign Affairs Cttee 1999–, Parl. Grand Cttee 1999–2003; Deputy mem. Finance Cttee April–Nov. 1991, Defence Cttee April–May 1991, Foreign Affairs Cttee 1991–94; Minister of Justice 1994–95; Parl. Gov. Bank of Finland 1991–92, mem. Supervisory Council Parl. Govs Bank of Finland 1991–94, 1995–2003, Second Deputy mem. Parl. Trustees 1991–93, 1995–99, First Deputy mem. Parl. Trustees Sept.–Nov. 1993, 1999–2000, mem. Trustees 1993–94; mem. and Vice-Chair. Finnish Del. to Parl. Ass. of Council of Europe 1996–2003, Deputy mem. 2003–; mem. Commrs to Govt Guarantee Fund 1996–99; mem. Finnish Del. to WEU Parl. Ass. 1999–2003; Parl. Speaker March–April 2003, Speaker's Council April 2003, Chancellery Comm. Speaker April 2003; Prime Minister of Finland April–June 2003; mem. European Parl. 2004–; mem. Equal Opportunities Comm. 1987–91, Advisory Bd for Prison Affairs 1988–91 (Chair. 1991–94), Helsinki Inst. for Criminal Policy (HEUNI) 1996–; Deputy Chair. Paasikivi Soc. 1994–. *Publications:* Oikeus Voittaa (Justice Wins) 1999, Sillanrakentaja 2002. *Leisure interests:* history, literature, art, sports. *Address:* European Parliament, Rue Wiertz, ASP 096242, 1047 Brussels, Finland (office). *Telephone:* (2) 284-56-14 (office). *Fax:* (2) 284-96-14 (office). *E-mail:* anneli.jaatteenmaki@europarl.europa.eu (office). *Website:* www .annelijaatteenmaki (office).

JACAMON, Jean-Paul; French business executive; *Senior Adviser, COG-NETAS SA;* b. 5 Aug. 1947, Thaon-les-Vosges; m. Colette Jacquier; four c.; ed Ecole Polytechnique de Paris and Ecole des Mines de Paris; mem. staff Ministry of Industry 1975, sr civil servant, French Regional Land Use Planning Comm. (DATAR) –1981; Exec. Asst Groupe Schneider 1981, various positions with Spie Batignolles (electrical eng construction subsidiary) 1983–, Man. of 'Ferrière la Grande' plant, Vice-Pres. Eng and Gen. Contracting Div., Vice-Pres. Electric and Nuclear Power Div. 1988, Vice-Pres. responsible for electrical contracting activities, Chair. and CEO Spie-Trindel (local contracting for electrical and electromechanical projects) –1993, COO Spie Batignolles 1993–94; Exec. Vice-Pres. European Div., Schneider Electric 1995, COO 1996–2002, Vice-Chair. 1999–2002; ind. consultant 2002–; Chair. (non-exec.)

Bonna Sabla 2003–05, Gardiner 2003–06, CPI 2006–; Dir (non-exec.) AMEC PLC 2002–06, Péchiney 2002–04, Carbonne Lorraine 2003–, Alcan 2004–07; currently Sr Adviser, COGNETAS SA; Chevalier, Ordre nat. du Mérite 1994. *Leisure interests:* golf, bridge. *Address:* Marly conseil, 23 rue d'Aumale, 75009 Paris (office); 64 route de l'Etang la Ville, 78750 Mareil-Marly, France (home). *Telephone:* 1-56-68-97-83 (office). *Fax:* 1-39-16-89-21 (office). *E-mail:* jp .jacamon@wanadoo.fr (home).

JACK, Ian; British writer and journalist; b. 7 Feb. 1945, Farnworth, Lancs.; s. of Harry Jack and Isabella Jack (née Gillespie); m. 1st 1979; m. 2nd Rosalind Sharpe 1998; one s. one d.; newspaper journalist in Scotland 1960s; variously reporter, feature writer, Foreign Corresp., Sunday Times 1970–86; co-f. Independent on Sunday 1986, Ed. 1991–95; Ed. Granta magazine 1995–2007; currently writes for The Guardian newspaper; Journalist of the Year 1986, Editor of the Year 1992. *Publications include:* Before the Oil Ran Out 1987, The Crash that Stopped Britain 2001; various Granta anthologies. *Address:* The Guardian, 119 Farringdon Road, London, EC1R 3ER, England (office). *Telephone:* (20) 7278-2332 (office). *Fax:* (20) 7837-4530 (office). *E-mail:* ian .jack@guardian.co.uk (office); iangjack@blueyonder.co.uk (home). *Website:* www.guardian.co.uk (office).

JACK, James Julian Bennett, PhD, FRS, FRCP, FMedSci; New Zealand neurophysiologist; b. 25 March 1936, Invercargill; ed Univ. of Otago, Univ. of Oxford, UK; Rhodes Scholarship 1960–63; Foulerton Gift Researcher 1964–68; demonstrator, Univ. Lecturer then Reader, then Prof. of Cellular Neuroscience, Lab. of Physiology (now Dept of Physiology, Anatomy and Genetics), Univ. of Oxford 1968–; Fellow, Univ. Coll., Oxford, Acad. of Medical Sciences 1998–; Gov. Wellcome Trust 1987– (Deputy Chair. 1994–99); Hon. FRSNZ 1998; Hon. DSc (Univ. of Otago) 1999. *Address:* c/o Department of Physiology, Anatomy and Genetics, Le Gros Clark Building, South Parks Road, Oxford, OX1 3QX, England (office).

JACK, Kenneth Henderson, OBE, FRS; British professor of applied crystal chemistry; *Professor Emeritus, University of Newcastle-upon-Tyne;* b. 12 Oct. 1918, North Shields, Northumberland (now Tyne and Wear); s. of the late John Henderson Jack DSC and Emily Jack (née Cozens); m. Alfreda Hughes 1942 (died 1974); two s.; ed Tynemouth Municipal High School, King's Coll., Univ. of Durham, Fitzwilliam Coll., Univ. of Cambridge; Experimental Officer, Ministry of Supply 1940–41; Lecturer in Chem., Univ. of Durham 1941–45, 1949–52, 1953–57; Sr Scientific Officer British Iron and Steel Research Asscn 1945–49; Research at Cavendish Lab., Cambridge 1947–49; Research Engineer Westinghouse Electrical Corpn, Pittsburgh, Pa, USA 1952–53; Research Dir Thermal Syndicate Ltd, Wallsend 1957–64; Prof. of Applied Crystal Chem. Univ. of Newcastle-upon-Tyne 1964–84, Prof. Emer. 1984–; Dir Wolfson Research Group for High-Strength Materials 1970–84; Leverhulme Research Fellow 1984–87; Consultant Cookson Group PLC 1986–94; Fellow, American Ceramic Soc. 1984; mem. Acad. of Ceramics 1989; Hon. Prof., Univ. of Wales, Swansea 1996–; Hon. mem. Soc. Française de Métallurgie 1984, Materials Research Soc. (India) 1991, Ceramic Soc. of Japan 1991; numerous awards and prizes, including Saville-Shaw Medal from Soc. of Chemical Industry 1944, Sir George Beilby Memorial Award from Inst. of Metals, Royal Inst. of Chemistry and Soc. of Chemical Industry 1951, Kroll Medal and Prize from Metals Soc. 1979, Prince of Wales Award for Industrial Innovation and Production 1984, Royal Soc. Armourers and Brasiers Award 1988, World Materials Congress Award, ASM Int. 1988, Inst. of Metals Griffith Medal 1989, Centennial Award, Ceramic Soc. of Japan 1991; British Ceramic Soc. Mellor Memorial Lecturer 1973, Metals Soc. Harold Moore Memorial Lecturer 1984, Oxford Metallurgical Soc. W. Hume-Rothery Memorial Lecturer 1986, American Ceramic Soc. Sosman Lecturer 1989. *Publications:* papers on solid state chem., crystallography, metallurgy, ceramic science and glass tech. in scientific journals and conference proceedings. *Leisure interests:* walking, playing with great-grandchildren. *Address:* 147 Broadway, Cullercoats, North Shields, Tyne and Wear, NE30 3TA, England (home). *Telephone:* (191) 257-3664 (home). *E-mail:* kennethjack@ btinternet.com (home).

JACKAMAN, Michael Clifford John, MA; British business executive; b. 7 Nov. 1935; s. of Air Commodore Clifford Thomas Jackaman and Lily Margaret Jackaman; m. Valerie Jane Pankhurst 1960; one s. one d.; ed Felsted School, Essex, Jesus Coll., Cambridge; with Yardley Ltd 1959–60, Beecham Foods Ltd 1960–63, John Harvey & Sons Ltd 1963–65, Findus Ltd 1965, Harveys of Bristol 1966–92 (Chair. 1984–93); Marketing Dir Allied Breweries Ltd 1978–80, Deputy Man. Dir 1978–83; Chair. Allied Vintners Ltd 1983–88; Chair. and CEO Hiram Walker-Allied Vintners Ltd 1988–91; Chair. Allied-Lyons (now Allied Domecq) PLC 1991–96; Chair. Grand Appeal, Royal Hosp. for Sick Children, Bristol 1996–; Dir Rank Group PLC 1992–97, Kleinwort Benson Group 1994–98, Theatre Royal, Bath 1999–; Hon. DBA (Univ. of West of England). *Leisure interests:* opera, gardening, tennis, walking, oriental antiques, theatre. *Address:* c/o Appeal Office, Royal Hospital for Children, 24 Upper Maudlin Street, Bristol, BS2 8DJ, England. *Telephone:* (117) 927-3888. *Fax:* (117) 929-3718.

JACKLIN, Anthony (Tony), CBE; British fmr professional golfer; b. 7 July 1944, Scunthorpe; s. of Arthur David Jacklin and Doris Lillian Jacklin; m. Vivien Jacklin 1966 (died 1988); two s. one d.; m. 2nd Astrid May Waagen 1988; one s. one step-s. one step-d.; Lincolnshire Open champion 1961; professional 1962–85, 1988–; won British Asst Professionals' title 1965; won Dunlop Masters 1967, 1973; first British player to win British Open since 1951 1969; US Open Champion 1970; first British player to win US Open since 1920 and first since 1900 to hold US and British Open titles simultaneously; Greater Greensboro Open champion, USA 1968, 1972; won Italian Open 1973, German Open 1979, Venezuelan Open 1979, Jersey Open 1981, British Professional Golfers' Asscn (PGA) champion 1982 and 15 major tournaments in various parts of the world; played in eight Ryder Cup matches and four times for England in World Cup; Capt. of 1983 GB and Europe Ryder Cup Team; Capt. of victorious European Ryder Cup team 1985 (first win for Europe since 1957), 1987; BBC TV golf commentator; moved to Sotogrande, Spain from Jersey 1983; Commr of Golf, Las Aves Club, Sotogrande 1983–; Dir of Golf, San Roque Club 1988–; now golf course designer; Hon. Life Pres. British Professional Golfers' Asscn; Hon. Fellow, Birmingham Polytechnic 1989. *Publications:* Golf With Tony Jacklin 1969, The Price of Success 1979, Jacklin's Golfing Secrets (with Peter Dobereiner), The First Forty Years (with Renton Laidlaw) 1985, Your Game and Mine (with Bill Robertson) 1999, Jacklin: The Autobiography 2006. *Address:* Tony Jacklin Golf Academy, 222 Haben Blvd, Palmetto,, FL 34221, USA (office). *Telephone:* (941) 722-4895.

JACKLIN, Bill, MA, RA; British artist and painter; b. (Walter William Burke-Jacklin), 1 Jan. 1943, Hampstead, London; s. of Harold Jacklin and Alice Jacklin; m. 1st Lesley Berman 1979 (divorced 1993); m. 2nd Janet Russo 1993; ed Walthamstow School of Art, London and Royal Coll. of Art; teacher at numerous art colls. 1967–75; moved to New York 1985; elected Royal Acad. 1990; Bursary Award, Arts Council, London 1975. *Publications:* numerous Marlborough catalogues 1980–2005. *Leisure interests:* walking, reading. *Address:* c/o Marlborough Fine Art, 6 Albemarle Street, London, W1X 4BY, England (home). *Telephone:* (401) 848-0774 (Newport, RI, USA) (office). *Website:* www.bjacklin.com (office).

JACKMAN, Hugh; Australian actor; b. 12 Oct. 1968; m. Deborra-Lee Furness; one c.; ed Univ. of Tech. Sydney, Western Australian Acad. of Performing Arts. *Stage appearances include:* Beauty and the Beast (Australia), Sunset Boulevard (Australia), Oklahoma (UK). *Films include:* Paperback Hero 1999, Erskineville Kings 1999, X-Men 2000, Someone Like You 2001, Swordfish 2001, Kate and Leopold 2001, X-Men 2 2003, Standing Room Only 2004, Van Helsing 2004, X-Men: The Last Stand 2006, Scoop 2006, The Fountain 2006, The Prestige 2006, Flushed Away (voice) 2006, Happy Feet (voice) 2006, Uncle Jonny 2008, Deception 2008, Australia 2008, X-Men Origins: Wolverine 2009. *Television includes:* Correlli 1995, Snowy River: The McGregor Saga 1996, Hey, Mr Producer! 1998, Halifax F. P. 1998, Oklahoma 1999. *Leisure interests:* piano, guitar, golf, windsurfing. *Address:* c/o Penny Williams Management, Level 2, 181 Glebe Point Road, Glebe, NSW 2037, Australia. *Telephone:* (2) 9552-1701. *Fax:* (2) 9660-0434. *Website:* www .pennywilliamsmgt.com.au.

JACKSON, Alan Robert, AO; Australian business executive; b. 30 March 1936, Drovin, Vic.; m.; four d.; ed Hemmingway Robertson Inst., Harvard School of Business, USA; clerk, accountant, Co. Sec., then Finance Dir and Man. Dir Mather & Platt Pty Ltd 1952–77; Man. Dir BTR Nylex Ltd 1977–91, Chair. 1991–97; Dir BTR PLC 1984–97, Man. Dir and Chief Exec. 1991–96, Chair. BTR Inc. USA 1991–96; Chair. Sanshin Holdings, Japan 1985–95, Nylex Malaysia Berhad 1985–96, CGPC Group, Taiwan 1986–96; Chair. and Chief Exec. Austrim Nylex Ltd 1990–2001 (retd); Chair. ACI Glass Co. Ltd 1993–96, ACI Guandong Glass Co. Ltd 1994–96, Dir Reserve Bank of Australia 1991–2001, Seven Network Ltd 1995–, Titan Petrochemicals and Polymers Berhad, Malaysia 1997–; Chair. Australian Trade Comm. 1995; mem. Econ. Planning Advisory Council 1990–; Dir St Frances Cabrini Hosp. 1995–; mem. Inst. of Chartered Accountants in Australia, Australian Soc. of Accountants, Australian Inst. of Man.; Advance Australia Award for Services to Industry 1990 and other awards. *Address:* Level 4 East Tower, 608 St Kilda Road, Melbourne, Vic. 3004, Australia.

JACKSON, Alphonso, BSc, LLB; American fmr government official; m. Marcia Jackson; two d.; ed Truman State Univ., Washington Univ. Law School; apptd Dir of Public Safety for City of St Louis 1977; fmr Exec. Dir St Louis Housing Authority; fmr Dir consultant services Laventhol and Howarth; fmr Special Asst to the Chancellor and Asst Prof., Univ. of Missouri; fmr Dir Dept of Public and Assisted Housing, Washington, DC, Chair. DC Redevelopment Land Agency Bd; Pres. and CEO Housing Authority City of Dallas, Tex. 1989–96; Pres. American Electric Power 1996–2001; Deputy Sec. and COO Dept of Housing and Urban Devt 2001–04, Sec. 2004–08 (resgnd). *Address:* c/o Department of Housing and Urban Development, 451 Seventh Street, SW, Washington, DC 20410, USA (office).

JACKSON, Betty, CBE, RDI; British couturier; b. 24 June 1949, Bacup, Lancs.; d. of Arthur Jackson and Phyllis Gertrude Jackson; m. David Cohen 1985; one s. one d.; ed Bacup and Rawtenstall Grammar School and Birmingham Coll. of Art and Design; Chief Designer Quorum 1975–81; f. Betty Jackson Ltd 1981, Dir 1981–; opened Betty Jackson retail shop 1991; Part-time tutor RCA 1982–, Visiting Prof. 1999; Fellow, Birmingham Univ. 1988–, Univ. of Cen. Lancashire 1992; Trustee, Victoria and Albert (V&A) Museum 2005; Hon. Fellow, RCA 1989; Designer of the Year 1985, Royal Designer for Industry (Royal Soc. of Arts) 1988, 1989, Fil d'Or, Int. Linen 1989, Contemporary Designer of the Year 1999, Established Award for Arts by Preston City Council 2004. *Leisure interests:* reading, listening to music. *Address:* Betty Jackson Ltd, 1 Netherwood Place, Netherwood Road, London, W14 0BW, England (office). *Telephone:* (20) 7602-6023 (office). *Fax:* (20) 7602-3050 (office). *E-mail:* info@bettyjackson.com (office). *Website:* www .bettyjackson.com (office).

JACKSON, Colin Ray, CBE; British fmr professional athlete; b. 18 Feb. 1967, Cardiff; world-class 110m hurdler; holds the 60m world indoor record and 110m outdoor record (as at end of 2003); 110m hurdles achievements include: silver medal European Jr Championships 1985, gold medal World Jr Championships 1986, silver medal Commonwealth Games 1986, silver medal European Cup 1987, bronze medal World Championships 1987, silver medal Olympic Games 1988, silver medal World Cup 1989, gold medal European Cup 1989, 1993, gold medal Commonwealth Games 1990, gold medal World Cup 1992, gold medal (and new world record) World Championships 1993 (silver medal 4x100m relay); achievements (60m hurdles): silver medal World Indoor Championships 1989, 1993, gold medal European Indoor Championships 1989 (silver medal 1987), 1994, gold medals European and Commonwealth Championships 1994, gold medal European Championships 1998, 2002, gold medal World Championships 1999; in world's top ten at 110m each year from 1986–2003; over 70 int. caps (most capped British athlete); 23 major championships medals (13 gold, nine silver, one bronze); retd March 2003; mem. Brecon Athletics Club, UK Int. 1985–; numerous Welsh, UK, European and Commonwealth records; currently commentator BBC Sport; Hon. BA (Aberystwyth) 1994, Hon. BSc (Univ. of Wales) 1999; Athlete of the Decade, French Sporting Council, Hurdler of the Century, German Athletic Asscn (DLV), Athlete of the Year 1993–94, British Athletics Writers, Sportsman of the Year 1994, Sports Writers Asscn. *Address:* c/o MTC (UK) Ltd, 20 York Street, London, W1V 6PU, England; 4 Jackson Close, Rhoose, Vale of Glamorgan, CF62 3DQ, Wales. *Telephone:* (20) 7935-8000 (MTC). *Fax:* (1446) 710642 (home). *Website:* www.mtc-uk.com.

JACKSON, Daryl Sanders, AO, DipArch, BArch, LFRAIA, ARIBA; Australian architect; b. 7 Feb. 1937, Clunes, Victoria; s. of Cecil John Jackson and Doreen May Sanders; m. Kay Parsons 1960; one s. three d.; ed Wesley Coll., Melbourne, Royal Melbourne Inst. of Tech., Univ. of Melbourne; Asst, Edwards, Madigan and Torzillo, Sydney 1959, Don Henry Fulton, Melbourne 1960, Chamberlin, Powell and Bon, London 1961–63, Paul Rudolph, New Haven, Conn. 1963–64, Skidmore, Owings and Merrill, San Francisco 1964; Partner, Daryl Jackson, Evan Walker Architects, Melbourne 1965–79; Dir Daryl Jackson Pty Ltd Architects 1979–; Dir Daryl Jackson, Robin Dyke Pty Ltd (Sydney) 1985–; Assoc. Prof. of Architecture, Melbourne Univ. 1985–, Deakin Univ. 2001–; Pres. Wesley Coll. Council, Melbourne 1993–; Dir Daryl Jackson Alastair Swayn Pty Ltd (Canberra); Dir Daryl Jackson Int. Ltd (London) 1989–; Dir RAIA Victorian Chapter Housing Service 1966–69; mem. RAIA Victorian Chapter Council 1967–77, Victorian Tapestry Workshop Cttee 1975–84, Parl. House Construction Authority, Canberra 1985–89, Victorian Arts Centre Trust 1991, Melbourne Cricket Club 1992– (Vice-Pres. 1997–); Trustee, Nat. Gallery of Vic. 1983–95; Chair. Australian Film Inst. 1990–94, Melbourne Major Events Co. Ltd 1991–; Life Fellow Royal Australia Inst. of Architects; Hon. FAIA; Hon. Diploma and Bronze Medal (Third World Biennale of Architecture, Interarch 85, Sofia) 1985; Royal Australia Inst. of Architects Architecture Awards: Bronze Medal 1970, 1973, 1976, 1978, Press Award 1990, Canberra Medallion 1981, Sir Zehlman Cowen Award 1981, 1984, Robert Haddon Award 1982, Walter Burley Griffin Award for Urban Design, William Wardle Public Architecture Award, Sustainable Architecture Award; ACT Architecture Awards: 1984, 1985, 1987, 1991, Gold Medal 1987, Australian Council Nat. Trusts Heritage Award 1990, Int. Award 1991, MCG Southern Stand 1991, Georges Interior Architectural Award 1998, Masterplanner, Univ. of Melbourne 2000, County Court of Australia Award 2003. *Major works:* YWCA Community Resource Centre, Suva, Fiji 1973, Princes Hill High School, Melbourne 1973, Methodist Ladies' Coll., Library Resource Centre, Melbourne 1973, City Edge Housing Devt, Melbourne 1976, School of Music, Canberra 1976, Asscn for Modern Educ. School, Canberra 1977, Emu Ridge Govt Housing Devt, Canberra 1978, School of Art, Canberra 1980, McLachlan Offices, Canberra 1980, The Walter and Eliza Hall Inst. of Medical Research, Melbourne 1982, Nat. Sports Centre, Swimming Training Hall, Bruce, ACT 1982, Australian Chancery Complex, Riyadh, Saudi Arabia 1987, Hyatt Hotel, Canberra, Bond Univ., Gold Coast 1989, Commercial Union Office Bldg, Melbourne 1990, Melbourne Cricket Ground Southern Stand 1991, 120 Collins Street, Melbourne, Methodist Ladies' Coll. Music School, Kew 1994, Subiaco Oval Redevelopment, Perth 1994, Wesley Coll. Pre-Preparatory School, Prahran 1995, Brisbane Cricket Ground Redevelopment, 'The Gabba' 1995, Royal Melbourne Hosp. 1995, Colonial Stadium, Melbourne 2000, Sydney Conservatorium of Music (with Robin Dyke) 2001, Royal Brisbane Hosp. 2003, Victorian County Court 2003, UN Int. School, Hanoi 2004, Melbourne Cricket Ground Northern Stand Re-Development (with MCGS) 2005, Southern Cross Station Redevelopment (with Grimshaw Architects) 2006. *Publications:* Daryl Jackson Architecture: Drawings and Photos 1984, Daryl Jackson, The Master Architect 1996; numerous articles and papers. *Address:* 35 Little Bourke Street, Melbourne, Vic. 3000, Australia (office). *Telephone:* (3) 9662-3022 (office). *Fax:* (3) 9663-5239 (office). *E-mail:* djackson@jacksonarchitecture.com (office). *Website:* www.jacksonarchitecture .com (office).

JACKSON, Francis Alan, CBE, DMus, FRCO; British organist and composer; b. 2 Oct. 1917, Malton, Yorks.; s. of William Altham Jackson and Eveline May (née Suddaby); m. Priscilla Procter 1950; two s. one d.; ed York Minster Choir School and with Sir Edward Bairstow; Organist, Malton Parish Church 1933–40; war service with 9th Lancers in N Africa and Italy 1940–46; Asst Organist, York Minster 1946, Master of the Music 1946–82, Organist Emer. 1988–; Conductor York Musical Soc. 1947–82, York Symphony Orchestra 1947–80; now freelance organist and composer; Fellow Guild of Musicians and Singers; Patron, Whitlock Trust; Hon. Fellow, Royal School of Church Music, Westminster Choir Coll., Princeton, NJ, USA, Royal Northern Coll. of Music, Guild of Church Musicians 2005; Order of St William of York 1983; Hon. DUniv (York) 1983. *Music:* published works include Symphony in D minor 1957, Organ Concerto 1985, Eclogue for piano and organ 1987, Recitative and Allegro for trombone and organ 1989, organ music including six sonatas, three duets, church music, songs and monodramas, Sonatina Pastorale for recorder and piano 1999, Sonata for trumpet and organ 2003. *Publications:* Blessed

City: The Life and Works of Edward C. Bairstow 1996. *Leisure interests:* gardening, art and architecture. *Address:* Nether Garth, East Acklam, Malton, N Yorks., YO17 9RG, England (home). *Telephone:* (1653) 658395 (home).

JACKSON, Frank Cameron, AO, PhD, FAHA, FASSA, FBA; Australian philosopher and academic; *Visiting Professor, Princeton University;* b. 31 Aug. 1943, Melbourne; s. of Allan C. Jackson and Ann E. Jackson; m. Morag E. Fraser 1966; two d.; ed Melbourne and La Trobe Univs; Prof. of Philosophy, Monash Univ., Vic. 1978–86, 1991; Prof. of Philosophy, ANU 1986–90, 1992–2007, Dir Inst. of Advanced Studies 1998–2001, Dir Research School of Social Sciences 2004–07; Visiting Prof., Princeton Univ. 2007–; part-time Research Prof., La Trobe Univ. and ANU 2008–10; Locke Lecturer, Univ. of Oxford 1995, Blackwells Lecturer, Brown Univ. 2006. *Publications:* Perception 1978, Conditionals 1986, The Philosophy of Mind and Cognition (with David Braddon-Mitchell) 1996, From Metaphysics to Ethics 1998, Mind, Method and Conditionals 1998, Mind, Morality and Explanation (with Philip Pettit and Michael Smith) 2004. *Leisure interests:* reading, tennis. *Address:* Department of Philosophy, 1879 Hall, Princeton University, Princeton, NJ 08544, USA (office); 75 Napier Crescent, Montmorency 3094, Australia (home). *Telephone:* (3) 9439-4773 (home). *E-mail:* fjackson@princeton.edu (office). *Website:* www.princeton.edu (office).

JACKSON, Glenda, CBE; British politician and fmr actress; b. 9 May 1936, Birkenhead, Cheshire; d. of Harry and Joan Jackson; m. Roy Hodges 1958 (divorced 1976); one s.; ed Royal Acad. of Dramatic Art; fmr mem. Royal Shakespeare Co. where roles included Ophelia in Hamlet and Charlotte Corday in Marat/Sade (in London and New York); played Queen Elizabeth I in TV series Elizabeth R; Pres. Play Matters (fmrly Toy Libraries Asscn) 1976–; Dir United British Artists 1983–; Labour MP for Hampstead and Highgate 1992–; Parl. Under-Sec. of State, Dept for the Environment and Transport 1997–99; Adviser on Homelessness, GLA 2000–; Hon. Fellow, Liverpool Polytechnic 1987; Hon. DLitt (Liverpool) 1978; Hon. LLM (Nottingham) 1992. *Plays include:* Marat/Sade, New York and Paris 1965, The Investigation 1965, Hamlet 1965, US 1966, Three Sisters 1967, Collaborators 1973, The Maids 1974, Hedda Gabler 1975, The White Devil 1976, Antony and Cleopatra 1978, Rose 1980, Strange Interlude 1984, Phaedra 1984, 1985, Across from the Garden of Allah 1986, Strange Interlude 1986, The House of Bernarda Alba 1986, Macbeth 1988, Scenes from an Execution 1990, Mermaid 1990, Mother Courage 1990, Mourning Becomes Electra 1991. *Films include:* Marat/Sade 1966, Negatives 1968, Women in Love (Acad. Award 1970) 1969, The Music Lovers 1970, Sunday, Bloody Sunday 1971, The Boy Friend 1971, Mary, Queen of Scots 1971, The Triple Echo 1972, Bequest to the Nation 1972, A Touch of Class (Acad. Award 1974) 1973, The Romantic Englishwoman 1975, The Tempter 1975, The Incredible Sarah 1976, The Abbess of Crewe 1976, Stevie 1977, Hedda 1977, House Calls 1978, The Class of Miss McMichael 1978, Lost and Found 1979, Hopscotch 1980, The Return of the Soldier 1982, Giro City 1982, Summit Conference 1982, Great and Small 1983, And Nothing But the Truth 1984, Turtle Diary 1985, Beyond Therapy 1985, Business as Usual 1986, Salome's Last Dance 1988, The Rainbow 1989, The Secret Life of Sir Arnold Bax 1992. *Leisure interests:* gardening, reading, listening to music. *Address:* House of Commons, London, SW1A 0AA, England. *Telephone:* (20) 7219-4008. *Fax:* (20) 7219-2112. *E-mail:* jacksong@parliament.uk.

JACKSON, Janet Damita Jo; American singer and choreographer; b. 16 May 1966, Gary, Ind.; d. of Joseph Jackson and Katherine Jackson; m. James DeBarge 1984 (annulled 1985); m. 2nd Rene Elizondo Jr 1991 (separated 1999); ed Valley Professional School; singing debut at age seven with family singing group, The Jacksons; television actress 1977–81, appearing in series Good Times (CBS), Diff'rent Strokes, Fame, A New Kind of Family; solo recording artist 1982–; worldwide concerts and tours; American Music Awards for Best Female Soul Singer (for Nasty), Best Female Soul Video (for What Have You Done For Me Lately?) and Best Pop Video (for When I Think of You) 1986, for Best Dance Artist, Best Female Pop Rock Artist and Best Female Soul R & B Artist 1991, for Favorite Pop/Rock Female Artist 2002, MTV Video Vanguard Award 1990, MTV Award for Best Female Video (for If) 1993, Starlight Foundation Humanitarian of the Year Award 1991, Grammy Award for Best R&B Song (for That's the Way Love Goes) 1993. *Recordings include:* albums: Janet Jackson 1982, Dream Street 1984, Control 1986, Janet Jackson's Rhythm Nation 1989, Rhythm Nation Compilation 1990, Janet 1993, Design of a Decade 1986–96 1995, The Velvet Rope 1997, All For You 2001, Damita Jo 2004, 20 Y.O. 2006, Discipline 2008. *Films include:* Poetic Justice 1993, Nutty Professor II: The Klumps 2000, Why Did I Get Married? 2007. *TV includes:* Good Times 1977–79, A New Kind of Family, Diff'rent Strokes, Fame. *Address:* Johnny Wright, Wright Entertainment Group, 7680 Universal Boulevard, #500, Orlando, FL 32819, USA (office). *Telephone:* (407) 826-9100 (office). *Website:* www.wegmusic.com (office); www.janet-jackson.com (office).

JACKSON, Rev. Jesse Louis; American clergyman and civic leader; *President, Rainbow PUSH Coalition;* b. 8 Oct. 1941, Greenville, N Carolina; s. of Charles Henry and Helen Jackson; m. Jacqueline Lavinia Brown 1964; three s. two d. one d. by Karin Stanford; ed Univ. of Illinois, Illinois Agricultural and Tech. Coll., Chicago Theological Seminary; ordained to Ministry Baptist Church 1968; active Black Coalition for United Community Action 1969; Co-Founder Operation Breadbasket S Christian Leadership Conf.; Co-ordinating Council Community Orgs, Chicago 1966, Nat. Dir 1966–77; Founder and Exec. Dir Operation PUSH (People United to Save Humanity), Chicago 1971–96, Pres. Rainbow PUSH Coalition (formed with merger with Rainbow Coalition) 1996–; unsuccessful cand. for Democratic nomination for US Presidency 1983–84, 1987–88; TV Host, Voices of America 1990–; Pres. Award Nat. Medical Asscn 1969; Humanitarian Father of the Year Award Nat. Father's Day Cttee 1971. *Address:* Rainbow PUSH Coalition, 930 East 50th Street, Chicago, IL 60615, USA (office). *Telephone:* (773) 373-3366 (office). *Fax:* (773) 373-3571 (office). *E-mail:* jjackson@rainbowpush.org (office). *Website:* www.rainbowpush.org (office).

JACKSON, John B. H.; British business executive; *Chairman, Xenova Group PLC;* Dir (non-exec.) Hilton Group PLC 1980, Vice-Chair. 1991–94, Chair. 1994–; Chair. Celltech, Xenova, Wyndham Press; Chair. (non-solicitor) Mishcon de Reya; Dir (non-exec.) WPP Group, Billiton. *Address:* Xenova Group PLC, 957 Buckingham Avenue, Slough, SL1 4NL, England (office). *Telephone:* (1753) 706-6000 (office). *Fax:* (1753) 706-607 (office). *Website:* www.xenova.co.uk (office).

JACKSON, (Kevin) Paul, BA, FID; British media industry executive and television producer; *CEO, Granada America;* b. 2 Oct. 1947, London; s. of the late T. Leslie Jackson and Jo Spoonley; m. Judith E. Cain 1981; two d.; ed Gunnersbury Grammar School and Univ. of Exeter; stage man. Marlowe Theatre, Canterbury 1970, Thorndike Theatre, Leatherhead 1971; production work for BBC TV: Two Ronnies, Three of a Kind, Carrott's Lib, The Young Ones, Happy Families 1971–82; freelance Producer and Dir Canon and Ball, Girls on Top 1982–84; Producer and Chair. Paul Jackson Productions: Red Dwarf, Don't Miss Wax, Saturday Live 1984–86; Exec. Producer, Appointments of Dennis Jennings (Acad. Award 'Oscar' for Best Live Action Short 1989); Man. Dir NGTV 1987–91; Dir of Programmes, Carlton TV 1991–93, Man. Dir Carlton TV 1993–94, Carlton UK Productions 1994–96; Controller BBC Entertainment 1997–2000; Man. Dir Granada Australia and CEO Red Heart Productions 2000–03, Dir Granada Int. Production and Entertainment (UK) 2003, CEO Granada America 2003–; Visiting Prof., School of English, Exeter Univ.; mem. Exec. Cttee US Comedy Arts Festival; Chair. Timebank (UK charity); Chair. Comic Relief 1987–98; Vice-Chair. Charity Projects 1990–92, Chair. 1992–99; Chair. RTS 1994–96; Stanford Exec. Programme 1993; Fellow Inst. of Dirs, Royal TV Soc.; Hon. Fellow (Exeter) 1999, Dr hc (Exeter) 2004; BAFTA 1983, 1984. *Leisure interests:* theatre, rugby, travel, food and wine, friends and family. *Address:* Granada America, 15303 Ventura Boulevard, Building C, Suite 800, Sherman Oaks, CA 91403, USA (office). *Telephone:* (818) 455-4600 (office). *Fax:* (818) 455-4701 (office). *Website:* www.int.granadamedia.com/cs/international/index.asp (office).

JACKSON, Lisa P., BS, MEng; American government official; *Administrator, Environmental Protection Agency;* b. 8 Feb. 1962, New Orleans, La; m. Kenny Jackson; two s.; ed Tulane Univ., Princeton Univ.; worked in various roles with US Environmental Protection Agency (EPA), Washington, DC 1986–2002; Asst Commr of Compliance and Enforcement, NJ Dept of Environmental Protection 2002–05, Asst Commr for Land Use Man. 2005–06, Commr of Environmental Protection 2006–08; Chief of Staff to Gov of NJ 2008; Admin. EPA, Washington, DC 2009–. *Leisure interest:* cooking. *Address:* Office of the Administrator, Environmental Protection Agency, Ariel Rios Building, 1200 Pennsylvania Avenue, NW, Washington, DC 20460, USA (office). *Telephone:* (202) 272-0167 (office). *Website:* www.epa.gov (office).

JACKSON, Margaret Anne, AC, BEcons, MBA, FCA; Australian business executive; b. 17 March 1953, Vic.; d. of Wallace James Jackson and Dorothy Jean Jackson; m. Roger Donazzan 1977; one s. one d.; ed Monash Univ. and Univ. of Melbourne; accountant, Price Waterhouse Co. 1973–77; accountant, Nelson Parkhill BDO 1977–91, Partner 1983–90; Partner KPMG Peat Marwick 1990–92; Chair. Transport Accident Comm. (Vic.) 1993–2001; fmr Deputy Chair. Southcorp Ltd; Dir (non-exec.) Qantas Airways Ltd 1992–2007, Chair. 2000–07, also Chair. Remuneration and Nominations Cttees; Dir Telecom Australia 1983–90, Australian Wool Corp. 1986–89, Int. Wool Secr. 1986–89, Pacific Dunlop 1992–2000, The Broken Hill Pty Co. Ltd 1994–2000, Australia and New Zealand Banking Group Ltd 1994–, Billabong International Ltd 2000–; fmr Chair. Malthouse Pty Ltd; Chair. Flexigroup Ltd 2006–; Deputy Chair. People Telecom Ltd; mem. Exec. Cttee Australia Japan Business Co-operation Cttee; Dir Brain Imaging Research Inst.; Chair. Asia Pacific Business Coalition on HIV-AIDS 2006–; Pres. Australian Volunteers Int.; Deputy Chair. Baker Capital Campaign Task Force, Baker Medical Research Inst., St Vincent's Medical Research Inst. 1994–96; Chair. Playbox Theatre Co. Pty Ltd 1998–2000 (Dir 1991–98); mem. Bd of Dirs Australia Foundation for Culture and the Humanities Ltd; mem. Vic. State Council Inst. of Chartered Accountants 1985–93 (Chair. 1989–90), Pharmaceutical Remuneration Benefits Tribunal 1985–90, Foreign Affairs Council, Nat. Council 1988–91, Convocation Cttee Univ. of Melbourne 1988–91, Australian Science and Tech. Council 1990–93, Nat. Health and Medical Research Council 1991, French Australian Industrial Research Steering Cttee 1997–98, Business Council of Australia Chair.'s Panel, The Walter & Eliza Hall Inst. of Medical Research, Melbourne Univ. Business School Asscn; Fellow, Australian Inst. of Co. Dirs, Inst. of Chartered Accountants in Australia; Int. Trustee Carnegie Mellon Univ., S Australia; Patron Salvation Army Capital Appeal for Homeless Youth, Vic.; Hon. LLD (Monash) 2002; Inst. of Chartered Accountants Distinguished Service Award. *Leisure interests:* travel, bush-walking, fishing, reading, photography, gardening. *Address:* c/o Qantas Airways Ltd, Level 12, Exhibition Street, Melbourne, Vic. 3000, Australia (office).

JACKSON, Michael, BA; British broadcasting executive; b. 11 Feb. 1958; s. of Ernest Jackson and Margaret Jackson (née Kearsley); ed King's School, Macclesfield, Polytechnic of Cen. London; Organizer Channel 4 Group 1979; Producer The Sixties 1982; ind. producer Beat Productions Ltd 1983–87; Ed. The Late Show, BBC TV (BFI Award) 1988–90; with Late Show Productions 1990–91; Head of Music and Arts BBC TV 1991–93, Controller BBC2 1993–96, Controller BBC1 and BBC Dir of TV 1996–97; CEO Channel 4 1997–2001, Dir of Programmes 1997–98; Chair. Film Four Ltd 1997–2001; Dir (non-exec.) EMI Group 1999–; Pres., CEO USA Entertainment Group 2001–02; Chair.

Universal Television Group 2002–2004 (resgnd following merger Universal's merger with NBC 2004); Hon. DLitt (Westminster) 1995. *Programmes produced include:* Whose Town is it Anyway?, Open the Box, The Media Show, The Nelson Mandela Tribute, Tales from Prague (Grierson Documentary Award), Moving Pictures, The American Late Show (Public Broadcasting Service, USA), Naked Hollywood (BAFTA Best Factual Series Award), Sounds of the Sixties, The Lime Grove Story, TV Hell. *Leisure interests:* reading, walking. *Address:* c/o Universal Television Group, 100 Universal City Plaza, Bldg 1280/12th Floor, Universal City, CA 91608, USA (office).

JACKSON, Gen. Sir Michael David (Mike), Kt, GCB, CBE, DSO; British military officer (retd) and consultant; *Senior Advisor, PA Consulting Group;* b. 21 March 1944; s. of George Jackson and Ivy Jackson (née Bower); m. Sarah Coombe 1985; two s. one d.; ed Stamford School, Sandhurst Mil. Acad., Univ. of Birmingham; commissioned Intelligence Corps 1963; transferred to Parachute Regt 1970, attended Staff Coll. 1976, Chief of Staff Berlin Infantry Brigade 1977–78, commanded a parachute co., NI 1979–81, mem. Directing Staff, Staff Coll. 1981–83, Commdr 1st Bn Parachute Regt 1984–86; with Sr Defence Staff, Jt Service Defence Coll., Greenwich 1986–88; Services Fellow, Wolfson Coll. Cambridge 1989; Commdr 39 Infantry Brigade, NI 1989–92; Dir-Gen. of Personnel Services, Ministry of Defence (Army) 1992–94; Commdr 3rd Div. 1994–96, Commdr Implementation Force (IFOR) Multinational Div. SW, Bosnia and Herzegovina 1995–96; Dir-Gen. of Devt and Doctrine, Ministry of Defence 1996–97; rank of Lt-Gen. 1997; Commdr Allied Rapid Reaction Force 1997–2000; Commdr Kosovo Force (KFOR) March–Oct. 1999; C-in-C Land Command 2000–03; Chief of the Gen. Staff 2003–06; Sr Advisor, PA Consulting Group 2007–; adviser, Numis Securities 2007–, Risk Advisory Group 2007–; Freeman City of London 1988. *Publication:* Soldier: The Autobiography 2007. *Address:* PA Consulting Group, 123 Buckingham Palace Road, London, SW1W 9SR, England (office). *Telephone:* (20) 7730-9000 (office). *Fax:* (20) 7333-5050 (office). *E-mail:* info@paconsulting.com (office). *Website:* www.paconsulting.com (office).

JACKSON, Michael (Mike) J., BA; American automobile sales executive; *Chairman and CEO, AutoNation Inc.;* b. 7 Feb. 1949, NJ; m. Patricia Jackson; one d.; ed St Joseph's Univ.; Technician Specialist, Mercedes-Benz USA 1974; Man. Partner, Euro Motorcars, Bethesda, Md 1979–90; Sr Vice Pres. of Marketing, Mercedes-Benz USA 1990–97, Pres. 1997, Pres. and CEO 1997–98; mem. Bd Dirs and CEO AutoNation Inc. 1999–, Chair. 2003–; Chair. Museum of Art, Fort Lauderdale; included in Advertising Age Top Marketing 100 (four times), mem. Automotive News All-Star Team of automotive execs (five times), Industry Leader of the Year, Automotive Hall of Fame 2003. *Address:* AutoNation Inc., The Atrium, 110 South East 6th Street, Fort Lauderdale, FL 33301, USA (office). *Telephone:* (954) 769-6000 (office). *Fax:* (954) 769-6537 (office). *E-mail:* info@autonation.com (office). *Website:* www.autonation.com (office).

JACKSON, Michael Joseph; American singer; b. 29 Aug. 1958, Gary, Ind.; s. of Joseph W. Jackson and Katherine E. Jackson (née Scruse); m. 1st Lisa Marie Presley 1994 (divorced 1996); m. 2nd Debbie Rowe 1996 (divorced 1999); two s. one d.; ed privately; Founder mem. and lead singer, The Jackson Brothers, later renamed The Jackson 5 1962–76, renamed The Jacksons 1976–84; simultaneous solo career 1971–; numerous live and TV appearances, concerts and tours; has recorded with numerous artists, including Minnie Ripperton, Carol Bayer Sager, Donna Summer, Paul McCartney; Founder, Heal The World Foundation (children's charity); Owner, ATV Music Co. (including rights for John Lennon and Paul McCartney songs); Owner, MJJ record label; Hon. Dir Exeter City Football Club 2002–; numerous Grammy Awards 1980–, including seven awards 1984, Song of the Year 1986, Legend Award 1993; numerous American Music Awards 1980–, including 11 awards 1984, Special Award of Achievement 1989, Artist of the Century 2002; BRIT Awards for Best Int. Artist 1984, 1988, 1989, Artist of a Generation 1996, various Soul Train Awards 1988–, MTV Video Vanguard Award 1988, two NAACP Image Awards 1988, American Cinema Awards Foundation Entertainer of the Decade 1990, first recipient BMI Michael Jackson Award 1990, three World Music Awards 1993. *Film appearances include:* The Wiz 1978, Captain Eo 1986, Moonwalker 1988, Ghosts 1997. *Television appearances include:* The Jacksons 1976, The Simpsons (guest voice as John Jay Smith) 1991, Living with Michael Jackson (documentary, ITV 1) 2003. *Recordings include:* albums: with The Jackson 5: Diana Ross Presents The Jackson 5 1969, ABC 1970, Third Album 1970, The Jackson 5 Christmas Album 1970, Goin' Back To Indiana 1971, Maybe Tomorrow 1971, Lookin' Through The Windows 1972, Get It Together 1973, In Japan! (live) 1973, Skywriter 1973, Dancing Machine 1974, Moving Violation 1975, Joyful Jukebox Music 1976; with The Jacksons: The Jacksons 1976, Goin' Places 1977, Destiny 1978, Triumph 1980, The Jacksons Live 1981, Live 1982, Fliphits 1983, Victory 1984, 2300 Jackson Street 1989, Children of the Light 1993; solo: Got To Be There 1971, Ben 1972, Music And Me 1973, Forever Michael 1975, The Best Of Michael Jackson 1975, The Wiz (film soundtrack) 1978, Off The Wall 1979, Thriller 1982, BAD 1987, Dangerous 1991, HIStory – Past, Present and Future Book I 1995, Invincible 2001, Number Ones 2003, The Ultimate Collection 2004; singles: solo: Got To Be There 1971, Rockin' Robin 1972, Ain't No Sunshine 1972, Ben 1972, Don't Stop Till You Get Enough 1979, Off The Wall 1979, Rock With You 1980, One Day In Your Life 1981, She's Out of My Life 1980, The Girl Is Mine (duet with Paul McCartney) 1982, Billie Jean 1983, Beat It 1983, Wanna Be Startin' Somethin' 1983, Human Nature 1983, Say Say Say (duet with Paul McCartney) 1983, Thriller 1983, PYT 1984, Farewell My Summer Love 1984, I Can't Stop Loving You (duet with Siedah Garrett) 1987, Bad 1987, The Way You Make Me Feel 1988, The Man In The Mirror 1988, Dirty Diana 1988, Another Part Of Me 1988, Smooth Criminal 1988, Leave Me Alone 1989, Liberian Girl 1989, Black And White 1991, Remember The Time 1992, In The Closet 1992, Jam 1992, Heal The World 1992, Give In To Me 1992, Scream (with Janet Jackson) 1995, You Are Not Alone 1995, Earth Song 1995, They Don't Care About Us 1996, Ghosts 1997, Stranger In Moscow 1997, Blood On The Dance Floor 1997, You Rock My World 2001, Cry 2001, Butterflies 2002, Unbreakable 2002, One More Chance 2003. *Publications:* Moonwalk (autobiog.) 1988, Dancing the Dream: Poems and Reflections 1992. *Address:* MJJ Productions, 9255 Wilshire Boulevard, Los Angeles, CA 90024, USA (office). *Website:* www.michaeljackson.com (office).

JACKSON, Michael (Mike) L.; American retail executive; *President and Chief Operating Officer, Supervalu Inc.;* ed Univs of Wis. and Pa; worked as store man. for Red Owl Foods; joined Supervalu Inc. as retail counsellor 1979, Sr Vice-Pres. of Operations for Retail Food Cos 1999–2001, apptd Exec. Vice-Pres. and Pres. of Distribution Food Cos 2001–05 Pres. and COO 2005–; Vice-Chair. Nat. Grocers Assn; mem. Bd of Dirs Int. Grocers Assn USA, YMCA of Metropolitan Minneapolis; mem. Advisory Bd Carlson School of Man. Inst. for Research in Marketing; mem. Wholesale Advisory Bd, Food Marketing Inst.; Trustee Food for All. *Address:* Supervalu Inc., 11840 Valley View Road, Eden Prairie, MN 55344, USA (office). *Telephone:* (952) 828-4000 (office). *Fax:* (952) 828-8998 (office). *Website:* www.supervalu.com (office).

JACKSON, Peter; New Zealand film director; b. 31 Oct. 1961, Pukerua Bay, North Island. *Films:* Meet the Feebles, Bad Taste, Dead Alive, Heavenly Creatures, The Frighteners, Contact (special effects only), The Lord of the Rings: The Fellowship of the Ring (BAFTA Award for Best Dir) The Lord of the Rings: The Two Towers 2002, The Lord of the Rings: The Return of the King (Golden Globe Award, Best Dir 2004, Critics' Choice Award, Best Director 2004, Acad. Award, Best Dir, Best Picture 2004) 2003, King Kong 2005. *Publication:* Peter Jackson (autobiog., with Brian Sibley) 2005. *Address:* c/o ICM, 8942 Wilshire Boulevard, Beverly Hills, CA 90211, USA.

JACKSON, Peter John, BSc; British business executive; *Chairman, Kingfisher PLC;* b. 16 Jan. 1947, Sheffield; s. of Jack Jackson and Joan Jackson; m. Anne Campbell 1974; two s. one d.; ed Univ. of Leeds; personnel and industrial relations positions at British Steel, Comm. on Industrial Relations, Guthrie Industries 1968–76; Dir Personnel and Employee Relations, Deputy Man. Dir Perkins Engines (Shrewsbury), Perkins Engines Group 1976–87; Personnel Dir British Sugar PLC 1987–88, Deputy Man. Dir 1988–89, Man. Dir 1989–93, Chief Exec. 1994–99; Chief Exec. Associated British Foods PLC 1999–2005 (Dir 1992–2005); Chair. Kingfisher PLC 2006–. *Leisure interests:* garden, Sheffield United. *Address:* Kingfisher PLC, 3 Sheldon Square, Paddington, London, W2 6PX, England (office). *Telephone:* (20) 7372-8008 (office). *Fax:* (20) 7644-1001 (office). *E-mail:* info@kingfisher.co.uk (office). *Website:* www.kingfisher.co.uk (office).

JACKSON, Rashleigh Esmond; Guyanese diplomatist; b. 12 Jan. 1929, New Amsterdam, Berbice; two s. two d.; ed Queen's Coll., Georgetown, Univ. Coll., Leicester, UK, Columbia Univ., New York, USA; entered public service 1948; Master, Queen's Coll. 1957; Prin. Asst Sec., Ministry of Foreign Affairs 1965, Perm. Sec. 1969–73; Perm. Rep. to UN 1973–78; Minister for Foreign Affairs 1978–90; consultant 1992–; Pres. UN Council for Namibia 1974; Chair. Caribbean Task Force on Environment 1991–92; Man. Dir Public Affairs Consulting Enterprise (PACE) 1993–; mem. Bd of Dirs Environmental Protection Agency Guyana 1997–. *Address:* c/o Ministry of Foreign Affairs, Takuba Lodge, 254 South Road and New Garden Street, Georgetown (office); 182 Republic Park, East Bank, Demerara, Guyana. *Telephone:* (2) 72847. *Fax:* (2) 55512.

JACKSON, Samuel L., BA; American actor; b. 21 Dec. 1948, Washington, DC; m. LaTanya Richardson; one d.; ed Morehouse Coll., Atlanta; Co-founder and mem. Just Us theatre co., Atlanta. *Stage appearances:* Home, A Soldier's Story, Sally/Prince, Colored People's Time, Mother Courage, Spell No. 7, The Mighty Gents, The Piano Lesson, Two Trains Running, Fences. *Films include:* Together for Days 1972, Ragtime 1981, Eddie Murphy Raw 1987, Coming to America 1988, School Daze 1988, Do The Right Thing 1989, Sea of Love 1989, A Shock to the System 1990, Def by Temptation 1990, Betsy's Wedding 1990, Mo' Better Blues 1990, The Exorcist III 1990, GoodFellas 1990, Return of the Superfly 1990, Jungle Fever 1991 (Best Actor Award, Cannes Int. Film Festival, New York Film Critics' Award), Strictly Business 1991, Juice 1992, White Sands 1992, Patriot Games 1992, Johnny Suede 1992, Jumpin' at the Boneyard 1992, Fathers and Sons 1992, National Lampoon's Loaded Weapon 1 1993, Amos & Andrew 1993, Menace II Society 1993, Jurassic Park 1993, True Romance 1993, Hail Caesar 1994, Fresh 1994, The New Age 1994, Pulp Fiction 1994, Losing Isaiah 1995, Kiss of Death 1995, Die Hard With a Vengeance 1995, Fluke (voice) 1995, The Great White Hype 1996, A Time to Kill 1996, The Long Kiss Goodnight 1996, One Eight Seven 1996, Trees Lounge 1996, Hard Eight 1996, Eve's Bayou (also producer) 1997, Jackie Brown 1997, Out of Sight 1998, The Negotiator 1998, Sphere 1998, Star Wars Episode I: The Phantom Menace 1999, Deep Blue Sea 1999, Rules of Engagement 1999, Any Given Wednesday 2000, Shaft 2000, Unbreakable 2000, The Caveman's Valentine 2001, The 51st State 2001, Changing Lanes 2002, Star Wars Episode II: Attack of the Clones 2002, The House on Turk Street 2002, XXX 2002, Basic 2003, S.W.A.T. 2003, Country of My Skull 2003, Kill Bill Vol. 2 2004, Twisted 2004, The Incredibles (voice) 2004, Coach Carter (Image Award for Best Actor 2006) 2005, The Man 2005, Freedomland 2005, Snakes on a Plane 2006, Home of the Brave 2006, Black Snake Moan 2006, Resurrecting the Champ 2007, 1408 2007, Star Wars: The Clone Wars 2008, Lakeview Terrace 2008, Soul Men 2008, The Spirit 2008, Inglourious Basterds (voice) 2009. *Television appearances:* (series) Movin' On 1972, Ghostwriter 1992; (films) The Trial of the Moke 1978, Uncle Tom's Cabin 1987, Common Ground 1990, Dead and Alive: The Race for Gus Farace 1991, Simple Justice 1993, Assault at West Point 1994, Against the Wall 1994, Afro Samurai: Resurrection (voice) 2009. *Address:* 12400 Wilshire Blvd, Suite 850, Los

Angeles, CA 90025-1055; c/o Toni Howard, ICM, 8942 Wilshire Boulevard, Beverly Hills, CA 90211, USA. *Website:* samueljackson.com.

JACKSON-NELSON, Marjorie, AC, CVO, MBE; Australian state official and fmr athlete; *Governor of South Australia;* b. 13 Sept. 1931, Coffs Harbour, NSW; d. of William Alfred Jackson and Mary Robinson; m. Peter Nelson 1953 (died 1977); one s. two d.; popularly known as 'The Lithgow Flash'; winner gold medal 100m and 200m (world record), Olympic Games 1952; winner four gold medals, Commonwealth Games 1950, three gold medals 1954; broke world sprint records on ten occasions; Man. Women's Section, Australian Commonwealth Games Teams 1982, 1986, 1990; Deputy Chair. Adelaide's bid to host 1998 Commonwealth Games 1990–92; Gen. Team Man. Commonwealth Games (first woman in position) 1994; fmr Pres. S Australia Div., Australian Olympic Fed.; Athletes Liaison Officer, Commonwealth Games 1998; f. Peter Nelson Leukaemia Research Fellowship 1977–; Gov. of S Australia 2001–; mem. S Australian Olympic Council 1997–, SOCOG 1998–2000; honoured by Australia Post on stamp celebrating Olympic legends 1998; featured on Olympic coin produced by Perth Mint 1999; Bearer, Olympic Flag at Opening Ceremony of Olympic Games, Sydney 2000; Hon. PhD (Charles Sturt Univ., Bathurst, NSW) 2001; Australian Sportsman of the Year 1952, Outstanding Athlete, Helms Foundation, USA 1952, Outstanding Athlete, Int. Amateur Athletics Asscn 1986, nominated by Gov.-Gen. and Prime Minister as one of twenty living mems of 200 Great Australians 1988, named Legend in Australian Sport 1995, Paul Harris Fellow Rotary 1995, inducted into Australian Sporting Hall of Fame 1995, Int. Women's Hall of Fame, New York, USA 2000, Australian Sports Medal 2000. *Address:* Government House Adelaide, GPO Box 2373, Adelaide, S Australia, 5001, Australia (office). *Telephone:* (8) 8203-9800 (office). *Fax:* (8) 8203-9899 (office). *E-mail:* governor@saugov.sa.gov.au (office). *Website:* www.governor.sa.gov.au.

JACOB, Christian; French politician; b. 4 Dec. 1959, Rozay-en-Brie, Seine-et-Marne; ed Sainte-Maure dans l'Aube School of Agric.; farmer and dairy producer at Vaudoy-en-Brie 1982–; Pres. Young Farmers Local Admin (Département) Centre of Seine-et-Marne 1986–89, Regional Centre for Northern France 1987–90, Nat. Centre 1992; mem. Nat. Social and Econ. Council 1992; elected MEP 1994, Chair. European Parl. Comm. on Agric. and Rural Devt 1994–97; elected Deputy for Seine-et-Marne, Nat. Ass. 1995–2002, 2007–; elected Mayor of Provins 200102, 2006–; Minister-Desig. of Family Affairs, Health and Disabled People 2002–04, of Small and Medium Enterprises, Commerce, Craftsmen, Liberal Professions and Consumption 2004; Minister of the Economy, Finance and Industry 2004–05, of the Civil Service 2005–07; Chair. Rassemblement pour la Repub. (RPR) Fed. of Seine-et-Marne 1998–2000 (mem. Parl. Group 1997–2002); Chair. Union for a Popular Movt (UMP) Fed. of Seine-et-Marne 2002–; mem. Del. to EU 1997; mem. Bd of Dirs SOPEXA (Soc. for the Expansion of Sales of Agricultural and Grocery Products) 1996–. *Publications:* La clé des champs 1994, Le pari du bon sens, un paysan en politique 1999. *Address:* Hôtel de Ville, 77160 Provins, France (office). *Telephone:* 1-64-60-38-33 (office). *Fax:* 1-64-00-61-27 (office). *E-mail:* cjacob@assemblee-nationale.fr (office). *Website:* www.assemblee-nationale.fr (office).

JACOB, François, MD, DSc; French geneticist and academic; *Professor Emeritus, Collège de France;* b. 17 June 1920, Nancy; m. 1st Lise Bloch 1947 (died 1984); three s. one d.; m. 2nd Geneviève Barrier 1999; ed Lycée Carnot and Univ. of Paris (Sorbonne); Officer Free French Forces 1940–45; with Inst. Pasteur 1950–, serving as Asst 1950–56, Head of Laboratory 1956–60, Head of Cellular Genetics Unit 1960–91, Pres. 1982–88; Prof. of Cellular Genetics, Collège de France 1965–92; mem. Acad. des Sciences 1977, Acad. française 1996; Foreign mem. Royal Danish Acad. of Sciences and Letters 1962, American Acad. of Arts and Sciences 1964; Foreign Assoc. NAS 1969; Foreign mem. Royal Soc., London 1973, Acad. Royale Médicale Belgique 1973, Acad. of Sciences of Hungary 1986, Royal Acad. of Sciences of Madrid 1987; Dr hc of several univs; Prix Charles Léopold Mayer, Acad. des Sciences 1962, Nobel Prize for Medicine (jointly with A. Lwoff and J. Monod) 1965; Croix de la Libération, Grand-Croix Légion d'honneur. *Publications:* The Logic of Life 1970, The Possible and the Actual 1981, The Statue Within 1987, La Souris, la mouche et l'homme 1997; and over 200 scientific papers. *Address:* Institut Pasteur, 25 rue de Dr Roux, 75724 Paris Cedex 15 (office); 64 rue Bonaparte, 75006 Paris, France (home). *Telephone:* 1-45-68-84-87 (office). *Fax:* 1-40-61-31-16 (office). *E-mail:* fjacob@pasteur.fr (office). *Website:* www.pasteur.fr/english (office).

JACOB, Gilles; French film director and producer and film festival director; *President, Festival de Cannes;* b. 1930; Gen. Del. Cannes Film Festival 1978–2000, Pres. 2000–; Commander of the Ordre National de la Légion d'Honneur 2005. *Films include:* Le Cinéma dans les yeux (dir and producer) 1987, Liberté (producer) 1989, Histories de festival (dir and producer)2002, Les Marches etc... (une comédie musicale) (dir and producer) 2003, Épreuves d'artistes (dir and producer) 2004. *Address:* Association française du festival international du film, 3 rue Amélie, 75007 Paris, France (office). *Telephone:* 1-53-59-61-00 (office). *Fax:* 1-53-59-61-10 (office). *E-mail:* festival@festival-cannes.fr (office). *Website:* www.festival-cannes.fr (office); www.festival-cannes.org (office).

JACOB, Lt-Gen. J.F.R., MSc; Indian politician and army officer; b. 2 May 1921, Calcutta; s. of E. Jacob; ed Madras Univ., Fort Sill, USA; commissioned into Indian Artillery 1942; active service in Middle East, Burma, Sumatra; fmrly commanded infantry and artillery brigades, the Artillery School, an infantry div., a corps and the Eastern Army; Chief of Staff Eastern Army during intervention in East Pakistan (now Bangladesh); retd 1978; Gov. of Goa 1998–99, of Punjab 1999–. *Address:* Raj Bhavan, Chandigarh, Punjab, India (office). *Telephone:* (172) 740740 (office); (172) 740768 (home).

JACOB, Mathew Mundakaal, BEcons, LLB, MA; Indian politician; *Governor of Meghalaya;* b. 9 Aug. 1928, Ramapuram; s. of Mathew Jacob; m. Achamma Jacob (deceased); four d.; advocate High Court of Cochin, specializing in taxation; involved in youth training in various parts of India for Bhoodan Movt for redistribution of land; Sec. Gen. Bharat Sevak Samaj org. to encourage popular participation in nat. Devt, Kerala 1956–66; led youth Work Camp Movt in India and co-leader int. work camps in Bangalore and Calcutta overseen by UNESCO; Indian Rep. World Youth Festival, Moscow 1957, World Ass. of Youth Confs., Delhi 1958; Convenor Student and Youth Affairs Cttee for Nat. Defence, Kerala State Govt 1962; State Sec. Sadachar Samiti, Kerala; mem. Exec. Cttee India Red Cross, Kerala State; Organizer Youth Hostel Movt, Kerala State and served as Sec. Gen. Youth Hostel Asscn of India; experience as social worker; mem. Bd of Govs. Inst. of Social Work directly after inception; Chair. Plantation Corpn of Kerala 1974–78; first Chair. Oil Palm India Ltd (Jt PCK-Govt initiative); Pres. Kerala State Co-operative Rubber Marketing Bd, Cochin for six years; Dir Indian Overseas Bank 1976–82; f. and Dir, then Chair. Chitralekha Film Cooperative, Trivandrum; Publr Bharat Sevak social work journal 1958–67; Man. Dir and Publr Congress Review newspaper 1977–86; Man. Dir Veekshanam (Malayalam daily) newspaper 1978–82; fmr Sec. Gen. Congress Party, Kerala State; fmr mem. All India Congress Cttee (AICC); mem. Indian Parl. (Senate) 1982–94; Chair. Parl. Cttee on Subordinate Legislation 1983–85; Deputy Chair. Senate 1986–87; Minister of State for Parl. Affairs 1987–93, Minister of State for Water Resources 1988–89, Minister of State for Home Affairs, Council of Ministers 1991–93, Chair. Parl. Standing Cttee on Home Affairs 1993–94; Gov. of Meghalaya, Shillong 1995–, of Arunachal Pradesh 1996; Del. to UN Gen. Ass. 1985, 1993, to UN/IPU World Disarmament Symposium 1985, UN World Human Rights Conf. 1993, to Commonwealth, IPU and rubber producers' confs. *Address:* Office of the Governor of Meghalaya, Raj Bhavan, Shillong -793001, India. *Telephone:* (364) 223001 (office); (364) 225352 (home). *Fax:* (364) 223338 (office). *Website:* meghalaya.nic.in (office).

JACOBI, Sir Derek George, Kt, CBE, MA; British actor; b. 22 Oct. 1938, London; s. of Alfred George Jacobi and Daisy Gertrude Masters; ed Leyton County High School and St John's Coll., Cambridge; Birmingham Repertory Theatre 1960–63 (first appeared in One Way Pendulum 1961); National Theatre 1963–71; Prospect Theatre Co. 1972, 1974, 1976–78, Artistic Assoc. 1976–91; Old Vic Co. 1978–79; joined RSC April 1982; Vice-Pres., Nat. Youth Theatre 1982–; Artistic Dir Chichester Festival Theatre 1995–96; Hon. Fellow St John's Coll., Cambridge; Variety Club Award 1976, British Acad. Award 1976, Press Guild Award 1976, Royal Television Soc. Award 1976, Hamburg Shakespeare Award 1998. *Television appearances include:* She Stoops to Conquer, Man of Straw, The Pallisers, I Claudius, Philby, Burgess and Maclean, Tales of the Unexpected, A Stranger in Town, Mr. Pye, Brother Cadfael 1994, Inquisition 2002, Mr. Ambassador 2003, The Long Firm 2004, London 2004, The Long Firm 2004, Marple: The Murder at the Vicarage 2004, Pinochet in Suburbia 2006, Mist: Sheepdog Tales (voice) 2007. *Films include:* Odessa File, Day of the Jackal, The Medusa Touch, Othello, Three Sisters, Interlude, The Human Factor, Charlotte 1981, The Man who went up in Smoke 1981, The Hunchback of Notre Dame 1981, Inside the Third Reich 1982, Little Dorrit 1986, The Tenth Man 1988, Henry V, The Fool 1990, Dead Again, Hamlet 1996, Love is the Devil (Evening Standard Award for Best Actor 1998) 1997, Gladiator 2000, Gosford Park 2001, The Revengers Tragedy 2002, Night's Noontime 2002, Two Men Went to War 2002, Cloud Cuckoo Land 2004, Bye Bye Blackbird 2005, Underworld Evolution 2005, Nanny McPhee 2005, Project Huxley 2005, Arritmia 2007, The Riddle 2007, Anastezsi 2007, The Golden Compass 2007. *Plays include:* The Lunatic, Lover and the Poet 1980, The Suicide 1980, Much Ado about Nothing, Peer Gynt, The Tempest 1982, Cyrano de Bergerac 1983, Breaking the Code 1986, Richard II 1988, Richard III 1989, Kean 1990, Becket 1991, Mad, Bad and Dangerous to Know, Ambassadors 1992, Macbeth 1993, Hadrian VII, Playing the Wife 1995, Uncle Vanya 1996, God Only Knows 2000; Dir Hamlet 1988, 2000. *Leisure interests:* gardening, reading, looking for the next job. *Address:* c/o ICM Ltd, Oxford House, 76 Oxford Street, London, W1N 0AX, England. *Telephone:* (20) 7636-6565. *Fax:* (20) 7323-0101.

JACOBOVITS DE SZEGED, Adriaan; Dutch diplomatist; *EU Special Representative for Moldova;* b. 27 Dec. 1935, Vienna, Austria; s. of Giulio Jacobovits de Szeged and Eveline Tak van Poortvliet; m. Françoise S. Montant 1968; two s.; ed Univ. of Leiden; Master of Netherlands Law; Ministry of Finance 1963; joined Foreign Service 1964; postings at Embassy, Moscow, Perm. Mission to UN and other int. orgs, Geneva, Embassy, London, Embassy, Nairobi, Perm. Del. to EC, Brussels; Dir Econ. Co-operation, Ministry of Foreign Affairs 1978–82; Dir-Gen. Political Affairs 1982–86; Perm. Rep. to UN, New York 1986–89; Perm. Rep. to NATO, Brussels 1989–93; Amb. to USA 1993–97; Pres. Int. Comm. for the Protection of the River Rhine 1999–2001; Personal Rep. of the OSCE Chair.-in-Office for Moldova 2002–03; EU Special Rep. for Moldova 2005–; Kt, Order of the Netherlands Lion; Grosses Verdienstkreuz (Germany); Commdr Légion d'honneur. *Address:* European Commission's Delegation to the Republic of Moldova, Kogalniceanu Street nr 12, MD 2001 Chisinau, Moldova (office); Riouwstraat 76, 2585 HD The Hague, Netherlands. *Telephone:* (2) 50-52-10 (office). *Fax:* (2) 27-26-22 (home). *E-mail:* Delegation-Moldova@cec.eu.int (office). *Website:* www.delmda.cec.eu.int/en (office).

JACOBS, Adrianus Gerardus, MEcon; Dutch business executive; b. 28 May 1936, Rotterdam; m. C.M.M. de Haas 1963; two s. one d.; ed Univ. of Rotterdam; joined De Nederlanden van 1845 1962 (Nationale-Nederlanden since 1963), Gen. Man. 1979, mem. Exec. Bd 1988, mem. Exec. Bd ING Group 1991, Vice-Chair. Exec. Bd ING Group 1992, Chair. 1992; Chair. Exec. Bd ING Insurance NV July 1992; Dir Nederlandse Participatie Mij. NV, NV Struktongroep, Nat. Investeringsbank NV; Kt Order of Netherlands Lion.

JACOBS, Rt Hon. Sir Francis Geoffrey, DPhil, KCMG, QC; British lawyer; *Professor of Law, King's College, London;* b. 8 June 1939, Cliftonville; s. of the late Cecil Sigismund Jacobs and Louise Jacobs (née Fischhof); m. 1st Ruth Freeman 1964; m. 2nd Susan Felicity Gordon Cox 1975; two s. three d.; ed City of London School, Christ Church, Oxford and Nuffield Coll., Oxford; lecturer in Jurisprudence, Univ. of Glasgow 1963–65; lecturer in Law, LSE 1965–69; Prof. of European Law, King's Coll., London 1974–88, Prof. of Law 2006–, Fellow, King's Coll. 1990; Secr. European Comm. of Human Rights and Legal Directorate, Council of Europe 1969–72; Legal Sec. Court of Justice of the EC 1972–74, Advocate Gen. 1988–2006; Barrister, Middle Temple 1964, QC 1984, Bencher 1990; Gov. Inns of Court School of Law 1996–2001; apptd to Privy Council 2005; Commdr, Ordre de Mérite 1983; Hon. LLD (Birmingham) 1996, (Glasgow) 2006; Hon. DCL (City Univ., London) 1997. *Publications include:* several books on European law and Yearbook of European Law (founding ed.) 1981–88. *Address:* School of Law, King's College, Strand, London, WC2R 2LS (office); Fountain Court Chambers, Temple, London, EC4Y 9DH (office); Wayside, 15 St Alban's Gardens, Teddington, Middx, TW11 8AE, England (home). *E-mail:* francis.jacobs@kcl.ac.uk (office).

JACOBS, Georges, MEconSc, DJur; Belgian business executive; *Chairman, Delhaize Group;* ed UCL Belgium, Univ. of Calif., Berkeley, USA; economist IMF 1966; joined UCB Group 1970, Chair. Exec. Cttee 1987–2004, currently Chair. Bd of Dirs; Chair. Bd of Dirs Delhaize Group 2005–; mem. Bd of Dirs Belgacom, Bekaert, SN Brussels Airlines; Pres. Union of Industrial and Employers' Confeds of Europe (UNICE) 1998–2003; mem. Man. Cttee Fed. of Belgian Cos (also Hon. Chair.). *Address:* Delhaize Group, Rue Osseghem-straat 53, Molenbeek-St-Jean, 1080 Brussels, Belgium (office). *Telephone:* (2) 412-21-11 (office). *Fax:* (2) 412-21-94 (office). *Website:* www.delhaize.com (office).

JACOBS, Marc; American fashion designer; b. 9 April 1963, New York City; ed High School of Art and Design, New York, Parsons School of Design; f. Jacobs Duffy Designs (with Robert Duffy) 1984; initiated Marc Jacobs design label 1986; Vice-Pres. Women's Design, Perry Ellis 1989; promoted 'grunge' fashion, early 1990s; Artistic Dir Louis Vuitton 1997–; CFDA Perry Ellis Award for New Talent 1987, CFDA Women's Designer of the Year Award 1992, VH1 Women's Designer of the Year Award, CFDA Accessory Designer of the Year, Best New Retail Concept Award, British Fashion Awards 2007. *Address:* 163 Mercer Street, New York, NY 10012, USA (office). *Telephone:* (212) 343-0222 (office). *Fax:* (212) 343-2960 (office). *Website:* www.marcjacobs.com (office).

JACOBS, Peter Alan, BSc; British business executive; b. 22 Feb. 1943, Ayrshire, Scotland; m. Eileen Dorothy Naftalin 1966; two s. one d.; ed Glasgow and Aston Univs; Production Man. Pedigree Petfoods 1981–83; Sales Dir Mars Confectionery 1983–86; Man. Dir British Sugar PLC 1986–91; Dir S. and W Berisford PLC 1986–91; CEO British United Provident Asscn 1991–98; Chair. Healthcall 1998–2001; Chair. L. A. Fitness 1999–, W.T. Foods; Dir (non-exec.) Hillsdown Holdings 1998–99, Bank Leumi (UK) 1998–2003, Allied Domecq 1998–2004, RAF Strike Command 2005–; Chair. abc media 2005–. *Leisure interests:* tennis, squash, music, theatre, fund-raising. *Address:* 2 Norfolk Road, London, NW8 6AX, England (home). *E-mail:* jacobs@peatonhouse.co.uk (office).

JACOBS, René, BPhil; Belgian conductor and singer (countertenor); *Artistic Director, Innsbrucker Festwochen der alten Musik;* b. 30 Oct. 1946, Ghent; ed Univ. of Ghent, studied singing with Louis Devos in Brussels, Lucie Frateur in The Hague; recitals in Europe, Canada, USA, Mexico and the Philippines; performances with madrigal ensembles and with early music groups, including the Leonhardt Consort, Il Complesso Barocco, La Petite Bande and groups led by Alan Curtis and Nikolaus Harnoncourt; sings Baroque music and directs his own ensemble, Concerto Vocale; best known in operas by Monteverdi, Cesti, Handel, Gluck and Cavalli; sacred music by Charpentier and Couperin; teacher of performing practice in Baroque singing, Schola Cantorum, Basle; appointments at the Int. Summer School for Early Music, Innsbruck, and the Aston Magna Acad. for Baroque Music, USA; regularly invited by Brussels La Monnaie and Berlin Staatsoper Unter den Linden; conducted Cavalli's Giasone, La Calisto, Eliogabalo, Gassmann's Opera seria, Handel's Flavio, Agrippina, Rinaldo, Semele, Giulio Cesare, Monteverdi's L'Incoronazione de Poppea, L'Orfeo, Il ritorno d'Ulisse patria, Madrigals, Graun's Cleopatra e Cesare, Scarlatti's Griselda, Haydn's Il mondo della luna, Conti's Don Chisciotte, Telemann's Orpheus, Der geduldige Sokrates, Keiser's Croesus, Mozart's Nozze di Figaro, Così fan tutte, Don Giovanni, Die Zauberflöte; Artistic Dir Innsbrucker Festwochen der alten Musik; Dr hc (Univ. of Ghent) 2008; Acad. Charles Cros Prix in Honorem 2001, Deutsche Schallplattenpreis Ehrenurkunde 2004, MIDEM Classical Award for Artist of the Year 2005, Gramophone Award for Musical Personality of the Year 2006, Partituren Dirigent des Jahres 2007, Telammann Prize 2008. *Recordings:* Cesti's L'Orontea (from the 1982 Holland Festival), Arias by Monteverdi and Benedetto Ferrari, Motets by Charpentier, Bach's St Matthew Passion, Handel's Admeto and Partenope, Lully's Bourgeois Gentilhomme, Gluck's Orfeo ed Euridice and Echo et Narcisse, Giasone and La Calisto by Cavalli, Handel's Alessandro and Tamerlano, Charpentier's David et Jonathas, Handel's Flavio (Deutsche Schallplattenkritik Jahrespreis 1991), Telemann's Orpheus (Deutsche Schaalplattenkritik Jahrespreis 1998), Scarlatti's Il primo omicidio, Keiser's Croesus, Handel's Giulio Cesare, Handel's Rinaldo (Cannes Classical Award 2004), Mozart's Così fan tutte, Mozart's Le nozze di Figaro (Echo Klassik 2005, MIDEM Classical Music Award for Recording of the Year 2005, Grammy Award for Best Opera 2007) 2004, Handel's Saul (MIDEM Classical Music Award Baroque category 2006, Gramophone Award for Best Baroque Vocal Recording 2006, Echo Klassik 2006) 2005, Haydn's Symphonies Nos 91 & 92 2005, Handel's Messiah 2006, La Clemenza di Tito (Deutsche Schallplattenkritik Jahrespreis 2006, Abendzeitung Stern des Jahres 2006, Classical BRIT Award Critics' Award 2007, Echo Klassik 2007, Opernwelt 2007), Mozart's Don Giovanni. *Address:* Double Bande, 94 rue La Fayette, 75003 Paris, France (office). *E-mail:* doublebande@aol.com (office).

JACOBSON, Dan, BA, FRSL; British (b. South African) writer; *Professor Emeritus of English, University College London;* b. 7 March 1929, Johannesburg; s. of Hyman Michael and Liebe Jacobson (née Melamed); m. Margaret Pye 1954; two s. one d.; ed Boys' High School, Kimberly, Univ. of Witwatersrand, S Africa; worked in business and journalism in SA, settled in England 1955; Fellow in Creative Writing, Stanford Univ., Calif. 1956–57; Prof. of English, Syracuse Univ., New York 1965–66; Visiting Fellow, State Univ. of NY 1971, Humanities Research Centre, ANU, Canberra 1981; Lecturer, Univ. Coll. London 1975–79, Reader in English, Univ. of London 1979–87, Prof. of English, Univ. Coll. London 1988–94, Prof. Emer. 1995–, Fellow 2005–; Hon. DLitt (Witwatersrand) 1997; John Llewelyn Rhys Award 1958, W. Somerset Maugham Award 1961, Jewish Chronicle Award 1971, H.H. Wingate Award 1978, J.R. Ackerley Award for Autobiography 1986, Mary Eleanor Smith Poetry Prize 1992. *Publications:* fiction: The Trap 1955, A Dance in the Sun 1956, The Price of Diamonds 1957, The Evidence of Love 1960, The Beginners 1965, The Rape of Tamar 1970, The Wonder-Worker 1973, Inklings (short stories) 1973, The Confessions of Josef Baisz 1977, Her Story 1987, Hidden in the Heart 1991, The God-Fearer 1992, All For Love 2005; non-fiction: The Story of the Stories (criticism) 1982, Time and Time Again (autobiog.) 1985, Adult Pleasures (criticism) 1988, The Electronic Elephant (travel) 1994, Heshel's Kingdom (travel) 1998, A Mouthful of Glass (trans.) 2000, Ian Hamilton in Conversation with Dan Jacobson (interview) 2002. *Address:* c/o A.M. Heath & Co., 79 St Martin's Lane, London, WC2N 4RE, England (office). *Telephone:* (20) 7836-4271 (office).

JACOBSON, Nina; American film industry executive; ed Brown Univ.; began film career as documentary researcher; joined Disney as story analyst in 1987; joined Silver Pictures as Dir of Film Devt 1988; fmr Head of Devt, MacDonald/Parkes Productions; fmr Sr Vice-Pres. of Production, Universal Pictures; fmr Sr Film Exec., DreamWorks SKG; joined Walt Disney in 1998, responsible for developing scripts and overseeing film production for Walt Disney Pictures, Touchstone Pictures and Hollywood Pictures, Pres. Buena Vista Motion Pictures Group –2006; returned to DreamWorks SKG signing film agreement 2007–; Co-founder (with Bruce Cohen) Out There (collection of gay and lesbian entertainment industry activists) 1995; ranked 94th by Forbes magazine amongst 100 Most Powerful Women 2005. *Address:* c/o DreamWorks Studios, 100 Universal City Plaza, Building 5125, Universal City, CA 91608, USA (office). *Telephone:* (818) 733-9988 (office). *Fax:* (818) 733-9987 (office). *Website:* www.dreamworks.com (office).

JACOBY, Ruth; Swedish diplomatist, international civil servant and organization official; *Ambassador to Germany;* b. 13 Jan. 1949, New York, USA; d. of Erich Jacoby and Lotte Jacoby; m. Bjorn Meidal 1976; two s.; ed Univ. of Uppsala; First Sec., Ministry for Foreign Affairs, Stockholm 1972, Deputy Asst Under-Sec. 1984–88, Asst Under-Sec. and Head of Dept 1990–94, Dir-Gen. for Devt Co-operation 2002–; mem. Swedish del. to OECD, Paris 1980–84; Deputy Asst Under-Sec., Ministry of Finance 1988–90; Exec. Dir World Bank 1994–97; Amb. for Econ. and Social Affairs, Perm. Mission of Sweden to the UN 1997–2002; Co-Chair. Preparatory Cttee of the Int. Conf. on Financing for Devt (FfD) 2001–02; Amb. to Germany 2006–. *Address:* Embassy of Sweden, Rauchstrasse 1, 10787 Berlin, Germany (office). *Telephone:* (30) 50506610 (office). *E-mail:* ruth.jacoby@foreign.ministry.se (home). *Website:* www.ud.se (office).

JACOMB, Sir Martin Wakefield, Kt, MA; British banker and business executive; *Chairman, Share PLC;* b. 11 Nov. 1929, Chiddingfold, Surrey; s. of Felise Jacomb and Hilary W. Jacomb; m. Evelyn Heathcoat Amory 1960; two s. one d.; ed Eton Coll. and Worcester Coll. Oxford; practised at the Bar 1955–68; Kleinwort, Benson Ltd 1968–85, Vice-Chair. 1976–85; Dir Hudson's Bay Co., Canada 1971–86; Chair. The Merchants Trust PLC 1974–85, Transatlantic Fund Inc. 1978–85; Dir Christian Salvesen PLC 1974–88, British Gas PLC 1981–88; Deputy Chair. Securities and Investments Bd Ltd 1985–87; a Deputy Chair. Barclays Bank PLC 1985–93; Chair. Barclays de Zoete Wedd 1986–91, British Council 1992–98; Dir Commercial Union Assurance Co. PLC 1984–93 (Deputy Chair. 1988–93); Dir Bank of England 1986–95, Daily Telegraph 1986–95, RTZ Corpn PLC (now Rio Tinto PLC) 1988–2000; Chair. Postel Investment Man. Ltd 1991–95; Dir Marks and Spencer 1991–2000, Canary Wharf Group PLC 1999– (Chair. 2004–), Minorplanet Systems PLC 2000–04; Deputy Chair. (non-exec.) Delta PLC 1993–94, Chair. 1993–2004; Chair. Prudential Corpn 1995–2000 (Dir 1994–2000), Share PLC 2001–; Dir Royal Opera House Covent Garden Ltd 1987–92, Oxford Playhouse Trust Ltd 1994, Oxford Playhouse Ltd 1994; External mem., Finance Cttee, Oxford University Press 1971–95; Hon. Master of the Bench of the Inner Temple 1987; Trustee, Nat. Heritage Memorial Fund 1982–97; Chancellor Univ. of Buckingham 1998–; Hon. Fellow, Worcester Coll. Oxford 1994; Dr hc (Buckingham) 1997, (Oxford) 1997. *Leisure interests:* theatre, family bridge. *Address:* Share PLC, The Share Centre, Oxford House, Oxford Road, Aylesbury, Bucks., HP21 8SZ (office); Office of the Chancellor, University of Buckingham, Hunter Street, Buckingham, MK18 1EG, England (office). *Website:* www.share.co.uk (office); www.buckingham.ac.uk (office).

JACQUEMARD, Simonne; French novelist, poet and essayist; b. 6 May 1924, Paris; d. of André Jacquemard and Andrée Jacquemard (née Raimondi); m. 2nd Jacques Brosse 1955; ed Inst. Saint-Pierre, Univ. of Paris; teacher of music; collaborator, Laffont-Bompiani Dictionaries; contrib. to Figaro Littéraire, La Table Ronde; travelled in USSR, Egypt, Greece, Italy, N Africa and Spain; Officier Ordre des Arts et des Lettres 1993, Chevalier Légion d'honneur 1999; Prix Renaudot 1962, Grand prix Thyde-Monnier 1984. *Dance:* Sacred dances of India; flamenco dance shows 1982–2000. *Publications:* Les fascinés 1951, Sable 1952, La leçon des ténèbres 1954, Planant sur les airs 1960, Compagnons insolites 1961, Le veilleur de nuit 1962 (Prix Renaudot 1962), L'orangerie 1963, Les derniers rapaces 1965, Dérive au zénith 1965, Exploration d'un corps 1965, Navigation vers les îles 1967, A l'état sauvage 1967, L'éruption du Krakatoa 1969, La thessalienne 1973, Des roses pour mes chevreuils 1974, Le mariage berbère 1975, Danse de l'orée 1979, Le funambule 1981, Lalla Zahra 1983, La fête en éclats 1985, Les belles échappées 1987, L'huître dans la perle 1993, Le Jardin d'Hérodote 1995, L'Éphèbe couronné de lierre 1995, La Gloire d'Ishwara 1996, Vers l'estuaire ébloui 1996, Trois mystiques grecs 1997, Orphée ou l'initiation mystique (jtly) 1998, L'Oiseau 1963, 1998 (Prix Jacques Lacroix, l'Académie française 1999), Héraclite d'Ephèse 2003, Rituels 2004, Pythagore et l'Harmonie des Sphères 2004. *Leisure interests:* studies on music (with Lucette Descave and Henriette Casadesus) and on bird life and observation of wild animals. *Address:* Le Verdier, 24620 Sireuil, France.

JACQUES, Paula; French author and broadcaster; b. 8 May 1949, Cairo; d. of Jacques Abadi and Esther Sasson; m. (divorced 1970); worked as comedienne in Africa; joined Radio France Internationale as reporter, worked on Après-midi de France-Culture, L'Oreille en coin 1975–90; presenter, Nuits-noires France-Inter radio 1997–, Cosmopolitaine 2000–; sometime writer, F Magazine; mem. jury Prix Femina 1996–, Prix des Cinq Continents. *Play:* Zanouba. *Publications:* Lumière de l'oeil 1980, Un baiser froid comme la lune 1983, L'Heritage de Tante Carlotta 1987, Deborah et les anges dissipés (Prix Femina 1991), La Déscente au Paradis (Prix Nice Baie des Anges) 1995, Les femmes avec leur amour 1997, Gilda Stambouli souffre et se plaint... (Prix Europe 1) 2001, Rachel-Rose et l'officier arabe (Prix des Sables d'Olonne) 2006. *Address:* France-Inter, 116 avenue du Président Kennedy, 75220 Paris cédex 16, France.

JACQUET, Luc; French filmmaker and writer; b. 5 Dec. 1967, Bourg-en-Bresse; fmr biologist. *Films:* Le congès des pingouins (cinematographer) 1993, Le printemps des phoques de Weddell (Ancre de bronze, Festival Int. du Film Maritime et d'Exploration, Toulon 1996, Coup de coeur du jury, Festival Int. du Film Montagne et Aventure, Autrans 1996) 1996, Le léopard de mer: la part de l'ogre (Palme d'Argent & Prix de la Meilleure Composition Musicale, Festival Mondial de l'Image Sous-Marine, Antibes 1999, Prix pour l'Excellente Qualité des Prises de Vues Sous-marines & Prix pour la Musique, Festival Int. du Film sur la Vie Sauvage, Missoula, Mont., USA 2000, Prix de la Meilleure Réalisation, Ekofilm – Festival Int. du Film de l'Environnement, Prague 2000) 1999, Killer Whales: Up Close and Personal (cinematographer) 2000, Une plage et trop de manchots (Primé au Festival Int. du Film Ornithologique de Ménigoute 2001) 2001, La tique et l'oiseau (Prix Nature et Découvertes, Festival Int. du Film Ornithologique de Ménigoute 2002, Prix du meilleur commentaire, Festival Valvert, Brussels 2002, Prix de la côte Picarde, Festival de l'oiseau d'Abbeville 2002) 2001, Sous le signe du serpent 2004, Antarctique printemps express (Prix Spécial Meilleur son, Festival Vertical de Moscou 2006) 2004, Des manchots et des hommes (Of Penguins and Men) (One Planet Award, Wildlife Film Festival, Toyama 2005, Grand prix du public Festival Grandeur Nature, Val d'Isère 2005, Best Film, Prix Jules Verne du Public, Prix Jules Verne de la Jeunesse, Festival Jules Verne 2005, Grand Prix, Festival de l'oiseau, Abbeville 2005, Ancre d'Argent, Prix des collégiens, Festival Int. du Film Maritime et d'Exploration, Toulon 2005, Edelweiss d'Argent, Festival du film de montagne de Torello 2005, Prix Adventura Homme et environnement, Mountain Film Festival, Canada 2005) 2004, La marche de l'empereur (The Emperor's Journey, aka March of the Penguins, USA) (Best Film Documentary, Las Vegas Film Critics Soc. Awards 2005, Nat. Board of Review (USA) 2005, Southeastern Film Critics Asscn Awards (USA) 2005, Broadcast Film Critics Asscn Awards (USA) 2006, Golden Trailer Awards (USA) 2006, Camie, Character and Morality in Entertainment Awards (co-recipient) 2006) 2005, Academy Award for Best Documentary, Features 2006, and numerous other awards) 2005, Le renard et l'enfant (The Fox and the Child) 2007. *E-mail:* contact@luc-jacquet.com (office). *Website:* www.luc-jacquet.com (office).

JACQUET, Michel Antoine Paul Marie; French business executive; b. 28 March 1936, Dijon; s. of André Jacquet and Marie-Antoinette Baut; m. 2nd Marie-Agnès Corbière 1976; one s. and one s. one d. by first m.; ed Lycée Rouget de Lisle, Lons-le-Saulnier, Lycée du Parc, Lyons and Ecole Polytechnique; Dir-Gen. Crédit Lyonnais d'Espagne 1971–77; Dir-Gen. Paribas Gabon and Pres. Sogapar 1977–79; Deputy Dir Banque Paribas 1980–84; CEO Paribas New York 1985–88; Pres. Nord-Est and Magnésia 1989–95, Hon. Pres. Nord-Est 1995–; currently Chair. Ledo-Salina; Vice-Chair. Supervisory Bd EDF Partenaires Capital Investissement; mem. Supervisory Bd Poincaré Investissements; mem. Bd of Dirs Lombard Int. Assurance, Texavenir, Renaissance Holdings, Cinq A Sec Holdings, LCIE Landaver;; Croix de valeur militaire, Chevalier Légion d'honneur. *Address:* Ledo-Salina, 46–48 rue Lauriston, 75116 Paris (office); 15 rue Raynouard, 75016 Paris, France (home).

JAEGER, Heinrich Martin, PhD; German physicist and academic; *Director, James Franck Institute, University of Chicago;* b. 15 May 1957, Flensburg; m. Julie Jaeger; one c.; ed Univ. of Kiel, Germany, Univ. of Minnesota, USA; Postdoctoral Fellow, Univ. of Chicago 1987–88, Asst Prof. 1991–96, Assoc. Prof. 1996–2000, Prof. 2000, Dir Materials Research Center 2001–06, Argonne Consortium for Nanoscience Research 2001–, James Franck Inst. 2007–, Chair. Physical Sciences Div. Cttee on Diversity 2005–; Sr Researcher, Centre for Submicron Tech., Delft Univ. of Tech., The Netherlands 1989–91; mem. Tech. Advisory Bd Atomworks 2003–; mem. Scientific Advisory Cttee, Argonne Center for Nanoscale Materials 2003–; mem. Essential Science Task Force, Chicago Museum of Science and Industry 2003–; mem. External Advisory Bd Centro para la Investigación Interdisciplinaria Avanzada en Ciencias de los Materiales, Chile 2004–; Fellow, American Physical Soc. 2002; Fulbright Scholarship 1981–82, Univ. of Minnesota Dissertation Fellowship 1986–87, James Franck Fellowship, Univ. of Chicago 1987–88, David and Lucile Packard Fellowship 1991–96, Alfred P. Sloan Research Fellowship 1992–94, Research Corpn Cottrell Scholarship 1994–96, Outstanding Achievement Award, Univ. of Minnesota 2002, Quantrell Award for Excellence in Undergraduate Teaching. *Publications:* author or co-author of over 130 scientific publs. *Address:* James Franck Institute, Center for Integrative Science, E229, University of Chicago, 929 East 57th Street, Chicago, IL 60637, USA (office). *Telephone:* (773) 702-6074 (office). *Fax:* (773) 834-0471 (office). *E-mail:* h-jaeger@uchicago.edu (office). *Website:* jfi.uchicago.edu (office).

JAEGER, Marc; Luxembourg judge; *President, Court of First Instance of the European Communities;* b. 1954; fmr attaché de justice, Public Attorney's Office; fmr Judge and Vice-Pres. Luxembourg Dist Court; Lecturer, Centre Univ. de Luxembourg; Legal Sec. Court of Justice of the European Communities 1986–; Judge, Court of First Instance 1996–, Pres. 2007–. *Address:* Court of the First Instance of the European Communities, rue du Fort Niedergrünewald, 2925 Luxembourg, Luxembourg (office). *Telephone:* 4303-1 (office). *Fax:* 4303-2100 (office). *Website:* www.curia.eu.int (office).

JAENICKE, Lothar, DPhil, DiplChem; German biochemist; b. 14 Sept. 1923, Berlin; s. of Johannes Jaenicke and Erna Jaenicke (née Buttermilch); m. Dr Doris Heinzel 1949 (died 2005); two s. two d.; ed Univs of Marburg, Tübingen; taught Univ. of Marburg 1946–57, Munich 1957–62, Cologne 1962, apptd. Prof. Cologne Univ. 1963, also Dir Inst. of Biochem. 1988, now Prof. Emer.; Visiting Scientist All India Inst. of Medicine, New Delhi 1961, Univ. of Texas, Austin 1977, 1992, 1994, 1996; Visiting Prof. American Univ. of Beirut 1971, Ain Shams Univ., Cairo 1974, Indian Inst. of Science, Bangalore 1980; mem. Rheinisch-Westfälische Akademie der Wissenschaften, Deutsche Akademie der Naturforscher Leopoldinae; Corresp. mem. Bayerische Akad. der Wissenschaften, Academia Europea; Fellow, Wissenschaftskolleg Berlin 1986–87; Hon. mem. Gesellschaft für Biochemie und Molekular Biologie, Gesellschaft der Naturforschung und Ärzte; Paul Ehrlich/Ludwig-Darmstaedter-Preis 1963, Otto Warburg Medal 1979, Richard Kuhn Medal 1984, Lorenz Oken Medal 2000. *Publications:* around 270 original papers on enzymology and biochemical signalling in scientific journals. *Address:* Kaesenstr. 13, 50677 Cologne (home); University of Cologne Institute of Biochemistry, Zülpicherstr. 47, 50674 Cologne, Germany (office). *Telephone:* (221) 4706425 (office); (221) 315725 (home). *Fax:* (221) 4706431 (office).

JAFFE, Harold W., AB, MD; American epidemiologist and academic; *Chairman, Department of Public Health, University of Oxford;* b. 26 April 1946, Newton, Mass.; ed Univ. of California at Berkeley and at Los Angeles; Jr doctor at Univ. of Calif. at LA Hosp. 1971–74; Clinical Research Investigator, Venereal Disease Control Div., Centers for Disease Control (CDC), Atlanta 1974–77, 1980–81, Epidemic Intelligence Service Officer for AIDS Activity 1981–83, f. (with James W. Curran and others) Kaposi's Sarcoma-Opportunistic Infections Task Force, Center for Infectious Diseases to study causes of immune-deficiency disease in homosexual men 1981, Chief, Epidemiology Br. of AIDS Programme, CDC 1983–, Dir Div. AIDS, STD and TB Laboratory Research –2001, Acting Dir Nat. Center for HIV, STD, and TB Prevention (NCHSTP) 2001, Dir 2002–03; Chair. Dept of Public Health, Oxford Univ. 2003–; Fellow in Infectious Diseases, Univ. of Chicago 1977–80; Visiting Prof., Chester Beatty Labs, Inst. of Cancer Research and Dept of Medicine, Hammersmith Hosp., London, 1988–90; Clinical Instructor of Medicine, Emory Univ. School of Medicine, Atlanta; Assoc. Ed. American Journal of Epidemiology, mem. Editorial Bd AIDS journal; Commendation Medal for work on HIV/AIDS, US Public Health Service 1984, Meritorious Service Medal 1986, Distinguished Service Medal 1992. *Publications:* book chapters and over 90 articles in scientific journals, including Epidemiologic Aspects of the Current Outbreak of Kaposi's Sarcoma and Opportunistic Infections, in New England Journal of Medicine Jan. 1982, The Epidemiology of AIDS: Current Status and Future Prospects, in Science Sept. 1985 (co-author), HIV Infection and AIDS in the United States, in Science Feb. 1989 (co-author). *Address:* Department of Public Health, University of Oxford, Old Road Campus, Headington, Oxford, OX3 7LF, England (office). *Telephone:* (1865) 226603 (office). *Website:* www.dphpc.ox.ac.uk (office).

JAFFE, Stanley Richard, BEcons; American film producer and director; b. 31 July 1940, New Rochelle, New York; s. of Leo Jaffe and Dora Bressler; m. Melinda Long; two s. two d.; ed Wharton School, Univ. of Pennsylvania; with Seven Arts Assoc. Corpn 1962–67, exec. Asst to Pres. 1964; Dir East Coast Programming, Seven Arts TV 1963–64, Dir Programming 1965–67; Exec. Vice-Pres., Chief Corp. Officer, Paramount Pictures Corpn 1969–70, Pres. Corpn also Pres. Paramount TV 1970–71; Pres. Jaffilms Inc. 1971; Exec. Vice-Pres. Worldwide Production, Columbia Pictures Corpn 1965–76; Pres. and COO Paramount Communications, New York 1991–94; Gov., Pres., COO New York Knicks 1991–94; Gov. New York Rangers 1991–94; owner Jaffilms LLC 1994–. *Films include:* The Professionals 1963, Goodbye Columbus 1968, Bad Company 1971, Man on A Swing 1973, Bad News Bears 1974, Kramer vs Kramer 1979, Taps 1981, Without a Trace 1983, Racing with the Moon 1984, Firstborn 1984, Fatal Attraction 1987, The Accused 1988, Black Rain 1989, School Ties 1992, The Firm 1993, Madeleine 1998, I Dreamed of Africa 2000, Four Feathers 2002.

JAFFRELOT, Christophe, PhD; French political scientist and academic; *Director, Centre d'Études et de Recherches Internationales (CERI);* ed Institut d'études politiques, Univ. Paris I – Sorbonne, Institut nat. des langues et civilisations orientales; Lecturer in South Asian Politics, Institut d'études politiques, Univ. Paris I – Sorbonne and Institut nat. des langues et civilisations orientales; Dir Centre d'études et de recherches internationales

(CERI); Ed. Critique internationale. *Publications:* The Hindu Nationalist Movement and Indian Politics 1996, L'Inde contemporaine de 1950 à nos jours (ed.) 1997, La démocratie en Inde – Religion, caste et politique 1998, BJP – The Compulsions of Politics (co-ed.) 1998, Le Pakistan, carrefour de tensions régionales (ed.) 1999, Démocraties d'ailleurs: démocraties et démocratisations hors d'Occident (ed.) 2000, Le Pakistan (ed.) 2000, Dr Ambedkar 2000, Inde: La Démocratie par la caste 2005. *Address:* CERI, 56 rue Jacob, 75006 Paris, France (office). *Telephone:* 1-58-71-70-00 (office). *Fax:* 1-58-71-70-91 (office). *E-mail:* info@ceri-sciences-po.org (office). *Website:* www.ceri-sciences-po.org (office).

JAGAT, Gurbachan; Indian politician and fmr police officer; *Governor of Manipur;* joined Indian Police Service 1966, Sr Supt, Amritsar 1978–81, Deputy Insp. Gen. Intelligence/Security Div., Punjab Police Force 1982–90, Man. Dir Punjab Police Housing Corpn 1990–95, Dir Gen. of Admin 1995–97; Dir Gen. of Police, Jammu and Kashmir 1997–2000; Dir Gen. Border Security Force 2000–02; Chair. Union Public Service Comm. 2002–08; Gov. of Manipur 2008–; Padma Shri 1987; Indian Police Medal for Meritorious Service 1982, Police Officer of the Year Award (Govt of Jammu and Kashmir) 2001, Pres.'s Police Medal for Distinguished Service 1992, Pashchimi Star, Sangram Medal, Special Duty Medal, Aantrik Seva Suraksha Medal. *Address:* Raj Bhawan, Imphal 795 001 Manipur, India (office). *Telephone:* (385) 2221444 (office). *Fax:* (385) 2220278 (office). *E-mail:* info@manipur.nic.in (office). *Website:* manipur.nic.in (office).

JAGDEO, Bharrat, MEconSc; Guyanese politician and head of state; *President;* b. 23 Jan. 1964, Unity Village, East Coast Demerara; ed Moscow State Univ.; mem. People's Progressive Party, elected to Cen. Cttee 1993, later mem. Exec. Cttee; worked as economist in State Planning Secr. 1990–92; Special Advisor to Minister of Finance 1992–93; Jr Minister of Finance 1993; fmrly Dir Guyana Water Authority; Dir Caribbean Devt Bank, Nat. Bank of Industry and Commerce, Gov. for Guyana, World Bank; Sr Finance Minister 1995–99; Prime Minister of Guyana 9–11 Aug. 1999; Pres. of Guyana 1999–. *Address:* Office of the President, New Garden Street, Bourda, Georgetown, Guyana (office). *Telephone:* 225-1330 (office). *Fax:* 227-3050 (office). *E-mail:* opmed@op.gov.gy (office). *Website:* www.op.gov.gy (office).

JAGENDORF, André Tridon, PhD; American biologist and academic; *Liberty Hyde Bailey Emeritus Professor of Plant Physiology, College of Agriculture and Life Sciences, Cornell University;* b. 21 Oct. 1926, New York; s. of Moritz A. Jagendorf and Sophie S. Jagendorf; m. Jean Whitenack 1952; two d. one s.; ed Cornell and Yale Univs.; Postdoctoral Fellow, Univ. of Calif., Los Angeles 1951–53; Asst Prof., Johns Hopkins Univ. 1953–58, Assoc. Prof. 1958–65, Prof. of Biology 1966; Prof. of Plant Physiology, Cornell Univ. 1966–, Liberty Hyde Bailey Prof. of Plant Physiology 1981–96, Emer. Prof. 1997–; mem. NAS 1980; Pres. American Soc. of Plant Physiologists; Merck Fellow in Natural Sciences 1951–53; Weizmann Fellow 1962; AAAS Fellow 1964; Fellow American Acad. of Arts and Sciences 1972; Distinguished Fellow, American Soc. of Plant Physiologists 2006; Outstanding Young Scientist Award, Md Acad. of Sciences 1961, Kettering Research Award 1963, C. F. Kettering Award in Photosynthesis, American Soc. of Plant Physiologists 1978, Charles Reid Barnes Award 1989. *Publications:* 162 papers in scientific journals. *Leisure interests:* music, ballet, art. *Address:* Plant Biology Department, 261 Plant Sciences Building, Cornell University, Ithaca, NY 14853 (office); 455 Savage Farm Drive, Ithaca, NY 14850, USA (home). *Telephone:* (607) 255-8940 (office); (607) 255-8826 (laboratory) (office). *Fax:* (607) 255-5407 (office); (607) 266-8703 (home). *E-mail:* atj1@cornell.edu (office). *Website:* www.plantbio.cornell.edu (office).

JAGGER, Bianca, MA; British (b. Nicaraguan) artist, film director and human rights activist; b. 2 May 1950, Managua, Nicaragua; d. of Carlos Perez-Mora and Dora Macias Somassiba; m. Michael P. Jagger 1971 (divorced 1979); one d.; ed Inst. of Political Sciences, Paris and New York Univ.; lecturer on Cen. America at several colls and univs; Co-Founder Iris House, New York; has campaigned for human rights in Cen. America, mem. several US Congressional dels and dels from int. human rights orgs; visited the Fmr Yugoslavia to document alleged human rights violations and testified before Helsinki Comm. on Human Rights and US Congressional Human Rights Caucus; has helped to evacuate children from Bosnia 1993–; works to protect rainforests in Honduras, Nicaragua and Brazil and indigenous peoples in Brazil; headed AIDS campaign 2001; contribs to New York Times; mem. Exec. Dir's Leadership Council, Amnesty Int. USA, Advisory Cttee Human Rights Watch America, Bd of Dirs Action Council for Peace in the Balkans, Bd Hispanic Fed., New York; Special Adviser Indigenous Devt Int., Cambridge, UK; Hon. DH (Stone Hill Coll., MA) 1983; UN Earth Day Int. Award 1994, Humanitarian Award, Hispanic Fed. of New York City 1996, 1996 Woman of the Year, Boys Town, Italy, Abolitionist of the Year Award, Nat. Coalition to Abolish the Death Penalty 1996, Right Livelihood Award 2004. *Films include:* Flesh Color, Success, Cannonball Run, Chud II. *TV includes:* Hotel, Miami Vice, The Colby's, The Rattles. *Leisure interests:* horse-riding, water-skiing. *Address:* 530 Park Avenue, 18D, New York, NY 10021, USA. *Telephone:* (212) 512-5328. *Fax:* (212) 512-7474.

JAGGER, Sir Michael (Mick) Philip, Kt, KBE; British singer, songwriter and actor; b. 26 July 1943, Dartford, Kent; s. of the late Joe Jagger and Eva Jagger; m. 1st Bianca Pérez Morena de Macías 1971 (divorced 1979); one d.; m. 2nd Jerry Hall (q.v.) 1990 (divorced 1999); two s. two d.; one d. by Marsha Hunt; one c. by Luciana Morad; ed London School of Econs, Univ. of London; began singing career with Little Boy Blue and the Blue Boys while at LSE; appeared with Blues Inc. at Ealing Blues Club, singer with Blues Inc. at London Marquee Club 1962; Founder-mem. and lead singer, Rolling Stones 1962–; wrote songs with Keith Richards under pseudonyms Nanker, Phelge until 1965, without pseudonyms 1965–; first own composition to reach No. 1 in

UK charts The Last Time 1965; first major UK tour 1964; tours to USA, Europe; fmrly lived in France; Pres. LSE Students' Union 1994–; Nordoff-Robbins Silver Clef 1982, Grammy Lifetime Achievement Award 1986, Ivor Novello Award for Outstanding Contribution to British Music 1991, Golden Globe Award for Best Original Song (for Old Habits Die Hard, with Dave Stewart, for film Alfie) 2005. *Films:* Ned Kelly (actor) 1969, Performance (actor) 1969, Gimme Shelter (actor) 1972, Free Jack (actor) 1991, Freejack (actor) 1992, Bent (actor) 1996, Enigma (prod.) 2001, Shine a Light 2007. *Recordings include:* albums: with The Rolling Stones: The Rolling Stones 1964, The Rolling Stones No. 2 1965, Out Of Our Heads 1965, Aftermath 1966, Between The Buttons 1967, Their Satanic Majesties Request 1967, Beggar's Banquet 1968, Let It Bleed 1969, Get Yer Ya-Ya's Out 1969, Sticky Fingers 1971, Exile On Main Street 1972, Goat's Head Soup 1973, It's Only Rock And Roll 1974, Black And Blue 1976, Some Girls 1978, Emotional Rescue 1980, Tattoo You 1981, Still Life 1982, Undercover 1983, Dirty Work 1986, Steel Wheels 1989, Flashpoint 1991, Voodoo Lounge 1994, Stripped 1995, Bridges to Babylon 1997, Forty Licks 2002, Live Licks 2004, A Bigger Bang 2005; solo: She's The Boss 1985, Primitive Cool 1987, Wandering Spirit 1993, Goddess In The Doorway 2001. *Publication:* According to the Rolling Stones (autobiography, jtly) 2003. *Address:* Munro Sounds, 5 Wandsworth Plain, London, SW18 1ES, England (office). *Telephone:* (20) 8877-3111 (office). *Fax:* (20) 8877-3033 (office). *Website:* www.rollingstones.com.

JAGIELIŃSKI, Roman; Polish politician; *Chairman, Peasant Democratic Party;* b. 2 Jan. 1947, Wichradz, Radom Prov.; m.; two s.; ed Horticulture Dept Main School of Farming, Warsaw; runs fruit farm in village of Świniokierz Dworski, Piotrków Trybunalski Prov.; Pres. Polish Fruit-Growers' Union; mem. United Peasants' Party (ZSL) 1970–89; mem. Polish Peasants' Party 'Rebirth' 1989–90; mem. Polish Peasants' Party (PSL) 1990–97; Co-Founder and Leader Peasant Democratic Party 1997–, Chair. 1998–; Deputy to Sejm (Parl.) 1991–, Vice-Chair. Parl. Comm. for Small and Medium Enterprises 1997–, Deputy Head of Agric. Cttee 2001–; Vice-Pres. Polish Peasants' Party Parl. Club 1991-96; Deputy Prime Minister and Minister of Agric. and Food Economy 1995–97; Chair. Soc. of Econ. and Educ. Initiatives. *Address:* Sejm RP, ul. Wiejska 4/6/8, 00-902 Warsaw, Poland (office). *Telephone:* (22) 6941602 (office). *E-mail:* Roman.Jagielinski@sejm.pl (home). *Website:* www.sejm.gov.pl (office).

JAGLAND, Thorbjørn; Norwegian politician; *Chairman, Parliamentary Standing Committee on Foreign Affairs;* b. 5 Nov. 1950; m. Hanne Grotjord 1975; two c.; ed Univ. of Oslo; Exec. Sec. Norwegian Labour League of Youth (AUF) 1977–81; Project and Planning Officer, Norwegian Labour Party 1981–86, Acting Gen. Sec. 1986, Gen. Sec. 1987, Chair. 1992–; mem. Storting; Chair. Labour Party Parl. Group; Prime Minister of Norway 1996–97; Minister of Foreign Affairs 2000–01; Chair. Parl. Standing Cttee on Foreign Affairs 2001–. *Publications include:* Min europeiske drøm 1990, Ny solidaritet 1993, Brev 1995, Vår sårbare verden 2002, For det blir for sent (co-author) 1982, Ti tescr om EU og Norge 2003; articles on defence, nat. security and disarmament. *Address:* Stortinget, 0026 Oslo, Norway (office). *Telephone:* 23313055 (office). *Fax:* 23313818 (office). *E-mail:* thorbjorn.jagland@stortinget.no (office).

JAGNE, Baboucarr-Blaise Ismaila, MA; Gambian diplomatist; *Head, United Nations Political Affairs Division, African Union;* b. 11 Feb. 1955, Banjul; m.; four c.; ed Univ. of Dakar and Univs of Grenoble and Paris, France; Asst Sec., Foreign Ministry 1980–84, Sec. to Pres. of Gambia, Chair. Islamic Peace Cttee on Iran–Iraq War 1984–88, Sr Asst Sec. for Political Legal Affairs 1986–89, Prin. Asst Sec. 1989–92; Deputy Perm. Sec. for Educ. 1992–93, for Political Affairs 1993–95; Minister of External Affairs 1995–97; Amb. to Saudi Arabia 1997–98; Perm. Rep. to UN 1998–2001; Sec. of State for Foreign Affairs 2001–05; Head, UN Political Affairs Div., African Union HQ, Addis Abba. *Address:* UN Political Affairs Division, African Union, POB 3243, Addis Ababa, Ethiopia (office). *Telephone:* (1) 51-7700 (office). *Fax:* (1) 51-7844 (office). *E-mail:* webmaster@africa-union.org (office). *Website:* www.africa-union.org (office).

JAGNE, Dodou Bammy; Gambian diplomatist; m.; five c.; ed Abingdon Coll., UK, London Chamber of Commerce, Int. Law Inst., Washington, DC, USA; various postings in Dept of State for Finance and Econ. Affairs, including Prin. Loans Officer responsible for External Public Debt and Loans Admin 1983–93, Deputy Perm. Sec. with responsibility for Macro-econ. Man., aid coordination and Chairing the Major Tender Bd 1997–98, Perm. Sec. 1998–2003; consultant, Int. Procurement Agency, UK, Gambia Public Works and Capacity Building Agency 1995–96; Nat. Authorizing Officer European Devt Fund Program 1983–2003; Amb. to USA 2004–07. *Publications:* author of various studies, reports and legislation. *Address:* c/o Department of State for Foreign Affairs, 4 Col. Muammar Ghadaffi Avenue, Banjul, Gambia.

JÁGR, Jaromír; Czech professional ice hockey player; b. 15 Feb. 1972, Kladno, Czechoslovakia (now Czech Repub.); s. of Jaromír Jágr; began skating aged three; was playing at highest level of competition in Czechoslovakia aged 16; first Czechoslovakian player drafted by NHL (Nat. Hockey League) without first defecting to West; taken by Pittsburgh Penguins with fifth overall pick in NHL Entry Draft 1990–2001; won five NHL scoring titles with the Penguins 1994–95 to 2000–01, including four in a row 1997–98 to 2000–01; team gold medal (Capt.), Winter Olympics, Nagano 1998; youngest player in NHL history (aged 19) to score a goal in Stanley Cup finals; traded to Washington Capitals 2001–03, to New York Rangers 2003–; played for Kladno, Czech Repub. 2004–05 (during NHL players strike), later for Avangard ice-hockey team, Omsk, Russia; captained Czech Repub. Gold Medal-winning team, World Hockey Championships, Austria 2005; scored 1,400th point 2 March 2006; leading active point scorer among European-born NHL players, second on all-time points list for European players; announced as new capt. of New York Rangers Oct. 2006–; scored his 600th career NHL goal Nov. 2006; wears no. 68 in honour of Prague Spring rebellion in Czechoslovakia in 1968, also the year in which his grandfather died while in prison; mem. Triple Gold Club (players who have won a Stanley Cup, a World Hockey Championship and an Olympic gold medal), Stanley Cup Winner 1991,1992, NHL All-Rookie Team 1991, Golden Stick Award 1995, 1996, 1999, 2000, 2002, 2005, 2006, Art Ross Trophy (Leading Point Scorer) 1995, 1998, 1999, 2000, 2001, NHL First Team All-Star 1995, 1996, 1998, 1999, 2000, 2001, 2006, NHL Second Team All-Star 1997, ranked 37th on The Hockey News' list of 100 Greatest Hockey Players 1998, Hart Trophy 1999, Lester B. Pearson Award 1999, 2000, 2006, Czech Sportsman of the Year 2005, IIHF World Championship All-Star Team 2005. *Address:* New York Rangers, 2 Pennsylvania Plaza, New York, NY 10121, USA (office). *Telephone:* (212) 465-6000 (office). *E-mail:* newyorkrangers@thegarden.com (office). *Website:* www.newyorkrangers.com (office).

JAHAN, Ismat, BA, MA; Bangladeshi lawyer and diplomatist; *Permanent Representative, United Nations;* ed Dhaka Univ., Fletcher School, Tufts Univ., with cross-registered course works at Harvard Univ., USA; career diplomat 1982–; fmr Fellow, School of Foreign Service, Georgetown Univ., Washington, DC; served in various capacities at Ministry of Foreign Affairs as well as missions abroad including Perm. Missions to UN in New York and Geneva, and High Comm. in New Delhi; Dir-Gen. Int. Orgs, UN and Multilateral Econ. Affairs, Ministry of Foreign Affairs –2005; Amb. to the Netherlands 2005–07; Amb. and Perm. Rep. to UN, New York 2007–. *Address:* Permanent Mission of Bangladesh, 227 East, 14th Floor, 45th Street, New York, NY 10017, USA (office). *Telephone:* (212) 867-3434 (office). *Fax:* (212) 972-4038 (office). *E-mail:* bangladesh@un.int (office). *Website:* www.un.int/bangladesh (office).

JAHANGIR, Asma, BA, BLL; Pakistani lawyer and human rights activist; *Special Rapporteur on Freedom of Religion or Belief, United Nations;* b. 27 Jan. 1952, Lahore; d. of Malik Jilani; sister of Hina Jilani; ed Kinnard Coll., Lahore, Pubjab Univ.; qualified as lawyer 1978; Advocate of the High Court 1982–; Co-founder (with Hina Jilani) and Pnr, AGHS Law Assocs (all-women law firm), Lahore 1980–, also Founder and Dir AGHS Legal Aid Cell (first free legal aid centre in Pakistan), Lahore 1984–; Advocate of the Supreme Court 1992–; Founding mem. and Chair. Human Rights Comm. of Pakistan, Lahore 1993–; mem. Women's Action Forum, Punjab Women Lawyers Asscn; mem. Comm. of Enquiry for Women (est. by Govt of Pakistan) 1994–97; UN Special Rapporteur on Extra Judicial, Summary or Arbitrary Executions 1998–2004, Special Rapporteur on Freedom of Religion or Belief 2004–; Commr Int. Comm. of Jurists, Geneva 1998–; Prof. of Law, Quaid-e-Azam Law Coll., Lahore; Co-chair South Asians for Human Rights 2000–; Council Mem. Minority Rights Group Int. 2002–04; mem. Bd of Dirs UN Research Inst. for Social Devt, Commonwealth Lawyers' Asscn, London 1997–2002, Interights, London 1997–2002, Asia Pacific Forum on Women Law and Devt, Kuala Lumpur 1988–2000; Exec. mem. Int. Crisis Group 2002–; placed under house arrest 2007; Hon. LLD (Univ. of St Gallen, Switzerland) 1998, (Queen's Univ., Canada) 1998, (Amherst Coll.) 2003; ABA Int. Human Rights Award 1992, Sitara-I-Imtiaz 1995, King Baudouin Int. Devt Prize 1998, Human Rights Award, Lawyers Cttee for Human Rights 1999, Millennium Peace Prize 2001, Ramon Magsaysay Award for Public Service 2002. *Achievements include:* led student protest against mil. dictator Ayub Khan 1969; filed a constitutional petition in Supreme Court challenging arrest of her father and questioning legality of Bhutto's govt 1972, won case 1982. *Publications include:* Divine Sanction? The Hadood Ordinance 1988, Children of a Lesser God: Child Prisoners of Pakistan 1992; numerous publs on topics ranging from child labour to electoral processes in Pakistan. *Address:* 131-E/1, Gulberg-III, Lahore (office); c/o Human Rights Commission of Pakistan, Aiwan-i-Jahmoor, 107 Tipu Block, New Garden Town, Lahore 54600, Pakistan (office). *Telephone:* (42) 5763234 (office). *Fax:* (42) 5763236 (office). *E-mail:* law@aghs.brain.net.pk (office). *Website:* www2.ohchr.org/ENGLISH/ISSUES/RELIGION/index.htm (office); www.hrcp-web.org.

JAHANGIRI, Guissou Jeannot, BA; French/Iranian international organization official; *Director, Open Asia France;* b. Iran; ed American Univ., Paris, Ecole des Hautes Etudes en Sciences Sociales, Paris; journalist (responsible for Iran, Cen. Asia and Afghanistan), Courier International 1990–, mem. Bd 1990–; Co-Founder and Dir Open Asia France (fmrly called The Asscn for Research and Information on Cen. Asia), Paris 1994–; Rep. of Human Rights Watch, Helsinki and Tajikistan 1995–96; Consultant to World Bank, Tajikistan 1996; Consultant and NGO Liaison Officer, UN Office for the Coordination of Humanitarian Affairs 1997–98. *Publications include:* articles in professional journals, UN reports. *Address:* Open Asia France, 12 rue Victor Letalle, 75020 Paris, France (office). *Telephone:* 1-47-97-32-97 (office). *Fax:* 1-47-97-32-97 (office). *E-mail:* Jeannot@enpc.fr (office); openasia@asia-mail.com (office). *Website:* oainternational.free.fr (office).

JAHN, Helmut, FAIA; German architect; b. 4 Jan. 1940, Nuremberg; s. of Wilhelm Anton Jahn and Karolina Wirth; m. Deborah Lampe 1970; one s.; ed Technische Hochschule, Munich and Illinois Inst. of Tech.; C.F. Murphy Assocs 1967–73, Exec. Vice-Pres. and Dir of Planning and Design 1973; corp. mem. American Inst. of Architects 1975; registered architect, NCARB 1975; mem. German Chamber of Architects, State of Hesse 1986; Prin. Murphy/Jahn 1981, Pres. 1982, Pres. and CEO 1983–; Visiting Prof. Harvard Univ. 1981, Yale Univ. 1983; numerous lectureships at univs and professional socs 1989–93; participant in numerous architectural exhbns; completed bldgs include libraries, exhbn halls, court bldgs, office and leisure bldgs, univ. bldgs, hotels, apartments and airport terminals in USA, Europe and Far East; Fellow American Inst. of Architects 1987; Hon. DFA (St Mary's Coll. Notre Dame, Ind.); Chevalier des Arts et des Lettres (France), Bundesverdienstkreuz Erster Klasse (Germany); numerous professional awards. *Major completed projects include:* Kemper Arena, Kansas City, Mo. 1974, Xerox Centre, Chicago, Ill. 1980, Argonne Program Support Facility, Argonne, Ill. 1981, 11 Diagonal Street, Johannesburg, SA 1983, James R. Thompson Center, Chicago, Ill. 1985, 362 West Street, Durban, SA 1986, Park Avenue Tower, NY 1986, United Airlines Terminal One Complex, O'Hare Airport, Chicago, Ill. 1987, One Liberty Place, Phila 1987, Northwestern Atrium Center, Chicago 1987, Wilshire/Westwood, LA 1988, Bartnett Center, Jacksonville, Fla 1990, Messeturm, Frankfurt, Germany 1991, 120 North LaSalle, Chicago 1992, One America Plaza, San Diego 1992, Mannheimer Lebensversicherung, Mannheim, Germany 1992, Hyatt Regency Roissy, Paris, France 1992, Munich Order Center, Munich, Germany 1993, Hitachi Tower, Singapore 1993, Caltex House, Singapore 1993, Hotel Kempinski, Munich, Germany 1994, Pallas, Stuttgart, Germany 1994, Kurfürstendamm 70, Berlin, Germany 1994, Principal Mutual Life Insurance Company, Des Moines, Ia 1996, RCID Administration Building, Orlando, Fla 1997, JC Decaux Bus Shelter 1998, New European Union Headquarters, Belgium, Brussels 1998, Munich Airport Center, Munich, Germany 1999. *Leisure interests:* sailing, skiing. *Address:* Murphy/Jahn, Inc., Suite 300, 35 East Wacker Drive, Chicago, IL 60601, USA. *Telephone:* (312) 427-7300. *Fax:* (312) 332-0274. *Website:* www.murphyjahn.com.

JAHN, Martin, MBA; Czech politician and business executive; b. 20 Jan. 1970, Prague; s. of Vladimír Jahn and Hana Jahn; m. Karolina Jahn; two d.; ed Prague School of Econs, DePaul Univ., Chicago, USA; Dir American Operations, Czechinvest 1996–99, CEO 1999–2004; Deputy Prime Minster, responsible for the Economy 2004–06; mem. Bd CMC Celákovice; mem. Czech-American Chamber of Commerce, Czech-Canadian Chamber of Commerce 2000–. *Leisure interests:* tennis, squash, skiing, film, literature, music. *Address:* c/o Office of the Government of the Czech Republic, nábř. E. Beneše 4, 118 01 Prague 1, Czech Republic (office).

JAHN, Robert George, BSE, MA, PhD; American aerospace scientist and academic; *Professor of Aerospace Science and Dean Emeritus, School of Engineering and Applied Science, Princeton University;* b. 1 April 1930, Kearny, NJ; s. of George Jahn and Minnie Holroyd; m. Catherine Seibert 1953; one s. three d.; ed Princeton Univ.; teaching asst, Princeton Univ. 1953–55; Instructor, Lehigh Univ. Bethlehem, Pa 1955–56, Asst Prof. 1956–58; Asst Prof. of Jet Propulsion, Calif. Inst. of Tech., Pasadena 1958–62; Asst Prof. of Aeronautical Eng, Princeton Univ. 1962–64, Assoc. Prof. 1964–67, Prof. of Aerospace Sciences 1967–2005, Dean, School of Eng and Applied Science 1971–86, now Dean Emer.; currently Program Dir Princeton Eng Anomalies Research; Pres. Int. Consciousness Research Labs 1996–2001, Chair. 2001–; mem. various NASA research cttees; numerous professional appointments etc.; Fellow, American Physical Soc., AIAA; Hon. ScD (Andhra) 1986; Curtis W. McGraw Award, American Soc. for Eng Educ. 1969, Medal for Outstanding Achievement in Electric Propulsion 2005, Edgar Mitchell Award for Noetic Achievement 2006. *Publications:* Physics of Electric Propulsion 1968, Margins of Reality (with B. J. Dunne) 1987; numerous articles on aeropspace science. *Leisure interests:* his dog, sports, music, home crafts. *Address:* Mechanical and Aerospace Engineering Department, Princeton University, Princeton, NJ 08544-5263 (office); Princeton Engineering Anomalies Research (PEAR), D-334, Engineering Quadrangle, Princeton University, Princeton, NJ 08544-5263, USA (office). *Telephone:* (609) 258-4550 (office). *E-mail:* rgjahn@princeton.edu (office); pearlab@princeton.edu (office). *Website:* www.princeton.edu/~pear/jahn (office).

JAHNÁTEK, Ľubomír, CSc; Slovak academic and politician; *Minister of the Economy;* b. 16 Sept. 1954, Nitra; m.; two c.; ed Slovak Tech. Univ.; worked for VÚSPAL (Plastics Processing and Application Research Inst.) 1978–98; Dir Gen. Production–Tech. Dept, Plastika Nitra a.s. 1992–2003; Strategy Dir Duslo Šala a.s. 2003–05; Lecturer, Faculty of Material Sciences and Tech., Slovak Tech. Univ. 2004–06, Head of Field Div. 2005–06; Minister of the Economy 2006–. *Address:* Ministry of the Economy, Mierová 19, 827 15 Bratislava, Slovakia (office). *Telephone:* (2) 4854-1111 (office). *Fax:* (2) 4333-7827 (office). *E-mail:* info@economy.gov.sk (office). *Website:* www.economy.gov.sk (office).

JAHUMPA, Bala Ibrahima Muhamadu Garba, BA, MA; Gambian diplomatist and politician; b. 20 July 1958, Banjul; ed Vassar Coll., USA and Birmingham Univ., UK; Adviser Dept of State for Agric. 1981–82, Dept of State for Foreign Affairs 1982–83; transferred to Gambian Embassy, Washington, DC, USA 1984–85; Asst Commr Upper River Div. 1986–87; Sr Asst Sec., Dept of State for Agric. 1987–90; Prin. Asst Sec., Dept of State for Local Govt and Lands 1990–94; Sec. of State for Finance and Econ. Affairs 1994–97; Deputy High Commr, Gambian Embassy, London 1997–99, Acting High Commr 1999–2001; Amb. to Cuba June–Sept. 2003; Sec. of State for Works, Construction and Infrastructure 2003–06, was fired alongside three other govt ministers Oct. 2006, reappointed following protest action by Banjulians appealing for their reinstatement Oct. 2006; Sec. of State for Foreign Affairs 2006–07. *Address:* c/o Department of State for Foreign Affairs, 4 Col Muammar Ghadaffi Avenue, Banjul, The Gambia (office).

JAIM-ETCHEVERRY, Guillermo, MD; Argentine university administrator and neurobiologist; *President, University of Buenos Aires;* Titular Prof. and Dir Dept of Cellular Biology and Histology, Faculty of Medicine, Univ. of Buenos Aires 1986–90, Pres. Univ. of Buenos Aires 2002–; Prin. Investigator, CONICET, IBRO/UNESCO, John Simon Guggenheim Memorial Foundation; mem. Nat. Acad. of Educ., Argentina Acad. of Communication Arts and Sciences; Corresp. mem. Acad. of Medical Sciences of Córdoba;; Bernardo Houssay Prize 1987, Master of Medicine, Nat. Acad. of Medicine, Argentina 2001. *Publications:* The Educational Tragedy. *Address:* University of Buenos Aires, Calle Viamonte 430/444, 1053 Buenos Aires, Argentina (office). *Telephone:* (11) 4511-8120 (office). *Website:* www.uba.ar (office).

JAIME, Aguinaldo; Angolan politician; *Deputy Prime Minister;* fmr Pres. Banco Africano de Investimentos; Gov. Nat. Bank of Angola 1999–2002; Deputy Prime Minister of Angola 2002–. *Address:* c/o Ministry of Information, Avenida Comandante Valódia, Luanda, Angola.

JAKHAR, Bal Ram, BA; Indian politician; *Governor of Madyha Pradesh;* b. 23 Aug. 1923, Panjkosi, Ferozepur Dist, Punjab; s. of Chaudhri Raja Ram Jakhar; m. Rameshwari Jakhar; three s. two d.; ed Forham Christian Coll., Lahore; elected to Punjab Ass. 1972, Deputy Minister of Co-operatives and Irrigation 1972–77, Leader of Opposition 1977–79; Speaker, Lok Sabha (House of the People) 1980–89, Pres. Indian Parl. Group, mem. Exec. Cttee Indian Group of IPU 1983–; mem. Indian Br., CPA 1979–, Chair. Exec. Cttee 1984–87; Gen. Sec. AICC 1990; Minister of Agric. 1991–96; Gov. Madhya Pradesh 2004–; Chair. Bharat Krishak Samaj 1979; Chair. Rules Cttee, Business Advisory Cttee, Gen. Purposes Cttee; Man. Cttee Jallianwala Bagh Memorial Trust; contributed to establishment of Parl. Museum and Archives (PMA) and Hall of Nat. Achievements; led numerous Indian parl. dels overseas 1980; Hon. DrSc (Haryana Agricultural Univ.); Vidya Martand, Gurukul Kangri Vishwa Vidyalay. *Publication:* People, Parliament and Administration. *Address:* 11 Race Course Road, New Delhi 110011, India.

JAKOBSEN, Mimi; Danish international organization official and fmr politician; *Secretary-General, Save the Children Denmark;* b. 19 Nov. 1948, Copenhagen; d. of Erhard Jakobsen; Lecturer in German Philology and Phonetics, Univ. of Copenhagen; elected mem. Parl. 1977; Minister for Cultural Affairs 1982–86, for Social Affairs 1986–88, of Business Affairs 1993–96, of Industry 1994–96; Leader, Centre Democrats party 1989–2005; joined Socialdemokraterne (Social Democrats) 2006; currently Sec.-Gen. Save the Children Denmark (Red Barnet). *Address:* Red Barnet, Rosenørns Allé 12, 1634 Copenhagen V, Denmark (office). *Telephone:* 35-36-55-55 (office). *Fax:* 35-39-11-19 (office). *Website:* www.redbarnet.dk (office).

JAKSITY, György, BEcons; Hungarian stockbroker; b. 1968; m. Kinga Jaksity; two c.; ed Karl Marx Univ. of Econs; Financial Adviser, Ministry of Finance 1989; consultant for several cos including Girozentrale Investment, Ibusz and Fotex, Budapest 1989–92; training with Price Waterhouse 1992; Chair. and Man. Dir Concorde Securities 1993–; Chair. Budapest Stock Exchange 2002–04; f. The Self Reliance Foundation. *Leisure interest:* reading. *Address:* c/o Budapest Stock Exchange, Deak Ferenc u.5, Budapest, 1052, Hungary (office). *Telephone:* (1) 429-6700 (office). *Fax:* (1) 429-6800 (office). *E-mail:* info@bse.hu (office).

JAKUBISKO, Juraj, MFA; Slovak film director, producer, scriptwriter and artist; b. 30 April 1938, Kojšov; m. Horváthová Jakubisko; one s. one d.; ed Prague Film Acad.; films censored by Communist regime late 1970s (Birds, Orphans and Fools, See You in Hell, My Friends); blacklisted and banned from producing films for ten years; retrospective tour of his work in USA, Canada and Europe 1991; mem. Twentieth Century Acad. 1999–; Pribina Cross, Second Class (Slovakia) 2003; more than 80 nat. and int. awards, including Maverick Award for vision in filmmaking, Taos Talking Picture Festival, USA 1998, Award in Recognition of Outstanding Achievement in the Art of the Film, Denver Int. Film Festival, USA 1998, Golden Seal Award of Yugoslavian Cinematheque for outstanding contrib. to world cinema, Belgrade 2000, Best Slovak Director Award in survey of the best Slovak and int. artists of 20th century conducted by Slovak film journalists and critics 2000, Lifetime Achievement Award, Masaryk Acad. of Art, Prague 2001, ČFTA Award: Czech Lion for Best Film Poster of the Year 2000, ČFTA Award: Czech Lion for Lifetime Artistic Contrib. 2002, Crystal Globe for Outstanding Artistic Contrib. to World Cinema, Karlovy Vary 2007. *Films:* Silence (Brussels Film Acad. Award, Knokke Experimental Film Festival, Belgium), Waiting for Godot (Best Short Film Award, Oberhausen, Simone Dubroilh Award, Mannheim) 1968, Birds, Orphans and Fools (banned 1968, Fipresci Prize 1991), The Bee Millennium (Golden Phoenix Award, Venice Film Festival) 1983, The Feather Fairy 1985, Frankenstein's Aunt 1986, A Rosy Story 1990, See You in Hell, My Friends (originally made in 1968 but banned by political censors) 1991, It's Better to Be Wealthy and Healthy Than Poor and Ill 1992 (re-released 2002), An Ambiguous Report About the End of the World (also TV series) 1999, Post Coitum 2004, Bathory 2008. *Leisure interests:* painting, golf. *Address:* Jakubisko Film Asscn Ltd, Palác Lucerna, Vodičkova 36, 116 02 Prague 1, Czech Republic (office). *Telephone:* (2) 9623-6353 (office). *Fax:* (2) 9623-6389 (office). *E-mail:* info@jakubiskofilm.com (office). *Website:* www.jakubiskofilm.com.

JALAL, Masooda; Afghan paediatrician and fmr government official; b. Gulbahar, Kapisa Prov.; m.; three c.; ed Gulbahar High School, medical school in Kabul; began medical career as physician at Maiwand Hosp., then served at Kabul Medical Inst. and Ataturk Hosp.; pvt. practice in paediatrics 1988–92; worked for UNHCR then health adviser to WFP 1993–2004; presidential cand. in Afghanistan 2004, 2008; Minister of Women's Affairs 2004–06. *Address:* c/o Ministry of Women's Affairs, beside Cinema Zainab, Shar-i-Nau, Kabul, Afghanistan. *Telephone:* (20) 2201378. *E-mail:* info@mowa.gov.af. *Website:* www.mowa.gov.af.

JALAL KHAN, Zubaida, MA; Pakistani politician; b. 31 Aug. 1959, Kuwait; ed Univ. of Balochistan; est. Girls Primary School, Mand, Balochistan 1982; volunteer, Family Planning Asscn of Pakistan 1986–; Del. to World Conf. on Women, People's Repub. of China 1995; Minister of Social Welfare and Women's Affairs 1999–2000, of Educ. 2000–04, of Women's Devt, Social Welfare and Special Educ. 2004–07; travelled to Nepal, Repub. of Korea and Philippines to study primary educ. systems. *Address:* c/o Ministry of Women Development, Social Welfare and Special Education, State Life Building (SLIC), 1st Floor, No. 5, Blue Area, China Chowk, F-6/4, Islamabad, Pakistan. *Telephone:* (51) 9206328.

JALALI, Ali Ahmad; Afghan/American politician; b. Kabul; m.; one s. one d.; mil. studies in Afghanistan, UK and Turkey; army col, Afghan Armed Forces –1978; Dir Islamic Unity of Afghan Mujahidin and Sr Mil. Commdr during rebellion against Soviet occupation 1980s; obtained American citizenship 1987; Dir, Broadcaster and Head of Pashto and Persian Services, Voice of America (int. radio station), Washington, DC –2003; Minister of Interior Affairs, Afghan Transitional Authority 2003–04, of Afghanistan 2004–05 (resgnd). *Publications include:* The Other Side of the Mountain (co-author) 1998, three-vol. mil. history of Afghanistan, several other books. *Address:* c/o Ministry of Interior Affairs, Shar-i-Nau, Kabul, Afghanistan (office).

JALAN, Bimal, PhD; Indian economist and politician; *Chairman, Public Interest Foundation;* ed Univ. of Calcutta, Univs of Cambridge and Oxford, UK; various positions at IMF, World Bank, Pearson Comm. 1964–70; Chief Economist, Industrial Credit and Investment Corpn of India 1970–73; Econ. Adviser, Ministry of Finance and of Industry, India 1973–79; Chief Econ. Adviser, Ministry of Finance 1981–88, Sec. for Banking 1985–88; Dir Econ. Affairs, Commonwealth Secr., London 1979–81; Exec. Dir IMF 1988–90; fmr Exec. Dir IBRD (India); Gov. Reserve Bank 1997–2003; mem. Parl. for Rajya Sabha 2003–; Chair. Public Interest Foundation, New Delhi 2008–. *Publications include:* India's Economic Crisis: The Way Ahead 1991; The Future of India: Politics, Economics and Governance 2005. *Address:* 4 Babar Road, New Delhi 110001, India (office). *Telephone:* (11) 2378-2037 (office). *Fax:* (11) 2378-2037 (office). *E-mail:* bjalan@nic.in (home). *Website:* www.bimaljalan.com (office).

JALANG'O, Bob Francis, BSc; Kenyan diplomatist and information technology specialist; b. 5 Feb. 1945, Siaya; two s. four d.; ed Makerere Univ., Kampala, Uganda; systems programmer, Olivetti Co. 1970–74; with Caltex Oil Kenya, Computer Systems Man. for six East African countries 1974–88; MP 1988–92; Amb. to Zambia, Malawi, Botswana, Italy, Greece, Poland 1993–2000; Perm Rep. to UN, New York 2000–03; Moran of the Burning Spear, Presidential Award 2000. *Leisure interests:* international travel, sports. *Address:* 643 Sore Drive, PO Box 41553, Nairobi, Kenya (home). *E-mail:* balozinewyork@hotmail.com (home).

JALEEL, Mohamed, MA; Maldivian politician; b. 19 Nov. 1959, Malé; s. of Ahmed Jaleel and Mariyam Waheeda; fmr Minister of State for Finance and Treasury, Minister of Finance and Treasury 2004–05, Minister of Econ. Devt and Trade 2005–08 (resgnd); Vice-Gov., then Gov. Maldives Monetary Authority. *Address:* M. Faamudheyrige, Orchid Magu, Malé, Maldives (home). *Telephone:* 3323888 (home). *Fax:* 3324432 (home).

JALILI, Saeed, PhD; Iranian government official; *Secretary, Shura-ye Ali-ye Amniyyat-e Melli (Supreme National Security Council);* b. 1965, Mashhad; ed Univ. of Science and Industry, Tehran; veteran of the 1980–88 Iran-Iraq war; Dir-Gen. Office of Supreme Leader Ayatollah Ali Khamenei 2001–05; adviser to Pres. Mahmoud Ahmadinejad 2005–; Deputy Foreign Minister for European and American Affairs 2005–07; Sec., Shura-ye Ali-ye Amniyyat-e Melli (Supreme Nat. Security Council) 2007–, role includes being Iran's chief nuclear negotiator. *Address:* Office of the Secretary, Shura-ye Ali-ye Amniyyat-e Melli, Tehran, Iran.

JALLAD, Farid al-; Palestinian lawyer and politician; trained as lawyer; Head of Arab Lawyers' Cttee in the W Bank; apptd to High Judiciary Council by the late Pres. Arafat 2003; Deputy Minister of Justice –2005, Minister of Justice 2005; Pres. Palestinian Bar Asscn; mem. Palestinian Legal Group, Inst. for the Study and Devt of Legal Systems (ISDLS), Calif. *Address:* c/o Ministry of Justice, POB 267, Ramallah, Palestinian Autonomous Areas (office).

JALLOUD, Maj. Abd as-Salam; Libyan politician and army officer; *Second-in-Command to Revolutionary Leader;* b. 15 Dec. 1944; ed Secondary School, Sebha, Mil. Acad., Benghazi; mem. of Revolutionary Command Council 1969–77, Gen. Secr. of Gen. People's Congress 1977–79; Minister of Industry and the Econ., Acting Minister of the Treas. 1970–72; Prime Minister 1972–77; Second-in-Command to Revolutionary Leader Col Gaddafi 1997–. *Address:* c/o General Secretariat of the General People's Congress, Tripoli, Libya.

JALLOW, Hassan Bubacar, LLB, LLM; Gambian lawyer; *Chief Prosecutor, Criminal Tribunal for Rwanda;* b. 14 Aug. 1951, Bansang; ed Univ. of Dar es Salaam, Tanzania, Nigerian Law School, Univ. Coll., London; State Attorney, Attorney-Gen.'s Chamber, Gambia 1976–82, Solicitor Gen. 1982–84, Attorney-Gen. and Minister of Justice 1984–94, Judge, Supreme Court 1998–2002; Judge, Appeals Chamber, Special Court for Sierra Leone 2002; Prosecutor, UN Int. Criminal Tribunal 1998–, carried out judicial evaluation for Yugoslavia, Chief Prosecutor, Int. Criminal Tribunal for Rwanda (ICTR) 2003–, also UN Under-Sec.-Gen.; legal expert for OAU and Commonwealth; Chair. Commonwealth Governmental Working Group of Experts in Human Rights; Commdr, Nat. Order of the Repub. of Gambia. *Achievements:* worked on drafting and conclusion of African Charter on Human Rights, adopted 1981. *Publications:* Law, Justice and Governance – Selected Papers 1998, The Law of Evidence in The Gambia 1998. *Address:* Office of the Prosecutor, International Criminal Tribunal for Rwanda, Arusha International Conference Centre, PO Box 6016, Arusha, Tanzania (office). *Telephone:* (27) 2504369/72 (office). *Fax:* (27) 2504000/4373 (office). *Website:* www.ictr.org (office).

JALLOW, Tamsir; Gambian diplomatist; *Ambassador to USA;* m. Mariama Jallow; one s. one d.; ed St Augustine's and Swedru Secondary School in Ghana, Univ. of Cape Coast, Ghana, Univ. of Birmingham, UK, Univ. of Kenya; fmr Head, Gambia Teacher's Union; fmr Publicity Sec. for ruling Alliance for Patriotic Reorientation and Construction party; fmr Deputy and House Majority Leader, Nat. Ass.; fmr Dir-Gen. Immigration Dept; Acting

High Commr to UK 2005–07 (also Chargé d'affaires a.i., Stockholm 2006–07), Perm. Rep. to UN, New York 2007, Amb. to USA 2007–. *Address:* Embassy of Gambia, 1424 K Street, NW, Suite 600, Washington, DC 20005, USA (office). *Telephone:* (202) 785-1399 (office). *Fax:* (202) 785-1430 (office). *E-mail:* www .gambiaembassy.us (office).

JALOLOV, Abdulkhafiz, DPhil; Uzbekistan politician and philosopher; b. 1 June 1947, Namangan; m. Jalolova Zarifahon; two s. one d.; ed Tashkent State Univ.; mil. service 1969–71; Lecturer of Philosophy, Tashkent Univ. 1971–72; researcher, Philosophy and Law Inst., Uzbekistan Acad. of Sciences 1972–77, Dir 1993–2001; Chair. of Philosophy, State Inst. of Physical Culture 1977–81; Asst Prof., Deputy Dir Social Science Lecturers' Skills Level Raising Inst., Tashkent State Univ. 1981–93; Second Sec. of Gen. Council, People's Democratic Party of Uzbekistan (PDP) 1991–94, First Sec. 1994–2003; unsuccessful PDP cand. in presidential elections 2000. *Publications include:* Mustakillik Mas'uliyati 1996, Istikbol Ufklari 1998, Demokratiya: mashakkatli surur 2000. *Address:* c/o People's Democratic Party of Uzbekistan, pl. Mustakillik, 5/1, 100029 Tashkent, Uzbekistan (office). *Telephone:* (71) 139-83-11 (office). *Fax:* (71) 133-59-34 (office).

JAMAL, Ahmad; American composer and pianist; b. 2 July 1930, Pittsburgh, Pa; (divorced); one d.; ed pvt. master-classes with Mary Cardwell Dawson and James Miller; George Hudson Orchestra nat. tour 1949; mem. The Four Strings 1949; accompanist to The Caldwells 1950; trio The Three Strings 1950–; many concert tours, including with Philip Morris; exclusive Steinway artist 1960s–; appeared on film soundtracks of Mash 1970, Bridges of Madison County 1995; Duke Ellington Fellow, Yale Univ.; Officier, Ordre des Arts et des Lettres 2007; NEA American Jazz Master, Pittsburgh Mellon Jazz Festival dedication 1994. *Television:* The Sound of Jazz 1962. *Compositions:* six works for Asai Quartet 1994, New Rhumba, Ahmad's Blues, Night Mist Blues, Extensions, The Awakening, Excerpts From The Blues, Tranquility, Manhattan Reflections. *Recordings include:* Poinciana, But Not For Me (including Bridges of Madison County) 1995, Essence Part 1 (Django D'Or Award, Paris) 1996, Olympia 2000, Live in Baalbeck (DVD) 2003, After Fajr 2005. *Address:* c/o Ellora Management, PO Box 755, 11 Brook Street, Lakeville, CT 06039, USA (office). *Telephone:* (860) 435-1305 (office). *Fax:* (860) 435-9916 (office). *E-mail:* elloramanagement@aol.com (office); elloradesigns@aol.com (home). *Website:* www.ahmadjamal.net (home).

JAMAL, Amir Habib, BComm (Econs); Tanzanian politician; b. 26 Jan. 1922, Dar es Salaam; s. of Habib Jamal and Kulsum Thawer; m. 1st Zainy Kheraj; m. 2nd Shahsultan Cassam 1967; three s. one d.; ed primary school, Mwanza, secondary school, Dar es Salaam and Univ. of Calcutta, India; elected mem. Tanganyika Legis. Council 1958; Minister of Urban Local Govt and Works 1959, of Communication, Power and Works 1960; Minister of State, President's Office, Directorate of Devt 1964; re-elected MP 1965; Minister of Finance 1965–72; Minister for Commerce and Industries 1972–75, of Finance and Econ. Planning 1975–77, of Communications and Transport 1977–79, of Finance 1979–83, without Portfolio 1983–84, Minister of State for Cabinet Affairs, Pres.'s Office 1984–85; Head, Perm. Mission to the UN, Geneva 1985–; Chair. Interpress Service, Third World, Rome; Chair. Governing Council Sokoine Univ. of Agric., Morogoro; Hon. Exec. Dir South Centre, Geneva; mem. Nat. Exec. CCM Party; mem. Brandt Comm. 1977–80, Trustee Dag Hammarskjöld Foundation; mem. Advisory Panel, World Inst. for Devt Economics Research; Dr hc (Uppsala) 1973, (Dar es Salaam) 1980. *Leisure interests:* gardening, reading, bridge, swimming.

JAMALI, Mir Zafarullah Khan, MA; Pakistani politician; b. 1 Jan. 1944, Rowjhan, Balochistan; s. of Mir Zafarullah Khan Jamali; m.; four s. one d.; ed Murree Royal Coll., Aitchison Coll., Lahore, Punjab Univ.; tribal elder from SW Prov. of Balochistan; joined Pakistan People's Party1970s; elected mem. Prov. Ass., Balochistan 1977; fmr Minister for Food and Information; Minister for Food and Agric. 1982, for Local Govt, for Water and Power 1985, for Railways 1986; mem. Nat. Ass. 1985–89; Chief Minister for Balochistan 1988–89; Rep. to UN 1991; elected ind. mem. Nat. Ass. 1993–, mem. Cabinet 1997–2004; Senator for Balochistan 1997–2006; Sr mem. Pakistan Muslim League –1999; mem. Pakistan Muslim League—Quaid-e-Azam; Prime Minister of Pakistan 2002–04 (resgnd); fmr mem. Nat. Security Council. *Leisure interest:* hockey. *Address:* c/o Office of the Prime Minister, Constitution Avenue, Islamabad, Pakistan (office).

JAMBREK, Peter, MA, PhD; Slovenian judge, legal consultant and author; b. 14 Jan. 1940, Ljubljana; ed Grammar School, Ljubljana, Ljubljana Univ. and Univ. of Chicago, USA; Prof., Dept of Theory of Law and State, Ljubljana; Judge, Constitutional Court of Repub. of Slovenia 1990, Pres. 1991–95; Judge, European Court of Human Rights 1993–99; Dean, Grad. School of Govt and European Affairs, Univ. of Ljubljana 2003; mem. Venice Comm. 2003; currently ind. consultant and author. *Publications:* Development and Social Change in Yugoslavia: Crises and Perspectives of Building a Nation 1975, Participation as a Human Right and as a Means for the Exercise of Human Rights 1982, Contributions for the Slovenian Constitution 1988, Constitutional Democracy 1992. *Address:* c/o University of Ljubljana, Kongresni trg 12, 1000 Ljubljana; Ceste v Megre 4, 64260 Bled, Slovenia (home). *Telephone:* (64) 77449 (home).

JAMEEL, Hon. Fathulla, BA; Maldivian politician and international organization official; *Senior Minister;* b. 5 Sept. 1942, Malé; m. 1st Aishath Ibrahim (divorced); two s. (one deceased); m. 2nd Fathimath Moosa Didi; one step-d.; ed Al-Azhar and Ein Shams Univs, Cairo, Egypt; foreign service training, Ministry of Foreign Affairs, Canberra, Australia; teacher, Majeediyya School, Malé 1969–73; Under-Sec., Ministry of External Affairs; Acting Under-Sec., Dept of Foreign Aid, Office of the Prime Minister 1974; Acting Under-Sec., Ministry of Transport 1975; Deputy Head Dept of External Affairs 1976–77; Perm. Rep. to UN, New York 1977–78; Minister of External (later Foreign) Affairs 1978–2005; Acting Minister of Planning and Devt 1982–83; mem. Parl. (Pres.'s nominee) 1989–; Sr Minister 2008–; mem. Nat. Educ. Council 1989–; Minister of State for Planning and Devt 1990–91; Gov. of Maldives to IMF 1979–83, to Asian Devt Bank 1979–83, to World Bank (IBRD) 1979–, to Islamic Devt Bank 1980–; Chair. Nat. Youth Council 1979–81, DHIRAAGU (Nat. Telecommunication Co.) 1988–, Maldives Fisheries Corpn 1990–91; mem. Fisheries Advisory Bd 1979–, Nat. Planning Council 1981–, Bd of Dirs Maldives Monetary Authority 1981–, Tourism Advisory Bd 1981–, Bd MNSL (Nat. Shipping Co.) 1979–; mem. Supreme Council for Islamic Affairs 1997–; mem. Commonwealth Consultative Group on issues related to small states; recipient of first Commonwealth Award from Oxford Centre for Islamic Studies 1999. *Address:* c/o President's Office, Boduthakurufaanu Magu, Malé, 20–05, Maldives (office). *Telephone:* 3320701 (office). *Fax:* 3325500 (office). *E-mail:* info@presidencymaldives.gov.mv (office). *Website:* www .presidencymaldives.gov.mv (office).

JAMES, Clive Vivian Leopold; Australian writer, broadcaster, journalist and poet; b. 7 Oct. 1939, Kogarah, NSW; s. of Albert A. James and Minora M. Darke; ed Sydney Technical High School, Sydney Univ. and Pembroke Coll. Cambridge; Asst Ed. Morning Herald, Sydney 1961; Pres. of Footlights at Cambridge, UK; TV critic, The Observer 1972–82, feature writer 1972–; Dir Watchmaker Productions 1994–; as lyricist for Pete Atkin, record albums include Beware of the Beautiful Stranger, Driving Through Mythical America, A King at Nightfall, The Road of Silk, Secret Drinker, Live Libel, The Master of the Revels; also songbook, A First Folio (with Pete Atkin). *Television series include:* Cinema, Up Sunday, So It Goes, A Question of Sex, Saturday Night People, Clive James on Television, The Late Clive James, The Late Show with Clive James, Saturday Night Clive, Fame in the 20th Century, Sunday Night Clive, The Clive James Show, Clive James on Safari; numerous TV documentaries including Clive James meets Katharine Hepburn 1986, Clive James meets Jane Fonda, Clive James meets Mel Gibson 1998, Clive James meets the Supermodels 1998, Postcard series 1989–. *Publications:* non-fiction: The Metropolitan Critic 1974, The Fate of Felicity Fark in the Land of the Media 1975, Peregrine Prykke's Pilgrimage through the London Literary World 1976, Britannia Bright's Bewilderment in the Wilderness of Westminster 1976, Visions Before Midnight 1977, At the Pillars of Hercules 1979, First Reactions 1980, The Crystal Bucket 1981, Charles Charming's Challenges on the Pathway to the Throne 1981, From the Land of Shadows 1982, Glued to the Box 1982, Flying Visits 1984, Snakecharmers in Texas 1988, The Dreaming Swimmer 1992, Clive James on Television 1993, Fame 1993, The Speaker in Ground Zero 1999, Even as We Speak (essays) 2000, Reliable Essays 2001, The Meaning of Recognition: New Essays 2001–2005 2005, North Face of Soho 2006, Alone in the Café 2007, Cultural Amnesia 2007; novels: Brilliant Creatures 1983, The Remake 1987, The Silver Castle 1996; autobiography: Unreliable Memoirs 1980, Falling Towards England: Unreliable Memoirs Vol. II 1985, Unreliable Memoirs Vol. III 1990, May Week was in June 1990, Brrm! Brrm! or The Man from Japan or Perfume at Anchorage 1991, Fame in the 20th Century 1993, The Metropolitan Critic 1993, North Face of Soho: Unreliable Memoirs Vol. IV; poetry: Fanmail 1977, Poem of the Year 1983, Other Passports: Poems 1958–85 1986, The Book of My Enemy: Collected Verse 1958–2003 2004, Opal Sunset: Selected Poems, 1958–2008 2008; contribs to numerous publs including Commentary, Encounter, Listener, London Review of Books, Nation, New Review, New Statesman, New York Review of Books, New Yorker, TLS. *Address:* United Agents, 12–26 Lexington Street, London, W1F 0LE, England (office). *Telephone:* (20) 3214-0800 (office). *Fax:* (20) 3214-0801 (office). *E-mail:* info@unitedagents.co.uk (office). *Website:* unitedagents.co.uk (office); www.clivejames.com.

JAMES, Rt Rev. Colin Clement Walter, MA; British ecclesiastic; b. 20 Sept. 1926, Cambridge; s. of the late Canon Charles C. H. James and Gwenyth M. James; m. Margaret J. (Sally) Henshaw 1962 (deceased); one s. two d.; ed Aldenham School, King's Coll., Cambridge and Cuddesdon Theological Coll.; Asst Curate, Stepney Parish Church 1952–55; Chaplain, Stowe School 1955–59; BBC Religious Broadcasting Dept 1959–67; Religious Broadcasting Organizer, BBC South and West 1960–67; Vicar of St Peter with St Swithin, Bournemouth 1967–73; mem. Gen. Synod 1970–95; Bishop Suffragan of Basingstoke 1973–77; Canon Residentiary of Winchester Cathedral 1973–77; Bishop of Wakefield 1977–85; Bishop of Winchester 1985–95; Pres. Woodward Corpn 1978–93, RADIUS 1980–93; Chair. Church Information Cttee 1976–79, Cen. Religious Advisory Cttee, BBC and IBA 1979–84, United Soc. for the Propagation of the Gospel 1985–88, Liturgical Comm. 1986–93; Hon. DLitt (Southampton) 1996. *Leisure interests:* theatre, travelling. *Address:* Long Meadow, 3 Back Street, St Cross, Winchester, SO23 9SB, England (home). *Telephone:* (1962) 868874 (home). *E-mail:* colinjames@btinternet.com (home).

JAMES, Sir Cynlais (Kenneth) Morgan, KCMG, MA; British diplomatist (retd); b. 29 April 1926, Resolven; s. of Thomas Ellis James and Lydia Ann (Morgan) James; m. Teresa Girouard 1953; two d.; ed St Marylebone Grammar School, Univ. of Durham, Trinity Coll., Cambridge; served with RAF 1944–47; Sr Branch of Foreign Service 1951, in Tokyo 1953, Brazil 1956, Cultural Attaché, Moscow 1959, Foreign Office 1962, Paris 1965, Saigon 1969; FCO, Head of Western European Dept 1971–75; NATO Defence Coll. 1975–76; Minister, Paris 1976–81; Amb. to Poland 1981–83; Asst Under-Sec. of State 1983; Amb. to Mexico 1983–86; Dir Thomas Cook Group 1986–91; Dir-Gen. Canning House 1987–92; Dir Darwin Instruments, Latin American Investment Trust 1991–96; Foreign and Colonial Emerging Markets Investment Trust PLC 1991–98, Polish Investment Trust (SECAV), Euro Principals Ltd; Adviser to Amerada Hess; Chair. British-Mexican Soc. 1987–90, Inst. of Latin-American Studies 1992–99; mem. Franco-British Council 1986–99, Young Concert Artists' Trust; Order of the Aztec Eagle (Mexico), Order of Andrés Bello (Venezuela), Order of Merit (Chile), Chevalier, Légion d'honneur; Dr hc

(Mexican Acad. of Int. Law). *Leisure interests:* history, music, tennis, cricket. *Address:* 64 The Atrium, 30 Vincent Square, London, SW1P 2NW, England. *Telephone:* (20) 7828-8527.

JAMES, Edison Chenfil, MSc; Dominican politician and agronomist; *Leader, Dominica United Workers Party (UWP);* b. 18 Oct. 1943, Marigot; s. of David James and Patricia James; m.; one s. two d.; ed North East London Polytechnic, Univ. of Reading, Imperial Coll., Univ. of London; teacher, St Mary's Acad. Sept.–Dec. 1973; agronomist Ministry of Agric. 1974–76; Farm Improvement Officer, Caribbean Devt Bank (attached to Dominica Agricultural and Industrial Devt Bank) 1976–80, Loans Officer 1976–80; Co-ordinator Coconut Rehabilitation and Devt Project; Chief Exec. (Gen. Man.) Dominica Banana Marketing Corpn 1980–87; Adviser to Dirs Bd of Windward Islands Banana Growers Asscn (WINBAN) 1980–87; Man. Dir Agricultural Man. Corpn Ltd (AMCROP) 1987–95; Leader Dominica United Workers Party (UWP) and Parl. Leader of the Opposition 1990–95, 2000–; Prime Minister of Dominica 1995–2000, also Minister of Legal and Foreign Affairs and Labour; leading negotiator with several int. aid agencies; served on numerous public service cttees. *Leisure interests:* cricket, football, int. affairs, politics, table tennis. *Address:* Dominica United Workers Party, 37 Cork Street, Roseau, Dominica (office).

JAMES, Geraldine, OBE; British actress; b. 6 July 1950; d. of Gerald Trevor Thomas and Annabella Doogan Thomas; m. Joseph Sebastian Blatchley 1986; one d.; ed Downe House, Newbury, Drama Centre London Ltd; Royal TV Soc. Award for Best Actress 1978, Venice Film Festival Award for Best Actress 1989, Drama Desk (New York) Award for Best Actress 1990. *Stage appearances:* repertory, Chester 1972–74, Exeter 1974–75, Coventry 1975, Passion of Dracula 1978, The White Devil 1981, Turning Over 1984, When I was a Girl I used to Scream and Shout 1987, Cymbeline 1988, Merchant of Venice 1989 (and Broadway 1990), Death and the Maiden 1992, Lysistrata 1993, Hedda Gabler 1993, Give Me Your Answer Do 1998, Faith Healer 2001–02, The Cherry Orchard 2003, Home 2004, The UN Inspector 2005. *Radio:* The Hours 2000, King Lear 2001, Whale Music 2003, Richard III 2003, The Raj Quartet 2004. *TV series:* The History Man 1980, Jewel in the Crown 1984, Blott on the Landscape 1985, Echoes 1988, Stanley and the Women 1991, Kavanagh QC 1995, Band of Gold 1995, Over Here 1995, Band of Gold 1996, Drovers' Gold 1996, Gold 1997, Kavanagh QC 1997, The Sins 2000, White Teeth 2002, Hearts of Gold 2002, Jane Hall's Big Bad Bus Ride 2006. *Television films:* Dummy 1977, She's Been Away 1989, Inspector Morse 1990, The Doll's House 1991, Ex 1991, The Healer 1994, Doggin Around 1994, Rebecca 1996, See Saw 1997, Hans Christian Andersen 2001, Crime and Punishment 2002, The Hound of the Baskervilles 2002, State of Play 2003, He Knew He Was Right 2003, Poirot 2005, A Harlot's Progress 2006, Caught in a Trap 2008, Phoo Action 2008, Heist 2008. *Films:* Sweet William 1978, Night Cruiser 1978, Gandhi 1981, The Storm 1985, Wolves of Willoughby Chase 1988, The Tall Guy 1989, If Looks Could Kill 1990, The Bridge 1990, Losing Track 1991, Prince of Shadows 1991, No Worries 1992, Words on the Window Pane 1993, Moll Flanders 1996, The Man Who Knew Too Little 1996, Testimony of Taliesin Jones 1999, First Love 1999, The Luzhin Defence 2000, Tom and Thomas 2001, Odour of Chrysanthemums 2002, An Angel for May 2002, Calendar Girls 2002, The Fever 2004. *Leisure interest:* music. *Address:* c/o Julian Belfrage Associates, Adam House, 14 New Burlington Street, London, W1S 3BQ, England (office). *Telephone:* (20) 7287-8544 (office).

JAMES, Ioan Mackenzie, MA, DPhil, FRS; British academic; *Professor Emeritus of Geometry, St. John's College, University of Oxford;* b. 23 May 1928; s. of Reginald D. James and Jessie A. James; m. Rosemary G. Stewart 1961; ed St Paul's School and Queen's Coll. Oxford; Commonwealth Fund Fellow, Princeton, Univ. of Calif. Berkeley and Inst. for Advanced Study 1954–55; Tapp Research Fellow, Gonville & Caius Coll. Cambridge 1956; Reader in Pure Math., Univ. of Oxford 1957–69, Sr Research Fellow, St John's Coll. 1959–69, Savilian Prof. of Geometry 1970–95, Prof. Emer. 1995–, Fellow, New Coll. 1970–95, Emer. Fellow 1995–, Leverhulme Emer. Fellow 1996–98; Ed. Topology 1962–; Hon. Prof. Univ. of Wales 1989; Hon. Fellow St John's Coll., Oxford 1988, New Coll., Oxford 1996; Hon. DSc (Aberdeen) 1993; Whitehead Prize and Lecturer 1978. *Publications:* The Mathematical Works of J.H.C. Whitehead 1963, The Topology of Stiefel Manifolds 1976, Topological Topics 1983, General Topology and Homotopy Theory 1984, Aspects of Topology 1984, Topological and Uniform Spaces 1987, Fibrewise Topology 1988, Introduction to Uniform Spaces 1989, Handbook of Algebraic Topology 1995, Fibrewise Homotopy Theory 1998, Topologies and Uniformities 1999, History of Topology 1999, Remarkable Mathematicians 2003, Remarkable Physicists 2004, Asperger's Syndrome and High Achievement 2006; numerous papers in mathematical journals. *Address:* Mathematical Institute, 24–29 St Giles, Oxford, OX1 3LB, England (office). *Telephone:* (1865) 735389 (office). *Fax:* (1865) 273583 (office). *E-mail:* imj@maths.ox.ac.uk (office). *Website:* www .maths.ox.ac.uk (office).

JAMES, LeBron Raymone; American professional basketball player; b. 30 Dec. 1984, Akron, OH; s. of Gloria James; two s. with Savannah Brinson; ed St Vincent-St Mary High School, Akron; selected at age 18 with first overall pick in 2003 NBA (Nat. Basketball Asscn) draft by Cleveland Cavaliers, becoming only second high school player taken at the number one draft position; played in bronze medal-winning Team USA at Olympic Games, Athens 2004; played in bronze medal-winning US Nat. Team at FIBA World Championships, Japan 2006; played in gold medal-winning US Nat. Team at FIBA Americas Championships, Las Vegas 2007; played in gold medal-winning Team USA ('Redeem Team') at Olympic Games, Beijing 2008; youngest player to register a triple-double and youngest player to score 50 points in one game 2004–05; youngest player in NBA history to average at least 30 points per game in a season 2005–06; named as one of three capts for US Men's Basketball Nat. Team for 2006–08; named Ohio's Mr Basketball and selected to the USA Today All-USA First Team (three times) 2001–03, named Gatorade Nat. Boys Basketball Player of the Year 2001–02, Rookie of the Year 2003–04, NBA MVP (Most Valuable Player) 2009, NBA All-Star Game MVP (Most Valuable Player) 2006, 2008, five-time NBA All-Star, three-time All-NBA selection, The Sporting News NBA Co-MVP 2005–06, Best Male Athlete Award, BET Award for Best Male Athlete 2006, 2007, NBA Scoring Champion 2008; ranked No. 1 in Forbes Top 20 Earners Under 25 with annual earnings of $27 million Dec. 2007. *Address:* Cavaliers Operating Company, LLC, 1 Center Court, Cleveland, OH 44115-4001; LeBronJames.com, 1507 W Market Street, Akron, OH 44313, USA. *Telephone:* (216) 420-2000 (Cavaliers). *Fax:* (216) 420-2101 (Cavaliers). *Website:* www.clevelandcavaliers.com; www.lebronjames.com.

JAMES, Michael Leonard, (Michael Hartland, Ruth Carrington), MA, FRSA; British government official, writer and broadcaster; b. 7 Feb. 1941, Cornwall; s. of the late Leonard James and Marjorie James; m. Jill Tarján 1975; two d.; ed Christ's Coll., Cambridge; entered govt service (GCHQ) 1963; Pvt. Sec. to Rt Hon. Jennie Lee, Minister for the Arts 1966–68; DES 1968–71; Planning Unit of Rt Hon Margaret Thatcher, Sec. of State for Educ. and Science 1971–73, Asst Sec. 1973; Deputy Chief Scientific Officer 1974; served in London, Milan, Paris 1973–78; Dir, IAEA Vienna 1978–83; Adviser, Int. Relations to Comm. of the European Union, Brussels 1983–85; a Chair. Civil Service Selection Bds 1983–93; Chair. The Hartland Press Ltd 1985–2001, Wade Hartland Films Ltd 1991–2000; Gov. East Devon Coll. of Further Educ., Tiverton 1985–91, Colyton Grammar School 1985–90, Sidmouth Community Coll. 1988–2004, Chair. Bd of Govs 1998–2001; Chair. Gen. Medical Council Professional Conduct Cttee 2000–06; mem. Immigration Appeal Tribunal 1987–2005, Devon and Cornwall Rent Assessment Panel 1990–, Asylum and Immigration Tribunal 2005–; feature writer and book reviewer, The Times (thriller critic 1989–90), travel corresp. 1993–), Daily Telegraph (thriller critic 1993–2000), Sunday Times, Guardian; Hon. Fellow, Univ. of Exeter 1985–. *TV and radio include:* Seven Steps to Treason (BBC Radio 4) 1990, Sonja's Report (ITV documentary) 1990, Masterspy: interviews with KGB defector Oleg Gordievsky (BBC Radio 4) 1991. *Publications:* Internationalization to Prevent the Spread of Nuclear Weapons (co-author) 1980; novels as Michael Hartland: Down Among the Dead Men 1983, Seven Steps to Treason (South West Arts Literary Award) 1985, The Third Betrayal 1986, Frontier of Fear 1989, The Year of the Scorpion 1991, The Verdict of Us All (short stories) (jtly) 2006; other: Masters of Crime – Lionel Davidson and Dick Francis 2006; novel as Ruth Carrington: Dead Fish 1998. *Address:* Cotte Barton, Branscombe, Devon, EX12 3BH, England.

JAMES, Thomas Garnet Henry, CBE, MA, FBA; British museum curator (retd); b. 8 May 1923, Neath, Wales; s. of Thomas Garnet James and Edith James (née Griffiths); m. Diana Margaret Vavasseur-Durell 1956 (died 2002); one s.; ed Neath Grammar School and Exeter Coll. Oxford; served in army (RA) 1942–45; Asst Keeper, British Museum 1951–74; Laycock Student, Worcester Coll. Oxford 1954–60; Keeper of Egyptian Antiquities, British Museum 1974–88; Chair. Egypt Exploration Soc. 1983–89, Vice-Pres. 1990; Chair. Advisory Cttee, Freud Museum 1987–98; Wilbour Fellow, The Brooklyn Museum 1964; Visiting Prof., Collège de France 1983, Memphis State Univ. 1990; Pres. Asscn for the Study of Travellers in Egypt and the Near East 1998–; mem. German Archaeological Inst.; Correspondant Etranger de l'Institut de France 2000; Hon. Fellow, Exeter Coll. Oxford 1998. *Publications:* The Mastaba of Khentika 1953, The Hekanakhte Papers 1962, Hieroglyphic Texts in the British Museum, I (revised) 1961, 9 1970, Archaeology of Ancient Egypt 1972, Corpus of Hieroglyphic Inscriptions in The Brooklyn Museum, 1 1974, Pharaoh's People 1984, Egyptian Painting 1985, Ancient Egypt: The Land and Its Legacy 1988, Egypt: The Living Past 1992, Howard Carter: The Path to Tutankhamun 1992, A Short History of Ancient Egypt 1995, Egypt Revealed: Artist-Travellers in an Antique Land 1997, Tutankhamun: The Eternal Splendour of the Boy Pharaoh 2000, Ramesses II 2002, The British Museum Concise Introduction: Ancient Egypt 2005. *Leisure interests:* music, cooking. *Address:* 113 Willifield Way, London, NW11 6YE, England (home). *Telephone:* (20) 8455-9221 (home). *Fax:* (20) 8731-6303 (home).

JAMES OF HOLLAND PARK, Baroness (Life Peer), cr. 1991, of Southwold in the County of Suffolk; **Phyllis Dorothy (P. D.) James,** OBE, JP, FRSL, FRSA; British author; b. 3 Aug. 1920, Oxford, England; d. of Sidney Victor James and Dorothy Amelia Hone; m. Ernest Connor Bantry White 1941 (deceased 1964); two d.; ed Cambridge Girls' High School; Admin., Nat. Health Service 1949–68; Prin., Home Office 1968; Police Dept 1968–72; Criminal Policy Dept 1972–79; JP, Willesden 1979–82, Inner London 1984; Chair. Soc. of Authors 1984–86, Pres. 1997–; mem. BBC Gen. Advisory Council 1987–88, Gov. BBC 1988–93; Assoc. Fellow, Downing Coll., Cambridge 1986; mem. Bd of British Council 1988–93, Arts Council; Chair. Arts Council Literary Advisory Panel 1988–92; mem. Detection Club; mem. Church of England Liturgical Comm. 1991–; Hon. Fellow, St Hilda's Coll., Oxford 1996, Downing Coll., Cambridge 2000, Girton Coll., Cambridge 2000; Hon. DLitt (Buckingham) 1992, (Herts.) 1994, (Glasgow) 1995, (Durham) 1998, (Portsmouth) 1999; Hon. LitD (London) 1993; Dr hc (Essex) 1996; Grand Master Award, Mystery Writers of America 1999. *Publications:* Cover Her Face 1962, A Mind to Murder 1963, Unnatural Causes 1967, Shroud for a Nightingale 1971, The Maul and the Pear Tree (with T. A. Critchley) 1971, An Unsuitable Job for a Woman 1972, The Black Tower 1975, Death of an Expert Witness 1977, Innocent Blood 1980, The Skull Beneath the Skin 1982, A Taste for Death 1986, Devices and Desires 1989, The Children of Men 1992, Original Sin 1994, A Certain Justice 1997, Time To Be in Earnest 1999, Death in Holy Orders 2001, The Murder Room 2003, The Lighthouse 2005, The Private Patient 2008. *Leisure interests:* exploring churches, walking by the sea. *Address:* c/o

Greene & Heaton Ltd, 37A Goldhawk Road, London, W12 8QQ, England (office).

JAMIR, S. C., BA, LLB; Indian politician; *Governor of Maharashtra;* b. 17 Oct. 1931, Ungma, Nagaland; s. of Shri Senayangba; m. Alemia Jamir 1959; three s. two d.; ed Univ. of Allahabad; mem. Interim Body of Nagaland, then Jt Sec. Naga People's Convention; Vice-Chair. Mokokchung Town Cttee 1959–60; MP 1961–70, MP Rajya Sabha 1987–89; Parl. Sec., Ministry of External Affairs, Govt of India 1961–67; Union Deputy Minister of Railways, of Labour and Rehabilitation, of Community Devt and Co-operation, Food and Agric. 1968–70; elected mem. to Nagaland Legis. Ass. 1971–73, re-elected mem. from Aonglenden Constituency 1974; subsequently apptd Minister of Finance, Revenue and Border Affairs; re-elected 1977 and apptd Deputy Chief Minister in UDF Ministry; Chief Minister of ULP Ministry April 1980; resgnd when NNDP Ministry came to power June 1980; Leader of Opposition Congress (I) in State Legis. Ass. 1980–82; elected from 26 Aonglenden Constituency, Gen. Elections 1982; unanimously elected Leader Congress (I) Legislature Party, Chief Minister Nagaland 1982–86, 1989–92, 1993–2003; Gov. of Goa 2004–08, of Maharashtra 2008–. *Address:* The Raj Bhavan, Maharashtra State Government, Malabar Hill, Mumbai 400 035, Maharashtra, India (office). *Telephone:* (22) 23630635 ext 231 (office). *Fax:* (22) 2363 3272 (office). *E-mail:* rajbhavan@maharashtra.gov.in (office). *Website:* www.maharashtra.gov.in (office).

JAMMEH, Col Yahya A. J. J.; Gambian head of state and fmr army officer; *President;* b. 25 May 1965, Kanilai Village, Foni Kansala Dist, Western Div.; m. Zineb Yahya-Jammeh (née Soumah); one d.; ed Gambia High School; joined fmr Gambia Nat. Gendarmerie as pvt. 1984; with Special Intervention Unit, Gambia Nat. Army 1984–86, Sergeant 1986, Escort Training Instructor, Gendarmerie Training School 1986–89, Cadet Officer 1987, commissioned 1989, Second Lt 1989, in charge of Presidential Escort, Presidential Guards 1989–90, CO Mobile Gendarmerie Jan.–June 1991, Mil. Police Unit June–Aug. 1991, Lt 1992, Commdr Gambia Nat. Army Mil. Police Aug.–Nov. 1992, Capt. 1994, Col 1996; became Chair. Armed Forces Provisional Ruling Council, Head of State 1994–; retd from army 1996; elected Pres. of The Gambia 1996–; Chair., Pres. Alliance for Patriotic Reorientation and Construction (APRC) 1996–; Chair. Inter-states Cttee for Control of Drought in the Sahel 1997–2000; 1st Vice-Chair. Org. of the Islamic Conf. 2000–; Grand Commdr, Order of Al-Fatah (Libya) 1995; Order of Distinction (Liberia) 2000; Grand Master of the Repub. of The Gambia 2001; Pan-African Humanitarian Award 1997 and numerous other awards. *Leisure interests:* playing tennis, soccer, hunting, reading, correspondence, driving and riding motorcycles, music, films and animal rearing. *Address:* Office of the President, State House, Banjul, The Gambia (office); Alliance for Patriotic Reorientation and Construction, GAMSTAR Building, Banjul. *Telephone:* 4223811 (office). *Fax:* 4227034 (office). *E-mail:* info@statehouse.gm (office). *Website:* www.statehouse.gm (office); www.jammeh2001.org (office).

JANABIL; Chinese party official; *Chairman, Xinjiang Uygur Autonomous Regional Committee, Chinese People's Political Consultative Conference;* b. April 1934, Habahe (Kaba) Co., Xinjiang Uygur Autonomous Region; s. of Simagul Janabil and Ajikhan Janabil; m. Zubila Janabil 1955; two s. two d.; joined CCP 1953; Vice-Chair. Revolutionary Cttee, Xinjiang Autonomous Region 1975–79; Chair. Revolutionary Cttee and First Sec. CCP Cttee, Ili Autonomous Kazakh Pref. 1975–80; Deputy Sec. CCP Cttee, Xinjiang 1977–83, Sec. 1983–85; Vice-Chair. Xinjiang 1979–83; Deputy Sec. then Sec. CCP 4th Xinjiang Uyghur Autonomous Regional Cttee 1985–; Chair. CPPCC 7th Xinjiang Uygur Autonomous Regional Cttee 1993–; Alt. mem. 10th CCP Cen. Cttee 1972–77, 11th CCP Cen. Cttee 1977–82, 12th CCP Cen. Cttee 1982–87, 13th Cen. Cttee 1987–92, 14th Cen. Cttee 1992–97; mem. 8th CPPCC Nat. Cttee 1993–98, 9th CPPCC Nat. Cttee 1998–2003; Del., 15th CCP Nat. Congress 1997–2002; Pres. Xinjiang Br. Futurology Soc. 1980. *Address:* c/o Xinjiang Autonomous Regional Chinese Communist Party, Urumqi, Xinjiang, People's Republic of China.

JANCSÓ, Miklós; Hungarian film director; b. 27 Sept. 1921, Vác; s. of Sándor Jancsó and Angela Poparád; m. 1st Katalin Wowesny 1949; one s. one d.; m. 2nd Márta Mészáros 1958; one s.; m. 3rd Zsuzsa Csákány 1981; one s.; studied legal sciences and ethnography at Kolozsvár (now Cluj), Romania and Budapest Coll. of Cinematographic Art; worked at newsreel studio 1953–58; documentary film studio 1962; Chief Producer, Hunnia Film Studio 1963–; Grand Prix of San Francisco 1961, Prix of Fédération Internationale de la Presse Cinématographique (FIPRESCI), Balázs Béla prize 1965, Merited artist 1970, Eminent Artist of the Hungarian People's Repub. 1980, Best Dir Award, Cannes Festival 1972, Kossuth Prize (2nd Degree) 1973, Prize for Oeuvre Complet (Cannes) 1982, Prize for Oeuvre Complet (Venice) 1990, Best Dir Award, Montreal 1992, Kossuth Prize 2006. *Films:* A harangok Rómába mentek (The Bells Have Gone to Rome) 1959, Oldás és Kötés (Cantata) 1963, Igy Jöttem (My Way Home) 1965, Szegény Legények (The Round-Up) 1966, Csillagosok–Katonák (The Red and the White) 1967, Csend és Kiáltás (Silence and Cry) 1968, Fényes Szelek (The Confrontation) 1969, Sirókkó (Winter Wind) 1969, La Pacifista (The Pacifist) 1970, Égi bárány (Agnus Dei, UK) 1971, Még kér a nép (Red Psalm) 1971, Elektreia (Electra) 1975, Private Vices, Public Virtues 1976, Életünket és vérünket: Magyar rapszódia 1 (Hungarian Rhapsody) 1979, Allegro Barbaro 1978, The Tyrant's Heart or Boccaccio in Hungary 1981, Omega, Omega (TV) 1983, Muzsika (Budapest) (TV) 1984, L'Aube (The Dawn) 1985, Harmadik jelenlét 1986, Szörnyek évadja (Season of Monsters) 1987, Jézus Krisztus horoszkópja (Jesus Christ's Horoscope) 1988, The Isten hátrafelé megy (God Walks Backwards) 1991, Kékk Duna keringö (The Blue Danube Waltz) 1992, Szeressük egymást gyerekek! 1996, Játssz, Félix, játssz! 1997, Sír a madár 1998, Nekem lámpást adott kezembe az Úr, Pesten (Lord's Lantern in Budapest) 1999, Anyád! A szúnyogok (Mother! The Mosquitos) 2000, Utolsó vacsora az Arabs Szürkénél (Last Supper of the Arabian Gray Horse) 2001, Kelj fel, komám, ne aludjál (Wake up Mate, Don't You Sleep) 2002, A Mohácsi vész (The Mohacs Disaster) 2004, Európából Európába 2006, Ede Megevé Ebédem 2006; for Italian TV: Il Tecnico e il Rito, Roma rivuole Cesare. *Stage productions:* Jack the Ripper (Budapest) 1977, Nostoi (Seoul) 1988. *Opera directed:* Otello (Florence) 1980. *Television:* Doktor Faustus 1983. *Address:* Eszter u. 17, 1022 Budapest, Hungary (home). *Telephone:* (1) 3165761 (home). *E-mail:* csakany@jancso.hu (home).

JANCSÓ, Péter, BEng; Hungarian business executive; *CEO, Graboplast Rt.;* ed Budapest Tech. Univ.; Man., Graboplast Győr Cotton-mill and Artificial Leather Manufacturing Co. 1979–88, CEO 1988–95, now CEO Graboplast Rt.; Chair. Rába Automotive Group; Dir State Privatization and Holding Co. 1995–98; Chair. Chamber of Commerce and Trade of N Trans-Danubia 1997–2000. *Address:* Graboplast Rt., Fehérváti út 16/b, 9023 Győr, Hungary (office). *Telephone:* (96) 506-147 (office). *Fax:* (96) 414-586 (office). *E-mail:* jancsop@graboplast.hu (office); jancso@graboplast.hu. *Website:* www.graboplast.hu (office).

JANDA, Krystyna; Polish actress and film and theatre director; b. 18 Dec. 1952, Starachowice; m.; two s. one d.; ed State Higher School of Drama, Warsaw; actress, Atheneum Theatre, Warsaw 1976–88, Powszechny Theatre, Warsaw 1988–; opened Theatre Polonia, Warsaw 2005; acting on TV and performing in cabaret; numerous awards in Poland and abroad; over 50 leading roles in classic and contemporary plays and over 50 leading roles in film and TV; Best Actress 40th Int. Film Festival, San Sebastián, Golden Duck Award 2007. *Films include:* Man of Marble 1976, Without Anaesthetic 1978, The Border 1978, The Conductor 1979, Die Grünen Vögel 1979, Golem 1979, Mephisto 1980, War Between Worlds 1980, Man of Iron 1981, Espion lève toi 1981, Interrogation 1982, Ce fut un bel été 1982, Bella Donna 1983, Gluth 1983, Der Bulle und das Mädchen 1984, Vertige 1985, My Mother's Lovers 1985, Laputa 1986, Short Film About Killing 1987, II Decalogue, V Decalogue 1988, Ownership 1989, Polish Kitchen 1991, Relieved of the Life 1992, As 1995, Pestka (actress and Dir) 1996, Mother's Mother 1996, Unwritten Principles 1997, Last Chapter 1997, David Weissen 1999, Żółtyszalik (Yellow Muffler) 2000, Przedwiośnie 2000, Życie jako śmiertelna choroba prienoszona drogą płciową (Life as a Fatal Sexually Transmitted Disease) 2000. *Stage appearances include:* Bal manekinów 1974, Edukacja Rity 1984, Z życia glist 1984, Biała bluzka 1987, Medea 1988, Shirley Valentine 1990, Kobieta zawiedziona 1996, Kotka na gorącym blaszanym dachu 1997, Maria Callas – Lekcja śpiewu (Song Lesson) 1997, Harry i ja (Harry and Me) 1998, Opowiadania zebrane (Collected Stories) 2001, Siedem grzechów głównych 2001, Mała Steinberg (Spoonface Steinberg) 2001, Kto się boi Virginii Woolf (Who's Afraid of Virginia Woolf) 2002, Mewa 2003, Czego nie Widać 2003, Janosik albo na Szkle Malowane 2004, Namiętność 2005, Lekcje stepowania 2005. *Plays directed include:* Hedda Gabler 1999, Związek otwarty (Friendship Opened) 2000, Zazdrość (Jealousy) 2001. *TV series:* Mierzejewska 1989, From Time to Time 1999. *Address:* Theater Polonia, 00-545 Warsaw, ul.Marszałkowska 56, Poland (office). *Telephone:* (22) 6216141 (office). *E-mail:* info@teatrpolonia.pl (office). *Website:* www.teatrpolonia.pl (office); www.krystynajanda.net.

JANDOSOV, Oraz; Kazakhstani economist and politician; *Chairman, National Economic Development Centre;* b. 26 Oct. 1961, Almaty; ed M.V. Lomonsonov State Univ., Moscow; worked as economist and govt adviser 1990s; First Deputy Minister for the Economy 1991–94; Deputy Gov. Bank of Kazakhstan 1994–96, Gov. 1996–98; First Deputy Prime Minister 1998–99, Deputy Prime Minister and Minister of Finance 1999; Head of nat. electricity grid operator 1999–2000; Deputy Prime Minister 2000–01, resgnd following protest by Prime Minister Kasimzhomart Tokayev regarding his membership of Democratic Choice of Kazakhstan (DCK) party which he co-founded in 2001; Founder and Co-Chair. Ak Zhol (Light Road) Democratic Party of Lazakhstan following disintegration of DCK March 2002–; Adviser to Pres. of Kazakhstan 2003; Head, State Monopolies and Competition Agency 2003–04; Chair. Nat. Econ. Devt Centre 2005–. *Leisure interests:* tennis, soccer, skiing. *Address:* Zenkov str. 70, Ap. 2, Almaty, Kazakhstan (office). *Telephone:* (7172) 91-59-58 (office). *Fax:* (7172) 91-46-91 (office). *E-mail:* nedc@nursat.kz (office). *Website:* www.nedc.kz (office).

JANDROKOVIĆ, Gordan; Croatian politician and diplomatist; *Minister of Foreign Affairs and European Integration;* b. 2 Aug. 1967, Bjelovar; m.; three c.; ed Faculties of Civil Eng and Political Science, Univ. of Zagreb, Diplomatic School, Ministry of Foreign Affairs, The Netherlands Inst. of Int. Relations, Clingendael, Erasmus Universiteit, Rotterdam; pvt. construction co. 1989–94; with Ministry of Foreign Affairs 1994–2000; Man. Stanić Co., Zagreb 2000–02; Gen. Man. Beming Co., Bjelovar 2002–03; mem. Croatian Democratic Union (HDZ) 1992–, Chair. HDZ Cttee for Small and Medium-Size Enterprises 2002–, HDZ Cttee for Bjelovar-Bilogora Co. 2003–, mem. HDZ Presidency 2004–; mem. Parl. 2003–, Chair. Parl. Cttee for the Economy, Devt and Reconstruction 2003–04, Parl. Foreign Policy Cttee 2004–07, Head of Parl. Del. to Croatia-EU Jt Parl. Cttee 2004–07; Minister of Foreign Affairs and European Integration 2008–; Man. Ed. The Witnesses to History series 1997–2002. *Leisure interests:* tennis, football, reading. *Address:* Ministry of Foreign Affairs and European Integration, trg Nikole Šubića Zrinskog 7–8, 10000 Zagreb, Croatia (office). *Telephone:* (1) 4569964 (office). *Fax:* (1) 4569977 (office). *E-mail:* mvpei@mvpei.hr (office). *Website:* www.mvpei.hr (office).

JANEWAY, Richard, AB, MD; American physician, academic and medical school administrator; *Executive Vice-President Emeritus for Health Affairs, School of Medicine, Wake Forest University;* b. 12 Feb. 1933, Los Angeles, Calif.; s. of VanZandt Janeway and Grace Eleanor Bell Janeway; m. Katherine Esmond Pillsbury 1955; one s. two d.; ed Colgate Univ., Univ. of Pennsylvania

JAN THE INTERNATIONAL WHO'S WHO 2010 JAN

School of Medicine; Instructor in Neurology, Bowman Gray School of Medicine of Wake Forest Univ. (now Wake Forest Univ. School of Medicine) 1966–67, Asst Prof. 1967–70, Assoc. Prof. 1970–71, Prof. 1971–, Dean 1971–85, Exec. Dean 1985–94, Vice-Pres. for Health Affairs 1983–90, Exec. Vice-Pres. 1990–97, Univ. Prof. of Medicine and Man. 1997–, Exec. Vice-Pres. Emer. for Health Affairs 1997–; mem. Winston-Salem Foundation Bd 1994–2002 (Chair. 1997–98); Dir Idealliance 1999–; Chair. Asscn of American Medical Colls. 1984–85; mem. Bd of Dirs B&T Corpn 1995– (Exec. Cttee 2000–, Chair. 2001–), S. Nat. Corpn 1989–95; mem. Nat. Asscn for Biomedical Research 1993–96, Americans for Medical Progress Inc. 1993–97; mem. Bd of Trustees Colgate Univ., 1988–95, Winston-Salem State Univ. 1991–95; mem. Inst. of Medicine of NAS, American Medical Asscn, American Heart Asscn, American Neurological Asscn, Soc. for Neuroscience, Soc. of Medical Admins., American Clinical and Climatological Asscn; Fellow American Acad. of Neurology; Life Fellow American Coll. of Physicians; John and Mary R. Markle Scholar in Academic Medicine 1968–73; Distinguished Service mem. Asscn of American Medical Colls. 1991; Medallion of Merit, Wake Forest Univ. 2000. *Leisure interests:* golf, photography, gardening, travel. *Address:* Wake Forest University, School of Medicine, Medical Center Blvd., Winston-Salem, NC 27157 (office); 2710 Old Town Club Road, Winston-Salem, NC 27106, USA (home). *Telephone:* (336) 716-1825 (office); (336) 727-7537 (home). *Fax:* (336) 716-1822. *E-mail:* djaneway@wfubmc.edu (office).

JANG, Ha Sung, PhD; South Korean academic; *Professor of Finance and Dean of the Business School, Korea University;* b. 19 Sept. 1953, Kwangju; ed Wharton School, Univ. of Pennsylvania, USA; joined in pro-democracy protests early 1970s; moved to USA to study for doctorate 1980s; taught finance at Wharton School and Univ. of Houston; returned to S Korea 1990; special adviser to Lazard's Korea Corp. Governance Fund; int. adviser to Chinese Security Regulatory Comm.; currently Prof. and Dean of the Business School, Korea Univ.; Exec. Dir Asian Inst. of Corp. Governance; Chair. Inst. of Dirs in E Asia Network; helped est. Center for Good Corp. Governance 2001; runs advocacy group, People's Solidarity for Participatory Democracy, to attempt to make S Korea's chaebol (large conglomerates) more accountable to minority shareholders, has won several milestone court victories; Int. Corp. Governance Network Excellence in Corp. Governance Award, Financial Analyst Journal Graham and Dodd Award, Maekyung Business Daily Maekyung Economist Award, Korea Univ. Granite Teaching Award, Korea Univ. Business School Prof. of the Year Award. *Publications:* numerous articles in professional journals. *Address:* Korea University Business School, 5 Anam-dong, Seongbuk-Gu, Seoul, 136-701 South Korea (office). *Telephone:* (2) 3290-1929 (office). *E-mail:* jangya@korea.ac.kr (office). *Website:* biz.korea.ac .kr/~jangya (office).

JANICOT, Daniel Claude Emmanuel, LenD; French international official; *Member, Conseil d'Etat;* b. 20 May 1948, Neuilly; s. of François-Xavier Janicot and Antoinette Mauxion; m. 2nd Catherine Lachenal 1991; one s.; two d. from previous marriage; ed Ecole Nat. d'Admin, Inst. d'Etudes Politiques and Faculté de Droit, Paris; Auditeur, Conseil d'Etat 1975–, Deputy Sec.-Gen. 1978–82, Maître des requêtes 1979; Maître de Conférences, Instituts d'Etudes Politiques, Paris and Bordeaux and Ecole Nat. des Ponts et Chaussées; mem. Admin. Council, Public Information Library, Beaubourg 1979; Del.-Gen. American Center 1980–90; Vice-Pres. Bibliothèque Nationale 1981; Maître de séminaire, Ecole Nat. d'Admin 1982–83; Del.-Gen. Union Centrale des Arts Décoratifs 1982–86; Special Adviser Office of Dir-Gen. of UNESCO 1990–91, Dir of Exec. Office of Dir-Gen. 1991–94, Asst Dir-Gen. 1994–99; mem. Conseil d'état 1995–; Chair. Bd, Centre Nat. d'Art Contemporain de Grenoble 1995–; Vice-Chair. Bd, Institut Français de Gestion 1996–; Dir Musée des arts premiers; mem. Bd of Dirs Artcurial Holding SA; Chevalier, Ordre nat. du Mérite, Ordre des Arts et Lettres, Légion d'honneur. *Address:* Conseil d'Etat, 1 place du Palais-Royal, 75100 Paris 01 SP (office); 6 rue Casimir-Périer, 75007 Paris, France (home). *Telephone:* 1-40-20-80-50 (office). *Fax:* 1-40-20-80-08 (office). *E-mail:* webmestre@conseil-etat.fr (office). *Website:* www .conseil-etat.fr (office).

JANIK, Krzysztof, PhD; Polish politician; *Head of Parliamentary Caucus, Democratic Left Alliance (SLD);* b. 11 June 1950, Kielce; m. Jadwiga Cisło; one s.; ed Jagiellonian Univ., Kraków; Sec. Voiv. Bd Union of Rural Youth (ZMW) 1971–75; researcher Silesian Univ. 1975–81; Vice-Chair. Polish Socialist Youth Union 1981–86; mem. Cen. Cttee Polish United Workers' Party (PZPR) 1986–90; mem. Social Democracy of the Rep. of Poland (SdRP) 1990–99; Deputy to Sejm (Parl.) 1993–; Under-Sec. of State Chancellery of the Pres. of Poland 1995–97; Gen. Sec. Democratic Left Alliance (SLD) 1999–, Head of SLD Parliamentary Caucus 2004–; Minister of Interior Affairs and Admin 2001–04. *Leisure interests:* bridge, books. *Address:* ul. Wielska 4–6–8, 00-902 Warsaw, Poland (office).

JANION, Maria, PhD; Polish academic; *Lecturer, Institute of Literary Research, Polish Academy of Sciences;* b. 24 Dec. 1926, Mońki; d. of Cyprian Janion and Ludwika Kudryk; ed Łódź Univ., Warsaw Univ.; researcher, Inst. of Literary Research, Polish Acad. of Sciences (PAN), Warsaw 1946–96, mem. Scientific Bd 1957–, Lecturer, Inst. of Philosophy and Sociology School of Social Research, PAN 1992–, mem. Cttee of Literary Sciences 1996–; Asst, Warsaw Univ. 1951–52, Lecturer 1981–87, apptd. Prof. 1987; researcher, Higher Pedagogic School, Gdańsk 1957–69, Prof. 1963–70; Prof., Inst. of Polish Studies, Gdańsk Univ. 1970–81, 1984–90; Ed.-in-Chief Historia i teoria literatury Studia (series) 1968–78, Bibliteka Romanistyczna (series) 1978–; Ordinary mem. Polish Acad. of Arts and Sciences 1990–; Corresp. mem. PAN 1991, mem. 1998–; mem. jury, Nike Literature Award 1997–, Chair. 2000–; Dr hc (Gdańsk Univ.) 1994; Alfred Jurzykowski Foundation Award 1980, Culture Foundation Great Prize for the Year 1998, Chair. of Council of Ministers Award 2001, Kazimierz Wyka Award 2001. *Publications include:* Romantism—Studies of Ideas and Style 1969, Gorączka romantyczna (Romantic Fever) 1975, Romantyzm i historia (with M. Żmigrodzka) 1978, Renewing of Meanings 1980, Transgresje (seven-vol. series, also co-ed.) 1981–88, Wobec zła 1989, Życie Pośmiertne Konrada Wallenroda 1990, Kobiety i duch inności (Women and the Spirit of Strangeness) 1996, Płacz generała. Eseje o wojnie 1998, Do Europy tak, ale razem z naszymi umarłymi (To Europe, Yes, but with Our Dead) 2000, Żyjąc tracimy życie. Niepokojące tematy egzystencji 2001, Niesamowita słowiańszczyzna 2006. *Address:* Institute of Literary Research, Polish Academy of Sciences, 00-330 Warsaw, ul. Nowy Świat 72, Poland (office). *Telephone:* (22) 6572764 (office). *Fax:* (22) 8269945 (office). *E-mail:* ibadlit@ibl.waw.pl (office). *Website:* www.ibl.waw.pl (office).

JANKLOW, William John, BS, JD; American politician and lawyer; b. 13 Sept. 1939, Chicago, Ill.; s. of Arthur Janklow and LouElla Gulbranson; m. Mary Dean Thom 1960; one s. two d.; ed Flandreau High School, South Dakota, Univ. of South Dakota; Staff Attorney and Chief Officer, S Dakota Legal Services 1966–67; Directing Attorney and Chief Officer, S Dakota Legal Services 1967–72; Chief Trial Attorney, S Dakota Attorney Gen.'s Office 1973–74; Attorney Gen. of S Dakota 1975–79; Gov. of S Dakota 1979–87, 1995–2003; elected US House of Reps 2003–04 (resgnd); convicted of second-degree manslaughter and reckless driving 2004; Dir Nat. Legal Services Corpn; fmr mem. Exec. Cttee of the Nat. Governors' Asscn; Republican; Nat. award for legal excellence and skill 1968; various awards. *Leisure interests:* waterskiing, collecting 1950s music.

JANKOVIĆ, Zoran, BEcons; Slovenian business executive; *President and CEO, Mercator d.d.;* ed Univ. of Ljubljana; Pres. and CEO, Mercator d.d. 1997–; Chair. Supervisory Bd, Pokojninska družba A. d.d. (pension fund); mem. Exec. Bd, Mans' Asscn; mem. Exec. Bd, Chamber of Commerce and Industry of Slovenia; Pres., Alumni Club of Faculty of Econs, Univ. of Ljubljana; Pres. Slovenian Handball Fed. 1996–2004, Hon. Pres. 2004–; Hon. Pres. Handball Club Krim Mercator. *Address:* Mercator d.d., Dunajksa 107, 1001 Ljubljana, Slovenia (office). *Telephone:* (1) 5601196 (office). *E-mail:* zoran .mercator@mercator.si (office). *Website:* www.mercator.si (office).

JANKOWITSCH, Peter, DDL; Austrian diplomatist and politician; *Secretary-General, Franco-Austrian Centre for East–West Encounters;* b. 10 July 1933, Vienna; s. of Karl Jankowitsch and Gertrude Jankowitsch (née Ladstaetter); m. 1st Odette Prevor 1962 (divorced); one s.; m. 2nd Silvia Lahner 2001; ed Vienna Univ. and The Hague Acad. of Int. Law; fmr lawyer; joined foreign service 1957, worked in Int. Law Dept; Pvt. Sec., Cabinet of Minister of Foreign Affairs 1959–62; posted to London 1962–64; Chargé d'affaires, Dakar, Senegal 1964–66; Head of Office of Bruno Kreisky, Chair. Austrian Socialist Party 1967; Chief of Cabinet of Fed. Chancellor (Kreisky) 1970–72; Perm. Rep. to UN 1972–78; Chair. UN Cttee on Peaceful Uses of Outer Space 1972–91; Vice-Chair. of Bd, Int. Energy Agency 1979–83; Rep. for Austria to UN Security Council 1973–75, Pres. Security Council 1973, Vice-Pres. 29th Gen. Assembly; Vice-Pres. 7th Special Session of Gen. Assembly 1975; mem. UN Security Council Mission to Zambia 1973; Perm. Rep. to OECD 1978–82; Deputy Perm. Under-Sec., Chief of Cabinet, Fed. Ministry of Foreign Affairs 1982–83; Fed. Minister for Foreign Affairs 1986–87; mem. Austrian Nat. Ass. (Nationalrat) 1983–90 (Chair. Foreign Relations Cttee 1987–90), 1992–93; Minister of State for Integration and Devt Co-operation 1990–92; Perm. Rep. to OECD and ESA 1993–98; Chair. OECD Devt Centre 1994–98; Chair. Jt Cttee European Parl.–Austrian Parl.; Sec.-Gen. Franco-Austrian Centre for East–West Encounters 1998–; Int. Sec. Soc. Dem. Party of Austria 1983–90; Chair. Human Rights Cttee Socialist Int. 1987–97, Vice-Chair. Socialist Int. Cttee on Econ. Affairs 1997–99; Pres. Cttee of Parliamentarians of EFTA 1989–90; Hon. Pres., Austrian Soc. for European Policy 1996–; mem. Bd Austrian Foreign Policy Soc, Austrian Inst. for Int. Politics, Vienna Inst. for Devt, Austrian UN League (fmrly Vice-Pres.), Int. Acad. of Astronautics 1998; Pres. Austrian Nat. Cttee for Unispace 1999; Chair. Austrian Space Agency 1998–; Pres. Austria-Viet Nam Soc. 1999–, Jerusalem Foundation, Austria 2002–; Assoc. Ed. Acta Astronomica 2003–; Hon. mem. Bd Int. Inst. of Space Law; Commdr Légion d'honneur; Allan D. Emil Memorial Award for Int. Co-operation in Astronautics 1981, Social Sciences Award, Int. Acad. of Astronautics 2001, and many other awards. *Publications:* Kreisky's Era in Austrian Foreign Policy (co-ed. with E. Bielka and H. Thalberg) 1982, Red Markings–International (co-ed. with H. Fischer) 1984, The European Integration Process and Neutral Austria 1994, Austria and the Non-Aligned 2002; and papers and articles on Austria and on econ. and political devt of the Third World; contrib. to Wörterbuch des Völkerrechts 1960. *Leisure interests:* history and baroque music. *Address:* Franco-Austrian Centre for East–West Encounters, Salzgries 19, 1010 Vienna, Austria (office). *Telephone:* (1) 5352335 (home); (1) 5338927 (office). *Fax:* (1) 5338927 (office). *E-mail:* jankowitsch@nextra.at (office). *Website:* www.peter-jankowitsch.net (home); www.oefz.at (office).

JANKULOVSKA, Gordana, MA; Macedonian lawyer and politician; *Minister of Internal Affairs;* b. 12 Oct. 1975, Ohrid; ed SS Cyril and Methodius Univ., Skopje and Univ. of Kent, UK; early career as lawyer in pvt. law firm 1999–2000; Head of Cabinet, Minister of Finance 2000–02; Gen.-Sec. Internal Macedonian Revolutionary Org.—Democratic Party for Macedonian Nat. Unity (Vnatrešno-Makedonska Revolucionerna Organizacija–Demokratska Partija za Makedonsko Nacionalno Edinstvo, IMRO—DPMNU) 2004–06; Minister of Internal Affairs 2006–; Special Achievement in Law Award, Univ. of Kent 2004. *Address:* Ministry of Internal Affairs, 1000 Skopje, Dimitar Mirchev bb, Former Yugoslav Republic of Macedonia (office). *Telephone:* (2) 3117222 (office). *Fax:* (2) 3112468 (office). *Website:* www.mvr.gov.mk (office).

JANNEH, Abdoulie, MA; Gambian international organization executive; *Under-Secretary-General and Executive Secretary, United Nations Economic Commission for Africa;* ed Fourah Bay Coll., Sierra Leone, Univs of

Nottingham and Bradford, UK, Econ. Devt Inst., World Bank (Project Man.); joined UNDP from Govt of Gambia as Programme Adviser 1979, Adviser, Office to Combat Desertification and Drought (UNSO), Burkina Faso 1979–80, Programme Officer, UNSO, New York 1981–83, Deputy Resident Rep. in Guinea 1984–86, Sierra Leone 1987–89, Deputy Exec. Sec. UN Capital Devt Fund 1990–93, Resident Coordinator and Resident Rep., Niger 1993–96, Ghana 1996–99, reassigned to New York to lead Transition Team 1999, Asst Sec.-Gen. and UNDP Regional Dir for Africa 2000–05, Under-Sec.-Gen. and Exec. Sec. UN Econ. Comm. for Africa, Addis Ababa, Ethiopia 2005–. *Address:* United Nations Economic Commission for Africa, Africa Hall, PO Box 3001, Addis Ababa, Ethiopia (office). *Telephone:* (1) 517200 (office). *Fax:* (1) 514416 (office). *E-mail:* ecainfo@uneca.org (office). *Website:* www.uneca.org (office).

JÁNOS, Kóka, PhD; Hungarian business executive and politician; *Leader, Parliamentary Group, Alliance of Free Democrats;* b. 5 July 1972, Budapest; m. (divorced); one d.; ed Esztergom Pelbárt Timisoara Franciscan High School, Faculty of Gen. Medicine, Semmelweis Univ. of Medical Sciences; CEO Elender Computer Ltd (Elender Computer Kft.) 1996–2004 (and CEO of legal successors of co.); European Deputy Pres. PSINet Inc. 1999–2001; Pres. Asscn of Information Tech. Enterprises 2003–; Chair. Information Tech. Program, Cttee of the Office for Nat. Research, Devt and Tech. 2004–; Minister of Economy and Transport 2004–08; mem. Parl. 2006–, currently Leader of Parl. Group of Alliance of Free Democrats; Chair. Szabad Demokraták Szövetsége (SzDSz—Alliance of Free Democrats) 2007–08; IT Manager of Year Award 2000. *Leisure interests:* aviation, sailing, travel. *Address:* Szabad Demokraták Szövetsége, 1143 Budapest, Gizella u. 36, Hungary (office). *Telephone:* (1) 223-2050 (office). *Fax:* (1) 222-3599 (office). *E-mail:* szerkesztoseg@szdsz.hu (office). *Website:* www.szdsz.hu (office); kokajanos.hu.

JANOWITZ, Gundula; Austrian singer (soprano); b. 2 Aug. 1937, Berlin, Germany; d. of Theodor Janowitz and Else Janowitz (née Neumann); m.; one d.; ed Acad. of Music and Performing Arts, Graz; debut with Vienna State Opera 1960; perm. mem. Deutsche Oper, Berlin 1966; sang with Metropolitan Opera, New York 1967, Salzburg Festival 1968–81, Teatro Colón, Buenos Aires 1970, Munich State Opera 1971, Grand Opera, Paris 73, Covent Garden Opera 1976, La Scala 1978; concerts in maj. cities throughout the world, appearances at Bayreuth, Aix-en-Provence, Glyndebourne, Spoleto, Salzburg, Munich Festivals; Opera Dir at Graz 1990–91; mem. Vienna State Opera, Deutsche Oper, Berlin; mem. Main Prize Jury, BBC Cardiff Singer of the World Competition 2003, 2005, 2007; Hon. Mem. Vienna State Opera, Acad. of Music, Graz, RAM, London. *Leisure interest:* modern literature. *Address:* 3072 Kasten 75, Austria.

JANOWSKI, Gabriel, DAgric; Polish politician; b. 22 April 1947, Konstantów; s. of Jan Janowski and Józefa Nocuń; m. Elżbieta Radomyska 1974; one s. two d.; ed Lycée Błonie, Warsaw Agricultural Univ., Int. Agric. Center, Wageningen, Netherlands, Georgetown Univ., Washington, DC; scientific worker and tutor, Warsaw Agricultural Univ. 1971–80, 1983–91; Founder and Vice-Pres. Solidarity Workers' Union of Farmers 1980–81, Pres. 1989–91; interned 1981–82; co-organizer Farmers' Pastorate 1983–89; lecturer, people's univs 1983–89; Co-organizer and Vice-Pres. Warsaw Econ. Soc. 1986; Founder and Vice-Chair. Econ. Union 1989; Senator 1989–91; Vice-Pres. Citizens' Parl. Caucus 1989–91; Founder Bank of Econ. Union 1991; Deputy to Sejm (Parl.) 1991–93, 1997–; Minister of Agric. and Food Economy 1991–93; Pres. Polish Peasants' Party–People's Alliance (PSL–PL) 1992–2001; Chair. Parl. Cttee on Agric. and Rural Devt 1997–2001; mem. Parl. Cttee on European Integration 1997–2001, Parl. European Cttee 2001–05, Cttee of Treasury 2001–05; Pres. Alliance for Poland (PdP) 2001–05, merged with four other parties to form League of Polish Families 2001; mem. Parl. Ass. of the Council of Europe 1997–2000, 2001–03; Pres. Patriotic Movement 2005–. *Leisure interests:* history, gardens. *Address:* Faszczyce Stare 18, 05-870 Błonie, Poland (home). *Telephone:* (22) 7254754 (home).

JANOWSKI, Marek; German conductor; *Artistic and Music Director, Orchestre de la Suisse-Romande;* b. 18 Feb. 1939, Warsaw, Poland; ed Cologne Musikhochschule and studied in Siena, Italy; fmrly Asst Conductor in Aachen, Cologne and Düsseldorf opera houses; Music Dir, Freiburg and Dortmund Operas 1973–79; Artistic Adviser and Conductor Royal Liverpool Philharmonic Orchestra 1983–86; Music Dir and Chief Conductor Orchestre Philharmonique de Radio France 1984–2000; Chief Conductor Gurzenich-Orchester, Cologne 1986–90; Artistic Dir Monte Carlo Philharmonic Orchestra 1999, Music Dir and Chief Conductor 2000–05; Principal Conductor and Artistic Dir Dresden Philharmonic Orchestra 2001–04; Chief Conductor and Artistic Dir Rundfunk Sinfonieorchester Berlin 2001–; Artistic and Music Dir Orchestre de la Suisse-Romande, Geneva 2005–; Endowed Guest Conductor Chair Pittsburgh Symphony Orchestra 2005–; regular guest conductor in Paris, West Berlin, Hamburg, Cologne and Munich opera houses; has also conducted at Metropolitan Opera (New York), Chicago, San Francisco (American opera debut 1983), Dresden and Vienna State Operas, Teatro Colón (Buenos Aires), Orange Festival (France) and Théâtre du Châtelet (Paris); has conducted concerts with Berlin Philharmonic, Chicago Symphony, London Symphony Orchestra, Philharmonia, NHK (Tokyo), Dresden Staatskapelle, Boston Symphony Orchestra, Stockholm Philharmonic and BBC Symphony Orchestra. *Recordings include:* Wagner's Der Ring des Nibelungen (with the Dresden Staatskapelle), Weber's Euryanthe, Strauss's Die Schweigsame Frau, Penderecki's The Devils of Loudun, Korngold's Violanta, Hindemith's Die Harmonie der Welt, Bruckner Symphonies No. 4 and No. 6 (with Orchestre Philharmonique de Radio France), Roussel four symphonies (with Orchestre Philharmonique de Radio France) (Diapason D'Or 1996), Weber's Oberon 1997, Strauss's Four Last Songs (Gramophone magazine Editor's Choice Award 2002). *Address:* c/o Jessica Ford, Intermusica Artists' Management Ltd, 16 Duncan Terrace, London, N1 8BZ, England (office); Orchestre de la Suisse Romande, Rue Bovy-Lysberg 2, 1204 Geneva, Switzerland (office). *Telephone:* (20) 7278-5455 (office). *Fax:* (20) 7278-8434 (office). *E-mail:* mail@intermusica.co.uk (office). *Website:* www.intermusica.co.uk (office); www.osr.ch.

JANŠA, Janez; Slovenian politician; *President, Slovenian Democratic Party;* b. 17 Sept. 1958, Ljubljana; ed Univ. of Ljubljana; intern at Republican Secr. for Defence; apptd Pres. Cttee for Basic People's Defence and Social Self Protection, Alliance of Socialist Youth of Slovenia 1982; wrote paper critical of conditions within Yugoslav People's Army labelled counter-revolutionary 1983, indicted by mil. prosecutor 1985; served as Defence Minister in newly formed Repub. of Slovenia early 1990s; Pres. Slovenian Democratic Party 1993–; Prime Minister 2004–08. *Publications:* several books including On My Own Side 1988, Premiki (Movements) 1992, Okopi (The Barricades) 1994, Seven Years Later 1995, Eight Years Later 1996; hundreds of articles, commentaries, essays and scientific discussions; also several poems and literary compositions. *Address:* Slovenian Democratic Party, 1000 Ljubljana, Komenskega 11, Slovenia (office). *Telephone:* (1) 4345450 (office). *Fax:* (1) 4345452 (office). *E-mail:* sekretar@sds.si (office). *Website:* www.sds.si (office).

JANSEN, Jan Kristian Schøning, DrMed; Norwegian physiologist and academic; *Senior Research Fellow, Research Council of Norway;* b. 16 Jan. 1931, Oslo; s. of Jan Jansen and Helene Schøning; m. Helen Troye 1981; three s. two d.; ed Oslo Univ.; Rockefeller Foundation Research Fellow, Univ. of Oxford 1959–60; Asst Prof., Dept of Physiology, Oslo Univ. 1968–79, Prof. of Physiology 1979–96; Visiting Prof., Harvard Medical School 1970–71; Sr Research Fellow, Research Council of 1995–; Anders Jahres Prize 1967, Monrad Krohn Legat 1982, Fridtjof Nansen Award 1996. *Publications:* articles in professional journals. *Address:* Research Council of Norway, POB 2700 St. Hanshaugen, 0131 Oslo, Norway.

JANSONS, Mariss; Latvian conductor; *Chief Conductor, Royal Concertgebouw Orchestra;* b. 14 Jan. 1943, Riga; s. of Arvid Jansons and Erhaida Jansons; m. Irina Jansons 1967; one d.; ed studied with father, Leningrad Conservatory with N. Rabinovich, Vienna Conservatory with Hans Swarovsky, Salzburg with von Karajan; Prin. Guest Conductor Leningrad (now St Petersburg) Philharmonic Orchestra; Chief Conductor Oslo Philharmonic 1979–2002; Guest Conductor Welsh Symphony Orchestra 1985–88; Salzburg debut with the Vienna Philharmonic 1994; Prin. Guest Conductor London Philharmonic Orchestra –1997; Prof. of Conducting, St Petersburg Conservatory 1995–; Music Dir Pittsburgh Symphony Orchestra 1995, Chief Conductor 1997–2002; Chief Conductor Symphonieorchester des Bayerischen Rundfunks and the Bavarian Radio Choir 2003–; Chief Conductor Royal Concertgebouw Orchestra 2004–; has appeared all over world, with Baltimore Symphony Orchestra, Berlin Philharmonic, Boston Symphony Orchestra, Chicago Symphony Orchestra, Cleveland Orchestra, London Philharmonia Orchestra, New York Philharmonic, Philadelphia Orchestra; winner Herbert von Karajan Competition 1971, Anders Jahre Cultural Prize (Norway), RSFSR People's Artist 1986, Royal Philharmonic Soc. Conductor of the Year Award 2004, Midem Classical Music Award for Artist of the Year 2006; Commdr with Star Royal Norwegian Order of Merit. *Recordings include:* Shostakovich Symphony No. 7 (BBC Music Magazine Orchestral Award 2007) 2006. *Leisure interests:* arts, theatre, films, sports. *Address:* Opus 3 Artists, 470 Park Avenue South, 9th Floor North, New York 10016, USA (office); Royal Concertgebouw Orchestra, Jacob Obrechtstraat 51, 1071 KJ Amsterdam, Netherlands (office). *Telephone:* (212) 584-7500 (office); (20) 3051010 (home). *Fax:* (646) 300-8200 (office); (20) 3051001 (office). *E-mail:* info@opus3artists.com (office); info@concertgebouworkest.nl (office). *Website:* www.opus3artists.com (office); www.concertgebouworkest.nl (office).

JANSSEN, Baron Daniel, IngLic, MBA; Belgian business executive; *Chairman, Solvay SA;* b. 15 April 1936, Brussels; s. of Baron Charles-Emmanuel Janssen and Marie-Anne (née Boël) Janssen; m. Thérèse Bracht 1970; three s.; ed Univ. of Brussels, Harvard Univ., USA; Asst Sec. Euratom Comm., Brussels 1959–60; Prof. Brussels Univ. 1965–71; mem. Club of Rome 1968–87; Bd of Dirs Brussels Univ. 1969–70; mem. of Bd Inst. pour l'Encouragement de la Recherche Scientifique dans l'Industrie et l'Agriculture (IRSIA) 1971–77, Vice-Chair. 1974–77; mem. of Bd Belgian Fed. of Chemical Industries 1972–76, Chair. 1976–79; mem. European Cttee for R & D, EEC 1974–79; Chair. Exec. Cttee UCB 1975–84, Fed. of Belgian Enterprises 1981–84; CEO, Solvay & Cie (now Solvay) SA 1986–, now Chair. Bd of Dirs; holds non-exec. positions on numerous bds; Alumni Achievement Award, Harvard Business School. *Leisure interests:* tennis, skiing, shooting. *Address:* Solvay SA, 33 rue du Prince Albert, 1050 Brussels (office); La Roncière, 108 avenue Ernest Solvay, 1310 La Hulpe, Belgium (home). *Telephone:* (2) 509-69-37 (office). *Fax:* (2) 509-72-40 (office). *Website:* www.solvay.com (office).

JANSSEN, Baron Paul-Emmanuel, LLD; Belgian banker; *Honorary Chair, Générale de Banque;* b. 22 Feb. 1931, Brussels; s. of Baron Charles-Emmanuel Janssen and Marie-Anne Janssen (née Boël); m. Cecilia Löfgren; one s. one d.; ed Univ. Libre de Bruxelles, Harvard Business School, USA; fmr Chair. Générale de Banque SA (now Hon. Chair.), Belgium, Belgian Banking Asscn; fmr Dir Solvay, Solvac, Boël, Atlas Copco, European Banking Fed., Belgian Fed. of Enterprises; Commdr Ordre de la Couronne, Commdr Ordre de Léopold, Officier Légion d'honneur. *Leisure interests:* riding, hunting, forestry, music. *Address:* Le Bonnier, 79 rue Gaston, Bary B, 1310 La Hulpe, Belgium (home). *Telephone:* (2) 653-88-08 (office); (2) 652-03-50 (home). *Fax:* (2) 652-12-29 (office); (2) 652-07-38 (home). *E-mail:* lebonnier@skynet.be (home).

JANVIER, Gen. Bernard Louis Antonin; French army officer; b. 16 July 1939, La Voulte-sur-Rhône, Ardèche; s. of Pierre Janvier and Eugénie Bernard; m. Denise Diaz 1963; two s. one d.; ed Lycée de Nice, Coll. d'Orange,

Lycée Bugeaud, Algiers, Univ. of Rennes and Ecole Spéciale Militaire de Saint-Cyr; commissioned 2nd Lt 1960; served in Algeria 1962–64, Madagascar and Comoros 1964–67; Co. Commdt 9th Parachute Regt 1968–70; Commdt in charge of trainee officers, Ecole Spéciale Militaire de Saint-Cyr 1970–72; Bn Chief 1974; training course, Ecole Supérieure de Guerre 1974–76; Lt-Col 1978; Second-in-Command, Bureau of Operations-Instruction 1981; Col 1982; Chef de Corps, 2nd Overseas Parachute Regt 1982–84; Head, Office of Personnel, Chief of Ground Forces 1984–87; Deputy to Gen. Commdt 6th Armoured Div. 1987–89; Brig.-Gen. 1988; Chief. Org.-Logistic Div. of Army Chief of Staff 1989–91; Commdt Operation Requin, Port Gentil, Gabon 1991; Commdt Daguet Div. Saudi Arabia and Iraq 1991; Div. Gen. 1991; Commdt 6th Armoured Div. Nîmes 1991–93; Army Chief of Staff, Operational Planning (Emia) 1993–95; Gen. Army Corps 1994; apptd Army Chief of Staff 1995; Dir Centre des hautes études militaires, Inst. des hautes études de la défense nat. 1996–98; Commdt UN Peace Forces in Fmr Yugoslavia 1995–96; Commdr Légion d'honneur, Ordre nat. du Mérite, Legion of Merit (USA); numerous other decorations including medals from Kuwait and Saudi Arabia. *Leisure interests:* history of Provence, running. *Address:* 6 place de l'Eglise, 83310 Grimaud, France (home).

JANZEN, Daniel Hunt, PhD; American biologist and academic; *Professor of Biology and Thomas G. and Louise E. DiMaura Term Chair, University of Pennsylvania;* b. 18 Jan. 1939, Milwaukee, Wis.; s. of Daniel Hugo Janzen and Floyd Foster Janzen; m. twice, divorced twice; one s. one d. from 1st marriage; ed Univ. of Minnesota and Univ. of California, Berkeley; Asst and Assoc. Prof., Univ. of Kansas 1965–68; Assoc. Prof., Univ. of Chicago 1969–72; Assoc. Prof. and Prof. of Ecology and Evolutionary Biology, Univ. of Michigan 1972–76; Prof. of Biology, Thomas G. and Louise E. DiMaura Term Chair Univ. of Pennsylvania, Philadelphia 1976–; teacher, Org. for Tropical Studies in Costa Rica 1965–; field research in tropical ecology, supported mainly by grants from NSF, USA 1963; MacArthur Fellow 1989; Gleason Award, American Botanical Soc. 1975; Crafoord Prize, Coevolutionary Ecology, Swedish Royal Acad. of Sciences 1984. *Publications:* Herbivores (co-ed., with G. A. Rosenthal) 1979, Costa Rican Natural History (ed.) 1983 and over 250 papers in scientific journals. *Leisure interest:* tropical ecology. *Address:* 301 Leidy Laboratories, Department of Biology, University of Pennsylvania, Philadelphia, PA 19104, USA (office); Parque Nacional Santa Rosa, Apdo. 169, Liberia, Guanacaste Province, Costa Rica. *Telephone:* (215) 898-5636 (office). *Fax:* (215) 898-8780 (office). *E-mail:* djanzen@sas.upenn.edu (office). *Website:* janzen.sas.upenn.edu (office); www.bio.upenn.edu/faculty/janzen (office).

JAOUI, Agnès; French actress, screenwriter and director; b. 19 Oct. 1964, Antony, Hauts-de-Seine; d. of Hubert Jaoui and Josiane Jaoui (née Zerah); m. Jean-Pierre Bacri; ed Lycée Henri IV, Paris, Théâtre des Amandiers, Nanterre. *Films:* as actor: Le Faucon (The Hawk) 1983, Hôtel de France 1987, L'Amoureuse 1987, Canti 1991, Cuisine et Dépendances (Kitchen with Apartment) 1993, Un Air de Famille (Family Resemblances) (Lumiere Award: Best Screenplay 1997) 1996, Le Déménagement 1997, On Connaît la Chanson (Same Old Song) (César: Best Supporting Actress 1998) 1997, Le Cousin 1997, La Méthode 1997, On the Run 1999, Une Femme d'Extérieur (Outgoing Woman) 2000, Le Goût des Autres (The Taste of Others) 2000, 24 Heures de la Vie d'une Femme (24 Hours in the Life of a Woman) 2002, Le Rôle de sa Vie 2004, Comme une Image (Look at Me) 2004, La Maison de Nina 2004, Le Rôle de sa vie 2004, La Maison de Nina 2005; as screenwriter: Cuisine et Dépendances, Smoking/No Smoking 1993, On Connaît la Chanson, Un Air de Famille; as screenwriter and dir: Le Goût des Autres (Grand Prix des Amériques 2000, César: Best Film and Best Original Adaptation 2001, David di Donatello Award: Best Foreign Film 2001, European Film Award: Best Screenwriter, Lumiere Award: Best Director 2001) 2000, Comme une Image (Bodil Award, Palme D'Or: Best Screen Play 2004, European Film Award: Best Screenwriter 2004) 2004, Parlez-moi de la pluie (Let's Talk About the Rain) 2008. *Address:* c/o Zelig, 57, rue Réaumur, 75002 Paris, France (office). *Website:* www.agnes-jaoui.over-blog.com.

JAPAN, H.M. Emperor of (see Akihito).

JAPARIDZE, Tedo, PhD; Georgian politician and diplomatist; b. 18 Sept. 1946, Tbilisi; m. Tamar Japaridze; one s.; ed Tbilisi State Univ., Inst. of USA and Canadian Studies, Moscow, Russia; fmr teacher, Dept of Int. Relations and Int. Law, Tbilisi State Univ.; with Ministry of Foreign Affairs 1989–92, positions include Head of Political Dept, Deputy Foreign Minister, First Deputy Foreign Minister, Vice-Chair. Council for UNESCO Affairs 1989–92, Nat. Security Adviser to Head of State 1992–94; Amb. to USA, Canada and Mexico 1995–2002; Sec. Nat. Security Council 2002–03; Minister of Foreign Affairs 2003–04; Hon. Chair. Transcaucasus Foundation and Special Advisor to Washington Strategic Advisors, LLC –2004; Sec.-Gen. Org. of the Black Sea Econ. Cooperation (BSEC), Perm. Int. Secr. (PERMIS) 2004–06. *Publications include:* White House: Mechanism of Decision-Making 1985, American Political Institutions: History and Currrent State (co-author) 1987; numerous articles on US domestic and foreign policy. *Address:* c/o Organization of the Black Sea Economic Cooperation Permanent International Secretariat, İstinye Caddesi, Müşir Fuad Paşa Yalısı, Eski Tersane, 80860İstinye-İstanbul, Turkey (office).

JAPAROV, Tuvakmammed; Turkmenistani politician; *Deputy Prime Minister, responsible for Economic Affairs;* Chair. Supreme Control Chamber of Turkmenistan –2009; Deputy Prime Minister, responsible for Econ. Affairs 2009–. *Address:* Office of the President and the Council of Ministers, 744000 Aşgabat, Presidential Palace, Turkmenistani (office). *Telephone:* (12) 35-45-34 (office). *Fax:* (12) 35-51-12 (office). *Website:* www.turkmenistan.gov.tm (office).

JARA, Alejandro; Chilean diplomatist and international organization executive; *Deputy Director-General, World Trade Organization;* b. 1949,

Santiago; m. Daniela Benavente; one s. two d.; ed high schools in Rio de Janeiro, Brazil and Santiago, Chile, Universidad de Chile, Law School, Univ. of California, Berkeley, USA (Fulbright Scholarship); joined Chilean Foreign Service 1976, specialized in int. econ. relations, served in Del. to GATT, Geneva 1979–84, seconded as Co-ordinator for Trade Policy Affairs to Econ. System for Latin America (SELA), Caracas, Venezuela, Dir for Bilateral Econ. Affairs 1993–94, Dir for Multilateral Econ. Affairs 1994–99, Sr Official to APEC and Deputy Chief Negotiator for the Chile–Canada Free Trade Agreement 1996–97, Chief Negotiator for the Chile–Mexico Free Trade Agreement 1997–98, Dir-Gen. for Int. Econ. 1999–2000, Amb. and Perm. Rep. to WTO, Geneva 2000–05, Chair. WTO Cttee on Trade and Environment 2001, Chair. Special Session of the Council for Trade in Services 2002; Deputy Dir-Gen. WTO 2005–. *Publications:* numerous articles and papers on int. trade. *Address:* World Trade Organization, Centre William Rappard, rue de Lausanne 154, 1211 Geneva, Switzerland (office). *Telephone:* (22) 7395111 (office). *Fax:* (22) 7314206 (office). *E-mail:* enquiries@wto.org (office). *Website:* www.wto.org (office).

JÁRAI, Zsigmond; Hungarian economist and banker; b. 29 Dec. 1951, Biharkeresztes; m. Marianna Kiss; one s. one d.; ed Univ. of Econs, Budapest; banker, State Devt Bank, Hungary 1976–89; Deputy Minister of Finance and Dir of State Bank Supervision 1989–90; Sr Exec. for Eastern Europe, James Capel & Co., London 1990–92; Man. Dir Samuel Montagu Financial Consult-ant and Securities Co., Budapest 1993–95; Chair. and CEO ABN AMRO (Magyar) Bank (fmrly Hungarian Credit Bank) 1995–98; Chair. Hungarian Stock Exchange 1996–98; Minister of Finance 1998–2000; Pres. Nat. Bank of Hungary 2001–07. *Address:* c/o National Bank of Hungary (Magyar Nemzeti Bank), Szabadság tér 8–9, 1850 Budapest, Hungary.

JARDIM GONÇALVES, Jorge Manuel, BCE; Portuguese banker; *Chairman, Senior Board, Banco Comercial Português (BCP);* b. 4 Oct. 1935, Funchal, Madeira Island; ed Univ. of Oporto; military service, Army Eng Corps 1960–63; engineer in Angola; lecturer, Eng School of Oporto –1970; joined Banco de Agricultura 1970, later apptd. to Bd of Dirs; employee Compañia de Gestion de Industrias (subsidiary of Banco Popular Español) 1975–76; Exec. Dir Banco Português do Atlântico 1977, Chair. 1979–85; Chair. Banco Comercial de Macao and Dir Companhia de Seguros de Macao 1979–85; CEO Banco Comercial Português (BCP) 1985–2005, Chair. Sr Bd 1985–; Deputy Pres. of Man. Bd, Union of Portuguese Banks; mem. Bd of Dirs Eureko 1993–; mem. Int. Monetary Conference (IMC); mem. Supervisory Bd Bank Millennium, Poland; mem. Sr Bd Novabank, Greece. *Address:* Banco Comercial Português (BCP), Praça D. João I, 28, 4000-295 Porto, Portugal (office). *Telephone:* 707-502424 (office). *Fax:* (21) 0066858 (office). *Website:* www.bcp.pt (office).

JARDINE, Al; American musician (guitar) and singer; b. 3 Sept. 1942, Lima, OH; mem., The Beach Boys 1961–62, 1963–; numerous tours and concerts, festival appearances; band est. Brother Records label 1967–; American Music Awards Special Award of Merit 1988, Grammy Lifetime Achievement Award 2001. *Recordings include:* albums: Surfin' Safari 1962, Surfer Girl 1963, Little Deuce Coupe 1963, Shut Down Vol. 2, All Summer Long 1964, Christmas Album 1964, The Beach Boys Today! 1965, Summer Days (and Summer Nights) 1965, Beach Boys Party 1966, Pet Sounds 1966, Smiley Smile 1967, Wild Honey 1968, Friends 1968, 20/20 1969, Sunflower 1970, Surf's Up 1971, Carl and the Passions – So Tough 1972, Holland 1973, The Beach Boys in Concert 1973, Endless Summer 1974, 15 Big Ones 1976, The Beach Boys Love You 1977, M.I.U. 1978, LA (Light Album) 1979, Keepin' The Summer Alive 1980, The Beach Boys 1985, Still Cruisin' 1989, Two Rooms 1991, Summer in Paradise 1992, The Sounds of Summer – The Very Best of The Beach Boys 2003. *Address:* c/o Elliott Lott, Boulder Creek Entertainment Corporation, 4860 San Jacinto Circle W, Fallbrook, CA 92028, USA (office); c/o Capitol Records, 1750 North Vine Street, Hollywood, CA 90028, USA. *Website:* www.thebeachboys.com; www.aljardine.com.

JARISLOWSKY, Stephen A., CC, MBA; Canadian business executive; *Chairman and CEO, Jarislowsky, Fraser Limited;* b. Sept. 1925, Berlin, Germany; m. Gail Jarislowsky; four c.; ed Cornell Univ., Univ. of Chicago, Harvard Business School; served in US Army during World War Two, in counter-intelligence in Japan after the war; engineer, Alcan Aluminum, Montreal 1949–52; f. Jarislowsky, Fraser Ltd (investment co.) 1955, fmr Pres., currently Chair. and CEO; Founder and Pres. The Jarislowsky Foundation; Chair. Learning Assocs, Goodfellow Lumber Inc.; mem. Bd of Dirs C. D. Howe Research Inst., Fraser Brothers Ltd, Growth Oil & Gas Investment Fund of Canada Ltd (also Pres.), Slocan Forest Products, Velan Inc.; Co-founder Canadian Coalition for Good Governance 2002; mem. Advisory Bd McGill Univ. Medical School, Queen's Univ. School of Business; has endowed eleven eponymous univ. chairs in Canada; Grand Officer, Nat. Order of Quebec; Hon. LLD (Queen's Univ., Univ. of Alberta, McMaster Univ., Université Laval, Concordia Univ., Univ. of Windsor, Université de Montréal). *Publications:* The Investment Zoo: Taming the Bulls and the Bears (co-author) 2005. *Address:* Jarislowsky, Fraser Limited, 1010 Sherbrooke Street West, Suite 2005, Montreal, PQ H3A 2R7, Canada (office). *Telephone:* (514) 842-2727 (office). *Fax:* (514) 842-1882 (office). *E-mail:* plapointe@jfl.ca (office). *Website:* www.jfl.ca (office).

JARMAN, Sir Brian, Kt, OBE, MA, PhD, FRCP, FRCGP, FMedSci, FFPH; British medical scientist and academic; *Professor Emeritus of Medicine, Faculty of Medicine, Imperial College;* b. London; ed Univ. of Cambridge, Imperial Coll. London; began career as exploration geophysicist with Shell Oil Co., Sahara; worked at St Mary's Hosp. Medical School and Harvard in hosp. posts; pioneered devt of research on socio-economic indicators of health status (Under Privileged Area scores or Jarman Index); Head Dept of Primary Health Care and Gen. Practice and Head Div. of Primary Care and Population

Health Sciences, Imperial Coll. School of Medicine, London –1998, Prof. Emer. of Medicine 1998–, also currently Dir Dr Foster Unit; Pres. BMA 2003–04; currently part-time Sr Fellow, Inst. for Healthcare Improvement, Boston, USA; mem. London Strategic Review Panel to advise Dept of Health 1998; medical mem. Bristol Royal Infirmary Enquiry 1999–2001; fmr mem. Council, Royal Coll. of Physicians; European Ed. Journal Watch (mem. Editorial Bd 1982–2004); frequent participant in nat. and int. advisory work. *Publications include:* numerous books and articles linking socio-economic variables to health status and quality of medical care. *Address:* 62 Aberdare Gardens, London, NW6 3QD, England (home). *Telephone:* 7786-431691 (mobile) (office). *E-mail:* b.jarman@imperial.ac.uk (office). *Website:* wwwfom.sk.med.ic.ac.uk/medicine/about/divisions/pcphs/phcgp/people/b.jarman.html (office).

JARMUSCH, Jim; American film director and screenwriter; b. 22 Jan. 1953, Akron, OH; ed Medill School of Journalism, Northwestern Univ., Evanston, Ill., Colombia Coll., SC; teaching asst to Nicholas Ray at New York Univ. Graduate Film School 1976–79; has worked on several films as sound recordist, cameraman and actor. *Films:* Permanent Vacation (writer, dir) 1980, You Are Not I (writer) 1981, The New World (dir) 1982, Stranger Than Paradise (writer, dir) (Camera d'Or Award, Cannes Film Festival 1984) 1983, Down By Law (writer, dir) 1986, Coffee and Cigarettes (short film, writer and dir) 1986, Mystery Train (writer, dir) 1989, Coffee and Cigarettes II (short film, writer and dir) 1989, Night on Earth (writer, dir) 1992, Coffee and Cigarettes III (short film, writer and dir) 1993, Dead Man (writer, dir) 1995, Year of the Horse (dir) 1997, Ghost Dog: The Way of the Samurai (writer, dir) 1999, Ten Minutes Older: The Trumpet (writer, dir) 2002, Coffee and Cigarettes (writer, dir) 2003, Broken Flowers 2005. *Music videos directed include:* The Lady Don't Mind (Talking Heads) 1986, Sightsee MC! (Big Audio Dynamite) 1987, It's Alright With Me (Tom Waits) 1991, I Don't Wanna Grow Up (Tom Waits) 1992, Dead Man Theme (Neil Young) 1995, Big Time (Neil Young and Crazy Horse) 1996. *Address:* c/o Bart Walker, Creative Artists Agency LLC, 162 5th Avenue, 6th Floor, New York, NY 10010, USA (office). *Telephone:* (212) 277-9000 (office).

JAROCKI, Jerzy; Polish theatre director; b. 11 May 1929, Warsaw; s. of Bohdan Jarocki and Leokadia Jarocka; m. 1st 1962; one d.; m. 2nd Danuta Maksymowicz 1980; ed State Higher School of Drama, studies in drama production in Kraków and in USSR; debut with Bruno Jasienski's Ball of the Dummies, Stanislaw Wyspianski Theatre of Silesia 1957; Dir Teatr Śląski, Katowice 1957–62, Stary Teatr, Kraków 1962–98; scientific worker, State Higher Dramatic School, Kraków 1965–; Dir Teatr Polski, Wrocław 1998–2000, Teatr Narodowy, Warsaw 2000–; directs plays mainly by Polish writers S. Witkiewicz, W. Gombrowicz, T. Różewicz and S. Mrożek, also by Shakespeare and Chekhov; mem. Presidential Council for Culture 1992–95; mem. Polish Acad. of Arts and Science, Kraków 1994–; productions abroad, including Amsterdam, Zürich, Munich, Chelyabinsk, Nuremberg, Wuppertal, Belgrade, Novi Sad, Bonn; teacher, State Higher School of Drama, Kraków 1963–, Asst Prof. 1965–85, Extraordinary Prof. 1985–; Gold Cross of Merit 1968, Commdr's Cross, Order of Polonia Restituta 1996; Dr hc (Jagiellonian Univ., Kraków) 2000; Schiller Award 1967, Gold Award of City of Kraków, Minister of Culture and Arts Prize (1st Class) 1971, 1997, Konrad Swinarski Award 1977, Contact-Int. Theatre Festival (3rd Prize) 1994, and others. *Plays directed:* has directed over 100 plays including: Ślub (The Wedding) 1960, 1973, 1974, 1991, Cymbeline 1967, Moja córeczka (My Little Daughter) 1968, Stara kobieta wysiaduje (Old Woman Brooding) 1969, Three Sisters 1969, 1974, Pater Noster 1971, Szewcy (The Shoemakers) 1972, On All Fours 1972, Matka (The Mother) 1966, 1974, The Trial 1973, The Cherry Orchard 1975, Rzeźnia (The Slaughterhouse) 1975, Bal manekinów (Mannequins Ball) 1976, King Lear 1977, White Glove 1978, Twilight 1979, The Dream of the Sinless 1979, The Inspector General 1980, Murder in the Cathedral 1982, Pieszo (On Foot) 1981, La Vida es Sueño 1983, Sceny z Jaffy (Scenes from Jaffa) 1984, Samobójca (The Suicide) 1987, Portret (Portrait) 1988, (in Germany) 1996, Słuchaj Izraelu (Listen, Israel) 1989, Pułapka (Trap) 1992, Sen srebrny Salomei (Silver Dream of Salome) 1993, Płatonow 1993, Kasia z Heilbronnu (Kate from Heilbronn) 1994, Grzebanie 1996, Płatonow akt pominięty (Płatonov, The Deleted Act) (Baltic House Int. Film Festival, St Petersburg 1997) 1996, Faust 1997, Historia PRL wg Mrożka (PPR History by Mrożek) 1998. *Address:* ul. Moniuszki 33, 31-523 Kraków, Poland.

JARQUÍN CALDERÓN, Edmundo, MA, JD; Nicaraguan economist and politician; b. Sept. 1946, Ocotal, Nuevo Segovia; ed Universidad Centroamericana, Managua, Universidad de Chile Law School; joined Juventud Democráta Cristiana 1965; student secretary Christian Democratic Youth of Latin America 1966–67; forced to leave academic studies in Chile following Gen. Augusto Pinochet's coup against Pres. Salvador Allende 1973; co-founder Unión Democrática de Liberación (UDEL) 1974; Minister for Foreign Cooperation 1981–84; Amb. to Mexico 1984–88, to Spain 1988–90; mem. Parl. for Frente Sandinista de Liberación Nacional (FSLN) and mem. Bd of Dirs, Nat. Ass. 1990–92; co-founder Movimiento Renovador Sandinista (MRS) (dissident group that split from FSLN) 1992; specialist in public policy IDB 1992–2005; cand. for Vice Pres. with Herty Lewites (MRS) 2006, cand. for Pres. upon death of Lewites July 2006. *Address:* Movimiento Renovador Sandinista (MRS), Tienda Katty 1 c. abajo, Apdo 24, Managua, Nicaragua (office). *Telephone:* (2) 78-0279 (office). *Fax:* (2) 78-0268 (office).

JARRATT, Sir Alexander Anthony, Kt, CB, BCom; British fmr business executive; b. 19 Jan. 1924, London; s. of Alexander Jarratt and Mary Jarratt; m. (Mary) Philomena Keogh 1946; one s. two d.; ed Royal Liberty Grammar School, Essex and Univ. of Birmingham; mil. service in Fleet Air Arm 1942–46; Asst Prin. Ministry of Power 1949–53, Prin. 1953–54; Treasury 1954–55; Prin. Pvt. Sec. to Minister of Fuel and Power 1955–59; Asst Sec. in Oil Div. of Ministry 1959–63, Under-Sec. in Gas Div. 1963–64; Cabinet Office 1964–65; First Sec., Nat. Bd for Prices and Incomes 1965–68; Deputy Under-Sec. of State, Dept of Employment and Productivity 1968; Deputy Sec., Ministry of Agric. 1970; mem. Bds of IPC and Reed Int. Ltd 1970; Man. Dir IPC 1970–74, Chair. 1974, also of IPC Newspapers 1974; Chair. and CEO Reed Int. Ltd 1974–85; Chair. CBI Econ. Policy Cttee 1972–74, Industrial Soc. 1975–79; mem. Supervisory Bd, Thyssen-Bornemisza 1972–89; Dir (non-exec.) ICI Ltd 1975–91, Smith's Industries 1984–96 (Chair. (non-exec.) 1985–91); Dir and Deputy Chair. Midland Bank 1980–91; Jt Deputy Chair. Prudential Corpn 1987–91, 1992–94 (Dir 1985–94); Chair. Admin. Staff Coll., Henley 1976–89, Centre for Dispute Resolution 1990–2000 (Pres. 2001–); Pres. Advertising Asscn 1979–83; mem. Council CBI, Chair. CBI Employment Policy Cttee 1982–86; Pres. Periodical Publishers Asscn 1983–85; Vice-Pres. Inst. of Marketing 1982; Chancellor Univ. of Birmingham 1983–2002; Gov. Ashridge Man. Coll.; Hon. DSc (Cranfield); Hon. DUniv (Brunel, Essex); Hon. DLL (Birmingham). *Leisure interests:* countryside pursuits, theatre, music, reading. *Address:* Barn Mead, Fryerning, Essex, CM4 0NP, England (home).

JARRAUD, Michel; French international organization executive and meteorologist; *Secretary-General, World Meteorological Organization;* b. 1952, Châtillon-sur-Indre; m.; two c.; ed Ecole Polytechnique, Ecole de la Météorologie Nationale; researcher, Météo-France 1976–78, Dir Weather Forecasting Dept 1986–89; researcher in numerical weather prediction, European Centre for Medium-Range Weather Forecasts (ECMWF) 1978–85, Dir Operational Dept 1990–91, Deputy Dir ECMWF 1991–95; Deputy Sec.-Gen. WMO 1995–2003, Sec.-Gen. 2004–; mem. Soc. Météorologique de France, Royal Meteorological Soc. (UK), African Meteorological Soc.; Fellow, American Meteorological Soc.; Hon. mem. Chinese Meteorological Soc., Cuban Meteorological Soc.; Commdr, Ordre nat. du Lion (Senegal) 2005; Hon. DSc (Universidad Nacional Agraria 'La Molina', Peru) 2004; First Class Distinction, Civil Defence of Venezuela 1999. *Address:* World Meteorological Organization, 7 bis, avenue de la Paix, CP 2300, 1211 Geneva 2, Switzerland (office). *Telephone:* (22) 7308111 (office). *Fax:* (22) 7308181 (office). *E-mail:* wmo@wmo.int (office). *Website:* www.wmo.ch (office).

JARRE, Jean Michel André, LèsL; French composer, musician (synthesizer, keyboard) and record producer; b. 24 Aug. 1948, Lyons; s. of Maurice Jarre and France Jarre (née Pejot); m. 2nd Charlotte Rampling (q.v.) 1978; m. 3rd Anne Parillaud 2005; one s. and one d. from previous marriage; ed Lycée Michelet, Université de la Sorbonne, Conservatoire de musique de Paris; composer of electronic music 1968–; int. concerts include shows in China, Europe and USA; shows incorporate state-of-the-art sound and vision tech.; composer for ballet Aor and Opéra de Paris 1971; UNESCO Goodwill Amb. 1993–; spokesperson European Music Industry 1998–, Int. Fed. for Phonographic Industry 1998–2000; Soc. des auteurs, compositeurs et éditeurs de musique Gold Medal 1980, Grand Prix de l'Acad. Charles Cros 1985; Officier, Ordre des Arts et des Lettres, Officer, Legion d'honneur. *Major live performances:* Place de la Concorde, Paris 1979 (record audience of one million); Peking, Shanghai 1981; Rendez-vous Houston (record audience of 1.3 million), Rendez-vous Lyons 1986; Destination Docklands, London 1988; Paris–La Défense: A City in Concert 1990 (2.5 million audience); Europe in Concert 1993; Hong Kong 1994; Eiffel Tower, Paris 1995 (one million audience); Moscow 1997 (record audience of 3.5 million); Electronic Night, Eiffel Tower, Paris 1998; Millennium Concert, Pyramids of Cairo (televised worldwide, estimated 2,000m. viewers) 1999; 2001 Rendez-vous in Space, Okinawa, Japan 2001; Akropolis Athens 2001; Aero, Aalborg, Denmark 2002; Forbidden City and Tiananmen Square, Beijing 2004; Gdansk Shipyard, Poland 2005. *Film scores:* Des Garçons et des filles 1968, Deserted Palace 1972, Les Granges brulées 1973, Die Hamburger Krankheit 1978, music and lyrics for numerous songs. *Recordings include:* albums: Oxygène 1976, Equinoxe 1978, Magnetic Fields 1980, The China Concerts (live) 1982, Zoolook (Grand Prix Academie du Disque 1985) 1984, Rendez-vous 1986, Cities in Concert: Houston/Lyons (live) 1987, Revolutions 1988, Jarre Live (Victoire de la Musique Best Instrumental Album 1986) 1989, Waiting for Cousteau 1990, Images (compilation) 1991, Chronologie 1993, Hong Kong (live) 1994, Oxygène 7–13 1997, Odyssey Through 02 (interactive) 1998, Metamorphoses 2000, Aero 2004, Téo & Téa 2007. *Publications:* Concert d'Images 1989, Paris-la-Défense, une ville en concert 1990, Europe in Concert 1994, Paris-Tour Eiffel, Concert pour la Tolérance 1995, The Millennium Concert at the Great Pyramids of Egypt 2000, Akropolis 2001, Jean Michel Jarre à Pékin 2004. *Address:* Fiona Commins, Aero Productions, 8 rue de Lévis, 75017 Paris, France (office). *Telephone:* (1) 44-90-91-70 (office). *Fax:* (1) 44-90-91-77 (office). *E-mail:* contactaero@wanadoo.fr (office). *Website:* www.jeanmicheljarre.com (office).

JARRETT, Keith; American pianist and composer; b. 8 May 1945, Allentown, PA; ed Berklee School of Music; gave first solo concert aged 7, followed by professional appearances; two-hour solo concert of own compositions 1962; led own trio in Boston; worked with Roland Kirk, Tony Scott and others in New York; joined Art Blakey 1965; toured Europe with Charles Lloyd 1966, with Miles Davis 1970–71; soloist and leader of own groups 1969–; Guggenheim Fellowship 1972; Prix du Prés. de la République 1991, Royal Swedish Acad. of Music Polar Prize 2003; Officier, Ordre des Arts et des Lettres. *Recordings include:* albums: Bach's Well-Tempered Klavier, Personal Mountains 1974, Luminessence 1974, Mysteries 1975, Changeless 1987, Nude Ants, The Cure 1990, Bye Bye Black 1991, At the Dear Head Inn 1992, Bridge of Light 1993, At the Blue Note 1994, La Scala 1995, Tokyo '96 1998, The Melody at Night With You 1999, Whisper Not 2000, Inside Out 2001, Always Let Me Go 2002, Selected Recordings 2002, Radiance 2005, The Carnegie Hall Concert 2006, Dmitri Shostakovich: 24 Preludes and Fugues 2006. *Address:* Vincent Ryan, 135 W 16th Street, New York, NY 10011, USA (office).

JARRETT, Valerie Bowman, BA, JD; American lawyer, business executive, civic leader and government official; *White House Senior Advisor and*

Assistant to the President for Intergovernmental Affairs and Public Liaison; b. 14 Nov. 1956, Shiraz, Iran; d. of Dr James E. Bowman; great-grandfather was first African-American to graduate from MIT, grandfather was first black man to head Chicago Housing Authority, father was first black resident at St Luke's Hosp., great-uncle is Vernon Jordan; m. Dr William Robert Jarrett 1983 (divorced 1988, died 1991); one d.; ed Northfield Mount Hermon School, Mass, Stanford Univ., Calif., Univ. of Michigan Law School; father ran hosp. for children in Shiraz, Iran; moved with family to London, UK aged five 1962–63, returned to Chicago 1963; began career in Chicago politics working for Mayor Harold Washington as Deputy Corpn Counsel for Finance and Devt 1987, continued to work in Mayor's Office in 1990s, Deputy Chief of Staff for Mayor Richard Daley, Commr Dept of Planning and Devt 1992–95, Chair. Chicago Transit Bd 1995–2003; Exec. Vice-Pres. The Habitat Company (real estate devt and man. co.) 1995–2007, Pres. and CEO 2007–09; mem. Bd Chicago Stock Exchange 2000–07, Chair. 2004–07, Chair. Chicago Stock Exchange Holdings, Inc. 2005–07; Finance Chair. US Senatorial Campaign for Barack Obama 2004, first Treas. of Senator's PAC, the Hopefund, also served as a Sr Advisor to the Obama for America Presidential Campaign; Co-Chair. Obama-Biden Transition Project 2008–09; White House Sr Advisor and Asst to the Pres. for Intergovernmental Affairs and Public Liaison 2009–, manages White House Office of Public Liaison, Office of Intergovernmental Affairs, and Chairs White House Comm. on Women and Girls; Chair. Bd of Trustees, Univ. of Chicago Medical Center, Vice-Chair. Bd of Trustees, Univ. of Chicago; Vice-Chair. Chicago 2016 Olympic Cttee, Metropolis 2020; mem. Bd of Dirs Fed. Reserve Bank of Chicago 2006–07, USG Corpn, Inc., Chicago, Navigant Consulting, Inc., RREEF America II; Dir Local Initiative Support Corpn, The Joyce Foundation, The Metropolitan Planning Council, Cen. Area Cttee; Trustee, Museum of Science and Industry. *Address:* The White House, 1600 Pennsylvania Avenue NW, Washington, DC 20500, USA (office). *Telephone:* (202) 456-1111 (office). *Fax:* (202) 456-2461 (office). *E-mail:* info@whitehouse.gov (office). *Website:* www.whitehouse.gov/administration/staff/valerie_jarrett (office).

JARRIN, Gen. (retd) Oswaldo; Ecuadorean government official, academic and fmr army officer; *Minister of National Defence;* Chair. Jt Chiefs of Staff –2003; fmr Sec. Nat. Security Council; Minister of Nat. Defence 2005–; Prof. Latin American Faculty of Social Sciences. *Address:* Ministry of National Defence, Exposición 208, Quito, Ecuador (office). *Telephone:* (2) 221-6150 (office). *Fax:* (2) 256-9386 (office). *E-mail:* paginaweb@fuerzasarmadasecuador.org (office). *Website:* www.fuerzasarmadasecuador.ec-gov.net (office).

JARUZELSKI, Gen. Wojciech; Polish politician and army officer; b. 6 July 1923, Kurów, Lublin Prov.; s. of Władysław Jaruzelski and Wanda Jaruzelska; m. Barbara Jaruzelska 1961; one d.; ed Infantry Officers' School and Karol Świerczewski Gen. Staff Acad., Warsaw; served with Polish Armed Forces in USSR and Poland 1943–45; various sr army posts 1945–57; Commdr Armoured Div. 1957–60; Chief of Cen. Political Bd of the Armed Forces 1960–65; Chief of Gen. Staff 1965–68; Minister of Nat. Defence 1968–83; Chair. Council of Ministers 1981–85; First Sec. Cen. Cttee PZPR 1981–89; Brig.-Gen. 1956, Divisional-Gen. 1960, Gen. of Arms 1968, Gen. of Army 1973; mem. PZPR 1948–90, mem. PZPR Cen. Cttee 1964–89, mem. Political Bureau 1971–89; Deputy to Sejm (Parl.) 1961–89; Vice-Pres. Chief Council of Union of Fighters for Freedom and Democracy 1972–88; Chair. Comm. for Econ. Reform 1981–86; Chair. Mil. Council for Nat. Salvation 1981–83; mem. Presidium All-Poland Cttee of Nat. Unity Front 1981–83, Provisional Nat. Council of Patriotic Movt for Nat. Rebirth (PRON) 1982–83, mem. Nat. Council PRON 1983–89; Chair. Country Defence Cttee 1983–90, Supreme Commdr of the Armed Forces of Polish People's Repub. for Wartime 1983–90; Chair. Council of State (Head of State) 1985–89, Pres. of Polish People's Repub. (Polish Repub.) 1989–90; charged with murder of shipyard workers in 1970, 2001; decorations include Order of Builders of People's Poland, Order of Banner of Labour (First Class), Kt's Cross of Order of Polonia Restituta, Silver Cross of Virtuti Militari and Cross of Valour, Medals of 30th and 40th Anniversary of People's Poland, Hon. Miner of People's Repub., Order of Lenin 1968, 1983, Commdr's Cross Order of the Crown (Belgium) 1967, Order of the October Revolution (USSR) 1973, Scharnhorst Order (GDR) 1975, Grand Cross Order of Henry the Navigator (Portugal) 1975, Order of the State Banner (Democratic People's Repub. of Korea) 1977, Order of Suche Bator (Mongolia) 1977, Order of the Red Banner (Hungary) 1977, Order of the Red Banner (USSR) 1978, Order of the White Lion (Czechoslovakia) 1979, Order of Klement Gottwald (Czechoslovakia) 1983, Karl Marx Order (GDR) 1983, Order of the Star of the Socialist Repub. (First class with Riband) (Romania) 1983, Order of the Golden Star (Vietnam) 1983, Order of Georgi Dimitrov (Bulgaria) 1983, Order of the Red Battle Banner (Mongolia) 1983, Order of the Banner (First Class with Diamonds) (Hungary) 1983, Order of José Martí (Cuba) 1983, Grand Cross of Order of the Holy Saviour (Greece) 1987, Officier Légion d'honneur 1989. *Publications:* Stan Wojenny: Dlaczego 1993, Różnić się mądrze 2000. *Leisure interests:* history, military affairs. *Address:* Biuro Byłego Prezydenta RP Wojciecha Jaruzelskiego, Al. Jerozolimskie 91, 02-001 Warsaw, Poland (office). *Telephone:* (22) 6289942 (office). *Fax:* (22) 6875773 (office).

JÄRVI, Neeme; Estonian conductor; *Musical Director, New Jersey Symphony Orchestra;* b. 7 June 1937, Tallinn; s. of August Järvi and Elss Järvi; m. Liilia Järvi 1961; two s. one d.; ed Tallinn Music School, Leningrad Conservatorium and Leningrad Postgraduate Studium, studied with N. Rabinovich and Y. Mravinsky; Conductor Estonian Radio Symphony Orchestra –1963; Chief Conductor Estonian State Opera House 1963–76, Estonian State Symphony Orchestra 1976–80; emigrated to USA 1980; Prin. Guest Conductor City of Birmingham Symphony Orchestra, UK 1981–83; Prin. Conductor Royal Scottish Nat. Orchestra 1984–88, Conductor Laureate for Life 1990–; Prin. Conductor Gothenburg Orchestra, Sweden 1982–; Music Dir Detroit Symphony Orchestra, USA 1990–2005, Music Dir Emer. 2006–; Music Dir, New Jersey Symphony Orchestra 2005–; Chief Conductor Residentie Orchestra, The Hague 2005–09; First Prin. Guest Conductor Japan Philharmonic Orchestra; guest conductor of many int. symphony orchestras, including New York Philharmonic, Boston, Chicago, Royal Concertgebouw, Philharmonia, London Symphony, London Philharmonic; conducted Eugene Onegin 1979, 1984, Samson and Delilah 1982 and Khovanshchina 1985 at Metropolitan Opera House, New York; has held int. master-classes in summer resort town of Pärnu, Estonia 2000–; Hon. Mem. Royal Swedish Acad. of Music, Estonian Composers Union 1989; Hon. Citizen, City of Gothenburg 1987, State of Michigan 1992; Kt Commdr of North Star Order, Sweden 1990, Sash, Order of Nat. Coat of Arms 1996, Insignia, Coat of Arms, Tallinn 1997; Dr hc (Royal Swedish Acad. of Music) 1988, 1990, (Estonian Music Acad.) 1989, (Aberdeen |) 1990, (Gothenburg) 1985, 1991, (Tallinn Music Conservatory), Wayne State Univ., USA) 1994, (Michigan) 1999; First Prize, Young Conductors' Competition, Leningrad 1957, Estonian Soviet Socialist Repub. (ESSR) Honoured Artist 1965, First Prize, Accademia Nazionale di Santa Cecilia Conductors' Competition 1971, ESSR Peoples' Artist 1971, USSR State Prize 1978, Sibelius Soc. Medal 1986, Gramophone Magazine's Artist of the Year 1990, Gold Record, Chandos recording co. 1992, Toblach's Mahler Prize (for recording of Mahler's Third Symphony) 1993, Grande Prix du Disque, Charles Gros Record Acad. of Paris (for CD of Stravinski's Symphony of Psalms) 1993. *Recordings include:* more than 350 CDs including all Prokoviev, Sibelius, Grieg, Nielsen, Dvorak, Shostakovich, Franz Berwald and Stenhammar symphonies since 1983. *Address:* Harrison Parrott, 5–6 Albion Court, London, W6 0QT, England (office); New Jersey Symphony Orchestra, 60 Park Place, 9th Floor, Newark, NJ 07102, USA. *Telephone:* (20) 7229-9166 (office); (973) 624-3713. *Fax:* (20) 7221-5042 (office); (973) 624-2115. *E-mail:* info@harrisonparrott.co.uk (office). *Website:* www.harrisonparrott.com (office); www.njsymphony.org; www.neemejarvi.com.

JARVIK, Robert Koffler, MD; American physician and business executive; *President and CEO, Jarvik Heart, Inc.;* b. 11 May 1946, Midland, Mich.; s. of Norman Eugene and Edythe Jarvik (née Koffler); m. Marilyn vos Savant 1987; one s. one d.; ed Syracuse Univ., New York, Univ. of Bologna, New York Univ., Univ. of Utah; research Asst, Div. of Artificial Organs, Univ. of Utah 1971–77; Acting Dir Old St Mark's Hosp., Div. of Artificial Organs 1977–78, Asst Dir 1978–82; Asst Research Prof. of Surgery, Univ. of Utah 1979–87; Pres. Symbian Inc., Salt Lake City 1981–87; Pres. and CEO Jarvik Research Inc. (now Jarvik Heart Inc.) 1987–; mem. American Soc. for Artificial Internal Organs, Int. Soc. for Artificial Organs; Hon. DSc (Syracuse) 1983, (Hahnemann Univ.) 1985; awards include Inventor of the Year 1983, Outstanding Young Men of America 1983, Gold Heart Award 1983, Par Excellence Award (Univ. of Utah). *Publication:* Ed. (US Section) The International Journal of Artificial Organs. *Address:* Jarvik Heart, Inc., 333 West 52nd Street, New York, NY 10019, USA (office). *Telephone:* (212) 397-3911 (office). *Fax:* (212) 397-3919 (office). *Website:* www.jarvikheart.com (office).

JASCHINSKI, Siegfried; German banking executive; *Chairman of the Board of Managing Directors, Landesbank Baden-Württemberg;* b. 21 Aug. 1954, Leverkusen; ed Universität zu Köln; began banking career with Trinkaus und Burkhardt 1982; joined Deutschen Bank AG, Frankfurt 1986; fmr mem. Bd of Man. Dirs SüdwestLB, Deputy Chair. Landesbank Baden-Württemberg (after merger with SüdwestLB) 2004–05, Chair. 2005–; mem. Advisory Bd Baden-Württemberg Int. Agency for Int. Econ. and Scientific Cooperation. *Address:* Landesbank Baden-Württemberg, Am Hauptbahnhof 2, Stuttgart 70173, Germany (office). *Telephone:* (711) 127-0 (office). *Fax:* (711) 12743544 (office). *E-mail:* kontakt@lbbw.de (office). *Website:* www.lbbw.de (office).

JASKIERNIA, Jerzy Andrzej, DJur; Polish diplomatist, politician and professor of law; b. 21 March 1950, Kudowa Zdrój; s. of Zofia Jaskiernia and Mieczysław Jaskiernia; m. Alicja Słowińska 1980; one s. one d.; ed Jagiellonian Univ., Kraków; teacher, Law and Admin. Faculty of Jagiellonian Univ., Kraków 1972–81; mem. Main Bd Socialist Youth Union 1973–76; mem. Polish Socialist Youth Union (ZSMP) 1976–85; mem. Main Arbitration Bd 1976–80, Chair. 1980–81, Chair. ZSMP Gen. Bd 1981–84; mem. Polish United Workers' Party (PZPR) 1970–90, Deputy mem. PZPR Cen. Cttee 1982–86, Vice-Chair. Youth Comm. of PZPR Cen. Cttee 1981–86; mem. Inter-party Problems Comm. of PZPR Cen. Cttee 1986–88, Nat. Council of Patriotic Movt for Nat. Rebirth 1983–89, Sec.-Gen. 1984–87; Adviser to Minister of Foreign Affairs 1987–88; Counsellor, Embassy in Washington, DC 1988–90; mem. Scientific Bd Research Inst. of Youth Problems (Warsaw) 1984–89; mem. Social Democracy of the Repub. of Poland (SdRP) 1990–99, SdRP Cen. Exec. Cttee 1991–92 (Head of Parl. and Self-Govt Affairs Dept 1990–91), SdRP Presidium of the Main Council 1993–97, Chair. Cttee on Int. Co-operation 1998–99; Deputy to Sejm (Parl.) 1985–89, 1991–; mem. Nat. Ass. Constitutional Cttee 1992–95; Chair. Legis. Cttee of the Sejm 1993–95, 1996–97, Foreign Affairs Cttee 2001–; Minister of Justice and Attorney-Gen. 1995–96; Prof., Świętokrzyska Acad., Kielce 1995–; Deputy Chair. Democratic Left Alliance (SLD), Parl. Caucus 1996–2001, Chair. 2001–04; mem. Parl. Ass. of Council of Europe 1994–, Chair. Sub-cttee on Human Rights 1998–2001, Chair. Sub-cttee on Criminal Law and Criminology 2001–03, Deputy Chair. Cttee on Legal Affairs and Human Rights 2003–; Chair. Polish-British Parl. Group 1993–, Deputy Chair. Cttee on European Integration 1997–2001; mem. SLD Nat. Cttee 1999–, SLD Nat. Exec. Bd 2000–04; mem European Parl (Group of the Party of European Socialists) 2004–, mem. Cttee on Foreign Affairs, Human Rights, Common Security and Defence Policy 2004–; Corresp. mem. European Acad. of Science, Arts and Literature, Paris 2002–; Chair. Inst. for Strategic Issues (IPS) 2002–. *Publications:* Pozycja stanów w systemie federalnym USA 1979, Dylematy młodych 1984, Dialog naszą szansą 1985, (co-author) System polityczny PRL w procesie przemian 1988, Problemy pluralizmu, porozumienia narodowego i consensusu w systemie politycznym PRL 1989, Stany Zjednoczone a współczesne procesy i koncepcje integracji europejskiej 1992, Zasada równości w prawie wyborczym USA 1992, Wizja parlamentu w nowej Konstytucji Rzeczypospolitej Polskiej 1994, Zasady demokratycznego państwa prawnego w sejmowym postepowaniu ustawodawczym 1999, Zgromadzenie Parlamentarne Rady Europy (English trans.: The Parliamentary Assembly of the Council of Europe 2003) 2000, Członkostwo Polski w Unii Europejskiej a Problem Nowelizagi Konstytagi RP 2004. *Address:* European Parliament, Rue Wiertz, 1047 Brussels, Belgium (office). *Telephone:* (2) 284-21-11 (office). *Fax:* (2) 284-69-74 (office); (2) 230-69-33 (office).

JASON, Sir David, Kt, OBE; British actor; b. (David White), 2 Feb. 1940; s. of Arthur White and Olwyn Jones; m. 2005; one d.; started acting career in repertory; awards include Best Actor Award, BAFTA 1988, Best Comedy Actor Award, BAFTA 1997, BAFTA Fellowship 2003. *Theatre includes:* Under Milk Wood 1971, The Rivals 1972, No Sex Please ... We're British! 1972, Darling Mr London (tour) 1975, Charley's Aunt (tour) 1975, The Norman Conquests 1976, The Relapse 1978, Cinderella 1979, The Unvarnished Truth (Mid/Far East tour) 1983, Look No Hans! (tour and West End) 1985. *Films:* Under Milk Wood 1970, Royal Flash 1974, The Odd Job 1978, Only Fools and Horses, Wind in the Willows (voice) 1983, The BFG (voice) 1989. *Television includes:* Do Not Adjust Your Set 1967, The Top Secret Life of Edgar Briggs 1973–74, Mr Stabbs 1974, Ronnie Barker Shows 1975, Open All Hours 1975, Porridge 1975, Lucky Feller 1975, A Sharp Intake of Breath 1978, Del Trotter in Only Fools and Horses 1981–2003, Porterhouse Blue 1986, Jackanory 1988, A Bit of A Do 1988–89, Single Voices: The Chemist 1989, Amongst Barbarians 1989, Pa Larkin in The Darling Buds of May 1990–92, A Touch of Frost 1992–2008, The Bullion Boys 1993, All the King's Men 1999, Micawber 2001, The Quest 2002, The Second Quest 2004, The Final Quest 2004, Ghostboat 2006, Hogfather 2006, The Colour of Magic 2008. *Voice work:* Dangermouse, Count Duckula, The Wind in the Willows, The B.F.G. *Leisure interests:* diving, flying, motorcycles. *Address:* c/o Richard Stone Partnership, 2 Henrietta Street, London, WC2E 8PS, England.

JATOI, Ghulam Mustafa; Pakistani politician and landowner; *Chairman, National People's Party;* b. 14 Aug. 1932, New Jatoi; s. of Ghulam Rasool Jatoi; m. 1st 1951; m. 2nd 1965; five s. three d.; elected Pres. Nawabshah Dist Council 1954, Sindh Prov.; elected mem. W Pakistan Ass. 1956, Nat. Ass. of Pakistan 1962, 1965, 1970, 1977, 1989, 1990, 1993, 1997; del. to UN Gen. Ass. 1962, 1965, to IPU Conf., Ottawa (elected Vice-Pres. of Conf.) 1965; Fed. Minister for Communications, Political Affairs, Railways and Natural Resources 1971; Special Envoy of Pres. to Indonesia, Malaysia, Japan 1972, of Prime Minister to Turkey 1976; Founder-mem. People's Party; fmr aide to the late Zulfikar Ali Bhutto, Prime Minister of Pakistan; fmr Chief Minister of Sindh; imprisoned for political activities 1977; led Movt for Restoration of Democracy against mil. regime; Founder Nat. People's Party; Leader of Opposition 1988; Leader of Combined Opposition Parties 1989–90, currently Chair.; Leader of Islamic Democratic Alliance for 1990 election; caretaker Prime Minister of Pakistan Aug.–Nov. 1990; Chair. Grand Nat. Alliance for 2002 election. *Leisure interest:* hunting. *Address:* National People's Party (NPP), Jatoi House, 18 Khayaban-e-Shamsheer Defence Housing Authority, Phase V, Karachi, Pakistan (office). *Telephone:* (21) 5854522 (office). *Fax:* (21) 5873753 (office).

JATUSRIPITAK, Somkid, BA, MBA, PhD; Thai government official; b. 15 July 1953, Bangkok; m. Anurachanee Jatusripitak; ed Thammasart Univ., Nat. Inst. of Devt Admin, Northwestern Univ., USA; previous positions include Sec. to Minister of Finance, Adviser to Minister of Foreign Affairs, Minister of Commerce, Vice-Pres., Stock Exchange; Minister of Finance 2001, 2002–03, 2004–; Deputy Prime Minister 2001–02, 2003–04, 2005–06; Knight Grand Cross Second Class 1994, First Class 1997. *Address:* c/o Ministry of Finance, Thanon Rama VI, Phaya Thai, Rajatevi, Bangkok, 10400, Thailand (office).

JAUHO, Pekka Antti Olavi; Finnish scientist and consultant; b. 27 April 1923, Oulu; s. of Antti Arvid Jauho and Sylvi Jauho (née Pajari); m. Kyllikki Hakala 1948; one s.; ed Univ. of Helsinki; Chief Mathematician, Insurance Co. Kansa 1951–54; Assoc. Prof., Tech. Univ. of Helsinki 1955–57 (now Helsinki Univ. of Tech.), Prof. of Tech. Physics 1957–70; Dir-Gen. The State Inst. for Tech. Research (Tech. Research Centre of Finland since 1972) 1970–87; consultant to many Finnish and foreign cos; mem. Acad. of Finland, American Nuclear Soc., European Physical Soc., RILEM, Finnish Acad. of Sciences, IVA (Swedish Acad. of Tech. Sciences) and several Finnish socs; Commdr Order of White Rose, Order of Lion (First Class, Finland), Commdr des Palmes académiques, Officier, Légion d'honneur; Hon. Prize of YDIN Power Asscn, Hon. Prize of VILAMO Foundation 1996. *Publications:* about 140 articles. *Leisure interests:* music, tennis. *Address:* Otakaari 1, 02150 Espoo 15 (office); Tuohikuja 9E, 02130 Espoo, Finland (home). *Telephone:* (9) 4513132 (office); (9) 427705 (home). *Fax:* (9) 427705 (home). *E-mail:* pekka.jauho@kolumbus.fi (home).

JAUMOTTE, Baron André; Belgian university official and mechanical engineer; b. 8 Dec. 1919, Jambes; s. of Jules Jaumotte and Marie Braibant; m. Valentine Demoulin 1946; ed Free Univ. of Brussels; Head Depts of Applied Mechanics and Aerodynamics, Free Univ. of Brussels 1958–86, Rector 1968–73, Pres. 1974–81; Chair. von Karman Inst. of Fluid Dynamics 1994–2004; Pres. A-VN 1981–2002; mem. Bd UN Univ., Tokyo 1980–86; Hon. Pres. Asscn des Universités partiellement ou entièrement de langue française (AUPELF) 1981–84; mem. Royal Acad., Belgium, Royal Acad. of Overseas Science, European Acad. of Sciences, Letters and Arts, Int. Acad. of Astronautics, Academia Europaea; mem. Nat. Acad. of Air and Space, France; Foreign mem. Acad. des Sciences (Paris) 1989, Romanian Acad. 1994; Commdr, Légion d'honneur 1981, Grand Officier, Ordine al Merito della Repubblica Italiana 1973, Commdr, Ordre du Mérite (Gabon), Grand Officier, Ordre de la Couronne (Belgium) 1983, Grand Officier, Ordre de Léopold 1988, Order of the Sacred Treasure, Gold and Silver Stars (Japan); Dr hc (Free University (VUB), Brussels), (Laval Univ., Québec), (Univ. of Cluj, Romania), (Tech. Univ., Bucharest). *Publications:* Rocket Propulsion 1967, Choc et Ondes de Choc 1971, 1973, La science au service du pays 1985, Un demi-siècle de nucléaire en Belgique 1994, Mosaïque: Fragments du tout 2000; 300 articles on internal aerodynamics and thermodynamics of turbomachines; report to King Baudouin Foundation. *Leisure interests:* painting and sculpture. *Address:* Université Libre de Bruxelles, avenue Franklin Roosevelt 50, CP 131/1, 1050 Brussels; 33 avenue Jeanne Bte. 17, 1050 Brussels, Belgium (home). *Telephone:* (2) 650-32-71 (office); (2) 647-54-13 (home). *Fax:* (2) 6504965 (home). *E-mail:* andre.jaumotte@ulb.ac.be (office).

JAVED MIANDAD KHAN; Pakistani fmr professional cricketer; b. 12 June 1957, Karachi; m.; ed CMS Secondary School, Karachi; Asst Vice-Pres. Habib Bank of Pakistan; right-hand middle-order batsman, leg-break and googly bowler; played for Karachi 1973–76, Sind 1973–76, Sussex 1976–79, Habib Bank 1976–94, Glamorgan 1980–85; 124 Test matches for Pakistan 1976–94, 34 as Capt., scoring 8,832 runs (average 52.5) including 23 hundreds; scored over 28,000 first-class runs (80 hundreds); toured England 1975, 1979 (World Cup), 1982, 1983 (World Cup), 1987, 1992 (Capt.); 233 limited-overs ints. scoring 7,381 runs (average 41.7); Pakistan Nat. Team Coach 1998–99, 2000–01, 2003–04; Wisden Cricketer of the Year 1982. *Leisure interests:* hockey, soccer, swimming, reading sports books, television, spending time with family. *Address:* National Stadium, National Stadium Road, Karachi, Pakistan.

JAWARA, Hon. Alhaji Sir Dawda Kairaba, Kt, FRCVS, DTVM; Gambian politician and fmr Head of State; b. 16 May 1924, Barajally; s. of Almamy Jawara and the late Mama Jawara; ed Achimota Coll., Glasgow Univ.; Principal Veterinary Officer, Gambian Civil Service 1957–60; entered politics 1960; Minister of Educ. 1960–61; Premier 1962–65; Prime Minister 1965–70; Pres. of Repub. of The Gambia 1970–94 (overthrown in coup); Vice-Pres. of Confed. of Senegambia 1982; Minister of Defence 1985; Pres. Comité Inter-Etats de Lutte contre la Sécheresse du Sahel; mem. Board Peutinger Coll. (FRG); Hon. GCMG 1974; decorations from Senegal, Mauritania, Lebanon, Grand Master Nat. Order of the Repub. of Gambia 1972, Peutinger Gold Medal 1979; numerous other decorations. *Leisure interests:* golf, gardening, sailing. *Address:* 15 Birchen Lane, Haywards Heath, West Sussex, RH16 1RY, England (office). *Telephone:* (1444) 456168 (home). *E-mail:* dawda@kjawara.freeserve.co.uk (home).

JAWORSKI, HE Cardinal Marian, DTheol, DPhil, DPhilR; Ukrainian (b. Polish) ecclesiastic; *Metropolitan Archbishop of Lviv;* b. 21 Aug. 1926, Lwów, Poland (now Lviv, Ukraine); ed Theological Acad., Kraków, Catholic Univ. of Lublin, Warsaw Theological Acad.; ordained priest, Kraków 1950; taught for several years at Catholic Theological Acad. of Warsaw and later at Pontifical Theological Faculty of Kraków (First Rector 1981–87); lectured in metaphysics and philosophy of religion at seminaries of various religious orders; consecrated Titular Bishop of Lambaesis and Apostolic Admin. of Lubaczów 1984; apptd. Metropolitan Archbishop of Lviv 1991; cr. Cardinal (secretly) 1998, (openly) (Titular Church of St Sixtus) 2001; Pres. Ukrainian Episcopal Conf. 1992–; Order of Prince Yaroslav the Wise (Fifth Rank) 2004; Dr hc (Bohum) 1985, (Cardinal Stefan Wysujnski Univ., Warsaw) 2002; Award 'For Great Contributions to Strengthening Peace and International Accord in Ukraine' 2004. *Publications:* three books, 31 monographs, two textbooks, more than 160 scientific articles. *Address:* Metropolis Curia of Archdiocese of Lviv of the Roman Catholic Church, Ploscha Katedralny 1, 79008 Lviv, Ukraine (office). *Telephone:* (322) 76-94-15 (office). *Fax:* (322) 96-61-14 (office). *E-mail:* AB@rkc.lviv.ua (office). *Website:* www.rkc.lviv.ua (office).

JAY, Martin, BA; British engineering industry executive; *Chairman, Invensys PLC;* b. July 1939; m.; two d. one s.; ed Winchester Coll. and New Coll. Oxford; began career with British Petroleum; Man. Dir and mem. Man. Bd GEC Electronic Components –1989; CEO Vosper Thornycroft PLC (now VT Group PLC) 1989–2002, Chair. (non-exec.) 2002–03; apptd Dir (non-exec.) Invensys PLC Jan. 2003, Chair. July 2003–. *Address:* Invensys PLC, Invensys Group Headquarters, Carlisle Place, London, SW1P 1BX, England (office). *Telephone:* (20) 7834-3848 (office). *Fax:* (20) 7834-3879 (office). *Website:* www.invensys.com (office).

JAY, Sir Michael Hastings, GCMG, KCMG, MA, MSc; British diplomatist (retd); b. 19 June 1946, Shawford, Hants.; s. of the late Alan Jay and of Felicity Vickery; m. Sylvia Mylroie 1975; ed Winchester Coll., Magdalen Coll., Oxford and School of Oriental and African Studies, Univ. of London; Ministry of Overseas Devt 1969–73, 1976–78; UK Del. IMF, IBRD, Washington, DC 1973–75; First Sec. New Delhi 1978–81; FCO 1981–85; Cabinet Office 1985–87; Counsellor, Paris 1987–90; Asst Under-Sec. of State for EC Affairs, FCO 1990–93, Deputy Under-Sec. of State (Dir for EC (now EU) and Econ. Affairs) 1994–96; Amb. to France 1996–2001; Perm. Under-Sec., FCO and Head of Diplomatic Service 2002–06. *Address:* c/o Foreign and Commonwealth Office, King Charles Street, London, SW1A 2AH, England. *Telephone:* (20) 7008-2150.

JAY, Peter, MA; British economic journalist and fmr diplomatist; b. 7 Feb. 1937, London; s. of the late Lord Jay; m. 1st Margaret Ann Callaghan (now Baroness Jay, q.v.), d. of Lord Callaghan, q.v.), 1961 (divorced 1986); one s. two d.; one s. by Jane Tustian; m. 2nd Emma Thornton 1986; three s.; ed Winchester Coll. and Christ Church, Oxford; Midshipman and Sub-Lt, RNVR 1956–57; Asst Prin., HM Treasury 1961–64, Pvt. Sec. to Jt Perm. Sec. 1964, Prin. 1964–67; Econs Ed. The Times 1967–77, Assoc. Ed. Times Business

News 1969–77; Presenter, Weekend World, ITV 1972–77, The Jay Interview 1975–77; Amb. to USA 1977–79; Consultant, Economist Group 1979–81; Dir The Economist Intelligence Unit (EIU) 1979–83; Columnist The Times 1980; Dir New Nat. Theatre, Washington, DC 1979–81; Chair. TV-AM 1980–83, TV-AM News 1982–83, Pres. TV-AM 1983; Presenter, A Week in Politics, Channel 4 1983–86; Chief of Staff to Robert Maxwell 1986–89; Econs Ed., BBC 1990–2001; Sr Ed. Consultant, Man. Dir Banking World BPCC, Editor Banking World 1983–86, Supervising Ed. 1986–89; Chair. United Way of GB 1982–83, Feasibility Study 1982–83; Chair. Nat. Council for Voluntary Orgs 1981–86; Visiting Scholar, Brookings Inst., Washington, DC 1979–80; Copland Memorial Lecturer, Australia 1980; Gov. Ditchley Foundation 1982–; Hon. DH (Ohio State Univ.) 1978; Political Broadcaster of Year 1973, Royal TV Soc.'s Male Personality of Year (Pye Award) 1974, Shell Int. TV Award 1974, Wincott Memorial Lecturer 1975. *Publications:* The Budget 1972, Foreign Affairs, America and the World 1979 (contrib.) 1980, The Crisis for Western Political Economy and other essays 1984, Apocalypse 2000 (with Michael Stewart) 1987, Road to Riches, or The Wealth of Man 2000; numerous newspaper and magazine articles. *Leisure interest:* sailing. *Address:* Hensington Farmhouse, Woodstock, Oxon, OX20 1LH, England. *Telephone:* (1993) 811222. *Fax:* (1993) 812861. *E-mail:* peter@jay.prestel.co.uk (office).

JAY OF PADDINGTON, Baroness (Life Peer), cr. 1992, of Paddington, in the City of Westminster; **Margaret Ann Jay,** PC, BA; British politician and business executive; b. 18 Nov. 1939; d. of the late James Callaghan (Lord Callaghan of Cardiff, Prime Minister 1976–79); m. 1st Peter Jay (q.v.) 1961 (divorced 1986); one s. two d.; m. 2nd M. W. Adler 1994; ed Somerville Coll., Oxford; began career as producer and journalist with BBC TV 1961–77, producer and reporter, ABC TV and Nat. Public Radio, USA 1979–82, Panorama, BBC TV 1982–86, This Week, Thames TV 1986–88; served as mem. various London Health Authorities 1974–97; Founder-Dir Nat. AIDS Trust 1988–92; apptd Labour Life Peer, House of Lords 1992–; Prin. Opposition Spokesperson on Health, House of Lords 1995–97, Minister of State, Dept of Health 1997–98, Leader, House of Lords and Minister for Women 1998–2001, currently serves as back-bench Privy Councillor, House of Lords; Dir (non-exec.) London Broadcasting Co. 1992–93, Carlton TV 1995–97, Scottish Power 1996–97; Dir (non-exec.) British Telecommunications (BT) PLC 2001–08, mem. Corp. Social Responsibility Cttee 2008–; Sr Ind. Dir and mem. Int. Advisory Bd, Independent Media Group 2002–; mem. Kensington, Chelsea and Westminster Health Authority 1992–97; Chair. Nat. Asscn Leagues of Hosp. Friends 1994–97; political consultant and Chair. Overseas Devt Inst. 2002–07; Sr Political Consultant, Currie & Brown, Amey Ltd 2002–07; Co-Chair. Iraq Comm. set up by Foreign Policy Centre and Channel 4 TV 2007; Hon. Fellow, Somerville Coll. Oxford; Dr hc (South Bank Univ.) 1999, (Sunderland Univ.) 2002. *Television:* reporter, contrib. or producer: Panorama (BBC TV) 1982–86, This Week (Thames TV) 1986, The Social History of Medicine (BBC TV) 1991, Hilary Clinton: The Extra President (BBC TV) 1992, Richard Leakey and the new Kenyan Opposition (BBC TV) 1996. *Publication:* Battered – The Story of Child Abuse (co-author) 1986. *Address:* House of Lords, Westminster, London, SW1A 0PW, England (office).

JAY-Z; American rap artist; b. (Shawn Carter), 4 Dec. 1969, Brooklyn, NY; m. Beyoncé Knowles 2008; co-founder, Roc-A-Fella Records 1995–, later expanding to incl. Roc-A-Wear clothing line and film co. (purchased by Universal 2004); collaborations with Puff Daddy, Lil' Kim, Foxy Brown, Notorious BIG, Mary J. Blige, Mariah Carey, Timbaland; numerous live performances; Pres. Def Jam label 2005–08; MTV Video Music Award for Best Rap Video (for Can I Get A. . .) 1999, for Best Video from a Film (for Can I Get A. . .) 1999, Source Awards for Lyricist of the Year 1999, for Best Hip Hop Artist 2001, Billboard Music Award for Rap Artist of the Year 1999, MOBO Award for Best Int. Hip Hop Act 1999, Soul Train Award for Sammy Davis Jr Entertainer of the Year 2001, Grammy Awards for Best Rap Performance by Duo or Group (for Big Pimpin') 2001, (for Swagga Like Us with T.I) 2009, for Best Rap/Sung Collaboration (for Numb/Encore with Linkin Park) 2006, MOBO Award for Best Int. Male 2006, Michael Jackson Award for Best Video, Soul Train Awards (for Show Me What You Got) 2007. *Film:* Streets Is Watching (writer and dir) 1998. *Recordings include:* albums: Reasonable Doubt 1996, In My Lifetime Vol. 1 1997, Vol. 2 Hard Knock Life 1999, Vol. 3 Life And Times Of S. Carter (Grammy Award for Best Rap Album 2001) 1999, The Dynasty—Roc La Familia 2000, The Blueprint (Soul Train Award for Album of the Year 2002) 2001, The Best Of Both Worlds (with R. Kelly) 2002, The Blueprint 2: The Gift And The Curse 2002, S Carter Collection 2002, The Black Album 2003, Collision Course (with Linkin Park) 2004, Kingdom Come 2006, American Gangster 2007, Blueprint 3 2008. *Address:* Roc-A-Fella Records, 825 Eighth Avenue, New York, NY 10019-7472, USA. *Website:* www.rocafella.com.

JAYAKUMAR, Shanmugam, LLM; Singaporean diplomatist and government official; *Deputy Prime Minister and Co-ordinating Minister for National Security;* b. 12 Aug. 1939, Singapore; m. Dr Lalitha Rajahram 1969; two s. one d.; ed Univ. of Singapore and Yale Univ., USA; Dean, Law Faculty, Univ. of Singapore 1974–80, Prof. of Law; Perm. Rep. of Singapore to UN 1971–74, High Commr to Canada 1971–74; MP 1980–; Minister of State for Law and Home Affairs 1981–83, Minister of Labour 1983–85, of Home Affairs 1985–94, of Foreign Affairs 1994–2004, of Law 1988–2008, Deputy Prime Minister and Co-ordinating Minister for Nat. Security 2004–; Public Service Star (BBM) 1980. *Publications:* Constitutional Law Cases from Malaysia and Singapore 1971, Public International Law Cases from Malaysia and Singapore 1974, Constitutional Law (with documentary material) 1976 and articles in journals. *Leisure interests:* jogging, golfing and in-line skating. *Address:* The Cabinet, Orchard Road, Istana Office Wing, Singapore Tel: Fax: Singapore 238823 (office). *Telephone:* 67375133 (office). *Fax:* 68356261 (office). *Website:* www.cabinet.gov.sg (office).

JAYALALITHA, C. Jayaram; Indian politician and fmr film actress; *Leader, All-India Anna Dravida Munnetra Kazhagam;* b. 24 Feb. 1948, Mysore City; d. of R. Jayaram; has appeared in over 100 films; joined All-India Anna Dravida Munnetra Kazhagam 1982, Propaganda Sec. 1983, Deputy Leader, currently Leader; elected mem. Rajya Sabha (Parl.) 1984; Chief Minister, Tamil Nadu 1991–96, 2001–06; Kalaimamani Award 1971–72. *Publications:* numerous publs. *Address:* All-India Anna Dravida Munnetra Kazhagam (AIADMK), 226 Avvai Shanmugam Salai, Royapet, Chennai 600 014, India (office). *Telephone:* (44) 28132266 (office). *Fax:* (44) 28133510 (office). *E-mail:* aiadmk@vsnl.net (office).

JAYASUNDERA, P. B., BA, MA, PhD; Sri Lankan civil servant, government official and airline industry executive; *Chairman, SriLankan Airlines Ltd;* ed Univ. of Colombo, Boston Univ. and Williams Coll., USA; held several sr positions in Cen. Bank of Sri Lanka –1980; with civil service since 1980, econ. adviser 1990, Dir-Gen. Dept of Fiscal Policy and Econ. Affairs 1995, Deputy Sec. to Treasury 1997–99, Sec. to Treasury 1999–2008; Chair. SriLankan Airlines Ltd 2008–; fmr Chair. Public Enterprises Reform Comm.; fmr Sr Policy Advisor, Ernst & Young; fmr consultant to IMF and World Bank on country assignments; found guilty by Supreme Court of acting with dishonest intent in sale of Lanka Marine Services Ltd shares and of misleading Bd of Investment, ordered to pay Rs 500,000 compensation July 2008. *Address:* Head Office, SriLankan Airlines Ltd, Level 22, East Tower, World Trade Centre, Echelon Square, Colombo 1, Sri Lanka (office). *Telephone:* (19) 7335555 (office). *Fax:* (19) 7335122 (office). *E-mail:* ulweb@srilankan.aero (office). *Website:* www.srilankan.aero (office).

JAYASURIYA, Sanath Teran; Sri Lankan professional cricketer; b. 30 June 1969, Matara; divorced; left-hand batsman and slow left-arm orthodox spin bowler; played for Sri Lanka, ACC Asian XI, Bloomfield Cricket and Athletic Club, Colombo Cricket Club, Somerset 2005; Sri Lanka's highest Test run-scorer; served as Sri Lanka's Capt. 1999–2003; Test debut: New Zealand vs Sri Lanka, Hamilton, NZ 1991, One-day Int. (ODI) debut: Australia vs Sri Lanka, Melbourne, Australia 1989; mem. Sri Lankan team that won World Cup 1996; First-class span: 1988/89–2005/06; List A span: 1989/90–2005/06; Twenty-20 span: 2004–05/06; Test batting and fielding averages: 100 matches, 170 innings, 6,580 runs, 42.17 average, 14 centuries, 29 half-centuries; Test bowling averages: 100 matches, 7,397 balls, 3,016 runs, 92 wickets, 5/34 best bowling in an innings, 9/74 best bowling in a match, 32.78 average; holds record for highest test score made by a Sri Lankan: 340 against India 1997; also holds world's third highest ODI score: 189 runs against India; currently has the fastest 50 in ODIs; became only the fourth batsman to score 10,000 runs in one-day cricket, Indian Oil Cup 2005; first Sri Lankan to play 100 Tests; nicknamed the 'Master Blaster'; Wisden Cricketer of the Year 1997, World Cup Most Valuable Player Award; stadium named in his honour in Matara. *Address:* c/o Sri Lanka Cricket, 35 Maitland Place, Colombo 07, Sri Lanka (office). *Telephone:* (11) 2681601-4 (office); (11) 2679568 (office). *Fax:* (11) 2697405 (office). *E-mail:* info@srilankacricket.lk (office). *Website:* www.srilankacricket.lk (office); content-uk.cricinfo.com/srilanka/content/player/49209.html.

JAYAWARDENA, Amarananda Somasiri, BA, MSc, MPA; Sri Lankan economist, academic, civil servant and banker; b. 3 Aug. 1936, Matale, Sri Lanka; s. of P. de S. Jayawardena and Emaline Weerasinghe; m. Lalitha Subasinghe 1968; one s. one d.; ed Univ. of Ceylon, London School of Econs, UK, Harvard Univ., USA; joined Cen. Bank of Sri Lanka 1958, Gov. and Chair. Monetary Bd 1995–2004; Visiting Lecturer, Univ. of Vidyodaya, Colombo 1968–75; Gen. Man. Bank of Ceylon 1977, Chair. 1989; Alt. Exec. Dir IMF 1981–86; Sec. Ministry of Industries, Science and Tech. 1989–93, Ministry of Finance and Planning 1994–95. *Radio:* frequent commentator on radio and TV. *Publications:* numerous publs on econs of world tea industry, evaluation of public enterprise performance and econ. aspects of privatization. *Leisure interests:* gardening, reading, the arts. *Address:* c/o Central Bank of Sri Lanka, World Trade Centre, West Tower, Echelon Square, PO Box 590, Colombo 1 (office).

JAYAWARDENA, D. H. S.; Sri Lankan business executive; *Chairman, Aitken Spence & Company;* Founder-Dir, Man. Dir Stassen Group; Man. Dir Distilleries Co. of Sri Lanka, Lanka Milk Foods (CWE) Ltd; Dir Hatton Nat. Bank; fmr Chair. Air Lanka (now Sri Lankan Airlines); Chair. Sri Lanka Insurance Corpn; Chair. Aitken Spence & Co. 2003–; mem. Bd Dirs Colombo Stock Exchange; Sr Advisor to Pres. on Int. Trade and Investment; Dir Bd of Investment of Sri Lanka. *Address:* Aitken Spence & Company Ltd., Vauxhall Towers, 305 Vauxhall Street, POB 5, Colombo 2, Sri Lanka (office). *Telephone:* (11) 2308308 (office). *Fax:* (11) 2445406 (office). *E-mail:* dhsjayawardena@aitkenspence.lk (office). *Website:* www.aitkenspence.com (office).

JAYSTON, Michael, FGSM; British actor; b. 29 Oct. 1935, Nottingham; s. of Aubrey Jayston and Edna Myfanwy Llewelyn; m. 1st Lynn Farleigh 1965 (divorced 1970); m. 2nd Heather Mary Sneddon (divorced 1977); m. 3rd Elizabeth Ann Smithson 1978; three s. one d.; with the RSC 1965–69, Nat. Theatre 1976–79. *Films include:* A Midsummer Night's Dream 1968, Cromwell 1970, Nicholas and Alexandra 1971, Follow Me! 1972, Alice's Adventures in Wonderland 1972, Craze 1973, A Bequest to the Nation 1973, Tales That Witness Madness 1973, The Homecoming 1973, The Internecine Project 1974, Dominique 1978, Zulu Dawn 1979, From a Far Country 1981, Highlander III: The Sorcerer 1994, Element of Doubt 1996. *TV includes:* The Power Game (series) 1965, The Edwardians (miniseries) 1972, Mr. Rolls and Mr. Royce 1972, Jane Eyre (miniseries) 1973, The Merchant of Venice 1974, The Importance of Being Earnest 1974, Ring Once for Death 1974, Coffin for the Bride 1974, Quiller (series) 1975, She Fell Among Thieves 1978, Gossip from the Forest 1979, Tinker, Tailor, Soldier, Spy (miniseries) 1979, Flesh and Blood (series) 1980, Dust to Dust 1985, Doctor Who (series) 1986, Still Crazy Like a Fox 1987, A Guilty Thing Surprised 1988, Shake Hands Forever 1988, Somewhere to Run 1989, A Bit of a Do (series) 1989, Cluedo (series) 1990, The Darling Buds of May 1993, A Dinner of Herbs (miniseries) 2000, Eastenders 2002; numerous appearances in series episodes. *Theatre appearances include:* Private Lives 1980, Sound of Music 1981, Way of the World 1984–85, Woman in Mind, Beethoven Readings with Medici String Quartet 1989, Dancing at Lughnasa 1992, Wind in the Willows, Nat. Theatre 1994, Racing Demon, Chichester Prod. in Toronto 1998, Easy Virtue, Chichester 1999. *Leisure interests:* cricket, darts, chess. *Address:* c/o Michael Whitehall Ltd, 125 Gloucester Road, London, SW7 4TE, England. *Telephone:* (20) 7244-8466. *Fax:* (20) 7244-9060.

JAZ, Awad Ahmad al-; Sudanese politician; *Minister of Finance and National Economy;* Minister of Energy and Mining –2008, of Finance and Nat. Economy 2008–; mem. Nat. Congress. *Address:* Ministry of Finance and National Economy, PO Box 735, Khartoum, Sudan (office). *Telephone:* (183) 777563 (office). *Fax:* (183) 775630 (office). *E-mail:* info@mof-sudan.net (office). *Website:* mof-sudan.com (office).

JAZAIRY, Idriss, MA, MEcons, MPA; Algerian international administrator and diplomatist; *Special Delegate of the President;* b. 29 May 1936, Neuilly-sur-Seine, France; four s. one d.; ed Univ. of Oxford, UK, Ecole Nat. d'Admin, Paris, France, Harvard Univ., USA; Chief Econ. and Social Dept Algiers 1963–71; Dir Int. Co-operation, Ministry of Foreign Affairs 1963–71; Adviser to Pres. of Repub. 1971–77; Under-Sec.-Gen. Ministry of Foreign Affairs 1977–79; Amb. to Belgium, Luxembourg and EEC 1979–82; Amb.-at-large specializing in int. econ. affairs, Ministry of Foreign Affairs 1982–84; Pres IFAD Rome 1984–93; Exec. Dir Agency for Co-operation and Research in Devt (ACORD), London 1993–99; Sr Consultant to UNDP 1994–98; Amb. to USA 1999–2004; currently Special Del. of Pres. of Algeria; mem. Bd of Dirs South Centre, Geneva 2002–; Pres. Bd of Govs African Devt Bank 1971–72; Chair. UN Gen. Ass. Cttee of the Whole on North–South Dialogue 1978–79; organized first World Summit on the Econ. Advancement of Rural Women, Geneva 1992; Grand Officer Order of Merit (Italy), Officer of the Wissam Alaouite (Morocco), Officer of the Order of Merit (Mauritania); Medal of Independence (Jordan); numerous other foreign decorations and awards. *Publication:* The State of World Rural Poverty 1992. *Leisure interests:* jogging, skiing, riding. *Address:* Office of the President, Présidence de la République, el-Mouradia, Algiers, Algeria. *Telephone:* (21) 69-15-15. *Fax:* (21) 69-15-95. *Website:* www.el-mouradia.dz.

JAZI, Dali; Tunisian politician; fmr Minister of Higher Educ.; Minister of Nat. Defence 2001–04. *Address:* c/o Ministry of National Defence, boulevard Bab Menara, 1030 Tunis, Tunisia (office).

JEAMBAR, Denis; French journalist; *CEO, Editions du Seuil;* mem. staff, Paris-Match 1970–73, Le Point 1973–95 (Ed. 1993–95); Ed. Radio station Europe 1 1995–96; Ed.-in-Chief weekly L'Express 1996–2006; CEO Editions du Seuil 2006–. *Publications:* Sur la route de Flagstaff 1980, George Gershwin 1982, Le PC dans la maison 1984, Dieu s'amuse 1985, Eloge de la trahison (with Yves Roucaute) 1988, Le Poisson pourrit par la tête (with José Frèches) 1992, Le Self-service électoral (with Jean-Marc Lech) 1993, Le Jour ou la girafe s'est assise 1994, La Grande Lessive: anarchie et corruption (with Jean-Marc Lech) 1995, L'Inconnu de Goa 1996, Questions de France 1996, Un Secret d'état 1997, Les Dictateurs à penser et autres donneurs de leçons 2004, Accusé Chirac, levez vous! 2005, Le Défi du monde avec Claude Allègre 2006, Nos enfants nous haïront (with Jacqueline Rémy) 2006. *Leisure interests:* painting, cinema, literature, travel. *Address:* Editions du Seuil, 27 rue Jacob, 75006 Paris, France (office).

JEAN, Michaelle; Canadian (b. Haitian) journalist, broadcaster, documentary film producer and public servant; *Governor-General of Canada;* b. Port-au-Prince, Haiti; m. Jean-Daniel Lafond; one d.; ed Univ. of Montréal, Univs of Florence, Milan and Perugia, Italy; fled Haiti 1968, moved to Canada; joined Radio-Canada 1988, reporter, Actuel, Montréal ce soir 1989; Host, Virages 1991–92, Le Point 1992–95; Host, RDI channel 1995, fmr programmes include Le Monde ce soir, L'Edition quebecoise, Horizons francophones, le Journal RDI, Host, Grands Reportages; Host, The Passionate Eye, Rough Cuts, CBC Newsworld; Gov.-Gen. of Canada 2005–; Anik Prize for information reporting 1994, Amnesty Int. Journalism Award 1995, Galaxi Award for best information program host 2000. *Documentary films:* Tropique Nord 1994, Haiti dans tous nos rêves 1995, L'heure de Cuba 1999. *Address:* Rideau Hall, 1 Sussex Drive, Ottawa, ON K1A 0AI, Canada (office). *Telephone:* (613) 993-8200 (office). *E-mail:* info@gg.ca (office). *Website:* www.gg.ca (office).

JEAN BENOÎT GUILLAUME MARIE ROBERT LOUIS ANTOINE ADOLPHE MARC D'AVIANO, HRH, fmr Grand Duke of Luxembourg (Duke of Nassau, Prince of Bourbon-Parma); b. 5 Jan. 1921, Colmar Berg; s. of Felix, Prince of Bourbon-Parma and Prince of Luxembourg and Charlotte, Grand Duchess of Luxembourg; m. Princess Josephine-Charlotte of Belgium 1953 (died 2005); three s. (including HRH Grand Duke Henri) two d.; Lt-Rep. of Grand Duchess 1961–64; became Grand Duke of Luxembourg on abdication of Grand Duchess Charlotte Nov. 1964, abdicated Oct. 2000; Col of the Irish Guards; mem. Int. Olympic Cttee; Chief Scout, Luxembourg Boy Scouts' Asscn; Col Regt Irish Guards 1984–; Dr hc (Strasbourg, Miami); numerous decorations. *Leisure interests:* photography and natural history. *Address:* Grand Ducal Palace, 2013 Luxembourg, Luxembourg (office). *Website:* www .gouvernement.lu.

JEANCOURT-GALIGNANI, Antoine; French property industry executive; *Director, Gecina Group;* b. 12 Jan. 1937, Paris; s. of Paul Jeancourt-Galignani and Germaine Verley; m. 1st Brigitte Auzouy 1961 (divorced 1983); three s. one d.; m. 2nd Hannelore Wagner 1983; one d.; ed Mount St Mary's Coll. Spinkhill, UK, Ecole St Louis de Gonzague, Faculté de Paris, Ecole Nat. d'Admin; Inspecteur de Finances 1965; Asst Sec., Office of Minister of Finance 1968–70, Treasury Dept of Ministry of Finance 1970–71; with Chase Manhattan Bank, New York 1972; Sr then Exec. Vice-Pres. in charge of int. and corp. banking, Crédit Agricole 1973–79; joined Banque Indosuez 1979, Pres. 1980–81, 1982–88, Chair. and CEO 1981–82, 1988–94; Chair. Assurances Générales de France 1994–2001; Chair. Gecina 2001–05, Dir 2005–; Dir Société Générale, Total 1994–, Euro Disney (Chair. Supervisory Bd 1995–), AGF, Kaufman & Broad SA; Officier, Légion d'honneur, Commdr, Ordre nat. du Mérite, Chevalier du Mérite agricole, Croix de la valeur militaire. *Publication:* La Finance Déboussolée 2001. *Address:* Board of Directors, Gecina Group, 14/16, rue des Capucines, 75084 Paris, Cedex 02; 3 avenue Bosquet, 75007 Paris, France (home). *Telephone:* 1-40-40-50-50 (office). *E-mail:* actionnaire@gecina.fr (office). *Website:* www.gecina.fr (office).

JEANMAIRE, Renée Marcelle (Zizi); French actress, dancer and singer; b. 29 April 1924, Paris; d. of Marcel Jeanmaire; m. Roland Petit (q.v.) 1954; one d.; student, Paris Opera Ballet 1933–40, Dancer 1940–44; with Ballets de Monte-Carlo, Ballets Colonel de Basil, Ballets Roland Petit; Dir (with Roland Petit) Casino de Paris 1969–; leading role in three concerts, Zénith 1995, nine concerts, Opéra Bastille 2000; music hall appearances; Chevalier de la Légion d'honneur, Chevalier des Arts et des Lettres, Officier, Ordre nat. du Mérite. *Films:* Hans Christian Andersen, Anything Goes, Folies Bergère, Charmants Garçons, Black Tights, La Revue, Zizi je t'aime; musical: The Girl in Pink Tights (Broadway). *Leading roles in:* Aubade, Piccoli, Carmen, La Croqueuse de Diamants, Rose des Vents, Cyrano de Bergerac, La Dame dans la Lune, La Symphonie Fantastique 1975, Le loup, La chauve-souris 1979, Hollywood Paradise Show 1985, Java for ever 1988, Marcel et la Belle Excentrique 1992. *Address:* c/o Editions Assouline, 26 rue Danielle Casanova, 75002 Paris, France.

JEANNENEY, Jean-Marcel, LèsL, DenD; French politician and economist; b. 13 Nov. 1910, Paris; s. of Jules Jeanneney (fmr Pres. of the Senate and Minister); m. Marie-Laure Monod 1936; two s. (and one s. deceased) five d.; ed Ecole Libre des Sciences Politiques, Paris; Prof. of Political Economy, Grenoble Univ. 1937–51, Dean of Law Faculty 1947–51; Prof. of Social Econs, Univ. of Paris 1951–56, of Financial Econs 1957–59, of Political Econs 1970–80; Dir du Cabinet of his father, Jules Jeanneney, Minister of State, de Gaulle Prov. Govt 1944–45; mem. Admin. Council, Ecole nat. d'admin. 1945–58; Dir Econ. Activity Study Service, Fondation Nat. des Sciences Politiques 1952–58; Consultant to OEEC 1953; mem. Rueff Cttee 1958; Rapporteur and del. to numerous confs; Minister of Industry, (Debré Cabinet) 1959–62; Amb. to Repub. of Algeria 1962–63; Chair. French Cttee on Co-operation with Developing Countries 1963; mem. and French Rep. to UN Econ. and Social Council 1964–66; Minister of Social Affairs 1966–68; Deputy June 1968; Minister of State 1968–69; Pres. L'Observatoire français des Conjonctures économiques 1981–89; Dir Nat. Foundation for Political Sciences (Sciences Po) 1981–; Commdr Légion d'honneur, Grand-Croix Ordre Nat. du Mérite, Commdr des Palmes académiques. *Publications:* Essai sur les mouvements des prix en France depuis la stabilisation monétaire (1927–1935) 1936, Economie et droit de l'électricité (with C. A. Colliard) 1950, Les commerces de détail en Europe occidentale 1954, Forces et faiblesses de l'économie française 1945–1956, Textes de droit économique et social français 1789-1957 (with Perrot), Documents économiques (2 Vols) 1958, Economie politique 1959, Essai de comptabilité interrégionale française pour 1954, 1969, Régions et sénat 1969, A mes amis gaullistes 1973, Pour un nouveau protectionnisme 1978, Les économies occidentales du XIXème siècle à nos jours 1985, L'Economie française depuis 1967, La traversée des turbulences mondiales 1989, Vouloir l'emploi 1994, Ecoute la France qui gronde 1996, Une Mémoire Républicaine 1997, Que vive la constitution de la cinquième république 2002. *Address:* Sciences Po, 27 rue Saint-Guillaume, 75337 Paris Cedex 07 (office); 102 rue d'Assas, 75006 Paris (home); Rioz 70190, France (home). *Telephone:* 1-45-49-50-50 (office); 3-84-91-82-52 (Rioz). *Fax:* 1-45-49-50-50 (office).

JEANNENEY, Jean-Noël, DèsLettres; French politician and academic; *Professor in Modern History, Institut d'études politiques de Paris (Sciences Po);* b. 2 April 1942, Grenoble; s. of Jean-Marcel Jeanneney (q.v.) and Marie-Laure Jeanneney (née Monod); m. 2nd Annie-Lou Cot 1985; two s.; ed Lycées Champollion and Louis-le-Grand, Ecole normale supérieure, Inst. d'études politiques de Paris; Lecturer in Contemporary History, Univ. de Paris X 1969–77, Lecturer 1968; Univ. Prof. in Modern History, Inst. d'études politiques de Paris (Sciences Po) 1977–; Pres., Dir-Gen. Radio-France and Radio-France Int. 1982–86; Pres. Bicentenary of the French Revolution 1988–89; mem. Bd of Dirs, Agence France-Presse 1982–84, Télédiffusion de France 1982–86, La Sept 1986, Seuil Publs 1987–91, 1993–2002; Chair. Scientific Council, Inst. d'Histoire du Temps Présent 1991–2000; Sec. of State for External Trade 1991–92, for Communication 1992–93; Regional Councillor, Franche-Comté 1992–98; Chair. Advisory Cttee for 'Histoire' (cable TV) 1997–2004; Pres. Europartenaires 1998–, Bibliothèque nationale de France 2002–07; Chevalier, Légion d'honneur, Commdr, Ordre nat. du Mérite; Dr hc (Université Libre de Belgique) 2005. *Radio:* Concordance des temps (weekly programme on French culture) 1999–. *Television:* historical films for French TV: Léon Blum ou la fidélité 1973, Eamon de Valera 1975, Le Rhin 1996, Les Grandes Batailles de la République 1996–2006, Senghor entre deux mondes 1998, Histoire des présidentielles 1965–1995 2002. *Publications:* Le Riz et le Rouge, cinq mois en Extrême-Orient 1969, Le Journal politique de Jules Jeanneney 1939–42 1972, François de Wendel en République, l'Argent et le Pouvoir 1976, Leçon d'histoire pour une gauche au pouvoir, La Faillite du Cartel 1924–26 1977, Le Monde de Beuve-Méry ou le métier d'Alceste (co-author) 1979, L'argent caché, milieux d'affaires et pouvoirs politiques dans la France du XXe Siècle 1981, Télévision nouvelle mémoire, les magazines de grand reportage 1959–68 (with others) 1982, Echec à Panurge, l'audiovisuel public au service de la différence 1986, Concordances des temps, chroniques sur l'actualité du passé 1987, Georges Mandel, l'Homme qu'on attendait 1991, L'avenir vient de loin (essay) 1994, Une histoire des médias des origines à nos jours 1996–2000, Le Passé dans le prétoire, l'historien, le juge et le journaliste 1998, L'Echo du siècle, Dictionnaire historique de la radio et de la télévision en France 1999, La République a besoin d'histoire, interventions 2000, L'Histoire va-t-elle plus vite? Variations sur un vertige 2001, Le duel, une passion française 2004, Clemenceau 2005, Concordance des temps: Dialogues radiophoniques 2005, Quand Google défie l'Europe: Plaidoyer pour un sursaut 2006, La Proverbe et l'étamine, lectures historiques et politiques 2007. *Address:* 48 rue Galande, 75005 Paris, France (home). *E-mail:* jean-noel .jeanneney@orange.fr (office).

JEANNIOT, Pierre Jean, OC, CQ, LLD, DSc; Canadian/French air transport official (retd); *Chairman, THALES Canada Inc.;* b. 9 April 1933, Montpellier, France; ed Sir George Williams Univ., McGill Univ. and Univ. de Montréal; designer of aircraft and marine instrumentation, Sperry Gyroscope of Canada 1952–55; various positions in research, Devt and man., Air Canada 1955–68; contributed to Devt of the 'black box'; Vice-Pres. Computers and Communications, Univ. du Québec 1969; Vice-Pres. Computer and Systems Services, Air Canada 1970–76; subsequently held other sr positions in Air Canada; Exec. Vice-Pres. and COO Air Canada 1983, Pres. and CEO 1984–90; Dir-Gen. and CEO IATA 1992–2002, Dir-Gen. Emer., Montreal; Chair. THALES Canada, Inc. 2003–; Dir Bank of Nova Scotia Subsidiary Bds; Dir Jet Airways 2006–; Chair. Bd Univ. of Québec 1971–77, Chancellor 1996–; Chair. Thales Canada Inc.; Pres. and CEO JINMAG Inc.; Chair. Travel Success Group; Chevalier, Légion d'honneur 1991, Independence Medal of First Order (Jordan) 1995; Dr hc (Québec) 1988, (Concordia) 1997, DSc (McGill) 2006; Man. Achievement Award, McGill Univ. 1989. *Publications:* numerous technical papers. *Address:* 800 Place Victoria, Suite 1148, PO Box 113, Montreal, PQ H4Z 1M1, Canada (office). *Telephone:* (514) 874-0202 (office). *E-mail:* jeanniotp@iata.org (office). *Website:* www.pierrejeanniot.com (office).

JEANTET, Pierre; French newspaper industry executive; b. 14 May 1947, Neuilly-sur-Seine; ed Université Droit à Paris-II Assas; started career at Agence France-Presse 1972, served as Chief, Econ. Service 1980–82, Asst Sec.-Gen. 1984, Sec.-Gen. 1984–85, Sales Man. 1985–87, Asst Dir-Gen. 1987–90; Chair. Intermonde Presse 1989–91; Dir-Gen. Eurexpansion 1990–93; Dir-Gen. Sud-Ouest press group 1993–2006; Dir-Gen. Le Monde newspaper and Deputy Chair. Le Monde Group 2006–07, Chair. Le Monde Group June–Dec. 2007; Vice-Pres. Syndicat de la Presse Quotidienne Régionale 2001–; Pres. Bd of Trustees Pyrénées Presse 2002–, Charente Libre 2003–, Société des Gratuits de Guyenne et Gascogne 2004–; Chevalier de la Légion d'honneur, Chevalier de la l'Ordre national du Mérite. *Address:* Société des Gratuits de Guyenne et Gascogne, rue Walter Scott, 33600 Pessac, France (office). *Telephone:* 5-57-89-19-00 (office). *Fax:* 5-59-89-19-16 (office). *Website:* www .s3g.fr (office).

JEEVES, Malcolm Alexander, CBE, MA, PhD, FMedSci, FBPsS, PPRSE; British psychologist, academic and writer; *Professor Emeritus of Psychology, University of St Andrews;* b. 16 Nov. 1926, Stamford; s. of Alexander Frederic Thomas Jeeves and Helena May Jeeves (née Hammond); m. Ruth Elisabeth Hartridge 1955; two d.; ed Stamford School, St John's Coll., Cambridge, Harvard Univ. USA; Commd. Royal Lincs. Regt, served with 'Desert Rats' in First Bn Sherwood Foresters, BAOR 1945–48; Research Exhibitioner, St John's Coll., Cambridge 1952; Rotary Foundation Fellow, Harvard Univ. 1953; Lecturer, Univ. of Leeds 1956; Prof. of Psychology, Adelaide Univ. 1959–69, Dean 1962–64; Vice-Prin. Univ. of St Andrews 1981–85, Dir MRC Cognitive Neuroscience Research Group, St Andrews 1984–89, now Prof. Emer. of Psychology; Ed.-in-Chief Neuropsychologia 1990–93; mem. Psychology Cttee SSRC 1972–76, Biology Cttee SERC 1980–84, Science Bd 1985–89, Council 1985–89, Neuroscience and Mental Health Bd, MRC 1985–89, Manpower Sub-cttee, ABRC 1991–93, Council Royal Soc. of Edin. 1984–88, Exec. 1985–87, Vice-Pres. Royal Soc. of Edin. 1990–93, Pres. 1996–99; Pres. Section J, BAAS 1988; Founding Fellow, Acad. of Medical Sciences 1998; Hon. Research Prof., Univ. of St Andrews 1993–; Hon. Sheriff Fife 1986–; Hon. DUniv (Stirling); Hon. DSc (Edin.) 1993, (St Andrews) 2000; Abbie Memorial Lecture, Adelaide Univ. 1981, Cairns Memorial Lecture, 1986, 1987, Burney Student, Cambridge, Kenneth Craik Award, St John's Coll., Cambridge, Gregg Bury Prize, Cambridge, Cairns Medal 1986. *Publications:* Thinking in Structures (with Z.P. Dienes) 1965, The Effects of Structural Relations upon Transfer (with Z.P. Dienes) 1968, The Scientific Enterprise and Christian Faith 1969, Experimental Psychology: An Introduction for Biologists 1974, Psychology and Christianity: The View Both Ways 1976, Analysis of Structural Learning (with G. B. Greer) 1983, Free To Be Different (with R.J. Berry and D. Atkinson) 1984, Behavioural Science: a Christian Perspective 1984, Psychology – Through the Eyes of Faith (with D.G. Myers) 1987, Mind Fields 1994, Callosal Agenesis (ed. with M. Lassonde) 1994, Human Nature at the Millennium 1997, Science, Life and Christian Belief (co-ed. with R.J. Berry) 1998, From Cells to Souls – and Beyond (ed. and contrib.) 2004, Human Nature (ed. and contrib.) 2005, Neuroscience, Psychology and Religion (co-author with Warren Brown) 2009; papers on neuropsychology and cognition in scientific journals. *Leisure interests:* music, fly fishing, walking. *Address:* School of Psychology, University of St Andrews, St Andrews, Fife, KY16 9JU (office); 7 Hepburn Gardens, St Andrews, Fife, KY16 9DE, Scotland (home). *Telephone:* (1334) 462072 (office); (1334) 473545 (home). *Fax:* (1334) 477441 (office); (1334) 472539 (home). *E-mail:* maj2@st-andrews.ac.uk (office). *Website:* www.psy.st-andrews.ac.uk (office).

JEEWOOLALL, Sir Ramesh, Kt, LLB; Mauritian politician and lawyer; b. 20 Dec. 1940; m.; two c.; ed Middle Temple, London, UK; lawyer 1969–71; magistrate 1971–72; Chair. Tea Devt Authority 1976; elected to Legis. Ass. (Labour Party) 1976, Deputy Speaker 1976–79, Speaker 1979–82, 1996–2001; elected to Legis. Ass. (Alliance Party) 1987; Minister of Housing, Lands and Environment 1987–90. *Address:* c/o National Assembly, Port Louis; 92 Belle Rose Avenue, Quatre Bornes, Mauritius.

JEFFERSON, Sir George Rowland, Kt, CBE, FREng, FIEE, FRAeS, FRSA, CBIM, FCGI; British/Australian business executive; b. 26 March 1921; s. of Harold Jefferson and Eva Elizabeth Ellen; m. 1st Irene Watson-Browne 1943 (died 1998); three s.; m. 2nd Bridget Anne Reilley 1999; ed Dartford Grammar School, Kent; eng apprentice, Royal Ordnance Factory, Woolwich 1937–42; with RAOC and REME 1942; Anti-Aircraft Command and Armament Design Dept, Fort Halstead 1942–45; Ministry of Supply, Fort Halstead 1945–52; joined Guided Weapons Div., English Electric Co. Ltd 1952, Chief Research Engineer 1953, Deputy Chief Engineer 1958; Dir English Electric Aviation Ltd 1961; with British Aircraft Corpn (BAC), Dir and CEO, BAC (Guided Weapons) Ltd 1963, Deputy Man. Dir 1964, mem. Bd 1965–77; Dir British Aerospace, Chair. and CEO its Dynamics Group 1977–80; Chair. BAC (Anti-Tank) 1968–78; Deputy Chair. Post Office 1980–87; Chair. British Telecommunications 1981–87, CEO –1986; Dir Babcock Int. 1980–87, Lloyds Bank 1986–89; Chair. Matthew Hall PLC 1987–88; Chair. City Centre Communications Ltd 1988–90, Videotron Corpn 1990–97; Dir AMEC PLC 1988–90; mem. Nat. Enterprise Bd 1979–80, Governing Council Business in the Community Ltd 1984–87; Freeman of the City of London; Hon. FIMechE; Hon. BSc (Eng); Hon. DSc (Bristol); Hon. DUniv (Essex). *Address:* 12 Ocean Shore's Edge, Connolly, Perth, WA 6027, Australia. *Telephone:* (8) 9300-6414 (home). *Fax:* (8) 9300-8777. *E-mail:* georgejefferson@dingoblue.net.au (home).

JEFFERTS SCHORI, Katharine, BSc, MSc, MDiv, PhD; American ecclesiastic; *Presiding Bishop and Primate, Episcopal Church of the USA;* b. 26 March 1954, Pensacola, Fla; m. Richard Schori; one c.; ed Stanford Univ., Oregon State Univ.; qualified oceanographer, worked with Nat. Marine Fisheries Service; ordained priest 1994, served at Church of the Good Samaritan, Corvallis, Ore. with special responsibility for Hispanic congregation; consecrated Bishop of Nev. 2001; elected Presiding Bishop and Primate of Episcopal Church 2006–, also serves as Bishop of the Convocation of American Churches in Europe; Hon. DD (Church Divinity School of the Pacific). *Publications:* A Wing and a Prayer: A Message of Faith and Hope 2007. *Address:* Office of the Presiding Bishop, 815 Second Avenue, New York, NY 10017, USA (office). *Telephone:* (212) 716-6273 (office). *Fax:* (212) 697-5892 (office). *E-mail:* sjones@ episcopalchurch.org (office). *Website:* www.episcopalchurch.org (office).

JEFFERY, Maj.-Gen. (Philip) Michael, AC, CVO, MC; Australian government official and army officer (retd); b. 12 Dec. 1937, Wiluna, WA; m. Marlena Kerr 1967; three s. one d.; ed Cannington School, E Victoria Park State School, Kent Street High School, Royal Mil. Coll., Duntroon, Canberra; comm. as Lt in Royal Australian Infantry Corps 1958; Platoon Commdr, 17 Nat. Service Training Co., Swanbourne, WA, Reconnaissance Officer, 1 Special Air Service (SAS) Co., Swanbourne 1959; promoted Temporary Capt., 1 SAS Co., Swanbourne 1962; Signal Platoon Commdr, Second Bn, Royal Australian Regt (2 RAR), Malaya 1962; promoted Capt., 2 RAR, Malaya 1962; Signal Platoon Commdr, 3 RAR, Malaya 1963; ADC to Chief of Gen. Staff, Lt-Gen. Sir John Wilton, Army HQ, Canberra, ACT 1964; SAS Regt, Swanbourne 1965; Operations Officer, SAS HQ, Labuan, Borneo 1965; Adjutant, SAS Regt, Swanbourne 1966; promoted Temporary Maj. 1966; Co. Commdr, First Bn, Pacific Islands Regt (1 PIR), Papua New Guinea (PNG); promoted Maj. 1968; Co. Commdr, 8 RAR, Enoggera, Viet Nam (Phuoc Tuy Prov.) and Enoggera 1969–70; Instructor, Battle Wing, Jungle Training Centre, Canungra, Queensland 1971; Student, Royal Mil. Coll. of Science, Schrivenham and British Army Staff Coll., Camberley, UK 1971; Staff Officer, Grade 2 Operations, Directorate of Operations, Army HQ, Canberra 1973; promoted Temporary Lt-Col 1973; Staff Officer Grade 1, Jt Warfare, Directorate of Operations, Army HQ, Canberra; Staff Officer Grade 1, Land Operations, HQ, PNG Defence Force, Port Moresby 1974; promoted Lt-Col 1974; CO Second Bn, Pacific Islands Regt (2 P1R), Wewak, PNG 1975; CO Special Air Service Regt, Swanbourne 1976; Student, Jt Services Staff Coll., Canberra 1978; Mil. Sec.'s Pool of Lt-Cols, Office of the CGS, Canberra 1978; Staff Officer Grade 1, Special Warfare, Operations Br., Army HQ, Canberra 1978; promoted Col and Dir Special Action Forces, Operations Br., Army Office, Canberra 1979; promoted Brig. and Head of Protective Services Co-ordination Centre, Dept of Admin. Services, Canberra 1981; Commdr 1 Brigade, Holsworthy, NSW 1983; Student, Royal Coll. of Defence Studies, UK 1984; promoted Maj. Gen. and Commdr 1 Div., Paddington, NSW 1985; Asst Chief of Gen. Staff, Logistics, Army Office, Canberra 1989; Deputy Chief of Gen. Staff, Army Office, Canberra 1990 Asst Chief of Gen. Staff, Material, Army Office, Canberra, 1991; transferred to Inactive Australian Army Reserve 1993; Gov. of Western Australia 1993–2000; Gov.-Gen. of Commonwealth of Australia 2003–08; Founder and Chair. Future Directions International, Perth, WA 2000–03; Citizen of Western Australia; Hon. Life mem. Returned and Services League; AO (Mil.) 1988; KStJ; Grand Companion of the Order of Logohu (Papua New Guinea) 2005; AASM with Bars, Malaysia, Thai/Malay, Borneo and Viet Nam 1945–75, GSM with Bars Borneo and Malay Peninsula 1962, Viet Nam Service Medal, ASM with Bars, Papua New Guinea and South East Asia 1945–75, Australian Centenary Medal, Defence Force Service Medal with four Bars, Nat. Medal with Bar, Papua New Guinea Independence Medal, Mil. Cross and S Vietnamese Cross of Gallantry with Gold Star, S Viet Nam Campaign Medal, Vietnamese Cross of Gallantry Unit Citation, Pingat Jasa Medal Malaysia 2006; Hon. DTech (Curtin Univ.) 2000; Paul Harris Fellow, The Rotary Foundation 1996, Citizen of Western Australia (CitWA) 2000.

Leisure interests: golf, cricket, fishing, reading, music. *Address:* c/o Government House, Dunrossil Drive, Yarralumla, ACT 2600, Australia (office).

JEFFORDS, James (Jim) Merrill, BS, LLB; American politician (retd); b. 11 May 1934, Rutland, Vt; s. of Olin M. Jeffords and Marion Hausman; m. Elizabeth Daley (died 2007); one s. one d.; ed Yale and Harvard Univs.; admitted to Vermont Bar 1962; law clerk, Judge Ernest Gibson, Vt District 1962; Pnr Bishop, Crowley & Jeffords 1963–66, Kinney, Carbine & Jeffords 1967–68; mem. Vt Senate 1967–68; Attorney-Gen. State of Vt 1969–73; Pnr, George E. Rice, Jr and James M. Jeffords 1973–74; mem. 94th–100th Congresses from Vt; Senator from Vermont 1989–2007 (retd); Chair. Environment Cttee 2001–07; Republican –2001, Ind. 2001–. *Address:* c/o 728 Hart Building, Washington, DC 20510-4503, USA (office).

JEFFREY, Robin Campbell, BSc, PhD, FREng, FIChemE, FIMechE; British engineer, business executive and academic (retd); b. 19 Feb. 1939; s. of Robert Jeffrey and Catherine McSporran; m. Barbara Robinson 1962; two s. one d.; ed Kelvinside Acad., Royal Tech. Coll. Glasgow, Pembroke Coll., Cambridge; with Babcock Int. 1956–79; with South of Scotland Electricity Bd 1979–89, Project Man. Torness AGR Station 1980–88, Chief Engineer, Generation Design and Construction 1988–89; Man. Dir Eng Resources, Scottish Power 1990–92; CEO Scottish Nuclear Ltd 1992–98, Chair. 1995–98; Jt Deputy Chair. British Energy PLC 1995–2001, Chair., CEO 2001–02; fmr Visiting Prof. of Eng, Univ. of Strathclyde; fmr mem. London Transport Bd; Canadian Nuclear Asscn's Int. Award 2002. *Address:* Brambles, Spring Copse, Oxford, OX1 5BJ, England (home). *E-mail:* robin.jeffrey1@btinternet.com (office).

JEFFREYS, Sir Alec John, Kt, BA, MA, DPhil, FRCPath, FRS, FLS, FMedSci, CBiol; British geneticist and academic; *Royal Society Wolfson Research Professor, University of Leicester;* b. 9 Jan. 1950, Oxford; s. of Sidney Victor Jeffreys and Joan Jeffreys (née Knight); m. Susan Miles 1971; two d.; ed Luton Grammar School, Luton Sixth Form Coll., Merton Coll., Oxford; European Molecular Biology Org. Postdoctoral Research Fellow, Univ. of Amsterdam 1975–77; Lecturer, Dept of Genetics, Univ. of Leicester 1977–82, Lister Inst. Research Fellow 1982–91, Reader in Genetics 1984–87, Prof. of Genetics 1987–, Royal Soc. Wolfson Research Prof. 1991–; Howard Hughes Int. Research Scholar 1993–97; Inventor of Genetic Fingerprinting; Fellow, Forensic Science Soc. of India 1989–, Int. Inst. of Biotechnology 1990–, Linnean Soc. of London 1994–; Founder Fellow, Acad. of Medical Sciences 1998; Foreign Assoc. NAS 2005; Hon. Freeman (Leicester) 1993; Hon. FRCP 1993; Hon. mem. Dept of Biochemistry, Univ. of Oxford 1997, Int. Soc. for Forensic Haemogenetics 1997, American Acad. of Forensic Sciences 1998, Biochemical Soc. 2003, NAS 2006; Hon. Life mem. Leicestershire Medico-Legal Soc. 1999; Hon. FRSM 2001; Hon. Fellow, Forensic Science Soc. 2005; Hon. DUniv (Open Univ.) 1991; Hon. Fellow (Luton) 1995, (Swansea) 2005; Hon. DSc (St Andrews) 1996, (Strathclyde) 1998, (Hull) 2004, (Oxford) 2004, (Leicester) 2004, (Kingston) 2005, (Liverpool) 2006, (King's Coll., London) 2007, (Teesside) 2007; Hon. DIur (Dundee) 2008; Gibbs Prize in Honours Biochemistry 1972, Colworth Medal for Biochemistry, Biochemical Soc. 1985, Linnean Bicentenary Medal for Zoology 1987, Carter Medal, Clinical Genetics Soc. 1987, 2003, Davy Medal, Royal Soc. 1987, Analytica Prize, German Soc. of Clinical Chemistry 1988, Australia Prize 1998; Midlander of the Year Award, 1988, Achievement of the Year Award, Leicester Publicity Asscn 1989, P. W. Allen Memorial Award, Forensic Science Soc. 1992, Milano Award 1992, Allan Award, American Soc. of Human Genetics 1992, Lloyd of Kilgerran Prize, Foundation for Science and Tech. 1993, Illuminated Address, Bedfordshire Co. Council 1994, Gold Medal for Zoology, Linnean Soc. 1994, Sir Frederick Gowland Hopkins Memorial Medal, Biochemical Soc. 1996, Albert Einstein World of Science Award, World Cultural Council Award, Baly Medal, Royal Coll. of Physicians 1997, Soc. of Chemical Industry Medal 1997, Australia Prize 1998, Sir George Stokes Medal, Royal Soc. of Chem. 2000, Edward Buchner Prize, Soc. for Biochem. and Molecular Biology (Germany) 2001, Nat. Historic Chemical Landmark plaque, Royal Soc. of Chem. 2002, Terence J Green Award, Int. Homicide Investigators Asscn 2003, Howard Steel Medal, British Orthopaedic Asscn 2003, AMP Award for Excellence in Molecular Diagnostics, Asscn for Molecular Pathology, USA 2003, Hon. Medal, Royal Coll. of Surgeons 2004, Daily Mirror Pride of Britain Lifetime Achievement Award 2004, Louis-Jeantet Prize for Medicine, Fondation Louis-Jeantet de Médecine, Switzerland 2004, Royal Medal, Royal Soc. 2004, Induction, Inventors Hall of Fame, Washington, DC 2005, Adelaide Medal, Int. Asscn of Forensic Sciences, Hong Kong 2005, Lasker Prize (for clinical medical research) 2005, Thomson Scientific Laureate Physiology/Medicine, USA 2006, Dr H.P. Heineken Prize for Biochemistry and Biophysics, Royal Netherlands Acad. of Arts and Sciences 2006, Morgan Stanley Great Briton Award 2006, Morgan Stanley Great Briton in Science and Innovation Award 2007, Millennium Laureate, Millennium Foundation, Helsinki 2008, Asscn of Colls Gold Award for Further Educ. Alumni 2008. *Publications:* numerous articles on human molecular genetics. *Leisure interests:* walking, swimming, postal history, reading unimproving novels. *Address:* Department of Genetics, Adrian Building, University of Leicester, University Road, Leicester, LE1 7RH, England (office). *Telephone:* (116) 252-3435 (office). *Fax:* (116) 252-3378 (office). *E-mail:* ajj@le.ac.uk (office). *Website:* www.le.ac.uk/ge/pages/staff/staff_pages/jeffreys (office).

JEFFRIES, Lionel; British actor and director; b. (Lionel Charles Jeffries), 10 June 1926; s. of Bernard Jeffries and Elsie Jeffries (née Jackson); m. Eileen Walsh; one s. two d.; ed Queen Elizabeth's Grammar School, Wimborne, Dorset, Royal Acad. of Dramatic Art; Burma Star, Kendal Award, Royal Acad. of Dramatic Art. *Stage appearances include:* (London) Hello Dolly 1983–84, See How They Run, Two into One 1984–85, The Wild Duck 1990, (New York) Pygmalion 1989. *Films include:* Will Any Gentleman? 1953, The Black Rider 1954, Jumping for Joy 1955, All for Mary 1955, No Smoking 1955, Windfall

1955, The Colditz Story 1955, The Quatermass Xperiment 1955, Up in the World 1956, The Baby and the Battleship 1956, Eyewitness (1956, Bhowani Junction 1956, Lust for Life 1956, High Terrace 1956, Hour of Decision 1957, The Man in the Sky 1957, The Vicious Circle 1957, Blue Murder at St. Trinian's 1957, Doctor at Large 1957, Barnacle Bill 1957, Behind the Mask 1958, Life Is a Circus 1958, Up the Creek 1958, Further Up the Creek 1958, Girls at Sea 1958, Dunkirk 1958, The Revenge of Frankenstein 1958, Orders to Kill 1958, Law and Disorder 1958, Please Turn Over 1959, Idle on Parade 1959, The Nun's Story 1959, Let's Get Married 1960, Bobbikins 1960, The Trials of Oscar Wilde 1960, Tarzan the Magnificent 1960, Jazz Boat 1960, Two Way Stretch 1960, The Hellions 1961, Fanny 1961, Mrs. Gibbons' Boys 1962, The Notorious Landlady 1962, Operation Snatch 1962, Kill or Cure 1962, The Long Ships 1963, The Scarlet Blade 1963, The Wrong Arm of the Law 1963, Call Me Bwana 1963, The Truth About Spring 1964, Murder Ahoy! 1964, First Men in the Moon 1964, You Must Be Joking! 1965, The Secret of My Success 1965, The Spy with a Cold Nose 1966, Arrivederci, Baby! 1966, Oh Dad, Poor Dad, Mama's Hung You in the Closet and I'm Feeling So Sad 1967, Rocket to the Moon 1967, Chitty Chitty Bang Bang 1968, Twinky 1969, 12 + 1 1969, Eyewitness 1970, Whoever Slew Auntie Roo? 1971, What Changed Charley Farthing? 1974, Wombling Free 1977, The Prisoner of Zenda 1979, Better Late Than Never 1982, A Chorus of Disapproval 1988; films directed include The Railway Children (also writer) 1970, The Amazing Mr. Blunden (also writer) 1972, Baxter! 1973, Wombling Free (also writer) 1977, The Water Babies 1978. *TV includes:* Room at the Bottom (series) 1964, Cream in My Coffee 1980, Shillingbury Tales (series) 1981, Father Charlie (series) 1982, Tom, Dick and Harriet (series) 1982, First and Last 1989, Ending Up 1989, Danny the Champion of the World 1989, Jekyll & Hyde 1990, Look at It This Way (miniseries) 1992, Woof! (series) 1993, Bed 1995, Heaven on Earth 1998; numerous appearances in series episodes. *Leisure interest:* painting. *Address:* c/o Liz Hobbs, Liz Hobbs Group Ltd, 65 London Road, Newark, Notts., NG24 1RZ, England. *Telephone:* (8700) 702702. *Website:* www.lizhobbsgroup.com.

JEKER, Robert A.; Swiss business executive; *Chairman, MCH Messe Schweiz AG;* b. 26 Aug. 1935, Basel; m. Vreni Jeker 1967; one s. two d.; ed Univ. of Mass, Amherst, USA; Head, Spalenberg br. Credit Suisse, Basel 1968–72, Head Credit Suisse, Basel 1972–76, mem. Exec. Bd 1976–83, Pres. 1983–93; Man. Dir Unotec, Anova and Nueva Holdings 1993–96; now Chair. Bd Batigroup AG, Basel, MCH Messe Schweiz AG, Basel; fmr Chair., now Vice-Chair. Swiss Steel, Emmenbrücke. *Leisure interests:* sports, concerts, travel. *Address:* MCH Messe Schweiz AG, 4005 Basel (office); Waldrain 2, 4103 Bottmingen, Switzerland (home). *Telephone:* (58) 2062010 (office); (61) 4013067 (home). *Fax:* (58) 2062009 (office); (61) 4013075 (home). *E-mail:* robertjeker@messe.ch (office). *Website:* www.messe.ch (office).

JEKSHENKULOV, Alikbek; Kyrgyzstani diplomatist and politician; b. 25 May 1957; m.; two s. one d.; ed Diplomatic Acad., Ministry of Foreign Affairs, Moscow; worked in Presidential Admin and Govt Office 1980–92; mem. Supreme Council, Chair. Cttee for Int. Relations of Parl. 1990–94; First Deputy Minister and Deputy Minister of Foreign Affairs 1994–2000; Amb. to Austria, Hungary, Czech Repub., Slovakia and Israel 2000–04; Perm. Rep. to OSCE, UN and int. orgs in Vienna 2000–04; Deputy Head of the Presidential Admin and Chief of Foreign Policy Div. 2004–05; Minister of Foreign Affairs 2005–06 (resgnd); Del. to UN Meeting on Ecology, NY 1997; Speaker at Carnegie Endowment for Int. Peace 2005; Peace and Accord Between Nations Award, Int. Rukhaniyat Asscn 2002. *Address:* c/o Ministry of Foreign Affairs, 720040 Bishkek, bul. Erkindik 57, Kyrgyzstan (office).

JELAŠIĆ, Radovan, MA, MBA; Serbian economist and central banker; *Governor, Narodna banka Srbije (National Bank of Serbia);* b. 19 Feb. 1968, Baja, Hungary; ed Univ. of Belgrade, Univ. of Illinois at Chicago, USA; Regional Man. for Cen. and Eastern Europe and positions in Corp. Banking Dept, Deutsche Bank, Frankfurt, Germany 1995–99; Sr Assoc., McKinsey & Co. Inc., Frankfurt, working on banking projects in Germany, Poland and Bulgaria 1999–2000; Vice-Gov. Nat. Bank of Yugoslavia/Serbia 2000–03, Gov. Narodna banka Srbije (Nat. Bank of Serbia) 2004–; fmr mem. Bd of Dirs Banking Rehabilitation Agency, Belgrade. *Address:* Narodna banka Srbije, PO Box 1010, Kralja Petra 12, 11000 Belgrade, Serbia (office). *Telephone:* (11) 3027100 (office). *Fax:* (11) 3027113 (office). *E-mail:* radovan.jelasic@nbs.yu (office). *Website:* www.nbs.yu (office).

JELE, Khiphusizi Josiah; South African diplomatist; b. 1 May 1930, Johannesburg; m. 1976; one s. two d.; ed Mil. Acad., Odessa and Moscow Political Science Acad., USSR; studied public admin, Great Britain and USA; African Nat. Congress (ANC) Political Commissar, Dir of Broadcasting, Chief Rep., Dar es Salaam, Tanzania 1967–71, ANC Rep., World Peace Council Secr., Helsinki, Finland 1971–77, Dir ANC Int. Affairs Dept, Lusaka, Zambia 1978–83, Chair. ANC Political Cttee, Lusaka 1983–85, Sec. to ANC Political Mil. Council, Lusaka 1985–91, mem. ANC Nat. Elections Comm. 1991–92, mem. ANC Civil Service Unit 1992–94; mem. ANC Exec. Cttee 1977–94; MP 1994; Perm. Rep. of South Africa to UN 1994–99; mem. Hon. Ambassadorial Cttee, Congress of Racial Equality; Phelps-Stokes Fund Annual Award 1995 (Hon. mem. Bd of Fund); Freedom of City of Memphis. *Publications:* (papers) Racism in South Africa 1973, Population Explosion in Africa 1974; Western Military Collaboration with South Africa (booklet). *Leisure interests:* soccer, boxing, jazz, classical music, reading. *Address:* c/o Ministry of Foreign Affairs, Union Building, E Wing, Government Avenue, Pretoria 0002, South Africa.

JELIMO, Pamela; Kenyan athlete; b. 5 Dec. 1989; d. of Rodah Jeptoo Keter (fmr 200m and 400m runner); ed Koyo Secondary School, Kapsabet; women's middle distance runner; started running as sprinter aged 13 in 2003; Kenyan High School Champion at 400m and 400m hurdles 2005; finished fifth in 400m race at Kenyan Championships 2007; Gold Medal, African Jr Championships 2007; ran 200m Kenyan nat. jr record (24.68); ran her first 800m race at

Kenyan trials for African Championships April 2008 (2:01.02); has been recruited by Kenyan Police, where she trains with Janeth Jepkosgei; at African Championships in Athletics 2008 set new nat. jr record of 1:58.70; won 800m at Hengelo Grand Prix May 2008 (new Jr World Record and Kenyan record of 1:55.76); ran 400m personal best of 52.78 in Nairobi June 2006; won Internationales Stadionfest (ISTAF) Golden League 2008 (set new African record time of 1:54.99); bettered record to 1:54.97 at Int. Asscn of Athletics Feds (IAAF) Golden League, Paris July 2008; Gold Medal, women's 800m, Olympic Games, Beijing 2008 (record time of 1:54.87; first Kenyan woman to win Olympic gold medal); ran personal best of 1:54.01 at Weltklasse Golden League meeting, Zurich 29 Aug. 2008 (third fastest time ever); coached by Zaid Aziz. *Address:* c/o Kenya Athletics Federation, PO Box 46722, Aerodrome Road, Riadha House, 00100 Nairobi West, Kenya. *Telephone:* (2) 605021. *Fax:* (2) 605020. *E-mail:* athleticskenya@gt.co.ke. *Website:* www.athleticskenya .org.

JELINEK, Elfriede; Austrian writer, dramatist and poet; b. 20 Oct. 1946, Mürzzuschlag, Styria; m. Gottfried Hüngsberg; ed Vienna Conservatory, Albertsgymnasium, Vienna and Univ. of Vienna; mem. Graz Writers' Asscn; The Young Austrian Culture Week Poetry and Prose Prize 1969, Austrian Univ. Students' Poetry Prize 1969, Austrian State Literature Stipendium 1972, City of Stadt Bad Gandersheim Roswitha Memorial Medal 1978, West German Interior Ministry Prize for Film Writing 1979, West German Ministry of Education and Art Appreciation Prize 1983, City of Cologne Heinrich Böll Prize 1986, Province of Styria Literature Prize 1987, City of Vienna Literature Appreciation Prize 1989, City of Aachen Walter Hasenclever Prize 1994, City of Bochum Peter Weiss Prize 1994, Rudolf Alexander Schroder Foundation Bremen Prize for Literature 1996, Georg Büchner Prize 1998, Berlin Theatre Prize 2002, City of Düsseldorf Heinrich Heine Prize 2002, Mülheim and der Ruhr Festival of Theatre Dramatist of the Year 2002, 2004, Else Lasker Schüler Prize, Mainz 2003, Lessing Critics' Prize, Wolfenbüttel 2004, Stig Dagerman Prize, Älvkarleby 2004, The Blind War Veterans' Radio Theatre Prize, Berlin 2004, Franz Kafka Prize 2004, Nobel Prize for Literature 2004. *Screenplays:* Die Ausgesperrten (TV) 1982, Malina (from novel by Ingeborg Bachmann) 1991. *Plays include:* Raststätte, Wolken. Heim, Das Werk, Totenauberg: ein Stück, Ein Sportstück, Das Lebewohl, In den Alpen. *Radio:* numerous pieces for radio, including wenn die sonne sinkt ist für manche schon büroschluss (radio play) 1974. *Publications:* Lisas Schatten (poems) 1967, wir sind lockvögel baby! (novel) 1970, Michael: ein Jugendbuch für die Infantilgesellschaft (novel) 1972, Die Liebhaberinnen (novel, trans. as Women as Lovers) 1975, bukolit (novel) 1979, Die Ausgesperrten (novel, trans. as Wonderful, Wonderful Times) 1980, ende: gedichte von 1966–1968 1980, Die endlose Unschuldigkeit (essays) 1980, Was geschah, nachdem Nora ihren Mann verlassen hatte oder Stützen der Gesellschaft 1980, Die Klavierspielerin (novel, trans. as The Piano Teacher) 1983, Burgtheater 1984, Clara S 1984, Oh Wildnis, oh Schutz vor ihr (non-fiction) 1985, Krankeit oder moderne Frauen 1987, Lust (novel) 1989, Wolken. Heim 1990, Die Kinder der Toten (novel) 1995, Macht nichts: eine kleine Trilogie des Todes 1999, Gier: ein Unterhaltungsroman 2000, Der Tod und das Mädchen I–V: Prinzessinnendramen 2003, Greed (novel) 2006; translations of other writers' works, including Thomas Pynchon, Georges Feydeau, Eugène Labiche, Christopher Marlowe; film scripts and an opera libretto. *Address:* Jupiterweg 40, 1140 Vienna, Austria. *Website:* www.elfriedejelinek.com.

JELINEK, Otto John; Canadian politician, business executive and fmr figure skater; *Chairman, Deloitte & Touche Central Europe;* b. 1940, Prague, Czechoslovakia; m. Leata Mary Bennett 1974; two s.; ed Oakville, Ont., Swiss Alpine Business Coll., Davos, Switzerland; business exec.; MP 1972–93; apptd Parl. Sec. to Minister of Transport 1979; fmr mem. Caucus Cttee on Trade, Finance, Econ. Affairs, fmr mem. Standing Cttee on Transport and Communications, on External Affairs; fmr mem. Parl. Cttee on Miscellaneous Estimates, Minister of State (Fitness and Amateur Sport) 1984–88, for Multiculturalism 1985–86, of Supply and Services and Receiver Gen. of Canada 1988–89; Acting Minister of Public Works 1988–89, Minister of Nat. Revenue 1989–93; Pres. Jelinek Int. Inc. 1993–; currently Chair. Deloitte & Touche Central Europe, also Chair. Deloitte Czech Repub.; mem. Int. Advisory Bd Soho Resources 2005–; fmr mem. Bd Dirs Hummingbird Communications Ltd, Canbra Foods Ltd; mem. Academic Council of Univ. of Econs Prague; fmr Chair. Canada-Taiwan Friendship Cttee; Hon. Pres. Canada-Czech Republic Chamber of Commerce; mem. Big Brothers' Asscn of Canada, Olympic Club of Canada, Canadian Sports Hall of Fame; Fed. Progressive Conservative Party; former pairs figure skating world champion 1962. *Address:* Deloitte Czech Republic, Týn 641/4, 110 00 Prague 1, Czech Republic (office). *Telephone:* (2) 24895500 (office). *Fax:* (2) 24895555 (office). *Website:* www.deloitte.com (office).

JELUŠIČ, Ljubica, MSc, PhD; Slovenian academic and government official; *Minister of Defence;* b. 16 June 1960, Koper; ed Faculty of Sociology, Political Science and Journalism, Royal Mil. Acad., Belgium; has held several academic positions since 1985 at Faculty of Social Sciences, Univ. of Ljubljana including Researcher, Asst, Asst Prof. and Assoc. Prof., Prof. of Defence Studies 2005–; Visiting Lecturer, Univ. of Zagreb, Centre for Civil-Mil. Relations, Belgrade; Deputy Dean, Faculty of Social Sciences, Command and Staff School 1995–97, Chair. Defence Studies Dept 1999–2007; Minister of Defence 2008–; Leader, Defence Restructuring and Conversion research project, COST Programme of the EC 1996–2001; Exec. Sec., Research Cttee on Armed Forces and Conflict Resolution, Int. Sociological Asscn 2006–08; mem. Editorial Bd Theory and Practice (Teorija in praksa) Magazine, Bulletin of the Slovenian Armed Forces (Bilten Slovenske vojske); reviewer for Security and Peace (Sicherheit und Frieden) magazine; mem. Int. Advisory Cttee, Geneva Centre for Democratic Control of Armed Forces. *Publication* Legitimacy of the Modern Military 1997. *Address:* Ministry of Defence, 1000 Ljubljana, Vojkova 55, Slovenia (office). *Telephone:* (1) 4712211 (office). *Fax:* (1) 4712978 (office). *E-mail:* info@mors.si (office). *Website:* www.mors.si (office).

JELVED, Marianne, MEd; Danish politician; *Leader, Social Liberals;* b. 5 Sept. 1943, Charlottenlund; m.; teacher in public schools 1967–89, Royal Danish School of Educ. Studies 1979–87; Deputy Mayor of Gundsø 1982–85; mem. Folketing 1988–; Chair. Social Liberal mems of Parl. 1988, currently Leader; Minister for Econ. Affairs 1993–2001, also for Nordic Cooperation 1994–2001, also Deputy Prime Minister. *Publications:* BRUD: Radikale vaerdier i en forandret tid (co-author) 1994. *Address:* Folketing, Christiansborg, 1240 Copenhagen K, Denmark (office). *Telephone:* 33-37-55-00 (office). *Fax:* 33-32-85-38 (office). *E-mail:* folketinget@folketinget.dk (office). *Website:* www.folketinget.dk (office).

JEMISON, Mae Carol, MD; American physician, business executive and fmr astronaut; *President and CEO, BioSentient Corporation;* b. 17 Oct. 1956, Decateur, Ala; d. of Charlie Jamison and Dorothy Jamison; ed Morgan Park High School, Chicago, Stanford Univ., Cornell Univ. Medical Coll., LA County/ Univ. of Southern Calif. (USC) Medical Center; gen. practitioner, Insurance N America (INA)/Ross Loos Medical Group LA 1982; Area Peace Corps Medical Officer to Sierra Leone and Liberia 1983–85; gen. practitioner, CIGNA Health Plans Calif. 1985–87; astronaut, NASA 1987–93, co-investigator, Bone Cell Research experiment, part of Endeavor space mission 1992; f. The Jemison Group Inc., Houston 1993; Prof. of Environmental Studies Dartmouth Coll. 1995–2002; Founder, Pres. and CEO BioSentient Corpn 1999–; A.D. White Prof.-at-Large, Cornell Univ. 1999–2005; f. The Earth We Share (TEWS) 1994; Founder and Chair. The Dorothy Jemison Foundation for Excellence 1994–; elected to NAS Inst. of Medicine 2001; Nat. Science Literary Advocate, Bayer Corpn; Moderator, IEEE-USA Tech. Symposia Space Techs. for Disaster Mitigation and Global Health; Dir Jemison Inst. for Advancing Tech. in Developing Countries; mem. American Medical Asscn, ACS, AAAS; mem. Bd Gen-Probe 2004–, World Sickle Cell Foundation, Scholastic Inc., Valspar Corpn, Texas Gov.'s State Council for Science and Bio Tech. Devt; Hon. mem. Center for Prevention Childhood Malnutrition, Montgomery Fellow, Dartmouth Coll.; Dr hc (Princeton Univ. and others); Essence Award 1988, Gamma Sigma Gamma Woman of the Year Award 1989, Johnson Publs Black Achievement Trailblazers Award, Kilby Science Award, Nat. Medical Asscn Hall of Fame, Texas Science Hall of Fame, Rotary Club Chicago's ROTARY/ One Award. *Television includes:* World of Wonder (Discovery Channel) 1994–95; guest appearances: Star Trek: The Next Generation 1993; as subject: The New Explorers (PBS-TV). *Achievements include:* first African-American woman in space 1992. *Publications:* Find Where the Wind Goes: Moments from My Life 2001. *Address:* Jemison Group, Inc., 4119 Montrose Blvd, Suite 230, Houston, TX 77006, USA. *Telephone:* (713) 528-9000 (home). *E-mail:* info@biosentient.com (office). *Website:* www.biosentient.com (office); www.maejemison.com (home).

JENCKS, Charles Alexander, BA, MA, PhD, FRSE; American architectural historian and designer; b. 1939, Baltimore, Md; m. Maggie Keswick (deceased); three s. one d.; ed Harvard Univ., Univ. of London, UK; studied under Siegfried Giedon and Reyner Banham; with Architectural Asscn 1968–88; Lecturer, UCLA 1974–; has lectured at over forty univs including Univs of Peking, Shanghai, Paris, Tokyo, Milan, Venice, Frankfurt, Montréal, Oslo, Warsaw, Barcelona, Lisbon, Zurich, Vienna, Edinburgh, Columbia, Princeton, Yale and Harvard; producer of furniture designs for Sawaya & Moroni, Milan 1986–; currently Ed. Consultant Architectural Design and Ed. Academy Editions, London; contrib. to Sunday Times Magazine, Times Literary Supplement, The Observer, The Independent (all UK); mem. Selection Cttee Venice Biennale 1980; Juror for Phoenix City Hall 1985; Curator Wight Art Centre, LA and Berlin 1987; mem. RSA, London, Acad. Forum of Royal Acad., London; Fulbright Scholarship (Univ. of London) 1965–67, NARA Gold Medal for Architecture 1992. *Furniture designs include:* 'Architecture in Silver': Tea and Coffee Service, Alessi, Italy 1983, Symbolic Furniture exhbn, Aram Designs, London 1985; other furniture and drawings collected by museums in Japan and Victoria & Albert Museum, London. *Architectural works include:* Garagia Rotunda, Truro, MA 1976–77, The Elemental House (with Buzz Yudell), LA, The Thematic House (with Terry Farrell), London 1979–84, The Garden of Six Senses 1998, The Garden of Cosmic Speculation, Scotland 2001, Landform Veda, Scottish Gallery of Modern Art, Edinburgh 2002, Portello Park, Milan 2003. *Television includes:* two feature films written for BBC on Le Corbusier and Frank Lloyd Wright. *Publications include:* Meaning in Architecture (co-ed.) 1969, Architecture 2000: Predictions and Methods 1971, Adhocism (co-author) 1972, Modern Movements in Architecture 1973, Le Corbusier and the Tragic View of Architecture 1974, The Language of Post-Modern Architecture 1977, The Daydream Houses of Los Angeles 1978, Bizarre Architecture 1979, Late-Modern Architecture 1980, Signs, Symbols and Architecture (co-author) 1980, Skyscrapers-Skycities 1980, Architecture Today 1982, Kings of Infinite Space 1983, Towards a Symbolic Architecture 1985, What is Post-Modernism? 1987, Post-Modernism – The New Classicism in Art and Architecture 1987, The Prince, The Architects and New Wave Monarchy 1988, The New Moderns 1990, The Post-Modern Reader (ed.) 1992, The Architecture of the Jumping Universe 1995, Theories and Manifestos of Contemporary Architecture 1997, New Science – New Architecture? 1997, The Chinese Garden (with Maggie Keswick), Le Corbusier and the Architecture of Continual Revolution 2000, The New Paradigm in Architecture 2002, The Garden of Cosmic Speculation 2003. *Address:* c/o Royal Academy Forum, Royal Academy of Arts, Burlington House, Piccadilly, London, W1J 0BD, England (office). *Website:* www .charlesjencks.com.

JENCKS, William Platt, MD; American biochemist and academic; *Professor Emeritus, Brandeis University;* b. 15 Aug. 1927, Bar Harbor, Me; s. of Gardner

Jencks and Elinor Melcher Cheetham; m. Miriam Ehrlich Jencks 1950; one s. one d.; ed Harvard Coll. and Harvard Medical School; Intern, Peter Bent Brigham Hosp., Boston, Mass. 1951–52; mem. staff, Dept of Pharmacology, Army Medical Service Graduate School 1953–54, Chief, Dept of Pharmacology 1954–55; Life Insurance Medical Research Fund Postdoctoral Fellow, Mass. Gen. Hosp. 1955–56; US Public Health Service Postdoctoral Fellow, Dept of Chem., Harvard 1956–57; Asst Prof. of Biochem., Brandeis Univ. 1957–60, Assoc. Prof. of Biochem. 1960–63, Prof. of Biochem. 1963–96, of Biochem. and Molecular Pharmacodynamics 1977–96, Prof. Emer. 1996–; Guggenheim Memorial Foundation Fellow 1973–74; Fellow AAAS, American Acad. of Arts and Sciences; mem. Nat. Acad. of Sciences, American Soc. of Biological Chemists, American Philosophical Soc.; Foreign mem. Royal Soc. (UK); American Chem. Soc. Award in Biological Chem. 1962, American Soc. of Biological Chemists Merck Award 1993, James Flack Norris Award 1995, Repligen Award 1996. *Publications:* Catalysis in Chemistry and Enzymology 1969, Biochemistry (co-author) 1992; and over 380 articles in journals. *Leisure interest:* music. *Address:* Brandeis University, Graduate Department of Biochemistry, Waltham, MA 02254 (office); 11 Revere Street, Lexington, MA 02420, USA (home). *Telephone:* (781) 736-2315 (office); (781) 862-8875 (home). *Fax:* (781) 736-2349. *Website:* www.bio.brandeis.edu (office).

JENKIN OF RODING, Baron (Life Peer), cr. 1987, of Wanstead and Woodford in Greater London; **(Charles) Patrick (Fleeming) Jenkin,** PC, MA; British politician; *President, Foundation for Science and Technology;* b. 7 Sept. 1926, Edin.; s. of the late C. O. F. Jenkin and Margaret E. Jenkin (née Sillar); m. Alison Monica Graham 1952; two s. two d.; ed Clifton Coll., Bristol, Jesus Coll., Cambridge; called to the Bar, Middle Temple 1952; Adviser Distillers Co. Ltd 1957–70; Hornsey Borough Council 1960–63; MP for Wanstead and Woodford 1964–87; Opposition Spokesman on Finance, Econs and Trade 1965–66, 1967–70; Financial Sec. to Treasury 1970–72, Chief Sec. 1972–74; Minister for Energy Jan.–March 1974; mem. Shadow Cabinet 1974–79; Opposition Spokesman on Energy 1974–76, on Social Services 1976–79; Sec. of State for Social Services 1979–81, for Industry 1981–83, for the Environment 1983–85; mem. House of Lords Select Cttee on Science and Tech. 1997–2001 (Chair. Sub-Cttee II on Science and Soc. 1999–2000); Dir (non-exec.) Tilbury Contracting Group Ltd 1974–79, Royal Worcs. Co. Ltd 1975–79; Dir Continental and Industrial Trust Ltd 1975–79; Adviser Arthur Andersen 1985–96; Dir Friends Provident Life Office 1986–88, Chair. 1988–98; Chair. Lamco Paper Sales Ltd 1987–93; Dir UK-Japan 2000 Group 1986–99 (Chair. 1986–90); Chair. Crystalate Holdings PLC 1988–90, Target Finland Ltd 1991–96 (Dir 1989–91); Vice-Pres. Local Govt Asscn 1987–, Nat. Asscn of Local Councils 1987–2000, Greater London Area Conservatives 1987–89, Pres. 1989–92; mem. UK Advisory Bd Nat. Econ. Research Assocs. Inc. 1985–98; Dir UK Council for Econ. and Environmental Devt Ltd 1987–2004; Council mem. Guide Dogs for the Blind Asscn 1987–97; Chair. Westfield Coll. Trust 1988–2000; Adviser Sumitomo Trust and Banking Co. Ltd 1989–; Pres. British Urban Regeneration Asscn 1990–96; Chair. Forest Healthcare NHS Trust 1991–97; mem. Advisory Bd PPRU, Queen Mary and Westfield Coll. 1991–97 (Fellow 1991–), Supervisory Bd Achmea Holding NV 1991–98; Council mem. Imperial Cancer Research Fund 1991–97 (Deputy Chair. 1994–97); Patron St Clare West Essex Hospice Care Trust 1991–; Jt Pres. MIND (Nat. Asscn of Mental Health) 1991–93, Asscn of London Govt 1995–; Vice-Pres., Nat. Housing Fed. 1991–99; Sr Vice-Pres. World Congress on Urban Growth and Devt 1992–94; Pres. London Boroughs Asscn 1992–95; Adviser Thames Estuary Airport Co. Ltd 1992–; mem. Int. Advisory Bd Marsh & McLennan Cos Inc. (US) 1993–99, Nijenrode Univ., Netherlands 1994–98; Vice-Pres. Foundation for Science and Tech. 1996–97, Chair. 1997–2006, Pres. 2006–; Pres. Asscn for Science Educ. 2002–03; Conservative; Freeman City of London; Hon. Freeman London Borough of Redbridge; Hon. Fellow, Queen Mary Coll., Univ. of London 1991–, Coll. of Optometrists 2003; Hon. FRSE 2001–; Hon. mem. BAAS 2001–; Hon. LLD (Univ. of the South Bank) 1997; Hon. DSc (Univ. of Ulster) 2001. *Leisure interests:* music, gardening, sailing, DIY . *Address:* House of Lords, Westminster, London, SW1A 0PW (office); Foundation for Science and Technology, 10 Carlton House Terrace, London, SW1Y 5AH, England. *Telephone:* (20) 7219-6966 (Westminster) (office). *Fax:* (20) 7219-0759 (Westminster) (office). *E-mail:* jenkinp@parliament.uk (office). *Website:* www.foundation.org.uk.

JENKINS, Sir Brian Garton, GBE, MA, FCA; British charity administrator and fmr business executive; *Prior of the Priory of England and the Islands, St John Ambulance;* b. 3 Dec. 1935, Beckenham; m. (Elizabeth) Ann Jenkins; one s. one d.; ed Tonbridge, Trinity Coll., Oxford; with RA, Gibraltar 1955–57; Partner, Coopers & Lybrand 1960–95; Chair. Woolwich PLC 1995–2000; Deputy Chair. Barclays PLC 2000–04; Pres. Inst. of Chartered Accountants in England and Wales 1985–86, London Chamber of Commerce and Industry 1996–98, British Computer Soc. 1997–98; Chair. Charities Aid Foundation 1998–2003, Prior of Priory of England and Islands, St John Ambulance 2004–; Lord Mayor of London 1991–92; Hon. Bencher Inner Temple, Hon. mem. Baltic Exchange. *Publication:* An Audit Approach to Computers 1978. *Address:* St John Ambulance, 27 St John's Lane, London, EC1M 4BU, England (office). *Telephone:* (8700) 104950 (office). *Fax:* (8700) 104065 (office). *Website:* www.sja.org.uk (office).

JENKINS, Charles H., Jr, BA, PhD; American retail executive; *Chairman, Publix Super Markets Inc;* b. 1944; m. Dorothy Jenkins; ed Goizueta Business School, Emory Univ., Harvard Univ.; Asst to Real Estate Vice-Pres., Publix Super Markets Inc. 1969–74, Dir 1974–, Vice-Pres. 1974–88, Exec. Vice-Pres. 1988–90, Chair. Exec. Cttee 1990–2000, COO 2000–01, CEO 2001–08, Chair. Bd of Dirs 2008–; fmr Pres. Lakeland Chamber of Commerce; fmr mem. Bd of Overseers, Boston Symphony Orchestra; Distinguished Alumni Achievement Award, Goizueta Business School, Emory Univ. *Address:* Publix Super Markets Inc., 3300 Publix Corporate Parkway, Lakeland, FL 33811, USA (office). *Telephone:* (863) 688-1188 (office). *Fax:* (863) 284-5532 (office). *Website:* www.publix.com (office).

JENKINS, Rt Rev. David Edward, MA; British ecclesiastic; b. 26 Jan. 1925, London; s. of Lionel C. Jenkins and Dora K. Jenkins (née Page); m. Stella M. Peet 1949; two s. two d.; ed St Dunstan's Coll., Catford, Queen's Coll., Oxford, Lincoln Theological Coll.; Capt. RA 1945–47; priest 1954; Succentor Birmingham Cathedral 1953–54; Fellow and Chaplain and Praelector in Theology, Queen's Coll., Oxford 1954–69, Hon. Fellow 1990; Dir Humanum Studies, WCC, Geneva 1969–73; Dir William Temple Foundation, Manchester 1973–78; Prof. of Theology, Univ. of Leeds 1979–84, Prof. Emer. 1984–; Bishop of Durham 1984–94; Asst Bishop of Ripon 1994–; Hon. Prof. of Divinity, Univ. of Durham 1994–; Hon. Fellow, Queen's Coll. Oxford, Univ. of Sunderland; Hon. DD (Durham, Aberdeen, Trinity Coll., Toronto, Leeds, Birmingham); Hon. DLit (Teesside); Hon. DCL (Northumbria). *Publications:* The Glory of Man 1967, Living With Questions 1969, What is Man? 1970, The Contradiction of Christianity 1979, God, Miracles and the Church of England 1987, God, Politics and the Future 1988, God, Jesus and Life in the Spirit 1988, Still Living With Questions 1990, Free to Believe (with Rebecca Jenkins) 1991, Market Why and Human Wherefores 2000, The Calling of a Cuckoo 2003. *Leisure interests:* opera and church music, walking, birdwatching, nature and conservation, travel, books. *Address:* Ashbourne, Cotherstone, Barnard Castle, Co. Durham, DL12 9PR, England (home). *Telephone:* (1833) 650804 (home). *Fax:* (1833) 650714 (home).

JENKINS, Hugh, CBE, FRICS; British business executive; b. 9 Nov. 1933, Port Talbot, S Wales; m. Beryl Kirk 1988; ed Llanelli Grammar School, Coll. of Estate Man.; valuer, London Co. Council 1956–62; Asst Controller Coal Industry (Nominees) Ltd 1962–68, Man. Dir 1968–72; Dir-Gen. Investments, Nat. Coal Bd 1972–85; Vice-Chair. Nat. Asscn of Pension Funds 1979–80; CEO Heron Financial Corpn 1985–86; Group Investment Dir, Allied Dunbar Asscn 1986–89; Deputy Chair. and Chief Exec. Allied Dunbar Unit Trusts 1986–89; Chair. and Chief Exec. Allied Dunbar Asset Man. 1987–89; Chair. Dunbar Bank 1988–89; Chair. and Chief Exec. Prudential Portfolio Mans 1989–95; Dir Prudential Corpn 1989–95; Chair. Falcon Property Trust 1995–2003, Devt Securities PLC 1999–2003; Deputy Chair. Thorn PLC 1996–97, Chair. 1997–98; Dir Unilever Pensions Ltd 1985–89, IBM Pensions Trust PLC 1985–89, Heron Int. 1985–89, EMI 1995–2002, Rank Org. 1995–2002, Johnson Matthey 1996–2003; Chair. Property Advisory Group, Dept of the Environment 1990–96; mem. City Capital Markets Cttee 1982, Pvt. Financial Panel 1994–95; Lay mem. Stock Exchange 1984–85; Fellow Pensions Man. Inst. *Leisure interests:* golf, theatre, travel. *Address:* 15 Walpole Street, London, SW3 4QP, England (home). *Telephone:* (20) 7730–1631 (home). *Fax:* (20) 7730–2723 (home). *E-mail:* berylandhughjenkins@btinternet.com (home).

JENKINS, Dame (Mary) Jennifer, DBE; British conservation and consumer organizer and campaigner; b. 18 Jan. 1921; d. of the late Sir Parker Morris; m. Roy Jenkins, the late Lord Jenkins of Hillhead 1945; two s. one d.; ed St Mary's School, Calne, Girton Coll., Cambridge; with Hoover Ltd 1942–43; Ministry of Labour 1943–46; Political and Econ. Planning 1946–48; part-time extra-mural lecturer 1949–61; part-time teacher, Kingsway Day Coll. 1961–67; Chair. Consumers Asscn 1965–76; mem. Exec. Bd British Standards Inst. 1970–73, Design Council 1971–74, Cttee of Man. Courtauld Inst. 1981–84, Exec. Cttee, Nat. Trust 1985–91 (Chair. 1986–90), Ancient Monuments Bd 1982–84, Historic Bldgs and Monuments Comm. 1984–85; Chair. Historic Bldgs Council for England 1975–84, Royal Parks Review Group 1991–96, Architectural Heritage Fund 1994–97, Expert Panel, Heritage Lottery Fund 1995–99, Civic Trust 2003–04; Pres. Ancient Monuments Soc. 1985– (Sec. 1972–75); Chair. N Kensington Amenity Trust 1974–77; Trustee, Wallace Collection 1977–83; Dir J. Sainsbury Ltd 1981–86, Abbey Nat. PLC 1984–91; JP London Juvenile Courts 1964–74; Hon. Fellow, Landscape Inst. 1995; Hon. FRIBA; Hon. FRICS; Hon. mem. Royal Town Planning Inst.; Hon. LLD (London) 1988, (Bristol) 1990; Hon. DCL (Newcastle-upon-Tyne) 1992, (Oxford) 2003; Hon. DUniv (York) 1990, (Strathclyde) 1993; Hon. DArch (Oxford Brookes) 1993, (Greenwich) 1998; Hon. DSc (St Andrews) 2006. *Publications:* From Acorn to Oak Tree: The Growth of the National Trust (with Patrick James) 1994, Remaking the Landscape: The Changing Face of Britain (Ed.) 2002. *Address:* 11 Hereford Mansions, Hereford Road, London, W2 5BA; St Amand's House, East Hendred, Oxon., OX12 8LA, England.

JENKINS, Sir Michael Romilly Heald, KCMG, BA, CRAeS; British diplomatist and business executive; *Chairman, Matra Petroleum plc;* b. 9 Jan. 1936, Cambridge; s. of Prof. Romilly Jenkins and Celine J. Jenkins (née Haeglar); m. Maxine L. Hodson 1968; one s. one d.; ed King's Coll., Cambridge; entered Foreign (subsequently Diplomatic) Service 1959; served in Paris, Moscow and Bonn; Deputy Chef de Cabinet 1973–75, Chef de Cabinet to George Thomson, EEC 1975–76; Prin. Adviser to Roy Jenkins, the late Lord Jenkins of Hillhead, Jan.–Aug. 1977; Head, European Integration Dept (External), FCO 1977–79; Head, Cen. Advisory Group, EEC 1979–81; Deputy Sec.-Gen., Comm. of the European Communities 1981–83; Asst Under-Sec. of State (Europe), FCO 1983–85; Minister, British Embassy, Washington 1985–87; Amb. to the Netherlands 1988–93; Exec. Dir Kleinwort Benson Group PLC 1993–96, Vice-Chair. Dresdner Kleinwort Benson 1996–2000, Dresdner Kleinwort Wasserstein 2001–03; Chair. British Group, Trilateral Comm. 1995–99, Action Centre for Europe (ACE) 1995–2003, DataRoam Ltd 2000–02, MCC 2000–02 (Trustee 2002–07), Matra Petroleum plc 2007–; Dir Aegon NV 1994–2001, Frontiers Capital Ltd 2006–07 (Chair. 2008–), GeoPark Holdings Ltd 2006–; adviser, Sage Int. Ltd (later SELS Ltd) 1998–2002; Pres. Boeing UK Ltd 2003–05, Adviser 2005–07; Commr Royal Hosp., Chelsea 2007–; mem. Council Britain in Europe 2000–, The Pilgrims 2001–, Advisory Council Prince's Trust 2002–; Companion, Royal Aeronautical Soc. 2004. *Publications:* Arakcheev,

Grand Vizir of the Russian Empire 1969, A House in Flanders 1992. *Address:* Frontiers Capital Ltd, 75 Wells Street, London, W1T 3HQ, England (office). *Telephone:* (20) 7182-7700 (office). *Fax:* (20) 7182-7701 (office). *Website:* www.frontierscapital.com (office).

JENKINS, Sir Simon David, Kt, BA; British journalist and organization offical; *Chairman, The National Trust;* b. 10 June 1943, Birmingham; s. of Daniel Jenkins; m. Gayle Hunnicutt 1978; one s. one step-s.; ed Mill Hill School, St John's Coll., Oxford; worked for Country Life Magazine 1965; News Ed. Times Educ. Supplement 1966–68; leader-writer, columnist, features ed. Evening Standard 1968–74; Insight Ed., Sunday Times 1974–76; Ed. Evening Standard 1977–78; Political Ed. The Economist 1979–86; columnist, Sunday Times 1986–90, The Spectator 1992–95, The Times 1992–, The Guardian; Ed. The Times 1990–92; Dir Faber and Faber Ltd (publr) 1981–90; mem. Bd Old Vic Co. 1979–81; part-time mem. British Rail Bd 1979–90, London Regional Transport Bd 1984–86; Founder and Dir Railway Heritage Trust 1985–90; Gov. Museum of London 1984–87, Bryanston School 1986–94; Chair. Comm. for Local Democracy 1993–95, Bldg Books Trust 1994–, Booker Prize Judges 2000, The National Trust 2008–; Deputy Chair. Historic Bldgs and Monuments Comm. 1985–90, English Heritage; Trustee, World Monuments Funds 1995–; Dir The Municipal Journal 1980–90; mem. South Bank Bd 1985–90; mem. Millennium Comm. 1994–2000; mem. Human Fertilization and Embryology Authority 2001–; Hon. DLitt (Univ. of London, City Univ.); Edgar Wallace Prize 1997, Rio Tinto David Watt Memorial Prize 1998; Journalist of the Year, Granada Awards 1988, Columnist of the Year 1993. *Publications:* A City at Risk 1971, Landlords to London 1975, Newspapers: The Power and the Money 1979, The Companion Guide to Outer London 1981, Images of Hampstead 1982, The Battle for the Falklands 1983, With Respect, Ambassador 1985, The Market for Glory 1986, The Selling of Mary Davies and other writings 1993, Against the Grain 1994, Accountable to None: The Tory Nationalization of Britain 1995, England's Thousand Best Churches 1999, England's Thousand Best Houses 2003, Big Bang Localism 2004, Thatcher and Sons 2006, Wales: Churches, Houses, Castles 2008. *Leisure interests:* architecture, history of London. *Address:* The National Trust, 32 Queen Anne's Gate, London SW1H 9AB, England (office). *Telephone:* (1793) 817400 (office). *Website:* www.nationaltrust.org.uk (office).

JENNINGS, Hon. Mr Justice John R. R., BA, LLB, QC; Canadian judge; b. 10 July 1937, Toronto, Ont.; s. of Robert D. Jennings and Mary Rogers; m. Eyton Margaret Embury 1964; two s.; ed Upper Canada Coll., Univ. of Toronto and Osgoode Hall Law School, Toronto; past mem. York Co. Legal Aid Area Cttee; mem. and past mem. Council, Medico-Legal Soc.; Chair. Nat. Family Law Section 1974–76; Pres. Co. of York Law Assen 1976; Chair. Bd, Windsor-Essex-Mediation Centre 1981–85; Dir Canadian Bar Insurance Assen 1987–89; Pres. Advocates' Soc. 1987, Canadian Bar Assen 1989–90, Canadian Bar Foundation 1989–90, CBANET Inc. 1989–90; Judge, Superior Court of Justice, Ont., Pres. Canadian Superior Courts Judges' Assen 2001–02; Hon. mem. Law Soc. of England & Wales; Fellow, American Coll. of Trial Lawyers. *Leisure interests:* tennis, travel. *Address:* Osgoode Hall, 130 Queen Street W, Toronto, Ont., M5H 2N5 (office); 70 Montclair Avenue, Apartment 703, Toronto, Ont., M5P 1P7, Canada (home). *Telephone:* (416) 327-5284 (office). *Fax:* (416) 327-5417 (office). *E-mail:* jjennings@judicom.cc.ca (office).

JENNINGS, Sir John (Southwood), Kt, CBE, PhD, FRSE, FGS; British business executive; b. 30 March 1937, Oldbury, Worcs.; s. of the late George Southwood Jennings and of Irene Beatrice (née Bartlett) Jennings; m. 1st Gloria Ann Griffiths 1961 (divorced 1996); one s. one d.; m. 2nd Linda Elizabeth Baston 1997; ed Oldbury Grammar School, Univs. of Birmingham and Edin.; joined Royal Dutch/Shell 1958, various posts, including Gen. Man. and Chief Rep. of Shell cos in Turkey 1976–78, Man. Dir Shell UK Exploration and Production 1979–84, Exploration and Production Co-ordinator, Shell Internationale Petroleum Mij., The Hague 1985–90; Dir The Shell Transport and Trading Co. PLC 1987–2001 (Man. Dir Royal Dutch/Shell Group of Cos. 1987–97, Chair. Shell Transport and Trading Co. 1993–97); Chair. EME (Emerging Market Econs) 2000–, Intelligent Energy 2001, Spectron 2002–; Dir Det Norske Veritas 1997–2001, Robert Fleming Holdings Ltd 1998–2000, the Mitie Group 1998–, Norseman Tectonics 1998–; Vice-Chair. Governing Body London Business School 1993–97 (mem. 1992–97); Vice-Pres. Liverpool School of Tropical Medicine 1991–97; mem. Council Royal Inst. of Int. Affairs 1994–97; Adviser JPMorgan Chase 2000–; Trustee, Edin. Univ. Devt Trust 1996, Exeter Univ. Council 1997–2000, Int. Advisory Bd Toyota Corpn 1997–, Bd of Counsellors Bechtel Corpn 1997–; Hon. DSc (Edin.) 1991, (Birmingham) 1997; Commdr, Ordre Nat. du Mérite (Gabon). *Leisure interests:* fishing, travel, music, wine. *Address:* South Kenwood, Kenton, Exeter, EX6 8EX, England (office).

JENRETTE, Richard Hampton, MBA; American business executive; b. 5 May 1929, Raleigh, NC; s. of Joseph M. Jenrette and Emma Love; ed Univ. of N Carolina and Harvard Grad. School of Business Admin.; New England Life Insurance Co. 1951–53; Brown Bros. Harriman & Co. 1957–59; with Donaldson, Lufkin & Jenrette Inc. (acquired by Credit Suisse Group 2000) 1959–96, Chair. 1986–96; Chair. Bd of Dirs Equitable Life Assurance Soc. 1987–94, Chair Exec. Cttee 1994–96, Chair., CEO Equitable Investment Corpn (now Credit Suisse First Boston) 1986–90; Dir Advanced Micro Devices, Sunnyvale, Calif.; Trustee, Duke Endowment; fmr Trustee The Rockefeller Foundation; Hon. DLitt (Univ. of SC) and other awards. *Publications:* Adventures With Old Houses 2000. *Address:* c/o Board of Trustees, The Duke Endowment, 100 North Tryon Street, Suite 3500, Charlotte, NC 28202-4012 (office); 67 East 93rd Street, New York, NY 10128, USA (home).

JENS, Walter, (Walter Freiburger, Momos), DPhil; German critic, philologist and novelist; *Honorary President, Akademie der Künste Berlin-Brandenburg;* b. 8 March 1923, Hamburg; s. of Walter Jens and Anna Jens (née Martens); m. Inge Puttfarcken 1951; two s.; ed Hamburg and Freiburg im Breisgau Univs; Asst, Univs of Hamburg and Tübingen 1945–49; Dozent, Univ. of Tübingen 1949–56, Prof. of Classical Philology and Rhetoric 1956–88, Prof. Emer. 1988–; Visiting Prof., Univ. of Stockholm 1964, Univ. of Vienna 1984; Dir Seminar für Allgemeine Rhetorik (Tübingen) 1967–; mem. Gruppe 47 1950, German PEN 1961– (Pres. 1976–82, Hon. Pres. 1982–), Berliner Akad. der Künste 1961–, Deutsche Akad. für Sprache und Dichtung 1962–, Deutsche Akad. der Darstellenden Künste (Frankfurt) 1964–, Freie Akad. der Künste (Hamburg) 1964; Pres. Akad. der Künste Berlin-Brandenburg 1989–97, Hon. Pres. 1997–; Hon. DPhil; Prix Amis de la Liberté 1951, Schleussner Schüller Prize 1956, Kulturpreis der deutschen Industrie 1959, Lessing Prize 1968, DAG Prize 1976, Tübinger Universitätsmedaille 1979, Heinrich-Heine Prize 1981, Adolf-Grimme 1984, Theodor-Heuss Prize (with I. Jens) 1988, Alternativer Büchnerpreis 1989, Hermann-Sinsheimer Prize 1989, Österreichischer Staatspreis für Kulturpublizistik 1990, Frankfurter Poetik-Vorlesungen 1992, Österreichisches Verdienstzeichen 1993, Bruno-Snell-Plakette, Univ. of Hamburg 1997, Ernst-Reuter-Plakette 1998, Deutscher Predigtpreis 2002, Corine Int. Buchpreis (with I. Jens) 2003. *Publications include:* Nein–Die Welt der Angeklagten (novel) 1950, Der Blinde (novel) 1951, Vergessene Gesichter (novel) 1952, Der Mann, der nicht alt werden wollte (novel) 1955, Die Stichomythie in der frühen griechischen Tragödie (diss.) 1955, Hofmannsthal und die Griechen 1955, Das Testament des Odysseus (novel) 1957, Statt einer Literaturgeschichte (Essays on Modern Literature) 1957, Moderne Literatur—moderne Wirklichkeit (essay) 1958, Die Götter sind sterblich (Diary of a Journey to Greece) 1959, Deutsche Literatur der Gegenwart 1961, Zueignungen 1962, Herr Meister (Dialogue on a Novel) 1963, Euripides-Büchner 1964, Von deutscher Rede 1969, Die Verschwörung (TV play) 1970, Am Anfang der Stall, am Ende der Galgen 1973, Fernsehen-Themen und Tabus 1973, Der tödliche Schlag (TV play) 1974, Der Prozess Judas (novel) 1975, Der Ausbruch (libretto) 1975, Republikanische Reden 1976, Eine deutsche Universität, 500 Jahre Tübinger Gelehrtenrepublik 1977, Zur Antike 1979, Die Orestie des Aischylos 1979, Warum ich Christ bin (ed.) 1979, Ort der Handlung ist Deutschland (essays) 1979, Die kleine grosse Stadt Tübingen 1981, Der Untergang (drama) 1982, In letzter Stunde (ed.) 1982, Aufruf zum Frieden 1983, In Sachen Lessing 1983, Kanzel und Katheder 1984, Momos am Bildschirm 1984, Dichtung und Religion (with H. Küng) 1985, Roccos Erzählung 1985, Die Friedensfrau 1986, Theologie und Literatur 1986, Das A und das O–die Offenbarung der Johannes 1987, Deutsche Lebensläufe 1987, Feldzüge eines Republikaners 1988, Juden und Christen in Deutschland 1988, Reden 1989, Schreibschule 1991, Die sieben letzten Worte am Kreuz 1992, Die Friedensfrau 1992, Mythen der Dichter 1993, Am Anfang das Wort 1993, Menschenwürdig sterben 1995, Macht der Erinnerung 1997, Aus gegebenem Anlass 1998, Wer am besten red't ist der reinste Mensch 2000, Der Römerbrief 2000, 'Der Teufel lebt nicht mehr, mein Herr': Erdachte Monologe – imaginäre Gespräche 2001, Pathos und Präzision, Texte zur Theologie 2002, Frau Thomas Mann: Das Leben der Katharina Pringsheim (with I. Jens) 2003, Katias Mutter: Das ausserordentliche Leben der Hedwig Pringsheim (with I. Jens) 2005, Auf der Suche nach dem verlorenen Sohn. Die Südamerika-Reise der Hedwig Pringsheim (with I. Jens) 2006, Psalm 104 (to G. Klebe, Composition 104 Psalm) 2007. *Address:* Sonnenstrasse 5, 72076 Tübingen, Germany (home). *Fax:* (7071) 600693 (home). *E-mail:* danielseger@web.de.

JENSEN, Arthur Robert, PhD; American educational psychologist and academic; *Professor Emeritus, Graduate School of Education, University of California, Berkeley;* b. 24 Aug. 1923, San Diego, Calif.; s. of Arthur Alfred Jensen and Linda Schachtmayer; m. Barbara Jane Delarme 1960; one d.; ed Calif. (Berkeley), Columbia and London Univs; Asst in Medical Psychology, Univ. of Maryland 1955–56; Research Fellow, Inst. of Psychiatry, London Univ. 1956–58; Asst Prof. to Prof. of Educational Psychology, Univ. of Calif., Berkeley 1958–94, Prof. Emer. 1994–; Research Psychologist, Inst. of Human Learning 1962–; Guggenheim Fellow 1964–65; Fellow, Center for Advanced Study in the Behavioral Sciences 1966–67; Visiting Lecturer, Melbourne, La Trobe, Adelaide and Sydney Univs. 1977, various univs in India 1980, China and Taiwan 2002; Galton Lecture, London 1999; Distinguished Research Contrib. Award, Int. Soc. for the Study of Individual Differences 2003, Kistler Prize 2003, 2004. *Publications:* Genetics and Education 1972, Educability and Group Differences 1973, Educational Differences 1973, Bias in Mental Testing 1980, Straight Talk About Mental Tests 1981, The *g* Factor 1998, Clocking the Mind 2006. *Leisure interests:* classical music, swimming. *Address:* School of Education, 4511 Tolman, University of California, Berkeley, CA 94720-1670 (office); 30 Canyon View Drive, Orinda, CA 94563, USA. *Telephone:* (510) 642-4201 (office). *E-mail:* jep@socrates.berkeley.edu (office). *Website:* www-gse.berkeley.edu (office).

JENSEN, Elwood V., PhD; American academic and cancer researcher; *George and Elizabeth Wile Chair for Cancer Research, University of Cincinnati;* b. 13 Jan. 1920, Fargo, ND; s. of Eli A. Jensen and Vera Morris Jensen; m. 1st Mary Collette 1941 (died 1982); one s. one d.; m. 2nd Hiltrud Herborg 1983; ed Wittenberg Coll. and Univ., of Chicago; Guggenheim Fellowship E.T.H. Zürich 1946–47; Asst Prof. Dept of Surgery, Univ. of Chicago 1947–51, Asst Prof. Ben May Lab. for Cancer Research and Dept of Biochemistry 1951–54, Assoc. Prof. 1954–60, Prof. Ben May Lab. for Cancer Research 1960–63, American Cancer Soc. Research Prof. Ben May Lab. and Dept of Physiology 1963–69, Prof. Dept of Physiology 1969–73, Dept of Biophysics and Theoretical Biology 1973–84, Dept of Physiological and Pharmacological Sciences 1977–84, Dept of Biochemistry 1980–90, Dir Ben May Lab. for Cancer Research 1969–82, Charles B. Huggins Distinguished Service Prof. Univ. of Chicago 1981–90, Prof. Emer. 1990–; Research Dir Ludwig Inst. for Cancer Research, Zürich 1983–87; scholar-in-residence Fogarty Int. Center NIH 1988–2001, Cornell Univ. Medical Coll. 1990–91;

Visiting Scientist Inst. for Hormone and Fertility Research, Hamburg, Germany 1991–97; Visiting Prof. Karolinska Inst., Sweden 1998–2001, STINT Visiting Scientist 1998–99, Prof. Emer. 1999–2001; Visiting Scientist Nat. Inst. of Child Health and Human Devt (NICH/NIH) 2001; Visiting Prof. Univ. of Cincinnati Medical Centre 2002–, now George and Elizabeth Wile Chair for Cancer Research; Nobel Ass. Fellowship 1998; mem. Research Advisory Bd Clinical Research Inst., Montreal 1987–96; mem. Scientific Advisory Bd Klinik für Tumorbiologie, Freiburg 1993–2002, Strang Cancer Prevention Center, New York 1994–98; mem. NAS (mem. Council 1981–84), American Acad. of Arts and Sciences; Hon. DSc (Wittenberg Univ.) 1963, (Acadia Univ.) 1976, (Medical Coll. Ohio) 1991; Hon. MD (Hamburg Univ.) 1995, (Univ. of Athens) 2005; American Asscn for Cancer Research Dorothy P. Landon Prize 2002, Albert Lasker Award for Basic Medical Research (jtly) 2004. *Publications:* 236 articles and reviews since 1945. *Leisure interests:* tennis, squash, riding. *Address:* Department of Cell Biology, University of Cincinnati, Vontz Center for Molecular Studies, 3125 Eden Avenue, Cincinnati, OH 45267-0521 (office); 216 East Martin Luther King Drive, Apartment C, Cincinnati, OH 45219, USA (home). *Telephone:* (513) 558-5750 (office); (513) 961-1808 (home). *Fax:* (513) 558-4454 (office). *E-mail:* elwood.jensen@uc.edu (office). *Website:* cna.uc.edu (office).

JENSEN, Hans Peter, PhD, DSc; Danish chemist and researcher; *Research Director, Danish Institute for Food and Veterinary Research;* b. 11 June 1943, Copenhagen; m. Helle Rønnow Olesen 1965; two s. one d.; ed Univ. of Copenhagen, Chalmers Univ. of Tech., Gothenburg; Asst Prof. Tech. Univ. of Denmark 1969, Assoc. Prof. 1972, Head of Chem. Dept A. 1980–83, Dean of Chem. Faculty 1983–86, Rector 1986–2001; Deputy Dir Inst. of Food Safety and Nutrition 2001–04; Research Dir Danish Inst. for Food and Veterinary Research 2004–; Research Assoc. Univ. of Oregon 1974–75, Visiting Prof. 1978, 1984; mem. Danish Natural Science Research Council 1984–92, Danish Acad. of Tech. Sciences, Cttee on Higher Educ. and Research (Council of Europe) 1986–2001, Evaluation Group of European Postgrad. Training Programme 1989–93, Cultural Foundation between Denmark and Finland 1989–97, Fulbright Comm. of Denmark 1990–2001; mem. Advisory Forum European Food Safety Authority 2003–, Velux Foundation 2004–; Chair. Danish Rectors' Conf. 1993–2000; Chair. Asscn of Nordic Univ. Rectors' Confs. 1995–2001; mem. Bd of Govs, Jt Research Centre of EU 2001–; Commdr Order of Dannebrog 1999; Dr hc (Shenandoah Univ., USA) 1993, (Helsinki Univ. of Tech.) 1998, (State Univ. of NY) 1998. *Publications:* General Chemistry (textbook) 1985; articles in professional journals. *Leisure interests:* music, literature. *Address:* Danish Institute for Food and Veterinary Research, Bülowsvej 27, 1790 Copenhagen (office); Jagtvej 172, 2100 Copenhagen Ø, Denmark (home). *Telephone:* 72-34-61-04 (office); 39-65-34-29 (home). *Fax:* 72-34-60-01 (office). *E-mail:* hpj@dfvf.dk (office). *Website:* www.dfvf.dk (office).

JENSEN, Ole Vig; Danish politician; b. 17 May 1936, Frederikssund; fmr teacher; mem. Folketing (Parl.) 1971–73, 1978–, mem. Presidium 1984–; mem. Gen. Council, Social Liberal Party 1968–, Exec. Council 1974–, Deputy Chair. Parl. Group 1979–; mem. Cen. Land Bd 1983–; Chair. Parl. Cttee for Agric. and Fisheries 1979–84; Deputy Chair. Parl. Educ. Cttee 1979–82; Minister of Cultural Affairs 1988–90, of Educ. 1993–98. *Address:* c/o Ministry of Education and Research, Frederiksholms Kanal 21, 1220 Copenhagen K, Denmark.

JENSSEN, Olav Christopher; Norwegian artist; *Professor of Painting, Hochschule fur Bildende Kunst, Hamburg;* b. 1954, Sortland, Vesteraland; ed Statens Kunstakademi, Oslo; Prof. of Painting, Hochschule fur Bildende Kunst, Hamburg 1996–; official artist, Offshore Northern Seas Int. Conf. (ONS) 2000. *Exhibitions include:* anti-smoking poster for WHO; mural, Nordic Embassy, Berlin; mosaic, Telenor Hovedkvarter, Fornebu, Norway; Vongole (Malmo Konsthall, Sweden) 1997, The Empty Drawing Room (Göttingen, Germany) 2000, Bergen Int. Festival 2000, Palindrome (Bergens Kunstforening, Norway) 2001, Anthony Wilkinson Gallery, London 2001, Baltic Gallery, Gateshead 2003; works on show in numerous public collections in Europe and USA. *Address:* c/o Hochschule fur Bildende Kunst, Lerchenfeld 2, 22081 Hamburg, Germany.

JENTSCH, Thomas J., PhD, MD; German neuropathologist and academic; *Professor and Director, Institute for Molecular Neuropathology, Zentrum für Molekulare Neurobiologie Hamburg;* ed Free Univ., Berlin and Fritz-Haber-Institut, Max-Planck-Gesellschaft; Postdoctoral Researcher, Institut für Klinische Physiologie, Free Univ., Berlin and Whitehead Inst. for Biomedical Research, MIT, USA; Research Group Leader, Zentrum für Molekulare Neurobiologie Hamburg (ZMNH), Hamburg Univ., Prof. and Dir Institute for Molecular Neuropathology, ZMNH 1993–, Dir ZMNH 1995–98, 2001–03; mem. Int. Scientific Advisory Bd, Instituto de Ciencias Biomédicas de la Universidad de Chile; mem. Academia Europaea 2000, European Molecular Biology Org. (EMBO) 2000, Berlin-Brandenburg Acad. of Sciences and Humanities 2001; Wilhelm Vaillant Prize for Biomedical Research 1992, Gottfried Wilhelm Leibniz Prize, Deutsche Forschungsgemeinschaft 1995, Alfred Hauptmann Prize for Research on Epilepsy 1998, Franz Volhard Prize for Research in Nephrology 1998, Zülch Prize, Gertrud-Reemtsma Foundation 1999, Feldberg Prize, Feldberg Foundation for Anglo-German Scientific Exchange 2000, Familie Hansen Prize 2000, Prix Louis-Jeantet de médecine 2000, Ernst Jung Prize for Medicine 2001, Adolf-Fick Prize for Physiology 2004, Homer W. Smith Award for Nephrology 2004. *Publications:* numerous articles in scientific journals. *Address:* Institut für Molekulare Neuropathobiologie, Zentrum für Molekulare Neurobiologie Hamburg, University of Hamburg, Falkenried 94, 20251 Hamburg, Germany (office). *Telephone:* (40) 42803-4741 (office). *Fax:* (40) 42803-4839 (office). *E-mail:* Jentsch@zmnh.uni-hamburg.de (office). *Website:* www.zmnh.uni-hamburg.de (office).

JEONG, Se-hyun; South Korean politician; *Minister of Unification;* ed Seoul Nat. Univ.; entered Ministry of Unification 1977, Vice-Minister of Unification 1998–99, Minister 1999–; represented S Korea during inter-Korean talks on Seoul's provision of fertilizer aid to N Korea and reunion of separated families 1998; Special Adviser to Head of Nat. Intelligence Service 2001–. *Address:* Ministry of Unification, 77-6, Sejong-no, Jongno-gu, Seoul 110-760, Republic of Korea (office). *Telephone:* (2) 720-2424 (office). *Fax:* (2) 720-2149 (office). *Website:* www.unikorea.go.kr (office).

JEREMIĆ, Vuk, PhD, MPA; Serbian politician; *Minister of Foreign Affairs;* b. 3 July 1975, Belgrade; m.; ed Univ. of Cambridge, Imperial Coll., London, UK and Harvard Univ., USA; fmr Financial Analyst, Deutsche Bank, Dresdner Kleinwort Benson Bank and AstraZeneca Pharmaceuticals, London; Adviser to Minister of Telecommunications 2000–03; Adviser to Minister of Defence of Serbia and Montenegro 2003–04; Adviser on Int. Relations and Head, Office of the Pres. of Serbia 2004–07; Minister of Foreign Affairs 2007–; f. Org. of Serbian Students Abroad (OSSI); mem. Demokratska Stranka (Democratic Party), Pres. Bd of Int. Relations 2004–06, mem. Exec. Bd 2006–. *Address:* Ministry of Foreign Affairs, 11000 Belgrade, Kneza Miloša 24–26, Serbia (office). *Telephone:* (11) 3616333 (office). *Fax:* (11) 3618366 (office). *E-mail:* msp@smip.sv.gov.yu (office). *Website:* www.mfa.gov.yu (office).

JERUSALEM, Siegfried; German singer (tenor), academic and university administrator; *Rector, Hochschule für Musik Nürnberg-Augsburg;* b. 17 April 1940, Oberhausen; m. 1980; one s. one d.; ed studied violin and piano at Folkwang Hochschule, Essen, studied singing with Hertha Kalcher, Stuttgart; played bassoon in German orchestras, including Stuttgart Radio Symphony Orchestra 1961–77; made singing debut in Zigeunerbaron 1975; debut Bayreuth Festival 1977, Metropolitan Opera, New York 1980, La Scala 1981, Vienna State Opera 1979; sang Loge and Siegfried, Wagner's Ring Cycle, Metropolitan New York 1990, Tristan, Bayreuth 1993, Wagner's Ring Cycle, Vienna 1994, Wagner's Rienzi, Vienna 1997, Tristana, Berlin Staatsoper 2000; Prof., Hochschule für Musik Nürnberg-Augsburg 2000–, Rector 2001–; Order of Merit (Germany) 1997; Grammy Award for Wagner's Ring Cycle 1982, for Rheingold 1991, Bundesverdienstkreuz (1st Class) 1996, Bambi Award 1996. *Leisure interests:* video, tennis, photography, golf. *Address:* Hochschule für Musik Nürnberg-Augsburg, Veilhofstr. 34, 90489 Nürnberg, Germany (office). *Telephone:* (911) 2318443 (office). *Fax:* (911) 2317697 (office). *E-mail:* hfm-rektorat@stadt.nuernberg.de (office). *Website:* www.hfm-n-a.de (office).

JERVIS, Robert, BA, PhD; American political scientist and academic; *Adlai E. Stevenson Professor of International Affairs, Columbia University;* ed Oberlin Coll., Univ. of Calif. at Berkeley; Asst Prof. of Govt, Harvard Univ. 1968–74, Assoc. Prof. 1972–74; Prof. of Political Science, Univ. of Calif. at LA 1974–80; fmr Prof. Yale Univ., Hebrew Univ.; currently Adlai E. Stevenson Professor of Int. Affairs, Columbia Univ.; Vice-Pres. American Political Science Asscn (APSA) 1988–89, Pres. 1999–2000; Co-Ed. Security Studies Series, Cornell Univ. Press; Fellow AAAS, American Acad. of Arts and Sciences; mem. bd of eight scholarly journals; Career Achievement Award, Security Studies Section, Int. Studies Asscn 1996, Nevitt Sanford Award for Distinguished Professional Contrib. to Political Psychology 1998, Lionel Trilling Award for Best Book by Columbia Faculty Mem. 1998; NAS Award for Behavioral Science Research Relevant to the Prevention of Nuclear War 2006. *Publications:* The Logic of Images in International Relations 1970, Perception and Misperception in International Politics 1976, The Illogic of American Nuclear Strategy 1984, Psychology and Deterrence (co-author) 1985, The Meaning of the Nuclear Revolution (Grawemeyer Award for Ideas Improving World Order 1990) 1989, Systems Effects: Complexity in Political and Social Life 1997, International Politics; Enduring Concepts and Contemporary Issues (co-ed.) 1999, The Origins of Major War (co-ed.) 2000, American Foreign Policy in a New Era 2005; numerous articles in professional journals and chapters in books. *Address:* Department of Political Science, International Affairs Building, Floor 7, 420 West 118th Street, New York, NY 10027, USA (office). *Telephone:* (212) 854-4616 (office). *Fax:* (212) 864-1686 (office). *E-mail:* rlj1@columbia.edu (office). *Website:* www.columbia.edu/cu/polisci (office).

JERVIS, Simon Swynfen, MA, FSA; British art historian; b. 9 Jan. 1943, Yoxford; s. of the late John Swynfen Jervis and of Diana Parker (née Marriott); m. Fionnuala MacMahon 1969; one s. one d.; ed Downside School, Corpus Christi Coll., Cambridge; with Leicester Museum and Art Gallery 1964–66; Asst Keeper, Furniture Dept, Vic. and Albert Museum 1966–75, Deputy Keeper 1975–79, Acting Keeper 1989, Curator 1989–90; Dir Fitzwilliam Museum, Cambridge 1990–95; Dir of Historic Bldgs, Nat. Trust 1995–2002; mem. Council, Soc. of Antiquaries 1986–88 (Pres. 1995–2001), Royal Archaeological Inst. 1987–91, Walpole Soc. 1990–95 (Chair. 2004–), Kelmscott Cttee 2001–; Chair. Nat. Trust Arts Panel 1987–95; Ed. Furniture History Soc. 1987–91, Chair. 1998–; Dir Burlington Magazine 1993–, Trustee 1997–; Guest Scholar, J. Paul Getty Museum 1988–89; Trustee, Royal Collection Trust 1993–2001, Leche Trust 1995–, Sir John Soane's Museum 1999– (Life Trustee 2002–); Iris Foundation Award for Outstanding Contributions to the Decorative Arts 2002. *Publications:* Victorian Furniture 1968, Victorian and Edwardian Decorative Art: the Handley Read Collection 1972, Printed Furniture Designs Before 1650 1974, High Victorian Design 1974, The Penguin Dictionary of Design and Designers 1984, Furniture from Austria and Hungary in the Victoria and Albert Museum 1986. *Leisure interests:* churches, tennis. *Address:* 45 Bedford Gardens, London, W8 7EF, England (office). *Telephone:* (20) 7727-8739 (home). *Fax:* (20) 7727-8739 (home).

JESIH, Boris, PhD; Slovenian artist and poet; b. 8 Aug. 1943, Škofja Loka; s. of Svetoslav and Kristina Jesih; m. Bojana Žokalj 1970 (divorced 1981); one s. one d.; ed Acad. of Fine Arts, Ljubljana, Berlin; works appear in numerous collections; has published several books of poetry; Ed.-in-Chief Razprave in Gradivo, Inst. of Ethnic Studies, Ljubljana; 10 nat. and 10 int. awards. *Publications include:* The Apple Tree and the Grafts 1979. *Leisure interests:* basketball, fishing. *Address:* Department of Fine Arts Education, University of Ljubljana, Kardeljeva Ploscad 16, 1000 Ljubljana (office). *Telephone:* (1) 589-22-00 (office). *Fax:* (1) 589-22-33 (office). *Website:* www.pef.uni-lj.si/index_en.html (office).

JESSEN-PETERSEN, Søren; Danish UN official; m.; four c.; trained as lawyer and journalist; served in Africa UNHCR 1972–77, Chief of Secr. UNHCR Exec. Cttee 1981–82, Exec. Sec. Second Int. Conf. on Assistance to Refugees in Africa 1983–84, Exec. Sec. Intergovernmental Conf. on Asylum Seekers and Refugees in Europe 1985, opened UNHCR Regional Office for Nordic Countries, Stockholm 1986, served as High Commr's Regional Rep. 1986–89; Special Adviser to UN Under-Sec.-Gen. for Political Affairs 1989; mem. UN Sec.-Gen.'s Task Force on Namibia 1989; Chef de Cabinet of High Commr UNHCR 1990–93, Dir External Relations 1992–94, Dir UNHCR Liaison Office at UN HQ, NY 1994–98, UN Special Envoy to fmr Yugoslavia 1995–96, Asst High Commr UNHCR, Geneva 1998–2001; Chair. EU Stability Pact's Migration, Asylum, Refugees Regional Initiative (MARRI), Chair. MARRI Steering Cttee 2002–04; EU Special Rep. in Skopje 2004; Special Rep. of UN Sec.-Gen. and Head, UN Interim Admin Mission in Kosovo (UNMIK) 2004–06. *Address:* c/o Ministry of Foreign Affairs, Asiatisk Pl. 2, 1448 Copenhagen K, Denmark.

JESZENSZKY, Géza, PhD; Hungarian historian and politician; b. 10 Nov. 1941, Budapest; s. of Zoltán Jeszenszky and Pálma Miskolczy-Simon; m. Edit Héjj; one s. one d.; ed Eötvös Loránd Univ., Budapest; banned from higher educ. for two years 1956–57; subject specialist with Nat. Széchényi Library 1968–76; Sr Lecturer, Budapest Univ. of Econs (now Corvinus Univ. of Budapest) 1976–81, Reader 1981–, Dean of the School of Political and Social Sciences 1989–90, Head, Faculty of Int. Relations 1990–91; Guest Scholar, Woodrow Wilson Center, USA 1985; Visiting Fulbright Prof., Univ. of Santa Barbara, Calif. 1984–86 and UCLA, USA 1986; Helen De Roy Visiting Prof., Univ. of Michigan, Ann Arbor, USA 1996; Visiting Prof., Coll. of Europe, Warsaw-Natolin, Babes-Bolyai Univ., Cluj-Napoca/Kolozsvár, Romania; Founding mem. Hungarian Democratic Forum 1988–96, Head Foreign Affairs Cttee 1988–90, mem. Presidency 1990–94; Minister of Foreign Affairs 1990–94; mem. Parl. 1994–98; Pres. Hungarian Atlantic Council 1995–98; Amb. to USA 1998–2002; Pres. Hungarian Carpathian Asscn; numerous decorations; C.I.E.S. Fulbright Grant 1984–86. *Publications:* Prestige Lost, The Changing Image of Hungary in Great Britain 1894–1918 1986, The Hungarian Question in British Politics 1848–1914 1986, István Tisza: Villain or Tragic Hero? 1987, Lessons of Appeasement 1994, More Bosnias? National and Ethnic Tensions in the Post-Communist World 1997; other studies in Hungarian and English. *Leisure interests:* literature, jazz, skiing, rowing, mountaineering. *Address:* c/o Ministry of Foreign Affairs, Bem rkp. 47, 1027 Budapest, Hungary (office).

JETER, Derek Sanderson; American professional baseball player; b. 26 June 1974, Pequannock, NJ; s. of Charles Jeter and Dorothy Jeter; ed Kalamazoo Central High School, Mich.; drafted by NY Yankees in first round amateur draft 1992; Major League Baseball (MLB) debut 29 May 1995; Capt. NY Yankees; shortstop on Yankees team that won four World Series titles in five years; apptd Capt. 2003; 1,290 career runs; Founder and Pres. Turn2 Foundation 1996–; American Baseball Coaches Asscn High School Player of the Year 1992; American League Rookie of the Year 1996; selected for American League All-Star Team 1998–2002, 2004, 2006; Most Valuable Player (MVP) World Series 2000; MVP All-Star Game 2000. *Publications:* The Life Yyou Imagine 2001, Game Day—My Life On and Off the Field 2001. *Address:* c/o New York Yankees, Yankee Stadium, East 161st Street and River Avenue, New York, NY 10452, USA. *Telephone:* (718) 293-4300. *Fax:* (718) 293-8431. *Website:* derekjeter.mlb.com/players/jeter_derek/index.jsp; newyork.yankees.mlb.com; www.turn2foundation.org.

JETTOU, Driss; Moroccan politician; b. 24 May 1945, El Jadida; m.; four c.; ed Lycée El Khawarizmi de Casablanca, Univ. of Rabat, Cordwainers Coll., London, UK; fmr Pres. Moroccan Fed. of Leather Industries (FEDIC); fmr Vice-Pres. Moroccan Asscn of Exporters (ASMEX); Minister of Trade and Industry 1994–95, of Culture and Foreign Trade 1995–97, of Trade, Industry and Culture 1997–98, of the Interior 1998–2002; Prime Minister of Morocco 2002–07; apptd Pres. Office Cherifien des Phosphates (OCP) 2002; fmr mem. Gen. Confed. of Moroccan Enterprises (CGEM); Grande Chevalier, Wissam du Trône. *Address:* c/o Office of the Prime Minister, Palais Royal, Le Méchouar, Rabat, Morocco (office).

JEUNET, Jean-Pierre; French film director; b. 1955, Roanne; worked as telecommunications engineer; dir of TV commercials and short films. *Films:* L'évasion 1978, Le manège (César Award) 1980 (both co-dir with Marc Caro), Le bunker de la dernière rafale 1981, Pas de repos pour Billy Brakko 1984, Foutaises (César Award) 1989, Delicatessen (César Award) 1991, Le cité des enfants perdus 1995, Alien: Resurrection 1997, Le fabuleux destin d'Amélie Poulain (Amélie) (Amanda Award, American Screenwriters Asscn Award, Bafta Film Award, David Lean Award for Direction, Canberra Int. Film Festival Audience Award, Chicago Int. Film Festival Audience Award, Czech Lion, César Award) 2001, Un long dimanche de fiançailles 2004. *Address:* c/o Artmédia, 20 Avenue Rapp, 75 007 Paris, France. *Telephone:* 1-43-17-33-00 (office). *Website:* www.jpjeunetlesite.online.fr.

JEWISON, Norman Frederick, BA, CC, DD; Canadian film director; b. 21 July 1926, Toronto; s. of Percy Joseph and Dorothy Irene (née Weaver) Jewison; m. Margaret Dixon 1953; two s. one d.; ed Malvern Collegiate High School, Toronto, Victoria Coll., Univ. of Toronto; stage actor, Toronto; TV actor

1950–52; TV director for CBC 1953–58, CBS 1958–61; film director 1961–; Faculty mem. Inst. for American Studies, Salzburg, Austria 1969; Pres. D'Avoriaz Film Festival 1981–; Dir Centre for Advanced Film Studies 1987–; director TV shows for Harry Belafonte, Andy Williams, Judy Garland and Danny Kaye; mem. Electoral Bd, Dirs Guild of America; mem. Canadian Arts Council; Chair. Canadian Film Centre 2002; Chancellor Victoria Coll., Univ. of Toronto 2004; Hon. LLD (Univ. of Western Ont.) 1974; Acad. of Canada Special Achievement Award 1988, Emmy Award 1960, Golden Globe Award 1966, Best Dir, Berlin Film Festival for Moonstruck 1988, Irving Thalberg Memorial Prize 1999. *Films include:* Forty Pounds of Trouble, The Thrill of It All 1963, Send Me No Flowers 1964 (all for Universal Studios), Art of Love, The Cincinnati Kid 1965, The Russians are Coming (also producer) 1966, In the Heat of the Night (Acad. Award 1967), The Thomas Crown Affair (also producer) 1967, Gaily, Gaily 1968, The Landlord (producer) 1969, Fiddler on the Roof (also producer) 1970, Jesus Christ Superstar (also producer) 1972, Billy Two Hats (producer) 1972, Rollerball 1974, F.I.S.T. (also producer) 1977, And Justice for All 1979, Best Friends 1982, A Soldier's Story 1984, Agnes of God 1985, Moonstruck 1987, In Country 1989, Other People's Money 1991, Only You 1994, Bogus 1996, The Hurricane 1999, Dinner with Friends (tv) 2001, The Statement 2003. *Leisure interests:* skiing, yachting, tennis. *Address:* 18 Gloucester Lane, Toronto, Ont. M4Y IL5, Canada. *Telephone:* (416) 923-2787 (office). *Fax:* (416) 923-8580 (office).

JEWKES, Sir Gordon Wesley, Kt, KCMG; British diplomatist; b. 18 Nov. 1931, Langley Moor, Co. Durham; s. of the late Jesse Jewkes; m. 1st Joyce Lyons 1954 (died 2005); two s.; m. 2nd Estelle Heime 2008; ed Barrow Grammar School, Magnus Grammar School, Newark-on-Trent; joined Colonial Office 1948; with army 1950–52; with Gen. Register Office 1950–63, 1965–68; mem. Civil Service Pay Research Unit 1963–65; joined FCO 1968; Commercial Consul, Chicago 1969–72, Consul-Gen. 1982–85; Deputy High Commr, Port of Spain 1972–75; Head of Finance Dept, FCO and Finance Officer of Diplomatic Service 1975–79; Consul-Gen. Cleveland 1979–82; Gov. Falkland Islands, Commr S Georgia and S Sandwich Islands, High Commr British Antarctic Territory 1985–88; Consul-Gen., New York and Dir-Gen. Trade and Investment, USA 1989–91; mem. Bd of Dirs Hogg Group PLC 1992–94, Slough Estates PLC 1992–2002; Exec. Dir The Walpole Cttee 1992–96; mem. Council Univ. of Buckingham 1996–2001, Marshall Aid Commemoration Comm. 1996–99, Salvation Army London Advisory Bd 1996–2001; Hon. DUniv (Buckingham) 2007. *Leisure interests:* music, travel, walking. *Address:* 23 Crabtree Close, Beaconsfield, Bucks., HP9 1UQ, England (home).

JHA, Nagendra Nath, BA; Indian diplomatist and politician; b. 5 Jan. 1935; ed Delhi Univ., Univ. of Cambridge, UK; joined Foreign Service 1957, Amb. to Ireland 1977–79, to Turkey 1979–1981, to Kuwait 1984–89, to Yugoslavia 1989–1990, to Sri Lanka 1990–93; Lt-Gov. Union Territories of Andaman and Nicobar Islands 2001–04; Lt-Gov. Pondicherry Jan.–June 2004; mem. Bharatiya Janata Party (BJP) Nat. Exec. 1994, Convenor BJP Foreign Affairs Cttee 1998. *Address:* c/o Bharatiya Janata Party, 11 Ashok Road, New Delhi, 110 001, India (office). *Telephone:* (11) 23382234 (office). *Fax:* (11) 23782163 (office). *E-mail:* bjpco@del3.vsnl.net.in (office). *Website:* www.bjp.org (office).

JHA, Parmanand, LLM, MA; Nepalese lawyer and politician; *Vice-President;* b. 20 April 1945, Mauaha, Saptari; s. of the late Madan Jha; m.; two s. two d.; ed Tribhuvan Univ., Kathmandu, Vrije Univ. Brussels, Belgium; joined civil service as Section Officer 1972, becoming Jt Sec., Ministry of Justice 1976; Judge, Kathmandu Dist Court, Zonal and Appellate courts, later Ad Hoc Justice, Supreme Court –2007 (resgnd); mem. Madhesi Jana Adhikar Forum Nepal (Madhesi People's Rights Forum Nepal); Vice-Pres. of Nepal 2008–. *Address:* Office of the Vice President, Kathmandu (office); Boudh Dwar Marg, Kumarigal 446/14, Ward No. 8, Kathmandu, Nepal (home). *Telephone:* 4228199 (office); 4486118 (home). *Fax:* 4228284 (office); 4486118 (home). *E-mail:* vicepresidentnp@gmail.com (office); Kumarigal 2062@hotmail.com (office).

JHA, Sanjay K., BSc, PhD; British/American computer engineer and business executive; *Co-CEO, Motorola, Inc.;* b. India; ed Univs of Liverpool and Strathclyde, UK; moved to US from UK 1994; held lead design eng roles with Brooktree Corpn, San Diego, and GEC Hirst Research Labs, London, UK; joined Qualcomm as Sr Engineer with VLSI (very large-scale integration) Group 1994–97, Vice-Pres. of Eng 1997–98, Sr Vice-Pres. of Eng 1998–2002, led formation of Qualcomm Technologies & Ventures 2002, managed both tech. investment portfolio and new tech. group as Sr Vice-Pres. and Gen. Man. 2002–03, Exec. Vice-Pres. Qualcomm and Pres. Qualcomm CDMA Technologies (chipset and software div.) 2003–06, COO Qualcomm Inc. 2006–08, oversaw Corp. Research and Devt and Qualcomm Flarion Technologies; joined Motorola, Inc. in 2008, mem. Bd of Dirs and Co-CEO 2008–, also CEO Motorola Mobile Devices business. *Address:* Motorola, Inc., 1303 East Algonquin Road, Schaumburg, IL 60196, USA (office). *Telephone:* (847) 576-5000 (office). *Fax:* (847) 576-5372 (office). *E-mail:* info@motorola.com (office). *Website:* www.motorola.com (office).

JHABVALA, Ruth Prawer, CBE, MA; British/American author and screenwriter; b. 7 May 1927, Cologne, Germany; d. of Marcus Prawer and Eleonora Cohn; sister of Siegbert Salomon Prawer (q.v.); m. C. S. H. Jhabvala 1951; three d.; ed Hendon Co. School and London Univ.; born in Germany of Polish parentage; refugee to England 1939; lived in India 1951–75, in USA 1975–; Neill Gunn Int. Fellowship 1979; Booker Award for best novel 1975, MacArthur Foundation Award 1984, Acad. Award for Best Screenplay 1986, 1992. *Film screenplays:* Shakespeare-Wallah 1965, The Guru 1969, Bombay Talkie 1970, Autobiography of a Princess 1975, Roseland 1977, Hullabaloo over Georgie and Bonnie's Pictures (TV) 1978, The Europeans 1979, Jane Austen in Manhattan 1980, Quartet 1981, The Courtesans of Bombay (TV)

1983, The Bostonians 1984, A Room with a View 1986, Madame Sousatzka 1988, Mr & Mrs Bridge 1989, Howards End 1992, The Remains of the Day 1993, Jefferson in Paris 1995, Surviving Picasso 1996, A Soldier's Daughter Never Cries 1998, The Golden Bowl 2000, Le Divorce 2003. *Publications:* novels: To Whom She Will 1955, Nature of Passion 1956, Esmond in India 1958, The Householder (also screenplay) 1960, Get Ready for Battle 1962, A Backward Place 1962, A New Dominion 1971, Heat and Dust (also screenplay) 1975, In Search of Love and Beauty 1983, Three Continents 1987, Poet and Dancer 1993, Shards of Memory 1995, My Nine Lives 2004; short story collections: A Stronger Climate 1968, An Experience of India 1970, How I Became a Holy Mother 1976, Out of India: Selected Stories 1986, East into Upper East 1998. *Address:* 400 East 52nd Street, New York, NY 10022, USA (home).

JI, Chaozhu, BSc; Chinese diplomatist (retired); b. 30 July 1929, Shanxi Prov.; s. of Prof. Chi Kungchuan; m. Wang Xiangtong 1957; two s.; ed Harvard Univ., USA, Tsinghua Univ., Beijing; stenographer and typist at Panmunjom, Korea for Chinese People's Volunteers 1952–54; English interpreter for Mao Zedong, Zhou Enlai and others 1955–73; Counsellor at Liaison Office of China in Washington, DC 1973–75; Deputy Dir Dept for Int. Orgs and Confs, Ministry of Foreign Affairs 1975–79, Deputy Dir of American and Oceanic Affairs 1979–82; Minister-Counsellor of Chinese Embassy in Washington, DC 1982–85; Amb. to Fiji, Kiribati and Vanuatu 1985–87; Amb. to UK 1987–91; UN Under-Sec. for Tech. Co-operation for Devt 1991–92; Under-Sec.-Gen., Dept of Econ. Devt 1992–96 (now Dept for Devt, Support and Man. Services); Vice-Chair. All-China Fed. of Returned Overseas Chinese 1997–2005; Sr Consultant China Inst. of Int. Strategic Studies 1997–; Patron Int. Managers Org. *Publications:* The Man on Mao's Right: From Harvard Yard to Tiananmen Square, My Life Inside China's Foreign Ministry (memoir) 2008. *Leisure interests:* swimming, archaeology, history. *Address:* c/o All–China Federation of Returned Chinese, 112-01 Queens Boulevard, Apartment 18, Huatian Mansion, 26th Floor, Lianhuachi East Road, Haidian District, Beijing 100038, People's Republic of China.

JI, Xianlin; Chinese university professor; b. 6 Aug. 1911, Shandong Prov.; one s. one d.; ed Tsinghua Univ., Beijing, Univ. of Göttingen, FRG; Prof., Dir Dept of Oriental Languages, Beijing Univ. 1946; disappeared during Cultural Revolution; Vice-Pres. Beijing Univ. 1978–84; Dir South Asian Inst., Chinese Acad. of Social Sciences 1978–85; Pres. Foreign Languages Research Soc. 1981; Pres. Soc. of Linguistics 1986, Soc. for Study of Africa and Asia, Dunhuang-Turpan Soc.; Vice-Pres. China Educ. Asscn for Int. Exchanges 1988–; Adviser, Chinese Writers' Asscn 1996–; Lifetime Achievement Award, Govt of China, for contribs to translation 2006; Padma Bhushan (India) 2008. *Publications include:* Collected Papers on the History of Cultural Relations Between China and India 1982, Studying the Ramayana 1981, Selected Papers on the Languages of Ancient India 1982 and trans. of various Indian classics including seven vols of Valmiki's Ramayana 1980, Problems of the Language of Primitive Buddhism 1985. *Address:* Department of Oriental Studies, Beijing University, Beijing, People's Republic of China. *Telephone:* 2501578.

JI, Yunshi; Chinese politician; *General Director, State Administration of Foreign Experts Affairs;* b. 26 Sept. 1945, Haimen, Jiangsu Prov.; m. Lu Guohong; one d.; ed Shandong Univ.; sent to do manual labour in Xishan Coal Mine, Suzhou City, Jiangsu Prov. 1970; worker, man. clerk and workshop dir Suzhou Light Industrial Electrical Machinery Plant 1971, Deputy Dir then Dir 1978–80; joined CCP 1975; Deputy Dir then Dir No. 2 Light Industry Bureau, Suzhou City 1980–82 (Deputy Sec. CCP Party Cttee 1980–82); Deputy Sec. then Sec. Jiangsu Prov. Cttee CCP Communist Youth League 1980–82; Sec. CCP Jiangsu City Cttee, Jiangsu Prov. 1984; apptd Vice-Gov. Jiangsu Prov. 1989–93, elected Vice-Gov. 1993–98, Acting Gov. 1998–2002; Gov. Hebei Prov. 2002–06; Alt. mem. 15th CCP Cen. Cttee 1997–2002, mem. 16th CCP Cen. Cttee 2002–07; Deputy Sec. CCP Jiangsu Prov. Cttee 2001, mem. Standing Cttee 2001; Gen. Dir State Admin of Foreign Experts Affairs 2006–. *Address:* State Administration of Foreign Experts Affairs, Room 50307, No.1 South Zhongguancun Street, Beijing 100873, People's Republic of China (office).

JIA, Chunwang; Chinese state official; b. 1938, Beijing; ed Tsinghua Univ., Beijing; joined CCP 1962; Sec. CCP Communist Youth League (CYL) and mem. Standing Cttee, CCP Party Cttee, Tsinghua Univ. (in charge of student affairs) 1964; fmr Sec. Beijing Municipal Cttee, CCP CYL; fmr mem. Standing Cttee, CCP CYL; fmr Sec. CCP Haidian Dist Cttee, Beijing; fmr Sec. Comm. for Discipline Inspection, CCP Beijing Municipal Cttee; Minister of State Security 1985–98; Minister of Public Security 1998–2003; mem. Cen. Comm. of Political Science and Law 1991–; ranked Commr-Gen. 1992; apptd First Political Commissar, Chinese People's Armed Police Force 1998; apptd Dir Nat. Narcotics Control Comm. 1999; Vice-Procurator-Gen., Supreme People's Procuratorate 1998–2003, Procurator-Gen. 2003–08; mem. 12th CCP Cen. Cttee 1982–87, 13th Cen. Cttee 1987–92, 14th CCP Cen. Cttee 1992–97, 15th CCP Cen. Cttee 1997–2002, 16th CCP Cen. Cttee 2002–07. *Address:* c/o Chinese Communist Party Central Committee, Quanguo Renmin Daibiao Dahui, Zhongguo Gongchan Dang, 1 Zhongnanhai, Beijing, People's Republic of China (office).

JIA, Pingwa; Chinese writer; b. 21 Feb. 1952, Danfeng Co., Shaanxi Prov.; s. of Jia Yanchun and Zhouzhue; m.; one d.; ed Dept of Chinese Language, Northwest Univ., Xian; Ed., Shaanxi People's Publishing House 1975–; Chief Ed. magazine Mei Wen (Beautiful Essays); mem. Writers' Asscn 1979–; Prize for Nat. Literature (three times), Pegasus Prize for Literature. *Publications:* more than 60 works, including novels Feidu (Defunct Capital) 1993, Turbulence, The Corrupt and Waning, White Night, The Abandoned Capital, Neighbours' Wives 2005, Impetuous 2005, Qin Opera 2005, Gaoxing (Happy) 2007; short stories and essays; works have been translated into many languages. *Leisure interest:* painting, collecting antiques. *Address:* No. 2 Lian Hu Xiang, Xian City, Shaanxi, People's Republic of China.

JIA, Qinglin; Chinese government official and engineer; *Chairman, National Committee, 11th Chinese People's Political Consultative Conference;* b. 1940, Botou, Hebei Prov.; ed Shijiazhuang Industrial Man. School, Hebei Coll. of Eng; joined CCP 1959; technician, Complete Plant Bureau, First Ministry of Machine-Building Industry 1958–62 (Deputy Sec. CCP 1962–69), Policy Research Office of the Gen. Office 1971–73, Chief, Product Man. Bureau, First Ministry of Machine-Building Industry 1973–78; sent to do manual labour, May 7th Cadre School, Fengxin Co., Jiangxi Prov. 1969–71; Gen. Man. China Nat. Machinery and Equipment Import and Export Corpn 1978–83; Dir Taiyuan Heavy Machinery Plant 1983–85 (Sec. CCP Party Cttee 1983–85); Deputy Sec. Standing Cttee, Fujian CCP Prov. Cttee 1986–93, Sec. 1993–96; Head, Org. Dept, CCP Fujian Prov. Cttee 1986–88; Pres. Party School, CCP Fujian Prov. Cttee 1988–90; Sec. Work Cttee of Depts, CCP Fujian Prov. Cttee 1988–90; Deputy Gov. (also Acting Gov.) of Fujian Prov. 1990–91, Gov. 1991–94; Vice-Mayor (also Acting Mayor) of Beijing 1996–97, Mayor 1997–99; Chair. Standing Cttee Fujian Prov. 8th People's Congress 1994–; Sec. CCP Beijing Municipal Cttee 1997–; mem. 14th CCP Cen. Cttee 1992–97, 15th CCP Cen. Cttee 1997–2002 (mem. Politburo 1997–2002), 16th CCP Cen. Cttee 2002–07 (mem. Standing Cttee of the Politburo 2002–07), 17th CCP Cen. Cttee 2007– (mem. Standing Cttee of the Politburo 2007–); Chair. 10th CPPCC Nat. Cttee 2003–08, Chair. 11th CPPCC Nat. Cttee 2008–. *Address:* Chinese People's Political Consultative Conference, No. 23, Taipingqiao Street, Beijing 100811 (office); Standing Committee, Chinese Communist Party Politburo, Quanguo Renmin Diabiao Dahui, Zhongguo Gongchan Dang, 1 Zhongnanhai, Beijing, People's Republic of China. *Website:* www.cppcc.gov.cn (office).

JIA, Zhijie; Chinese party and government official; b. 1935, Fuyu Co., Jilin Prov.; ed in USSR; joined CCP 1960; Dir Lanzhou Petrochemical Machinery Plant; Deputy Sec. Plant CCP Cttee; Deputy Sec. Gansu Prov. CCP Cttee 1983–92; Gov. Gansu Prov. 1986–92; Gov. of Hubei Prov. 1992–94; Sec. CCP Cttee Hubei Prov. 1994–2001; Sec.-in-Chief Hubei Mil. District CCP Cttee 1994; Alt. mem. CCP 13th Cen. Cttee 1987–92, mem. 14th CCP Cen. Cttee 1992–97, 15th CCP Cen. Cttee 1997–2002; Deputy 9th NPC 1998–2003. *Address:* c/o Office of Provincial Governor, 1 Beihuan Road, Wuhan, Hubei Province, People's Republic of China. *Telephone:* (27) 87814585. *Fax:* (27) 87816148.

JIANG, Baolin; Chinese artist; b. 20 Jan. 1942, Penglai Co., Shandong Prov.; s. of the late Jiang Chunfu and Dai Shuzhi; m. Ling Yunhua 1970; one s. one d.; ed Dept of Traditional Chinese Painting, Inst. of Fine Arts, Zhejiang, Cen. Acad. of Fine Arts, Beijing; worked in Cultural House, Fenghua Co. 1967–79; Dir Zhejiang Artists' Gallery 1982–84; Vice-Pres. Zhejiang Landscape Painting Research Inst. 1982–; mem. Council of Zhejiang Br. of Chinese Painters' Asscn 1984–; mem. Bd Zhejiang Painting Acad. 1984–; Visiting Prof., Beijing Cen. Fine Arts Acad. 1996–; Tutor, Acad. of Arts, Tsinghua Univ., Beijing, mem. Council, Cui Zifan Art Foundation Int.; mem. Chinese Artists' Asscn; numerous exhbns 1987–, including Contemporary Chinese Paintings in celebration of Hong Kong's return to China, Beijing, Shanghai, Tianjin 1997; Silver Medal, 9th Nat. Art Exhbn 1999. *Publications:* Collections of Jiang Baolin's Paintings 1984, Jiang Baolin's ink-wash paintings 1989, Signatur Objekt 15, Jiang Baolin 1991, Jiang Baolin's Paintings (published in France) 1991, A selection of Jiang Baolin's Bird and Flower Paintings 1992, The World of Jiang Baolin's Ink & Wash Painting 1994, The Art World of Jiang Baolin (published in Korea) 1996, Series on Modern Chinese Artists 2000. *Leisure interests:* Beijing Opera, literature, music, gardening. *Address:* 201 Building 11, 2nd District, Nandu Huayuan Wenyi Road, Hangzhou, People's Republic of China. *Telephone:* (571) 8850096. *Fax:* (571) 8850096.

JIANG, Boju; Chinese mathematician and academic; *Professor of Mathematics, Peking University;* b. 4 Sept. 1937, Tianjin City; m. Chuanrong Xu 1968; two d.; ed Peking Univ.; Assoc. Prof. of Math., Peking Univ. 1978–82, Prof. 1983–, Dean School of Math. Sciences 1995–98; mem. Chinese Acad. of Sciences 1980; Fellow, Third World Acad. of Sciences 1985; Nat. Scientific Award of China 1982, 1987, S. S. Chern Mathematics Award 1988, Ho Leung Ho Lee Foundation Math. Prize 1996, L. K. Hua Math. Award 2002, Hua LuoGeng Maths Prize 2005. *Address:* Department of Mathematics, Peking University, 5 Yiheyuan Road, Hai Dian, Beijing 100871, People's Republic of China (office). *Telephone:* (10) 62751804 (office). *Fax:* (10) 62751801 (office). *Website:* www.pku.edu.cn (office).

JIANG, Chunyun; Chinese party official; b. April 1930, Laixi Co., Shandong Prov.; ed Teachers Training Coll., Laixi Co., Chinese Language and Literature Self-Study Univ.; fmr primary school teacher; Clerk of CCP Maren Dist Cttee, Sec., CCP Laixi Co. Cttee 1946–49; joined CCP 1947; Dir of Gen. Office Laixi Co. CCP Cttee 1949–57; Deputy Section Chief, Qingdao br., China Export Corpn for Local Products 1957–60; with Foreign Trade Bureau, Qingdao City 1957–60; Instructor and Chief Insp. and Deputy Dir of Gen. Office, Propaganda Dept Shandong Prov. CCP Cttee 1960–66; manual work in village in Huimin Co. during Cultural Revolution, sent to cadre school, Qihe Co. 1969; worked under Revolutionary Cttee Shandong Prov. 1970–75; Deputy Dir, Gen. Office, Shandong Prov. CCP Cttee 1975–77, Deputy Sec.-Gen., then Sec.-Gen. 1977–83, Deputy Sec. 1983–84; Sec., Ji'nan Municipal CCP Cttee 1984–87; Acting Gov., Shandong Prov. 1987–88, Gov. 1988–89; Pres. Shandong Prov. Party School 1989–92; First Sec., Shandong Mil. Dist CCP Cttee 1989–94; Sec., CCP Shandong Prov. Cttee 1993–94; Vice-Premier State Council (in charge of agricultural work) 1995–98; Head of State Flood-Control and Drought Relief HQ; mem. 13th CCP Cen. Cttee, 14th CCP Cen. Cttee 1992–97 (mem. Secr. of Politburo 1992–97), 15th CCP Cen. Cttee

1997–2002; Deputy, 7th NPC 1988–93, 8th NPC 1993–98, Vice-Chair. Standing Cttee of 9th NPC 1998–2003; Pres. China Family Planning Asscn 1998–; Prof. (part-time), Shandong Univ.; Hon. Prof., China Agric. Univ. *Address:* Standing Committee of National People's Congress, Beijing, People's Republic of China.

JIANG, Enzhu; Chinese diplomatist; *Chairman, 10th NPC Foreign Affairs Committee;* b. 14 Dec. 1938, Jiangsu Prov.; s. of Jiang Guohua and Yu Wen Guizhen; m. Zhu Manli; one s.; ed Beijing Foreign Languages Univ.; joined Ministry of Foreign Affairs as translator 1964; Attaché, Third and Second Sec., Embassy in London during 1970s; Deputy Dir-Gen., then Dir-Gen. Dept of West European Affairs, Ministry of Foreign Affairs 1984–90, Asst Foreign Minister 1990–91, Vice-Minister 1991–95; Chief Negotiator for People's Repub. of China in Sino-British talks over future of Hong Kong; Deputy Head of Preliminary Working Cttee of Preparatory Cttee of Hong Kong Special Admin. Region; Amb. to UK 1995–97; Dir Hong Kong br., Xinhua News Agency 1997–99; Dir (Minister) Liaison Office of People's Repub. of China to Hong Kong SAR 2000–03; mem. 15th CCP Cen. Cttee 1997–2002; mem. Standing Cttee 9th NPC 1998–2003; Chair. 10th NPC Foreign Affairs Cttee 2003–. *Address:* c/o Ministry of Foreign Affairs, 225 Chaoyangmen Nan Dajie, Chaoyang Qu, Beijing 100701, People's Republic of China.

JIANG, Gen. Futang; Chinese army officer; *Political Commissar, Shenyang Military Area Command, People's Liberation Army;* b. Oct. 1941, Rongcheng Co., Shandong Prov.; ed Political Acad. of the Chinese PLA; joined PLA 1959, CCP 1960; Dir Political Section, Regt 1969–70; Deputy Div. Political Commissar 1974–76; Dir Army Political Dept 1976–80; Political Commissar, 46th Army, Army (or Ground Force), PLA Services and Arms, 1983–85; Dir Political Dept of PLA Jinan Mil. Area Command 1985–93; Deputy Political Commissar and Dir Political Dept of PLA Chengdu Mil. Area Command 1993–95; Political Commissar, PLA Shenyang Mil. Area Command 1995–; rank of Maj.-Gen. 1988–93, Lt-Gen. 1993–2002, Gen. 2002–; mem. 15th CCP Cen. Cttee 1997–2002, 16th CCP Cen. Cttee 2002–07. *Address:* PLA Shenyang Military Area Command, Shenyang City, Liaoning Province, People's Republic of China.

JIANG, Jianqing, MEng, PhD; Chinese banker; *Executive Director and Chairman, Industrial and Commercial Bank of China Ltd;* b. Feb. 1953; ed Shanghai Univ. of Finance and Econs, Jiaotong Univ., Shanghai; Dir Shanghai City United Bank (now Bank of Shanghai) 1995–97; Dir Shanghai Br., Industrial and Commercial Bank of China (ICBC) 1997–99, Group Vice-Pres. 1999–2000, Pres. 2000–05, Exec. Dir and Chair. 2005–; Alt. mem. 16th CCP Cen. Cttee 2002–07, 17th CCP Cen. Cttee 2007–; Prof. (part-time), Man. Inst., Jiaotong Univ. (also Doctorate Adviser and Researcher); mem. Monetary Policy Comm., People's Bank of China. *Publications:* Analytical View on Foreign Financial Agitation, Thoughts on Financial Agitation, Technical Revolution in American Banking. *Address:* Industrial and Commercial Bank of China Ltd, Tianyin Building, 55 Fuxingmennai Dajie, Xicheng Qu, 100032 Beijing, People's Republic of China (office). *Telephone:* (10) 66106071 (office). *Fax:* (10) 66106053 (office). *E-mail:* webmaster@icbc.com.cn (office). *Website:* www.icbc.com.cn (office).

JIANG, Jiemin; Chinese petroleum industry executive; *President, China National Petroleum Corporation (CNPC);* b. 1954; ed Shandong Univ.; Deputy Dir Shengli Petroleum Admin Bureau 1993–94; Sr Exec. Qinghai Petroleum Admin Bureau 1994, Dir 1994–99; Asst to Gen. Man. and Team Leader of Restructuring, China Nat. Petroleum Corpn (CNPC) 1999, Dir and Vice-Pres. PetroChina Co. Ltd 1999–2000, Vice-Chair. and Pres. 2004–07, Chair. 2007–, also Vice-Pres. CNPC 2004–06, Pres. 2006–; Deputy Prov. Gov. Qinghai Prov. 2000–04, also mem. Prov. Party Cttee 2000, 2003; Alt. mem. 17th CCP Cen. Cttee 2007–. *Address:* China National Petroleum Corporation, 6 Liupukang Street, Xicheng District, Beijing 100724, People's Republic of China (office). *Telephone:* (10) 62094114 (office). *Fax:* (10) 62095148 (office). *Website:* www .cnpc.com.cn (office).

JIANG, Li-Jin, PhD; Chinese organic chemist and academician; b. 15 April 1919, Beijing; d. of Jiong-Shang Jiang and Shu-Duan Li; m. Guo-Zhi Xu 1954; two s.; ed Univ. of Minnesota, USA; Prof. and Sr Research Fellow, Inst. Photographic Chem. (renamed Technical Inst. of Physics and Chemistry 1999), Acad. Sinica 1978–; mem. Standing Cttee 6th CPPCC 1982–87, 7th CPPCC 1987–92, 8th CPPCC 1992–97; mem. Standing Cttee of Chem. Div., Acad. Sinica 1981–93, mem. Academia Sinica 1994–. *Publications:* The Chemistry and Phototherapeutic Mechanism of Hypocrellins (Second Prize, Natural Science Award, Acad. Sinica 1990), The Relationship between the Structures of the Phycobiliproteins and the Evolution of the Algal Species, The Study of the Mechanism of Energy Transfer (Second Prize, Natural Science Award, Acad. Sinica 1993), The Photochemical, Photophysical and Photodynamical Actions of the Naturally Occurring Perylenohydroxylquinones (Second Prize, Natural Science Award, Acad. Sinica 1996). *Address:* Technical Institute of Physics and Chemistry, Academia Sinica, Bei Sha Tan, De Wai, Beijing 100101 (office); Apartment 804, Building 812, Huang Zhuang, Haidian Qu, Beijing 100080, People's Republic of China (home). *Telephone:* (10) 64888068 (office); (10) 62569291 (home). *Fax:* (10) 62029375.

JIANG, Minkuan; Chinese party and state official; *Vice-President, China Association of Inventions;* b. 1930, Suzhou City, Jiangsu Prov.; ed Shanghai Polytechnic School; joined CCP 1961; fmr technician, workshop dir, factory dir and chief engineer, Southwest China Aluminium Processing Factory 1966–79; Deputy Sec. CCP Cttee, Sichuan Prov. 1982–85; Vice-Gov. Sichuan 1983–85, Gov. 1985–88; Vice-Chair. State Science and Tech. Comm. 1988–90; Dir State Patent Bureau 1988–89; Deputy Dir United Front Work Dept, CCP Cen. Cttee 1990–95, Exec. Deputy Head 1995–98; Vice-Pres. China Asscn of Inventions 1991–; Vice-Chair. 7th Exec. Cttee All China Fed. of Industry and Commerce

1993, China Chamber of Commerce 1993–; mem. 12th CCP Cen. Cttee 1982–87, 13th CCP Cen. Cttee 1987–92, 14th Cen. Cttee CCP 1992–97, 15th Cen. Cttee 1997–2002; mem. Standing Cttee 7th to 9th CPPCC Nat. Cttees 1988–2003; Vice-Chair. Science, Educational Culture, Public Health and Physical Culture Cttee, 9th Nat. Cttee of CPPCC 1998–2003. *Address:* c/o National Committee of Chinese People's Political Consultative Conference, 23 Taipingqiao Street, Beijing, People's Republic of China.

JIANG, Wen; Chinese actor and film director; b. 1963, Tangshan, Hebei Prov.; m. 1st Sandrine Chenivisse, one d.; m. 2nd Zhou Yun, one s.; ed Cen. Acad. of Drama; joined China Youth Arts Theatre 1984; actor at Cen. Acad. of Drama. *Films include:* Fu rong zhen 1984, Moot doi wong hau 1986, Hong gao liang (Red Sorghum) 1987, Ben ming nian 1990, Da taijian Li Lianying (Li Lianying, the Imperial Eunuch) 1991, Yangguang Canlan de Rizi (In the Heat of the Sun) (dir, actor) 1994, Qin song 1996, Song jia huang chao 1997, The Soong Sisters (Hong Kong Film Award for Best Supporting Actor 1998) 1997, Guizi lai le (Devils on the Doorstep) (dir, producer) (Cannes Film Festival Grand Prix 2000) 2000, Xun qiang (The Missing Gun) (producer) 2002, Tian di ying xiong (Warriors of Heaven and Earth) 2003, Lü cha (Green Tea) 2003, Yi ge mo sheng nu ren de lai xin (A Letter from an Unknown Woman) 2004, Mo li hua kai (Jasmine) 2004, The Sun Also Rises (actor, director and writer) 2007, Connected 2008. *Address:* Central Academy of Drama, 39 East Mianhua Lane, Dongcheng District, Beijing 100710, People's Republic of China (office).

JIANG, Xi; Chinese government official; b. (Qing Jong), Jan. 1923, Shanghai; fmr Vice-Minister of Commerce; Pres. China Gen. Commercial 1994–, World Asscn of Chinese Cuisine; currently Sr Adviser Sino-Japan Food Devt Cttee; Hon. Pres., China Cuisine Asscn. *Address:* China Chamber of Commerce, 45 Fuxingmennei Street, Beijing 100801, People's Republic of China. *Telephone:* (10) 66094602 (office); (10) 63467719 (home). *Fax:* (10) 66062700 (office). *E-mail:* wacc@ccas.com.cn (office). *Website:* www.ccas.com.cn.

JIANG, Xinxiong; Chinese party and government official; b. 6 July 1931; ed Nankai Univ., Tianjin; joined CCP 1956; Dir nuclear fuel plant 1979–82; Vice-Minister of Nuclear Industry 1982–83, Minister 1983; Chair. Bd of Dirs, China Isotopes Co. 1983–98; Pres. Nat. Nuclear Corpn 1988–98; Chair. China Atomic Energy Authority 1994–99; Deputy Head Leading Group for Nuclear Power Plants; Vice-Chair Finance and Econ. Cttee of 9th NPC 1998–2003; Pres. China-Canada Friendship Asscn of NPC 1998–2003; Alt. mem. 12th CCP Cen. Cttee 1982–87, 13th CCP Cen. Cttee 1987–92, 14th CCP Cen. Cttee 1992–97. *Address:* c/o Standing Committee of National People's Congress, Beijing, People's Republic of China. *Telephone:* (10) 68533923.

JIANG, Zemin; Chinese fmr head of state; b. 17 Aug. 1926, Yangzhou City, Jiangsu Prov.; ed Jiaotong Univ., Shanghai; joined CCP 1946; worked in Shanghai Yimin No. 1 Foodstuffs Factory, Shanghai Soap Factory, First Ministry of Machine-Bldg Industry; trainee, Stalin Automobile Plant, Moscow, USSR 1955–56; Deputy Chief Power Div., Deputy Chief Power-Engineer, Dir, Power Plant, Changchun No. 1 Auto Works 1957–62; Deputy Dir Shanghai Electric Equipment Research Inst., Dir and Acting Party Sec. Wuhan Thermo-Tech. Machinery Research Inst., Deputy Dir, Dir Foreign Affairs Bureau of First Ministry of Machine-Bldg Industry 1962–80; Vice-Chair. and Sec.-Gen. State Comm. on Admin of Imports and Exports, State Comm. on Admin of Foreign Investment 1980–82; First Vice-Minister Electronics Industry 1982–83, Minister 1983–85; Mayor of Shanghai 1985–88; Deputy Sec., Sec. Shanghai Municipal Party Cttee 1985–89; mem. 12th Nat. Congress CCP Cen. Cttee 1982, Politburo 1st Plenary Session of 13th Cen. Cttee 1987, Gen. Sec. 4th Plenary Session 1989, Chair. Mil. Cttee 5th Plenary Session 1989; mem. Standing Cttee Politburo, Gen. Sec. and Chair. Mil. Cttee 14th and 15th CCP Cen. Cttees 1992–2002; Chair. Cen. Mil. Comm. of CCP Cen. Cttee 1990–2004, Cen. Mil. Comm. of People's Repub. of China 1998–2005; Pres. People's Repub. of China 1993–2003; Hon. Chair. Red Cross Soc. of China; Hon. Pres. Software Industry Asscn. *Address:* Chinese Communist Party, Zhongguo Gongchan Dang, 1 Zhongnanhai, Beijing, People's Republic of China.

JIANG, Zhenghua; Chinese politician; *Vice-Chairman, Standing Committee, 10th National People's Congress;* b. Oct. 1937, Hangzhou City, Zhejiang Prov.; ed Xi'an Jiaotong Univ., Int. Demography Acad., Bombay, India; Lecturer, Auto Control Dept and Dir Population Research Centre, Inst. of Systematic Eng 1958–78; Dir Population and Econs Inst. 1958–78; Prof., Xi'an Jiaotong Univ. 1978–91; Visiting Prof., Univ. of Paris, France, Stanford Univ., USA; Specialist, India Int. Devt Centre 1986; fmr Tech. Advisor, State Census Office; Vice-Minister, State Family Planning Comm. 1991–99; joined Chinese Peasants' and Workers' Democratic Party 1992; Vice-Chair. Cen. Cttee 11th Chinese Peasants' and Workers' Democratic Party (CPWDP) 1992–97, Chair. Cen. Cttee 12th CPWDP 1997–2002; mem. 7th CPPCC Nat. Cttee 1988–93, Standing Cttee 8th CPPCC Nat. Cttee 1993–98 (mem. Sub-cttee of Educ., Science, Culture, Health and Sports 1993–98); Vice-Chair. Standing Cttee of 9th NPC 1998–2003, of 10th NPC 2003–; mem. Macao Hand-Over Ceremony Govt Del., Macao Special Admin. Region Preparatory Cttee 1999; now Prof. of Systems Eng, Econometrics and Demography; fmr Pres. China Soc. of Tech. and Demography; fmr Vice-Pres. Demographic Inst., Shaanxi Prov.; fmr adviser to and mem. Exec. Council Demography Soc. of China; mem. Council Int. Demography Soc. 1993–; Gold Medal, Bombay Int. Demography Acad., India 1981, Outstanding Expert at Nat. Level of China 1985, Nat. Advanced Worker of China 1989, First Class Nat. Science and Tech. Progress Prize 1987. *Publications:* Economic Development Planning Models 1981, Country Report on Population of China 1997, Sustainable Development of China 1999, Population – Systematic and Quantitative Study and its Application (First Class Award, State Scientific and Technological Advancement), Analysis and Planning of Population, Programming Regional Population and Coordination Development of Economy. *Address:* Standing Committee of National People's

Congress, Beijing 100805 (office); 11 Min Zu Yuan Road, Room 601, Beijing 100029, People's Republic of China (home). *Telephone:* (10) 63091615 (office); (10) 62357120 (home). *Fax:* (10) 63091614 (office). *E-mail:* jenjenny@sina.com (office).

JIANG, Zhuping; Chinese engineer and administrator; b. 1937, Yixing Co., Jiangsu Prov.; ed Faculty of Missile Eng, Harbin Mil. Eng Inst.; joined CCP 1960; with Design Inst. of Ministry of Nat. Defence 1963–65; Deputy Dir Design Inst. of Nanchang Aircraft. Mfg Plant 1978–82, Deputy Sec. plant's Party Cttee 1982–84; Sec. Party Cttee of Depts under Ministry of Aeronautics Industry 1984–85; Vice-Gov. of Jiangxi Prov. 1985–88; Deputy Sec. CCP Jiangxi Prov. Cttee 1988–95; Gov. of Hubei Prov. 1995–2001; Sec. CCP Hubei Prov. Cttee 2001; Deputy to 9th NPC 1998–2003, Vice-Chair. NPC Educ., Science, Culture and Health Cttee 2001; mem. 14th CCP Cen. Cttee 1992–97, 15th CCP Cen. Cttee 1997–2002; Deputy Dir Civil Aviation Gen. Admin. of China 1991–95. *Address:* c/o National People's Congress, Tiananmen Square, Beijing, People's Republic of China.

JIANG, Zilong; Chinese writer; *Vice-Chairman, Chinese Writers' Association;* b. 2 June 1941, Cang Xian, Hebei; s. of Jiang Junsan and Wei Huanzhang; m. Zhang Qinglian 1968; one s. one d.; worker Tianjin Heavy Machinery Plant 1958; navy conscript 1960–65; Vice-Chair. Chinese Writers' Asscn 1996–; Nat. Short Story Prize 1979. *Publications:* A New Station Master 1965, One Day for the Chief of the Bureau of Electromechanics 1976, Manager Qiao Assumes Office 1979, Developer 1980, Diary of a Plant Secretary 1980, All the Colours of the Rainbow 1983, Yan-Zhao Dirge 1985, Serpent Deity 1986, Jiang Zilong Works Collection (eight vols) 1996, Human Vigour 2000, Ren Qi 2000, Empty Hole 2001. *Leisure interests:* swimming, Beijing opera. *Address:* No. 7 Dali Road, Heping District, Tianjin (home); Tianjin Writers' Association, Tianjin, People's Republic of China. *Telephone:* (22) 23304153 (office); (22) 23306250 (home). *Fax:* (22) 23304159 (office); (22) 23306250 (home). *E-mail:* jzltj@hotmail.com (home).

JIČÍNSKÝ, Zdeněk, DJur; Czech politician, academic and jurist; *Chairman, Parliamentary Permanent Commission on the Constitution;* b. 26 Feb. 1929, Ostřešany; m. Naďa Jičínská 1961; two s.; ed Charles Univ., Prague; mem. Czech. CP 1951–69; on staff of Inst. of Social Sciences, Cen. Cttee of Czech. CP 1954–60; Prof., Law Faculty, Charles Univ. 1964–70; mem. Scientific Law Council, Charles Univ. 1962–69; mem. Legal Comm., Cen. Cttee of Czech. CP 1964; mem. Expert Comm. of Govt Cttee for Constitutional Regulation of Repub. 1968; Deputy Chair. Czech. Nat. Council 1968; mem. Chamber of Nations, Fed. Ass. of CSSR 1969; forced to leave public life and university 1969; lawyer in insurance co. 1969–77; signed Charter 77; Rep. Civic Forum 1989; Deputy Chair. Fed. Ass. 1989–90, First Deputy Chair. 1990–92; Deputy and mem. Presidium Fed. Ass. 1992–; mem. Civic Movt 1991–92; mem. Czechoslovak Social Democratic Party 1992–; mem. Parl. 1996–2002, 2003–, Deputy Chair. Parl. Constitutional Juridical Cttee 1996–2002; mem. Standing Del. to Inter parl. Union 1996–98, Chair. Parl. Perm. Comm. on the Constitution 2007–; mem. Scientific Law Council Charles Univ. 2006–; political commentator, Právo newspaper (fmrly Rudé Právo) 1992–. *Publications:* Political Ideology of the First Czechoslovak Republic 1961, On the Development of Thinking in Czechoslovakia in the Sixties 1991, Developments in Czechoslovak Parliament since November 1989 1993, The Extinction of Czechoslovakia in 1992 from a Constitutional Viewpoint 1993, Problems of Czech Politics 1994, Charter 77 and Society Governed by the Law 1995, Constitutional and Political Problems of the Czech Republic 1995, The Constitution of the Czech Republic in Political Practice 2007; numerous works on politics, theory of state and law and institutional law. *Leisure interests:* skiing, cycling, jazz. *Address:* Pařížská 12, 110 00 Prague 1, Czech Republic (home). *Telephone:* (2) 22312560 (home). *E-mail:* jicinskyz@psp.cz (office); a2@jicinsky.cz (office). *Website:* www.jicinsky.cz (office).

JIHAD, Abdullah; Maldivian economist, central banker and politician; held several positions in Ministry of Finance, including Minister of State; Gov. Maldives Monetary Authority (first ind. gov.) 2007–08; Minister of Finance and Treasury 2008. *Address:* c/o Ministry of Finance and Treasury, Block 379, Ameenee Magu, Malé 20-379, Maldives (office).

JILANI, Hina; Pakistani lawyer and human rights activist; b. 1951; sister of Asma Jahangir; qualified as lawyer 1974; Advocate of the High Court 1981–; co-f. (with Asma Jahangir) AGHS Law Assocs (all-women law firm), Lahore 1981, also co-f. AGHS Legal Aid Cell (first free legal aid centre in Pakistan) 1984; Advocate of the Supreme Court 1992–; Founding mem. Human Rights Comm. of Pakistan, Lahore 1986–, Women's Action Forum; apptd UN Special Rep. on the Situation of Human Rights Defenders 2000–08; involved with UN Center for Human Rights, the Carter Centre, UN Conf. of Women; awards from ABA, Human Rights Watch, Millennium Peace Prize 2001. *Address:* c/o Human Rights Commission of Pakistan, Aiwan-i-Jahmoor, 107 Tipu Block, New Garden Town, Lahore 54600, Pakistan (office). *Telephone:* (42) 5838341 (office). *Fax:* (42) 5883582 (office). *E-mail:* hrcp@hrcp-web.org (office). *Website:* www.hrcp-web.org (office).

JIMENEZ, Menardo R., BSc (Com); Philippine business executive; b. 6 Dec. 1932, Manila; s. of the late Marcelo A. Jimenez and Emiliana Rodriguez-Jimenez; m. Carolina L. Gozon 1962; two s. two d.; ed Far Eastern Univ., qualified as certified accountant; worked for Abaca Corpn of Philippines (Abacorp) 1956–70; Pres. and CEO Repub. Broadcasting Inc. (now GMA-Radio TV Arts, GMA-7) –2000; Chair. MA Jimenez Enterprises Inc., Majalco Finance & Investment Corpn, Cable Entertainment Corpn; Pres. Albay-Agro Industrial Devt Corpn, Justitia Realty & Devt Corpn, GMA Marketing & Productions Inc.; Dir many cos; Chair. and Trustee Kapwa Ko Mahal Ko Foundation; Chair. Bd Philippine Constitution Asscn; Chair. Prison Fellowship Philippines Inc.; Gov. Philippine Nat. Red Cross; Dir Philippine Chamber of Commerce and Industry; Dir or Trustee many other bodies. *Leisure interest:* stamp collection. *Address:* c/o GMA Network Center, EDSA corner Timog Avenue, Diliman, Quezon City, Philippines.

JIMÉNEZ-BELTRÁN, Domingo; Spanish international organization executive; b. 2 April 1944, Zaragoza; s. of Mariano Jiménez and María Gloria Beltrán; m. Elin Solem; one c.; ed High Tech. School of Industrial Engineers and Polytechnic Univ., Madrid; Lecturer, Polytechnic Univ., Madrid 1978–86; Exec. Adviser to Minister for Public Works and Planning 1983–85; Deputy Dir-Gen. for Int. and EU Relations and with Ministry of Public Works and Urban Planning 1985–86; Attaché for Environment and Public Works, Perm. Mission to EU, Brussels 1986–87; Head of Div. Health, Physical Safety and Quality, Consumers Policy Service, EC 1987–91; Dir-Gen. for Environmental Policy, Sec. of State for Environment and Housing, Ministry of Public Works, Transport and Environment 1991–94; Exec. Dir European Environment Agency, Copenhagen 1994–2002; Founder and fmr Dir Observatorio de la Sostenibilidad en España (Spanish Observatory of Sustainability); currently Adviser to the Prime Minister; Nat. Prize on Environment (Spain) 2008, Emisoft Sustainability Prize 2008. *Publications:* Late Lessons From Early Warnings: The Precautionary Principle 1896–2000 (co-author) 2001; author or ed. of various publs and articles. *Address:* c/o Observatorio de la Sostenibilidad en España (OSE), Universidad de Alcalá, Plaza San Diego s/n – Casa Anexa al Rectorado, 2ª planta, 28801 Alcalá de Henares, Madrid; Prime Minister's Chancellery, Complejo de la Moncloa, 28071 Madrid, Spain. *Telephone:* (91) 8854039 (OSE); (91) 3353535 (Chancellery). *E-mail:* juancarlos.ochoa@uah.es. *Website:* www.sostenibilidad-es.org; www.mpr.es.

JIMÉNEZ PUERTO, Milton Danilo; Honduran government official and lawyer; b. 8 Nov. 1961; m. D. Alba María Soto Quezada; ed Universidad Nacional Autónoma de Honduras; joined Partido Liberal de Honduras 1985; fmr Dir Colegio de Abogados Honduras; Co-Dir Consultorio Jurídico Popular; fmr Legal Adviser Cen. Nacional de Trabajadores del Campo; Minister of Foreign Affairs 2006–07 (resgnd). *Address:* Partido Liberal, Col. Miramonte, Teguucigalpa, Honduras (office). *Telephone:* 232-0520 (office). *Fax:* 232-0797 (office). *Website:* www.partidoliberal.net (office).

JIN, Chongji; Chinese historian; b. 13 Dec. 1930, Qingpu, Jiangsu Prov.; ed Fudan Univ.; joined CCP 1948; Lecturer, Admin., Fudan Univ. 1951–65; researcher, Ministry of Culture 1965–73; Deputy Chief Ed., Chief Ed. Cultural Relics Press 1973–81; researcher, Assoc. Exec. Dir, Exec. Dir CCP Cen. Cttee Historical Documents Research Office 1981–; Vice-Dir Cultural and Historical Documents Cttee, CPPCC; Chair. All-China Asscn of Historians. *Publications:* Xinhai Geming de Qian Qian Hou Hou (A History of the 1911 Revolution), Sun Zhongshan he Xinhai Geming (Sun Yat-sen and the 1911 Revolution), Biography of Zhou En-lai (1898–1976), Biography of Mao Zedong (1893–1949). *Leisure interest:* reading. *Address:* Historical Documents Research Office of Chinese Communist Party Central Committee, 1 Maojiawan, Xisi Bei Qian, Beijing 100017 (office); Wanshoulu Jia-15, 7th Zone, 4th Building, 101th Room, Beijing 100036, People's Republic of China (home). *Telephone:* (10) 63095701 (office); (10) 68218172 (home). *Fax:* (10) 63094431 (office).

JIN, Ha, BA, MA, PhD; American/Chinese writer, poet and academic; *Professor, Department of English, Boston University;* b. (Jin Xuefei), 21 Feb. 1956, Jinzhou, China; m. Lisah Bian 1982; one c.; ed Heilongjian Univ., Harbin, Shangdong Univ., Jinan, Brandeis Univ.; faculty mem. Dept of English, Emory Univ. 1993–2002, Boston Univ. 2002–; wrote libretto for opera (with Tan Dun), The First Emperor (Metropolitan Opera, New York) 2006; Fellow, American Acad. of Arts and Sciences 2006; PEN/Hemingway Award 1997, Flannery O'Connor Award 1997, Nat. Book Award 1999, PEN/Faulkner Award 2000, 2005, Asian American Literary Award 2001, Townsend Prize for Fiction 2002. *Publications:* fiction: Ocean of Words: Army Stories 1996, Under the Red Flag 1997, In the Pond 1998, Waiting 1999, The Bridegroom (short stories) 2000, The Crazed 2002, War Trash (novel) 2004, A Free Life 2007; poetry: Between Silences 1990, Facing Shadows 1996, Wreckage 2001; essays: The Writer as Migrant 2008. *Address:* c/o Department of English, College of Arts and Sciences, Boston University, 236 Bay State Road, Boston, MA 02215, USA (office). *Telephone:* (617) 353-2506 (office). *Fax:* (617) 353-3653 (office). *E-mail:* xjin@bu.edu (office). *Website:* www.bu.edu/english (office).

JIN, Nyum; South Korean politician; b. 1940; ed Coll. of Commerce, Seoul Nat. Univ., Washington Univ., Stanford Univ.; with Econ. Planning Bd (EPB); fmr Minister of Labour; fmr Minister of Energy and Resources, of Maritime Affairs and Fisheries; Deputy Prime Minister for Finance and the Economy 2000–02 (resgnd). *Address:* c/o Ministry of Finance and Economy, 1 Jungang-dong, Gwacheon City, Gyeonggi Province, Republic of Korea (office).

JIN, Puqing; Chinese business executive; *President and Executive Director, China Railway Construction Corporation;* b. 1950; ed Jinzhou Communist Party School; joined China Railway Construction Corpn Group 1968, Dir 2005–, Gen. Man., Pres. and Exec. Dir 2007–; Deputy Head of 12th Eng Bureau, Ministry of Railways 1993–98, also Chair., Gen. Man. and Deputy Sec., China Railway 12th Bureau Group Co. Ltd CCP Cttee 1998–2005. *Address:* China Railway Construction Corpn, No. 40, Fuxing Road, Beijing, 100855, People's Republic of China (office). *Telephone:* (10) 51888114 (office). *Fax:* (10) 68217382 (office). *E-mail:* info@crcc.cn (office). *Website:* www.crcc.cn (office).

JIN, Renqing; Chinese politician; b. July 1944, Suzhou, Jiangsu Prov.; ed Cen. Inst. of Finance and Banking; staff mem. Grain Bureau, Yongsheng Co., Yunnan Prov. 1968–97, Deputy Dir 1977–80; joined CCP 1972; Deputy Dir Financial Office, Yongsheng Co. 1977–80; mem. Standing Cttee CCP Yongsheng Co. Cttee 1980–82 (Vice-Chair. CCP Revolutionary Cttee 1980–82), Deputy Sec. CCP Yongsheng Co. Cttee 1982–83; Deputy Magistrate, Yongsheng Co. (Dist) People's Court 1980–82, Acting Magistrate and Magistrate 1982–83; mem. CCP Lijiang Prefectural Cttee, Yunnan Prov. 1985–91; Deputy Commr Lijiang Prefectural Admin. Office 1985–91; Vice-Gov. Lijiang 1985–91; Vice-Minister of Finance 1991–95; Deputy Sec.-Gen. State Council 1995; apptd Vice-Mayor of Beijing 1995, elected Vice-Mayor 1998; mem. Standing Cttee CCP Beijing Municipal Cttee 1995; Deputy Sec. CCP Beijing Municipal Cttee 1997, Deputy Dir Planning and Construction Cttee 1997; Dir State Tax Bureau 1998–2003; Alt. mem. CCP 15th Cen. Cttee 1997–2002, mem. CCP 16th Cen. Cttee 2002–07; Minister of Finance 2003–07; Hon. Chair. Exec. Cttee All-China Fed. of Industry and Commerce 1996–97. *Address:* c/o Zhongguo Gongchan Dang (Chinese Communist Party), Beijing, People's Republic of China (office).

JIN, Shangyi; Chinese artist; b. 1934, Jiaozuo City, Henan Prov.; ed Cen. Fine Arts Acad., Beijing; known as the forerunner of classicism in Chinese Art; Pres. Cen. Inst. of Fine Arts 1987–; Chair. Chinese Artists' Asscn; Vice-Chair. China Fed. of Literary and Art Circles 2001; Guest lecturer, Art Dept, New York Municipal Univ. 1982. *Works include:* Seeing People Off 1959, The December Meeting 1961, Mao Zedong at the December Conference 1961, Mao Zedong Leads the Red Army on the Long March 1964, Spring of the Rivers 1977, Oil Workers 1978, A Maiden 1981, A Tajik Girl 1983, Qu Qiubai 1984, Prayer 1987, Ascending Peak Mushitago, Our Friends are All Over the World, Summer Ranch. *Address:* Central Institute of Fine Arts, 5 Xiaowei Hutong, East District, Beijing 100730, People's Republic of China (office). *Telephone:* (10) 65254731 (office).

JIN, Xiangwen; Chinese administrator; b. Oct. 1939, Shanghai; ed Wuhan Surveying and Mapping Inst.; joined CCP 1966; Dir State Bureau of Surveying and Mapping 1988–2000. *Address:* c/o State Bureau of Surveying and Mapping, Beijing, People's Republic of China.

JIN, Yong; Chinese writer, journalist and newspaper publisher; b. (Louis Cha Liang Yong), 6 Feb. 1924, Haining, Zhejiang Prov.; m. three times; ed Dongwu Law School; writer, Ta Kung Pao newspaper, Shanghai, later Hong Kong; later became film reviewer and screenwriter; first martial arts novel serialised in Xin Wan Bao newspaper, Hong Kong 1955; f. newspaper Ming Bao Daily, Hong Kong; ceased writing novels in 1972; several hon. degrees; Chevalier de la Légion d'Honneur 1992, Commdr de l'Ordre des Arts et des Lettres 2004. *Publications:* (titles translated) Legend of the Book and the Sword 1955, The Sword Stained With Royal Blood (Vol. I Crimson Sabre Saga) 1956, Flying Fox of the Snowy Mountain 1959, The Young Flying Fox, Legend of the Condor Heroes (Vol. I Condor trilogy) 1957, Return of the Condor Heroes (Vol. II Condor trilogy) 1959, Heavenly Sword Dragon Sabre (Vol. III Condor trilogy) 1961, Demi Gods Semi Devils 1963, Way of the Heroes, Requiem of Ling Sing, The Proud Smiling Wanderer 1967, The Duke of Mount Deer (Vol. II Crimson Sabre Saga), The Deer and the Cauldron 1969, Sword of the Yue Maiden 1970. *Address:* c/o The Chinese University Press, The Chinese University of Hong Kong, Sha Tin, N.T., Hong Kong Special Administrative Region, People's Republic of China (office). *Website:* www.chineseupress.com (office).

JIN, Yongjian; Chinese diplomatist and national organization official; b. 15 Sept. 1934; s. of Jin Zhiying and Bo Canzhang; m. Wang Youping 1955; two s.; ed Beijing Univ. of Foreign Studies; officer, People's Inst. of Foreign Affairs of China 1954–63; Attaché, Embassy in Nairobi 1964–67; officer, African Dept Ministry of Foreign Affairs, Beijing 1967–71, Deputy Dir-Gen., Dir-Gen. 1984–88, Dir-Gen. Dept of Int. Orgs and Confs 1988–90; Third Sec., Second Sec. Embassy in Lagos 1971–76; Second Sec., First Sec. then Counsellor, Perm. Mission to UN, New York, Alt. Rep. to UN Security Council, Rep. to Security Council Special Cttee on Decolonization, UN Council for Namibia 1977–84, Deputy Perm. Rep., Amb. to UN, Deputy Rep. to Security Council 1990–92; Amb. and Perm. Rep. to UN, Geneva, also accred to Other Int. Orgs in Switzerland 1992–96; Under-Sec.-Gen. for Devt Support and Man. Services, UN 1996–97, for Gen. Ass. Affairs and Conf. Services 1997–2001; Pres. UN Asscn of China 2001–07; Adjunct Prof., Nankai Univ. 2005–. *Leisure interests:* walking, Chinese chess, bridge. *Address:* 71 Nanchizi, Beijing 100 006, People's Republic of China (office).

JIN LUXIAN, Mgr Louis; Chinese Catholic ecclesiastic; *Bishop of Shanghai;* b. 20 June 1916, Shanghai; s. of Luc Jin and Lucy Chang; ed Xuhui seminary in Shanghai, Pontifical Gregorian Univ., Rome; first ordained 1945; convicted of counter-revolutionary activities 1960, spent 22 years under house arrest, in re-education camps, and in prison, released 1982; Bishop, Shanghai Diocese 1984–; Dir Sheshan Catholic Seminary in Shanghai 1985–; mem. Standing Cttee CPPCC 8th Nat. Cttee 1993–98. *Leisure interest:* collecting stamps. *Address:* Bishop's Residence, 158 Pu Xi Road, Shanghai 200030, People's Republic of China. *Telephone:* (21) 64398913. *Fax:* (21) 64398913.

JINASENA, Deshamanya T. N., BTech (Eng), DIC (Hons), CEng, FIESL; Sri Lankan company director; *Managing Director, Jinasena Group of Companies;* b. 13 July 1940, Colombo; ed Loughborough Univ., UK; apptd Chair. Jinasena Group 1965–, Man. Dir 1965–, business ventures in hotel industry, agricultural machinery, tyres, garments, pumps, seafood, tractors; Dr hc (Loughborough); Hon. DTech. *Leisure interests:* photography, sailing, motor racing. *Address:* Jinasena Group, 4 Hunupitiya Road, PO Box 196, Colombo 2 (office); 9 Gampaha Road, Ekala, Ja Ela, Sri Lanka (home). *Telephone:* (1) 2448848 (office); (1) 2232383 (home). *Fax:* (1) 2448815 (office); (1) 2232383 (home). *E-mail:* nihal@jinasena.com.lk (office); tnjhome@eureka.lk (home). *Website:* www.jinasena.com (home).

JINDAL, Bobby, ScB, MLitt; American politician; *Governor of Louisiana;* b. (Piyush Jindal), 10 June 1971, Baton Rouge, La; s. of Amar Jindal and Raj Jindal of New Delhi, India; m. Supriya Jolly; three c.; ed Baton Rouge High School, Brown Univ., Providence, RI, Univ. of Oxford, UK (Rhodes Scholar); consultant for McKinsey & Co., Washington, DC 1994–95; Sec., La Dept of Health and Hosps 1996–98; Exec. Dir Nat. Bipartisan Comm. on the Future of Medicare 1998–99; volunteer in Gov. of La Office and State Legislature 1999; Pres. Univ. of Louisiana System 1999–2001; Asst Sec. for Planning and Evaluation of Health and Human Services 2001–03; cand. for Gov. of La 2003; elected to US Congress for La's First Dist 2004, re-elected 2006, mem. House Cttee on Homeland Security, House Cttee on Natural Resources; Gov. of Louisiana 2008– (state's first ethnic minority gov. since Reconstruction and youngest current-serving gov. in USA); mem. Bd of Dirs Our Lady of the Lake Hosp., Baton Rouge 2000–01, Educ. Comm. of States 2000–01, Nat. Conf. Cttee and Justice, Baton Rouge chapter 2000–01; mem. Salvation Army, Baton Rouge 1986–87, Better Business Bureau, Baton Rouge 1987–88, Teach for America, Baton Rouge chapter 1997–98; Republican; named to All-USA First Acad. Team, USA Today 1992, named La's Most Outstanding Young Man, Jr Chamber of Commerce 1995, Jefferson Award, Nat. Inst. of Public Service 1998, chosen by Scholastic Update magazine as "one of America's top 10 extraordinary young people for the next millennium", India Abroad Person of the Year 2005. *Leisure interest:* tennis. *Address:* Office of the Governor, PO Box 94004, Baton Rouge, LA 70804-9004, USA (office). *Telephone:* (225) 342-0991 (office). *Fax:* (225) 342-7099 (office). *E-mail:* info@bobbyjindal.com (office). *Website:* www.gov.state.la.us (office); www.bobbyjindal.com (office).

JING, Shuping; Chinese industrialist; *Honorary Chairman, China Minsheng Banking Corporation;* b. 1918, Shangyu Co., Zheijiang Prov.; ed St John's Univ., Shanghai; Deputy Man. Xinzhong Factory, Shanghai 1940–42; Man. Changxing Trade Co. 1943–50; Deputy Sec.-Gen. Fed. of Industry and Commerce 1963; mem. Bd of Dirs China Int. Trust and Investment Corpn 1979, Vice-Pres. 1984–89, Exec. Dir, Chair. Bd Dirs 1988; Chair. Bd Dirs China Minsheng Banking Corpn 1993, currently Hon. Chair.; Pres. China Int. Econ. Consultants Inc. 1981–; Vice-Chair. Exec. Cttee of All-China Fed. of Industry and Commerce 1988–93, also fmr Chair.; mem. Standing Cttee 6th NPC 1986; mem. 2nd CPPCC Nat. Cttee 1954–59, 3rd CPPCC Nat. Cttee 1959–64, 4th CPPCC Nat. Cttee 1964–78, 5th CPPCC Nat. Cttee 1978–83, Standing Cttee 6th CPPCC Nat. Cttee 1983–88, Deputy Sec.-Gen. 7th CPPCC Nat. Cttee 1988–93, Deputy Sec.-Gen. 8th CPPCC Nat. Cttee 1993–98, Vice-Chair. 9th CPPCC Nat. Cttee 1998–2003; mem. NPC Preliminary Working Cttee of Preparatory Cttee of Hong Kong Special Admin. Region (SAR) 1993–97; mem. Hong Kong Hand-Over Ceremony Govt Del., Hong Kong SAR Preparatory Cttee 1997, Macao Hand-Over Ceremony Govt Del., Macao SAR Preparatory Cttee 1999; Vice-Chair. Asscn for Relations Across the Taiwan Straits 1991–; Vice-Pres. Taiwan Studies Soc. 1988–. *Address:* China Minsheng Banking Corporation, 2 Fuxingmen Nei Street, Xicheng District, Beijing 100031, People's Republic of China (office).

JINGILI, Ali Ahmad Jama; Somali politician; Minister for Information 2007–08, of Foreign Affairs and Int. Co-operation 2008 (resgnd). *Address:* c/o Ministry of Foreign Affairs and International Co-operation, Mogadishu, Somalia (office).

JIRICNA, Eva Magdalena, CBE, DipArch, RIBA; British architect; *Principal, Eva Jiricna Architects;* b. 3 March 1939, Zlin, Czechoslovakia; d. of the late Josef Jiricny and Eva Jiricna; ed Univ. of Prague, Prague Acad. of Fine Arts; worked with GLC's School Div. 1968; Louis de Soissons Partnership 1969–78, Project Architect; practice with David Hodges 1978; team leader at Richard Rogers Partnership 1982–84; f. own practice 1984, re-formed as Eva Jiricna Architects 1986–; External Examiner for RCA and Schools of Architecture at Leicester, Sheffield, Oxford, Bath, Humberside and Plymouth Univs and for RIBA; Pres. Architectural Asscn, London 2004–05; mem. RIBA Gold Medal Jury 2005–06, RIBA Regional Awards Jury (Chair.) 2005, Design Review panel CABE 2005–07; Adviser Civic Trust Nat. Awards panel 2005–06; Trustee, London Open House; Hon. Fellow, RCA 1990, RDI 1991, RSA 1993, Royal Incorporation of Architects in Scotland 1996, RA 1997, AIA 2006; Hon. Prof. of Architecture and Design, Univ. of Applied Arts, Prague 2000; Hon. DTech (Southampton, Brno, Czech Repub.) 2000; Hon. DLitt (Sheffield) 2000; Design Prize, RA 1994. *Television includes:* Tales from Prague, BBC 2, Architecture of the Imagination: Staircases, BBC 2 1990, The Late Show: Czech Modernism 1994, Wideworld, Anglia TV 1997, The Dome: Trouble at the Big Top, BBC 2 1999. *Publications include:* Eva Jiricna: Design in Exile, The Joseph Shops: Eva Jiricna, Staircases, In/Ex Terior: The Works of Eva Jiricna 2005. *Address:* Eva Jiricna Architects, Third Floor, 38 Warren Street, London, W1T 6AE, England (office). *Telephone:* (20) 7554-2400 (office). *Fax:* (20) 7388-8022 (office). *E-mail:* mail@ejal.com (office). *Website:* www.ejal.com (office).

JISCHKE, Martin C., PhD; American engineer and academic administrator; b. 7 Aug. 1941, Chicago, Ill.; m. Patricia Fowler Jischke; one s. one d.; ed Illinois Tech. Inst. Chicago, Massachusetts Inst. of Tech.; Asst to Transportation Sec. US Dept of Transportation, Washington, DC 1975–76; Dir and Prof., School of Aerospace, Mechanical and Nuclear Eng., Univ. of Okla 1977–81, Dean of Eng Coll. 1981–86, Acting Pres. 1985; Chancellor Mo.-Rolla Univ. 1986–91; Pres. Iowa State Univ. 1991–2000, Purdue Univ. 2000–07; Pres. Asscn of Big Twelve Univs 1994; mem. Bd of Dirs Bankers Trust 1995–, American Council on Educ. 1996–, Nat. Merit Scholarship Corpn 1997–; Founding Pres. Global Consortium of Higher Educ. and Research for Agric. 1999; Fellow, AAAS, AIAA; numerous awards including Centennial Medallion of American Soc. for Eng Educ., Ukraine Medal of Merit, Professional Achievement Award from Ill. Inst. of Tech., Justin Smith Morrill Award from US Dept of Agriculture 2004. *Publications:* articles in specialist journals. *Leisure interests:* golf, reading, travel. *Address:* 500 McCormick Road, West Lafayette, IN 47906, USA (home).

JOANNOU, Dakis, MCE, DArch; Greek business executive; *Chairman, J&P-Avax SA;* b. 1939, Nicosia, Cyprus; s. of Stelios Joannou and Ellie Joannou; m. Lietta Joannou; two s. two d.; ed Cornell Univ., Ithaca, NY, USA, Univ. of

Rome, Italy; Chair. J&P-AVAX SA, Pres. Exec. Bd J&P Group of Cos, J&P (Overseas); Chair. Athenaeum InterContinental Hotel & Touristic Enterprises SA, Yes! Hotels & Restaurants; f. Deste Foundation 1983, currently Pres.; mem. Int. Dir's Council Solomon R.F. Guggenheim Foundation, New York; mem. Tate Modern, London, UK; mem. Bd of Trustees, New Museum of Contemporary Art, New York. *Leisure interest:* collecting contemporary art. *Address:* 9 Fragoklissias Street, Marousi 15125, Greece (office). *Website:* www.deste.gr; www.jp-avax.gr.

JOBIM, Nelson Azevedo; Brazilian lawyer and politician; *Minister of Defence;* b. 12 April 1946, Santa Maria; ed Universidade Federal do Rio Grande do Sul; practised as lawyer 1969–94; Assoc. Prof. of Law, Universidade Federal de Santa Maria, Universidade de Brasília 1973–87; Pres. Santa Maria section, Bar Asscn 1977–78, Vice-Pres. Rio Grande Do Sul section 1984–86; mem. Partido do Movimento Democrático Brasileiro (PMDB), Leader PMDB in Nat. Ass. 1988; elected mem. of Parl. for Rio Grande do Sul 1987–91, re-elected 1991; Minister of Justice 1995–97, Minister of Defence 2007–; served as judge and Pres. Supreme Fed. Court. *Address:* Ministry of Defence, Esplanada dos Ministérios, Bloco Q, 70049-900 Brasília, DF, Brazil (office). *Telephone:* (61) 3312-4000 (office). *Fax:* (61) 3225-4151 (office). *E-mail:* faleconosco@defesa.gov.br (office). *Website:* www.defesa.gov.br (office).

JOBS, Steven Paul; American computer industry executive; *CEO, Apple Computer, Inc.;* b. 24 Feb. 1955, San Francisco, Calif.; adopted s. of Paul J. Jobs and Clara J. Jobs; m. Laurene Powell 1991; three c.; ed Homestead High School, Los Altos, Calif., Reed Coll., Portland, Ore.; summer employee, Hewlett-Packard, Palo Alto, Calif. while in high school; video game designer, Atari Inc. 1974; co-f. (with Stephan Wozniak) Apple Computer, Inc., Cupertino, Calif., Chair. 1975–85, Consultant 1997–, Interim CEO 1997–2000, mem. Bd of Dirs and CEO 2000–; Pres. NeXT Inc., Calif. 1985–96; acquired Pixar Animation Studios from George Lucas, Chair. and CEO 1986–2006, mem. Bd of Dirs The Walt Disney Co. (after Disney acquisition of Pixar 2005); Pres. Mozilla Foundation 2005–; Co-designer (with Stephan Wozniak) Apple I 1976, Apple II 1977; Nat. Medal of Tech. *Address:* Apple Computer Inc., 1 Infinite Loop, Cupertino, CA 95014, USA (office). *Telephone:* (408) 996-1010 (office). *Fax:* (408) 974-2113 (office). *E-mail:* media.help@apple.com (office). *Website:* www.apple.com (office).

JOČIĆ, Dragan; Serbian lawyer and politician; b. 1960, Belgrade; ed Faculty of Law, Univ. of Belgrade; est. pvt. law practice, Belgrade; founding mem., Democratic Party of Serbia (DSS) 1992, mem. Exec. Bd 1992–, currently Vice-Pres.; elected Deputy to Serbian Parl. 1992–97; mem. Belgrade City Council 2000–; Pres. Parl. Comm. for Defence and Security 2002; Minister of Internal Affairs 2004–08. *Address:* Democratic Party of Serbia (Demokratska stranka Srbije), 11000 Belgrade, Pariska 13, Serbia (office). *Telephone:* (11) 3204719 (office). *Fax:* (11) 3204743 (office). *E-mail:* info@dss.org.yu (office). *Website:* www.dss.org.yu (office).

JODICE, Mimmo; Italian photographer and professor of fine arts; b. 29 March 1934, Naples; m. Angela Jodice; two s. one d.; Prof. Acad. of Fine Arts, Naples 1970–96; first photographic exhbn in Milan (with text of Cesare Zavattini) 1970; exhibited in many major museums including San Francisco Museum of Art, Philadelphia Museum of Art, Museo di Capodimonte, Cleveland Museum of Art, Castello di Rivoli, Turin 1970–; Prix Accad. dei Lincei for Photography 2004. *Publications include:* La Città Invisibile 1990, Mediterranean 1995, Paris 1998, Eden 1998, Isolario Mediterraneo 2000, Anni Settanta 2000, Boston 2001, Mare 2003. *Leisure interest:* classical music. *Address:* Baudoin Lebon Gallery, 38 rue St Croix de la Bretonnerie, 75004 Paris, France (office); Salita Casale 24, 80123 Naples, Italy (office). *Telephone:* (081) 2466144 (office). *Fax:* (081) 2466144 (office). *E-mail:* mimmo.jodice@inwind.it (office).

JOEL, William (Billy) Martin; American singer, songwriter and musician (piano); b. 9 May 1949, Bronx, NY; s. of Howard Joel and Rosalind Nyman; m. 2nd Christie Brinkley 1985 (divorced 1994); one d.; m. 3rd Kate Lee 2004; solo recording artist 1972–; first tour of USSR by American popular music artist 1987; numerous tours, live appearances world-wide; Dr hc (Fairfield Univ.) 1991, (Berklee Coll. of Music) 1993; Hon. DHL (Hofstra Univ.) 1997; Hon. DMus (Long Island Univ.) 2000; Grammy Awards for Record of the Year (for Just the Way You Are) 1978, for Song of the Year (for Just the Way You Are) 1978, Grammy Legend Award 1990, ASCAP Founders' Award 1997, numerous American Music Awards, including American Music Award of Merit 1999, RIAA Diamond Award 1999, James Smithson Bicentennial Medal of Honor 2000. *Recordings include:* albums: Cold Spring Harbor 1971, Piano Man 1973, Streetlife Serenade 1974, Turnstiles 1976, The Stranger 1977, 52nd Street (Grammy Awards for Album of the Year, for Best Pop Vocal Performance) 1979, Glass Houses (Grammy Award for Best Pop Vocal Performance) 1980, Songs In The Attic 1981, The Nylon Curtain 1982, An Innocent Man 1983, Greatest Hits Volume I & II 1985, The Bridge 1986, Kohuept 1987, Storm Front 1989, River Of Dreams 1993, Greatest Hits Volume III 1997, 2000 Millennium Concert 2000, The Essential Billy Joel 2001, Fantasies and Delusions 2001, Movin Out 2002,. *Publication:* Goodnight My Angel: A Lullabye (juvenile fiction) 2004. *Address:* c/o Columbia Records, Sony BMG Music, 550 Madison Avenue, New York, NY 10022-3211, USA (home). *Website:* www.sonybmg.com (office); www.billyjoel.com.

JOERRES, Jeffrey (Jeff) A., BS; American business executive; *Chairman, President and CEO, Manpower Inc.;* ed Marquette Univ., Milwaukee, Wis.; fmr Man. IBM; Vice-Pres. of Sales and Marketing ARI Network Services –1993; Vice-Pres. of Marketing, Manpower Inc. 1993, becoming Sr Vice-Pres. of European Operations, Global Account Man. and Devt, Pres. and CEO 1999–, Chair. 2001–; Dir Artisan Funds, Johnson Controls Inc., Nat. Asscn of Mfrs; Co-Chair. CEO Diversity Cttee of Greater Milwaukee Cttee, NAACP Nat. Convention, Milwaukee 2005; Trustee, Cttee for Econ. Devt (CED). *Address:* Manpower Inc., 100 Manpower Place, Milwaukee, WI 53212, USA (office). *Telephone:* (414) 961-1000 (office). *Fax:* (414) 906-7985 (office). *E-mail:* info@manpower.com (office). *Website:* www.manpower.com (office).

JÕERÜÜT, Jaak; Estonian politician and diplomatist; *Ambassador to Latvia;* b. 9 Dec. 1947, Tallinn; m.; ed Faculty of Econs, Tallinn Technical Inst.; Ed. Eesti Raamat publishing house 1976–77; Sec. and Deputy Chair. Estonian Writers' Union 1977–89; Deputy Minister, Ministry of Culture 1989–90; mem. Parl. 1990–92, Chair. Standing Cttee on Research, Educ. and Culture; Amb. to Finland 1993–97; Dir-Gen. Protocol Dept, Ministry of Foreign Affairs 1997–98; Amb. to Italy 1998–2002, to Malta 1999–2002, to Cyprus 1999–2004; Inspector-Gen., Ministry of Foreign Affairs 2002–04; Special Adviser to the Govt 2002–03; Perm. Rep. to UN, New York July–Nov. 2004; Minister of Defence 2004–05; Amb. to Latvia 2006–; mem. Estonian Writers' Union, Estonian PEN. *Address:* Embassy of Estonia, Skolas iela 13, Rīga 1010, Latvia (office). *Telephone:* 6781-2020 (office). *Fax:* 6781-2029 (office). *E-mail:* embassy.riga@mfa.ee (office). *Website:* www.estemb.lv (office).

JOFFE, Josef, PhD; German journalist, editor and international relations scholar; *Publisher-Editor, Die Zeit;* b. 15 March 1944, Łódź, Poland; m. Dr Christine Joffe; two d.; ed Swarthmore Coll., Johns Hopkins Univ., Harvard Univ., USA; Foreign and Editorial Page Dir Suddeutsche Zeitung 1985–2000; Publr-Ed. Die Zeit newspaper 2000–; Professorial Lecturer, Johns Hopkins Univ. 1982–84; Adjunct Prof. of Political Science, Stanford Univ. 2004–, Fellow, Inst. for Int. Studies, Stanford 2004, now Sr Fellow; Fellow, Hoover Inst.; Visiting Prof. of Govt, Harvard Univ. 1999–2000, Assoc., Olin Inst. for Strategic Studies; Visiting Lecturer, Princeton Univ., Dartmouth Univ.; Founding Bd mem. The National Interest 1995–2005, The American Interest; mem. Editorial Bd International Security, Prospect; Order of Merit, Germany 1998; hon. degree (Swarthmore Coll.) 2002, (Lewis and Clark Coll.) 2005; Theodor-Wolff-Prize in Journalism (Germany), Ludwig Börne Prize in Essays/Literature (Germany). *Publications include:* The Limited Partnership: Europe, the United States and the Burdens of Alliance 1987, The Great Powers 1998, Überpower: The Imperial Temptation of America 2006; numerous articles in scholarly journals and chapters in books. *Address:* Die Zeit, Speersort 1, 20095 Hamburg, Germany (office). *Telephone:* (40) 328-00 (office). *Fax:* (40) 3280-596 (office). *E-mail:* gentsch@zeit.de (office). *Website:* www.zeit.de (office).

JOFFE, Roland I. V.; British film director; b. 17 Nov. 1945, London; m. Jane Lapotaire (divorced); one s.; ed Carmel Coll., Berks. and Univ. of Manchester; Prix Italia 1978, Prix de la Presse, Prague 1978, Premio San Fidele 1985. *Films:* The Killing Fields 1984, The Mission 1986, Fat Man and Little Boy 1989, City of Joy 1991, Super Mario Bros (producer only), The Scarlet Letter 1995, Goodbye Lover 1999, Vatel 2000, Captivity 2007. *Television includes:* Spongers 1978, No Mama No 1980, United Kingdom 1981, 'Tis Pity She's a Whore 1982, Shadow Makers 1990, The Stars Look Down (series). *Address:* William Morris Agency, 151 South El Camino Drive, Beverly Hills, CA 90212, USA.

JÓHANNESSON, Jón Ásgeir; Icelandic retail executive; *President and CEO, Baugur Group hf;* b. 1968, Reykjavík; s. of Jóhannes Jónsson; ; ed Commercial Coll. of Iceland; with father f. Bonus discount grocery chain 1989, merged with rival Hagkaup to form Baugur Group hf, has served as Man. Dir, CEO, and Chair., currently Pres. and CEO; has acquired several UK retail cos including Oasis, Karen Millen, Whistles, Warehouse and Principles, Hamleys, Goldsmiths, Big Food Group, House of Fraser; mem. Bd of Dirs Straumur-Burdaras (Icelandic investment bank). *Address:* Baugur Group hf, Túngötu 6, 101 Reykjavík, Iceland (office). *Telephone:* 5307800 (office). *Fax:* 5307801 (office). *E-mail:* jon.asgeir@baugurgroup.com (office). *Website:* www.baugurgroup.com (office).

JOHANNS, Michael (Mike) Owen, BA, JD; American lawyer and politician; *Senator from Nebraska;* b. 18 June 1950, Osage, Ia; s. of John Robert Johanns and Adeline Lucy Johanns (née Royek); m. 1st Constance J. Weiss 1972 (divorced 1985); one s. one d.; m. 2nd Stephanie Suther 1986; ed St Mary's Coll., Creighton Univ.; law clerk, Neb. State Supreme Court 1974–75; Assoc., Cronin and Hannon (law firm) 1975–76; Pnr, Nelson, Johanns, Morris, Holdeman and Titus, Lincoln, Neb. 1976–91; Commr Lancaster Co., Neb. 1982–86; mem. Lincoln City Council 1989–91, Mayor of Lincoln 1991–98; Gov. of Neb. 1999–2005; Sec., US Dept of Agric., Washington, DC 2005–09; Senator from Neb. 2009–; fmr Chair. Gov.'s Ethanol Coalition; fmr Co-Chair. Gov.s' Biotechnology Partnership, Gov.s' Public Power Alliance; fmr Vice-Chair. Midwest Gov.s' Asscn; fmr mem. League of Nebraska Municipalities, Midwest Govs Conf., Nat. Govs Asscn, Republican Govs Asscn, US Conf. of Mayors, Western Govs Asscn; Republican. *Address:* 404 Russell Senate Office Building, Washington, DC 20510, USA (office). *Telephone:* (202) 224-4224 (office). *Fax:* (202) 228-0436 (office). *E-mail:* mike_johanns@johanns.senate.gov (office). *Website:* johanns.senate.gov (office).

JÓHANNSSON, Kjartan, CE, PhD; Icelandic politician and diplomatist; b. 19 Dec. 1939, Reykjavik; s. of Jóhann and Astrid Dahl Thorsteinsson; m. Irma Karlsdóttir 1964; one d.; ed Reykjavik Coll., Tech. Univ. of Stockholm, Sweden, Univ. of Stockholm, Illinois Inst. of Tech., Chicago; Consulting Eng in Reykjavik 1966–78; Teacher in Faculty of Eng and Science, later Prof. in Faculty for Econs and Business Admin, Univ. of Iceland 1966–78, 1980–89; Chair. Org. for Support of the Elderly, Hafnarfjördür; mem. Bd of Dir Icelandic Aluminium Co. Ltd 1970–75; Chair. Fisheries Bd of Municipal Trawler Co., Hafnarfjördür 1970–74; mem. Municipal Council, Hafnarfjördür 1974–78; mem. Party Council and Exec. Council, Social Democratic Party 1972–89, Vice-Chair. of Social Democratic Party 1974–80, Chair. 1980–84; mem. Althing (Parl.) 1978–89, Speaker of the Lower House 1988–89; Minister of Fisheries 1978–80, also Minister of Commerce 1979–80; Amb. and Perm. Rep. to UN and other int. orgs Geneva 1989–94; Sec.-Gen. EFTA 1994–2001; mem. staff External Trade Department, Ministry of Foreign Affairs 2002; Amb. to Belgium, Liechtenstein, Luxembourg and Chief of Mission to the EU 2002–05. *Address:* c/o Ministry of Foreign Affairs, Raudarárstíg 25, 150 Reykjavík (office); Vatusstig 21, 101 Reykjavík, Iceland (home). *Telephone:* 5459900 (office); 5342597 (home). *Fax:* 5622373 (office). *E-mail:* postur@utn .stjr.is (office); kjartan.johannsson@gmail.com (home). *Website:* utanrikisraduneyti.is.

JOHANSEN, Hans Christian, DrOec; Danish professor of economic history; b. 27 June 1935, Århus; s. of Vilhelm Johansen and Clara Andersen; m. Kirstine Madsen 1967; one s. one d.; ed Univ. of Århus; Danish Foreign Service 1963–64; Sr Lecturer, Univ. of Århus 1964–70; Prof. of Econ. History, Univ. of Odense 1970–2003; Dir Danish Centre for Demographic Research 1998–2002. *Publications:* books and articles on Danish and int. econ. and social history in the 18th, 19th and 20th centuries. *Address:* Anne Maries Alle 4A, 5250 Odense SV, Denmark (home). *Telephone:* 66-17-21-05 (home). *E-mail:* hcj@hist.sdu.dk (office).

JOHANSEN, John MacLane, MArch; American architect; b. 29 June 1916, New York; s. of John C. and Jean MacLane Johansen; m. 1st Mary Lee Longcope 1945; m. 2nd Beate Forberg 1981; one s. one d.; ed Harvard Coll. and Harvard Grad. School of Design; self-employed architect 1947, est. office in New York 1950, est. firm of Johansen-Bhavnani 1973, pvt. practice, New York 1989–; Pres. Architectural League 1968–70; Prof., Pratt Inst.; Prof. of Architecture at Yale Univ. at various times and has taught for short periods at MIT, Columbia and Harvard Univs and Univ. of Pa; Architect in Residence, American Acad. in Rome 1975; mem. American Acad. of Arts and Letters; Hon. DFA (Maryland Inst. and Clark Univ.); Brunner Award 1968, Honor Award, AIA 1972, Gold Medal, New York Chapter, AIA 1976, Bard Award, City Club of NY 1977. *Publications:* An Architecture for the Electronic Age, The Three Imperatives of Architecture, Observations and Deductions, John M. Johnnsen: A Life in the Continuum of Modern Architecture 1995. *Leisure interests:* painting, writing, music, building construction, sport, travel. *Address:* 821 Broadway, New York, NY 10003, USA.

JOHANSEN, Peter, DrPhil; Danish computer scientist and academic; *Professor of Computer Science, University of Copenhagen;* b. 29 Jan. 1938, Copenhagen; s. of Paul Johansen and Grethe Johansen (née Smith); m. Jytte Jepsen 1963; one s. two d.; ed Univ. of Copenhagen; Asst Prof. Tech. Univ. 1964–67; mem. Research Staff, MIT 1967–69; Asst Prof. of Computer Science, Univ. of Copenhagen 1969–74, Prof. 1974–, Dean of Faculty 1988–90; Visiting Prof., Univ. of Manoa, Hawaii, USA 1977–78; mem. Danish Natural Science Research Council 1981–84, Royal Danish Acad. of Sciences 1984–; Kt (First Class) Order of Dannebrog. *Publications:* An Algebraic Normal Form for Regular Events 1972, The Generating Function of the Number of Subpatterns 1979, Representing Signals by their Toppoints in Scale Space 1986, Inductive Inference of Ultimately Periodic Sequences 1988, On the Classification of Toppoints in Scale Space 1994, On-line string matching with feedback 1995, Adaptive Pattern Recognition 1997, Branch Points in One-dimensional Gaussian Scale Space 2000, Products of Random Matrices 2002. *Address:* Ørnebakken 72, 2840 Holte (home); Datalogisk Institut, Room S203, Universitetsparken 1, 2100 Copenhagen, Denmark (office). *Telephone:* 35-32-14-42 (office). *Website:* www.diku.dk/~peterjo (office).

JOHANSON, Donald Carl, PhD; American physical anthropologist and academic; *Director, Institute of Human Origins, Arizona State University;* b. 28 June 1943, Chicago, Ill.; s. of Carl Torsten and Sally Eugenia Johanson (née Johnson); m. 1st Chris Boner 1967 (divorced); m. 2nd Susan Whelan 1981 (divorced); one step-s. one step-d.; m. 3rd Lenora Carey 1988 (divorced); one s.; ed Univ. of Illinois, Univ. of Chicago; mem. Dept of Physical Anthropology, Cleveland Museum of Natural History 1972–81, Curator 1974–81; Adjunct Prof. Case Western Reserve Univ. 1982; Prof. of Anthropology, Stanford Univ. 1983–89; Prof. of Anthropology and Dir Inst. of Human Origins, Ariz. State Univ. 1997–; host, Nature (series), Public Broadcasting Service TV 1982, host-narrator three-part Nova series In Search of Human Origins 1994; Pres. Inst. of Human Origins, Berkeley 1981–97; Fellow, AAAS, Royal Geographical Soc., California Acad. of Sciences; Hon. DSc (John Carroll) 1979, (The Coll. of Wooster) 1985, (Case Western Reserve) 2009; Fregene Prize 1987, American Book Award 1982, Distinguished Service Award, American Humanist Asscn 1983, Golden Plate, American Acad. of Achievement 1976, Professional Achievement Award 1980, Outstanding Achievement Award 1979, Golden Mercury Int. Award 1982, Alumni Achievement Award, Univ. of Ill. 1995, Anthropology in Media Award, American Asscn of Anthropologists 1999. *Television:* The First Family 1981, Lucy in Disguise 1982, In Search of Human Origins 1994. *Publications:* The Beginnings of Humankind (with M. A. Edey) (American Book Award) 1981, Blueprints: Solving the Mystery of Evolution (with M. A. Edey) 1989, Lucy's Child: The Discovery of a Human Ancestor (with James Shreeve) 1989, Journey from the Dawn (with Kevin O'Farrell) 1990, Ancestors: In Search of Human Origins (with L. E. Johanson and Blake Edgar) 1994, From Lucy to Language (with Blake Edgar) 1997, Ecce Homo (co-ed. with G. Ligabue) 1999, The Skull of Australopithecus afarensis (with W. H. Kimbel and Y. Rak) 2004, Lucy's Legacy: The Quest for Human Origins (with Kate Wong) 2009; many scientific articles, papers and reviews. *Leisure interests:* photography, tennis, fly-fishing, classical music (including opera), golf. *Address:* Institute of Human Origins, Arizona State University, PO Box 874101, Tempe, AZ 85287, USA (office). *Telephone:* (480) 727-6580 (office). *Fax:* (480) 727-6570 (office). *E-mail:* johanson.iho@asu.edu (office). *Website:* www.becominghuman.org (office); iho.asu.edu (office).

JOHANSSON, (Erik) Lennart Valdemar; Swedish business executive; b. 3 Oct. 1921, Gothenburg; s. of Waldemar and Alma Johansson (née Nordh); m.

Inger Hedberg 1944; two s. one d.; ed Tech. Coll.; Production Engineer AB SKF 1943, Man. of Mfg 1961, Gen. Man. 1966, Deputy Man. Dir 1969, Pres. and Group CEO 1971–95, Chair. 1985–92, Hon. Chair. 1992–; mem. Royal Swedish Acad. of Eng Sciences 1971; D Tech. hc (Chalmers Univ. of Tech., Gothenburg) 1979; Hon. DTech (Sarajevo) 1983; King of Sweden's Medal, John Ericsson Medal 1986; Commdr Merito della Repub. Italiana, Commdr Royal Order of Vasa, Yugoslav Star Medal with Golden Garland, Das grosse Bundesverdienstkreuz, Kt Commdr's Cross (1st Class), Finnish Order of the Lion. *Leisure interests:* sailing, swimming. *Address:* Berzeliigatan 11-65, 412 53 Gothenburg, Sweden (home).

JOHANSSON, Leif, MSc (Eng); Swedish business executive; *President and CEO, AB Volvo;* b. 30 Aug. 1951, Gothenburg; s. of Lennart Johansson (q.v.) and Inger Johansson; m. Eva Birgitta Fjellman; two s. three d.; ed Ed. Chalmers Univ. of Tech.; joined Electrolux 1978, Chief Exec. 1994; mem. Bd Dirs, Pres. and CEO AB Volvo, Gothenburg 1997–; mem. Bd Dirs Bristol-Myers Squibb Co., Svenska Cellulosa AB SCA, Confed. of Swedish Enterprise, Asscn of Swedish Eng Industries; Dir Confed. of Swedish Enterprise; mem. Royal Swedish Acad. of Eng Sciences; Order of the Seraphim 2001, Chevalier de la Légion d'honneur. *Address:* AB Volvo, 405 08 Göteborg, Sweden (office). *Telephone:* (31) 66-00-90 (office). *Fax:* (31) 54-33-72 (office). *E-mail:* leif .johansson@volvo.com. *Website:* www.volvo.com (office).

JOHANSSON, Olof; Swedish business executive and fmr politician; b. 1937, Ljungby, Kalmar; m. Inger Johansson; two s.; non-commissioned reserve officer 1959; farm-worker, journalist, office worker, teacher 1953–65; mem. Stockholm City Council 1966–70; Sec. Centre Party's Parl. Group 1966–69, Chair. Youth League 1969–71; mem. Parl. 1971–76, 1978–79, 1982–98; mem. Nat. Bd Centre Party 1971–87, Asst Deputy Leader 1979–86, Deputy Leader 1986–87, Leader 1987; Minister for Energy and Tech. Devt 1976–78, for Civil Service Affairs and Personnel 1979–82, for the Environment 1991–94; mem. Council of Europe 1986–97, Nordic Council 1986–97, Advisory Council on Foreign Affairs 1987–97; Chair. Systembolaget 2002–08. *Address:* c/o System-bolaget, Kungsträdgårdsgatan 14, 103484 Stockholm, Sweden.

JOHANSSON, Scarlett; American actress; b. 22 Nov. 1984, New York; m. Ryan Reynolds 2008; ed Professional Children's School, Manhattan; face of Eternity Moment perfume 2004. *Films include:* North 1994, Just Cause 1995, If Lucy Fell 1996, Manny & Lo 1996, Home Alone III 1997, The Horse Whisperer (Hollywood Reporter Young Star Award) 1998, My Brother the Pig 1999, Ghost World (Best Supporting Actress, Toronto Film Critics Asscn) 2000, The Man Who Wasn't There 2001, An American Rhapsody 2001, Eight Legged Freaks 2002, Lost in Translation (Countercurrent Prize for Best Actress, Venice Film Festival, Best Actress, BAFTA Awards, Best Actress, Boston Soc. of Film Critics) 2003, Girl with a Pearl Earring 2003, The Perfect Score 2004, A Love Song for Bobby Long 2004, The SpongeBob SquarePants Movie (voice) 2004, In Good Company 2004, Match Point 2005, A Good Woman 2005, The Island 2005, Scoop 2006, The Black Dahlia 2006, The Prestige 2006, The Nanny Diaries 2007, The Other Boleyn Girl 2008, Vicky Cristina Barcelona 2008. *Recording:* album: Anywhere I Lay my Head 2008. *Address:* c/o Marcel Pariseau, True Public Relations, 6725 W Sunset Boulevard, Suite 570, Los Angeles, CA 90028, USA (office).

JOHANSSON-HEDBERG, Birgitta, BA; Swedish psychologist and business executive; *Chairman, Vinnova;* b. 1947; ed Lund Univ.; Chair. AB Lindex 1993–2004; fmr Resident Dir for Scandinavia, Wolters Kluwer; CEO FöreningsSparbanken (Swedbank) (formed by merger of Föreningsbanken AB and Sparbanken Sverige 1997) –2003; Pres. and CEO Svenska Lantmännen (Swedish Farmers' Supply and Crop Marketing Asscn) 2004–06; Chair. Vinnova 2007–; Deputy Chair. A-banan; mem. Bd of Dirs Svea Skog 2002–, Fortum Corpn 2004–, Swedish Financial Supervisory Authority, NAXS Nordic Access Buyout Fund, Forest Co. Ltd 2008–, TeliaSonera AB 1993–2001, Skandia 2004–05; Chair. Umeå Univ.; mem. Aktiemarknadsnämnden, Swedish Securities Council; ranked by Fortune magazine amongst 50 Most Powerful Women in Business outside the US (32nd) 2002. *Address:* Vinnova, 101 58, Stockholm, Sweden (office). *Telephone:* (8) 473-30-00 (office). *E-mail:* vinnova@vinnova.se (office). *Website:* www .vinnova.se (office).

JOHN, Sir David Glyndwr, Kt, KCMG, MA, MBA; British business executive; *Chairman, Premier Oil PLC;* b. 20 July 1938, Pontypridd; s. of William G. John and Marjorie John; m. Gillian Edwards 1964; one s. one d.; ed Christ's Coll., Cambridge, Columbia Univ., New York and Harvard Univ., USA; trainee man. British Steel; later worked for RTZ and Redland; joined Gray Mackenzie (Inchcape Group) 1981, Chief Exec. 1986; Chief Exec. Inchcape Berhad 1987, Chair. 1990; mem. Bd Inchcape PLC 1988–95; Exec. Chair. Inchcape Toyota Motors 1995, BSI Group 2002–; Chair. (non-exec.) Premier Oil PLC 1998–; Dir (non-exec.) BOC Group PLC 1993– (Chair. (non-exec.) 1996–2002), The St Paul Cos Inc., Minn., USA 1996–2003, Balfour Beatty PLC 2000– (Chair. 2003–), Welsh Devt Agency 2001–02; Dr hc (Univ. of Glamorgan). *Leisure interests:* reading, gardening. *Address:* Premier Oil PLC, 23 Lower Belgrave Street, London, SW1W 0NR, England (office). *Telephone:* (20) 7730-1111 (office). *Fax:* (20) 7730-4696 (office). *E-mail:* premier@premier-oil.com (office). *Website:* www.premier-oil.com (office).

JOHN, Sir Elton, Kt, CBE; British musician (piano), singer and songwriter; b. (Reginald Kenneth Dwight), 25 March 1947, Pinner, Middx; s. of Stanley Dwight and Sheila Farebrother; m. Renata Blauel 1984 (divorced 1988); pnr David Furnish; ed Pinner Co. Grammar School, Royal Acad. of Music; began piano lessons 1951; played piano in Northwood Hills Hotel bar 1964; mem. local group Bluesology 1961–67; worked for Mills Music Publishers; began writing songs with Bernie Taupin 1967; solo recording contract with DJM Records 1967; concerts in Los Angeles 1970; formed Rocket Record Co. with

Bernie Taupin 1973, first album released 1976; f. publishing co., Big Pig Music 1974; frequent tours in UK, USA, Japan, Australia 1971–76; Vice-Pres. Nat. Youth Theatre of GB 1975–; first int. star to perform concerts in USSR 1979; produced records with Clive Franks for Kiki Dee, Blue, Davey Johnstone's China 1976–77; Chair. Watford Football Club 1976–90, 1997–, Life Pres. 1990–; f. Elton John AIDS Foundation 1993, Rocket Pictures; Trustee Wallace Collection 1999–; Chair. The Old Vic Theatre Trust 2002–; Fellow, British Acad. of Composers and Songwriters 2004–; Officier, Ordre des Arts et des Lettres 1993; Hon. mem. RAM 1997; Dr hc (RAM) 2002; Ivor Novello Awards (for Daniel) 1974, (for Don't Go Breaking My Heart, with Kiki Dee) 1977, (for Song for Guy) 1979, (for Nikita) 1986, (for Sacrifice) 1991, American Music Awards for Favorite Male Artist, Favorite Single 1977, Silver Clef Award 1979, BRIT Awards for Outstanding Contribution to British Music 1986, Best British Male Artist 1991, MTV Special Recognition Trophy 1987, Grammy Awards 1987, 1991, 1998, 2000, Grammy Lifetime Achievement Award 2000, Nat. Acad. of Popular Music Hitmaker Award 1989, Q Magazine Merit Award 1993, Acad. Award for Best Original Song (for Can You Feel the Love Tonight?) 1995, recipient of Kennedy Center Honors 2004. *Films:* Goodbye to Norma Jean 1973, Tommy 1973, To Russia with Elton 1980, The Rainbow 1989, The Lion King (music) 1994. *Stage productions:* The Lion King (musical) 2001, Billy Elliot (musical) 2004, Lestat (musical, with Bernie Taupin) 2006. *Recordings include:* albums: Empty Sky 1969, Elton John 1970, Tumbleweed Connection 1971, Friends (film soundtrack) 1971, 17-11-70 1971, Madman Across the Water 1972, Honky Chateau 1972, Don't Shoot Me, I'm Only the Piano Player 1973, Goodbye Yellow Brick Road 1973, Caribou 1974, Captain Fantastic and the Brown Dirt Cowboy 1975, Rock of the Westies 1975, Here and There 1976, Blue Moves 1976, A Single Man 1978, Victim of Love 1979, Lady Samantha 1980, 21 at 33 1980, The Fox 1981, Jump Up 1982, Too Low for Zero 1983, Breaking Hearts 1984, Ice on Fire 1985, Leather Jackets 1986, Reg Strikes Back 1988, Sleeping with the Past 1989, The One 1992, Made in England 1995, Love Songs 1995, The Big Picture 1997, Aida 1999, El Dorado 2000, Songs from the West Coast 2001, Peachtree Road 2004, The Captain and the Kid 2006, Rocket Man 2007. *Leisure interests:* football, collecting records, tennis, all sports. *Address:* Sanctuary Artist Management, Sanctuary House, 45–53 Sinclair Road, London, W14 0NS, England (office). *Telephone:* (20) 7602-6351 (office). *Fax:* (20) 7603-5941 (office). *Website:* www.eltonjohn.com.

JOHN, Patrick; Dominican politician; b. 7 Jan. 1937; Leader Dominica Labour Party 1974–83, Deputy Leader 1983–84; Minister of Communications and Works 1970–73, Deputy Premier and Minister of Finance 1974, Premier of Dominica 1974–78, Prime Minister 1978–79, Minister for Housing, Security and Devt 1978–79; Gen. Sec. Labour Party of Dominica 1985; mem. Parl. July–Nov. 1985; arrested 1981, tried and acquitted May 1982, re-tried Oct. 1985; sentenced to 12 years' imprisonment for conspiracy to overthrow govt.

JOHN, Sajeev O., BSc, PhD, FRSC; Canadian physicist and academic; *Professor of Physics, University of Toronto;* ed Massachusetts Inst. of Tech., Harvard Univ.; Natural Sciences and Eng Research Council of Canada Postdoctoral Fellow, Univ. of Pennsylvania 1984–86; Asst Prof. of Physics, Princeton Univ. 1986–89; joined Dept of Physics, Univ. of Toronto 1989, Prof. of Physics and Govt of Canada Research Chair 2001–; fmr Prin. Investigator, Photonics Research Ontario; lab. consultant, Corp. Research Science Labs, Exxon Research and Eng 1985–89; lab. consultant, Bell Communications Research, Red Bank, NJ 1989; mem. Max-Planck Soc. (Germany); Fellow, Canadian Inst. for Advanced Research, American Physical Soc., Optical Soc. of America; C.V. Raman Chair Professorship, Govt of India 2007; Herzberg Medal 1996, McLean Fellowship, Univ. of Toronto 1996, Steacie Prize in Science and Eng, Nat. Research Council of Canada 1997, Killam Fellowship, Canada Council for the Arts, Guggenheim Fellowship, Japan Soc. for the Promotion of Science Fellowship, Humboldt Sr Scientist Award (Germany) 2000, King Faisal Int. Prize for Science (co-recipient) 2001, first ever winner of Premier's Platinum Medal for Science and Medicine 2002, Rutherford Medal, Royal Soc. of Canada (co-recipient) 2004, IEEE LEOS Int. Quantum Electronics Award 2007, Brockhouse Medal for Condensed Matter and Materials Physics, Canadian Asscn of Physicists 2007. *Achievement:* co-invented concept of photonic band gap materials 1987. *Address:* Department of Physics, University of Toronto, 60 St George Street, Toronto, Ont. M5S 1A7, Canada (office). *Telephone:* (416) 978-3459 (office). *Fax:* (416) 978-2537 (office). *E-mail:* john@physics.utoronto.ca (office). *Website:* www.physics.utoronto.ca (office).

JOHNOVÁ, Adriena; Czech painter; b. 6 Aug. 1926, Prague; d. of the late Václav Šimota and Milena Šimota; m. Jiři John 1923 (died 1972); one s.; ed Univ. of Industrial Arts; Grand Prix for Graphics, Ljubljana 1979, Grand Prix Int. for Drawings, Wrocław, Gottfried von Herder Prize, Vienna, Medal of Merit, Prague 1997. *Leisure interests:* human relations, literature, music, nature. *Address:* Na Podkovce 14, 140 00 Prague 4; Nad Královskou oborou 15, 170 00 Prague 7, Czech Republic. *Telephone:* (2) 41430393.

JOHNS, Andrew; Australian professional rugby league player (retd); b. 19 May 1974, Cessnock, NSW; halfback/hooker; player for Newcastle Knights 1994–2007, New South Wales 1995–2007, Australia 1995–2007; 212 appearances (62 as Capt.), 75 tries, 1,952 points, for Newcastle Knights, 21 appearances for New South Wales in State of Origin fixtures, 23 tests for Australia (apptd capt. in 2002); mem. of Australia's World Cup winning teams 1995 (named Player of the Tournament and Man of the Match in final) and 2000; winner Rugby League World Golden Boot Award 1999, 2001; winner Nat. Rugby League Player of the Year award three times; captained Newcastle Knights to Premiership title 1997, 2001. *Leisure interests:* surfing, horse racing. *Address:* The Fordham Company, POB 820, Woollahra, NSW 1350, Australia (office). *Telephone:* (02) 93329111 (office).

JOHNS, Anthony Hearle, PhD, FAHA; Australian/British professor of Islamic studies; *Professor Emeritus and Visiting Fellow, Research School of Asian and Pacific Studies, Australian National University;* b. 28 Aug. 1928, Wimbledon, UK; s. of the late Frank Charles Johns and of Ivy Doris Kathleen Johns (née Hearle); m. Yohanni Bey 1956; four s. one d.; ed St Boniface's Coll., Plymouth, UK and School of Oriental and African Studies, Univ. of London; lecturer Ford Foundation-sponsored Training Project, Indonesia 1954–58; Sr Lecturer in Indonesian Languages and Literatures, Australian Nat. Univ. 1958–63, Prof. 1963–, now Prof. Emer., Chair. and Head. Dept 1963–83, Dean Faculty of Asian Studies 1963–64, 1965–67, 1975–79, 1988–91, Head Southeast Asia Centre 1983–88; Visiting Prof., Univ. of Toronto (Dept of Religious Studies and Dept of Middle East and Islamic Studies) 1989; Special Foreign Visiting Prof. in Islamic Studies Chiba Univ., Tokyo 1991; Visiting Scholar, Oxford Centre for Hebrew and Jewish Studies, UK 1993–94; Visiting Fellow, Research School Pacific and Asian Studies, Australian Nat. Univ., Canberra 1994–96, 1997–2000, 2005–; Fellow Inst. for Advanced Studies, Hebrew Univ. of Jerusalem 1984–85; Univ. of London Sr Studentship 1953–54; Rhuvon Guest Prize in Islamic Studies, SOAS 1953–54, Centenary Medal for Service to Australian Society and the Humanities 2003. *Publications:* The Gift Addressed to the Spirit of the Prophet 1965, A Road with No End (trans. and Ed.) 1968, Cultural Options and the Role of Tradition 1981, Islam in Asia II Southeast and East Asia (Ed. and contrib. with R. Israeli) 1984, Reflections on the Dynamics and Spirituality of Sūrat al-Furqān in Literary Structures of Religious Meaning in the Qur'an (contrib.) 2000, Islam in World Politics (Ed. and contrib. with Nelly Lahoud) 2005. *Leisure interests:* music, literature. *Address:* Division of Pacific and Asian History, Research School of Pacific and Asian Studies, Australian National University, Canberra, ACT 0200 (office); 70 Duffy Street, Ainslie, Canberra, ACT 2602, Australia (home). *Telephone:* (2) 6125-3106 (office); (2) 6249-6574 (home). *Fax:* (2) 6125-5525 (office). *E-mail:* ahyj@coombs.anu.edu.au (office); ah_yjohns@netspeed.com.au (home). *Website:* rspas.anu.edu.au (office).

JOHNS, Jasper; American painter; b. 15 May 1930, Augusta; s. of Jasper Johns, Sr and Jean Riley; ed Univ. of South Carolina; works in following collections: Tate Gallery, London, Museum of Modern Art, New York, Albright-Knox Art Gallery, Buffalo, NY, Museum Ludwig, Cologne, Hirshhorn Museum and Sculpture Garden, Washington, DC, Whitney Museum of American Art, Stedelijk Museum, Amsterdam, Moderna Museet, Stockholm, Dallas Museum of Fine Arts, Art Inst. of Chicago, Baltimore Museum of Art, Kunstmuseum Basel, Cleveland Museum of Art, Nat. Gallery of Art, Washington, DC, San Francisco Museum of Modern Art, Va Museum of Fine Arts, Walker Art Center, Minneapolis; mem. American Acad. of Arts and Letters; Hon. RA (London); Prize, Pittsburgh Int. 1958, Wolf Foundation Prize 1986, Gold Medal (American Acad. and Inst. of Arts and Letters) 1986, Int. Prize, Venice Biennale 1988, Nat. Medal of Arts 1990, Officier, Ordre des Arts et Lettres 1990, Praemium Imperiale Award (Japan) 1993. *Address:* PO Box 642, Sharon, CT 06069, USA.

JOHNS, Air Chief Marshal Sir Richard Edward, Kt, GCB, KCVO, CBE, FRAeS; British air force officer; b. 28 July 1939, Horsham, Sussex; s. of the late Lt Col Herbert Edward Johns and Marjory Harley Johns (née Everett); m. Elizabeth Naomi Anne Manning 1965; one s. two d.; ed Portsmouth Grammar School, RAF Coll., Cranwell; commissioned 1959; Night Fighter/Fighter Reconnaissance Squadrons, UK, Cyprus, Aden 1960–67; Flying Instructor 1968–71, Flying Instructor to HRH the Prince of Wales 1970–71; Officer Commanding 3 (Fighter) Squadron (Harrier) 1975–77; Dir Air Staff Briefing 1979–81; Station Commdr and Harrier Force Commdr, RAF Gütersloh 1982–84; ADC to HM The Queen 1983–84; at Royal Coll. of Defence Studies 1985; Sr Air Staff Officer, HQ RAF, Germany 1985–88; Sr Air Staff Officer HQ Strike Command 1989–91; Air Officer Commanding No. 1 Group 1991–93; Chief of Staff, Deputy C-in-C Strike Command and UK Air Forces 1993–94; Air Officer Commanding in Chief Strike Command 1994; C-in-C Allied Forces NW Europe 1994–97; Chief of Air Staff and Air ADC to HM The Queen 1997–2000; Constable and Gov. of Windsor Castle 2000–08; Pres. Windsor Festival 2001–08, Windsor and Eton Choral Soc. 2001–08, Royal Windsor Rose and Horticultural Soc. 2000–08; Nat. Pres. Hearing Dogs for Deaf People 2002–; Chair. Bd of Trustees, RAF Museum 2000–06; Patron Labrador Life Line Trust 2001–; Gov. Portsmouth Grammar School 1996–; mem. Council St George's House 2000–08; Trustee, The Prince Philip Trust Fund 2000–08, Foundation of the Coll. of St George 2007–; Freeman City of London 1999, Liveryman GAPAN 1999–, Hon. Air Commodore, RAF Regt 2000–; Hon. Col 73 Engineer Regt (V) 1994–2001. *Leisure interests:* military history, rugby, cricket, equitation. *Address:* Norman Tower, Windsor Castle, Windsor, SL4 1NJ, England (office). *Telephone:* (1753) 868286 (office); (1753) 856106 (home). *Fax:* (1753) 854910 (office).

JOHNSON, Abigail P., BS, MBA; American business executive; b. 1962, Mass; d. of Edward C. (Ned) Johnson III; m.; two c.; ed Hobart Coll., William Smith Coll. and Harvard Univ.; with Booz Allen Hamilton 1984–86; Analyst and Portfolio Man., Fidelity Management & Research Corpn, Boston (better known as Fidelity Investments, founded by her grandfather in 1946) 1988–97, Assoc. Dir Investment Div. 1997–2001, Pres. 2001–05, currently head of Fidelity Institutional Retirement Services; ranked by Fortune magazine amongst 50 Most Powerful Women in Business in the US (eighth) 2004, (eighth) 2005, (18th) 2006, (30th) 2007, ranked by Forbes magazine amongst 100 Most Powerful Women (15th) 2004, (37th) 2005, ranked 12th by Forbes magazine amongst The 400 Richest Americans 2005, ranked by Forbes magazine amongst The World's Richest People (28th) 2004, (25th) 2005, (28th) 2006, ranked by Forbes magazine fifth Richest Woman 2006. *Address:* FMR Corpn, 82 Devonshire Street, Boston, MA 02109, USA (office). *Telephone:* (617) 563-7000 (office). *Fax:* (617) 476-6150 (office). *Website:* www.fidelity.com (office).

JOHNSON, Rt Hon. Alan; British government official; *Secretary of State for Health;* b. May 1950; ed Sloane Grammar School; postman, London 1968, Slough 1969; elected to Branch Cttee Union of Communication Workers 1973, apptd Chair. Slough Branch 1976, elected to Nat. Exec. Council 1981, became full-time Officer 1987, elected (youngest ever) Gen. Sec. 1992, apptd Jt Gen. Sec. after merger of Union of Communication Workers and Nat. Communication Union 1995; mem. Gen. Council and Nat. Exec. Cttee of TUC; fmr Dir Unity Trust Bank; MP for Kingston-upon-Hull West and Hessle 1997–; mem. Trade and Industry Select Cttee; apptd Parl. Pvt. Sec. to Financial Sec. to Treasury 1997, to Paymaster Gen. 1998; Minister for Competitiveness, Dept of Trade and Industry 1999–2001, Minister of State for Employment Relations and Regions 2001, Industry added to Portfolio 2002; Minister of State for Lifelong Learning, Higher and Further Educ., Dept for Educ. and Skills 2003–04; Sec. of State for Work and Pensions 2004–05, for Productivity, Energy and Industry 2005–06, for Educ. and Skills 2006–07, for Health 2007–. *Address:* Department of Health, Richmond House, 79 Whitehall, London, SW1A 2NS (office); Goodwin Resource Centre, Icehouse Road, Hull, HU3 2HQ, England (office). *Telephone:* (20) 7210-4850 (London) (office); (1482) 219211 (Hull) (office). *Fax:* (20) 7210-5523 (London) (office); (1482) 219211 (Hull) (office). *E-mail:* dhmail@dh.gsi.gov.uk (office); johnsona@parliament.uk (office). *Website:* www.dh.gov.uk (office); www.alanjohnson.org (office).

JOHNSON, Allen; American athlete; b. 1 March 1971, Washington, DC; one d.; ed Lake Braddock High School, Burke, VA and North Carolina Coll.; sprint hurdler; 110m hurdles personal best 12.92 seconds (Brussels, Belgium Aug. 1996); winner: World Championships 110m hurdles 1995, 1997, 2001, 2003, US Indoor Championships 60m hurdles 1995, 2002, 2003, World Indoor Championships 60m hurdles 1995, 2003, US Championships 100m hurdles 1996, 1997, 2000, 2001, 2002, 2003, World Championships 4×400m 1997 (with US team), Olympic Games 110m hurdles 2001, Nat. Indoor Championships 60m 2002, 2003; runner-up: World Cup 110m hurdles 1994, 2002, World Cup 4×100m 1996 (with US team), International Amateur Athletics Federation Grand Final 110m 1995, 2001; 4th: Olympic Games 110m hurdles 2000; ranked 1st in 2003; eight runs of under 13 seconds in 110m hurdles; North American record holder 110m hurdles; coached by Curtis Frye; Jesse Owens Award 1997. *Address:* c/o HSInternational, Inc., 2600 Michelson Drive, Suite 680, Irvine, CA 92612, USA (office). *E-mail:* hsi@hsi.net (office). *Website:* www.hsi.net (office).

JOHNSON, Antonia Ax:son; Swedish business executive; *Chairman, Axel Johnson Group;* b. 1943; four c.; succeeded father as Chair. of family-owned A. Johnson & Co. (now Axel Johnson Group), conglomerate that includes business in food retailing and telecommunications; mem. City Council Täby Municipality; mem. Liberal Party; ranked by Forbes magazine amongst 100 Most Powerful Women (65th) 2004, (61st) 2005, (71st) 2006, (69th) 2007, ranked by the Financial Times amongst Top 25 Businesswomen in Europe (fourth) 2005, (fourth) 2006, (third) 2007. *Address:* Axel Johnson AB, Villagatan 6, PO Box 26008, 100 41 Stockholm, Sweden (office). *Telephone:* (8) 7016100 (office). *Fax:* (8) 213026 (office). *Website:* www.axel-johnson.se (office); www.axeljohnson.com (office).

JOHNSON, Ben, MA, RCA; British artist; b. 24 Aug. 1946, Llandudno, Wales; s. of Harold Johnson and Ivy Lloyd Jones; m. Sheila Kellehar 1976; two s.; ed Royal Coll. of Art; has exhibited internationally since 1969; has undertaken direct comms from Centre Pompidou, Paris and Museum of London; work represented in public and corp. collections at Boymans van Beuningen Museum, Rotterdam, British Council, London, Tate Gallery, London, Contemporary Arts Soc., London, RIBA, London, City Art Gallery, Glasgow, Whitworth Gallery, Manchester, Centre Pompidou, Paris, Victoria & Albert Museum, London, Deutsche Bank, British Petroleum, Guildhall Art Gallery, Corpn of London, Special Admin. Regional Govt of Hong Kong, New Convention & Exhbn Centre, Hong Kong, Regional Services Council Museum, Hong Kong, British Museum, London; commissioned by Nat. Museums of Liverpool to make portrait of Liverpool, European Capital of Culture 2008; Hon. FRIBA. *Publications:* Cityscape: Ben Johnson's Liverpool. *Leisure interests:* architecture, cities. *Address:* 4 St Peter's Wharf, Chiswick Mall, London, W6 9UD, England (office). *Telephone:* (20) 8563-8768 (office). *Fax:* (20) 8741-2707 (office). *E-mail:* benjohnson@benjohnsonartist.com (office). *Website:* www.benjohnsonartist.com (office).

JOHNSON, Ben; Canadian (b. Jamaican) fmr athlete; b. 30 Dec. 1961, Falmouth, Jamaica; emigrated with family to Canada 1976; began athletics career coached by Charlie Francis 1977; finished last, Commonwealth Games 100 metres trial, Canada 1978; won Canadian Jr title, became Canadian citizen 1979; selected for Olympic Games, Moscow, but Canada boycotted Games 1980; came sixth in 100m, Pan-American Jr Games 1980, second, Commonwealth Games 1982; semi-finalist, World Championships 1983; bronze medallist, Olympic Games, LA, USA; won World Cup 1985, Commonwealth title 1986, indoor 60m record 1987; gold medallist, World Championships, with time of 9.83 seconds, Rome 1987; came first in final, Olympic Games, in world record 9.79 seconds, Seoul 1988; medal withdrawn after allegations concerning drug-taking; stripped of world record Sept. 1989, life ban from Canadian nat. team lifted Aug. 1990; failed second drugs test and banned from athletics for life March 1993; IAAF rejected petition for reinstatement Aug. 1999.

JOHNSON, Betsey Lee, BA; American fashion designer; b. 10 Aug. 1942, Hartford, Conn.; d. of John Herman Johnson and Lena Virginia Johnson; m. 1st John Cale 1966; one d.; m. 2nd Jeffrey Olivier 1981; ed Pratt Inst., New York, Syracuse Univ.; Editorial Asst. Mademoiselle magazine 1964–65; pnr and co-owner Betsey, Bunky & Nini, New York 1969–; shops in New York, LA, San Francisco, Coconut Grove, Fla, Venice, Calif., Boston, Chicago, Seattle; Prin. Designer for Paraphernalia 1965–69; designer Alvin Duskin Co., San Francisco 1970; Head Designer Alley Cat by Betsey Johnson (div. of LeDamor, Inc.) 1970–74; freelance designer for Jr Womens' div., Butterick Pattern Co. 1971, Betsey Johnson's Kids Children's Wear (div. of Shutterbug Inc.) 1974–77, Betsey Johnson for Jeanette Maternities, Inc. 1974–75; designer for Gant Shirtmakers Inc. (women's clothing) 1974–75, Tric-Trac by Betsey Johnson (women's knitwear) 1974–76, Butterick's Home Sewing Catalog 1975– (children's wear); Head Designer Jr sportswear co.; designed for Star Ferry by Betsey Johnson and Michael Miles (children's wear) 1975–77; owner and Head Designer B.J., Inc., designer wholesale co., New York 1978; Pres. and Treas. B.J. Vines, New York; opened Betsey Johnson store, New York 1979; mem. Council of Fashion Designers, American Women's Forum; Hon. Chair. Fashion Targets Breast Cancer initiative; Merit Award, Mademoiselle magazine 1970, Coty Award 1971, two Tommy Print Awards 1971. *Address:* Betsey Johnson, 498 7th Avenue, 21st Floor, New York, NY 10018-6798; 110 East 9th Street, Suite A889, Los Angeles, CA 90079, USA. *Telephone:* (212) 244-0843. *Website:* pr@betseyjohnson.com; www.betseyjohnson.com.

JOHNSON, (Alexander) Boris (de Pfeffel); British politician and journalist; *Mayor of London;* b. 19 June 1964, New York City USA; s. of Stanley Patrick Johnson and Charlotte Fawcett; m. 1st Allegra Mostyn-Owen; m. 2nd Marina Wheeler 1993; two s. two d.; ed Eton Coll. and Balliol Coll., Oxford; journalist with The Times 1987–88; EC Corresp., The Daily Telegraph 1989–94, Asst Ed. and Chief Political Columnist 1994–99, currently columnist; Ed. The Spectator 1999–2005; MP (Conservative) for Henley 2001–08; Vice-Chair. Conservative Party 2003–04; Shadow Minister for the Arts 2004; Shadow Minister for Higher Educ. 2005–07; Mayor of London 2008–; What the Papers Say Award for Columnist of the Year 2006. *Television:* The Dream of Rome (BBC2) 2006. *Publications:* Friends, Voters, Countrymen 2001, Seventy-Two Virgins (novel) 2004, The Dream of Rome 2006, The British 2007, Life in the Fast Lane: The Johnson Guide to Cars 2007. *Address:* The Mayor's Office, Greater London Authority, City Hall, The Queen's Walk, London, SE1 2AA, England (office). *Telephone:* (20) 7983-4100 (office). *Fax:* (20) 7983-4057 (office). *E-mail:* mayor@london.gov.uk (office). *Website:* www.london.gov.uk (office); www.boris-johnson.com (office).

JOHNSON, Brian Frederick Gilbert, PhD, FRS, FRSC, FRSE; British chemist and academic; *Master of Fitzwilliam College, University of Cambridge;* b. 11 Sept. 1938; s. of Frank Johnson and Mona Johnson; m. Christine Draper 1962; two d.; ed Northampton Grammar School, Univ. of Nottingham; Reader in Chem., Univ. of Cambridge 1978–90, Fellow Fitzwilliam Coll. 1970–90, Hon. Fellow 1990–, Master 1999–; Crum Brown Prof. of Inorganic Chem., Univ. of Edin. 1991–95; Prof. of Inorganic Chem., Univ. of Cambridge 1995–; Tilden Lecturer, RSC; Corday Morgan Medal, RSC, Frankland Medal and Prize, RSC. *Publications:* Transition Metal Clusters 1982, over 1,000 academic papers and review articles. *Leisure interests:* walking, painting, riding, gardening. *Address:* Department of Chemistry, Lensfield Road, CB2 1EW, Cambridge; Fitzwilliam College, Cambridge, CB3 0DG, England (home). *Telephone:* (1223) 336337. *E-mail:* bfgj1@cus.cam.ac.uk (office).

JOHNSON, Charles Richard, BS, MA, PhD; American author and academic; *Professor, Department of English, University of Washington, Seattle;* b. 23 April 1948, Evanston, Ill.; m. Joan New 1970; one s. one d.; ed Southern Illinois Univ., State Univ. of NY, Stoneybrook; fmr cartoonist and filmmaker; Lecturer, Univ. of Washington, Seattle 1975–79, Assoc. Prof. of English 1979–82, Prof. 1982–; Co.-Dir Twin Tigers (martial arts studio); recipient of US Nat. Book Award for Middle Passage 1990. *Publications include:* novels: Faith and the Good Thing 1974, Oxherding Tale 1982, Middle Passage 1990; The Sorcerer's Apprentice (short stories); Being and Race: Black Writing Since 1970 1988, The Middle Passage 1990, All This and Moonlight 1990, In Search of a Voice (with Ron Chernow) 1991; Black Humor, Half-Past Nation Time (drawings); Booker, Charlie Smith and the Fritter Tree (broadcast plays); numerous reviews, essays and short stories. *Address:* University of Washington, Department of English, Engl. G N-30, Seattle, WA 98105 (office); c/o Atheneum Publishers, Macmillan Publishing Company, 866 3rd Avenue, New York, NY 10022, USA. *Telephone:* (206) 543-4233 (office). *Website:* depts.washington.edu/engl (office).

JOHNSON, David T., BEcons; American diplomatist; *Minister and Deputy Chief of Mission, US Embassy in London;* b. Georgia; m. Scarlett M. Swan; two d. one s.; ed Emory Univ., Canadian National Defence Coll.; Asst Nat. Trust Examiner, Treasury Dept; joined US Foreign Service 1977; Vice-Consul, Consulate-Gen., Ciudad Juárez, Mexico 1978–79; Econ. Officer, US Embassy, Berlin 1981–83; Deputy Dir, State Dept Operations Center 1987–89; Consul.-Gen., Vancouver 1990–93; Deputy Spokesman, State Dept; Dir State Dept Press Office 1993–95; Deputy Press Sec. for Foreign Affairs at the White House and Spokesman for Nat. Sec. Council 1995–97; Chief (with rank of Amb.), US Mission to OSCE 1998, Minister and Deputy Chief of Mission, US Embassy, London 2003–. *Address:* Embassy of the USA, 24–32 Grosvenor Square, London, W1A 1AE, England (office). *Telephone:* (20) 7499-9000 (office). *Fax:* (20) 7629-9124 (office). *Website:* www.usembassy.org.uk (office).

JOHNSON, David Willis, BEcons, MBA; Australian business executive; b. 7 Aug. 1932, Tumut, NSW; s. of Alfred Ernest Johnson and Eileen Melba Johnson (née Burt); m. Sylvia Raymonda Wells 1966; three s.; ed Univs of Sydney and Chicago; Exec. Trainee Ford Motor Co., Geelong; Man. Trainee Colgate-Palmolive, Sydney 1959–60, Product Man. 1961, Asst to Man. Dir 1962, Brands Man. 1963, Gen. Products Man. 1964-65; Asst Gen. Man. and Marketing Dir, Colgate-Palmolive, Johannesburg 1966, Chair. and Man. Dir 1967–72; Pres. Warner-Lambert/Parke Davis Asia, Hong Kong 1973–76, Personal Products Div., Warner-Lambert Co., Morris Plains, NJ 1977, Exec. Vice-Pres. and Gen. Man. Entenmann's Div., Bay Shore, NY 1979, Pres. Speciality Foods Group, Morris Plains, NJ 1980-81, Vice-Pres. 1980–82; Pres. and CEO Entenmann's Div., Bay Shore 1982, Vice-Pres. Gen. Foods Corpn,

White Plains, NY 1982–87, Pres., CEO Entenmann's Inc., Bay Shore 1982–87; Chair., Pres. and CEO Gerber Products Co., Fremont, Mich. 1987–89, Chair. and CEO 1989–90; Pres., CEO and Dir Campbell Soup Co., Camden, NJ 1990–97, 2000–01, Chair. Bd of Dirs 1993–2001; mem. Bd of Dirs Colgate-Palmolive Co., Exec. Advisory Bd Donaldson, Lufkin & Jenrette Merchant Banking Partners; mem. Advisory Council Univ. of Notre Dame Coll. of Business Admin., Univ. of Chicago Grad. School of Business; fmr Dir American Bakers Asscn, Nat. Food Producers' Asscn, Grocery Mfrs America; Distinguished Alumnus Award, Univ. of Chicago 1992; Dir of Year Award, Nat. Asscn of Corp. Dirs 1997. *Address:* c/o Campbell Soup Company World Headquarters, Campbell Place, Camden, NJ 08103, USA.

JOHNSON, Earvin, Jr. (Magic); American fmr professional basketball player and business executive; *Chairman and CEO, Johnson Development Corporation;* b. 14 Aug. 1959, Lansing, Mich.; s. of Earvin Johnson and Christine Johnson; m. Cookie Kelly; one s.; ed Lansing Everett High School, Mich. State Univ.; led Mich. State Univ. to NCAA Men's Basketball Championship 1979; drafted by Los Angeles Lakers Nat. Basketball Asscn (NBA) first overall 1979, played 1979–91 (retd after announcing he was HIV-positive); Vice-Pres., co-owner Los Angeles Lakers 1994–, Head Coach 1994, resumed playing career Feb. 1996, retd July 1996; Chair. Johnson Devt Corpn 1993–, Magic Johnson Entertainment 1997–; presenter TV show The Magic Hour 1998; mem. NBA All-Star Team 1980, 1982–89, mem. LA Lakers NBA championship teams 1980, 1982, 1985, 1987, 1988 (Finals Most Valuable Player 1980, 1982, 1987), US Olympic team 1992 (Gold Medal); NBA Most Valuable Player 1987, 1989, 1990; fmr mem. Nat. Aids Asscn, rejoined 1993; commentator NBC-TV 1995–96; f. Magic Johnson Foundation 1991; Player of the Year (Sporting News) 1987, J. Walter Kennedy Citizenship Award 1992, voted One of 50 Greatest Players in NBA History 1996, elected Naismith Memorial Basketball Hall of Fame 2002. *Publications:* Magic 1983, What You Can Do to Avoid AIDS 1992, My Life (autobiog.) 1992. *Address:* Johnson Development Corporation, 9100 Wilshire Blvd., Suite 710 East, Beverly Hills, CA 90212, USA (office). *Telephone:* (310) 247-1994 (office). *Fax:* (310) 247-0733 (office). *Website:* www.magicjohnson.org (office); www.johnsondevelopmentcorp.com (office).

JOHNSON, Edward C. (Ned), III, BA; American financial services executive; *Chairman and CEO, Fidelity Investments;* m.; three c.; ed Harvard Univ.; research analyst, Fidelity Management & Research (FMR) Co. 1957, Man. Trend Fund 1960, Pres. FMR Corpn 1972, currently Chair. and CEO Fidelity Investments. *Address:* Fidelity Investments, 82 Devonshire Street, Boston, MA 02109, USA (office). *Telephone:* (617) 563-7000 (office). *Fax:* (617) 476-3876 (office). *Website:* www.fidelity.com (office).

JOHNSON, F(rederick) Ross, BComm, MBA; Canadian business executive; *Chairman, AuthentiDate, Inc;* b. 13 Dec. 1931, Winnipeg, Man.; s. of Frederick H. Johnson and Caroline Green; m. Laurie A. Graumann 1979; two s. (from previous marriage); ed Univs of Manitoba and Toronto; Vice-Pres. Merchandising, T. Eaton Co. (Canada) 1965–66; Exec. Vice-Pres. and COO, GSW Ltd 1966–71; Pres. and CEO, Standard Brands Ltd, Canada 1971–74; Dir Standard Brands Inc. 1974–, Sr Vice-Pres. 1974–75, Pres. 1975–76, Chair. and CEO 1977–81; Pres. and COO Nabisco Brands Inc. 1981–83, Vice-Pres. and CEO 1984–85, Chief Exec. RJR Nabisco 1987–89 (after takeover of Nabisco by Reynolds), Pres. and COO R. J. Reynolds Industries 1985–87, Pres. and CEO 1987–89; Chair. and CEO RJM Group Inc. (investment advisory firm) 1989–; mem. Bd of Dirs AuthentiDate 2003–, Chair. 2005–; fmr Dir American Express, Power Corpn of Canada, Wosk's Ltd, Vancouver, Bank of Nova Scotia, Toronto; mem. Advisory Council, Columbia Univ., New York; Trustee, Econ. Club of New York (fmr Chair.); Chair. Multiple Sclerosis Soc., New York; mem. Int. Advisory Council, Power Corpn of Canada; Dr hc (St Francis Xavier Univ., Antigonish, NS) 1978, (Univ. of Newfoundland) 1980. *Leisure interests:* golf, skiing, tennis. *Address:* c/o Board of Directors, AuthentiDate, Inc., 2 World Financial Center, 225 Liberty Street, 43rd Floor, New York, NY 10281; RJM Group, 200 Galleria Parkway, Suite 970, Atlanta, GA 30339, USA.

JOHNSON, Gabriel Ampah, DD'État; Togolese biologist, academic and university administrator; *Professor and Chair of Biology, National University of Ivory Coast;* b. 13 Oct. 1930, Aneho; s. of William K. A. Johnson and Rebecca A. Ekue-Hettah; m. Louise Chipan 1962; three s. three d.; ed Univ. of Poitiers, France; Teaching Asst, Univ. of Poitiers –1956; Research Fellow, CNRS, France 1958–60; Deputy Dir of Educ., Togo 1959-60; Asst Prof., Nat. Univ. of Ivory Coast, Abidjan 1961–64, Assoc. Prof. 1965–66, Prof., Chair. of Biology 1966–, Asst Dean, Faculty of Science 1963–68, Founding Dir Nat. Centre for Social Services 1964–68; Founding Rector, Univ. du Bénin, Lomé, Togo 1970–86; Dir of Higher Educ., Togo 1970–75; Pres. Nat. Planning Comm. of Togo 1973; Pres. Asscn of African Univs 1977–80; mem. Exec. Bd UNESCO 1997–; mem. Bd of Admin., Asscn of Partially or Fully French-Speaking Univs 1975–, Pan African Inst. for Devt 1977–, Int. Cttee of Bioethics 2001, Admin. Council Int. Fund for the Promotion of Culture (UNESCO) 2003; mem. Cen. Cttee Togo People's Rally (ruling party) 1976–; Founding Pres. Africa Club for an Integrated Devt 1980–; mem. Zoological Soc. of France 1956, Biological Soc. of France 1962, Endocrinological Soc. of France 1966, French Nat. Acad. of Pharmacy 2003; Hon. Vice-Pres. Gold Mercury Int. 1983; Chevalier, Ordre nat. de la Côte d'Ivoire 1966; Officier Légion d'honneur 1971; Commdr Order of Cruzeiro do Sul (Brazil) 1976; Commdr Order of Merit (France) 1983; Commdr, Ordre des Palmes Académiques, (France) 1986; Commdr, Ordre du Mono (Togo) 2000; Dr hc Sherbrooke, (Canada) 1979, (Lille) 1983, (Bordeaux) 1986; Medal of Honour, Univ. of São Paulo, Brazil 1980; Gold Mercury Int. Award 1982, Gold Medal of Honour, Univ. of Benin. *Publications:* several articles in scientific journals. *Leisure interests:* reading, classical and modern

music, swimming, farming (cattle breeding). *Address:* BP 7098, Lomé, Togo. *Telephone:* (2) 21-53-65 (home).

JOHNSON, Gary Earl, BA; American business executive and politician; b. 1 Jan. 1953, Minot, ND; s. of Earl W. Johnson and Lorraine B. Bostow; m. Dee Sims 1976; one s. one d.; ed Univ. of New Mexico; Pres. and CEO Big J Enterprises, Albuquerque 1976–99; Gov. of New Mexico 1995–2003; mem. Bd Dirs Entrepreneurship Studies programme Univ. of NM 1993–95, Albuquerque Chamber of Commerce 1993–95; Republican; Entrepreneur of the Year 1995. *Leisure interests:* rock and mountain-climbing, skiing, flying, athletics. *Address:* c/o Office of the Governor, Room 400, State Capitol, Santa Fe, NM 87503, USA.

JOHNSON, Graham Rhodes, OBE, FRAM, FGSM; British pianist; b. 10 July 1950, Bulawayo, Rhodesia (now Zimbabwe); s. of the late John Edward Donald Johnson and of Violet May Johnson; ed Hamilton High School, Bulawayo, Rhodesia, Royal Acad. of Music, London; Artistic Adviser, accompanist Alte Oper Festival, Frankfurt 1981–82; Prof. of Accompaniment, Guildhall School of Music 1986–; Song Adviser, Wigmore Hall 1992–; Artistic Dir The Songmakers' Almanac; guest lecturer in several countries; writer, presenter BBC Radio 3 series on Poulenc, BBC TV series on Schubert 1978, Liszt 1986; concert début, Wigmore Hall 1972; has accompanied numerous singers including Dame Elisabeth Schwarzkopf, Jessye Norman, Victoria de los Angeles, Dame Janet Baker, Sir Peter Pears, Dame Felicity Lott, Ann Murray, Matthias Goerne, Christine Schäfer, Dorothea Roeschmann, François Le Roux; has appeared at festivals in Edin., Munich, Hohenems, Salzburg, Bath, Hong Kong, Bermuda; Chair. Jury Wigmore Hall Int. Singing Competition 1997, 1999, 2001; mem. Royal Swedish Acad. of Music 2000; numerous recordings; Chevalier, Ordre des Arts et des Lettres 2002; Gramophone Award 1989, 1996, 1997, Royal Philharmonic Prize for Instrumentalist 1998. *Publications:* contrib. The Britten Companion 1984, Gerald Moore: The Unashamed Accompanist, The Spanish Song Companion 1992, The Songmakers' Almanac Reflections and Commentaries 1996, A French Song Companion 2000, articles and reviews. *Leisure interests:* dining out, book collecting. *Address:* Askonas Holt Ltd, Lincoln House, 300 High Holborn, London, WC1V 7JH, England (office); 83 Fordwych Road, London, NW2 3TL, England. *Telephone:* (20) 7400-1700 (office); (20) 8452-5193. *Fax:* (20) 7400-1799 (office); (20) 8452-5081 (home). *E-mail:* info@askonasholt.co.uk (office). *Website:* www.askonasholt.co.uk (office).

JOHNSON, Hugh Eric Allan, OBE, MA; British writer, editor and broadcaster; b. 10 March 1939, London; s. of the late Guy F. Johnson CBE and Grace Kittel; m. Judith Eve Grinling 1965; one s. two d.; ed Rugby School, King's Coll., Cambridge; feature writer, Condé Nast Magazines 1960–63; Ed. Wine and Food Magazine 1963–65; Wine Corresp., Sunday Times 1965–67, Travel Ed. 1967; Ed. Queen Magazine 1968–70; Wine Ed., Gourmet Magazine 1971–72, Cuisine Magazine, New York 1983–84; Chair. Winestar Productions Ltd 1984–, The Hugh Johnson Collection Ltd, The Movie Business; Pres. Sunday Times Wine Club 1973–, Circle of Wine Writers 1997–2007; Founder-mem. Tree Council 1974; Founder The Plantsman (quarterly) 1979; Dir Château Latour 1986–2001; Editorial Consultant, The Garden (Royal Horticultural Soc. Journal) 1975–2005; columnist, Tradescant's Diary 1975–; Sec. Wine and Food Soc. 1962–63; Gardening Corresp., New York Times 1986–87; Hon. Chair. Wine Japan 1989–93; Hon. Pres. Int. Wine and Food Soc. 2004–08, Wine & Spirit Educ. Trust 2009–; Fellow Commoner, King's Coll. Cambridge 2001; Hon. Freeman of the Vintner's Co. 2003; Chevalier, Ordre nat. du Mérite 2003; Dr hc (Acad. du Vin de Bordeaux) 1987, (Essex) 1998; André Simon Prize 1967, 1989, 2005, Glenfiddich Award 1972, 1986, 1990, Marqués de Cáceres Award 1984, Wines and Vines Trophy 1982, Grand Prix de la Communication de la Vigne et du Vin 1992, 1993, Decanter Magazine Man of the Year 1995, Von Rumor Award, Gastronomische Akad., Germany 1998, Gold Veitch Memorial Medal, Royal Horticultural Soc. 2000. *Television includes:* Wine – A User's Guide (series) 1986, Vintage – A History of Wine (series) 1989, Return Voyage 1992. *Publications:* Wine 1966, Frank Schoonmaker's Encyclopaedia of Wine (ed. of English edn) 1967, The World Atlas of Wine 1971 (sixth edn with Jancis Robinson 2007), The International Book of Trees 1973, The California Wine Book (with Bob Thompson) 1976, Understanding Wine (Sainsbury Guide) 1976, Hugh Johnson's Pocket Wine Book (annually since 1977), The Principles of Gardening 1979 (revised edn with new title, Hugh Johnson's Gardening Companion 1996), Hugh Johnson's Wine Companion 1983 (sixth edn with Stephen Brook 2009), How to Handle a Wine (video) 1984, Hugh Johnson's Cellar Book 1986, The Atlas of German Wines 1986, How to Enjoy Your Wine 1985, The Wine Atlas of France (with Hubrecht Duijker) 1987, The Story of Wine 1989, The Art and Science of Wine (with James Halliday) 1992, Hugh Johnson on Gardening: The Best of Tradescant's Diary 1993, Tuscany and Its Wines 2000, Wine: A Life Uncorked 2005, Hugh Johnson in the Garden 2009. *Leisure interests:* travel, trees, gardening, pictures. *Address:* 73 St James's Street, London, SW1A 1PH (home); Saling Hall, Great Saling, Essex, CM7 5DT, England (home). *Telephone:* (1371) 850243 (home). *Website:* www.salinghall.com; www.tradsdiary.com.

JOHNSON, Adm. Jay; American naval officer (retd); b. 1946, Great Falls, Mont.; m. Garland Hawthorne; one c.; ed US Naval Acad.; joined USN 1968; fmr Asst to Chief of Naval Personnel; fmr Commdr Naval Group Eight, Theodore Roosevelt Battle Group 1992; Commdr Second Fleet Striking Fleet Atlantic, Jt Task Force 120 1994; fmr Vice-Chief Naval Operations; aircraft-carrier combat pilot during Viet Nam War; Chief of Naval Operations 1996–2000 (retd); numerous medals and awards. *Address:* c/o The Pentagon, Washington, DC 20350, USA.

JOHNSON, John D., BBA; American business executive; *President and CEO, CHS;* b. Rhame, ND; ed Black Hills State Univ.; grew up in Spearfish, SDak;

began his career with fmr Harvest States as feed consultant in GTA Feeds Div. 1976, then Regional Sales Man., then Dir of Sales and Marketing, then Gen. Man. GTA Feeds, Group Vice-Pres. Harvest States Farm Marketing & Supply for Harvest States Cooperatives 1992–95, Pres. and CEO Harvest States 1995–98, Pres. and Gen. Man. CHS (following merger of Cenex and Harvest States June 1998) 1998–2000, Pres. and CEO CHS 2000–; mem. Bd of Dirs GoldKist, Inc., Ventura Foods, LLC, CF Industries, Nat. Council of Farmer Cooperatives; CEO Communicator of the Year, Cooperative Communicators Asscn 2003. *Address:* CHS, PO Box 64089, St Paul, MN 55164-0089 (office); CHS, 5500 Cenex Drive, Inver Grove Heights, MN 55077, USA (office). *Telephone:* (651) 355-6000 (office). *E-mail:* info@chsinc.com (office). *Website:* www.chsinc.com (office).

JOHNSON, Joseph Eggleston, III, MD; American professor of medicine and administrator; b. 17 Sept. 1930, Elberton, Ga; s. of Joseph Eggleston Johnson and Marie Johnson (née Williams); m. Judith H. Kemp 1956; one s. two d.; ed Vanderbilt Univ., Nashville, Tenn., Johns Hopkins Univ., Baltimore, Md; Instructor in Medicine, Johns Hopkins Univ. School of Medicine 1961–62, physician, Johns Hopkins Hosp. 1961–66, Asst Prof. of Medicine 1962–66, Asst Dean for Student Affairs 1963–66; Assoc. Prof. of Medicine, Univ. of Fla Coll. of Medicine 1966–68, Chief, Div. of Infectious Disease 1966–72, Prof. of Medicine 1968–72, Assoc. Dean 1970–72; Prof. and Chair. Dept of Medicine, Bowman Gray School of Medicine 1972–85; Chief of Medicine, NC Baptist Hosp. 1972–85; Dean, Univ. of Mich. Medical School 1985–90, Prof. of Internal Medicine 1985–93; Sr Vice-Pres. American Coll. of Physicians 1993–, interim exec. Vice-Pres. 1994–95; mem. accreditation comm. on grad. medical educ. 1988–93; Markle Scholar, Royal Soc. of Medicine; mem. Johns Hopkins Soc. of Scholars, Int. Soc. of Internal Medicine (Pres. 2000–02. *Publications:* 100 articles and book chapters on infectious disease, immunology and internal medicine. *Address:* American College of Physicians, Independence Mall West, Sixth Street at Race, Philadelphia, PA 19106 (office); 15-C-44, The Philadelphian, 2401 Pennsylvania Avenue, Philadelphia, PA 19130, USA (home). *Telephone:* (215) 351-2690 (office).

JOHNSON, Linton Kwesi, BA; British poet and writer; b. 24 Aug. 1952, Chapeltown, Jamaica; ed Goldsmiths Coll., London; family emigrated to London 1963; involved in Black Panther movement, London; wrote for NME and Melody Maker in 1970s and 1980s; regular TV/radio apppearances as an authority on reggae; C. Day-Lewis Fellowship 1977, Assoc. Fellow, Warwick Univ. 1985; founder LKJ Records and LKJ Music Publishers; trustee, George Padmore Inst.; Hon. Fellow, Wolverhampton Polytechnic 1987, Goldsmiths Coll., London 2002; Hon. Visiting Prof., Middlesex Univ. 2004; Italian literary awards 1990, 1998, Silver Musgrave Medal Inst. of Jamaica 2005. *Recordings include:* Dread Beat An' Blood, Forces of Victory, More Time, LKJ Live in Paris. *Publications:* Voices of the Living and the Dead 1974, Dread Beat an' Blood 1975, Inglan is a Bitch 1980, Tings an' Times: Selected Poems 1991, Mi Revalueshanary Fren: Selected Poems 2002; contrib. to recordings, television. *Address:* PO Box 623, Herne Hill, London, SE24 OLS, England (office). *Telephone:* (20) 7738-7647 (office). *Fax:* (20) 7738-7647 (office). *E-mail:* info@lkjrecords.com (office). *Website:* www.lkjrecords.com (office).

JOHNSON, Dame Louise Napier, DBE, PhD, FRS; British scientist and academic; *Professor Emerita, University of Oxford;* b. 26 Sept. 1940, Worcester; d. of George Edmund Johnson and Elizabeth Johnson (née King); m. Abdus Salam (deceased); one s. one d.; ed Wimbledon High School, Univ. Coll. London, Royal Institution, London; Research Asst, Yale Univ. 1996; demonstrator, Zoology Dept, Univ. of Oxford 1967–73, Lecturer in Molecular Biophysics 1973–90, David Phillips Prof. of Molecular Biophysics 1990–2007, Dir of Life Sciences, Diamond Light Source 2003–07, Additional Fellow, Somerville Coll. 1973–90, Hon. Fellow 1991, Professorial Fellow, Corpus Christi Coll. 1990–2007, currently Prof. Emer., works at Lab. of Molecular Biophysics, Dept of Biochemistry; Life Science Dir Diamond Light Source, Oxford 2003, now Diamond Fellow; mem. European Molecular Biology Org. 1991–; Assoc. Fellow, Third World Acad. of Sciences 2000–; mem. Council, Royal Soc. 1998–2001, Scientific Advisory Council, European Molecular Biology Lab. 1994–2000, Council for the Central Lab. of the Research Councils 1998–2001; Trustee Cambridge Crystallographic Data Centre; Gov. Westminster School 1994–2001; mem. American Acad. of Arts and Sciences 2007–; Hon. DSc (St Andrews) 1992; Linderström-Lang Prize 1989, Charmian Medal, Royal Soc. of Chem. 1997, Datta Medal, Fed. of European Biochemical Soc. 1998, Novartis Medal and Prize 2009. *Publications:* Protein Crystallography (with T. L. Blundell) 1976, Glycogen Phosphorylase (co-author) 1991; more than 150 scientific papers on lysozyme, phosphorylase protein kinases, allosteric mechanisms, cell cycle proteins, protein crystallography. *Leisure interests:* family, horses. *Address:* Laboratory of Molecular Biophysics, Department of Biochemistry, University of Oxford, Oxford, OX1 3QU, England (office). *Telephone:* (1865) 275365 (office). *Fax:* (1865) 285353 (office). *E-mail:* louise@biop.ox.ac.uk (office). *Website:* www .bioch.ox.ac.uk/aspsite/research/brochure/Johnson (office).

JOHNSON, Luke; British television executive; *Chairman, Channel Four Television Corporation;* s. of Paul Johnson; ed Oxford Univ.; started career with BMP (advertising firm); media analyst Kleinwort Benson Securities; fmr Chair. PizzaExpress PLC; Chair. Signature Restaurants PLC; Chair. Channel Four Television Corpn 2004–; co-Man. Intrinsic Value PLC; f. and Dir NewMedia SPARK PLC; mem. Bd of Dirs Nightfreight PLC, Integrated Dental Holdings PLC; Gov. London Inst. *Address:* Channel Four Television Corporation, 124 Horseferry Road, London, SW1P 2TX, England (office). *Telephone:* (20) 7396-4444 (office). *Website:* www.channel4.com (office).

JOHNSON, Manuel H., Jr; American economist, academic and fmr government official; *Chairman and Senior Partner, Johnson Smick International;* b. 10 Feb. 1949, Troy, Alabama; s. of Manuel Holman Johnson Sr and

Ethel Lorraine Jordan; m. Mary Lois Wilkerson 1972; two s.; ed Troy State Univ., Fla State Univ., George Mason Univ., Fairfax, Va; Asst Sec. of Treasury for Econ. Policy 1982–86; mem. Fed. Reserve Bd 1985–90, Vice-Chair. 1986–90; Dir Centre for Global Market Studies, George Mason Univ. 1990–94; Co-Chair. and Sr Partner, Johnson Smick International, Washington, DC 1990–; Distinguished Alumni Award, Coll. of Social Sciences, Fla State Univ. 2003. *Publications:* co-author: Political Economy of Federal Government Growth 1980, Better Government at Half Price 1981, Deregulating Labor Relations 1981. *Address:* Johnson Smick International, 1133 Connecticut Avenue, NW, #901, Washington, DC 20036, USA.

JOHNSON, Martin O., CBE; British professional rugby union player and rugby manager; *Manager, England rugby union team;* b. 9 March 1970, Solihull; joined Leicester 1988, won Premiership honours 1999–2001; toured Australia with England Schoolboys side 1990; int. debut England versus France 1993; captained British Lions on SA tour 1997, winning 2–1 Test series; apptd Capt. England team in Six Nations Championships 2000; first player ever to captain two British Lions tours; won Heineken Cup (with Leicester) 2001, 2002; 84 caps (39 as Capt.) as at Dec. 2003; captained England to Grand Slam and World Cup wins in 2003; retd from int. rugby after World Cup 2003; apptd Manager, England team 2008. *Publication:* Agony and Ecstasy, Martin Johnson: The Autobiography (British Book Awards Sports Book of the Year 2004). *Address:* c/o Rugby Football Union, Rugby House, Rugby Road, Twickenham, Middlesex TW1 1DS, England (office). *Telephone:* (20) 8892-2000 (office). *E-mail:* media@therfu.com (office). *Website:* www.rfu .com (office); www.england-rugby.com (office).

JOHNSON, Michael; American fmr professional athlete; b. 13 Sept. 1967, Dallas; m. Kerry Doyen 1998; one s.; ed Baylor Univ.; world champion 200m. 1991, 400m and 4×400m 1993, 200m, 400m and 4×400m (world record) 1995, 400m 1997, 400m (world record) and 4×400m . 1999; Olympic champion 4×400m (world record) 1992, 200m, 400m 1996, world record holder 400m (indoors) 44.63 seconds 1995, 4×400m (outdoors) 2:55.74 1992, 2:54.29 1993; undefeated at 400m from 1989–97; first man to be ranked World No. one at 200m and 400m simultaneously 1990, 1991, 1994, 1995; Olympic champion 200m (world record), 400m, Atlanta 1996; Olympic Champion 400m and 4×400m, Sydney 2000; announced retirement 2001; currently TV commentator; Jesse Owens Award (three times), Track and Field US Athlete of the Year (four times), Asscn of American Univs. (AAU)/Sullivan Award 1996. *Publications:* Slaying The Dragon (autobiog.) 1996, Michael Johnson: Sprinter Deluxe. *Leisure interest:* piano. *Address:* IMG, 600 17th Street, Suite 2420 South, Denver, CO 80202 (office); USA Track and Field, P.O. Box 120, Indianapolis, IN 46206, USA. *Telephone:* (303) 573-0600 (office). *Fax:* (303) 573-0605 (office).

JOHNSON, Paul Bede, BA; British journalist, historian and broadcaster; b. 2 Nov. 1928, Barton; s. of William Aloysius and Anne Johnson; m. Marigold Hunt 1957; three s. one d.; ed Stonyhurst and Magdalen Coll., Oxford; Asst Exec. Ed. Réalités, Paris 1952–55; Asst Ed. New Statesman 1955–60, Deputy Ed. 1960–64, Ed. 1965–70, Dir 1965; DeWitt Wallace Prof. of Communications, American Enterprise Inst., Washington, DC 1980; mem. Royal Comm. on the Press 1974–77, Cable Authority 1984–90; freelance writer; Book of the Year Prize, Yorkshire Post 1975, Francis Boyer Award for Services to Public Policy 1979, King Award for Excellence (Literature) 1980, Pilkington Literary Award 2003, Presidential Medal of Freedom, USA 2006. *Publications:* The Offshore Islanders 1972, Elizabeth I: a Study in Power and Intellect 1974, Pope John XXIII 1975, A History of Christianity 1976, Enemies of Society 1977, The National Trust Book of British Castles 1978, The Civilization of Ancient Egypt 1978, Civilizations of the Holy Land 1979, British Cathedrals 1980, Ireland: Land of Troubles 1980, The Recovery of Freedom 1980, Pope John Paul II and the Catholic Restoration 1982, Modern Times 1983 (revised 1991), History of the Modern World: From 1917 to the 1980s 1984, The Pick of Paul Johnson 1985, Saving and Spending 1986, The Oxford Book of Political Anecdotes (ed.) 1986, The History of the Jews 1987, Intellectuals 1988, The Birth of the Modern: World Society 1815–1830 1991, Wake Up Britain! 1994, The Quest for God 1996, To Hell with Picasso and other essays 1996, A History of the American People 1997, The Renaissance 2000, Napoleon 2002, Art: A New History 2003, The Vanished Landscape: A 1930s Childhood in the Potteries 2004, Creators: From Chaucer to Walt Disney 2006, Heroes: From Alexander the Great to Mae West 2009. *Leisure interests:* painting, hill walking. *Address:* 29 Newton Road, London, W2 5JR; The Coach House, Over Stowey, nr Bridgwater, Somerset TA5 1HA, England. *Telephone:* (20) 7229-3859 (London); (1278) 732393 (Somerset). *Fax:* (20) 7792-1676 (London).

JOHNSON, Pierre Marc, BA, LLL, MD, FRSC; Canadian politician and lawyer; b. 5 July 1946, Montreal; s. of the late Daniel Johnson and Reine (née Gagné) Johnson; m. Marie-Louise Parent 1973; one s. one d.; ed Collège Jean-Brébeuf, Montreal, Univ. of Montreal and Univ. of Sherbrooke; called to Québec Bar 1971; admitted Québec Coll. of Physicians and Surgeons 1976; elected to Québec Nat. Ass. 1976; mem. Nat. Exec. Council, Parti Québécois 1977–79, Pres. Parti Québécois 1985–87; Minister of Labour and Manpower, Québec 1977–80, of Consumer Affairs, Cooperatives and Financial Insts 1980–81, of Social Affairs 1981–84, of Justice, Attorney-Gen. and Minister Responsible for Canadian Intergovernmental Affairs 1984–85; Premier of Québec Oct.–Dec. 1985; Leader of Opposition, Québec Nat. Ass. 1985–87; Sr Counsel Heenan Blaikie Attorneys, Montreal; Dir Unimedia, Innovitech Inc., CRC Sofema, EETINA (Mexico), Int. Union for Conservation of Nature (Geneva); Hon. PhD (Lyon). *Publication:* The Environment and NAFTA: implementing and understanding New Continental Law 1995. *Leisure interests:* skiing, swimming, music. *Address:* 1250 René Levesque blvd West, Suite 2500, Montreal, Québec, H3B 4Y1, Canada. *Telephone:* (514) 846-2200. *Fax:* (514) 846-3427.

JOHNSON, Richard Keith; British actor and producer; b. Upminster, Essex; s. of Keith Holcombe Johnson and Frances Louisa Olive Johnson (née Tweed); m. 1st Sheila Ann Sweet 1957 (divorced); one s. one d.; m. 2nd Kim Novak 1965 (divorced); m. 3rd Marie-Louise Nordlund 1982 (divorced); one s. one d.; m. 4th Lynne Gurney 2004; ed Parkfield School, Felsted School, Royal Acad. of Dramatic Art (RADA); Nat. Theatre Player, Assoc. Artist RSC; first stage appearance in Hamlet, Opera House, Manchester 1944; Founder, Chair. and CEO United British Artists 1982–90; mem. Council British Acad. Film and Television Arts 1976–78, Council Royal Acad. of Dramatic Art 2001–; Best Actor Guild of Broadcasting Writers 1992. *Plays:* major parts include Marius Tertius (The First Victoria) 1950, Pierre (The Madwoman of Chaillot) 1951, Demetrius (A Midsummer Night's Dream) 1951, George Phillips (After My Fashion) 1952, Beauchamp, Earl of Warwick (The Lark) 1955, Laertes (Hamlet) 1955, Jack Absolute (The Rivals) 1956, Lord Plynlimmon (Plaintiff in a Pretty Hat) 1956, Orlando (As You Like It), Mark Antony (Julius Caesar), Leonatus (Cymbeline), Ferdinand (The Tempest), Romeo (Romeo and Juliet), Sir Andrew Aguecheek (Twelfth Night), title-role in Pericles, Don Juan (Much Ado About Nothing) 1957–58, Ferdinand (The Tempest) 1957, Romeo (Romeo and Juliet), Sir Andrew Aguecheek (Twelfth Night), Moscow and Leningrad 1959, The Prince (Ondine), Grandier (The Devils), RSC 1960–62, Charles (Blithe Spirit), Pinchwife (The Country Wife), Pilate (The Passion), title-role in The Guardsman all at Nat. Theatre 1975–78; UK tour, Death Trap 1982, An Inspector Calls 1992, The Rivals 1994, Long Day's Journey Into Night 1996, Uncle Vanya 1996, Staying On 1997, To Kill a Mockingbird 1997, Plenty 1999, The Seagull (RSC) 2000, Tales From Hollywood 2001, Gates of Gold 2002, Mrs Warren's Profession 2003–04. *Films:* Never so Few 1959, The Haunting 1963, The Pumpkin Eater 1964, Operation Crossbow 1965, Khartoum 1966, Deadlier Than the Male 1966, Oedipus the King 1967, Hennessy 1975, Turtle Diary 1984, Treasure Island 1989, Milk 1998, Tomb Raider 2001. *TV films:* Man for All Seasons 1988, Voice of the Heart 1988, The Camomile Lawn, Anglo-Saxon Attitudes 1992, Heavy Weather 1995, The Echo 1998, The Whistle Blower 2000; leading roles in productions including Rembrandt, Antony and Cleopatra, Hamlet (Claudius), The Member for Chelsea (Sir Charles Dilke), Cymbeline. *Productions include:* The Biko Inquest, Serjeant Musgrave's Dance, The Playboy of the Western World, Old Times, Turtle Diary, Castaway, The Lonely Passion of Judith Hearne, Tales From Hollywood 2001, Hock and Soda Water 2001, Gates of Gold 2002. *Publication:* Hennessy 1974. *Leisure interests:* photography, music, travel, cooking, gardening. *Address:* c/o Conway, Van Gelder, Robinson Ltd, 18–21 Jermyn Street, London, SW1Y 6HP, England. *Telephone:* (20) 7287-0077. *Fax:* (20) 7287-1940.

JOHNSON, Robert L., MA; American media executive; *Founder, Chairman and CEO, Black Entertainment Television (BET);* b. 1946, Hickory, MS; m. Sheila Johnson; two c.; ed Univ. of Ill., Woodrow Wilson School, Princeton Univ.; held positions at Washington, DC Urban League and Corpn for Public Broadcasting; Press Sec. to Hon. Walter E. Fauntroy, Congressional Del. from DC 1973–76; Vice-Pres. of Govt Relations, Nat. Cable & Telecommunications Asscn (NCTA) 1976–79; Founder, Chair. and CEO Black Entertainment TV (BET) 1980– (since 1998 a subsidiary of Viacom), est. BET Pictures and BET Arabesque 1998, BET Interactive 2000; owns a dozen US hotels and a number of lottery licences on Antigua, Anguilla and St Kitts; majority owner of Charlotte (NC) Bobcats professional basketball team; mem. Bd US Airways, Hilton Hotels Corpn, General Mills, United Negro Coll. Fund, Nat. Cable TV Asscn, American Film Inst.; mem. Bd Govs Rock and Roll Hall of Fame, Cleveland, OH, Brookings Inst.; Broadcasting & Cable Magazine Hall of Fame Award 1997, Cable & Telecommunications Asscn for Marketing (CTAM) Grand Tam Award, Cablevision magazine 20/20 Vision Award, National Association for the Advancement of Colored People (NAACP) Image Award, Nat. Women's Caucus Good Guys Award, Princeton Nat. Distinguished Alumni Award, Nat. Cable & Telecommunications Pres.'s Award. *Address:* BET, 2000 M Street, NW, Suite 602, Washington, DC 20036, USA (office). *Website:* www.bet.com.

JOHNSON, Stephen L., BA, MS; American scientist and fmr government official; b. 21 March 1951, Washington, DC; ed Taylor Univ., George Washington Univ.; fmr Dir of Operations Hazelton Labs Corpn, Litton Bionetics Inc.; fmr positions at US Environmental Protection Agency (EPA) include Dir Field Operations Div., Office of Pesticide Programs (OPP), Deputy Dir Hazard Evaluation Div., OPP, Exec. Sec. Scientific Advisory Panel for the Fed. Insecticide, Fungicide and Rodenticide Act, Deputy Dir OPP 1997–99, Acting Deputy Asst Admin. 1999–2000, Deputy Asst Admin. 2000, Prin. Deputy Asst Admin., Acting Asst Admin. Office of Prevention, Pesticides and Toxic Substances 2001, Asst Admin. 2001–03, Acting Deputy Admin. EPA 2003–04, Deputy Admin. 2004–05, Acting Admin. Jan.–May 2005, Admin. 2005–09; Presidential Rank Award 1997, 2001, EPA Excellence in Man. Award, Vice-Pres.'s Hammer Award, seven bronze medals, one silver medal. *Address:* c/o Environmental Protection Agency, Ariel Rios Building, 1200 Pennsylvania Avenue, NW, Washington, DC 20460, USA.

JOHNSON, Suzanne M. Nora, BA, JD; American lawyer and business executive; ed Univ. of Southern Calif. and Harvard Law School; attorney with Simpson Thacher & Bartlett; served as law clerk on US Court of Appeals –1985; joined Goldman Sachs in 1985, Pnr 1992, Head of Global Healthcare Business in Investment Banking Div. 1994–2002, Head of Global Investment Research Div. 2002–07, Chair. Global Markets Inst. April 2004–07, Vice-Chair. Goldman Sachs Group, Inc. Nov. 2004–07; mem. Bd Carnegie Inst. of Washington, Univ. of Southern Calif., RAND Health, Technoserve, Women's World Banking; Trustee Brookings Inst., Council for Excellence in Govt; ranked 34th by Forbes magazine amongst 100 Most Powerful Women 2006. *Address:* 365 North Rockingham Ave, Los Angeles, CA 90049, USA (office).

JOHNSON, Thomas S., AB, MBA; American bank executive; b. 19 Nov. 1940, Racine, Wis.; s. of H. Norman Johnson and Jane Agnes McAvoy; m. Margaret Ann Werner 1970; two s. one d.; ed Trinity Coll., Harvard; Head Graduate Business Program, Instructor Finance and Control Ateneo de Manila Univ. 1964–66; Special Asst to Controller, Dept of Defense 1966–69; with Chemical Bank and Chemical Banking Corpn 1969–89, Exec. Vice-Pres. 1979, Sr Exec. Vice-Pres. 1981, Pres. 1983–89; Pres., Dir Corp. and Mfrs Hanover Trust Co. 1989–91, Olympia and York Devts Ltd 1992–; Chair. Pres. CEO GreenPoint Financial Corpn, GreenPoint Savings Bank, Flushing, NY 1993–2004, now mem. Bd of Dirs North Fork Bankcorporation Inc. (acquired GreenPoint 2004); Chair. Bd of Dirs. Union Theological Seminary, Harvard Business School Club of Greater New York; Bank Capital Market Asscn.'s Cttee for Competitive Securities Market; Dir Bond Club of New York Inc.; Vice-Pres. and Bd mem. Cancer Research Inst. of America; mem. Bd of Dirs Alleghany Corpn, R.R. Donnelley & Sons Co., The Phoenix Cos Inc., Freddie Mac 2004–; fmr Dir Texas Commerce Bancshares Inc., Pan Atlantic Re, Inc., Phelps Stokes Fund, Montclair Art Museum; mem. Council on Foreign Relations, Financial Execs Inst., Asscn of Reserve City Bankers, The Group of Thirty; Trustee Trinity Coll.; mem. Business Cttee, Museum of Modern Art, Consultative Group on Int. Econ. and Monetary Affairs. *Address:* Board of Directors, North Fork Bankcorporation Inc., 275 Broadhollow Road, Melville, NY 11747, USA.

JOHNSON, Timothy Peter, MA, JD; American politician; *Senator from South Dakota;* b. 28 Dec. 1946, Canton, SDak; s. of Vandal Johnson and Ruth Ljostveit; m. Barbara Brooks 1969; two s. one d.; ed Univ. of South Dakota and Michigan State Univ.; called to Bar, S Dakota 1975, US Dist Court, S Dakota 1976; fiscal analyst, Legis. Fiscal Agency, Lansing, Mich. 1971–72; sole practice, Vermillion, S Dakota 1975–86; mem. S Dakota House of Reps 1978–82, S Dakota Senate 1982–86; mem. 101st–103rd US Congresses 1987–97; Senator from S Dakota 1997–; Democrat. *Address:* 324 Hart Senate Office Building, Washington, DC 20510-0001, USA (office). *Telephone:* (202) 224-5842. *Fax:* (202) 228-5765. *Website:* johnson.senate.gov.

JOHNSON, Sir Vassel Godfrey, Kt, CBE, JP; British banking executive and business executive; b. 18 Jan. 1922, Cayman Islands; s. of the late Charles McKintha Johnson and of Theresa Virginia Johnson (née McDoom); m. Rita Joanna Hinds 1952; three s. (one deceased) four d.; ed Govt Secondary School, Grand Cayman and Bennet Coll., Wolsey Hall, Univ. of Sussex, UK; entered civil service, Cayman Islands 1942; with Cayman Co. of Jamaica Home Guard 1942–45; clerical officer, Dept of Treasury, Customs and PO 1945–55; Asst to Deputy Treas. 1955–59; Clerk of Courts 1959–60; Public Recorder 1962–76; Treas. and Collector of Taxes 1965–82; Head of Exchange Control 1966–80; Insp. of Banks and Trust Cos 1966–73; Chair. Cayman Islands Currency Bd 1971–82; mem. Exec. Council, responsible for Finance and Devt 1972–82; Acting Gov. of Cayman Islands 1977; Chair. Govt Vehicles Funding Scheme 1977–82; retd from civil service 1982; Dir British American Bank 1983–; Chair. Public Service Comm. 1983–84; MLA, George Town 1984–88; mem. Exec. Council, responsible for Devt and Nat. Resources 1984–88; Founding Dir Cayman Airways Ltd 1968, Chair. 1971–77, 1984–85; Chair. Cayman Islands Corpn (Airways) 1969–77; Trustee Swiss Bank & Trust Corpn 1983–97; Man. Dir Montpellier Properties (Cayman) Ltd 1983–97; Chair. Bd of Govs Cayman Preparatory School 1982–84, 1993–95; Silver Jubilee Medal 1977. *Publications include:* Cayman Islands Economic and Financial Review 1904–1981 1982, As I See It: How the Cayman Islands Became a Leading Financial Centre (autobiog.) 2001. *Leisure interests:* bridge, church-related activities (Sr Elder, United Church). *Address:* POB 78G, Grand Cayman, Cayman Islands (office). *Telephone:* 9499217 (office). *Fax:* 9459326 (office).

JOHNSON, W. Bruce, BA, MBA, JD; American business executive; *President and Interim CEO, Sears Holdings Corporation;* ed Duke Univ.; spent 16 years at Colgate-Palmolive Co. in various roles; worked as a man. consultant at Booz Allen & Hamilton and at Arthur Andersen & Co. –1998; Dir, Org. and Systems, Carrefour SA 1998–2003; Sr Vice-Pres., Supply Chain and Operations, Kmart 2003, Exec. Vice-Pres., Supply Chain and Operations for combined co. following merger with Sears, Chair. 2005–06, took on store operations 2006–08, Pres. and Interim CEO Sears Holdings Corpn 2008–. *Address:* Sears Holdings Corpn, 3333 Beverly Road, Hoffman Estates, IL 60179, USA (office). *Telephone:* (847) 286-2500 (office). *E-mail:* info@searsholdings.com (office). *Website:* www.searsholdings.com (office).

JOHNSON, Wesley Momo, MBA, CPA; Liberian politician and diplomatist; *Ambassador to UK;* b. 27 May 1944, Monrovia; m.; eight c.; ed Monrovia Coll., St Francis Coll., Brooklyn, NY, Long Island Univ., NY, USA; Baptist Licentiate and Deacon, Zion Grove Baptist Church, Brewerville; fmr Auditor, Old Colony Newport Nat. Bank, Providence, RI, USA; Auditor, Treasury Dept of Liberia (now Ministry of Finance) 1968–72; Sr Bookkeeper (Class-I) and Brokerage Man., Skyline Shipping Co. 1972–77; Founding mem. and Vice-Chair. Progressive Alliance of Liberia 1973, Progressive People's Party 1980; Founding mem. United People's Party 1984, Chair. 1999–; fmr Amb. to Egypt, Consul Gen. to New York 1981; mem. Interim Legis. Ass. 1990–94, Chair. House Standing Cttee on Banking and Currency, Cttee on Ways, Means, Finance and Maritime Affairs, Co-Chair. Cttee on Rules, Cttee on Order and Executive, Sec.-Gen. Liberian Parl. Union; Vice-Chair. Nat. Transitional Govt 2003–07; Amb. to UK 2007–; led Liberian del. to several int. confs including 36th Gen. Ass. of UN (Chair. Cttee on Disarmament) 1981, African Pacific Caribbean Comm., Rosenberg 1992, mem. del. to Inter-Parl. Union, New Delhi, India; Partner, Nimley & Assocs, CPA Inc.; Lecturer, Univ. of Liberia, United Methodist Univ., AME Zion Univ. Coll.; mem. numerous accounting firms and financial insts, including Liberian Certified Public Accountants, Inst. of Certified Internal Auditors, Inc., Atlanta, Ga, American Banking Asscn, RI, MBA Executive, NY USA. *Leisure interests:* playing soccer, athletics, reading, teaching, hard work. *Address:* Embassy of Liberia, 23 Fitzroy Square, London, W1 6EW, England (office). *Telephone:* (20) 7388-5489 (office). *Fax:* (20) 7380-1593 (office). *E-mail:* liberianembassy@yahoo.co.uk (office). *Website:* www.embassyofliberia.org.uk (office).

JOHNSON, William, DSc, FRS, FREng, FIMechE; British professor of engineering (retd); *Professor Emeritus, University of Cambridge;* b. 20 April 1922, Manchester; s. of James Johnson and Elizabeth Riley; m. Heather Marie Thornber 1946 (died 2004); three s. two d.; ed Univ. of Manchester and Univ. Coll. London; Prof. of Mechanical Eng UMIST 1960–75, Visiting Prof. of Mechanical Eng and History of Science 1992–94; Prof. of Mechanics, Eng Dept Univ. of Cambridge 1975–82, Prof. Emer. 1982–; Visiting Prof., Industrial Eng Dept, Purdue Univ., Ind., USA 1984–85, United Technologies Distinguished Prof. of Eng 1988–89; Founder, Ed. Int. Journal of Mechanical Sciences 1960–87, Int. Journal of Impact Eng 1983–87; Foreign Fellow Acad. of Athens 1982; Foreign mem. Russian Acad. of Science (Ural Br.) 1993, Indian Nat. Acad. of Eng 1999; Fellow of Univ. Coll. London 1981; Hon. DTech (Bradford) 1976, Hon. DEng (Sheffield) 1986, (UMIST) 1995; T. Bernard Hall Prize 1965, 1966, James Clayton Fund Prize 1972, 1977, Safety in Mechanical Eng Prize 1980, 1990, James Clayton Prize, Inst. Mechanical Engineers 1987, Silver Medal Inst. Sheet Metal 1987, AMPT Gold Medal, Dublin 1995, American Soc. of Mechanical Engineers Engineer-Historian Award 2000. *Publications:* (with various co-authors) Plasticity for Mechanical Engineers 1962, Mechanics of Metal Extrusion 1962, Bibliography of Slip Line Fields 1968, Impact Strength of Materials 1972, Engineering Plasticity 1973, Engineering Plasticity: Metal-Forming Processes 1978, Crashworthiness of Vehicles 1978, A Source Book of Plane Strain Slip Line Fields 1982, Collected Works on B. Robins and C. Hutton 2003, Record and Services Satisfactory (memoir) 2003. *Leisure interests:* gardening, walking, music, reading. *Address:* 62 Beach Road, Carlyon Bay, St Austell, Cornwall, PL25 3PJ, England. *Telephone:* (1726) 813179.

JOHNSON-LAIRD, Philip Nicholas, PhD, FRS, FBA; British/American psychologist and academic; *Stuart Professor of Psychology, Princeton University;* b. 12 Oct. 1936, Leeds, Yorks.; s. of Eric Johnson-Laird and Dorothy Johnson-Laird (née Blackett); m. Maureen Mary Sullivan 1959; one s. one d.; ed Culford School, Univ. Coll., London; left school aged 15 and worked as quantity surveyor and in other jobs before univ.; Asst Lecturer, Dept of Psychology, Univ. Coll., London 1966, Lecturer 1967–73; Visiting mem. Inst. for Advanced Study, Princeton, NJ USA 1971–72; Reader in Experimental Psychology, Univ. of Sussex 1973, Prof. 1978–82; Asst Dir, MRC Applied Psychology Unit, Cambridge 1982–89; Fellow Darwin Coll. Cambridge 1984–89; Visiting Fellow, Cognitive Science, Stanford Univ., USA 1980, Visiting Prof. of Psychology 1985; Visiting Prof. of Psychology, Princeton Univ., USA 1986, Prof. 1989–, Stuart Prof. of Psychology 1994–; mem. American Philosophical Soc., NAS; Dr hc (Gothenburg) 1983; Laurea hc (Padua) 1997, (Palermo) 2005, (Univ. Ca' Foscari, Venice) 2008; Hon. DSc (Univ. of Dublin Trinity Coll.) 2000, (Sussex) 2007; Hon. DPsych, (Univ. Nacional de Educación a Distancia, Madrid) 2000, (Ghent) 2002; Rosa Morison Memorial Medal, Univ. Coll. London, James Sully Scholarship; Spearman Medal, British Psychological Soc. 1974, Pres.'s Award 1985, Fyssen Foundation Int. Prize 2002. *Publications:* Thinking and Reasoning (co-ed. with P. C. Wason) 1968, Psychology of Reasoning (with P. C. Wason) 1972, Language and Perception (with G. A. Miller) 1976, Thinking (co-ed. with P. C. Wason) 1977, Mental Models 1983, The Computer and the Mind 1988, Deduction (with R. M. J. Byrne) 1992, Human and Machine Thinking 1993, How We Reason 2006; numerous articles in psychological journals; reviews. *Leisure interests:* arts, composing music, talking and arguing. *Address:* Department of Psychology, 3-C-3 Green Hall, Princeton University, Princeton, NJ 08544, USA (office). *Telephone:* (609) 258-4432 (office). *Fax:* (609) 258-1113 (office). *E-mail:* phil@princeton.edu (office). *Website:* weblamp.princeton.edu/~psych/psychology/home/index.php (office).

JOHNSON-SIRLEAF, Ellen, BBA, MPA; Liberian politician and head of state; *President;* b. 29 Oct. 1938; four s.; ed Coll. of West Africa, Monrovia, Madison Business Coll., Madison, Wis., Univ. of Colorado and Harvard Univ., USA; Asst Minister of Finance 1972–78, Deputy Minister of Finance 1979–80; Sr Loan Officer, IBRD, Washington, DC 1973–77, 1980–81; sentenced to ten years' imprisonment for speech that was critical of mil. ruler Samuel Doe; briefly detained twice in prison before fleeing country; fmr Pres. Liberian Bank for Devt Investment; Vice-Pres. Citibank Regional Office for Africa, Nairobi 1982–85; Vice-Pres. and mem. Bd Dirs Equator Holders, Hong Kong Equator Bank Ltd, Washington, DC –1992; Asst Admin. UNDP and Dir Regional Bureau for Africa 1992–97; Chair. and CEO Kormah Investment and Devt Corpn; Leader Unity Party (UP), Presidential Cand. 1997; charged with treason by Taylor regime and forced into political exile; Chair. Open Soc. Inst. West Africa (part of Soros Foundation Network); External Adviser, UN Econ. Comm. for Africa; mem. Advisory Bd Modern Africa Growth and Investment Co.; Sr Adviser and W/Cen. Africa Rep. of Modern Africa Fund Mans; Founder Measuagoon (Liberian NGO); rep. Liberia on bds of IMF, IBRD and African Devt Bank; selected by OAU to investigate Rwanda genocide 1999; elected Pres. of Liberia (world's first elected black female pres. and Africa's first elected female head of state) 2005–; Chair. Comm. on Good Governance (Liberia) 2004–05; Founding mem. Int. Inst. for Women in Political Leadership; mem. Bd Dirs Synergos Inst. 1988–99; Distinguished Fellow, Claus M. Halle Inst. for Global Learning, Emory Univ. 2006; Grand Commdr, Star of Africa Redemption of Liberia; Commdr de l'Ordre du Togo; Franklin Delano Roosevelt Freedom of Speech Award 1988, Ralph Bunche Int. Leadership Award, Common Ground Award 2006, Laureate of the Africa Prize for Leadership for the Sustainable End of Hunger 2006, ranked by Forbes magazine amongst the 100 Most Powerful Women (51st) 2006, (100th) 2007, (66th) 2008, Bishop John T. Walker Distinguished Humanitarian Service Award, Africare 2007. *Publications:* From Disaster to Development 1991, The Outlook for Commercial Bank Lending to Sub-Saharan Africa 1992, Women, War and Peace: The Independent Experts' Assessment on the Impact of Armed Conflict on Women and Women's Role in Peace-building (co-author) (project of UNIFEM) 2002, This Child Will be Great: Memoir of a Remarkable Life by Africa's First Woman President 2009. *Address:* Executive Mansion, PO Box 10-9001, Capitol Hill, 1000 Monrovia 10, Liberia (office).

JOHNSSON, Anders B., LLM; Swedish international organization official; *Secretary-General, Inter-Parliamentary Union;* b. 1948, Lund; m.; three c.; ed Univs of Lund and New York; mem. staff UNHCR, posts in Honduras, Pakistan, Sudan and Viet Nam, then Prin. Legal Adviser to High Commr, Geneva 1976–91; Under-Sec.-Gen. IPU 1991–94, Deputy Sec.-Gen. and Legal Adviser 1994–98, Sec.-Gen. 1998–. *Address:* Inter-Parliamentary Union, CP 330, 1218 Le Grand-Saconnex/ Geneva, Switzerland (office). *Telephone:* (22) 9194150 (office). *Fax:* (22) 9194160 (office). *E-mail:* postbox@mail.ipu.org (office). *Website:* www.ipu.org (office).

JOHNSSON, Finn, MBA; Swedish business executive; *Chairman, AB Volvo;* b. 1946, Gothenburg; worked for Machine Div., Swedish Match, fmr Pres. Swedish Match Europe and Swedish Match Asia; fmr Pres. Arenco Machine Co., USA; fmr Pres. Tarkett AB; fmr Exec. Vice-Pres. Stora AB; fmr Pres. Industri AB Euroc; Deputy Chief Exec. and COO United Distillers, UK –1998; Pres. and CEO Mölnlycke Health Care AB –2005, Chair. 2005–; mem. Bd of Dirs AB Volvo 1998–, Chair. 2004–, also Chair. Remuneration Cttee; Chair. West Sweden Chamber of Commerce and Industry, Luvata Oy, Thomas Concrete Group AB, KappAhl AB, City Airline, EFG European Furniture Group AB; mem. Bd of Dirs Guinness 1994–, Skanska AB 1998–, AB IndustriVärden 2000–, Bilisten. *Address:* AB Volvo, 405 08 Gothenburg, Sweden (office). *Telephone:* (31) 660000 (office). *Fax:* (31) 545772 (office). *E-mail:* marten.wikforss@volvo.com (office). *Website:* www.volvo.com (office).

JOHNSTON, David Lloyd, CC, LLB; Canadian legal scholar and university administrator; *President, University of Waterloo;* b. 28 June 1941, Sudbury, Ont.; s. of Lloyd Johnston and Dorothy Stonehouse; m. Sharon Downey 1964; five d.; ed Sault Collegiate Inst., Sault Ste. Marie, Ont., Harvard Univ., Univ. of Cambridge and Queen's Univ., Kingston; Asst Prof. Faculty of Law, Queen's Univ., Kingston; 1966–68; Asst Prof. Faculty of Law, Univ. of Toronto 1968–69, Assoc. Prof. 1969–72, Prof. 1972–74; Dean and Prof. Faculty of Law, Univ. of W Ont. 1974–79; Prof. of Law, McGill Univ. 1979–, Prin. and Vice-Chancellor 1979–94; Pres. and mem. Bd. of Governors, Univ. of Waterloo 1999–; Pres. Harvard Univ. Bd of Overseers 1997–98; recipient of 12 hon. degrees. *Publications:* Computers and the Law 1968, Canadian Securities Regulation 1977, The Law of Business Associations (with R. Forbes) 1979, Canadian Companies and the Stock Exchange 1980, If Québec Goes: The Real Cost of Separation (with Marcel Côté) 1995, Getting Canada On Line: Understanding the Information Highway (co-author) 1995, Cyberlaw 1997, Communications Law of Canada 1999; numerous articles in academic journals. *Leisure interests:* jogging, skiing. *Address:* University of Waterloo, 200 University Avenue W, Waterloo, Ont., N2L 3G1 (office); R. R. #1, St Clements, Ont., N0B 2M0, Canada (home). *Telephone:* (519) 888-4400 (office); (519) 699-4877 (home). *Fax:* (519) 888-6337 (office). *E-mail:* president@waterloo.ca (office). *Website:* www.uwaterloo.ca (office).

JOHNSTON, Hon. Donald James, PC, OC, QC, BA, BCL; Canadian politician, lawyer, international civil servant, consultant and academic; *Counsel, Heenan Blaikie LLP;* b. 26 June 1936, Cumberland, Ont.; s. of Wilbur Austin Johnston and Florence Jean Moffat Tucker; m. Heather Bell Maclaren; four d.; ed McGill Univ. and Univ. of Grenoble; joined Stikeman, Elliott (int. law firm) 1961; subsequent f. own law firm, Johnston, Heenan & Blaikie; taught fiscal law at McGill Univ. 1963–76; MP 1978–88; Pres. Treasury Bd 1980–82; Minister for Econ. Devt and Minister of State for Science and Tech. 1982–83; Minister of State for Econ. Devt and Tech. 1983–84; Minister of Justice and Attorney-Gen. June–Sept. 1984; elected Pres. Liberal Party of Canada 1990, re-elected 1992; Counsel, Heenan, Blaikie (law firm), Montreal 1988–96, Heenan Blaikie LLP (law firm) 2006–; Sec.-Gen. OECD 1996–2006; consultant, McCall MacBain Foundation, Geneva 2006–; Chair. Int. Risk Governance Council (IRGC), Geneva 2006–; Visiting Prof., Yonsei Univ., Seoul, S Korea; Grand Cordon, Order of the Rising Sun (Japan) 2006, Commdr's Cross with Star, Order of Merit (Hungary) 2006, Order of the White Double Cross (Slovakia) 2006, Grand Croix, Ordre de Léopold II (Belgium) 2007; four hon. degrees in econs and law; Gold Medallist, McGill Univ. 1958. *Films:* As Exec. Producer: Seizure 1974. *Publications:* Up the Hill (political memoirs) 1986; several books and numerous articles on taxation, law and public affairs in professional journals. *Leisure interests:* tennis, piano, writing. *Address:* Heenan Blaikie LLP, 1250 René-Lévesque Blvd West, Suite 2500, Montreal, PQ H3B 4Y1, Canada (office); 537 Courser Road, Glensutton, PQ D0E 2K0 (home). *Telephone:* (514) 846-2280 (office); (450) 538-5124 (home). *Fax:* (514) 921-1280 (office); (450) 538-0304 (home). *E-mail:* djohnston@heenan.ca (office); donaldjames.johnston@gmail.com (home). *Website:* www.heenanblaikie.com (office).

JOHNSTON, Jennifer; Irish writer; b. 12 Jan. 1930, Dublin; d. of Denis Johnston and Shelah Richards; m. 1st Ian Smyth; two s. two d.; m. 2nd David Gilliland; ed Park House School, Dublin, Trinity Coll., Dublin; Hon. Fellow Trinity Coll., Dublin; Hon. DLitt (New Univ. of Ulster, Queen's Univ., Belfast, Trinity Coll., Dublin, Nat. Univ. of Ireland); Whitbread Prize 1980, Giles Cooper Award 1989, Premio Giuseppe Acerbi 2003. *Plays:* The Desert Lullaby, Moonlight and Music; several radio and TV programmes. *Publications:* How Many Miles to Babylon?, The Old Jest, The Christmas Tree, The Invisible Worm 1991, The Illusionist 1995, Two Moons, The Railway Station Man 1986, Shadows on Our Skin, The Gingerbread Woman, The Porch 1986, The Invisible Man 1986, The Desert Lullaby 1996, This is Not a Novel 2003, Grace and Truth 2005, Foolish Mortals 2008. *Leisure interests:* reading, theatre, cinema. *Address:* Brook Hall, Culmore Road, Derry, BT48 8JE, Northern Ireland (home). *Telephone:* (28) 7135-1297 (home).

JOHNSTON, J(ohn) Bennett; American consultant and fmr politician; *CEO, Johnston & Associates LLC;* b. 10 June 1932, Shreveport, La; s. of J. Bennett Johnston; m. Mary Gunn; two s. two d.; ed Byrd High School, Washington and Lee Univ., US Mil. Acad. and La State Univ. Law School; mil. service in Judge Advocate Gen. Corps La; State Senator 1968–72; Senator from La 1972–96; Chair. Democratic Senatorial Campaign Cttee 1975–76; mem. Senate Cttee on Energy and Natural Resources, on Appropriations, Senate Budget Cttee, mem. Senate Bldg Cttee; CEO Johnston & Assocs LLC 1996–; co-Chair. American Iranian Council; mem. Bd of Dirs Freeport-McMoRan Copper & Gold, Inc., Chevron, Nexant, Fundacion Amistad, US China Business Council; Vice-Pres. US Pacific Econ. Cooperation Council; Democrat; Hon. DIur (Louisiana State Univ., Tulane Univ., Centenary Coll., Univ. of Louisiana, Southern Univ., Xavier Univ., Louisiana Tech. Univ.). *Leisure interest:* tennis. *Address:* Johnston & Associates LLC, 1330 Connecticut Avenue, NW, Washington, DC, 20036, USA. *Telephone:* (202) 659-8400 (office). *Fax:* (202) 659-1340 (office).

JOHNSTON, Lawrence (Larry) R., BBA; American retail executive; ed Stetson Univ., Deland, Fla; began career as Man. Trainee, Gen. Electric Co. 1972, various man. positions 1979–84, Merchandising Man., Washington DC 1984, later Regional Man., Cleveland, Corp. Vice-Pres. 1989, Vice-Pres. Sales and Distribution, GE Appliances, Pres. and CEO GE Medical Systems Europe 1997–99, Sr Vice-Pres. 1999–2001, Pres. and CEO GE Appliances 1999–2001; Chair., CEO and Pres. Albertson's Inc. 2001–06; mem. Bd of Dirs Home Depot Inc.; fmr mem. Bd of Dirs World Food Forum, Paris, Food Marketing Inst., Washington, DC. *Address:* c/o Board of Directors, Home Depot Inc., 2455 Paces Ferry Road, Atlanta, GA, 30339-4024, USA (office).

JOHNSTON, Michael F., BA, MBA; American business executive; *Chairman and CEO, Visteon Corporation;* b. 21 May 1947; m.; three c.; ed Univ. of Mass at Lowell, Mich. State Univ.; various man. positions with Micropol –1989; joined Johnson Controls Inc. 1989, Gen. Man. SLI Battery Div. 1991–93, Vice-Pres. and Gen. Man. Johnson Controls Battery Group 1993–97, Vice-Pres. and Gen. Man. ASG Interior Systems Business 1997, Pres. Americas Automotive Group 1997–99, Pres. N America/Asia Pacific, Automotive Systems Group 1997–99, Pres. of e-Business 1999–2000; Pres. and COO Visteon Corpn 2000–04, apptd Dir 2002, Pres. and CEO 2004, Chair. and CEO 2005–; mem. Bd of Dirs Flowserve Corpn, Whirlpool Corpn. *Address:* Visteon Corporation, 17000 Rotunda Drive, Dearborn, MI 48120, USA (office). *Telephone:* (313) 755-2800 (office). *Fax:* (313) 755-7983 (office). *Website:* www.visteon.com (office).

JOHNSTON, Ronald John, MA, PhD, FBA; British geographer and academic; *Professor of Geography, University of Bristol;* b. 30 March 1941, Swindon; s. of Henry Louis Johnston and Phyllis Joyce Johnston (née Liddiard); m. Rita Brennan 1963; one s. one d.; ed The Commonweal Co. Secondary Grammar School, Swindon, Univ. of Manchester, Monash Univ., Australia; Teaching Fellow, then Lecturer, Dept of Geography, Monash Univ. 1964–66; Lecturer then Reader, Dept of Geography, Univ. of Canterbury, NZ 1967–74; Prof. of Geography, Univ. of Sheffield 1974–92, Pro-Vice-Chancellor for Academic Affairs 1989–92; Vice-Chancellor Univ. of Essex 1992–95; Prof. of Geography, Univ. of Bristol 1995–; Co-Ed. Environment and Planning 1979–2005, Progress in Human Geography 1979–2007; mem. Acad. of Learned Socs for the Social Sciences; Hon. DUniv (Essex) 1996; Hon. LLD (Monash) 1999; Hon. DLitt (Sheffield) 2002; Hon. DLH (Bath) 2005; Murchison Award, Royal Geographical Soc. (RGS) 1984, Victoria Medal (RGS) 1990, Hons Award for Distinguished Contribs, Asscn of American Geographers 1991, Prix Vautrin Lud 1999. *Publications:* author or co-author of more than 50 books, including Geography and Geographers, Philosophy and Human Geography, City and Society, The Geography of English Politics, A Nation Dividing?, Bell-ringing: The English Art of Change-Ringing, An Atlas of Bells; ed. or co-ed. of more than 20 books, including Geography and the Urban Environment (six vols), The Dictionary of Human Geography; author or co-author of more than 800 articles in academic journals. *Leisure interests:* bell-ringing, walking. *Address:* School of Geographical Sciences, University of Bristol, Bristol, BS8 1SS, England (office). *Telephone:* (117) 928-9116 (office). *Fax:* (117) 928-7878 (office). *E-mail:* r.johnston@bris.ac.uk (office). *Website:* www.ggy.bris.ac.uk/staff/staff_johnston.html (office).

JOHNSTONE, D(onald) Bruce, Jr, PhD; American university administrator and academic; *Professor Emeritus and Director, International Comparative Finance and Accessibility Project, University at Buffalo;* b. 13 Jan. 1941, Minneapolis, Minn.; s. of Donald Bruce Johnstone and Florence Elliott Johnstone; m. Gail Eberhardt 1965; one s. one d.; ed Harvard Univ. and Univ. of Minnesota; Admin. Asst to Senator Walter F. Mondale (q.v.) 1969–71; Project Specialist, Ford Foundation 1971–72; Exec. Asst to Pres. and Vice-Pres., Univ. of Pennsylvania 1972–77, Adjunct Assoc. Prof. of Educ. 1976–79, Vice-Pres. for Admin. 1977–79; Pres. State Univ. Coll., Buffalo 1979–88; Chancellor State Univ. of New York 1988–94; apptd Univ. Prof. of Higher and Comparative Educ., Univ. at Buffalo 1994, now Prof. Emer. and Dir Int. Comparative Finance and Accessibility Project, also Distinguished Service Prof. and Distinguished Scholar Leader, Fulbright New Century Scholars Program; Dr hc (D'Youville Coll.) 1995, (Towson State Univ.) 1995, (Calif. State Univ.) 1997; Golden Quill Award, Nat. Asscn of Student Financial Aid Admins. *Publications:* Financing Higher Education: Cost-Sharing In International Perspective; other works on the econs and man. of higher educ. in domestic and int. perspectives. *Leisure interests:* writing, wilderness canoeing, wildflower botany. *Address:* 428 Baldy Hall, University at Buffalo, Buffalo, NY 12246 (office); 284 Rivermist Drive, Buffalo, NY 14202, USA (home). *Telephone:* (716) 645-1078 (office). *Fax:* (716) 645-2481 (office). *E-mail:* dbj@buffalo.edu (office). *Website:* www.gse.buffalo.edu/FAS/johnston (office).

JOHNSTONE, L. Craig, BA; American diplomatist and UN official; *Deputy High Commissioner, United Nations High Commissioner for Refugees;* b. 1 Sept. 1942, Seattle, Wash.; m. Silke Johnstone; four c.; ed Univ. of Maryland, Harvard Univ.; worked in Viet Nam for USAID and as US Foreign Service Officer 1965–70; also held positions embassy in Ottawa, on the staff of Sec. of State Henry Kissinger; coordinator with UN Gen. Ass.; fmr Deputy Asst Sec. of State for Latin America; Amb. to Algeria 1985–88; held several sr man. positions at Cabot Corpn, Brussels 1989–94; Dir for Resources, Plans and Policy, Office of the Sec. of State 1994–99; fmr Sr Vice-Pres. US Chamber of Commerce; European Vice-Pres. and Gen. Man. The Boeing Co. –2007; Deputy High Commr, UNHCR 2007–; mem. Bd of Dirs Vital Voices Global Partnership; mem. Bd of Trustees Humanitarian Aid Foundation; fmr Fellow, Council on Foreign Relations, New York, Inst. of Politics, Harvard. *Address:* United Nations High Commissioner for Refugees, Case Postale 2500, 1211 Geneva 2 Dépôt, Switzerland (office); 2068 42nd Avenue East, Seattle, WA 98112, USA (home). *Telephone:* (22) 7398111 (office). *E-mail:* johnstone@unhcr.org (office). *Website:* www.unhcr.org (office).

JOHNSTONE, Peter; British diplomatist and administrator; b. 30 July 1944; m. Diane Claxton 1969; one s. one d.; joined Foreign Office 1962, postings abroad include Berne 1965–66, Benin City 1966–68, Budapest 1968–69, Maseru 1969–72, Dhaka 1977–79; First Sec. Dublin 1979–82, Harare 1986–89; Consul-Gen. Edmonton 1989–91; Counsellor for Commercial Devt, Jakarta 1995–2000; Gov. of Anguilla and Chair. Exec. Council 2000–04. *Address:* c/o Foreign and Commonwealth Office, King Charles Street, London, SW1A 2AH, England. *Telephone:* (20) 7008-1500. *Website:* www.fco.gov.uk.

JOHOR, HRH The Sultan of; Tuanku Mahmood Iskandar ibni al-Marhum Sultan Ismail; Malaysian; b. 8 April 1932, Johore Bahru, Johore; s. of Sultan Tengku Ismail of Johore; m. 1st Josephine Trevorrow 1956; m. 2nd Tengku Zanariah Ahmad Zanariah Ahmad 1961; ed Sultan Abu Bakar English Coll., Johore Bahru, Trinity Grammar School, Sydney, Australia, Devon Tech. Coll., Torquay, UK; Tengku Makota (Crown Prince) 1959–61, 1981; Raja Muda (second-in-line to the throne) 1966–81; fifth Sultan of Johore 1981–; Col-in-Chief, Johore Mil. Forces 1981–; Yang di-Pertuan Agung (Supreme Head of State) 1984–89; f. Mado's Enterprises and Mados-Citoh-Daiken (timber cos). *Leisure interests:* hunting, tennis, golf, flying, water sports.

JOKIĆ, Ljubiša; Montenegrin military officer; b. 24 Sept. 1958, Plav; m.; two s.; fmr pilot and flight instructor; positions held include Commdr Golubovci Airfield, Podgorica, Sec. Supreme Defense Council, head of military cabinet of Pres. of Serbia and Montenegro, head personnel department Defense Ministry; Chief of Staff Army of Serbia and Montenegro 2005–06. *Leisure interests:* football, skiing, hunting, reading. *Address:* c/o Ministry of Defence, Birčaninova 5, 11000 Belgrade, Serbia (office). *Fax:* (11) 3651430 (home).

JOKLIK, Wolfgang Karl (Bill), DPhil; American microbiologist and academic; *James B. Duke Distinguished Professor Emeritus, Department of Molecular Genetics and Microbiology, Duke University;* b. 16 Nov. 1926, Vienna, Austria; s. of Karl F. Joklik and Helene Joklik (née Giessl); m. 1st Judith V. Nicholas 1955 (died 1975); one s. one d.; m. 2nd Patricia H. Downey 1977; ed Sydney Univ. and Univ. of Oxford; Research Fellow, ANU 1954–56, Fellow 1957–62; Assoc. Prof. of Cell Biology, Albert Einstein Coll. of Medicine, New York 1962–65, Siegfried Ullman Prof. 1966–68; Prof. and Chair. Dept of Microbiology and Immunology, Duke Univ. 1968–92, James B. Duke Distinguished Prof. 1972–96, James B. Duke Distinguished Prof. Emer. 1996–; Pres. Virology Div. American Soc. for Microbiology 1966–69; Chair. Virology Study Section NIH 1973–75; Pres. American Medical School Microbiology Chairs' Asscn 1979, American Soc. for Virology 1982–83; Ed.-in-Chief Virology 1975–93, Microbiological Reviews 1991–95; Assoc. Ed. Journal of Biological Chem. 1978–88; mem. NAS, mem. NAS Inst. of Medicine; Humboldt Prize 1986, ICN Int. Prize in Virology 1992, Distinguished Faculty Award, Duke Univ. Medical Center Alumni Asscn 2005. *Publications:* contrib. to and sr ed. specialist books, including Zinsser Microbiology, Principles of Animal Virology, The Reoviridae; more than 200 articles in specialist journals. *Leisure interests:* travel, photography, music, golf, tennis and squash. *Address:* Department of Molecular Genetics and Microbiology, Box 3020, Duke University Medical Center, Durham, NC 27710, USA. *Website:* mgm.duke.edu (office).

JOKŪBONIS, Gediminas; Lithuanian sculptor; b. 8 March 1927, Kupiškis; s. of Albinas Jokūbonis and Domicėlė Jokūbonienė; m. Bronė Valantinaitė 1953; two s. one d.; ed Kaunas Inst. of Decorative and Applied Arts, Inst. of Arts, Lithuanian SSR; Lecturer, Vilnius Inst. of Arts (now Acad. of Arts) 1965–, Prof. 1974–; mem. USSR (now Russian) Acad. of Arts 1983; author of monumental sculptures in Lithuania, including Mother (Memorial Complex, Pirciupiai) 1960, Monuments to the singer Kipras Petrauskas, Vilnius 1974, to the poet Maironis, Kaunas 1977, to A. Miczkevic, Vilnius 1984, to poet Vienažindys Mažeikiai 1987, to Grand Duke of Lithuania Vytautas, Vytautas church in Kaunas 1991, to Martynas Mažvydas, Nat. Library, Vilnius 1996, to the poet Antanas Baranauskas, Seinai, Poland 1999; People's Artist of Lithuania 1977; Lithuanian State Prize, Lenin Prize. *Leisure interests:* archaeology, history. *Address:* VDA, Maironio Str. 6, 2600 Vilnius (office); V. Kudirkos 4–3, 2009 Vilnius, Lithuania. *Telephone:* (2) 253632 (office); (2) 330714 (home).

JOLIE, Angelina; American actress; b. 4 June 1975, Los Angeles; d. of Jon Voight (q.v.) and the late Marcheline Bertrand; m. 1st Jonny Lee Miller 1996 (divorced 1999); m. 2nd Billy Bob Thornton 2000 (divorced 2003); one d. (with Brad Pitt) two adopted s. one adopted d.; ed Lee Strasberg Inst., New York

Univ.; apptd Goodwill Amb. by UNHCR 2001–; mem. Council on Foreign Relations 2007–; UN Global Humanitarian Action Award 2005. *Films include:* Lookin' to Get Out 1982, Cyborg II: Glass Shadow 1995, Hackers 1995, Foxfire 1996, Mojave Moon 1996, Love is All There is 1996, True Women 1997, George Wallace (Golden Globe 1998) 1997, Playing God 1997, Hell's Kitchen 1998, Gia (Golden Globe 1999, Screen Actors Guild Award 1999) 1998, Playing by Heart 1999, Girl, Interrupted (Acad. Award for Best Supporting Actress 2000) 1999, Tomb Raider 2001, Original Sin 2001, Life or Something Like It 2002, Lara Croft Tomb Raider: Cradle of Life 2003, Beyond Borders 2003, Taking Lives 2004, Shark Tale (voice) 2004, Sky Captain and the World of Tomorrow 2004, Alexander 2004, Mr & Mrs Smith 2005, The Good Shepherd 2006, A Mighty Heart 2007, Beowulf (voice) 2007, Kung Fu Panda (voice) 2008, Wanted 2008, Changeling 2008. *Address:* c/o Geyer Kosinski, Media Talent Group, 9200 Sunset Blvd, Suite 810, West Hollywood, CA 90069; c/o Richard Bauman & Associates, Suite 473, 5757 Wilshire Boulevard, Los Angeles, CA 90036, USA (office).

JOLIOT, Pierre Adrien, DèsSc; French scientist and academic; *Honourary Professor, Collège de France;* b. 12 March 1932, Paris; s. of Frédéric Joliot and Irène Joliot (née Curie); m. Anne Gricouroff 1961; two s.; ed Faculté des Sciences de Paris; researcher, CNRS 1954–81, Dir of Research 1974–; Prof., Collège de France 1981–2002, Hon. Prof. 2002–; Chef de Service, Institut de Biologie Physico-Chimique 1975–94, Admin. 1994–97; Dir Dept of Biology, Ecole Normale Supérieure 1987–92; Scientific Adviser to Prime Minister 1985–86; Pres. Science Ethics Cttee, CNRS 1998–2001; mem. Comité nat. d'évaluation de la recherche, CNER, 1989–92; mem. de l'Institut (Acad. des Sciences, Paris) 1982; mem. NAS, Academia Europaea, Acad. Européenne des Sciences, des Arts et des Lettres; Officier, Légion d'honneur; Commdr de l'Ordre nat. du mérite; Prix André Policard-Lacassagne 1968, Charles F. Kettering Award for excellence in photosynthesis 1970, Prix du Commissariat à l'Energie Atomique 1980, CNRS Gold Medal 1982. *Publications:* La recherche passionnément 2001, scientific works on bioenergetics and photosynthesis. *Leisure interests:* tennis, sailing, skiing. *Address:* Collège de France, 11, place Marcelin Berthelot, 75231 Paris Cedex 05 (office); 16 rue de la Glacière, 75013 Paris, France (home). *Telephone:* 1-44-27-12-11 (office); 1-43-37-22-56 (home). *E-mail:* message@college-de-france.fr (office).

JOLLY, Robert Dudley, BVSc, PhD, DSc, FRSNZ, MNZM; New Zealand veterinary pathologist and academic; *Research Fellow and Professor Emeritus, Institute of Veterinary, Animal and Biomedical Science, Massey University;* b. 1 Oct. 1930, Hamilton; s. of Thomas D. Jolly and Violet Mills; m. Aline C. Edwards 1958; two s. two d.; ed King's Coll., NZ, Univs of Auckland and Sydney, Australia; mixed veterinary practice, Rotorua 1955–59; Teaching Fellow, Univ. of Sydney 1960–63; Assoc. Prof., Univ. of Guelph, Canada 1963–65; Sr Lecturer, Massey Univ. 1965–68, Reader 1968–85, Prof. in Veterinary Pathology and Public Health 1985–96, Research Fellow and Prof. Emer. 1997–; Hon. mem. American Coll. of Veterinary Pathologists; Hon. Fellow, Australian Coll. of Veterinary Science; Hon. FRCPA; mem. NZ Order of Merit 2005; Hector Medal 1996. *Publications:* 150 publs in scientific books and journals. *Leisure interests:* gardening, trout fishing. *Address:* 136 Buick Crescent, Palmerston North (home); Institute of Veterinary, Animal and Biomedical Science, Massey University, Palmerston North, New Zealand (office). *Telephone:* (6) 356-9099 (office); (6) 354-5852 (home). *E-mail:* r.d.jolly@massey.ac.nz (office). *Website:* ivabs.massey.ac.nz (office).

JOLOWICZ, John Anthony, QC, MA; British professor of law and barrister (retd); *Professor Emeritus of Comparative Law, University of Cambridge;* b. 11 April 1926, London; s. of H. F. Jolowicz and Ruby Wagner; m. Poppy Stanley 1957; one s. two d.; ed Oundle School and Trinity Coll., Cambridge; army service 1944–48; called to the Bar 1952; QC 1990; Fellow, Trinity Coll. Cambridge 1952–; Asst Lecturer, Lecturer in Law, Univ. of Cambridge 1955–72, Reader in Common and Comparative Law 1972–76, Prof. of Comparative Law 1976–93, Prof. Emer. 1993–, Chair. Faculty of Law 1985–87; Pres. Soc. of Public Teachers of Law 1986–87; Visiting Prof. in Chicago 1957, Mexico 1965, 1968, Paris 1976, Bologna 1992, Trento 1995; Bencher, Gray's Inn, London; Vice-Pres. Int. Acad. of Comparative Law 1999–; Corresp. Acad. des Sciences Morales et Politiques; Chevalier, Légion d'honneur 2002; Dr hc (Nat. Univ. Mexico) 1985, (Buckingham) 2000. *Publications:* Winfield & Jolowicz on Tort, H. F. Jolowicz's Lectures on Jurisprudence 1963, Public Interest Parties and the Active Role of the Judge (with M. Cappelletti) 1975, Droit Anglais (with others) 1992, Recourse Against Judgments in the European Union (with others, also Man. Ed.) 1999, On Civil Procedure 2000 (trans. into Chinese 2008); numerous legal articles. *Leisure interests:* music, reading, travel, grandchildren. *Address:* Trinity College, Cambridge, CB2 1TQ (office); West Green House, 20 West Green, Barrington, Cambs., CB22 7SA, England (home). *Telephone:* (1223) 338400 (office); (1223) 870495 (home). *Fax:* (1223) 338564 (office); (1223) 872852 (home). *E-mail:* jaj1000@cam.ac.uk (home). *Website:* www.law.cam.ac.uk/staff/view_staff.php?profile=jaj1000 (office).

JOLY, Alain; French business executive; *Chairman and CEO, L'Air Liquide SA;* b. 18 April 1938, Nantes; s. of Albert Joly and Yvonne Poyet Rolin; m. Marie-Hélène Capbern-Gasqueton 1966; two s. one d.; ed Lycée Louis Le Grand, Paris and Ecole Polytechnique Paris; engineer, L'Air Liquide 1962–67; Dir of Operations, Canadian Liquid Air 1967–73; Dir Corp. Planning, Soc. L'Air Liquide 1973–76, Regional Man. 1976–78, Gen. Sec. 1978–81, Vice-Pres. 1981, Dir 1982, Chair. and CEO 1995–, Chair. Supervisory Bd 2001–; Dir Lafarge Coppée (now Lafarge) 1993–, Banque Nat. de Paris 1995–; mem. Int. Council, JP Morgan; Croix de la Valeur Militaire, Officier, Légion d'honneur. *Leisure interests:* sailing, golf. *Address:* L'Air Liquide SA, 75 Quai d'Orsay, 75321 Paris cedex 7, France. *Telephone:* 1-40-62-55-55. *Website:* www.airliquide.com.

JOLY, Eva, DenD; Norwegian judge; b. (Gro Eva Farseth), 5 Dec. 1945, Oslo; m. Paschal Joly (died 2001); one s. one d.; moved to Paris at 18 to work as au pair; legal counsellor in a psychiatric hosp.; apptd regional judge, Orleans 1981, Asst to Public Prosecutor 1981–83; High Court Judge, Evry 1983–89, then First Examining Judge; legal specialist, Interministerial Cttee for Industrial Reconstruction, Ministry of Finance, Paris 1989, Deputy Sec.-Gen. –1993; investigating magistrate for financial affairs, Palais de Justice, Paris 1993, led to conviction of Bernard Tapie 1994, Roland Dumas 1998, forty exec. mem. of Elf Aquitaine including Chair. Lok Le Floch-Prigent 1995–2002, employees of Pechiney, Crédit Lyonnaise and other high-ranking politicians and businessmen; returned to Norway as special adviser to Norwegian Ministry of Justice with mandate to help strengthen Norway's work internationally against corruption and money laundering Oslo 2002–05; Special Adviser Norwatch (monitors Norwegian businesses in developing countries) 2005; Special Adviser to Iceland's Minister of Justice (assisting in investigation into bank crisis in Iceland) 2009–; Transparency Int. Integrity Award 2001, European of the Year, Reader's Digest 2002. *Publication:* Notre Affaire à Tous (This Concerns All of Us) (autobiog.) 2000, Is This the World We Want To Live In? 2003, Justice Under Siege: One Woman's Battle Against a European Oil Giant (memoir) 2006. *Address:* c/o Ministry of Justice and Ecclesiastical Affairs, Skuggasundi, 150 Reykjavík, Iceland. *Telephone:* 5459000. *Fax:* 5527340. *E-mail:* postur@dkm.stjr.is. *Website:* www.domsmalaraduneyti.is.

JONAH, Samuel (Sam) Kwesi Esson, MSc, DSc; Ghanaian mining industry executive; *Chairman, Jonah Capital;* b. 19 Nov. 1949, Kibi; m. Theodora Rosemond Arthur 1973; three s. two d.; ed Adisadel Coll., Camborne School of Mines, Imperial Coll. of Science and Tech., UK; shovel boy, Obuasi Gold Mine 1969; CEO Ashanti Goldfields Co. Ltd 1986–2004, Exec. Pres. and Dir AngloGold Ashanti (following acquisition) 2004–05, Non-Exec. Pres. and Dir 2005; Chair. Limestone Products Ghana, First Atlantic Merchant Bank Ltd, Equator Exploration Ltd 2005–, Equinox Minerals Ltd 2005–, Jonah Capital 2005–; Dir Lonmin plc, Defiance Mining Corpn, Anglo American Corpn of South Africa, Anglo American Platinum Corpn Ltd; mem. Ghana Investors' Advisory Council, Int. Investment Advisory Council of South Africa, Global Compact Advisory Council; Hon. KBE; Order of the Silver Guard; Hon. DSc (Camborne School of Mines and Univ. of Exeter) 1966. *Address:* 31A Killarney Road, Sandhurst, Sandton 2146 (home); Jonah Capital, 1st Floor, AMB Capital Holdings, 18 Fricker Street, Illovo Boulevard, Johannesburg 2196, South Africa (office). *Telephone:* (11) 215-2282 (office). *Fax:* (11) 268-6868 (office). *E-mail:* sam@jonahcapital.com (office). *Website:* www.jonahcapital.com (office).

JONAS, Sir Peter, Kt, CBE, BA, LRAM, FRSA; British arts administrator, opera company director and university lecturer; b. 14 Oct. 1946, London; s. of Walter Adolf and Hilda May Jonas; m. Lucy Hull 1989 (divorced 2001); ed Worth School, Univ. of Sussex, Royal Northern Coll. of Music, Manchester, Royal Coll. of Music, London, Eastman School of Music, Univ. of Rochester, USA; Asst to Music Dir, Chicago Symphony Orchestra 1974–76, Artistic Admin. 1976–85; Dir of Artistic Admin., The Orchestral Asscn, Chicago 1977–85; Gen. Dir ENO 1985–93; Staatsintendant (Gen. and Artistic Dir) Bavarian State Opera, Munich 1993–2006 (retd); mem. Bd of Man. Nat. Opera Studio 1985–93; mem. Council Royal Coll. of Music 1988–95; mem. Council of Man., London Lighthouse 1990–92; mem. Kuratorium Richard Strauss Gesellschaft 1993–; mem. Advisory Bd Bayerische Vereinsbank 1994–2004; mem. Rundfunkrat, Bayerische Rundfunk, Athenaeum 1999–2006; mem. Governing Bd, Berlin State Opera Trust 2004–; mem. Advisory Bd, Tech. Univ., Munich 2006–; Queen's Lecture, Berlin 2001; Visiting Lecturer, St Gallen Univ. 2003–, Univ. of Zurich 2004–, Bavarian Theatre Acad., Univ. of Munich; Hon. FRCM; Hon. FRNCM; Bayerische Verdienstorden (Germany) 2003, Maximiliansorden (Germany) 2007; Hon. DMus (Sussex) 1993; Bavarian Constitutional Medal 2003, City of Munich Kulturellen Ehrenpreis 2004, Karl Valentinorden (Germany) 2006. *Publications:* Powerhouse (with M. Elder and D. Pountney) 1993, Eliten und Demokratie 1999. *Leisure interests:* 20th century architecture, cinema, theatre, skiing, mountain hiking, long distance walking, old master paintings. *Address:* Einsiedlerstrass 15a, 8820 Wädenswil, Switzerland (home). *Telephone:* 434779871 (office). *Fax:* 434779872 (office). *E-mail:* sirpeterjonas@hispeed.ch (home).

JONATHAN, Goodluck Ebele, BSc, MSc, PhD; Nigerian politician; *Vice-President;* b. 20 Nov. 1957, Rivers (now Bayelsa) State; m.; ed Univ. of Port Harcourt; Preventative Officer, Dept of Customs and Excise 1975–77; Science Insp. of Educ., Rivers State Ministry of Educ. 1982–83; Lecturer in Biology, Rivers State Coll. of Educ. 1983–93; Asst Dir and Head of Sub-Dept of Environment Protection, Oil Mineral Producing Area Devt Comm. 1993–98; Deputy Gov. Bayelsa State 1999–2007; Vice-Pres. of Nigeria 2007–; mem. People's Democratic Party; Fellow, Nigeria Environmental Soc., Inst. of Public Admins, Int. Asscn for Impact Assessment; mem. Science Teachers Asscn of Nigeria, Fisheries Soc. of Nigeria; Inst. of Public Admins Award 2002. *Address:* Office of the Head of State, New Federal Secretariat Complex, Shehu Shagari Way, Central Area District, Abuja, Nigeria (office). *Telephone:* (9) 5233536 (office).

JONES, Alan Stanley, OBE; Australian fmr racing driver; b. 2 Nov. 1946, Melbourne; s. of Stan Jones (fmr Australian champion racing driver); m. Beverly Jones 1971; one adopted s.; ed Xavier Coll., Melbourne; began racing in 1964 in Australia, raced in Britain from 1970; World Champion 1980, runner-up 1979; CanAm Champion 1978; Grand Prix wins: 1977 Austrian (Shadow-Ford), 1979 German (Williams-Ford), 1979 Austrian (Williams-Ford), 1979 Dutch (Williams-Ford), 1979 Canadian (Williams-Ford); 1980 Argentine (Williams-Ford), 1980 French (Williams-Ford), 1980 British (Williams-Ford), 1980 Canadian (Williams-Ford), 1980 US (Williams-Ford),

1981 US (Williams-Ford); announced retirement in 1981; began competng in Australian Touring Car Championships 1990, established own team Pack Leader Racing, 1996, and sold the team in 1997; participated in launch of Australian Motor Sports Acad.; apptd to Bd Australian Grand Prix Corpn 1995; TV commentator. *Leisure interests:* collecting interesting cars, farming in Australia, boating.

JONES, Allen, RA, FRBS; British artist; b. 1 Sept. 1937, Southampton; s. of William Jones and Madeline Jones; m. 1st Janet Bowen 1964 (divorced 1978); two d.; m. 2nd Deirdre Morrow 1994; ed Hornsey School of Art, Royal Coll. of Art; Sec., Young Contemporaries, London 1961; lived in New York 1964–65; Tamarind Lithography Fellowship, Los Angeles 1966; Guest Prof., Dept of Painting, Univ. of S Florida 1969; Hochschule für Bildende Künste, Hamburg 1968–70, Hochschule der Künste, Berlin 1982–83; Guest Lecturer, Univ. of Calif. 1977; first solo exhbn, London 1963, solo exhbns in UK, USA, Switzerland, Germany, Italy, Australia, Japan, Netherlands, Belgium, Austria, Spain, China, Argentina, Brazil, Czech Repub., Cyprus, Norway, Finland, Estonia 1963–; many group exhbns of paintings and graphic work, world-wide 1962–; first travelling retrospective, Europe 1979–80; Welsh Arts Council-sponsored sculpture exhbn 1992; British Council Print Retrospective 1995–98; Commercial Mural Project, Basel 1979; designs for TV and stage in Germany and UK; sculptures commissioned for Liverpool Garden Festival 1984, Cotton's Atrium, Pool of London 1987, Sterling Hotel, Heathrow 1990, Riverside Health Authority, Chelsea and Westminster Hosp., London 1993, Swire Properties, Hong Kong 1997, 2002, Goodwood 1998, GSK World HQ, London 2001–02, Estouteville, Va, USA 2004–05, Yuzi Paradise Sculpture Parks, Guilin and Shanghai, China 2005–06, Chatsworth House 2008; works in many public and pvt. collections in UK and elsewhere, including Tate Gallery, London, Victoria & Albert Museum, London, Museum of 20th Century, Vienna, Stedelijk Museum, Amsterdam, Museum of Modern Art, New York, Hirshhorn Museum, Washington, DC, Chicago Museum of Art, Moderna Museet, Stockholm, Yale Center for British Art, Whitney Museum of American Art, New York; Trustee, British Museum 1990–99, now Trustee Emer.; Hon. Dr of Arts (Southampton) 2007 Prix des Jeunes Artistes, Paris Biennale 1963, Art and Work Award, Wapping Arts Trust 1989, Heitland Foundation Award 1995. *Publications:* Allen Jones Figures 1969, Allen Jones Projects 1971, Waitress 1972, Ways and Means 1977, Sheer Magic (Paintings 1959–79) 1979, UK 1980, Allen Jones (painting and sculpture) 1963–93 1993, Allen Jones Prints 1995, Allen Jones 1997, Allen Jones Sculptures 1965–2002 2002, Allen Jones Works 2006. *Leisure interest:* gardening. *Address:* 41 Charterhouse Square, London, EC1M 6EA, England (home). *Telephone:* (20) 7606-2984 (home). *Fax:* (20) 7600-1204 (home). *E-mail:* dm@allenjonestheartist.com (home).

JONES, Arthur (Alun) Gwynne (see CHALFONT).

JONES, Hon. Barry Owen, AO, MA, LLD, DSc, DLitt, DUniv, FAA, FAHA, FTSE, FASSA, FRSA, FRSV, FAIM; Australian politician, fmr public servant, university lecturer and lawyer; *Professorial Fellow, University of Melbourne;* b. 11 Oct. 1932, Geelong, Vic.; s. of Claud Edward Jones and Ruth Marion Jones (née Black); m. Rosemary Hanbury 1961 (died 2006); ed Melbourne High School, Melbourne Univ.; MP, Victorian Parl. 1972–77, House of Reps 1977–98; Minister for Science 1983–90, for Tech. 1983–84, Minister Assisting the Minister for Industry, Tech. and Commerce 1984–87, Minister for Science, Customs and Small Business 1988–90; Minister Assisting the Prime Minister for Science and Tech. 1989–90; Visiting Prof., Wollongong Univ. 1991–98, Victoria Univ. of Tech. 1994–; Adjunct Prof., Monash Univ. 1999–; Chair. Port Arthur Historic Site, Tasmania 2000–, Victorian Schools Innovation Comm. 2001–05; mem. Nat. Comm. for UNESCO 1990–99, Exec. Bd of UNESCO, Paris 1991–95; Chair. House of Reps Cttee on Long Term Strategies 1990–96; Nat. Pres. Australian Labor Party 1992–2000, 2005–06, Vice-Pres. 2004–05, 2006–07; Chair. Australian Film and TV School 1973–75, Australian Film Inst. 1974–80, Vision 2020 Australia 2002–; Deputy Chair. Australian Council for the Arts 1969–73, Australian Constitutional Convention 1997–98; Vice-Pres. World Heritage Cttee, Paris 1995–96, Australia ICOMOS Inc. 1998–2000; mem. Australian Film Devt Corpn 1970–75, Australian Nat. Library Council 1996–98; mem. Bd Australian Stem Cells Centre 2002–08; Visiting Fellow, Trinity Coll., Cambridge, UK 1999–; Vice-Chancellor's Fellow, Univ. of Melbourne 2005–07, Professorial Fellow 2007–; Silver Jubilee Medal 1977, Longford Life Achievement Award, Australian Film Inst. 1986, Redmond Barry Award, Australian Library and Information Asscn 1996, Living Nat. Treasure, Nat. Trust 1997, John Curtin Medal 2001, Centenary Medal 2003. *Television:* host, Encounter 1968–69. *Publications include:* Macmillan Dictionary of Biography 1981, Sleepers, Wake!: Technology and the Future of Work 1982, Managing Our Opportunities 1984, Living by Our Wits 1986, Dictionary of World Biography 1994, Coming to the Party (ed.) 2006, A Thinking Reed (autobiography) 2006. *Leisure interests:* films, music, travel, collecting autographed documents, antique terracottas and paintings, reading. *Address:* GPO Box 496, Melbourne, Victoria 3001, Australia. *Telephone:* (3) 8344-8628 (office); (418) 399196 (home). *E-mail:* bojones@unimelb.edu.au (home).

JONES, Bill T.; American dancer and choreographer; *Artistic Director, Bill T. Jones/Arnie Zane Dance Company;* b. 15 Feb. 1952, Bunnell, Fla; ed State Univ. of New York, Binghamton; Co-founder American Dance Asylum 1973; Co-founder and Artistic Dir Bill T. Jones/Arnie Zane Dance Co. 1982–; collaborations with Toni Morrison, Max Roach, Jessye Norman, Sir Peter Hall; dir Guthrie Theatre, Minneapolis 1994; Assoc. Choreographer, Lyons Opera Ballet 1995–; MacArthur Foundation Grant; Dr hc (Bard Coll.) 1996; New York Dance and Performance (Bessie) Award (with Arnie Zane) 1986, Bessie Award for D-Man in the Waters 1989, Dorothy B. Chandler Performing Arts Award 1991, Dance Magazine Award 1993, Edin. Festival Critics' Award (presented to Jones/Zane Dance Co.) 1993, Dorothy and Lillian Gish Prize 2003, Harlem Renaissance Award 2005, Samuel H. Scripps American Dance Festival Award for Lifetime Achievement 2005, Wexner Prize 2005, Eileen Harris Norton Fellowship 2007. *Dance:* choreographer (with Arnie Zane) Pas de Deux for Two 1974, Across the Street 1975, Whosedebabedoll? Baby Doll 1977, Monkey Run Road 1979, Blauvelt Mountain 1980; Choreographer Negroes for Sale (soloist) 1973, Track Dance 1974, Everybody Works/All Beasts Count 1976, De Sweet Streak to Loveland 1977, The Runner Dreams 1978, Stories, Steps and Stomps 1978, Progresso 1979, Echo 1979, Naming Things Is Only the Intention to Make Things 1979, Floating the Tongue 1979, Sisyphus Act I and II 1980, Open Spaces 1980, Tribeca, Automation, Three Wise Men, Christmas 1980, Secret Pastures 1984, History of Collage 1988, D-Man in the Waters 1989, Dances 1989, Last Supper at Uncle Tom's Cabin/The Promised Land 1991, Love Defined 1991, Aria 1992, Last Night on Earth 1992, Fête 1992, Still/Here 1993 (Edin. Festival 1995), Achilles Loved Patroclus 1993, War Between the States 1993, Still/Here 1994, We Set Out Early . . . Visibility Was Poor 1997, Out Some Place 1998, The Breathing Show 1999, You Walk? 2000, Fantasy in C Major 2000, The Table Project 2001, Verbum 2002, WORLDWITHOUT/IN 2002, Black Suzanne 2002, WORLD II 2002, There Were. . . 2002, Power/Full 2002, Another Evening 2003, Reading, Mercy and The Artificial Nigger 2003, Mercy 10 x 8 on a Circle 2003, and before. . . 2003, Blind Date 2005, As I Was Saying. . . 2005, Another Evening: I Bow Down 2006, Chapel/Chapter 2006, The Seven (Lucille Lortel Award) 2006, Spring Awakening (Joseph Callaway Award 2006, Tony Award for Best Choreography 2007, Obie Award 2007) 2006; has also choreographed for Alvin Ailey American Dance Theater, Axis Dance Co., Boston Ballet, Lyon Opera Ballet, Berlin Opera Ballet, Dayton Contemporary Dance Co., Diversions Dance Co.; dir and choreographer of operas including: New Year 1990 (Co-Dir BBC TV production), The Mother of Three Sons, Lost in the Stars; theatre productions include Perfect Courage (co-dir), Dream on Monkey Mountain (dir). *Publication:* Last Night on Earth 1995. *Address:* Bill T. Jones/Arnie Zane Dance Company, 27 West 120th Street., Suite 1, New York, NY 10027, USA (office). *Telephone:* (212) 426-6655 (office). *Fax:* (212) 426-5883 (office). *E-mail:* info@billtjones.org (office). *Website:* www.billtjones.org (office).

JONES, Bobby Louis, BS, BEd, MA, PhD; American gospel singer, television broadcaster and lecturer; *Presenter and Producer, The Bobby Jones Gospel Hour;* b. 1938, Henry, TN; m. Ethel Williams Jones; ed Tenn. State Univ. and Vanderbilt Univ., Nashville, Tenn.; teacher, elementary schools in Tenn. and Missouri; textbook consultant for educational publr; Instructor in Reading and Study Skills, Tenn. State Univ. 1973–85; began performing as gospel singer 1970s; Producer and Host Fun City 5 (children's programme), WTBF, Nashville; formed gospel group 'New Life' 1975; cr. first Black Expo, Nashville 1976; signed contract for first TV gospel show (Channel 4) 1976; Producer and Host The Bobby Jones Gospel Hour (BET) 1980–, Bobby Jones World (BET) 1978–84, Video Gospel (BET) 1989, Bobby Jones Gospel Explosion (BET) 1989–, Bobby Jones Presents... Gospel on Stage, Bobby Jones Presents... Gospel on Classics (Word Network) 2001–, radio programme The Bobby Jones Gospel Countdown (Sheridan Network); composed and acted in gospel opera 'Make a Joyful Noise' (Gabriel Award, Int. Film Festival Award) 1980; co-ordinator Exec. Int. Record Label Gospel Artists Retreat; Hon. PhD (Payne Theological Seminary, Wilberforce, Ohio) 1991; Commonwealth Award, Gospel Music Asscn 1990, 352 honours and awards housed at Indiana Univ. *Recordings include:* New Life albums: Sooner or Later 1976, There Is Hope in This World 1978, Caught Up 1979, Tin Gladje 1981, Soul Set Free 1982, Come Together (Dove Award, Gospel Music Asscn) 1984, I'll Never Forget 1990, Bring It to Jesus 1993, Another Time 1996, Just Churchin' (featuring the Nashville Superchoir) 1998; singles: I'm So Glad I'm Standing Here Today (with Barbara Mandrell, Grammy Award) 1984. *Television includes:* Sister Sister (film) 1982. *Plays:* Yes God is Real. *Radio:* The Bobby Jones Gospel Countdown, The Bobby Jones Gospel Radio Show. *Publication:* Touched by God: Stories of Nineteen Gospel Artists 1998, Make a Joyful Noise: My 25 Years in Gospel Music (autobiog.) 2000. *Leisure interests:* TV, basketball, tennis, football. *Address:* c/o Millennium Entertainment, 1314 Fifth Avenue N, Nashville, TN 37208, USA (office). *Website:* www.bobbyjonesgospel.com (office).

JONES, Bryn Terfel (see TERFEL (JONES), Bryn).

JONES, David A., BA, JD; American health care industry executive; *Chairman, Humana Inc.;* b. Louisville, Ky; ed Univ. of Louisville, Yale Univ.; certified public accountant 1954; served in USN 1954–57; mem. Faculty of Econs, Yale Univ. 1958–60; Co-founder Humana Corpn 1961, CEO 1961–97, Dir Humana Inc. (health benefits co. cr. following separation of Humana Corpn into two cos 1993) 1993–, Vice-Chair. 1996–2005, Chair. 2005–; Chair. and Man. Dir Chrysalis Ventures 1993–; Chair. Hospira; fmr Chair. Healthcare Leadership Council, Nat. Cttee for Quality Health Care; mem. Bd Dirs Abbott Labs, Glenview Trust Co.; mem. The Business Roundtable, Bd American Asscn of Health Plans; Founding Chair. Bd of Visitors, Peter F. Drucker Grad. Man. Centre; Hon. PhD (Chicago Medical School, Univ. of Louisville, Transylvania Univ., Claremont Grad. School); Alumnus of the Year, Univ. of Louisville 2004. *Address:* Humana Inc., 500 West Main Street, Louisville, KY 40202, USA (office). *Telephone:* (502) 580-1000 (office). *Fax:* (502) 580-3677 (office). *E-mail:* info@humana.com (office). *Website:* www.humana.com (office).

JONES, Gen. David Charles, DFC; American fmr air force officer; b. 9 July 1921, Aberdeen, SDak; s. of Maurice Jones and Helen Meade; m. Lois M. Tarbell 1942; one s. two d.; ed Univ. of North Dakota and Minot State Coll., ND, USAF Flying School, Nat. War Coll.; Commdr 22nd Air Refueling Squadron 1953–54, 33rd Bomb Squadron 1954; Operations Planner, Bomber Mission Branch, HQ Strategic Air Command Sept.–Dec. 1954, Aide to C-in-C,

SAC 1955–57; Dir of Material, later Deputy Commdr for Maintenance, 93rd Bomb Wing 1957–59; Chief, Manned Systems Branch, Deputy Chief and later Chief, Strategic Div., DCS/Operations, HQ USAF 1960–64; Commdr 33rd Tactical Fighter Wing March–Oct. 1965; Insp.-Gen. HQ United States Air Forces in Europe 1965–67, Chief of Staff Jan.–June 1967, Deputy Chief of Staff, Plans and Operations 1967–69; Deputy Chief of Staff, Operations, HQ 7th Air Force, Repub. of Viet Nam 1969, Vice-Commdr 7th Air Force, Tan Son Nhut Airfield, Repub. of Viet Nam 1969; Commdr 2nd Air Force 1969–71; Vice-C-in-C USAFE (US Air Forces in Europe), later C-in-C USAFE and Commdr 4th Allied Tactical Air Forces, Ramstein Air Base, FRG 1971–74; Chief of Staff USAF 1974–78, Chair. Jt Chiefs of Staff 1978–82; fmr Dir USAir, Radio Corpn of America, Nat. Broadcasting Co., Kemper Group 1982, US Steel, Nat. Educ. Corpn; fmr Chair. Bd Hay Systems Inc.; Distinguished Service Medal with Oak Leaf Cluster, Legion of Merit, Bronze Star Medal, Air Medal W/I OLC and many other decorations; Hon. DHumLitt (Nebraska) 1974; Hon. DLaws (Louisiana Tech. Univ.) 1975. *Leisure interests:* jogging, skiing, racquetball, flying, historical novels. *E-mail:* dcji@aol.com (office).

JONES, Dean Mervyn; Australian fmr professional cricketer; b. 24 March 1961, Coburg, Vic.; m. Jane Jones 1986; one d.; ed Mt. Waverley High School, Vic.; right-hand batsman; played for Victoria 1981–82 to 1997–98; (Capt. 1993–94 to 1995–96), Durham 1992, Derbyshire (Capt.) 1996 to 1997, resigning mid-way through season and returning home; played in 52 Tests for Australia 1983–84 to 1992–93, scoring 3,631 runs (average 46.5) including 11 hundreds; toured England 1989; scored 19,188 first-class runs (55 hundreds); 164 limited-overs ints; Wisden Cricketer of the Year 1990. *Publication:* Deano: My Call 1995. *Leisure interests:* golf, baseball, looking after his two Rottweilers.

JONES, Douglas Samuel, MBE, MA, DSc, CMath, CEng, FRS, FRSE, FIMA, FIEE; British academic; *Professor Emeritus of Mathematics, University of Dundee;* b. 10 Jan. 1922, Corby, Northants.; s. of Jesse Dewis Jones and Bessie Streather; m. Ivy Styles 1950; one s. one d.; ed Wolverhampton Grammar School, Corpus Christi Coll., Univ. of Oxford; Flight Lt, RAF Volunteer Reserve 1941–45; Commonwealth Fellow, Mass. Inst. of Tech. 1947–48; Asst Lecturer, then Lecturer, Univ. of Manchester 1948–54, Sr Lecturer 1955–57; Visiting Prof., New York Univ. 1955, 1962–63; Prof. of Math., Univ. of Keele 1957–64; Ivory Prof. of Math., Univ. of Dundee 1965–92, Emer. Prof. 1992–; mem. Univ. Grants Cttee 1976–86, Chair. Math. Sciences sub-Cttee 1976–86; mem. Computer Bd 1976–82; mem. Open Univ. Visiting Cttee 1982–87; mem. Council, Inst. of Math. and its applications 1982–97 (Pres. 1988–90); Hon. Fellow, Corpus Christi Coll., Univ. of Oxford; Hon. DSc (Strathclyde) 1975; Keith Prize, RSE 1974, Marconi Prize, IEE 1974, Van Der Pol Gold Medal, Int. Scientific Radio Union 1981; Naylor Prize of London Math. Soc. 1987. *Publications include:* Electrical and Mechanical Oscillations 1961, The Theory of Electromagnetism 1964, Generalised Functions 1966, Introductory Analysis (vol.1) 1969, (vol.2) 1970, Methods in Electromagnetic Wave Propagation 1979, 1994, Elementary Information Theory 1979, The Theory of Generalised Functions 1982, Differential Equations and Mathematical Biology 1983, Acoustic and Electromagnetic Waves 1986, Assembly Programming and the 8086 Microprocessor 1988, 80x86 Assembly Programming 1991, Introduction to Asymptotics 1997. *Leisure interest:* avoiding e-mail. *Address:* Department of Mathematics, The University, Dundee, DD1 4HN (office); 1 The Nurseries, St Madoes, Glencarse, Perth, PH2 7NX, Scotland (home). *Telephone:* (1382) 344486 (office); (1738) 860544 (home). *Fax:* (1382) 345516 (office). *E-mail:* dross@mcs.dundee.ac.uk (office). *Website:* www.maths.dundee.ac.uk (office).

JONES, Edward P.; American writer; b. Washington, DC; ed Holy Cross Coll., Univ. of Virginia; PEN/Hemingway Award 1993, Nat. Book Critics' Circle Award for Fiction, Lannan Foundation grant. *Publications:* Lost in the City (short stories) 1992, The Known World (novel) (Pulitzer Prize for Fiction 2004, Int. IMPAC Dublin Literary Award 2005) 2003, All Aunt Hagar's Children 2006. *Address:* c/o HarperCollins Publishers Inc., 10 East 53rd Street, New York, NY 10022, USA (office). *Website:* www.harpercollins.com.

JONES, George; American country music singer; b. 12 Sept. 1931, Saratoga, Texas; s. of George Jones and Clara Washington Jones; m. 3rd Tammy Wynette 1969 (divorced 1975, died 1998); m. 4th Nancy Sepulvado 1983; began singing for money on streets in Beaumont aged 11; performed on local radio and bars; began recording career with single No Money in This Deal 1954; mem. Grand Ole Opry 1969–; Grammy Award for Best Male Country Vocal Performance (for Choices) 1999, Nat. Medal of Arts 2002, Kennedy Center Honor 2008. *Recordings:* Grand Ole Opry's New Star 1957, Hillbilly Hit Parade 1958, Long Live King George 1958, Country Church Time 1959, White Lightning and other Favorites 1959, George Jones Salutes Hank Williams 1960, Songs from the Heart 1962, Sings Country and Western Hits 1962, George Jones Sings Bob Wills 1962, Homecoming in Heaven 1962, I Wish Tonight Would Never End 1963, What;s In Our Hearts 1963, A King and Two Queens 1964, Bluegrass Hootenanny 1964, George Jones Sings Like The Dickens! 1964, For the First Time! Two Great Singers (with Gene Pitney) 1965, Mr Country and Western Music 1965, New Country Hits 1965, Old Brush Arbors 1965, Country Heart 1966, I'm a People 1966, It's Country Time Again 1966, Live Bug 1966, We Found Heaven Right Here on Earth at 4033 1966, Hits by George 1967, Walk Through this World With Me 1967, If My Heart Had Windows 1968, Sings the Songs of Dallas Frazier 1968, I'll Share My World With You 1969, Where Grass Won't Grow 1969, Will You Visit Me on Sunday? 1970, George Jones with Love 1971, We Go Together 1971, A Picture of Me (Without You) 1972, Me and the First Lady 1972, We Loce to Sing About Jesus 1972, Let's Build a World Together 1973, Nothing Ever Hurt Me 1973, We're Gonna Hold On 1973, In a Gospel Way 1974, The Grand Tour 1974, George and Tammy and Tina 1975, Memories of Us 1975, Alone Again 1976, Golden Ring 1976, The Battle 1976, Bartender's Blues 1978, Double

Trouble 1980, I Am What I Am 1980, Together Again 1981, Still the Same Ole Me 1981, A Taste of Yesterday's Wine 1982, Jones Country 1983, Shine On 1983, You've Still Got a Place in My Heart 1984, Ladies' Choice 1984, By Request 1984, First Time Live 1984, Who Gonna Fill Their Shoes? 1985, Wine Colored Roses 1986, Too Wild Too Long 1987, One Woman Man 1989, You Oughta Be Here With Me 1990, Friends in High Places 1991, And Along Came Jones 1991, Walls Can Fall 1992, High Tech Redneck 1993, Bradley Barn Sessions 1994, One 1995, I Lived to Tell It All 1996, It Don't Get Any Better Than This 1998, Cold Hard Truth 1999, The Rock: Stone Cold Country 2001, The Gospel Collection 2003, Hits I Missed...And One I Didn't 2004, God's Country 2006, Kicking Out the Footlights ...Again 2006, Burn Your Playhouse Down 2008. *Publication:* I Lived to Tell It All (autobiog.). *E-mail:* info@ georgejones.com (office). *Website:* www.georgejones.com.

JONES, Grace; American singer, model and actress; b. 19 May 1952, Spanishtown, Jamaica; d. of Robert and Marjorie P. Jones; one s.; m. Atila Altaunbay 1996 (divorced); moved to New York at age of 12; abandoned Spanish studies at Syracuse Univ. for first stage role, Phila; became fashion model in New York, then Paris; made first album, Portfolio, for Island Records 1977; debut as disco singer New York 1977; opened La Vie en Rose restaurant, New York 1987; Q Idol Award 2008. *Films include:* Gordon's War 1973, Attention Les Yeux! 1976, Deadly Vengeance 1981, Conan the Destroyer 1984, A View to a Kill 1985, Vamp 1986, Straight to Hell 1987, Siesta 1987, Boomerang 1992, Cyber Bandits 1995, McCinsey's Island 1998, Palmer's Pick Up 1999, Falco 2008. *Recordings:* albums: Fame, Muse, Island Life, Slave to the Rythym, Hurricane 2008. *Address:* c/o Wall of Sound, 338A Ladbroke Grove, London W10 5AH, England (office). *Website:* www.wallofsound.net (office).

JONES, Dame Gwyneth, DBE, FRCM, ARCM; British/Swiss singer (soprano); b. 7 Nov. 1936, Pontnewynydd, Mon., Wales; d. of the late Edward George Jones and Violet Webster; one d.; ed Royal Coll. of Music, London, Accad. Chigiana, Siena, Zürich Int. Opera Centre; with Zürich Opera House 1962–63; a Prin. Dramatic Soprano, Royal Opera House, Covent Garden 1963–; with Vienna State Opera House 1966–, Deutsche Oper Berlin 1966–, Bavarian State Opera 1967–; guest performances in numerous opera houses throughout the world including La Scala, Milan, Rome Opera, Berlin State Opera, Munich State Opera, Hamburg, Paris, Metropolitan Opera, New York, San Francisco, Los Angeles, Zürich, Geneva, Dallas, Chicago, Teatro Colón, Buenos Aires, Tokyo, Beijing, Hong Kong, Seoul, Bayreuth Festival, Salzburg Festival, Arena di Verona, Edin. Festival and Welsh Nat. Opera; known for many opera roles including Leonora, Il Trovatore, Desdemona, Otello, Aida, Aida, Leonore, Fidelio, Senta, The Flying Dutchman, Medea, Medea (Cherubini), Sieglinde, Die Walküre, Lady Macbeth, Macbeth, Elizabeth, Don Carlos, Madame Butterfly, Tosca, Donna Anna, Don Giovanni, Salome, Eva in Die Meistersinger, Kundry, Parsifal and Isolde, Tristan und Isolde, Helena, Aegyptische Helena (R. Strauss), Färberin, Frau ohne Schatten, Elektra, Elektra (R. Strauss), Elisabeth/Venus, Tannhäuser, Marschallin, Octavian, Der Rosenkavalier, Brünnhilde, Der Ring des Nibelungen, Ortrud, Lohengrin, Minnie, Fanciulla del West, Norma (Bellini), Erwartung (Schoenberg), La voix humaine (Poulenc), Kabanicha, Katia Kabanowa (Janacek), Kostelnicka Küsterin, Jenůfa (Janacek), Herodias, Salome (Richard Strauss), Klytämnestra, Elektra (Richard Strauss), Queen of Hearts, Alice in Wonderland (Unsuk Chin), Begbick, Mahagonny (Kurt Weill); Pres. Richard Wagner Soc., London 1990; masterclasses in UK, Germany, France, Netherlands, Canada and Switzerland; debut as Stage Dir with new production of Der Fliegende Holländer by Richard Wagner at Deutsches Nat. Theater, Weimar; recordings for Decca, DGG, Philips, Chandos, EMI, CBS, Claves, Orfeo; Fellow, Royal Welsh Coll. of Music and Drama 1992; Kammersängerin in Austria and Bavaria; Hon. mem. RAM 1980, Vienna State Opera 1989; Bundesverdienstkreuz (FRG) 1988, Commdr des Arts et des Lettres 1993, Österreichische Ehren Kreuz für Wissenschaft und Kunst, 1. Klasse 1998; Hon. DMus (Glamorgan) 1995, (Wales) 1998; Shakespeare Prize, Hamburg 1987, Golden Medal of Honour, Vienna 1991, Premio Pucci Award Torre del Lago 2003, Cymry for the World Honour, Wales Millennium Centre, Cardiff 2004. *Television films:* Fidelio, Aida, Flying Dutchman, Leonore, Beethoven 9th Symphony, Elisabeth and Venus in Tannhäuser, Poppea (Monteverdi), Rosenkavalier (R. Strauss), Die Walküre, Siegfried, Götterdämmerung, Die lustige Witwe, Don Carlos, Tristan und Isolde, La voix humaine (Mahagonny), Begbick (Mahagonny), Turandot, Senta (Der fliegende Holländer), Queen of Hearts (Alice in Wonderland). *Address:* PO Box 2000, 8700 Küsnacht, Switzerland.

JONES, (David) Huw, MA, FRTS; British broadcasting executive; *Chairman, Skillset Cymru;* b. 5 May 1948, Manchester; s. of late Idris Jones and of Olwen Edwards; m. Siân Marylka Miarczynska 1972; one s. one d.; ed Cardiff High School for Boys, Jesus Coll., Oxford; pop singer, recording artist, TV presenter 1968–76; Dir, Gen. Man. Sain Recording Co. 1969–81; Chair. Barcud Cyf (TV Facilities), Caernarfon 1981–93; Man. Dir, Producer Teledu'r Tir Glas Cyf (ind. production co.) 1982–93; first Chair. Teledwyr Annibynnol Cymru (Welsh Ind. Producers) 1984–86; Chief Exec. S4C (Welsh Fourth Channel) 1994–2005; Chair. Skillset Cymru; Dir Sgrin Cyf, SDN Ltd, Skillset Ltd, Nat. Ass. of Wales Broadcasting Co. Ltd, mem. British Screen Advisory Council; Hon. Fellow, Univ. of Wales, Aberystwyth 1997. *Leisure interests:* reading, cycling, walking. *Address:* Skillset, Prospect House, 80–110 New Oxford Street, London, WC1A 1HB, England (office). *Telephone:* (20) 7520-5757 (office). *Fax:* (20) 7520-5758 (office). *E-mail:* info@skillset.org (office). *Website:* www.skillset.org (office).

JONES, Ieuan Wyn, LLB; British politician and lawyer; *Deputy First Minister, National Assembly for Wales;* b. 22 May 1949, Denbigh, Wales; s. of the late John Jones and of Mair Jones; m. Eirian Llwyd; three c.; ed Liverpool

Polytechnic; practised as solicitor 1974–87; MP for Ynys Môn 1987–2001, mem. Nat. Ass. for Wales (AM) for Ynys Môn 1999–, Deputy First Minister 2007–; Chair. Plaid Cymru—The Party of Wales 1980–82, 1990–92, Pres. and Leader 2000–03, Leader Ass. Group 2003–06, Leader 2006–. *Publications:* Europe: The Challenge Facing Wales 1996, Thomas Gee (biog.) 1998. *Leisure interests:* history, sport. *Address:* C2.13, National Assembly for Wales, Pierhead Street, Cardiff Bay, CF99 1NA, Wales (office). *Telephone:* (29) 2089-8414 (office). *Fax:* (29) 2089-8269 (office). *E-mail:* ieuan.wynjones@wales .gov.uk (office). *Website:* www.wales.gov.uk (office).

JONES, J. Steve, PhD; British geneticist and writer; *Professor of Genetics, University College London;* b. 24 March 1944, Aberystwyth, Wales; ed Wirral Grammar School, studied in Edinburgh and Chicago; currently Prof. of Genetics, Univ. Coll. London; UCL representative to London Regional Science Centre; Pres. Galton Inst.; several visiting professorships, including Harvard Univ., Univ. of Chicago, Univ. of California at Davis, Univ. of Botswana, Fourah Bay Coll., Sierra Leone and Flinders Univ., Adelaide; Royal Soc. Faraday Medal for public understanding of science 1997, BP Natural World Book Prize 1999, 2000, Inst. of Biology Charter Medal 2002. *Radio and television includes:* gave Reith Lectures on 'The Language of the Genes' 1991, Blue Skies (BBC Radio 3), In the Blood (six-part TV series on human genetics) 1996. *Publications:* Genetics for Beginners (with B. van Loon) 1991, The Cambridge Encyclopedia of Human Evolution (ed. with R. D. Martin, D. Pilbeam) 1992, The Language of the Genes (Rhone-Poulenc Book Prize, Yorkshire Post First Book Prize 1994) 1993, In The Blood 1995, Almost like a Whale: The Origin of Species Updated (aka Darwin's Ghost) 1999, Y: The Descent of Men 2002, The Single Helix: A Turn Around the World of Science 2005; also around 100 scientific papers in a variety of journals and contrib. column, View from the Lab, to The Daily Telegraph. *Address:* Department of Biology, University College London, Gower Street, London, WC1E 6BT, England (office). *E-mail:* j.s.jones@ucl.ac.uk (office). *Website:* www.ucl.ac.uk/biology/academic-staff/jones/jones.htm (office).

JONES, James Earl; American actor; b. 17 Jan. 1931, Arkabutla, Miss.; s. of Robert Earl Jones and Ruth Williams; m. Cecilia Hart 1982; ed Univ. of Mich.; numerous stage appearances on Broadway and elsewhere include Master Harold . . . And the Boys, Othello, King Lear, Hamlet, Paul Robeson, A Lesson From Aloes, Of Mice and Men, The Iceman Cometh, A Hand is on the Gate, The Cherry Orchard, Danton's Death, Fences; frequent TV appearances; cast as voice of Darth Vader in films Star Wars, The Empire Strikes Back and The Return of the Jedi; Hon. DFA (Princeton, Yale, Mich.); Tony Award for role in stage version and Golden Globe Award for role in screen version of The Great White Hope, Lifetime Achievement Award, Screen Actor's Guild 2008, numerous other awards. *Films include:* Matewan, Gardens of Stone, Soul Man, My Little Girl, The Man, The End of the Road, Dr Strangelove, Conan the Barbarian, The Red Tide, A Piece of the Action, The Last Remake of Beau Geste, The Greatest, The Heretic, The River Niger, Deadly Hero, Claudine, The Great White Hope, The Comedians, Coming to America, Three Fugitives, Field of Dreams, Patriot Games, Sommersby, The Lion King (voice), Clear and Present Danger, Cry the Beloved Country, Lone Star, A Family Thing, Gang Related, Rebound, Summer's End 1998, Undercover Angel 1999, Quest for Atlantis 1999, Our Friend Martin (voice) 1999, On the Q.T. 1999, Finder's Fee 2001, Recess Christmas: A Miracle on Third Street (voice) 2001, 2004: A Light Knight's Odyssey (voice) 2004, Robots (voice) 2005, The Sandlot 2 2005, The Benchwarmers (voice) 2006, Welcome Home, Roscoe Jenkins 2008. *Address:* Horatio Productions, PO Box 610, Pawling, NY 12564-0610, USA.

JONES, Gen. (retd) James L., BSc; American diplomatist and army officer (retd) and government official; *National Security Adviser;* b. 19 Dec. 1943, Kansas City, Mo.; m. Diane Jones (née Johnson); four c.; ed Georgetown Univ. School of Foreign Service, Basic and Amphibious Warfare Schools, Quantico, Virginia, Nat. War Coll., Washington, DC; Second Lt, US Marine Corps 1967, Platoon Commdr and Co. Commdr Co. G, 2nd Bn, 3rd Marines, Viet Nam 1967–68, rank of First Lt 1968, Co. Commdr Camp Pendleton, Calif. 1968–70, Marine Barracks, Washington, DC 1970–73, Co. H, 2nd Bn, 9th Marines, 3rd Marine Div., Okinawa 1974–75; served in Officer Assignments Section, HQ Marine Corps, Washington, DC 1976–79; rank of Maj. 1977; Marine Corps Liaison Officer to US Senate 1979–84; rank of Lt-Col 1982; Commdr 3rd Bn, 9th Marines, 1st Marine Div., Camp Pendleton 1985–87; Sr Aide to Commdr of Marine Corps 1987–89; rank of Col 1988; Mil. Sec. to Commdt 1989–90; CO 24th Marine Expeditionary Unit, Camp Lejeune, NC 1990–92; rank of Brig.-Gen. 1992; Deputy Dir J-3, US European Command, Stuttgart, Germany 1992–94; Chief of Staff Jt Task Force Provide Promise, Operations in Bosnia and Herzegovina and Macedonia 1992–94; rank of Maj.-Gen. 1994; Commanding Gen. 2nd Marine Div., Marine Forces Atlantic, Camp Lejeune 1994–96; Dir Expeditionary Warfare Div., Office of the Chief of Naval Operations 1996; Deputy Chief of Staff for Plans, Policies and Operations, HQ Marine Corps 1996; rank of Lt-Gen. 1996; Mil. Asst to Sec. of Defense 1997–99; rank of Gen. 1999; 32nd Commdt Marine Corps 1999–2003; Commdr US European Command and 14th Supreme Allied Commdr Europe, NATO 2003–06; Chair. US Ind. Comm. on the Security Forces of Iraq 2007; Pres. and CEO US Chamber of Commerce Inst. for 21st Century Energy 2007–09; apptd by US State Dept to act as Special Envoy for Middle East Security 2007–09; Nat. Security Adviser to the Pres., The White House 2009–; fmr mem. Bd of Dirs Invacare Corpn; numerous decorations; Dr hc (Georgetown Univ.) 2002; Defense Distinguished Service Medal, Silver Star Medal, Legion of Merit with 4 Gold Stars, Bronze Star Medal with Combat V, Combat Action Ribbon and numerous other awards. *Address:* National Security Council, Eisenhower Executive Office Building, 17th Street and Pennsylvania Avenue, NW, Washington, DC 20504, USA (office). *Telephone:* (202) 456-9371 (office). *Website:* www.whitehouse.gov/nsc (office).

JONES, James Robert, LLB; American diplomatist and attorney; *Chairman and CEO, Manatt Jones Global Strategies;* b. 5 May 1939, Muskogee, Okla; s. of Robert Jones and Margaret Wich; m. Olivia Barclay 1968; two s.; ed Univ. of Oklahoma and Georgetown Univ.; Asst to Pres. Johnson, White House, Washington, DC 1965–69; practising lawyer and business consultant, Tulsa, Okla 1969–73; mem. US Congress 1973–87; partner, Dickstein, Shapiro & Moran (law firm), Washington, DC 1987–89; Chair. and CEO American Stock Exchange, New York 1989–93; Amb. to Mexico 1993–97; Pres. Warnaco Int. 1997–98; Sr Counsel to Manatt, Phelps and Phillips 1998–99; Chair. and CEO Manatt Jones Global Strategies 1999–; Steiger Award 1979, Humanitarian Award, Anti Defamation League 1990, Aztec Eagle Award (Mexico) 1997. *Leisure interests:* golf, reading. *Address:* 700 12th Street, NW, Suite 1100, Washington, DC 20005, USA. *Telephone:* (202) 585-6560. *Fax:* (202) 585-6600. *E-mail:* jjones@manatt.com (office). *Website:* www.manattjones.com (office).

JONES, Rt Rev. James Stuart, BA; British ecclesiastic; *Bishop of Liverpool;* b. 18 Aug. 1948; s. of Maj. James Stuart Anthony Jones and Helen Deans Dick Telfer (née McIntyre); m. Sarah Caroline Rosalind Marrow 1980; three d.; ed Univ. of Exeter and Wycliffe Hall, Oxford; Asst Master Sevenoaks School 1971–74; producer, Scripture Union 1975–81; asst curate, Christ Church, Clifton 1982–84, Assoc. Vicar 1984–90; Vicar Emmanuel Church, Croydon 1990–94; Bishop of Hull 1994–98; Bishop of Liverpool 1998–; Hon. DD (Hull) 1999; Hon. DLitt (Univ. of Lincolnshire and Humberside) 2001. *Television:* The Word on the Street 1999. *Publications include:* Following Jesus 1984, Finding God 1987, Why Do People Suffer? 1993, The Power and the Glory 1994, The People of the Blessing 1998, The Moral Leader 2002, Jesus and the Earth 2003. *Leisure interests:* swimming, opera, holidays in France. *Address:* Bishop's Lodge, Woolton Park, Woolton, Liverpool, L25 6DT, England (office). *Telephone:* (151) 421-0831 (office). *Fax:* (151) 428-3055 (office). *E-mail:* bishopslodge@liverpool.anglican.org (office). *Website:* www.liverpool.anglican .org (office).

JONES, (Everett) Le Roi, (Amiri Baraka); American poet and dramatist; *Editor, Unity & Struggle Newspaper;* b. 7 Oct. 1934, Newark, NJ; s. of Coyette L. Jones and Anna Lois (Russ) Jones; m. 1st Hettie R. Cohen 1958 (divorced 1965); two d.; m. 2nd Sylvia Robinson (Bibi Amina Baraka) 1966; five c.; two step-c.; ed Howard Univ., New School and Columbia Univ.; served with USAF; taught poetry at New School Social Research, drama at Columbia Univ., literature at Univ. of Buffalo; Visiting Prof., San Francisco State Univ.; began publishing 1958; f. Black Arts Repertory Theater School, Harlem 1964, Spirit House, Newark 1966; Whitney Fellowship 1963, Guggenheim Fellowship 1965; Fellow, Yoruba Acad. 1965; Visiting Lecturer, Afro-American Studies, Yale Univ. 1977–78; Asst Prof. of African Studies, State Univ. of New York 1980–83, Assoc. Prof. 1983–85, Prof. 1985–; Ed. Unity & Struggle Newspaper; mem. Int. Co-ordinating Cttee of Congress of African Peoples; mem. Black Acad. of Arts and Letters; Fellow, American Acad. of Arts and Letters; Poet Laureate of NJ 2002–04; James Weldon Johnson Medal for outstanding contribution to the Arts. *Publications include:* Preface to a Twenty Volume Suicide Note 1961, Dante 1962, Blues People 1963, The Dead Lecturer 1963, Dutchman 1964, The Moderns 1964, The System of Dante's Hell 1965, Home 1965, Jello 1965, Experimental Death Unit 1965, The Baptism–The Toilet 1966, Black Mass 1966, Mad Heart 1967, Slave Ship 1967, Black Music 1967, Tales 1968, Great Goodness of Life 1968, Black Magic, Four Black Revolutionary Plays 1969, Black Art 1969, In Our Terribleness 1970, Junkies are Full of Shhh ..., Bloodrites 1970, Raise 1971, It's Nation Time 1971, Dutchman + the Slave 1971, Kawaida Studies 1972, Spirit Reach 1972, Afrikan Revolution 1973, Hard Facts: Excerpts 1975, Spring Song 1979, AM/TRAK 1979, In the Tradition: For Black Arthur Blythe 1980, Reggae or Not! Poems 1982, The Autobiography of Le Roi Jones/Amiri Baraka 1984, Thornton Dial: Images of the Tiger 1993, Shy's, Wise, Y's: The Griot's Tale 1994, Transbluesency 1996, Funk Lore 1996, Home 1998, Black Music 1998, The Essence of Reparations 2003, Somebody Blew up America 2004, Tales of the Out and Gone (Pen Faulkner Award 2008) 2006, Digging: Afro American Soul of American Classical Music 2009, Razor: Revolutionary Art for Cultural Revolution 2009; several film scripts; ed. Hard Facts 1976. *Address:* Celeste Bateman and Associates, PO Box 4071, Newark, NJ 07114-4071, USA (office); 808 South 10th Street, Newark, NJ 07108, USA (office). *Telephone:* (973) 705-8253 (office); (973) 242-1572 (office). *E-mail:* celestebateman@aol.com (office); Amirib@aol.com. *Website:* www.celestebateman.com (office); www .amiribaraka.com (home). *Fax:* (973) 242-1509 (office).

JONES, Marion; American professional athlete; b. 12 Oct. 1975, Los Angeles; m. C. J. Hunter 1998 (divorced); pnr Tim Montgomery; one s.; ed Rio Mesa High School, Thousand Oaks High School, Calif., N Carolina Coll.; gold medal (100m), World Championships 1997, 1999; three gold medals (100m, 200m and 4×400m relay) and two bronze medals (long-jump and 4×100m relay), Olympic Games, Sydney 2000; gold medal (200m), World Championships 2001, gold medal (100m) World Cup 2002; stripped of medals won at Sydney Olympic Games after admitting to use of illicit performance enhancing drugs Dec. 2007; sentenced to six months imprisonment on charges of lying to federal prosecutors Jan. 2008; Jesse Owens Award (three times), Associated Press Female Athlete of the Year 2000, Laureus World Sportswoman of the Year 2000. *Address:* c/o USA Track and Field, 1 RCA Dome, Suite 140, Indianapolis, IN 46225-1023, USA (office).

JONES, Mark Ellis Powell, MA, FSA, FRSE; British museum administrator; *Director, Victoria and Albert Museum;* b. 5 Feb. 1951; s. of John Ernest Powell-Jones and Ann Paludan; m. Ann Camilla Toulmin 1983; two s. two d.; ed Eton Coll., Worcester Coll., Oxford and Courtauld Inst. of Art; Asst Keeper Dept of Coins and Medals, British Museum 1974–90, Keeper 1990–92; Dir Nat. Museums of Scotland 1992–2001; Dir Victoria and Albert Museum, London 2001–; Ed. The Medal 1983–94; Pres. Féd. Int. de la Médaille 1994–2000,

British Art Medal Soc. 1998–2004 (Sec. 1982–94); co-f. Scottish Cultural Resources Access Network 1994–96, mem. Bd 1996–2006; mem. Royal Mint Advisory Cttee 1994–2004, Arts and Humanities Data Service Steering Cttee 1997–99, Focus Group Nat. Cultural Strategy 1999–2000; Dir Edin. and Lothians Tourist Bd 1998–2000; mem. Bd Resource (Museums, Libraries and Archives Council) 2000–05; mem. Council RCA 2001–; Trustee, Nat. Trust 2005–, Pilgrim Trust 2006–; mem. Advisory Bd Dept for Culture, Media and Sport 2006–; Hon. Prof., Univ. of Edin. 1997; Chevalier de l'Ordre des Arts et des Lettres; Hon. DLitt (Royal Holloway) 2002. *Publications include:* The Art of the Medal 1977, Impressionist Painting 1979, Contemporary British Medals 1986, Fake?: the Art of Deception (ed.) 1990, Why Fakes Matter (ed.) 1992, Designs on Posterity (ed.) 1994. *Address:* The Victoria and Albert Museum, Cromwell Road, South Kensington, London, SW7 2RL, England (office). *E-mail:* mark.jones@vam.ac.uk (office). *Website:* www.vam.ac.uk (office).

JONES, Mervyn Thomas, BA; British diplomatist; b. 23 Nov. 1942; s. of William Clifford Jones and Winifred Mary Jones (née Jenkins); m. Julia Mary Newcombe 1965; two s.; ed Univ. Coll., Swansea; entered Diplomatic Service 1964; FCO 1964–66; Calcutta 1966, Bonn 1966–70, Warsaw 1970–73, FCO 1973–77, Oslo 1977–80; First Sec. (Man.), then Head of Chancery, Bangkok 1981–85; on secondment to Commonwealth Secr. as Asst Dir Int. Affairs Div. 1985–90; Deputy Consul Gen. and Consul (Commercial), LA 1990–94; Asst Head, Migration and Visa Dept, FCO 1994–96; Counsellor (Commercial and Econ.), Brussels (also accred to Luxembourg) 1996–99; Consul Gen. and Deputy Head of Mission, Brussels 1999; Gov. Turks and Caicos Islands 2000–02. *Leisure interests:* reading, walking, cinema, music. *Address:* c/o Foreign and Commonwealth Office, King Charles Street, London, SW1A 2AH, England (office).

JONES, Michael Frederick; British journalist; b. 3 July 1937, Gloucester; s. of the late Glyn F. Jones and Elizabeth Coopey; m. Sheila Dawes 1959; three s.; ed Crypt Grammar School, Gloucester; reporter on prov. newspapers 1956–64; Financial Times 1964–65; Daily Telegraph 1965–67; Business News Asst Ed. The Times 1967–70; Man. Ed. The Asian, Hong Kong 1971; News Ed. Sunday Times 1972, Political Corresp. 1975, Political Ed. 1984, Assoc. Ed. 1990–95, Assoc. Ed. (Politics) 1995–2002; Chair. Parl. Press Gallery, House of Commons 1989–91; Media Adviser, Memorial to the Women of World War II, London 2004–05; Visiting Fellow, Goldsmith's Coll., Univ. of London 2000–02; currently Research Asst to Baroness Boothroyd. *Publication:* Betty Boothroyd: The Autobiography (collaborated) 2001. *Leisure interest:* researching modern history. *Address:* 43 Hillview Road, Orpington, Kent, BR6 0SE, England (home). *Telephone:* (1689) 820796 (home). *E-mail:* micjon1937@hotmail.com (home).

JONES, Monty Patrick, BSc, MSc, PhD; Sierra Leone plant breeder; *Executive Director, Forum for Agricultural Research in Africa;* b. 5 Feb. 1951, Freetown; m. Geraldine Bamidele Jones; ed Univ. of Sierra Leone, Univ. of Birmingham, UK; began career with West Africa Rice Devt Agency (WARDA) 1975, worked as rice breeder and researcher 1980s, Head of Upland Rice Breeding Program, Côte d'Ivoire 1991; Exec. Dir Forum for Agricultural Research in Africa (FARA), Ghana 2002–; mem. Bd AGRA; Grand Officer, Order of the Rokel (Sierra Leone) 2004, Nat. Order of Merit of Cote d'Ivoire; Hon. DSc (Birmingham) 2005, Hon. PhD (Ghent); World Food Prize 2004, World's 100 Most Influential Men 2007. *Achievements include:* made breakthrough in combining Asian and African rice varieties to develop Nerica, a 'New Rice for Africa', uniquely suited to poor African rice farmers 1994. *Publications:* numerous specialist papers, including The Rice Plant and its Environment 1996, Biotechnology Application in Agriculture: Challenges and Opportunities for Africa 2007, A New Green Revolution: An Answer to the Challenge for Africa? 2007, Priorities for Sustainable Agriculture and Food Security 2007. *Address:* FARA Secretariat, PMB CT 173 Cantonments, #2 Gowa Close, Roman Ridge, Accra, Ghana (office). *Telephone:* (21) 772823 (office); (21) 779421 (office). *Fax:* (21) 773676 (office). *E-mail:* MJones@fara-africa.org (office). *Website:* www.fara-africa.org (office).

JONES, Norah; American singer and pianist; b. (Geetali Norah Jones Shankar), 30 March 1979, New York, NY; d. of Ravi Shankar and Sue Jones; ed Booker T. Washington High School for the Performing and Visual Arts, Dallas, North Texas Univ.; mem. Wax Poetic; formed band with Jesse Harris, Lee Alexander and Dan Rieser; solo artist 2001–; also mem. live band, The Little Willies; MOBO Award for Best Jazz Act 2002, VH1 Best Young Female Singer Award 2002, Grammy Awards for Best New Artist, for Record of the Year, for Best Female Pop Vocal Performance (both for Don't Know Why) 2003, BRIT Award for Int. Breakthrough Artist 2003, World Music Awards for Best Female Artist, Best Pop Female Artist 2004, Grammy Awards for Best Female Pop Vocal Performance (for Sunrise), for Record of the Year (for Here We Go Again, with Ray Charles) 2005. *Film appearance:* My Blueberry Nights 2007. *Recordings include:* albums: solo: Come Away With Me (Grammy Awards for Album of the Year, Best Pop Vocal Album 2003) 2002, Feels Like Home 2004, Not Too Late 2007; with The Little Willies: The Little Willies 2006. *Address:* Macklam Feldman Management, Suite 200, 1505 W Second Avenue, Vancouver, BC V6H 3Y4, Canada (office); c/o Blue Note Records, 304 Park Avenue S, Third Floor, New York, NY 10010, USA (office). *Website:* www.norahjones.com.

JONES, Quincy; American composer, arranger, conductor and musician (trumpet); b. 14 March 1933, Chicago; s. of Quincy Delight and Sarah Jones; m. 2nd Peggy Lipton; two d.; three c. by previous m.; one d. with Nastassja Kinski (q.v.); ed Seattle Univ., Berklee School of Music and Boston Conservatory; musician and arranger, Lionel Hampton Orchestra 1950–53; arranger for orchestras and singers including Frank Sinatra, Dinah Washington, Count Basie, Sarah Vaughan and Peggy Lee; organizer and trumpeter, Dizzy Gillespie Orchestra, Dept of State tour of Near and Middle East and S. America 1956; Music Dir Barchlay Disques, Paris; led own European tour 1960; Music Dir Mercury Records 1961, Vice-Pres. 1964; conductor of numerous film scores; composer, actor in film Blues for Trumpet and Koto; producer recordings of Off the Wall 1980 by Michael Jackson (q.v.), Thriller 1982, Bad, videotape Portrait of An Album: Frank Sinatra with Quincy Jones and Orchestra 1986; composer The Oprah Winfrey Show 1989–; producer, Fresh Prince of Bel Air 1990–; Dr hc (Berklee Music Coll.) 1983; (Hebrew Univ.) 1993, (Clark Univ.) 1993; German Jazz Fed. Award, Edison Int. Award (Sweden), Downbeat Critics' Poll Award, Downbeat Readers' Poll Award, Billboard Trendsetters Award 1983, Martell Foundation Humanitarian Award 1986, Nat. Acad. of Songwriters Lifetime Achievement Award 1989, Jean Hersholt Humanitarian Award 1995, several Grammy Awards, Scopus Award, Producers' Guild of America Award 1999, World Econ. Forum Crystal Award 2000, Marian Anderson Award 2001, Nat. Foundation for Advancement in the Arts Ted Arison Prize 2001, Kennedy Center Honor 2001, BBC Jazz Lifetime Achievement Award 2006, Ivor Novello Special Int. Award 2007. *Recordings include:* albums: Body Heat 1974, The Dude 1981, Back on the Block 1989. *Publication:* The Complete Quincy Jones: My Journey and Passions 2008. *Address:* Quincy Jones Music Company, 6671 Sunset Blvd, #1574A, Los Angeles, CA 90028, USA (office). *Telephone:* (323) 957-6601 (office). *Fax:* (323) 962-5231 (office). *E-mail:* info@quincyjonesmusic.com (office). *Website:* www.quincyjonesmusic.com (office); www.quincyjones.com (office).

JONES, Randall Todd, Sr; American retail executive; *President, Publix Super Markets;* joined Publix Super Markets 1980, Regional Dir of Retail Operations 1999–2003, Vice-Pres. 2003–05, Sr Vice-Pres. 2005–08, Pres. 2008–. *Address:* Publix Super Markets Corporate Office, PO Box 407, Lakeland, FL 33802-0407 (office); 525 East Christina Blvd, Lakeland, FL 33813, USA. *Telephone:* (863) 688-1188 (office). *Fax:* (863) 284-5532 (office). *E-mail:* info@publix.com (office). *Website:* www.publix.com (office).

JONES, Roy, Jr; American professional boxer; b. 16 Jan. 1969, Pensacola, Fla; three s.; professional career record of 49 wins, three defeats, 38 knockouts; voted Outstanding Boxer Olympic Games 1988; won IBF (Int. Boxing Fed.) middleweight crown beating Bernard Hopkins 1993; moved up to super middleweight, won IBF title from James Toney 1994; moved up to light heavyweight div. winning WBC (World Boxing Council) (1997), WBA (World Boxing Asscn) (1998) and IBF (1999) titles; winner WBA heavyweight title 2003 (first fmr middleweight champion since 1897 to win title); winner WBC light heavyweight title 2003, defeated by Glen Johnson losing IBF light heavyweight title 2004, lost to Antonio Tarver losing WBC and WBA light heavyweight title 2004; minor league professional basketball player for five years with the Sarasota Sun Dogs; f. Body Head Entertainment 1998; has appeared in numerous films and TV programmes; currently boxing analyst and commentator for Home Box Office (HBO); Boxing Writers' Asscn of America Fighter of the Decade (for 1990s), The Ring Fighter of the Year 1994, WBC Lifetime Achievement Award 2001. *Leisure interests:* music, basketball, hunting, fishing, raising livestock. *Address:* c/o Home Box Office Inc., 1100 Avenue of the Americas, New York, NY 10036, USA (office). *Telephone:* (212) 512-1000 (office). *Fax:* (212) 512-1182 (office). *Website:* www.hbo.com/boxing (office).

JONES, Stephen John Moffat, BA; British milliner; b. 31 May 1957, West Kirby, Cheshire; s. of Gordon Jones and Margaret Jones; ed Liverpool Coll., St Martin's School of Art; milliner 1980–, collaborating with int. designers including Jean-Paul Gaultier, Comme des Garçons, Claude Montana, John Galliano, Christian Dior (Paris) 1997–; colour creator for Shiseido Cosmetics; licences in Japan for gloves, sunglasses, kimonos, scarves, handkerchiefs, handbags; hats in perm. collections of Victoria and Albert Museum, London, Brooklyn Musuem, New York, Kyoto Costume Inst., Australian Nat. Gallery, Canberra; Accessory Designer of the Year 2005; Chevalier des Chapeaux de Caussade, France 2005. *Leisure interest:* sculpture. *Address:* Stephen Jones Millinery Ltd, 36 Great Queen Street, London, WC2B 5AA, England (office). *Telephone:* (20) 7242-0770 (office). *Fax:* (20) 7242-0796 (office). *Website:* www.stephenjonesmillinery.com (office).

JONES, Sir Tom, Kt; British singer; b. (Thomas Jones Woodward), 7 June 1940, Treforest, Glamorgan, Wales; s. of Thomas Woodward and Freda Woodward (née Jones); m. Melinda Trenchard 1956; one s.; fmr bricklayer, factory worker; sang in clubs and dance halls billing himself as Tommy Scott, singing with the Senators and with self-formed group The Playboys; changed his name to Tom Jones, signed contract with Decca as solo artist 1963; first hit record It's Not Unusual 1965; toured USA 1965; appeared in Ed Sullivan Show at Copacabana, New York and in variety show This Is Tom Jones in UK and USA 1969; other TV appearances include Beat Room, Top Gear, Thank Your Lucky Stars, Sunday Night at the London Palladium, The Right Time (series) 1992; score for musical play Matador 1987; acted and sang in live performance of Dylan Thomas' Under Milkwood 1992; performed in Amnesty Int. 40th Anniversary Special 2001, Pavarotti and Friends 2001, Prince's Trust Party in the Park 2001; Hon. Fellow Welsh Coll. of Music and Drama 1994; mem. Screen Actors Guild, American Fed. of TV and Radio Artists, American Guild of Variety Artists; Britain's Most Popular Male Singer in Melody Maker Poll 1967, 1968; Hon. Fellow, Welsh Coll. of Music and Drama 1994; MTV Video Award 1988, BRIT Award for Best British Male Solo Artist 2000, Nodnoff Robbins Music Therapy Silver Clef Award 2001, Q Magazine Merit Prize 2002, Brit Award for Outstanding Contrib. to Music 2003. *Films:* The Jerky Boys – The Movie 1995, Mars Attacks! 1996, Agnes Browne 1999, The Emperor's New Groove (voice) 2000. *Albums:* Along Came Jones 1965, A-Tom-Ic Jones 1966, From The Great 1966, Green Green Grass Of Home 1966, Live At The Talk Of The Town 1967, Delilah 1968, Help Yourself 1968, Tom Jones Live In Las

Vegas 1969, This Is Tom Jones 1969, Tom 1970, I Who Have Nothing 1970, Tom Jones Sings She's A Lady 1971, Tom Jones Live At Caesar's Palace, Las Vegas 1971, Close Up 1972, The Body And Soul Of Tom Jones 1973, Somethin' 'Bout You Baby I Like 1974, Memories Don't Leave Like People 1975, Say You'll Stay Until Tomorrow 1977, Rescue Me 1980, Darlin' 1981, Matador: The Musical Life Of El Cordorbes 1987, At This Moment 1989, After Dark 1989, Move Closer 1989, Carrying A Torch 1991, The Lead And How To Swing It 1994, Reload 1999, Mr Jones 2002, Reload 2 2002, 24 Hours 2008. *Singles include:* It's Not Unusual 1965, What's New Pussycat 1965, Thunderball 1966, Green Green Grass of Home 1966, Detroit City 1967, Funny Familiar Forgotten Feelings 1967, I'll Never Fall In Love Again 1967, I'm Coming Home 1967, Delilah 1968, Help Yourself 1968, Love Me Tonight 1969, Without Love 1969, Daughter of Darkness 1970, I Who Have Nothing 1970, She's A Lady 1971, Till 1971, The Young New Mexican Puppeteer 1972, Can't Stop Loving You, Letter To Lucille 1973, Somethin' 'Bout You Baby I Like 1974, Say You Stay Until Tomorrow 1976, A Boy From Nowhere 1987, Kiss (with Art of Noise) 1988, All You Need Is Love 1993, If I Only Knew 1994, Burning Down The House (with The Cardigans) 1999, Baby It's Cold Outside (with Cerys Matthews) 1999, Mama Told Me Not To Come (with Stereophonics) 2000, Sex Bomb (with Mousse T) 2000, You Need Love Like I Do (with Heather Small) 2000, Tom Jones International 2002. *Publications:* The Fantasticks (screenplay) 2000. *Leisure interests:* history, music. *Address:* c/o Rosie Hartnell, Valley Music Ltd, 11 Cedar Court, Fairmile, Henley on Thames, Oxon RG9 2JR, England (office); Tom Jones Enterprises LLC, 1801 Avenue of the Stars, Suite 200, Los Angeles, CA 90067, USA (office). *Telephone:* (1491) 845840 (office); (310) 552-0044 (office). *E-mail:* rosie@valleymusicuk.com (office); office@tomjones.com (office). *Fax:* (310) 552-0714 (office). *Website:* www.tomjones.com.

JONES, Tommy Lee; American actor; b. 15 Sept. 1946, San Saba, Tex.; s. of Clyde L. Jones and Lucille Marie Scott; m. 1st Kimberlea Cloughley 1981; m. 2nd Dawn Laurel 2001; ed Harvard Univ.; Broadway debut in A Patriot for Me; other Broadway appearances include Four in a Garden, Ulysses in Night Town, Fortune and Men's Eyes; Emmy Award for TV role as Gary Gilmon in The Executioner's Song. *Films include:* Love Story 1970, Eliza's Horoscope, Jackson County Jail, Rolling Thunder, The Betsy, Eyes of Laura Mars, Coal Miner's Daughter, Back Roads, Nate and Hayes, River Rat, Black Moon Rising, The Big Town, Stormy Monday, The Package, Firebirds, JFK, Under Siege, House of Cards, The Fugitive, Blue Sky, Heaven and Earth, Natural Born Killers, The Client, Blue Sky, Cobb, Batman Forever, Men In Black 1997, Volcano 1997, Marshals 1997, Small Soldiers (voice) 1998, Rules of Engagement 1999, Double Jeopardy 1999, Space Cowboys 2000, Men in Black II 2002, The Hunted 2003, Man of the House 2005, The Three Burials of Melquiades Estrada (also dir) 2005, A Prairie Home Companion 2006, No Country for Old Men 2007, In the Valley of Elah 2007. *Television appearances include:* The Amazing Howard Hughes, Lonesome Dove, The Rainmaker, Cat on a Hot Tin Roof, Yuri Nosenko, KGB, April Morning. *Address:* William Morris Agency, One William Morris Place, Beverly Hills, CA 90212, USA (office). *Telephone:* (310) 859-4000 (office). *Fax:* (310) 859-4462 (office). *Website:* www.wma.com (office).

JONES, Vaughan Frederick Randal, DèsSc, FRS; New Zealand mathematician and academic; *Professor of Mathematics, University of California, Berkeley;* b. 31 Dec. 1952, Gisborne; ed Auckland Grammar School, Univ. of Auckland, Univ. of Geneva, Switzerland; fmr Asst Lecturer, Univ. of Auckland; at Ecole de Physique, Geneva 1974–76, Ecoles Mathématiques 1976–79, taught as asst; E. R. Hedrick Asst Prof. of Math., UCLA 1980–81; Asst Prof., Univ. of Pennsylvania 1981–84, Assoc. Prof. 1984–85; Prof., Univ. of California, Berkeley 1985–; mem. American Acad. of Arts and Sciences 1993–; Hon. DSc (Univ. of Auckland) 1992, (Univ. of Wales) 1993; Univ. Entrance Scholarship 1970, Gilles Scholarship, Phillips Industries Bursary 1970, Swiss Gov. Scholarship 1973, F. W. W. Rhodes Memorial Scholarship, Vacheron Constantin Prize 1980, Guggenheim Fellowship 1986, Fields Medal, Int. Congress of Mathematicians, Kyoto, Japan 1990, New Zealand Gov. Science Medal 1991. *Publications:* numerous articles in math. journals on functional analysis, knot theory and Von Neumann algebras. *Address:* Department of Mathematics, 925 Evans Hall, University of California, Berkeley, CA 94720-3840, USA (office). *Telephone:* (510) 642-4196 (office). *E-mail:* vfr@math.berkeley.edu (office). *Website:* www.math.berkeley.edu (office).

JONES-MORGAN, Judith, LLB, LLM; Saint Vincent and the Grenadines attorney-at-law; *Attorney-General;* b. 7 Sept. 1957, Trinidad and Tobago; d. of Rita Jones; m. Desmond Carlos Richardson Morgan; ed Univ. of E London and Jesus Coll. Cambridge, UK; accounts technician Ministry of Finance and Treasury, Trinidad and Tobago 1976–80; legal clerk, Nat. Energy Corpn, Trinidad and Tobago 1980–84; legal asst, Graham Ritchie & Co., UK 1988–89; pupil barrister Chancery/Commercial Chambers, UK 1991; Crown Counsel in Chambers of Attorney-Gen., Saint Vincent and the Grenadines 1992–93, Sr Crown Counsel 1993–99; registrar, High Court 2000–01, Attorney-Gen. of Saint Vincent and the Grenadines 2001–; mem. Interim Study Programme for Judicial Educators 2000; mem. Bar of England and Wales, Saint Vincent and the Grenadines, Trinidad and Tobago; mem. Hon. Soc. of the Middle Temple, UK; Fellow, Cambridge Commonwealth Soc. 1990; Cambridge Commonwealth Award, Maxwell Law Prize, UKCOSA Essay Competition. *Leisure interests:* politics, drama, public speaking, cricket, jogging, travel. *Address:* Attorney-General's Chambers, Methodist Building, Granby Street, Kingstown (office); PO Box 78, Mount Pleasant, Argyle, Saint Vincent and the Grenadines, West Indies (home). *Telephone:* (784) 457-2807 (office); (784) 458-2010 (home). *Fax:* (784) 457-2898 (office). *E-mail:* att.gen.chambers@vincysurf.com (office); judithmorgan_ag@hotmail.com (home).

JONES OF BIRMINGHAM, Baron (Life Peer), cr. 2007, of Alvechurch and of Bromsgrove in the County of Worcestershire; **Digby Marritt,** LLB, FRSA, CIMgt; British lawyer, government minister and fmr business consultant; b. 28 Oct. 1955, Birmingham; s. of Derek Jones and Bernice Jones; m. Patricia Mary Jones; ed Bromsgrove School, Univ. Coll. London; joined Edge & Ellison (corp. law firm) 1978, Pnr 1984, Deputy Sr Pnr 1990, Sr Pnr 1995; joined KPMG as Vice-Chair. Corp. Finance 1998; Dir-Gen. CBI 2000–06; Sr Adviser to Deloitte 2006–07; Sr Adviser, Barclays Capital 2006–07, Ford (Europe) 2006–07, JCB 2006–07; UK Skills Envoy 2006–07; Minister of State for Trade and Investment, Dept for Business, Enterprise and Regulatory Reform (jtly with FCO) 2007–08, also Labour whip in House of Lords 2007–08; Dir (non-exec.) Alba PLC 2003–07; Dir Leicester Tigers 2005–, Königswinter 2003–07; mem. Advisory Bd Commonwealth Educ. Fund 2000–07; fmr Pres. Tourism Alliance 2001–06; Commr Comm. for Racial Equality 2002–07; fmr mem. Nat. Learning and Skills Council 2004–06, Skills Alliance 2002; Companion Inst. of Man. 2000; Chair. Birmingham Univ. Business School Advisory Bd 2004; full mem. Aston Reinvestment Trust 2003; Fellow, RSA 2001, Royal Inst. 2002, Univ. Coll. London 2004; Pres. Univ. Coll. London Campaign 2004–; Hon. Fellow, Cardiff Univ. 2004; Dr hc (Univ. of Central England) 2002, (Univ. of Birmingham) 2002, (Univ. of Manchester), (Inst. of Science and Tech.) 2003, (Univ. of Herts.) 2004, (Middx Univ.) 2005, (Sheffield Hallam Univ.) 2005, (Univ. of Warwick) 2006, (Univ. of Aston) 2006, (Univ. of Bradford) 2006, (Univ. of Hull) 2006, (Queens Univ., Belfast) 2006, (Univ. of Loughborough) 2007, (Univ. of Nottingham) 2007, (Thames Valley Univ.) 2007, (Univ. of Wolverhampton) 2007,. *Leisure interests:* Aston Villa, theatre, skiing, cycling, rugby, military history. *Address:* House of Lords, London, SW1A 0PW (office); 58 Elizabeth Court, 1 Palgrave Gardens, London, NW1 6EJ, England (home). *Telephone:* (20) 7219-5353 (office). *Website:* www.sirdigbyjones.com (office).

JONES PARRY, Sir Emyr, KCMG, PhD; British diplomatist; *President, University of Aberystwyth;* b. 21 Sept. 1947, Carmarthen, Wales; s. of Hugh Jones Parry and Eirwen Jones Parry; m. Lynn Jones Parry; two s.; ed Gwendraeth Grammar School, Univ. Coll., Cardiff, St Catharine's Coll., Cambridge; joined FCO 1973; Deputy Chef du Cabinet and Pres. of the European Council 1987–89; Head EC Dept (External) FCO 1989–93; Minister, Embassy in Madrid 1993–96; Deputy Political Dir FCO 1996–97; Dir EU, FCO 1997–98; Political Dir FCO 1998–2001; Perm. Rep. to N Atlantic Council, NATO 2001–03, to UN 2003–07; Pres., Univ. of Aberystwyth 2007–. *Leisure interests:* gardening, theatre, reading, sport. *Address:* Aberystwyth University, Old College, King Street, Aberystwyth, Ceredigion, SY23 2AX, Wales (office). *Telephone:* (1970) 623111 (office). *Website:* www.aber.ac.uk (office).

JONG, Erica Mann, BA, MA; American writer and poet; b. 26 March 1942, New York; d. of Seymour Mann and Eda Mann (née Mirsky); m. 1st Michael Worthman 1963 (divorced 1965); m. 2nd Allan Jong 1966 (divorced 1975); m. 3rd Jonathan Fast 1977 (divorced 1983); one d.; m. 4th Kenneth David Burrows 1989; ed Barnard Coll. and Columbia Univ., New York; studied poetry with Mark Strand and Stanley Kunitz; Lecturer in English, City Coll. of New York 1965–66, 1969–70; Poetry Instructor, Poetry Center of the 92nd Street Y 1966–69; Lecturer in English, Overseas Div., Univ. of Md, Heidelberg, Germany 1970–72; Bread Loaf Writers Conf., Middlebury, Vt 1970–73; mem. Literature Panel, NY State Council on Arts 1972–74; mem. of Faculty, Salzburg Seminar, Austria 1993; Visiting Writer, Ben Gurion Univ., Beersheva, Israel 1998, Bennington Coll. 1998, Marymount Coll. Writers Workshop Poetry Seminar 2007; Hon. Fellow, (Welsh Coll. of Music and Drama) 1994; New York State Council on the Arts Grants 1971, Nat. Endowment of the Arts grant 1973; Hon. PhD (CUNY) 2006; Acad. of American Poets Prize 1971, Poetry magazine Bess Hokin Prize 1971, Poetry Soc. of America Alice Faye di Castagnola Award 1972, Freud Award for Literature, Italy 1975, UN Award for Excellence in Literature 1995, Prix Littéraire de Deauville Film Festival, France 1998. *Publications:* poetry: Fruits and Vegetables 1971, Half-Lives 1973, Loveroot 1975, At the Edge of the Body 1979, Ordinary Miracles 1983, Becoming Light: Poems New and Selected 1991, Love Comes First 2009; novels: Fear of Flying 1973, How to Save Your Own Life 1977, Fanny: Being the True History of Fanny Hackabout-Jones 1980, Parachutes and Kisses 1984, Serenissima: A Novel of Venice (aka Shylock's Daughter: A Novel of Love in Venice) 1987, Any Woman's Blues 1990, Inventing Memory: A Novel of Mothers and Daughters 1997, Sappho's Leap 2004; non-fiction: Witches 1981, Megan's Book of Divorce (for children) 1984, The Devil at Large: Erica Jong on Henry Miller 1993, Fear of Fifty: A Midlife Memoir 1994, Composer Zipless: Songs of Abandon from the Erotic Poetry of Erica Jong 1995, What Do Women Want? Bread. Roses. Sex. Power. 1998, Seducing the Demon: Writing for my Life 2006. *Leisure interests:* sailing, flying, blogging for the Huffington Post. *Address:* 205 East 68th Street, Suite T3G, New York, NY 10021, USA (office). *Website:* www.writershouse.com (office); www.ericajong.com (home). *E-mail:* officejongleur@rcn.com (office).

JONG, Petrus J. S. de, DSC; Dutch politician and naval officer; b. 3 April 1915, Apeldoorn; m. Anna Geertriida Jacoba Henriette Bartels; three c.; ed Royal Naval Coll.; entered Netherlands Royal Navy 1931, commissioned 1934; submarine Commdr during Second World War; Adjutant to Minister for Navy 1948; Capt. of frigate De Zeeuw 1951; Staff Officer on staff Allied Commdr-in-Chief, Channel, Portsmouth 1953; Adjutant to Queen of Netherlands 1955; Capt. of destroyer Gelderland 1958; State Sec. for Defence 1959–63; Minister of Defence 1963–67; Prime Minister and Minister of Gen. Affairs 1967–71; mem. First Chamber (Parl.) 1971–74; Catholic Party.

JONSEN, Albert R., MA, PhD, STM; American academic; *Co-Director and Senior Scholar in Residence, Program in Medicine and Human Values, California Pacific Medical Center;* b. 4 April 1931, San Francisco, Calif.; s. of Albert R. Jonsen and Helen C. Sweigert; m. Mary E. Carolan 1976; ed

Gonzaga Univ., Spokane, Wash., Santa Clara Univ., Calif. and Yale Univ.; Instructor in Philosophy, Loyola Univ. of Los Angeles 1956–59; Instructor in Divinity, Yale Univ. 1966–67; Asst, Assoc. Prof. in Philosophy and Theology, Univ. of San Francisco 1968–73, Pres. 1969–72; Prof. of Ethics in Medicine and Chief, Div. of Medical Ethics, Univ. of Calif., San Francisco 1973–87; Prof. of Ethics in Medicine, Chair. Dept of Medical History and Ethics, Univ. of Wash., Seattle 1987–99, Prof. Emer. 1999–; currently Co-Dir and Sr Scholar in Residence, Program in Medicine and Human Values, Calif. Pacific Medical Center; Commr US Nat. Comm. for Protection of Human Subjects of Biomedical and Behavioral Research 1974–78; Commr President's Comm. for Study of Ethical Problems in Medicine and in Biomedical and Behavioral Research 1979–82; mem. Artificial Heart Assessment Panel, Nat. Heart and Lung Inst. 1972–73, 1984–86; mem. Nat. Bd of Medical Examiners 1985–88; Consultant American Bd of Internal Medicine 1978–84; mem. NAS Inst. of Medicine; mem. NAS Cttee on AIDS Research; Chair. NRC Cttee on the Social Implications of AIDS 1987–92, Nat. Advisory Bd on Ethics and Reproduction 1992–97; Pres. Soc. for Health and Human Values 1986; Guggenheim Fellowship 1986–87; Visiting Prof., Yale Univ. 1999–2000, Stanford Univ. School of Medicine 2002, Univ. of Va Law School 2002; mem. Ethics Advisory Bd GERON Corpn 2000–; Guggenheim Fellowship 1982; Davies Award, American Coll. of Physicians 1987, Convocation Medal, American Coll. of Surgeons 1988, Annual Award, Soc. for Health and Humanities 1993, Lifetime Achievement Award, American Soc. for Bioethics and Humanities 1999. *Publications:* Responsibility in Modern Religious Ethics 1968, Ethics of Newborn Intensive Care 1976, Clinical Ethics (with M. Siegler and W. Winslade) 1982, The Abuse of Casuistry (with S. Toulmin) 1986, The Old Ethics and the New Medicine 1990, The Impact of AIDS on American Society (with J. Stryker) 1993, The Birth of Bioethics 1997, A Short History of Medical Ethics 2000, Bioethics Beyond the Headlines 2005. *Leisure interests:* sketching, swimming, walking, music. *Address:* 1333 Jones Street, #502, San Francisco, CA 94109, USA (home). *Telephone:* (415) 600-1647 (office). *E-mail:* arjonsen@aol.com (office); jonsena@sutterhealth.com (office). *Website:* depts .washington.edu/mhedept/facres/aj_bio.html (office).

JONZE, Spike; American film director, film producer, actor and screenwriter; b. (Adam Spiegel), 1969, Rockville, MD; s. of Arthur Spiegel III and Sandy Granzow; m. Sofia Coppola 1999 (divorced 2003); fmr Ed., Freestylin', Go, BMX Action, Homeboy, Grand Royal magazines; f. Dirt magazine with Andy Jenkins and Mark Lewman 1991; began directing skating films and music videos. *Music videos as director:* California by Wax, Sure Shot by the Beastie Boys, Sabotage by the Beastie Boys, Drop by the Pharcyde, Cannonball by The Breeders, What's Up Fatlip? by Fatlip, Undone (The Sweater Song) by Weezer, Buddy Holly by Weezer (MTV Video Music Award for Best Direction 1995), Feel The Pain by Dinosaur Jr, If I Only Had A Brain by MC 900ft Jesus, Sky's The Limit by The Notorious B.I.G., Crush with Eyeliner by R.E.M., It's Oh So Quiet by Björk, Da Funk by Daft Punk, Praise You by Fatboy Slim, Weapon of Choice by Fatboy Slim, Elektrobank by The Chemical Brothers, Wonderboy by Tenacious D (as Spike Jones). *Films:* Video Days (dir) 1991, Mi Vida Loca (actor) 1994, How They Get There (dir) 1997, The Game (actor) 1997, Amarillo by Morning (dir) 1998, Being John Malkovich (dir, actor) (New York Film Critics Circle Award for Best First Film, Broadcast Film Critics Asscn Breakthrough Performer, Online Film Critics Soc. Award for Best Debut) 1999, Three Kings (actor) 1999, Torrance Rises (dir, as Richard Coufey) 1999, Human Nature (producer) 2001, Adaptation (dir) (Berlin Film Festival Silver Bear 2003) 2002, Jackass: The Movie (writer, producer) 2002, Yeah Right! (dir, producer) 2003, Jackass Number Two (producer) 2006. *Television:* Jackass (series writer and producer) 2000. *Address:* c/o Creative Artists Agency, Inc., 9830 Wilshire Blvd, Beverly Hills, CA 90212-1825, USA (office).

JOPLING, Jay; British art dealer and gallery owner; *Owner, White Cube gallery;* b. 1963; s. of Lord Jopling, fmr Minister of Agric., Fisheries and Food; m. Sam Taylor-Wood; ed Eton Coll., Univ. of Edinburgh; began by selling fire extinguishers before starting to deal in post-war American art; formed friendship with artist Damien Hirst 1991, arranged financing for production of new work; supported small list of artists, including Hirst and Marc Quinn organizing exhbns in warehouses; opened White Cube gallery, St James's, London 1993, gallery moved to larger space in Hoxton 2000, Mason's Yard gallery located off Duke Street, St James's opened in Sept. 2006; acquired representation of further young British artists, including wife Sam Taylor-Wood, Chapman Brothers, Tracey Emin and Antony Gormley. *Address:* White Cube, 48 Hoxton Square, London, N1 6PB (office); White Cube, 25–26 Mason's Yard (off Duke Street), St James's, London, SW1Y 6BU, England. *Telephone:* (20) 7930-5373 (office). *Fax:* (20) 7749-7470 (Hoxton Square) (office); (20) 7749-7480 (Mason's Yard) (office). *E-mail:* enquiries@whitecube.com (office). *Website:* www.whitecube.com (office).

JOPLING, Baron (Life Peer), cr. 1997, of Ainderby Quernhow in the County of North Yorkshire; **(Thomas) Michael Jopling,** PC, BSc; British politician and farmer; *Member of Parliamentary Assembly, NATO;* b. 10 Dec. 1930, Ripon, Yorks.; s. of Mark Bellerby Jopling; m. Gail Dickinson 1958; two s.; ed Cheltenham Coll. and King's Coll., Newcastle-upon-Tyne; mem. Thirsk Rural Dist Council 1958–64; Conservative MP for Westmorland 1964–83, Westmorland and Lonsdale 1983–97; Jt Sec. Conservative Parl. Agric. Cttee 1966–70; Parl. Pvt. Sec. to Minister of Agric. 1970–71; an Asst Govt Whip 1971–73; Lord Commr of the Treasury 1973–74; an Opposition Spokesman on Agric. 1974–75, 1976–79; Shadow Minister of Agric. 1975–76; Parl. Sec. to HM Treasury and Chief Whip 1979–83; Minister of Agric., Fisheries and Food 1983–87; mem. Nat. Council, Nat. Farmers' Union 1962–64, UK Exec., Commonwealth Parl. Asscn 1974–79, 1987–97, Vice-Chair. 1977–79, Int. Exec. 1988–89; Chair. Select Cttee on Sittings of the House 1991–92; mem. Select Cttee on Agric. 1967–69, on Foreign Affairs 1987–97; mem. NATO Parl. Ass. 1987–97, 2001–; Leader UK Del. to Parl. Ass., OSCE 1990–97, mem. 2000–01; mem. Lords Sub-Cttee 'C' European Defence and Security 1999–2003 (Chair. 2000–03); Pres. Auto-Cycle Union 1989–2003, Pres. Emer. 2003–; DL Cumbria 1991–97, N Yorks. 1998–2006; Hon. Sec. British American Parl. Group 1987–2001; Hon. DCL (Newcastle) 1992. *Address:* Ainderby Hall, Thirsk, North Yorks., YO7 4HZ, England. *Telephone:* (1845) 567224.

JORDA, Claude Jean Charles; French judge and international official; *Judge, International Criminal Court;* b. 16 Feb. 1938, Bône, Algeria; ed Institut d'Etudes Politiques and School of Law, Univ. of Toulouse, Ecole Nat. de la Magistrature (ENM); called to Bar, Toulouse 1961; Auditeur de Justice (magistrate in training) 1963–66; Magistrate, Cen. Admin. Services Dept, Ministry of Justice 1966–70, Deputy Dir for Legal Org. and Regulations 1976–78, Dir Legal Services 1982–85; Sec.-Gen. ENM 1970–76; Vice-Pres. Tribunal de Grande Instance, Paris 1978–82; Prosecutor-Gen. Court of Appeals, Bordeaux 1985–92, Paris 1992–94; Judge at Int. Criminal Tribunal for Fmr Yugoslavia (ICTY) 1994–96, Pres. Trial Chamber I 1995–99, Pres. ICTY 1999–2003; Judge, Int. Criminal Court 2003–Aug. 2007 (resgnd); Officier, Légion d'honneur 1993, Commdr, Ordre nat. du Mérite 2000, Commdr des Palmes académiques, Commdr du Mérite agricole; Médaille de l'Educ. Surveillée (for services to young people in difficulty and in prison). *Publications include:* Un nouveau statut pour l'accusé dans le procédure du Tribunal pénal international pour l'ex-Yougoslavie (essays) 2000; academic contribs, book chapters and conf. proc., articles on ICTY . *Address:* International Criminal Court, Maanweg 174, 2516 AB, The Hague, The Netherlands (office). *Telephone:* (70) 5158065 (office). *Fax:* (70) 5158789 (office). *E-mail:* claude.jorda@icc-cpi.int (office). *Website:* www.icc-cpi.int/php/index .php (office).

JORDAN, Michael Hugh, MSChemE; American broadcasting and media executive; *Chairman, EDS (Electronic Data Systems Corporation);* b. 15 June 1936, Kansas City, Mo.; m. Kathryn Hiett 1961 (divorced); one s. one d.; m. Hilary Cecil 2000; ed Yale and Princeton Univs; consultant prin. McKinsey & Co. 1964–74; Dir Financial Planning PepsiCo 1974–76, Sr Vice-Pres. Planning and Devt 1976–77, Sr Vice-Pres. Mfg Operations Frito-Lay Div. PepsiCo Int. 1977–82, Pres., CEO 1983–85, Pres. PepsiCo Foods Int. 1982–83, Exec. Vice-Pres., Chief Financial Officer PepsiCo Inc. 1985–86, Pres. 1986, also Bd Dirs., Pres., CEO PepsiCo Worldwide 1987–92; Chair., CEO Westinghouse Electric Corpn 1993–98; Chair. Centre for Excellence in Ed. 1988–92; Chair., Bd Dirs and Partner, Clayton, Dubilier and Rice 1992–93; Chair. CBS –1998; Chair. and CEO Electronic Data Systems (EDS) 2003–07, Chair. 2007–; mem. Bd Dirs Melville Corpn, Rhone-Poulenc Rorer, Aetna, Dell Computers Inc., United Negro Coll. Fund 1986–. *Address:* EDS Headquarters, 5400 Legacy Drive, Plano, TX 75024-3199, USA (office). *Telephone:* (972) 604-6000 (office). *Fax:* (972) 605-2643 (office). *Website:* www.eds.com (office).

JORDAN, Michael Jeffery; American business executive and fmr professional basketball player; b. 17 Feb. 1963, Brooklyn, NY; s. of the late James Jordan and of Delores Jordan; m. Juanita Vanoy 1989 (divorced 2006); two s. one d.; ed Univ. of North Carolina; player for Univ. of North Carolina (won NCAA championship 1982); drafted by Nat. Basketball Asscn (NBA) Chicago Bulls in first round 1984, played 1984–93, 1995–98 (NBA Champions 1991, 1992, 1993, 1996, 1997, 1998); mem. US Olympic basketball team 1984, 1992; mem. NBA All-Star team 1985, 1987-93, 1996–98, 2003; played for Birmingham Barons minor league baseball team 1993, Nashville Sounds 1994–95; scored 32,292 points during career (third highest in NBA history), holds record for most points in NBA playoff game with 63, for highest points-scoring average (30.12) and many other records; named world's highest paid athlete, Forbes Magazine 1992; retd from Chicago Bulls 1998; Pres. Basketball Operations, Washington Wizards NBA professional basketball team 1999–2003, came out of retirement to play for Washington Wizards 2001–03; extensive business interests include Michael Jordan's: The Restaurant 1993, Jordan Brand Clothing 1997; f. Jordan Motorsports/Suzuki 2004; supports numerous children's charities; part owner Bobcats Basketball Holdings, LLC (NBA's Charlotte Bobcats basketball franchise) 2006–; Seagram's NBA Player of the Year 1987; Most Valuable Player, NBA All-Star Game 1988, NBA Most Valuable Player 1988, 1991, 1992, 1996, 1998. *Publications:* Rare Air: Michael on Michael (autobiography) 1993, I Can't Accept Not Trying: Michael Jordan on the Pursuit of Excellence, Driven From Within (co-author) 2004. *Address:* Bobcats Basketball Holdings, LLC, 333 East Trade Street, Suite 700, Charlotte, NC 28202; Jordan Brand, c/o Nike World Headquarters, One Bowerman Drive, Beaverton OR, 97005-6453, USA (office). *Telephone:* (704) 424-4120 (Charlotte). *Fax:* (704) 388-8734. *Website:* www.nba.com/bobcats; www.jumpman23.com (office).

JORDAN, Neil Patrick, BA; Irish writer and film director; b. 25 Feb. 1950, Sligo; three s. two d.; ed St Paul's Coll. Raheny, Dublin and Univ. Coll. Dublin; co-f. Irish Writers' Co-operative, Dublin 1974; Dr hc (Univ. Coll. Dublin) 2005; London Film Critics' Circle Award 1984, London Evening Standard Most Promising Newcomer Award 1982, Los Angeles Film Critics' Circle Award 1992, NY Film Critics' Circle Award 1992, Writers Guild of America Award 1992, BAFTA Awards 1992, 2000, Golden Lion, Venice Film Festival 1996, Silver Bear, Berlin Film Festival 1997. *Films directed:* Angel 1982, Company of Wolves 1984, Mona Lisa 1986, High Spirits 1988, We're No Angels 1989, The Miracle 1990, The Crying Game 1992, Interview with the Vampire 1994, Michael Collins (Golden Lion, Venice 1996) 1995, The Butcher Boy 1997, In Dreams 1999, The End of the Affair 1999, Not I 2000, The Good Thief 2002, Breakfast on Pluto (Best Dir, Best Writer, Irish Film and Television Awards 2007) 2005, The Brave One 2007. *Publications:* Night in Tunisia and Other Stories (Guardian Fiction Award 1979) 1976, The Past 1979, The Dream of a Beast 1983, Sunrise with Sea Monster 1994, Nightlines 1995, Shade (novel)

2004. *Leisure interest:* music. *Address:* 2 Sorrento Terrace, Dalkey, Co. Dublin, Ireland (home).

JORDAN, Mgr Thierry; French ecclesiastic; *Archbishop of Rheims;* b. 31 Aug. 1943, Shanghai, China; ed Lycée Hoche, Grand Séminaire de Versailles, Institut catholique de Paris, Gregorian Univ., Rome, Italy; ordained priest, Versailles 1966; chaplain, Church of Saint-Louis-des-Français, Rome, then Sec. to Cardinal Jean Villot, Vatican 1967–79; curate, Vésinet, Versailles 1980–84; Vicar-Episcopal, Saint-Quentin-en-Yvelines 1984–87; Vicar-Gen. Versailles diocese 1986–88; Bishop of Pontoise (Val-d'Oise) 1988–99; Archbishop of Rheims 1999–; Chair. Comm. épiscopale de la vie consacrée of Conf. of French Bishops 1993–96. *Address:* Archevéché de REIMS, secrétariat et Chancellerie, 3, rue du Cardinal de Lorraine, BP.2729, 51058 Rheims, France (office). *Telephone:* 3-26-47-05-33 (office). *Fax:* 3-26-84-94-66 (office). *Website:* catholique-reims.cef.fr (office).

JORDAN, Vernon Eulion, Jr; American lawyer and investment banker; *Senior Managing Director, Lazard Freres & Company LLC;* b. 15 Aug. 1935, Atlanta; s. of Vernon Eulion Jordan and Mary Jordan (née Griggs); m. 1st Shirley M. Yarbrough 1958 (died 1985); one c.; m. 2nd Ann Dibble Cook 1986; ed DePauw Univ., Howard Univ.; mem. Bar, Ga 1960, Ark. 1964; law practice, Atlanta 1960–61; Ga Field Dir NAACP 1961–63; law practice, Pine Bluff, Ark. 1964–65; Dir Voter Educ. Project Southern Regional Council 1964–68; Attorney, Office of Econ. Opportunity, Atlanta 1969; Exec. Dir United Negro Coll. Fund 1970–71; Pres. Nat. Urban League 1972–81; Sr Partner, Akin, Gump, Strauss, Hauer & Feld 1981–2000, of Counsel Akin, Gump, Strauss, Hauer & Feld LLP 2000–; Chair. Clinton Pres. Transition Bd; joined Lazard Freres and Co. LLC 2000, Sr Man. Dir 2000–; mem. Bd Dirs American Express Co., Asbury Automotive Group, Inc., Lazard Ltd, Xerox Corpn; mem. Int. Advisory Bd Barrick Gold; mem. American Bar Asscn, Nat. Bar Asscn, Council on Foreign Relations, The Bilderberg Meetings and Bars of Ark., DC, Ga, US Supreme Court; Trustee Howard Univ.; Pres. Econ. Club of Washington, DC; fmr Dir Voter Educ. Project of Southern Regional Council; fmr Ga Field Dir, Nat. Asscn for the Advancement of Colored People (NAACP); Presidential appointments have included mem. Pres.'s Cttee for the Points of Light Initiative Foundation, Sec. of State's Advisory Cttee on SA, Advisory Council on Social Security, Presidential Clemency Bd, American Revolution Bicentennial Comm., Nat. Advisory Cttee on Selective Service, Council White House Conf. 'To Fulfill These Rights'; mem. Iraq Study Group, US Inst. of Peace 2006; over 60 hon. degrees, including Princeton Univ., Harvard Univ. *Publication:* Vernon Can Read! A Memoir 2001. *Leisure interests:* golf, tennis, yoga. *Address:* Lazard Freres & Co. LLC, 30 Rockefeller Plaza, New York, NY 10112-0002 (office). *Telephone:* (212) 632-6190 (office). *Fax:* (212) 332-1640 (office). *E-mail:* jeannie.adashek@lazard.com (office). *Website:* www.lazard.com (office).

JORDAN, (Zweledinga) Pallo, PhD; South African politician; *Minister of Arts and Culture;* b. 22 May 1942, Kroonstad, OFS; s. of Dr Archibald Jordan and Priscilla Ntantala; m. Carolyn Roth 1972; one d.; ed Athlone High School, Cape Town, Univs of Cape Town and Wisconsin and London School of Econs; joined African Nat. Congress (ANC) 1960; worked full time for ANC in London 1975–77; Head, Radio Freedom, Luanda, Angola 1977–79; in Lusaka, Zambia 1980–90; Mem. ANC Nat. Exec. Cttee (NEC) 1985–, Deputy Sec. of Information 1985, Admin. Sec. of NEC Secr. –1988, Head of Dept. of Information and Publicity 1989–; MP 1994–; Minister of Posts, Telecommunications and Broadcasting 1994–96, of Environmental Affairs and Tourism 1996–99, of Arts and Culture 2004–; Head of Foreign Affairs Cttee 2002–04. *Publications:* articles and papers on South African political questions. *Address:* Ministry of Arts and Culture, Department of Arts and Culture, Nassau Building, Room 7060, 188 Schoeman Street, Pretoria 0002, South Africa (office). *Telephone:* (12) 32440968 (office). *Fax:* (12) 3242687 (office). *E-mail:* andile.xaba@dac.gov.za (office). *Website:* www.dac.gov.za (office).

JORDAN OF BOURNVILLE, Baron (Life Peer), cr. 2000, of Bournville in the County of West Midlands; **William Brian Jordan,** CBE; British trade union official; b. 28 Jan. 1936, Birmingham; s. of Walter Jordan and Alice Jordan; m. Jean Livesey 1958; three d.; ed Secondary Modern School, Birmingham; machine-tool fitter 1961; joined eng union and served as shop steward; convenor of shop stewards, Guest Keen & Nettlefolds 1966, later Dist Pres.; Div. Organizer for West Midlands AUEW 1977; Pres. Amalgamated Eng and Electrical (fmrly Amalgamated and Eng) Union 1986–95; mem. TUC Gen. Council 1986–95 (Chair. Cttee on European Strategy 1988–95); mem. NEDC (Chair. Eng Industry Cttee) 1986–92, Energy Industry Training Bd 1986–91, Council, Industrial Soc. 1987–, Advisory, Conciliation & Arbitration Service (ACAS) 1987–95, Nat. Training Task Force 1989–92, Eng Training Authority 1991–, Foundation for Manufacturing and Industry; Gen. Sec. ICFTU 1994–2002; fmr Pres. European Metalworkers' Fed.; fmr Exec. mem. Int. Metalworkers' Fed.; fmr mem. European Trade Union Confed., Bd Govs BBC, Nat. Advisory Council for Educ. and Training Targets, UK Skills Council; mem. Victim Support Advisory Cttee, Bd English Partnership, Winston Churchill Trust; a Gov. of LSE, Ashridge Man. Coll.; mem. Royal Soc. of Arts; Dr hc (Univ. of Cen. England) 1993, (Univ. of Cranfield) 1995. *Leisure interests:* reading, sports (especially football, Birmingham City Football Club supporter). *Address:* c/o ICFTU, Boulevard Emile Jacqmain 155, 1210 Brussels, Belgium.

JORDÁN-PANDO, Roberto; Bolivian diplomatist and economist; b. 21 Feb. 1930; m.; five c.; ed Universidad Real y Pontífica San Francisco Xavier, Sucre, Universidad Mayor San Andrés, La Paz; Deputy Minister for Rural and Farming Affairs 1955–56, Minister 1960–63; Amb.-del. to UN Gen. Ass. 1956–57, to first UN Conf. on Law of the Sea 1958; Head Bolivian del. to UNCTAD 1964; fmr consultant FAO, OAS, UNDP and other orgs; Pres. Financial de Consultoria Srl 1984–; consultant on investment projects, PEMECO Ltd 1993–95; Prof., Latin American Faculty of Social Sciences 1990–91; Rector Universidad Privada Franz Tamayo 1996–98; Perm. Rep. to UN 1998–2001. *Address:* c/o Ministry of Foreign Affairs, Calle Ingavi, esq. Junin, La Paz, Bolivia (office).

JORDANOV, Minco; Macedonian politician; b. 1 July 1944, Stip; ed Univ. of Belgrade; Gen. Man. Rudnici i Zelezarnica Co., Skopje 1983–89; Man. Techometal-Vardar Rep. Office, Moscow 1989–92; Man. Duferko SA 1992–94, mem. Bd of Dirs 1994–2004, also responsible for countries of fmr USSR 1994–97; Pres. Bd of Dirs Makstil A.D. 1997–2004; Deputy Prime Minister in Charge of Econ. Reforms 2004–06; Pres. Man. Bd, Nat. Entrepreneurship and Competitiveness Council 2006–; mem. Social Democratic Alliance of Macedonia. *Address:* c/o Office of the Prime Minister, 1000 Skopje, Ilindenska bb, Macedonia (office).

JORDANOVSKI, Ljupco, PhD; Macedonian fmr head of state, politician and diplomatist; b. 13 Feb. 1953, Štip; Pres. Sobranie (Ass.); Acting Pres., Fmr Yugoslav Repub. of Macedonia Feb.–May 2004; Amb. to USA July–Dec. 2006 (recalled); mem. Social Democratic Alliance of Macedonia (Socijaldemokratski Sojuz na Makedonije–SDSM). *Address:* c/o Office of the President, 11 Oktomvri bb, 1000 Skopje, Republic of Macedonia (office).

JØRGENSEN, Anker; Danish politician and trade union official; b. 13 July 1922, Copenhagen; s. of Johannes Jørgensen; m. Ingrid Jørgensen 1948; four c.; ed School for Orphans and evening classes; messenger, shipyard worker, warehouse worker 1936–50; Vice-Pres. Warehouse Workers' Union 1950, Pres. 1958–62; Group Sec. Transport and Gen. Workers' Union 1962–68, Pres. 1968–72; mem. Folketing (Parl.) 1964–94; mem. Bd of Dirs, Workers' Bank of Denmark 1969–; Prime Minister 1972–73; Parl. Leader, Social Democratic Group 1973–75; Prime Minister 1975–82; Chair. Social Democratic Party, Social Democratic Parl. Group 1972–87; mem. European Cttee Against Racism 1994–. *Publication:* Memoirs (Vol. I) 1994. *Address:* Borgbjergsvej 1, 2450 S.V. Copenhagen, Denmark.

JØRGENSEN, Bo Barker, PhD; Danish biologist and academic; *Professor of Geology, University of Bremen;* b. 22 Sept. 1946, Copenhagen; s. of Carl C. B. Jørgensen and Vibeke Balslev Smidt; m. Inga M. Vestergaard 1971; two s. one d.; ed Univs of Copenhagen and Århus; Lecturer, Dept of Ecology and Genetics, Univ. of Århus 1973–77, Sr Lecturer 1977–87, Prof. 1987–92; Dir Max Planck Inst. for Marine Microbiology, Bremen, Germany 1992–; Prof., Univ. of Bremen 1993–; Adjunct Prof., Univ. of Århus 1993–; researcher, Marine Biology Lab., Eilat, Israel 1974, 1978, NASA–ARC, Moffett Field, Calif. 1984–85. *Publications:* more than 200 scientific publs in int. journals in the fields of ecology, microbiology and geochemistry. *Leisure interests:* photography, music. *Address:* Auf den Hornstücken 25, 28359 Bremen, Germany (home). *Telephone:* (421) 242336 (home). *E-mail:* bjoergen@mpi-bremen.de (office). *Website:* www.mpi-bremen.de (office).

JØRGENSEN, Sven-Aage, MA; Danish professor of German philology; b. 22 July 1929, Herstedvester; s. of Aage Julius Jørgensen and Emma Lydia Jørgensen (née Eriksen); m. Elli Andresen 1957 (divorced 1985); two s. one d.; ed Birkerød Statsskole, Univ. of Copenhagen, Univ. of Würzburg and Warburg Inst., London; Lecturer, Univ. of Copenhagen 1961, Prof. of German Philology 1968; Research Prof., Univ. of Bielefeld 1980–81; Visiting Prof., Heidelberg 1973, Regensburg 1985, Kiel 1986, Cologne 1990; Visiting Fellow, ANU 1975; mem. Royal Danish Acad. of Sciences and Letters 1986, Akad. der Wissenschaften in Göttingen 1998; Kt, Order of Dannebrog; Alexander von Humboldt Prize 1995, Univ. Gold Medal 1957. *Publications:* J. G. Hamann's Fünf Hirtenbriefe 1962, J. G. Hamann's Sokratische Denkwurdigkeiten und Aesthetica in Nuce 1962, Th. Fontane's Unwiederbringlich 1971, J. G. Hamann 1976, Deutsch-dänische Literaturbeziehungen im 18. Jhdrt. (co-ed.) 1977, Dänische 'guldalderliteratur' und deutsche Klassik (co-ed.) 1982, Tysk et sprog Fire Stater–Fire Kulturer 1989, Wieland's Oberon 1990, Geschichte der deutschen Literatur 1740–1789 (co-author) 1990, Zentrum der Aufklärung: Kopenhagen–Kiel Altona (co-ed.) 1992, Verfilmte Litteratur (co-ed.) 1993, Fortschritt ohne Ende–Ende des Fortschritts? (ed.) 1994, Wieland Epoche-Werk-Wirkung (co-author) 1994, C. M. Wieland's Die Abenteuer des Don Sylvio von Rosalva 2001; numerous articles. *Leisure interests:* jogging, swimming. *Address:* Valby Gade 16, 3200 Helsinge, Denmark (home). *Telephone:* 33-15-76-04 (home). *E-mail:* sven.aage@get2net.dk (home).

JORGENSON, Dale W., PhD; American economist and academic; *Samuel W. Morris University Professor, Harvard University;* b. 7 May 1933, Bozeman, Mont.; s. of Emmett B. Jorgenson and Jewell T. Jorgenson; m. Linda Ann Mabus 1971; one s. one d.; ed Reed Coll., Portland, Ore. and Harvard Univ.; Asst Prof. of Econs, Univ. of Calif., Berkeley 1959–61, Assoc. Prof. 1961–63, Prof. 1963–69; Ford Foundation Research Prof. of Econs, Univ. of Chicago 1962–63; Prof. of Econs, Harvard Univ. 1969–80, Frederic Eaton Abbe Prof. of Econs 1980–2002, Samuel W. Morris Univ. Prof. 2002–, Frank William Taussig Research Prof. of Econs 1992–94, Chair. Dept of Econs 1994–97; Dir Program on Tech. and Econ. Policy, Kennedy School of Govt, Harvard Univ. 1984–; mem. Science Advisory Cttee, Gen. Motors Corpn 1996–2002; Visiting Prof. of Econs, Hebrew Univ., Jerusalem, Israel 1967, Stanford Univ. 1973; Visiting Prof. of Statistics, Univ. of Oxford, UK 1968; Chair. Section 54, Econ. Sciences, Nat. Acad. of Sciences 2000–03; Founding mem. Bd on Science, Tech. and Econ. Policy, Nat. Research Council 1991–98, Chair. 1998–; Consulting Ed., North-Holland Publishing Co., Amsterdam, Netherlands 1970–2002; Fellow, American Statistical Asscn 1965, AAAS 1982, Econometric Soc. 1984 (Pres. 1987); mem. American Acad. of Arts and Sciences 1969, NAS 1978, American Econ. Asscn (Pres. 2000, Distinguished Fellow 2001), Royal Econ. Soc., Econ. Study Soc., Conf. on Research in Income and Wealth, Int. Asscn for Research in Income and Wealth, American Philosophical Soc. 1998; Foreign mem. Royal Swedish Acad. of Sciences 1989; several fellowships including

NSF Sr Postdoctoral Fellowship, Netherlands School of Econs, Rotterdam 1967–68; lectures include Shinzo Koizumi, Keio Univ., Tokyo, Japan 1972, Fisher-Schultz, 3rd World Congress, Econometric Soc. 1975, Frank Paish, Asscn of Univ. Teachers of Econs Conf., UK 1980, Erik Lindahl Lectures, Uppsala Univ. 1987, Inst. Lecture, Inst. of Industrial Econs, Univ. of Toulouse 2001, Astra Zeneca/Ericsson Lecture, Research Inst. of Industrial Econs, Stockholm 2002; Dr hc (Uppsala, Oslo) 1991, (Keio) 2003, (Mannheim) 2004, (Rome) 2006, (Stockholm School of Econs) 2007, (Chinese Univ. of HK) 2007, (Kansai) 2009; John Bates Clark Medal, American Econ. Asscn 1971, Outstanding Contrib. Award, Int. Asscn of Energy Economists 1994. *Publications:* Optimal Replacement Policy (co-author) 1967, Measuring Performance in the Private Economy of the Federal Republic of Germany 1950–1973 (co-author) 1975, Econometric Studies of U.S. Energy Policy (ed.) 1976, Technology and Economic Policy (co-ed. with R. Landau) 1986, Productivity and U.S. Economic Growth (co-author) 1987, Technology and Capital Formation (co-ed. with R. Landau) 1989, General Equilibrium Modeling and Economic Policy Analysis (co-ed.) 1990, Technology and Agricultural Policy (co-ed.) 1990, Tax Reform and the Cost of Capital (with Kun-Young Yun) 1991, Tax Reform and the Cost of Capital: An International Comparison (co-ed. with R. Landau) 1993, Postwar U.S. Economic Growth (Productivity, Vol. 1) 1995, International Comparisons of Economic Growth (Productivity, Vol. 2) 1995, Capital Theory and Investment Behavior (Investment, Vol. 1) 1996, Tax Policy and the Cost of Capital (Investment, Vol. 2) 1996, Improving the Performance of America's Schools: The Role of Inventives (co-author) 1996, Aggregate Consumer Behavior (Welfare, Vol. 1) 1997, Measuring Social Welfare (Welfare, Vol. 2) 1997, Econometric General Equilibrium Modeling (Growth, Vol. 1) 1998, Energy, the Environmental and Economic Growth (Growth, Vol. 2) 1998, Economic Modeling of Producer Behavior (Econometrics, Vol. 1) 2000, Lifting the Burden: Tax Reform, the Cost of Capital and U.S. Economic Growth (Investment, Vol. 3) (with Kun-Young Yun) 2001, Industry-Level Productivity and International Competitiveness Between Canada and the United States (co-ed. with Franck C. Lee) 2001, Economic Growth in the Information Age (Econometrics, Vol. 3) 2002, Measuring and Sustaining the New Economy (co-ed. with C. Wessner) 2002; over 232 papers and contribs to learned journals and collections of essays. *Address:* Department of Economics, 122 Littauer Center, Harvard University, Cambridge, MA 02138-3001 (office); 1010 Memorial Drive, Cambridge, MA 02138, USA (home). *Telephone:* (617) 495-4661 (office); (617) 491-4069 (home). *Fax:* (617) 495-4660 (office); (617) 491-4105 (home). *E-mail:* djorgenson@harvard.edu (office). *Website:* post.economics.harvard.edu/faculty/jorgenson (office).

JORTNER, Joshua, PhD; Israeli chemist and academic; *Professor Emeritus of Chemistry, Tel-Aviv University;* b. 14 March 1933, Tarnow, Poland; s. of Arthur Jortner and Regina Jortner; m. Ruth Sanger 1960; one s. one d.; ed Hebrew Univ. of Jerusalem; Instructor, Dept of Physical Chem., Hebrew Univ. of Jerusalem 1961–62, Sr Lecturer 1963–65; Research Assoc., Univ. of Chicago 1962–64, Prof. 1965–71; Assoc. Prof. of Physical Chem., Tel-Aviv Univ. 1965–66, Prof. 1966–, Head of Inst. of Chem. 1966–72, Deputy Rector 1966–69, Vice-Pres. 1970–72, Heinemann Prof. of Chem. 1973–2003, Prof. Emer. 2003–; Visiting Prof. of Chem., H.C. Orsted Inst., Univ. of Copenhagen 1974; Visiting Prof., Univ. of Calif., Berkeley 1975; Vice-Pres. Israeli Acad. of Sciences and Humanities 1980–86, Pres. 1986–95, mem. Council 1996–; Vice-Pres. IUPAC 1996–97, Pres. 1998–99, Past Pres. 2000–01; Int. Acad. of Quantum Science Award 1972, Weizmann Prize 1973, Rothschild Prize 1976, Kolthof Prize 1976, Israel Prize in Chem. 1982, Wolf Prize 1988, Hon. J. Hejrovsky Gold Medal 1993, August Wilhelm von Hofmann Medal 1995, Joseph O. Hirschfelder Prize in Theoretical Chem. 1999, Maria Sklodowska-Curie Medal 2003, Medal of Israeli Chemical Soc. 2004, EMET Prize 2008. *Publications:* author or co-author of over 720 scientific articles in professional journals; author or ed. of 29 books; Intramolecular Radiationless Transitions (with M. Bixon) 1968, Energy Gap Law for Radiationless Transitions (with E. Englman) 1970, Electronic Excitations in Condensed Rare Gases (with N. Schwentner and E. E. Koch) 1985, Cluster Size Effects 1992; The Jerusalem Symposia on Quantum Chemistry and Biochemistry (co-ed. with Bernard Pullman) Vols 15–27 1982–93. *Leisure interest:* science policy. *Address:* School of Chemistry, Tel-Aviv University, Ramat Aviv, 69978 Tel-Aviv, Israel (office). *Telephone:* 3-6408322 (office); 3-6415218 (office). *Fax:* 3-6415054 (office). *E-mail:* jortner@chemsg1.tau.ac.il (office); jortner@chemsg1.tau.ac.il (office). *Website:* www.tau.ac.il/chemistry/jortner (office).

JORY, Edward John, PhD, FAHA; British/Australian professor of classics; *Senior Honorary Research Fellow, Department of Classics and Ancient History, University of Western Australia;* b. 20 June 1936, England; s. of E. B. A. Jory; m. Marie McGee 1965; three s.; ed Humphry Davy Grammar School, Penzance and Univ. Coll., London; Lecturer, Dept of Classics and Ancient History, Univ. of Western Australia 1959–65, Sr Lecturer 1966–73, Assoc. Prof. 1974–78, Dean of Faculty of Arts 1976–79, Prof. and Head of Dept 1979–84, 1988–89, Head of Div. of Arts and Architecture 1990–93, Exec. Dean Faculty of Arts 1994–2000, currently Sr Hon. Research Fellow; Visiting Prof., Inst. of Classical Studies, Univ. of London 1990; Alexander von Humboldt Fellow 1974, 1980, Kommission für Alte Geschichte und Epigraphik, Munich 1974, T. B. L. Webster Fellow, Inst. of Classical Studies 2000. *Publications:* contrib. to Corpus Inscriptionum Latinarum 1974, 1989; numerous articles on the Roman theatre. *Leisure interests:* cricket, skin diving, golf. *Address:* Department of Classics and Ancient History, University of Western Australia, Crawley, WA 6009 (office); 36 Marita Road, Nedlands, WA 6009, Australia (home). *Telephone:* (8) 6488-7073 (office); (8) 9380-1638 (office); (8) 9386-2714 (home). *Fax:* (8) 9380-1009 (office). *E-mail:* ejjory@arts.uwa.edu.au (office). *Website:* www.classics.uwa.edu.au (office).

JOSEFSSON, Lars-Göran, BEng; Swedish energy industry executive; *President and CEO, Vattenfall AB;* b. 29 Oct. 1950; m.; four c.; ed secondary school in Ulricehamn, Chalmers Inst. of Tech.; began career as systems engineer at Defence Electronics Div. L.M. Ericsson 1974, several exec. posts until Pres. Chemtronics 1984, Ericsson Radio Systems Head, Radar Div. 1985, Vice-Pres. and head of Surface Sensor Div. 1987, Schrack Telecom AG (later named Ericsson Schrack AG 1994 and Ericsson Austria 1996), Vienna, 1993–97; Pres. and CEO Celsius Corpn 1997–2000; Pres. and CEO Vattenfall AB 2000–, Deputy Dir 2008–, also Chair. Vattenfall Europe AG, Vattenfall Europe Mining AG; mem. Supervisory Bd Bohler-Uddeholm AG, Eskom Holdings Ltd; mem. Royal Swedish Mil. Acad., Royal Swedish Soc. of Naval Sciences. *Leisure interests:* tennis, skiing, hunting. *Address:* Vattenfall AB, Jamtlandsgaten 99, 162 87 Stockholm, Sweden (office). *Telephone:* (8) 739-50-00 (office). *Fax:* (8) 37-01-70 (office). *E-mail:* info@vattenfall.com (office). *Website:* www.vattenfall.com (office).

JOSEPH, Cedric Luckie, MA; Guyanese diplomatist (retd) and historian; b. 14 May 1933, Georgetown; s. of the late Frederick McConnell Joseph and Cassie Edith Joseph, née Austin; m. Dona Avril Barrett 1973; two s.; ed London School of Econs, Univ. Coll. of Wales, Aberystwyth; taught history at a London comprehensive school 1962–66; Lecturer in History, Univ. of the W Indies, Kingston, Jamaica 1966–71; Prin. Asst Sec., Ministry of Foreign Affairs, Guyana 1971–74; Deputy High Commr to Jamaica 1974–76; Counsellor, Embassy in Washington, DC 1976; Deputy Perm. Rep., Perm. Mission of Guyana to the UN, New York 1976–77; High Commr to Zambia (also accred to Angola, Botswana, Mozambique, Tanzania and Zimbabwe) 1977–82, to UK (also accred as Amb. to France, the Netherlands, Yugoslavia and UNESCO) 1982–86; Chair. Commonwealth Cttee on Southern Africa 1983–86; Head of the Presidential Secr. 1986–91; Sec. to Cabinet 1987–91; Sr Amb., Ministry of Foreign Affairs 1991–94; foreign policy analyst/consultant with reference to Guyana's frontiers 1995–; Cacique's Crown of Honour 1983. *Publications include:* Reconstruction of the Caribbean Community 1994, Dependency and Mendicancy 1995, Transition and Guyana 1995, Caribbean Community – Security and Survival 1997, Intervention, Border and Maritime Issues in CARICOM (tech. ed.) 2007, Anglo-American Diplomacy and the Reopening of the Guyana/Venezuela Boundary Controversy 1961–1966 1998 (revised edn 2008), The British West Indies Regiment 1914-1918 2008; several articles in professional journals. *Leisure interests:* the fine arts, reading, walking. *Address:* 332 Republic Park, Peter's Hall, East Bank Demerara, Guyana (home). *E-mail:* clmdj@networksgy.com (home).

JOSEPH, Martin, MSc; Trinidadian politician; *Minister of National Security and Rehabilitation;* b. 1 Oct. 1949, Trinidad; ed Univ. of Maryland, USA; mem. Senate of Trinidad and Tobago; fmr Minister of Public Utilities and the Environment; Minister of Housing –2003; Minister of Nat. Security and Rehabilitation 2003–. *Address:* Ministry of National Security, Temple Court, 31–33 Abercromby Street, Port of Spain, Trinidad and Tobago (office). *Telephone:* 623-2441 (office). *Fax:* 627-8044 (office). *E-mail:* msn@tstt.net.tt (office). *Website:* nationalsecurity.gov.tt (office).

JOSEPH, Robert G., MA, PhD; American academic and diplomatist; *Senior Scholar, National Institute for Public Policy;* b. 1949, Williston, North Dakota; ed US Naval Acad., St. Louis Univ., Univ. of Chicago, Columbia Univ.; several positions in US State Dept including Commr to Standing Consultative Comm., Amb. to US-Russian Consultative Comm. on Nuclear Testing, Prin. Deputy Asst, Sec. of Defense for Int. Security Policy, Deputy Asst, Sec. for Nuclear Forces and Arms Control Policy; Prof. of Nat. Security Studies and Founder/Dir, Center for Counterproliferation Research, Nat. Defense Univ. 1992–2001; Special Asst to Pres. and Sr Dir for Proliferation Strategy, Counterproliferation and Homeland Defense, Nat. Security Council –2005; UnderSec. for Arms Control and Int. Security 2005–07 (resgnd); Dir of Studies, Nat. Inst. for Public Policy 2004–05, Sr Scholar 2004–; mem. Nat. Security Advisory Council, Center for Security Policy; fmr Research Consultant, Inst. for Foreign Policy Analysis. *Address:* National Institute for Public Policy, 9302 Lee Highway, Suite 750, Fairfax, VA 22031, USA (office). *E-mail:* Amy.joseph@nipp.org (office). *Website:* www.nipp.org (office).

JOSEPHSON, Brian David, PhD, FRS, FInstP; British physicist and academic; *Professor Emeritus of Physics, University of Cambridge;* b. 4 Jan. 1940, Cardiff, Wales; s. of Abraham Josephson and Mimi Josephson; m. Carol Anne Olivier 1976; one d.; ed Cardiff High School, Univ. of Cambridge; Fellow, Trinity Coll., Cambridge 1962–; Research Asst, Prof., Univ. of Illinois 1965–66; Asst Dir of Research, Univ. of Cambridge 1967–72, Reader in Physics 1972–74, Prof. of Physics 1974–2007, Prof. Emer. 2007–; Hon. mem. IEEE; Foreign Hon. mem. American Acad. of Arts and Sciences; Hon. DSc (Univ. of Wales, Univ. of Exeter); Hon. PhD (Bar Ilan Univ.); New Scientist Award 1969, Research Corpn Award 1969, Fritz London Award 1970, Hughes Medal Royal Soc. 1972, Guthrie Medal 1972, van der Pol 1972, Elliott Cresson Medal 1972, Holweck Medal 1972, Nobel Prize for Physics (jtly) 1973, Faraday Medal 1982, Sir George Thomson Medal 1984, Computing Anticipatory Systems Award 2000. *Music:* Sweet and Sour Harmony 2007. *Publications:* Consciousness and the Physical World (co-ed.) 1980, The Paranormal and the Platonic Worlds (in Japanese) 1997; research papers on superconductivity, critical phenomena, theory of intelligence, science and mysticism. *Leisure interests:* walking, ice skating, photography, astronomy. *Address:* Cavendish Laboratory, J.J. Thomson Avenue, Cambridge, CB3 0HE, England (office). *Telephone:* (1223) 337254 (office). *Fax:* (1223) 337356 (office). *E-mail:* bdj10@cam.ac.uk (office). *Website:* www.tcm.phy.cam.ac.uk/~bdj10 (office).

JOSEPHSON, Erland; Swedish actor and theatre director; b. 15 June 1923, Stockholm; at Municipal Theatre, Helsingborg 1945–49, Gothenburg 1949–56, Royal Dramatic Theatre, Stockholm 1956–; Dir Royal Dramatic Theatre, Stockholm 1966–75; American stage debut in The Cherry Orchard 1988. *Films include:* Sceningång (1956, Som man bäddar 1957, Nära livet 1958, Ansiktet 1958, Vargtimmen 1968, Flickorna 1968, Eva: den utstötta

1969, En Passion 1969, Viskningar och rop 1972, Scener ur ett äktenskap 1973, Monismanien 1995 1975, Ansikte mot ansikte 1976, Den Allvarsamma leken 1977, Al di là del bene e del male 1977, Io ho paura 1977, En och en 1978, Höstsonaten 1978, Die Erste Polka 1979, Marmeladupproret 1980, Kärleken 1980, Dimenticare Venezia 1980, Variola vera 1981, Samo jednom se ljubi 1981, Sezona mira u Parizu 1981, Montenegro 1981, La Casa del tappeto giallo 1982, Fanny och Alexander 1982, Eva 1983, Nostalghia 1983, Bella Donna 1983, Angelas krig 1984, Bakom jalusin 1984, Dirty Story 1984, De Flyvende djævle 1985, Saving Grace 1985, Amorosa 1986, Offret 1986, La Coda del diavolo 1986, Il Giorno primal 1987, The Legendary Life of Ernest Hemingway 1988, Una Donna spezzata 1988, The Unbearable Lightness of Being 1988, Le Testament d'un poète juif assassiné 1988, Hanussen 1988, Seobe 1989, Il Sole buio 1990, God afton, Herr Wallenberg: En Passionshistoria från verkligheten 1990, Cattiva 1991, Prospero's Books 1991, Meeting Venus 1991, Oxen 1991, Den Ofrivillige golfaren 1991, Holozän 1992, Sofie 1992, C'è Kim Novak al telefono 1994, Drømspel 1994, Zabraneniat plod 1994, Pakten 1995, Kristin Lavransdatter 1995, To Vlemma tou Odyssea 1995, Magnetisörens femte vinter 1999, Trolösa 2000, Nu 2003, Dag och natt (voice) 2004, Dobro ustimani mrtvaci 2005. *Television includes:* Svarta handsken 1957, Beslut i morgondagen 1968, Reservatet 1970, Brända tomten 1974, Ett Drömspel 1980, Dubbelsvindlarna (miniseries) 1982, Savannen 1983, Un Caso d'incoscienza 1984, Efter repetitionen 1984, L'Ultima mazurka 1986, Storm, der Schimmelreiter 1986, Il Giudice istruttore 1987, Garibaldi il generale (miniseries) 1987, Rosenbaum (miniseries) 1991, The Last Witness 1993, Vendetta (miniseries) 1995, Som löven i Vallombrosa (miniseries) 1995, Magisk cirkel 1995, Larmar och gör sig till 1997, Den Tatuerade änkan 1998, Från regnormarnas liv 1998, Ivar Kreuger 1998, En Liten film (miniseries) 1999, Il Papa buono, Il 2003, Saraband 2003. *Publications include:* Cirkel 1946, Spegeln och en portvakt 1946, Spel med bedrövade artister 1947, Ensam och fri 1948, Lyssnarpost 1949, De vuxna barnen 1952, Utflykt 1954, Sällskapslek 1955, En berättelse om herr Silberstein 1957, Kungen ur leken 1959, Doktor Meyers sista dagar 1964, Kandidat Nilssons första natt 1964, Lejon i Övergångsåldern (pjas Dromaten) 1981, En talande tystnad (pja's Dramaten) 1984, Loppaus Kvållsvard 1986, Kameleonterna 1987, Järgen 1988, Rollen 1989, A Story about Mr. Silberstein 2001. *Address:* c/o Royal Dramatic Theatre, Nybroplan, Box 5037, 102 41 Stockholm, Sweden.

JOSHI, Aravind Krishna, BE, DIISc, MS, PhD, FIEEE; American (b. Indian) computer scientist and academic; *Henry Salvatori Professor of Computer and Cognitive Sciences, University of Pennsylvania;* b. 5 Aug. 1929, Poona, India; m. Susan Joshi; two d.; ed Pune Univ., Poona, Indian Inst. of Science, Bangalore, Univ. of Pennsylvania; Research Asst, Indian Inst. of Science, Bangalore 1952; Research Asst, Tata Inst. of Fundamental Research, Bombay 1953; engineer, Radio Corpn of America, Camden, NJ 1954–58; Research Asst, Dept of Linguistics, Univ. of Pennsylvania, Philadelphia 1958–61, Asst Prof. of Electrical Eng 1961–67, Asst Prof. of Linguistics 1964–67, Assoc. Prof. of Electrical Eng and mem. Grad. Group in Linguistics 1967–72, Prof. of Computer and Information Science and mem. Grad. Group in Linguistics 1972–83, Chair. Dept of Computer and Information Science 1972–85, Henry Salvatori Prof. of Computer and Cognitive Sciences with Secondary appointment in Dept of Linguistics, Secondary appointment in Dept of Psychology and Dir Artificial Intelligence Center 1983–, Co-Dir Cognitive Science Program 1979–2002, Co-Dir Inst. for Research in Cognitive Science 1990–2002, Co-Dir NSF Science and Tech. Center for Research in Cognitive Science 1991–2002; Distinguished Visitor, IEEE Computer Group 1970; mem. Inst. for Advanced Study, Princeton, NJ 1971–72; mem. NSF Advisory Panel for Computer Science and Eng 1976–79, NSF Advisory Panel for Div. of Information, Robotics, and Intelligent Systems 1988–; mem. Int. Jt Cttee on Computational Linguistics 1994, Perm. mem. 1995–; Visiting Prof., Univ. of Paris VII, France May–June 1994; mem. Nat. Acad. of Eng 1999–, Asscn for Computing Machinery (mem. Special Interest Group on Theory of Computation, Fellow 1998–), American Math. Soc., Linguistic Soc. of America, Asscn for Computational Linguistics (ACL, mem. Exec. Cttee, Pres. ACL 1975), Cognitive Science Soc.; Founding Fellow, American Asscn for Artificial Intelligence 1990–; Hon. Chair. ACL 2000, Hong Kong 2000; Dr hc (Univ. of Paris VII) 2002; Guggenheim Fellow 1971–72, Best Paper Award, Nat. Conf. on Artificial Intelligence 1987, Research Excellence Award, Int. Jt Conf. of Artificial Intelligence 1997, ACL Lifetime Achievement Award 2002, David Rumelhart Prize, Cognitive Science Soc. 2003, Benjamin Franklin Medal for Cognitive Science, The Franklin Inst. 2005. *Publications:* Elements of Discourse Understanding (co-ed.) 1981, Special Issue of journal Computational Intelligence (ed.) 1994, Centering on Discourse (co-ed.) 1998, Supertagging (co-ed.) 2007; numerous scientific papers in professional journals. *Address:* University of Pennsylvania, IRCS, Suite 476A, 3401 Walnut Street, Philadelphia, PA 19104-6228 (office); Department of Computer and Information Science, 506 Levine Bldg, 200 S 33rd Street, Philadelphia, PA 19104-6389 (office); 919 South 48th Street, Philadelphia, PA 19143, USA (home). *Telephone:* (215) 898-0359 (IRCS) (office); (215) 898-8540 (Computer and Information Science) (office); (215) 727-0513 (home). *Fax:* (215) 573-9247 (IRCS) (office); (215) 898-0587 (Computer and Information Science) (office). *E-mail:* joshi@cis.upenn.edu (office). *Website:* www.cis.upenn.edu/~joshi (office).

JOSHI, B. L.; Indian diplomatist and politician; *Governor of Uttarakhand;* b. village in Rajasthan; ed Scottish Church Coll., Kolkata, Univ. Law Coll., Kolkata; began career with police service 1975, worked with Intelligence Bureau on subjects including Interpol, counterfeiting, narcotics, industrial security, UN correctional work and juvenile delinquency; worked in Prime Minister's office with Lal Bahadur Shastri and then with Indira Gandhi for over four years, and with Ministry of External Affairs as First Sec. in High Comms of India in Islamabad and London and as Head of Chancery in Embassy in Washington, DC; took voluntary retirement from IPS in 1991 and became involved in social work; also worked as adviser in a large industrial group; moved to USA in 1993, where he was dir with two large cos and also Exec. Dir Foundation for Excellence, Inc., Calif.; returned to India in 2000; apptd mem. Rajasthan State Human Rights Comm., with rank of High Court Judge, for four years; Lt Gov. of Delhi 2004–07; Gov. of Meghalaya April–Aug. 2007, of Uttarakhand Aug. 2007–. *Address:* Raj Bhawan, Dehradun, Uttarakhand, India (office). *E-mail:* he-ua@nic.in (office). *Website:* gov.ua.nic.in (office).

JOSPIN, Lionel Robert; French politician; b. 12 July 1937, Meudon, Hauts-de-Seine; s. of Robert Jospin and Mireille Dandieu; m. 2nd Sylviane Agacinski 1994; one s. one d. (from previous m.), one step-s.; ed Institut d'études politiques de Paris, École nat. d'admin; Sec. Ministry of Foreign Affairs 1965–70; Prof., Econ. Inst. universitaire de tech. de Paris-Sceaux, also attached to Univ. de Paris XI 1970–81; Nat. Sec. Socialist Party, mem. Steering Cttee 1973–75, spokesman on Third World Affairs 1975–79, Int. Relations 1979–81, First Sec. 1981–88, Head 1995–97; Councillor for Paris (18E arrondissement) 1977–86; Socialist Deputy to Nat. Ass. for Paris (27E circ.) 1981–86, for Haute-Garonne 1986–88; mem. Gen. Council Haute-Garonne 1988–; Conseiller régional, Midi-Pyrénées 1992–98; Minister of State, Nat. Educ., Research and Sport May–June 1988; Minister of State, Nat. Educ., of Youth and Sport 1988–91, Minister of Nat. Educ. 1991–92; presidential cand. 1995, 2002; Prime Minister of France 1997–2002; Grand Officier, Légion d'honneur 2008; Trombinoscope Politician of the Year 1997. *Publications:* L'Invention du Possible 1991, 1995–2000: Propositions pour la France 1995, Le Temps de répondre 2002, Le Monde comme je le vois 2005. *Leisure interests:* basketball, tennis. *Address:* c/o Parti Socialiste, 10 rue de Solférino, 75333 Paris, Cédex 07, France.

JOSS, Robert L., PhD; American business executive, academic and university administrator; ed Univ. of Washington, Stanford Univ.; Deputy to Asst Sec. for Econ. Policy, US Treasury Dept, Washington, DC 1968–71; joined Wells Fargo Bank 1971, Vice-Chair. 1987–93, Dir Wells Fargo and Co. 1999–; CEO and Man. Dir Westpac Banking Corpn, Sydney, Australia 1993–99; Philip H. Knight Prof. and Dean, Grad. School of Business, Stanford Univ. 1999–2009; mem. Bd of Dirs Agilent Technologies Inc. 2003–; fmr mem. Bd of Dirs Westpac, BEA Systems, E.piphany Inc., Makena Capital, Shanghai Commercial Bank; Sloan Fellow, Stanford Business School 1965–66; fmr White House Fellow. *Address:* c/o Graduate School of Business, Stanford University, 450 Serra Mall, Stanford, CA 94305, USA (office).

JOSSELIN, Charles, LenD; French economist and politician; b. 31 March 1938, Pleslin-Trigavou; s. of Charles Josselin and Marie Hamoniaux; m. 2nd Evelyne Besnard 1987; four c.; fmr attaché, financial secr., Banque de l'Union Parisienne, economist, Soc. centrale pour l'équipement du territoire; Parti Socialiste (PS) Nat. Ass. Deputy for 2nd Côtes d'Armor Constituency (Dinan) 1973–78, 1981–97 1; Minister of State for Transport 1985–86, for the Sea 1992–93; Sec. of State attached to Minister of Foreign Affairs, with responsibility for Co-operation 1997, for Co-operation and Francophonie 1997–98, Deputy Minister for Co-operation and Francophonie 1998–2002, Minister of State 1998–2002; Mayor of Pleslin-Trigavou 1977–97; mem. European Parl. 1979–81; Chair. Nat. Council for Regional Economies and Productivity 1982–86, Nat. Ass.'s EC Select Cttee 1981–85, 1988–92, Vice-Chair. EU Select Cttee 1993–; Chair. Parl. Study Group on int. aid orgs; mem. Côtes d'Armor Gen. Council for Ploubalay canton 1973–, Chair. 1976–97, Vice-Chair. 1997–; mem. Nat. Council for Town and Country Planning, Local Finance Cttee, EU Cttee of the Regions; Vice-Pres. High Comm. Int. Co-operation 2003–; Chair. Cités Unies France (twin city org.) 2004–; Senator representing, Côtes d'Armor 2006–. *Address:* 12 Bis Rue de Brest, 22100 Dinan (office); c/o Le Sénat, Casier de la Poste, 15 Rue de Vaugirard, 75291 Paris Cedex 06, France (office). *Telephone:* 2-96-85-43-52 (office). *E-mail:* c.josselin@senat.fr (office); charles-josselin@orange.fr (home). *Website:* www.senat.fr (office); www.cites-unies-france.org (office).

JOUANNEAU, Daniel, LLM; French diplomatist; *Ambassador to Canada;* b. 15 Sept. 1946, Vendôme; m.; one d.; ed French Inst. of Political Studies, École nationale d'admin (French Nat. School of Public Admin); worked in Legal Adviser's Office, Ministry of Foreign Affairs 1971–74; First Sec. in Egypt 1974–76; Office of Econ. and Financial Affairs (multilateral commercial matters) 1976–80; Consul Gen., Salisbury, Rhodesia 1980; Chargé d'affaires, Zimbabwe 1980–81; Asst-Dir for Western Europe, then European Correspondent 1981–85, Ministry of Foreign Affairs; Chief of Mission (ODA), Guinea 1985–87; Consul Gen., Québec, Canada 1987–89; Chief of European-Union Dept 1989–90; Amb. to Mozambique, non-resident Amb. in Lesotho and Swaziland 1990–93; Chief of Protocol 1993–97; Amb. to Lebanon 1997–2000; Inspector Gen. of Foreign Affairs 2000–04; Amb. to Canada 2004–. *Address:* Embassy of France, 42 Sussex Drive, Ottawa, ON K1M 2C9, Canada (office). *Telephone:* (613) 789-1795 (office). *Fax:* (613) 562-3735 (office). *E-mail:* politique@ambafrance-ca.org (office). *Website:* www.ambafrance-ca.org (office).

JOULWAN, Gen. George Alfred, BS, MA; American army officer (retd); b. 16 Nov. 1939, Pottsville, Pa; m. Karen E. Jones; three d.; ed US Mil. Acad. West Point, Loyola Univ., Chicago, US Army War Coll., Washington, DC; served in Viet Nam as Co. Commdr and Operations Officer, 1st Bn, 26th Infantry, 1st Infantry Div. and as Brigade Operations Officer and Deputy Div. Operations Officer, 101st Airborne Div. (Air Assault); Aide-de-Camp to Vice-Chief of Staff, US Army; Special Asst to the Pres. 1973–74, to Supreme Allied Commdr, Europe 1974–75; Bn Commdr, US Army, Europe 1975–77; Dir Political and Economic Studies, US Army War Coll., Pa 1978–79; Commdr 2nd Brigade, 3rd Infantry Div. (Mechanized), US Army, Europe 1979–81, Chief of Staff 1981–82; Exec. Officer to Chair., Jt Chiefs of Staff, Washington, DC

1982–85; Dir Force Requirements (Combat Support Systems), Office of Deputy Chief of Staff for Operations and Plans, Washington, DC 1985–86; Deputy Chief of Staff for Operations, US Army, Europe and Seventh Army 1986–88, Commdg Gen., 3rd Armored Div. 1988–89, V Corps, 1989–90; C-in-C, US Southern Command, Quarry Heights, Panama 1990–93, US European Command, Stuttgart/Vaihingen, Germany 1993–97; Supreme Allied Commdr, Europe, SHAPE, Belgium 1993–97 (retd); Pres. One Team Inc. 2002–05; Hon. Col 26th Infantry Regiment Asscn; numerous decorations including Defense Distinguished Service Medal (with Oak Leaf Cluster), Defense Superior Service Medal, Silver Star (with Oak Leaf Cluster); numerous orders including Légion d'honneur, Hessian Order of Merit (Germany). *Telephone:* (703) 486-8173 (office). *Fax:* (703) 486-8176 (office).

JOURDA, Françoise Hélène; French architect and academic; b. 26 Nov. 1955, Lyon; teacher various schools in Europe including Ecole d'Architecture de Lyon 1979–83, Ecole d'Architecture de Saint Etienne 1985–89, Ecole d'Architecture d'Oslo, Norway 1990, Cen. London Polytechnic, UK, Univ. of Minnesota, USA 1992, Tech. Univ. of Kassel, Germany 1998; Prof. Inst. of Spatial Design, Vienna Univ. of Tech. 1999–; mem. Acad. of Architecture, Acad. of Arts, Germany, Nat. Comm. on Historical Monuments; Co-founder Jourda & Perraudin Architectural Agency (now Jourda Architectes); Hon. mem. German Acad. of Architecture; Chevalier, Legion d'honneur, Ordre nat. du Mérite, des Arts et des Lettres. *Architectural works include:* Acad. of the Ministry of the Interior, Herne Sodigen 1993, Palace of Justice, Melun 1994, Greenhouse, Potsdam 1995, European Hosp., Lyon 1998, Décathlon Store, Hannover 1999, French Pavilion for Expo 2000, Lille Police station 2001, office block, Vienna 2003, Commercial Centre, Athens 2004. *Address:* Jourda Architectes Paris, 4 cité de Paradis, 75010 Paris, France (office); Institute of Spatial Design, Vienna University of Technology, Karlsplatz 13, 1040 Vienna, Austria (office). *Telephone:* 1-55-28-82-20 (Paris) (office). *Fax:* 1-55-28-85-18 (office). *E-mail:* archi@jourda-architectes.com (office); fhjourda@nerim.com (office). *Website:* www.jourda-architectes.com (office).

JOVANOVIĆ, Vladislav, LLB; Serbian diplomatist; b. 9 June 1933, Prokuplje; s. of Milorad Jovanović and Dragica Jovanović; m. Mirjana Jovanović (née Borić) 1985; one s.; ed Belgrade Univ.; joined Foreign Service 1957; served in Belgium, Turkey and UK 1960–79, Amb. to Turkey 1985–89; various sr posts in Fed. Ministry for Foreign Affairs 1990–91; Head, Yugoslav Dels to Disarmament and Human Dimension confs of CSCE 1990–91; Minister of Foreign Affairs, Repub. of Serbia 1991–92; Fed. Minister for Foreign Affairs of Yugoslavia 1992, 1993–95; Amb. and Perm. Rep. of Yugoslavia to UN 1995–2000; Chevalier de la Légion d'honneur and other decorations. *Publications:* two books of poetry In Search for Searches 1991, Butterfly and Light 1994. *Leisure interest:* chess. *Address:* c/o Ministry of Foreign Affairs, 11000 Belgrade, Kneza Milosa 24, Serbia (office).

JOVANOVIĆ, Živadin; Serbian politician and diplomatist; *President, Belgrade Forum for the World of Equals;* b. 14 Nov. 1938, Oparic, Rekovać Dist; ed Belgrade Univ.; legal adviser, Novi Beograd Dist Council 1961–64; with Ministry of Foreign Affairs 1964–, diplomatic service in Toronto, Canada 1966–70, Nairobi, Kenya 1974–78; Yugoslavian Amb. to Angola 1988–93; Asst to Minister of Foreign Affairs 1994–97; mem. Narosna Skuptina of Serbia (Parl.) 1997–; Deputy Chair. Socialist Party of Serbia 1997–, Acting Pres. 2001; Minister of Foreign Affairs of Yugoslavia 1998–2000; Founder and Pres. Belgrade Forum for World of Equals 1999–; numerous Nat. and foreign decorations. *Publications include:* Abolishment of the State 2003, National Minorities 2004, Intellectuals and Society 2005, Foreign Policy 2006, Critical Analyses of the Serbian Constitution 2007. *Address:* Socialist Party of Serbia, bul. Lenjina 6, 11000 Belgrade (office); Ilijê Garasanina 8, St 6, 11000 Belgrade, Serbia (home). *Telephone:* (11) 2455822 (office); (11) 2452071 (office); (11) 3237074 (office). *Fax:* (11) 2445421 (office). *E-mail:* bedforum@gmail.com (office); jovanovici@beotel.yu (home). *Website:* www.bedforum.com (office).

JOVIĆ, Ivo Miro; Bosnia and Herzegovina politician; b. 15 July 1950, Trebizat, Capljina; s. of Mio Jović and Mara Bukovac; m. Lucija; three c.; ed Sarajevo Dept of History; fmr Prof. Ilijas, Kiseljak; fmr Dir adult educ. center, Kiseljak; fmr Prin. secondary school, Kiseljak; Deputy Minister of Educ., Science, Culture and Sport, Canton of Middle Bosnia 1997–99; Deputy Minister of Educ., Science, Culture and Sport of Bosnia and Herzegovina Fed. 1999–2001; mem. House of Reps 2002–05; Mem. of the Presidency June 2005–06, Chair. June 2005–Feb. 2006. *Address:* c/o Office of the State Presidency, Musala 5, 71000 Sarajevo, Bosnia and Herzegovina (office).

JOWELL, Rt Hon. Tessa Jane Helen Douglas, PC, MA; British politician; *Minister for the Olympics and Minister for London;* b. 17 Sept. 1947, London; d. of Kenneth Palmer and Rosemary Palmer; m. 1st Roger Jowell 1970 (divorced 1978); m. 2nd David Mills 1979; one s. one d. and one step-s. two step-d.; ed St Margaret's School, Aberdeen, Univs of Aberdeen and Edinburgh; childcare officer, social worker, community care Dir; Asst Dir MIND 1974–86; Dir Community Care Special Action Project 1987–90, Joseph Rowntree Foundation Community Care Programme 1990–92; mem. Labour Party 1969–; Councillor, London Borough of Camden 1971–86; MP for Dulwich 1992–97, for Dulwich and W. Norwood 1997–; Opposition Whip, responsible for Trade and Industry 1994–95, Opposition Spokeswoman on Women 1995–96, on Health 1996–97; Minister of State for Public Health 1997–99, for Employment 1999–2001; Minister for Women, House of Commons 1998–2001; Sec. of State for Culture, Media and Sport 2001–07; Minister for the Olympics 2005–, for London (Paymaster Gen.) 2007–; Chair. Social Services Cttee, Housing Man. Cttee, Staff Cttee, Asscn of Metropolitan Authorities 1978–86; mem. Mental Health Act Comm. 1985–90, Health Select Cttee 1992–94; Gov. Nat. Inst. of Social Work 1985–97; Visiting Fellow, Nuffield Coll., Oxford. *Publications:* numerous papers on social policy and

community care. *Address:* House of Commons, London, SW1A 0AA, England (office). *Telephone:* (20) 7219-3409 (office). *Fax:* (20) 7219-2702 (office). *E-mail:* jowellt@parliament.uk (office). *Website:* www.tessajowell.net (office).

JOXE, Pierre Daniel, LenD; French politician; *Member, Conseil Constitutionnel;* b. 28 Nov. 1934, Paris; s. of Louis Joxe and Françoise-Hélène Halevy; m. 3rd Valérie Cayeux 1981; two s. two d. from previous m.; ed Lycée Henri IV, Faculté de droit and Ecole Nat. d'Admin; mil. service 1958–60; auditor, later Counsellor Cour des Comptes; mem. Exec. Bureau and Exec. Cttee, Socialist Party 1971–93; Deputy for Saône and Loire 1973, 1978, 1981, 1986, 1988; Minister of Industry and Admin May–June 1981, of the Interior, Decentralization and Admin July 1984 and March 1986, of the Interior 1988–91, of Defence 1991–93; First Pres. Cour des Comptes (audit court) 1993–2001; mem. Conseil Constitutionnel 2001–; mem. European Parl. 1977–79; Pres. Regional Council, Burgundy 1979–82, Socialist Parl. Group 1981–84, 1986–88; Hon. KBE; Commdr, Ordre nat. du Mérite. *Publications:* Parti socialiste 1973, Atlas du Socialisme 1973, L'édit de Nantes (Literary Prize, Droits de l'homme) 1998, A propos de la France 1998, Pourquoi Mitterrand 2006. *Address:* Conseil Constitutionnel, 2 rue de Montpensier, 75100 Paris, France (office). *Telephone:* 1-40-15-30-00 (office). *Fax:* 1-40-20-93-27 (office). *E-mail:* relations-exterieures@conseil-constitutionnel.fr (office). *Website:* www.conseil-constitutionnel.fr (office).

JOY-WAY ROJAS, Victor, BEng, MA, MEcon; Peruvian politician; ed Univ. Nac. de Ingeniería, Escuela Superior de Admin. Pública, Peru, Williams Coll., Mass and Harvard Univ., USA; Man. Dir number of overseas trade and int. business cos; consultant to UN and OAS on foreign trade; Head Andean Plan for the Promotion of Exports, Cartagena Accord Group; Pres. Org. of Peruvian Importers and Exporters; Co-ordinator China-Latin America Econ. Cooperation Programmes; Dir Corpn Andina de Fomento; Ministry of Industry, Tourism, Integration and Int. Commercial Negotiations 1991–92; mem. Democratic Constituent Congress 1992–, Third Vice-Pres. 1993, Second Vice-Pres. 1994–95, First Vice-Pres. 1995–96, Pres. 1996–97, 1998; fmr Vice-Pres. Amazonian Parl.; Pres. Council of Ministers and Minister of the Economy 1999; under investigation for fraud allegedly committed while in office, 2001; Rep. of Pres. of Peru to External Debt Cttee; Pres. Econ. Comm. 1995–96, Foreign Affairs Comm. 1997–98, Peruvian Congress; Pres. Peru-China Friendship League, Peru-Brazil Friendship League; mem. Privatization Cttee (COPRI). *Address:* c/o Oficina del Presidente, Lima, Peru.

JOYA, Malalai; Afghan politician; *Director, Organization for Promoting Afghan Women's Capabilities (OPAWC);* b. 25 April 1979, Farah Prov.; family fled to Iran and Pakistan 1982, returned to Afghanistan and est. secret school for women in Herat 1998; f. Malalai Health Clinic and Orphanage 2002; Del. to Constitutional Loya Jirga 2003; mem. Parl. for Farah Prov. 2005–07 (suspended from parl. on the grounds that she had insulted fellow reps in a TV interview, suspension currently being appealed); Dir Org. for Promoting Afghan Women's Capabilities (OPAWC); Hon. Citizen of Commune of Provincia di Arezzo 2007, Comune di Bucine 2007, Comune di Supino 2007; Malalai of Maiwand Award 2004, Int. Women of the Year Award, Valle d'Aosta Prov. of Italy 2004, Gwangju Award for Human Rights, May 18th Foundation, S Korea 2006, Women of Peace Award, Women's Peacepower Foundation 2006, named amongst 1000 Women for the Nobel Peace Prize 2005, named by World Econ. Forum amongst 250 Young Global Leaders for 2007, certificate of honour from Mayor of Berkeley, Calif. 2007, Golden Fleur-de-Lis (Giglio d'Oro) Award, Town Council of Toscana Region of Italy 2007, Mare Nostrum Award, Commune of Palazzo in Viareggio, Italy 2007, Anna Politkovskaya Award 2008, Int. Anti-Discrimination Award 2009, and others. *Address:* OPAWC, Str. 1, Qala-e-Najara, Sec. 2, Khairkhana Mina 144, Kabul, Afghanistan (office). *Telephone:* (799) 9544358 (office). *E-mail:* dcmj.afg@gmail.com (office); mj@malalaijoya.com (home). *Website:* www.geocities.com/opawc (office); www.malalaijoya.com (home).

JOYNER-KERSEE, Jacqueline, BA; American fmr athlete; b. 3 March 1962, E St Louis, Ill.; d. of Alfred Joyner and the late Mary Joyner; m. Bobby Kersee 1986; ed Univ. of California, Los Angeles; specialized in heptathlon; coached by husband; world record heptathlon scores: 7,158 points, Houston, 1986; 7,215 points, USA Olympic trial, Indianapolis 1988 (still world record as at Dec. 2003); 7,291 points, Seoul 1988; 7,044 points (gold medal), Olympic Games, Barcelona 1992; three Olympic gold medals, four world championships; long jump: gold medal, World Championships 1987, gold medal, Olympic Games, Seoul 1988, bronze medal, Olympic Games, Barcelona 1992, bronze medal, Olympic Games, Atlanta 1996; winner IAAF Mobil Grand Prix 1994; Chair. St Louis Sports Comm. 1996–; played basketball for Richmond Rage, American Basketball League 1996; business interests include Gold Medal Rehab (sports medicine); CEO Elite Int. Sports Marketing; f. Jackie Joyner-Kersee Gold Medal Scholarship program (now Jackie Joyner-Kersee Youth Foundation) 1988, currently mem. Bd of Dirs; Hon. DHL (Spellman Coll.) 1998, (Howard Univ.) 1999, (George Washington Univ.) 1999; numerous honours including Associated Press Female Athlete of the Year 1988, first woman to win Sporting News Man of the Year Award, Jim Thorpe Award 1993, Jackie Robinson Robie Award 1994, Jesse Owens Humanitarian Award 1999, World Women and Sport Trophy for the Americas, IOC 2007. *Publication:* A Kind of Grace (autobiog.) 1997. *Address:* c/o Jackie Joyner-Kersee Youth Foundation, 101 Jackie Joyner-Kersee Circle, East St. Louis, IL 62204; Elite International Sports Marketing Inc., 1034 South Brentwood Boulevard, Suite 1530, St Louis, MO 63117, USA. *Telephone:* (618) 274-5437 (Foundation). *Fax:* (618) 274-1868 (Foundation). *Website:* www.jackiejoyner-kerseefoundation.org.

JOYON, Francis; French yachtsman; b. 28 May 1956, Hanches, Eure-et-Loire; m. Virginie Joyon; two s.; worked at Glénans Nautical Centre, working as boat-builder, later sailing instructor; first major race 1988 Route of

Discovery (finished in third place); other races include 1989 Round Europe Race, 1990 Route du Rhum, 1992 OSTAR, Route du Cafe, 2000 Europe 1 Newman Star race (first major win, on board Eure et Loir), 2000 Transat (winner), 2001 Fastnet Race (winner); became fastest world non-stop solo yachtsman 2004; solo North Transatlantic record 2005; set new solo round-the-world record on board IDEC II 2008. *Address:* c/o Les Glénans, Quai Louis Blériot, 75016 Paris, France (office). *Website:* www.trimaran-idec.com.

JÓZEFIAK, Marek, MSc; Polish business executive; *Chairman, Telekomunikacja Polska (TP S.A);* b. 1958; m.; two c.; ed Wrocław Tech. Univ.; sr man. for several cos; mem. Supervisory Bd BIAZET –1997; mem. Supervisory Bd TP S.A 1996–97, Chair. 2001–; Chair.'Primus Inter Pares' foundation 1990–97; Dir-Gen. PTK Centertel 1997–2001; mem. Business Centre Club, Polish Industry, Commerce and Finance Asscn, Asscn of Managers in Poland. *Leisure interests:* tennis, skiing, literature, theatre. *Address:* Nowy Świat 6/12 Str., 00–400 Warsaw, Poland (office). *Telephone:* (22) 8275630 (office). *Fax:* (22) 8265559 (office). *E-mail:* emer@mailer.cst.tpsa.pl (office). *Website:* www .tpsa.pl (office).

JU, Gen. Sang-song; North Korean army officer and politician; *Minister of People's Security;* career in Korean People's Armed Forces; attained rank of Gen. 1997; commdr of army unit stationed on border with S Korea 2000; cand. mem. Korean Worker's Party 1970–90, full mem. 1990–; mem. Supreme People's Parl. 1990–98; Minister of People's Security and mem. Nat. Defence Comm. 2004–. *Address:* Ministry of Defence, Pyongyang, Democratic People's Republic of Korea (office).

JU MING; Taiwanese sculptor; b. 20 Jan. 1938, Miaoli Tunghsiao; s. of Lee-chi Chu and Ai Wang; apprenticeship with Master Chin-chuan Lee 1953–57; trained in modern sculpture by Yu Yu Yang 1968–76; moved to USA and made debut in int. arena 1981; produced two series: Taichi Series in wood and bronze and Living World Series in wood, bronze, sponge and stainless steel; Hon. Dr of Art (Fu Jen Catholic Univ.) 2003; Sculpture Award Chinese Sculptors and Artists Asscn 1976, Nat. Culture Award, Repub. of China Nat. Culture Foundation 1976, Award for Ten Outstanding Young People 1987, Achievement Award of Fok Ying Tung, Hong Kong 1998, The Second Enku Award Japan 2002. *Publications:* Juming Sculptures – The Living World 1, 2, 3, Juming – Mixed Media, Juming – Oil Paintings, Juming Sculpture 1976–1993, Taichi in Wood, Ju Ming Wood Sculptures – Buffalo, Ju Ming Paintings, Ju Ming On Art, Carving for Humanity (biog.), Secret Garden of Ju Ming, Ju Ming. *Leisure interest:* tai-chi. *Address:* 208 No. 2 She-shi-hu, Chin-shan, Taipei (office); 111 No. 28, Lane 460, Sec. 2, Chih-shan Road, Taipei, Taiwan (home). *Telephone:* (2) 24989940 (office); (2) 28412011 (home). *Fax:* (2) 24988529 (office); (2) 28413000 (home). *E-mail:* rese1502@juming.org.tw (office); www.juming.org.tw (office).

JUAN, Alexis Raymond, LLD; French banking executive; *Chairman, Komercni Banka;* b. 1943, Algeria; ed Political Studies Inst., Grenoble; joined Société Générale 1968, various man. roles including positions with subsidiary cos in Tokyo, Japan 1973–76, Athens, Greece 1980–84, Seoul, Repub. of Korea as Dir, Korean French Banking Corpn 1978–80, Deputy CEO, Société Générale, UK Div., London 1984–87, various man. roles with Société Générale in France 1987–98, mem., Bd of Dirs Comm. 1998–, Chair., Komercni Banka, Prague, Czech Repub. *Address:* Komercni Banka, Na Prikope 33, 11047 Prague 1, Czech Republic (office). *Website:* www.kb.cz (office).

JUAN CARLOS I, HM The King of Spain; b. 5 Jan. 1938, Rome, Italy; s. of the late HRH Don Juan de Borbón y Battenberg, Count of Barcelona and of the late HRH Doña María de las Mercedes de Borbón y Orleans and grandson of King Alfonso XIII and Queen Victoria Eugenia of Spain; m. Princess Sophia, d. of the late King Paul of the Hellenes and of Queen Frederica, 1962; one s., HRH Prince Felipe, The Prince of Asturias, b. Jan. 1968; two daughters, Princess Elena, Princess Cristina; ed privately in Fribourg, Switzerland, Madrid, San Sebastián, Inst. of San Isidro, Madrid, Colegio del Carmen, Gen. Mil. Acad., Zaragoza and Univ. of Madrid; spent childhood in Rome, Lausanne, Estoril and Madrid; commissioned into the three armed forces and undertook training in each of them 1957–59; studied the org. and activities of various govt ministries; named by Gen. Franco as future King of Spain 1969, inaugurated as King of Spain 22 Nov. 1975, named as Capt.-Gen. of the Armed Forces Nov. 1975; Foreign mem. Acad. des sciences morales et politiques, Assoc. mem. 1988; Dr hc (Strasbourg) 1979, (Madrid), (Harvard) 1984, (Sorbonne) 1985, (Oxford) 1986, (Trinity Coll., Dublin) 1986, (Bologna) 1988, (Cambridge) 1988, (Coimbra) 1989, (Tokyo, Bogotá, Limerick, Tufts, Chile) 1990, (Toronto) 1991, (Jerusalem) 1993; Charlemagne Prize 1982, Bolívar Prize (UNESCO) 1983, Gold Medal Order 1985, Candenhove Kalergi Prize, Switzerland 1986, Nansen Medal 1987, Humanitarian Award Elie Wiesel, USA 1991, shared Houphouët Boigny Peace Prize (UNESCO) 1995, Franklin D. Roosevelt Four Freedoms Award 1995. *Address:* Palacio de la Zarzuela, 28071 Madrid, Spain. *Website:* www.casareal.es.

JUANTORENA, Alberto; Cuban sports administrator, fmr athlete and politician; b. 3 Dec. 1950, Santiago; m.; five c.; moved to Havana to train under Polish coach Zgymunt Zabierzowski 1971; gold 400m (45.36) Dominica Cen. American Games 1974; gold 800m (1:43.50), gold 400m (44.26) Montreal Olympic Games 1976; gold 800m (1:44.01), gold 400m (45.36) Dusseldorf World Cup 1977; gold 400m (44.27), gold 800m (1:47.78) Columbia Cen. American Games 1978; fmr Vice-Minister of Sports for Cuba, Vice-Pres. Cuban Olympic Cttee, Vice-Pres. for Latinamerica UNESCO, Sr Vice-Pres. Cuban Olympic Cttee; mem. Council IAAF; Track & Field News Athlete of the Year 1976, 1977; Olympic Order. *Address:* c/o Cubadeportes S.A., Calle 20 No. 710 e/ 7ma y 9na, Miramar, Playa, Havana, Cuba (office). *Telephone:* 24-09-45 (office). *Fax:* 24-19-14 (office). *E-mail:* cdp@inder.co.cu (office).

JUBEIR, Adel bin Ahmed al-, BA, MA; Saudi Arabian diplomatist; *Ambassador to USA;* b. 1 Feb. 1962, Riyadh; ed Univ. of N Texas and Georgetown Univ., USA; fmr Special Asst to Amb., Embassy in Washington, DC; fmr Dir Saudi Arabian Information and Congressional Affairs Office; Foreign Affairs Advisor, Crown Prince's Court 2000–05; Custodian of the Two Holy Mosques, Advisor, Royal Court 2005–07; Amb. to USA 2007–; served in Jt Information Bureau in Dhahran during Operation Desert Shield/Desert Storm 1990–91; Visiting Diplomatic Fellow, Council of Foreign Relations, New York 1994–95; Hon. DHumLitt (N Texas) 2006. *Address:* Embassy of Saudi Arabia, 601 New Hampshire Avenue, NW, Washington, DC 20037, USA (office). *Telephone:* (202) 342-3800 (office). *Fax:* (202) 944-6750 (office). *E-mail:* info@ saudiembassy.net (office). *Website:* www.saudiembassy.net (office).

JUDEH, Nasser, BSc; Jordanian government official and politician; *Minister of Foreign Affairs;* ed Georgetown Univ., USA; Pvt. Sec. and Press Sec. to HRH Prince Hassan 1985–92; Dir Jordan Information Bureau, London 1992–94; Dir Jordan TV Corpn 1994–98, Dir-Gen. 1998; Minister of Information 1998–99, Official Govt Spokesman 1998–99, 2005–07; Chair. Bd of Information and Communication Expertise 1999–2005; Minister of State for Media Affairs and Communication 2007; Minister of Foreign Affairs 2009–; media adviser to Royal Jordanian Airlines 2003; Grand Cordon of the Order of Al Kawkab, Grand Cordon of the Order of Al- Istiklal, Officier, Légion d'honneur, Grand Officer, Order of Orange-Nassau (Netherlands). *Leisure interests:* underwater sports, hunting, reading, tennis. *Address:* Ministry of Foreign Affairs, POB 35217, Amman 11180, Jordan (office). *Telephone:* (6) 5735150 (office). *Fax:* (6) 5735163 (office). *E-mail:* inquiry@mfa.gov.jo (office). *Website:* www.mfa.gov.jo (office).

JUDGE, Sir Paul, Kt, MA, MBA, LLD; British business executive; *Chairman, Royal Society of Arts;* b. 1949, London; m. Barbara Judge; two s.; ed St Dunstan's Coll., Trinity Coll. Cambridge, Wharton Business School, Univ. of PA, USA; joined Cadbury Schweppes 1973, various positions in Overseas Group finance dept 1973–78, Group Deputy Finance Dir 1978, Man. Dir Cadbury Schweppes Kenya 1980–82, Man. Dir Cadbury Typhoo 1982–84, Group Planning Dir and mem. Exec. Cttee 1984–85, led buyout of Cadbury Schweppes food cos to form Premier Brands 1985; apptd mem. Milk Marketing Bd and Chair. of Food for Britain, UK Govt 1989; Dir-Gen. Conservative Party 1992–95; Ministerial Adviser, Cabinet Office 1995–96; Chair. Royal Soc. for Arts, Manufactures and Commerce (RSA) 2003–; fmr Dir Boddington Group PLC, Grosvenor Devt Capital PLC, WPP Group PLC; currently Dir Standard Bank Group Ltd; Chair. Schroder Income Growth Fund PLC; Chair. Tempur Pedic Inc., mem. Advisory Bd Barclays Pvt. Bank, Lynka Promotional Products, Krakow, Poland, Int. Advisory Bd Inst. for the Study of Europe, Columbia Univ. NY, USA; Chair. Marketing Standards Setting Body, Businessdynamics Trust, Govs of St Dunstan's Coll., Wharton Exec. Bd for Europe, Africa and the Middle E; UK Chair. of British-N American Cttee; Pres. Asscn of MBAs; Pres.-Elect Chartered Man. Inst.; Vice-Pres. Marketing Council, Chartered Inst. of Marketing; Deputy Chair. Globe Theatre Devt Council; Treasurer Imperial Soc. of Knights Batchelor, British Food Trust; Trustee The Cambridge Foundation, Deputy Chair. The American Man. Asscn; Past Master Worshipful Co. of Marketers. *Leisure interests:* photography, travel. *Address:* 152 Grosvenor Road, London, SW1V 3JL, England (office). *Telephone:* (20) 7834-9041 (office). *E-mail:* paul@paulrjudge.com (office). *Website:* www.rsa.uk (office).

JUGNAUTH, Rt Hon. Sir Anerood, KCMG, PC, QC; Mauritian politician, lawyer and head of state; *President;* b. 29 March 1930, Palma; m. Sarojni Devi Ballah; one s. one d.; ed Church of England School, Palma, Regent Coll., Quakre, Borneo, Lincoln's Inn, London; called to Bar 1954; won seat on Legis. Ass., Mauritius 1963; Minister of State and Devt 1965–67, of Labour 1967; Dist Magistrate 1967; Crown Counsel and Sr Crown Counsel 1971; co-founder and Pres. Mouvement Militant Mauricien with Paul Bérenger (q.v.) Dec. 1971–; Leader of Opposition 1976; Prime Minister of Mauritius 1982–95, other portfolios include Minister of Finance 1983–84, of Defence and Internal Security and Reform Insts, of Information, Internal and External Communications and the Outer Islands, of Justice; Prime Minister and Minister of Defence and Home Affairs and of External Communications Sept. 2000–03; Pres. 2003–; Order of the Rising Sun (Japan) 1988, Grand Officier, Légion d'honneur 1990; Hon. DCL (Mauritius) 1985; Hon. LLD (Madras) 2001; Dr hc (Aix-en-Provence) 1985. *Leisure interests:* football, reading. *Address:* President's Office, Clarisse House, Vacoas, Port Louis; La Caverne No. 1, Vacoas, Mauritius (home). *Telephone:* 697-0077 (office). *Fax:* 697-2347 (office). *E-mail:* statepas@intnet.mu (office). *Website:* ncb.intnet.mu/president.htm (office).

JUGNAUTH, Pravind Kumar, LLB; Mauritian politician and barrister; *Leader, Mouvement Socialiste Militant;* b. 25 Dec. 1961; m.; three c.; ed Univ. of Buckingham, UK; joined Mouvement Socialiste Militant 1987, Deputy Leader 1999–2003, Leader 2003–; Councillor, Municipality of Vacoas/Phoenix 1996; mem. Parl. for Constituency No. 11 (Vieux Grand Port and Rose Belle); Minister of Agric., Food, Trade and Natural Resources 2000–03, Deputy Prime Minister and Minister of Finance Sept.–Dec. 2003, Deputy Prime Minister and Minister of Finance and Econ. Devt Dec. 2003–05. *Address:* Mouvement Socialiste Militant, Sun Trust Building, 31 Edith Cavell Street, Port Louis (office); La Caverne No. 1, Vacoas, Mauritius (home). *Telephone:* 212-8787 (office). *Fax:* 208-9517 (office). *E-mail:* request@msmsun.com (office). *Website:* www.msmparty.org (office).

JUGNOT, Gérard; French actor, writer, director and producer; b. 4 May 1951, Paris; one s. with Cécile Magna; Chevalier de la Légion d'honneur 2004. *Films include:* L'an 01 (The Year 01) 1973, Salut l'artiste (Hail the Artist) (uncredited)) 1973, Que la fête commence... (Let Joy Reign Supreme) (uncredited) 1974, Les valseuses (Getting It Up) 1974, Le bol d'air (also writer) 1975, C'est pas parce qu'on a rien à dire qu'il faut fermer sa gueule (also writer) 1975, Vous ne l'emporterez pas au paradis 1975, Pas de problème! (No Problem!) 1975, Calmos (Cool, Calm and Collected) 1976, Oublie-moi, Mandoline (Forget Me, Mandoline) 1976, Le juge et l'assassin (The Judge and the Assassin) (uncredited) 1976, Le locataire (The Tenant) 1976, On aura tout vu (The Bottom Line) 1976, Dracula père et fils (Dracula and Son) 1976, Monsieur Klein 1976, Le jouet (The Toy) 1976, Le chasseur de chez Maxim's (Maxim's Porter) 1976, Casanova & Co. (aka Some Like It Cool, USA), Herbie Goes to Monte Carlo 1977, Des enfants gâtés (Spoiled Children) 1977, Vous n'aurez pas l'Alsace et la Lorraine (You Won't Have Alsace-Lorraine 1977, La septième compagnie au clair de lune (The Seventh Company Outdoors) 1977, Les petits câlins (The Little Wheedlers) 1978, Pauline et l'ordinateur 1978, Les bronzés (French Fried Vacation, USA) (also writer) 1978, Les héros n'ont pas froid aux oreilles (Heroes Are Not Wet Behind the Ears, USA) (also writer) 1979, Un si joli village… (The Investigation) 1979, le coup de sirocco 1979, Les bronzés font du ski (also writer) 1979, Retour en force (Return in Bond) 1980, Le coup du parapluie (Umbrella Coup) 1980, Les Charlots contre Dracula 1980, Pourquoi pas nous? 1981, Pour 100 briques t'as plus rien… (For 200 Grand, You Get Nothing Now) 1980, Le Père Noël est une ordure (also writer) 1982, Le quart d'heure américain (also writer) 1982, La fiancée qui venait du froid 1983, Papy fait de la résistance 1983, Le garde du corps 1984, Pinot simple flic (also writer and dir) 1984, Just the Way You Are 1984, Tranches de vie (Slices of Life) 1985, Les rois du gag 1985, Scout toujours… (also writer and dir) 1985, Nuit d'ivresse 1986, Le beauf 1987, Tandem 1987, Tant qu'il y aura des femmes (uncredited) 1987, Sans peur et sans reproche (Without Fear or Blame) (also writer and dir) 1988, Les cigognes n'en font qu'à leur tête 1989, Les 1001 nuits (1001 Nights, aka Scheherazade, UK) 1990, Les secrets professionnels du Dr Apfelglück 1991, Une époque formidable…(Wonderful Times) (also writer and dir) 1991, Les clés du paradis (The Keys to Paradise) 1991, Voyage à Rome 1992, Grosse fatigue (Dead Tired) 1994, Casque bleu (Blue Helmet) (also writer and dir) 1994, Les faussaires (The Impostors) 1994, 3,000 scénarios contre le virus (3,000 Scenarios to Combat a Virus) (dir segment 'La pharmacie') 1994, Fantôme avec chauffeur 1996, Fallait pas!… (also writer and dir) 1996, Marthe 1997, Au bain… Mari! 1999, Trafic d'influence (Influence Peddling) 1999, L'ami du jardin 1999, Meilleur espoir féminin (Most Promising Young Actress) (also writer and dir) 2000, Oui, mais… (Yes, But…) 2001, Monsieur Batignole (also writer, dir and producer) 2002, Le raid (The Race) 2002, Les clefs de bagnole (The Car Keys) 2003, Les choristes (Chorists) (also dir and assoc. producer) 2004, The Magic Round-about (voice) 2005, Boudu (also dir and co-producer) 2005, Il ne faut jurer… de rien! 2005, Les bronzés amis pour la vie (also writer) 2006, Les brigades du tigre 2006. *Television includes:* Pierrot mon ami (Pierrot My Friend) 1979, Merci Bernard (series) 1982, L'adieu aux as (mini-series) 1982, Le Père Noël est une ordure (also writer) 1985, Restauratec 2002, Volpone 2003, Trois petites filles 2004.

JUHÁSZ, Ferenc; Hungarian politician; b. 6 Jan. 1960, Nyíregyháza; m.; two c.; ed Lajos Kossuth Vocational School, György Bessenyei Teachers' Training Coll., Nyíregyháza, Coll. of Finance and Public Accountancy, Univ. of Pécs; Head of Co. Office, HSP (Magyar Szocialista Párt—MSZP) 1991–94; elected mem. of Parl. 1994, mem. Defence Cttee 1994–96, Vice-Chair. 1996–98; apptd Vice-Chair. Defence Cttee on Legislation, Chair. Control Comm. 1998; Head, Working Group of HSP faction for Defence and Nat. Security 1998–2002, Deputy Head of faction for Parl. 1999–2000; Deputy Chair. HSP 2000–; Minister of Defence 2002–. *Address:* Hungarian Socialist Party, Köztársaság tér 26, 1081 Budapest, Hungary (office). *Telephone:* (1) 210-0046 (office). *Fax:* (1) 210-0081 (office). *E-mail:* info@mszp.hu (office); ferenc.juhasz@mszp.hu. *Website:* www.mszp.hu (office).

JUILLET, Alain; French intelligence officer and fmr business executive; *Senior Officier, Secrétariat Général de la défense nationale (SGDN);* b. 1943; ed Centre de perfectionnement des affaires, Institut des hautes études de défense nationale, Paris, Stanford Univ., USA; fmr employee, Pernod-Ricard, Jacobs-Suchard, Union Laitière Normande, France Champignon; Chief Exec. French Operations, Marks & Spencer Ltd –2001; Head of Information, Direction Générale de la Sécurité Extérieure (DGSE) 2002–03; Sr Officer responsible for econ. intelligence, Secrétariat général de la défense nationale (SGDN) 2004–. *Address:* Secrétariat Général de la défense nationale (SGDN), 51, boulevard de la Tour-Maubourg, 75700 Paris 07 SP, France (office).

JUKNEVIČIENĖ, Rasa; Lithuanian physician and politician; *Minister of National Defence;* b. 26 Jan. 1958, Panevėžio raj. Tiltagalių km; m. Zenonas Juknevičius; ed Kaunas Medical Inst.; pediatrician, Cen. Hosp., Poswolu 1984–90; mem. Supreme Council, Reconstituent Seimas 1990–92; Deputy in Seimas 1996–, Vice-Pres. Parl. Del. to NATO Parl. Ass. 1999–2000, mem. Comm. for NATO Affairs 2004–08 (Deputy Chair. 2005–08); mem. Homeland Union—Lithuanian Christian Democrats (Tėvynės Sąjunga); Lithuanian Grand Duke Gediminas Order of the Commdr's Cross of Lithuania's 10th Anniversary of Independence. *Leisure interests:* reading, growing flowers. *Address:* Ministry of National Defence, Totorių 25/3, Vilnius 01121, Lithuania (office). *Telephone:* (5) 262-4821 (office). *Fax:* (5) 212-6082 (office). *E-mail:* vis@kam.lt (office). *Website:* www.kam.lt (office).

JULIAN, Louise; Swedish business executive; *CEO, EF Education;* ed Univ. of Stockholm, Sweden, Sorbonne Univ., Paris, France; spent childhood in Singapore; joined EF Education in 1986, has served as Pres. EF Travel, EF Foundation, EF Language Travel, later CEO EF North America, CEO EF Education 2002–; ranked by Fortune magazine amongst 50 Most Powerful Women in Business outside the US (35th) 2004. *Address:* EF Education First Boston, One Education Street, Cambridge, MA 02141, USA (office). *Telephone:* (617) 619-1000 (office). *Fax:* (617) 619-1495 (office). *E-mail:* louise.julian@ef .com (office). *Website:* www.ef.com (office).

JULIEN, Michael Frederick, FCA, FCT; British business executive and accountant (retd); b. 22 March 1938, London; s. of the late Robert A. F. Julien and Olive R. Evans; m. Ellen Martinsen 1963; one s. two d.; ed St Edward's School, Oxford; Price Waterhouse & Co. 1958–67; other commercial appointments 1967–76; Group Finance Dir BICC (now Balfour Beatty PLC) 1976–83; Exec. Dir Finance and Planning, Midland Bank (now HSBC Bank PLC) 1983–86; Man. Dir Finance and Admin. Guinness PLC (now Diageo PLC) 1987–88, Dir (non-exec.) 1988–97; Group Chief Exec. Storehouse PLC (now Mothercare PLC) 1988–92; Chair. Owners Abroad PLC (now First Choice Holidays PLC) 1993–97; Dir Medeva PLC 1993–98; fmr Deputy Chair. Oxford Professional Training Ltd. *Leisure interests:* family, travel, computing (including video editing). *Address:* Glenhaven, 1 Beechwood Avenue, Weybridge, Surrey, KT13 9TF, England (home). *Telephone:* (1932) 831286 (home). *Fax:* (7092) 040900 (home). *E-mail:* michael@julienco.com (home). *Website:* www.julienco.com (home).

JULIUS, Anthony Robert, PhD; British lawyer; *Consultant, Mishcon de Reya;* b. 16 July 1956; s. of Morris Julius and Myrna Julius; m. 1st Judith Bernie 1979 (divorced 1998); two s. two d.; m. 2nd Dina Rabinovitch 1999; one s.; ed City of London School, Jesus Coll., Cambridge, Univ. Coll. London; articled Victor Mishcon & Co., qualified 1981, partner Mishcon de Reya 1984–, (Head of Litigation 1987–98), Consultant 1998–; Solicitor Advocate 1999; Teacher (part–time), Law Faculty, Univ. Coll. London 1995–97; Dir Inst. of Jewish Policy Research (reporting on Holocaust Denial Legislation) 1995–97 (Deputy Chair. Research Bd 1995–97); f., Trustee and Chair. Diana, Princess of Wales Memorial Trust, Vice-Pres. 1997–2003; Chair. Man. Bd Centre for Cultural Analysis, Theory and History, Univ. of Leeds 2001–. *Publications:* T. S. Eliot, Anti-Semitism and Literary Form 1995, Art Crimes (chapter in Law and Literature) 1999, Idolising Pictures 2000, Transgressions 2002. *Leisure interest:* cooking. *Address:* Mishcon de Reya, Summit House, 12 Red Lion Square, London, WC1R 4QD, England (office). *Telephone:* (20) 7440-7000 (office). *Fax:* (20) 7404-8171 (office). *E-mail:* anthony.julius@mishcon.co.uk (office).

JULIUS, DeAnne, CBE, PhD; American/British economist; *Chairman, Chatham House;* b. 14 April 1949; d. of Marvin Julius; m. Ian A. Harvey 1976; one s. one d.; ed Iowa State Univ. and Univ. of California, Davis; Econ. Adviser for Energy, World Bank 1975–82; Man. Dir Logan Assocs, Inc. 1983–86; Dir of Econs Royal Inst. of Int. Affairs (RIIA), London 1986–89; Chief Economist Shell Int. Petroleum Co., London 1989–93, British Airways 1993–97; mem. Monetary Policy Cttee, Bank of England 1997–2001, Dir Bank of England Court 2001–04; Chair. British Airways Pension Investment Man. Ltd 1995–97; Dir (non-exec.) Lloyds TSB 2001–07, BP (British Petroleum) 2001–, Serco Group 2001–, Roche 2002–, Jones Lang LaSalle 2008–; Chair. Royal Inst. of Int. Affairs (now Chatham House) 2003–; Dr hc (Warwick) 2000, (South Bank) 2001, (Bath) 2002, (Birmingham) 2006. *Publications:* The Economics of Natural Gas 1990, Global Companies and Public Policy: The Growing Challenge of Foreign Direct Investment 1990, Is Manufacturing Still Special in the New World Order? (jtly) 1993 (Amex Bank Prize); numerous articles on int. econs. *Leisure interests:* skiing, windsurfing, bonsai. *Address:* Chatham House, 10 St James's Square, London, SW1Y 4LE, England (office). *Telephone:* (137) 245-1878 (office). *Fax:* (137) 245-4770 (office). *E-mail:* chairman@chathamhouse.org.uk (office). *Website:* www .chathamhouse.org.uk (office).

JULLIEN, François, DèsSc; French academic; *Professor of Philosophy, University de Paris VII-Denis Diderot;* b. 2 June 1951, Embrun, Hautes-Alpes; s. of Raymond Jullien and Marie Cler; m. Odile Sournies 1974; one s. two d.; ed Ecole normale supérieure, Univs of Peking and Shanghai, China, Univ. Paris-Sorbonne; Head French Sinology Unit, Hong Kong 1978–81; Resident Maison franco-japonaise, Tokyo 1985–87; Sr Lecturer, Univ. de Paris VIII-Saint-Denis 1981–87; Prof. 1987–90; Prof. Univ. de Paris VII-Denis Diderot 1990–, Dir l'UFR Asie orientale 1990–2000; Pres. Asscn française des études chinoises 1988–90; Pres. Collège Int. de philosophie 1995–98; Dir Oriental collection, Presses Univ. de France (PUF), Dir Inst. de la Pensée Contemporaine, des collections Orientales et Libelles, currently Dir Agenda de la Pensée Contemporaine, PUF, Dir Centre Marcel Granet; sr mem. Inst. Universitaire de France 2001–; mem. Editorial Cttee Critique journal. *Publications:* Fleurs du matin cueillies le soir 1976, Sous le dais fleuri 1978 (both translations of the Chinese texts of Lu Xun), La Valeur allusive 1985, Procès ou création 1989, Eloge de la fadeur 1991, La Propension des choses 1992, Figures de l'immanence 1993, Le Détour et l'accès 1995, Fonder la morale 1995, Traité de l'efficacité 1997, Un sage est sans idée ou l'autre de la philosophie 1998, De l'essence ou du nu 2000, Penser d'un dehors (la Chine) 2000, Du "temps": éléments d'une philosophie du vivre 2001, La Grande image n'a pas de forme 2003 (trans. into Vietnamese, Italian, Castillian, German), L'Ombre au tableau 2004, Nourrir sa vie, à l'écart du bonheur 2005, Conférence sur l'efficacité 2005. *Address:* Université Paris VII-Denis Diderot, 2 place Jussieu, 75251 Paris Cedex 05 (office); 8 rue Tournefort, 75005 Paris, France (home). *Telephone:* 1-44-27-82-95 (office).

JULLIEN, Mgr Jacques; French ecclesiastic; b. 7 May 1929, Brest; s. of Pierre Jullien and Jeanne Maudon; ed Grand-Séminaire de Quimper, Univ. Catholique d'Angers, Univ. Catholique de Paris et Hautes-Etudes, Paris; ordained priest 1954; Vicar, Locmaria-Quimper; Prof. of Moral Theology, Grand-Séminaire de Quimper 1957–69; Curé, Saint-Louis de Brest 1969–78; Bishop of Beauvais 1978–84; Coadjutor Bishop to HE Cardinal Gouyon 1984; Archbishop of Rennes, Dol and Saint-Malo 1985–98, Archbishop Emer. 1998–; Chevalier, Légion d'honneur. *Publications:* Le Chrétien et la politique 1963, Les Chrétiens et l'état (co-author) 1967, La régulation des naissances, Humanae Vitae 1968, Pour vous, qui est Jésus-Christ? (co-author) 1968, Faire vivre, livre blanc sur l'avortement (co-author) 1969, Les prêtres dans le combat politique 1972, L'homme debout 1980, En paroles et en actes 1983, La Procréation artificielle: des motifs d'espérer (co-author), Demain la Famille 1992, Trop petit pour ta grâce 1996. *Address:* 45 rue de Brest, 35042 Rennes; Communauté des Augustines, 4 rue Adolphe Leray, 35044 Rennes cedex, France. *Website:* catholique-rennes.cef.fr.

JULY, Serge; French journalist; b. 27 Dec. 1942, Paris; one s.; journalist Clarté 1961–63; Vice-Pres. Nat. Union of Students 1965–66; French teacher Coll. Sainte-Barbe, Paris 1966–68; Asst Leader Gauche prolétarienne 1969–72 (disbanded by the Govt); co-f. newspaper, Libération 1973, Chief Ed. 1973–2006, Publishing Dir 1974–75, Jt Dir 1981, Man. Dir 1987–2006; Reporter Europe 1983; mem. Club de la presse Europe 1976–. *Publications:* Vers la guerre civile (with Alain Geismar and Erlyne Morane) 1969, Dis maman, c'est quoi l'avant-guerre? 1980, Les Années Mitterrand 1986, La Drôle d'Année 1987, Le Salon des artistes 1989, La Diagonale du Golfe 1991, Entre quatre z'yeux (with Alain Juppé).

JUMAGULOV, Apas; Kyrgyzstani diplomatist, politician and business executive; b. Sept. 1934, Arashan; s. of Jumagul Jumagulov; ed Moscow Inst. of the Petrochemical and Gas Industry; began working as geologist in state oil industry; actively participated in activities of local CP br.; Chief Engineer, Kyrgyzneft (state oil and gas co.) –1973; apptd Head of Industry and Transportation Dept, Cen. Cttee of CP of Kyrgyz SSR 1973; later took on several other admin. posts at regional and nat. levels; Head of Govt of Kyrgyzia 1986–91; nominated himself as a cand. in presidential elections 1990; Admin. Head of his native region of Chu 1990–93; Prime Minister 1993–98 (retd); Amb. to Germany 1998–2003, also accred to Holy See and Scandinavian countries 1999–2003; withdrew from politics and became intermediary and consultant; Chair. Moscow br. of Postnoff co. 2003–; entered leadership ranks of Eurasian Movt 2004–; Amb. to Russian Fed. 2005–07; Order of Merit (Germany) 2003. *Address:* c/o Ministry of Foreign Affairs, 720040 Bishkek, bul. Erkindik 57, Kyrgyzstan.

JUMBE, (Mwinyi) Aboud; Tanzanian politician (retd); b. 14 June 1920, Zanzibar; s. of Jumbe Mwinyi and Sanga Mussa; m. Khadija Ibrahim 1947, Zeyena Rashid 1976, Fatma Muhammed 1980; fourteen s. four d.; ed secondary school, Zanzibar and Makerere Univ. Coll., Uganda; Teacher 1946–60; fmr mem. Zanzibar Township Council; mem. Afro-Shirazi Party (ASP) 1960–77, later Organizing Sec., Head 1972–77; Vice-Chair. Chama Cha Mapinduzi (formed by merger of TANU and ASP) 1977–84; mem. Nat. Assembly of Zanzibar (ASP) 1961–84; Opposition Whip 1962–64; Minister of Home Affairs, Zanzibar Jan.–April 1964; Minister of State, First Vice-President's Office, Tanzania 1964–72, concurrently responsible for Ministry of Health and Social Services 1964–67; First Vice-Pres. of Tanzania 1972–77, Vice-Pres. 1977–84; Chair. Zanzibar Revolutionary Council 1972–84; fmr Vice-Chair. Revolutionary Party of Tanzania; has resgnd all Govt and party positions and now resides as a villager; engaged in small-scale fishing, animal husbandry and land cultivation. *Leisure interests:* reading and writing Islamic materials. *Address:* Mjimwema, PO Box 19875, Dar es Salaam, Tanzania. *Telephone:* 33969; 31359.

JUMBE, Philbert Alexander; Zimbabwean business executive; b. 22 Oct. 1946, Bindura; m. Bernadette Stembeni 1974; one s. five d.; ed Bradley Inst., Bindura; Man. Dir Zimbabwe Bearings (Pvt) Ltd, Harare 1980; currently Chair. Powerspeed Electrical Ltd; Chief Exec. PAJ Holdings (Pvt) Ltd, Zimbabwe Bearings Manufacturing (Pvt) Ltd; Pres. Zimbabwe Nat. Chamber of Commerce (ZNCC) 1989–90, 1990–91 (Chair. Harare Branch 1986); mem. Council, Zimbabwe Asscn of Pension Funds 1980–81; Chair. Machembere Creche, Highfield 1978; Chair. and Founder-mem. Rusununguko School Students' Asscn 1987; Life mem. Jairosi Jiri Asscn 1985, Zimbabwe Council for Welfare of Children 1986; Award for Outstanding Services to ZNCC 1985, 1989. *Leisure interests:* tennis, squash, jogging. *Address:* Powerspeed Electrical Ltd., PO Box 942, Granietside, Harare, Zimbabwe.

JUNCKER, Jean-Claude, LLM; Luxembourg politician; *Prime Minister and Minister of State and of Finance;* b. 9 Dec. 1954, Redange-sur-Attert; s. of Jos Juncker and Marguerite Hecker; m. Christiane Frising 1979; ed Univ. of Strasbourg; Parl. Sec. to Christian Social Party 1979–82; Sec. of State for Labour and Social Affairs 1982–84, Minister of Labour, Minister in charge of Budget 1984–89, Minister of Labour, of Finance 1989–94; Prime Minister of Luxembourg 1995–, also Minister of State, of Finance and the Treasury, of Labour and Employment 1995–99, of State and of Finance 1999–; Chair. Christian Social Party 1990–95; Chair. Social Affairs and Budget Councils 1985; Gov. IBRD 1989–95, fmr Gov. IMF, EBRD; elected first Perm. Pres. Eurogroup 2005; Int. Karlspreis, Aachen 2006. *Leisure interest:* reading. *Address:* Hôtel de Bourgogne, 4 rue de la Congrégation, 1352 Luxembourg, Luxembourg (office). *Telephone:* 478-21-00 (office). *Fax:* 46-17-20 (office). *E-mail:* ministere.etat@me.etat.lu (office).

JUNG, Andrea, BA; American retail executive; *Chairman and CEO, Avon Products Inc.;* b. 18 Sept. 1958, Toronto, Canada; eldest child of Chinese immigrants; m. 2nd Michael Gould; one adopted s. one d. from previous m.; ed Princeton Univ.; grew up in Wellesley, Mass; joined man. trainee programme at Bloomingdale's 1979; fmr Sr Vice-Pres. Gen. Merchandising, I. Magnin, San Francisco; Exec. Vice-Pres. Neiman Marcus –1994; consultant for Avon Products 1993, Pres. Product Marketing Group Marketing, Avon US 1994–96, Sr Vice-Pres. Global Marketing, Avon Products Inc. 1996–97, mem. Bd of Dirs 1998–, Pres. and COO 1998–2000, CEO 1999–, Chair. 2001–; Chair. The Cosmetic, Toiletry and Fragrance Asscn (first woman) 2001–05; mem. Bd of Dirs Gen. Electric Co., Princeton Univ., Fashion Inst. of Tech., Fragrance Foundation, Cosmetic Exec. Women, Sales Corpn Donna Karan Int., Catalyst; mem. Int. Advisory Council, Salomon Smith Barney; Trustee New York Presbyterian Hosp.; ranked by Fortune magazine amongst 50 Most Powerful Women in Business in the US 1998–2001, (fifth) 2002, (third) 2003, (third) 2004, (fifth) 2005, (seventh) 2006, (ninth) 2007, named by BusinessWeek magazine as one of Best Managers of the Year 2003, ranked by Forbes magazine amongst 100 Most Powerful Women (61st) 2004, (35th) 2005, (37th) 2006, (30th) 2007, (19th) 2008, named by Newsweek magazine as one of 10 Prominent People to Watch in 2005 2004, ranked third by The Wall Street Journal amongst its 50 Women to Watch in Business 2005. *Leisure interest:* playing the piano. *Address:* Avon Products Inc. Headquarters, 1345 Avenue of the Americas, New York, NY 10105-0302, USA (office). *Telephone:* (800) 367-2866 (office). *Website:* www.avoncompany.com (office).

JUNG, Franz Josef, DJur; German lawyer and politician; *Minister of Defence;* b. 5 March 1949, Erbach, Rheingau-Taunus Dist, Hesse; m.; three c.; ed Rheingau School, Geisenheim, Univ. of Mainz; legal training at Wiesbaden Dist Court 1974–76; solicitor in Eltville 1976–, public notary 1983–; mem. Dist Ass. of Rheingau-Taunus 1972–87; mem. Nat. Exec., CDU German Youth Union 1973–93, Vice-Chair. 1981–83; elected to Hessen State Parl. (Landtag), Wiesbaden 1983–2005; Hessian State Minister for Fed. and European Affairs and Head of Hessian State Chancellory 1999–2000; Gen. Sec. of CDU in Hessen 1987–91, CDU Parl. Sec., Hessen Landtag 1987–99; CDU Parl. Whip in Hessen Landtag 2003–05; mem. CDU Nat. Exec. Cttee 1998–; elected to Fed. Parl. (Bundestag), Berlin 2005–; Minister of Defence 2005–; Chair. Producers' Asscn Research Inst. of Geisenheim 1999, Friends of ZDF TV 2002; mem. Rheingau Music Festival Cttee 1989–, ZDF TV Advisory Bd 1999, Eintracht Frankfurt e.V. Man. Bd 1999, Eintracht Frankfurt AG Supervisory Bd 2003–05. *Address:* Ministry of Defence, Arbeitsbereich 2, Stauffenbergstrasse 18, 10785 Berlin, Germany (office). *Telephone:* (18) 8820048000 (office). *Fax:* (18) 8820048004 (office). *E-mail:* sabrinakluemper@bmvg.bund400.de (office). *Website:* www.bundeswehr.de (office); www.franz-josef-jung.de (office).

JUNG, Man-won, BA, MBA; South Korean energy industry executive; *President and CEO, SK Networks;* ed Yonsei Univ., NY Univ.; served in Korean Ministry of Energy and Resources 1980–94; consultant SKC Chemical Business Group (fmrly Yukong Oxichemical) 1994–96, Vice-Pres. Man. and Planning Office 1996–2000, Vice-Pres. SK Customer Service Devt Div. 2000–01, Vice-Pres. Wireless Internet Business Div. Group and Finance Business Div., SK Telecom 2001–02, Pres. SK Global Energy Sales Group and Head SK Global Normalization Process Task Force 2002–03, Pres. and CEO SK Networks 2003–. *Address:* SK Networks, 99 Seorin-Dong, Jongru-Gu, Seoul 110-110, Republic of Korea (office). *Telephone:* (2) 2121-5114 (office). *Fax:* (2) 2121-7001 (office). *E-mail:* Byc778@skcorp.com (office). *Website:* www.skcorp.com (office).

JUNG, Roland Tadeusz, BChir, MA, MB, MD, FRCP, FRCPE; British physician; b. 1948, Glasgow; m.; one d.; ed Pembroke Coll., Cambridge, St Thomas' Hosp. Medical School, London; MRC Clinical Scientist, Dunn Nutrition Unit, Cambridge 1977–80; Sr Registrar, Royal Postgrad. Medical School, London 1980–82; Consultant Physician, Ninewells Hosp. and Medical School, Dundee 1982–91, Clinical Dir of Medicine 1991–94; Dir Tayside Research & Devt NHS Consortium, Dundee 1997–2000; Chair. Scottish Hosp. Endowments Research Trust 2000–01; Chief Scientist, Scottish Exec. Health Dept 2001–07 (retd); mem. Innogen Centre Advisory Cttee; Sr Distinction Advisor, Eastern Region for Scottish Advisory Cttee for Distinction Award 2004; Card Medal, Asscn of Physicians of GB and Ireland 1987. *Publications:* Endocrine Problems in Oncology 1984, Colour Atlas of Obesity 1990. *Leisure interest:* gardening, walking, reading, visiting gardens. *Address:* c/o Innogen Centre Advisory Committee, ESRC Innogen Centre, Technology Faculty, Development Policy and Practice Group, The Open University, Walton Hall, Milton Keynes, MK7 6AA, England.

JUNG, Volker, PhD; German business executive; *Chairman of the Supervisory Board, MAN Aktiengesellschaft;* b. 1939; Exec. Vice-Pres. Siemens AG 2001–03; currently Chair. Supervisory Bd, MAN AG; also Chair. Supervisory Bd EPCOS AG, Infinion Technologies AG, Siemens AE, Athens, Greece, Siemens Ltd, Johannesburg, SA; mem. Supervisory Bd Direkt Anlage Bank AG; Vice-Pres. Bundesverbandes der Deutschen Industrie (Fed. Asscn of German Industries). *Address:* MAN Aktiengesellschaft, Ungererstrasse 69, 80805 Munich, Germany (office). *Telephone:* 89360980 (office). *Fax:* 893609868299 (office). *Website:* www.man.de (office).

JÜNGEL, Eberhard Klaus, DTheol; German professor of theology; b. 5 Dec. 1934, Magdeburg; s. of Kurt Jüngel and Margarete Rothemann; ed Humboldtschule, Magdeburg, Katechetisches Seminar, Naumburg/Saale, Kirchliche Hochschule, Berlin and Univs of Zürich and Basel, Switzerland; asst, Kirchliche Hochschule (Sprachenkonvikt), East Berlin 1959–61, Lecturer in New Testament 1961–63, Lecturer in Systematic Theology 1963–66; ordained priest of the Evangelical Church 1962; Prof. of Systematic Theology and History of Dogma, Univ. of Zürich 1966–69; Prof. of Systematic Theology and Philosophy of Religion and Dir Inst. für Hermeneutik (interpretation of scripture), Univ. of Tübingen 1969–2003, Dean, Faculty of Evangelical Theology 1970–72, 1992–94; Ephorus Evangelisches Stift, Tübingen 1987–2005; Guest Prof. of Systematic Theology, Univ. of Halle-Wittenberg 1990–93, Univ. of Berlin 1994; Fellow Inst. for Advanced Study, Berlin; various appointments within Evangelical Church, etc.; mem. Heidelberg and Norwegian Acads, Academia Scientiarum et Artium Europaea, Salzburg, Akad. der Wissenschaften, Göttingen; Ordre pour le mérite 1992; Grosses Verdienstkreuz mit Stern des Verdienstordens 1994; Verdienstmedaille des Landes Baden-Württemberg; Hon. DD (Aberdeen) 1985; Dr hc (Greifswald) 2000; Karl Barth Prize 1986. *Publications:* more than 20 books including Paulus und Jesus 1962, Gottes Sein ist im Werden 1965, Unterwegs zur Sache 1972, Gott als Geheimnis der Welt 1977, Entsprechungen 1980, Glauben und Verstehen, Zum Theologiebegriff Rudolf Bultmanns 1985, Wertlose Wahrheit.

Zur Identität und Relevanz des christlichen Glaubens 1990, Das Evangelium von der Rechtfestigung des Gottlosen als Zentrum des Glaubens 1998, Indikative der Gnade-Imperative der Freiheit 2000, Ed. Religion in Geschichte und Gegenwart and five vols of sermons. *Address:* c/o Institut für Hermeneutik, Liebermeisterstrasse 12, 72076 Tübingen (office); Schwabstrasse 51, 72074 Tübingen, Germany (home).

JUNGERIUS, Pieter Dirk, DSc; Dutch professor of geography; b. 10 June 1933, Rÿnsburg; ed Gymnasium B, Leiden and Univ. of Amsterdam; Asst Univ. of Amsterdam 1955–59; Scientific Officer, Soil Survey of England and Wales 1959–63; on secondment to Soil and Land Use Survey, Ghana 1959, Ministry of Agric. E Nigeria 1960–63; Sr Lecturer in Physical Geography, Univ. of Amsterdam 1963–70; seasonal staff mem. Ministry of Mines and Tech. Surveys, Canada 1965–67; Prof. of Physical Geography, Climatology and Cartography, Univ. of Amsterdam 1970–; mem. Royal Netherlands Acad. of Sciences 1987. *Publications:* Soil Evidence of Tree Line Fluctuations, Alberta, Canada 1969, Quarternary Landscape Developments, Río Magdalena, Colombia 1976, Soils and Geomorphology 1985, Perception and Use of the Physical Environment in Peasant Societies 1986, Dunes of the European Coast: Geomorphology, Hydrology, Soils. *Address:* c/o Royal Netherlands Academy of Sciences, Het Trippenhuis, Kloveniersburgwal 29, 1011 JV Amsterdam, Netherlands.

JUNIPER, Tony, BSc, MSc; British environmental campaigner, ecologist and environmental writer; b. 24 Sept. 1960, Oxford; s. of the late Austin Wilfred Juniper and Constance Margaret Elliston; m. Sue Sparkes; three c.; ed Univ. of Bristol, Univ. Coll. London; began career with Birdlife Int. (conservation network); joined Friends of the Earth 1990, fmr campaigns and policy Dir, Dir Ilisu Dam campaign, Vice-Chair. Friends of the Earth International 2000–08, Exec. Dir Friends of the Earth, England, Wales and NI 2003–08; Founding Bd mem. Stop Climate Chaos 2005–; Special Adviser to Prince of Wales' Rainforest Project; Sr Assoc., Univ. of Cambridge Programme for Industry; sits on several advisory panels. *Publications:* Deserts of Trees: The Environmental and Social Impacts of Large-scale Tropical Reforestation in Response to Global Climate Change (co-author) 1992, Whose Hand on the Chainsaw? UK Government Policy and the Tropical Rainforests (co-author) 1992, Wildlife Bill 1995, Threatened Planet 1996, Parrots: A Guide to Parrots of the World (Juniper and Parr) (McColvin Medal for Outstanding Work of Reference, Library Asscn 1999) 1998, Spix's Macaw: The Race to Save the World's Rarest Bird 2002, How Many Light Bulbs Does It Take to Change A Planet? 2007, Saving Planet Earth 2007. *Leisure interests:* natural history, fishing, walking, writing. *Address:* c/o Friends of the Earth, 26–28 Underwood Street, London, N1 7JQ, England (office). *Website:* www.tonyjuniper.com.

JUNZ, Helen B., PhD; American economist and consultant; d. of Samson Bachner and Dobra Bachner (née Mandelbaum); ed Univ. of Amsterdam, Netherlands and New School of Social Research; Acting Chief, Consumer Price Section, Nat. Industrial Conf. Bd, New York 1953–58; Research Officer, Nat. Inst. of Social and Economic Research, London 1958–60; Economist, Bureau of Economic Analysis, US Dept of Commerce, Washington, DC 1960–62; Adviser, Div. of Int. Finance, Bd of Govs, US Fed. Reserve System, Washington, DC 1962–77; Adviser, OECD, Paris 1967–69; Sr Int. Economist, Council of Econ. Advisers, The White House, Washington, DC 1975–77; Deputy Asst Sec., Office of Asst Sec. for Int. Affairs, US Dept of the Treasury, Washington, DC 1977–79; Vice-Pres. and Sr Adviser, First National Bank of Chicago 1979–80; Vice-Pres. Townsend Greenspan and Co. Inc., New York 1980–82; Sr Adviser, European Dept, IMF, Washington, DC 1982–87, Deputy Dir Exchange and Trade Relations Dept 1987–89, Special Trade Rep. and Dir, Geneva Office 1989–94, Dir Gold Econ. Service, World Gold Council, Geneva and London 1994–96; Pres. HBJ Int. (consultancy), London 1996–; Consulting Research Dir, Financial Assets, Presidential Advisory Comm. on Holocaust Assets in the USA 1998–2000; Contrib., Ind. Cttee of Eminent Persons (Volcker Cttee) 1996–99; Researcher, Int. Comm. on Holocaust Era Insurance Claims; mem. Ind. Comm. of Experts, Switzerland (Bergier Comm.) 2001–02; Charles H. Revson Foundation Fellow, Center for Advanced Holocaust Studies, US Holocaust Memorial Museum 2003–04; Claims Resolution Tribunal Special Master, Holocaust Victim Assets Litigation (Swiss Banks), New York 2004–08; currently Researcher, Jerusalem Center for Public Affairs. *Publications:* Where Did All the Money Go? 2002; numerous articles in professional journals. *Address:* HBJ International, 39 Chalcot Square, London, NW1 8YP, England (office).

JUPPÉ, Alain Marie; French politician and fmr government official; *Mayor of Bordeaux;* b. 15 Aug. 1945, Mont-de-Marsan, Landes; s. of Robert Juppé and Marie Juppé (née Darroze); m. 1st Christine Leblond 1965; one s. one d.; m. 2nd Isabelle Legrand-Bodin 1993; one d.; ed Lycée Louis-le-Grand, Paris, Ecole normale supérieure, Inst. d'études politiques, Paris and Ecole Nat. d'Admin; Insp. of Finance 1972; Office of Prime Minister Jacques Chirac (q.v.) June–Aug. 1976; tech. adviser, Office of Minister of Cooperation 1976–78; Nat. del. of RPR 1976–78, Nat. Sec. of RPR with responsibility for econ. and social recovery 1984–88, Sec.-Gen. 1988–95, Acting Pres. 1994–95, Pres. 1995–97; tech. adviser, Office of Mayor of Paris (Jacques Chirac) 1978; Dir-Gen. with responsibility for finance and econ. affairs, Commune de Paris 1980; Councillor, 18th arrondissement, Paris 1983–95; Second Asst to Mayor of Paris in charge of budget and financial affairs 1983–95; Deputy to Nat. Ass. from Paris 1988–97, from Gironde 1997–; Mayor of Bordeaux 1995–2001, 2001–04, 2006–; mem. European Parl. 1984–86, 1989–93; Deputy to Minister of Economy, Finance and Privatization with responsibility for budget 1986–88; Minister of Foreign Affairs 1993–95; Prime Minister of France 1995–97; cleared of embezzlement charges 1999; Pres. Union pour la majorité presidentielle (UMP) 2002–04 (resgnd); Minister of State for Ecology and Sustainable Devt May–June 2007; Grand Officier, Légion d'honneur 2009, Grand Cross of Merit, Sovereign Order of Malta. *Publications:* La Tentation de Venise 1993, Entre Nous 1996, Montesquieu, Le moderne 1999, Entre quatre z'yeux (with Serge July q.v.) France mon pays – Lettres d'un voyageur 2006, Je ne mangerai plus de cerises en hiver 2009. *Address:* Mairie, place Pey-Berland, 33077 Bordeaux, France (office). *Website:* www.bordeaux.fr (office).

JURGENSEN, William G. (Jerry), BCom, MBA; American insurance industry executive; *CEO, Nationwide Mutual Insurance Company;* m. Patty Jurgensen; two c.; ed Creighton Univ., Omaha, Neb.; 17 years with Norwest Corpn, various man. positions including Pres. and CEO, Norwest Investment Services and later Exec. Vice-Pres., Corp. Banking; Man. First Chicago NBD Corpn –1998, Exec. Vice-Pres. Bank One Corpn (following merger) 1998–2000; CEO Nationwide Mutual Insurance Co. 2000–; mem. Bd Dirs Achieve, Inc., ConAgra Foods, Inc.; Dir Greater Columbus Chamber of Commerce, Law Enforcement Foundation of Ohio, Nationwide Children's Hosp.; Chair. Gov.'s Comm. on Teaching Success 2001–03; Chair. 2002 Campaign for United Way of Cen. Ohio; Co-Chair. Ohio Gov.'s Public-Private Collaborative Comm.; mem. Columbus Downtown Devt Corpn, Ohio Business Roundtable, Financial Services Roundtable, Columbus Partnership, Ohio State Univ. Hosp., Business Higher Educ. Forum; Trustee, Loyola Univ., Newberry Library. *Address:* Nationwide Mutual Insurance Co., One Nationwide Plaza, Columbus, OH 43215-2220, USA (office). *Telephone:* (614) 249-7111 (office). *Fax:* (614) 249-7705 (office). *E-mail:* info@nationwide.com (office). *Website:* www.nationwide.com (office).

JÜRGENSON, Sven, BSc; Estonian diplomatist; *Foreign Policy Adviser to the President of Estonia;* b. 2 April 1962; m.; three c.; ed Tallinn Tech. Univ., Institut Internationale d'Admin Publique, Paris, Ingenieurhochschule, Dresden; Jr Research Assoc. and Lecturer in Data Processing, Tallinn Tech. Univ. 1987–90; Sr Assoc., Estonian Inst. 1990–91; Counsellor, Chargé d'affaires, Helsinki, Counsellor, Office for Estonian Culture, Helsinki 1991–93; Minister-Counsellor, Chargé d'affaires, Embassy, Vienna 1993–95; Deputy Political Dir, Ministry of Foreign Affairs, then Dir Div. for Int. Orgs and Security Policy 1995–96, Dir-Gen. Political Dept 1996–98; Amb. to Turkey 1996–98; Perm. Rep. to UN 1998–2000; Amb. to USA 2000–03; Under-Sec. for Political Affairs and for EU Affairs, Ministry of Foreign Affairs 2004–06; Foreign Policy Adviser to the Pres. of Estonia 2006–. *Address:* Office of the President, A. Weizenbergi 39, 15050 Tallinn, Estonia (office). *Telephone:* 6316202 (office). *Fax:* 6316250 (office). *E-mail:* vpinfo@vpk.ee (office). *Website:* www.kadriorg.ee (office).

JURINAC, Srebrenka (Sena); Austrian singer (soprano); b. 24 Oct. 1921, Travnik, Yugoslavia; d. of Dr Ljudevit Jurinac and Christine Cerv-Jurinac; m. Dr Josef Lederle (died 2005); ed Gymnasium and Music Acad., Zagreb, Yugoslavia; studied under Maria Kostrenćić; first appearance as Mimi, Zagreb 1942; mem. Vienna State Opera Co. 1944–82; now works as voice teacher; has sung at Salzburg, Glyndebourne Festivals, etc.; sang in Der Rosenkavalier 1966 and 1971, Tosca 1968, Iphigénie en Tauride 1973, Covent Garden; Austrian State Kammersängerin 1951; Ehrenkreuz für Wissenchaft und Kunst 1961, Grosses Ehrenzeichen für Verdienste um die Republik Österreich 1967, Ehrenring der Wiener Staatsoper 1968, Ehrenmitglied der Wiener Staatsoper 1971, Silver Rose of the Vienna Philharmonic Orchestra 2001. *Films:* Lisinski 1943, Der Rosenkavalier 1960. *Television:* Schwester Angelica (Puccini) (ORF) 1959, Otello (Verdi) (ORF) 1965, Wozzeck (Berg) (ZDF) 1970, Hänsel und Gretel (ORF) 1981. *Recordings:* Fidelio, Orfeo, Così fan tutte, Don Giovanni, Idomeneo, Le Nozze di Figaro, Ariadne auf Naxos, Der Rosenkavalier, Eugene Onegin, Lieder by Schumann and Richard Strauss, Sena Jurinac at the Vienna State Opera 2006. *Leisure interests:* gardening, cats. *Address:* c/o Ursula Tamussino, Wehrgasse 11A, 1050 Vienna, Austria (office). *Telephone:* (1) 5879295 (home). *Fax:* (1) 5879295 (office). *E-mail:* ursula.tamussino@chello.at (office).

JURKOVIĆ, Pero, PhD; Croatian economist; b. 4 June 1936, Brštanica, Neum, Bosnia and Herzegovina; ed Univs of Sarajevo, Skopje and Zagreb; chief accountant, construction materials industry Neretva, Čapljina 1956–57; Officer for Planning, Municipality of Čapljina 1960–61, Chief Officer for Agric. 1961–63; Dir Inst. of Economy, Mostar 1963–67; Assoc. to Adviser, Econ. Inst., Zagreb (also Assoc. Prof., Foreign Trade School and Faculties of Econs Zagreb and Mostar) 1967–80; Prof., Faculty of Econs, Zagreb 1980–92; currently lectures at Univ. of Zagreb Grad. School of Econs and Business; Gov. Nat. Bank of Croatia 1992–96; apptd Chief Econ. Adviser to Pres. of Croatia 1997; mem. Int. Inst. for Financing, Saarbrücken, Int. Asscn of Economists; Guest Lecturer, Univs of Rotterdam, London, Lexington and Florida; B. Adžija and M. Mirković awards. *Publications:* more than 150 publs including System of Public Financing (with Ksente Bogoev) 1977, Introduction to the Theory of Economic Policy 1984, Fundamentals of the Economics of Public Services 1987, Commercial Finances 1987, Fiscal Policy 1989. *Address:* University of Zagreb Graduate School of Economics and Business, Room 101, Trg. J. F. Kennedy 6, 10000 Zagreb, Croatia (office). *Telephone:* (1) 238-3199 (office). *Fax:* (1) 233-5633 (office). *E-mail:* pero.jurkovic@efzg.hr (office). *Website:* www.efzg.hr (office).

JUROWSKI, Vladimir; Russian conductor; *Principal Conductor, London Philharmonic Orchestra;* b. 1972, Moscow; ed Music Acad., Berlin and Dresden, Germany; chief conductor, Sibelius Orchestra, Berlin 1993–96; founder and conductor, United Berlin ensemble, performing modern music; int. debut conducting May Night by Rimsky-Korsakov, Wexford Festival 1995; fmr prin. guest conductor, Orchestra Sinfonica Verdi, Milan; prin. guest conductor Teatro Comunale, Bologna 2001; Music Dir Glyndebourne Festival Opera 2001–07; Prin. Guest Conductor London Philharmonic Orchestra 2003–06, Prin. Conductor 2007–; Music Dir Russian Nat. Orchestra 2006–; has conducted in major venues worldwide, including Metropolitan Opera

(New York), Opera Bastille (Paris), Komische Oper (Berlin), Teatro Comunale (Bologna), Teatro Real (Madrid), Royal Opera House (London), Welsh Nat. Opera (Cardiff), ENO (London), Edin. Festival; Royal Philharmonic Soc. Conductor Award 2007. *Recordings include:* Werther by Massenet, Shostakovich Symphonies 1 and 6 2006. *Address:* Stage Door, Via Marconi 71, 40122 Bologna, Italy (office); London Philharmonic Orchestra, 89 Albert Embankment, London, SE1 7TP, England (office); Russian National Orchestra, Orchestrion Garibaldi, 19 Moscow 117335, Russia (office). *Telephone:* (051) 19984750 (office). *Fax:* (051) 19984779 (office). *E-mail:* info@stagedoor.it (office). *Website:* www.stagedoor.it (office); www.lpo.co.uk (office); www.rno .ru.

JURŠĖNAS, Česlovas; Lithuanian journalist, editor and politician; b. 18 May 1938, Panižiškė village, Švenčioniai Co. (now Ignalina Dist); m. Jadvyga Juršėnas; one s.; ed Ignalina Secondary School, Vilnius Univ., Higher Party School, Leningrad (now St Petersburg); awarded journalist diploma 1960, worked as journalist for 15 years, first in editorial offices of weekly newspaper Statyba (Construction) and daily newspaper Tiesa (Truth), int. reviewer at Lithuania Radio and Television from 1964, Ed.-in-Chief TV Information broadcasts, later edited TV programme Atgimimo Banga (Wave of Revival) and other broadcasts; worked at Cen. Cttee and Council of Ministers of Lithuanian CP 1973–78; Head of editorial office of Vakarinės Naujienos (Evening News) 1978–83; first Press Officer for Govt of Lithuania 1989, later responsible for relations with Supreme Council; with others, signed Act on the Re-establishment of the State of the Repub. of Lithuania 11 March 1990; stood for elections as ind. cand. of LCP, worked in Comm. on State Re-establishment and the Constitution, elected to Supreme Council – Reconstituent Seimas 1990–92, elected Deputy Elder of the Parl. 1992, mem. Seimas (Parl.) for Ignalina-Švenčioniai single-member constituency No. 53 1992–, Deputy Chair. 6th Seimas, later Chair., worked on Cttee on Legal Affairs and headed Opposition parl. group of Lithuanian Democratic Labour Party (LDLP) during 7th Seimas, Deputy Chair. 8th Seimas 2000–02, First Deputy Chair. 2002–04, July–Nov. 2004, Acting Chair. Seimas April–July 2004, Chair. Seimas Del. to Ass. of Lithuanian and Ukrainian Parls, Chair. Parl. Group for Relations with the People's Repub. of China, Speaker of the Seimas 2008; mem. Council of Švenčioniai Dist 1997–2000; active participant in separation of LCP from CPSU and ind. reorganization of LCP; mem. Presidium of LDLP Council 1990–, Chair. of party 1996–2001, First Deputy Chair. Lithuanian Social Democratic Party (LSDP—Lietuvos Socialdemokratų Partija) following unification of Social Democrats (SDPL) and LDLP 2001–; mem. Journalists' Union of Lithuania; mem. Editorial Science Council of the Lithuanian General Encyclopaedia and the Courts Council; Pres. Lithuanian Chess Fed.; Citizen of Honour of the Švenčionių Dist; Grand Cross of the Order of Vytautas the Great; Dr hc (Univ. of Lithuania); Gold Medal, Ignalina Secondary School. *Publications:* has published several books on politics and world affairs. *Leisure interests:* playing chess, collecting writings and caricatures of famous contemporary politicians. *Address:* Seimas, 01109 Vilnius, Gedimino pr. 53, Lithuania (office). *Telephone:* (5) 239-6626 (office). *Fax:* (5) 239-6077 (office). *E-mail:* Ceslovas.Jursenas@lrs.lt (office); cejurs@lrs.lt (office). *Website:* www .lrs.lt (office).

JUSKO, Marián, DPhil; Slovak banker; b. 24 March 1956, Prešov; m.; one c.; ed Univ. of Econs, Bratislava; lecturer Univ. of Econs, Bratislava 1979–90, adviser, Slovak Nat. Council 1990; Head of Banking Analyses and Prognoses, State Bank of Czechoslovakia 1991; Deputy Minister, Ministry of Admin. and Privatization of Nat. Property of Slovak Repub.; Chair. Bd Nat. Property Fund 1991–92; mem. man. team State Bank of Czechoslovakia for Slovakia, Bratislava 1992; Vice-Gov. Nat. Bank of Slovakia 1993–99, Gov. 1999–2004. *Address:* c/o National Bank of Slovakia, Imricha Karvaša 1, 813 25 Bratislava, Slovakia (office). *E-mail:* igor.barat@nbs.sk (office).

JUSYS, Oskaras; Lithuanian diplomatist; *Undersecretary, Ministry of Foreign Affairs;* b. 13 Jan. 1954, Anyksciai Region; m.; one s.; ed Vilnius Univ., V. Lomonosov Univ., Moscow; Sr Lecturer, Faculty of Law, Vilnius Univ. 1981–1985, Assoc. Prof. 1986–90; Scientific Scholarship, IREX Exchange Programme, Law School, Columbia Univ., New York, USA 1985–86; Dir Legal Dept, Ministry of Foreign Affairs 1990–92, Counsellor to Minister of Foreign Affairs 1993–94; Amb., Perm. Rep. of Lithuania to UN 1994–2000; Deputy Minister of Foreign Affairs 2000–01, currently Undersec.; fmr Perm. Rep. to EU; Dir Lithuanian Br. of US law firm McDermott, Will & Emery 1993–94. *Leisure interests:* jazz, basketball. *Address:* Ministry of

Foreign Affairs, J. Tumo-Vaižganto 2, Vilnius 01511, Lithuania (office). *Telephone:* (5) 236-2444 (office). *Fax:* (5) 231-3090 (office). *E-mail:* urm@urm.lt (office). *Website:* www.urm.lt (office).

JUTTERSTRÖM, Christina, BA; Swedish journalist, broadcasting executive and academic; *Chairman, Statens museer för världskultur (National Museums of World Culture);* b. 27 March 1940, Stockholm; d. of Siri Lewell and Gosta Lewell; m. 1st Stig Jutterstroem 1961; m. 2nd Ingemar Odlander 1978; two d.; ed Uppsala Univ.; political reporter, Swedish Radio and TV 1967–75, Africa Corresp. 1975–77, Man. Ed. Radio News and Commentaries 1977–81; Ed.-in-Chief Dagens Nyheter 1982–95, Expressen 1995–96; Prof. of Journalism, Univ. of Gothenburg 1997; Dir-Gen. Sveriges Television (SVT), Sweden's public service TV broadcaster 2001–06; Chair. Bd of Dirs Statens museer för världskultur (Nat. Museums of World Culture), Göteborg 2007–. *Address:* National Museums of World Culture, Box 5306, 402 27 Göteborg, Sweden (office). *Telephone:* (31) 63-27-00 (office). *Fax:* (31) 63-27-10 (office). *E-mail:* info@smvk.se (office). *Website:* www.smvk.se (office).

JUVENALY, Metropolitan (Vladimir Poyarkov); Russian ecclesiastic; b. 22 Sept. 1935, Yaroslavl; ed Leningrad Seminary, Moscow Theological Acad.; hieromonk 1960; Sec. Dept of Foreign Relations, Moscow Patriarchy 1960; teacher, Moscow Seminary 1961–62; Ed. Golos Pravoslavia (magazine) 1962–63; Dean Russian Orthodox Church in West Berlin 1962–63; ordained as archimandrite 1963; Chief Russian Holy Mission in Jerusalem 1963–64; Deputy Chair. Dept of Foreign Relations, Moscow Patriarchy 1964–72, Chair. 1972–81; consecrated Bishop 1965; Bishop of Zaraisk, Vicar of Moscow Diocese 1965–69; Bishop of Tula and Belev, Archbishop, Metropolitan 1969–77; Perm. mem. Holy Synod 1972–; Metropolitan of Krutitsy and Kolomna 1977–; Chair. Synodal Comm. on Canonization of Saints; Hon. Citizen of Moscow region, Podolsk, Kolomna, Dmitrov; Hon. mem. Leningrad (now St Petersburg) Theological Seminary 1973–, Moscow Theological Seminary 1974–; Order of Peoples' Friendship 1985, Order of Honour 2000, Order of Services to the Fatherland 2006 and numerous other state and church decorations. *Publications:* numerous articles in Journal of Moscow Patriarchate. *Address:* Moscow Diocese, Novodevichy Proezd 1/1, 119435 Moscow, Russia. *Telephone:* (495) 246-08-81.

JYOTI, Roop, MBA MPA; Nepalese business executive and fmr politician; *Vice-Chairman, Jyoti Group;* b. Sept. 1948; s. of the late Shri Maniharsha Jyoti; ed Indian Inst. of Tech., Bombay, Harvard Univ.; qualified as chemical engineer; exec. positions at several Jyoti Group enterprises (family-owned), then Vice-Chair. (following death of his father); fmrly Nat. Advisor to Resident Rep. of UNDP in Nepal; mem. Tariff Bd, Govt of Nepal; Minister of Finance 2005–06; mem. Senate, Tribhuvan Univ.; mem. Trust of Nepal Vipassana Centre. *Address:* Jyoti Group, Jyoti Bhawan, Kantipath, Kathmandu, Nepal (office). *E-mail:* info@jyotigroup.org (office). *Website:* www.jyotigroup.org (office).

JYRÄNKI, Antero, DIur; Finnish professor of constitutional law; *Professor, University of Turku;* b. 9 Aug. 1933, Hamina; two s. one d.; ed Univ. of Helsinki; Assoc. Prof. of Public Law, Univ. of Tampere 1966–70; Gen. Sec. to the Pres. of the Repub. 1970–73; Sr Research Fellow, Acad. of Finland 1974–77; Vice-Chair., Comm. on the Revision of the Constitution 1970–74; Assoc. Prof. of Public Law, Univ. of Tampere 1977–79; Prof. of Constitutional and Int. Law, Univ. of Turku 1980–, Dean, Law Faculty 1981–83, 1991–93; Research Prof., Acad. of Finland 1983–87; Pres. Finnish Asscn of Constitutional Law 1982–88; mem. Council of the Int. Asscn of Constitutional Law 1983–, mem. Exec. Cttee 1993–; mem. Admin. Bd Finnish Broadcasting Corpn 1983–99, Finnish Acad. of Science 1987–; Perm. Expert for the Constitutional Comm. of Parl. 1982–. *Publications:* Sotavoiman ylin päällikkyys (The Commander-in-Chief of the Armed Forces) 1967, Yleisradio ja sananvapaus (The Freedom of Expression and Broadcasting) 1969, Perustuslaki ja yhteiskunnan muutos (The Constitution and the Change of Society) 1973, Presidentti (The President of the Republic) 1978, Lakien laki (The Law of the Laws) 1989, Kolme vuotta linnassa (Three Years in the Presidential Castle) 1990, Valta ja vapaus (Power and Freedom) 1994, Uusi perustuslakimme (Our New Constitution) 2000. *Leisure interests:* languages, literature, problems of mass communication. *Address:* Faculty of Law, Room 315, University of Turku, 20014 Turku, Finland (office). *Telephone:* (2) 3335522 (office). *E-mail:* antero.jyranki@utu.fi (office). *Website:* www.law.utu.fi/english (home).

K

KA, Ibra Deguène; Senegalese diplomatist; b. 4 Jan. 1939, Koul-Mecke, Thies Region; ed Ecole Nationale d'Admin et de Magistrature; Chief Div. of UN Affairs, Ministry of Foreign Affairs 1969–72, Chef de Cabinet 1972–73, Exec. Sec. Senegalo-Gambian Interministerial Cttee 1973–78; Amb. to several countries, including Algeria, Tunisia, Liberia, USA, Argentina, Mexico and Switzerland 1978–96; Perm. Rep. to UN, New York 1996–2001; Chair. UN Group of Experts to monitor Security Council arms embargo against Democratic Republic of the Congo 2005; mem. UN Special Cttee investigating Israeli activities in the Occupied Territories 1994; Founding mem. UN Asscn Senegal; Commdr Nat. Order of Merit and other decorations. *Address:* c/o Ministry of Foreign Affairs, place de l'Indépendance, BP 4044, Dakar, Senegal.

KÄÄRIÄINEN, Seppo, PhD; Finnish politician; b. 29 March 1948, Ilisalmi, Kirma; m. Pirjo Terttu Tuulikki (née Kolehmainen) 1975; one s.; Party Sec., Finnish Centre Party 1980–90, Chair. Party Parl. Group 1991–93, Vice-Pres. 1994–2000; mem. Suomen Eduskunta (Parl.) 1987–, mem. Foreign Affairs Cttee 1987–93, 1999–2000, Finance Cttee 1990–91, 1999–2003, Vice-Chair. Commerce Cttee 1995–99, Chair. Defence Cttee 2003; Minister of Trade and Industry 1993–95; Minister, Ministry for Foreign Affairs 1993–95; Minister of Defence 2004–07; First Deputy Speaker, Eduskunta 2007–; Chair. Del. to Jt Comm. of European Parl. and Eduskunta 1993; Pres. Bd of Dirs Itä-Suomen Ammattitaito Ry 2003–; Vice-Pres. Bd of Dirs Finnvera Oy 1999–2003. *Publications:* Suomen oma tie (Finland's Own Way) 1986, Haastaja (The Contender) 1989, The Strategic Choices of the Centre Party 1964–2001 2002. *Leisure interests:* walking, marathons. *Address:* Suomen Eduskunta, Mannerheimintie 30, 00102 Helsinki, Finland (office). *Telephone:* (9) 4321 (office). *Fax:* (9) 4322274 (office). *E-mail:* eduskunta@eduskunta.fi (office). *Website:* www.eduskunta.fi (office).

KAAS, Patricia; French singer; b. 5 Dec. 1966, Stiring Wendel, nr Forbach; tea-dance and night-club appearances aged 13; first single, Jalouse aged 17; first major success with Mademoiselle Chante le Blues; toured Viet Nam and Cambodia 1994; tours world-wide; six Victoires de la Musique, two World Music Awards; de Gaulle-Adenauer Prize 2001. *Recordings include:* albums: Mademoiselle Chante 1988, Scène de Vie 1990, Carnet de Scène (live) 1991, Je Te Dis Vous 1993, Tour de Charme (live) 1994, Café noir 1996, Dans Ma Chair 1997, Rendez-vous 1998, Le mot de passe 1999, Patricia Kaas Live 2000, Rien ne s'arrête 2001, Piano bar 2002, Sexe fort 2004, Toute la Musique 2005, Kabaret 2008. *Publications:* Patricia Kaas – Tour de Charme 1994. *Address:* Attitude, 71 rue Robespierre, 93100 Montreuil, France. *Website:* www.kabaretkaas.com/kabaret.

KABA, Sidiki; Senegalese human rights organization executive and lawyer; *President, International Federation for Human Rights;* human rights lawyer assoc. with cases in Senegal, Chad, Côte d'Ivoire, Guinea; Pres. Nat. Org. for Human Rights, Senegal; Vice-Pres. Int. Fed. of the League for Human Rights, Paris, Pres. 2001–. *Address:* Fédération Internationale des Droits de l'Homme, 17 Passage de la Main d'Or, 75011 Paris, France (office). *Telephone:* 1-43-55-25-18 (office). *Fax:* 1-43-55-18-80 (office). *E-mail:* fidh@fidh.org (office). *Website:* www.fidh.org (office).

KABAKOV, Alexander Abramovich; Russian writer and journalist; *Departmental Editor, Commersant Publishing;* b. 22 Oct. 1943, Novosibirsk; m.; one d.; ed Dniepropetrovsk Univ.; engineer, space rocket production co. 1965–70; journalist, Gudok 1972–88; columnist, then Deputy Ed.-in-Chief Moscow News 1988–97; special corresp., Commersant Publishing 1997–2000, Departmental Ed. 2000–; columnist, New Media Publishing Group 2002–; Chief Ed. journal Sak Voyazh; Chair. jury for Russian Booker Prize 2006; first literary publ. 1975; Moscow Journalists' Union Prize 1989, Best Pens of Russia Award 1999, Short Story of the Year Award 1999. *Publications:* Cheap Novel 1982, Cafe Yunost 1984, Oil, Comma, Canvas 1986, Approach of Kristapovich (trilogy) 1985, Obviously False Fabrications (collection of short stories) 1989, No Return 1989, Story-Teller 1991, Imposter 1992, The Last Hero (novel) 1995, Selected Prose 1997, One Day from the Life of a Fool 1998, The Arrival Hall 1999, Youth Café 2000, The Journey of an Extrapolator 2000, The Tardy Visitor 2001, Qualified as Escape 2001, Survivor 2003, Everything Corrected (novel) (Apollon Grigoryev Prize 2005, Big Book Prize 2006) 2004, Moscow Stories (Prose of the Year Prize 2005, Ivan Bunin Prize 2006) 2005. *Leisure interest:* jazz. *Address:* New Media Publishing Group, Pyatnitzkaya str. 55, Moscow, Russia (office). *Telephone:* (495) 411-63-90 (office); (495) 994-83-45 (home); (495) 101-77-24.

KABARITI, Abdul Karim A., BA; Jordanian banking executive and fmr politician; *Chairman and CEO, Jordan Kuwait Bank;* b. 15 Dec. 1949, Amman; m.; two c.; ed St Edward's Univ., Austin, Tex., USA, American Univ. of Beirut, Lebanon; licensed financial adviser, New York –1986; proprietor of a money exchange co.; mem. bd of dirs of many cos; mem. House of Reps for Governorate of Ma'an 1989–93, 1993–95, Minister of Tourism 1989–92, of Labour 1992–93, of Foreign Affairs 1995–96, Prime Minister, Minister of Defence and of Foreign Affairs 1996–97; currently Chair. and CEO Jordan Kuwait Bank; mem. Bd of Dirs Burgan Bank; fmr Chair. Foreign Relations Cttee of House of Reps; fmr Head, Royal Court; Chair. Bd Social Security Corpn 1992–93; Chair. Bd Vocational Training Corpn 1992–93. *Leisure interests:* water skiing, music. *Address:* Jordan Kuwait Bank, POB 9776, Amman 11194, Jordan (office). *Telephone:* (6) 5629400 (office). *Fax:* (6) 5687452 (office). *E-mail:* webmaster@jkbank.com.jo (office). *Website:* www.jordan-kuwait-bank.com (office).

KABBAH, Alhaji Ahmed Tejan, BEcons; Sierra Leonean fmr head of state; b. 16 Feb. 1932, Pendembu, Kailahun Dist, Eastern Prov.; m. Patricia Tucker (deceased); four c.; ed St Edward's School, Freetown, Cardiff Coll. of Tech., Univ. Coll. Aberystwyth, Wales; called to the Bar (Gray's Inn), London; fmr Dist Commr Moyamba, Kono, Bombali and Kambia Dists., Deputy Sec., Ministry of Social Welfare and Perm. Sec., Ministries of Educ. and of Trade and Industry; joined staff of UN, served as UNDP Rep. Lesotho 1973, Tanzania and Uganda 1976, temporarily assigned to Zimbabwe 1980, apptd head of Eastern and Southern Africa Div. 1979, Deputy Personnel Dir, then Dir, Div. of Admin. and Man. 1981–92; mem. Sierra Leone People's Party (SLPP) 1954–; Chair. Nat. Advisory Council 1992–96; Pres. of Sierra Leone 1996–97, March 1998–2007, also Minister of Defence and C-in-C of Armed Forces; fmr Chancellor Univ. of Sierra Leone; Grand Commdr Order of the Repub. of Sierra Leone; Hon. LLD (Univ. of Sierra Leone), (Southern Connecticut State Univ.) 2001. *Address:* Sierra Leone People's Party, 29 Rawdon Street, Freetown, Sierra Leone (office). *Telephone:* (22) 228222 (office). *Fax:* (22) 228222 (office). *E-mail:* sq-slpp@hotmail.com (office). *Website:* www.slpp.ws (office).

KABBAJ, Omar; Moroccan international organization official; b. 15 Aug. 1942, Rabat; s. of Ahmed Kabbaj and Khadija Moulato; m. Saida Lebbar; four s.; ed Ecole Supérieure de Commerce et d'Administration des Entreprises de Toulouse, France; mem. Exec. Bd IMF and World Bank; fmr Minister of Econ. Affairs Minister; Exec. Pres. and Chair. Bd of Dirs African Devt Bank (ADB) and African Devt Fund (ADF) 1995–2005, now Hon. Pres.; fmr mem. UN Comm. on HIV/AIDS and Governance in Africa (CHGA); Kt of the Order of the Throne of Morocco, Grand Officer of the Nat. Order of Tunisia, Officer of the Nat. Order of Burkina Faso. *Publications:* The Challenge of African Development 2003. *Address:* c/o African Development Bank, rue Joseph Anoma, 01 BP 1387, Abidjan 01, Côte d'Ivoire (office).

KABBARAH, Mohammad Bashar, PhD; Syrian central banker and economist; b. 1944, Damascus; s. of M. Jamil and Hikmat Kouatly; m. 1968; three c.; ed American Univ. Washington, DC, Western Illinois Univ. and American Univ. of Beirut; Section Head, Office of Gen. Studies, The Presidency 1973–74; Economist, Econ. Bureau, The Presidency 1974–77, Sr Economist 1977–82; Adviser/Dir Econ. Bureau of Pres. of Syria 1982–95; Gov. Cen. Bank of Syria 1995–2004; Arab Monetary Fund; Chief Ed. The Syrian Econ. Journal 1975–84; Alt. Gov. IMF; Alt. Exec. Dir Arab Fund for Econ. and Social Devt, Programme for Financing Arab Trade; mem. Syrian Higher Planning Bd; Washington-Lincoln Honor Award 1968, Hall of Nations Award 1969–70, Union of Arab Banks Award 1996. *Publications:* more than 20 papers and articles in professional journals and contribs. to The Arabic Encyclopedia. *Leisure interests:* historical reading, antiquities, agronomy, sports. *Address:* c/o Central Bank of Syria, PO Box 2254, At-Tajrida al-Mughrabia Square, Damascus, Syria. *Telephone:* (11) 2220550.

KABERUKA, Donald, MPhil, PhD; Rwandan economist, politician and international organization official; *Executive President and Chairman, African Development Bank;* ed Tanzania, Glasgow Univ., LSE; early career in banking industry; fmr State Minister for Budget and Planning; Minister of Finance and Econ. Planning 1997–2005; Exec. Pres. and Chair. African Devt Bank 2005–; Chair. Bd of Govs Africa Trade Insurance Agency (ATI) 2003–; Chair. Nat. Africa Peer Review Comm. 2004–; Chair. PTA Bank (East, Central and Southern Africa devt bank) 2001-02; Vice-Chair. Nat. AIDS Comm. 2002–03. *Address:* African Development Bank, rue Joseph Anoma, 01 BP 1387, Abidjan 01, Côte d'Ivoire (office). *Telephone:* 20-20-44-44 (office). *Fax:* 20-20-49-59 (office). *E-mail:* afdb@afdb.org (office). *Website:* www.afdb.org (office).

KABILA KABANGE, Maj.-Gen. Joseph, BA; Democratic Republic of the Congo army officer and head of state; *President;* b. 4 June 1970, Sud-Kivu Prov.; s. of the late Laurent-Désiré Kabila; m. Olive Lembe; one d.; ed Nat. Defence Univ., People's Repub. of China; Deputy Chair. Jt Chiefs of Staff, Congolese Armed Forces 1998–2000, Army Chief of Staff 2000–01; Pres. Democratic Repub. of the Congo 2001–, fmrly Minister of Defence; Dr hc (Hankuk Univ., S Korea). *Address:* Office of the President, Hôtel du Conseil Exécutif, ave de Lemera, Kinshasa-Gombé, Democratic Republic of the Congo (office). *Telephone:* (12) 30892 (office). *E-mail:* pr@presidentrdc.cd (office). *Website:* www.presidentrdc.cd (office).

KABIRI, Muhiddin; Tajikistani politician; *Chairman, Islamic Rebirth Party of Tajikistan;* b. (Muhiddin Tilloyevich Kabirov), 1966, Fayzobod dist; m.; five c.; ed Tajik Nat. Univ., Sane Univ., Yemen, Diplomatic Acad., Moscow; aide to Chair. Islamic Rebirth Party of Tajikistan 1997–2000, Deputy Chair. 2000–04, First Deputy Chair. 2004–06, Chair. 2006–; mem. Majlisi Namoyandagon (Ass. of Reps) 2005–, mem. Cttee on Science, Educ., Culture and Youth Police. *Address:* Islamic Rebirth Party of Tajikistan, 734000 Dushanbe, pos. Kalinina, Kuchai Tukhagul 55, Tajikistan (office). *Telephone:* (372) 27-25-30 (office). *Fax:* (372) 27-53-93 (office).

KABORÉ, Roch Marc-Christian; Burkinabè politician; *President, Congrès pour la démocratie et le progrès;* Minister of State in charge of Relations with Insts 1990–94; Prime Minister of Burkina Faso 1994–96; mem. Organisation pour la démocratie populaire/Mouvement du travail (ODP/MT), First Vice-Pres., then Pres. Congrès pour la démocratie et le progrès (CDP) (f. 1996 as successor to ODP/MT) 1996–. *Address:* Congrès pour la démocratie et le progrès, 1146 ave Dr Kwamé N'Krumah, 01 BP 1605, Ouagadougou 01, Burkina Faso (office). *Telephone:* 50-31-50-18 (office). *Fax:* 50-31-43-93 (office).

E-mail: contact@cdp-burkina.org (office). *Website:* www.cdp-burkina.org (office).

KAC, Eduardo, BA, MFA, PhD; Brazilian/American artist and writer; *Professor of Art and Technology, School of Art, Art Institute of Chicago;* b. 1962, Rio de Janeiro, Brazil; ed Pontifícia Universidade Católica do Rio de Janeiro, School of the Art Institute of Chicago, Univ. of Wales, UK; pioneer of holopoetry, telepresence art, biotelematics, transgenic art; moved to Chicago 1989; Prof. of Art and Tech., School of Art, Art Inst. of Chicago 1997–; mem. Editorial Bd Leonardo (journal); Shearwater Foundation Holography Award 1995, Leonardo Award for Excellence 1998, award for telepresence work Uirapuru, InterCommunication Centre Biennale, Tokyo 1999. *Publications:* New Media Poetry: Poetic Innovation and New Technologies (anthology) 1996; Luz & Letra, Ensaios de arte, literatura e comunicação 2004; Telepresence and Bio Art: Networking Humans, Rabbits and Robots 2005, Signs of Life: Bio Art and Beyond 2007; articles in periodicals. *Address:* Art and Technology Department, School of the Art Institute of Chicago, 37 South Wabash Avenue, Chicago, IL 60603, USA (office). *Telephone:* (312) 899-5100 (office). *E-mail:* ekac@artic.edu (office). *Website:* www.ekac.org (office).

KACHORNPRASART, Maj.-Gen. Sanan; Thai politician; *Leader, Mahachon Party;* b. 7 Sept. 1944, Phichit; ed Chulachomklao Royal Mil. Acad.; aide-de-camp to Gen. Chalard Hiranyasiri; involved in attempted coup 1981; mem. Parl. (Democrat Party) for Phichit 1983, 1986, 1988; Deputy Communications Minister 1986; Minister of Agric. and Co-operatives 1989, of the Interior 1998–2000; Deputy Prime Minister 1990–91; Sec.-Gen. Democrat Party –2004; Leader, Mahachon Party 2004–. *Address:* Mahachon, Bangkok, Thailand.

KACZMAREK, Jan, DTechSc; Polish scientist and academic; b. 2 Feb. 1920, Pabianice; s. of Władysław Kaczmarek and Zofia Kaczmarek; m. Olga Steranka 1946; one s. one d.; ed Acad. of Mining and Metallurgy, Kraków; Asst to Asst Prof. Acad. of Mining and Metallurgy, Kraków 1947–58; Head, Dept of Metal Working, Kraków Tech. Univ. 1958–68, Asst Prof. 1958–62, Prof. 1962–89, Pro-Rector and Rector 1966–68; with Research Inst. of Metal Cutting (IOS) 1949–68, Dir 1958–68; Pres. State Cttee for Science and Tech. 1968–72; Deputy to Sejm (Parl.) 1972–75, 1985–89; Minister of Science, Higher Educ. and Tech. and mem. Govt Presidium 1972–74; Prof. Inst. for Fundamental Problems of Tech. 1978–, Head Dept of Mechanical Systems 1980–90, Leader State research projects 1975–2001, Head Lab. for Surface Layer of Solids 1990–95; Pres. Supervisory Bd SIGMA-NOT Ltd (publrs), Warsaw 1991–; Corresp. mem. Polish Acad. of Sciences (PAN) 1962, Ordinary mem. 1971–, Scientific Sec. 1972–80, mem. Presidium 1972–80, 1984–87, Chair. Scientific Cttee of Machines Construction 1982–93; mem. Gen. Council Fed. of Polish Scientific-Tech. Asscns. (NOT) 1972–90, Vice-Chair. 1976–80, Chair. 1980–82, Vice-Pres. 1982–84, Pres. 1984–90; mem. Polish Acad. of Knowledge and Art, Cracow (PAU) 1989–, Polish Acad. of Eng 1991– (mem. Exec. Cttee 1991–, Vice-Pres. 1992–97, Hon. mem. 1998–); Ed.-in-Chief Advances in Manufacturing Science and Tech. 2001–; Foreign mem. Nat. Acad. of Eng (USA) 1976–, Bulgarian Acad. of Sciences 1977–, Royal Acad. of Sciences, Literature and Arts, Belgium 1978–, Cen. European Acad. of Science and Arts 1998; Foreign Hon. mem. Groupement pour l'Avancement des Mécaniques Industrielles (GAMI), France 1979–; mem. Int. Inst. for Production Eng Research (CIRP) 1961–, Pres. 1973–74, mem. Senate 1975–, Hon. mem. 1990–; mem. numerous other Polish, foreign and int. scientific socs; Hon. mem. Polish Soc. of Mechanical Eng 1976– (Hon. Pres. 1998); Kt's and Commdr's Cross of Order of Polonia Restituta, Gold Order of Palmes académiques 1971, Grand Officier Légion d'honneur 1972, Hon. Citizen of City of Pabianice 2002, and other decorations; Dr hc (Tech. Univ. Chemnitz) 1973, (Moscow Tech. Univ.) 1974, (Tech. Univ. of Poznań) 2001, (Tech. Univ. of Kosralin) 2002; N. Copernicus Medal 1980. *Publications:* numerous publs on production eng and theory of machining and science of science, including (in Polish) Principles of Metals Cutting 1956, Theory of Machining by Cutting: Abrasion and Erosion 1970, (in English) 1976, On Principles of Science Policy 1972, (in French) 1972. *Leisure interests:* gardening, classical music. *Telephone:* (22) 8269806 (office). *E-mail:* jankacz@interia.pl (office). *Website:* www .sigma-not.pl (office).

KACZMAREK, Janusz; Polish lawyer and politician; b. 25 Dec. 1961, Gdynia; m.; two s.; ed Univ. of Gdańsk; started legal training in Dist Prosecutor's Office, Elbląg 1985–88, in Gdańsk 1988; Dist Prosecutor, Gdynia 1993–2000; Regional Prosecutor, Gdańsk 2000–01; Deputy Prosecutor Gen. 2001; Deputy Dir Preparatory Proceedings Dept, Nat. Prosecutor's Office 2001–03; Appellate Prosecutor, Gdańsk 2003–05; Head, Nat. Prosecutor's Office 2005–07; Minister of Internal Affairs and Admin Feb.–Aug. 2007; lecturer on material criminal law to public prosecutor's trainees 1992–; Chair. Editorial Bd Prokuratura i Prawo, Kwartalnik Apelacji Gdańskiej, Kwartalnik Krajowego Centrum Szkolenia Kadr Sadów Powszechnych i Prokuratury; co-organizer Razem przeciw przemocy (Together Against Violence) program; mem. Law and Justice (PiS) (Prawo i Sprawiedliwość); arrested Polish anti-corruption agency Aug. 2007. *Publications:* author of numerous book and articles on law. *Address:* Prawo i Sprawiedliwość, ul. Nowogrodzka 84/86, 02-018 Warsaw, Poland (office). *Telephone:* (22) 6215035 (office). *Fax:* (22) 6216767 (office). *E-mail:* biuro@pis.org.pl (office). *Website:* www.pis.org.pl (office).

KACZMAREK, Wiesław; Polish politician; b. 1 Jan. 1958, Wrocław; m.; two d.; ed Warsaw Univ. of Technology; Sr Asst, Mechanics and Tech. Dept, Warsaw Univ. of Tech. 1984–89; Deputy Dir Industrial & Commercial Chamber of Foreign Investors 1989–91; Co-founder and mem. Social Democracy of the Repub. of Poland (SdRP) 1990–99; Deputy in Sejm (Parl.) 1989–; Man. Warsaw Br., First Commercial Bank SA, Lublin 1991–93; Minister of Privatization 1993–96, of the Economy 1997, of the Treasury 2001–03; mem.

Nat. Bd Democratic Left Alliance (SLD) 1999–2004; mem. Polish Social Democracy (Socjaldemokracja Polski—SDPL, splinter group of SLD) 2004–. *Leisure interests:* diving, sailing (Pres. Polish Sailing Asscn), hunting, skiing, photography. *Address:* c/o Polish Social Democracy (Socjaldemokracja Polski—SDPL), 02-904 Warsaw, ul. Bernardyńska 14a, Poland (office). *Telephone:* (22) 8406008 (office). *E-mail:* sdpl.wybory@onet.pl (office). *Website:* www.sdpl.pl (office); www.kaczmarek.pl.

KACZMAREK, Zdzisław; Polish scientist and academic; *Professor, Warsaw University of Technology;* b. 7 Aug. 1928, Poznań; s. of Edward and Klara Kaczmarek; m. Imelda Kaczmarek 1950; two s. one d.; ed Warsaw Univ. of Tech.; scientific worker in Warsaw Univ. of Tech. 1947–78, Doctor of Tech. Sciences 1958, Assoc. Prof. 1961–67, Extraordinary Prof. 1967–72, Ordinary Prof. 1972–; fmr Dir of Inst. of Environmental Eng in Dept of Water and Sanitary Eng; Chief of Div. in the State Hydro-Meteorological Inst. (PIH-M), Warsaw 1957–60, Vice-Dir 1960–63, Gen. Dir of Hydro-Meteorological Inst. 1963–66; Dir of Inst. for Meteorology and Water Economy, Warsaw 1976–80; Head, Water Resources Dept, Inst. of Geophysics, Warsaw 1981–2004; Chair. of Cttee of Water Economy, Polish Acad. of Sciences (PAN); mem. Polish United Workers' Party (PZPR) 1951–90; Deputy mem. of Warsaw Cttee of PZPR 1955–57, worked in Dept of Science and Educ. of Central Cttee. of PZPR, Deputy Chief of Dept 1966–71; mem. of Comm. of Science in Cen. Cttee of PZPR, mem. of Cen. Cttee 1986–89; former mem. of Gen. Bd of Polish Teachers' Asscn (ZNP); First Deputy Minister of Science, Higher Educ. and Tech. 1972–74; Project Leader, Int. Inst. of Applied Systems Analysis, Austria 1974–76, 1989–91; Deputy Chair. of Cen. Qualifying Comm. for Scientific Personnel, attached to Chair. of Council of Ministers 1989; Chair. State Council for Environmental Protection 1981–86; Poland 2000 Cttee for Prognosis on Country Devt 1984–88, Cttee on Water Resources, Cttee on Global Change 1996–; mem. Comm. for Hydrology, WMO 1993–, Nat. Council for Water Resources 2002–; Corresp. mem. Polish Acad. of Sciences 1969–, mem. 1980–, Deputy Scientific Sec. Polish Acad. of Sciences 1971–72, Sec. of VII Dept of Polish Acad. of Sciences 1978–80, Sec.-Gen. Polish Acad. of Sciences 1981–88; Silver and Gold Cross of Merit, Commdr's Cross and Officer's Cross of Order of Polonia Restituta, Order of Banner of Labour (1st Class), Order of Friendship of Nations (USSR), Silver Star of Order of Friendship (GDR) and other decorations; Int. Hydrological Prize 1990. *Publications:* numerous works on hydrology and water resources, on impacts of climate change and variability, on organization of scientific research and on co-operation of science and national economy. *Leisure interests:* sightseeing and tourism. *Address:* c/o Water Resources Department, Institute of Geophysics, Polish Academy of Sciences, ul. Ks. Janusza 64, 01-452, Warsaw (office); al. J. Ch. Szucha 16 m. 51, 00-582 Warsaw, Poland (home). *Telephone:* (22) 6915851 (office); (22) 6291057 (home). *Fax:* (22) 6915915 (office). *E-mail:* kaczmar@igf.edu.pl (office).

KACZYŃSKI, Jarosław Aleksander, DJur; Polish politician and lawyer; *Leader, Law and Justice (PiS) (Prawo i Sprawiedliwość);* b. 18 June 1949, Warsaw; s. of Rajmund Kaczyński and Jadwiga Kaczyńska; brother of Lech Kaczyński (q.v.); ed Warsaw Univ.; Asst, Sr Asst in Inst. of Science and Higher Educ. 1971–76; collaborator, Workers' Defence Cttee (KOR) 1976–80; scientific worker, Białystok br. of Warsaw Univ. 1977–81; ed. Głos (independent magazine) 1980–82; warehouseman 1982; mem. Solidarity Trade Union 1980–90; Sec. Nat. Exec. Comm. of Solidarity 1986–87; took part in Round Table talks in Comm. for Political Reforms Feb.–April 1989; Ed.-in-Chief Tygodnik Solidarność (weekly) 1989–90; Deputy to Senate 1989–91; Dir Office of Pres. and Minister of State 1990–92; Deputy to Sejm (Parl.) 1991–93, 1997–, mem. Ethics Comm. 2001–; Founder and Chair. Centre Alliance 1990–98; Co-Founder with his brother and mem. Main Bd Law and Justice (Prawo i Sprawiedliwość—PiS) 2001–, Pres. Law and Justice Parl. Club 2001–03, Pres. PiS and Chair. Main Bd 2003–, Prime Minister of Poland 2006–07; mem. Helsinki Comm. in Poland 1982–89. *Leisure interests:* animals (especially cats), reading, history of Poland. *Address:* Law and Justice (PiS) (Prawo i Sprawiedliwość), 02-018 Warsaw, ul. Nowogrodzka 84/86 (office); Sejm RP, 00-902 Warsaw, ul. Wiejska 4/6/8, Poland. *Telephone:* (22) 6215035 (office). *Fax:* (22) 6216767 (office). *E-mail:* biuro.organizacyjne@pis.org.pl (office). *Website:* www.pis.org.pl (office).

KACZYŃSKI, Lech Aleksander, PhD; Polish politician, trade union official, lawyer and head of state; *President;* b. 18 June 1949, Warsaw; s. of Rajmund Kaczyński and Jadwiga Kaczyńska; brother of Jarosław Kaczyński (q.v.); m. Maria Mackiewicz 1978; one d.; ed Warsaw, Gdańsk Univ.; Asst, Sr Asst in Labour Law Dept, Gdańsk Univ. 1971–97; adviser to striking workers in Gdańsk Aug. 1980; mem. Solidarity Ind. Self-governing Trade Union 1980–; head Group for Current Analysis and Intervention Bureau of Founding Cttee of Solidarity Trade Union, then head regional Centre for Social and Professional Work, Gdańsk 1980–81; mem. Regional Bd of Solidarity, Gdańsk 1981; interned 1981–82; assoc. of Lech Wałęsa (q.v.) 1982–91 and Provisional Co-ordinating Comm. of Solidarity 1983–84, its rep. in Gdańsk Jan.–July 1986, Sec. 1986–87; sec. Nat. Exec. Comm. of Solidarity 1988–90; took part in Round Table talks in Comm. for Trade Union Pluralism Feb.–April 1989; mem. Presidium Nat. Exec. Comm. of Solidarity 1989–90, First Deputy Chair. Nat. Comm. May 1990–91, Assoc. Workers' Defence Cttee (KOR) 1977–78, Free Trade Unions on the Seacoast 1978–80; Citizens' Cttee of Solidarity Chair. 1988–91; Senator 1989–91, Minister of State for Nat. Security Affairs in Chancellery of Pres. of Poland March–Nov. 1991; Pres. Cen. Audit Comm. 1992–95; Deputy to Sejm (Parl.) 1991–93, 2001–, Chair. Comm. of Admin. and Interior Affairs 1991–93; Vice-Leader Programme Bd of Public Affairs Inst., Warsaw 1996–; mem. EUROSAI Governing Bd 1993–95, Admin. Bd of ILO; Prof., Acad. of Catholic Theology (now Cardinal S. Wyszyński Univ.), Warsaw 1998–; Minister of Justice and Prosecutor-Gen. 2000–01; Co-Founder and Chair. Nat. Cttee Law and Justice (Prawo i Sprawiedliwość—PiS) Party

2001–03, Chair. Political Bd 2003–; Mayor of Warsaw 2002–05; Pres. of Poland 2005–. *Publications:* Social Pension 1989 and some 15 works on labour law and social insurance. *Leisure interests:* reading, family, history, philosophy. *Address:* Chancellery of the President, 00-902 Warsaw, ul. Wiejska 10, Poland (office). *Telephone:* (22) 6952900 (office). *Fax:* (22) 6952238l (office). *E-mail:* listy@prezydent.pl (office). *Website:* www.prezydent.pl (office).

KADAKIN, Alexander Mikhailovich; Russian diplomatist; *Ambassador to Sweden;* b. 22 July 1949, Kishinev, Moldova; ed Moscow Inst. of Int. Relations; translator Special Construction Bureau Vibpribor, Kishinev 1966–67; joined diplomatic service 1972; with USSR Embassy, India 1972, Attaché 1972–75, Third Sec. 1975–78; Second Sec. Secr., First Deputy to USSR Minister of Foreign Affairs 1978–80, First Sec., Secr. 1980–83, Asst 1983–86, Asst to Deputy Minister 1986–88, Asst First Deputy Minister 1988–89; Minister-Counsellor USSR Embassy, India 1989–91; First Deputy Head of Dept USSR Ministry of Foreign Affairs 1991; Counsellor Embassy, India 1991–93; Amb. to Nepal 1993–97; mem. Collegium, Dir of Linguistic Support Dept, Ministry of Foreign Affairs 1997–99; Amb. to India 1999–2004, to Sweden 2004–; Asst Prof., Dept of Indian Studies, Moscow State Inst. of Int. Relations 1979–85. *Address:* Embassy of the Russian Federation, Gjörwellsgt. 31, 112 60 Stockholm, Sweden (office). *Telephone:* (8) 13-04-41 (office). *Fax:* (8) 618-27-03 (office). *E-mail:* rusembassy@telia.com (office). *Website:* www.ryssland.se (office).

KADANNIKOV, Vladimir Vasilievich; Russian politician and business executive; b. 3 Sept. 1941, Gorky (now Nizhny Novgorod); m.; two d.; ed Gorky Polytech. Inst.; fitter, foreman, then area man., Gorky Automotive Plant 1959–67; Deputy Workshop Man., Volga Automotive Works 1967–76; Deputy Dir-Gen. PO AvtoVAZ in charge of production 1976–86, First Deputy Dir-Gen., then Dir R&D Centre 1986–88, Dir-Gen. PO AvtoVAZ 1988–93, Pres. and Dir-Gen. joint stock co. AvtoVAZ Inc. 1993–96; First Deputy Prime Minister of Russia Jan.–Aug. 1996; Chair. Bd Dirs AvtoVAZ Inc. 1996–2005, GM-AvtoVAZ –2005; Chair. Council for Industrial Policy; mem. Presidential Consultative Council; mem. Int. Eng Acad., Russian Eng Acad.; fmr People's Deputy of the USSR; Hon. Prof. Samara State Univ.; Hero of Socialist Labour. *Publications:* book chapters and scientific articles on cold sheet stamping by stretch forming. *Leisure interests:* reading, basketball. *Address:* Yuzhnoe Shosse 36, 445633 Togliatti, Russia. *Telephone:* (8482) 37-71-25. *Fax:* (848) 378-74-50.

KADANOFF, Leo Philip, PhD; American physicist and academic; *John D. MacArthur Distinguished Service Professor Emeritus, University of Chicago;* b. 14 Jan. 1937, New York; s. of Abraham Kadanoff and Celia (Kibrick) Kadanoff; m. Ruth Ditzian 1979; four d.; ed Harvard Univ.; postdoctoral research at Bohr Inst. for Theoretical Studies, Copenhagen, Denmark 1960–62; Asst Prof. of Physics, Univ. of Ill. 1962–63, Assoc. Prof. 1963, Prof. 1965–69; Visiting Prof., Univ. of Cambridge, UK 1965; Univ. Prof. of Physics, Brown Univ. 1969–78, Prof. of Eng 1971–78; Prof. of Physics, Univ. of Chicago 1978–82, John D. MacArthur Distinguished Service Prof. of Physics and Math. 1982–, now Emer.; Alfred P. Sloan Foundation Fellow 1962–67; mem. Editorial Bd Annals of Physics 1982–, Nuclear Physics 1980–; mem. NAS 1978 American Philosophical Soc. 1997; Fellow American Acad. of Arts and Sciences, American Physical Soc.; Ryerson Lectureship, Univ. of Chicago 2000; Buckley Prize, American Physical Soc. 1977, Onsager Prize, American Physical Soc. 1998; Wolf Foundation Award 1980, Elliott Cresson Medal, Franklin Inst. 1986, IUPAP Boltzmann Medal 1989, Quantrell Award, Univ. of Chicago 1990, Centennial Medal, Harvard Univ. 1990, Grande Médaille d'or, Acad. des Sciences de l'Inst. de France 1998, Nat. Medal of Science 2000. *Publications:* Quantum Statistical Mechanics (with G. Baym) 1962, From Order to Chaos: Essays Critical Chaotic and Otherwise 1993, Statistical Physics: Statics, Dynamics and Renormalization 2000. *Address:* 5421 South Cornell Avenue, Chicago, IL 60615 (home); James Franck Institute, University of Chicago, 5640 South Ellis Avenue, Chicago, IL 60637, USA (office). *Telephone:* (773) 702-7189 (office). *Fax:* (773) 702-2172 (office). *E-mail:* l-kadanoff@uchicago.edu (office); leop@uchicago.edu (office). *Website:* physics.uchicago.edu/t_cond.html#Kadanoff (office); jfi.uchicago.edu/~leop/ (office).

KÁDÁR, Béla, PhD, DSc; Hungarian politician, economist and academic; b. 21 March 1934, Pécs; s. of Lajos Kádár and Teréz Schmidt; m. Patricia Derzső; one s.; ed Budapest Univ. of Economy; worked for Int. Econ. Dept, Nat. Bank of Hungary, Elektro-impex Foreign Trading Co.; fmr dept head and research man., Business and Market Research Inst.; with Hungarian Acad. of Sciences Research Inst. of World Economy 1965–88; Lecturer, Eötvös Loránd Univ. of Budapest; Visiting Prof., Santiago de Chile and San Marcos Univ. of Lima; Dir Econ. Planning Inst. 1988–90; Minister of Int. Econ. Relations 1990–94; mem. Parl. 1994–98, Chair. Cttee on Budget and Finances; Vice-Chair. Hungarian Asscn of Economists 1990–2000, Chair. 2002–; Univ. Prof. 1998–; Pres. Hungarian Export-Import Bank 1998–99; Vice-Pres. Hungarian Soc. of Foreign Affairs 1998–; Amb. to OECD 1999–2003; mem. Monetary Council of Hungarian Nat. Bank 1999–; Chair. Hungarian Group in Trilateral Comm. 1999–; Academician, Hungarian Acad. of Sciences; Dr hc (San Marcos Univ., Lima) 1970, (Budapest) 1999; Grand Prix, Hungarian Acad. of Sciences 1984, Econ. Policy Club (Bonn) Prize for Social Market Econs 1993. *Publications:* author of eight books and more than 400 papers. *Leisure interests:* music, literature. *Address:* Mártonhegyi u. 38/B, Budapest 1124, Hungary. *Telephone:* (1) 355-7987. *Fax:* (1) 355-7987.

KADARÉ, Ismail; Albanian writer; b. 28 Jan. 1936, Gjirokastër; s. of Halit Kadaré; m. Elena Gushi 1963; two d.; ed Univ. of Tirana and Gorky Inst., Moscow; full-time writer since 1963; works translated into more than 30 languages; sought political asylum in Paris 1990; mem. Albanian Acad.; Corresponding, then Assoc. Foreign mem. Acad. des sciences morales et politiques; mem. Acad. of Arts, Berlin, Acad. Mallarmé; Dr hc (Grenoble III) 1992, (St Etienne) 1997; Prix Mondial Cino del Duca 1992, Int. Booker Prize 2005. *Plays:* Mauvaise saison pour Olymp. *Publications:* fiction: Gjenerali i ushtërisë së vdekur (trans. as The General of the Dead Army) 1963, Kështjella (trans. as The Castle, later as The Siege) 1970, Kronikë në gur (trans. as Chronicle in Stone) 1971, The Great Winter (novel, in trans.) 1973, Ura më tri harque (trans. as The Three-Arched Bridge) 1978, The Twilight (in trans.) 1978, The Niche of Shame (in trans.) 1978, Kush e solli doruntinen (trans. as Who Brought Back Doruntine?) 1980, Prilli i thyer (trans. as Broken April) 1980, Nëpunësi I pallatit të ëndrrave (trans. as The Palace of Dreams) 1980, Nje dosje per Homerin (trans. as The H Dossier) 1980, Koncert në fund të dimrit (trans. as The Concert) 1985, Eschyle or The Eternal Loser (in trans.) 1988, Albanian Spring (in trans.) 1991, Le Monstre (in trans.) 1991, Piramida (trans. as The Pyramid) 1992, La Grande muraille 1993, Le Firman aveugle 1993, Clair de Lune 1993, L'Ombre 1994, L'Aigle 1996, Spiritus 1996, Oeuvres 1993–97 (12 vols) 1997, Temps barbares, de l'Albanie au Kosovo 1999, Il a fallu ce deuil pour se retrouver 2000, Froides fleurs d'avril (trans. as Spring Flowers, Spring Frost) 2000, L'envol du migrateur 2001, Vie, jeu et mort de Lul Mazrek 2002, La fille d'Agamemnon 2003, Le successeur 2003; six vols of poetry 1954–80, criticism, essays. *Address:* c/o Librairie Arthème Fayard, 75 rue des Saints Pères, 75006 Paris (office); 63 blvd Saint-Michel, 75005 Paris, France (home). *Telephone:* (1) 43-29-16-20 (home).

KADDOUMI, Farouk, (Abu Lutef); Palestinian politician; *President of the Executive Committee, Fatah (The Palestine National Liberation Movement);* b. 1931, Qalqilyah; ed Cairo Univ.; moved to Nablus during Arab–Israeli War 1948; worked for Arab–American Petroleum Co. (ARAMCO), Saudi Arabia early 1950s; joined Baath Party, Egypt 1954; joined Fatah in UAE 1960; with Ministry of Health, Kuwait 1965–66; expelled from Kuwait for anti-governmental activities connected with Palestinian Liberation Org. (PLO) 1966; became key figure in PLO 1969, apptd Head of Political Dept, Damascus, Syria 1973; participated in activities of Said al-Muraghi (Aba Musa) Group 1980s; opposed signing of Oslo Peace Accords with Israel 1993; apptd Dir of Palestinian Econ. Council for Reconstruction and Devt (PEDCAR) by Yasser Arafat; Pres. Exec. Cttee, Palestine Nat. Liberation Movt (al-Fatah) 2004–. *Address:* Fatah (The Palestine National Liberation Movement), Palestinian Autonomous Areas (office). *Website:* www.fateh.net (office).

KADEGE, Alphonse Marie; Burundian politician; Vice-Pres. of Burundi 2003–04; acquitted on charges of coup plot 2007; mem. Union pour le progrès national (UPRONA). *Address:* c/o Union pour le progrès national (UPRONA), BP 1810, Bujumbura, Burundi (office).

KADHAFI, Col Mu'ammar Muhammed al- (see GADDAFI, Col Mu'ammar Muhammed al-).

KADOMATSU, Masahiro; Japanese business executive; *President and CEO, Asahi Glass Company;* b. 29 Oct. 1942, Tokyo; ed Keio Univ.; joined Asahi Glass Co. 1965, numerous man. positions 1965–98 including Gen. Man. Sales, Gen. Man. Electronic Products Div. 1998–2000, Man. Dir and Gen. Man., Display Glass 2000–02, Sr Exec. Officer and Pres. Display Co. 2002–03, Sr Exec. Vice Pres. and Pres. Display Co. 2003–04, CEO and Pres. Asahi Glass Co. 2004–; Counsellor, The Energy Conservation Centre, Japan, Int. Centre for the Study of East Asian Devt. *Address:* Asahi Glass Company, 1-12-1 Yuraku-cho, Chiyoda-ku, Tokyo 100-8405, Japan (office). *Telephone:* (3) 3218-5096 (office). *Website:* www.agc.co.jp (office).

KADOORIE, Hon. Sir Michael, Kt; Hong Kong business executive; *Chairman, CLP Holdings Limited;* b. 1941, Hong Kong; s. of the late Lawrence, Lord Kadoorie and of Muriel Gubbay; m.; three c.; ed Institut Le Rosey, Switzerland; family roots in business in the Far East go back to his grandfather, who made a fortune in Shanghai, mostly lost in 1949, and later, in Hong Kong through finance, real estate and utilities; Chair. CLP Group, Hong Kong (electricity provider); Chair. Hong Kong & Shanghai Hotels, owners and operators of Peninsula Hotel Group; controls and is a mem. Bd of Dirs Metrojet Ltd, Heliservices (Hong Kong) Ltd; mem. Bd of Dirs Sir Elly Kadoorie & Sons Ltd, Hutchison Whampoa Ltd; Alternate Dir Hong Kong Aircraft Engineering Co. Ltd 1989–; Founder CLP Research Inst. (subsidiary of CLP Holdings); fmr mem. Council of Univ. of Hong Kong; Trustee, Kadoorie Charitable Foundation; Grand Bauhinia Star; Officier, Légion d'honneur; Commdr, Order of Léopold II (Belgium); Hon. LLD (Univ. of Hong Kong) 2004. *Leisure interests:* photography, helicopter pilot, collecting classic cars. *Address:* CLP Holdings, 147 Argyle Street, Kowloon, Hong Kong Special Administrative Region, People's Republic of China (office). *Telephone:* 2678-8111 (office). *Fax:* 2760-4448 (office). *E-mail:* clp_info@clp.com.hk (office). *Website:* www.clpgroup.com (office).

KADUMA, Ibrahim Mohamed, BSc (Econs), BPhil; Tanzanian politician and economist; *Chancellor, Mzumbe University;* b. 1937, Mtwango Njombe, Iringa Region; s. of the late Mohamed Maleva Kaduma and of Mwanaidza Kaduma; m. Happiness Y. Mgonja 1969; four s. one d.; ed Makerere Univ. Coll. Uganda and Univ. of York, UK; Accounts Clerk, the Treasury 1959–61, Accounts Asst 1961, Asst Accountant 1962–65, Economist 1965–66, Dir of External Finance and Technical Co-operation 1967–69, Deputy Sec. Treasury 1969–70; Principal Sec. Ministry of Communications, Transport and Labour, 1970–72, Treasury 1972–73; Dir Inst. of Devt Studies, Univ. of Dar es Salaam 1973–75, Centre on Integrated Rural Devt for Africa 1982–85; Minister for Foreign Affairs 1975–77, of Trade 1980–81, of Communications and Transport 1981–82; Vice-Chancellor Univ. of Dar es Salaam 1977–80; fmr Gen. Man. Tanzania Sisal Devt Bd; currently Chancellor Mzube Univ.; Arts Research Prize, Makerere Univ., Uganda 1964–65. *Leisure interests:* tennis, squash, gardening, dairy farming. *Address:* Mzumbe University, PO Box 1, Mzumbe, Tanzania (office). *Telephone:* (23) 2604380 (office). *Fax:* (23) 2604382 (office). *E-mail:* mu@mzumbe.ac.tz (office). *Website:* www.mzumbe.ac.tz (office).

KADYROV, Ramzan Akhmadovich; Russian government official; *President, Chechen (Nokchi) Republic;* b. 5 Oct. 1976, Tsenteroi, Checheno-Ingush ASSR (now Chechen—Nokchi Repub.); s. of the late Pres. Akhmed Kadyrov; m.; seven c.; fmr Commdr of 'Kadyrovtsy' militia (Presidential security service); fmr Head of Security, Chechen (Nokchi) Repub.; First Deputy Chair. of Govt, Chechen (Nokchi) Repub. 2004–05, Acting Chair. of Govt 2005–06, Chair. of Govt 2006–07, Pres. 2007–; Chair. Ramzan boxing club, Terek Grozny football club; Hon. mem. Russian Acad. of Natural Sciences; Hero of Russia Medal, Order of Courage, Order of Akhmad Kadyrov, Caucasus Service Medal, Defender of the Chechen Repub. Medal. *Leisure interests:* football, horses. *Address:* Office of the President, 364000 Chechen (Nokchi) Republic, Groznyi, ul. Garazhnaya 10a, Russian Federation (office). *Telephone:* (8712) 22-20-01 (office); (8712) 22-20-09 (office). *Fax:* (8712) 22-20-14 (office). *E-mail:* secretariat_chr@mail.ru (office). *Website:* www.chechnya.gov.ru (office); www.ramzan-kadyrov.ru.

KADYSHEVSKY, Vladimir G.; Russian physicist; *Scientific Leader, Joint Institute for Nuclear Research;* b. 5 May 1937, Moscow; widowed; one d.; ed Moscow State Univ.; Jr, then Sr Researcher, Head of Sector, then Dir Lab. of Theoretical Physics, Jt Inst. for Nuclear Research 1987–92, Dir Jt Inst. for Nuclear Research 1992–2005, Scientific Leader 2006–; mem. Presidium of Russian Acad. of Sciences (RAS), Corresp. mem. RAS 1991–2000, mem. 2000–; Hon. Citizen of Moscow Region 2001; N.M. Krylov Prize 1990 and N.N. Bogolubov Prize 2001 from Acad. of Sciences of Ukraine, Gold Medal, Int. Asscn of Acads of Sciences 2002, Gold Medal, Inst. of European Integration 2003. *Publications include:* numerous scientific papers on particle physics, quantum field theory, math. physics, and group theoretical and geometrical methods in field theory. *Leisure interests:* art, cinema, theatre, music. *Address:* Joint Institute for Nuclear Research, 6 Joliot-Curie str., 141980 Dubna, Moscow region (office); 2 Vekslera str., 141980 Dubna, Moscow region, Russia (home). *Telephone:* (495) 632-78-67 (office); (09621) 6-22-43 (office); (09621) 6-22-16 (home). *Fax:* (495) 632-78-80 (office); (09621) 6-58-92 (office). *E-mail:* kadyshev@jinr.ru (office). *Website:* www.jinr.ru (office).

KAFELNIKOV, Yevgeny Aleksandrovich; Russian fmr professional tennis player; b. 18 Feb. 1974, Sochi; m. two d.; ed Krasnodar Pedagogical Inst.; ATP professional 1992; won ATP tournaments including Milan, St Petersburg, Gstaad, Long Island; won French Open (singles and doubles) 1996; won Moscow Kremlin Cup 1997, 1999; won Australian Open 1999; mem. Russian Fed. Davis Cup Championship Team 1993, winner (with Russian team) 2002; runner-up World Championship, Hanover 1997; highest ATP rating 1st (May 1999); Olympic champion (singles), Sydney 2000; winner of 26 singles titles and 27 doubles titles; retd 2004; currently professional poker player, won Korona Russian Poker Championships, Moscow 2004. *Leisure interests:* fishing, flying, golf. *Address:* c/o All-Russian Tennis Association, Luzhnetskaya nab. 8, 119871 Moscow, Russia.

KAFKA, Alexandre; Brazilian economist, academic and international finance consultant; b. 25 Jan. 1917; s. of the late Bruno Kafka and Jana Kafka (née Bondy de Bondrop); m. Rita Petschek 1947 (died 2006); two d.; ed Law School German Univ., Prague, Grad. School of Int. Studies, Geneva, Balliol Coll. Oxford, England; Prof. of Econs, Univ. de São Paulo 1941–46; Adviser to Brazilian Del. to Preparatory Cttee and Conf. of Int. Trade Org. 1946–48; Asst Div. Chief, Int. Monetary Fund (IMF) 1949–51, Exec. Dir 1966–98, Vice-Chair. Deputies of Cttee on Reform of Int. Monetary System and Related Matters 1972–74; Adviser, Superintendency of Money and Credit (now Banco Central do Brasil); Dir of Research, Brazilian Inst. of Econs 1951–56, Dir 1961–63; Chief Financial Inst. and Policies Section, UN 1956–59; Prof. of Econs, Univ. of Va, US 1959–60, 1963–75, lecturer Law School 1977–87; Lecturer, George Washington Univ. 1989, Visiting Prof. of Econs, Boston Univ. 1975–79; Adviser to Minister of Finance 1964; Comendador Ordem do Rio Branco (Brazil) 1973, Grand Cross (Colombia), Order de Boyaca (Colombia), Grand Officer (Peru), Order del sol (Peru). *Publication:* IMF Governance, in G-24: commemorating 50th year after Bretton Woods Conf. 1994. *Address:* 4201 Cathedral Avenue, NW, Apt. 805E, Washington, DC 20016, USA. *Telephone:* (202) 623-7870 (office); (202) 362-1737 (home).

KAFRAWY, Hasaballah Mohamed al-, BEng; Egyptian politician; b. 22 Nov. 1930, Kafr Saad Area, Damitta Governorate; s. of Mohamed al-Kafrawy; m. Elham Abd al-Aziz Fouad 1961; three s.; ed Alexandria Univ.; with southern region of High Dam electricity lines until 1966; Chair. Canal Gen. Contracting Co.; Vice-Pres. exec. organ for reconstruction of Suez Canal region 1974, Pres. 1975; Gov. of Damietta 1976; Deputy Minister for Reconstruction, then Minister of Devt, Housing and Land Reclamation 1977–86; supervised planning of satellite cities and public utilities of Sadat, Ramadan 10, October 6, May 15, Cairo Sanitary Project, Damietta Port etc.; Minister of Devt, New Communities, Housing and Public Utilities 1986–93; mem. Egyptian People's Ass. 1979–93; Chair. and CEO El rehab Saudi-Egyptian Group of cos 1997; Pres. Egyptian Eng Asscn 1990; Perm. mem. Int. Org. of Metropolis; Chair. New Communities Authority; Vice-Chair. Int. Asscn of Major Metropolises (Metropolis); mem. Egyptian Specialized Nat. Councils, Egyptian Acad. for Scientific Research and Tech. (Chair. New Communities Research Council Acad.), Gen. Authority for Investment and Free Zones; Head, Egyptian Engineers Syndicate, Univ. Councils of Alexandria, Helwan and Mansoura, Cairo Univ. Centre for Devt and Technological Planning Research; referred to as "Imhotep of Modern Egypt"; Egyptian Order of Merit (First Class) 1964, 1975, 1980, Medal for Championship of Labour (USSR) 1964, Order of Merit (First Class) (France) 1983, Nile Wishah 1994; UN Habitat Prize for Housing 1992. *Address:* 21 Gamal Eldin Aboulmahasen Street, Garden City, PO Box 11451, Cairo, Egypt. *Telephone:* (2) 3555505. *Fax:* (2) 3556255. *Website:* www.hkafrawy.org.

KAGAME, Maj.-Gen. Paul; Rwandan politician, army officer and head of state; *President;* b. 1957; m.; four c.; ed Fort Leavenworth, USA; escaped to Uganda with family from anti-Tutsi persecution 1960; joined Ugandan Rebel Army 1982, Chief of Intelligence Ugandan Army 1986; formed rebel army of Rwandan exiles 1990, Leader campaign in Rwanda 1990–94, helped broker cease-fire 1993; Vice-Pres. and Minister of Nat. Defence 1994–2000, Pres. of Rwanda April 2000–; Head Rwandan Patriotic Front Party (FPR) 2000; Young Presidents' Org. 2003, Africa Gender Award 2007. *Leisure interests:* tennis, reading. *Address:* Office of the President, BP 15, Kigali, Rwanda (office). *Telephone:* (590) 62007 (office). *Fax:* 752431 (office). *E-mail:* pkagame@gov.rw (office). *Website:* www.gov.rw (office).

KAGAN, Elena, MPh, JD; American lawyer, academic and government official; b. 28 April 1960, New York, NY; ed Hunter Coll. High School, Princeton Univ., Worcester Coll., Oxford, UK, Harvard Law School; Law Clerk for Judge Abner Mikva, US Court of Appeals, DC Circuit 1986–87, for Justice Thurgood Marshall, US Supreme Court 1987–88; Assoc., Williams & Connolly (law firm), Washington, DC 1989–91; Asst Prof., Univ. of Chicago Law School 1991–95, Tenured Prof. of Law 1995; Assoc. Counsel to the Pres., The White House 1995–96, Deputy Asst to Pres. for Domestic Policy and Deputy Dir of Domestic Policy Council 1997–99; Visiting Prof., Harvard Law School 1999–2001, Prof. of Law 2001–03, Charles Hamilton Houston Prof. of Law 2003–, Dean of Faculty of Law 2003–; nominated as Solicitor Gen. US Dept of Justice, Washington, DC 2009. *Publications:* contribs to journals including Harvard Law Review, Supreme Court Review, Univ. of Chicago Law Review, Texas Law Review, Law and Social Inquiry. *Address:* Office of the Dean, Harvard Law School, 1563 Massachusetts Avenue Cambridge, MA 02138; c/o Department of Justice, 950 Pennsylvania Avenue, NW, Washington, DC 20530-0001, USA. *Website:* www.law.harvard.edu; www.usdoj.gov.

KAGAN, Henri B., PhD; French chemist and academic; *Professor Emeritus, University of Paris South;* b. 15 Dec. 1930, Boulogne-sur-Seine; s. of Alexandre Kagan and Adeline Celmiker; m. Claude Vignon 13 Aug. 1960; three d.; ed Sorbonne, École Nat. Supérieure de Chimie, Paris; Research Assoc., Collège de France 1962–67; Visiting Researcher, Univ. of Tex., Austin, USA 1965, Visiting Prof. 1980; Asst Prof., Univ. of Paris S, Orsay 1967–73, Prof. 1973–99, Prof. Emer. 1999–; Prof., Institut Universitaire de France 1993–99; mem. Acad. des Sciences 1991–; Foreign mem. Polish Acad. of Sciences 1994–; Visiting Prof. at several int. univs including Fort Collins, Colo, USA 1976, Uppsala, Sweden 1998, Weizmann Inst., Israel 1988; JSPS, Japan 1977, 2001–03; Hon. Fellow, Chemical Research Soc. of India 2000, Royal Soc. of Chem. 2003; Chevalier, Ordre Nat. du Mérite 1996, Chevalier, Légion d'honneur 2002; Dr hc (Bucharest) 1999, (Basilicata) 2004, (Montréal) 2008; numerous awards including French Chemical Soc. Le Bel Award 1967, Academie des Sciences Cahours Award 1968, Prelog Medal ETH 1990, Chaire Francqui, Louvain 1994, August-Wilhelm von Hofmann Medal 1991, Yamada Prize 1998, Nagoya Medal for Organic Chem. 1998, Tetrahedron Prize 1999, Wolf Prize in Chem. 2001, Grand Prix de la Fondation de la Maison de la Chimie 2002, Ryoji Noyori Prize 2002, Bower Award and Prize for Achievement in Science, Franklin Inst. 2005, Horst-Pracejus Prize 2007. *Publications:* more than 300 publs 1955–2005; books include: Stéréochimie organique 1975. *Leisure interest:* history. *Address:* ICMMO, Building 420, Université Paris-Sud, 91405 Orsay (office); 10 rue Georges Clemenceau, 91400, Orsay, France (home). *Telephone:* 1-69-15-78-95 (office). *Fax:* 1-69-15-46-80 (office). *E-mail:* kagan@icmo.u-psud.fr (office). *Website:* www.icmo.u-psud.fr/w-kagan/home.htm (office).

KAGARLITSKY, Boris Yuliyevich, PhD; Russian journalist and writer; *Director, Institute of Globalization Studies and Social Movements;* b. 1958, Moscow; ed State Inst. of Theatrical Art; Ed. Leviy povorot (samizdat journal) 1978–82; Co-ordinator Moscow People's Front 1988; Deputy, Moscow city Soviet (prov. Parl.) 1990–93; Founding mem. Party of Labour 1992; fmr adviser to Chair., Fed. of Ind. Trade Unions of Russia; Sr Research Fellow, Inst. of Comparative Political Studies, Russian Acad. of Sciences 1994–2002; Dir Inst. of Globalization Studies 2003–07, Inst. of Globalization Studies and Social Movts 2007–; columnist, The Moscow Times, ZNet. *Publications:* The Thinking Reed (Deutscher Memorial Prize) 1988, The Dialectic of Hope 1989, Farewell Perestroika: A Soviet Chronicle 1990, Disintegration of the Monolith 1993, Square Wheels: How Russian Democracy Got Derailed 1994, The Mirage of Modernisation 1995, Restoration in Russia 1995, New Realism, New Barbarism: Socialist Theory in the Era of Globalization 1999, The Twilight of Globalization: Property, State and Capitalism 1999, The Return of Radicalism: Reshaping the Left Institutions 2000, Russia under Yeltsin and Putin: Neo-liberal Autocracy 2002, The Politics of Empire: Globalisation in Crisis (co-ed.) 2004; contribs Novaya Gazeta, The Progressive, Red Pepper, Green Left Weekly. *Address:* Institute of Globalization Studies and Social Movements, Gazetny per. 5, Moscow, Russia (office). *E-mail:* kagarlitsky@narod.ru. *Website:* kagarlitsky.narod.ru (office); www.iprog.ru (office).

KAGERMANN, Henning, PhD; German software industry executive; *Chairman of the Executive Board and CEO, SAP AG;* b. 1948; Lecturer in Theoretical Physics and Computer Science, Tech. Univ. of Braunschweig and Univ. of Mannheim 1982–92; joined SAP (business-application software co.) AG 1982, apptd to Exec. Bd 1991, Co-Chair. 1998–2002, Co-Chair. and CEO 2002–03, Chair. and CEO 2003–; mem. Supervisory Bd Deutsche Bank AG, Daimler-Chrysler Services AG, Münchener Rückversicherungs-Gesellschaft AG; Trustee Tech. Univ. of Munich. *Address:* SAP AG, Neuroffstrasse 16, 69190 Walldorf, Germany (office). *Telephone:* (6227) 747474 (office). *Fax:* (6227) 757575 (office). *E-mail:* info.germany@sap.com (office). *Website:* www.sap.com (office).

KAGEYAMA, Mahito; Japanese business executive; *Executive Vice-President, Toyota Tsusho Corporation;* b. 28 Jan. 1949; joined Sanwa Bank

Ltd (later UFJ Bank Ltd) 1972, Exec. Officer 1999–2002, Sr Exec. Officer 2002–03 (resgnd); Sr Advisor, Tomen Corpn Feb.–June 2003, Pres. June 2003–2006, Exec. Vice-Pres. Toyota Tsusho Corp. (after merger of Tomen with Toyota Tsusho Corp.) 2006–. *Address:* Toyota Tsusho Corporation, 9-8, Meieki, 4-chome, Nakamura-ku, Nagoya 450-8575, Japan (office). *Telephone:* (52) 584-5000 (office). *Fax:* (52) 584-5663 (office). *Website:* www.toyota-tsusho.com (office).

KAHIN, Dahir Riyale; Somali politician; *President of "Republic of Somaliland";* Vice-Pres. self-proclaimed Repub. of Somaliland (NW Somalia) –2002, Pres. May 2002–. *Address:* Office of the President of the Republic of Somaliland, Hargeysa, Somalia (office). *Website:* www.somalilandgov.com.

KAHN, Alfred Edward, AB, PhD; American professor of economics and government official; *Robert Julius Thorne Professor of Political Economy Emeritus, Cornell University;* b. 17 Oct. 1917, Paterson, NJ; s. of the late Jacob M. Kahn and Bertha Orlean Kahn; m. Mary Simmons 1943; one s. two d.; ed New York Univ. and Graduate School, Univ. of Missouri, Yale Univ.; Research Staff of Brookings Inst. 1940, 1951–52; US Govt Service with Antitrust Div., Dept of Justice, Dept of Commerce, War Production Bd 1941–43; Research Staff, 20th Century Fund 1944–45; Prof., Dept of Econs, Ripon Coll., Wis. 1945–47; Dept of Econs, Cornell Univ., Ithaca, NY 1947–89, Robert Julius Thorne Prof. of Political Economy Emer. 1989–, Dean Coll. of Arts and Sciences 1969–74; mem. Econ. Advisory Bd, AT & T 1968–74; Chair. New York Public Service Comm. 1974–77, US Civil Aeronautics Bd 1977–78; Adviser to the Pres. (Carter) on Inflation 1978–80; Special Consultant, Nat. Econ. Research Associates 1957–64, 1980–; mem. Int. Inst. for Applied Systems Analysis Advisory Cttee on Price Reform and Competition in the USSR 1990–92; Chair. Blue Ribbon Panel to Study Pricing in the Calif. Electricity Market 2000; Vice-Pres. American Econ. Asscn 1981–82; mem. Advisory Cttee The Digital Age Communications Act Project 2005; mem. American Acad. of Arts and Sciences, Fellow 1977–; Hon. LLD (Colby Univ., Ripon Coll., Univ. of Mass., Northwestern Univ., Colgate Univ.); Hon. DHL (State Univ. of New York) 1985; numerous awards including Distinguished Alumni Award, Univ. of New York 1976, Harry E. Salzberg Hon. Medallion 1986, Burton Gordon Feldman Award, Brandeis Univ. 1989, L. Welch Pogue Award for Lifetime Contribs to Aviation 1997, Sovereign Fund Award 1997, J. Rhoads Foster Award for achievements in econ. regulation 1999, Wilbur Cross Medal, Yale Univ. 1995, AEI-Brookings Jt Center for Regulatory Studies First Distinguished Lecturer 1999, American Antitrust Inst. Award for Lifetime Achievement in Antitrust 2003. *Publications:* Great Britain in the World Economy (co-author) 1946, Fair Competition: The Law and Economics of Antitrust Policy (co-author) 1954, Integration and Competition in the Petroleum Industry 1959, The Economics of Regulation (two vols) 1970, 1971 (reprinted 1988), Letting Go: Deregulating the Process of Deregulation 1998, Whom the Gods Would Destroy, or How Not to Deregulate 2001, Lessons from Deregulation: Telecommunications and Airlines After the Crunch 2004; around 100 articles in professional journals and some 250 testimonies before Federal and State agencies etc. *Leisure interests:* sports, dramatics, music. *Address:* 308 N Cayuga Street, Ithaca, NY 14850, USA (office). *Telephone:* (607) 277-3007 (office). *Fax:* (607) 277-1581 (office). *E-mail:* alfred.kahn@nera.com (office).

KAHN, C. Ronald, BA, MD, MS; American medical scientist and academic; *Senior Investigator and Head of the Section on Obesity and Hormone Action, Mary K. Iacocca Professor of Medicine and Vice Chairman of the Board, Elliott P. Joslin Diabetes Center, Harvard Medical School;* b. Louisville, Ky; ed Univ. of Louisville; Intern and Resident, Barnes Hosp., Ward Medicine Saint Louis, Mo. 1968–70; Clinical Assoc. and Sr Clinical Assoc., Clinical Endocrinology Br., Nat. Insts of Arthritis, Metabolism and Digestive Diseases, NIH, Bethesda, Md 1970–73, Diabetes Br. 1973–78 (Chief of Section on Cellular and Molecular Physiology 1979–81), Admitting and Attending Physician, Clinical Center 1972–81; Visiting Scientist, Center de Moleculaire, CNRS, Gif-Sur-Yvette, France 1979–80; Adjunct Prof. of Genetics, George Washington Univ., Washington, DC 1980–81; Clinical Assoc. Prof. of Medicine, Uniformed Services Univ. of Health Sciences, Bethesda 1981; Assoc. Prof. of Medicine, Harvard Univ. Medical School Boston, Mass 1981–84, Prof. of Medicine 1984–, Mary K. Iacocca Prof. of Medicine 1986–, also Sr Investigator and Head, Section on Obesity and Hormone Action, Dir Elliot P. Joslin Research Lab., Joslin Diabetes Center, Boston 1981–, Sr Staff, Joslin Clinic 1985–, Exec. Vice-Pres. and Dir Joslin Diabetes Center 1997–2000, Pres. 2000, now Vice Chair of the Bd; Assoc. Staff, Dept of Endocrinology and Internal Medicine, New England Deaconess Hosp., Boston 1981–85, Active Staff 1986–; Physician, Brigham and Women's Hosp., Boston 1981–91, Chief, Div. of Diabetes and Metabolism, Dept of Medicine 1981–92, Sr Physician 1992–, Sr Consultant in Diabetes and Metabolism 1993–; Prof. in Endocrinology and Metabolism, The Hosp. of the Good Samaritan, Los Angeles, CA 1985; Visiting Prof., Royal Postgraduate Hosp., London, UK 1985; Overseas Visiting Prof., Royal Melbourne Hosp., Melbourne, Australia 1985; Roerig Visiting Professorship in Diabetes, Univ. of Colorado Health Sciences Center, Denver, Colo 1990; Visiting Scientist, Dana Farber Cancer Inst., Dept of Cellular and Molecular Biology, Boston 1990–91; Visiting Research Scientist, Brandeis Univ., Waltham, Mass 1998–99; Exec. Ed. Trends in Endocrinology and Metabolism 1989–90; Consulting Ed. The Journal of Clinical Investigation 1992–; Assoc. Ed. Diabetes 1996–; mem. Editorial Bd Diabetes and Metabolism Reviews 1984–, Receptor 1989–, Trends in Endocrinology and Metabolism 1991–, Journal of Receptor Research 1992–, Proceedings of the Association of American Physicians 1997–, American Journal of Medicine 1998–; mem. Advisory Bd Endocrine Reviews 2001–; mem. American Fed. for Clinical Research 1972–, The Endocrine Soc. 1975– (mem. Council 1990–93), American Diabetes Asscn (ADA) 1976–, American Soc. for Clinical Investigation 1979– (Pres. 1988–89), American Soc. of Biological Chem. 1982–, Asscn of American Physicians 1983–, Nat. Council of American Soc. for Clinical Investigation 1985–, NAS 1999–, NAS Insts of Medicine 1999–; Fellow, American Acad. of Arts and Sciences 1991–, American Asscn for the Advancement of Science 1994–; Alumni Fellow, Univ. of Louisville 1993–; Hon. DSc (Louisville) 1984, (Université de Paris Pierre et Marie Curie) 1990; Hon. MA (Louisville) 1984; David Rumbough Memorial Award for Scientific Achievement, Juvenile Diabetes Foundation 1977, ADA Eli Lilly Award for Research 1981, Award for Outstanding Clinical Research Under Age 40, American Fed. for Clinical Research 1983, Pfizer Biomedical Research Award 1986, Cristobal Diaz Award, Int. Diabetes Foundation 1988, Top 100 Most-Cited Scientists for 1973–84 and 1981–88, The Scientist 1990, ADA Banting Medal for Distinguished Scientific Achievement 1993, Distinguished Scientist Award, Clinical Ligand Assay Soc. 1997, ADA Albert Renold Award 1998, Dorothy Hodgkin Award, British Diabetes Asscn 1999, Int. Soc. of Endocrinology Award, CCISE 2000, Fred Conrad Koch Award, The Endocrine Soc. 2000, and other awards. *Publications:* more than 440 articles in medical and scientific journals. *Address:* Kahn Lab, Harvard Medical School, Joslin Diabetes Center, One Joslin Place, Room 705, Boston, MA 02215, USA (office). *Telephone:* (617) 732-2635 (office). *Fax:* (617) 732-2540 (office). *E-mail:* c.ronald.kahn@joslin.harvard.edu (office). *Website:* www.joslin.org (office).

KAHN, Eugene (Gene) S.; American retail executive; b. 1950; ed City Coll. of NY; began retail career at Gimbel's 1971; joined The May Dept Stores Co. 1990, Pres. and CEO G. Fox Div. 1990–92, Pres. and CEO Filene Div. 1992–96, apptd to Bd of Dirs 1996, Vice-Chair. 1996–97, Exec. Vice-Chair. 1997–98, Pres. and CEO 1998, Chair. and CEO –2005; fmr Treas., Mary Inst. and St Louis Country Day School (MICDS); mem. Bd of Trustees, Wash. Univ. at St Louis. *Address:* c/o The May Department Stores Company, 611 Olive Street, St Louis, MO 63101, USA (office).

KAHN, Jacob Meyer, BA (Law), MBA; South African business executive; *Chairman, SABMiller plc;* b. 29 June 1939, Pretoria; m. Lynette Sandra Asher 1968; two d.; ed Univ. of Pretoria; Dir South African Breweries Ltd 1981, Group Man. Dir 1983, Exec. Chair. 1990–, Group Chair. 1999–; Chair. SABMiller plc 1999–; Chief Exec. South African Police Service 1997–99; fmr Pres. SA Foundation; Prof. Extraordinaire 1989; Hon. DComm (Univ. of Pretoria) 1990; Marketing Man of the Year 1987, Business Man of the Year 1990, Award for Business Excellence 1991, South African Police Star of Excellence for Outstanding Service 2000. *Leisure interests:* reading, golf. *Address:* SABMiller plc, PO Box 1099, Johannesburg (office); SABMiller plc, 2 Jan Smuts Avenue, Johannesburg; 4 East Road, Morningside, Sandton, Johannesburg, South Africa (home). *Telephone:* (11) 4071800 (office); (11) 7836061 (home). *Fax:* (11) 4031857 (office); (11) 7836061 (home). *E-mail:* carol.decastro@sabmiller.com (office). *Website:* www.sabmiller.com (office).

KAHN, Robert E., PhD; American computer scientist and electrical engineer; *Chairman, CEO and President, Corporation for National Research Initiatives;* ed City Coll. of New York, Princeton Univ.; fmr mem. Tech. Staff Bell Labs; later Asst Prof. of Electrical Eng MIT; joined US Defense Advanced Research Projects Agency (DARPA) 1972, later Dir Information Processing Techniques Office; co-inventor TCP/IP protocols, Knowbot programs, originated concept of architecture networking; f. Corpn for Nat. Research Initiatives (CNRI) 1986, currently Chair., CEO and Pres.; Fellow IEEE, AAAI, ACM; mem. Nat. Acad. of Eng; Hon. Fellow Univ. Coll. London; hon. degree (Princeton Univ., Univ. of Pavia, ETH Zurich, Univ. of Maryland, George Mason Univ., Univ. of Cen. Fla); AFIPS Harry Goode Memorial Award, Marconi Award, ACM SIGCOMM Award, ACM Pres.'s Award, ACM Software Systems Award, IEEE Koji Kobayashi Computer and Communications Award, IEEE Alexander Graham Bell Medal, IEEE Third Millennium Medal, Computerworld/Smithsonian Award, ASIS Special Award, Computing Research Bd Public Service Award, Sec. of Defense Civilian Service Award (twice), Nat. Medal of Tech. 1997, Nat. Acad. of Eng Charles Stark Draper Prize 2001, Prince of Asturias Award 2002, Digital ID World Award 2003, Asscn for Computing Machinery A. M. Turing Award 2004. *Address:* Corporation for National Research Initiatives, 1895 Preston White Drive, Suite 100, Reston, VA 20191-5434, USA (office). *Telephone:* (703) 620-8990 (office). *Fax:* (703) 620-0913 (office). *E-mail:* web-comments@cnri.reston.va.us (office). *Website:* www.cnri.reston.va.us (office).

KAHNEMAN, Daniel, PhD; Israeli/American psychologist and academic; *Eugene Higgins Professor of Psychology and Professor of Public Affairs, Woodrow Wilson School, Princeton University;* b. 1934, Tel-Aviv; m. Anne Treisman; ed The Hebrew Univ., Jerusalem, Univ. of Calif., Berkeley; Lecturer in Psychology The Hebrew Univ. 1961–66, Sr Lecturer 1966–70, Assoc. Prof. 1970–73, Prof. 1973–78; Lecturer in Psychology, Harvard Univ. 1966–67; Prof. of Psychology, Univ. of British Columbia, Canada 1978–86; Prof. of Psychology, Univ. of Calif., Berkeley 1986–94; Eugene Higgins Prof. of Psychology, Princeton Univ. 1993–, Prof. of Public Affairs, Woodrow Wilson School 1993–; Visiting Scientist, Univ. of Michigan 1965–66, Applied Psychological Research Unit, Cambridge, UK 1968–69; Fellow Centre for Cognitive Studies 1966–67, Centre for Advanced Studies in the Behavioural Sciences 1977–78, Centre for Rationality, The Hebrew Univ. 2000–; Assoc. Fellow Canadian Inst. for Advanced Research 1984–86; Visiting Scholar, Russell Sage Foundation 1991–92; Fellow American Acad. of Arts and Sciences, Econometric Soc., American Psychological Asscn, American Psychological Soc., Canadian Psychological Asscn; mem. NAS, Soc. of Experimental Psychologists, Psychonomic Soc., Soc. for Econ. Science, Soc. for Judgement and Decision Making (Pres. 1992–93); mem. Ed. Bd Journal of Behavioral Decision Making, Journal of Risk and Uncertainty, Thinking and Reasoning, Economics and Philosophy; pioneered integration of research about decision-making into field of econs; Hon. DrSc (Univ. of Pennsylvania Contrib.) 2001; Distinguished Scientific Contrib. Award, American Psychological Soc. 1982, Distinguished Scientific Contrib. Award, Soc. of Consumer Psychology 1992, Warren Medal, Soc. of Experimental Psychologists 1995, Hilgard Award for

Lifetime Contrib. to General Psychology 1995, Nobel Prize for Econ. Sciences 2002. *Publications include:* Attention and Effort 1973, Human Engineering of Decisions in Ethics in an Age of Uncertainty 1980, Well-Being: Foundations of Hedonic Psychology (co-ed.) 1999, Choices, Values and Frames (co-ed.) 2000, Heuristics and Biases: The Psychology of Intuitive Judgement (co-ed.) 2002; author or co-author of over 120 articles in professional journals and chapters in books. *Address:* 332 Wallace Hall, Woodrow Wilson School, Princeton University, Princeton, NJ 08544-1013, USA (office). *Telephone:* (609) 258-2280 (office). *Fax:* (609) 258-5974. *E-mail:* kahneman@princeton.edu (office). *Website:* www.wws.princeton.edu (office).

KAI-BANYA, Melrose; Sierra Leonean diplomatist; *Ambassador to Russia;* b. Freetown; fmr staff mem., Human Resources Man., Cen. Bank of Sierra Leone; fmr teacher, Milton Margai Teacher's Coll., Freetown; Amb. to Russia (also accred to Albania, Armenia, Serbia and Montenegro, Croatia, Kosovo, Azerbaijan, Belarus, Estonia, Georgia, Kazakhstan, Kyrgyzstan, Latvia, Lithuania, Moldova, Tajikistan, Ukraine, Uzbekistan, Czech Repub., Slovakia, Poland, Hungary and Bulgaria) 1996–; head of Group of African Ambs in Moscow. *Leisure interests:* theatre, museums, literature. *Address:* Embassy of Sierra Leone, 121615 Moscow, 26 Rublyovskoye shosse 26/1/58–59, POB 141, Russia (office). *Telephone:* (495) 415-41-66 (office). *Fax:* (495) 415-29-85 (office).

KAIFU, Toshiki; Japanese politician; b. 2 Jan. 1931, Nagoya City; m. Sachiyo Kaifu; ed Waseda Univ.; elected to House of Reps (LDP) 1960 and served 13 terms; Parl. Vice-Minister of Labour; Chair. Steering Cttee of House of Reps; various posts in admin. of the late Takeo Miki 1974–76, including Deputy Chief Cabinet Sec. 1974–76, Chair. of Diet Policy Cttee of Liberal Democratic Party (LDP); Minister of Educ. 1976–77, 1985–86; Prime Minister of Japan 1989–91 (resgnd); Leader New Frontier Party (opposition coalition) 1994–95; currently Chair. 21st Century World Expo Promotion Parliamentary League. *Address:* House of Representatives, National Diet Building, 1-7-1 Nagatacho, Chiyoda-ku, Tokyo, Japan.

KAIN, Karen, CC; Canadian ballet dancer and arts administrator; *Artistic Director, National Ballet of Canada;* b. 28 March 1951, Hamilton, Ont.; d. of Charles A. Kain and Winifred Mary Kelly; m. Ross Petty 1983; ed Nat. Ballet School; joined Nat. Ballet 1969, Prin. 1970; has danced most of major roles in repertoire; appeared as Giselle with Bolshoi Ballet on USSR tour, Aurora in the Sleeping Beauty with London Festival Ballet in UK and Australia, in Swan Lake with Vienna State Opera Ballet; toured Japan and Korea with Ballet national de Marseille 1981; cr. roles of Chosen Maiden in The Rite of Spring for Nat. Ballet 1979, Giuletta in Tales of Hoffman for Ballet national de Marseille 1982, the Bride in The Seven Daggers/Los Siete Puñales and roles in Glen Tetley's Alice 1986, La Ronde 1987, Daphnis and Chlöe 1988, Tagore 1989, Musings 1991, James Kudelka's The Actress 1994; appeared in CBC-TV productions of Giselle, La Fille Mal Gardée, The Merry Widow, Alice, La Ronde; Pres. The Dancer's Transition Centre; Artistic Assoc., Nat. Ballet of Canada 1999–2005, Artistic Dir 2005–; Officier des Arts et Lettres; hon. degrees from York, McMaster and Trent Univs; Silver Medal, Second Int. Ballet Competition, Moscow 1973, Int. Emmy Award for Karen Kain: Dancing in the Moment, Gov.-Gen.'s Award for Lifetime Achievement in the Performing Arts, Barbara Hamilton Memorial Award 2007. *Publication:* Movement Never Lies (autobiog.) 1994. *Address:* The Walter Carsen Centre for The National Ballet of Canada, 470 Queens Quay West, Toronto, ON M5V 3K4, Canada (office). *Telephone:* (416) 345-9686 (office). *Fax:* (416) 345-8323 (office). *E-mail:* info@national.ballet.ca (office). *Website:* www.national.ballet.ca (office).

KAINE, Timothy Michael; American politician; *Chairman, Democratic National Committee;* b. 26 Feb. 1958, St Paul, MN; m. Anne Holton; two s. one d.; ed Univ. of Missouri, Harvard Law School; worked as missionary in Honduras; fmr attorney; mem. City Council of Richmond, Va, later Mayor of Richmond; Lt Gov. and Pres. of the Senate of Va 2002–; Gov. of Va 2005–09; Chair. Democratic Nat. Cttee 2009–. *Leisure interests:* camping, hiking, cycling, canoeing. *Address:* Democratic National Committee, 430 South Capitol Street, SE, Washington, DC 20003, USA (office). *Telephone:* (202) 863-8000 (office). *Website:* www.democrats.org (office).

KAISER, Karl, PhD; German professor of political science; *Ralph I. Straus Visiting Professor, John F. Kennedy School of Government, Harvard University;* b. 8 Dec. 1934, Siegen; s. of Walther Kaiser and Martha Müller; m. Deborah Strong 1967; two s. one d.; ed Univs of Cologne, Bonn and Grenoble and Nuffield Coll., Oxford, UK; Lecturer, Harvard Univ. 1963–67, Univ. of Bonn 1968–69, Johns Hopkins Univ. Bologna Center 1968–69; Prof. of Political Science, Univ. of the Saarland 1969–74, Univ. of Cologne 1974–91, Univ. of Bonn 1991–; Otto-Wolf Dir Research Inst. of German Soc. for Foreign Affairs, Bonn and Berlin 1973–2003; currently Ralph I. Straus Visiting Prof., John F. Kennedy School of Govt., Harvard Univ.; mem. German Council of Environmental Advisors; mem. Bd of Dirs Foreign Policy, Internationale Politik, Asian-Pacific Review; mem. Advisory Bd American-Jewish Cottee, Berlin; mem. Bd Fed. Acad. of Security Policy, Berlin; Hon. CBE 1989; Officier, Légion d'honneur, Bundesverdienstkreuz Erster Klasse 1999; Prix Adolphe Bentinck 1973; NATO Atlantic Award 1986. *Publications:* EEC and Free Trade Area 1963, German Foreign Policy in Transition 1968, Europe and the USA 1973, New Tasks for Security Policy 1977, Reconciling Energy Needs and Proliferation 1978, Western Security: What Has Changed, What Can be Done? 1981, Atomic Energy Without Nuclear Weapons 1982, German–French Security Policy 1986, British–German Co-operation 1987, Space and International Politics 1987, Germany's Unification, The International Aspects 1991, Germany and the Iraq Conflict 1992, Foreign Policies of the New Republics in Eastern Europe 1994, Germany's New Foreign Policy, Vol. 1 1994, Vol. 2 1995, Vol. 3 1996, The Foreign Policies of the New Democracies in Central and Eastern Europe 1994, Acting for Europe, German-French Co-operation in a Changing World 1995, World Politics in a New Era 1996, Interests and Strategies 1996, Institutions and Resources 1998, The Future of German Foreign Policy 1999. *Leisure interests:* music, sailing. *Address:* Kennedy School of Government, Belfer-G-3, Mailbox 40, 79 JFK Street, Cambridge, MA 02138-5801, USA. *Telephone:* (617) 495-1899 (office). *Fax:* 617) 495-8292 (office). *E-mail:* karl_kaiser@ksg.harvard.edu (office). *Website:* ksgfaculty.harvard.edu/karl_kaiser (office).

KAISER, Michael M., BA, SM; American arts administrator; *President, John F. Kennedy Center for Performing Arts;* ed Brandeis Univ. and Sloan School of Man., MIT; Founder and Dir Michael M. Kaiser Assocs (consultancy) 1981–85, Kaiser/Engler (arts man. consultancy) 1994, Pres. 1994–95; Exec. Dir Alvin Ailey Dance Theater Foundation 1991–93, American Ballet Theatre 1995–98, Royal Opera House, London 1998–2000; Pres. John F. Kennedy Center for Performing Arts, Washington DC 2001–; Adjunct Prof. of Business Admin., Rockhurst Coll., Kan. 1985–86; Adjunct Prof. of Arts Admin., New York Univ.; US Del. to Advisory Comm. on Arts Funding Policies of S African Govt 1994–95; Visiting Prof. of Arts Admin., Univ. of Witwatersrand 1995; Assoc. Dir State Ballet of Mo. 1985–87, Pierpoint Morgan Library 1987–89; mem. Bd of Dirs New York Foundation for the Arts; fmr Dir Washington Opera, Ensemble Studio Theater, PS 122; Order of the Mexican Eagle 2006; Dance Magazine Award 2001, Capezio Award 2002, Helen Hayes Washington Post Award for Innovative Leadership in the Theater Community 2003, St Petersburg 300 Medal 2004, Washingtonian of the Year 2004, US Dept of State Citation 2005, Blacks in Dance Award 2005, Award for Cultural Exchange (China) 2005, Impresario of the Year by Musical America 2006. *Publications:* Understanding the Competition: A Practical Guide to Competitive Analysis 1981, Developing Industry Strategies: A Practical Guide to Industry Analysis 1983, Strategic Planning in the Arts: A Practical Guide 1995, The Art of the Turnaround 2008. *Address:* John F. Kennedy Center for Performing Arts, 2700 F Street, NW, Washington, DC 20566, USA (office). *Telephone:* (202) 416-8000 (office). *Website:* www.kennedy-center.org (office).

KAJANTIE, Keijo Olavi, PhD; Finnish physicist and academic; *Professor of Physics, University of Helsinki;* b. 31 Jan. 1940, Hämeenlinna; m. Riitta Erkiö 1963; one s. one d.; ed Univ. of Helsinki; Visiting Scientist CERN, Geneva 1966–67, 1969–70, 1995–98; Assoc. Prof. of Physics, Univ. of Helsinki 1970–72, Prof. 1973–, currently Head, Theoretical Physics Div.; Visiting Prof., Univ. of Wis., Madison 1975; Research Prof. Acad. of Finland 1985–90; Sr Scientist, Acad. of Finland 2002–03. *Publications:* more than 180 publs in the field of elementary particle physics. *Address:* Department of Physics, PO Box 64, 00014 University of Helsinki, Helsinki, Finland; Liisankatu 12D 26, 00170 Helsinki, Finland (home). *Telephone:* (9) 19150622 (Univ.); (9) 1352232 (home). *E-mail:* keijo.kajantie@helsinki.fi (office). *Website:* www.helsinki.fi/~kajantie (office).

KAJIYAMA, Tisato, PhD, DEng; Japanese polymer chemist, university administrator and academic; *President, Kyushu University;* ed Univ. of Massachusetts, USA, Kyushu Univ.; Prof., Dept of Applied Chem., Faculty of Eng, Kyushu Univ., currently Pres. Kyushu Univ. and Head, Kyushu Univ. User Science Inst. *Publications:* New Developments in Construction and Functions of Organic Thin Films 1996, Polymer Science and Industrial Research in the Fast-Changing Age: 7th SPSJ International Polymer Conference (ed.) 2000, Macromolecular Symposia 159: Polymer Science and Industrial Research (ed.); numerous scientific papers in professional journals on polymer chemistry. *Address:* Kyushu University, 6-10-1 Hakozaki, Higashi-ku, Fukuoka 812-8581, Japan (office). *Telephone:* (92) 642-2100 (office). *Fax:* (92) 642-4236 (office). *Website:* www.kyushu-u.ac.jp (office).

KAKÁ; Italian (b. Brazilian) professional footballer; b. (Ricardo Izecson dos Santos Leite), 15 May 1982, Brasilia; m. Caroline Celico 2005; began career as jr football player with São Paulo FC 1990, turned professional 2002; first match for nat. Brazilian team 2002; joined AC Milan, Italy, as midfielder 2003–; Jr Championship Winner, São Paulo 2000, UEFA Best European Midfielder 2005, FIFPro World Player of the Year 2007, UEFA Top Forward of the 2006–07 CL season and Club Footballer of the Year 2007, France Football Magazine Ballon D'Or for European Footballer of the Year 2007, FIFA World Player of the Year 2007, World Soccer Player of the Year 2007. *Address:* AC Milan, Via Filippo Turati 3, 20121 Milan, Italy (office). *Telephone:* (02) 62281 (office). *Fax:* (02) 6598876 (office). *Website:* www.acmilan.com (office).

KAKARAYA, Sir Pato; Papua New Guinea government official; b. Sambakmanda village, Enga Prov.; MP for Wapenamanda 1972–1987; fmr Minister; f. Peoples Democratic Movt; Gov.-Gen. of Papua New Guinea 2004. *Address:* c/o Government House, POB 79, Port Moresby 121, Papua New Guinea (office).

KAKLAMANIS, Apostolos; Greek politician and lawyer; b. 7 Sept. 1936, Lefkas; s. of Christos Kaklamanis and Evageloula Kaklamanis; m. Athina-Anna Gavera 1972; one s. one d.; ed Univ. of Athens; Gen. Sec. Ministry of Welfare 1964–65; political prisoner during colonels' dictatorship; Founding mem. Pasok and mem. Cen. Cttee and Exec. Cttee; mem. Vouli (Parl.) for Athens B 1974–; Minister of Labour 1981–82, of Educ. and Religious Affairs 1982–86, of Justice 1986–87, Minister in charge of the Prime Minister's Office 1987–88, Minister of Health, Welfare and Social Services 1988–89, of Labour 1989–90; Speaker of Parl. 1993–2004. *Address:* Vouli, Parliament Bldg, Syntagma Square, 100 21 Athens (office); Solomou 58, 106 82 Athens, Greece (office). *Telephone:* (210) 3608640 (office); (210) 3708200 (office). *Fax:* (210) 3708210 (office). *E-mail:* apkaklamanis@parliament.gr (office); ak@apkaklamanis.gr (office). *Website:* www.parliament.gr (office); www.apkaklamanis.gr (office).

KAKOURIS, Constantine; Greek judge; b. 16 March 1919, Pyrgos; s. of Nicolas and Helen Kakouris; ed Univs of Athens and Paris; called to Bar, Athens 1942; Auxiliary Judge, Supreme Admin. Court 1951–62, Asst Judge 1962–70, Judge 1970–83; Judge, Court of Justice of EEC 1983–97; several times mem. or Pres. High Council of the Judiciary and High Council of Diplomatic Corps, Chief Inspector for Admin. Tribunals; Pres. or mem. several cttees.; Corresp. mem. Acad. of Athens 1996–; Dr hc (Univ. of Athens Law School) 1992. *Publications:* A study of General Theory of Law on Judiciary Power and the Mission of the Courts; articles and reviews in legal and philosophical journals. *Leisure interest:* philosophy. *Address:* 52, Skoufa Street, 106 72 Athens, Greece. *Telephone:* (1) 3635588.

KALAM, Aavul Pakkiri Jainulabidin Abdul, PhD; Indian fmr head of state and nuclear scientist; b. 15 Oct. 1931, Dhanushkodi, Rameswaram Dist; ed Madras Inst. of Tech.; mem. staff Space Dept 1960s and 1970s, later Defence Lab., Hyderabad; launched India's first satellite 1980, masterminded integrated guided missile devt and nuclear programmes, developed Agni, Trishul and Prithvi missiles, responsible for carrying out underground nuclear tests 1998; fmr Cabinet Minister and Prin. Scientific Adviser to Govt 1999–2001; Chair. Tech. Information, Forecasting and Assessment Council; head of an agricultural devt agency; Pres. of India 2002–07; Padma Bhusan 1981, Padma Vibhushan 1990, Bharat Ratna 1997. *Publications include:* Yenudaya Prayana (Tamil poems), Wings of Fire (bestselling autobiog.) 1999, Eternal Quest (children's novel), Ignited Minds: Unleashing the Power Within India 2001. *Address:* c/o President's Office, Rashtrapati Bhavan, New Delhi 110 004 (office); 10 Rajaji Marg, New Delhi, India (home).

KALAMANOV, Vladimir Avdashevich, DrHist; Russian politician; *Representative of Russian Federation, United Nations Educational, Scientific and Cultural Organization (UNESCO);* b. 1951, Moscow; ed Moscow State Inst. of Int. Relations; Head of Dept Ministry of Problems with Nationalities; Plenipotentiary Rep. of Pres. in Repubs. of N Ossetia and of Ingushetia 1997–99; Dir Fed. Migration Service of Russian Fed. 1999–2002; Special Rep. of Pres. to supervise observance of human rights and freedom in Chechen Repub. 2000; Rep. of Russian Fed. at UNESCO 2002–. *Address:* 1 rue Miollis, 75732, Paris, Cedex 15, France. *Telephone:* 1-45-68-26-82; 1-45-04-37-52. *Fax:* 1-42-67-51-99. *E-mail:* unerus@club-internet.fr.

KALANTARI, Issa, PhD; Iranian scientist and agriculturalist; *Director, Farmers' House;* b. 1952, Marand; s. of Mohammad Hussein Kalantari and Kobra Kalantari (née Esfandi); m. 1982; one s. one d.; ed Univ. of Urmiya, Univ. Nebraska and Iowa State Univ., USA; Dir Farmers' House (agricultural union) 1981–; Head of Agricultural Extension Org. 1982, Plant and Seed Improvement Research Inst. 1983, Deputy Minister for Agricultural Research, Educ. and Extension 1983–85, Man. Dir and Head of Bd of Dirs Moghan Stock-farming and Agro-Industry Complex, Ministry of Agric. 1985–88; Minister of Agric. 1988–2001; Pres. World Food Council 1991–95. *Publications:* A Policy for Reforming Nutrition Patterns: Nutrition Physiology and Foodstuff Economics 1997; series of articles in journal Agricultural Economics and Development. *Leisure interests:* reading, sport. *Address:* Farmers' House, 21, 33rd Street, JahanAra Avenue, Tehran (office); 5, Morshed, Sheidai Street, Gholhak, Tehran, Iran (home). *Telephone:* (21) 886390612 (office); (21) 22001057 (home). *Fax:* (21) 88639060 (office). *E-mail:* issakalantari@gmail.com (home).

KALASHNIKOV, Lt-Gen. Mikhail Timofeyevich, DTechSc; Russian military engineer; b. 10 Nov. 1919, Kuria, Altai Territory; s. of Timofei Alexandrovich Kalashnikov and Alexandra Frolovna; m. (deceased); one s. two d.; served during World War II, wounded; inventor of new types of armaments since 1940s, of AK, AKM carbines RPK-74, RPKS-74, 5.45 mm light machine guns, AK-74, AKS-74, AKS-74U assault rifles (total number of machine carbines produced designed by Kalashnikov exceeds 55 million); Chief constructor Head of Constructor's Bureau at Izhmash; Deputy of USSR Supreme Soviet 1950–54, 1966–69, 1970–73, 1974–78, 1979–88; Order of the Red Star 1949; Order of Banner of Labour 1957; Hero of Socialist Labour 1958, 1976; Order of Lenin 1958, 1969, 1976; Order of Great October Socialist Revolution 1974; Order of Peoples' Friendship 1982; Order of Patriotic War, First Class 1985; Order for Distinguished Services to the Motherland, Second Class 1994; Andrei Pervozvanny Order 1998; Order 'Pashany' (Badge of Honour) (Belarus) 1999; Peter the Great Order 2001; Order 'Doslyk' First Class (Peoples' Friendship) (Kazakhstan 2003; USSR State Prize 1949, Lenin Prize 1964, State Prize 1998; Pres. of Russian Fed. Prize 2003. *Publications:* Memories of a Weapon Designer, From a Stranger's Doorstep to the Kremlin's Gates, We Went With You by One Road. *Leisure interests:* hunting, fishing, gardening, reading historical books. *Address:* AO 'Izhmash', 426006 Izhevsk; Sovetskaya ul. 21A –46, 426076 Izhevsk, Russia (home). *Telephone:* (3412) 49-52-49 (office); (3412) 52-41-85 (home). *Fax:* (3412) 78-17-80.

KALASHNIKOV, Sergey Vyacheslavovich, DPsych; Russian politician; b. 3 July 1951, Akmolinsk, Kazakh SSR; m. Natalia Kalashnikova; three c.; ed Leningrad State Univ., Inst. of Psychology, USSR (now Russian) Acad. of Sciences, Acad. of Nat. Econs USSR Council of Ministers, Russian Diplomatic Acad.; Head, Social-Psychological service of the Research Inst., USSR Ministry of Defence Industry, concurrently Chair. Inst. of Advanced Studies, USSR Ministry of Oil and Chemical Industry, Dir Intermanager State Enterprise 1979–91; Chair. European-Asian Bank; concurrently Dir-Gen. Asscn of Defence against Unemployment and Poverty, Chair. Cttee on Labour and Social Policy in the State Duma, Deputy of the Duma, Chair. Perm. Cttee on Social Policy, Interparliamentary Ass. of CIS 1993–98; Minister of Labour and Social Devt 1998–2000; Deputy Sec.-Gen. Union of Russia and Belarus 2000–03; Head, Dept of Social Devt, Office of the Govt 2003–; Pres. Russian Fed. of the Sports Lover, Russian Asscn of Professional Golf; Chair. Nat. Council for Political and Social Reform; Co-Chair. Int. Forum 'World Experience and the Russian Economy'; mem. Bd Moscow English Club, Jury All-Russian Competition 'Best Russian Firms'; mem. Int. Acad. of Informatics, Russian Acad. of Science; Order of Friendship; Badge of Excellence for Border Services, Distinguished Worker of the Russian Ministry of Labour, Laureate, Nat. Peter the Great Prize. *Publications:* more than 50 works including two monographs and textbook Social Psychology of Management. *Address:* Office of the Government, Krasnopresnenskaya nab. 2, 103274 Moscow, Russia (office). *Telephone:* (495) 205-57-35 (office). *Fax:* (495) 205-42-19 (office). *Website:* www.government.ru (office).

KALBFELL, Karl-Heinz; German automotive industry executive; b. 29 Dec. 1949; ed FH Druck Univ.; fmr boxer; responsible for advertising at Eriba/Hymer, camper and caravan builder 1975–77; Head of Marketing, BMW GmbH 1977, Man. 1988, Sr Vice-Pres. BMW Group Marketing, Dir Rolls-Royce Project 2001, Dir (non-exec.) 2003, Chair. and CEO Rolls-Royce Motor Cars June–Oct. 2004; Head, Alfa Romeo Jan.–Sept. 2005, CEO Maserati SpA 2005–06 (resgnd), Chair. Fiat Polo Sportivo planning comm. *Address:* c/o Maserati SpA, Viale Ciro Menotti 322, 41100 Modena, Italy (office).

KALETSKY, Anatole, MA; British journalist; *Associate Editor and Economic Commentator, The Times (UK);* b. 1 June 1952, Moscow, Russia; s. of Jacob Kaletsky and Esther Kaletsky; m. Fiona Murphy 1985; two s. one d.; ed Melbourne High School, Australia, Westminster City School and King's Coll., Cambridge, UK and Harvard Univ., USA; Hon. Sr Scholar, King's Coll., Cambridge 1973–74; Kennedy Scholar, Harvard Univ., USA 1974–76; financial writer, The Economist 1976–79; leader writer, Financial Times 1979–81, Washington Corresp. 1981–83, Int. Econs Corresp. 1984–86, Chief, New York Bureau 1986–90, Moscow Assignment 1990; Econs Ed. The Times 1990–96, Assoc. Ed. and econ. commentator 1992–; Dir Kaletsky Econ. Consulting 1997–; mem. Advisory Bd UK Know-How Fund for E Europe and fmr Soviet Union 1991–, Royal Econs Soc. 1999–; Specialist Writer of the Year, British Press Awards 1980, 1992, Press Awards Commentator of the Year 1995, What the Papers Say 1996, Financial Journalist of the Year, Wincott Foundation Award 1997. *Publications:* The Costs of Default 1985, In the Shadow of Debt 1992. *Leisure interests:* playing the violin, cinema, family life. *Address:* The Times, 1 Pennington Street, London, E1 9XY, England (office). *Telephone:* (20) 7782-5000 (office). *Fax:* (20) 7782-5046 (office). *Website:* www.timesonline.co.uk (office).

KALFIN, Ivailo Georgiev, MSc; Bulgarian politician; *Deputy Prime Minister and Minister of Foreign Affairs;* b. 30 May 1964, Sofia; m.; one d.; ed French Language School, Sofia, Univ. of Nat. and World Economy, Sofia, Business Univ., Vienna, Austria, Univ. of Loughborough, UK, Coll. of Europe, Bruges, Belgium; scholarship student under Chevening program, UK and German Marshall Fund, USA; taught Finance at Int. Univ., Sofia; worked for Machinoexport as well as in pvt. sector in the field of foreign trade, finance and consulting; mem. Municipal Council of Bulgarian Socialist Party (BSP), Supreme Council of BSP, Political Council of the Bulgarian Euroleft; Spokesperson for pre-election coalition 'Together for Bulgaria' 1996; mem. Parl. for Sofia (Parl. Group of the Democratic Left) 1994–97, 2000–01, 2005–, mem. Foreign Policy Cttee, Budgeting and Finance Cttee, Deputy Chair. Bulgarian-EU Jt Parl. Cttee; Sec. for Econ. Affairs to the Pres. 2002–05; Deputy Prime Minister and Minister of Foreign Affairs 2005–; Founder Social Democrats Political Movt; Man. and Sr Partner in consulting cos 1990–94, 1997–2000; Sr Prof., Univ., Sofia 2000–; observer of elections in Kosovo as mem. OSCE Missions 2001, 2003; mem. Advisory Bd Bulgarian Nat. Bank 2004–, Bulgaria Beyond the Facts Early Warning System implemented by UNDP and USAID; Founding mem. Bulgarian Macroeconomics Asscn; mem. Asscn of British Alumni in Bulgaria, Bd Dirs Inst. for Econs and Int. Relations, Fellows Network of the German Marshall Fund of the USA, Asscn of Scholarship Fellows of the Chevening programme, UK. *Publications:* Bulgaria 2010: Economic Challenges (report to Pres. of Bulgaria) (co-author) 2005, Factors of Economic Growth in Bulgaria (co-author) 2000; numerous articles in Bulgaria and in int. trade journals on EU and macroeconomic issues. *Address:* Ministry of Foreign Affairs, 1040 Sofia, ul. Al. Zhendov 2, Bulgaria (office). *Telephone:* (2) 971-14-08 (office). *Fax:* (2) 870-30-41 (office). *E-mail:* iprd@mfa.government.bg (office). *Website:* www.mfa.government.bg (office); www.kalfin.eu (home).

KALICHSTEIN, Joseph, MSc; American/Israeli pianist; b. 15 Jan. 1946, Tel-Aviv; s. of Isaac Kalichstein and Mali Kalichstein; m. Rowain (née Schultz) Kalichstein; two c.; ed Juilliard School, New York; New York debut 1967; European debut 1970; appearances with all the world's leading orchestras; engagements include Nat. Symphony Orchestra, Washington, DC, Cincinnati Symphony, US tour with Jerusalem Symphony and Lawrence Foster, and return tours to Japan and Scandinavia; mem. Piano Faculty of Juilliard School 1985–; First Prize, Leventritt Int. Competition 1969, Edward Stevermann Memorial Prize 1969. *Leisure interests:* reading, chess. *Address:* Opus 3 Artists, 470 Park Avenue South, 9th Floor North, New York, NY 10016, USA (office); Harrison Parrott, 5–6 Albion Court, London, W6 0QT, England (office). *Telephone:* (212) 584-7500 (office); (20) 7229-9166 (office). *Fax:* (646) 300-8200 (office); (20) 7221-5042 (office). *E-mail:* info@opus3artists.com (office); info@harrisonparrott.co.uk (office). *Website:* www.opus3artists.com (office); www.harrisonparrott.com (office).

KALILOMBE, Rt Rev. Patrick-Augustine, STL, SSL, PhD; Malawi ecclesiastic and lecturer; *Bishop Emeritus of Lilongwe;* b. 28 Aug. 1933, Dedza; s. of Pierre Kalilombe and Helena Mzifei; ed Kasina Seminary, Kachebere Theological Coll., Gregorian Univ., Rome, Graduate Theological Union, Berkeley, USA; trained as White Father, Algeria and Tunisia 1954–58; ordained priest 1958; teacher and Rector, Kachebere Major Seminary 1964–72; Bishop of Lilongwe 1972–79 (resgnd), now Bishop Emer.; Fellow and Lecturer in Third World Theologies, Selly Oak Colls, Univ. of Birmingham, UK 1982–86, Dir Centre for Black and White Christian Partnership, Selly Oak Colls 1985, Sr Lecturer, Third World Theologies 1982–87; Vice-Pres. East African Episcopal Confs 1974–76, Ecumenical Asscn of Third World Theologians 1976–78, Ecumenical Asscn of African Theologians 1985; Cttee mem. Symposium of Episcopal Confs of Africa and Madagascar 1974–76; mem. Council, Malawi Univ. 1974–76. *Publications:* Christ's Church in Lilongwe 1973, From Outstations to Small Christian Communities 1983, Doing Theology at the Grassroots 2000. *Address:* c/o Diocese of Lilongwe, PO Box 33, Lilongwe, Malawi.

KALIMBETOVA, Tazhikan B.; Kyrgyzstani politician; b. 1964; Deputy Minister of Finance –2007, also head of financial intelligence service 2005–07, Minister of Finance 2007–09, Chair. Iran-Kyrgyzstan Jt Econ. Comm.; Deputy Chair. EurAsian Group 2006–07; Chair. Social Fund 2007–. *Address:* c/o Ministry of Finance, 720040 Bishkek, pr. Erkindik 58, Kyrgyzstan.

KALIŇÁK, Robert; Slovak lawyer and politician; *Deputy Prime Minister and Minister of the Interior;* b. 11 May 1971, Bratislava; ed Faculty of Law, Comenius Univ., Bratislava; Man. ACE Press (legal publrs) 1991; Asst, Commercial Law Office 1992–95; Articled Clerk, Maríková and Pnrs (law firm), Bratislava 1995–99; Attorney, MKKT (law firm) 1999–2002; mem. Národná rada Slovenskej republiky (Parl.) 2002–, Chair. Cttee for Defence and Security 2002–04, Special Supervision Cttee of Nat. Security Office 2004–06; mem. Regional Council of Bratislava 2005–; Deputy Prime Minister and Minister of Interior 2006–; mem. Slovak Bar Asscn. *Address:* Ministry of the Interior, Pribinova 2, 812 72 Bratislava, Slovakia (office). *Telephone:* (2) 5094-1111 (office). *Fax:* (2) 5094-4397 (office). *E-mail:* tokmv@minv.sk (office). *Website:* www.minv.sk (office).

KALINOWSKI, Jarosław; Polish politician; b. 12 April 1962, Wyszków; m.; two d. three s.; ed Warsaw Agricultural Univ., Inst. of Law Sciences of the Polish Acad. of Sciences; owner of farm in Jackowo Górne; mem. Union of Rural Youth (ZMW) 1981–89; Admin. Somianka village 1990–97; Deputy to Sejm (Parl.) 1993–; Deputy Prime Minister and Minister of Agric. and Food Economy (later Rural Devt) 1997, 2001–03; mem. and fmr Pres. Polish People's Party (Polskie Stronnictwo Ludowe—PSL) 1997–, Chair. PSL Parl. Club 2000–, Chair. Caucus 2000–01; cand. in Polish presidential election 2000; Deputy to Local Ass. of the Voivodship of Mazovia 1998–2000. *Leisure interests:* culture and folk music. *Address:* Polskie Stronnictwo Ludowe, ul. Grzybowska 4, 00-131 Warsaw, Poland (office). *Telephone:* (22) 654-38-49 (office); (22) 620-60-20 (office). *Fax:* (22) 620-60-26 (office). *E-mail:* psl@psl.org .pl (office). *Website:* www.psl.org.pl (office).

KALLA, Yusuf, BEcons; Indonesian politician and business executive; *Vice-President;* b. 15 May 1942, Watampone, South Sulawesi; ed Hassanudin Univ., Makassar (fmrly Ujungpandang), South Sulawesi; began career as Chair. Advisory Council of Indonesian Chamber of Commerce and Industry (KADIN) at prov. level (South Sulawesi) and Coordinator of KADIN for Eastern Indonesia; Rep. of South Sulawesi in Peoples' Consultative Ass.; served in House of Reps for four consecutive terms (including chair. of communication forum for reps at regional level); apptd Chief of Nat. Logistics Agency (Bulog) 1999–2000; Minister of Trade and Industry 1999–2000 (forced to resign by Pres. Wahid on suspicion of corruption); Coordinating Minister for People's Welfare 2001–04; Vice-Pres. of Indonesia 2004–; mem. Partai Golongan Karya (Golkar), Pres. and Chair. 2004–; Chair. PT Makassar Mina Usaha, PT Kalla Inti Karsa and NV Hadji Kalla Trading Co. *Address:* Office of the Vice-President, Jalan Merdeka Selatan 6, Jakarta (office); Partai Golongan Karya (Golkar), Jalan Anggrek Nellimurni, Jakarta 11480, Indonesia. *Telephone:* (21) 363539 (Office of Vice-Pres.) (office); (21) 5302222. *Fax:* (21) 5303380. *E-mail:* info@golkar.or.id. *Website:* www.golkar .or.id.

KALLAS, Siim; Estonian politician and banker; *Vice-President for Administrative Affairs, Audit and Anti-Fraud, European Commission;* b. 2 Oct. 1948, Tallinn; s. of Udo Kallas and Rita Kallas; m. Kristi Kallas (née Kartus) 1972; one s. one d.; ed Tartu State Univ.; Chief Specialist Ministry of Finance Estonian SSR 1975–79; Gen. Man. Estonian Savings Banks 1979–86; Deputy Ed. Rahva Hääl 1986–89; Chair. Asscn of Estonian Trade Unions 1989–91; Pres. Eesti Pank (Bank of Estonia) 1991–95; Founder and Chair. Estonian Reform Party (Eesti Reformierakond) 1994–2004; elected to Riigikogu (Parl.) 1995–99, also mem. Parl. Nat. Defence Cttee and Parl. Foreign Affairs Cttee 2003–04; Minister of Foreign Affairs 1995–96; Minister of Finance 1999–2002; Prime Minister of the Repub. of Estonia 2002–03; Visiting Prof., Tartu State Univ.; EU Commr without Portfolio 2004, Vice-Pres. for Admin. Affairs, Audit and Anti-Fraud 2004–; Cross of the Order of Merit (Germany) 2000, Grand Officier, Légion d'honneur 2001, Order of the Nat. Coat of Arms 2003. *Leisure interests:* history, reading, opera, tennis, cycling. *Address:* European Commission, 200 Rue de la Loi, Berlaymont, 1040 Brussels, Belgium (office). *Telephone:* (2) 298-87-62 (direct line) (office); (2) 298-87-63 (office). *Fax:* (2) 298-84-92 (office). *E-mail:* siim.kallas@ec.europa.eu (office). *Website:* ec .europa.eu/commission_barroso/kallas (office).

KALLASVUO, Olli-Pekka, LLM; Finnish telecommunications executive; *President and CEO, Nokia Corporation;* b. 13 July 1953, Lavia; ed Univ. of Helsinki; fmrly with Union Bank of Finland; Corp. Counsel Nokia 1980, Asst Vice-Pres. Legal Dept 1987, Asst Vice-Pres. Finance 1988–90, mem. Group Exec. Bd 1990–, Sr Vice-Pres. Finance 1990–91, Exec. Vice-Pres. and Chief Financial Officer Nokia 1992–96, 1999–2003, Corp. Exec. Vice-Pres. Nokia Americas 1997–98, Exec. Vice-Pres. and Gen. Man. of Mobile Phones 2004–05, Pres. and COO Nokia 2005–06, Pres. and CEO 2006–, mem. Bd Dirs 2007–; Chair. Nokia Siemens Networks BV; mem. Bd of Dirs EMC Corpn. *Leisure interests:* golf, tennis, political history. *Address:* Nokia Corporation, Keilalahdentie 4, 00045 Espoo, Finland (office). *Telephone:* (7180) 08000 (office). *Fax:* (7180) 38226 (office). *E-mail:* info@nokia.com (office). *Website:* www .nokia.com (office).

KALLIO, Heikki Olavi, LLM, DrPhil; Finnish historian, writer and fmr organization official; b. 9 June 1937, Turku; m. 1st Liisa Toivonen 1961 (divorced 1995); three s. one d.; m. 2nd Anneli Hämäläinen 1997; ed Helsinki Univ., Tallinn Univ.; Chief Admin. Officer, Univ. of Turku 1963–71; Admin. Dir Acad. of Finland 1971–72, Exec. Vice-Pres. (Admin.) 1973–2002; Admin. Dir State Tech. Research Centre 1973; historian and writer 2002–; Dr hc (Tallinn); Finnish Order of White Cross, Kt 1st Class, Hungarian Order of Merit, Kt Commdr, Order of Templars, Kt Grand Cross, Medal of Honour, Merited Service of the State of Finland. *Publications:* Finnish–Estonian Scientific Relations with Special Focus on the Occupation Years 1940–91. *Leisure interests:* sailing, navigation, safety and security at sea, historiography. *Address:* Rapakivenkuja 2 D 33, 00710 Helsinki, Finland (home). *Telephone:* (40) 5569755 (home). *E-mail:* heikki.kallio@pp1.inet.fi (office).

KALLIOMÄKI, Antti Tapana; Finnish politician; b. 8 Jan. 1947, Siikainen; m. Helena Marjatta Kalliomäki 1969; two s.; physical training teacher, Hämeenkylä Upper Comprehensive School 1973–91; Project Man. Finnish Sports Asscn 1981–83; mem. Vantaa City Council 1984–2000; Chair. Vantaa Municipal Org. 1988–92; mem. Parl. 1983–, Chair. SDP Parl. Group 1991–95, 1999–2003, Vice-Chair. Cttee for the Future 1993–95, mem. Parl. Cttee on Defence Policy 1986–87, Cttee on Sports 1988–90, Parl. Advisory Bd on Defence Policy 1989–91; Chair. Parl. Security Policy Monitoring Group 2002–03; mem. SDP Party Cttee/Party Exec. 1990–2002; Vice-Chair. European SDP 2001–; Sec. to Prime Minister 1986–87; Minister of Trade and Industry 1995–99; Deputy Prime Minister and Minister of Finance 2003–05; Minister of Educ. 2005–07; mem. Parl. Supervisory Council, Bank of Finland 1987–91, Admin. Council, Finnish Broadcasting Co. (YLE) 2002–03 (Vice-Chair. 2002–03); Chair. Supervisory Bd Neste 1994–95. *Address:* c/o Suomen Sosialidemokraattinen Puolue (SDP) (Finnish Social Democratic Party), Saariniemenkatu 6, 00530 Helsinki, Finland (office).

KALLIS, Jacques Henry; South African cricketer; b. 16 Oct. 1975, Pinelands, Cape Province; ed Wynberg Boys High School; right-handed batsman and right-arm fast-medium bowler; teams played for various age-group teams (Western Province Under-13, Under-19, South Africa Schools, Under-17, Under-19, Under-24), Western Province 1994–, Middlesex 1997, Glamorgan 1999, South Africa 1995– (test debut versus England at Durban, 1995, one-day int. debut versus England at Cape Town, 1996); scored 6,656 runs (average 55.46, with 19 hundreds) and taken 167 wickets (average 31.23) in 85 tests; 7,267 runs (average 45.99) and 189 wickets in 203 one-day ints; 12,692 runs (average 52.88, with 35 hundreds) and 301 wickets in 171 first-class matches; in 2004 became first batsman since Sir Donald Bradman to hit five centuries in consecutive test innings; selected for World XI team 2005; ranked world's number one batsman for the first time in January 2005; Founder Jacques Kallis Scholarship Foundation 2006; South Africa Cricketer of the Year 1999, 2000, 2004, Int. Cricket Council (ICC) Player of the Year 2004, Sir Garfield Sobers Trophy 2004. *Leisure interest:* golf. *Address:* c/o United Cricket Board of South Africa, Gauteng, South Africa. *Telephone:* (11) 8802810. *E-mail:* proteas@cricket.co.za. *Website:* www.cricket.co.za; www .kallis.co.za.

KALLSBERG, Anfinn; Faroe Islands politician; b. 19 Nov. 1947; s. of Gunnar Kallsberg and Katrina Kallsberg; with J. F. Kjølbro 1964–74; self-employed bookkeeper, Vidareidi 1974–96; Mayor of Vidareidi 1974–80; mem. Faroese Rep. Council 1980–, Chair. 1991–93, Chair. Finance Cttee 1989–91, 2004–, mem. Foreign Affairs Cttee 2004; Prime Minister and Minister of Constitutional Affairs, Foreign Affairs and Municipal Affairs 1998–2004; one of two reps of Faroe Islands in Danish Folketing (Parl.) 2005–; mem. Nordic Council 1991, 1994–98; mem. Man. Cttee Klaksvik Hosp. 1991–96; mem. Fólkaflokkurin (People's Party). *Address:* FO-750, Vidareidi; c/o Fólkaflokkurin (People's Party), Jónas Broncksgøta 29, 100 Tórshavn, Faroe Islands. *Telephone:* 451032. *Fax:* 451032. *E-mail:* anfinn.kallsberg@ft.dk; folkaflokkurin@logting.fo. *Website:* www.kallsberg.fo; folkaflokkurin.fo.

KALMAN, Jozef, RSDr; Slovak politician and trade union official; *Chairman, Left-wing Bloc (Ľavicový blok);* b. 18 April 1951, Pohorelá, Banská Bystrica Dist; s. of Jozef Kalman and Lucia Kalmanová; m. Mária Kalmanová 1972; two d.; official of Metal Workers' Trade Union; Deputy Prime Minister of Slovak Repub. 1994–98; Vice-Chair. Movt for a Democratic Slovakia (HZDS) 2000–02; Chair. Left-wing Bloc (Ľavicový blok) 2002–; unsuccessful cand. for Pres. 2004. *Address:* Left-wing Bloc (Ľavicový blok), Nevädzova 5, 821 01 Bratislava, Slovakia (office). *E-mail:* aparat@lavicovyblok.sk (office). *Website:* www.lavicovyblok.sk (office).

KÁLMÁN, Rudolf Emil, BEng, MEng, ScD; Hungarian/American mathematician and academic; *Professor Emeritus, Eidgenössische Technische Hochschule Zürich (ETH Zürich);* b. 19 May 1930, Budapest; m. Constantina Stavrou; one s. one d.; ed Massachusetts Inst. of Tech., Columbia Univ.; Research Mathematician, Research Inst. for Advanced Study, Baltimore 1958–64; Prof., Stanford Univ. 1964–71; Grad. Research Prof. and Dir Center for Math. System Theory, Univ. of Florida, Gainesville 1971–92; Chair. for Math. System Theory, Eidgenössische Technische Hochschule Zürich (ETH Zürich) 1973–; mem. NAS, Nat. Acad. of Eng, American Acad. of Arts and Sciences; Foreign mem. Hungarian, French and Russian Acads of Science; numerous hon. doctorates; IEEE Medal of Honor 1974, IEEE Centennial Medal 1984, Inamori Foundation Kyoto Prize in High Tech. 1985, American Math. Soc. Steele Prize 1987, Richard E. Bellman Control Heritage Award 1997, Nat. Acad. of Eng Charles Stark Draper Prize 2008. *Achievements include:* inventor of Kalman filter, optical digital technique used in control systems and avionics. *Publications:* over 50 technical articles. *Address:*

Eidgenössische Technische Hochschule Zürich (ETH Zürich), WEN B 17, Weinbergstrasse 94, 8092 Zürich, Switzerland (office). *Telephone:* (44) 632-3470 (office). *E-mail:* rudolf.kalman@math.ethz.ch (office). *Website:* www.math.ethz.ch (office).

KALMS, Baron (Life Peer), cr. 2004, of Edgware in the London Borough of Barnet; **(Harold) Stanley Kalms;** British business executive; *President, DSG International plc;* b. 21 Nov. 1931; s. of Charles Kalms and Cissie Kalms; m. Pamela Jimack 1954; three s.; ed Christ's Coll., Finchley; began career with Dixons 1948 working in father's photographic store; opened 16 shops; Dixons Photographic floated 1962, Man. Dir 1962–72, Chair. Dixons Group PLC (now DSG International plc) 1972–2002, Pres. 2002–; Dir British Gas 1987–97; Chair. (non-exec.) Volvere plc; Chair. King's Healthcare NHS Trust 1993–96; Dir Centre for Policy Studies 1991– (Treas. 1993–98), Business for Sterling 1998–; Treas. Conservative Party 2001–03; Founder and sponsor Dixons Bradford City Tech. Coll.; Visiting Prof., Business School, Univ. of N London 1991; fmr Visiting Prof., Univ. of London Business School; Gov. Nat. Inst. of Econ. and Social Research 1995; Trustee, Econ. Educ. Trust; Hon. Fellow, London Business School 1995; Hon. DLitt (CNAA) 1991, Hon. DUniv (N London) 1994, Hon. DEcon (Richmond) 1996. *Leisure interests:* ballet, communal activities, opera. *Address:* DSG International plc, Maylands Avenue, Hemel Hempstead, Herts., HP2 7TG, England (office). *Telephone:* (870) 850-3333 (office). *Fax:* (1442) 233-218 (office). *Website:* www.dixons-group-plc.co.uk (office).

KALNIETE, Sandra, MA; Latvian politician and diplomatist; b. 22 Dec. 1952, Togur, Tomsk Region, Russia; m. (divorced); ed Latvian Acad. of Art, Univ. of Leeds, UK and Univ. of Geneva, Switzerland; Sec.-Gen. Latvian Artists' Union 1987–88; f. Latvian Popular Front 1988, Sec.-Gen., Deputy Chair. Co-ordinating Council 1988–90; Chief of Protocol Dept, Deputy Foreign Minister, Ministry of Foreign Affairs 1990–93, Minister of Foreign Affairs 2002–04; Amb. to UN, Geneva, Switzerland 1993–97, to France 1997–2000, to UNESCO 2000–02; EU Commr without Portfolio May–Nov. 2004; mem. Saeima (Parl.) (New Era—Jaunais laiks) 2006–; Patron, Prix Europa 2005; Commdr, Order of the Three Stars 1995, Commdr, Légion d'honneur 2001, Commdr des Palmes académiques 2002, Cross of Commdr of the Order of the Grand Duke Gediminas 2005; Latvian Cabinet Ministers' Award. *Publications:* Latviesu tekstilmaksla (Latvian Textile Art) 1989, Es lauzu, tu lauzi, mes lauzam. Vini luza (I Broke, You Broke, We Broke. They Fell Apart) 2000, Ar balles kurpem Sibirijas sniegos (With Dancing Shoes in Siberian Snows) 2001. *Address:* Saeima (Parliament), Jekaba iela 11, Rīga 1811, Latvia (office). *Telephone:* 6708-7111 (office). *Fax:* 6708-7100 (office). *E-mail:* Sandra.Kalniete@saeima.lv (office). *Website:* www.saeima.lv (office).

KALOMOH, Tuliameni; Namibian diplomatist and international organization official; b. 18 Feb. 1948, Onamutai; m.; three c.; ed Indian Acad. of Int. Law and Diplomacy, New Delhi, India; Special Asst to Regional Election Dir, Oshakati; Chief Rep. to W Africa, SW Africa People's Org. (SWAPO) 1976–81, Chief Rep. to France 1981–86, SWAPO Amb. to India 1986–90; Amb. to USA (concurrently High Commr to Canada) 1991–96; Under-Sec. for Political and Econ. Affairs 1990–91, Acting Minister for Foreign Affairs 2000–01, Deputy Minister for Foreign Affairs 2001–02; UN Special Rep. for Liberia 1997–2002; UN Asst Sec.-Gen. for Political Affairs 2002–07. *Address:* c/o Department of Political Affairs, United Nations, New York, NY 10017, USA. *Telephone:* (212) 963-1234.

KALORKOTI, Panayiotis, BA, MA; British artist; b. 11 April 1957, Cyprus; one s.; ed Univ. of Newcastle-upon-Tyne, RCA, Koninklijke Akad. voor Kunst en Vormgeving, 's-Hertogenbosch; Artist in Residence, Leeds Playhouse 1985, Cleveland Co. 1992, The Grizedale Soc., Cumbria 1994; Bartlett Fellow in Visual Arts, Univ. of Newcastle-upon-Tyne 1988; commissioned by Imperial War Museum, London 1988, Nat. Garden Festival, Gateshead 1989–90; now part-time tutor and visiting lecturer at various art depts; Granada Prize for Northern Young Contemporaries, Whitworth Art Gallery, Manchester 1983. *Publications include:* Kalorkoti 1988, A Retrospective of Etchings and Screenprints 1990, A Retrospective View 1985–91 1992, Etchings and Drawings 1992, Retrospective (Etchings 1983–93) 1994, Reflections of Grizedale (Acrylics, Watercolours, Etchings) 1995, An Exhibition of Acrylics, Watercolours and Etchings 1997, Heads, Faces and Figures 1998. *Leisure interests:* music, films, malt whisky, travel. *E-mail:* panayiotis@kalorkoti.fsnet.co.uk.

KALOSIL, Moana Carcasses; Ni-Vanuatu politician; mem. Parl. (Green Party), currently Deputy Leader of Opposition; Minister of Foreign Affairs 2003–04, for Finance and Econ. Devt 2004–05; Leader, Green Party 2001–. *Address:* Parliament House, Port Vila, Vanuatu (office).

KALOUSEK, Miroslav; Czech politician; *Minister of Finance;* b. 17 Dec. 1960, Tábor; m.; two c.; ed Inst. of Chemical Tech., Prague; Head of Investment, Mitas Praha (tyre mfrs) 1985–90; Econ. Adviser to Vice-Chair. of Czech Govt 1990–92, Dir Dept of Advisers 1992–93, Govt Rep. on Advisory Cttee, South-Bohemian Brewery 1991–92; mem. Parl. (Christian Democratic Party, KDU-ČSL) 1993–, Deputy Minister of Defence 1993–98, Chair. Parl. Budget Cttee 2002–05, Vice-Chair. 2006–, Minister of Finance 2007–; Chair. Christian Democratic Party (KDU-ČSL) 2003–06; mem. Bd of Dirs West-Bohemian Brewery 1992–94, Land Fund of the Czech Republic 1994–96. *Address:* Ministry of Finance, Letenská 15, 118 00 Prague 1, Czech Republic (office). *Telephone:* 257042100 (office). *Fax:* 257043114 (office). *E-mail:* ministr@mfcr.cz (office). *Website:* www.mfcr.cz (office).

KALPOKAS, Donald; Ni-Vanuatu politician and diplomatist; *Permanent Representative, United Nations;* ed Univ. of South Pacific; fmr Minister of Educ. and Judicial Services; Pres. Vanuaaku Pati (VP), now Hon. Pres.; Prime Minister of Vanuatu Sept.–Dec. 1991, 1998–99, also Minister of Comprehensive Reform Programme 1998–99, the Public Service, of Foreign Affairs and acting Minister of Agric., Forestry and Fisheries, Deputy Prime Minister and Minister of Educ. 1996–97, –2004; unsuccessful cand. for Pres. 2004; Perm. Rep. to UN, New York 2007–. *Address:* Permanent Mission of Vanuatu to the United Nations, 866 United Nations Plaza, 3rd Floor, New York, NY 10017, USA (office). *Telephone:* (212) 425-9600 (office). *Fax:* (212) 425-9653 (office). *E-mail:* vanuatu@un.int (office).

KALTONGA, Bakoa; Ni-Vanuatu politician; *Minister of Foreign Affairs and External Trade;* First Political Adviser, Ministry of Infrastructure and Public Utilities –2008; Minister of Foreign Affairs and External Trade 2008–; mem. Vanuaaku Pati (Our Land Party). *Address:* Ministry of Foreign Affairs, PMB 051, Port Vila, Vanuatu (office). *Telephone:* 27750 (office). *Fax:* 27832 (office).

KALUGIN, Maj.-Gen. Oleg Danilovich; Russian/American intelligence officer and politician; b. 6 Sept. 1934, Leningrad; m.; two d.; ed Leningrad Univ., Columbia Univ.; on staff of KGB 1958–89; corresp., Soviet Radio, New York 1959–65; Second, then First Sec., Embassy in Washington, DC 1965–70; Chief, Dept of External Intelligence Service, KGB 1973–80; First Deputy Chief of KGB for City of Leningrad and Leningrad Region 1980–87; returned to Moscow 1987, forced to retire for participation in democratic movt and criticism of KGB 1989, deprived of all decorations and titles by order of Pres. Gorbachev 1990; prosecuted, all charges lifted at end of 1991; USSR People's Deputy 1990–91; gave evidence on activities of KGB in courts and mass media; consultant, Information Service Agency; mem. Fed. Democratic Movt 1995–; has lived in USA 1996–; sentenced in absentia by Russian court to 15 years' imprisonment for treason after disclosing Russian agents in USA 2001; mem. Advisory Bd Dirs, Int. Spy Museum, Washington, DC; acquired US citizenship 2003; Man. Dir Cannistraro Assocs (security consulting firm) 1998–; numerous decorations. *Publications:* The First Directorate: My 32 Years in Intelligence and Espionage Against the West (autobiog.) 1994; numerous articles. *Leisure interests:* hunting, fishing, swimming. *Address:* c/o Cannistraro Associates, PO Box 854, McLean, VA 22101, USA (office). *Telephone:* (202) 257-1621 (office). *Fax:* (703) 506-4620 (office). *Website:* intelligencebrief.net (office).

KALULE, Ayub; Ugandan fmr professional boxer; b. 6 Jan. 1954, Kampala; m.; three d.; amateur boxer 1967–76; lightweight gold medal, Commonwealth Games 1974; inaugural winner of world amateur light-welterweight championship 1974; professional boxer April 1976–86; won Commonwealth middleweight title May 1978 (first Ugandan to win a Commonwealth championship); defended it Sept. 1978; won World Boxing Asscn version of world light-middleweight title from Masashi Kudo, Akita, Japan Oct. 1979; retained title v. Steve Gregory Dec. 1979, Emiliano Villa April 1980, Marijan Benes June 1980 and Bushy Bester Sept. 1980; first Ugandan to win a world title; won all 35 fights before losing to Sugar Ray Leonard (q.v.) 1981; career record: 46 wins, 4 defeats; now lives in Denmark. *Leisure interest:* table tennis. *Address:* c/o Palle, Skjulet, Bagsvaert 12, Copenhagen 2880, Denmark.

KALUMBA, Katele, PhD; Zambian politician; *National Secretary, Movement for Multi-party Democracy;* ed Univ. of Zambia (UNZA), Washington Univ., U.S.A., Univ. of Toronto, Canada; health consultant to govts. and int. orgs.; Minister of Health 1991–98, of Home Affairs and of Tourism 1998–99, of Finance and Econ. Devt. 1999–2002, of Foreign Affairs 2002 (resgnd); mem. Nat. Ass. (Movt for Multi-party Democracy—MMD) 2002–; currently Nat. Sec., MMD. *Address:* Movement for Multi-party Democracy (MMD), POB 30708, Lusaka, Zambia (office).

KALVĪTIS, Aigars, MSc; Latvian politician; b. 27 June 1966, Rīga; m.; three s.; ed Univ. of Wisconsin, USA, Latvian Univ. of Agric., Univ. Coll. Cork, Ireland; milkman and tractor driver, Alamnas Bruk AB, Sweden 1990–91; Dir Agro Biznesa Centrs 1992–94; Chair. Bd Zemgales piens 1994; Chair. Comm. of the Cen. Union of Latvian Dairying 1994–98; mem. Saeima (Parl.) 1998–99, 2002–04, mem. Budget and Finance (Taxation) Cttee, Public Expenditure and Audit Cttee; Minister of Agric. 1999–2000, of Econs 2000–02; Prime Minister 2004–07 (resgnd); mem. People's Party (Tautas partija), Chair. of Parl. Group 2002–04. *Leisure interest:* ice hockey. *Address:* Saeima, Jekaba str. 11, Rīga 1811, Latvia (office). *Telephone:* 67087222 (office). *Fax:* 67087100 (office). *E-mail:* tautpart@saeima.lv. *Website:* www.saeima.lv (office); www.tautaspartija.lv.

KALYAGIN, Aleksander Aleksandrovich; Russian actor; b. 25 May 1942, Malmysh, Kirov Region; m. Glushenko Yevgeniya Konstantinovna; one s. one d.; ed Shchukin Higher School of Theatre Art; actor Taganka Theatre and Yermolova Theatre in Moscow 1966–71; Moscow Art Theatre 1971–93; master classes in Russia and in Europe; Chair. Union of Theatre Workers of Russia 1996–; f. and Artistic Dir Et Cetera Theatre in Moscow 1992–; People's Artist of Russia 1983, State Prize 1981, 1983. *Roles in productions:* Dark Lady of the Sonnets by G. B. Shaw, Don Quixote by A. Morfov after Cervantes, Old New Year by M. Roshchin, Notes of the Lunatic and Marriage by Gogol, Galileo by Brecht, Tartuffe by Molière, several plays by A. Gelman, M. Shatrov, A. Galin and other contemporary dramatists; in cinema since 1967. *Films include:* Untimely Man 1973, One's Own Among Strangers 1974, Slave of Love 1976, Interrogation 1979, Aesop 1982, Prokhindiada or Run on the Spot 1985, How Are You Doing, Crucians? 1992, Moi Ivan, toi Abraham 1993, Deti chugunnykh bogov 1993, Prokhindiada 2 1994, Foto 2003. *Television:* Bednaya Nastya (series) 2003. *Leisure interests:* collecting art books, museums. *Address:* Union of Theatre Workers, Strastnoy blvd 10, 103031 Moscow (office); 1905 Goda str., 3 Apt 91, 123100 Moscow, Russia (home). *Telephone:* (495) 209-28-46 (office); (495) 205-26-54 (home). *Fax:* (495) 230-22-58 (office). *E-mail:* stdrf@rc.ru.

KALYUZHNY, Victor Ivanovich; Russian diplomat and politician; *Ambassador to Latvia;* b. 18 April 1947, Birsk, Bashkiria; ed Ufa Inst. of Oil; Mgr, then Deputy Head Tomskneft Co. 1970–78, First Deputy Dir.-Gen. 1993–97; Chief Engineer Dept of Oil and Gas Vasyuganneft Co., Strezhevoy; Sec. CP Cttee Strezhevoyneft Co. 1980–84, later Deputy Dir; Second Sec. Strezhevoy Town CP Exec. Cttee 1984–86; Deputy Dir USSR Ministry of Oil Industry 1986; Chief Engineer, then Dir Priobneft Co., Nizhevartovsk Tumen 1986–90; Dir Vietsovpetro, Vu Tan, Viet Nam 1990–93; First Vice-Pres. Vostochnaya Neftyanaya Komapniya, Tomsk 1997–98; First Deputy Minister of Fuel and Power Industry 1998–99, Minister 1999–2000; Special Rep. of Pres. for Caspian Sea with rank of Deputy Minister of Foreign Affairs 2000–; Amb. to Latvia 2004–. *Address:* Embassy of the Russian Federation, Antonijas iela 2, Rīga, 1010, Latvia (office). *Telephone:* 733-2151 (office). *Fax:* 783-0209 (office). *E-mail:* rusembas@delfi.lv (office). *Website:* www.latvia.mid.ru (office).

KAMAL, Fida M.; Bangladeshi barrister; ed Univ. of Dhaka, Punjab Univ., Pakistan, Inner Temple, London, UK; called to the Bar 1979, enrolled as lawyer of High Court 1979, of Appellate Div. 1986; ex-officio Chair. Bangladesh Bar Council; Additional Attorney-Gen. 2002–07, Acting Attorney-Gen. Jan.–Feb. 2007, Attorney-Gen. 2007–08. *Address:* c/o Office of the Attorney-General, Supreme Court Building, Ramna, Dhaka 1000, Bangladesh (office).

KAMAL, Yousuf bin Hussein, BBA; Qatari government official; *Minister of Finance, and of Economy and Trade;* b. 1948; ed Cairo Univ.; previous positions in Ministry of Finance include Asst Deputy Dir, Deputy Dir, Gen. Dir, Deputy Minister, Minister of Finance 1998–, also Acting Minister of Economy and Trade 2006–; fmr Deputy Head, Bd of Dirs Qatar Petroleum; fmr mem. Bd of Dirs Qatar Cen. Bank, Q-Tel; fmr Head, Bd of Dirs Ras Laffan LNG. *Address:* Ministry of Finance, POB 3322 Doha, Qatar (office). *Telephone:* 4461444 (office). *Fax:* 4431177 (office). *E-mail:* webmaster@mec.gov.qa (office). *Website:* www.mec.gov.qa (office).

KAMALASABEYSON, K.C.; Sri Lankan lawyer; b. Trincomalee; ed St Thomas's Coll., Mount Lavinia, Sri Lanka Law Coll., Univ. of Colombo, King's Coll., London, UK; enrolled as Advocate of Supreme Court 1972; practised at unofficial Bar for two years 1972–74; joined Attorney-Gen.'s Dept as State Counsel 1974, Sr State Counsel 1984, Deputy Solicitor-Gen. 1990–96, Additional Solicitor-Gen. 1996–98, Pres.'s Counsel 1997, Solicitor-Gen. 1998–99, Attorney-Gen. 1999–2007; engages in legal research and has taught law on a visiting basis at Faculty of Law, Univ. of Colombo and Sri Lanka Law Coll.; mem. Council of Legal Educ. of Sri Lanka 1998–. *Address:* c/o Chamber 52, Attorney General's Department, Colombo 12, Sri Lanka (office).

KAMALI, Norma, BFA; American fashion designer; b. 27 June 1945, New York; d. of Sam Arraez and Estelle Galib; m. M. H. Kamali (divorced); ed Fashion Inst. of Tech., New York; ind. fashion designer, New York 1965–; opened first shop in East 53rd Street 1968, moving to Madison Avenue 1974; retitled business OMO (On My Own) and moved to 56th Street 1978; second boutique opened Spring Street, New York 1986; OMO Home opened 1988; collaboration with Bloomingdale's on production of exclusive collections 1988–; OMO Tokyo opened 1990; Coty American Fashion Critics' Winnie Award 1981, 1982, Outstanding Women's Fashion Designer of the Year Award, Council of Fashion Designers of America 1982, Coty Hall of Fame Award 1983, American Success Award 1989, Pencil Award 1999, Fashion Outreach Style Award 1999, Business Outreach Award, Manhattan Chamber of Commerce 2001, Entrepreneur Award, The Fashion Group 2002, inducted Fashion Walk of Fame 2002, Bd of Dirs Special Tribute Award, Council of Fashion Designers of America 2006. *Address:* OMO Norma Kamali, 11 West 56th Street, New York, NY 10019, USA. *Website:* www.normakamalicollection.com; www.normakamalivintage.com.

KAMALUDHEEN, Abdullah, BSc; Maldivian politician; b. 12 July 1954; m.; five c.; ed Majeediyya School and Almeda Univ., USA; clerk, Ministry of Foreign Affairs 1972; Admin. Sec., Office of the Pres. 1972–76; Under-Sec., Port Comm. and Public Works Dept, Ministry of Finance 1976–77, Dir 1977–82; Dir Dept of Tourism and Foreign Investment, Office of the Pres. 1978, Dir Dept of Public Works and Labour 1982–89, Dir Islamic Centre 1984–93; Minister of Public Works and Labour 1989–93; Chair. and Man. Dir Maldives Ports Authority 1990–93; Chair. Bank of Maldives Ltd 1990–93, Maldives Electricity Board 1991–93; Exec. Dir, Maldives National Ship Man. Ltd 1991–93; mem. Parl. 1992–; mem. Constitutional Ass. 1995–; Minister of Human Resources, Employment and Labour 1998–2003, of Fisheries, Agric. and Marine Resources 2003–07, of Home Affairs 2007–08. *Address:* c/o Ministry of Home Affairs, Huravee Bldg, 3rd Floor, Ameer Ahmed Magu, Malé 20-05, Maldives (office).

KAMANDA, Kama Sywor, DipHumLit, BJ, BA, LèsL; Democratic Republic of the Congo writer, poet, novelist, playwright and essayist and lecturer; b. 11 Nov. 1952, Luebo; s. of the late Malaba Kamenga and Kony Ngalula; ed Journalism School, Kinshasa, Univ. of Kinshasa, Univ. of Liège, Belgium; political leader; freelance journalist; lecturer at various univs, schools, etc.; literary critic for several newspapers; mem. French Soc. of Men of Letters, Conseil Int. d'Etudes Francophones, Belgian Soc. of Authors, Composers and Editors (SABAM), Maison de la poésie (MAPI – Dakar, Senegal), SCAM; Acad. française Paul Verlaine Award 1987, Acad. française Théophile Gautier Award 1993, Louise Labé Award 1990, Black Africa Asscn of French-Speaking Writers Award 1991, Acad. Inst. of Paris Special Poetry Award 1992, Silver Jasmine for Poetic Originality 1992, Gen. Council Agen Special Prize for French-Speaking Countries 1992, Greek Poets and Writers Asscn Melina Mercouri Award 1999, Int. Poets Acad. India Poet of the Millennium Award 2000, Joal Fadiouth hon. citation, Senegal 2000, Int. Soc. of Greek Writers Poetry Award 2002, Int. Council for French Studies Maurice-Cagnon Exceptional Contribution Honour Certificate 2005, World Acad. of Letters Master Diploma for Specialty Honors in Writing, USA 2006, United Cultural Convention Int. Peace Prize, USA 2006. *Publications:* Les Contes des veillées africaines 1967, Chants de brumes 1986, Les Résignations 1986, Éclipse d'étoiles 1987, Les Contes du griot Vol. 1 1988, Vol. 2: La Nuit des griots 1991, Vol. 3: Les Contes des veillées africaines 1998, La Somme du néant 1989, L'Exil des songes 1992, Les Myriades des temps vécus 1992, Les Vents de l'épreuve 1993, Quand dans l'âme les mers s'agitent 1994, Lointaines sont les rives du destin 1994, L'Étreinte des mots 1995, Œuvre poétique 1999, Les Contes du crépuscule 2000, Le Sang des solitudes 2002, Contes (édition illustrée) 2003, Contes (œuvres complètes) 2004, La Traversée des mirages 2006, La Joueuse de Kora 2006, Contes africains (Grund) 2006, Au-delà de Dieu, au-delà des chimères 2007, Oeuvres poétiques complètes 2008. *Leisure interests:* travel, reading. *Address:* 18 Am Moul, 7418 Buschdorf, Luxembourg (office). *Telephone:* 621-47-46-96 (mobile) (office). *E-mail:* kamanda@pt.lu (office). *Website:* www.kamanda.net (office); www.kamasyworkamanda.info (office); http://webplaza.pt.lu/public/kamanda (office).

KAMANDA WA KAMANDA, Gérard, LenD; Democratic Republic of the Congo politician, administrator and lawyer; b. 10 Dec. 1940, Kikwit; s. of Raphaël Kamanda and Germaine Kukikidika; two s. one d.; ed Coll. St Ignace de Kiniati, Coll. Notre Dame de Mbansa Boma, Univ. Lovanium, Kinshasa; lawyer, Court of Appeal 1964; Legal Adviser, Fédération congolaise des travailleurs 1964–65; Prof., Inst. Nat. d'Etudes Politiques 1965–66; Legal Adviser to Presidency of Repub. 1965–66, Sec.-Gen. 1966–67; Prin. Adviser with responsibility for legal, admin., political and diplomatic affairs to Presidency of Repub.; Dir de Cabinet to Sec.-Gen. of OAU 1967–72, Asst Sec.-Gen. 1972–78; Perm. Rep. to UN 1979–82; State Commr for Foreign Affairs and Int. Co-operation 1982–83, for Justice 1983–84; Deputy Sec.-Gen. MPR 1987; f. Mouvement populaire de la revolution (MPR) 1997; Assoc. mem. Office Nat. de la Recherche Scientifique et du Développement; Vice-Pres. Zairian section, Soc. Africaine de la Culture; del. to several int. confs; Deputy Prime Minister 1994–97, in charge of Institutional Reforms, Justice and Keeper of the Seals 1994–96, of Interior 1996–97, of Minister of Scientific Research 1997–2004. *Publications:* Essai-critique du système de la criminalité d'emprunt 1964, Négritude face au devenir de l'Afrique 1967, L'université aujourd'hui en Afrique 1969, L'intégration juridique et le développement harmonieux des nations africaines 1969, L'incidence de la culture audio-visuelle sur le phénomène du pouvoir 1970, Les organisations africaines Vol. I: L'OUA ou la croisade de l'unité africaine 1970, Vol. II: 1970, Le défi africain: une puissance économique qui s'ignore 1976, L'enracinement: culture et progrès 1976. *Address:* c/o Ministry of Scientific Research, Immeuble Dungo, Avenue Golonel Ebeya, 54, Kinshasa, Democratic Republic of the Congo (office).

KAMARCK, Andrew Martin, BS, MA, PhD; American international bank official, economist and writer; b. 10 Nov. 1914, Newton Falls, New York; s. of Martin Kamarck and Frances Earl; m. Margaret Goldenweiser Burgess 1941; one s. two d.; ed Harvard Univ.; Int. Section, Fed. Reserve Bd 1939–40; US Treasury 1940–42; US Army 1942–44; Allied Control Comm., Italy 1943–44; Allied Control Council, Germany 1945; Office of Int. Finance, US Treasury, Chief of Nat. Advisory Council on Int. Monetary and Financial Problems (NAC) Div., Financial Policy Cttee preparing Marshall Plan 1945–48; US Treasury Rep., Rome 1948–50; Chief of Africa section, Econ. Dept, World Bank 1950–52; Econ. Adviser, Dept of Operations, Europe, Africa and Australasia, World Bank, Chief of Econ. Missions to 14 countries, 1952–64; Dir Econ. Dept, World Bank 1965–71; Dir Econ. Devt Inst. 1972–77, Sr Fellow 1977–78; mem. American Econ. Asscn, Council on Foreign Relations; Dir African Studies Asscn 1961–64; Visiting Fellow, Harvard Inst. Int. Devt 1977–86; Regents Prof., Univ. of Calif. 1964–65; mem. Council, Soc. for Int. Devt 1967–70, 1973–76; Pres. Housing Assistance Corpn of Cape Cod 1980–83; US War Dept Certificate of Merit 1945. *Publications:* The Economics of African Development 1967, Capital Movements and Economic Development (co-author) 1967, The Tropics and Economic Development 1976, La Politica Finanziaria degli Alleati in Italia 1977, Economics and the Real World 1983, Health, Nutrition and Economic Crises (co-author) 1988, The Role of the Economist in Government (co-author) 1989, The Bretton Woods-GATT System (co-author) 1995, Economics for the Twenty-First Century 2001, Economics as a Social Science 2002. *Leisure interests:* walking, music. *Address:* 118 Pine Ridge Road, Brewster, MA 02631, USA (home). *Telephone:* (508) 385-8221 (home). *E-mail:* kamarck@post.harvard.edu (home).

KAMAT, Digambar V., BSc; Indian politician; *Chief Minister of Goa;* b. 8 March 1954, Margao, Goa; s. of Shri Vasant Kamat; m.; Councillor, Margao Municipal Council 1985–90; mem. Legis. Ass. of State of Goa 1994–, mem. Cttee on Govt Assurances 1995–96, 1996–97, 1997–98, 1999–2000 (fmr Chair.), Select Cttee on Bill No. 29 of Goa Advocates Welfare Fund Bill 1995, Business Advisory Cttee 1996–97, House Cttee to study Model Rent Control Legislation, Panel of Presiding Mems 1997–98, Cttee on Public Undertakings, Chair. Public Accounts Cttee 1999–2000; Minister for Power, Protocol, and Art and Culture 1999; mem. Town and Country Planning Bd; Minister for Power, Urban Devt and Mines 2002; Chief Minister of Goa 2007–; Chair. Produce Market Cttee 1979–91; mem. Southern Planning and Devt Authority 1986–89; mem. Exec. Cttee Nat. Council of State Agricultural Marketing Bd, New Delhi 1992–94; Vice-Chair. COSAMB 1994–96; mem. State Consumer Protection Council 1993–96; Founder-mem. Damodar Educ. Soc.; Sec. Model Educ. Soc.; mem. Advisory Cttee for Parshuram Girijan Samaj; Treas., Margao Cricket Club 1973; Pres. Sparkling Stars Asscn, Margao 1973–74; Founder-Pres. Rotary Club of Margao 1973, Samrat Club; mem. Goa, Daman and Diu State Council of Sports 1976–78; Vice-Pres. Goa Badminton Asscn 1980–83, Pres. 1999–2000; mem. and Trustee, Margao Ambulance Trust; Hon. Sec. Goa Badminton Asscn; COSAMB Award, Nat. Council of State Agricultural Marketing Bd, New Delhi; Bakshi Jivabadada Kerkar State Award, Govt of Goa. *Leisure interests:* helping needy people, reading, playing badminton, swimming, cricket. *Address:* Goa Legislature Secretariat, Alto-Porvorim, Goa, 403521 (office); Sanrit Apartments, 1st Floor, nr Masjid, Malbhat, Margao, Goa, India (home). *Telephone:* (832) 2224845 (office); (832) 2730432 (home). *Fax:* (832) 2411054 (office). *E-mail:* mla-marg.goa@nic.in (office). *Website:* goavidhansabha.gov.in (office).

KAMATA, Michisada; Japanese energy industy executive; *Chairman, Kyushu Electric Power Company Incorporated;* joined Kyushu Electric Power Co. Inc. 1958, served as Man. Dir., Vice-Pres. and Pres., Chair. 2003–; Vice Chairman Kyushu Tourism Promotion Org.; Chair. Kyushu-Yamaguchi Econ. Fed.; Vice-Chair. Fed. of Electric Power Cos 2001–03; Dir Japan Nuclear Fuel Ltd, Kyushu-Yamaguchi Econ. Fed. (Kyukeiren), Japan Productivity Center for Socio-Econ. Devt (JPC-SED), Energy Conservation Center of Japan; Trustee, Int. Center for the Study of E Asian Devt (ICSEAD). *Address:* Kyushu Electric Power Company Incorporated, 1–82 Watanabe Dori 2-chome, Chuo-ku, Fukuoka 810–8720, Japan (office). *Telephone:* (92) 761–3031 (office). *Fax:* (92) 733–1435 (office). *Website:* www.kyuden.co.jp (office).

KAMATARI, Esther; Burundian model and politician; b. 1951; ed Nat. School of Admin; mem. of Burundi royal family, fled Burundi 1970 after assassination of family mems; became fashion model in Paris; mem. Asscn of People of Burundi in France; unsuccessful cand. in 2005 Burundi presidential election, Parti pour la restitution de la monarchie et du dialogue (PRMD) (Abuhuza). *Publications:* Princesse des Rugo: Mon Histoire (autobiography) 2001. *Address:* c/o Parti pour la restitution de la monarchie et du dialogue (PRMD) (Abuhuza), Bujumbura, Burundi.

KAMATH, K. V., BSc, MBA; Indian banker; *CEO and Managing Director, Industrial Credit and Investment Corporation of India Ltd (ICICI);* b. 2 Dec. 1947, Mangalore, Karnataka; m.; one s. one d.; ed Karnataka Regional Educational College, Indian Inst. of Man.; mem. of staff, Industrial Credit and Investment Corpn of India Ltd (ICICI) 1971–88, Man. Dir and CEO 1996–; Adviser, Asian Devt Bank, Manila 1988–96; mem. Man. Cttee, Associated Chambers of Commerce and Industry; mem. Nat. Council Confed. of Indian Industry; mem. Governing Bd Indian Inst. of Man., Ahmedabad, Indian School of Business, Nat. Inst. of Bank Man., Manipal Acad. of Higher Educ.; Asian Business Leader of the Year, CNBC 2001, Businessman of the Year, Business India magazine 2005, Outstanding Business Leader of the Year, CNBC-TV18 2006. *Address:* ICICI Bank Limited, ICICI Bank Towers, Bandra-Kurla Complex, Mumbai 400051, India (office). *Telephone:* (22) 26531414 (office). *Fax:* (22) 26531167 (office). *E-mail:* info@icicibank.com (office). *Website:* www.icicibank.com (office).

KAMATH, M. V., BSc; Indian journalist and broadcasting executive; *Chairman, Prasar Bharati (Broadcasting Corporation of India);* b. 1921, Udupi; upon graduation from univ. worked for five years as chemist; changed careers and became reporter, then special adviser, then Ed. Free Press Journal, Mumbai 1946–54; Foreign Corresp. Times of India reporting from Germany and France, Ed. Sunday Times 1967–69, US Corresp. Times of India, Washington DC 1969–78; Ed. Illustrated Weekly 1978–81; columnist in numerous newspapers and magazines 1981–; mem. Bd of Dirs Prasar Bharati (Broadcasting Corpn of India) 2002, Chair. 2003–; Padma Bhushan 2004. *Publications:* over 40 books including The United States and India 1776–1976 1976, Philosophy of Death and Dying 1978, The Other Face of India 1988, A Banking Odyssey: The Canara Bank Story 1991, Ganesh Vasudeo Mavalankar 1992, Management Kurien-Style: The Story of the White Revolution, Points and Lines, Charat RAM: A Biography 1994, Journalist's Handbook 1995, Gandhi's Coolie: Life and Times of Ramkrishna Bajaj 1995, Professional Journalism 1996, Some of Us are Lucky 1996, Milkman from Anand: The story of Verghese Kurien 1996, Sai Baba of Shirdi: A Unique Saint (jtly) 2005. *Address:* Prasar Bharati, Doordarshan Bhavan, Copernicus Marg, New Delhi 110001 (office); Kalyanpur House, 3rd Road, Near Railway Station, Kar, Mumbai, India (home). *Telephone:* (22) 26483418 (home). *Website:* www.ddindia.com (office).

KAMBA, Walter Joseph, BA, LLB, LLM; Zimbabwean administrator and academic; *Professor Emeritus of Law, University of Namibia;* b. 6 Sept. 1931, Marondera; s. of Joseph Mafara and Hilda Kamba; m. Angeline Saziso Dube 1960; three s. (one deceased); ed Univ. of Cape Town, Yale Law School; attorney, High Court of Rhodesia (now Zimbabwe) 1963–66; Research Fellow, Inst. of Advanced Legal Studies, London Univ. 1967–68; Lecturer then Sr Lecturer in Comparative Law and Jurisprudence, Univ. of Dundee 1969–80, Dean Faculty of Law 1977–80; Legal Adviser ZANU (PF) 1977–80; Prof of Law, Univ. of Zimbabwe 1980–, Vice-Prin. 1980–81, Vice-Chancellor 1981–91; Vice-Chair. Zimbabwe Broadcasting Corpn 1980–87, Chair. 1987; Inaugural UNESCO Africa Prof., Univ. of Utrecht 1992–96; Founding Dean and UNESCO Prof. of Human Rights, Democracy and Law, Univ. of Namibia 1994–2000, legal adviser, Prof. 1995, now Prof. Emer.; Trustee, Zimbabwe Mass Media Trust 1981–, Conservation Trust of Zimbabwe 1981–87, Zimbabwe Cambridge Trust 1987–; mem. Bd Gov.'s Rauche House Coll. Harare 1980–; mem. Working Party on Future Policy of Asscn of Commonwealth Univs 1981; mem. Council, Exec. Cttee and Budget Review Cttee Asscn of Commonwealth Univs 1981–83; mem. Council UN Univ. for Peace, Costa Rica 1982–86, Univ. of Zambia 1982–86, Commonwealth Standing Cttee on Student Affairs 1982–88, UN Univ., Tokyo 1983–89, Zimbabwe Nat. Comm. for UNESCO 1987–, Bd of Govs Zimbabwe Inst. of Devt Studies 1982–, Chair. 1986–, Exec. Bd Asscn African Univs 1984–; Chair. Electoral Supervisory Comm. 1984, Kingston's (Booksellers and Distributors) 1984–, Asscn of Eastern and Southern African Univs 1984–87; Chair. Council UN Univ., Tokyo 1985–87; Vice-Pres. Int. Asscn of Univs 1985–90, Pres. 1990–; Trustee, African-American Inst. (New York) 1985–; mem. Int. Bd, United World Colls 1985–87, Bd of Govs, Int. Devt Research Centre, Canada 1986–, Nat. Cttee Law and Population Studies Project 1986–, Swaziland Univ. Planning Comm.

1986, Bd, Commonwealth of Learning 1988, Int. Cttee for Study of Educ. Exchange 1988–; Patron, Commonwealth Legal Education Asscn 1986–; Hon. LLD (Dundee) 1982, (Natal) 1995, (Zimbabwe) 1998; Officer, Ordre des palmes académiques. *Publications:* articles in law journals. *Leisure interest:* tennis. *Address:* Faculty of Law, University of Zimbabwe, PO Box MP 167, Mount Pleasant, Harare, Zimbabwe (office); International Association of Universities, 1 rue Miollis, 75732 Paris, cedex 15, France (office).

KAMEI, Shizuka; Japanese politician; Parl. Vice-Minister of Transport, Minister 1994–95, of Construction 1996; mem. House of Reps for Hiroshima 1977–; Chair. LDP Nat. Org. Cttee and Acting Chair. LDP Policy Research Council. *Address:* c/o Liberal-Democratic Party, 1-11-23, Nagata-cho, Chiyoda-ku, Tokyo 100, Japan. *Website:* www.shugiin.go.jp (office); www.kamei-shizuka.net (home).

KAMEL, Sheikh Saleh Abdullah, BA, MBA; Saudi Arabian business executive; *Chairman, ART (Arab Radio and Television);* m.; ed King Abdulaziz Univ.; est. business based on contracts with Saudi Arabian Govt; est. real-estate devts in Buhairat, Tunisia and Durat al-Arous, Jeddah; f. MBC (Middle Eastern Broadcasting Center) and ART (Arab Radio and TV); majority owner and Chief Exec. Dallah al Baraka Group, Chair. and Man. Dir Al Baraka Banking Group, Chair. Al Baraka Investment and Devt; Deputy Chair. Al Jazira Bank; mem. Bd Al Baraka Investment and Devt Co., Savola, Jeddah Chamber of Commerce and Industry, Saudi Research and Publishing Ltd. *Address:* Dallah al Baraka Group, Dallah Tower, Palestine Street, Jeddah 21452 (office); PO Box 430, Jeddah 21411, Saudia Arabia (office). *Telephone:* (2) 671-0000 (Dallah al Baraka) (office); (2) 667-3316 (office). *Fax:* (2) 617-0347 (Dallah al Baraka) (office); (2) 671-7056 (office). *Website:* www.albaraka.com (office).

KAMEL AHMED, Kamal ad-Din, MB, ChB, MD, DMSc; Egyptian pathologist and academic; *Professor Emeritus, Mansoura Medical School;* b. 20 Jan. 1927, Mehella El-Kobra; m. Naguia Abd-El Khalek Safwat 1954; one s.; ed medical schools of Cairo and Ain Shams Univs and Max Planck Inst., Germany; fmly with WHO mission in Iran; Prof. and Head of Dept of Pathology, Mansoura Medical School 1969–80, Dean of Medical School 1971–80; Vice-Pres. Mansoura Univ. 1980–82, Pres. 1983–87, Prof. Emer., Mansoura Medical School 1987–; Distinguished Service Medal 1987, Mansoura Univ. Award 1988. *Publications:* A Study of Carcinoma of the Urinary Bladder 1958, A New Application of Van Gieson Stain in the Diagnosis of Tumours of the Nervous System 1962, A Scheme for the Histological Diagnosis of Tumours of the Nervous System during Operations 1965, Modern Pathology 1989. *Leisure interest:* member of Gezira Sporting Club, Cairo. *Address:* 33 Ramsis Street, Apartment 144, Cairo, Egypt. *Telephone:* 5741307.

KAMEN, Dean; American inventor, physicist and engineer; *President, DEKA Research and Development Corporation;* ed Worcester Polytechnic Inst.; while undergrad. invented wearable infusion pump; f. AutoSyringe Inc. 1976; developed first portable pump to dispense insulin 1978; est. Science Enrichment Encounters (SEE) museum 1985; developed portable dialysis machine 1993; created the Segway Human Transporter (motorized, low-energy scooter) 2001; mem. Nat. Acad. of Eng; Owner and Pres. DEKA Research and Devt Corpn 1992–; f. US FIRST (For Inspiration and Recognition of Science and Tech.) Foundation 1989; Hon. DSc (Rensselear Polytechnic Inst.), (Worcester Polytechnic Inst.); Engineer of the Year (Design News Magazine) 1994, Hoover Medal 1995, NH Business Leader of the Year 1996, Heinz Award in Tech., the Economy and Employment 1998, Nat. Medal of Tech. 2000, Lemelson-MIT Prize 2002; inducted into Nat. Inventors Hall of Fame 2005. *Achievements include:* holds more than 100 US patents. *Address:* DEKA Research and Development Corporation, Technology Center, 340 Commercial Street, Manchester, NH 03101, USA (office). *Telephone:* (603) 669-5139 (office). *Fax:* (603) 624-0573 (office). *E-mail:* contactdeka@dekaresearch.com (office). *Website:* www.dekaresearch.com (office); www.usfirst.org.

KAMIJO, Kiyofumi, BSc; Japanese business executive; *Chairman, Tokyu Corporation;* ed Waseda Univ.; joined Tokyu Corpn 1958, Vice-Pres. –June 2001, Pres. and CEO June 2001–05, Chair. 2005–; Dir Tokyu Land Corpn, Japan-Fiji Friendship Soc. *Address:* Tokyu Corporation, 5–6 Nanpeidai-cho, Shibuya-ku, Tokyo 150–8511, Japan (office). *Telephone:* (3) 3477–6111 (office). *Fax:* (3) 3462–1690 (office). *Website:* www.tokyu.co.jp (office).

KAMIKAWA, Yoko; Japanese politician; b. 1 March 1953, Shizuoka; two c.; ed Coll. of Arts and Sciences, Tokyo Univ., John F. Kennedy School of Govt, Harvard Univ., USA; Researcher, Mitsubishi Research Inst. 1977; est. policy consultancy 1977; served on policymaking staff of US Senator Max Baucus; ran for election to House of Reps as ind. cand. 1996, was not elected; joined LDP 1997; elected to House of Reps 2000, representing Shizuoka Pref., Dir of Women's Affairs Div., LDP 2000, Parl. Sec. for Internal Affairs and Communication 2005, Minister of State for Gender Equality, Population and Social Affairs 2007–08 (resgnd). *Address:* Liberal-Democratic Party (LDP), 1-11-23, Nagata-cho, Chiyoda-ku, Tokyo, 100-8910, Japan. *Telephone:* (3) 3581-6211 (office). *E-mail:* koho@ldp.jimin.or.jp (office). *Website:* www.kamikawayoko.net (office); www.jimin.jp (office).

KAMILOV, Abdulaziz H., PhD; Uzbekistan diplomatist; *Ambassador to USA;* b. 16 Nov. 1947, Yangiyul; m.; one s.; ed Moscow Inst. of Oriental Languages; served at Diplomatic Acad., USSR Ministry of Foreign Affairs; joined USSR diplomatic service 1972, Attaché, USSR Embassy in Beirut 1973–76, Second Sec., Damascus 1980–84, mem. Div. of Near East, USSR Ministry of Foreign Affairs 1984–88; Sr Researcher, Inst. of World Econs and Int. Affairs, USSR Acad. of Sciences 1988–91; Counsellor, Uzbekistan Embassy in Moscow 1991–92; Deputy Chair. Security Service of Uzbekistan Repub. 1992–94; First Deputy Minister of Foreign Affairs Jan.–Aug. 1994, Minister of Foreign Affairs 1994–2003, Amb. to USA 2003–. *Address:* Embassy of Uzbekistan, 1746 Massachusetts Avenue, NW, Washington, DC 20036-1903, USA (office). *Telephone:* (202) 887-5300 (office). *Fax:* (202) 293-6804 (office). *E-mail:* root@relay.tiv.uz (office). *Website:* www.uzbekistan.org (office).

KAMINSKI, Janusz, BA; Polish cinematographer and film director; b. 27 June 1959, Ziembice; m. Holly Hunter (q.v.) 1995; ed Columbia Coll., Chicago, American Film Inst., Washington, DC; mem. American Soc. of Cinematographers. *Films include:* All the Love in the World 1990, The Rain Killer 1990, The Terror Within II 1990, Grim Prairie Tales 1990, Pyrates 1991, Killer Instinct 1991, Cool as Ice 1991, Mad Dog Coll 1992, Trouble Bound 1993, The Adventures of Huck Finn (dir of photography) 1993, Schindler's List (Acad. Award for Best Cinematographer 1994) 1993, Little Giants 1994, Tall Tale 1995, How to Make an American Quilt 1995, Jerry Maguire 1996, Amistad 1997, The Lost World: Jurassic Park 1997, Saving Private Ryan 1998, Lost Souls 2000, AI: Artificial Intelligence 2001, Minority Report 2002 (dir of photography), Catch Me If You Can 2002, The Terminal 2004, Jumbo Girl 2004, War of the Worlds 2005, Munich 2005, Mission Zero (dir of photography) 2007, Le Scaphandre et le Papillon (Prize Vulcain de l'Artiste-Technicien, Cannes Film Festival 2007) 2007. *Address:* 1223 Wilshire Boulevard, #645 Santa Monica, CA 90403, USA (office).

KAMIŃSKI, Gen. Józef; Polish army officer and politician; b. 3 March 1919, Brzeżany, Tarnopol Dist; s. of Antoni Kamiński and Tekla Kamińska (née Szpakowska); m. Krystyna Kamińska (née Podlaszewska); one s. one d.; ed Infantry Training Centre, Rembertów; during Second World War in USSR, served in Red Army unit in the Far East 1940–43 in Polish Army 1943–, soldier of Tadeusz Kościuszko First Infantry Div. Platoon Commdr, subsequently Co. and Battalion Commdr; Deputy C-in-C, 34th Infantry Regt, 8th Infantry Div.; took part in fighting against armed underground Ukrainian org. in Bieszczady Mountains 1946; Commdr of Regt then of Infantry Div. and Armoured Div.; Brig.-Gen. 1954; Armoured Corps Commdr 1954–64; Commdr, Pomeranian Mil. Dist 1964–71, Silesian Mil. Dist 1971–76; rank of Gen. 1974; Deputy Chief of Staff of United Armed Forces of Warsaw Treaty, then Commdt of Karol Świerczewski Gen. Staff Acad. of Polish Army, Warsaw; mem. Union of Fighters for Freedom and Democracy (ZBoWiD), fmr mem. ZBoWiD Voivodship Bd, Bydgoszcz, mem. ZBoWiD Chief Council, Pres. ZBoWiD Gen. Bd; Pres. Union of Veterans of Polish Repub. and Former Political Prisoners 1990–99, Hon. Pres. 1999–; Order of Banner of Labour (1st and 2nd Class), Grunwald Cross (3rd Class), Order Polonia Restituta (4th and 5th Class), Order of Lenin, Order of Friendship among the Nations, Virtuti Militari Cross (5th Class). *Leisure interest:* military history. *Address:* ul. Szarkowników 12, 04-410 Warsaw, Poland. *Telephone:* (2) 6119680 (office).

KAMIŃSKI, Marek; Polish explorer; b. 24 March 1964, Gdańsk; s. of Zdzisław Kamiński and Maria Kamińska; Founder, Game San SA and Marek Kamiński Foundation; mem. The Explorers Club 1996–; Hon. mem. Polar Research Cttee Polish Acad. of Sciences; Kt's Cross Order of Polonia Restituta; Finalist, World Young Business Achiever 1994, Man of the Year 1995, Życie Warszawy daily, Gold Medal for Outstanding Achievments in Sport, Chopin Award, Super Kolos Award 2004, Caritas Reward, Pope John Paul II 2005. *Expeditions to:* Mexico, Guatemala, crossing of Spitsbergen, crossing of Greenland (twice); attempted solo crossing of Antarctica; first man who reached alone both North and South Poles in the same year 1995; climbed Mount Vinson (Antarctica) 1998; crossed Gibson Desert 1999; sailed yacht across the Atlantic (twice); participated in expedition to sources of the Amazon 2000 and North Pole expedition 2001, 2002. *Publications:* Not Only a Pole 1996, My Poles: Diaries from Expeditions 1990–98 (Artus Award for the Best Book of the Year) 1998, My Expeditions 2001, Razem na biegun (Together to the Pole) 2005. *Leisure interests:* travelling to the coldest places in the world, sailing, philosophy. *Address:* c/o Marek Kamiński Foundation, ul. Grunwaldzka 212, 80-266 Gdańsk, Poland. *Telephone:* (58) 5544522. *Fax:* (58) 5523315. *E-mail:* mkaminski@gamasan.pl (office). *Website:* www.kaminski.pl (home).

KAMLANG-EK, Gen. Arthit; Thai politician and fmr military officer; b. 31 Aug. 1925, Bangkok; m.; four c.; ed Chulachomklao Royal Mil. Acad.; Supreme Commdr of Armed Forces and C-in-C of the Army 1983–86; Senator 1977, 1986; Thai People's Party mem. Senate for Loei 1988–, Chair. Senate Standing Cttee on Military Affairs (SSCMA); Deputy Defense Minister 1990–91; Dr hc (Srinakharinwirto Univ.), (Pepperdine Univ.); Kt Grand Cordon (Special Class) of the Most Exhalted Order of the White Elephant. *Address:* c/o Government House, Nakhom Pathan Road, Bangkok 10300, Thailand. *E-mail:* sen188@parliament.go.th. *Website:* www.senate.go.th.

KAMOSHITA, Ichirō, MD; Japanese physician and politician; b. 16 Jan. 1949, Adachi, Tokyo; ed Nihon Univ.; Dir Hibiya Kokusai Clinic 1981–88; Head Dir Kamoshita-gakuen Acad., Educational Corpn 1988–93, Aojuji-kai, Healthcare Corpn 1993; mem. House of Reps (originally for Japan New Party; joined LDP 1997) 1993–, has served as dir of numerous parl. cttees including Judicial Affairs 1996, 1998, Election Law 1998, Finance 1998, Audit and Oversight 1998, 2006, Political Ethics and Election Law 1999, Health and Welfare 2000, Health, Labour and Welfare 2002–06; Sr Vice-Minister of Health, Labour and Welfare 2002–03, Minister of the Environment 2007–08, Minister in Charge of Global Environmental Problems 2007–08. *Address:* Liberal-Democratic Party (LDP), 1-11-23, Nagata-cho, Chiyoda-ku, Tokyo 100-8910, Japan (office). *Telephone:* (3) 3581-6211 (office). *E-mail:* koho@ldp .jimin.or.jp (office). *Website:* www.jimin.jp (office).

KAMOUGUÉ, Gen. Wadal Abdelkader; Chadian politician and army officer; *Minister of National Defence;* b. 20 May 1939, Bitam, Gabon; s. of Terkam Kamougue and Jeannette Kinel; m. 1st Eve-Marie Baba 1967; m. 2nd Martine Rondoh 1983; nine c.; Minister of Foreign Affairs and Co-operation,

mem. of Supreme Mil. Council in Govt of Brig.-Gen. Félix Malloum 1975–78; Commdr of Gendarmerie 1978–79; mem. Provisional State Council following Kano peace agreement March–May 1979, in charge of Agric. and Animal Resources; Leader, Front Uni du Sud (later Forces Armées Tchadiennes, Forces Unifiées) 1979; Vice-Pres. Transitional Gov. of Nat. Unity (GUNT) 1979–82; Pres. State Council 1980–82; fled to Cameroon, then Gabon Sept.–Oct. 1982, after defeat by forces of FAN; Leader, Mouvement révolutionnaire du peuple, Brazzaville, Congo 1983–87; returned to N'Djamena Feb. 1987; Minister of Agric. 1987–89, of Justice 1989–90, of Trade and Industry 1990, of Civil Service and Labour 1993–94, of Nat. Defence 2008–; Pres. Assemblée Nat. (Parl.) 1997; Pres. Union pour le renouveau et la démocratie (URD) 1992–; Général de Brigade 1992–; mem. Conseil Provisoire de la République (CPR) 1991–92; Commdr Ordre nat. avec Palme d'Or Chevalier du Mérite Civique, Commdr Ordre nat. du Tchad, Chevalier Ordre nat. du Mérite (France), Commdr Ordre nat. Centrafricain (Central African Repub.), Commdr Ordre Coréen (Repub. of Korea). *Leisure interests:* volleyball, basketball, reading, table tennis, athletics. *Address:* Ministry of National Defence, BP 916, N'Djamena (office); Union pour le renouveau et la démocratie, BP 92, N'Djamena, Chad. *Telephone:* 52-35-13 (Ministry) (office); 51-44-23. *Fax:* 52-65-44 (Ministry) (office); 51-41-87.

KAMP, Henricus (Henk) Gregorius Jozeph; Dutch politician; b. 23 July 1952, Hengelo; ed Tax and Customs Admin Centre, Utrecht; worked as investigator Fiscal Information and Investigation Service 1980–86; mem. Borculo Municipal Council 1976–94, alderman 1986–94; mem. Gelderland Provincial Council 1987–94; mem. House of Reps 1994–; apptd Minister of Housing, Planning and Environment 2002; Minister of Defence 2003–06. *Address:* c/o Volkspartij voor Vrijheid en Democratie (VVD) (People's Party for Freedom and Democracy—Netherlands Liberal Party), POB 30836, 2500 GV The Hague, Netherlands. *Telephone:* (70) 3613061 (office). *Fax:* (70) 3608276 (office). *E-mail:* alg.sec@vvd.nl (office). *Website:* www.vvd.nl (office).

KAMPELMAN, Max M., JD, PhD; American diplomatist and lawyer; *Of Counsel, Fried, Frank Harris, Shriver and Jacobson LLP;* b. 7 Nov. 1920, New York; s. of Joseph Kampelmacher and Eva Gottlieb; m. Marjorie Buetow 1948; two s. three d.; ed New York and Minnesota Univs; Partner, Fried, Frank Harris, Shriver and Kampelman, Washington 1956–85, Fried, Frank Harris, Shriver and Jacobson 1989–91, Counselor 1991–; Visiting Prof. Political Science, Claremont Coll., Calif. 1963; Sr Adviser, US Del. to the UN 1966–67; Chair. Emer., Greater Washington Telecommunications Asscn (WETA-TV), American Acad. of Diplomacy, Inst. for the Study of Diplomacy; Co-Chair., US Del. to observe the Elections in El Salvador 1984; Bd of Dirs, US Inst. of Peace 1985–86; Amb., Head of US Del. to the Negotiations on Nuclear and Space Arms 1985–89; Counselor Dept of State 1987–89; Amb. and Chair. US Del. to the Conf. on Security and Co-operation in Europe (CSCE), Madrid 1980–83; Amb., Head US del. to Geneva Meeting on Ethnic Minorities of the CSCE 1991; Amb., Head US del. to Moscow Meeting of Conf. on Human Dimension of the CSCE 1991; Legis. Counsel to Senator H. H. Humphrey 1949–55; Bd of Trustees Woodrow Wilson Int. Center for Scholars 1979–90 (Chair. 1979–81); Chair. Freedom House 1983–85, 1989–; Kt Commdr's Cross of the Order of Merit (FRG) 1984; Dr hc (Hebrew Univ. of Jerusalem) 1982, (Hebrew Union Coll.) 1984, (Georgetown Univ.) 1984, (Bates Coll.) 1986, (Minn.) 1987, (Bar Ilan) 1987, (Adelphi Univ.) 1988, (Yeshiva Univ.) 1990, (Ben Gurion Univ.) 1992, (Florida Int. Univ.) 1993, (Brandeis Univ.) 1993; Hon. DIur (Jewish Theological Seminary of NY) 1988, (NY Univ.) 1988; The Anatoly Scharansky Award 1981; Vanderbilt Gold Medal, New York Univ. Law Center 1982; Human Rights Award, American Fed. of Teachers 1983; Masaryk Award, Czechoslovak Nat. Council of America 1983; Golden Plate Award, American Acad. of Achievement 1984; Henry M. Jackson Award (JINSA) 1987; Sec. of State's Distinguished Service Award 1988; Trainar Award for Distinction in the Conduct of Diplomacy, Georgetown Univ. 1988 Pres.'s Citizens' Medal 1989, Library of Congress Living Legend Award 2000. *Publications:* The Communist Party vs. the C.I.O.: A Study in Power Politics 1957, Three Years at the East-West Divide 1983; Co-Author: The Strategy of Deception 1963; contrib. to Congress Against the President 1976, Entering New Worlds: The Memoirs of a Private Man in Public Life 1991. *Address:* Fried, Frank Harris, Shriver and Jacobson LLP, Suite 800, 1001 Pennsylvania Avenue, NW, Washington, DC 20004 (office); 3154 Highland Place, NW, Washington, DC 20008, USA (home). *Telephone:* (202) 639-7020 (office). *Fax:* (202) 639-7008 (office). *E-mail:* Max_Kampelman@friedfrank.com (office). *Website:* www.ffhsj .com (office).

KAMPFNER, John; British writer and journalist; *CEO, Index on Censorship;* fmr foreign corresp. with Reuters and Daily Telegraph; Chief Political Corresp., Financial Times mid-1990s; fmr political commentator, Today programme (BBC Radio 4); Political Ed. New Statesman 2002–05, Ed. 2005–08; CEO, Index on Censorship 2008–; Chair. Turner Contemporary Operating Trust 2008–; regular appearances on radio and TV; British Soc. of Magazine Eds. Ed. of the Year Award for Current Affairs Magazines 2006. *Television documentary films:* (all for BBC) Israel Undercover 2002, The Ugly War: Children of Vengeance (Foreign Press Asscn Award for Film of the Year and Journalist of the Year) 2002, War Spin 2003, Robin Cook: The Lost Leader (profile) 2003, Clare Short: The Conscientious Objector (profile) 2003, Who Runs Britain (series) 2004. *Publications:* Inside Yeltsin's Russia: Corruption, Conflict, Capitalism 1995, Robin Cook: The Life and Times of Tony Blair's Most Awkward Minister 1999, Blair's Wars 2003, Dangerous Liaisons: Blair, Britain and the Failure of Europe 2007; contrib. to The Herald, The Observer, The Independent, The Guardian, Daily Express, The Times, Sunday Times, Daily Mail, Financial Times, Los Angeles Times, Daily Telegraph, Evening Standard,. *Address:* Knight Ayton Management, 114 St Martin's Lane, London, WC2N 4BE, England (office); Index on Censorship, 6–8 Amwell Street, London EC1R 1UQ, England (office). *Telephone:* (20) 7836-5333 (office); (20) 7279-2313 (office). *Fax:* (20) 7836-8333 (office). *E-mail:* info@ knightayton.co.uk (office); john@jkampfner.net (office). *Website:* www .knightayton.co.uk (office); www.indexoncensorship.org (office); www .jkampfner.net.

KAMPOURIS, Emmanuel Andrew, MA; Greek business executive; b. 14 Dec. 1934, Alexandria, Egypt; s. of Andrew G. Kampouris and Euridice A. Caralli; m. Myrto Stellatos 1959 (deceased); two s.; ed King's School, Bruton, UK, Oxford Univ. and N Staffs. Coll. of Tech.; Plant Man. and Dir KEREM, Athens 1962–64; Dir HELLENIT, Athens 1962–65; Vice-Pres. and Group Exec. (Int. and Export), American Standard Inc., Piscataway, NJ 1979–84, Sr Vice-Pres. (Bldg Products) 1984–89; Pres. and CEO American Standard Inc. 1989–99, Chair. 1993–99; mem. Bd of Dirs Click Commerce Inc., Horizon Blue Cross Blue Shield of NJ, Stanley Works, Alticor Inc., SmartDisk Corpn; fmr mem. of Bd Nat. Endowment for Democracy (continues as Chair. Budget and Audit Cttee); Trustee Emer., Hudson Inst.; mem. Econ. Club of NY, Oxford Univ. Council for School of Man. Studies, Oxford Law Soc.; mem. Bd US Chamber of Commerce 1994–2001; Democracy Service Medal, Nat. Endowment for Democracy 2007. *Leisure interests:* golf, tennis, classical music. *Address:* c/o Board of Directors, National Endowment for Democracy, 1025 F Street, NW, Suite 800, Washington, DC 20004, USA (office).

KAMPRAD, Ingvar; Swedish home furnishings executive; *Head, IKEA International A/S;* b. 30 March 1926, Småland; m. Margaretha Kamprad; three s.; f. IKEA home furnishings co. 1943. *Publication:* The History of IKEA 1998. *Address:* POB 640, 251 06 Helsingborg, Sweden (home). *Telephone:* (42) 26-71-00 (office). *Fax:* (42) 13-28-05 (office). *Website:* www.ikea.com (office).

KAMU, Okko; Finnish conductor and violinist; b. 7 March 1946, Helsinki; m. Susanne Kamu 1987; three s. three d.; ed Sibelius Acad.; leader, Suhonen Quartet 1964; began professional career with Helsinki Philharmonic Orchestra 1965; subsequently appointed leader, Finnish Nat. Opera Orchestra 1966–69, Third Conductor 1967; guest conductor, Swedish Royal Opera, Stockholm 1969; Chief Conductor, Finnish Radio Symphony Orchestra 1971–77; Music Dir Oslo Philharmonic 1975–79, Helsinki Philharmonic 1981–89; Prin. Conductor, Netherlands Radio Symphony 1983–86; Prin. Guest Conductor, City of Birmingham Symphony Orchestra 1985–88; Prin. Conductor, Sjaelland Symphony Orchestra, Copenhagen 1988–94; Music Dir Stockholm Sinfonietta 1989–93; Prin. Conductor Helsingborg Symphony Orchestra 1991–2000; First Guest Conductor, Singapore Symphony Orchestra 1995–2001; Music Dir Finnish Nat. Opera, Helsinki 1996–2000; Prin. Guest Conductor Lausanne Chamber Orchestra 1999–2002; conducted world premières of Sallinen's operas The Red Line and The King Goes Forth to France; numerous engagements with orchestras and opera houses worldwide; mem. Royal Swedish Acad. of Music 1996; First Prize, First Int. Karajan Conductor Competition, Berlin 1969. *Leisure interests:* sailing, fishing, underwater photography, diving, golf, gastronomy, family life. *Address:* Villa Arcadia, Calle Mozart 7, Rancho Domingo, 29639 Benalmedina Pueblo, Spain.

KAMYNIN, Mikhail Leonidovich; Russian diplomatist; *Director of the Information and Press Department, Ministry of Foreign Affairs;* b. 13 Aug. 1956, Moscow; m.; one d. one s.; ed Moscow Inst. of Int. Relations, Diplomatic Acad. of Ministry of Foreign Affairs; various positions, Embassy in Mexico 1978–82, 1987–91; Press Sec., Ministry of Foreign Affairs 1991–92; Counsellor, Embassy in Spain 1992–97; Asst Dir of Press and Information, Ministry of Foreign Affairs 1997–99; Minister Counsellor, Embassy in Cuba 1999–2002; Asst Dir European Affairs, Ministry of Foreign Affairs 2002; Amb. to Spain 2002–05; Dir of Information and Press Dept, Ministry of Foreign Affairs 2005–; del. to numerous int. meetings; mem. Russian Union of Journalists. *Address:* Ministry of Foreign Affairs, 119200 Moscow, Smolenskaya-Sennaya pl. 32/34, Russia (office). *Telephone:* (495) 244-41-19 (office). *Fax:* (495) 230-41-12 (office). *E-mail:* dip@mid.ru (office); pressdept@mid.ru (office). *Website:* www.mid.ru (office).

KAN, Naoto; Japanese politician; *Acting President, Democratic Party of Japan;* fmr patent attorney; Minister of Health and Welfare Jan.–Nov. 1996; mem. House of Reps; mem. New Party Sakigake (NPS), now Sakigake; Founder mem. Democratic Party of Japan 1998, Pres. 1998–99, 2002–04 (resgnd), Sec.-Gen. 2000–02, Acting Pres. 2006–. *Address:* Democratic Party of Japan, 1-11-1 Nagata-cho, Chiyoda-ku, Tokyo 100-0014, Japan. *Telephone:* (3) 3595-8601 (office); (3) 3595-9960 (office). *Fax:* (3) 3595-7318 (office). *E-mail:* dpjenews@dpj.or.jp (office). *Website:* www.dpj.or.jp (office).

KAN, Yuet Wai, MD, DSc, FRCP, FRS; American physician, investigator and academic; *Louis K. Diamond Professor of Hematology, Departments of Laboratory Medicine and Medicine, University of California, San Francisco;* b. 11 June 1936, Hong Kong; s. of Tong Po Kan and Lai Wai Li; m. Alvera Lorraine Limauro 1964; two d.; ed Wah Yan Coll., Hong Kong and Univ. of Hong Kong Medical School; Asst Prof. of Pediatrics, Harvard Medical School, USA 1970–72; Assoc. Prof., Dept of Medicine, Univ. of Calif., San Francisco 1972–77, Prof., Depts of Lab. Medicine, Medicine 1977–, Louis K. Diamond Prof. of Hematology 1991–, Investigator, Howard Hughes Medical Inst. 1976–; Head Div. of Molecular Medicine and Diagnostics 1989–; Dir and Hon. Prof. Inst. of Molecular Biology, Univ. of Hong Kong 1991–94; mem. Research Grants Council, Hong Kong 1990–94; mem. NIH Blood Diseases and Resources Advisory Cttee 1985–89, Nat. Inst. of Digestive and Kidney Disease Advisory Council, NIH 1991–95; mem. Scientific Advisory Bd, St Jude's Children's Hosp. 1994–97, Qiu Shi Science and Technologies Foundation, Hong Kong 1994–, Nat. Heart, Lung & Blood Inst. 1995–96, Thalassemia Int. Fed. 1995–; Trustee Croucher Foundation 1992–, Chair. 1997–; mem. Scientific Advisory Bd and Exec. Cttee, Qiu Shi Foundation on Science and Tech., Hong Kong; mem. NAS (currently Council Mem.), Academia Sinica, Assoc. Fellow, Third World Acad. of Sciences; Foreign mem. Chinese Acad. of

Sciences; Dr hc (Univ. of Cagliari, Sardinia, Italy) 1981, (Chinese Univ. of Hong Kong) 1981, (Univ. of Hong Kong) 1987, (Open Univ. of Hong Kong) 1998; Damashek Award, American Soc. of Hematology 1979, Stratton Lecture Award, Int. Soc. of Hematology 1980, George Thorn Award, Howard Hughes Medical Inst. 1980, Gairdner Foundation Int. Award 1984, Allan Award, American Soc. of Human Genetics 1984, Lita Annenberg Hazen Award for Excellence in Clinical Research 1984, Waterford Award in Biomedical Sciences 1987, NIH Merit Award 1987, American Coll. of Physicians Award 1988, Sanremo Int. Award for Genetic Research 1989, Warren Alpert Foundation Prize 1989, Albert Lasker Clinical Medical Research Award 1991, Christopher Columbus Discovery Award in Biomedical Research 1992, City of Medicine Award 1992, Cotlove Award, Acad. of Clinical Lab. Physicians and Scientists 1993, Merit Award, Fed. of Chinese Canadians Educ. Foundation 1994, Helmut Horten Research Award 1995, Shaw Prize, Hong Kong 2004. *Publications:* more than 240 articles and chapters in many scientific journals and books. *Address:* HSW 901E, Box 0793, University of California, 533 Parnassus Avenue, San Francisco, CA 94143-0793, USA. *Telephone:* (415) 476-5841 (office). *Fax:* (415) 476-2956 (office). *E-mail:* yw .kan@ucsf.edu (office). *Website:* labmed.ucsf.edu (office).

KAN-DAPAAH, Albert; Ghanaian politician and chartered accountant; b. 14 March 1953, Maase-Boaman, Ashanti Region; ed Acherensua Secondary School, Inst. of Professional Studies, North East London Polytechnic and Emile Woolf Coll. of Accountancy, UK; Audit Sr with Pannel Kerr Forster, transferred to Monrovia, Liberia and London, UK offices 1978–86; Head of Audit, Social Security and Nat. Insurance Trust Jan.–Sept. 1987; Dir of Audit, Electricity Co. of Ghana 1987, later Dir of Finance for six years; Pnr, Kwesie, Kan-Dapaah & Baah Co., Accra; Man. Consultant Kan-Dapaah and Assocs; fmr part-time Lecturer in Auditing, School of Admin, Univ. of Ghana, Inst. of Professional Studies; Pres. Inst. of Chartered Accountants (Ghana) 1996; Vice-Pres. Asscn of Accountancy Bodies in West Africa 1996; mem. Bd of Dirs SSB Consumer Credit Ltd 1987–95; Alt. Bd mem. Kabel Metal Ghana Ltd 1987–95, New Times Corpn 1987–95; Ashanti Regional Rep. on Nat. Council of the New Patriotic Party, mem. Finance and Econ. Affairs Cttee 1992–96; mem. Parl. for Afigya Sekyere West 1997–; Minister for Energy 2000–03, for Communications and Tech. 2003–07, for Interior 2006–07, of Defence 2007–09; mem. Ghana Inst. of Chartered Accountants; Fellow, Chartered Asscn of Certified Accountants (UK). *Address:* c/o New Patriotic Party, C912/2 Duade Street, Kokomlemle, POB 3456, Accra, Ghana (office). *Telephone:* (21) 227951 (office). *Fax:* (21) 224418 (office). *E-mail:* npp@africanonline.com.gh (office).

KANAAN, Taher Hamdi, PhD; Jordanian business consultant and organization official; *Managing Director, Jordan Center for Policy Research and Dialogue;* b. 1 March 1935, Nablus, Palestine; s. of Hamdi and Najiah (née Quttainah) Kanaan; m. Ilham Kahwaji 1960; three s.; ed American Univ. of Beirut, Trinity Coll., Cambridge, UK; Econ. Adviser, Ministry of Planning, Iraq 1964–65; Dir of Programmes at Arab Fund for Econ. and Social Devt, Kuwait 1973–76; Consultant in Industrial Devt, Ministry of Planning, Morocco 1977–78; Chief External Financing and Devt, UNCTAD, Geneva 1979–83; Dir and Econ. Adviser Arab Fund 1983–85; Minister of Occupied Territories Affairs 1985, of Planning 1986–89, Deputy Prime Minister for Devt 1998–99; Gen. Man. Industrial Devt Bank of Jordan 1989–92; mem. Bd of Higher Educ., Jordan; mem. Bd of Govs World Bank, Arab Fund for Econ. and Social Devt 1985–89; mem. Bd of Trustees Center for Arab Unity Studies, Beirut, Econ. Research Forum, Cairo, Arab Anti-Corruption Org.; Man. Dir Jordan Center for Policy Research and Dialogue, Amman 2003–; mem. Advisory Group Arab Human Devt Report. *Leisure interest:* swimming, music, history, philosophy, surfing the Internet. *Address:* Jordan Center for Policy Research and Dialogue, PO Box 830825, Zahran, Amman 11183, Jordan (office). *Telephone:* (6) 5923676 (office). *Fax:* (6) 5923368 (office). *E-mail:* info@ jcpprd.org (office); taher.kanaan@gmail.com (home). *Website:* www.jcpprd.org (office).

KANAI, Tsutomu, MS, PhD; Japanese electronics industry executive; *Chairman Emeritus, Hitachi Ltd;* b. 1930; ed Univ. of Tokyo; trained as mechanical engineer; joined Hitachi Ltd 1958, worked on devt of nuclear reactors in Cen. Research Lab., sr positions include Exec. Man.-Dir and Group Exec. Power Group 1985–87, Sr Exec. Man.-Dir 1987–89, Exec. Vice-Pres. and Dir 1989–91, Pres. and Rep. Dir 1991–99, Chair. and Rep. Dir 1999–2005, now Chair. Emer.; Singapore Honorary Citizen Award 2005. *Address:* Hitachi Ltd, 4-6 Kanda-Surugadai, Chiyoda-ku, Tokyo 101-8010, Japan (office). *Telephone:* (3) 3258-1111 (office). *Fax:* (3) 3258-2375 (office). *Website:* www.hitachi.com (office).

KANANIN, Roman Grigorevich; Russian architect; b. 19 June 1935, Moscow; s. of Grigoriy Kananin and Maria Kananin; m. 1959; one d.; ed Moscow Architectural Inst.; Head of Atelier No. 3. of Public Jt Stock Co. Mosproject 1972–; mem. Russian Acad. of Architecture and Bldg Sciences 2005–; Lenin Prize 1984, Honoured Builder of Moscow 1999, People's Architect 2005. *Works include:* Patrice Lumumba Univ. (now Univ. of People's Friendship), Moscow (with others) 1969–73, residential blocks on Lenin Prospekt, Moscow 1965–70, multi-storey brick residential complex, Noviye Cheremushky 1973–84, memorial complex to war veterans in Novorossiysk 1982, various monuments in Moscow and Magnitogorsk, including monument to Gerzen and Ogarev, Vorobyevy Hils, Moscow, Palace of Youth, Moscow 1978, IRIS Pulman Hotel and apartments, Moscow 1991, Parus Business Centre, Tverskaya-Yamskaya St, Moscow 1994, exclusive multi-storey residential bldgs, Krasnoproletarskaya str., vl. 7 1999, Dolgorukovskaya str., vl. 24–30 2001, B. Gruzinskaya str., vl. 37 2001, residential complexes, Petrovsko-Razumkovsky proezd, B Academicheskaya St, Moscow. *Leisure interests:* sport, travelling. *Address:* Joint-Stock Company Mosproject, 13/14,

1-st Brestkaya str., GSP, 125190 Moscow, Russia. *Telephone:* (495) 209-61-22; (495) 250-46-99. *Fax:* (495) 209-50-02.

KANAPLYOU, Uladzimir; Belarusian politician; *Chairman, Palata Predstaviteley (House of Representatives);* Deputy Chair. Palata Predstaviteley 2000–04, Chair. 2004–. *Address:* Palata Predstaviteley, 220010 Minsk, vul. Savetskaya 11, Belarus (office). *Telephone:* (17) 227-25-14 (office). *Fax:* (17) 222-31-78 (office). *E-mail:* admin@gov.house.by (office). *Website:* house.gov.by (office).

KANAWA, Dame Kiri (see TE KANAWA, Dame Kiri).

KANBUR, Ravi, MA, DPhil; British economist and academic; *T. H. Lee Professor of World Affairs, International Professor of Applied Economics and Management and Professor of Economics, Cornell University;* b. 28 Aug. 1954, Dharwar, India; s. of Prof. M. G. Kanbur and M. M. Kanbur; m. Margaret S. Grieco 1979; ed King Edward VII Camp Hill School, Birmingham, Gonville & Caius Coll. Cambridge and Merton and Worcester Colls. Oxford; Prize Fellow, Nuffield Coll. Oxford 1978–79; Fellow in Econs, Clare Coll. Cambridge 1979–83; Prof. of Econs, Univ. of Essex 1983–85; Visiting Prof., Princeton Univ. 1985–87; Prof. of Econs and Dir Devt Econs Research Centre, Univ. of Warwick 1987–89, Hon. Prof. 1994; Sr Adviser and Ed. World Bank Economic Review and World Bank Research Observer, IBRD, Washington, DC 1989–92; World Bank Resident Rep. in Ghana 1992–94, World Bank Chief Economist for Africa 1994–96, Prin. Adviser to Sr Vice-Pres. and Chief Economist 1996–97; T. H. Lee Prof. of World Affairs, Int. Prof. of Applied Econs and Man. and Prof. of Econs, Cornell Univ., Ithaca, NY 1997–; American Agricultural Econs Asscn Research Award (jtly with L. Haddad) 1991. *Publications:* articles in learned journals. *Leisure interest:* watching TV. *Address:* 309 Warren Hall, Cornell University, Ithaca, NY 14853-7801, USA (office). *Telephone:* (607) 255-7966 (office). *Fax:* (607) 255-9984 (office). *E-mail:* sk145@cornell.edu (office). *Website:* people.cornell.edu/pages/sk145 (office).

KANCHELI, Giya (Georgy); Georgian composer; b. 10 Aug. 1935, Tbilisi; s. of Alexander Kancheli and Agnessa Kancheli; m. Valentina Djikia; one s. one d.; ed Tbilisi State Conservatory with I. Tuskia; Prof. Tbilisi Conservatory 1970–90; Music Dir Rustaveli Drama Theatre 1971–; First Sec. Georgian Composers' Union 1984–89; Composer in Residence, Berlin (German Academic Exchange Service) 1991–92; Composer in Residence, Royal Flemish Philharmonic Orchestra, Antwerp 1995–96; USSR State Prize 1976, USSR People's Artist 1988, State Prize of Georgia 1982, Nika Prize for film music 1987, Triumph Prize Moscow 1998. *Compositions include:* symphonies: First 1967, Second 1970, Third 1973, Fourth (in Memoriam Michelangelo) 1975, Fifth 1977, Sixth (In Memory of Parents) 1980, Seventh (Epilogue) 1986; other symphonic works: Mourned by the Wind for orchestra and viola 1989, Lament (in memory of Luigi Nono), for violin, soprano and orchestra 1995; opera: Music for the Living 1984; chamber works: Life Without Christmas 1989–90 (cycle of four works for chamber ensembles), Magnum Ignotum, for wind ensemble and tape 1994, Exil, for soprano, small ensemble and tape 1994; music to plays by Shakespeare, including King Lear, Richard III and other productions of Rustaveli Drama Theatre, incidental music. *Address:* Consience Straat 14, 2018 Antwerp, BelgiumTovstonogov str. 6, 380064 Tbilisi, Georgia. *Telephone:* (3) 295-03-39 (Tbilisi); (3) 230-85-53 (Antwerp).

KANDBORG, Lt-Gen. Ole Larson; Danish army officer (retd) and consultant; *Military Adviser, DCS Group;* b. 16 May 1941, nr Skanderborg; m. Lis Kandborg; two c.; ed Viborg, Army Officers' Acad., Copenhagen, Canadian Forces' Staff Coll., Toronto, Canada, NATO Defence Coll., Rome, Italy; nat. service with Prince's Life Regt, Viborg, Sergeant, Lt; First Lt, Capt. of mechanized infantry Bn 1966–72; Instructor, Danish Combat Arms School 1974–77; Staff Officer, HQ of the UN Peace-keeping Force in Cyprus 1977–78; Co. Commdr, Skive, G3 of Mechanized Brigade 1978–82; at Faculty of Danish Defence Coll. 1982–84; Instructor, annual Nordic UN Staff Officers' Course (Sweden), Chief Instructor; Lt-Col, Commdr of 1st Tank Bn, Jutland Dragoon Regt, Holstebro 1984–85; Public Information Adviser and Deputy to Chief of Defence, Defence HQ, Copenhagen 1986–89; Deputy Chief of Staff for Plans and Policy 1992; Col, Commdr 2nd New Zealand Brigade, Vordingborg 1989–90; Maj.-Gen., Commdr Jutland Div., Fredericia 1990–92; Commdr of Danish Operational Command based in Århus and Kamp 1993–96; Danish Mil. Rep. to NATO Mil. Cttee April–Sept. 1996, Dir Int. Mil. Staff, NATO 1996–2001 (retd); currently Mil. Adviser on strategic and NATO matters, DCS Group; Commdr, Order of Dannebrog, Mil. Good Service Medal, Reserve Officers' Asscn's Good Service Medal, Commdr 1st Degree, Order of the Swedish North Star, Legion of Merit (Degree of Commdr); UN Medal 7. *Address:* c/o DCS Group, Virkelyst 10, 9400 Noerresundby, Denmark (office). *Telephone:* 70-23-13-70. *Fax:* 98-19-07-00. *Website:* www.dcsgroup.dk.

KANDEL, Eric Richard, BA, MD; American psychiatrist, biochemist and academic; *Professor of Neuroscience, Columbia University;* b. 7 Nov. 1929, Vienna, Austria; m. 1956; two c.; ed Harvard Coll., New York Univ.; New York Univ. (NYU) School of Medicine 1956; Resident in Psychiatry, Harvard Medical School 1960–64, staff psychiatrist 1964–65; Assoc. Prof. of Physiology, NYU 1965–74; Prof. of Physiology and Psychiatry, Columbia Univ. 1974–, Prof. of Biochemistry 1992, now Prof. of Neuroscience; Sr Investigator, Howard Hughes Medical Inst. 1983–; mem. NAS, American Acad. of Arts and Sciences, Soc. of Neurosciences (Pres. 1980–81), Int. Brain Research Org., New York Acad. of Sciences; numerous awards and prizes including Nat. Medal of Science 1988, Warren Triennial Prize 1992, Harvey Prize 1993, Mayor Award for Excellence in Science and Tech. 1994, New York Acad. of Medicine Award 1996, Wolf Foundation Prize in Medicine 1999, Heineken Prize 2000, Nobel Prize for Medicine (jt recipient) 2000. *Publications:* In Search of Memory (Los Angeles Times Book Prize for Science and Technology) 2006; numerous articles in academic journals. *Address:* Howard Hughes

Medical Institute, Columbia University, 1051 Riverside Drive, New York, NY 10032, USA (office). *Telephone:* (212) 543-5204 (office). *Fax:* (212) 543-5474 (office). *E-mail:* erk5@columbia.edu (office). *Website:* www.excalibur.cpmc.columbia.edu (office).

KANEKO, Hisashi, MSc; Japanese business executive and foundation executive; *President, NEC Foundation of America;* b. 19 Nov. 1933, Tokyo; s. of Shozo Kaneko and Toshi Kaneko; m. Mokoto Washino; three c.; ed Tokyo Univ., Univ. of Calif., Berkeley; joined NEC Corpn 1956, Pres. NEC America 1989–91, NEC Corpn 1994–99 (resgnd), Counselor 1999–; currently Pres. and mem. Bd of Dirs NEC Foundation of America. *Address:* NEC Foundation of America, 2950 Express Drive South, Suite 102, Islandia, NY 11749-1412, USA (office). *Telephone:* (631) 232-2212 (office). *Website:* www.necfoundation.org (office).

KANEKO, Isao; Japanese airline industry executive; *Senior Adviser, Japan Airlines Corporation;* b. 1 March 1938; m.; one d.; ed Tokyo Univ.; joined Japan Airlines (JAL) 1960, worked in Int. Cargo Dept then joined Industrial Relations Dept; posted to American Region HQ, New York 1968–72; Deputy Vice Pres. Industrial Relations 1985–95, mem. Bd of Dirs 1991–, Man. Dir and Sr Vice Pres., Human Resources 1995–97, Sr Man. Dir and Sr Vice Pres., Human Resources 1997–98, Pres. JAL 1998–2002, Pres. and CEO Japan Airlines and concurrently Pres. and CEO Japan Airlines System Corpn 2002–04, Chair. and CEO Japan Airlines Corpn (JAL Group holding co.) and concurrently Chair. Japan Airlines Int. and Japan Airlines Domestic System 2004–05, Sr Adviser 2005–; Chair. Japan-Asia Exchange Cttee, Keiza Doyukai (Japan Asscn of Corp. Execs). *Address:* Japan Airlines Corporation, 2-4-11, Higashi-Shinagawa, Shinagawa-ku, Tokyo 140-8605, Japan. *Telephone:* (3) 5769-6098. *Website:* www.jal.co.jp.

KANEKO, Ryotaro; Japanese insurance executive; b. 20 June 1941; Man. Dir Meiji Life Insurance Co. 1994–97, Sr Man. Dir 1997–98, Pres. 1998–2004, Pres. and Dir Meiji Yasuda Life Insurance Co. (following merger with Yasuda Mutual Life) 2004–05 (resgnd); Dir Mitsubishi Tokyo Financial Group 2003–05. *Address:* c/o Meiji Yasuda Life Insurance Company, 19–1 Nishi-Shinjuku, Shinjuku-ku, Tokyo 169-8701, Japan (office).

KANERVA, Ilkka Armas Mikael, MPolSc; Finnish politician; b. 28 Jan. 1948, Lokalahti; mem. Turku City Council 1972–; Party Man., Nat. Coalition Party 1972–93 (mem. Exec. Cttee 1975–93), Chair. Nat. Coalition Party Youth League 1972–76; mem. Suomen Eduskunta (Parl.) 1975–, mem. Foreign Affairs Cttee 1979-1987, 1995–99, Chair. Parl. Supervisory Bd, Bank of Finland 1995–99, Chair. Defence Cttee 1999–2003, Deputy Speaker 2003–07; Minister of State (attached to Office of the Council of State) 1987–90, Minister at the Ministry of Finance 1989–91, 1991, Minister of Transport and Communications 1990–91, of Labour 1991–94, of Foreign Affairs 2007–08 (resgnd); Chair. Comm. of State Guarantee Fund 1996–; Chair. Supervisory Bd, Veikkaus Oy (Nat. Lottery Co.) 1996–; Pres. Finnish Athletics Fed.; Pres. Helsinki 2005 World Championships Organising Cttee; Council mem. Int. Asscn of Athletics Fed. 2003–. *Address:* c/o Kansallinen Kokoomus (Kok) (National Coalition Party), Pohjoinen Rautatiekatu 21b, 00100 Helsinki, Finland. *Telephone:* (20) 7488488. *Fax:* (20) 7488505. *E-mail:* jori.arvonen@kokoomus.fi. *Website:* www.kokoomus.fi; www.ilkkakanerva.net.

KANG, Chang-oh; South Korean business executive; *President and Representative Director, POSCO;* Sr Man.-Dir and Gen. Superintendent, Pohang Works, Pohang Iron & Steel Corpn (POSCO) 1988, apptd Dir 1995, Sr Exec. Vice-Pres. and Chief Financial Officer 2002–03, Pres. and Rep. Dir 2003–. *Address:* POSCO, POSCO Centre 892, Daechi-dong, Kangnam-ku, Seoul 135–777, Republic of Korea (office). *Telephone:* (2) 3457-0114 (office). *Fax:* (2) 3457-1999 (office). *Website:* www.posco.co.kr (office).

KANG, Chung-won, BA, MA; South Korean banking executive; *President and CEO, Kookmin Bank;* b. 19 Dec. 1950; ed Dartmouth Coll., Fletcher School of Law and Diplomacy, Tufts Univ., USA; held numerous exec. positions for Citibank including in New York 1979, in Repub. of Korea 1979–83; with Bankers Trust Group, Seoul 1983–92, Chief Rep. Bankers Trust Securities Corpn 1992–96, Chief Country Officer, Korea Bankers Trust Group 1996–99; Chief Country Officer, Deutsche Bank Group, Korea 1999–2000; Pres. and CEO Seoul Bank 2000–02; Adviser, Kim & Chang (law firm) 2003–04, World Bank Group 2003–04; Pres. and CEO Kookmin Bank 2004–; Dir (non-exec.) LG Investment & Securities Co. 2003–04. *Address:* Kookmin Bank, 9-1, 2-ga, Namdaemoon-ro, Jung-gu, Seoul 100-703, Republic of Korea (office). *Telephone:* (2) 2073-7114 (office). *Fax:* (2) 2073-8360 (office). *E-mail:* info@kbstar.com (office). *Website:* www.kbstar.com (office).

KANG, Dong-suk; American violinist; b. 28 April 1954, Seoul, Repub. of Korea; m. Martine Schittenhelm; one s. one d.; ed Juilliard School, New York and Curtis Inst. Philadelphia (under Ivan Galamian); went to New York to study 1967; won San Francisco Symphony Foundation Competition and Merriweather Post Competition, Washington, DC 1971; winner at other competitons including Queen Elisabeth, Brussels, Montreal, and Carl Flesch, London; has appeared with maj. orchestras throughout USA, UK, Europe and Far East and at music festivals around the world including BBC Promenade concerts (debut 1987). *Recordings include:* complete repertoire for violin and orchestra by Sibelius, Nielsen Violin Concerto, Elgar Violin Concerto, Bruch Violin Concerto, Walton Violin Concerto. *Address:* 17 rue du Lieutenant Heitz, 94300 Vincennes, France (office).

KANG, Gum-sil; South Korean civil rights lawyer and politician; b. 1957; ed Seoul Nat. Univ.; admitted to Bar 1981; served as judge 1983–96 (under S Korean mil. rule, defied common practice of jailing student activists by releasing them on bail); led group of judges advocating reform of outdated legal system 1994; attorney 1996–; Vice-Pres. Lawyers for a Democratic Soc.

(Minbyun) 2000–; Minister of Justice (first woman) 2003–04; Chief Attorney, Horizon Law Group, Seoul –2006; unsuccessful cand. for Mayor of Seoul (Uri Party) 2006. *Leisure interests:* amateur singer and dancer. *Address:* c/o Uri Party, National Assembly, 1 Yeouido-dong, Yeongdeungpo-gu, Seoul 150-701, Republic of Korea (office).

KANG, Man-soo; South Korean civil servant and politician; b. 1945, Hapcheon, S Gyeongsang Prov.; began career at Ministry of Finance 1970, Vice-Minister of Finance 1997–98 (resgnd over Asian financial crisis); econ. affairs adviser to Pres. Lee for several years, Head of Econ. Affairs Sub-cttee on Lee's Transition Cttee –2008; Pres. Seoul Devt Inst. during Lee's tenure as Mayor of Seoul; co-ordinated Lee's economy-related pledges during presidential campaign; Minister of Strategy and Finance 2008–09. *Address:* c/o Ministry of Strategy and Finance, Government Complex II, 88 Gwanmunro, Gwacheon City, Gyeonggi Province, 427-725, South Korea (office).

KANG, Sok-ju; North Korean politician; *Vice-Minister of Foreign Affairs;* b. 4 Aug. 1939, Pyongwan, S Pyongan Prov.; First Vice-Minister, Admin. Council, Ministry of Foreign Affairs 1986–87, First Vice-Minister of Foreign Affairs 1987–, del. to UN following N Korean accession to UN 1991, Head of Del. to negotiations with USA 1993, attended meeting of Kim Il Sung and US Pres. Jimmy Carter 1994, signed nuclear agreement with USA, Geneva 1994, accompanied Kim Jong Il to Russia 2001, to summit with Japanese Prime Minister Junichiro Koizumi 2002; mem. Cen. Cttee Korean Workers' Party 1991–. *Address:* Ministry of Foreign Affairs, Pyongyang, Democratic People's Republic of Korea (office).

KANG, Young-hoon, MA, PhD; South Korean politician and diplomatist; *Chairman, UNEP (United Nations Environment Programme) Korea Committee;* b. 30 May 1922; m. Hyo-Soo Kim 1947; two s. one d.; ed Univs of Manchuria, Univ. of Southern California, USA; Mil. Attaché to Embassy, Washington, DC 1952–53; Div. Commdr 1953, Corps Commdr 1959–60; retd rank of Lt-Gen. 1961; Asst Minister of Defence 1955–56; Staff mem. Research Inst. on Communist Strategy and Propaganda, Univ. of S. California 1968–69; Dir Research Inst. on Korean Affairs, Silver Spring, Md 1970–76; Dean Grad. School, Hankuk Univ. of Foreign Studies 1977–78; Chancellor Inst. of Foreign Affairs and Nat. Security, Ministry for Foreign Affairs 1978–80; Amb. to UK 1981–84, to the Holy See 1985–88; Prime Minister of the Repub. of Korea 1988–91; currently Chair. UNEP Korea Cttee; fmr Chair. Sejong Foundation; numerous mil. medals. *Address:* c/o UNEP Korea Committee, 509 Suwoon Hall, 88 Kyungwoon-dong, Jongno-gu, Seoul, 110-775, Korea. *E-mail:* unep@unep.or.kr. *Website:* www.unep.or.kr/bbs.

KANGAS, Edward A. (Ed), BA, MBA, CPA; American accountant and health care industry executive; *Chairman, Tenet Healthcare Corporation;* b. 22 May 1944; ed Univ. of Kansas; began career as staff accountant Touche Ross 1967, Pnr 1975, Man.-Dir 1985–89, Man.-Pnr Deloitte & Touche USA (following merger of Deloitte Haskins & Sells and Touche Ross 1989) 1989–94, Chair. and CEO Deloitte Touche Tohmatsu (DTT) 1989–2000, Consultant 2000–03; Chair. Tenet Healthcare Corpn 2003–; mem. Bd of Dirs Hovnavian Enterprises Inc., Electronic Data Systems Corpn (EDS), Eclipsys Corpn; Chair. Nat. Multiple Sclerosis Soc. 2000–; mem. Policy Cttee, Cttee for Econ. Devt (also Trustee); mem. Bd of Advisers Univ. of Kansas Business School, now Emer. Bd mem.; mem. Bd of Overseers Wharton School, Univ. of Pa, Bd of Trustees, Univ. of Kansas Endowment Foundation; CPA in New York and Conn.; Distinguished Alumni Award, Univ. of Kansas School of Business 2000. *Address:* Tenet Healthcare Corporation, 3820 State Street, Santa Barbara, CA 93105, USA (office). *Telephone:* (805) 563-7000 (office). *Fax:* (805) 563-7070 (office). *Website:* www.tenethealth.com (office).

KANI, John; South African actor; b. 1943; fmrly worked on a car ass. line; began acting in amateur production; many stage tours abroad and appearances in S. Africa particularly at Market Theatre, Johannesburg; appeared in Sizwe Banzi is Dead, Royal Court Theatre, London 1973, Nat. Theatre, London 2007, Waiting for Godot, Miss Julie, Othello 1987; fmr Exec. Trustee, Market Theatre, Foundation, currently mem. Exec. Council; Dr hc (Cape Town) 2006; Tony Award for Broadway performance in Athol Fugard's Sizwe Banzi is Dead, Hiroshima Foundation for Peace & Culture Award 2000. *Films:* Marigolds in August 1980, Gräset sjunger 1981, Saturday Night at the Palace 1987, An African Dream 1987, Options 1988, A Dry White Season 1989, The Native Who Caused All the Trouble 1989, Sarafina! 1992, Soweto Green 1995, The Ghost and the Darkness 1996, Kini and Adams 1997, The Tichborne Claimant 1998, Final Solution 2001, Nothing But The Truth (Fleur de Cap Award for Best Actor and Best New South African Play, Olive Schreiner Prize 2005) 2002. *Address:* The Market Theatre, PO Box 8656, Johannesburg, 2000 South Africa (office). *Telephone:* (11) 8321641 (office). *Website:* www.markettheatre.co.za (office).

KANN, Peter Robert; American publisher, business executive and journalist; b. 13 Dec. 1942, New York; s. of Robert Kann and Marie Kann (née Breuer); m. 1st Francesca Mayer 1969 (died 1983); m. 2nd Karen House 1984; one s. three d.; ed Harvard Univ.; with The Wall Street Journal 1964–; journalist, New York 1964–67, Viet Nam 1967–68, Hong Kong 1968–75, Publr and Ed. Asian Edn 1976–79, Assoc. Publr 1979–88; Exec. Vice-Pres. Dow Jones & Co. 1986, Pres. int. and magazine groups 1986–89, mem. Bd of Dirs 1987; Publr and Editorial Dir The Wall Street Journal 1989–2002; Pres. Dow Jones & Co. New York 1989–91, Chair. 1991–2007 (retd), CEO 1991–2006; Chair. Bd Far Eastern Econ. Review 1987–89; Trustee Asia Soc. 1989–94, Inst. for Advanced Study, Princeton 1990–, Aspen Inst. 1994–98; mem. Pulitzer Prize Bd 1987–96; Pulitzer Prize for int. reporting 1972. *Address:* c/o Dow Jones & Company, 1 World Financial Center, 200 Liberty Street, New York, NY 10281, USA (office).

KANTOR, Mickey; American corporate lawyer; *Partner, Mayer, Brown, Rowe & Maw LLP;* b. 1939; m. 1st (died 1978); two s. (died 1988) one d.; m. 2nd 1982; one d.; ed Vanderbilt Univ., Georgetown Univ. Law School; served in USN; began career as lawyer protecting rights of migrant farm workers; pnr LA law firm 1993; mem. Bd of Legal Services Corpn in Carter Admin; mem. Comm. investigating LA Riots 1992; Chair. Clinton Presidential Campaign 1992; US Trade Rep. 1993–97; Sec. of Commerce 1996–97; Partner, Mayer, Brown, Rowe & Maw, Washington 1997–; also mem. Bd Dirs Korea First Bank, Int. Advisory Bd Fleishman-Hillard, Bd of Visitors, Georgetown Univ. Law Center; Chief Negotiator, NAFTA, Uruguay Round, Free Trade Areas of America, APEC, ING USA, CB Richard Ellis Group; Order of Southern Cross (Brazil); Distinguished Public Service Medal, Center for Study of Presidency. *Address:* Mayer, Brown LLP, 1909 K Street, NW, Washington, DC 20006, USA (office). *Telephone:* (202) 263-3000 (office). *Fax:* (202) 263-3300 (office). *E-mail:* mkantor@mayerbrown.com (office). *Website:* www.mayerbrown.com (office).

KANYA, Mary Madzandza; Swazi diplomatist; *High Commissioner to UK;* m. Leo Kanya; ed Zombodze Nat. School; fmr teacher, Swaziland Teacher Training Coll., Univ. of Swaziland; tutored children of King Sobhuza II; f. royal school; fmr Sr Insp. of Schools; became Swaziland's first female Amb. 1990, High Commr to Canada 1990–94, Amb. to USA 1994–2005, High Commr to UK 2005–. *Address:* Swaziland High Commission, 20 Buckingham Gate, London, SW1E 6LB, England (office). *Telephone:* (20) 7630-6611 (office). *Fax:* (20) 7630-6564 (office). *E-mail:* enquiries@swaziland.org.uk (office); swaziland@swaziland.btinternet.com (office).

KANZAKI, Takenori, LLB; Japanese politician; *Standing Adviser, New Komeito party;* b. 15 July 1943, Tien-Tsin, People's Repub. of China; ed Tokyo Univ.; public prosecutor 1968–76; lawyer 1982–; mem. House of Reps; mem. Komeito party (now New Komeito party), Chair. Foreign Affairs Cttee, Chief Rep. 1998–2006, now Standing Adviser; Chair. Diet Policy Cttee; Minister of Posts and Telecommunications 1993–94. *Publication:* Prohibition of Profit Granting (co-author). *Leisure interests:* shogi (Japanese chess), reading, travelling, theatre. *Address:* New Komeito Headquarters, 17 Minami-Motomachi, Shinjuku-ku, Tokyo 160-0012 (office); Room No. 201, No. 6 Green Building, 2-12-7 Hakata-Ekimae, Hakata-ku, Fukuoka-shi 812, Fukuoka Prefecture, Japan (home). *Telephone:* (3) 3353-0111 (office); (3) 3581-5111. *Fax:* (3) 3353-9746 (office); (3) 3503-2388. *Website:* www.komei.or.jp (office); www.kanzakitakenori.org.

KAO, Charles, CBE, PhD, FRS, FREng; American (b. Chinese) electrical engineer and academic (retd); b. (Kao Kuen), 4 Nov. 1933, Shanghai, China; s. of the late Chun-Hsian and Tsing-Fong King; m. May-Wan Wong 1959; one s. one d.; ed Univ. of London; engineer, Standard Telephones and Cables Ltd, UK 1957–60, Research Scientist/Research Man., Standard Telecommunications Labs Ltd/ITT Cen. European Lab., Essex, UK 1960–70; Chair. Dept of Electronics, Chinese Univ. of Hong Kong 1970–74; Chief Scientist and Dir of Eng, Electro-Optical Products Div., ITT, Roanoke, Va 1974–81, Vice-Pres. and Dir of Eng 1981–88; Exec. Scientist and Corp. Dir of Research, ITT Advanced Tech. Centre, Conn. 1983–87; Vice-Chancellor The Chinese Univ. of Hong Kong 1987–96; Chair. and CEO Transtech Services Ltd 1996–2001, ITX Services Ltd 2000–04; Hon. CBE 1993; Hon. DSc (Chinese Univ. of Hong Kong) 1985, (Sussex) 1990, (Durham) 1994, (Hull) 1998, (Yale) 1999, (Princeton) 2002, (Toronto) 2005; Dr hc (Soka) 1991; Hon. DEng (Glasgow) 1992; Hon. Dr of Telecommunications Eng (Padova, Italy) 1996; numerous awards and prizes including IEEE Alexander Graham Bell Medal 1985, Marconi Int. 1985, IEEE Faraday Medal (UK) 1989, Japan Prize 1996, Charles Stark Draper Prize, Nat. Acad. of Eng (USA) 1999, Asian of the Century in Science and Tech., Asiaweek (magazine) 1999. *Publications:* Optical Fiber Technology II 1981, Optical Fiber Systems: Technology, Design and Applications 1982, Optical Fibre 1988, A Choice Fulfilled – The Business of High Technology 1991. *Leisure interests:* tennis, hiking, pottery-making. *Address:* c/o S. K. Yee Foundation, Unit 1708, Office Tower, Convention Plaza, 1 Harbour Road, Wan Chai, Hong Kong Special Administrative Region, People's Republic of China (office). *Telephone:* 26037643 (office). *Fax:* 26037663 (office). *E-mail:* ckao@ie.cuhk.edu.hk (home).

KAO, Chin-Yen; Taiwanese business executive; *Chairman and CEO, UNI–President Enterprises Corporation;* b. 24 May 1929, Taiwan; m. Lai-Kwan Kao; one d.; ed Tainan Co. Tienchow Elementary School; Sales Man. Tainan Fabric Corpn 1957–67; f. Pres. Enterprises Group (now UNI-Pres. Enterprises Corpn) 1968, Vice-Chair., Pres. and CEO 1989, now Chair. and CEO; Chair. Pres. Enterprises Chain Store Corpn 1986–; Chair. Ztong Yee Industrial Co. Ltd 1977–, Ton Yi Industrial Corpn 1979–, ScinoPharm Taiwan Ltd; Chair. Bd of Trustees Southern Taiwan Univ. of Tech.; mem. Cen. Standing Cttee, Kuomintang 1994–; Chair. Taiwan Industrial Mfrs Asscn 1999; Hon. PhD (Lincoln) 1983. *Address:* UNI–President Enterprises Corporation, 301 Jhongjheng Road, Yongkang City, Tainan County 710, Taiwan (office). *Telephone:* (6) 2532121 (office). *Fax:* (6) 2532661 (office). *Website:* www.uni-president.biz (office).

KAPARTIS, Costas, MA; Cypriot labour relations official; b. 28 Sept. 1933, Nicosia; m. Anna Kapartis; three c.; ed Webster and Cornell Univs, USA; various positions in Ministry of Labour and Social Insurance 1957–65; Dir-Gen. Cyprus Employers' Fed. 1965–75; Exec. Sec. Int. Org. of Employers 1975, Deputy Sec.-Gen. 1980–90, Sec.-Gen. 1990–2001. *Address:* 9 chemin A. Pasteur, 1209 Geneva, Switzerland (home).

KAPIL DEV; Indian fmr professional cricketer; b. (Kapildev Ramlal Nikhanj), 6 Jan. 1959, Chandigarh; m. Romi Dev; ed Punjab Univ.; right-hand middle-order batsman, right-arm fast-medium bowler; played for Haryana 1975–76 to 1991–92, Northamptonshire 1981–83, Worcestershire

1984–85; played in 131 Tests for India 1978–79 to 1993–94, 34 as Capt., scoring 5,248 runs (average 31.0) including 8 hundreds and taking record 434 wickets (average 29.6); youngest to take 100 Test wickets (21 years 25 days); hit four successive balls for six v. England, Lord's 1990; scored 11,356 runs (18 hundreds) and took 835 wickets in first-class cricket; toured England 1979, 1982, 1983 (World Cup), 1986 and 1990; 225 limited-overs internationals; Indian Nat. Coach 1999–2000; founding mem. and Acad. mem. Laureus World Sports Foundation 2000; Wisden Cricketer of the Year 1983, Electrolux Kelvinator Wisden Indian Cricketer of the Century 2002. *Publication:* Kapil Dev: Triumph of the Spirit 1995. *Leisure interests:* hunting, riding, dancing. *Address:* 39 Sunder Nagar, New Delhi 110 003, India. *Telephone:* (11) 4698333. *Fax:* (11) 3719776.

KAPITSA, Sergey Petrovich, DPhysMathSc; Russian physicist and academic; *Professor of Physics, Moscow Institute of Physics and Technology;* b. 14 Feb. 1928, Moscow; s. of the late Pyotr Kapitsa; m. Tat'yana Alimovna Kapitsa; one s. two d.; ed Moscow Aviation Inst.; engineer Cen. Inst. of Aerohydrodynamics 1949–51; Jr researcher Inst. of Geophysics 1951–53; researcher, head of lab., leading researcher, chief researcher, Kapitsa Inst. of Physical Problems, USSR (now Russian) Acad. of Sciences 1953–; Prof., Head of Dept Moscow Inst. of Physics and Tech. 1965–; mem. Russian Acad. of Natural Sciences 1990, Vice-Pres. 1995, now Hon. Vice-Pres.; mem. World Acad. of Sciences and Arts, European Acad.; Pres. Eurasian Physical Soc., Int. Inst. of Sciences, Int. Fed. of Aeronautics, Manchester Literary and Philosophical Soc.; mem. Ed. Bd Public Understanding of Science, Sceptical Inquirer and other Publs; Kalinga Prize of UNESCO 1979; USSR State Prize 1989. *Television:* broadcaster Obvious-Unbelievable (series) 1973–94, Obvious-Unbelievable XXI century 1997–. *Leisure interest:* underwater swimming. *Address:* Russian Academy of Sciences, 117901 Moscow, Leninsky pr. 14, Moscow, Russia (office). *Telephone:* (495) 954-29-05 (office). *Fax:* (495) 954-33-20 (office).

KAPLAN, Jonathan Stewart; American film writer, film director, television producer and television director; b. 25 Nov. 1947, Paris, France; s. of Sol Kaplan and Frances Heflin; m. Julie Selzer 1987 (divorced 2001); one d.; ed Univ. of Chicago, New York Univ.; mem. tech. staff, Bill Graham's Fillmore East, New York 1969–71; appeared in The Dark at the Top of the Stairs, Broadway 1956–57; Best Male Vocal Concept Video, Billboard 1986. *Films:* Night Call Nurses 1972, Student Teachers 1973, The Slams 1973, Truck Turner 1974, White Line Fever 1974, Mr Billion 1976, Over the Edge 1978, 11th Victim 1979, Muscle Beach 1980, Gentleman Bandit 1981, White Orchid 1982, Heart Like a Wheel 1983, Project X 1986, The Accused 1987, Immediate Family 1989, Love Field 1990, Unlawful Entry 1992, Bad Girls 1994, Rebel Highway 1994, Picture Windows 1995, Fallen Angels 1996, Brokedown Palace 1999. *Video films:* directed 15 music videos for John Mellencamp, two for Rod Stewart (q.v.), one for Barbra Streisand (q.v.) and one for Paula Abdul (q.v.). *TV includes:* JAG (writer) 1995, ER (producer/dir) 1999–2005, The Court (Dir) 2002, Inconceivable (Dir) 2005, Crossing Jordan (Dir) 2005, Law & Order (Dir) 2005–06, Without a Trace (Dir) 2006–07. *Address:* Industry Entertainment, 953 Carillo Drive, Suite 300, Los Angeles, CA 90048, USA (office).

KAPLINSKI, Jaan; Estonian poet, writer, linguist and translator (retd); b. 22 Jan. 1941, Tartu (Dorpat); s. of Jerzy Kaplinski and Nora Raudsepp; m. Tiia Toomet 1969; one s. one d.; three s. one d. with Tiia Toomet; ed Univ. of Tartu; mem. Riigikogu (State Ass.) 1992–95; Lecturer in History of Western Civilization, Univ. of Tartu; columnist at various Estonian and Scandinavian newspapers; has written around 900 poems, 20 stories and some plays; mem. Universal Acad. of Cultures, Estonian Writers' Union, European Acad. of Poetry; IV Class Order of Nat. Coat of Arms 1997, Chevalier, Légion d'honneur 2000, Order of the Lion of Finland 2003. *Publications include:* poetry: Ma vaatasin päikese aknasse 1976, Uute kivide kasvamine 1977, The New Heaven & Earth of Jaan Kaplinski 1981, Raske on kergeks saada 1982, Tule tagasi helmemänd 1984, Õhtu toob tagasi kõik 1985, Käoraamat: Luulet 1956–80 1986, The Wandering Border 1987, The Same Sea in Us All 1990, Sjunger näktergalen än i Dorpat?: En brevväxling 1990, I Am The Spring in Tartu and other poems in English 1991, Non-Existent Frontier 1995, Võimaluste võimalikkus 1997, Öölinnud, öömõtted yölintuja, yöajatuksia: Luuletusi 1995–97 1998, Evening Brings Everything Back 2004. *Leisure interests:* gardening, forestry, astronomy. *Address:* Nisu 33–9, 50407 Tartu, Estonia (home); c/o Bloodaxe Books Ltd, Highgreen, Tarset, Northumberland NE48 1RP, England (office). *Telephone:* (56) 645-9489 (home). *E-mail:* jaan .kaplinski@gmail.com (home). *Website:* http://jaan.kaplinski.com (home).

KAPOOR, Anil; Indian actor and producer; b. 24 Dec. 1959, Tilak Nagar, Mumbai; s. of Surinder Kapoor and Nirmal Kapoor; m. Sunita Kapoor (née Bhambhani) 1984; one s., two d.; ed Our Lady of Perpetual Succour High School, Chembur; Nata Kalaratna by Government of Andhra Pradesh 1997, Avadh Samman by Government of Uttar Pradesh 2002 Performer with All-Round Comic Excellence, Vodafone Comedy Honors 2008, Special Award, Stardust Awards 2009. *Films include:* Hamare Tumhare 1979, Ex Baar Kaho 1980, Vamsa Vriksham 1980, Hum Paanch 1981, Shakti 1982, Pallavi Anu Pallavi 1983, Who Saat Din 1983, Mashaal (Filmfare Best Supporting Actor Award) 1984, Andar Baahar 1984, Laila 1984, Love Marriage 1984, Saaheb 1985, Yudh 1985, Mohabbat 1985, Meri Jung 1985, Kahan Kahan Se Guzar 1986, Pyaar Ka Sindoor 1986, Chameli Ki Shaadi 1986, Aap Ke Saath 1986, Janbaaz 1986, Pyar Kiya Hai Pyar Karenge 1986, Karma 1986, Insaaf Ki Awaaz 1986, Itihaas 1987, Mr India 1987, Hifazat 1987, Thikana 1987, Kasam 1988, Ram-Avtar 1988, Vijay 1988, Sone Pe Suhaaga 1988, Tezaab (Filmfare Best Actor Award) 1988, Inteqam 1988, Ram Lakhan 1989, Joshilay 1989, Eeshwar 1989, Rakhwala 1989, Abhimanyu 1989, Aag Se Khelenge 1989, Kala Bazaar 1989, Parinda 1989, Awaargi 1990, Kishen Kanhaiya 1990, Ghar Ho Ta Aisa 1990, Jeevan Ek Sangharsh 1990, Amba 1990, Jamai Raja 1990, Jigarwala 1991, Benaam Badsha 1991, Pratikar 1991, Lamhe 1991, Beta (Filmfare Best Actor Award) 1992, Zindagi Ek Jua 1992, Humlaa 1992, Khel 1992, Heer Ranjha 1992, Apradhi 1992, Roop Ki Rani Choron Ka Raja 1993, Guru Deev 1993, Laadla 1994, Andaz 1994, 1942: A Love Story 1994, Mr. Azaad 1994, Trimurti 1995, Rajkumar 1996, Loafer 1996, Mr. Bechara 1996, Virasat (Filmfare Critics Award for Best Performance, Star Screen Award Best Actor) 1997, Deewana Mastana 1997, Kabhi Na Kabhi 1998, Gharwali Baharwali 1998, Jhooth Bole Kauwa Kaate 1998, Hum Aapke Dil Mein Rehte Hain 1999, Biwi No. 1 (Best Comedian Award, Int. Indian Film Acad. Awards) 1999, Mann 1999, Taal (Filmfare Best Supporting Actor Award, Best Supporting Actor Award, Int. Indian Film Acad. Awards, Star Screen Award Best Supporting Actor, Zee Cine Award, Best Actor in a Supporting Role – Male) 1999, Bulandi 2000, Pukar (National Film Award for Best Actor, Bollywood Movie Award for Most Sensational Actor) 2000, Hamara Dil Aapke Paas Hai 2000, Karobaar 2000, Lajja 2001, Nayak 2001, Badhaai Ho Badhaai 2002, Om Jai Jagadish 2002, Rishtey 2002, Armaan 2003, Calcutta Mail 2003, Musafir 2004, Bewafaa 2004, My Wife's Murder 2005, No Entry 2005, Chocolate 2005, Humko Deewana Kar Gaye 2006, Darna Zaroori Hai 2006, Salaam-e-Ishq: A Tribute to Love 2007, Welcome (Best Role as a Comedian, German Public Bollywood Awards) 2007, My Name is Anthony Gonsalves 2008, Black & White 2008, Race 2008, Tashan (Best Actor in a Negative Role Award, Stardust Awards) 2008, Slumdog Millionaire (Screen Actors Guild Award for Outstanding Performance by a Cast in a Motion Picture) 2008, Yuvvraaj 2008; as producer: Badhaai Ho Badhaai 2002, My Wife's Murder 2005, Gandhi, My Father (Hottest Film Producer Award, Stardust Awards) 2007. *Address:* c/o 31 Shringar, Presidency Society, 7th Road, JVPD Scheme, Mumbai, 400 049, India (office). *Website:* www.anilkapoor.net (office).

KAPOOR, Anish, CBE, MA; British sculptor; b. 12 March 1954, Bombay; s. of Rear-Adm. Kapoor and Mrs D. C. Kapoor; m. Susanne Spicale 1995; one d. one s.; ed Hornsey Coll. of Art, Chelsea Coll. of Art and Design, London; teacher, Wolverhampton Polytechnic 1979; Artist-in-Residence, Walker Art Gallery, Liverpool 1982; one-man exhbns in Paris 1980, 1998, London 1981, 1982, 1983, 1985, 1988, 1989–90, 1990–91 (Anish Kapoor Drawings, Tate Gallery, London), 1993, 1995–96, 1998, 2000, 2002, 2003 (Unilever Series, Tate Modern), Liverpool 1982, 1983, Rotterdam, Lyon 1983, New York 1984, 1986, 1989, 1990, 1993, 1998, 2001, 2004, Basel 1985, Oslo, Univ. of Mass. Amherst 1986, Sydney 1987, Nagoya, Japan 1989, 1994, Venice 1990, Grenoble 1990–91, Madrid 1991, 1992, Hanover 1991, Ushimado, Japan 1991, Cologne 1991, 1996–97, Los Angeles 1992, San Diego 1992–93, Tel Aviv 1993, Ljubljana 1994, Tokyo 1995, 1999, Tilburg 1995, Milan 1995–96, Turku, Finland 1996, Cambridge, England 1996, Brescia, Italy 1996, 1998, 2004, San Francisco 1996, Bordeaux 1999, Santiago de Compostela, Spain 1998, Helsinki, Finland 2001, Seoul, South Korea 2003, Bregenz, Austria 2003, San Gimignano and Naples, Italy 2003, Chicago (Millennium Park) 2004, Mons, Belgium 2004; travelling exhbn USA and Canada 1992–93; and has participated in group exhbns since 1974 throughout Britain and in Europe, North America, Japan, Australia, New Zealand, Mexico, Morocco, Korea and Brazil; works in public collections including Tate Gallery, London, Hirshhorn Museum and Sculpture Garden, Washington, DC, Museum of Modern Art, New York, Art Gallery of NSW, Australia, Contemporary Art Soc., London, Nat. Gallery, Ottawa, Hara Museum of Contemporary Art, Tokyo, Auckland City Art Gallery, NZ, Tel-Aviv Museum of Art, Groenningen Exhbn, Neues Museum, Bremen, Lyon Biennale, Lisson Gallery, London and many others; public comms: Cast Iron Mountain, Tachikawa Art Project, Tokyo 1994; outdoor comms: Toronto 1995, Israel Museum, Jerusalem 1997, Bordeaux 1998–99, Chicago 2004; designed set for Idomeneo, Glyndebourne 2003; selected by British Memorial Garden Trust to create memorial in NY to British victims of the 11 Sept. 2001 attacks on World Trade Center 2004; Hon. Fellow London Inst. 1997; Hon. DLitt (Leeds) 1993; Hon. Fellow London Inst. 1997; Premio Duemila, Venice Biennale 1990, Turner Prize, Tate Gallery, London 1991. *Address:* c/o Lisson Gallery, 67 Lisson Street, London, NW1 5DA, England. *Telephone:* (20) 7724-2739. *Fax:* (20) 7724-7124.

KAPOOR, Gen. Deepak, MA, MBA; Indian army officer; *Chief of Army Staff;* b. 1948; m. Kirti Kapoor; one s. one d.; ed Sainik School, Kunjpara, Defence Services Staff Coll., Wellington, Nat. Defence Coll., New Delhi, Indira Gandhi Nat. Open Univ., New Delhi; commissioned into Regt of Artillery 1967, veteran of Indo-Pak War in eastern theatre (Bangladesh) 1971, Chief Operations Officer for UNOSOM II (UN Operation in Somalia – Phase 2) 1994–95, commanded 161 Infantry Brigade in Uri, Jammu and Kashmir, 22nd Mountain Div. (as part of a Strike Corps during Operation Parakram) 2001–02, Chief of Staff of 4 Corps in Tezpur (involved in counter-insurgency operations in Assam), promoted to Lt-Gen., commanded 33 Corps at Siliguri, West Bengal, commanded Army Training Command (ARTRAC) in Shimla, Commdr Northern Army, apptd Hon. ADC to Pres. of India, Sr Col Commdt Regt of Artillery, Vice-Chief of Army –2007, Chief of Army Staff 2007–, Hon. Col of Brigade of the Guards 2008–; Vishisht Seva Medal 1996, Sena Medal 1998, Ati Vishisht Seva Medal 2006, Param Vishisht Seva Medal 2007. *Leisure interest:* golf. *Address:* Additional Directorate General of Public Information B 30, South Block, Integrated HQ of MoD (Army), DHQ PO, New Delhi 110 011, India (office). *Telephone:* (11) 23018531 (office). *Fax:* (11) 23015403 (office). *E-mail:* a_l_c@vsnl.com (office). *Website:* indianarmy.nic.in (office).

KAPOOR, Shashi; Indian actor and producer; b. (Balbirraj Kapoor), 18 March 1938, Calcutta; s. of the late Prithviraj Kapoor; m. Jennifer Kendal 1958 (died 1984); three c.; joined Shakespeareana co. 1955 and toured India, Pakistan and Malaysia; producer with Junoon 1978–. *Films include:* Meena 1944, Tadbir 1945, Renuka 1947, Bhakta Dhruva 1947, Bhakta Gopalbhaiya 1948, Bhakta Bilwamangal 1948, Aag 1948, Patanga 1949, Veer Babruwahan 1950, Samadhi 1950, Ram Darshan 1950, Awaara 1951, Sanskar 1952,

Mordhwaj 1952, Dana Paani 1953, Dharmputra 1961, Char Diwari 1961, Prem Patra 1962, Mehendi Lagi Mere Hath 1962, Yeh Dil Kisko Doon 1963, Jab Se Tumhe Dekha Hai 963, Holiday in Bombay 1963, The Householder 1963, Benazir 1964, Waqt 1965, Mohabbat Isko Kahete Hain 1965, Jab Jab Phool Khile 1965, Shakespeare-Wallah 1965, Pyaar Kiye Jaa 1966, Neend Hamari Khwab Tumhare 1966, Biradari 1966, Dil Ne Pukara 1967, Aamne Samne 1967, Pretty Polly 1967, Juaari 1968, Haseena Maan Jayegi 1968, Raja Saab 1969, Pyar Ka Mausam 1969, Kanyadaan 1969, Jahan Pyar Mile 1969, Ek Shriman Ek Shrimati 1969, Suhana Safar 1970, Rootha Na Karo 1970, My Love 1970, Abhinetri 1970, Bombay Talkie 1970, Sharmeelee 1971, Patanga 1971, Janwar Aur Insaan 1972, Siddhartha 1972, Naina 1973, Aa Gale Lag Jaa 1973, Roti Kapada Aur Makaan 1974, Paap Aur Punya 1974, Mr. Romeo 1974, Jeevan Sangram 1974, Insaniyat 1974, Chor Machaye Shor 1974, Salaakhen 1975, Prem Kahani 1975, Deewaar 1975, Chori Mera Kaam 1975, Anari 1975, Shankar Dada 1976, Naach Utha Sansar 1976, Koi Jeeta Koi Haara 1976, Jai Bajrang Bali 1976, Deewangee 1976, Aap Beeti 1976, Kabhi Kabhie: Love Is Life (1976, Fakira 1976, Hira Aur Patthar 1977, Farishta Ya Qatil 1977, Doosra Aadmi 1977, Chor Sipahi 1977, Chakkar Pe Chakkar 1977, Immaan Dharam 1977, Mukti 1977, Rahuketu 1978, Rahuketu 1978, Phaansi 1978, Muqaddar 1978, Junoon 1978, Heeralal Pannalal 1978, Atithee 1978, Apna Khoon 1978, Amar Shakti 1978, Aahuti 1978, Satyam Shivam Sundaram: Love Sublime 1978, Trishul 1978, Do Musafir 1978, Ahsaas 1979, Gautam Govinda 1979, Kaala Patthar 1979, Duniya Meri Jeb Mein 1979, Suhaag 1979, Swayamvar 1980, Kalyug 1980, Ganga Aur Suraj 1980, Kali Ghata 1980, Do Aur Do Paanch 1980, Neeyat 1980, Shaan 1980, Maan Gaye Ustad 1981, Krodhi 1981, Bezubaan 1981, Kranti 1981, Silsila 1981, Baseraa 1981, Ek Aur Ek Gyarah 1981, Vijeta 1982, Sawaal 1982, Namak Halaal 1982, Vakil Babu 1982, Heat and Dust 1983, Door-desh 1983, Ghungroo 1983, Bandhan Kuchchey Dhaagon Ka 1983, Yaadon Ki Zanjeer 1984, Utsav 1984, Pakhandi 1984, Ghar Ek Mandir 1984, Zameen Aasmaan 1984, Bhawani Junction 1985, Bepanaah 1985, Alag Alag 1985, Swati 1986, New Delhi Times 1986, Maa Beti 1986, Ek Main Aur Ek Tu 1986, Aurat 1986, Abodh 1986, Ilzaam 1986, Pyaar Ki Jeet 1987, Naam O Nishan 1987, Ijaazat 1987, Anjaam 1987, Sindoor 1987, Sammy and Rosie Get Laid 1987, Hum To Chale Pardes 1988, The Deceivers 1988, Meri Zabaan 1989, Jaaydaad 1989, Clerk 1989, Farz Ki Jung 1989, Gair Kanooni 1989, Touhean 1989, Oonch Neech Beech 1989, Raeeszada 1990, Akayla 1991, In Custody 1993, Aag Ka Toofan 1993, Vivekananda 1994, Gulliver's Travels (TV) 1996, Jinnah 1998, Side Streets 1998. *Films produced include:* Junoon 1978 (Nat. Award), Kalyug 1980, 36 Chowringhee Lane 1981, Vijeta 1982, Utsav 1984, Ajooba 1991. *Address:* 112, Atlas Apartments, Mumbai 400006, India (home); Film Walas, Janki Kutir, Juhu Church Road, Mumbai 400049. *Telephone:* (22) 6142922 (office); (22) 3697710 (home).

KAPOR, Mitchell David, BA; American computer industry executive; *President and Chairman, Open Source Applications Foundation;* b. 1950, New York; m. Freada Kapor Klein; ed Campus-Free Coll., Yale Univ., Massachusetts Inst. of Tech.; early career as disc jockey with WHCN-FM, Hartford, Conn.; teacher of transcendental meditation, Cambridge, Mass, Fairfield, Iowa; entry level computer programmer in Cambridge; mental health counsellor, New England Memorial Hosp., Stoneham, Mass; ind. software consultant 1978, co-developed Tiny Troll program; Product Man. Personal Software Inc.; Publr VisiCalc software, designer and programer of VisiPlot and VisiTrend; f. Lotus Devt Corpn 1982, Pres. then Chair. and CEO 1982–86; Chair. and CEO ON Tech. 1987–90; Co-founder and Chair. Electronic Frontier Foundation 1990–94; Chair. Mass Comm. on Computer Tech. and Law 1992–93; Adjunct Prof., MIT Media Lab. 1994–96; Pnr, Accel Pnrs 1999–2001; Founder and Chair. Open Source Applications Foundation 2001–; Lecturer, Univ. of Calif., Berkeley 2005–06, Adjunct Prof., School of Information 2006–; mem. Computer Science and Tech. Bd, Nat. Information Infrastructure Advisory Council; Founding investor, UUNET and Real Networks; Chair. Bd Linden Research; fmr mem. Bd of Dirs Groove Networks, Ximian, Reactivity; Trustee, Kapor Family Foundation 1984–98; f. Mitchell Kapor Foundation 1997; Founding Chair. Mozilla Foundation 2003; Trustee, Level Playing Field Inst. *Publications:* numerous articles on impact of personal computing and networks on society information infrastructure policy, intellectual property issues, anti-trust in the digital era. *Address:* Open Source Applications Foundation, 543 Howard Street, Suite 500, San Francisco, CA 94105, USA (office). *Telephone:* (415) 946-3016 (office). *Fax:* (415) 946-3001 (office). *E-mail:* mitch@kapor.com. *Website:* www .osafoundation.org (office); www.kapor.com (office).

KAPPA, Yarka, MA; Papua New Guinea politician and diplomatist; ed Univ. of Wollongong, Australia; fmr Chargé d'affaires and Perm. Rep. UNESCO, Paris; mem. Parl. (Ind.) for Lagaip-Pogera Open Electorate, Enga Prov. 2002–07, fmr Head, Perm. Parl. Cttee on Law and Order; Minister of Defence 2004–06. *Address:* c/o Murray Barracks, Free Mail Bag, Boroko, NCD 111, Papua New Guinea (office).

KAPPES, Stephen R., BS, MS; American government official; *Deputy Director of Operations, Central Intelligence Agency;* b. 22 Aug. 1951, Cincinnati; m. Kathleen Kappes (née Morgan); two c.; ed Athens High School, Ohio Univ., Ohio State Univ.; served as Officer in US Marine Corps 1976–81; worked at CIA 1981–2004, 2006–, various positions including Chief of Counterintelligence Center, Assoc. Deputy Dir for Operations for Counter-intelligence, Asst Deputy Dir of Operations 2002–04, Deputy Dir of Operations 2004, 2006–; Exec. Vice-Pres. for Global Strategy, ArmorGroup Int. 2005–06, COO 2006. *Address:* Central Intelligence Agency, Office of Public Affairs, Washington, DC 20505, USA (office). *Telephone:* (703) 482-0623 (office). *Fax:* (703) 482-1739 (office). *Website:* www.cia.gov (office).

KAPSE, Ramchandra Ganesh, LLB, MA; Indian government official; b. 1 Dec. 1933, Nasik, Maharashtra; ed Univ. of Bombay; fmr Head, Dept of Marathi Literature, D. G. Ruparel Coll., Mumbai; mem. Bharatiya Jan Sangh 1955–; mem. Kalyan Municipality 1962–74; mem. Maharashtra Legis. Ass. 1978–89, Leader Bharatiya Janata Group 1985–89; Chair. CIDCO, Maharashtra 1979–80; mem. Lok Sabha 1989–96, Rajya Sabha 1996–98; Lt Gov. of Andaman and Nicobar Islands 2004–06 (resgnd); Chair. Standing Cttee on Food, Civil Supplies and Consumer Protection 1998–99, Railway Passengers Services Cttee; Pres. Pragati Pratishthan non-governmental org.; Founder-Sec. Rambhau Mhalgi Prabodhini; Hon. Advisor, Bureau of Parl. Studies and Training 1998–. *Address:* c/o Office of the Lieutenant-Governor, Administration of the Andaman and Nicobar Islands, Raj Nivas, Port Blair 744 101, India (office).

KAPTEYN, Paul Joan George, LLD; Dutch lawyer; b. 31 Jan. 1928, Laren, NH; s. of Paul J. Kapteyn and Picaine (Schröder) Kapteyn; m. Ieteke Streef 1956; one s. one d.; ed Univ. of Leiden, Inst. des Hautes Etudes Int., Paris; Asst Prof. of Int. Law, Univ. of Leiden 1953–60; with Foreign Office, The Hague 1960–63; Prof. of Law of Int. Orgs, Univ. of Utrecht 1963–74, Univ. of Leiden 1972–76; mem. Council of State 1976–90, Pres. Judicial Section 1984–90; mem. Int. Comm. of Jurists 1976–90; Pres. Netherlands Asscn of Int. Law 1987–93; Judge, Court of Justice of the EC 1990–2000; mem. Royal Netherlands Acad. of Sciences. *Publications:* The Common Assembly of the European Coal and Steel Community 1960, An Introduction to the Law of the European Communities 4 edns. (co-author) 1970–87. *Leisure interests:* tennis, reading, travelling.

KAPUR, Shekhar, CA; Indian film director; b. 1945, Lahore, Pakistan; m. Suchitra Krishnamurthy; one d. *Films include:* Masoom 1983, Mr India 1987, Bandit Queen 1994, Dil Se Dushmani 1998, Elizabeth 1998, The Four Feathers 2002, The Guru (exec. producer) 2002, Elizabeth: The Golden Age 2007. *Television includes:* Tahqiqat (series) 1994). *Address:* c/o CAA, 2000 Avenue of the Stars, Los Angeles, CA 90067, USA; 42 New Sital Apartments, A. B. Nair Road, Juhu, Mumbai 400449, India (home). *Telephone:* (22) 6204988 (home). *Website:* www.shekharkapur.com.

KAPUTIN, Sir John, CMG; Papua New Guinea politician and international organization official; *Secretary-General, African, Caribbean and Pacific Group of States (ACP Group);* b. (John Rumet), 11 July 1941; s. of the late Daniel ToKaputin and Rellie Iakirara; ed Rockhampton Boys Grammar School, Queensland, Australia, Univ. of Hawaii, USA; trained as teacher and bureaucrat 1960s; mem. House of Ass. (Rabaul constituency) 1972–2002; mem. Constitutional Planning Cttee that developed PNG Constitution 1972; Minister for Justice 1973–74, for Nat. Planning and Devt 1978–80, for Finance and Planning 1980–82, for Minerals and Energy 1985–88, for Foreign Affairs 1992–94, 1999–2000, for Mining and Petroleum 1994; Deputy Speaker 1975–77; Chair. Bipartisan Cttee on Bougainville Crisis 1988–90, Special State Negotiator for Bougainville 1998; Co-Pres. African, Caribbean and Pacific (ACP) Group of States–EU Jt Ass., Brussels, Belgium 1995–97, Sec.-Gen. ACP Secr. 2005–; Special Ministerial Envoy for Int. Financial Insts, responsible for negotiations with IMF, World Bank, EU and Asian Devt Bank 2000–02; led ACP Ministerial Missions to Burundi, Rwana, Equitorial Guinea, Togo Fiji and Solomon Islands; Hon. Pres. ACP/EU Jt Parliamentary Ass. 1997; Togolese Medal of Freedom and Liberty, Govt of Repub. of Togo. *Address:* Secretariat of the African, Caribbean and Pacific Group of States, Avenue Georges Henri 451, 1200 Brussels, Belgium (office). *Telephone:* (2) 743-06-00 (office). *Fax:* (2) 735-55-73 (office). *E-mail:* info@acp.int (office). *Website:* www.acpsec.org (office).

KAPUYA, Hon. Juma Athumani, BSc MSc PhD; Tanzanian academic and politician; *Minister of Labour, Employment and Youth Development;* b. 22 June 1945; ed Tabora Boys' Secondary School, Univ. of Dar es Salaam; Tutorial Asst, Univ. of Dar es Salaam 1971–74, Asst Lecturer 1974–76, Lecturer 1976–78, Sr Lecturer 1978–83, Assoc. Prof. 1983–87, Prof. 1987–95; adviser, Tanganyika Youth League (Univ. of Dar es Salaam) 1971–77, Chama Cha Mapinduzi (CCM) Youth 1977–82; Leader, CCM, Univ. of Dar es Salaam 1983–95; mem. Parl. (CCM) for Urambo Magharibi; Minister of Defence and Nat. Service 2006–08; Minister of Labour, Employment and Youth Devt 2008–; Dir Tobacco Authority, Sugar Authority; Dir and Rep. OTTU, Univ. of Dar es Salaam, Inst. of Adult Educ. *Address:* Ministry of Labour, Employment and Youth Development, POB 1422, Dar es Salaam, Tanzania (office). *Telephone:* (22) 2120419 (office). *Fax:* (22) 2113082 (office).

KARA-MURZA, Alexei Alexeyevich, Dr rer. pol, DPhil; Russian politician and academic; *Deputy Chairman, Union of Rightist Forces (SPS);* b. 1956; ed Moscow State Univ.; Dir Cen. for Theoretical Studies of Russian Reforms, Inst. of Philosophy, Russian Acad. of Sciences; Co-Pres. Moscow Foundation of Freedom and Human Rights (now Moscow Liberal Fund) 1992–; worked as scientific researcher; Head of Dept of Social and Political Philosophy, Russian Acad. of Sciences 1995–; also currently Prof. of Political Science Moscow State Univ.; Deputy Chair. Union of Rightist Forces party 2000–; mem. Council of Trustees Obshchaya Gazeta (weekly); Ed.-in-Chief Pravoe Delo newspaper. *Publications:* scientific publs on modern philosophy and politology. *Address:* Union of Rightist Forces (URF) (Soyuz pravykh sil) (SPS), ul. M. Andronyevskaya 15, 109544 Moscow (office); Centre for Theoretical Studies of Russian Reforms, Russian Academy of Sciences, Volkhonka str. 14 Bldg 5, 119842 Moscow, Russia (office). *Telephone:* (495) 203-91-09 (office); (495) 956-29-09 (SPS) (office). *E-mail:* edit@sps.ru (office). *Website:* www.sps.ru (office).

KARABAYEV, Ednan Oskonovich, PhD; Kyrgyzstani academic and government official; b. 17 Jan. 1953, Talas; ed Kyrgyz State Univ., Inst. of History of Kyrgyz SSR Acad. of Sciences; early career as history teacher, Frunze (now Bishkek); Minister of Foreign Affairs 1992–93, 2007–09; Head Int. Relations

Dept, Kyrgyz-Russian Slavic Univ. 1994–2007, also fmr Dean; Advisor to Pres. 2000; Pres. UNA of Kyrgyzstan; mem. Cyril-Mefody Acad. of Slavic Enlightenment; Honoured Worker of Educ. in Kyrgyz Repub. *Publications:* more than 200 scientific and other articles and contribs to monographs. *Address:* c/o Ministry of Foreign Affairs, 720040 Bishkek, bul. Erkindik 57, Kyrgyzstan. *Telephone:* (312) 62-05-45. *E-mail:* gendep@mfa.gov.kg.

KARACHENTSOV, Nikolai Petrovich; Russian actor; b. 24 Oct. 1944, Moscow; m. Svetlana Porgina; one s.; ed Studio School, Moscow Art Theatre; with Lenkom Theatre 1967–; People's Artist of Russia 1989. *Films include:* Elder Son, Déjà Vu, Underground of the Witches, A Woman for All, Petersburg Secrets. *Theatre includes:* Til in Til Eulenspiegel, Zvonarev in Sorry, Lev Zudin in Czech Photo, Rezanov in Yunona and Avos. *Address:* Voznesensky per. 16/4, Apt. 59, 103009 Moscow, Russia. *Telephone:* (495) 229-30-65. *Website:* www.karachentsov.info.

KARADJORDJEVIC, HRH Crown Prince Alexander (see ALEXANDER KARADJORDJEVIC, HRH Crown Prince).

KARADŽIĆ, Radovan; Serbian political leader, psychiatrist and poet; b. 19 June 1945, Petnjica, nr Šavnik, Montenegro; s. of Vuk Karadžić; m. Lilijana Zelen Karadžić; one s. one d.; ed Univ. of Sarajevo, Columbia Univ., New York, USA; moved to Sarajevo, Bosnia and Herzegovina in 1960; worked in state hosps, including Koševo Hosp. (specialized in neuroses and depression); team psychologist for Red Star Belgrade football club 1983; with Unis Co.; Co.-founder and Pres. Serbian Democratic Party 1989; leader of self-declared Serb Repub. (in Bosnia and Herzegovina), elected Pres., resgnd 1996, int. arrest warrant issued for him July 1996; attended ceasefire talks in London Aug. 1992, Geneva Jan. 1993, after outbreak of hostilities; named as war crimes suspect by UN Tribunal for Fmr Yugoslavia April 1995; formally charged with genocide and crimes against humanity by Int. War Crimes Tribunal for Fmr Yugoslavia 1995; in hiding 1996–2008; arrested in Belgrade 21 July 2008, brought before Belgrade's War Crimes Court, had been working at pvt. clinic in Belgrade specializing in alternative medicine and psychology; Order of St Dionysus of Xanthe (First Rank); Risto Ratković Prize for Literature, Mikhail Sholokhov Prize for Poetry, Russian Writers' Union 1994. *Publications include:* Slavic Guest (poems) (main literary award of Montenegro 1993), There Are Miracles, There Are No Miracles (poems for children), Miraculous Chronicles of the Night (novel), Under the Left Breast of the Century (poems) 2005. *Leisure interest:* composes music.

KARAGANOV, Sergei Aleksandrovich, DHist; Russian defence and foreign affairs specialist; *Chairman of the Presidium, Council of Foreign and Defence Policy, Russian Academy of Sciences;* b. 12 Sept. 1952, Moscow; m.; one d.; ed Moscow State Univ., postgraduate study in USA; Jr Fellow, Sr Fellow, Head of Section, USA and Canada Studies Inst. 1978–88; Research Fellow, Perm. Mission of USSR at UN 1976–77; Head of Dept, Deputy Dir Inst. of Europe of Russian Acad. of Sciences 1988–; mem. Foreign Policy Council, Ministry of Foreign Affairs of Russia 1991; Founder and Chair. of the Presidium, Council of Foreign and Defence Policy, Russian Acad. of Sciences 1991–; mem. Presidential Council of Russia 1992–99; Adviser to Presidential Admin.; mem. Consulting Council to Security Council of Russia 1993–; mem. Consultative Council of Fed. 1996–; Chair. Dept on World Politics, State Univ. Higher School of Econs 2002–, Dean, School of Int. Econs and Foreign Affairs 2006–; Chair. Editorial Bd Russia in Global Affairs magazine 2002–; mem. Pres.'s Public Council for Assisting the Devt of Civil Society and Human Rights 2004–, Ministry of Defence Public Council 2006–; mem. IISS, London. *Publications:* 18 books and brochures, including Russia: State of Reforms 1993, Security of the Future Europe (ed.; in Russian) 1993, Harmonization the Evolution of U.S. and Russian Defense Policies (co-ed. with F. Ikle; also published in Russian) 1993, Where Russia Goes? Foreign and Defense Policy in the New Era 1994, Damage Limitation or Crisis? Russia and the World (co-ed. with Robert D. Blackwill) 1994, Wither Western Aid to Russia" (ed. and dir of the study; also published in Russian) 1994, Russia's Economic Role in Europe. Report of the Commission for the Greater Europe, Vol. II (co-authored with O. Lambsdorf; also published in Russian) 1995, Geopolitics Change in Europe, Policies of the West and Russia's Alternatives (ed. and head of the study) 1995, Towards a New Democratic Commonwealth (co-authored with Graham Allison and Karl Kaiser) 1996, Russian-American Relations on the Threshold of Two Centuries (co-author) 2000, Strategy for Russia: Agenda for the President-2000 (ed.; in Russian) 2000, Strategy for Russia: Ten Years of CFDP (ed.) 2002; more than 350 articles in Russian on econs of foreign policy, arms control, nat. security strategy, Russian foreign and defence policies. *Leisure interests:* athletics, literature, cooking. *Address:* Mokhovaya Street 11-3B, 125993 Moscow (office); Chernyahovskogo, 9/5 Apt 387, 125139 Moscow, Russia (home). *Telephone:* (495) 692-84-72 (office); (495) 152-99-82 (home). *Fax:* (495) 609-92-98 (office). *E-mail:* cfdp@online.ru (office); cfdp@mail.ru (home). *Website:* www.svop.ru.

KARAGEORGHIS, Vassos, PhD, FSA, FRSA; Cypriot archaeologist; *Director, Foundation Anastasios G. Leventis;* b. 29 April 1929, Trikomo; s. of George Karageorghis and Panagiota Karageorghis; m. Jacqueline Girard 1953; one s. one d.; ed Pancyprian Gymnasium, Nicosia, Univ. Coll. and Inst. of Archaeology, Univ. of London; Asst Curator, Cyprus Museum 1952–60, Curator 1960–63, Acting Dir, Dept of Antiquities, Cyprus 1963–64, Dir 1964–89; Dir Archaeological Research Unit, Prof. of Archaeology, Univ. of Cyprus 1992–96; excavations at Salamis 1952–73, Akhera and Pendayia 1960, Kition 1962–81, Maa-Palaeokastro, Pyla-Kokkinokremos 1979–87, Prof. Emer. 2004–; Dir d'Etudes, Ecole Pratique des Hautes Etudes, Sorbonne, Paris 1983–84; Adjunct. Prof. of Classical Archaeology, State Univ. of New York, Albany 1973–; Geddes-Harrower Prof. of Classical Art and Archaeology, Univ. of Aberdeen 1975; Visiting Mellon Prof., Inst. for Advanced Study, Princeton 1989–90; adviser to the Pres. of Cyprus on cultural heritage 1989–92; mem. Council, Anastasios G. Leventis Foundation (Dir 1996–), Cultural Foundation of the Bank of Cyprus; mem. Royal Swedish Acad., Accad. dei Lincei, Acad. des Inscriptions et Belles Lettres, German Archaeological Inst., Acad. of Athens; Corresp. mem. Austrian Acad. of Sciences, Royal Acad. of Spain 1997; Hon. mem. Soc. for Promotion of Hellenic Studies, Archaeological Inst. of America, Council of Greek Archaeological Soc., ICOMOS 2005; Visiting Fellow, Merton Coll., Oxford 1979, 1988, Sr Research Fellow 1980, Hon. Fellow 1990; Visiting Fellow, All Souls Coll., Oxford 1982; Visiting Scholar Harvard Univ. 1997–; Fellow, Royal Soc. of Humanistic Studies, Lund, Univ. Coll., London; Corresp. Fellow, British Acad.; mem. Nat. Olympic Cttee Greece 1998; Hon. Fellow, Soc. of Antiquaries, London; Hon. Citizen of Plovdiv (Bulgaria) 2003; Order of Merit (1st Class), FRG 1980, Commdr, Royal Order of Polar Star (Sweden) 1990, Commdr, des Arts et des Lettres 1990, Commdr, Order of Merit (Italy) 1990, Austrian Decoration for Arts and Sciences 1997, Officier, Légion d'honneur 1998, Commdr of the Order of Honour (Greece) 2008; Dr hc (Lyon, Göteborg, Athens, Birmingham, Toulouse, Brock, Brussels, Oxford, Dublin, Mariupolis—Ukraine); Prix de la Soc. des Etudes Grecques, Sorbonne 1966, R. B. Bennett Commonwealth Prize 1978, Onassis Prize 'Olympia' 1991, Premio Internazionale 'I Cavalli d'Oro di San Marco' 1996, Award for Excellence in Science and Arts, Govt of Cyprus 1998, G. Maraslis Medal (Odessa) 2003. *Publications include:* Treasures in the Cyprus Museum 1962, Corpus Vasorum Antiquorum 1963, 1965, Nouveaux documents pour l'étude du bronze récent à Chypre 1964, Sculptures from Salamis, Vol. I 1964, Vol. II 1966, Excavations in the Necropolis of Salamis, Vol. I 1967, Vol. II 1970, Vol. III 1973, Vol. IV 1978, Mycenaean Art from Cyprus 1968, Cyprus (Archaeologia Mundi) 1968, Salamis in Cyprus 1969, Altägäis und Altkypros (with H. G. Buchholz) 1971, Cypriot Antiquities in the Pierides Collection, Larnaca, Cyprus 1973, Fouilles de Kition I 1974, Kition, Mycenaean and Phoenician discoveries in Cyprus 1976, The Civilization of Prehistoric Cyprus 1976, La céramique chypriote de style figuré Indash;III (with Jean des Gagniers) 1974–79, Vases et figurines de l'Age du Bronze (with Jean des Gagniers) 1976, Fouilles de Kition II (with J. Leclant and others) 1976, Hala Sultan Tekké I (with P. Åström, D. M. Bailey) 1976, Fouilles de Kition III (with M. G. Guzzo Amadasi) 1977, Two Cypriot sanctuaries of the end of the Cypro-Archaic period 1977, The Goddess with Uplifted Arms in Cyprus 1977, Cypriot Antiquities in the Medelhavsmuseet, Stockholm (with C. G. Styrenius and M.-L. Winbladh) 1977, Mycenaean Pictorial Vase Painting (with Emily Vermeule) 1981, Excavations at Kition IV (with J. N. Coldstream and others) 1981, Cyprus from the Stone Age to the Romans 1982, Palaepaphos-Skales. An Iron Age Cemetery in Cyprus 1983, Pyla-Kokkinokremos–A late 13th Century BC fortified settlement in Cyprus (with M. Demas) 1984, Cyprus at the close of the Late Bronze Age (co-ed. with J. D. Muhly) 1984, Ancient Cypriot Art in the Pierides Foundation Museum (with others) 1985, Archaeology in Cyprus 1960–85 (ed.) 1985, Excavations at Kition V (with M. Demas) 1985, La Nécropole d'Amathonte III: Les Terres Cuites 1987, Excavations at Maa-Palaeokastro 1979–86, 1988 (with M. Demas), Blacks in Ancient Cypriot Art 1988, The End of the Late Bronze Age in Cyprus 1990, Tombs at Palaepaphos 1990, Les anciens Chypriotes: entre orient et occident 1990, The Coroplastic Art of Ancient Cyprus (Vol. I) 1991, (Vol. II) 1993, (Vol. III) 1993, (Vol. IV) 1995, (Vol. VI) 1996, Cyprus in the Eleventh Century BC (ed.) 1994, Cyprus and the Sea (co-ed. with D. Michaelides) 1995, The Evolution of the Economy of Cyprus from the Prehistoric Period to the Present Day (co-ed. with D. Michaelides) 1996, The Potters' Art of Ancient Cyprus (with Y. Olenik) 1997, Greek Gods and Heroes in Ancient Cyprus 1998, Cypriot Archaeology Today: Achievements and Perspectives 1998, Excavating at Salamis in Cyprus, 1952–74 1999, Ayia Paraskevi Figurines in the Univ. of Pennsylvania Museum (with T. P. Brennan) 1999, Die Sammlung zyprischer Antiken im Kunsthistorischen Museum 1999, Ancient Cypriot Art in the Severis Collection 1999, The Art of Ancient Cyprus in the Fitzwilliam Museum, Cambridge (with E. Vassilika and P. Wilson) 1999, Ancient Art from Cyprus. The Cesnola Collection (with J. R. Mertens, M. E. Rose), Céramiques mycéniennes Ras Shamra – Ougarit XIII (with M. Yon, N. Hirschfeld), Ancient Cypriot Art in Copenhagen. The Collections of the Nat. Museum of Denmark and the New York Carlsberg Glyptotek (with Bodil Bundgaard Rasmussen et al.), Defensive Settlements of the Aegean and Eastern Mediterranean after c. 1200 B.C. (with Christine Morris), Italy and Cyprus in Antiquity, 1500-450 B.C. (with L. Bonfante), Ancient Cypriot Art in Berlin (with S. Brehme et al.), Greek and Cypriot Antiquities in the Archaeological Museum of Odessa (with V. P. Vanchugov et al.), Early Cyprus, Crossroads of the Mediterranean, Ancient Cypriote Art in the National Archaeological Museum Athens, The Cyprus Collections in the Medelhausmuseet (with S. Houby-Nielsen et al.), Ancient Cypriot Art in the Musée d'Art et d'Histoire, Geneva (with J. Chamay et al.), Cypriot Antiquities in the Royal Ontario Museum (with Paul Denis et al.), Ancient Cypriot Art in Russian Museums (with A. Bukina et al.), Early Cyprus: Crossroads of the Mediterranean, Aspects of Everyday Life in Ancient Cyprus: Iconographic Representations 2006, and more than 380 articles in Greek, German, American, English and French journals. *Leisure interests:* gardening, photography. *Address:* 16 Kastorias Str., Nicosia 1055 (home); Foundation Anastasios G. Leventis, 40 Gladstonos Street, Nicosia 1095, Cyprus (office). *Telephone:* (2) 2667706 (home); (2) 2674018 (home). *Fax:* (2) 2675002 (home). *E-mail:* leventcy@zenon.logos.cy.net (office). *Website:* www.leventisfoundation.org (office).

KARAMANLIS, Konstantinos (Kostas), PhD; Greek politician and lawyer; *Prime Minister;* b. Sept. 1956; m. Natasha Pazaitis 1998; one d. one s.; ed Athens Univ. Law School, Deree Coll., Fletcher School of Law and Diplomacy, Tufts Univ.; served in Greek Navy 1977–79; Lecturer in Political Science, Diplomatic History and Corp. Law, Deree Coll.; mem. Parl. 1989, 1990, 1993, 1996, 2000; Pres. Nea Demokratia (New Democratic Party) 1997; Vice-Pres. European People's Party 1999–; Prime Minister of Greece 2004–; Vice-Pres. Int. Democratic Union 2002–; Chair. European Democrat Union Party

Leaders Conf. 2003. *Publications:* Eleftherios Venizelos and Greek Foreign Relations 1928–32 1986, Spirit and Era of Gorbachev 1987. *Address:* Office of the Prime Minister, Maximos Mansion, Herodou Atticou 19, 106 74 Athens, Greece (office). *Telephone:* (210) 3385491 (office). *Fax:* (210) 3238129 (office). *E-mail:* primeminister@primeminister.gr (office). *Website:* www.primeminister.gr (office).

KARAMANOV, Alemdar Sabitovich; Ukrainian/Crimean Tatar composer; b. 10 Sept. 1934, Simferopol; ed Moscow State Conservatory (pupil of S. Bogatyrev and D. Kabalevsky); author of numerous symphonic compositions including 24 symphonies 1954–94, vocal-orchestral compositions of secular and religious character, including Requiem 1991, Mysteria of Khersones 1993, 3 piano concertos, 2 violin concertos, Nat. Anthem of Crimea Repub. 1992, chamber ensembles, piano music, choruses and vocal compositions; most of his music not performed up to late 1980s. *Address:* Voykova str. 2, Apt. 4, Simferopol, Crimea, Ukraine (home).

KARAMARKO, Tomislav; Croatian politician; *Minister of the Interior;* b. 25 May 1959, Zadar; m.; two c.; ed Univ. of Zagreb; archivist, Nat. Archives of Croatia 1987–88; Head, Office of the Prime Minister 1991–92, Cabinet Chief 1992–93; Chief of Police Admin, Zagreb 1993–96; Deputy Minister of the Interior 1996–98; Nat. Security Adviser to Pres. of Croatia 2000; Head, Office for Nat. Security 2000–02; Head, Counter-Intelligence Agency 2004–06; Dir Intelligence-Security Agency 2006–08; Minister of the Interior 2008–. *Address:* Ministry of the Interior, 10000 Zagreb, Savska cesta 39, Croatia (office). *Telephone:* (1) 6122129 (office). *Fax:* (1) 6122299 (office). *E-mail:* pitanja@mup.hr (office). *Website:* www.mup.hr (office).

KARAMI, Omar; Lebanese lawyer and politician; b. 7 Sept. 1934, An Nouri; s. of the late Abdul Hamid Karami; brother of Rashid Karami; elected mem. Parl. 1991; fmr Minister of Educ. and the Arts; Prime Minister of Lebanon 1990–92 (resgnd), Oct. 2004–Feb. 2005 (resgnd). *Address:* c/o Majlis Alnwab, Beirut, Lebanon (office).

KARAN, Donna, BFA; American fashion designer; *Chief Designer, LVMH;* b. (Donna Faske), 2 Oct. 1948, Forest Hills, New York; m. 1st Mark Karan (divorced 1978); one d.; m. 2nd. Stephan Weiss 1983 (died 2001); ed Parsons School of Design, New York; designer, Anne Klein & Co., then Addenda Co. –1968; returned to Anne Klein 1968, Assoc. Designer 1971, Dir of Design (in collaboration with Louis Dell'Olio q.v.) 1974–84; Owner and Designer, Donna Karan Co., New York 1984–96, Chair. and Head Designer, Donna Karan Int. (public co.) 1996–2001; Chief Designer, LVMH 2001–; Co-Chair. Kids for Kids Events, Pediatric AIDS Foundation 1993–, Ovarian Cancer Research 'Super Saturday' Event, East Hampton, NY 1998–; mem. Bd of Dirs Council of Fashion Designers of America Design Industries Foundation for AIDS (DIFFA), Parsons School of Design; Coty Awards 1977, 1981, Council of Fashion Designers of America Designer of the Year 1985, 1990, 1996, Council of Fashion Designers of America Menswear Designer of the Year 1992, FIFI Award for Best Women's Fragrance 1993, DIFFA Divine Design Award 1995, Parsons Fashion Critics Award 1996, Fashion Designers of America Women's Wear Award 1996, FEMMY Designer of the Year Award 1999, FIFI Best Nat. Advertising Campaign of the Year Award 2001, Fashion Group Int. Superstar Award (first American designer) 2003, Lifetime Achievement Award, Council of Fashion Designers of America 2004. *Address:* Donna Karan International, 550 Seventh Avenue, 15th Floor, New York, NY 10018, USA (office). *Telephone:* (212) 789-1509 (office). *Website:* www.donnakaran.com.

KARAOSMANOGLU, Attila, PhD; Turkish economist; b. 20 Sept. 1932, Manisa; s. of Ibrahim Ethem Karaosmanoglu and Fatma Eda Karaosmanoglu; m. Sukriye Ozyet 1960; one s.; ed Univs of Ankara and Istanbul, Harvard and New York Univs, USA; mem. Faculty, Middle East Tech. Univ. and Ankara Univ. 1954–63; Head, Econ. Planning Dept, State Planning Org. of Turkey 1960–62; Adviser, Fed. of Turkish Trade Unions and consultant to Turkish Scientific and Tech. Research Council 1963–65; Consultant, Directorate for Scientific Affairs, OECD 1965–66; Economist, then Sr Economist, World Bank 1966–71, Chief Economist 1973–75, Dir of Devt Policy 1975–79, Dir of Europe, Middle East and N Africa Region Country Programmes 1979–82, Vice-Pres. E Asia and Pacific Region 1983–87, Asia Region 1987–91 Man. Dir World Bank 1991–95 (retd); Deputy Prime Minister in Charge of Econ. Affairs and Chair. High Planning Council, Turkish Govt 1971; mem. Exec. Bd Is Bank, Turkey 1972; Chief Adviser, Istanbul Chamber of Industry 1995–; mem. Bd Scientific and Technological Research Council of Turkey 1995–; Alt., Bank of Turkey 1996–; Chair. Bd Nat. Inst. of Metrology 1997–. *Publications:* Towards Full Employment and Price Stability (OECD publ., co-author) 1977, Poverty and Prosperity – The Two Realities of Asian Development 1989, Diversity and Consensus – The Emergence of an Asian Development Paradigm 1991. *Address:* c/o Istanbul Chamber of Industry, Meşrutiyet Cad. No:62, Istanbul; Dr. Faruk Ayanoglu Cad. 37 D.5, 81030 Fenerbahce, Istanbul, Turkey.

KARASIN, Grigory Borisovich; Russian diplomatist; *Deputy Minister of Foreign Affairs;* b. 23 Aug. 1949, Moscow; m.; two d.; ed Moscow Inst. of Oriental Languages, Moscow State Univ.; diplomatic service since 1972; translator, attaché USSR Embassy, Senegal 1972–76; attaché First African Div., USSR Ministry of Foreign Affairs 1976–77; sec. to Deputy Minister of Foreign Affairs 1977–79; Second, First Sec. Embassy, Australia 1979–85; First Sec., Counsellor Second European Div. Ministry of Foreign Affairs 1985–88; Counsellor USSR Embassy, UK 1988–92; Head of Dept of Africa, Ministry of Foreign Affairs of Russia 1992–93, Head. Dept of Information and Press 1993–96; Deputy Minister of Foreign Affairs 1996–2000; Amb. to UK 2000–05; Deputy Minister of Foreign Affairs 2005–. *Address:* Ministry of Foreign Affairs, 119200 Moscow, Smolenskaya-Sennaya pl. 32/34, Russia (office). *Telephone:* (495) 244-16-06 (office). *Fax:* (495) 230-21-30 (office). *E-mail:* ministry@mid.ru (office). *Website:* www.mid.ru (office).

KARDASHEV, Nikolai Semenovich; Russian astronomer; *Deputy Director, Astro Space Centre, Lebedev Physical Institute, Russian Academy of Sciences;* b. 25 April 1932; m.; one d.; ed Moscow State Univ.; lab., sr lab., jr, sr researcher State Astronomical Inst. 1955–67; head of lab., Deputy Dir Inst. of Space Studies USSR Acad. of Sciences 1967–90; Dir Astro Space Cen., Lebedev Physical Inst., USSR Acad. of Sciences 1990–; corresp. mem. USSR (now Russian) Acad. of Sciences 1976, mem. 1994; research in radiophysics, radioastronomy, radio radiation of galaxies and quasars; USSR State Prize. *Publications include:* Pulsars and nonthermal Radio Sources 1970, Strategy and Future Projects 1977; numerous articles in scientific journals. *Address:* Astro Space Centre, Lebedev Physical Institute, Russian Academy of Sciences, Profsoyuznaya str. 84/32, 117997 Moscow, Russia (office). *Telephone:* (495) 333-21-89 (office). *E-mail:* nkardash@asc.rssi.ru (office). *Website:* www.asc.rssi.ru (office).

KAREFA-SMART, John Musselman, BA, BSc, MD, CM, DTM, MPH, FRSH, FAPHA, FRSA; Sierra Leonean politician and physician; b. 17 June 1915, Rotifunk; s. of Rev. James Karefa-Smart and May Karefa-Smart (née Caulker); m. Rena Joyce Weller 1948; one s. two d.; ed Fourah Bay and Otterbein Colls., McGill and Harvard Univs.; lecturer, Union Coll., Bunumbu 1936–38; ordained Elder of Evangelical United Brethren Church 1938; Medical Officer, RCAMC 1943–45; Sierra Leone Missions Hosps 1946–48; Lecturer, Ibadan Univ. Coll. (Nigeria) 1949–52; Health Officer, WHO 1952–55, Leader del. to WHO 1956 and 1959; mem. House of Reps 1957–64; Minister of Lands and Survey 1957–59; Africa Consultant, World Council of Churches 1955–56; Minister for External Affairs 1960–64; Asst Prof. Columbia Univ. 1964–65; Asst Dir-Gen. WHO, Geneva 1965–70; Visiting Prof. of Int. Health, Harvard Univ. 1971–73, Lecturer Harvard Medical School 1973–81; Medical Dir Roxbury Health Centre 1973–78, Health and Devt Consultant 1978–; Clinical Prof. Boston Univ. 1976–; Visiting Prof., Harvard Univ. 1977–; returned to Sierra Leone 1990; f. United Democratic Party; Pres. United Nat. People's Party (UNPP) –1997; mem. Parl., Leader of Opposition 1996–99; mem. Bd of Dirs Albert Schweitzer Fellowship, Population Inst., HMI Inc.; Hon. LLD (Otterbein, McGill, Boston), Hon. DSc (Sierra Leone); Commdr Order of Star of Africa (Liberia), Kt Grand Band, Order of African Redemption (Liberia), Grand Cordon, Order of the Cedar (Lebanon). *Publications:* The Halting Kingdom 1959, Evaluating Health Program Impact 1974. *Leisure interests:* photography, stamps, the internet, travel. *Address:* 20 Damba Road, Freetown, Sierra Leone. *Telephone:* (22) 272163. *E-mail:* tonkolili@aol.com.

KAREKIN II, His Holiness (Ktritch Narssisian); Armenian ecclesiastic; *Supreme Patriarch and Catholicos of All Armenians;* b. 16 Aug. 1951, Etchmiadzin; ed Kevorkian Theological Seminary, Univ. of Vienna, Univ. of Bonn; Asst Dean, Kevorkian Theological Seminary; ordained priest 1972; pastor in Germany 1975; Asst to Vicar-Gen. of Araratian Patriarchal Diocese 1980, Vicar-Gen., Bishop 1983, later Archbishop; mem. Supreme Spiritual Council of Catholicosate of All Armenians 1990–; Supreme Patriarch and Catholicos of All Armenians 1999–; f. Vazkenian Seminary, Sevan 1989, Christian Educ. Centre 1990; Dr hc (Artsakh); Kawkab Medal (First Class) Jordan 2000, Bethlehem 2000 Award (Palestinian Nat. Authority) 2000, Star of Romania 2000;. *Address:* Residence of the Catholicosate of all Armenians, Vagharshapat, Monastery of St Etchmiadzin, Armenia (office). *Telephone:* (10) 28-57-37 (office). *Fax:* (10) 15-10-77 (office). *E-mail:* holysee@etchmiadzin.am (office). *Website:* www.holyetchmiadzin.am (office).

KARELIN, Col Aleksander Aleksandrovich; Russian politician and fmr professional wrestler; b. 19 Sept. 1967, Novosibirsk; m. Olga Karelina; two s. one d.; ed Novosibirsk Pedagogical Inst., Motor-Transport Tech. Coll., Omsk Inst. of Physical Culture, Lesgaft Acad. of Physical Culture; turned professional 1978; unbeaten for 12 years until the Sydney Olympics; world champion (nine times), European champion (12 times); Olympic champion 1988, 1992, 1996; Olympic silver medallist, Sydney 2000; mem. of team Dynamo; specialist, Fed. Tax Police Service 1995–99, Col of the Tax Police 1995; co-founder and co-leader Yedinstvo; Chair. Interregional Co-ordinating Council, Unity (Yedinstvo) party in Siberian Fed. Dist; mem. State Duma 1999–, Deputy Chair. Cttee for Int. Affairs 2003–; currently mem. Supreme Council, United Russia party; USSR Merited Master of Sports, Hero of Russia 1997. *Leisure interests:* poetry, literature, classical music. *Address:* State Duma, Yedinstvo Faction, Okhotny Ryad 1, 103265 Moscow, Russia (office). *Telephone:* (495) 292-56-97 (office).

KARELOVA, Galina Nikolaevna, BEcons, BEng; Russian politician; b. 29 June 1959, Sverdlovsk Region; Deputy Speaker Sverdlovsk Regional Legis. Ass. 1993–95; Rep. of Sverdlovsk Region in Russian Fed. Council 1993–95, also Head of Cttee of Social Issues, Upper Chamber; elected to State Duma 1995, Head of Sub-Cttee on Int. Cooperation in Science, Culture and Humanitarian Fields; apptd to Ministry of Labour and Social Devt 1997; First Deputy Minister of Labour and Social Devt 1997–2003, also Chair. Women's Issues Comm. of the Fed. Council; Deputy Prime Minister in Charge of Social Issues 2003–04; First Deputy Minister of Health and Social Devt 2004–07; Chair. Social Insurance Fund of Russia 2007; Deputy Head of the Russian State Duma, mem. United Russia (Yedinaya Rossiya); mem. Bd of Dirs Pervyi Kanal 2004–. *Address:* Gosudarstvennaya Duma (State Duma), 103265 Moscow, Okhotnyi ryad 1, Russia. *Telephone:* (495) 692-80-00. *Fax:* (495) 203-42-58. *E-mail:* stateduma@duma.ru. *Website:* www.duma.ru.

KARGBO, Tom Obakeh, DipEd, MSc, PhD; Sierra Leonean diplomatist and academic; b. 17 July 1945, Mabonto; s. of Pa Yamba Kargbo and Leah Susannah Kargbo; m. Mary Kargbo 1980; one s. two d.; ed Fourah Bay Coll., Univ. of Sierra Leone and Univ. of Salford, Manchester, UK; Lecturer, St Augustine's Teachers' Coll., Makeni 1969–72; Sr Teacher, Muslim Brotherhood Secondary School, Freetown 1973–75; Lecturer, Dept of Environmental

Studies and Geography, Njala Univ. Coll., Univ. of Sierra Leone 1984–87; Perm. Rep. of Sierra Leone to UN, New York 1987–92; Amb. to USA 1993–97; UN appointments in peacekeeping in South Africa, Baranja-Croatia, and Bosnia, and head UN Mission in Bosnia and Herzegovina's Political and Humanitarian Affairs Training Unit, Sarajevo; fmr Lecturer in African and Afro-American Studies, State Univ. of NY Coll. (SUNY) at Brockport; currently Chair. and Project Coordinator for activities of Org. for the Advancement of Literacy (OFAL), Sierra Leone. *Publications:* numerous papers including two for UNICEF (on disability) and one for FAO (on rural issues). *Leisure interests:* reading, games (outdoor). *Address:* Organization for the Advancement of Literacy (OFAL), 44 East Lower Pipe Line, Freetown, Sierra Leone (office). *Telephone:* (22) 230453 (office). *Website:* www.ofal.org (office).

KARIBZHANOV, Zhanybek Salimovich; Kazakhstani agronomist, economist, diplomatist and government official; b. 23 Nov. 1948, Aybas village of Sherbakulsky rayon, Omsk region, Russia; ed Omsk Agricultural Inst.; Head of Lab. and Sr Scientific Officer, All-Union Research and Design Tech. Inst. Cybernetics, Moscow 1979–82; Chief Economist, Zarya kommunizma (state farm), October rayon, Turgayski region and Dir Panfilov state farm, Oktyabrski rayon 1982–87; Chief of Cen. Admin of Social and Econ. Devt Planning of Agric., State Agro-Industrial Cttee of Kazakh SSR, Alma-Ata 1987–89; Head, Agrarian Dept of Cen. Cttee, CP of Kazakhstan 1989–92; Head, Kokchetav regional admin 1992–93; Deputy Prime Minister and Chair. State Cttee on State Property 1993–94; Minister of Agric. 1994–96; Deputy Prime Minister 1996–97; Akim, Akmolinsk region July–Dec. 1997; Deputy Prime-Minister and Minister of Agric. 1997–99; Adviser to the Pres. of Kazakhstan 1999–2001; Amb. to People's Repub. of China 2001–07; Akim, Eastern Kazakhstan Oblast Admin. Jan.–May 2008. *Address:* c/o Eastern Kazakhstan Oblast Administration, 070000 Eastern Kazakhstan obl., Ust-Kamenogorsk, ul. M. Gorkogo, Kazakhstan.

KARIEVA, Bernara; Uzbekistan ballet dancer; *Artistic Director, Bolshoi Navoi Theatre of Opera and Ballet;* b. 28 Jan. 1936, Tashkent; d. of Rakhim Kariev; m. Kulakhmat Rizaev; two d.; ed Tashkent Choreography School (under N.A. Dovgelli and L.A. Zass) 1947–51 and Moscow School of Choreography (under M. A. Kozhukhova); Prin. Ballerina with Navoi Theatre, Tashkent 1955–96, Bolshoi Ballet Moscow 1957–, Artistic Dir Bolshoi Navoi Theatre of Opera and Ballet, Tashkent 1994–; mem. CPSU 1967–91; frequently perfomrances with Bolshoi Ballet, Moscow and has given many performances abroad; Prof. of Choreography; USSR People's Deputy 1989–91; mem. UNESCO Nat. Comm. on Culture, Uzbekistan, Asscn of Actors of Uzbekistan 1984–98; Adviser to Minister of Culture 2003–; Dir, Master Class Centre 2004–; awards include Uzbek State Prize 1970, People's Artist of USSR 1973, USSR State Prize 1982; Uzbek Order of Dustlike; 200th Anniversary of Pushkin Medal. *Roles include:* Odette/Odile (Swan Lake by Tchaikovsky), Giselle (by Adan), Anna Karenina (by Shchedrin), Donna Anna (Don Juan), Zarriny (Love and the Sword by Ashrify), Dea (by Gugo), Madame Bovary (by Flaubert), Spartacus (by Khachaturian), Maskarad, Neznakomka (by Blok), Othello, Hamlet. *Ballets include:* Ballet Princess. *Film appearances:* I'm a Ballerina, Born Miniatures, Variations. *Leisure interests:* piano music, visually discovering the world. *Address:* Bolshoi Navoi Theatre of Opera and Ballet, 100017 Tashkent, 28 M. K. Otaturk street, Uzbekistan (office). *Telephone:* (71) 133-35-28 (office). *Fax:* (71) 133-33-44 (office). *Website:* bolshoi-uz.ferghana.ru/truppa/karieva_en.shtml (home).

KARIM-LAMRANI, Mohammed; Moroccan business executive and fmr politician; b. 1 May 1919, Fez; m.; four c.; econ. adviser to HM King Hassan II; Dir-Gen. Office Chérifien des Phosphates 1967–90; Chair. Crédit du Maroc; Minister of Finance April–Aug. 1971; Prime Minister 1971–72, 1983–86, 1992–94; Pres. Crédit du Maroc, Phosphates de Boucraa, Société Marocaine de Distillation et Rectification; Founder and Pres. Soc. Nat. d'Investissements 1966–; mem. Bd of Dirs SMEIA; mem. Hon. and Consultive Cttee, Int. Inst. for Promotion and Prestige, Geneva; Ouissam de Grand Officier de l'Ordre du Trône, Légion d'honneur, Order of Rising Sun (Japan). *Address:* c/o Board of Directors, SMEIA, SMEIA Building, 47 Boulevard Ba Hamad, Casablanca 20300; Rue du Mont Saint Michel, Anfa Supérieur, Casablanca 21300, Morocco. *E-mail:* contact@smeia.com.

KARIMOV, Dzhamshed Khilolovich, DEcon; Tajikistani politician; b. 4 Aug. 1940, Dushanbe; m.; two c.; ed Moscow Technological Inst. of Light Industry; researcher, Cen. Research Inst. of Econs and Math., USSR Acad. of Sciences; Asst Chair of Econ. of Industry Tajik State Univ., Jr researcher, Head of Div. of Optimal Planning Inst. of Econ., Tajik Acad. of Sciences 1962–72, Deputy Dir, Dir Research Inst. of Econ. and Econ.-Math. Methods of Planning, State Planning Cttee, Tajik SSR 1972–81; Corresp. mem. Tajik Acad. of Sciences; Deputy Chair. State Planning Cttee 1981–88; Deputy Chair. Council of Ministers, Chair. State Planning Cttee 1988–89; First Sec. Dushanbe City Cttee of CP Tajikistan 1989–91; USSR People's Deputy 1989–92; Deputy, First Deputy Chair. Council of Ministers Tajik Repub. 1991–92; represented Repub. of Tajikistan in Russia 1992–93; Chief Adviser on Econ. to Pres. Sept.–Nov. 1994; Prime Minister of Tajikistan 1994–96 (forced to resign after bloodless coup); Adviser to Pres. Rakhmonov 1996–97; apptd Amb. to People's Repub. China 1997. *Address:* c/o Ministry of Foreign Affairs, Rudaki prosp. 42, 734051 Dushanbe, Tajikistan.

KARIMOV, Islam Abduganiyevich, CandEconSc; Uzbekistani politician and head of state; *President;* b. 30 Jan. 1938, Samarqand, Uzbek SSR, USSR; m. Tatyana Karimova; two d.; ed Cen. Asian Polytechnic Inst. and Tashkent Econs Inst.; mem. CPSU 1964–91; Engineer, then Leading Engineer-Constructor in Tashkent aviation construction factory 1960–66; Chief Specialist, Head of Dept, First Deputy Chair. State Planning Cttee 1966–83, Chair. 1986; Minister of Finance, Deputy Chair. of Council of Ministers, Uzbek SSR 1983–86; First Sec., Qashqadaryo Viloyat Party Cttee 1986–89; First Sec., Uzbek SSR CP Cen. Cttee 1989–91; USSR People's Deputy 1989–91; mem. Cen. Cttee CPSU and Politburo 1990–91; Pres. of Uzbek SSR 1990; Chair. People's Democratic Party of Uzbekistan 1991–96; Pres. of Uzbekistan 1991– (elected by Supreme Soviet 24 March 1990, term of office extended by popular referendum 27 March 1995, re-elected 9 Jan. 2000 and 23 Dec. 2007); concurrently Chair. Cabinet of Ministers; mem. Acad. of Sciences of Uzbekistan; Hon. Chair. Fund of Friendship of Cen. Asia and Kazakhstan; Hon. DEcon; Dr hc and from nine foreign univs and acads; Mustakillik (Independence) Award, Amir Temur Award, Borobudur Gold Medal, UNESCO 2006. *Publications:* Uzbekistan: Its Own Model of Renovation and Progress 1992, Uzbekistan – A State with a Great Future 1992, On the Priorities of the Economic Policy of Uzbekistan 1993, Uzbek Model of Deepening Economic Reforms 1995, Uzbekistan's Way of Restoration and Progress, To Complete the Noble Cause, Stability and Reforms 1996, Uzbekistan on the Threshold of the Twenty-First Century 1997, Uzbekistan Striving Towards the 21st Century 1999, The Spiritual Path of Renewal 2000. *Leisure interest:* tennis. *Address:* Office of the President, 100163 Tashkent, O'zbekiston shox ko'ch. 43, Uzbekistan (office). *Telephone:* (71) 139-53-25 (office). *Fax:* (71) 139-54-04 (office). *E-mail:* presidents_office@press-service.uz (office). *Website:* www.press-service.uz.

KARIMOVA, Gulnora Islamovna; Uzbekistani business executive and diplomatist; *Permanent Representative, United Nations, Geneva;* b. 8 July 1972, Farg'ona; d. of Pres. of Uzbekistan, Islam Karimov; m. Mansur Maqsudi (divorced); one s. one d.; ed Tashkent State Univ., Univ. of World Economy and Diplomacy, Tashkent, Univ. of Information and Tech., Tashkent, New York, Univ., Fashion Inst. of Tech., Harvard Grad. School of Arts and Sciences, USA; early academic career at Univ. of World Economy and Diplomacy, Dept of Int. Studies, Tashkent; fmrly with Perm. Mission to UN, New York; returned to Uzbekistan and developed business interests in mobile cellular telephone operator and numerous industrial cos; consultant and adviser to Minister of Foreign Affairs; Minister-Counsellor, Embassy of Uzbekistan, Moscow 2003–08; Deputy Minister of Foreign Affairs, responsible for Cultural and Humanitarian Co-operation 2008; Perm. Rep. to UN and Int. Orgs, Geneva 2008–; Chair. Forum of Culture and Arts Foundation of Uzbekistan. *Film:* has performed in a music video under the stage name GooGoosha. *Publications:* Categories of Competitiveness of Countries with Transitional Economies: The Example of Uzbekistan 1998, Problems of Security in Central Asia: The Conditions, Tendency and Prospect of Development 2001. *Leisure interests include:* jewellery and accessory designer, singer, poet. *Address:* Forum of Culture and Arts Foundation of Uzbekistan, 100057 Tashkent, O'zbekistan shoh ko'ch. 80, Uzbekistan (office); Permanent Representation of Uzbekistan, PO Box 50036, 21523 Geneva, Switzerland (office). *Telephone:* (71) 239-27-74 (office). *Fax:* (71) 239-27-71 (office). *E-mail:* fonduz@mail.ru (office). *Website:* www.fondforum.uz (office); www.googoosha.uz (office); www.guli.uz.

KARIMULLAH, Adm. Shahid; Pakistani naval officer (retd); *Ambassador to Saudi Arabia;* ed Nat. Defence Coll., US War Coll.; joined navy operations br. 1965, Pakistan Fleet Commdr, apptd Admiral 2002, Chief of Naval Staff 2002–05; currently Amb. to Saudi Arabia; mem. Nat. Security Council; Sitara-i-Jurrat, Sitara-i-Imtiaz (mil.), Hilal-i-Imtiaz (mil.), Medal of Merit of the Turkish Armed Forces 2003. *Address:* Embassy of Pakistan, POB 94007, Riyadh 11693, Saudi Arabia (office). *Telephone:* (1) 488-7272 (office). *Fax:* (1) 488-7953 (office).

KARINA, Anna; French actress; b. (Hanne Karen Blarke Bayer), 22 Sept. 1940, Fredriksburg, Solbjerg, Denmark; d. of Carl Johann Bayer and of Elva Helvig Frederiksen; m. 1st Jean-Luc Godard (q.v.) (divorced); m. 2nd Pierre-Antoine Fabre 1968 (divorced); m. 3rd Daniel Georges Duval 1978; Prix Orange. *Films include:* She'll Have To Go 1961, Une femme est une femme 1961, Vivre sa vie 1962, Le petit soldat 1963, Bande à part 1964, Alphaville 1965, Made in the USA 1966, La religieuse 1968, The Magus 1968, Before Winter Comes 1968, Laughter in the Dark 1969, Justine 1969, The Salzburg Connection 1972, Living Together 1974, L'assassin musicien 1975, Les oeufs brouillés 1976, Boulette chinoise 1977, L'ami de Vincent 1983, Ave Maria 1984, Dernier été à Tanger 1987, Cayenne Palace 1987, L'Oeuvre au noir 1988, Last Song 1989, L'Homme qui voulait être coupable 1990, Une Histoire d'amour 2000, The Truth About Charlie 2002, Moi César, 10 ans 1/2, 1m39 2003. *Album:* Une histoire d'amour 2000. *Publications:* Golden City 1983, On n'achète pas le soleil (novel) 1988. *Address:* c/o Ammédia, 20 avenue Rapp, 75007 Paris; Orban éditions, 76 rue Bonaparte, 75006 Paris, France.

KARKARIA, Bachi; Indian editor; *Consulting Editor, The Times of India;* m.; two s.; ed Loreto Coll., Calcutta, Calcutta Univ.; began career at Illustrated Weekly of India 1969; Asst Ed. The Statesman, Calcutta (first woman) 1980; Group Editorial Dir, Mid Day Multimedia Ltd 2000–02; Ed. Sunday Times of India 1998–2000, Resident Ed. The Times of India 2003, in charge of Delhi section, then Nat. Metro Ed., now Consulting Ed. and columnist; mem. Int. Women's Media Foundation; mem. Bd World Editors' Forum 2002–, India AIDS Initiative of Bill and Melinda Gates Foundation; Jefferson Fellow, East West Center, Honolulu; mem. Professional Women's Advisory Bd, American Biographical Inst.; Media India Award (for human interest stories) 1992, Mary Morgan-Hewitt Award for Lifetime Achievement 1994. *Publications include:* Dare to Dream: The Life of M.S. Oberoi 2007. *Address:* The Times of India, 7 Bahadur Shah Zafar Marg, New Delhi 110 002, India (office). *Telephone:* (11) 23492049 (office). *Fax:* (11) 23351606 (office). *Website:* www.timesofindia.com (office).

KARLE, Isabella Helen, PhD; American physicist and academic; *Physicist, Naval Research Laboratory;* b. 2 Dec. 1921, Detroit, Mich.; d. of Zygmunt A. Lugoski and Elizabeth Lugoski (née Graczyk); m. Jerome Karle (q.v.) 1942; three d.; ed Univ. of Mich.; Assoc. Chemist, Univ. of Chicago 1944; Instructor in Chem., Univ. of Mich. 1944–46; physicist, Naval Research Lab., Washington, DC 1946–; mem. NAS, American Crystallographic Asscn, ACS, American Physical Soc., American Biophysical Soc., American Peptide Soc., American Philosophical Soc.; Hon. DSc (Michigan) 1976, (Wayne State) 1979, (Maryland) 1986, (Athens) 1997, (Pennsylvania) 1999, (Harvard) 2001, (Jagiellonian Univ., Kraków) 2002; Hon. DHumLitt (Georgetown) 1984; Women in Science and Eng Lifetime Achievement Award 1986, Swedish Royal Acad. of Sciences Gregori Aminoff Prize 1988, Bijvoet Medal, Univ. of Utrecht, Netherlands 1990, Franklin Inst. Bower Award in Science 1993, NAS Chemical Sciences Award 1995, Nat. Medal of Science, Pres.'s Award, USA 1995, Merrifield Award, American Peptide Soc. 2007, and other awards and honours. *Publications:* over 350 scientific articles, chapters and reviews. *Leisure interests:* swimming, ice skating, needlework. *Address:* Naval Research Laboratory, Code 6030, 4555 Overlook Avenue, SW, Washington, DC 20375 (office); 6304 Lakeview Drive, Falls Church, VA 22041, USA (home). *Telephone:* (202) 767-2624 (office). *Fax:* (202) 767-6874 (office). *Website:* www.nrl.navy.mil (office).

KARLE, Jerome, PhD; American scientist; *Chief Scientist, Laboratory for the Structure of Matter, Naval Research Laboratory;* b. 18 June 1918, Brooklyn, New York; s. of Louis Karfunkle and Sadie Helen Kun; m. Isabella Karle (née Lugoski) 1942; three d.; ed Abraham Lincoln High School, City Coll. of New York, Harvard Univ. and Univ. of Mich.; Head, Electron Diffraction Section, Naval Research Lab. 1946–58, Head, Diffraction Branch 1958–68, Chief Scientist, Lab. for the Structure of Matter 1968–; Prof. (part-time), Univ. of Maryland 1951–70; Pres. American Crystallographic Asscn 1972; Chair. US Nat. Cttee for Crystallography of NAS and Nat. Research Council 1973–75; Pres. Int. Union of Crystallography 1981–84; Charter mem. Sr Exec. Service 1979; Fellow, American Physical Soc.; mem. NAS; jt recipient of Nobel Prize for Chem. 1985, for devt of methods to determine the structures of crystals and several other awards. *Publications:* one book and about 200 research and review articles on theoretical and experimental topics associated with the study of the structures of materials by diffraction methods. *Leisure interests:* stereo-photography, swimming, ice-skating. *Address:* Naval Research Laboratory for the Structure of Matter, Building 35, Room 201, Code 6030, 4555 Overlook Avenue, SW, Washington, DC 20375, USA (office). *Telephone:* (202) 767-2665. *Website:* www.nrl.navy.mil (office).

KARLIC, HE Cardinal Estanislao Esteban, DTheol; Argentine ecclesiastic (retd); b. 7 Feb. 1926, Oliva; ed Pontifical Gregorian Univ.; ordained priest 1954; Auxiliary Bishop of Córdoba and Titular Bishop of Castrum 1977–83; Coadjutor Archbishop of Paraná 1983–86; Archbishop of Paraná 1986–2003 (retd), Archbishop Emer. 2003–; cr. Cardinal 2007, Cardinal-Priest of Beata Maria Vergine Addolorata a piazza Buenos Aires 2007–; fmr Pres. Exec. Comm. of Episcopal Conf. of Argentina; fmr mem. Special Council for America of Gen. Secr. of Synod of Bishops, served as Co-Sec.; mem. comm. appointed by Pope John Paul II to write the Catechism of the Roman Catholic Church 1986–92. *Address:* c/o Archdiocese of Paraná, Monte Caseros 77, 3100 Paraná [Entre Rios], Argentina.

KARLOV, Nikolai Vasilyevich; Russian physicist; *Adviser, Russian Academy of Sciences;* b. 15 Oct. 1929, Leningrad; m.; one s. one d.; ed Moscow State Univ.; worker aviation plant, Moscow 1943–47; Jr, then Sr researcher, then Head of Sector Lebedev Physical Insts, USSR Acad. of Sciences 1955–83, Head of Sector, then Head of Div. Inst. of Gen. Physics 1983–87; Rector Moscow Inst. of Physics and Tech. 1987–97; USSR People's Deputy 1989–91; Chair. Higher Attestation Cttee 1992–98; Corresp. mem. Russian Acad. of Sciences 1984, Adviser 1999–; mem. American Physical Soc.; Order of Friendship 1995; USSR State Prize 1976. *Publications:* 15 scientific books including Intense Resonant Interactions in Quantum Electronics (with V. M. Akulin) 1992, Lectures on Quantum Electronics 1993, Oscillations, Waves, Structures (with N. A. Kirichenko) 2001, Initial Chapters on Quantum Mechanics (with N. A. Kirichenko) 2004; more than 300 articles in scientific journals. *Leisure interests:* history of Russia, old Russian literature, foreign languages. *Address:* Moscow Institute of Physics and Technology, Institutsky per. 9, 141700 Dolgoprudny, Moscow (office); Acad. Zelinsky str. 3818135, 119334 Moscow, Russia (home). *Telephone:* (495) 408-81-54 (office); (495) 135-13-86 (home). *Fax:* (495) 408-81-54 (office); (495) 135-13-86 (home). *E-mail:* nkarlov@mfti.ru (office).

KARLSSON, Jan O., BA; Swedish politician, international organization official and fmr civil servant; b. 1 June 1939, Stockholm; ed Univ. of Stockholm; Admin. Officer, Head of Section, Ministry of Agric. 1962–68; Political Adviser, Cabinet Office 1968–73, Co-ordinating Adviser 1990–91; Sec. to City Commr, Stockholm City Council 1973–77; Deputy Sec. to Presidium, Nordic Council 1977–82; Under-Sec. of State to Minister for Nordic Co-operation 1982–85; Under-Sec. of State, Ministry of Finance 1985–88; Chair. Comm. on Metropolitan Problems 1988–90; Prime Minister's Personal Rep. on Nordic Co-operation in connection with membership of European Environment Agency and EU 1991–92; Negotiator and Adviser, SDP 1992–94; Dir-Gen. Ministry for Foreign Affairs 1994; Minister for Devt Co-operation, Migration and Asylum Policy 2002–03; Acting Minister for Foreign Affairs and Minister (Devt Co-operation, Migration and Asylum Policy), Ministry of Foreign Affairs 2003; mem. European Court of Auditors 1995, Pres. 1999–; mem. editorial staff, TIDEN periodical 1974–82, Ed.-in-Chief 1978–82; mem. Bd Nordic Investment Bank 1983–89, Nat. Pharmacy Corpn 1986–91; Chair. Bd Swedish Nat. Housing Finance Corpn 1986–89; Chair. OECD Project Group on Housing, Social Integration and Liveable Environments in Cities 1991–93; fmr mem. Bd Stockholm Philharmonic. *Address:* c/o Ministry for Foreign Affairs, 10339 Stockholm, Sweden (office).

KARLSTRÖM, Johan; Swedish construction industry executive; *President and CEO, Skanska AB;* ed Royal Inst. of Tech., Stockholm, Advanced Man. Program, Harvard Univ., USA; began career as Regional Man., Skanska Northern Sweden, later Exec. Vice-Pres. Skanska, Nordic region, Exec. Vice-Pres. Skanska USA –2008, Pres. and CEO Skanska AB 2008–; fmr Pres. BPA (Bravida). *Address:* Skanska AB, Klarabergsviadukten 90, 111 91 Stockholm, Sweden (office). *Telephone:* (8) 753-88-00 (office). *Fax:* (8) 755-12-56 (office). *E-mail:* info@skanska.com (office). *Website:* www.skanska.com (office).

THE KARMAPA, (Urgyen Trinley Doje); Tibetan Buddhist leader; Living Buddha of the White Sect, Tibet; Seventeenth Incarnation; enthroned 1992; now living in exile in Dharamsala, India.

KARMAZIN, Melvin (Mel) Alan, BS; American media executive; *President and CEO, Sirius Satellite Radio Inc.;* b. 24 Aug. 1943, New York; m. Sharon Karmazin (divorced 1994); one s. one d.; ed Pace Univ.; stage man. CBS Radio 1960–70, Chair., CEO CBS Station Group 1996–, now Pres., COO CBS Corpn; Vice-Pres., Gen. Man. Metromedia Inc. 1970–81; Pres. Infinity Broadcasting Corpn 1981–96, CEO 1988–96; Pres., COO Viacom Inc. 2000–04 (resgnd); Pres. and CEO Sirius Satellite Radio Inc. 2004–; fmr mem. Bd of Dirs Westwood One, Blockbuster, New York Stock Exchange; Vice-Chair. Bd of Trustees, Museum of TV and Radio; numerous awards including Nat. Asscn of Broadcasters Nat. Radio Award and IRTS Gold Medal Award; inducted into Broadcasting Hall of Fame. *Address:* Sirius Satellite Radio Inc., 1221 Avenue of the Americas, 36th Floor, New York, NY 10020, USA (office). *Telephone:* (212) 584-5100 (office). *Fax:* (212) 584-5200 (office). *Website:* www.siriusradio.com (office).

KARMI, Ram, RIBA; Israeli architect; b. 13 Sept. 1931, Jerusalem; m. Rivka Edery; three s. three d.; ed Architectural Asscn School, London, UK; joined father's architectural office in partnership Karmi-Meltzer-Karmi 1956–67; est. (with sister) office of Karmi Assoc. Architects 1967–92, est. br. offices Tel-Aviv, New York 1972; Chief Architect, Ministry of Housing 1975–79; Pnr, Karmi Architects & Co., Tel-Aviv 1979–92; various teaching posts at Faculty of Architecture and Town Planning, Technion 1964, Assoc. Prof. 1987–94; Visiting Prof., Princeton Univ. 1969, MIT 1972, 1983, Columbia Univ. 1969–70; projects include univ. bldgs (Faculty of Humanities, Hebrew Univ., Mt Scopus), schools, hotels (Holyland Compound, Jerusalem), pvt. homes, large housing projects (Gilo, Jerusalem), public bldgs (Museum of Children of the Holocaust, Supreme Court, Jerusalem, Habima Theater, renovation Tel-Aviv), Ben Gurion Airport (main terminal, landside and industrial complexes) 2000 and industrial complexes; won competition for Prime Minister's Office Bldg 1996; mem. Israel Inst. of Architects and Engineers, Architectural Asscn, London; Rokach Prize for El Al Bldg, Tel-Aviv 1965, Rechter Prize for Negev Center–Combined Commercial Center and Housing, Beer Sheba 1967, Reinholds Prize for Commercial Center and Housing, Beer Sheba 1969, Rokach Prize for Residential Bldgs, Be'eri Street, Tel-Aviv 1970, Asscn of Architects and Engineers in Israel Prize for Supreme Court Bldg (with Ada Karmi-Melamede) 1998, Rechter Prize for Yad Layeled Museum, Kibbutz Lohamei Hagetaot 1999, Israel Prize for Architecture 2002. *Publications:* numerous articles in professional journals. *Address:* c/o Ada Karmi-Melamede Architects, 17 Kaplan Street, Tel-Aviv 64734 (office); 2 Yehoshua Ben-Noon Street, Herzeliya Pituah, Israel (home). *Telephone:* (3) 6912112 (office); (9) 9586767 (home). *Fax:* (3) 6913508 (office). *E-mail:* ada@akmp.co.il (office). *Website:* adakarmimelamede.com (office).

KARMOKOV, Khachim Mukhamedovich, DEcon; Russian economist and politician; *Chairman, Federation Accounts Chamber;* b. 2 May 1941, Zayukovo, Kabardin-Balkar Autonomous Repub.; m.; one d.; ed Kabardin-Balkar State Univ., Moscow Inst. for Eng and Econs; Eng and managerial posts in construction industry 1963–67, 1978–81; teacher, docent Kabardin-Balkar State Univ. 1967–78; Financial Dir Trust Kabbalpromstroi 1981–90; Deputy Chair. Council of Ministers, Kabardin-Balkar Repub. 1990–91; Chair. Supreme Soviet Kabardin-Balkar Repub. 1991–93; Chair. Accounts Chamber of Russian Fed. 1994–; mem. State Duma Russian Fed. 1993–95; Rep. of Kabardino-Balkan Repub. in Council of Fed. 2001–; mem. Russian Acad. of Natural Sciences, Int. Acad. of Informatization. *Leisure interest:* hunting. *Address:* Federation Council, ul. B. Dmitrovka 26, 103426 Moscow (office); Lenina Prospect 27, Suite 327, 360028 Nalchik, Kabardino-Balkaria, Russia (office). *Telephone:* (495) 203-90-74 (Moscow) (office); (86622) 74050 (Nalchik) (office). *Fax:* (495) 203-46-17 (Moscow) (office). *E-mail:* post_sf@gov.ru (office). *Website:* www.council.gov.ru (office).

KARMOUL, Akram Jamil, PhD; Jordanian business executive and consultant; *Chairman and Managing Director, Rawda Company for Info, Tech and E-Commerce;* b. 13 Aug. 1939, W Bank; m. Huda Abu-Errub 1964; two s. two d.; ed Assiut Univ., Univ. of Strathclyde and Imperial Coll., London, UK; geologist, geophysicist and mining engineer 1961–72; Dir Industry, later Dir Science and Tech. Ministry of Planning 1972–80; Dir Gen. of Industry Ministry of Industry and Trade 1980–87; Dir, Man. Industrial, Commercial and Agric. Co. 1987; Exec. Dir and Asst Man. Dalla-Al-Baraka Saudi Group, Jeddah 1988–89; Dir of Industry Dept UN-ECWA Comm. for W Asia 1989–93; Gen. Man. United Textile Group 1995; Assoc. Consultant, Arab Consulting Centre and Assignments UNDP 1996; currently Chair. and Man. Dir Rawda Co. for Info, Tech and E-Ccommerce; mem. Arab Knowledge Man. Soc.; Science Award for Outstanding Persons. *Publications:* numerous works on mineral wealth and industrial tech. of Jordan, public enterprises. *Leisure interests:* reading, swimming. *Address:* Rawda Company for Info, Tech and E-Commerce, PO Box 960555, Amman, Jordan (office). *Telephone:* (6) 5660155 (office). *Fax:* (6) 5660366 (office). *E-mail:* info@e-ritt.com (office).

KARNAD, Girish, MA; Indian playwright, filmmaker and actor; b. 19 May 1938, Matheran; s. of Raghunath Karnad and Krishnabai Karnad; m. Saraswarthy Ganapathy 1980; one s. one d.; ed Karnatak Coll., Dharwad and Univ. of Oxford; Rhodes Scholar, Oxford 1960–63; Pres. Oxford Union Soc.

1963; Asst Man. Oxford Univ. Press, Madras 1963–69, Man. 1969–70; Homi Bhabha Fellow 1970–72; Dir Film & TV Inst. of India, Pune 1974, 1975; Visiting Prof. and Fulbright Scholar-in-Residence, Univ. of Chicago 1987–88; Indian Co-Chair., Media Cttee, Indo-US Subcomm. 1984–93; Chair. Sangeet Natak Akademi (Nat. Acad. of Performing Arts) 1988–93; Dir The Nehru Centre, London 2000; World Theatre Amb., Int. Theatre Inst. of UNESCO 2008; Fellow, Sangeet Natak Acad. 1994; Hon. DLitt (Univ. of Karnataka) 1994; several awards for film work; Padma Bhushan 1992, Bharatiya Jnanapith Award 1999, Sahitya Acad. Award 1994. *Plays include:* Yayati 1961, Tughlaq 1964, Hayavadana 1971, Anjumallige 1976, Nagamandala 1988, Taledanda 1990, Agni Mattu Male 1995, Tipu Sultan Kanda Kanasu 2000, Bali 2002, Wedding Album. *Films include:* Vamsha Vriksha 1971, Kaadu 1973, Tabbaliyu Neenade Magane 1977, Ondanondu Kaaladalli 1978, Utsav 1984, Cheluvi 1992, Kanooru Heggadithi 1999, Iqbal (as actor) 2005, Dor (as actor) 2006. *Radio:* Ma Nishada 1986, The Dreams of Tipu Sultan 1997. *TV:* Antaraal 1996, Swarajnama 1997, Kanooru Ki Thakurani 1999, wrote and presented The Bhagavad Gita for BBC Two 2002. *Address:* 697, 15th Cross, JP Nagar Phase II, Bangalore 560 078, India (home). *Telephone:* (80) 659 0463. *Fax:* (80) 659-0019. *E-mail:* gkarnad38@aol.com (home).

KARNIK, Kiran; Indian business executive; b. March 1947; various positions at Indian Space Research Org. including Dir Devt and Educational Communication Unit 1983–91; Dir Consortium for Educational Communication 1991–95; Man. Dir Discovery Networks India 1995–2001; Pres. Nat. Asscn of Software and Service Cos (NASSCOM) 2001–07. *Address:* c/o NASSCOM Head Office, International Youth Centre, Teen Murti Marg, Chanakyapuri, New Delhi 110021, India. *Telephone:* (11) 23010199. *Fax:* (11) 23015452. *E-mail:* info@nasscom.in. *Website:* www.nasscom.in.

KAROUI, Hamed, PhD; Tunisian physician and politician; *First Vice-Chairman, Rassemblement constitutionnel démocratique;* b. 30 Dec. 1927, Sousse; m.; four c.; ed Faculté de Médecine de Paris, France; worked as physician at Sousse Regional Hosp. 1957–; active in Destour Movt 1942–, including responsibility for Al Kifah journal; Pres. Féd. Destourienne de France; Municipal Councillor, Sousse 1957–72, elected Mayor 1985; Deputy to the Nat. Ass. 1964, re-elected 1981 and 1989; Vice-Pres. Chamber of Deputies 1983–86; Minister for Youth and Sports 1986–87; Dir Parti Socialiste Destourien (renamed Rassemblement constitutionnel démocratique 1988) 1987, First Vice-Chair. 1999–; Minister for Justice 1988–89; Prime Minister 1989–99; Grand Cordon Ordre de l'Indépendance, Ordre de la République (Tunisia), Ordre du 7 Novembre. *Leisure interest* shooting. *Address:* Rassemblement constitutionnel démocratique, blvd 9 avril 1938, Tunis, Tunisia. *E-mail:* info@rcd.tn (office); maherkar@hexabyte.tn (home). *Website:* www.rcd.tn (office).

KARP, Richard Manning, AB, SM, PhD; American computer scientist and academic; *Senior Research Scientist, International Computer Science Institute;* b. 3 Jan. 1935, Boston, Mass; s. of Abraham Karp and Rose Karp; ed Harvard Univ.; Researcher, IBM Thomas J. Watson Research Center 1959–68; Prof. of Computer Science, Math. and Operations Research, Univ. of California, Berkeley 1968–94, 1999–; Research Scientist, Int. Computer Science Inst. 1988–95, Sr Research Scientist 1999–; Prof., Univ. of Washington 1995–99; Fellow, American Acad. of Arts and Sciences, AAAS, Asscn for Computing Machinery, Inst. for Operations Research and Man. Science; mem. NAS, Nat. Acad. of Eng, American Philosophical Soc., French Acad. of Sciences; eight hon. degrees; numerous awards including Turing Award 1985, Nat. Medal of Science 1996, Israel Inst. of Tech. Harvey Prize 1998, Benjamin Franklin Medal in Computer and Cognitive Science 2004, Inamori Foundation Kyoto Prize 2008. *Achievements include:* co-developer with Jack Edmonds of Edmonds-Karp algorithm 1971. *Address:* International Computer Science Institute, 1947 Center Street, Suite 600, Berkeley, CA 94704, USA (office). *Telephone:* (510) 666-2900 (office). *Fax:* (510) 666-2956 (office). *E-mail:* karp@icsi.berkeley.edu (office). *Website:* www.eecs.berkeley .edu/~karp/biography.html (office).

KARPLUS, Martin, PhD; American/Austrian chemist and academic; *Theodore William Richards Professor Emeritus of Chemistry, Harvard University;* b. 15 March 1930, Vienna, Austria; s. of Hans Goldstern and Isabella Goldstern; m. Marci Hazard 1981; one s. two d.; ed Harvard Univ. and California Inst. of Tech.; NSF Postdoctoral Fellow, Math. Inst., Oxford, UK; Asst Prof., Dept of Chem., Univ. of Illinois 1955–59; Assoc. Prof. 1960; Prof. of Chem., Columbia Univ., New York 1960–66; Prof. of Chem., Harvard Univ., Cambridge, Mass 1966–, Theodore William Richards Prof. of Chem. 1979–99, Theodore William Richards Research Prof. 1999–2007, Emer. 2007–; Visiting Prof., Univ. of Paris 1972–73, 1980–81 (Prof. 1974–75), Collège de France 1980–81, 1987–88; Prof. Conventionné, Louis Pasteur Univ. 1992, 1994–; Eastman Prof., Univ. of Oxford 1999–2000; mem. European Acad. of Arts, Sciences and Humanities, NAS, American Acad. of Arts and Sciences, Int. Acad. of Quantum Molecular Science; Foreign mem. Netherlands Acad. of Arts and Science, Royal Soc. (UK); Dr hc (Sherbrooke) 1998, Ehrendoktorat (Zürich) 2006; Joseph O. Hirschfelder Prize in Theoretical Chem., Univ. of Wisconsin 1995, ACS Harrison Howe Award, Rochester Section 1967, Award for Outstanding Contrib. to Quantum Biology, Int. Soc. of Quantum Biology 1979, Distinguished Alumni Award, Calif. Inst. of Tech. 1986, Irving Langmuir Award, American Physical Soc. 1987, Nat. Lecturer, Biophysical Soc. 1991, ACS Theoretical Chem. Award (first recipient) 1993, Anfinsen Award, Protein Soc. 2001, Pauling Award, Northwest Section ACS 2004. *Publications:* Atoms and Molecules (with R. N. Porter) 1970, A Theoretical Perspective of Dynamics, Structure and Thermodynamics (with C. L. Brooks III and B. M. Pettitt) 1988, A Guide to Biomolecular Simulations (with O. M. Becker) 2006; over 750 articles in the field of theoretical chem. *Address:* Department of Chemistry and Chemical Biology, Harvard University, 12 Oxford Street, Cambridge, MA 02138, USA (office); Laboratoire de Chimie Biophysique, ISIS, Université Louis Pasteur, 67000 Strasbourg, France (office). *Telephone:* (617) 495-4018 (office). *Fax:* (617) 496-3204 (office). *E-mail:* marci@tammy.harvard.edu (office). *Website:* www.chem.harvard .edu/research/faculty/martin_karplus.php (office).

KARPOV, Anatolii Yevgenievich, DEcon; Russian chess player; b. 23 May 1951, Zlatoust; s. of Yevgeniy Stepanovich Karpov and Nina Karpov; m. 1st Irina Karpov; one s.; m. 2nd Natalia Bulanova; one d.; ed Leningrad Univ.; mem. CPSU 1980–91; USSR Candidate Master 1962, Master 1966; European Jr Champion 1967, 1968, World Jr Champion 1969; Int. Master 1969, Int. Grandmaster 1970; USSR Champion 1976, 1983, 1988; world champion 1975–85; became world champion when the holder Bobby Fischer refused to defend the title and he retained his title against Viktor Korchnoi in 1978 and in 1981; defended against Garry Kasparov (q.v.) in Moscow Sept. 1984; the match later adjourned due to the illness of both players; lost to the same player in 1985; unsuccessfully challenged Kasparov 1986, 1987, 1990; won World Championship title under FIDE after split in chess orgs 1993, 1996, 1998; has won more tournaments than any other player (over 160); first player to become a millionaire from playing chess; People's Deputy of USSR 1989–91; Pres. Soviet Peace Fund (now Int. Asscn of Peace Funds) 1982–; Pres. Chernobyl-Aid org. 1989–; UNICEF Amb. for Russia and E Europe 1998–; Chair. Council of Dirs Fed. Industrial Bank, Moscow; mem. Soviet (now Russian) UNESCO Affairs Comm.; mem. Bd Int. Chess Fed.; Ed.-in-Chief Chess Review 64 (magazine) 1980–91; Winner of Oscar Chess Prize 1973–77, 1979–81, 1984, 1994, Fontany di Roma Prize for humanitarian achievements 1996; Hon. Texan, Hon. Citizen of Tula, Zlatoust, Orsk and other cities in Russia, Belarus and Ukraine. *Publications:* Chess is My Life 1980, Karpov Teaches Chess 1987, Karpov on Karpov 1991, How to Play Chess and 47 other books. *Leisure interest:* philately. *Address:* International Peace Fund, Prechistenka 10, Moscow, Russia. *Telephone:* (495) 202-41-71; (495) 202-42-36.

KARPOV, Vladimir Vasilyevich; Russian author and editor; b. 28 July 1922, Orenburg; s. of Vasiliy Karpov and Lydia Karpov; m. Evgenia Vasilievna Karpov 1956; one s. two d.; ed Military Acad., Moscow and Gorky Literary Inst.; arrested 1941, sent to camp, released to join a penal Bn, subsequently distinguishing himself in mil. reconnaissance work; mem. CPSU 1943–91; started publishing (novels, stories, essays) 1948–; Deputy Ed. of Oktyabr 1974–77; Sec. of Presidium of USSR Union of Writers 1981–86, First Sec. 1986–91; Chief Ed. of Novy mir 1981–86; Deputy to the Presidium of the USSR Supreme Soviet 1984–89; mem. CPSU Cen. Cttee 1988–90, USSR People's Deputy 1989–91; mem. Acad. of Mil. Sciences; Hon. DLitt (Strathclyde Univ.); State Prize 1986, Hero of Soviet Union 1944. *Publications:* The Marshal's Baton 1970, Take Them Alive 1975, The Regimental Commander 1982–84, The Eternal Struggle 1987, Marshal Zhukov, (Vol. I) 1989, (Vol. II) 1992, (Vol. III) 1995, Selected Works (3 Vols), The Destiny of a Scout (novel) 1999, The Executed Marshals 2000. *Leisure interests:* collecting books, especially on mil. history. *Address:* Kutozovsky prosp. 26, Apt. 94, Moscow, Russia. *Telephone:* (495) 249-26-12. *Fax:* (495) 200-02-93.

KARRUBI, Mahdi; Iranian cleric and politician; *Secretary-General, Hezb-e Etemad-e Melli (National Confidence Party—NCP);* b. 1937, Aligoudarz, Lorestan; mem. Majles (Parl.) and Speaker 1989–92, 2000–04; unsuccessful cand. for Pres. 2005; Founder and Sec.-Gen. Hezb-e Etemad-e Melli (Nat. Confidence Party—NCP) 2005–; mem. Asscn of Militant Clerics –2005 (fmr Sec.-Gen.), Expediency Discernment Council of the System –2005 (resgnd); f.. Etemad-e Melli (daily newspaper) 2006. *Address:* Hezb-e Etemad-e Melli (National Confidence Party—NCP), Tehran, Iran (office). *Telephone:* (21) 88373306 (office). *E-mail:* Ravabet_Omomi@Etemademelli.ir (office). *Website:* www.etemademelli.ir (office).

KARSENTI, René, MS, MBA, PhD; French international finance official; *Executive President, International Capital Market Association;* b. 27 Jan. 1950, Tlemcen, Algeria; s. of Leon Karsenti and Mireille Benhaim; m. Hélène Dayan 1978; two d.; ed ESCIL, Lyons; Paris Business School and Sorbonne, Paris; researcher in finance and econs, Univ. of Calif. Berkeley 1973; investment analyst/portfolio man. Caisse des Dépôts, Paris 1975–79; Finance Officer, World Bank (IBRD), Washington, DC 1979–83, Financial Adviser 1983–85, Div. Chief 1985–87, Sr Man. Finance Dept, Treasury 1987–89; Treas., Dir Financial Policy Dept, Int. Finance Corp, World Bank Group, Washington, DC 1989–91; Treas. EBRD 1991–95; Dir-Gen. Finance, European Investment Bank 1995–2006; Exec. Pres. and mem. Bd of Dirs Int. Capital Market Asscn, Zürich and London 2006–; Chair. Euro Debt Market Asscn 2004–; mem. Man. Selection Cttee, French Pensions Reserve Fund (FRR) and Strategic Cttee, Agence France Trésor (French Ministry of Finance); mem. Investment Advisory Cttee, FAO, Rome; Chevalier Légion d'honneur. *Publications:* Research in Pharmaceutical Industry 1977; various financial lectures and articles on int. finance, capital markets and European Monetary Union. *Leisure interests:* swimming, antiques, opera. *Address:* International Capital Market Association, Talacker 29, 8001 Zurich, Switzerland (office). *Telephone:* 443634222 (office). *Fax:* 443637772 (office). *E-mail:* rene.karsenti@icmagroup.org (office). *Website:* www.icmagroup.org (office).

KARTASHKIN, Vladimir Alekseevich, DJur; Russian politician; *Editor-in-Chief, International Lawyer Magazine;* b. 4 March 1934; m. Elena Kovanova 1991; one s. one d.; ed Moscow State Univ.; Chief Scientific Researcher, Inst. of State and Law 1957–63, Chief Researcher, Prof. 1985–; with Div. of Human Rights UN 1969–73; consultant, UN Dir-Gen. on Juridical Problems 1979–85; Chair. Comm. on Human Rights, Russian Presidency 1996–2002; Prof., Int. Inst. of Human Rights, Strasbourg, Cornell Univ., Santa-Clair Univ., Univ. of Peoples' Friendship, Moscow; Ed.-in-Chief International Lawyer Magazine 2003–; Meritorious Lawyer of Russia. *Publications:* over 200 books and articles including Human Rights in International and State Law. *Leisure interests:* tennis, swimming. *Address:* Institute of State and Law, Russian Academy of Sciences, Znemaenka str. 10, 119841, Moscow, Russia (office). *Telephone:* (495) 291-34-90 (office); (495) 242-37-63 (home). *E-mail:* kartashkin@comtv.ru (office).

KARTOMI, Margaret Joy, AM, BA, BMus, DrPhil, FAHA, AUA; Australian musicologist and academic; *Professor of Music, School of Music, Monash University;* b. (Margaret Joy Hutchesson), 24 Nov. 1940, Adelaide; d. of George Hutchesson and Edna Hutchesson; m. Hidris Kartomi 1961; one d.; ed Univ. of Adelaide, Humboldt Univ.; Lecturer, Music Dept, Monash Univ. 1969–70, Sr Lecturer 1971–73, Reader 1974–88, Prof. of Music 1989–, Head of Music School 1989–2001, currently Coordinator of Research and Ethnomusicology; Dir Inst. of Contemporary Asian Studies, Monash Univ. 1989–91; Dir Monash-ANZ Centre for Int. Briefing 1988–90, Monash Asia Inst. 1988–90; Dir-at-large Int. Musicology Soc. 1993–; mem. Nat. Cttee Musicological Soc. of Australia (Nat. Pres. 1978-92), American Musicological Soc., Int. Council for Traditional Music, Council Soc. for Ethnomusicology; Visiting Prof., Univ. of California, Berkeley 1986–87; Dir Symposium of Int. Musicological Soc., Melbourne 1988, 2004; Program Chair. and Chair. E. Wachsmann Prize Cttee 2005–06; mem. Editorial Bd Journal of Musicological Research, Ethnomusicology Forum, Wacana Seni, Musicology Australia 2008–; Alexander Clarke Prize for Pianoforte Performance 1960, Dr Ruby Davy Prize for Musical Composition 1961, Fed. German Record Critics' Prize 1983, 1998, 2007, Australian Centenary Medal 2001, presented with a Festschrift in the Journal of Musicological Research Vol. 24, Nos 3–4 in honour of her 65th birthday 2005. *Publications:* On Concepts and Classifications of Musical Instruments 1990, The Gamelan Digul and the Prison Camp Musician Who Built It: An Australian Link with the Indonesian Revolution 2003; author or ed. of 12 other books; numerous articles and 300 articles in the New Grove Dictionary of Musical Instruments 1989. *Leisure interests:* tennis, badminton, concerts, theatre. *Address:* School of Music, Monash University, Wellington Road, Clayton, Vic. 3168, Australia (office). *Telephone:* (03) 9905-3238 (office). *Fax:* (3) 9905-3241 (office). *E-mail:* margaret.kartomi@arts.monash.edu.au (office). *Website:* www.arts.monash.edu.au/music/staff/mkartomi.php (office).

KARUKUBIRO-KAMUNANWIRE, Perezi, PhD; Ugandan diplomatist and academic; *Ambassador to USA;* b. 25 July 1937, Mbarara; m.; two c.; ed Columbia Univ., New York, USA; Chair. Uganda People's Congress Youth League 1958–63; Pres. and Chair. Pan-African Students' Org. in the Americas 1965–70; Prof., CUNY, USA 1974–86, fmr Prof., Black Studies Program; Amb. to Austria (also accred to FRG and the Holy See) and Perm. Rep. to Int. Orgs in Vienna 1986–88, Perm. Rep. to UN, New York 1988–95, Chair. UN Gen. Ass. Special Political Cttee 1990–95; Adjunct Prof., Center for Conflict Man. and Organizational Research, Sophia Univ., Bulgaria 2003–06; Amb. to USA 2006–. *Publications:* A Study Guide to Uganda (co-ed.) 1970; numerous articles in the field of int. relations. *Address:* Embassy of Uganda, 5911 16th Street, NW, Washington, DC 20011, USA (office). *Telephone:* (202) 726-4758 (office). *Fax:* (202) 726-1727 (office). *E-mail:* pkamunanwire@ugandaembassyus.org (office). *Website:* www.ugandaembassy.com (office).

KARUME, Amani Abeid; Tanzanian accountant and politician; *President and Chairman, Supreme Revolutionary Council of Zanzibar;* b. 1 Nov. 1948, Zanzibar; s. of the late Abeid Amani Karume; m. Shadya Amani Karume; six c.; ed Lumumba Coll. Zanzibar; accountant, Zanzibar Treasury 1969–70, Chief Accountant 1970–71, Prin. Sec., Ministery of Finance 1971–74, Prin. Sec., Ministry of Planning 1974–78, Prin. Sec., Ministry of Communications and Transport 1978–80, Zanzibar; Pvt Business Consultant Rep., G.E.C. of UK, Zanzibar 1980–90; mem. House of Reps 1990–2000, served as Minister of Trade and Industries and Minister of Communications and Transport; Chair. and Pres. Supreme Revolutionary Council of Zanzibar 2000–, also Minister of Finance and Econ.Planning; mem. Chama Cha Mapunduzi (CCM – Revolutionary Party of Tanzania); mem. Bd of Dirs East African Harbours Corpn –1973. *Address:* State House, PO Box 776, Zanzibar, Tanzania (office). *Telephone:* (24) 2230814 (office). *Fax:* (24) 2233722 (office).

KARUME, Hon. (James) Njenga; Kenyan politician and business executive; b. 1929, Nakuru dist.; farmer and business exec.; fmrly Chair. Gikuyu, Embu and Meru Asscn (GEMA); MP for Kiambaa 1979–; Asst Minister, Ministry of Lands, Local Govt, Energy and Co-operative Devt and Marketing 1979–91; Special Programmes Minister 2004–05; Minister of State for Defence, Office of the Pres. 2005–08; mem. Democratic Party of Kenya –1992, mem. KANU Party 1992–; Elder of the Order of the Golden Heart of Kenya. *Address:* PO Box 30594-00100, Nairobi, Kenya (home).

KARUNANIDHI, Muthuvel, (Kalaignar); Indian politician and playwright; *Chief Minister of Tamil Nadu; Leader, Dravida Munnetra Kazhagam;* b. 3 June 1924, Thirukkuvalai, Thanjavur; s. of Muthuvel Karunanidhi and Anjuham Karunanidhi; m. Dayalu Karunanidhi; four s. two d.; ed Thiruvarur Bd High School; Ed.-in-Charge Kudiarasu; journalist and stage and screen playwright in Tamil, acting in his own plays staged to collect party funds; has written over 35 film-plays including the screen version of the Tamil classic Silappadhikaram, stage plays and short stories; started first student wing of the Dravidian movt called Tamilnadu Tamil Manavar Mandram; one of founder-mems of Dravida Munnetra Kazhagam Legis. Party (DMK) 1949, Treas. 1961, Deputy Leader 1962–67, Pres. 1969–; Founder-; mem. Tamil Nadu Legis. Ass. 1957–; led the Kallakkudi Agitation and was imprisoned for six months; State Minister of Public Works 1967–69; Chief Minister of Tamil Nadu (Madras) 1969–76 (presidential rule imposed), 1989–90, 1996–2001, 2006–; arrested on corruption charges 2001, then released; Thamizha Vell (Patron of Tamil), Asscn of Research Scholars in Tamil 1971; Ed. DMK Murasoli (Tamil daily organ), Kudiyarasu; Founder Mutharam (journal), State Govt News Reel, Arau Studio, Tamil Arasu (govt journal); Hon. DLitt

(Annamalai Univ., Tamil Nadu) 1971. *Publications include:* Thenpandi Singham (Raja Rajan Award) and over 100 books of prose and poetry; also screenplays. *Leisure interests:* reading, writing, discussion. *Address:* Office of the Chief Minister, Government of Tamil Nadu, Secretariat, Fort St George, Chennai 600 009 (office); Dravida Munnetra Kazhagam, Anna Arivalayam, Teynampet, Chennai 600 018 (office); 7A S. Gopalapuram, IV Street, Chennai 600 086, India (home). *Telephone:* (44) 25672345 (office); (44) 28115225 (home). *Fax:* (44) 25671441 (office). *E-mail:* cmcell@tn.nic.in (office). *Website:* www.tn.gov.in (office).

KARVE, Priyadarshini; Indian scientist and business executive; *Founder-Director, Samuchit Enviro Tech Pvt. Ltd;* Founder-Dir Samuchit Enviro Tech Pvt. Ltd; co-ordinated project 'Commercialisation of Improved Biomass Fuels and Cooking Devices in India – Pilot Project' funded by Household Energy and Health Programme of Shell Foundation in state of Maharashtra with help of 10 local NGOs 2003–05, scaled-up project 2006–; World Tech. Award in Environment, The World Tech. Network 2005. *Achievements include:* developed technique for converting agro-waste into char briquettes using environment-friendly process and scaled it up for economically feasible rural tech.; also involved in various R&D activities to develop cleaner wood-burning stoves and other energy appliances for rural households. *Address:* Appropriate Rural Technology Institute, c/o Samuchit Enviro Tech Pvt. Ltd, Flat No. 6, Ekta Park Co-op Housing Society, Behind Nirmitee Showroom, Law College Road, Pune 411004, India (office). *Telephone:* (20) 25460138 (office). *Fax:* (20) 25460138 (office). *E-mail:* pkarve@arti-india.org (office). *Website:* www.arti-india.org (office).

KARVINEN, Jouko, MSc (Eng); Finnish business executive; *CEO, Stora Enso Oyj;* b. 31 Aug. 1957, Helsinki; m.; two c.; ed Tampere Univ. of Tech.; various positions in Traction Div., Stromberg OY 1982–87, Man. Advanced Devt Allen-Bradley Stromberg Inc., Wis., USA 1987–88; Profit Centre Man. LV AC Drives 1988–90; Vice-Pres. Power Electronics Div., ABB Drives OY 1990–93, Vice-Pres. Business Unit Drives Products & Systems, Zürich 1993–98, Sr Vice-Pres. Business Area Automation Power Products 1998–2000, Exec. Vice-Pres. ABB Group Ltd 2000–02, also Head of Automation Tech. Products Div. and mem. Group Exec. Cttee 2000–02; CEO Medical Systems Div., Royal Philips Electronics, Boston, USA 2002–06, also Sr Vice-Pres. and mem. Group Man. Cttee 2002–06, CEO Philips Medical Systems Div., Amsterdam 2006, also Exec. Vice-Pres. and mem. Bd of Man. 2006; mem. Bd Dirs and CEO Stora Enso Oyj 2007–. *Address:* Stora Enso Oyj, Kanavaranta 1, PO Box 309, 00101 Helsinki, Finland (office). *Telephone:* (20) 46131 (office). *Fax:* (20) 4621471 (office). *E-mail:* info@storaenso.com (office). *Website:* www.storaenso.com (office).

KARZAI, Hamid, MA; Afghan politician and head of state; *President;* b. 24 Dec. 1954, Karz, Qandahar; s. of the late Abdul-Ahad Karzai, Chief of Popolzai tribe, assassinated in Quetta 1999; m. Zeenat Karzai 1999; one s.; ed Habibia High School, Simla Univ., India; Dir of Information, Nat. Liberation Front 1985–86, Deputy Dir, Political Office 1986–89; Dir Foreign Relations Dept, Office of Interim Pres. 1989–91; fmr official rep. of deposed Afghan king, Zahir Shah; Deputy Foreign Minister 1992–96; went into exile 1996–2001; Chief of Popolzai tribe, S Afghanistan 1999–; served as consultant to Union Oil Co. of Calif. (UNOCAL), USA; mem. Del. to Future of Afghanistan Govt Talks, Bonn Nov. 2001; Chair. Afghan Interim Authority Dec. 2001–June 2002; Pres. of Transitional Authority (elected by Loya Jirga) June 2002–Nov. 2004, elected Pres. of Afghanistan Nov. 2004–; Hon. KCMG 2003; Hon. DLitt (Himachal Univ.) 2003, Hon. DLit (Nebraska Univ.) 2005, Hon. DJur (Georgetown Univ.) 2006; Int. Rescue Cttee Freedom Award 2002, American Bar Asscn Asia Rule of Law Award 2003, Int. Republican Inst. Freedom Award 2003, Philadelphia Liberty Medal 2004, Int. Der Steiger Award 2007. *Address:* Office of the President, Gul Khana Palace, Presidential Palace, Kabul, Afghanistan (office). *E-mail:* president@afghanistangov.org (office). *Website:* www.president.gov.af (office).

KASAHARA, Yukio, BEng; Japanese business executive; b. 27 Jan. 1925, Tokyo; m. Yuri Tsumura 1983; ed Tokyo Univ.; joined Nippon Mining Co. 1949, mem. Bd of Dirs 1974, Man. Dir and Gen. Man. Petroleum Group 1976, Sr Man. Dir and Gen. Man. Petroleum Group 1979, Exec. Vice-Pres. and Gen. Man. of Planning and Devt Group and Petroleum Group 1981, Pres. and Rep. Dir 1983–89, Chair. and Rep. Dir (co. renamed Japan Energy Corpn 1993) June 1989, then Adviser. *Leisure interests:* reading, model railroading. *Address:* c/o Japan Energy Corporation, 2-10-1, Toranomon, Minato-ku, Tokyo 105-8407; 3–6–1201, Okubo 2-chome, Shinjuku-ku, Tokyo 169, Japan (home). *Telephone:* (3) 202-3119 (home).

KASAI, Yoshiyuki, MEconSc; Japanese transport industry executive; *Chairman, Central Japan Railway Company (JR Central);* ed Faculty of Law, Univ. of Tokyo, Univ. of Wis., USA; joined Japanese Nat. Railways (JNR) 1963, becoming Deputy Dir-Gen. –1987, apptd Pres. and Rep. Dir Central Japan Railway Company (JR Central) (following JNR privatization) 1987, currently Chair.; Visting Prof., Research Center for Advanced Science and Tech., Univ. of Tokyo; Univ. of Wis. Distinguished Alumnus Award 1999. *Publications:* Japanese National Railways: Its Break-up and Privatization 2003. *Address:* Central Japan Railway Company, 1-1-4 Meiki, Nakamura-ku, Nagoya 450-6101, Japan (office). *Telephone:* (5) 2564-2413 (office). *Fax:* (5) 2587-1300 (office), (3) 5255-6780 (office). *E-mail:* kasai.secretary@rcast.u-tokyo.ac.jp. *Website:* www.jr-central.co.jp (office).

KASAL, Jan; Czech politician; *Vice-Chairman, Poslanecká sněmovna (Chamber of Deputies);* b. 6 Nov. 1951, Nove Město na Moravě; m. Jaroslava Ranecká; three c.; ed Czech Tech. Univ.; ind. research worker in hydraulic systems 1975–90; mem. Czechoslovak People's Party 1986–89; First Vice-Chair. Christian Democratic Union–Czechoslovak People's Party 1992–99,

2001–06, Chair. 1999–2001; mem. Poslanecká sněmovna (Chamber of Deputies) 1990–, Vice-Chair. Poslanecká sněmovna 1990–98, 2002–; Pres. European Acad. for Democracy 1993–. *Leisure interests:* history, literature, music. *Address:* Poslanecká sněmovna (Chamber of Deputies), Parliament Buildings, Sněmovni 4, 118 26 Prague 1, Czech Republic (office). *Telephone:* (2) 57172095 (office). *Fax:* (2) 57173637 (office). *E-mail:* kasal@psp.cz (office). *Website:* www .psp.cz (office).

KASASBEH, Hamad al-, PhD; Jordanian economist and politician; *Minister of Finance;* b. 1956, Karak; ed Columbia Univ., USA; Econ. Researcher and Adviser, Cen. Bank of Jordan –1996; Gen. Man. Cities and Villages Devt Bank 1996–99; Sec.-Gen. Accounting Bureau 1999–2003, Sec.-Gen., Ministry of Finance 2003–07, Minister of Finance 2007–; fmr Lecturer, Univ. of Jordan; Chair. Jordanian Free Zones Corpn; Dir Royal Jordanian Airline. *Publications:* 14 publs in the field of finance. *Address:* Ministry of Finance, POB 85, Amman 11118, Jordan (office). *Telephone:* (6) 4636321 (office). *Fax:* (6) 4618528 (office). *E-mail:* info@mof.gov.jo (office). *Website:* www.mof.gov.jo (office).

KASATKINA, Natalya Dmitriyevna; Russian ballet dancer and choreographer; b. 7 June 1934, Moscow; d. of Dmitriy A. Kasatkin and Anna A. Kardashova; m. Vladimir Vasilyov 1956; one s.; ed Bolshoi Theatre Ballet School; with Bolshoi Theatre Ballet Company 1954–76, main roles including Frigia (Spartacus), Fate (Carmen), The Possessed (The Rite of Spring); Choreographer (with V. Vasilyov) of Vanina Vanini 1962, Geologists 1964, The Rite of Spring 1965, Tristan and Isolde 1967, Preludes and Fugues 1968, Our Yard 1970, The Creation of the World 1971, Romeo and Juliet 1972, Prozrienie 1974, Gayane 1977, Mayakovsky (opera) 1981, Adam and Eve (film ballet) 1982, The Magic Cloak 1982, The Mischiefs of Terpsichore 1984, Blue Roses for a Ballerina (film ballet) 1985, Pushkin 1986, The Faces of Love 1987, Petersburg's Twilights 1987, The Fairy's Kiss 1989, Don Quixote (film ballet) 1990, Sleeping Beauty 2004; TV Film: Choreographic Novels; Head (with V. Vasilyov); Moscow State Classical Ballet Theatre 1977–; wrote libretto and produced operas Peter I 1975, Così fan Tutte (with V. Vasilyov) 1978; choreographed (with V. Vasolyov) Spartacus (Khachaturian) 2002; State Prize of USSR 1976, People's Actress of RSFSR 1984. *Television:* Ballet Ballet, Bolshoi Legends. *Leisure interests:* drawing, cooking. *Address:* 103006 Moscow, Karetny Riad 5/10, Apt. 37, Russia. *Telephone:* (495) 299-95-24. *Fax:* (495) 921-31-27.

KASDAN, Lawrence Edward, BA, MA; American film director, screenwriter and producer; b. 14 Jan. 1949, Miami Beach, Fla; s. of Clarence Norman Kasdan and Sylvia Sarah Kasdan (née Landau); m. Meg Goldman 1971; two s.; ed Univ. of Mich.; copywriter W. B. Doner and Co. (advertising co.), Detroit 1972–75, Doyle, Dane Berbach, LA 1975–77; freelance screenwriter 1977–80; film dir, screenwriter, LA 1980–,; mem. Writers Guild, American West, Dirs Guild, American West; Clio awards for Advertising, Writers Guild Award for The Big Chill 1983, Distinguished Screenwriter Award, Austin Film Festival 2001, Laurel Award for Screen Writing Achievement, Writers Guild of America 2006. *Films include:* The Empire Strikes Back (co-writer) 1980, Continental Divide (writer) 1981, Raiders of the Lost Ark (writer) 1981, Body Heat (writer and dir) 1981, Return of the Jedi (co-screenwriter) 1982, The Big Chill (writer, dir and exec. producer) 1983, Silverado (writer, dir and producer) 1985, Cross My Heart (producer) 1987, The Accidental Tourist (screenplay, dir and producer) 1989, Immediate Family (exec. producer) 1989, I Love You to Death (dir) 1989, Grand Canyon (dir and writer, Golden Bear, Berlin Film Festival 1992) 1991, Jumpin' at the Boneyard (exec. producer) 1992, The Body Guard (writer and producer) 1992, Wyatt Earp (dir, co-producer, writer) 1994, French Kiss (dir) 1995, Home Fries (producer) 1998, Mumford (writer and dir) 1999, Dreamcatcher (screenplay and dir) 2003. *Address:* c/o CAA, 2000 Avenue of the Stars, Los Angeles, CA 90067, USA.

KASEL, Jean-Jacques, DenD; Luxembourg diplomatist; *Maréchal and Chef de Cabinet at the Court of the Grand Duke of Luxembourg;* b. 17 Jan. 1946, Luxembourg; m. Jacqueline Vandervorst; one s., two d.; ed Inst. d'Etudes Politiques, Paris; joined Foreign Ministry 1973, Embassy in Paris (also Deputy Perm. Rep. to OECD) 1976–79; Pvt. Sec. to Gaston Thorn 1979–81; Dir for Budget and Staff Regulation, Gen. Secr. EC Council 1981–84; Chargé, Special Missions, Perm. Mission of Luxembourg to EC 1984–86; Dir Political and Cultural Affairs, Foreign Ministry 1986–89; Amb. to Greece (resident in Luxembourg) 1989; Perm. Rep. to EU 1991–98, Chair. Perm. Reps Cttee of Council of Ministers of EU 1997–98; Perm. Rep. to NATO 1998–2003; Amb. to Belgium 1998; Maréchal at the Court of Grand Duke of Luxembourg and Chef de Cabinet 2002–; Grand-Croix Ordre Civil et Militaire d'Adolphe de Nassau, Grand Officier Ordre de la Couronne de Chêne, Officier Ordre de Mérite, Grand Croix Ordre de la Couronne (Belgium), Grand Croix Ordre de Léopold II (Belgium), Grand Croix Ordre du Phoenix (Greece), Grand Croix Ordre de Mérite (Italy), Grand Croix Ordre de Danebrog (Denmark), Grand Croix Ordre Infant Henrique (Portugal),Grand Croix Ordre Nat. (Romania), Grand Officier Mérite (Austria), Grand Officier Mérite (Sweden), Grand Officier Mérite (Norway), Grand Officier Faucon (Iceland), Grand Officier Mérite (Germany), Commdr Ordre de Mérite (France), Commdr Ordre de Mérite (Spain). *Leisure interests:* horseriding, tennis, skiing, cycling, gardening, the press. *Address:* Palais Grand-Ducal, Luxembourg, Luxembourg (office).

KASER, Michael Charles, MA, DLitt; British economist; b. 2 May 1926, London; s. of Joseph Kaser and Mabel Blunden; m. Elizabeth Anne Mary Piggford 1954; four s. one d.; ed King's Coll., Cambridge; with Econs Section Ministry of Works, London 1946–47; HM Foreign Service 1947–51, Second Sec., Moscow 1949; UN Econ. Comm. for Europe, Geneva 1951–63; Lecturer in Soviet Econs, Univ. of Oxford 1963–72, Chair. Faculty Bd 1974–76, mem. Gen. Bd of Faculties 1972–78, Chair. Advisory Council of Adult Educ. 1972–78, Univ. Latin Preacher 1982; Gov. Plater Coll., Oxford 1968–95, Gov. Emer.

1995–; Visiting Prof. of Econs, Univ. of Mich., USA 1966; Visiting Lecturer, European Inst. of Business Admin, Fontainebleau 1959–82, 1988–92, Univ. of Cambridge 1967–68, 1977–78, 1978–79; Reader in Econs and Professorial Fellow, St Antony's Coll., Oxford 1972–93, Sub-Warden 1986–87, Reader Emer. 1993–; Dir Inst. of Russian, Soviet and E European Studies, Univ. of Oxford 1988–93; Assoc. Fellow, Templeton Coll., Oxford 1983–; Visiting Faculty mem. Henley Man. Coll. 1987–2002; mem. Centre for Euro-Asian Studies, Univ. of Reading 1997–; Vice-Chair. Social Science Research Council Int. Activities Cttee 1980–84; Special Adviser House of Commons Foreign Affairs Cttee 1985–87; Chair. Co-ordinating Council, Area Studies Asscns 1986–88 (mem. 1980–93, 1995), Wilton Park Academic Council, FCO 1986–92 (mem. 1985–2001); Pres. British Asscn of Slavonic and E European Studies 1988–91, Vice-Pres. 1991–93; Prin. Charlemagne Inst., Edin. 1993–94, Hon. Fellow, Divinity Faculty, Univ. of Edin. 1993–96; mem. Int. Social Science Council, UNESCO 1980–91, Council of Royal Inst. of Int. Affairs 1979–85, 1986–92 (mem. Meetings Cttee 1976-88, Chair. Cen. Asian and Caucasus Advisory Bd 1993–2004), Royal Econ. Soc. 1975–86, 1987–90, Council School of Slavonic and E European Studies 1981–87, Cttee Nat. Asscn for Soviet and E European Studies 1965–88, Steering Cttee Königswinter Anglo-German Confs 1969–90, Exec. Cttee Int. Econ. Asscn 1974–83, 1986– (Gen. Ed.), also various editorial bds, Anglo-Soviet, British-Mongolian, Anglo-Polish, British-Bulgarian, British-Yugoslav (Chair.), Canada-UK, British-Romanian and UK-Uzbek Round Tables, British-Polish Mixed Comm.; Sec. British Nat. Cttee of AIESEE 1988–93; Pres. British Asscn of Fmr UN Civil Servants 1994–2001 (Hon. Vice-Pres. 2001–), Albania Soc. of Britain 1992–95; Chair. Council, the Keston Inst., Oxford 1994–2002; Trustee, Foundation of King George VI and Queen Elizabeth, St Catharine's 1987–2006 (Chair. Academic Consultative Cttee 1987–2002), Sir Heinz Koeppler Trust 1987–2001 (Chair. 1992–2001); mem. Higher Educ. Funding Council for England Advisory Bd on E European Studies 1995–2000, CAFOD E Europe Cttee 2001–06; Hon. Prof., Inst. for German Studies, Univ. of Birmingham 1994–; Kt Order of St Gregory the Great 1990, Order of Naim Frashëri (Albania) 1995, Kt Order of Merit (Poland) 1999; Hon. DSocSc (Birmingham) 1996. *Publications:* Comecon: Integration Problems of the Planned Economies 1965, Planning in East Europe (with J. Zielinski) 1970, Soviet Economics 1970, Health Care in the Soviet Union and Eastern Europe 1976, Economic Development for Eastern Europe 1968, Planning and Market Relations (with R. Portes) 1971, The New Economic Systems of Eastern Europe (jointly) 1975, The Soviet Union since the Fall of Khrushchev (with A. H. Brown) 1975, Soviet Policy for the 1980s (with A. H. Brown) 1982, Economic History of Eastern Europe, Vols I–III (with E. A. Radice) 1985–86, Early Steps in Comparing East-West Economies (with E. A. G. Robinson) 1991, Reforms in Foreign Economic Relations of Eastern Europe and the Soviet Union 1991, The Macroeconomics of Transition in Eastern Europe (with D. Morris) 1992, The Central Asian Economies after Independence (with S. Mehrotra) 1992, 1996, Education and Economic Change in Eastern Europe and the Former Soviet Union (with D. Phillips) 1992, Cambridge Encyclopedia of Russia and the Former Soviet Union (jtly) 1994, Privatization in the CIS 1996, The Economies of Kazakstan and Uzbekistan 1997, The Prudential Management of Hydrocarbon Revenues in Resource-Rich Transition Economies (co-author) 2006; articles in econ. and Slavic journals. *Address:* 31 Capel Close, Oxford, OX2 7LA, England (home). *Telephone:* (1865) 515581 (home). *Fax:* (1865) 515581 (home). *E-mail:* michael .kaser@economics.ox.ac.uk (office).

KASHIO, Kazuo; Japanese business executive; b. 9 Jan. 1929, Tokyo; ed Nihon Univ.; currently Pres. and CEO Casio Computer Co. Ltd, Tokyo. *Address:* Casio Computer Company Ltd, 6-2, Hon-machi 1-chome, Shibuya-ku, Tokyo 151-8543, Japan (office). *Telephone:* (3) 5334-4111 (office). *Website:* www.casio.co.jp (office).

KASHIO, Toshio; electronics industry executive; *Chairman, Casio Computer Company Ltd;* b. Tokyo; began career working for Kashio Seisakusho (now Casio Computer Co. Ltd) f. by brother Tadao Kashio 1946, fmr Pres. now Chair.; introduced first electric calculator 1957; Lifetime Achievement Award, Consumer Electronics Asscn 2000. *Address:* Casio Computer Company Ltd, 1-6-2 Hon-machi, Shibuya-ku, Tokyo 151-8543, Japan (office). *Telephone:* (3) 5334-4111 (office). *Fax:* (3) 5334-4669 (office). *Website:* www.casio.co.jp (office).

KASHLEV, Yuriy Borisovich, DHist; Russian diplomatist; *First Vice-Rector, Diplomatic Academy of the Ministry of Foreign Affairs;* b. 13 April 1934, Tejen; s. of Boris and Olga Kashlev; m. 1957; one s. one d.; ed Moscow Inst. of Int. Relations; fmr mem. CPSU; worked for Soviet Cttee for Youth Orgs. 1961–65; CPSU Cen. Cttee 1965–68; Counsellor, USSR Ministry of Foreign Affairs 1968–70; served in Embassy, UK 1970–71, Counsellor, Head of Sector, Deputy Head, Dept of Information, Ministry of Foreign Affairs 1971–78, Head Dept 1982–86; Sec.-Gen. USSR Comm. for UNESCO 1978–82; Head Dept of Humanitarian and Cultural Relations 1986–89, Deputy First Vice-Minister, USSR Ministry of Foreign Affairs 1986–90; mem. or head of Soviet dels to CSCE confs Geneva, Berne, Vienna, Paris; Russian Amb. to Poland 1990–96; Rector and Prof., Diplomatic Acad. of the Ministry of Foreign Affairs 1996–2000, First Vice-Rector 2001–; 11 state awards (orders and medals), from USSR, Mongolia, Poland and Bulgaria. *Publications:* Détente in Europe: from Helsinki to Madrid, International Information Exchange, After Fourteen Thousand Wars, Mass Media and International Relations, Ideological Struggle or Psychological War, Information and PR in International Relations, Manyfaced Diplomacy: Confessions of an Ambassador, The Helsinki Process 1975–2005: Lights and Shadows through the Eyes of a Participant 2005, Information, Mass Communication and international relations 2005; other books on int. affairs. *Leisure interests:* tennis, journalism. *Address:* Diplomatic Academy of the Ministry of Foreign Affairs, Ostozhenka str. 53/2, 119021 Moscow, Russia (office); Dolgorukowskaya Str. 22, App. 38, Moscow (home). *Telephone:* (495) 973-07-74 (also fax) (home); (495) 245-39-43 (office). *Fax:*

(495) 244-18-78 (office). *E-mail:* yuri.kashlev@dipacademy.ru (office). *Website:* www.dipacademy.ru/english (office).

KASICH, John R., BA; American fmr politician; *Chairman, New Century Project;* b. 13 May 1952, McKees Rocks, Pa; ed Ohio State Univ.; Admin. Asst, Ohio State Senate 1975–77; mem. Ohio Legislature 1979–82; mem. 98th–104th Congress from 12th Ohio Dist, Washington 1983–2001, mem. Nat. Security Cttee, mem. House Budget Cttee, then Chair.; Chair. New Century Project, Columbus, Ohio 2001–; currently Man. Dir, Investment Banking Div. Lehman Brothers; host, FoxNews current affairs TV show Heartland with John Kasich; Guest Lecturer, Fisher Coll. of Business, Ohio State Univ.; fmr Guest Fellow, George Bush School of Govt and Public Service, Texas A&M Univ., Annenberg School for Communication, Univ. of Pennsylvania. *Publications:* Courage is Contagious 1999, Stand for Something 2006. *Address:* New Century Project, 2021 East Dublin-Granville Road, Suite 161, Columbus, OH 43229, USA. *Telephone:* (614) 785-1600. *Fax:* (614) 785-1611. *Website:* www.newcenturyproject.org; johnkasich.com.

KAŠICKÝ, František; Slovak government official and diplomatist; *Permanent Representative, NATO;* b. 18 Nov. 1968, Gelnica; m.; two c.; ed Mil. Pedagogical Acad., Bratislava, Akademie der Bundeswehr fur Information und Kommunikation, Strausberg, Germany; Sr Officer for Social Man., Ministry of Defence 1991–93; Ed. Specialist, OBRANA (mil. newspaper) 1993–98, also Press Sec. for Minister of Defence; Asst Sec. of State, Ministry of Defence 1998–2000; Defence Ministry Spokesman, Office Dir and Dir of Communications Dept 2001–03; Dir Mil. Defence Intelligence 2003–04; Sec. Parl. Cttee of Nat. Council for Defence and Security, Special Control Cttee of Nat. Council for Control of Activities of Nat. Security Authority, Cttee of Nat. Council for Control of Information Tech. 2004–06; Minister of Defence 2006–08 (resgnd); Perm. Rep. to NATO, Brussels May 2008–; mem. Direction-Social Democracy (Smer-Sociálna demokracia). *Address:* Office of the Permanent Representative of Slovakia, blvd Léopold III, 1110 Brussels, Belgium (office). *Telephone:* (2) 707-41-11 (office). *Fax:* (2) 707-45-79 (office). *E-mail:* natodoc@hq.nato.int (office). *Website:* www.nato.int (office).

KASIM, Marwan al-, PhD; Jordanian politician; b. 12 May 1938, Amman; ed Eastern Michigan, Columbia and Georgetown Univs, USA; joined Ministry of Foreign Affairs 1962; Consul-Gen., New York 1964–65; Deputy Dir of Protocol 1966; Political Officer, Embassy in Beirut 1967–68, in USA 1968–72; Sec. to Crown Prince Hassan 1972–75; Dir-Gen. Royal Hashemite Court 1975–76, Chief 1988; Minister of State 1976; Minister of Supply 1977–79; Minister of State for Foreign Affairs 1979–80, Minister of Foreign Affairs 1980–83; Deputy Prime Minister and Minister of Foreign Affairs 1988–90; Jordanian, Syrian, Mexican, Lebanese, Chinese and Italian decorations. *Address:* c/o Ministry of Foreign Affairs, Amman, Jordan.

KASIRER, Nicholas, FRSC, BCL, LLB, DEA, BA; Canadian professor of law and university administrator; *Dean, Faculty of Law, McGill University;* ed Univ. of Toronto, McGill Univ., Univ. Paris I, France; law clerk to Hon. Jean Beetz, Supreme Court of Canada, Ottawa 1987–88; Asst Prof., Faculty of Law, McGill Univ., Montréal 1989–94, Assoc Prof. 1994–2000, Prof. 2000–, James McGill Prof. 2002–, Dean, Faculty of Law 2003–, Dir Québec Research Centre for Pvt. and Comparative Law 1996–2003; mem. Editorial Bd Canadian Journal of Law and Society, The Philanthropist, The Estates and Trusts Reports, Canadian Legal Education Annual Review; mem. Québec Bar; American Soc. of Comparative Law, Hessel Yntema Award in Comparative Law; Prix de la Fondation du Barreau, Law Students' Asscn John W. Durnford Teaching Excellence Award, McGill Alumni Asscn David Johnston Medal. *Address:* Office of the Dean, Faculty of Law, Chancellor Day Hall, Room 15, 3644 Peel Street, Montréal, PQ H3A 1W9, Canada (office). *Telephone:* (514) 398-6604 (office). *Fax:* (514) 398-4659 (office). *E-mail:* nicholas.kasirer@mcgill.ca (office). *Website:* people.mcgill.ca/nicholas.kasirer (office).

KASIT, Piromya, BSc, MSc; Thai diplomatist and politician; *Minister of Foreign Affairs;* b. 15 Dec. 1944, Bangkok; m. Chintana Piromya (née Wajanabukka); one s. (died 1994) one d.; ed Chulalongkorn Univ., Georgetown Univ., Inst. of Social Studies, The Hague, Nat. Defence Coll.; Third Sec., Dept of Int. Orgs, Ministry of Foreign Affairs 1968, News Analysis Div., Dept of Information 1969–72, SEATO Div., Dept of Int. Orgs 1972–75; Third, then Second Sec., Embassy in Brussels and Perm. Mission to EU 1975–79; Second Sec., Int. Econ. Affairs Div., Dept of Econ. Affairs, Ministry of Foreign Affairs, then First Sec., Office of the Dir-Gen. 1979–81, Dir Econ. Information Div. 1983–84, Deputy Dir-Gen. 1985–88, Dir Commerce and Industry Div., ASEAN Dept 1981–83, Dir Policy and Planning Div., Office of the Perm. Sec., Dir-Gen. Dept of Int. Orgs 1988–91; Amb. to USSR (also accred to Mongolia) 1991, to Russian Fed. 1991–93, to Indonesia (also accred to Papua New Guinea) 1994–96, to Germany 1997–2001, to Japan 2001–04, to USA 2004–08; Minister of Foreign Affairs 2008–; Commdr (Fourth Class), Most Exalted Order of the White Elephant 1974, Kt Commdr (Second Class) 1987, Kt Grand Cross (First Class) 1991, Kt Grand Cordon (Special Class) 1999, Commdr (Third Class) Most Noble Order of the Crown of Thailand 1977, Kt Commdr (Second Class) 1982, Kt Grand Cross (First Class) 1988, Kt Grand Cordon (Special Class) 1994, Grand Cross of the Order of Merit (Germany) 2001, Grand Cordon of the Order of the Rising Sun (Japan) 2004; Chakrabarti Mala Medal 1993. *Address:* Ministry of Foreign Affairs, Thanon Sri Ayudhya, Bangkok 10400, Thailand (office). *Telephone:* (2) 643-5000 (office). *Fax:* (2) 225-6155 (office). *E-mail:* information@mfa.go.th (office). *Website:* www.mfa.go.th (office).

KASKARELIS, Vassilis, BSc, LLB; Greek diplomatist; *Permanent Representative, European Union;* b. 26 Nov. 1948, Athens; m. Anna Kaskarelis; two s.; ed Univ. of Thessalonoki, Univ. of Athens; Embassy Attaché, Ministry of Foreign Affairs 1974; Third Sec. in Ankara, Turkey 1976; Consul in Venice, Italy 1979; First. Sec. in Nicosia, Cyprus 1984; Head of Mil. Mission in Berlin, Germany 1987, Consul-Gen. in Greece 1990; Deputy Dir. Turkish Desk, Ministry of Foreign Affairs 1991, Minister Plenipotentiary, Head of Cabinet of Sec.-Gen. 1993; Deputy Perm. Rep. to UN, New York 1995; Perm. Rep. to NATO, Brussels 2000–04; currently Perm. Rep. to EU, Brussels; Grand Commdr, Order of the Phoenix (Greece), Chevalier, Ordre nat. du Mérute. *Address:* Office of the Permanent Representative, rue Montoyer 25, 1000 Brussels, Belgium (office). *Telephone:* (2) 551-56-37 (office). *Fax:* (2) 512-79-12 (office). *E-mail:* brp.kaskarelis@rp-grece.be (office). *Website:* www.greekembassy-press.be (office).

KASMIN, John; British art dealer; *Managing Director, Kasmin Ltd;* b. 24 Sept. 1934, London; s. of David Kosminsky and Vera D'Olzewski; m. Jane Nicholson 1959 (divorced 1975); two s.; ed Magdalen Coll. School, Oxford; worked for Gallery One, Soho, London; Dir New London Gallery, Bond St 1960–61; f. Kasmin Gallery, Man. Dir Kasmin Ltd 1961–, Knoedler Kasmin Ltd 1977–92. *Leisure interests:* literature, art, walking, museums. *Address:* Kasmin Ltd, 34 Warwick Avenue, London, W9 2PT, England. *Fax:* (20) 7289-0746.

KASPAROV, Garry Kimovich; Russian-Armenian fmr chess player and political activist; *Leader, United Civil Front;* b. (Garry Weinstein), 13 April 1963, Baku, Azerbaijan SSR; s. of the late Kim Weinstein and of Klara Kasparova; m. 1st Maria Arapova (divorced); one d.; m. 2nd Yulia Vovk 1996; one s.; ed Azerbaijan Pedagogical Inst. of Foreign Languages; started playing chess in 1967; Azerbaijan Champion 1976; USSR Jr Champion 1976; Int. Master 1978, Int. Grandmaster 1980; World Jr Champion 1980; won USSR Championship 1981, subsequently replacing Anatolii Karpov (q.v.) at top of world ranking list; won match against Viktor Korchnoi, challenged Karpov for World Title in Moscow Sept. 1985, the match being adjourned due to the illness of both players; won rescheduled match to become the youngest-ever world champion in 1985; successfully defended his title against Karpov 1986, 1987, 1990; series of promotional matches in London Feb. 1987; won Times World Championship against Nigel Short 1993; stripped of title by World Chess Fed. 1993; winner Oscar Chess Prize 1982–83, 1985–89, World Chess Cup 1989; highest-ever chess rating of over 2800 1992–; f. Professional Chess Asscn (PCA) 1993; won PCA World Championship against V. Anand 1995, lost title against V. Kramnik 2000; won match against Deep Blue computer 1996, lost 1997; defeated in four-game match of rapid chess against Karpov, New York 2002; retd from professional chess 2005; Deputy Leader Democratic Party of Russia 1990–91; f. The Kasparov Foundation, Moscow; actively promotes use of chess in schools as an educational subject; f. Kasparov Int. Chess Acad.; Founder and Leader United Civil Front 2005–; Order of Red Banner of Labour. *Publications:* New World Chess Champion 1985, The Test of Time 1986, Child of Change (with Donald Trelford) 1987, London-Leningrad Championship Games 1987, Unlimited Challenge 1990, How Life Imitates Chess 2007. *Leisure interests:* history (new chronology), politics, computers, literature, walking, weight training, swimming, rowing, most sports. *Address:* 119002 Moscow, Gagarinskii per. 26 office 3, (office); 119002 Moscow, Gagarinskii per. 26/12, Russia (home). *Telephone:* (499) 241-16-92 (office); (499) 241-82-80 (home). *Fax:* (499) 241-16-92 (office); (499) 241-95-96 (home). *E-mail:* maiavia@dol.ru (office). *Website:* www.rufront.ru (office).

KASPER, HE Cardinal Walter Josef, DTheol; German ecclesiastic and Catholic theologian; *President, Pontifical Council for Promoting Christian Unity;* b. 5 March 1933, Heidenheim/Brenz; s. of Josef Kasper and Theresia Bacher; ed Univs of Tübingen and Munich; ordained priest 1957; Prof. of Dogmatic Theology, Univ. of Münster 1964–70, Univ. of Tübingen 1970–89; Bishop of Rottenburg-Stuttgart 1989–99; Chair. Comm. for World Church Affairs 1991–99, Comm. for Doctrine of Faith, German Bishops Conf. 1996–99; Special Sec. Synod of Bishops 1985; mem. Heidelberger Akad. der Wissenschaften, Academia Scientiarum et Artium Europaea; mem. Congregation for the Doctrine of Faith, Pontifical Council for Culture 1998; Sec. Pontifical Council for Promoting Christian Unity 1999, Pres. 2001–; cr. Cardinal (Cardinal-Deacon of Ognissanti in Via Appia Nuova) 2001; Hon. Prof. (Eberhard-Karls Univ., Tübingen) 2001; Bundesverdienstkreuz; Dr hc (Catholic Univ. of America, Washington, DC) 1990, (St Mary's Seminary and Univ., Baltimore) 1991, (Marc Bloch Univ., Strasbourg 2000; Landesverdienstmedaille. *Publications:* Die Tradition in der Römischen Schule 1962, Das Absolute in der Geschichte 1965, Glaube und Geschichte 1970, Einführung in den Glauben 1972 (An Introduction to Christian Faith 1980), Jesus der Christus 1974, Der Gott Jesu Christi 1982, Theologie und Kirche 1987 (Theology and Church 1989), The Christian Understanding of Freedom and the History of Freedom in the Modern Era 1988, Wahrheit und Freiheit in der Erklärung über die Religionsfreiheit des II. Vatikanischen Konzils 1988, Lexikon für Theologie und Kirche 1993–2001, Theologie und Kirche II 1999. *Leisure interest:* climbing. *Address:* Pontificio Consiglio per l'Unita dei Cristiani, Via dell'Erba 1, 00193, Città del Vaticano, Rome, Italy. *Fax:* (06) 69885365 (office). *E-mail:* office@christianunity.va. *Website:* www.vaticano.va.

KASPSZYK, Jacek; Polish conductor; *Artistic and General Director, Polish National Opera;* b. 1952; ed Acad. of Music, Warsaw; conducting debut at age 14; debut Warsaw Nat. Opera 1975; Prin. Guest Conductor Deutsche Oper am Rhein, Düsseldorf 1976–77; Prin. Conductor Polish Nat. Radio Symphony Orchestra 1978–80, Music Dir 1980–82; debut Berlin Philharmonic and New York 1978, London (with Philharmonia) 1982; conducted French Nat., Stockholm Philharmonic, Bavarian Radio Symphony, Rotterdam, Czech Philharmonic Orchestras; conducted Detroit Opera and San Diego Symphony Orchestra 1982; concerts at La Scala, Milan 1982; Australian tour with Chamber Orchestra of Europe 1983; conducted UK orchestras 1982–; debut Henry Wood Promenade Concerts 1984; Prin. Conductor and Artistic Adviser

North Netherlands Orchestra 1991–95; Prin. Guest Conductor English Sinfonia 1992–; has toured with the Yomiuri Nippon Symphony and performed with Tokyo and Hong Kong Philharmonics, New Zealand, San Diego, Cincinnati, Winnipeg, Calgary Symphonies, and Detroit Opera; Prin. Guest Conductor Polish Philharmonic 1996-; Artistic and Musical Dir Polish National Opera, Warsaw 1998–2005, Artistic and Gen. Dir 2005–; III Prize, Karajan Competition 1977. *Music:* operas conducted include: Queen of Spades (Düsseldorf) 1977, Haunted Manor (Detroit) 1982, A Midsummer Night's Dream (Lyon) 1983, Eugene Onegin (Bordeaux) 1985, The Magic Flute (Opéra Comique, Paris and Stockholm) 1986, Seven Deadly Sins (Lyon) 1987, Die Fledermaus (Scottish Opera), Flying Dutchman (Opera North, UK) 1988, Barber of Seville (English Nat. Opera) 1992, Der Rosenkavalier (Warsaw) 1997, Don Giovanni (Warsaw) 1999, The Nutcracker (Zürich) 2000; many productions and recordings with Teatr Wielki, Warsaw, including performances in Luxembourg, Lvov, Beijing, Paphos, Japan (tour) and Bolshoi Theatre in Moscow; recordings with London Symphony Orchestra, London Philharmonic Orchestra, Royal Philharmonic, Philharmonic Orchestras, Warsaw Symphony Orchestra; several other recordings. *Address:* c/o The Music Partnership Limited, 41 Aldebert Terrace, London SW8 1BH, England (office); Teatr Wielki, pl. Teatralny 1, 00-950, Warsaw, Poland (office). *Telephone:* (20) 7840-9590 (office); (22) 6920500 (office). *Fax:* (20) 7735-7595 (office); (22) 8260423 (office). *E-mail:* office@musicpartnership.co.uk (office); office@teatrwielki.pl (office); dyrnacz@teatrwielki.pl (office). *Website:* www.musicpartnership.co.uk (office); www.teatrwielki.pl (office).

KASRASHVILI, Makvala; Georgian singer (soprano); *Artistic Director, Bolshoi Theatre Opera;* b. 13 March 1948, Kutaisi; d. of Nina Nanikashvili and Filimon Kasrashvili; m. (divorced); ed Tbilisi Conservatory; joined Bolshoi Co., Moscow 1968, Artistic Dir Bolshoi Theatre Opera Dept 2000–; has performed internationally, including Covent Garden, London, Metropolitan Opera, New York, Verona, Vienna State Opera; Grand Prix, Montreal Vocal Competition 1973, Merited Artist of Russian Fed. 1975, People's Artist of Georgian SSR 1980, Zakhar Paliashvili Georgian SSR State Prize 1983, People's Artist of the USSR 1986, State Prize of Russia 1998. *Roles include:* Lisa, Tatyana, Maria, Tosca, Lauretta, Donna Anna, Leonora, Aida, Turandot, Amelia. *Leisure interest:* car driving. *Address:* Bolshoi Theatre, Teatralnaya Pl. 1, Moscow, Russia. *Telephone:* (495) 200-58-00 (home). *Website:* www.bolshoi.ru (office).

KASRAWI, Farouk, MSc, MPhil; Jordanian diplomatist; b. 1942; ed American Univ. of Beirut, Lebanon, London Univ., UK, George Washington Univ., USA; with Embassy in London 1971–76; Counselor, Embassy in Washington DC 1977–81; Dir Int. Orgs Dept, Ministry of Foreign Affairs 1981–83; Deputy Perm. Rep. to UN, New York 1983–86; Perm. Rep. to UN Office and Specialized Agencies, Geneva 1986–90; Amb. to Japan 1990–2000, to Germany 2000–02; Pres. Jordan Inst. of Diplomacy 2002–05; Minister of Foreign Affairs April–Nov. 2005; Special Advisor on Foreign Affairs to HM King Abdullah II of Jordan 2006–. *Address:* Ministry of Foreign Affairs, POB 35217, Amman 11180, Jordan (office). *Telephone:* (6) 5735150 (office). *Fax:* (6) 5735163 (office). *E-mail:* inquiry@mfa.gov.jo (office). *Website:* www.mfa.gov.jo (office).

KASRIEL, Bernard L. M.; French business executive; *Managing Partner, LBO France;* b. 1946; three c.; ed Ecole Polytechnique, Institut Européen d'Admin des Affaires (INSEAD), Fontainbleau, Harvard Univ., USA; several man. positions with industrial cos 1970–77; joined Lafarge SA 1977, with Sanitaryware Div. 1977–81, Group Exec. Vice-Pres. 1982–87, Sr Exec. Vice-Pres. 1987–89, seconded as Pres. and COO Nat. Gypsum, Dallas, Tex. 1987–89, Group Man.-Dir 1989–95, Vice-Chair. and COO 1995–2003, CEO 2003–06, Vice-Chair. 2006; Man. Pnr, LBO France (pvt. equity fund) 2006–; mem. Bd of Dirs Lafarge SA, L'Oréal, Arkema, Nucor Corpn, Sonoco Products Co. 1995–; Chevalier de la Légion d'honneur 1996. *Leisure interests:* tennis. *Address:* LBO France, 148 rue de l'Université, 75007 Paris, France (office). *Telephone:* 1-40-62-77-67 (office). *Fax:* 1-40-62-75-55 (office). *E-mail:* elizabeth.oreilly@lbofrance.com (office). *Website:* www.lbofrance.com (office).

KASSEBAUM BAKER, Nancy Landon, MA; American fmr politician; b. 29 July 1932, Topeka; d. of Alfred (Alf) M. Landon and Theo Landon; three s. one d.; m. 2nd Howard Baker (q.v.) 1996; ed Univs of Kansas and Michigan; mem. Washington, DC staff of Senator James B. Pearson of Kansas 1975–76; Senator from Kansas 1978–97, Chair. Labor and Human Resources Cttee (first woman Chair. of major Senate Cttee), mem. several other Senate cttees including Foreign Relations Cttee; first Mary Louise Smith Chair in Women and Politics, Iowa State Univ. 1996–97; mem. Bd of Dirs Int. Crisis Group, Nat. Cttee on US-China Relations; mem. Advisory Bd Partnership for a Secure America, It's My Party Too PAC; fmr mem. Bd Trustees Robert Wood Johnson Foundation; fmr Co-Chair. The Presidential Appointee Initiative Advisory Bd, Brookings Inst.; mem. Comm. for Africa 2005; Republican; Hon. Chair. Vital Voices Global Partnership; Benjamin Rush Medal, William and Mary Law School 2004. *Address:* 2750 Z Ave, Burdick, KS 66838-9534, USA.

KASSEM, Abdul-Rauf al-, DArch; Syrian architect and politician; b. 1932, Damascus; ed Damascus Univ. School of Arts, Istanbul Univ., Turkey and Geneva Univ., Switzerland; teacher of architecture, School of Fine Arts Damascus, Dean 1964–70, Head, Architecture Dept, School of Civil Engineering Damascus Univ. 1970–77, Rector 1977–79; concurrently engineer 1964–77; Gov. of Damascus 1979–80; elected mem. Baath party Regional Command Dec. 1979, Cen. Command of Progressive Nat. Front April 1980; Prime Minister 1980–87; mem. Higher Council for Town Planning 1968–; mem. Nat. Union of Architects' Perm. Comm. on Town Planning 1975–; Hon. Prof. Geneva Univ. 1975–. *Address:* c/o Office of the Prime Minister, Damascus, Syria.

KASSOMA, António Paulo; Angolan politician; *Prime Minister;* b. 6 June 1951, Luanda; s. of Paulo Kassoma and Laurinda Katuta; mil. techniques instructor 1975; Tech. Dir Base Central de Reparações 1976–78; Vice Minister of Defence for Armament and Technique 1978–79, of Transports and Communication 1988–89; Minister of Territory Admin 1991–92; Sr Officer, Angolan Armed Forces 2001–; mem. People's Movt for Liberation of Angola (MPLA) 2003–; Gov. Huambo prov. 2004–08; Prime Minister of Angola 2008–. *Address:* Office of the Prime Minister, Luanda, Angola.

KASTEN, Robert (Bob) Walter, Jr., BA; American fmr politician; *President, Kasten & Company;* b. 19 June 1942, Milwaukee, Wis.; s. of Robert W. Kasten and Mary Kasten (née Ogden); m. Eva J. Nimmons 1986; one d.; ed Univ. of Arizona and Columbia Univ., New York; with Genesco, Nashville, Tenn. 1966–68; Dir and Vice-Pres. Gilbert Shoe Co., Thiensville, Wis. 1968–75; mem. Wis. State Senate 1972–75, mem. Jt Finance Cttee 1973–75, Chair. Jt Survey Cttee on Tax Exemptions 1973–80; Designee, Eagleton Inst. of Politics 1973; mem. US House of Reps from Wis. 9th Dist 1975–79, mem. Govt Operations Cttee, Small Businesses Cttee, Appropriations, Budget, Commerce, Science and Transportation Cttee; Alt. del. Republican Nat. Convention 1972, del. 1976, Co-Chair. 1988; Senator from Wis. 1980–93; Founder and Pres. Kasten & Co (consulting firm), Washington, DC 1993–; Sr Assoc., Center for Strategic and Int. Studies, Washington, DC 1993–. *Address:* Kasten & Co., 1629 K Street, NW, Washington, DC 20006, USA. *Telephone:* (202) 223-9151 (office). *E-mail:* kastenco@aol.com (office).

KASTNER, Elliott; American film producer; b. 7 Jan. 1933, New York; s. of Jack Kastner and Rose Kastner; m. Tessa Kennedy; four s. one d. *Films include:* Harper (The Moving Target), Kaleidoscope 1965, The Bobo, Laughter in the Dark, Night of the Following Day, Where Eagles Dare 1968, The Walking Stick, A Severed Head, When Eight Bells Toll, Tam Lin, Villain, X Y and Zee, The Nightcomers, Big Truck and Poor Clare, Face to the Wind, Fear is the Key, The Long Goodbye, Cops and Robbers, Jeremy, 11 Harrowhouse, Spot, Rancho Deluxe, 92 in the Shade, Farewell My Lovely, Russian Roulette, Breakheart Pass, The Missouri Breaks, The Swashbuckler, A Little Night Music, Equus, Black Joy, The Stick-Up, The Medusa Touch, The Big Sleep, Absolution, Golden Girl, Yesterday's Hero, North Sea Hijack, The First Deadly Sin, Death Valley, Man Woman and Child, Oxford Blues, Garbo Talks, Nomads, White of the Eye, Heat, Angel Heart, Zits, The Blob, Jack's Back, Never on Tuesday, Zombie High, A Chorus of Disapproval, Homeboy, The Last Party, Love is All There Is, Sweet November, Opal. *Address:* Cinema Seven Productions Ltd, Pinewood Studios, Iver Heath, Iver, Bucks., SL0 0NH, England.

KASTNER, Marc A., MS, PhD; American (b. Canadian) physicist and academic; *Donner Professor of Science and Head, Department of Physics, Massachusetts Institute of Technology;* b. 20 Nov. 1945, Toronto; m.; two d.; ed Univ. of Chicago; Research Fellow, Harvard Univ. 1972–73; Asst Prof. of Physics, MIT, Cambridge, MA 1973–77, Assoc. Prof. 1977–83, Head, Dept of Physics, Div. of Atomic Condensed Matter and Plasma Physics 1983–87, Prof. of Physics 1983–89, Asst Dir, MIT Consortium for Superconducting Electronics 1989–92, Donner Prof. of Science 1989–, Head, Dept of Physics 1998–; Dir NSF Materials Research Science and Eng Center, Center for Materials Science and Eng 1993–98; Dir, Brookhaven Science Associates 2000–; Chair. several confs and cttees; mem. Nat. Research Council Solid State Sciences Cttee 1995–2001; Fellow Hertz Foundation, American Physical Soc., AAAS; American Physical Soc. Oliver E. Buckley Prize 2000. *Address:* Department of Physics, Massachusetts Institute of Technology, Room 6-113, 77 Massachusetts Avenue, Cambridge, MA 02139-4301, USA (office). *Telephone:* (617) 253-4801 (office). *Fax:* (617) 253-8554 (office). *E-mail:* mkastner@mit.edu (office). *Website:* web.mit.edu/physics/facultyandstaff/marc_kastner.html (office).

KASTRUP, Dieter; German diplomatist (retd); *Chairman, Stiftung Erinnerung, Verantwortung und Zukunft;* b. March 1937, Bielefeld; m.; two c.; ed Univ. of Cologne; Third Sec. to First Sec., Embassy in Tehran 1967–71, Counsellor, then Deputy Div. Head, Ministry of Foreign Affairs, Bonn 1971–75, served in Embassy in Washington, DC 1975–78, Perm. Rep., Consulate-Gen., Houston, Tex. 1978–80, Head Div., Ministry of Foreign Affairs 1980–85, Head Directorate 1985–88, Dir-Gen. 1988–91, State Sec. 1991–95; Amb. to Italy 1995–98; Perm. Rep. to UN, New York 1998–2001; Foreign and Security Policy Adviser to Fed. Chancellor 2002; currently Chair. Stiftung Erinnerung, Verantwortung und Zukunft (Remembrance, Responsibility and Future Fund Foundation). *Address:* Stiftung Erinnerung, Verantwortung und Zukunft, Markgrafenstrasse 12–14, 10969 Berlin, Germany. *Telephone:* (30) 25929780. *Fax:* (30) 25929742. *E-mail:* info@stiftung-evz.de. *Website:* www.fonds-ez.de.

KASURI, Khurshid Mehmoud, BA, DPhil; Pakistani politician; b. 1941, Lahore; s. of Mahmud Ali Kasuri; ed Punjab Univ., Univs of Cambridge and Oxford, UK; fmr Sec.-Gen. Tehrik-e-Istiqlal; first Sec.-Gen. People's Democratic Alliance 1990–93; Fed. Minister for Parl. Affairs, Interim Govt 1991–93; mem. Pakistan Muslim League 1997–; mem. Nat. Ass. 1997–; Minister of Foreign Affairs 2002–07, also of Law, Justice and Human Rights 2002–04; cand. in parl. elections 2008; mem. Nat. Security Council. *Address:* c/o Ministry of Foreign Affairs, Constitution Avenue, Islamabad, Pakistan. *Telephone:* (51) 9210335.

KASYANOV, Mikhail Mikhailovich; Russian politician; *Leader, Russian People's Democratic Union;* b. 8 Dec. 1957, Solntsevo, Moscow Oblast; ed Moscow Inst. of Automobile Transport; held sr positions at RSFSR State Planning Comm., then Ministry of Econs 1981–90; Chief of Section for Foreign Econ. Relations, Russian State Cttee for Econs 1990–91; Head, Dept for Foreign Econ. Relations, Ministry of Finance 1991–93, Head, Dept of Overseas Credits 1993–95, Deputy Minister of Finance 1995–99, First Deputy

Minister, then Minister 1999–2000; main negotiator with Western financial orgs on questions of Russian liabilities; Deputy Man. for Russian Fed., EBRD 1999; First Deputy Prime Minister Jan. 2000, Acting Chair. of Govt, then Chair. of Govt (Prime Minister) 2000–04; mem. Presidium of Russian Govt 1999–2004, Security Council 1999–2004; f. MK-Analytics (consultancy) 2005; currently Leader, Russian People's Democratic Union; barred by Cen. Election Comm. of Russia from being cand. in presidential election on grounds of alleged forged signatures in support of him 2008. *Address:* Russian People's Democratic Union (Rossiiskii narodno-demokraticheski soyuz), 117279 Moscow, ul. Profsoyuznaya 93, korp. 4, Russia (office). *Telephone:* (495) 429-61-70 (office). *Fax:* (495) 429-63-10 (office). *E-mail:* newtypeparty@mail.ru (office). *Website:* nardemsoyuz.ru (office); kasyanov.ru.

KATAINEN, Jyrki, MScS; Finnish politician; *Deputy Prime Minister and Minister of Finance;* b. 14 Oct. 1971, Siilinjärvi; m. Mervi Katainen; mem. Siilinjärvi Municipal Council 1993–; Vice-Chair. Regional Council of Pohjois-Savo 1994–95; mem. Parl. (Finnish Nat. Coalition Party—Kokoomus) 1999–, Vice-Chair. Kokoomus Youth League 1994–95, Vice-Chair. Kokoomus 2001–04, Chair. 2004–; Chair. Cttee for the Future 2003–; mem. Finnish Del. to W European Union Parl. Ass. 2004–; Deputy mem. Finnish Del. to OSCE Parl. Ass. 2003–; mem. Admin. Bd Finnish Broadcasting Corpn 2003–; Deputy Prime Minister and Minister of Finance 2007–; named among World Econ. Forum's Global Leaders for Tomorrow 2003. *Address:* Ministry of Finance, Snellmaninkatu 1, PO Box 28, 00023 Helsinki, Finland (office). *Telephone:* (9) 16033004 (office). *Fax:* (9) 16034712 (office). *E-mail:* jyrki.katainen@vm.fi (office). *Website:* www.vm.fi (office); www.jyrkikatainen.fi (office).

KATANANDOV, Sergey Leonidovich; Russian politician; *Head of the Republic of Karelia;* b. 21 April 1955, Petrozavodsk; m.; two s.; ed Petrozavodsk State Univ., NW Acad. of State and Municipal Service; worked as Head of Sector, Sr Engineer, Petrozavodskstroi 1977–91; mem. Petrozavodsk City Exec. Cttee, Chair. City Soviet 1991–98, Mayor of Petrozavodsk 1994–98; elected Chair. Karelian Govt 1998–2002; Head of the Repub. of Karelia 2002–; Merited Worker of Nat. Economy of Repub. of Karelia 1995, Order of Honour of Russian Fed. 2000, Medal of Merits 2004. *Publications include:* articles in Russian and Finnish journals and newspapers. *Leisure interests:* fishing, hunting, swimming, reading. *Address:* Government of Karelia, Lenina prosp. 19, Petrozavodsk 185020, Karelia (office); Andropova av. 30, Petrozavodsk, Karelia, Russia. *Telephone:* (8142) 79-93-00 (office). *Fax:* (8142) 79-93-91 (office). *E-mail:* government@karelia.ru (office). *Website:* www.gov.karelia.ru.

KATAYAMA, Mikio; Japanese business executive; *President and COO, Sharp Corporation;* b. 1958; ed Univ. of Tokyo; joined Sharp Corpn 1981, Group Gen. Man. Liquid Crystal Display (LCD) Div. 2002, Dir 2003–, Exec. Dir 2005–, Corp. Sr Exec. Dir for LCD Business –2006, Pres. Sharp Corpn 2006–07, Pres. and COO 2007–. *Address:* Sharp Corpn, 22 Nagaike-cho, Abeno-ku, Osaka 545-8522, Japan (office). *Telephone:* (6) 6621-1221 (office). *Fax:* (6) 6627-1759 (office). *E-mail:* info@sharp.co.jp (office). *Website:* www.sharp.co.jp (office); sharp-world.com (office).

KATEGAYA, Eriya; Ugandan lawyer and politician; *First Deputy Prime Minister and Minister in Charge of East African Affairs;* b. 4 July 1945, Kyamate, Ntungamo Dist; ed Dar es Salaam Univ.; mem. Front for Nat. Salvation (FRONASA), political org. in exile in Tanzania during 1970s; Founder-mem. Uganda Patriotic Movt 1980; served with Nat. Resistance Army during armed struggle against govt of Milton Obote during 1980s; Sec. for Diplomatic Affairs and later Nat. Political Commissar, Nat. Resistance Movt (NRM); fmr Minister of Foreign Affairs, of Internal Affairs 2001–03; after removal from Cabinet worked as pvt. lawyer; Founder-mem. Forum for Democratic Change (political party) 2004; Deputy Prime Minister and Minister in Charge of East African Affairs 2006–, rejoined NRM; Chair. Council of Ministers, East African Community. *Address:* c/o East African Community, Arusha International Conference Centre Building, Kilimanjaro Wing, 5th Floor, POB 10965, Arusha, Tanzania (office). *E-mail:* eac@eachq.org (office).

KATEN, Karen L., BA, MBA; American pharmaceutical industry executive (retd); b. Kansas City, Mo.; ed Univ. of Chicago; work in sales at office supply co.; joined Pfizer in 1974, Vice-Pres. Marketing 1983–86, Vice-Pres. and Dir of Operations 1986–91, Vice-Pres. and Gen. Man. 1991–93, Exec. Vice-Pres. Pfizer Pharmaceuticals Group 1993, Pres. Pfizer US Pharmaceuticals 1995–2002, Sr Vice-Pres. 1999–2001, mem. Pfizer Leadership Team, Exec. Vice-Pres. Pfizer Inc. and Pres. Pfizer Global Pharmaceuticals 2001–05, Pres. Pfizer Human Health and Vice-Chair. Pfizer Inc. 2005–07 (retd), Chair. Pfizer Foundation 2006–08; Sr Advisor Essex Woodlands Health Ventures 2007–; mem. Bd of Dirs General Motors Corpn 1997–, Air Liquide, Harris Corpn, Home Depot 2007–; fmr mem. Pharmaceutical Research and Mfrs Asscn of America, Bd European Fed. of Pharmaceutical Industry Asscns, Int. Council JP Morgan Chase & Co., Council for US and Italy, Nat. Bd Trustees for the American Cancer Soc. Research Foundation, American Diabetes Asscn Bd of Corp. Advisors; mem. Bd of Dirs Nat. Alliance for Hispanic Health, Catalyst; mem. RAND Corpn Health Bd of Advisors; apptd to US-Japan Pvt. Sector/Govt Comm. and Nat. Infrastructure Cttee; fmr Treas. PhRMA (Pharmaceutical Research and Mfrs of America); mem. Healthcare Leadership Council; Trustee, Univ. of Chicago and mem. Council Grad. School of Business; Trustee, Economic Club of New York; ranked by Fortune magazine amongst 50 Most Powerful Women in Business in the US 1998–2001, (seventh) 2002, (sixth) 2003, (10th) 2004, (ninth) 2005, ranked by Business Week magazine's annually amongst 25 Top Executives, 11 separate Woman of the Year or similar awards from civic groups, nat. asscns and univs, Hallene Lecturer, Univ. of Illinois 2004, Dolan Lecturer, Fairfield Univ., Conn. 2004. *Address:* 425 East 58th Street, Apt 22–D, New York, NY 10022-2300.

KATES, Robert William, PhD; American geographer, academic and editor; b. 31 Jan. 1929, Brooklyn, New York; s. of Simon J. Kates and Helen G. Brener; m. Eleanor C. Hackman 1948; one s. two d.; ed Univ. of Chicago; Asst Prof., Grad. School of Geography, Clark Univ. 1962–65, Assoc. Prof. 1965–67, Prof. 1968–92, Univ. Prof. 1974–80, Univ. Prof. and Dir Alan Shawn Feinstein World Hunger Program 1986–92, Prof. Emer., Watson Inst. for Int. Studies 1992–; Visiting Research Scholar, Belfer Center for Science and Int. Affairs, Harvard Univ., now Sr Research Fellow; Exec. Ed. Environment Magazine; Dir Bureau of Resource Assessment and Land Use Planning, Univ. Coll., Dar es Salaam 1967–68; Hon. Research Prof., Univ. of Dar es Salaam 1970–71; Fellow, Woodrow Wilson Int. Center for Scholars 1979; mem. Asscn of American Geographers (Pres. 1993–94); Co-Convener, Initiative on Science and Tech. for Sustainability; mem. NAS, AAAS. *Publications include:* Risk Assessment of Environmental Hazard 1978, The Environment as Hazard (with Ian Burton and Gilbert F. White) 1978; co-ed. of 18 books; monographs and articles on environmental topics. *Address:* Initiative on Science and Technology for Sustainability, 33 Popple Point, Trenton, ME 04605, USA. *Telephone:* (207) 667-5450. *Fax:* (207) 664-0375. *E-mail:* rwkates@verizon.net.

KATHRADA, Ahmed, BA; South African fmr politician; *Chairman, Robben Island Museum Council;* b. 21 Aug. 1929, Schweizer Reneke; joined Young Communist League 1941; first imprisoned for participation in Passive Resistance 1946, subsequently imprisoned several times during 1950s and 1960s; first banned in 1954, accused in treason trial 1956–61, placed under house arrest Oct. 1962; sentenced to life imprisonment, Rivonia Trial 1964, unconditionally released 1989; rep. SA in World Fed. of Democratic Youth 1951–52; involved in Defiance Campaign 1952, Congress of People's Campaign 1955; Sec. first Free Mandela Cttee 1962; mem. African Nat. Congress (ANC) Del. to Talks about Talks with South African Govt 1990, Nat. Exec. Cttee ANC 1991–99, Internal Leadership Cttee of ANC, Head Public Relations Dept; MP Govt of Nat. Unity 1994–99; Parl. Counsellor in Office of Pres. 1994–99; Chair. Robben Island Museum Council; Chair. Ex-Political Prisoners' Cttee; Fellow, Mayibuye Centre, Univ. of Western Cape; Patron, Trauma Centre, Cape Town; Pravasi Bharatiya Samman, Ministry of Overseas Indian Affairs 2005. *Address:* Robben Island Museum, Private Bag, Robben Island, Cape Town 7400, South Africa. *Telephone:* (21) 4095100. *Fax:* (21) 4111059. *Website:* www.robben-island.org.za.

KATILI, John (Younis) Ario, DSc; Indonesian geologist, academic and politician; b. 9 June 1929, Gorontalo, Sulawesi; m. Iliana Syarifa Uno; one s. one d.; ed Univ. of Indonesia, Inst. of Tech., Bandung, Univ. of Innsbruck, Austria; fmr Prof. of Structural and Tectonic Geology, Head Dept of Geology and Dean Faculty of Mineral Tech., Inst. of Tech. Bandung (ITB); Vice-Pres. of ITB 1961; Deputy Chair. Indonesian Inst. of Sciences –1973; Dir-Gen. of Mines 1973-84, of Geology and Mineral Resources 1984–89; fmr Sr Adviser to State Minister of Research and Tech. and to Minister of Mines and Energy; fmr Vice-Chair. Indonesian Nat. Research Council; Vice-Speaker House of Reps (Parl.) and Vice-Chair. People's Consultative Ass. 1992–97; Amb. to Russian Fed., Turkmenistan, Kazakhstan and Mongolia 1999–2004; First Pres. Southeast Asia Union of Geological Sciences 1984; Vice-Pres. Indonesian Acad. of Sciences 1998; mem. Nat. Geographic Soc.; Foreign mem. Russian Acad. of Natural Sciences 2000; Fellow, Islamic Acad. of Sciences; Hon. mem. RGS, Indonesian Asscn of Geologists, Geological Soc. of Sweden, Royal Geological Soc. and Mining Soc. of the Netherlands; Commdr Ordre Nat. du Mérite 1988, Order of Orange Nassau 1995; Dr hc (Stockholm) 1988; Van Waterschoot van der Gracht Medal 1995. *Publications:* 12 books; over 150 scientific and policy papers in English and Indonesian. *Address:* c/o IAGI Secretariat, Mineral and Batubara Building, 6th Floor, No.10, Jakarta 12870, Indonesia (office).

KATIN, Peter Roy, FRAM, ARCM; British pianist and teacher; b. 14 Nov. 1930, London; s. of the late Jerrold Katin and Gertrude Katin; m. Eva Zweig 1954; two s.; ed Henry Thornton School, Royal Acad. of Music, Westminster Abbey; London debut, Wigmore Hall 1948; extensive concert tours in UK, Europe, Africa, Canada, USA and Far East; special interest in Chopin; recordings for Decca, EMI, Unicorn, Everest, Philips, CFP, Lyrita and Pickwick Int., Claudio, Olympia, Simax, Athene; Prof., RAM 1956–60, Univ. of Western Ont. 1978–84, Royal Coll. of Music 1992–2001; Founder Katin Centre for Advanced Piano Studies 1991, Katin Trio 1997; Pres. Camerata of London 1994–; Hon. DMus (De Montfort) 1994; Eric Brough Memorial Prize 1944, Chopin Arts Award (New York) 1977. *Leisure interests:* writing, tape-recording, theatre, reading, photography. *Address:* 41 First Avenue, Bexhill-on-Sea, East Sussex TN40 2PL, England (home). *Telephone:* (1424) 211167 (home). *E-mail:* rpmusic@btinternet.com (office); peter.katin@btinternet.com (home). *Website:* www.peterkatin.com.

KATO, Ryozo; Japanese diplomatist; b. 1941, Saitama Pref.; m. Hanayo Kato; three c.; ed Univ. of Tokyo; joined Ministry of Foreign Affairs 1965, Dir Security Affairs Div. 1981–84, Dir Treaties Div. 1984–87, Dir-Gen. Affairs Div. 1990–92, Deputy Dir N American Affairs Bureau 1992–94, Dir-Gen. Asian Affairs Bureau 1995–97, Dir-Gen. Foreign Policy Bureau 1997–99, Minister, Washington, DC 1987, Consul-Gen., San Francisco 1994, Deputy Minister for Foreign Affairs 1999–2001, Amb. to USA 2001–08. *Address:* Ministry of Foreign Affairs, 2-11-1, Shiba-Koen, Minato-ku, Tokyo 105-8519, Japan (office). *Telephone:* (3) 3580-3311 (office). *Fax:* (3) 3581-2667 (office). *E-mail:* webmaster@mofa.go.jp (office). *Website:* www.mofa.go.jp (office).

KATO, Susumu; Japanese business executive; *President and CEO, Sumitomo Corporation;* b. 21 May 1947, Kyoto; ed Kobe Univ.; joined Sumitomo Corpn 1970, Asst Man. Sumitomo Corpn of America, LA 1979–85, Asst Man.,

Rolled Steel Import-Export Dept 1985–89, Man. Sumitomo Corpn of America, Detroit 1989–96, Deputy Gen. Man. Steel Sheets Int. Trade Dept 1996–97, Gen. Man. 1997–99, Corp. Officer and Deputy Gen. Man., Iron and Steel Div. 1999–2000, Man., Personnel and Gen. Affairs Div. 2000–03, mem. Bd of Dirs 2000–, also Gen. Man. Corp. Planning and Co-ordination 2001–03, Man. Exec. Officer 2003–05, Sr Man. Exec. Officer 2005–07, Pres. and CEO Sumitomo Corpn of America, NY 2005–07, also Gen. Man. for the Americas 2005–07, Exec. Vice-Pres. Sumitomo Corpn, Tokyo 2007, Pres. and CEO 2007–. *Address:* Sumitomo Corpn, 8-11 Harumi 1-chome, Chuo-ku, Tokyo 104-8610, Japan (office). *Telephone:* (3) 5166-5000 (office). *E-mail:* info@sumitomocorp.co.jp (office). *Website:* www.sumitomocorp.co.jp (office).

KATO, Susumu, PhD; Japanese physicist and academic; *Professor Emeritus of Atmospheric Physics, Kyoto University;* b. 27 Aug. 1928, Saitama; s. of the late Nimpei Kato and Minoru Kato; m. Kyoko Kojo; ed Kyoto Univ.; Lecturer, Faculty of Eng, Kyoto Univ. 1955–61, Asst Prof., Ionosphere Research Lab. 1961–62, Assoc. Prof. 1964–67, Prof. 1967–81, Dir and Prof., Radio Atmospheric Science Centre 1981–92, Prof. Emer. 1992–; Research Officer, Upper Atmosphere Section, CSIRO, NSW, Australia 1962–64; Visiting Scientist, High Altitude Observatory, NCAR, Colo 1967–68, 1973–74; Visiting Prof., Dept of Meteorology, UCLA, LA 1973–74, Bandung Inst. of Tech., Indonesia 1994–97; Vice-Chair. Japan-Indonesia Science and Tech. Forum 1992–96; AGU Fellow 1991; Foreign Assoc. Nat. Acad. of Eng, USA 1995–; Fellow, Int. Inst. for Advanced Studies 1998; Tanakadate Prize 1959, Yamaji Science Prize 1974, Appleton Prize 1987, Hasegawa Prize 1987, Fujiwara Prize 1989, Japan Acad. Award 1989. *Publications:* Dynamics of the Upper Atmosphere 1980, Dinamika Atmosfer 1998; over 100 scientific papers on atmospheric tidal theory, observation of atmospheric waves by MST radar. *Leisure interests:* reading, music, jogging, swimming, Japanese calligraphy. *Address:* 22-15 Fujimidai, Otsu, Shiga Prefecture, 520-0846, Japan (home). *Telephone:* (77) 534-1177 (home). *Fax:* (77) 533-4013 (home). *E-mail:* kato@rish.kyoto-u.ac.jp (office).

KATOH, Nobuaki; Japanese business executive; *President and CEO, DENSO Corporation;* ed Keio Univ., Tokyo; joined DENSO Corpn in 1971, served as Gen. Man. Air-Conditioning Planning and Gen. Planning Depts, Man. Officer 2004–05, Pres. DENSO's European HQ 2005–07, Sr Man. Dir responsible for Corp. Center and Thermal Systems Business Group 2007–08, Pres. and CEO DENSO Corpn 2008–. *Address:* DENSO Corpn, 1-1 Showa-cho, Kariya, Aichi 448-8661, Japan (office). *Telephone:* (556) 25-5511 (office). *Fax:* (566) 25-4509 (office). *E-mail:* info@globaldenso.com (office). *Website:* www.globaldenso.com (office).

KATONA, Tamás; Hungarian diplomat, politician and historian; *Chairman, Manfred Wörner Foundation;* b. 2 Feb. 1932, Budapest; s. of Tibor Katona and Magdolna Halász; m. Klára Barta; one s. two d.; ed Archiepiscopal High School (Rákóczianum), Budapest, Eötvös Loránd Univ., Budapest; head of public libraries 1954–61; Ed. Magyar Helikon Publishing House and Európa Publishing House 1961–86; Lecturer in 19th-century Hungarian History, Eötvös Coll. 1980–85, József Attila Univ. of Szeged 1986–90; mem. Parl. 1990–98; Sec. of State for Foreign Affairs 1990–92; Sec. of State, Prime Minister's Office 1992–94; First Vice-Pres. IPU, Hungary; Mayor, Castle Dist, Budapest 1994–98; Prof., Károli Gáspár Protestant Univ. 1998–2000; Amb. to Poland 2000–03; Chair. Hungarian Scout Asscn 1994–98, Manfred Wörner Foundation 1998–; Scientific Adviser, Inst. of History, Hungarian Acad. of Sciences 2003–; Ed. serial publs Bibliotheca Historica and Pro Memoria (pocket library of history and cultural history); Grand Officer, Order of Merit (Poland), Grand Officer, Order of Merit of the Sovereign Order of St John, Hungarian Defence Cross (First Class). *Publications:* Az aradi vértanúk (The Martyrs of Arad) 1979, 1983, 1991, 2003, A korona kilenc évszázada (Nine Centuries of the Crown) 1979, A tatárjárás emlékezete (The Mongol Invasion) 1981, 1987, Budavár bevételének emlékezete, 1849 (Capture of Fort Buda in 1849) 1991, Csány László erdélyi főkormánybiztos (László Csány High Commissioner of Transylvania) 1991. *Leisure interests:* tennis, music. *Address:* Fortuna-utca 13, 1014 Budapest, Hungary (home). *Telephone:* (1) 201-13-65 (home). *Fax:* (1) 225-32-93 (home). *E-mail:* fortunau13@hotmail.com (home).

KATORI, Hidetoshi, BA, MA, PhD; Japanese physicist and academic; ed Univ. of Tokyo; currently Assoc. Prof., Dept of Applied Physics, Grad. School of Eng, Univ. of Tokyo; Prize of French Soc. of Chronometry 2005, Prize of Japan Soc. for the Promotion of Science 2005, Julius Springer Prize for Applied Physics 2005. *Publications:* numerous scientific papers in professional journals. *Address:* Department of Applied Physics, School of Engineering, University of Tokyo, Hongo 7-3-1, Bunkyo-ku, Tokyo 113-865, Japan (office). *Telephone:* (3) 5841-6800 (office). *E-mail:* katori@ap.t.u-tokyo.ac.jp (office). *Website:* www.ap.t.u-tokyo.ac.jp (office).

KATRENKO, Vladimir Semenovich, DEcon; Russian politician; *First Deputy Chairman, State Duma;* b. 11 Nov. 1956, Mineralnye Vody, Stavropol Krai; m.; two d., one s.; ed Mineralnye Vody Railway-Tech. Inst. no.4, Rostov Inst. of Railway Engineers, All-Union Corresp. Legal Inst.; worked as carpenter; served in army 1976–78; trained as electrical mechanic, qualified as engineer mechanic; driver Soviet Auto Transport, Mineralnye Vody, manager of convoys, apptd Gen. Dir 1988, 1996, Sec. Communist Party Cttee; elected to State Duma 1993, 1999, 2003, First Deputy Chair. 2004–, First Deputy Head United Russian faction, mem. Cttee for Ethnic Affairs, head of Comm. on North Caucasus; head of state admin, Mineralnye Vody 1996–99; fmr deputy head Govt of Stavropol Krai province, Sec. Political Council; mem. Gen. Council United Russia party; Hon. Transport Worker of Russian Fed. 1994, Award for Services to the Devt of Physical Culture and Sport 1998, Esteemed Railwayman 2003, Friendship Order 2003. *Leisure interests:* playing guitar, poetry, arts, mini-football. *Address:* Russian State Duma,

Okhotniy Ryad 1, 103265 Moscow, Russia (office). *Telephone:* (495) 292-80-00 (office). *Website:* www.katrenko.ru (office); www.duma.ru (office).

KATRITZKY, Alan Roy, MA, DPhil, PhD, ScD, FRS; British/American chemist, researcher, academic and consultant; *Kenan Professor of Chemistry and Director, Florida Institute of Heterocyclic Compounds, University of Florida;* b. 18 Aug. 1928, London; s. of Frederick C. Katritzky and Emily C. Katritzky (née Lane); m. Agnes Kilian 1952; one s. three d.; ed Univs of Oxford and Cambridge; Univ. Lecturer, Univ. of Cambridge 1958–63; Fellow Churchill Coll., Cambridge 1959–63; Prof. of Chem., Univ. of East Anglia 1963–80, Dean, School of Chemical Sciences 1963–70, 1976–80; Kenan Prof., Univ. of Florida 1980–, Dir Florida Inst. of Heterocyclic Compounds 1986–; Assoc. Ed. Journal für praktische Chemie 1997-99; foreign mem. Polish Acad. of Sciences, Royal Catalan Acad. of Sciences, Slovenian Acad. of Arts and Sciences, Russian Acad. of Science, Siberian Section 2003, Indian Nat. Acad. of Science 2003; Fellow American Asscn for Advancement of Science 2000, World Innovation Foundation 2003; Hon. Fellow, Italian Chem. Soc., Polish Chem. Soc., Chemical Research Foundation of India (2003); Hon. Prof. Beijing Inst. of Tech., Xian Modern Univ.; Cavaliere ufficiale (Italy); Hon. DSc (Madrid, Poznań, Gdańsk, E Anglia, Toulouse, St Petersburg, Bucharest, Rostov, Ghent, Bundelkhand); Dr hc (Timisoara, Romania) 2003, (Wroclaw, Poland) 2004; Heterocyclic Award, Royal Soc. of Chem., Sr Humboldt Award (Germany), Heyrowsky Medal, Czech Acad. of Science 1997, Hillier Medal, Latvian Acad. of Sciences 1999, Kametani Prize (Japan) 1999, Gold Medal, Partnership for Peace Foundation, Moscow 2001, ACS Cope Sr Scholar Award 2001, Tilden Lecturer, Chem. Soc., Cope Senior Scholar Award, ACS 2002, Lifetime Achievement Award, Indian Chemical Soc. 2003. *Publications:* author or co-author of seven books and more than 1700 papers in heterocyclic chemistry; Ed. Advances in Heterocyclic Chemistry (80 vols) and Comprehensive Heterocyclic Chemistry, 1st edn (eight vols), 2nd edn (ten vols), Organic Functional Group Transformations (seven vols). *Leisure interests:* walking, wind surfing. *Address:* Department of Chemistry, University of Florida, PO Box 117200, Gainesville, FL 32611 (office); 1221 SW 21st Avenue, Gainesville, FL 32601, USA (home). *Telephone:* (352) 392-0554 (office); (352) 378-1221 (home). *Fax:* (352) 392-9199 (office). *E-mail:* katritzky@chem.ufl.edu (office). *Website:* ark.chem.ufl.edu (office).

KATSAV, Moshe; Israeli politician; b. 5 Dec. 1945, Iran; m. Gila Katsav; four s. one d.; ed Hebrew Univ. of Jerusalem; reporter for Yediot Aharonot (newspaper) 1966–68; Mayor of Kiryat Malachi 1969, 1974–81; mem. Knesset 1977–99; mem. Interior and Educ. Cttees 1977–81; Deputy Minister of Housing and Construction 1981–84; Minister of Labour and Social Affairs 1984–88, of Transportation 1988–92; mem. Cttee on Defence 1988–92, 1996–99; Chair. Likud faction in the Knesset, Parl. Cttee of Chinese–Israeli Friendship League 1992–96; Deputy Prime Minister 1996–99, also Minister of Tourism, for Israeli Arab Affairs; Pres. of Israel 2000–07 (resgnd); Chair. Cttee for Nat. Events 1996–99; mem. Foreign Affairs and Defence Cttee 1999–2000; mem. Bd of Trustees Ben-Gurion Univ. 1978–; Dr hc (Univ. of Nebraska) 1998, (George Washington Univ.) 2001, (Hartford Univ., Conn.) 2001, (Yeshivah Univ., NY) 2002, (Bar Ilan Univ., Israel) 2003, (China Agricultural Univ., Beijing) 2003, (Sorbonne, Paris) 2004, (ELTE Univ. of Budapest) 2004; Bene Merito Medal of the Acad. of Science of Austria 2004. *Address:* c/o Office of the President, Beit Hanassi, 3 Hanassi Street, Jerusalem 92188, Israel (office).

KATSONGA, Davies Chester, BA, MBA; Malawi politician; *Minister of Labour and Vocational Training;* b. 6 Aug. 1955, Mwanza; m.; two s.; ed Schiller Int. Univ., Inst. of Marketing, South-Bank Univ., London, UK; MP for Mwanza Cen. Constituency 1999–; Minister of Mines, Natural Resources and Environmental Affairs, then Speaker of Parl. 1999–2004; Minister of Natural Resources 2004–05, of Foreign Affairs 2005–06, of Defence 2006–07, for Presidential and Parl. Affairs 2007–08, of Labour and Vocational Training 2008–; mem. Democratic Progressive Party 2005–. *Leisure interests:* playing and watching soccer, reading political autobiographies, travel, angling, carpentry, environmental affairs and computers. *Address:* Ministry of Labour, Private Bag 344, Capital City, Lilongwe 3, Malawi (office). *Telephone:* 1772080 (office). *Fax:* 1773803 (office). *E-mail:* labour@malawi.net (office); dkatsonga@yahoo.co.uk (home). *Website:* www.malawi.gov.mw/Labour/Home%20%20Labour.htm (office).

KATSUMATA, Nobuo; Japanese business executive; b. 1943; m. Fusae Katsumata; joined Marubeni Corpn 1966, various man. positions, mem. Bd of Dirs 1996–, fmr Chief Dir of Paper Pulp, Sr Man. Dir –2003, Pres. and CEO 2003–08, Chair. 2008–; Chair. Japan Foreign Trade Council, Inc.; Commdr of the Lion of Finland 2003. *Leisure interest:* sailing. *Address:* Marubeni Corpn, 42 Ohtemachi 1-chome, Chiyoda-ku, Tokyo 100-8088, Japan (office). *Telephone:* (3) 3282-2111 (office). *Fax:* (3) 3282-4241 (office). *E-mail:* info@marubeni.com (office). *Website:* www.marubeni.com (office).

KATSUMATA, Tsunehisa; Japanese energy industry executive; *Chairman, Tokyo Electric Power Company (TEPCO), Inc.;* b. 1940; ed Univ. of Tokyo; joined Tokyo Electric Power Co. (TEPCO), Inc. as grad. trainee, held various man. positions, including Man., Corp. Planning Dept, Exec. Vice-Pres. for Corp. Planning –2002, Pres. 2002–08, Chair. 2008–; Vice-Chair. Bd of Councillors, Nippon-Keidanren; Dir Japan Nuclear Fuels Ltd, Japan Productivity Center for Socio-Econ. Devt, Japan Investor Relations Asscn; mem. Bd Dirs KDDI Corp.; Chair. Fed. of Electric Power Cos of Japan. *Leisure interests:* reading, Go (traditional Japanese strategy game).

KATTAN, Naïm, OC, FRSC; Canadian writer; b. 26 Aug. 1928, Baghdad, Iraq; s. of the late Nessim and Hela Kattan; m. Gaetane Laniel 1961; one s.; ed Univ. of Baghdad and Sorbonne, Paris; newspaper corresp. in Near East and Europe, broadcaster throughout Europe; emigrated to Canada 1954; Int.

Politics Ed. for Nouveau Journal 1961–62; fmr teacher at Laval Univ.; fmr Sec. Cercle Juif de langue française de Montreal; freelance journalist and broadcaster; Prof., Univ. of Québec, Montreal; Assoc. Dir Canada Council; mem. Académie Canadienne-Française; Pres. Royal Soc. of Canada; Chevalier Légion d'honneur; Officier des Arts et Lettres de France; Chevalier Ordre nat. du Québec; Dr. hc (Middlebury Coll.). *Publications:* (novels) Adieu Babylone 1975, Les Fruits arrachés 1981, La Fiancée promise 1983, La Fortune du passager 1989, La Célébration 1997, L'Anniversaire 2000; (essays) Le Réel et le théâtral 1970, Ecrivains des Amériques, Tomes I-III, Le Repos et l'Oubli 1987, Le Père 1990, Farida 1991, La Reconciliation 1992, A. M. Klein 1994, La Distraction 1994, Culture: Alibi ou liberté 1996, Idoles et images 1996, Figures bibliques 1997, L'Amour reconnu 1999, Le Silence des adieux 1999, Le gardien de mon frère 2003, La Parole et le lieu 2004, Les Villes de naissance, L'Ecrivain migrant, Farewell Babylon: Coming of Age in Jewish Baghdad 2007; also numerous short stories and criticisms. *Address:* 2463 rue Sainte Famille No. 2114, Montreal, PQ, H2X 2K7, Canada. *Telephone:* (514) 499-2836. *Fax:* (514) 499-9954. *E-mail:* kattan.naim@uqam.ca.

KATUWAL, Lt-Gen. Rukmangad; Nepalese army officer; *Chief of Army Staff;* b. 1944, Okahldhunga dist; Deputy Chief of Army Staff –Aug. 2006, Acting Chief of Army Staff Aug.–Sept. 2006, Chief of Army Staff (first commoner officer) Sept. 2006–. *Address:* Office of the Chief of Army Staff, Ministry of Defence, Singha Durbar, Kathmandu, Nepal (office). *Telephone:* (1) 4211290 (office). *Fax:* (1) 4211294 (office). *E-mail:* mod@mos.com.np (office).

KATZ, Daryl, LLB; Canadian lawyer and business executive; *Chairman and CEO, Katz Group;* b. 1962, Edmonton; s. of Barry Katz; m.; two c.; ed Univ. of Alberta Law School; fmr lawyer; Founder, Katz Group, group of pharmacy cos that includes Rexall, Guardian IDA, Medicine Shop and Pharm Plus drugstore chains, Chair. and CEO 1996–. *Address:* The Katz Group, Suite 1702 Bell Tower, 10104 103rd Avenue, Edmonton, Alberta T5J 0H8, Canada (office). *Telephone:* (780) 990-0505 (office). *Fax:* (780) 702-0647 (office). *E-mail:* esilverman@katzgroup.ca (office). *Website:* www.katzgroup.ca (office).

KATZ, Michael, AB, MD, FAAP; American paediatrician and academic; *Senior Vice-President for Research and Global Programs, March of Dimes Foundation;* b. 13 Feb. 1928, Lwów, Poland; s. of Edward Katz and Rita Gluzman; m. Robin J. Roy 1986; one s.; ed Univ. of Pennsylvania, State Univ. of New York, Brooklyn, Columbia Univ. School of Public Health; Intern, UCLA Medical Center 1956–57; Resident, Presbyterian Hosp. New York 1960–62, Dir Pediatric Service 1977–92; Hon. Lecturer in Paediatrics, Makerere Univ. Coll., Kampala, Uganda 1963–64; Instructor in Pediatrics, Columbia Univ. 1964–65, Prof. in Tropical Medicine, School of Public Health 1971–92, Prof. Emer. 1992–, Prof. of Pediatrics, Coll. of Physicians and Surgeons 1972–77, Reuben S. Carpentier Prof. and Chair. Dept of Pediatrics 1977–92, Prof. Emer. 1992–; Asst Prof. of Pediatrics, Univ. of Pennsylvania 1966–71; Sr Vice-Pres. for Research and Global Programs, March of Dimes Foundation 1992–; Pres. World Alliance of Orgs for the Prevention of Birth Defects 1995–; Assoc. mem. Wistar Inst., Philadelphia 1965–71; Consultant, WHO regional offices, Guatemala, Venezuela, Egypt, Yemen; mem. US Del. to 32nd World Health Ass., Geneva 1979; Consultant, UNICEF, New York and Tokyo; mem. numerous medical socs including Inst. of Medicine of NAS; Fellow, American Acad. of Pediatrics, AAAS; Jurzykowski Foundation Award in Medicine 1983, Alexander von Humboldt Foundation Sr US Scientist Award 1987. *Publications:* contributions to numerous journals and medical works. *Leisure interest:* music. *Address:* 1 Griggs Lane, Chappaqua, NY 10514 (home); March of Dimes Foundation, 1275 Mamaroneck Avenue, White Plains, NY 10605, USA (office). *Telephone:* (914) 997-4555 (office). *Fax:* (914) 997-4560 (office). *E-mail:* mkatz@marchofdimes.com (office); robinroy@optonline.net (home). *Website:* www.marchofdimes.com (office).

KATZ, Samuel Lawrence, MD, DSc; American paediatrician, vaccinologist and academic; *Wilburt C. Davison Professor and Chairman Emeritus, Department of Pediatrics, Medical Center, Duke University;* b. 29 May 1927, Manchester, NH; s. of Morris Katz and Ethel Lawrence Katz; one sister Maxine Morse; m. 1st Betsy Jane Cohan 1950 (divorced 1971); four s. (one s. deceased) three d.; m. 2nd Catherine Minock Wilfert 1971; two step-d.; ed Dartmouth Coll. and Harvard Univ.; hosp. appointments, Boston, Mass 1952–56; Exchange Registrar, Paediatric Unit, St Mary's Hosp. Medical School, London, UK 1956; Research Fellow in Pediatrics, Harvard Medical School at Research Div. of Infectious Diseases, Children's Hosp. Medical Center, Boston 1956–58, Research Assoc. 1958–68; Pediatrician-in-Chief, Beth Israel Hosp., Boston 1958–61, Visiting Pediatrician 1961–68; Assoc. Physician, Children's Hosp. Medical Center, Boston 1958–63, Sr Assoc. in Medicine 1963–68, Chief, Newborn Div. 1961–67; Instructor in Pediatrics, Harvard Medical School, Boston 1958–59, Assoc. 1959–63, Tutor in Medical Sciences 1961–63, Asst Prof. of Pediatrics 1963–68; Co-Dir Combined Beth Israel Hosp.-Children's Hosp. Medical Center, Infectious Disease Career Training Program 1967–68; Prof. and Chair. Dept of Pediatrics, Duke Univ. School of Medicine, Durham, NC 1968–90, Wilburt C. Davison Prof. of Pediatrics 1972–97, Wilburt C. Davison Prof. Emer. 1997–; prin. activities involve research on children's vaccines and on pediatric AIDS; mem. Bd Dirs Georgetown Univ. 1987–93, Hasbro Foundation 1988–, Burroughs Wellcome Fund 1991–99 (Chair. 1995–99), Scientific Advisory Bd, St Jude Children's Research Hosp.; Consultant, NIH AIDS Exec. Cttee 1986–89, mem. NIH Pediatric AIDS Exec. Cttee 1994–97; mem. Editorial Bd Pediatric Infectious Diseases Report; fmr mem. Editorial Bd Annual Review in Medicine, Postgraduate Medicine, Reviews of Infectious Diseases, Current Problems in Pediatrics, Ped Sat (TV Educ.); Chair. Bd of Trustees, Int. Vaccine Inst., Seoul, S Korea 2004–; Co-Chair. Indo-US Vaccine Action Program 1999–2004; mem. Soc. for Pediatric Research, American Soc. for Microbiology, American

Asscn of Immunologists, American Public Health Asscn, American Soc. for Clinical Investigation, American Pediatric Soc., American Epidemiological Soc., American Soc. for Virology, American Fed. for Clinical Research, Inst. of Medicine; Fellow, American Acad. of Pediatrics, Infectious Diseases Soc. of America, AAAS; Hon. DSc (Georgetown Univ.) 1996, (Dartmouth Coll.) 1998; Presidential Medal of Dartmouth Coll. for Leadership and Achievement 1991, Distinguished Physician Award, Pediatric Infectious Diseases Soc. 1991, Bristol Award and Soc. Citation, Infectious Diseases Soc. of America 1993, Needleman Medal and Award, American Public Health Asscn 1997, Howland Award, American Pediatric Soc. 2000, Gold Medal, Sabin Vaccine Inst. 2003, Founders Medal, Duke Univ. 2004 and other awards. *Publications:* numerous articles in scientific journals, textbooks of paediatrics and infectious diseases. *Leisure interests:* jazz drumming (Joe Butterfield Dixieland Jazz Concert 1994–2003), cycling, reading, opera. *Address:* Duke University Medical Center, Box 2925, Durham, NC 27710, USA (office). *Telephone:* (919) 668-4852 (office); (919) 968-0008 (home). *Fax:* (919) 681-8934 (office); (919) 968-0447 (home). *E-mail:* katz0004@mc.duke.edu (office); slkatz@mindspring.com (home). *Website:* www.mc.duke.edu (office).

KATZAROV, Lt-Gen. Anguel, MSc; Bulgarian business executive and fmr army officer; *CEO, Industrial Holding Bulgaria (IHB) AD;* b. 1942; ed Nat. Military Univ. Vassil Levski, Veliko Tarnovo, Staff Coll. Frunze and Gen. Staff Coll., Moscow, Russia; fmr army officer, attached to Ministry of Defence and Gen. Staff of Bulgarian Army; joined Industrial Holding Bulgaria (IHB) AD 2002, CEO and mem. Man. Bd 2003–. *Address:* Industrial Holding Bulgaria (IHB) AD, 47 Vassil Levski Blvd, 1000 Sofia, Bulgaria (office). *Telephone:* (2) 9807101 (office). *Fax:* (2) 9807072 (office). *E-mail:* office@bulgariaholding.com (office). *Website:* www.bulgariaholding.com (office).

KATZENBACH, Nicholas deBelleville; American lawyer, fmr government official and business executive (retd); b. 17 Jan. 1922, Philadelphia; s. of Edward Katzenbach and Marie Katzenbach; m. Lydia King Phelps Stokes 1946; two s. two d.; ed Philips Exeter Acad., Princeton and Yale Univs. and Balliol Coll., Oxford, UK; US Army Air Force 1941–45; admitted to NJ Bar 1950, Conn. Bar 1955, New York Bar 1972; with firm Katzenbach Gildea and Rudner, Trenton, NJ 1950; Attorney-Adviser, Office of Gen. Counsel, Air Force 1950–52, part-time Consultant 1952–56; Assoc. Prof. of Law, Yale Univ. 1952–56; Prof. of Law, Univ. of Chicago 1956–60; Asst Attorney-Gen., US Dept of Justice 1961–62, Deputy Attorney-Gen. 1962–64, Attorney-Gen. 1965–66; Under-Sec. of State 1966–69; Sr Vice-Pres. and Gen. Counsel, IBM Corpn 1969–86; Pnr, Riker, Danzig, Scherer, Hyland and Perretti 1986–91, Counsel 1991–94; Chair. (non-exec.) MCI Group March 2004–05; mem. ABA, American Judicature Soc., American Law Inst.; Democrat; hon. degrees from Rutgers Univ., Univ. of Bridgeport (Conn.), Tufts Univ., Georgetown Univ., Princeton, Northeastern Univ., Brandeis Univ., Bard Coll. *Publications:* The Political Foundations of International Law (with Morton A. Kaplan) 1961, Legal Literature of Space (with Prof. Leon Lipson) 1961, Some of it was Fun: Working with RFK and LBJ 2008. *Address:* 33 Greenhouse Drive, Princeton, NJ 08540, USA (home). *Telephone:* (609) 924-8536 (home). *Fax:* (609) 924-6610 (home).

KATZENBERG, Jeffrey; American film industry executive; *CEO, Dreamworks Animation SKG;* b. 21 Dec. 1950; m. Marilyn Siegal; one s. one d.; Asst to Chair., CEO Paramount Pictures, New York 1975–77; Exec. Dir Marketing, Paramount TV, Calif. 1977, Vice-Pres. Programming 1977–78; Vice-Pres. feature production, Paramount Pictures 1978–80, Sr Vice-Pres. production, motion picture div. 1980–82, Pres. production, motion pictures and TV 1982–94; Chair. Walt Disney Studios, Burbank, Calif. –1994; Co-founder and Prin. Dreamworks SKG 1995–2005, CEO Dreamworks Animation SKG 1994–. *Address:* Dreamworks Animation SKG, 1000 Flower Street, Glendale, CA 91201, USA (office). *Telephone:* (818) 695-5000 (office). *Fax:* (818) 695-9944 (office). *Website:* www.dreamworksanimation.com (office).

KATZIR, Ephraim, MSc, PhD; Israeli scientist, academic, administrator and fmr head of state; *Professor, Department of Biological Chemistry, Weizmann Institute of Science;* b. (Ephraim Katchalski), 16 May 1916, Kiev, Russia; s. of Yehuda and Tsila Katchalski; m. Nina Gotlieb 1938 (deceased); one s.; ed Hebrew Univ., Jerusalem; Prof. and Head, Dept of Biophysics, Weizmann Inst. of Science 1951–73; Chief Scientist, Ministry of Defence 1966–68; Pres. of Israel 1973–78; Prof. Weizmann Inst. of Science 1978–, Prof. Tel-Aviv Univ. 1978–; first incumbent Herman F. Mark Chair in Polymer Science, Polytechnic Inst. of New York 1979; Pres. World ORT Union (Org. for Rehabilitation Through Training) 1987–90, COBIOTECH Int. Scientific Cttee for Biotech. 1989–95; mem. Israel Acad. of Sciences and Humanities, NAS, USA, Leopoldina Acad. of Science, German Democratic Repub., The Royal Soc. of London (Foreign mem.), Int. Union of Biochemistry, Acad. des Sciences, France (Foreign mem.), American Acad. of Microbiology and many other orgs.; mem. American Soc. of Biological Chemists (Hon.), American Acad. of Arts and Sciences (Foreign Hon. mem.), Royal Inst. of Great Britain (Hon. mem.); Hon. Prof. Polytechnic Inst., New York; Commdr Légion d'honneur 1990; Hon. PhD (Brandeis, Michigan, Harvard, Northwestern, Jerusalem Hebrew, McGill, Thomas Jefferson, Oxford, Miami Univs., Weizmann Inst., Israel Technion and Hebrew Union Coll., Jerusalem, Eidgenossische Technische Hochschule, Univ. of Buenos Aires); Tchernikhovski Prize 1948; Weizmann Prize 1950; Israel Prize Natural Sciences 1959; Rothschild Prize Natural Sciences 1961; first recipient of Japan Prize, Science and Tech. Foundation of Japan 1985; Underwood Prescott Award, MIT 1982; Enzyme Eng Award 1987; Linderstrøm-Lang Gold Medal 1969; Hans Krebs Medal 1972. *Publications:* numerous papers and articles on proteins and polyamino acids, polymers structure and function of living cells and enzyme engineering. *Leisure interest:* swimming. *Address:* Department of Biological Chemistry, Weizmann Institute of Science, PO Box 26, Rehovot 76100, Israel (office). *Telephone:* 8-

9343947 (office); 8-9343525 (home). *Fax:* 8-9468256 (office). *E-mail:* ephraim.katzir@weizmann.ac.il (office). *Website:* www.weizmann.ac.il/Biological_Chemistry (office).

KAUFMAN, Charles (Charlie) Stewart; American screenwriter; b. Nov. 1958, W Hartford, Conn.; m. Denise Kaufman; one d.; ed Boston Univ., New York Univ.; worked in newspaper circulation dept, The Star Tribune, Minneapolis, Minn. 1986–90; contrib. to National Lampoon 1991; began scriptwriting 1991; cr. short films shown on Late Night with David Letterman TV show 1990s; writer 30 episodes for TV shows 1991–96; Producer, Misery Loves Company (TV series) 1995. *Screenplays include:* films: Being John Malkovich 1999, Human Nature 2001, Adaptation (Best Screenplay, Broadcast Film Critics Asscn, Chicago Film Critics Asscn, Nat. Bd of Review, Toronto Film Critics Asscn) 2002, Confessions of a Dangerous Mind 2002, Eternal Sunshine of the Spotless Mind (Nat. Bd of Review Best Original Screenplay Award 2004, BAFTA Award 2005, Writers' Guild of America Award for Best Original Screenplay 2005, Acad. Award for Best Original Screenplay 2005) 2004, Synecdoche, New York 2008; TV: Get A Life 1991–92, The Edge 1992–93, The Trouble with Larry 1993, Ned and Stacey 1996–97, The Dana Carvey Show 1996. *Leisure interest:* reading. *Address:* United Talent Agency, 9560 Wilshire Boulevard, Fifth Floor, Beverly Hills, CA 90212, USA (office).

KAUFMAN, Sir Gerald Bernard, Kt, PC, MA, MP; British politician; b. 21 June 1930; s. of Louis Kaufman and Jane Kaufman; ed Leeds Grammar School and Queen's Coll., Oxford; Asst Gen. Sec. Fabian Soc. 1954–55; political staff, Daily Mirror 1955–64; Political Corresp., New Statesman 1964–65; Parl. Press Liaison, Labour Party 1965–70; MP for Manchester, Ardwick 1970–83, for Manchester, Gorton 1983–; Under-Sec. of State for the Environment 1974–75, for Industry 1975; Minister of State, Dept of Industry 1975–79; mem. Parl. Cttee of Labour Party 1980–92; Opposition Spokesman for Home Affairs 1983–87; Shadow Foreign Sec. 1987–92; Chair. House of Commons Nat. Heritage Select Cttee 1992–97, Culture, Media and Sport Select Cttee 1997–2005; mem. Labour Party Nat. Exec. Cttee 1991–92; mem. Royal Comm. on House of Lords Reform 1999; Chair. Booker Prize Judges 1999; Hillai-e-Pakistan 1999. *Publications:* How to Live under Labour (co-author) 1964, To Build the Promised Land 1973, How to Be a Minister 1980 (revised edn 1997), Renewal: Labour's Britain in the 1980s 1983, My Life in the Silver Screen 1985, Inside the Promised Land 1986, Meet Me in St Louis 1994. *Leisure interests:* cinema, opera, records, theatre, concerts, travel. *Address:* House of Commons, Westminster, London, SW1A 0AA (office); 87 Charlbert Court, Eamont Street, London, NW8, England (home). *Telephone:* (20) 7219-5145 (office). *Fax:* (20) 7219-6825 (office).

KAUFMAN, Henry, BA, MS, PhD; American banker and investment manager; *President, Henry Kaufman & Company Inc.;* b. 20 Oct. 1927, Wenings, Germany; s. of Gustav and Hilda (née Rosenthal) Kaufman; m. Elaine Reinheimer 1957; three s.; ed New York and Columbia Univs; emigrated to USA 1937; Asst Chief Economist, Research Dept, Fed. Reserve Bank of New York 1957–61; with Salomon Bros., New York 1962–88, Gen. Pnr 1967–88, mem. Exec. Cttee 1972–88, Man. Dir 1981–88, also Chief Economist, in charge Bond Market Research, Industry and Stock Research and Bond Portfolio Analysis Research Depts.; f. Henry Kaufman & Co. Inc., NY 1988–; Pres. Money Marketeers, New York Univ. 1964–65; Dir Lehman Bros. 1995–, Statue of Liberty-Ellis Island Foundation, Inc., W.R. Berkley Corpn, Federal Home Loan Mortgage Corpn; Trustee, New York Univ., Whitney Museum of American Art, Hudson Inst.; mem. Bd of Govs, Tel-Aviv Univ.; mem. American Econ. Asscn, American Finance Asscn, Conf. of Business Economists, Econ. Club, New York (also Dir), UN Asscn (also Dir), Council on Foreign Relations; mem. Int. Advisory Cttee, Federal Reserve Bank of New York, Advisory Cttee to Investment Cttee for the IMF Staff Retirement Plan; Trustee Inst. of Int. Educ. 1982–, Chair. 1989–2003, Chair. Emer. 2003–; George S. Eccles Prize for excellence in economic writing, Columbia Business School 1987. *Publication:* Interest Rates, the Markets and the New Financial World 1986, On Money and Markets, A Wall Street Memoir 2000. *Address:* Henry Kaufman & Co., 590 Madison Avenue, 5, New York, NY 10022, USA (office). *Telephone:* (212) 758-7100 (office).

KAUFMAN, Philip; American screenwriter and film director; b. 23 Oct. 1936, Chicago, Ill.; s. of Nathan Kaufman and Betty Kaufman; m. Rose Kaufman; one s.; ed Univ. of Chicago and Harvard Law School; fmr teacher in Italy. *Films:* Goldstein (co-screenplay, co-dir and co-producer) (Prix de la Nouvelle Critique, Cannes 1964), Fearless Frank 1965, The Great Northfield Minnesota Raid 1971, The White Dawn (dir only) 1973, Invasion of the Body Snatchers (dir only) 1977, The Wanderers (co-screenplay and dir) 1979, The Right Stuff (dir and screenplay) 1983 (winner of four Acad. Awards), The Unbearable Lightness of Being (dir and co-screenplay) 1988, (Orson Welles Award for Best Filmmaker-Writer/Dir 1988, Nat. Soc. of Film Critics Award for Best Dir 1988), Henry & June (dir and co-scriptwriter) 1990, Rising Sun (dir and co-screenplay) 1993, China: The Wild East (narrator and exec. producer) 1995, Quills 2000, Twisted 2004. *Address:* c/o William Morris Agency, 151 South El Camino Drive, Beverly Hills, CA 90212, USA.

KAUFMANN, Jonas; German singer (tenor); b. 1969, Munich; ed Munich Hochschule für Musik, masterclasses with Hans Hotter and James King; sang with Saarbrucken Opera 1994–96; Salzburg Festival debut in Busoni's Dr Faust 1999; engagements from 1999, including Stuttgart, Chicago, Milan and Salzburg; season 2002 appearances included Flamand in Capriccio at Turin, Don Ottavio in Don Giovanni at Munich, Fierrabras at Zürich Oper; season 2003 appearances included Alfredo Germont in La Traviata at Chicago Opera, Rinaldo in Armida at Zürich Oper, Faust in La Damnation de Faust at Geneva, Belmonte in Die Entfuhrung aus dem Serail at Salzburg Festival, Tannhauser, Die Zauberflote and Die Entfuhrung aus dem Serail at Zürich Oper, and a recital at the Wigmore Hall, London; season 2004 included Max in Der Freischutz at Berlin, Fidelio at Zürich Oper, Cassio in Otello at Paris, Die Schopfung at Naples, and a recital in Brussels; other roles include Mozart's Ferrando, Belmonte, Tamino, Titus, Jacquino in Fidelio, Rossini's Almaviva, Alfredo in Otello; prizewinner Meistersinger Competition, Nuremberg 1993. *Recordings include:* Carl Loewe's The Three Wishes, R. Strauss's Lieder (Gramophone Award for Best Solo Vocal Recording) 2007. *Address:* Zemsky/Green Artists Management, 104 West 73rd Street, Suite 1, New York, NY 10023, USA (office). *Telephone:* (212) 579-6700 (office). *Fax:* (212) 579-4723 (office). *Website:* www.zemskygreen.com (office).

KAUL, Hans-Peter, JD; German , judge and diplomatist; *Judge and President, Pre-Trial Division, International Criminal Court;* b. 25 July 1943; m.; four c.; ed Int. Peace Acad., Vienna, Austria, Max Planck Inst., Heidelberg, Acad. of Int. Law, The Hague, The Netherlands, Ecole Nat. d'Admin, Paris, France, Univs of Heidelberg and Lausanne; mil. service in German army 1963–67, attained rank Capt.; Consul and Press Attaché, Embassy in Oslo, Norway 1977–80; with Office for UN Affairs, Fed. Foreign Office, Bonn 1980–84; Press Counsellor and Spokesman, Embassy in Tel-Aviv, Israel 1984–86; Political Counsellor, Embassy in Washington, USA 1986–90; Deputy Dir, Office of Nr Eastern Affairs, Fed. Foreign Office, Bonn 1990–93; First Counsellor, Perm. Mission to UN, NY 1993–96; Dir Office for Public Int. Law, Fed. Foreign Office, Bonn and Berlin 1996–2002; Amb. and Commr of Fed. Foreign Office for Int. Criminal Court (ICC) 2002–03; Judge, ICC 2003–, Pres. Pre-Trial Div. 2004–; Head of German Dels to Preparatory Cttee for ICC 1996–98, 1999–2002; mem. Nat. Advisory Cttee of German Red Cross Soc. on Int. Humanitarian Law 1996–; mem. German Soc. for Int. Law, German Soc. for the UN, German Soc. for Foreign Policy, Int. Criminal Law Network. *Publications:* chapters in books, country reports, articles in professional journals in German, English, Spanish, Portuguese and Arabic languages. *Address:* International Criminal Court, Maanweg 174, 2516 AB The Hague, The Netherlands (office); Buchsweildrstr. 16, 14195, Berlin, Germany (office). *Telephone:* (70) 5158237 (office); 84418040 (home). *Fax:* (70) 5158789 (office). *E-mail:* hanspeter.kaul@icc-cpi.int (office). *Website:* www.icc-cpi.int.

KAULA, Prithvi Nath, MA, MLibrSc; Indian library scientist and academic; *UGC Professor Emeritus, Lucknow University;* b. 13 March 1924, Srinagar; s. of Damodar Kaula; m. Asha Kaula 1941; two s. three d.; ed S.P. Coll., Srinagar, Punjab Univ., Delhi Univ., Banaras Hindu Univ.; mem. Council, Indian Library Asscn 1949–53, 1956–62, Pres. 1996–98; Man. Ed. Annals, Bulletin and Granthalayas of Indian Library Asscn 1949–53; Sec. Ranganathan Endowment for Library Science 1951–61; Founder, Gen. Sec. Delhi Library Asscn 1953–55, 1958–60, Vice-Pres. 1956–58; Visiting lecturer in Library Science, Aligarh Muslim Univ. 1951–58; Reader Dept of Library Science, Univ. of Delhi 1958–60; Vice-Pres. Govt of India Libraries Asscn 1958–61; mem. Review Cttee on Library Science, Univ. Grants Comm. 1961–63, mem. Panel on Library and Information Science 1978–80, 1982–84, Chair. 1990–92; Chair. Curriculum Devt Cttee (UGC) 1991–93; Visiting Prof. Documentation, Research and Training Centre, Bangalore 1962, 1965; Ed. Library Herald 1958–61, Herald of Library Science 1962–; Pres. Fed. of Indian Library Asscns. 1966–83; mem. Governing Council, Nat. Library of India 1966–69; UNESCO Expert, UNESCO Regional Centre in the Western Hemisphere for Latin American countries, Havana 1967–68; Founder and Gen. Sec. Indian Asscn of Teachers of Library Science 1969, Pres. 1973–85, Patron 1986–; Ed. Granthalaya Vijnana 1970–; Librarian, Banaras Hindu Univ. and Prof. and Head, Dept of Library Science 1971–78, Dean Faculty of Arts 1980–82; Prof. Emer. Kashi Vidyapith 1983–, UGC Prof. Emer. Lucknow Univ. 1985–; Ed. Research Journal of the Banaras Hindu Univ. 1980–, Ed. Progress in Library and Information Science 1980–; Ed.-in-Chief International Information, Communication and Education 1982–; Chair. Council of Literacy and Adult Educ. 1971–; Pres. Indian Library Asscn 1996–98; Vice-Pres. Indian Asscn of Special Libraries and Information Centres; UNESCO expert and consultant, UNESCO Regional Centre for the Western Hemisphere (Latin American countries) 1967–68; Dir, UNESCO Training Programme on Library Science and Documentation, Havana, Cuba 1968, Modernisation of Library and Information Service, Nat. Library, Bangkok, Thailand 1978; Bureau for Promotion of Urduo Library Science 1980–84; mem. State Library Cttee, Uttar Pradesh 1981–85, Acad. Council, Aligarh Muslim Univ. 1996–2000, Acad. Council, Dr Ambedkar Univ. 1997–99; mem. Raja Rammohun Roy Library Foundation 1974–77, 1996–99; Bd of Studies in Library and Information Science of 16 univs; Expert mem. UNESCO Advisory Group on Comparability of Higher Degrees in Library Science 1973–75, Nat. Review Cttee on Univ. and Coll. Libraries 1996–; Dir Int. Inst. of Higher Studies in Educ., Knowledge and Professional Training 1992–; mem. Bd Trustees, Nat. Book Trust 1999–; Patron Indian Coll. Library Asscn, Nat. Music Acad., Library Council; Visiting Prof. 38 Indian Univs, 11 American Univs, Univ. of Havana, Hebrew Univ., Jerusalem and Univs in France, Cuba, Canada, Germany, Denmark, Italy, Hungary, Mexico, Spain, Thailand, Brazil, Singapore, the former USSR and the UK; Consultant and Adviser on Library Science to several int. orgs and nat. asscns; Organizing Sec. and Pres. of numerous confs; f. several professional bodies and trusts; est. Kaula Endowment for Library and Information Science 1975; Regional Pres. World Council of Vocational Educ. 1995–; Founder-Ed. of six journals, currently Ed. of three journals; Founder Delhi Library Asscn 1953, Jammu and Kashmir Library Asscn 1966, Indian Asscn for Teachers of Library and Information Science 1969, Nat. Book Museum 2000, Ranganathan Soc. for Book Culture, Library and Informatics Studies 2002; Fellow Raja Rammohun Roy Foundation 2002–; Hon. Adviser, Libraries, AP Govt 1972–79; Hon. Fellow Int. Council for Professional Educ. 1992, RRR Library Foundation 2001; Int. Kaula Gold Medal awarded to 22 recipients 1975–, Ranganathan-Kaula Gold Medal to 12 recipients 1980–, honoured by Int. Festschrift Cttee 1974, 1984, 1994, Indian

Library Movt Award 1974, Pro Mundi Beneficio Medal (India) 1975, Deutsche Bücherei Medal (Germany) 1981, Commemorative Medal of Honour (USA) 1985, Kaula Gold Medal instituted at six univs; Kaula-Bashiruddin Chair instituted at Aligarh Univ., PADMASHRI Award, Govt. of India 2004; numerous other awards. *Films:* documentary: P.N. Kaula: Kitabon Massihah (God's Messenger for Books) 2003. *Publications:* 60 books and monographs and numerous other publs including over 1,000 technical papers and book reviews on library science, labour problems and student unrest. *Leisure interests:* reading, writing, the study of library and information science. *Address:* Lucknow University, C-239 Indira Nagar, Lucknow 226016, India (office). *Telephone:* (522) 351172 (office). *E-mail:* kaula@endowment.org (office). *Website:* www.lkouniv.ac.in/univ_administration.asp (office); www .kaulaendowment.org (office).

KAUNDA, Kenneth David; Zambian fmr politician; *Chairman, Kenneth Kaunda Children of Africa Foundation;* b. (Buchizya), 28 April 1924, Lubwa; m. Betty Banda 1946; six s. (two s. deceased) two d. one adopted s.; ed Lubwa Training School and Munali Secondary School; schoolteacher at Lubwa Training School 1943, Headmaster 1944–47; Sec. Chinsali Young Men's Farming Asscn 1947; welfare officer, Chingola Copper Mine 1948; school teaching 1948–49; Founder-Sec. Lubwa branch, African Nat. Congress (ANC) 1950, district organizer 1951, prov. organizer 1952, Sec.-Gen. for N Rhodesia 1953; imprisoned for possession of prohibited literature Jan.–Feb. 1954; broke away from ANC to form Zambia African Nat. Congress 1958; imprisoned for political offences May 1959–Jan. 1960; Pres. United Nat. Independence Party 1960–92, 1995–2000; Minister of Local Govt and Social Welfare, N Rhodesia 1962–64; Prime Minister of N Rhodesia Jan.–Oct. 1964; Pres. Pan-African Freedom Movt for East, Central and South Africa (PAFMECSA) 1963; First Pres. of Zambia 1964–91 and Minister of Defence 1964–70, 1973–78; Head of Sub-Cttee for Defence and Security 1978–91; Minister of Foreign Affairs 1969–70, also of Trade, Industry, Mines and State Participation 1969–73; Chair. Mining and Industrial Devt Corpn of Zambia 1970; Chair. Org. of African Unity (OAU) 1970–71, 1987–88, Non-Aligned Nations Conf. 1970–73, fmr Chair. ZIMCO; Chancellor, Univ. of Zambia 1966–91, Copperbelt Univ. 1988; f. Peace Foundation 1992; charged with 'misprison of treason' over alleged involvement in attempted coup d'état 1997; freed after six months of house arrest after charges dropped June 1998; deprived of citizenship March 1999; citizenship restored by Supreme Court 2000; Founder and Chair. Kenneth Kaunda Children of Africa Foundation 2000–; Freeman of the Municipality of Chipata 1994; Order of the Collar of the Nile, Kt of the Collar of the Order of Pius XII, Order of the Queen of Sheba; Hon. LLD (Fordham, Dublin, Windsor (Canada), Wales, Sussex, York and Chile Univs); Dr hc (Humboldt State Univ., Calif.) 1980; Jawaharlal Nehru Award for Int. Understanding, Quaide Azam Human Rights Inst. Prize (Pakistan) 1976; honoured for his Keynote Address on Conflict Resolution in Africa and for Distinguished Leadership of African People for Over Half A Century, African Studies Coalition, Calif. State Univ., Sacramento 1995, WANGO Universal Peace Award 2004. *Publications:* Black Government 1961, Zambia Shall Be Free 1962, A Humanist in Africa (with Colin Morris) 1966, Humanism in Zambia and a Guide to its Implementation 1967, Humanism Part II 1977, Letter to my Children 1977, Kaunda On Violence 1980. *Address:* Office of the First President of the Republic of Zambia, 21 A Serval Road, PO E 501, Lusaka, Zambia. *Telephone:* (1) 260327 (office); (1) 260323 (home). *Fax:* (1) 220805 (office); (1) 220805 (home). *Website:* www.kkcaf.org.

KAUR, Prabhjot (see Prabhjot Kaur).

KAURISMÄKI, Aki; Finnish filmmaker; b. 4 April 1957; co-founder film production co-operative Filmtotal; Man. Dir and Jt owner (with brother Mika Kaurismäki) film production co. Villealfa; jtly runs distribution co. Senso Film. *Films:* (Co-writer and Asst Dir) The Liar 1980, The Worthless 1982, The Clan: Tale of the Frogs 1984, Rosso 1985; (Co-Dir) The Saimaa Gesture 1981; (Dir) Crime and Punishment 1985, Calamari Union (Special Award, Hong Kong Int. Film Festival) 1985, Shadows in Paradise (Jussi Award for Best Finnish Film) 1986, Hamlet 1987, Ariel 1988, Leningrad Cowboys Go Home 1989, The Match Factory Girl 1989, I Hired a Contract Killer 1990, La Vie Bohème, Leningrad Cowboys Meet Moses 1993, Take Care of Your Scarf, Tatiana 1995, Drifting Clouds 1996, The Man Without a Past (Cannes Film Festival Best Actress Award 2002) 2002, Ten Minutes Older: The Trumpet (segment) (also producer, writer, editor) 2002, Visions of Europe (also writer, producer) 2004, Laitakaupungin valot (Lights in the Dark) 2006. *Rock videos:* Rock'y VI, Thru', The Wire, LA Woman 1986. *Address:* c/o The Finnish Film Foundation, K.13, Kanavakatu 24, SF-00160 Helsinki, Finland.

KAUZMANN, Walter Joseph, PhD; American chemist and academic (retd); *David B. Jones Professor Emeritus of Chemistry, Princeton University;* b. 18 Aug. 1916, Mount Vernon, New York; s. of Albert Kauzmann and Julia Kahle; m. Elizabeth Flagler 1951 (died 2004); two s. one d.; ed Cornell and Princeton Univs; Research Fellow, Westinghouse Co.; with Nat. Defense Council Explosives Research Lab.; worked on Manhattan Project, Los Alamos Labs, NM 1944–46; Asst Prof., Princeton Univ. 1946–51, Assoc. Prof. 1951–60, Prof. 1960–83, David B. Jones Prof. of Chem. 1963–83, Chair. Dept of Chemistry 1963–68, Prof. Emer. 1968–, Chair. Dept of Biochemical Sciences 1980–82; Visiting Scientist, Nat. Resources Council of Canada, Halifax 1983; mem. NAS, American Acad. of Sciences 1964–, ACS, American Physical Soc., AAAS, Fed. of American Scientists, American Soc. of Biochemists, American Geophysical Union; Guggenheim Fellow 1957, 1974–75; Visiting Lecturer, Kyoto Univ., Japan 1974, Ibadan Univ., Nigeria 1975; Hon. PhD (Stockholm Univ.) 1992; Stein and Moore Award from Protein Soc. 1993, first recipient Kaj Ulrik Linderstrøm-Lang Medal 1966. *Publications:* Introduction to Quantum Chemistry 1957, Thermal Properties of Matter (two vols) 1966, 1967, Structure and Properties of Water 1969. *Address:* 301 North Harrison Street, PMB 152, Princeton, NJ 08540 (home); c/o Department of Chemistry, Princeton University, Princeton, NJ 08544, USA (office).

KAVAN, Jan Michael, CH, BSc; Czech politician and journalist; *Foreign Policy Adviser to the President of the Chamber of Deputies;* b. 17 Oct. 1946, London; s. of Pavel Kavan and Rosemary Kavanová (née Edwards); m. Lenka Mázlová 1991 (divorced 2005); one s. three d.; ed Charles Univ., Prague, London School of Econs, Univ. of Reading and St Antony's Coll., Oxford, UK; journalist, Univerzita Karlova, Prague 1966–68; Ed. East European Reporter, London 1985–90; Dir Palach Press Ltd, London 1974–90, Deputy Dir Jan Palach Information and Research Trust 1982–90; Vice-Pres. East European Cultural Foundation, London 1985–90; mem. Parl. Fed. Ass. of Czech Repub. 1990–92, 2002–, mem. Foreign Affairs Cttee; mem. Czech Social Democratic (CSSD) Party 1993–, mem. Foreign Affairs Comm. 1994–98, Spokesman on Foreign Affairs 1996–98, elected to Presidium of Cen. Exec. Cttee 1997; Chair. Helsinki Citizens' Ass. in Czech Rep. 1990–95, Policy Centre for the Promotion of Democracy, Prague 1992–98; Senator, Parl. of Czech Repub. 1996–2000; Minister of Foreign Affairs 1998–2002, Deputy Prime Minister 1999–2002; Deputy Chair. Cen. and East European Cttee of the Socialist International 1997, State Security Council 1999–2002; Chair. Council for Intelligence Activities 1999–2002; Pres. UN Gen. Ass. 2002–03; mem. Parl. 2002–06, Deputy Chair. Foreign Affairs Cttee 2004–06, Deputy Leader of Parl. Group of Soc. Democratic Party (CSSD), mem. Presidium of Party of European Socialists (PES) 2006–; foreign policy advisor to Pres. of Chamber of Deputies, Czech Repub.; foreign policy adviser to Prime Minister of Slovakia; Visiting Prof. of Politics and History, Adelphi Univ., New York 1993–94; Karl Loewenstein Fellow in Politics and Jurisprudence, Amherst Coll., Mass 1994; lectured at Columbia and Stanford Univs, Wellesley Coll., Harvard Center for European Studies; taught at London Adult Educ. Inst. for 15 years; Pres. 57th Session UN Gen. Ass. 2002–03; Hon. Prof., Faculty of Int. Relations, Mongolia State Univ. 1999; Hon. Fellow LSE 2001; Companion of Honour 2003, Int. Order of Merit 2003; Hon. DHumLitt (Adelphi) 2001; TGM Medal of Honour 2001. *Publications:* Czechoslovak Socialist Opposition 1976, Voices of Czechoslovak Socialists 1977, Voices from Prague 1983, Justice with a Muzzle 1996, McCarthyism Has a New Name: Lustration, Transition to Democracy in Eastern Europe and Russia 2002; more than 100 articles. *Leisure interests:* int. politics, good literature, film, theatre. *Address:* Parliament of the Czech Republic, Snemovni 4, 118 26 Prague 1 (office); Klausova 13c, Prague 5, 155 00, Czech Republic (home). *Telephone:* (257) 173013 (office). *Fax:* (257) 534403 (office). *E-mail:* kavanjm@seznam.cz (home).

KAVANAGH, Dan (see Barnes, Julian Patrick).

KAVÁNEK, Pavel; Czech banker; *Chairman and CEO, Ceskolovenská Obchodni Banka;* two c.; ed Prague School of Econs Georgetown Univ., USA; staff mem., Foreign Exchange Dept, Ceskolovenská Obchodni Banka 1972–76, Chief Dealer of Dept 1977–90, mem. Bd of Dirs 1990–93, Chair. and CEO 1993–; with Zivnostenská Banka, London, UK 1976–77; Vice-Pres. Asscn of Banks, Prague; Pew Econ. Freedom Fellowship, Georgetown Univ. 1992. *Address:* Ceskolovenská Obchodni Banka, Na Prikope 14, 11520 Prague 1, Czech Republic (office). *Telephone:* (26) 1351000 (office). *Fax:* (22) 4225282 (office). *E-mail:* pkavanek@csob.cz (home). *Website:* www.csob.cz (office).

KAVINDELE, Enoch Percy; Zambian politician; Vice-Pres. Movt for Multi-Party Democracy; Minister of Health –2001; Vice-Pres. of Zambia 2001–03; mem. Nat. Assembly for Kabompo West. *Address:* c/o National Assembly, Lusaka, Zambia (office).

KAWADA, Kenji; Japanese banking executive; *President and Representative Director, Saitama Resona Bank Ltd;* fmr Exec. Officer, Resona Holdings Inc., Dir, Pres. and Rep. Exec. Officer 2003, now Pres. and Rep. Dir Saitama Resona Bank Ltd. *Address:* Saitama Resona Bank Ltd, 4-1 Tokiwa 7-chome, Saitama-shi, Saitama City, Japan (office). *Telephone:* (4) 8824-2411 (office). *Website:* www.resona-gr.co.jp/saitamaresona (office).

KAWAGUCHI, Fumio; Japanese energy industry executive; *Chairman and Representative Director, Chubu Electric Power Company, Inc.;* b. 8 Sept. 1940; Aichi Pref.; ed Waseda Univ. School of Commerce; joined Chubu Electric Power Co., Inc. 1964, Man. Nagoya Office 1999, Man. Dir 1999–2001, Pres. 2001–06, Chair. and Rep. Dir 2006–; Chair. Chubu Econ. Fed., Chubu Industrial Advancement Center; mem. Bd of Councillors, Japan Co-operation Center for the Middle East; Hon. Consul of FRG in Nagoya 2007. *Address:* Chubu Electric Power Co., Inc., 1 Higashi-shincho, Higashi-ku, Nagoya 461-8680, Japan (office). *Telephone:* (52) 951-8211 (office). *Fax:* (52) 962-4624 (office). *E-mail:* info@chuden.co.jp (office). *Website:* www.chuden.co.jp (office).

KAWAGUCHI, Yoriko, BA, MPh; Japanese economist and politician; b. 14 Jan. 1941, Tokyo; m.; two c.; ed Univ. of Tokyo, Yale Univ., USA; at Ministry of Int. Trade and Industry 1965–76, 1979–90, Dir-Gen. Global Environmental Affairs 1992–93; economist, World Bank (IBRD) 1976–78; Minister, Embassy in Washington, DC 1991–92; Man. Dir Suntory Ltd 1993–2000; Minister of the Environment 2000–02, of Foreign Affairs 2002–04; Special Adviser to the Prime Minister responsible for Foreign Affairs 2004–05; mem. House of Councillors (Liberal Democratic Party) 2005–, mem. Cttee on the Environment, Dir Special Cttee on Political Ethics and the Electoral System, Dir Research Cttee on Int. Issues and Climate Change; Chair. Research Comm. on Environment, Policy Research Council, Liberal Democratic Party, Vice-Chair. Econ. and Industry Cttee, Vice-Chair. Special Cttee on Regional Vitalization, Vice-Chair. Special Cttee on Women, Adviser Research Comm. on Int. Competitiveness, Chair. Cttee on Water Resource Security; Sec.-Gen. Comm. to Promote Global-Warming Countermeasures, Policy Research Council; Co-Chair. Int. Cttee on Nuclear Non-Proliferation and Disarmament; Chair. Asia-Pacific Forum for Environment and Devt; mem. Foundation Bd of Forum of Young Global Leaders, World Econ. Forum; Councillor Int. Cttee,

Parliamentarians for Global Action; mem. Hon. Advisory Cttee, UN Univ.; Vice-Chair. GLOBE Japan, GLOBE Int.; mem. Pres.'s Council of Int. Activities; mem. Bd of Trustees, US-Japan Foundation; Band, Order of the Aztec Eagle (Mexico) 2003, Extraordinary Grand Cross, Nat. Order of Merit (Paraguay) 2004; Dr hc (Nat. Univ. of Mongolia) 2004; Wilbur Cross Medal (Yale Univ.) 2008. *Address:* Room 418, Saingiin-kaikan, 2-1-1 Nagata-cho, Chiyoda-ku, Tokyo 100-8962, Japan (office). *Telephone:* (3) 3508-8418 (office). *Fax:* (3) 5512-2418 (office). *E-mail:* yoriko_kawaguchi3@sangiin.go.jp (office). *Website:* www.yoriko-kawaguchi.jp (office).

KAWAI, Masanori; Japanese freight company executive; *President and CEO, Nippon Express Company;* Exec. Vice Pres. Nippon Express Co. –2005, Pres. and CEO 2005–. *Address:* Nippon Express Company Ltd, 1-9-3, Higashi Shimbashi, Minato-ku, Tokyo 105-8322, Japan (office). *Telephone:* (3) 6251-1111 (office). *Website:* www.nittsu.co.jp (office).

KAWAI, Ryoichi; Japanese business executive; b. 18 Jan. 1917; s. of Yoshinari Kawai and Chieko Kawai; m. 1st Kiyoko Kawai 1942 (died 1973); three s.; m. 2nd Junko Kawai 1976; ed Tokyo Univ.; joined Komatsu Ltd 1954, Pres. 1964–82, Chair. 1982–95, Dir and Counsellor 1995, Counsellor 1997–; mem. Bd of Dirs Nomura School of Advanced Man. *Leisure interest:* golf. *Address:* c/o Komatsu Building, 2-3-6, Akasaka, Minato-ku, Tokyo 107-8414, Japan.

KAWAKUBO, Rei; Japanese couturier; b. 1942, Toyko; m. Adrian Joffe; ed Keio Univ., Tokyo; joined Asahikasei 1964; freelance designer 1966; est. Comme des Garçons Label 1969, Founder and Pres. Comme des Garçons Co. Ltd,Tokyo 1973–; opened first overseas Comme des Garçons Boutique in Paris 1982; opened Dover Street Market, first London store October 2004; joined Fed. Française de la Couture 1982; Japan Comme des Garçons Collection presented twice a year, Tokyo; 395 outlets in Japan, five Comme des Garçons shops and 550 outlets outside Japan; currently has 11 lines of clothing, one line of furniture and a perfume; f. Six magazine 1988; cr. costumes and stage design for Merce Cunningham's Scenario 1997; mem. Chambre Syndicale du Pret-a-Porter; Chevalier de L'Ordre des Arts et des Lettres; Dr hc (RCA, London) 1997; Mainichi Newspaper Fashion Award 1983, 1988, Excellence in Design Award, Harvard Univ. 2000. *Address:* c/o Comme des Garçons Co. Ltd, 5-11-5 Minamiaoyama, Minato-ku, Tokyo 107, Japan. *Telephone:* (3) 3407-2480. *Fax:* (3) 5485-2439.

KAWAMATA, Tadashi, MFA; Japanese visual artist; b. 1953, Hokkaido; ed Tokyo Nat. Univ. of Fine Art and Music; works exhibited at Venice Biennale 1982, Int. Youth Triennale of Drawing, Nuremberg 1983, Documenta 8 1987, São Paulo Biennale 1987, Tyne Int. Exhbn for Contemporary Art, Newcastle-upon-Tyne and Gateshead, UK 1990; apartment projects: Takara House Room 205, Tokyo 1982, Slip in Tokorozawa 1983, Tetra House N-3 W-26, Sapporo 1983; construction site projects: Spui Project, The Hague 1986, La Maison des Squatters, Grenoble 1987, Nove de Julho Cacapave, São Paulo 1987, Fukuroi Project 1988; urban projects: P.S.1 Project, New York 1985, Destroyed Church, Kassel 1987, Toronto Project at Colonial Tavern Park, Toronto 1989, Project at Begijnhof St Elisabeth, Kortrijk, Belgium 1989–90, Documente 9 1992, Biennale d' Art Contemporain, Lyon 1993, Münster Skulptor Projekt 1997, 11th Biannale of Sydney 1989, Echigo Tsumari Art Triennial 2000, 4th Shanghai Bienniale 2002, Busan Bienniale 2002, Bienal de Valencia 2003; Prof. Tokyo Univ. of Fine Art and Music 1999–2005; mem. Program Advisory Cttee Space Shower TV 2002–05; Dir Yokohama Triennale 2005; Asian Cultural Council Fellowship Grant (worked in New York 1984–86); Grand Prix Int. Youth Triennale 1983. *Address:* c/o Annely Juda Fine Art, 4th Floor, 23 Dering Street, London, W1S 1AW, England. *Website:* www.tk-onthetable.com; www.cafetalk.net.

KAWAR, Karim Tawfik, BSc; Jordanian business executive and fmr diplomatist; *President, Kawar Group;* b. 14 June 1966, Anman; m. Luma Kawar; one s. two d.; ed Boston Coll., USA; founding mem. several business asscns and non-governmental orgs, including Jordan American Business Asscn, Young Entrepreneurs Asscn, Jordanian Intellectual Property Asscn; est. computer co. and headed an umbrella group encompassing 10 information systems and software cos; apptd to Econ. Consultative Council by King Abdullah II 1999; Head of REACH Initiative (led team of 40 Jordanian information tech. professionals to launch the IT industry in Jordan) 1999; Amb. to USA (also accred to Mexico) 2002–07; fmr Network Coordinator UN Information and Communication Technologies Task Force–Arab Regional Network; fmr Chair. Information Tech. Asscn of Jordan (INTAJ); Vice-Chair. Jordan River Foundation; mem. Young Presidents Org.; Pres. Kawar Group 2007–; Eisenhower Fellow 2000; named Global Leader for Tomorrow by World Econ. Forum. *Address:* Kawar Group, PO Box 222, Amman 11118, Jordan (office). *Telephone:* (6) 5609500 (office). *Fax:* (6) 569 8322 (office). *E-mail:* president@kawar.com.jo (office). *Website:* www.kawar.com (office).

KAWARA, Tsutomu; Japanese politician; mem. House of Reps; fmr Deputy Chief Cabinet Sec.; fmr Dir.-Gen. Defence Agency; fmr Construction Minister; Dir.-Gen. Defence Agency 1999–2000. *Address:* c/o Defence Agency, 9-7-45, Akasaka, Minato-ku, Tokyo 107-8513, Japan (office).

KAWASAKI, Jiro; Japanese politician; b. 15 Nov. 1947, Mie; s. of Hideji Kawasaki; ed Keio Univ.; with Matsushita Electric Industrial Co. 1973–80; mem. House of Reps for Mie dist 1980–, Parl. Vice-Minister, Ministry of Posts and Telecommunications 1990, Minister of Transport 1998–99, of Hokkaido Devt Agency 1999, of Economy, Trade and Industry 2004–05, of Health, Labour and Welfare 2005–06; fmr Head, Public Relations Dept of LDP. *Leisure interests:* reading, tennis. *Address:* c/o Liberal-Democratic Party—LDP (Jiyu-Minshuto), 1-11-23, Nagata-cho, Chiyoda-ku, Tokyo 100-8910, Japan. *Telephone:* (3) 3581-6211. *E-mail:* koho@ldp.jimin.or.jp. *Website:* www.jimin.jp.

KAWAWA, Rashidi Mfaume; Tanzanian politician; b. 1929, Songea; ed Tabora Secondary School; fmr Pres. Tanganyikan Fed. of Labour; Minister of Local Govt and Housing 1960–61; Minister without Portfolio 1961–62; Prime Minister Jan.–Dec. 1962, Vice-Pres. 1962–64; Second Vice-Pres., United Repub. of Tanzania 1964–77, also Prime Minister 1972–77; Minister of Defence and Nat. Service 1977–80, Minister without Portfolio 1980; fmr Vice-Pres. TANU (Tanganyika African Nat. Union); mem. Chama Cha Mapinduzi (CCM—Revolutionary Party of Tanzania), Sec.-Gen. 1982–93. *Address:* c/o Chama Cha Mapinduzi (CCM) (Revolutionary Party of Tanzania), Kuu Street, POB 50, Dodoma, Tanzania.

KAY, Alan, MS, PhD; American computer scientist and academic; *President, Viewpoints Research Institute;* ed Univs of Colorado and Utah; fmr professional jazz guitarist, composer and theatrical designer; worked for Univ. of Utah Advanced Research Project Agency (ARPA) research team that designed or developed 3D-graphics, the FLEX machine (an early interactive object-oriented personal computer), the Dynabook (notebook-sized laptop computer for children), and participated in original design of the ARPANet (later became the Internet) late 1960s; Co-founder Xerox Palo Alto Research Center (PARC) early 1970s; fmr Chief Scientist, Atari; fmr Fellow, Apple Computer; fmr Vice-Pres. Research and Devt, The Walt Disney Co.; Founder and Pres. Viewpoints Research Inst., Inc., Glendale, Calif. 2001–; Sr Fellow, Hewlett-Packard Co. 2002–; Sr Scientist, Div. of Information Tech., Univ. of Wis. 2005–; currently Adjunct Prof., UCLA; Visiting Prof., Kyoto Univ., Japan 2005; Fellow, American Acad. of Arts and Sciences, Nat. Acad. of Eng (NAE), Royal Soc. of Arts (UK), Computer Museum History Center; Dr hc (Kungl Tekniska Hoegskolan, Stockholm, Columbia Coll., Chicago); A.M. Turing Award, Asscn of Computing Machinery (ACM), Kyoto Prize, Inamori Foundation, ACM Software Systems Award, ACM Outstanding Educator Award, J-D Warnier Prix d'lnformatique, NEC C&C Prize 2001, Funai Prize, ZeroOne Award, Univ. of Berlin, inducted into Utah Information Tech. Asscn Hall of Fame 2003, NAE Charles Stark Draper Prize 2004. *Publications:* numerous articles in scientific journals. *Leisure interest:* classical pipe organist. *Address:* Viewpoints Research Institute, Inc., 1209 Grand Central Avenue, Glendale, CA 91201, USA (office). *Telephone:* (818) 332-3001 (office). *Fax:* (818) 244-9761 (office). *E-mail:* kim.rose@vpri.org (office). *Website:* www.viewpointsresearch.org (office).

KAY, John Anderson, FBA, FRSE; British economist; b. 3 Aug. 1948, Edinburgh; s. of the late James Kay and Allison Kay; m. Deborah Freeman 1986 (divorced 1995); ed Royal High School, Edinburgh, Univ. of Edinburgh and Nuffield Coll., Oxford; Fellow, St John's Coll. Oxford 1970–; Lecturer in Econs, Univ. of Oxford 1971–79; Research Dir Inst. for Fiscal Studies 1979–82, Dir 1982–86; Dir Centre for Business Strategy, London Business School 1986–91; Chair. London Econs 1986–96; Dir Said Business School, Univ. of Oxford 1997–99, Undervalued Assets Trust PLC 1994–2005; Dir (non-exec.) Halifax Bldg Soc. 1991–97, Foreign & Colonial Special Utilities Investment Trust PLC 1993–2003, Value and Income Trust PLC 1994–, Halifax PLC 1997–2000, Clear Capital Ltd 2004–08; Law Debenture Corpn 2004–, Scottish Mortgage Investment Trust PLC 2008–. *Publications:* The British Tax System 1989, Foundations of Corporate Success 1993, Why Firms Succeed 1995, The Business of Economics 1996, The Truth about Markets 2003, Everlasting Light Bulbs 2004, Culture and Prosperity 2005, The Hare and the Tortoise 2006, The Long and the Short of It 2008; co-author: Concentration in Modern Industry, The Reform of Social Security, The Economic Analysis of Accounting Profitability; articles in scholarly journals. *Leisure interests:* walking, travel. *Address:* The Erasmus Press Ltd, PO Box 4026, London, WIA 6NZ, England (office). *Telephone:* (20) 7224-8797. *Fax:* (20) 7402-1368. *E-mail:* johnkay@johnkay.com (office). *Website:* www.johnkay.com (office).

KAYE, Carol; American musician (electric bass guitar, guitar); b. 24 March 1935, Everett, Wash.; one s. two d.; teacher of guitar 1949–, electric bass 1969–; on the road, big band 1954–55; played bebop jazz, night clubs 1956–61; special records, studio guitarist 1957–66; studio electric bassist 1963–; invented 16th note bass recording styles; over 10,000 sessions; television credits, playing bass include M.A.S.H, Mission Impossible, Hawaii 5-O, Brady Bunch, Soap; film credits, playing bass include Thomas Crown Affair, Heat of the Night, Valley of the Dolls, Shaft (theme), columnist, Bassics Magazine; mem. Musicians' Union; Women in Music Award 2000, Lifetime Achievement Award, Duquesne Univ. Pittsburgh Jazz Soc. 2000, Los Angeles Composers–Arrangers Award 2004, Lifetime Achievement Award, Bass Player Magazine 2008. *Television:* First Lady of Bass TV (documentary). *Recordings:* albums: Carol Kaye: Bass, Thumbs Up, Carol Kaye Guitars '65; credits on guitar include: Zippity Doo Dah, Batman Theme, Birds and Bees, The Beat Goes On, You've Lost That Lovin Feelin, La Bamba; credits on bass guitar include: Way We Were, Feelin' Alright, Good Vibrations, Help Me Rhonda, Wouldn't It Be Nice, Can't Help Myself, Heat of Night, I Don't Need No Doctor, Little Green Apples, Baby Love, River Deep Mountain High, Something Stupid, This is My Song, Mission Impossible, Pet Sounds, Smile. *Publications:* writer, composer of over 30 tutorials; How to Play the Electric Bass, Jazz Improvisation for Bass. *Leisure interests:* reading, teaching. *Address:* 25852 McBean Parkway, Suite 200, Valencia, CA 91355, USA (office). *Telephone:* (661) 288-6551 (office). *E-mail:* carol@carolkaye.com. *Website:* www.carolkaye.com.

KAYE, Harvey Jordan, PhD; American academic and writer; *Ben and Joyce Rosenberg Professor of Social Change and Development and Director, Center for History and Social Change, University of Wisconsin-Green Bay;* b. 9 Oct. 1949, Englewood, NJ; s. of Murray N. Kaye and Frances Kaye; m. Lorna Stewart 1973; two d.; ed Paramus High School, Rutgers Univ., Univ. of Mexico, Univ. of London, UK and Louisiana State Univ.; Asst Prof. of Interdisciplinary Studies, St Cloud Univ., Minn. 1977–78; Asst Prof. of Social Change and Devt, Univ. of Wis., Green Bay 1978–83, Assoc. Prof. 1983–86,

Head of Dept 1985–88, Prof. 1986–, Ben and Joyce Rosenberg Prof. of Social Change and Devt 1990–, Dir Center for History and Social Change 1991–; Visiting Fellow, Univ. of Birmingham, UK 1987; mem. Editorial Bd Marxist Perspectives 1978–80, The Wisconsin Sociologist, Wis. Sociological Asscn 1985–87, Rethinking History 1996–; Consulting Ed., Verso Publishers, London 1988–94, NYU Press 1996–; Series Ed., American Radicals (Routledge) 1992–98; columnist, Times Higher Educational Supplement 1994–2001, Tikkun magazine 1996–97, Index on Censorship 1996–, The Guardian Unlimited 2007–; mem. Exec. Bd, Center for Democratic Values 1996–2000, Scholars, Artists and Writers for Social Justice 1997–2000; mem. American Historical Asscn, American Sociological Asscn, Org. of American Historians, PEN; Nat. Endowment for the Humanities Fellowship 2002–03; Historical Adviser, Remix America 2008–, Thomas Paine documentary; Founders' Award for Scholarship 1985, Isaac Deutscher Memorial Prize 1993, Best Book for the Teen Age, New York Public Library 2001, Best Book 2006, Wisconsin Library Asscn. *Publications:* The British Marxist Historians 1984, The Powers of the Past 1991, The Education of Desire 1992, Why do Ruling Classes Fear History? 1996, Thomas Paine 2000, Are We Good Citizens? 2001, Thomas Paine and the Promise of America 2005; (Ed.) History, Classes and Nation-States 1988, The Face of the Crowd: Studies in Revolution, Ideology and Popular Protest 1988, Poets, Politics and the People 1989, E. P. Thompson: Critical Perspectives (with K. McClelland) 1990, The American Radical (with M. Buhle and P. Buhle) 1994, Imperialism and its Contradictions 1995, Ideology and Popular Protest 1995; numerous articles on history and historians. *Leisure interests:* travel, films, friendship and conversation. *Address:* Social Change and Development Department, University of Wisconsin-Green Bay, 2420 Nicolet Drive, Green Bay, WI 54311, USA (office). *Telephone:* (920) 465-2355 (office); (920) 465-2755 (office). *Fax:* (920) 465-2791 (office). *E-mail:* kayeh@uwgb.edu (office). *Website:* www.uwgb.edu/centerhsc (office).

KAYSEN, Carl, AB, MA, PhD; American economist and academic; *Professor Emeritus, Massachusetts Institute of Technology;* b. 5 March 1920, Philadelphia; s. of Samuel and Elizabeth Resnick; m. 1st Annette Neutra 1940 (died 1990); two d.; m. 2nd Ruth A. Butler 1994; ed Overbrook High School, Philadelphia, Univ. of Pennsylvania and Harvard Univ.; Nat. Bureau of Econ. Research 1940–42; Office of Strategic Services, Washington, DC 1942–43; US Army (Intelligence) 1943–45; Teaching Fellow in Econs, Harvard Univ. 1947, Jr Fellow, Soc. of Fellows 1947–50, Asst Prof. in Econs 1950–55, Assoc. Prof. 1955–57, Prof. 1957–66, Assoc. Dean, Grad. School of Public Admin 1960–66, Lucius N. Littauer Prof. of Political Economy 1964–66; Dir Inst. of Advanced Study, Princeton 1966–76, Dir Emer. 1976–, Prof. of Social Science 1976–77; David W. Skinner Prof. of Political Econ., MIT 1976–90, Prof. Emer. 1990–, Sr Research Scientist 1992–, Dir Program in Science, Tech. and Soc. 1981–86, now Faculty Emer.; Vice-Chair. and Dir Research, Sloan Comm. on Govt and Higher Educ. 1977–79; Sr Fulbright Research Scholar, LSE 1955–56; Econ. Consultant to Judge Wyzanski, Fed. Dist. Court of Mass 1950–52; Deputy Special Asst to Pres. for Nat. Security Affairs 1961–63. *Publications:* United States v. United Shoe Machinery Corporation, an Economic Analysis of an Anti-Trust Case 1956, The American Business Creed (with others) 1956, Anti-Trust Policy (with D. F. Turner) 1959, The Demand for Electricity in the United States (with Franklin M. Fisher) 1962, The Higher Learning, the Universities and the Public 1969, Nuclear Power, Issues and Choice, Nuclear Energy Policy Study Group Report (with others) 1977, A Program for Renewed Partnership, Report of the Sloan Commission on Government and Higher Education (with others) 1980, Emerging Norms of Justified Intervention 1993, Peace Operations by the United Nations (with George Rathjens) 1996, The American Corporation Now (ed.) 1996, The United States and the International Criminal Court (co-ed. with S. Sewall) 2000, War in Iraq (co-author) 2002, Alternatives, Costs, and Consequences. *Address:* Massachusetts Institute of Technology Program in Security Studies, 292 Main Street, E38-614 Cambridge, MA 02139, USA (office). *Telephone:* (617) 253-4054 (office). *Fax:* (617) 253-9330 (office).

KAZANNIK, Aleksei Ivanovich, DIur; Russian lawyer; b. 26 July 1941, Perepis, Chernigov Region; m.; two s.; ed Irkutsk Univ.; teacher Irkutsk Univ. 1975–79; Prof., Head of Chair, Omsk Univ. 1979–89, 1994–; forbidden to give public lectures because of criticism of Soviet invasion of Afghanistan; USSR People's Deputy 1989–91; fmr mem. USSR Supreme Soviet; active participant Movt Democratic Russia; mem. Interregional Group of Deputies; mem. Cttee on ecology problems and rational use of natural resources, USSR Supreme Soviet; mem. Pres.'s Council 1993–94; Prosecutor-Gen. of Russia 1993–94 (resgnd); founder and Chair. Party of People's Conscience 1995–; Chair. Cttee on problems of nationalities, religions and public orgs of Omsk Region 1996–; Deputy Gov. Omsk Region 1999–. *Publications:* legal aspects of regional problems of nature preservation, numerous articles on ecology, law, pamphlets. *Address:* Administration of Omsk Region, Krasny Put str. 1, 644002 Omsk; Omsk State University, Mira Prosp. 55A, 644077 Omsk, Russia. *Telephone:* (3812) 23-49-26 (Administration). *E-mail:* eshish@univer.omsk.ru.

KAZANTSEV, Col-Gen. Victor Germanovich; Russian army officer; b. 22 Feb. 1946, Kokhanovo, Vitebsk Region, Belarus; m. Tamara Valentinovna Kazantseva; ed Leningrad Higher School of Gen. Army, M. Frunze Mil. Acad., Mil. Acad. of Gen. Staff; officer in Caucasian, Middle-Asian, Turkestan, Baikal Mil. Commands, Cen. Army Group in Czechoslovakia, First Deputy Commdr of Army N Caucasian Mil. Command; Chief of Staff to Commdr of troops N Caucasian Mil. Command 1996–97, Commdr 1997–99; Commdr group of Fed. forces in N Caucasus 1999–2000; Rep. of Pres. to S Fed. Dist 2000–04; Hero of Russia for operations in Dagestan and Chechnya 1999. *Address:* c/o Office of the Representative of the President to Southern Federal District, Bolshaya Sadovaya str. 73, 344006 Rostov-on-Don, Russia (office).

KAZARNOVSKAYA, Lubov Yurievna; Russian singer (soprano); b. 18 July 1956; m. Robert Roszik; ed Moscow Gnessin School of Music and Moscow State Conservatory; as student became soloist, Moscow Stanislavsky and Nemirovich-Danchenko Musical Theatre 1981–86; soloist, Leningrad Kirov (now Mariinsky) Opera Theatre 1986–89; debut outside USSR in Un Ballo in Maschera, Zürich Opera 1989, Desdemona in Otello, Covent Garden, London March 1990; moved to Vienna 1989; has performed in major opera houses of the world, in opera productions with Herbert von Karajan, Carlos Kleiber, Claudio Abbado, Riccardo Muti, Daniel Barenboim, James Conlon; also performs in concerts, including Requiem (Verdi), La Voix humaine by Poulenc and at festivals in Salzburg, Bregenz, Edin. and others; Chair. Comm. on Cultural and Humanitarian Co-operation, Asscn of Russian Municipal Formations; Chair. Russian Musical Educational Soc.; f. Lubov Kazarnovskaya Fund (supports Russian opera); winner, All-Union Competition of Singers 1981, int. competition in Bratislava 1984; Gramophone Critic's Award for CD anthology of romances 2008. *Music:* operatic roles include leading parts in Eugene Onegin, Iolanthe, La Bohème, Pagliacci, Faust, Marriage of Figaro, Falstaff, Force of Destiny, Boris Godunov, La Traviata, Salome. *Address:* Hohenbergstrasse 50, 1120 Vienna, Austria. *Telephone:* (1) 839106 (Vienna) (home); (495) 249-17-13 (Moscow) (home).

KAZHEGELDIN, Akezhan Magzhan-Uly; Kazakhstani politician and economist; b. 27 March 1952, Georgiyevka, Semipalatinsk Region; m. Bykova Natalia Kazhegeldina; one s. one d.; ed Kazakh State Univ., Moscow Inst. of Oriental Studies; Chair. Regional Exec. Cttee of Semipalatinsk 1983; Dir Ore-enriching Factory, Deputy Gov. Admin. of Semipalatinsk Region 1991–94; Pres. Kazakhstan Union of Industrialists and Entrepreneurs 1992–; apptd First Deputy Prime Minister of Kazakhstan 1994, Prime Minister 1994–97; Adviser to Pres. Nazarbayev May–Oct. 1998; disbarred from presidential election in 1998; f. Republican People's Party of Kazakhstan 1998, Chair. Bd 1998–2001; mem. Politburo Bd United Democratic Party 2001; in opposition to Pres. Nazarbayev 1999–, now lives abroad, sentenced to 10 years imprisonment in absentia 1999. *Publications include:* six books including Kazakhstan in the Conditions of Reforms, Problems of State Regulation in the Conditions of Socio-Economic Transformation, Socio-Economic Problems of Development of Kazakhstan in the Conditions of Reforms 1999, Opposition to Middle Ages 2000. *Address:* c/o Republican Independent Political Club Association (Assotsiatsiya Respublianskogo Nezavisimogo Politicheskogo Kluba–RNPK), ul. Zhestoksan 12/514–515, 480050, Almaty, Kazakhstan. *Telephone:* (7172) 32-59-58. *Fax:* (7172) 32-39-85. *E-mail:* akkz@inbox.ru.

KAZIBWE, Speciosa Wandira, MD, ChB; Ugandan physician, politician and government official; *Chairman, Microfinance Support Centre Ltd;* b. 1 July 1955, Iganga Dist; ed Makerere Univ., Kampala; mem. Nat. Resistance Movt (NRM)); MP for Kigulu S Iganga Dist; Deputy Minister for Industry 1989–91; fmr Minister for Gender and Community Devt; fmr Minister of Agric., Animal Industry and Fisheries; Vice-Pres. of Uganda 1994–2003 (resgnd to attend Harvard Univ. School of Public Health, USA); Chair. Microfinance Support Centre Ltd, Uganda 2008–; Co-founder Concave International Ltd. (agricultural co-op consulting co.); fmr Chair. African Women's Cttee on Peace and Devt; mem. Bd of Dirs African Science Acad. Devt Initiative; Chair. Sr Women's Advisory Group on the Environment; mem. Uganda Women Entrepreneurs Asscn, Uganda Women Doctors Asscn, UN Comm. on the Status of Women 2006; fmr Co-Chair. Study Panel on Agricultural Productivity in Africa, InterAcademy Council; mem. Global Bd, Hunger Project. *Address:* Microfinance Support Centre Ltd, Plot 46, Windsor Crescent, Kololo, PO Box 33711, Kampala, Uganda (office). *Telephone:* (41) 233665 (office). *Fax:* (41) 233673 (office).

KAZMIN, Andrei Ilyich, PhD; Russian banker; *Chairman and CEO, Sberbank;* b. 1958, Moscow; m.; ed Moscow Inst. of Finance; Economist, State Bank of the USSR 1982–83; Asst Prof., then Deputy Dean Faculty of Credit, Moscow Inst. of Finance 1983–88; Sr Researcher USSR (now Russian) Acad. of Sciences 1988–91; Sr Research Fellow Alexander von Humboldt Foundation, Inst. for Int. Politics and Security, Ebenhausen, Germany 1991–93; training at German Ministry of Finance and German banks 1992–93; Deputy Minister of Finance, Russian Fed. 1993–96; Chair. of Bd and CEO Savings Bank of Russian Fed. (Sberbank) 1996–; Vice-Pres. World Savings Banks Inst. 2000–; mem. Bd of Dirs MasterCard Europe 2000–; Order of Honour 2002. *Publications:* more than 40 publs. *Leisure interest:* theatre, literature, sports. *Address:* Sberbank, Vavilova str. 19, 117997 Moscow, Russia (office). *Telephone:* (495) 957-57-58 (office). *Fax:* (495) 747-37-58 (office). *E-mail:* sbrf@sbrf.ru (office). *Website:* www.sbrf.ru (office).

KAZULIN, Alyaksandr, PhD; Belarusian mathematician, university rector and politician; *Chairman, Assembly (Hramada)—Belarusian Social-Democratic Party;* b. 25 Nov. 1955, Minsk; m. Iryna Kazulina (died 2008); two d.; ed Belarusian State Univ.; mil. service in Soviet Navy as Marine 1974–76; Lecturer and Instructor, Youth Communist League (Komsomol), later Dean, Belarusian State Univ. 1980–88, Rector 1996–2003; Dept Chief, then First Deputy Minister, Educ. Ministry 1988–96; Minister of Educ. 1998–2001; f. People's Will political movt 2005; joined Belarusian Social-Democratic Party, March 2005, elected Chair. Assembly (Hramada)—Belarusian Social-Democratic Party following merger of parties in April 2005; sentenced to five-and-a-half years' imprisonment on charges of hooliganism and inciting mass disorder July 2006, granted early release following pressure by US Govt 16 Aug. 2008. *Address:* Assembly (Hramada)—Belarusian Social-Democratic Party, 220035 Minsk, vul. Drozda 8/52, Belarus (office). *Telephone:* (17) 226-74-37 (office). *Fax:* (17) 226-74-37 (office). *E-mail:* bsdggramada@tut.by (office). *Website:* www.bsdp.org (office).

KE, Bingsheng, BS, MA, PhD; Chinese agricultural economist and university administrator; *President, China Agricultural University;* ed Univ. of Hohenheim, Germany, Peking Univ., China Agric. Univ.; economist with Ministry of Agric., becoming Dir Centre for Rural Economy Studies 1997–2007; Prof., China Agricultural Univ., also fmr Deputy Dean, Grad. School, Dean Coll. of Econs and Man., Vice-Pres. China Agric. Univ., Pres. 2008–; adviser to Chinese Govt on agricultural policy issues. *Publications:* China's Grain Market and Policy 1995. *Address:* Office of the President, China Agricultural University, 17 Qinghua Donglu, Haidian District, Beijing 100083, People's Republic of China (office). *Telephone:* (10) 6273 6482 (office). *Fax:* (10) 6273 7704 (office). *E-mail:* cauie@cau.edu.cn (office). *Website:* www.cau.edu.cn (office).

KEACH, Stacy; American actor and director; b. 2 June 1941, Savannah, Ga; s. of Walter Edmund Keach and Dora Stacy; m. Malgossia Tomassi 1986; two d.; stage debut in Joseph Papp's production of Hamlet, Cen. Park 1964; other stage appearances include A Long Day's Journey into Night, Macbird (Vernon Rice Drama Desk Award), Indians, Deathtrap, Hughie, Barnum, Cyrano de Bergerac, Peer Gynt, Henry IV (Parts I & II), Idiot's Delight, The King and I 1989, Love Letters 1990–93, Richard III 1991, Stieglitz Loves O'Keefe 1995; Dir Incident at Vichy and Six Characters in Search of an Author for TV; mem. Artists Cttee Kennedy Center Honors 1986–; Hon. Chair. American Cleft Palate Foundation 1995–; recipient of three Obie Awards, Pasadena Playhouse Alumni Man of the Year 1995, Pacific Pioneers Broadcasters' Asscn Diamond Circle Award 1996. *Films include:* The Heart is a Lonely Hunter, End of the Road, The Travelling Executioner, Brewster McCloud, Doc, Judge Roy Bean, The New Centurions, Fat City, The Killer Inside Me, Conduct Unbecoming, Luther, Street People, The Squeeze, Gray Lady Down, The Ninth Configuration, The Long Riders, Road Games, Butterfly, Up in Smoke, Nice Dreams, That Championship Season, The Lover, False Identity, The Forgotten Milena, John Carpenter's Escape from LA 1996, Prey of the Jaguar 1996, The Truth Configuration 1998, American History X 1998, Icebreaker 1999, Unshackled 2000, Militia 2000, Mercy Streets 2000, Sunstorm 2001, When Eagles Strike 2003, Jesus, Mary and Joey 2003, Caught in the Headlights 2004, Galaxy Hunter 2004, El Padrino 2004, The Hollow 2004, Man with the Screaming Brain 2005, Keep Your Distance 2005, Come Early Morning 2006, Jesus, Mary and Joey 2006, Death Row 2006, W. 2008, Chicago Overcoat 2009, The Portal 2009, The Boxer 2009. *Television includes:* Mike Hammer, Private Eye (series) 1997, The Courage to Love 2000, Titus (series) 2000, Lightning: Fire From the Sky 2001, Rods! (series) 2002, The Santa Trap 2002, Miracle Dogs 2003, Frozen Impact 2003, Desolation Canyon 2006, Fatal Contact: Bird Flu in America 2006, Washington the Warrior (voice, miniseries) 2006, Blackbeard (miniseries) 2006, Prison Break (series) 2005–07. *Publication:* Keach, Go Home! 1996 (autobiog.). *Address:* William Morris Agency, 1 William Morris Place, Beverly Hills, CA 90212; c/o Palmer & Associates, #950, 23852 Pacific Coast Highway, Malibu, CA 90265, USA (office).

KEAN, Thomas H., MA; American academic administrator and fmr politician; b. 21 April 1935, New York; m. Deborah Bye; two s. one d.; ed Princeton Univ., Columbia Univ. Teachers' Coll.; fmr teacher of history and Govt; mem. NJ Ass. 1967–77, Speaker 1972, Minority Leader 1974; Acting Gov. of NJ 1973, Gov. 1982–90; Pres. Drew Univ., Madison, NJ 1990–2005 (retd); mem. White House Conf. on Youth 1970–71; fmr Chair. Carnegie Corpn of New York, Educate America, Nat. Environmental Educ. and Training Foundation; Chair. Newark Alliance, Nat. Campaign to Prevent Teen Pregnancy, Nat. Comm. on Terrorist Attacks upon the US (9-11 Comm.) 2002–04; mem. Bd Robert Wood Johnson Foundation, Nat. Council World Wildlife Fund; regular columnist, The Star Ledger. *Publications include:* The Politics of Inclusion, Without Precedent: The Inside Story of the 9/11 Commission (with Lee H. Hamilton) 2006. *Address:* c/o Office of the President, Drew University, 36 Madison Avenue, Madison, NJ 07940, USA.

KEANE, Fergal Patrick, OBE; Irish journalist and broadcaster; b. 6 Jan. 1961; s. of the late Eamon Brendan Keane and of Mary Hasset; m. Anne Frances Flaherty 1986; one s.; ed Terenure Coll., Dublin and Presentation Coll., Cork; trainee reporter with Limerick Leader 1979–82; reporter Irish Press Group, Dublin 1982–84, Radio Telefis Eireann, Belfast 1986–89 (Dublin 1984–86); NI Corresp. BBC Radio 1989–91, South Africa Corresp. 1991–94, Asia Corresp. 1994–97, Special Corresp. Radio 4 1997–; presenter, Fergal Keane's Forgotten Britain (BBC) 2000; columnist The Independent newspaper; Hon. DLitt (Strathclyde) 2001, (Staffs.) 2002; James Cameron Prize 1996, Bayeux Prize for war reporting 1999; Reporter of the Year Sony Silver Award 1992 and Sony Gold Award 1993, Int. Reporter of the Year 1993, Amnesty Int. Press Awards, RTS Journalist of the Year 1994, BAFTA Award 1997. *Publications:* Irish Politics Now 1987, The Bondage of Fear 1994, Season of Blood: A Rwandan Journey 1995, Letter to Daniel 1996, Letters Home 1999, A Stranger's Eye 2000, There will be Sunlight Later: A Memoir of War 2004, All of These People (memoir) 2005. *Leisure interests:* fishing, golf, poetry. *Address:* BBC Radio, Broadcasting House,.Portland Place, London, W1A 1AA, England. *Website:* www.bbc.co.uk/radio4/presenters/fergal_keane.shtml.

KEAT CHHON, PhD; Cambodian politician; *Senior Minister and Minister of the Economy and Finance;* b. 11 Aug. 1934, Kratie Prov.; m. Lay Neari; one s. one d.; ed Charles Stuart Univ., Australia; naval architect, marine engineer and nuclear engineer; fmr Gov. Bank of Cambodia; elected mem. of Parl.; currently Sr Minister, Minister of the Economy and Finance and Sr Minister in charge of Rehabilitation and Devt; Coordinator Working Group for Govt Pvt. Sector Forum; Vice Chair. Council for the Devt of Cambodia; Vice-Chair. Cambodian Inst. for Cooperation and Peace, Phnom-Penh; Commdr Légion d'honneur, Grand Cross Order of Sowathara (Cambodia), Grand Cross Order of Kingdom of Cambodia. *Publications:* Cambodia's Economic Development: Policies, Strategies and Implementation 1999. *Address:* Ministry of the Economy and Finance, 60 rue 92, Phnom-Penh, Cambodia (office). *Telephone:*

(23) 723164 (office). *Fax:* (23) 723164 (office). *E-mail:* mef@mef.gov.kh (office). *Website:* www.mef.gov.kh (office).

KEATING, Francis (Frank) Anthony, II, JD; American lawyer and fmr politician; *President and CEO, American Council of Life Insurers;* b. 10 Feb. 1944, St Louis, Mo.; s. of Anthony Francis Keating and Anne Martin; m. Catherine Dunn Heller 1972; one s. two d.; ed Georgetown Univ., Univ. of Oklahoma; called to the Bar, Okla 1969; Special Agent with FBI 1969–71; Asst Dist Attorney, Tulsa Co. 1971–72; mem. Okla House of Reps 1972–74, Okla Senate 1974–81; attorney, Northern Dist, Okla 1981–84; Asst Sec., US Treasury Dept, Washington, DC 1985–88, Assoc. Attorney-Gen., US Dept of Justice 1988–89, Gen. Counsel and Acting Deputy Sec., US Dept of Housing and Urban Devt 1989–93; attorney in pvt. practice, Tulsa 1993–95; Gov. of Okla 1995–2003; Pres. and CEO American Council of Life Insurers 2003–; mem. Okla Bar Asscn; mem. Bd Dirs Nat. Archives Foundation, Mt Vernon; Pres. Fed. City Council; hon. degrees from Marymount Univ., Groves Coll., Univ. of Tulsa, LaRoche Coll., Regentes Univ.; Order of Malta, Fed. Asscn. *Publications:* for children: Will Rogers (Spur Award, Western Writers of America 2003), Theodore (Int. Children's Book Award for Non-fiction 2007). *Address:* American Council of Life Insurers, 101 Constitution Avenue, NW, Washington, DC 20001-2133, USA (office). *Telephone:* (202) 624-2000 (office). *Fax:* (202) 572-4840 (office). *E-mail:* Media@acli.com (office). *Website:* www.acli.com (office).

KEATING, Henry Reymond Fitzwalter, (Evelyn Hervey), FRSL; British writer; b. 31 Oct. 1926, St Leonards-on-Sea, Sussex; s. of John Hervey Keating and Muriel Keating; m. Sheila Mary Mitchell 1953; three s. one d.; ed Merchant Taylors' School, Trinity Coll., Dublin; journalist 1952–59; Chair. Crime Writers Asscn 1970–71, Soc. of Authors 1983, 1984; Pres. The Detection Club 1985–2001; Gold Dagger Award 1964, 1980, Diamond Dagger Award 1996. *Publications:* Death and the Visiting Firemen 1959, Zen There Was Murder 1960, A Rush on the Ultimate 1961, The Dog It Was That Died 1962, Death of a Fat God 1963, The Perfect Murder 1964, Is Skin Deep, Is Fatal 1965, Inspector Ghote's Good Crusade 1966, Inspector Ghote Caught in Meshes 1967, Inspector Ghote Hunts the Peacock 1968, Inspector Ghote Plays a Joker 1969, Inspector Ghote Breaks an Egg 1970, Inspector Ghote Goes by Train 1971, The Strong Man 1971, Inspector Ghote Trusts the Heart 1972, Bats Fly Up for Inspector Ghote 1974, The Underside 1974, A Remarkable Case of Burglary 1975, Murder Must Appetize 1976, Filmi, Filmi Inspector Ghote 1976, Agatha Christie: First Lady of Crime (ed) 1977, A Long Walk to Wimbledon 1978, Inspector Ghote Draws a Line 1979, Sherlock Holmes, the Man and his World 1979, The Murder of the Maharajah 1980, Go West, Inspector Ghote 1981, The Lucky Alphonse 1982, The Sheriff of Bombay 1983, Under a Monsoon Cloud 1984, Mrs Craggs, Crimes Cleaned Up 1985, Writing Crime Fiction 1986, The Body in the Billiard Room 1987, Dead on Time 1988, Inspector Ghote, His Life and Crimes 1989, The Iciest Sin 1990, Cheating Death 1992, The Rich Detective 1993, Doing Wrong 1994, The Good Detective 1995, Asking Questions 1996, In Kensington Gardens Once 1997, The Soft Detective 1997, Bribery, Corruption Also 1999, Jack, the Lady Killer 1999, The Hard Detective 2000, Breaking and Entering 2000, A Detective in Love 2001, A Detective Under Fire 2002, The Dreaming Detective 2003, A Detective at Death's Door 2004, One Man and His Bomb 2006, Rules, Regs and Rotten Eggs 2007, Inspector Ghote's First Case 2008. *Address:* 35 Northumberland Place, London, W2 5AS, England. *Telephone:* (20) 7229-1100.

KEATING, Michael, BA, MA, PhD, FRSE; Canadian/British/Irish political scientist and academic; *Professor of Political and Social Sciences, European University Institute;* b. 2 Feb. 1950; s. of Michael Joseph Keating and Margaret Watson Keating; m. Patricia Ann Patrick; ed Univ. of Oxford, Council for Nat. Academic Awards, Inst. of Linguists; grad. student and part-time Lecturer in Politics and Econs, Glasgow Coll. of Tech. 1972–75; Sr Research Officer in Govt, Univ. of Essex 1975–76; Lecturer in Politics, North Straffordshire Polytechnic 1976–79; Sr Lecturer in Politics, Univ. of Strathclyde 1979–88; Prof. of Political Science, Univ. of Western Ontario, Canada 1988–99; Chair in Scottish Politics, Univ. of Aberdeen 1999–; Prof. of Political and Social Sciences, European Univ. Inst., Florence, Italy 2000–; Visiting Prof. of Political Science, Virginia Polytechnic Inst. and State Univ., USA 1987–88, Univ. of Sunderland, UK 1995–2000; Visiting Prof. of Govt, Univ. of Strathclyde 1988–99; Visiting Prof., Institut d'Etudes Politiques, Paris 1991; Univ. of Santiago de Compostela, Spain 1992; Scholar in Residence, Rockefeller Foundation Center, Bellagio, Italy 1997; Norman Chester Sr Visiting Research Fellow, Nuffield Coll., Oxford 1998; Visiting Fellow, Schuman Centre, European Univ. Inst. 1999, McQuarie Univ., Sydney, Australia 2005; Founder and Co-Dir European Consortium for Political Research Standing Group on Regionalism; Jt Ed. Regional and Federal Studies; mem. editorial bds Environment and Planning, Government and Policy, Space and Polity, Modern and Contemporary France, Spanish Cultural Studies, Regional Studies, Politique et Sociétés. *Publications include:* State and Regional Nationalism: Territorial Politics and the European State 1988, Comparative Urban Politics: Power and the City in the United States, Canada, Britain and France 1991, The Politics of Modern Europe: The State and Political Authority in the Major Democracies 1993, The European Union and the Regions (co-ed.) 1995, Nations Against the State: The New Politics of Nationalism in Quebec, Catalonia and Scotland 1996, The New Regionalism in Western Europe: Territorial Restructuring and Political Change 1998, Paradiplomacy in Action: The External Activities of Subnational Governments 1999, The Government of Scotland 2005, Methodologies and Approaches in the Social Sciences (co-ed.) 2008. *Address:* Department of Political and Social Sciences, European University Institute, Via dei Roccettini, 9, 50014 San Domenico di Fiesole (FI), Italy (office). *Telephone:* (055) 4685250 (office). *Fax:* (055) 4685279 (office). *E-mail:* Michael.Keating@eui.eu (office). *Website:* www.iue.it/SPS (office).

KEATING, Hon. Paul John; Australian politician; b. 18 Jan. 1944, Sydney; s. of Matthew Keating and Min Keating; m. Anna Van Iersel 1975; one s. three d.; ed De la Salle Coll., Bankstown; Research Officer, Federated Municipal and Shire Council Employees' Union of Australia 1967; mem. House of Reps for Fed. Seat of Blaxland 1969–96; Minister for N Australia Oct.–Nov. 1975; Opposition Spokesman on Agric. Jan.-March 1976, on Minerals and Energy 1976–83, on Treasury Matters Jan.–March 1983; Fed. Treas. 1983–91; Leader, Australian Labour Party 1991–96; Deputy Prime Minister 1990–91, Prime Minister of Australia 1991–96; Chair. Australian Inst. of Music 1999–2005; Bd of Architects of NSW 2000–04; Hon. LLD (Keio Univ., Tokyo) 1995, (Nat. Univ. of Singapore) 1999, (Univ. NSW) 2003. *Publication:* Engagement: Australia Faces the Asia Pacific 2000. *Leisure interests:* classical music, architecture, swimming, fine arts. *Address:* PO Box 1265, Potts Point, 1335 NSW, Australia. *Telephone:* (2) 9358 5466 (office). *Fax:* (2) 9358 5477 (office). *Website:* www.keating.org.au (office).

KEATING, Roly; British broadcasting executive; *Director of Archive Content, BBC;* joined BBC as trainee 1983, Series Ed. Bookmark 1992–97, Head of Programming for UKTV 1997–2001, Controller of Digital Channels 1999–2001, Controller of Arts Commissioning 2000–01, Controller of BBC 4 2001–04, of BBC 2 2004–08, Dir of Archive Content 2008–; BAFTA Award for Best Arts Programme (Bookmark) 1993. *Address:* BBC Television Centre, Wood Lane, White City, London, W12 7RJ, England (office). *Telephone:* (20) 8743-8000 (office). *Fax:* (20) 8225-7821 (office). *Website:* www.bbc.co.uk/bbctwo (office).

KEATING, Ronan; Irish singer and songwriter; b. 3 March 1977, Dublin; s. of Gerry Keating and the late Marie Keating; m. Yvonne Keating; one s. one d.; mem. Boyzone 1993–2001, 2007–; solo artist 1999–. *Recordings include:* albums: with Boyzone: Said and Done 1995, A Different Beat 1996, Where We Belong 1998, By Request 1999, Back Again... No Matter What 2008; solo: Ronan 2000, Destination 2002, Bring You Home 2006, Songs for My Mother 2009. *Publications:* No Matter What 2000, Life is a Rollercoaster 2000. *Address:* The Outside Organisation, Butler House, 177–178 Tottenham Court Road, London, W1T 7NY, England (office). *Telephone:* (20) 7436-3633 (office). *Fax:* (20) 7436-3632 (office). *E-mail:* pressoffice@outside-org.co.uk (office). *Website:* www.ronankeating.com.

KEATON, Diane; American actress; b. 5 Jan. 1946, Calif.; student Neighbourhood Playhouse, New York; New York stage appearances in Hair 1968, Play It Again Sam 1971, The Primary English Class 1976; f. Blue Relief Productions (film production co.). *Films include:* Lovers and Other Strangers 1970, Play It Again Sam 1972, The Godfather 1972, Sleeper 1973, The Godfather Part 2 1974, Love and Death 1975, I Will-I Will–For Now 1975, Harry and Walter Go To New York 1976, Annie Hall 1977, (Acad. Award for Best Actress and other awards), Looking for Mr. Goodbar 1977, Interiors 1978, Manhattan 1979, Reds 1981, Shoot the Moon 1982, Mrs Soffel 1985, Crimes of the Heart 1986, Trial and Error 1986, Radio Days 1987, Heaven (Dir) 1987, Baby Boom 1988, The Good Mother 1988, The Lemon Sisters 1989, Running Mates 1989, The Godfather III, Wildflower (Dir) 1992, Secret Society (Dir), Manhattan Murder Mystery 1993, Unsung Heroes (Dir) 1995, Father of the Bride 2 1995, Marvin's Room, The First Wives Club 1996, The Only Thrill 1997, The Other Sister 1999, Hanging Up (also Dir) 2000, Town and Country 2001, Plan B 2001, Sister Mary Explains It All 2001, Wildflower 2002, Something's Gotta Give (Golden Globe Award, Best Actress Musical or Comedy 2004) 2003, The Family Stone 2005, Because I Said So 2007, Mama's Boy 2007, Mad Money 2008. *Publications:* Reservations, Still Life (Ed.). *Address:* Blue Relief Productions, 301 North Canyon Drive, Suite 205, Beverly Hills, CA 90210; c/o The Gersh Agency, 232 North Canyon Drive, Suite 201, Beverly Hills, CA 90210, USA. *Telephone:* (310) 275-7900 (Blue Relief).

KEATON, Michael; American actor; b. 9 Sept. 1951, Pittsburgh, Pa; m. Caroline MacWilliams (divorced); one s.; ed Kent State Univ.; with comedy group, Second City, LA. *Films:* Night Shift 1982, Mr Mom 1983, Johnny Dangerously 1984, Touch and Go 1986, Gung Ho 1986, The Squeeze 1987, Beetlejuice 1988, Clean and Sober 1988, The Dream Team 1989, Batman 1989, Pacific Heights 1990, One Good Cop 1991, Batman Returns 1992, Much Ado About Nothing 1992, My Life, The Paper 1994, Speechless 1994, Multiplicity 1996, Jackie Brown 1997, Desperate Measures 1998, Out of Sight 1998, Jack Frost 1999, Shot at Glory 2000, Quicksand 2001, First Daughter 2004, White Noise 2005, Game 6 2005, Herbie Fully Loaded 2005, Cars (voice) 2006, The Last Time 2006, The Merry Gentleman (also dir) 2009. *Television appearances include:* All in the Family, Maude, Mary Tyler Moore Show, Working Stiffs, Report to Murphy, Roosevelt and Truman (TV film), Body Shots (producer) 1999, Live from Baghdad 2002. *Address:* c/o ICM Management, 8942 Wilshire Boulevard, Beverly Hills, CA 90211, USA.

KEAVENEY, Raymond, MA; Irish gallery director and art historian; *Director, National Gallery of Ireland;* b. 1947, Carlanstown, Co. Meath; ed Franciscan Coll., Gormanston, University Coll. Dublin; worked and studied abroad 1975–78; Curator, Nat. Gallery of Ireland, Dublin 1979–81, Asst Dir 1981–88, Dir 1988–; specializes in Italian art and Old Master drawings. *Publications:* Master European Drawings 1983, Views of Rome 1988. *Address:* National Gallery of Ireland, Merrion Square West, Dublin 2, Ireland. *Telephone:* (1) 6615133 (office); (1) 6615133. *Fax:* (1) 6615372. *E-mail:* rkeaveney@ngi.ie (office). *Website:* www.nationalgallery.ie (office).

KEBICH, Vyacheslau Frantsavich; Belarusian politician; b. 10 June 1936, Konyushevshchina, Minsk Dist; s. of Frants Karlovich Kebich and Tatyana Vasilyevna Kebicha; m. Yelena Kebicha 1970; one s. one d.; ed Belarus Polytechnic Inst., Higher Party School; mem. CPSU 1962–91, Cen. Cttee 1980–91; engineer, man. in Minsk 1973–80; party official 1980–85; Deputy Chair. Council of Ministers, Chair. State Planning Cttee 1985–90; USSR People's Deputy 1989–91; Chair. Council of Ministers (Prime Minister) of Byelorussia (now Belarus) 1990–94; Presidential cand. 1994; Pres. Belarus Trade and Finance Union 1994; mem. Supreme Soviet (Parl.) 1980–96, MP 1996; Corresp. mem. Int. Eng Acad.; Belarus State Prize. *Leisure interest:* fishing. *Address:* c/o National Assembly, K. Marksa str. 38, Dom Urada, 220016 Minsk, Belarus.

KECHICHE, Abdellatif; Tunisian actor, screenwriter and director; b. 7 Dec. 1960, Tunis; stage acting debut in Sans titre by Garcia Lorca 1978; followed by Un balcon sur les Andes by Eduardo Manet, Nat. Odeon Theatre; film debut in Le thé à la menthe; directing debut with La faute à Voltaire 2000. *Films include:* as actor: Le thé à la menthe 1984, Les innocents (The Innocents) 1987, Bezness (Acting Prize, Festival du Film Francophone de Namur 1992, Acting Prize, Festival de Damas 1993) 1992, Un vampire au paradis (A Vampire in Paradise) 1992, La boîte magique (The Magic Box) 2002, Sorry, Haters 2005; as writer and dir: La faute à Voltaire (Blame It on Voltaire) (Golden Lion, Venice Film Festival 2000, Distribution Prize, Munich Int Film Festival 2002) 2000, L'esquive (Special Jury Prize, Istanbul Int Film Festival 2004, César Award for Best Film, Best Dir, Best Screenplay 2005) 2003, La Graine et le mulet (Couscous) (Special Jury Prize, Venice Film Festival 2007, César Award for Best Film, Best Dir, Best Screenplay 2008, Prix Louis Delluc) 2007.

KECHICHE, Muhammad Rachid; Tunisian politician; *Minister of Finance;* fmr Sec.-Gen. of the Govt; Minister of Finance 2004–. *Address:* Ministry of Finance, place du Gouvernement, 1008 Tunis, Tunisia (office). *Telephone:* (71) 571-888 (office). *Fax:* (71) 963-959 (office). *E-mail:* mfi@ministeres.tn (office).

KEDAH, HRH The Sultan of; Tuanku Haji Abdul Halim Mu'adzam Shah ibni al-Marhum Sultan Badlishah, DK, DKH, DKM, DMN, DUK, DK (Kelantan), DK (Pahang), DK (Selangor), DK (Perlis), DK (Johore), DK (Trengganu), DP (Sarawak), SPMK, SSDK, DHMS; Malaysian; *Timbalan Yang di-Pertuan Agong (Deputy Supreme Head of State)*b. 28 Nov. 1927, Alor Setar; m. Tuanku Bahiyah binti Al-Marhum Tuanku Abdul Rahman, d. of 1st Yang di Pertuan Agong of Malaya, 1956; three d.; ed Sultan Abdul Hamid Coll., Alor Setar and Wadham Coll., Oxford; Raja Muda (Heir to Throne of Kedah) 1949, Regent of Kedah 1957, Sultan 1958–; Timbalan Yang di Pertuan Agong (Deputy Head of State of Malaysia) 1965–70, Yang di Pertuan Agong (Head of State) 1970–75; Col Commdt Malaysian Reconnaissance Corps 1966; Col-in-Chief of Royal Malay Regiment 1975; Timbalan Yang di-Pertuan Agong (Deputy Supreme Head of State) 2006–; Kt St J. First Class Order of the Rising Sun (Japan) 1970, Bintang Maha Putera, Klas Satu (Indonesia) 1970, Kt Grand Cross of the Bath (UK) 1972, Most Auspicious Order of the Rajamithrathorn (Thailand) 1973. *Leisure interests:* golf, billiards, photography, tennis. *Address:* Istana Anak Bukit, Alor Setar, Kedah, Darul Aman, Malaysia.

KEDDAFI, Col Mu'ammar al- (see Gaddafi, Col Mu'ammar al-).

KEDIKILWE, Ponatshego, MA; Botswana politician; *Minister of Minerals, Energy and Water Affairs;* b. 4 Aug. 1938, Sefhophe; ed Univ. of Connecticut, Syracuse Univ.; joined Govt 1970; Prin. Finance Officer, Finance Ministry 1974–76; Sec. for Financial Affairs 1976; Perm. Sec., Ministry of Works, Transport and Communications 1977–79; Dir Public Service Man., Office of the Pres. 1979–84; mem. Parl. 1984–; Deputy Minister of Finance 1984; Minister of Presidential Affairs and Public Admin 1985–89, 1994–98, of Commerce and Industry 1989–94, of Finance and Devt Planning 1998, of Educ. 1999–2000, of Minerals, Energy and Water Affairs 2007–; fmr Chair. Botswana Democratic Party; Presidential Order of Honour 1992. *Leisure interests:* soccer, ranching, debating, gardening, speech writing, traditional music, folklore and poetry. *Address:* PO Box 2, Sefhophe (home); Ministry of Minerals, Energy and Water Affairs, Khama Cres., Private Bag 0018, Gaborone, Botswana (office). *Telephone:* 3656600 (office). *Fax:* 3972738 (office). *Website:* www.gov.bw/government/ministry_of_minerals_energy_and_water_affairs (office).

KEE, Robert, CBE, MA; British journalist, writer and broadcaster; b. 5 Oct. 1919, Calcutta, India; s. of late Robert Kee and Dorothy F. Kee; m. 1st Janetta Woolley 1948 (divorced 1950); one d.; m. 2nd Cynthia Judah 1960 (divorced 1989); one s. (and one s. deceased) one d.; m. 3rd Catherine M. Trevelyan 1990; ed Rottingdean School, Stowe School and Magdalen Coll., Oxford; journalist, Picture Post 1948–51; picture ed. Who 1952; foreign corresp. Observer 1956–57, Sunday Times 1957–58; literary ed. Spectator 1957; TV reporter Panorama, BBC 1958–62; TV Reporters Int., This Week, Faces of Communism (four parts, also for Channel 13, USA) ITV 1962–78; Ireland: a TV history (13 parts, also for Channel 13, USA), Panorama, BBC 1979–82; TVam 1982–83, Presenter 7 Days (Channel 4), ITV 1984–88; numerous BBC radio broadcasts 1946–97; BAFTA Richard Dimbleby Award 1976. *Publications:* A Crowd Is Not Company 1947, The Impossible Shore 1949, A Sign of the Times 1955, Broadstrop in Season 1959, Refugee World 1960, The Green Flag 1972, Ireland: A History 1980, The World We Left Behind 1984, The World We Fought For 1985, Trial and Error 1986, Munich: The Eleventh Hour 1988, The Picture Post Album 1989, The Laurel and the Ivy: Parnell and Irish Nationalism 1993. *Leisure interests:* swimming, music. *Address:* c/o Rogers, Coleridge and White, 20 Powis Mews, London, W11 1JN, England. *Telephone:* (20) 7221-3717. *E-mail:* info@rcwlitagency.co.uk.

KEEFFE, Barrie Colin; British dramatist, novelist, director and university tutor; *Tutor, City University London;* b. 31 Oct. 1945, London; s. of the late Edward Thomas Keeffe and Constance Beatrice Keeffe (née Marsh); m. 1st Sarah Dee (Truman) 1969 (divorced 1975); m. 2nd Verity Eileen Bargate 1981 (died 1981); two step-s.; m. 3rd Julia Lindsay 1983 (divorced 1991); ed East Ham Grammar School; fmr actor with Nat. Youth Theatre, journalist; has written plays for theatre, TV and radio; fmr Resident Writer, Shaw Theatre, London, RSC; Assoc. Writer, Theatre Royal, Stratford East, also mem. Bd;

Assoc. Soho Theatre Co.; Writers' Mentor, Nat. Theatre 1999–2002; Tutor, City Univ., London 2001–; Bye-Fellow, Christ's Coll., Cambridge 2003–04; UN Amb., 50th Anniversary Year 1995; mem. Soc. des auteurs et compositeurs dramatiques; French Critics' Prix Révélation 1978, Thames TV Playwright Award 1979, Giles Cooper Award Best Radio Plays, Mystery Writers of America Edgar Allan Poe Award 1982. *Theatre plays include:* Only a Game 1973, A Sight of Glory 1975, Scribes 1975, Here Comes the Sun 1976, Gimme Shelter 1977, A Mad World My Masters 1977, Barbarians 1977, Frozen Assets 1978, Sus 1979, Heaven Scent 1979, Bastard Angel 1980, She's So Modern 1980, Black Lear 1980, Chorus Girls 1981, Better Times 1985, King of England 1988, My Girl 1989, Not Fade Away 1990, Wild Justice 1990, I Only Want to Be With You 1995, Shadows on The Sun 2001. *Plays directed include:* A Certain Vincent, A Gentle Spirit, Talking of Chekov (Amsterdam and London), My Girl (London and Bombay), The Gary Oldman Fan Club (London). *Film:* The Long Good Friday (screenplay). *Television plays include:* Substitute 1972, Not Quite Cricket 1977, Gotcha 1977, Nipper 1977, Champions 1978, Hanging Around 1978, Waterloo Sunset 1979, No Excuses (series) 1983, King 1984. *Radio plays include:* Good Old Uncle Jack 1975, Pigeon Skyline 1975, Self- Portrait 1977, Paradise 1990, On the Eve of the Millennium 1999, Tales 2000, Feng Shui and Me 2000, The Five of Us 2002. *Publications:* novels: Gadabout 1969, No Excuses 1983; screenplay: The Long Good Friday 1998; Barrie Keeffe Plays I 2001. *Leisure interests:* playing tennis, watching soccer. *Address:* 110 Annandale Road, London, SE10 0JZ, England. *E-mail:* barriekeeffe@aol.com (office).

KEEFFE, Bernard, BA; British conductor, broadcaster and academic; b. 1 April 1925, London; s. of Joseph Keeffe and Theresa Keeffe (née Quinn); m. Denise Walker 1954; one s. one d.; ed St Olave's Grammar School and Clare Coll., Cambridge; served in Intelligence Corps 1943–47; mem. Glyndebourne Opera Co. 1951–52; BBC Music Staff 1954–60; Asst Music Dir, Royal Opera House 1960–62; Conductor BBC Scottish Orchestra 1962–64; Prof., Trinity Coll. of Music 1966–89; freelance conductor and broadcaster on radio and TV, concerts with leading orchestras 1966–; mem. int. juries, competitions in Sofia, Liège, Vienna and London; Warden solo performers section, Inc. Soc. of Musicians 1971; Chair. Anglo-Austrian Music Soc.; Hon. Fellow, Trinity Coll. of Music 1968. *Radio:* Music in Japan (BBC World Service). *Television:* Elgar and the Orchestra (Best Music Programme of the Year) (BBC) 1979. *Publications:* Harrap's Dictionary of Music and Musicians (Ed.), ENO Guide to Tosca. *Leisure interests:* photography, languages. *Address:* 153 Honor Oak Road, London, SE23 3RN, England. *Telephone:* (20) 8699-3672.

KEEGAN, Sir John, Kt, OBE; British military historian and journalist; b. 15 May 1934, London; s. of Francis Joseph Keegan and Eileen Mary Bridgman; m. Susanne Keegan; two s. two d.; ed privately and Balliol Coll. Oxford; awarded travel grant to study American Civil War in USA; writer of political reports for US Embassy, London 1957–59; Lecturer, then Sr Lecturer, War Studies Dept, Royal Mil. Acad., Sandhurst 1959–86; war corresp. for Atlantic Monthly Telegraph, Beirut 1984; Defence Ed. Daily Telegraph 1986–; Delmas Prof. of History, Vassar Coll. 1997–98; Contributing Ed. US News and World Report 1986–; Dir E Somerset NHS Trust 1991–97; Commr Commonwealth War Graves Comm. 2000–; Trustee, Heritage Lottery Fund 1994–2000; Fellow, Princeton Univ. 1984; Hon. Fellow, Balliol Coll. Oxford 1995; Hon. LLD (New Brunswick) 1997; Hon. LittD (Queen's Univ. Belfast) 2000; Hon. DLitt (Bath) 2001; Samuel Eliot Morrison Prize, US Soc. for Mil. History 1996, BBC Reith Lecturer 1998. *Publications include:* The Face of Battle 1976, The Nature of War 1981, Six Armies in Normandy: From D-Day to the Liberation of Paris 1982, Zones of Conflict: An Atlas of Future Wars 1986, Soldiers: A History of Men in Battle 1986, The Mask of Command 1987, Who's Who in Military History (with A. Wheatcroft) 1987, The Price of Admiralty: The Evolution of Naval Warfare 1989, The Second World War 1990, Churchill's Generals (ed.) 1991, A History of Warfare 1993, Warpaths: Travels of a Military Historian in North America 1995, Who's Who in World War 2 1995, The Battle for History: Re-fighting World War II 1995, Warpaths 1996, The First World War 1998, The Penguin Book of War 1999, Winston Churchill 2002, Intelligence in War 2003, The Iraq War 2004; ed. and co-ed. of several mil. reference works. *Address:* The Manor House, Kilmington, nr Warminster, Wilts., BA12 6RD, England. *Telephone:* (1985) 844856.

KEEGAN, Kevin Joseph, OBE; British professional football manager, fmr professional football player and business executive; b. 14 Feb. 1951, Armthorpe; s. of the late Joseph Keegan; m. Jean Woodhouse 1974; two s.; player Scunthorpe United, Liverpool 1971–77 (won League Championship three times, FA Cup 1974, European Cup 1977, UEFA Cup 1973, 1976), SV Hamburg 1977–80, Southampton 1980–82, Newcastle United 1982–84 (retd); scored 274 goals in approx. 800 appearances; capped for England 63 times (31 as Capt.), scoring 21 goals; Man. Newcastle United 1992–97, Fulham 1998–99, Manchester City 2001–05, Newcastle United 2008; Man. England nat. team 1999–2000; f. Soccer Circus (interactive football training games), Glasgow 2006; Footballer of the Year 1976, European Footballer of the Year 1978, 1979. *Publications:* Kevin Keegan 1978, Against the World: Playing for England 1979, Kevin Keegan: My Autobiography 1997. *Address:* Soccer Circus, Xscape, Kings Inch Road, Renfrew, Glasgow, PA4 8XU, Scotland (office). *Telephone:* (141) 885-1222. *E-mail:* info@soccercircus.com. *Website:* www.soccercircus.com.

KEEGAN, Robert (Bob) J., BS, MBA; American business executive; *Chairman, President and CEO, Goodyear Tire & Rubber Company;* m. Lynn Keegan; two c.; ed LeMoyne Coll., Syracuse, NY, Univ. of Rochester, NY; joined Eastman Kodak Co. 1972, various man. positions in Distribution and Marketing Depts, Rochester, NY, Gen. Man. Kodak NZ 1986–87, Dir of Finance, Rochester 1987–90, Gen. Man. Kodak Spain 1990–91, Gen. Man. of Consumer Imaging, Kodak Europe, Middle E and Africa 1991–93, Corp. Vice-

Pres. 1993–95, Pres. Kodak Professional and Corp. Vice-Pres. July–Oct. 1997, Pres. of Consumer Imaging and Sr Vice-Pres. 1997–2000, Exec. Vice-Pres. 2000–03; Exec. Vice-Pres. and Global Strategy Officer, Avery Dennison Corpn 1995–97; Pres. and CEO Goodyear Tire & Rubber Co. Jan. 2003–, Chair. July 2003–. *Address:* Goodyear Tire & Rubber Company, 1144 East Market Street, Akron, OH 44316-0001, USA (office). *Telephone:* (330) 796-2121 (office). *Fax:* (330) 796-2222 (office). *E-mail:* info@goodyear.com (office). *Website:* www.goodyear.com (office).

KEEL, Alton G., Jr, BS, PhD; American diplomatist, civil servant, engineer and banker; *Chairman and Managing Director, Atlantic Partners LLC;* b. 8 Sept. 1943, Newport, Va; s. of Alton G. Keel and Ella Kennedy; m. 1st Franmarie Kennedy-Keel 1982; one d.; m. 2nd Lynn Matti Keel; ed Univ. of Virginia and Univ. of California, Berkeley; Facility Man. Naval Weapons Center 1971–77; Sr Official Senate Armed Services Cttee, US Senate 1977–81; Asst Sec., US Air Force for Research, Devt and Logistics, The Pentagon 1981–82; Assoc. Dir Nat. Security and Int. Affairs, Exec. Office of Pres. 1982–86; Exec. Dir and Pres. Comm. on Space Shuttle Challenger Accident 1986; Acting Asst to the Pres. for Nat. Security Affairs 1986; Perm. Rep. to NATO 1987–89; Pres., Man. Dir Carlyle Int., The Carlyle Group 1992–94; Chair. Carlyle SEAG 1994–95, Chair., Man. Dir Atlantic Pnrs LLC (pvt investment group), Washington, DC 1992; Chair., CEO Land-5 Corpn 1999–2002; mem. Dean's Advisory Bd, Univ. of Va 1996–; CEO InoStor Corpn 2002–05; Nat. Congressional Science Fellow, AIAA 1977; Youth Scientist Award 1976, Air Force Decoration for Exceptional Civilian Service 1982; NASA Group Achievement Award 1987, Distinguished Alumnus Award (Univ. of Va) 1987. *Publications:* numerous scientific and tech. articles, foreign policy and nat. security publs. *Leisure interests:* running, golf, sailing, physical fitness. *Address:* Fairhill Farm, 2891 South River Road, Stanardsville, VA 22973, USA. *Telephone:* (434) 990-9504. *Fax:* (434) 990-9503. *E-mail:* Fairhillfarm@hughes.net. *Website:* www.fairhillfarmusa.com.

KEELER, HE Cardinal William Henry, DCL; American ecclesiastic (retd); b. 4 March 1931, San Antonio, Tex.; s. of Thomas L. Keeler and Margaret T. Keeler (née Conway); ed Lebanon Catholic High School, Pa, St Charles Seminary, Overbrook, Phila, Pontifical Gregorian Univ., Rome, Italy; ordained priest 1955; Asst Pastor, Our Lady of Good Counsel Church, Marysville 1956–58, 1961–64, Pastor 1964; Sec. Diocesan Tribunal 1956–58; Sec. to Bishop Leech during Second Vatican Council, Rome 1962–65; apptd Peritus or 'Special Advisor' to the Council by Pope John XXIII, served on staff of Council Digest (daily communication service sponsored by US Bishops), named Papal Chamberlain (with title of Mgr) by Pope Paul VI 1965; Vice-Chancellor Harrisburg Diocese 1965–69, Chancellor 1969, later Vicar Gen.; apptd Auxiliary Bishop of Harrisburg and Titular Bishop of Ulcinium (Dulcigno) 1979; Admin. Diocese of Harrisburg 1983; Bishop of Harrisburg 1983–89; Chair. Nat. Conf. of Catholic Bishops (NCCB)'s Cttee for Ecumenical and Interreligious Affairs 1984–87, Vice-Pres. NCCB 1989–92, Pres. 1992–95; Archbishop of Baltimore 1989–2007 (retd); cr. Cardinal (Titular Church of St Mary of the Angels) 1994; Pres. American Div. Catholic Near East Welfare Asscn, Cathedral Foundation; Chair. Black and Native American Missions Bd, Bd of Catholic Charities; mem. Bd Basilica of the Nat. Shrine of the Immaculate Conception, Washington, DC, Mount St Mary's Coll.; Publr The Catholic Review; mem. Bd of Trustees Catholic Univ. 1989–93, Advisory Panel for Father Michael McGivney Fund for New Initiatives in Catholic Educ. 1993, Pontifical Council for Promoting Christian Unity 1994; named Prelate of Honor by Pope Paul VI 1970; hon. degrees from Lebanon Valley Coll., Mount St Mary's Coll., Gettysburg Coll., Susquehanna Univ., Gannon Univ., Pa 1993, Loyola Coll., Baltimore, St Mary's Coll. of Minnesota, Shippenburg State Univ., Pa, Elizabethtown Coll., Pa, Univ. of Notre Dame, Ateneo Univ., The Philippines, Coll. of Notre Dame of Maryland, Franciscan Univ., Steubenville, OH, Viterbo Univ., Wis. *Address:* c/o Catholic Center, 320 Cathedral Street, Baltimore, MD 21201 (office); 408 North Charles Street, Baltimore, MD 21201, USA (home). *Fax:* (410) 727-8234 (home).

KEILIS-BOROK, Vladimir Isaakovich, DSc; Russian geophysicist and applied mathematician; *Honorary Director, International Institute of Earthquake Prediction Theory and Mathematical Geophysics;* b. 31 July 1921, Moscow; s. of Isaak Moiseyevich and Kseniya Ruvimovna Keilis-Brook; m. L. N. Malinovskaya 1955; one d.; ed S. Ordzhonikidze Inst. of Geological Prospecting, O. Schmidt Inst. of Earth Physics, USSR Acad. of Sciences; Chair. Dept of Computational Geophysics 1960–89; Dir Int. Inst. Earthquake Prediction Theory and Mathematical Geophysics 1989–98, Hon. Dir 1998–; mem. USSR (now Russian) Acad. of Sciences 1987–; Foreign Assoc. NAS; Foreign Hon. mem. American Acad. of Arts and Sciences; Assoc. Royal Astronomical Society; mem. Bd of several int. journals 1987–91; fmr Pres. Int. Union of Geodesy and Geophysics. *Publications:* Computational Seismology series, Vols 1–24 1966–91; other works on global seismology and tectonics. *Leisure interests:* mountaineering, sociology. *Address:* International Institute of Earthquake Prediction Theory and Mathematical Geophysics, Moscow 113556, Warshavskoye sh. 79, Kor. 2, Russia. *Telephone:* (495) 110-77-95 (office); (495) 936-55-88 (home). *Fax:* (495) 956-70-95.

KEILLOR, Garrison Edward, BA; American writer and broadcaster; b. (Gary Edward Keillor), 7 Aug. 1942, Anoka, MN; s. of John P. Keillor and Grace R. (Denham) Keillor; m. 1st Mary Guntzel (divorced 1976, died 1998); one s.; m. 2nd Ulla Skaerved (divorced); m. 3rd Jenny Lind Nilsson; one d.; ed Anoka High School and Univ. of Minn.; journalist 1962–63; radio announcer and presenter 1969–73; creator and host A Prairie Home Companion radio show 1974–87, 1993–; host American Radio Co. 1989–93; staff writer The New Yorker 1987–92; George Foster Peabody Award 1980, Ace Award for best musical host (A Prairie Home Companion) 1988, Best Music and Entertainment Host Awards 1988, 1989, American Acad. and Institute of Arts and

Letters Medal 1990, Music Broadcast Communications Radio Hall of Fame 1994, Nat. Humanities Medal 1999, John Steinbeck Award 2007. *Film:* A Prairie Home Companion 2006. *Publications:* Happy to Be Here 1982, Lake Wobegon Days (Grammy Award for best non-musical recording 1987) 1985, Leaving Home 1987, We Are Still Married: Stories and Letters 1989, WLT: A Radio Romance 1991, Wobegon Boy The Book of Guys 1993, Cat, You Better Come Home (children's book) 1995, The Old Man Who Loved Cheese 1996, The Sandy Bottom Orchestra 1996, Wobegon Boy 1997, ME by Jimmy (Big Boy) Valente as told to Garrison Keillor 1999, Lake Wobegon Summer 1956 2001, Love Me 2004, Pontoon 2007, Liberty: A Lake Wobegon Novel 2008; contrib. to newspapers and magazines. *Address:* A Prairie Home Companion, Minnesota Public Radio, 45 Seventh Street E, St Paul, MN 55101, USA (office). *Website:* prairiehome.publicradio.org (office).

KEINÄNEN, Eino, MPolSc; Finnish fmr civil servant and business executive; b. 17 Nov. 1939; ed Univ. of Helsinki; credit official, Kansallis-Osake-Pankki 1962–64; Head of Section, Finnish State Computer Centre and Planning Organ for State Accounting 1965–68; various posts, Budget Dept, Ministry of Finance 1969–85, Head Budget Dept 1985–87, Perm. Under-Sec. 1987–89, Perm. State Sec. 1989–95; Gen. Man. and mem. Bd Postipankki Ltd 1995–96, Chair and Chief Exec. 1996–2000; mem. Bd of Dirs Finnish State Treasury 1985–89, Finnish Tourist Bd 1985–89, Finnish Foreign Trade Asscn 1985–89, Cen. Statistical Office of Finland 1985–89; mem. Investment Fund of Finland 1985–89; Vice-Pres. Supervisory Bd Finnish Export Credit Ltd 1987–, Finnish Fund for Industrial Devt Co-operation Ltd (Finnfund) 1994–; Pres. Bd of Dirs State Computer Centre 1988–; mem. Supervisory Bd Slot Machine Asscn 1989–, Regional Devt Fund of Finland Ltd 1989–, Finnish Grain Bd 1989–; mem. Bd of Admin Alko Ltd 1989–; Pres. Supervisory Bd Finnish Ice-Hockey Asscn 1989–.

KEINO, Kipchoge A. (Kip); Kenyan fmr athlete; b. 1940, Kipsamo; m. Phyllis Keino; fmr physical training instructor in police force; began int. running career in 1962; set two world records at 3000m and 5000m 1964; winner 1500m and 5000m, African Games 1964, 1965; winner one mile and three miles, Commonwealth Games 1966; gold medallist 1500m, silver medallist 5000m, Olympic Games, Mexico City 1968; gold medallist 3000m steeplechase, silver medallist 1500m, Olympic Games, Munich 1972; retd from int. running 1973; Pres. Kenyan Olympic Cttee; mem. IOC; helped establish high-altitude training as a technique to improve running time at any altitude; helped coach Kenyan track-and-field teams; ran in London Marathon for Oxfam 2002; f. Kip Keino Foundation, acquired a farm in Kenya (with wife Phyllis), est. Kip Keino School and orphanage on farm land; apptd by Athletics Kenya to lead investigation into country's poor performance at World Championships 2003 and to find a new head coach for Kenya's Olympic team Sept. 2003–; Laureus World Sports Acad. 'Sport for Good' Award. *Address:* Kip Keino School, Eldoret, Kenya; Kip Keino Foundation Inc., 14 Redwood Lane, B-101, Ithaca, NY 14850, USA. *Website:* www.kipkeinotraining.org/donations.htm.

KEITA, Ibrahima Boubacar; Malian politician; *President, National Assembly;* Minister of Foreign Affairs 1993–94; Prime Minister of Mali 1994–2000; fmr Chair. of External Relations, Alliance pour la démocratie au Mali (ADEMA); Leader, Rassemblement pour le Mali 2001–, presidential cand. 2002; currently Pres. Nat. Ass. *Address:* Assemblée nationale, BP 284, Bamako, Mali (office). *Telephone:* 221-57-24 (office). *Fax:* 221-03-74 (office). *E-mail:* mamou@blonba.malinet.ml (office). *Website:* www.animali.org (office).

KEITA, Modibo, DScS; Malian academic, psychologist and adviser on development issues; *Managing Director, Cabinet d'Etudes Keita-Kala Saba;* b. 13 Jan. 1953, Bamako; m.; three s.; ed Tübingen Univ., Germany; Prof. of Higher Educ., École normale supérieure de Bamako 1984–86; f. Cabinet d'Etudes pour l'Education et le Développement (CED) 1987 (renamed Cabinet d'Etudes Keita-Kala Saba—CEK-Kala Saba 1997–); Dir Boutique de Gestion, d'Echanges et de Conseils – Promotion de l'Artisanat 1993–94; Co-ordinator of Urban Waste Expertise Programme in W Africa 1996–, Making Decentralization Work/Mali 2001. *Publications:* numerous articles in magazines. *Leisure interests:* art, culture, sport. *Address:* Cek-Kala Saba, BP 9014, Bamako (office); 868 Rue Faladié Sema, Porte 66, Bamako, Mali (home). *Telephone:* 220-94-12 (office); 220-12-60 (home). *Fax:* 220-94-13 (office). *E-mail:* cek@afribone.net.ml (office); mokesn@yahoo.fr (home). *Website:* www.cek.com.ml (office).

KEITA, Salif; Malian singer; b. 25 Aug. 1949, Djoliba; began musical career in Bamako 1967; joined govt-sponsored group Super Rail Band; moved to Paris to begin solo career as a singer 1984; performances at festivals, tours of Japan, Australia, Canada, USA, Africa (including South Africa); annual European tour including summer festivals; Chevalier, Ordre des Arts et des Lettres, Chevalier, Order of the Nation (Mali), Nat. Order of Guinea 1977; Grammy Award. *Recordings include:* albums: Soro 1987, Ko-Yan 1989, Destiny of a Noble Outcast 1991, Amen 1991, L'Enfant Lion 1992, Mansa of Mali 1994, Folon 1995, Rail Band 1996, Seydou Bathili 1997, Papa 1999, Sosie 2001, Compilation 1969–80 2001, Moffou 2002, Salif Keita: The Lost Album (with Kante Manfila) 2005, M'Bemba 2005. *Address:* c/o Universal Jazz France, 22 rue des Fossés St Jacques, 75005 Paris, France. *E-mail:* lau.bizot@wanadoo.fr. *Website:* salifkeita.artistes.universalmusic.fr.

KEITEL, Hans-Peter, DrIng; German business executive; *Member of the Supervisory Board, Hochtief AG;* b. 1947; ed Stuttgart Technical Univ., Tech. Univ. of Munich; various sr and man. positions with Lahmeyer Int. (consulting engineers) 1975–87; tech. consultant to banking consortium involved in Channel Tunnel project 1986–87; joined Hochtief AG, Essen 1988, Dir and Head of Int. Business 1988–90, mem. Man. Bd 1990–92, CEO and Head of Construction Service Europe 1992–99, Chair. and CEO 1999–2007, now mem. Supervisory Bd; Pres. Fed. of the German Construction Industry 2005–; Vice-Pres. Fed. of German Industries 2005–; fmr mem. Supervisory Bd Lahmeyer AG, Cen. Advisory Bd Commerzbank AG; mem. Bd of Dirs RWE AG 1999–. *Address:* Hochtief AG, Opernplatz 2, 45128 Essen, Germany (office). *Telephone:* 2018240 (office). *Fax:* 2018242777 (office). *Website:* www.hochtief.de (office).

KEITEL, Harvey, BFA; American actor and producer; b. 13 May 1939; m. Lorraine Bracco (divorced); one d.; ed The Actors Studio, New School Univ.; served in US Marines; starred in Martin Scorsese's student film Who's That Knocking at My Door?; stage appearances in Death of a Salesman, Hurlyburly; co-Pres. The Actors Studio; f. The Goatsingers (production co.). *Films:* Mean Streets, Alice Doesn't Live Here Anymore, That's the Way of the World, Taxi Driver, Mother Jugs and Speed, Buffalo Bill and the Indians, Welcome to LA, The Duellists, Fingers, Blue Collar, Eagle's Wing, Deathwatch, Saturn 3, Bad Timing, The Border, Exposed, La Nuit de Varennes, Corrupt, Falling in Love, Knight of the Dragon, Camorra, Off Beat, Wise Guys, The Men's Club, The Investigation, The Pick-up Artist, The January Man, The Last Temptation of Christ, The Two Jakes, Two Evil Eyes (The Black Cat), Thelma & Louise, Tipperary, Bugsy, Reservoir Dogs, Bad Lieutenant, The Assassin, The Young Americans, The Piano, Snake Eyes, Rising Sun, Monkey Trouble, Clockers, Dangerous Game, Pulp Fiction, Smoke, Imaginary Crimes, Ulysses' Gaze 1995, Blue in the Face 1995, City of Industry, Cop Land 1996, Head Above Water, Somebody to Love 1996, Simpatico 1999, Little Nicky 2000, U-571 2000, Holy Smoke 2000, Nailed 2001, Taking Sides 2001, Grey Zone 2001, Nowhere 2002, Ginostra 2002, Red Dragon 2002, Beeper 2002, Crime Spree 2003, Galindez File 2003, Dreaming of Julia 2003, Puerto Vallarta Squeeze 2003, National Treasure 2004, The Bridge of San Luis Rey 2004, Shadows in the Sun 2005, Be Cool 2005, A Crime 2006, The Stone Merchant 2006, Arthur and the Invisibles (voice) 2006, My Sexiest Year 2007, National Treasure Book of Secrets 2007, The Ministers 2009. *Television:* The Path to 9/11 2006, Life on Mars (series) 2008–09. *Address:* c/o The Endeavor Agency, 9601 Wilshire Blvd., 10th Floor, Beverly Hills, CA 90212,; The Goatsingers, 179 Franklin Street, 6th Floor, New York, NY 10013, USA. *Telephone:* (212) 966-3045 (Goatsingers). *Fax:* (212) 966-4362 (Goatsingers).

KEITH, Rt Hon. Sir Kenneth James, KBE, PC, LLB, LLM, QC; New Zealand judge; *Judge, International Court of Justice;* b. 19 Nov. 1937; s. of Patrick James Keith and Amy Irene Keith (née Witheridge); m. Jocelyn Margaret Buckett 1961; two s. two d.; ed Auckland Grammar School, Univ. of Auckland, Victoria Univ. of Wellington, Harvard Law School; with Dept of External Affairs, Wellington 1960–62; with Law Faculty, Vic. Univ. 1962–64, 1966–91, Prof. 1973–91, Dean 1977–81; UN Secr. Office of Legal Affairs 1968–70; with NZ Inst. of Int. Affairs 1971–73; Judge, Courts of Appeal of Samoa 1982–, Cook Islands 1982–, Niue 1995–, NZ 1996–2003; Judge, Supreme Court of Fiji 2003–05, Supreme Court of NZ 2004–05, Int. Court of Justice 2006–; mem. NZ Law Comm. 1986–91, Pres. 1991–96; mem. NZ Nat. Group of Perm. Court of Arbitration 1985–, panel of arbitrators, Int. Centre for Settlement of Investment Disputes 1994–, Inst. of Int. Law 2003–; Pres. NZ Inst. of Int. Affairs 2000–; Commemoration Medal 1990; Hon. LLD (Auckland) 2001, (Victoria) 2004. *Publications:* Advisory Jurisdiction of the International Court 1971, Essays on Human Rights (ed.) 1968; numerous Law Comm. publs and papers on constitutional and int. law in legal journals. *Leisure interests:* family, walking, reading. *Address:* International Court of Justice, Peace Palace, 2517 KJ, The Hague, Netherlands (office); 11 Salamanca Road, Kelburn, Wellington, New Zealand (home). *Telephone:* (70) 3022323 (office); (4) 472-6664 (home). *Fax:* (70) 3649928 (office); (4) 472-6664 (home). *E-mail:* k.keith@icj-cij.org (office). *Website:* www.icj-cij.org (office).

KEITH, Penelope Anne Constance, OBE, CBE; British actress; b. (Penelope Anne Constance Hatfield), 2 April 1940, Sutton, Surrey; d. of Frederick Hatfield and Constance Mary Keith; m. Rodney Timson 1978; ed Annecy Convent, Seaford, Sussex, Convent Bayeux, Normandy, Webber Douglas School, London; first professional appearance, Civic Theatre, Chesterfield 1959; repertory, Lincoln, Salisbury, Manchester 1960–63, Cheltenham 1967; RSC, Stratford 1963, Aldwych 1965; Pres. Actors Benevolent Fund 1990–; Gov. Queen Elizabeth's Foundation for the Disabled 1989–, Guildford School of Acting 1991–; Trustee Yvonne Arnaud Theatre 1992–; High Sheriff of Surrey 2002; Best Light Entertainment Performance (British Acad. of Film and TV Arts) 1976, Best Actress 1977, Show Business Personality (Variety Club of GB) 1976, BBC TV Personality 1979, Comedy Performance of the Year (Soc. of West End. Theatre) 1976, Female TV Personality, T.V. Times Awards 1976–78, BBC TV Personality of the Year 1978–79, TV Female Personality (Daily Express) 1979–82. *Stage appearances include:* Suddenly at Home 1971, The Norman Conquests 1974, Donkey's Years 1976, The Apple Cart 1977, The Millionairess 1978, Moving 1980, Hobson's Choice, Captain Brassbound's Conversion 1982, Hay Fever 1983, The Dragon's Tail 1985, Miranda 1987, The Deep Blue Sea 1988, Dear Charles 1990, The Merry Wives of Windsor 1990, The Importance of Being Earnest 1991, On Approval 1992, Relatively Speaking 1992, Glyn and It 1994, Monsieur Amilcar 1995, Mrs Warren's Profession 1997, Good Grief 1998, Star Quality 2001. *TV includes:* Kate (series) 1970, The Good Life 1974–77, Private Lives 1976, The Norman Conquests 1977, Much Ado About Nothing 1978, The Hound of the Baskervilles 1978, To the Manor Born 1979–2007, Spider's Web 1982, On Approval 1982, Waters of the Moon 1983, Sweet Sixteen (series) 1983, Tickle on the Tum (series) 1984, Moving (series) 1985, Executive Stress (series) 1986, Growing Places, No Job for a Lady (series) 1990, Law and Disorder (series) 1994, Next of Kin (series) 1995, Coming Home 1998, Margery and Gladys 2003. *Radio includes:* Agatha Raison series. *Films include:* Every Home Should Have One 1970, Take a Girl Like You 1970, Rentadick 1972, Penny Gold 1973, Ghost Story 1974, Priest of Love 1981. *Leisure interest:* gardening.

Address: London Management, 2–4 Noel Street, London, W1V 3RB, England. *Telephone:* (20) 7287-9000. *Fax:* (20) 7287-3036.

KEKE, Kieren Aedogan, MD; Nauruan physician and politician; *Minister of Foreign Affairs and Trade, Transport and Telecommunications;* b. 1971, Yaren; s. of Ludwig Keke; fmr Parl. Speaker; mem. Naoero Amo (Nauru First) party; Minister of Health and Transport –2007 (resgnd), led breakaway opposition faction following vote of no-confidence in Prime Minister Nov. 2007, Minister of Foreign Affairs and Trade, Transport and Telecommunications Nov. 2007–; fmr Pres. Nat. Youth Council for Nauru. *Address:* Ministry of Foreign Affairs and Trade, Yaren, Nauru (office). *Website:* www.naoeroamo.com (office).

KEKILBAYEV, Abish Kekilbayevich, (Abish Tagan); Kazakhstani politician and writer; b. 6 Dec. 1939, Ondy, Mangystau Region; s. of Kekilbay Kokimov and Aysaule Kokimova; m. Klara Zhumabaeva; four c.; ed Kazakh State Univ.; schoolteacher of Kazakh language; worked for newspapers Kazakh Adebieti and Leninshil Zhas; Ed.-in-Chief Studio Kazakhfilm; CP official in Alma-Ata; Deputy Minister of Culture Kazakh SSR; Sec. Man. Cttee Kazakh Writers' Union; Chair. Presidium of Kazakh Soc. for Protection of Monuments of History and Culture 1962–89; Chair. Cttee on Nat. Policy, Language and Culture Devt, Kazakhstan Supreme Soviet 1991–93; Ed.-in-Chief Egemen Kazakhstan (newspaper) 1992–93; State Counsellor 1993–94; Chair. Supreme Council of Repub. 1994–95; State Counsellor to Pres. of Repub. 1995–; Deputy to Majlis (Parl.) 1995–; State Sec. Rep. of Kazakhstan 1996–2002; Senator (Parl.) 2002–. *Publications:* author of novels, short stories, critical reviews, translations. *Address:* House of Parliament, Abai Ave 33, 010000 Astana (office); 14 Magistralnaya 1, Apt 98, 473000 Astana, Kazakhstan (home). *Telephone:* (7172) 15-35-20 (office). *Fax:* (7172) 32-69-55 (office). *E-mail:* sarsenova@parlam.kz.

KELAM, Tunne; Estonian politician and historian; b. 10 July 1936, Taheva, Valgamaa Region; m. Mari-Ann Kelam; one d.; ed Tartu State Univ.; Sr Researcher, Cen. History Archives 1959–64; Sr Ed. Estonian Encyclopaedia 1965–75; Sr Bibliographer, F. R. Kreutzwald State Library of Estonian SSR 1975–79; employee, Ranna State farm 1980–88; with journal Akadeemia 1988–90; mem. Bd Int. Policy Forum 1991; mem. Riigikogu (Parl.) 1992–2004, Vice-Pres. Riigikogu (Parl.) 1992–2003, Chair. European Affairs Cttee 1997–2003, Co-Chair. EU–Estonia Jt Parl. Cttee 1997–2003; Chair. Supervisory Bd Nat. Library 1996–99; mem. Tallinn City Council 1999, Viimsi Parish Council 2002–04; f. Eesti Rahvusliku Sõltumatuse (Estonian Nat. Independence Party) 1988, Chair. 1993–95; mem. Isamaaliit Party 1995–, Chair. 2002–; Chair. Estonian Nat. Group, Inter-Parl. Union 1992–95; Chair. Estonian Del. to Parl. Ass. of the Council of Europe 1992–95, Vice-Pres. Parl. Ass. of the Council of Europe 1994–95, mem. Europe Monitoring Cttee and Rapporteur for Ukraine 1996–2000; Rep. of Estonian Parl. at Convention on the Future of Europe 2002–03; mem. European Parl. (Erakond Isamaaliit—Pro Patria Union) 2004–, mem. Cttee on Regional Devt, Sub-cttee on Security and Defence, Del. to EU–Russia Parl. Cooperation Cttee; Pres. Estonian Scout Asscn 1996–; Deputy Chair. Estonian European Movt 1998–; mem. Bd of Dirs Inst. for Human Rights 1997–, Kistler-Ritso Foundation 1998–, Estonian Nat. Opera 2003–; Chair. Nat. Citizens' Cttee of Estonia 1989–90), Cttee of Estonia (perm. organ of Congress of Estonia) 1990–92; fmr mem. Constitutional Ass.; Hon. Citizen of Maryland, USA, Hon. Pres. Estonian Scout Asscn 1996–; Officier, Ordre nat. du Mérite, Badge of the Order of the Nat. Coat of Arms (Second Class) 2001, I Class Order of the Nat. Coat of Arms 2006; Paul Harris Fellowship, Rotary Int. Award, Estonian Newspapers' Union Award 1996, Baltic Ass. Award, Schuman Medal 2006. *Publications:* Tunne Kelam (autobiog.) 1999, Estonian Way to Freedom, Tallinn 2002; numerous articles and trans from English, French, Polish, German, Italian and Russian. *Address:* ASP 10E146, European Parliament, Bâtiment Altiero Spinelli, 60 rue Wiertz, 1047 Brussels, Belgium (office); Liiva tee 6, 74 001 Haabneeme, Estonia. *Telephone:* (2) 284-7279 (office). *Fax:* (2) 284-9279 (office). *E-mail:* ttkelam@europarl.europa.eu (office); tunne.kelam@irl.ee. *Website:* www.kelam.ee (office).

KELANTAN, HRH The Sultan of; Tuanku Ismail Petra ibni al-Marhum Sultan Yahaya Petra; Malaysian s. of the late al-Marhum Tengku Yahaya Petra Ibni al-Marhum Sultan Ibrahim and al-Marhum Tengku Zainab binti Tengku Mohamed Petra; mem. The Conf. of Rulers, Malaysia; Sultan of Kelantan 1979–;*Website:* www.kelantan.gov.my.

KELCHE, Gen. Jean-Pierre; French army officer; *Le Grand Chancelier de la Légion d'honneur;* b. 19 Jan. 1942, Macon; m.; two c.; ed Mil. Acad., Saint Cyr; served in Côte d'Ivoire, then Djibouti 1971–73, Jr Staff Course, Staff Coll., then with French Caribbean and Guiana Territorial Command 1979–81; Commdr 5th Combined Bn, Djibouti 1985–87; Staff Officer, Doctrine and Devt Div., rank of Brig.-Gen. 1991; Deputy Commdr 5th Armoured Div., Landau, Germany 1991; Chief Plans, Programmes and Evaluation Div., Gen. Staff 1992–95; Chief of Prime Minister's Mil. Cabinet 1995–96; Vice-Chief of Defence Staff 1996–98, Chief of Defence Staff, rank of Gen. 1998–2002; Le Grand Chancelier de la Légion d'honneur 2004–; Commdr, Légion d'honneur, Officier, Ordre nat. du Mérite. *Address:* c/o Le Musée national de la Légion d'honneur, 2, rue de la Légion d'honneur, 75007 Paris; Palais de Salm, 64 rue de Lille, Paris, France (office). *Website:* www.legiondhonneur.fr.

KELDYSH, Leonid Veniaminovich, DrPhysMathSc; Russian physicist and academic; *Professor, Department of Physics, Texas A&M University;* b. 7 April 1931, Moscow; s. of Benjamin L. Granovskii and Lyudmila V. Keldysh; m. Galina S. Krasnikova 1983 (deceased); one s.; ed Moscow State Univ., P.N. Lebedev Physics Inst., Russian Acad. of Sciences; Jr then Sr Researcher, Head of Sector, Head of Dept, Lebedev Physical Inst., USSR (now Russian) Acad. of Sciences 1954–89, Dir 1989–93, Sr Researcher 1993–, now Vice-Chair.; Prof., Moscow State Univ. 1965–; Prof., Dept of Physics, Texas A&M Univ. 2005–; Röntgen Prof., Univ. of Würzburg 1997; Pres. Physical Soc. of Russian Fed. 1998–; Corresp. mem. USSR (now Russian) Acad. of Sciences 1968, Full mem. 1976, Academic-Sec., Dept of Gen. Physics 1991–96; fmr Visiting Miller Prof., Miller Inst., Univ. of California, Berkeley; Ed. Solid State Communications, Fyzika i Tekhnika Poluprovodnikov; main research on quantum many body theory, solid state theory, physics of semiconductors, interaction of electromagnetic radiation with matter; Foreign Assoc. NAS (USA) 1995–; Lomonosov Prize, USSR Acad. of Sciences 1965, Hewlett-Packard Prize, European Physics Soc. 1975, Lenin Prize 1976, A.V. Humboldt Research Award 1994, Triumph Prize (Russian Fed.) 2001, S.I. Vavilov Gold Medal, Russian Acad. of Sciences 2006. *Publications:* Coherent Exciton States 1972, Electron-Hole Drops in Semiconductors 1976; numerous articles in scientific journals 1957–. *Address:* P.N. Lebedev Physical Institute, Leninski Prospect 53, 117924 Moscow V-333, Russia (office); Department of Physics, Texas A&M University, 4242 TAMU, College Station, TX 77843-4242, USA (office). *Telephone:* (495) 135-30-33 (Moscow) (office). *Fax:* (495) 938-22-51 (Moscow) (office). *E-mail:* keldysh@physics.tamu.edu (office). *Website:* www.physics.tamu.edu (office); www.lebedev.ru (office).

KELETI, György; Hungarian politician and army officer; b. 18 May 1946, Losonc; m. Erzsébet Petrik; three c.; ed Toldy Ferenc Secondary School, Budapest, Zalka Máté Mil. Tech. Coll., Zrinyi Miklós War Coll.; co. commdr, then later deputy commdr of a bn in Vác Dist 1969–74; posts in Ministry of Defence 1980; Press Spokesman, Ministry of Defence 1977; mem. Hungarian Socialist Workers' Party (MSZMP) 1969–89; mem. Oroszlány org. of HSP (MSZP) 1992–, mem. nat. presidium of party 1996–2003; mem. Parl. for Constituency 3, Kisbér, Komárom-Esztergom Co. 1992–, Chair. Nat. Security Cttee 1998–2002, Defence Cttee 2002–, Deputy Parl. Group Leader 2004–, mem. Cttee on Standing Orders 2004–; Minister of Defence 1994–98; Chair. Regional Asscn of Komárom-Esztergom Co. 1998, Chair. Election Cttee at 7th Congress 2000; rank of Col in army reserve; Order of Star (with swords), Silver Cross of Merit. *Address:* Hungarian National Assembly, Kossuth tér 1-3, PO Box 1357, 1055 Budapest, Pf.: 2, Hungary (office). *Telephone:* (1) 441-4000 (office). *E-mail:* gyorgy.keleti@parlament.hu (office). *Website:* www.parlament.hu (office).

KELLENBERGER, Jakob, DPhil; Swiss diplomatist and international organization official; *President, International Committee of the Red Cross;* b. 19 Oct. 1944, Heiden; m. Elisabeth Kellenberger-Jossi 1973; two d.; ed Univ. of Zürich, with stays at Univs of Tours, Granada; joined Swiss diplomatic service 1974, diplomatic postings in Madrid, Brussels and London; Head of Office in Charge of European Integration, Berne 1984–92, Minister 1984, Amb. 1988, State Sec. Fed. Dept of Foreign Affairs 1992–99; Pres. Int. Cttee of the Red Cross and Red Crescent (ICRC) 2000–; Dr hc (Basle Univ.) 2003. *Address:* International Committee of the Red Cross and Red Crescent, 19 avenue de la Paix, 1202 Geneva, Switzerland (office). *Telephone:* (22) 7302246 (office). *Fax:* (22) 7349057 (office). *Website:* www.icrc.org (office).

KELLER, Bill, BA; American newspaper editor; *Executive Editor, The New York Times;* b. 18 Jan. 1949; m. Emma Gilbey; one s. two d.; ed Pomona Coll., Wharton School Univ. of PA; reporter The Portland Oregonian 1970–79, Congressional Quarterly Weekly Report, Washington, DC 1980–82, The Dallas Times Herald 1982–84; domestic corresp. The New York Times 1984–86, Russian Corresp. and Bureau Chief, Moscow 1986–91, Bureau Chief, Johannesburg, SA 1992–95, Foreign Ed., NY 1995–97, Man. Ed. 1997–2001, Op-Ed. Columnist and Sr Writer 2001–03, Exec. Ed. July 2003–; Trustee, Pomona Coll.; Pulitzer Prize for coverage of the USSR 1989. *Publication:* Tree Shaker: the Story of Nelson Mandela 2008. *Address:* The New York Times, 620 Eight Avenue, New York, NY 10018, USA (office). *Telephone:* (212) 556-1234 (office). *E-mail:* executive-editor@nytimes.com (office). *Website:* www.nytimes.com (office).

KELLER, Evelyn Fox, PhD; American historian, philosopher of science and academic; *Professor of History and Philosophy of Science, Massachusetts Institute of Technology;* b. 20 March 1936, New York; d. of Albert and Ray Fox; m. Joseph B. Keller 1964 (divorced); one s. one d.; ed Radcliffe Coll., Brandeis and Harvard Univs; Asst Research Scientist, New York Univ. 1963–66, Assoc. Prof. 1970–72; Assoc. Prof., State Univ. of New York, Purchase 1972–82; Prof. of Math. and Humanities, Northwestern Univ. 1982–88; Prof., Univ. of Calif., Berkeley 1988–92; Prof. of History and Philosophy of Science, MIT 1992–; mem. Inst. of Advanced Studies, Princeton 1987–88; Visiting Fellow, later Scholar, MIT 1979–84, Visiting Prof. 1985–86; Pres. West Coast History of Science Soc. 1990–91; mem. American Philosophical Soc. 2006, American Acad. of Arts and Sciences 2007; Dr hc (Mount Holyoke Coll.) 1991, (Univ. of Amsterdam) 1993, (Simmons Coll.) 1995, (Rensslaer Polytechnic Inst.) 1995, (Tech. Univ. of Luleå, Sweden) 1996, (New School Univ.) 2000, (Allegheny Coll.) 2000, (Wesleyan Univ.) 2001, (Dartmouth Coll.) 2007; MacArthur Fellow 1992–97, Guggenheim Fellowship 2000–01, Moore Scholar, Calif. Inst. Tech. 2002, Winton Chair, Univ. of Minnesota 2002–05, Dibner Fellow 2003, Radcliffe Inst. Fellow 2005, Rothschild Lecturer, Harvard Univ. 2005, Plenary Speaker, Int. History of Science Congress, Beijing 2005; numerous awards, including Mina Shaughnessey Award 1981–82, Radcliffe Grad. Soc. Medal 1985, Medal of the Italian Senate 2001, Chaire Blaise Pascal 2005–07. *Publications include:* A Feeling for the Organism 1983, Reflections on Gender and Science 1985, Secrets of Life, Secrets of Death 1992, Keywords in Evolutionary Biology (ed.) 1994, Refiguring Life 1995, Feminism and Science (co-author) 1996, The Century of the Gene 2000, Making Sense of Life 2002. *Address:* Massachusetts Institute of Technology, E51-171, 77 Massachusetts Avenue, Cambridge, MA 02139, USA (office). *Telephone:* (617) 324-2095 (office). *Fax:* (617) 253-8118 (office). *E-mail:* efkeller@mit.edu (office). *Website:* web.mit.edu.sts (office).

KELLER, Joseph Bishop, PhD; American mathematician and academic; *Professor Emeritus of Mathematics and Mechanical Engineering, Stanford University;* b. 31 July 1923, Paterson, NJ; s. of Isaac Keller and Sally Bishop; m. Evelyn Fox 1963 (divorced 1976); one s. one d.; ed New York Univ.; ed New York Univ.; Prof. of Math. Courant Inst. of Math. Sciences, New York Univ. 1948–79, Chair. Dept of Math., Univ. Coll. of Arts and Sciences and Graduate School of Eng and Sciences 1967–73; Prof. of Math. and Mechanical Eng Stanford Univ. 1979– now Prof. Emer.; Research Assoc. Woods Hole Oceanographic Inst. 1965–; mem. NAS, Foreign mem. Royal Soc.; Hon. Prof. of Math. Sciences (Univ. of Cambridge) 1990; Hon. DTech (Tech. Univ. of Denmark) 1979, Hon. DSc (Northwestern Univ.) 1988, (Crete) 1993, (New Jersey Inst. Tech.) 1995, (Carlos Tercero de Madrid) 1995, (New York Univ.) 2002, (Univ. Notre Dame) 2005; Nemmers Prize 1996, shared Wolf Prize 1997, Nat. Medal of Science 1988, NAS Award in Applied Math. and Numerical Analysis 1995, numerous awards and lectureships. *Publications:* over 400 articles in professional journals. *Leisure interests:* hiking, skiing. *Address:* Department of Mathematics, Stanford University, Stanford, CA 94305 (office); 820 Sonoma Terrace, Stanford, CA 94305, USA (home). *Telephone:* (650) 723-0851 (office). *Fax:* (650) 725-4066 (office). *E-mail:* keller@math.stanford.edu (office).

KELLER, Samuel; Swiss museum administrator and foundation executive; *Head, Fondation Beyeler;* joined Art Basel 1994, Dir 2000–07, currently Chair. Advisory Bd, launched sister fair Art Basel Miami Beach 2002; Head, Fondation Beyeler, Riehen 2008–, also Chair. Art Kunstmesse AG; Young Global Leader, World Econ. Forum 2005. *Address:* Fondation Beyeler, Baselstrasse 101, 4125 Riehen, Switzerland (office). *Telephone:* 616459700 (office). *Fax:* 616459719 (office). *E-mail:* fondation@beyeler.com (office). *Website:* www.beyeler.com (office).

KELLER, Thomas A.; American chef; b. 1955, Southern Calif.; fmr chef, La Reserve and Restaurant Raphael, New York; served an estagiere apprentice in France in restaurants of Guy Savoy, Michael Pasquet, Gerard Besson, also Taillevant, Le Toit de Passey, Chiberta and Le Pre Catalan; est. restaurant Rakel, New York; Exec. Chef, Checkers Hotel, Los Angeles; acquired The French Laundry, Yountville, Calif. 1994, currently Chef and Owner; Founder and Owner EVO Inc. (retail line of olive oils and vinegar); spokesperson for Calif. Milk Advisory Bd 1997–98; Owner Bouchon 1998, Bouchon Bakery 2003, Per Se 2004, Bouchon at the Venetian 2004; Ivy Award, Restaurants and Insts 1996; named Best American Chef: Calif., James Beard Foundation 1996; Oustanding Chef: America 1997; World's Best Chef, Wedgewood 2002. *Publication:* Under Pressure 2008. *Address:* c/o Kristine Kester, Public Relations, The French Laundry, 6640 Washington Street, Yountville, CA 94559, USA (office). *Telephone:* (707) 944-8979 (office). *Fax:* (707) 944-1974 (office). *Website:* frenchlaundry.com.

KELLEY, Mike, BFA, MFA; American musician and artist; b. 1954, Wayne, Mich.; ed Univ. of Michigan, California Inst. of the Arts, Valencia; fmr mem. band Destroy All Monsters, Detroit; moved to Los Angeles 1978; was also in band Poetics; works inspired by history, philosophy, politics, underground rock music, decorative arts and working-class artistic expression; often takes up class and gender issues as well as issues of normality, criminality and perversion; currently Faculty mem. Grad. Dept of Fine Art, Art Center Coll. of Design, Pasadena; Publr X-TRA; mem. Project X Foundation for Art and Criticism; lives and works in Los Angeles; Louis Comfort Tiffany Foundation Grant 1984, Visual Artists Fellowship Grant, Nat. Endowment for the Arts 1985, Artists Space Interarts Grant 1986, Awards in the Visual Arts Grant 1987, Museum Program Exhbn Grant, Nat. Endowment for the Arts 1990, Skowhegan Medal in Mixed Media 1997, Distinguished Alumnus Award, Univ. of Michigan School of Art and Design 1998 Distinguished Alumnus Award, California Inst. of the Arts 2000, John Simon Guggenheim Memorial Foundation Fellowship 2003. *Works in public collections:* Carnegie Museum, Pittsburgh, Centre Georges Pompidou, Paris, Detroit Inst. of Art, Fonds Nat. d'Art Contemporain, Fundación "la Caixa", Madrid, Los Angeles Co. Museum of Art, Louisiana Museum, Humleback, Germany, Metropolitan Museum of Art, New York, Museum Abteiberg Mönchengladbach, Mönchengladbach, Germany, Museum Moderner Kunst, Vienna, Museum of Contemporary Art, Chicago, Museum of Contemporary Art, Los Angeles, Museum of Fine Arts, Boston, Museum of Modern Art, New York, Solomon R. Guggenheim Museum, New York, Statens Museum for Kunst, Copenhagen, Stedelijke Museum, Eindhoven, Art Inst. of Chicago, Van Abbe Museum, Eindhoven, Walker Art Center, Cincinnatti, Whitney Museum of American Art, New York. *Address:* c/o Marianne Boesky Fine Art, 535 West 22nd Street, New York, NY 10011, USA. *Telephone:* (212) 680-9889. *Fax:* (212) 680-9887. *E-mail:* info@marianneboeskygallery.com. *Website:* www.artcenter.edu; www.mikekelley.com.

KELLNER, Lawrence W. (Larry), BS; American business executive; *Chairman and CEO, Continental Airlines Inc.;* m. Susan Kellner; four c.; ed Univ. of South Carolina; Exec. Vice-Pres. and Chief Financial Officer American Savings Bank –1995; Sr Vice-Pres. and Chief Financial Officer Continental Airlines Inc. 1995–96, Exec. Vice-Pres. and Chief Financial Officer 1996–2001, Dir 2001–, Pres. 2001–04, COO 2003–04, Chair. and CEO 2004–; Dir Marriott International, Air Transport Assen, Greater Houston Partnership, Methodist Hosp., Cen. Houston Inc., Spring Br. Educ. Foundation; mem. Nat. Exec. Bd Boy Scouts of America; mem. Advisory Bd March of Dimes; Univ. of South Carolina Distinguished Alumni Award 1998. *Address:* Continental Airlines Inc., PO Box 4607, Houston, TX 77210, USA (office). *Telephone:* (713) 324-2950 (office). *Fax:* (713) 324-2687 (office). *Website:* www.continental.com (office).

KELLY, Alfred F., Jr., MBA; American financial services industry executive; *President, American Express Company;* m. Margaret P. Kelly; two s. three d.; ed Iona Coll.; Asst Prof., Iona Coll. 1980–85; fmr Head of Information Systems, Exec. Office of the Pres., The White House; fmrly with Information Systems and Strategic and Financial Planning Dept, PepsiCo; joined Strategic Planning Dept, American Express Co. 1987, Vice-Pres. of Technologies 1988, Exec. Vice-Pres. and Gen. Man., Consumer Marketing 1997–98, Pres. Consumer Card Services Group 1998–2000, Group Pres., Consumer, Small Business and Merchant Services 2000–07, Pres. 2007–; Chair. Wall Street Charity Golf Classic; mem. Bd of Dirs The Hershey Co. 2005–07 (resgnd), Concern Worldwide USA, Carvel Children's Rehabilitation Center; Trustee, Iona Coll., NY-Presbyterian Hosp.; mem. Council on Foreign Relations. *Address:* American Express Company, World Financial Center, 200 Vesey Street, New York NY 10285, USA (office). *Telephone:* (212) 640-2000 (office). *Fax:* (212) 640-2428 (office). *Website:* www.americanexpress.com (office).

KELLY, Donald P.; American business executive; b. 24 Feb. 1922, Chicago; s. of Thomas Nicholas Kelly and Ethel M. Healy; m. Byrd M. Sullivan 1952; two s. one d.; ed De Paul, Loyola and Harvard Univs; Man. Data Processing, Swift & Co. 1953, Asst Controller 1965, Controller 1967, Vice-Pres. Corp. Devt 1968, Financial Vice-Pres. and Dir 1970–; Financial Vice-Pres. and Dir Esmark April–Oct. 1973, Pres., COO 1973–77, Pres. and CEO 1977–82, Chair., Pres. and CEO 1982–84; Chair. Kelly Briggs and Assocs, Inc. 1984–86; Chair., CEO BCI Holdings Corpn 1986–87; Chair. and CEO EII Holdings Inc. 1987–88; Chair. Beatrice Co., Chicago March–Oct. 1988; Pres. and CEO D.P. Kelly Assocs L.P. 1988–; Dir, Chair., Pres., CEO Envirodyne Industries Inc. 1989–96. *Address:* D.P. Kelly and Associates, 701 Harger Road, Suite 190, Oak Brook, IL 60523, USA.

KELLY, Edmund F.; American insurance industry executive; *Chairman, President and CEO, Liberty Mutual Holding Company Inc.;* b. 1946, Co. Armagh, Northern Ireland; Man. Aetna Life and Casualty Co. 1974–92; Pres. and COO Liberty Mutual Insurance Co. 1992–98, Pres. and CEO Liberty Mutual Holding Co. Inc. 1998–, Chair. 2001–. *Address:* Liberty Mutual Holding Co. Inc., 175 Berkeley Street, Boston, MA 02116, USA (office). *Telephone:* (617) 357-9500 (office). *Fax:* (617) 574-6688 (office). *E-mail:* info@libertymutual.com (office). *Website:* www.libertymutual.com (office).

KELLY, Ellsworth; American painter and sculptor; b. 31 May 1923, Newburgh, NY; ed Pratt Inst., Brooklyn, Boston Museum Fine Arts School and Ecole des Beaux Arts, Paris, France; mil. service 1943–45; works exhibited at Salon de Réalités Nouvelles, Paris 1950, 1951, Carnegie Int. 1958, 1961, 1964, 1967, São Paulo Biennale 1961, Tokyo Int. 1963, Documenta III and IV, Germany 1964, 1968, Venice Biennale 1966, Guggenheim Int. 1967, Corcoran Annual, Washington, DC 1979, etc.; works in numerous perm. collections including Museum of Modern Art, Whitney Museum, Carnegie Inst., Chicago Art Inst., Guggenheim Museum, Tate Gallery, London, Musée d'Art Moderne, Paris, Stedelijk Museum, Amsterdam; mem. Nat. Inst. of Arts and Letters; Chevalier Ordre des Arts et des Lettres 1993; Mayor of Barcelona Medal 1993 and numerous other awards and prizes. *Address:* c/o Matthew Marks Gallery, 523 West 24th Street, New York, NY 10011, USA. *E-mail:* info@matthewmarks.com. *Website:* www.matthewmarks.com.

KELLY, Gail P., BA, MBA; South African banking executive; *CEO and Managing Director, Westpac Banking Corporation;* b. 25 April 1956, Pretoria; m. Allan Kelly 1977; ed Univ. of Cape Town, Charles Sturt Univ., Australia; worked as a teacher in Rhodesia and SA; began banking career with Nedcor Bank, Head of Human Resources 1990–97; joined Commonwealth Bank, Sydney, Australia as Gen. Manager of Strategic Marketing 1997, later served as Head, Customer Service Div.; CEO St George Bank 2002–07; CEO and Man. Dir Westpac Banking Corpn (only woman CEO of a top 20 Australian co.) 2008–, announced plans to merge bank with St George Bank May 2008, also Dir, Westpac New Zealand Ltd; mem. Bd Dirs Melbourne Business School Ltd; Best Financial Services Exec., Australian Banking & Finance magazine 2003, 2004, ranked by Forbes magazine amongst 100 Most Powerful Women (11th) 2008. *Address:* Westpac Banking Corpn, Level 20, 275 Kent Street, Sydney 2000, Australia (office). *Telephone:* (2) 8253-0390 (office). *Fax:* (2) 8253-1888 (office). *E-mail:* info@westpac.com.au (office). *Website:* www.westpac.com.au (office).

KELLY, Gregory Maxwell, PhD, FAA; Australian professor of pure mathematics; *Professor Emeritus, University of Sydney;* b. 5 June 1930, Sydney; s. of Owen S. Kelly and Rita M. (née McCauley) Kelly; m. Constance Imogen Kelly 1960; three s. one d.; ed Univs of Sydney and Cambridge, England; Lecturer in Pure Math. Univ. of Sydney 1957–60, Sr Lecturer 1961–65, Reader 1965–66; Prof. of Pure Math. Univ. of NSW 1967–72, Univ. of Sydney 1973–94, Prof. Emer. and Professorial Fellow 1994–; Ed. Journal of Pure and Applied Algebra 1971–, Applied Categorical Structures 1992–, Theory and Applications of Categories 1995–; Australian Centenary Medal 2003. *Publications:* An Introduction to Algebra and Vector Geometry 1972, Basic Concepts of Enriched Category Theory 1981; numerous learned papers. *Leisure interests:* bridge, music, swimming. *Address:* University of Sydney, School of Mathematics and Statistics, FO7, Sydney, NSW 2006 (office); 5 Bolton Place, Pymble, NSW 2073, Australia (home). *Telephone:* (2) 9351-3796 (office); (2) 9983-9985 (home). *Fax:* (2) 9351-4534 (office). *E-mail:* maxk@maths.usyd.edu.au (office). *Website:* www.maths.usyd.edu.au (office).

KELLY, James A., BS, MBA; American fmr government official; *Senior Advisor and CSIS Distinguished Alumni, Center for Strategic and International Studies (CSIS);* m. Audrey Pool Kelly; two c.; ed Harvard Univ., US Naval Acad., Nat. War Coll.; served in USN 1959–83, retd from active duty as Capt., Supply Corps; Deputy Asst Sec. of Defence for Int. Security Affairs (East Asia and Pacific), Pentagon 1983–86; Special Asst for Nat. Security Affairs to Pres. Ronald Reagan and Sr Dir of Asian Affairs, Nat. Security Council 1986–89; Pres. EAP Assocs Inc. (int. business consultants), Honolulu

1989–94; Pres. The Pacific Forum, Center for Strategic and Int. Studies, Honolulu 1994–2001; Asst Sec. of State for East Asian and Pacific Affairs 2001–05; currently Sr Advisor, Center for Strategic and Int. Studies. *Address:* c/o Center for Strategic and International Studies (CSIS), 1800 K Street, NW, Suite 400, Washington, DC 20006, USA (office). *Telephone:* (202) 887-0200 (office). *Fax:* (202) 775-3199 (office). *Website:* www.csis.org (office).

KELLY, Jim; American journalist; *Managing Editor, Time Inc.;* b. 15 Dec. 1953, Brooklyn, New York; m. Lisa Henricksson; one s.; ed Princeton Univ.; joined Time magazine 1977, as writer in Nation section, Foreign Ed. early 1990s, Deputy Man. Ed. 1996–2000, Man. Ed. 2001–06, Man. Ed. Time Inc. 2006–; Ed. Corporate Welfare series 1998, Visions 21 series 1999–2000; mem. Bd of Visitors Columbia Univ. Grad. School of Journalism. *Address:* Time Inc., Time-Life Building, Rockefeller Center, 1271 Avenue of the Americas, New York, NY 10020-1393, USA (office). *Telephone:* (212) 522-1212 (office). *Fax:* (212) 522-0323 (office). *Website:* www.time.com (office).

KELLY, John Hubert, BA; American diplomatist; *Ambassador-in-Residence, Center for International Strategy, Technology and Policy, Sam Nunn School of International Affairs, Georgia Institute of Technology;* b. 20 July 1939, Fond du Lac, Wis.; m. Helena Marita Ajo; one s. one d.; ed Emory Univ., Atlanta; Second Sec. US Embassy, Ankara 1966–67; American Consul, Songkhla, Thailand 1969–71; First Sec. US Embassy, Paris 1976–80; Deputy Exec. Sec., Dept of State, Washington DC 1980–81, Sr Deputy Asst Sec. of State for Public Affairs 1982–83, Prin. Deputy Asst Sec. of State for European Affairs 1983–85; Amb. to Lebanon 1986–88, to Finland 1991–94; Prin. Deputy Dir of Policy Planning Staff 1988–89; Asst Sec. for Near Eastern and SE Asian Affairs 1989–93; Man. Dir Int. Equity Partners, Atlanta 1995–98; Pres. John Kelly Consulting Inc. 1999–; Dir Finnish-American Chamber of Commerce 1998, American Int. Petroleum Co. 1999; Trustee, Lebanese American Univ. 1997; Amb.-in-Residence, Sam Nunn School for Int. Affairs, Georgia Inst. of Tech. 1999–; mem. Council on Foreign Relations, American-Turkish Council, Middle East Inst., Southern Center for Int. Studies. *Address:* Sam Nunn School of International Affairs, Georgia Tech, 781 Marietta Street, NW, Atlanta, GA 30332-1610; John Kelly Consulting, Inc., 1808 Over Lake Drive SE, Suite D, Conyers, GA 30013, USA (office). *Telephone:* (770) 918-9957 (office). *Fax:* (770) 483-3090 (office). *Website:* www.cistp.gatech.edu.

KELLY, John Philip, CMG, LVO, MBE; British diplomatist; *Vice-President, Victoria League for Commonwealth Friendship;* b. 25 June 1941, Tuam, Ireland; s. of William Kelly and Norah Kelly (née Roche); m. Jennifer Anne Buckler 1964; one s.; ed Oatlands Coll., Dublin, Open Univ.; joined HM Diplomatic Service 1959; worked at Embassies in Kinshasa (fmrly Léopoldville) 1962–65, Cairo 1965–67, Bonn 1967–70; with FCO 1970–73, 1986–89, 1994–96; with High Comm. Canberra 1973–76, Consulate-Gen. Antwerp 1977–78; with Dept of Trade 1980–82; Rep. to Grenada 1982–86; Deputy Gov. of Bermuda 1989–94; Gov. Turks and Caicos Islands 1996–2000; Chair. Victoria League for Commonwealth Friendship 2002–07, Vice-Pres. 2007–. *Leisure interests:* family, Rotary International, cruise lecturing, golf, reading, walking. *Address:* The Laurels, 56 Garden Lane, Royston, Herts., SG8 9EH, England (home). *Telephone:* (1763) 245128 (home). *E-mail:* johnandjenniferkelly@btinternet.com (home).

KELLY, Michael Joseph, BS, MS, MA, PhD, ScD (Cantab.), CEng, CPhys, FRS, FREng, FInstP, FIEE; New Zealand/British engineer, physicist and academic; *Professor and Director, Centre for Solid State Electronics, University of Surrey;* b. 14 May 1949, New Plymouth, NZ; m.; one d.; ed Victoria Univ. of Wellington, Univ. of Cambridge; Visiting Fellow, Dept of Physics, Victoria Univ. of Wellington 1974; Research Fellow in Physics, Trinity Hall, Cambridge 1974–77, Staff Fellow in Theoretical Physics 1977–81, Staff Fellow in Physics 1989–92; Visiting Researcher, KFA-IFF, Julich, FRG 1975; IBM Research Fellow, Dept of Physics, Univ. of California, Berkeley 1975–76; SRC Advanced Fellow, Cavendish Lab., Cambridge 1977–81, Visiting Fellow 1988–92, Royal Soc./Science and Eng Research Council Industrial Fellow 1989–91; Visiting Fellow, Max Planck Institut für Festkorperforschung, Stuttgart, FRG 1980; mem. research staff, GEC Hirst Research Centre 1981–92, Man. Superlattice Research Group 1984–90, Coordinator GEC Superlattice Research 1984–1992, Man. EEC, Dept of Trade and Industry, Ministry of Defence and GEC Research Contracts 1984–92; Prof. of Physics and Electronics, Dept of Physics, Univ. of Surrey 1992–96, Acting Head of Dept Jan.–April 1995, Head of Dept of Electronic and Electrical Eng 1996–97, Head of School of Electronic Eng, Information Tech. and Math. 1997–2001, Dir Centre for Solid State Electronics 2000–, mem. Senate Univ. of Surrey 1996–, Council Univ. of Surrey 1997–, Planning and Resources Cttee 1997–; Dir (non-exec.) Surrey Satellite Technology Ltd 1996–; Vice-Pres. Inst. of Physics 2001–05; mem. Council Royal Soc. 2001–02; mem. or fmr mem. numerous professional and govt cttees; Assoc. Ed. International Journal of Electronics 1996–; mem. American Inst. of Physics, IEEE; Hon. Fellow, Royal Soc. of NZ 1999; GEC Publs Prizewinner 1986, 1987, 1988, Paterson Medal and Prize, Inst. of Physics 1989, Nelson Gold Medal, GEC 1991, Silver Medal, Royal Acad. of Eng 1999, Hughes Medal, Royal Soc. 2006. *Publications:* The Physics and Fabrication of Microstructures and Microdevices (co-ed.) 1986, Technology Foresight Panel Report #8 on 'IT and Electronics' (co-author) 1995, Low Dimensional Semiconductors 1995, Advanced Materials in the Market Place (co-ed.) 1995, The Current Status of Semiconductor Tunnelling Devices (co-ed.) 1996; more than 210 papers and review articles, book chapters etc. in refereed journals, and in conf. proceedings etc.; 13 patents on semiconductor devices (seven patents still active). *Address:* School of Electronic Engineering, Information Technology and Mathematics, University of Surrey, Guildford, GU2 5XH, Surrey, England (office). *Telephone:* (1483) 259410 (office). *Fax:* (1483) 534139 (office). *E-mail:* M.Kelly@eim.surrey.ac.uk (office). *Website:* www.ee.surrey.ac.uk (office).

KELLY, Most Rev. Patrick Altham, STL, PhL; British ecclesiastic; *Roman Catholic Archbishop of Liverpool and Metropolitan of the Northern Province;* b. 23 Nov. 1938, Morecambe; s. of John Kelly and Mary Kelly (née Altham); ed Preston Catholic Coll., Venerable English Coll., Rome; Asst Priest, Lancaster Cathedral 1964–66; Prof. of Dogmatic Theology, Oscott Coll., Birmingham 1966–79, Rector 1979–84; Bishop of Salford 1984–96; Archbishop of Liverpool, Metropolitan of the Northern Prov. 1996–. *Address:* Archbishop's House, Lowood, Carnatic Road, Mossley Hill, Liverpool L18 8BY, England. *Telephone:* (151) 724-6398. *Fax:* (151) 724-6405. *E-mail:* archbishop.liverpool@rcaolp.co.uk (office). *Website:* www.archdiocese-of-liverpool.co.uk (office).

KELLY, Ros, AO, BA,; Australian fmr politician; *Executive Director, Environmental Resources Management;* b. 25 Jan. 1948, Sydney; d. of M. Raw and P. Raw; m. David Morgan; one s. one d.; ed Univ. of Sydney; high-school teacher, NSW and ACT 1969–74; consultant and mem. ACT Consumer Affairs Council 1974–79; mem. ACT Legal Aid Comm. 1976–79; fmr mem. ACT Legis. Ass.; mem. Fed. Parl. 1980–95; Sec. Fed. Labor Party Parl. Caucus 1981–87; Minister for Defence, Science and Personnel 1987–89, for Telecommunications and Aviation Support 1989–90, for Sport, the Environment and Territories 1990–94, for the Arts 1990–93, Assisting the Prime Minister for the Status of Women 1993–94; mem. Int. Advisory Council Normandy Mining Ltd 1995–2001; Group Exec. Dames & Moore 1995–2001; Exec. Dir Environmental Resources Management (consulting firm) 2001–; Dir (non-exec.) Theiss Pty Ltd 1998–, Thiess Environmental Services 1998–, External Sustainable Devt Advisory Group, The Rescue Helicopter Service; Chair. NSW Premiers Environmental Mining Awards 1999–, Minerals Council of Australia's External Advisory Group on Sustainability, Nat. Breast Cancer Foundation of Australia 2005–; mem. Advisory Council Sustainable Minerals Inst., Int. Council of Normandy Minerals, Nat. Advisory Council Greenfleet; Trustee, Worldwide Fund for Nature. *Leisure interests:* reading, films, aerobics. *Address:* National Breast Cancer Foundation, GPO Box 4126, Level 3, 18–20 York Street, Sydney, NSW 2000 (office); Environmental Resources Management, Building C, 33 Saunders Street, Pyrmont, NSW 2009, Australia. *E-mail:* info@nbcf.org.au (office); rkelly3@bigpond.net.au (home).

KELLY, Rt Hon. Ruth Maria, BA, MSc; British economist and politician; b. 9 May 1968, Limavady, Northern Ireland; d. of Bernard James Kelly and Gertrude Anne Kelly; m. Derek John Gadd 1996; one s. three d.; ed Sutton High School, Westminster School, Queen's Coll., Oxford, London School of Econs; econs writer, The Guardian newspaper 1990–94; economist, Bank of England 1994–97, Deputy Head of Inflation Report Div. 1994–96, Man. Financial Stability 1996–97; MP (Labour) Bolton W 1997–; Parl. Pvt. Sec. to Nicholas Brown MP 1998–2001; Econ. Sec. to HM Treasury 2001–02; Financial Sec. to HM Treasury 2002–04; Deputy, Cabinet Office 2004; Sec. of State for Educ. and Skills 2004–06, for Communities and Local Govt 2006–07, for Transport 2007–08 (resgnd); Minister for Women 2006–07; elected to Royal Econ. Soc. Council 1999–2001; mem. House of Commons Treasury Select Cttee 1997–98; mem. Fabian Soc., Council of Man. Nat. Inst. for Econ. and Social Research 1998–2001; Minister to Watch, Zurich/Spectator Party Awards 2001. *Publications include:* Taxing the Spectator 1993, Hedging Your Futures (co-author) 1994, The Wrecker's Lamp (co-author) 1994, The Case for Universal Payment (chapter in Time Off with the Children: Paying for Parental Leave) 1999, Europe (chapter in Beyond 2000: Long-Term Policies for Labour) 1999, Reforming the Working Family Tax Credit: How An Integrated Child Credit Could Work for Children and Families 2000; chapters in New Gender Agenda 2000, The Progressive Century 2001. *Leisure interests:* family, chess, walking. *Address:* House of Commons, London, SW1A 0AA; 2–4 Wilbraham Street, Westhoughton, Bolton, BL5 3RA, England. *Telephone:* (1942) 813468. *E-mail:* kellyr@parliament.uk. *Website:* www.ruthkellymp.com.

KELMAN, James; British writer; b. 9 June 1946, Glasgow; m. Marie Connors; two d.; ed Greenfield Public School, Govan; Spirit of Scotland Award. *Plays:* Hardie and Baird, The Last Days 1991, One, Two – Hey (R and B musical, toured 1994). *Radio:* The Art of the Big Bass Drum (play, BBC Radio 3) 1998. *Publications include:* novels: The Bus Conductor Hines 1984, A Chancer 1985, A Disaffection (James Tait Black Memorial Prize) 1989, How Late It Was, How Late (Booker Prize) 1994, Translated Accounts 2001, You Have to be Careful in the Land of the Free 2004, Kieron Smith, Boy (Saltire Soc's Book of the Year) 2008; short stories: An Old Pub Near the Angel 1973, Short Tales from the Nightshift 1978, Not Not While the Giro 1983, Lean Tales 1985, Greyhound for Breakfast (Cheltenham Prize) 1987, The Burn (short stories, Scottish Arts Council Book Award) 1991, Busted Scotch 1997, The Good Times (Scottish Writer of the Year Award) 1998; plays: The Busker 1985, In the Night 1988; other: And the Judges Said (essays) 2002. *Address:* Rodgers, Coleridge and White Ltd, 20 Powis Mews, London, W11 1JN, England (office). *Telephone:* (20) 7221-3717 (office). *E-mail:* info@rcwlitagency.com (office). *Website:* www.rcwlitagency.com (office).

KELNER, Simon; British newspaper editor; *Managing Director and Editor-in-Chief, The Independent and The Independent on Sunday;* b. 9 Dec. 1957, Manchester; ed Bury Grammar School, Preston Polytechnic; Trainee Reporter, Neath Guardian 1976–79; Sports Reporter, Extel 1979–80; Sports Ed., Kent Evening Post 1980–83; Asst Sports Ed., The Observer 1983–86; Deputy Sports Ed., The Independent 1986–89; Sports Ed., Sunday Corresp. 1989–90; Sports Ed., The Observer 1990–91, Ed. 1991–93; Sports Ed., The Independent on Sunday 1993–95, Night Ed., The Independent 1995, Features Ed. 1995–96; Ed. Night and Day Magazine, Mail on Sunday 1996–98; Ed.-in-Chief, The Independent 1998–, The Independent on Sunday 1998–, Man. Dir 2008–; Patron The Journalism Soc. 2004–; Hon. Fellowship, Univ. of Cen. Lancashire; Ed. of the Year, What the Papers Say Awards 1999, 2003, Newspaper Ed. of the Year, What the Papers Say Awards 2004, Edgar Wallace

Award 2000, 2004, Newspaper of the Year, British Press Awards 2004, GQ Editor of the Year 2004, Media Achiever of the Year, Campaign Media Awards 2004, Marketeer of the Year, Marketing Week Effectiveness Awards 2004. *Publications:* To Jerusalem and Back 1996. *Address:* The Independent, Independent House, 191 Marsh Wall, London, E14 9RS, England (office). *Telephone:* (20) 7005-2000 (office). *Fax:* (20) 7005-2022 (office). *E-mail:* s.kelner@independent.co.uk (office). *Website:* www.independent.co.uk (office).

KELSO, Adm. Frank Benton II; American naval officer; b. 11 July 1933, Fayetteville, Tenn.; s. of Thomas Benton Kelso and Wista Muse; m. Landess McCown 1956; four c.; ed US Naval Acad.; graduated from US Naval Acad. 1956; attended Submarine School 1958; Office of Program Appraisal 1983; Office, Sec. for the Navy 1985; attained rank of Adm. 1986; Commdr US Sixth Fleet 1985–86; Commdr-in-Chief, US Atlantic Fleet, Norfolk, Va 1986–88; Supreme Allied Commdr, Atlantic Commdr-in-Chief, Atlantic Command, Norfolk 1988–90; Chief of Naval Operations, Washington, DC 1990–94; Acting Sec. of Navy 1993; retd 1994.

KELTOŠOVÁ, Olga, BSc; Slovak politician; *Mayor of Lamač, Bratislava;* b. (Olga Suchalová), 27 Feb. 1943, Pezinok; m. (divorced); one s. one d.; ed Komenský Univ. Bratislava; collaborated with various students' magazines later banned in 1968; worked as translator and interpreter 1970–89; Press Sec. Democratic Party 1989; Deputy Chair. to Nat. Council 1990–92; expelled from Democratic Party 1991, joined Movt for Democratic Slovakia (now Political Party for Democratic Slovakia) 1991; Minister of Labour, Social Affairs and Family Matters 1992–94, 1995–98; Chair. Co-ordination Cttee for Issues of Handicapped 1995, Co-ordinating Body for Problems of Women 1996; elected mem. Parl. 1998; Mayor of Lamač, Bratislava 2006–; A. Hlinka Order 1998. *Leisure interests:* classical ballet, gardening. *Address:* Miestny úrad Lamač, Heyrovského 2, 841 03 Bratislava (office). *Telephone:* (2) 6478-0065 (office). *Fax:* (2) 6478-0689 (office). *E-mail:* starostka@lamac.sk (office). *Website:* www.lamac.sk (office).

KEMAKEZA, Sir Allan; Solomon Islands politician; b. 1951, Panueli village, Central Prov.; joined Royal Solomon Islands Police Force 1972, apptd Asst Superintendent 1988; Minister for Housing and Govt Service, Solomon Islands 1989–1993; Minister for Forests, Environment and Conservation 1995–96; Deputy Prime Minister for Peace and Nat. Reconciliation; Prime Minister 2001–06 (resgnd). *Address:* c/o Office of the Prime Minister, POB G1, Honiara, Solomon Islands (office).

KEMAL, Yaşar; Turkish writer and journalist; b. (Kemal Sadık Gökçel), 1926, Adana; m. 1st Thilda Serrero 1952 (deceased); one s.; m. 2nd Ayse Semiha Baban 2002; self-educated; mem. Académie Universelle des Cultures, Paris; Commdr, Légion d'honneur 1984; Dr hc (Strasbourg) 1991, (Akdeniz Univ., Antalya) 1991, (Mediterranean Univ.) 1992, (Free Univ., Berlin) 1998, (Bilkent Univ.) 2002; Prix Mondial Cino del Duca 1982, VIII Premi Internacional Catalunya, Barcelona 1996, Hellman-Hammett Award, New York 1996, Peace Prize of German Book Trade 1997, Prix Nonino, Percoto, Italy 1997, Stig Dagerman Prize, Sweden 1997, Norwegian Authors Union Prize 1997, Prix Ecureuil de littérature étrangère, Bordeaux 1998, Z. Homer Poetry Award 2003, Soranos Prize (Thessalonika, Greece) 2003, Turkish Publisher's Asscn Lifetime Achievement Award 2003. *Publications:* (in English) Memed, My Hawk 1961, The Wind from the Plain 1963, Anatolian Tales 1968, They Burn the Thistles 1973, Iron Earth, Copper Sky 1974, The Legend of Ararat 1975, The Legend of the Thousand Bulls 1976, The Undying Grass 1977, The Lords of Akchasaz (Part I), Murder in the Ironsmiths' Market 1979, The Saga of a Seagull 1981, The Sea-Crossed Fisherman 1985, The Birds Have Also Gone 1987, To Crush the Serpent 1991, Salman the Solitary 1997, The Story of an Island Vols I–IV 1998; novels, short stories, plays and essays in Turkish. *Leisure interest:* folklore. *Address:* P.K. 14, Basinköy, Istanbul, Turkey. *Website:* www.yasarkemal.net.

KEMMER, Michael; German banking executive; *Chairman of the Board of Management, Bavaria BayernLB;* b. 30 April 1957, Nördlingen; ed Ludwig-Maximilians Univ., Munich; Bank Officer, Bayerische Vereinsbank 1977–79, Cen. Accounts Div. 1988–94; Research Asst, Univ. of Munich 1984–87; Head, Main Finance Dept, DG Bank, Frankfurt 1994–96; Head, Cen. Div., Group Accounts, Bayerische Vereinsbank (now Bayerische Hypo- und Vereinsbank AG) 1996–2003, Head, Accounts and Taxes Div. 2003; mem. Bd of Man. and Chief Risk Officer HVB Group 2003–05; Chief Financial Officer Bavaria BayernLB 2006–08, Chair. Bd of Man. 2008–. *Address:* Bavaria BayernLB, Brienner Strasse, 80333 Munich, Germany (office). *Telephone:* (89) 2171-01 (office). *E-mail:* presse@bayernlb.de (office). *Website:* www.bayernlb.de (office).

KÉMOULARIA, Claude de; French international administrator, diplomatist and banker; *Executive Vice-President, Institut D'Etudes Politiques Mediterraneennes- Club de Monaco;* b. 30 March 1922, Paris; s. of Joseph de Kémoularia and Marguerite Eichenlaub; m. Chantal Julia de Kémoularia 1951; one d. two s.; ed Lycée de Fontainbleau, Faculté de Droit, Univ. de Paris and Ecole Libre des Sciences Politiques; Personal Asst to Minister of Interior 1944–45; sr Adviser, Office of Gov.-Gen., French Zone of Occupied Germany 1946–47; Parliamentary Sec. to Minister of Finance 1948; Parl. Sec. to Chair. CEO Pres. Paul Reynaud 1948–56; Personal Asst to Sec.-Gen. of UN, Dag Hammarskjöld 1957–61, in charge of World Refugee Year 1960; Dir European Information Services of UN 1961; entered pvt. business 1962; Dir Forges de Chatillon-Commentry 1962–64, Paribas North America 1979–82, S. G. Warburg 1980–82; Sr Consultant to Administrator, UN Devt Programme 1964–80; Dir of Cabinet and Pvt. Adviser to Prince Rainier of Monaco 1965–67; adviser Chair. CEO Pres. int. operations (Banque de Paris et des Pays-Bas) 1968–82; Hon. Chair. Soc. Néo-Calédonienne de Dévt. et Participations, Soc. Gabonaise de Participations; Amb. to Netherlands 1982–84; Perm. Rep. to UN 1984–87; UN Goodwill Amb. for Population Matters 1987–92, Vice-Chair. SGS Holding France 1994–2004; Dir Société générale de surveillance 1987–94, Aerospaitiale, Nina Ricci, Eurocopter; mem. Bd Bank Dhofar Al Omani Al-Fransi, Oman 1975–98, Baiduri Bank Berhad, Brunei 1991–, Bank of Sharjah, UAE; Pres. Paribas Netherlands 1988–92, Hon. Pres. 1992; Pres. Advisory Cttee Revue politique et parlementaire 1989–; Admin., Institut d'Etudes Politiques Mediterranéennes (IEPM) 1999, Co-founder and Vice Pres. IEPM-Club de Monaco 2000–; Hon. Pres. French UN Asscn; Chair. Friends of the French Repub. Asscn; Pres. French Omani Business Club, Qatari French Business Club (French section); mem. Nat. Council, Mouvement Européen, American Club of Paris, France-Amérique, France-Grande Bretagne; Officier Légion d'honneur, Commdr des Arts et Lettres, Grand Officier Orange Nassau and other decorations. *Leisure interest:* international affairs. *Address:* Club de Monaco, 73 Champs Elysées, 75008 Paris (office); 41 boulevard du Commandant Charcot, 92200 Neuilly-sur-Seine, France (home). *Telephone:* 1-56-43-36-10 (office); 1-47-22-90-90 (home). *Fax:* 1-56-43-36-11 (office). *E-mail:* iepm@wanadoo.fr (office).

KEMP, Rt Rev. Eric Waldram, MA, DD, DLitt, FRHistS; British ecclesiastic (retd); b. 27 April 1915, Grimsby; s. of Tom Kemp and Florence L. Waldram; m. Leslie Patricia Kirk 1953; one s. four d.; ed Brigg Grammar School, Lincs., Exeter Coll., Oxford and St Stephen's House; ordained Deacon 1939, priest 1940; curate, St Luke's, Southampton 1939–41; Librarian Pusey House, Oxford 1941–46; Chaplain Christ Church, Oxford 1941–46; Acting Chaplain St John's Coll., Oxford 1943–45; Fellow, Chaplain, Tutor and Lecturer in Theology and Medieval History, Exeter Coll. Oxford 1946–69, Fellow Emer. 1969; Dean of Worcester 1969–74; Lord Bishop of Chichester 1974–2001; Canon and Prebendary of Caistor in Lincoln Cathedral 1952–2000; Chaplain to the Queen 1967–69; Hon. Prov. Canon of Cape Town 1960; Chanoine d'honneur, Chartres Cathedral 1998; Hon. Fellow, Univ. Coll. Chichester 2001; Hon. DLitt (Sussex) 1986; Hon. DD (Berne) 1987; Bampton Lecturer 1959–60. *Publications:* Canonization in the Western Church 1948, 25 Papal Decretals Relating to the Diocese of Lincoln 1954, N.P. Williams 1954 (biog.), An Introduction to Canon Law in the Church of England 1957, Life and Letters of K. E. Kirk 1959, Counsel and Consent 1961, Man: Fallen and Free 1969, Square Words in a Round World 1980. *Leisure interests:* music, travel and medieval history. *Address:* 5 Alexandra Road, Chichester, W Sussex, PO19 7LX, England. *Telephone:* (1243) 780-647.

KEMP, Martin John, MA, DLitt, FBA, FRSA, FRSE; British art historian, academic, author and exhibition curator; *Emeritus Professor, University of Oxford;* b. 5 March 1942, Windsor; s. of Frederick Maurice Kemp and Violet Anne (née Tull) Kemp; m. Jill Lightfoot 1966 (divorced 2003); one s. one d.; ed Windsor Grammar School, Downing Coll., Cambridge and Courtauld Inst. of Art, London; Lecturer in History of Western Art, Dalhousie Univ., NS, Canada 1965–66; Lecturer in History of Fine Art, Univ. of Glasgow 1966–81; Prof. of Fine Arts, Univ. of St Andrew's 1981–90; Prof. of History, Royal Scottish Acad. 1985–; Prof. of History and Theory of Art, Univ. of St Andrew's 1990–95; Prof. of History of Art, Univ. of Oxford 1995, now Emer. Prof. and Head of Dept; Fellow Trinity Coll. Oxford 1995–; Provost St Leonard's Coll., Univ. of St Andrew's 1991–95; mem. Inst. for Advanced Study, Princeton, NJ, USA 1984–85; Slade Prof., Univ. of Cambridge 1987–88; Benjamin Sonenberg Visiting Prof., Inst. of Fine Arts, New York Univ. 1988; Wiley Visiting Prof., Univ. of N Carolina, Chapel Hill 1993; British Acad. Wolfson Research Prof. 1993–98; Trustee, Nat. Galleries of Scotland 1982–87, Victoria and Albert Museum, London 1986–89, British Museum 1995–, Ashmolean Museum 1995–; Pres. Leonardo da Vinci Soc. 1988–97; Chair. Asscn of Art Historians 1989–92; mem. Exec. Scottish Museums Council 1990–95; Dir and Chair. Graeme Murray Gallery 1990–92; Dir Wallace Kemp/Artakt 2001; mem. Bd Interalia 1992–, Bd Museum Training Inst. 1993–98, Council British Soc. for the History of Science 1994–97; mem. Visual Arts Advisory Panel, Arts Council of England 1996–; Visiting mem., Getty Center, Los Angeles 2002; Mellon Sr Fellow, Canadian Centre for Architecture, Montreal 2004; Fellow, Royal Soc. of Sciences, Uppsala 1995; Hon. mem. American Acad. of Arts and Sciences 1996–, Hon. Fellow, Downing Coll. 1999, Trinity Coll. Oxford 2008; Hon. DLitt (Heriot Watt) 1995, (Uppsala) 2009; Mitchell Prize 1981; Armand Hammer Prize for Leonardo Studies 1992; Pres.'s Prize, Italian Asscn of America 1992. *Publications:* Leonardo da Vinci: The Marvellous Works of Nature and Man 1981, Leonardo da Vinci (co-author) 1989, Leonardo on Painting (co-author) 1989, The Science of Art: Optical Themes in Western Art from Brunelleschi to Seurat 1990, Behind the Picture: Art and Evidence in the Italian Renaissance 1997, Immagine e Verità 1999, The Oxford History of Western Art (ed.) 2000, Spectacular Bodies (with Marina Wallace) 2000, Visualizations The Nature Book of Science and Art 2001, Leonardo 2004, Leonardo da Vinci: Experience, Experiment and Design 2006, Seen/Unseen 2006, The Human Animal 2007; regular column on Science in Culture in Nature 1997–. *Leisure interests:* sport, music. *Address:* Trinity College, Oxford, OX1 3BH (home). *Telephone:* (20) 3214-0882 (office); (1993) 811364 (office). *E-mail:* CDawnay@unitedagents.co.uk (office); martin.kemp@trinity.ox.ac.uk (office). *Website:* www.martinjkemp.co.uk (office).

KEMP-WELCH, Sir John, Kt, FRSA; British fmr stock exchange executive; b. 31 March 1936, Hertford; s. of Peter Kemp-Welch and Peggy Kemp-Welch; m. Diana Leishman 1964; one s. three d.; ed Winchester Coll.; Hoare & Co. 1954–58; Cazenove & Co. 1959–93, Jt Sr Partner 1980–93; Dir Savoy Hotel PLC 1985–98; Dir London Stock Exchange 1991–2000, Chair. 1994–2000; Chair. Scottish Eastern Investment Trust 1994–99, Claridge's Hotel 1995–97; Deputy Chair. Financial Reporting Council 1994–2000; Vice-Chair. Fed. of European Stock Exchanges 1996–98; Dir Royal and Sun Alliance Insurance Group PLC 1994–99, British Invisibles 1994–98, Securities and Futures Authority 1994–97, ProShare 1995–97, Accountancy Foundation 2000–, HSBC Holdings 2000–06; Gov. The Ditchley Foundation 1980–; Trustee,

Farmington; Hon. Fellow, Securities Inst.; Hon. DBA (London Guildhall Univ.) 1998. *Leisure interests:* the hills of Perthshire, Impressionist paintings, champagne.

KEMPSTON DARKES, V. Maureen, OC, BA, LLB; Canadian lawyer and automotive industry xecutive; *Group Vice President and President, Latin America, Africa and Middle East, General Motors Corporation;* b. 31 July 1948, Toronto, Ont.; m. Lawrence J. Darkes; ed Victoria Coll., Univ. of Toronto and Univ. of Toronto Law School; called to Bar of Toronto; mem. Legal Staff, General Motors (GM) of Canada Ltd 1975–79, Asst Counsel 1979, Head of Tax Staff 1980–84, Gen. Dir Public Affairs 1987, Vice-Pres. of Corp. Affairs and mem. Bd of Dirs 1991, Gen. Counsel and Sec. 1992, Pres. (first woman) and Gen. Man. 1994–2001, Vice-Pres. GM Corpn (one of only two female vice-pres) 1994–2001, Pres. GM Latin America, Africa and the Middle East and mem. GM Automotive Strategy Bd and Group Vice-Pres. 2002–; mem. Legal Staff, General Motors Corpn, Detroit, Mich., USA 1979–80, mem. staff, Treas.'s Office, New York 1985–87, Vice-Pres. 1994–2001; mem. Bd of Dirs Hughes Aircraft of Canada, CAMI Automotive, CN Rail, Brascan Ltd, Thomson Corpn, Nat. Quality Inst., Nat. Research Council, Vehicle Mfrs Asscn, Ont. Govt Educ. Quality and Accountability Bd, Ont. Minister of Health's Women's Health Council; apptd to Free Trade Agreement Automotive Select Panel 1989, Transportation Equipment Sectoral Advisory Group on Int. Trade 1994; mem. Arts and Science Advisory Bd Univ. of Toronto, Bd of Govs Univ. of Waterloo, Business School Advisory Cttee Univ. of Western Ontario, Bd of Dirs Women's Coll. Hosp. Foundation, Chancellor's Council of Victoria Coll., Bd New Directions, Council of Advisory Govs for the YMCA of Greater Toronto; fmr Co-Chair. BC Cancer Foundation's Millennium Campaign; Order of Ontario 1997, Officer of the Order of Ontario 2000; Hon. DComm (St Mary's Univ.) 1995; Hon. LLD Univ. of Toronto) 1996, (Univ. of Victoria, McMaster Univ., Dalhousie Univ., Wilfrid Laurier Univ., Law Soc. of Upper Canada); Women's Automotive Asscn Int. Professional Achievement Award 1997, ABA Margaret Brent Women Lawyers of Achievement Award 1998, Automotive Hall of Fame Distinguished Service Citation 1999, Gov. Gen.'s Awards in Commemoration of the Persons Case 2006; ranked by Fortune magazine amongst 50 Most Powerful Women in Business outside the US (seventh) 2002, (sixth) 2003; named to International Power 50, Forbes magazine 2008. *Address:* General Motors Latin America, Africa and Middle East Region, 2901 SW 149th Ave., Suite 400, Miramar, FL 33027, USA (office). *Telephone:* (954) 392-3500 (office). *Website:* www.gm.com (office).

KEMPTHORNE, Dirk Arthur, BS; American government official and fmr politician; b. 29 Oct. 1951, San Diego, Calif.; s. of James Henry Kempthorne and Maxine Jesse Kempthorne (née Gustason); m. Patricia Jean Merrill 1977; one s. one d.; ed Univ. of Idaho; Exec. Asst to Dir Idaho Dept Lands, Boise 1975–78; Exec. Vice-Pres. Idaho Home Builders' Asscn 1978–81; Campaign Man., Batt for Gov., Boise 1981–82; Idaho Public Affairs Man. FMC Corpn, Boise 1983–86; Mayor of Boise 1986–93; Senator from Idaho 1993–99; Gov. of Idaho 1999–2006; US Sec. of Interior 2006–09; Chair. US Conf. of Mayors Standing Cttee on Energy and Environment 1991–93, mem. Advisory Bd 1991–93; Sec. Nat. Conf. of Republican Mayors and Municipal Elected Officials 1991–93; mem. Bd of Dirs Parents and Youth Against Drug Abuse 1987–; Republican; numerous awards. *Address:* c/o Department of the Interior, 1849 C Street, NW, Washington DC 20240, USA.

KEMULARIA, Konstantine; Georgian diplomatist and politician; b. 4 April 1954, Khobi; m.; three c.; ed Tbilisi State Univ.; worked as investigator in Sukhumi Prosecutor's Office 1975–76; Chief Investigator Kutaisi Prosecutor's Office 1976–79; Jr Research Officer, Acad. of Sciences of Georgia 1979; Research Officer, Union Acad. of Sciences, State and Jurisprudence Inst. 1980–83, Head Research Officer 1983–87; various positions 1987–92 in Prosecutor's Office Bd of Georgia including Prosecutor, Prosecutor of Chiatura, Deputy Head of Div., and Head of Bd; Minister of Justice 1992–93; Leader, Moscow Juridicial Service 1994–95; elected mem. Tbilisi Sakrebulo 1998; mem. Parliament 1999–2004; Amb. to Russian Fed. Feb.–June 2004; Chair. Supreme Court 2004–05; Deputy Prime Minister and Minister of Justice Feb.–Dec. 2005; apptd Nat. Security Adviser to Pres. and Sec., Nat. Security Council 2005; currently Asst on Energy and Transportation Coordination Issues. *Address:* c/o Office of the President, 0105 Tbilisi, P. Ingorovka 7, Georgia. *Telephone:* (32) 99-00-70. *Fax:* (32) 99-88-87. *E-mail:* secretariat@admin.gov.ge. *Website:* www.president.gov.ge.

KENDAL, Felicity, CBE; British actress; b. 25 Sept. 1946; d. of Geoffrey Kendal and Laura Kendal; m. 1st (divorced); one s.; m. 2nd Michael Rudman 1983 (divorced 1991); one s.; ed six convents in India; first appeared on stage 1947, at age nine months in A Midsummer Night's Dream; grew up touring India and Far East with parents' theatre co., playing pageboys at age eight and Puck at age nine, graduating to roles such as Viola in Twelfth Night, Jessica in The Merchant of Venice and Ophelia in Hamlet; returned to England 1965; Variety Club Most Promising Newcomer 1974, Best Actress 1979, Clarence Derwent Award 1980, Evening Standard Best Actress Award 1989, Variety Club Best Actress Award 2000. *Stage roles include:* London debut as Carla in Minor Murder, Savoy Theatre 1967, Katherine in Henry V, Lika in The Promise, Leicester 1968, Amaryllis in Back to Methuselah, Nat. Theatre, Hermia in A Midsummer Night's Dream, Hero in Much Ado About Nothing, Regent's Park, London 1970, Anne Danby in Kean, Oxford 1970, London 1971; Romeo and Juliet, 'Tis Pity She's a Whore and The Three Arrows 1972; The Norman Conquests, London 1974, Viktosha in Once Upon a Time, Bristol 1976, Arms and The Man, Greenwich 1978, Mara in Clouds, London 1978; Constanza Mozart in Amadeus, Desdemona in Othello; On the Razzle 1981, The Second Mrs. Tanqueray, The Real Thing 1982, Jumpers 1985, Made in Bangkok 1986, Hapgood 1988, Ivanov 1989, Much Ado About Nothing 1989, Hidden Laughter 1990, Tartuffe 1991, Heartbreak House 1992, Arcadia 1992, An Absolute Turkey 1994, Indian Ink 1995, Mind Millie for Me 1996, The Seagull 1997, Waste 1997, Alarms and Excursions 1998, Fallen Angels 2000, Humble Boy 2002, Happy Days 2003, Amy's View 2006, The Vortex 2008. *TV appearances include:* four series of The Good Life; Solo; The Mistress; The Woodlanders; Edward VII; plays and serials including Viola in Twelfth Night 1979, The Camomile Lawn 1992, The Mayfly and the Frog, Boy meets Girl, The Tenant of Wildfell Hall, Crimes of Passion, The Dolly Dialogues, Now is Too late, Deadly Earnest, The Marriage Counsellor, Home and Beauty, Favourite Things, How Proust Can Change Your Life 2000, Rosemary and Thyme 2003, Dr Who 2007. *Films include:* Shakespeare Wallah 1965, Valentino 1976, Parting Shots. *Publication:* White Cargo (memoirs) 1998. *Address:* c/o Chatto and Linnit, 123A Kings Road, London, SW3 4PL, England (office). *Telephone:* (20) 7352-7722 (office). *Fax:* (20) 7352-3450.

KENDALL, David William, FCA; British business executive; b. 8 May 1935; s. of William Jack Kendall and Alma May Kendall; m. 1st Delphine Hitchcock 1960 (divorced); one s. one d.; m. 2nd Elisabeth Rollison 1973; one s. one d.; ed Enfield Grammar School, Southend High School; with Elles Reeve & Co. 1955–62, Shell-Mex & BP Ltd 1963–68; Finance Dir Irish Shell & BP Ltd 1969–70; Crude Oil Sales Man. British Petroleum Co. Ltd 1971–72, Man. Bulk Trading Div. 1973–74, mem. Org. Planning Cttee 1975; Gen. Man. BP NZ Ltd 1976–79, Man. Dir and CEO 1980–82; Chair. BP South West Pacific 1979–82; Finance and Planning Dir BP Oil Ltd 1982–85, Man. Dir and CEO 1985–88; Dir BP Chemicals Int. 1985–88, BP Oil Int. 1985–88, BP Detergents Int. 1985–88; Deputy Chair. British Coal Corpn 1989–90; Chair. Ruberoid PLC 1993–2000, Whitecroft PLC 1993–1999, Meyer Int. PLC 1994–95, Celtic Energy Ltd 1994–2003, Wagon PLC 1997–2005, G-T-P Group Ltd 2006–; Dir STC PLC 1988–90, Danka Business Systems PLC 1993–2000 (Chair. 1998–2000), Gowrings 1993–2004, South Wales Electricity PLC 1993–96; Dir (non-exec.) Bunzl PLC 1988–90 (Chair. 1990–93), Blagden Industries PLC 1993–94 (Chair. 1994–2000), British Standards Inst. 2000–05; Pres. UK Petroleum Industries Asscn 1987–88, Oil Industries Club 1988. *Leisure interests:* golf, music. *Address:* 41 Albion Street, London, W2 2AU, England. *Telephone:* (20) 7258-1955.

KENEALLY, Thomas Michael, AO, FRSL; Australian writer; b. 7 Oct. 1935, Sydney; s. of Edmund Thomas and Elsie Margaret Keneally; m. Judith Mary Martin 1965; two d.; ed St Patrick's Coll., Strathfield, NSW; Lecturer in Drama, Univ. of New England, Armidale, NSW 1968–70; Visiting Prof. Univ. of Calif., Irvine 1985, Prof. Dept of English and Comparative Literature 1991–95; Berg Prof. Dept of English, New York Univ. 1988; Pres. Nat. Book Council of Australia –1987; Chair. Australian Soc. of Authors 1987–90, Pres. 1990–; mem. Literary Arts Bd 1985–; mem. Australia-China Council; mem. American Acad. of Arts and Sciences; Founding Chair. Australian Republican Movt 1991–93; Hon. DLit (Univ. of Queensland), (Nat. Univ. of Ireland) 1994; Hon. DLitt (Fairleigh Dickenson Univ., USA) 1996, (Rollins Coll., USA) 1996; Royal Soc. of Literature Prize, Los Angeles Times Fiction Prize 1983. *Publications:* The Place at Whitton 1964, The Fear 1965, Bring Larks and Heroes 1967, Three Cheers for the Paraclete 1968, The Survivor 1969, A Dutiful Daughter 1970, The Chant of Jimmie Blacksmith 1972, Blood Red, Sister Rose 1974, Gossip from the Forest 1975, Moses and the Lawgiver 1975, Season in Purgatory 1976, A Victim of the Aurora 1977, Ned Kelly and the City of Bees 1978, Passenger 1978, Confederates 1979, Schindler's Ark (Booker Prize 1982) 1982, Outback 1983, The Cut-Rate Kingdom 1984, A Family Madness 1985, Australia: Beyond the Dreamtime (contrib.) 1987, The Playmaker 1987, Towards Asmara 1989, Flying Hero Class 1991, Now and in Time to Be: Ireland and the Irish 1992, Woman of the Inner Sea 1992, The Place Where Souls Are Born: A Journey into the American Southwest 1992, Jacko: The Great Intruder 1993, The Utility Player – The Story of Des Hassler (non-fiction) 1993, Our Republic (non-fiction) 1993, A River Town 1995, Homebush Boy: A Memoir 1995, The Great Shame: And the Triumph of the Irish in the English-Speaking World 1998, Bettany's Book 2000, An American Scoundrel: The Life of the Notorious Civil War General Dan Sickles (non-fiction) 2002, An Angel in Australia 2002, Abraham Lincoln (biog.) 2003, The Office of Innocence 2003, The Tyrant's Novel 2004, The Commonwealth of Thieves: The Story of the Founding of Australia (non-fiction) 2006, The Widow and Her Hero 2007, Searching for Schindler: A Memoir 2008. *Leisure interest:* cross-country skiing, swimming, hiking. *Address:* Curtis Brown (Australia) Pty Ltd, PO Box 19, Paddington, NSW 2021, Australia (office).

KENILOREA, Rt Hon. Sir Peter, KBE, PC, DipEd; Solomon Islands politician; *Speaker, National Parliament;* b. 23 May 1943, Takataka, Malaita; m. Margaret Kwanairara 1971; eight c.; ed Teachers' Coll. in New Zealand; Schoolmaster, King George VI Secondary School 1968–70; Asst Sec. Finance 1971; Admin. Officer, Dist admin. 1971–73; Lands Officer 1973–74; Deputy Sec. to Cabinet and to Chief Minister 1974–75; District Commr, Eastern Solomons 1975–76; mem. Legis. Ass. 1976–78; MP for East Are-Are 1976–; f. United Democratic Party 1980, Pres. 1989–; Chief Minister of the Solomon Islands 1976–78; Prime Minister of the Solomon Islands 1978–81, 1984–86; Deputy Prime Minister 1986–89, Minister of Foreign Affairs 1988–89, of Foreign Affairs and Trade Relations 1990; Speaker of Nat. Parl. 2001–; Ombudsman 1996–; Dir S Pacific Forum Fisheries Agency 1991–94; Co-Chair. Peace Negotiation and Chair. Peace Monitoring Council 2000–; Order of Brilliant Star with Special Grand Cordon (China Taiwan) 1985; Queen's Silver Jubilee Medal 1977, Solomon Islands Ind. Medal 1978. *Publications:* numerous articles for political and scientific publs. *Leisure interests:* reading, sports. *Address:* Rara Village, East Are'Are, Malaita Province (home); National Parliament, POB G19, Honiara (office); PO Box 1674, Honiara, Solomon Islands. *Telephone:* 21751 (office). *Fax:* 23866 (office). *Website:* www .parliament.gov.sb.

KENNARD, Olga, OBE, ScD, FRS; British research scientist; *Trustee, British Museum;* b. 23 March 1924, Budapest, Hungary; d. of Joir Weisz and Catherina Weisz; m. 1st David Kennard 1948 (divorced 1961); two d.; m. 2nd Sir Arnold Burgen (q.v.) 1993; ed schools in Hungary, Prince Henry VIII Grammar School, Evesham and Newnham Coll. Cambridge; Research Asst, Cavendish Lab., Cambridge 1944–48; MRC Scientific Staff, London 1948–61; MRC External Scientific Staff, Univ. of Cambridge 1961–89; Dir Cambridge Crystallographic Data Centre 1965–97; MRC Special Appt. 1969–89; Visiting Prof., Univ. of London 1988–90; mem. Academia Europaea, Council, Royal Soc. 1995–97; Trustee of British Museum 2004; Hon. LLD Univ. of Cambridge 2003; Royal Soc. of Chem. Prize for Structural Chem. 1980. *Publications:* about 200 papers in scientific journals and books on X-ray crystallography, molecular biology, information technology; 20 scientific reference books. *Leisure interests:* swimming, music, modern architecture and design. *Address:* Keelson, 8A Hills Avenue, Cambridge, CB1 7XA, England. *Telephone:* (1223) 415381.

KENNARD, William E.; American business executive, lawyer and fmr government official; *Managing Director, Global Telecommunications and Media Investment Strategy, The Carlyle Group LLC;* b. 19 Jan. 1957, Los Angeles; s. of Robert A. Kennard and Helen Z. King; m. Deborah D. Kennedy 1984; ed Stanford Univ., Yale Law School.; fmrly with Nat. Asscn of Broadcasters; fmr Pnr and mem. Bd Dirs Verner, Liipfert, Bernhard, McPherson and Hand law firm; Gen. Counsel to Fed. Communications Comm. 1993–97, Chair. 1997–2001; Man. Dir Global Telecommunications and Media Investment Strategy The Carlyle Group LLC 2001–; mem. Bd of Dirs Insight Communications, Hawaiian Telcom, NY Times Co.; fmr mem. Bd of Dirs Nextel Communications, Dex Media East LLC, eAccess Ltd; Dr hc (Howard Univ.), (Gallaudet Univ.), (Long Island Univ.). *Address:* The Carlyle Group LLC, 1001 Pennsylvania Ave NW, Washington, DC 20004, USA (office). *Telephone:* (202) 347-2626 (office). *E-mail:* inquiries@thecarlylegroup.com (office). *Website:* www.thecarlylegroup.com (office).

KENNEDY, Alison Louise (A. L.), BA; British writer; b. 22 Oct. 1965, Dundee, Scotland; ed Univ. of Warwick; community arts worker for Clydebank & Dist 1988–89; Writer-in-Residence, Hamilton & East Kilbride Social Work Dept 1989–91, for Project Ability, Arts & Special Needs 1989–95, Copenhagen Univ. 1995; book reviewer for The Scotsman, Glasgow Herald, BBC, STV, The Telegraph 1990–; Ed. New Writing Scotland 1993–95; part-time Lecturer, St Andrews Univ. 2002–07; Assoc. Prof., Creative Writing Programme, Univ. of Warwick 2007–; columnist, The Guardian; stand-up comedian 2005–; Hon. DLit (Glasgow); DSc hc; Somerset Maugham Award, Encore Award, SAC Book Award, Best of Young British Novelists (twice), Lannan Literary Award for Fiction 2007. *Films:* Stella Does Tricks (writer) 1997. *Television:* Ghostdancing (BBC TV drama/documentary, writer and presenter) 1995, Dice (series I and II, with John Burnside, Canadian TV). *Radio:* Born a Fox (BBC Radio 4 drama) 2002, Like an Angel (BBC Radio 4 drama) 2004. *Plays:* The Audition (Fringe First Award) 1993, Delicate (performance piece for Motionhouse dance co.) 1995, True (performance project for Fierce Productions and Tramway Theatre) 1998. *Publications:* Night Geometry and the Garscadden Trains 1991, Looking for the Possible Dance 1993, Now That You're Back 1994, So I Am Glad 1995, Tea and Biscuits 1996, Original Bliss 1997, The Life and Death of Colonel Blimp 1997, Everything You Need 1999, On Bullfighting 1999, Indelible Acts 2002, Paradise 2004, Day (Saltire Scottish Book of the Year Award 2007, Costa Book of the Year Award 2007) 2007. *Address:* Antony Harwood Ltd, 103 Walton Street, Oxford, OX2 6EB, England (office). *Telephone:* (1865) 559615 (office). *Fax:* (1865) 554173 (office). *Website:* www.a-l-kennedy.co.uk.

KENNEDY, Anthony M., BA, LLB; American judge; *Associate Justice, Supreme Court;* b. 23 July 1936, Sacramento, Calif.; s. of Anthony J. Kennedy and Gladys Kennedy; m. Mary Davis; two s. one d.; ed Stanford Univ., LSE and Harvard Univ. Law School; mem. Calif. Bar 1962, US Tax Court Bar 1971; Assoc., Thelen, Marrin, Johnson & Bridges (law firm), San Francisco 1961–63; sole practice, Sacramento 1963–67; Pnr, Evans, Jackson & Kennedy (law firm) 1967–75; Prof. of Constitutional Law, McGeorge School of Law, Univ. of Pacific 1965; Judge US Court of Appeals, 9th Circuit, Sacramento 1976–88; Judge, Supreme Court of USA 1988–. *Address:* United States Supreme Court, One First Street, NE, Washington, DC 20543, USA (office). *Telephone:* (202) 479-3211 (office). *Website:* www.supremecourtus.gov (office).

KENNEDY, Rt Hon. Charles Peter, MA, PC; British politician, journalist and broadcaster; b. 25 Nov. 1959, Inverness, Scotland; s. of Ian Kennedy and Mary McVarish MacEachen; m. Sarah Gurling 2002; one s.; ed Lochaber High School, Fort William and Univ. of Glasgow; journalist, BBC Highland, Inverness 1982; Fulbright Scholar and Assoc. Instr, Dept of Speech Communication, Indiana Univ. Bloomington Campus 1982–83; MP for Ross, Cromarty and Skye 1983–97, for Ross, Skye and Inverness W 1997–; mem. Social Democratic Party 1983–88, Liberal Democrats 1988– (Spokesperson on Trade and Industry 1988–89, on Health 1989–92, on Europe and East–West relations 1992–97, on Agric. and Rural Affairs 1997–99); Pres. Liberal Democrats 1990–94, Leader 1999–2006 (resgnd); Vice-Pres. Liberal Int.; Visiting Parl. Fellow, St. Antony's College, Oxford; Dr hc (Glasgow) 2002. *Publication:* The Future of Politics 2000. *Address:* 5 MacGregor's Court, Dingwall IV15 9HS, Scotland; House of Commons, London, SW1A 0AA, England. *Telephone:* (20) 7219-6226 (office). *Fax:* (20) 7219-4881 (office). *E-mail:* kennedy@parliament.uk (office); charles@highlandlibdems.org.uk; info@charleskennedy.org.uk. *Website:* www.charleskennedy.org.uk (office).

KENNEDY, Donald, MA, PhD; American biologist, academic, editor and fmr university administrator; *President Emeritus, Stanford University;* b. 18 Aug. 1931, New York; s. of William D. Kennedy and Barbara (Bean) Kennedy; m. 1st Barbara J. Dewey 1953; two d.; m. 2nd Robin Beth Wiseman 1987; two step-s.; ed Harvard Univ.; Asst Prof., Syracuse Univ. 1956–59, Assoc. Prof. 1959–60; Asst Prof., Stanford Univ. 1960–62, Assoc. Prof. 1962–65, Prof. 1965–77, Chair. Dept of Biological Sciences 1965–72, Benjamin Crocker Prof. of Human Biology 1974–77, Vice-Pres. and Provost 1979–80, Pres. 1980–92, Pres. Emer. and Bing Prof. of Environmental Science Emer. 1992–; Sr Consultant, Office of Science and Tech. Policy, Exec. Office of the Pres. 1976–77; Commr of Food and Drug Admin. 1977–79; Ed.-in-Chief Science Magazine 2000–; Fellow, American Acad. of Arts and Sciences; mem. NAS; Hon. DSc (Columbia Univ., Williams Coll., Michigan, Rochester, Ariz., Whitman Coll., Coll. of William and Mary); Dinkelspiel Award 1976. *Publications:* The Biology of Organisms (with W. M. Telfer) 1965, Academic Duty 1997; over 60 articles in scientific journals. *Leisure interests:* skiing, fly fishing, natural history. *Address:* Stanford University, Encina Hall E401, Stanford, CA 94305 (office); 532 Channing Avenue, #302, Palo Alto, CA 94301, USA (home). *E-mail:* kennedyd@stanford.edu (office). *Website:* fsi.stanford .edu/people/donaldkennedy (home).

KENNEDY, Edward Moore, AB, LLB; American politician and lawyer; *Senator from Massachusetts;* b. 22 Feb. 1932, Boston, Mass; s. of the late Joseph Kennedy and Rose Elizabeth Kennedy (née Fitzgerald); brother of the late Pres. John F. Kennedy and Senator Robert Kennedy; m. 1st Virginia Joan Bennett 1958 (divorced 1982); two s. one d.; m. 2nd Victoria Anne Reggie 1992; ed Milton Acad., Harvard Coll. and Univ. of Virginia Law School; served in US Army, Infantry, Private 1st Class 1951–53; Man. Western States, John F. Kennedy Presidential Campaign 1960; fmr Asst Dist Attorney, Mass.; Senator from Mass. 1962–; Asst Majority Leader, US Senate 1969–71; Chair. Senate Judiciary Comm. 1979–81; current Chair. Senate Cttee on Health, Educ., Labor and Pensions; Trustee, John F. Kennedy Center for the Performing Arts; Fellow, American Acad. of Arts and Sciences; Democrat; Hon. KBE 2009; numerous hon. degrees; named as one of 10 Outstanding Young Men, US Jaycees 1967. *Publications:* Decisions for a Decade 1968, In Critical Condition: The Crisis in Americ's Health Care 1972, Our Day and Generation 1979, Freeze: How You Can Help Prevent Nuclear War (with Senator Mark Hatfield q.v.) 1979, America Back on Track 2006, My Senator and Me 2006. *Address:* 317 Russell Senate Building, Washington, DC 20510, USA (office). *Telephone:* (202) 224-4543 (office). *Fax:* (202) 224-2417 (office). *E-mail:* senator@kennedy.senate.gov (office). *Website:* kennedy.senate.gov (office).

KENNEDY, Eugene Patrick, BSc, PhD; American scientist and academic; *Hamilton Kuhn Professor of Biological Chemistry and Molecular Pharmacology, Emeritus, Harvard University Medical School;* b. 4 Sept. 1919, Chicago; s. of Michael Kennedy and Catherine Frawley Kennedy; m. Adelaide Majewski 1943; three d.; ed De Paul Univ. and Univ. of Chicago; Asst Prof., Ben May Lab., Univ. of Chicago 1952–55, Assoc. Prof. 1955–56, Prof. of Biological Chem. 1956–60; Prof. and Head, Dept of Biological Chem., Harvard Medical School 1960–65, Hamilton Kuhn Prof. of Biological Chem. and Molecular Pharmacology, Harvard Medical School 1960, now Prof. Emer.; Assoc. Ed. Journal of Biological Chemistry 1969; Pres. American Soc. of Biological Chemists 1970–71; mem. NAS, American Acad. of Arts and Sciences 1961–, American Philosophical Soc.; Hon. DSc (Chicago) 1977; George Ledlie Prize (Harvard) 1976, Heinrich Wieland Prize 1986; Glycerine Research Award 1956; Paul-Lewis Award, American Chem. Soc. 1959, Lipid Chem. Award of the American Oil Chemists Soc. 1970, Josiah Macy, Jr Foundation Faculty Scholar Award 1974, Gairdner Foundation Award 1976, Sr US Scientist Award, Alexander von Humboldt Foundation 1983, Passano Award 1986. *Address:* Department of Biological Chemistry, Harvard Medical School, 25 Shattuck Street, Boston, MA 02115; 221 Mount Auburn Street, Cambridge, MA 02138, USA (office). *Telephone:* (617) 432-1861 (office). *E-mail:* eugene_kennedy@hms.harvard.edu (office). *Website:* bcmp.med.harvard.edu (office).

KENNEDY, George Danner, BA; American business executive; *Founding Managing Partner, Berkshires Capital Investors;* b. 30 May 1926, Pittsburgh, Pa; s. of Thomas Reed Kennedy and Lois Kennedy (née Smith); m. Valerie Putis 1972; three s. one d.; ed Williams Coll.; with Scott Paper Co. 1947–52, Champion Paper Co. 1952–65; Pres. Brown Co. 1965–71; Exec. Vice-Pres. IMCERA (fmrly Int. Minerals & Chemical Corpn) 1971–78, Dir 1975, Pres. 1978–86, CEO 1983–93, Chair. of IMCERA (now Mallinckrodt Group) 1986; Founder and Man. Pnr, Berkshires Capital Investors 1996–; mem. Bd of Dirs Kemper National and and Kemper Foundation 1982–, Brunswick Corpn 1979–, Ill. Tool Works, Inc, Scotsman Industries Inc., American National Can Co., Stone Container Corpn; Dir SCM Corpn 1978–82; Bd Chair. Children's Memorial Hosp., Chicago; Vice-Pres. and Dir NE Ill. Boy Scout Council; Trustee, Nat. Comm. Against Drunk Driving, Chicago Symphony. *Address:* Berkshires Capital Investors, 430 Main Street, Suite 4, Williamstown, MA 01267 (office); P.O. Box 559, Winnetka, IL 60093, USA. *Telephone:* (413) 458-9683 (office). *Fax:* (413) 458-5603 (office). *E-mail:* info@berkshirescap.com. *Website:* www.berkshirescap.com (office).

KENNEDY, Geraldine; Irish journalist; *Editor, The Irish Times;* b. 7 Sept. 1951, Tramore, Co. Waterford; d. of James Kennedy and Nora McGrath; m. David J. Hegarty; two d.; ed Convent S.H.M., Ferrybank, Waterford; Political Corresp. The Sunday Tribune 1980–82, The Sunday Press 1982–87; mem. Dáil Éireann (Irish Parl.) 1987–89; Public Affairs Corresp. The Irish Times 1990–93, Political Corresp. 1993–99, Political Ed. 1999–2002, Duty Ed. 2000–02, Ed. 2002–, Dir Irish Times Ltd 2002–; Dr hc (Queen's Univ., Belfast); Journalist of the Year 1994. *Leisure interests:* travel, reading, food. *Address:* The Irish Times, PO Box 74, 24–28 Tara Street, Dublin 2, Ireland (office). *Telephone:* (1) 6758000 (office). *Fax:* (1) 6758035 (office). *E-mail:* editor@irish -times.ie (office). *Website:* www.ireland.com (office).

KENNEDY, James C., BBA; American publishing and media executive; *Chairman and CEO, Cox Enterprises Inc.;* b. 1947, Honolulu; m.; ed Univ. of

Denver; with Atlanta Newspapers 1976–79; Pres. Grand Junction Newspapers 1979–80, Publr Grand Junction Daily Sentinel 1980–85; Vice-Pres. Newspaper Div. Cox Enterprises Inc. 1985–86, Exec. Vice-Pres. then Pres. 1986–87, COO then Chair. 1987–; Chair. and CEO Cox Enterprises Inc. 1988–, also Chair. Cox Communications and Cox Radio. *Cycling achievements:* past Masters Nat., Pan American and World Champion in 3000 meter pursuit; served as capt. of four-man team that won Race Across AMerica (RAAM) 1992, setting world record. *Address:* Cox Enterprises Inc., 6205 Peachtree Dunwoody Road, Atlanta, GA 30328 (office); 1601 W Peachtree Street NE, Atlanta, GA 30309, USA (home). *Telephone:* (678) 645-0000 (office). *Fax:* (678) 645-1079 (office). *Website:* www.coxenterprises.com (office).

KENNEDY, Sir Ludovic Henry Coverley, Kt, MA, FRSL; Scottish broadcaster and writer; b. 3 Nov. 1919, Edinburgh; s. of late Capt. E. C. Kennedy, RN and of Rosalind Kennedy; m. Moira Shearer King 1950 (died 2006; one s. three d.; ed Eton Coll., Christ Church, Oxford; served in RN 1939–46 (attained rank of Lt); Pvt. Sec. and ADC to Gov. of Newfoundland 1943–44; Librarian, Ashridge (Adult Educ.) Coll. 1949; Ed., feature, First Reading (BBC Third Programme) 1953–54; Lecturer for British Council, Sweden, Finland, Denmark 1955, Belgium, Luxembourg 1956; contested Rochdale by-election 1958, gen. election 1959 as Liberal candidate; Pres. Nat. League of Young Liberals 1959–61, mem. Liberal Party Council 1965–67; TV and radio: introduced Profile, ATV 1955–56; newscaster, ITV 1956–58; introducer On Stage, Associated Rediffusion 1957, This Week, Associated Rediffusion 1958–59; Chair. BBC features: Your Verdict 1962, Your Witness 1967–70; commentator BBC's Panorama 1960–63, Television Reports Int. (also producer) 1963–64; introducer BBC's Time Out 1964–65, World at One 1965–66; presenter Liberal Party's Gen. Election TV Broadcasts 1966, The Middle Years, ABC 1967, The Nature of Prejudice, ATV 1968, Face The Press, Tyne-Tees 1968–69, 1970–72, Against the Tide, Yorkshire TV 1969, Living and Growing, Grampian TV 1969–70, 24 Hours, BBC 1969–72, Ad Lib, BBC 1970–72, Midweek, BBC 1973–75, Newsday, BBC 1975–76, Tonight, BBC 1976–80, A Life with Crime BBC 1979, presenter Lord Mountbatten Remembers 1980, Change of Direction 1980, Did You See? BBC 1980–88, Great Railway Journeys of the World BBC 1980, Chair. Indelible Evidence BBC 1987, 1990, A Gift of the Gab BBC 1989, Portrait BBC 1989; mem. Council Navy Records Soc. 1957–70; Pres. Sir Walter Scott Club, Edin. 1968–69; Chair. Royal Lyceum Theatre Co. of Edin. 1977–84; Chair. Judges, NCR Book Award 1990–91; Pres. Voluntary Euthanasia Soc. 1995–; FRSA 1974–76; Voltaire Memorial Lecturer 1985; Hon. DL (Strathclyde) 1985, (Southampton) 1993; Dr hc (Edin.) 1990, (Stirling) 1991; Richard Dimbleby Award (BAFTA) 1989, Bar Council Special Award 1992; Cross First Class, Order of Merit (Fed. Repub. of Germany). *Films include:* The Sleeping Ballerina, The Singers and the Songs, Scapa Flow, Battleship Bismarck, Life and Death of the Scharnhorst, U-Boat War, Target Tirpitz, The Rise of the Red Navy, Lord Haw-Haw, Who Killed the Lindbergh Baby?, Elizabeth: The First Thirty Years, A Life of Richard Dimbleby, Happy Birthday, dear Ma'am, Murder in Belgravia: The Lucan Affair, Princess to Queen. *Publications:* Sub-Lieutenant 1942, Nelson's Band of Brothers 1951, One Man's Meat 1953, Murder Story 1956, Ten Rillington Place 1961, The Trial of Stephen Ward 1964, Very Lovely People 1969, Pursuit: the Chase and Sinking of the Bismarck 1974, A Presumption of Innocence: the Amazing Case of Patrick Meehan 1975, The Portland Spy Case 1978, Wicked Beyond Belief: The Luton Post Office Murder Case 1980, Menace: The Life and Death of the Tirpitz 1979, The Airman and the Carpenter: The Lindbergh Case and the Framing of Richard Hauptmann 1985, On My Way to the Club (autobiog.) 1989, Euthanasia: The Good Death 1990, Truth to Tell (collected writings) 1991, In Bed with an Elephant: A Journey through Scotland's Past and Present 1995, All in the Mind: A Farewell to God 1999; Gen. Ed. The British at War 1973–77; Ed. A Book of Railway Journeys 1980, A Book of Sea Journeys 1981, A Book of Air Journeys 1982, 36 Murders and Two Immoral Earnings 2002. *Address:* c/o Rogers, Coleridge and White, 20 Powis Mews, London, W11 1JN, England (office).

KENNEDY, (George) Michael (Sinclair), CBE, MA, CRNCM, FIJ; British journalist and music critic; b. 19 Feb. 1926, Chorlton-cum-Hardy, Manchester; s. of Hew G. Kennedy and Marian F. Kennedy; m. 1st Eslyn Durdle 1947 (died 1999); m. 2nd Joyce Bourne, 10 Oct. 1999; ed Berkhamsted School; staff music critic, The Daily Telegraph 1941–50, Northern Music Critic 1950–60, Northern Ed. 1960–86, Jt Chief Music Critic 1986–89; Chief Music Critic, The Sunday Telegraph 1989–2005; Gov. Royal Northern Coll. of Music; Hon. mem. Royal Manchester Coll. of Music 1971, Hon. mem. Royal Philharmonic Soc. 2006; Hon. MA (Manchester) 1975; Hon. MusD (Manchester) 2003. *Publications:* The Hallé Tradition: A Century of Music 1960, The Works of Ralph Vaughan Williams 1964, Portrait of Elgar 1968, Elgar: Orchestral Music 1969, Portrait of Manchester 1970, History of the Royal Manchester College of Music 1971, Barbirolli: Conductor Laureate 1971, Mahler 1974, The Autobiography of Charles Hallé, with Correspondence and Diaries (ed.) 1976, Richard Strauss 1976, Britten 1980, Concise Oxford Dictionary of Music (ed.) 1980, The Hallé 1858–1983 1983, Strauss: Tone Poems 1984, Oxford Dictionary of Music (ed.) 1985, Adrian Boult 1987, Portrait of Walton 1989, Music Enriches All: The First 21 Years of the Royal Northern College of Music, Manchester 1994, Richard Strauss: Man, Musician, Enigma (French critics prize for musical biog. 2003) 1999, The Life of Elgar 2004, Buxton: an English Festival 2004; contrib. to newspapers and magazines, including Gramophone, Listener, Musical Times, Music and Letters, The Sunday Telegraph, BBC Music Magazine. *Leisure interest:* cricket. *Address:* The Bungalow, 62 Edilom Road, Manchester, M8 4HZ, England (home). *Telephone:* (161) 740-4528 (home). *E-mail:* majkennedy@bungalow62.fsnet.co.uk.

KENNEDY, Nigel Paul, ARCM; British violinist; b. 28 Dec. 1956, Brighton, England; s. of John Kennedy and Scylla Stoner; m. Agnieska Kennedy; one s.; ed Yehudi Menuhin School, Juilliard School of Performing Arts, New York; debut playing Mendelssohn's Violin Concerto at the Royal Festival Hall with the London Philharmonic Orchestra under Riccardo Muti 1977; subsequently chosen by the BBC as the subject of a five-year documentary on the devt of a soloist; other important debuts include with the Berlin Philharmonic 1980, New York 1987; has made appearances at all the leading UK festivals and in Europe at Stresa, Lucerne, Gstaad, Berlin and Lockenhaus; tours to Australia, Austria, Canada, Denmark, Germany, Hong Kong, India, Ireland, Italy, Japan, Republic of Korea, New Zealand, Norway, Poland, Spain, Switzerland, Turkey and the USA; has given concerts in the field of jazz with Stephane Grappelli, including at the Edinburgh Festival and Carnegie Hall; runs his own jazz group; five-year sabbatical 1992–97; Artistic Dir, Polish Chamber Orchestra 2002–; Sr Vice-Pres. Aston Villa Football Club 1990–; Hon. DLitt (Bath) 1991; Golden Rose of Montreux 1990, Variety Club Showbusiness Personality of the Year 1991, BRIT Award for Outstanding Contribution to British Music 2000, Male Artist of the Year 2001, Echo Klassik Award for Instrumentalist of the Year 2008. *Television:* Coming Along Nicely (BBC documentary on his early career) 1973–78. *Recordings include:* Strad Jazz 1984, Elgar Sonata with Peter Pettinger 1985, Elgar's Violin Concerto with the London Philharmonic and Vernon Handley (Gramophone magazine Record of the Year, BPI Award for Best Classical Album of the Year) 1985, Vivaldi's Four Seasons, Bartók Solo Sonata and Mainly Black (arrangement of Ellington's Black Brown and Beige Suite), Sibelius Violin Concerto with the City of Birmingham Symphony Orchestra conducted by Sir Simon Rattle, Walton's Violin Concerto with the Royal Philharmonic Orchestra and André Previn, Bruch and Mendelssohn concertos with the English Chamber Orchestra conducted by Jeffrey Tate, Kafka (Kennedy's compositions), Tchaikovsky's Chausson Poème with the London Philharmonic Orchestra 1988, Brahms Violin Concerto with the London Philharmonic under Klaus Tennstedt 1991, Beethoven Violin Concerto with the NDR-Sinfonieorchester and Klaus Tennstedt 1992, chamber works by Debussy and Ravel, Berg's Violin Concerto, Vaughan Williams' The Lark Ascending with Sir Simon Rattle and the CBSO, works by Fritz Kreisler 1998, The Kennedy Experience, chamber works by Bach, Ravel and Kodaly (with Lynn Harrell) 1999, Classic Kennedy with the English Chamber Orchestra 1999, Bach's Concerto for Two Violins in D Minor, Concerto for Oboe and Violin in D Minor and the A Minor and E Major violin concertos the Berlin Philharmonic 2000, Nigel Kennedy Plays Bach 2006, Inner Thoughts 2006, Blue Note Sessions 2006, Polish Spirit 2007, Beethoven and Mozart Violin Concertos 2008, A Very Nice Album 2008. *Publication:* Always Playing 1991. *Leisure interests:* cricket, golf, football. *Address:* c/o John Stanley, Kennedy, 90–96 Brewery Road, London, N7 9NT, England. *Website:* www.kennedyjazz.com.

KENNEDY, Patrick J.; Irish business executive; *Chairman of the Executive Board, SHV Holdings NV;* b. 22 Sept. 1953, Galway; joined Calor Gas Ltd (subsidiary of SHV Energy NV) 1982, becoming man. of various SHV cos in Eastern Europe, UK and Brazil, including Probugas, Slovakia 1993–94, Pamgas 1994–96, Dir Supergasbras Distribuidora de Gás, Brazil 1996–98, Dir Calor Gas Ltd 1998–2000, Chair. SHV Gas 2000–01, mem. Exec. Bd SHV Holdings 2001–, Chair. 2006–. *Address:* SHV Holdings NV, Rijnkade 1, 3511 LC Utrecht, Netherlands (office). *Telephone:* (30) 233-88-33 (office). *Fax:* (30) 233-83-04 (office). *E-mail:* info@shv.nl (office). *Website:* www.shv.nl (office).

KENNEDY, Rt Hon. Sir Paul (Joseph Morrow), PC, MA, LLB; British judge (retd); b. 12 June 1935, Sheffield; m. Virginia Devlin 1965; two s. two d.; ed Ampleforth Coll., York, Gonville & Caius Coll., Cambridge; called to Bar Gray's Inn 1960, Bencher 1982, Treas. 2002; Recorder of Crown Court 1972–83; QC 1973; Judge, High Court of Justice, Queen's Bench Div. (QBD) 1983–92, Vice-Pres. QBD 1997–2002; Presiding Judge, NE Circuit 1985–89; Lord Justice of Appeal 1992–2005 (retd); Chair. Criminal Cttee Judicial Studies Bd 1993–96; mem. Sentencing Guidelines Council –2005, Court of Appeal of Gibraltar 2006–, Interception of Communications Comm. 2006–; Hon. Fellow, Gonville & Caius Coll. Cambridge 1998; Hon. LLD (Sheffield) 2000. *Leisure interests:* family, walking, occasional golf. *Address:* c/o Court of Appeal Civil Division, The Royal Courts of Justice, Strand, London, WC2A 2LL, England.

KENNEDY, Paul Michael, CBE, MA, DPhil, FRHistS, FBA; British historian and academic; *J. Richardson Dilworth Professor of History and Director, International Security Studies, Yale University;* b. 17 June 1945, Wallsend; s. of John Patrick Kennedy and Margaret (née Hennessy) Kennedy; m. 1st Catherine Urwin 1967 (died 1998); three s.; m. 2nd Cynthia Farrar 2001; ed St Cuthbert's Grammar School, Newcastle-upon-Tyne, Univ. of Newcastle and Oxford Univ.; Research Asst to Sir Basil Liddell Hart 1966–70; Lecturer, Reader and Prof., Univ. of E Anglia 1970–83; J. Richardson Dilworth Prof. of History, Yale Univ. 1983–, Dir Int. Security Studies 1988–; Visiting Fellow, Inst. for Advanced Study, Princeton 1978–79; Fellow, Alexander von Humboldt Foundation, American Philosophical Soc., American Acad. of Arts and Sciences; Hon. DHL (New Haven, Alfred, Long Island, Connecticut); Hon. DLitt (Newcastle, East Anglia); Hon. LLD (Ohio); Hon. MA (Yale, Union, Quinnipiac); Dr hc (Leuven). *Publications:* The Samoan Tangle 1974, The Rise and Fall of British Naval Mastery 1976, The Rise of the Anglo-German Antagonism 1980, The Realities Behind Diplomacy 1981, Strategy and Diplomacy 1983, The Rise and Fall of the Great Powers 1988, Grand Strategy in War and Peace 1991, Preparing for the Twenty-First Century 1993, Pivotal States: A New Framework for US Policy in the Developing World (ed.) 1998, The Parliament of Man: The United Nations and the Quest for World Government 2006. *Leisure interests:* soccer, hill-walking, old churches. *Address:* Department of History, Yale Univ., PO Box 208353, New Haven, CT 06520-8353, USA (office). *Telephone:* (203) 432-6242 (office). *Fax:* (203) 432-6250 (office). *E-mail:* paul.kennedy@yale.edu (office). *Website:* www.yale.edu/iss (office).

KENNEDY, William Joseph, BA; American author and academic; *Professor of Creative Writing and Director, New York State Writers' Institute, University at Albany, State University of New York;* b. 16 Jan. 1928, Albany, New York; s. of William J. Kennedy and Mary E. McDonald; m. Ana Segarra 1957; one s. two d.; ed Siena Coll., New York; Asst Sports Ed. and columnist, Glens Falls Post Star, New York 1949–50; reporter, Albany Times-Union, New York 1952–56, special writer 1963–70; Asst Man. Ed. and columnist, P.R. World Journal, San Juan 1956; reporter, Miami Herald 1957; corresp., Time-Life Publs, Puerto Rico 1957–59; reporter, Knight Newspapers 1957–59; Founding Man. Ed. San Juan Star 1959–61; Lecturer, State Univ. of New York, Albany 1974–82, Prof. of English 1983–; Visiting Prof., Cornell Univ. 1982–83; Exec. Dir and Founder, NY State Writers' Inst. 1983–; Nat. Endowment for Arts Fellow 1981, MacArthur Foundation Fellow 1983; several hon. degrees; Gov. of New York Arts Award 1984, Creative Arts Award, Brandeis Univ. 1986. *Publications include:* The Ink Truck 1969, Legs 1975, Billy Phelan's Greatest Game 1978, Ironweed (Pulitzer Prize and Nat. Book Critics Circle Award 1984) 1983, O Albany! (non-fiction) 1983, Charlie Malarkey and the Belly Button Machine (children's book) 1986, Quinn's Book 1988, Very Old Bones 1992, Riding the Yellow Trolley Car 1993, Charlie Malarkey and the Singing Moose (children's book) 1994, The Flaming Corsage 1996, Grand View (play) 1996, Roscoe 2002; film scripts, The Cotton Club 1984, Ironweed 1987; also short stories, articles in professional journals. *Address:* Department of English, University at Albany, State University of New York, Humanities 333, 1400 Washington Avenue, Albany, NY 12222; New York State Writers Institute, New Library, LE 320, University at Albany, State University of New York, Albany, NY 12222, USA (office). *Telephone:* (518) 442-4055 (office). *Fax:* (518) 442-4599 (office). *E-mail:* writers@uamail.albany.edu (office). *Website:* www.albany.edu/writers-inst (office); www.albany.edu/english (office).

KENNEDY OF THE SHAWS, Baroness (Life Peer) cr. 1997, of Cathcart in the City of Glasgow; **Helena Ann Kennedy,** QC, FRSA; British lawyer; b. 12 May 1950, Glasgow; d. of Joshua Kennedy and Mary Jones; pnr (Roger) Iain Mitchell 1978–84; one s.; m. Dr Iain L. Hutchison 1986; one s. one d.; ed Holyrood Secondary School, Glasgow and Council of Legal Educ.; called to the Bar, Gray's Inn 1972; mem. Bar Council 1990–93; mem. CIBA Comm. into Child Sexual Abuse 1981–83; mem. Bd City Limits Magazine 1982–84, New Statesman 1990–96, Counsel Magazine 1990–93; mem. Council, Howard League for Penal Reform 1989–, Chair. Comm. of Inquiry into Violence in Penal Insts for Young People (report 1995); Commr BAFTA inquiry into future of BBC 1990, Hamlyn Nat. Comm. on Educ. 1991–; Visiting lecturer, British Postgrad. Medical Fed. 1991–; Adviser, Mannheim Inst. on Criminology, LSE 1992–; Leader of inquiry into health, environmental and safety aspects of Atomic Weapons Establishment, Aldermaston (report 1994); Chancellor, Oxford Brookes Univ. 1994–2001; Chair. British Council 1998–2004, Human Genetics Comm. 2000–; author of official report (Learning Works) for Further Educ. Funding Council on widening participation in further educ. 1997; Pres. School of Oriental and African Studies, London Univ. 2002–; mem. Advisory Bd, Int. Centre for Prison Studies 1998; Chair. London Int. Festival of Theatre, Standing Cttee for Youth Justice 1992–97; Chair. Charter 88 1992–97; Pres. London Marriage Guidance Council, Birth Control Campaign, Nat. Children's Bureau, Hillcroft Coll.; Vice-Pres. Haldane Soc., Nat. Ass. of Women; mem. British Council's Law Advisory Cttee Advisory Bd for Study of Women and Gender, Warwick Univ., Int. Bar Asscn's Task Force on Terrorism; presenter of various programmes on radio and TV and creator of BBC drama series Blind Justice 1988; Patron, Liberty; mem. Acad. de Cultures Internationales; Hon. Fellow Inst. of Advanced Legal Studies, Univ. of London 1997; Hon. mem. Council, Nat. Soc. for Prevention of Cruelty to Children; 18 hon. LLDs from British and Irish Univs; Women's Network Award 1992, UK Woman of Europe Award 1995; Campaigning and Influencing Award, Nat. Fed. of Women's Insts 1996, Times Newspaper Lifetime Achievement Award in the Law (jtly) 1997; Spectator Magazine's Parl. Campaigner of the Year 2000. *Publications:* The Bar on Trial (jtly) 1978, Child Abuse within the Family (jtly) 1984, Balancing Acts (jtly) 1989, Eve was Framed 1992, Just Law: the Changing Face of Justice and Why it Matters to Us All 2004; articles on legal matters, civil liberties and women. *Leisure interests:* theatre, spending time with family and friends. *Address:* House of Lords, London, SW1A 0PW, England (office). *Telephone:* (20) 7219-5353 (office); (1708) 379482 (home). *Fax:* (200 7219-5979 (office); (1708) 379482 (home). *E-mail:* info@helenakennedy.co.uk (home). *Website:* www.parliament.uk (office); www.helenakennedy.co.uk (home).

KENNETT, B(rian) L. N., FRS, PhD, ScD; British seismologist and academic; *Director and Distinguished Professor of Seismology, Research School of Earth Sciences, Australian National University;* ed Univ. of Cambridge; Research Fellow, Emmanuel Coll., Univ. of Cambridge 1972–76, Sr Research Asst, Dept of Geodesy and Geophysics 1975–76, Asst Lecturer, Dept of Applied Math. and Theoretical Physics 1976–79, Lecturer 1979–84; Professorial Fellow and Group Leader, Seismology Group, Research School of Earth Sciences, ANU 1984–91, Prof. 1991–, Pro-Vice-Chancellor and Chair. Inst. of Advanced Studies 1994–97, 2001–03, Deputy Dir Australian Nat. Seismic Imaging Resource (ANSIR) 1997–2002, Dir, ANSIR Nat. Research Facility for Earth Sounding 2002–, Coordinator, Earth Physics, Research School of Earth Sciences 2002–06, Dir and Distinguished Prof. of Seismology, Research School of Earth Sciences 2006–; Lindemann Trust Fellow, Visiting Asst Research Geophysicist, Univ. of California, San Diego 1974–75; fmr Pres., Int. Asscn of Seismology and Physics of the Earth's Interior; Fellow, American Geophysical Union 1988–, Australian Acad. of Sciences 1994–; Assoc., Royal Astronomical Soc. 1996–; numerous awards including Commonwealth of Australia Centenary Medal, Australian Acad. of Sciences Jaeger Medal for Australian Earth Sciences 2005, Geological Soc. of London Murchison Medal 2006, European Geosciences Union Gutenberg Medal 2007, Royal Astronomical Soc. Gold

Medal for Geophysics 2008. *Publications:* Seismic Wave Propagation in Stratified Media 1983, The Seismic Wavefield: Introduction and Theoretical Development 2001, The Seismic Wavefield: Interpretation of Seismograms on Regional and Global Scales 2002, Geophysical Continua: Deformation in the Earth's Interior (co-author). *Address:* Research School of Earth Sciences, Australian National University, Canberra, ACT 0200, Australia (office). *Telephone:* (2) 6125-4621 (office). *Fax:* (2) 6257-2737 (office). *E-mail:* brian@rses.anu.edu.au (office). *Website:* rses.anu.edu.au/~brian (office).

KENNEY, Edward John, MA, FBA; British academic; *Professor Emeritus of Latin, University of Cambridge;* b. 29 Feb. 1924, London; s. of George Kenney and Emmie Carlina Elfrida Schwenke; m. Gwyneth Anne Harris; ed Christ's Hosp. and Trinity Coll. Cambridge; served in Royal Signals, UK and India 1943–46; Asst Lecturer, Univ. of Leeds 1951–52; Research Fellow, Trinity Coll., Cambridge 1952–53, Fellow of Peterhouse 1953–91, Asst Lecturer in Classics, Univ. of Cambridge 1955–60, Lecturer 1960–70, Reader in Latin Literature and Textual Criticism 1970–74, Kennedy Prof. of Latin 1974–82, Prof. Emer. 1982–; Jt Ed. Classical Quarterly 1959–65; Jt Ed. Cambridge Greek and Latin Classics 1970–; Pres. Jt Asscn of Classical Teachers 1977–79, Classical Asscn 1982–83, Horatian Soc. 2003–07; Treas. and Chair. Council of Almoners, Christ's Hosp. 1984–86; Foreign mem. Royal Netherlands Acad. of Arts and Sciences. *Publications:* P. Ovidi Nasonis Amores, etc. 1961 (second edn 1995), Lucretius, De Rerum Natura III 1971, The Classical Text 1974 (Italian trans. 1995), The Cambridge History of Classical Literature, Vol. II, Latin Literature (ed. and contrib.) 1982, The Ploughman's Lunch (Moretum) 1984, Ovid, Metamorphoses–Introduction and Notes 1986, Ovid, The Love Poems – Introduction and Notes 1990, Apuleius, Cupid & Psyche 1990, Ovid, Sorrows of an Exile (Tristia) – Introduction and Notes 1992, Ovid, Heroides xvi–xxi 1996, Apuleius, The Golden Ass –Trans. with Introduction and Notes 1998; numerous articles and reviews. *Leisure interests:* cats, books. *Address:* Peterhouse, Cambridge, CB2 1RD, England (office).

KENNEY, Jason; Canadian politician; *Minister for Citizenship, Immigration and Multiculturalism;* b. 30 May 1968, Oakville, Ont.; fmr Exec. Dir Sask. Taxpayers Asscn and Pres. Canadian Taxpayers Fed.; fmr mem. Sask. Liberal Party, mem. Reform Party of Canada 1997–2000, Canadian Alliance 2000–03, Conservative Party of Canada 2003–; mem. Parl. for Calgary Southeast 1997–; served in Shadow Cabinet 1997–2005, positions included Deputy House Leader for the Official Opposition, critic for Canada–US relations, for Nat. Revenue and for Finance; Minister for Citizenship, Immigration and Multiculturalism 2008–. *Address:* Citizenship and Immigration Canada, Jean Edmonds Towers, 21st Floor, 365 Laurier Avenue West, Ottawa, ON K1A 1L1, Canada (office). *Telephone:* (613) 954-1064 (office). *Fax:* (613) 957-2688 (office). *E-mail:* minister@cic.gc.ca (office). *Website:* www.cic.gc.ca (office).

KENNICUTT, Robert C., Jr, BS, MS, PhD; American astronomer and academic; *Plumian Professor of Astronomy, University of Cambridge;* b. 4 Sept. 1951, Baltimore; m. Norma Kennicutt 1976; one d.; ed Rensselaer Polytechnic Inst., Univ. of Washington; Adjunct Research Fellow, Calif. Inst. of Tech. 1978–80, also Carnegie Postdoctoral Fellow, Hale Observatories, Pasadena, Calif. 1978–80; Asst Prof., Dept of Astronomy, Univ. of Minnesota 1980–85, Assoc. Prof. 1985–88; Assoc. Prof. and Astronomer, Steward Observatory, Univ. of Arizona 1988–1992, Deputy Head, Dept of Astronomy 1991–98, Prof. and Astronomer, Steward Observatory 1992–2006; Beatrice M. Tinsley Centennial Prof., Univ. of Texas 1994; Plumian Prof. of Astronomy and Experimental Philosophy, Univ. of Cambridge 2005–, Professorial Fellow, Churchill Coll. 2007–; Ed.-in-Chief The Astrophysical Journal 1999–2006; Adriaan Blaauw Prof., Univ. of Groningen, The Netherlands 2001; Chair. Science Oversight Cttee (SOC), NASA Next Generation Space Telescope Study 1996–1998, SOC Co-Chair. Science with Next Generation Space Telescope Conf. 1997, SOC Chair. Aspen Workshop, Star Formation, ISM Physics, and Galaxy Evolution 1997–98, Next Generation Space Telescope Science Preliminary Non-Advocate Review Cttee 1998–99, NSF Astronomy Early Career Award Selection Cttee 2003, Space Telescope Science Inst. Dir Search Cttee 2004–05; Panellist, NRC Space Studies Board Task Group on Space Astronomy and Astrophysics 1996; mem. Int. Advisory Cttee, Chinese Journal of Astronomy and Astrophysics 2002–, Gemini Observatory Visiting Cttee 2004–; mem. NAS, American Astronomical Soc. (Vice-Pres. 1998–2001), Int. Astronomical Union, Astronomical Soc. of the Pacific, American Acad. of Arts and Sciences, Spitzer Legacy Science Working Group 2001–, NSF Nat. Virtual Observatory Advisory Cttee 2002–; Fellow, American Acad. of Arts and Sciences 2001–; numerous lectureships including Dept of Astrophysical Sciences, Princeton Univ. 1990, Canary Islands Winter School in Astronomy 1991, 26th Saas Fee Advanced Course 1996, Les Houches Summer School 1996, 3rd Latin American Conf. on Extragalactic Astronomy, Cordoba, Argentina 1996, Jerusalem Winter School in Theoretical Physics 1997–98, Intelligence Agents Group Advanced School on Star Formation, Sao Paulo, Brazil 1998, Dept of Astronomy, Univ. of Wis. 2002, Faculty, 9th Vatican Summer School in Observational Astronomy and Astrophysics 2002–03; Carnegie Fellowship 1978–80; Visiting Fellow, Leiden Observatory, Univ. of Leiden 1982; Alfred P. Sloan Fellowship 1983–87. *Publications:* as co-author: Galaxies: Interactions and Induced Star Formation 1998, Hubble's Science Legacy: Future Optical/Ultraviolet Astronomy from Space 2002; numerous contribs to science journals. *Address:* Institute of Astronomy, University of Cambridge, Madingley Road, Cambridge, CB3 0HA, England (office). *Telephone:* (1223) 765844 (office). *Fax:* (1223) 766658 (office). *E-mail:* robk@ast.cam.ac.uk (office). *Website:* www.ast.cam.ac.uk/~robk (office).

KENNY, Sir Anthony John Patrick, Kt, DPhil, FBA; British philosopher and university teacher; *President, Royal Institute of Philosophy;* b. 16 March 1931, Liverpool; s. of John Kenny and Margaret Kenny (née Jones); m. Nancy Caroline Gayley 1966; two s.; ed Gregorian Univ., Rome, Italy, St Benet's Hall,

Oxford; ordained Catholic priest, Rome 1955; curate, Liverpool 1959–63; returned to lay state 1963; Asst Lecturer, Univ. of Liverpool 1961–63; Lecturer in Philosophy, Exeter and Trinity Colls, Oxford 1963–64; Tutor in Philosophy, Balliol Coll., Oxford 1964, Fellow 1964–78, Sr Tutor 1971–72, 1976–77, Master 1978–89; Warden Rhodes House 1989–99; Professorial Fellow, St John's Coll., Oxford 1989–99; Pro-Vice-Chancellor, Univ. of Oxford 1984–99, Pro-Vice Chancellor for Devt 1999–2001; Wilde Lecturer in Natural and Comparative Religion, Oxford 1969–72; Jt Gifford Lecturer, Univ. of Edinburgh 1972–73; Stanton Lecturer, Univ. of Cambridge 1980–83; Speaker's Lecturer in Biblical Studies, Univ. of Oxford 1980–83; Visiting Prof., Stanford and Rockefeller Univs and Univs of Chicago, Washington, Michigan and Cornell; Vice-Pres. British Acad. 1986–88, Pres. 1989–93; Chair. Bd British Library 1993–96 (mem. Bd 1991–96); Pres. Royal Inst. of Philosophy 2005–; Del. and mem. of Finance Cttee, Oxford Univ. Press 1986–93; Ed. The Oxford Magazine 1972–73; mem. Royal Norwegian Acad. 1993–, American Philosophical Soc. 1994–, American Acad. of Arts and Sciences 2003–; Hon. Bencher, Lincoln's Inn 1999; Hon. DLitt (Bristol) 1982, (Denison Univ.) 1986, (Liverpool) 1988, (Glasgow) 1990, (Lafayette) 1990, (Trinity Coll., Dublin) 1992, (Hull) 1993, (Belfast) 1994; Hon. DCL (Oxford) 1987; Hon. DLit (London) 2002; Aquinas Medal 1996. *Publications:* Action, Emotion and Will 1963, Responsa Alumnorum of English College, Rome (two vols) 1963, Descartes 1968, The Five Ways 1969, Wittgenstein 1973, The Anatomy of the Soul 1974, Will, Freedom and Power 1975, Aristotelian Ethics 1978, Freewill and Responsibility 1978, The God of the Philosophers 1979, Aristotle's Theory of the Will 1979, Aquinas 1980, The Computation of Style 1982, Faith and Reason 1983, Thomas More 1983, The Legacy of Wittgenstein 1984, A Path from Rome 1985, The Logic of Deterrence 1985, The Ivory Tower 1985, Wyclif – Past Master 1985, Wyclif's De Universalibus 1985, Rationalism, Empiricism and Idealism 1986, Wyclif in His Times 1986, The Road to Hillsborough 1986, Reason and Religion (essays) 1987, The Heritage of Wisdom 1987, God and Two Poets 1988, The Metaphysics of Mind 1989, Mountains 1991, What is Faith? 1992, Aristotle on the Perfect Life 1992, Aquinas on Mind 1992, The Oxford Illustrated History of Western Philosophy (ed.) 1994, Frege 1995, A Life in Oxford 1997, A Brief History of Western Philosophy 1998, Essays on the Aristotelian Tradition 2001, Aquinas on Being 2002, The Unknown God 2003, A New History of Western Philosophy (one vol.) 2003, A New History of Western Philosophy Vol. 1: Ancient Philosophy 2004, Vol. 2: Medieval Philosophy 2005, Arthur Hugh Clough: A Poet's Life 2005, What I Believe 2006, Life, Liberty and the Pursuit of Utility (with C. Kenny) 2006, The Rise of Modern Philosophy 2006. *Address:* St John's College, Oxford, OX1 3JP, England (office). *Telephone:* (1865) 764174 (home). *E-mail:* ajpk@f2s.com (home).

KENNY, Gen. Sir Brian (Leslie Graham), Kt, GCB, CBE; British army officer (retd); b. 18 June 1934; s. of late Brig. James W. Kenny, CBE and Aileen A. G. Swan; m. Diana C. J. Mathew 1958; two s.; ed Canford School; commissioned into 4th Hussars (later Queen's Royal Irish Hussars) 1954; served British Army of the Rhine (BAOR), Aden, Malaya, Borneo and Cyprus; pilot's course 1961; Ministry of Defence 1966–68; Instructor Staff Coll. 1971–73; CO Queen's Royal Irish Hussars (QRIH), BAOR and UN, Cyprus 1974–76; Col G.S. 4 Armoured Div. 1977–78; Command, 12 Armoured Brigade (Task Force D) 1979–80; Royal Coll. of Defence Studies 1981; Commdr 1st Armoured Div. 1982–83; Dir Army Staff Duties, Ministry of Defence 1983–85; Command, 1st British Corps 1985–87; C-in-C BAOR and Commdr NATO's Northern Army Group 1987–89; Deputy Supreme Allied Commdr Europe 1990–93; Col Commandant RAVC 1983–95; Col QRIH 1985–93; Col Commandant RAC 1988–93; Gov. Royal Hosp. Chelsea 1993–99, Gov. Canford School 1988–; Chair. ABF 1993–99; Dir (non-exec.) Dorset Ambulance Trust 2000–; Bath King of Arms 1999–. *Leisure interests:* theatre, cricket, tennis, golf, shooting, racing. *Address:* c/o Lloyds Bank, Camberley, Surrey, GU15 3SE, England (office).

KENT, Bruce Eric, PhD; Australian historian and academic; *Distinguished Fellow, National Europe Centre, Australian National University;* b. 15 Feb. 1932, Melbourne; s. of Rev. Eric Deacon Kent and Beatrice Maude Kent; m. Ann Elizabeth Garland 1966; two s.; ed Geelong Grammar School, Melbourne Univ., Univ. of Oxford, UK, Australian Nat. Univ.; Tutor in History, Univ. of Melbourne 1954–55; Lecturer in History, ANU 1962–70, Sr Lecturer 1970–90, Reader 1990–, Acting Head of History Dept 1984, Visiting Fellow, Dept of Econ. History 1998, now Distinguished Fellow, Nat. Europe Centre; Fulbright Visiting Fellow, Hoover Inst., Stanford Univ. and History Dept, Princeton Univ., USA 1970; Visiting Lecturer, E China Normal Univ., Shanghai 1975–76; Pres. Australian Asscn of European Historians 1984–86; Visiting Fellow, Center of Int. Studies, Princeton Univ., USA, 1996; Victorian Rhodes Scholar 1955. *Publication:* The Spoils of War: The Politics, Economics and Diplomacy of Reparations, 1918–1932 1989. *Leisure interests:* violin, cricket, surfing. *Address:* 4/3 Tasmania Circle, Forrest, ACT 2603 (home); National Europe Centre, 1 Liversidge Street, Building 67C, Australian National University, Canberra, ACT 0200, Australia (office). *Telephone:* (2) 6273-1019 (home); (2) 6260-6222 (home); (2) 6125-6697 (office). *Fax:* (2) 6125-5792 (office). *E-mail:* bruce.kent@anu.edu.au (office). *Website:* www.anu.edu.au/NEC (office).

KENT, HRH The Duke of (Prince Edward George Nicholas Paul Patrick), Earl of St Andrew's, Baron Downpatrick, KG, GCMG, GCVO, ADC; b. 9 Oct. 1935; s. of the late Duke of Kent (fourth s. of King George V) and Princess Marina (d. of the late Prince Nicholas of Greece); m. Katherine Worsley 1961; two s. (George, Earl of St Andrew's and Lord Nicholas Windsor) one d. (Lady Helen Windsor); ed Eton Coll. and Le Rosey, Switzerland; Second Lt, Royal Scots Greys 1955; attended Army Staff Course 1966, later on staff, GOC Eastern Command, Hounslow, Major 1967; Lt-Col Royal Scots Dragoon Guards 1972, Maj. Gen. 1983, Deputy Col-in-Chief 1993–; rank of Field

Marshal 1993; Ministry of Defence 1972–76; Chair. Nat. Electronics Council 1977–; Vice-Chair. British Overseas Trade Bd 1976–; Pres. All-England Lawn Tennis Club 1969–, Commonwealth War Graves Comm., RNLI 1969–, Football Asscn 1971–, Automobile Asscn 1973–, RAF Benevolent Fund 1974–, Scout Asscn 1975–, Royal Inst. of Great Britain 1976–, Business and Technicians Educ. Council 1984–, Eng Council 1989–, British Menswear Guild 1989–; Hon. Pres. Royal Geographical Soc. 1969–; Dir Vickers; Chancellor Univ. of Surrey 1977–; Patron Inst. of Export 1977–, Kent Opera 1978–, The London Philharmonic 1980–, Anglo-Jordanian Soc. 1982–, The Hanover Band 1992–, Anglo-German Asscn 1994; as Queen's Special Rep. has visited Sierra Leone 1961, Uganda 1962, The Gambia 1965, Guyana and Barbados 1966, Tonga 1967; ADC to HM The Queen 1967; Grand Master of the United Grand Lodge of England 1967–; Col-in-Chief Royal Regt of Fusiliers 1969–, Devonshire and Dorset Regt 1978–, Lorne Scots Regt 1978–; Col Scots Guards 1974; Hon. DCL (Durham), Hon. LLD (Leeds), DUniv (York); Colonel-in-Chief, The Royal Regiment of Fusiliers 1969, Colonel, Scots Guards 1974, Colonel-in-Chief, The Devonshire and Dorset Regiment 1977, Colonel-in-Chief, The Lorne Scots (Peel, Dufferin and Hamilton Regiment) 1977, Hon. Air Vice Marshal, Royal Air Force 1985, Colonel-in-Chief, The Royal Scots Dragoon Guards 1994, Honorary Air Commodore, RAF Leuchars 1993, Hon. Air Chief Marshal, RAF 1996; King George VI and Queen Elizabeth Coronation Medal 1937, Queen Elizabeth II Coronation Medal 1953, Queen Elizabeth II Golden Jubilee Medal 2002; The Order of St George and St Constantine, 1st class (Greece), The Most Illustrious Order of Tri Shakti Patta, 1st class (Nepal) 1960, Knight Grand Band, the Order of the Star of Africa (Liberia) 1962, Grand Cordon, the Order of the Renaissance (Jordan) 1966, Grand Cross, the Order of St Olav (Norway) 1988, Grand Cross, the Order of Merit of the Republic of Poland (Poland) 1999. *Leisure interests:* skiing, shooting, photography, opera. *Address:* York House, St James's Palace, London, SW1A 1BQ, England.

KENT, Francis William, PhD, DipEd, FAHA; Australian academic; *Australian Professorial Fellow, School of Historical Studies, Monash University;* b. 30 March 1942, Melbourne; m. 1st Dale V. Kent 1964 (divorced 1984); one d.; m. 2nd Carolyn James 1987; one s. one d.; ed Univ. of Melbourne and Univ. of London; Lecturer, Sr Lecturer and Reader in History, Monash Univ. 1971–, Personal Chair. 1989–, Prof. of History 1989–, now Australian Professorial Fellow, School of Historical Studies; Dir Monash Univ. in Prato 2000–2004; Fellow Harvard Univ. at Centre for Italian Renaissance Studies, Florence 1977–78, Visiting Scholar 1982, Visiting Prof. 1986–87; Robert Lehman Visiting Prof. 1995–96; Shouler Lecturer in History, Johns Hopkins Univ. 1999; Foundation Co-Ed. I Tatti Studies: Essays in the Renaissance 1982; Gen. Ed. Correspondence of Lorenzo de' Medici 2001–; Socio Straniero Deputazione di Storia Patria per la Toscana. *Publications:* Household and Lineage in Renaissance Florence 1977, A Florentine Patrician and His Palace (with others) 1981, Neighbours and Neighbourhood in Renaissance Florence (with D. V. Kent) 1982, Patronage, Art and Society in Renaissance Italy (ed. with P. Simons) 1987, Bartolomeo Cederni and his Friends (with G. Corti) 1991, Lorenzo de Medici and the Art of Magnificence 2004; numerous articles. *Leisure interests:* reading, gardening, travel. *Address:* 19 Downshire Road, Elsternwick, Vic. 3185, Australia (home).

KENT, Jonathan; theatre and opera director; b. 1951, Cape Town, SA; ed Cen. School of Speech and Drama, London; began career as actor, Glasgow Citizens 1970s; Jt Artistic Dir (with Ian McDiarmid) The Almeida Theatre, London 1990–2002; freelance dir 2002–; Artistic Dir Man of La Mancha (Broadway, New York), Hamlet (Japan), Katya Kabanova (Santa Fe, Calif.), The Paris Letter (New York) 2003, The False Servant (London) 2004. *Plays directed include:* Richard II, Coriolanus, Hamlet, The Tempest, Platonov, As You Desire Me, Faith Healer, Racine, King Lear, The Country Wife, The Sea. *Operas directed include:* Katya Kabanova 2003, A Child of Our Time 2005, Lucio Silla 2005, The Tempest 2006, Tosca 2006, The Turn of the Screw 2006. *Address:* c/o St John Donald, United Agents, 12–26 Lexington Street, London, W1F 0LE, England (office). *Telephone:* (20) 3214-0800 (office). *Fax:* (20) 3214-0801 (office). *E-mail:* info@unitedagents.co.uk (office). *Website:* www .unitedagents.co.uk (office).

KENT, Muhtar A., BSc, MSc; Turkish/American business executive; *President and CEO, Coca-Cola Company;* b. 1952, New York City; m. Defne Kent; two c.; ed Univ. of Hull, London City Univ., UK; joined Coca-Cola Co., Atlanta, Ga 1978, Gen. Man. Coca-Cola Turkey and Cen. Asia 1985–89, Pres. East Cen. Europe Div. and Sr Vice-Pres. Coca-Cola Int. 1989–95, Man. Dir Coca-Cola Amatil-Europe 1995–98, Pres. and CEO Efes Beverage Group (majority owner of Turkish bottler Coca-Cola Icecek) 1999–2005, Pres. and COO Coca-Cola N Asia, Eurasia and Middle East Group 2005–06, Pres. Coca-Cola Int. Jan.–Dec. 2006, Pres. and COO Coca-Cola Co., Atlanta 2006–08, Pres. and CEO 2008–. *Address:* The Coca-Cola Co., 1 Coca-Cola Plaza, Atlanta, GA 30313-2499, USA (office). *Telephone:* (404) 676-2121 (office). *Fax:* (404) 676-6792 (office). *E-mail:* info@thecoca-colacompany.com (office). *Website:* www.thecoca-colacompany .com (office).

KENTRIDGE, Sir Sydney, Kt, KCMG, QC, MA; British lawyer; b. 5 Nov. 1922, Johannesburg, South Africa; s. of Morris Kentridge and May Kentridge; m. Felicia Geffen 1952; two s. two d.; ed King Edward VII School, Johannesburg, Univ. of the Witwatersrand and Exeter Coll., Oxford; war service with S African forces 1942–46; Advocate, SA 1949, Sr Counsel 1965; called to Bar, Lincoln's Inn, London 1977, Bencher 1986; Queen's Counsel, England 1984; Judge, Court of Appeal, Jersey and Guernsey 1988–92; mem. Court of Appeal, Botswana 1981–89, Constitutional Court, SA 1995–97; Roberts Lecturer, Univ. of Pa 1979; Hon. Fellow American Coll. of Trial Lawyers 1998; Hon. Fellow Exeter Coll., Oxford 1986; Hon. mem. Bar Asscn New York City 2001; Hon. LLD (Leicester) 1985, (Cape Town) 1987, (Natal) 1989, (London) 1995,

(Sussex) 1997, (Witwatersrand) 2000; Granville Clark Prize, USA 1978. *Leisure interests:* opera, theatre. *Address:* 7–8 Essex Street, London, WC2R 3LD, England. *Telephone:* (20) 7379-3550. *Fax:* (20) 7379-3558.

KENWORTHY, Duncan, OBE, MA, FRSA; British film producer; *Managing Director, Toledo Productions Ltd;* b. 9 Sept. 1949; s. of Bernard Kenworthy and Edna Muriel Kenworthy (née Calligan); ed Rydal School, Christ's Coll., Cambridge, Annenberg School, Univ. of Pennsylvania, USA; Children's Television Workshop, New York 1973–76; Consulting Producer, Arabic Sesame Street, Kuwait 1977–79; Producer and Exec., Jim Henson Productions, London 1979–95; Producer and Man. Dir Toledo Productions Ltd 1995–; Dir DNA Films Ltd 1997–2008; mem. Council BAFTA 1996–, Chair. BAFTA Film Cttee 2002–04, Chair. BAFTA 2004–06; Chair. Film Policy Review Group 1997–99, Film Advisory Cttee, British Council 1999–2008, UK-China Forum 2000–01; Dir Film Council 1999–2003; Gov. Nat. Film and TV School 2001–; British Producer of the Year, London Film Critics 1994. *Films include:* The Dark Crystal (assoc producer) 1980, Four Weddings and a Funeral (Best Film, and Lloyds Bank Peoples' Choice Award, BAFTA 1994, Best Foreign Film, Cesar Award 1994) 1994, Lawn Dogs 1997, Notting Hill (BAFTA Orange Audience Award 2000) 1999, The Parole Officer 2001, Heartlands (exec. producer) 2002, Love Actually 2003. *Television includes:* Fraggle Rock (Emmy Award for Outstanding Children's Programming 1983) 1982, The Storyteller (BAFTA Award for Best Children's Programme 1989) 1986–88; Living with Dinosaurs (Emmy Award for Best Children's Programme 1990) 1988, Monster Maker 1988, Greek Myths (BAFTA for Best Children's Fictional Programme 1991) 1990, Gulliver's Travels (Emmy Award for Outstanding Mini-series 1996) 1996. *Address:* Toledo Productions Ltd, Suite 44, 10 Richmond Mews, London, W1D 3DD, England (office). *Telephone:* (20) 7851-6677 (office). *Fax:* (20) 7437-7740 (office). *E-mail:* info@toledoproductions.com (office).

KENWRIGHT, Bill, CBE; British theatre producer; b. 4 Sept. 1945; s. of Albert Kenwright and Hope Kenwright (née Jones); ed Liverpool Inst.; actor 1964–70; theatre producer 1970–; Vice-Chair. Everton Football Club; Dr hc (Liverpool John Moores) 1994; numerous awards. *Films directed include:* Stepping Out, Don't Go Breaking My Heart 1999. *Plays directed include:* Joseph and The Amazing Technicolor Dreamcoat 1979, The Business of Murder 1981, A Streetcar Named Desire 1984, Stepping Out 1984, Blood Brothers 1988, Shirley Valentine 1989, Travels With My Aunt 1993, Piaf 1993, Lysistrata 1993, Medea 1993, Pygmalion 1997, A Doll's House, An Ideal Husband, The Chairs 2000, Ghosts, The Female Odd Couple. *Leisure interest:* football. *Address:* Bill Kenwright Ltd, 106 Harrow Road, London, W2 1RR, England (office). *Telephone:* (20) 7446-6200 (office). *Fax:* (20) 7446-6222 (office). *Website:* www.kenwright.com (office).

KENYATTA, Uhuru; Kenyan politician; *Minister of Finace;* b. 1961; s. of the late fmr Pres. Jomo Kenyatta; Chair. Kenya Tourism Bd 1999; nominated MP by Pres. Daniel arap Moi (q.v.); apptd Minister of Local Govt 2001; Vice-Chair. Kenya African Nat. Union (KANU) 2002, then Acting Pres., Pres. 2005–06, 2007–; named heir apparent by Pres. Moi July 2002, failed to be elected in presidential elections Dec. 2002; Deputy Prime Minister and Minister of Trade 2008–09, Minister of Finance 2009–. *Address:* Ministry of Finance, Treasury Building, Harambee Avenue, POB 30007, Nairobi, Kenya (office). *Telephone:* (20) 252299 (office). *Fax:* (20) 310833 (office). *Website:* www .treasury.go.ke (office); www.kanuonline.com.

KENYON, Sir Nicholas Roger, Kt, CBE, BA; British broadcasting executive; *Managing Director, Barbican Centre;* b. 23 Feb. 1951, Altrincham, Cheshire; s. of Thomas Kenyon and Kathleen Holmes; m. Marie-Ghislaine Latham-Koenig 1976; three s. one d.; ed Balliol Coll., Oxford; music critic, The New Yorker 1979–82, The Times 1982–85, The Observer 1985–92; Music Ed. The Listener 1982–87; Ed. Early Music 1983–92; programme adviser, Mozart Now Festival, South Bank, London 1991; Controller, BBC Radio 3 1992–98, Dir BBC Proms 1996–2007, Controller BBC Millennium Programmes 1998–2000, BBC Live Events and TV Classical Music 2000–07; Man. Dir Barbican Centre, London 2007–; mem. Bd ENO 2005–; Gov. Wellington School; Royal Philharmonic Soc. Awards for Fairest Isle (BBC Radio 3) 1996 and Sounding the Century 2000. *Publications:* The BBC Symphony Orchestra 1930–80 1981, Simon Rattle: The Making of a Conductor (revised edn as Simon Rattle: From Birmingham to Berlin 2001), Authenticity and Early Music (ed.) 1988, The Viking Opera Guide (co-ed.) 1993, The Penguin Opera Guide (co-ed.) 1995, Musical Lives (ed.) 2001, The BBC Proms Guide to Great Concertos (ed.) 2003, The BBC Proms Pocket Guide to Great Symphonies (ed.) 2003, The Faber Pocket Guide to Mozart 2005. *Address:* Barbican Centre, Silk Street, London, EC2Y 8DS, England (office). *Website:* www.barbican.org.uk (office).

KENZO; Japanese fashion designer; b. (Kenzo Takada), 1940, Kyoto; ed Bunka Fashion Coll., Tokyo; after graduating designed patterns for a Tokyo magazine; moved to Paris 1964; created own freelance collections and sold designs to Louis Féraud 1964–70; opened own shop Jungle Jap 1970; noted for translating traditional designs into original contemporary garments and for ready-to-wear knitwear; Head of Kenzo fashion house until retirement in 1999; cr. Yume label 2002. *Film:* Yume, Yume no Ato (dir and writer) 1981. *Address:* c/o KENZO, 1 rue de Pont Neuf, 75001 Paris, France (office).

KEOBOUNPHAN, Gen. Sisavath; Laotian politician; b. 1 May 1928, Houaphanh Prov.; Political Chief, then Head of mil. force, Rassavong armed unit 1949–52; Founding mem. Lao People's Revolutionary Party (LPRP) 1955, mem. Cen. Cttee 1955, 1972–75; Party Sec., Samneua Rallying Zone 1956–60; mem. Admin. Bd for Supreme Command and Chief of Supreme Gen. Staff of Lao People's Army 1960–72; Minister attached to Prime Minister's Office and Minister of the Interior 1975–91; Maj. of Vientiane Municipality Admin 1975–91; Minister of Agric. and Forestry 1991–96; Vice-Pres. of Laos 1996–98, Prime Minister of Laos 1998–2001. *Address:* c/o Lao People's Revolutionary Party, Vientiane, Laos (office).

KEOGH, Lainey; Irish knitwear designer; b. 20 Sept. 1957; d. of Peter Keogh and Patricia Byrne; worked in medical sciences –1983; began to work with yarn in 1983; recognized for work by Int. Wool 1987; mem. Secr. Int. Festival du Lin 1989, British Fashion Council 1994; Man. Dir Lainey Keogh 1986–; developed fabrics for Dior couture studio 1998, collected by Metropolitan Museum of Art, New York; Prix De Coeur (France) 1987; Cable Ace Award for Costume Design for film Two Nudes Bathing 1995, People of the Year Award (Ireland) 1997, Prix de Coeur (France) 1997. *Leisure interests:* sky, walking, painting, meditation. *Address:* 42 Dawson Street, Dublin 2, Ireland. *Telephone:* (1) 6793299. *Fax:* (1) 6794975. *E-mail:* laineykeogh@eircom.net; info@ laineykeogh.com. *Website:* www.laineykeogh.com.

KEOHANE, Nannerl O., PhD; American academic and fmr university president; *Laurance S. Rockefeller Distinguished Visiting Professor of Public Affairs in the Woodrow Wilson School and University Center for Human Values, Princeton University;* b. 18 Sept. 1940, Blytheville, Ark.; d. of James Arthur Overholser and Grace Overholser (née McSpadden); m. 1st Patrick Henry, III 1962 (divorced 1969); m. 2nd Robert O. Keohane 1970; three s. one d.; ed Wellesley Coll., St Anne's Coll., Univ. of Oxford, Yale Univ.; mem. faculty, Swarthmore Coll. 1967–73, Stanford Univ. 1973–81, Fellow, Center for Advanced Study in the Behavioral Sciences, Stanford Univ. 1978–79, 1987–88; Pres. and Prof. of Political Sciences, Wellesley Coll. 1981–93, Duke Univ. 1993–2004; Laurance S. Rockefeller Distinguished Visiting Prof. of Public Affairs in the Woodrow Wilson School and the Univ. Center for Human Values, Princeton Univ. 2004–; mem. Harvard Corpn (Pres. and Fellows of Harvard Coll.) and Fellow, Harvard Coll. 2005–; mem. Bd of Dirs IBM 1986–, Bd Trustees The Colonial Williamsburg Foundation 1988–2001, Center for the Advanced Study of the Behavioral Sciences 1991–97, The Nat. Humanities Center 1993–; mem. MIT Corpn 1992–97, Doris Duke Charitable Foundation 1996–, Overseers Cttee to Visit the John F. Kennedy School of Govt 1996– (Chair. 2001–03); Fellow, American Acad. of Arts and Sciences, American Philosophical Soc.; Marshall Scholar 1961–63; Dr hc from several univs and colleges; Wilbur Cross Medal, Yale Univ., Nat. Women's Hall of Fame 1995, Golden Plate Award, American Acad. of Achievement 1998. *Leisure interests:* travel, jogging, theatre, music. *Address:* Woodrow Wilson School, 437 Robertson Hall, Princeton University, Princeton, NJ 08544-1013, USA. *Telephone:* (609) 258-8974 (office). *Fax:* (609) 258-0390 (office). *E-mail:* nkeohane@princeton.edu (office). *Website:* www.wws.princeton.edu (office); www.princeton.edu/~uchv (office).

KEOHANE, Robert Owen, BA, MA, PhD; American political scientist and academic; *Professor of International Affairs, Woodrow Wilson School, Princeton University;* b. 3 Oct. 1941, Chicago, Ill.; s. of Robert Emmet Keohane and Marie Irene Keohane (née Pieters); m. Nannerl Overholser 1970; three s. one d.; ed Shimer Coll., Illinois, Harvard Univ.; Fellow, Harvard Univ., Woodrow Wilson School of Public and Int. Affairs, Princeton Univ. 1961–62; mem. Woodrow Wilson Award Cttee 1982, Chair. Nominating Cttee 1990–91, Chair. Minority Identification Project 1990–92; Instructor, then Assoc. Prof., Swathmore Coll. 1965–73; Assoc. Prof., then Prof., Stanford Univ. 1973–81; Ed. Int. Org. 1974–80, mem. Bd Eds 1968–77, 1982–88, 1992–97, 1998–, Chair. 1986–87; Prof., Brandeis Univ. 1981–85; Pres. Int. Studies Assn 1988–89, Chair. Nominations Cttee 1985; Prof., then Stanfield Prof. of Int. Peace, Harvard Univ. 1985–96, Chair. Dept of Govt 1988–92; James B. Duke Prof. of Political Science, Duke Univ. –2004; Prof. of Int. Affairs, Woodrow Wilson School, Princeton Univ. 2004–; Sherill Lecturer, Yale Univ. Law School 1996; Pres. American Political Science Assn 1999–2000; mem. NAS 2005; Fellow, American Acad. of Arts and Sciences 1983–, Center for Advanced Study in Behavioral Sciences 1977–78, 1987–88, 2004–05; Frank Kenan Fellow, Nat. Endowment for the Humanities 1995–96; Bell Research Fellow, German Marshall Fund 1977–78; Fellow, Council on Foreign Relations 1967–69, Guggenheim Foundation 1992–93, Sr Foreign Policy Fellow, Social Science Research Council 1986–88; Bellagio Resident Fellow 1993; Hon. PhD (Univ. of Århus, Denmark) 1988; Grawemeyer Award for Ideas Improving World Order 1989, First Mentorship Award, Soc. for Women in Int. Political Economy 1997, Skytte Prize, Johan Skytte Foundation, Uppsala, Sweden 2005. *Publications include:* After Hegemony: Cooperation and Discord in the World Political Economy 1984, Neorealism and Its Critics 1986, International Institutions and State Power: Essays in International Relations Theory 1989; (as co-author): Power and Interdependence: World Politics in Transition 1977, Institutions for the Earth: Sources of Effective International Environmental Protection 1993, After the Cold War: State Strategies and International Institutions in Europe, 1989–91 1993, Designing Social Inquiry: Scientific Inference in Qualitative Research 1994; (as co-ed.): Transnational Relations and World Politics 1972, The New European Community: Decision-Making and Institutional Change 1991, Ideas and Foreign Policy 1993, From Local Commons to Global Interdependence 1994, Institutions for Environmental Aid: Pitfalls and Promises 1996, Internationalization and Domestic Politics 1996, Imperfect Unions: Security Institutions Across Time and Space 1999, Exploration and Contestation in the Study of World Politics 1998, Legalization and World Politics 2000. *Address:* Woodrow Wilson School, 408 Robertson Hall, Princeton University, Princeton, NJ 08544-1013, USAUSA (office). *Telephone:* (609) 258-1856 (office). *Fax:* (609) 258-0019 (office). *E-mail:* rkeohane@princeton.edu (office). *Website:* www.wws.princeton.edu/rkeohane (office).

KEOUGH, Donald (Don) Raymond, BS; American business executive; *Chairman, Allen & Company Inc.;* b. 4 Sept. 1926, Maurice, Ia; s. of Leo H. Keough and Veronica Keough (née Henkels); m. Marilyn Mulhall 1949; three s. three d.; ed Creighton Univ.; with Butter-Nut Foods Co., Omaha 1950–61,

Duncan Foods Co., Houston 1961–67; Vice-Pres. and Dir Marketing Foods Div., The Coca-Cola Co., Atlanta, Ga 1967–71, Pres. 1971–73; Exec. Vice-Pres. Coca-Cola USA 1973–74, Pres. 1974–76; Exec. Vice-Pres. The Coca-Cola Co., Atlanta, Ga 1976–79, Sr Exec. Vice-Pres. 1980–81, Pres., COO and Dir 1981–93; Chair. Bd of Dirs Coca-Cola Enterprises Inc., Atlanta, Ga 1986–93, Adviser to Bd 1993–98; returned as mem. Bd 2004; Chair. Bd Allen & Co., Inc. 1993–, Convera 2002–; fmr Chair. Bd of Trustees, Univ. of Notre Dame, now Chair. Emer.; Fellow, American Acad. of Arts and Sciences 2002; Laetare Medal, Univ. of Notre Dame 1993; Dr hc (Univ. of Notre Dame), (Creighton Univ.), (Emory Univ.), (Trinity Univ. Dublin, Ireland), (lark Univ.). *Address:* Allen & Company Inc., 711 5th Avenue, 9th Floor, New York, NY 10022, USA (office). *Telephone:* (212) 832-8000 (office). *Fax:* (212) 832-8023 (office).

KERAVNOS, Makis, MSc; Cypriot banker and government official; *CEO, Hellenic Bank Public Co. Ltd;* b. 1951, Larnaka; m. Niki Keravnos; three c.; ed Pancyprian Gymnasium of Kykkos, Nat. and Kapodistrian Univ. of Athens, Pantion Univ., Brooks Univ., Oxford, UK; various sr exec. positions in private cos; various positions Human Resources Devt Authority including Sr Officer; apptd Minister of Labour 2003; Minister of Finance 2004–05 (resgnd); CEO Hellenic Bank 2005–; founding mem. and Pres. Pancyprian Asscn of Economists; mem. Bd of Dirs Cyprus Asscn of Quality; Vice-Pres Cyprus Inst. of Political Research and European Affairs. *Address:* Hellenic Bank Public Co. Ltd, Digeni Akrita Avenue 92, PO Box 24747, 1394 Nicosia, Cyprus (office). *Telephone:* (22) 860000 (office). *Website:* www.hellenicbank.com (office).

KERDEL-VEGAS, Francisco, MSc, MD; Venezuelan dermatologist, physician and diplomatist; b. 3 Jan. 1928, Caracas; s. of Osvaldo F. Kerdel and Sofia Vegas de Kerdel; m. Martha Ramos de Kerdel 1977; two s. four d.; ed Liceo Andrés Bello, Caracas, Universidad Cen. de Venezuela, Harvard Univ. and New York Univ., USA; Prof. of Dermatology, Universidad Cen. de Venezuela 1954–77; Visiting Scientist, Dept of Experimental Pathology, ARC Inst., Cambridge, UK, mem. Trinity Coll. Cambridge; Scientific Attaché, Venezuelan Embassy, London, UK 1966–67; Vice-Chancellor Simón Bolívar Univ. 1969–70; Amb. to UK 1987–92, to France (also accred to UNESCO) 1995–99; Visiting Prof., United Medical and Dental Schools of Guy's and St Thomas's Hosps, Univ. of London 1990; mem. Nat. Research Council, Venezuela 1969–79; mem. Bd Universidad Metropolitana, Caracas 1970, Int. Soc. of Dermatology 1987– (Pres. 1984–89, now Hon. Pres.); Co-Chair. Pan-American Medical Asscn 1990; Prosser White Oration, Royal Coll. of Physicians 1972; Fellow, Venezuelan Acad. of Medicine, Venezuelan Acad. of Sciences, American Coll. of Physicians, American Acad. of Dermatology; Hon. Fellow, Acad. of Medicine, Brazil, Chile; Hon. mem. Royal Soc. of Medicine, British Asscn of Dermatologists and Socs of Dermatology of 15 other countries; Hon. DSc (Calif. Coll. of Podiatric Medicine) 1975, (Cranfield Inst. of Tech., UK) 1991; Orders of Andrés Bello, Cecilio Acosta, Francisco de Miranda, Diego de Losada, El Libertador; Hon. CBE; Chevalier, Légion d'honneur. *Publications:* Tratado de Dermatología 1959; chapters in textbooks on dermatology. *Leisure interests:* travelling, swimming, photography, reading. *Address:* c/o Sociedad Venezolana de Dermatología y Cirugía Dermatológica, Avda. Francisco de Miranda, Edif. Menegrande, Piso 6, Ofic. 6-4. Urb, Los Palos Grandes, Caracas 1080, Venezuela (office).

KÉRÉKOU, Brig.-Gen. Mathieu (Ahmed); Benin politician and army officer; b. 2 Sept. 1933, Natitingou; ed Saint-Raphael Mil. School, France; served French Army until 1961; joined Dahomey Army 1961; Aide-de-camp to Pres. Maga 1961–63; took part in mil. coup d'état which removed Pres. Christophe Soglo 1967; Chair. Mil. Revolutionary Council 1967–68; continued studies at French mil. schools 1968–70; Commdr Ouidah Paratroop Unit and Deputy Chief of Staff 1970–72; leader of the mil. coup d'état which ousted Pres. Ahomadegbe Oct. 1972; Pres. and Head of Mil. Revolutionary Govt, Minister of Nat. Defence 1972–91, fmr Minister of Planning, of Co-ordination of Foreign Aid, Information and Nat. Orientation; Pres. of Benin 1996–2006; Chair. Cen. Cttee Parti de la révolution populaire du Bénin. *Leisure interests:* cycling, football. *Address:* c/o Présidence de la république, PO Box 1288, Cotonou, Benin.

KERESZTESI, János; Hungarian business executive; *CEO, FreeSoft Nyrt.;* b. 1958; m.; two c.; began career with SZÁMALK; later with Digital Equipment Hungary; Pnr Relationships Man. and later Indirect Sales Man., Oracle Hungary 1995–99; Operations Man., Sun Microsystems Hungary 1999–2004; CEO FreeSoft Nyrt. 2004–; mem. Bd, Asscn of IT Cos 2005–; Asscn of IT Cos IT Man. of the Year 2001. *Address:* FreeSoft Nyrt., Neumann Janos u. 1/C, Iunfopark Budapest, 1117 Budapest, Hungary (office). *Telephone:* (61) 371-2910 (office). *Fax:* (61) 371-2911 (office). *E-mail:* fs.inf@freesoft.hu (office). *Website:* www.freesoft.hu (office).

KERGIN, Michael Frederick, BA, MA (Econs); Canadian government official, academic and fmr diplomatist; *Premier of Ontario's Special Adviser on Border Issues;* b. Canadian Mil. Hosp., Bramshott, UK; m. Margarita Fuentes Kergin; three s.; ed Univ. of Toronto, Magdalen Coll. Oxford, UK; joined Dept of Foreign Affairs and Int. Trade (fmrly Dept of External Affairs) as Foreign Services Officer 1967, positions include Sr Dept Asst to Sec. of State for External Affairs 1984–86, Asst Deputy Minister responsible for Political and Int. Security Affairs 1994–96, and for the Americas and Security and Intelligence Affairs 1996–98; Amb. to Cuba 1986–89, to USA 2000–05; Premier of Ont.'s Special Adviser on Border Issues 2005–; currently Adjunct Prof., Faculty of Political Studies, Univ. of Ottawa, also Sr Fellow, Grad. School of Public and Int. Affairs; Visiting Scholar, Western Michigan Univ., Kalamazoo 2006–07; Foreign Policy Adviser to the Prime Minister and Asst Sec. to the Cabinet for Foreign and Defence Policy 1998–2000; mem. Del. to Inter-American Devt Bank; fmr Embassy Minister, Washington, DC, USA, Santiago, Chile and Yaoundé, Cameroon; fmr Deputy Head of Mission to UN,

New York. *Address:* 55, Laurier Avenue East, Desmarais Building, Room 11129a, University of Ottawa, Ottawa, ON K1N 6N5; c/o Office of the Premier, Legislative Building, Queen's Park, Toronto, ON M7A 1A1, Canada (office). *Telephone:* (613) 562-5800, ext. 4691 (Ottawa) (office). *Fax:* (613) 562-5241 (Ottawa) (office). *E-mail:* Michael.Kergin@uottawa.ca (office). *Website:* www .premier.gov.on.ca (office); www.governance.uottawa.ca/api/eng/ word_director.asp.

KERIM, Srgjan, PhD; Macedonian diplomatist, politician and academic; *Secretary-General's Special Envoy for Climate Change, United Nations;* b. 12 Dec. 1948, Skopje; m.; three c.; ed Belgrade Univ., fmr Yugoslavia; Asst then Prof. of Int. Econ. Relations, Belgrade Univ. 1972–91; Visiting Prof., Univ. of Hamburg, Germany and New York Univ., USA 1972–91; mem. Presidency of Youth Fed. of Yugoslavia, also Chair. Foreign Policy Cttee 1976–78; Minister for Foreign Econ. Relations 1986–89; Asst Minister and Spokesman, Ministry of Foreign Affairs 1989–91; Vice-Pres. Copechim–France Co., Paris 1992–94; Amb. to Germany 1994–2000, to Liechtenstein and Switzerland 1995–2000; Minister of Foreign Affairs 2000–01; Perm. Rep. to UN, New York 2001–04, Pres. 62nd Session UN Gen. Ass. 2007–08, UN Sec.-Gen.'s Special Envoy for Climate Change 2008–; Gen. Man. Media Print Macedonia (part of WAZ Media Group) and Gen. Man. for South-Eastern Europe, WAZ Media Group 2003; Chair. Politika Newspapers and magazines, Belgrade 2004; Pres. Macedonian-German Econ. Asscn 2003–06, Hon. Pres. 2006; UN Millennium Devt Goals Award 2008. *Publications:* nine books and more than 100 scientific works on int. politics, int. economic and youth issues. *Address:* United Nations, New York, NY 10017, USA (office). *Telephone:* (212) 963-1234 (office). *Fax:* (212) 963-4879 (office). *Website:* www.un.org (office).

KERIMKULOV, Medetbek Temirbekovich; Kyrgyzstani politician; b. 28 Jan. 1949; Mayor of Bishkek 1999–2005; Interim Prime Minister June–July 2005; First Deputy Prime Minister 2005–06; Acting Minister of Industry, Commerce and Tourism 2006–07. *Address:* c/o Ministry of Industry, Commerce and Tourism, 720002 Bishkek, pr. Chui 106, Kyrgyzstan (office).

KERIMOV, Makhmud; Azerbaijani physicist and academic; *President, Azerbaijan National Academy of Sciences;* b. 18 Oct. 1948, Baku; m.; two c.; ed Baku State Univ.; mem. staff Inst. of Physics, Azerbaijan Nat. Acad. of Sciences 1979–, Prof. 2000–, mem. 2001, Pres. 2001–; mem. Int. Eco-Energy Acad. *Publications:* over 116 scientific papers and patents on chemical physics, radiation physics, chem. of condensed matter, electron spin resonance spectroscopy, environmental studies. *Address:* Azerbaijan National Academy of Sciences, Istiglaiyyat str. 10, 370001 Baku, Azerbaijan (office). *Telephone:* (12) 492-35-29 (office). *Fax:* (12) 492-56-99 (office). *E-mail:* president@aas.ab .az (office).

KERIN, John Charles, AM, BA, BEcons; Australian politician; b. 21 Nov. 1937, Bowral, NSW; s. of the late Joseph Sydney Kerin and Mary Louise Kerin (née Fuller); m. 1st Barbara Elizabeth Large (divorced 1981); one d.; m. 2nd Dr June Rae Verrier 1983; ed Univ. of New England, Australian Nat. Univ.; Econs Research Officer in wool marketing, Bureau of Agricultural Econs 1971, 1975–78; MP for Macarthur 1972–75, for Werriwa 1978–93; Minister for Primary Industry 1983–87, for Primary Industries and Energy 1987–91, Treas. for Trade and Overseas Devt 1991–93; resgnd from Parl. 1993; Chair. Australian Meat and Livestock Corpn 1994–97; Dir Coal Mines Australia Ltd 1994–2001; Chair. Biologic Int. Ltd 1996–98; fmr Deputy Chancellor Univ. of Western Sydney, now mem. Bd of Trustees and Chair. Macarthur Council of the Univ.; Chair. NSW Forestry Comm.; Chair. or mem. of various pvt. and public orgs; Bd mem. CSIRO 2008–; Fellow, Australian Inst. of Agricultural Science and Tech., Australian Acad. of Tech. Sciences and Eng; Australian Labor Party; Dr hc (New England) 1992, (Western Sydney) 1995, (Tasmania) 2001. *Leisure interests:* opera, bush-walking, classical music, reading. *Address:* PO Box 3, Garran, ACT 2605, Australia (home). *Telephone:* (6) 285-2480 (home). *Fax:* (6) 282-5778 (home). *E-mail:* kerrier1@bigpond.net.au (home).

KERKAVOV, Rovshen Bairamnazarovich; Turkmenistani politician and economist; b. 1961, Ashgabat; ed Novosibirsk Inst. of Electrotechnology; engineer, Turkmenpromsvyazstroi Co. 1983–84; engineer, Ashgabat GPO 1986; economist and Head of Div., Ashgabat Glavpochtamt Co. 1991–93; First Deputy Dir-Gen., then Dir-Gen. State Co. of Post Communications, Turkmenpochta 1995–97; Minister of Telecommunications Repub. of Turkmenistan 1997–2001; Deputy Chair. Cabinet of Ministers 2001; Order of Galkynysh. *Address:* c/o Cabinet of Ministers, Ashgabat, Turkmenistan (office).

KERKELING, Hans-Peter (Hape); German comedian, writer, actor and television broadcaster; b. 9 Dec. 1964, Recklinghausen; ed Marie Curie Gymnasium, Recklinghausen; presenter, writer WDR TV 1985–87, BR TV 1988–89, RB TV 1989–91; actor, Dir NDR TV 1991–94; presenter, writer RTL TV 1994–95, SAT 1 TV 1998–; host SAT 1 show Darüber lacht die Welt; Verdienstkreuz des Landes NordRheinWestfalen 2006; Golden Camera, Golden Rose of Montreux, Adolf Grimme Prize, Tele-star, Golden Gong, Europa 1991–93, Peter Frankenfeld Prize 2002, Deutscher Fernsehpreis 2003, 2004, Bayerischer Fernsehpreis 2004, Comedy Prize 2004, Golden Camera for Best TV Entertainer 2005, Comedy Prize for Best Comedian 2005, 2006, Adolf-Grimme Honour Award 2007. *Films:* Vorwärts (cinema) 1990, Club Las Piranjas (NDR TV) 1995, Willi und die Windzors (NDR TV) 1996, Die Oma ist tot (NDR TV) 1997, Alles wegen Paul (producer) 2002, Samba in Mettmann (cinema) 2004. *Television:* comedy: Kerkelings Kinderstunde 1984, Känguru 1985–86, Total Normal 1989, Cheese 1994, Warmumsherz 1995, Zappenduster 1997, Gisbert 1998, Darüber lacht die Welt 1998, Hape's halbe Stunde 2001; presenter: Eurovisioin Song Contest 1989–91, German TV Awards 2001, Stars in der Manege 2001, Golden Europa Awards 2002, Aids-

Gala 2002, 2003, Die 70-er Show 2003, 2004, Der grosse Deutschtest 2004, 2005, Hape trifft 2005. *Recordings include:* Hawaii 1984, Hannilein & Co 1986, Erwarten Se nix 1990, Das ganze Leben ist ein Quiz 1991, Hurz (film soundtrack) 1991, Vorsicht Telefon 1993, Der kleine Vampir (film soundtrack) 1993, Sportreporter Rap 1993, Helsinki is Hell 1999, Junge, Junge 2000, Das Ding muss rein 2000, Die 70 min. Show 2003, Tanze Sambe mit mir 2004; (albums) Ariola 1984,. *Publications:* Hannilein & Co. 1992, Kein Pardon 1993, Cheese 1994, Ich bin dann mal weg 2006. *Address:* Büro Hape Kerkeling, Postfach 32 06 30, 40421 Düsseldorf, Germany. *Website:* www.hapekerkeling .de.

KERKORIAN, Kirk; American business executive; *Co-Chairman, President and CEO, Tracinda Corporation;* b. 6 June 1917, Fresno, Calif.; m. 1st Hilda Schmidt 1942 (divorced 1951); m. 2nd Jane Hardy 1954 (divorced); two d.; m. 3rd Lisa Bonder 1998 (divorced 1998); one d.; commercial airline pilot 1940; Capt. Transport Command, RAF 1942–44; f. LA Air Services (later Trans Int. Airlines Group) 1948, Int. Leisure Corpn 1968; CEO MGM Inc. 1973–74, Chair. Exec. Cttee, Vice-Chair. MGM 1974–79, controlling stockholder MGM/ UA Communications Co. and MGM Mirage; Co-Chair., Pres. CEO Tracinda Corpn 1979–; majority shareholder MGM Grand casino, fmr fmr minority shareholder DaimlerChrysler AG; ranked 19th by Forbes magazine among The 400 Richest Americans 2005. *Address:* Tracinda Corporation, 150 Rodeo Drive, Suite 250, Beverly Hills, CA 90212, USA. *Telephone:* (310) 271-0638. *Fax:* (310) 271-3416. *Website:* www.mgmmirage.com.

KERMODE, Sir (John) Frank, Kt, MA, FBA, FRSL; British writer and academic; b. 29 Nov. 1919, Douglas, Isle of Man; s. of John Pritchard Kermode and Doris Kennedy; m. Maureen Eccles 1947 (divorced); one s. one d.; ed Univ. of Liverpool; John Edward Taylor Prof., Univ. of Manchester 1958–65; Winterstoke Prof., Univ. of Bristol 1965–67; Lord Northcliffe Prof., Univ. Coll., London 1967–74; King Edward VII Prof., Univ. of Cambridge 1974–82; Julian Clarence Levi Prof., Humanities Dept, Univ. of Columbia, New York 1983, 1985; Charles Eliot Norton Prof. of Poetry, Harvard Univ. 1977–78; Foreign mem. American Acad. of Arts and Sciences, Accad. dei Lincei, Rome 2002; Hon. mem. American Acad. of Arts and Letters 1999–; Officier, Ordre des Arts et des Sciences; Hon. DHL (Chicago); Hon. DLitt (Liverpool) 1981, (Amsterdam), (Yale) 1995, (Wesleyan) 1997, (London) 1997, (Columbia) 2002, (Harvard) 2004. *Publications:* Romantic Image 1957, Wallace Stevens 1960, The Sense of an Ending 1967, Lawrence 1973, The Classic 1975, The Genesis of Secrecy 1979, The Art of Telling 1983, Forms of Attention 1985, History and Value 1988, The Literary Guide to the Bible (ed. with Robert Alter) 1989, An Appetite for Poetry 1989, Poetry, Narrative, History 1989, The Uses of Error 1991, The Oxford Book of Letters (with Anita Kermode) 1995, Not Entitled: A Memoir 1995, Shakespeare's Language 2000, Pleasing Myself 2001, Pieces of My Mind 2003, The Age of Shakespeare 2004, Pleasure and Change 2004. *Leisure interest:* music. *Address:* 9 The Oast House, Grange Road, Cambridge, CB3 9AP, England. *Telephone:* (1223) 357931. *E-mail:* frankkermode@lineone .net (home).

KERNAN, Roderick Patrick, PhD, DSc, MRIA; Irish professor of physiology; *Professor Emeritus, University College Dublin;* b. 20 May 1928, Dublin; s. of Dermod Kernan and Pauline Kernan (née Hickey); m. Mary Cecily Kavanagh 1956; one s. one d.; ed Synge Street Boys' School and Univ. Coll. Dublin; Research Assoc., Dept of Reproductive Physiology, Rockefeller Inst., New York, USA 1957–58; Sr Fellow Medical Research Council of Ireland 1958–66; Rae Prof. of Biochemistry, Royal Coll. of Surgeons in Ireland 1965–67; Assoc. Prof. of Gen. Physiology, Univ. Coll. Dublin 1966–93, Prof. Emer. 1993–; Visiting Prof. of Physiology, George Washington Univ., Washington, DC 1969–70; elected mem. Royal Irish Acad. 1965, mem. Council 1977–81, 1986–90, 1993–, Vice-Pres. 1978, 1986, Sec. for Science 1993–2000; mem. Physiological Soc. 1963. *Publications:* Cell K 1965, Cell Potassium 1980. *Leisure interests:* hill walking, photography, gardening, painting, music. *Address:* 37 Templeville Drive, Dublin 6W (home); c/o Royal Irish Academy, 19 Dawson Street, Dublin 2, Ireland (office). *Telephone:* (1) 4906323 (office). *Fax:* (1) 6762346 (home). *E-mail:* roddy_kernan@yahoo.com (home).

KERNAN, Gen. William F., MA; American army officer (retd) and business executive; *Senior Vice President and General Manager, International Group, MPRI Inc.;* b. Fort Sam Houston, Tex.; m. Marianne Purnell; one s.; ed US Army Command and Gen. Staff Coll., US Army War Coll.; commissioned Infantry Officer 1968; commanded two Airborne Cos, two Ranger Cos, an Airborne Infantry Battalion, the 75th Ranger Regt; exchange officer 3rd Battalion, Parachute Regt, UK; Asst Div. Commdr (Manoeuvre) 7th Infantry Div.; Dir Plans, Policy and Assessments, J5, US Special Operations Command; Commdr 101st Airborne Div. (Air Assault), XVIII Airborne Corps and Fort Bragg; combat tours Viet Nam, Grenada, Panama; rank of Gen. 2000; Supreme Allied Commdr, Atlantic (SACLANT) and C-in-C US Jt Forces Command, Norfolk, Va 2000–02; Sr Vice Pres. and Gen. Man. Int. Group, MPRI Inc., Alexandria, Va 2002–; Legion of Merit (with 3 oak leaf clusters), Kt Commdr's Cross of the Order of Merit of the Fed. Repub. of Germany 2003; Defense Distinguished Service Medal, Distinguished Service Medal (with oak leaf cluster), Bronze Star Medal (with V device), Bronze Star Medal (with oak leaf cluster), Purple Heart, Meritorious Service Medal (with 3 oak leaf clusters), Air Medal and other mil. medals and badges; Outstanding Achievement Award, North Carolina Tech. Asscn 2006. *Address:* MPRI Inc., International Group, 1201 East Abingdon Drive, Suite 425, Alexandria, VA 22314, USA (office). *Telephone:* (703) 684-0853 (office). *Website:* www.mpri .com/main/internationalgroup.html (office).

KERR, David Nicol Sharp, CBE, MSc, FRCP, FRCPE; British physician; *Vice-President, National Kidney Research Fund;* b. 27 Dec. 1927, London; s. of William Kerr and Elsie Ransted; m. (Mary) Eleanor Jones 1960; two s. one d.; ed George Watson's Boys' School and Univs of Edinburgh and Wisconsin;

Surgeon-Lt RNVR 1953–55; Surgeon Lt-Commdr RNR 1993–95; Prof. of Medicine, Univ. of Newcastle-upon-Tyne 1968–83; Dean, Royal Postgrad. Medical School 1984–91; Prof. of Renal Medicine, Univ. of London 1986–93, Prof. Emer. 1993–; medical adviser and trustee Nat. Kidney Research Fund 1999–2003, Chair. 2000–03, Vice-Pres. 2003–; Postgrad. Medical Adviser, North Thames Regional Health Authority, later Nat. Health Service (NHS) Exec. N Thames Regional Office 1991–97; Medical Awards Admin. Commonwealth Scholarships Comm. 1993–98; Ed. Journal of Royal Coll. of Physicians 1994–98; mem. Council, British Heart Foundation 1991–97; Hon. consultant renal physician, Hammersmith Hosp.; Volhard Medal (German Medical Foundation), Distinguished Overseas Medal (Nat. Kidney Foundation of USA) etc. *Publications:* Oxford Textbook of Clinical Nephrology (ed.); other books, book sections and articles in professional journals. *Leisure interests:* walking, theatre, opera, church. *Address:* 22 Carbery Avenue, London, W3 9AL, England (home); National Kidney Research Fund, Kings Chambers, Priestgate, Peterborough, PE1 1FG, England (office). *Telephone:* (20) 8992-3231 (home); (1733) 704-664 (office). *Fax:* (20) 8992-3231; (1733) 704-660 (office). *E-mail:* enquiries@nkrf.org.uk (office); DNSKerr@aol.com (home). *Website:* www.nkrf.org.uk (office).

KERR, Philip Ballantyne, LLM; British writer; b. 22 Feb. 1956, Edinburgh, Scotland; s. of William Kerr and Ann Brodie; m. Jane Thynne 1991; two s. one d.; ed Northampton Grammar School and Birmingham Univ.; film critic, New Statesman; Prix de Romans L'Aventures, Deutsches Krimi Prize. *Play:* Bluesbreakers 2002. *Publications:* adult fiction: March Violets 1989, The Pale Criminal 1990, The Penguin Book of Lies (ed.) 1990, A German Requiem 1991, A Philosophical Investigation 1992, The Penguin Book of Fights, Feuds, and Heartfelt Hatreds: An Anthology of Antipathy (ed.) 1992, Dead Meat 1993, Gridiron (aka The Grid) 1993, Esau 1996, A Five-Year Plan 1997, The Second Angel 1998, The Shot 1999, Dark Matter 2002, The One from the Other 2007; juvenile fiction (as P.B. Kerr): Children of the Lamp: The Akhenaten Adventure 2004, Children of the Lamp: The Blue Djinn of Babylon 2005, A Quiet Flame 2007. *Leisure interest:* cinema. *Address:* A. P. Watt Literary Agents, 20 John Street, London, WC1N 2DR, England (office). *Telephone:* (20) 7405-6774 (office). *Fax:* (20) 7430-1952 (office). *Website:* www.apwatt.co.uk (office); www.pbkerr.com. *E-mail:* pbk@pbkerr.com.

KERR OF KINLOCHARD, Baron (Life Peer), cr. 2004, of Kinlochard in Perth and Kinross; **John Olav Kerr,** GCMG, BA; British business executive, fmr diplomatist and fmr international public servant; *Deputy Chairman, Royal Dutch Shell plc;* b. 22 Feb. 1942, Grantown-on-Spey, Scotland; s. of the late Dr Kerr and Mrs J. D. O. Kerr; m. Elizabeth Kalaugher 1965; two s. three d.; ed Glasgow Acad. and Pembroke Coll., Oxford; entered diplomatic service 1966; served Moscow and Rawalpindi; Pvt. Sec. to Perm. Under-Sec. FCO 1974–79; Head DM1 Div. HM Treasury 1979–81; Prin. Pvt. Sec. to Chancellor of Exchequer 1981–84; Head of Chancery, Washington, DC 1984–87; Asst Under-Sec. of State, FCO 1987–90; Amb. and Perm. Rep. of UK to EC (now EU), Brussels 1990–95; Amb. to USA 1995–97; Perm. Under-Sec. of State and Head of HM Diplomatic Service 1997–2002; Sec.-Gen. European Convention 2002; mem. House of Lords 2004–; EU Select Cttee 2006–; Deputy Chair. Royal Dutch Shell plc 2005–; Dir Scottish American Investment Co. 2002–, Shell Transport and Trading 2003–05, Rio Tinto Ltd 2003–, Rio Tinto plc 2003–, Scottish Power 2007–; Trustee, Rhodes Trust, Oxford, Nat. Gallery, London, Fulbright Comm., Carnegie Trust for the Univs of Scotland; mem. Council Centre for European Reform, Business for New Europe; Chair. of Court and Council, Imperial Coll. London 2006–; Hon. LLD (St Andrews) 1996, (Glasgow) 1999. *Address:* House of Lords, Westminster, London, SW1A 0PW, England (office). *Telephone:* (20) 7219-5353 (office).

KERREY, J. Robert (Bob), BS; American university administrator and fmr politician; *President, The New School;* b. 27 Aug. 1943, Lincoln, Neb.; s. of James Kerrey and Elinor Kerrey; m. 1st; one s. one d.; m. 2nd Sarah Paley 2001; one s.; ed Univ. of Nebraska; served in USN in Viet Nam 1966–69; Owner and Founder of Grandmother's Skillet Restaurant outlets in Omaha and Lincoln, Neb. 1972–75; Owner and Founder of fitness enterprises, including Sun Valley Bowl and Prairie Life Fitness Center, Lincoln; Gov. of Neb. 1983–87; Pnr, Printon, Kane & Co. (law firm), Lincoln 1987; Senator from Neb. 1989–2001; Pres. The New School (fmrly New School Univ.), New York 2001–; mem. Nat. Comm. on Terrorist Attacks Upon the US (9/11 Comm.) 2004; Democrat; Dr hc (New York Law School); Medal of Honor; Bronze Star; Purple Heart; Robert L. Haig Award for Distinguished Public Service, New York State Bar Asscn, Distinguished Nebraskan Award. *Publications:* When I Was a Young Man: A Memoir 2002. *Address:* The New School, Johnson and Kaplan Building, 66 W 12th Street, New York, NY 10011, USA (office). *Telephone:* (212) 229-5600. *Website:* www.newschool.edu/admin/ pres/index.html.

KERRY, John Forbes, JD; American lawyer and politician; *Senator from Massachusetts;* b. 11 Dec. 1943, Denver; s. of Richard J. Kerry and Rosemary Kerry (née Forbes); m. 1st Julia S. Thorne 1970; two d.; m. 2nd Teresa Heinz Kerry 1995; ed Yale Univ. and Boston Coll.; served in USN 1966–70; called to Bar, Mass 1976; Nat. Co-ordinator, Vietnam Veterans Against the War 1969–71; Asst Dist Attorney, Middx Co., Mass 1976–79; Pnr, Kerry & Sragow (law firm), Boston 1979–82; Lt-Gov. of Mass 1982–84; Senator from Mass 1985–; unsuccessful Democratic cand. for US Pres. 2004; awarded Bronze Star, Silver Star, 3 Purple Hearts. *Publications:* The New Soldier 1971, The New War: The Web of Crime That Threatens America's Security 1997, This Moment on Earth (with Teresa Heinz Kerry) 2007. *Address:* 304 Russell Senate Office Building, Washington, DC 20510, USA (office). *Telephone:* (202) 224-2742 (office). *Fax:* (202) 224-8525 (office). *Website:* kerry.senate.gov (office).

KERTÉSZ, Imre; Hungarian writer and translator; b. 9 Nov. 1929, Budapest; m. 2nd Magda Kertész; deported to Auschwitz, then Buchenwald during World War II 1944; worked for newspaper Világosság, Budapest 1948–51 (dismissed when it adopted CP line); mil. service 1951–53; ind. writer and trans. of German authors such as Nietzsche, Schnitzler, Freud, Roth, Wittgenstein and Canetti 1953–; has also written theatre musicals; works have been translated into German, Spanish, French, English, Czech, Russian, Swedish and Hebrew; Brandenburg Literary Prize 1995, Leipzig Book Prize for European Understanding 1997, WELT-Literaturpreis 2000, Ehrenpreis der Robert-Bosch-Stiftung 2001, Hans-Sahl-Preis 2002, Nobel Prize in Literature 2002. *Publications include:* Sorstalanság (trans. as Fatelessness) (Jewish Quarterly Wingate Literary Prize 2006) (made into film 2005) 1975, A nyomkeresö (The Pathfinder) 1977, Detektívtörténet (Detective Story) 1977, A kudarc (Fiasco) 1988, Kaddis a meg nem születetett gyermekért (Kaddish for a Child not Born 1997) 1990, Az angol labogó (The English Flag) 1991, Gályanapló (Galley Diary) 1992, A Holocaust mint kultúra (The Holocaust as Culture) 1993, Jegyzökönyv 1993, Valaki más: a változás kró'nikája (I, Another: Chronicle of a Metamorphosis) 1997, A gondolatnyi csend, amig kivégzöoztag újratölt (Moment of Silence while the Execution Squad Reloads) 1998, A számüzött nyelv (The Exiled Language) 2001, Felszámolás: regény (Liquidation) 2003. *Address:* c/o Magvetõ Press, Balassi B.U. 7, 1055 Budapest, Hungary (office); c/o Northwestern University Press, 625 Colfax Street, Evanston, IL 60208-4210, USA (office).

KERTZER, David I., PhD; American historian, anthropologist, writer and academic; *Provost, Brown University;* b. 20 Feb. 1948, New York City; s. of Morris Kertzer and Julia Hoffman Kertzer; m. Susan; one d. one s.; ed Brown Univ., Brandeis Univ.; Asst Prof. of Anthropology, Bowdoin Coll. 1973–79, Assoc. Prof. 1979–84, Prof. 1984–89, William R. Kenan, Jr Prof. 1989–92, Chair. Dept of Sociology and Anthropology 1979–81, 1984–86, 1987–88, 1992; Paul Dupee, Jr Univ. Prof. of Social Science, Brown Univ. 1992–, also Prof. of Anthropology 1992–, of History 1992–2001, of Italian Studies 2001–, Provost Brown Univ. 2006–; Fulbright Sr Lecturer, Univ. of Catania 1978; Professore a contratto, Univ. of Bologna 1987; Visiting Fellow Trinity Coll., Cambridge, UK 1991; Visiting Scholar, Posthumous Inst. and Univ. of Amsterdam 1994; Visiting Dir of Studies, Ecole des Hautes Etudes en Sciences Sociales, Paris 1994; Prof. of Educ., American Acad. of Rome 1999; Fulbright Chair, Univ. of Bologna 2000; Visiting Prof., Ecole Normale Superieure, Paris 2002; guest lecturer at over 40 univs world-wide; Co-Founder and Co-Ed. Journal of Modern Italian Studies 1994–; Ed. Book Series: New Perspectives in Anthropological and Social Demography 1996–2007; Pres. Soc. for the Anthropology of Europe 1994–96; mem. Editorial Bd Social Science History 1987–96, 2001–04, Journal of Family History 1990–, Continuity and Change 1996–2000, Int. Studies Review 1998–2002; mem. Jury Lynton History Prize 2000–01; mem. Exec. Bd American Anthropological Asscn 1995–96, NIH Population Review Cttee 1996–99, Nat. Research Council Cttee on Population 1999–2005, German Marshall Fund Advisory Bd 2000–02; Vice-Pres. Social Science History Asscn 2005–06, Pres. 2006–07; Fellow, American Acad. of Arts and Sciences 2005–; Fellowship Center for Advanced Studies, Stanford 1982–83, Guggenheim Fellowship 1986, Nat. Endowment for the Humanities Fellowship 1995, Rockefeller Foundation Fellowship, Bellagio, Italy 2000. *Publications include:* Comrades and Christians: Religion and Political Struggle in Communist Italy 1980, Famiglia Contadina e Urbanizzazione 1981, Family Life in Central Italy 1880–1910: Sharecropping, Wage Labour and Coresidence (Marraro Prize, Soc. for Italian Historical Studies 1985) 1984, Ritual, Politics and Power 1988, Family, Political Economy and Demographic Change (Marraro 1990) 1989, Sacrificed for Honor: Italian Infant Abandonment and the Politics of Reproductive Control 1993, Politics and Symbols: The Italian Communist Party and the Fall of Communism, 1996, The Kidnapping of Edgardo Mortara (Nat. Jewish Book Award 1997, Best Books of the Year, Publishers Weekly, Toronto Globe and Mail 1997; stage version 'Edgard Mine' by Alfred Uhry premiered 2002) 1997, The Popes Against the Jews (UK edn The Unholy War 2002) 2001, Prisoner of the Vatican 2004, Amelia's Take 2008; contrib. to numerous nat. and state newspapers, contrib., ed. or co-ed. of numerous books, author of over 60 journal articles and 50 academic papers. *Address:* Office of the Provost, University Hall, Room 114, One Prospect Street, Box 1862, Brown University, Providence, RI 02912, USA (office). *Telephone:* (401) 863-2706 (office). *Fax:* (401) 863-1928 (office). *E-mail:* provost@brown.edu (office). *Website:* www .davidkertzer.com (office).

KERZNER, Solomon (Sol); South African business executive; *Chairman and CEO, Kerzner International Resorts Inc.;* b. 23 Aug. 1935, Johannesburg; s. of Morris Kerzner; two s. three d.; ed Athlons High School, Univ. of Witwatersrand; Founder and CEO Southern Sun Hotels 1969–83; CEO Sun Int. Hotels (now Kerzner Int. Resorts Inc.) 1983–87, Chair. and CEO 1993–, Pres. 1993–2003; Chair. World Leisure Group 1989–94; rep. Univ. of Witwatersrand for boxing and wrestling 1954–55; Inst. of Marketing Man. Marketing Award of the Year 1978–80, Jewish Businessman of the Year 1993, elected US Gaming Hall of Fame, Lifetime Achievement Award by FEDHASA, South Africa's major tourism agency. *Address:* Kerzner International Resorts, Inc., The Crown Building, 730 Fifth Avenue, Fifth Floor, New York, NY 10019, USA (office). *Telephone:* (212) 659-5184 (office). *Fax:* (212) 659-5201 (office). *E-mail:* MediaRelations@Kerzner.com (office). *Website:* www.kerzner.com (office).

KESHTMAND, Sultan Ali; Afghan politician; b. 1935; ed univ.; mem. of Hazara ethnic minority; Founder-mem. People's Democratic Party of Afghanistan (PDPA) and mem. Cen. Cttee 1965; with Parcham faction when PDPA split 1967; Minister of Planning April–Aug. 1978; tried on charges of conspiracy and sentenced to death 1978; sentence commuted by Pres. Amin. Oct. 1978; fmr Vice-Pres. of Revolutionary Council; Deputy Prime Minister and Minister of Planning after Soviet intervention 1979–81; Prime Minister of Afghanistan and Chair. Council of Ministers 1981–88, 1989–90; First Vice-Pres. 1990–91.

KESSLER, Heinz; Austrian banking executive; *President of the Supervisory Board, Erste Bank Group;* fmr CEO Erste Bank der österreichischen Sparkassen AG, Pres. Supervisory Bd 1998–; Chair. Nettingsdorfer Papierfabrik Man. AG, Reform-Werke Bauer & Co. GmbH, Reform-Werke Bauer & Co. Holding AG; Deputy Chair. Austria Versicherungsverein auf Gegenseitigkeit Privatstiftung, Duropack AG, Rath AG, UNIQA Versicherungen AG; mem. Die Erste österreichische Spar-Casse Privatstiftung. *Address:* Erste Bank der österreichischen Sparkassen AG, Graben 21, 1010 Vienna, Austria (office). *Telephone:* (50) 100-10100 (office). *Fax:* (50) 100-13112 (office). *E-mail:* investor.relations@erstebank.at (office). *Website:* www.erstebank.com/investorrelations (office).

KESSLER, Ronald, BA, MA, PhD; American sociologist and academic; *Professor of Health Care Policy, Harvard Medical School;* b. 26 April 1947, Bristol, Pa; m. Vicki Shahly; two s. two d.; ed Temple Univ., New York Univ., York Univ.; Pre-doctoral Fellow, Health Service Research, Montefiore Hosp., Bronx, New York 1972–74; Research Assoc., New York State Psychiatric Inst. 1975–76; Research Assoc., Center for Policy Research 1976–77; Postdoctoral Fellow, Dept of Psychiatry, Univ. of Wis. 1977–79; Asst Prof., Dept of Sociology, Univ. of Mich. 1979–81, Assoc. Prof., Dept of Sociology and Assoc. Research Scientist, Survey Research Center 1981–88, Prof., Dept of Sociology and Program Dir Survey Research Center 1988–96; Prof., Dept of Health Care Policy, Harvard Medical School 1996–; mem. Editorial Bd Journal of Health and Social Behavior 1978–81, 1992–94, Public Opinion Quarterly 1981–84, American Sociological Review 1982–85, 1989–92, Sociological Methods and Research 1983–, Psychological Medicine 1994–, Women's Health: Research on Gender, Behavior, and Policy 1994–, Psychological Methods 1996–, Journal of Evaluation in Clinical Practice 1997–, International Journal of Methods in Psychiatric Research 1998–, Health Services Research 1998–, Journal of Affective Disorders 2003–, Culture, Medicine and Psychiatry 2003–, Archives of General Psychiatry 2003–, Psychiatry and Clinical Neurosciences 2004–, Journal of Health & Productivity 2006–; mem. Scientific Advisory Bd Anxiety Disorders Asscn of America 2000–05, Nat. Depressive and Manic-Depressive Asscn 2001–, Nat. Alliance for the Mentally Ill Scientific Council 2003–; mem. Medical Advisory Bd Jed Foundation 2005–; mem. Inst. of Medicine 1999, American Sociological Asscn, American Public Health Asscn, Sociological Research Asscn, Society of Behavioral Medicine Research; Fellow, American Psychopathological Asscn; Hon. Fellow, American Psychiatric Asscn 1999; Research Scientist Devt Award, Nat. Inst. of Mental Health (NIMH) 1984–94, NIMH MERIT Award 1987–97, NIMH Research Scientist Award 1995–99, Paul Hoch Award, American Psychopathological Asscn 1997, Rema Lapouse Mental Health Epidemiology Award, American Public Health Asscn 1997, Presidential Citation, American Psychological Asscn 2005. *Publications:* Linear Panel Analysis: Models of Quantitative Change (co-author) 1981, Television and Aggression: A Panel Study (co-author) 1982, Methodological Issues in AIDS Behavioral Research (co-ed.) 1993, Measuring Stress: A Guide for Health and Social Scientists (co-ed.) 1995, How Healthy Are We?: A National Study of WellBeing at Midlife (co-ed.) 2003, Health and Work Productivity: Making the Business Case for Quality Health Care (co-ed.) 2006; numerous articles in medical journals. *Address:* Department of Health Care Policy, Harvard Medical School, 180 Longwood Avenue, Boston, MA 02115-5899, USA (office). *Telephone:* (617) 630-8043 (home); (617) 432-3587 (office). *Fax:* (617) 432-3588 (office). *E-mail:* kessler@hcp.med.harvard.edu (office). *Website:* www.hcp.med.harvard.edu (office).

KESTELMAN, Sara; British actress; b. 12 May 1944, London; d. of late Morris Kestelman and Dorothy Mary Creagh; ed Cen. School of Speech and Drama; joined Liverpool Playhouse; subsequently moved to Library Theatre, Manchester; roles included Abigail in The Crucible and Cecily in The Importance of Being Earnest; joined Royal Shakespeare Co. (RSC) 1969; roles for RSC included Mariana in Measure for Measure, Jessie Tate in The Silver Tassle, Margaret in Much Ado About Nothing, Cassandra in Troilus and Cressida, Natasha in Subject to Fits, Titania in A Midsummer Night's Dream and Cleopatra in Gorky's Enemies; other stage appearances have included Messalina in I Claudius (Queen's Theatre, London), Lady Macbeth and Ruth in The Homecoming (Birmingham Repertory Theatre), Prudence in Plunder and Ilyena in Uncle Vanya (Bristol Old Vic), Nine (Donmar) 1996, Hamlet 2000. *Films include:* Zardoz 1974, Lisztomania 1975, Break of Day 1977, Lady Jane 1986, Star Wars: Knights of the Old Republic II: The Sith Lords (voice) 2004, Ex Memoria 2006. *Television includes:* Jack Flea's Birthday Celebration 1975, Under Western Eyes 1975, Kean 1978, The Walls of Jericho (miniseries) 1980, Lady Windermere's Fan 1985, Somewhere to Run 1989, The Last Romantics 1991, Cabaret 1993, Brazen Hussies 1996, The History of Tom Jones, a Foundling (miniseries) 1997, Invasion: Earth (miniseries) 1998, The Going Wrong 1998, Anna Karenina (miniseries) 2000, Mind Games 2001, Trial and Retribution VII 2003, Trial and Retribution VIII 2004; appearances in series Dixon of Dock Green 1996, The Rivals of Sherlock Holmes 1973, The New Avengers 1976, Bergerac 1981, Van der Valk 1991, Kavanagh QC 1997, Relic Hunter 2000, Casualty 2004, Midsomer Murders 2005, Instinct 2007. *Publication:* A Two Hander (poems, with Susan Penhaligon) 1996. *Leisure interests:* drawing, photography, writing.

KESWICK, Sir (John) Chippendale (Chips) Lindley, Kt; British merchant banker; b. 2 Feb. 1940; s. of the late Sir William Keswick and of Mary Lindley; brother of Henry N. L. Keswick and Simon L. Keswick; m. Lady Sarah Ramsay 1966; three s.; ed Eton Coll., Univ. of Aix-Marseilles; with Glyn Mills & Co. 1961–65; Jt Vice-Chair. Hambros PLC 1986, Jt Deputy Chair. 1990–97, Group Chief Exec. 1995–97; Chair. Hambros Bank Ltd 1986–95,

Chair. (non-exec.) 1995–98, Chair. Hambros PLC 1997–98; Sr Banking and Capital Markets Adviser Société Générale 1998–; mem. Bd of Dirs Persimmon PLC 1984–, De Beers 1993–, Bank of England 1993–2000, Edin. Investment Trust PLC 1992–, IMI PLC 1994–, Anglo American Corpn of S Africa Ltd 1995; Vice-Counsellor Cancer Research Campaign 1992–; Sr Ind. Dir Investec Ltd 2002–; Hon. Treas. Children's Country Holidays Fund; mem. Queen's Body Guard for Scotland, Royal Co. of Archers 1976–. *Leisure interests:* bridge, country pursuits. *Address:* c/o Board of Directors, Investec Limited, 100 Grayston Drive, 2nd Floor, Sandown Sandton, Gauteng 2196, South Africa; 17 Charterhouse Street, London, EC1N 6RA (office). *Telephone:* (20) 7430-3553 (office). *Fax:* (20) 7430-8670 (office).

KESWICK, Henry Neville Lindley; British business executive; *Chairman, Jardine Matheson Holdings Limited;* b. 29 Sept. 1938; s. of the late Sir William Keswick and of Mary Lindley; a brother of Sir (John) Chippendale Keswick (and of Simon Lindley Keswick q.v.); m. Lady Tessa Reay 1985; ed Eton Coll., Univ. of Cambridge; Nat. Service 1956–58; joined Matheson & Co. 1961, Chair. 1975–, mem. Bd Dirs Jardine Matheson Holdings Ltd, Hong Kong 1967–, Chair. 1972–75, 1989–, Jardine Strategic Holdings 1989– (Dir 1988–); Dir Sun Alliance and London Insurance PLC 1975–96, Sun Alliance Group PLC 1989, Deputy Chair. 1993–96, Dir Royal and Sun Alliance Insurance Group PLC 1996–2000; mem. Bd of Dirs Robert Fleming Holdings Ltd 1975–2000, Rothmans Int. 1988–94, Hongkong Land Co. 1988–, Mandarin Oriental Int. 1988–, Dairy Farm Int. Holdings 1988–, The Daily Telegraph 1990–2001, Hong Kong Land, Mandarin Oriental, Rothschilds Continuation Holdings; Chair. Hong Kong Asscn 1988–2001, now Vice-Chair.; mem. 21st Century Trust 1987–97; Propr The Spectator 1975–81; Trustee, Nat. Portrait Gallery 1982–2001 (Chair. 1994–2001). *Leisure interest:* country pursuits.

KESWICK, Simon Lindley, FRSA; British business executive; *Chairman, Hongkong Land Holdings Ltd;* b. 20 May 1942; s. of the late Sir William Keswick and of Mary Lindley; brother of Henry Neville Lindley Keswick and Sir John Chippendale Lindley Keswick (q.v.); m. Emma Chetwode 1971; two s. two d.; ed Eton Coll. and Trinity Coll., Cambridge; Dir Fleetways Holdings Ltd, Australia 1970–72, Greenfriar Investment Co. 1979–82; Dir Matheson & Co. Ltd 1978–82, Chair. Jardine Matheson Insurance Brokers 1978–82, Dir Jardine Matheson & Co. Ltd, Hong Kong 1972–, Man. Dir 1982, Chair. 1983–89, Jardine Matheson Holdings Ltd 1984–89 (Dir 1972–), Jardine Strategic Holdings Ltd 1987–89, (Dir 1987–), Jardine Int. Motor Holdings 1990–97; Chair. Hongkong Land Holdings Ltd 1983–, Hongkong & Shanghai Banking Corpn 1983–88, Mandarin Oriental Int. Ltd 1984–, Dairy Farm Int. Holdings Ltd 1984–, Fleming Mercantile Investment Trust 1990– (Dir 1988–), Trafalgar House PLC 1993–96; Dir Hanson PLC 1991–, Jardine Lloyd Thomson Group PLC 2001–; Dir (non-exec.) Wellcome 1995–; Trustee, British Museum 1989–. *Leisure interests:* country pursuits, Tottenham Hotspur Football Club. *Address:* Rockcliffe, Upper Slaughter, Cheltenham, Glos., GL54 2JW, England; May Tower 1, 5–7 May Road, Hong Kong Special Administrative Region; Hongkong Land Ltd, 8th Floor, One Exchange Square, Central, Hong Kong Special Administrative Region, People's Republic of China (office). *Telephone:* (1451) 30648 (England); 2842-8428 (Hong Kong) (office). *Fax:* 2845-9226 (Hong Kong) (office). *E-mail:* gpobox@hkland.com (office). *Website:* www.hkland.com (office).

KESWICK, Hon. Tessa; British administrator and fmr civil servant; *Deputy Chairman, Centre for Policy Studies;* b. (Annabel Therese Fraser), 15 Oct. 1942, Beauly, Scotland; d. of 15th Lord Lovat and Rosamund Broughton; m. 1st Lord Reay 1964 (divorced 1978); two s. one d.; m. 2nd Henry Keswick (q.v.) 1985; ed Sacred Heart Convent, Woldingham, Surrey; Conservative Councillor, Royal Borough of Kensington and Chelsea 1982–86; Conservative cand. for Inverness 1987; special policy adviser to Rt Hon. Kenneth Clarke (q.v.) at Dept of Health 1989, Dept of Educ., Home Office, Treasury –1995; Dir Centre for Policy Studies 1995–2004, Deputy Chair. Centre for Policy Studies 2004–; Fellow, King's Coll. London. *Leisure interests:* art, music, breeding horses. *Address:* Centre for Policy Studies, 57 Tufton Street, London, SW1P 3QL, England (office). *Telephone:* (20) 7222-4488 (office). *Fax:* (20) 7222-4388 (office). *E-mail:* tessa@cps.org.uk (office). *Website:* www.cps.org.uk (office).

KETO, Aila, AO; Australian conservationist and academic; *President, Australian Rainforest Conservation Society Inc.;* b. Tully, Queensland; m. Keith Scott; Adjunct Prof., School of Agronomy and Horticulture, Univ. of Queensland 2002–; helped develop Centre for Native Floriculture at Univ. of Queensland Gatton; Co-founder and Pres. Rainforest Conservation Soc. (now Australian Rainforest Conservation Soc. Inc.) 1982–; helped negotiate SE Queensland Forests Agreement with Queensland Govt, conservation groups and Queensland Timber Bd 1999; Hon. Life mem. Australian Conservation Foundation 1990; Hon. DSc (Queensland) 2003; BHP Bicentennial Award for the Pursuit of Excellence (Environment), Advance Australia Foundation Award, UNEP Global 500 Roll of Honour 1988, Avon Spirit of Achievement Award, World Class Achievers, Telecom Australia, Golden Gecko Award, Gold Coast and Hinterland Environment Council 1990, Special Award for Outstanding Environmental Achievement, Sunshine Coast Environment Council 1990, Fred M. Parkard Int. Parks Merit Award, Int. Union for Conversation of Nature 1992, Queenslander of the Year Award 2000, Premier's Millennium Award for Excellence 2000, Centenary Medal 2003, selected as a Queensland Great 2005, Volvo Environment Prize (co-recipient) 2005. *Achievements include:* work led to protection of more than 1.5 million hectares of Queensland's rainforest; helped achieve closure of rainforest timber industry in North Queensland 1987, and subsequent end of all rainforest-logging on Queensland public land 1994; negotiated Springbrook Rescue programme 2006, Delbessie Agreement 2008. *Publications:* numerous publs in scientific journals. *Address:* Australian Rainforest Conservation Society, 19 Colorado Avenue, Bardon, Queensland 4065, Australia (office). *Telephone:* (7) 33681318 (office). *Fax:* (7) 33683938 (office). *E-mail:* aila.keto@rainforest.org.au (office). *Website:* www.rainforest.org.au (office).

KETTANI, M. Ali, PhD; Moroccan electrical engineer and academic; b. 27 Sept. 1941, Fez; m.; four c.; ed Swiss Fed. Inst. of Tech., Geneva and Lausanne Univs., Carnegie Mellon Univ.; instructor, Ecole d'Ingenieurs, Rabat 1964; Asst Prof., Electrical Eng Dept, Univ. of Pittsburgh 1966–68; Assoc. Prof., Electrical Eng Dept, Univ. of Riyadh 1968–69, Univ. of Petroleum and Minerals, Dhahran 1969–73, Head of Dept 1972–74, Prof. 1973–82; Visiting Prof., MIT 1975–76; Dir Gen. Islamic Foundation for Science, Tech. and Devt 1981–89; Fellow, Sec. Gen. Islamic Acad. of Sciences 1986–94, Vice-Pres. 1994–; f. Ibn Rushd Int. Islamic Univ., Córdoba; mem. Bd Int. Fed. of Insts of Advanced Studies, Stockholm; mem. Energy Research Group, Ottawa, Exec. Cttee Islamic Educ., Science and Culture Org. 1982–86, Arab Thought Forum, Amman. *Publications:* 12 books in English and Arabic and more than 150 articles on energy issues. *Address:* Academy of the Kingdom of Morocco, Charia Imam Malik, Km 10 B.P., 1380 Rabat, Morocco. *Telephone:* (3) 7755199 (office). *Fax:* (3) 7755101 (office). *E-mail:* alacademia@iam.net.ma (office).

KETTERLE, Wolfgang, MSc, PhD; German physicist and academic; *John D. MacArthur Professor of Physics, Massachusetts Institute of Technology;* b. 21 Oct. 1957, Heidelberg; m., divorced; three c.; ed Univ. of Heidelberg, Tech. Univ. of Munich, Univ. of Munich, Max-Planck Inst. for Quantum Optics, Garching; Research Asst, Max-Planck Inst. for Quantum Optics, Garching 1982–85, Staff Scientist 1985–88; Research Scientist, Dept of Physical Chem., Univ. of Heidelberg 1989–90; Research Assoc., Dept of Physics, MIT, Mass. 1990–93, Asst Prof. of Physics 1993–97, Prof. of Physics 1997–98, John D. MacArthur Prof. of Physics 1998–; Fellow, American Physical Soc. 1997, American Acad. of Arts and Sciences 1999, Inst. of Physics 2002, Optical Soc. of America 2006; mem. German Physical Soc., Optical Soc. of America, European Acad. of Sciences and Arts 2002, Acad. of Sciences in Heidelberg 2002, Bavarian Acad. of Sciences 2003, German Acad. of Natural Scientists Leopoldina 2005; Foreign Assoc., NAS 2002; Officier, Légion d'honneur 2002, Medal of Merit of the State of Baden-Würtemburg (Germany) 2002, Kt Commdr's Cross (Badge and Star), Order of Merit (Germany) 2002; Michael and Philip Platzman Award, MIT 1994, David and Lucille Packard Fellowship 1996, Gustav-Hertz Prize, German Physical Soc. 1997, Rabi Prize, American Physical Soc. 1997, Discover Magazine Award for Tech. Innovation 1998, Fritz London Prize 1999, Dannie-Heineman Prize, German Acad. of Sciences 1999, Benjamin Franklin Medal in Physics (jt recipient) 2000, Nobel Prize in Physics (jt recipient) 2001, Killian Award, MIT 2004. *Address:* 80 Clifton Street, Belmont, MA 02478 (home); Massachusetts Institute of Technology, Room 26–243, 77 Massachusetts Avenue, Cambridge, MA 02139, USA (office). *Telephone:* (617) 489-2421 (home); (617) 253-6815 (office). *Fax:* (617) 253-4876 (office). *E-mail:* ketterle@mit.edu (office). *Website:* cua.mit.edu/ketterle_group (home).

KEUTCHA, Jean; Cameroonian politician, civil servant and diplomatist; b. June 1923, Bangangté; m.; three c.; ed École supérieure d'agriculture de Yaoundé; Chef de Cabinet, Minister of State with Special Responsibilities 1957, subsequently Chef de Cabinet, Sec. of State with responsibility for Information, Posts and Telecommunications; Asst to Chief of Bamiléké Region 1959; Sub-Prefect, Bafoussam 1960; Prefect of Mifi, subsequently of Menoua 1962–64; Sec. of State for Public Works 1964, subsequently Sec. of State for Rural Devt and Sec. of State for Educ.; Minister of Foreign Affairs 1971–72, 1975–80, of Agric. 1972–75; Amb. to EEC 1984–85, to People's Repub. of China 1985–88; Pres. Caisse nationale de réassurances (CNR); Commdr, Ordre Camerounais de la Valeur, Grand Officier, Légion d'honneur, Grand Officier de l'Ordre Nat. Gabonais, etc. *Publication:* Le Guide pratique pour la taille du Cafétier Arabica. *Address:* Caisse nationale de réassurances, avenue Foch, BP 4180, Yaoundé, Cameroon. *Telephone:* 22-37-99. *Fax:* 23-36-80.

KÉVÉS, György; Hungarian architect; *President, Kévés Architects Inc.;* b. 20 March 1935, Osi; s. of Sándor Kévés and Ványi Piroska; m. Éva Földvári 1966; ed Tech. Univ., Budapest; designer for firms, Agroterv and Eliti, Budapest 1959–61, Iparterv, Budapest 1961–69, Studio 'R' 1983–; private practice with Éva Földvári 1966–; teacher, Faculty of Architecture, Tech. Univ., Budapest 1966–73; Sr Architect and Prof., Architectural Masterschool, Budapest 1974–; with Káva Architects 1987–, Kévés Architects Inc.; organizes confs and exhbns Masterschool, including exhbns of post-modern architecture and Mario Bottá's works 1980–; organized lectures by Rob Krier and Mario Bottá, Hungary 1980; Visiting Lecturer, Washington Univ., St Louis, USA 1981; exhbns: Budapest, Milano Triennale 1973, Stuttgart 1977, Canada 1978, Washington Univ. St Louis 1983; Ybl Prize, Hungarian State Prize, several first prizes in architecture competitions. *Major works include:* Orczy Forum City Centre, Budapest. *Publications include:* Architecture of the 70s, Architecture of the 20th century; numerous articles in architectural magazines. *Leisure interest:* all kinds of art. *Address:* Kévés és Építésztársai Rt., Melinda u. 21, 1121 Budapest, Hungary. *Telephone:* (1) 275-6002 (office). *Fax:* (1) 395-7623 (office). *E-mail:* kava21@axelero.hu.

KEY, John, BComm; New Zealand politician; *Prime Minister;* b. 9 Aug. 1961, Auckland; m. Bronagh Key; two c.; ed Burnside High School, Univ. of Canterbury; early career as investment banker in mid 1980s, then worked in Singapore, London and Sydney for Merrill Lynch in 1990s; mem. Foreign Exchange Cttee Fed. Reserve Bank of New York 1999–2001; returned to New Zealand 2001; mem. Parl. (Nat. Party) for Helensville 2002–, Nat. Party Deputy Finance Spokesman 2002–04, Finance Spokesman 2004-06, Leader 2006–; Prime Minister of New Zealand 2008–. *Address:* Parliament Buildings, Molesworth Street, Wellington 6011 New Zealand (office). *Telephone:* (4) 471-9307 (office). *Fax:* (4) 473-3689 (office). *E-mail:* john.key@national.org.nz (office); john.key@parliament.govt.nz (office). *Website:* www.national.org.nz (office); www.johnkey.co.nz (home).

KEYFITZ, Nathan, PhD, FRSC; American demographer and academic; *Professor Emeritus, Harvard University;* b. 29 June 1913, Montreal, Canada; s. of Arthur Keyfitz and Anna Keyfitz (née Gerstein); m. Beatrice Orkin 1939; one s. one d.; ed McGill Univ. and Univ. of Chicago, USA; Statistician, then Sr Research Statistician, Dominion Bureau of Statistics, Ottawa 1936–56; Lecturer in Sociology, McGill Univ. 1948–51; Adviser to Indonesian Planning Bureau, Jakarta 1952–53; Prof. of Sociology, Univ. of Montreal 1962–63, Univ. of Toronto 1959–63, Univ. of Chicago 1963–68, Chair. Dept of Sociology 1965–67; Prof. of Demography, Univ. of Calif., Berkeley 1968–72; Andelot Prof. of Sociology and Demography, Harvard Univ. 1972–83, Prof. Emer. 1983–, Chair. Dept of Sociology 1978–80; Lazarus Prof. of Social Demography, Ohio State Univ. 1981–83, Prof. Emer. 1983–; Visiting Fellow Statistics Canada 1983–; Leader Population Programme, Deputy Dir, Int. Inst. for Applied Systems Analysis, Laxenburg, Austria 1984–93; Consultant, Dept of Finance, Jakarta, Indonesia 1984–90; researcher Initiatives on Children, American Acad. of Arts and Sciences 1994–2000; mem. NAS, Int. Statistical Inst.; Fellow American Statistical Asscn; Pres. Population Asscn of America 1970; Life Trustee, Nat. Opinion Research Center; Hon. mem. Canadian Statistical Soc. 1980–; Hon. MA (Harvard), Hon. LLD (Western Ont., Montreal, McGill, Alberta, Edmonton, Siena, Carleton). *Publications:* Applied Mathematical Demography 1985, Introduction to the Mathematics of Population 1977, Population Change and Social Policy 1982, World Population Growth and Aging (jtly) 1990. *Leisure interests:* computers, foreign languages. *Address:* 1580 Massachusetts Avenue, Apt. 7C, Cambridge, MA 02138, USA (home). *Telephone:* (617) 491 2845 (home).

KEYNES, Richard Darwin, CBE, MA, PhD, ScD, FRS; British physiologist and fmr academic; b. 14 Aug. 1919, London; s. of the late Sir Geoffrey Keynes and Margaret Elizabeth Darwin; m. Anne Pinsent Adrian; four s. (one deceased); ed Oundle School and Trinity Coll., Cambridge; Temporary Experimental Officer, Anti-Submarine Establishment and Admiralty Signals Establishment 1940–45; Demonstrator, later Lecturer in Physiology, Univ. of Cambridge 1949–60; Research Fellow, Trinity Coll., Cambridge 1948–52; Fellow of Peterhouse, Cambridge and Dir of Studies in Medicine 1952–60, Hon. Fellow 1989–; Head of Physiology Dept, Agricultural Research Council Inst. of Animal Physiology, Babraham 1960–65, Dir Inst. 1965–73; Prof. of Physiology, Univ. of Cambridge 1973–86; first person to trace movements of sodium and potassium during transmission of nerve impulses; Sec.-Gen. Int. Union for Pure and Applied Biophysics 1972–78, Vice-Pres. 1978–81, Pres. 1981–84; Chair. ICSU/UNESCO Int. Biosciences Networks 1982–93; Pres. Fed. European Physiological Socs 1991–94; Foreign mem. Royal Danish Acad. 1971, American Philosophical Soc. 1977, American Acad. of Arts and Sciences 1978, Acad. Brasileira de Ciências 1995; Fellow, Churchill Coll. Cambridge 1961–, Eton Coll. 1963–78; Ordem Nacional do Mérito Científico (Brazil) 1997; Dr hc (Brazil) 1968, (Rouen) 1995, (Nairobi) 1999. *Publications:* The Beagle Record (ed.) 1979, Nerve and Muscle (with D. J. Aidley) 1981, Charles Darwin's Beagle Diary 1988, Lydia and Maynard: the letters between Lydia Lopokova and John Maynard Keynes (co-ed.) 1989, Charles Darwin's Zoology Notes and Specimen Lists from HMS Beagle 2000, Fossils, Finches and Fuegians: Charles Darwin's Adventures and Discoveries on the Beagle, 1832–1836 2002. *Leisure interest:* pre-Columbian antiquities. *Address:* 4 Herschel Road, Cambridge, CB3 9AG, England (home). *Telephone:* (1223) 353107 (home). *E-mail:* rdk12@cam.ac.uk (home).

KEYS, Alicia; American singer, songwriter and musician (piano); b. 25 Jan. 1981, New York; ed Professional Performing Arts School, Manhattan; classically trained pianist; solo artist; numerous live appearances, festivals; collaborations with Angie Stone, Jimmy Cozier; Grammy Awards for Best New Artist 2001, for Song of the Year, Best Female R&B Vocal Performance, Best R&B Song (all for Fallin') 2001, for Best R&B Song (for You Don't Know My Name) 2005, for Best Female R&B Vocal Performance (for No One) 2008, (for Superwoman) 2009, American Music Award Favorite New Artist, Pop/Rock, Favourite New Artist, Soul/R&B 2002, MTV Award Best R&B Act 2002, American Music Award for Best Female Soul/R&B Artist 2004, Source Hip Hop Music Award for Female Artist of the Year 2004, MTV Award for Best R&B Video 2005, Lady of Soul Award for Best R&B/Soul or Rap Song (for If I Ain't Got You) 2005, MTV Europe Music Award for Best R&B 2005, Image Awards for Top Female Musical Artist, for Best Song, for Best Video (for Unbreakable) 2006, World Music Award for Best R&B Act 2008. *Recordings include:* albums: Songs In A Minor (Grammy Award for Best R&B Album 2001, MOBO Award for Best Album 2002) 2001, The Diary of Alicia Keys (Grammy Award for Best R&B Album 2005) 2003, Unplugged 2005, As I Am 2007. *Films:* Smokin' Aces 2006, The Nanny Diaries 2007, The Secret Life of Bees 2008. *Address:* William Morris Agency, 1325 Avenue of the Americas, New York, NY 10019, USA (office). *Telephone:* (212) 586-5100 (office). *Fax:* (212) 246-3583 (office). *Website:* www.wma.com (office); www.aliciakeys.net.

KEZERASHVILI, Davit; Georgian politician and government official; b. 22 Sept. 1978, Tbilisi; m.; two s.; ed Ivane Javakhishvili Tbilisi State Univ.; Sr Inspector, Penitentiary Dept, Ministry of Justice April–Sept. 2001; Head of Information and Analysis Div., Dept of Informatics, Ministry of Justice 2001–02; Asst to Chair. Tbilisi City Council 2002–04; Head of Finance Police, Ministry of Finance 2004–06; Minister of Defence 2006–08. *Address:* c/o Ministry of Defence, 0112 Tbilisi, Gen. Kvinitadze 20, Georgia.

KHACHATRIAN, Vardan; Armenian politician; *Minister of Finance and the Economy;* b. 6 April 1959, Jermuk City; m.; two c.; ed Yerevan Polytech. Inst., Moscow Supreme Tech. Univ.; engineer Mineral Waters of Armenia Industrial Union 1980–83, Yerevan Polytech. Inst. 1983–85; Sr Engineer in Tech. Div., Div. Head, then Head of Production Tech. Div., Industrial Bakery Union of Armenia 1985–90; Workshop Head in Zovk Production Unit, then Dir Zovk Factory, Food Ministry of ASSR 1990–92; mem. Privatization Cttee, Repub. of Armenia 1992–95; mem. Nat. Ass. and Deputy Head Standing Cttee for Finance, Credit, Fiscal and Econ. Affairs 1995–98, Head Standing Cttee 1999–2000; Head of Finance, Budgetary Dept, Ministry of Defence 1998–99; Minister of Finance and the Economy 2000–. *Address:* Ministry of Finance and the Economy, Melik-Adamian St 1, 375010 Yerevan, Armenia (office). *Telephone:* (10) 52-70-82 (office). *Fax:* (10) 52-37-45 (office). *Website:* mfe.gov.am (office).

KHACHATRYAN, Armen; Armenian politician and philologist; b. 13 Aug. 1957, Yerevan; s. of Avag Khachatryan and Johanna Hovakimyan; m. Larisa Khachatryan; one s. two d.; ed Yerevan State Pedagogical Inst.; Instructor, Shaumyan Regional CP Cttee and Yerevan City Comsomol Cttee 1981–87; Dir Yerevan School 191 1987–90; Founder and Vice-Pres. for Science and Educ. Yerevan Univ. of Hrachya Asharyan, Prof. 1991–99; elected Deputy and apptd Speaker, Nat. Ass. 1999–2002, also fmr Chair. Standing Cttee on Foreign Relations; Prof. and Academician, New York Acad. of Sciences; est. Barcelona restaurant 2004; Sodruzhestvo Award, Council Inter-Parl. Ass. of CIS 2001; Saint Andreas Order, Patriarch of Constantinople. *Address:* c/o National Assembly, 19 M. Baghramyan Avenue, 375095 Yerevan, Armenia (office).

KHADDAM, Abd al-Halim; Syrian lawyer and politician; *Leader, National Salvation Front in Syria;* b. 15 Sept. 1932, Baniyas; early career as lawyer in Damascus 1954–64; Gov. of Damascus 1967–69; Minister of the Economy and Foreign Trade 1969–70; Deputy Prime Minister and Minister of Foreign Affairs 1970–84; mem. Regional Command, Baath Party 1971–84; Vice-Pres. for Political and Foreign Affairs 1984–2005 (resgnd); moved to Paris 2005; charged with treason by Syrian Parl. and expelled from Baath Party, announced govt-in-exile 2006; Founding Assembly Mem. and Leader, Nat. Salvation Front in Syria, opposition group based in Washington, DC. *E-mail:* info@SaveSyria.org. *Website:* www.savesyria.org.

KHADER, Naser, MA; Danish politician; *Leader, Ny Alliance;* b. 1 July 1963, Damascus, Syria; s. of Ahmed Khader and Sada Abu Khader; ed univs of Copenhagen, Århus, Odense; worked as Arabic interpreter and trans. 1983–98; trans. and consultant, Radio Denmark 1989–97; consultant for DAB (housing soc.) 1996–97; mem. Social Liberal Party 1984–2007, mem. Cen. Bd 1996–2007; mem. Parl. for Western Copenhagen 1994–99, Eastern Copenhagen 2000–; City Councillor 1997–2000; Founder and Leader Ny Alliance (New Alliance) party 2007; UNICEF Amb. 2000–; Danish Authors' Asscn Award for Peace and Int. Understanding 1998, Cultural Award, Union of Commercial and Clerical Employees 1998, AFS-Interkultur Intercultural Award 1999, Modermål-Selskabets, Native Language Asscn Award 2000, Junior Chamber's Award for The Outstanding Young Person of 2001, Heiberg Award 2002, Life Award (Lifeforum, a Danish business Asscn) 2006, Free Speech Award (JyllandsPosten newspaper) 2006, Int. Award, Comité Laïcité République, France 2007. *Publications:* Ære og Skam (Honour and Shame) 1996, khader.dk (with Jakob Kvist) 2000, Modsætninger Mødes (Opposites Unite) (with Bent Melchior) 2003, Tro mod Tro (Belief Against Belief) (with Kathrine Lilløer) 2005. *Address:* Ny Alliance, Kompagnistræde 6, 2nd Floor, 1208 Copenhagen K, Denmark (office). *Telephone:* 29-37-93-14 (office). *E-mail:* nyalliance@nyalliance.dk (office); naser.khader@ft.dk (office). *Website:* www.nyalliance.dk (office); www.khader.dk (office).

KHADJIEV, Salambek Naibovich, DChemSc; Russian/Chechen professor of chemistry and politician; b. 7 Jan. 1941, Shali, Chechen Repub.; m.; one s. two d.; ed Grozny Oil Inst., Moscow Univ.; Sr Researcher and Hon. Dir Inst. of Oil 1983–87; Dir Scientific Production Union Grozneftekhim 1987-91; USSR People's Deputy 1989-91; Minister of Petroleum Refining and Petrochemicals, USSR 1991; Chair. Democratic Reforms Movt in Chechen Rep. 1991–93, Prime Minister of Chechen Rep. (apptd by Russian govt) March–Oct. 1995; Chair. State Cttee of Industrial Policy, Russian Fed. 1995–96, Vice-Pres. Asscn of Financial and Industrial Groups 1996; Chair. Ecotec-oil Co. Moscow; Corresp. mem. Russian Acad. of Sciences 1990–, currently with A.V. Topchiev Inst. of Petrochemical Synthesis, Moscow; Co-chair. Bd of Trustees Fund for Humanitarian Assistance to the Chechen Repub.; Ed.-in-Chief Petroleum Chemistry magazine; Chair. Scientific Bd of Petrochemistry, Russian Acad. of Sciences; Fellow, Islamic Acad. of Sciences in Amman; Labour Veteran 1988, Hon. Oil-Chemist of the USSR 1990, Honoured Worker of Science & Technology, Chechen Repub., Honoured Worker of Ministry of Fuel & Energy of Russia 2001. *Publications:* Cracking of Oil – Fractions over Zeolite Catalysts; more than 250 scientific publs and more than 120 inventions. *Address:* A.V. Topchiev Institute of Petrochemical Synthesis, Russian Academy of Sciences, 29 Leninsky Prospekt, Moscow 117912 (office); bld. 12 42/44 Mytnaya Street, 115035 Moscow, Russia. *Telephone:* (495) 236-41-29 (office). *Fax:* (495) 236-12-62 (office). *E-mail:* ecotek@dol.ru (office); khadzhiev@ips.ac.ru (office). *Website:* www.ips.ac.ru (office).

KHADKA, Purna Bahadur; Nepalese politician; b. 1955; Nepali Congress Dist Pres. 1988–91; elected to House of Reps 1991, 1994, 1999; Minister of Youth, Sports and Culture 1998–99, of Information and Communication and Industry 1999; Minister of Industry, Commerce and Supplies; Minister of Home Affairs 2004–05; mem. Nepali Congress Party—Democratic. *Address:* c/o Ministry of Home Affairs, Singha Durbar, Kathmandu, Nepal (office).

KHAI, Phan Van; Vietnamese politician; b. 25 Dec. 1933, Thong Hoi village, Cu Chi Dist, Saigon (now Ho Chi Minh City); involved in revolutionary activities from 1947, in N Viet Nam 1954–60; joined CP 1959; student, Moscow Nat. Univ. of Econs 1960–65; fmrly with Gen. Dept of State Planning Cttee, fmr econ. researcher; in communist-controlled areas of S Viet Nam 1973; Deputy Dir Aid Planning Dept of Nat. Reunification Cttee 1974–75; Deputy Dir Planning Dept, Ho Chi Minh City 1976–78, Dir 1979–80; Deputy Mayor, Ho Chi Minh City 1979–80, Perm. Deputy Mayor 1981–84, Mayor 1985–89; Chair. People's Cttee of Ho Chi Minh City 1985–89; Perm. mem. Ho Chi Minh

City CP Cttee 1979–80, Deputy Sec. 1981–84; Alt. mem. CP Cen. Cttee 1982–84, mem. 1984–, mem. Political Bureau 1991–; Chair. State Planning Cttee 1989–91; Deputy Chair. Council of Ministers 1991–92; Perm. Deputy Prime Minister of Viet Nam 1992–97; Prime Minister of Viet Nam 1997–2006. *Address:* c/o Office of the Prime Minister, Hanoi, Viet Nam.

KHAIN, Viktor Yefimovich, DSc; Russian geologist and academic; *Senior Associate, Institute of the Lithosphere of Marginal Seas, Russian Academy of Sciences;* b. 26 Feb. 1914, Baku; s. of Sophia and Yefim Khain; m. Valentina Kuzmina 1949; two s.; ed Azerbaijan Industrial Inst.; geologist at oil fields, Azerbaijan 1935–39; Assoc. Azerbaijan Oil Research Inst. 1939–41; army service 1941–45; mem. CPSU 1943–90; Sr Assoc., Inst. of Geology, Acad. of Sciences, Azerbaijan SSR 1945–54; Prof. Azerbaijan Industrial Inst. 1949–54; Head of Dept Museum of Earth Sciences, Moscow Univ. 1954–60; Senior Assoc., Vernadsky Inst. of Geochemistry and Analytical Chem., USSR Acad. of Sciences 1957–71; Prof. Geology Dept, Moscow Univ. 1961–94, Prof. Emer. 1994–; Sec.-Gen. Subcomm. for the Tectonic Map of the World, Int. Geological Congress 1972–87, Pres. 1988–; Senior Assoc., Geological Inst., USSR Acad. of Sciences 1972–91, Inst. of the Lithosphere, Russian Acad. of Sciences 1991–; Corresp. mem. USSR Acad. of Sciences 1966–87, mem. 1987; mem. New York Acad. of Sciences 1994; Hon. mem. Moscow Soc. of Naturalists, Bulgarian Geological Soc., Acad. Europaea 1994; Foreign mem. Soc. Géologique de France, Geological Soc. of London, Georgian Acad. of Sciences 1996; Hon. Prof. of Earth Sciences, Changchun Univ. 1996; Hon. DSc (Univ. P. et M. Curie, Paris) 1977; State Prize, USSR 1987, Prestwich Prize, Soc. Géologique de France 1990, Steinmann Medaille, Geologische Vereinigung (GDR) 1991, Karpinsky Gold Medal (USSR Acad. of Sciences) 1991, Fourmarier Medaille d'Or (Acad. Royale de Belgique) 1993, Lomonosov Prize (Moscow Univ.) 1993, State Prize, Russia 1995. *Publications include:* Geotectonic Principles of Oil Prospecting 1954, The Geology of Caucasus (with E. E. Milanovsky) 1963, General Geotectonics 1964, Regional Geotectonics (5 Vols) 1971–85, Geology of USSR 1985, General Geology 1988 (co-author), Historical Geotectonics (Vol. 1) 1988 (with N. A. Bozhko), (Vol. 2) 1991 (with K. B. Seslavinsky), (Vol. 3) 1993 (with A. .N Balukhovsky), Geology of Northern Eurasia 1994, Main Problems of Modern Geology 1994, Geotectonics and Principles of Geodynamics (with M. G. Lomize) 1995, History and Methodology of Geological Sciences (with A. G. Ryabunkin) 1996, Historical Geology (with N. V. Koronovsky and N. A. Yasamanov) 1997. *Address:* Institute of the Lithosphere of Marginal Seas, 22 Staromonetny per., 109180 Moscow (office); 54 Frunzenskaya emb., apt. 18, 119270 Moscow, Russia (home). *Telephone:* (495) 939-11-09; (495) 203-81-23 (office); (495) 242-44-47 (home). *Fax:* (495) 233-55-90.

KHAIRI, Haziq-ul-, BA, MA, LLB; Pakistani judge and writer; *Chief Justice, Federal Shari'a Court of Pakistan;* b. 5 Nov. 1931, Delhi, India; s. of the late Raziq-ul-Khairi, Ed. of Ismat; ed Anglo-Arabic Higher Secondary School, Darya Ganj Delhi and in Karachi, Univ. of Karachi; migrated with family upon partition of India; apptd Judge of Sindh High Court, Prov. Ombudsman (Sindh); fmr mem. Council of Islamic Ideology; currently Chief Justice Fed. Shari'a Court of Pakistan; Chair. Thinker's Forum (Hamdard Shura), Karachi; ex-officio mem. Nat. Judicial Policy Making Cttee, Law and Justice Comm., Advisory Bd Al-Mizan Foundation, Admin Cttee of Al-Mizan Foundation, Bd of Govs, Bd of Trustees, Council of Trustees and Selection Bd Int. Islamic Univ., Islamabad; Chief Patron SAARC Health, Pakistan; mem. Syndicate, Baqai Medical Univ.; Pres., Cen. and West Asian Studies, Univ. of Karachi; mem. Human Rights Comm. of Pakistan; Pres. Anglo-Arabic School and Coll. Old Boys Asscn; Trustee, Transparency International (Pakistan). *Address:* Federal Shari'a Court, Islamabad, Pakistan (office).

KHAIRULLAYEV, Saidullo Khairullayevich; Tajikistani politician; *President, Majlisi Namoyandagon (Assembly of Representatives);* b. 10 Aug. 1945, Garm dist; ed Tashkent Higher CPSU School, Tajik Inst. of Agric.; Engineer, Chief Engineer, then Head of Div. Garm irrigation system 1969–75; Chair. Exec. Cttee Garm Regional Soviet of People's Deputies 1975–77, Chair. Regional Soviet 1979–85; First Sec., Soviet region CP of Tajikistan 1985–88; Sec. Ktalon Regional CP Cttee 1988–90; Deputy Prime Minister of Tajikistan 1991–92; Minister of Environmental Protection, then Minister of Nature Protection 1992–94; Chair. Govt Cttee on Precious Metals 1994–95, Govt Cttee on Land Construction and Land Reform 1999–2000; Pres. Majlisi Namoyandagon (Ass. of Reps) 2000–; Merited Worker of Tajikistan, Order of Nishoni Fakhri. *Address:* Majlisi Oli, Majlisi Namoyandagon, 734051 Dushanbe, Xiyoboni Rudaki 42, Tajikistan (office). *Telephone:* (372) 21-23-66 (office). *Fax:* (372) 21-92-81 (office). *E-mail:* mejparl@parliament.tojikiston.com (office).

KHAKAMADA, Irina Mutzuovna, Cand. Econ.; Russian politician; b. 13 April 1955, Moscow; m. 3rd Vladimir Sirotinsky; three c.; ed Univ. of Friendship of Peoples in Moscow; mem. Research Inst. State Planning Cttee 1981–85; teacher, Tech. Inst. of Automobile Factory 1985–89; Sr expert, Russian Stock Exchange of Raw Materials 1990; mem. Party of Econ. Freedom 1992, Sec.-Gen and Co-Chair. 1992–94; Pres. Liberal Women's Foundation 1994; mem. State Duma 1993–97, 1999–2003, Head of Right Forces faction, Deputy Chair. 2000–; Leader, pre-election union Obshcheye Delo 1995; Chair. State Cttee for Support of Small Enterprises 1997–98; Founder and Co-Leader pre-election union Pravoye Delo, transformed later into Union of Right Forces party 1999, Co-Chair. 2000–2004 (resgnd); cand. for Pres. of Russian Fed. 2004 (ind.). *Publications:* The Maiden Name, Peculiarities of National Politics; and numerous articles. *Address:* c/o State Duma, Okhotny ryad 1, 103265 Moscow, Russia (office). *Website:* www.duma.ru (office).

KHALATNIKOV, Isaac Markovich, DPhysMathSc; Russian theoretical physicist and academic; *Honorary Director, L.D. Landau Institute of Theoretical Physics, Russian Academy of Sciences;* b. 17 Oct. 1919, Dniepropetrovsk;

two d.; ed Dniepropetrovsk State Univ.; Jr Researcher, Sr Researcher, Head of Div., Inst. of Physical Problems, USSR Acad. of Sciences 1945–65, Dir L.D. Landau Inst. of Theoretical Physics, USSR (now Russian) Acad. of Sciences 1965–92, Hon. Dir 1992–, Adviser Russian Acad. of Sciences 1993–; Prof., Moscow Inst. of Physics and Tech. 1954–; Prof., Tel-Aviv Univ. School of Physics and Astronomy 1993–2003; Corresp. mem. USSR Acad. of Sciences 1972, mem. 1984; Foreign mem. Royal Soc. 1994; Hon. Pres. Landau Network Centro Volta, Como, Italy 1995; USSR State Prize 1953, Landau Prize in Physics 1976, Alexander von Humboldt Award 1989, Kiwani Club Int. Prize 1999, Blaise Pascal Medal, European Acad. of Sciences 2005. *Publications:* more than 200 papers on solid state physics, relativistic cosmology, quantum field theory. *Leisure interest:* chess. *Address:* Landau Institute of Theoretical Physics, Kosygina str. 2, 119334 Moscow, Russia (office). *Telephone:* (495) 137-32-44 (office); (495) 702-93-17 (office); (496) 522-10-41 (home). *Fax:* (495) 938-20-77 (office). *E-mail:* khalat@itp.ac.ru (office).

KHALED; Algerian singer, musician (keyboard, accordion) and songwriter; b. (Khaled Hadj Brahim), 29 Feb. 1960, Wahrane; mem., The Five Stars; first recording aged 14; first hit Trigue Al Lissi (The Way To School) 1975; lyrics censored in Algeria until 1983; relocated to Paris 1990; first int. rai hit Didi 1992; collaborations with Chaba Zahouania, Rachid Taha and Faudel; crowned 'King of Rai' at the first rai festival, Oran 1985, BBC Radio 3 World Music Award for Middle East/North Africa region 2005. *Recordings include:* albums: Rai King of Algeria 1985, Fuir Mais Ou? 1991, Khaled 1992, N'ssi N'ssi (César Award for Best Soundtrack) 1993, Sahra 1996, Kenza 1997, Les Monstres Sacrés du Rai, Ya Taleb (with Chaba Zahouania), Best Of The Early Years 2002, Ya Rayi 2004. *Address:* c/o AZ/Universal Music France, 20, rue des Fossés St-Jacques, 75005 Paris, France (office). *Website:* khaled-lesite.artistes.universalmusic.fr.

KHALED, Mohamed Sidiya Ould Mohamed; Mauritanian politician; *Minister of Finance;* Dir-Gen. of the Treasury –2004; Minister of Finance 2004–07. *Address:* c/o Ministry of Finance, BP 181, Nouakchott, Mauritania (office).

KHALEEL, Ahmed; Maldivian diplomatist; *Permanent Representative, United Nations;* b. 17 March 1962; m.; one d.; Third Sec., High Comm. in Colombo, Sri Lanka 1981–83; Third Sec., Perm. Mission to UN, New York 1984–88; Sr Sec., Dept of External Resources, Ministry of Foreign Affairs 1988–90; Second Sec., Perm. Mission to UN, New York 1990–91; Deputy Dir Protocol Div., Ministry of Foreign Affairs 1992–93; First Sec., Perm. Mission to UN, New York 1994–2002, Counsellor, 2002–06, Deputy Perm. Rep. 2005–06; Minister-Counsellor, Embassy in Tokyo 2006–07; Perm. Rep. to UN, New York 2008–. *Address:* Permanent Mission of the Maldives to the United Nations, 820 Second Avenue, Suite 800c, New York, NY 10017, USA (office). *Telephone:* (212) 599-6195 (office). *Fax:* (212) 661-6405 (office). *E-mail:* mdv@undp.org (office). *Website:* www.un.int/maldives (office).

KHALID, Mansour, LLD; Sudanese diplomatist and lawyer; *Minister of Foreign Trade;* b. 13 Dec. 1931, Omdurman; s. of Khalid Mohammed and Sara Sawi; ed Univs of Khartoum, Pennsylvania, USA and Paris, France; began his career as attorney, Khartoum 1957–59; Legal Officer, UN, New York 1962–63; Deputy UN Resident Rep., Algeria 1964–65; with Bureau of Relations with Member States, UNESCO, Paris 1965–69; Visiting Prof. of Int. Law, Univ. of Colo 1968, Univ. of Khartoum 1982; Minister of Youth and Social Affairs, Sudan 1969–71; Chair. Del. of Sudan to UN Gen. Ass., Special Consultant and Personal Rep. of UNESCO Dir-Gen. for UNRWA fund-raising mission 1970; Perm. Rep. to UN, New York 1971, Pres. UN Security Council; Minister of Foreign Affairs 1971–75, of Educ. 1975–77, of Foreign Affairs Feb.–Sept. 1977; Asst to Pres. for Co-ordination and Foreign Affairs 1976, Asst to Pres. for Co-ordination 1977; fmr mem. Political Bureau and Asst Sec.-Gen., Sudan Socialist Union 1978; resgnd from all political posts July 1978 but remained mem. of Gen. Congress of the Sudan Socialist Union; Chair. Bureau of Trilateral Co-operation, Khartoum 1978–80; Personal Rep. for Exec. Dir of UNEP Anti-desertification Programme 1981–82; UN Special Consultant on Co-ordination of UN Information System 1982; Chair. Univ. Devt Cttee, Univ. of Khartoum 1982; Fellow, Woodrow Wilson Center, Smithsonian Inst. 1978–80; financial and investment consultant 1980–; adviser to Pres. Omar Al Bashir –2007; Minister of Foreign Trade 2007–; Loyal Son of Sudan and numerous foreign decorations. *Publications include:* Private Law in Sudan 1970, The Nile Basin, Present and Future 1971, Solution of the Southern Problem and its African Implications 1972, The Decision-Making Process in Foreign Policy 1973, Sudan Experiment with Unity 1973, A Dialogue with the Sudanese Intellectuals, Nimeiri and the Revolution of Dis-May 1985, 1985, The Government They Deserve: The Role of the Elite in Sudan's Political Evolution 1990, War and Prospects of Peace in Sudan 2003. *Leisure interests:* music, gardening. *Address:* Ministry of Foreign Trade, Khartoum (office); PO Box 2930, Khartoum, Sudan (home). *Telephone:* (183) 772793 (office). *Fax:* (183) 773950 (office).

KHALIFA, HE Sheikh Abdullah bin Khalid al-; Bahrain government official; s. of HE Sheikh Isa bin Salman al-Khalifa; Pres. of Historical Documents Centre, Govt of Bahrain; Minister of Justice and Islamic Affairs 2001–06, Deputy Prime Minister 2002–06; Pres. Bahrain Red Crescent Soc.; Hon. Pres. Wisdom Home Soc.; Man.-Dir Lightspeed Communications Co., Manama. *Publications:* Bahrain Through the Ages 1993; articles in journals including Al Watheeqa. *Leisure interests:* historical documents, sports. *Address:* c/o Ministry of Islamic Affairs, POB 450, Diplomatic Area, Manama, Bahrain (office).

KHALIFA, Sheikh Ali bin Khalifa al-; Bahraini politician; *Deputy Prime Minister;* s. of Sheikh Khalifa Bin Salman Al Khalifa; m.; four c.; Asst Under-Sec. for Immigration and Passports 1983–93; Minister of Transportation

1993–; Deputy Prime Minister 2005–; fmr Chair. Bahrain Telecommunications Co.; fmr Chair. Gulf Air Co. GSC, Bahrain Airport Services Co.; mem. Bahrain Econ. Devt Bd 2002–. *Address:* c/o Office of the Prime Minister, PO Box 1000, Government House, Government Road, Manama, Bahrain.

KHALIFA, HM Sheikh Hamad bin Isa al-, (King of Bahrain); b. 28 Jan. 1950, Bahrain; s. of the late Sheikh Isa bin Salman al-Khalifa; m. Sheikha Sabeeka bint Ibrahim al-Khalifa 1968; six s. (including HH Sheikh Salman bin Hamad al-Khalifa) four d.; ed Secondary School, Manama, Bahrain, Leys School, Cambridge Univ., Mons Officer Cadet School, Aldershot, England and US Army Command and Gen. Staff Coll., Fort Leavenworth, Kan., USA; formed Bahrain Defence Force 1968, Commdr-in-Chief 1968–, also C-in-C Nat. Guard, raised Defence Air Wing 1978; mem. State Admin. Council 1970–71; Minister of Defence 1971–88; Deputy Pres. Family Council of Al-Khalifa 1974–; succeeded as Ruler on the death of his father March 1999; introduced constitutional monarchical system and assumed title of King Feb. 2002; created Historical Documents Centre 1976; Founder mem. and Pres. Bahrain High Council for Youth and Sports 1975–; initiated Al-Areen Wildlife Parks Reserve 1976; f. Salman Falcon Centre 1977, Amiri Stud, Bahrain 1977; f. Bahrain Equestrian and Horse Racing Asscn, Pres. 1977–; f. Bahrain Centre for Studies and Research 1989; hon. mem. Helicopter Club of GB; Orders of the Star of Jordan (1st Class) 1967, Al-Rafidain of Iraq (1st Class) 1968, National Defence of Kuwait (1st Class) 1970, Al-Muhammedi of Morocco (1st Class) 1970, Al-Nahdha of Jordan (1st Class) 1972, Qiladat Gumhooreeya of Egypt (1st Class) 1974, The Taj of Iran (1st Class) 1973, King Abdul-Aziz of Saudi Arabia (1st Class) 1976, Repub. of Indonesia (1st Class) 1977, Repub. of Mauritania (1st Class) 1969, El-Fateh Al-Adheem of Libya (1st Class) 1979, Kuwait Liberation 1994, Hon. KCMG (UK), Ordre nat. du Mérite de la République française (1st Class) 1980, Grand Cross of Isabel la Católica of Spain (1st Class) 1981; Freedom of the City of Kansas 1971, US Army Certificate of Honour 1972. *Leisure interests:* horse riding, golf, study of ancient history and prehistory of Bahrain, water skiing, swimming, fishing, falconry, shooting, football, tennis. *Address:* PO Box 555, Ritala Palace, Manama, Bahrain. *Website:* www.bahrainembassy.org/rulingfam (office).

KHALIFA, Sheikha Haya Rashed al-, LLB; Bahraini lawyer, international organization executive and diplomatist; b. 18 Oct. 1952; ed Univ. of Kuwait, Univ. of Paris I (Panthéon-Sorbonne), France, Alexandria Univ. and Ain Shams Univ., Egypt; admitted as a lawyer to both Court of Cassation and Constitutional Court of Bahrain 1979; one of the first two women to practise law in Bahrain; fmr counsel at Bahrain Ministry of State for Legal Affairs as well as a sr attorney at a major Bahraini law firm; Prin. and Founding Partner, Haya Rashed Al Khalifa Law Firm; has held many sr positions, including Vice-Chair. Arbitration and Dispute Resolution Cttee Int. Bar Asscn 1997–99; Amb. to France (also accred to Belgium, Switzerland and Spain) 2000–04; Perm. Rep. to UNESCO 2000–04; Legal Adviser to Royal Court of Bahrain; Pres. 61st Session UN Gen. Ass. 2006–07; Rep. of Bahrain to ICC Int. Court of Arbitration; fmr Vice-Pres. Bahrain Bar Soc.; fmr mem. WIPO Arbitration Centre Consultative Cttee, Supreme Council of Culture, Art and Literature; mem. Bahrain Bar Asscn, Child Devt Soc., Arab Women's Legal Network; Bath for Peace Award. *Address:* Office of the President, United Nations General Assembly, United Nations Plaza, New York, NY 10017, USA (office); Haya Rashed Al Khalifa, Attorneys at Law & Legal Consultants, First Floor, Bahrain Development Bank Building, PO Box 1188, Diplomatic Area, Manama, Bahrain. *Telephone:* (212) 963-1234 (office); (17) 537771. *Fax:* (212) 963-4879 (office); (17) 531117. *E-mail:* h.alkhalifa@hraklf.com (home). *Website:* www.un.org (office); www.hraklf.com/l1.htm.

KHALIFA, Sheikh Isa bin Ali al-; Bahraini government official; fmr Minister of Oil. *Address:* c/o Ministry of Oil, POB 1435, Manama, Bahrain (office). *Telephone:* 17291511 (office). *Fax:* 17293007 (office).

KHALIFA, Sheikh Khalid bin Ahmad al-, BSc; Bahraini diplomatist; *Minister of Foreign Affairs;* b. 4 April 1960; m. Shaikha Wesal bint Mohamed Al Khalifa; ed Islamic Scientific Coll., Amman, Jordan, Univ. of Texas, USA; served at Embassy in Washington, DC 1985–94; Chief Liaison Officer, Office of Deputy Prime Minister of Foreign Affairs 1995–2000; Amb. to UK 2001–05 (also accred to Netherlands 2002–05, to Ireland 2002–05, to Norway 2002–05, to Sweden 2003–05); Minister of Foreign Affairs 2005–; Bahrain Medal 2001. *Leisure interests:* history, politics, social affairs, literature, travel. *Address:* Ministry of Foreign Affairs, POB 547, Government House, Government Road, Manama, Bahrain (office). *Telephone:* 17227555 (office). *Fax:* 17212603 (office). *Website:* www.mofa.gov.bh.

KHALIFA, Maj.-Gen. Khalifa bin Ahmed al-; Bahraini army officer and government official; b. 20 June 1945, Muharraq, Bahrain; ed Royal Mil. Acad., Sandhurst, UK; platoon commdr; training co. commdr; infantry co. commdr; bn second in command; battalion commdr; fmr Chief of Staff, Bahrain Defence Force; Minister of Defence 1988–06. *Address:* c/o Ministry of Defence, PO Box 245, West Rifaa, Bahrain. *Telephone:* 17653333 (office). *Fax:* 17663923 (office).

KHALIFA, Sheikh Khalifa bin Sulman al-; Bahraini politician; *Prime Minister;* b. 1935; s. of the late Sheikh Sulman and brother of the ruler, Sheikh Isa; Dir of Finance and Pres. of Electricity Bd 1961; Pres. Council of Admin 1966–70; Pres. State Council 1970–73, Prime Minister 1973–; fmr Chair. Bahrain Monetary Agency; UN Special Citation of the Habitat Scroll of Honour Award 2006. *Address:* Office of the Prime Minister, PO Box 1000, Government House, Government Road, Manama, Bahrain. *Telephone:* 17253361. *Fax:* 17533033.

KHALIFA, Sheikh Mohammed bin Abdulla al-; Bahraini politician; Minister of State for Defence Affairs 2006–. *Address:* c/o Office of the Prime Minister, PO Box 1000, Government House, Government Road, Manama, Bahrain.

KHALIFA, Sheikh Muhammad bin Mubarak bin Hamad al-, BA; Bahraini government official; *Deputy Prime Minister;* b. 1935; s. of Sheikh Mubarak bin Hamad al-Khalifa; m.; two c.; ed American Univ. of Beirut, Lebanon, Univ. of Oxford and Univ. of London, UK; attended Bahrain Courts as cand. for the bench, Dir of Information 1962; Head of Political Bureau 1968 (now Dept of Foreign Affairs); State Council 1970; Minister of Foreign Affairs 1971–2005; currently Deputy Prime Minister with additional responsibilities for ministerial cttees. *Address:* c/o Office of the Prime Minister, POB 1000, Government House, Government Road, Manama, Bahrain.

KHALIFA, Sahar, BA, MA, PhD; Palestinian writer and feminist; b. 1941, Nablus; m. 1959 (divorced); two d.; ed Rosary Coll. and Bir Zeit Univ., Univ. of North Carolina and Univ. of Iowa, USA; began writing 1967–; moved to USA to study; returned to Nablus 1988; f. Women's Affairs Center, Nablus, Gaza City 1991, Amman 1994; Fulbright Scholar 1980; Naguib Mahfouz Prize. *Publications include:* novels (in trans.): We Are Not Your Slave Girls Anymore 1974, Wild Thorns 1975, The Sunflower 1980, Memoirs of an Unrealistic Woman 1986, The Door of the Courtyard 1990, The Inheritance 1997. *Address:* c/o Pontas Literary and Film Agency, Sèneca, 31, 08006 Barcelona, Spain.

KHALIFA, HH Sheikh Salman bin Hamad al-, BPA, MA; Bahraini government official; *Crown Prince and Deputy Commander in Chief, Bahrain Army;* s. of HM Sheikh Hamad bin Isa al-Khalifa, King of Bahrain; ed American Univ., Washington, DC, USA, Univ. of Cambridge, UK; Chair. Bahrain Centre for Studies and Research 1992–95; Under-Sec. for Defence 1995–99, Crown Prince and C-in-C Bahrain Defence Force 1999–2008; Deputy C-in-C Bahrain Army 2008–; Chair. Bd of Trustees Bahrain Centre for Studies and Research 1995–99; Chair. Supreme Council of Youth and Sport; CEO Econ. Development Bd. *Address:* Ministry of Defence, PO Box 245, West Rifa'a (office); Crown Prince Court, POB 29091, Bahrain (office). *Telephone:* 17662100. *Fax:* 17661200. *Website:* www.bahrainembassy.org/rulingfam (office).

KHALIL, Idriss, PhD; Moroccan mathematician and academic; b. 20 Dec. 1936, El Jadida; m.; two c.; ed Rabat Univ., Univs of Bordeaux, Nancy and Paris, France; Asst Lecturer, Univ. of Bordeaux 1963–65; Asst Lecturer, then Sr Lecturer, then Prof., Univ. Mohammed V, Rabat Univ. 1966–; Jr Lecturer, Univ. of Nancy 1968–70; Research Asst, CNRS 1968–72; Lecturer, Bielefeld Univ. 1973; Dean, Faculty of Sciences, Univ. Mohammed V, Rabat Univ. 1974–85; Prof., Univ. of Nancy, MIT, Ecole Polytechnique, Paris and Paris-Sud Univ. 1979–85; fmr Minister of Educ. and Higher Educ.; Ed. Afrika Mathematika 1979; Founder-mem. Math. Africa Union 1976, African Asscn for the Advancement of Science and Tech.; Corresp. mem. Int. Asscn for Peace (PUGWASH) 1979; mem. Royal Acad. of Morocco 1982, Int. Asscn of French-Speaking Communities; Founding Fellow, Islamic Acad. of Sciences; Chevalier des Palmes académiques 1979, Ordre nat. du Mérite 1982, Ordre du Trône (Morocco) 1982. *Address:* c/o Academy of the Kingdom of Morocco, Charia Imam Malik, Km 10, B.P. 1380, Rabat; Université Mohammed V, BP 554, 3 rue Michlifen, Agdal, Rabat, Morocco (office). *E-mail:* alacademia@iam.net.ma.

KHALILI, Abdul Karim; Afghan politician; *Second Vice-President;* Leader Hizb-i Wahadat i Islami (Unity Party), an alliance of anti-Taliban fighters from Hazara ethnic minority, located in Bamian prov.; driven out of Cen. Afghanistan by Taliban 1998; Leader Bamian prov. 2001–; apptd Vice-Pres. Transitional Authority 2002, elected Second Vice-Pres. 2004–. *Address:* c/o Office of the President, Gul Khana Palace, Presidential Palace, Kabul, Afghanistan (office). *Website:* www.president.gov.af (office).

KHALILOV, Erkin Khamdamovich, DJur, CandJur; Uzbekistan politician; b. 1955, Buxoro; m.; three s.; ed Tashkent State Univ.; engineer, Research-Production Unit Cybernetics 1977–79; Jr, then Sr Researcher, Head of Div. Inst. of Philosophy and Law Uzbek Acad. of Sciences, 1979–90; Deputy, then Chair. Cttee on Law, Deputy Chair. (Speaker) Supreme Soviet (Oliy Majlis) 1990–93, Acting Chair. 1993–95, Chair. 1995–1999, re-elected 2000, Speaker Qoqunchilik palatasi Kengashi (Legis. Chamber) 2005–08; Order Mehnat Shuhrati 1999. *Publications:* about 100 articles on law and politics. *Leisure interests:* lawn tennis, football. *Address:* c/o Qoqunchilik palatasi Kengashi, Oliy Majlis, 100008 Tashkent, Xalqlar Do'stligi shoh ko'ch. 1, Uzbekistan (office). *Telephone:* (71) 139-87-07 (office); (71) 139-41-51 (office). *Website:* www.parliament.gov.uz (office).

KHALILZAD, Zalmay; American (b. Afghan) diplomatist; b. 22 March 1951, Mazar-i-Sharif, Afghanistan; m. Cheryl Benard; two s.; ed American Univ. of Beirut, Lebanon, Univ. of Chicago; Asst Prof. of Political Science, School of Int. and Public Affairs, Columbia Univ. 1979–85; received Council on Foreign Relations fellowship to join US State Dept 1984, Special Advisor on Afghanistan to Under-Sec. of State 1985–89, Under-Sec. of Defence for Policy Planning 1990–92; Defence Analyst Rand Corpn 1993–2000; headed Bush-Cheney transition team for US Dept of Defense, also served as Counselor to Sec. of Defense, also Special Asst to Pres. and Sr Dir for Southwest Asia, Near East, and North African Affairs, Nat. Security Council 2001; Special Envoy to Kabul, Afghanistan 2002, to Iraqi Nat. Congress, Iraqi Opposition 2003; Amb. to Afghanistan 2003–05, to Iraq 2005–07; Perm. Rep. to UN, New York 2007–09; King Ghazi Ammanullah Medal, Afghanistan, Defense Dept Medal for Outstanding Public Service (twice). *Publications include:* The Government of God: Iran's Islamic Republic (with Cheryl Benard) 1984, Sources of Conflict in the 21st Century: Strategic Flashpoints and US Strategy 1998, Strategic Appraisal: United States Air and Space Power in the 21st Century (with Jeremy Shapiro) 2002; numerous articles in journals and books. *Address:* c/o Permanent Mission of the United States to the UN, 799 United Nations Plaza, New York, NY 10017, USA.

KHAMA, Lt-Gen. (Seretse) Ian; Botswana politician and head of state; *President;* s. of the late Sir Seretse Khama, Pres. of Botswana 1966–80; fmr Commdr Botswana Defence Force; Minister of Presidential Affairs and Public Admin March–July 1998; elected mem. Nat. Ass. 1998; Vice-Pres. of Botswana 1998–2008, Pres. 2008–. *Address:* Office of the President, Private Bag 001, Gaborone, Botswana (office). *Telephone:* 3950825 (office). *Fax:* 3950858 (office). *E-mail:* op.registry@gov.bw (office). *Website:* www.gov.bw/government/ministry_of_state_president.html#office_of_the_president (office).

KHAMENEI, Ayatollah Sayyed Ali; Iranian politician and religious leader; *Wali Faqih (Supreme Religious Leader);* b. 17 July 1939, Mashad, Khorassan; s. of the late Ayatullah Sayyid Jawad Husaini Khamenei; m. 1964; four s. one d.; ed Qom; studied in Islamic seminary of Najaf 1957, in Islamic seminary of Qom 1958–64, returned to Mashad 1964; joined Revolutionary Movt of Imam Khomeini 1962; imprisoned six times 1964–78, once exiled in 1978; Co-founder Islamic Republican Party 1979, Sec.-Gen. and Pres. Cen. Cttee 1980–87; Sec. of Defense, Supervisor of Islamic Revolutionary Guards, Leader of the Friday Congregational Prayer, Tehran Rep. in Consultative Ass. 1980; Imam Khomeini's Rep. in High Security Council 1981; Pres. of Iran 1981–89; mem. Revolutionary Council until its dissolution Nov. 1979; survived assassination attempt June 1981; Pres. Expedience Council 1988; Wali Faqih (Supreme Religious Leader) 1990–. *Leisure interests:* reading, art, literature. *Address:* Office of the Wali Faqih, Shoahada Street, Qom, Iran. *E-mail:* info@leader.ir; istiftaa@wilayah.org. *Website:* www.leader.ir.

KHAMTAY, Gen. Siphandone; Laotian army officer, politician and fmr head of state; b. 8 Feb. 1924, Houa Khong Village, Champassak Prov.; m.; five c.; mil. officer 1947–48, rep. of Lao Itsala 1948, mem. Front Cen. Cttee 1950–52, Chair. Control Cttee 1952–54; Gen. Staff mem. Pathet Lao 1955–56, Head Cen. Cttee 1957–59, propaganda and training officer 1959–60, mem. Cen. Cttee 1957, C-in-C 1960, mem. Politburo 1972–2006; mem. Lao People's Revolutionary Party (LPRP) 1972, Leader 1992–2006; mem. Secr. LPRP 1982; Deputy Prime Minister and Minister of Nat. Defence 1975–91; Prime Minister of Laos 1991–98; fmr Supreme Commdr Lao People's Army; Pres. of Laos 1998–2006. *Address:* c/o Office of the President, Vientiane, Laos.

KHAN, Aamir Hussain; Indian actor; b. 14 March 1965, Mumbai; s. of Tahir Hussain and Zeenat Hussain; m. Reena Khan; one s. one d.; ed Bombay Scottish and N. M. Coll. *Films include:* Yaadon Ki Baaraat, Daulat Ki Jang, Holi, Parampara, Dil Hai Ki Manta Nahin, Qayamat Se Qayamat Tak 1988, Raakh, Jawani Zindabad, Love Love Love, Hum Hain Rahi Pyar Ke 1994, Jo Jeeta Wohi Sikander, Baazi, Dil, Rangeela, Deewana Mujhsa Nahin, Raja Hindustani (Best Actor Award) 1996, Ishq (Romancing with Music) 1997, Ghulam 1998, Sarfarosh (Best Actor Award) 1999, Mann, 1947 Earth 1999, Mela 1999, Lagaan (Best Actor Award) 2001, Dil Chahta Hai 2001, The Rising Ballad of Mangal Pandey 2005, Rang De Basanti (Paint It Yellow) 2006, Fanaa 2006, Taare Zameen Par 2007. *Address:* 11 Bella Vista Apartments, Pali Hill, Bandra (West), Mumbai 400 050, India. *Telephone:* (91) 22 6463744. *Website:* www.aamirkhan.com.

KHAN, Abdul Qadeer, PhD; Pakistani scientist; b. 1935, Bhopal, India; m.; two d.; ed Univ. of Karachi, Catholic Univ. of Leuven, Belgium; mem. of staff, Physical Dynamics Research Lab., Amsterdam 1972–76; est. Eng Research Labs (now Dr A. Q. Khan Research Labs), Kahuta 1976, Chair. –2001; Pres.'s Special Science and Tech. Adviser with Ministerial Rank 2001–04; Patron-in-Chief Dr A. Q. Khan Inst. of Tech. and Man.; Hilal-e-Imtiaz 1989, Nishan-e-Imtiaz 1996. *Address:* Dr A. Q. Khan Institute of Technology and Management, ICCTS Plaza 81, F-7/G-7 Markaz, Blue Area, Islamabad, Pakistan (office). *Telephone:* (51) 9268141 (office). *Fax:* (51) 9268156 (office). *E-mail:* stcd@comsats.net.pk (office). *Website:* www.krl.com.pk (office).

KHAN, Makhdoom Ali, LLM; Pakistani lawyer; ed Univ. of Karachi, Univ. of Cambridge and London School of Econs, UK; enrolled as Advocate, High Court of Sindh 1977; barrister, England and Wales, Society of Lincoln's Inn 1978; enrolled as Advocate, Supreme Court of Pakistan 1989, Sr Advocate 2001–; Lecturer in Law, Univ. of Keele, UK 1979–80; Prof. of Law, Univ. of Karachi, Sindh Muslim Govt Law Coll. 1980–88; Attorney-Gen. for Pakistan 2001–07 (resgnd); Chair. Pakistan Bar Council 2001–07; fmr Chair. Pakistan Electronic Media and Regulatory Authority, Pakistan Telecommunications Authority; fmr mem. Law and Justice Comm. of Pakistan. *Address:* Supreme Court of Pakistan, Constitution Avenue, Islamabad (office). *Telephone:* (51) 9220581 (office). *Fax:* (51) 9213452 (office). *Website:* www.supremecourt.gov.pk (office).

KHAN, Ali Akbar; Indian classical musician; b. 14 April 1922, Shivpur (now in Bangladesh); s. of Dr Allauddin Khan and Medina Khan; m. Mary J. Khan; debut in Allahabad 1936 with world tours since 1955; Founder Ali Akbar Coll. of Music, Calcutta 1956, San Rafael, Calif. 1968, Basel, Switzerland 1982; musical dir for numerous films including award-winning Hungry Stones; numerous appearances at concerts and maj festivals, world-wide; musical collaboration with Yehudi Menuhin, Ravi Shankar (q.v.), Duke Ellington and others; lecture recitals at maj univs, including Montreal, McGill, Washington, San Diego and Tennessee; composer of concerti, orchestra pieces and several ragas, notably Chandranandan, Gauri Manjari, Alamgiri, Medhavi; Propr Alam Madina Music Productions (record co.); f. Ali Akbar Khan Foundation 1994; MacArthur Foundation Fellowship 1991; Nat. Heritage Fellowship 1997; recipient Meet the Composer/Arts Endowment Commissioning Music grant 1996; Hon. DLitt (Rabindra Bharati Univ., Calcutta) 1974; Dr hc (Calif. Inst. of Arts) 1991, (Viswa Bharati Univ., Shantiniketan, India) 1998, (New England Conservatory of Music) 2000; Pres. of India Award 1963, 1966, Grand Prix du Disque 1968, Padma-bhibhushan Award 1989, Kalidas Award 1992, Bill Graham Lifetime Award, BAM 1993, Asian Paints Shiromani Award 1997, Nat. Acad. of Recording Arts and Science Gov.'s Award for Outstanding Achievement 1998, Asiatic Soc. of Calcutta Indira Gandhi Gold Plaque 1998; Ustad Ali Akbar Khan Day est. in San Francisco, 18 Oct. 1998. *Address:* Ali Akbar College of Music, 215 West End Avenue, San Rafael, CA 94901, USA. *Telephone:* (415) 454-6264. *E-mail:* office@aacm.org; info@ammp.com. *Website:* www.aacm.org; www.ammp.com.

KHAN, Amjad Ali; Indian musician (sarod) and composer; b. 9 Oct. 1945, Gwalior, Madhya Pradesh; s. of the late Hafiz Ali Khan and Rahat Jahan Begum; m. Subhalakshmi Barooah 1976; two s.; ed Modern School, New Delhi; numerous concert performances and festival appearances worldwide; mem. World Arts Council, Geneva; Founder-Pres. Ustad Hafiz Ali Khan Memorial Soc. (promotion of Indian classical music and dance); Visiting Prof. Univ. of York, UK 1995, Univ. of Pa, Univ. of NM; Padma Shree 1975, Padma Bhusan 1991, Sarod Samrat, Gwalior 1993, Padma Vibhushan 2001, Commdr, Ordre des Arts et des Lettres; Hon. Citizen Nashville, Tenn. 1997, Houston, Tex. 1997, Mass, Atlanta; Hon. DUniv (York) 1997, (Delhi) 1998; UNESCO Award, Ghandi UNESCO Medal, Int. Music Forum 1970, 1975, Special Honour, Sahitya Kala Parishad, Delhi 1977, Musician of Musicians, Bhartiya Vidhya Bhavan, Nagpur 1983, Amjad Ali Khan Day (Mass.) 1984, Acad. Nat. Award (Tirupathi) 1987, Raja Ram Mohan Roy Teacher's Award 1988, Sangit Natak Acad. Award 1989, Tansen Award, Nat. Cultural Org., New Delhi 1989, Vijaya Ratna Award, India Int. Friendship Soc., New Delhi 1990, Crystal Award, World Econ. Forum 1997, Fukuoka Cultural Grand Prize (Japan). *Compositions include:* many ragas; music for Kathak ballets Shan E. Mughal, Shahajahan Ka Khwab, Ganesh; orchestral compositions Ekta Se Shanti, Ekta Ki Shakti, Tribute to Hong Kong (for Hong Kong Philharmonic Orchestra). *Radio includes:* promenade concert, BBC 1995. *Recordings include:* Raag Bhairav (named one of best CDs in world, BBC Music Magazine 1996), Moksha 2005. *Publications:* The World of Amjad Ali Khan, ABBA – God's Greatest Gift to Us. *Leisure interests:* music, light reading, long walks. *Address:* c/o Askonas Holt, Lincoln House, 300 High Holborn, London, WC1V 7JH, England (office); 3 Sadhna Enclave, Panchsheel Park, New Delhi 110 017, India; 25 Hillhouse Lane, Old Brooksville, NY 11545-2503, USA. *Telephone:* (20) 7400-1700 (office); (11) 6017062 (India) (office); (516) 671-1615 (USA). *Fax:* (20) 7400-1799 (office); (11) 6018011 (India). *E-mail:* info@askonasholt.co.uk (office); music@sarod.com. *Website:* www.askonasholt.co.uk (office); www.sarod.com (office).

KHAN, Sardar Attiq Ahmed, MA; Pakistani politician and writer; b. 1 Jan. 1955, Ghaziabad, Tehsil Dheerkot, Bagh Dist; s. of Sardar Abdul Qayyum Khan; ed Madina Univ., Saudi Arabia; fmr Chair. youth and student wing All Jammu and Kashmir Muslim Conf., later Chief Organizer, All Jammu and Kashmir Muslim Conf., Pres. 2002–06; elected mem. Legis. Ass. three times; Prime Minister of Azad Jammu and Kashmir 2006–09. *Address:* All Jammu and Kashmir Muslim Conference, PO Box 184, Satellite Town, Rawalpindi 46300, Pakistan.

KHAN, Gen. Besmellah; Afghan military officer; *Chief of Army Staff;* fought with Northern Alliance against Taliban; fmr Deputy Minister of Defence, Chief of Staff, Ministry of Defence; fmr Chief Commdr Kabul garrison; currently Chief of Gen. Staff, Afghanistan Nat. Army. *Address:* Afghanistan National Army Headquarters, Kabul, Afghanistan (office).

KHAN, Hameed Ahmed, PhD; Pakistani physicist and academic; *Executive Director, COMSATS;* b. 1 May 1942, Rangoon, Burma; ed Punjab Univ., Univ. of Birmingham, UK; joined Pakistan Atomic Energy Comm. (PAEC) 1965; helped to commission country's first research reactor; on staff of teaching and research faculties, Univ. of Birmingham –1974; Chief Scientist, Pakistan Atomic Energy Commission 1965–72, Sr Scientific Officer 1972–77, Principal Scientific Officer 1977–86, Chief Scientific Officer 1986–94, Head, Radiation Physics Div. 1992–94, Assoc. Dir 1994–96; Visiting Prof. Bahauddin Zakarayia Univ., Multan 1994; Dir –Gen. Pakistan Institute of Nuclear Science and Technology (PINSTECH) 1996–2000; Exec. –Dir COMSATS (Comm. on Science and Tech. for Sustainable Devt in the South) 2000–; fmr Chief Ed. Nucleus; Fellow Islamic Acad. of Sciences, Pakistan Acad. of Sciences, Alexander von Humboldt (AVH), Philips University,; First Prize in Physics (Nat. Book Foundation of Pakistan) 1991, 1992, 1993, Khawarizmi Prize (Iranian Research Org. for Science and Tech.) 1993, Prize in Tech. (Third World Network of Scientific Orgs) 1998, Sitara-i-Imtiaz Award, Int. ISESCO Science Prize 2006. *Address:* COMSATS, 4th Floor, Shahrah-e-Jamhuriat, G-5/2, Islamabad, Pakistan (office). *Telephone:* (51) 9204900 (office). *Fax:* (51) 9216539 (office). *E-mail:* drhakhan@comsats.net.pk (office). *Website:* www.comsats.org.pk (office).

KHAN, Rear Adm. Hasan Ali; Bangladeshi naval officer; b. 11 Feb. 1950, Hat-Lakshmipur, Gaibandha; m. Afsana Khan; two d.; ed Defence Service Command and Staff Coll., Nat. Defence Coll., Mirpur; Officer Cadet Navy 1969, mem. Exec. Br. 1972, has commanded several ships, fmr positions include Asst Chief of Naval Staff, Naval Sec., Naval Admin. Authority Dhaka –2005, Chief of Naval Staff 2005–07. *Address:* c/o Ministry of Defence, Old High Court Building, Dhaka, Bangladesh (office). *Telephone:* (2) 259082 (office).

KHAN, Imran (see KHAN NIAZI, Imran).

KHAN, Irene Zubaida; Bangladeshi international organization executive; *Secretary-General, Amnesty International;* b. 24 Dec. 1956, Dhaka; one d.; ed Victoria Univ. of Manchester, UK and Harvard Law School, USA; joined Office of UNHCR 1980, adviser to local project offices, worked in Pakistan, SE Asia, UK, Ireland and numerous crisis deployments 1980–90, Sr Exec. Officer to Sadako Ogata 1991–95, Chief of Comm. in India 1995, Head of Documentation and Research Centre 1998–99, Head of Comm. in Fmr Yugoslav Repub. of Macedonia 1999, Deputy Dir Dept for Int. Legal Protection; Sec.-Gen.

Amnesty Int. 2001–; Dr hc (Ferris State Univ.) 2005, (Ghent Univ.) 2007; Pilkington Woman of the Year 2002, Sydney Peace Prize 2006; Ford Foundation Fellowship. *Address:* Amnesty International, 1 Easton Street, London, WC1X 0DN, England (office). *Telephone:* (20) 7413-5500 (office). *Fax:* (20) 7956-1157 (office). *E-mail:* secgen@amnesty.org (office). *Website:* www .amnesty.org (office).

KHAN, Ishratul Ebad; Pakistani government administrator; Gov. of Sindh Prov. 2002–. *Address:* Office of the Governor of Sindh, Karachi, Pakistan (office). *Telephone:* (21) 9201201-3 (office). *E-mail:* governor@governorsindh .gov.pk (office). *Website:* www.sindh.gov.pk (office).

KHAN, Jemima; British charity fund-raiser; *UK Special Representative, United Nations International Children's Emergency Fund (UNICEF);* b. 30 Jan. 1974, London; d. of Sir James Goldsmith and Lady Annabel Vane Tempest Stewart; m. Imran Khan 1995 (divorced 2004); two s.; ed Bristol Univ.; moved to Lahore, Pakistan with husband Imran Khan 1995; developed own brand of tomato ketchup; Jemima Khan Designs (fashion label) 1996–2001; campaigner to improve literacy levels in Pakistan; UK Special Rep. UNICEF 2001–; travelled to refugee camps across Pakistan; f. Jemima Khan Appeal; reporter and news presenter, Channel 5, Bangladesh 2002–04; fund-raiser, Shaukat Khanum Memorial Cancer Hosp.; Rover People's Award for Best Dressed Female Celebrity, British Fashion Awards 2001. *Address:* c/o UNICEF, 3 United Nations Plaza, New York, NY 10017, USA (office).

KHAN, Khurshed Alam, MA; Indian politician; b. 5 Feb. 1919, Kaimganj; s. of Jan Alam; elected to Rajya Sabha 1974, 1980, Lok Sabha 1984; Minister of State for Commerce 1980, for Tourism and Civil Aviation 1982, 1983–84, for Tourism 1982–83, for External Affairs 1984, for Commerce 1985, for Textiles 1985–86, Gov. of Goa 1989–91, of Karnataka 1991–99; fmr Chancellor Jamia Milia Islamia; Vice-Pres. Zakir Hussain Educ. and Cultural Foundation; mem. Zakir Hussain Memorial Trust. *Address:* Pitaura (Kaimganj), Farrukhabad District, Uttar Pradesh, India (home).

KHAN, M. Morshed, BEng; Bangladeshi politician; b. 8 Aug. 1940, Chittagong; m.; one s. four d.; ed Tokyo Univ. of Tech. and Agric. and Sofia Univ., Japan; fmr Alt. Gov. ILO; Founder-Chair. Arab Bangladesh Bank Ltd; Chair. Pacific Group of Industries, Pacific Bangladesh Telecom Ltd, Bangladesh Asscn of Banks; co-f. Global Foundation for Christian–Muslim Partnership; elected mem. Standing Cttee, Int. Conf. of Asian Political Parties; Pres. Metropolitan Chamber of Commerce and Industries, Bangladesh Employers' Fed.; elected mem. of Parl. several times; Chair. Special Cttee on Foreign Affairs 1991–96; apptd Special Envoy of the Prime Minister 1996, subsequently mem. Advisory Council, Vice-Chair. Bangladesh Nationalist Party; Minister of Foreign Affairs 2001–06. *Address:* c/o Ministry of Foreign Affairs, Segunbagicha, Dhaka 1000, Bangladesh (office).

KHAN, Maj. Gen. (retd) Mohammad Anwar; Pakistani army officer; fmr Vice-Chief Pakistan Army; Pres. of Azad Kashmir 2001–06.

KHAN, Gen. Mohammed Ismail; Afghan politician; *Minister of Water and Energy;* b. 1954, Herat; ed Kabul Mil. Coll.; served as officer in Afghan army; fmr Mujahidin Commdr during Soviet occupation; joined Jamiat-i Islami (Islamic Soc.) 1979; led uprising and liberated Herat from Soviet control; Gov. of Herat 1993–97, 2001–04; taken prisoner by Taliban following re-occupation of Herat 1997, escaped in 2000; Mil. Commdr Herat –2003; Minister of Water and Energy 2004–; mem. Northern Alliance. *Address:* Ministry of Water and Energy, Kabul, Afghanistan (office).

KHAN, Rahat; Bangladeshi writer and editor; *Editor, Dainik Ittefaq;* b. 1940, Kishoregonj; ed Univ. of Dhaka; taught for eight years in colls including Nasirabad Coll. of Mymensingh, Jagannath Coll. of Dhaka, Commerce Coll. of Chittagong; apptd Asst Ed. Dainik Ittefaq (daily) 1969, now Ed.; Ekushe Padak 1996; Bangla Acad. Award 1973, Suhrid Literary Award 1975, Sufi Motahar Hossain Award 1979, Mahbubullah Zebunnesa Trust Award 1979, Abul Mansur Memorial Award 1980, Humayun Qadir Memorial Award 1982, Shuhrid Literary Award 1975, Trayi Literary Award 1988, Cetana Literary Award 1989. *Publications include:* short story collections: Onischito Lokaloy (Uncertain Human Habitation) 1972, Ontohin Jatra (The Eternal Journey) 1975, Bhalo Monder Taka (Money for Good and Evil) 1981, Apel Songbad (News of the Apple) 1983, and others; novels: Omol Dhobol Chakuri (Milk-White Service) 1982, Ek Priyodorshini (A Beautiful Woman) 1983, Chayadompoti (A Shadow Couple) 1984, Sangharsha (Clash) 1984, Shahar (The City) 1984, Hey Onanter Pakhi (O, Bird of Infinity) 1989, Modhyomather Khelowar (The Forward Footballer) 1991, Akhanksha (Desire), Kayekjan (A Few Persons), Ognidaho (Conflagration), Hey Maton Bongo (O, Mother Bangla). *Address:* Dainik Ittefaq, 1 Ramkrishna Mission Road, Dhaka, Bangladesh (office). *Telephone:* (2) 7122660 (office). *Fax:* (2) 7122651-3 (office). *E-mail:* rahat.khan@ittefaq.com (office). *Website:* www.ittefaq.com (office).

KHAN, Raja Zulqarnain, BA; Pakistani politician; *President of Azad Kashmir;* b. 15 March 1936, Gujrat; s. of the late Khan Bahadur Raja Muhammad Afzal Khan (fmr Gov. and Minister); ed New Delhi Modern High School, Aitcheson Coll., Lahore, Govt Coll., Lahore; Co-founder Jammu Kashmir Liberation League 1960; Minister in cabinet of Pres. Maj.-Gen. Abdul Rehman of Azad Jammu Kashmir (AJK) 1969; elected mem. AJK Legis. Ass. from Samani constituency (then in Mirpur Dist, now in Bhimbher Dist) 1975, elected mem. AJK Legis. Ass. from Bhimbher constituency 1985; Minister for Finance, Planning and Devt, Health and Revenue 1985–91, for Finance and Planning and Devt 1991–96; elected mem. Jammu and Kashmir Council 1996–2001; adviser to Chair. AJK Council and to the Prime Minister; cand. of All Jammu Kashmir Muslim Conf. in presidential elections Aug. 2006; Pres. Azad Kashmir 2006–. *Address:* Office of the President, Azad Kashmir

Government, Muzaffarabad, Pakistan (office). *Website:* www.ajk.gov.pk (office).

KHAN, Shah Rukh; Indian film actor and producer; b. 2 Nov. 1965, New Delhi; s. of the late Mir Taj Mohammed Khan and Fatima Begum; m. Gauri Chibber Khan 1991; one s. one d.; ed St Columba's High School, New Delhi, Hansraj Coll., Jamiya Miliya Islamiya, New Delhi; TV debut in role of Abhimanyu in war drama series Fauji (Soldier) 1988; film debut in Deewana 1992; Co-owner Dreamz Unlimited production co., Red Chilies Entertainments production co.; Best Indian Citizen Award 1997, Jade Magazine Award for Sexiest Man in Asia 2001, Rajiv Gandhi Award for Excellence in the Field of Entertainment 2002, named by Time Magazine one of their 20 Asian Heroes under 40 2004, MSN Search Personality of the Year Award 2004, Sabse Tez Personality of the Year Award 2004, Chhoton Ka Funda Award 2004, 'F-Awards' for Excellence in Indian Fashion Celebrity Model of the Year 2004, Pepsi Sabsey Favourite Star Kaun Award Favourite Hero 2004, Asian Guild Awards Bollywood Star of the Decade 2004, Padma Shri Award, Govt of India 2005, awarded the title 'Hammer-e-Hind' by Hindi newspaper DeshBakht 2006; 13 Filmfare Awards, 10 Rupa Cinegoers Awards, six Star Screen Videocon Awards, six Sansui Viewers Choice Movie Awards, four Zee Cine Awards, four People's Choice Movie Awards, three IIFA Awards, three Zee Gold Bollywood Awards, two AFJA Awards, one Aashirwad Award, one Disney Kids Channel Award, one MTV Immies Indian Music Excellence Award, one Sports World Film Award. *Films include:* Deewana (Crazy) (Filmfare Best Debut Award) 1992, Raju Ban Gaya Gentleman 1992, Maya 1992, Chamatkar 1992, Dil Aashna Hai (The Heart Knows the Truth 1992, King Uncle 1993, Kabhi Haan Kabhi Naa (Sometimes Yes, Sometimes No) (Filmfare Critics Award for Best Performance) 1993, Darr (Fear) 1993, Baazigar (Filmfare Best Actor Award) 1993, Anjaam (Filmfare Best Villain Award) 1994, Zamaana Deewana 1995, Trimurti 1995, Ram Jaane 1995, Oh Darling Yeh Hai India 1995, Karan Arjun 1995, Guddu 1995, Dilwale Dulhania Le Jayenge (Lovers Will Walk off with the Bride, UK) (Filmfare Best Actor Award) 1995, English Babu Desi Mem 1996, Chaahat 1996, Army 1996, Dushman Duniya Ka 1996, Pardes 1997, Gudgudee 1997, Koyla 1997, Yes Boss 1997, Dil To Pagal Hai (The Heart is Crazy) (Filmfare Best Actor Award) 1997, Duplicate 1998, Dil Se… (From the Heart, USA) 1998, Kuch Kuch Hota Hai (Something is Happening, UK) (Filmfare Best Actor Award) 1998, Baadshah 1999, Phir Bhi Dil Hai Hindustani 2000, Hey Ram 2000, Josh 2000, Har Dil Jo Pyar Karega… 2000, Mohabbatein (Love Stories) (Filmfare Critics Award for Best Performance) 2000, Gaja Gamini 2000, One 2 Ka 4 2001, Asoka 2001, Kabhi Khushi Kabhie Gham… (Sometimes Happy, Sometimes Sad) 2001, Devdas (Filmfare Best Actor Award 2003) 2002, Hum Tumhare Hain Sanam 2002, Shakti: The Power 2002, Saathiya 2002, Chalte Chalte 2003, Kal Ho Naa Ho (Tomorrow May Never Come, USA) 2003, Yeh Lamhe Judaai Ke 2004, Main Hoon Na 2004, Veer-Zaara 2004, Swades (Our Country, USA) (Filmfare Best Actor Award) 2004, Kaal (song) 2005, Silsiilay 2005, Paheli 2005, Alag (song) 2006, Kabhi Alvida Naa Kehna (Never Say Goodbye) 2006, Don – The Chase Begins Again 2006, Khazan 2006. *Television includes:* Fauji (series) 1988, In Which Annie Gives It Those Ones 1989, Circus (series) 1989, Idiot (mini-series) 1991. *Leisure interests:* computer games, hi-tech gadgets, acting. *Address:* 603 Amrit Bandar (West), Mumbai 400050, India (office). *Telephone:* (22) 6486116 (office); (22) 6281413 (office). *E-mail:* dreamzandfilms@hotmail.com (office).

KHAN, Sikander Mustafa, MSc; Pakistani automotive industry executive; *Chairman, Millat Tractors Limited;* ed NED Eng Coll., Karachi, Imperial Coll. of Science and Tech., London, Univ. of Newcastle upon Tyne; arranged financial package and structured deal that lead to employee buyout of nationalized Millat Tractors Ltd from Govt 1992, currently Chair.; Chair. Tech. Educ. and Vocational Training Authority 1999–, Punjab Vocational Training Council 1999–; mem. and Hon. Sec., Pakistan Chapter, Inst. of Mechanical Engineers. *Address:* Millat Tractors Limited, Sheikhupura Road, Shahdra, 54950 Lahore, Pakistan (office). *Telephone:* (42) 7914786 (office). *Fax:* (42) 7925835 (office). *E-mail:* smkhan@millat.com.pk (office). *Website:* www.millat.com.pk (office).

KHAN, Zaffar Ahmad; Pakistani engineer and business executive; *Chairman, Pakistan International Airlines Corporation;* ed Peshawar Univ., one-year training programme in Japan, Advanced Man. Program, Univ. of Hawaii, short courses at INSEAD, Paris and Harvard Business School, USA; joined Esso Pakistan Fertilizer Co. (later known as Exxon Chemical) 1969, was transferred overseas to serve Exxon Chemical in Hong Kong, USA and Singapore 1973–82, Vice-Pres. Marketing and Dir of Exxon Chemical Pakistan Ltd 1982, held various posts in all divs including Marketing, Manufacturing, Finance and Corp. Services 1982–91, played role in the first employee-led buyout in corp. history of Pakistan which resulted in Engro Chemical Pakistan Ltd 1991, Pres. and CEO 1997–2004; Chair. Pakistan Int. Airlines Corpn 2007–; Chair., mem. or fmr mem. various pvt. and public sector bds, including Engro Asahi, Engro Vopak, United Bank, Sui Southern Gas Co., PTML (Ufone), PTCL, Pakistan Steel, Unilever Pakistan, Karachi Stock Exchange, Nat. Commodity Exchange, Pakistan Inst. of Corp. Governance, Acumen Fund, State Bank of Pakistan; Pres. Overseas Chamber of Commerce and Industry; has also served on numerous advisory cttees of Govt of Pakistan, including Econ. Advisory Bd, Pay and Pension Cttee, Cttee that developed Nat. Environment Quality Standards; mem. Pakistan Centre for Philanthropy; Chair. fund-raising cttee of Agha Khan Univ.; Sitara-e-Imtiaz. *Address:* Pakistan International Airlines Corporation, Head Office, Jinnah International Airport, Karachi 75200, Pakistan (office). *Telephone:* 111-786-786 (office); (21) 457-2011 (office). *Fax:* (21) 457-2225 (office); (21) 457-0419 (office). *E-mail:* info@piac.com.pk (office). *Website:* www.piac.com.pk (office).

KHAN HOTI, Amir Haider; Pakistani politician and government official; *Chief Minister of North West Frontier Province;* b. 1971, Mardan; s. of Muhammad Azam Khan Hoti, fmr Fed. Minister of Communication; grand s. of Khan Abdul Wali Khan, nephew of Asfandiyar Wali Khan, Pres. of Awami Nat. Party, of Begum Naseem Wali Khan, grand s. of Amir Muhammad Khan; ed Atchison Coll., Lahore, Working Edwards Coll.; began political career from platform of Awami Nat. Party; fought his first election in 2002 from PF 23 Mardan 1; Chief Minister NW Frontier Prov. 2008–. *Address:* Office of the Chief Minister, North West Frontier Province, Peshawar, Pakistan (office). *E-mail:* info@nwfp.gov.pk (office). *Website:* www.nwfp.gov.pk (office).

KHAN NIAZI, Imran; Pakistani politician and fmr professional cricketer; *Chairman, Tehreek-e-Insaf;* b. 25 Nov. 1952, Lahore; m. Jemima Goldsmith 1995 (divorced 2004); two s.; ed Aitchison Coll. and Cathedral School, Lahore, Worcester Royal Grammar School and Keble Coll. Oxford, UK; right-arm fast bowler, middle-order right-hand batsman; played for Lahore 1969–71, Worcs. 1971–76, Univ. of Oxford 1973–75 (Capt. 1974), Dawood 1975–76, PIA 1975–81, Sussex 1977–88, NSW 1984–85; 88 Test matches for Pakistan 1971–92, 48 as Capt., scoring 3,807 runs (average 37.6) and taking 362 wickets (average 22.8); toured England 1971, 1974, 1975 (World Cup), 1979 (World Cup), 1982, 1983 (World Cup), 1987; scored 17,771 first-class runs and took 1,287 first-class wickets; 175 limited-overs ints, 139 as Capt. (including 1992 World Cup victory); second player to score a century and take 10 wickets in a Test 1983; third player to score over 3,000 Test runs and take 300 wickets; Special Rep. for Sports, UNICEF 1989; Ed.-in-Chief Cricket Life 1989–90; f. Imran Khan Cancer Hosp. Appeal 1991–; f. Tehreek-e-Insaf (Movt for Justice) 1996, Chair. 1996–; mem. Nat. Ass. for Mianwali 2002–07; Hon. Fellow, Keble Coll. Oxford 1988; Wisden Cricketer of the Year 1983, Hilal-e-Imtiaz 1993. *Film appearance:* Kidnap 2008. *Publications:* Imran 1983, All-Round View (autobiography) 1988, Indus Journey 1990, Warrior Race 1993; writes syndicated newspaper column. *Leisure interests:* shooting, films, music. *Address:* Tehreek-e-Insaf, Central Secretariat, H-07, Parliament Lodges, Islamabad, Pakistan (office). *Telephone:* (51) 2270744 (office). *Fax:* (51) 2873893 (office). *E-mail:* info@insaf.org.pk (office). *Website:* www.insaf.org.pk (office).

KHAN WILLIAMS, Mehr, MA; Pakistani UN official; *Special Adviser to the Executive Director, United Nations Children's Fund (UNICEF);* b. 1945, India; m.; one c.; ed Univ. of Karachi; fmrly with Univ. of Karachi, United Press Int., Associated Press of Pakistan, World Bank, Washington, DC; joined UN 1976, Deputy Dir UNICEF Programme Funding Office, Dir UNICEF Div. of Communication 1989–96, Acting Dir UN Information Centre, Sydney, Dir UNICEF Innocenti Research Centre, Florence 1998–2000, Regional Dir East Asia and the Pacific, UNICEF Bangkok –2004, Special Adviser to Exec. Dir of UNICEF 2004, 2006–, Deputy High Commr for Human Rights, UN 2004–06, fmr Chair. Jt UN Information Cttee; fmr Trustee, TV Trust for the Environment, London. *Address:* Office of the Executive Director, UNICEF, 3 United Nations Plaza, New York, NY 10017, USA (office). *Telephone:* (212) 326-7000 (office). *Fax:* (212) 887-7465 (office). *E-mail:* info@unicef.org (office). *Website:* www.unicef.org (office).

KHANDOHIY, Volodymyr; Ukrainian diplomatist and government official; *Minister of Foreign Affairs;* b. 21 Feb. 1953, Cherkasy; m.; two c.; ed T.G. Shevchenko Kyiv State Univ.; attaché, Third Sec., Ministry of Foreign Affairs 1976–79; attaché, Perm. Mission to UN, New York 1979–83; Second Sec., Dept of Int. Orgs, Ministry of Foreign Affairs 1983–85, First Sec., Secr. Gen. 1985–88; First Sec., Perm. Mission to UN, New York 1988–92, Deputy Perm. Rep., then Acting Perm. Rep. 1992–94; Head of Dept Int. Relations, Ministry of Foreign Affairs 1994–95, Deputy Minister of Foreign Affairs and Chair. Nat. Comm. on UNESCO Affairs 1995–98; Rep. to UNESCO Exec. Council 1996–98; Amb. to Canada 1998–2000, to Netherlands 2000–02, to Belgium 2000–05 (also accred to Luxembourg); Rep. to ICAO 1998–2000, to OPCW 2000–02; Dir Dept for NATO, Ministry of Foreign Affairs 2005–06, Deputy Minister for Foreign Affairs 2006–07, First Deputy Minister 2007–09, Minister of Foreign Affairs 2009–. *Address:* Ministry of Foreign Affairs, 01018 Kiev, pl. Mykhailivska 1, Ukraine (office). *Telephone:* (44) 238-15-06 (office). *Fax:* (44) 226-31-69 (office). *Website:* www.mfa.gov.ua (office).

KHANDU, Dorjee; Indian politician; *Chief Minister of Arunachal Pradesh;* b. 3 March 1955, Gyangkhar village; s. of the late Leki Dorjee; m.; four s. two d.; began career in Intelligence Corps, Indian Army; mem. Arunachal Pradesh State Ass. 1990–; Minister of State for Co-operation 1995–96; State Cabinet Minister of Animal Husbandry and Veterinary and Dairy Devt 1996–98, of Power 1998–2006, of Mines, Relief and Rehabilitation 2002–03, of Relief and Rehabilitation and Disaster Man. 2003–04; Chief Minister of Arunachal Pradesh 2007–. *Address:* Office of the Chief Minister, Government of Arunachal Pradesh, Naharlagun, 791110, India (office). *Telephone:* (360) 2212173 (office); (360) 2214306 (home). *Website:* arunachalipr.gov.in (office).

KHANDURI, Maj.-Gen. Bhuwan Chandra, BSc, BE, MIE; Indian engineer and army officer (retd), politician and management consultant; *Chief Minister of Uttarakhand;* b. 1 Oct. 1934, Dehradun, Uttaranchal; s. of the late Shri Jai Ballabh Khanduri and Smt. Durga Devi Khanduri; m. Smt. Aruna Khanduri 1964; one s. one d.; ed Allahabad Univ., College of Mil. Eng, Pune, Inst. of Engineers, New Delhi and Inst. of Defence Man., Secunderabad; served in Corps of Engineers, Indian Army 1954–1990; mem. Parl. (Garhwal constituency, Uttarakhand) 1991–96, 1998–; mem. Bharatiya Janata Party (BJP), Chief Whip, Parl. Party 1991–96, 1998–99, 2004, mem. Nat. Exec. 1992–97, 2000–, Vice-Pres. Uttar Pradesh State 1996–97; Minister of State (with ind. charge) for Roads, Transport and Highways 2000–03, Minister with Cabinet rank 2003–04; Chief Minister of Uttarakhand 2007–; mem. Cttee on Public Accounts 1998–99, on Rules, Business Advisory 1998–99, 1999–2000, 2004, on Home Affairs 1998–99, 1999–2000 and Convenor of sub-Cttee on Personnel Policy of Cen. Para-Mil. Forces, Consultative Cttee, Ministry of Defence, Cttee on Public Undertakings 1999–2001, on Ethics; Chair. Cttee on Finance 2004; mem. Cttee on Gen. Purposes, Consultative Cttee Ministry of Petroleum and Natural Gas; Patron, Parvatiya Sanskriti Parishad, Dehradun 1990–93, Chandra Ballabh Trust; Founder and Pres. Poorva Sainik Seva Parishad, Uttar Pradesh 1992–2000, Uttarakhand Pradesh Sangarsh Samsiti 1994–96; mem. Wild Life Soc. of India 1990–2000, G.B. Pant Himalaya Environment and Devt Cttee 1998–2000; Ati Vishisht Seva Medal for Distinguished Service in the Indian Army 1982. *Leisure interests:* sports, reading. *Address:* Jai Durga Niwas, 12, Vikas Marg, Pauri Garhwal, 246001 (home); Office of the Chief Minister, Camp Office, Annexe Circuit House, New Cantt Road, Dehradun, 248001, India (office). *Telephone:* (135) 2755100 (office). *Fax:* (135) 2755102 (office). *E-mail:* bc.khanduri@nic.in (office). *Website:* www.uttara.in (office).

KHANE, Abd-El Rahman, MD; Algerian physician, government official and international organization official; b. 6 March 1931, Collo; m. 1955; three s. one d.; ed Univ. of Algiers; served as officer in Nat. Liberation Army until Algerian independence 1962; mem. Nat. Council Algerian Revolution (CNRA) 1957–60; Sec. of State, provisional Govt (GPRA) 1958–60; Gen. Controller Nat. Liberation Front 1960–61; Head of Finance Dept, GPRA 1961–62; Pres. Algerian-French tech. org. for exploiting wealth of Sahara sub-soil 1962–65; Pres. Electricité et Gaz d'Algérie July–Oct. 1964; mem. Bd of Dirs Nat. Petroleum Research and Exploitation Co. 1965–66; Minister of Public Works and Pres. Algerian-French Industrial Co-operation Org. 1966–70; physician in Cardiology Dept, Univ. Hosp. of Algiers 1970–73; Sec.-Gen. OPEC 1973–74; Exec. Dir UNIDO 1975–85; Founding mem. and mem. Bd Worldwatch Inst., now mem. Emer. *Address:* 42 chemin B. Brahimi, El Biar, Algiers, Algeria (home). *Telephone:* (21) 924483 (home).

KHANFAR, Wadah; Jordanian journalist; *Director-General, Al-Jazeera Satellite Network;* ed Univ. of Jordan; joined Al-Jazeera 1999, fmr corresp. Africa Bureau, New Delhi corresp. on war in Afghanistan 2002, Baghdad Bureau Chief 2003, Man. Dir Al-Jazeera 2003–06, Dir-Gen. Al-Jazeera Satellite Network 2006–. *Address:* Al-Jazeera Satellite Network, POB 23123, Doha, Qatar (office). *Telephone:* 4890881 (office). *Fax:* 4885333 (office). *Website:* english.aljazeera.net (office).

KHANH, Emmanuelle, (pseudonym of Renée Nguyen); French fashion designer; b. 12 Sept. 1937, Paris; m. Manh Khanh Nguyen 1957; one s. one d.; fmr fashion model for various Paris houses including Balenciaga and Givenchy 1957–63; designer of jr sportswear for Cacharel, Paris 1962–67; est. own co., launching Missoni knitwear and other products, Paris 1970; f. own label, specializing in embroidered clothes, accessories 1971; Chevalier des Arts et des Lettres 1986. *Leisure interest:* music. *Address:* Emanuelle Khanh, 36 rue du Faubourg Saint-Honoré, 75008 Paris, France (office). *Telephone:* 1-42-68-01-77 (office). *Fax:* 1-42-66-95-82 (office).

KHANH, Lt-Gen. Nguyen; Vietnamese politician and fmr army officer; *Chief of State, 'Government of Free Viet Nam';* b. 8 Nov. 1927, Tra Vinh Province; ed Viet Nam Mil. Acad., Dalat, Army Staff Schools, Hanoi and France and US Command and Gen. Staff Coll., Fort Leavenworth; served in French Colonial Army 1954, Vietnamese Army 1954; Chief of Staff to Gen. Duong Van Minh 1955; took part in coup against Pres. Diem Nov. 1963; Prime Minister Jan.–Oct. 1964; Chair. Armed Forces Council 1964–65; led coup Jan. 1965; Roving Amb. 1965; moved to US 1977; mem. Secr. CP of Viet Nam; Vice-Prime Minister and Gen. Sec. Council of Ministers 1987; Lecturer, US Army War Coll., US Air Force Special Operations Command, Texas Tech Univ., Univ. of Denver 1993–; apptd Chief of State of Govt of Free Vietnam (anti-communist group located in Calif.) 2005–. *Address:* Government of Free Vietnam, 12755 Brookhurst Street, Suite 104, Garden Grove, CA 92840, USA (office). *Telephone:* (714) 636-9514 (office). *Fax:* (714) 636-9513 (office). *Website:* www.gfvn.org (office).

KHANNA, Tejendra, MSc, MA; Indian business executive and civil servant; *Lieutenant-Governor of the National Capital Territory of Delhi;* b. 16 Dec. 1938; ed Patna Univ., Univ. of Calif., Berkeley, USA; joined Indian Admin. Service 1961; Prin. Sec. to Chief Minister of Punjab, Sec. of Science, Tech. and Environment, of Food Supplies and of Labour Employment 1970s; fmr Man. Dir for Punjab, State Industrial Devt Corpn; Sec. to Govt of Punjab for Irrigation, Power and Public Works 1983–86, Financial Commr for Revenue 1986–89; Chief Controller of Imports and Exports, Ministry of Commerce, Govt of India 1989–91; Chief Sec. to Govt of Punjab, Head of Civil Service, Chief Co-ordinator of Govt Programmes 1991–92; Sec. for Food, Govt of India 1992–93, for Commerce 1993–96; Prin. Civil Service Co-ordinator of Bilateral, Multilateral and Regional Trade Relations 1993–96; Lt-Gov. and Admin. Nat. Capital Territory of Delhi 1997–98, 2007–; Chair. Ranbaxy Laboratories Ltd 1999–2007; mem. Advisory Bd Standard Chartered Bank, UK 1999–2003; Trustee, Popular First; mem. Indian Inst. of Public Admin 1978–; Life Mem. Bhartiya Vidya Bhawan. *Address:* Office of the Lieutenant-Governor, National Capital Territory of Delhi, Raj Niwas, Delhi 110054, India (office). *Telephone:* (11) 23975022 (office). *Fax:* (11) 23937099 (office). *E-mail:* webupdate@nic.in (office). *Website:* delhigovt.nic.in (office).

KHARE, V. N., BA, LLB; Indian judge; b. 2 May 1939; enrolled as advocate, Allahabad High Court 1961, fmr Chief Standing Counsel for State Govt at Allahabad Bench, Judge 1983–1996; Chief Justice Kolkata High Court 1996–97; Judge Supreme Court of India 1997–2002, Chief Justice 2002–04 (retd); Padma Vibhushan 2006. *Leisure interests:* cricket, music and reading books. *Address:* 5 Krishna Menon Marg, 110011 New Delhi, India. *Telephone:* (11) 23015290 (home); (11) 23388942. *Fax:* (11) 23010056 (home); (11) 23383792.

KHARITONOV, Mark Sergeyevich; Russian writer; b. 31 Aug. 1937, Zhitomir, Ukraine; m. Galina Edelman; one s. two d.; ed Moscow Pedagogical Inst.; teacher of secondary school; exec. sec. of newspaper; of publishing house 1960–69; freelance 1969–; trans. Kafka, Stefan Zweig, Elias Canetti, Herman Hesse, Thomas Mann and others; works banned in official press until 1988; first Booker Russian Novel Prize for Lines of Fate or Milashevich's Trunk 1992, Prix du Meilleur Livre Etranger Essai (France) 1997. *Publications include:* Prokor Menshutin 1971 (published 1988), Provincial Philosophy 1977 (published 1993), Two Ivans 1980 (published 1988), Lines of Fate or Milashevich's Trunk 1985 (published 1992), Storozh 1994, The Voices 1994, Return from Nowhere 1995, Seasons of Life 1998, A Mode of Existence 1998, The Approach 1998, Amores Novi 1999, The Conveyor 2000, Stenography of the End of the Century 2002, A Professor of Lie 2002, Stenography of the Beginning of the Century 2003, Playing with Yourself 2004. *Address:* Bazhova str. 15, corp. 1, Apt. 182, 129128 Moscow, Russia (home). *Telephone:* (495) 187-56-92 (home). *Fax:* (495) 187-56-92 (home). *E-mail:* mkharitonov@mail.ru (home).

KHARITONOV, Col Nikolai Mikhailovich; Russian politician; b. 31 Oct. 1948, Rezino, Novosibirsk Region; m.; four d.; ed Novosibirsk Inst. of Agric., Acad. of Nat. Econs; agronomist sovkhoz Novosibirsk Region 1972–76; Dir sovkhoz 1976–94; deputy Novosibirsk Regional Exec. Cttee; RSFSR People's Deputy, mem. Cttee on Agrarian Problems Supreme Soviet Russian Fed. 1990–93, mem. faction Agrarian Union 1990; mem. State Duma 1993–; leader Agrarian Group (later Agrarian-Industrial Group) 1994–2003; re-elected to Duma as ind. cand. 2003–; Deputy Chair. Agrarian Party of Russia 1993–2000; mem. Parl. Ass. of European Council; cand. for Pres. of Russian Fed. (Communist Party) 2004. *Leisure interest:* sports. *Address:* State Duma, Okhotnyi ryad 1, 103265 Moscow, Russia (office). *Telephone:* (495) 292-83-10 (office). *Fax:* (495) 292-94-64 (office). *E-mail:* www@duma.ru (office). *Website:* www.duma.ru (office).

KHARKAVETS, Andrey Mikhailovich; Belarusian politician; *Minister of Finance;* First Deputy Minister of Finance 2006–08, Minister of Finance 2008–. *Address:* Ministry of Finance, vul. Savetskaya 7, 220048 Minsk, Belarus (office). *Telephone:* (17) 227-27-26 (office). *Fax:* (17) 222-45-93 (office). *E-mail:* minfin@minfin.gov.by (office). *Website:* www.minfin.gov.by (office).

KHARRAT, Edwar al-, LLB; Egyptian author; b. 16 March 1926, Alexandria; s. of Kolta Faltas Youssef al-Kharrat; m. 1958; two s.; ed Alexandria Univ.; storehouse asst, Royal Navy Victualling Dept, Alexandria 1944–46; clerk, Nat. Bank of Egypt 1946–48; clerk, Nat. Insurance Co. 1950–55; Dir of Tech. Affairs Afro-Asian People's Solidarity Org. 1959–67, Asst Sec.-Gen. 1967–73, Pres. 1967–; mem. Afro-Asian Writers' Asscn (Asst Sec.-Gen. 1967–72), Egyptian Writers' Union, Egyptian PEN; trans. and broadcaster for Egyptian Broadcasting Service; Assoc. Sr mem. St Antony's Coll., Oxford 1979; Ed. The Lotus, Afro-Asian Writings; Franco-Arab Friendship Prize 1991, Ali Al Owais Award (for fiction) 1996, Cavifis Prize 1998, State Merit Award 2000. *Publications include:* short stories: High Walls 1959, Hours of Pride 1972 (State Prize), Suffocations of Love and Mornings 1983; novels: Rama and the Dragon 1979, The Railway Station 1985, The Other Time 1985, Saffron Dust 1986, The Ribs of Desert 1987, Girls of Alexandria 1990, Creations of Flying Desires 1990, Waves of the Nights 1991, Stones of Bobello 1992, Penetrations of Love and Perdition 1993, My Alexandria 1994, Ripples of Salt Dreams 1994, Fire of Phantasies 1995, Soaring Edifices 1997, Certitude of Thirst 1997, Throes of Facts and Folly 1998, Boulders of Heaven 2000, Path of Eagle; poetry: Cry of the Unicorn 1998, Seven Clouds 2000; literary criticism: Transgeneric Writing 1994, The New Sensibility 1994, From Silence to Rebellion 1994, Hymn to Density 1995, Beyond Reality 1998, Voices of Modernity in Fiction 1999, Modernist Poetry in Egypt 2000, Fiction and Modernity 2003, The Fiction Scene 2003. *Leisure interest:* travel. *Address:* 45 Ahmad Hishmat Street, Zamalek, Cairo, Egypt. *Telephone:* (2) 7366367. *Fax:* (2)7366367.

KHARRAZI, Kamal, PhD; Iranian diplomatist and fmr academic; *Chairman, Strategic Council on Foreign Relations;* b. 1 Dec. 1944, Tehran; s. of Mehdi Kharrazi and Kobra Kharrazi; m. Mansoureh Kharrazi; two c.; ed Tehran Univ., Univ. of Houston, USA; Teaching Fellow, Univ. of Houston 1975–76; Man. of Planning and Programming, Nat. Iranian TV 1979; Man. Dir Centre for Intellectual Devt of Children and Young Adults 1979–81; Deputy Foreign Minister for Political Affairs 1979–80, Minister of Foreign Affairs 1997–2005; Chair., Strategic Council on Foreign Relations 2006–; Man. Dir Islamic Repub. News Agency 1980–89; mem. Supreme Defence Council, Head War Information HQ 1980–89; Prof. of Man. and Psychology, Tehran Univ. 1983–89; Perm. Rep. to UN, New York 1989–97; Founding mem. Islamic Research Inst., London; mem. American Asscn of Univ. Profs. *Publications:* numerous textbooks and journal articles on psychology and foreign affairs. *Leisure interest:* mountain climbing. *Address:* Kashani Alley 1, Keshvardust Street, Jomhuri Avenue, Tehran, Iran (office). *Telephone:* (21) 64413131 (office); (21) 64413178 (office). *Fax:* (21) 66466270 (office). *E-mail:* kharrazi@imam-khamenei.ir (office). *Website:* www.leader.ir.

KHASAWNEH, Awn Shawkat al-, MA, LLM; Jordanian judge; *Vice-President, International Court of Justice;* b. 22 Feb. 1950, Amman; ed Islamic Educational Coll. of Amman, Queens' Coll. Cambridge, England; entered diplomatic service 1975; with Perm. Mission to UN 1976–80, later as First Sec.; with Ministry of Foreign Affairs 1980–90, Head of Legal Dept 1985–90; Legal Adviser to Crown Prince 1990–95, Adviser to the King 1995, Chief of the Royal Hashemite Court 1996–98; mem. (Judge) Int. Court of Justice Feb. 2000–, Vice-Pres. 2006–; mem. Arab Int. Law Comm. 1982–89; mem. Subcomm. on Prevention of Discrimination and Protection of Minorities (Chair. 1993), Comm. on Human Rights 1984–93, Special Rapporteur of Comm. on Human Rights on the human rights dimensions of forcible population transfer; mem. Int. Law Comm. 1986–; mem. Royal Jordanian Comm. on Legislative and Admin. Reform 1994–96; mem. Bd of Eds Palestine Yearbook of Int. Law; mem. Int. Law Asscn, Chair. Cttee on Islamic Law and Int. Law 2003–; mem. Council of the Centre of Islamic and Middle Eastern Law, SOAS; Istiqlal Order 1st Class 1993, Kawkab Order 1st Class 1996, Nahda Order 1st Class 1996, Grand Officier Légion d'honneur 1997. *Address:* International Court of Justice, Peace Palace, Carnegieplein 2, 2517 KJ The Hague, Netherlands (office). *Telephone:* (70) 302-23-23 (office). *Fax:* (70) 364-99-28 (office). *E-mail:* information@icj-cij.org (office). *Website:* www.icj-cij.org (office).

KHASBULATOV, Ruslan Imranovich, DEconSc; Chechen politician, economist and academic; *Chair of International Economic Relations Department, Plekhanov Academy of Economics;* b. 22 Nov. 1942, Grozny; s. of Imran Khasbulatov and Govzan Khasbulatova; m.; one s. one d.; ed Kazakh State Univ., Moscow State Univ.; instructor, Cen. Cttee of Comsomol 1970–72, Head of Information Sector Inst. of Social Sciences, USSR Acad. of Sciences 1972–74, Head of Sector, Research Inst. of Higher Educ. 1974–79, Lecturer, Prof., Head, Chair of Int. Econ. Relations Dept, Plekhanov Inst. (now Acad.) of Econs 1979–90, 1995–; Deputy of Supreme Soviet in Russia 1990–93, First Vice-Chair., then Acting Chair. Supreme Soviet 1990–91, Chair. 1991–93; Chair. Interparl. Ass. of CIS 1992–93; charged with fraud and imprisoned Sept.–Oct. 1993, released by State Duma Feb. 1994; one of the leaders of opposition to Pres. Dudaev-Mashadof in Chechen crisis 1991–96 and to mil. policy of Kremlin; Corresp. mem. Russian Acad. of Sciences 1991. *Publications:* Bureaucracy and Socialism 1989, Russia: Time of Change 1991, International Economic Relations (two vols) 1991, Power 1992, The Struggle for Russia 1993, Les Ombres au-dessus de la Maison Blanche (France) 1993, Great Russian Tragedy (two vols) 1994, World Economy 1994, World Economy (two vols) 2001, Crisis of Commonwealth of Independent States and Positive Experience of European Union 2002, The Great American Tragedy and What Should the World Do to Prevent Terrorism? 2001–02, The Kremlin and Russian–Chechen War (five vols): Vol. 1 Exploded Life 2002, Vol. 2 Power: Sword and Guile 2002, Vol. 3 Thoughts of War and Peace 2002, Vol. 4 A Big Strategic Game 2003, Vol. 5 Aliens 2003, Which Policy is Needed for Russia from the Point of View of the World Scientific Community? 2004, Fairy Tales About Reforms 2004, The Principle of Optimum in the Economic System and Social Functions of the State 2005, States and Revolutions 2005, The World Economy and International Economic Relations, Vols 1 and 2 2006. *Leisure interests:* fishing, hunting, playing chess. *Address:* Plekhanov Academy of Economics, Stremyanny per. 36, 113054 Moscow (office); Granatnay per. 10/35, Moscow, Russia (home). *Telephone:* (495) 958-50-15 (office); (495) 697-53-92 (home). *Fax:* (495) 958-46-22 (office). *E-mail:* hasbulatov@rea.ru (home).

KHATAMI, Hojatoleslam Sayed Muhammad, BPhil; Iranian cleric, politician and fmr head of state; b. 1943, Ardkan, Yazd; s. of Ayatollah Seyyed Rooh Allah Khatami (religious scholar); m. 1974; one s. two d.; ed Qom and Isfahan seminaries and Univ. of Tehran; Man. Islamic Centre, Hamburg; mem. for Ardakan and Meibod, first Islamic Consultative Ass. (Parl.); rep. of Imam Khomeini and Dir Kayhan newspaper; fmr Minister of Culture and Islamic Guidance; Cultural Deputy HQ of C-in-C and Head Defence Publicity Cttee; fmr Minister of Culture and Islamic Guidance; fmr Adviser to Pres. Rafsanjani and Pres. Nat. Library of Iran; fmr mem. High Council of Cultural Revolution; Pres. of Iran 1997–2006; apptd mem. UN group Alliance of Civilizations 2005–; Head, Int. Center of Dialogue Among Civilizations; numerous hon. degrees. *Publications:* Fear of Wave, From World of City to World City, Faith and Thought Trapped by Selfishness; and numerous articles and speeches. *Address:* c/o Office of the President, Pastor Avenue, Tehran, Iran. *Website:* www.khatami.ir.

KHATIB, Hisham, PhD, FIEE, FIEEE; Jordanian energy and environmental consultant and fmr politician; *Chairman, Jordan Electricity Regulatory Commission;* b. 5 Jan. 1936, Acre, Palestine; s. of Mohamed Khatib and Fahima Khatib; m. Maha Khatib 1968; two s. one d.; ed Univs of Cairo, Birmingham, London; Chief Engineer Jerusalem Electricity Co. 1965–73; Deputy Dir Gen. Jordanian Electricity Authority 1974–76; Sr Energy Expert, Arab Fund, Kuwait 1976–80; Dir Gen. Jordan Electricity Authority 1980–84; Minister of Energy and Mineral Resources 1984–89; Vice-Chair. World Energy Council 1989–92; int. energy consultant 1990–93; Minister of Water and Irrigation 1993–94, of Planning 1994–95; Chair. Int. Cttee for Developing Countries World Energy Council 1992–95; int. consultant 1995–; currently Chair. Jordan Electricity Regulatory Comm.; Hon. Vice-Chair. World Energy Council; decorations from Jordan, Sweden, Italy, Indonesia, Austria and the Vatican; Achievement Medal, IEEE (UK) 1998, Global Energy Award, World Energy Council Rome 2007. *Publications:* Economics of Reliability 1978, Financial and Economic Evaluation of Projects 1997, Palestine and Egypt Under the Ottomans: Paintings, Books, Photographs, Maps and Manuscripts 2003, Economic Evaluation of Projects in the Electricity Supply Industry 2003; numerous articles in professional journals. *Leisure interest:* collecting nineteenth-century Jerusalem and Holy Land artefacts. *Address:* PO Box 410, Amman 11831 (home); PO Box 925387, Amman 11119, Jordan (home). *Telephone:* (6) 5815316 (home); (6) 5805001 (office). *Fax:* (6) 5827392 (home). *E-mail:* khatib36@wanadoo.jo (home); khatib@nets.com.jo (office).

KHATTAK, Vice-Adm. Taj Muhammad, MSc; Pakistani naval officer; *Chairman, Port Qasim Authority;* b. 20 Feb. 1948, Sahiwal; s. of Karra Khan Khattak and Gul Begum; m. Nasim Khattak; two s.; ed Cadet Coll., Hassan Abdal; joined Pakistan Navy 1965, fought during Indo-Pak War 1971 (POW in India for two years), appointments include Flag Officer of Sea Training, Additional Sec./Dir-Gen. Ports and Shipping Wing, Ministry of Communications, Commdr Pakistan Fleet, Deputy Chief of Naval Staff (Projects), Deputy Chief of Naval Staff (Material), Chief of Staff, Naval HQ, Islamabad; apptd

Rear Adm. 1997, Vice-Adm. 2002; currently Chair. Port Qasim Authority, Karachi; Sword of Honour 1969, Sitara-e-Jurrat (Gallantry Award) 1971, Sitara-e-Imtiaz 1996, Hilal-e-Imtiaz 2001. *Publications include:* Amphibious Threat to Pakistan, Indian Nuclear Threat. *Leisure interests:* reading, golf. *Address:* Office of the Chairman, Port Qasim Authority, Bin Qasim, Karachi 75020 (office); 12 B/1 3rd Gizri Street, DHA, Phave-IV Karachi 75020, Pakistan (home). *Telephone:* (21) 9204271 (office); (21) 5898382 (home). *E-mail:* tajmkhattak@hotmail.com (home). *Website:* www.portqasim.org.pk (office).

KHATUN, Sahara, BA, LLB; Bangladeshi politician; *Minister of Home Affairs;* b. 1 March 1943, Dhaka; mem. Awami League, currently Legal Sec.; mem. Jatiya Sangsad (Parl.) for Dhaka-18 constituency; Minister of Home Affairs 2009–; Founder and Pres. Bangladesh Awami Ainjibi Parishad (advocacy group); Gen. Sec. Bangladesh Mahila Samity (women's asscn); mem. Int. Women Lawyers' Asscn, Int. Women's Alliance. *Address:* Ministry of Home Affairs, Bangladesh Secretariat, School Bldg, 2nd and 3rd Floors, Dhaka, Bangladesh (office). *Telephone:* (2) 7169076 (office). *Fax:* (2) 7164788 (office). *E-mail:* info@mha.gov.bd (office). *Website:* www.mha.gov.bd (office).

KHAVIN, Vladimir Yosifovich; Russian architect; b. 29 July 1931, Moscow; s. of Yosif Efimovich Khavin and Sophya Danilovna Khavina; m. Nadezhda Ermakova; one s.; ed Moscow Architectural Inst.; Head of Workshop no. 12 of Mosproekt-1; teacher, Moscow Inst. of Architecture 1976–; Corresp. mem. Int. Acad. of Architecture 1999; Lenin Prize 1984; Honoured Architect of Russia 1988. *Works include:* Circus Bldg on Vernadsky St, Moscow 1963–71, October Square 1972, Intourist Hotel Complex by Kakhovskaya Metro Station 1980, Monument to Frunze, Frunze 1965, The Rear to the Front Monument, Magnitogorsk 1972–79, memorial complex To the Heroes of the Civil War and the Great Patriotic War, Novorosiysk 1982, Moscow town-building exhbn, Brestskaya St 1985, Palace of Youth on Komsomolskaya Avenue, Moscow 1988, new residential Dist Yushnoye Buruvo 1990–, reconstruction of Cheryomushkinski Dist, Moscow 1990–, Russian Jt-Stock Co. complex GASPROM 1995, apt houses, Namyotkina str. 1997. *Leisure interest:* painting. *Address:* Glavmosarchitektura, Triumfalnaya Square 1, 103001 Moscow (office); Novocheryomushkinskaya str. 71/82, Apt 259, 123056 Moscow, Russia (home). *Telephone:* (495) 251-61-72 (office); (495) 719-97-16 (home). *Fax:* (495) 251-61-72.

KHAYOYEV, Izatullo; Tajikistani politician and economist; b. 22 June 1936, Khodzhaikhok, Kulyab Dist, Tajik SSR; m. several s.; ed Tajik Univ., Higher Party School; mem. CPSU 1961–91; worked in financial insts 1954–61; Head of Dept, Ministry of Agric. 1961–63; Chair. of collective farm 1963–65; Sr posts in state and CP insts 1966–78; Minister of Meat and Dairy Industry, Tajik SSR 1978–83; First Sec. Kulyab Dist 1983–86; Deputy, USSR Supreme Soviet 1984–89; cand. mem. CPSU Cen. Cttee 1986–91; Chair. Council of Ministers, Tajik SSR 1986–90, Vice-Pres. Tajik SSR 1990–91; Prime Minister 1991–92; Minister of Foreign Econ. Relations 1992–94; Head of Staff of Pres. Rakhmonov 1994–96; in pvt. business 1999–; orders and medals of USSR and Repub. of Tajikistan. *Leisure interests:* saddle-horse riding, reading fiction, science fiction and literature. *Address:* Prospect Rudaki, 1 proezd k. 75/2, Dushanbe, Tajikistan (home). *Telephone:* 24-75-35 (home).

KHAYRULLOYEV, Maj.-Gen. Sherali; Tajikistani government official and fmr army officer; *Minister of Defence;* b. 8 Nov. 1949, Dangarin Dist, Kulob Viloyat; m.; c.; ed Tajikistan State Univ.; conscripted to serve in USSR Ministry of Internal Affairs 1970, served in various positions including Platoon Commdr 1970–77, subsequently served in various Ministry depts; Deputy Internal Affairs Minister 1988–95; Minister of Defence 1995–. *Address:* Ministry of Defence, 734025 Dushanbe, Kuchai Bokhtar 59, Tajikistan (office). *Telephone:* (372) 23-18-97 (office). *Fax:* (372) 23-19-37 (office).

KHAZANOV, Gennady Viktorovich; Russian comedian and actor; b. 1945, Moscow; m. Zlata Khazanov; one d.; ed State High School of Circus and Variety Actors; worked in radio equipment factory; debut as actor Moscow Univ. Students' Theatre Nash Dom; compere L. Utyosov Orchestra; on professional stage since 1969 in solo productions, first production Trifles of Life 1981; variety programmes Evident and Unbelievable 1987, Little Tragedies 1987, Selected 1988; leading role Gamblers of XXI Century Moscow Art Theatre; leading role in film Little Giant of Large Sex; performed in America, Australia, Israel, Germany, Canada; Artistic Dir Variety Theatre Mono 1991–96; Dir, Artistic Dir Moscow Variety Theatre 1997–; First Prize All-Union Competition of Variety Artists; State Prize 1995. *Address:* Variety Theatre, Bersenevskaya Nab. 20/2, 109072 Moscow, Russia. *Telephone:* (495) 230-18-68.

KHEIFETS, Leonid; Russian stage director; b. 4 May 1934, Minsk, Belarus; ed Belarus Polytech. Inst., Moscow State Inst. of Theatre Arts; stage dir Moscow Theatre of the Soviet Army 1963–71, chief stage dir 1988–94; stage dir Moscow Maly Theatre 1971–88; teacher, then Prof. Moscow State Inst. of Theatre Arts 1980–; State Prize of the Russian Federation 1991. *Plays:* The One Who Made Miracle 1962, My Poor Marat 1965, The Death of Ivan the Terrible 1966, Masters of Time (Moscow Theatre of the Soviet Army) 1967, Wedding of Krechinsky 1971, Before the Sunset 1973, King Lear 1979, Retro (with Galin, Moscow Maly Theatre) 1981, Western Tribune (Sovremennik Theatre) 1983, Cherry Garden, Rudin (on TV), Antigona in New York (Moscow Theatre of the Modern Play) 1995, Running Stranger (Moscow Mossoviet Theatre) 1996.

KHELEF, Abdelaziz, Licence in Econ. Sciences, High Diploma in Econ. Sciences; Algerian economist and banker; *Director-General, Arab Bank for Economic Development in Africa (Banque arabe pour le développement économique en Afrique—BADEA);* ed in Algeria and Paris, France; has held numerous high-ranking positions in Algerian Govt, including Minister of Commerce, Minister of Finance, State Sec. in charge of Maghreb Affairs, Amb. to Tunisia and Sec.-Gen. of the Presidency; joined Islamic Devt Bank (IDB) in 1994 where he held several high-ranking positions, including Advisor to Pres. and IDB Regional Dir for Northern and Western Africa; Dir-Gen. Arab Bank for Econ. Devt in Africa (Banque arabe pour le développement économique en Afrique—BADEA) 2006–. *Address:* Arab Bank for Economic Development in Africa, Sayed Abd ar-Rahman el-Mahdi Street, PO Box 2640, Khartoum 11111, Sudan (office). *Telephone:* (1) 83773646 (office). *Fax:* (1) 83770600 (office). *E-mail:* badea@badea.org (office). *Website:* www.badea.org (office).

KHELIL, Chakib, PhD; Algerian engineer, economist and government official; *Minister of Energy and Mining;* b. 8 Aug. 1939, Oujda, Morocco; m.; two c.; ed Texas A&M Univ., USA; engineer with Shell and Phillips Petroleum, Okla and with McCord and Assocs, Dallas; returned to Algeria as Head of Petroleum Eng Dept Sonatrach 1971, also Pres. Alcore (jt venture between Sonatrach and Corelab); Chair. Valhyd Group (oil recovery co.) 1973–76, also Tech. Adviser to Pres. of Algeria; with World Bank 1980–99 (retd), positions included petroleum projects in Africa, Latin America and Asia, then Head of Energy Unit for Latin America then Petroleum Adviser; Minister of Energy and Mines 1999–; Pres. OPEC 2001, 2008; Chair. African Energy Comm. 2001; Pres. Org. of Arab Petroleum Exporting Countries 2002, Asscn of African Petroleum Producers 2004; Medal of the Order of the Sun of Peru 2002. *Address:* Ministry of Energy and Mining, BP 677, Tower A, Val d'Hydra, Alger-Gare, Algiers, Algeria (office). *Telephone:* (21) 48-85-26 (office). *Fax:* (21) 48-85-57 (office). *E-mail:* info@memalgeria.org (office). *Website:* www.mem-algeria.org (office).

KHER, Anupam; Indian actor; b. 7 March 1955; fmr Chair. Indian Film Certification Bd; Padma Shri 2004 8 Filmfare Awards. *Films include:* Saaransh 1984, Utsav 1984, Hum Naujawan 1985, Wafadaar 1985, Arjun 1985, Aitbaar 1985, Kala Dhanda Goray Log 1986, Aakhree Raasta 1986, Karma 1986, Samundar 1986, Raosaheb 1986, Jeeva 1986, Insaaf Ki Awaaz 1986, Duty 1986, Allah Rakha 1986, Uttar Dakshin 1987, Zevar 1987, Sansar 1987, Dozakh 1987, Falak 1988, Hatya 1988, Zakhmi Aurat 1988, Agnee 1988, Vijay 1988, Tezaab 1988, Sone Pe Suhaaga 1988, Pestonjee 1988, Kabzaa 1988, Ghar Mein Ram Gali Mein Shyam 1988, Bees Saal Baad 1988, Ladaai 1989, Zakhm 1989, Paap Ka Anth 1989, Tridev 1989, Ram Lakhan 1989, Parinda 1989, Nigahen 1989, Main Tera Dushman 1989, Mahadev 1989, Kanoon Apna Apna 1989, Deshwasi 1989, Chaal Baaz 1989, Aakhri Gulam 1989, Krodh 1990, Dil 1990, Jeevan Ek Sangharsh 1990, Aaj Ka Arjun 1990, Nyay Anyay 1990, Muqaddar Ka Badshah 1990, Khatarnak 1990, Jeene Do 1990, Izzatdaar 1990, Awaargi 1990, Hum 1991, Saudagar 1991, Saathi 1991, Phoolwathi 1991, Mast Kalandar 1991, Lamhe 1991, Khel 1991, Haque 1991, Dil Hai Ki Manta Nahin 1991, Sarphira 1992, Humlaa 1992, Ek Ladka Ek Ladki 1992, Deedar 1992, Vansh 1992, Umar Pachpan Ki Dil Bachpan Ka 1992, Heer Ranjha 1992, Beta 1992, Apradhi 1992, Phoolan Hasina Ramkali 1993, Aaj Ki Aurat 1993, Baaghi Sultana 1993, Roop Ki Rani Choron Ka Raja 1993, Dil Ki Baazi 1993, Izzat Ki Roti 1993, Gumrah 1993, Sainik 1993, Dil Tera Aashiq 1993, Tadipaar 1993, Kasam Teri Kasam 1993, Shreeman Aashiq 1993, Parampara 1993, Meri Jaan 1993, Lootere 1993, Khalnayak 1993, 1942 A Love Story 1993, Baali Umar Ko Salaam 1994, Saajan Ka Ghar 1994, Pyaar Ka Rog 1994, Pehla Pehla Pyaar 1994, Ikke Pe Ekka 1994, Laadla 1994, Insaniyat 1994, HAHK 1994, Eena Meena Deeka 1994, Darr 1994, Janam Kundli 1995, Dilwale Dulhania Le Jayenge 1995, Ram Shastra 1995, Zamana Deewana 1995, Taqdeerwala 1995, Raghuveer 1995, Oh Darling! Yeh Hai India 1995, Dushmani 1995, Dil Ka Doctor 1995, Tu Chor Main Sipahi 1996, Papa Kahte Hain 1996, Prem Granth 1996, Shohrat 1996, Maahir 1996, Mr Bechara 1996, Vishwasghaat 1996, Shastra 1996, Nirbhay 1996, Chaahat 1996, Zor 1997, Agni Chakra 1997, Ziddi 1997, Mere Sapno Ki Rani 1997, Aflatoon 1997, Uff! Yeh Mohabbat 1997, Sanam 1997, Judwaa 1997, Gudgudee 1997, Deewana Mastana 1997, Hazaar Chaurasi Ki Maa 1998, Keemat 1998, Salaakhen 1998, Aunty No. 1 1998, Jab Pyaar Kisise Hota Hai 1998, Puraido 1998, Kuch Kuch Hota Hai 1998, Prem Aggan 1998, Hum Aapke Dil Mein Rehte Hain 1999, Sooryavansham 1999, Haseena Maan Jaayegi 1999, Jhooth Bole Kauwe Kaate 1999, Kaho Naa... Pyar Hai 1999, Kya Kehna 2000, Refugee 2000, Dhadkan 2000, Hamara Dil Aapke Paas Hai 2000, Dhaai Akshar Prem Ke 2000, Aaghaaz 2000, Mohabbatein 2000, Ghaath 2000, Aashiq 2001, Jodi No. 1 2001, Kyo Kii 2001, Bend it Like Beckham 2002, Yeh Hai Jalwa 2002, Jaal: The Trap 2003, Banana Brothers 2003, Shart: The Challenge 2004, Bride and Predjudice 2004, Jaan-E-Mann 2006, Hope and a Little Sugar 2006, Khosla Ka Ghosla 2006, It's a Mismatch 2006, Vivah 2006, Meerabai Not Out 2007, Zamaanat 2007, Shakalaka Boom Boom 2007, Gandhi Park 2007, Jaane Bhi Do Yaaron 2007, Buddha Mar Gaya 2007, Se, jie 2007, Victoria No. 203 2007, Dhokha 2007, Apna Asmaan 2007, Kuch Khatta Kuch Meetha 2007.

KHIATI, Mostéfa, PhD; Algerian professor of medicine and academic administrator; *President, FOREM (Fondation pour la Promotion de la Santé et le Développement de la Recherche);* ed Algerian Medical Inst.; fmr Head, Dept of Pediatrics, El-Harrach Hosp.; Chef de service de pédiatrie, Hôpital Zmirli 1989–99, Hôpital Belfort 1999–; Pres. Nat. Foundation for Health Progress and Medical Research Devt in Algeria 1990–; Président du Conseil Médical de l'hôpital Belfort 2003–; mem. Medical Soc. of Algeria, Algerian Soc. of Pediatrics 1983–86, Int. Asscn of Pediatrics, Int. Asscn of Pediatrics; Pres. FOREM (Fondation pour la Promotion de la Santé et le Développement de la Recherche) 1990–; fmr consultant, Ministry of Health; Fellow, Islamic Acad. of Sciences; Dr hc (l'Université de Tiaret) 2002 Shoman Award for Clinical Sciences 1984, Maghrebian Medicine Award 1986, Chadli Benjedid Award 1989, Union of Arab Physicians Award, Prix Maghrébin de Médecine et du Président de la République Tunisienne (Tunis) 1997, Humanitarian price, XIIe World congress, Wadem (Lyon, France) 2001. *Address:* 41, Cité du 20

Août, Oued Errouman, 16 403 El Achour, Algeria (office). *Telephone:* (61) 50-70-95 (office). *Fax:* (21) 52-25-94 (office). *E-mail:* mkhiati@voila.fr.

KHIEM, Pham Gia, DSc; Vietnamese politician and government official; *Minister of Foreign Affairs;* b. 6 Aug. 1944, Hanoi; ed Hanoi Univ. of Tech. and postgraduate studies in Czechoslovakia; Lecturer, Bac Thai Univ. of Mechanical Eng and Electronics 1967–70; worked at Ministry of Investment and Planning 1976–96, positions included Head, Industrial Div. and Dir Dept of Science, Educ. and Environment, then Deputy Minister of Investment and Planning, Minister of Science, Tech. and Planning 1996–97; Deputy Prime Minister 1997–2006; Minister of Foreign Affairs 2006–; Deputy Nat. Ass.; mem. CP of Viet Nam Central Cttee (CPVCC), Politburo. *Address:* Ministry of Foreign Affairs, 1 Ton That Dam, Ba Dinh District, Hanoi, Viet Nam (office). *Telephone:* (4) 1992000 (office). *Fax:* (4) 8445905 (office). *E-mail:* banbientap@mofa.gov.vn (office). *Website:* www.mofa.gov.vn (office).

KHIEU, Samphan; Cambodian politician; b. 1932, Svay Rieng Prov.; m. Khieu Ponnary; ed Univ. of Paris; f. French-language journal, Observer, Cambodia; Deputy Nat. Ass. in Prince Sihanouk's party, Sangkum Reastr Nyum (Popular Socialist Community); served as Sec. of State for Commerce; left Phnom Penh to join Khmer Rouge 1967; Minister of Defence in Royal Govt of Nat. Union of Cambodia (GRUNC) 1970–76, Deputy Prime Minister 1970–76 (in exile 1970–75, in Phnom Penh 1975–76); mem. Politburo Nat. United Front of Cambodia (FUNC) 1970–79; C-in-C Khmer Rouge High Command 1973–79; Pres. of State Presidium (Head of State) 1976–79; Prime Minister of the Khmer Rouge opposition Govt fighting Vietnamese forces 1979–91; Vice-Pres. of Govt of Democratic Kampuchea (in exile) June 1982–91 (responsibility for Foreign Affairs); Pres. Khmer Rouge 1985–91, returned to Cambodia Nov. 1991; apptd 'Prime Minister' of illegal Provisional Govt of Nat. Unity (fmrly Khmer Rouge) 1994; Chair. Party of Democratic Kampuchea; Pres. and founder Nat. Solidarity Party May 1997; mem. Supreme Nat. Council 1991–97; Vice-Pres. in charge of Foreign Affairs, Nat. Govt of Cambodia 1991; Chair. Cambodian Nat. Union Party (CNUP) 1993–97; surrended to govt Dec. 1997; arrested Nov. 2007.

KHIN NYUNT, Lt-Gen.; Myanma politician and army officer; b. 1940, Kyauktan; m. Khin Win Shwe; one d. two s.; Chief of Military Intelligence 1984–2003; Prime Minister of Myanmar 2003–04; mem. Mil. Council; sentenced to 44 years (suspended) in jail on eight charges including corruption and bribery 2005.

KHIZHA, Georgy Stepanovich, DTechSc; Russian politician and manager; b. 2 May 1938, Ashkhabad; m.; two d.; ed Leningrad Polytech. Inst., Acad. of Nat. Econ.; engineer, head of div., Chief Engineer, Dir-Gen. Leningrad Engels Factory (now Svetlana Asscn) 1961–91; Deputy Mayor of Leningrad 1991–92; Deputy Prime Minister of Russia 1992–93, Chair. Expert Council of Govt 1993–, Int. Cttee for Econ. Reforms and Co-operation 1993–96. *Publications:* more than 60 papers and about 50 licensed inventions. *Leisure interests:* hunting and diving. *Address:* Expert Council, Krasnopresnenskaya nab. 2, 103274 Moscow, Russia. *Telephone:* (495) 205-59-67; (495) 205-56-32.

KHLOPONIN, Aleksander Gennadyevich; Russian politician and banking official; *Governor of Krasnoyarsk;* b. 6 March 1965, Colombo, Sri Lanka; m.; one d.; ed Moscow Inst. of Finance; army service 1983–85; with Vneshtorgbank 1989–92; Deputy, First Deputy Chair., Chair., Pres., Commercial Bank Int. Financial Co. 1992–; Acting Deputy Chair., mem. Bd of Dirs then Dir-Gen. Norilsky Nikel 1996–2001; mem. Advisory Council, Fed. Comm. 1997–; mem. Bd of Dirs Kolskaya Mine Co., Murmansk 1998–; Gov. Taimyr Autonomous Territory 2001–02; Gov. Krasnoyarsk Territory 2002–; Order of Honour 1998. *Address:* Office of the Governor, Mira prosp. 110, 660009 Krasnoyarsk, Russia (office). *Telephone:* (3912) 22-22-63 (office). *Fax:* (3912) 22-11-78 (office). *E-mail:* kds@adm-kr.krasnoyarsk.su (office). *Website:* www.krskstate.ru (office).

KHLYSTUN, Viktor Nikolayevich, DEcon; Russian agricultural engineer and politician; b. 19 March 1946, Dmitrievka, Kokchetav Region, Kazakhstan; m.; two c.; ed Moscow Inst. of Agric. Eng (MIIZ); metalworker, worker sovkhoz 1963–65; Asst, Sr teacher, docent, Prof., Dean Moscow Inst. of Agric. Eng 1971–90, 1998–, Sec. CP Bureau 1977–80, Pro-rector 1980–90; Chair. RSFSR State Cttee on Land Reform 1990–91; Minister of Agric. 1991–93, 1995–98; Deputy Chair. Agroprombank 1994–96; Deputy Chair. of Russian Govt responsible for agric. problems 1997–98; Dir-Gen. Inst. of Agrarian Market Research, Moscow 1998–; Corresp. mem. Russian Acad. of Agricultural Sciences; Vice-Pres. Razgulyai-Ukzross Corpn 1998–. *Address:* Institute of Agricultural Engineering, 2nd Institutskaya str. 6, 109428 Moscow, Russia (office). *Telephone:* (495) 171-29-50. *Fax:* (495) 171-29-50.

KHODAKOV, Aleksander Georgyevich; Russian diplomatist; b. 8 March 1952, Moscow; m.; two s.; ed Moscow State Inst. of Int. Relations, Algiers Univ., Algeria; worked in USSR Embassy, Gabon 1974–79; Legal and Treaty Dept, Ministry of Foreign Affairs 1980–85, Deputy Dir Legal Dept 1992–94, Dir 1994–97; First Sec., then Second Sec. Perm. Mission of USSR to UN, New York 1985–91; Perm. Rep. to Org. for banning Chemical Armaments, The Hague; Amb. to the Netherlands 1997–2003; mem. of staff Ministry of Foreign Affairs 2003–. *Address:* Ministry of Foreign Affairs, Smolenskaya-Sennaya pl. 32/34, 121200 Moscow, Russia (office). *Telephone:* (095) 244-16-06 (office). *Fax:* (095) 230-21-30 (office). *E-mail:* ministry@mid.ru (office). *Website:* www.mid.ru (office).

KHODJAMYRAT, Annagurbanov; Turkmenistani government official; *Minister of Internal Affairs;* b. 1959, Akhal velayat; ed Turkmen State Univ.; Head, Police Dept of Aşgabat 2004–07; Deputy Minister of Internal Affairs Jan.–April 2007, Minister of Internal Affairs April 2007–. *Address:*

Ministry of Internal Affairs, 744000 Aşgabat, pr. 2076 85, Turkmenistan (office). *Telephone:* (12) 35-59-23 (office).

KHODORKOVSKII, Mikhail Borisovich; Russian business executive; b. 26 June 1963, Moscow; m. 1st Yelena Khodorkovskaya; one s.; m. 2nd Inna Khodorkovskaya; two s. one d.; ed Moscow Mendeleyev Inst. of Chemistry and Tech., G. V. Plekhanov Inst. of Nat. Econs; Head of Centre of Interfield Research Programmes (NTTM), USSR State Cttee for Science and Tech. (now Menatep Asscn) 1986–93; Chair. Menatep Bank 1993–; Chair. Commercial Innovation Bank of Scientific Progress 1989–90; Econ. Counsellor to Chair. of Russian Council of Ministers 1990–91; Deputy Minister of Fuel and Energy Industry 1991; Chair. Rosprom 1995–; Vice-Pres. YUKOS Asscn 1996, Chair. United Bd Rosprom-YUKOS Co. 1997–2000, Chair. Exec. Cttee OAO NK YUKOS, Man. Cttee YUKOS-Moscow 2000–03, CEO YUKOS –2003; Owner, Moskovskiye Novosti newspaper 2003–; charged with fraud and tax evasion Oct. 2003, convicted May 2005 and sentenced to nine years in prison, sentence later reduced to eight years, moved into prison camp no. 13 in Krasnokamensk, Zabaykalsky Krai Oct. 2005. *Address:* 105215 Moscow, a/ya 'Press-Tsentr', Russia. *Website:* www.khodorkovsky.ru.

KHOO, Eric; Singaporean filmmaker; *Head Filmmaker, Zhao Wei Films;* b. 27 March 1965; dir, producer, writer and cinematographer of short films; Head Filmmaker, Zhao Wei Films (production co.); has participated in festivals in Venice, Berlin, Cannes, San Francisco, Montreal, Moscow, London, Rotterdam and the Golden Horse Film Festival in Taipei; Young Artist Award for Film, Nat. Arts Council 1997, Singapore Youth Awards 1999. *Films directed include:* Barbie Dogs Joe 1990, Hope and Requiem 1991, August 1991, The Punk Rocker and... 1992, The Watchman 1993, Symphony 92.4 FM 1993, Pain (also Ed. and Cinematographer) 1994, Mee Pok Man (Fukuoka and Pusan Prizes) 1995, Shier lou (Twelve Stories: Fed. of Int. Film Critics Award, UOB Young Cinema Award, Singapore Int. Festival, Golden Maile Award for Best Picture, Hawaii Int. Film Festival) 1997, Home VDO 2000, One Leg Kicking 2001, Be With Me 2005, Digital Sam in Sam Saek 2006: Talk to Her 2006, F. (Cinematographer) 2007. *Films produced include:* Pain 1994, Liang Po Po 1999, Stories About Love 2000, One Leg Kicking 2001, 15 2003, Zombie Dogs 2004, 4:30 2005. *Films written include:* Hope and Requiem 1991, August 1991, Pain 1994, Shier lou (Twelve Stories) 1997, Be With Me 2005. *Television:* as exec. producer: Drive 1998, Seventh Month 2004. *Publications:* One Fine Day (graphic novel) 2005. *Address:* Zhao Wei Films, 22 Scotts Road, No. 01–38, Singapore 228221 (office). *Telephone:* 67357124 (office). *Fax:* 67351181 (office). *E-mail:* info@zhaowei.com (office). *Website:* www.zhaowei.com (office).

KHOO-OEI, Mavis; Singaporean business executive; *Chairman and Managing Director, Goodwood Park Hotel Limited;* b. (Khoo Bee Geok), d. of the late Khoo Teck Puat; m. Humphrey Oei (deceased); ed Nat. Univ. of Singapore; an heir to banking and hotel fortune of her father; Chair. and Man. Dir Goodwood Park Hotel; involved with running Khoo Teck Puat Foundation; mem. Bd of Dirs Khoo Teck Puat Hosp., Yishun. *Address:* Goodwood Park Hotel, 22 Scotts Road, Singapore 228221 (office). *Telephone:* 6737-7411 (office). *Fax:* 6732-8558 (office). *E-mail:* enquiries@goodwoodparkhotel.com (office). *Website:* www.goodwoodparkhotel.com (office).

KHORANA, Har Gobind, BS, MSc, PhD; American (b. Indian) scientist and academic; *Alfred P. Sloan Professor of Biology and Chemistry Emeritus and Senior Lecturer, Massachusetts Institute of Technology;* b. 9 Jan. 1922, Raipur; s. of Sri Ganpat Rai and Shiramati Krishna Khorana; m. Esther Elizabeth Sibler 1952; one s. two d.; ed Punjab Univ., Univ. of Liverpool; began career as organic chemist; worked with Sir Alexander Todd on building nucleotides, Cambridge 1950–52; later worked with Nat. Research Inst., Canada, until 1960; Prof. and Co-Dir Inst. of Enzyme Chem., Univ. of Wis. 1960–64, Conrad A. Elvehjem Prof. in Life Sciences 1964–70; Andrew D. White Prof.-at-Large, Cornell Univ., Ithaca 1974–80; Alfred P. Sloan Prof., MIT 1970–97, Prof. Emer. and Sr Lecturer 1997–; Visiting Prof., Rockefeller Inst. 1958–; mem. NAS; Foreign Academician USSR (now Russian) Acad. of Sciences 1971; Foreign mem. Royal Soc. London 1978, Pontifical Acad. of Sciences 1978; numerous hon. degrees,; Nobel Prize for Medicine and Physiology (with Holley and Nirenberg) for interpretation of genetic code and its function in protein synthesis 1968, Louisa Gross Horwitz Prize for Biochem. 1968, ACS Award for creative work in Synthetic Chem. 1968, Lasker Foundation Award 1968, American Acad. of Achievement Award 1971, Willard Gibbs Medal 1974, Gairdner Foundation Annual Award 1980, Nat. Medal of Science 1987, Paul Kayser Int. Award of Merit 1987. *Publications:* Some Recent Developments in the Chemistry of Phosphate Esters of Biological Interest 1961; articles on Biochemistry in various journals. *Leisure interests:* music, hiking. *Address:* Department of Chemistry, Massachusetts Institute of Technology, 77 Massachusetts Avenue, Room 68-680, Cambridge, MA 02139, USA (office). *Telephone:* (617) 253-1871 (office). *Fax:* (617) 253-0533 (office). *E-mail:* khorana@mit.edu (office). *Website:* web.mit.edu/chemistry/www/faculty/khorana.html (office).

KHOSLA, Ashok, BA, MA, AM, PhD; Indian scientist, environmentalist, academic and international organization official; *President, International Union for Conservation of Nature (IUCN);* b. 31 March 1940; m.; ed St Lawrence Coll., Kent and Peterhouse, Univ. of Cambridge, UK, Harvard Univ., USA; refugee from Kashmir 1947; studied at 16 schools in 10 countries; Faculty mem., Harvard Univ. 1963–70; man. various businesses in USA 1965–70; Dir Office of Environmental Planning, Govt of India, New Delhi 1972–76; Dir Infoterra, UNEP, Nairobi, Kenya 1976–82; Chair. and CEO various social enterprises in India 1985–; Founder and Chair. Development Alternatives, New Delhi 1983–; Special Advisor to Brundtland Comm. (WCED), mem. evaluation teams for GEF pilot phase, World Bank's 25 Years of Environmental Programmes, and Sec.-Gen.'s Task Force to Restructure the

Environmental Activities of the United Nations; Chair. NGO Forum at Earth Summit, Rio de Janeiro 1992; has served on bds of several environment and conservation orgs, including Int. Union for Conservation of Nature (IUCN), Worldwide Fund for Nature, Centre for Our Common Future, Int. Inst. for Sustainable Devt, Stockholm Environment Inst., Zero Emissions Research and Initiatives, Alliance for a New Humanity, EnergyGlobe, EXPO 2000, Toyota Environmental Awards and Planet2025; first elected Councillor to IUCN, representing Govt of India, at Kinshasa Gen. Ass. 1975, UNEP Rep. at Council 1978, participated in Council as Deputy Chair. and later as Chair. Comm. on Environmental, Econ. and Social Policy (then CEP, later CESP), re-elected Regional Councillor 1988, 1990, Pres. IUCN 2008–; Pres. Club of Rome 2006–; mem. Int. Advisory Council, Criteria CaixaCorp, Barcelona 2008–; Chair. Int. Council for Science/Scientific Cttee on Problems of the Environment Programme on Environmental Information 1984–87; mem. UNEP Governing Council 1972–76; Teaching Fellow, with Prof. Roger Revelle, designed and taught Nat Sci 118, 'Population, Resources and the Environment', Harvard Univ. (first university course on the environment) 1965; Order of the Golden Ark (Netherlands) 1999, Stockholm Challenge Award 2001, UN Sasakawa Environment Prize 2002, Schwab Foundation Award for Outstanding Social Entrepreneur 2004. *Publications:* has published extensively on environmental issues. *Address:* International Union for Conservation of Nature, Rue Mauverney 28, Gland 1196, Switzerland (office). *Telephone:* (22) 999-0000 (office). *Fax:* (22) 999-0002 (office). *E-mail:* webmaster@iucn.org (office). *Website:* www.iucn.org (office); www.devalt.org.

KHOSLA, Vinod, BTech, MSc, MBA; Indian/American investment industry executive; *Owner, Khosla Ventures;* b. 28 Jan. 1955, Pune, India; m. Neeru Khosla; one s. three d.; ed Indian Inst. of Tech., Delhi, Carnegie Mellon Univ., Stanford Univ. Grad. School of Business; started soy milk co. to service people in India who did not have refrigerators 1975; came to USA to study; one of three founders of Daisy Systems (first significant computer aided design system for electrical engineers) 1980; started Sun Microsystems to build workstations for software developers 1982, pioneered 'open systems' and RISC processors, left co. 1985; Gen. Partner, Kleiner, Perkins, Caufield & Byers (venture capital firm) 1986–; f. Khosla Ventures 2004; Co-founder The Indus Entrepreneurs; assists or serves on bds of eASIC (programmable ASIC platform), Infinera (optical communications), Kovio (printed electronics), Skyblue (internet PC), Spatial Photonics (Micromirror displays), Xsigo (datacentre switch), Grameen Foundation, MetricStream, moka5, Ausra, Zettacore, iSkoot, among others; Charter mem. TiE (not-for-profit global network of entrepreneurs and professionals); Founding Bd mem. Indian School of Business; Hon. Chair. DonorsChoose San Francisco Bay Area Advisory Bd. *Address:* Khosla Ventures, 3000 Sand Hill Road, Building 3, Suite 170, Menlo Park, CA 94025, USA (office). *Telephone:* (650) 376-8500 (office). *Fax:* (650) 926-9590 (office). *E-mail:* kv@khoslaventures.com (office). *Website:* www.khoslaventures.com (office).

KHOSROKHAVAR, Farhad; Iranian/French sociologist and academic; *Professor of Sociology and Director of Studies, Ecole des Hautes Etudes en Sciences Sociales (EHESS);* b. 21 March 1948, Tehran; Asst Prof., Bou Ali Univ. Hamadan, Iran 1977–79; Assoc. Prof., Center for Science Policy, Ministry of Culture and Higher Educ., Iran, 1979–90; Rockefeller Fellow 1990–91; Assoc. Prof. of Sociology, Ecole des Hautes Etudes en Sciences Sociales–Cadis (EHESS), Paris 1991–98, Prof. of Sociology 1998–, currently also Dir of Studies; Visiting Scholar, Yale Univ. 2008, Harvard Univ. 2009. *Publications include:* La Foulard et la République (with Françoise Gaspard) 1995, Sous le voile islamique (with Chala Chafiq) 1995, Anthropologie de la révolution iranienne 1997, L'islam des jeunes 1997, L'Iran, comment sortir d'une révolution religieuse? (with Oliver Roy) 1999, La recherche de soi, dialogues sur le sujet (with Alain Touraine) 2000, L'Instance du sacré 2001, Les Nouveaux martyrs d'Allah (trans. with additional chapter as Suicide Bombers: Allah's New Martyrs 2005) 2002, L'Islam en prison 2004, Muslims in Prison (with James A. Beckford and Danièle Joly) 2005, Avoir vingt ans dans le pays des ayatollahs (with Amir Nikpey) 2009, Jihadism Worldwide 2009. *Address:* EHESS–Paris, 54 boulevard Raspail, 75006 Paris, France (office). *Telephone:* 1-49-54-25-63 (office). *E-mail:* cavard@ehess.fr (office). *Website:* www.ehess.fr (office).

KHOTINENKO, Vladimir I.; Russian film director and producer, actor, scriptwriter and artist; b. 20 Jan. 1952, Slavgorod, Altai territory; m.; one d.; ed Sverdlovsk Inst. of Architecture; constructor at Pavlodar tractor production factory 1969–70; artist Sverdlovsk film studio 1978–82; freelance 1982–; All-Union Film Festival Prize 1988, Kinoshok Prizes 1992, 1993, Nika Prizes for Best Film 1993, for Best Film Dir 1993. *Films:* Races with Pursuit (production designer) 1979, The Smoke of the Home Country (production designer) 1980, Kinfolk (as actor) 1981, Vot takaya muzyka (production designer) 1981, Kazachya zastava (actor, production designer) 1982, Alone and Unarmed (dir) 1984, V strelyayushchej glushi (dir) 1986, Mirror for a Hero (dir) 1987, Who is the Singer Married To? (actor) 1988, Vagon lit (dir) 1989, The Swarm (dir, writer) 1990, Patriotic Comedy (dir, writer) 1992, Makarov (dir, producer) 1993, A Muslim (dir, producer) 1995, The Arrival of a Train (dir, producer) 1995, Road (producer, actor, dir) 1996, 72 metra (dir, writer) 2004, Vecherniy zvon (dir) 2004. *Television:* Po tu storonu volkov (dir, mini series) 2002, Gibel imperii (mini series) 2005. *Address:* Fadeyeva str. 6, apt 269, Moscow 125047, Russia (office). *Telephone:* (495) 250-47-38 (office).

KHOUNA, Cheikh el Avia Ould Mohamed; Mauritanian politician; b. 1956; mem. Democratic and Social Republican Party (replaced by Republican Party for Democracy and Renewal—RPDR 2005); fmr Minister of Fisheries and Marine Economy; Minister of Foreign Affairs 1998, 2008; Prime Minister of Mauritania 1996–97, 1998–2003. *Address:* Republican Party for Democracy and Renewal (RPDR), ZRB, Tevragh Zeina, Nouakchott, Mauritania (office). *Telephone:* 529-18-36 (office). *Fax:* 529-18-00 (office). *E-mail:* info@prdr.mr (office). *Website:* www.prdr.mr (office).

KHOURY, Elias; Lebanese novelist and literary critic; b. 1948, Ashrafiyyeh, nr Beirut; ed Lebanese Univ., Beirut, Univ. of Paris, France; with PLO Research Centre, Beirut 1973–79; Publr Su'un filastiniya (Palestinian Affairs) journal 1976–79; Editorial Dir Al-Karmel 1981–82; Ed. culture section of As-Safir journal 1983-90, Al-Mulhaq cultural supplement of an-Nahar daily newspaper 1992–; Dir Masrah Beyrut theatre 1993–98; Global Distinguished Prof. of Middle Eastern and Islamic Studies, New York Univ. 2004–05; fmr Prof., Columbia Univ., Lebanese Univ., American Univ. of Beirut, and Lebanese American Univ.; Lettre Ulysses Award 2005. *Publications:* An 'ilaqat al-da'irah (novel) 1975, Al-Jabal al-Saghir (novel) 1977, Dirasat fi naqd al-shi'r (criticism) 1979, Abwab al-Madinah (novel) 1981, Al-wujuh al-baida' (novel) 1981, Al-dhakira al-mafquda (criticism) 1982, Al-mubtada' wa'l-khabar (short stories) 1984, Tajribat al-ba'th 'an ufq (criticism) 1984, Zaman al-ihtilal (criticism) 1985, Rahlat Gandhi al-Saghir (novel) 1989, Mamlakat al-Ghuraba (novel) 1993, Majma' al-Asrar (novel) 1994, Bab al-Shams (novel) (Palestine Prize 1998) 1998, Ra'ihat al-Sabun (novel) 2000, Yalo (novel) 2002, Ka'anaha Nae'ma (novel) 2007. *Address:* c/o An-Nahar (The Day), Immeuble An-Nahar, place des Martyrs, Marfa', Beirut 2014 5401, Lebanon. *Telephone:* (1) 994888. *Fax:* (1) 996777. *E-mail:* webmaster@annahar.com.lb. *Website:* www.annaharonline.com.

KHOURY-GHATA, Vénus; Lebanese/French novelist and poet; b. 1937, Bsherre; m. 1st (divorced); three c.; m. 2nd Jean Ghata (died 1981); one d.; ed Etude de Lettres, Liban; fmr journalist; moved to France 1973; fmr contrib. and trans., Europe magazine; Pres. Prix des Cinq Continents, Prix Yvon Goll, Prix France Liban; mem. selection cttee, Prix Mallarmé, Prix Max-Pol-Fouchet, Prix Max-Jacob; frequent radio broadcaster; Chevalier, Légion d'honneur 2000, Officier, Ordre nat. du Mérite 2003; Prix Mallarmé, Prix Apollinaire 1981, Prix Supervielle 1997, Grand Prix, Soc. des Gens de Lettres. *Publications:* poetry: (first collection) 1966, Les Ombres et leurs cris (Prix Guillaume-Apollinaire) 1980, Monologue du mort (Prix Mallarmé) 1987, Fable pour un peuple d'argile (Grand Prix de la Société des gens de lettres) 1992, Anthologie person-elle 1997, Elle dit 1999, Here There Was Once a Country (anthology in trans.) 2001, La Compassion des pierres 2001, She Says (trans.) 2003, À quoi sert la neige – Poèmes pour enfants 2008; novels: Vacarme pour une lune morte 1983, Bayarmine 1990, Mortemaison 1992, La maitresse du notable (Liberaturpreis) 1992, La Maestra 1994, Les Fiancées du Cap Ténès 1995, Une maison au bord des larmes 1998, Privilège des morts 2001, La Compassion des pierres 2001, Le Moine, l'ottoman et la femme du grand argentier 2003, A House on Edge of Tears 2006, La Maison aux orties 2006, Sept pierres pour la femme adultère 2007, Quelle est la nuit parmi les nuits 2007, Les obscurcis 2008; contrib. in trans. to Ambit, Banipal: A Journal of Modern Arab Literature, Columbia, Field, Contemporary Poetry and Poetics, Gobshite Quarterly, Jacket, Luna, The Manhattan Review, Metre, The New Yorker, Poetry, Shenandoah, Verse, Poetry London. *Address:* 16 avenue Raphael, 75016 Paris, France. *Telephone:* 1-45-04-06-37. *Fax:* 1-45-04-06-37.

KHRISTENKO, Viktor Borisovich, BSc, DEcon; Russian politician; *Minister of Industry and Trade;* b. 28 Aug. 1957, Chelyabinsk; m. 2nd Tatyana Golikova; three c.; ed Chelyabinsk Polytechnical Inst. and Acad. of Nat. Economy; sr teacher and Lecturer, Faculty of the Econs of Machine Construction, Chelyabinsk Polytechnical Inst. 1979–90; Chair. Perm. Comm., First Deputy Chair. Econs Cttee, Chair. Property Man. Cttee, Chelyabink City Exec. Cttee 1990–91; Deputy Head Admin of Chelyabinsk Oblast 1991–94, First Deputy Head 1994–96; Plenipotentiary Rep. of the Pres. of the Russian Fed. in Chelyabinsk Oblast 1997; Deputy Minister of Finances, Russian Fed. June 1997, First Deputy Minister 1998; mem. Presidium May–Aug. 1998; Deputy Chair. of Govt (Deputy Prime Minister) April–Sept. 1998, 2000, First Deputy Chair. (First Deputy Prime Minister) 1999, 2000–04, Acting Chair. (Acting Prime Minister) 24 Feb.–5 March 2004; Minister of Industry and Energy (now Minister of Industry and Trade) 2004–; Special Presidential Envoy for Integration with CIS 2004–; Chair. Comm. on Chechnya 2000, on Housing Policy 2001, on Reform of the Electrical Enery Sector 2001. *Address:* Ministry of Industry and Trade, 109074 Moscow, Kitaigorodskii proyezd 7, Russia (home). *Telephone:* (495) 710-55-00 (office). *Fax:* (495) 710-57-22 (office). *E-mail:* info@mte.gov.ru (office). *Website:* www .minprom.gov.ru (office).

KHRUSHCHOV, Nikolai Grigoryevich; Russian biologist; *Director, Koltsov Institute of Biology of Development, Russian Academy of Sciences;* b. 23 June 1932; m.; one d.; ed 2nd Moscow Inst. of Medicine; Jr, then Sr Researcher, Head of Div. Deputy Dir, currently Dir Koltsov Inst. of Biology of Devt USSR (now Russian) Acad. of Sciences; corresp. mem. Russian Acad. of Sciences 1979, mem. 1990, mem. Presidium 1994, Academician Sec. Dept of Gen. Biology; Mechnikov Prize. *Publications:* main scientific research and numerous scientific publs on problems of biology of devt of tissue and cellular systems. *Address:* Koltsov Institute of Biology of Development, Russian Academy of Sciences, Vavilova str. 26, 117808 Moscow, Russia (office). *Telephone:* (495) 938-16-91 (office); (495) 938-51-90 (Acad.) (office).

KHRZHANOVSKY, Andrei Yurevich; Russian filmmaker, scriptwriter and teacher; b. 30 Nov. 1939, Moscow; s. of Yuriy Borisovich Khrzhanovsky and Vera Mihayilovna Khrzhanovsky; m. Mariya Newman 1972; one s.; ed VGIK; worked with 'Soyuzmultfilm' since 1962; Chair. Bd Higher Refresher Animation School-Studio 'Shar'; Prof. VGIK; Hon. Artist of Russia; State Prize 1986, 1999, Prizes of Russian Acad. of Cinema 1995, 1998, 2004. *Films include:* Once upon a time there lived a man by the name of Kozyavin 1966, The Glass Harmonica 1968, The Cupboard 1971, The Butterfly 1972, In the World of Fables 1973, A Wonderful Day 1975, The House that Jack Built 1976, I Fly to You in Memory (trilogy of films based on Pushkin's doodles) 1977,

1981, 1982, The King's Sandwich 1985, The School of Fine Arts (part 1 – A Landscape with Juniper 1987, part 2 – The Return 1990), The Lion with the Grey Beard 1994, Oleg Kagan: Life After Life (documentary) 1996, The Long Journey (based on Federico Fellini's drawings) 1997, The Dreams About MKHAT (documentary) 1999, Studys About Pushkin, Lullaby for Cricket 1999, Pushkin Take-off 2002, I Love You 2002, A Cat and a Half (based on Joseph Brodsky's drawings) 2002. *Publications:* Der ambivalente Charme des Surrealismus: Go East, Frankfurt am Main 2002 (Subversionen des Surrealen un mittel, und osteuropäishen Film), The Pupil of the Wizard: V. S. Meierhold and Erast Garin (ed and contrib.) 2004. *Address:* Vasilyevskaya str. 7, Apt 56, 123056 Moscow, Russia (home). *Telephone:* (495) 254-51-75 (home). *E-mail:* harmonic@umail.ru (home).

KHUB DASS, Rt Rev. Smart, MA; Pakistani educator and religious leader; b. 20 Dec. 1938, Lahore; s. of the late Rev. Khub Dass; ed Univ. of Punjab, Univ. of Nashville, Tenn., USA; fmr youth leader; fmr Prin. Intermediate Colls, Co-ordinator of Educ.; fmrly Gen. Sec. (Synod) Church of Pakistan, now Moderator; Bishop of Hyderabad 1997; Exec. mem. World Methodist Conf., mem. Educ. Cttee. *Publications include:* History of the Church of Pakistan, Seven Words on the Cross, Sunday School Lessons (Sarmaya-I-Hayat). *Leisure interest:* reading. *Address:* 27 Liaqat Road, Civil Lines, Hyderabad 71000, Sindh, Pakistan (office). *Telephone:* (221) 780-221 (office). *Fax:* (221) 28772 (office). *E-mail:* dohcop@hyd.netasia.co.pk (office).

KHUBLARYAN, Martin Gaykovich, PhD; Russian hydrologist and academic; *Director, Water Problems Institute, Russian Academy of Sciences;* b. 5 March 1935; m. Servenik A. Gabrielyan 1968; two d.; ed Armenian Inst. of Agric., Erevan; Sr Researcher, Head of Lab., Deputy Dir Inst. of Water Problems, USSR Acad. of Sciences 1968–88, Dir 1988–; Corresp. mem. USSR (now Russian) Acad. of Sciences 1984, mem. and Adviser 1994; mem. American Soc. of Hydrology; Ed.-in-Chief Water Resources Journal; Russian Acad. of Sciences Award for Terrestrial Waters Sciences. *Publications include:* Chemical substance transport in soil and its effect on groundwater quality 1989, Water Streams: Models of flow and quality surface water 1991, The Caspian Sea Phenomenon 1995, The Application of Non-linear Models to the Analysis of Water Level Fluctuations in Reservoirs 1996; numerous other publs on hydromechanics, hydrology and hydrogeology. *Leisure interests:* classical music, chess, museums, literature. *Address:* Water Problems Institute, Russian Academy of Sciences, 3 ul. Gubkina, 117971 Moscow (office); Proffsouznaya str. 43-1-84, 117420 Moscow, Russia (home). *Telephone:* (495) 135-54-56 (office); (495) 135-40-04 (office); (495) 331-32-60 (home). *Fax:* (495) 135-54-15 (office). *E-mail:* martin@aqua.laser.ru (office).

KHUDAIBERDYEV, Narmankhonmadi Dzhurayevich; Uzbekistan politician; b. 1928; ed Uzbek Agricultural Inst.; mem. CPSU 1948–91; dept head, sec. of a regional Uzbek Komsomol Cttee; Lecturer, Asst Prof. Agric. Inst., Samarkand 1943–54; leading CPSU and state posts 1954–; Sec. Bukhara Dist Cttee of Uzbek CP, Head Agric. Dept of Cen. Cttee of Uzbek CP; Second Sec. Bukhara Dist Cttee 1956–60; Deputy to Supreme Soviet of Uzbek SSR 1959–63, 1967; mem. Cen. Cttee of Uzbek CP 1960; Deputy Chair. Council of Ministers of Uzbek SSR 1960–61; First Sec. Surkhan-Darya Dist Cttee of Uzbek CP 1961–62; Prime Minister of Uzbekistan 1971–85; cand. mem. Cen. Cttee of CPSU 1961–66, mem. 1971; mem. Foreign Affairs Comm. of Soviet of the Union, USSR Supreme Soviet 1962–66; Sec. and mem. Presidium of the Cen. Cttee of the Uzbek CP 1962–65, Chair. Agric. Bureau 1962–64; Chair. Council of Ministers of Uzbek SSR 1971–84; mem. Politburo of Cen. Cttee of Uzbek CP 1971–84; sentenced to nine years in a labour camp for bribery Sept. 1989, released 1992.

KHUDONAZAROV, Davlatnazar; Tajikistani film director and politician; b. 13 March 1944; ed All-Union Inst. of Cinematography; film dir and cameraman in documentary cinema 1965–77; debut in feature film The First Morning of Youth 1979; Chair. Confed. of Cinema Unions 1990–; USSR People's Deputy, mem. of Supreme Soviet 1989–91; mem. Inter-regional Deputies' Group; cand. for Pres. of Tajikistan 1991; moved to Moscow after civil war 1992; adviser, Social and Political Union Focus 1999–; Rudaki State Prize of Tajikistan 1972, Distinguished Contributor to Tajik Culture 1977, Badge of Honor and other awards. *Films include:* Dzura Sarkor, Tale about Rustam, Rustam and Sokhrab, One Life is not Enough, Tale about Siyavush, A Brook Ringing in Melted Snow (Prize of All-Union Film Festival 1983). *Address:* Confederation of Cinema Unions, 123825 Moscow, Vasilyevskaya str. 13, Russia. *Telephone:* (495) 250-41-14 (office).

KHUDYAKOV, Konstantin Pavlovich; Russian film director; b. 13 Oct. 1938, Moscow; m. Irina Mikhailovna Ivanova; one s.; ed All-Union Inst. of Cinematography; film Dir 1970–; with Mosfilm Studio 1970–; mem. Union of Cinematographers 1975; Prof., Head of Studio Higher Courses of Film Dirs.; Prof. All-Union Inst. of Cinematography 1995–; Chair. State Attestation Comm. of Russian Inst. of Cinematography 1998–; Crystal Box for Pages of Life 1971, Prize Moscow Film Festival for Who Will Pay for Luck 1980, Grand Prix Barcelona Film Festival 1986, Golden Tulip Prize Istanbul Film Festival 1986, Prize of the 1st Washington Film Festival 1986, Prize of the Royal Acad. of Cinema (Stockholm) for Success 1986, Prize of European Community for From Evening to Noon (TV), 1983, Prize of the Jerusalem Film Festival for Mother of Jesus 1988. *Films include:* Pages of Life, To Live Your Own Way, Ivatsov, Petrov, Sidorov, Success, From Evening to Noon, Death in Cinema, Contender, Mother of Jesus, Without the Return Address, Michel, The Shadows of Fabergé. *Televisions productions:* Presence, Behind the Stone Wall, The Sun of the Wall, Such a Long Short Life, Girl without Dowry, Game, Tango for Two Voices, Impostors. *Leisure interests:* avant-garde and jazz music. *Address:* 1812 Iear str. 3, Apt 40, 121293 Moscow, Russia (home). *Telephone:* (495) 148-33-37 (home).

KHURSHID, Ahmed, MA, LLB, PhD; Pakistani economist and politician; *Chairman, Institute of Policy Studies;* b. 22 March 1932, Delhi, India; Chair. Inst. of Policy Studies, Islamabad 1979–; Vice-Pres. Islamic Research Acad. 1979–; Fed. Minister of Planning Devt and Statistics 1978–79, mem. Hiira Cttee 1978–83; Senator 1985–97; Chair. Islamic Foundation, UK 1978–, Int. Inst. of Islamic Econs ., Int. Islamic Univ. 1983–87; mem. Bd Trustees, Islamic Centre, Nigeria 1976–, Bd Trustees, Int. Islamic Univ., Islamabad 1980–, Foundation Council, Royal Acad. for Islamic Civilization, Jordan 1987–, and numerous academic advisory cttees.; Islamic Devt Bank Award 1988, King Faisal Int. Prize for Services to Islam 1990, 5th Annual Prize, American Finance House 1998. *Address:* Institute of Policy Studies, Nasr Chambers, Block-19, Markaz F-7, Islamabad 44000, Pakistan (office). *Telephone:* (51) 2650971 (office). *Fax:* (51) 2650704 (office). *E-mail:* khurshid@ips.net.pk (office). *Website:* www.ips.org.pk (office).

KHUSH, Gurdev Singh, PhD, FRS; Indian agronomist and academic; b. 22 Aug. 1935, Rurkee; s. of Kartar Singh and Pritam Kaur; m. Harwant Kaur Grewal 1961; one s. three d.; ed Punjab Univ., Chandigarh, Univ. of California, Davis, USA; Research Asst, Univ. of Calif., Davis 1957–60, Asst Geneticist 1960–67; Plant Breeder, Int. Rice Research Inst., Manila, Philippines, 1967–72, Head of Plant Breeding, Genetics and Biochem. Div. 1972–2001; mem. Indian Nat. Science Acad., Third World Acad. of Sciences, NAS (USA); Borlaug Award 1977, Japan Prize 1987, Int. Agronomy Award 1989, World Food Prize 1996, Rank Prize 1998, Wolf Prize for Agriculture 2000, China Int Scientific and Tech Cooperation Award 2001. *Achievements:* noted for his role in developing high-yielding varieties of rice, which led to doubling of world rice production between 1966 and 1990. *Publications:* Cytogenetics of Aneuploids 1974, Plant Breeding Lectures 1984, Host Plant Resistance to Insects 1995; 152 research papers and 40 book chapters. *Leisure interests:* world history, human rights. *Address:* c/o International Rice Research Institute, P.O. Box 3127, Makati City 1271, Philippines (office). *Telephone:* (2) 845-0563, ext. 734 (office); (2) 845-0563, ext. 251 (home). *Fax:* (2) 891-1292 (office); (2) 891-1292 (home). *E-mail:* g.khush@cgiar.org (office).

KHUSSAIBY, Salim Bin Mohammed Bin Salim al-; Omani diplomatist; b. 11 March 1939; m.; three c.; ed Teachers Coll., Zanzibar and Police Officers Coll., Kenya; teacher Secondary School, Dubai 1964–70; joined Royal Omani Police 1970, apptd Deputy Inspector Gen. of Police and Customs; Minister Plenipotentiary, Ministry of Foreign Affairs 1976, later Chargé d'affaires Embassy in Nairobi; Consul Gen. Bombay 1979; Amb. to Kuwait 1980–82, to Pakistan, (also Accred to Nepal, Bangladesh, Brunei, Darussalem, Indonesia and Malaysia) 1982–87; Perm. Rep., UN, New York 1987–99, Pres. Security Council 1995. *Address:* c/o Ministry of Foreign Affairs, POB 252, Muscat 113, Oman.

KHUWA, Mohammed Khair; Afghan diplomatist; Amb. to Ukraine –2004; Gov. of Herat Prov. 2004–. *Address:* c/o Governor's House, Herat, Afghanistan.

KHUWEITER, Abd al-Aziz al-Abdallah al-, PhD; Saudi Arabian politician; *Minister of State and Cabinet Minister;* b. 1927, Onaizah; s. of Abdullah Khuweiter and Moodi al-Khuweiter; m. Fatima al-Khuweiter 1963; one s. three d.; Vice-Rector King Saud Univ.; Head, Directorate Supervision and Follow-up; fmr Minister of Health; Minister of Educ. 1987–95, Minister of State and Cabinet Member 1995–; King Abdulaziz Order of Merit (Second Class), Republican Order, Sudan (First Class). *Publications:* Fi Turuk al Bahth, Tarikh Shafi Ibn Ali (ed.), Al-Malik al-Zahir Baybars (in Arabic and English), Al-Rawd al Zahir (ed.), Min Hatab al-Layl, Ayy-Bunayy, Qiraah Fi Diwan al-Sha'ir Muh. Uthaymin, Ayy Bonayy (five vols), Itlala Ala Al-Turath, Yowman Wa Malik (two vols), Mal'al-Sallah min Thamar al- Majallah (three vols), Hadeeth al-Rokbatain, Iamhat Min Tareekh al-Ta'leem, Dam'aton Harra, Wasmon Ala Adim al-Zarman (ten vols), Rasd Leseyaha al-Fikr, Nazz al-Yara ', Al-Salamo' Alykum. *Leisure interests:* reading, writing. *Address:* Council of Ministers, Qasar al-Yamamah (office); POB 539, Riyadh 11421, Saudi Arabia (home). *Telephone:* (1) 4882404 (office); (1) 4910033 (home). *Fax:* (1) 4930466 (office); (1) 4882622 (office).

KHVOSTOV, Mikhail Mikhaylovich; Belarusian diplomatist; *Ambassador to USA;* b. 27 June 1949, Vytebsk Region; m.; two c.; ed Minsk Inst. of Foreign Languages, Belarussian State Univ.; with Ministry of Foreign Affairs 1982–91; Sr Diplomatic Officer, Perm. Mission of Belarus to UN, New York 1991–92, at Embassy in Washington, DC 1992–93; Head, State Protocol Dept, Legal Dept, Ministry of Foreign Affairs 1993–94, Deputy Minister of Foreign Affairs 1994–97; Amb. to Canada 1997–2000; Asst to Pres. for Foreign Policy Issues Aug.–Nov. 2000; Deputy Prime Minister and Minister of Foreign Affairs 2000–01, Minister of Foreign Affairs 2001–03; Amb. to USA 2003–. *Address:* Embassy of Belarus, 1619 New Hampshire Avenue, NW, Washington, DC 20009, USA (office). *Telephone:* (202) 986-1604 (office). *Fax:* (202) 986-1805 (office). *E-mail:* usa@belarusembassy.org (office). *Website:* www.belarusembassy.org (office).

KIAMAKOSA, Mutombo; Democratic Republic of the Congo politician; Minister of Finance –2004; currently Pres. Autorité de Régulation de la Poste et des Télécommunications du Congo. *Address:* Autorité de Régulation de la Poste et des Télécommunications du Congo, Immeuble GECAMINES Boulevard du 30 juin, Kinshasa, Democratic Republic of the Congo (office). *Telephone:* (13) 92491 (office). *Fax:* (13) 92492 (office). *E-mail:* info.arptc@arptc.cd (office). *Website:* www.arptc.cd (office).

KIAROSTAMI, Abbas, BA; Iranian film director, producer, writer and photographer; b. 22 June 1940, Tehran; m. (divorced); two s.; ed Tehran Coll. of Fine Arts; worked as designer and illustrator (commercials, film credit titles and children's books); involved in establishment of film making Dept at Inst. for Intellectual Devt of Children and Young Adults (Kanoon); ind. film maker from early 1990s; has made over 20 films, including shorts, educational films, documentaries; more than 50 int. prizes including special prize of the Pasolini Foundation 1995, UNESCO Fellini Medal 1997, Lifetime Achievment Award, Yerevan Int. Film Festival 2005. *Films directed:* Nan va koucheh (Bread and Alley, short) (debut production of Kanoon film Dept) 1970, Zangu-e tafrih (Breaktime) 1972, Tajrobeh (The Experience) 1973, Mossafer (The Traveller) 1974, Man ham mitoumam (So Can I, short) 1975, Do rah-e hal baraye yek massaleh (Two Solutions for One Problem, short) 1975, Lebasi bara-ye arusi (A Wedding Suit) 1976, Rang-ha (Colours, short) 1976, Bozorgdasht-e mo'allem (Tribute to the Teachers, documentary) 1977, Az oghat-e faraghat-e khod chegouneh estefadeh konim: Rang-zanie (How to Make Use of Leisure Time: Painting, short) 1977, Gozarech (The Report) 1977, Rah-e hal (Solution, short) 1978, Ghazieh-e shekl-e aval, ghazieh-e shekl-e douuom (First Case, Second Case) 1979, Dandan-dard (Toothache, short) 1979, Beh tartib ya bedoun-e tartib (Orderly or Disorderly, short) 1981, Hamsorayan (The Chorus, short) 1982, Hamshahri (Fellow Citizen) 1983, Avali-ha (First-Graders, documentary) 1984, Khaneh-je doost kojast? (Where Is the Friend's House?, first film of the 'Koker trilogy') 1987, Mashq-e shab (Homework, documentary) 1989, Namay-eh nazdik (Close-Up, documentary) 1990, Zendegi va digar hich (And Life Goes On..., second film of the 'Koker trilogy') (aka Va zendegi edemah darad—Life and Nothing More) (Cannes Film Festival Rossellini Prize) 1991, Zir-e darakhtan-e zeyton (Through the Olive Trees, final film of the 'Koker trilogy') 1994, Tavalod-e noor (Plus Dinner for One, short) 1996, Ta'am-e gilas (The Taste of Cherry) (Cannes Film Festival Palme d'Or) 1997, Bad mara khahad bourd (The Wind Will Carry Us) (Venice Film Festival Grand Jury Prize) 1999, ABC Africa (documentary) 2001, Ta'ziyeh 2002, 10 (also writer) 2002, Five (also writer) 2003, Ten Minutes Older (short) 2003, 10 on Ten (also writer) 2004, Tickets (with others, also writer) 2004, Kargaran mashghoole karand (also writer) 2006, Roads of Kiarostami (also writer) 2006, Kojast jaye residan (also writer) 2007. *Film screenplays:* The Key 1987, The Journey 1995, Badkonak-e sefid (The White Balloon) (Cannes Film Festival Caméra d'Or) 1995, Istgah-e matrouk (The Deserted Station) 2002, Talaye sorgh (Crimson Gold) 2003. *Publications:* Walking with the Wind: Poems 2001. *Address:* c/o Zeitgeist Films Ltd, 247 Center Street, Second Floor, New York, NY 10013, USA.

KIBAKI, Mwai, BA, BSc (Econs); Kenyan politician and head of state; *President and Commander-in-Chief of the Armed Forces;* b. 15 Nov. 1931, Gatuyaini, Othaya Div., Nyeri Dist, Cen. Prov.; s. of the late Kibaki Githinji and Teresia Wanjiku; m. M. Lucy Muthoni; three s. one d.; ed Mang'u High School, Makerere Univ., London School of Econs, UK; Lecturer in Econs, Makerere Univ. Coll. 1959–60; Nat. Exec. Officer, Kenya African Nat. Union (KANU) 1960–64; elected by Legis. Council as one of Kenya's nine reps in E African Legis. Ass. of E African Common Services Org. 1962; mem. House of Reps for Nairobi Doonholm 1963–78; Parl. Sec. to Treasury 1963–65; Asst Minister of Econ. Planning and Devt 1964–66; Minister for Commerce and Industry 1965–69, of Finance 1969–70, of Finance and Econ. Planning 1970–78, of Finance 1978–82, of Home Affairs 1978–88, of Health 1988–91; Vice-Pres. of Kenya 1978–88; Vice-Pres. KANU 1978–88; Pres. Democratic Party 1991–2002; Leader of the Official Opposition 1998–2002; Pres. of Kenya and C-in-C of the Armed Forces Dec. 2002–; mem. Party of Nat. Unity—PNU (coalition of several parties); Chief, Order of the Golden Heart; Hon. DrIng (Nairobi), Hon. DLitt (Jomo Kenyatta Univ. of Science and Tech.); Gandhi-King Award for Non-Violence 2003, FDI Personality of the Year Award 2004. *Leisure interests:* reading, golf. *Address:* State House, PO Box 40530, 00100 Nairobi, GPO, Kenya (office). *Telephone:* (20) 227436 (office). *Fax:* (20) 2720572 (office). *E-mail:* pps@statehousekenya.go.ke (office). *Website:* www .statehousekenya.go.ke (office).

KIBEDI, Wanume, LLB; Ugandan politician and lawyer; b. 3 Aug. 1941, Busesa; s. of Mr and Mrs E. M. Kibedi; m. Elizabeth Kibedi (née Amin) 1970; one d.; ed Busoga Coll. and Univ. of London; articled with Waterhouse and Co., London 1961–66, admitted solicitor 1966; worked in office of Attorney-Gen., Uganda 1968; Pnr, Binaisa and Co. (advocates) 1969–70; Minister of Foreign Affairs 1971–73 (resgnd); del. to UN Gen. Ass. 1971; Perm. Rep. to the UN 1986–89. *Leisure interests:* chess, tennis, reading. *Address:* c/o Ministry of Foreign Affairs, POB 7048, Kampala, Uganda.

KIBEDI VARGA, Aron, PhD; Dutch/Hungarian academic and poet; *Professor of French Literature, Vrije Universiteit, Amsterdam;* b. 4 Feb. 1930, Szeged, Hungary; m. 1st T. Spreij 1954; m. 2nd K. Agh 1964; m. 3rd S. Bertho 1991; four s. one d.; ed Univs of Amsterdam, Leiden, Sorbonne; Lecturer in French Literature, Vrije Universiteit, Amsterdam 1954–66, Prof. of French Literature 1971–; Prof. of French Literature, Univ. of Amsterdam 1966–71; Visiting Prof. Iowa Univ. 1971, Yale Univ. 1975, Princeton Univ. 1980, Rabat Univ. 1985, Coll. de France 1992; mem. Cttee Int. Soc. for the History of Rhetoric 1979–83; Pres. Int. Asscn Word and Image Studies 1987–93; mem. Royal Netherlands Acad. of Sciences 1981–; mem. Hungarian Acad. of Sciences 1990–; Dr hc (Pécs) 1994. *Publications:* criticism: Les Constantes du Poème 1963, Rhétorique et Littérature 1970, Théorie de la Littérature (ed.) 1981, Discours récit, image 1989, Les Poétiques du classicisme (ed.) 1990, Le Classicisme 1998, Szavak, világok 1998, Noé könyvei 1999, Amszterdami krónika 2000, És felébred aminek neve van 2002, A jelen 2003; poetry (in Hungarian): Kint és Bent 1963, Téged 1975, Szépen 1991, Hántani, fosztani 2000, Oldás 2004. *Address:* Department of French, Vrije Universiteit, Amsterdam, Netherlands (office). *Telephone:* (20) 4446456 (office). *Fax:* (20) 4446500 (office).

KIBIROV, Timur Yuryevich; Russian poet; b. (Zapoyev), 15 Feb. 1955, Shepetovka, Ukraine; m. Yelena Ivanovna Borisova; one d.; ed Krupskaya Moscow Regional Pedagogical Inst.; jr researcher All-Union Research Inst. of Arts 1981–93; ed. Tsikady (Publr) 1993–; first poems published in Yunost and

Continent 1989; Pushkin Prize (Germany) 1993, Prize of Druzhba Narodov (magazine) 1993. *Publications:* collections of poetry: Calendar 1990, Verses about Love 1993; Sentiments 1994; verses in leading literary journals. *Address:* Ostrovityanova str. 34, korp. 1, Apt. 289, Moscow, Russia (home). *Telephone:* (495) 420-6175 (home).

KIBRICK, Anne, EdD; American nurse and academic; *Professor Emerita of Nursing, College of Nursing, University of Massachusetts;* b. 1 June 1919, Palmer, Mass; d. of Martin Karlon and Christine Grigas Karlon; m. Sidney Kibrick 1949; one s. one d.; ed Boston Univ., Columbia Univ., Harvard Univ.; Head Nurse, Worcs. Hahnemann Hosp. 1941–43; Staff Nurse, Children's Hosp. Medical Center, Boston 1943–45; Educ. Dir, Charles V. Chapin Hosp., Providence, RI 1945–47; Asst Educ. Dir, Veterans Admin. Hosp. 1948–49; Asst Prof., Simmons Coll., Boston 1949–55; Dir Grad. Programs in Nursing, Boston Univ. 1958–63, Prof. and Dean 1963–70; Dir Grad. Programs in Nursing, Boston Coll. 1970–74; Chair. School of Nursing, Boston State Coll. 1974–82; Dean Coll. of Nursing, Univ. of Massachusetts, Boston 1982–88, Prof. 1988–93, Prof. Emer. 1993–, now mem. Advisory Council; Consultant Nat. Student Nurses Asscn 1985–88; Consultant, Hadassah Medical Org., Israel, Cumberland Coll. of Health Sciences, NSW, Australia, Menonfia Univ., Shebin El-Kam, Egypt; Fellow, American Acad. of Nursing 1973–; mem. Inst. of Medicine, NAS 1972–, Brookline Town Meeting 1995–2000; Charter mem. Nat. Acads of Practice 1985–; mem. Bd of Dirs Post-Grad. Medical Inst., Mass Medical Soc. 1983–96, Exec. Cttee 1988–96; Dir Landy-Kaplan Nurses Council 1992– (Treas. 1994–98); Hon. DHL (St Joseph's Coll.); Mary Adelaide Nutting Award, Distinguished Service Award and Isabel Stewart Award, Nat. League for Nursing, Service Award, Nat. Hadassah Org. and other awards; Chancellor's Medal, Univ. of Massachusetts, Boston 1992, Hall of Fame, Nursing, Teacher's Coll., Univ. of Columbia 1999, Living Legend, Massachusetts Nurses Asscn, Massachusetts Nurses Asscn Award 2006. *Publications:* Explorations in Nursing Research (with H. Wechsler) 1979; numerous professional articles. *Leisure interests:* reading, travel. *Address:* 130 Seminary Avenue, #312, Auburndale, MA 02466, USA (home). *Telephone:* (617) 969-3225 (home).

KIDD, Hon. Douglas Lorimer (Doug), DCNZM, LLB; New Zealand politician and lawyer; b. 12 Sept. 1941, Levin; s. of Lorimer Edward Revington Kidd and Jessie Jean Kidd (née Mottershead); m. Jane Stafford Richardson 1964; one s. two d.; ed Horowhenua Coll., Vic. Univ., Wellington; Pnr, Wisheart Macnab & Pnrs (law firm) 1964–78; fmr part-time mussel farmer, Marlborough Sounds; Nat. Party MP for Marlborough/Kaikoura 1978–99; Minister of State-Owned Enterprises and Assoc. Minister of Finance 1990–91; Minister of Fisheries 1990–96; Minister of Maori Affairs 1991–93; Minister of Energy, of Labour and for Accident Rehabilitation and Compensation Insurance 1993–96; Speaker of House of Reps and Chair. of Parl. Service Comm. 1996–99; fmr Foundation Pres. Marlborough Forest Owners' Asscn; Nat. Party List MP 1999–2002; Opposition Spokesman on Fisheries; Chair. Regulations Review Select Cttee; mem. Privileges and Maori Affairs Select Cttee 1999–2002; mem. Waitangi Tribunal 2004–; Hon. Col of Canterbury, Nelson, Marlborough, West Coast Regt 1997–2003; Commemoration Medal 1990, Chief of Gen. Staff's Commendation for Outstanding Service to NZ Army 1999. *Leisure interests:* fishing, reading, travel. *Address:* 6 Elgin Way, Wellington 6035, New Zealand (home). *Website:* www.waitangitribunal.govt.nz.

KIDJO, Angélique; Benin singer and songwriter; b. 14 July 1960, Cotonou; d. of Frank Kidjo and Yvonne Kidjo; m. Jean Hébrail 1987; one d.; ed in Cotonou; began performing in her mother's theatre co. aged six; joined Kidjo Brothers Band, Alafia, Pili Pili and later Parakou; moved to Paris, France 1983; solo artist 1986–; numerous tours and live appearances; collaborations with Carlos Santana, Manu Dibango, Branford Marsalis, Alicia Keys, Peter Gabriel, Joss Stone; UNICEF Goodwill Amb. 2002–; f. Batonga Foundation 2007; Commdr, Nat. Order of Merit 2008, Medal of the Presidency of the Italian Republic 2008; African Musician of the Year 1991, Best African Singer, Kora Awards 1997, MOBO Award for Best World Music Act 2002, Grammy Award for Best World Music album 2008, NAACP Image Award for Outstanding World Music Album 2008. *Recordings include:* albums: Pretty 1980, Ninive, Ewa Kadjo 1985, Parakou 1989, Logozo 1991, Ayé 1994, Fifa 1996, Oremi 1998, Black Ivory Soul 2002, Oyaya! 2004, Djin Djin (Grammy Award for Best Contemporary World Music Album 2008) 2007. *Address:* Madison House Inc., East 628 Broadway, Suite 502, New York, NY 10012, USA (office). *E-mail:* kevin@scifidelity.com (office). *Website:* www.kidjo.com (home).

KIDMAN, Dame Fiona Judith, DCNZM, OBE; New Zealand writer; b. 26 March 1940, Hawera; d. of Hugh Eric Eakin and Flora Cameron Eakin (née Small); m. Ian Kidman 1960; one s. one d.; ed small rural schools in the north of NZ; Founding Sec./Organizer NZ Book Council 1972–75; Sec. NZ Centre, PEN 1972–76, Pres. 1981–83; Pres. NZ Book Council 1992–95, Pres. of Honour 1997–; f. Writers in Schools, Words on Wheels (touring writing co.), Writers Visiting Prisons, Randell Cottage Writers Trust; mem. Bd of Dirs Randell Cottage Writers Trust; Deputy Chair. French Cultural Trust; numerous literary prizes including NZ Book Awards (fiction category), Queen Elizabeth II Arts Council Award for Achievement, Victoria Univ. Writers' Fellow; NZ Scholarship in Letters; A. W. Reed Award for Lifetime Achievement 2001, Meridian Energy Katherine Mansfield Fellow 2006, Creative NZ Michael King Fellowship 2008. *Publications:* A Breed of Women 1979, Mandarin Summer 1981, Mrs. Dixon and Friend (short stories) 1982, Paddy's Puzzle 1983, The Book of Secrets 1986, Unsuitable Friends (short stories) 1988, True Stars 1990, Wakeful Nights (poems selected and new) 1991, The Foreign Woman (short stories) 1994, Palm Prints (autobiog. essays) 1995, Ricochet Baby 1996, The House Within 1997, The Best of Fiona Kidman's Short Stories 1998, New Zealand Love Stories; An Oxford Anthology (ed.) 1999, A Needle in the Heart (short stories) 2002, Songs from the Violet Café (novel) 2003, Captive Wife 2004; The Best New Zealand Fiction Vols 1, 2 and 3 (ed.) 2004, 2005, 2006, At the End of Darwin Road: A Memoir 2008. *Leisure interests:* theatre, film, family pursuits. *Fax:* (4) 386-1895 (home); (9) 444-7524 (office). *E-mail:* fionakidman@yahoo.com; fiona@fionakidman.co.nz; admin@randomhouse.co.nz (office). *Website:* www.fionakidman.co.nz. *Address:* Random House NZ Ltd, Private Bag 102950, North Shore Mail Centre, Auckland, New Zealand (office). *Telephone:* (9) 444-7197 (office).

KIDMAN, Nicole, AC; Australian actress; b. 20 June 1967, Hawaii, USA; d. of Dr Antony Kidman and Janelle Glenny; m. 1st Tom Cruise 1990 (divorced 2001); one adopted s. one adopted d.; m. 2nd Keith Urban 2006; one d.; ed St Martin's Youth Theatre, Melbourne, Australian Theatre for Young People, Sydney and Philip Street Theatre; acting debut in Australian film aged 14; Australian Film Inst. Best Actress Award for role in TV mini-series Bangkok Hilton; voted Best Actress of Year in Australia for role in Vietnam. *Films include:* The Emerald City, The Year My Voice Broke, Flirting, Dead Calm 1989, Days of Thunder 1990, Far and Away 1992, Billy Bathgate 1992, Malice 1993, My Life 1993, Batman Forever 1995, To Die For 1995, Portrait of a Lady 1996, The Peacemaker 1997, Eyes Wide Shut 1998, Practical Magic 1999, Moulin Rouge (Golden Globe for Best Actress in a Musical) 2001, The Others 2001, Birthday Girl 2001, The Hours (Golden Globe for Best Dramatic Actress 2003, BAFTA Award for Best Actress in a Leading Role 2003, Acad. Award for Best Actress 2003) 2002, Cold Mountain 2003, The Human Stain 2003, Dogville 2003, The Stepford Wives 2004, Birth 2004, The Interpreter 2005, Bewitched 2005, Fur: An Imaginary Portrait of Diane Arbus 2006, Happy Feet (voice) 2006, I Have Never Forgotten You (voice) 2007, The Invasion 2007, Margot at the Wedding 2007, The Golden Compass 2007, Australia 2008. *Play:* The Blue Room 1998–99. *Address:* PMK Public Relations, 1775 Broadway, Suite 701, New York, NY 10019, USA (office).

KIDWA, Nasser al-; Palestinian diplomatist; ed Cairo Univ.; mem. Fatah 1969–, mem. PLO Cen. Council 1981–86, 1999–; mem. Palestine National Council 1975–; Amb. and Perm. Observer to UN, New York 1991–2005; Minister of Foreign Affairs, Palestinian Authority (PA) 2005. *Address:* c/o Ministry of Foreign Affairs, POB 4017, Ramallah, Gaza, Palestinian Autonomous Areas (office).

KIDWAI, Akhlaq R., BA, MS, PhD; Indian politician, academic, scientist and administrator; *Governor of Haryana and Rajasthan;* b. 1 July 1920, Baragaon, Barabanki Dist, UP; s. of the late Shri Ashfaq-ur-Rahman Kidwai and Smt. Nasimunnisa; m. Shrimati Jadmila Kidwai (deceased); two s. four d.; ed Jamia Millia Islamia, New Delhi, Univ. of Illinois and Cornell Univ., USA; research and devt chemist, Cipla Labs, Bombay 1941–45; Prof. and Head of Dept of Chem., Dean Faculty of Science, Aligarh Muslim Univ. 1951–67, Dir, Dept of Research Plant Products, Chancellor 1983–92; Chair. Union Public Service Comm. 1967–79; Gov. of Bihar 1979–85, 1993–98, of W Bengal 1998–99; Chair. Dr Ambedkar Centre for Biomedical Research, Univ. of Delhi 1998–2003; Nat. Chair. Inst. of Marketing and Devt 2000–; Chair. Bombay Mercantile Cooperative Bank 1999–2003; mem. Rajya Sabha (Upper House of Parl.) 2000–04, mem. Consultative Cttee for Ministries of Science and Tech., Environment and Forest 2000–04, mem. Standing Cttee on Agric., Water Resources and Food Processing Industries 2000–04; Gov. of Haryana 2004–, also of Rajasthan 2007–; mem. Nat. Cttee on Science and Tech. 1968–75, Perspective Science and Tech. Plan Cttee, Dept of Science and Tech. and the Planning Comm., Council and Governing Body of Indian Council of Agricultural Research 1970–73, Bd of Council of Scientific and Industrial Research, Regional Imbalances Enquiry Comm., Jammu and Kashmir State 1979, State Planning Bd and Heavy Industries Plan Cttee, Govt of Uttar Pradesh, Univ. Grants Comm. and Chair. Sub-cttee on Non-Formal Methods of Educ., mem. and Patron Delhi Public School Soc. 1968–, Chair. Review Cttee on Unani Medicine, Ministry of Health, Govt of India, Chair. Selection Bd of Scientists Pool 1968–79, Chair. Bd of Assessment of Educational and Tech. Qualification for Employment, Ministry of Educ., Govt of India 1967–79; Pres. Vocational Educ. Soc. for Women 1985–; mem. AAAS; Hon. Fellow, Inst. of Engineers, India; Dr hc (Vidhya Vajaspati, Inst. of Tibetan Studies, Sarnath) 1997. *Publications:* more than 40 research papers in organic chem. and biochemistry. *Leisure interests:* gardening, sports. *Address:* 196 Zakir Bagh, Okhla Road, New Delhi 110 025 (home); Haryana Raj Bhavan, Chandigarh 160 019, India (office). *Telephone:* (172) 2740643 (home); (172) 2740654 (office). *Fax:* (172) 2740557 (office). *E-mail:* arkidwai@sansad.nic.in (office); governor@hry.nic.in (office).

KIDWAI, Naina Lal, MBA; Indian banker; *CEO, HSBC (India);* b. 1957; m.; ed Harvard Business School, USA (first Indian woman grad. 1982); began career at ANZ Grindlay's Bank; joined Morgan Stanley (India) 1994, Vice-Chair. and Head of Investment Banking, JM Morgan Stanley –2002; Exec. Vice-Chair. and Man. Dir HSBC Securities and Capital Markets (India) Pvt. Ltd 2002–, Deputy CEO HSBC (India) 2004–06, CEO 2006–; Chair. Capital Market Cttee, Fed. of Indian Chambers of Commerce and Industry; Chair. Govt of India Science and Tech. Bd, Governing Body of Nat. Council of Applied Econ. Research, Econ. Policy and Reforms Council for the State of Rajasthan, Governing Body of Lady Shri Ram Coll. for Women, Delhi Univ., Governing Council of India Habitat Centre; Dir Int. Bd of Digital Pnrs Foundation, USA, SEWA (non-profit org. for self-employment of underprivileged women); adviser, Nat. Entrepreneurship Network; ranked third by Fortune magazine in first ever listing of The World's Top Women in Business in Asia 2000, ranked by Fortune magazine amongst 50 Most Powerful Women in Business outside the US 2001, (50th) 2002, (47th) 2003, (41st) 2006, (38th) 2007, honoured by Time Magazine as one of their 15 Global Influentials 2002, ranked 34th by The Wall Street Journal in list of World's Top 50 Businesswomen 2004, recipient of several Awards for Business in India, Padma Shri 2007. *Leisure interests:* listening to Indian and Western classical music, wildlife tours. *Address:* HSBC Securities and Capital Markets (India) Pvt. Ltd, New Delhi, India (office). *Telephone:* (22) 22681247 (office). *Fax:* (22) 22631984 (office). *Website:* www.hsbc.co.in (office).

KIEBER, Walter, DJur; Liechtenstein politician and lawyer; b. 20 Feb. 1931, Feldkirch, Austria; s. of Alfons Kieber and Elisabeth Kieber; m. Selma Ritter 1959; one s. one d.; ed Grammar School in Bregenz, Austria, Univ. of Innsbruck; lawyer in Vaduz 1955–59, 1981–; entered civil service as Head of Govt Legal Office 1959; Chief of Presidential Office 1965–; Sec.-Gen. of Govt 1969, Deputy Head of Govt 1970–74, Head of Govt 1974–78, Deputy Head of Govt 1978–80; Pres. Liechtenstein Bar Asscn 1993–; mem. Progressive Citizens' Party; Grand Cross, Liechtenstein Order of Merit, Grosses Goldenes Ehrenzeichen am Bande für Verdienste um die Republik Österreich (Austria). *Address:* Pflugstrasse 12, 9490 Vaduz; Landstrasse 22, 9494 Schaan, Liechtenstein (home). *Telephone:* 399-49-49 (office).

KIEBER-BECK, Rita; Liechtenstein politician; b. 27 Dec. 1958, Nenzing, Austria; m. Manfred Kieber; ed Oberstufenrealgymnasium, Feldkirch, Univ. of Fribourg, Switzerland, Univ. of Innsbruck, Austria, Chulalongkorn Univ. of Bangkok and Chiang Mai, Thailand; Instructor in German, Business, Political Science and Econs, Commercial Business School, Buchs, Switzerland 1979–81; full-time instructor, Realschule (Upper School) Balzers 1982–90; with Liectenstein Inst., Bendern 1990–94, Man. Dir 1991–94; Man. Dir Adiuvaris Treuunternehmen reg. (Fiducary), Triesen 1993, 2001; Consulting mem. Parl. Group of Progressive Citizens' Party (Fortschritte Bürgerpartei, FBP) 1997–2000, mem. Presidency 1997–, Chair. Educ. Working Group 1997–, mem. Man. Presidency and Financial Adviser 2000–01; Deputy Prime Minister with responsibility for Educ., Justice, Transport and Telecommunications 2001–05; Minister of Foreign Affairs, Cultural Affairs and Family and Equal Opportunity 2005–09; Pres. Liechtenstein Upper School Teachers' Asscn 1988–90; mem. Educational Comm., Upper Schools, Liechtenstein 1984–88, Adult Educ. Comm. 1992–98. *Address:* c/o Progressive Citizens' Party, Aeulestr. 56, Postfach 1213, 9490 Vaduz, Liechtenstein (office).

KIEFER, Anselm; German artist; b. 8 March 1945, Donaueschingen; m.; three c.; ed Univ. of Freiburg and Freiburg Acad., Karlsruhe Acad.; first one-man exhbn, Galerie am Kaiserplatz, Karlsruhe 1969; first one-man exhbn in USA, Marian Goodman Gallery, New York; retrospective exhbns Städtische Kunsthalle, Düsseldorf, Musée d'Art Moderne, Paris and Israel Museum, Jerusalem 1984, Stedelijk Museum, Amsterdam 1986, US tour 1987–89; first group exhbn, Deutscher Künstlerbund, Kunstverein, Hanover 1969; has also exhibited Kunstverein, Frankfurt 1976, Kassel Documenta 1977, 1982, 1987, Biennale de Paris 1977, Venice Biennale 1980, White Cube, London 2005, 2006, Royal Acad., London 2007; other group exhbns include Expressions: New Art from Germany, touring exhbn USA 1983–84, touring exhbn Moscow and Leningrad 1983, 1984 Museum of Modern Art survey of int. art, Fifth Biennale of Sydney, Australia 1984; works in many pvt collections including Saatchi Collection, London and in many public galleries including Art Inst. of Chicago, Museum of Modern Art, Phila Museum of Art, Hirshhorn Museum, Washington, DC, LA Museum of Contemporary Art and San Francisco Museum of Modern Art, Praemium Imperiale 1999; Wolf Foundation Prize 1990. *Publication:* A Book by Anselm Kiefer 1988. *Address:* c/o American-European Fine Art, 1100 Madison Avenue, New York, NY 10028, USA. *E-mail:* gallery@aefineart.com.

KIELHOLZ, Walter B., BA; Swiss banking executive; *Chairman, Credit Suisse Group;* b. 25 Feb. 1951, Zurich; m. Daphne Kielholz-Pestalozzi; ed Univ. of St Gallen; began career with Gen. Reinsurance Corpn, Zurich 1976 with assignments in USA, UK and Italy, Head of European Marketing –1986; opened art gallery and picture framing business with his wife 1983; Head of Client Relations, Multinational Services Dept, Credit Suisse 1986–89, mem. Bd Dirs 1999–, Chair. Audit Cttee 1999–2002, Chair. Credit Suisse Group 2003–, also Chair. Chairman's and Governance Cttee, joined Swiss Re, Zurich 1989, apptd mem. Exec. Bd 1993, CEO 1997–2002, mem. Bd of Dirs 1998–, Chair. Audit Cttee 1999–2002, Exec. Vice-Chair. Swiss Re 2003–07, Vice-Chair. 2007–; Pres. Int. Monetary Conf. 2006–07; Chair. Supervisory Bd Avenir Suisse (think tank); mem. Int. Asscn for the Study of Insurance Econs, European Financial Roundtable 2004–, Center for Strategic and Int. Studies 2005–; mem. Bd Dirs Geneva Asscn 1999–, economiesuisse 2003–; Chair. Zürcher Kunstgesellschaft; mem. Soc. of Zurich Friends of the Arts, Lucerne Festival Foundation Board; inducted into Insurance Hall of Fame 2005. *Leisure interests:* sailing, skiing, tennis, golf, reading, opera, concerts, art. *Address:* Credit Suisse Group, PO Box 1, 8070 Zurich (office); Credit Suisse Group, Paradeplatz 8, 8001 Zurich, Switzerland (office). *Telephone:* (44) 212-16-16 (office). *Fax:* (44) 333-25-87 (office). *E-mail:* info@credit-suisse.com (office). *Website:* www.credit-suisse.com (office).

KIELY, Leo, BEcons, MBA; American brewing industry executive; *CEO, MillerCoors;* b. 16 Jan. 1947; ed Harvard Univ., Wharton School of Business, Univ. of Pa; Brand Asst and Asst Brand Man., Procter & Gamble, Cincinnati 1971–73; various posts at Wilson Sporting Goods Co. including Vice-Pres. of Marketing and Sr Business Man., Chicago 1973–79; Pres. Ventura Coastal Corpn (div. of Seven-Up) 1979–82; Vice-Pres. Brand Man., Frito-Lay Inc. 1982–83, Vice-Pres. Marketing 1983–84, Marketing and Sales 1984–89, Sr Vice-Pres. Field Operations 1989–91, served as Vice-Pres. and Gen. Man., Cen. Div., Div. Pres. 1991–93; joined Coors Brewing Co. 1993, mem. Bd of Dirs 1998–, Pres. and CEO Molson Coors Brewing Co. (after merger of Coors and Molson cos) 2005–07, CEO MillerCoors (after merger of SABMiller and Molson Coors US operations) 2007–; mem. Bd of Dirs Nat. Asscn of Mfrs, SEI Center for Advanced Studies, Wharton School of Finance, Denver Center for the Performing Arts; mem. Foundation Bd Metropolitan State Coll.; Chair. Mile High United Way, Denver; Nat. Trustee Boys and Girls Clubs of America.

Address: Molson Coors Brewing Company, 1225 17th Street, Denver, CO 80202, USA (office). *Telephone:* (303) 279-6565 (office). *Fax:* (303) 277-5415 (office). *E-mail:* consumers@coors.com (office). *Website:* www.molsoncoors.com (office).

KIELY, Rory; Irish politician; *Chairman of Seanad Éireann;* b. May 1934; m. Eileen Kiely (née O'Connor); two s. two d.; ed Univ. Coll. Cork; Senator 1977–82, 1983–; elected Cathaoirleach (Chair.) of Seanad Éireann 2002–. *Address:* Cathaoirleach, Seanad Eireann, Leinster House, Kildare Street, Dublin 2, Ireland (office). *Telephone:* (1) 6183227 (office). *Fax:* (1) 6184101 (office). *E-mail:* rory.kiely@oireachtas.ie (office). *Website:* www.oireachtas.ie (office).

KIEP, Walther Leisler; German politician, business executive and consultant; b. 5 Jan. 1926, Hamburg; s. of the late Louis Leisler Kiep and Eugenie vom Rath; m. Charlotte ter Meer 1950; three s. (one deceased) two d.; ed Hamburg, Istanbul, Frankfurt; with Ford Motor Co., then Insurance Co. of North America 1948–55, joined Gradmann and Holler 1954, Man. Pnr 1968–98; mem. Advisory Council of Deutsche Bank 1972–2001; mem. CDU 1961–, mem. Bundestag 1965–76, 1980–82; fmr Chair. Parl. Cttee on Foreign Aid, Treas., mem. Exec. Cttee 1971–92; Lower Saxony Minister for Econs and Finance 1976–80, concurrently Special Envoy for Turkish aid; Deputy to Leader of Opposition 1980–82; Chair. Atlantik-Brücke Berlin 1984–2000; mem. Int. European Advisory Bd Fuji-Wolfensohn, New York 1989–98; Chair. ZENECA GmbH, Plankstadt 1993–98; Chair. Int. Advisory Bd, Marsh & McLennan New York 1993–2000; Chair. Supervisory Bd IABG, Ottobrunn 1994–2000; Pres. European Business School, Oestrich-Winkel 1994–2000; mem. Int. Advisory Bd, Columbia Univ., New York 1997–, Int. Advisory Bd, Fuji Bank Ltd, Tokyo 1999–2002; Hon. Chair. Atlantik-Brücke eV, Berlin 2004–; Bundesverdienstkreuz mit Stern und Schulterband, Grosses Verdienstkreuz des Niedersächsischen Verdienstordens; Hon. CBE; Dr hc. *Publications:* Goodbye Amerika – Was Dann? 1972, A New Challenge for Western Europe 1974, Was bleibt ist grosse Zuversicht 1999, Brücken meines Lebens 2006. *Leisure interest:* history. *Address:* Holzhecke 31, 60528 Frankfurt a.M., Germany (office). *Telephone:* (69) 67-73-38-84 (office). *Fax:* (69) 67-73-38-72 (office). *E-mail:* kiep_consultant@t-online.de (office).

KIERES, Leon; Polish politician and professor of law; *President, Institute of National Remembrance;* b. 26 May 1948, Kolonia Zielona; s. of Józef Kieres and Helena Kieres; m. Anna Kieres; one s. one d.; ed Wrocław Univ.; Jr Librarian, Wrocław Univ. 1970, Research Asst 1971–73, Sr Asst 1973–75, Lecturer in Law 1975–85, Asst Prof. 1985–91, Extraordinary Prof. 1991–96, Ordinary Prof., Faculty of Law and Admin. 1996–; councillor, Wrocław Town Council 1990–98; Pres. Self-governmental Council of Wrocław Voivodship 1990–98; mem. Local Govt Council at the Chancellory of the Pres. 1994; Vice-Pres. Congress of Local and Regional Authorities of Council of Europe 1995, mem. Parl. Ass. 1998–2000, involved in Council of Europe mission in Bosnia and Herzegovina 1998; Senator (Wrocław Voivodship), Vice-Pres. Senate Local Govt and Public Admin. Cttee, mem. Foreign Affairs and European Integration Cttee; Pres. int. group of local govt observers in Croatia 1997; councillor, Dolnoslaskie Voivodship Council, Pres. Culture, Science and Educ. Cttee 1998–2002; Pres. Inst. of Nat. Remembrance 2000–05, The Club of Rome 2000; Vice-Pres. Polish-German Co-operation Foundation 1993; mem. Polish Teachers' Asscn 1970–80, NSZZ Solidarnosc 1980–2000, Cttee on Legal Sciences, Polish Acad. of Sciences 2003–, Warsaw Scientific Asscn 2003, Regional Studies Asscn 2003; Bronze Cross of Merit 1978; Kt's Cross, Order of Polonia Restituta 1996; St Silvester Order of the Pope 1998; Walerian Panka Award 1997, St George Medal 2002, 'Lumen Gentium' Medal, Lublin Archdiocese 2004, Lawyer of the Year Award, Gazeta Pranna 2004. *Publications include:* Zalecenia RWPG w sprawie koordynacji narodowych planów gospodarczych i ich realizacja w PRL (Recomendations of Council for Mutual Economic Aid on Coordination of National Economic Schemes and Their Realization in Poland) 1978, Zagraniczne przedsiebiorstwo socjalistyczne w Polsce (Foreign Socialist Enterprises in Poland) 1986, Struktura Centralnego aparatu gospodarczego i jego funkcje (Structure of Central Economic Machinery and its Functions, ed.) 1989, Tworzenie i funkcjonowanie spólek: zagadnienia cywilnoprawne i administracyjne (Establishment and Functioning of Companies: Civil and Administrative Law Issues, ed.) 1989, Region samorzadowy (Local-governmental Region) 1991, Podejmowanie dzialalnosci gospodarczej przez inwestorów zagranicznych (Foreign Investors' Establishment) 1993, Prawo administracyjne (Administrative Law, co-author), Administracyjne prawo gospodarcze (Administrative Economic Law, co-author) 2003; over 40 scientific publs and numerous articles in nat. and foreign magazines on public admin. law, econ. law and law of local govt. *Leisure interests:* supporting football teams, watching good films. *Address:* ul. Obornicka 34 m. 15, 51-113 Wrocław, Poland (home).

KIIR MAYARDIT, Salva; Sudanese politician and fmr military leader; *President of Southern Sudan and Vice-President of Sudan;* b. 1951; joined Anyanya separatist movt. during First Sudanese Civil War, early 1960s, later becoming an officer, joined regular army after peace settlement 1972; with Army of Sudan 1972–83, attaining rank of Capt.; Founding mem. Sudan People's Liberation Movt (SPLM) 1983, later Deputy Party Leader, Chief of Staff Sudan Peoples Liberation Army (mil. wing of SPLM) 1999, Chair. SPLM after death of John Garang) 2005, C-in-C SPLA 2005–; Vice-Pres. of Southern Sudan 2005, Pres. 2005–, Pres. of Southern Sudan 2005–. *E-mail:* webmaster@splmtoday.com (office). *Website:* www.splmtoday.com (office).

KIKABIDZE, Vakhtang Konstantinovich; Georgian actor and singer; b. 19 July 1938, Tbilisi; s. of Konstantin Kikabidze and Manana Bagrationi; m. Irene Kebadze 1964; one s.; soloist and leader of Georgian pop-group Orera 1966–; film début in 1967 with Meeting in the Hills; solo career since 1988; USSR State Prize 1978, People's Artist of Georgian SSR 1980, Order of Honour, special award (Georgia) 1994, Order of Konstantine (Russia) 1997, Order of St Nicholaus 1998, Golden Gramophone Prize 1998, Leonid Utesov Prize for Achievement in field of Music 2000. *Films include:* Meeting in the Hills 1967, Don't Grieve 1968, I'm a Detective 1969, The Stone of the First Water 1970, Pen-name Lukach, The Melodies of Verikysky Block 1973, Lost Expedition 1973, Completely Gone 1972, Mimino 1978, TASS is Authorized to Inform, Hi! Friend (TV film) 1981, To Your Health Dear (Dir, scriptwriter, actor) 1983, Man and all the Others (scriptwriter, producer, actor) 1985, Fortuna (actor) 2000. *Music:* albums: My Years, My Wealth 1994, Larisa Ivanovna Please! 1995, Letter to Friend 1996, Tango of Love 1999, Greatest Hits 2000. *Leisure interest:* fishing. *Address:* S. Chikovani Street 20, Apt. 38, 380015 Tbilisi, Georgia. *Telephone:* (32) 98-90-14; 23-08-67 (home). *Website:* www.buba.diaspora.ru.

KIKOIN, Konstantin Abramovich, PhD, DrSci; Israeli (b. Russian) theoretical physicist, academic, poet and essayist; *Professor, School of Physics and Astronomy, Tel-Aviv University;* b. 9 Aug. 1945, Kalinin (now Tver); s. of Abraham Kikoin and Ekaterina Sosenkova; m. Larisa Markina 1969; one s. one d.; ed Ural State Univ. (Sverdlovsk/Ekaterinburg), Physical-Tech. Inst. Moscow; Jr Scientific Researcher, Inst. of Optical-Physical Measurements, Moscow 1971–74; Sr Scientific Researcher I.V. Kurchatov Inst. of Atomic Energy, Moscow 1974–85, Leading Scientific Researcher and Vice-Head of Solid State Theory Dept 1985–96; Research Fellow, Dept of Physics, Ben Gurian Univ. of the Negev, Israel 1997–2006; Prof., School of Physics and Astronomy, Tel-Aviv Univ. 2006–; Deputy Chair. Exec. Bd Moscow Physical Soc. 1989–96, Assoc. Ed. Journal of Moscow Physical Soc. 1990–96, Journal of Experimental and Theoretical Physics 1991–; Rep. of American Inst. of Physics in Moscow 1992–94; mem. Expert Council of Supreme Attestation Cttee 1994–96; mem. Israeli Federation of Writers' Unions 2008–; Kapitza Fellowship, Royal Soc. (UK) 1995. *Publications:* two monographs, seven reviews and more than 150 papers in scientific journals, two books of collected verses. *Leisure interest:* translating poetry from Russian into English. *Address:* School of Physics and Astronomy, Tel-Aviv University, Tel-Aviv 69978, Israel (office). *E-mail:* konstk@post.tau.ac.il (office). *Website:* www.tau.ac.il (office).

KIKUTAKE, Kiyonori, BA, FAIA; Japanese architect; b. 1 April 1928, Kurume; s. of Kiyoshi and Masue Kikutake; m. Norie Sasaki 1953; one s. two d.; ed Waseda Univ.; est. Kiyonori Kikutake & Assocs (Architects) 1953, now Rep. Dir; Prof. Dept of Architecture, Waseda Univ. 1959; Prof. Emer. Beijing Polytechnic Univ.; Vice-Pres. Japan Fed. of Professional Architects Asscns, Tokyo Professional Architects' Asscn, Japan Architects' Asscn 1982–; Exec. Dir Tokyo YMCA Inst. of Design; mem. Bd Architectural Inst. of Japan 1962–, Japan Inst. of Macro-Engineering Soc. (fmr Pres.) Tokyo Soc. of Architects Bldg Engineers ((fmr Pres. now Hon. Pres.); mem. French Academie D'Architecture; Visiting Prof. Univ. of Hawaii 1971, Univ. Aachen, Germany 1980, Univ. of Virginia 1980, Univ. of Vienna, Austria; del. to UNESCO Int. Conf., Zürich 1970; currently Pres. Hyper Building Research Cttee; Hon. Fellow, American Inst. of Architects 1971; Hon. Mem. Bulgarian Inst. of Architecture, Japan Inst. of Architects; Hon. Citizen, Kurume city; Ministry of Educ. Arts Award 1964, Architectural Inst. of Japan Award 1964, Pan Pacific Architectural Citation of the Hawaii Chapter, AIA 1964, Japan Academy of Architecture Prize 1970, Cultural Merits of Kurume City 1975, Auguste Perret Award UIA 1978, XXI Mainichi Art Awards 1979, The 31th Building Constructors Society Prize 1990, Shimane Prefecture Grand Prize for Beautiful Scenery 2000. *Major works include:* Shimane Prefectural Museum 1958, Sky House 1958, Admin. Building for Izumo Shrine, Tatebayashi City Hall 1963, Hotel Tokoen, Yonago-City, Miyakonojo City Hall, Pacific Hotel, Chigasaki 1966, Iwate Prefectural Library 1967, Shimane Prefectural Library, Hagi Civic Centre 1968, Kurume Civic Centre 1969, Expo Tower for Expo 70, Osaka 1970, Pasadena Heights (tiered mass housing) 1974, Aquapolis (floating module for ocean), Ocean Expo 75 1975, Hagi City Hall 1975, Redevelopment of Yamaga city centre 1975, Tsukuba Academic New Town, Pedestrian Deck Network and the Symbol Tower 1976, Otsu Shopping Centre 1976, branches of Kyoto Community Bank 1971–, Tanabe Museum, Matsue City 1979, Darumaya-Seibu Dept Store 1980, Treasury of Izumo Shrine 1981, Seibu-Yaow Shopping Centre 1981, Karuizawa Art Museum 1981, Kuamoto Pref. Arts and Crafts Centre 1982, Fukuoka City Hall (Ass. Hall) 1982, Edo Tokyo Museum 1992, Kurume City Hall 1994, Nagano Winter Olympic Games, Opening and Closing Ceremony Stadium Installation 1998, Shimane Art Museum, Japan 1999, Kyushu National Museum, Japan 2004, World Expo, Aichi, Japan 2005. *Publications:* Metabolism 1960 1960, Taisha Kenchiku-ron (Metabolic Architecture) 1968, Ningen-no-Kenchiku (Human Architecture) 1970, Ningen-no-Toshi (A Human City) 1970, Essence of Architecture 1973, Floating City 1973, Kiyonori Kikutake–Works and Methods 1956–70 1973, Community and Civilization 1978, Kiyonori Kikutake-Concepts and Planning 1978, Ningen-no-Kankyo (Human Environment) 1978, Community and City 1978, Tight Spaces, Macro-Engineering 1982. *Leisure interests:* swimming, photography, reading, travel. *Address:* Kikutake Architects, 1-10-1 Otsuka, Bunkyo-ku, Tokyo 112-0012, Japan (office). *Telephone:* (3) 5976-6161 (office); (3) 5976-6166 (office). *E-mail:* info@kikutake.co.jp (office). *Website:* www.kikutake.co.jp (office).

KIKWETE, Lt-Col Jakaya Mrisho; Tanzanian politician and head of state; *President;* b. 7 Oct. 1950, Msoga village; after graduation joined Tanzania African Nat. Union (now Chama Cha Mapinduzi (CCM) party); seconded to Tanzania People's Defence Forces as Chief Political Instructor at Monduli Cen. Mil. Acad.; commissioned as Lt and retd Col 1992; Deputy Minister, Ministries of Finance, of Water and Livestock Devt, of Energy and Minerals 1987–90, Minister 1990–94; Chair. Council of Ministers of the E African Community; Minister of Foreign Affairs and Int. Co-operation 1995–2005; Pres. 2005–; Chair. African Union Ass. 2008–; Patron Tanzania Nat.

Basketball Asscn. *Address:* Office of the President, State House, PO Box 9120, Dar es Salaam, Tanzania (office). *Telephone:* (22) 2116679 (office). *Fax:* (22) 2113425 (office). *Website:* www.tanzania.go.tz/poffice (office).

KILAR, Wojciech; Polish composer; b. 17 July 1932, Lwów (now Lviv, Ukraine); m. Barbara Pomianowska; ed State Higher School of Music, Katowice, (student of B. Woytowicz) Nadia Boulanger School; mem. Cttee Int. Festival of Contemporary Music Warszawska Jesień 1975, Polish Composers Union 1953–; mem. Polish Acad. of Arts and Sciences 1998–; Dr hc (Opole Univ.) 1999; Lili Boulanger Memorial Fund Award, Boston 1960, Jurzykowski Foundation Award, New York 1983, State Award Grade I 1980, Award of Minister of Culture 1967, 1976, 1975, Prize of Polish Composers' Union 1975, ASCAP Award for his score from Coppola's Dracula in Los Angeles in 1992. *Works include:* Sonatina for flute and piano 1951, Woodwind Quintet 1952, Mała uwertura 1955, I Symfonia 1955, II Symfonia 1956, Oda Bela Bartok in Memoriam 1957, Riff 62 1962, Générique 1963, Springfield Sonnet 1963, Diphthongs 1964, Solenne 1967, Training 68 for clarinet, trombone, and piano 1968, Upstairs Downstairs for soprano choir and orchestra 1971, Przygrywka i Kolęda 1972, Krzesany 1974, Bogurodzica 1975, Kościelec 1909 1976, Hoary Bog [Siwa Mgła] for baritone and orchestra 1979, Exodus 1981, Victoria for mixed choir and orchestra 1983, Angelus for soprano, for mixed choir and orchestra 1984, Orawa for string orchestra 1986, Choralvorspiel for string orchestra 1988, Requiem Father Kolbe for symphony orchestra 1994, Concerto for Piano and Orchestra 1996, Missa pro pace 2000; music for about 30 plays and 150 films including Illumination 1973, The Promised Land 1974, Dracula (ASCAP Award, Los Angeles 1992) 1991, Death and the Maiden 1994, Life at a Gallop 1995, The Portrait of a Lady 1996, The Ninth Gate 1999, Pamietam 2002, The Supplement 2002, The Pianist 2002, The Revenge 2002, Vendetta 2003. *Leisure interests:* books about mountains and cats, travels, home, cars. *Address:* ul. Kościuszki 165, 40-524 Katowice, Poland. *Telephone:* (32) 2514965.

KILGUS, Martin A., MA, PhD; German journalist; *Editor, SWR Public Radio, Television & Internet;* b. 15 March 1963, Stuttgart; s. of Alfred Kilgus and Charlotte-Pauline Hofmann; ed Wirtemberg-Gymnasium, Stuttgart, Univ. of Stuttgart and The American Univ., Washington, DC, USA; traineeship, NBC Radio; joined Dept for Ethnic Broadcasting, SDR Radio & TV, Stuttgart 1989; worked as ed. for migrants' audio broadcasts 1991; now Ed. with SWR (fmrly SDR) Radio, TV & Internet; Chair. Int. Educ. Information Exchange (IEIE e.V.), Stuttgart 1996–; Vice-Chair. German Asscn for the UN BW; special field of research and activity include Digital Audio Broadcasting (DAB) and multi-lingual broadcasts; Caritas Prize for Journalism. *Leisure interests:* arts, literature, cooking, snowboarding. *Address:* SWR Public Radio, TV & Internet, Neckarstrasse 230, 70190 Stuttgart, Germany (office). *Telephone:* (711) 9292648 (office). *Fax:* (711) 929182648 (office). *E-mail:* martin.kilgus@swr.de (office). *Website:* www.swr.de/international (office).

KILLINGER, Kerry K., MBA; American banking executive; ed Univ. of Iowa; fmr Investment Analyst, Banker's Life Insurance, NE; Exec. Vice-Pres. Murphey Favre Inc. –1982, joined Washington Mutual Inc. (following takeover of Murphey Favre) 1982, Exec. Vice-Pres. and later Sr Vice-Pres., Pres. 1988–2005, CEO 1990–2008, Chair. 1991–2008 (following acquisition of Washington Mutual by JP Morgan Chase); Dir Financial Services Roundtable, Washington Roundtable, Washington Financial League, SAFECO Corpn, Simpson Investment Co., Achieve, Partnership for Learning, Greater Seattle Chamber of Commerce; mem. NY Stock Exchange Listed Cos Advisory Cttee, Cttee to Encourage Corp. Philanthropy; American Banker Magazine Banker of the Year 2001. *Publications:* Middle Market Mortgages...Then More 2003. *Address:* c/o Washington Mutual Inc., 1301 Second Avenue, Seattle, WA 98101, USA. *Telephone:* (206) 461-2000.

KILLION, Redley (Rere), MA (Econs); Micronesian politician and economist; b. 23 Oct. 1951, Weno, Chuuk State; m. Jacinta Killion; nine c.; ed Mizpah High School, Weno, Marist High School, Eugene, Oregon, Univ. of Hawaii, Vanderbilt Univ., Nashville, Tenn., USA; economist, Dept of Resources and Devt, Trust Territory Govt 1974–79; Dir Dept of Resources and Devt, Chuuk State Govt 1979–86; Nat. Senator 1987–99, Vice-Pres. Federated States of Micronesia 1999–2007; Congress of Micronesia Scholarship Awards 1969–70; UN Fellowship for Graduate Studies at Vanderbilt Univ. 1977–78. *Address:* c/o PO Box PS-53, Palikir, Pohnpei State, FSM 96941 (office); PO Box PS 237, Palikir, Pohnpei State, FSM 96942, Micronesia (home). *Telephone:* (691) 320-2833 (home). *Fax:* (691) 320-2930 (home).

KILLIP, Christopher David; British photographer; *Professor of Visual Studies, Harvard University;* b. 11 July 1946, Isle of Man; s. of Allen Killip and Mary Quirk; one s.; ed Douglas High School for Boys; photography in Isle of Man 1969–71; Prof. of Visual Studies, Harvard Univ. 1991–; ACGB Photography Awards 1973–74, Northern Arts Photography Fellow 1975–76, ACGB Bursary Award 1977, Henri Cartier-Bresson Award, Paris 1989. *Publications:* Isle of Man (portfolio), Isle of Man (book) 1980, In flagrante 1988, Fifty-five 2001, The Pirelli Work 2006. *Address:* Harvard University, 24 Quincy Street, Cambridge, MA 02138, USA.

KILLY, Jean-Claude; French business executive and fmr Olympic skier; b. 30 Aug. 1943, St-Cloud, Seine-et-Oise; s. of Robert Killy and Madeleine de Ridder; m. Danièlle Gaubert 1973 (died 1987); one d., two step-c.; ed Ecole de Val-d'Isère, Lycées in Chambéry, Grenoble, Saint-Jean-de-Maurienne, Bourg-Saint-Maurice; French champion 1964, 1965, 1966; won three gold medals at Winter Olympics, Grenoble, France 1968; retd from competitive skiing 1968 but returned in 1972 to become professional world champion in 1973; customs officer 1965–68; Publicity Agent Gen. Motors 1968; Marketing Consultant (concerning skiing information) United Air Lines 1969; settled in Geneva 1969 and moved into the sports clothing business with the co. Veleeda-Killy; Tech. Adviser Dynamic 1981; mem.Exec. Bd Alpine Cttee of the Int. Skiing Fed. 1977–94; Pres. World Sport Marketing (now Amaury Sport Org.) 1992–2000, Société du Tour de France 1992–2001; Co-Pres. Winter Olympics, Albertville 1992; fmr Chair. Coca-Cola France, mem. Admin Bd Coca-Cola 1993, Coca-Cola Enterprises 1997, Int. Olympic Cttee 1995–; Dir Rolex Watch Co.; Pres. Co-ordination Cttee for 2006 Olympic Games in Turin 2000–06, Organizing Cttee for the 2009 Alpine FIS Ski World Championships 2002–07 (resgnd); Commdr, Légion d'honneur; IOC Olympic Order; Export Oscar 1982. *Film:* Snow Job 1972. *Publications:* Skiez avec Killy 1969, Le Ski 1978. *Leisure interests:* flying, reading, cycling, walking, swimming, snowboarding. *Address:* 13 chemin Bellefontaine, 1223 Cologny -GE, Switzerland.

KILMER, Val Edward; American actor; b. 31 Dec. 1959, Los Angeles; m. Joanne Whalley (q.v.) 1988 (divorced 1996); one d.; ed Hollywood's Professional School, Juilliard; began career in theatre then film debut in 1984; f. Blessed Films (production co.). *Films:* Top Secret 1984, Real Genius 1985, Top Gun 1986, Willow 1988, Kill Me Again 1989, The Doors 1991, Thunderheart 1991, True Romance 1993, The Real McCoy 1993, Tombstone 1993, Wings of Courage 1995, Batman Forever 1995, Heat 1995, The Saint 1996, The Island of Dr. Moreau 1996, The Ghost and the Darkness 1996, Dead Girl 1996, Joe the King 1999, At First Sight 1999, Planet Red 2000, Pollock 2000, Salton Sea 2002, Run for the Money 2002, Masked and Anonymous 2003, Wonderland 2003, Spartan 2004, Blind Horizon 2004, Mindhunters 2004, Alexander 2004, Kiss, Kiss, Bang, Bang 2005, Moscow Zero 2006, 10th & Wolf 2006, Played 2006, Summer Love 2006, Deja Vu 2006, The Ten Commandments: The Musical 2006. *Stage appearances include:* Electra and Orestes, Henry IV Part One 1981, As You Like It 1982, Slab Boys (Broadway debut) 1983, Hamlet 1988, 'Tis Pity She's A Whore 1992, The Postman Always Rings Twice (Playhouse Theatre, London) 2005. *Address:* c/o William Morris Agency, 1 William Morris Place, Beverly Hills, CA 90212, USA. *Telephone:* (310) 859-4000. *Fax:* (310) 859-4462. *Website:* www.wma.com; www.valkilmer.org (office).

KIM, Anatoly Andreyevich; Russian writer; b. 15 June 1939, S Kazakhstan; ed Literary Inst., Moscow; freelance writer 1973–; Prof. of Russian Language and Literature, Inst. of Journalism, Moscow; lecturer in S Korea 1991–95. *Publications include:* more than 20 books including novels: Gatherers of Herbs 1976, Litis 1980, Squirrel 1984, Forest-Father 1989, Onlyrya 1995, Mushroom Picking with Bach's Music 1997, The Wall 1998, Twins 2000; numerous short stories; film scripts: My Sister Lucy, Revenge, To Go Out of the Forest. *Address:* Akademika Pavlova str. 36, apt. 112, 121552 Moscow, Russia (home). *Telephone:* (495) 140-15-31 (home).

KIM, Chang-keun, BA, MBA; South Korean business executive; ed Yonsei Univ., Univ. of Southern Calif., USA; joined SK Corpn (refinery and petrochemical mfr) 1974, held positions successively as staff mem. Ulsan Plant, SK Chemicals Co. Ltd, Sr Man. Treasury Dept, Dir of Strategic Services, Office of Corp. Planning, 1994–96, Dir of Finance 1996–97, Man.-Dir SK Group Office of Corp. Man. and Planning (OCMP) 1997–2000, Exec. Dir 2000, Head of Restructuring HQ, fmr Pres. and CEO SK Corpn; convicted of accounting irregularities by Seoul Dist Court 2003. *Address:* c/o SK Corporation, 99 Seorin-dong, Jongno-gu, Seoul 110-110, Republic of Korea (office).

KIM, Dae-jung, MA, PhD; South Korean politician; b. 3 Dec. 1925, Hugwang-ri, S Jeolla Prov.; m. Lee Lee Ho; ed Mokpo Commercial High School, Korea and Kyunghee Univs, Diplomatic Acad. of Foreign Ministry of Russia; Pres. Mokpo Merchant Ship Co. 1948; arrested by N Korean Communists, escaped from jail 1950; Pres. Mokpo Daily News 1950; Deputy Commdr S Jeolla Region, Maritime Defence Force 1950; Pres. Heungkuk Merchant Shipping Co. 1951; Pres Dae-yang Shipbldg. Co. 1951; mem. Cen. Cttee Democratic Party 1957, Spokesman 1960, Spokesman, Nat. Alliance to Protect Human Rights 1958; elected to 5th Nat. Ass. 1961, 6th Nat. Ass. 1963; Spokesman, People's Party 1965, Chair. Policy Planning Council and mem. Cen. Exec. Bd 1966; Spokesman, New Democratic Party and mem. of Party Cen. Exec. Bd 1967; elected to 7th Nat. Ass. 1967, 8th Nat. Ass. 1971; injured in assassination attempt 1971; in exile, organized anti-dictatorship movts in Japan and USA 1972; abducted from Japan by Korean CIA agents, survived two assassination attempts, forcibly returned to Seoul, placed under house arrest 1973; arrested for criticizing Constitution 1976; sentenced to five years' imprisonment 1977; sentence suspended; released from jail, placed under house arrest 1978; house arrest lifted 1979; amnesty granted, civil rights restored; rearrested, charged with treason, sentenced to death 1980; sentence commuted to life imprisonment 1981; sentence reduced to 20 years, later suspended 1982; went into exile in USA 1982; f. Korean Inst. for Human Rights, Va 1983; returned to Korea 1985; under intermittent house arrest 1985–87; Co-Chair. Council for Promotion of Democracy 1985; Standing Adviser, Reunification Democratic Party 1987; f. Party for Peace and Democracy, Pres. 1987–91; reappointed to 13th Nat. Ass. 1988; f., Pres. New Democratic Party April–Sept. 1991; f. Democratic Party, Co.-Chair. 1991–92; reappointed to 14th Nat. Ass., later retd from politics 1992; f. Kim Dae-Jung Peace Foundation for Asia-Pacific Region, Chair. Bd of Dirs 1994; ended retirement from politics 1995; f. Nat. Congress for New Politics 1995; Pres. of Repub. of Korea 1997–2003; Pres. Millennium Democratic Party 2000–01; Co-Pres. Forum of Democratic Leaders in Asia-Pacific 1994; Visiting Fellow, Clare Hall Coll., Univ. of Cambridge, UK 1993, Life Fellow 1993; mem. Int. Ecological Acad. Moscow 1994–; Adviser, Int. Cttee for Relief of Victims of Torture, USA 1984–, Union Theological Seminary, USA 1984–; Visiting Fellow, Centre for Int. Affairs, Harvard Univ., USA 1983–84; Trustee, Fed. of Unions of Korean Shipbldg Agents 1951; Ed.-in-Chief, Centre for Study of Korean Labour 1995; Hon. Prof. (Moscow Univ.) 1992, (Chinese Acad. of Social Sciences, Nankai Univ., Fudan Univ., People's Repub. of China) 1994; Hon. LLD (Emory Univ., USA) 1983, (Catholic Univ. of America) 1992; Hon. Dr of

Political Science (Wonkwang Univ.) 1994; numerous honours and awards including Bruno Kreisky Human Rights Award, Austria 1981, Union Medal, Union Theol. Seminary, USA 1994; awarded Nobel Peace Prize 2000. *Publications include:* Conscience in Action 1985, Prison Writings 1987, Building Peace and Democracy 1987, Kim Dae-jung's Views on International Affairs 1990, In the Name of Justice and Peace 1991, Korea and Asia 1994, The Korean Problem: Nuclear Crisis, Democracy and Reunification 1994, Unification, Democracy and Peace 1994, Mass Participatory Economy: Korea's Road to World Economic Power 1996. *Address:* c/o Office of the President, Chong Wa Dae, 1 Sejongno, Jongno-gu, Seoul, Republic of Korea (office).

KIM, Dong-jin, BEng, PhD; South Korean automotive industry executive; *Vice-Chairman and Co-CEO, Hyundai Motor Company;* b. 4 Dec. 1950; m.; two c.; ed Seoul Nat. Univ., Finlay Eng Coll., USA; research engineer, Korea Inst. of Science and Tech. 1972; sr research engineer, Agency for Defence Devt 1973–78; Man. Hyundai Heavy Industries Co. Ltd 1978–79, Sr Exec. Vice-Pres. Hyundai Precision & Industry Co. Ltd 1979–98, Pres. and CEO Hyundai Space & Aircraft Co. Ltd 1998–99, apptd Pres. Hyundai Motor Co. 2000, currently Vice-Chair. and Co-CEO; Chair. Korea Geospatial Information and Tech. Asscn 1999–; Pres. e-HD.com Inc. 2000–; Order of Nat. Security Merit (Samil-Jang) 1985; Prize of Devotion Merit, Seoul Nat. Univ. School of Eng 1998. *Address:* Hyundai Motor Company, 231 Yangjae-dong, Seocho-gu, Seoul 137-938, Republic of Korea (office). *Telephone:* (2) 3464-1114 (office). *Fax:* (2) 3463-3484 (office). *Website:* www.hyundai-motor.com (office).

KIM, Gen. Dong-shin, BA, MS; South Korean politician and army general (retd); b. 13 March 1941, Kwangju City; ed Seoul Nat. Univ., Korean Mil. Acad. and Hannam Univ.; Regimental Commdr, Army of Repub. of Korea 1983; apptd Chief, Foreign Policy Div., Ministry of Nat. Defence 1984; Deputy Dir of Strategic Planning, Jt Chief of Staff 1989–90; Commanding Gen. 51st Infantry Div. 1990–92; Dir of Force Planning 1992–93; Commanding Gen. Capital Corps, 3rd Army 1993–94; Chief Dir of Operations, Jt Chiefs of Staff 1995–96; Deputy C-in-C, Repub. of Korea–US Combined Forces Command 1996–98; Army Chief of Staff 1998–99; Adviser, Nat. Security Cttee 2000; Minister of Nat. Defence 2001–02; Visiting Scholar, RAND Center for Asia Pacific Policy 2002–03; Silver Star Medal 1972, Order of Nat. Security Merit (Samil Medal 1983, Gukson Medal 1993, Tangil Medal 1997), Order of Mil. Merit 1991, US Army Meritorious Service Medal 1999, Legion of Merit 2001. *Address:* c/o Ministry of National Defence 1, 3-ga, Yonsan-don, Yongsan-gu, Seoul, Republic of Korea (office).

KIM, Gye-kwan; North Korean politician and diplomatist; *Deputy Minister of Foreign Affairs;* b. 1943; participated in Pyongyang-Washington negotiations and Geneva talks as working-level rep. of N Korea; close confidante of Pres. Kim Jong-il; one of N Korea's most experienced negotiators; travelled widely in Europe before 1993; served as Amb.-at-Large and maintained ties with socialist parties in Western Europe; designated Deputy Negotiator in first nuclear talks with USA, later Chief Negotiator; head of del. to four-party talks between N and S Korea, China and USA to address Korean peninsula issues; currently Deputy Minister of Foreign Affairs. *Address:* Ministry of Foreign Affairs, Pyongyang, Democratic People's Republic of Korea (office).

KIM, Hak-su, BA, MA, PhD; South Korean international civil servant, economist and academic; *Distinguished Visiting Professor, Graduate School of International Studies, Yonsei University;* b. 27 Feb. 1938, Wonju, Kangwon; ed Yonsei Univ., Univ. of Edinburgh, UK, Univ. of S Carolina, USA; economist, Cen. Bank 1960; Sec. to Minister of Commerce and Industry 1969; London Rep., Bank of Korea 1971–73; Exec. Dir Daewoo Corpn 1977, later Pres.; Chief Planning Officer, Chief Tech. Advisor UN Dept for Tech. Co-operation and Devt 1980s; Sr Research Fellow, Korea Inst. for Int. Econ. Policy 1989–93; Pres. Hanil Banking Inst. 1993–95; Sec.-Gen. of the Colombo Plan, Sri Lanka 1995–99; Korean Amb. for Int. Econ. Affairs 1999; UN Under-Sec.-Gen. and Exec. Sec. UN ESCAP 2000–07 (appointment renewed 2005); Distinguished Visiting Prof., Grad. School of Int. Studies, Yonsei Univ., Seoul 2007–. *Leisure interests:* classical music, trekking, walking. *Address:* Graduate School of International Studies, Yonsei University, 134 Sinchon-dong Seodamun-gu, Seoul 120-749 (office); 319-1601 Hanyong Apt, Bundang, Kyunggi, South Korea (home). *Telephone:* (2) 2123-6297 (office); (2) 656-7556 (home). *E-mail:* magkim16@hotmail.com (office). *Website:* gsis.yonsei.ac.kr (office).

KIM, Vice-Marshal Il-chol; North Korean politician; *Minister of People's Armed Forces;* b. 1928, Pyongyang; ed Mangyongdae Revolutionary School, Navy Acad., USSR; apptd Commdr East Sea Fleet 1970; mem. Party Cen. Cttee 1980–; Deputy in Supreme People's Ass. 1982; apptd Commdr of Navy 1982; rank of Lt-Gen. 1982, Col-Gen. 1985, Gen. 1992, Vice-Marshal 1997; First Minister of the People's Armed Forces 1997–98, Minister 1998–; Vice-Chair. Nat. Defence Comm. 1998–; Kim Il Sung medal 1982, Nat. Flag Order, Nat. Hero title 1995. *Address:* Office of the Minister, Ministry of the People's Armed Forces, Pyongyang, Democratic People's Republic of Korea (office).

KIM, Gen. Jang-soo; South Korean army officer and government official; b. 1948, Gwangju; m. Park Hyo-sook; one s. one d.; ed Korea Mil. Acad., Yonsei Univ.; served in several key posts in Army including Deputy Commdr Korea-US Combined Forces Command and Chief Operations and Strategy Dir Jt Chiefs of Staff; Army Chief of Staff 2005–06; Minister of Nat. Defence 2006–08. *Address:* c/o Ministry of National Defence, 1, 3-ga, Yeongsan-dong, Yeongsan-gu, Seoul 140-701, Republic of Korea (office).

KIM, Ji-woon; South Korean filmmaker and screenwriter; b. 6 July 1964, Seoul. *Films:* Choyonghan kajok (The Quiet Family, writer, dir) 1998, Banchikwang (The Foul King, writer, dir) 2000, Coming Out (writer, dir) 2001, Saam gaang (Three, segment 'Memories', dir, writer) 2002, Janghwa, Hongryeon (A Tale of Two Sisters, writer, dir) 2003, Dalkomhan insaeng (A Bittersweet Life, writer, dir) 2005.

KIM, Jim Yong, MD, PhD; physician and international health organization official; *Director, Department of HIV/AIDS, World Health Organization;* ed Brown Univ., Harvard Univ.; Founding Trustee Partners in Health (Harvard–affiliated nonprofit org.) 1987, mem. Bd of Dirs; apptd by WHO to help lead int. response to drug-resistant tuberculosis by establishing pilot MDR TB treatment programs and organizing effective delivery systems for antibiotics 1999; co-Chief Div. of Social Medicine and Health Inequalities, Brigham and Women's Hospital, Boston 2001–; currently Assoc. Prof. of Medicine and Medical Anthropology, Dir Program in Infectious Disease and Social Change, Harvard Medical School; also currently Dir Dept of HIV/AIDS and Sr Advisor to Dir Gen., WHO 2003–; John D. and Catherine T. MacArthur Foundation Genius Fellowship 2003. *Publication:* Dying for Growth: Global Inequality and the Health of the Poor (co-ed.). *Address:* World Health Organization, Department of HIV/AIDS, 20 Avenue Appia, 1211 Geneva 27, Switzerland (office); Partners in Health, 641 Huntington Avenue, 2nd Floor-Program in Infection and Social Change, Boston, MA (office); Harvard Medical School, 25 Shattuck Street, Boston, MA 02115, USA (office). *Telephone:* (22) 791 4530 (Switzerland) (office); (617) 432-2575 (USA) (office). *Fax:* (22) 791 4834 (Switzerland) (office); (617) 432-6045 (USA) (office). *E-mail:* kimj@who.int (office); hiv-aids@who.int (office). *Website:* www.who.int/hiv/en (office); www.brighamandwomens.org/socialmedicine (office); www.hms.harvard.edu/dsm (office); www.pih.org/index.html (office).

KIM, Jin-pyo, MA; South Korean politician; b. 4 May 1947, Suwon, Gyeonggi Prov.; ed Gyeongbok High School, Seoul Nat. Univ., Univ. of Wisconsin, USA; Dir Consumption Tax Bureau, Ministry of Finance 1983, Dir Tax Policy Section 1988, Dir-Gen. Tax Systems Bureau 1993, Dir-Gen. Foreign Trade Affairs Bureau 1995, Asst Minister, Taxations, Ministry of Finance and Economy 1999, Vice Minister of Finance and Economy 2001; Sr Presidential Sec. for Policy and Planning Jan.–June 2002; Minister of Govt Policy Co-ordination 2002–03; Deputy Prime Minister and Minister of Finance 2003–04; mem. Nat. Ass. 2004–; Deputy Prime Minister and Minister of Educ. and Human Resources Devt –2006; Hon. Dr Public Admin (Univ. of the Cumberlands). *Publication:* Looking on the Bright Side: Korean Economy 2004. *Address:* c/o Ministry of Education and Human Resources Development, 77, 1-ga, Sejong-no, Jongno-gu, Seoul 110-760, Republic of Korea (office). *E-mail:* jp311@assembly.go.kr (home).

KIM, Marshal Jong-il; North Korean supreme head of state; *General Secretary, Workers' Party of Korea, Chairman, National Defence Commission, Supreme Commander of Korean People's Army and Marshal of the Democratic People's Republic of Korea;* b. 16 Feb. 1942, secret camp on Mt Paekdu; s. of the late Kim Il-sung (named Eternal Pres. 1998) and Kim Jong-suk; ed Kim Il-sung Univ., Pyongyang; Officer, then Section Chief, then Deputy Dir, then Dir a Dept of Cen. Cttee Workers' Party of Korea 1964–73, mem. Cen. Cttee 1972, Sec. 1973; mem. Political Comm. Cen. Cttee 1974, mem. Presidium of Politburo of Cen. Cttee of Workers' Party of Korea 1980–, Gen. Sec. 1997–; First Vice-Chair. Nat. Defence Comm. 1990–93, Chair. (Head of State) April 1993–; mem. Mil. Comm. Cen. Cttee at Sixth Party Congress 1980; Deputy to Supreme People's Ass. 1982–; Supreme Commdr Korean People's Army 1991–; Marshal of the Democratic People's Repub. of Korea 1992–; Hon. Dr (Inca Garsilaso de la Vega Univ., Peru) 1986, (Chiclayo Univ., Peru) 1986; Kim Il Sung Order (three times), title of Marshal; Orden de Solidaridad, Cuba, Grand Croix de l'Ordre Nat. des Mille Collines, Rwanda, Necklace Order of Egypt; Kim Il Sung Prize; Hero of Democratic People's Repub. of Korea (three times), and many other foreign and domestic awards and honours. *Publications include:* Kim Jong Il Selected Works (15 vols), For the Completion of the Revolutionary Cause of Juche (10 vols). *Address:* Central Committee of the Workers' Party of Korea, Pyongyang, Democratic People's Republic of Korea.

KIM, Brig.-Gen. Jong-pil; South Korean politician; b. 7 Jan. 1926, Puyo; m. Park Young Ok (niece of the late Pres. Park Chung Hee); one s. one d.; ed High School, Gyeongju, Seoul Nat. Univ. and Korean Military Acad.; served in Korean war; Dir Korean Cen. Intelligence Agency 1961–63; mem. Nat. Assembly 1963–68, 1971–80; Chair. Democratic Republican Party 1963–68; Sr Adviser to Pres. 1970; Vice-Pres. Democratic Republican Party 1971, Pres. 1979–80 (banned from political activity 1980); Pres. New Democratic Republican Party 1987; Jt Pres. Democratic Liberal Party (DLP) 1990–93, Chair. 1993; Hon. Chair. United Liberal Democrats, Pres. 2000–04; Prime Minister 1971–75, 1998–99; mem. Spanish Nat. Acad., Korean Acad.; Hon. LLD (Long Island Univ., NY) 1964, (Chungang Univ., Seoul) 1966, (Fairleigh Dickinson Univ.) 1968; Hon. DHumLitt (Westminster Coll., Fulton, Mo.) 1966; Hon. PhD (Hongik Univ.) 1974; numerous awards from Korean and foreign govts. *Leisure interests:* painting, music. *Address:* 340-38, Shindang 4-dong, Jung-gu, Seoul, Republic of Korea (home). *Telephone:* (2) 783-7061-2 (home). *Fax:* (2) 782-9185 (home).

KIM, Jung-tae, BSc; South Korean banker; ed Seoul Nat. Univ.; began career with Daehan Merchant Bank 1969; with Daeshin Securities 1975; Exec. Dir Dongwon Securities 1982, Dir of Venture Capital 1991, Vice-Pres. –1997, CEO 1997–98; Vice-Chair., Pres. and CEO Housing and Commercial Bank 1998–2001, Pres. and CEO Kookmin Bank (cr. after merger of Housing and Commercial Bank with Kookmin) 2001–04. *Address:* c/o Kookmin Bank, 9-1 Namdaemunro 2-ga, Jung-gu, Seoul, Republic of Korea (office).

KIM, Jung-won; South Korean business executive; *Chairman, Hanhyo Development Company Ltd.;* b. 3 March 1948; ed Kyungnam Sr High School, Guilford Coll., New York; joined Hanil Synthetic Fiber Ind. Co. Ltd 1972, Exec. Man. Dir 1974, Vice-Pres. 1975, Pres. 1979–; Pres. Hanhyo Co. Ltd 1977, Chair. 1984–; Pres. Hanhyo Devt Co. Ltd 1978, Chair. 1984–; Pres. Kyungnam

Woollen Textile Co. Ltd 1979; First Chair. Hanhyo Acad. 1982; Pres. Korean Amateur Volleyball Asscn 1983, Vice-Pres. Asian Volleyball Asscn 1983; awarded Saemaul Decoration 1974; First Hon. Consul Kingdom of the Netherlands 1985. *Address:* Kukje-ICC Corpn, C.P.O. Box 747, Seoul, Republic of Korea.

KIM, Mahn-je, DEcon; South Korean politician and economist; b. 3 Dec. 1934, Sonsan; ed Univs of Denver and Missouri, USA; Assoc. Prof., Sogang Univ., Seoul 1965–70, Prof. 1982–; mem. Legis. Ass. 1980–; Minister of Finance 1983–86; Deputy Prime Minister and Minister of Econ. Planning 1986–88; Pres. Korean Devt Inst. 1971–82, Korean Int. Econ. Inst. (KIEI) 1981, KorAm Bank 1983–84; apptd. CEO Pohang Iron & Steel Co. 1994, Chair. 1996–98, sentenced by Seoul Dist Court to 30 million won in fines on embezzlement charges 1999; Sr Policy Researcher, Policy Research Inst. of Democratic Justice Party (DJP) 1982; mem. Monetary Bd 1975–, Econ. Planning Bd Advisory Cttee 1982; currently mem. Bd of Dirs Korea Forum for Progress, East-West Center Foundation. *Address:* c/o East-West Center, 1601 East-West Road, Honolulu, HI 96848, USA.

KIM, Man-bok; South Korean fmr government official; b. 1946, Busan; ed Seoul Nat. Univ., Konkuk Univ.; joined Agency for Nat. Security Planning (now Nat. Intelligence Service) 1974; Councillor, Embassy in Washington, DC 1993–96; fmr Chief, Information Man. Bureau, Nat. Security Council; Chief Office of Planning and Coordination –April 2006, Deputy Dir overseeing overseas operations April–Nov. 2006, Nat. Intelligence Security Chief Nov. 2006–08, resgnd after being accused of leaking classified inter-Korean documents to media. *Address:* c/o National Intelligence Service, Central Government Complex, 77-6 Sejongno, Jongno-gu, Seoul, Republic of Korea (office).

KIM, Seong-kyu; South Korean government official; Minister of Justice –2005; Dir Nat. Intelligence Service 2005–06 (resgnd). *Address:* c/o National Intelligence Service, Central Government Complex, 77-6, Sejongno, Jongno-gu, Seoul, Republic of Korea (office).

KIM, Soo-bong, PhD; South Korean particle physicist and academic; *Assistant Professor of Physics, Seoul National University;* fmr mem. Michigan CDF group studying proto/anti-proton collisions at Fermilab; currently Asst Prof., Dept of Physics, Seoul Nat. Univ.; involved in research at Super-Kamiokande underground project to search for neutrino mass and proton decay, Kamioka, Japan, and at Large Hadron Collider (LHC) at CERN, Geneva, Switzerland. *Publications:* numerous articles in scientific journals. *Address:* Department of Physics, Seoul National University, Shilim-dong, Kwanak-ku, Seoul 151-742, Republic of Korea (office). *Telephone:* (2) 880-5755 (office). *Fax:* (2) 884-3002 (office). *E-mail:* sbkim@phya.snu.ac.kr (office). *Website:* physics.snu.ac.kr/~sbkim/ (office).

KIM, Ssang-su; South Korean electronics executive; *Vice-Chairman and CEO, LG Electronics Inc.;* b. 2 Jan. 1945, Gimcheon, N Gyeongsang Prov.; m. Shin Kyung-sook; two d. one s.; ed Coll. of Eng and Science, Hanyang Univ.; joined LG Electronics (fmrly named Goldstar) as engineer 1969, various sr positions include Factory Head in Refrigerator Div., Pres. of Living System Co., and Pres. of Digital Appliance Co. –2000, Vice-Chair. and CEO 2003–; named The Star of Asia, US Business Week 2003. *Leisure interests:* mountain-climbing, golf, reading. *Address:* LG Electronics Inc., 20 Yeouido-dong, Yeoungdeungpo-gu, Seoul 150-721, Republic of Korea (office). *Telephone:* (2) 3777-3427 (office). *Fax:* (2) 3777-3428 (office). *Website:* www.lge.com (office); www.kimssangsu.com (home).

KIM, Suk-joon, BA; South Korean business executive; *Chairman and CEO, SsangYong Corporation;* b. 9 April 1955, Gyeongsang Prov.; m.; two s. one d.; ed Korea Univ., Seoul; mil. service Repub. of Korea Marine Corps 1972–75; planning office SsangYong Corpn 1977–79, NY and LA br. offices SsangYong (USA) Inc. 1979–82, Dir Planning and Project Man. Div. SsangYong Eng and Construction Co. Ltd 1982–83, CEO 1983–95, Pres. 1983–92, Chair. 1992–95, Vice-Chair. SsangYong Business Group (later SsangYong Corpn) 1991–93, 1994–95, CEO 1991–93, 1994–, Chair. 1995–, Chair., CEO SsangYong Motor Co. 1994–95, Chair., CEO SsangYong Cement Industrial Co. 1995–; Co-Chair. Korean Party Korea-France High-Level Businessmens' Club, Korean Party Korea-Singapore Econ. Co-operation Cttee; Vice-Chair. Korea-Japan Econ. Asscn, Fed. of Korean Industries, Korean Employers' Fed.; mem. Korea Chamber of Commerce and Industries; Dir Bd of Trustees Kookmin Univ.; Baden-Powell World Fellow, World Scout Foundation; Order of Industrial Service Merit Gold Tower 1991. *Address:* SsangYong Corporation, SsangYong Global Centre, 64, 2–ga, Jeo-dong, Jung-gu, Box 409 Seoul 100-748, Republic of Korea (office). *Telephone:* (2) 270-8114 (office). *Fax:* (2) 273-0981 (office). *Website:* www.ssy.co.kr (office).

KIM, Suk-soo; South Korean lawyer, politician and judge; b. 20 Nov. 1932; ed Yonsei Univ., Seoul; admitted to Korean Bar 1958; Judge Advocate, Repub. of Korea Army HQ 1960–63; judge, Masan Br., Court of Pusan Dist Court 1963–67, Pusan Dist Court 1967–69, Incheon Br., Court of Seoul Civil and Criminal Dist Court 1969–70, Seoul Criminal Dist Court 1970–71, Seoul High Court 1971–73; Research Judge, Supreme Court 1973–74; Presiding Judge, Pusan Dist Court 1974–77, Sungbook Br., Court of Seoul Dist Court 1977–79, Seoul Civil Dist Court 1979–80; Chief Judge, Incheon Br., Court of Suwon Dist Court 1980–81; Presiding Judge, Seoul High Court and Chief Judge Nambu Br., Seoul Dist Court 1981–83; Sr Presiding Judge, Seoul High Court 1983–86; Chief Judge, Pusan Dist Court 1986–88; Vice-Minister of Court Admin 1988–91; Supreme Court Justice 1991–97; Chair. Nat. Election Comm. 1993–97; Chair. Judicial Officers' Ethics Cttee of Supreme Court 1997–2001; Chair. Korea Press Ethics Comm. 2000–02; Chair. Govt Public Service Ethics Cttee 2002; Prime Minister of Repub. of Korea 2002–03; Auditor Bd of Dirs Yonsei Univ. Foundation 1997–2002; Dir Samsung Electronics Co. 1999–2001, Yonsei Law Promotion Foundation 2002; Order of Service Merit (Blue Stripes) 1997; Hon. PhD (Yonsei Univ.) 1997. *Address:* c/o Office of the Prime Minister, 77 Sejong-no, Jongno-gu, Seoul, Republic of Korea (office).

KIM, Sun-dong, MBA; South Korean petroleum industry executive; *Chairman, S-Oil Corporation;* b. 1942; ed Seoul Nat. Univ.; with Korea Oil Corpn 1963–74; Man. SsangYong Cement Industrial Co. Ltd 1974–76, Dir SsangYong Corpn 1978–80; Man. Dir S-Oil Corpn 1980–84, Exec. Dir 1984–87, Vice-Pres. 1987–91, Pres. and CEO 1991–98, Vice-Chair. and CEO 1998–2000, Chair. and CEO 2000–07, Chair. 2007–; mem. Korea Petroleum Asscn (Chair. 1997). *Address:* S-Oil Corporation, PO Box 758, 60 Yoido-dong, Yeongdungpo-gu, Seoul 150-607, Republic of Korea (office). *Telephone:* (2) 3772-5151 (office). *Fax:* (2) 783-7993 (office). *Website:* www.s-oil.com (office).

KIM, Taek-jin, MSc; South Korean computer engineer and business executive; *Chairman, President and CEO, NCSoft Corporation;* ed Seoul Nat. Univ.; co-author of Hangul (Korean-language word-processing program) while at Univ. 1989; cr. Hanmesoft (computer software) 1989; staff mem. Research and Devt Centre, Hyundai Electronics Industries Co. (now Hynix) 1991–92, Head of Devt Team for Shinbiro (S Korea's first internet service provider), 1994; cr. Lineage (online fantasy computer game) 1997, expanded to Taiwan markets 2000, has signed up five million users –2002; Founder, Chair., Pres. and CEO NCSoft Corpn 1997–, est. subsidiaries and jt ventures in USA, Japan, Hong Kong and China; Regional Dir Microsoft Corpn 1998; Man of the Year, Computer Reporters Asscn 1989, New Venture Age Leader, Naeway Economic Daily 2000, Industrial Medal, Soft Expo/Digital Contents Fair 2001, Best Contrib. to Cultural Industry, Ministry of Culture and Tourism 2001. *Address:* NCSoft Corpn, 157-33 Oksan Bldg., Samsung-dong, Gangnam-gu, Seoul 135-090, Republic of Korea (office). *Telephone:* (2) 2186-3300 (office). *Website:* www.ncsoft.co.kr (office).

KIM, Vladimir, MBA, PhD; Kazakhstani mining industry executive; *Executive Chairman, Kazakhmys PLC;* b. 1961; m.; three c.; ed Alma-Ata Architectural Inst.; joined Kazakhmys Group 1995, apptd Man. Dir and CEO JSC Zhezkazgantsvetmet 1995, Chair. Bd of Dirs Kazakhmys PLC 2000–, currently also Exec. Chair. *Address:* Kazakhmys PLC, 6th & 7th Floor, Cardinal Place, 100 Victoria Street, London, SW1E 5JL, England (office). *Telephone:* (20) 7901-7800 (office). *Fax:* (20) 7901-7859 (office). *Website:* www.kazakhmys.com (office).

KIM, Wan-su; North Korean central banker; *President, Central Bank of the Democratic People's Republic of Korea;* Deputy Minister of Finance –2004; Pres. Cen. Bank of Democratic People's Repub. of Korea 2004–. *Address:* Central Bank of the DPRK, Munsudong, Seungri Street 58-1, Central District, Pyongyang, Democratic People's Republic of Korea (office). *Telephone:* (2) 3338196 (office). *Fax:* (2) 3814624 (office). *E-mail:* kcb_idkb@co.chesin.com (office).

KIM, Woo-choong, BA; South Korean business executive; b. 19 Dec. 1936, Daegu; s. of Yong-Ha Kim and In-Hang Chun; m. Hrrja Chung 1964; four c.; ed Kyunggi High School, Seoul, Yonsei Univ.; with Econ. Devt Council; with Hansung Industrial Co. Ltd, Dir –1967 (resgnd); Founder, Daewoo Industrial Co. Ltd (textile co.) 1967, Chair. Daewoo Group, includes Daewoo Shipbldg & Heavy Machinery Ltd, Daewoo Motor Co., etc.; Founder, Daewoo Foundation 1978; under investigation for fraud and fled 1999, returned to South Korea and arrested 2005, convicted of charges including embezzlement and accounting fraud, sentenced to 10 year in jail 2006; Commdr, Légion d'honneur 1996; Dr hc (Yonsei Univ., Korea Univ., George Washington Univ., USA, Univ. of South Carolina, Russian Econ. Acad., Univ. Santiago de Cali/Univ. del Valle, Colombia; numerous honours and awards including Int. Business Award, Int. Chamber of Commerce 1984. *Publications:* It's Big World and There's Lots To Be Done 1989, Every Street is Paved With Gold: The Road to Real Success.

KIM, Gen. Yong-chun; North Korean army official; *Vice-Chairman, National Defence Commission;* b. 1922; Assoc. mem. Workers' Party Cen. Cttee (WPCC) –1980, Deputy Chief of Dept, WPCC 1980–83; rank of Gen. 1992, Vice Marshall 1995; Chief of Staff, North Korean People's Party 1995–07; Vice-Chair. Nat. Defence Comm. 2007–; mem. Nat. Defence Comm. 1998–. *Address:* National Defence Commission, Pyongyang, People's Republic of Korea (office).

KIM, Yong-il; North Korean politician; *Prime Minister;* b. 2 May 1944; ed Rajin Univ. of Marine Transport; served in army 1961–70; various positions in Ministry of Land and Marine Transport 1980–94, including Instructor and Deputy Dir, Minister for Marine and Land Transport 1994–2007; Prime Minister 2007–. *Address:* Office of the Premier, Pyonyang, Democratic People's Republic of Korea (office).

KIM, Yong-nam; North Korean politician; *President, Presidium of the Supreme People's Assembly;* b. 1925, North Hamgyong prov.; ed Kim Il Sung Univ., Moscow Univ.; mem. Cen. Cttee Workers' Party of Korea (WPK) 1970, Political Commissar 1977, mem. Political Bureau 1980–; Vice-Premier and Minister of Foreign Affairs 1983–98; Del. to Supreme People's Ass.; Pres. Presidium of the Supreme People's Ass. 1998–. *Address:* Choe ko in min hoe ui (Supreme People's Assembly), Pyongyang, Democratic People's Republic of Korea (office).

KIM, Young-sam, BA; South Korean politician; b. 20 Dec. 1927, Koje-gun, South Gyeongsang Prov.; s. of Kim Hong-Jo and late Park Bu-ryon; m. Sohn Myoung-Soon; two s. three d.; ed Kyongnam High School, Busan and Seoul Nat. Univ.; mem. Nat. Ass. 1954–79; Founder-mem. Democratic Party 1955; re-elected Pres. New Democratic Party 1974, 1979; expelled from Nat. Ass. for opposition to regime of Pres. Park. 1979; arrested under martial law 1980–81;

banned from political activity Nov. 1980; again under house arrest 1982–83; staged 23-day hunger strike demanding democracy May–June 1983; Co-Chair. Council for Promotion of Democracy 1984; played leading role in org. of New Korea Democratic Party (absorbing Democratic Korea Party) which won large number of seats in 1985 election; political ban lifted May 1985; Presidential Cand. 1987 elections; Founder-Pres. Reunification Democracy Party 1987–90; Exec. Chair. Democratic Liberal Party (DLP) 1990–97, Pres. 1992–97; Pres. of Repub. of Korea 1992–97; Dr hc (Towson State Univ., Baltimore) 1974; Martin Luther King Peace Prize 1995. *Publications:* There is No Hill We Can Depend On, Politics is Long and Political Power is Short, Standard-Bearer in his Forties, My Truth and My Country's Truth 1984, My Resolution 1987, Democratization, the Way of Salvation of my Country 1987, New Korea 2000. *Leisure interests:* calligraphy, mountain climbing, jogging, swimming. *Address:* 7-6 Sangdo 1-dong, Dongjak-gu, Seoul, Republic of Korea.

KIM, Young-se, BFA, MA, PhD; South Korean industrial designer and business executive; *CEO, INNODESIGN;* b. 1950, Seoul; ed Seoul Nat. Univ. and Univ. of Illinois; began career as designer at Mel Boldt and Assocs., Chicago and Hari and Assocs., Skokie, Ill.; fmr Design Consultant, DuPont; Asst Prof. of Industrial Design, Univ. of Illinois 1980–82; Founder and CEO INNODE-SIGN Inc., Palo Alto, Calif. 1986, INNODESIGN Korea 1999, INNODESIGN China 2004; Silver Medal, Industrial Design Excellence Awards 2005, Grand Prix, Korea Industrial Design Awards, winner of Gold, Silver and Bronze Industrial Design Awards. *Publications:* Innovator, The Trendsetter 1999, Design A to Z 2000, A Napkin Worth 12 Hundred Millions 2001, Design, Start from Love! 2001; regular contributor to The Economist. *Address:* INNODE-SIGN, 577 College Avenue, Palo Alto, CA 94306, USA (office); INNO Tower, 11–13F 61-3, Nonhyun-dong, Gangnam-gu, Seoul, South Korea (office); Beijing Lufthansa Center, C401 50 Liangmaqiao Road, Chaoyang District, Beijing 100016, People's Republic of China (office). *Telephone:* (650) 493-4666 (Palo Alto) (office); (2) 344-56481 (Seoul) (office); (10) 64639490 (Beijing) (office). *Fax:* (650) 493-6198 (Palo Alto) (office); (2) 344-75465 (Seoul) (office); (10) 64639489 (Beijing) (office). *E-mail:* info@innodesign.com (office); innokr@innodesign.com (office); innochina@innodesign.com (office). *Website:* global.innodesign.com (office).

KIMBALL, Warren Forbes, PhD; American historian and academic; *Robert Treat Professor of History, Rutgers University;* b. 24 Dec. 1935, Brooklyn, New York; s. of Cyril S. Kimball and Carolyn F. Kimball; m. Jacqueline Sue Nelson 1959; one s. two d.; ed Villanova and Georgetown Univs.; served USNR 1958–65; Instructor, US Naval Acad. 1961–65; Asst Prof., Georgetown Univ. 1965–67, Univ. of Georgia 1967–70; Assoc. Prof., Rutgers Univ. 1970–85, Prof. II 1985–93, Robert Treat Prof. of History 1993–; Pitt Prof. of American History, Corpus Christi, Cambridge Univ., UK 1988–89; Arthur Link Prize, Soc. for Historians of American Foreign Relations 2001. *Publications:* 'The Most Unsordid Act': Lend-Lease, 1939–1941 1969, Swords or Ploughshares? The Morgenthau Plan 1976, Churchill and Roosevelt: The Complete Correspondence (3 Vols) 1984, The Juggler: Franklin Roosevelt as Wartime Statesman 1991, Forged in War: Roosevelt, Churchill and the Second World War 1997. *Address:* 2540 Otter Lane, John's Island, SC 29455 (home); Department of History, 175 University Avenue, Rutgers University, Newark, NJ 07102-1814, USA (office). *Telephone:* (843) 768-3879 (home). *E-mail:* wkimball@andromeda.rutgers.edu (office). *Website:* andromeda.rutgers.edu/~history (office).

KIMUNYA, Amos Muhinga, BA, CPA,; Kenyan accountant and politician; *Minister of Trade;* b. 6 March 1962, Embu; ed Univ. of Nairobi; early career as accountant; mem. Parl. for Kipipiri, Minister for Lands and Settlement 2003–06, of Finance 2006–08 (resgnd), of Trade 2009–; Chair. Inst. of Certified Accountants of Kenya 1999–2001; mem. Nat. Rainbow Coalition. *Address:* Ministry of Trade, Teleposta Towers, Kenyatta Avenue, POB 30430, Nairobi, Kenya (office). *Telephone:* (20) 331030 (office). *Fax:* (20) 248722 (office). *E-mail:* ps@tradeandindustry.go.ke (office). *Website:* www.tradeandindustry.go.ke (office).

KIMURA, Hiroshi; Japanese business executive; *Representative Director, President and CEO, Japan Tobacco Inc.;* b. 23 April 1953, Yamaguchi Prov.; ed Kyoto Univ.; early career with Japan Tobacco Inc. and Salt Public Corpn, fmr Exec. Vice-Pres. and Asst to CEO JT International Holding BV (subsidiary of Japan Tobacco Inc.), Dir of Business Planning and Head, Overseas Operations, Japan Tobacco Inc. 1999–2006, mem. Bd of Dirs 2005–, Rep. Dir, Pres. and CEO 2006–. *Address:* Japan Tobacco Inc., 2-1, Toranomon 2-chome, Minato-ku, Tokyo, 105-8422, Japan (office). *Telephone:* (3) 3582-3111 (office). *Fax:* (3) 5572-1441 (office). *E-mail:* info@jti.com (office). *Website:* www.jti.com (office).

KIMURA, Yaichi; Japanese petroleum industry executive; *President, Cosmo Oil Company Limited;* b. 1940; joined Daikyo Oil Co. 1963, Gen. Man. Corp. Planning Dept, Cosmo Oil Co. Ltd (after merger of Daikyo Oil, Maruzen Oil and Cosmo Oil) 1988–90, Gen. Man. Finance Dept 1990–94, mem. Bd of Dirs 1993–, Dir-Gen. Corp. Planning Dept 1994–96, Man. Dir 1996–98, Sr Man. Dir 1998–2001, Exec. Vice-Pres. 2001–04, Pres. 2004–. *Address:* Cosmo Oil Co. Ltd, 1-1-1, Shibaura, Minato-ku, Tokyo 105-8528, Japan (office). *Telephone:* (3) 3798-3211 (office). *Fax:* (3) 3798-3841 (office). *E-mail:* info@cosmo-oil.co.jp (office). *Website:* www.cosmo-oil.co.jp (office).

KINAKH, Col Anatoliy Kyryllovych; Ukrainian politician; *Chairman, Party of Industrialists and Entrepreneurs;* b. 4 Aug. 1954, Bratuşani, Moldovan SSR; m. Marina Volodymyrivna Kinakh 1960; three d.; ed Leningrad (now St Petersburg) Vessel Construction Inst.; worked on vessel construction and in vessel repair plants in Tallinn and Nikolayev 1978–90; elected to Mykolayiv Oblast Parl. 1990; mem. Comm. on Econ. Reform and Nat. Econ. Man. 1990; Presidential Rep. in Mykolayiv Oblast, then Head of Mykolayiv Regional Admin. 1992–94; Head, Mykolayiv Regional Council of People's Deputies 1994–95; mem. Political Council People's Democratic Party of Ukraine, Deputy Chair. 1996; Deputy Prime Minister of Ukraine in charge of Industrial Policy 1995–96; Presidential Adviser on Industrial Policy, then Pres. Ukrainian Union of Businessmen 1996–97; First Deputy Head, Council of Int. Congress of Businessmen 1997–; mem. Higher Econ. Council at Ukrainian Presidency, Head of Co-ordination Council on Privatization of Industrial Enterprises of Strategic Importance 1997–; mem. Nat. Council of Ukraine on Quality Issues 1997–2001; Head, Verkhovna Rada Cttee on Industrial Policy 1998–2001; Chair. Nat. Cttee of Int. Trade Chamber 1998–2001; First Deputy Prime Minister of Ukraine Aug.–Dec. 1999, Jan.–Sept. 2005; Prime Minister of Ukraine 2001–02; mem. Parl. 2002–; presidential cand. 2004; Chair. Nat. Security and Defence Council 2005–06; Minister of the Economy 2007; currently Chair. Party of Industrialists and Entrepreneurs of Ukraine; mem. Acad. of Cybernetics; Hon. Prof., Mykolaiv Govt Humanitarian Univ. *Leisure interest:* classical music. *Address:* Party of Industrialists and Entrepreneurs, 01203 Kyiv, vul. Sh. Rustaveli 11, Ukraine (office). *Telephone:* (44) 590-17-44 (office). *Fax:* (44) 590-17-44 (office). *E-mail:* info@uspp.org.ua (office). *Website:* www.pppu.info (office); www.kinakh.com.ua.

KINCAID, Jamaica; Antigua and Barbuda writer; b. (Elaine Potter Richardson), 25 May 1949, St John's; d. of Annie Richardson; m. Allen Shawn; one s. one d.; staff writer, The New Yorker 1976; currently Visiting Lecturer on African and African American Studies and on English and American Literature and Language, Harvard Univ.; mem. American Acad. of Arts and Letters; numerous hon. degrees; Lila Wallace-Reader's Digest Fund Annual Writer's Award 1992. *Publications include:* At the Bottom of the River (short stories; American Acad. and Inst. of Arts and Letters Morton Dauwen Zabel Award) 1983, Annie John (novel) 1985, A Small Place (non-fiction) 1988, Lucy (novel) 1990, The Autobiography of My Mother 1995, My Brother 1997, My Favorite Plant 1998, Poetics of Place (with Lynn Geesaman) 1998, My Garden (non-fiction) 1999, Talk Stories 2001, Mr Potter 2002, Among Flowers: A Walk in the Himalaya 2005. *Leisure interest:* gardening. *Address:* Harvard University, Department of African and African American Studies, 12 Quincy Street, Cambridge, MA 02138 (office); c/o Farrar Straus & Giroux, 19 Union Square West, New York, NY 10003, USA. *Telephone:* (617) 496-8543 (office). *E-mail:* jkincaid@fas.harvard.edu (office). *Website:* aaas.fas.harvard.edu (office).

KINCSES, Veronika; Hungarian singer (soprano); d. of György Kincses and Etelka Angyal; m. József Vajda; one s.; ed Liszt Ferenc Music Acad. Budapest and Accademia Santa Cecilia, Rome; soloist, State Opera, Budapest; song-recitals, also oratorio performances; guest performances in USA, Argentina, Venezuela, Hong Kong, Singapore etc. 1997–98; operatic roles include Madame Butterfly, Mimi in La Bohème, Manon Lescaut, Liu in Turandot, Le Villi (Puccini), Contessa in Le Nozze di Figaro, Fiordiligi in Così fan Tutte, Vitellia in La Clemenza di Tito, Elvira in Don Giovanni, Amelia in Simone Boccanegra, Leonora in La Forza del destino, Micaela in Carmen, Marguerita in Faust, Silvana in Fiamma–Respighi, Eva in Meistersinger von Nürnberg, Adriana in Adriana Lecouvreur, Tosca, Judit in Bluebeard's Castle; Winner, Dvořák Int. Singing Competition, Prague 1971, Liszt Prize, Kossuth Prize (Hungary), Prix de l'Acad. du Disque, Paris (four times). *Recordings:* Die Königin von Saba, Haydn's Der Apotheker and La Fedeltà Premiata, Songs by Bellini, Liszt's Hungarian Coronation Mass, Madame Butterfly, Orfeo ed Euridice, La Bohème (also DVD), Suor Angelica, Le Nozze di Figaro, etc. *Leisure interest:* teaching singers. *Address:* International Management of the Hungarian State Opera, Andrássy ut 22, 1061 Budapest, Hungary (office); Robert Lombardo Associates, 61 West 62nd Street, New York, NY 10023, USA (office). *Telephone:* (1) 332-7372 (Hungary) (office); (212) 586-4453 (New York) (office).

KIND, Dieter Hans, DrIng, FIEEE; German electrical engineer; *Professor Emeritus, Technical University, Braunschweig;* b. 5 Oct. 1929, Reichenberg, Bohemia; s. of Hans Kind and Gerta Kind; m. Waltraud Wagner 1954; three c.; ed Technical Univ., Munich; Prof. and Dir High-Voltage Inst., Technical Univ., Braunschweig 1962–75, Prof. Emer. 1975–; Pres. Physikalisch-Technische Bundesanstalt, Braunschweig and Berlin 1975–95, Comité Int. des Poids et Mesures, Sèvres/Paris 1975–95; Ehrenring VDE 1988, Dong-Baeg Medal (Korea) 1988, Ordem do Mérito Científico (Brazil) 1995, Grosses Bundesverdienstkreuz; Dr hc (Tech. Univ. Munich). *Publications:* An Introduction to High-Voltage Experimental Technique 1978, High-Voltage Insulation Technology 1985, Herausforderung Metrologie 2002, Naturforscher und Festeller der Technik 2006; about 50 scientific articles. *Leisure interests:* sport, literature. *Address:* Knappstrasse 4, 38116 Braunschweig, Germany. *Telephone:* (531) 511497. *Fax:* (531) 5160239.

KINDELAN MESA, Mario Cesar; Cuban boxer; b. 10 Aug. 1971, Holgu; m.; ed Physical Culture and Sport, ISCFM Fasardo, Havana; began boxing aged 14 years, competed as lightweight; trained by Julian R. Gonzalez since 1990; won Pan-American Games 1999, 2003; gold medals World Championships 1999, 2001, 2003; gold medals Olympic Games 2000 (Sydney), 2004 (Athens); undefeated since winning Pan-American Games in 1999; retd after winning second Olympic gold medal 2004, returned to fight Amir Khan in a professional fight 2005 (lost on points), again retd; Best Boxer in Cuba 1999, Russell Cup for Best Boxer at World Championships 2001, Cuban Sportsman of the Year 2001. *Address:* c/o Comité Olímpico Cubano, Zona Postal 4, Calle 13, No. 601, Vedado, Havana, CP 10400, Cuba.

KINDLE, Fred, MBA; Liechtenstein/Swiss business executive; b. 25 March 1959; ed Swiss Fed. Inst. of Tech., Northwestern Univ., USA; Marketing Project Man. Hilti AG, Liechtenstein 1984–86; Assoc. and Engagement Man. McKinsey & Co. (New York and Zurich) 1988–92; Head, Mass Transfer Dept

Sulzer Chemtech AG, Switzerland 1992–96, Head, Product Div. 1996–99, CEO Sulzer Industries 1999–2001, CEO Sulzer Ltd 2001–04; CEO ABB Ltd 2005–08, also fmr Pres.; mem. Bd of Dirs VZ Holding Ltd, Zurich Financial Services; mem. Swiss American Chamber of Commerce. *Address:* c/o ABB Ltd, Affolternstrasse 44, 8050 Zurich, Switzerland (office).

KINDLER, Jeffrey B., BA, JD; American lawyer and pharmaceutical industry executive; *Chairman and CEO, Pfizer Inc.;* b. 13 May 1955, Montclair, New Jersey; m. Sharon Sullivan, one s. one d.; ed Tufts Univ., Harvard Law School; worked at Fed. Communications Comm.; served as law clerk to US Supreme Court Justice William J. Brennan, Jr and to Judge David L. Bazelon, US Court of Appeals, DC Circuit; fmr Partner, Williams & Connolly (law firm), Washington, DC; fmr Vice-Pres. and Sr Counsel, Litigation and Legal Policy, General Electric Co.; Sr Vice-Pres. and Gen. Counsel, McDonald's Corpn 1996–97, Exec. Vice-Pres. for Corp. Relations and Gen. Counsel 1997–2001; Chair. and CEO Boston Market Corpn –2002, Pres. Partner Brands –2002; Sr Vice-Pres. and Gen. Counsel, Pfizer Inc. 2002–04, Exec. Vice-Pres. and Gen. Counsel 2004–05, Vice-Chair. and Gen. Counsel 2005–06, CEO 2006–, mem. Bd of Dirs and Chair. 2006–, also Chair. Exec. Cttee and mem. Pfizer Exec. Leadership Team; mem. Bd of Dirs Ronald McDonald House Charities, US-Japan Business Council, US Chamber of Commerce, Manhattan Theater Club, New York Philharmonic, Partnership for New York City; mem. Bd of Trustees Ronald McDonald House Charities, Tufts Univ.; numerous awards including Stephen E. Banner Award, Lawyers Div. of UJA Fed. of New York 2002. *Address:* Pfizer Inc., 235 East 42nd Street, New York, NY 10017-5755, USA (office). *Telephone:* (212) 573-2323 (office). *E-mail:* leaddirector@pfizer.com (office). *Website:* www.pfizer.com (office).

KINELEV, Vladimir Georgiyevich, DTechSc; Russian politician; *Director, Institute for Information Technologies in Education, United Nations Educational, Scientific and Cultural Organization (UNESCO);* b. 28 Jan. 1945, Ust-Kalmanka, Altay Region; m.; one d.; ed Bauman Higher Tech. School; worked Cen. Bureau of Experimental Machine-Construction, Asst, Prof., Pro-rector Bauman Higher Tech. School; First Deputy Chair. State Cttee on Science and Higher School 1990–91; Chair. Cttee on Higher School Ministry of Science, Higher School and Tech. Policy of Russian Fed., concurrently First Deputy Minister 1992–93; Chair. State Cttee on Higher Educ. 1993–96; Deputy Chair. Russian Govt 1996; Minister of Gen. and Professional Educ. 1996–98; Dir UNESCO Inst. for Information Technologies in Educ. (IITE) 1998–; Academician Russian Acad. of Educ., Russian Eng Acad.; Prize of USSR Govt 1990, State Prize of Russia 1997; Order of Honour, Russian Fed. 1995. *Publications:* The Objective Necessity 1995, Education and Culture in the History of Civilization 1998. *Address:* UNESCO Institute for Information Technologies in Education, Kedrova str. 8, 117292 Moscow, Russia (office). *Telephone:* (495) 129-19-98 (office). *Fax:* (495) 718-07-66 (office). *E-mail:* kinelev@iite.ru (office). *Website:* www.iite.ru.

KING, Angus S., Jr, BA, JD; American lawyer, broadcaster and fmr politician; *Of Counsel, Bernstein, Shur, Sawyer & Nelson P.A;* b. 31 March 1944; m. Mary J. Herman; four s. one d.; ed Dartmouth Coll. and Univ. of Pennsylvania; called to the Bar, Maine 1969; staff attorney Pine Tree Legal Assistance, Showhegan, Me 1969–72; Chief Counsel, Office of Senator William D. Hathaway, US Senate Sub cttee on Alcoholism and Narcotics, Washington 1972–75; fmr Pnr, Smith, Lloyd & King (law firm), Brunswick, Me; Gov. of Maine 1995–2003; Distinguished Lecturer, Bowdoin Coll. 2004–; Of Counsel, Bernstein, Shur, Sawyer & Nelson P.A., Portland 2004–; Vice-Chair. Medicaid Advisory Comm., US Dept of Health and Human Services 2005–; TV host Maine Watch 1977–96; Vice-Pres. and Gen. Counsel Swift River/Hafslund Co. 1983; Founder and Pres. NE Energy Man. Inc. 1989–94; John Bernotavich Award 2005. *Address:* Bernstein, Shur, Sawyer & Nelson P.A, 100 Middle Street, POB 9729, Portland, ME 04104, USA (home). *Telephone:* (207) 774-1200 (office). *Fax:* (207) 774-1127 (office). *E-mail:* aking@bernsteinshur.com (office). *Website:* bernsteinshur.com (office).

KING, Anthony Stephen, DPhil; Canadian political scientist and academic; *Professor of Government, University of Essex;* b. 7 Nov. 1934, Toronto; s. of the late Harold King and Marjorie King; m. 1st Vera Korte 1965 (died 1971); m. 2nd Jan Reece 1980; ed Queen's Univ., Kingston, Ont., Magdalen and Nuffield Colls, Oxford; Fellow, Magdalen Coll., Oxford 1961–65; Sr Lecturer, Univ. of Essex 1966–68, Reader 1968–69, Prof. of Govt 1969–; Visiting Prof., Univ. of Wis. 1967, Princeton Univ. 1984; Fellow, Center for Advanced Study in Behavioral Sciences, Stanford Univ., Calif. 1977–78; elections commentator for BBC, various periodicals; mem. Cttee on Standards in Public Life 1994–98, Royal Comm. on House of Lords Reform 1999; Chair. RSA Comm. on Illegal Drugs, Communities and Public Policy 2005–07; mem. Academia Europaea 1998; Hon. Foreign mem. American Acad. of Arts and Sciences 1993, Hon. Life Fellow, RSA. *Publications:* The British General Election of 1964 (co-author) 1965, The British General Election of 1966 (co-author) 1966, British Politics: People, Parties and Parliament (ed.) 1966, The British Prime Minister (ed.) 1969, Westminster and Beyond (co-author) 1973, British Members of Parliament: A Self-portrait 1974, Why is Britain Becoming Harder to Govern? (ed.) 1976, Britain Says Yes: The 1975 Referendum on the Common Market 1977, The New American Political System (ed.) 1978, Both Ends of the Avenue: the Presidency of the Executive Branch and Congress in the 1980s (ed.) 1983, Britain at the Polls 1992 (ed.) 1992, SDP: The Birth, Life and Death of the Social Democratic Party (co-author) 1995, Running Scared: Why America's Politicians Campaign Too Much and Govern Too Little 1997, New Labour Triumphs: Britain at the Polls (ed.) 1997, British Political Opinion 1937–2000 (ed.) 2001, Does the United Kingdom Still Have a Constitution? 2001, Britain at the Polls 2001 (ed.) 2001, Leaders' Personalities and the Outcomes of Democratic Elections (ed.) 2002, Britain at the Polls 2005 (ed.) 2006, The British Constitution 2007; numerous papers in British and American

journals. *Leisure interests:* holidays, music, theatre, walking. *Address:* Room 5.022, Department of Government, University of Essex, Wivenhoe Park, Colchester, Essex, CO4 3SQ (office); The Mill House, Lane Road, Wakes Colne, Colchester, Essex, CO6 2BP, England (home). *Telephone:* (1206) 873393 (office); (1787) 222497 (home). *Fax:* (1787) 224221 (home). *Website:* www.essex .ac.uk/government (office).

KING, Riley B. (B. B.); American singer and musician (guitar); b. 16 Sept. 1925, Itta Bena, Miss.; began teaching himself guitar 1945; later studied Schillinger System; fmr disc jockey and singer, Memphis, Tenn. radio stations; cut his first record in 1949, Miss Martha King; numerous int. appearances; Co-Chair. Foundation for Advancement of Inmate Rehabilitation and Recreation 1972–; toured USSR 1979; performance at closing ceremonies, Summer Olympics, Atlanta, Ga 1996; Hon. LHD (Tougaloo Coll. Miss.) 1973, Hon. DMus (Yale) 1977; Grammy Lifetime Achievement Award 1987, Kennedy Center Honors 1995, Living Legend Award, Trumpet Awards 1997, Royal Swedish Acad. of Music Polar Music Prize 2004, Presidential Medal of Freedom 2006. *Films include:* When We Were Kings 1996, Blues Brothers 1998, 2000. *Recordings include:* albums: Completely Well 1970, The Incredible Soul of B. B. King 1970, Indianola Mississippi Seeds 1970, Live In Cook County Jail 1971, Live At The Regal 1971, B. B. King In London 1971, LA Midnight 1972, Guess Who 1972, The Best Of.... 1973, To Know You Is To Love You 1973, Friends 1974, Lucille Talks Back 1975, King Size 1977, Midnight Believer 1978, Take It Home 1979, Now Appearing At Ole Miss 1980, There Must Be A Better World Somewhere 1982, Love Me Tender 1982, Blues 'n' Jazz 1984, Six Silver Strings 1986, Live At San Quentin 1991, Blues Summit (Grammy Award for Best Traditional Blues Album 1994) 1993, Lucille and Friends 1995, Live in Japan 1999, Makin' Love Is Good For You 2000, A Christmas Celebration of Hope 2001, Anthology 2001, Reflections 2003, 80 (Grammy Award for Best Traditional Blues Album 2006) 2005, One Kind Favor (Grammy Award for Best Traditional Blues Album 2009) 2008. *Address:* Lieberman Management, 1414 Avenue of the Americas, Suite 202, New York, NY 10019, USA (office). *Telephone:* (212) 421-2021 (office). *Website:* www.liebermanmgt.com (office); www.bbking.com.

KING, Billie Jean; American fmr tennis player; *Chair, USA Tennis High Performance Committee, United States Tennis Association;* b. 22 Nov. 1943, Long Beach, Calif.; d. of Willard J. Moffitt; m. Larry King 1965 (divorced); ed Los Angeles State Univ.; amateur player 1958–67, turned professional 1967; Australian champion 1968; Italian champion 1970; French champion 1972; Wimbledon champion 1966, 1967, 1968, 1972, 1973, 1975; US Open champion 1967, 1971, 1972, 1974; FRG champion 1971; South African champion 1966, 1967, 1969; won record 20 Wimbledon titles (six singles, 10 doubles, four mixed) and played more than 100 matches; had won 1,046 singles victories by 1984; sports commentator, ABC-TV 1975–78; f. Women's Tennis Asscn 1973; Publisher, Women Sports 1974–; Commr, US Tennis Team 1981–; CEO World TeamTennis 1985–; Capt. US Fed. Cup Team 1995–2004; Chair US Tennis Asscn (USTA) Tennis High Performance Cttee 2005–; Women's Olympic Tennis Coach 1996, 2000; Consultant, Virginia Slims Championship Series; nat. amb. for AIM children's charity; Top Woman Athlete of the Year Award 1973; Lifetime Achievement Award, March of Dimes 1994, Sarah Palfrey Danzig Award 1995, Flo Hyman Award 1997. *Publications:* Tennis to Win 1970, Billie Jean (with Kim Chapin) 1974, We Have Come a Long Way: The Story of Women's Tennis 1988. *Leisure interests:* ballet, movies. *Address:* USA Tennis High Performance Program, Home Depot Center, 18400 Avalon Boulevard, Suite 600, Carson, CA 90746, USA. *Website:* www .highperformance.usta.com/home/default.sps.

KING, Sir David Anthony, Kt, BSc, MA, PhD, ScD, FRS, FRSC, FInstP; British academic and research scientist; *Director, Smith School of Enterprise and the Environment, University of Oxford;* b. 12 Aug. 1939, Durban, South Africa; s. of Arnold King and Patricia Vardy; m. Jane Lichtenstein 1983; three s. one d.; ed St John's Coll., Johannesburg, Univ. of Witwatersrand, Johannesburg, Imperial Coll. London; Lecturer in Chemical Physics, Univ. of E Anglia, Norwich 1966–74; Brunner Prof. of Physical Chem., Univ. of Liverpool 1974–88, Head, Dept of Inorganic, Physical and Industrial Chem. 1983–88; 1920 Prof. of Physical Chem., Dept of Chem., Univ. of Cambridge 1988–, Head, Dept of Chem. 1993–2000; Fellow, St John's Coll. 1988–95, Queen's Coll. 2001–; Master of Downing Coll. 1995–2000; Chief Scientific Adviser to UK Govt and Head, Office of Science and Tech. 2000–07; Dir Smith School of Enterprise and the Environment, Univ. of Oxford 2008–; Ed. Chemical Physics Letters 1990–2001; Pres. Asscn of Univ. Teachers 1976–77; Chair. British Vacuum Council 1982–85; mem. Comité de Direction, Centre Cinétique et Physique, Nancy 1974–81, Research Awards Advisory Cttee Leverhulme Trust 1980–91 (Chair. 1995–2001), Direction Cttee (Beirat) Fritz Haber Inst., Berlin 1981–93; Chair. European Science Foundation Programme 'Gas–Surface Interactions' 1991–96, Kettle's Yard Gallery, Cambridge 1989–2001; Sr Scientific Adviser to UBS; Pres. BAAS; Assoc. Fellow, Third World Acad. of Sciences 2000; Foreign mem. American Acad. of Arts and Sciences 2002; Hon. Fellow, Indian Acad. of Sciences, Downing Coll., Univ. of Cardiff 2001; Hon. Prof., Qingdao Univ., People's Repub. of China; Hon. Life Fellow, Royal Soc. of Arts 2006; Hon. DSc (Liverpool) 2001, (East Anglia) 2001, (Stockholm) 2003, (Genoa) 2002, (Leicester) 2002, Cardiff (2002), (Witwatersrand) 2003, (St Andrews) 2003, (York) 2004, (Oxford Brookes) 2007; Shell Scholar 1963–66, RSC Awards, Surface Chem. 1978, RSC Tilden Lecturer 1988, Medal for Research, British Vacuum Council 1991, Liversidge Lectureship and Medal 1997–98, Royal Soc. Rumford Medal 2003. *Publications:* The Chemical Physics of Solid Surfaces and Heterogeneous Catalysis (seven vols) (co-ed. with D. P. Woodruff) 1980–94, The Hot Topic: How to Tackle Global Warming and Still Keep the Lights On (with Gabrielle Walker) 2008; over 450 original pubs in the scientific literature. *Leisure interests:* photography, art, philosophy. *Address:* Smith School of Enterprise and the Environment, Hayes

House, 75 George Street, Oxford, OX1 2BQ (office); Department of Chemistry, University of Cambridge, Lensfield Road, Cambridge, CB2 1EN (office); 20 Glisson Road, Cambridge, CB1 2EW, England (home). *Telephone:* (1865) 614964 (Oxford) (office); (1223) 336338 (Cambridge) (office); (1223) 315629 (Cambridge) (home). *Fax:* (1865) 614960 (Oxford) (office); (1223) 762829 (Cambridge) (office). *E-mail:* director.smithschool@admin.ox.ac.uk (office); director@smithschool.ox.ac.uk (office); dak10@cam.ac.uk (office). *Website:* www.smithschool.ox.ac.uk (office); www.ch.cam.ac.uk (office).

KING, Don; American boxing promoter; b. 20 Aug. 1931, Cleveland; s. of Clarence King and Hattie King; m. Henrietta King; two s. one d.; convicted of manslaughter and justifiable homicide; boxing promoter 1972–; owner Don King Productions Inc. 1974–; fighters promoted include: Muhammad Ali (q.v.), Sugar Ray Leonard (q.v.), Mike Tyson (q.v.), Ken Norton, Joe Frazier, Larry Holmes (q.v.), Roberto Durán (q.v.), Tim Witherspoon, George Foreman (q.v.), Evander Holyfield (q.v.); f. The Don King Foundation and actively supports other charities including The Martin Luther King Jr Foundation; Int. Boxing Hall of Fame 1997. *Address:* c/o Don King Productions Inc., 501 Fairway Drive, Deerfield Beach, FL 33441, USA (office). *E-mail:* info@donking.com. *Website:* www.donking.com.

KING, Francis Henry, (Frank Cauldwell), CBE, OBE, MA, FRSL; British writer; b. 4 March 1923, Adelboden, Switzerland; s. of the late Eustace Arthur Cecil King and Faith Mina Read; ed Shrewsbury School and Balliol Coll., Oxford; served in British Council 1948–62, Regional Dir, Kyoto, Japan 1958–62; theatre critic Sunday Telegraph 1978–88; Pres. English PEN 1978–86, Int. PEN 1986–89, Vice-Pres. Int. PEN 1989–; Somerset Maugham Prize 1952, Katherine Mansfield Short Story Prize 1965, Yorkshire Post Prize 1984. *Publications:* novels: To the Dark Tower 1946, Never Again 1947, The Dividing Stream 1951, The Widow 1957, The Man on the Rock 1957, The Custom House 1961, The Last of the Pleasure Gardens 1965, The Waves Behind the Boat 1967, A Domestic Animal 1970, Flights 1973, A Game of Patience 1974, The Needle 1975, Danny Hill 1977, The Action 1978, Act of Darkness 1983, Voices in an Empty Room 1984, Frozen Music (novella) 1987, The Woman Who Was God 1988, Punishments 1989, The Ant Colony 1991, Secret Lives 1991, The One and Only 1994, Ash on an Old Man's Sleeve 1996, Dead Letters 1997, Prodigies 2001, The Nick of Time 2003; short stories: So Hurt and Humiliated 1959, The Japanese Umbrella 1964, The Brighton Belle 1968, Hard Feelings 1976, Indirect Method 1980, One is a Wanderer 1985, A Hand at the Shutter 1996, The Sunlight on the Garden 2006; biog.: E. M. Forster and His World 1978, My Sister and Myself: The Diaries of J. R. Ackerley 1982; travel: Florence 1982, Florence: A Literary Companion 1991, Yesterday Came Suddenly (autobiog.) 1993. *Leisure interests:* ikebana, pictures and music. *Address:* 19 Gordon Place, London, W8 4JE, England (home). *Telephone:* (20) 7937-5715 (home). *E-mail:* fhk@dircon.co.uk (home).

KING, Ivan Robert, PhD; American astronomer and academic; *Research Professor, Astronomy Department, University of Washington;* b. 25 June 1927, New York; s. of Myram King and Anne King (née Franzblau); m. Alice Greene 1952 (divorced 1982); two s. two d.; ed Woodmere Acad., Hamilton Coll., Harvard Univ.; served in USNR 1952–54; Methods Analyst, US Dept of Defence 1952–56; Asst Prof., then Assoc. Prof., Univ. of Ill. 1956–64; Assoc. Prof. of Astronomy, Univ. of Calif., Berkeley 1964–66, Prof. 1966–93, Prof. Emer. 1993–, Chair. Astronomy Dept 1967–70; Research Prof., Astronomy Dept., Univ. of Washington 2002–; Pres. American Astronomical Soc. 1978–80; mem. AAAS, Fellow, Chair. Astronomy Section 1973; mem. NAS. *Publications:* The Universe Unfolding 1976, The Milky Way as a Galaxy 1990; 100 articles in scientific journals. *Address:* Astronomy Department, University of Washington, Physics-Astronomy Bldg., B372, 3910 15th Aveneue NE, Seattle, WA 98195, USA (office). *Telephone:* (206) 685-9010 (office). *E-mail:* king@astro.washington.edu (office). *Website:* www.astro.washington.edu/king (office).

KING, Justin; British business executive; *CEO, J Sainsbury plc;* b. 1961; involved in marketing campaigns for Häagen-Dazs, Pepsi-Cola and Mars; fmr Man. Dir Häagen-Dazs UK; held various sr positions at Asda Hypermarkets in trading and human resources divs, including Retail Man.-Dir 1994–2001; Dir of Food, Marks & Spencer plc 2001–04; CEO J Sainsbury plc 2004–, also Chair. Operating Bd; Dir (non-exec.) Staples, Inc. 2007–. *Address:* J Sainsbury plc, 33 Holborn, London, EC1N 2HT, England (office). *Telephone:* (20) 7695-6000 (office). *Fax:* (20) 7695-7610 (office). *E-mail:* info@j-sainsbury.co.uk (office). *Website:* www.j-sainsbury.co.uk (office).

KING, Larry; American broadcaster; b. (Lawrence Harvey Zeiger), 19 Nov. 1933, Brooklyn; s. of Eddie Zeiger and Jennie Zeiger; m. 1st Frida Miller 1952; m. 2nd Alene Akins 1961 (divorced 1963, remarried 1967, divorced 1971); one d.; m. 3rd Mickey Sutphin 1993 (divorced 1993); m. 4th Sharon Lepore 1976 (divorced 1984); m. 5th Julia Alexander 1989, (divorced 1992); one s.; m. 6th Shawn Southwick 1997; two c.; disc jockey with various radio stations, Miami, Fla 1957–71; freelance writer and broadcaster 1972–75; radio personality, Station WIOD, Miami 1975–78; writer, entertainment sections of Miami Herald for seven years; host, The Larry King Show (radio talk show) 1978–94, WLA-TV Let's Talk, Washington, DC; host Larry King Live (TV) 1985–; columnist, USA Today, Sporting News; f. Larry King Cardiac Foundation; Dr hc (George Washington Univ.), (New England Inst. of Tech.), (Brooklyn Coll.), (Pratt Inst.); Talk Show Host of the Year, Nat. Asscn of Radio Talk Show Hosts 1993, Scopus Award, American Friends of Hebrew Univ. 1994, Golden Plate Award, American Acad. of Achievement 1996, Mahoney Award, Harvard Univ. 2000, March of Dimes' Franklin Delano Roosevelt Award 2000. *Films:* appeared as himself in films Ghostbusters 1984, Lost in America 1985, Crazy People 1990, Exorcist III 1990, Dave 1993, Spin 1995, Open Season 1996, Contact 1997, The Jackal 1997, Primary Colors 1998, Bulworth 1998, Enemy of the State 1998, The Kid 2000, The Contender 2000, America's Sweethearts 2001, John Q 2002, Marilyn's Man 2004, Shrek 2 (voice) 2004, The Stepford Wives 2004, Mr 3000 2004, Shrek the Third (voice) 2007. *Publications:* Mr King, You're Having a Heart Attack (with B. D. Colen) 1989, Larry King: Tell Me More, When You're from Brooklyn, Everything Else is Tokyo 1992, On the Line (jtly) 1993, Daddy Day, Daughter Day (jtly) 1997, My Remarkable Journey (with Cal Fussman) 2009. *Address:* c/o CNN Larry King Live, 820 1st Street, NE, Washington, DC 20002, USA (office). *Website:* www.cnn.com/CNN/anchors_reporters/king.larry.html (office).

KING, Mary Elizabeth; British horse rider; b. 8 June 1961, Newark, Notts.; d. of Lt-Commdr M. D. H. Thomson; m. David King 1995; one s. one d.; ed Manor House School, Honiton, King's Grammar School, Ottery St Mary, Evendine Court (Cordon Bleu); team gold medals 1991, 1994, 1995, 1997, 2007; rep. GB in Equestrian Eventing Team at Olympic Games in Barcelona 1992, Atlanta 1996, Sydney 2000, Athens 2004, Beijing 2008, Team Silver Medal, Athens 2004, Team Bronze Medal, Beijing 2008; British Open champion 1991, 1992, 1996, 2007; winner Badminton Horse Trials 1992, 2000, Burghley Horse Trials 1996; broke her neck in 2001, but has made full recovery; mem. winning GBI team at Burghley Horse Trials 2001; Watch Leader 'Sir Winston Churchill'; Team Silver Medal, World Equestrian Games 2006; Team Gold and Individual Silver at European Championships, Italy 2007. *Publications:* Mary Thomson's Eventing Year 1993, All the King's Horses 1997, William and Mary 1998. *Leisure interests:* tennis, snow and water skiing. *Address:* Old Barn Cottage, Salcombe Regis, Sidmouth, Devon, EX10 0JQ, England (office). *Telephone:* (1395) 514882 (office). *Fax:* (1392) 258846 (office). *E-mail:* maryking1a@aol.com (home).

KING, Maurice Athelstan, QC, LLB; Barbadian politician and lawyer; b. 1 Jan. 1936; s. of James Cliviston King and Caroline Constance King; m. Patricia A. Williams; one s. one d.; ed Harrison Coll., Barbados, Univ. of Manchester and Gray's Inn, London; lawyer in pvt. practice 1960–; Chair. Natural Gas Corpn 1964–76; mem. Barbados Senate 1967–75; Gen. Sec. Democratic Labour Party 1968–69; Amb. to USA and Perm. Rep. to OAS Jan.–Sept. 1976; mem. Parl. 1981–; Attorney-Gen. and Minister of Legal Affairs 1986–91, Attorney-Gen. 1991–94 and Minister of Foreign Affairs 1991–93, of Justice and CARICOM Affairs 1993–94. *Leisure interests:* music, tennis, reading, swimming. *Address:* Law Chambers, Suite 209, Dowell House, Roebuck Street, Bridgetown, Barbados (office). *Telephone:* 429-9010 (office). *Fax:* 228-7560 (office).

KING, Mervyn Allister, BA, FBA; British economist, academic and central banker; *Governor, Bank of England;* b. 30 March 1948; s. of Eric Frank King and Kathleen Alice Passingham; ed Wolverhampton Grammar School, King's Coll., Cambridge; Jr Research Officer, Dept of Applied Econs, Cambridge Univ., mem. Cambridge Growth Project 1969–73, Research Officer 1972–76, Lecturer, Faculty of Econs 1976–77; Esmée Fairbairn Prof. of Investment, Univ. of Birmingham 1977–84; Prof. of Econs, LSE 1984–95; Exec. Dir Bank of England 1991–98, Chief Economist 1991–98, Deputy Gov. (Monetary Policy) 1998–2003, Gov. 2003–; Pres. Inst. of Fiscal Studies 1999–2003; Research Officer, Kennedy School at Harvard Univ., USA 1971–72, Visiting Prof. of Econs 1982–; Visiting Prof. of Econs MIT 1983–84, LSE 1996–; Co-Dir LSE Financial Markets Group 1987–91; Man. Ed. Review of Economic Studies 1978–83; founder mem. Monetary Policy Cttee 1997; mem. City Capital Markets Cttee 1989–91; Bd mem. The Securities Asscn 1987–89; mem. Council and Exec. Cttee Royal Econ. Soc. 1981–86, 1992–97; Fellow, Econometric Soc. 1982–; mem. Acad. Europaea 1992; mem. Council, European Econ. Asscn (Pres. 1993); Research Assoc. Nat. Bureau of Econ. Research; Assoc. mem. Inst. of Fiscal and Monetary Policy, Ministry of Finance, Japan 1986–91; mem. The Group of Thirty 1997, Advisory Council of the London Symphony Orchestra 2001; Chair. of OECD's Working Party 3 (WP3) Cttee 2001–03; Visiting Fellow, Nuffield Coll. Oxford 2002–03; mem. Cttee All England Lawn Tennis and Croquet Club; Patron, Worcester Co. Cricket Club; Trustee Nat. Gallery; Hon. Sr Scholarship and Richards Prize, King's Coll. Cambridge 1969; Hon. Fellow, St John's Coll., Cambridge 1997, King's Coll. Cambridge 2004; Foreign Hon. Mem. American Acad. of Arts and Sciences 2000; Hon. Life Mem. Inst. for Fiscal Studies 2006; Dr hc (London Guildhall Univ.) 2001, (Birmingham) 2002, (City Univ., London) 2002, (LSE) 2003, (Wolverhampton) 2003, (Edin.) 2005, (Helsinki) 2006, (Cambridge) 2006; Wrenbury Scholarship, Univ. of Cambridge 1969, Stevenson Prize, Univ. of Cambridge 1970, Kennedy Scholarship and Harkness Fellowship 1971, Medal of Univ. of Helsinki 1982. *Publications:* Public Policy and the Corporation 1977, The British Tax System (with J. A. Kay), Indexing for Inflation (co-ed. with T. Liesner) 1975, The Taxation of Income from Capital Growth (co-author) 1984; numerous articles in various journals. *Address:* Bank of England, Threadneedle Street, London, EC2R 8AH, England. *Telephone:* (20) 7601-4444 (office). *Fax:* (20) 7601-4953 (office). *E-mail:* nicole.morey@bankofengland.co.uk (office). *Website:* www.bankofengland.co.uk (office).

KING, Phillip, CBE, MA (Cantab.); British sculptor; *Professor Emeritus, Royal College of Art;* b. 1 May 1934, Tunis, Tunisia; s. of the late Thomas J. King and Gabrielle Liautard; m. 1st Lilian Odelle 1957 (divorced 1987); one s. (deceased); m. 2nd Judith Corbalis 1991; ed Mill Hill School, Christ's Coll., Cambridge, St Martin's School of Art, London; Asst to Henry Moore 1957–59; taught at St Martin's School of Art 1959–74; Prof. of Sculpture, Royal Coll. of Art 1980–90, Prof. Emer. 1991–; Prof. of Sculpture, RA 1990–99, Pres. 1999–2004; Trustee, Tate Gallery 1967–69; mem. Art Panel, Arts Council 1977–79; Hon. Fellow Christ Coll., Cambridge 2002–; 1st Prize Int. Sculpture exhbn, Piestany (Czechoslovakia) 1968. *Leisure interest:* holidays in Corsica close to both land and sea. *Address:* c/o Royal College of Art, Kensington Gore, London, SW7 2EU, England.

KING, Stephen Edwin, (Richard Bachman), BS; American writer and screenwriter; b. 21 Sept. 1947, Portland, ME; s. of Donald King and Nellie R.

(née Pillsbury) King; m. Tabitha J. Spruce 1971; two s. one d.; ed Univ. of Maine; teacher of English, Hampden Acad., ME 1971–73; writer-in-residence, Univ. of Maine at Orono 1978–79; mem. Authors' Guild of America, Screen Artists' Guild, Screen Writers of America, Writers' Guild; Medal for Distinguished Contribution to American Letters, Nat. Book Foundation 2003. *Television:* Kingdom Hospital. *Publications:* novels: Carrie 1974, Salem's Lot 1975, The Shining 1976, The Stand 1978, The Dead Zone 1979, Firestarter 1980, Cujo 1981, Different Seasons 1982, The Dark Tower I: The Gunslinger 1982, Christine 1983, Pet Cemetery 1983, The Talisman (with Peter Straub) 1984, It 1986, The Eyes of the Dragon 1987, Misery 1987, The Dark Tower II: The Drawing of the Three 1987, Tommyknockers 1987, The Dark Half 1989, The Dark Tower III: The Waste Lands 1991, Needful Things 1991, Gerald's Game 1992, Dolores Claiborne 1992, Insomnia 1994, Rose Madder 1995, Desperation 1996, The Green Mile (serial novel) 1996, The Dark Tower IV: Wizard and Glass 1997, Bag of Bones 1997, The Girl Who Loved Tom Gordon 1999, Hearts in Atlantis 1999, Riding the Bullet 2000, The Plant (serial novel) 2000, Dreamcatcher 2001, Black House (with Peter Straub) 2001, From a Buick 8 2002, The Dark Tower V: Wolves of the Calla 2003, The Dark Tower VI: Song of Susannah 2004, The Dark Tower VII: The Dark Tower 2004, The Colorado Kid 2005, Cell 2006, Lisey's Story 2006, Duma Key 2008; other: Night Shift (short stories) 1978, Danse Macabre (non-fiction) 1980, Different Seasons (short stories) 1982, Creepshow (comic book) 1982, Cycle of the Werewolf (illustrated novel) 1984, Skeleton Crew (short stories) 1985, Four Past Midnight (short stories) 1990, Nightmares and Dreamscapes (short stories) 1993, Head Down (story) 1993, Six Stories (short stories) 1997, Storm of the Century (screenplay) 1999, On Writing: A Memoir of the Craft (revised edn as Secret Windows) 2000, Everything's Eventual: 14 Dark Tales (short stories) 2002, Faithful (non-fiction, with Stewart O'Nan) 2005, Just After Sunset (short stories) 2008, numerous short stories, screenplays and television plays; as Richard Bachman: Rage 1977, The Long Walk 1979, Roadwork 1981, The Running Man 1982, Thinner 1984, The Regulators 1996, Blaze 2007. *Address:* 49 Florida Avenue, Bangor, ME 04401, USA (office). *Website:* www.stephenking.com (office).

KING, Stephenson; Saint Lucia politician; *Prime Minister and Minister of Finance (including International Financial Services), External Affairs, Home Affairs and National Security;* MP for Castries North 2006–; Minister for Health and Labour Relations 2006–07, of Finance (including Int. Financial Services), External Affairs, Home Affairs and Nat. Security 2007–, Prime Minister 2007–; mem. United Workers Party. *Address:* Office of the Prime Minister, Greaham Louisy Administrative Bldg, 5th Floor, Waterfront, Castries, Saint Lucia (office). *Telephone:* 468-2111 (office). *Fax:* 453-7352 (office). *E-mail:* admin@pm.gov.lc (office). *Website:* www.pm.gov.lc (office).

KING AKERELE, Olu Banke (Bankie), BA, MA; Liberian politician; *Minister of Foreign Affairs;* b. 11 May 1946, granddaughter of fmr Liberian Pres. Charles D. B. King; ed Univ. of Ibadan, Nigeria, Brandeis Univ., Northeastern Univ., Colombia Univ., USA; Sr Planning Officer, Ministry of Planning and Econ. Affairs 1968–69, Deputy Dir Nat. Social Security and Welfare Corpn 1975–1980; Deputy Dir UNIFEM 1982–89, Deputy Resident Rep. of UN in Senegal 1989–91, UNDP Rep. in Mauritius and the Seychelles 1991–94, Man. Dir Country Strategy and Program Devt Div., UNIDO 1994–1996, Chief, E and Cen. Africa Div. Regional Bureau for Africa, UNDP 1996–1997, Country Programme Advisor UNDP Africa 1998, UNDP Resident Rep. and Resident Co-ordinator UN System Operational activities for Devt in Zambia 1998–2003, Programme Co-ordinator UNDP-UNESCO Project Foundations for Africa's Future Leadership, UNESCO's Regional Officer for Educ. in Africa, 2006; Minister of Commerce and Industry 2006–07, of Foreign Affairs 2007–; Order Distinguished Services, Second Div. (Zambia); Liberian Business Asscn Award. *Address:* Ministry of Foreign Affairs, Mamba Point, PO Box 10-9002, 1000 Monrovia 10, Liberia (office). *Telephone:* 226763 (office). *Website:* www.mofa.gov.lr (office).

KING-HELE, Desmond George, MA, FRS; British writer and scientist; b. 3 Nov. 1927, Seaford, Sussex; s. of late S. G. King-Hele and Mrs B. King-Hele; m. Marie Newman 1954 (separated 1992); two d.; ed Epsom Coll. and Trinity Coll., Cambridge; Royal Aircraft Establishment, Farnborough 1948–88 (research on earth's gravity field and upper atmosphere by analysis of satellite orbits), Deputy Chief Scientific Officer, Space Dept 1968–88; mem. Int. Acad. of Astronautics 1961–; Chair. British Nat. Cttee for the History of Science, Medicine and Tech. 1985–89, History of Science Grants Cttee 1990–93; Ed. Notes and Records of the Royal Soc. 1989–96; Bakerian Lecturer, Royal Soc. 1974, Wilkins Lecturer, Royal Soc. 1997; Hon. DSc (Univ. of Aston) 1979, Hon. DUniv (Univ. of Surrey) 1986; Soc. of Authors' Medical History Prize 1999; Eddington Medal, Royal Astronomical Soc. 1971, Chree Medal, Inst. of Physics 1971, Nordberg Medal, Int. Cttee on Space Research 1990. *Radio:* dramas: A Mind of Universal Sympathy 1973, The Lunaticks 1978. *Publications:* Shelley: His Thought and Work 1960, Satellites and Scientific Research 1960, Erasmus Darwin 1963, Theory of Satellite Orbits in an Atmosphere 1964, Observing Earth Satellites 1966, Essential Writings of Erasmus Darwin 1968, The End of the Twentieth Century? 1970, Poems and Trixies 1972, Doctor of Revolution 1977, Letters of Erasmus Darwin 1981, Animal Spirits 1983, Erasmus Darwin and the Romantic Poets 1986, Satellite Orbits in an Atmosphere 1987, The R.A.E. Table of Earth Satellites 1957–1989, 1990, A Tapestry of Orbits 1992, John Herschel 1992, Erasmus Darwin: A Life of Unequalled Achievement 1999, Antic and Romantic 2000, Charles Darwin's The Life of Erasmus Darwin 2002, The Collected Letters of Erasmus Darwin 2006; more than 300 scientific or literary papers in various learned journals. *Leisure interests:* playing tennis, savouring the beauties of nature, writing verse. *Address:* 7 Hilltops Court, 65 North Lane, Buriton, Hants., GU31 5RS, England (home). *Telephone:* (1730) 261646 (home).

KING OF BRIDGWATER, Baron (Life Peer), cr. 2001, of Bridgwater in the County of Somerset; **Thomas (Tom) Jeremy King,** PC, CH, MA; British politician; b. 13 June 1933, Glasgow; s. of John H. King and Mollie King; m. Elizabeth J. Tilney 1960; one s. one d.; ed Rugby School and Emmanuel Coll., Cambridge; in packaging and printing industry 1958–70; MP for Bridgwater 1970–2001; Parl. Pvt. Sec. to Rt Hon Christopher Chataway 1970–74; Shadow Spokesman for Energy 1976–79; Minister for Local Govt 1979–83; Sec. of State for the Environment Jan.–June 1983 for Transport June–Oct. 1983, for Employment 1983–85, for NI 1985–89, for Defence 1989–92; Chair. Intelligence and Security Cttee 1994–97; Chair. London Int. Exhbn Centre, Docklands; Dir (non-exec.) Electra Investment Trust 1992–; mem. Nolan Cttee on Standards in Public Life 1994–97; Conservative. *Leisure interests:* cricket, skiing, forestry. *Address:* House of Lords, Westminster, London, SW1A 0PW, England (office).

KINGMAN, Sir John Frank Charles, Kt, ScD, CStat, FRS; British mathematician, statistician and academic; b. 28 Aug. 1939, Beckenham; s. of the late Frank E. T. and Maud Elsie (née Harley) Kingman; m. Valerie Cromwell 1964; one s. one d.; ed Christ's Coll., Finchley, London, Pembroke Coll., Cambridge; Asst Lecturer in Math., Univ. of Cambridge 1962–64, Lecturer 1964–65; Reader in Math. and Statistics, Univ. of Sussex 1965–66, Prof. 1966–69; Prof. of Math., Univ. of Oxford 1969–85; Chair. Science and Eng Research Council 1981–85; Vice-Chancellor Univ. of Bristol 1985–2001; Chair. Statistics Comm. 2000–03; N M Rothschild Professorship of Mathematical Sciences and Dir Isaac Newton Inst. for Mathematical Sciences, Univ. of Cambridge 2001–06; mem. council British Tech. Group 1984–92; mem. Bd British Council 1986–91; Pres. London Math. Society 1990–92; Hon. Fellow, St Anne's Coll., Oxford, Pembroke Coll., Cambridge; Hon. DSc (Sussex) 1983, (Southampton) 1985, Hon. LLD (Bristol) 1989, (Queen's Univ., Ont.) 1999; Officier des Palmes académiques. *Publications:* Introduction to Measure and Probability (with S. J. Taylor) 1966, The Algebra of Queues 1966, Regenerative Phenomena 1972, Mathematics of Genetic Diversity 1980, Poisson Processes 1993. *Address:* c/o Isaac Newton Institute for Mathematical Sciences, 20 Clarkson Road, Cambridge, CB3 0EH (office).

KINGSDOWN, Baron, (Life Peer), cr. 1993, of Pemberton in the County of Lancashire; **Robert (Robin) Leigh-Pemberton,** KG, PC, MA, DCL; British banker and barrister; b. 5 Jan. 1927, Lenham; s. of the late Robert Douglas Leigh-Pemberton, MBE, MC and Helen Isabel Payne-Gallwey; m. Rosemary Davina Forbes 1953; five s. (one deceased); ed St Peter's Court, Broadstairs, Eton Coll., Trinity Coll., Oxford; Oppidan Scholar, Eton 1940–45; Grenadier Guards 1945–48; practised at the Bar 1953–60; Dir Univ. Life Assurance Soc. 1968–78; Dir Birmid-Qualcast PLC, Deputy Chair. 1970–75, Chair. 1975–77; Dir Redland PLC 1972–83, Equitable Life Assurance Soc. 1978–83, Vice-Pres. 1982; Dir Nat. Westminster Bank PLC 1972–74, Deputy Chair. 1974–77, Chair. 1977–83; Gov. Bank of England 1983–93; Dir BIS 1983–2003; mem. Kent Co. Council 1961–77, Leader 1964–69, Chair. 1972–75; JP for Kent 1961–76; Deputy Lt for Kent 1969, Vice-Lord Lt 1972–82, Lord Lt 1982–2002; Gov. Wye Coll., Univ. of London 1968–77; Deputy Pro-Chancellor Univ. of Kent 1969–78, Pro-Chancellor 1977–83; mem. Medway Ports Authority 1972–77, SE Econ. Planning Council 1971–74, Prime Minister's Cttee on Standards in Local Govt 1973–74, Cttee of Enquiry into Teachers' Pay 1974, Cttee to review Police Conditions of Service 1977–79, NEDC 1981–92; Chair. City Communications Centre 1979–82, Cttee of London Clearing Bankers 1982–83; Pres. Royal Agric. Soc. of England 1989–90; Dir (non-exec.) Glaxo Wellcome 1993–96, (non-exec.) Hambros 1993–98, Redland 1972–83, 1993–98, (non-exec.) Foreign & Colonial Investment Trust 1993–98; Seneschal Canterbury Cathedral 1982–; Privy Councillor 1988; Hon. Master of the Bench, Inner Temple 1983; KStJ 1983, Order of Aztec Eagle, Mexico (First Class) 1985, Kt of the Garter 1994; Hon. DCL (Kent) 1983; Hon. MA (Trinity Coll., Oxford) 1984; Hon. DLitt (City of London) 1988, (Loughborough) 1989, (City Polytechnic) 1990. *Leisure interests:* English country life, the arts. *Address:* Torry Hill, Sittingbourne, Kent, ME9 0SP, England (home). *Telephone:* (1795) 830258 (home). *Fax:* (1795) 830268 (home).

KINGSLEY, Sir Ben, Kt; British actor; b. (Krishna Bhanji), 31 Dec. 1943, Scarborough, Yorks.; s. of Rahimtulla Harji Bhanji and Anna Leina Mary Bhanji; m. Daniela Barbosa de Carneiro 2007; three s. one d. from previous relationships; ed Manchester Grammar School; with RSC 1970–80; Nat. Theatre 1977–78; Assoc. Artist, RSC; Hon. MA (Salford Univ.); awarded Padma Shri (Govt of India); Evening Standard Best Film Actor 1983, European Film Awards Best European Actor 2001. *Stage appearances include:* A Midsummer Night's Dream, Occupations, The Tempest, Hamlet (title role), The Merry Wives of Windsor, Baal, Nicholas Nickleby, Volpone, The Cherry Orchard, The Country Wife, Judgement, Statements After An Arrest, Othello (title role), Caracol in Melons, Waiting for Godot. *Television appearances include:* The Love School 1974, Kean, Silas Marner, The Train 1987, Murderous Amongst Us 1988, Sweeney Todd 1998, Anne Frank (Screen Actors' Guild Award for Best Actor 2002) 2001, several plays. *Films:* Gandhi (two Hollywood Golden Globe Awards 1982, New York Film Critics' Award, two BAFTA Awards, Acad. Award, Los Angeles Film Critics' Award 1983), Betrayal 1982, Harem 1985, Turtle Diary 1985, Without A Clue 1988, Testimony 1988, Pascali's Island 1988, Bugsy 1991, Sneakers 1992, Innocent Moves 1992, Dave 1992, Schindler's List 1993, Death and the Maiden 1994, Species 1995, Twelfth Night 1996, Photographing Fairies 1997, The Assignment 1998, Weapons of Mass Destruction 1998, The Confession 1999, Parting Shots 1999, Spooky House 2000, What Planet Are You From? 2000, Rules of Engagement 2000, Sexy Beast (Best Actor, British Ind. Film Awards 2001) 2000, The Triumph of Love 2001, A.I. (voice) 2001, Tuck Everlasting 2002, House of Sand and Fog 2003, Thunderbirds 2004, Suspect Zero 2004, A Sound of Thunder 2005, Oliver Twist 2005, Lucky Number Slevin 2005, BloodRayne 2005, I Have Never Forgotten You The Life and Legacy of Simon Wiesenthal

2006, You Kill Me 2007, The Last Legion 2007, The Ten Commandments (voice) 2007, Elegy 2007, The Wackness 2007, Transsiberian 2008, War, Inc. 2008, The Love Guru 2008, Fifty Dead Men Walking 2008. *Address:* c/o ICM, 76 Oxford Street, London, W1N 0AX, England. *Telephone:* (20) 7636-6565. *Fax:* (20) 7323-0101.

KINGSMILL, Baroness (Life Peer), cr. 2006, of Holland Park in the London Borough of Kensington and Chelsea; **Denise Patricia Byrne Kingsmill,** CBE; British lawyer; b. 24 April 1947, New Zealand; d. of Patrick Henry Byrne and Hester Jean Byrne; m. David Gordon Kingsmill 1970 (divorced 2002); one s. one d.; ed Girton Coll., Cambridge; admitted as solicitor 1980; with ICI Fibres then Int. Wool Secr. 1968–75; Robin Thompson & Pnrs 1979–82; Russell Jones & Walker 1982–85; Denise Kingsmill & Co. 1985–90; Pnr D. J. Freeman 1990–93; Consultant, Denton Hall 1994–2000; Chair. Optimum Health Services NHS Trust 1992–99; Deputy Chair. Competition Comm. (fmrly Monopolies and Mergers Comm.) 1997–2003; apptd Head Ind. Review into Women's Employment and Pay, Dept of Trade and Industry 2001, Chair. Accounting For People Task Force –2003; currently Sr Adviser, Royal Bank of Scotland; Chair. Sadler's Wells 2003–04; Deputy Chair. MFI Furniture Group 1999–2001; mem. Bd of Dirs British Airways 2004–; fmr mem. Bd of Dirs Home Office, Rainbow UK 1993–94, MFI Furniture Group, Norwich and Peterborough Building Soc. 1997–2001, Telewest Communications, Manpower UK; Trustee, Design Museum 2000; mem. Devt Cttee, Judge Inst., Cambridge Univ. Business School 2001–; Gov. Coll. of Law 1992–2001; fmr Pro-Chancellor Brunel Univ.; Hon. Fellow, Univ. of Wales, Cardiff; Hon. LLD (Brunel) 2001. *Publications include:* Women's Employment and Pay Review 2001. *Address:* House of Lords, London, SW1A 0PW, England (office).

KINGSOLVER, Barbara, MS; American writer; b. 8 April 1955, Annapolis, Md; m. Steven Hopp; two d.; ed DePauw Univ., Indiana, Univ. of Arizona; scientific writer, Office of Arid Land Studies, Univ. of Ariz. 1981–85; freelance journalist 1985–87, novelist 1987–; book reviewer, New York Times 1988–, Los Angeles Times 1989–, San Francisco Chronicle, The Nation, The Progressive, The Washington Post, Women's Review of Books and others; Woodrow Wilson Foundation/Lila Wallace Fellowship 1992; est. The Bellwether Prize for Fiction: In Support of a Literature of Social Change 1997; Hon. LittD (DePauw) 1994; Nat. Writers Union Andrea Egan Award 1998, Arizona Civil Liberties Union Award 1998, Nat. Humanities Medal 2000, Best American Science and Nature Writing 2001, Gov.'s Nat. Award in the Arts, Ky 2002, John P. McGovern Award for the Family 2002, Physicians for Social Responsibility Nat. Award 2002. *Publications:* The Bean Trees (Enoch Pratt Library Youth-to-Youth Books Award) 1988, Holding the Line 1989, Homeland and Other Stories 1989, Animal Dreams (Edward Abbey Award for Ecofiction, PEN/USA West Fiction Award) 1990, Another America 1992, Pigs in Heaven (Mountains and Plains Booksellers Award for Fiction, Los Angeles Times Fiction Prize) 1993, High Tide in Tucson 1995, The Poisonwood Bible (Village Voice Best Books 1998, New York Times Top Ten Books 1998, Los Angeles Times Best Books for 1998, Independence Publisher Brilliance Audio 1999, Booksense Prize 1999, Nat. Book Award (SA) 2000) 1998, Prodigal Summer 2000, Small Wonder 2002, Last Stand 2002, Animal, Vegetable, Miracle: Our Year of Seasonal Eating (American Booksellers Book of the Year Award, James Beard Foundation Award) 2007. *Leisure interests:* human rights, environmental conservation, natural history, farming. *Address:* PO Box 160, Meadowview, VA 24361 (office); c/o Harper Collins, 10 East 53rd Street, New York, NY 10022, USA.

KINGSTON, Arthur Edward, PhD, FRAS, FInstP, MRIA; British physicist and academic; *Professor Emeritus, Queen's University Belfast;* b. 18 Feb. 1936, Armagh, N Ireland; s. of Arthur Kingston and Henrietta Duff; m. Helen McCann 1962; one s. one d.; ed Royal School Armagh and Queen's Univ. Belfast; Research Fellow, Queen's Univ. 1959–60, Sr Research Fellow 1960–61; Asst Lecturer, Liverpool Univ. 1961–62, Lecturer 1962–63; Visiting Fellow, Univ. of Colorado, USA 1963–64; Lecturer, Queen's Univ. 1964–68, Sr Lecturer 1968–71, Reader 1971–83, Prof. of Theoretical Atomic Physics 1983, Dean, Faculty of Science 1989–94, Provost for Science and Agric. 1994, Prof. Emer. 2000–; mem. Int. Acad. of Astronautics. *Publications:* more than 260 papers in atomic physics and astro-physics. *Address:* Dept of Applied Mathematics and Theoretical Physics, David Bates Building, The Queen's University of Belfast, University Road, Belfast, BT7 1NN (office); 25 Cadogan Park, Belfast, BT9 6HH, Northern Ireland (home). *Telephone:* (28) 9027-3175 (office); (28) 9066-9658 (home). *Fax:* (28) 9023182 (office). *E-mail:* a.kingston@qub.ac.uk (office). *Website:* www.qub.ac.uk/mp/amtpt (office).

KINGSTON, Maxine Hong, BA; American author and academic; *Professor Emerita, Department of English, University of California, Berkeley;* b. 27 Oct. 1940, Stockton, Calif.; d. of Tom Kingston and Ying Lan Hong (née Chew); m. Earll Kingston 1962; one s.; ed Univ. of California, Berkeley; taught English, Sunset High School, Hayward, Calif. 1965–66, Kahuku High School, Hawaii 1967, Kahaluu Drop-In School 1968, Kailua High School 1969, Honolulu Business Coll. 1969, Mid-Pacific Inst., Honolulu 1970–77; Prof. of English, Visiting Writer, Univ. of Hawaii, Honolulu 1977; Thelma McCandless Distinguished Prof., Eastern Mich. Univ., Ypsilanti 1986; Chancellor's Distinguished Prof., Univ. of California, Berkeley 1990–, now Prof. Emer.; Mademoiselle Magazine Award 1977, Anisfield-Wolf Book Award 1978, Stockton (Calif.) Arts Comm. Award 1981, Hawaii Award for Literature 1982, NEA Writing Fellow 1980, Guggenheim Fellow 1981, named Living Treasure of Hawaii 1980, American Acad. and Inst. Award in Literature 1990, Nat. Humanities Medal 1997, Fred Cody Lifetime Achievement Award 1998, John Dos Passos Prize 1998, Ka Palapola Po'okela Award 1999, Commonwealth Club Silver Medal 2001, California State Library Gold Medal 2002, Spirituality and Health Book Award, KPFA Peace Award 2005, Red Hen Press Lifetime Achievement Award 2006, Los Angeles Times Book Festival Lifetime Achievement Award 2007, Nat. Book Foundation Medal for Distinguished ContribS to American Letters 2008. *Publications:* The Woman Warrior: Memoirs of a Girlhood Among Ghosts (Nat. Book Critics Circle Award for non-fiction) 1976, China Men (Nat. Book Award) 1981, Hawaii One Summer (Ka Palapola Po'okela Award 1999) 1987, Through The Black Curtain 1988, Tripmaster Monkey – His Fake Books (PEN USA West Award in Fiction) 1989, The Literature of California (ed.) 2001, To Be The Poet 2002; The Fifth Book of Peace 2004, Veterans of War, Veterans of Peace (ed., Northern California Book Award 2007, Pacific Justice and Reconciliation Center Peace Book Award) 2006; short stories, articles and poems. *Leisure interests:* roller-blading, gardening. *Address:* Department of English, University of California, 413 Wheeler Hall, Berkeley, CA 94720, USA (office). *Telephone:* (510) 643-5127 (office). *E-mail:* yinglan@berkeley.edu (office). *Website:* english.berkeley.edu (office).

KINIGI, Sylvie; Burundian politician and civil servant; b. 1952; fmr exec. officer of structural adjustment programme; Prime Minister of Burundi 1993–94; fmr mem. Union pour le progrès nat. (UPRONA); currently Sr Political Advisor and Coordinator of Programs, Special Rep. of the UN Sec. Gen. to the Great Lakes Region in Africa. *Address:* c/o Bureau de Coordination des Affaires Humanitaires des Nations Unies, Immeuble Losonia, blvd du 30 juin, Kinshasa, Democratic Republic of the Congo.

KINKEL, Klaus, LLD; German politician and lawyer; b. 17 Dec. 1936, Metzingen; s. of Ludwig Kinkel and Charlotte Klaus; m. Ursula Vogel 1961; one s. three d.; ed Bonn, Cologne, Tübingen Univs; lawyer 1962–70; Personal Aide to Hans Dietrich Genscher (q.v.) 1970–79; State Sec. Justice Ministry 1982–83, 1987–91, Justice Minister 1991–92; Minister of Foreign Affairs 1992–98; Fed. Vice-Chancellor 1992–99; Head of External Intelligence Service 1983–87; mem. Bundestag (Parl.) 1994–2002, Chair. Free Democratic Party 1993–95; Sr Adviser, Lehman Brothers Europe 2003–; mem. Advisory Bd EnBW Energie Baden-Wuerttemberg AG; mem. Int. Advisory Cttee, Robert Bosch GMBH. *Leisure interests:* jogging, tennis. *Address:* c/o Lehman Brothers, Rathenauplatz 1, 60313 Frankfurt, Germany (office). *Telephone:* (69) 153070 (office). *Fax:* (69) 153076599 (office). *Website:* www.lehman.com (office).

KINNEAR, Greg; American actor; b. 17 June 1963, Logansport, Ind.; s. of Edward Kinnear and Suzanne Kinnear; m. Helen Labdon 1999; ed Univ. of Ariz.; began career as marketing asst, Empire Entertainment, Los Angeles; worked as reporter for MTV; creator, co-exec. producer and host Best of the Worst TV show 1990–91; host Talk Soup TV show 1991–95, Later with Greg Kinnear 1994; Male Discovery of the Year, Golden Apple Awards 1996. *Television:* host: Best of the Worst, Talk Soup (Daytime Emmy Award (jtly) 1995), Later with Greg Kinnear; actor: Murder in Mississippi 1990, Dillinger 1991, Based on an Untrue Story 1993, Dinner with Friends 2001. *Films:* Blankman 1994, Sabrina (Most Promising Actor, Chicago Film Critics Asscn Awards 1996) 1995, Dear God 1996, A Smile Like Yours 1997, As Good as It Gets (Best Supporting Actor, NBR Awards 1997, Southeastern Film Critics Asscn Awards 1998, Golden Satellite Awards 1998) 1997, You've Got Mail (Best Supporting Actor in Comedy/Romance, Blockbuster Entertainment Awards 1999) 1998, Mystery Men 1999, What Planet Are You From? 2000, Nurse Betty 2000, Loser 2000, The Gift 2000, Someone Like You 2001, We Were Soldiers 2002, Stuck On You 2003, Godsend 2004, Robots (voice) 2005, Bad News Bears 2005, The Matador 2005, Fast Food Nation 2006, Little Miss Sunshine 2006, Invincible 2006, Unknown 2006, Feast of Love 2007, Baby Mama 2008, Ghost Town 2008, Flash of Genius 2008, Green Zone 2009. *Address:* Creative Artists Agency, 2000 Avenue of the Stars, Los Angeles, CA 90067, USA (office). *Telephone:* (424) 288-2000 (office). *Fax:* (424) 288-2900 (office). *Website:* www.caa.com (office).

KINNELL, Galway, MA; American writer and academic; *Chancellor, The Academy of American Poets;* b. 1 Feb. 1927, Providence, RI; s. of James S. Kinnell and Elizabeth Mills; m. 1st Inés Delgado de Torres 1965; (divorced) one s. two d.; m. 2nd Barbara K. Bristol 1997; ed Princeton Univ. and Univ. of Rochester; Guggenheim Fellow 1963–64, 1974–75, MacArthur Fellow 1984; Dir Writing Programme New York Univ. 1981–84, Samuel F. B. Morse Prof. of Arts and Sciences 1985–92, Erich Maria Remarque Prof. of Creative Writing 1992–2005; currently Chancellor The Academy of American Poets; named Vt State Poet 1989–93; mem. Nat. Inst., Acad. of Arts and Letters; Award of Nat. Inst. of Arts and Letters 1962, Cecil Hemley Poetry Prize 1969, Medal of Merit 1975, Pulitzer Prize 1983, Nat. Book Award 1983, Frost Medal 2001. *Publications:* poetry: What a Kingdom it Was 1960, Flower Herding on Mount Monadnock 1963, Body Rags 1966, The Book of Nightmares 1971, The Avenue Bearing the Initial of Christ into the New World 1974, Mortal Acts, Mortal Words 1980, Selected Poems 1982, The Past 1985, Imperfect Thirst 1994; novel: Black Light 1966; children's story: How the Alligator Missed Breakfast 1982; trans.: The Poems of François Villon 1965, On the Motion and Immobility of Douve by Yves Bonnefoy 1968, The Lackawanna Elegy by Yvan Goll 1970, The Essential Rilke; interviews: Walking Down the Stairs 1977. *Address:* 1218 Town Road 16, Sheffield, VT 05866 (home); c/o The Academy of American Poets, 584 Broadway, Suite 604, New York, NY 10012-5243, USA (office).

KINNEY, Catherine R.; American securities industry executive; b. 1952; m.; ed Iona Coll., New Rochelle, Harvard Graduate School of Business; joined NY Stock Exchange 1974, responsible for trading-floor operations and tech. 1986–95, Group Exec. Vice-Pres. 1995–2002, Pres., Co-COO, Exec. Vice-Chair. and mem. Bd of Dirs 2002–06, Pres. and Co-COO NYSE Group (after merger of NYSE and Archipelago) 2006–07, Pres. and Co-COO NYSE Euronext Inc., Paris (after acquisition of Euronext by NYSE) 2007, Group Exec. Vice-Pres. and Head of Global Listings 2007–09, also mem. Man. Bd; mem. Bd Securities Industry Automation Corpn 1988–97, mem. exec. Cttee

1994–97; mem. Bd Catholic Charities of New York, New York Univ. Downtown Hosp., Bd of Regents, Georgetown Univ.; Trustee Iona Coll.; Woman of the Year (Financial Women's Asscn) 2001, ranked by the Financial Times amongst Top 25 Businesswomen in Europe (18th) 2007. *Address:* c/o New York Stock Exchange, 11 Wall Street, New York, NY 10005, USA (office).

KINNOCK, Baron (Life Peer), cr. 2005, of Bedwellty; **Neil Gordon Kinnock,** PC, BA; British politician; *Chairman, British Council;* b. 28 March 1942, Tredegar, S Wales; s. of Gordon Kinnock and Mary Howells; m. Glenys Elizabeth Parry 1967; one s. one d.; ed Lewis School, Pengam, Univ. Coll., Cardiff; Pres. Univ. Coll., Cardiff Students' Union 1965–66; Tutor Organizer in Industrial and Trade Union Studies, Workers' Educational Asscn 1966–70; MP for Bedwellty 1970–83, for Islwyn 1983–95; mem. Welsh Hosp. Bd 1969–71; Parl. Pvt. Sec. to Sec. of State for Employment 1974–75; mem. Gen. Advisory Council BBC 1976–80; mem. Nat. Exec. Cttee, Labour Party 1978–94 (Chair. 1987–88); Leader of Labour Party 1983–92; Leader of the Opposition 1983–92; EU Commr with responsibility for Transport 1995–99, Vice-Pres. European Comm. 1999–2004; Pres. Cardiff Univ. 1998–; Chair. British Council 2004–; Hon. LLD (Wales) 1992, Alexis de Tocqueville Prize 2003. *Publications:* Wales and the Common Market 1971, Making Our Way 1986, Thorns and Roses 1992; contribs to newspapers, periodicals and books including The Future of Social Democracy 1999. *Leisure interests:* male voice choral music, opera, theatre, reading, grandchildren, rugby, soccer, cricket. *Address:* British Council, 10 Spring Gardens, London SW1, England (office). *Telephone:* (20) 7389-4887 (office). *Website:* www.britishcouncil.org (office).

KINSCH, Joseph, MSc; Luxembourg business executive; *Chairman, Arcelor-Mittal SA;* b. 2 May 1933, Esch-sur-Alzette; m. Ruth Lauxen; two s.; began career with Arbed, Burbach, Saar, Germany 1961, moved to Luxembourg HQ 1962, Dir of Accounting and Finance 1977–79, Head of Steel Processing Firms 1979–85, Group Chief Financial Officer 1985–92, apptd mem. Bd of Man. 1985, Pres. and CEO 1992–93, Chair. and CEO 1993–1998, Chair. 1998–2002, Chair. Arcelor SA (following merger of Arbed, Aceralia and Usinor and now Arcelor-Mittal) 2002–; Pres. honoraire Union of Luxembourg Enterprises, Chamber of Commerce of the Grand-Duchy of Luxembourg; Hon. Consul of Brazil in Luxembourg; Grand Officer of the Oak Crown, Officer of the Crown, Civil and Mil. Order of Adolph of Nassau (Luxembourg), Grand Cross of Civil Merit (Spain), Grand Officer of the Order of Leopold II (Belgium), Grand Officer of the Order of Merit of the Portuguese Repub., Officier Légion d'honneur, Grand Cross of the Order of Merit of the FRG, Commdr of Cruzeiro do Sul (Brazil), Commdr of the Order of the Polar Star (Sweden), Order of Industrial Merit (S Korea); Dr hc (Sacred Heart Univ., Luxembourg). *Leisure interests:* art, golf, reading. *Address:* Arcelor-Mittal SA, 19 avenue de la Liberté, 2930 Luxembourg, Luxembourg (office). *Telephone:* 47-92-23-60 (office). *Fax:* 47-92-26-58 (office). *E-mail:* contact@arcelor.com (office). *Website:* www.arcelor.com (office).

KINSELLA, John; Australian poet, writer, editor and publisher; *Editor, Salt;* b. 1963, Perth, WA; ed Univ. of Western Australia; Writer-in-Residence, Churchill Coll., Cambridge 1997; Ed. Salt literary journal; Publr and Ed. Folio (Salt) Publishing; Richard L. Thomas Prof. of Creative Writing, Kenyon Coll., USA 2001, then Prof. of English; Adjunct Prof., Edith Cowan University, Western Australia, and Prin. of the Landscape and Language Centre; Consultant Ed. Westerly (journal); Int. Ed. The Kenyon Review; Fellow, Churchill Coll., Cambridge; Western Australia Premier's Award for Poetry 1993, Harri Jones Memorial Prize for Poetry, Adelaide Festival John Bray Poetry Award 1996, Sr Fellowships Literature Bd of the Australia Council, Young Australian Creative Fellowship, Grace Leven Poetry Prize, The Age Poetry Book of the Year. *Publications:* poetry: The Frozen Sea 1983, Night Parrots 1989, The Book of Two Faces 1989, Poems 1991, Ultramarine (with Anthony Lawrence) 1992, Eschatologies 1991, Full Fathom Five 1993, Syzygy 1993, Erratum/Frame(d) 1995, Intensities of Blue (with Tracy Ryan) 1995, The Silo: A Pastoral Symphony 1995, The Radnoti Poems 1996, The Undertow: New and Selected Poems 1996, Lightning Tree 1996, Graphology (ed.) 1997, Poems: 1980–1994 1997, voice-overs (with Susan Schultz) 1997, The Hunt 1998, Kangaroo Virus (with Ron Sims) 1998, Sheep Dip 1998, Pine (with Keston Sutherland) 1998, alterity: poems without tom raworth 1998, The Benefaction (ed.) 1999, Fenland Pastorals 1999, Visitants 1999, Counter-Pastorals 1999, Wheatlands 2000, Zone 2000, Zoo (with Coral Hull) 2000, The Hierarchy of Sheep 2001, Auto 2001, Speed Factory (with Bernard Cohen, McKenzie Wark and Terri-ann White) 2002, Rivers (with Peter Porter and Sean O'Brien) 2002, Outside the Panopticon 2002, Lightning Tree 2003, Peripheral Light: New and Selected Poems (Western Australian Premier's Book Award for Poetry 2004) 2003, Four Australian Poets (with others) 2003, Doppler Effect 2004, The New Arcadia 2005, Shades of the Sublime and Beautiful 2008; prose: Genre (novel) 1997, Grappling Eros (short stories) 1998, Crop Circles (play in verse) 1998, Paydirt (play), The Wasps (play), From Poetry to Politics and Back Again 2000, Divinations: Four Plays 2003, Peter Porter in Conversation with John Kinsella (with Peter Porter) 2003. *Address:* Salt Publishing Ltd, PO Box 937, Great Wilbraham, Cambridge, CB21 5JX, England (office). *Telephone:* (1223) 882220 (office). *Fax:* (1223) 882260 (office). *Website:* www.saltpublishing.com (office); www.johnkinsella.org.

KINSELLA, Hon. Noël A., BA, LPh, STL, PhD, STD; Canadian human rights advocate, public servant, politician and academic; *Speaker of the Senate;* b. 28 Nov. 1939, Saint John, NB; m. Ann Kinsella (née Conley); ed Univ. Coll., Dublin, Ireland, St Thomas Aquinas Univ. and Pontifical Lateran Univ., Rome, Italy; spent 42 years as faculty mem. St Thomas Univ., Fredericton, NB where he taught psychology, philosophy and human rights; Assoc. Under-Sec. of State of Canada –1990; Senator 1990–, Opposition Whip 1994–99, Deputy Leader of the Opposition 1999–2004, Leader of the Opposition 2004–06, Speaker of the Senate 2006–, fmr mem. several Senate Standing Cttees,

including Human Rights, Social Affairs, Science and Tech., and Nat. Finance; Chair. New Brunswick Human Rights Comm. 1967–88; licensed mem. Coll. of Psychologists of New Brunswick; fmr Pres. Canadian Human Rights Foundation; mem. Advisory Council, Canadian Museum for Human Rights; mem. Bd of Govs St Thomas Univ.; Hon. Captain (Navy); Kt of the Order of Malta 1984, Commdr, Order of St John 2008; Dr hc (Dominican Univ. Coll., Ottawa) 2006, Hon. LLD (St Thomas Univ.) 2007. *Publications:* three books, several monographs and more than 50 articles on psychology and human rights. *Address:* Office of the Speaker of the Senate, 280-F Centre Block, Parliament Buildings, Ottawa, ON K1A 0A4, Canada (office). *Telephone:* (613) 992-4416 (office). *Fax:* (613) 992-9772 (office). *E-mail:* kinsen@sen.parl.gc.ca (office). *Website:* www.sen.parl.gc.ca/nkinsella (office).

KINSELLA, Thomas; Irish poet; b. 4 May 1928, Dublin; s. of John Paul Kinsella and Agnes Casserly Kinsella; m. Eleanor Walsh 1955; one s. two d.; with Irish Civil Service 1946–65, resgnd as Asst Prin. Officer, Dept of Finance 1965; Artist-in-Residence, Southern Ill. Univ. 1965–67, Prof. of English 1967–70; Prof. of English, Temple Univ., Philadelphia 1970–90; Dir Dolmen Press Ltd, Cuala Press Ltd, Dublin; f. Peppercanister (pvt. publishing co.) Dublin 1972; mem. Irish Acad. of Letters 1965–, American Acad. of Arts and Sciences 2000–; Guggenheim Fellowship 1968–69, 1971–72; Hon. DLitt (Nat. Univ. of Ireland) 1985; Hon. Sr Fellow, School of English, Univ. Coll. Dublin 2003; Guinness Poetry Award 1958, Irish Arts Council Triennial Book Award 1960, Denis Devlin Memorial Award 1966, 1969, 1992, First European Poetry Award 2001. *Publications:* Poems 1956, Another September (poems) 1958, Downstream (poems) 1962, Nightwalker and Other Poems 1966, Notes from the Land of the Dead (poems) 1972, Butcher's Dozen 1972, New Poems 1973, Selected Poems 1956–1968 1973, Song of the Night and Other Poems 1978, The Messenger (poem) 1978, Fifteen Dead (poems) 1979, One and Other Poems 1979, Poems 1956–1973, Peppercanister Poems 1972–1978 1979; Songs of the Psyche (poems) 1985, Her Vertical Smile (poem) 1985, St Catherine's Clock (poem) 1987, Out of Ireland (poems) 1987, Blood and Family (collected poems from 1978) 1988, Poems from Centre City 1990, Personal Places (poems) 1990, One Fond Embrace (poem) 1990, Madonna and other Poems 1991, Open Court (poem) 1991, Butcher's Dozen (anniversary reissue) 1992, From Centre City (collected poems from 1990) 1994, The Dual Tradition: an Essay on Poetry and Politics in Ireland 1995, Collected Poems 1956–94, The Pen Shop (poem) 1997, The Familiar (poems) 1999, Godhead (poems) 1999, Citizen of the World (poems) 2001, Littlebody (poem) 2001, Marginal Economy (poems) 2006, Readings in Poetry (essays) 2006, A Dublin Documentary (poems) 2006; The Táin (trans.) 1969; Selected Poems of Austin Clarke 1976; co-ed. Poems of the Dispossessed 1600–1900 (with 100 translations from the Irish) 1981; Ed.: Ireland's Musical Heritage: Sean O'Riada's Radio Talks on Irish Traditional Music 1981, The New Oxford Book of Irish Verse (including all new trans from the Irish) 1986. *Leisure interests:* history, publishing.

KINSELLA, William Patrick, OC, BA, MFA; Canadian writer and poet; b. 25 May 1935, Edmonton, Alberta; s. of John M. Kinsella and Olive M. Elliot; m. 1st Myrna Salls 1957; m. 2nd Mildred Heming 1965; m. 3rd Ann Knight 1978; m. 4th Barbara L. Turner 1999, three d.; ed Eastwood High School, Edmonton and Univs of Victoria and Iowa; recipient Houghton Mifflin Literary Fellowship 1982; Order of BC 2005; Hon. DLitt. (Univ. of Victoria) 1991; Books in Canada First Novel Award 1982; Canadian Authors' Asscn Award for Fiction 1982; Writers Guild Alberta Award for Fiction 1982, 1983; Vancouver Award for Writing 1987; Stephen Leacock Award for Humour 1987; Canadian Booksellers Asscn Author of the Year 1987. *Publications:* stories: Dance Me Outside 1977, Scars 1978, Shoeless Joe Jackson Comes to Iowa 1980, Born Indian 1981, The Moccasin Telegraph 1983, The Thrill of the Grass 1984, The Alligator Report 1985, The Fencepost Chronicles 1986, Five Stories 1987, Red Wolf, Red Wolf 1987, The Further Adventures of Slugger McBatt (reissued as Go the Distance 1995) 1988, The Miss Hobbema Pageant 1988, Dixon Cornbelt League 1993, Brother Frank's Gospel Hour 1994, The Secret of the Northern Lights 1998, The Silas Stories 1998, Japanese Baseball 2000; novels: Shoeless Joe 1982, The Iowa Baseball Confederacy 1986, Box Socials 1991, The Winter Helen Dropped By 1995, If Wishes Were Horses 1996, Magic Time 1998; other works: The Ballad of the Public Trustee 1982, The Rainbow Warehouse (poetry, with Ann Knight) 1989, Two Spirits Soar: The Art of Allen Sapp 1990, Even at this Distance (poetry, with Ann Knight) 1993. *Leisure interests:* baseball, sumo wrestling, Scrabble. *Address:* #201, 14881 Marine Drive, White Rock, BC, V4B 1C2, Canada (office); PO Box 3067 Sumas, WA 98295, USA.

KINSKI, Nastassja; German actress; b. (Nastassja Nakszynski), 24 Jan. 1961, W Berlin; d. of the late Klaus Kinski and of Ruth Brigitte Kinski; m. Ibrahim Moussa 1984 (divorced 1992); one s. one d.; one d. by Quincy Jones (q.v.); film début in Falsche Bewegung 1975; Bundespreis 1983. *Films include:* Stay As You Are 1978, Tess 1978, One From The Heart 1982, Cat People 1982, Moon In The Gutter 1983, Spring Symphony 1983, Unfaithfully Yours 1984, The Hotel New Hampshire 1984, Maria's Lovers 1984, Paris, Texas 1984, Revolution 1985, Harem, Torrents of Spring 1989, On a Moonlit Night 1989, Magdalene 1989, The King's Future 1989, The Secret, Night Sun 1991, Faraway, So Close!, Terminal Velocity 1994, One Night Stand 1997, Little Boy Blue 1997, Father's Day 1997, Somebody is Waiting 1997, Sunshine 1998, Your Friends and Neighbors 1999, The Magic of Marciano 1999, The Intruder 1999, Town and Country 1999, The Lost 1999, The Claim 2000, The Day the World Ended 2001, An American Rhapsody 2001, Say Nothing 2001, Diary of a Sex Addict 2001, Beyond the City Limits 2001, .com for Murder 2002, Paradise Found 2003, À ton image 2004, Inland Empire 2006. *Address:* c/o Peter Levine, William Morris Agency, One William Morris Place, Beverly Hills, CA 90212 (office); 888 Seventh Avenue, New York, NY 10106, USA.

KINSLEY, Michael, BA, JD; American journalist; b. 9 March 1951, Detroit, Mich.; m. Patty Stonesifer; ed Cranbrook Kingswood School, Mich., Harvard Univ., Magdalen Coll., Oxford, UK and George Washington Univ.; journalist, The New Republic (magazine), Ed. 1978–95, writing 'TRB from Washington' column; editorial posts at Washington Monthly, Harper's, The Economist; Co-host Crossfire TV program (CNN) 1989–95; Founding Ed. Slate online magazine 1995–2002, columnist 2002–04; Editorial and Opinion Ed. Los Angeles Times 2004–05; columnist Time magazine 2006–; fmr columnist Wall Street Journal, The Times (London), Washington Post; contrib. to New Yorker, Reader's Digest, Condé Nast Traveler, Vanity Fair; American Ed. Guardian Unlimited (London) 2006; Columbia Journalism Review Editor of the Year 1999. *Publication:* Please Don't Remain Calm: Provocations and Commentaries 2008, Creative Capitalism (ed) 2009. *Address:* Time, Inc., 1271 Avenue of the Americas, New York, NY 10020, USA. *Telephone:* (212) 522-1212. *Fax:* (212) 522-0602. *Website:* www.time.com.

KINZLER, Kenneth W., PhD; American oncologist and academic; *Professor of Oncology, Johns Hopkins Oncology Center, Johns Hopkins University School of Medicine;* b. 30 Jan. 1962, Philadelphia, Pa; ed Philadelphia Coll. of Pharmacy and Science (PCPS) and Johns Hopkins Univ. School of Medicine (JHUSM), Baltimore, Md; Postdoctoral Fellow in Oncology, JHUSM 1988–90, Asst Prof. 1990–94, Assoc. Prof. and Co-Dir Molecular Genetics Lab. 1994–99, Prof. of Oncology 1999–, also Prof. of Oncology, McKusick-Nathans Inst. of Genetic Medicine, Johns Hopkins Univ.; Alumni Award for Highest Average in Toxicology Curriculum, PCPS 1983, David Israel Macht Award for Excellence in Research, JHUSM 1988, Sandoz Award for Superior Academic Achievement and Contribution to Health Care, JHUSM 1988, Postdoctoral Award in Basic Science, JHUSM 1990, Young Alumnus Award, PCPS 1993. *Publications:* more than 220 articles in scientific journals. *Address:* Johns Hopkins Oncology Center, Room 588, Cancer Research Building, 1650 Orleans Street, Baltimore, MD 21231, USA (office). *Telephone:* (410) 955-2928 (office). *Fax:* (410) 955-0548 (office). *E-mail:* kinzlke@welch.jhu.edu (office); kinzlke@jhmi.edu (office). *Website:* www.hopkinsmedicine.org/pharmacology/research/kinzler.html (office).

KIPCHOGE, Eliud; Kenyan athlete; b. 5 Nov. 1984, Kapsisiywa, nr Kapsabet, Nandi Dist, Rift Valley Prov.; ed Kaptel Secondary School; distance runner; based in Nijmegen, Netherlands during track season; began racing in local cross-country events 2001; won jr race in nat. cross country trials 2002 and selection to nat. team; won 5,000m at trials for World Jr Championship, but did not travel to event due to illness; won jr nat. cross country trials and world event in Lausanne 2003; broke world jr 5,000m record, Oslo 2003; Gold Medal, 5,000m, World Championships, Paris 2003 (championship record time); won nat. cross country trials 2004, 2005 over 12 kilometres; won Kenya's 2004 Olympic Trials at 5,000m; Bronze Medal, 5,000m, Olympic Games, Athens 2004, World Indoor Championships, Moscow 2006; Silver Medal, 5,000m, World Championships, Osaka 2007, Olympic Games, Beijing 2008; Men's 3,000m Best Year Performance 2004–05, Head of State's Commendation 2006. *Address:* Athletics Kenya, Riadha House, PO Box 46722, 00100 Nairobi, Kenya. *E-mail:* athleticskenya@gt.co.ke.

KIPKETER, Wilson; Kenyan/Danish professional athlete; b. 12 Dec. 1970, Kapchemoiywo, Kenya; m. Pernille Kipketer 2000; ed St Patrick's High School, Iten, Kenya; world outdoor record-holder for 800m (1 minute 41.11 seconds) 1997 and indoor record (1 minute 42.67 seconds) 1997; set new world indoor record for 1000m (2 minutes 14.36 seconds), Birmingham, UK 2000; coached by Slawomir Nowak; resident in Denmark since 1990, qualified to compete for Denmark May 1995; gold medal, World Championships 1995, 1997, 1999; gold medal, World Indoor Championships 1997; Olympic silver medal 800m, Sydney 2000; European champion 800m, Munich 2002; silver medal, World Indoor Championships 2003; unbeaten over 800m for 28 races in 1996–97; retd 2005; currently Amb., Int. Asscn of Athletics Feds. *Address:* c/o International Association of Athletics Federations, 17 rue Princesse Florestine, BP 359, 98007, Monaco. *E-mail:* info@iaaf.org.

KIPPENHAHN, Rudolf; German astronomer; b. 24 May 1926, Bärringen, Czechoslovakia; s. of Rudolf Kippenhahn and Alma Belz; m. Johanna Rasper 1955; three d.; ed Graslitz and St Joachimsthal Schools, Univs of Halle and Erlangen; Scientific Asst, Bamberg Observatory 1951–57; staff mem., Max-Planck-Inst. für Physik und Astrophysik, Inst. für Astrophysik 1957–65, mem. of Directorate 1963, Dir 1975–91, now Prof. Emer.; Visiting Prof., Caltech, Pasadena and Princeton Univ. 1961–62; Prof., Univ. Observatory, Göttingen 1965–75; Visiting Prof., UCLA 1968, Ohio State Univ. 1979, Univ. Observatory, Hamburg 1986–87; Hon. Prof., Univ. of Munich 1975–; Assoc. mem. Royal Astronomical Soc., London; mem. Bayerische Akademie der Wissenschaften, Munich; Corresp. mem. Austrian Acad. of Sciences;; Verdienstkreuz (1st Class) (FRG); Carus-Medal, Leopoldina, Halle, Carus Prize, City of Schweinfurt, Lorenz-Oken-Medal, Gesellschaft Deutscher Naturforscher und Ärzte, Eddington Medal, Royal Astronomical Soc. 2005. *Publications:* One Hundred Billion Suns: The Birth, Life and Death of the Stars 1983, Licht vom Rande der Welt 1984, Light from the Depth of Time 1987, Unheimliche Welten 1987, Stellar Structure and Evolution 1990, Der Stern von dem wir Leben 1990, Abenteuer Weltall 1991, Discovering the Secrets of the Sun 1994; and numerous articles in astronomical and astrophysical journals. *Address:* Rautenbreite 2, 37077 Göttingen, Germany. *Telephone:* (551) 24714. *Fax:* (551) 22902.

KIRALY, Charles Frederick (Karch); American professional volleyball player; b. 3 Nov. 1960, Jackson, Mich.; s. of Lazlo Kiraly; m. Janna Miller; two s.; ed UCLA; led UCLA to Nat. Collegiate Athletic Asscn (NCAA) championships 1979, 1981, 1982; played on nat. team, winning gold medals, Olympic Games 1984, 1988, world championship titles 1982, 1986; won inaugural gold medal for Olympic beach volleyball (with Kent Steffes) 1996; record for most pro beach titles (148); f. Karch Kiraly Volleyball Acad., Karch Kiraly Scholarship Fund; Fédération Internationale de Volleyball (FIVB) Player of the Century; Asscn of Volleyball Professionals (AVP) Sportsman of the Year 1995, 1997, 1998, AVP Most Valuable Player 1990, 1992, 1993, 1994, 1995, 1998. *Publications include:* co-author (with Byron Shewman) Beach Volleyball, The Sand Man (autobiog.). *Address:* c/o Karch Kiraly Volleyball Academy, 1360 East 9th Street, Suite 850, Cleveland, OH 44114, USA. *Telephone:* (216) 363-1650. *Fax:* (216) 696-7748. *E-mail:* info@karchacademy.com. *Website:* www.karchacademy.com.

KIRANANDANA, Khunying Suchada, BComm, PhD; Thai university professor; *Professor Emeritus, Chulalongkorn University;* b. Bangkok; m. Thienchay Kiranandana; two s.; ed Chulalongkorn Univ., Bangkok, Harvard Univ., USA; several positions in Faculty of Commerce and Accountancy, Chulalongkorn Univ. 1979–99, Grad. School 1999–2004, Pres. Chulalongkorn Univ. 2004–08, now Prof. Emer.; mem. Sasin Steering Cttee, Sasin Advisory Bd 2004–08; mem. Test of English as a Foreign Language (TOEFL) Policy Council 1997–2000; Dir Kasikornbank PLC 2000–, Serm Suk Public Co. Ltd; Chair. Phufa Shop Operations Cttee 2001–; mem. Thai Red Cross Soc. Cttee 2006–, Nat. Legislature Council 2006–08; Dir Serm Suk Co. Ltd 2008–; Kt, Grand Cordon (Special Class), Most Exalted Order of the White Elephant, Kt, Grand Cordon, Most Noble Order of the Crown of Thailand, Most Illustrious Order (Fourth Class) of Chula Chom Klao. *Publications:* Inferential Statistics, an Introduction 1982, Theory of Sample Surveys 1995, Statistical Information Technology: Data in Information Systems 1998, Statistics in Everyday Life 2004. *Leisure interest:* reading. *Address:* Faculty of Commerce and Accountancy, Chulalongkorn University, 254 Phyathai Road, Patumwan, Bangkok 10330, Thailand (office). *Telephone:* (2) 218-5715 (office). *Fax:* (2) 218-5715 (office). *E-mail:* suchada.ki@chula.ac.th (office). *Website:* www.chula.ac.th (office).

KIRBY, Anthony John, PhD, FRS, FRSC; British chemist, academic and research scientist; b. 18 Aug. 1935, Welwyn Garden City, Herts.; s. of Samuel A. Kirby and Gladys R. Kirby (née Welch); m. Sara Nieweg 1962; one s. two d.; ed Eton Coll., Gonville and Caius Coll., Cambridge; Fellow, Gonville and Caius Coll. 1962–, Demonstrator, Lecturer in Organic Chem., Univ. of Cambridge 1968–85, Reader 1985–95, Prof. of Bio-organic Chem. 1995–2002, Tutor 1967–75, Dir of Studies in Natural Sciences, Gonville and Caius Coll., Cambridge 1968–96; NATO Research Fellow, Brandeis Univ., Mass, USA 1963–64; Coordinator European Network on Artificial Nucleases 2000–04; Hon. DPhil (Turku) 2006; Award in Organic Reaction Mechanisms, Royal Soc. of Chem. (RSC) 1983, RSC Tilden Lecturer 1987, RSC Ingold Lecturer 1996, Marin Drinov Medal, Bulgarian Acad. of Sciences 2003. *Publications:* The Organic Chemistry of Phosphorus (with S. G. Warren) 1967, Stereoelectronic Effects at Oxygen 1983, Stereoelectronic Effects 1996; over 300 articles on mechanistic bio-organic chemistry. *Address:* University Chemical Laboratory, Cambridge, CB2 1EW (office); 87 Holbrook Road, Cambridge, CB1 2SX, England (home). *Telephone:* (1223) 336370 (office); (1223) 210403 (home). *Fax:* (1223) 336362 (office). *E-mail:* ajk1@cam.ac.uk (office). *Website:* www.ch.cam.ac.uk/staff/ajk.html (office).

KIRBY, Hon. Justice Michael Donald, AC, CMG, BA, BEcons, LLM; Australian judge; *Justice, High Court;* b. 18 March 1939, Sydney; s. of Donald Kirby and the late Jean Kirby (née Knowles); partner Johan van Vloten 1969; ed Fort Street Boys' High School and Univ. of Sydney; Fellow, Senate, Univ. of Sydney 1964–69; mem. NSW Bar Council 1974; Deputy Pres., Australian Conciliation & Arbitration Comm. 1975–83; Chair. Australian Law Reform Comm. 1975–84, OECD Expert Group on Privacy and Int. Data Flows 1978–80, Cttee of Counsellors, Human and People's Rights UNESCO 1985, UNESCO Expert Group on the Rights of Peoples 1989; mem. Admin. Review Council of Australia 1976–84; mem. Council, Univ. of Newcastle, NSW 1977–83, Deputy Chancellor 1978–83; mem. Australian Nat. Comm. for UNESCO 1980–84, 1997– (Hon. mem. 1997–2007), Australian Inst. of Multicultural Affairs 1979–83; Judge, Fed. Court of Australia 1983–84; mem. Exec. CSIRO 1983–86; Chancellor, Macquarie Univ., Sydney 1984–93; Pres. Court of Appeal, Supreme Court of NSW 1984–96; Acting Chief Justice of NSW 1988, 1990, 1993, 1995, 2007, 2008; Admin. (Acting Gov.) NSW 1991; Justice, High Court of Australia 1996–; Acting Chief Justice of Australia 2007–08; Commr WHO Global Comm. on AIDS 1989–91; mem. Int. Comm. of Jurists, Geneva 1985–99, mem. Exec. Cttee 1989–95, Chair. 1992–95, Pres. 1995–98, Pres. Australian Section 1989–96; Special Rep. of Sec.-Gen. of UN on Human Rights for Cambodia 1993–96; Pres. Court of Appeal of Solomon Islands 1995–96; Pres. Australian Acad. of Forensic Sciences 1987–89; mem. Ethics Cttee of Human Genome Org. 1995–2003; mem. Council of the Australian Opera; mem. ILO Fact-Finding and Conciliation Comm. on Freedom of Asscn Inquiry on South Africa 1991–92; mem. Perm. Tribunal of Peoples' Session on Tibet 1992; Trustee, AIDS Trust of Australia 1987–93; Gov. Int. Council for Computer Communications, Washington 1984–; mem. UNESCO Jury for Prize for Teaching of Human Rights 1994–96, UNESCO Int. Bioethics Cttee 1996–2006; Rapporteur Int. Group on Judicial Integrity (UNHCR) 2001–, UNAIDS Global Panel on HIV/AIDS and Human Rights 2003–; Co-Chair. Expert Group on Bioethics and Human Rights, High Commr of Human Rights 2002–; Chair. UNAIDS Expert Group on HIV Testing in UN Peacekeeping Operations 2001–02, Jt UNAIDS/High Commr for Human Rights Expert Group on Revision of UN Guidelines on HIV/AIDS and Human Rights 2002–; Chair. Group of Experts, UNESCO IBC drafting of Declaration of Universal Norms in Bioethics 2004–05; mem. Judicial Reference Group, High Commr for Human Rights 2007–; mem. Advisory Bd Int. Human Rights Inst., De Paul Univ., Chicago, USA; Hon. Fellow, NZ Research Foundation, Australian Acad. of Social Sciences 1996, Acad. of Social Sciences in Australia 2004, Australian Acad. of Humanities 2006; Hon. Bencher, Inner Temple (London) 2006; Hon. mem. American Law Inst. 2000, Soc. of Legal Scholars (UK) 2007; Hon. DLitt

(Newcastle, NSW) 1987, (Ulster) 1998, (James Cook Univ.) 2003, Hon. LLD (Macquarie Univ.) 1995, (Sydney Univ.) 1996, (Buckingham Univ.) 2000, (ANU) 2004, Hon. DUniv (S Australia) 2001, (Southern Cross Univ.) 2007; Loewenthal Medal, Sydney Univ., Australian Human Rights Medal 1991, Laureate, UNESCO Prize for Human Rights Educ. 1998. *Publications:* Industrial Index to Australian Labour Law 1978, 1984, Reform the Law 1983, The Judges 1984, A Touch of Healing 1986 (co-ed.), Through the World's Eye 2000, Judicial Activism (Hamlyn Lectures 2003) 2004. *Leisure interest:* work. *Address:* Lvl 7 195 Macquarie Street, Sydney, NSW 2000, Australia (home). *E-mail:* mail@michaelkirby.com.au (office). *Website:* www .michaelkirby.com.au.

KIRBY, Peter Maxwell, MA, MBA; Australian business executive; *Chairman, Medibank Private Limited;* b. 2 Aug. 1947, South Africa; s. of Robert Maxwell Kirby and May Kirby; m. Erica Anne Ebden; one s.; ed Rhodes Univ., Natal Univ., Univ. of Manchester, UK, Univ. of the Witwatersrand, Harvard Business School, USA; Man. Dir Dulux Paints 1991–92; CEO ICI Paints Asia Pacific 1992–95, ICI Paints 1995–98; Man. Dir and CEO CSR Ltd 1998–2003; mem. Bd Dirs Macquarie Bank Ltd 2003–, ORICA Ltd 2003–; currently Chair. Medibank Private Ltd; Centenary Medal 2003. *Leisure interests:* boating, cars. *Address:* Macquarie Group, 1 Matin Place, Sydney, Australia (office). *Telephone:* (2) 8232-3333 (office). *Fax:* (2) 8232-4330 (office). *Website:* www .macquarie.com.au (office).

KIRBY, Ronald Hubert, BArch; Zambian architect and urban designer; b. 3 Jan. 1936, Lusaka, N Rhodesia; s. of Hubert Rowland Kirby and May Elizabeth Kirby (née Hinds); m. Davina Anne Roderick 1985; one d.; ed Muir Coll., Uitenhage, Univ. of Cape Town, Univ. of Witwatersrand; architect, commissions include: Queen Victoria Memorial Library, Zimbabwe 1960, Ndola Civic Centre, Zambia 1975, UAE Nat. Ass., Abu Dhabi 1977, Oppenheimer Life Sciences Bldg, Johannesburg 1979, Zimbabwe Parl. Bldg, Harare 1984; external examiner Univs of Cape Town and Pretoria 1985, rep. Zambia and Africa at confs in various countries; Chair. Transvaal Prov. Inst. of Architecture PR and Press Communication 1985–87; Prof. of Architecture and Head of Dept Univ. of Witwatersrand 1991–94; Dir Zambia Nat. Housing Authority 1991–92; mem. S Africa Council of Architects Educational Inspection Comm. to Univ. of Witwatersrand 1985–, Transvaal Prov. Inst. of Architecture Commn. 1983–87; fmr Pres. Zambia Inst. of Architecture; Zambia Inst. of Architecture Industrial Award 1964, Commercial Awards 1964, 1968, Civic Award 1968, Institutional Awards 1971, 1973, 1983, Inst. of S African Architecture Awards of Merit 1983, 1987, RIBA Bronze Medal, Rhodesia 1963, Habitation Space Int. Award 1981. *Publications:* numerous articles in professional journals. *Address:* P.O. Box 337, Melville, 2109 Johannesburg, South Africa. *Telephone:* (271) 482-2323. *Fax:* (271) 482-1218. *E-mail:* plandesign@icon.co.za (office).

KIRCHNER, Alfred; German theatre director; b. 22 May 1937, Göppingen; s. of Julius Kirchner and Alice Kirchner (née Bonatz); two d.; ed Max Reinhardt Schule, Berlin; Chief Producer, Staatstheater, Stuttgart 1972–79; mem. Bd of Dirs and Chief Producer, Schauspielhaus, Bochum 1979–86, Burgtheater, Vienna 1986–89; Gen. Dir Staatliche Schauspielbühnen, Berlin 1990–97; guest producer at Residenztheater, Munich, Hamburg Schauspielhaus, Hamburg State Opera, Frankfurt Opera, Holland Festival, Brussels Opera, Vienna State Opera, Santa Fé Opera, etc.; has directed operas by Udo Zimmermann, Bernd Alois Zimmermann, Hans Zender, Hans Werner Henze, Mozart, Verdi, Mussorgsky, Tchaikovsky; Dir Der Ring des Niebelungen, Bayreuth 1994–98, La Bohème, Frankfurt 1998, Rosenkavalier, Leipzig 1998, Rigoletto, Leipzig 1999, Peter Grimes, Strasbourg 1999, Manon Lescaut, Frankfurt 1999; producer of work for radio and TV.

KIRCHNER, Néstor Carlos; Argentine lawyer, politician and fmr head of state; *President, Partido Justicialista (PJ);* b. 25 Feb. 1950, Río Gallegos, Santa Cruz; m. Cristina Fernandez de Kirchner; one s. one d.; ed La Plata Nat. Univ.; fmr lawyer; jailed briefly during 1976–83 mil. dictatorship; Pres. Fund for Social Provision 1983–84; Mayor of Río Gallegos 1987–91; Gov. Prov. of Santa Cruz 1991–2003; mem. Partido Justicialista (Peronist party), Pres. 2008–; Pres. of Argentina 2003–07; Pres. Pres. Fed. Org. for Producers of Hydrocarbons 1992–. *Address:* Partido Justicialista (PJ), Domingo Matheu 130, 1082ABD Buenos Aires, Argentina (office). *Telephone:* (11) 4954-2450 (office). *Fax:* (11) 4954-2421 (office). *E-mail:* contacto@pj.org.ar (office). *Website:* www.pj.org.ar (office).

KIRCHSCHLAGER, Angelika; Austrian singer (mezzo-soprano); b. 1965, Salzburg; ed Musisches Gymnasium, Salzburg and Vienna Music Acad.; studied with Walter Berry in Vienna 1984; first performance in Die Zauberflöte, Vienna Kammeroper; concert performances in Austria, France, Germany, Italy, Czech Repub., Denmark, USA and Japan; recitals in London, Edinburgh, Amsterdam, Cologne, Frankfurt, Hohenems, Graz, Bilbao and in Scandinavia; composed Jonathan Miller production, Lausanne Opera 1998–99; sang with London Symphony Orchestra, New York Chamber Orchestra and Vienna Symphony Orchestra 1999–2000; feature broadcasts on Austrian Nat. Radio and TV (ORF); participated in film production about Hugo Wolf in role of Frieda Zerny 1992; operatic title roles include Le nozze di Figaro, Schloss Schönbrunn, Vienna, Der Rosenkavalier, Geneva, Hänsel und Gretel, Graz, The Merry Widow, Vienna, Palestrina, Vienna, Don Giovanni, Ravenna and Milan, Les Contes d'Hoffman, Paris, Ariadne auf Naxos, London; three prizes Int. Belvedere Competition, Vienna 1991. *Recordings include:* album of lieder by Alma Mahler, Gustav Mahler and Erich Wolfgang Korngold (solo debut) 1997; featured on recording of Mendelssohn with Claudio Abbado and Berlin Philharmonic; When Night Falls (solo recital). *Address:* c/o Sony BMG, Bedford House, 67–69 Fulham High Street, London, SW6 3JW, England (office). *Website:* www.sonyclassical.com/artists/ kirchschlager (office).

KIRIENKO, Sergey Vladilenovich; Russian economist, politician, government official and energy industry executive; *Head, State Atomic Energy Corporation (Rosatom);* b. 26 July 1962, Sukhumi; m. Maria Kirienko; one s. two d.; ed Inst. of Naval Engineers, Gorky (now Nizhy Novgorod), Acad. of Nat. Econ., Moscow; served in Soviet arm 1984–86; worked as Master in Krasnoe Sormovo shipbuilding facility, Nizhy Novgorod; elected Sec. of regional Komsomol org. 1986, then Sec., Krasnoye Sormovo Komsomol Cttee, First Sec., Gorky regional Komsomol Cttee, mem. All-Union Leninist Communist Youth League (Komsomol) Cen. Cttee; Founder and Chair. Garantia Bank, Nizhy Novgorod 1993–96; Pres. NorSea Oil Co., Nizhy Novgorod 1996–97; First Deputy, Ministry of Fuel and Energy May–Oct. 1997, also apptd Deputy Chair. Governmental Comm. for Coordination of Implementation of Production-Sharing Agreements (between fed. exec. bodies and regional authorities), Head Interdepartmental Comm. for ind. entities' access to Gazprom's gas transportation network, also became mem. panel of state reps in Transneft; Minister of Fuel and Energy 1997–98; Prime Minister, Russian Fed. April—Aug. 1998; Founder and Co-Chair. Novaya Sila party 1998; mem. State Duma representing Right Force Alliance 1999–2000, Leader Parl. faction Union of Right Forces; Presidential Rep. Volga Fed. Dist 2000–05; Chair. State Comm. on Chemical Weapons Destruction 2001–05; Head, Fed. Agency for Atomic Energy 2005–08; Head, State Atomic Energy Corpn (Rosatom) 2007–. *Address:* c/o RosEnergoAtom, 119017 Moscow, Bolshaya Ordynka, 24/26, Russia (office). *Telephone:* (495) 239-2422 (office). *Fax:* (495) 239-4603 (office). *E-mail:* npp@rosatom.ru (office). *Website:* www .rosatom.com/en (office).

KIRILL I, His Holiness Patriarch; Russian ecclesiastic; *Patriarch of Moscow and All Russia;* b. (Vladimir Mikhailovich Gundyayev), 20 Nov. 1946, Leningrad (now St Petersburg); s. of Mikhail Gundyayev; ed Leningrad Theological Acad.; ordained as Hierodeacon 1969, Hieromonk 1969; Prof. of Dogmatic Theology and Aide to Insp., Leningrad Theological Acad. 1970; Personal Sec. to Metropolitan Nikodim, Leningrad 1970; ordained Archimandrite 1971; Rector, Leningrad Acad. and Seminary 1974; consecrated Bishop of Vyborg 1976, Archbishop 1977; Archbishop (later Metropolitan), Smolensk and Vyazma 1984–89, Archbishop, Smolensk and Kaliningrad 1989–91, Metropolitan, Smolensk and Kaliningrad 1991–2009; Patriarch of Moscow and All Russia 2009–; Deputy Chair. Dept for External Church Relations, Moscow Patriarchate 1978–89, Chair. 1989–; Perm. mem. Holy Synod 1989–; fmr Russian Orthodox Church Rep. to WCC, mem. WCC Cen. Cttee and Exec. Cttee 1975–; fmr Man. Patriarch's parishes, Finland. *Television:* host of weekly programme, ORT/Channel One 1994–. *Address:* Danilov monastery DECR, MP, 115191 Moscow, 22 Danilovsky val, Russia (office). *Telephone:* (495) 633-8428 (office). *Fax:* (495) 633-8428 (office). *E-mail:* cs@mospatr.ru (office). *Website:* www.mospat.ru (office).

KIRK, David Edward, MBE, MB, ChB; New Zealand media executive and fmr rugby union player; *CEO, Fairfax Media Ltd;* b. 5 Oct. 1961, Wellington; ed Wanganui Collegiate School, Univ. of Otago, Univ. of Oxford, UK; played prov. rugby for Otago, toured with New Zealand Colts and first toured with All Blacks in 1983, refused to join rebel "Cavaliers" team on moral grounds when planned 1986 All Black tour to SA was cancelled, captained so-called "Baby Blacks", was made capt. of NZ team in inaugural Rugby World Cup in 1987 and led team to victory over France in final, retd from competitive rugby aged 25 and took up Rhodes Scholarship at Worcester Coll., Oxford 1987; returned to NZ becoming coach of Wellington NPC team 1993, media commentator 1994; worked as staffer for Prime Minister Jim Bolger and as man. consultant McKinsey & Co.; CEO Fairfax Media Ltd (publr of The Sydney Morning Herald, The Age and The Australian Financial Review in Australia, and The Dominion Post and The Christchurch Press in NZ) 2005–. *Address:* Fairfax Media Ltd, Level 19, Darling Park, Sussex Street, Sydney, NSW 2000, Australia (office). *Telephone:* (2) 9282-3046 (office). *Fax:* (2) 9282-3065 (office). *E-mail:* info@fxj.com.au (office). *Website:* www.fxj.com.au (office).

KIRK, Kent Sand; Danish politician and fishing captain; b. 29 Aug. 1948, Esbjerg; s. of Sand Kirk and Brynhild Kirk; m. Ruth Henriksen 1971; three s. one d.; Master's certificate, capt. of fishing boat 1971; Gen. Man. K. and K. Kirk Ltd 1973; Chair. Bd Fishermen's Asscn, Esbjerg 1975; mem. Bd Danish Deep Sea Fishing Fed., Danish Fishermen's Producers' Org., Esbjerg Harbour Council 1976; mem. European Parl. 1979–84; mem. Folketing 1984–98; Minister for Fisheries 1989–93; mem. Bd Danish Conservative Party 1980–84; Vice-Pres. European Democratic Group 1981–83; Pnr, Esvagt Ltd (stand-by vessels) 1981; Chair. Bd Int. School, Esbjerg 1982; currently with DR TV. *Leisure interests:* skiing, reading. *Address:* DR TV, TV-Byen, 2860 Søborg, Denmark. *Telephone:* 35-20-30-40. *Fax:* 35-20-26-44. *E-mail:* dr-kontakten@ dr.dk. *Website:* www.dr.dk.

KIRK, Matthew; British diplomatist and business executive; *Director of External Relationships, Vodafone Group plc;* m. Anna Kirk; two d.; ed St John's Coll., Oxford, Ecole Nat. d'Admin, Paris; joined FCO 1982, overseas assignments to New York, Belgrade, Gibraltar and Paris, Head of Investments in Information and Communications Tech., Cabinet Office, European Secr., FCO –2002, Amb. to Finland 2002–06; Dir of External Relationships, Vodafone Group 2006–. *Address:* Vodafone Group plc, Vodafone House, The Connection, Newbury, Berks., RG14 2FN, England (office). *Telephone:* (1635) 33251 (office). *Website:* www.vodafone.com (office).

KIRK, Paul Grattan, Jr, AB, LLB; American political official and lawyer; *Retired Partner, Sullivan & Worcester LLP;* b. 18 Jan. 1938, Newton, Mass.; s. of Paul G. Kirk and Josephine Kirk (née O'Connell); m. Gail Loudermilk 1974; ed Harvard Univ.; Pnr, Sullivan & Worcester LLP (law firm), Boston and Washington, DC 1977–90, Counsel 1990–, now Retd Pnr; Chair. Kirk & Assocs Inc. 1990–; Special Asst to Senator Edward Kennedy (q.v.); Nat. Political Dir Kennedy for Pres. Cttee 1980; Treas. Democratic Nat. Cttee 1983–85, Chair.

1985–89; Visiting Lecturer, Mass. Continuing Legal Educ. Program, New England Law Inst., J. F. Kennedy Inst. of Politics, Harvard Univ.; Chair., Bd of Dirs J. F. Kennedy Library Foundation, Nominating Cttee Harvard Bd of Overseers 1993, Nat. Democratic Inst. for Int. Affairs 1992–2001; mem. Bd of Dirs ITT Corpn 1989–97, Bradley Real Estate Inc. 1992–99, Hartford Life Insurance Co. 1995–2000, Hartford Financial Services Group 1994–, Rayonier Corpn 1993–; mem. Bd of Trustees, Stonehill Coll. 1984–, St Sebastian's School 1992–; Co-Chair. Comm. on Pres. Debates 1987–; Chair. Visiting Comm. on Harvard Athletics 2000–; Hon. LLD (Stonehill Coll.) 2002, Hon. LLD (Southern New England School of Law) 2003; W. Averell Harriman Democracy Award 1988. *Leisure interest:* athletics. *Address:* Sullivan & Worcester LLP, One Post Office Square, Suite 2400, Boston, MA 02109, USA (office). *Telephone:* (617) 338-2987 (office). *Fax:* (617) 338-2880 (office). *E-mail:* pkirk@sandw.com (office). *Website:* www.sandw.com (office).

KIRK, Ronald, BA, JD; American lawyer, government official and fmr politician; *United States Trade Representative;* b. 27 June 1954, Austin, Tex.; m. Matrice Kirk; two d.; ed Austin Coll., Univ. of Texas; Legis. Asst to US Senator Lloyd Bentsen, Washington, DC 1981–83; Asst City Attorney for Intergovernmental Relations and Chief Lobbyist, City of Dallas, Tex. 1983–89; shareholder, Johnson & Gibbs P.C. (law firm) Dallas 1990–94; Pnr, Gardere Wynne Sewell LLP (law firm) 1994–2004; Sec. of State, State of Texas 1994–95; Mayor of Dallas 1995–2001; Pnr, Vinson & Elkins LLP, Dallas 2005–09; US Trade Rep., Washington, DC 2009–; mem. ABA, Nat. Bar Asscn, Tex. State Bar, JL Turner Legal Asscn, Austin Coll. Alumni Asscn, Univ. of Texas Alumni Asscn (Pres.-elect 2008–09); Democrat; Hon. LHD (Austin Coll.) 2006; CB Bunkley Community Service Award, JL Turner Legal Asscn 1994, Woodrow Wilson Center Award 2000, Jurisprudence Award, Anti-Defamation League 2004, Justinian Award, Dallas Lawyers Auxiliary 2008; named one of The 50 Most Influential Minority Lawyers in America by The National Law Journal 2008. *Address:* Office of the United States Trade Representative, Winder Bldg, 600 17th St, NW, Washington, DC 20508, USA. *Telephone:* (202) 395-3230. *Fax:* (202) 395-4549. *E-mail:* contactustr@ustr.eop.gov. *Website:* www.ustr.gov.

KIRKBY, Dame (Carolyn) Emma, DBE, MA; British singer (soprano); b. 26 Feb. 1949, Camberley, Surrey; d. of the late Capt. Geoffrey Kirkby and of Beatrice Daphne Kirkby; one s. with Anthony Rooley; ed Sherborne School for Girls and Somerville Coll., Oxford and pvt singing lessons with Jessica Cash; specialist singer of renaissance, baroque and classical repertoire; debut London concert 1974; full-time professional singer 1975–; since mid-1970s involved in revival of performances with period instruments and the attempt to recreate the sounds the composers would have heard; performances at the Proms from 1977; freelance work with many groups and orchestras in the UK and Germany, including Consort of Musicke, Taverner Players, Academy of Ancient Music, London Baroque, Florilegium, Freiburger Barockorchester, Fretwork, Orchestra of the Age of Enlightenment, Concerto Copenhagen, Purcell Quartet; appearances at festivals, including Bruges, Utrecht, Luzern, Mosel, Rheingau, Passau, Schleswig-Holstein, Saintes, Beaune, Ottawa, Elora, Tanglewood, Mostly Mozart (New York) and many others; Hon. DLitt (Salford) 1985, Hon. DMus (Bath) 1994, (Sheffield) 2000; Hon. Fellow, Guildhall School of Music, Royal Acad. of Music, Royal Coll. of Music, Trinity Coll. of Music; Handel Prize, Halle, Germany 1997, Classic FM Artist of the Year 1999. *Recordings include:* Complete songs of John Dowland 1976–77, Messiah (Handel) 1979, 1988, Madrigals by Monteverdi, Wert, Scarlatti and other Italians, Schütz, Grabbe, Wilbye, Ward and other English composers, Monteverdi Vespers, Mass in B Minor (Bach), Handel's Athalia, Joshua, Judas Maccabaeus, Sequences by Hildegarde of Bingen (Hyperion), Arie Antiche and Songs of Maurice Greene, Dido and Aeneas, Handel's German Arias, Italian Cantatas, Songs by Arne and Handel, Stabat Mater (Pergolesi), Haydn's Creation, Mozart Motets, Mozart Concert Arias, Vivaldi Opera Arias, Handel Opera Arias, Christmas Music with Westminster Abbey Choir, Christmas Music with London Baroque, with Bell'Arte Salzburg, Bach Cantatas with Freiburger Barockorchester and with Purcell Quartet, Byrd Consort Songs with Fretwork, Handel: Sacred Contatas, Handel Gloria 2001, Lute song recitals with Anthony Rooley and with Jakob Lindberg. *Address:* c/o Consort of Musicke, 13 Pages Lane, London, N10 1PU, England (office). *Telephone:* (20) 8444-6565 (office). *Fax:* (20) 8444-1008 (office). *E-mail:* consort@easynet.co.uk (office). *Website:* www.emmakirkby.com.

KIRKILAS, Gediminas; Lithuanian politician; b. 30 Aug. 1951, Vilnius; m. Liudmila Kirkilienė; one s. one d.; ed Vilnius Teachers' Training Coll., Vilnius Higher School of Politics, Vilnius Univ.; interior restorer, Monument Restoration Trust 1972–78; worked within CP 1982–90; Asst to First Sec. of Cen. Cttee of Lithuanian CP, later to Deputy of Supreme Council–Reconstituted Seimas (Parl.), Repub. of Lithuania 1989–92; Ed. and Publr Golos Litvy (The Voice of Lithuania) daily newspaper 1991–95; mem. Seimas 1992–; fmr Chair. Cttee on Nat. Security and Defence, Cttee on Foreign Affairs, Deputy Chair. Cttee on European Affairs, Head of Seimas Del. to NATO Parl. Ass.; Elder Group of Lithuanian Social Democratic Labour Party 1993–96; head, Presidential working group to develop nat. security strategy 1993–96; Special Rep. of Pres. for matters related to transportation between Lithuania and Kaliningrad region of Russian Fed. 2002; given rank of Amb. 2003; Minister of Nat. Defence and mem. Cttee on Nat. Security and Defence 2004–06; Prime Minister of Lithuania 2006–08; acting Sec. of Ind. Cen. Cttee of Lithuanian CP 1990; elected Deputy Chair. Constitutive Ass. of Lithuanian Democratic Labour Party (LDLP) 1990, first Asst to the Sec. 1991–96, temporary Chair. 1993, mem. Presidium 1996–2001; following absorption of LLDP in 2001, Deputy Chair. Lithuanian Social Democratic Party 2001–; Cross of Officer of the Lithuanian Grand Duke Vytautas, Order of the Cross of Vytis, Commdr Cross of the Repub. of Poland, Grand Cross of Portugal. *Publications:* Political Commentary for the Period 1995, numerous articles on policy and public life. *Leisure interests:* fishing, tennis, philosophy, literature, arts, cycling, pipe smoking. *Address:* Lithuanian Social Democratic Party, Barboros Radvilaites g. 1, Vilnius 01124, Lithuania (office). *Telephone:* (5) 261-3907 (office). *Fax:* (5) 261-5420 (office). *E-mail:* info@lsdp.lt (office). *Website:* www.lsdp.lt (office).

KIRKINEN, Heikki, PhD; Finnish academic (retd); b. 22 Sept. 1927, Liperi; s. of Sulo A. Kirkinen and Anna Hirvonen; m. Maire Mirjam Rehvonen 1953; one s.; ed Joensuu Lycée, Univ. of Helsinki; Lecturer in History and Finnish, Orthodox Seminary of Finland 1953–59; Lecturer in History, Univ. of Jyvaskyla 1960–62; Researcher, Acad. of Finland 1962–66; Assoc. Prof., Sorbonne, Paris 1966–70; Prof. of History, Univ. of Joensuu 1970, Rector 1971–81, Prof. and Dir Inst. of History 1981–90; Assoc. Prof., Sorbonne Nouvelle 1984–85; Assoc. Dir of Studies, Ecole Pratique des Hautes Etudes, Paris 1988–89; mem. History Soc., Finnish Literature Soc., Acad. of Sciences of Finland; mem. Acad. Européenne des Sciences, des Arts et des Lettres; Hon. mem. Kalevala Soc., Foundation for Promotion of Karelian Culture; Commdr, Order of the White Rose; Commdr, Ordre des Palmes académiques, Officier, Ordre Nat. du Mérite. *Publications:* Les Origines de la conception moderne de l'homme-machine 1960, Karelia between East and West, I. Russian Karelia in the Renaissance (1478–1617) 1970, Karelia on the Battlefield. Karelia Between East and West, II 1976, Problems of Rural Development in Finland and in France (ed.) 1982, Europas födelse. Bonniers varldshistoria 7 1984, The Kalevala, an Epic of Finland and all Mankind (with H. Sihvo) 1985, History of Russia and the Soviet Union (ed.-in-chief) 1986, Le Monde kalévaléen en France et en Finlande avec un regard sur la tradition populaire et l'épopée brétonnes (ed. with Jean Perrot) 1987, Byzantine Tradition and Finland 1987, Structures and Forces in History 1987, The Roots of the Kalevala Tradition in North Karelia 1988, Europe of Regions and Finland 1991, History of the Karelian People (co-author) 1994, Provincial Government 1996, Termite or Angel? – Reflections on Cultural Evolution 2002, A la frontière entre l'est et l'ouest en Europe: revue de l'AMOPA 2004. *Leisure interests:* music, fishing. *Address:* Roskildenkatu 4D7, 80140 Joensuu (home); University of Joensuu, BP 111, 80101 Joensuu, Finland (office). *Telephone:* (13) 801143 (home).

KIRKLAND, Gelsey; American ballet dancer and ballet teacher; b. 29 Dec. 1952, Bethlehem, Pa; m. Greg Lawrence; ed School of American Ballet; youngest mem. of New York Ballet at 15 in 1968, Soloist 1969–72, Prin. Dancer 1972–74; with American Ballet Theater 1974–81, 1982–84, teacher, coach American Ballet Theatre 1992; Guest Dancer, Royal Ballet, London 1980–86, Stuttgart Ballet 1980; currently mem. Guest Faculty Broadway Dance Center, New York. *Ballets include:* Firebird, The Goldberg Variations, Scherzo fantastique, An Evening's Waltzes, The Leaves are Fading, Hamlet, The Tiller in the Field, Four Bagatelles, Stravinsky Symphony in C, Song of the Nightingale Connotations, Romeo and Juliet and others. *Publications:* Dancing on My Grave (autobiog.) 1987, The Shape of Love (with Greg Lawrence) 1990, The Little Ballerina and Her Dancing Horse 1993. *Address:* c/o Broadway Dance Center, 322 West 45th Street, 3rd Floor, New York, NY 10036, USA. *Telephone:* (212) 582-9304. *E-mail:* info@bwydance.com. *Website:* www.bdcnyc.com/faculty/bios/kirkland_gelsey.shtml.

KIRKWOOD, Thomas (Tom) Burton Loram, CBE, BA, MSc, PhD, FMedSci; British medical scientist and academic; *Professor of Medicine and Head, Department of Gerontology, Institute for Ageing and Health, University of Newcastle-upon-Tyne;* b. 6 July 1951; s. of the late Kenneth Kirkwood and of Deborah Burton Kirkwood (née Collings); m. 1st Betty Rosamund Bartlett 1973 (divorced 1975); one s. one d.; m. 2nd Jane Louise Bottomley 1995; ed Dragon School, Oxford, Magdalen Coll. School, Oxford, St Catharine's Coll., Cambridge, Worcester Coll., Oxford; initially qualified as a mathematician; developed 'disposable soma' theory of ageing; Scientist, Nat. Inst. for Biological Standards and Control, London 1973–79, Staff Scientist 1979–81; Staff Scientist, Computing Lab., MRC Nat. Inst. for Medical Research, London 1981–87, Sr Staff Scientist 1987–88, Head, Lab. of Math. Biology 1988–93; Prof. of Biological Gerontology, Univ. of Manchester 1993–99 (first in GB); Prof. of Medicine and Head of Dept of Gerontology, Univ. of Newcastle-upon-Tyne 1999–; Chair. British Soc. for Research on Ageing 1992–99; Dir Jt Centre on Ageing, Univs of Manchester and Newcastle upon Tyne 1996–; Gov. Research Advisory Council, Research into Ageing 1998–2001, Chair. 1999–2000; Chair. Foresight Task Force on Health Care of Older People 1999–2001; mem. WHO Expert Advisory Panel on Biological Standardization 1985–, UK Human Genome Mapping Project Cttee 1991–93, Basic Scis Interest Group, Wellcome Trust 1992–97, Bio tech. and Biological Sciences Research Council 2001–; Co-Ed. Mechanisms of Ageing and Devt 2000–; Pres. Int. Biometric Soc. (British Region) 1998–2000; Fellow, Inst. for Advanced Study, Budapest 1997; Heinz Karger Prize 1983, Fritz Verzár Medal 1996, British Geriatrics Soc. Dhole-Eddlestone Prize 2001, Royal Inst. Henry Dale Prize 2002. *Radio:* BBC Reith Lectures 2001. *Publications:* (jtly): Accuracy in Molecular Processes: Its Control and Relevance to Living Systems 1986, Time of Our Lives: The Science of Human Ageing 1999, Sex and Longevity: Sexuality, Gender, Reproduction, Parenthood 2001; (with C.E. Finch): Chance, Development and Aging 2000, The End of Age 2001; numerous scientific articles in learned journals. *Leisure interests:* gardening, hill-walking, running, pottery. *Address:* Newcastle University, Institute for Ageing and Health, Henry Wellcome Laboratory for Biogerontology Research, Newcastle General Hospital, Newcastle-upon-Tyne, NE4 6BE (office); Roughlees, Ewesley, Morpeth, Northumberland, NE61 4PH, England (home). *Telephone:* (191) 256-3319 (office). *Fax:* (191) 256-3445 (office). *E-mail:* tom.kirkwood@ncl.ac.uk (office). *Website:* www.ncl.ac.uk/medi/research/gerontology (office).

KIRMANI, Tariq, MBA; Pakistani business executive; ed Inst. of Business Admin, Karachi; spent seven years working in USA, UAE and Australia; served in oil sector in various marketing, operations and finance man.

positions, first Pakistani to be elected a co. dir of a multinational oil co. 1991; Deputy Man. Dir (Marketing) Pakistan State Oil 1999–2001, Man. Dir 2001–05; Chair. and CEO Pakistan Int. Airlines 2005–07 (resgnd); mem. Bd of Dirs Pakistan Refinery Ltd, Pak Grease, Attock Petroleum Ltd, Pakistan Telecommunication Company Ltd, Pvt. Power Infrastructure Bd, Railway Bd, Asia Petroleum Ltd, Pak-Arab Pipeline Co. Ltd, Petroleum Inst. of Pakistan, Cupola Pakistan Foundation; Chair. Oil Cos Advisory Cttee 2001–; Vice-Chair. Pakistan Advertisers Soc.; mem. Bd Govs Shaukat Khanum Memorial Trust; mem. Selection Bd Inst. of Business Admin; mem. Corp. Governance Cttee Karachi Stock Exchange; Pres. Pakistan Hockey Fed. 2005–06. *Address:* c/o Pakistan International Airlines Corporation, Head Office, Quaid-e-Azam International Airport, Karachi 75200, Pakistan (office).

KIRPICHNIKOV, Mikhail Petrovich, DBiolSc; Russian politician, scientist and academic; *Pro-Rector and Head, Innovation Policy and Innovation Project Management Department, Lomonosov Moscow State University;* b. 9 Nov. 1945, Moscow; m.; one d.; ed Moscow Inst. of Physics and Tech.; with Inst. of Molecular Biology 1972–89; Deputy Head, Head of Div., USSR Cttee on Science and Tech. 1989–91; Head of Div., Head of Dept, Ministry of Science and Tech. Policy of Russian Fed. 1991–93; Head, Div. of Science, Educ., High School and Tech., Russian Govt 1993–94, Head, Dept of Science and Educ. 1994–98; First Deputy Minister of Science and Tech. July–Sept. 1998, Minister 1998–2001; Prof. and Head, Protein Eng Lab., Inst. of Bio-organic Chemistry, Russian Acad. of Sciences 2000–; Pro-Rector andf Head, Innovation Policy and Innovation Project Management Dept, Lomonosov Moscow State Univ. 2004–; mem., Russian Acad. of Sciences 1997–. *Publications:* over 200 books, articles and papers on biology. *Address:* Innovation Policy and Innovatiion Project Management Department, Lomonosov Moscow State University, GSP-2, Leninskie Gory, Moscow, 119992; Institute of Bio-organic Chemistry, Mirlukho-Maklaya str. 16/10, GSP-7 Moscow, 117871, Russia. *Telephone:* (495) 335-28-88 (office).

KIRPICHNIKOV, Valery Aleksandrovich; Russian politician; b. 29 June 1946, Rostov-on-Don; m.; two c.; ed Leningrad Polytech. Inst.; Lt in air defence forces 1969–71; engineer, sr engineer, Deputy Head of lab., S. Vavilov State Inst. of Optics, Leningrad Region br. 1971–81; Chief Engineer, Research Inst. of Complex Tests 1981–88; Deputy Chair., Chair., Exec. Cttee Sosnovy Bor Town Soviet 1988–92; RSFSR Peoples' Deputy 1990, mem. Supreme Soviet 1990–93; mem. State Duma 1993–98; Deputy Gov. Leningrad Region 1996–98; Pres. Union of Russian Towns 1993–98; Minister of Regional Policy of Russian Fed. 1998–99; First Deputy Minister of Fed., Nat. and Migration Policy 2000–01; f. Russian Union of Local Self-Man. *Publications:* scientific works, patents.

KIRSCH, Philippe, QC, LLM; Canadian judge and fmr diplomatist; *President, International Criminal Court;* b. 1 April 1947, Quebec; ed Stanislas Coll., Montreal, Univ. of Montreal, Acad. of Int. Law, The Hague, The Netherlands, Int. Peace Acad., Vienna, Austria; called to the Bar, Quebec 1970; apptd QC 1988; joined diplomatic service, assignments with Bureau of Legal Affairs and US Div., Dept of Foreign Affairs and Int. Trade, Ottawa, with Embassy in Peru, Perm. Mission to the UN, New York –1985; Dir Legal Operations Div., Dept of External Affairs, Ottawa 1983–88; Amb. and Deputy Perm. Rep. to UN, New York 1988–92; Deputy Legal Adviser and Dir-Gen., Bureau of Legal Affairs, Dept of Foreign Affairs and Int. Trade 1992–94, Asst Deputy Minister for Legal and Consular Affairs 1994–96, Legal Adviser 1994–99; Amb. to Sweden 1999–2003; Judge, Int. Criminal Court (ICC), The Hague 2003–, Pres. 2006–; Amb. and Agent of Canada in legal disputes 1985–86, 1995–98, 1999–2003; Chair. Preparatory Comm. for ICC 1999–2002; Rep. of Canada to various int. orgs and confs; Chair. UN Legal Ad Hoc Cttees 1993–94, 1997–99; mem. Perm. Court of Arbitration 1995–99; Robert S. Litvack Human Rights Memorial Award 1999, Minister of Foreign Affairs Award for Foreign Policy Excellence 1999, William J. Butler Human Rights Medal 2001. *Publications:* chapters in books, articles in professional journals. *Address:* International Criminal Court, Maanweg 174, 2516 AB The Hague, The Netherlands (office). *Telephone:* (70) 5158515 (office). *Fax:* (70) 5158555 (office). *E-mail:* pio@icc-cpi.int (office). *Website:* www.icc-cpi.int/presidency/president.html (office).

KIRSCH, Wolfgang; German banking executive; *CEO, DZ Bank AG;* b. 19 March 1955, Bensberg; m.; two c.; ed Univ. of Cologne; banking apprenticeship at Deutsche Bank 1975–77, Corp. Customers Man. and Authorised Officer, Deutsche Bank, Düsseldorf 1981–88, Gen. Man. Deutsche Bank, Viersen 1988–93, Deputy Man. and Head of Corp. Customers Business, Deutsche Bank, Düsseldorf 1993–96, Deputy Head of Credit Line Man. for Corp. Customers Business Germany, Deutsche Bank, Frankfurt am Main 1996–98, Gen. Man. and Chief Country Officer, Deutsche Bank, Singapore 1998–2000, Man. Dir and Sr Credit Exec. of the Corporates and Real Estate Div. and CIB Corp. and Investment Bank Div., Deutsche Bank, Frankfurt am Main 2000–02; mem. Bd of Man. Dirs and Dir Risk Man. and Int. Business Devt, Deutsche Zentral-Genossenschaftsbank (DZ Bank) AG 2002–05, Deputy Chair. 2005–06, CEO 2006–, also Chair. Supervisory Bd of R + V Versicherung AG, Bausparkasse Schwäbisch Hall AG, Union Asset Man. Holding AG; mem. Supervisory Bd Südzucker AG. *Address:* Deutsche Zentral-Genossenschaftsbank AG, Platz der Republik, 60265 Frankfurt am Main, Germany (office). *Telephone:* (69) 7447-01 (office). *Fax:* (69) 7447-1685 (office). *E-mail:* mail@dzbank.de (office). *Website:* www.dzbank.de (office).

KIRSCHNER, Marc W., PhD; American cell biologist and academic; *Professor and Chairman, Department of Systems Biology, Harvard Medical School;* ed Northwestern Univ., Univ. of California, Berkeley; postdoctoral research at Univ. of California, Berkeley and Univ. of Oxford, UK; Asst Prof. of Biochemical Sciences, Princeton Univ. 1972; Assoc. Prof. of Biochemical Sciences, Princeton Univ. 1976–78, Prof. of Biochemical Sciences 1978; Prof. of Biochemistry and Biophysics, Univ. of California, San Francisco 1978–93; Carl W. Walter Prof. and Chair. Dept of Cell Biology, Harvard Medical School 1993–2003, Founder and Chair. Dept of Systems Biology 2003–, Co-Founder Inst. for Chem. and Cell Biology, Harvard Univ. 1999; mem. NAS, American Acad. of Arts and Sciences; Foreign mem. Royal Soc. 1999–, Academia Europaea; William C. Rose Award, American Soc. for Biochemistry and Molecular Biology 2001, Gairdner Foundation Int. Award (Canada) 2001, E.B. Wilson Medal, American Soc. for Cell Biology 2003, Dickson Prize for Science, Carnegie Mellon Univ. 2004. *Publication:* Cells, Embryos and Evolution (with John C. Gerhart) 1997, The Plausibility of Life: Resolving Darwin's Dilemma (with John C. Gerhart) 2005. *Address:* Department of Systems Biology, Harvard Medical School, 200 Longwood Avenue, Boston, MA 02115, USA (office). *Telephone:* (617) 432-2250 (office). *Fax:* (617) 432-0420 (office). *E-mail:* marc@hms.harvard.edu (office). *Website:* sysbio.med.harvard.edu/faculty/kirschner (office); (office).

KIRSCHSTEIN, Ruth L., AB, MD; American physician and administrator; *Senior Advisor to the Director, National Institutes of Health (NIH);* b. 12 Oct. 1926, Brooklyn, New York; d. of Julius Kirschstein and Elizabeth Kirschstein (née Berm); m. Alan S. Rabson 1950; one s.; ed Long Island Univ., New York and Tulane Univ., New Orleans, La; hosp. intern and resident 1951–54; Instructor in Pathology, Tulane Univ. 1954–55; Medical Officer, Resident in Pathology, then Pathologist, Lab. of Viral Products, NIH 1956–60, Chief, Section of Pathology, Lab. of Viral Immunology 1960–62, Asst Chief, Lab. of Viral Immunology 1962–64, Acting Chief, Lab. of Pathology 1964–65, Chief 1965–72; Asst Dir Div. of Biologics Standards, NIH 1971–72, Acting Deputy Dir, Bureau of Biologics 1972–73, Deputy Assoc. Commr for Science 1973–74; Dir Nat. Inst. of Gen. Medical Sciences, NIH (first woman to head an Inst.) 1974–93; Deputy Dir NIH 1993–2002, Acting Dir 1993, 2000–02, currently Sr Advisor to Dir; mem. Inst. of Medicine of NAS, American Acad. of Arts and Sciences; Co-Chair. PHS Co-ordinating Comm. on Women's Health Issues 1990–; Co-Chair. Special Emphasis Oversight Comm. on Science and Tech. 1989–; Hon. LLD (Atlanta) 1985; Hon. DSc (Mount Sinai School of Medicine) 1984, (Medical Coll. of Ohio) 1986; Dr hc (School of Medicine, Tulane Univ.) 1997; Presidential Meritorious Exec. Rank Award 1980, Distinguished Exec. Service Award Sr Exec. Asscn 1985, Presidential Distinguished Exec. Rank Award 1985, 1995, Asscn for Women in Science Mentorship Award 1997, Women of Achievement Award, Jewish Anti-Defamation League 2000, and numerous other awards; mem. Md Women's Hall of Fame. *Publications:* numerous scientific papers. *Address:* National Institutes of Health, Office of the Director, 9000 Rockville Pike, Bethesda, MD 20892 (office); 6 West Drive, Bethesda, MD 20814, USA (home). *Website:* www.nih.gov (office).

KIRST, Michael W., MPA, PhD; American academic; *Professor Emeritus of Education and Business Administration, Stanford University;* b. 1 Aug. 1939, West Reading, Pa; s. of Russell Kirst and Marian Kirst (née Weile); m. Wendy Burdsall 1975; one s. one d.; ed Dartmouth Coll. and Harvard Univ.; Assoc. Dir President's Comm. on White House Fellows, Nat. Advisory Council on Educ. of Disadvantaged Children 1966; Dir Program Planning and Evaluation, Bureau of Elementary and Secondary Educ., US Office of Educ. 1967; Staff Dir US Senate Sub-cttee on Manpower, Employment and Poverty 1968; Prof. of Educ. and Business Admin., Stanford Univ. 1968, now Prof. Emer., also affiliated with Stanford Center on Adolescence; Pres. Calif. State Bd of Educ. 1977–81; Chair. Bd of Int. Comparative Studies in Educ., NAS 1994–; Dir, Policy Analysis for Calif. Educ.; Dir, Consortium for Policy Research in Educ.; mem. Nat. Acad. of Educ., USA, Int. Acad. of Educ. and numerous other educ. bds, cttees, etc. *Publications include:* Schools in Conflict: Political Turbulence in American Education (with F. Wirt) 1992, Contemporary Issues in Education: Perspectives from Australia and USA (with G. Hancock and D. Grossman) 1983, Who Controls Our Schools: American Values in Conflict 1984, Political Dynamics of American Education 2001, From High School to College 2004. *Address:* School of Education, Stanford University, 485 Lasuen Mall, Stanford, CA 94305-3096, USA (office). *Telephone:* (650) 723-4412 (office). *Fax:* (650) 725-7412 (office). *E-mail:* mwk@stanford.edu (office). *Website:* www.michaelwkirst.com.

KIRWAN, William E., PhD; American university administrator, academic and mathematician; *Chancellor, University System of Maryland;* b. 14 April 1938, Louisville, Ky; s. of Albert Dennis Kirwan and Elizabeth H. Kirwan; m. Patricia Harper 1960; one s. one d.; ed Univ. of Kentucky, Rutgers Univ.; Asst Instructor, Rutgers Univ. 1963–64; Asst Prof., Dept of Math., Univ. of Maryland 1964–68; Visiting Lecturer, Royal Holloway Coll., Univ. of London, UK 1966–67; Assoc. Prof., Dept of Math., Univ. of Md at Coll. Park 1968–72, Prof. 1972–, Chair. Dept of Math. 1977–81, Vice-Chancellor for Academic Affairs 1981–88, Acting Chancellor 1982, Vice-Pres. for Academic Affairs and Provost 1986–88, Acting Pres. 1988–89, Pres. 1989–98; Pres. Ohio State Univ. 1998–2002; Chancellor Univ. System of Md 2002–; Chair. Nat. Asscn of State Univs and Land Grant Colls 1995–; mem. Knight Comm. on Intercollegiate Athletics (Co-Chair 2007–), American Math. Soc., Math. Asscn of America; American Acad. of Arts and Sciences 2002–; mem. Editorial Bd Journal of Diversity in Higher Education 2007–; Ed. Proceedings of the American Mathematical Society 1979–85; NDEA Fellow 1960–63; NSF Grants 1965–82; mem. Bd Dirs Council for Higher Educ. Accreditation; Greater Baltimore Cttee, Econ. Alliance of Greater Baltimore, Md Business Roundtable for Educ., Wendy's Int; Officier, Order of Leopold II, Belgium 1989; Hall of Distinguised Alumni, Univ. of Kentucky, Md House of Dels Speaker's Medallion 2007. *Publications:* Advances in Complex Analysis (co-ed. with L. Zalcman) 1976; numerous published research articles and seminar talks. *Leisure interests:* classical music, tennis. *Address:* Office of the Chancellor, University System of Maryland, 3300 Metzerott Road, Adelphi, MD 20783-1690, USA (office). *Telephone:* (301) 445-1901 (office). *Fax:* (301) 445-1931 (office). *E-mail:* bkirwan@usmd.edu (office). *Website:* www.usmd.edu/usm/chancellor (office).

KISELEV, Anatoly Ivanovich; Russian aviation engineer; b. 29 April 1938, Moscow; m.; one s. one d.; ed Moscow I nst. of Aviation Tech.; fmr electrician, then Eng, tester, head of lab., head of workshop, Deputy Dir Moscow Khrunichev Machine Construction Factory 1956–72, Dir 1975–93, involved in merger of Moscow Khrunichev Machine Construction Factory and Salut Construction Bureau, Dir M.V. Khrunichev State Space Scientific Production Cen. 1993–; Deputy Head, then First Chief of Dept USSR Ministry of Gen. Machine Construction 1972–75; Dir-Gen. Russian-American Lokhid-Khrunichev (Int. Launch Services) 1994–2001, mem. Bd Dirs 2001–; Lenin Prize; Order for Service to Motherland, Hero of Socialist Labour and numerous other orders and medals. *Address:* M.V. Khrunichev State Space Scientific Production Center, Novozavodskaya str. 18, 121309 Moscow, Russia (office). *Telephone:* (495) 145-88-54 (office). *Fax:* (495) 142-59-00 (home). *Website:* www.khrunichev.ru.

KISELEV, Oleg Vladimirovich, CandTechSci; Russian politician and engineer; *Chairman, Renaissance Capital;* b. 1 June 1953, Divnoye, Stavropol territory; m.; one s.; ed Moscow State Inst. of Construction; teacher Inst. of Steel and Alloys 1981–86; Deputy Dir Inst. of Chem. Physics USSR (now Russian) Acad. of Sciences 1986–88; Founder and Head Alfa-Eco co-operative, then Jt Venture Alfa-Eco, then Alfa production-finance co. including Alfa Bank and other affiliates 1988–91; Founder, Pres. and Chair. Bd Dirs Mosexpo Co. 1991–; co-f. IMPEX Bank 1993, Pres. and Chair. Bd Dirs 1993–2001; mem. Bd Dirs Russian Bank of Reconstruction and Devt 2001–; Man. Dir, Chair. Bd Metalloinvest (holding co.) 2001–; Chair. Bd of Dirs Renaissance Capital 2004–; Vice-Pres. Russian Union of Industrialists & Entrepreneurs; mem. Int. Asscn of Business Dirs 1989–; Chair. Council on Foreign Econ. Relations, Ministry of Foreign Affairs 1992; mem. Govt Union on Business 1993–94, Pres. Council 1994, Bd Dirs Russian-American Foundation of Support of Business 1994–, Public Council on Foreign and Defence Policy, Bd Asscn of Russian Banks 1999–. *Address:* Metalloinvest Co., Yefremova str. 12a, 119048 Moscow, Russia (office). *Telephone:* (495) 245-72-10 (office).

KISELEV, Yevgenii Alekseyevich; Russian broadcaster and journalist; b. 15 June 1956, Moscow; s. of Aleksei Kiselev and Anna Kiselev; m. Masha Shakhova 1974; one s.; ed Inst. of Asian and African Studies, Moscow State Univ.; teacher of Persian (Farsi) language, Higher School of KGB 1981–84; corresp., Radio Moscow Middle Eastern Dept 1984–86; TV journalist 1987–; regular host '120 Minutes' breakfast show 1987–90, staff corresp. news div. Gosteleradio (fmr USSR State Cttee for TV and radio broadcasting) 1989–90; made series of documentaries on everyday life in Israel 1989, 1990; joined newly founded Russian TV 1991, anchorman 'Vesti' late-night news programme; joined Ostankino State TV co. 1992; started 'Itogi' weekly news and current affairs programme 1992, on TNT station 2001–; Co-Founder and Vice-Pres. NTV independent broadcasting co. 1993–2000, Gen. Dir 2000–01; Co-founder, NTV-Plus Co. (direct satellite broadcasting) 1996; Gen. Dir TV-6 Independent Broadcasting Co. 2001–02; Ed.-in-Chief TVS Broadcasting 2002–2003; Ed.-in-Chief Moskovskiye Novosti (Moscow News) newspaper Oct. 2003–2005 (resgnd); reportedly joined Free Choice 2008 in early 2004; radio programme presenter Ekho Moskvy 2005–; mem. Acad. of Russian TV; Journalist of the Year, Moscow Journalistic Union 1993; included on list of 100 most influential people in Russia, publ monthly by Nezavisimaya Gazeta 1993–; Int. Press Freedom Award, Cttee to Protect Journalists, New York 1995. *Leisure interest:* playing tennis. *Address:* Ekho Moskvy, ul. Novyi Arbat 11, 119992, Moscow, Russia (office). *Telephone:* (495) 202-92-29 (office). *E-mail:* info@echo.msk.ru (office). *Website:* www.echomsk.ru (office).

KISHIDA, Fumio; Japanese politician; b. 29 July 1957; mem. House of Reps representing Hiroshima Pref. First Dist 1993–; fmr Vice-Minister for Construction, fmr Sr Vice-Minister of Educ.; Minister of State for Okinawa and Northern Territories Affairs, Quality-of-Life Policy, Science and Tech. Policy, Challenge Again, and Regulatory Reform 2007–08 (resgnd); mem. LDP (Liberal Democratic Party). *Address:* Jiyu-Minshuto (Liberal Democratic Party), 1-11-23, Nagata-cho, Chiyoda-ku, Tokyo 100-8910, Japan (office). *Telephone:* (3) 3581-6211 (office). *E-mail:* koho@ldp.jimin.or.jp (office). *Website:* www.jimin.jp (office); www.kantei.go.jp (office).

KISHIDA, Katsuhiko; Japanese business executive; *Chairman and Representative Director, Yamaha Corporation;* b. 19 Nov. 1941; joined Nippon Gakki Co. Ltd (now Yamaha Corpn) 1966, Gen. Man. Piano Div. 1992, Dir 1994, Man. Dir 1998, Sr Man. Dir 2000, Chair. and Rep. Dir 2004–. *Address:* Yamaha Corporation, 10-1 hakazawa-cho, Hamamatsu, Shizuoka 430-8650, Japan (office). *Telephone:* (5) 3460-2800 (office). *Fax:* (5) 3460-2802 (office). *Website:* www.global.yamaha.com (office).

KISHIMOTO, Tadamitsu, MD, PhD; Japanese immunologist, academic and fmr university president; *Visiting Professor, Laboratory of Immune Regulation, Graduate School of Frontier Biosciences, Osaka University;* b. 7 May 1939, Osaka; s. of Tadanobu Kishimoto and Yasuko Kishimoto; ed Osaka Univ. Medical School; Research Fellow, Dept of Medicine, Johns Hopkins Univ. School of Medicine 1970–73, Asst Prof. 1973–74; Asst Prof., Dept of Medicine III, Osaka Univ. Medical School 1974–79, Prof. and Chair. 1991–98, Prof., Dept of Pathology and Medicine 1979–83, Prof., Inst. for Molecular and Cellular Biology 1983–91, Dean, Osaka Univ. Medical School 1995–97, Pres. Osaka Univ. 1997–2003, now Visiting Prof., Lab. of Immune Regulation, Grad. School of Frontier Biosciences; Foreign Assoc. NAS 1991–; mem. Japan Acad. 1995–; Chair. 7th Int. Congress on AIDS in Asia and the Pacific 2005; fmr Chair. Cabinet Office Biotechnology Strategy Council; Hon. mem. American Asscn of Immunologists 1992, American Soc. of Hematology 1997; Order of Culture 1998; Asahi Prize 1988, Imperial Prize, Japan Acad. 1992, Person of Cultural Merit 1990, Robert Koch Gold Medal 2003, Royal Swedish Acad. of Sciences Crafoord Prize 2009. *Address:* Laboratory of Immune

Regulation, Graduate School of Frontier Biosciences, Osaka University, 1-3 Yamadaoka, Suita, Osaka 565-0871 (office); 3-5-31, Nankano-cho, Tondabayashi City, Osaka, Japan (home). *Telephone:* (6) 6879-4431 (office); (7) 2124-0532 (home). *Fax:* (6) 6879-4437 (office). *E-mail:* kishimot@imed3.med.osaka-u.ac.jp (office). *Website:* www.fbs.osaka-u.ac.jp/eng/labo/32a.html (office).

KISHLANSKY, Mark Alan, PhD, FRHistS; American historian and academic; *Frank Baird, Jr Professor of History, Harvard University;* b. 10 Nov. 1948, Brooklyn, NY; s. of Morris Kishlansky and Charlotte Katz; m. Jeanne Thiel 1975; two s.; ed Commack High School, State Univ. of New York at Stony Brook and Brown Univ.; Prof. of History, Univ. of Chicago 1975–91, Northwestern Univ. 1983; Prof. of History, Harvard Univ. 1991–97, Frank Baird, Jr Prof. of History 1997–; Mellon Visiting Prof. of History, California Inst. of Tech. 1990; mem. Cttee on Social Thought 1990–91; various research awards and other distinctions. *Publications:* The Rise of the New Model Army 1979, Parliamentary Selection: Social and Political Choice in Early Modern England, Early Modern Europe: The Crisis of Authority (co-ed. with C. M. Gray and E. Cochrane) 1987, Civilization in the West (with P. Geary and P. O'Brien) 1991, Sources of the West (ed.) 1991, Societies and Cultures in World Civilizations (with P. Geary, P. O'Brien, R. B. Worg) 1995, A Monarchy Transformed 1996. *Leisure interests:* Shakespeare, baseball, comedy. *Address:* Department of History, Robinson M-01, Harvard University, Cambridge, MA 02138, USA (office). *Telephone:* (617) 496-3427 (office). *Fax:* (617) 496-3425 (office). *E-mail:* mkishlan@fas.harvard.edu (office). *Website:* www.courses.fas.harvard.edu/~history (office).

KISLOV, Aleksander Konstantinovich, DHist; Russian political scientist; *Head, Peace Research Centre, Institute of World Economy and International Relations (IMEMO), Russian Academy of Sciences;* b. 11 Sept. 1929, Moscow; m.; one s. two d.; ed Moscow Inst. of Int. Relations; corresp., Head of Div., Head of Sector, Deputy Ed.-in-Chief Foreign Information Dept, TASS News Agency 1956–71; Head of Sector, Inst. for USA and Canadian Studies, USSR Acad. of Sciences 1971–86, Deputy-Dir Inst. of World Econs and Int. Relations 1986–96; Dir Peace Research Inst., Inst. of World Economy and Int. Relations (IMEMO), Russian Acad. of Sciences 1990–96, Head Peace Research Centre 1996–; fmr consultant Dept of Planning Int. Events, USSR Ministry of Foreign Affairs; mem. editorial bd numerous journals; mem. Russian Acad. of Nat. Sciences 1992–. *Publications:* USA and the Islamic World, Contemporary Foreign Policy of the USA (two vols, ed. and co-author). *Address:* Institute of World Economy and International Relations (IMEMO), Profsoyuznaya str. 23, 117997 Moscow (office); Apt 374, prospekt Vernadskogo 127, 117571 Moscow, Russia (home). *Telephone:* (495) 128-93-89 (office); (495) 438-61-59 (home). *Fax:* (495) 120-65-75 (office). *E-mail:* imemoran@online.ru (office). *Website:* www.imemo.ru (office).

KISLYAK, Sergey Ivanovich; Russian diplomatist; *Ambassador to USA and Permanent Observer, Organization of American States;* b. 1950; ed Moscow State Inst. of Eng and Tech., Acad. of Foreign Trade; joined Ministry of Foreign Affairs 1977, has served in numerous positions, including Dir Dept of Security and Disarmament 1995–98, Amb. to Belgium, concurrently Perm. Rep. to NATO, Brussels 1998–2003, Deputy Minister of Foreign Affairs 2003–08, Amb. to USA and Perm. Observer, OAS, Washington, DC 2008–; fmr mem. Coll. of Ministry of Foreign Affairs. *Address:* Embassy of the Russian Federation, 2650 Wisconsin Avenue, NW, Washington, DC 20007, USA (office). *Telephone:* (202) 298-5700 (office). *Fax:* (202) 298-5749 (office). *E-mail:* rusembus@erols.com (office). *Website:* www.russianembassy.org (office).

KISSIN, Evgeny Igorevich; Russian pianist; b. 10 Oct. 1971, Moscow; s. of Igor Kissin and Emilia Kissin; ed Moscow Gnessin Music School, studied piano with Anna Kantor; debut playing Mozart's D-minor concerto aged 10; appeared with Moscow Philharmonic, playing Chopin concertos 1984; tour of Japan with the Moscow Virtuosi; debut in Western Europe with the Berlin Radio orchestra 1987; British debut at the Lichfield Festival with the BBC Philharmonic 1987; London Symphony Orchestra concert 1988; concerts with the Royal Philharmonic and Yuri Temirkanov 1990; promenade concert debut with the BBC Symphony, playing Tchaikovsky's First Concerto 1990; US debut with the New York Philharmonic and a solo recital at Carnegie Hall 1990, subsequent US tour included Tanglewood 1991; Grammy Award ceremony and performances with the Chicago Symphony and Philadelphia Orchestra 1991–92; performed with the Boston Symphony; London recital debut and concert with the Philharmonia 1992–93; Prokofiev Concertos with the Berlin Philharmonic 1992–93; played Chopin and Schumann at the Royal Festival Hall, London 1997; first pianist to perform a recital at the London Proms 1997; Chopin's First Concerto at the London Proms with the Bavarian State Orchestra 1999; first concerto soloist to play in the Proms Opening concert 2000; 10th anniversary tour of recitals in the USA, including Carnegie Hall 2000–01; appearances with the Warsaw Philharmonic, Philharmonia Orchestra, Bavarian Staatskapelle, Chicago Symphony, Boston Symphony, Metropolitan Opera, Bayerische Rundfunk, and the Leipzig Gewandhaus 1999–2001; Brahms' Concerto No. 2 in B flat major at the London Proms 2002; Hon. mem. Royal Acad. of Music; Hon. DMus (Manhattan School of Music) 2001; Diapafon d'Or (France), Grand Prix Nobel Academie de Disque (France), Edison Klassiek Award (Netherlands) 1990, Chigiana Acad. Musician of the Year (Sienna) 1991, Musical America's Instrumentalist of the Year 1995, Triumph Award for outstanding contribution to Russia's culture 1997, Echo Award (Germany) 2002, Shostakovich Award (Moscow) 2003, Herbert von Karajan Award 2005, Distinguished Artistic Leadership Award, Atlantic Council 2008. *Recordings include:* Tchaikovsky Concerto No.1 with Berlin Philharmonic cond. Herbert von Karajan; live recording of Chopin Conertos with Moscow Philharmonic cond. by Dmitri Kitaenko 1984, Rachmaninov 2nd Concerto and Etudes Tableaux with the London Symphony conducted by Gergiev, Rachmaninov Concerto No. 3, Chopin Vols I and II live recital from

Carnegie Hall, Prokofiev Piano Concertos 1 and 3 with Berlin Philharmonic conducted by Claudio Abbado, Haydn and Schubert Sonatas 1995, Beethoven: Moonlight Sonata, Franck: Prelude, Choral et Fugue, Brahms: Paganini Variations 1998, Chopin: 4 Ballades, Berceuse op 57, Barcarolle op 60, Scherzo No. 4 op 54 1999, Chopin recital including 24 Preludes Op. 28, Sonata No, 2 and Polonaise in A-flat, Brahms 2003, Scriabin, Medtner, Stravinsky (Grammy Award for Best Instrumental Soloist Performance, without orchestra 2006) 2005, Schubert: Piano Music for Four Hands (with James Levine) 2006, Schumann's Piano Concerto and Mozart's Piano Concerto No. 24 2007, Beethoven's Complete Piano Concertos 2008. *Leisure interests:* friends, reading, theatre, walking. *Address:* Askonas Holt Ltd, Lincoln House, 300 High Holborn, London, WC1V 7JH, England (office). *Telephone:* (20) 7400-1700 (office). *Fax:* (20) 7400-1799 (office). *E-mail:* info@askonasholt.co.uk (office). *Website:* www.askonasholt.co.uk (office); www.kissinmusic.com.

KISSINGER, Henry Alfred, MA, PhD; American academic, international consultant and fmr government official; *Chairman, Kissinger McLarty Associates;* b. 27 May 1923, Fuerth, Germany; s. of Louis Kissinger and Paula Stern; m. 1st Anne Fleisher 1949 (divorced 1964); one s. one d.; m. 2nd Nancy Maginnes 1974; ed George Washington High School, Harvard Coll., Harvard Univ.; went to USA 1938; naturalized US Citizen 1943; US Army 1943–46; Dir Study Group on Nuclear Weapons and Foreign Policy, Council of Foreign Relations 1955–56; Dir Special Studies Project, Rockefeller Brothers Fund 1956–58; Consultant, Weapons System Evaluation Group, Joint Chiefs of Staff 1956–60, Nat. Security Council 1961–63, US Arms Control and Disarmament Agency 1961–69, Dept of State 1965–68 and to various other bodies; Faculty mem. Harvard Univ. 1954–69; Dept of Govt and Center for Int. Affairs; faculty Harvard Univ. Center for Int. Affairs 1960–69; Dir Harvard Int. Seminar 1951–69, Harvard Defense Studies Program 1958–69, Asst to Pres. of USA for Nat. Security Affairs 1969–75; Sec. of State 1973–77; prominent in American negotiations for the Viet Nam settlement of Jan. 1973 and in the negotiations for a Middle East ceasefire 1973, 1974; Trustee, Center for Strategic and Int. Studies 1977–; Chair. Kissinger Assocs Inc. (since 1999 Kissinger McLarty Assocs Inc.) 1982–; mem. Pres.'s Foreign Intelligence Advisory Bd 1984–90; Chair. Nat. Bipartisan Comm. on Cen. America 1983–84; fmr Chair. US Comm. investigating Sept. 11 attacks; Counsellor to J. P. Morgan Chase Bank and mem. of its Int. Advisory Council; Hon. Gov. Foreign Policy Asscn; Sr Fellow, Aspen Inst., syndicated columnist LA Times 1984–; Adviser to Bd of Dirs American Express, Forstmann Little & Co., Dir Emer. Freeport McMoran Copper and Gold Inc., Conti Group Cos Ltd, The TCW Group, US Olympic Cttee, Int. Rescue Cttee; Chair. American Int. Group, Int. Advisory Bd; mem. Exec. Cttee Trilateral Comm.; Chair. Eisenhower Exchange Fellowships; Chancellor The Coll. of William and Mary; Hon. Chair. World Cup USA 1994; Woodrow Wilson Book Prize 1958, American Inst. for Public Service Award 1973, Nobel Peace Prize 1973, American Legion Distinguished Service Medal 1974, Wateler Peace Prize 1974, Presidential Medal of Freedom 1977, Medal of Liberty 1986, Hon. KCMG 1995, and many other awards and prizes. *Publications:* Nuclear Weapons and Foreign Policy 1956, A World Restored: Castlereagh, Metternich and the Restoration of Peace 1812–22 1957, The Necessity for Choice: Prospects of American Foreign Policy 1961, The Troubled Partnership: A Reappraisal of the Atlantic Alliance 1965, American Foreign Policy (3 essays) 1969, White House Years 1979, For the Record 1981, Years of Upheaval 1982, Observations: Selected Speeches and Essays 1982–84 1985, Diplomacy 1994, Years of Renewal 1999, Does America Need a Foreign Policy? 2001, Ending the Vietnam War 2003, Crisis 2003; and numerous articles on US foreign policy, international affairs and diplomatic history. *Address:* 350 Park Avenue, New York, NY 10022; Suite 400, 1800 K Street, NW, Washington, DC 20006, USA. *Telephone:* (212) 759-7919 (NY); (202) 822-8182 (DC). *Website:* www.kmaglobal.com.

KISTLER, Darci; American ballet dancer; b. 4 June 1964, Riverside, Calif.; d. of Jack B. Kistler and Alicia Kistler (née Kinner); m. Peter Martins (q.v.) 1991; ed School of American Ballet; studied with Irina Kosmovska in Los Angeles; joined corps de ballet, New York City Ballet as prin. dancer under Balanchine 1980, announced retirement in 2009; injured 1982–85; mem. perm. faculty School of American Ballet 1994–; New York Women's Award, Golden Plate Award, Dance Magazine Award. *Ballets:* performances include prin. role in Haydn Concerto 1979, Swan Queen in Lev Ivanov's choreographing of Swan Lake 1979, leading roles in Brahms-Schönberg Quartet, Divertimento no. 15, Symphony in C, Raymonda Variations, Walpurgisnacht Ballet, Valse fantaisie, Tchaikovsky Suite no. 3, Dew Drop and the Sugar Plum Fairy in The Nutcracker 1980; new roles created for her in Suite from Soldier's Tale and Tchaikovsky Symphony no. 1 1980; leading roles in Who Cares?, Balanchine's Chaconne, Jacques d'Amboise's Irish Fantasy, Robbins' Prélude à l'après-midi d'un Faune, Martin's The Magic Flute 1981–82; shepherdess in Jacques d'Amboise's Pastorale 1982, siren in Peter Martins' Piano Rag-Music 1982; returned to New York Theater in Prélude à l'après-midi d'un Faune 1985; subsequent roles include: Titania in Balanchine's A Midsummer Night's Dream and the siren in his Prodigal Son, strip-tease girl in Slaughter on Tenth Avenue, man-eating door in Variations pour une porte et un soupir, title role in La Sonnambula 1986, Balanchine's Serenade, Ivesiana, Danses Concertantes, Mozartiana and Jewels 1988–89; Jerome Robbins' The Four Seasons 1989; Balanchine's Allegro brillante, Tchaikovsky Suite no. 3, Robbins' The Goldberg Variations, Other Dances, Dances at a Gathering, In G Major 1989–90, Balanchine Celebration 1993, Symphonic Dances 1994, Apollo 1994; debut in Balanchine's La Valse 1991, Peter Martins' The Sleeping Beauty, Peter Martins' Swan Lake (full length) 1999. *Films:* Balanchine's Ballerinas – Ann Belle 1988, The Nutcracker 1993. *Publication:* Ballerina: My Story 1993. *Leisure interests:* piano, painting, tennis, skiing, cooking. *Address:* School of American Ballet, 70 Lincoln Center

Plaza, New York, NY 10023-4897, USA (office). *Telephone:* (212) 769-6600 (office). *Fax:* (212) 769-4897 (office). *Website:* www.sab.org (office).

KITAGAWA, Kazuo, LLB; Japanese politician; b. 2 March 1953; ed Faculty of Law, Soka Univ.; began career as lawyer 1981–90; licensed tax accountant 2000; elected to House of Reps for Osaka Constituency 1990–; Dir Standing Cttee on Audit 1990–93, on Security 1990–93, on Finance 1994–96, on Budget 1998–99, Nat. Basic Policies 2000; Parl. Vice-Minister for Finance 1993–94; Chair. Standing Cttee on Science and Tech. 1999–2000, New Komeito Policy Research Council 2000–03; Minister of Land, Infrastructure and Transport 2004–06. *Address:* c/o Liberal-Democratic Party—LDP (Jiyu-Minshuto), 1-11-23, Nagata-cho, Chiyoda-ku, Tokyo 100-8910, Japan. *Telephone:* (3) 3581-6211. *E-mail:* koho@ldp.jimin.or.jp. *Website:* www.jimin.jp.

KITAJIMA, Kosuke; Japanese swimmer; b. 22 Sept. 1982, Tokyo; ed Nippon Sport Science Univ., Tokyo; fourth place in 100m breaststroke, Olympic Games, Sydney 2000; broke oldest swimming world record (200m breaststroke) at Asia Games 2002; Gold Medal, 100m and 200m breaststroke (set two world records), World Championships, Barcelona 2003, 100m and 200m breaststroke, Olympic Games, Athens 2004 (first Japanese Olympic swimmer to win two individual gold medals), 200m breaststroke, World Championships, Melbourne 2007, 100m (world record time of 58.91) and 200m breaststroke, Olympic Games, Beijing 2008; Silver Medal, 100m breaststroke, FINA Short Course World Championships, Moscow 2002, 100m breaststroke, World Championships, Melbourne 2007; Bronze Medal, 100m breaststroke, World Championships, Fukuoka 2001, 4×100m Medley Relay, World Championships, Barcelona 2003, 4×100m Medley Relay, Olympic Games, Athens 2004, 4×100m Medley Relay, Olympic Games, Beijing 2008; set world record time of 2:07.51 for 200m breaststroke June 2008; Medal with Purple Ribbon; Most Valuable Player, Asian Games 2002, Tokyo Medal of Honor, World Pacific Swimmer of the Year 2003, 2007. *Leisure interests:* fashion, driving. *Address:* c/o Sunny Side Up Inc., 4-12-8 Sendagaya, Shibuya-ku, Tokyo 151-0051, Japan (office); c/o Japan Swimming Fed., Kishi Memorial Hall, 1-1-1 Jinnan, Shibuya-ku, Tokyo 150-8050, Japan. *Telephone:* (3) 6825-3201 (office); (3) 3481-2306. *Fax:* (3) 5413-3051 (office); (3) 3481-0942. *Website:* www.ssu.co.jp (office); www.frogtown.jp. *E-mail:* jpn-swimming@japan-sports.or.jp.

KITAJIMA, Yoshitoshi; Japanese business executive; *Chairman, President and CEO, Dai Nippon Printing Company Ltd;* joined Dai Nippon Printing Co. Ltd 1963, has served in several exec. positions including Man. Dir, Sr Man. Dir and Vice Pres., currently Chair., Pres. and CEO; mem. Bd of Dirs TV Asahi Corpn, The Japan Forum; mem. EU-Japan Fest Cttee, Advisory Cttee Asia Pacific Univ.; Order of the Knight of Dannebrog (Denmark). *Address:* Dai Nippon Printing Company Limited, 1-1 Ichigaya Kagacho1-chome, Shinjuku-ku, Tokyo 162-8001, Japan (office). *Telephone:* (3) 3266-2111 (office). *Fax:* (3) 5225-8239 (office). *Website:* www.dnp.co.jp (office).

KITAMURA, Hiroshi, KBE; Japanese diplomatist and university president; b. 20 Jan. 1929, Osaka; m. Sachiko Kitamura 1953; two d.; ed Tokyo Univ., Fletcher School of Law and Diplomacy, Tufts Univ., Mass., USA; joined Foreign Affairs Ministry 1953, served in Washington, DC, New York, Delhi; First Sec., Embassy in London 1963–66; with Mission to OECD, Paris 1971–74; Exec. Asst to Prime Minister 1974–76; Deputy Dir-Gen. American Affairs Bureau 1977–79, Dir-Gen. 1982–84, Deputy Vice-Minister of Foreign Affairs 1984–87, Deputy Minister 1987–88; Consul-Gen. San Francisco 1979–82, Amb. to Canada 1988–90, to the UK 1991–94; Corp. Adviser, Mitsubishi Corpn 1994–99; Pres. Shumei Univ. 1998–2001; Prime Minister's Personal Rep. to Venice Summit 1987, Toronto Summit 1988; Fellow, Center for Int. Affairs, Harvard Univ. 1970; Chair. Japan–British Soc. 1994–2003; Gold and Silver Star, Order of the Rising Sun 1999; Hon. LLD (Northumbria) 1993. *Publications include:* Psychological Dimensions of US–Japanese Relations 1971, Between Friends (co-author) 1985, The UK Seen through an Ambassador's Eyes (in Japanese), Diplomacy and Food (in Japanese), An Ambassador and his Lhasa Apso (in Japanese). *Leisure interests:* Japanese classical music, food and wine, golf. *Address:* 1-15-6 Jingumae, Shibuya-ku, Tokyo, Japan. *Telephone:* (3) 3470-4630. *Fax:* (3) 3470-4830.

KITAMURA, Norio; Japanese business executive; *Chairman and CEO, Japan Post Service Co. Ltd;* b. 1942; ed Kagoshima Univ.; joined Toyota Motor Corpn, becoming Pres. Toyota Motor Italia 1996–2006; joined Japan Post Service Co. Ltd 2006, Chair. and CEO (following privatization Oct. 2007) 2007–. *Address:* Japan Post Service Co. Ltd, 1-3-2 Kasumigaseki, Chiyoda-ku, Tokyo 100-8798, Japan (office). *Telephone:* (03) 3504-4411 (office). *Website:* www.post.japanpost.jp (office).

KITAMURA, So; Japanese playwright; b. 5 July 1952, Ohtsu-shi; m. Konomi Kitamura; one d.; Leader, Project Navi 1986–; awards include Kishida Gikyoku-sho 1984, Kinoleuni-ya engeki-sho 1989. *Publications:* plays include: Hogiuta, So-Ko Gingatetsudo no yoru. Novels include: Kaijin nijumenso den (Shincho sha), Seido no majin (Shincho sha), Kenji (Kadokawa). *Leisure interest:* movies. *Address:* Project Navi, 11–13 Imaike-Minami, Chikusa-ku, Nagoya-shi, Aichi 464, Japan. *Telephone:* (52) 731-2867.

KITANO, Takeshi; Japanese film director, actor, comedian and screenwriter; b. 18 Jan. 1947, Tokyo; ed Meiji Univ. *Films:* Makoto-chan (actor) 1980, Danpu wataridori (actor) 1981, Manon (actor) 1981, Sukkari... sono ki de! (actor) 1981, Merry Christmas, Mr. Lawrence (actor) 1983, Jukkai no mosquito (actor) 1983, Kanashii kibun de joke (actor) 1985, Yasha (actor) 1985, Komikku zasshi nanka iranai! (actor) 1986, Anego (actor) 1988, Sono otoko, kyobo ni tsuki (writer, director, actor) 1989, Hoshi tsugu mono (actor) 1990, 3-4x jugatsu (writer, director, actor) 1990, Ano natsu, ichiban shizukana umi (writer, director) 1991, Sakana kara daiokishin! (actor) 1992, Erotikkuna kankei (actor) 1992, Sonatine (writer, director, actor) 1993, Kyôso tanjô (writer, actor) 1993, Minnâ-yatteruka! (writer, director, actor) 1995, Johnny

Mnemonic (actor) 1995, Gonin (actor) 1995, Kidzu ritan (writer, director) 1996, Hana-bi (writer, director, actor) (Venice Film Festival Golden Lion) 1997, Tokyo Eyes (actor) 1998, Kikujiro no natsu (writer, director, actor) 1999, Gohatto (actor) 1999, Brother (writer, director, actor) 2000, Batoru rowaiaru (Battle Royale) (actor) 2000, Dolls (writer, director) 2002, Asakusa Kid (writer) 2002, Battle Royale II (actor) 2003, Zatôichi (writer, director, actor) (Venice Film Festival Silver Lion) 2003, Izô: Kaosu mataha fujôri no kijin (actor) 2004, Chi to hone 2004, Takeshis' 2005, Gegege no Kitano 2007. *Leisure interest:* writing. *Address:* Office Kitano Inc., Tokyo, Japan. *E-mail:* office@ office-kitano.co.jp. *Website:* www.office-kitano.co.jp.

KITARO; Japanese musician; b. (Takahashi Masanori), 1953, Toyohashi; self-taught electric guitar player; began music career during school studies; founding mem. rock band The Far East Family Band –1976; abandoned rock for new age music and released first solo album Astral Voyage 1978; composed musical score for TV documentary series Silk Road 1980; signed with Geffen Records 1986; first live tour of N America leading to sales of two million albums in US 1987; featured as key artist and composer in Japan's Millennium celebration event; composed soundtrack for Chinese drama The Soong Sisters 2002; performs annual televised concerts from mountain location of his Japanese home and studio base in Nagano Pref. *Albums include:* Astral Voyage 1978, Millennia 1978, Ten Kai Astral Trip 1978, Full Moon Story 1979, Ki 1979, Oasis 1979, Silk Road Suite (Vols 1–4) 1980–83, Ten Huang 1980, Queen of Millennia 1982, India 1983, Tenjiku 1983, Tenku 1986, Silver Cloud 1986, Toward the West 1986, The Light of the Spirit 1987, Kojiki 1990, Kitaro Live in America 1991, Dream 1992, Mandala 1994, Peace on Earth 1996, Cirque Ingenieux 1998, Heaven and Earth 1997, Gaia 1998, Thinking of You 1999, Ancient 2001, An Ancient Journey 2002, Mizuniinorite 2002, The Soong Sisters 2002, Sacred Journey of Ku-Kai 2003, Shikoku 88 Kasho 2004. *Address:* c/o Domo Records Inc., 11340 West Olympic Boulevard, Suite 270, Los Angeles, CA 90064, USA (office). *Website:* domo.com/kitaro (office).

KITAYAMA, Teisuke, BA; Japanese banking executive; *President and Representative Director, Sumitomo Mitsui Financial Group;* b. 26 Oct. 1946; ed Univ. of Tokyo; joined Mitsui Bank 1969, Gen. Man. Yokohama-Ekimae Br., Sakura Bank (fmrly Mitsui Taiyo Kobe Bank) 1992–95, Gen. Rep. in Thailand and Gen. Man. of Bangkok Br. 1995–97, Dir and Gen. Man. Planning Div. 1997–2000, Man. Dir 2000, Man. Dir Sumitomo Mitsui Banking Corpn (formed by merger of Sakura Bank and Sumitomo Bank) 2001–02, Sr Man. Dir 2002–03, Sr Man. Dir Sumitomo Mitsui Financial Group, Inc. (holding co. of Sumitomo Mitsui Banking Corpn) 2003–04, Deputy Pres. 2004–05, Pres. and Rep. Dir 2005–, also Chair. and Rep. Dir Sumitomo Mitsui Banking Corpn. *Address:* Sumitomo Mitsui Financial Group, Inc., 1-2, Yurakucho 1-Chome, Chiyoda-ku, Tokyo 100-0006, Japan (office). *Telephone:* (3) 5512-3411 (office). *Fax:* (3) 5512-4429 (office). *E-mail:* info@smfg.co.gp (office). *Website:* www.smfg.co.jp (office).

KITAYENKO, Dmitriy Georgievich; Russian conductor; b. 18 Aug. 1940, Leningrad; ed Leningrad Conservatory; postgrad. study Moscow Conservatory (under Khazanov and Ginzburg); further study at Acad. of Music, Vienna 1966–67; conductor, Nemirovich-Danchenko Theatre 1969–, prin. conductor 1970–76; chief conductor, Moscow Philharmonic 1976–89; numerous appearances in Europe and USA; teacher at Moscow Conservatory 1969–, Prof. 1986–90; Music Dir, Frankfurt Radio Orchestra 1990–95; apptd Conductor, Bern Symphony Orchestra 1994; Perm. Conductor, Music Adviser, Bergen Philharmonic Orchestra 1991–; USSR People's Artist 1984; RSFSR State Prize 1988. *Address:* Chalet Kalimor, 1652 Botterens, Switzerland (home).

KITBUNCHU, HE Cardinal Michael Michai; Thai ecclesiastic; *Archbishop of Bangkok;* b. 25 Jan. 1929, Samphran, Nakhon Pathom; ordained priest, Bangkok 1959; Archbishop of Bangkok 1973–; elevated to Cardinal, apptd Cardinal-Priest of S. Lorenzo in Panisperna 1983. *Address:* Assumption Cathedral, 40 Thanon Charoenkrung, Bangrak, Bangkok 10500 (office); Bishop's Conference of Thailand, 122/6-7 Soi Naaksuwan, Thanon Nonsi, Yannawa, Bangkok 10120, Thailand. *Telephone:* (2) 233-8712 (office); (2) 681-5361. *Fax:* (2) 237-1033 (office); (2) 681-5370. *E-mail:* cbct@ksc.th.com (office).

KITE, Thomas (Tom) O., Jr; American professional golfer; b. 9 Dec. 1949, Austin, Tex.; m. Christy Kite; two s. one d.; ed Univ. of Texas; won Walker Cup 1971; professional golfer, PGA 1972–2000; won Ryder Cup 1979, 1981, 1983, 1985, 1987, 1989, 1993, European Open 1980, US Open, Pebble Beach, Calif. 1992; LA Open 1993; 14 US PGA Tour wins; apptd Capt. US team for 1997 Ryder Cup, Valderrama, Spain; joined Sr PGA Tour 2000, wins include The Countryside Tradition 2000, MasterCard Championship 2002; currently plays on Champions Tour; spokesman for Chrysler Jr Golf Scholarship program; f. Tom Kite Design (golf course design co.); Bob Jones Award 1979, Player of the Year (Golf Writers) 1981, 1989, Vardon Trophy 1981, 1982, PGA Player of the Year 1989, elected to World Golf Hall of Fame 2004. *Leisure interest:* landscaping. *Address:* c/o PGA Tour, 112 Tpc Boulevard Ponte Vedra Beach, FL 32082, USA. *Telephone:* (512) 983-5483. *E-mail:* info@tomkitedesign.com.

KITONGA, Nzamba; Kenyan senior counsel and judge; *President, Court of Justice, Common Market for Eastern and Southern Africa (COMESA);* b. 1956; fmr Chair. Law Soc. of Kenya; fmr Pres. and Chair. East African Law Soc.; fmr Vice-Chair. Goldenberg Comm. of Inquiry; Judge of Appellate Div., Common Market for Eastern and Southern Africa (COMESA) Court of Justice 2005–, Pres. Court of Justice 2005–. *Address:* COMESA Secretariat, Ben Bella Road, PO Box 30051, 101101 Lusaka, Zambia (office). *Telephone:* (1) 229725 (office). *Fax:* (1) 225107 (office). *E-mail:* comesa@comesa.int (office). *Website:* www.comesa.int (office).

KITSIKIS, Dimitri, MA, PhD, FRSC; Canadian/French/Greek poet, historian and academic; *Professor Emeritus, Department of History, University of* Ottawa; b. 2 June 1935, Athens, Greece; s. of the late Nikolas Kitsikis and Beata Petychakis; m. 1st Anne Hubbard 1955 (divorced 1973); one s. one d.; m. 2nd Ada Nikolaros 1975; one s. one d.; ed American Coll. Athens, Ecole des Roches, Normandy, Lycée Lakanal and Lycée Carnot, Paris and Sorbonne, Paris; Research Assoc. Grad. Inst. of Int. Studies, Geneva 1960–62, Centre for Int. Relations, Nat. Foundation of Political Science, Paris 1962–65, Nat. Centre for Scientific Research, Paris 1965–70; Assoc. Prof. of History of Int. Relations, Univ. of Ottawa 1970–83, Prof. 1983–96, Emer. Prof. 1996–; Sr Research Scholar, Nat. Centre of Social Research, Athens 1972–74; Founder, Ed. Intermediate Region (journal) 1996–; adviser to Govts of Greece and Turkey; numerous visiting professorships and other appointments; f. Dimitri Kitsikis Public Foundation and Library, Athens 2006; First Prize in Poetry, Abdi Ipekçi Peace and Friendship Prize 1992. *Publications include:* 34 books including, Propaganda and Pressure in International Politics 1963, The Role of the Experts at the Paris Peace Conference of 1919 1972, A Comparative History of Greece and Turkey in the 20th Century 1978, History of the Greek-Turkish Area 1981, The Ottoman Empire 1985, The Third Ideology and Orthodoxy 1990, The Old Calendarists 1995, Turkish-Greek Empire 1996, The Byzantine Model of Government 2001, J.-J. Rousseau and the French Origins of Fascism 2006, Bektashism and Alevism 2006, A Comparative History of Greece and China 2007; co-author of 35 other books; six vols of poetry, including Omphalos 1977, L'Orocc dans l'age de Kali 1985, Le Paradis Perdu sur les Barricades 1993, two vols of poetry and painting; more than 150 scholarly articles. *Leisure interests:* art, science fiction, study of languages. *Address:* Department of History, University of Ottawa, ON K1N 6N5, Canada (office); Dimitri Kitsikis Foundation, Hagiou Ioannou Theologou 22, Zographou, Athens 15772, Greece (office); 2104 Benjamin Avenue, Ottawa, ON K2A 1P4, Canada (home); 29 Travlantoni, Zographou, Athens 15772, Greece (home). *Telephone:* (613) 562-5735 (Ottawa) (office); (210) 778-0225 (Athens) (office); (613) 729-9814 (Ottawa) (home); (210) 777-6937 (Athens) (home); (27310) 83096 (Pikoulianika, Greece) (home); 1-40-31-32-34 (Paris) (home); (613) 834-4634 (Ottawa) (home). *Fax:* (613) 562-5995 (Ottawa) (office). *E-mail:* dimitri.kitsikis@uottawa.ca (office); dkitsiki@rogers.com (home). *Website:* ca .geocities.com/dimitri-kitsikis@rogers.com (office).

KITTEL, Charles, PhD; American physicist, academic and writer; *Professor Emeritus, Department of Physics, University of California, Berkeley;* b. 18 July 1916, New York; s. of George Paul Kittel and Helen Kittel; m. Muriel Agnes Lister 1938; two s. one d.; ed Massachusetts Inst. of Tech., Univ. of Cambridge, UK and Univ. of Wisconsin; Prof. of Physics, Univ. of California, Berkeley 1951–78, Prof. Emer. 1978–; mem. NAS, American Acad. of Arts and Sciences; Buckley Prize for Solid State Physics, Berkeley Distinguished Teaching Award, Oersted Medal, American Asscn of Physics Teachers. *Publications:* Quantum Theory of Solids 1963, Thermal Physics 1980, Introduction to Solid State Physics 1996. *Leisure interests:* friends, wine. *Address:* Department of Physics, University of California, 559 Birge, Berkeley, CA 94720-7300, USA (office). *Telephone:* (510) 643-9473 (office). *E-mail:* kittel@berkeley.edu (office). *Website:* www.physics.berkeley.edu (office).

KITTIKHOUN, Alounkèo; Laotian diplomatist; *Assistant Minister of Foreign Affairs;* b. 10 Oct. 1951, Pakse, Champasark; m. Dr Kongpadith Kittikhoun; two s.; ed Royal Inst. of Law and Admin, Vientiane, Univ. of Paris I (Panthéon-Sorbonne), Int. Inst. of Public Admin, Paris, France; joined Foreign Ministry 1977; Second Sec., then First Sec. and Counsellor, Perm. Mission to UN 1980–90, Perm. Rep. 1993–2007; Chair. Landlocked Developing Countries Group at the UN 1999–2003 and of numerous other UN bodies and cttees; Deputy Dir Dept of Int. Orgs, Foreign Ministry 1990–92, Dir 1992–93; Assistant Minister of Foreign Affairs 2007–. *Leisure interests:* golf, reading, eating, relaxing with family. *Address:* Ministry of Foreign Affairs, rue That Luang 01004, Ban Phonxay, Vientiane, Laos (office). *Telephone:* (21) 413148 (office). *Fax:* (21) 414009 (office). *E-mail:* cabinet@mofa.gov.la (office); alkktk@hotmail.com (home). *Website:* www.mofa.gov.la (office).

KITZHABER, John Albert, BS, MD; American physician, academic and fmr politician; *President, Estes Park Institute;* b. 5 March 1947, Colfax, WA; s. of Albert Raymond Kitzhaber and Annabel Reed Wetzel; ed Dartmouth Coll. and Univ. of Ore.; intern Gen. Rose Memorial Hosp., Denver 1976–77; Emergency Physician Mercy Hosp., Roseburg, Ore. 1974–75; mem. Ore. House of Reps 1979–81, Ore. Senate 1981–95, Pres. 1985, 1987, 1989, 1991; Gov. of Ore. 1995–2003; Pres. Estes Park Inst. 2003–Pres. The Kitzhaber Center, Lewis and Clark Law School 2005–; Assoc. Prof., Ore. Health & Science Univ. 1986–, now also Dir for the Center for Evidence Based Policy; Chair on Health Care Policy with Foundation for Medical Excellence; f. Archimedes Movt 2006–; mem. American Coll. of Emergency Physicians, Physicians for Social Responsibility, American Council of Young Political Leaders; Democrat. *Address:* The Archimedes Movement, c/o The Foundation for Medical Excellence, 1 SW Columbia, Suite 860, Portland, OR 97258, USA (office). *Telephone:* (503) 709-8574 (office). *E-mail:* kitz@wecandobetter.org (office). *Website:* wecandobetter.org (office); www.estespark.org (office).

KITZINGER, Sheila Helena Elizabeth, MBE, MLitt; British birth educator, writer, social anthropologist and lecturer; b. 29 March 1929, Taunton, Somerset; d. of Alex Webster and Clare Webster; m. Uwe Kitzinger (q.v.) 1952; five d.; ed Bishop Fox's Girls' School, Taunton, Ruskin Coll. and St Hugh's Coll., Oxford; Research Asst Dept of Anthropology, Univ. of Edin. 1952–53; Course Team Chair. Open Univ. 1981–83; Man. Cttee Midwives' Information and Resource Service 1985–87, Editorial Cttee 1987–; Chair. Steering Cttee Int. Homebirth Movt; mem. Bd Int. Caesarean Awareness Network; Consultant, Int. Childbirth Educ. Asscn; Adviser, Baby Milk Coalition, Maternity Alliance; Patron of the Seattle School of Midwifery; Dir Birth Crisis Network; frequent appearances internationally on TV and film productions on midwifery educational and health-care activism, internationally; Hon. Prof., Thames Valley Univ. 1993–; Hon. Pres. Birth Companions; Joost de Blank Award for Research 1971–73. *Publications:* The Experience of Childbirth 1962, Education and Counselling for Childbirth 1977, Women as Mothers 1978, The Place of Birth (co-ed. with John Davis) 1978, Birth at Home 1979, The Good Birth Guide 1979, The Experience of Breastfeeding 1979, Pregnancy and Childbirth 1980, Some Women's Experiences of Episiotomy (with Rhiannon Walters) 1981, 1983, Episiotomy: physical and emotional aspects 1981, The New Good Birth Guide 1983, Women's Experience of Sex 1983, (ed. with Penny Simkin) Episiotomy and the Second Stage of Labor 1984, Being Born 1986, Celebration of Birth 1987, Freedom and Choice in Childbirth 1987, Some Women's Experiences of Epidurals 1987, Giving Birth: How it Really Feels 1987, The Midwife Challenge (ed.) 1988, The Crying Baby 1989, Breastfeeding Your Baby 1989, Talking with Children about Things that Matter (with Celia Kitzinger) 1989, Pregnancy Day by Day (with Vicky Bailey) 1990, Homebirth and Other Alternatives to Hospital 1991, Ourselves as Mothers 1993, Birth over Thirty-Five 1994, The Year after Childbirth 1994, The New Pregnancy and Childbirth 1997, Becoming a Grandmother 1997, Breastfeeding 1998, Rediscovering Birth 2000, Midwifery Guidelines on Water Birth (with Ethel Burns) 2000, Birth Your Way: Choosing Birth at Home or in a Birth Centre 2002, Pregnancy and Childbirth: Choices and Challenges 2003, The New Experience of Childbirth 2004, The Politics of Birth 2005, Understanding Your Crying Baby 2005, Birth Crisis 2006. *Leisure interest:* painting. *Address:* The Manor, Standlake, Oxon., OX29 7RH, England. *Telephone:* (1865) 300266. *Fax:* (1865) 300438. *E-mail:* sheila@sheilakitzinger.com (home). *Website:* www.sheilakitzinger.com (office).

KITZINGER, Uwe, CBE, MLitt, MA; British academic; b. 12 April 1928, Nuremberg, Germany; s. of the late Dr G. and Lucy Kitzinger; m. Sheila Helena Elizabeth Webster (Sheila Kitzinger (q.v.)) 1952; five d.; ed Watford Grammar School, Balliol and New Colls, Oxford; Foundation Scholar, New Coll., Oxford; Pres. of Oxford Union 1950; Econ. Section, Council of Europe 1951–58; Research Fellow, Nuffield Coll., Oxford 1956–62, Official Fellow and Investment Bursar 1962–76, Emer. Fellow 1976–; Dean, European Inst. of Business Admin. (INSEAD), Fontainebleau 1976–80; Dir Oxford Centre for Man. Studies 1980–84; first Pres. Templeton Coll., Oxford 1984–91; Founding Ed., Journal of Common Market Studies 1962–; Visiting Prof. Univ. of West Indies 1964–65; Visiting Prof. of Govt and Assoc., Centre for Int. Affairs, Harvard 1969–70; Visiting Prof. Univ. of Paris VIII 1970–73; Adviser to the late Lord Soames (Vice-Pres. Comm. of the European Communities), Brussels 1973–75; Sr Research Fellow Atlantic Council 1993–; Visiting Scholar Harvard Univ. 1993–; Founding Chair. Cttee on Atlantic Studies 1967–70; Founding Chair. Major Projects Asscn 1981–86; Pres. Int. Asscn of Macro-Eng Socs. 1987–92, 1996–, Féd. Britannique des Alliances Françaises 1998–2004; Council mem. European Movt 1974–76, Royal Inst. of Int. Affairs 1976–85, Oxfam 1981–84, Fondation Jean Monnet 1990–; Chair. Oxfordshire Radio Ltd 1988; mem. Conflict Man. Group, Cambridge, Mass., Inst. for Transition to Democracy, Zagreb, Asian Disaster Preparedness Centre, Bangkok; co-f. Lentils for Dubrovnik 1991; Hon. Fellow, Templeton Coll. 2001; Order of Morning Star (Croatia) 1997; Hon. LLD 1986. *Publications:* German Electoral Politics 1960, The Challenge of the Common Market 1961, Britain, Europe and Beyond 1964, The Second Try 1968, Diplomacy and Persuasion 1973, Europe's Wider Horizons 1975, The 1975 Referendum (with David Butler) 1976, Macro-Engineering and the Earth (jt ed. with Ernst Frankel) 1998. *Leisure interest:* cruising under sail. *Address:* The Manor, Standlake, Oxon., England; La Rivière, 11100 Bages d'Aude, France. *Telephone:* (1865) 300702 (England) (office); (1865) 300266 (England) (home); 4-68-41-70-13 (France). *Fax:* (1865) 300702 (England); 4-68-41-70-13 (France). *E-mail:* kitzing@fas.harvard.edu (office); uwe_kitzinger@yahoo.com (home).

KIVEJINJA, Kirunda; Ugandan politician; *Minister of Internal Affairs;* mem. Parl. (Nat. Resistance Movt —NRM) for Bugweri –2007; Minister of Transport and Communications –1999 (resgnd), Minister in charge of the Presidency 2003, Third Deputy Prime Minister and Minister of Information and Nat. Guidance 2006–09; Minister of Internal Affairs 2009–; Dir of External Affairs, NRM Secr. 1999–2003. *Address:* Ministry of Internal Affairs, Plot 75 Jinja Road, POB 7191 Kampala, Uganda (office). *Telephone:* (41) 4231059 (office). *Fax:* (41) 4231063 (office). *E-mail:* info@mia.go.ug (office). *Website:* www.mia.go.ug (office).

KIVRIKOGLU, Gen. Huseyin; Turkish army officer; b. Dec. 1934, Bozuyuk, Bilecik; m.; one s.; ed Isiklar Mil. School, Army Acad., Army War Coll., Armed Forces Coll., NATO Defence Coll., Rome, Italy; served as platoon and battery commdr in various artillery units 1957–65, Staff Officer 9th Infantry Div. in Sarikamis 1967–70; Planning Officer, Allied Forces S Europe Operations Div., Italy 1979–72; Instructor, Army War Coll. 1972–73; Section Chief of Gen. Staff and Br. Chief of Land Forces Command; Commdr of Cadet Regt, Army Acad., Ankara 1978–80; rank of Brig.-Gen. 1980; Chief of Operations Centre, Supreme HQ Allied Powers in Europe (SHAPE), Belgium 1980–83; Commanding Officer 3rd and 11th Brigades 1983–84; rank of Maj. Gen. 1984; Chief of Staff NATO Allied Land Forces SE Europe (CLSE), Izmir 1984–86; Commanding Officer 9th Infantry Div. 1986–88; rank of Lt-Gen. 1988; Asst Chief of Staff, Gen. Staff HQ; Commanding Officer 5th Corps and Under-Sec. Ministry of Nat. Defence 1990–93; promoted to Four Star 1993; Commdr CLSE 1993–96, First Army, Istanbul 1996–97, Land Forces 1997–98; C-in-C Armed Forces and Chief of Gen. Staff 1998–2002; Armed Forces Distinguished Service Medal, Grand Cross and Golden Honour Medal (Turkey), Star of Romania, Order of Merit (USA), Order of Distinction Medal (Pakistan); numerous Army Acad. Badges, NATO Service Badge, Commdr Armed Forces Identification Badge. *Address:* c/o Ministry of National Defence, Milli Savunma Bakanligi, 06100 Ankara, Turkey (office).

KIYANI, Gen. Ashfaq Pervez; Pakistani army officer; *Chief of Army Staff;* b. April 1952, Jehlum; m.; one s. one d.; ed Mil. Coll., Jhelum, Command and Staff Coll., Quetta, Command and Gen. Staff Coll., Fort Leavenworth, USA, Nat. Defence Coll., Islamabad; commissioned in Baloch Regt 1971, commanded infantry bn, infantry brigade, infantry div. and corps; Deputy Mil. Sec. for Benazir Bhutto 1988–89; fmr Dir-Gen. of Mil. Operations; Corps Commdr of Rawalpindi 2003–04; Dir-Gen. Inter-Services Intelligence 2004–07; chosen to carry out investigations of two assassination attempts on Gen. Pervaiz Musharraf; Vice-Chief of Army Staff (also promoted to four-star Gen.) Oct.–Nov. 2007, Chief of Army Staff Nov. 2007–; Pres. Pakistan Golf Fed. 2004–. *Leisure interest:* golf. *Address:* Ministry of Defence, Pakistan Secretariat, No. II, Rawalpindi 46000, Pakistan (office). *Telephone:* (51) 9271107 (office). *Fax:* (51) 9271113 (office). *E-mail:* tahir@mod.gov.pk (office).

KIYONGA, Crispus, MD; Ugandan physician and politician; *Minister of Defence;* b. Kasese; ed Johns Hopkins Univ., USA; mem. Parl. for Bukonzo West; posts have included Minister for Cooperatives and Marketing 1986, Minister of Finance 1986–92, Minister of Health –2001, Minister without Portfolio Nat. Political Commissar, Nat. Resistance Movt 2001–06, Minister of Defence 2006–; apptd Chair Transitional Working Group for Establishment of Global AIDS and Health Fund by UN Sec.-Gen. 2001. *Address:* Ministry of Defence, Bombo, POB 7069, Kampala, Uganda (office). *Telephone:* (41) 2270331 (office). *Fax:* (41) 2245911 (office). *E-mail:* spokesman@defenceuganda.mil.ug (office). *Website:* www.defenceuganda.mil.ug (office).

KIZIM, Col.-Gen. Leonid Denisovich, CandMilSc; Russian cosmonaut; b. 5 Aug. 1941, Krasny Liman, Ukraine; m.; one s. one d.; ed Chernigov Higher Mil. Aviation School, Gagarin Mil. Aircraft Acad., Mil. Gen. Staff Acad.; with cosmonaut team 1965–87; took part in space flights on Soyuz-3, orbital station Salyut-6 1980, Soyuz T-10, T-11, orbital station Salyut-7, orbital complex Mir 1984; Chair. NW Regional Br. Russian Fed. of Cosmonauts; Deputy Commdr of Space Mil. Forces, Ministry of Defence 1987–99; Head A. F. Mozhaisky Mil. Acad. of Space and Eng 1999–2001 (retd); Order of Lenin (3), other decorations. *Address:* c/o A. F. Mozhaisky Military Academy of Space Engineering, Kadetskiy Bulvar, 6/42, St. Petersburg, Russia (office).

KJAERSGAARD, Pia; Danish politician; *Chairwoman, Danish People's Party;* b. 23 Feb. 1947, Copenhagen; d. of Poul Kjaersgaard and Inge Munch Jensen; m. Henrik Thorup; two c.; ed Gentofte Lower Secondary School, Copenhagen School of Commerce; office asst for insurance and advertising co. 1963–67; home care asst 1978–84; mem. Folketing (Parl.) for Progress Party in Copenhagen Co. constituency 1984–87, in Funen Co. constituency 1987–95, for Danish People's Party in Funen Co. constituency 1995–98, in Copenhagen Co. constituency 1998–2007, in Zealand Greater constituency 2007–; Leader of Fremskridtspartiet (Progress Party) 1985–94; mem. Ministry of Justice's Road Safety Comm. 1986–87; Chair. Parl.'s Health Cttee 1988–91; mem. Council of Reps Danmarks Nationalbank 1989–96; mem. Nordic Council 1990–94, 1998–2000, Vice-Chair. Liberal Group 1990–94; Del. to 49th, 54th and 57th UN Gen. Ass., New York 1995, 2000, 2003; mem. Defence Comm. of 1997 1997–98; Progress Party cand. in Ryvang Nomination Dist 1979–81, in Ballerup and Gladsaxe Nomination Dist 1981–84, in Hvidovre Nomination Dist 1983–84, in Middelfart Nomination Dist 1984–95; Co-founder and Chair. Danish People's Party 1995–; Danish People's Party cand. in Hellerup and Gentofte Nomination Dists 1997–2000, in Glostrup Nomination Dist 1997–2007, in Kalundborg Nomination Dist 2007–; Deputy Chair. Council of Foreign Affairs; mem. Bd Political Foreign Affairs and OSCE; mem. Comm. of the Intelligence Service, Political-Econ. Bd; mem. Justice Comm.; mem. Man. Cttee Danish-Taiwanese Asscn; Kt (First Class), Order of Dannebrog 2002; Kosan Prize 1986, Politician of the Year 1989, Golden Post Horn, Dansk Postordre Forening (Danish Mail-Order Asscn) 1992, Medal of Honour of the Friends of Overseas Chinese Asscn 1999, Special Medal of Diplomacy (Taiwan) 2003, named Politician of the Year by the Landsforeningen for Erhvervsinteresser (Nat. Asscn of Business Interests), Medal of Brilliant Star (Taiwan) 2008. *Publication:* ...men udsigten er god (...but the View is Good) 1998, Digteren og Partiformanden (co-author) 2006. *Leisure interests:* gardening, music, physical fitness. *Address:* Kaermindevej 31, 2820 Gentofte (home); Dansk Folkeparti, Christiansborg, 1240 Copenhagen K, Denmark (office). *Telephone:* 33-37-51-07 (office). *Fax:* 33-37-51-93 (office). *E-mail:* dfkala@ft.dk (office). *Website:* (office).

KJELLÉN, Bo, MPolSc; Swedish diplomatist; *Senior Research Fellow, Stockholm Environment Institute;* b. 8 Feb. 1933, Stockholm; s. of John Kjellen and Elsa Kjellen; m. 1st Margareta Lindblom 1959 (died 1978); m. 2nd Gia Boyd 1980; four c.; ed Univ. of Stockholm; entered Foreign Service 1957, posted to Rio de Janeiro, Brussels, Stockholm 1959–69; Prin. Pvt. Sec. to Sec.-Gen., OECD 1969–72; Deputy Head of Mission Del. to EEC, Brussels 1972–74; Amb. to Viet Nam 1974–77; Head Multilateral Dept for Devt Co-operation, Ministry of Foreign Affairs 1977–81; Under-Sec. Admin. and Personnel 1981–85; Amb. to OECD and UNESCO 1985–91; Chief Negotiator, Ministry of Environment 1991–98; Negotiator Climate Convention 1991–2001; Chair. Swedish Research Council for Environment, Agricultural Sciences and Spatial Planning 2001–04; Visiting Fellow, Tyndall Centre, Univ. of E Anglia 2003, 2005; Sr Research Fellow, Stockholm Environment Inst. 2005–; Hon. DSc (Cranfield, UK) 1997; Hon. PhD (Gothenburg) 1999; Hon. DTech (Mälardalen Univ., Sweden) 2005; Elizabeth Haub Prize for Environmental Diplomacy 1999, GEF Award for Environmental Leadership 1999. *Publications:* several articles in academic publs and in the press on environment and sustainable devt. *Address:* Stockholm Environment Institute, Kräftriket 2 B, 10691 Stockholm, Sweden (office). *Telephone:* (8) 674-74-00 (office); (18) 71-03-07 (home). *E-mail:* bo.kjellen@sei.se (office). *Website:* www.sei.se (office).

KJETSAA, Geir, DPhil; Norwegian professor of Russian literature; *Professor, University of Oslo;* b. 2 June 1937, Oslo; s. of Thorleif Kjetsaa and Marit

Kjetsaa; m. Gerd Margit 1959; one d.; ed Univ. of Oslo and Moscow State Univ., USSR; Asst Dept of Slavic and Baltic Studies, Univ. of Oslo 1966–70, Prof. 1971–; Pres. Asscn of Norwegian Slavists 1977–80, 1982–87, Asscn of Scandinavian Slavists 1984–87; Vice-Pres. Int. Dostoevsky Soc. 1983–; mem. Norwegian Acad. of Sciences and Letters 1984–; Bastian Prize 1978, Fritt Ords Honnør 2000, Premija imeni F.M. Dostoevskogo 2001, Faculty Prize 2003, Anders Jahre's Kulturpris 2004. *Publications:* Evgenij Baratynskij 1973, The Authorship of The Quiet Don 1984, Dostoevsky and His New Testament 1984, Prinadlezhnost Dostoevskomu 1986, Fyodor Dostoevsky: A Writer's Life 1987, Nikolaj Gogol: Den gåtefulle dikteren 1990, Maxim Gorki: Eine Biographie 1996, Lew Tolstoj: Dichter und Religionsphilosoph 2001, Anton Chekhov – Life and Works 2004; about 40 trans. from Russian into Norwegian including War and Peace (Leo Tolstoy). *Address:* Universitetet i Oslo, PO Box 1030, Blindern, 0315 Oslo (office); Lybekkveien 12A, 0772 Oslo, Norway (home). *Telephone:* 22856798 (office). *E-mail:* geir.kjetsaa@east.uio.no (office). *Website:* www.hf.uio.no/east (office).

KJØNSTAD, Asbjørn, DJur; Norwegian legal scholar and academic; *Professor of Social Law, University of Oslo;* b. 6 Feb. 1943, Levanger; s. of the late Arne Kjønstad and of Nelly Stavern Kjønstad; m. 1st Lise-Lena Stubberød 1971–81 (divorced); one d.; m. 2nd Ayala Orkan 1995 (divorced 2002); Legal Adviser, Nat. Insurance Admin. 1970–72; Research Fellow, Univ. of Oslo 1972–78, Prof. of Pvt. Law 1978–84, Head, Inst. of Pvt. Law 1983–84, Prof. of Social Law 1985–, Dean of Faculty of Law 1986–88, mem. Bd of Univ. of Oslo 1986–88, 1999–2001; Chair. Royal Comm. on Social Security Law 1982–90; Chair. Governmental Comm. on Co-ordination of Pension Schemes 1991–95, on Transfer of Pension Rights 1999–2000, on Industrial Injuries Compensation 2001–04; Guest Scholar Boston Univ., USA 1995–96; Guest Prof. Leuven Univ., Belgium 1997; Vice-Pres. European Inst. of Social Security 1993–97; mem. Bd Nat. Council on Tobacco and Health 1972–93, 1997–2003, Head Research Project on Tobacco Products Liability 1998–2000; Ed. Student Law Journal 1969, Norwegian Journal of Law 1991–2000, Tort Law Journal 2004–; mem. Norwegian Acad. of Science 1987; Hon. JuD (Lund Univ., Sweden) 1996; Hon. Prize Smokefree 2004. *Publications:* 45 scientific reports and books and some 190 articles on social security law, medical law and tort law including: Social Security and Compensation for Personal Injuries 1977, The Industrial Injuries Insurance 1979, Constitutional Protection of Social Security 1984, Medical Law 1987, Norwegian Social Law 1987, A Simplified National Insurance Act 1990, The National Insurance Disablement Pension 1992, Health Priority and Patient's Rights (co-ed.) 1992, Social Services and the Rule of Law (co-author) 1993, Constitutional Protection of Social Security Benefits (co-author) 1994, Aspects of Health Law (co-author) 1994, Welfare Law I (co-author) 1997, Law, Power and Poverty (co-ed.) 1997, Introduction to Social Security Law 1998, Social Security Act with commentary (ed.) 1998, European Social Security Law (ed.) 1999, Social Services and the Rule of Law (co-author) 2000, Welfare Law (Vol. I, co-author) 2000, Confidentiality About Children 2001, Welfare Law II – Social Services (co-author and co-ed.) 2003, Law and Poverty (co-author and co-ed.) 2003, The Development of Tort Law 2003, Health Law – The Legal Position of Patients and Health Workers 2005. *Leisure interests:* outdoor exercise, skiing, jogging, mountain walking. *Address:* University of Oslo, Karl Johann gs 47, PO Box 6706, 0130 Oslo (office); Lillevannsveien 37C, 0788 Oslo, Norway (home). *Telephone:* 22-85-94-80 (office); 22-13-80-75 (home). *Fax:* 22-85-94-20 (office); 22-49-64-51 (home). *E-mail:* asbjorn.kjonstad@jus.uio.no (office). *Website:* www.jus.uio.no (office).

KLACKENBERG, Dag, LLB, MBA; Swedish business executive; *Managing Director, Svensk Handel (Swedish Trade Federation);* b. 5 Jan. 1948, Stockholm; s. of Gunnar Klackenberg and Brita Klackenberg; ed Stockholm School of Econs, Stockholm Univ.; trainee, Ministry of Foreign Affairs 1974, becoming Dir-Gen. for Admin. Affairs 1993–2001; Chair. Vattenfall AB 2001–08; Man. Dir Svensk Handel (Swedish Trade Fed.) 2001–; Chair. Handelsbanken Regionbank Mellansverige 2003–07; Chair. Swedish Export Credits Guarantee Bd 2008–; mem. Bd Atrium Ljungberg Gruppen AB 2004–. *Address:* Svensk Handel, Regeringsgatan 60, 103 29 Stockholm, Sweden (office). *Telephone:* (10) 4718500 (office). *Fax:* (10) 4718665 (office). *E-mail:* dag.klackenberg@svenskhandel.se (office). *Website:* www.svenskhandel.se (office).

KLAG, Michael J., BS, MD, MPH, FACP; American epidemiologist and academic; *Dean, Bloomberg School of Public Health, Johns Hopkins University;* ed Juanita Coll., Univ. of Pennsylvania, Johns Hopkins School of Hygiene and Public Health; Asst Clinical Prof., State Univ. of New York Upstate Medical Center 1982–84; Surgeon, Commissioned Corps, US Public Health Service 1982–84; joined Johns Hopkins Hosp. staff 1987, Dir Clinical Track, Preventative Medicine Residency, Johns Hopkins Univ. School of Hygiene and Public Health 1987–88, Instructor of Medicine, Jt Appointment in Epidemiology and Health Policy and Man., Johns Hopkins Univ. School of Medicine 1987–88, Asst Prof. of Medicine 1988–92, Assoc. Prof. 1992–97, Prof. 1998, Acting Dir Div. of Gen. Internal Medicine, Dept of Medicine, Johns Hopkins Univ. School of Medicine 1994–96, Dir 1996–2002, Assoc. Dir for Gen. Medicine 1996–2001, Interim Dir Dept of Medicine 2000–01, Vice Dean for Clinical Investigation 2001–05 Interim Dir Welch Center for Prevention, Epidemiology and Clinical Research, Johns Hopkins Medical Insts 1996–97 Interim Physician-in-Chief, Johns Hopkins Hosp. 2000–01, Dean, Johns Hopkins Bloomberg School of Public Health 2005–; Dir Precursors Study 1988–; Fellow, American Coll. of Physicians; mem. American Heart Asscn; David M. Levine Excellence in Mentoring Award 2003, Champion of Public Health Award 2004. *Publications:* more than 120 articles. *Address:* Johns Hopkins Bloomberg School of Public Health, 615 North Wolfe Street, Baltimore, MD 21205, USA (office). *Telephone:* (410) 955-3540 (office). *Fax:* (410) 955-0121 (office). *E-mail:* mklag@jhsph.edu (office). *Website:* faculty.jhsph.edu (office).

KLAMMER, Franz; Austrian fmr skier; b. 3 Dec. 1953, Mooswald; m.; two d.; 26 World Cup race wins, including downhill titles 1975, 1976, 1977, 1978, 1983; gold medal, downhill race, Winter Olympics 1976; retd from skiing 1985; took up car racing; won European Championship Touring Car race, Nurburgring, Germany; f. Franz Klammer Foundation; UN Goodwill Amb.; mem. Laureus World Sports Acad. *Leisure interests:* golf. *Address:* Franz Klammer Foundation, Singerstrasse 27/17, 1010 Vienna, Austria. *Telephone:* 699-100-25-735. *Fax:* (1) 479-90-55. *E-mail:* charity@franzklammerfoundation.com. *Website:* www.franzklammerfoundation.com.

KLAS, Eri; Estonian conductor; b. 7 June 1939, Tallinn; s. of Eduard Klas and Anna Klas; m.; one d.; ed Tallinn State Conservatory, studied at Leningrad State Conservatory with Nikolai Rabinovich; percussionist, Estonian State Symphony Orchestra 1959–65; Asst Conductor to Boris Khaikin Bolshoi Theatre, Moscow 1969–72; Conductor Orchestra of Estonian Radio 1964–70; Conductor Nat. Opera Theatre Estonia 1965–94, Music Dir 1975–94, Laureate Conductor 1994–; conducted more than 100 symphony orchestras in 40 different countries; Music Dir Royal Opera, Stockholm 1985–89; Prin. Guest Conductor Finnish Nat. Opera 1990–; Chief Conductor Århus Symphony Orchestra, Denmark 1991–96; Prof., Sibelius Acad. Helsinki 1994–; Music Dir Orchestra of Dutch Radio 1996–; Artistic Dir and Prin. Conductor Tampere Philharmonic Orchestra 1998–; Musical Adviser, Israel Sinfonietta 1999–; Chair. Bd Estonia Nat. Cultural Foundation 1991–; conducted at the Nobel Prize Ceremonial Concert in Stockholm 1989; Order of Nordstjernen (Sweden), Order of the Finnish Lion, Order of the White Star (Estonia); Dr hc (Estonian Acad. of Music) 1994. *Repertoire includes:* more than 50 operas, operettas, musicals and ballets. *Address:* Nurme str. 54, 11616 Tallinn, Estonia. *Telephone:* (2) 504-3444. *Website:* www.erkf.ee (office).

KLASSEN, Cindy; Canadian speed skater; b. 12 Aug. 1979, Winnipeg, Man.; ed Mennonite Brethren Collegiate Inst., Winnipeg; began sports career as ice hockey player; played for Canadian Nat. Youth Team; switched to speed skating when she failed to be selected for Winter Olympics in 1998; bronze medal, 3000m, Winter Olympics, Salt Lake City 2002; World All-round Champion 2003; missed 2003–04 season due to serious injury; gold medal, 1500m and 3000m, World Single Distance Championships 2005; silver medal, World All-round Championships 2005; gold medal, 1500m, Winter Olympics, Turin 2006, silver medal, 1000m and Team Pursuit, bronze medal, 3000m and 5000m; World All-round Champion 2006; holder of world records at 1000m, 1500m and 3000m distances; Canada's all-time most decorated Olympian (five gold and one bronze medals); named flag-bearer for closing ceremony of Winter Olympics at Turin 2006, Lou Marsh Award as Canadian Athlete of the Year, Toronto Star 2006, Bobbie Rosenfeld Award as Canadian Female Athlete of the Year 2005, 2006. *Address:* c/o Landmark Sport Group, 1 City Centre Drive, Suite 605, Mississauga, ON L5B 1M2, Canada. *Telephone:* (905) 949-1910. *Fax:* (905) 949-4984. *E-mail:* admin@landmarksport.com (office). *Website:* www.cindyklassen.com (office).

KLATTEN, Susanne, BSc, MBA; German business executive; *Deputy Chairwoman, Supervisory Board, Altana AG;* b. (Susanne Quandt), 28 April 1962, Bad Homburg; d. of Herbert Quandt and Johanna Quandt; m. Jan Klatten; three c.; ed Univ. of Buckingham, UK, Int. Inst. for Man. Devt, Lausanne, Switzerland; trained as advertising exec.; man. asst Burda GmbH 1989–90; work experience in USA 1991; inherited share of BMW Group and majority of shares of Altana AG; mem. Bd of Dirs BMW Group 1997–, Byk Gulden Lomberg GmbH; Deputy Chair. Supervisory Bd Altana AG; Chair. Bd of Counsellors Herbert Quandt Foundation, Bad Homburg; ranked by Forbes magazine amongst 100 Most Powerful Women (41st) 2004, (71st) 2005. *Address:* Altana AG, Herbert-Quandt-Haus, Am Pilgerrain 15, 61352 Bad Homburg, Germany (office). *Telephone:* (6172) 17120 (office). *Fax:* (6172) 1712365 (office). *Website:* www.altana.de (office).

KLAUS, Václav, PhD; Czech politician, economist and head of state; *President;* b. 19 June 1941, Prague; s. of Václav Klaus and Marie Klausová; m. Livia Klausová 1968; two s.; ed Prague School of Econs, Cornell Univ., Czech Acad. of Sciences; researcher, Inst. of Econs Czechoslovak Acad. of Sciences –1970; various positions Czechoslovak State Bank 1971–86; head Dept of Macroeconomic Policy, Inst. of Forecasting, Acad. of Sciences 1987–; f. Civic Forum Movt (Chair. 1990–91); Minister of Finance 1989–92; Chair. Civic Democratic Party 1991–2002; Deputy Prime Minister 1991–92; Prime Minister of the Czech Republic 1992–97; Chair. State Defence Council 1993–97; Chair. Govt Cttee for Integration of Czech Repub. in NATO 1997; Chair. Chamber of Deputies 1998–2002; Pres. of Czech Republic 2003–; serves as a Nat. Centre for Policy Analysis Distinguished Leader; mem. Scientific Council, Palacký Univ. 1997–; Hon. Prof. Univ. Guadalajara 1993; Hon. Chair. ODS (Civic Democratic Party) 2002–; Hon. DHumLitt (Suffolk Univ.) 1991, Dr hc (Rochester Inst. of Tech.) 1991, (Univ. Francisco Marroquín, Guatemala) 1993, (Jacksonville, USA) 1995, (Buckingham, UK) 1996, (Prague School of Econs) 1994, (Belgrano Univ., Argentina) 1994, (Tufts Univ., USA) 1994, (Univ. of Aix-Marseilles) 1994, (Tech. Univ. of Ostrava) 1997, (Toronto, Canada) 1997, (Arizona) 1997, (Dallas) 1999, (Chicago) 1999; Schumpeter Prize for Econs, Freedom Award (New York) 1990, Max Schmidheiny Freedom Prize, St Gallen 1992, Ludwig Erhard Prize, Germany 1993, Poeutinger Collegium Prize 1993, Hermann Lindrath Prize (Hanover) 1993, Konrad Adenauer Prize (Prague) 1993, Club of Europe Award 1994, Prix Transition (Fondation du Forum Universal) 1994, Adam Smith Award (Libertas, Copenhagen) 1995, Int. Democracy Medal (Center for Democracy, Washington, DC) 1995, Transatlantic Leadership Award (European Inst., Washington, DC) 1995, Prognos Award (Prognos Forum, Basel) 1995, James Madison Award (James Madison Inst., Jacksonville, USA) 1995, Karel Engliš Prize (Universitas Masarykiana Foundation, Brno) 1995, European Prize for Craftsmanship, Germany 1996, Goldwater Medal for Econ. Freedom, Phoenix, USA 1997, Bernhard Harms Medal (Kiel Inst. of World Econs) 1999. *Publications:* A Road to Market Economy 1991, Tomorrow's Challenge 1991, Economic Theory and Economic Reform 1991, Why am I a Conservative? 1992, Dismantling Socialism: A Road to Market Economy II 1993, The Year–How much is it in the History of the Country? 1993, The Czech Way 1994, Rebirth of a Country: Five Years After 1994, Counting Down to One 1995, Between the Past and the Future: Philosophical Reflections and Essays 1996, The Defence of Forgotten Ideas 1997, Tak pravil Václav Klaus (So Said Václav Klaus, conversations with J. Klusáková), Why I Am Not a Social Democrat 1998, Země, kde se již dva roky nevládne (The Land that has not been Governed for 2 years) 1999, Cesta z pasti (The Way Out of the Trap) 1999 From the Opposition Treaty to the Tolerance Patent 2000, Evropa pohledem politika a pohledem ekonoma (Europe, The View of the Politician and the View of the Economist) 2001, Conversations with Václav Klaus 2001, Klaus v Bruselu (Klaus in Brussels) 2001, On the Road to Democracy–The Czech Republic From Communism to Free Society 2005; numerous articles. *Leisure interests:* tennis, skiing, basketball, volleyball, jazz, music, reading fiction. *Address:* Office of the President, Pražský hrad, 119 08 Prague 1, Czech Republic (office). *Telephone:* 224371111 (office). *Fax:* 224373300 (office). *E-mail:* ladislav.jakl@hrad.cz (office). *Website:* www.hrad.cz (office); www.klaus.cz (home).

KLAVER, Piet C.; Dutch business executive; *Member, Supervisory Board, SHV Holdings NV;* b. 1945; Chair. Makro Group –2006; Chair. of Exec. Bd, SHV Holdings NV 1998–2006, now mem. Supervisory Bd; mem. Int. Advisory Bd RAI Foundation, Advisory Bd KidsRights; mem. Supervisory Bd ING Group 2006–, Jaarbeurs Holding B.V.; mem. Bd of Dirs Stichting Maatschappij en Onderneming (SMO); Chair. African Parks Foundation, Utrecht School of Arts; mem. Bd of Recommendation, BIG Int. Study Project, Univ. of Groningen. *Address:* SHV Holdings NV, Rijnkade 1, 3511 LC Utrecht, The Netherlands (office). *Telephone:* (30) 2338833 (office). *Fax:* (30) 2338304 (office). *E-mail:* info@shv.nl (office). *Website:* www.shv.nl (office).

KLEBANOV, Ilya Iosifovich; Russian politician; *Presidential Envoy to the Northwest Federal District;* b. 7 May 1951, Leningrad; m. Yevgenya Yakovlevna Klebanova; one s. one d.; ed Leningrad Polytech. Inst.; Eng electrophysicist Electron scientific production unit 1974–77; engineer, then Sr master, Head of Construction Bureau, later Head of Div. Leningrad Optical-Mechanical Complex (LOMO) 1977–92, Dir-Gen. 1992–97; First Vice-Gov. St Petersburg 1997–98; Deputy Chair. of Russian Govt 1999–2002, Minister of Industry, Science and Tech. (Minpromnauki) 2001–03; Presidential Envoy to the NW Fed. Dist 2003–; mem. Russian Security Council 2003–. *Leisure interest:* classical music. *Address:* Office of the Plenipotentiary Representative of the President, Shpalernaya str. 47, 193015 St Petersburg, Russia (office). *Telephone:* (495) 206-65-50 (office). *Fax:* (812) 323-75-87 (office). *E-mail:* szfo@saint-petersburg.ru (office).

KLEBE, Giselher; German composer; b. 28 June 1925, Mannheim; s. of Franz Klebe and Gertrud Michaelis Klebe; m. Lore Schiller 1946; two d.; ed Berlin Conservatoire and with Boris Blacher; Composer in Berlin until 1957; Prof. of Composition and Theory of Music, Nordwestdeutsche Musik-Akad., Detmold 1957–; mem. Acad. of Arts, Berlin and Hamburg, Bavarian Acad. of Fine Arts 1978; Pres. Berlin Acad. of Arts 1986–89; Bundesverdienstkreuz (1st Class) 1975, Grosses Bundesverdienstkreuz 1999; Berliner Kunstpreis 1952, Preis Musik im XX Jahrhundert, Rome 1954, Mauricio Fürst Prize (Sweden) 1959, Rompreis Villa Massimo 1962, Premio Marzotto, Valdiagno 1964. *Principal works:* operas: Die Räuber (Schiller) 1957, Die tödlichen Wünsche (Balzac) 1959, Die Ermordung Cäsars (Shakespeare) 1959, Alkmene (Kleist) 1961, Figaro lässt sich scheiden (Ödön von Horvath) 1963, Jacobowsky und der Oberst (Werfel) 1965, Das Märchen von der Schönen Lilie (nach Goethe) 1969, Ein wahrer Held (Synge/Böll) 1975, Das Mädchen aus Domrémy (Schiller) 1976, Rendezvous (Sostshenkov) 1977, Der jüngste Tag (Ödön von Horwath) 1980, Die Fastnachtsbeichte (nach Zuckmayer) 1983, Gervaise Macquart (after Zola) 1995, Chlestakows Wiederkehr (after Gogol) 2008; ballets: Signale 1955, Menagerie 1958, Das Testament (nach F. Villon) 1970; orchestral works: Zwitschermaschine 1950, Deux Nocturnes 1952, 7 symphonies 1952, 1953, 1967, 1971, 1977, 1995, 2003, Adagio und Fuge (with theme from Wagner's Walküre) 1962, Herzschläge (for Beatband and Symphony Orchestra), Konzert für Cembalo mit elektrischen Klangveränderungen und kleines Orchester 1972, Orpheus (Dramatic scenes for orchestra) 1976, Salutations 1981, Boogie Agitato 1981, Concerto for clarinet and orchestra op. 92; songs: Fünf Lieder 1962, Vier Vocalisen für Frauenchor 1963, La Tomba di Igor Stravinsky (for oboe and chamber orch.) 1979, Concerto for organ and orchestra 1980, Concerto for harp and orchestra 1988, Concerto for cello and orchestra 1989, Poema Drammatico 1999, Mignon, concerto for violin and orchestra 2000; church music: Missa (Miserere Nobis) 1964, Stabat Mater 1964, Messe (Gebet einer armen Seele) 1966, Beuge dich, du Menschenseele (after S. Lagerlöf) for baritone and organ, Choral und Te deum for solo soprano, choir and orchestra 1978, Weihnachtsoratorium 1989; chamber music: Three String Quartets 1949, 1963, 1981, Two Solo Violin Sonatas 1952 and 1955, Two Sonatas for Violin and Piano 1953 and 1974, 'Römische Elegien' 1953, Piano Trio Elegia Appassionata 1955, Introitus, Aria et Alleluja for Organ 1964, Quintet for Piano and Strings quasi una fantasia 1967, Fantasie und Lobpreisung (for organ) 1970, Variationen über ein Thema von Hector Berlioz (for organ and three drummers) 1970, Sonate für Kontrabass und Klavier 1974, 'Nenia' for solo violin 1975, Der Dunkle Gedanke for clarinets and piano 1980, Klavierstücke für Sonya (piano) 1980, Feuersturz für Klavier (Op. 91) 1983, Otto canti con rime di Michelangelo 2000, Poema Drammatico, Concerto per due pianoforti ed orchestra (Op. 130) 2000, Poema Lirico per violino e pianoforte con orchestra d'archi (Op. 136) 2001, Dorneukrőning after Tizian (for mezzo-soprano and orchestra) 2003. *Leisure interest:* photography. *Address:* Bruchstrasse 16, 32756 Detmold, Germany (home). *Telephone:* (30) 3900070 (office); (5231) 23414 (home).

KLEIN, Calvin Richard; American fashion designer; b. 19 Nov. 1942, Bronx, New York; s. of Leo Klein and Flore Klein (née Stern); m. 1st Jayne Centre 1964 (divorced 1974); one d.; m. 2nd Kelly Rector 1986 (divorced 2006); ed Fashion Inst. of Tech., New York and High School of Art and Design; started fashion business 1968; Pres./Designer Calvin Klein Ltd 1968–2002 (co. sold to Phillips-Van Heusen Corpn); Consultant Fashion Inst. of Tech. 1975–; mem. Council of Fashion Designers; Coty Award 1973, 1974, 1975; Coty Hall of Fame, FIT Pres.'s Award, Outstanding Design Council of Fashion Designers of America (four womenswear, two menswear). *Address:* c/o Calvin Klein, Phillips-Van Heusen Corporation, 200 Madison Avenue, New York, NY 10016, USA. *Website:* www.calvinklein.com.

KLEIN, George, MD, DSc, PhD; Swedish tumour biologist; *Research Group Leader, Microbiology and Tumour Biology Centre, Karolinksa Institute;* b. 28 July 1925, Budapest, Hungary; s. of Henrik Klein and Ilona Engel; m. Eva Fischer 1947; one s. two d.; ed medical schools at Pécs, Szeged and Budapest, Hungary and Stockholm, Sweden; Instructor Histology, Budapest Univ. 1945, Pathology 1946; Research Fellow, Karolinska Inst. 1947–49, Asst Prof. of Cell Research 1951–57; Prof. of Tumour Biology and Head of the Dept for Tumour Biology, Karolinska Inst. Med. School, Stockholm 1957–93, Research Group Leader, Microbiology and Tumour Biology Centre, Karolinksa Inst. 1993–; Guest Investigator, Inst. for Cancer Research, Philadelphia, Pa 1950; Visiting Prof., Stanford Univ. 1961; Fogarty Scholar, NIH 1972; Dunham Lecturer, Harvard Medical School 1966; Visiting Prof., Hebrew Univ., Jerusalem 1973–93; Harvey Lecturer 1973; Donald Wae Waddel Lecturer, Univ. of Arizona 1991; mem. Scientific Advisory Council of Swedish Medical Bd, Royal Swedish Acad. of Sciences; mem. Bioethics Cttee, UNESCO; Corresp. mem. American Asscn of Cancer Research; Foreign Assoc. NAS; Fellow, New York Acad. of Science; Ed. Advances in Cancer Research; Hon. mem. American Asscn of Immunologists, of Cancer Research, French Soc. of Immunology, Hungarian Acad. of Sciences, American Acad. of Arts and Sciences; Hon. DSc (Univ. of Chicago) 1966, (Univ. of Neb.) 1991; Hon. MD (Univ. of Debrecen) 1988; Hon. PhD (Hebrew Univ., Jerusalem) 1989, (Tel-Aviv Univ.) 1994, (Osaka Univ.) 2001; Bertha Goldblatt Teplitz Award (jtly) 1960, Rabbi Shai Shacknai Prize in Tumour Immunology 1972, Bertner Award 1973, Award of American Cancer Soc. 1973, Prize of Danish Pathological Soc., Harvey Prize 1975, Prize of Cancer Research Inst. 1975, Gairdner Prize 1976, Behring Prize 1977, Annual Award Virus Cancer Program 1977, Gen. Motors Sloan Prize for Cancer Research, Björkén Award of Uppsala Univ. 1979, Award of the Santa Chiara Acad., Italy, 1979, Erik Fernström Prize (with Eva Klein) 1983, Anniversary Prize of the Swedish Med. Asscn 1983, Letterstedt Prize, Royal Swedish Acad. of Sciences 1989, Doblong Prize, Swedish Acad. of Literature 1990, Lisl and Leo Eitinger Prize, Oslo Univ. 1990, Robert Koch Gold Medal 1998, Lifetime Achievement Award, Inst. of Human Virology 1998, Brupbacher Foundation Prize, Zürich 1999, Paracelsus Medal 2001, Wick R. Williams Memorial Lecture Award 2001, Ingemar Hedenius Prize 2002, G.J. Mendel Hon. Medal for Merit in the Biological Sciences 2005, IARC Medal of Honour 2006. *Publications include:* more than 1,000 papers in fields of experimental cell research and cancer research; The Atheist and the Holy City 1990, Hack i häl på Minerva (with Lars Gyllensten) 1993, Pietà 1993, Live Now 1997, Korpens Blick 1998. *Address:* MTC, Karolinska Institutet, Box 280, 171 77 Stockholm (office); Kottlavagen 10, 181 61 Lidingo, Sweden (home). *Telephone:* (8) 728-67-30 (office). *Fax:* (8) 33-04-98 (office). *Website:* www.mtc.ki.se/groups/klein_g (office).

KLEIN, Herbert George; American journalist and fmr government official; b. (Herbert George Klein), 1 April 1918, Los Angeles; s. of George J. and Amy Cordes Klein; m. Marjorie Galbraith 1941; two d.; ed Univ. of Southern California; journalist 1940–42; USNR 1942–46; Political Reporter and News Ed., Post Advocate 1946; Feature Writer, San Diego Evening Tribune 1950, Editorial Writer 1951; Chief Editorial Writer, San Diego Union 1951, Ed. 1959; mem. office staff of Vice-Pres. Nixon 1959–60; Dir of Communications for the Exec. Branch 1969–73; publicist and press sec. for many of Richard Nixon's election campaigns; Vice-Pres. Corp. Relations Metromedia Inc. 1973–77; Pres. H.G. Klein Media Consultants 1977–80; Ed.-in-Chief, Vice-Pres. Copley Newspapers, San Diego 1980–2003; Trustee, Univ. S Calif., LA; Nat. Fellow, American Enterprise Inst., Washington, DC 2004–; Pres. Holiday Bowl (American football) 1987; Dr hc (Univ. of San Diego) 1998, (Univ. of Southern California) 2006; ASA V. Call Award, Univ. of Southern California 1982, 'Mr San Diego' 2002. *Television:* guest in numerous public affairs programmes, including Meet the Press, Face the Nation, 20-20 with Barbara Walters, Johnny Carson, Merv Griffin. *Publication:* Making It Perfectly Clear 1980. *Leisure interests:* golf, reading, gardening, spectator sports. *Address:* 750 B Street, Suite 2380, San Diego, CA 92101 (office); 5110 Saddlery Square, PO Box 8935, Rancho, Santa Fe, CA 92067, USA (home). *Telephone:* (619) 702-1141 (office). *Fax:* (619) 702-1145 (office). *E-mail:* hklein.hgk@sdcoxmail.com (office).

KLEIN, Maj.-Gen. Jacques Paul; American air force officer (retd) and international organization official; m. Dr Margrete Siebert Klein; two c.; fmr Air Force Officer (retd as Maj.-Gen.); joined Foreign Service in Operations Center of Exec. Secr. of Sec. of State 1971; Consular Officer, Consulate-Gen., Bremen; Political Officer, Office of Southern European Affairs, Dept of State; Counsellor Officer, Berlin; Political Officer, Embassy in Bonn; Man. Analysis Officer, Office of Dir-Gen. of Foreign Service; seconded to Dept of Defense as Adviser on Int. Affairs to Sec. of Air Force with rank of Deputy Asst Sec.; Dir Office of Strategic Tech. Matters, Bureau of Politico-Mil. Affairs, Dept of State; Asst Deputy Under-Sec. of Air Force for Int. Affairs, Dept of Defense 1989–90; Prin. Adviser to Dir-Gen. Foreign Service 1990–93; Political Adviser to C-in-C, US European Command, Stuttgart 1993–96; Prin. Deputy High Rep., Bosnia and Herzegovina 1997–99; UN Transitional Admin. for Eastern Slavonia, Baranja and Western Sirmium, rank of Under-Sec.-Gen. 1996–97; Special

Rep. of Sec.-Gen. to Bosnia and Herzegovina, rank of Under-Sec.-Gen. 1999–2003; UN Special Rep. for Liberia 2003–05; Visiting Lecturer in Int. Affairs and Frederick Schultz Visiting Prof. of Public and Int. Affairs, Woodrow Wilson School, Princeton Univ. 2005–06 (retd); mem. Cosmos Club and Army and Navy Clubs of Washington, DC, Acad. d'Alsace, Council on Foreign Relations; Grand Officer, Order of the Crown (Belgium), Grand Cross of Merit (Germany), Order of King Dmitar Zvonimir with Sash and Morning Star (Croatia), Commdr, Aeronautical Order of Merit (Brazil), Commdr, Order of the Lion (Senegal), Officier, Légion d'honneur, Kt Great Band of the Humane Order of African Redemption (Nat. Transitional Govt of Liberia); Air Force Distinguished Service Medal, Legion of Merit (with oak leaf cluster), Bronze Star, Distinguished Honor Award, Dept of State, Defense Medal for Outstanding Public Service, Dept of the Air Force Award for Exceptional and Meritorious Civilian Service. *Address:* c/o Cosmos Club, 2121 Massachusetts Avenue, NW, Washington, DC 20008, USA.

KLEIN, Jonathan D.; American business executive; *CEO, Getty Images Inc.;* b. South Africa; with Hambros Bank Ltd, London 1983–93, Dir 1989–93; Co-f. Getty Investment Holdings 1993–95; Jt Chair. Getty Communications PLC 1995–96, CEO and Dir 1996–98; co-f., CEO and Dir Getty Images 1998–; mem. Bd of Dirs Getty Investments LLC, Real Networks Inc.,, The Global Business Coalition on HIV/AIDS, Friends of the Global Fight against AIDS, Tuberculosis and Malaria; Trustee, Groton School; Int. Center of Photography Trustee's Award (with Mark Getty) 2006. *Address:* Getty Images Inc., 601 North 34th Street, Seattle, WA 98103, USA (office). *Telephone:* (206) 925-5000 (office). *Fax:* (206) 925-5001 (office). *Website:* corporate.gettyimages.com (office).

KLEIN, Lawrence Robert, PhD; American economist and academic; *Benjamin Franklin Professor Emeritus of Economics, University of Pennsylvania;* b. 14 Sept. 1920, Omaha, Neb.; s. of Leo Byron Klein and Blanche Monheit; m. Sonia Adelson 1947; one s. three d.; ed Univ. of California, Berkeley, Massachusetts Inst. of Tech., Lincoln Coll., Oxford, UK; mem. Faculty, Univ. of Chicago 1944–47; Research Assoc., Nat. Bureau of Econ. Research, Cambridge, Mass 1948–50; mem. Faculty, Univ. Michigan 1949–54; Research Assoc., Survey Research Center 1949–54; Oxford Inst. Statistics 1954–58; Prof., Univ. of Pennsylvania 1958–64, Univ. Prof. 1964–68, Benjamin Franklin Prof. 1968–, now Prof. Emer.; Visiting Prof., Osaka Univ. 1960, Univ. of Colorado 1962, CUNY 1962–63, Hebrew Univ. of Jerusalem 1964, Princeton Univ. 1966, Stanford Univ. 1968, Univ. of Copenhagen 1974; Ford Visiting Prof., Univ. of Calif., Berkeley 1968; Visiting Prof., Inst. for Advanced Studies, Vienna 1970–74; Econ. Consultant to Canadian Govt 1947, UNCTAD 1966, 1967, 1975, McMillan Co. 1965–74, E. I. du Pont de Nemours 1966–68, State of NY 1969, American Telephone and Telegraph Co. 1969, Fed. Reserve Bd 1973, UNIDO 1973–75, Congressional Budget Office 1977–82, Council of Econ. Advisers 1977–80; Adviser State Planning Comm., People's Repub. of China; Chair. Bd of Trustees, Wharton Econometrics Forecasting Assoc. Inc. 1969–80, Chair. Professional Bd 1980–92; Dir Uni-Coll Corpn; Dir W. P. Carey & Co. 1984–; Trustee, Maurice Falk Inst. for Econ. Research, Israel, 1969–75; mem. Advisory Council, Inst. for Advanced Studies, Vienna 1977–; Chair. Econ. Advisory Cttee Gov. of Pa 1976–78; mem. Cttee on Prices, Fed. Reserve Bd 1968–70; Prin. Investigator, Econometric Model Project of Brookings Inst., Washington, DC 1963–72, Project LINK 1968–, Sr Adviser Brookings Panel on Econ. Activity 1970–; coordinator Jimmy Carter's Econ. Task Force 1976; mem. Advisory Bd, Strategic Studies Center, Stanford Research Inst. 1974–76; Ed. International Economic Review 1959–65, Assoc. Ed. 1965–92; mem. Editorial Bd Empirical Economics 1976–; Fellow, Econometrics Soc., American Acad. of Arts and Sciences, NAS, Social Sciences Research Council, American Econs Asscn, Eastern Econ. Asscn; Corresp. Fellow, British Acad. 1991; Hon. Prof., Shanghai Acad. of Social Sciences 1994, Univ. of Nankai, People's Repub. of China 1993, Chinese Acad. of Social Science 2000; Hon. Fellow, Lincoln Coll. Oxford 2004; Hon. LLD (Mich.) 1977, (Dickinson) 1981, (Pennsylvania) 2006; Hon. DLitt (Glasgow) 1991; Hon. ScD (Widener Coll.) 1977; Hon. DSc (Elizabeth Town) 1981, (Ball State) 1982, (Technion) 1982, (Nebraska) 1983, (Nat. Cen., Taiwan) 1985, (Rutgers) 1991; Hon. DHumLitt (Bard) 1986, (Bilkent) 1989, (St Norbert) 1989; Hon. Dr Ed. (Villanova) 1978; Dr hc (Vienna) 1977, (Bonn, Free Univ. of Brussels, Univ. of Paris) 1979, (Madrid) 1980, (Helsinki) 1986, (Łodz) 1990, (Bar Ilan) 1994, (Carleton, Canada) 1997, (Piraeus, Greece) 2000, (Acad. of Econ. Studies, Romania) 1999, (Toronto) 2002, (Konan Univ., Japan) 2002, (Keio Univ., Japan) 2002, (Universidad del Estaod de Mexico) 2004, (Univ. of Costa Rica) 2005, (Univ. of Slovenia) 2005); J.B. Clark Medal, American Econ. Asscn 1959, William F. Butler Award, New York Asscn of Business Economists 1975; Golden Slipper Club Award 1977; Nobel Prize in Econ. Science for work on econometric models 1980. *Publications:* The Keynesian Revolution 1947, Textbook of Econometrics 1953, An Econometric Model of the United States 1929–1952 1955, Wharton Econometric Forecasting Model 1967, Essay on the Theory of Economic Prediction 1968, Brookings Quarterly Econometric Model of U.S. Econometric Model Performance (author-ed.) 1976, The Economics of Supply and Demand 1983, Lectures in Econometrics 1983, Comparative Performance of US Econometric Models 1991. *Address:* University of Pennsylvania, McNeil Building, Room 335, 3718 Locust Walk, Philadelphia, PA 19104-6297 (office); 1400 Waverly Road, B035, Gladwyne, PA 19035, USA (home). *Telephone:* (215) 898-7713 (office). *Fax:* (215) 573-2057 (office). *E-mail:* lrk@econ.upenn.edu (office). *Website:* www.econ.upenn.edu (office).

KLEIN, Michael L., BSc, PhD, FRS; British chemist and academic; *Director, Laboratory for Research on the Structure of Matter, University of Pennsylvania;* b. 13 March 1940, London; ed Univ. of Bristol; Ciba-Geigy Fellow, Univ. of Genoa, Italy 1964–65; ICI Fellow, Univ. of Bristol, Dept of Theoretical Chemistry 1965–67; Research Assoc., Rutgers Univ., Physics Dept 1967–68;

Assoc. Research Officer, Nat. Research Council of Canada, Chemistry Div., Ottawa, Canada 1968–74, Sr Research Officer 1974–85, Prin. Research Officer 1985–87; Adjunct Prof. of Physics, Univ. of Waterloo, Ont. 1977–83; Prof. of Chemistry, McMaster Univ., Ont. 1977–88; Visiting Prof., Univ. of Amsterdam, Netherlands 1985; Neel Visiting Prof., École Normale Supérieure, Lyons, France 1988; William Smith Prof. of Chemistry, Univ. of Pa 1991–93, Hepburn Prof. of Physical Science 1993, Dir, Lab. for Research on the Structure of Matter 1993–, also Dir, Center for Molecular Modelling 1995–; Visiting Prof., Univ. of Florence, Italy 1993; mem. Editorial Bd several journals including Journal of Physics Condensed Matter 1993–97, Molecular Physics 1993–99, Computational Materials Science 1993–, Journal of Chemical Physics 2003–, Chemical Physics Letters 2003–; mem. Royal Soc. of Chemistry, Faraday Div., American Chemical Soc. 1998–, American Physical Soc. 1999–, American Acad. of Arts and Science 2003–; Fellow Guggenheim Foundation 1989–90; Hon. Fellow Chemical Inst. of Canada 1979–, Royal Soc. of Canada 1984–; American Chemical Soc. Phila Section Award 1998, American Physical Soc. Aneesur Rahman Prize 1999. *Address:* Laboratory for Research on the Structure of Matter, University of Pennsylvania, 3231 Walnut Street, 102 LRSM, Philadelphia, PA 19104-6202, USA (office). *Telephone:* (215) 898-8571 (office). *Fax:* (215) 898-8296 (office). *E-mail:* klein@lrsm.upenn.edu (office). *Website:* www.sas.upenn.edu/chem/faculty/klein/klein.html (office).

KLEIN, Naomi; Canadian writer, journalist and social critic; b. 1970, Montréal; syndicated columnist for The Globe and Mail, Canada and The Guardian, UK; contrib. to numerous publs including The Nation, The Guardian, New Statesman, Newsweek International, New York Times, Village Voice and Ms. Magazine; campaigner on issues of devt econs, corp. accountability and consumer affairs; has travelled throughout N America, Asia, Latin America and Europe giving lectures and workshops on corp. branding and econ. globalization 1996–; frequent media commentator; guest lecturer at Harvard Univ., Yale Univ., McGill Univ. and New York Univ.; Canadian Nat. Business Book Award 2001, Le Prix Médiations, France 2001, Ms. Magazine's Women of the Year Award 2001. *Publication:* No Logo: Taking Aim at the Brand Bullies (translated into 22 languages) 2000, The Shock Doctrine: The Rise of Disaster Capitalism (Warwick Prize for Writing 2009) 2007. *Address:* c/o Random House of Canada Ltd, 1 Toronto Street, Unit 300, Toronto, ON M5C 2V6, Canada (office). *E-mail:* admin@nologo.org (office). *Website:* www.nologo.org (office).

KLEIN, Peter Wolfgang, PhD; Dutch historian and academic; *Professor of Early Modern History, State University of Leiden;* b. 10 Dec. 1931, Vienna, Austria; ed Netherlands School of Econs, Rotterdam; Asst Prof. of Econ. History 1959–65; Reader in Social History 1965–67; Prof. of Econ. and Social History, Erasmus Univ., Rotterdam 1969–85, Part-time Prof. of Econ. History 1969–74, Vice-Chancellor 1974–75, Dean Faculty of Econs 1977–78, Head History Dept 1979–81; Prof. of Early Modern History, State Univ. Leiden 1985–, Head History Dept 1986–88; Pres. Dutch Historical Soc. 1987–; mem. State Cttee for Nat. History 1981–, Bd State Inst. for History Second World War 1972–89, Scientific Cttee Inst. of Econ. History Francesco Datini 1986–, Cttee Int. Asscn of Econ. History 1985–, Royal Netherlands Acad. of Arts and Sciences 1979 (Chair. Arts Dept); Founding mem. Academia Europaea. *Publication:* Dr. Trippen in de 17e. eeuw 1965. *Address:* Vakgroep Geschiedenis, Doelensteeg 16, 2311VL Leiden (office); Oude Herengracht 24, Leiden, Netherlands (home); Universitet Leiden, Stationsweg 46, P.O. Box 9500, 2399 RA Leiden. *Telephone:* (71) 272759 (office); (71) 5272727. *Fax:* (71) 5273118.

KLEIN, Hon. Ralph; Canadian politician; b. 1 Nov. 1942, Calgary; m. Coleen Klein; public relations positions with Alberta Div., Red Cross and United Way of Calgary and Dist 1963–69; Sr Civic Affairs reporter CFCN TV and Radio 1969–80; Mayor of Calgary 1980–89; MLA for Calgary-Elbow 1989–, Minister of Environment 1989, Leader Progressive Conservative Party 1992–2006, Premier of Alberta 1992–2006; Dr hc (Southern Alberta Inst. of Tech.) 1998, (Olds Coll.) 2000, (Kangwon Nat. Univ., South Korea) 2004; hon. chief Kainai Chieftainship 1996; Alberta Achievement Award 1988, Lion's Club Medal of Distinction for Service to Humanity 1988, Calgarian of the Decade by Calgary Herald 1989, Gov. Gen.'s Award 1992, adopted into Siksika (Blackfoot) Nation 1993, Man of the Year, Int. Young Entrepreneurs Org. 1994, Colin M. Brown Freedom Medal, Nat. Citizens' Coalition 1994, B'nai B'rith's Citizen of the Year 1994; Order of St. John in 1986, Olympic Order 1988. *Address:* c/o Alberta Progressive Conservatives Party, 9919 106 Street NW, Edmonton, Alberta T5K 1E2, Canada.

KLEINBERG, Jon M., AB, SM, PhD; American computer scientist and academic; *Professor of Computer Science, Cornell University;* ed Cornell Univ., Massachusetts Inst. of Tech.; researcher, IBM Theory and Computation Group 1995, Computer Science Principles and Methodologies Group 1996–97, mem. Visiting Faculty Program, IBM Almaden Research Center 1998–; mem. faculty, Dept of Computer Science, Cornell Univ. 1996–, currently Prof. of Computer Science; NSF Career Award, Office of Naval Research Young Investigator Award, MacArthur Foundation Fellowship, Packard Foundation Fellowship, Sloan Foundation Fellowship, grants from NSF, Faculty of the Year Award, Cornell Univ. Asscn of Computer Science Undergraduates 2002, Nevanlinna Prize 2006. *Achievement:* devised the HITS algorithm for ranking Web pages. *Publications:* Algorithm Design (co-author) 2005; numerous scientific papers in professional journals. *Address:* Department of Computer Science, Upson Hall, Cornell University, Ithaca, NY 14853, USA (office). *Telephone:* (607) 255-3600 (office), (607) 255-5331 (office). *Fax:* (607) 255-7316 (office). *E-mail:* kleinber@cs.cornell.edu (office). *Website:* www.cs.cornell.edu/home/kleinber (office).

KLEINFELD, Klaus, Dr rer. pol, Dipl.-Kfm; German business executive; *CEO, Alcoa Inc.;* b. 6 Nov. 1957, Bremen; ed Georg-August Univ., Göttingen, Univ.

of Würzburg; Researcher Inst. of Foundation for Empirical Social Research, Nuremberg 1982–86; Product Man. Pharmaceuticals Div., Ciba-Geigy AG, Basel 1986–87; joined Corp. Sales and Marketing Siemens AG, Advertising and Design Man. 1987, Corp. Strategies Man. 1988–94, Head, Corp. Projects 1994–95, Head, Siemens Corp. Consulting 1995–98, Head, Angiography, Fluoroscopic and Radiographic Systems Div. 1998–2000, mem. Group Exec. Man., Medical Solutions Group, COO Siemens Corpn, USA 2001–02, CEO 2002–04, mem. Man. Bd Siemens AG 2002–07, mem. Corp. Exec. Cttee 2004–07, Deputy Chair. Man. Bd 2004, Pres. and CEO 2005–07; Pres. and COO Alcoa Inc. 2007–08, CEO 2008–. *Publication:* Corporate Identity und strategische Unternehmensführung 1994.

KLEINROCK, Leonard, BEE, MS, PhD; American computer scientist and academic; *Professor of Computer Science, Henry Samueli School of Engineering and Applied Science, University of California, Los Angeles;* b. 13 June 1934, New York; ed Bronx High School of Science, City Coll. of New York, Massachusetts Inst. of Tech.; Prof. of Computer Science, Henry Samueli School of Eng and Applied Science, UCLA 1963–, Chair. Dept 1991–95, currently Distinguished Prof. of Computer Science; Co-founder and first Pres. Linkabit Corpn; Co-founder Nomadix, Inc.; Founder and Chair. TTI/Vanguard (advanced tech. forum org.); mem. Nat. Acad. of Eng, American Acad. of Arts and Sciences; Fellow, IEEE, Asscn for Computing Machinery, INFORMS (Inst. For Operations Research and The Man. Sciences), Int. Electrotechnical Comm.; Founding mem. Computer Science and Telecommunications Bd of Nat. Research Council; hon. doctorates from around the world; Guggenheim Fellow, L.M. Ericsson Prize, NAE Charles Stark Draper Prize, Marconi Int. Fellowship Award, Okawa Prize, IEEE Internet Millennium Award, ORSA Lanchester Prize, ACM SIGCOMM Award, NEC Computer and Communications Award, Sigma Xi Monie A. Ferst Award, Townsend Harris Medal and Electrical Eng Award, City Coll. of New York, UCLA Outstanding Faculty Mem. Award, UCLA Distinguished Teaching Award, UCLA Faculty Research Lecturer, INFORMS Pres.'s Award, ICC Prize Paper Award, IEEE Leonard G. Abraham Prize Paper Award, IEEE Harry M. Goode Award, listed by Los Angeles Times amongst "50 People Who Most Influenced Business This Century" 1999, listed by Atlantic Monthly amongst 33 most influential living Americans Dec. 2006, Nat. Medal of Science 2007. *Achievements include:* known as a "father of the Internet"; developed math. theory of packet switching networks, tech. underpinning the Internet, while a grad. student at MIT 1960–62; wrote first paper and published first book on the subject; also directed transmission of first message ever sent over Internet. *Publications:* six books and more than 250 papers in professional journals on packet switching networks, packet radio networks, local area networks, broadband networks, gigabit networks, nomadic computing, performance evaluation and peer-to-peer networks. *Address:* Computer Science Department, Unversity of California, Los Angeles, 3732G Boelter Hall, Los Angeles, CA 90095, USA (office). *Telephone:* (310) 825-2543 (office). *Fax:* (310) 825-7578 (office). *E-mail:* lk@cs.ucla.edu (office). *Website:* www.lk.cs.ucla.edu (office); www.engineer.ucla.edu (office).

KLEISTERLEE, Gerard J.; Dutch business executive; *Chairman, President and CEO, Royal Philips Electronics;* b. 1946; ed Eindhoven Tech. Univ., Netherlands; joined Philips in Medical Systems Div. 1974, several posts in mfg man., Gen. Man. Professional Audio Systems product group (now part of Consumer Electronics) 1981, joined Philips Components 1986, later Gen. Man. Philips Display Components for Europe, Man. Dir Philips Display Components Worldwide 1994, Pres. Philips Taiwan and Regional Man. Philips Components in Asia-Pacific 1996, responsible for Philips Group in China 1997–98, Pres. and CEO Philips Components 1999–2000, mem. Group Man. Cttee 1999–, apptd Exec. Vice-Pres. Royal Philips Electronics (also mem. Bd of Man.) 2000, COO Philips 2000–01, Chair. Bd of Man. and Group Man. Cttee, Pres. and CEO Royal Philips Electronics 2001–; mem. Supervisory Bd De Nederlandsche Bank NV 2006–, Rotterdam Philharmonic Orchestra; mem. European Table of Industrialists 2001–, mem. Exec. Cttee and Chair. Competitiveness Working Group 2007–; mem. Asia Business Council, Trans Atlantic Business Dialogue, Dutch Innovation Platform; Chair. Supervisory Bd Eindhoven Tech. Univ. 2001–, Foundation of the Cancer Centre Amsterdam; mem. Exec. Cttee IMD, Lausanne 2007–; Dr hc (Leuven). *Address:* Royal Philips Electronics, Breitner Center, HBT 14.12, Amstelplein 2, 1096 BC Amsterdam, Netherlands (office). *Telephone:* (20) 5977122 (office). *Fax:* (20) 5977120 (office). *Website:* www.philips.com (office).

KLEMPERER, Paul David, BA, MBA, PhD, FBA; British economist and academic; *Edgeworth Professor of Economics, University of Oxford;* b. 15 Aug. 1956; s. of the late Hugh G. Klemperer and Ruth Jordan; m. Margaret Meyer 1989; two s. one d.; ed King Edward's School, Birmingham, Peterhouse, Cambridge, Stanford Univ., USA; Consultant, Andersen Consulting (now Accenture) 1978–80; Harkness Fellow of Commonwealth Fund 1980–82; Lecturer in Operations Research and Math. Econs, Univ. of Oxford 1985–90, Reader in Econs 1990–95, Edgeworth Prof. of Econs 1995–, John Thomson Fellow and Tutor, St Catherine's Coll. 1985–95, Fellow, Nuffield Coll. 1995–; Visiting Lecturer, MIT 1987, Univ. of Calif., Berkeley 1991, 1993, Stanford Univ. 1991, 1993, Yale Univ. 1994, Princeton Univ. 1998; consultant to Dept of Trade and Industry 1997–2000, US Fed. Trade Comm. 1999–2001, Dept for Energy, Transport and the Regions 2000–01, Dept for the Environment, Food and Rural Affairs 2001–02 and pvt. cos; mem. UK Competition Comm. 2001–05; Ed. RAND Journal of Economics 1993–99; Assoc. or mem. Editorial Bd Oxford Economic Papers 1986–, Review of Economic Studies 1989–97, Journal of Industrial Economics 1989–96, International Journal of Industrial Organization 1993–2000, European Economic Review 1997–2001, Review of Economic Design 1997–2000, Economic Policy 1998–99, Economic Journal 2000–04, Frontiers in Economics 2000–, Journal of Economic Analysis and Policy 2001–, Journal of Competition Law and Economics 2004–; mem.

Council, Royal Econ. Soc. 2001–, Econometric Soc. 2001– (Fellow 1994), European Econ. Asscn 2002–; Hon. Fellow, ELSE 2001–, Foreign Hon. mem. American Acad. of Arts and Sciences 2005–. *Publications:* The Economic Theory of Auctions 1999, Auctions: Theory and Practice 2004; articles in econs journals. *Address:* Nuffield College, Oxford, OX1 1NF, England (office). *Telephone:* (1865) 278588 (office). *E-mail:* paul.klemperer@economics.ox.ac.uk (office). *Website:* www.economics.ox.ac.uk/index.php/staff/klemperer (office); www.paulklemperer.org (home).

KLEMPERER, William, PhD; American chemist and academic; *Research Professor, Department of Chemistry and Chemical Biology, Harvard University;* b. 6 Oct. 1927, New York; s. of Paul Klemperer and Margit Klemperer (née Freund); m. Elizabeth Cole 1949; one s. two d.; ed New Rochelle High School, NY, Harvard Univ. and Univ. of California, Berkeley; US Navy Air Corps 1944–46; Instructor, Berkeley Feb.–June 1954; Instructor, Harvard Univ. 1954–57, Asst Prof. 1957–61, Assoc. Prof. 1961–65, Research Prof. 1965–; Asst Dir NSF (for math. and physical sciences) 1979–81; mem. American Physical Soc. (APS), NAS, American Acad. of Arts and Sciences, ACS; several memorial lectures; Hon. Citizen of Toulouse, France 2000; Hon. DSc (Univ. of Chicago) 1996; Wetherill Medal, Franklin Inst., ACS Irving Langmuir Award, APS Earle Plyler Award, NSF Distinguished Service Medal, Bomem Michelson Award, Coblentz Soc., Remsen Award, Maryland Section of ACS, ACS Peter Debye Award in Physical Chem., Faraday Medal, Royal Soc. of Chem., ACS E. Bright Wilson Award in Spectroscopy 2001, Ionnes Marcus Marci Medal, Prague 2004. *Address:* 53 Shattuck Road, Watertown, MA 02172 (home); Department of Chemistry and Chemical Biology, Harvard University, 12 Oxford Street, Cambridge, MA 02138, USA (office). *Telephone:* (617) 924-5775 (home); (617) 495-4094 (office). *Fax:* (617) 496-5175 (office). *E-mail:* billk@otto.harvard.edu (office). *Website:* www.chem.harvard.edu/research/faculty/william_klemperer.php (office).

KLEPPE, Johan; Norwegian politician and veterinarian; b. 29 Sept. 1928, Bjørnskinn, Andøya; s. of Jon Kleppe and Alvhild Caroliussen Kleppe; m. Inger Johansen 1961; one s. one d.; ed Veterinary Coll. of Norway; Veterinarian 1954–63, Dist Veterinarian, Andøy 1963–76, Supervisory Veterinarian 1966–76; Regional Veterinary Officer of North Norway 1976–94; mem. Bjørnskinn Municipal Council 1956–64; Deputy Mayor of Andøy 1964–66, Mayor 1966–68, 1975–78, mem. Exec. Cttee Andøy municipality 1964–78; Deputy mem. of Parl. 1967; Parl. Under-Sec. of State, Ministry of Agriculture 1968–69; Liberal mem. of Parl. for Nordland 1969–73, mem. Bd of Liberal Parl. faction 1969–73; mem. Liberal Party's Cttee on Oil Policy and EC Cttee, mem. Prin. Planning Cttee; Minister of Defence 1972–73; mem. Liberal Nat. Exec. 1966–72; Leader, Norwegian del., FAO confs, Rome and Malta 1969; Norwegian Del., UN Gen. Ass., New York 1971; fmr Bd mem. Nordland Co. Liberal Asscn; fmr Chair. Students Liberal Asscn, Oslo and Bjørnskinn and Andøy Liberal Asscn; Chair. of Board, Directorate of State Forests 1969–77, Chair. Nat. Council on Sheep-breeding 1969–82; Chair. of Bd Nordlandsbanken A/S, 8480 Andenes 1974–90, State Veterinary Laboratory for Northern Norway 1976–91, Vesteraalen Intermunicipal Planning Office 1978–88; Vice-Chair. Cttee Norwegian Veterinary Asscn 1981–84, Chair. 1984–91; Chair. of Bd Andøyposten a/s 1981–90, Troms Population Acad. Asscn 1987–94; mem. Bd Norwegian Nat. Programme for Sea Ranching 1990–94. *Address:* 8484 Risøyhamn, Norway. *Telephone:* 76-14-76-30. *Fax:* 76-14-76-30.

KLEPPER, Kenneth O.; American business executive; *President and Chief Operating Officer, Medco Health Solutions Inc.;* m. Connie Klepper; several fmr exec. man. positions with Cigna, NPM, Empire BlueCross BlueShield, WellChoice Inc.; Exec. Vice-Pres. and COO Medco Health Solutions Inc. 2003–06, Pres. and COO 2006–; mem. USN Corporate Exec. Panel. *Address:* Medco Health Solutions Inc., 100 Parsons Pond Drive, Franklin Lakes, NJ 07417-2603, USA (office). *Telephone:* (201) 269-3400 (office). *Fax:* (201) 269-1109 (office). *Website:* www.medco.com (office).

KLEPPNER, Daniel, PhD; American physicist and academic; *Lester Wolfe Professor of Physics and Associate Director, Research Laboratory of Electronics, Massachusetts Institute of Technology;* ed Williams Coll., Williamstown, Mass, Univ. of Cambridge, UK, Harvard Univ.; Fulbright Fellow, Univ. of Cambridge 1953–55; NSF Postdoctoral Fellow 1959–60; Alfred E. Sloan Foundation Fellow 1962–64; Asst Prof. of Physics, Harvard Univ. 1962–66; Assoc. Prof. of Physics, MIT 1966–73, Prof. of Physics 1974–, Head, Div. of Atomic, Plasma Condensed Matter Physics, Dept of Physics 1976–79, Lester Wolfe Prof. of Physics and Assoc. Dir Research Lab. of Electronics (RLE) 1985–, Dir NSF MIT-Harvard Center for Ultracold Atoms 2000–, Prin. Investigator, RLE Atomic, Molecular and Optical Physics Group; mem. NAS; Fellow, American Physical Soc. (APS), American Asscn for the Advancement of Science, American Acad. of Arts and Sciences; APS Davisson-Germer Prize 1985, APS Julius Edgar Lilienfeld Prize 1990, William F. Meggers Award, Optical Soc. of America 1990, James Rhyne Killian, Jr Faculty Achievement Award, MIT, Oersted Award, American Asscn of Physics Teachers, Wolf Prize for Physics, Wolf Foundation (Israel) 2005. *Publications:* numerous articles in scientific journals. *Address:* Room 26-237, 77 Massachusetts Avenue, Massachusetts Institute of Technology, Cambridge, MA 02139-4307, USA (office). *Telephone:* (617) 253-6811 (office). *E-mail:* Kleppner@mit.edu (office). *Website:* rleweb.mit.edu (office).

KLEPSCH, Egon Alfred, DPhil; German politician; *Honorary President, Europa-Union Deutschland;* b. 30 Jan. 1930, Bodenbach/Elbe; s. of Egon Klepsch and Hermine Hölzl; m. Anita Wegehaupt 1952; three s. three d.; joined CDU 1951, mem. Bureau 1977–94; Fed. Chair. Young Christian Democrats 1963–69; Chair. EU of Young Christian Democrats 1964–70; mem. Bundestag 1965–80; mem. Parl. Ass of Council of Europe and of WEU 1969–80; mem. European Parl. (not directly elected) 1973–79, elected mem. European Parl. 1979–94, Vice-Pres. 1982–84, Pres. 1992–94; Vice-Pres.

European People's Party (EPP) 1977–92, mem. Bureau 1992–94, Chair. EPP Group 1977–82, 1984–92; Pres. Europa-Union Deutschland 1989–97, Hon. Pres. 1997–; Vice-Chair. German Council of European Movt 1990–99 (Hon. mem. 1999–); mem. Bd of Govs Deutschlandfunk 1991; Bundesverdienstkreuz mit Stern und Schulterband and decorations from Italy, Luxembourg, Argentina, Chile and Greece. *Publications:* several books on European policy and military topics. *Leisure interest:* chess. *Address:* c/o Europa-Union Deutschland e.V. Sophienstraße 28/29, 10178 Berlin, Germany.

KLERIDES, Takis; Cypriot accountant, business consultant and fmr government official; *Chairman, Tufton Oceanic Finance Group;* b. 21 Aug. 1951, Nicosia; m. Nancy Hak 1976; one s. one d.; ed Birmingham Polytechnic, UK; joined KPMG Cyprus 1977, Pnr 1983–97, Sr Pnr 1997–; Minister of Finance 1999–2003, also apptd a Gov. of the IMF and EBRD 1999–2003; pvt. business consultant 2003–; mem. Monopolies Comm. 1998–99, Cyprus Olympic Cttee 1996–99; Chair. Cyprus Basketball Fed. 1988–98; Chair. Tufton Oceanic Finance Group; mem. Bd of Dirs Logicom Public Ltd; Fellow, Chartered Asscn of Certified Accountants; mem. Inst. of Certified Public Accountants of Cyprus (mem. Council 1991–99). *Leisure interest:* sports. *Address:* Tufton Oceanic Finance Group, 3 Thalia Street, PO Box 51309, 3504 Limassol, Cyprus (office). *Telephone:* 25840300 (office). *Fax:* 25575895 (office). *Website:* www.tuftonoceanic.com (office).

KLESSE, William R. (Bill), BSc, MSc; American business executive; *Chairman and CEO, Valero Energy Corporation;* ed West Tex. A&M Univ., Univ. of Dayton; numerous exec. positions with Valero Energy Corpn and its predecessors for almost 40 years including Vice-Pres. of Logistics and Strategy 1982–84, then Dir of Corporate Devt, Sr Vice-Pres., Exec. Vice-Pres., Exec. Vice-Pres. Ultramar Diamond Shamrock (refining operations) 1996–99, Exec. Vice-Pres. of Operations and Chair. Shamrock Logistics LLC 1999–2001, Exec. Vice-Pres. of Refining and Commercial Operations (after merger of Ultramar Diamond Shamrock and Valero) 2001–03, Exec. Vice-Pres. and COO Valero Energy Corpn 2003–06, CEO and Vice-Chair. 2006–07, Chair. and CEO 2007–. *Address:* Valero Corporate Headquarters, PO Box 696000, One Valero Way, San Antonio, TX 78269-6000, USA (office). *Telephone:* (210) 345-2000 (office). *Fax:* (210) 345-2646 (office). *E-mail:* info@valero.com (office). *Website:* www.valero.com (office).

KLEY, Karl-Ludwig, PhD; German lawyer and business executive; *Chairman of the Executive Board and General Partner, Merck KGaA;* b. 11 June 1951, Munich; ed Ludwig-Maximilians Univ., Munich; completed industrial business apprenticeship at Siemens AG then trained as lawyer in Hamburg and Johannesburg; joined Bayer AG as Asst to Chair. of Man. Bd 1982, then Chief Financial Officer, Japan 1987–91, then numerous exec. positions in Pharmaceuticals Div. including Head, Pharmaceuticals, Italy 1994–97, then Head Corp. Finance and Investor Relations 1998; Chief Financial Officer and mem. Exec. Bd Lufthansa AG 1998–2008; Vice-Chair. Exec. Bd Merck KGaA 2006–07, Chair. Exec. Bd 2007–, also mem. Exec. Bd E. Merck OHG; mem. Supervisory Bd Bertelsmann AG, WestLB AG; fmr mem. Supervisory Bd Vattenfall Europe AG, MAN AG; mem. Presidential Council of German Chemical Industry Asscn (VCI); Hon. Prof., Otto Beisheim School of Man. 2006. *Address:* Merck KGaA, Frankfurter Str. 250, 64293 Darmstadt, Germany. *Telephone:* (6151) 720. *Fax:* (6151) 722000. *Website:* www.merck.de.

KLEY, Max Dietrich; German business executive; *Chairman of the Supervisory Board, Infineon Technologies AG;* b. 1940, Berlin; m.; three c.; ed Univs of Munich and Heidelberg; joined Legal Dept BASF AG 1969, Head of Tax Dept 1977–82, CEO Gewerkschaft Auguste Vic., Marl 1982–87, Pres. Energy and Coal Div. 1987–90, mem. Bd of Exec. Dirs 1990–2003, Deputy Chair. 1999–2003, mem. Supervisory Bd 2003–; Chair. Supervisory Bd. Infineon Technologies AG 2002–, Interim CEO March–Aug. 2004; mem. Supervisory Bd Bayerische Hypo- und Vereinsbank AG 1990–, Gerling Konzern Speziale-Kreditversicherungs-AG 1992–, Landesbank Rheinland-Pfalz 1993–, Lausitzer Braunkohle AG 1995–, Mannesmann Demag Krauss Maffei AG 1995–, Winterhall AG 1996–, BASF Coatings AG 1999–; Chair. Industrial Energy and Power Asscn 1991–97; mem. Bd of Trustees Accounting Standards Cttee Foundation 2003–; Pres. German Inst. for Share Promotion 1998–. *Address:* Infineon Technologies AG, Am Campeon 1-12 Neubiberg, Munich 85579 DEU +49- (Phone), Germany (office). *Telephone:* (89) 23402166 (office). *Website:* www.infineon.com (office).

KLIBI, Chedli, BA; Tunisian politician and international official; b. 6 Sept. 1925, Tunis; s. of Hassouna Klibi and Habiba Bannani; m. Kalthoum Lasram 1956; one s. two d.; ed Sadiki Coll., Tunis, Sorbonne, Paris; successively high school teacher, Lecturer, Univ. of Tunis and journalist 1951–57; Dir-Gen. Tunisian Radio and TV 1958–61; Minister of Information and Cultural Affairs 1961–64, 1969–73, of Cultural Affairs 1976–78, of Information Sept. 1978; Minister, Dir Cabinet of Pres. 1974–76; Sec.-Gen. League of Arab States 1979–90; Mayor of Carthage 1963–90; mem. Political Bureau and Cen. Cttee, Neo Destour (Parti Socialiste Destourien) 1979–; mem. Cairo Arabic Language Acad.; Grand Officier Légion de Honneur 1972, Grand Cordon, Order of Independence and Order of Repub. (Tunisia) and several foreign decorations. *Publications include:* The Arabs and the Palestinian Question, Islam and Modernity, Culture is a Civilisational Challenge, Orient–Occident, la paix violente. *Leisure interest:* reading. *Address:* 9 rue Ibn Kaldoun, Carthage, Tunisia (home). *Telephone:* 734-535 (home). *Fax:* 734-820 (home).

KLICH, Bogdan, MA; Polish physician, politician and academic; *Minister of National Defence;* b. 8 May 1960, Kraków; ed Kraków Medical Acad., Jagiellonian Univ.; Adviser to Chief Negotiator of Poland with EU 1989–99; doctoral studies, Dept of Historical Philosophy 1991–95; mem. Parl. 2001–04, Vice-Chair. Cttee on Foreign Affairs, mem. Cttee on Nat. Defence; Deputy Minister of Nat. Defence 1999–2000; Observer to European Parl. 2003–04; Polish Rep. and mem. Policy Cttee of Parl. Ass. of Council of Europe 2001–04; mem. European Parl. (Group of European People's Party (Christian Democrats) and European Democrats) 2004–07, Chair. Del. for Relations with Belarus 2004–07, mem. Cttee on Foreign Affairs, Human Rights, Common Security and Defence Policy 2004–07, Conf. of Del. Chairmen 2004–07; Minister of Nat. Defence 2007–; Pres. Inst. of Strategic Studies 1997–; mem. IISS, London; Lecturer, Centre for European Studies, Jagiellonian Univ.; Order of Merit for Defence of Lithuania, Gold Medal of Merit, Ministry of Foreign Affairs, Slovakia. *Address:* Ministry of National Defence, ul. Klonowa 1, 00-909 Warsaw, Poland (office). *Telephone:* (22) 6280031 (office). *Fax:* (22) 8455378 (office). *E-mail:* bpimon@wp.mil.pl (office). *Website:* www.wp.mil.pl (office).

KLÍMA, Ivan, MA; Czech author and dramatist; b. 14 Sept. 1931, Prague; s. of Vilém Klíma and Marta Klíma; m. Helena Malá-Klímová 1958; one s. one d.; ed Charles Univ., Prague; Ed. Československy spisovatel (publishing house) 1958–63; Ed. Literární noviny 1963–67, Literární Listy 1968, Listy 1968–69; Visiting Prof., Univ. of Michigan, Ann Arbor 1969–70, Univ. of Calif., Berkeley 1998; freelance author publishing abroad 1970–89; columnist, Lidove Noviny newspaper; mem. Council, Czech Writers 1989–, Ed.'s Council, Lidové noviny 1996–97; Exec. Pres. Czech PEN Centre 1990–93, Deputy Pres. 1993–; Hostovský Award, New York 1985, George Theiner Prize (UK) 1993, Franz Kafka Prize 2002, Medal for Outstanding Service to the Czech Repub. 2002. *Publications:* Ship Named Hope 1968, A Summer Affair 1972, My Merry Mornings (short stories) 1979, My First Loves (short stories) 1985, Love and Garbage 1987, Judge on Trial 1987, My Golden Trades (short stories) 1992, The Island of Dead Kings 1992, The Spirit of Prague (essays, jtly) 1994, Waiting for the Dark, Waiting for the Light 1996, The Ultimate Intimacy (novel) 1997, No Saints or Angels 1999, Between Security and Insecurity: Prospects for Tomorrow 2000, Lovers for a Day: New and Collected Stories on Love 2000, Karel Capek: Life and Work 2002, The Premier and the Angel (in Czech) 2004; plays: The Castle 1964, The Master 1967, The Sweetshop Myriam 1968, President and the Angel, Klara and Two Men 1968, Bridegroom for Marcela 1968, The Games 1975, Kafka and Felice 1986; contribs to magazines. *Leisure interests:* tennis, gathering mushrooms. *Address:* České Centrum Mezinárodního, PEN Klubu, ul. 28, října 9, 11000 Prague 1 (office); Na Dubině 5, 14700 Prague 4, Czech Republic (home). *Telephone:* (2) 24221926 (office).

KLIMA, Viktor; Austrian politician and business executive; *Chief Representative, South American Operations and President, Volkswagen Argentina;* b. 4 June 1947, Vienna; s. of Viktor Klima and Anna Varga; m. Sonja Holzinger 1995; one s. one d.; ed Vienna Tech. Univ., Univ. of Vienna; worked at Inst. for Automation and Scientific Business Consultancy; joined staff of Österreichische Mineralöl-Verwaltungs AG (ÖMV) 1970, Head Organizational Div. 1980–85, Dir Cen. Personnel Office and group's Prokuriet (holder of a gen. power of attorney) 1986, mem. Man. Bd with responsibility for finance, control, accountancy and acquisitions (subsequently also chemical div.) 1990–92; Minister of Public Economy and Transport 1992–96, of Finance 1996–97, Fed. Chancellor of Austria 1997–2000; Chief Rep., South America Operations and Pres. Volkswagen Argentina 2000–; fmr mem. several supervisory and advisory bds, Governing Bd Fed. of Public Economy and Utility Enterprises; fmr Chair. Fed. Econ. Chamber's Petroleum Industry Labour Law Cttee, Cttee on Public and Utility Enterprises. *Address:* Volkswagen Argentina S.A., Avda. Henry Ford y Delcasse, 1617 General Pacheco, Buenos Aires, Argentina (office). *Telephone:* (11) 4317-9000 (office). *Fax:* (11) 4317-9001 (office). *Website:* www.volkswagen.com.ar (office).

KLIMMT, Reinhard; German politician and historian; b. 16 Aug. 1942; elected mem. of Landtag 1975; Chair. SPD Landtag Party, mem. SPD Party Exec., Chair. Media Comm. of SPD Party Exec. –1998; Minister-Pres. of Saarland 1998–99; Minister of Regional Planning, Urban Devt, Construction and Transport 1999–2000; consultant to Bd of Deutsche Bahn AG 2002–. *Publication:* überall und irgendwo: Aus der Welt der Bücher 2006. *Address:* c/o Board of Directors, Deutsche Bahn Aktiengesellschaft, Potsdamer Platz 2, 10785 Berlin, Germany. *Telephone:* (30) 297-0. *Fax:* (30) 297-6-19-19. *Website:* www.db.de.

KLIMOV, Dmitri Mikhailovich; Russian mechanical engineer; *Councillor, Institute for Problems in Mechanics, Russian Academy of Sciences;* b. 13 July 1933; m.; ed Moscow State Univ.; researcher Research Inst. of Applied Mech. 1958–67; head of lab., head of div.; Deputy Dir Inst. for Problems in Mechanics USSR Acad. of Sciences 1967–89, Dir 1989, now Councillor Corresp. mem USSR (now Russian) Acad. of Sciences 1981, mem. 1992, Academician-Sec. Div. for Problems of Machine Engineering, Mechanics and Control Processes 1996–; main research in mechanics, gyroscopic and navigation systems, gen. and analytical mechanics, mechanics of deformable solid bodies; Deputy Chair. Scientific Council on Problems of Man. of Navigation Movt; USSR State Prize 1976, Russian State Prize 1994. *Publications:* Inertial Navigation on the Sea 1984, Applied Methods in Oscillations Theory 1988, Methods of Computer Algebra in Problems of Mechanics 1989; numerous articles. *Leisure interest:* chess. *Address:* Institute for Problems in Mechanics, Vernadskogo prosp. 101, block 1, 119526 Moscow, Russia (office). *Telephone:* (495) 434-46-10 (office); (495) 938-14-04 (Academy). *Fax:* (495) 938-20-48 (office). *E-mail:* ipm@ipmnet.ru (office). *Website:* www.ipmnet.ru (office).

KLIMOVSKI, Savo, LLD, PhD; Macedonian politician and academic; b. 1947, Skopje; m. Radmila Klimovski; one s. one d.; ed Skopje Univ., Ljubljana Univ.; Lecturer, Asst Prof., Prof., Dean of Law Faculty, Pres., St Cyril and Methodius Univ., Skopje; mem. Exec. Council, Macedonian Ass. 1986–90; Pres. Macedonian Cttee for Educ., Culture and Physical Culture; f. Democratic Alternative (political party) 1998; mem. Govt Coalition For Changes; Speaker, Ass. of Repub. of Macedonia 1998–2000, Pres. Cttee for Constitutional Issues,

Council for Interethnic Relations; Pres. Repub. of Macedonia Nov.–Dec. 1999. *Publications:* Constitutional and Political System, Politics and Institutions, Political Philosophy, Parliamentary Law. *Address:* c/o Democratic Alternative (DA) (Demokratska Alternativa), 1000 Skopje, ul. Dame Gruev 1; Bul. 'Patizanski odredi' nr. 3/II-19, Skopje (home); Sobranje, Oktomyri blvd 11, 91000 Skopje, Macedonia. *E-mail:* klimovski@eccf.ukim.edu.mk. *Website:* www.klimovski.com.mk (home).

KLIMUK, Col-Gen. Piotr Ilyich, DTechSc; Russian cosmonaut; b. 10 July 1942, Komarovka, Brest Region; m. Lilia Vladimirovna Klimuk; one s.; ed Chernigov Higher Mil. Aviation School, Air Force Acad., Lenin Mil. Political Acad.; three space flights 1973–78; Deputy Head, Head Political Dept Yuriy Gagarin Centre for Cosmonauts Training 1978–91, Head 1991–2003 (retd); USSR People's Deputy 1989–91; Hero of Soviet Union 1973, 1975; Tsiolkovsky Gold Medal, USSR State Prize 1978, 1981, Gold Medal (Polish Acad. of Sciences); Order of Fatherland of the 2nd class 2002. *Publications:* Next to the Stars, Attacking Weightlessness. *Address:* c/o Yuriy Gagarin Centre for Cosmonauts Training, Zvezdny Gorodok, Moscow Region, Russia.

KLINE, Kevin Delaney, BA; American actor and director; b. 24 Oct. 1947, St Louis; s. of Robert J. Kline and Peggy Kirk; m. Phoebe Cates 1989; one s. one d.; ed Indiana Univ. and Juilliard School Drama Div. New York; founding mem. The Acting Co. New York 1972–76; Obie Award for sustained achievement, Will Award for classical theatre; Joseph Papp Award 1990, John Houseman Award 1993, Gotham Award 1997. *Films include:* Sophie's Choice 1982, Pirates of Penzance 1983, The Big Chill 1983, Silverado 1985, Violets are Blue 1985, Cry Freedom 1987, A Fish Called Wanda (Acad. Award for Best Supporting Actor 1989) 1988, The January Man 1989, I Love You to Death 1989, Soapdish 1991, Grand Canyon 1991, Consenting Adults 1992, Chaplin 1992, Dave 1993, Princess Caraboo 1994, French Kiss 1995, The Hunchback of Notre Dame (voice) 1996, Fierce Creatures 1996, The Ice Storm 1997, In and Out 1997, A Midsummer Night's Dream 1999, Wild Wild West 1999, The Road to El Dorado (voice) 2000, The Anniversary Party 2001, Life as a House 2001, Orange County 2002, The Emperor's Club 2002, The Hunchback of Notre Dame II (voice) 2002, De-Lovely 2004, Pink Panther 2006, A Prairie Home Companion 2006, As You Like It 2006, Trade 2007, Definitely, Maybe 2008. *Theatre:* Broadway appearances in On the Twentieth Century 1978 (Tony Award 1978), Loose Ends 1979, Pirates of Penzance 1980 (Tony Award 1980), Arms and the Man 1985; off-Broadway appearances in Richard III 1983, Henry V 1984, Hamlet (also Dir) 1986, 1990, Much Ado About Nothing 1988, Measure for Measure 1995, The Seagull 2001. *Television includes:* Freedom: A History of Us (series) 2003, As You Like It (Outstanding Performance by a Male Actor in a Television Movie or Miniseries 2008) 2007. *Address:* c/o William Morris Agency, 1325 Avenue of the Americas, New York, NY 10019, USA.

KLINE, Lowry F., BA, JD; American beverage industry executive; *Chairman, Coca-Cola Enterprises Inc.;* b. 1941, Louden, Tenn.; m. Jane Kline; three c.; ed Univ. of Tennessee; Pnr, Miller & Martin (law firm) 1970–95; Gen. Counsel, Johnston Coca-Cola Bottling Group 1981–91; Sr Vice-Pres. and Gen. Counsel, Coca-Cola Enterprises Inc. (bottler) 1996–97, Exec. Vice-Pres. and Gen. Counsel, 1997–99, Exec. Vice-Pres. and Chief Admin. Officer 1999–2000, Dir 2000–, Vice-Chair. 2000–02, CEO 2001–04, 2005–06, Chair. 2002–; mem. Bd of Dirs The Dixie Group, Inc., Jackson Furniture Industries; fmr Pres. Chattanooga Bar Asscn, Tenn. Bd of Law Examiners; fmr Chair. Tenn. Bar Foundation. *Address:* Coca-Cola Enterprises Incorporated, POB 723040, Atlanta, GA 31139-0040, USA (office). *Telephone:* (770) 989-3000 (office). *Fax:* (770) 989-3788 (office). *Website:* www.cokecce.com (office).

KLINGENBERG, Wilhelm, PhD; German academic (retd); b. 28 Jan. 1924, Rostock; s. of Paul Klingenberg and Henny Klingenberg; m. Christine Kob 1953; two s. one d.; ed Kiel Univ.; Asst, Hamburg Univ. 1952–55; Asst Prof., then Assoc. Prof. Göttingen Univ. 1955–63; Prof., Univ. of Mainz 1963–66; Prof. of Math., Univ. of Bonn 1966, now retd; mem. Acad. of Science and Literature, Mainz; Dr hc (Leipzig) 2001. *Publications:* A Course in Differential Geometry 1978, Lectures on Closed Geodesics 1978, Riemannian Geometry 1982, 1995, Der weite Weg zum Kailas 1992, Tibet 1997, Klassische Differentialgeometrie 2004. *Leisure interests:* piano, horseback riding, Chinese art, art of Albrecht Dürer. *Address:* c/o Mathematics and Natural Science, University of Bonn, Beringstrasse 1, 53115 Bonn (office); Am Alten Forsthaus 42, 53125 Bonn, Germany (home). *Telephone:* (228) 737785 (office); (228) 251529 (home). *Fax:* (228) 737298 (office). *E-mail:* klingenb@math.uni-bonn.de (office). *Website:* www.math.uni-bonn.de/people/klingenb (office).

KLINSMANN, Jürgen; German football coach and fmr professional footballer; b. 30 July 1964, Göppingen; m. Debbie Klinsmann (née Chin) 1995; one s. one d.; centre-forward, began career with Stuttgarter Kickers before moving to VfB Stuttgart 1984–89 (79 goals); mem. winning team, World Cup 1990, UEFA Cup with Inter Milan 1991 and Bayern Munich 1996; with Inter Milan 1989–92 (34 goals); AS Monaco 1992–94 (29 goals) with Tottenham Hotspur 1994–95, 1997–98; played for Bayern Munich 1995–97 (31 goals), Sampdoria 1997; scored 47 goals in 108 int. games for Germany; f. children's care charity AGAPEDIA; Vice-Pres. SoccerSolutions (sports marketing and business devt consultancy); fmr Tech. Advisor, Los Angeles Galaxy (Major League Soccer); Int. Spokesman Mastercard; Int. Amb. for FIFA World Cup, Germany 2006; Head Coach, German Nat. Football Team 2004–07; Coach FC Bayern Munich 2008–09; German Footballer of the Year 1988, 1994, English Footballer of the Year 1995. *Leisure interests:* travel, cinema, music, languages, family. *Address:* Soccer Solutions LLC, 744 SW Regency Place, Portland, OR 97225, USA. *Telephone:* (503) 297-0844. *Website:* www.soccersolutions.com.

KLITSCHKO, Vitali, PhD; Ukrainian fmr professional heavyweight boxer; b. 19 July 1971, Belovodsk, Kyrgyzstan; s. of Col Wladimir Rodionovich

Klitschko and Nadezhda Ulyanovna Klitschko; m. Natalia Egorova 1996; one s. s., one d.; ed Pereyaslav-Khmelnitsky Pedagogical Inst., Kiev Univ.; six-times world kickboxing champion (four times as professional); three times Ukrainian heavyweight boxing champion; heavyweight champion of World Mil. Games 1995; silver medallist World Boxing Championship 1995; turned professional 1996 (with Universum Box-Promotion), debut bout versus Tony Bradham 16 Nov. 1996 in Hamburg, Germany; World Boxing Org. (WBO) Intercontinental Champion 2 May 1998 to 26 June 1999; European Champion 24 Oct. 1998 to 26 June 1999 and 25 Nov. 2000 to 29 Sept. 2002; WBO World Champion 26 June 1999 to 1 April 2000; World Boxing Asscn Intercontinental Champion 27 Jan. 2001 to 21 June 2003; defeated Corrie Sanders to claim vacant World Boxing Council title 24 April 2004; vacated title and retd Nov. 2005; professional boxing career record: 34 wins (33 knock-outs) and 2 defeats; Dir of Sports, XXI Century (fund for sports devt) 1995–; with his brother (Wladimir Klitschko) endorses Klitschko BoxPower fitness programme; appeared in film Ocean's Eleven; rep. UNICEF 2002–; Ukrainian Man of the Year 2000, awarded Kiev Arts Patron medal 2003. *Publications:* Our Fitness (with Wladimir Klitschko). *Address:* c/o SPORTFIVE S.A., 70 rue du Gouverneur Général Eboué, 92130 Issy-Les-Moulinequx, France. *Website:* www.klitschko.com.

KLOBUCHAR, Amy, BA, JD; American lawyer and politician; *Senator from Minnesota;* b. 25 May 1960, Plymouth, Minn.; d. of Jim Klobuchar and Rose Klobuchar; m. John Bessler 1993; one d.; ed Yale Univ. and Univ. of Chicago Law School; practised law in Minn. and worked closely with fmr Vice-Pres. Walter Mondale; Assoc. Pnr, Dorsey & Whitney LLP (law firm) 1985–93; Pnr, Gray Plant Mooty LLP 1993–98; Attorney and Chief Prosecutor, Hennepin Co., Minn. 1998–2007; Senator from Minnesota 2007–, mem. Cttee on Agric., Nutrition and Forestry, Cttee on Environment and Public Works, Cttee on Commerce, Science and Transportation, US Congress Jt Econ. Cttee; Pres. Minnesota Co. Attorneys Asscn 2002–03; Democrat; '40 Under 40' Award, CityBusiness, named by Minnesota Lawyer magazine "Lawyer of the Year" 2001. *Publication:* Uncovering the Dome. *Address:* 302 Hart Senate Office Building, Washington, DC 20510, USA (office). *Telephone:* (202) 224-3244 (office). *Fax:* (202) 228-2186 (office). *Website:* klobuchar.senate.gov (office); www.amyklobuchar.com (office).

KLOCHKOVA, Yana; Ukrainian swimmer; b. 7 Aug. 1982, Simferopol; began swimming at age seven; Silver Medal 400m. Medley, European Championships 1997, World Championships 1997; Gold Medal 200m. Individual Medley (IM), 400m. IM, European Championships 1999, 2000, 2002, 2004; Gold Medal 400m. IM, 400m. Freestyle, World Championships 2001, 200m. IM, 400m. IM, World Championships 2003; Gold Medal 200m. IM, 400m. IM, Sydney Olympics 2000, Athens Olympics 2004 (first swimmer to win both Individual Medleys in consecutive Olympics); holds world record in 400m. IM; Ukraine Sports Personality of the Year, Swimming World Female Swimmer of the Year 2005, World Swimmer of the Year 2005. *Address:* c/o National Olympic Committee of Ukraine, Esplanadna St. 42, 01023 Kiev, Ukraine (office). *E-mail:* info@noc-ukr.org (office). *Website:* www.noc-ukr.org (office).

KLOKKARIS, Lt-Gen. Phivos; Cypriot military officer and government official; b. 1946, Yeroskipou, Paphos; m. Niki Klokkaris; one s. one d.; ed Kykkos Gymnasium of Nicosia, Mil. Acad., Nat. Defence Acad. of Greece, Armoured Vehicles Officers' Acad.; served as officer in Greek army –1993; joined Cyprus Nat. Guard with rank of Col 1993, served in various army staff units and admin. posts to rank of Lt-Gen., second-in-command of Nat. Guard 2002–06; Minister of Defence June–Sept. 2006 (resgnd); Rep. of Cyprus, EU Mil. Cttee 2002–03. *Address:* c/o Ministry of Defence, 4 Emmanuel Roides Avenue, 1432 Nicosia, Cyprus (office).

KLOPPERS, Marius, BE (Chem.), MBA, PhD; South African engineer and mining industry executive; *CEO, BHP Billiton Limited;* b. 26 Aug. 1962; m. Carin Kloppers; three c.; ed Univ. of Pretoria, Massachusetts Inst. of Tech., USA, Institut Européen d'Admin des Affaires (INSEAD), France; early career with Sasol Ltd, S Africa; fmr man. consultant with McKinsey & Co., Netherlands; joined Billiton (BHP Billiton after 2001) 1993, held several man. positions including Gen. Man. Hillside Aluminium, COO Aluminium, CEO Samancor Managanese, Group Exec. Billiton plc, Chief Marketing Officer and Chief Commercial Officer, BHP Billiton Group, Group Pres. Non-ferrous Materials Group and Exec. Dir BHP Billiton –2007, CEO BHP Billiton 2007–. *Address:* BHP Billiton Ltd, BHP Billiton Centre, 180 Lonsdale Street, Melbourne, Vic. 3000, Australia (office). *Telephone:* 1300-55-4757 (office). *Fax:* (3) 9609-3015 (office). *E-mail:* webmaster@bhpbilliton.com (office). *Website:* www.bhpbilliton.com (office).

KLOSE, Hans-Ulrich; German politician and lawyer; *Vice-Chairman, Foreign Affairs Committee, Bundestag;* b. 14 June 1937, Breslau; two s. two d.; ed gymnasium in Bielefeld High School, Clinton, Iowa USA and Univs of Freiburg and Hamburg; fmr lawyer in Hamburg; mem. Social Democratic Party (SPD) 1964–; mem. Public Services and Transport Workers' Union 1968; mem. Hamburgische Bürgerschaft 1970, Chair. SPD Parl. Group 1972; Senator of the Interior 1973; Mayor of Hamburg 1974–81 (resgnd); mem. (Constituency 18, Hamburg-Harburg) Bundestag 1983–, Chair. SPD Parl. Party 1991–94, Vice-Pres. Bundestag 1994–98, Chair. Foreign Affairs Cttee 1998–2002, Vice-Chair. 2002–; Chair. German-American Parl. Group 2003–; Treas. SPD 1987–91; Hon. Citizen of Lima 1981. *Publications:* Das Altern der Gesellschaft 1993, Altern hat Zukunft 1993, Charade (poems) 1997, Charade 2 (poems) 1999. *Leisure interests:* early American cultures, art and antiques, painting, literature. *Address:* Bundeshaus, Platz der Republik 1, 11011 Berlin, Germany (office). *Telephone:* (30) 22771876 (office). *Fax:* (30) 22770110 (office). *E-mail:* hans-ulrich.klose@bundestag.de (office). *Website:* klose.spd-hamburg.de (office).

KLOSSON, Michael, MA, MPA; American diplomatist and academic; b. 22 Aug. 1949, Washington; s. of Boris H. Klosson and Harriet F. C. Klosson; m. Boni Klosson; two d.; ed Hamilton Coll. and Princeton Univ.; teacher of English and modern Chinese History, Hong Kong Baptist Coll. 1971–72; joined Foreign Service 1972, served with Bureau of E Asian and Pacific Affairs, State Dept, Washington and Taipei and with Office of Japanese Affairs 1975–81; Special Asst to Secs of State Alexander Haig and George Schultz 1981–83; Deputy Dir Office of European Security and Political Affairs, Dir Secr. Staff, Office of Sec. of State 1984–90; Deputy Chief of Mission and Chargé d'Affaires, US Embassy, Stockholm and The Hague 1990–96; Prin. Deputy Asst Sec. of State for Legis. Affairs 1996–99; Consul-Gen. for Hong Kong and Macao 1999–2002; Amb. to Cyprus 2002–05; State Dept Chair, Industrial Coll. of the Armed Forces 2005–06; Visiting Lecturer, Hamilton Coll., 2006–07; Herbert H. Lehman Fellowship, Winston Churchill Fellowship; six Superior Honor Awards, US Dept of State. *Music:* Behold the Word 1968. *Leisure interests:* photography, music, running, scuba diving. *Address:* c/o Government Department, Hamilton College, 198 College Hill Road, Clinton, NY 13323, USA.

KLOSTER, Einar, BA; Norwegian business executive; b. 22 Sept. 1937, Oslo; s. of Knut Utstein Kloster and Ingeborg Kloster (née Ihlen); m. Elizabeth Blake (née Haüan) 1961; two d.; ed Dartmouth Coll. and Harvard Univ., USA; Marketing Man. Philips Norway 1961–68, Philips Head Office, Netherlands 1968–70; Marketing Dir Philips Japan 1970–74; CEO Philips East Africa 1974–77, Philips Norway 1978–82, Philips Brazil 1982–85; Exec. Vice-Pres. North American Philips Corpn 1985–86, Pres. 1989; Chair. and CEO Kloster Cruise Ltd 1986–88, Pres. and CEO 1989–2004; Chair. Norsk Hydro 1997–2001. *Leisure interests:* golf, tennis, skiing. *Address:* PO Box 1365, Vika, 0114 Oslo, Norway (office). *Telephone:* 22-40-31-30 (office). *Fax:* 22-40-31-31 (office). *E-mail:* einar.kloster@online.no (office).

KLÜFT, Carolina Evelyn; Swedish athlete; b. 2 Feb. 1983, Boras; d. of Johnny Kluft and Ingalill Kluft; m. Patrik Klüft 2007; ed Växjö Katedralskola, Växjö Univ.; heptathlete; took up athletics in 1995, int. debut in Santiago 2000; gold medals: European Jr Championships 2000, 2002, World Jr Championships 2000, European Championships 2002 (broke her own world junior record), 2006, European Indoor Championships 2005, 2007, World Championships 2003 (became third athlete to score over 7,000 points), 2005, 2007 and Olympic Games 2004; also won gold medal at the pentathlon at World Indoor Championships 2003, bronze medal at Long Jump at World Indoor Championships 2004; mem. IFK Växjö club; European Athletic Asscn Athlete of the Year 2003, 2006, Swedish Sports Fed. Sportswoman of the Year 2003. *Leisure interests:* friends and family. *Address:* Norgatan 24, 352 31 Växjö, Sweden (office). *Telephone:* (470) 70-35-32 (office). *Fax:* (470) 70-35-39 (office). *E-mail:* johnny.kluft@euroaccident.com (home). *Website:* www.rf.se (home).

KLUG, Sir Aaron, Kt, OM, ScD, FRS; British biochemist; *Group Leader, Division of Structural Studies, MRC Laboratory of Molecular Biology, Cambridge;* b. 11 Aug. 1926; s. of Lazar Klug and Bella Silin; m. Liebe Bobrow 1948; two s. (one deceased); ed Durban High School and Univs of the Witwatersrand, Cape Town and Cambridge; Jr Lecturer 1947–48; Research Student, Cavendish Lab., Univ. of Cambridge 1949–52, Rouse-Ball Research Studentship, Trinity Coll., Cambridge 1949–52, Colloid Science Dept, Cambridge 1953; Nuffield Research Fellow, Birkbeck Coll., London 1954–57; Dir Virus Structure Research Group, Birkbeck Coll. 1958–61; mem. of staff and Group Leader, MRC Lab. of Molecular Biology, Cambridge 1962–, Jt Head, Div. of Structural Studies 1978–86, Dir 1986–96; Pres. Royal Soc. 1995–2000; Fellow of Peterhouse 1962–93; Foreign Assoc. NAS; Foreign mem. Max Planck Gesellschaft 1984, Acad. des Sciences, Paris 1989, Japan Acad. 1999; Foreign Hon. mem. American Acad. of Arts and Sciences; Hon. Fellow, Trinity Coll., Cambridge, Royal Coll. of Physicians 1987, Royal Coll. of Pathologists 1991, Peterhouse, Cambridge 1993–, Birkbeck Coll. 1994; Hon. Prof., Univ. of Cambridge 1989; Hon. DSc (Chicago) 1978, (Columbia) 1978, (Witwatersrand 1984), (Hull) 1985, (Jerusalem) 1985, (St Andrews) 1987, (Western Ont.) 1991, (Warwick) 1994, (Cape Town) 1997, (London) 1999, (Oxford) 2001; Dr hc (Strasbourg) 1978, (Stirling) 1998; Hon. Dr Fil. (Stockholm) 1980; Hon. LittD (Cantab.) 1998; Hon. DLitt (Cambridge) 1998; Heineken Prize, Royal Netherlands Acad. of Science 1979, Louisa Gross Horwitz Prize, Columbia Univ. 1981, Nobel Prize for Chem. 1982, Copley Medal, Royal Soc. 1985, Harden Medal, Biochemical Soc. 1985, Baly Medal, Royal Coll. of Physicians 1987; William Bate Hardy Prize, Cambridge Philosophical Soc. 1996, Croonian Prize Lecture, Royal Soc. 2007. *Publications:* articles in scientific journals. *Leisure interests:* reading, ancient history. *Address:* MRC Laboratory of Molecular Biology, Cambridge, CB2 2QH, England (office). *Telephone:* (1223) 248011 (office). *E-mail:* akl@mrc-lmb.cam.ac.uk (office). *Website:* www2.mrc-lmb.cam.ac.uk/SS (office).

KLUGE, John Werner, BA; American broadcasting and advertising company executive; *Chairman and President, Metromedia Company;* b. 21 Sept. 1914, Chemnitz, Germany; s. of Fritz Kluge and Gertrude Kluge (née Donj); one s. one d.; ed Wayne State Univ., Detroit and Columbia Univ.; with Otten Bros Inc., Detroit 1937–41; served in US Army 1941–45; Pres., Dir WGAY Radio Station, Silver Spring, Md 1946–59, St Louis Broadcasting Corpn, Brentwood, Mo. 1953–58, Pittsburgh Broadcasting Co. 1954–59; Pres., Treas., Dir Capitol Broadcasting Co., Nashville 1954–59, Assoc. Broadcasters Inc., Fort Worth, Dallas 1957–59; pnr, Western NY Broadcasting Co., Buffalo 1957–60; Pres., Dir Washington Planagraph Co. 1956–60, Mid-Fla Radio Corpn, Orlando 1952–59; Treasurer, Dir Mid-Fla TV Corpn 1957–60; owner, Kluge Investment Co., Washington, DC 1956–60; pnr, Nashton Properties, Nashville 1954–60, Texworth Investment Co., Fort Worth 1957–60; Chair. Bd Seaboard Service System Inc. 1957–58; Pres. New England Fritos, Boston 1947–55, New York Inst. of Dietetics 1953–60; Chair. Bd, Treas., Dir, Kluge, Finkelstein & Co., Baltimore; Chair. Bd, Treas., Tri-Suburban Broadcasting Corpn, Washington, Kluge & Co.; Chair. Bd, Pres., Treas., Silver City Sales Co., Washington; Dir Marriott-Hot Shoppes Inc., Nat. Bank Md, Waldorf Astoria Corpn and other cos; Vice-Pres. Bd of Dirs United Cerebral Palsy Research and Educational Foundation 1972–; Chair. Bd, Pres., CEO Metromedia Inc., Secaucus, NJ 1959–86 (after sale of TV stations to News Corpn); now Chair. Pres. Metromedia Co., E Rutherford, NJ; f. John W. Kluge Foundation; Library of Congress Living Legend Award. *Address:* Metromedia Company, 1 Meadowlands Plaza, East Rutherford, NJ 07073, USA (home). *Telephone:* (201) 531-8000 (office). *Fax:* (201) 531-2804 (office).

KLUTSE, Kwassi; Togolese politician; fmr Minister of Planning and Territorial Devt; Prime Minister, Minister of Planning and Territorial Devt 1996–99. *Address:* c/o Office of the Prime Minister, Lomé, Togo.

KLUZA, Stanisław, PhD; Polish economist and government official; *Chairman, Komisji Nadzoru Finansowego (Polish Financial Supervision Authority);* b. 2 June 1972, Warsaw; m.; ed Warsaw School of Econs, Washington Univ., St Louis, USA, Univ. of Glasgow, UK; early positions included working at Higher School of Int. Commerce and Finance (GSBE-HSICF and Computerland shop; worked at Unilever Polska 1994–98, McKinsey & Co. 1998–99; Head, Econ. Analysis Team, Office for Strategic Planning, Bank Gospodarki Żymnościowej SA (BGŻ) 2002–03, Chief Economist and Adviser to Pres. of Man. Bd 2003–06; Second Sec. of State and Deputy Minister of Finance May–July 2006, Minister of Finance July–Sept. 2006; Chair. Komisji Nadzoru Finansowego (Polish Financial Supervision Authority) 2006–; Asst Prof., Inst. of Statistics and Demography, Warsaw School of Econs; mem. Supervisory Bd, Siersza Power Generation Plant; mem. Soc. of Polish Economists, Hon. Council of Experts of AISEC Poland, Club 01; Fulbright Scholar, Dekaban-Liddle Scholar; Prime Minister's Award for Doctoral Thesis, Foundation for Polish Science Award. *Publications:* numerous articles in professional publications. *Address:* Komisji Nadzoru Finansowego, Plac Powstańców, Warszawy 1, 00-950 Warsaw, Poland (office). *Telephone:* (22) 3326600 (office). *Fax:* (22) 3326793 (office). *Website:* www.knf.gov.pl (office).

KNACKSTEDT, Günter Wilhelm Karl, PhD; German diplomatist; *Correspondent, Börsen-Zeitung;* b. 29 July 1929, Berlin; s. of Willi Knackstedt and Anni Knackstedt; m. (divorced); two s.; m. 2nd Marianne Fischbach 1984; ed Univs. of Frankfurt, Paris, Cincinnati and Harvard; Ed. Cincinnati Enquirer daily newspaper 1958–59; Chief Ed. You and Europe, Wiesbaden 1959–61; joined diplomatic service 1961; Press Attaché, Havana 1963, Caracas 1963–66; Ministry of Foreign Affairs 1966–74; Sec. for Parl. Affairs 1976–79; Political Counsellor, Madrid 1974–76; Amb. to Luxembourg 1979–84, to Council of Europe, Strasbourg 1985–88, to Chile 1988–89, to Poland 1989–92, to Portugal 1992–94; Corresp. Börsen-Zeitung financial newspaper. *Publications:* Compendium of World History 1954, Living with Venezuelans 1968. *Leisure interests:* skiing, tennis, collecting old clocks. *Address:* 7 val Ste Croix, 1371 Luxembourg. *Telephone:* 453701 (office); 225530 (home). *Fax:* 453706 (office).

KNAIFEL, Alexander Aronovich; Russian composer; b. 28 Nov. 1943, Tashkent; s. of Aron Iosifovich Knaifel and Muza Veniaminovna Shapiro-Knaifel; m. Tatiana Ivanovna Melentieva 1965; one d.; ed Moscow and Leningrad Conservatoires; freelance composer; mem. Composers' Union 1968–, Cinematographers' Union 1987–; Order of Friendship 2004; DAAD Honoured Grant-Aided Composer, Berlin 1993, Honoured Art Worker of Russia 1996. *Compositions:* Sonata on a Fairy Tale 1961, A Sling 1962, Diada 1962, Burlesca 1963, Non stop 1963, Marching and Dancing Two-voice Textures 1963, A Toast by Robert Burns 1963, A Flower 1963, A Classical Suite 1963, Ostinati 1964, An Angel and Five Poems by Mikhail Lermontov 1964; Musique militaire 1964, A Plain-air-fugue, a Fugue-interior 1964, An Anthem to Foolishness 1964, Turno a turno 1964, In via 1964, In Memory of Samuil Marshak 1964, Those Seeking the City to Come 1964–65, Passacaglia 1965, The Canterville Ghost 1965–66, Disarmament 1966, 150 000 000 1966, Lamento 1967, Salve! 1967, Tertium non datur 1967, Petrograd Sparrows 1967, A Little One and a Black One 1968, Monodia 1968, Medea 1968, Argumentum de jure 1969, Jeanne 1970–78, Baby Songs in Sleep 1972, A prima vista 1972, Appelli 1972, Status nascendi 1973–75, Two Times 1975, Vampampet 1975, Ainana 1978, FFPh 1978–2004, Rafferty Jazz Chorus 1980, Vera (Faith) 1980, A Call 1980, Solaris 1980, Da (Yes) 1980, A Silly Horse 1981, A Chance 1982, Barbarian Rock 1982, Nika 1983–84, Churiki 1984, Epitaphs 1984, God 1985, Agnus Dei 1985, A Kholop's Wing 1986, Insanity 1987, Through the Rainbow of Involuntary Tears 1987–88, Litania 1988, Notturno 1988, Shramy marsha (Scars of marching) 1988, Voznosheniye (The Holy Oblation) 1991, Svete Tikhiy (O Gladsome Light) 1991, Once Again on the Hypothesis 1992, Scalae Iacobis 1992, Chapter Eight 1992–93, Cantus 1993, Maranatha 1993, Butterfly 1993, In Air Clear and Unseen 1994, Alice in Wonderland 1994–2002, O Havenly King 1994, O Comforter 1995, Psalm 51 (50) 1995, Amicta sole 1995, Blazhenstva 1996, Bliss 1997, With the White on the White 1997–98, Lux aeterna 1997, This Child 1997, The Tabernacle 1998, Snowflake on a Spiderthread 1998, A Day 1999, Small Blue Feathers 2001, Morning Prayers 2001, Petia i Folk 2001, A Fairy Tale of a Fisherman and a Little Fish 2002, Lukomoriye 2002–03, A Confession 2003, Nativity 2003, The Cherubimic Hymn 2004, Gee! 2004, Chalice 2004, Old Photos 2004, The Little Beads for Niua 2004, Of the Pope and of His Workman Balda 2004, O Spirit of Truth 2005, Tzarevna 2005, The Lord's Prayer 2006, Bridge 2006–07, O Master of My Days 2007, A Mad Tea-Party 2007, For Tatiana and Annushka 2007, Pleno Dolcissimo 2007, E.F. 2008; incidental music for 40 films. *Publications:* Musique militaire 1974, Diada (Two Pieces) 1975, Classical Suite 1976, The Canterville Ghost 1977, Five Poems by Mikhail Lermontov 1978, Lamento 1979, The Petrograd Sparrows 1981, A Silly Horse 1985,

Medea 1989, Vera (Faith) 1990, Passacaglia 1990, Da (Yes) 1991, O Comforter 1997, Bliss 1997. *Leisure interests:* photography, shooting video films. *Address:* Skobelevski pr. 5, Apt 130, 194214 St Petersburg, Russia (home). *Telephone:* (812) 293-82-68 (home). *Fax:* (812) 293-53-97 (home). *E-mail:* knaifel@hotmail.com (office); knaifel@mail.ru (home). *Website:* www.ceo.spb.ru/rus/music/knaifel.a.a (office).

KNAPP, Charles, MA, PhD; American economist, academic, fmr university administrator and fmr government official; *Distinguished Public Service Fellow, Institute of Higher Education, University of Georgia;* b. 13 Aug. 1946, Ames, Ia; s. of Albert B. Knapp and Anne Marie Knapp; m. Lynne Vickers Knapp 1967; one d.; ed Iowa State Univ. and Univ. of Wisconsin; Asst Prof. of Econs, Univ. of Tex., Austin 1972–76; Special Asst to US Sec. of Labor 1976–79; Deputy Asst Sec. of Labor for Employment Training 1979–81; Visiting Faculty, George Washington Univ. 1981–82; Sr Vice-Pres. Tulane Univ. 1982–85, Exec. Vice-Pres. 1985–87; Pres. and Prof. of Econs, Univ. of Georgia 1987–97, Pres. Emer. 2004–, Distinguished Public Service Fellow, Inst. of Higher Educ.2005–; fmr Pres. Aspen Inst. 1997–99; Sr Fellow, Asscn of Governing Bds of Univs and Colls 1999–2000; Pnr, Heidrick & Struggles Int. Inc., Atlanta 2000; Dir AFLAC, Inc. *Publications:* A Human Capital Approach to the Burden of the Military Draft 1973, Earnings and Individual Variations in Postschool Human Investment 1976, Employment Discrimination 1978. *Address:* Institute of Higher Education, Meigs Hall, University of Georgia, Athens, GA Athens, GA 30602, USA (office). *Telephone:* (706) 542-0620 (office). *E-mail:* cknapp@uga.edu (office). *Website:* www.uga.edu/ihe/knapp.html (office).

KNAPP, Oscar, PhD; Swiss economist and diplomatist; *Ambassador to Austria;* m.; ed Univ. of St Gall; fmr Head of Financial, Econ. and Trade Div., Embassy in Washington, DC; Amb. to Brazil 1996–2000; Exec. mem., State Secr. of Econ. Affairs, mem. Bd of Dirs and Head, Econ. Devt Co-operation Office 2003–06; Amb. to Austria 2006–. *Address:* Embassy of Switzerland, Prinz-Eugen-Str. 7, 1030 Vienna, Austria (office). *Telephone:* (1) 795-05-0 (office). *Fax:* (1) 795-05-21 (office). *E-mail:* vie.vertretung@eda.admin.ch (office). *Website:* www.eda.admin.ch/wien (office).

KŇAŽKO, Milan; Slovak politician, actor and broadcast industry executive; b. 28 Aug. 1945, Horné Plachtince, Velký Krtíš Dist; m. Eugenia Kňažková; three s.; ed Acad. of Performing Arts, Bratislava, Univ. of Nancy, France; mem. Theatre on the Promenade (drama co.), Bratislava 1970–71; actor, New Theatre, Bratislava 1971–85; mem. Slovak Nat. Theatre Drama Co. Bratislava, 1985–; Co-founder, Public Against Violence (political movt) Nov. 1989, rally speaker 1989–90; adviser to Pres. of Czechoslovakia 1989–90; Deputy Fed. Ass. 1990–92; Minister for Foreign Affairs, Govt of Slovak Repub. 1990–91; mem. and Vice-Chair. Movt for Democratic Slovakia 1991–93 (resgnd); Deputy Prime Minister, Slovak Repub. 1992–93, Minister for Foreign Affairs 1992–93; apptd Minister of Culture 1998; Chair. Govt Council of Slovak Repub. for Ethnic Groups 1992–93; Chair. Alliance of Democrats 1993–94, Ind. Deputies Club 1993–; First Deputy Chair. Democratic Union of Slovakia 1994–2000; Vice-Chair. Slovak Democratic and Christian Union (SDCHU) 2000–; Dir Gen. Televízia JOJ (pvt. TV network) 2003–07; numerous roles on stage, in films, on TV, on radio; Merited Artist Award 1986 (returned award 1989). *Film roles include:* Nevesta hôl (The Bride of the Mountains, UK) 1972, Kohút nezaspieva 1986, Svet nic neví 1987, Maria Stuarda (TV) 1988, Dobrí holubi se vracejí 1988, Omyly tradicnej moralky (TV) 1989, Dlouhá míle (TV mini-series) 1989, Devet kruhu pekla 1989, Svedek umírajícího casu 1990, Poslední motýl (The Last Butterfly) 1991, Bel ami (TV) 2005. *Leisure interests:* family, sport, culture, theatre, golf. *Address:* c/o Televízia JOJ, PO Box 33, 830 07 Bratislava 37, Slovakia (office).

KNEALE, (Robert) Bryan (Charles), RA, RWA, FRBS; British sculptor; b. 19 June 1930, Douglas, Isle of Man; s. of the late William Kneale and Lilian Kewley; m. Doreen Lister 1956 (died 1998); one s. (deceased) one d.; ed Douglas High School, Douglas School of Art, Isle of Man, Royal Acad. Schools; Tutor, RCA Sculpture School 1964, Sr Tutor 1980–85, Head Dept of Sculpture 1985–90; Head of Sculpture School, Hornsey 1967; Assoc. Lecturer, Chelsea School of Art 1970; Fellow RCA 1972, Sr Tutor 1980–85, Head of Sculpture Dept 1985–90; Prof. of Drawing, Royal Coll. of Art 1990–95, Sr Fellow 1995; Master of Sculpture RA 1982–85, Prof. 1985–90; mem. Fine Art Panels, Nat. Council for Art Design 1964–71, Arts Council 1971–73, CNAA 1974–82; Chair. Air and Space 1972–73; organized Sculpture '72, RA 1972, Battersea Park Silver Jubilee Sculpture 1977, Sade exhbn, Cork 1982, Sculpture for Westminster Cathedral 1999; comms include Bronze Doors, Portsmouth Cathedral 1999, sculpture for Villa Marina Douglas and Nobles Hosp., Isle of Man 2004, Capt. Quilliam Memorial, Castletown, Isle of Man 2005, Illiam Dhone Memorial, Malew Church, Isle of Man 2006; Rome Prize 1949, Leverhulme Award 1952, Young Artist Competition Prize 1955, Arts Council Purchase Award 1978. *Address:* 10A Muswell Road, London, N10 2BG, England. *Telephone:* (20) 8444-7617. *Fax:* (20) 8444-7617.

KNEŽEVIĆ, Stojan, DenM, DèsSc; Croatian professor of internal medicine; *Professor of Medicine, University of Zagreb-Croatia;* b. 6 Dec. 1923, Split; s. of Stevo Knežević and Marija Knežević; m. Jelena Konstantinović 1947; one s. one d.; ed Univ. of Zagreb; country doctor, DZ-Sisak 1952–54; Specialist in Internal Medicine 1954–57; Asst Clinic for Internal Medicine, Zagreb 1957–63; intern, St Antoine Hosp., Paris; Asst Prof., then Prof. of Medicine, Univ. of Zagreb-Croatia 1963–; Head of Gastroenterology Inst., Univ. of Zagreb; Ed.-in-Chief, Acta Medica Croatica 1996–; Pres. Zbor liječnika Hrvatske 1965–74; Pres. Acad. Medicinskl znanosti Hrvatske 1982–92; mem. Senate; mem. Soc. européene de culture; Hon. mem. Croatian Acad. of Medical Sciences, Hrvatski Liječnički Zbor, Czecho-Slovak Medical Asscn, Croatian Anthropological Soc.; Order of Danice Hrvatske (Rudjer Bošković) 2001; Award of the City of Zagreb 1966, Gold Medal, Bologna. *Publications:* Klinička medicina 1959, Interna medicina 1970, Etika i medicina 1976, San je java snena 1977 (literary), Medicinske razglednice 1985, Slike koje pamtim 1989 (poetry), Medicinski susreti 1990, Medicina Starije Dobi 1990, Udžbenik Interne Medicine 1991, Veliki Medicinski Savjetnik, Misli i Poruke (Aforizmi) 1998, Izronci iz Tmine (poetry) 1999, Moje Dvorište u Ratu 2002, Navoji Vatre i Dima 2003, Iskre i Iskrice 2003, Potomci Aforizama 2004, Draga Ženo... (poetry) 2007. *Leisure interests:* writing, poetry, philosophy. *Address:* Smičiklasova 19, 10000 Zagreb, Croatia (home). *Telephone:* (1) 4614856 (home).

KNIAZEV, Alexander A.; Russian cellist; b. 21 April 1961; s. of Alexandre S. Schwarzmann and Ludmila P. Kniazeva; m. (deceased); ed Moscow State Conservatory, Nyzhny-Novgorod State Conservatory; Prof. Moscow State Conservatory 1995; masterclasses in France, Spain, Republic of Korea, Philippines; concerts 1978–, in Russia, UK, France, Germany, Italy, Spain, Belgium, Austria, USA, S Africa, S America, Republic of Korea, Japan and elsewhere; performed with partners V. Afanasyev, S. Milstein, E. Leonskaya, B. Engerer, Kun Woo Oark, V. Spivakov, V. Tretyakov, M. Brunello, Yu. Bashmet, Yu. Milkis; First Prize Nat. Competition, Vilnius, Lithuania 1977, Third Prize G. Cassado Int. Competition, Florence, Italy 1979, First Prize Int. Chamber Music Competition, Trapani, Italy 1987, Second Prize Tchaikovsky Int. Competition, Moscow, Russia 1990, First Prize Unisa Int. Competition, Pretoria, S Africa. *Leisure interest:* chess. *Address:* Skornyzhny per. 1, apt 58, Moscow 107078, Russia (home).

KNIGHT, Andrew Stephen Bower, MA; British editor and business executive; *Chairman, J. Rothschild Capital Management;* b. 1 Nov. 1939; s. of M. W. B. Knight and S. E. F. Knight; m. 1st Victoria Catherine Brittain 1966 (divorced); one s.; m. 2nd Begum Sabiha Rumani Malik 1975 (divorced 1991); two d.; m. 3rd Marita Georgina Phillips Crawley 2006; ed Ampleforth Coll., York, Balliol Coll., Oxford; Ed. The Economist 1974–86; Chief Exec. Daily Telegraph 1986–89, Ed.-in-Chief 1987–89; Chair. News Int. PLC 1990–94; Chair. Ballet Rambert 1984–87; Chair. Times Newspaper Holdings 1990–94; Dir News Corpn 1991–; Dir Rothschild Investment Trust CP 1996–, Chair. J. Rothschild Capital Management 2008–; Chair. Shipston Home Nursing 1996–2006; Chair. Jerwood Charity 2003–06; mem. Advisory Bd Center for Econ. Policy Research, Stanford Univ., USA 1981–; Gov. mem. Council of Man. Ditchley Foundation 1982–; Founder-Trustee Spinal Muscular Atrophy Trust; now farms in Warwicks. and Dannevirke, NZ. *Address:* J. Rothschild Capital Management Ltd, 27 St James's Place, London, SW1A 1NR (office); Compton Scorpion Manor, Shipston-on-Stour, Warwicks., CV36 4PJ, England (home).

KNIGHT, Gladys Maria; American singer; b. 28 May 1944, Atlanta, Ga; d. of Merald Knight and Elizabeth Knight (née Woods); m. 2nd Barry Hankerson 1974 (divorced 1979); one s. and two c. (from previous marriage); tours with Morris Brown Choir 1950–53; formed Gladys Knight and The Pips 1953–89; mem. Lloyd Terry Jazz Ltd 1959–61; numerous tours and live appearances, TV and film appearances; solo artist 1989–; four Grammy Awards, American Music Awards 1984, 1988. *Film and TV appearances:* Pipe Dreams 1976, Charlie & Co. (series) 1985, Desperado (TV film) 1987, An Enemy Among Us (TV film) 1987, Twenty Bucks 1993, Hollywood Homicide 2003, Unbeatable Harold 2005. *Recordings include:* albums: Letter Full of Tears 1961, Gladys Knight and The Pips 1964, Everybody Needs Love 1967, Feelin' Bluesy 1968, Silk & Soul 1968, Nitty Gritty 1969, All in a Knight's Work 1970, If I Were Your Woman 1971, Standing Ovation 1971, All I Need Is Time 1973, Imagination 1973, Help Me Make It Through The Night 1973, It Hurt Me So Bad 1973, Neither One Of Us 1973, Claudine (OST) 1974, I Feel A Song 1974, Knight Time 1974, 2nd Anniversary 1975, A Little Knight Music 1975, Bless This House 1976, Pipe Dreams 1976, Love Is Always On Your Mind 1977, Still Together 1977, Miss Gladys Knight 1978, The One And Only 1978, Gladys Knight 1979, Memories 1979, About Love 1980, Midnight Train To Georgia 1980, That Special Time of Year 1980, Teen Anguish 1981, Touch 1980, Visions 1983, Life 1985, All Our Love 1988, Christmas Album 1989, Good Woman 1991, Just For You 1994, Many Different Roads 1998, At Last 2000, Christmas Celebrations 2002, The Best Thing That Ever Happened To Me 2003, One Voice 2005. *Address:* Newman Management Inc, 2110 East Flamingo Road, Suite 300, Las Vegas, NV 89119, USA (office).

KNIGHT, Sir Harold Murray, Kt, KBE, DSC, MComm; Australian banker; b. 13 Aug. 1919, Melbourne; s. of W.H.P. Knight; m. Gwenyth Catherine Pennington 1951; four s. one d.; ed Scotch Coll., Melbourne and Melbourne Univ.; Commonwealth Bank of Australia 1936–40, 1946–55; served Australian Imperial Forces and Royal Australian Navy 1940–45 (awarded DSC); Statistics Div., Research and Statistics Dept of IMF 1955–59, Asst Chief 1957–59; Research Economist, Reserve Bank of Australia 1960, Asst Man. Investment Dept 1962–64, Man. Investment Dept 1964–68, Deputy Gov. Reserve Bank of Australia and Deputy Chair. of Bank's Bd 1968–75, Gov. and Chair. of Bd 1975–82; Dir Western Mining Corpn 1982–91, Mercantile Mutual Group 1983–89, Chair. 1985–89; Chair. I.B.J. Australia Bank Ltd 1985–92; Dir Angus and Coote Holdings Ltd 1986–93; mem. Police Bd, NSW 1988–89, 1991–93; Pres. Scripture Union, NSW 1983–2002; Hon. Visiting Fellow, Macquarie Univ. 1983–86, Councillor 1984–87, 1990–93; Hon. DLitt (Macquarie Univ.) 1995. *Publication:* Introducción al Análisis Monetario 1959. *Address:* 26 Cardigan Street, Stanmore, NSW 2048, Australia.

KNIGHT, Keith Desmond St. Aubyn, BA, QC; Jamaican lawyer and politician; b. Brompton, St Elizabeth; m.; two c.; ed Howard Univ. and Univ. of Pittsburgh, USA; admitted to Bar, Grays Inn, London, UK 1973, admitted to Inner Bar as QC 1995; entered elective politics 1989; MP for E Cen. St Catherine, Minister of Nat. Security and Justice 1989–2001, of Foreign Affairs and Foreign Trade 2001–06; Council Pres., UN Security Council Meeting concerning Afghanistan 2001; Co-founder and Sr Pnr, Knight, Junor &

Samuels, Kingston (law firm) 2006–; Exec. mem. People's Nat. Party; mem. Advocate Asscn, Jamaican Bar Asscn; Founder-Pres. Jamaica Nat. Asscn; fmr Pres. Caribbean Asscn of Students. *Address:* Upstairs Bog Walk Post Office, St. Catherine, Jamaica (office). *Telephone:* 985-1192 (office). *Fax:* 985-1192 (home).

KNIGHT, Malcolm D., MSc, PhD; Canadian economist; b. Windsor, Ont.; m.; three d.; ed Univ. of Toronto and London School of Econs, UK; teacher of econs, Univ. of Toronto and LSE 1971–75; joined Research Dept, IMF 1975, served successively as economist in Financial Studies Div., Chief of External Adjustment Issues, Asst Dir of Research Dept for Developing Country Studies, Deputy Dir of Middle East Dept, Monetary and Exchange Affairs Dept, European Dept; fmrly COO Bank of Canada, Sr Deputy Gov. 1999–2003, mem. Bd of Dirs; Gen. Man. BIS 2003–09; fmrly Adjunct Prof., Centre for Canadian Studies, Johns Hopkins Univ. School of Advanced Int. Studies, Virginia Polytechnic and State Univ.; Academic Visitor, Centre for Labour Econs, LSE 1985–86; mem. Editorial Bd IMF Staff Papers 1987–97; Trustee, Int. Accounting Standards Cttee Foundation, Per Jacobsson Foundation; mem. Bd of Patrons of the European Asscn for Banking and Financial History, Johns Hopkins Univ. Soc. of Scholars. *Publications include:* numerous publs in fields of macroeconomics, int. finance and banking. *Address:* c/o Bank for International Settlements, Centralbahnplatz 2, 4052 Basel, Switzerland (office).

KNIGHT, Philip H(ampson), MBA; American business executive; *Chairman, Nike Inc.;* b. 24 Feb. 1938, Portland, Ore.; s. of William W. Knight and Lota Hatfield; m. Penelope Parks 1968; two s.; ed Univ. of Ore., Stanford Univ.; First Lt US Army 1959–60; CEO Nike Inc., Beaverton, Ore. 1969–2004, Chair. 1969–; Dir US–Asian Business Council, Washington; mem. American Inst. of Certified Public Accountants; Ore. Businessman of the Year 1982. *Leisure interests:* sports, reading, movies. *Address:* One Bowerman Dr., Beaverton, OR 97005 (home); Nike Inc., 1 SW Bowerman Drive, Beaverton, OR 97005, USA (office). *Telephone:* (503) 671-3598 (office). *Fax:* (503) 644-6655 (office). *E-mail:* lisa.mckillips@nike.com (office). *Website:* www.nike.com (office).

KNIPPING VICTORIA, Eladio, LLB; Dominican Republic diplomatist; b. 28 June 1933, Santiago de los Caballeros; s. of Elpidio Knipping and Luz Victoria; m. Soledad Knipping 1963; one s. one d.; ed Autonomous University of Santo Domingo, Diplomatic School of Spain, School of Int. Affairs, Madrid; Asst to Madrid Consulate 1963–65, Econ. Attaché, Netherlands 1966–68; Sec. Consultative Comm. Ministry of Foreign Affairs; Minister-Counsellor and Deputy Chief of Div. of UN Affairs, OAS and Int. Orgs 1966–68, 1969–74; Minister-Counsellor Perm. Mission to UN, New York 1968–69, Amb. to Honduras 1974–78; Perm. Rep. to OAS 1979–83, 1987–95; Amb. (non-resident) to Barbados, Jamaica, St Lucia and Trinidad and Tobago 1990–, to Haiti 1995–97, to Panama 1997–2001, to Honduras 2001; Perm. Rep. to UN, New York 1983–87; Pres. Juridical and Political Comm., OAS Perm. Council 1981–82, 1992–93; Dominican mem. Int. Court of Arbitration, The Hague; Del. UN III Conf. of Law of the Sea; Lecturer in Int. Law Pedro Henríquez Ureña Univ. 1969; f. Inst. Comparative Law; mem. Spanish-Portuguese-American and Philippine Inst. of Int. Law (Pres. 1990–92); UN Adlai Stevenson Fellow. *Leisure interests:* reading, listening to music. *Address:* c/o Secretariat of State for External Relations, Avda Independencia 752, Santo Domingo, DN, Dominican Republic (office).

KNÍŽÁK, Milan; Czech multimedia artist, writer, art theorist and musician; *Director-General, National Gallery, Prague;* b. 19 April 1940, Plzeň; s. of Karel Knížák and Emilie Knížáková; m. 1st Soňa Švecová 1967; m., 2nd Jarka Charvátová 1970; m., 3rd Marie Geislerová 1975; ed Acad. of Fine Arts, Charles Univ., Prague; f. Aktual group; prosecuted and imprisoned on numerous occasions 1957–89 mostly for his art activities; in USA (at invitation of Fluxus group of artists) 1968–70; Univ. Prof.; Rector Acad. of Fine Arts, Prague 1990–97; Dir Gen. Nat. Gallery Prague 1999–; mem. Czech TV Council 2001–03; awards include DAAD Berlin, Barkenhoff Worpswede, Germany, Schloss Bleckede, Germany, Schloss Solitude, Germany, 5th Inter-Triennale Wrocław, Poland; Medal 1st Degree, Ministry for Educ. and Physical Training 1997. *Films:* Stone Ceremony, Material Events, Kill Yourself and Fly. *Albums:* Broken Music 1979, Obřad hořící mysli (The Rite of a Burning Mind) 1992, Navrhuju krysy (I Propose the Rats) 2002. *Plays:* Also in my Belly Grows a Tree, Heads. *Radio Play:* Adamits. *Television:* Kill Yourself and Fly (a film about M. Knížák) 1991. *Publications:* Zeremonien 1971, Action as a Life Style 1986, Neo Knížák 1991, Nový ráj (New Paradise) 1996, Bez důvodu (Without Reason) 1996, Jeden z možných postojů, jak být s umění (One Way to Exist with Art) 1998, Skutečnost, že jsem se narodil, beru jako výzvu (The Fact I was Born I Take as a Challenge) 1999, Tady ve Skotsku (Here in Scotland) (with J. Lancaster) 2000, Básně 1974–2001 (Poems 1974–2001) 2001, Vedle umění (Close to the Arts) 2002, and many others. *Leisure interests:* collecting old marionettes and scientific research on them. *Address:* AVU, U Akademie 4, 17000 Prague 7; Národní galerie v Praze, Palác Kinských, Staroměstské náměstí 12, 11015 Prague 1, Czech Republic (office). *Telephone:* (22) 2329331 (office); (602) 321208 (home). *Fax:* (22) 2324641 (office); (22) 4919782 (home). *E-mail:* genreditel@ngprague.cz (office). *Website:* www.ngprague.cz (office); www.avu.cz (office).

KNOBLOCH, Bernd, BBA, LLB; German business executive; b. 20 Nov. 1951, Munich; ed Ludwigs-Maximilians-Universität, Munich; admitted to German Bar 1979; mem. Bd of Man. Dirs Eurohypo AG 1992–, Deputy Chair. of Man. Bd, Eurohypo AG (cr. following merger of Deutsche Hyp AG, Rheinhypo AG and Eurohypo AG 2002) 2002–04, Chair. of Man. Bd 2004–08; mem. Bd of Man. Dirs Commerzbank AG 2006–08; mem. Supervisory Bd, Hypo Real Estate Holding AG 2008–; mem. Städel Admin, Frankfurt 2005; mem. Bd Hertle Foundation, VINCI Deutschland GmbH, Ludwigshafen, DB Real Estate Investment GmbH, Europäische Hypothekenbank SA, Luxembourg. *Address:* Ludolfusstrasse 13, D-60487 Frankfurt-am-Main (office); Frauenlobstrasse 60A, 60487 Frankfurt-am-Main, Germany (home). *Telephone:* 697706-2001 (office); 69707-5555. *Fax:* 697706-2015 (office). *Website:* www.eurohypo.com (office).

KNOLL, József; Hungarian pharmacologist; *Professor Emeritus, Department of Pharmacology and Pharmacotherapy, Semmelweis University;* b. 30 May 1925, Kassa; s. of Jakab Knoll and Blanka Deutscher; m. Dr Berta Knoll; one d.; ed Semmelweis Univ., Budapest; Asst Lecturer Univ. Pharmacological Inst.; Lecturer Medical Univ. 1958, Prof. and Head 1962–95, Vice-Rector 1964–70; currently Prof. Emer., Dept of Pharmacology and Pharmacotherapy, Semmelweis Univ.; Corresp. mem. Hungarian Acad. of Sciences 1970, mem. 1979–; Gen. Sec. Hungarian Pharmacological Soc. 1962–67, Pres. 1967–83, Hon. Pres. 1984–; Chair. Nat. Drug Admin. Cttee and Drug Research Cttee of the Acad. of Sciences; Vice-Pres. Medical Sciences Section, Hungarian Acad. of Sciences 1967–76; mem. Leopoldina Deutsche Akad. der Naturwissenschaften, Halle 1974–; councillor, Int. Union of Pharmacological Sciences 1981–84, First Vice-Pres. 1984–87; Foreign mem., Polish Acad. of Arts and Sciences 1995; mem. editorial bd of numerous int. pharmacological periodicals;; Hon. mem. Pharmacological Socs of Czech Repub., Bulgaria, Poland and Italy; Hon. FRSM 1990; Dr hc (Medizinische Akad., Magdeburg) 1984, (Bologna Univ.) 1989; Nat. Prize of Hungary 1985, Award for Distinguished Service in European Pharmacology 1999, Award for Outstanding Contribs to Anti-Aging Medicine 2001, Nat. Prize (Széchenyi) Hungary 2003. *Achievements include:* developed (-)-deprenyl (Selegiline), a drug used world-wide. *Publications:* Theory of Active Reflexes 1969, Handbook of Pharmacology, nine edns since 1965, The Brain and Its Self Springer 2005; over 800 papers in int. trade journals; 53 patents. *Leisure interest:* visual arts. *Address:* Semmelweis University, Faculty of General Medicine, Department of Pharmacology and Pharmacotherapy, Budapest 1089, Nagyvárad tér 4, Hungary. *Telephone:* (1) 210-4405 (office); (1) 329-3805 (home). *Fax:* (1) 210-4405. *E-mail:* jozsefknoll@hotmail.com (office). *Website:* http://xenia.sote.hu/depts/pharmacology/staff/knoll.htm.

KNOPFLER, Mark, OBE, BA; British musician (guitar), singer, songwriter and record producer; b. 12 Aug. 1949, Glasgow, Scotland; s. of late Erwin Knopfler and of Louisa Knopfler; brother of David Knopfler; m. Lourdes Salomone 1983; two s.; ed Leeds Univ.; fmr music journalist Yorkshire Evening Post; fmr mem. bands, Brewer's Droop, Cafe Racers; f. mem., Dire Straits 1977–88, 1991–95; group toured world-wide; first-ever CD single, Brothers In Arms 1985; formed own ad hoc band, Notting Hillbillies 1989; solo artist 1984–, guest on numerous albums by other artists; Hon. DMus (Leeds) 1995; Ivor Novello Awards for Outstanding British Lyric 1983, Best Film Theme 1984, Outstanding Contribution to British Music 1989, Nordoff-Robbins Silver Clef Award for Outstanding Services to British Music 1985, Grammy Awards for Best Country Performance (with Chet Atkins) 1986, 1991. *Film music composition:* Local Hero 1983, Cal 1984, Comfort and Joy 1984, Alchemy Live (television) 1984, The Princess Bride 1987, Last Exit to Brooklyn 1989, Tishina 1991, Wag the Dog 1998, Hooves of Fire (television) 1999, Metroland 1999, A Shot at Glory 2001, songs for numerous other films. *Recordings include:* albums: with Dire Straits: Dire Straits 1978, Communiqué 1979, Making Movies 1980, Love Over Gold 1982, Extendedanceplay 1983, Alchemy: Dire Straits Live 1984, Brothers In Arms 1985, Money For Nothing 1988, On Every Street 1991, On The Night 1993, Live at the BBC 1995, Sultans of Swing 1998; solo: Comfort and Joy 1984, Neck and Neck (with Chet Atkins) 1990, Golden Heart 1996, Sailing To Philadelphia 2000, The Ragpicker's Dream 2002, Shangri-La 2004, All the Roadrunning (with Emmylou Harris) 2006, Kill to get Crimson 2007; with Notting Hillbillies: Missing... Presumed Having a Good Time 1990. *Address:* William Morris Agency, 1325 Avenue of the Americas, New York, NY 10019, USA (office). *Telephone:* (212) 586-5100 (office). *Fax:* (212) 246-3583 (office). *Website:* www.mark-knopfler.com.

KNOPOFF, Leon, BS, MS, PhD; American physicist, geophysicist and academic; *Professor Emeritus of Physics and Geophysics, UCLA;* b. 1 July 1925, Los Angeles, California; m. Joanne Van Cleef 1961; one s. two d.; ed California Inst. of Tech; Asst Prof., Assoc. Prof. of Physics, Miami Univ. 1948–50; mem. staff Univ. of Calif. (LA) 1950–, Prof. of Geophysics 1957–, of Physics 1961–, now Emer., Research Musicologist 1963–, Assoc. Dir Inst. of Geophysics and Planetary Physics 1972–86; Prof. of Geophysics, Calif. Inst. of Tech. 1962–63; Visiting Prof. Technische Hochschule, Karlsruhe (Germany) 1966; Chair. US Upper Mantle Cttee 1963–71, Sec.-Gen. Int. Upper Mantle Cttee 1963–71; Nat. Science Foundation Sr Postdoctoral Fellow 1960–61; Guggenheim Foundation Fellowship (Cambridge) 1976–77; Visiting Prof., Harvard Univ. 1972, Univ. of Chile, Santiago 1973; Chair. Int. Cttee on Mathematical Geophysics 1971–75; H. Jeffreys Lecturer, Royal Astronomical Soc. 1976; mem. NAS, American Philosophical Soc., American Physical Soc.; Fellow, American Acad. of Arts and Sciences, American Geophysical Union; Foreign Assoc., Royal Astronomical Soc.; Hon. mem. Seismological Soc. of America, Hon. Prof., China Earthquake Admin, Beijing Dr hc (Univ. Louis Pasteur, Strasbourg); Int. Co-operation Year Medal (Canada) 1965, Wiechert Medal, German Geophysical Soc. 1978, Gold Medal of the Royal Astronomical Soc. 1979, Medal of the Seismological Soc. of America 1990. *Publications:* The Crust and Upper Mantle of the Pacific Area (co-ed.) 1968, The World Rift System (co-ed.); chapters in Physics and Chemistry of High Pressures (ed. R. L. Bradley) 1963, Physical Acoustics (ed. W. P. Mason) 1965, The Earth's Mantle (ed. T. Gaskell) 1967, The Megatectonics of Oceans and Continents (ed. H. Johnson and B. L. Smith); more than 300 papers in professional journals. *Leisure interests:* mountaineering, gardening, playing piano and harpsichord. *Address:* Department of Earth and Space Sciences, Geology 1809, UCLA, 595 Charles Young Drive East, Box 951567, Los Angeles, CA

90095-1567, USA (office). *Telephone:* (310) 825-1885 (office). *Fax:* (310) 206-3051 (office). *E-mail:* knopoff@physics.ucla.edu (office). *Website:* www.ess.ucla.edu/faculty/knopoff/index.asp (office).

KNORRE, Dmitri Georgievich; Russian chemist and biochemist; b. 28 July 1926, Leningrad; s. of Georgy F. Knorre and Elena A. Knorre; m. Valeria L. Knorre 1959 (died 1996); one s. two d.; ed Moscow Chemical-Technological Inst.; worked in USSR (now Russian) Acad. of Sciences Inst. of Chemical Physics 1947–61, then in all grades to Head Dept of Biochem. at Acad. of Sciences, Inst. of Organic Chem. 1961–84, Dir at Acad. Sciences Inst. of Bio-organic Chem., Novosibirsk 1984–96, Adviser to Pres. Acad. of Sciences 1996–; also Prof. of Univ. of Novosibirsk 1961–, Dean 1961–83; Corresp. mem. of Acad. 1968–81, mem. 1981, Acad.-Sec. Dept of Biochem. and Biophysics 1988–99; Hon. PhD Chem. Science (Novosibirsk Univ.) 1967; Lenin Prize, M. Shemyakin Prize and other awards. *Publications:* Chemical Kinetics, Physical Chemistry, Biological Chemistry. *Leisure interest:* hiking. *Address:* Institute of Bio-organic Chemistry, Prospekt Lavrenteva 8, 630090 Novosibirsk (office); ul. Voyevodskogo 7, 630090 Novosibirsk, Russia (home). *Telephone:* (3832) 36-06-32 (office); (3832) 35-57-03 (home). *Fax:* (3832) 33-36-77 (office). *Website:* www.ibch.ru (office).

KNOTT, John Frederick, OBE, BMet, PhD, ScD, FRS, FREng, FRSA; British materials scientist and academic; *Feeney Professor of Metallurgy and Materials, University of Birmingham;* ed Univs of Sheffield and Cambridge; currently Feeney Prof. of Materials and Metallurgy, Univ. of Birmingham; mem. Health and Safety Comm., Nuclear Safety Advisory Cttee; Past Pres. Birmingham Metallurgical Asscn; Pres. Int. Congress on Fracture 1993–97; mem. Governing Body and Fellow, Churchill Coll. Cambridge; Fellow, Inst. of Materials, Welding Inst.; Foreign mem. Acad. of Sciences of Ukraine; Hon. Prof., Beijing Univ. of Aeronautics and Astronautics, Xi'an Jiatong Univ., People's Repub. of China; Inst. of Metals Lecturer 2005, Robert Franklin Mehl Award 2005, Leverhulme Medal, Royal Soc. 2005. *Publications:* numerous scientific articles in professional journals on the quantitative scientific understanding of fracture processes in metals and alloys and its eng applications. *Address:* Department of Metallurgy and Materials, School of Engineering, Elms Road, Edgbaston, Birmingham, B15 2TT (office); 5 Mildmay Close, Stratford-upon-Avon, Warwicks., CV37 9FR, England (home). *Telephone:* (121) 414-6729 (office); (1789) 261977 (home). *Fax:* (121) 414-7080 (office). *E-mail:* J.F.Knott@bham.ac.uk (office). *Website:* www.eng.bham.ac.uk/metallurgy (office).

KNOWLES, Anthony (Tony) Carroll, BA; American fmr politician; b. 1 Jan. 1943, Tulsa, Okla; m. Susan Morris; two s. one d.; ed Yale Univ.; served in US Army, Vietnam 1961–65; Owner and Man. restaurants The Works, Anchorage 1968, Downtown Deli, Anchorage 1978; Mayor of Anchorage 1981–87; Gov. of Alaska 1994–2002; unsuccessful cand. for US Senate 2004, for Gov. of Alaska 2006; mem. Citizen's Cttee for Planned Growth and Devt of Anchorage 1972, Borough Ass., Anchorage 1975–79; fmr mem. Bd of Dirs KAKM TV Station, Anchorage Chamber of Commerce; Child Advocate of the Year, American Child Welfare League 1999. *Address:* c/o Office of the Governor, PO Box 110001, Juneau, AK 99811, USA.

KNOWLES, Beyoncé (see Beyoncé).

KNOWLES, William S.; American scientist; b. 1 June 1917, Taunton, Mass; m. Nancy Knowles 1945; ed Harvard and Columbia Univs; chemist with Monsanto Co. 1942–86; during career made breakthrough in devt of drug treatment for Parkinson's Disease; IR 100 Awards for Asymmetric Hydrogenation 1974, St. Louis ACS Section Award 1978, Monsanto Thomas and Hochwalt Award 1981, ACS Award for Creative Invention 1982, Organic Reactions Catalysis Soc. Paul N. Rylander Award 1996, Nobel Prize in Chem. 2001 (jt recipient). *Leisure interests:* cycling, environmental issues. *Address:* c/o Monsanto Company, 800 North Lindbergh Boulevard, St Louis, MO 63167, USA (office). *Telephone:* (314) 694-1000 (office). *Website:* www.monsanto.com (office).

KNOWLING, Robert E., Jr, BA, MBA; American computer engineer and business executive; *CEO, Vercuity Solutions Inc.;* b. 1955, Ind.; m.; four c.; ed Wabash Coll., Northwestern Univ. Kellogg Graduate School of Man.; staff mem. Indiana Bell (now part of Ameritech) 1970s; Head of Eng Devt Team Ameritech 1992, later Vice-Pres. Network Operations; Exec. Vice-Pres. of Operations and Techs US West; Pres. and CEO Covad Communications, Calif. 1998–2001; Chair. and CEO Information Access Technologies Inc. 2001–03; CEO New York Leadership Acad., New York City Bd of Educ. 2003–05; CEO Vercuity Solutions, Inc. 2005–; mem. Bd Dirs Hewlett-Packard Co., Ariba Inc., Heidrick & Struggles Int., Immune Response Corpn (now Chair.), Juvenile Diabetes Foundation Int.; mem. Advisory Bd Ontologent, Inc., Northwestern Univ. Kellogg Graduate School of Man., Univ. of Mich. Graduate School of Business. *Leisure interest:* YMCA volunteer. *Address:* Vercuity Solutions Inc., 5889 South Greenwood Plaza Blvd., Suite 300, Greenwood Village, CO 80111, USA (office). *E-mail:* info@vercuity.com (office). *Website:* www.vercuity.com (office).

KNOX, Selby Albert Richard, PhD, DSc, CChem, FRSC; British chemist and academic; b. 24 Sept. 1944, Newcastle-upon-Tyne; s. of George H. Knox and Elsie Knox; m. Julie D. Edwards 1979; one s. two d.; ed Rutherford Grammar School, Newcastle-upon-Tyne and Univ. of Bristol; Research Fellow, UCLA 1970–71; Lecturer, Univ. of Bristol 1972–83, Reader 1983–90, Prof. of Inorganic Chem. 1990–96, Head Dept of Chem. 1992–2001, Head Inorganic and Materials Chem. 2001–04, Alfred Capper Pass Prof. of Chem. 1996–2004, Pro-Vice-Chancellor 2004–08; Corday-Morgan Medal and Prize 1980, Award for Chem. of Noble Metals and Their Compounds, Royal Soc. of Chem. (RSC) 1986, RSC Tilden Lecturer 1992–93. *Publications:* more than 160 scientific papers on organometallic chem. *Leisure interests:* fly fishing, sailing, skiing.

KNUDSEN, Eric Ingvald, BA, MA, PhD; American neuroscientist and academic; *Professor of Neurobiology, School of Medicine, Stanford University;* ed Univ. of California, Santa Barbara, George August Univ., Göttingen, Germany, Woods Hole Marine Biological Lab., Univ. of California, San Diego; Postdoctoral Research Fellow, California Inst. of Tech. 1976–79; Asst Prof., Dept of Neurobiology, Stanford Univ. School of Medicine 1979–85, Assoc. Prof. 1985–88, Prof. 1988–, Assoc. Chair. Dept of Neurobiology 1997–2000, Chair. 2001–05, Chair. Stanford Medical Student Scholars Program 1986–90, mem. Cttee on Courses and Curriculum 1994–96, mem. School of Medicine Appointments and Promotions Cttee 1995–98, Dir Neurosciences Grad. Program 1998–2000, mem. Research Planning Cttee Medical School Strategic Planning 2001–02, Exec. Cttee Neuroscience Inst. 2001–; Assoc. Ed. Journal of Neuroscience 1986–88, Journal of Neurophysiology 1986–89; mem. Editorial Cttee Annual Review of Neuroscience 1988–92; Co-organizer Int. Meeting: Advances in Auditory Neuroscience, San Francisco; mem. Satellite of the IUPS 1986, NSF Advisory Panel: Sensory Physiology and Perception 1986; Councillor, Int. Soc. for Neuroethology 2002–; mem. Core research network on early experience and brain development, MacArthur Foundation 2002–, Nat. Scientific Council on the Developing Child 2003–; mem. NAS 2002–; Fellow, American Acad. of Arts and Sciences 1996–; AAAS Newcomb Cleveland Prize 1978, Young Investigator Award, Soc. for Neuroscience 1984, NAS Troland Research Award 1988, Claude Pepper Award, Nat. Inst. of Deafness and Communicative Disorders 1991, Edward C. and Amy H. Sewall Professorship, Stanford Univ. School of Medicine 1995, Givaudan-Roure Award, Asscn for Chemoreception Sciences 1996, W. Alden Spencer Award, Coll. of Physicians and Surgeons, Columbia Univ. 2002, Kuffler Lecturer, Harvard Medical School 2004, Gruber Neuroscience Prize, The Peter and Patricia Gruber Foundation 2005. *Publications:* more than 70 scientific papers, book chapters and reviews on the mechanisms of attention, learning and strategies of information processing in the central auditory system of developing and adult barn owls, using neurophysiological, pharmacological, anatomical and behavioural techniques. *Address:* Stanford University School of Medicine, 300 Pasteur Drive, Stanford, CA 94305, USA (office). *Telephone:* (650) 723-5492 (office). *E-mail:* eknudsen@stanford.edu (office). *Website:* med.stanford.edu/profiles/Eric_Knudsen (office).

KNUDSON, Alfred G., Jr, MD, PhD; American geneticist, physician and academic; *Distinguished Scientist, Fox Chase Cancer Center;* b. 9 Aug. 1952, Los Angeles, Calif.; m. Anna T. Meadows MD; ed Calif. Inst. of Tech., Columbia Univ., New York; intern, Huntington Memorial Hosp., Pasadena, Calif. 1947–48; Asst Resident in Pediatrics, New York Hosp. 1948–49; Resident in Pediatrics, Los Angeles Childrens' Hosp., 1949–50, Research Fellow 1950–51; Pediatrician (1st Lt, MC, USAR) USAH Fort Riley, Kansas 1951–53; on staff, City of Hope Medical Center 1956–66, Chair. Dept of Pediatrics 1956–62, Chair. Dept of Biology 1962–66; Assoc. Dean for Basic Sciences, State Univ. of New York at Stony Brook 1966–69; Prof. of Biology and Pediatrics, M.D. Anderson Hospital and Tumor Inst., Houston, Texas 1969–76, Assoc. Dir (Educ.) 1969–70; Dean and Prof. of Medical Genetics, Univ. of Texas Grad. School of Biomedical Sciences, Health Science Center, 1970–76, Prof. of Pediatrics, Medical School, 1972–76; Sr mem. Scientific Research Staff, Fox Chase Cancer Center 1976–, Dir Inst. for Cancer Research 1976–83, Pres. Fox Chase Cancer Center 1980–82, Leader Molecular Oncology Program 1989–98, Fox Chase Distinguished Scientist and Sr Adviser to Pres. 1992–; Special Adviser to Dir Nat. Cancer Inst. and Acting Dir Human Genetics Program, Div. of Cancer Epidemiology and Genetics 1995–98; mem. NAS, American Philosophical Soc., American Acad. of Arts and Sciences, Asscn of American Physicians, American Soc. of Human Genetics (Pres. 1978), AAAS (Fellow 1987–), American Pediatric Soc., American Asscn for Cancer Research, Int. Soc. of Pediatric Oncology; Guggenheim Fellowship 1953–54, Nat. Foundation – March of Dimes Fellowship 1954–56, Charles S. Mott Prize, General Motors Cancer Research Foundation 1988, Medal of Honor, American Cancer Soc. 1989, Founders' Award, Chemical Industry Inst. for Toxicology 1990, Janeway Medal, American Radium Soc. 1990, Katharine Berkan Judd Award, Memorial Sloan-Kettering Cancer Center 1990, William Allan Memorial Award, American Soc. of Human Genetics 1991, Bertner Award, M.D. Anderson Cancer Center 1995, Charles Rodolphe Brupbacher Foundation Award (Switzerland) 1995; Robert J. and Claire Pasarow Foundation Award 1996, Selikoff Cancer Award, Ramazzini Inst. for Occupational and Environmental Health Research 1996, Durham City of Medicine Award 1996, Strang Award, Strang Cancer Prevention Center, New York 1996; Gairdner Foundation Int. Award 1997, IBM-Princess Takamatsu Cancer Research Fund Lectureship and Award, Tokyo 1997, Karnofsky Memorial Lecture Award, American Soc. of Clinical Oncology 1997, Trondheim Millennium Lecturer (Norway) 1997, Albert Lasker Award for Clinical Medical Research (jtly) 1998, Distinguished Career Award, American Soc. of Hematology/Oncology, Int. John Scott Award, City of Philadelphia 1999, Lila Gruber Memorial Cancer Research Award, American Acad. of Dermatology 2000, Pediatric Oncology Lectureship, American Soc. of Clinical Oncology 2002, Kyoto Prize in Basic Science 2004, Bristol-Myers Squibb Award in Cancer Research 2005. *Publications:* Genetics and Disease 1965; contrib. numerous articles to scientific and medical journals. *Leisure interests:* travel, tennis, reading. *Address:* Fox Chase Cancer Center, 7701 Burholme Avenue, Philadelphia, PA 19111, USA (office). *Telephone:* (215) 728-3642 (office). *Fax:* (215) 214-1623 (office). *E-mail:* AG_Knudson@fccc.edu (office). *Website:* www.fccc.edu (office).

KNUSSEN, (Stuart) Oliver, CBE; British composer and conductor; b. 12 June 1952, Glasgow; s. of Stuart Knussen and Ethelyn Jane Alexander; m. Susan Freedman 1972; one d.; ed Watford Field School, Watford Boys Grammar School, Purcell School; pvt. composition study with John Lambert 1963–68; conducted first performance of his First Symphony with London

Symphony Orchestra 1968; Fellowships to Berkshire Music Center, Tanglewood, USA 1970, 1971, 1973; Caird Travelling Scholarship 1971; Head of Contemporary Music Activities, Tanglewood Music Center 1986–93; Co-Artistic Dir Aldeburgh Festival 1983–98; Music Dir London Sinfonietta 1998–2002, Conductor Laureate 2002–; Hon. mem. American Acad. of Arts and Letters 1994, Royal Philharmonic Soc. 2002; Dr hc (Royal Scottish Acad. of Music and Drama) 2002; Countess of Munster Awards 1964, 1965, 1967; Peter Stuyvesant Foundation Award 1965; Watney-Sargent Award for Young Conductors 1969; Arts Council Bursaries 1979, 1981; winner, first Park Lane Group Composer Award 1982, Michael Ludwig Nemmers Prize in Musical Composition 2006. *Compositions include:* operas: Where the Wild Things Are 1979–81, Higglety Pigglety Pop! 1984–85; symphonies: Symphony in one movement 1969, No. 2 (soprano and small orchestra) (Margaret Grant Composition Prize, Tanglewood 1971); 1970–71, No. 3 1973–79; other works for chamber ensemble and for voice and ensemble, for orchestra and for piano. *Leisure interests:* cinema, record collecting, whale watching. *Address:* Harrison Parrott, 5–6 Albion Court, London, W6 0QT, England (office); c/o Faber Music Ltd, 74–77 Great Russell Street, London, WC1B 3DA, England (office). *Telephone:* (20) 7229-9166 (office). *Fax:* (20) 7221-5042 (office). *E-mail:* info@harrisonparrott.co.uk (office). *Website:* www.harrisonparrott.com (office); www.fabermusic.com (office).

KNUTH, Donald Ervin, MS, PhD; American computer scientist and academic; *Professor Emeritus of The Art of Computer Programming, Stanford University;* b. 10 Jan. 1938, Milwaukee, Wis.; s. of Ervin Henry Knuth and Louise Marie Knuth (née Bohning); m. Nancy Jill Carter 1961; one s. one d.; ed Case Inst. of Tech., California Inst. of Tech.; Asst Prof. of Math., Calif. Inst. of Tech. 1963–66, Assoc. Prof. 1966–68; Prof. of Computer Science, Stanford Univ. 1968–77, Fletcher Jones Prof. of Computer Science 1977–89, Prof. of The Art of Computer Programming 1990–93, Prof. Emer. 1993–; mem. NAS, Nat. Acad. of Eng; Foreign mem. French, Norwegian, Bavarian Science Acads, Royal Soc. of London; 33 hon. degrees, including Paris 1986, Oxford 1988, St Petersburg 1992, Harvard 2003; Nat. Medal of Science 1979, Steele Prize, American Math. Soc. 1986, Franklin Medal, Franklin Inst. of Philadelphia 1988, Harvey Prize, Israel Inst. of Tech. 1995, John Von Neumann Medal, IEEE 1995, Kyoto Prize 1996, and numerous other awards. *Publications:* The Art of Computer Programming (Vol. 1) 1968, (Vol. 2) 1969, (Vol. 3) 1973, Surreal Numbers 1974, Mariages Stables 1976, Computers and Typesetting (five Vols) 1986, Concrete Mathematics 1988, 3:16 Bible Texts Illuminated 1990, Literate Programming 1992, The Stanford GraphBase 1993, Selected Papers on Computer Science 1996, Digital Typography 1999, MMIXware 1999, Selected Papers on Analysis of Algorithms 2000, Things a Computer Scientist Rarely Talks About 2001, Selected Papers on Computer Languages 2003, Selected Papers on Discrete Mathematics 2003. *Leisure interests:* piano and organ playing, browsing in libraries. *Address:* Computer Science Department, Gates 477, Stanford University, Stanford, CA 94305, USA (office). *Telephone:* (650) 723-4367 (office). *Website:* www-cs-faculty.stanford.edu/~knuth (office).

KOBAYASHI, Eizo; Japanese business executive; *President and CEO, ITOCHU Corporation;* joined ITOCHU Corpn 1972, various sr positions including mem. Exec. Bd 2000, COO of Information Tech. and Telecommunications Div. 2001–02, Man. Dir and Chief Information Officer 2002–03, Sr Man. Dir 2003–04, Pres. and CEO 2004–; Vice-Chair. Japan Foreign Council Inc.; Exec. Dir Bank of Japan 2004–. *Address:* ITOCHU Corpn, 5-1 Kita-Aoyama 2-chome, Minato-ku, Tokyo 107-8077, Japan (office). *Telephone:* (3) 3497-2121 (office). *Fax:* (3) 3497-4141 (office). *E-mail:* info@itochu.co.jp (office). *Website:* www.itochu.co.jp (office).

KOBAYASHI, Makoto, PhD; Japanese physicist; *Professor Emeritus, High Energy Accelerator Research Organization (KEK);* b. 7 April 1944, Nagoya; ed Nagoya Univ.; Research Assoc., Kyoto Univ. 1972–79; Asst Prof., Nat. Lab. of High Energy Physics 1979–89, Prof. 1989–97, Head of Physics Div. II 1989–97; Prof., Inst. of Particle and Nuclear Science, High Energy Accelerator Research Org. (KEK) 1997–2006, Prof. Emer. 2006–, Dir Inst. of Particle and Nuclear Science 2003–; Nishina Memorial Prize 1979, J.J.Sakurai Prize (American Physical Soc.) 1985, Japan Acad. Prize 1985, Asahi Prize 1995, Chunichi Cultural Prize 1995, Person of Cultural Merit Award 2001, Nobel Prize for Physics 2008. *Address:* High Energy Accelerator Research Organization, 1-1 Oho, Tsukuba, Ibaraki 305-0801, Japan (office). *Telephone:* (9) 864-5379. *Fax:* (9) 879-6049. *E-mail:* Makoto.Kobayashi.exp@kek.jp. *Website:* www.kek.jp/intra-e.

KOBAYASHI, Shu, PhD; Japanese chemist and academic; *Professor, Graduate School of Pharmaceutical Sciences, University of Tokyo;* ed Univ. of Tokyo; Asst Prof., Science Univ. of Tokyo 1987–91, Lecturer, Dept of Applied Chem., Faculty of Science 1991–92, Assoc. Prof. 1992–98, Special Promoted Researcher 1997; Prof., Grad. School of Pharmaceutical Sciences, Univ. of Tokyo 1998–; Visiting Prof., Université Louis Pasteur, Strasbourg, France 1993, Kyoto Univ. 1995, Nijmegen Univ., Netherlands 1996, Philipps-Universität Marburg, Germany 1997; CREST Investigator, Japan Science and Tech. Agency, 1997–2001, SORST Investigator 2002–04, ERATO Investigator 2003–; Assoc. Ed. Journal of Combinatorial Chemistry 1999–, Advanced Synthesis and Catalysis 2000–; mem. Editorial Advisory Bd Molecules Online 1997–2000, Synthesis 1999–, Chemical Reviews 2000–; Expert Analyst, CHEMTRACTS-Organic Chemistry 1999–; Chemical Soc. of Japan Award for Young Chemists 1991, Teijin Award in Synthetic Organic Chem. 1992, New Chem. Inst. Research Award 1992, Nissan Science Foundation for Younger Generation Award 1993, Ciba-Geigy Research Foundation Award 1994, Kurata Research Foundation Award 1995, first Springer Award in Organometallic Chem. 1997, Bio-Mega/Boehrinder Ingelheim Lecturer 1999, Merck-SFC Lectureship 1999, Wyeth-Ayerst Lec-

tureship 1999, Novartis Chem. Lectureship 2000, MIT/Wyeth-Ayerst Lectureship 2000, Nagoya Lectureship 2000, Roche Lectureship 2001, NPS Distinguished Lecturer 2001, IBM Science Award 2001, Organic Reactions Lecturer 2002, Nagoya Silver Medal 2002, Novo-Nortis Lectureship 2003, Manchester-Merck Lecturer 2004, Mitsui Chemical Catalysis Science Award 2005, JSPS Prize 205, Arthur C. Cope Scholar Award 2006, Howard Memorial Lecturer 2006. *Publications:* numerous articles in scientific journals on devt of new synthetic methods, novel catalysts, organic synthesis in water, solid-phase organic synthesis, total synthesis of biologically interesting compounds and organometallic chem. *Address:* Department of Chemistry, School of Science, University of Tokyo, Hongo, Bunkyo-ku, Tokyo 113-0033, Japan (office). *Telephone:* (3) 5841-4790 (office). *Fax:* (3) 5684-0634 (office). *E-mail:* admin@tokyo.jst.go.jp (office). *Website:* www.jst.go.jp/EN (office); utsc2.chem.s.u-tokyo.ac.jp/%7Esynorg/index_E.html (office).

KOBAYASHI, Takashi; Japanese particle physicist and academic; currently Assoc. Prof., Neutrino Group, 4th Physics Div., Inst. for Particle and Nuclear Studies, High Energy Accelerator Research Org. (KEK), Tsukuba. *Publications:* numerous articles in scientific journals on neutrino physics. *Address:* The 4th Physics Division, Institute for Particle and Nuclear Studies, High Energy Accelerator Research Organization (KEK), 1-1 Oho, Tsukuba 305-0801, Japan (office). *Telephone:* (29) 864-5414 (office); (29) 864-5200 ext. 4669 (KEK local cell phone) (office). *Fax:* (29) 864-7831 (office). *E-mail:* takashi.kobayashi@kek.jp (office). *Website:* jnusrv01.kek.jp/~kobayasi (office).

KOBAYASHI, Yoshimitsu, MSc, PhD; Japanese business executive; *Representative Director, President and CEO, Mitsubishi Chemical Holdings Corporation;* b. 18 Nov. 1946, Yamanashi; ed Univ. of Tokyo, Hebrew Univ., Jerusalem; joined Mitsubishi Chemical Industry Ltd (later Mitsubishi Chemical Corpn), Tokyo 1974, Gen. Man. Information Storage Products Dept, Pres. Mitsubishi Kagaku Media 1996, CEO 2001–03, Exec. Officer, Chief Tech. Officer and Man. Exec. Officer, Mitsubishi Chemical Corpn, Man. Exec. Officer and Chief Tech. Officer –2007, Rep. Dir, Pres. and CEO 2007–, Pres. Mitsubishi Chemical Group Science and Tech. Research Center Inc. 2005–06, mem. Bd Dirs and Rep. Dir, Mitsubishi Chemical Holdings Corpn 2006–, Pres. and CEO 2007–, Chair. Mitsubishi Kagaku Inst. of Life Sciences 2006, Rep. Dir, Pres. and CEO 2007–. *Address:* Mitsubishi Chemical Holdings Corpn, 3-8 Shiba 5-chome, Minato-ku, Tokyo 108-0014, Japan (office). *Telephone:* (3) 6414-3730 (office). *Fax:* (3) 6414-3745 (office). *E-mail:* info@mitsubishichem-hd.co.jp (office). *Website:* www.mitsubishichem-hd.co.jp (office).

KÖBBEN, André J. F., PhD; Dutch professor of cultural anthropology and administrator; b. 3 April 1925, 's-Hertogenbosch; m. Agatha H. van Vessem 1953; one s. two d.; ed Municipal Gymnasium and Univ. of Amsterdam; Prof. of Cultural Anthropology, Univ. of Amsterdam 1955–76; Visiting Prof., Univ. of Pittsburgh 1972; Cleveringa Prof., Univ. of Leiden 1980–81; Prof., Erasmus Univ. 1981–90; Dir Centre for the Study of Social Conflicts 1976–90; Curl Bequest Prize, Royal Anthropological Inst. 1952; mem. Royal Netherlands Acad. of Science 1975; Hon. mem. Anthropological Soc. 1986. *Publications:* Le Planteur noir 1956, Van primitieven tot medeburgers 1964, Why exceptions? The logic of cross-cultural analysis 1967, Why Slavery? 1997, De Onwelkome Boodschap (The Unwelcome Message) 1999, Goldhagen Versus Browning 2002, Het Gevecht met de Engel (The Struggle with the Angel) 2003, and many others. *Address:* Libellenveld 2, 2318 VG Leiden, Netherlands. *Telephone:* (71) 5215369 (home). *E-mail:* ajkobben@planet.nl (home).

KOBEH GONZÁLEZ, Roberto; Mexican engineer, public servant and international organization official; *President, Council, International Civil Aviation Organization;* ed Nat. Polytechnic Inst. of Mexico; fmr Prof. of Aeronautical Electronics, Nat. Polytechnic Inst.; 40 years of experience as public servant in Mexican Govt, occupying various posts in Civil Aeronautics Directorate, including Deputy Dir-Gen. for Admin and Air Transport, Dir-Gen. Air Navigation Services of Mexico (SENEAM) 1978–97; Rep. of Mexico on Council of ICAO, serving as First Vice-Pres., Chair. Finance Cttee. and as mem. Air Transport and Unlawful Interference Cttees 1998–2006, Pres. Council 2006–; Emilio Carranza Medal, Award for Extraordinary Service, Fed. Aviation Admin (USA), honoured by Cen. American Corpn of Aerial Navigation Services for his contrib. to devt of aviation in Cen. America. *Address:* International Civil Aviation Organization, External Relations and Public Information Office, 999 University Street, Montréal, PQ H3C 5H7, Canada (office). *Telephone:* (514) 954-8220 (office); (514) 954-8221 (office). *Fax:* (514) 954-6376 (office). *E-mail:* icaohq@icao.int (office). *Website:* www.icao.int (office).

KOBIA, Rev. Samuel, MA, DD; ecclesiastic and international organization official; *General Secretary, World Council of Churches;* b. 20 March 1947, Miathene, Meru; m. Ruth Kobia; two d. two s.; ed St Paul's United Theological Coll., Nairobi, McCormick Theological Seminary, Indianapolis, Ind., Christian Theological Seminary, Massachusetts Inst. of Tech., USA; ordained minister in Methodist Church, Kenya; Exec. Sec. for Urban Rural Mission, WCC 1978–84, Chair. Frontier Internship in Mission, Int. Coordination Cttee 1981–85, Vice-Moderator Comm. to Combat Racism 1984–91, Exec. Dir Justice, Peace and Creation Unit 1993–99, Dir Cluster on Issues and Themes 1999–2002, Dir and Special Rep. for Africa 2002–04, Gen.-Sec. WCC 2003–; Dir Church Devt Activities, Nat. Council of Churches Kenya (NCCK), 1984–87, Gen.-Sec. NCCK 1987–93; helped est. Zimbabwe Christian Council 1980–81; Co-founder Nairobi Peace Group 1987, Fellowship of Councils of Churches in E and S Africa (FOCCESA) 1991; Chair. Peace Talks for Sudan 1991; Chair. Kenya Nat. Election Monitoring Unit 1992; Fellow, Centre for the Values in Public Life, Divinity School, Harvard Univ., USA 2000; Chancellor St Paul's Univ., Limuru, Kenya 2007–; Hon. Prof., Univ. of Buenos Aires, Argentina 2004; Nat. Ecumenical Award (Kenya) 2007. *Publications include:*

Origins of Squatting and Community Organization in Nairobi 1985, Together in Hope 1990, The Quest for Democracy in Africa 1993, The Courage to Hope 2003. *Address:* World Council of Churches, PO Box 2100, 150 Route de Ferney, 1211 Geneva, Switzerland (office). *Telephone:* (22) 791-6111 (office). *Fax:* (22) 791-0361 (office). *Website:* www.wwc-coe.org (office).

KOBZON, Iosif Davydovich, DPhil; Russian singer and politician; *Chairman, Commission on Culture;* b. 11 Sept. 1937, Chasov Yar, Ukraine; m. Nelly Kobzon; one s. one d.; ed Moscow Gnessin Pedagogical Inst. of Music; army service 1956–59, soloist Ensemble of Dance and Song of Caucasian Mil. command 1957–59; soloist All-Union Radio and TV Co. 1959–62; soloist Moskonzert 1962–89; Artistic Dir and Chair., Vocal and Variety Show Faculty Gnessin Inst. (now Acad.) of Music 1989–, Prof. 1992; soloist and Artistic Dir Concert Co. Moskva; retd from concert activity 1997; Pres. Jt Stock Co. Moscovit 1990–97; USSR People's Deputy 1989–92; mem. State Duma (Parl.) 1997–98 (suspended membership), 1999–2003. re-elected (Yedinaya Rossiya faction) 2003–; Deputy Chair. Comm. on Culture 1999–2003, Chair. 2004–; Order of Courage 2002, Order of Friendship 2003; People's Artist of USSR, Russia, Ukraine, Checheno-Ingushetia and Dagestan Autonomous Repub.; USSR State Prize 1984. *Address:* State Duma, Okhotny ryad 1, 103265 Moscow, Russia (office). *Telephone:* (495) 292-17-53 (office); (495) 292-17-53 (home). *Fax:* (495) 292-73-85 (office).

KOÇ, Mustafa Vehbi, BA; Turkish business executive; *Chairman, Koç Holding AŞ;* b. 29 Oct. 1960, Istanbul; s. of Rahmi M. Koç; m. Caroline N. Koç; two d.; ed George Washington Univ., USA; Chair. Koç Holding AŞ, Istanbul; Chair. TÜSİAD High Advisory Council; fmr Chair. Turkish-American Business Council; Vice-Chair. Bd Turkish Industrialists and Businessmen's Asscn, American-Turkish Council; mem. Istanbul Chamber of Industry, Foreign Econ. Relations Bd, Young Presidents' Org., JP Morgan Int. Council 2004–, Rolls-Royce Int. Advisory Bd, Nat. Bank of Kuwait Int. Advisory Council, Bd of Vehbi Koç Foundation, Bd of Trustees of Educational Volunteers Foundation; Hon. Consul-Gen. of Finland in Istanbul; Grande Ufficiale (Italy); Hadrian Award, World Monuments Fund 2008. *Address:* Koç Holding AŞ, Nakkastepe, Azizbey Sok. No. 1, Kuzguncuk, 34674 Istanbul, Turkey (office). *Telephone:* (216) 5310272 (office). *Fax:* (216) 3414519 (office). *E-mail:* stephenk@koc.com.tr (office). *Website:* www.koc.com.tr (office).

KOÇ, Rahmi M., BA; Turkish business executive; *Honorary Chairman, Koç Holding AŞ;* divorced; three s.; ed Johns Hopkins Univ., USA; joined family business Koç Group 1958 working for Otokoç Co., Ankara, Chair. Exec. Cttee Koç Holding AŞ 1970–75, Deputy Chair. Bd of Man. 1975–80, Chair. Man. Cttee 1980, Chair. Koç Holding AŞ 1984–2003, now Hon. Chair.; fmr Pres. ICC 1995–96; Founder and Chair. Rahmi M Koç Museum, Istanbul; Grosses Verdienstkreuz (Germany), Order of High Merit of the İtalian Repub. 2001; Dr hc (Johns Hopkins) 1998, (Anadolu Üniversitesi) 1998, (Ege Üniversitesi) 1999, (Bilkent Üniversitesi) 1999, (Ovidius Univ., Romania) 2001. *Address:* Koç Holding AŞ, Nakkaştepe Aziz Bey Sok. 1, Kuzguncuk, 34674 Istanbul, Turkey (office). *Telephone:* (216) 5310000 (office). *Fax:* (216) 5310099 (office). *E-mail:* info@koc.com.tr (office). *Website:* www.koc.com.tr (office); www.rmk-museum.org.tr (office).

KOČÁRNÍK, Ivan, CSc; Czech politician and business executive; b. 29 Nov. 1944, Třebonín, Kutna Hora Dist; m.; two d., one s.; ed Prague Inst. of Econs; worked at Research Inst. of Financial and Credit System until 1985; Dir Research Dept, Fed. Ministry of Finance 1985–89; Deputy Minister of Finance of Czechoslovakia 1990; mem. Civic Democratic Party (ODS); Vice-Premier and Minister of Finance of Czech Repub. 1992–97; Chair. Council of Econ. and Social Agreement 1992–97; Chair. Bd Czech Insurance Co. 1997–2001, Chair. Supervisory Bd 2000–07; Vice-Chair. of Supervisory Bd Unipetrol 2006–; Advisor to Minister of Finance 2007–; Chair. Supervisory Bd Czech Airlines (ČSA) 2007–; Central European magazine Best Minister of Finance in 1994 1995. *Leisure interests:* tennis, skiing, hiking, music. *Address:* ČSA—České aerolinie (Czech Airlines), Ruzyně Airport, 160 08 Prague 6, Czech Republic. *Telephone:* (2) 20116220 (office). *Fax:* (2) 20115397 (office). *E-mail:* mailbox.com@csa.cz (office). *Website:* www.csa.cz (office).

KOCH, Edward (Ed) I., LLB; American lawyer, fmr politician and fmr local government official; *Partner, Bryan Cave LLP;* b. 12 Dec. 1924, New York; s. of Louis Koch and Joyce Silpe; ed City Coll. of New York and New York Univ. Law School; served Second World War in US Army; admitted to New York bar 1949; sole practice law, New York 1949–64; Sr Pnr Koch, Lankenau, Schwartz & Kovner 1965–69; mem. Council, New York 1967–68, Mayor 1978–90; pnr Robinson, Silverman, Pearce, Aronsohn and Berman (now Bryan Cave LLP), New York 1990–; mem. US House of Reps from New York, 17th Dist 1969–72, 18th Dist 1973–77, mem. House Appropriations Cttee; Sec. New York Congressional Del.; Democratic Dist Leader, Greenwich Village 1963–65, mem. Village Ind. Democrats; Visiting Fellow, Urban Research Center, New York Univ. 1990–91; TV commentator for Fox 5; columnist New York Post 1990–; film critic for 4 newspapers; mem. US Holocaust Memorial Council. *Publications:* Mayor (autobiog.) 1984, Politics 1985, His Eminence and Hizzoner (with HE Cardinal J. O'Connor) 1989, All the Best: Letters from a Feisty Mayor 1990, Citizen Koch 1991, Ed Koch on Everything 1994, Murder at City Hall 1995, Murder on Broadway 1996, Murder on 34th Street 1997, The Senator Must Die 1998, Giuliani Nasty Man 1999, New York: A State of Mind 1999, I'm Not Done Yet 2000, Eddie, Harold's Little Brother 2004. *Address:* Bryan Cave LLP, 1290 Avenue of the Americas, New York, NY 10104-3300, USA (office). *Telephone:* (212) 541-2100 (office). *Fax:* (212) 541-1321 (office). *E-mail:* eikoch@bryancave.com (office). *Website:* www.bryancave.com (office).

KOCH, Roland; German politician and lawyer; *Minister-President, Hessen;* b. 24 March 1958; m.; two c.; ed Johann Wolfgang Goethe-Universität, Frankfurt am Main; co-f. Junge Union, youth org. of Christian Democratic Party (CDU) 1972, Deputy Nat. Chair. 1983–87; Town Councillor Eschborn 1997–94; Chair. CDU Main-Taunus Dist 1979–1990; mem. State Parl., Hessen 1987–; Fed. State Chair. CDU Hessen 1998–; Minister-Pres. Hessen 1999–; Pres. Bundesrat 1999; Fed. Vice-Chair. of CDU 2006–; mem. Weißer Ring charitable org.; initiator Darmstadt Manifesto for promotion of arts and culture; EWS Award, European Econ. Affairs Council 2005. *Publications:* Chancengsellschaft (Hrsg.) 1996, Vision 21 1998, Aktive Bürgergesellschaft (Hrsg.) 1998, Die Zukunft der Bürgergesellschaft, Gemeinsam Chancen nutzen 2001. *Leisure interests:* cooking, art museums, tennis. *Address:* Georg-August-Zinn Str. 1, 65183 Wiesbaden, Germany (home). *Telephone:* (611) 323900 (office). *Fax:* (611) 323698 (office). *E-mail:* roland.koch@stk.hessen.de (office). *Website:* www.staatskanzlei.hessen.de (office); www.roland-koch.de (office).

KOCHARIAN, Robert S.; Armenian politician and fmr head of state; b. 31 Aug. 1954, Xankandi (Stepanakert), Nagornyi Karabakh Autonomous Oblast; s. of Sedrack S. Kocharian and Emma A. Ohanian; m. Bella L. Kocharian; two s. one d.; ed Yerevan Polytechnic Inst.; served in Soviet Army 1972–74; engineer and electrotechnician Electro-Tech. plant, Stepanakert 1981–87; concurrently sec. factory CP Cttee 1987–89; Co-founder Karabakh Movt 1988; Deputy to Armenian Supreme Council 1989–94; left CP 1989; after proclamation of 'Repub. of Nagornyi Karabakh' in Azerbaijan 2 Sept. 1991 and Referendum 10 Dec. 1991 elected to Supreme Council 'Nagornyi Karabakh Repub.', Chair. State Cttee of Defence and Leader of Repub. 1992–94; apptd First Pres. of 'Nagornyi Karabakh Repub.' by Supreme Council 1994–97; Prime Minister 1997–98; Pres. of Armenia 1998–2008. *Leisure interests:* basketball, jazz. *Address:* c/o Office of the President, 0077 Yerevan, Marshal Baghramian Avenue 26, Armenia.

KOCHERGA, Anatoly Ivanovich; Ukrainian singer (bass); b. 9 July 1947, Vinnitsa; s. of Ivan Kocherga and Maria Kocherga; m. Lina Kocherga 1985; one d.; ed Kiev Conservatoire and studied at La Scala, Milan; soloist, Shevchenko Opera and Ballet, Kiev 1972–, also Vienna State Opera 1990–; Glinka Prize 1971, Tchaikovsky Prize 1974, USSR People's Artist 1983. *Major roles include:* Boris Godunov, Galitsky (Borodin's Prince Igor), Don Basilio (Barber of Seville), Mephistopheles (Gounod's Faust), Don Carlos (Verdi), Don Giovanni (Mozart), Khovanshchina (Mussorgsky), Dosiphey (Khovanshchina), Nilakanta (Lakmé); USSR People's Artist 1983. *Leisure interest:* tennis. *Address:* Gogolevskaho 37, Korp. 2, Apt. 47, Kiev 254053, Ukraine.

KOCHERGIN, Eduard Stepanovich; Russian theatrical designer; b. 22 Sept. 1937, Leningrad; s. of Stepan Kochergin and Bronislava (née Odinets) Kochergina; m. Inna Gabai 1962; one s.; ed Leningrad Theatre Art Inst., theatre production faculty (pupil of N. Akimov and T. Bruni); chief set-designer in various Leningrad theatres 1960–; chief set-designer at Gorky (now Tovstonogov) Bolshoi Drama Theatre 1972; worked as set-designer, Maly Drama Theatre and in Japan, USA, Poland, Germany, Finland, Canada, France; Prof. Y.I. Repin Inst. of Painting 1983–; mem. Russian Acad. of Fine Arts 1991; Fatherland's Decoration of Merit (4th Order), State Prize 1974, 1978; three Golden and two Silver awards, int. exhbns theatre design Novisad 1975, 1978, Prague 1975, 1979, 1987; Honoured Artist of Russia. *Publications:* Angel's Doll 2003. *Leisure interest:* research in Russian pre-Christian culture and symbolism. *Address:* Tovstonogov Bolshoi Drama Theatre, Fontanka 65, 191023 St Petersburg, Russia. *Telephone:* (812) 352-89-33 (office); (812) 351-23-79 (home). *Fax:* (812) 110-47-10.

KOCHETKOV, Nikolay Konstantinovich; Russian chemist and academic; *Director Emeritus, Zelinsky Institute of Organic Chemistry, Russian Academy of Sciences;* b. 18 May 1915, Moscow; s. of Konstantin Kochetkov and Marie Kochetkova; m. Dr. Vera Volodina 1945; one s. one d.; ed M. V. Lomonosov Inst. of Fine Chem. Tech.; Asst, Chemistry Dept of Moscow Univ. 1945–52, Dozent 1952–56, Prof. 1956–60; Head of Dept of Organic Synthesis, Inst. of Pharmacology 1953–60; Deputy Dir, Head of Nucleic Acids and Carbohydrates Laboratory, Inst. of Natural Products 1960–66; Dir, Head of Carbohydrates Laboratory, Zelinsky Inst. of Organic Chem. 1966–88, Dir Emer. 1988–; Corresp. mem. USSR (now Russian) Acad. of Medical Sciences 1957–; Corresp. mem. USSR (now Russian) Acad. of Sciences 1960–79, mem. 1979–; mem. Soc. de Chimie 1972–, Polish Acad. of Sciences 1988; Haworth Medal (Royal Soc. of Chem.) 1989, Lenin Prize 1989, Nat. Prize of Demidov Foundation 1993, Hero of Socialist Labour, Lomonosov Great Gold Medal, Russian Acad. of Science 1995 and other decorations; Order of Lenin. *Publications:* Chemistry of Natural Products 1961, Chemistry of Carbohydrates 1967, Organic Chemistry of Nucleic Acids 1970, Radiation Chemistry of Sugars 1973, Carbohydrates in the Synthesis of Natural Products 1984, Synthesis of Polysaccharides 1995. *Address:* Zelinsky Institute of Organic Chemistry, Leninsky Prospekt 47, Moscow 117913, Russia. *Telephone:* (495) 137-61-48 (office); (495) 237-48-16 (home). *Fax:* (495) 135-53-28. *Website:* www.ioc.ac.ru.

KOCHHAR, Chanda, MA, MBA; Indian banker and accountant; *Joint Managing Director, ICICI Bank Ltd;* m.; one s. one d.; ed Jamnalal Bajaj Inst. of Man. Studies, Mumbai; joined Project Appraisal Div., ICICI in 1984, handled various projects in various industries and was actively involved in the bank's computerization initiatives, deputed to newly formed ICICI Bank as a part of core group for setting up and conceptualizing strategic direction for the bank 1993, served as first Head of Credit 1993–96 returned to ICICI to become part of initiatives such as infrastructure lending, structured products group and major clients group 1996–2000, Man. Dir ICICI Home Finance Ltd and ICICI Personal Financial Services 2000–01, Exec. Dir ICICI Bank 2001–06, Deputy Man. Dir 2007–07, Jt Man. Dir 2007–; J. N. Bose Gold Medal in Cost Accountancy and Wockhardt Gold Medal for Excellence in Man. Studies, Jamnalal Bajaj Inst. of Man. Studies, Retail Banker of the Year in Asia 2004,

Economic Times Award for Corporate Excellence as the Businesswomen of the Year 2005, ranked by Fortune magazine amongst 50 Most Powerful Women in Business outside the US (47th) 2005, (37th) 2006, (33rd) 2007. *Address:* ICICI Bank Ltd, ICICI Bank Towers, Bandra-Kurla Complex, Mumbai 400051, India (office). *Telephone:* (22) 2653-1414 (office). *Fax:* (22) 2653-1167 (office). *Website:* www.icicibank.com (office).

KOCHI, Jay K., BS, PhD; American chemist and academic; *Robert A. Welch Professor, Department of Chemistry, University of Houston;* b. 17 May 1927, Los Angeles; s. of Tsuruzo Kochi; m. Marion K. Kiyono 1961; one s. one d.; ed Univ. of Calif. and Iowa State Univ.; Instructor, Harvard Univ. 1952–55; Nat. Inst. of Health Special Fellow, Univ. of Cambridge, UK 1955–56; Shell Devt Co. Emeryville, Calif. 1956–62; Case Western Univ., Cleveland, Ohio 1962–69; Earl Blough Prof., Ind. Univ. 1969–84; Robert A. Welch Distinguished Prof. of Chem., Univ. of Houston, Tex. 1984–; chemical consultant 1964–; mem. NAS; J. F. Norris Award, ACS 1981, Sr von Humboldt Award 1986; A. C. Cope Scholar Award, ACS 1988, Houston Section Award, ACS 2001, Southwest Region Award, ACS 2002. *Publications:* three books and more than 650 research papers. *Address:* Department of Chemistry, University of Houston, University Park, Houston, TX 77204-5641 (office); 4372 Faculty Lane, Houston, TX 77004, USA (home). *Telephone:* (713) 743-3293 (office). *Fax:* (713) 743-2709 (office). *E-mail:* jkochi@mail.uh.edu (office). *Website:* www .chem.uh.edu/Faculty/Kochi/Index.html (office).

KOCIJANČIČ, Andreja; Slovenian physician and university administrator; b. 1942; m. Janez Kocijančič; one s. one d.; ed Univ. of Ljubljana; worked at Mil. Medical Acad. 1969–71; Asst Prof., Faculty of Medicine, Univ. of Ljubljana 1978–84, Assoc. Prof. 1984–89, Prof. of Medicine 1989–1995, Sr Counselor for Health 1995, Pres. Comm. for Postgraduate and Doctoral Studies 1995–2003, Rector Univ. of Ljubljana 2005–09; Deputy Dir Internal Zaloška Clinic, Clinical Centre Ljubljana 1982–87; Pres. Yugoslavia Endocrinology Asscn 1972–76; mem. Exec. Cttee Int. Soc. of Endocrinology 1979–89; mem. Cen. Cttee European Fed. of Endocrine Socs 1987–95; mem. Bd of Dirs European Foundation for Osteoporosis 1995–2000; Chair. Health Council of Slovenia 1982–86; Vice-Pres. Council for Higher Educ. of the Repub. of Slovenia 1998–2002; Pres. 2002–04; Vice-Pres. Medical Chamber of Slovenia 2004–08. *Address:* University of Ljubljana, Kongresni trg 12, 1000 Ljubljana, Slovenia (office). *Telephone:* (1) 2418600 (office). *Fax:* (1) 2418650 (office). *E-mail:* rektor@uni-lj.si (office). *Website:* www.uni-lj.si (office).

KOCK, Manfred; German ecclesiastic; b. 14 Sept. 1936, Burgsteinfurt; s. of Walter Kock and Erika Braunschweig; m. Gisela Stephany 1960; two s. one d.; ed Univs of Bethel, Münster and Tübingen; pastor, Recklinghausen 1962–70, Cologne 1970–97; Chair. Evangelical Church in the Rhineland 1997–2003 (resgnd), Council of the Evangelical Church in Germany (EKD) 1997–2003 (resgnd). *Address:* c/o Evangelical Church in Germany, Herrenhäuser Str. 12, 30419 Hanover, Germany (office).

KOCSIS, Zoltán; Hungarian pianist, conductor and composer; *General Music Director, Hungarian National Philharmonic Orchestra;* b. 30 May 1952, Budapest; s. of Ottó Kocsis and Mária Mátyás; m. 1st Adrienne Hauser 1986; one s. one d.; m. 2nd Erika Tóth 1997; one s. one d.; ed Budapest Music Acad. (under Pál Kadosa); Asst Prof., Music Acad. Budapest 1976–79, Prof. 1979–; Producer of Archive Section of Hungaroton (record co.); Co-founder and Artistic Co-Dir Budapest Festival Orchestra 1983–96; Gen. Music Dir Hungarian Nat. Philharmonic Orchestra 1997–; First Prize, Beethoven Piano Competition, Hungarian Radio and Television 1970, Liszt Prize 1973, Kossuth Prize 1978, Merited Artist's Title 1984, Lifetime Achievement Award, MIDEM, Cannes 2004, Kossuth Prize 2005. *Performances:* has appeared with Berlin Philharmonic Orchestra and performed in Germany, USSR, Austria and Czechoslovakia 1971; toured USA together with Dezsö Ranki and Budapest Symphony Orchestra (under George Lehel) 1971; recitals in Netherlands, Paris, London and Ireland 1972; concerts in Norway, with Svyatoslav Richter in France and Austria, with Claudio Abbado and London Symphony Orchestra and at BBC Promenade Concerts in London and Festival Estival, Paris 1977, Edin. Festival 1978, Verbier Festival, Ferrara Festival, La Roque D'Antheron, with Chicago Symphony, Atlanta Symphony and Minnesota orchestras. *Publications:* Miscellaneous Publications, Arrangements for Piano and 2 Pianos, etc. *Leisure interest:* photography. *Address:* c/o IMG Artists, The Light Box, 111 Power Road, London, W4 5PY, England (office); Hungarian National Philharmonic Orchestra, Komor Marcell u. 1, 1095 Budapest, Hungary (office). *Telephone:* (20) 7957-5800 (office); (1) 4116620 (office). *Fax:* (20) 7957-5801 (office); (1) 4116624 (office); (1) 424-5917 (home). *E-mail:* artistseurope@imgartists.com (office); kocsis.z@ filharmonikusok.hu (office). *Website:* www.imgartists.com (office); www .filharmonikusok.hu (office).

KODAMANOĞLU, Nuri, MSc; Turkish politician; b. 16 Aug. 1923, Ulukişla-Niğde; s. of Fazil and Hatice Kodamanoğlu; m. Ayten Unal Kodamanoğlu 1951; ed Istanbul Univ.; fmr civil servant, Ministry of Educ.; later Under-Sec. Ministry of Educ.; Deputy to Grand Nat. Assembly; Minister of Energy and Natural Resources 1972; Adviser to the Prime Minister 1988; Chief Adviser to the Pres. 1991; mem. Business Admin. Inst., Faculty of Political Science, Univ. of Ankara; mem. Ataturk Research Centre; mem. Bd of Dirs. Turkish Petroleum Corpn; mem. Consultative Cttee Asscn of Turkish Parliamentarians 1995–; Consultant, Asscn of Turkish Chambers of Commerce, Chambers of Ind. and Exchange. *Publications:* Principles of New Education 1954, Education in Turkey 1963; various articles and reports. *Leisure interests:* handicrafts, gardening. *Address:* Bükreş Sokak No. 6 Daire 8, Cankaya, 06680 Ankara, Turkey. *Telephone:* (312) 427-15-15.

KODEŠ, Jan; Czech fmr tennis player; b. 1 March 1946, Prague; s. of Jan Kodeš and Vlasta Richterová-Kodešová; m. 1st Lenka Rösslerová-Kodešová 1967 (divorced 1988); one s. one d.; m. 2nd Martina Schlonzová; one d.; ed Univ. of Econs, Prague; first Czech national to win a Grand Slam title; Wimbledon Singles Champion 1973, French Open Singles Champion 1970, 1971, runner-up US Championships 1971, 1973, Italian Championships 1970, 1971, 1972; mem. Czechoslovak Davis Cup Team 1964–80, including 1975 (runners-up), 1980 (winners), non-playing Capt. 1982–87; Czechoslovak No. 1 player 1966–77; Bd mem. Czechoslovak Tennis Asscn 1982–98; mem. ETA Men's Cttee 1990–93; mem. ITF Davis Cup European Cttee 1997–98; Founder and Tournament Dir Czech Open, Prague 1987–98; Pres. Czech Tennis Asscn 1994–98; Dir Czechoslovak Tennis Centre 1986–92; mem. ITF/ITHF Golden Achievement Award Cttee 2006–, ITHF Enshrinee Nominating Cttee 2008–; part-owner and CEO Prague CZ Fashion sro 1994–2003; Meritorious Master of Sports 1971, State Decoration for Outstanding Work 1973, ITF Award for Services to the Game 1988, Int. Tennis Hall of Fame 1990. *Publication:* Tennis Was My Life 2006. *Leisure interests:* football, other sports, stamp collecting, films, history. *Address:* Pro-Tennis International Consulting JK, Na Beránce 20, Prague 6, 160 00 Czech Republic (office). *Telephone:* (2) 33321536 (office); (2) 33321536 (home). *Fax:* (2) 33321535 (home). *E-mail:* jan@kodes-tennis.com (office). *Website:* www.kodes-tennis.com (office).

KODJO, Edem; Togolese politician and administrator; *Chairman, Coalition des forces démocrates (CFD);* b. 23 May 1938, Sokodé; m. 1962; two s. two d.; ed Coll. St Joseph, Univ. of Rennes, Ecole Nat. d'Admin, Paris, France; worked as admin. for Office de Radiodiffusion-Télévision Française (ORTF) 1964–67; returned to Togo 1967; Sec.-Gen., Ministry of Finance, Economy and Planning 1967–72; Admin., Banque Centrale des Etats de l'Afrique de l'Ouest 1967–76, Pres. of Admin. Council 1973–76; Dir-Gen. Soc. Nat. d'Investissement 1972–73; Minister of Finance and Economy 1973–76, of Foreign Affairs 1976–77, of Foreign Affairs and Co-operation 1977–78; Sec.-Gen. of the OAU 1978–84; Assoc. Prof. Sorbonne, Paris 1985–90; Prime Minister of Togo 1994–96, 2005–06; Founder and Chair. Pan-African Inst. of Int. Relations (IPRI); Ed. Afrique 2000; mem. Rassemblement du Peuple Togolaise (RPT), RPT Political Bureau (Sec.-Gen. 1967–71); Leader Togolese Union for Democracy (UTD) –1999, Pres. Convergence patriotique panafricaine 1999–2003, then merger with several other parties to form Coalition des forces démocrates (CFD), currently acting Chair; mem. Club of Rome; Gov. for Togo, IMF 1973–76; fmr Chair. OAU Council of Ministers, Afro-Arab Perm. Comm. on Co-operation, OAU Cttee of Ten; Commdr, Ordre du Mono, Togo, Officier, Légion d'honneur; Dr hc (Univ. of Bordeaux I); Univ. of Sorbonne Medal. *Address:* Coalition des forces démocrates (CFD), Lomé, Togo (office).

KODJO, Messan Abgéyomé; Togolese politician; b. 12 Oct. 1954, Tokpli, Yoto Pref.; m.; ed Higher School of Sciences and Tech., Univ. of Benin, Univ. of Poitiers, France; fmr Sales Man. SONACOM; Minister for Youth, Sports and Culture 1988–91, for Territorial Admin and Security 1992; organized Constitutional Referendum; Gen. Man. Port Authority of Lomé 1993–99; elected Deputy 1999; Prime Minister of Togo 2000–02. *Address:* c/o Bureau du Premier Ministre, BP 5618, Lomé, Togo (office).

KOEDA, Itaru, BEng; Japanese motor industry executive; *Co-Chairman, Nissan Motor Co. Ltd;* b. 25 Aug. 1941; ed Univ. of Tokyo; joined Nissan Motor Co. Ltd 1965, becoming Gen. Man. of several corp. depts, fmr Vice-Pres. and Dir Nissan UK, mem. Bd of Dirs Nissan Motor Co. Ltd 1993–, Exec. Vice-Pres. –2003, Exec. Vice-Pres. and Co-Chair. 2003–; mem. Bd of Dirs Renault SA 2003–; Chair. Japan Automobile Mfrs Asscn 2004–06; Chair. Japan-Mexico Econ. Cttee, Keidanren (Japan Business Fed.). *Address:* Nissan Motor Co. Ltd, 17-1 Ginza 6 chome Chuo-Ku, Tokyo 104 8023, Japan (office). *Telephone:* (3) 3543-5523 (office). *Fax:* (3) 5565-2228 (office). *Website:* www.nissan.co.jp (office).

KOEPP, David; American screenwriter; b. 9 June 1963, Pewaukee, Wis. *Film screenplays:* Apartment Zero 1989, Bad Influence 1990 (with Martin Donovan), Toy Soldiers (with Daniel Petrie, Jr) 1991, Death Becomes Her (with Martin Donovan) 1992, Jurassic Park (with Michael Crichton) 1993, Carlito's Way 1993, The Paper (with Stephen Koepp) 1994, The Shadow 1994, Suspicious 1994, Mission: Impossible 1996, Lost World: Jurassic Park 1997, Snake Eyes 1998, Stir of Echos 1999, Panic Room 2002, Spider-Man 2002, Secret Window 2004, War of the Worlds 2005, Zathura: A Space Adventure 2005, Ghost Town (also dir) 2008, Indiana Jones and the Kingdom of the Crystal Skull 2008, Angels & Demons 2009. *Address:* 10 West 83rd Street, New York, NY 10024; UTA, 9560 Wilshire Boulevard, Beverly Hills, CA 90212, USA.

KOFFIGOH, Joseph Kokou; Togolese politician; *President, Coordination nationale des forces nouvelles;* b. 1948, Kpele Dafo; m.; three s. one d.; ed Univs of Abidjan and Poitiers, France; called to the Bar, Poitiers, France; joined Viale Chambers, Togo; f. Togo Bar Asscn 1980, Pres. 1990; founder mem. Observatoire panafricain de la démocratie (OPAD) 1991, Ligue togolaise des droits de l'homme 1990; founder mem. and Vice-Pres. FAR (Asscn for reform); Vice-Pres. Nat. Sovereign Conf.; Prime Minister of Togo 1991–94, also Minister of Defence, Minister of Foreign Affairs and Co-operation 1999–2001; apptd Minister of Regional Integration responsible for relations with Parl. 2001; Pres. Coordination nat. des forces nouvelles. *Leisure interests:* lawn tennis, basketball, shadow-boxing. *Address:* Coordination nationale des forces nouvelles, Lomé, Togo (office).

KOFLER, Georg; German (b. Italian) television executive; b. 26 April 1957, Brunico, Italy; m. José Kofler; two s.; ed Univ. of Vienna; fmrly mem. staff Austrian state broadcasting co. Österreichischer Rundfunk (ORF); with Eureka TV 1987–89; co-founder (with Gerhard Ackermans and Thomas Kirch) and Chair. Pro 7 TV network 1989–2000; CEO KirchPayTV (now Premiere Fernsehen GmbH and Company KG), Munich 2002–07. *Address:* c/o

Premiere Fernsehen GmbH and Company KG, Medienallee 4, 85767 Unterföhring, Germany.

KOGA, Nobuyuki; Japanese business executive; *President and CEO, Nomura Holdings Inc.;* b. 22 Aug. 1950; joined Nomura Holdings 1974, Dir 1995–, Man. Dir 1999–2000, Exec. Vice-Pres. and COO 2000–03, Pres. and CEO 2003–, Pres. Nomura Securities 2003–. *Address:* Nomura Holdings Inc., 1-9-1, Nihonbashi, Chuo-ku, Tokyo 103-8645, Japan (office). *Telephone:* (3) 3211-1811 (office). *Fax:* (3) 3278-0420 (office). *Website:* www.nomura.com (office).

KOGAN, Pavel Leonidovich; Russian violinist and conductor; *Music Director and Chief Conductor, Moscow State Symphony Orchestra;* b. 6 June 1952, Moscow; s. of Leonid Kogan and Elizaveta Gilels; m. (divorced); one s.; ed Moscow State Conservatory; studied conducting in Leningrad with I. Mussin and in Moscow with Leo Ginzburg; performances 1970–; Conductor Moscow Chamber Orchestra 1980–83; Chief Conductor and Music Dir Zagreb Philharmonic 1988–90, Moscow State Symphony Orchestra, Mosow 1988–; Prin. Guest Conductor, Utah Symphony Orchestra, USA 1998–99; winner Int. Jean Sibelius Competition Helsinki, 1970. *Performances:* performed in maj. concert halls of Europe, America and Japan as soloist, also in ensembles with parents and pianist Nina Kogan (sister); performed with symphony orchestras in USSR (Russia), USA and countries of Europe and Asia since 1983. *Leisure interest:* automobiles. *Address:* Moscow State Symphony Orchestra, Spartakovskaya sq., 1/2, Moscow (office); Bryusov per. 8/10, Apt. 19, 103009 Moscow, Russia (home). *Telephone:* (495) 267-52-23 (office); (495) 292-13-95 (home). *E-mail:* msso@yandex.ru (office). *Website:* msso.ru (office).

KOGAN, Richard Jay, MBA; American business executive; *Principal, Kogan Group LLC;* b. 6 June 1941, New York; s. of Benjamin Kogan and Ida Kogan; m. Susan Linda Scher 1965; ed City Coll. of City Univ. of New York and Stern School of Business, New York Univ.; fmr Pres. US Pharmaceuticals Div., Ciba-Geigy Corpn; Exec. Vice-Pres. Pharmaceutical Operations, Schering-Plough Corpn 1982–86, Pres. and COO 1986–95, CEO 1996–2003 (retd); currently Prin. Kogan Group LLC; mem. Bd Dirs Colgate-Palmolive Co., Bank of New York Co. Inc., St Barnabas Medical Center and Corpn; mem. Council on Foreign Relations; Trustee, New York Univ. *Address:* Kogan Group LLC, Suite 415, 51 JFK Parkway, Short Hills, NJ 07078-2702, USA (office). *Telephone:* (973) 379-6560 (office). *Fax:* (973) 379-7050 (office). *E-mail:* RJK@RJKogan.com (office). *Website:* www.thekogangroupllc.com (office).

KOGURE, Gohei, BEcons; Japanese business executive; *Senior Adviser and Counselor, Dentsu Inc.;* b. 19 Sept. 1924, Gunma Pref.; s. of Goro Kogure and Hiro Kogure; m. Noriko Shigehara 1951; one s. one d.; ed Univ. of Tokyo; joined Dentsu Inc. 1947, Exec. Dir 1971–73, Man. Dir 1973–79, Sr Man. Dir 1979–85, Pres. and CEO 1985–93, Chair. 1993–97, now Sr Corp. Adviser and Couselor; Chair. Japan Advertising Agencies Asscn 1987, now Adviser; Trustee Keizai Doyukai (Japan Asscn of Corp. Execs); fmr Vice-Pres. Int. Advertising Asscn Japan Chapter; Hon. Life mem. Int. Advertising Asscn; Kt Commdr Order of St Sylvester Pope with Star (Vatican), Grand Cordon of the Order of the Sacred Treasure 2001; All Japan Advertising Award 1989. *Film:* Madadayo (producer) 1993. *Leisure interests:* golf, haiku. *Address:* Dentsu Inc., 1-8-1 Higashi-shimbashi, Minato-ku, Tokyo 105-7001, Japan (office). *Telephone:* (3) 6216-5111 (office). *Website:* www.dentsu.com.

KOH, Harold Hongju, AB, BA, MA, JD; American lawyer, academic, university administrator and fmr government official; *Dean and Gerard C. and Bernice Latrobe Smith Professor of International Law, Yale University Law School;* b. 8 Dec. 1954, Boston; m. Mary-Christy Fisher; one s. one d.; ed Harvard Univ., Magdalen Coll., Oxford Univ., UK, Harvard Law School; Teaching Fellow, First-Year Legal Methods Program, Harvard Law School (Contracts and Civil Procedure) 1978–79; Clerk to Judge Malcolm Richard Wilkey, DC Circuit Court 1980–81; Clerk to Justice Harry A. Blackmun, US Supreme Court 1981–82; Assoc., Covington & Burling (pvt. law firm), Washington, DC 1982–83; Adjunct Asst Professorial Lecturer in Law, George Washington Univ. Nat. Law Center 1982–85; Attorney-Advisor, Office of Legal Counsel, US Dept of Justice 1983–85; Assoc. Prof., Yale Law School 1985–90, Prof. 1990–93, Gerard C. and Bernice Latrobe Smith Prof. of Int. Law 1993–, Dir Orville H. Schell, Jr. Center for Int. Human Rights 1993–98, Dean, Yale Law School 2004–; Asst Sec. of State for Democracy, Human Rights and Labor, US State Dept 1998–2001; Visiting Prof. of Int. Law, Faculty of Law, Univ. of Toronto 1990, 2002; Visiting Prof., Hague Acad. of Int. Law 1993; Visiting Fellow, All Souls College and Waynflete Lecturer, Magdalen Coll., Oxford Univ. 1996–97; fmr Ed. American Journal of International Law, Foundation Press Casebook Series; Fellow, American Acad. of Arts and Sciences; mem. Bd Harvard Univ., Brookings Inst., Nat. Democratic Inst., Human Rights First, Human Rights in China; Hon. Fellow, Magdalen Coll., Oxford; Dr hc (CUNY Law School); Asian American Bar Asscn of New York's Outstanding Lawyer of the Year Award 1997, Wolfgang Friedmann Award, Columbia Law School 2003, Louis B. Sohn Award, American Bar Asscn. *Publications:* has written more than 80 articles and authored or co-authored eight books including National Security Constitution (Richard E. Neustadt Award from American Political Science Asscn as best book on American Presidency 1991) 1990, Transnational Legal Problems (with H. Steiner and D. Vagts) 1994, International Business Transactions in United States Courts 1998, Deliberative Democracy and Human Rights (with Ronald C. Slye 1999. *Address:* Office of the Dean, Yale Law School, PO Box 208215, New Haven, CT 06520, USA (office). *Telephone:* (203) 432-1660 (office). *Fax:* (203) 432-7117 (office). *E-mail:* harold.koh@yale.edu (office). *Website:* www.law.yale.edu/about/officeofthedean.asp (home).

KOH, Tommy Thong Bee, LLD; Singaporean diplomatist and law professor; b. 12 Nov. 1937, Singapore; s. of Koh Han Kok and Tsai Ying; m. Siew Aing 1967; two s.; ed Univ. of Singapore, Harvard Univ., USA and Univ. of Cambridge, UK; Asst Lecturer, Univ. of Singapore 1962–64, Lecturer 1964–71, Sub-Dean, Faculty of Law, Univ. of Singapore 1965–67, Vice-Dean 1967–68, Assoc. Prof. of Law and Dean, Faculty of Law 1971–74, currently Prof. of Law; Perm. Rep. of Singapore to UN 1968–71, concurrently High Commr to Canada 1969–71; Perm. Rep. to UN, (also accred to Canada and Mexico) 1974–84; Amb. to USA 1984–90; Amb.-at-Large, Ministry of Foreign Affairs 1990–; Dir Inst. of Policy Studies 1990–97; Exec. Dir Asia–Europe Foundation 1997–; Pres. Third UN Law of the Sea Conf. (Chair. Singapore Del. to Conf.) 1981–82; Chair. Preparatory Cttee, Chair. Main Cttee UN Conf. on Environment and Devt 1990–92; UN Sec.-Gen.'s Special Envoy to Russian Fed., Latvia, Lithuania and Estonia Aug.–Sept. 1993; Chair. Nat. Arts Council 1991–96; Chair. Nat. Heritage Bd 2002–; Commdr Order of the Golden Ark, The Netherlands 1993, Grand Cross of Order of Bernardo O'Higgins, Chile 1997; Hon. LLD (Yale) 1984; Adrian Clarke Memorial Medal 1961, Leow Chia Heng Prize 1961, Public Service Star 1971, Meritorious Service Medal 1979, Wolfgang Friedman Award 1984, Jackson H. Ralston Prize 1985, Annual Award of the Asia Soc., New York, 1985, Int. Service Award, Fletcher School of Law and Diplomacy, Tufts Univ., USA 1987, Jit Trainor Award for Distinction in Diplomacy, Georgetown Univ., USA 1987, Distinguished Service Order Award 1990, Elizabeth Haub Prize, Univ. of Brussels and Int. Council on Environmental Law 1997, Fok Ying Tung Southeast Asia Prize, Hong Kong 1998. *Publications:* United States and East Asia: Conflict and Cooperation 1995, The Quest for World Order: Perspectives of a Pragmatic Idealist 1998. *Leisure interests:* sport, reading, music. *Address:* c/o Faculty of Law, National University of Singapore, Eu Tong Sen Building, 469G Bukit Timah Road, Singapore 259776, Singapore (office). *Telephone:* 65161305 (office). *Fax:* 67790979 (office). *E-mail:* lawkohtb@nus.edu.sg (office). *Website:* law.nus.edu.sg (office).

KOHÁK, Erazim, BA, MA, PhD; Czech philosopher, academic and author; *Senior Research Fellow, Centre for Global Studies, Philosophical Institute, Academy of Science of Czech Republic;* b. 21 May 1933, Prague; s. of Dr Miloslav Kohák and Dr Zdislava Koháková; m. 3rd Dorothy Koháková; three d. from 1st m.; ed Yale Univ.; exiled with parents to USA 1948; Lecturer, Boston Univ. 1960–72, Prof. 1972–90, Prof. Emer. 1995–; returned to Czechoslovakia 1990; Prof. Ordinarius, Inst. of Philosophy and Religious Studies, Charles Univ., Prague 1990–2001, Prof. Emer. 2000–; currently Sr Research Fellow, Centre for Global Studies, Philosophical Inst., Acad. of Science of Czech Republic; mem. American Philosophical Asscn, Husserl Circle, Ethical Panel, Nat. Public TV 2005–; mem. Czech TV Council 2001–05; Medal of Merit (Czech Repub.) 1998; Josef Vavroušek Prize for Ecology 1997, Great Gold Medal, Charles Univ., Hlávka Medal, Czechoslavak Acad. of Science. *Publications:* The Victors and the Vanquished 1973, Na vlastní kuži 1973, Národ v nás 1978, Idea and Experience 1978, The Embers and the Stars 1984, Ohen a hvezdy (trans. by Milan Šimečka) 1985, Krize rozumu a prirozený svet 1986, Jan Patocka: His Thought and Writings (Jan Patočka: Mšlení a dílo) 1989, Dopisy pres oceán (Letters Across the Ocean) 1992, Jan Patocka: filosofický životopis (trans. by Josef Moural) 1993, P.S.: Psové 1993, Pražské přednášky: Život v pravě a moderní skepse (Life in Truth and Modern Scepsis) 1992, Clovek, dobro a zlo 1993, Hesla Erazima Koháka 1995, Pruvodce po demokracii 1997, Pravda a pestrost 1997, Zelená svatozář: Přednášky z ekologické etiky 1998, Hesla mladých svišťů 1999, The Green Halo: Bird's Eye View of Ecological Ethics (trans. from the Czech by the author) 2000, Erazim Kohák, Poutník po hvezdách 2001, Orbis bene vivendi (Vybral a uspořádal Roman Šantora) 2001, P.S. Psové 2002, Dary noci 2003, Erazim Kohák: Zorným úhlem filosofa 2004, Svoboda, svedomí, soužití 2004, Buď Bohu sláva za vše kropenaté 2005, Kopí Don Quijota 2008, Hearth and Horizon: Ethnic Identity and Global Humanity in Czech Philosophy 2008; numerous articles in professional and popular journals. *Leisure interests:* hiking, railways, ecology. *Address:* Philosophy Institute AVČR, Room 209a, Jilská 1, 110 00 Prague 1 (office); Babákovă 2200, 148 00 Prague 414, Czech Republic (home). *Telephone:* 604-484220 (mobile) (office); (2) 72935568 (home). *E-mail:* kohak.e@ecn.cz (home).

KOHL, Herbert H. (Herb), BA, MBA; American politician and retail executive; *Senator from Wisconsin;* b. 7 Feb. 1935, Milwaukee; ed Univ. of Wis., Harvard Business School; served in Army Reserve 1958–64; worked in family-owned Kohl's grocery and dept stores, Pres. 1970–79; Chair. Wis. Democratic Party 1975-77; bought Milwaukee Bucks professional basketball team 1985; currently Pres. Herb Kohl Investments; Senator from Wis. 1988–, serves on Senate Appropriations Cttee, Judiciary Cttee, Special Cttee on Aging, Agric. Appropriations Sub cttee, Judiciary Sub cttee on Antitrust, Business Rights and Competition; f. Herb Kohl Educational Foundation Achievement Award Program 1990; Democrat; Food Research and Action Center Distinguished Service Award, Wis. Farm Bureau Fed. Distinguished Service to Agric. Award. *Address:* Office of Senator Herb Kohl, United States Senate, 330 Hart Senate Office Building, Washington, DC 20510 (office); Office of Senator Herb Kohl, 310 West Wisconsin Avenue, Suite 950, Milwaukee, WI 53203, USA (office). *Telephone:* (202) 224-5653 (Washington) (office); (414) 297-4451 (Milwaukee) (office). *Fax:* (202) 224-9787 (Washington) (office); (414) 297-4455 (Milwaukee) (office). *Website:* kohl.senate.gov.

KÖHLER, Horst, Dr rer. pol; German banker, politician and head of state; *Federal President;* b. 22 Feb. 1943, Skierbieszow, Poland; m.; two c.; ed Univ. of Tübingen; began career as scientific research asst, Inst. for Applied Econ. Research, Univ. of Tübingen, 1969–76; held various positions in Germany's Ministries of Econs and Finance 1976–89; Sec. of State, Ministry of Finance, Bonn 1990–93; Pres. Deutsche Sparkassen- und Giroverband, Bonn 1993–98; Deputy German Gov. IBRD and EBRD, Pres. EBRD 1998–2000; Pres. European Asscn of Savings Banks 1994–97; Man. Dir IMF 2000–04; Fed. Pres. of Germany 2004–; Hon. Prof., Univ. of Tübingen 2003; Grosses

Verdienstkreuz der Bundesrepublik Deutschland 1992; Commdr de l'Ordre Grand-ducal de la Couronne de Chêne 1994; Officier, Légion d'honneur 1995; Verdienstmedaille des Landes Baden-Württemberg 2002. *Address:* Office of the Federal President, 11010 Berlin, Germany (office). *Telephone:* (30) 20000 (office). *E-mail:* poststelle@bpra.bund.de (office). *Website:* www.bundespraesident.de (office).

KOHLHAUSSEN, Martin; German business executive; *Chairman of the Supervisory Board, Commerzbank AG;* b. 6 Nov. 1935, Marburg/Lahn; m.; three c.; ed Univs of Frankfurt am Main, Freiburg and Marburg; bank training, Deutsche Bank, Frankfurt am Main; Man. Lloyds Bank, Frankfurt am Main 1974–76; Man. Tokyo Br. Westdeutsche Landesbank Girozentrale 1976–78, New York Br. 1979–81; mem. Bd Man. Dirs Commerzbank AG 1982–2001, Chair. Exec. Cttee 1991–2001, Chair. Supervisory Bd 2001–; Chair. Supervisory Bd HOCHTIEF AG, Heraeus Holding GmbH; Pres. Int. Monetary Conf. 1999, 2000; Pres. Bundesverband Deutscher Banken 1997–2000; mem. Supervisory Bd ThyssenKrupp AG, Intermediate Capital Group, Nat. Pensions Reserve Fund, Schering AG, Verlagsgruppe Georg von Holtzbrinck GmbH; mem. Bd of Dirs Bayer AG 1992–, Intermediate Capital Group 2004–; Hon. Dr rer. pol (Technische Univ., Chemnitz) 1998. *Address:* Commerzbank AG, Kaiserplatz, 60311 Frankfurt am Main, Germany (office). *Telephone:* (69) 136-20 (office). *Fax:* (69) 28-53-89 (office). *E-mail:* info@commerzbank.com (office). *Website:* www.commerzbank.com (office).

KOHN, Walter, BA, MA, PhD; American physicist, chemist and academic; *Research Professor of Physics and Chemistry, University of California, Santa Barbara;* b. 9 March 1923, Vienna, Austria; s. of Salomon Kohn and Gusti Rappaport; m. 1st Lois Mary Adams 1948 (divorced); three d.; m. 2nd Mara Schiff 1978; ed Harvard Univ. and Univ. of Toronto, Canada; served with Canadian Infantry 1944–45; Instructor Harvard Univ. 1948–50; Asst Prof., Assoc. Prof., then Prof., Carnegie Mellon Inst. of Tech. 1950–60; Prof. Univ. of Calif. at San Diego 1960–79, Chair. Dept of Physics 1961–63, Dir Inst. for Theoretical Physics 1979–84; Prof. of Physics, Univ. of Calif. at Santa Barbara 1984–91, Prof. Emer. and Research Prof. 1991–, Research Prof. of Physics and Chem.; mem. revision cttee reactor div. NIST, Md 1994–; Visiting Prof., Univs of Mich. and Pa 1957–58, Imperial Coll. of Science and Tech., London 1960; Nat. Research Council Fellow, Inst. of Theoretical Physics, Copenhagen 1951–52; Guggenheim Fellow and Visiting Prof., Ecole Normale Supérieure, Paris 1963–64; NSF Sr Postdoctoral Fellow, Univ. of Paris 1967; Councillor-at-Large, American Physical Soc. 1968–72; Visiting Prof., Hebrew Univ., Jerusalem 1970 and Univs of Washington, Paris, Copenhagen, ETH, Zürich; mem. Bd of Govs Weizmann Inst. 1996–; mem. Int. Acad. of Quantum Molecular Sciences, NAS; Foreign mem. Royal Soc.; Fellow, American Acad. of Arts and Sciences, AAAS; Hon. LLD (Toronto) 1967, Hon. DSc (Univ. of Paris) 1980, (Queen's Univ., Canada) 1986, Hon. DPhil (Brandeis Univ.) 1981, (Hebrew Univ. of Jerusalem) 1981; Oliver E. Buckley Prize in Solid State Physics 1960, Davisson-Germer Prize in Surface Physics 1977, Nat. Medal of Science 1988, Feenberg Medal 1991, Nobel Prize in Chem. (jt winner) 1998, Neils Bohr/UNESCO Gold Medal 1998. *Publications:* 205 scientific articles in professional journals 1945–2005. *Leisure interests:* music, reading, sports. *Address:* Department of Physics, University of California, Santa Barbara, CA 93106 (office); 236 La Vista Grande, Santa Barbara, CA 93103, USA (home). *Telephone:* (805) 893-3061 (office); (805) 962-1489 (home). *Fax:* (805) 893-5816 (office); (805) 962-1489 (home). *E-mail:* kohn@physics.ucsb.edu (office). *Website:* www.physics.ucsb.edu/~kohn (office).

KOHONEN, Teuvo Kalevi, DEng, FIEEE; Finnish physicist, computer scientist and academic; *Professor, Laboratory of Computer and Information Science, Helsinki University of Technology;* b. 11 July 1934, Lauritsala; s. of Väinö Kohonen and Tyyne E. Koivunen; m. Elvi Anneli Trast 1959; two s. two d.; ed Helsinki Univ. of Tech.; Teaching Asst in Physics, Helsinki Univ. of Tech. 1957–59, Asst Prof. in Physics 1963–65, Prof. of Tech. Physics 1965–93, Prof., Lab. of Computer and Information Science; Research Assoc., Finnish Atomic Energy Comm. 1959–62; Visiting Prof., Univ. of Washington, Seattle 1968–69; Research Prof., Acad. of Finland 1975–78, 1980–99, Prof. Emer. 1999–; Pres. European Neural Network Soc. 1991–92; Vice-Chair. Int. Asscn for Pattern Recognition 1982–84; mem. Acad. Scientiarum et Artium Europaea, Académie Européenne des Sciences, des Arts et des Lettres, Finnish Acad. of Sciences, Finnish Acad. of Eng Sciences; Commdr, Order of Lion of Finland, Kt, Order of White Rose of Finland; Dr hc (Univ. of York, Åbo Akademi, Univ. of Dortmund); Emil Aaltonen Prize 1983, Cultural Prize, Finnish Commercial TV (MTV) 1984, IEEE Neural Networks Pioneer Award 1991, Int. Neural Network Soc. Lifetime Achievement Award 1992, Finnish Cultural Foundation Prize 1994, Tech. Achievement Award, IEEE Signal Processing Soc. 1995, King-Sun Fu Prize, Int. Asscn for Pattern Recognition 1996, Centennial Prize, Finnish Asscn of Grad. Engineers (TEK) 1996, Medal of Finnish Acad. of Eng Sciences 1997, SEFI Leonardo da Vinci Medal, European Soc. for Eng Educ. 1998, Jubilee Prize Finnish Foundation of Tech. 1999, Italgas Prize 1999, Caianiello Int. Award 2000, Third Millennium Medal, IEEE Signal Processing Soc. 2000, Academician 2000, IEEE Frank Rosenblatt Award 2008. *Publications:* Digital Circuits and Devices 1972, Associative Memory: A System Theoretical Approach 1977, Content-Addressable Memories 1982, Self-Organization and Associative Memory 1984, Self-Organizing Maps (Springer Series in Information Sciences, Vol. 30) 1995. *Leisure interests:* philosophy of music, literature. *Address:* Laboratory of Adaptive Informatics, Helsinki University of Technology, PO Box 5400, 02015 HUT (office); Mellsteníntie 9 C 2, 02170 Espoo, Finland (home). *Telephone:* (9) 451-3268 (office). *E-mail:* teuvo.kohonen@tkk.fi (office). *Website:* www.cis.hut.fi/teuvo (office).

KOIKE, Yuriko, BA; Japanese politician and fmr broadcaster; b. 15 July 1952; ed Faculty of Sociology, Kwansei Gakuin Univ., Cairo Univ. and American Univ. of Cairo, Egypt; began career as interpreter and translator of Arabic 1977; Sec.-Gen. Japan–Arab Asscn 1977–78, 1990–92; interviewer and coordinator, Nippon TV Special Col Qadaffi and Yasser Arafat 1978; Anchor, Current Issues, Nippon TV 1979–88; Anchor, World Business Satellite and Top Business Execs, TV Tokyo 1988–90; elected to House of Councillors (Japan New Party) 1998; elected to House of Reps for Hyogo Pref. 1993–, Vice-Minister Man. and Coordination Agency 1992–94, Chair. Standing Cttee on Science and Tech. 1997–98, mem. Standing Cttee on Trade and Industry 1998–99, Dir Standing Cttee on Finance 1998–2000, mem. Standing Cttee on Health and Welfare 2000–03; Vice-Pres. Japan New Party 1994; Founding mem. New Frontier Party 1994, Asst to Sec.-Gen. 1995–96, Dir Public Relations Bureau 1996–97; Founding mem. Liberal Party 1998, mem. Cttee on Public Relations 1999–2000; Vice-Chair. Policy Planning Cttee, Conservative Party 2000–03; Minister of Environment 2003–06; Minister of State for Okinawa and Northern Territories Affairs 2004–06, in Charge of Global Environmental Problems 2005–06; Adviser to Prime Minister on Nat. Security 2006–07; Minister of Defence (first woman) June–Aug. 2007; currently mem. LDP; Visiting Prof., Chuo Univ. Grad. School 2009–. *Address:* 2-12-5 Minamiikebukuro, Toshima-ku, Tokyo; 2-2-1 Nagata-cho,Chiyoda-ku, Tokyo, Japan. *E-mail:* koike@yuriko.or.jp. *Website:* www.yuriko.or.jp.

KOIRALA, Anuradha, BA; Nepalese activist and organization official; *Founding Chairperson, Maiti Nepal;* b. 14 April 1949; d. of the late Col Pratap Singh Gurung and Laxmi Gurung; one s.; ed St Xavier's Coll., Kolkata, India; fmr schoolteacher; Founder and Chair. Maiti Nepal (Mother's Home – shelter, educational facility, hospice and lobbying org. to fight domestic abuse, rape, child prostitution, child labour and trafficking of girls for sex trade) 1993–; Asst Minister for Women, Children and Social Welfare 2002–03; Distinguished Social Worker Award, Nepal 1997–98, 1999, Noted Social Worker Award, Nepal 1997–98, 100 Heroines Award 1998, Best Social Worker of the Year Award, Social Welfare Council, Nepal 1998–99, 2000, Prabal Gorkha Dakshin Bahu Medal, Nepal 1999–2000, Everest Foundation Nepal Felicitation 2000, Best Social Worker, Women's Asscn Nepal 2000, Int. Children's Award 2002, Trishaktipatta 2002, Birendra Aiswarya Padak 2002. *Leisure interests:* singing, dancing. *Address:* PO Box 9599, Katmandu; Maiti Nepal Central Office, 83–Maiti Marg, Pingalsthan, Gaushala, Nepal (office). *Telephone:* (1) 4492904 (office); (1) 4478401 (home). *Fax:* (1) 4489978 (office). *E-mail:* maiti@ccsl.com.np (office); info@maitinepal.org (office); anuradha@maitinepal.org (office). *Website:* www.maitinepal.org (office).

KOIRALA, Girija Prasad; Nepalese politician; b. 1925; s. of the late K.P. Koirala and the late Divya Koirala; one d.; Founding mem. and Pres. Nepal Trade Union Congress 1948; Pres. Morang Dist, Nepali Congress 1952–60; imprisoned after 1960 coup 1960–67, exiled in India with sr Nepali Congress Party leaders and workers 1968, returned to Nepal 1975; Gen. Sec. Nepali Congress Party 1975–91; Sr Leader Satyagraha (civil disobedience movt) and put under house arrest for nine months 1987; Sr Leader and Nepali Congress Party Gen. Sec. Jana Andolan (Mass Movt) that restored multi-party system in Nepal 1990; mem. House of Reps and Leader Parl. Party of Nepali Congress Party 1991; Prime Minister of Nepal 1991–94, 1998–99, 2000; Interim Prime Minister 2006–08 (resgnd), also Minister of Defence, of Health and Population and of the Royal Palace; Pres. Nepali Congress Party 2001–. *Address:* Nepali Congress Party, Bhansar Tole, Teku, Kathmandu, Nepal (office). *Website:* www.nepalicongress.org (office).

KOIRALA, Sushil; Nepalese politician; mem. Parl.; fmr Gen. Sec. Nepali Congress Party. *Address:* c/o Nepali Congress Party, Bhansar Tole, Teku, Kathmandu, Nepal (office).

KOIVISTO, Mauno Henrik, PhD; Finnish fmr head of state and politician; b. 25 Nov. 1923, Turku; s. of Juho Koivisto and Hymni Sofia Koivisto (née Eskola); m. Taimi Tellervo Kankaanranta 1952; one d.; ed Turku Univ.; Man. Dir Helsinki Workers' Savings Bank 1959–67; Gov. Bank of Finland 1968–82, Gov. for Finland IBRD 1966–69, IMF 1970–79; Minister of Finance 1966–67; Prime Minister 1968–70, 1979–82; Minister of Finance and Deputy Prime Minister Feb.–Sept. 1972; Pres. of Finland 1982–94; Chair. Bd of Postipankki 1970–82, Mortgage Bank of Finland Ltd 1971–82, Bd of Admin. of Co-operative Soc. ELANTO 1966–82; mem. Bd of Admin., Co-operative Union KK 1964–82. *Publications:* Sosiaaliset suhteet Turun satamassa (doctoral thesis) 1956, Landmarks: Finland in the World 1985, Foreign Policy Standpoints 1982–92: Finland and Europe 1992, Witness to History 1997; 11 books on econs and social politics. *Leisure interest:* volleyball. *Address:* c/o Presidential Palace, Mariankatu 2, 00170 Helsinki, Finland.

KOIVULEHTO, Jorma Juhani, PhD; Finnish professor of Germanic philology; *Professor Emeritus, University of Helsinki;* b. 12 Oct. 1934, Tampere; m. Marja-Liisa Pakarinen 1963; one s. one d.; ed Univ. of Helsinki and German Dialect Research Centre of Marburg/Lahn, Fed. Repub. of Germany; Assoc. Prof. of Germanic Philology, Univ. of Helsinki 1973–83, Prof. 1983–98, Prof. Emer. 1998–; Research Prof., Acad. of Finland 1988–93; mem. Finnish Acad. of Sciences; corresp. mem. Akad. der Wissenschaften, Gottingen, Österreichische Akad. der Wissenschaften; Hon. mem. Finno-Ugrian Soc. (Helsinki) 1997–. *Publications include:* 'Jäten' in deutschen Mundarten 1971, Idg. Laryngale und die finnisch-ugrische Evidenz 1988, Uralische Evidenz für die Laryngaltheorie 1991, Indogermanisch-Uralisch: Lehnbezie-hungen oder (auch) Urverwandtschaft? 1994, Verba mutuata 1999, Finno-Ugric Reflexes of North-West Indo-European and Early Stages of Indo-Iranian 2000, The Earliest Contacts Between Indo-European and Uralic Speakers in the Light of Lexical Loans 2001, Frühe Kontakte zwischen Uralisch und Indogermanisch im nordwestindogermanischen Raum 2003. *Address:* Sallatunturintie 1 D 24, 00970 Helsinki, Finland (home). *Telephone:* (9) 19124027 (office); (9) 3256081 (home). *Fax:* (9) 19123069 (office). *E-mail:* jorma.koivulehto@helsinki.fi (office).

KOIZUMI, Junichiro; Japanese fmr politician; b. 8 Jan. 1942, s. of Junya Koizumi; m. Kayoko Miyamoto 1978 (divorced 1982); three s.; mem. House of Reps from Kanagawa 1972–2006; fmr Parl. Vice-Minister of Finance and of Health and Welfare; Minister of Posts and Telecommunications 1992–93; Chair. House of Reps Finance Cttee; mem. Mitsuzuka Faction of LDP; Minister of Health and Welfare 1996–98, Prime Minister of Japan 2001–06; Pres. Jiyu Minshuto (Liberal-Democratic Party) 2001–06. *Address:* c/o Jiya Minshuto, 1-11-23, Nogata-che, Chiyoda-ku, Tokyo 100-8910, Japan (office).

KOJIMA, Kiyoshi, PhD; Japanese economist and academic; *Professor Emeritus of Economics, Hitotsubashi University;* b. 22 May 1920, Nagoya; m. Keiko Kojima 1947; ed Tokyo Univ. of Commerce and Econs, Leeds Univ., UK and Princeton Univ., USA; Asst Prof. of Int. Econs, Hitotsubashi Univ. 1945–60, Prof. 1960–84, Prof. Emer. 1984–; Secr. (Dir) for UN Conf. on Trade and Devt 1963; Prof. Int. Christian Univ. 1984–91, Surugadai Univ. 1991–97; mem. Science Council of Japan 1985; British Council Scholarship 1952–53, Rockefeller Foundation Fellowship 1953–55; Second Order of the Sacred Treasure 1996. *Publications:* (in Japanese): Theory of Foreign Trade 1950, Japan's Economic Development and Trade 1958, Japan in Trade Expansion for Developing Countries 1964 (in English), Japan and a Pacific Free Trade Area 1971, Japan and a New World Economic Order 1977, Direct Foreign Investment 1978, Japanese Direct Investment Abroad 1990, Trade, Investment and Pacific Economic Integration 1996, The Flying-Geese Theory of Economic Development 2003; Ed. Papers and Proceedings of a Conference on Pacific Trade and Development 1968, 1969, 1973; also articles in English on int. trade. *Leisure interests:* golf, Noh (Utai). *Address:* 3-24-10 Maehara-cho, Koganei-shi, Tokyo 184-0013, Japan. *Telephone:* (3) 381-1041.

KOJIMA, Yorihiko; Japanese business executive; *President and CEO, Mitsubishi Corporation;* b. 1941, Tokyo; ed Univ. of Tokyo; joined Mitsubishi 1965, assigned to heavy machinery section of machinery group, worked at Olayan Saudi Holdings in Al-Khobar, Saudi Arabia 1978–80, fmr Man. Dir Merchant Banking Group, Mitsubishi Corpn, mem. Bd of Dirs 1995–, CEO New Business Initiative Group 2000, Exec. Vice-Pres. –2004, Pres. 2004–, also CEO, Chief Innovation Officer of Internal Audit 2005–; Vice-Chair. Japan Asscn of Corp. Execs (Keizai Doyukai) 2003–. *Address:* Mitsubishi Corporation, 6-3, Marunouchi 2-chome, Chiyoda-ku, Tokyo 100-8086, Japan (office). *Telephone:* (3) 3210-2121 (office). *Fax:* (3) 3210-8583 (office). *E-mail:* info@mitsubishicorp.com (office). *Website:* www.mitsubishicorp.com (office).

KOK, Willem (Wim); Dutch fmr politician; b. 29 Sept. 1938, Bergambacht; m.; three c.; ed Nijenrode Business School; Asst Int. Officer Netherlands Fed. of Trade Unions (Construction Sectors) 1961–67, Sec. 1967–69; Sec. Netherlands Fed. of Trade Unions (NVV) 1969–73, Chair. (later renamed Fed. of Netherlands Trade Unions, FNV) 1973–85; Chair. European Trade Union Confed. 1979–82; mem. Parl. 1986–2002, Party Leader Labour Party 1986–2002; Deputy Prime Minister and Minister of Finance 1989–94; Prime Minister of the Netherlands and Minister for Gen. Affairs 1994–2002; apptd Deputy Chair. Socialist Int. 1989; Vice-Chair. De Nederlandsche Bank; Adviser to European Comm.; mem. Supervisory Bd KLM 2003–, Royal Dutch/Shell, ING 2003–, TPG 2003–. *Address:* Dijsselhofplantsoen 12, 1077 BL, Amsterdam, Netherlands.

KOKH, Alfred Reingoldovich, CandEconSci; Russian media executive; b. 28 Feb. 1961, Zyryanovsk, Kazakhstan; m.; two d.; ed Leningrad Inst. of Finance and Econs; Sr Researcher Prometey Inst.; Asst Leningrad Polytech. Inst. 1987–90; elected Chair. Sestroretsk Dist Exec. Cttee, Leningrad 1990–91; Deputy Dir Cttee on Man. of State Property of St Petersburg 1991–93; First Deputy Chair. State Cttee on Property in Russian Fed. 1993–96, Chair. 1996–97; Vice-Chair. Russian Fed. Govt responsible for Privatization and Budget 1997 (resgnd); Chair. Bd of Dirs Montes Auri Investment Co. 1997–; Dir-Gen. Gasprom-Media 1998–2001 (resgnd); Chair. Bd of Dirs NTV Broadcasting 2001–03; mem. Exec. Cttee Union of Rightist Forces (SPS) party, man. parliamentary election campaign for Union of Right Forces party 2003, editor-in-chief Pravoe Delo (party newspaper). *Publications:* History of Privatization in Russia (with A. Chubais and M. Boyko) 1997, Sale of Soviet Empire 1998. *Address:* c/o Union of Rightist Forces (URF) (Soyuz pravykh sil) (SPS), ul. M. Andronyevskaya 15, 109544 Moscow; Montes Auri Co., Gazetny per. 3, 103918 Moscow, Russia (office). *Telephone:* (495) 229-03-04 (office).

KOKJE, Vishnu Sadashiv, LLB, MA; Indian lawyer and government official; b. 6 Sept. 1939, Dahi village, Tehsil Kukshi Dist, Dhar, Madhya Pradesh (MP); m. Leena Vishnu Kokje; two d.; ed secondary educ. in Dhar MP, Holkar Coll., Indore, MP, Govt Arts and Commerce Coll., Indore, Christian Coll., Indore; practised in various legal fields, including civil law, labour and industrial law, co. matters and constitutional writs 1964–90; appeared before several Enquiry Comms and in election petitions; apptd Judge of MP High Court 1990; Pres. MP State Consumer Disputes Redressal Comm. 1992–94; Admin. Judge, Rajasthan High Court 1998–2001, Acting Chief Justice of Rajasthan High Court 2001; Sr Advocate, Supreme Court of India 2002–03; Gov. of Himachal Pradesh 2003–08. *Leisure interests:* reading, travelling, long motor drives, computers and Internet surfing, badminton and cricket. *Address:* c/o Raj Bhawan, Shimla, Himachal Pradesh (office); 201 Park Residency, 24 Bapna Compound, Race Course Road No. 2, Indore 452 003, Madhya Pradesh, India. *Fax:* (177) 2624440 (home).

KOKOSHIN, Andrei Afanasievich, DHisSc; Russian political scientist, politician and academic; *Professor and Dean of School of World Politics, Lomonosov Moscow State University;* b. 26 Oct. 1945, Moscow; m.; two d.; ed Bauman Moscow Higher Tech. Univ.; scientific researcher, Head of Dept, Deputy Dir Inst. of USA and Canada Acad. of Sciences 1974–92; First Deputy Minister of Defence of the Russian Fed. 1992–97; Chair. Interagency Cttee on Defence Security, Security Council of the Russian Fed. 1993–97; mem. Govt Council on Industrial Policy 1993–97; Sec. Council of Defence of Russian Fed. 1993–97; Chief Military Inspector of Russian Fed.; Sec. Security Council of Russian Fed. 1997–98; mem. State Duma 1999– (mem. Otechestvo–All Russia faction –2003, United Russia faction 2003–), Vice-Chair. Cttee on Industry, Construction and High Technologies 1999–2003, Chair. Cttee on Nat. Security, CIS and Compatriot Affairs 2003–; mem. Russian Acad. of Sciences 1987 (Acting Vice-Pres. 1998–99, Dir Inst. of Int. Security 2000–), Russian Acad. of Social Sciences 1993, Russian Acad. of Artillery and Rocket Science and Eng 1993–, Russian Acad. of Natural Sciences; Chair. Bd High Tech. Foundation/Gorbachev Project 2001, Russian Public Bd for Educ. Devt 2001; mem. Scientific Advisory Council, Inst. for Int. Studies, Stanford Univ. 2000, Gen. Council United Russia Party 2001–, Bd Dirs Nuclear Threat Initiative 2001–, Bd of Trustees Russian–American Business Council 2002, Nat. Anticorruption Comm. 2002; Dean School of World Politics, Prof., Lomonosov's Moscow State Univ. (MGU) 2003–; Hon. Chair. Russian Rugby Football League 1992–; Services for the Fatherland, Mark of Honour, Military Comradeship 1987, 1997, 2000. *Publications:* 20 books (including six as co-author) on nat. security, int. affairs, Russian nat. industrial policy and econs including Forecasting and Foreign Policy 1975, The USA in the System of International Relations in the 1980s 1984, Weapons in Space: Security Dilemma 1986, National Industrial Policy of Russia 1992, Soviet Strategic Thought 1918–1991 1999, The National Industrial Policy and the National Security of Russia (jtly) 2001, Deterrence in the Second Nuclear Age (jtly) 2001, Types and Categories of Nuclear Conflicts in the XXI Century 2003, Strategic Governance 2003; more than 150 articles and papers. *Address:* State Duma, Okhotny Ryad 1, 103265 Moscow, Russia. *Telephone:* (495) 292-52-18 (office); (495) 938-18-92 (office). *Fax:* (495) 292-99-91 (office); (495) 938-18-93 (office).

KOKOYEV (KOKOITI), Eduard Dzhabeyevich; Georgian politician; *'President', 'Republic of South Ossetia';* b. 31 Oct. 1964, Tskhinvalis Bordeli N45, S Ossetian Autonomous Oblast, Georgian SSR, Soviet Union; fmr mem. Russian nat. wrestling team; First Sec. Tskhinvali Br. of Komsomol 1989–92; business activities, Moscow 1992–2001; 'Rep.' of 'Repub. of South Ossetia', Moscow 1997–99; 'Pres.' of 'Repub. of South Ossetia' 2001–; mem. Kleta Partia party. *Address:* Office of the 'President of the Republic of South Ossetia', 7300 Shida Kartli Mkhare, Tskhinvali, Georgia (office).

KOŁAKOWSKI, Leszek, DPhil, FBA; Polish/British academic (retd); b. 23 Oct. 1927, Radom; s. of Jerzy Kołakowski and Lucyna Kołakowska (née Pietrusiewicz); m. Tamara Dynenson 1949; one d.; ed Łódź and Warsaw Univs; Asst (logic), Łódź Univ. 1947–49; Asst Warsaw Univ. 1950–54, Chair. Section of History of Philosophy 1959–68 (expelled by govt for political reasons); Visiting Prof., McGill Univ., Montréal 1968–69; Prof., Univ. of Calif., Berkeley 1969–70; Sr Research Fellow, All Souls Coll., Oxford Univ. 1970–1995, Fellow, Emer.; Prof., Yale Univ. 1975, Univ. of Chicago 1981–94; mem. American Acad. of Arts and Sciences, British Acad., Bayerische Akad. der Künste, Institut Int. de Philosophie, Acad. Europaea, Acad. Universelle des Cultures, Polish Acad. of Sciences; mem. PEN Club, Polish Philosophical Soc., Polish Writers Asscn, Philosophical Soc., Oxford; Hon. Fellow, All Souls Coll., Oxford; Dr hc (Bard Coll., New York, Reed Coll., Portland, USA, State Univ. of New York, Adelphi Univ., New York, Łódź, Gdańsk, Sczecin, Wroclaw); Alfred Jurzykowski Award 1969, Friedenpreis des deutschen Buchhandels 1977, Prix Européen d'Essai Zurich 1980, Prix d'Erasme and McArthur Foundation Prize 1983, Jefferson Award 1986, Prix Tocqueville 1994, Bloch Prize 1995, White Eagle Order 1997, Premio Nonino 1998, John W. Kluge Prize 2003, Jerusalem Prize 2007. *Publications include:* Individual and Infinity (in Polish) 1958, Marxism and Beyond 1968, Chrétiens sans église 1968, Positivist Philosophy 1970, Conversations with the Deveil 1972, Positivist Philosophy 1972, Die Gegenwärtigkeit des Mythos 1973, Husserl and the Search for Certitude 1975, Leben trotz Geschichte 1977, Main Currents of Marxism 1976–78 (three vols), Religion If There Is No God 1982, Bergson 1985, Metaphysical Horror 1988, Modernity on Endless Trial 1990, God Owes Us Nothing 1994, Freedom, Fame, Lying and Betrayal 1999, My Correct Views on Everything (in Polish) 1999, Mini-Lectures on Maxi-Issues (three vols in Polish, trans in various languages), In Praise of Inconsistency (three vols in Polish), What the Greek Philosophers Ask Us About (in Polish, Vol. 1), The Eyes of Spinoza 2004; several fairy tales, dramas and Biblical stories. *Address:* 77 Hamilton Road, Oxford, OX2 7QA, England (home).

KOLDING, Eivind, LLM; Danish lawyer and business executive; *Partner, A.P. Møller – Maersk Group;* b. 1959; ed Copenhagen Univ.; admitted to Bar in 1986; lawyer, Corp. Secr., A.P. Møller, Copenhagen 1989, later Sr Vice-Pres. and Head of Secr., Man. Dir Maersk Hong Kong Ltd 1996–98, Chief Financial Officer, A.P. Møller – Maersk Group 1998–2006, mem. Exec. Bd and Pnr, A.P. Møller – Maersk and Co-CEO Container Business, A.P. Moller – Maersk Group 2006–, CEO Maersk Line 2007–; Vice-Chair. Danske Bank, Danmarks Skibskredit (Denmark Ship Finance); Chair. Safmarine Container Lines NV; Deputy Chair. Danske Bank mem. Bd of Dirs Maersk China Ltd, Maersk Inc, Maersk BV The Maersk Co. Ltd, London, Dansk Supermarked. *Address:* A.P. Møller, Esplanaden 50, 1098 Copenhagen K, Denmark (office). *Telephone:* 3363-3363 (office). *Fax:* 3363-4108 (office). *E-mail:* grphrhqhrd@maersk.com (office). *Website:* www.apmoller.com (office); www.maersk.com (office).

KOLESNIKOV, Gen. Mikhail Petrovich; Russian army officer; b. 30 June 1939, Yeisk, Krasnodar Dist; m.; one s.; ed Omsk Tank Tech. School, Gen. Staff Acad.; started mil. service as Commdr of platoon 1975, then Commdr of co., Bn, Regt 1975–77, Head of Staff and Deputy Commdr of Div. 1977–79, Commdr of tank div. 1979–83, Commdr of corps, Commdr of Army in Transcaucasian Command 1983–87, Head of Staff and First Deputy Commdr of troops in Siberian Command 1987–89, Head of Staff and First Deputy C-in-C of Southern Command 1988–90, Head of Gen. Staff and First Deputy C-in-C of land troops 1990–91, Deputy Head of Staff of Armed Forces of Russian Fed. 1991–92, First Deputy Minister of Defence, Head of Gen. Staff of Russian Fed. 1992–96; Chair. Cttee Heads of Staff CIC Armed Forces 1996–98, Pres.'s State Tech. Comm. 1998–2000. *Address:* c/o Gostekhkomissiya, Znamenka str. 19, 103160 Moscow, Russia. *Telephone:* (495) 924-68-08 (office).

KOLESNIKOV, Lt-Gen. Vladimir Ilyich; Russian criminal investigator; *Deputy Prosecutor General;* b. 1938; m.; two c.; ed Rostov State Univ., Acad. of Ministry of Internal Affairs; worked as investigator, Deputy Head, Dept of Criminal Investigation; Deputy Head, Dept of Internal Affairs; Head, Main Dept of Criminal Investigation 1991–; First Deputy Minister of Internal Affairs 1995–2000; Adviser to Prosecutor Gen. of Russia 2000, currently Deputy Prosecutor Gen. *Address:* Prosecutor General's Office, Bolshaya Dmitrovka str. 15A, 103793 Moscow, Russia. *Telephone:* (495) 292-88-69 (office). *Website:* www.genproc.gov.ru.

KOLEV, Gen. Nikola Ivanov; Bulgarian government official and fmr air force commander; *Head of the Office to the President of the Republic;* b. 9 Aug. 1951, Karadzhalovo, Plovdiv Region; m. Velichka Asenova Koleva; two d.; ed Electrical Eng Tech. School, Plovdiv, Air Force Acad., G. S. Rakovski Nat. War Coll., Gen. Staff Coll., Moscow, Russia, Defence Language Inst., San Antonio, USA; Asst Chief of Staff for Plans, 19th Fighter Air Regiment HQ 1975–76; Asst Chief Operations Dept, 10th Mixed Air Corps HQ 1976–78; Chief of Staff, 19th Fighter Air Regt 1982–85; Sr Asst Chief of Operations Dept, Air Defence and Air Force HQ 1985–88; Chief of Staff, 1st Air Defence Div. 1990–92; Mil. Adviser for Air Force and Air Defence to Pres. of Bulgaria 1992–96; First Deputy Chief of Air Force HQ 1996–98; Deputy Chief of Gen. Staff for Resources 1998–2000, for Operations 2000–02; Chief of Gen. Staff, Bulgarian Armed Forces 2002–06; Head of Office to Pres. of Repub. 2006–; mem. NATO Mil. Cttee 2002–06; apptd Maj.-Gen. 1996, Lt-Gen. 1997, Gen. 2002; eight medals and awards presented by Ministry of Defence. *Address:* Office of the President, 1123 Sofia, bul. Dondukov 2, Bulgaria (office). *Telephone:* (2) 923-93-33 (office). *E-mail:* press@president.bg (office). *Website:* www.president.bg (office).

KOLLER, Arnold, DrIur, LicOec; Swiss politician and academic; b. 29 Aug. 1933, Appenzell; m. Erica Brauder 1972; two c.; ed Univ. of St Gallen, Freiburg Univ., Univ. of Berkeley, USA; fmr Univ. Prof. of Law, Univ. of St Gallen; mem. Swiss Parl. 1971–85; Pres. Nat. Council 1984–85; mem. Bundesrat (Fed. Council) 1986–99, Head of Fed. Mil. (Defence) Dept 1986–89; Head Fed. Dept of Justice and Police 1989–99; Pres. of Switzerland 1990, 1997; Pres. Int. Conf. on Federalism 2002; Chair. Forum of Feds; DrIur hc (Bern) 2002. *Publications:* Grundfragen einer Typuslehre im Gesellschaftsrecht 1967, Die unmittelbare Anwendbarkeit völkerrechtlicher Verträge und des EWG-Vertrags 1971, Für eine starke und solidarische Schweiz 1999, Zur Entstehung der neuen Bundesverfassung 2002. *Leisure interests:* skiing, tennis. *Address:* Steinegg, Gschwendes 8, 9050 Appenzell, Switzerland (home). *Telephone:* (71) 7872290 (home). *Fax:* (71) 7875590 (home). *E-mail:* arnold.koller@bluemail.ch (home). *Website:* www.forumfed.org (office).

KOLLER, Daphne, BSc, MSc, PhD; Israeli/American computer scientist and academic; *Professor of Computer Science, Stanford University;* b. Jerusalem, Israel; m. Dan Avida; ed Hebrew Univ. of Jerusalem, Stanford Univ.; Postdoctoral Researcher, Computer Science Div., Univ. of California, Berkeley 1993–95; Asst Prof., Dept of Computer Science, Stanford Univ. 1995–2001, Assoc. Prof. 2001–06, Arthur G. Villard Fellow for Undergraduate Teaching 2004–, Prof. 2006–; Fellow, American Asscn for Artificial Intelligence 2004; Rothschild Grad. Fellowship 1989–90, Univ. of California Pres.'s Postdoctoral Fellowship 1993–95, Arthur L. Samuel Award for best thesis in the Computer Science Department, Stanford Univ. 1994, Sloan Foundation Research Fellowship 1996, Office of Naval Research Young Investigator Award 1999, Presidential Early Career Award for Scientists and Engineers 1999, IJCAI Computers and Thought Award 2001, MacArthur Foundation Fellowship 2004, World Tech. Award in Information Tech. (Software), The World Tech. Network 2004, ACM/Infosys Award 2007. *Publications:* numerous scientific papers in professional journals. *Leisure interests:* reading, listening to music, hiking, travelling to exotic locations with her husband. *Address:* Room 142, Gates Building 1A, Computer Science Department, Stanford University, Stanford, CA 94305-9010, USA (office). *Telephone:* (650) 723-6598 (office). *Fax:* (650) 723-6598 (office). *E-mail:* koller@cs.stanford.edu (office). *Website:* ai.stanford.edu/~koller/bio.html (office).

KOLLO, René; German singer (tenor); b. 20 Nov. 1937, Berlin; s. of the late Willi Kollodzieyski and of Marie-Louise Kollodzieyski; m. 1st Dorthe Larsen 1967; one d.; m. 2nd Beatrice Bouquet 1982; began career with Staatstheater, Brunswick 1965; First Tenor, Deutsche Oper am Rhein 1967–71; Dir Metropol Theater, Berlin 1996–97; guest appearances with numerous leading opera cos and at annual Bayreuth Wagner Festival; Bundesverdienstkreuz, Goldene Kamera Award, Hörzu 2000. *Performances include:* The Flying Dutchman 1969, 1970, Lohengrin 1971, Die Meistersinger von Nürnberg 1973, 1974, Parsifal 1975, Siegfried 1976, 1977, Tristan (Zürich) 1980, (Bayreuth) 1981. *Publication:* Imre Fabian im Gespräch mit René Kollo 1982. *Leisure interests:* sailing, tennis, flying. *Address:* c/o Pran Event GmbH, Ralf Sesselberg, An der Brücke 18, 26180 Rastede, Germany (office). *Telephone:* (4) 402-8687 (office). *Website:* www.kollo.com.

KOLODKIN, Anatoliy Lazarevich, DCL; Russian judge, maritime law scholar and academic; *Professor of Law of Sea, Institute of State and Law, Russian Academy of Sciences;* b. 27 Feb. 1928, Leningrad; m.; one s.; ed Leningrad Univ.; mem. numerous USSR dels to int. confs on maritime affairs; headed USSR dels at confs of Int. Maritime Satellite Org. (INMARSAT) 1981; participated in creation of Russian maritime satellite org. 'Morsvyassputnik'; Deputy Dir Gen., Prof., Scientific Research Inst. of Maritime Transport 1981–; Spokesman and Co-ordinator Group D, Eastern European states, at UN Conf. for elaboration, UN Convention on conditions of registration of ships 1982–86; co-author draft Convention on legal status of Ocean Data Acquisition Systems; Prof. of Law of Sea, Inst. of State and Law, Russian Acad. of Sciences 1994–, Head of Int. Law Div.; mem. Perm. Court of Arbitration, The Hague 1990–; mem. (Judge) UN Int. Tribunal for Law of Sea 1996–; has lectured extensively on law of sea in Russia and abroad; Pres. Maritime Law Asscn of USSR (now CIS) 1981–, Russian Int. Law Asscn 1994–; Chair. Nat. Cttee of Russian Fed. on UN Decade of Int. Law 1996–2001; Co-Chair. Scientific Expert Council of State Duma (Parl.) for Int. Law 1996–; Chair. Asscn of Lawyers of Russia Int. Law Comm. 2007–; Hon. Vice-Pres. Int. Maritime Cttee 1994–; mem. Council, Int. Oceanic Inst. 'Pacem in Maribus', Malta 1971–; mem. Acad. Councils, Inst. of State and Law, Russian Acad. of Sciences 1993–; mem. Higher Degree Cttee, Expert Council on Legal Sciences of Russian Fed. 1985–2001; mem. World Acad. of Science and Art 1989–; mem. Council, Law of the Sea Inst. (USA) 1989–95; mem. group of experts of State Duma for elaboration of new Russian marine legislation, internal waters, the State Frontier, Territorial Sea and Contiguous Zone, Continental Shelf, Exclusive Econ. Zone, Merchant Shipping Code, UNESCO Underwater Cultural Heritage Conversion 1993–; mem. Scientific Expert Council of the Council of Russian Fed. (Parl.) 2003, Scientific Council of the Marine Bd of the Govt, Russia; several decorations of Russia; Hon. Medal, Free Univ. of Brussels 1993–2002. *Publications:* 270 scientific articles, books and manuals (co-authorship) in Russia, USA, UK, FRG, Belgium, Italy, Poland and other countries. *Address:* Bolshoi Koptevsky per. 3a, 125319 Moscow; Leningradsky prospect 66,60a, 125167 Moscow, Russia (home). *Telephone:* (495) 151-75-88 (office); (495) 151-54-54 (home). *Fax:* (495) 152-09-16. *E-mail:* kolodkin@smniip.ru.

KOŁODKO, Grzegorz Witold, PhD; Polish economist, academic, author and politician; *Founding Director and Professor, Transformation, Integration and Globalization Economic Research;* b. 28 Jan. 1949, Tczew; m.; two d.; ed Kozminski Univ., Warsaw; Prof., Warsaw School of Econs 1972–2001, Dir Inst. of Finance 1989–94; Prof. of Econs, Kozminski Univ. (ALK), Warsaw 2000–; fmr consultant, World Inst. for Devt Econs Research of UN, Helsinki; IMF and World Bank expert 1991–92, 1999–2000; First Deputy Prime Minister 1994–97, 2002–03; Minister of Finance 1994–97, 2002–03; Founding Dir and Prof., Transformation, Integration and Globalization Econ. Research (TIGER) 2000–; Visiting Prof., Yale Univ., UCLA; John C. Evans Prof. in European Studies, Univ. of Rochester, NY 1998–2004; Visiting Prof. Universita di Trento, Italy 2007–, Moscow School of Econs, Lomonosov Univ. 2005–; Hon. Prof., Indian Inst. of Finance 2004, Tianjin Univ., China 2005, Moscow Acad. of Econs and Law 2005; Commdr's Medal, Order of Polonia Restituta 1997; Dr hc (Univ. of Lvov) 2003, (Univ. of Chengdu) 2004; numerous prizes and awards including Polish Broadcasting Award 1985, Man of the Year Award 1994, Polish TV Best Politician Award 1997, Award of Minister for Science 2002. *Publications:* more than 400 publs in 24 languages on econ. theory and policy, including books in English: Strategy for Poland 1994, The Polish Alternative: Old Myths, Hard Facts and New Strategies in Successful Transformation of the Polish Economy 1997, From Shock to Therapy: The Political Economy of Postsocialist Transformations 2000, Post-Communist Transition: The Thorny Road 2000, Globalization and Transformation: Illusions and Reality 2001, Globalization and Catching-up in Transition Economies 2001, Emerging Market Economies: Globalization and Development 2003, Globalization and Social Stress 2005, The Polish Miracle: Lessons for Emerging Markets 2005, The World Economy and Great Post-Communist Change 2006, World on the Move 2009. *Leisure interests:* contemporary literature, ancient civilizations, nature, sport, marathon runner (best time 3:38), travelling (more than 140 countries), nature. *Address:* Transformation, Integration and Globalization Economic Research (TIGER), 59 Jagiellonska Street, 03-301 Warsaw, Poland (office). *Telephone:* (22) 5192108 (office). *Fax:* (22) 5192265 (office). *E-mail:* kolodko@tiger.edu.pl (office). *Website:* www.tiger.edu.pl (office); www.kolodko.net (home).

KOLOKOLOV, Boris Leonidovich; Russian diplomatist; *Ambassador and Consultant, Ministry of Foreign Affairs;* b. 9 Nov. 1924; m. (wife deceased); one d.; ed Moscow Inst. of Int. Relations; army service, took part in mil. operations 1942–45; diplomatic service, UN, Geneva 1956–62; mem. Protocol Dept USSR Ministry of Foreign Affairs 1962–69, Chief of Protocol Dept 1969–73; Amb. to Tunisia 1973–81; Deputy Minister of Foreign Affairs of RSFSR (now Russia) 1981–96, Amb. Extraordinary and Plenipotentiary and consultant on int. problems, Ministry of Foreign Affairs 1996–; Prof., Academician Int. Science Acad. of Information, Information Processes and Technologies; numerous nat. and int. honours and awards, including Honoured Diplomatist of the Russian Fed. 1999. *Publication:* Profession – Diplomatist (memoirs) 2000, 2006. *Address:* Ministry of Foreign Affairs, Smolenskaya-Sennaya pl. 32/34, 119200 Moscow, Russia (office). *Telephone:* (495) 244-92-30 (office). *Fax:* (495) 253-90-81 (office). *E-mail:* ministry@mid.ru (office). *Website:* www.mid.ru (office).

KOLOMOISKY, Igor; Israeli (b. Ukrainian) business executive; b. Dnipropetrovsk; ed Dnipropetrovsk Metallurgical Inst.; currently Co-owner Privat Dnepropetrovsk business group; Co-f. Sentosa Ltd (oil supplier) 1991, currently mem. Bd of Dirs; controlling shareholder and mem. Supervisory Bd PrivatBank; mem. Supervisory Bd Ukrnafta oil and gas co. 2003–; invested $110 million in Cen. European Media Enterprises (CME) 2007, mem. Bd of Dirs. *Address:* CME Development Corporation, Aldwych House, 81 Aldwych, London WC2B 4HN, England (office). *Telephone:* (20) 7430-5357 (office). *Fax:* (20) 7430-5402 (office). *E-mail:* romana.tomasova@cme-net.com (office). *Website:* www.cetv-net.com (office); www.privatbank.ua (office).

KOLPAKOVA, Irina; Russian ballerina (retd) and ballet teacher; *Ballet Master, American Ballet Theatre;* b. 22 May 1933, Leningrad; m. Vladilen

Semenov 1955; one d.; ed Leningrad Choreographic School, Leningrad Conservatory; Prima Ballerina, Kirov Theatre of Opera and Ballet, Leningrad (now Mariinsky Theatre, St Petersburg) 1957–91; Ballet master, American Ballet Theatre 1991–; fmr Ballet master, Ballet Internationale, Indianapolis Ind. 1997, then Asst Artistic Dir; Prof., Acad. of Russian Ballet 1995–; Order of Lenin 1967; People's Artist of the USSR 1965, Grand Prix de Ballet, Paris 1966, USSR State Prize 1980, Hero of Socialist Labour 1983. *Main ballet roles:* Aurora (Sleeping Beauty), Juliet (Romeo and Juliet), Desdemona (Othello), Tao Khao (The Red Poppy), Maria (Fountain of Bakhchisarai), title roles in Giselle, Cinderella, Raymonda and La Sylphide, Chopiniana (Les Sylphides), Kitri (Don Quixote), Natalie Pushkin (Pushkin), Eve (Creation of the World); cr. role of Katerina (The Stone Flower) and Shirin (Legend of Love). *Television:* main roles: The Lady (The Lady and the Hooligan), Woman (The House by the Roadside), Aurora (Sleeping Beauty), Raymonda (Raymonda). *Address:* American Ballet Theatre, 890 Broadway, New York, NY 10003, USA (office). *Telephone:* (212) 477-3030 (office). *Fax:* (212) 254-5938 (office). *E-mail:* irinakolpakova@hotmail.com. *Website:* www.abt.org (office).

KOLTAI, Ralph, CBE FRSA; British stage designer; b. 31 July 1924, Berlin, Germany; s. of Alfred Koltai and Charlotte Koltai (née Weinstein); m. Annena Stubbs 1954 (divorced 1976); ed Cen. School of Art and Design, London; served in Royal Army Service Corps and with British Intelligence 1945–47; Assoc. Designer RSC 1963–66, 1976–; Head, Dept of Theatre Design, Cen. School of Art and Design 1965–72; elected Royal Designer for Industry, Royal Soc. of the Arts 1984; Opera Dir The Flying Dutchman, Hong Kong Arts Festival 1987 and La Traviata 1990; over 200 productions of opera, drama and dance throughout Europe, the USA, Canada and Australia; Fellow, Acad. of Performing Arts, Hong Kong 1994, London Inst., Rose Bruford Coll. Art 1999; Hon. Fellow, London Inst. 1996; Dr hc (Liverpool Inst. for Performing Arts) 2007; Royal Design for Industry, London Drama Critics' Award (for As You Like It) 1967, Gold Medal (Prague Quadriennale) 1975, Soc. of West End Theatres Designer of the Year (for Brand) 1978, Golden Triga (Prague) 1979, 1991, 2003, London Drama Critics' Award (for The Love Girl and The Innocent) 1981, Designer of the Year Award (for Cyrano de Bergerac) 1989, Silver Medal, Prague (for Othello) 1987, Distinguished Service to Theater, US Inst. of Theater Tech. 1993. *Designs include:* musical Metropolis 1989 (London), The Planets (Royal Ballet) 1990, The Makropulos Affair (Norwegian Opera) 1992, My Fair Lady (New York) 1993, La Traviata (Stockholm) 1993, Hair (London) 1993, Othello (Essen) 1994, (Tokyo) 1995, Madame Butterfly (Tokyo) 1995, Twelfth Night (Copenhagen) 1996, Carmen (Royal Albert Hall, London) 1997, Simon Boccanegra (Wales) 1997, Timon of Athens (Chicago) 1997, Nabucco (Festival Orange, France) 1998, Suddenly Last Summer (also Dir, Nottingham Playhouse) 1998, Dalibor (Edin. Festival) 1998, A Midsummer Night's Dream (Copenhagen 1998), Don Giovanni (St Petersburg) 1999, Genoveva (Edin. Festival) 2000, Katya Kabanova (La Fenice, Venice) 2003. *Publication:* Ralph Koltai: Designer for the Stage 1997. *Leisure interest:* wildlife photography. *Address:* c/o Rachel Daniels, Berlin Associates, 14 Floral Street, London WC2E 9DH; Suite 118, 78 Marylebone High Street, London, W1U 5AP, England. *Telephone:* (20) 7836-1112. *Fax:* (20) 7632-5280. *Website:* www.ralphkoltai.com.

KOLYADA, Nikolai Vladimirovich; Russian actor, writer and playwright; b. 4 Dec. 1957, Presnogorkovka, Kustanai region, Kazakhstan; ed Sverdlovsk Higher School of Theatre Arts; actor Sverdlovsk Drama theatre 1972–77; mem. USSR Writers' Union 1989–; teacher Yekaterinburg Inst. of Theatre Arts 1998–; Ed.-in-Chief Ural Journal 1999–; Sverdlovsk Komsomol Cttee Prize 1978, Teatralnaya Zhizn (magazine) Prize 1988, Schloss Solitude Academy Award, Stuttgart, Germany 1992. *Plays:* Forfeits, Our Unsociable Sea or A Fool's Vessels, Barakb Lashkaldak, Parents' Day, Slingshot, Chicken, Polonaise, Mannequin, A Tale About the Dead Tsarina, Persian Lilac; *Theatre:* Chicken Blindness. *Publications:* Plays for Beloved Theatre 1994. *Address:* Ural Journal, Malysheva str. 24, 620219 GSP 352, Yekaterinburg, Russia. *Telephone:* (3432) 759754. *Fax:* (3432) 769741. *E-mail:* editor@mail.ru. *Website:* www.koljada.uralinfo.ru/.

KOMAROV, Igor Sergeyevich, DrSc; Russian geologist; *Professor of Engineering Geology, Moscow Geological Prospecting Academy;* b. 29 Jan. 1917, Kiev; s. of Sergey Ivanovich Komarov and Nathalia Yosifovna Komarova; m. Nathalya Khaime 1968; one s. one d.; ed Moscow Geological Prospecting Inst.; prospecting work 1938–43; served in Soviet Army 1943–47; on staff of Moscow Geological Prospecting Inst. (now Acad.), Asst Prof., Dean, then Prof. of Eng Geology 1948–; Lenin Prize for work on Eng Geology of the USSR (8 Vols) 1982. *Publications:* Multimeasured Statistical Analysis in Engineering Geology 1976, Application of Aeromethods in Engineering Geology 1978, Engineering Geology of the USSR (8 Vols) 1976–80, Engineering Geology of the Earth 1989, Engineering Geology of Platform Regions of the USSR 1991. *Leisure interests:* skiing, bridge. *Address:* Moscow Geological Prospecting Academy, 23 Micklucho–Macklai Street, 117873 Moscow (office); Millionshchikova Street 15, Apt. 198, 115487 Moscow, Russia (home). *Telephone:* (495) 433-64-66 (office); (495) 112-05-90 (home). *E-mail:* ikomarov@space.ru (home).

KOMATSU, Koh, BEcons; Japanese banker; b. 14 March 1921, Kobe City; s. of Masanori Komatsu and Sumi Komatsu; m. Setsuko Itoh 1948; one s. two d.; ed Univ. of Tokyo; joined Sumitomo Bank Ltd 1946, Dir 1971–, Man. Dir 1973–77, Sr Man. Dir 1977–81, Deputy Pres. 1981–83, Pres. 1983–87, Deputy Chair. 1987; Dir Fed. of Bankers Asscn of Japan 1983; Standing Dir Kansai Econ. Fed. 1984. *Leisure interest:* literature. *Address:* 301 Higashimatsubara Terrace, 24-15, Daita 4-chome, Setagaya-ku, Tokyo, Japan (home). *Telephone:* (3) 323-3154 (home).

KOMBO YAYA, Dieudonné; Central African Republic politician; fmr Deputy Dir Org. for African Unity, fmr Sr Political Officer, Africa Union Comm.; Minister of Foreign and Francophone Affairs and Regional Integration 2008–09. *Address:* c/o Ministry of Foreign and Francophone Affairs and Regional Integration, Bangui, The Central African Republic (office).

KOMISARJEVSKY, Christopher, BS, MBA; American public relations executive; *Member, International Advisory Council, APCO Worldwide;* b. 16 Feb. 1945, New Haven, Conn.; m. Reina Komisarjevsky;; ed Union Coll., Univ. of Freiburg, Univ. of Connecticut School of Business, Wharton School; Capt. US Army (helicopter pilot) 1967–72, combat service in Viet Nam, 1st Cavalry Div. 1969–70; Sr Vice-Pres. Hill & Knowlton 1974–85, Deputy Man. Dir Hill & Knowlton Int. 1985–86, COO 1986–87, Pres. and CEO of Europe/Middle East/Africa operations 1987–88, Exec. Vice-Pres. and Man. Dir Corp. and Financial Counselling Office, USA 1990–91, Exec. Vice-Pres. and Gen. Man., New York and Eastern USA, 1991–93; Pres. and CEO Carl Byoir and Assocs 1988–90; Pres. and CEO Gavin Anderson & Co. 1993–95; Pres. and CEO Burson Marsteller, USA 1995–98, Pres. and CEO Burson Marsteller (Worldwide) 1998–2004 (retd); ad interim Harold Burson Faculty Chair Boston Univ. Coll. of Communication 2006; with APCO Worldwide, New York, mem. APCO Worldwide Int. Advisory Council and Sr Counselor 2006–; Trustee, EQ Advisors Trust; mem. Univ. of Miami Rosenstiel School, Asscn for the Help of Retarded Children; mem. Arthur Page Soc.; lectured on communications and business in Spain, Switzerland and New York; Ellis Island Medal of Honor 1996. *Publications:* Peanut Butter & Jelly Management 2000 (with Reina Komisarjevsky); numerous articles on public relations topics. *Address:* APCO Worldwide, 51 Madison Avenue, Suite 2510, New York, NY 10100, USA (office). *Telephone:* (212) 300-1800. *Fax:* (212) 300-1819. *Website:* www.apcoworldwide.com.

KOMIYAMA, Hiroshi, MEng, PhD; Japanese chemical engineer, university administrator and academic; *President, University of Tokyo;* b. 15 Dec. 1944, Tochigi Pref., Tokyo; ed Toyama High School, Tokyo, Univ. of Tokyo; mem. staff, Univ. of Tokyo 1972–, Lecturer 1977–81, Asst Prof. 1981–88, Prof., Dept of Chemical System Eng 1988–2005, Dean School of Eng 2000–02, Vice-Pres. Univ. of Tokyo 2003–04, Exec. Vice-Pres. 2004–05, Pres. 2005–; Pres. Soc. of Chemical Engineers of Japan 2002–03; Best Paper of the Year, Soc. of Chemical Engineers of Japan 1979, Best Research of the Year 1992, Society Award of the Year 2003. *Publications:* Technology to Sustain the Earth 1999, Answering to the Issues of Global Warming 1999, Structuring the Knowledge 2004; numerous scientific papers in professional journals. *Address:* Office of the President, University of Tokyo, 7-3-1 Hongo, Bunkyo-ku, Tokyo 113-8654, Japan (office). *Telephone:* (3) 3812-2111 (office). *Fax:* (3) 5689-7344 (office). *E-mail:* kokusai@ml.adm.u-tokyo.ac.jp (office). *Website:* www.u-tokyo.ac.jp (office).

KOMLEVA, Gabriela Trofimovna; Russian ballerina; *Rehearsal Mistress, Maryinski Theatre and Professor, Choreographic Department, St Petersburg Conservatoire;* b. 27 Dec. 1938, Leningrad; d. of Trofim Ivanovich Komlev and Lucia Petrovna Komleva; m. Arkady Andreevich Sokolov-Kaminsky 1970; ed Leningrad Ballet School (teacher Kostrovitskaya) and Leningrad Conservatoire; with Kirov (now Mariinsky) Ballet 1957–, teacher 1978–; teacher, Leningrad Conservatoire 1987–, Prof. 1994; regular masterclasses in Europe and USA 1994–; Presenter, Terpsichore's Finest Points, Leningrad TV 1985–89; currently Rehearsal Mistress, Maryinski Theatre and Prof., Choreographic Dept, St Petersburg Conservatoire; numerous awards including People's Artist of USSR 1983. *Major roles:* Odette-Odile in Swan Lake, Aurora in Sleeping Beauty, Nikiya in La Bayadère, Raymonda, Giselle, Kitry in Don Quixote, Cinderella, Sylphide, Sylphides, Firebird, Paquita, Pas de Quatre and many modern ballets. *Films:* Don Quixote, La Bayadère, The Sleeping Beauty, Paquita, Pas de Quatre, Cinderella, The Moor's Pavane, The Firebird, Leningrad Symphony, Furious Isadora. *Radio:* as presenter: Saint-Petersburg Ballet: Events and Fates 2002–03. *Publications:* Dance – My Happiness and My Suffering, The Memoirs of a St Petersburg Ballerina 2000. *Leisure interests:* painting, music. *Address:* 190005 St Petersburg, Fontanka Nab. 116, Apt. 34, Russia (home). *Telephone:* (812) 110-10-83 (home). *Fax:* (812) 110-10-83 (home). *E-mail:* sokolov-kaminsky@zamblez.zu.

KOMLÓS, Péter; Hungarian violinist; *Professor of Violin, Liszt Ferenc Academy of Music, Budapest;* b. 25 Oct. 1935, Budapest; s. of László Komlós and Franciska Graf; m. 1st Edit Fehér 1960, two s.; m. 2nd Zsuzsa Árki 1984, one s.; ed Budapest Music Acad.; f. Komlós String Quartet 1957; First Violinist, Budapest Opera Orchestra 1960; Leader Bartók String Quartet 1963–; Prof. of Violin, Liszt Ferenc Acad. of Music, Budapest 1981–; first prize Int. String Quartet Competition, Liège 1964, Liszt Prize 1965, Gramophone Record Prize of Germany 1969, Kossuth Prize 1970, 1997, Eminent Artist Title 1980, UNESCO Music Council Plaque 1981; Order of Merit, Middle Cross of Repub. of Hungary 1995. *Performances:* extensive concert tours to USSR, Scandinavia, Italy, Austria, German Democratic Repub. Czechoslovakia 1958–64, USA, Canada, NZ and Australia 1970, including Human Rights Day concert, UN HQ New York, Japan, Spain and Portugal 1971, Far East, USA and Europe 1973; performed at music festivals of Ascona, Edin., Adelaide, Spoleto, Menton, Schwetzingen, Lucerne, Aix-en-Provence. *Recordings:* recordings of Beethoven's string quartets for Hungaroton, Budapest and of Bartók's string quartets for Erato, Paris. *Leisure interest:* watching sports. *Address:* 2083 Solymár, Sport-u. 6, Hungary. *Telephone:* (6) 26-360-697. *Fax:* (6) 26-360-772. *E-mail:* stradivari@axelero.hu (office). *Website:* www.lfze.hu (office).

KOMMANDEUR, Jan, PhD; Dutch professor of physical chemistry (retd); b. 29 Nov. 1929, Amsterdam; s. of Jan Kommandeur and Rika Jorna; m. Elizabeth Eickholz 1951; two s.; ed Univ. of Amsterdam; Postdoctoral Fellow, Research Council, Ottawa, Canada 1955–57; Research Scientist, Union Carbide Corpn, Cleveland, Ohio 1958–61; Prof. of Physical Chem., Univ. of Groningen 1961–94; mem. Royal Netherlands Acad. of Science 1981, Science

KOM THE INTERNATIONAL WHO'S WHO 2010 KON

Advisory Council of the Netherlands; Kt Order of Lion 1993. *Publications:* Photoconductivity in Aromatic Hydrocarbons 1958, Electric Conductivity in Organic Complexes 1961, Ions in Iodine 1966, Natural Gas in Europe: How much, for how long? 1977, Radiationless Transitions 1988. *Leisure interests:* literature, theatre, popularizing science. *Address:* P. J. Noel Baker Straat 180, 9728 WG, Groningen, Netherlands (home). *Telephone:* (50) 5267053. *Fax:* (50) 5267053. *E-mail:* j.kommandeur@home.nl (home).

KOMORI, Shigetaka, BEcons; Japanese business executive; *President and CEO, Fujifilm Holdings Corporation;* ed Univ. of Tokyo; joined Fuji Photo Film Co. Ltd 1963, held various sr positions in Graphic Arts and Printing Div., Industrial Products Dept and Corp. Planning Office, Head of Fuji Photo Film Europe GmbH, Düsseldorf, Dir Fuji Photo Film Co. Ltd 1995, Man.-Dir 1999, Pres. 2000–03, Rep. Dir, Pres. and CEO Fujifilm Holdings Corpn 2003–; Pres. Photo-Sensitized Materials Mfrs Asscn, Japan-German Soc., Japan-Netherlands Soc.; Chair. Japan Asscn of Graphic Arts Suppliers and Mfrs; Grand Cross of the Order of Merit (Germany) 2006; Medal with Blue Ribbon by HM the Emperor of Japan 2004, Leadership Award, Int. Imaging Industry Asscn (I3A) 2004, inducted into Photo Marketing Asscn Int. Hall of Fame 2006. *Address:* Fujifilm Holdings Corpn, 26–30 Nishiazabu 2-chome, Minato-ku, Tokyo 106-8620, Japan (office). *Telephone:* (3) 3406-2111 (office). *Fax:* (3) 3406-2173 (office). *E-mail:* info@fujifilm.com (office). *Website:* www.fujifilm.com (office).

KOMOROWSKI, Bronisław; Polish politician; *Marshal of the Sejm;* b. 4 June 1952, Oborniki Śląskie; s. of the late Count Zygmunt Leon Komorowski and of Jadwiga from Szalkowski; m. Anna Dembowska; two s. three d.; ed Cyprian Kamil Norwid High School, Varsovian Univ.; belonged to 75th Mazovian Scout Team in Pruszków, scout instructor in 208 WDHiZ scout team, Mokotów; ed., 'General Word' 1977–80; acted as underground publr at Polish People's Repub. (PRL), co-operated with Antoni Macierewicz in monthly publ. Voice; sentenced with activists of Movt of Defence Say the Man to one month's imprisonment for organizing demonstration of 11 Nov. 1979 1980; worked in Centre of Social Investigations of NSZZ 'Solidarity' 1980–81; a signatory of founder's declaration of Clubs Service Independence 27 Sept. 1981; internee during 1980s; taught in Lower Seminar in Niepokalanów 1981–89; Man. Minister Alexander Hall's office 1989–90; Civil Vice-Minister of Nat. Defence in govts of Tadeusz Mazowiecki, Jan Krzysztof Bielecki and Hanna Suchocka 1990–93; connected to Democratic Union and Freedom Union Unia Wolności early 1990s, Gen. Sec. of these parties 1993–95; elected to Parl. for Democratic Union 1991, 1993; co-f. Koło Konserwatywno-Ludowe 1997, joined with newly created Stronnictwo Konserwatywno Ludowe and Akcja Wyborcza Solidarność (AWS); won parl. mandate as cand. of AWS 1997, Chair. Parl. Cttee of Nat. Defence 1997–2000; Minister of Nat. Defence 2000–01; became mem. of Civic Platform 2001; re-elected to Sejm 2001, 2005; mem. Nat. Civic Platform Bd 2001–; Deputy Chair. Parl. Cttee of Nat. Defence and mem. Parl. Cttee of Foreign Matters, Vice-Marshal of the Sejm 2005–07, Marshal of the Sejm 2007–. *Address:* Sejm, 00-902 Warsaw, ul. Wiejska 4/6, Poland (office). *Telephone:* (22) 285927 (office). *E-mail:* zjablon@sejm.gov.pl (office). *Website:* www.sejm.gov.pl (office).

KOMOROWSKI, Stanislaw, DSc; Polish diplomatist; *Under Secretary of State, Ministry of Foreign Affairs;* b. 18 Dec. 1953, Warsaw; s. of Henryk Komorowski and Helena Komorowska; m. Ewa Komorowska; three s.; ed Warsaw Univ.; researcher, Inst. of Physical Chem., Polish Acad. of Sciences 1978–90, lecturer 1987–89; lecturer, Univ. of Utah, USA 1989; Dir Dept of Western Europe, Ministry of Foreign Affairs 1991–94; Amb. to The Netherlands 1994–98, to UK 1999–2004; Dir Secr. of Minister of Foreign Affairs 1998–99; Dir Asia Pacific Dept, Ministry of Foreign Affairs 2004–05, UnderSec. of State 2005–; Grand Cross of the Order of Orange Nassau 1988, Hon. KCVO. *Leisure interests:* tennis, photography, skiing. *Address:* Ministry of Foreign Affairs, Al. 7 ch. Szucha 23, 00580 Warsaw, Poland (office). *Telephone:* (22) 5239302 (office). *Fax:* (22) 5239599 (office). *E-mail:* stanislaw.komorowski@msz.gov.pl (office). *Website:* www.msz.gov.pl (office).

KOMRIJ, Gerrit; Dutch poet, novelist, essayist and playwright; b. 30 March 1944, Winterswijk; ed Univ. of Amsterdam; fmr Ed. Maatstaf (literary magazine); Founder Poetry Club and Awater poetry magazine; Ed. the Sandwich series of poetry anthologies; has written under pseudonyms Gerrit Andriesse, Joris Paridon, Mr Pennewip and Griet Rijmrok; Dichter des Vaderlands (Dutch Poet Laureate) 2000–04 (resgnd post early); Dr hc (Univ. of Leiden) 2000; Cestoda Prize 1975, Kluwer-prijs 1983, P. C. Hooft-prijs 1993. *Publications:* Maagdenburgse halve bollen 1968, Alle vlees is als gras of Het knekelhuis op de dodenakker (Poetry Prize of Amsterdam 1970) 1969, Ik heb Goddank twee goede longen 1971, Tutti-frutti 1972, Daar is het gat van de deur 1974, Fabeldieren 1975, Horen, zien en zwijgen. Vreugdetranen over de treurbuis 1977, Capriccio 1978, Dood aan de grutters 1978, Heremijntijd, exercities en ketelmuziek 1978, Papieren tijgers (Busken Huet Prize 1979) 1978, De Nederlandse poëzie van de negentiende en twintigste eeuw in duizend en enige gedichten 1979, De stankbel van de Nieuwezijds 1979, Het schip De Wanhoop 1979, Averechts 1980, Verwoest Arcadië 1980, De os op de klokketoren (Herman Gorter Prize 1982) 1981, Onherstelbaar verbeterd 1981, De phoenix spreekt 1982, Gesloten circuit 1982, Het chemisch huwelijk 1982, De paleizen van het geheugen 1983, Dit helse moeras 1983, Het boze oog 1983, Alles onecht 1984, Schrijfrecept 1984, De gelukkige schizo 1985, Verzonken boeken 1986, Lof der simpelheid 1988, Humeuren en temperamenten 1989, De pagode 1990, Over de bergen 1990, Met het bloed dat drukinkt heet 1991, Over de noodzaak van tuinieren 1991, De ondergang van het regenwoud 1993, Dubbelster 1993, Intimiteiten 1993, Alle gedichten tot gisteren 1994, De Nederlandse poëzie van de twaalfde tot en met de zestiende eeuw in duizend en enige bladzijden 1994, De buitenkant 1995, Een zakenlunch in Sintra en andere Portugese verhalen 1996, In liefde bloeyende: de Nederlandse poëzie van de 12de tot de 20ste eeuw in tien gedichten: een voorproefje 1996, Kijken is bekeken worden 1996, Niet te geloven 1997, Pek en zwavel 1997, In liefde bloeyende: de Nederlandse poëzie van de twaalfde tot en met de twintigste eeuw in honderd en enige gedichten (Gouden Uil prize 1999) 1998, Lood en hagel 1998, De Afrikaanse poëzie in duizend en enige gedichten 1999, De Afrikaanse poëzie: 10 gedichten en een lexicon 1999, 52 sonnetten bij het verglijden van de eeuw 2000, Poëzie is geluk 2000, De klopgeest 2001, Hutten en paleizen 2001, Luchtspiegelingen 2001, Trou moet blycken, of Opnieuw in liefde bloeyende: de Nederlandse poëzie van de twaalfde tot en met de eenentwintigste eeuw in honderd en enige gedichten 2001, Vreemd pakhuis 2001, Vreemde melodieën 2001, Lang leve de dood 2003, Alle gedichten tot gisteren 2004, Gouden woorden 2005, Spaans benauwd 2005, Fata morgana 2005, Kakafonie 2006; contrib. to Vrij Nederland magazine, NRC Handelsblad newspaper. *Address:* Bas Pauw, Singel 464, 1017 Amsterdam, Netherlands (office). *Telephone:* (20) 620 62 61 (office). *Fax:* (20) 620 71 79 (office). *E-mail:* b.pauw@nlpvf.nl (office).

KOMŠIĆ, Željko; Bosnia and Herzegovina lawyer and politician; *Member of the Tripartite State Presidency;* b. 20 Jan. 1964, Sarajevo; m.; one d.; ed Univ. of Sarajevo, Edmund A. Walsh School of Foreign Service at Georgetown Univ., Washington, DC, USA; served in Army of Repub. of Bosnia and Herzegovina during Bosnian War; embarked on political career during which he served as Deputy Mayor of Sarajevo, twice as Head of Municipal Govt of Novo Sarajevo 2000–06, and Amb. to Fed. Repub. of Yugoslavia 2001–02; Vice-Pres Social Democratic Party of Bosnia and Herzegovina (SDP BiH) (Socijaldemokratska Partija BiH) 2006–; Croat mem. Tripartite State Presidency 2006–, Chair. 2007–08; Golden Lily, Bosnian Govt. *Address:* Office of the State Presidency, 71000 Sarajevo, Musala 5, Bosnia and Herzegovina (office). *Telephone:* (33) 664941 (office). *Fax:* (33) 472491 (office). *Website:* www.predsjednistvobih.ba (office).

KON, Igor Semenovich, DPhil; Russian psychologist and sexologist; *Chief Researcher, N. Miklukho-Maklai Institute of Ethnology and Anthropology, Russian Academy of Sciences;* b. 21 May 1928, Leningrad; ed Leningrad Pedagogical Inst.; Asst Prof. Vologoda Pedagogical Inst. 1950–52; Asst Prof. Leningrad Chemical-Pharmaceutical Inst. 1953–56; Prof. Dept of Philosophy, Leningrad State Univ. 1956–67; Head of Div. Inst. of Sociological Research, USSR Acad. of Sciences 1967–72; Prof. Inst. of Social Sciences 1972–74; Chief Researcher, N. Miklukho-Maklai Inst. of Ethnography (now Inst. of Ethnology and Anthropology), Russian Acad. of Sciences 1974–; mem. Russian Acad. of Educ. 1989; Hon. Prof. (A. D. White Prof.-at-Large) Cornell Univ. 1989, Dr hc (Univ. of Surrey) 1992 Gold Medal, World Asscn of Sexology 2004. *Publications:* Philosophy of History in the 20th Century 1959, Positivism in Sociology 1962, Sociology of Personality 1967, Friendship (4th edn 2005), In Search of the Self 1984, Adolescent Pschology (4th edn 1989), Child and Society (2nd edn 2003), Sexual Revolution in Russia 1995, Faces and Masks of the Same-Sex Love (2nd edn 2003), Male Body in the History of Culture 2003, Sexology 2004, Sexual Culture in Russia (2nd edn 2005); numerous articles and edited books. *Address:* N. Miklukho-Maklai Institute of Ethnology and Anthropology, Leninsky prosp. 32a, korp. B, 117334 Moscow, Russia (office). *Telephone:* (495) 938-17-47 (office). *Fax:* (603) 688-8417 (office). *E-mail:* igor_kon@mail.ru (office). *Website:* www.neuro.net.ru/sexology (office); sexology.narod.ru (office).

KONARÉ, Alpha Oumar, PhD; Malian international organization official and fmr head of state; b. 2 Feb. 1946, Kayes; m. Adame Ba Konaré; four c.; ed Ecole nat. supérieure, Univ. of Warsaw, Poland; fmr teacher; Dir Inst. for Human Sciences, Bamako 1974, Historic and Ethnographic Div., Ministry of Culture 1975–78; Minister for Youth, Sports and Culture 1978–80 (resgnd); Research Fellow, Institut supérieur de formation et de recherche appliquée, Bamako 1980–89; consultant, UNESCO and UNDP 1981–92; f. Jamana, a cultural co-operative 1983; f. daily Les Echos, monthly for young people, Grin Grin and news service on tape cassettes for rural population 1989; Pres. of Mali 1992–2002; Chair. African Union Comm. 2003–08; mem. ADEMA-PASJ party, Club of Madrid. *Publications:* Le Concept du pouvoir en Afrique, Bibliographie archéologique du Mali, Les grandes dates du Mali (with Adam Ba), Sikasso Tata, Les Constitutions du Mali, Les Partis politiques au Mali. *Address:* c/o Office of the Secretary-General of the Government, BP 14, Koulouba, Bamako, Mali.

KONATÉ, Gen. Sékouba; Guinean politician; *Minister at the Presidency, in charge of National Defence;* b. 1966, Kissidougou; m.; four c.; joined Guinean Army 1985, Lt 1993–2000, Capt. 2000–06, Commdr 2006–08, Lt Col 2008–09, Gen. 2009–; Commdr, Macenta Parachute Detachment 2000–06; Deputy Commdr Guekedou Ind. Batallion 2007–08; Commdr Autonomous Air Transport Battalion (BATA) 2008–09; Minister at the Presidency, in charge of Nat. Defence 2009–. *Address:* Ministry of National Defence, Camp Samory-Touré, Conakry, Guinea (office). *Telephone:* 41-11-54 (office).

KONDIĆ, Novak, MBA, PhD; Bosnia and Herzegovina economist, academic and fmr government official; *Professor of Economics, University of Banja Luka;* b. 20 July 1952, Stratinska, Banja Luka; s. of Vlado Kondić and Gospa Kondić; m. Nevenka Predragović 1980; two s.; ed Univ. of Banja Luka; Prof., Univ. of Banja Luka; Head Co. Accountancy Dept, Serbian Devt Bank, Banja Luka 1977–86, Head of Inspectorate Control and Information Analysis 1986–90, Dir Municipal Admin. of Public Revenues 1990–92, mem. Municipal Exec. Bd 1990–92; Deputy Dir-Gen. Payment Transaction Services for Repub. of Srpska 1992–95, for Banja Luka 1997; Minister of Finance, Repub. of Srpska 1995–97, 1998–2000; Rep. of Bosnia and Herzegovina to IMF 1998; Exec. Dir Razvojna Banka, Gen. Dir 2004–06; currently Prof. of Econs, Univ. of Banja Luka; Medal for Mil. Valour. *Leisure interests:* beekeeping, gardening, vineyard cultivation, fruit farming. *Address:* Faculty of Economics, University of Banja Luka, Trg srpskih vladara 2, 78000 Banja Luka, Bosnia and Herzegovina. *Telephone:* (51) 218-997. *Fax:* (51) 315-694. *E-mail:* uni-bl@blic.net. *Website:* unibl.org.

KONDO, Seiichi, BA; Japanese government official and diplomatist; *Permanent Representative, United Nations Educational, Scientific and Cultural Organization (UNESCO);* m.; one d.; ed Univ. of Tokyo, St Catherine's Coll., Oxford, UK; seconded by Foreign Ministry to Ministry of Int. Trade and Industry 1977–80, to Int. Energy Agency, OECD 1980–83; Deputy Dir OECD Desk, Foreign Ministry 1983–86, Deputy Head Korea Desk 1986–87, Chef de Cabinet, Vice-Minister of Foreign Affairs 1987–88, Dir Int. Press Div. 1988–90; Head of Chancery, Manila 1990–92; Counsellor for Public Affairs, Washington, DC 1992–95, Minister 1996; Head Co-ordination and Logistics Office for G8 Summits, Asia-Pacific Econ. Co-operation and Asia-Europe Meeting 1996–97; Deputy Dir-Gen. Econ. Affairs Bureau 1998–99; Deputy Sec.-Gen. OECD 1999–2003; Dir-Gen. for Public Diplomacy, Ministry of Foreign Affairs 2003–06; Perm. Rep. to UNESCO, Paris 2006–; Chevalier, Légion d'honneur. *Publications:* Image of Japan in the American Media 1994, The Distorted Image of Japan – The Perception Game Inside The Beltway 1997; many articles in Japanese and English-language magazines. *Leisure interests:* reading, music, tennis, golf, horse riding. *Address:* Permanent Delegation of Japan to UNESCO, 148, rue de l'Université, 75007 Paris, France (office); 1-11-16 Kamiosaki, Shinagawa-ku, Tokyo 141-0021, Japan (home). *Telephone:* 1-53-59-27-00 (office); (3) 5501-8136 (office). *Fax:* 1-53-59-27-27 (office). *E-mail:* deljpn.ambr@unesco.org (office). *Website:* www.unesco.emb-japan.go.jp (office).

KONDO, Shiro; Japanese business executive; *Representative Director, President and CEO, Ricoh Company Ltd;* b. 1950; joined Ricoh Co. Ltd 1973, Deputy Gen. Man. Imaging System Business Group 2000, Sr Vice-Pres. 2000–02, Exec. Vice-Pres. 2002–07, Man. Dir 2003, Dir 2005–07, Rep. Dir 2007–, Pres. and CEO 2007–; mem. Bd of Dirs Sindo Ricoh Co. Ltd.

KONDRATYEV, Col-Gen. Georgy Grigorievich; Russian army officer; *Chief Military Expert, Ministry of Emergencies and Natural Disasters;* b. 17 Nov. 1944, Klintsy, Bryansk Region; m.; two c.; ed Kharkov Guards Tank School, Mil. Acad. of Armoured Forces, USSR Gen. Staff Acad.; served as Commdr of tank platoon, Bn, Commdr Regt, Gen. Staff 1973–74; Regt Commdr 1974–76; Deputy Commdr, Div. Commdr 1976–85; Deputy C-in-C Turkestan Army Mil. Command 1985–87, Commdr 1987–89; First Deputy C-in-C Turkestan Mil. Command 1989–91, Commdr 1991–92; Deputy Minister of Defence of Russian Fed. 1992–95; Deputy Minister Ministry of Emergencies and Natural Disasters 1995–99, Chief. Mil. Expert 1999–. *Address:* Ministry of Emergencies and Natural Disasters, Teatralny per. 4, 103012 Moscow, Russia. *Telephone:* (495) 926-38-57 (office).

KONDRUSEVIC, Tadeusz Ignatyevich, DTheol; Russian ecclesiastic; *Titular Archbishop of Hippo Diarrhytus and Apostolic Administrator for Catholics of the Latin Rite in Northern European Russia;* b. 3 Jan. 1946; ed Vilnius Polytech. Inst., Kaunas Ecclesiastical Seminary; with St Therese Church, Ostra Brama Church, Vilnius 1981–87; Dean Cathedral of God's mother–Angels' Tsarina, Grodno 1988–89; Titular Bishop and Apostle Admin. of Minsk, First Bishop of Belarus Catholics 1989; currently Titular Archbishop of Hippo Diarrhytus and Apostolic Admin. for Catholics of the Latin Rite in Northern European Russia, Moscow. *Address:* Church of St Ludovic, 101000 Moscow, M. Lubyanka str. 12, Russia (office). *Telephone:* (495) 925-20-34 (office).

KONG, Jiesheng; Chinese writer; b. 1952, Guangzhou City, Guangdong Prov.; Vice-Chair. Guangzhou Br. of Writers' Asscn 1985; travelled to USA and co-f. literary magazine; joined Editorial bd of Today magazine 1990. *Publications:* My Marriage 1978, On the Other side of the Stream 1979, A Life and Death Ordeal 1981, The Southern Bank 1982, The Big Jungle 1984, Story Investigations 1985. *Address:* Guangzhou Branch of Writers' Association, Guangzhou City, Guangdong Province, People's Republic of China.

KONGANTIYEV, Moldomusa; Kyrgyzstani police officer and politician; *Minister of Internal Affairs;* Chief of Police, Bishkek *c.* 2006; Minister of Internal Affairs 2008–. *Address:* Ministry of Internal Affairs, 720040 Bishkek, Frunze 469, Kyrgyzstan (office). *Telephone:* (312) 66-24-50 (office). *Fax:* (312) 68-20-44 (office). *E-mail:* mail@mvd.bishkek.gov.kg (office). *Website:* www.mvd.kg (office).

KONI, Gen. Allafouza; Chadian army officer and politician; career in Chadian Armed Forces; fmr presidential adviser; Minister of Nat. Defence, Veterans and Victims of War 2004. *Address:* c/o Ministry of National Defence, Veterans and Victims of War, BP 916, N'Djamena, Chad (office).

KONIDARIS, Ioannis (John), DrIur; Greek professor of law; *Professor of Ecclesiastical Law, University of Athens;* b. 10 Sept. 1948, Chios; s. of Marinos Konidaris and Ioanna Konidaris; m. Ersi Mantakas 1975, one d.; ed Univs of Athens, Thessaloniki and Munich; mil. service 1971–73; mem. Bar Asscn of Athens 1974–; Asst Faculty of Law, Univ. of Frankfurt, Germany 1978–81; Lecturer in Ecclesiastical Law 1985; mem. Editorial Bd of official journal of Bar Asscn of Athens 1985–2006; Prof. of Ecclesiastical Law, Univ. of Athens 1989–; Research Scholarship, Max Planck Inst. for European History of Law, Frankfurt am Main 1989–90; Dir Research Centre for the History of Greek Law, Acad. of Athens 1994–2000, Ed. the Centre's Yearbook (Vol. 31) 1995, (Vol. 32) 1996, (Vol. 33) 1997, (Vol. 34) 1998; columnist on ecclesiastical issues, BHMA newspaper 1992–; adviser on religious subjects to Minister of Foreign Affairs 1996–99, 2001; Sec.-Gen. for Religious Affairs, Ministry of Nat. Educ. and Religious Affairs 2001–04; Founder and Ed. Nomokanonika 2002–. *Publications include:* Monastic Property Law Between 9th and 12th Centuries 1979, Legal Aspects of Monastery 'Typika' 1984, 2003, Legal Theory and Praxis concerning Jehovah's Witnesses in Greece 1987, 1988, 1991, 2005, Law 1700/1987 and the Recent Crisis Between the Orthodox Church and the Greek State 1988, 1991, Issues of Byzantine and Ecclesiastical Law Vol. I 1990, Church and State in Greece 1993, The Conflict Between Law and Canon and the Establishment of Harmony Between Them 1994, Ekklesiastika Atakta 1999, Basic Legislation of State-Church Relations 1999, 2006, A Manual of Ecclesiastical Law 2000, 2008, Regulations of the Church of Greece 2001, Regulations of the Monasteries of the Church of Greece (two vols) 2002, Mount Athos Avaton 2003, Issues of Byzantine and Ecclesiastical Law Vol. II 2008; numerous articles on ecclesiastical law and history of law, especially Byzantine law. *Address:* University of Athens, 45 Akadimias Street, 10672 Athens (office); 107 Asklipiou Street, 11472 Athens (pvt. office) (office); 20 Bizaniou Street, 15237 Filothei/ Athens, Greece (home). *Telephone:* (210) 3688607 (office); (210) 3630391 (pvt. office) (office); (210) 6742896 (home). *Fax:* (210) 6772225 (home); (210) 3630391 (pvt. office) (office). *E-mail:* imkonidaris@law.uoa.gr (office). *Website:* www.law.uoa.gr (office).

KONISHI, Masakazu (Mark), PhD; Japanese neurobiologist and academic; *Bing Professor of Behavioral Biology, California Institute of Technology;* ed Hokkaido Univ., Sapporo, Univ. of California, Berkeley; held posts at Univ. of Tubingen and Max-Planck Inst., Germany, Univ. of Wisconsin and Princeton Univ., USA; Prof. of Biology, Calif. Inst. of Tech. 1975–80, Bing Prof. of Behavioral Biology 1980–; Coues Award 1983, Dana Award 1992, inaugural Edward M. Scolnick Prize in Neuroscience Research, McGovern Inst. 2004, and numerous other awards. *Publications:* The Harvey Lectures: Series 86, 1992 (The Harvey Lectures) (co-author) 1994; numerous articles in scientific journals. *Address:* Division of Biology, 156-29, California Institute of Technology, 1200 E California Boulevard, Pasadena, CA 91125, USA (office). *Telephone:* (626) 395-4951 (office). *Fax:* (626) 449-0756 (office). *E-mail:* konishim@caltech.edu (office). *Website:* biology.caltech.edu/Members/Konishi (office).

KONJANOVSKI, Zoran; Macedonian engineer and politician; *Minister of Defence;* b. 3 March 1967, Bitola; ed St Kliment Ohridski Univ.; engineer, Strezevo Public Enterprise 1999–; mem. Vnatrešno-Makedonska Revolucionerna Organizacija—Demokratska Partija za Makedonsko Nacionalno Edinstvo (VMRO—DPMNE) 1993–, mem. Exec. Cttee 2005–; Pres. Municipal Council of Bitola 2005–; Minister for Local Self-Govt 2006–08, for Defence 2008–. *Address:* Ministry of Defence, Orce Nikolov bb, Skopje 1000, former Yugoslav Republic of Macedonia (office). *Telephone:* (2) 3282042 (office). *Fax:* (2) 3282042 (office). *E-mail:* info@morm.gov.mk (office). *Website:* www.morm.gov.mk (office).

KONO, Eiko, BA; Japanese business executive; *Senior Adviser, Recruit Co. Ltd;* b. 1 Jan. 1946; ed Waseda Univ.; joined Nippon Recruit Center Co. Ltd (now Recruit Co. Ltd) 1969, Dir and Deputy Gen. Man. Advertising Business Div. April–Nov. 1984, Dir and Gen. Man. 1984–85, Man. Dir 1985–86, Sr Man. Dir 1986–94, Exec. Vice-Pres. 1994–97, Pres. and Bd Dir 1997–2003, Chair. and CEO 2003–04, Chair. 2004–05, Sr Adviser 2005–; External Dir Hoya Corpn 2003–, Japan Telework Asscn 2004–; Corp. Auditor, Mitsui Sumitomo Insurance Co. Ltd 2004, now Dir; Counsellor, Sasakawa Peace Foundation; Vice-Chair. Keizai Doyukai (Japan Asscn of Corp. Execs); mem. Council for Regulatory Reform; Trustee Waseda Univ. 2004–; ranked by Fortune magazine amongst 50 Most Powerful Women in Business outside the US (seventh) 2001, (10th) 2002, (ninth) 2003. *Address:* Recruit Co. Ltd, Corporate Headquarters, Recruit GINZA 8 Building, 8-4-17 Ginza, Chuo-ku, Tokyo 104-8001, Japan (office). *Telephone:* (3) 35751111 (office). *Website:* www.recruit.co.jp (office).

KONO, Yohei; Japanese politician; *Speaker, House of Representatives;* b. 15 Jan. 1937; ed Waseda Univ., Stanford Univ.; mem. House of Reps from Kanagawa; fmr Parl. Vice-Minister of Educ., Dir-Gen. Science and Tech. Agency; Chief Cabinet Sec. (State Minister) 1992–93; Chair. LDP Research Comm. on Foreign Affairs, Pres. 1993–99; Deputy Prime Minister and Minister of Foreign Affairs 1994–96, Minister of Foreign Affairs 1999–2001; Speaker, House of Reps 2003–; left LDP to co-found New Liberal Club (now defunct) 1976–86; mem. Miyazawa faction of LDP. *Address:* Office of the Speaker of the House of Representatives, National Diet Building, Chiyoda-ku, Tokyo, Japan (office); Liberal Democratic Party (Jiyu-Minshuto), 1-11-23, Nagata-cho, Chiyoda-ku, Tokyo 100-8910, Japan. *Telephone:* (3) 3581-6211. *E-mail:* koho@ldp.jimin.or.jp (office). *Website:* www.jimin.jp (office).

KONOVALOV, Aleksander Nikolayevich, MD; Russian neurosurgeon; *Director, N. N. Burdenko Institute of Neurosurgery, Russian Academy of Medical Sciences;* b. 12 Dec. 1933, Moscow; s. of Nikolai Konovalov and Ekaterina Konovalova; m. Inna Konovalova 1957, one s.; ed First Moscow Medical Inst.; intern, researcher, Deputy Dir N. N. Burdenko Research Inst. of Neurosurgery 1957–75, Dir 1975–; mem. Russian Acad. of Medical Sciences 1992, Russian Acad. of Sciences 2000; Pres. Asscn of Neurosurgeons of Russia 2003–; conducted unique operation on separation of the heads of Siamese twins 1989; Ed.-in-Chief Voprosi Neurochirurgii; Orden Druzba Narodov; USSR and Russian Fed. State Prizes. *Publications:* more than 215 works on problems of surgery. *Leisure interests:* tennis, skiing. *Address:* N. N. Burdenko Institute of Neurosurgery, 16 4th Tverskaya Yamskaya str, 125047 Moscow (office); Novoslobodskaya str. 57/65, Apt. 33, 127057 Moscow, Russia (home). *Telephone:* (495) 251-65-26 (office); (499) 978-76-18 (home). *Fax:* (495) 250-93-51 (office); (495) 975-22-28. *E-mail:* akonovalov@nsi.ru (office). *Website:* www.nsi.ru (office).

KONOVALOV, Aleksandr Vladimirovich, PhD; Russian lawyer and government official; *Minister of Justice;* b. 19 June 1968, Leningrad; ed Law Faculty, St Petersburg State Univ.; served in USSR Army 1986–88; joined St Petersburg Prosecutor's Office 1992, positions included Asst to Prosecutor of Vyborg Dist 1992, Investigator, Vyborg Dist Office 1992–94, Prosecutor, Fed.

Security Law Enforcement Supervision Dept 1994–97, Deputy Prosecutor of Moskovsky Dist 1997–98, Prosecutor of Moskovsky Dist 1998–2001, First Deputy Prosecutor, St Petersburg 2001–05; Prosecutor, Repub. of Bashkortostan 2005; Presidential Envoy to Volga Fed. Dist 2005–08; Minister of Justice 2008–; fmr mem. Security Council of Russian Fed. *Address:* Ministry of Justice, 119991 Moscow, ul. Zhitnaya 14, Russia (office). *Telephone:* (495) 955-59-99 (office). *Fax:* (495) 916-29-03 (office). *Website:* www.minjust.ru (office).

KONRÁD, György; Hungarian novelist and essayist; b. 2 April 1933, Berettyóújfalu, nr Debrecen; s. of József Konrád and Róza Klein; m. Judit Lakner; three s. two d.; ed Debrecen Reform Coll., Madách Gymnasium, Budapest, Eötvös Loránd Univ., Budapest; teacher at general gymnasium in Csepel; Ed. Életképek 1956; social worker, Budapest 7th Dist Council 1959–65; Ed. Magyar Helikon 1960–66; urban sociologist on staff of City Planning Research Inst. 1965–73; full-time writer 1973–; Pres. Akad. der Künste Berlin-Brandenburg 1997; Visiting Prof. of Comparative Literature, Colorado Springs Coll. 1988; Corresp. mem. Bayerische Akad., Munich; fmr Pres. Int. PEN; Herder Prize, Vienna-Hamburg 1984, Charles Veillon European Essay, Zürich 1985, Fredfonden Peace Foundation, Copenhagen 1986, Fed. Critics' Prize for Novel of the Year (FRG) 1986, Maecenas Prize 1989, Manès-Sperber Prize 1990, Kossuth Prize, Friedens-Preis des Deutschen Buchhandels 1991, Karlspreis zu Aachen 2001; numerous scholarships. *Publications include:* novels: A látogató (The Case Worker) 1969, A városlapító (The City Builder) 1977, A cinkos (The Loser) 1982, Kerti mulatság (Feast in the Garden) (Vol. 1 of trilogy Agenda) 1989, Kóóra (Stone Dial) (Vol. 2 of Agenda) 1995; essays: Új lakótelepek szociológiai problémái 1969, Az értelmiség utja az osztályhatalomhoz (The Intellectuals on the Road to Class Power) 1978, Az autonómia kisértése (The Temptation of Autonomy) 1980, Antipolitics 1986, Esszék 91–93 (Essays 1991–93) 1993, The Melancholy of Rebirth 1995, Várakozás (Expectation) 1995, Áramló leltár 1996, Láthatatlan hang (The Invisible Voice: Meditations on Jewish Themes) 2000. *Address:* Torockó utca 3, 1026 Budapest, Hungary. *Telephone:* (1) 560-425.

KONROTE, Maj.-Gen. Jioji (George); Fijian politician, diplomatist and retd army officer; *Minister of State for Immigration and Ex-Servicemen;* served in Fijian Armed Forces; Force Commdr UNFIL Peace-keeping Force, Lebanon 1999; Perm. Sec. for Home Affairs 2001; High Commr to Australia 2001–06; mem. Parl. representing Rotuman Communal Constituency 2006–; Minister of State for Immigration and Ex-Servicemen 2006–. *Address:* Office of the Minister of State for Immigration and Ex-Servicemen, New Wing, Govt Bldgs, PO Box 2349, Suva, Fiji (office). *Telephone:* 3211754 (office). *Fax:* 3300346 (office). *E-mail:* infohomaff@govnet.gov.fj (office). *Website:* www.parliament.gov.fj (office).

KONSTANTINOV, Boris A., Dr Med.; Russian cardiac surgeon; *Director, Russian Research Centre for Surgery at the Russian Academy of Medical Sciences;* b. Moscow; m.; three s.; ed Moscow Sechenov Med. Inst.; head of division, Research Centre for Surgery at the Russian Acad. of Medical Sciences 1968–88, Dir 1988–; mem. Presidium Pirogov Assoc. of Surgeons, Inst. Soc. of Cardiovascular Surgeons, European Acad. of Cardiac Surgeons, Russian Acad. of Medical Sciences; two State Prizes; two Orders of Friendship of People. *Publications include:* over 300 scientific papers on heart transplants and eight monographs, including Diseases in Early Age Children 1970, Physiological and Clinical Fundamentals of Surgical Cardiology 1981. *Address:* Russian Research Centre for Surgery, Russian Academy of Medical Sciences, Abrikosovsky per. 2, Moscow 119874, Russia (office). *Telephone:* (495) 246-95-63 (office).

KONTIĆ, Radoje, DTechSc; Montenegrin politician and engineer; b. 31 May 1937, Nikšić; s. of Milivoje Kontić and Vidoslava Kontić; m. Mara Kontić; three c.; ed High School of Chemical Eng; specialized in ferrous metallurgy while in France; Tech. Dir Niksic Steel Co.; Prof., School of Tech. and Metallurgy Univ. of Podgorica; Minister, Fed. Govt; Prime Minister of Yugoslavia 1993–97. *Publications include:* univ. textbook on metallurgy.

KONTOGEORGIS, Georgios; Greek politician and public servant; b. 21 Nov. 1912; m.; Prin. Admin., Ministry of Economy and of Trade 1941–52; Dir-Gen. Ministry of Trade until 1967; Sec. of State for Econ. Co-ordination and Planning 1974–77; mem. Parl. (New Democracy Party) 1977; Minister for Relations with the EEC 1977 (led negotiations for Greece's entry); Commr for Transport, Fisheries and Co-ordination of Tourism, Comm. of European Communities 1981–85; Minister for Nat. Economy and Tourism 1989–90. *Publication:* The Association of Greece with the European Community 1961, Greece in Europe 1985, The European Idea: The European Union, Greece: History, Present, Perspectives 1995. *Address:* c/o Ministry of Foreign Affairs, Odos Akadimias 3, 106 71 Athens; 26–28 Anagnostopoulou Street, 106 73 Athens, Greece. *Telephone:* 3616844.

KONTSEVICH, Maxim, PhD; Russian mathematician and academic; *Resident Professor, Institut des Hautes Etudes Scientifiques;* b. 25 Aug. 1964, Khimki; ed Moscow Univ. and Univ. of Bonn, Germany; began research at Inst. for Problems of Information Processing, Russian Acad. of Sciences, Moscow; held positions at Univ. of Bonn –1994 and Harvard Univ. and Inst. for Advanced Studies, Princeton, USA; Prof., Univ. of California, Berkeley 1993–95; Resident Prof., Institut des Hautes Etudes Scientifiques, Bures-sur-Yvette, France 1995–; Visiting Prof., Rutgers Univ., New Brunswick, NJ, USA 1997; mem. Acad. des sciences (France) 2002–; Otto Hahn Prize, Max-Planck Gesellschaf, Bonn 1992, Prix de la mairie de Paris 1992, Prix Iagolnitzer, Int. Asscn of Math. Physics 1997, Fields Medal, 23th Int. Congress of Mathematicians, Berlin (jtly) 1998, Crafoord Prize (jtly) 2008. *Publications:* Pseudoperiodic Topology 2000; numerous articles in math. journals on string theory, quantum field theory and knot theory. *Address:* Institut des Hautes Etudes Scientifiques, Le Bois-Marie 35, route de Chartres, 91440 Bures-sur-Yvette, France (office). *Telephone:* 1-60-92-66-00 (office). *Fax:* 1-60-92-66-09 (office). *E-mail:* maxim@ihes.fr (office). *Website:* www.ihes.fr (office).

KONUK, Nejat; Turkish-Cypriot politician, lawyer and writer; b. 1928, Nicosia; ed Turkish Lycée, Cyprus and Law Faculty of Ankara Univ., Turkey; Legal Adviser in Turkish Civil Service, Turkey; Sec.-Gen. and Acting Dir-Gen. of Turkish Communal Chamber, Cyprus; Under-Sec. to Rauf Denktaş (q.v.) 1968–69; Minister of Justice and Internal Affairs, Turkish Cypriot Admin. 1969–75; mem. for Nicosia, Turkish Communal Chamber, Constituent Ass., Turkish Cypriot Leg. Ass. 1970–; Co-founder Nat. Unity Party 1975, Leader 1976–78; Prime Minister 'Turkish Federated State of Cyprus' 1976–78; Leader of the Democratic People's Party 1979–82 (resgnd); Pres. Legis. Ass. 'Turkish Federated State of Cyprus' July–Dec. 1981, 1982–83; Prime Minister 'Turkish Repub. of N Cyprus' 1983–85. *Publications:* essays on literature, various papers on Cyprus, political articles 1953–77. *Leisure interests:* reading, swimming. *Address:* Kumsal, Lefkoşa, Mersin 10, Turkey.

KONUMA, Michiji, DS; Japanese physicist and academic; *Professor Emeritus of Physics, Keio University, and Professor Emeritus, Musashi Institute of Technology;* b. 25 Jan. 1931, Tokyo; s. of Haruo Konuma and Taka Konuma; m. Masae Shinohara 1960; one s. one d.; ed Musashi High School and Univ. of Tokyo; Research Assoc. Univ. of Tokyo 1958–67 (leave of absence 1963–67); Research Fellow, Consiglio Nazionale Ricerche, Italy and Visiting Prof. Scuola Normale Superiore, Pisa 1963–65; Visiting Prof., Catholic Univ. of Louvain, Belgium 1965–67; Assoc. Prof., Kyoto Univ. 1967–83; Prof., Keio Univ. 1983–96, Prof. Emer. 1996–; Prof. and Dean, Faculty of Environmental and Information Studies, Musashi Inst. of Tech., Yokohama 1996–2001, Adviser 2001–03, Prof. Emer. 2005–; Visiting Prof., Univ. of the Air 1992–2001; Visiting Researcher, Int. Peace Research Inst., Meiji Gakuin Univ., Tokyo 2004–; Chair. Special Cttee of Nuclear Physics, Science Council of Japan 1969–72; Assoc. Ed. Progress of Theoretical Physics 1976–84; Ed. Bulletin of the Physical Society of Japan 1986–87; mem. Physics Action Council, UNESCO 1994–96; mem. and fmr Pres. Physical Soc. of Japan; Pres. Asscn of Asia Pacific Physical Socs 1994–97, Special Adviser 2001–; mem. Council, Pugwash Confs on Science and World Affairs 1992–2002; Dir Tokyu Foundation for Better Environment 2001–; Councillor, Shimonaka Memorial Foundation 2006–08, Dir 2008–; other professional appointments; Hon. mem. Roland Eötvös Physical Soc., Hungary 1997, Hungarian Acad. of Sciences 1998; Soryushi Medal for Distinguished Service 2004. *Publications:* numerous books and articles on theoretical particle physics, history of modern physics and physics educ. *Address:* International Peace Research Institute, Meiji Gakuin University, 1-2-37 Shiroganedai, Minato-ku, Tokyo 224-0015, Japan (office). *Telephone:* (45) 891-8386 (home). *Fax:* (45) 891-8386 (home). *E-mail:* mkonuma254@m4.dion.ne.jp (home).

KONWICKI, Tadeusz; Polish writer, film director and screenwriter; b. 22 June 1926, Nowa Wilejka, USSR (now in Lithuania); m. Danuta Lenica (deceased); ed Jagiellonian Univ., Kraków, Warsaw Univ.; partisan with Home Army detachment 1944–45; mem. Polish Writers' Asscn 1949–, Polish Language Council; mem. editorial staff Nowa Kultura (weekly) 1950–57; Officer's Cross, Order of Polonia Restituta 1964; State Prize, 3rd Class 1950, 1954, 1st Class 1966; Mondello Prize for Literature 1981 and many other awards and prizes at int. film festivals, including Venice 1958. *Films directed:* Ostatni dzień lata (Last Day of Summer) 1958, Zaduszki 1962, Salto 1965, Jak daleko stąd jak blisko 1972, Dolina Issy 1982, Lawa 1989. *Publications:* novels: Władza 1954, Godzina smutku 1954, Z oblężonego miasta 1955, Rojsty 1956, Dziura w niebie 1959, Sennik współczesny (A Dreambook of Our Time) 1963, Ostatni dzień lata (filmscript) 1966, Wniebowstąpienie 1967, Zwierzoczłekoupiór 1969, Nic albo nic 1971, Kronika wypadków miłosnych 1974, Kalendarz i klepsydra (The Calendar and the Sand-Glass) 1976, Kompleks polski 1977, Mała apokalipsa 1979, Wschody i zachody Księżyca 1982, Rzeka podziemna, podziemne ptaki 1984; Nowy Świat i okolice 1986, Bohiń 1987, Zorze wieczorne 1991, Czytadło 1994, Pamflet na samego siebie (Slander Against Myself) 1995, Pamietam, ze bylo goraco (I Remember It Was Hot) 2001; filmscripts: Zimowy zmierzch (Winter Twilight), Matka Joanna od aniołów 1961, Faraon 1965, Jowita 1968, Austeria 1982, Chronicle of Amorous Incidents 1985. *Address:* ul. Górskiego 1 m. 68, 00-033 Warsaw, Poland.

KONYUKHOV, Fedor Filippovich; Russian explorer and artist; b. 12 Dec. 1951, Chkalovo, Zaporizhye Region, USSR (now Ukraine); m. Irina Konyukhov; three c.; ed Odessa Navigation Coll., Leningrad Arctic Coll., Kronstadt Marine Higher School, Bobruysk School of Arts; completed solo expedition to North Pole 1989; f. School of Travellers 1991; Head, Lab. for Remote Training under Extreme Conditions, Modern Humanitarian Acad., Moscow 1998–; Plenipotentiary Rep. of UNEP (UN programme on Environmental Protection) 1997–; mem. Russian Union of Artists 1983–, Moscow Union of Artists, Graphic Arts section 1996–, Union of Journalists of Russian Fed., Union of Writers of Russian Fed.; Hon. Citizen Terni, Italy 1991, Taipei, Taiwan 1995, Nakhodka, Russia 1996; Hon. Academician of Russian Arts Acad.; Order of Friendship of Peoples, UNESCO Order; Merited Master of Sports of Russia 1989, Gold Medal of the Russian Arts Acad. *Expeditions include:* North Geographical Pole (3 times), South Geographical Pole, Pole of considerable inaccessibility in Arctic Ocean, Mt. Everest (Alpinists pole), Cape Horn (Yachtsmen pole); within program Seven Summits of the World climbed highest mountains on each continent: Elbrus (Europe/Russia) 1992, Everest (Asia) 1992, Winson Massif (Antarctica) 1996, Aconcagua (South America) 1996, Kilimanjaro (Africa) 1997, Mt. Kosciusko (Australia) 1997, Mt. McKinley (North America) 1997. *Address:* Tourism and Sports Union of Russia, Studeniy proyezd 7, 129282 Moscow, Russia. *Telephone:* (495) 478-63-02 (office). *E-mail:* oscar75@yandex.ru. *Website:* www.konyukhov.ru.

KOO, Bon-moo; South Korean business executive; *Chairman and CEO, LG Group;* b. 10 Feb. 1945, Kyongsangnam-do Chinju; m.; three c.; ed Yonsei

Univ., Ashland Univ., Cleveland State Univ., USA; served in various man. roles at Lucky Co., Ltd 1975–80 including Gen. Man. Export Man. 1979, Gen. Man. 1979–81, Goldstar Electronics Co. Ltd 1981, Dir 1981–85, Man. Dir 1985, Exec. Dir Planning and Man. Office, Lucky Goldstar 1985–89, Vice Pres. Planning and Man. Office 1989, Vice Chair. 1989–95, Chair. Overseas Business Devt Cttee 1993, Vice Chair. and CEO Goldstar Electronics Co., Ltd 1993, Chair. and CEO LG Group (fmrly Lucky Goldstar Group) 1995–, Chair. and CEO LG Chemical Ltd 1998–, LG Electronics Inc. 1998–; CEO LG Evergreen Foundation, 1997; Vice-Chair. Fed. of Korean Industries 1989, Chair. Tax Revision Cttee 1999; Owner LG Twins professional baseball team 1990–. *Address:* LG Group, LG Twin Towers, 20 Yoido-dong, Youngdungpo-gu, Seoul 150-721, Republic of Korea (office). *Telephone:* (2) 3773-1114 (office). *Fax:* (2) 3773-7813 (office). *E-mail:* info@lg.net (office). *Website:* www.lg.net (office); www.lge.com (office); www.koobonmoo.pe.kr.

KOO, Jeffrey Len-song, Sr, MBA; Taiwanese business executive; *Chairman, Chinatrust Financial Holding Co., Ltd;* b. 8 Sept. 1933, Taipei; m. Mitzi Koo; three s. one d.; ed Soochow Univ., New York Univ., USA; f. China Securities and Investment Corpn (now Chinatrust Commercial Bank) 1966, Chair. 1988–92, currently Chair. Chinatrust Financial Holding Co., Ltd and Head, Koos Group (family conglomerate), Chair. Trust Holding Corpn, PT Bank Chinatrust Indonesia, Chinatrust Cultural Foundation, Taipei Pacific Econ. Cooperation Cttee of PECC, Overseas Investment and Devt Corpn, Taiwan Inst. of Econ. Research, Taiwanese–Japanese Econ. and Trade Foundation; Adviser, China Taipei Del. of Asia Pacific Econ. Cooperation; Del. Asian Devt Bank; mem. Cen. Standing Cttee Kuomintang; Nat. Policy Adviser to Pres. of Taiwan 1996–2004, Sr Adviser 2004–; Amb.-at-Large for Taiwan 1998–2002; fmr Chair. Chinese Nat. Asscn of Industry and Commerce (CNAIC), now Hon. Chair.; Hon. Chair. Taiwan-US Econ. Council; Trustee, New York Univ., De La Salle Univ., Philippines; Dr hc (De La Salle Univ., Philippines). *Address:* Chinatrust Financial Holding Co., Ltd, 3 Sung Shou Road, 18 Floor, Suite 3, Taipei 110, Taiwan (office). *Telephone:* (2) 2722-2002 (office). *Fax:* (2) 8780-3000 (office). *Website:* www.chinatrust.com.tw (office).

KOO, John, BEcons; South Korean electronics industry executive; *Chairman, LS Cable Ltd;* b. 11 Dec. 1946, Jinjoo, Namdo Prov.; ed Kyonggi High School, Princeton Univ., USA; joined LG Int. 1973, Import Section 1973–76, Man., Machinery and Electronics Div. 1976–79, Gen. Man. Hong Kong Office 1979–81, Singapore Office 1982–83, Chief, Singapore Office 1983–87, joined LG Electronics Co. Ltd (fmrly Goldstar Co. Ltd) 1987, Man. Dir Overseas Operations Div. 1987–88, Sr Man. Dir Overseas Operations Div. 1988–91, Vice-Pres. 1991–95, CEO 1994–2003, Pres. 1995–99, Vice-Chair. 1999–2003; Chair. LG Cable Ltd (now LS Cable) 2004–; Chair. Electronic Industries Asscn of Korea (EIAK), Industrial Design Cttee of Fed. of Korean Industries, Electronic Display Industrial Research Asscn; Chair. Zenith Electronics Corpn; Vice-Chair. Korea Industrial Tech. Asscn; mem. Korea Inst. for Industrial Econs and Trade; Iron Tower Order of Industrial Service Merit 1985, Gold Tower Order of Industrial Service Merit 1995. *Address:* LS Cable Ltd, Floor 19–21, ASEM Tower, 159, Samseong-dong, Gangnam-gu, Seoul 135-798, Republic of Korea (office). *Telephone:* (2) 2189-9114 (office). *Fax:* (2) 2189-9119 (office). *Website:* www.lscable.com (office); www.johnkoo.pe.kr.

KOOGLE, Timothy (Tim) A., BS, MS, DEng; American business executive; b. 1952; m. (divorced); ed Univ. of Virginia, Stanford Univ.; Pres. Intermec Corpn; Corp. Vice-Pres. Western Atlas Inc.; with Motorola Inc.; CEO Yahoo! Corpn 1992–99, Chair., CEO 1999–2001; Founder and CEO Serendipity Land Holdings LLC (pvt land development co.), developer of El Banco resort, Punta de Mita, Mexico; Founder and Man. Dir The Koogle Foundation; mem. Bd of Dirs Thomas Weisel Pnrs Group LLC 2006–; fmr Chair. Bd Dirs AIM. *Leisure interests:* vintage guitars, cars. *Address:* c/o Board of Directors, Thomas Weisel Partners, 1 Montgomery Street, San Francisco, CA 94104, USA (office). *Website:* www.elbancomexico.com.

KOOIJMANS, Pieter Hendrik, DJur; Dutch politician and lawyer; b. 6 July 1933, Heemstede; m. A. Kooijmans-Verhage; four c.; ed Free Univ. Amsterdam; mem. Faculty of Law, Free Univ. of Amsterdam 1960–65, Prof. of European Law and Public Int. Law 1965–73; State Sec. for Foreign Affairs 1973–77; Prof. of Public Int. Law, Univ. of Leiden 1978–92, 1995–97; Minister for Foreign Affairs 1993–94; mem. (Judge) Int. Court of Justice 1997–2006; Minister of State 2007–; Chair. or mem. numerous orgs including Chair. Bd Carnegie Foundation; Head Netherlands del. to UN Comm. on Human Rights 1982–85, 1992, Chair. Comm. 1984–85, Special Rapporteur on questions relevant to torture 1985–92; mem. Inst. of Int. Law; mem. various UN and CSCE missions to fmr Yugoslavia 1991–92. *Publications:* various textbooks and articles on int. law and human rights. *Address:* Prinsenweg 111, 2242 ED Wassenaar, Netherlands (home). *Telephone:* (70) 5141738 (home). *E-mail:* kooijmansverhage@planet.nl (home).

KOOLHAAS, Remment (Rem); Dutch architect and academic; *Professor in Practice, Department of Architecture, Graduate School of Design, Harvard University;* b. 1944; ed Architectural Asscn School; fmr journalist Haagse Post, Amsterdam; fmr screenplay writer; co.-f. Office of Metropolitan Architecture (OMA); f. Grosztstadt Foundation; Visiting Scholar, The Getty Center, LA 1993; now Prof. in Practice, Harvard Univ. Grad. School of Design; Chevalier, Légion d'honneur 2001; Progressive Architecture Award (jtly) 1974, Le Moniteur, Prix d'Architecture 1991, Antonio Gaudi Prize 1992, Pritzker Prize 2000, Praemium Imperiale 2003, Royal Gold Medal (RIBA) 2004, European Union Prize for Contemporary Architecture 2005. *Major works include:* Congrexpo, Lille, Kunsthal, Rotterdam, Educatorium, Univ. of Utrecht, Cardiff Bay Opera House, Wales, extension of the Tate Gallery, London, Miami Performing Arts Center, Hypo-Theatiner-Zentrum, Munich, Yokohama Urban Ring, Japan, New Seoul Int. Airport, extension of The Hague's Parl. Bldg, Guggenheim Heritage 2001, Guggenheim Las Vegas 2001, Summer Pavilion, Serpentine Gallery, London 2006. *Exhibitions include:* The Sparkling Metropolis, Guggenheim Museum 1978, OMA 1972–88, ArchitecturMuseum, Basel 1988, OMA: The First Decade, Boymans Museum, Rotterdam 1989, OMA, Museum of Modern Art, New York 1994, Light Construction, Museum of Modern Art, New York 1995. *Publications:* The Berlin Wall as Architecture 1970, Exodus, or the Voluntary Prisoners of Architecture 1972, OMA 30: 30 Colours 1999, OMA Rem Koolhaas Living, Vivre, Leben 1999, Mutations 2001. *Address:* OMA/AMO Rotterdam, 3032 AD Rotterdam (office); Harvard University Graduate School of Design, 48 Quincy Street, Cambridge, MA 02138, USA (office). *Telephone:* (10) 2438200; (617) 495-1000 (Harvard) (office). *Fax:* (10) 2438202 (office). *E-mail:* office@oma.nl (office); Jinaba@gsd.harvard.edu (office). *Website:* www.oma.nl (office); www.gsd.harvard.edu (office).

KOOLMAN, Olindo; Aruban politician; b. 1942; Gov. Gen. of Aruba 1992–2004. *Address:* c/o Office of the Governor, Plaza Henny Eman 3, Oranjestad, Aruba (office).

KOONS, Jeff; American artist; b. 21 Jan. 1955, York, Pa; m. 1st Ilona Staller (La Cicciolina) 1991 (divorced 1994); one s.; m. 2nd Justine Wheeler; one s.; ed School of the Art Inst. of Chicago, Maryland Inst. Coll. of Art; fmr commodity broker, Wall Street; Fellow, American Acad. of Arts and Sciences 2005. *Address:* c/o Daniel Weinberg Contemporary Art, 2900 Pacific Avenue, San Francisco, CA 94115, USA (office). *Telephone:* (415) 440-9696 (office). *Fax:* (415) 440-9699 (office). *Website:* www.jeffkoons.com.

KOONTZ, Dean Ray, (David Axton, Brian Coffey, Deanna Dwyer, K. R. Dwyer, John Hill, Leigh Nichols, Anthony North, Richard Paige, Owen West), BS; American writer; b. 9 July 1945, Everett, Pa; s. of Raymond Koontz and Florence Logue; m. Gerda Ann Cerra 1966; ed Shippensburg Univ.; fmr teacher of English; freelance author 1969–; work includes novels, short stories, science fiction/fantasy, social commentary/phenomena and journalism; Hon. DLitt (Shippensburg) 1989. *Publications include:* (under various names) Star Quest 1968, The Fall of the Dream Machine 1969, Fear That Man 1969, Anti-Man 1970, Beastchild 1970, Dark of the Woods 1970, The Dark Symphony 1970, Hell's Gate 1970, The Crimson Witch 1971, A Darkness in My Soul 1972, The Flesh in the Furnace 1972, Starblood 1972, Time Thieves 1972, Warlock 1972, A Werewolf Among Us 1973, Hanging On 1973, The Haunted Earth 1973, Demon Seed 1973, Strike Deep 1974, After the Last Race 1974, Nightmare Journey 1975, The Long Sleep 1975, Night Chills 1976, The Voice of the Night 1980, Whispers 1980, The Funhouse 1980, The Eyes of Darkness 1981, The Mask 1981, House of Thunder 1982, Phantoms 1983, Darkness Comes 1984, Twilight 1984, The Door to December 1985, Strangers 1986, Shadow Fires 1987, Watchers 1987, Twilight Eyes 1987, Oddkins 1988, Servants of Twilight 1988, Lightning 1988, Midnight 1989, The Bad Place 1990, Cold Fire 1991, Hideaway 1992, Dragon Tears 1992, Winter Moon 1993, The House of Thunder 1993, Dark Rivers of the Heart 1994, Mr Murder 1994, Fun House 1994, Strange Highways 1994, Icebound 1995, Intensity 1995, The Key to Midnight 1995, Ticktock 1996, Santa's Twin 1996, Sole Survivor 1996, Fear Nothing 1997, Seize the Night 1998, False Memory 1999, From the Corner of his Eye 2001, One Door Away From Heaven 2001, By the Light of the Moon 2002, The Face 2003, Odd Thomas 2003, Life Expectancy 2004, Frankenstein 2: City of Night (with Ed Gorman) 2004, Forever Odd 2005, The Husband 2006, Brother Odd 2006, The Good Guy 2007, The Darkest Evening of the Year 2007, Odd Hours 2008, Bliss to You 2008, In Odd We Trust 2008, Shadowfires 2008, The Bad Place 2008, Frankenstein: Prodigal Son (graphic novel series) 2008, Your Heart Belongs to Me 2008, Relentless 2009. *Address:* POB 9529, Newport Beach, CA 92658, USA (office). *E-mail:* dean@deankoontz.com (office). *Website:* www.deankoontz.com.

KOOP, C. Everett, AB, MD, ScD; American surgeon, fmr government official and academic; *Senior Scholar, C. Everett Koop Institute, Dartmouth College;* b. 14 Oct. 1916, New York; s. of J. Everett Koop and Helen Apel; m. Elizabeth Flanagan 1938; three s. one d.; ed Dartmouth Coll., Cornell Medical School and Grad. School of Medicine, Univ. of Pennsylvania; Surgeon-in-Chief, Children's Hosp. of Philadelphia 1948–81; Prof. of Pediatric Surgery, Univ. of Pa 1959–85; Prof. of Pediatrics 1976–85; US Surgeon Gen. 1981–89; Deputy Asst Sec. for Health and Dir Office of Int. Health, US Public Health Service (USPHS) 1982; Consultant, USN 1964–84; Ed. of various medical journals 1961–; Sr. Scholar C. Everett Koop Inst., Dartmouth Coll., McInerny Prof., Dartmouth Coll. 1994–; mem. Asscn Mil. Surgeons (Pres. 1982, 1987); special qualifications in pediatric surgery, American Bd. of Pediatric Surgery; Chevalier, Légion d'honneur 1980; 41 hon. degrees; Hon. FRCS; Hon. FRSM, Denis Browne Gold Medal, British Asscn of Paediatric Surgeons 1971, Duarte, Sanchez and Mella Award (Dominican Repub.), Drexel Univ. Eng and Science Day Award 1975, USPHS Distinguished Service Medal 1983, Sec.'s Recognition Award, US Dept of Health and Human Services 1986, Harry S Truman Award 1990, Presidential Medal of Freedom 1995, Heinz Foundation Award 1995, Medal of Honor, American Cancer Soc. 2000 and other USPHS awards; two Freddies Awards, Int. Science in Medicine Film Festival. *Television:* C. Everett Koop MD (Emmy Award). *Publications:* 235 papers and monographs; several books including Koop: The Memoirs of the Former Surgeon General 1991, Let's Talk 1992, Critical Issues in Global Health 2001. *Leisure interest:* lapidary art. *Address:* C. Everett Koop Institute at Dartmouth, 7025 Parker House, Hanover, NH 03755, USA (office). *Telephone:* (603) 646-9890 (office). *Fax:* (603) 646-9891 (office). *E-mail:* susan.a.wills@dartmouth.edu. *Website:* www.dartmouth.edu/dms/koop (office).

KOOPMAN, Antonius (Ton) Gerhardus Michael; Dutch musician, academic and conductor; *Professor of Harpsichord, Royal Conservatory, The Hague;* b. 2 Oct. 1944, Zwolle; m. Christine H. H. Mathot 1975; three d.; ed Amsterdam Conservatory and Univ. of Amsterdam; Prof. of Harpsichord,

Royal Conservatory, The Hague; f. Amsterdam Baroque Orchestra 1979, Amsterdam Baroque Choir 1992; appears on concert platforms around the world and on radio and TV; has made over 200 recordings of harpsichord and organ works by Bach, Handel etc.; f. his own record label Antoine Marchand (Sub-label of Challenge Classics); Hon. mem. RAM, London; Dr hc (Utrecht) 2000; winner of several prizes. *Publications:* Interpretation of Baroque Music 1985 and a small book about J. S. Bach 1985; The Harpischord in Dutch Paintings (co-), The World of the Bach Cantatas (co-ed with Christoph Wolff) 1996. *Leisure interests:* art and culture of the Renaissance and Baroque period. *Address:* Meerweg 23, 1405 BC Bussum, Netherlands. *Telephone:* (35) 6913676. *Fax:* (35) 6939752. *E-mail:* ton.koopman@wxs.nl (office). *Website:* www.tonkoopman.nl (office).

KOOPMANS, Lense; Dutch banking executive; *Chairman of the Supervisory Board, Rabobank Group;* b. 17 June 1943; Prof. Emer., Univ. of Groningen; mem. Bd of Dirs Rabobank Nederland 1996–2002, mem. Supervisory Bd 2002–, Chair. 2007–; Chair. Supervisory Bd Burgfonds BV –2004, Cordares NV, Siers Groep BV, Arriva Nederland BV; mem. Bd Dirs Stichting Administratiekantoor Unilever NV; mem. Supervisory Bd Nuon NV, Huntsman Holland BV, KIWA NV, Eureko BV 2005–; Chair. Bd of Supervision Fries Museum en Princessehof; mem. Bd of Supervision Univ. Medical Centre, Groningen, Stichting TNO. *Address:* Rabobank Group, Postbus 17100, Croeselaan 18, 3500 HG Utrecht, Netherlands (office). *Telephone:* (30) 216-00-00 (office). *Fax:* (30) 216-26-72 (office). *E-mail:* info@rabobank.com (office). *Website:* www.rabobank.com (office).

KÖÖRNA, Arno, PhD; Estonian economist; *Professor Emeritus, Eurouniversity, Tallinn;* b. 2 Feb. 1926, Tartu; s. of Artur Köörna and Anna Köörna; m. Eha Lind 1946; two c.; ed Tartu Univ.; lecturer Tartu Univ. 1953–65, Prof. 1971; Corresp. mem. Estonian Acad. of Sciences 1972, mem. 1975; Scientific Dir Inst. of Econs Estonian Acad. of Sciences 1965–66, Dir 1966–73; Chief Scientific Sec. Presidium of Estonian Acad. of Sciences 1973–82, Vice-Pres. 1978–82, Pres. 1990–94; Prof. Emer., Eurouniversity, Tallinn 1998–. *Publications:* Science in Estonia 1993, Introduction to the Theory of Innovation 1997, In the Service of Prometheus 2002. *Address:* Estonian Academy of Sciences, Kohtu str. 6, 10130 Tallinn (office); Kapi str. 9-22, 10136 Tallinn, Estonia (home). *Telephone:* (2) 6442129 (office); (2) 6620628 (home). *Fax:* (2) 6451805 (office). *E-mail:* riho@tan.ee (office); arno.koorna@mail.ee (home). *Website:* www.akadeemia.ee (office).

KOOSER, Theodore (Ted), BS, MA; American poet and writer; b. 25 April 1939, Ames, Ia; m. 1st Diana Tresslar 1962 (divorced 1969); one s.; m. 2nd Kathleen Rutledge 1977; ed Iowa State Univ., Univ. of Neb.; Underwriter, Bankers Life Neb. 1965–73; part-time instructor in creative writing 1970–, Sr Underwriter, Lincoln Benefit Life 1973–84, Vice-Pres. 1984–98; currently Prof., Univ. of Neb., Lincoln; Ed. and Publr, Windflower Press; Poet Laureate of the USA 2004–06; John H. Vreeland Award for Creative Writing 1964, Prairier Schooner Prizes in Poetry 1976, 1978, NEA Literary Fellowships 1976, 1984, Columbia Magazine Stanley Kunitz Poetry Prize 1984, Governor's Arts Award 1988, Mayor's Arts Award 1989, Poetry Northwest Richard Hugo Prize 1994, Nebraska Arts Council Merit Award 2000, Pushcart Prize, James Boatwright Prize. *Publications:* Official Entry Blank 1969, Grass County 1971, Twenty Poems 1973, A Local Habitation and a Name 1974, Shooting a Farmhouse: So This is Nebraska 1975, Not Coming to be Barked At 1976, Voyages to the Inland Sea (with Harley Elliott) 1976, Hatcher 1978, Old Marriage and New 1978, Cottonwood County (with William Kloefkorn) 1979, Windflower Home Almanac of Poetry (ed.) 1980, Sure Signs: New and Selected Poems (Soc. of Midland Authors Poetry Prize) 1980, One World at a Time 1985, The Blizzard Voices 1986, As Far as I Can See: Contemporary Writers of the Middle Plains (ed.) 1989, Etudes 1992, Weather Central 1994, A Book of Things 1995, A Decade of Ted Kooser Valentines 1996, Riding with Colonel Carter 1999, Winter Morning Walks: 100 Postcards to Jim Harrison (Nebraska Book Award for poetry 2001) 2000, Braided Creek: A Conversation in Poetry (with Jim Harrison) 2003, Local Wonders: Seasons in the Bohemian Alps (Friends of American Writers Chicago Award, ForeWord Magazine Gold Award for Autobiography, Nebraska Book Award for Nonfiction 2003) 2002, Delights and Shadows (Pulitzer Prize for Poetry 2005) 2004, The Poetry Home Repair Manual 2004, Flying at Night: Poems 1965–1985 2005, Valentines 2008; contrib. to The American Poetry Review, Antioch Review, Cream City Review, The Hudson Review, Kansas Quarterly, The Kenyon Review, Midwest Quarterly, The New Yorker, Poetry Northwest, Poetry, Prairie Schooner, Shenandoah, Tailwind. *Address:* Daniel Gillane, 203 Dunreath Street, Lafayette, LA 70506, USA (office); 1820 Branched Oak Road, Garland, NE 68360-9303, USA (home). *Telephone:* (402) 588-2272 (home). *E-mail:* kr84428@navix.net (home). *Website:* www.tedkooser.com.

KÖPECZI, Béla; Hungarian historian, academic and fmr politician; b. 16 Sept. 1921, Nagyenyed (Aiud in Romania); s. of Árpád Köpeczi and Anna Tomai; m. Edit Bölcskei 1951; ed Budapest and Paris Univs.; Publr 1949–53; Vice-Pres., Hungarian Council of Publishing 1953–55; Chair. Hungarian Bd of Publishing 1955; Head, Cultural Dept Hungarian Socialist Workers' Party 1964–66; Prof. Univ. of Budapest 1964, Vice-Rector 1967; mem. Hungarian Acad. of Sciences, Deputy Gen. Sec. 1970–72, Gen. Sec. 1972–75, Deputy Sec.-Gen. 1975–82; Minister of Culture and Educ. 1982–88; Hungarian State Decoration 2003, Commdr Palmes académiques; Dr hc (Paris) 1979, (Rome); State Prize 1980. *Publications:* La France et la Hongrie au début du XVIIIe siècle 1971, Révolté ou révolutionnaire 1973, L'Autobiographie d'un prince rebelle 1977, Staatsräson und christliche Solidarität 1983, Hongrois et Français de Louis XIV à la Révolution française 1983, A francia felvilágosodás (The Age of French Enlightenment) 1986, History of Transylvania (ed.) 1986, A bujdosó Rákóczi (Prince Rákóczi in exile) 1991, Histoire de la culture hongroise 1994, Nemzetképkutatás és XIX. századi román irodalom magyarság képe (The Search for National Identity and Hungarian Image in Romanian Literature of the 19th Century) 1995, Brenner Domokoos 1996, Az emberisors és a XX századi francia regény (The Human Condition and the French Novel in the 20th century) 1997, Correspondance diplomatique de François II Rákóczi 1711–1735 1999, Egy cselszövö diplomata, Klement János Mihály 2000, Vetési Kökenyesdi László 2001, Rákóczi Ferenc Kúlpolitikája (Foreign Policy of Rákóczi) 2002, Erdelyi történetek (Stories of Transylvania) 2002, Bercsényi Miklós válogatott levelei (Selected Letters of Miklós Bercsényi) 2003, Francia müvelődés-és irodalomtörténeti tanulmányok (Studies on French Culture and Literature) 2004. *Leisure interests:* literature, music, travelling. *Address:* Tulipán-u. 5, 1022 Budapest, Hungary (home). *Telephone:* 3265169 (home).

KOPELSON, Arnold, BS, JD; American film producer; *Co-Chairman and CEO, Kopelson Entertainment;* b. 14 Feb. 1935, New York; m. Anne Kopelson; ed New York Univ., New York Law School; with Anne Kopelson exec. producer, producer, packager, developer and distributor of over 100 films; Co-Chair. and CEO Kopelson Entertainment; mem. Bd of Dirs CBS Corpn 2007–; Variety Showbiz Expo Hall of Fame 1986, NATO/ShoWest Producer of the Year 1994, Cinema Expo Int. Lifetime Achievement in Film-making Award, Nat. Asscn of Theater Owners Producer of the Year Award, Publicists Guild of America Motion Picture Showmanship Award, New York Law School Distinguished Alumnus Award for Lifetime Achievement. *Television:* series: The Fugitive 2000, Thieves 2001. *Films produced:* Lost and Found (exec. producer) 1979, The Legacy (exec. producer) 1979, Night of the Juggler (exec. producer) 1980, Foolin' Around 1980, Final Assignment (exec. producer) 1980, Dirty Tricks (exec. producer) 1981, Platoon 1986 (Acad. Award for Best Picture), Warlock (exec. producer and int. distributor) 1989, Triumph of the Spirit 1989, Fire Birds (exec. producer) 1990, Out for Justice 1991, Falling Down 1993, The Fugitive 1993, Outbreak 1995, Seven 1995, Eraser 1996, Murder at 1600 1997, Mad City 1997, The Devil's Advocate 1997, U.S. Marshals 1998, Perfect Murder 1998, Don't Say a Word 2001, Joe Somebody 2001, Twisted 2004. *TV film:* Past Tense. *Address:* Kopelson Entertainment, 1900 Avenue of the Stars, Suite 500, Los Angeles, CA 90067, USA (office). *Telephone:* (310) 407-1500 (office). *Fax:* (310) 407-1501 (office).

KOPONEN, Harri; Finnish telecommunications industry executive; *CEO and General Manager, Wataniya Telecom;* b. 6 Dec. 1962, Lahti; s. of Onni Koponen and Aili Ikonen; m.; four c.; ed Commercial Coll. of Turku, Helsinki Univ., Helsinki School of Econs; fmr Educ. Officer, Finnish Defence Force; fmr Office Man. Oy Shell AB; fmr Head Telecom Sales, Hewlett-Packard; Global Account Exec., Ericsson, Exec. Vice-Pres. and Gen. Man. Ericsson Consumer Products in Americas, Man. Dir SonyEricsson Americas; Pres. and CEO Sonera, then Deputy CEO TeliaSonera and Head, TeliaSonera International (after merger of Swedish Telia and Sonera) 2002–04; CEO and Gen. Man. Wataniya Telecom, Kuwait 2005–; Defence Cross of Finland; Hon. PhD. *Achievement:* European Champion in American Football 1985. *Leisure interests:* hockey, golf, coaching. *Address:* Wataniya Telecom, PO Box 613, Safat 13007, Kuwait (office). *Telephone:* (965) 805555 (office). *Fax:* (965) 2441967 (office). *E-mail:* harri@wataniya.com (office). *Website:* www.wataniya.com (office).

KOPPEL, Ted, MA; American journalist and broadcaster; b. 8 Feb. 1940, Lancs., England; m. Grace A. Dorney; four c.; ed Syracuse and Stanford Univs; went to USA 1953; news corresp., writer, WMCA, New York 1963; with ABC (American Broadcasting Corpn) News 1963, fmr news corresp. Vietnam; Chief, Miami Bureau, ABC News; Chief, Hong Kong Bureau; diplomatic corresp. Hong Kong Bureau, ABC News, Washington; anchorman, ABC News Nightline 1980–2005, Ed. Man. 1980–2005; Man. Ed., Discovery Channel US 2005–08; corresp. for ABC TV specials including The People of People's China 1973, Kissinger: Action Biography 1974, Second to None 1979, The Koppel Reports 1988–90; co-author with Marvin Kalb, TV special: In the National Interest (Overseas Press Club Award); numerous awards. *Publications:* The Wit and Wisdom of Adlai Stevenson 1985, In The National Interest 1977, Nightline: History In the Making 1996. *Address:* c/o Discovery Channel, Discovery Communications Inc., 1 Discovery Place, Silver Spring, MD 20910, USA (office).

KOPPER, Hilmar; German banker; b. 13 March 1935, Oslanin, West Prussia; CEO Deutsche Bank AG –1997, Chair. Supervisory Bd 1997–99; Chair. of Supervisory Bd Daimler-Benz AG (now Daimler AG), Stuttgart 1990–2007; Chair. of Supervisory Bd Lincas GmbH, Hamburg; mem. Supervisory Bd Akzo, Arnhem, Netherlands, Bayer AG, Leverkusen, Deutsche Lufthansa AG, Cologne, Deutsche Bank, Frankfurt, Mannesmann AG, Düsseldorf, Municher Rückversicherungs-Gesellschaft, Munich, VEBA AG, Düsseldorf; Chair. Advisory Bd Brauerei Beck & Co., Bremen, Frowein GmbH & Co. KG, Wuppertal, Leopold Kostal GmbH & Co. KG, Lüdenscheid; mem. Advisory Bd Solvay & Cie SA, Brussels; fmr Deputy Chair. Bd Morgan Grenfell Group PLC, London; mem. Bd St Helens. *Leisure interests:* reading, collecting the wrappings that encase citrus fruits in greengrocers' shops. *Address:* c/o Supervisory Board, Daimler AG, Epplestrasse 225, 70546 Stuttgart, Germany (office).

KOPTEV, Yuri Nikolayevich, Cand Tech Sc; Russian engineer and manager; b. 13 March 1940, Stavropol; m.; two s.; ed Bauman Higher Tech. School; worked as engineer for Lavochkin Science-Tech. Corpn 1965–69; author of a number of space-rocket projects; Sr Engineer, Head of Dept, then Deputy Minister, Ministry of Gen. Machine Construction 1969–91; Vice-Pres. Rosobshchemash Corpn 1991–92; Dir-Gen. Russian Space Agency 1992–99, Russian Aviation and Space Agency 1999–2004; Chair. Tupolev Corpn 1999–; Co-Chair. Space Cttee Russian-American Comm. for Econ. and Tech. Co-operation 1993–; Prof., Bauman Moscow State Tech. Univ.; mem. Tsiolkovsky Acad. of Cosmonautics and Presidium, Cosmonautics Fed. of Russia and

Presidium, Int. Acad. of Eng; three state prizes 1997, 1993, 1999, four state awards. *Address:* c/o Russian Aviation and Space Agency, 129857 Moscow, 42 Shchepkina str., Russia (office).

KORA, Madhu; Indian politician and social worker; b. 6 Jan. 1971, Patahatu village, W Singhbhoom Dist; s. of Rasika Koda and Kuni Kui; m. 2004; ed Zilla school, Chaibasa, correspondence course with Utkal Univ., Orissa; began political career as activist with All Jharkhand Students Union early 1990s, later associated with Rashtriya Swayamsevak Sangh; elected to Jharkhand Legis. Ass. (Bharatiya Janata Party—BJP) for Jagannathpur constituency 2000, elected as ind. mem. for W Singhbhoom Dist 2005; Panchayati Raj Minister, Jharkhand 2000–03, Minister for Mines and Geology 2005–06; led rebellion that toppled BJP-led coalition govt of Arjun Munda Sept. 2006; Chief Minister of Jharkhand 2006–08 (resgnd). *Leisure interests:* cricket, football. *Address:* c/o Office of the Chief Minister, Ranchi, Jharkhand, India (office).

KORALEK, Paul George, CBE, RA, RIBA, FRAIA,; British architect; b. 7 April 1933, Vienna, Austria; s. of the late Ernest Koralek and Alice (née Müller); m. (Audrey) Jennifer Koralek 1956; one s. two d.; ed Aldenham, Architectural Asscn; Partner and Dir Ahrends, Burton & Koralek, Architects 1961–; Fellow, Royal Inst. of the Architects of Ireland; Winner Int. Competition for New Library, Trinity Coll., Dublin 1961, Competition for Nat. Gallery Extension 1982–85, Int. Competition for Devt Plan, Grenoble Univ. 1991, RIBA Architecture Award 1978, 1996, 1999, RIBA Housing Award 1977, Structural Steel Design Award 1976, 1980, 1985, Financial Times Award 1976 (Commendation 1986, 1987), Civic Trust Award 1986, 1992, Royal Inst. of the Architects of Ireland Award 1999. *Buildings include:* new British Embassy, Moscow 1999; Docklands Light Railway Extension Stations; Templeton Coll., Oxford 1969, Nebenzahl House, Jerusalem 1972, Warehouse and Showroom for Habitat, Wallingford 1974, residential bldg for Keble Coll., Oxford 1976, Arts Faculty bldg, Trinity Coll., Dublin 1979, factory for Cummins Engines, Shotts 1983, supermarket, J. Sainsbury, Canterbury 1984, Retail HQ, W.H. Smith, Swindon 1985, 1995, dept store John Lewis, Kingston 1990, St Mary's Hosp., Newport, Isle of Wight 1990, White Cliffs Heritage Centre, Dover 1991, Dublin Dental Hosp. 1998–, Techniquest Science Discovery Centre, Cardiff 1995, Insts of Tech. Tralee, Waterford, Blanchardstown 2002–, Offaly Co. Council HQ 2002, Tipperary N Riding County Offices 2000–, Convent Lands Devt Plan, Dublin 2000–, Trinity Coll. Dublin Arts Faculty extension 2002, Galway Co. Council offices extension, new library and HQ 2002, housing at Newcastle West, Co. Limerick 2004, John Wheatley Coll., Glasgow 2005. *Publications:* Ahrends, Burton & Koralek 1991, Collaborations – The Architecture of ABK 2002. *Address:* Unit 1, 7 Chalcot Road, London, NW1 8LH, England (office). *Telephone:* (20) 7586-3311 (office). *Fax:* (20) 7722-5445 (office). *E-mail:* abk@abklondon.com (office).

KORBA, Krzysztof; Polish business executive; *President of the Management Board, Softbank SA;* ed Warsaw Univ. of Tech.; Head of IT Systems, Nuclear Power Information Centre 1969–73; System Analyst and IT Systems Designer, ZETO-ZOWAR 1973–74, Head of Div. 1980–81; Sr Specialist, PESEL Govt Information Centre 1974–80; Deputy Dir, IT Dept, Social Security Authority 1981–83; Sales Dir and later Regional Dir ICL Poland/International Computers Ltd 1983–93; Pres. Exec. Bd, Bull Polska 1993–95; Pres. Exec. Bd and CEO Unisys Polska 1995–; currently Pres. Man. Bd Softbank SA. *Address:* Softbank SA, 17 Stycznia 72a Str., 02–146 Warsaw, Poland (office). *Telephone:* (22) 8786200 (office). *Fax:* (22) 8786300 (office). *E-mail:* ir@softbank.pl (office). *Website:* www.softbank.pl (office).

KÖRBER, Hans-Joachim; German retail executive; mem. Exec. Bd, Chair. and CEO, Metro AG 1999–2007; Dir SEB AB, Stockholm; mem. Global Advisory Bd, Egon Zehnder Int. *Address:* c/o Metro AG, Metro-Strasse 1, 40235 Dusseldorf, Germany (office).

KÖRBER, Manfred J.; German public relations executive and bank official; b. 15 Sept. 1939, Berlin; ed Univs of Bonn and Hamburg; with Mobil Oil Deutschland AG 1966–67; cen. staff Dept Hoechst AG 1967–73; with Deutsche Bundesbank 1973–98, Head of Press and Information, Public Relations Div. 1984–87, Head of Dept of Press and Public Relations, Library and Archives, Language Services, Press Spokesman 1987–98; Dir of Communications and Press Spokesman, European Cen. Bank, Frankfurt 1998–2003. *Address:* c/o European Central Bank, Kaiserstr. 29, Postfach 160319, 60066 Frankfurt am Main, Germany.

KORD, Kazimierz; Polish conductor; *Music Director, Teatr Wielki, Warsaw;* b. 18 Nov. 1930, Pogórze nr. Cieszyn; m.; ed Leningrad Conservatory with Wladimir Nilsen, Acad. of Music, Kraków, State Higher School of Music in Kraków with Artur Malawski; Artistic Man. Music Theatre, Kraków 1962–69; Man. and Music Man. Great Symphonic Orchestra of Polish Radio and TV in Katowice 1969–73; Artistic Dir and Prin. Conductor Warsaw Philharmonic 1977–2001; Chief Conductor Südwestfunk Orchestra in Baden Baden 1980–86; six years' co-operation with Metropolitan Opera, New York; Music Dir Teatr Wielki, Warsaw 2005–, Acting Gen. Dir. 2006; conducted in all important music centres of the world, toured in 57 countries; Critics' Award at Music Biennale Berlin 1971, Gold Orpheus Prize of Polish Musicians' Union 1972, Star of the Year, Munich 1975, Minister of Culture and Arts Prize (1st Class) 1977, 1998. *Recordings:* complete Beethoven symphonies, Górecki's Symphony No. 3 and works by J.S. Bach, Chopin, Lutoslawski, Penderecki, Panufnik, Schumann, Richard Strauss, Szymanowski and Szymański. *Leisure interest:* astronomy. *Address:* c/o Teatr Wielki, pl. Teatralny 1, Warsaw (office); ul. Nadarzyńska 37A, 05-805 Kanie-Otrebusy, Poland (home). *E-mail:* kama.kord@t-online.de (home). *Website:* www.teatrwielki.pl.

KORDA, Michael Vincent, BA; American publishing executive (retd); *Editor-in-Chief Emeritus, Simon & Schuster Inc.;* b. 8 Oct. 1933, London, England; s. of Vincent Korda and Gertrude Korda (née Musgrove); m. Carolyn Keese 1958; one s.; ed Magdalen Coll., Oxford, UK; served in RAF 1952–54; joined Simon and Schuster, New York 1958–, first as Ed., then Sr Ed., Man. Ed., Exec. Ed., Sr Vice-Pres. and Ed.-in-Chief, Ed.-in-Chief Emer. 2005–; mem. Nat. Soc. of Film Critics, American Horse Shows Asscn. *Publications:* Male Chauvinism: How It Works 1973, Power: How to Get It, How to Use It 1975, Success! 1977, Charmed Lives 1979, Worldly Goods 1982, The Fortune 1989, Man to Man: Surviving Prostate Cancer 1997, Another Life, 2000, Making the List 2001, Country Matters 2002, Horse People 2004, Ulysses S. Grant: The Unlikely Hero 2004, Marking Time: Collecting Watches and Thinking about Time 2004, Journey to a Revolution: A Personal Memoir and History of the Hungarian Revolution of 1956 2006, Cat People (with Margaret Korda) 2006, Ike: An American Hero 2007, With Wings Like Eagles 2009. *Address:* c/o Simon and Schuster, 1230 Avenue of the Americas, New York, NY 10020, USA.

KORDA, Petr; Czech professional tennis player; b. 23 Jan. 1968, Prague; s. of Petr Korda and Jana Korda; m. Regina Rajchrtová 1992; two d. one s.; coached by his father until aged 18; coached by Tomáš Petera 1991–; winner Wimbledon Jr Doubles 1986; turned professional 1987; runner-up French Open 1992; winner Grand Slam Cup 1993; winner Stuttgart Open 1997, Australian Open 1998, Qatar Open 1998; mem. Czechoslovak Davis Cup Team 1988, 1996; lives in Monte Carlo; received one-year ban after testing positive for nandrolone in Wimbledon Championship 1998; retd in 1999 having won 20 professional titles (including 10 singles titles); now plays in Srs Tour; runner-up to Guy Forget 2001; won Honda Challenge 2002; Chair. Bd of Supervisors Karlštejn golf resort, Czech Repub. 2000–. *Leisure interest:* golf. *Address:* c/o Czech Tenisova Asociace, Ostrov Stvanice 38, 170 00 Prague, Czech Republic.

KORHONEN, Keijo Tero, PhD; Finnish diplomatist and academic; b. 23 Feb. 1934, Paltamo; s. of Hannes Korhonen and Anna Korhonen (née Laari); m. 1st Anneli Korhonen (née Torkkila) 1958, three s.; m. 2nd Anita Korhonen (née Uggeldahl) 1990; ed Turku Univ.; Prof. of Int. Relations, Univ. of Arizona 1964, currently Adjunct Prof. of Political Science; Fellow, Weatherhead Center for Int. Affairs, Harvard Univ. 1969–70; Deputy Dir for Political Affairs, Ministry of Foreign Affairs 1971–74; Prof. of Political History, Univ. of Helsinki 1974–77; Minister of Foreign Affairs 1976–77; Under-Sec. of State for Political Affairs, Ministry of Foreign Affairs 1977–83; Perm. Rep. to UN 1983–88; Special Adviser to Prime Minister 1988–89; Ed.-in-Chief Kainuun Sanomat 1989–94; Presidential cand. (ind.) 1994; fmr Deputy Chair. Paasikivi Society; mem. Exec. Bd Tucson Cttee on Foreign Relations. *Publications:* four books about Finnish–Soviet and Finnish–Russian relations since 1808; Finland in the Russian Political Thought of the 19th century 1966, An Ambassador's Journal, Urho Kekkonen, the Leader and the Man, The Reverse Side of the Coin 1989, This Country Is Not For Sale 1991, An Accidental Corporal (memoir) 1999. *Leisure interests:* reading, jogging, horse riding. *Address:* Department of Political Science, Office 320, University of Arizona, POB 210027, Tucson, AZ 85721-0027, USA. *Telephone:* (520) 621-3980 (office). *E-mail:* keijok@email.arizona.edu (office). *Website:* web.arizona.edu/~polisci (office).

KORMILTSEV, Col-Gen. Nikolai Viktorovich; Russian army officer; b. 14 March 1946, Omsk; ed Omsk Higher Military General Army School, Moscow M.V. Frunze Military Acad., Moscow Military Acad. of General Staff; Commdr of Army corpus, Turkestan Mil. Command –1994; Deputy Commdr, then Commdr of Armed Forces, Baikal Mil. Command 1994–98; Commdr of Armed Forces, Siberian Mil. Command 1998–2001; C-in-C Land Armed Forces 2001–04; Deputy Minister of Defence 2001–04. *Address:* c/o Ministry of Defence, Znamenka str. 19, 103160 Moscow, Russia (office).

KORNAI, János, DrSc; Hungarian economist; *Allie S. Freed Professor Emeritus of Economics, Harvard University;* b. 21 Jan. 1928, Budapest; m. Zsuzsa Dániel 1971; two s. one d.; ed Univ. of Budapest; Econ. Ed. 1947–55; Research Assoc. Inst. of Econs, Hungarian Acad. of Sciences 1955–58, Inst. of Textile Industry 1958–63; Sr Research Assoc., Computer Centre, Hungarian Acad. of Sciences 1963–67; Research Prof., Inst. of Econs, Hungarian Acad. of Sciences 1967–; Allie S. Freed Prof. of Econs, Harvard Univ. 1986–2002, Allie S. Freed Prof. Emer. 2002–; Perm. Fellow, Collegium Budapest 1992–2002, Perm. Fellow Emer. 2002–; Distinguished Research Prof. Cen. European Univ. 2005–; Visiting Prof., LSE 1964, Univ. of Sussex 1966, Stanford Univ. 1968, Yale 1970, Princeton and Stanford 1972–73, Stockholm 1976–77, Geneva 1981, Munich 1983, Princeton 1983–84, Harvard 1984–85; Pres. Hungarian Social Science Asscn 1992, Int. Econ. Asscn 2002–05; mem. Hungarian Acad. of Sciences; Corresp. mem. British Acad.; Foreign mem. Royal Swedish Acad., Finnish Acad., Russian Acad. of Sciences, Bulgarian Acad. of Sciences; Hon. mem. American Acad. of Arts and Sciences 1972, American Econ. Asscn 1976, European Asscn for Comparative Econ. Studies 1996; Hon. Pres. Asscn of New Institutional Economists of Hungary 2004; Hon. Citizen of Budapest 2005; Officier, Légion d'honneur 1997, Order of Merit (Hungary), Commdr's Cross, Order of Merit (Hungary) 2002, Commdr's Cross with Star 2007; Dr hc (Paris) 1978, (Poznań) 1978, (London) 1990, (Amsterdam), (Budapest) 1992, (Wrocław) 1993, (Turin) 1993, (Debrecen) 2001, (Stockholm) 2001, (Varna) 2003, (Veszprem) 2003, (Pecs) 2003, (Cen. European Univ.) 2004, (Krakow) 2008; Seidman Award 1982, Hungarian State Prize 1983, Humboldt Prize 1983, Széchenyi Prize 1994, Prima Primissima Prize 2005, Lifetime Achievement Award 2008. *Publications:* Overcentralization in Economic Administration 1959, Mathematical Planning of Structural Decisions 1967, Anti-Equilibrium 1971, Rush versus Harmonic Growth 1972, Economics of Shortage 1980, Non-Price Control 1981, Growth, Shortage and Efficiency 1982, Contradictions and Dilemmas 1985, The Road to a Free Economy 1990, Vision and Reality 1990, The Socialist System 1992, Highways and Byways 1995, Struggle and Hope 1997, Welfare, Choice and

Solidarity in Transition (with K. Eggleston) 2001, By Force of Thought: Irregular Memoirs of an Intellectual Journey 2006, From Socialism to Capitalism 2008. *Address:* Collegium Budapest, Institute for Advanced Study, Szentháromság utca 2, 1014 Budapest, Hungary (office). *Telephone:* (1) 224-8312 (office). *Fax:* (1) 224-8328 (office). *E-mail:* kornai@colbud.hu (office).

KORNBERG, Sir Hans (Leo), Kt, MA, PhD, DSc, ScD, FRS, FRSA; British/American biochemist and academic; *University Professor and Professor of Biology, Boston University;* b. 14 Jan. 1928, Herford, Germany; s. of Max Kornberg and Margarete Kornberg (née Silberbach); m. 1st Monica M. King 1956 (died 1989); twin s. two d.; m. 2nd Donna Haber 1991; ed Queen Elizabeth Grammar School, Wakefield and Univ. of Sheffield; John Stokes Research Fellow, Univ. of Sheffield 1952–53; mem. MRC Cell Metabolism Research Unit, Univ. of Oxford 1955–61; Lecturer in Biochemistry, Worcester Coll., Oxford 1958–61; Prof. of Biochemistry, Univ. of Leicester 1961–75; Sir William Dunn Prof. of Biochemistry, Univ. of Cambridge 1975–95; Univ. Prof. and Prof. of Biology, Boston Univ., USA 1995–; Fellow, Christ's Coll., Cambridge 1975–, Master 1982–95; mem. SRC 1967–72, Chair. Science Bd 1969–72; Chair. Royal Comm. on Environmental Pollution 1976–81; mem. Agric. and Food Research Council 1980–84; mem. Priorities Bd for Research and Devt in Agric. 1984–90; Chair. Advisory Cttee on Genetic Modification 1986–95, Jt Policy Group Agric. and Environment 1986–89; mem. Bd NIREX 1986–95; Pres. Int. Union of Biochemistry and Molecular Biology 1991–94, The Biochemical Soc. 1990–95 (Hon. mem. 2001–); mem. Advisory Council for Applied Research and Devt 1982–85, Scientific Advisory Cttee Inst. for Molecular Biology and Medicine, Monash Univ. 1987–; Commonwealth Fund Fellow, Yale Univ. and Public Health Research Inst., New York 1953–55; Vice-Pres. Inst. of Biology 1969–72; Vice-Chair. European Molecular Biological Org. 1978–81; Pres. BAAS 1984–85 (Hon. mem. 2003–); Pres. Asscn for Science Educ. 1991–92; mem. German Acad. of Sciences Leopoldina 1982; Foreign Assoc. NAS 1986; mem. Academia Europaea 1988; Fellow, American Acad. of Microbiology 1992; Foreign mem. American Philosophical Soc. 1993, Accad. Nazionale dei Lincei, Italy 1997; Leeuwenhoek Lecturer, Royal Soc. 1972; Man. Trustee, Nuffield Foundation 1973–93; Gov. Wellcome Trust 1990–95; Hon. mem. Soc. for Biological Chem., USA 1972, Japanese Biochemistry Soc. 1981; Foreign Hon. mem. American Acad. of Arts and Sciences 1987; Hon. FRCP 1989; Hon. Fellow, Worcester Coll., Oxford, Brasenose Coll., Oxford, Wolfson Coll., Cambridge; Hon. FIBiol 2004; Hon. ScD (Cincinnati) 1974; Hon. DSc (Warwick) 1975, (Leicester) 1979, (Sheffield) 1979, (Bath) 1980, (Strathclyde) 1985, (South Bank) 1994, (Leeds) 1995, (La Trobe) 1997; Hon. DUniv (Essex) 1979; Hon. MD (Leipzig) 1984; Hon. LLD (Dundee) 1999; Colworth Medal, Biochemical Soc. 1963, Warburg Medal, Gesellschaft für biologische Chemie der Bundesrepublik, Germany 1973. *Publications:* numerous articles in scientific journals. *Leisure interests:* conversation, cooking. *Address:* Biology Department, Boston University, 5 Cummington Street, Boston, MA 02215 (office); The University Professors, Boston University, 745 Commonwealth Avenue, Boston, MA 02215 (office); 134 Sewall Avenue, #2, Brookline, MA 02446, USA (home). *Telephone:* (617) 358-1691 (office); (617) 739-6103 (home). *Fax:* (617) 353-5084 (office). *E-mail:* hlk@bu.edu (office). *Website:* www.bu.edu/biology/Faculty_Staff/hlk.html (office).

KORNBERG, Roger D., BS, PhD; American biochemist and academic; *Mrs. George A. Winzer Professor of Medicine, Department of Structural Biology, School of Medicine, Stanford University;* b. 1947, St Louis, Mo.; s. of the late Arthur Kornberg (winner of Nobel Prize in Medicine 1959) and Sylvy Kornberg; m. Yahli Lorch; two s. one d; ed Harvard Univ., Stanford Univ.; Postdoctoral Fellow and mem. of scientific staff, Lab. of Molecular Biology, Univ. of Cambridge, UK 1972–75; Asst Prof., Dept of Biological Chem., Harvard Medical School 1976–78; Prof., Dept of Structural Biology, School of Medicine, Stanford Univ. 1978–, now Mrs. George A. Winzer Prof. of Medicine, Dept Chair. 1984–92; Visiting Prof., Hebrew Univ. of Jerusalem 1986–; Ed. Annual Reviews of Biochemistry; mem. NAS, American Acad. of Arts and Sciences; Assoc. mem. European Molecular Biology Org.; Hon. mem. Japanese Biochemical Soc.; Dr hc (Hebrew Univ. of Jerusalem) 2001, (Univ. of Umeå) 2003; Eli Lilly Award 1981, Passano Award 1982, Harvey Prize 1987, Ciba-Drew Award 1990, Gairdner Int. Award (co-winner with Robert Roeder) 2000, Welch Award 2001, Gran Prix, French Acad. of Sciences 2002, Sloan Award 2005, Louisa Gross Horwitz Prize, Columbia Univ. 2006, Dickson Prize in Medicine, Univ. of Pittsburgh 2006, Nobel Prize in Chem. 2006. *Address:* Stanford University Medical School, Department of Structural Biology, Fairchild Building, 1st Floor, 299 Campus Drive, Stanford, CA 94305-5126, USA (office). *Telephone:* (650) 723-6988 (office); (650) 725-5390 (office). *E-mail:* kornberg@stanford.edu (office). *Website:* kornberg.stanford.edu (office).

KORNBLUM, John Christian, BA; American diplomatist and investment banker; *Chairman, Lazard & Co. GmbH;* b. 6 Feb. 1943, Detroit, Mich.; s. of Samuel Christian Kornblum and Ethelyn Kornblum (née Tonkin); m. Helen Sen 1987; two s.; ed Mich. State Univ., Georgetown Univ.; Officer-in-Charge of Berlin and Eastern Affairs, Bonn 1970–73; mem. policy planning staff Dept of State 1973–75, Officer-in-Charge of European Regional Political Affairs 1977–79, Dir of Cen. European Affairs 1981; political adviser to US mission, Berlin 1979–81, Minister and Deputy Commdt 1985; Deputy Rep. to NATO, Brussels 1987; Amb. and Rep. to CSCE 1991; Sr Deputy Asst Sec. of State for European Affairs 1994; Asst Sec. of State for European and Canadian Affairs 1996; Amb. to Germany 1997–2001; Chair. Lazard & Co. GmbH 2001–; mem. US Del. to Quadripartite Negotiations, Berlin 1970–72; co-ordinator meeting of 1977, Chair. US Del. to Helsinki 1992, Head US Del. to Vienna 1992; mem. Supervisory Bd ThyssenKrupp Technologies AG, Bayer AG 2002–; mem. Bd of Trustees American Inst. for Contemporary German Studies; mem. Bd of Dirs Int. Univ. Bremen Foundation of America Inc.; Distinguished Alumni Award, Michigan State Univ. 1999, Silver Award, American Chamber of Commerce (Germany) 2000; Kt's Cross, Germany 1991, Order of Merit, Austria 1994. *Leisure interests:* music, sports, gardening, travel. *Address:* Lazard & Co. GmbH, Pariser Platz 4A, 10117 Berlin, Germany (office). *Telephone:* (30) 72610190 (office). *Fax:* (30) 726101910 (office). *E-mail:* john.kornblum@lazard.com (office). *Website:* www.lazard.com (office).

KORNUKOV, Col-Gen. Anatoly Mikhailovich; Russian army officer (retd); *Officer, Ministry of Defence;* b. 10 Jan. 1942, Stakhanovo, Lugansk Region; m.; one s. one d.; ed Chernigov Higher Mil. Aviation School, Zhukov Mil. Acad., Mil. Gen. Staff Acad.; Commdr of fighter squadron, Aviation Regt of Fighter Div. in Far E; qualified as Mil. Pilot-Sniper; Commdr Anti-Aircraft Defence Forces of Moscow Command 1991–97; C-in-C Mil. Aircraft Forces of Russian Fed. 1998–2002 (resgnd); on staff of Ministry of Defence 2002–. *Leisure interests:* nature, music. *Address:* c/o General Air Force Staff, B. Pirogorskaya str. 23, K-160 Moscow, Russia (office). *Telephone:* (495) 296-18-00 (office).

KOROLEV, Mikhail Antonovich, DEconSc; Russian statistician; *President, Interstate Statistical Committee of the Commonwealth of Independent States;* b. 12 Sept. 1931, Almaty; s. of A. I. Korolev and T. A. Ivanova; m. Letalina Koroleva 1957; one d.; ed Moscow Plekhanov Inst. of Nat. Econ.; Asst Dean, Dept Head, Moscow Inst. of Econs and Statistics 1954–66, Rector 1966–72, Prof. 1967–; Deputy, First Deputy Dir Cen. Statistics Bd of USSR 1972–85, Dir 1985–87; Pres. USSR State Cttee on Statistics 1987–89; Adviser to Prime Minister of USSR 1991; Pres. Interstate Statistical Cttee of CIS 1992–; cand. mem. CPSU Cen. Cttee 1986–90; Deputy to USSR Supreme Soviet 1986–89; Chair. Statistical Comm. of UN 1979–81, Vice-Chair. 1976–79, 1989–91; mem. Int. Statistical Inst., Int. Informatics Acad.; Hon. Scientist; name "Korolev Mikhail Antonovich" given to star in the constellation Sagittarias. *Publications:* 20 books, numerous articles. *Leisure interests:* chess, art, tennis. *Address:* Interstate Statistical Committee of the Commonwealth of Independent States, 39, Bldg 1, Myasnitskaya Street, 107450 Moscow, Russia (office). *Telephone:* (495) 607-40-86 (office). *Fax:* (495) 207-45-92 (office). *E-mail:* korolev@cisstat.org (office); MKorolev@netscape.net (home). *Website:* www.cisstat.org (office); mikhailkorolev.narod.ru.

KOROLOGOS, Tom Chris, BA, MS; American journalist, business executive and diplomatist (retd); b. 1933, Salt Lake City, Utah; s. of Chris T. Korologos and Irene M. Kolendrianos; m. 1st Joy G. Korologos (died 1997); one s. two d.; m. 2nd Ann McLaughlin; ed Univ. of Utah and Columbia Univ. Grad. School of Journalism (Grantland Rice Fellowship and Pulitzer Fellowship); officer, USAF 1956–57; journalist, New York Herald Tribune, Long Island Press, Salt Lake Tribune, Associated Press; Co-founder, Pres. and Chair. Exec. Cttee, Timmons & Co., Washington DC 1975–2003; Dir Congressional Relations for Pres. Reagan's transition 1980–81, for Nat. Bipartisan (Kissinger) Comm. for Cen. America; Sr Advisor to Senator Bob Dole during his 1996 presidential campaign; mem. Bush-Cheney transition team 2001; served in the Nixon and Ford Admins as Deputy Asst to Pres. for Legis. Affairs (Senate); served for nine years under Senator Wallace F. Bennett (Republican, Utah) as his Chief of Staff in the Senate; served as a Sr Staff mem. in US Congress, as an asst to two Pres in the White House; Sr Counselor with Coalition Provisional Authority, Baghdad, Iraq May–Dec. 2003; Amb. to Belgium 2004–07; fmr mem. US Advisory Comm. on Public Diplomacy; fmr charter mem. Broadcasting Bd of Govs with jurisdiction over all non-mil. US Govt radio and TV broadcasting overseas; Republican. *Address:* c/o US Department of State, 2201 C Street NW, Washington, DC 20520, USA.

KOROMA, Abdul G.; Sierra Leonean diplomatist and lawyer; *Judge, International Court of Justice;* ed King's Coll., London, UK, Kiev State Univ., USSR (now Ukraine); barrister and Hon. Bencher (Lincoln's Inn) and legal practitioner, High Court of Sierra Leone; joined Sierra Leone Govt service 1964, Int. Div., Ministry of External Affairs 1969; del. to UN Gen. Ass.; mem. Int. Law Comm. (Chair. 43rd Session); mem. of dels to 3rd UN Conf. on the Law of the Sea, UN Conf. on Succession of States in Respect of Treaties, UN Comm. on Int. Trade Law, Special Cttee on the Review of the UN Charter and on the Strengthening of the Role of the Org. Cttee on the Peaceful Uses of Outer Space; Vice-Chair. UN Charter Cttee 1978; Chair. UN Special Cttee of 24; Deputy Perm. Rep. of Sierra Leone to the UN 1978–81, Perm. Rep. 1981–85; fmr Amb. to S Korea, to Cuba and to EEC and Perm. Del. to UNESCO; Amb. to France, Belgium, Netherlands, Luxembourg and to Ethiopia and OAU 1988; Perm. Rep. to UN –1994; Judge, Int. Court of Justice 1994–; fmr High Commr in Zambia, Tanzania and Kenya; Chair. UN 6th Cttee (Legal); Vice-Pres. African Soc. of Int. and Comparative Law, African Soc. of Int. Law; Pres. Henry Dunant Centre for Humanitarian Dialogue, Geneva; mem. Int. Planning Council of Int. Ocean Inst., Cttee of Experts on the Application of Conventions and Recommendations, ILO, Geneva; del. to numerous int. confs; Visiting Prof., Univ. of Bangalore, India; lecturer at numerous univs; mem. American Soc. of Int. Law, Inst. of Int. Law; Insignia of Commdr of Rokel 1991, Order of Grand Officer of Repub. of Sierra Leone; Hon. LLD. *Publications:* numerous articles on int. law. *Leisure interests:* reading, music, sports. *Address:* International Court of Justice, Peace Palace, Carnegieplein, 2517 KJ The Hague, Netherlands (office). *Telephone:* (70) 3022323 (office). *Fax:* (70) 3022409 (office). *E-mail:* information@icj-cij.org (office). *Website:* www.icj-cij.org (office).

KOROMA, Ernest Bai; Sierra Leonean politician and head of state; *President;* b. 23 Oct. 1953, Makeni, Bombali Dist; m. Sia Koroma; two c.; ed Univ. of Sierra Leone; began career as teacher, St Francis Secondary School, Makeni; joined Sierra Leone Nat. Insurance Co. 1978; joined Reliance Insurance Trust Corpn 1985, Man. Dir 1988–2002; represented All People's Congress (APC) in presidential and parl. elections 2002, lost presidential vote but elected to parl. representing Bombali Dist; Leader APC 2002–, temporarily stripped of leadership due to internal party dispute 2005; Pres. of Sierra

Leone 2007–; Fellow, West African Insurance Inst.; Assoc. Inst. of Risk Man., UK; mem. Inst. of Dirs, UK. *Address:* All-People's Congress, 137h Fourah Bay Road, Freetown, Sierra Leone (office). *E-mail:* info@new-apc.org (office). *Website:* apcparty.org (office).

KOROMA, Momodu, MSc; Sierra Leonean politician; b. 12 Sept. 1956; m.; five c.; ed Njala Univ. Coll., Univ. of Nairobi, Kenya, Univ. of Reading, UK, Int. Centre for Theoretical Physics, Trieste, Italy; govt minister 1996–, fmr Minister of Presidential Affairs; Minister of Foreign Affairs and Int. Cooperation 2002–07; mem. Sierra Leone Peoples Party (SLPP). *Leisure interests:* tennis, sight-seeing. *Address:* MQ8 Spur Road, Wilberforce, Freetown, Sierra Leone (home). *Telephone:* 232873 (home). *E-mail:* graceful@sierratel.se (home).

KOROTCHENYA, Ivan Mikhailovich; Belarusian politician; ed Minsk Agric. Acad.; worked as chief agronomist, then Chair. of collective farm; fmr Chair. Regional Union of Collective Farms then Chair. Viley Dist Soviet of People's Deputies; Deputy Belarus Supreme Soviet, mem. Accord faction 1994–96; mem. Presidium; Chair. Comm. on Problems of Glasnost, Mass Media and Human Rights 1990–92; elected coordinator of Workgroup at Council of Leaders of States and Leaders of Govts CIS Countries after disintegration of USSR 1992–98; Deputy Exec. Sec. CIS Secr. 1998–2001. *Address:* Secretariat of Russia and Belarus Union, Kirova str. 17, 220050 Minsk, Belarus (office).

KOROTEYEV, Anatoly Sazonovich, DTechSc; Russian physicist; *President, K. Tsiolkovsky Academy of Cosmonautics;* b. 22 July 1936, Moscow Region; s. of Sazon Z. Koroteyev and Maria P. Koroteyeva; m.; one s.; ed Moscow Aviation Inst.; engineer, Sr Engineer, Head of Div., First Deputy Dir Research Inst. of Thermal Processes (now Keldysh Research Centre) 1959–88, Dir 1988–; Corresp. mem. USSR (now Russian) Acad. of Sciences 1990, mem. 1994; Pres. K. Tsiolkovsky Acad. of Cosmonautics 2005–; scientific research includes propulsion and power systems of rocket and space complexes, generation and diagnostics of low-temperature plasma, creation of electric arc plasma generators and derivation of concentrated pulse electron flows in dense environments; Order for Service to Fatherland 1996, Rank III Order for Service to Fatherland 2006; USSR State Prize 1982, Russian Acad. of Science Prize 2001, Russian Fed. Govt Prize in Science and Eng 2001, State Prize of Russian Fed. 2002, Russian Pres.'s Prize 2005, Russian Fed. Honoured Scientist. *Publications:* Generator for Low-Temperature Plasma 1969, Applied Dynamics of Thermal Plasma 1975, Electric-arc Plasmotrons 1980, Plasmatrons: Structures, Characteristics, Calculation 1993, Electron-Beam Plasma 1993, Nuclear Rocket Engines 2001, Rocket Engines and Power Systems on the Basis of Nuclear Reactor 2002, Seventy Years at the Forefront of Rocket-Space Technics 2003, Gasdynamic and Thermophysical Processes in Solid Rocket Propulsion 2004, Manned Flight to Mars 2007; numerous articles. *Leisure interests:* history, skiing. *Address:* M. Keldysh Research Centre, Onezhskaya str. 8, 125438 Moscow, Russia (home). *Telephone:* (495) 456-46-08 (home). *Fax:* (495) 456-82-28 (home). *E-mail:* kerc@elnet.msk.ru (office); kerc@comcor.ru (office). *Website:* www.kerc.msk.ru (home).

KOROTYCH, Vitaliy Alekseyevich; Russian/Ukrainian writer and poet; *Editor, Boulevard magazine;* b. 26 May 1936, Kiev; s. of Aleksey Korotych and Zoa Korotych; m. Zinaida Korotych 1958; two s.; ed Kiev Medical Inst.; physician 1959–66; Ed. Ukrainian literary journal Ranok 1966–77; Ed.-in-Chief Vsesvit magazine 1978–86; Ed.-in-Chief Ogonyok weekly magazine 1986–91; Sec. of Ukrainian Writers' Union 1966–69; mem. USSR Writers' Union 1981–90; USSR People's Deputy 1989–91; Prof. Boston Univ., USA 1991–98, returned to Moscow; ed. Boulevard magazine and others 1998–; several Russian, Ukrainian, Polish and Bulgarian decorations and medals including two USSR State Prizes, A. Tolstoy Prize 1982, Int. Julius Fuchik Prize 1984, Wiental Prize, Georgetown Univ. (USA) 1987, Int. Ed. of the year, W P Revue (USA) 1989. *Publications include:* Golden Hands 1961, The Smell of Heaven 1962, Cornflower Street 1963, O Canada! 1966, Poetry 1967, Metronome (novel) 1982, The Face of Enmity (novel) 1984, Memory, Bread and Love 1986, Le Visage de la haine (travel essays) 1988, Glasnost und Perestroika 1990, The Waiting Room (memoirs, Vol. I) 1991, On My Behalf (memoirs, Vol. II) 2000, Selected Poems 2005, Selected Essays 2005; many translations from English into Ukrainian and other Slavonic languages. *Address:* Trifonovskaya str. 11, Apt. 256, 127018 Moscow, Russia (home). *Telephone:* (495) 689-03-84 (home). *Fax:* (495) 689-03-84 (home). *E-mail:* ziter@telecont.ru (home).

KORS, Michael; American fashion designer; b. 9 Aug. 1959, Mineola, NY; s. of William Kors and Joan L. Kors; ed Fashion Inst. of Tech.; early career designing for Lothar's boutique, New York; f. Kors Co. (now Michael Kors Inc.) 1981, Pres. 1981–; launched accessories 2001; launched Michael fragrance for women 2000, Island fragrance for men 2005 (FIFI Award for Best Bath and Body Collection 2006); Dupont American Original Award 1983, Elle/Cadillac Fashion Award for Excellence 1995, New York Award 1999, CFDA Award for Womenswear Designer of the Year 1999, CFDA Menswear Award 2003. *Publications:* articles in Vogue, The New York Times and other newspapers and magazines. *Leisure interests:* theatre, film, travel. *Address:* Corporate Headquarters, Michael Kors Inc., 11 West 42nd Street, New York, NY 10036, USA. *Website:* www.michaelkors.com.

KORTHALS ALTES, Frederik; Dutch lawyer and politician; *Chairman, Advisory Council on International Affairs;* b. 15 May 1931, Amsterdam; s. of Everhardus Joannes Korthals Altes and Mary s'Jacob; m. Henny Matthijssen; ed Leiden Univ.; practised as solicitor 1958–82; mem. First Chamber, States-Gen. 1981–82, 1991–2001; Minister of Justice 1982–89; Chair. Volkspartij voor Vrijheid en Democratie (VVD) 1975–81, Floor Leader in First Chamber, States-Gen. 1995–97, Pres. 1997–2001; currently Chair. Advisory Council on

Int. Affairs; Pnr, Nauta Dutilh (law firm) 1990–96; Hon. Minister of State 2001–; Grand Officier, Légion d'honneur 1984, Grosses Verdienskreuz des Verdienstordens 1985, Commdr, Order of Orange-Nassau, Grand Cross Ordem do Mérito 1989, Grand Cross Ordre nat. du Mérite, Grand Cross of Sacred Treasure (Japan) 2000; Prof. E.M. Meijers Medal of Law Faculty (Leiden) 1988, Nat. Police Award 1990. *Address:* Oudorpweg 9, 3062 RB, Rotterdam (home); Advisory Council on International Affairs, Bezuidenhoutseweg 67, Room 9E19, PO Box 20061, 2500 EB, The Hague, Netherlands (office). *Telephone:* (70) 3485325 (office); (10) 4526163 (home); 653-301424 (mobile) (home). *Fax:* (70) 3486256 (office); (10) 4529491 (home). *E-mail:* aiv@minbuza.nl (office); fka@planet.nl (home). *Website:* www.aiv-advies.nl (office).

KORTLANDT, Frederik H. H., PhD; Dutch academic; *Professor of Descriptive and Comparative Linguistics, University of Leiden;* b. 19 June 1946, Utrecht; ed Univ. of Amsterdam; Asst Prof. of Slavic Linguistics, Univ. of Amsterdam 1969–72; Assoc. Prof. of Balto-Slavic Languages, Univ. of Leiden 1972–74, Prof. 1974–; Prof. of Descriptive and Comparative Linguistics 1985–; mem. Royal Netherlands Acad. 1986–; Spinoza Prize 1997. *Publications:* Modelling the Phoneme 1972, Slavic Accentuation 1975; numerous articles on linguistics and Slavic, Baltic, Germanic, Celtic, Armenian, Japanese and other languages. *Leisure interest:* classical music. *Address:* Faculty of Letters, PO Box 9515, 2300 RA Leiden (office); Cobetstraat 24, 2313 KC Leiden, Netherlands (home). *Telephone:* (71) 527-2501 (office). *Fax:* (71) 527-7569 (office). *E-mail:* f.kortlandt@hum.leidenuniv.nl (office). *Website:* www.kortlandt.nl (office).

KORTÜM, Franz-Josef; German business executive; *Chairman of the Management Board, Webasto AG;* b. 18 Aug. 1950, Billerbeck, Coesfeld; m.; three c.; ed studies in Münster and Regensburg; employed in family car retailing co. Billerbeck 1975; car sales exec., Bielefeld subsidiary of Daimler-Benz AG 1976; Head, Passenger Car Field Sales, Used Vehicle Sales and Truck Sales, Berlin subsidiary of Daimler-Benz AG 1979; Asst to Dir of Sales Org. Germany, Daimler-Benz AG, Stuttgart-Untertürkheim 1985; Dir Saarbrücken subsidiary of Daimler-Benz AG 1987; Dir Cen. Admin. Daimler-Benz AG 1989; Man. Dir Mercedes-Benz-owned co. Rheinische Kraftwagengesellschaft (RKW), Bonn 1990; Man. Dir Webasto AG 1994, CEO 1999, currently Chair. Man. Bd; mem. Man. Bd Audi AG 1992, Chair. 1993–95. *Address:* Webasto AG, Kraillinger Strasse 5, Stockdorf 82131, Germany (office). *Telephone:* (49) 8985794 (office). *Website:* www.webasto.com (office).

KORZENIOWSKI, Robert; Polish athlete; b. 30 July 1968, Lubaczów; m. Agnieszka Fiedziukiewicz; one d.; ed Acad. of Physical Education, Kraków; winner gold medal 20 km walk Olympic Games, Atlanta 1996, 20 km walk and 50 km walk, Sydney 2000, 50 km walk Athens 2004; winner 20 km walk European Cup, La Coruña 1996; winner gold medal 50 km walk World Championships, Athens 1997, Edmonton 2001, Paris 2003; winner gold medal 50 km walk European Championships 1998, Munich 2002; Sport and Fair Play Amb. to European Council, Strasbourg 1997–; Officer's Cross, Order of Polonia Restituta 2000; Gold Medal for Outstanding Achievement in Sport 1996. *Publication:* Chodu sportowego. *Leisure interests:* books, cinema, cooking, history, politics. *Address:* Korzeniowski i Sport Promocja, ul. Bociana 6, 31-231 Kraków, Poland (office). *Telephone:* (12) 420-03-30 (office). *Fax:* (12) 415-88-65 (office). *E-mail:* korzeniowski@korzeniowski.pl (office). *Website:* www.korzeniowski.pl (office).

KORZHAKOV, Lt-Gen. Aleksander Vasilyevich; Russian army officer; b. 31 Jan. 1950, Moscow; m.; two d.; ed All-Union Inst. of Law; mem. Dept 9 State Security Cttee 1970–89; personal bodyguard of First Sec. Moscow CPSU Cttee Boris Yeltsin 1986–87; f. and Chief Security Service of Russian Supreme Soviet 1990–91; Head Security Service of Pres. of Russia 1991–96, Deputy Chief Main Admin. of Bodyguards 1992–96 (discharged); participated in suppression of attempted coup of Aug. 1991 and confrontation of Oct. 1993; mem. State Duma (Parl.) 1997–; joined Otechestvo-All Russia faction 2000. *Publication:* Boris Yeltsin: From Dawn to Decline (memoirs) 1997. *Leisure interest:* tennis. *Address:* State Duma, Okhotny Ryad 1, 103009 Moscow, Russia. *Telephone:* (495) 292-87-78. *Fax:* (495) 292-87-78.

KORZHAVIN, Naum; Russian author and poet; b. (Mandel Emmanuel Moiseyevich Korzhavin), 14 Oct. 1925, Kiev; ed Karaganda Mining Inst. and Gorky Inst. of Literature, Moscow 1959; first publication 1941; exiled to West (USA) 1974; revisited Moscow 1989; citizenship and membership of Writers' Union restored 1990. *Publications include:* The Years 1963, Where Are You? 1964, Bread, Children in Auschwitz, Autumn in Karaganda, Verse 1981, Selected Verse 1983, Interlacements 1987, Letter to Moscow 1991, The Time is Given 1992, To Myself 1998; contributor to émigré dissident journal Kontinent. *Address:* 28c Colborne Road, Apt 2, Brighton, MA 02135, USA.

KORZHEV-CHUVELYOV, Gely Mikhailovich; Russian artist; b. 7 July 1925, Moscow; ed Surikov State Inst. of Arts, Moscow; professional artist 1950–; participated in numerous Soviet and foreign exhbns 1950–; Prof. Moscow Higher Artist-Tech. Inst. 1966–; mem. USSR (now Russian) Acad. of Arts 1970; Chair. Bd Artists' Union of RSFSR (now Russia) 1968–75; Sec. Bd of Dirs Artists' Union of USSR (now Russia); Merited Worker of Arts of the RSFSR, Repin State Prize of USSR, People's Artist of the RSFSR 1972. *Address:* Bolshoi Devyatinski per. 5, Apt 45, Moscow, Russia. *Telephone:* (495) 212-55-29.

KORZHOVA, Natalya Artemovna; Kazakhstani politician; b. 8 April 1958, Sarkand; ed Alma-Ata (Almaty) Inst. of Nat. Economy; numerous positions at Ministry of Finance 1979–, including Deputy Minister of Finance 1999–2002, Vice-Minister, then First Deputy Minister of Econs and Budgetary Planning 2002–06, Minister of Finance 2006–07; mem. Cttee on Human Rights; Pres. Female Football and Mini-Football Fed. of Repub. of Kazakhstan. *Publica-*

tions: numerous articles in specialist publications and periodicals. *Address:* c/o Ministry of Finance, 010000 Astana, pl. Respubliki 60, Kazakhstan (office).

KOSACHEV, Konstantin, PhD; Russian diplomatist and politician; *Chairman, State Duma International Affairs Committee;* b. 17 Sept. 1962, Moscow region; ed Moscow State Inst. of Int. Relations; Deputy Dir Ministry of Foreign Affairs, Moscow 1984; fmr Counsellor, Embassy in Stockholm; mem. State Int. Affairs Council 1998; Deputy, State Duma (Parl.) 1999–, First Vice Chair., Fatherland All Russia Party, State Duma 2001–, Chair. State Duma Int. Affairs Cttee 2003–; Chair. Russian Del., Parl. Ass. of Council of Europe (PACE) 2004–, Vice-Pres. PACE 2005–; Order of Friendship (Russia), Royal Order of the N Star (Sweden). *Address:* International Affairs Committee, 103265 Moscow, Gosudarstvennaya Duma, Okhotnyi ryad 1, Russia (office). *Telephone:* (495) 292-83-10 (office). *Website:* www.duma.ru (office).

KOSAI, Akio, BA; Japanese business executive; *Counsellor, Sumitomo Chemical Company;* b. 19 April 1931, Okayama; ed Univ. of Tokyo; joined Sumitomo Chemical Co., Ltd 1954, Dir and Gen. Man. Industrial Chemicals and Fertilizers Div. 1983; Pres. Petrochemical Corpn of Singapore (Pte) Ltd 1984–87; Man. Dir Sumitomo Chemical Co., Ltd 1987, Sr Man. Dir 1991, Pres. 1993–2000, Chair. 2000, now Counsellor; Deputy Chair. Nippon-Keidanren (Japan Business Fed.) and Chair., Japanese Cttee of East Asia Businessmen's Conference; mem. Int. Advisory Council, Econ. Devt Bd (EDB) Singapore; mem. Bd of Dirs Sumitomo Bakelite Co., Ltd, Inabata and Co. Ltd. *Address:* Sumitomo Chemical Co. Ltd, 2-27-1, Shinkawa, Chuo-ku, Tokyo, 104-8260, Japan. *Telephone:* (3) 5543-5102. *Fax:* (3) 5543-5901. *Website:* www.sumitomo-chem.co.jp (office).

KOSCHNICK, Hans Karl-Heinrich; German politician; *Chairman of Steering Committee on Refugee Matters, Stability Pact for South Eastern Europe;* b. 2 April 1929, Bremen; m. Christel Risse; ed Mittelschule; Local Govt Official, Bremen 1945–51, 1954–63; Trade Union Sec. of the Union of Public Employees, Transport and Communications (ÖTV) 1951–54; mem. Social Democratic Party (SPD) 1950–, Fed. Exec. Council 1970–, Party Bd 1975–, Deputy Chair. SPD 1975–79; mem. Provincial Diet of Land Bremen (Landtag) and City Admin. 1955–63; Senator for the Interior 1963–67; Mayor of Bremen 1967–85; Pres. of the Senate, Bremen 1967–85; mem. Fed. Council (Bundesrat) 1965–, Pres. 1970–71, 1981–82; Nat. Vice-Chair. SPD 1975–79; Chair., German Union of Local Authorities (Deutscher Städtetag) 1971–77; mem. Bd Städtetag (Assoc. of German Municipalities) 1970–, Pres. 1971–77; mem. Exec. Cttee Int. Union of Local Authorities (IULA) 1972–77, 1980–85, Pres. 1981–85; mem. Parl. 1987–94; EU Admin. in Mostar 1994–95; Govt Rep. for Bosnia 1998–; currently Chair. Steering Cttee on Refugee Matters, Stability Pact for SE Europe; Hon. Citizen of Gdansk 1985, of Bremen 1999; Dr hc (Haifa Univ.) 1997. *Leisure interest:* chess. *Address:* Rudolstädterweg 9, 28329 Bremen, Germany. *Telephone:* 4673733.

KOSHIBA, Masatoshi, PhD; Japanese physicist and academic; *Senior Counselor, International Centre for Elementary Particle Physics, University of Tokyo;* b. 19 Sept. 1926, Toyohashi City, Aichi Pref.; ed Univ. of Tokyo, Univ. of Rochester, New York, USA; Prof., Dept of Physics, Univ. of Tokyo 1970–87, now Prof. Emer., Sr Counselor Int. Centre for Elementary Particle Physics 1987–; Prof., Tokai Univ. 1987–97; pioneer of neutrino-astronomy and cosmic-ray physics; led path-breaking experiments Kamiokande and Super-Kamiokande (massive detectors capturing neutrinos from the Sun and a distant supernova explosion 1987); Grosse Verdienstkreuz (Germany) 1985, Order of Culture 1988, Order of Cultural Merit 1997; Nishina Prize, Nishina Foundation 1987, Ashai Prize, Ashai Press 1988, 1999, Acad. Award, Acad. of Japan 1989, Fujuwara Science Foundation 1997, Wolf Prize, Govt of Israel 2000, Nobel Prize in Physics 2002. *Address:* International Centre for Elementary Particle Physics, University of Tokyo, 7-3-1 Hongo, Bunkyo-ku, Tokyo 113-0033, Japan (office). *Telephone:* (3) 3815-8384 (office). *Fax:* (3) 3814-8806 (office). *E-mail:* hisho@icepp.s.u--tokyo.ac.jp (office). *Website:* www.icepp.s.u-tokyo.ac.jp (office).

KOSHIRO, Matsumoto, IX; Japanese actor; b. (Teruaki Fujima), 1942; s. of the late Koshiro VIII; m.; one s.; debut in Kabuki (Japanese traditional theatre) when child; as child acted under name Kintaro, as young man Somegoro Ichikawa; became Koshiro IX 1980. *Plays include:* Kanjincho (and many other Kabuki plays), Man of La Mancha (included 10-week run on Broadway), The King and I (including 6-month run in West End), Half a Sixpence, Sweeney Todd, Fiddler on the Roof, Amadeus (Salieri). *Address:* c/o Kabukiza Theatre, No. 12–15 Ginza 4 chome, Chuo-ku, Tokyo 104, Japan.

KOSHMAN, Col-Gen. Nikolai Pavlovich; Russian politician; b. 5 April 1944, Mironovka; s. of Pavel Porfirievich Koshman and Maria Fiedoseevna Koshman; m.; two s.; ed Mil. Acad. of Home Front and Transport; numerous posts from Commdr of team to Commdr of corps, railway armed forces 1973–91, Deputy Commdr 1991–95; mem. of Mission of Plenipotentiary Rep. of Russian Pres. to Chechen Repub.; Chair. Govt of Chechen Repub. 1996, Plenipotentiary Rep. of Russian Govt in Chechen Repub. with rank of Deputy Prime Minister 1999–2000; Deputy Minister of Transport, Russian Fed. 1997–; Head Fed. Service of Special Construction Rosspetsstroy 1997–98; Adviser to the Pres. of the Russian Fed. 2001–02; Deputy Minister of Communications Jan.–Oct. 2002; Chair. State Cttee of Construction 2002–. *Publication:* Restoration of the Economy and Social Sphere of the Chechen Republic 1999. *Leisure interests:* theatre, sports (football, tennis), hunting, travelling. *Address:* Gosstroi Rosii, Stroiteley str. 8, korp. 2, 117987 Moscow (office); A. Zelynsky str. 6-37, 117534 Moscow, Russia (home). *Telephone:* (495) 930-17-55 (office); (495) 137-74-85 (home). *Fax:* (495) 939-27-02 (office).

KOSICE, Gyula; Argentine artist and poet; b. 26 April 1924, Košice, Czechoslovakia (now Slovakia); s. of Joseph F. Kosice and Eta Kosice (née Berger); m. Haydée Itaovit 1947; two d.; ed Acad. of Arts, Buenos Aires; co-f. Arturo magazine 1944, Concrete Art Invention 1945; f. Madí Art Movement 1946, f., Ed. Universal Madí Art magazine 1947; first use of neon gas in art 1946; introduction of water as essential component of his work 1948; creator Hydrospatial City (concept) 1948–; works include sculptures, hydrospatial courses, hydromurals; works in museums and pvt. collections in Argentina, Latin America, USA, Europe and Asia; Best Art Book, Asscn of Art Critics for Arte Madi 1982, Ordre des Arts et des Lettres 1989, Premio Trayectoria en el Arte, Nat. Arts Foundation 1994, Ciudadano Ilustre de la Ciudad de Buenos Aires 1997, Homenaje por Trayectoria de 62 Amős, Centro Recoleta 2003. *Publications:* Invención 1945, Madí Manifesto 1946, Golse-Se (poems) 1952, Peso y Medida de Alberto Hidalgo 1953, Antología Madí 1955, Geocultura de la Europa de Hoy 1959, Poème hydraulique 1960, Arte Hidrocinético 1968, La Ciudad Hidroespacial 1972, Arte y Arquitectura del Agua 1974, Arte Madí 1982, Obra Poética 1984, Entrevisiones 1984, Teoría sobre el Arte 1987, Arte y Filosofía Porvenirista 1996, Madí grafias 2001. *Leisure interests:* writing books on art, creating works of art. *Address:* Humahuaca 4662, Buenos Aires (office); República de la India 3135 6° A, 1425 Buenos Aires, Argentina (home). *Telephone:* (1) 867-1240 (office); (1) 801-8615 (home). *Fax:* (1) 807-0115 (home). *E-mail:* gyula@kosice.com.ar (home). *Website:* www.kosice.com.ar (office).

KOSOPKIN, Aleksandr Sergeevich; Russian government official; *Presidential Representative, State Duma;* b. 1 June 1957, Chita; m.; one s., one d.; ed Chelyabinsk Railway Transport Inst., Moscow State Legal Acad.; worked as train engine driver's asst and engine driver South Ural Railways, Zlatoust 1978–90; People's Deputy 1990–93, Chair. Sub Cttee in Russian Supreme Soviet's Social Policy Comm., mem. Democratic Russia, Working Union of Russia, Chernobly deputies groups; specialist Russian Fed. Ass.'s Information and Tech. Support Dept 1993–94; joined Presidential Admin 1994 working as consultant then group head then Deputy Dept Head and Head of Section responsible for relations with State Duma and mems of Fed. Council in Presidential Domestic Policy Dept 1996–2000, Deputy Head and Head of Dept responsible for relations with Fed. Ass. 2000–01, Head of Presidential Domestic Policy Dept 2001–04; Presidential Rep., State Duma 2004–. *Address:* State Duma, Okhotny Ryad 1, 103265 Moscow, Russia (office). *Telephone:* (495) 292-8000 (office). *Website:* www.duma.ru (office).

KOSOR, Jadranka, LLB; Croatian politician; *Deputy Prime Minister, Minister of Family, Veterans' Affairs and Intergenerational Solidarity;* b. 1 July 1953, Pakrac; one s.; ed Faculty of Law, Zagreb; worked as journalist 1972–1995, radio journalist covering war topics 1991–95; mem. of Parl. 1995–; apptd Vice Pres. of Parl. 1995; Vice Pres. Croatian Democratic Union (HDZ) 1995–97, 2002–; Minister of Family, Veterans' Affairs and Intergenerational Solidarity 2003–, Deputy Prime Minister 2004–; presidential cand. 2004; Hon. Pres. Deaf and Blind Asscn Dodir; Zlatno pero Award Croatian Journalists Asscn, EC Award for Humanitarian Work, Europski krug Award of Croatian European House, Lifetime Achievement Award Ivan Šibl Croatian Nat. TV. *Publications:* two books related to the Homeland War, two books of poetry. *Leisure interests:* music, dancing, reading. *Address:* Ministry of Family, Veterans' Affairs and Intergenerational Solidarity, 10000 Zagreb, Park Stara Trešnjevka 4 (office); Croatian Democratic Union (Hrvatska demokratska zajednica–HDZ), 10000 Zagreb, trg žrtava fašizma 4, Croatia (office). *Telephone:* (1) 3657800 (Ministry) (office); (1) 4553000 (HDZ) (office). *Fax:* (1) 3657852 (Ministry) (office); (1) 4552600 (HDZ) (office). *E-mail:* hdz@hdz.hr (office); ministrica@mobms.hr (Ministry) (office). *Website:* www.mhbdr.hr (office); www.hdz.hr (office).

KOSOVAN, Col-Gen. Alexander Davydovich; Russian army officer and construction engineer; b. 26 Oct. 1941, Akhtyrskaya, Krasnodar Territory, Russia; m.; one s. one d.; ed Novosibirsk Inst. of Eng and Construction; head of construction group, chief engineer, Deputy Head Dept of Eng Construction, Ministry of Defence 1966–84; Chief Eng, Deputy Head Construction Dept Volga Mil. Command 1984–88; Deputy Commdr Caucasus Mil. Command on construction and quartering of forces 1988–92; First Deputy Head of Dept on Construction and Quartering of Forces, Russian Ministry of Defence 1992–97, Deputy Minister of Defence in charge of military construction and housing 1997; currently First Deputy Head Dept of City Construction Policy Making, Devt and Reconstruction of Moscow; Order for Service to Motherland in Armed Forces 1989, Order of Labour Red Banner 1990, other Govt decorations. *Publications:* numerous articles on problems of mil. construction, text-books and methodical manuals for univ. and mil. schools. *Leisure interest:* fishing. *Address:* Department of City Construction Policy Making, Development and Reconstruction of Moscow, 5, Nikitsky Lane, Moscow, 103864, Russia (office). *Telephone:* (495) 202-09-11 (office). *Fax:* (495) 956-64-84 (office). *Website:* www.dgp.stroi.ru (office).

KOSSACK, Georg, FBA; German historian and academic; *Professor Emeritus, University of Munich;* b. 25 June 1923, Neuruppin; s. of Fritz Kossack and Franziska Kossack (née Unruhe); m. Ruth Kossack 1947; one s. one d.; Prof., Univ. of Kiel 1959–75, Univ. of Munich 1975–, now Prof. Emer.; mem. German Archaeological Inst., Bayerische Akademie der Wissenschaften; Fellow, British Acad., mem. Slovenian Acad. Ljubljana. *Publications:* Studien zum Symbolgut Urnenfelder und Hallstallzeit 1954, Südbayern während Hallstallzeit 1959, Graeberfelder Hallstallzeit 1979, Archsum auf Sylt I 1980, II 1987, Ed. Siedlungen im deutschen Küstengebiet 1984, Skythika 1987, Maoqinggou (with T. Höllmann) 1992, Towards Translating the Past: Selected Studies in Archaeology 1998, Religiöses Denken der Spàthrouze – ū. frühen Eisenzeit 1999. *Leisure interest:* reading nineteenth-century history. *Address:* Pietzenkirchen 56A, 83083 Riedering, Germany. *Telephone:* 08036-7342.

KOSSOWSKI, Marek, BE; Polish business executive; *President of the Management Board, PGNiG;* b. 1952; ed Silesian Univ., Katowice; with Wytwórnia Sprzętu Komunikacyjnego "PZE-Kalisz" (production plant) 1971–72; clerk, Silesian Univ., Katowice 1975–76; mem. Man. Bd, then

Vice-Chair., Socialist Union of Polish Students, Katowice 1976–80; Man., Regional Cttee, Polish United Workers' Party (PZPR), Katowice 1980–83; at Office of Council of Ministers, becoming Vice-Dir of Chair.'s Office 1983–86; Dir Minister's Cabinet, Ministry of Mining and Energy 1986–87; Deputy Dir-Gen., Warsaw Br., Coal Community 1988–90; Br. Dir and Mem. Man. Bd Państwowa Agencja Węgla Kamiennego SA (Govt Coal Agency) 1990–93; Dir Polski Bank Inwestycyjny SA, Warsaw 1993–94; Advisor to Pres. of Man. Bd, TUiR Warta SA (insurance co.) 1994–95, also Vice-Pres., Man. Bd Warta Vita SA; mem. Man. Bd Powszechny Bank Kredytowy SA 1995–99; Pres. Man. Bd PBK Nieruchomości SA 1999–2000; Dir, Przedsiębiorstwo Obsługi Cudzoziemców Dipservice (real estate co.) 2000–01; Under-Sec. of State, Ministry of the Economy, Labour and Social Policy 2001–03; Pres., Man. Bd, PGNiG 2003–. *Address:* PGNiG, ul. Krucza 6/14, 00-537 Warsaw, Poland (office). *Telephone:* (22) 5835000 (office). *Fax:* (22) 6917900 (office). *E-mail:* pr@pgnig.pl (office). *Website:* www.pgnig.pl (office).

KOSTABI, Kalev Marki (Mark); American artist and composer; b. 27 Nov. 1960, Los Angeles; ed Calif. State Univ., Fullerton; involved in East Village art movt, New York 1984; f. Kostabi World (studio, gallery, offices) 1988; retrospective exhbns, Mitsukoshi Museum, Tokyo 1992, Art Museum of Estonia, Tallinn 1998; represented in various perm. collections including Museum of Modern Art, New York, Metropolitan Museum of Art, New York, Guggenheim Museum, New York, Brooklyn Museum, Corcoran Gallery of Art, Washington, DC, Groninger Museum; has designed album covers including Guns 'n' Roses, Use Your Illusion, The Ramones' Adios Amigos; has also designed a Swatch watch, limited-edn vases, computer accessories; produces weekly cable TV show Inside Kostabi. *Albums:* I Did It Steinway 1998, Songs for Sumera 2003, New Alliance 2006. *Publications include:* Sadness Because the Video Rental Store Was Closed, Kostabi: The Early Years, Conversations With Kostabi, The Rhythm of Inspiration. *Address:* Kostabi World, 514 West 24th Street, New York, NY 10011, USA (office). *Telephone:* (212) 334-7442 (office). *E-mail:* kostabiworld@yahoo.com (office). *Website:* kostabi.com.

KOSTADINOVA, Stefka; Bulgarian high jumper (retd), government official and national organization official; *President, Bulgarian Olympic Committee;* b. 15 March 1965, Plovdiv; m. Nikolay Petrov (divorced 1999); one s.; ed Plovdiv Sports School; initially concentrated on gymnastics and swimming, later transferred to athletics; four-time European Indoor Champion: Athens 1985, Lievenne 1987, Budapest 1988, Paris 1994; European Outdoor Champion, Stuttgart 1986; set world high jump record (2.09m, still unbeaten Sept. 2005), Rome 1987; World Outdoor Champion 1987, 1995; won Silver Medal, Olympic Games, Seoul, S Korea 1988, Gold Medal, Olympic Games, Atlanta, Ga, USA 1996; five world indoor championship titles: Paris 1985, Indianapolis 1987, Budapest 1989, Toronto 1993, Paris 1997; has set altogether seven world records: three outdoors and four indoors, and has jumped over 2.00m more than 100 times, an achievement unequalled by any other athlete in the women's high jump; 1997 outdoor season curtailed due to foot injury requiring two operations, retd 1999; Vice-Pres. Bulgarian Athletics Fed. 1999–2005, Pres. 2005–; Deputy Minister of Sport and Youth 2003–; voted Sportsperson of the Year in Bulgaria 1985, 1987, 1995, 1996, voted Sportsperson of the Year in the Balkans five times, included by IAAF in the Top 10 of the Twentieth Century Female Athletes. *Address:* Bulgarian Olympic Committee, Sofia 1040, Angel Kanchev str. 4, Bulgaria (office). *Telephone:* (2) 987-56-95 (office). *Fax:* (2) 987-03-79 (office). *E-mail:* boc@bgolympic.org (office). *Website:* www.bgolympic.org (office).

KOSTELIĆ, Janica; Croatian professional skier; b. 5 Jan. 1982, Zagreb; d. of Ante Kostelić and Marica Kostelić; ed high school in Zagreb; began skiing aged three; competed at top level since age 15; competed for first time in World Cup race at Cortina d'Ampezzo, Italy 1998; competed in Olympics Games, Nagano, Japan 1998; severely damaged right knee aged 17 (at St Moritz Dec. 1999) whilst leading World Cup standings; returned to competition and won Overall World Cup title (First in Slalom and Combined), Are 2001; Gold Medals in Combined, Slalom, Giant Slalom at Winter Olympic Games, Salt Lake City, UT, USA 2002, Silver Medal at Super-G (first alpine skier to win four Olympic medals at the same Winter Games) 2002; won Slalom and Overall World Cups 2003; diagnosed with hyperthyroidism Oct. 2003; career interrupted by knee injury early 2004; third major comeback late 2004; won Slalom at Aspen, Colo Nov. 2004, Santa Caterina and San Sicario, Italy 2005; five victories in FIS World Cup in all five disciplines (Downhill, Combined, Giant Slalom, Super-G and Slalom) 2005; Gold Medal in Combined, Winter Olympic Games, Torino 2006, Silver Medal in Super-G 2006; brother Ivica Kostelic won Gold Medal in Slalom, Winter Olympics 2002; numerous nat. and int. sport awards, including Eurosport Award as World's Best Athlete 2006, Laureus Sportswoman of the Year 2006. *Leisure interests:* scuba diving, photography, music. *Address:* c/o Croatian Ski Association, Trg Krešimira Ćosića 11, 10000 Zagreb, Croatia. *Telephone:* (1) 3093-009. *Fax:* (1) 3093-008. *E-mail:* janica@croski.hr. *Website:* www.janica.hr.

KOSTELKA, Lt-Gen. Miroslav; Czech politician, diplomatist and army officer (retd); *Ambassador to Russia;* b. 31 Jan. 1951, Františkovy Lázně; m.; one s. two d.; ed Mil. Acad. of Brno, NATO Defence Coll., Rome, Italy; began mil. career as bn commdr; Deputy Chief of Nat. Rear Anti-Aircraft Defences 1987–92; Chief of Staff of Main Rear Service 1992–93; Inspector, Czech Repub. Army Logistics 1994–98; Mil. Attaché, Embassy in Ottawa, Canada 1998–2002; Deputy Chief of Gen. Staff 2002–03; Minister of Defence 2003–04; Dir Prime Minister Section 2004–05; Amb. to Russia 2005–; Ordre nat. du Mérite; Hon. Memorial Badge for services in IFOR, UN Peace Service Medal, Medal of Army of Czech Repub., Přemysl Otakar II Hon. Memorial Badge. *Address:* Velryslanectví ČR v Ruské federaci, J. Fučíka 12/14, 123056 Moscow 1, Russia (office). *Telephone:* (495) 251-05-44 (office). *Fax:* (045) 250-15-23 (office). *E-mail:* moscow@embassy.mzv.cz (office). *Website:* www.mfa.cz/moscow (office).

KOSTIĆ, Branko, PhD; Montenegrin politician and academic; *Professor of Economy, University of Montenegro;* b. 1939, Rvaši, Montenegro; s. of Vlado Kostić and Veúka Kostić (née Vukotić); m. Milica Kostić (née Pejović); two d.; ed Belgrade Univ.; joined CP 1957; Pres. Cen. Cttee of Montenegrin Youth 1963–69; Vice-Exec. and Gen. Exec. of Aluminium Combine, Titograd 1969–79; Prof. of Economy, Univ. of Montenegro 1979–; Vice-Pres. Montenegrin Govt 1986–89; Pres. of Presidency of Montenegro 1989–90; mem. Yugoslav Collective Presidency, Vice-Pres. 1991–92; Decoration, Work Achievements with Golden Wreath; Decoration, Mil. Achievements with Silver Swords; several honours and awards. *Publications include:* Aluminium and Technical Progress 1981, 1991: To be Remembered 1996, Memoirs 2005; several publs, articles and scientific papers. *Leisure interests:* reading, writing, viniculture, gardening. *Address:* University of Montenegro, Cetinjski, put b.b., 81000 Podgorica (office); Moskovska 16, 81000 Podgorica, Montenegro (home). *Telephone:* (81) 245-014 (office); (81) 244-096 (home). *Fax:* (81) 244-096 (home). *E-mail:* majak@cg.yu (home).

KOSTIKOV, Vyacheslav Vasilyevich; Russian politician, journalist and diplomatist; b. 24 Aug. 1940, Moscow; m. Marina Smirnova, one d.; ed Moscow State Univ., All-Union Acad. of Foreign Trade, Sheffield Univ., UK; staff-mem.; ed. Div. of Information UNESCO Secr. in Paris 1972–78, 1982–88; political reviewer Press Agency Novosti 1978–82; Press Sec. of Pres. Boris Yeltsin 1992–94; plenipotentiary rep. of Russia in Vatican City and Amb. to Malta 1995–96; Pres. Finance Group Moskovsky Delovoy Mir (MDM) 1996–97; Deputy Dir-Gen. Media-Most Holding 1997–2001; currently freelance journalist. *Publications:* numerous books including Romance with the President 1996; novels: The Heir, The Syzin's Dissonance, Bridges to the Left Bank; books on Russian emigration; numerous articles in dailies Izvestia, Ogonyok, reviews in Times of India. *Leisure interest:* classical music.

KOSTIN, Andrey Leonidovich; Russian banking executive; *Chairman and CEO, Vneshtorgbank;* b. 21 Sept. 1956, Moscow; m.; one s.; ed Moscow Lomonosov State Univ.; with Ministry of Foreign Affairs 1979–92, seconded to Russian Gen. Consulate, Australia 1979–82, Embassy in UK 1985–90; joined Investments and Finance Co. 1992; Deputy Head Dept of Foreign Investments, Imperial Bank 1993–95; First Deputy Chair. 1995, mem. Bd of Dirs, Nat. Reserve Bank 1994–96; Exec. Chair. Vnesheconombank 1996–2002, Chair. and CEO Vneshtorgbank (Bank for Foreign Trade) 2002–; mem. Business Advisory Council APEC 2007–; Order of Honour 1999, Russian Govt Hon. Diplomas 1998, 2001. *Address:* Vneshtorgbank, 190000 St Petersburg, ul. Bolshaya Morskaya 29, Russia (office). *Telephone:* (812) 314-60-59 (office). *Fax:* (812) 312-78-18 (office). *E-mail:* info@vtb.ru (office). *Website:* www.vtb.ru (office).

KOSTOV, Ivan Yordanov; Bulgarian politician; b. 23 Dec. 1949; m.; two d.; ed Karl Marx Higher Inst. of Econs, Sofia and Kliment Ohridski Univ., Sofia; fmr economist; Asst Prof., Karl Marx Higher Inst. of Econs 1974; Sr Asst Prof., Scientific Communism Dept, V. Iyich Lenin Higher Inst. of Mechanical and Electrical Eng, Sofia (now Tech. Univ.) 1979, Asst Prof. 1991; elected Deputy (Union of Democratic Forces—UDF) to 7th Grand Nat. Ass., Chair. Econ. Affairs Cttee 1990, Deputy to 36th Nat. Ass. 1991, 37th Ass. 1993, Deputy Floor Leader of UDF Parl. Group 1993, Deputy to 38th Ass. 1997, 39th Ass. 2001; Minister of Finance 1990–92; Chair. and Pres. Union of Democratic Forces (SDS) 1993; Prime Minister of Bulgaria 1997–2001; led group of deputies who split from UDF to form new parl. group (United Democratic Forces) and, later, found a new political party, Democrats for a Strong Bulgaria (Demokrati za silna Balgarija—DSB), Chair. 2004–07 resgnd). *Address:* Demokrati za silna Balgariya, ul. G. Ignatiyev 10A, 1000 Sofia, Bulgaria (office). *Telephone:* (2) 980-53-34 (office). *Fax:* (2) 987-17-51 (office). *E-mail:* mediacentre@dsb.bg (office). *Website:* www.dsb.bg (office).

KOSTRZEWSKI, Jan Karol, MD, MPH; Polish epidemiologist and academic; *Professor Emeritus of Epidemiology, National Institute of Hygiene, National Centre for Disease Prevention and Control;* b. 2 Dec. 1915, Kraków; s. of Jan Kostrzewski and Maria Sulikowska; m. Ewa Sobolewska 1948; one s. three d.; ed Jagiellonian Univ., Kraków and Harvard School of Public Health, Boston; Health Service Doctor 1939–51; Head of Epidemiology Dept, State Hygiene Inst., Warsaw 1951–78; Prof. of Epidemiology Warsaw Medical Acad. 1954–60; Under-Sec. of State, Ministry of Health and Social Welfare and Chief Sanitary Inspector 1961–68; Minister of Health and Social Welfare 1968–72; Scientist State Hygiene Inst. 1973–78, Head of Epidemiology Dept, Prof. Emer. of Epidemiology 1990–; Corresp. mem. Polish Acad. of Sciences (PAN) 1967–76, mem. 1976–, mem. Presidium 1971–89, Sec. Dept of Medical Sciences 1972–80, Vice-Pres. 1981–83, Pres. 1984–89; Chair. Cttee Nat. Health Protection Fund 1981–; Chair. Research Strengthening Group UNDP/World Bank/WHO Special Programme on Tropical Diseases Research; Vice-Chair. Nat. Council of Patriotic Movt for Nat. Rebirth 1983–89; Deputy to Sejm (Parl.) 1985–89; Chair. Presidium of Ecological Social Movt 1986–; fmr mem. Consultative Council attached to Chair. of Council of State; mem. Exec. Bd WHO 1973, Chair. 1975; mem. Council Int. Epidemiological Asscn 1974, Pres. 1977–81; Hon. mem. Mechnikov Soc. Microbiologists and Epidemiologists 1956–, later Pres.; Sec. Int. Comm. for Assessment of Smallpox Eradication in India, Nepal, Ethiopia, Horn of Africa and Bhutan 1977–79; Corresp. mem. Acad. Nat. de Médecine (Paris) 1979, Global Advisory Comm. for Medical Research 1980, Foreign mem. Acad. of Medical Sciences, USSR 1986, Foreign Fellow, Indian Nat. Science Acad. 1986; Visiting Prof., Centers for Disease Control and Prevention, Atlanta, Ga USA 1976; Heath Clark Lecturer, Univ. of London 1986–87; mem. External Review Team for Human Reproduction Research Program 1988–89; Order of Banner of Labour 1st and 2nd Class, Commdr and Kt's Cross, Order of Polonia Restituta, Cross of

Valour, Gold Cross of Merit, Warsaw Insurgent Cross and others; Dr hc (WAM, Łódź) 1979, (AM, Lublin) 1985. *Publications:* numerous works on epidemiology including Communicable Diseases and Their Control on the Territory of Poland in the XX Century (co-author and co-ed.). *Leisure interests:* sport, photography, skiing, fishing. *Address:* National Institute of Hygiene, ul. Chocimska 24, Warsaw (office); Al. Róz 10M6, 00-556, Warsaw, Poland (home). *Telephone:* (22) 8493104 (office); (22) 6284988 (home). *E-mail:* jan_kostrzewski@op.pl (home).

KOŠTUNICA, Vojislav, LLB; Serbian lawyer and politician; *Leader, Democratic Party of Serbia (Demokratska stranka Srbije);* b. 24 March 1944, Belgrade; s. of Jovan Koštunica and Radmila Arandjelovic; m. Dr Zorica Radović; ed Belgrade State Univ.; Lecturer in Law, Belgrade Univ. 1970–74; expelled for opposition to univ. admin. 1974; Sr Researcher, Inst. of Philosophy and Social Theories in Belgrade; took part in opposition movt from 1980s; Founder-mem. Democratic Party; left party in 1992 to form Democratic Party of Serbia (Demokratska stranka Srbije), now Chair.; remained outside mainstream politics until nominated by opposition parties to stand as a cand. against Slobodan Milošević; Pres. of the Fed. Repub. of Yugoslavia 2000–03; Prime Minister of Serbia 2004–08. *Publications include:* Political System of Capitalism and Opposition 1978, Party Pluralism or Monism (co-author) 1983, Between Force and the Law 2000, Freedom Endangered 2002. *Address:* Demokratska stranka Srbije, 11000 Belgrade, Pariska 13, Serbia (office). *Telephone:* (11) 3204719 (office). *Fax:* (11) 3204743 (office). *E-mail:* info@dss.org.yu (office). *Website:* www.dss.org.yu (office).

KOSTYUK, Platon Grigorievich, MD, PhD; Ukrainian neurophysiologist, physician and biologist; *Director, A.A. Bogomoletz Institute of Physiology, National Academy of Sciences of Ukraine;* b. 20 Aug. 1924, Kiev; s. of G. S. Kostyuk and M. F. Kostyuk; m. Liudmila V. Kostyuk 1950; two d.; ed Kiev State Univ. and Kiev Medical Inst.; mem. CPSU 1947–91; Head, Dept of Gen. Physiology of Nervous System, A. A. Bogomoletz Inst. of Physiology 1958–, Dir of Inst. 1966–, also Head, Scientific Council; Head, Dept of Membrane Biophysics, Moscow Physico-Tech. Inst. 1982–; mem. Ukrainian Acad. of Sciences 1966– (Vice-Pres. 1993–98), Ukrainian Acad. of Medical Sciences 1994, Russian, Czechoslovak and Hungarian Acads, Akad. Leopoldina; mem. Exec. Cttee European Neurosciences Asscn; Chair. United Scientific Council for Problems of Human and Animal Physiology; Pavlov Prize 1960, Sechenov Prize 1977, State Prize 1983, A. A. Bogomoletz Prize 1987. *Publications:* Intracellular Perfusion of Excitable Cells 1984, Role of Calcium Ions in Nerve Cell Function 1991, Calcium Signalling in the Nervous System 1995, Plasticity in Nerve Cell Function 1998. *Leisure interests:* tennis, downhill skiing. *Address:* A. A. Bogomoletz Institute of Physiology, National Academy of Sciences, 4 Bogomoletz Street, 01024 Kiev 24, Ukraine. *Telephone:* (44) 253-2909 (office); (44) 234-2071 (home). *Fax:* (44) 253-64-58 (office). *E-mail:* pkostyuk@serv.biph.kiev.ua (office). *Website:* www.biph.kiev.ua/departments/gphns/kostyuk (office).

KOSTYUK, Valery V., Dr Tech.; Russian mechanical engineer; b. 26 Aug. 1940, Zaporozhye, Ukraine; ed Chelyabinsk State Polytech. Inst.; eng. Chelyabinsk Polytech. Inst. 1962–63; jr, then sr researcher, Prof. Moscow Aviation Inst. 1963–78; Chief research dept, USSR Ministry of Secondary Education 1978–79; Deputy Dir-Gen. scientific division, USSR Ministry of Higher Education 1979–84; head of division USSR State Planning Comm. 1984–91; Vice-Pres., then Pres. Asscn of Int. Co-operation 1993–96; First Deputy Chair. State Cttee on Science and Tech. 1996–97; First Deputy Minister of Sciences and Technology 1997–99; Chief Scientific Sec. Russian Acad. of Sciences 2001; mem. Russian Acad. of Sciences (corresp. mem. 1991–97), Russian Acad. of Eng. and Tech.; USSR State Prize 1985. *Publications include:* numerous scientific papers on energy, thermal exchange and hydrodynamics in energy, cryogenics, rocket-space installations and nuclear reactors. *Address:* Russian Academy of Sciences, Leninsky prosp. 14, Moscow 119991, Russia (office). *Telephone:* (495) 954-32-76 (office).

KOSUMI, Bajram, DPhil; Kosovo politician and academic; b. 20 March 1960, Tuxhec, Kamenicë; m.; four c.; ed Univ. of Priština; student movement leader, Priština 1981; sentenced to 10 years for opposing communist govt of Yugoslavia; journalist 1991–93; mem. Alliance for Future of Kosova (AAK), Pres. Parl. Party 1994–96, Vice-Pres. AAK 2000–02; Minister of Public Information, Interim Govt of Kosovo 1999; mem. Ass. of Kosovo 2001–04, 2004–07, 2007–; Minister for Environment and Spatial Planning of Kosovo 2004–05; Prime Minister of Kosovo 2005–06 (resgnd); Prof., Univ. of Priština. *Publications:* A Concept on Sub-Policy 1995, Vocabulary of Barbarians 2000, A Concept on the New Political Thought 2001, Lyric of Fishta 2004, Literature from Prison 2006, A Decisive Year 2006. *Leisure interest:* mountain hiking. *Address:* Street Sylejman Vokshi H A, 9A Priština (home); c/o Government Building, Assembly of Republic of Kosovo, Mother Teresa Street, N.N., Priština, Kosovo (office). *E-mail:* bajram.kosumi@ks-gov.net (office); lamippk@yahoo.com (home).

KOSUTH, Joseph; American artist; b. 31 Jan. 1945, Toledo, Ohio; two d.; ed Toledo Museum School of Design, privately under the Belgian painter Line Bloom Draper, Cleveland Inst. of Art, School of Visual Arts, NY; a pioneer of conceptual art and installation art 1960s; moved to NY 1965; f. Museum of Normal Art, NY 1967; Prof. School of Visual Arts, NY 1967–85, Hochschule für Bildende Künste, Hamburg, Germany 1988–90, Staatliche Akad. der Bildende Künste, Stuttgart 1991–97, Kunstakademie Munich 2001–06, currently at Inst. Universitario di Architettura, Venice, Italy; Visiting and Guest Lecturer Yale Univ., Cornell Univ., New York Univ., Duke Univ., UCLA, Cal Arts, Cooper Union, Pratt Inst., The Musuem of Modern Art, NY, Art Inst. of Chicago, Royal Academy, Copenhagen, Ashmolean Museum, Oxford, of Rome, Berliln Kunstakademie, RCA, London, Glasgow School of Art, Hayward Gallery, London, The Sorbonne, Paris, Sigmund Freud Museum, Vienna; co-ed. The Fox magazine 1975–76; art ed. Marxist Perspectives 1977–78; Chevalier des Arts et Lettres 1993, Decoration of Honour in Gold (Austria) 2003; Dr hc (Bologna, Italy); Cassandra Foundation Grant 1968, Brandeis Univ. Creative Art Award 1990, Frederick R. Weisman Art Foundation Award 1991, Venice Biennale Menzione d'Onore 1993, 3 franc postage stamp issued in honour of his work in Figeac (France) 1999. *Publication:* Art After Philosophy and After (collected writings) 1991, Purloined (novel) 2001, Guide to Contemporary Art Special Edn 2003. *Address:* 591 Broadway, New York, NY 10012, USA (home); c/o Sean Kelly, 528 East 29th Street, New York, NY 10001 (office). *Telephone:* (212) 219-8984 (New York) (home); (6) 68809621 (Rome) (home).

KOTAITE, Assad, LLD; Lebanese lawyer and international aviation official (retd); b. 6 Nov. 1924, Hasbaya; s. of Adib Kotaite and Kamle Abousamra; m. Monique Ayoub 1983; ed French Univ., Beirut, Univ. of Paris and Acad. of Int. Law, The Hague; Head of Legal and Int. Affairs, Directorate of Civil Aviation, Lebanon 1953–56; Rep. of Lebanon, Council of ICAO 1956–70; Sec.-Gen. ICAO 1970–76, Pres. Council 1976–2006 (retd); Pres. Int. Court of Aviation and Space Arbitration, Paris 1995–; many decorations from academic insts and foreign states. *Address:* 5955 Wilderton Avenue, Apt O4A, Montreal, PQ, H3S 2V1 (home); c/o International Civil Aviation Organization, 999 University Street, Suite 12.20, Montreal, PQ H3C 5H7, Canada.

KOTAK, Uday, BCom, MMS; Indian business executive; *Vice-Chairman and Managing Director, Kotak Mahindra Bank;* s. of Suresh Kotak and Indira Kotak; m.; two c.; ed Sydenham Coll. amd Jamnalal Bajaj Inst. of Man. Studies, Bombay Univ.; Vice-Chair. and Man. Dir Kotak Mahindra Bank (fmrly Kotak Mahindra Finance Ltd) 2002–; Chair. Kotak Securities Ltd; Chair. and Dir Kotak Mahindra Primus Ltd; Dir of various subsidiary cos including Kotak Securities Ltd, Kotak Mahindra Asset Man. Co Ltd, Kotak Mahindra Capital Co Ltd, OM Kotak Mahindra Life Insurance Co Ltd; mem. Bd of Dirs Bajaj Hindustan Ltd, Dabur India Ltd, Ford Credit Kotak Mahindra Ltd, Kotak Forex Brokerage Ltd, Mahindra & Mahindra Financial Services Ltd, Hutchison Max Telecom Pvt. Ltd, Business Standard Ltd, Indiacar.com Pvt. Ltd, Blue Star Ltd –2002; mem. Advisory Cttee Nat. Stock Exchange of India Ltd; mem. Exec. Bd Indian School of Business; named Global Leader of Tomorrow by the World Econ. Forum 1996, Centre for Org. Devt V. Krishnamurthy Award for Excellence 2007. *Leisure interest:* cricket. *Address:* Kotak Mahindra Bank, 1st Floor, Bakhtawar 229, Nariman Point, Mumbai 400 021, India (office). *Telephone:* (22) 66341100 (office). *Website:* www.kotak.com (office).

KOTANKO, Christoph, PhD; Austrian editor; *Editor-in-Chief, Kurier;* b. 27 July 1953, Braunau am Inn; m. Ingrid Kotanko; one d.; ed Gymnasium, Braunau, studied Romance languages and journalism in Vienna and Paris; Domestic Ed., Wochenpresse 1979–86, Ed. news magazine profile 1986–88; Head of Domestic Policy and commentator for daily newspaper Kurier, with a special focus on European and security policy 1988–97, Deputy Ed.-in-Chief 1997–2003, Exec. Ed.-in-Chief 2003–05, Ed.-in-Chief 2005–; Goldenes Verdienstzeichen der Republik Österreich (für EU-Berichterstattung), Officier, Ordre nat. du Mérite 2005; Kurt-Vorhofer Prize 1999. *Address:* Kurier, Lindengasse 48–52, 1072 Vienna, Austria (office). *Telephone:* (1) 521-00 (office). *Fax:* (1) 521-00-22-57 (office). *E-mail:* leser@kurier.at (office). *Website:* www.kurier.at (office).

KOTCHEFF, Ted; Canadian film and stage director; b. 7 April 1931, Toronto; m. Laifun Chung; two c.; with CBC Television 1952–57; joined ABC-TV, London 1957; f. Panoptica Productions in Canada with wife Laifun Chung 1996. *Films include:* Life At The Top 1965, Two Gentlemen Sharing 1968, Wake In Fright 1971, The Apprenticeship of Duddy Kravitz (in Canada) 1973–74, Fun with Dick and Jane 1977, Who is Killing the Great Chefs of Europe? 1978, North Dallas Forty (directed and wrote) 1979, First Blood, Split Image, 1982–83, Uncommon Valour 1984, Joshua, Then and Now 1985, Switching Channels 1988, Weekend at Bernie's 1989, Winter People (dir) 1989, Folks! (actor) 1992, Hidden Assassin 1995. *Plays include:* Play With A Tiger, Maggie May, The Au Pair Man, Have You Any Dirty Washing, Mother Dear?. *Television includes:* The Human Voice 1966, Of Mice And Men 1968, Edna The Inebriate Woman 1971, What Are Families for? 1993, Love on the Run 1994, Family of Cops 1995, A Husband, a Wife and a Lover 1996, Borrowed Hearts 1997, Buddy Faro (series) 1998, Crime in Connecticut: The Story of Alex Kelly 1999, Law & Order (exec. producer) 1999–2007.

KOTELKIN, Maj.-Gen. Aleksander Ivanovich; Russian politician; *First Deputy Head, Department of Municipal Property, Moscow Government;* b. 19 Nov. 1954, Kiev; m.; one s.; ed Kiev Higher School of Eng and Aviation, Diplomatic Acad.; served in the army, engineer of aviation equipment Kiev Mil. command 1976–87; with USSR Mission in UN, New York 1988–90; on staff Ministry of External Econ. Relations 1991–94; Head Chief Dept on mil.-tech. co-operation 1993–94; Dir-Gen. State Co. Rosvooruzheniye 1994–97, Chief Adviser on Marketing 1997–; First Deputy Minister of Foreign Econ. Relations and Trade 1997–98; First Deputy Head Dept. of Municipal Property, Moscow Govt 1998–. *Address:* Karetny Ryad 2/1, 103006 Moscow, Russia. *Telephone:* (495) 299-55-37 (office).

KOTENKOV, Maj.-Gen. Aleksander Alekseyevich; Russian politician; *Representative of the President, Federation Council;* b. 23 Sept. 1952, Krasnodar Territory; m.; one s.; ed Rostov-on-Don Inst. of Agric. Machine Construction, Mil.-Political Acad. by corresp.; engineer Rostov Don Factory Rubin 1974–75; army service 1975–90; People's Deputy Russian Fed. 1990–93; Deputy Chair. Cttee Supreme Soviet on Defence and Security 1991; Deputy Head, Head State Law Dept, Russian Presidency, 1992–93; Head Provincial Admin, Martial Law Zone, N Ossetia and Ingushetia 1993–95; Deputy Minister of Nat. Policy 1995–96; mem. State Duma (Parl.)

1993–96; Rep. of President in State Duma 1996–2004, in Fed. Council 2004–. *Address:* c/o Office of the President, Staraya pl. 4, 103132 Moscow, Russia (office). *Telephone:* (495) 925-35-81 (office). *Fax:* (495) 206-07-66 (office). *E-mail:* president@gov.ru (office). *Website:* www.kremlin.ru (office).

KOTLER, Philip, MA, PhD; American professor of marketing; *S.C. Johnson & Son Distinguished Professor of International Marketing, Kellogg School of Management, Northwestern University;* b. 27 May 1931; s. of Maurice Kotler and Betty Kotler; three d.; ed Univ. of Chicago, Massachusetts Inst. of Tech.; post-doctoral research in math., Harvard Univ., in behavioural science, Univ. of Chicago; currently S.C. Johnson & Son Distinguished Prof. of Int. Marketing, Kellogg School of Man., Northwestern Univ., Evanston, IL; consultant for IBM, Gen. Electric, AT&T, Honeywell, Bank of America, Merck; fmr Chair. Coll. of Marketing, Inst. of Man. Sciences; fmr Dir American Marketing Asscn (AMA), MAC Group; fmr mem. Yankelovivh Advisory Bd; currently mem. Bd of Govs School of Art Inst., Chicago, Advisory Bd Drucker Foundation; fmr Trustee, Marketing Science Inst.; Hon. PhD (Stockholm Univ., Univ. of Zürich, Athens Univ. of Econs and Business, DePaul Univ., Kraków School of Business and Econs, HEC–Paris, Vienna Univ. of Econs and Business Admin, Budapest Univ. of Econ. Science and Public Admin, Catholic Univ. of Santo Domingo); Paul Converse Award, AMA 1978, Distinguished Marketing Educator Award, AMA 1985, Award for Marketing Excellence, European Asscn of Marketing Consultants and Sales Trainers, Annual Charles Coolidge Parlin Marketing Research Award 1989, Marketer of the Year, Sales and Marketing Execs Int. 1995, Marketing Educator of the Year, Acad. of Marketing Science 2002. *Publications include:* Marketing Management: Analysis, Planning, Implementation and Control 1967, Principles of Marketing, Marketing Models, Strategic Marketing for Non-Profit Organizations, The New Competition, High Visibility, Social Marketing, Marketing Places, Marketing for Congregations, Marketing for Hospitality and Tourism, The Marketing of Nations, Kotler on Marketing, Marketing Insights from A to Z 2003; over 100 articles in professional journals. *Address:* Kellogg School of Management, Northwestern University, 2001 Sheridan Road, Evanston, IL 60208, USA (office). *Telephone:* (847) 491-3522 (office). *Fax:* (847) 491-2498 (office). *E-mail:* kelloggmedia@kellogg.northwestern.edu (office). *Website:* www.kellogg.northwestern.edu (office).

KOTLYAKOV, Vladimir Mikhailovich, DrGeogSc; Russian geographer; *Director, Institute of Geography, Russian Academy of Sciences;* b. 6 Nov. 1931, Lobnya, Moscow Region; m. Valentina Alexeevna Bazanova; two s.; ed Moscow State Univ.; Jr Researcher, Sr Researcher, Head of Glaciology Dept, Inst. of Geography USSR (now Russian) Acad. of Sciences 1954–86, Dir 1986–; Corresp. mem., Russian Acad. of Sciences 1976, mem. 1991–; Vice-Pres. Russian Geographical Soc. 1980–2000, Hon. Pres. 2000–; People's Deputy of USSR 1989–91; mem. Academia Europaea, Earth Council 1993–, French Acad. of Sciences 2002–; Hon. mem. American, Mexican, Italian, Estonian and Georgian Geographical Socs, Int. Glaciological Soc.; Litke Gold Medal, Russian Geographical Soc. 1985, Przhevalsky Gold Medal, Russian Geographical Soc. 1995, State Prize of Russian Fed. 2002, Russian Ind. Prize 'Triumph' 2004, Berg Gold Medal, Russian Acad. of Sciences 2005. *Publications include:* Snow Cover of Antarctica 1961, Snow Cover of the Earth and Glaciers 1968, Glaciology Dictionary 1984, Elsevier's Dictionary of Glaciology 1990, World of Snow and Ice 1994, Science, Society, Environment 1997, World Atlas of Snow and Ice Resources 1997; Collection of Selected Works: Glaciology of Antarctica (Vol. 1) 2000, Snow Cover and Glaciers of the Earth (Vol. 2) 2004, Geography in the Changing World (Vol. 3) 2001, Ice, Love and Hypothesis (Vol. 4) 2001, In the World of Snow and Ice (Vol. 5) 2002, Science is a Life (Vol. 6) 2003. *Leisure interest:* travelling. *Address:* Profsoyuznaya str. 43-1-80, 117420 Moscow (home); Institute of Geography, Russian Academy of Sciences, Staromonetny per. 29, 119017 Moscow, Russia (office). *Telephone:* (495) 957-08-34 (home); (495) 959-00-32 (office). *Fax:* (495) 959-00-33 (office). *E-mail:* direct@igras.geonet.ru (office); igras@igras.geonet.ru (office). *Website:* igras.geonet.ru (office).

KÖTSCHAU, Gabriele, DrIur; German barrister, politician and international organization official; *Director of the Secretariat, Council of the Baltic Sea States;* b. (Gabriele Bögelsack), 1950, Berlin; m.; two c.; ed Free Univ. of Berlin, Univ. of Kiel; mem. Schleswig-Holstein Parl. 1988–2005, fmr Vice-Pres.; Dir Secr. Council of Baltic Sea States 2005–; Bundesverdienstkreuz. *Publications:* numerous lectures and articles on Baltic Sea cooperation and Eastern Europe. *Address:* Council of the Baltic Sea States, Strömsborg, PO Box 2010, Stockholm 103 11, Sweden (office). *Telephone:* (8) 440-19-20 (office). *Fax:* (8) 440-19-44 (office). *E-mail:* gabriele.koetschau@cbss.org (office). *Website:* www.cbss.org (office).

KOTTO, Yaphet Fredrick; American actor; b. 15 Nov. 1944, Harlem, New York; s. of Yaphet Mangobell Kotto and Gladys M. Kotto; m. Antoinette Pettyjohn 1975; six c. *Films include:* Nothing But a Man 1963, Liberation of Lord Byron Jones 1964, Across 110th Street 1973, Live and Let Die 1974, Report to the Commissioner 1974, Sharks Treasure 1974, Monkey Hustle 1975, Drum 1976, Blue Collar 1977, Alien 1978, Brubaker 1979, Hey Good Looking 1982, Fighting Back 1982, Star Chamber 1983, Warning Sign 1985, Terminal Entry 1986, Eye of the Tiger 1986, PrettyKill 1987, The Running Man 1987, Midnight Run 1988, Nightmare of the Devil (also dir), Terminal Entry 1986, Jigsaw Murders 1988, A Whisper to a Scream 1989, Ministry of Vengeance 1989, Tripwire 1990, Hangfire 1991, Freddy's Dead 1991, Almost Blue 1992, Extreme Justice 1993, Intent to Kill 1993, The Puppet Masters 1994, Dead Badge 1995, Out-of-Sync 1995, Two If By Sea 1996. *Theatre includes:* Great White Hope, Blood Knot, Black Monday, In White America, A Good Place to Raise a Boy, Fences (London) 1990. *Television includes:* Raid on Entebbe 1977, Rage 1980, Women of San Quentin 1983, In Self Defense 1987, Badge of the Assassin, Harem, Desperado, Perry Mason, Prime Target, After the Shock, Chrome Soldiers, It's Nothing Personal, Extreme Justice, The American Clock, Deadline For Murder, Homicide: Life on the Street (series) 1993–99, The Defenders: Payback 1997, Homicide: The Movie 2000, The Ride 2000, Stiletto Dance 2001. *Address:* 480 N. Westlake Boulevard, Malibu, CA 90265, USA (office).

KOUASSI, René Aphing; Côte d'Ivoirian government official; fmr magistrate; Minister of Defence 2006–07. *Address:* c/o Ministry of Defence, Camp Galliéni, côté Bibliothèque nationale, BP V241, Abidjan, Côte d'Ivoire (office).

KOUCHNER, Bernard, (Bernard Gridaine), KBE, DenM; French politician, physician and screenwriter; *Minister of Foreign and European Affairs;* b. 1 Nov. 1939, Avignon; two s. one d. by Evelyne Pisier; one s. by Christine Ockrent (q.v.); gastro-enterologist, Hôpital Cochin, Paris; Co-founder and Pres. Médecins sans Frontières 1971–79; Founder, Médecins du Monde 1980; has organized and undertaken numerous humanitarian missions world-wide since 1968; Sec. of State, Ministry of Social Affairs and Employment May 1988; Sec. of State responsible for Humanitarian Action, Office of Prime Minister 1988–91, Ministry of Foreign Affairs 1991–92; Minister of Health and Humanitarian Action 1992–93, 1997–99, Minister Del., Ministry of Health 2001–02; mem. European Parl. 1994–97; UN Chief Admin., Kosovo 1999–2001; Founder, Foundation for Humanitarian Action 1993–; radio broadcaster RTL 2 1995; Founder, Malades sans Frontières 2003; currently Prof. of Public Health and Devt, CNAM; Minister of Foreign and European Affairs 2007–; Dr hc (Durham, Pristina, Sarajevo, Ben Gurion, Erasmus Rotterdam); Dag Hammarskjöld Prize 1979, Louis Weiss Prize (European Parl.) 1979, Athinai Prize (Alexander Onassis Foundation) 1981, Prix Europa 1984, Nobel Peace Prize (with Médecin sans Frontières) 1999, Prix de la Tolerance 2003. *Television:* as Bernard Gridaine has written scripts for series including Médecins de Nuit, Hotel de Police, Bonjour Maitre. *Publications:* La France Sauvage, Les Voraces, L'Ile de Lumière, Charité Business, Le Devoir d'Ingérence (jtly) 1988, Les Nouvelles Solidarités 1989, Le Malheur des Autres 1991, Dieu et les Hommes (jtly) 1993, Vingt idées pour l'an 2000 1995, Ce que je crois 1995, La dictature médicale 1995, le Premier qui dit la Verité 2002, Les Guerres de la Paix 2004, Quand tu sera Président (jtly) 2004. *Address:* Ministry of Foreign Affairs, 37 quai d'Orsay, 75351 Paris Cedex 07, France (office). *Telephone:* 1-43-17-53-53 (office). *Fax:* 1-43-17-52-03 (office). *Website:* www.diplomatie.gouv.fr (office).

KOUDELKA, Josef; French (b. Czechslovak) photographer; b. 10 Jan. 1938, Boskovice; ed Technical Univ. of Prague; aeronautical engineer, Prague and Bratislava 1961–67; specialized in photography 1967–; extensive travel throughout Europe documenting lives of gypsies; exhibited in Prague 1961, 1967, MOMA, New York 1975, Amsterdam 1978, Stockholm 1980, Hayward Gallery, London 1984 etc. mem. Magnum Photos Inc. 1971–; mem. Union of Czechoslovakian artists 1965–; Chevalier des Arts et Lettres 1992; Prix Nadar 1978, Grand Prix Nat. de la Photographie (France) 1987, Hugo Erhurth Prize 1989, Prix Romanes 1989, Henri Cartier-Bresson Award 1991, Century Medal of the Royal Photographic Soc., UK, Medal of Merit 2002, and others. *Publications:* Gypsies 1975, Photopoche Josef Koudelka 1984, Exils 1 1988, Mission Photographique Transmanche 1989, Prague 1990, Z. Fotografickeho Dila 1958–1990 1990, Divaldo Za Branou 1965–1970 1993, Black Triangle 1994, Wales Reconnaissance 1998, Chaos 1999, Lime Stone 2001, Teatro del Tempo 2003. *Address:* c/o Magnum Photos, 19 rue Hégesippe Moneau, 75018 Paris, France.

KOULIBALY, Mamadou, PhD; Côte d'Ivoirian economist, academic and politician; *President of National Assembly;* b. 21 April 1957, Azaguié, Agboville; m.; three c.; Prof. of Econ. Science, Univ. of Abidjan; fmrly Minister of Economy and Finance; currently Pres. of Nat. Ass. *Address:* Assemblée Nationale, 01 BP 1381, Abidjan 01, Côte d'Ivoire (office). *Telephone:* 20-21-60-69 (office). *Fax:* 20-22-20-87 (office).

KOULOUMBIS, Evangelos; Greek politician and engineer; b. 1929, Athens; s. of Athanasios Kouloumbis and Anastasia Kouloumbis; m. Dimitra Lambrou; one s. one d.; ed Athens Polythechnic Univ.; Founder-mem. Civil Eng Asscn, mem. Gov. Council 1965–67, Pres. 1974–75; Pres. of Tech. Chamber 1974–81; Minister of Public Works in caretaker govt 1974; Pres. Greek Cttee for Balkan Agreement and Co-operation 1975–; mem. Parl. 1981–89; Chair. Council of Energy Ministers of EEC 1983 and many Greek and int. conventions, Perm. Conf. of Engineers of SE Europe (COPISEE) 1978–80; Hon. mem. League of Cypriot Engineers and Architects; mem. Greek Cttee UNESCO 1982–83; Minister without Portfolio 1981–82, for Energy and Nat. Resources 1982–84, of Physical Planning, Housing and Environment 1984, for Physical Planning, Housing, Public Works, Transport 1985–88, for the Environment, Physical Planning and Public Works 1985–88; Gov. Nat. Mortgage Bank of Greece 1993–95; Pres. Jt County Authorities of Athens and Piraeus 1995, Union of County Councils of Greece 1995. *Publications:* articles on economic, social and political matters. *Address:* 11 Kleomenous Street, 106 75 Athens, Greece. *Telephone:* (1) 7250333.

KOUMI, Margaret (Maggie); British journalist; b. 15 July 1942; d. of the late Yiasoumis Koumi and Melexidia Paraskeva; m. Ramon Sola 1980; ed Buckingham Gate, London; sec. Thomas Cook 1957–60; sub-ed., feature and fiction writer Visual Features Ltd 1960–66; sub-ed. TV World 1966–67; Production Ed. 19 Magazine 1967–69, Ed. 1969–86, concurrently Ed. Hair Magazine; Man. Ed. Practical Parenting, Practical Health, Practical Hair and Beauty 1986–87; Jt Ed. Hello! 1988–93, Ed. 1993–2001, Consultant Ed. 2001–; Jt Ed. of the Year Award 1991. *Publications:* Beauty Care 1981, Claridges – Within The Image 2004. *Leisure interests:* reading, travel, exploring markets. *E-mail:* anniebowman@hellomagazine.com (office).

KOUMURA, Masahiko, LLB; Japanese politician; b. Ehime; m.; two s. one d.; ed Chuo Univ.; Parl. Vice-Minister Defence Agency 1987, for Finance 1989, for

Foreign Affairs 1996; Minister of State, Dir-Gen. Econ. Planning Agency 1994–95; mem. House of Reps for Yamaguchi 1980–, Chair. Special Cttee on Disasters 1991, on Agric., Forestry and Fisheries 1991, on Prevention of Int. Terrorism and Japan's Cooperation and Support 2003, on Humanitarian Assistance for Reconstruction in Iraq 2003; Deputy Sec.-Gen. LDP, Dir Nat. Defence Div. 1991, Chair. Special Cttee on External Econ. Cooperation 2002; Minister of Foreign Affairs 1999, 2007–08, of Justice 2000–01, of Defence 2007. *Address:* Liberal-Democratic Party (LDP), 1-11-23, Nagata-cho, Chiyoda-ku, Tokyo 100-8910, Japan (office). *Telephone:* (3) 3581-6211 (office). *E-mail:* koho@ldp.jimin.or.jp (office). *Website:* www.jimin.jp (office).

KOURULA, Erkki, LLL, LLM, PhD; Finnish lawyer, diplomatist and judge; *Judge, International Criminal Court;* b. 12 June 1948; m. Pirkko Kourula; two c.; ed Univ. of Helsinki, Univ. of Oxford, UK; research posts at Univs of Oxford and Helsinki, Acad. of Finland, UN, Geneva 1972–82, 1984–85; Dist Judge 1979; Prof. of Int. Law, Univ. of Lapland, Rovaniemi 1982–83; Counsellor and Legal Adviser, Ministry of Foreign Affairs 1986–89, Dir Int. Law Div. 1989–91; Minister Counsellor and Legal Adviser, Perm. Mission to UN, NY 1991–95; Amb., Deputy Dir Gen. for Legal Affairs, Ministry of Foreign Affairs 1995–98, Dir Gen. for Legal Affairs 2002–03; Amb., Perm. Rep. to Council of Europe, Strasbourg 1998–2002; Judge, Int. Criminal Court (ICC), The Hague 2003–; Head Del. to Preparatory Cttee for ICC 1994–98; Agent of Finland to European Courts of Justice and Human Rights; mem. Del. to UN Gen. Ass. 1986–90, 1995–97; mem., chair. or del. to numerous int. orgs, cttees and confs. *Publications:* The Identification and Characteristics of Regional Arrangements for the Purpose of the United Nations Charter (doctoral thesis); contribs to publs and articles on activities of UN and ICC. *Address:* International Criminal Court, Maanweg 174, 2516 AB The Hague, Netherlands (office). *Telephone:* (70) 5158515 (office). *Fax:* (70) 5158555 (office). *E-mail:* pio@icc-cpi.int (home). *Website:* www.icc-cpi.int (office).

KÕUTS, Vice Adm. Tarmo; Estonian naval officer; b. 27 Nov. 1953, Saaremaa Island; m. Velina Kõuts; one s.; ed Tallinn Maritime Coll., Kaliningrad Tech. Inst., Nat. Defence Acad., Finland; held positions successively as officer, capt. and capt.-instructor on various ships, Estonian Shipping Co. 1973–90; Rector, Estonian Maritime Acad. 1990–93; Dir-Gen. Estonian Border Guard 1993–99; Commdr of Estonian Defence Forces 2000–06 (resgnd); mem. Riigikogu (State Ass.) 2007–, mem. Union of Pro Patria and Res Publica (IRL—Isamaa ja Res Publica Liit); Pres. Estonian Shooting Union; Order of the Cross of Eagle (2nd Class) 1998, Royal Norwegian Order of Merit 2002, Grand Cross Order of Prince Henry the Navigator (Portugal) 2003, Order of the National Coat of Arms (2nd Class) 2005, Commdr Grand Cross of Order of Viesturs (Latvia) 2005, Distinguished Service Decoration Estonian Defence Forces. *Leisure interests:* hunting, fishing, sailing. *Address:* Riigikogu (State Assembly) Lossi plats 1a, Tallinn 15165, Estonia (office). *Telephone:* 631-6331 (office). *Fax:* 631-6334 (office). *E-mail:* riigikogu@riigikogu.ee (office). *Website:* www.riigikogu.ee (office).

KOUYATÉ, Lansana; Guinean international organization official, diplomatist and politician; b. 1950, Koba; m.; three c.; joined diplomatic service 1983, Counsellor, Embassy in Cote d'Ivoire 1983–85; Head, Africa and OAU Dept, Ministry of Foreign Affairs 1985–87; Amb. to Egypt, Sudan, Turkey, Jordan, Syria and Lebanon 1987–92; Perm. Rep. to UN, New York 1992–97, Vice-Pres. ECOSOC 1992–93, Sec. Gen's Special Rep. to Somalia 1993–94, Under-Sec. Gen. in charge of Political Affairs for Africa, Western Asia and Middle East, UN Security Council 1994–97; Exec. Sec. Econ. Community of W African States (ECOWAS) 1997–2002; Perm. Rep. to Int. Org. of Francophone Countries 2002–07; Prime Minister of Guinea 2007–08; Commdr, Légion d'honneur, Commdr of the Mono Order (Togo), African Star (Liberia). *Publications include:* International Funding of State-owned Companies in Guinea: Problems and Prospects, The End of the Cold War and its Impact on Third-World Countries. *Address:* c/o Office of the Prime Miinister, National Assembly, Palais du Peuple, BP 414, Conakry, Guinea (office).

KOVAC, Caroline A., PhD; American business executive; *Venture Partner, Burrill & Company;* ed Oberlin Coll., Ohio, Univ. of Southern California; joined IBM 1983, held exec. man. positions at IBM Research, including Vice-Pres. Tech. Strategy and Div. Operations, Head of IBM Research Efforts in Computational Biology, Gen. Man. Life Sciences 2000–04, Gen. Man. Healthcare and Life Sciences 2004–06 (retd); Venture Pnr, Burrill & Company (venture capital firm) 2006–; mem. Bd of Dirs Chromatin, eMarkets, Wellpartner, Foundation for NIH, Africa Harvest; Dir Emer. Research!America; Trustee, Case Western Reserve Univ. 2006–; mem. Emer. IBM Acad. of Tech.; Women in Tech. Int.'s Hall of Fame, Turing Lecturer, British Computer Soc. 2003, ranked by Fortune magazine amongst 50 Most Powerful Women in Business in the US (50th) 2004. *Address:* Burrill & Company, One Embarcadero Center, Suite 2700, San Francisco, CA 94111, USA (office). *Telephone:* (415) 591-5400 (office). *Fax:* (415) 591-5401 (office). *E-mail:* burrill@b-c.com (office). *Website:* www.burrillandco.com (office).

KOVÁČ, Michal; Slovak politician, economist and banker; b. 5 Aug. 1930, Lubiša, E Slovakia; m. Emília Kováčová; two s.; ed Commercial Acad., Bratislava Univ. of Econs; Asst Lecturer, Bratislava Univ. of Econs 1954; joined staff State Bank of Czechoslvakia 1956; fmr financial adviser to Nat. Bank of Cuba; Deputy Dir Zivnostenska (trade bank), London 1967–69, recalled, expelled from CP and demoted to bank clerk 1969; researcher, lecturer 1970–78; elected to Fed. Ass. 1990; Minister of Finance, Slovak Repub. 1990, resgnd 1991; re-elected to Fed. Ass., Chair. Czech Fed. Ass. of Czech and Slovak Fed. Rep. June–Dec. 1992; Pres. of Slovak Repub. 1993–98; C-in-C the Armed Forces 1993–98; Chair. M. Kováč and V. Havel Foundation 1993–; fmr mem. Movt for a Democratic Slovakia, Deputy Chair. 1991–93; Grand Cross, Order of Merit (Poland) 1994, White Eagle Order (Poland) 1997, numerous Slovak decorations including White Double Cross Order, Ľudovít Štúr Order; CEELIA Award, American Bar Asscn 1995, Lions Club Award 1995. *Address:* c/o Office of the President, Hodžovo nám. 1, PO Box 128, 810 00 Bratislava, Slovakia.

KOVACEVICH, Richard (Dick) M., BEng, MEng, MBA; American banking executive; *Chairman, Wells Fargo & Company;* b. 1944; ed Stanford Univ.; Exec. Vice-Pres. Kenner Div., Gen. Mills Inc., Minneapolis 1967–72; Prin. Venture Capital 1972–75; Vice-Pres. Consumer Services Norwest Corpn, Minneapolis 1975, subsequently Sr Vice-Pres. New York banking group, Exec. Vice-Pres., Man. New York bank div., Exec. Vice-Pres., mem. Policy Cttee, Vice-Chair., COO banking group, Pres., COO, Vice-Chair., Chair. and CEO 1996–98; Pres. and CEO Wells Fargo & Co. (after merger with Norwest Corpn), San Francisco 1999–2005, Chair. and CEO 2005–06, Chair. 2006–; mem. Bd of Dirs Cargill, Inc., Cisco Systems, Inc., Target Corpn; mem. Gov. Arnold Schwarzenegger's California Comm. for Jobs and Econ. Growth; Vice-Pres. and mem. Bd of Govs of San Francisco Symphony; Vice-Chair. and mem. Bd of Trustees of San Francisco Museum of Modern Art. *Leisure interest:* playing basketball. *Address:* Wells Fargo & Co., PO Box 63750, San Francisco, CA 94163 (office); Wells Fargo & Co., 420 Montgomery Street, San Francisco, CA 94104, USA (office). *Telephone:* (800) 869-3557 (office); (866) 878-5865 (office). *Fax:* (415) 677-9075 (office); (626) 312-3015 (office). *E-mail:* BoardCommunications@wellsfargo.com (office). *Website:* www.wellsfargo.com (office).

KOVACEVICH, Stephen; American pianist; b. 17 Oct. 1940, San Francisco; s. of Nicholas Kovacevich and Loreta Kovacevich (née Zuban); ed Berkeley High School, Calif.; studied under Lev Shorr and Dame Myra Hess; London debut 1961; subsequently appeared at int. music festivals in Edin., Bath, Harrogate, Berlin, San Sebastián and Salzburg; a soloist at Henry Wood Promenade Concerts for 14 seasons; tours frequently in Europe, America and Australasia; fmr Prin. Guest Conductor of Australian Chamber Orchestra; fmr Music Dir of Irish Chamber Orchestra; has conducted City of Birmingham Symphony, BBC Philharmonic, Bournemouth Symphony, Royal Liverpool Philharmonic orchestras, Chamber Orchestra of Europe, London Mozart Players, Nat. Youth Chamber Orchestra; numerous recordings; winner of Kimber Award, Calif. 1959, Mozart Prize, London 1962, Edison Award (for recording of Bartok's 2nd Piano Concerto), Gramophone Award 1993 (for recording of Brahms' 1st Piano Concerto). *Publication:* Schubert Anthology. *Leisure interests:* tennis, chess, cinema, Indian food. *Address:* c/o Ekkehard Jung, Van Walsum Management Ltd, The Tower Building, 11 York Road, London, SE1 7NX, England (office). *Telephone:* (20) 7902-0532 (office). *Fax:* (20) 7902-0530 (office). *Website:* www.vanwalsum.com (office).

KOVACIC, Ernst; Austrian violinist and conductor; b. 12 April 1943, Kapfenberg; m. Anna Maria Schuster 1968; four s.; ed Acad. of Music, Univ. of Music, Vienna; teacher Univ. of Music, Vienna 1975–; prizewinner, int. competitions, Geneva 1970, Barcelona 1971, Munich 1972; appears throughout Europe, UK and USA with leading orchestras and has appeared at many festivals including Salzburg, Berlin, Vienna, Bath, Edin., Aldeburgh and London Proms; first performances of works by composers including H. K. Gruber, K. Schwertsik, E. Krenek, F. Cerhe, I. Erod, R. Holloway, B. Furrer, G. F. Haas, N. Osbourne, K. H. Essl, H. Eder; repertoire includes maj. works of baroque, classical and romantic periods and contemporary works; Artistic Dir Vienna Chamber Orchestra 1996–98; Pres. Ernst Krenek Privatstiftung. *Address:* Kriehuberpasse 29/5, 1050 Vienna, Austria (home).

KOVÁCS, András; Hungarian film director and scriptwriter; b. 20 June 1925, Kide (now in Romania); m. Gabriella Pongrác; one s. one d.; ed Győrffy Coll. and Acad. of Dramatic and Cinematic Arts; Drama reader, Hungarian Film Studio 1950, Drama Dept Head 1951–57, Film Dir 1960–; Chair. Parl. Curatorium of Public Foundation for Hungarian TV 1996–98; Pres. Fed. of Hungarian Film and TV Artists 1981–86; Balázs B. Prize, Kossuth Prize 1970, Master of the Hungarian Moving Pictures 2004; named Eminent Artist. *Films:* Zápor (Summer Rain) 1960, Pesti háztetők (On the Roofs of Budapest) 1961, Isten őszi csillaga (Autumn Star) 1962, Nehéz emberek (Difficult People) 1964, Hideg napok (Cold Days) 1966, Falak (Walls) 1968, Ecstasy from 7 to 10 1969, Staféta (Relay Race) 1971, A magyar ugaron (Fallow Land) 1973, Bekötött szemmel (Blindfold) 1975, Labirintus (Labyrinth) 1976, A ménesgazda (The Stud Farm) 1978, Októberi vasárnap (A Sunday in October) 1979, Ideiglenes Paradicsom (Temporary Paradise) 1981, Szeretők (An Afternoon Affair) 1983, A vörös grófnö (The Red Countess) 1985, Valahol Magyarországon (Rearguard Struggle) 1987, Az álommenedzser (The Dream Manager) 1994, Nehéz ember Kaliforniában, Egy 1996, A Nehéz emberek ma 1996. *TV films:* Menekülés Magyarországra (Flight to Hungary) 1980, György Lukács Portray 1986, Volt egyszer egy egyetem (Once Upon a University) 1995, Utak Vásárhelyröl (Roads from Vásárhely) 1996, Két szólamban 2000, Reggeltól hajnalig Válaszúton 2001, Film egy regényről 2002, Egy borértő ember 2003, Polixena and John 2005. *Publication:* Egy film forrásvidéke 1972. *Leisure interest:* gardening. *Address:* Magyar jakobinusok tere 2/3, 1122 Budapest, Hungary. *Telephone:* (1) 356-7227.

KOVÁCS, László; Hungarian politician; *Commissioner for Taxation and Customs Union, European Commission;* b. 3 July 1939; m.; one d.; ed Coll. of Politics, Univ. of Econ. Sciences, Petrik Lajos Tech. School; chemical technician, Medicolor, Kobánya Pharmaceutical Works 1957–66; youth and student movt 1966–75; consultant and Deputy Head, Dept for Int. Relations, Hungarian Socialist Workers' Party 1975–86; mem. Parl. 1990–2004, mem. Foreign Affairs Cttee 1990–93 (Chair. 1993–94); mem. Presidium Hungarian Socialist Party (MSZP) 1990–2004, Head of Parl. Faction 1998–2000, Chair. 1998–2004; Deputy Minister of Foreign Affairs 1986–89, State Sec. 1989–90, Minister of Foreign Affairs 1994–98, 2002–04; EU Commr for Taxation and Customs Union 2004–; Chair.-in-Office OSCE 1995; Vice-Chair. Socialist International 2003–05; Co-Chair. Cen. and East European Cttee 1996–2003;

mem. Council of Wise Men of Council of Europe 1997–99. *Address:* European Commission, 200 Rue de la Loi, 1049 Brussels, Belgium (office). *Telephone:* (2) 299-11-11 (office). *Fax:* (2) 295-01-38 (office). *E-mail:* Laszlo.Kovacs@ec.europa.eu (office). *Website:* ec.europa.eu/commission_barroso/kovacs (office).

KOVÁCS, László F., BEng, BEcons; Hungarian business executive; b. 1943; ed Chemical Univ. of Veszprém, Univ. of Econs, Budapest; Research Engineer, Hungarian Crude Oil and Natural Gas Research Inst. 1967–68; Production Engineer, Leuna Works, Borsodi Vegyi Kombinát, Germany 1968–70, Investment Man. 1971–81, Commercial Dir 1981–90; Man. Dir Müanyagfeldolgozó Kft. Jan.–April 1991; Commr Borsodchem April–Sept. 1991, CEO and Chair. 1991–2001, CEO 2001–06 (resgnd). *Address:* c/o Borsodchem, Bolyai tér 1, 3700 Kazincbarcika, Hungary (office).

KOVALEV, Col-Gen. Nikolai Dmitriyevich; Russian security officer; *Chairman, Committee on Veterans' Affairs;* b. 1949, Moscow; m.; one d.; ed Moscow Inst. of Electronic Machine Construction; on staff system of state security KGB 1974–; served for 2 years in Afghanistan; staff mem. Dept of Fed. Service of Counterespionage of Moscow and Moscow Region –1994; Deputy Dir Fed. Security Service (FSB) 1994–96; Acting Dir, then Dir 1996–98; mem. Security Council of Russia; mem. Comm. on Higher Mil. Titles and Posts, Council on Personnel Policy of Pres. of Russia; mem. to State Duma 1999–; mem. Otechestvo-All Russia faction; Chair. Comm. for Struggle Against Corruption 2000–05, Cttee on Veterans' Affairs 2005–. *Address:* State Duma, Okhotny ryad 1, 103265 Moscow, Russia. *Telephone:* (495) 292-89-19 (office). *Fax:* (495) 292-89-24 (office).

KOVALEV, Sergey Adamovich, PhD; Russian politician; b. 2 March 1930, Seredina-Buda, Ukraine; s. of Adam Vasil'evich Kovalev and Valentina Vasilerna Kovaleva; m. 1st Elena Viktorovna Tokareva 1949; m. 2nd Luydmila Uyr'evna Boitsova 1967; one s. two d.; ed Moscow State Univ.; worked as researcher, Moscow Univ.; active participant in movt for human rights since late 1960s; one of assocs of Academician A. Sakharov, one of founders Initiative Group for Human Rights 1969; ed. Samizdat Bulletin Chronicles of Current Events, expelled from Moscow Univ. 1969; arrested on charge of anti-Soviet propaganda 1974, sentenced to seven years' imprisonment and three years in exile 1974; lived in Kalinin, returned to Moscow 1987; mem. Project Group for Human Rights of Int. Foundation for Survival and Devt of Humanity, Engineer Inst. of Problems of Data Transmission USSR Acad. of Sciences 1987–90; People's Deputy of Russian Fed. 1990–93; Chair. Cttee for Human Rights of Supreme Soviet of Russia 1990–93; Co-Chair. Soviet Del. on Moscow Conf. on Human Rights 1991; Chief of Russian Del. to UN Comm. on Human Rights 1992–95; one of founders and leaders of Vybor Rossii; mem. State Duma (Parl.) 1993–95, 1999–; Chair. Pres.'s Cttee on Human Rights 1994–96; Ombudsman of Russian Fed. 1994–95; Kt of Honour of Chkezia 1997; Council of Europe Human Rights Prize 1995, Olof Palme Prize 2004. *Leisure interests:* hunting, fishing. *Address:* State Duma, Okhotny ryad 1, 103009 Moscow, Russia (office). *Telephone:* (495) 292-93-43 (office). *Fax:* (495) 292-94-64 (office). *E-mail:* www@duma.ru (office). *Website:* www.duma.ru (office).

KOVALEVSKY, Jean, DèsSc; French astronomer; *Astronomer, Observatoire de la Côte d'Azur;* b. 18 May 1929, Neuilly-sur-Seine; s. of Jean Kovalevsky and Hélène Pavloff; m. Jeannine Reige 1956 (died 2003); two s. one d.; ed Univ. of Paris and Ecole Normale Supérieure; Research Asst Paris Observatory 1955–59, Yale Univ. 1957–58; Head of Computing and Celestial Mechanics Service, Bureau des Longitudes 1960–71; Exec. Dir Groupe de Recherches de Geodésie Spatiale 1971–78; Founder and first Dir Centre d'Etudes et de Recherches Géodynamiques et Astronomiques 1974–82, 1988–92; astronomer, Observatoire de la Côte d'Azur, Grasse 1986–; Sec. Bureau Int. des Poids et Mesures 1991–97, Pres. 1997–2004; Pres. Bureau Nat. de Métrologie 1995–2005; mem. French Acad. of Sciences, Int. Acad. of Astronautics, Academia Europaea, Acad. of Sciences of Turin, French Acad. of Tech., Scientific Cttee European Space Agency 1979–81; Chevalier, Légion d'honneur, Commdr, Ordre du Mérite. *Publications:* Introduction to Celestial Mechanics 1967, Traité de Géodésie (with J. Levallois), Vol 4. 1971, Astrométrie moderne 1990, Modern Astronomy 1995 (reprint 2002), Fundamentals of Astrometry (with P.K. Seidelmann) 2004; about 250 scientific papers. *Leisure interests:* gardening, stamp collection. *Address:* 59 Boulevard Émile Zola, 06130 Grasse (home); Gemini, Observatoire de la Côte d'Azur, avenue Copernic, 06130 Grasse, France (office). *Telephone:* 4-93-70-60-29 (home); 4-93-40-53-87 (office). *Fax:* 4-93-40-53-33 (office). *E-mail:* jean.kovalevsky@obs-azur.fr (office). *Website:* www.obs-nice.fr (office).

KOVANDA, Karel, MBA, PhD; Czech diplomatist; *Deputy Director General of External Relations, European Commission;* b. 5 Oct. 1944, Gilsland, UK; s. of Oldřich Kovanda and Ivy Norman; m. Noemi Berová 1993; one s. two d.; ed Prague School of Agric., Massachusetts Inst. of Tech. and Pepperdine Univ., USA; leadership, Czech Nat. Student Union 1968–69; emigrated to USA 1970; lecturer in political science and freelance journalist 1975–80; man. positions in US pvt. sector 1980–90; returned to Czechoslovakia 1990; Czech Ministry of Foreign Affairs 1991–93, Political Dir 1993, Deputy Minister 1997–98; Perm. Rep. of Czech Repub. to UN 1993–97, to UN Security Council 1994–95, to NATO 1998–2005; Deputy Dir Gen. of External Relations, EC 2005–; Pres. ECOSOC 1997; Czech Order of Merit, First Class 2003. *Leisure interests:* literature, theatre, travel, stamp collecting. *Address:* Directorate-General External Relations, European Commission, 1049 Brussels, Belgium (office). *Telephone:* (2) 298-07-65 (office). *E-mail:* Karel.Kovanda@ec.europa.eu (office). *Website:* (office).

KOWALCZYK, Most Rev. Archbishop Józef, DCL; Polish ecclesiastic and diplomatist; *Apostolic Nuncio to Poland;* b. 28 Aug. 1938, Jadowniki Mokre; ed Hosianum Higher Ecclesiastic Seminary, Olsztyn, Catholic Univ. of Lublin, Pontifical Gregorian Univ., Rome, Roman Rota Studium; ordained priest 1962; employee, Roman Rota, Congregation for the Discipline of the Sacraments; organizer and Head of Polish Section, State Secr. 1978–89; Titular Archbishop of Heraclea and Apostolic Nuncio in Poland 1989–; Hon. mem. Soc. of Polish Canon Lawyers; Dr hc (Agric. Acad., Kraków 1999, Cardinal S. Wyszyński Univ. 2000, Catholic Univ. of Lublin 2001). *Publications:* Dojrzewanie czasu 1998, Na drodze konsekrowanej 1999, Służyć słowu 2000 and ed. of Karol Wojtyła's papers and Polish edition of papal teaching (14 vols). *Address:* Nuncjatura Apostolska, al. J. Ch. Szucha 12, Skr. poczt. 163, 00-582 Warsaw, Poland (office). *Telephone:* (22) 6288488 (office). *Fax:* (22) 6284556 (office).

KOWLESSAR, Saisnarine; Guyanese politician and banking executive; fmr Gov. of Bank for Guyana, IMF; Minister of Finance –2006. *Address:* c/o Ministry of Finance, Main and Urquhart Streets, Georgetown, Guyana (office).

KOWNACKI, Piotr, LLB; Polish civil servant and petroleum industry executive; *Chief of the Chancellery of the President of Poland;* b. 8 Oct. 1954, Warsaw; m. 1976; two d.; ed Univ. of Warsaw; with Inst. of Law Studies, Polish Acad. of Sciences 1979–83; Press Officer Sejm (Parl.) 1983–87; Adjudicating Counsellor, Office of the Constitutional Tribunal 1987–89; Dir Office of Govt Plenipotentiary for Reform of Local Govt Structures 1989–91; Under-Sec. of State in Office of Council of Ministers 1991; Vice-Pres. Supreme Chamber of Control 1991–99, 2001–06; Vice-Pres. Bank Ochrony Srodowiska (Bank for Environmental Protection) 1999–2001; Vice-Pres. for Auditing and Regulation, Deputy CEO and mem. Man. Bd Polski Koncern Naftowy (PKN) Orlen 2006–07, Pres. and CEO Jan.–July 2008; Chair. Supervisory Bd Unipetrol; Sec. of State and Deputy Chief of Chancellery of Pres. of Poland July–Sept. 2008–, Chief of Chancellery Sept. 2008–. *Address:* Chancellery of the President of the Republic of Poland, ul. Wiejska 10, 00-902 Warsaw, Poland (office). *Telephone:* (22) 695-29-00 (office). *Fax:* (22) 695-12-53 (office). *E-mail:* fnowaczynski@prezydent.pl (office). *Website:* www.president.pl (office).

KOYAMBOUNOU, Gabriel Jean Edouard; Central African Republic politician; b. Bangui; ed Univ. of Abidjan, École Nat. des Douanes, Françaises, Neuilly-sur-Seine, France; fmr Inspector Gen.; Prime Minister of Cen. African Repub. 1995–96; Minister of State in charge of Communication, Posts and Telecommunications, New Technologies and Francophone Affairs –2003; Second Vice-Pres. Mouvement pour la libération du peuple centrafricain (MLCP); Pres. Handball Fed.; Grand Officier, Ordre du Merite; Gold Medal in Sport. *Publication:* Mémoire sur le 'Droit Douanier'. *Leisure interest:* handball. *Address:* BP 42, Bangui, Central African Republic (home).

KOZACHENKO, Leonid Petrovich; Ukrainian engineer, economist and politician; *President, Ukrainian Agrarian Confederation;* b. 14 May 1955, Veprik, Kiev region; m.; two d.; ed Ukrainian Acad. of Agric., All-Union Acad. of Foreign Trade; worked in agric. enterprises in Fastov region 1972–86, head of collective farm in Fastiv dist 1979; party functionary CP of Ukraine 1986–88; Deputy Head of Dept, Ukrainian Ministry of Agric. 1991–2001, Dir Agroland 2000–01, Deputy Prime Minister of Agric. 2001–02; f. Ukrainian League of Businessmen 1993; Co-f. Ukrainian Asscn of Corn, Nat. Asscn of Stock Exchanges, Ukrainian Asscn for Ecology Protection; Founder and Pres. Ukrainian Agrarian Confed. 1998–; mem. Presidential Comm. on Agric., Presidium Ukrainian Union of Businessmen; mem. Co-ordination Council of Businessmen at Ministry of Agrarian Policy; Charter of Honour of Verkhovna Rada; Merited Worker of Agric. of Ukraine 1998. *Address:* Ukrainian Agrarian Confederation, Saksaganskogo str., 53/80, office 807, Kiev 01033, Ukraine (office). *Telephone:* (44) 284-32-38 (office). *E-mail:* agroconf@agroconf.org (office). *Website:* www.agroconf.org (office).

KOZAI, Toyoki, BS, MS, PhD; Japanese horticulturist, university administrator and academic; *President, Chiba University;* b. 25 Sept. 1943, Tokyo; ed Chiba Univ., Univ. of Tokyo; Research Asst, Dept of Agricultural Eng, Faculty of Agric., Univ. of Osaka Pref. 1973–77; Assoc. Prof., Dept of Horticulture, Faculty of Horticulture, Chiba Univ. 1977–90, Prof., Dept of Bioproduction Science 1990–2005, Dean Faculty of Horticulture 1999–2005, Pres. Chiba Univ. 2005–; Post-doctoral Fellow, Centre for Agro-Biological Research, Wageningen, Netherlands 1974–75; Visiting Researcher, Dept of Biological and Agricultural Eng, Cook Coll., Rutgers Univ., NJ, USA 1989; Prize for Academic Achievement, Soc. of Agricultural Meteorology of Japan 1982, Prize for Academic Achievement, Japanese Soc. of High Tech. in Agric. 1991, Prize for Academic Achievement, Japanese Soc. of Environment Control in Biology 1992, Prize for Academic Achievement, Japanese Acad. of Agricultural Sciences and Yomiuri Newspaper Co. 1997, Int. Scientific and Technological Award, Kunming City, People's Repub. of China 2002, Friendship Award, State Admin of Foreign Experts Affairs, People's Repub. of China 2002, Medal with Purple Ribbon, Japanese Govt 2002. *Publications:* numerous scientific papers in professional journals. *Address:* Office of the President, Chiba University, 1-33 Yayoi-cho, Inage-ku, Chiba-shi, Chiba 263-8522, Japan (office). *Telephone:* (43) 251-1111 (office). *Fax:* (43) 290-2041 (office). *E-mail:* kokusai@office.chiba-u.jp (office). *Website:* www.chiba-u.jp (office).

KOZAK, Dmitrii Nikolayevich; Russian lawyer and politician; *Deputy Chairman of the Government;* b. 7 Nov. 1958, Voroshylovhrad (now Kirovohrad) Oblast, Ukraine; m.; two s.; ed Vinnytsia Polytechnical Inst., Leningrad (now St Petersburg) State Univ.; Asst to Prosecutor of Leningrad; on staff, Asscn of Marine Trade Ports 1985–89; on staff, Exec. Cttee Leningrad City Council 1990–91; Head of Law Dept Office, St Petersburg 1991–94; Chair. Law Cttee Admin. St Petersburg; mem. Govt of St Petersburg, mem. Comm. on Human Rights 1994–96; apptd Deputy Gov. St Petersburg 1998, resgnd end of year; pvt. law practice 1998–99; Deputy Head of Admin. of Russian Pres. on Legal Problems May–Aug. 1999; First Deputy Head of Govt of

Russian Fed. 1999, Head 1999–2000; Deputy Head of Admin. of Russian Pres. 2000–03, First Deputy Head 2003–04; Head of Govt Admin. March–Sept. 2004; Presidential Rep. in Southern Fed. Okrug 2004–07; Minister of Regional Devt 2007–08; Deputy Chair. of Govt 2008–. *Address:* Office of the Government, 103274 Moscow, Krasnopresnenskaya nab. 2, Russia (office). *Telephone:* (495) 205-57-35 (office). *Fax:* (495) 205-42-19 (office). *Website:* www .government.ru (office).

KOZAK, Roman Ye.; Russian actor and stage director; *Artistic Director, Moscow Pushkin Drama Theatre;* b. 29 June 1957, Vinnitsa, Ukraine; ed Studio School of Moscow Art Theatre; actor Moscow Chekhov Art Theatre, concurrently Studio Theatre Chelovek 1983–89; f. and Artistic Dir fifth studio of Moscow Art Theatre 1989–92; Artistic Dir Moscow Stanislavsky Drama Theatre 1992–94; Stage Dir Moscow Art Theatre 1995–2000; Artistic Dir Moscow Pushkin Drama Theatre 2001–; teacher Studio School of Moscow Art Theatre; Grand Prix Int. Theatre Festival, Munich, Germany, Grand Prix Int. Theatre Festival, Riga, Latvia. *Plays as actor include:* Days of the Turbins, The Seagull, Amadeus (Moscow Art Theatre), Emigrants (Studio Theatre Chelovek). *Plays as stage director:* Cinzano (Studio Theatre Chelovek), Masquerade (fifth studio, Moscow Art Theatre), Don Quixote (Moscow Stanislavsky Drama Theatre), The Most Important, The Dance of Death, Othello (Riga Theatre of Russian Drama), Love in Crimea, Marriage, Forest Berry (Moscow Art Theatre), Birthday of Smirnova (Stary Theatre, Kraków, Poland), Cinzano (Troy Theatre, Glasgow, Scotland). *Address:* Moscow Pushkin Drama Theatre, Tverskoy blvd 23, Moscow 123104, Russia (office). *Telephone:* (495) 203-85-87 (office); (495) 203-23-86 (office).

KOZAKOV, Mikhail Mikhailovich; Russian actor and theatre director; b. 14 Oct. 1934, Leningrad; s. of Mikhail Kozakov; m. 1st; three c.; m. 3rd Anna Yampolskaya; one s. one d.; ed Moscow Art Theatre Studio School; actor Moscow Mayakovsky Theatre 1958–59, Sovremennik Theatre 1959–64, Moscow Art Theatre 1964–72; Theatre on Malaya Bronnaya 1972–81; worked in Israel as actor, Ghesher Theatre, Chamber Theatre Tel-Aviv 1991–96; returned to Russia 1996; actor, Moscow Mayakovsky Theatre 1996–; f. own theatre co.; gives poetic concerts; debut in film Murder on Dante Street 1956; Peoples' Artist of Russia 1980, USSR and Russian State Prizes. *Films include:* The Year 1918, Nine Days of a Year, Eugénie Grandet, An Amphibian Man, A Straw Hat, A Comedy of Errors. *Films directed include:* Anonymous Star, Prokrovsky Gates, If to Believe Lopotukhin, Shadow, Faustus. *Publications:* Third Call, Sketches in the Sand Actors' Book. *Address:* Mayakovsky Theatre, B. Nikitskaya str. 17, 103009 Moscow, Russia. *Telephone:* (495) 277-06-17 (home).

KOŽENÁ, Magdalena; Czech singer (mezzo-soprano); b. 26 May 1973, Brno; pnr Sir Simon Rattle; one s.; ed Conservatoire, Brno, Coll. of Performing Arts, Bratislava; guest singer, Janáček Opera, Brno 1991–; debut as soloist, Vienna Volksoper 1996–97; appearances include Bach's B Minor Mass at the QEH, London 2000, Salzburg Festival debut as Zerlina in Don Giovanni 2002, charity concerts following floods in Czech Repub. 2002, Idamante in Idomeneo at Glyndebourne 2003 and Salzburg Festival, Cherubino for Bavarian State Opera, Metropolitan Opera, Dorabella at Salzburg Easter Festival, Berlin, Varvara, Dorabella, Zerlina at Metropolitan Opera, Theatre des Champs Elysees, Covent Garden debut in La Cenerentola 2007; regular broadcasts for Czech radio and television; tours in Europe, USA, Japan, Venezuela, Taiwan, Hong Kong, Republic of Korea, Canada; roles include Dorabella in Così fan tutte, Isabella in Italiana in Algeri (Rossini), Venus in Dardanus (Rameau), Mercedes in Carmen, Annius in La Clemenza di Tito, Paris in Paride ed Elena, lead in Orfeo ed Eurydice (both Gluck), lead in Hermia (Britten), Poppea in L'Incoronazione di Poppea (Monteverdi), Mélisande (Debussy),; Chevalier, Ordre des Arts et des Lettres 2003; first place in Int. Scheider Competition 1992, first place in Int. Mozart Competition, Salzburg 1995, George Solti Prize (France), Youngster of Arts, Europe 1996, Orphée d'Or, L'Académie du Disque Lyrique (France) 1999, Diapason d'Or (France) 2000, Echo Klassik Best New Artist (Germany) 2000, Gramophone Award (London) 2001, Gramophone Artist of the Year 2004, Person of the Year in Culture (Czech Repub.) 2002, 2003. *Recordings include:* Bach Arias (Harmony Magazine Award 1998), Johann Sebastian Bach Cantatas 2000, G.F. Handel Italian Cantatas 2000, G.F. Handel Messiah 2001, Magdalena Kožená – Le belle imagini (Echo Klassik Award 2002, Gold Record of Universal 2003) 2002, Johann Sebastian Bach Arias (Gold Record of Universal 2003, Platinum Record of Universal 2003) 2003, G.F. Handel – Giulio Cesare 2003, Magdalena Kožená – French Arias (Gramophone Award 2003) 2003, Magdalena Kožená – Songs 2004, Magdalena Kožená – Lamento 2005, Paride ed Elena 2005, La Clemenza di Tito 2006, Enchantment 2006, Mozart Arias 2006, Ah! Mio Cor 2007. *Leisure interests:* philosophy, music, swimming, cycling. *Address:* Central European Music Agency, Kapucínské nám. 14, 602 00 Brno, Czech Republic (office); Askonas Holt Ltd, Lincoln House, 300 High Holborn, London, WC1V 7JH, England (office); Národní divadlo, Dvořákova 11, 600 00 Brno, Czech Republic (home). *Telephone:* (5) 42213053 (office); (20) 7400-1720 (office). *Fax:* (5) 42213056 (office); (20) 7400-1723 (office). *E-mail:* david@cema-music.com (office); peter.bloor@askonasholt.co.uk (office); obchodni.ndb@seznam. *Website:* www.cema-music.com (office); www.askonasholt.co.uk (office); www .ndbrno.cz; www.kozena.cz.

KOZHIN, Vladimir Igorevich; Russian business executive; b. 28 Feb. 1959, Troitsk, Chelyabinsk Region; m. Alla Kozhina; one s.; ed Leningrad Electrotech. Inst.; instructor, Head of Div., Petrograd Dist Comsomol Cttee; then on staff Research-Production Co. Azimuth, Dir-Gen. Russian-Polish Jt Co. Azimuth Int. Ltd 1991–93; Dir-Gen. St Petersburg Asscn of Jt Cos 1993–94; Head NW Cen. Fed. Dept of Currency and Export Control 1994–99, Head 1999–2000; Head, Office of Russian Pres. 2000–, Head Presidential Property Man. Asscn. *Address:* Office of the President, Staraya pl. 4, 103132

Moscow, Russia (office). *Telephone:* (495) 925-35-81 (office). *Fax:* (495) 206-07-66 (office). *E-mail:* president@gov.ru (office). *Website:* www.kremlin.ru (office).

KOZHOKIN, Mikhail Mikhailovich, CandHist; Russian journalist; b. 23 Feb. 1962, Moscow; ed Moscow State Univ.; Jr researcher, researcher, Sr researcher Inst. of USA and Canada, USSR (now Russian) Acad. of Sciences 1988–92, Sr researcher Cen. of Econ. and Political Studies, worked with G. Yavlinsky 1992–93; Head Information Dept ONEXIM bank 1993–96; Deputy Chair. Exec. Cttee 1996–; Asst to First Deputy Chair. of Russian Govt, mem. Govt Comm. on Econ. Reform 1997–; Dir Holding Co. Interros on work with mass media and public relations; Chair. Bd of Dirs Izvestia (newspaper) 1997–98, Ed.-in-Chief 1998–2003 (resgnd). *Leisure interests:* travelling, water tourism. *Address:* c/o Izvestia, Tverskaya str. 18, korp. 1, 127994 Moscow, Russia (office).

KOZHOKIN, Yevgeny Mikhailovich, DHist; Russian politologist and historian; *Director, Institute for Strategic Studies;* b. 9 April 1954, Moscow; m.; two d.; ed Moscow State Univ.; on staff Inst. of World History, USSR Acad. of Sciences 1984–90; People's Deputy of Russian Fed. 1990–93; Founder and Dir Inst. for Strategic Studies 1994. *Film:* Producer and idea's author for documentary A Lonely Battalion. *Publications:* The French Workers: From the Great French Revolution to the Revolution of 1848 1985, The State and the People: From the Fronde to the Great French Revolution 1989, The History of Poor Capitalism 2005, and more than 100 others. *Leisure interest:* swimming. *Address:* Institute for Strategic Studies, Flotskaya str. 15, 125413 Moscow, Russia (office). *Telephone:* (495) 454-92-64 (office). *Fax:* (495) 454-92-65 (office). *E-mail:* prime@riss.ru (office). *Website:* www.riss.ru (office); www .roscommira.ru (office).

KOZLÍK, Sergej; Slovak politician; b. 27 July 1950, Bratislava; ed Univ. of Econs; clerk with Price Authority 1974–88; Head Dept of Industrial Prices, Ministry of Finance 1988–90; Dir Exec. Dept of Antimonopoly Office 1990–92; Sec. Movt for a Democratic Slovakia (became political party 2000) 1992–; Vice-Premier, Govt of Slovakia 1993–94; Minister of Finance of Slovak Repub. 1994–97; Deputy to Nat. Council 1994–2004; mem. European Parl. (Non-attached Mems) 2004–, mem. Cttee on Budgets, Substitute mem. Cttee on Econ. and Monetary Affairs, mem. Del. to ACP-EU Jt Parl. Ass.; Gov. World Bank 1994–98 Alt. Gov. IMF 1994–98. *Address:* European Parliament, Bâtiment Altiero Spinelli, 01E252, 60 rue Wiertz, 1047 Brussels, Belgium (office). *Fax:* (2) 284-92-57 (office). *E-mail:* sergej_kozlik@nrsr.sk (office). *Website:* www.europa.eu (office).

KOZLOV, Alexey Semenovich; Russian composer, saxophone player and band leader; b. 13 Oct. 1935, Moscow; m. 1st; one s.; m. 2nd Lyalya Adburakhmanovna Absalyamova; ed Moscow Inst. of Architecture, Moscow Music Coll.; researcher, Inst. of Design 1963–76; started playing saxophone in youth clubs 1955; founder and leader of jazz quintet 1959, jazz band of café Molodezhnoye 1961–66; arranger and soloist orchestra VIO-66; teacher Moscow Experimental Studio of Jazz Music 1967–76; Founder and music Dir jazz-rock ensemble Arsenal 1973–, festivals and tours including Delhi and Bombay 1989, Woodstock 1990, Jazz Rally, Düsseldorf 1993, Carnegie Hall 1995, Bonn 1996, with Arsenal, Chamber Soloists of Moscow, the Shostakovich String Quartet, Ars Nova Trio; master classes in towns of Russia and Oklahoma City Univ. 1994; Gen.-Man. Jazz Div., Goskoncert 1995–97; mem. Musical Cttee under Pres. of Russia 1997–; Art Dir Radio Jazz, Moscow 2001–; author of TV programmes, All That Jazz, Improvisation; composer of jazz, film and theatre music; Merited Artist of Russia; his ensemble Arsenal awarded Ovation Prize as the best jazz band in Russia 1995. *Publications:* Rock: Roots and Development 1989, Memoirs—My 20th Century, He-Goat on the Saxophone 2000; numerous articles in music journals. *Address:* Shchepkin str. 25, Apt. 28, 129090 Moscow, Russia (home). *Telephone:* (495) 688-31-56 (home); (916) 183-88-82 (home). *E-mail:* askozlov@mtu-net.ru (home); askozlov1@ jandex.ru (home). *Website:* www:musiclab.ru (office); www:arsenalband.com (office).

KOZLOV, Valery Yassilyevich, DrSc; Russian politician; *Vice-President, Russian Academy of Sciences;* b. 1 Jan. 1950, Kostyly, Ryazan Region; ed Moscow State Univ.; Sr Researcher Moscow State Univ. 1972, Deputy Dean, Chief Scientific Sec. –1998; Adviser to Ministry of Gen. and Professional Educ. (later Ministry of Educ.) 1998–99, Deputy Minister 1999–; Corresp. mem. Russian Acad. of Sciences 1997–2000, mem. 2000–, Vice-Pres. 2002–; Founder, Ed.-in-Chief Int. Journal of Regular and Chaotic Dynamics; State Prize of the Russian Fed. 1994. *Address:* Russian Academy of Sciences, Leninsky prosp. 14, GSP-I, 117910 Moscow, Russia (office). *Telephone:* (495) 237-45-32 (office). *Fax:* (495) 954-26-21 (office). *E-mail:* kozlov@pran.ru (office). *Website:* www.pran.ru (office).

KOZOL, Jonathan, BA; American writer; b. 5 Sept. 1936, Boston; s. of Dr Harry L. Kozol and Ruth Massell Kozol; ed Harvard Coll. and Magdalen Coll., Oxford, UK; Rhodes Scholar 1958; teacher in Boston area 1964–72; lecturer at numerous univs 1973–2006; Guggenheim Fellow 1972, 1984; Field Foundation Fellow 1973, 1974; Rockefeller Fellow 1978, Sr Fellow 1983; f. Education Action! (non-profit org.); mem. Editorial Bd Greater Good Magazine. *Publications:* Death At An Early Age (Nat. Book Award 1968) 1967, Free Schools 1972, The Night Is Dark 1975, Children of the Revolution 1978, On Being a Teacher 1979, Prisoners of Silence 1980, Illiterate America 1985, Rachel and Her Children: Homeless Families in America (Robert F. Kennedy Book Award 1989, Conscience in Media Award of the American Soc. of Journalists and Authors 1989) 1988, Savage Inequalities: Children in America's Schools (New England Book Award 1992) 1991, Amazing Grace (Anisfield-Wolf Book Award 1996) 1995, Ordinary Resurrections 2000, The Shame of the Nation: The Restoration of Apartheid Schooling in America (Nation Magazine Book Award) 2005, Letters to a Young Teacher 2007. *Address:* PO Box 145, Byfield,

MA 01922; Education Action!, A Project of The Cambridge Institute for Public Education, 16 Lowell Street, Cambridge, MA 02138, USA (office). *Telephone:* (617) 945-5568 (office). *Fax:* (617) 945-5562 (office); (978) 462-8557 (home). *E-mail:* jonathankozol@gmail.com; educationactioninfo@gmail.com. *Website:* ed-action.org.

KOZYREV, Andrey Vladimirovich, CandHist; Russian politician; b. 27 March 1951, Brussels, Belgium; m. 2nd; one d.; ed Moscow State Inst. of Int. Relations; worker Kommunar factory, Moscow 1968–69; mem. staff USSR Ministry of Foreign Affairs, various posts, to Head of Sector 1974–86, Head of Dept of Int. Orgs 1986–90; Foreign Minister of Russian Fed. 1990–95; Deputy State Duma (Parl.) 1995–99; mem. Bd Dirs, Dir E European Div. ICN Pharmaceuticals 1998–; Lecturer, Moscow Inst. of Int. Relations 1996–. *Publications:* Transfiguration 1995; numerous articles on foreign policy. *Address:* ICN Pharmaceuticals, Uscheva str. 24, 119048, Moscow, Russia. *Fax:* (495) 383-66-00, ext. 2101.

KPOTSRA, Roland Yao; Togolese politician, diplomatist and civil servant; *Permanent Representative, United Nations;* b. 20 Feb. 1947, Lom; m.; two c.; joined Foreign Ministry as Desk Officer in Admin. Affairs Div. 1974, Dir Treaties and Legal Affairs Div. 1982–88, Dir Admin and Personnel 1987–90; Sec. Perm. Mission to UN, New York 1976–79, Counsellor 1979–, Chargé d'affaires April–Aug. 1980, Perm. Rep. to UN 1996–2002 and currently; Chargé de Mission, Ministry of Foreign Affairs and Co-operation 1992–93, Sec.-Gen. 1993–96, Minister of Foreign Affairs and Co-operation 2002–03; First Counsellor Embassy in Brazil 1980–82; Chargé d'affaires in Zimbabwe 1990–91; Leader of Del. to 63rd session of OAU Council of Ministers, 10th Ministerial Conf. of Movt of Non-Aligned Countries 1995; Deputy Head of Del. to OAU 50th Ass.; headed team at int. French-speaking conf. on conflict resolution from African perspective 1995; Lecturer in Diplomatic History, École Nat. d'Admin, Togo; Chevalier, Nat. Order of Merit 1984; Officer, Order of Mono 1996. *Address:* Permanent Mission of Togo to the UN, 112 East 40th Street, New York, NY 10016, USA (office). *Telephone:* (212) 490-3455 (office). *Fax:* (212) 983-6684 (office). *E-mail:* onu@republicoftogo.com (office); togo@un .int (home).

KRAAG-KETELDIJK, Lygia; Suriname politician; *Minister of Foreign Affairs;* b. 1941; Dir of Political Affairs, Cabinet of the Pres. 2000–05; Minister of Foreign Affairs 2005–. *Address:* Ministry of Foreign Affairs, 25 Lim A Po Street, POB 25, Paramaribo, Suriname (office). *Telephone:* 471209 (office). *Fax:* 410411 (office). *E-mail:* buza@sr.net (office).

KRABBE, Jeroen Aart; Dutch actor, artist and director; b. 5 Dec. 1944; m. Herma van Geemert; three s.; ed Acad. of Fine Arts and Toneel Drama School, Amsterdam; acted in repertory theatre and formed own acting co. within the Netherlands; Commdr, Order of the Lion (Netherlands) 1999; Best Actor Award, Madrid, Sorrento, Oxford 1984, Anne Frank Medal 1985, Golden Heart of Rotterdam 1986, Golden Calf Award 1996. *Theatre includes:* The Diary of Anne Frank, Clouds, Relatively Speaking, How the Other Half Lives, Cyrano de Bergerac, Danton's Death, Love's Labours Lost, Sleuth, A Day in the Death of Joe Egg, Sweet Bird of Youth, Love Letters, Amadeus 2005. *TV appearances:* William of Orange (Netherlands), Miami Vice, Dynasty, One for the Dancer, Sweet Weapon, Only Love, Jesus, Stalin (all American TV); host talkshows; numerous roles in plays and series. *Films include:* Soldier of Orange 1977, A Flight of Rainbirds 1981, The Fourth Man 1984, The Shadow of Victory 1985, Turtle Diary, No Mercy 1987, The Living Daylights, A World Apart, Crossing Delancey, Melancholia 1989, The Prince of Tides 1991, Stalin 1991, Kafka 1991, King of the Hill 1991, The Fugitive 1993, Farinelli 1994, Immortal Beloved 1994, The Disappearance of García Lorca 1995, Business for Pleasure 1996, The Honest Courtesan 1996, Cinderella 1997, Left Luggage (directorial debut; Berlin Film Festival award 1998) 1997, Dangerous Beauty 1998, Discovery of Heaven (actor and dir, Rembrandt Best Film Award 2001) 2001, Ocean's Twelve 2004, Deuce Bigalow 2004, Man with a Camera 2004, Snuff 2006. *Publications:* The Economy Cookbook. *Address:* Van Eeghenstraat 107, 1071 EZ Amsterdam, Netherlands.

KRAEHE, Graham J., AO; Australian business executive; *Chairman, Bluescope Steel Ltd;* fmr Man.-Dir Pacifica Ltd and WH Wylie Ltd (now Monroe); Man.-Dir Southcorp Ltd 1994–2001; apptd Dir Nat. Australian Bank Ltd 1997, Chair. 2004–05; mem. Bd of Dirs BHP Steel Ltd (now Bluescope Steel Ltd) 2002–, currently Chair; mem. Reserve Bank of Australia Bd 2007–; mem. Bd of Dirs Djerriwarrh Investments Ltd 2002–; fmr mem. Bd of Dirs Djerriwarrh Investments Ltd, Innovation Economy Advisory Bd for Vic.; fmr mem. Bd of Dirs Email Ltd, News Corpn, Brambles Ltd, Business Council of Australia; mem. Foundation Council, Australian Davos Connection; fmr Nat. Pres. Metal Trade Industry Asscn; Chair. Australian Future Directions Forum. *Address:* Bluescope Steel Ltd, Level 11, 120 Collins Street, Melbourne, Vic. 3000, Australia (office). *Telephone:* (3) 9666-4000 (office). *Fax:* (3) 9666-4111 (office). *Website:* www.bluescopesteel.com (office).

KRAEHENBUEHL, Pierre, BA; Swiss international organization executive; *Director of Operations, International Committee of the Red Cross;* b. 1966; m.; three c.; ed Univ. of Geneva; began a career in journalism and photography, but then began work at Lutheran World Fed.; joined Int. Cttee of Red Cross (ICRC) 1991, first served in field operations as del. in El Salvador and Peru, given managerial responsibilities in Afghanistan 1993–95, and subsequently in Bosnia and Herzegovina, served as Head of Operations for Cen. and South-Eastern Europe in Geneva, personal adviser to Jakob Kellenberger (Pres. ICRC) 2000–02, Dir of Operations 2002–. *Address:* International Committee of the Red Cross, 19 avenue de la Paix, 1202 Geneva, Switzerland (office). *Telephone:* (22) 734-60-01 (office). *Fax:* (22) 733-20-57 (office). *E-mail:* press .gva@icrc.org (office). *Website:* www.icrc.org (office).

KRAFT, Christopher Columbus, Jr., BS; American engineer and space agency administrator (retd); b. 28 Feb. 1924, Phoebus, Va; s. of Christopher Columbus Kraft and Vanda Olivia Kraft (née Suddreth); m. Elizabeth Anne Turnbull 1950; one s. one d.; ed Virginia Polytechnic Inst.; mem. Langley Aeronautical Lab., Nat. Advisory Cttee for Aeronautics 1945; selected to join Space Task Group on Project Mercury 1958; Flight Dir of all Mercury Missions: head of mission operations Gemini program; Dir of Flight Operations, Manned Spacecraft Center 1963–69; elected mem. Nat. Acad. of Eng 1970; Deputy Dir Johnson Space Center 1970–72; Dir NASA Johnson Space Center 1972–82; Fellow, American Inst. of Aeronautics and Astronautics 1966, American Astronautical Soc.; Hon. DEng (Indiana Inst. of Tech.) 1966, (St Louis Univ., Ill.) 1967, (Villanova) 1979; Arthur S. Fleming Award 1963, NASA Outstanding Leadership Award 1963, Spirit of St Louis Medal, American Soc. of Mechanical Engineers 1967, NASA Distinguished Service Medal (twice) 1969, Chevalier, Légion d'honneur 1976, Nat. Civil Service League Career Service Award 1976, W. Randolph Lovelace Award (American Astronautical Soc.) 1977, Daniel and Florence Guggenheim Award (Int. Astronautics Fed.) 1978, AAIA von Karman Lectureship Award 1979, Goddard Memorial Trophy 1979, Roger W. Jones Award 1979, inducted into Virginia Aviation Hall of Fame 1979. *Publications:* Flight: My Life in Mission Control 2001. *Address:* c/o Dutton Books, 375 Hudson Street, New York, NY 10014, USA.

KRAFT, Robert Paul, BS, MS, PhD; American astronomer and academic; *Professor Emeritus of Astronomy and Astrophysics and Astronomer Emeritus, UC Observatories / Lick Observatory, University of California, Santa Cruz;* b. 16 June 1927, Seattle, Wash.; s. of Victor P. Kraft and Viola E. Ellis; m. Rosalie A. Reichmuth 1949; two s.; ed Univ. of Washington and Univ. of California at Berkeley; Instructor in mathematics and astronomy, Whittier Coll. 1949–51; Asst Prof. of Astronomy, Indiana Univ. 1956–58; Asst Prof. of Astronomy, Univ. of Chicago 1958–59; mem. staff, Mt Wilson and Palomar Observatories 1960–67; Astronomer and Prof., Lick Observatory 1967–92, Astronomer and Prof. Emer. 1992–, Acting Dir Lick Observatory 1968–70, 1971–73, Dir 1981–91; Dir Univ. of California Observatories 1988–91; Visiting Fellow, Joint Inst. of Laboratory Astrophysics, Univ. of Colo 1970; Pres. American Astronomical Soc. 1974–76; Vice-Pres. Int. Astronomical Union 1982–88, Pres. 1997–2000; mem. NAS, American Acad. of Arts and Sciences; Nat. Science Foundation Fellow 1953–55, Fairchild Scholar, California Inst. of Tech. 1980; Beatrice Tinsley Visiting Prof., Univ. of Texas 1991–92; Henry Norris Russell Lecturer 1995; DSc hc (Ind. Univ.) 1995; Warner Prize, American Astronomical Soc. 1962, Distinguished Alumnus Award, Univ. of Wash. 1995, Bruce Medal 2005. *Publications:* articles in professional journals. *Leisure interests:* music (classical and rock), oenology, duplicate bridge. *Address:* Lick Observatory, University of California, Santa Cruz, CA 95064, USA (office). *Telephone:* (831) 459-3281 (office). *Fax:* (831) 426-3115 (office). *E-mail:* kraft@ucolick.org (office). *Website:* astro.ucsc.edu (office).

KRAFT, Vahur, BA; Estonian banker; *New Country Manager, Nordea Bank Finland Plc (Estonia Branch);* b. 11 March 1961, Tartu; s. of Ülo Kraft and Aime Kraft; m. Anne Kraft 1990; one s.; ed Tartu Univ.; with Eesti Hoiupank (Estonian Savings Bank), rising to Head of Br. 1984–90; Vice-Chair. Bd Dirs Eesti Sotsiaalpank (Estonian Social Bank) 1990–91; Deputy Gov. Eesti Pank (Bank of Estonia) 1991–95, Gov. 1995–2005, Vice-Gov. for Estonia of IMF 1992–95, Gov. 1995–2005; New Country Man. for Nordea Bank Findland Plc (Estonia Br.) 2005–; Chair. Bd of Trustees Tartu Univ. Foundation; Chair. Supervisory Bd Estonian Deposit Guarantee Fund; mem. Supervisory Council, Financial Supervision Authority, Council of the Stabilization Reserves, Bd Centre for Strategic Initiatives; Hon. mem. Tallinn Jr Chamber of Commerce; Order of White Star, Second Class. *Address:* Nordea Bank Finland Plc (Estonia Branch), Hobujaama 4, 15068 Tallinn, Estonia (office). *Telephone:* (2) 628-3200 (office). *Fax:* (2) 628-3201 (office). *E-mail:* tallinn@ nordea.com (office). *Website:* www.nordea.ee (office).

KRAGGERUD, Egil, DPhil; Norwegian academic; *Professor Emeritus of Classical Philology, University of Oslo;* b. 7 July 1939, S Höland; s. of John Kraggerud and Borghild Westeren; m. Beate Sinding-Larsen 1963; three s. one d.; ed ed Oslo Katedralskole and Oslo Univ.; Research Fellow, Univ. of Oslo 1965–67, Lecturer in Classics 1967–68, Prof. of Classical Philology 1969–92, now Prof. Emer.; Ed. Symbolae Osloenses 1972–94; mem. Norwegian Acad. of Science and Letters, Royal Norwegian Soc. of Sciences and Letters, Acad. Europaea; Thorleif Dahl's Literary Award 1992. *Publications:* Aeneisstudien 1968, Horaz und Actium 1984, Aeneiden (7 vols) 1983–89. *Leisure interests:* skiing, concerts. *Address:* Classical Department, University of Oslo, PO Box 1007, Blindern, 0316 Oslo (office); Bygdöy allé 13, 0257 Oslo, Norway (home). *Telephone:* 22-44-27-44 (home). *E-mail:* egil.kraggerud@kri .uio.no (home). *Website:* www.uio.no (office).

KRAGULY, Radovan; British artist; b. 10 Sept. 1935, Prijedor, Yugoslavia; s. of Dragoja Kraguly and Mileva Kraguly; ed Acad. of Fine Arts, Belgrade, Cen. School of Arts and Crafts, London; lecturer Cambridge School of Art and Tech. –1965, Manchester Coll. of Art 1965–67, London Coll. of Printing and Design 1967–69, Ecole des Beaux Arts, Mons 1969–78, Parson School of Art and Design 1978–88; represented in perm. and major collections at Museum of Modern Art, Paris, British Museum, Victoria and Albert Museum, Museum of Modern Art, New York, Leicester Univ. Library, Library of Congress, Washington, City Art Gallery, Sarajevo, Art Council of Wales, Cardiff, Power Gallery, Sydney, Prenten Cabinet, Brussels, Nat. Museum and Gallery of Wales, Cardiff, Fond Nat. d'Art Contemporain, Paris, Manchester City Art Gallery, City Art Gallery, Banja Luka, Nat. Library of Wales, Aberystwyth, The Whitworth Art Gallery, Manchester, South London Art Gallery; numerous prizes and awards including Printmaking Prize (Jazu-Zagreb) 1962, Yugoslav Trienale Prize 1967, Grafika Creativa Prize (Helsinki) 1975, Int.

Grand Prix Fondation Pierre Cornette de St Cyr (Paris) 1978, Int. Grand Prix, Drawing Biennial (Rijeka) 1980. *Publications include:* La Vache dans l'imaginaire 1989, The Imaginary Cow of Kraguly 1990, Kraguly–Gallery Vera Van Laer 1992, Hathor: Voies Lactées Kraguly 1995, Kraguly Hathor: VLK 1998. *Address:* Llwyngarth Fawr, Comin Coch, Builth Wells, Powys, LD2 3PP, Wales (home); 22 rue Quincampoix, 75004 Paris, France. *Telephone:* (1597) 860340 (Wales) (home); 1-42-74-70-47 (Paris). *Fax:* (1597) 860340 (Wales) (home); 1-42-74-70-47 (Paris). *E-mail:* nenak@free.fr (home).

KRAIJENHOFF, Jonkheer Gualtherus; Dutch business executive; b. 11 July 1922; s. of Albertus Kraijenhoff and Gualthera Kraijenhoff; m. Yvonne Kessler; one s. two d.; ed Switzerland; Royal Air Force (UK) pilot 1943–47; joined NV Organon, Oss 1947, Man. Dir 1957; mem. Bd of Man. NV Kon. Zwanenberg-Organon 1959, Pres. 1963; mem. Bd of Man., Kon. Zout-Organon NV 1967, Pres. 1969; Vice-Pres. AKZO NV, Arnhem 1969, Pres. 1971–78, mem. Supervisory Council May 1978– (fmr Chair.); Dir S. G. Warburg and Co. 1978–; Dir APV Holdings 1983–; Pres. Netherlands Red Cross 1966–86, Chair. Cen. Laboratories for Blood Transfusion, Red Cross 1990–; KtStJ Netherlands Lion. *Address:* Zomerland, Louiseweg 15, Nijmegen, Netherlands (home).

KRAINEV, Vladimir Vsevolodovich; Russian pianist; b. 1 April 1944, Krasnoyarsk; m. Tatyana Tarasova; ed Moscow State Conservatory with Heinrich Neuhaus and Stanislav Neuhaus; début with orchestra as child prodigy in Kharkov 1953, in Moscow 1963; prize winner of several int. competitions; soloist with maj. orchestras in many European cultural centres and festivals; played with Carlo Maria Giulini, Pierre Boulez, John Pritchard, Dmitry Kitayenko; teacher in Moscow Conservatory 1987–91, Hochschule für Musik in Hanover 1991–; People's Artist of Russia 1984, USSR State Prize 1986. *Repertoire includes:* most of classical concertos and all concertos by Mozart and Prokofiev. *Address:* Staatliche Hochschule für Musik und Theater, Walderseestrasse 100, Hanover, Germany. *Telephone:* (3212) 3641485 (Hanover); (495) 158-24-56 (Moscow).

KRAIRIKSH, Khun Sakthip, BA; Thai diplomatist; b. 5 Sept. 1947; m. M. R. Benchapa Krairiksh; three c.; ed Webb School, Calif., Boston Univ., Mass., USA, Nat. Defence Coll.; joined Ministry of the Interior 1971; Office of Nat. Security Council, Prime Minister's Office 1976–1979; Sec. to Minister of Foreign Affairs 1979–82; Dir-Gen. of Protocol Dept 1988–90, Dir-Gen. of Information Dept and Foreign Ministry Spokesman 1990–93; Deputy Chief of Mission in Washington, DC 1982–85; Amb. at Large 1986; Amb. to Cambodia 1993, to Japan 1999–2001, to USA (non–resident to Jamaica and Dominican Rep.) 2001–04; Perm. Sec. of Ministry of Tourism and Sports 2004–07; mem. Bd of Dirs Natural Park Public Co Ltd, Thai Beverage PCL 2005–, Tourism Authority and Nat. Cultural Cttee 1990–92, HRH Prince Mahidol Awards 1992; Grand Companion (Third Class), Most Illustrious Order of Chula Chom Klao 1996, Kt Commdr (Second Class) 1999, Kt Grand Cordon (Special Class) Most Exalted Order of the White Elephant 1997, Order of Sacred Treasure (Gold and Silver Star) 1991, Grand Cordon of Order of Rising Sun 2001 (Japan), Commdr of Most Distinguished Order of St Michael and St George (UK) 1996; Hon. PhD (Soka Univ., Japan). *Address:* c/o Board of Directors, Thai Beverage PCL, 14 Viphavadi Rangsit Rd., Chomphon, Chatuchak Bangkok, 10900, Thailand. *Website:* www.thaibev.com.

KRAJICEK, Richard; Dutch professional tennis player; b. 6 Dec. 1972, Rotterdam; s. of Petr Krajicek and Ludmilla Krajicek; m. Daphne Dekkers 1999; one s. one d.; started playing tennis aged three; turned professional 1989; reached semi-finals Australian Open 1992; Wimbledon Men's Singles Champion 1996; won 20 titles to retirement in June 2003; now competes on Masters Tour; f. Richard Krajicek Foundation 1993; Arthur Ashe Humanitarian of Year Award 2000. *Leisure interests:* basketball, golf. *Address:* c/o Richard Krajicek Foundation, Olympisch Stadion 3, 1076 DE Amsterdam, Netherlands (office). *Telephone:* (20) 6705400 (office). *Fax:* (20) 6705390 (office). *E-mail:* info@krajicek.nl (office). *Website:* www.krajicek.nl (office).

KRALL, Diana; Canadian singer, pianist and composer; b. 16 Nov. 1966, Nanaimo, BC; m. Elvis Costello 2003; twin s.; ed Berklee Coll., Boston; began classical piano aged four; regular tours of North America, Britain, Europe and the Far East. *Film appearance:* De-Lovely 2004. *Recordings include:* albums: Steppin' Out 1993, Only Trust Your Heart 1994, All For You 1995, Love Scenes 1997, When I Look In Your Eyes (Grammy Award Best Jazz Vocal) 1999, The Look Of Love 2001, Heartdrops: Vince Benedetti Meets Diana Krall 2003, The Girl in the Other Room 2004, Christmas Songs 2005, From This Moment On (Juno Award for Vocal Jazz Album Of The Year 2007) 2006, The Very Best Of Diana Krall 2007, Quiet Nights 2009. *Address:* S.L. Feldman and Associates, Stephen Macklam and Sam Feldman, 200–1505 West Second Avenue, Vancouver, BC V6H 3Y4, Canada (office). *Website:* www.dianakrall.com.

KRALL, Hanna; Polish journalist and writer; b. 20 May 1937, Warsaw; m. Jerzy Szperkowicz; one d.; ed Univ. of Warsaw; reporter, Życie Warszawy 1955–66, Polityka 1966–, corresp. in Moscow 1966–69; corresp., Tygodnik Powszechny, Gazeta Wyborcza; freelance writer early 1980s–; Solidarity Cultural Prize 1985, Prize of Minister of Culture and Art 1989, J. Shocken Literary Prize (Germany), Kulture Foundation Award 1999, Leipzig Book Fair Award 2000, Herder Prize 2005. *Publications include:* Na wschód od Arbatu (East of the Arbat) 1972, Zdążyć przed Panem Bogiem (Shielding the Flame) 1977, Sześć odcieni bieli (Six Shades of White) 1978, Sublokatorka (The Sub-tenant) 1985, Hipnoza (Hypnosis) 1989, Trudności ze wstawaniem (Difficulties Getting Up) 1990, Taniec na cudzym weselu (Dance at a Stranger's Wedding) 1993, Co się stało z naszą bajką (What's Happened to Our Fairy Tale) 1994, Dowody na istnienie (Proofs of Existence) 1996, Tam już nie ma żadnej rzeki (There is No River There Anymore) 1998, To ty jesteś Daniel (So You Are Daniel) 2001, Wyjątkowo długa linia (Incredible Long Line) 2004, Król kier znów na wylocie (King of Hearts) 2006 (books translated into over 18 languages). *Address:* Bacewiczówny 7/27, 02-786 Warsaw, Poland (home); Stowarzyszenie Pisarzy Polskich, ul. Krakowskie Przedmieście 87/89, 00-079 Warsaw, Poland (office). *Telephone:* (22) 6433164. *Fax:* (22) 6433164.

KRAMAR, Marjan, BEcons; Slovenian business executive; *President of the Management Board, Nova Ljubljanska Banka d.d.;* ed Univ. of Ljubljana; began career with Helios Domzale 1982; Dir of Planning, Analyses and Business Counselling, Ljubljanska Banka Trbovlje 1983–88; mem. Man. Bd Gradbeno Podjetje SGD Beton 1988–89; Adviser to Slovenian Rep., SFRY Presidency 1989–91; Head of Prime Minister's Cabinet 1991–94; mem. Man. Bd Slovene Export Corpn 1994–2004, Pres. 1998–2004; Pres. Man. Bd Nova Ljubljanska Banka d.d. 2004–; Chair. Supervisory Bd ETI Elektroelement Izlake; fmr Vice-Chair.Supervisory Bd Revoz. *Address:* Nova Ljubljanska Banka d.d., Trg republike 2, 1520 Ljubljana, Slovenia (office). *Telephone:* (1) 4250155 (office). *Fax:* (1) 4250331 (office). *E-mail:* info@nlb.si (office). *Website:* www.nlb.si (office).

KRAMER, Larry D., BA; American writer; b. 25 June 1935, Bridgeport, Conn.; ed Yale Univ.; Production Exec. Columbia Pictures Corpn, London 1961–65; Asst to Pres. United Artists, New York; producer-screenwriter, Women in Love 1970; Co-founder Gay Men's Health Crisis Inc., New York 1981; Founder ACT UP-AIDS Coalition to Unleash Power, New York 1988. *Publications:* Faggots 1978, The Normal Heart (play) 1985, Just Say No 1988, The Furniture of Home 1989, The Destiny of Me 1993, The People Themselves: Popular Constitutionalism and Judicial Review 2005.

KRAMER, Dame Leonie Judith, AC, DBE, DPhil, FAHA, FACE; Australian academic; *Professor Emerita of Australian Literature, University of Sydney;* b. 1 Oct. 1924; d. of the late A. L. Gibson and G. Gibson; m. Harold Kramer 1952 (deceased); two d.; ed Presbyterian Ladies Coll., Melbourne and Univs of Melbourne and Oxford; Tutor, St Hugh's Coll., Oxford 1949–52; Assoc. Prof. Univ. of NSW 1963–68; Prof. of Australian Literature, Univ. of Sydney, 1968–89, Prof. Emer. 1989–; Deputy Chancellor, Univ. of Sydney 1988–91, Chancellor 1991–2001; Vice-Pres. Australian Asscn for Teaching of English 1967–70; Vice-Pres. Australian Soc. of Authors 1969–71; mem. Nat. Literature Bd of Review 1970–73; mem. Council, Nat. Library of Australia 1975–81; Pres., then Vice-Pres. Australian Council for Educ. Standards 1973–; mem. Univs Comm. 1974–86; Commr Australian Broadcasting Comm. (ABC) 1977–81, Chair. 1982–83, Dir Australia and NZ Banking Group 1983–94, Western Mining Corpn 1984–96, Quadrant Magazine Co. Ltd 1986–99 (Chair. 1988–99); mem. Council Nat. Roads and Motorists' Asscn 1984–95, Council Foundation for Young Australians 1989–2000, Asia Soc. 1991–2000; Nat. Pres. Australia-Britain Soc. 1984–93, Order of Australia Asscn 2001–04; mem. Council ANU 1984–87; mem. Bd of Studies, NSW Dept. of Educ. 1990–2001; Chair. Bd of Dirs Nat. Inst. of Dramatic Art 1987–91, Deputy Chair. 1991–95; Sr Fellow, Inst. of Public Affairs 1988–96; Commr Electricity Comm. (NSW) 1988–95; mem. World Book Encyclopaedia Advisory Bd 1989–99, Int. Advisory Cttee Encyclopaedia Britannica 1991–99, NSW Council of Australian Inst. of Co. Dirs 1992–2001; Chair. Operation Rainbow Australia Ltd 1996–2003; mem. Governing Council Old Testament House, Canberra 1998–2001; Gov. Medical Benefits Fund 2005–; Hon. Fellow, St Hugh's Coll. Oxford 1994, St Andrew's Coll., Univ. of Sydney, Hon. Prof. Dept of English (Sydney) 2002, Janet Clarke Hall, Univ. of Melbourne 2005; Hon. DLitt (Tasmania), 1977 (Queensland) 1991, (NSW) 1992; Hon. LLD (Melbourne) 1983, (ANU) 1984; Hon. MA (Sydney) 1989; Britannica Award 1986. *Publications include:* (as L. J. Gibson): Henry Handel Richardson and Some of Her Sources 1954; (as Leonie Kramer): Australian Poetry 1961 (ed.) 1962, Companion to Australia Felix 1962, Myself When Laura 1966, A Guide to Language and Literature (with Robert D. Eagleson) 1977, A. D. Hope 1979, The Oxford History of Australian Literature (ed.) 1981, The Oxford Anthology of Australian Literature (ed. with Adrian Mitchell) 1985, My Country: Australian Poetry and Short Stories – Two Hundred Years (two vols) 1985, James McAuley: Poetry, Essays etc. (ed.) 1988, David Campbell: Collected Poems (ed.) 1989, Collected Poems of James McAuley 1995. *Leisure interests:* gardening, music. *Address:* A20–John Woolley, Room S365, University of Sydney, Sydney NSW 2006 (office); 12 Vaucluse Road, Vaucluse, NSW 2030 Australia (home). *Telephone:* (2) 93514164 (office). *Fax:* (2) 93514773 (office). *E-mail:* L.Kramer@staff.unisyd.edu.au (office).

KRAMMER, Peter H., MD; German immunologist and academic; *Speaker, Tumorimmunology Program, German Cancer Research Centre;* b. 2 April 1946, Rheydt; ed Univ. of Freiburg; Internship in Internal Medicine and Pathology, Univ. of Freiburg, Univ. Hosp. and Inst. of Pathology 1971–72, Study mem., Low Molecular Weight Nuclear RNA 1972, Internship in Surgery 1972–73; mem. Basel Inst. for Immunology, Switzerland 1973–75; Assoc., German Cancer Research Centre, Inst. for Immunology and Genetics, Heidelberg 1976, Acting Head, Div. of Immunogenetics 1981–88, Head 1989–, Acting Dir 1990–; mem. Max-Planck Inst. for Immunology, Freiburg 1976; Visiting Prof., Dept of Microbiology, Univ. of Texas Health Science Center at Dallas, Tex., USA 1981; Visiting Scientist, Centre for Molecular Biology, Heidelberg 1984–85; Speaker, Tumorimmunology Program, German Cancer Research Centre, Heidelberg 1993–; mem. German Immunological Soc. 1973, American Asscn for Cancer Research, European Molecular Biology Org. 1999, APOGENIX Foundation 2000; mem. Medical Faculty, Heidelberg Univ. 1978; mem. Scientific Cttee Health Research Council; mem. Scientific Bd German Cancer Research Centre 1978–83, 1990–94, 1995–97, 1997–2000; mem. Editorial Bd Immunology Letters, Immunobiology, Cell Death and Differentiation, Cancer Research, European Journal of Immunology, Journal of Clinical Investigation, International Journal of Cancer; Order of Merit (FRG) 1991; King Phillip Award for Leukemia Research 1991, Robert Koch Prize 1995, Behring Lecturer 1995, Meyenburg Prize 1996, Heinz-Ansmann

Prize 1996, Kitasato-Behring Prize 1996, German Cancer Prize 1996, Cancer Research Award, Wilhelm Warner Foundation 1997, Avery Landsteiner Prize 1998, Theodor Kocher Lecture 2000, Ludwick Hirszfeld Medal, Polish Soc. for Experimental and Clinical Immunology 2000, Ernst-Jung Prize for Medicine 2000, Norman Heatley Lecturer, Univ. of Oxford, UK 2000, Annual MRC Lecturer, SOT Meeting 2001, Genius Biotech Award APOGENIX 2001, Lautenschläger Research Prize 2003. *Publications:* more than 360 articles in medical and scientific journals. *Address:* Tumorimmunology Program, Deutsches Krebsforschungszentrum, Im Neuenheimer Feld 280, 69120 Heidelberg, Germany (office). *Telephone:* (6221) 423718 (office). *Fax:* (6221) 411715 (office). *E-mail:* p.krammer@dkfz.de (office). *Website:* www.sfb405.uni-hd.de/Krammer.html; www.zmbh.uni-heidelberg.de/mcb/Brochure/Krammer.html (office).

KRAMNIK, Vladimir Borisovich; Russian chess master; b. 25 June 1975, Tuapse, Krasnodar Territory, Russia; m.; started playing chess at age of 4; cand. for Master title 1986; Grandmaster title 1991; World Champion among young people 16–18 years of age, winner World Chess Olympiads Manila 1992, Moscow 1994, Yerevan 1996; winner maj. int. tournaments and matches; since 1995 holds place among the 3 highest-rated players of the world; took part in World Championship 1993; ranked number one world player 1996; won match against Gary Kasparov for World Championship Oct. 2000, won unified world chess championship 2006; winner of Chess Oscar 2000, 2001. *Publication:* Kramnik: My Life and Games (autobiog. with Takov Damsky). *Telephone:* (495) 495-32-72 (Moscow) (home). *Website:* www.kramnik.com.

KRANJC, Jože, LLB; Slovenian business executive; *President of the Management Board, Intereuropa Global Logistics Service Ltd;* ed Univ. of Ljubljana; joined Intereuropa Global Logistics Service Ltd 1969, with Legal Dept 1969–74, Man. of Gen. Admin. Services 1975–78, Dir of Forwarding Unit (TOZD) 1978–95, Pres., Man. Bd 1995–; Pres., Koper Regional Chamber of Commerce and Industry; mem., Bd of Transport and Communications Asscn, Slovenian Chamber of Commerce; mem. Supervisory Bd, several cos; Nat. Award for Outstanding Commercial and Entrepreneurial Achievements (Slovenian Chamber of Commerce and Industry) 2000. *Address:* Intereuropa Global Logistics Service Ltd, Vojkovo nabrezje 32, 6000 Koper, Slovenia (office). *Telephone:* (5) 6641000 (office). *Fax:* (5) 6642674 (office). *Website:* www.intereuropa.si (office).

KRANJEC, Marko, PhD; Slovenian economist, academic and central banker; *Governor, Banka Slovenije (Bank of Slovenia);* b. 12 April 1940, Novo mesto; ed Faculty of Econs, Univ. of Ljubljana; fmr Asst Prof., Faculty of Public Admin, Univ. of Ljubljana, Prof of Public Finance 2002–06; Head, Analysis Dept Ljubljanska Bank 1968–70; Researcher, Inst. of Econ. Research 1970–76, Research Advisor 1986–90; macroeconomist, OECD, Paris –1984; economist, World Bank, Washington, DC 1984–86; first Minister of Finance of ind. Slovenia 1990–91; Vice-Gov. Banka Slovenije (Bank of Slovenia) 1991–97, Gov. 2007–; mem. Governing Council European Cen. Bank, Govt's Strategic Council for Econ. Devt; fmr mem. Supervisory Bd Krka, Novo Mesto; Silver Order of Freedom of Repub. of Slovenia 2001. *Address:* Banka Slovenije, Slovenska 35, 1505 Ljubljana, Slovenia (office). *Telephone:* (1) 4719000 (office). *Fax:* (1) 2515516 (office). *E-mail:* bsl@bsi.si (office). *Website:* www.bsi.si (office).

KRANTZ, Judith, BA; American author; b. 9 Jan. 1928, New York City; d. of Jack David Tarcher and Mary Brager; m. Stephen Krantz 1954 (died 2007); two s.; ed Wellesley Coll.; contrib. to Good Housekeeping 1948–54, McCalls 1954–59, Ladies Home Journal 1959–71; Contributing Ed. Cosmopolitan 1971–79. *Publications:* Scruples 1978, Princess Daisy 1980, Mistral's Daughter 1982, I'll Take Manhattan 1986, Till We Meet Again 1988, Dazzle 1990, Scruples Two 1992, Lovers 1994, Spring Collection 1996, The Jewels of Teresa Kant 1998, Sex & Shopping: Confessions of a Nice Jewish Girl 2000. *Address:* c/o Esther Newberg, International Creative Management Inc. (ICM), 40 West 57th Street, New York, NY 10019, USA (office). *Telephone:* (212) 556-5600 (office). *Website:* www.icmtalent.com (office).

KRĄPIEC, Rev. Mieczysław Albert; Polish ecclesiastic and professor of philosophy; *Professor, Catholic University of Lublin;* b. 25 May 1921, Berezowica Mała n. Zbaraż (now Ukraine); ed Dominican Friars' Coll., Kraków, St Thomas Pontifical Univ., Rome, Italy, Catholic Univ. of Lublin; Dominican friar; ordained priest 1945, Lecturer in Philosophy, Dominican Friars' Coll., Kraków 1946–; teacher, Catholic Univ. of Lublin 1951, Prof. 1962–, Dean, Christian Philosophy Faculty 1959–62, 1969–70, Rector 1970–83, Head of Metaphysics Faculty; mem. Polish Acad. of Sciences 1994–, Polish Acad. of Arts and Crafts, St Thomas Aquinas Pontifical Univ., Rome, European Acad. of Sciences and Arts, Salzburg; fmr Chair. and mem. Catholic Univ. of Lublin Scientific Soc.; Commdr's Order of Polonia Restituta, Grand Officer's Cross of Order of Leopold II (Belgium), Order of Academic Insignia of the French Acad.; Dr hc (Pontifical Inst. of Medieval Studies, Toronto) 1989, (Catholic Univ. of Louvain, Belgium) 1991, (Tarnopol Univ. of Pedagogics, Ukraine) 1991, (Pedagogical Univ. of Tarnopol, Ukraine) 1993. *Publications:* Theory of the Analogy of Existence of Metaphysical Methodology (jtly) 1964, Metaphysics 1966, Aristotelian Concept of Substance 1966, I: A Man 1974, A Man and Natural Law 1975, Language and Real World 1985, About Understanding Philosophy 1991, At the Foundations of Understanding Culture 1991, Introduction to Philosophy (jtly) 1992, 1996, About Human Policy 1993, To Regain the Real World 1997, Considerations on the Nation 1998. *Leisure interests:* picking mushrooms, cooking. *Address:* ul. Złota 9, 20-112 Lublin, Poland. *Telephone:* (81) 5328727.

KRARUP, Thorleif, BSc, BComm; Danish business executive; *Chairman, Dangaard Telecom A/S;* b. 1952; Chair. Man. Bd Nykredit 1987–91; Group CEO Tryg Nykredit Holding 1991–92; Group CEO Unidanmark 1992–2000; Chair. Exec. Bd Unibank 1992–2000; Deputy CEO Nordic Baltic Holding 2000; Group CEO Nordea 2000–02, Sr Vice-Pres. 2002–2004; Chair. TDC –2006; Chair. Dangaard Telecom A/S 2006–; Deputy Chair. Lundbeck A/S, Lundbeck Foundation LFI A/S, ALK-Abello A/S; mem. Bd of Dirs Bang & Olufsen A/S, Lundbeckfonden, Scion DTU A/S, Group 4 Securicor. *Address:* Dangaard Telecom Holding A/S, Transitvej 12, 6330 Padborg, Denmark (office). *Telephone:* 73-30-30-80 (office). *Fax:* 73-30-30-94 (office). *Website:* www.dangaard.com/dangaardtelecomuk (office).

KRASHENINNIKOV, Pavel Vladimirovich, DJur; Russian lawyer; b. 21 June 1964, Polevskoye, Sverdlovsk Region; m.; one d.; ed Sverdlovsk Inst. of Law; teacher, Sverdlovsk Inst. of Law 1991–93; lecturer, Moscow State Univ. 1994–; Deputy Head, Chief Dept of Housing Policy, State Cttee on Construction of Russian Fed. 1993–; Head, Dept of Civil and Econ. Law, Ministry of Justice 1993–96; Deputy Chair. State Cttee on Antimonopoly Policy and Support of New Econ. Structures 1996–97; First Deputy Minister of Justice 1997–98, Acting Minister March 1998, Minister 1998–99; Co-ordinator, Pres., Comm. for Counteraction against Political Extremism in Russia 1998–99; mem. State Duma (Union of Right-Wing Forces faction) 1999, re-elected as ind. (later joined Yedinaya Rossiya faction) 2003–, Chair. Legislative Cttee. *Publications:* over 70 articles on civil law. *Address:* State Duma, Okhotny ryad 1, 103265 Moscow, Russia (office). *Telephone:* (495) 292-92-10 (office). *Fax:* (495) 292-97-82 (office).

KRASIKOV, Anatoly Andreyevich, DHist; Russian journalist and scholar; *Chief Researcher, Institute of Europe, Russian Academy of Sciences;* b. 3 Aug. 1931, Moscow; m.; one d.; ed Moscow Inst. of Int. Relations; on staff USSR Telegraph Agency TASS 1955–92; Deputy Dir-Gen. ITAR-TASS 1978–92; on staff of Pres. Yeltsin, Head of Press, Exec. Sec., Council on Interaction with Religious Orgs of Russian Presidency 1992–96; Chair. Int. Christianity Cttee 1996; Head, Centre for Studies of Problems of Religion and Soc.; Chief Researcher, Inst. of Europe, Russian Acad. of Sciences 1996–; Pres. Russian Chapter, Int. Religious Liberty Asscn 1997–2003, Hon. Pres. Euro-Asia Chapter, 2004–; Public Policy Scholar, Woodrow Wilson Center, Washington, DC 2000; Galina Starovoitova Fellow on Human Rights and Conflict Resolution, Kennan Inst., Washington, DC 2004. *Publications:* Church-State Relations in Russia 1998, Proselytism and Religious Liberty in Russia 1999, The Enigma of Liberty 2001, Russian Orthodoxy: Striving for Monopoly? 2004. *Leisure interests:* music, archives, tourism. *Address:* Institute of Europe, Mokhovaya str. 11, Bldg 3v, 103873 Moscow, Russia (office). *Telephone:* (495) 292-23-04 (office). *Fax:* (495) 200-42-98 (office). *E-mail:* ankras@ok.ru (office). *Website:* www.ieras.ru (office).

KRASIN, Yury Andreyevich, DSc; Russian politologist and academic; *Head, Department for Analysis of Socio-Political Processes, Institute of Sociology, Russian Academy of Sciences;* b. 7 June 1929, Penza; one d.; ed Leningrad State Univ.; Lecturer, Asst Prof., Leningrad State Pedagogical Inst. 1952–60; Asst Prof., Inst. of Professional Skill Improvement, Moscow State Univ. 1960–63; Sr Fellow, Inst. of Philosophy USSR (now Russian) Acad. of Sciences 1963; consultant, Int. Div. CP Cen. Cttee; Prof., Moscow Inst. of Professional Skill Improvement at Moscow State Univ. 1963–75; Prof., Head of Dept, Prorector, Acad. of Social Sciences at CPSU Cen. Cttee 1975–87; Rector Inst. of Social Sciences at CPSU Cen. Cttee 1987–91; Dir-Gen. Foundation of Social and Political Studies 1991–92; Dir Centre of Social Programmes, Int. Foundation of Social, Econ. and Politological Studies 1992–97; Adviser, Gorbachev Foundation 1997–; Head, Dept for Analysis of Socio-Political Processes, Inst. of Sociology, Russian Acad. of Sciences 1993–; mem. Presidium Acad. of Political Science; mem. Russian Acad. of Natural Sciences; Dr hc (Inst. of Sociology, Russian Acad. of Sciences) 2008; Lomonosov Prize of Moscow State Univ. 1968, USSR State Prize 1980, Pitirim Sorokin Silver Medal 2008. *Publications:* 20 books including Dialectic of the Revolutionary Process 1972, Capitalism Today: Paradoxes of Development (jtly) 1989, Russia at the Crossroads: Authoritarianism or Democracy 1998, Russia: Quo Vadis? (with A. Galkin) 2003, Public Policy in Russia (ed.) 2005, Social Inequality and Public Policy (ed.) 2007; articles on social movts, democratic reform in Russia, civil, social and political matters. *Leisure interests:* classical music, skiing. *Address:* Institute of Sociology, 117218 Moscow, Krzhizhanovskogo str. 24/35, korp. 5 (office); 121433 Moscow, Malaya Philevskaya str. 44, Apt 11, Russia (home). *Telephone:* (495) 719-09-40 (office); (499) 144-29-83 (home). *Fax:* (495) 945-74-01 (office). *E-mail:* krasinyua@mtu-net.ru (home). *Website:* www.spbrc.nw.ru (office).

KRASNIQI, Jakup; Kosovo politician; *President, Kosovo Assembly;* b. 1951, Negrofc-Drena; fmr political prisoner; apptd Press Spokesman of Kosovo Liberation Army (KLA, Ushtria Çlirimtare e Kosovës—UÇK) 1998; mem. Democratic Party of Kosovo (PDK), Sec.-Gen. 2005, currently Chair. Parl. Group of PDK, Pres. Kosovo Ass. 2007–. *Publications:* books: Kthesa e Madhe – Ushtria Çlirimtare e Kosovës, Kosova in a Historical Context 2007, Një luftë ndryshe për Kosovën 2007. *Address:* Kuvendi i Kosovës/Skupština Kosova (Kosovo Assembly), 10000 Prishtina, Rruga Nënë Terezë, Kosovo (office). *Telephone:* (38) 211186 (office). *Fax:* (38) 211188 (office). *E-mail:* info@assembly-kosova.org (office). *Website:* www.assembly-kosova.org (office).

KRASOVSKIY, Nikolay Nikolayevich, DrPhysMathSc; Russian mathematician and mechanician; *Chief Scientific Researcher, Institute of Mathematics and Mechanics, Ural Scientific Centre, Russian Academy of Sciences;* b. 7 Sept. 1924, Sverdlovsk (now Ekaterinburg); ed Ural Polytechnic Inst.; teaching and scientific work, Ural Polytechnic Inst. 1949–55, 1957–59; mem. CPSU 1954–91; Research worker, Inst. of Mechanics, USSR (now Russian) Acad. of Sciences 1955–57, Prof. Ural Univ. 1959–70; scientific and admin. work, Inst. of Math. and Mechanics of Ural Scientific Centre, USSR (now Russian) Acad. of Sciences 1970–, Dir 1970–77, Chief Scientific

Researcher 1977–; Corresp. mem. USSR (now Russian) Acad. of Sciences 1964–68, mem. 1968–; Hero of Socialist Labour 1974, Lenin Prize 1976, USSR State Prize 1984, Gold Medal of Liapunov, Russian Acad. of Sciences 1992, Great Gold Medal of Lomonosov, Russian Acad. of Sciences 1996, Order of Lenin, Order of the Red Banner, Order for Services to the Motherland (Second Class) and other decorations. *Publications:* works in field of stability of motion theory and theory of control systems, including Stability of Motion 1963, Game-Theoretical Control Problem (with A. I. Subbotin) 1988, Control under Lack of Information (with A. N. Krasovskiy) 1995. *Address:* c/o Institute of Mathematics and Mechanics, GSP-384, S. Kovalevskaya Str. 16, 620219 Ekaterinburg, Russia (office). *Telephone:* (343) 74-40-13 (office); (343) 59-41-73 (home). *Fax:* (343) 74-25-81 (office).

KRASTS, Guntars; Latvian politician and economist; b. 16 Oct. 1957, Riga, Latvia; m.; three s.; ed Latvian State Univ.; researcher Inst. of Agric. Econ. 1983–91; Chair. Exec. Bd RANG Ltd 1991–95; Minister of Econs 1995–97; Prime Minister of Latvia 1997–98; Vice-Prime Minister for EU Affairs 1998–99; Chair Saeima (Parl.) Foreign Affairs Cttee 1998–2002, European Affairs Cttee 2002–04; MEP 2004–, Vice-Chair. Cttee on Economic and Monetary Affairs. *Publications:* numerous publs in Latvia and abroad on econ. and foreign policy issues. *Leisure interests:* swimming, skiing. *Address:* European Parliament, rue Wiertz ASP A4F370. 1047 Brussels, Belgium. *Telephone:* (2) 284-59-09 (office). *Fax:* (2) 284-99-09 (office). *E-mail:* g.krasts@europarl.eu.int (office).

KRAUS, Andreas, DPhil; German historian and academic; *Professor Emeritus of Bavarian History, University of Munich;* b. 5 March 1922, Erding; s. of Karl Kraus and Katharina Mayer; m. Maria Kastner 1947; one d.; ed Univ. of Munich; teacher 1949–61; Extraordinary Prof. of History, Philosophical and Theological Hochschule, Regensburg 1961–67; Prof., Univ. of Regensburg 1967–77; Prof. of Bavarian History, Univ. of Munich 1977–, Prof. Emer. 1989–; mem. Bayerischen Akad. der Wissenschaften 1971; Bayerischer Verdienstorden 1983, Bundesverdienstkreuz 1993, Komtur des St Gregorius Ordens mit Stern 1995, Bayerische Volksstiftung 1998. *Publications:* Die historische Forschung an der bayerischen Akademie der Wissenschaften 1959, Vernunft und Geschichte 1963, Das päpstliche Staatssekretariat 1964, Civitas Regia 1972, Regensburg 1979, Die naturwissenschaftliche Forschung an der bayerischen Akademie der Wissenschaften 1979, Geschichte Bayerns 1983, Handbuch d. Bayerischen Geschichte Vol. II 1988, Maximilian I., Bayerns Grosser Kurfürst 1990, Handbuch d. Bayerischen Geschichte Vol. III 1-3, 1996–2001, Erding. Stadt mit vielen Gesichtern 1997, Das Gymnasium der Jesuiten in München (1558–1773) 2001, König Ludwig I, Handbuch d. Bayerischen Geschichte Vol. IV 2002. *Address:* Nederlingerstrasse 30A, 80638 Munich 19; Landsbergerstr. 74, 86938 Schondorf, Germany. *Telephone:* (89) 1575354 (home); (81) 92407 (Schondorf).

KRAUSS, Alison; American country and bluegrass singer and musician (fiddle); b. 23 July 1971, Champaign, IL; singer, musician since age 14; lead singer with Union Station 1987–; Int. Bluegrass Music Asscn Awards for Female Vocalist of the Year 1990, 1991, 1993, 1995, Country Music Television Award for Independent Video of the Year (for I've Got That Old Feeling) 1991, Entertainer of the Year 1991, 1995, Country Music Asscn Awards for Female Vocalist of the Year, Single of the Year (for When You Say Nothing At All), Vocal Event of the Year (for Somewhere In The Vicinity Of The Heart, with Shenandoah), and Horizon Award 1995, Grammy Award for Female Country Vocal Performance (for Baby, Now That I've Found You) 1995, Country Music Television Award for Rising Video Star of the Year 1995, GAVIN Americana Artist of the Year 1995, Great British Country Music Award for Int. Female Vocalist of the Year 1996, for Int. Bluegrass Band of the Year 1997, 1998, 1999, 2000, Grammy Awards for Best Country Performance by a Duo or Group (for Looking In The Eyes Of Love), for Best Country Instrumental Performance (for Little Liza Jane) 1997, Gospel Music Asscn Dove Award for Bluegrass Recorded Song of the Year (for Children of the Living God, with Fernando Ortega) 1998, Canadian Country Music Award for Vocal/Instrumental Collaboration (for Get Me Through December, with Natalie Mac Master) 2000, Int. Bluegrass Music Asscn Award for Gospel Recorded Event of the Year (for I'll Fly Away, with Gillian Welch) 2001, Grammy Award for Country Performance by a Duo or Group (for The Lucky One) 2001, Grammy Award for Best Country Instrumental Performance (for Cluck Old Hen) 2003, Country Music Asscn Award for Best Video and Music Event (for Whiskey Lullaby, with Brad Paisley) 2004, Grammy Awards for Best Country Performance by a Duo or Group with Vocal (for Restless, with Union Station), for Best Country Instrumental Performance (for Unionhouse Branch with Union Station) 2006, for Best Pop Collaboration with Vocals (for Gone Gone Gone with Robert Plant) 2008, (for Rich Woman with Robert Plant) 2009, for Record of the Year (for Please Read the Letter with Robert Plant) 2009, for Best Country Collaboration with Vocals (for Killing the Blues with Robert Plant) 2009, CMA Award for Musical Event of the Year (for Gone Gone Gone with Robert Plant) 2008. *Recordings include:* albums: Different Strokes 1985, Too Late to Cry 1987, Two Highways (with Union Station) 1989, I've Got That Old Feeling (Grammy Award for Bluegrass Recording 1990, Int. Bluegrass Music Asscn Award for Album of the Year 1991) 1990, Every Time You Say Goodbye (with Union Station) (Grammy Award for Bluegrass Recording 1992, Int. Bluegrass Music Asscn Award for Album of the Year 1993) 1992, I Know Who Holds Tomorrow (with The Cox Family) (Grammy Award for Southern, Country or Bluegrass Gospel Album) 1994, Now That I've Found You: A Collection 1995, So Long So Wrong (with Union Station) (GAVIN Americana Album of the Year, Grammy Award for Best Bluegrass Album) 1997, Forget About It 1999, New Favorite (with Union Station) (Grammy Award for Best Bluegrass Album) 2001, Live (with Union Station) (Int. Bluegrass Music Asscn Awards Album of the Year, Grammy Award for Best Bluegrass Album 2003) 2002, Lonely Runs Both Ways (Grammy Award for Best Country Album, with Union Station 2006) 2004, A Hundred Miles or More 2007, Raising Sand (with Robert Plant) (Grammy Awards for Album of the Year 2009, for Best Contemporary Folk/Americana Album 2009) 2007. *Address:* D. S. Management, 2814 12th Avenue S, Nashville, TN 37204, USA (office); Union Station Land Inc., PO Box 121711, Nashville, TN 37212, USA. *Website:* www.alisonkrauss.com.

KRAUSZ, Ferenc, DipEng, DrTechn; Hungarian/Austrian physicist and academic; *Director, Max Planck Institute of Quantum Optics;* b. 17 May 1962, Mór, Hungary; m.; two c.; ed Eötvös Loránd Univ., Budapest, Budapest Univ. of Tech., Vienna Univ. of Tech.; Asst Prof., Vienna Univ. of Tech. 1996–98, Prof. of Electrical Eng 1999–2004; Dir Max Planck Inst. of Quantum Optics, Garching, Germany 2003–; Prof. of Physics, also Chair. of Experimental Physics, Ludwig-Maximilians-Univ., Munich 2004–; mem. Austrian Acad. of Sciences 2003–; Dr hc (Tech. Univ. Budapest) 2005; Austrian Physical Soc. Fritz Kohlrausch Award 1994, Federal Ministry of Science and Educ. START Award 1996, Ernst Abbe Foundation Carl Zeiss Award 1998, Federal Ministry of Science and Educ. Wittgenstein Award 2002, Julius Springer Award in Applied Physics (USA) 2003, Gottfried Wilhelm Leibniz Award Deutsche Forschungsgemeinschaft 2006. *Publications:* one book (ed.), five book chapters and more than 100 papers on ultrashort-pulse laser physics, intense light–matter interactions, nonlinear optics, and atomic, plasma and x-ray physics. *Address:* Max Planck Institute of Quantum Optics, Hans-Kopfermann-Strasse 1, 85748 Garching (office); Lehrstuhl für Experimentalphysik, Department für Physik, Ludwig-Maximilians-University Munich, Am Coulombwall 1, 85748 Garching, Germany. *Telephone:* (89) 32905-602 (office). *Fax:* (89) 32905-649 (office); (89) 289-14141. *E-mail:* ferenc.krausz@mpq.mpg.de (office); ferenc.krausz@physik.uni-muenchen.de. *Website:* www.mpq.mpg.de/krausz/contact.html (office); www.atto.physik.uni-muenchen.de.

KRAUTHAMMER, Charles, MD; American psychiatrist and journalist; b. 13 March 1950, New York; s. of Shulim Krauthammer and Thea Krauthammer; m. Robyn Trethewey; one s.; ed McGill Univ., Balliol Coll. Oxford and Harvard Univs, Medical School; Resident in Psychiatry, Mass. Gen. Hosp. Boston 1975–78; Scientific Adviser, Dept of Health and Human Services, Washington, DC 1978–80; speech writer to Vice-Pres. Walter Mondale (q.v.), Washington, DC 1980–81; Sr Ed. The New Republic, Washington, DC 1981–88; essayist, Time Magazine 1983–; syndicated columnist, The Washington Post 1984–; mem. Bd of Advisers, The Nat. Interest, Public Interest; mem. President's Council on Bioethics 2002–; Nat. Magazine Award (for essays), American Soc. of Magazine Eds 1984, First Amendment Award, People for the American Way 1985, Pulitzer Prize (for commentary) 1987. *Publications:* Cutting Edges 1985; contribs. to psychiatric journals. *Leisure interest:* chess. *Address:* c/o The Washington Post Writers Group, 1150 15th Street, NW, Washington, DC 20071, USA. *Website:* www.washingtonpost.com.

KRAUZE, Andrzej; Polish painter, illustrator and political cartoonist; b. 1947, Warsaw; m. Małgosia Krauze; three s.; ed Acad. of Fine Art, Warsaw; worked as cartoonist for periodicals Szpilki, Kultura, Solidarity Weekly 1970s; moved to London 1981; cartoonist for The Guardian, Sunday Telegraph, The Bookseller, New Society, New Statesman, Rzeczpospolita (Polish daily) and numerous other publs in UK, France and USA. *Address:* c/o The Guardian, 119 Farringdon Road, London, EC1R 3ER, England (office). *Telephone:* (20) 7278-2332 (office).

KRAVCHENKO, Adm. Victor Andreyevich; Russian naval officer; b. 5 Dec. 1943, Bogdanovich, Sverdlovsk Region; m.; one d.; ed Higher Mil. Marine School, Mil. Marine Acad., Acad. of Gen. Staff; served as Sr Asst, submarine Commdr, Head of staff, submarine div. Commdr, First Deputy Head of Staff, Black Sea Fleet 1968–91; First Deputy Commdr, Baltic Fleet 1991–96; Commdr, Black Sea Fleet 1996–98; Head of Gen. Staff, First Deputy C-in-C Russian Navy 1998–; Russian Academy of Natural Sciences (RANS) Hon.'For Merits' Award; numerous other awards and decorations. *Address:* General Staff of the Russian Navy, B. Kozlovsky Per. 6, 103175 Moscow, Russia (office). *Telephone:* (495) 204-38-62.

KRAVCHUK, Leonid Makarovych, CandEconSc; Ukrainian politician; b. 10 Jan. 1934, Velykyi Zhytyn (Poland, now in Rivne Oblast, Ukraine); s. of Makar Olexiyovich and Khima Ivanivna Kravchuk; m. Antonina Mikhailivna 1957; one s.; ed Kyiv State Univ. and Acad. of Social Sciences, Moscow; teacher of Political Economy, Chernovitsky Tech. School; party work since 1960, on staff Ukrainian CP Cen. Cttee 1970–; Head, Propaganda Dept 1980–88, Ideology Dept 1988–89, Sec., Cen. Cttee, mem. Politburo 1990; Chair. Ukrainian Supreme Soviet 1990–91; Pres. of Ukraine 1991–94; C-in-C Armed Forces of Ukraine 1991–94; mem. Verkhovna Rada (Parl.) 1994–2006; f. Mutual Understanding Movt 1994; mem. Social Democratic Party; Head, All-Ukrainian Union of Democratic Forces Zlagoda 1999–; Chair. State Cttee for Admin. Reforms 1997–99; Protector Mohyla Acad.-Nat. Univ. of Kyiv 1991; Head, Trusteeship Council, Children and Youth Activity Cen. of Ukraine 1992; Hon. Pres. East European Asscn of Businessmen; Dr hc (La Salle Univ., Phila, USA) 1992. *Publications include:* State and Authorities: Experience of Administrative Reforms 2001, We Have What We Have 2002. *Leisure interests:* chess, books, cinema. *Address:* Verkhovna Rada, 01008 Kyiv, vul. M. Hrushevskoho 5, Ukraine (office). *Telephone:* (44) 255-21-15 (office). *Fax:* (44) 253-32-17 (office). *E-mail:* umz@rada.gov.ua (office). *Website:* www.rada.gov.ua (office).

KRAVIS, Henry R., BA, MBA; American investment banker; *Founding Partner, Kohlberg Kravis Roberts & Co.;* b. 6 Jan. 1944, Tulsa, Okla; s. of the late Raymond Kravis and Bessie Kravis (née Roberts); m. 1st the late Diane Shulman (divorced); two c.; m. 2nd Carolyn Roehm 1985 (divorced 1993); m. 3rd Marie-Josée Drouin 1994; ed Loomis Chaffee School, Clareomont McKenna Coll., Columbia Univ.; began career as Vice-Pres. Katy Industries,

New York; Pnr Bear Stearns & Co., New York 1969–76; Founding Pnr Kohlberg Kravis Roberts & Co. (investment bank), New York 1976–, Sr Pnr 1987–; Co-Chair. Bd of Overseers, Columbia Univ. Business School; Vice-Chair. Rockefeller Univ.; Trustee Mount Sinai Medical Center, Metropolitan Musuem of Art; Chair. Emer. WNET, New York (public TV station); mem. Bd of Dirs Partnership for New York City (fmr Co-Chair.), Council on Foreign Relations; Founder and Chair. New York City Investment Fund; Co-founder Republican Leadership Council; mem. Business Council. *Leisure interest:* collecting art. *Address:* Kohlberg Kravis Roberts & Co., 9 West 57 Street, Suite 4200, New York, NY 10019, USA (office). *Telephone:* (212) 750-8300 (office). *Website:* www.kkr.com (office).

KRAVITZ, Lenny; American singer, musician (piano, guitar), songwriter and producer; b. 26 May 1964, New York; m. Lisa Bonet (divorced); actor, as teenager; mem., Calif. Boys Choir and Metropolitan Opera; solo artist 1989–; numerous tours world-wide, TV and live appearances; f. Kravitz Design, Miami 2005; BRIT Award for Best Int. Male 1994, Grammy Awards for Male Rock Vocal Performance 2000, 2001, American Music Award for Favorite Pop/ Rock Male Artist 2002. *Recordings include:* albums: Let Love Rule 1989, Mama Said 1991, Are You Gonna Go My Way 1993, Circus 1995, 5 1998, Greatest Hits 2000, Lenny 2001, Baptism 2004, It Is Time For A Love Revolution 2008. *Address:* International Talent Booking, First Floor, Ariel House, 74a Charlotte Street, London, W1T 4QJ, England (office). *Telephone:* (20) 7637-6979 (office). *Fax:* (20) 7637-6978 (office). *E-mail:* mail@itb.co.uk (office); info@kravitzdesign.com. *Website:* www.lennykravitz.com; www.kravitzdesign.com.

KRAWCHECK, Sallie L., BA, MBA; American banker; b. 1965, Charleston, SC; m. Gary Appel; ed Univ. of N Carolina at Chapel Hill, Columbia Business School, New York; worked with Fortune magazine; worked for Salomon Brothers; worked for Donaldson, Lufkin & Jenrette; joined Sanford C. Bernstein stock research firm in 1994, Dir of Research 1998–2001, Chair. and CEO 2001–02; Chair. and CEO Smith Barney (div. of Citigroup) 2002–04, Chief Financial Officer and Head of Strategy 2004–07, Chair. and CEO Global Wealth Man. Div. 2007–08, mem. Man. Cttee Citigroup 2004–08; mem. The Morehead Foundation's Cen. Selection Cttee; ranked by Fortune magazine amongst 50 Most Powerful Women in Business in the US (14th) 2003, (seventh) 2004, (seventh) 2005, (ninth) 2006, (12th) 2007, ranked by Forbes magazine amongst 100 Most Powerful Women (48th) 2004, (seventh) 2005, (sixth) 2006, (64th) 2008, named a Time Magazine Global Business Influential. *Address:* c/o Citigroup, 399 Park Avenue, New York, NY 10043, USA (office).

KRAWIEC, Dariusz Jacek; Polish business executive; *President and CEO, PKN Orlen;* ed Poznań Univ. of Econs; with PEKAO SA (bank) 1992; Consultant, Man. Consulting Dept, Ernst & Young SA 1993; Asst, Sr Asst, Man. Asst and Man. in Corp. Finance Dept, Price Waterhouse Sp. z o.o. 1993–97; with Nomura International plc (investment bank), London, UK, responsible for Polish market 1997–2002; Pres. Man. Bd and Gen. Dir Impexmetal SA 1998–2002; Pres. Man. Bd Elektrim SA 2002; Man. Dir Sindicatum Ltd, London 2003–04; Pres. Man. Bd Action SA 2006–08; participant in PKN Orlen Man. Bd Mems' competition for a new term of office Feb. 2008, Vice-Pres. Man. Bd PKN Orlen June–Sept. 2008, Pres. Man. Bd and CEO Sept. 2008–; fmr Chair. Supervisory Bd Huta Aluminium 'Konin' SA, Metalexfrance SA, S and I SA, cemarket.com SA; mem. Supervisory Bd Impexmetal SA, Elektrim SA, PTC Sp. z o.o. (ERA GSM), Elektrim Telekomunikacja Sp. z o.o., Elektrim Magadex SA, Elektrim Volt SA, PTE AIG. *Address:* PKN Orlen, 09-411 Plock, ul. Chemikow 7, Poland (office). *Telephone:* (24) 3650000 (office). *Fax:* (24) 3654040 (office). *E-mail:* info@orlen.pl (office). *Website:* www.orlen.pl (office).

KRAYER, Georg F., LLD; Swiss banking executive; *Chairman, Bank Sarasin & Company Ltd;* b. 30 May 1943, Basel; m. Luise Krayer; two d.; ed Univ. of Basel; joined A. Sarasin & Cie (now Bank Sarasin & Co. Ltd), Basel 1970, vocational training in Paris, France and New York, apptd Pnr 1978, Chair. Bd of Admin 1997–2002, Chair. Bd of Dirs 1997–; mem. Basel Stock Exchange 1978–92, Pres. 1989–92; Vice-Chair.Bâloise Holding AG; Chair. Swiss Bankers Asscn 1992–2003;; Hon. Dr rer. pol 2004. *Leisure interest:* rowing. *Address:* Bank Sarasin & Company Ltd, Elisabethenstrasse 62, 4002 Basel, Switzerland (office). *Telephone:* (61) 2777777 (office). *Fax:* (61) 2727610 (office). *E-mail:* georg.krayer@sarasin.ch (office). *Website:* www.sarasin.ch (office).

KREBS, Edwin Gerhard, MD; American biochemist and academic; *Professor Emeritus, Departments of Pharmacology and Biochemistry, School of Medicine, University of Washington;* b. 6 June 1918, Lansing, Iowa; s. of William Krebs and Louise Stegeman; m. Virginia French 1945; one s. two d.; ed Univ. of Illinois and Washington Univ., St Louis; intern, Barnes Hosp. St Louis 1944–45; Research Fellow, Washington Univ., St Louis 1946–48; Asst Prof. of Biochemistry, Univ. of Washington, Seattle 1948–52, Assoc. Prof. 1952–57, Prof. 1957–66; Prof. and Chair. Dept of Biological Chem., School of Medicine Univ. of Calif., Davis 1968–76; Prof. and Chair. Dept of Pharmacology, Univ. of Washington, Seattle 1977–83, Prof. of Biochem. and Pharmacology 1984–91; Sr Investigator, Howard Hughes Medical Inst., Seattle 1983–90, Sr Investigator Emer. 1991–; mem. NAS, American Soc. of Biological Chemists, American Acad. of Arts and Sciences; Nobel Prize for Medicine (with Edmond Fischer q.v.) 1992, Albert Lasker Award for Basic Medical Research 1989. *Address:* Department of Pharmacology, University of Washington, K540 E, Health Sciences Building, Box 357750, Seattle, WA 98195-7750, USA (office). *Telephone:* (206) 543-8500 (office). *Fax:* (206) 685-9720 (office). *E-mail:* egkrebs@u.washington.edu (office). *Website:* depts.washington.edu/phcol/nobelprize/krebs (office).

KREBS, Baron (Life Peer), cr. 2007, of Wytham in the County of Oxfordshire; **John Richard Krebs,** MA, DPhil, FRS, FMedSci; British zoologist and scientific administrator; *Principal, Jesus College Oxford;* b. 11 April 1945, Sheffield; s. of Prof. Sir Hans Krebs and Margaret Fieldhouse; m. Katharine A. Fullerton 1968; two d.; ed City of Oxford High School, Pembroke Coll. Oxford; Departmental Demonstrator in Ornithology, Edward Grey Inst. of Field Ornithology and Oxford Lecturer in Zoology, Pembroke Coll. Oxford 1969–70, Lecturer in Zoology, Edward Grey Inst. 1976–88, E.P. Abraham Fellow in Zoology, Pembroke Coll. 1981–88, Fellow 1988–2005, Hon. Fellow 2005–; Asst Prof., Inst. of Resource Ecology, Univ. of British Columbia, Vancouver, Canada 1970–73; Lecturer in Zoology, Univ. Coll. of North Wales, Bangor 1973–74; SRC Research Officer, Animal Behaviour Research Group, Dept of Zoology, Oxford 1975–76; Fellow, Wolfson Coll. 1976–81; Royal Soc. Research Prof., Univ. of Oxford 1988–2005, Prin. Jesus Coll. Oxford 2005–; Chief Exec. NERC 1994–2000; Chair. Food Standards Agency 2000–05; Dir Agric. and Food Research Council (AFRC) Unit of Ecology and Behaviour and NERC Unit of Behavioural Ecology 1989–94; Sr Scientific Consultant and Chair. Animals Research Cttee, AFRC 1991–94; External Scientific mem. Max Planck Soc. 1985; Pres. Int. Soc. of Behavioural Ecology 1988–90, Asscn for Study of Animal Behaviour 1992–94; mem. Academia Europaea 1995; Foreign mem. American Philosophical Soc. 2000, American Acad. of Arts and Sciences 2000; Hon. Fellow, Univ. of Cardiff 1999, Univ. Wales Inst. Cardiff 2006, Univ. Wales Bangor 2007; Hon. Fellow, Deutsche Ornithologische Gesellschaft 2003; Hon. Fellow, Salters' Co. 2006; Hon. mem. British Ecological Soc. 1999; Foreign Hon. mem. NAS 2004; Kt Bachelor 1999; Hon. DSc (Sheffield) 1993, (Wales) 1997, (Birmingham) 1997, (Exeter) 1998, (Warwick) 2000, (Cranfield) 2001, (Kent) 2001, (Plymouth) 2001, (South Bank) 2003, (Heriot-Watt) 2002, (Queen's Univ., Belfast) 2002, (Lancaster) 2005, (Guelph) 2006; Dr hc (Stirling) 2000; Nuffield Foundation Science Fellowship 1981; Scientific Medal, Zoological Soc. 1981, Bicentenary Medal, Linnaean Soc. 1983, Frink Medal, Zoological Soc. 1996, Elliott Coues Award, American Ornithologists' Union 1999, Asscn for Study of Animal Behaviour Medal 2000, Benjamin Ward Richardson Gold Medal, Royal Soc. for Promotion of Health 2002, Wooldridge Medal, British Veterinary Asscn 2004, Croonian Lecture and Medal, Royal Soc., London 2004, Lord Raynor Medal & Lecture, Royal Coll. of Physicians 2005, Award for Outstanding Achievement, Soc. for Food Hygiene Tech. 2005, Harben Gold Medal, Royal Inst. of Public Health 2006. *Publications:* Behavioural Ecology: An Evolutionary Aproach (co-ed. with N. B. Davies) 1978, 1984, 1991, 1997, An Introduction to Behavioural Ecology (with N. B. Davies) 1981, 1986, 1993, Foraging Theory: Princeton Monographs in Behaviour and Ecology, No. 4 (with D. W. Stephens) 1987, Foraging Behaviour (co-ed. with A. Kamil and H. R. Pulliam) 1987, Behavioural and Neural Studies of Learning and Memory (co-ed. with G. Horn) 1991. *Leisure interests:* gardening, violin, running, walking. *Address:* Jesus College, Oxford, OX1 3DW, England (office). *Telephone:* (1865) 279701 (office). *E-mail:* principal@jesus.ox.ac.uk (office). *Website:* www.jesus.ox.ac.uk (office).

KREBS, Robert Duncan, MBA; American transport industry executive (retd); b. 2 May 1942, Sacramento, Calif.; s. of Ward C. Krebs and Eleanor B. Krebs (née Duncan); m. Anne Lindstrom 1971; two s. one d.; ed Stanford and Harvard Univs; Asst Gen. Man. S Pacific Transportation Co., Houston 1974–75, Asst Regional Operations Man. 1975–76, Asst Vice-Pres. San Francisco 1967–77, Asst to Pres. 1977–79, Gen. Man. 1979, Vice-Pres. Transportation 1979-80, Operations 1980–82, Pres. 1982–83; Dir and Pres. Santa Fe S Pacific Corpn (now Santa Fe Pacific Corpn) 1983–96, Pres., Chair. and CEO 1988–96, Pres. and CEO Burlington Northern Santa Fe Corpn 1995–2002, Chair. 2000–02; mem. Bd of Dirs Railpower Techs Corpn 2005, Phelps Dodge Corpn –2006, UAL Corpn 2006–, Fort Worth Symphony Orchestra; Vice Chair. Bd of Trustees Ravinia Festival. *Address:* c/o Board of Trustees, Ravinia Festival, 418 Sheridan Road, Highland Park, IL 60035, USA.

KREITZBERG, Peeter, DPhil; Estonian politician and academic; b. 14 Dec. 1948, Parnu; m. (divorced); one s. two d.; ed Tartu State Univ., Lund Univ., Sweden; Head of Students Bureau of Comprehensive Research, Tartu Univ. 1972–74, Lecturer, Sr Teacher, Asst Prof., then Prof. 1977–96; Prof., Tallinn Pedagogical Univ. 1977–; Minister of Culture and Educ. 1995; Deputy Mayor of Tallinn 1996–99; mem. Riigikogu (Parl.) 1999–, Vice-Chair. 2001–05, currently Chair., Cultural Affairs Cttee; mem. British Soc. of Educ. Philosophy; Grand Officier, Ordre nat. du Mérite 2001, Grand Oficial, Ordem do Infante Dom Henrique, Order of the Nat. Coat of Arms, Third Class (Estonia) 2003. *Publications include:* Principles of Classification and Concretising Targets in Education 1987, Legitimisation of Education Aims: Paradigms and Metaphors 1993. *Leisure interest:* fishing. *Address:* Riigikogu, Tompea Castle, Lossi plats 1A, 0100 Tallinn (office); Esku 3, Tallinn, Estonia (home). *Telephone:* (2) 631-64-80 (office); (2) 600-25-90 (home). *Fax:* (2) 631-64-85 (office). *E-mail:* peeter.kreitzberg@riigikogu.ee (office). *Website:* www.riigikogu.ee (office).

KREJČA, Otomar; Czech actor and director; b. 23 Nov. 1921, Skrýšov; s. of František Krejča and Ludmila Pechová; m. Marie Tomášová 1986; one s.; ed Charles Univ., Prague; mem. Prague Nat. Theatre 1951–69, Art Chief, Nat. Theatre Drama Section 1956–61; Founder and Artistic Dir of Divadlo za branou (Theatre Beyond the Gate) 1965–71, Dir 1971–72 (theatre shut 1972); Dir Theatre S.K.N. 1973–75; allowed to work only outside CSSR 1976–89; Artistic Dir Schauspielhaus Düsseldorf 1976–78, Atelier Théâtral de Louvain-la-Neuve 1979–81; Founder and Dir Divadlo za branou II, Prague 1990–94; Dir Prague Nat. Theatre 1997–98; Ordre des Arts et Lettres 1978, 1991, Medal for Merit 1998; Dr hc (Univ. of Prague) 2002, (AMU) 2002; State Prize 1951, 1968, Honoured Artist 1958, Kainz Medal (Austria) 1969, Int. Pirandello Prize (Italy) 1978, Distinction of Union of Soviet Asscns for Cultural Links and Friendship with Overseas 1991, K.I. Stanislavski Merit Award for World

Theatre (Russia) 1999, Czech Literary Fund Prize 2000, Special Prize for Lifelong Mastery 2001, Artis Bohemiae Amicis Medal 2001, German Language Festival Prize 2002. *Theatre roles:* Kreon in Oedipus (Sophocles), Prometheus (Aeschylus), Macbeth, Othello, Malvolio (Shakespeare), Don Juan (Molière), Protasov in Redemption (Tolstoy), Warwick in Saint Joan (Shaw), Tscheboutykin in Three Sisters (Chekhov). *Plays directed include:* all Chekhov's plays, Romeo and Juliet, Hamlet, Measure for Measure (Shakespeare), Antigone (Sophocles), Life Is A Dream (Calderón), Waiting for Godot (Beckett), Faust (Goethe), Minetti (Bernard) and other classical and modern dramas; Guest Dir for productions in Havana, Brussels, Cologne, Salzburg, Vienna, Stockholm, Paris, Avignon, Genoa, Berlin. *Films include:* Daleká cesta 1949, Zalobnici 1960, Vyssí princip (Higher Principle) 1960, Muz z prvniho století (Man in Outer Space, USA) 1961, Kohout plasí smrt 1961, Tereza 1961, Kocár nejsvetejsí svátosti (TV) 1962, Bez svatozáre 1963, Alibi na vode 1965, Cytri v kruhu 1967. *Address:* Kubišova 26, 18200 Prague 8, Czech Republic (home). *Telephone:* (2) 8468-1759 (home). *Fax:* (2) 8468-1759 (home).

KREMENYUK, Victor Aleksandrovich, DHist; Russian civil servant and scholar; *Deputy Director, Institute for the USA and Canadian Studies, Russian Academy of Sciences;* b. 13 Dec. 1940, Odessa (now in Ukraine); m. Lyudmila Agapova; one d.; ed Moscow Inst. of Int. Relations; army service 1963–68; with Mezdunarodnaya Zhizn magazine 1968–70; with Inst. of USA and Canada, USSR (now Russian) Acad. of Sciences 1970–; expert, Cttee on Int. Problems, USSR Supreme Soviet 1989–91; expert, State Duma 1993–; worked on project Process of Int. Negotiations in Int. Inst. of Applied System Analysis Austria, lectures and seminars in USA, Germany, Austria; Deputy Dir Inst. for USA and Canadian Studies 1989–; Chair. Expert Council of Political Sciences 1992–99; mem. Council on Higher Policy at Ministry of Foreign Affairs 1991–96; mem. Scientific Council, Russian Inst. of Strategic Studies 1995–; mem. Council of Social Sciences, Presidium of Russian Acad. of Sciences 1991–; mem. Nat. Geographical Soc., USA, Int. Asscn of Conflictology; mem. Consultative and Observation Councils Salzburg Seminar, Austria, Centre of Applied Studies on Negotiations, Switzerland; mem. Editorial Bds, magazines Econ., Politics and Ideology, Journal of Negotiations, USA 1990–2000, Journal of Peace Studies, USA; Nat. Prize for Science and Tech. (USSR) 1980, CPR Inst. for Dispute Resolution (New York) Book Award 2002. *Publications:* more than 100 articles and 12 scientific monographs; ed. more than 50 scientific works in Russian and English. *Address:* Institute for USA and Canadian Studies, Khlebny per. 2/3, 123995 Moscow, Russia (office). *Telephone:* (495) 291-14-83 (office); (495) 430-07-95 (home). *Fax:* (495) 203-70-17 (office). *E-mail:* vkremenyuk@yahoo.com (office). *Website:* (office).

KREMER, Gidon; Russian/German violinist; *Artistic Director, Kremerata Baltica;* b. 27 Feb. 1947, Riga, Latvia; ed Riga School of Music, Moscow Conservatory (with David Oistrakh); recitalist and orchestral soloist worldwide 1965–; has played in most major int. festivals including Berlin, Dubrovnik, Helsinki, London, Moscow, Prague, Salzburg, Tokyo and Zürich; has played with most major int. orchestras including Berlin Philharmonic, Boston Symphony, Concertgebouw, LA Philharmonic, New York Philharmonic, Philadelphia, San Francisco Symphony, Vienna Philharmonic, London Philharmonic, Royal Philharmonic, Philharmonia, NHK Symphony of Japan and all main Soviet orchestras; has worked with Bernstein, von Karajan, Giulini, Jochum, Previn, Abbado, Levine, Maazel, Muti, Harnoncourt, Mehta and Marriner; f. Kremerata Baltica (chamber orchestra) 1977, Artistic Dir 1977–; f. Lockenhaus Chamber Music Festival 1981; plays a Stradivarius; lives in Germany; prizewinner at Queen Elisabeth Competition, Brussels, Montreal Competition and Fourth Int. Tchaikovsky Competition (First Prize) 1970, Paganini Prize, Genoa; Grand Prix du Disque and Deutsche Schallplattenpreis. *Recordings:* has made more than 45 records. *Performances:* first performances include Henze, Stockhausen, Schnittke, Pärt, Astor Piazzola. *Address:* Opus 3 Artists, 470 Park Avenue South, 9th Floor North, New York, NY 10016, USA (office); Kremerata Baltica, R. Vagnera iela 4, 1050 Riga, Latvia (office). *Telephone:* (212) 584-7500 (office); 6722-4055 (office). *Fax:* (646) 300-8200 (office); 6721-3072 (office). *E-mail:* info@opus3artists.com (office); kremerata@tvnet.lv (office). *Website:* www.opus3artists.com (office); www.kremerata-baltica.com (office).

KREMP, Herbert, DPhil; German journalist; b. 12 Aug. 1928, Munich; s. of Johann Kremp and Elisabeth Kremp; m. Brigitte Steffal 1956; two d. (one deceased); ed Munich Univ.; reporter, Frankfurter Neue Presse 1956–57; Political Ed. Rheinische Post 1957–59; Dir Political Dept, Der Tag, Berlin 1959–61; Bonn Corresp. Rheinische Post 1961–63; Ed.-in-Chief Rheinische Post 1963–68; Ed.-in-Chief Die Welt 1969–77, Co-Ed. 1981, Co-Publr 1984–87, Chief Corresp. in Beijing 1977–81, Ed.-in-Chief 1981–85, apptd Chief Corresp. in Brussels 1987, Co-Ed., Springer Group newspapers 1984–87, commentator, Die Welt, Berliner Morgenpost, Welt am Sonntag, Bild, B.Z. Berlin, Hamburger Abendblatt; currently associated with Axel Springer publishing house; Bundesverdienstkreuz 1988; Konrad Adenauer Prize 1984, Theodor-Wolff Prize 1978, 2003. *Publications:* Am Ufer der Rubikon: Eine politische Anthropologie, Die Bambusbrücke: Ein asiatisches Tagebuch 1979, Wir brauchen unsere Geschichte 1988. *Address:* c/o Axel Springer Verlag AG, Axel-Springer-Str. 65, 10888 Berlin, Germany.

KRENS, Thomas, MA; American museum director; *Senior Adviser on International Affairs, Solomon R. Guggenheim Foundation;* b. 26 Dec. 1946, New York; ed Williams Coll., State Univ. of New York, Albany and Yale Univ.; Asst Prof. of Art, Williams Coll., Williamstown, Mass. 1972–80, Asst Prof. of History of Art, Grad. Program 1977–80, Adjunct Prof. of Art History 1988–; Dir Williams Coll. Museum of Art 1980–88; consultant, Solomon R. Guggenheim Museum, New York 1986–88, Dir 1988, Dir Guggenheim Museums Worldwide, Dir and Trustee Solomon R. Guggenheim Foundation

1988–2008, Sr Adviser on Int. Affairs 2008–; Dir The Peggy Guggenheim Collection, Venice 1988–; Hon. DHumLitt (State Univ. of NY). *Publications:* Jim Dine Prints: 1970–77 1977, The Prints of Helen Frankenthaler 1980, The Drawing of Robert Morris 1982, Robert Morris: The Mind/Body Problem 1994. *Address:* c/o Solomon R. Guggenheim Museum, 1071 Fifth Avenue, New York, NY 10128-0173, USA (office). *Telephone:* (212) 423-3500 (office). *Website:* www.guggenheim.org (office).

KRENZ, Egon; German politician; b. 1937; ed Teacher Training Inst. Putbus and Cen. Cttee of CPSU Party Univ. Moscow; joined Freie Deutsche Jugend (FDJ) 1953, Socialist Unity Party (SED) and Confed. of Free German Trade Unions 1955; various functions within FDJ and SED 1957–64; Sec. Ernst Thälmann Pioneer Org. 1967–74, Chair. 1971–74; First Sec. FDJ Cen. Council 1974–83; mem. Nat. Council of Nat. Front 1969–; cand. mem. Cen. Cttee of SED 1971–73, mem. 1973–90, Sec. 1989–90, cand. mem. Politburo 1976–83, mem. 1983–90, Gen. Sec. 1989–90; Deputy to Volkskammer 1971–90, mem. Presidium 1971–81, Chair. FDJ Faction 1971–76; mem. Council of State 1981–84, Deputy Chair. 1984–89, Chair. (Head of State) 1989–90; stripped of membership of CP (fmrly SED); now property developer, Berlin; faced charges of manslaughter for killings of persons fleeing over Berlin Wall and other borders 1994; on trial Aug. 1995, sentenced to six and a half years' imprisonment for the deaths of those trying to cross the Berlin Wall Aug. 1997, sentence upheld on appeal Nov. 1999, released Dec. 2003; decorations include Karl Marx Orden, Banner der Arbeit, Verdienstmedaille der DDR.

KRENZ, Jan; Polish conductor and composer; b. 14 July 1926, Włocławek; s. of Otton Krenz and Eleonora Krenz; m. Alina Krenz 1958; one s.; ed Higher School of Music; conducting debut, Łódź Philharmonic Orchestra 1946; Chief Conductor, State Poznań Philharmonic Orchestra 1947–49; Chief Conductor Polish Nat. Radio Symphony Orchestra of Katowice 1953–67; Chief Conductor Danish Radio Orchestra, Copenhagen 1960s; Leader, Grand Opera House Orchestra (Teatr Wielki), Warsaw 1968–73; conducted Berlin Philharmonic, Staatskapelle Dresden, Leningrad Philharmonic and all the major London orchestras; Gen. Dir of Music, Bonn Orchestra 1979–82; frequent collaboration with Yomiuri Nippon Symphony Orchestra; performing only as guest conductor 1983–; Diploma of Ministry of Foreign Affairs 1980; Hon. mem. Asscn of Polish Composers; Hon. Conductor Polish Nat. Radio Symphony Orchestra of Katowice; decorations include Order of Banner of Labour (First Class), Commdr's Cross with Star of Polonia Restituta Order; State Prize 1955, 1972, Prize of Asscn of Polish Composers 1968, Grand Prix du Disque, France 1972, Prize of Polish Artists' and Musicians' Asscn (SPAM) Orfeusz 1974. *Compositions include:* chamber, vocal and symphonic music, orchestral transcriptions of Polish classics, J. S. Bach (including Polyphonic suite on four fragments from Bach's Die Kunst der Fuge) and Szymanowski, film and stage music. *Leisure interest:* painting. *Address:* al. J. Ch. Szucha 16, 00-582 Warsaw, Poland.

KREPS, Juanita Morris, MA, PhD; American fmr government official, economist and academic; *Vice-President Emerita and Professor Emerita, Duke University;* b. 11 Jan. 1921, Lynch, Ky; d. of the late Elmer Morris and Cenia Blair Morris; m. Dr Clifton H. Kreps, Jr 1944 (deceased); one s. two d. (one deceased); ed Berea Coll., Duke Univ.; Instructor in Econs, Denison Univ., Ohio 1945–46, Asst Prof. 1947–50; Lecturer, Hofstra Univ., NY, 1952–54; Queens Coll., NY 1954–55; Visiting Asst Prof., Duke Univ., NC, Asst Prof. 1958–62, Assoc. Prof. 1963–68, Prof. 1968–72, Dean of Women's Coll., Asst Provost 1969–72, James B. Duke Prof. 1972–77, Vice-Pres. of Duke Univ. 1973–77, now Vice-Pres. Emer. and Prof. Emer.; US Sec. of Commerce 1977–79; Ford Faculty Research Fellow 1964–65; mem. Bd of Dirs NY Stock Exchange (first woman) 1972–77, AT&T 1980–91, Armco Inc. 1980–91, UAL Inc. 1979–92, Eastman Kodak Co. 1975–77, 1979–91, J. C. Penney Co. 1972–77, 1979–91, Zurn Industries Inc. 1982–93, Deere & Co. 1982–92, Chrysler Corpn 1983–91, Citicorp 1979–89, RJR Nabisco 1975–77, 1979–89; Chair. Bd of Trustees, Educational Testing Service 1975–76; Pres. American Asscn for Higher Educ. 1975–76; Pres. Bd of Overseers, Teachers Insurance and Annuity Asscn and Coll. Retirement Equities Fund 1992–96; mem. Comm. on Future of Worker-Man. Relations to advise Secs of Commerce and Labor 1993–95; Trustee Coll. Retirement Equities Fund 1972–77, 1985–92, Berea Coll. 1972–78, 1980–98, Duke Endowment 1979–, Kenan Inst. of Pvt. Enterprise, Univ. of NC, Chapel Hill 1995–; Fellow, American Acad. of Arts and Sciences 1988; 20 hon. degrees; NC Public Service Award 1976, Haskins Award 1984, Corp. Governance Award, Nat. Asscn of Corp. Dirs (first recipient) 1987, Duke Univ. Medal for Distinguished Meritorious Service and many others. *Publications:* ed.: Employment, Income and Retirement Problems of the Aged 1963, Technology, Manpower and Retirement Policy 1966; ed. and contrib.: Lifetime Allocation of Work and Income 1971, Sex in the Marketplace: American Women at Work 1971; co-author: Principles of Economics (with C. E. Ferguson) 1962, 1965, Contemporary Labor Economics 1974, Sex, Age and Work 1975, Women and the American Economy, a Look to the 1980s 1976; over 60 papers on ageing, retirement and econs. *Leisure interests:* music, art. *Address:* 115 East Duke Building, Duke University, Durham, NC 27708; 29 Forest at Duke Drive, Durham, NC 27705, USA. *Telephone:* (919) 684-2616 (office). *Fax:* (919) 684-8351 (office). *E-mail:* juanita.kreps@duke.edu (office).

KRESAL, Katarina; Slovenian lawyer and politician; *Minister of Internal Affairs;* b. 1973; ed Bezigrad High School, Faculty of Law, Univ. of Ljubljana; contractual work, Slovenian Chamber of Physiotherapists 1994–96; clerk trainee, High Court in Ljubljana 1996–98; Slovenian State Bar Exam 1999; Sr Clerk, Commercial Disputes Dept, Ljubljana Dist Court 1999–2000; Sr Consultant for Commercial and Corp. Law, Kapitalska družba d.d., Ljubljana 2000–01; mem. advisory bodies of Delo Tiskarna, BTC Terminal and Konstruktor (rep. of Kapitalska družba) 2000–01; Head of Legal Dept,

Western Wireless International d.o.o., Ljubljana and mem. Sr Man. Team 2001–03; Dir Legal Dept, Western Wireless International 2001–03; attorney cand., Attorneys at law Miro Senica in odvetniki, Ljubljana 2003–04, attorney at law 2004–08, Deputy Dir and Dir Econ. and Int. Affairs Dept 2005–08; Pres. Liberalna demokracija Slovenije (Liberal Democracy of Slovenia) 2007–; Minister of Internal Affairs 2008–; mem. advisory bodies of GV Zalozbe and lus Software; mem. Asscn of Young Laywers of Slovenia, European Young Bar Asscn. *Publications:* has published articles in foreign publs such as International Financial Review 1000 and The Guide to Mergers and Acquisitions. *Address:* Ministry of Internal Affairs, 1501 Ljubljana, Štefanova 2 (office); Liberalna demokracija Slovenije, Slovenska cesta 29, 1000 Ljubljana, Slovenia. *Telephone:* (1) 4325125 (office); (1) 200-03-10. *Fax:* (1) 2514330 (office); (1) 200-03-11. *E-mail:* gp.mnz@gov.si (office); katarina.kresal@lds.si. *Website:* www.mnz.gov.si (office); www.lds.si.

KRESS, Victor Melkhiorovich, Dr Econs; Russian politician; *Governor of Tomsk Region;* b. 16 Nov. 1948, Kostroma Region; m.; two c.; ed Novosibirsk Inst. of Agric., Russian Acad. of Man.; agronomist, agric. enterprises Tomsk Region; Deputy Chair., Agric.-Industrial complex Tomsk Region 1971–87; First Sec. Dist CP Cttee, Tomsk Region 1987–90; Chair. Tomsk Regional Soviet 1990–91, Interregional Asscn Siberian Agreement 1998–2001; Head, Admin. of Tomsk Region 1991–96, Gov. 1996–; mem. Council of Russian Fed. 1993–2000; Chair. Interregional Asscn Siberian Agreement; Order of The Sign of Respect (Znak Potcheta) 1986, Order of Merit to Russia of the IV Grade (Za Zaslugi pered Otetchestrom) 1998; Medal for Working Virtue (Za Trudovya Doblest) 1976. *Publications:* Tomsk Region: Today and Tomorrow (4 vols) 1997, Russia's Hard Time: View from the Province 1998, Tomsk Region: at the Crossroads of Centuries 1999, Tomsk Region: Beginning of the 21st Century 2002. *Address:* Office of the Governor, Lenina Square 6, 634050 Tomsk, Russia (office). *Telephone:* (3822) 51-05-05 (office); (3822) 51-06-86 (office). *Fax:* (3822) 51-03-23 (office); (3822) 51-07-30 (office). *E-mail:* ato@tomsk.gov.ru (office). *Website:* www.tomsk.gov.ru (office).

KRGOVIĆ, Ljubiša, MA; Montenegrin economist and central banker; *President of the Council, Central Bank of Montenegro;* b. 1957, Mojkovac; ed secondary school in Berane, Univ. of Montenegro, Belgrade Univ.; researcher, Econs Inst., Univ. of Montenegro 1983–91; Dir Montenegrin Employment Bureau 1991–92; Advisor to the Prime Minister in Govt of Montenegro 1992–94; Vice-Gov. Nat. Bank of Yugoslavia 1995–99; mem. Monetary Council, Nat. Bank of Montenegro 1999–2001; Deputy Prime Minister for financial system and public spending 2000–01; Pres. Montenegro Securities Exchange 2000–02; Pres. of Council, Centralna banka Crne Gore (Cen. Bank of Montenegro) 2001–. *Address:* Centralna Banka Crne Gore, 81000 Podgorica, bul. Svetog Petra Cetinjskog 7, Montenegro (office). *Telephone:* (81) 403191 (office). *Fax:* (81) 664140 (office). *E-mail:* info@cb-cg.org (office). *Website:* www.cb-mn.org (office).

KRIEL, Hermanus Jacobus, BA, LLB; South African politician and lawyer; b. 14 Nov. 1941, Kakamas; s. of Prof. Kriel and Mrs Kriel; one s. two d.; ed Hugenote Hoërskool, Univ. of Stellenbosch; conveyancer and notary 1968; Chair. Cape Div. Council 1976–77; mem. Cape Prov. Council 1977–84, Cape Exec. Cttee 1981–84; MP 1984–89; Minister of Planning, Prov. Affairs and Nat. Housing 1989–91, of Law and Order 1991–94; Premier of Western Cape Provincial Parl. 1994–97; F. C. Erasmus Award, Stella Officii Egregii. *Leisure interests:* golf, reading. *Address:* c/o Private Bag 9043, Cape Town 8000, South Africa.

KRIELE, Martin, DJur, LLM; German legal scholar and academic; *Professor Emeritus of Philosophy and Public Law, University of Cologne;* b. 19 Jan. 1931, Opladen; s. of the late Dr Rudolf Kriele and of Konstanze Henckels; m. 1st Christel Grothues 1960; one s. one d.; m. 2nd Alexa Michalsen; ed Freiburg, Münster, Bonn and Yale Univs, USA; admitted to the Court 1961; Prof. of Philosophy of Law and Public Law, Univ. of Cologne 1967–96, Prof. Emer. 1996–; currently Co-Publr Zeitschrift für Rechtspolitik (journal); Dir Inst. for Political Philosophy and Problems of Legislation 1967; Judge, Constitutional Court of North Rhine-Westphalia 1976–88. *Publications:* Kriterien der Gerechtigkeit 1963, Theorie der Rechtsgewinnung 1967, Einführung in die Staatslehre 1975, Legitimitätsprobleme der Bundesrepublik 1977, Die Menschenrechte zwischen Ost und West 1977, Recht und praktische Vernunft 1979, Befreiung und politische Aufklärung 1980, Nicaragua, das blutende Herz Amerikas 1985, Die Demokratische Weltrevolution 1987, Recht, Vernunft, Wirklichkeit (essays) 1990. *Leisure interest:* music (piano). *Address:* University of Cologne, Seminar für Staatsphilosophie und Rechtspolitik, Albertus-Magnus-Platz 1, 50923 Cologne, Germany (office); Dorf 11, 6900 Möggen, Austria (home). *Telephone:* (221) 4702230 (office); (5573) 3772 (home). *Fax:* (221) 4705010 (office); (5573) 3772 (home).

KRIER, Léon; Luxembourg architect, urban planner and designer; b. 7 April 1946, Luxembourg; ed Univ. of Stuttgart; Asst to James Stirling London 1968–70, 1973–74; project pnr with J.P. Kleihues, Berlin 1971–72; in pvt. practice in London 1974–; Lecturer, Architectural Asscn School, London 1973–76, Royal Coll. of Art, London 1977, Princeton Univ. 1977; Jefferson Prof. of Architecture, Univ. Va Charlottesville 1982; E. Saarinen Prof., Yale Univ. 2001, Davenport Prof. 2004; architectural and urban design adviser to HRH The Prince of Wales; works include numerous city centre and housing re devt plans, schools, univs, public bldgs etc. in UK, Germany, Luxembourg, Spain, Italy, Greece, Sweden, USA, Belgium, St Lucia, France and Portugal; City of Berlin Architecture Prize (with Rob Krier) 1975, Jefferson Medal for Architecture 1985, European Culture Prize 1995, Silver Medal Acad. Française 1997, first recipient of Richard H Driehaus Prize for Classical Architecture 2003. *Projects include:* masterplans for Poundbury 1988, 2004, Novoli, Florence 1993, Città Nuova, Alessandria, Italy 1997, Village Hall Windsor Florida USA 1997, Val d'Europe Brasserie Agape France 2000–03, Hardelot, France 2001, School of Architecture Auditorium Univ. of Miami USA 2001–04, Knokke Heuleburg Masterplan Belgium 2001–04; designs furniture for Giorgetti, Italy 1991–. *Publications include:* Buildings and Projects of James Stirling (ed.) 1974, The Reconstruction of the European City 1978, The City within the City (ed.) 1979, Architecture and Urban Design (ed. by Richard Economakis) 1967–92, Architecture: Choice or Fate 1997 (trans. into 7 languages). *Address:* 37 rue du X Octobre, 7243 Bereldange, Luxembourg.

KRIKALEV, Sergey Konstantinovich; Russian cosmonaut; b. 27 Aug. 1958, Leningrad; m.; one d.; ed Leningrad Mechanical Inst.; engineer Research Production Co. Energia 1981–85, took part in developing new samples of space tech.; Master of Sports in piloting; mem. Cosmonauts' team since 1985; flight engineer Soyuz TM-7 1988, Soyuz TM-12 1991–92, STS-60 (first joint U.S/Russian Space Shuttle Mission) 1994, STS-88 Endeavour 1998, Expedition-1 2000–01, Commdr Expedition-11 2005; spent 310 days in orbit on Soyuz TM-12 1991–92; Champion of Moscow 1983, Hero of the Soviet Union 1989, Hero of the Russian Fed. 1992, NASA Space Flight Medal 1994, 1998; Order of Lenin, Officier de la Légion d'Honneur. *Address:* Yuriy Gagarin Centre for Cosmonauts Training, Zvezdny Gorodok, Moscow Region, Russia. *Telephone:* (495) 971-86-16.

KRIM, Mathilde, BS, PhD; American medical researcher and organization official; *Founding Chairman, American Foundation for AIDS Research (amfAR);* b. 9 July 1926, Como, Italy; m. Arthur B. Krim (deceased); one d.; ed Univ. of Geneva, Switzerland; research scientist, Weizmann Inst. of Science, Israel 1953–59, Cornell Univ. Medical School 1959–62, Sloan-Kettering Inst. for Cancer Research 1962–81, Dir Interferon Lab. 1981–85; at Dept of Pediatrics, St Luke's Roosevelt Hosp. Center and Columbia Univ. 1986–90; Adjunct Prof. of Public Health and Man., Columbia Univ., New York 1990–; f. AIDS Medical Foundation (renamed American Foundation for AIDS Research 1985) 1983, Chair. 1983–2004, now Founding Chair.; 15 hon. doctorates including Dr hc (Dartmouth) 2005; Presidential Medal of Freedom 2000, Eleanor Roosevelt Val-Kill Medal 2001, ranked 86th by Forbes magazine amongst 100 Most Powerful Women 2004, and numerous other awards. *Publications:* 76 articles and papers in scientific and medical journals on cellular biology, virology and interferon research. *Leisure interests:* horticulture, zoology, visual arts. *Address:* American Foundation for AIDS Research, 120 Wall Street, 13th Floor, New York, NY 10005-3908 (office); Health Policy and Management, Mailman School of Public Health, Columbia University, 722 West 168th Street, New York, NY 10032-3702, USA (office). *Telephone:* (212) 806-1600 (amfAR) (office); (212) 988-7655 (Mailman School) (office). *Fax:* (212) 806-1601 (amfAR) (office). *Website:* www.amfar.org (office); mailman.hs.columbia.edu (office).

KRIPKE, Saul Aaron, BA, LHD; American philosopher and academic; *Distinguished Professor, Graduate Program in Philosophy, City University of New York;* b. 13 Nov. 1940, Bay Shore, New York; s. of Myer Samuel Kripke and Dorothy Kripke; m. Margaret P. Gilbert 1976 (divorced 1998); ed Harvard Univ.; Soc. of Fellows, Harvard Univ. 1963–66, concurrently Lecturer with rank of Asst Prof., Princeton Univ. 1964–66; Lecturer, Harvard Univ. 1966–68; Assoc. Prof., Rockefeller Univ. 1968–72, Prof. 1972–76; McCosh Prof. of Philosophy, Princeton Univ. 1977–98, now Emer.; currently Distinguished Prof., Grad. Program in Philosophy, CUNY; Fellow, American Acad. of Arts and Sciences; Corresp. Fellow, British Acad.; Fulbright Fellow 1962–63; Guggenheim Fellow 1968–69, 1977–78; Visiting Fellow, All Souls Coll., Oxford, UK 1977–78, 1989–90; Visiting Prof., The Hebrew Univ. 1998–; mem. American Philosophical Soc. 2004–; Hon. DHumLitt (Univ. of Neb. at Omaha) 1977, (Johns Hopkins Univ.) 1997, (Univ. of Haifa) 1998, (Univ. of Penn) 2005; Detur Prize 1960, Charles J. Wister Prize 1962, Howard Behrman Award 1988, Schock Prize in Logic and Philosophy 2001. *Publications:* Naming and Necessity 1980, Wittgenstein on Rules and Private Language 1982; numerous papers in professional journals and anthologies. *Address:* Graduate Program in Philosophy, CUNY Graduate Center, 365 Fifth Avenue, New York, NY 10016, USA (office). *Telephone:* (212) 817-8615 (home). *E-mail:* skripke@gc.cuny.edu (office). *Website:* web.gc.cuny.edu/philosophy/people/kripke.html (office).

KRISHNA, S. M., BA, BL, MCL; Indian lawyer, politician and professor of international law; b. 1 May 1932; s. of the late Shri S.C.Mallaiah; m. Smt. Prema 1964; two d.; ed Maharaja's Coll. Mysore, Govt Law Coll., Bangalore, Southern Methodist Univ. Dallas, George Washington Univ., Washington DC, USA; Prof. of Int. Law, Renukacharya Law Coll., Bangalore 1962–68; mem. Karnataka Legis. Ass. 1962–67, 1989–94; mem. Lok Sabha (Parl.) 1968–72; mem. Karnataka Legis. Council 1972–77, Minister of Commerce and Industries and Parl. Affairs 1972–77; returned to Parl. 1980, Minister of State for Industry 1983–84, for Finance 1984–85; Speaker, Karnataka Legis. Ass. 1989–1992; Deputy Chief Minister of Karnataka 1992–94; mem. Rajya Sabha 1996–99; Chief Minister of Karnataka 1999–2004; Gov. of Maharashtra 2004–08 (resgnd); fmr mem. del. to UN, New York 1982; Pres. KPCC 1999–2000; Del. Commonwealth Parl. Seminar, Westminster, UK 1990. *Leisure interests:* reading, designing men's clothes, sport. *Address:* c/o Raj Bhavan, Malabar Hill, Mumbai, Maharashtra, 400 035, India (office).

KRISHNAMOORTHY, V.; Sri Lankan diplomatist; *High Commissioner to Bangladesh;* fmr First Sec. and Head of Chancery, Perm. Rep. of Sri Lanka to Org. for Prohibition of Chemical Weapons, The Hague, Netherlands; currently High Commr to Bangladesh; Patron Sri Lanka-Bangladesh Chamber of Commerce and Industry. *Address:* High Commission of Sri Lanka, House 4A, Road 113, Gulshan Model Town, Dhaka 1212, Bangladesh (office). *Telephone:* (2) 9896353 (office). *Fax:* (2) 8823971 (office). *E-mail:* slhc@citechco.net (office).

KRISHNAMURTY, G. V. G., BA, BSc, BL; Indian election commissioner (retd) and lawyer; b. 19 Nov. 1934, Chirala, Andhra Pradesh; s. of G. V. Subbarao and Mrs G. Rajeswaramma; m. Mrs G. Padma 1957; one s. one d.; ed Andhra Univ.; pro-independence student activist and mem. Azad Hindu Fauz Youth League 1945–47; advocate, Andhra Pradesh High Court 1958; lecturer, Law Coll. Osmania Univ. 1958, 1962; Sr Research Officer, Indian Law Inst. 1962–63; advocate, Supreme Court; Deputy Legal Adviser, Comm. of Inquiry, Cabinet Secr. 1972–73; Additional Legal Adviser, Ministry of Law and ex-officio Govt Counsel, Delhi High Court 1973–76; Supreme Court of India 1978–79; Govt Arbitrator 1979–83; Jt Sec. and Legal Adviser 1983–87; Additional Sec. Govt of India 1987–88, Special Sec. 1988–89; Sec. Law Comm. of India 1989–92; Election Commr of India 1993–99; Int. Observer Sri Lanka Pres. Elections 1999, Kazakhstan Parl. Elections 2004; del. to various int. confs etc.; numerous professional appointments and other distinctions; Hon. LLD (Jhansi Univ.) 1996; National Citizen's Award 1990, Great Son of the Soil Award 1996, NRI Gold Int. Award 1996, Glory of India Int. Award 1998, Champion of Indian Democracy Award 2001, Pride of India Int. Award 2002. *Publications include:* Dynamics of Diplomacy 1968, Modern Diplomacy, Dialectics and Dimensions 1980; articles in legal journals. *Leisure interests:* reading, watching nature, cultural activities. *Address:* 1402 Kausumbhi, opp. Delhi Anand Vihar ISBT, Ghaziabad, Uttar Pradesh, India. *Telephone:* (120) 2778056 (office); (120) 2778056 (home). *Fax:* (120) 2778056 (office); (120) 2778056 (home).

KRISHNAN, Natarajan, BA (Econs); Indian diplomatist; b. 6 Oct. 1928, Mayuram, Tamil Nadu; s. of the late V. Natarajan; m. Lalitha Krishnan; one s. two d.; ed Univ. of Madras; joined Indian Foreign Service 1951; Third Sec., later Second Sec., Bangkok 1955–56; Second Sec., Chargé d'Affaires, Phnom Penh 1956–57; UnderSec. Ministry of External Affairs 1957–58; First Sec., Chargé d'Affaires, Buenos Aires 1959–62; Deputy Sec., Dir Ministry of External Affairs 1962–67; Consul-Gen. and Perm. Rep. to UN Offices, Geneva 1967–71; Joint Sec. Ministry of External Affairs 1971–76; Amb. to Yugoslavia 1976–79; Additional Sec. Ministry of External Affairs 1979–81; Amb. and Perm. Rep. to UN 1981–87; Dean, School of Int. Studies, Pondicherry Univ. 1988–90; Prime Minister's Special Envoy for Africa 1987–89; mem. Exec. Bd UNESCO 1989–93; mem. Commonwealth Observer Group, Presidential and Parliamentary Elections in United Repub. of Tanzania 1995. *Address:* Flat 2C, King's Crest Apts, No. 8 Millers Road, Bangalore 560046, India.

KRISHNAN, Tan Sri T(atparanandam) Ananda, BA, MBA; Malaysian business executive; *CEO, Usaha Tegas Sendirian Berhad;* b. 1938, Kuala Lumpur; m.; three c.; ed Victoria Inst., Kuala Lumpur, Univ. of Melbourne, Australia, Harvard Univ., USA; f. Exoil Trading; CEO Usaha Tegas Sendirian Berhad (investment and consulting org. with interests in communications, broadcasting, media, leisure, entertainment and energy); cos in which it has an interest include Maxis Communications (took pvt. in leveraged buyout 2007), MEASAT Broadcast Network Systems, Binariang Satellites Systems, Bumi Armada, Objektif Bersatu, Celestial Pictures Ltd, Hong Kong; Man. Usaha Tegas Entertainment Systems; Head of Astro All Asia Networks PLC; developer of Petronas Twin Towers, Kuala Lumpur. *Address:* Usaha Tegas Sendirian Berhad, Level 44, Menara MAXIS, Kuala Lumpur City Centre, 50088 Kuala Lumpur (office); Maxis Communications Berhad, Level 18, Menara Maxis, KLCC Off Jalan Ampang, 50088 Kuala Lumpur, Malaysia. *Telephone:* (3) 23807788 (office); (3) 23307000. *Fax:* (3) 23806677 (office); (3) 23300008. *E-mail:* corpinfo@maxis.com.my. *Website:* www.maxis.com.my.

KRISTAN, Ivan, BA, DJur; Slovenian politician, lawyer and academic; *Professor Emeritus, Faculty of Law, Ljubljana University;* b. 12 June 1930, Arnovo; ed Ljubljana Univ.; worked in trade unions 1956–67; Teacher, Faculty of Law, Ljubljana Univ. 1967–77, Prof. 1977–87, Dean 1983–85, Rector 1985–87, now Prof. Emer.; mem. Cttee for Constitutional Reforms of the Slovenian Repub. 1970–74, 1987–90; mem. Constitutional Court of Yugoslavia 1987–91; Pres. Nat. Council of Slovenian Repub. 1992–98; Pres. of Supervising Cttee, Int. Asscn for Constitutional Law (IACL); mem. Asscn of Fighters for the Liberation of Slovenia. *Publications:* moe than 200 books, articles and scientific papers on legal problems of human rights, federalism, self-determination and sovereignty of nations, including Constitutional Law of Socialist Fed. Repub. of Yugoslavia (co-author). *Address:* c/o Drustvo za ustavno pravo, Subiceva 4, 1000, Ljubljana, Slovenia (office). *E-mail:* ivan .kristan@siol.net.

KRISTEVA, Julia, DèsL; French psychoanalyst and writer; b. 24 June 1941, Silven, Bulgaria; m. Philippe Sollers 1967; one s; ed Univ. of Sofia and Ecole des Hautes Etudes en Sciences Sociales, Paris, Univ. of Paris VII; researcher in linguistics and French literature, Lab. of Social Anthropology, Ecole des Hautes Etudes en Sciences Sociales 1967–73; Prof., Univ. of Paris VII 1973–99, Prof. classe exceptionelle 1999–, Dir Ecole Doctorale Langue, Littérature, Image, civilisations et sciences humaines; Chargé de mission auprès du Pres. for the handicapped; Visiting Prof., Columbia Univ., New York 1974, Univ. of Toronto 1992; mem. Editorial Bd Telquel 1970–82; mem. Soc. psychanalytique de Paris, American Acad. of Arts and Sciences, Inst. Universitaire de France, British Acad., Acad. universelle des cultures; Chevalier, Ordre des Arts et des Lettres 1987, Chevalier, Légion d'honneur 1997, Officier, Ordre nat. du Mérite 2004, Officier de la Légion d'honneur 2008; Dr hc (Western Ont., Canada) 1995, (Victoria, Toronto) 1997, (Harvard) 1999, (Univ. Libre de Belgique) 2000, (Bayreuth) 2000, (Toronto) 2000, (Sofia) 2002, (New School, New York) 2003; Prix Henri Hertz Chancellerie des Universités de Paris 1989, Holberg Int. Memorial Prize, Norway 2004, Grande Médaille de Vermeil de la Mairie de Paris 2005, Award of Merit, Bucknell Univ. 2006. *Publications include:* Séméiotike: Recherches pour une sémana-lyse 1969, Le Texte du roman, approche sémiologique d'une structure discursive transformationnelle 1970, La Révolution du langage poétique:

l'avant-garde à la fin du XIXème siècle, Lautréamont et Mallarmé 1974, Des chinoises 1974, Polylogue 1977, Folle Vérité (with Jean Michel Ribettes) 1979, Pouvoirs de l'horreur: Essai sur l'abjection 1980, Le Langage, cet inconnu 1981, Histoires d'amour 1985, Au commencement était l'amour 1985, Soleil noir, dépression et mélancolie 1987, Etrangers à nous-mêmes (Prix Henri Hertz 1989) 1988, Les Samouraïs 1990, Lettre ouverte à Harlem Désir 1990, Le Vieil homme et les loups 1991, Les Nouvelles maladies de l'âme 1993, Le Temps sensible: Proust et l'expérience littéraire (essay) 1994, Possessions 1996, Sens et non-sens de la révolte 1996, La Révolte intime 1997, L'Avenir d'une révolte 1998, Le Génie féminin, Vol. 1: Hannah Arendt 1999, Vol. 2: Melanie Klein 2000, Colette 2002, Meurtre à Byzance 2004, La Haine et le Pardon: Pouvoirs et limites de la psychanalyse III 2005, Thérèse mon amour 2008. *Address:* Université de Paris VII, Grands Moulins, 7th Floor, bureau 777C, 16, rue Marguerite Duras, 75205 Paris cedex 13, France (office). *Telephone:* 1-57-27-64-42 (office). *Fax:* 1-57-27-64-44 (office). *E-mail:* julia .kristeva@univ-paris-diderot.fr (office). *Website:* www.kristeva.fr.

KRISTIANSEN, Kjeld Kirk, BSc, MBA; Danish business executive; *Vice-Chairman, LEGO Group;* b. 27 Dec. 1947, ; s. of Godtfred Kirk Christiansen and Edith Kirk Christiansen; grandson of Ole Kirk Christiansen, founder of LEGO; m. Camilla Kirk Christiansen 1974; one s. two d.; ed Århus Business School, IMD International, Lausanne, Switzerland; mem. Bd LEGO Toy Co. 1975–, inherited co. (majority shareholder) 1979, Vice-Chair. LEGO Group 1996–, Pres. and CEO 1979–2004, Chair. and Co-owner (with his three c.) LEGO A/S, Chair. and Co-owner (with sister Gunhild) KIRKBI A/S, Chair. LEGO Foundation, Ole Kirk's Foundation, Edith and Godtfred Kirk Christiansen's Foundation. *Leisure interests:* breeding Danish horses, sports cars. *Address:* LEGO Holding A/S, Aastvej 1, 7190 Billund, Denmark (office). *Telephone:* 79-50-60-70 (office). *Fax:* 75-33-27-25 (office). *Website:* www.lego .com (office).

KRIŠTO, Borjana; Bosnia and Herzegovina politician; *President, Federation of Bosnia and Herzegovina;* b. 13 Aug. 1961, Livno; m.; fmr Vice-Pres. of Parl.; fmr Vice-Pres., Fed. of Bosnia and Herzegovina; Minister of Justice 2003–07; Rep. to Council of Europe 2007–; Pres. Fed. of Bosnia and Herzegovina 2007–; mem. Croatian Democratic Union of Bosnia and Herzegovina. *Address:* Office of the President of the Federation of Bosnia and Herzegovina, 71000 Sarajevo, Alipašina 41, Bosnia and Herzegovina (office). *Telephone:* (33) 472618 (office). *Fax:* (33) 472618 (office). *E-mail:* info@fbihvlada.gov.ba (office). *Website:* www .fbihvlada.gov.ba (office).

KRISTO, Vladimir, CSc, DIur; Albanian politician; *President of the Consti-tutional Court;* b. 8 April 1947, Korça; ed Tirana Univ.; Chief of Studies' Dept, Gen. Attorney's Office 1983–92; Deputy Minister of Justice 1992–96, 2005–07; Legal Advisor to Prime Minister of Albania 1996–98; pvt. legal practice 1998–2005; mem. Constitutional Court 2007–, Pres. 2007–; fmr mem. High Council of Justice, Co-ordination and Legal Co-operation Cttee, Council of Europe. *Publications:* numerous articles and academic papers on law and public admin. *Address:* Constitutional Court, Bulevardi Dëshmorët e Kombit, Tirana, Albania (office). *Telephone:* (4) 228357 (office). *Fax:* (4) 228357 (office). *E-mail:* kujtim.osmani@gjk.gov.al (office). *Website:* www.gjk.gov.al (office).

KRISTOFFERSON, Kris, BA, PhD; American country singer, songwriter and actor; b. (Kris Carson), 22 June 1936, Brownsville, TX; m. 1st; one s. one d.; m. 2nd Rita Coolidge 1973 (divorced 1980); one d.; m. 3rd Lisa Meyers 1983; four s., one d.; ed Pomona Coll. and Univ. of Oxford; Capt. in US Army 1960–65; songwriter 1965–; solo recording artist 1969–; mem. of side project, The Highwaymen (with Willie Nelson, Johnny Cash, Waylon Jennings) 1985–; numerous concerts world-wide; actor 1972–; CMA Song of the Year (for Sunday Morning Coming Down) 1970, Grammy Awards for Best Country Song 1972, Best Country Vocal Performance (with Coolidge) 1973, 1976, Golden Globe for Best Actor 1976, ACM Single of the Year (for Highwayman, with The Highwaymen) 1986, two American Music Awards (with The Highwaymen) 1986, Americana Awards Free Speech Award 2003, Johnny Cash Visionary Award, CMT Music Awards 2007. *Films include:* Cisco Pike 1972, Pat Garrett and Billy the Kid 1973, Blume in Love 1973, Bring Me the Head of Alfredo Garcia 1974, Alice Doesn't Live Here Anymore 1974, The Sailor Who Fell From Grace With The Sea 1976, A Star is Born 1976, Vigilante Force 1976, Semi-Tough 1977, Convoy 1978, Heaven's Gate 1981, Rollover 1981, Welcome Home 1989, Millennium 1989, A Soldier's Daughter Never Cries 1998, Blade 1 1998, Come Dance with Me 1999, Payback 1999, Limbo 1999, Joyriders 1999, Comanche 2000, Planet of the Apes 2001, Chelsea Walls 2001, Wooly Boys 2001, D-Tox 2002, Blade II 2002, Where the Red Fern Grows 2003, Blade III 2003, The Jacket, Lives of the Saints, Where the Red Fern Grows, Dreamer 2005, Gun (voice) 2005, The Wendell Baker Story 2005, Fast Food Nation 2006, Disappearances 2006, Requiem for Billy the Kid (voice) 2006, Room 10 2006. *Television appearances include:* Freedom Road (TV film) 1979, Amerika (series) 1987, Rip 1989, Sandino, Christmas in Connecticut 1992, Tad 1995. *Recordings include:* albums: Kristofferson 1970, The Silver-Tongued Devil and I 1971, Border Lord 1972, Jesus Was a Capricorn 1973, Full Moon (with Rita Coolidge) 1973, Spooky Lady's Sideshow 1974, Who's to Bless and Who's to Blame 1975, Breakaway (with Rita Coolidge) 1975, A Star Is Born (soundtrack) 1977, Surreal Thing 1976, Songs of Kristofferson 1977, Easter Island 1978, Natural Act (with Rita Coolidge) 1979, Shake Hands With The Devil (with Rita Coolidge) 1979, Help Me Make It Through The Night 1980, To The Bone 1981, The Winning Hand 1983, Music From Songwriter (with Willie Nelson) 1984, Highwayman (with The Highwaymen) 1985, Repossessed 1986, Third World Warrior 1990, Highwaymen 2 (with The Highwaymen) 1992, A Moment of Forever 1995, The Austin Sessions 1999, Broken Freedom Song: Live from San Francisco 2003, Repossessed/Third World Warrior 2004, This Old Road 2006. *Address:* Gelfand, Rennert & Feldman, 1880 Century Park East, Suite 1600, Los Angeles, CA 90067 (office);

c/o One Way, 1 Prospect Avenue, PO Box 6429, Albany, NY 12206, USA. *Telephone:* (310) 553-1707 (office). *E-mail:* mwalsh@grfllp.com (office).

KRISTOPANS, Vilis; Latvian politician; b. 13 June 1954; m.; ed Riga State Tech. Univ.; basketball player, Latvian nat. team 1972–81; sports instructor Sports Cttee, Daugava Cen. Council 1977–83; coach, Head coach, basketball team VEF 1983–89; Chair. co-operative soc. Noster 1990; Dir-Gen. Jt Dardedze 1990–92; Vice-Pres. Interbaltija Ltd 1992–93; Minister of State Revenue 1993–94; Chair. Deutsche-Lettische Bank 1994–95; Minister of Transport Latvian Repub. 1995–98; Prime Minister of Latvia, also Minister of Agric. 1998–99; mem. Parl. (Seimas) 1993–98; mem. Bd Latvijas ceļš (Latvian Way); Pres. Latvian Basketball League 1992–97; mem. Ventspils Free Ports Bd 1994–. *Address:* Latvijas ceļš, Terbatas jela 4-9, 1011 Rīga, Latvia (office). *Telephone:* 6708-7111 (office).

KRIVINE, Alain; French journalist and politician; b. 10 July 1941, Paris; m. Michèle Martinet 1960; two d.; ed Lycée Condorcet and Faculté des Lettres de Paris; mem. Jeunesses communistes 1956, French CP 1958; Leader Union of Student Communists, Paris-Sorbonne Univ. 1964–65; f. Revolutionary Communist Youth 1966 (disbanded by the Govt 1968), Communist League 1969 (dissolved 1973); cand. presidential elections 1969, 1974; journalist, Rouge 1969–; mem. Political Bureau of Ligue Communiste Révolutionnaire 1974–2006; mem. European Parl. 1999–2004; mem. Secretariat UNIFI de la IVe Internationale. *Publications:* La Farce électorale 1969, Questions sur la révolution 1973, Mais si, rebelles et repentis (with Daniel Bensaid) 1988. *Address:* Ligue Communiste Révolutionnaire (LCR), 2 rue Richard-Lenoir, 93100 Montreuil, France. *Telephone:* 1-48-70-42-30. *Fax:* 1-48-59-23-28. *E-mail:* lcr@les-rouge.org. *Website:* www.lcr-rouge.org.

KRIVINE, Emmanuel; French violinist and conductor; b. 7 May 1947, Grenoble; s. of Henri Krivine and Rejla Krivine (née Weisbrod); one d.; ed Conservatoire Nat. Supérieur de Musique et de Danse, Paris, Conservatoire Royal de Bruxelles; pupil of Henryk Szeryng and Yehudi Menuhin; solo violinist, Paris 1964, Brussels 1965–68; Perm. Guest Conductor Radio-France 1976–83; Dir Lorraine-Metz Regional Orchestra 1981–83; Prin. Guest Conductor Orchestra of Lyon 1983; Artistic Dir French Nat. Youth Orchestra 1983–; Musical Dir Nat. Orchestra of Lyon 1987–2000; Conductor French Nat. Orchestra 2001–; Guest Conductor various int. orchestras including Berlin Philharmonic, Concertgebouw and Chamber Orchestra of Europe 1977–; Chevalier, Ordre nat. du Mérite, Officier des Arts et Lettres; Ginette-Neveu Medal 1971 and numerous other awards. *Leisure interests:* literature, philosophy. *Address:* c/o Askonas Holt, Lincoln House, 300 High Holborn, London, WC1V 7JH, England (office); 2 rue Hotel de Ville, 1800 Vevey, Switzerland. *Telephone:* (20) 7400-1700 (office). *Fax:* (20) 7400-1799 (office). *E-mail:* info@askonasholt.co.uk (office). *Website:* www.askonasholt.co.uk (office).

KRIVOKAPIĆ, Ranko; Montenegrin politician; *Speaker, Skupština Crne Gore (Parliament);* b. 17 Aug. 1961, Kotor; two c.; mem. Social Democratic Party of Montenegro (Socijaldemokratska Partija Crne Gore), currently Pres.; mem. Skupština Republike Crne Gore (Parl.) 1989–, Speaker 2003–; mem. Presidency of Union of Reform Forces of Montenegro 1990; fmr Head of Montenegrin Del. to Parl. Ass., OSCE. *Address:* Office of the Speaker, Skupština Crne Gore, 81000 Podgorica, Svetog Petra Cetinjskog 2, Montenegro (office). *Telephone:* (81) 242182 (office). *Fax:* (81) 242192 (office). *E-mail:* predsjednik@skupstina.mn.yu (office). *Website:* www.skupstina.cg.yu (office).

KRIWET, Heinz, Dr rer. pol; German business executive; b. 2 Nov. 1931, Bochum; ed Univs of Cologne and Freiburg; trainee, German Iron & Steel Fed. 1960–61; Personal Asst to Vice-Pres. Sales, Hüttenwerk Rheinhausen (Krupp) 1962–63, Man. Planning and Marketing Dept 1964–67; Gen. Man. Sales, Friedrich Krupp Hüttenwerke AG, Bochum 1968, mem. Exec. Bd in charge of Sales 1969–72; mem. Exec. Bd in charge of Sales, Thyssen AG, Düsseldorf 1973–83; Chair. Exec. Bd Thyssen Stahl AG, Duisburg 1983–91; Chair. Exec. Bd Thyssen AG, Düsseldorf 1991; Chair. Supervisory Bd ThyssenKrupp AG –2001, now mem.; fmr Chair. Thyssen Industrie AG, Thyssen Handelsunion AG, Thyssen Edelstahlwerke AG, Thyssen Stahl AG, Thyssen Wohnbau GmbH, Rheinische Kalksteinwerke GmbH, Fried. Krupp AG Hoesch-Krupp; mem. Supervisory Bd Allianz Lebensversicherungs AG, Commerzbank AG, Mannesmann-Röhrenwerke AG, Pechiney Int. Paris, RWE Energie AG, Gerling Group, Hapag Lloyd, Leipziger Messe GmbH; mem. Bd of Dirs The Budd Co. Troy, Mich., USA; mem. Man. Bd Inst. Int. du Fer et de l'Acier, Brussels; Chair. German Iron & Steel Fed. 1984–88. *Address:* Thyssen AG, August-Thyssen-Strasse 1, 40211 Düsseldorf, Germany.

KRIŽANIČ, Franc, MSc, PhD; Slovenian economist, academic and government official; *Minister of Finance;* b. 4 Dec. 1954, Ljubljana; ed Univ. of Ljubljana; Assoc. Prof., Faculty of Econs, Univ. of Ljubljana 2000–, Dir Law School, Econ. Inst. 2001–08; Pres. Council of Experts, Insurance Supervision Agency 2000–05; Pres. Supervisory Bd, Slovenian Red Cross 2007–08; Minister of Finance 2008–. *Publications:* The Investment Multiplier in Slovenia 1992, The Slovenian Economy: An Econometric Study of the Periods 1986–1992–1994 1995. *Address:* Ministry of Finance, 1502 Ljubljana, Župančičeva 3, Slovenia (office). *Telephone:* (1) 3696610 (office). *Fax:* (1) 3696619 (office). *E-mail:* gp.mf@gov.si (office). *Website:* www.mf.gov.si (office).

KROEMER, Herbert, PhD; American scientist and academic; *Professor of Electrical and Computer Engineering, University of California, Santa Barbara;* b. 25 Aug. 1928, Weimar, Germany; ed Univ. of Göttingen; carried out pioneering work in semi-conductor research; Prof. of Electrical and Computer Eng, Univ. of Calif., Santa Barbara 1985–; Nat. Lecturer, IEEE Electron Devices Soc.; mem. NAS, Nat. Acad. of Eng, IEEE, American Physics Soc.; Dr hc (Tech. Univ., Aachen) 1985, (Lund) 1998; J. Erbers Award 1973, Heinrich Welker Medal 1982, Jack Morton Award (IEEE) 1986, Alexander von Humboldt Research Award 1994, Nobel Prize for Physics (jt recipient) 2000. *Publications:* Quantum Mechanics: For Engineering, Materials Science and Applied Physics, Thermal Physics (jt author). *Address:* ECE Department and Materials Department 2205A Engineering Science Building, Electrical and Computer Engineering Department, University of California, Santa Barbara, CA 93106-9560, USA (office). *Telephone:* (805) 893-3078 (office). *Fax:* (805) 893-7990 (office). *E-mail:* kroemer@ece.ucsb.edu (office). *Website:* www.ece.ucsb.edu/Faculty/Kroemer/default.html (office).

KROES, Neelie, MSc (Econs); Dutch politician and economist; *Commissioner for Competition, European Commission;* b. 19 July 1941, Rotterdam; ed Erasmus Univ., Rotterdam; Asst Prof. of Transport Econs, Erasmus Univ. 1965–1971; mem. Rotterdam Municipal Council, Rotterdam Chamber of Commerce 1969–71; mem. Parl. 1971–77; Vice-Minister of Transport, Public Works and Telecommunication 1977–81, Minister of Transport, Public Works and Telecommunication 1982–89; Advisor to EU Commr for Transport 1989–91; EU Commr for Competition 2004–; Pres. Nijenrode Univ. 1991–2000; Chair. Supervisory Bd MeyerMonitor –2004, Nederlands Luchtvaart Overleg (Dutch Aviation Platform) –2004; mem. Supervisory Bd Cório, Royal P&O Nedlloyd NV, Ballast Nedam, New Skies Satellites, Lucent Technologies BV (Netherlands), Nederlandse Spoorwegen NV (Dutch Railways), Volvo Group, Thales Group –2004; Dir (non-exec.) MM02 plc –2004; mem. Bd of Trustees ProLogis International –2004; Chair. Governing Bd Delta Psychiatrical Hosp., Het Rembrandthuis Foundation, Poets of All Nations, Overlegorgaan Waterbeheer en Noordzee-aangelegenheden; fmr Chair. Nyenrode Fund, Supervisory Bd Port Support International BV, Governing Bd TBS Mental Hosp. De Kijvelanden, Governing Bd Bezinnings Groep Water, Supervisory Bd NIB Capital NV, Supervisory Bd Intis BV, Governing Bd Kunsthal; mem. Governing Bd Nelson Mandela Children Fund Member, Bd Dirs World Cancer Research Fund; fmr mem. Governing Bd Royal Trade Fair (Koninklijke Jaarbeurs), Governing Bd Stichting International Human Resources, Development VNO/NCW, Advisory Bd International Problems (AIV), Supervisory Bd Dirs Prologis European Properties, Advisory Bd PriceWaterhouseCooper, Supervisory Bd NCM Holding NV, Bd of Dirs Brambles Industries Ltd (Australia), Supervisory Bd McDonald's, Bd of Dirs SC Johnson Wax Euro Bd, Supervisory Bd Digital Equipment BV, Supervisory Bd Groeneveld Transport Efficiency, Raad van Toezicht Veerstichting, Competitiveness Group to Chair. EC, Governing Bd Insurance Authority, Governing Bd Conservation of Nature, High Level Group on the trans-European Network; fmr adviser, Monitor Group, Arcadis (Heidemij/Grabowsky); Kt, Order of the Dutch Lion 1981, Grand Officier, Légion d'honneur 1984, Bundesverdienstkreuz 1985, Grand Officer, Order of Orange Nassau 1989, Bintang Mahaputra Adiprana Order (Indonesia) 1993; Dr hc (Hull) 1989; Woman of the Year in Infrastructure, Int. Road Fed. 1993, ranked by Forbes magazine amongst 100 Most Powerful Women (44th) 2005, (38th) 2006, (59th) 2007, (47th) 2008. *Address:* European Commission, 200 rue de la Loi, 1049 Brussels, Belgium (office). *Telephone:* (2) 299-11-11 (office). *Fax:* (2) 295-01-38 (office). *E-mail:* Neelie.Kroes@cec.eu.int (office). *Website:* ec.europa.eu/comm/commission_barroso/kroes/index_en.html (office).

KROGSGAARD-LARSEN, Povl, PhD, DSc; Danish scientist and academic; *Professor, Department of Medicinal Chemistry, Danish University of Pharmaceutical Sciences;* b. 17 May 1941, Frøslev Mors; s. of Niels Saaby and Marie Saaby (née Krogsgaard) Larsen; m. Tove Krogsgaard-Larsen 1964; one s. one d.; ed Danish Univ. of Pharmaceutical Sciences; Asst Prof. Royal Danish School of Pharmacy (now Danish Univ of Pharmaceutical Sciences) 1970–75, Assoc. Prof. 1975–86, Prof. 1986–, Rector 2001–04; mem. Royal Danish Acad. of Sciences and Letters 1986, Danish Acad. of Natural Sciences 1987, Danish Acad. of Tech. Sciences 1987; mem. Bd Dirs Alfred Beuzon Foundation 1991– (currently Vice Chair.); mem. Bd Dirs Carlsberg Foundation 1993– (currently Chair.); Chair. Carlsberg A/S 1993–, Aūriga A/S 2002–; Paul Ehrlich Prize 1989, Lundbeck Foundation Prize 1989, H. C. Ørsted Award 1967, Ole Rømer Award 1983, Astra Award 1991, W. Th. Nauta Award 1996, Pharmaceutical Research Achievement Award 2004. *Publications:* 340 scientific articles, 80 scientific reviews, eight science books (ed.), one textbook (ed.). *Leisure interests:* history, sport. *Address:* Department of Medicinal Chemistry, Danish University of Pharmaceutical Sciences, 2 Universitetsparken, 2100 Copenhagen (office); 25 Elmevej, Blovstrød, 3450 Allerød, Denmark (home). *Telephone:* 35-30-65-11 (office); 48-17-12-15 (home). *Fax:* 35-30-60-40 (office); 48-17-55-50 (home). *E-mail:* pk@carlsbergfondet.dk (office); pk@carlsbergfondet.dk (office). *Website:* www.dfh.dk/uk (office).

KROHN DEVOLD, Kristin, MSc; Norwegian national organization official and fmr politician; *Secretary-General, Den Norske Turistforening (Norwegian Trekking Association);* b. 12 Aug. 1961, Ålesund; m.; two c.; ed Univ. of Bergen, Norwegian School of Econs, Univ. of Oslo, Norwegian Nat. Defence Coll.; mem. Oslo City Parl. 1991–93; mem. Parl. (Stortinget) for Oslo 1993–97, 1997–2001, 2001–05, Sec. of the Lagting (Presidium, Stortinget) 1993–97, mem. Standing Cttee on Business and Industry 1993–97, Election Cttee 1997–2001, 2001–05, Working Procedures Cttee 1997–2001, Extended Foreign Affairs Cttee 1997–2001, Chair. Standing Cttee on Justice 1997–2001; Minister of Defence 2001–05; Substitute mem. Del. to Consultation Organ for European Econ. Area Affairs, Brussels 1993–97; Group Sec. Parl. Group, Conservative Party 1987–92, mem. Bd Party 1996, Parl. Steering Cttee 1997–2001; Sec.-Gen. Norwegian Trekking Assen 2006–; mem. Bd Statistics Norway 1989–93, St Hanshaugen Residence for the Elderly and Nursing Home 1991–92, Main Cttee of World Handball Championship 1999, Save the Children Norway 1999–. *Address:* Den Norske Turistforening (Norwegian Trekking Association), Youngstorget 1, 0181 Oslo, Norway (office). *Telephone:* 40-00-18-68 (office). *E-mail:* info@turistforeningen.no (office). *Website:* www.turistforeningen.no (home).

KRÓL, Jan Władysław; Polish politician and economist; *Strategic Advisor, Ernst and Young Poland;* b. 24 June 1950, Mielec; four c.; ed Higher School of Econs, Kraków, Jagiellonian Univ., Kraków; Worker PAX Soc. 1974–81, Inco-Veritas 1982–83, Remo and Rovan cos. 1983–89; mem. Solidarity Independent Self-governing Trade Union (NSZZ Solidarność) 1980–; assoc. Dziekania Political Thought Club 1984–88; deputy Govt Plenipotentiary for Local Govt Reform 1989–90; Deputy to the Sejm (Parl.) 1989–2001, Vice-Leader Trade and Services Comm. 1989–97, Sec. Democratic Union (UD) Parl. Caucus 1989–91, leader Extraordinary Cttee for consideration of bills within the State Enterprise Pact 1991–93, Vice-Marshal of Sejm 1997–2001; (Speaker) Co-Chair. Polish Ass. of Sejms of Poland and Lithuania 1997–2001; co.-f. and mem. ROAD (Democratic Campaign Citizens' Movt) 1990–91; Chair Polish-Canadian Econ. Council 1990; co.-f. and mem. Democratic Union 1991–94; mem. Nat. Polish Bd of the Friends of Lithuania Club 1992; mem. Freedom Union (UW) 1994– (also mem. Nat. Bd); Chair. Programme Bd Foundation for Econ. Educ. 1999–; Deputy Pres., Council of the Bd, Foundation in Support of Local Democracy; currently Strategic Advisor Ernst and Young Poland, Warsaw. *Publications:* Świadectwo (Evidence) 1989, Przodem do przodu (Face forward) 1993, Z notatnika posła (From Deputy Notebook) 1997, W dialogu (In Dialogue) 1999, Pułapki polskiej demokracji (Polish Democracy Traps) 2001; and numerous articles. *Leisure interests:* tourism, horses. *Address:* Ernst and Young Poland, 39 Sienna Street, 00-121 Warsaw, Poland (office). *Telephone:* (22) 557-79-49 (office). *Fax:* (22) 557-70-01 (office). *E-mail:* fee@gdnet.pl (office); jan.krol@pl.ey.com (office). *Website:* www.europa.edu.pl (office).

KROL, John A., BS, MSc; American business executive (retd); b. 16 Oct. 1936, Ware, Mass.; m. Janet Valley; two d.; ed Tufts Univ., Bettis Nuclear Reactor Eng School; commissioned into USN 1959, worked as nuclear engineer Bureau of Ships Naval Reactors Br.; joined E.I. du Pont de Nemours & Company as chemist, Wilmington, Del. 1963, marketing and manufacturing positions with DuPont Fibers 1965–83, Vice-Pres. 1983, Sr Vice-Pres. 1990, Group Vice-Pres., Sr Vice-Pres. DuPont Agric. Products 1986, Vice-Chair. DuPont 1992–97, Chair. 1997–98, Pres. 1995–97, CEO 1995–98 (retd); mem. Nat. Agricultural Chemists Asscn, Bd of Dirs 1987–; mem. Bd of Dirs ACE Ltd, MeadWestvaco Corpn, Milliken & Company, Tyco Int. Ltd 2002–; fmr mem. Bd of Dirs Mead Corp., J. P. Morgan & Co., Nat. Asscn of Mfrs, Del. Art Museum, Wilmington 2000, Catalyst; Trustee Tufts Univ., Univ. of Del., Hagley Museum, US Council for Int. Business; mem. American Chemical Soc. Corp. Liaison Bd, Business Roundtable, Business Council; mem. exec. Cttee Del. Business Roundtable, Business/Public Educ. Council. *Leisure interests:* golf, tennis, squash, skiing. *Address:* c/o Board of Directors, Tyco International Ltd, 9 Roszel Road, Princeton, NJ 08540, USA.

KROLL, Alexander (Alex) S., BA; American advertising executive; *Chairman Emeritus, Young and Rubicam Inc.;* b. 1937, Leechburg, Pa; ed Rutgers Univ.; fmr player, NY Titans, American Football League; with Young & Rubicam, Inc., New York 1962–, copywriter 1962–68, Vice-Pres. 1968–69, Sr Vice-Pres. 1969–70, Exec. Vice-Pres. and Worldwide Creative Dir 1970–75, Pres. and COO 1982, CEO 1985, then Chair. and CEO 1986, also Dir, Chair. Emer. 1994–; Man. Dir Young & Rubicam USA 1975–77, Pres. 1977; Chair. Emer. The Advertising Council; Kodak Life Achievement Award 1985, Nat. Coll. Athletic Asscn Silver Anniversary Award 1987, Coll. Football Hall of Fame 1997. *Address:* c/o Young & Rubicam Brands, 285 Madison Avenue, New York, NY 10017, USA.

KROLL, Lucien; Belgian architect and town planner; b. 17 March 1927, Brussels; m. Simone Marti; two d.; ed Athénée Royal de Huy, Ecole Nat. Supérieure d'Architecture de la Cambre, Institut Supérieur d'Urbanisme de la Cambre, Institut Supérieur et Int. d'Urbanisme Appliqué, Brussels; numerous works in Belgium, France, Italy, Germany, Italy and Rwanda 1953–; Founder mem. Inst. d'Esthétique Industrielle 1956; own architectural practice 1952–; environmental research, Ecolonia, Netherlands; exhbns of work in Brussels, Hanover, Utrecht, Aubervilliers, Copenhagen, Aarhus, Luxembourg, Boston; organized confs including Habiter?, Brussels 1972; visiting prof. and lecturer many univs throughout Europe, USA and Japan; mem. Acad. française d'Architecture 1985–; Hon. mem. Bund der Deutschen Architekten; Commdr, Ordre des Arts et des Lettres; Médaille J.-F. Delarue, Acad. française d'Architecture 1980. *Works include:* houses, churches, schools, exhbns, industrial design, monasteries Ottignies and Rwanda; town-planning in Brussels and Kigali, Rwanda, Brussels (housing, with participation of future inhabitants) 1967, ministries and Pres.'s Palace, Rwanda, Medical Faculties Neighbourhood, Brussels 1970, Froidmont Dominican house 1970, housing, Cergy-Pontoise (with participation of future inhabitants) 1977, housing rehabilitation, Alençon 1978, Alma underground station, Brussels 1979, housing, Marne-la-Vallée 1980, Utrecht Acad., computer-aided design and creation of 'Landscape' program 1981, housing, Laroche-Clermault, France, Bordeaux, St-Germain, France, Haarlem, Netherlands, Knokke, Pessac-Bordeaux, Bethoncourt, Montbéliard, St.-Dizier, etc.; schools Saint-Germain, Cinais en Touraine, Faenza (Italy); tech. lycée Belfort; Maison de 3e âge, Ostend; extension to Univ. of St-Etienne; Maison de l'Environnement, Belfort; tech. lycée Caudry (High Environmental Quality). *Publications:* CAD-Architektur 1985, Architecture of Complexity 1986, Buildings and Projects (also in German and French) 1987, Componenten 1995, Bien vieillir chez soi 1995, Enfin chez soi 1996, Eco, Bio, Psycho about Urban Ecology 1996, Tutto e paesaggio (also in French 2001), Ecologie urbane 2002, Rassegna 'Lucien Kroll'; over 700 articles on industrial and urban architectural design and comparative architecture. *Address:* Atelier d'Urbanisme, d'Architecture et d'Informatique L. Kroll, Avenue Louis Berlaimont 20, Boîte 9, 1160 Brussels, Belgium (office). *Telephone:* (2) 673-35-39 (office). *Fax:* (2) 673-89-27 (office). *E-mail:* kroll@brutele.be (office). *Website:* homeusers.brutele.be/kroll (office).

KRON, Patrick; French manufacturing executive; *Chairman and CEO, Alstom;* b. 26 Sept. 1953, Paris; ed Ecole Polytechnique, Paris Ecole des Mines; with Ministry of Industry 1979–84; joined Pechiney Group 1984, various operational roles, Pechiney, Greece 1984–88, various sr financial roles, Paris 1988–93, becoming Pres., Electrometallurgy Div., mem. Exec. Cttee, Pechiney Group 1993–97, Chair. Carbone Lorraine Co. 1993–95, Head, Food and Healthcare Packaging Sector, Pechiney 1995–97, and COO, American Nat. Can Co., Chicago 1995–97; CEO Imerys 1998–2002; mem. Exec. Bd Alstom 2001–, CEO Jan. 2003–, Chair. March 2003–; mem. Bd Dirs Les Arts Florissants, Bouygues; Légion d'honneur 2004. *Address:* Alstom, 3 avenue André Malraux, 92309 Levallois-Perret Cedex, France (office). *Telephone:* 1-41-49-20-00 (office). *Fax:* 1-41-49-24-85 (office). *E-mail:* info@alstom.com (office). *Website:* www.alstom.com (office).

KRONKAITIS, Maj.-Gen. Jonas A., BS, MBA; Lithuanian army officer; m. Rūta Kronkaitis; one s. one d.; ed Univ. of Connecticut, Syracuse Univ., US Army War Coll., US Army Command and Gen. Staff Coll., USA; 27 years mil. service in US Armed Forces; held positions successively as infantry platoon leader, battalion commdr, G-4 of 1st Armoured Div., Instructor in Man. Studies Ordnance School and Centre, served with 4th Armoured Corps, 2nd Armoured Cavalry Regiment and 1st Armoured Div., Germany, with 1st Cavalry Div., Viet Nam, Insp.-Gen. US Army, Jt Project Man. (Army and Navy) Guided Projectiles and Cannon Artillery Weapons Systems; Man.-Gen. Rock Island Arsenal (state-owned armament mfg co.); Dir Dept of Defence Programs, Atlantic Research Corpn (co. mfg rocket motors), USA –1997; Vice-Minister of Defence, Repub. of Lithuania 1997–99; Commdr Lithuanian Armed Forces 1999–2004; apptd Brig.-Gen. 1999, Maj.-Gen. 2001; fmr mem. AIAA, Assoc. of US Army, Lithuanian–American Community, Nat. Security Industrial Asscn, Navy League; fmr Chair. Bd Trustees Baltic Inst.; Legion of Merit; Viet Nam Cross of Gallantry, three Bronze Stars, three Meritorious Service Medals, Army Commendation Medal, Air Medal. *Address:* c/o Ministry of National Defence, Šv. Ignoto 8/29, 2001 Vilnius, Lithuania.

KROON, Lt-Adm. Luuk; Dutch naval officer (retd); b. Dec. 1942, Ridderkerk; m. Annie Kroon; joined Royal Netherlands Navy 1961; apptd to destroyer HNLMS Amsterdam 1964, USS Zellars (naval exchange programme) 1967; commdr inshore and coastal minesweepers 1968–72; served in Directorate Material, Ministry of Defence, The Hague 1972–75; Commdg Officer HNLMS Staphorst 1975–77; Staff Officer Minewarfare, Naval HQ, The Hague 1978–81; Commdg Officer HNLMS Jaguar 1981–82, HNLMS Callenburgh 1982–84; Naval Staff Planner to Chief of Defence Staff 1984–89; Deputy Chief of the Naval Staff (Plans) 1989–92; Commdr Netherlands Task Group 1992–93; Admiral Netherlands Fleet, Commdr Maritime Forces BeneNorthWest and Admiral Benelux 1993–95; C-in-C of Royal Netherlands Navy 1995–98; Chief of Netherlands Defence Staff 1998–2004 (retd); apptd Rear Admiral 1992, Vice-Admiral 1993, Admiral 1998, now Lt-Adm. *Address:* c/o Ministry of Defence, Library, POB 20701 ES The Hague, The Netherlands (office).

KROPF, Susan J., BA, MBA; American retail executive; ed St John's Univ., New York Univ.; joined Avon Products Inc. 1970, Vice-Pres. Product Devt 1990–92, Sr Vice-Pres. US Marketing 1992–93, Sr Vice-Pres. Global Product Man. 1993–94, Pres. New and Emerging Markets Div. 1994–97, Pres. Avon US 1997–98, COO for N America 1999–2001, Co. Pres. and COO 2001–07 (retd); mem. Bd of Dirs MeadWestvaco Corpn, Sherwin Williams Co., Wallace Foundation, Fragrance Foundation, Coach, Inc. 2006–; mem. Cosmetic Exec. Women, Fashion Group Int; YWCA Acad. of Women Achievers Award 1997, Beautiful Apple Award, March of Dimes 2004, Lifetime Achievement Award, Cosmetic Exec. Women 2006. *Address:* c/o Avon Products, Inc. Headquarters, 1345 Avenue of the Americas, New York, NY 10105 USA (office).

KROPIWNICKI, Jerzy Janusz, DEcon; Polish politician and economist; *Mayor of Łódź;* b. 5 July 1945, Częstochowa; m.; one s.; ed Warsaw School of Econs; scientific worker, Łódź Univ. 1968–81 (dismissed); mem. Solidarity Ind. Self-governing Trade Union 1980–, Deputy Chair. Solidarity Łódź Region Br., mem. Solidarity Nat. Comm., co-organizer demonstration against martial law, arrested 13 Dec. 1981, sentenced to 6 years' imprisonment, released under amnesty July 1984; illegal activity 1984–90, co-organizer, Solidarity Regional Exec. Comm., Łódź 1984–86, co-organizer and activist, Working Group of Solidarity Nat. Comm. 1986–90; co-organizer and activist of Pastoral Care of Working People 1985–; lay worker, St Teresa's Roman Catholic Parish Church, Łódź 1986–89; scientific worker, Econ.-Sociological Faculty of Łódź Univ. 1989–; mem. Christian-Nat. Union (ZChN) 1989–, mem. Presidium of ZChN Gen. Bd 1989–93, Vice-Pres. 1991–93, 2000–; Deputy to Sejm (Parl.) 1991–93 and 1997–2001; Minister of Labour and Social Policy 1991–92; Minister-Head of Cen. Office of Planning 1992–93; Minister and Head of Governmental Centre for Strategic Studies 1997–2001; Minister of Regional Devt and Construction 2000–01; Mayor of Łódź 2004–. *Publications:* numerous articles on econs and four books. *Leisure interests:* mountain hiking, reading (history and science-fiction). *Address:* The City of Lodz Office, 104 Piotrkowska St., 90-926Łódź (office); Christian National Union, ul. Twarda 28, 00-853 Warsaw, Poland. *Telephone:* (42) 638-41-15 (office); (42) 638-41-24 (office). *Fax:* (22) 6280804. *E-mail:* tombush@polbox.com. *Website:* www.uml.lodz.pl (office).

KROTO, Sir Harold Walter, Kt, BSc, PhD, FRS, FRSC; British scientist and academic; *Francis Eppes Professor of Chemistry, Florida State University;* b. 7 Oct. 1939, Wisbech, Cambs.; s. of Heinz Kroto (fmrly Krotoschiner) and Edith Kroto; m. Margaret Henrietta Hunter 1963; two s.; ed Bolton School, Univ. of Sheffield; Postdoctoral Fellow, Nat. Research Council, Canada 1964–66; Research Scientist, Bell Telephone Labs, NJ, USA 1966–67; Tutorial Fellow, Univ. of Sussex 1967–68, Lecturer 1968–77, Reader 1977–85, Prof. of Chem. 1985–2005, Royal Soc. Research Prof. 1991–2001, Research Prof. Emer.

2001–; Francis Eppes Prof. of Chem., Florida State Univ. 2004–; Visiting Prof., Univ. of British Columbia 1973, Univ. of Southern California 1981, UCLA 1988–92, Univ. of California, Santa Barbara (Distinguished Visiting Prof. 1996–); Chair. Bd Vega Science Trust 1995–; Pres. Royal Soc. of Chem. (RSC) 2002–04; exec. producer of science programmes for network TV; fmr mem. Nat. Advisory Cttee on Cultural and Creative Educ.; Foreign mem. Finnish Acad. of Sciences, Academy of Sciences (Torino) 2005; Foreign Assoc. NAS 2007; Freeman, City of Torino; Hon. Foreign mem. Korean Acad. of Science and Tech. 1997; Hon. Fellow, Royal Microscopical Soc. 1998; Hon. FRSE 1998; Hon. Fellowship, Bolton Inst.; Order of Cherubini (Torino) 2005; 29 hon. degrees, including Univs of Brussels (Univ. Libre), Stockholm, Limburg, Sheffield, Kingston, Sussex, Helsinki, Nottingham, Yokohama City, Sheffield-Hallam, Hertfordshire (returned due to closure of Chem. Dept), Aberdeen, Leicester, Aveiro (Portugal), Bielefeld (Germany), Hull, Manchester Metropolitan, Exeter (returned due to closure of Chem. Dept), Hong Kong City, Gustavus Adolphus Coll. (USA), Univ. Coll. London, Patras (Greece), Dalhousie (Canada), Strathclyde, Manchester, Kraków, Durham, Queen's Belfast, Surrey, Polytechnico (Torino), Beijing, Liverpool; RSC Tilden Lectureship 1981, shared Int. Prize for New Materials, American Physical Soc. 1992, Italgas Prize for Innovation in Chem. 1992, shared Hewlett Packard Europhysics Prize 1994, Nobel Prize for Chem. (co-recipient) for discovery of C_{60}, Buckminsterfullerene 1996, RSC Longstaff Medal 1993, shared Medal for Achievement in Carbon Science, American Carbon Soc. 1997, Ioannes Marcus Marei Medal, Prague 2000, Prix Leonardo Bronze Medal 2001, Copley Medal, Royal Soc. 2004, Erasmus Medal, Academia Europaea, Kavli Lecturer 2008. *Publications:* Molecular Rotation Spectra 1975, 1983; more than 300 papers in chem., chemical physics and astronomy journals. *Leisure interests:* graphic design (winner Sunday Times Book Jacket Design Competition 1964, Möet Hennessy/Louis Vuitton Science pour l'Art Prize 1994), tennis. *Address:* Room 2007 CSL, Department of Chemistry and Biochemistry, The Florida State University, Tallahassee, FL 32306-4390, USA (office); School of Chemistry, Chichester 3 3r341, Physics and Environmental Science, University of Sussex, Brighton, BN1 9QJ, England (office). *Telephone:* (850) 644-8274 (Tallahassee) (office); (1273) 678329 (Brighton) (office). *Fax:* (850) 644-8274 (Tallahassee) (office). *E-mail:* kroto@chem.fsu.edu (office); h.w.kroto@sussex.ac.uk (office). *Website:* www.chem.fsu.edu (office); www.sussex.ac.uk/chemistry (office); www.kroto.info.

KROTOV, Mikhail Valentinovich; Russian government official; *Plenipotentiary Presidential Representative in the Constitutional Court;* b. 14 March 1963, Leningrad; ed A.A. Zhdanov Leningrad State Univ.; with St Petersburg Univ. 1986–2005, positions including Sr Lecturer, Head of Chair of Legal Protection for the Environment, Pro-Rector for Legal and Econ. Matters; First Deputy Gen. Dir Gazprom-Media 2005; Plenipotentiary Presidential Rep. in the Constitutional Court of the Russian Fed. 2005–; Educ. Prize of the Pres. of the Russian Fed. 2001. *Address:* c/o The Presidential Executive Office, Staraya Square 4, Moscow 103132, Russia. *Website:* www.kremlin.ru/eng/subj/97793.shtml (office).

KRUEGER, Anne Olive, PhD; American economist, international organization official and academic; *Professor of International Economics, Paul H. Nitze School of Advanced International Studies;* b. 12 Feb. 1934, Endicott, NY; d. of Leslie A. Osborn and Dora W. Osborn; m. James Henderson 1981; one d.; ed Oberlin Coll. and Univ. of Wisconsin; Asst Prof. of Econs, Univ. of Minnesota 1959–63, Assoc. Prof. 1963–66, Prof. 1966–82; Research Assoc., Nat. Bureau of Econ. Research 1969–82; Vice-Pres. Econs and Research, IBRD 1982–86; Univ. Arts and Sciences Prof. of Econs, Duke Univ. 1987–92; Sr Fellow (non-resident) Brookings Inst. 1988–94; Herald L. and Caroline L. Ritch Prof. of Humanities and Sciences, Stanford Univ. 1993–, Dir Center for Research on Econ. Devt and Policy Reform 1996–2001; First Deputy Man. Dir IMF 2001–06, Acting Man. Dir March–May 2004, Special Advisor to the Man. Dir 2006–; Prof. of Int. Econs, Paul H. Nitze School of Advanced Int. Studies, Washington, DC 2007–; visiting prof. at univs in USA, Denmark, Germany, France, Australia and Sweden; mem. editorial bds of several int. econ. journals; fmr Vice-Pres. American Econ. Asscn, Pres. 1996–97; mem. NAS; Fellow, American Acad. of Arts and Sciences, Econometric Soc.; Hon. Prof., Nat. Acad. of the Economy, Moscow 2004; Dr hc (Hacettepe Univ., Ankara) 1990; Hon. DHumLitt (Georgetown) 1993; Hon. DEcons (Monash Univ., Australia) 1995; Hon. Dr of Business (Melbourne Business School) 2004; Robertson Prize, NAS 1984, Bernhard-Harms Prize, Kiel Inst. 1990; Kenan Enterprise Award, Kenan Charitable Trust 1990, Frank E. Seidman Distinguished Award in Political Economy 1993. *Publications include:* Foreign Trade Regimes and Economic Development: Turkey 1974, The Benefits and Costs of Import Substitution in India: A Microeconomic Study 1975, Trade and Development in Korea (co-ed.) 1975, Growth, Distortions and Patterns of Trade Among Many Countries 1977, The Developmental Role of the Foreign Sector and Aid: Korea 1979, Trade and Employment in Developing Countries (co-ed.) 1981, Exchange Rate Determination 1983, The Political Economy of International Trade (co-ed.) 1989, Aid and Development (co-author) 1989, Perspectives on Trade and Development 1990, Political Economy of Policy Reform in Developing Countries 1993, American Trade Policy 1995, The WTO as an International Institution (ed.) 1998. *Address:* Bernstein-Offit 574, The Paul H. Nitze School of Advanced International Studies, The Johns Hopkins University, 1717 Massachusetts Avenue, NW Washington, DC 20036, USA (office). *Telephone:* (202) 587-3238 (office). *Fax:* (202) 663-5656 (office). *E-mail:* annekrueger@jhu.edu (office). *Website:* www.sais-jhu.edu (office).

KRÜGER, Hardy; German actor and writer; b. 12 April 1928, Berlin; s. of Max and Auguste (née Meier) Krüger; m. 1st Renate Damrow; one d.; m. 2nd Francesca Marazzi; one s. one d.; m. 3rd Anita Park 1978; German repertory theatre 1945–56, entered films in 1943; several awards and prizes. *Films include:* Der Rest ist Schweigen 1959, Blind Date 1959, Taxi pour Tobrouk 1961, Hatari 1961, Les Dimanches de Ville d'Avray 1962, Les Quatre Verités 1962, Le Gros Coup 1963, Le Chant du Monde 1964, Flight of the Phoenix 1965, The Defector 1966, La Grande Sauterelle 1966, The Battle of Neretva 1968, The Secret of Santa Vittoria 1969, Death of A Stranger 1972, Le Solitaire 1973, Barry Lyndon 1974, Paper Tiger 1974, Potato Fritz (Best Actor Award, Cannes) 1975, A Bridge Too Far 1976, L'Autopsie d'un Monster 1976, The Wild Geese 1978. *Publications:* Ein Farm in Afrika 1970, Sawimbulu 1971, Wer stehend stirbt, lebt länger 1973, Diè Schallmauer 1978, Die Frau des Griechen 1980, Junge Unrast 1983, Sibirienfahrt, Tagebuch einer Reise 1985, Frühstück mit Theodore 1990, Weltenbummler, Reisen zu Menschen und Göttern 1992, Weltenbummler, Willkommen auf funf Kontinenten 1994, Weltenbummler, Glückliche Tage auf dem Blauen Planeten 1996, Wanderjahre 1999, Szenen eines Clowns 2001. *Address:* Maximilianstrasse 23, 80539 Munich, Germany.

KRÜGER, Manfred Paul, DPhil; German writer, academic and editor; *Lecturer, Institute for Spiritual Science and Arts, Nuremberg and Fachhochschule Ottersberg;* b. 23 Feb. 1938, Köslin; s. of Paul Krüger and Hildegard Krüger; m. Christine Petersen 1962; three s. four d.; ed Oberrealschule Ansbach, Heidelberg Univ., Tübingen Univ.; Asst Prof., Erlangen Univ. 1966–73; Lecturer, Inst. for Spiritual Science and Arts, Nuremberg 1972–; Lecturer, Fachhochschule Ottersberg 1980–; Co-Ed. Goetheanum weekly 1984–96. *Publications:* Gérard de Nerval 1966, Wandlungen des Tragischen 1973, Nora Ruhtenberg 1976, Bilder und Gegenbilder 1978, Wortspuren 1980, Denkbilder 1981, Literatur und Geschichte 1982, Mondland 1982, Nah ist er 1983, Meditation 1983, Rosenroman 1985, Meditation und Karma 1988, Anthroposophie und Kunst 1988, Ästhetik der Freiheit 1992, Ichgeburt 1996, Das Ich und seine Masken 1997, Die Verklärung auf dem Berge 2003. *Address:* Rieterstrasse 20, 90419 Nuremberg, Germany. *Telephone:* (911) 338678.

KRUGMAN, Paul Robin, PhD; American economist and academic; *Professor of Economics and International Affairs, Princeton University;* b. 28 Feb. 1953, Albany, New York; s. of David Krugman and Anita Krugman; m. Robin Leslie Bergman 1983; ed Yale Univ., Massachusetts Inst. of Tech.; Asst Prof., Yale Univ. 1977–79; Asst Prof., MIT 1979–80, Assoc. Prof. 1980–82, Prof. 1983–2000; Sr Staff Economist, Council of Econ. Advisers 1982–83; Columnist, New York Times 1999–; Prof. of Econs and Int. Affairs, Princeton Univ. 2000–; John Bates Clark Medal 1991, Nobel Prize for Economics 2008. *Publications:* Market Structure and Foreign Trade (with E. Helpman) 1985, International Economics, Theory and Policy (with M. Obsfeld) 1988, The Age of Diminished Expectations 1990, Rethinking International Trade 1990, Geography and Trade 1991, Currencies and Crises 1992, Peddling Prosperity 1994, The Great Unravelling: From Boom to Bust in Three Short Years 2003, The Conscience of a Liberal 2007. *Leisure interest:* music. *Address:* Department of Economics, 414 Robertson Hall, Princeton University, Princeton, NJ 08544, USA (office). *E-mail:* pkrugman@princeton.edu (office). *Website:* www.princeton.edu/~pkrugman (office); www.econ.princeton.edu (office); topics.nytimes.com/top/opinion/editorialsandoped/oped/columnists/paulkrugman.

KRUMMACHER, Hans-Henrik, DPhil; German academic; *Professor Emeritus, University of Mainz;* b. 24 Aug. 1931, Essen-Werden; m. Eva Wentscher 1956; one s. four d.; ed Humboldt Univ. Berlin, Univs. of Heidelberg and Tübingen; Archivist, Schiller-Nationalmuseum, Marbach a.N. 1956–58; Asst Prof., Univ. of Cologne 1958–67; Prof. of German Literature, Univ. of Mainz 1967–99, Prof. Emer. 1999–; mem. Akademie der Wissenschaften und der Literatur zu Mainz 1984; Corresp. mem. Österreichische Akad. der Wissenschaften 1993. *Publications:* Das 'als ob' in der Lyrik 1965, Der junge Gryphius und die Tradition 1976; Ed. Eduard Mörike, Werke und Briefe 1967–, Neudrucke deutscher Literaturwerke 1975–. *Address:* Am Mainzer Weg 10, 55127 Mainz-Drais, Germany (home). *Telephone:* (6131) 477550 (home).

KRUMNOW, Jürgen, Dr rer. pol; German business executive; *Chairman of the Supervisory Board, TUI AG;* b. 18 May 1944, Grünberg, Silesia; m. Christiane Krumnow; ed Hamburg Univ.; trainee, Deutsche Bank AG, Bremen 1964–66, Accounting Dept, Frankfurt am Main 1970–74, Exec. Secr. 1974–78, Head, Reutlingen/Tübingen Br. 1978–82, Head, Cen. Accounting and Planning Dept 1982–86, Exec. Man. 1986–88, mem. Exec. Bd 1988–99, Consultant 1999–2004; mem. Supervisory Bd TUI AG 1997–, Chair. 2004–, Chair. Audit Cttee –2004; fmr mem. Supervisory Bd Volkswagen AG, Deutsche Bahn AG, Hapag Lloyd AG, Peek & Cloppenburg KG; Deputy Chair. Lenze Holding; fmr Chair. Deutsches Rechnungslegungs Standards Cttee (DRSC—German Accounting Standards Bd). *Address:* TUI AG, Postfach 610209, 30602 Hanover (office); TUI AG, Karl-Wiechert-Allee 4, 30625 Hanover, Germany (office). *Telephone:* (511) 566-00 (office). *Fax:* (511) 566-1901 (office). *E-mail:* info@tui-group.com (office). *Website:* www.tui-group.com (office).

KRUPP, Fred; American lawyer, environmental activist and national organization official; *President, Environmental Defense Fund;* m. Laurie Krupp; three c.; ed Yale Univ., Univ. of Michigan Law School; spent several years in pvt. law practice in New Haven, Conn. in several firms: Cooper, Whitney, Cochran & Krupp 1984; Pnr, Albis & Krupp 1978–84; Founder and Gen. Counsel, Connecticut Fund for the Environment 1978–84; Pres. Environmental Defense Fund 1984–; mem. Bd H. John Heinz III Center for Science, Econs and the Environment, John F. Kennedy School of Govt Environment Council, Leadership Council of the Yale School of Forestry and Environmental Studies; fmr mem. Pres.'s Advisory Cttee on Trade Policy and Negotiations for both Pres. Bill Clinton and Pres. George W. Bush; helped launch corp. coalition US Climate Action Partnership; Keystone Leadership in Environment Award 1999, Champion Award, Women's Council on Energy and the Environment 2002, among 16 people named America's Best Leaders by US

News and World Report 2007. *Achievements include:* won gold medal in FISA World Rowing Championships 2006. *Publication:* Earth: The Sequel: The Race to Reinvent Energy and Stop Global Warming (with Miriam Horn) (New York Times Best Seller) 2008. *Address:* Environmental Defense Fund, 257 Park Avenue South, New York, NY 10010, USA (office). *Telephone:* (212) 505-2100 (office). *Fax:* (212) 505-2375 (office). *E-mail:* info@edf.org (office). *Website:* www.edf.org (office).

KRUPP, Georg; German business executive; b. 15 July 1936; fmr Deputy mem. Bd of Man. Dirs Deutsche Bank; Chair. Supervisory Bd WMF AG, Geislingen, Kunz Holding GmbH & Co. KG, Gschwend; mem. Supervisory Bd IVECO Magirus AG, Ulm, Strabag AG, Cologne, Gerling-Konzern Versicherungs-Beteiligungs AG, Cologne, Rheinmetall AG, Düsseldorf, BHS Tabletop AG, Selb, Bizerba GmbH & Co. KG, Balingen, IVECO NV, Amstelveen, Netherlands. *Address:* WMF AG, Eberhardstrasse, Geislingen 73309, Germany.

KRYLOV, Sergey Borisovich; Russian diplomatist and business executive; *Head, International Relations Office, Sistema Corporation;* b. 26 Oct. 1949, Moscow; m.; two d.; ed Moscow State Inst. of Int. Relations, Diplomatic Acad. of Ministry of Foreign Relations; diplomatic service 1971–; translator, attaché Embassy, Zaire 1971–76; attaché, Third, Second Sec. Second Africa Dept, USSR Ministry of Foreign Affairs 1976–79; First Sec., Counsellor to Minister 1979–86, Asst to Deputy Minister 1986–89; Minister-Counsellor USSR Embassy, Portugal 1990–92; Dir of Dept, Exec. Sec. Ministry of Foreign Affairs of Russia 1992–93; Deputy Minister of Foreign Affairs, Russia 1993–96; Perm. Rep. to UN, New York and other int. orgs, Geneva 1997–98; Amb. to Germany 1998–2004; Head, Int. Relations Office, Sistema Corpn 2004–. *Address:* Sistema Corporation, 10 Leontievsky Pereulok, 125009 Moscow, Russian Federation (office). *Telephone:* (495) 629-06-00 (office). *Fax:* (495) 232-33-91 (office). *Website:* www.sistema.com (office).

KRZAKLEWSKI, Marian, DIng; Polish politician and trade union official; b. 23 Aug. 1950, Kolbuszowa; m.; two s.; ed Silesian Tech. Univ., Gliwice 1975; scientific worker Polish Acad. of Sciences (PAN) and Silesian Tech. Univ., Gliwice 1976–90; mem. Solidarity Trade Union (independent, self-governing union) 1980–; Chair. of Solidarity 1991–2002; mem. ICFTU 1991–; Co-founder and Leader Solidarity Election Action (AWS) 1996–2001; Deputy to Sejm (Parl.) 1997–2001; Chair. Solidarity Election Action Parl. Club 1997–2001; main negotiator and jt architect of parl. and govt coalition Solidarity Election Action–Freedom Union; Co-founder and Chair. Social Movt of Solidarity Election Action (RS AWS) 1997–2000 (merged with three other parties to form Solidarity Electoral Action of the Right 2000); Hon. Chair. Social Movt of Solidarity Election Action (RS AWS) 1999; Man of the Year, Zycie newspaper 1996, Kisiel Prize 1997, Platinum Laurel of Skills 1998. *Publication:* Solidarity's Revival and Polish Politics. *Leisure interests:* family life, tourism, sport, arts, literature. *Address:* Komisja Krajowa NSZ2 Solidarnose, ul. Wały Piastowskie 24, 80-855 Gdańsk, Poland. *Telephone:* (58) 308 44 72. *Fax:* (58) 305 90 44.

KRZYZEWSKI, Mike, BS; American basketball coach; *Head Basketball Coach and Executive-in-Residence, Duke University;* b. 13 Feb. 1947, Chicago, Ill.; m.; three d.; ed Weber High School, Chicago, US Mil. Acad., West Point; served as officer in US Army 1969–74; Grad. Asst Coach at Ind. Univ. 1974–75; Coach, US Mil. Acad., West Point 1976–80; Head Coach, Duke Univ. 1980–; has led Duke to over 700 wins and Nat. Collegiate Athletic Asscn (NCAA) Championships 1991, 1992, 2001, appeared in NCAA Final Fours ten times; Atlantic Coast Conf. (ACC) regular season championship eleven times, ACC Tournament Championships ten times; ranks first all-time in NCAA tournament wins (68); Olympic Trials Instructor 1984; coached US team in World Univ. Games 1987, World Championship Games and Goodwill Games 1990; Asst Coach US Gold Medal Team, Olympic Games 1992; Pres. Nat. Asscn of Basketball Coaches (NABC) 1998–99; coach of Team USA 2006 World Championships, 2008 Beijing Olympics; named Nat. Coach of the Year (eight times), ACC Coach of the Year (five times), named NABC Coach of the Decade (1990s) 2000, inducted into Basketball Hall of Fame 2001, named America's Best Coach by Time magazine/CNN 2001. *Publications include:* Leading with the Heart 2001, Beyond Basketball 2006. *Address:* Athletic Department, Duke University, Box 90555, Durham, NC 27708, USA (office). *Telephone:* (919) 613-7505 (office). *E-mail:* gbbrown@duaa.duke.edu (office). *Website:* www.coachk.com (office).

KSEŃ, Jacek, PhD; Polish banking executive; *President of the Management Board, Bank Zachodni WBK;* ed Poznan School of Econs, Higher School of Planning and Statistics; Financial Markets Operator, Bank Handlowy –1978; Vice-Dir, Foreign Currency Dept, Polska Kasa Opieka SA, Paris 1978, becoming Head, Foreign Exchange Deals, Head, Foreign Bonds Team 1985–87; Commercial Rep, Bond Dept, Lyonnaise de Banque, Paris 1987–90, also Vice-Dir for Int. Financial Markets 1989–90; Ind. Sr Dealer, Int. Futures Dept, Caisse Nat. Credit Agricole 1990–96, mem. Sr Man. Team 1991–96; Pres. Man. Bd, Wielkopolski Bank Kredytowy (WBK), Poland 1996–2001, Pres. Bank Zachodni WBK (following merger) June 2001–. *Address:* Bank Zachodni WBK, pl. Wl. Andersa 5, 61-894 Poznań, Poland (office). *Telephone:* (61) 856-40-00 (office). *Fax:* (61) 856-40-11 (office). *E-mail:* jacek.ksen@bzwbk.pl (office). *Website:* www.bzbk.pl (office).

KUBILIUS, Andrius; Lithuanian politician; *Prime Minister;* b. 8 Dec. 1956; m. Rosa Kabiliene; two s.; ed Vilnius Univ.; lab. technician, Vilnius Univ. 1979–90, then engineer, then scientific research asst; mem. Sajūdis Movt 1988–, Exec. Sec. Sajūdis Council 1990–92; mem. Seimas 1992–, First Vice-Chair. 1996–99, mem. Ass. of Elders 2000–03, 2005–, mem. Cttee on European Affairs 2004–, Cttee of Devt of Information Society 2004–05, Cttee on Rural Affairs 2005–, Leader of Opposition 2005–08; Prime Minister of Lithuania 1999–2000, 2008–; mem. Homeland Union, Chair. 2003–. *Address:* Office of the Prime Minister, Gedimino pr. 11, Vilnius 01103; Homeland Union—Conservatives, Political Prisoners and Deportees, Christian Democrats (HU) (Tėvynės Sąjunga) (TS), L. Stuokos-Gucevičiaus g. 11, Vilnius 01122; Seimas, Gedimino ave. 15, 2001 Vilnius, Lithuania (office). *Telephone:* (5) 266-3874 (office); (5) 212-1657 (Homeland Union); (5) 239-6658 (office). *Fax:* (5) 216-3877 (office); (5) 278-4722 (Homeland Union). *E-mail:* sekretoriatas@tsajunga.lt; info@tslk.lt (office); ankubi@lrs.lt; Andrius.Kubilius@lrs.lt. *Website:* www.ministraspirmininkas.lt (office); www.tsajunga.lt; www3.lrs.lt (office).

KUBILIUS, Jonas, DSc; Lithuanian mathematician and academic; *Professor, Faculty of Mathematics and Informatics, Vilnius University;* b. 27 July 1921, Fermos, Jurbarkas Dist; s. of Petras Kubilius and Petronėlė Giedraitytė; m. Valerija Pilypaitė 1950; one s. one d.; ed Vilnius and Leningrad Univs and Math. Inst. Moscow; Lab. Asst, Asst Prof., Vilnius Univ. 1945–48, Assoc. Prof., Prof., Faculty of Math. and Informatics 1951–, Rector 1958–91; mem. Lithuanian Acad. of Sciences 1962–, mem. Presidium 1962–92; People's Deputy of USSR 1989–91; mem. Seimas (Parl.) of Lithuania 1992–96; Pres. Lithuanian Soc. of Math.; several orders; Dr hc (Greifswald, Prague, Salzburg and Latvian Univs); State Prize in Science 1958, 1980. *Publications:* Probability Methods in the Theory of Numbers 1959, Real Analysis 1970, Probability and Statistics 1980, Limit Theorems 1998; book of essays 1996; several hundred papers. *Leisure interests:* music, history, bibliophilism. *Address:* Vilnius Universitetas, Universiteto 3, 01513 Vilnius (office); Kuosų 14, 10313 Vilnius, Lithuania (home). *Telephone:* (2) 332-228 (office). *E-mail:* jonas.kubilius@maf.vu.lt (office). *Website:* www.mif.vu.lt/en (office).

KUBIŠ, Ján; Slovak diplomatist and government official; *Executive Secretary, United Nations Economic Commission for Europe;* b. 12 Nov. 1952, Bratslavia; m.; one d.; ed Moscow State Inst. for Int. Affairs; served in Dept of Int. Econ. Orgs, Ministry of Foreign Affairs (Czechoslovakia) 1976–80, Head of Security and Arms Control Section 1985–88, Dir-Gen. Euro-Atlantic Section 1991–92; served in Embassy in Addis Ababa 1980–85; First Sec. Embassy in Moscow 1989–90, Deputy Head and Head of Political Dept 1990–91; Chair. CSCE Cttee of Sr Officials and Amb.-at-Large 1992; Perm. Rep. (for Slovakia), UN Office, GATT and other Int. Orgs, Geneva 1993–94; Chief Negotiator (for Slovakia) for Pact for Stability in Europe 1994; Dir OSCE Conflict Prevention Centre 1994–98; Special Rep. of UN Sec.-Gen. for Tajikistan and Head, UN Mission of Mil. Observers 1998–99; Sec.-Gen. OSCE 1999–2005, Personal Rep. of Chair.-in-Office for Cen. Asia 2000; EU Special Rep. for Cen. Asia 2005–06; Minister of Foreign Affairs 2006–09; Exec. Sec., UN Econ. Comm. for Europe 2009–; OSCE Medal 1998. *Address:* Economic Commission for Europe, Palais des Nations, 1211 Geneva 10, Switzerland (office). *Telephone:* 229171234 (office). *Fax:* 229170505 (office). *E-mail:* info.ece@unece.org (office). *Website:* www.unece.org (office).

KUBUABOLA, Ratu Jone; Fijian politician; elected MP for SW Urban (Fijian Communal) Constituency; Minister for Finance, Nat. Planning and Communications –2006; mem. Soqosoqo ni Duavata ni Lewenivanua Party. *Address:* c/o Soqosoqo ni Duavata ni Lewenivanua Party Office, Edinburgh Drive, Suva, Fiji (office).

KUČAN, Milan; Slovenian politician and lawyer; b. 14 Jan. 1941, Križevci, Prekmurje; m. Štefka Kučan; two d.; ed Ljubljana Univ.; joined Fed. of Communists of Slovenia 1958; mem. Cen. Cttee Fed. of Communists of Slovenia; Chair. Comm. on Educational Problems of Cen. Cttee, Youth Union of Slovenia 1963–65; Chair. Cen. Cttee 1968–69; mem. Cen. Cttee Communist Union of Slovenia 1973–78, Chair. 1986–89; Sec. Republican Conf. of Socialist Union of Slovenia 1973–78; Chair. Slovenian Skupščina (Parl.) 1978–86; Pres. of Slovenia 1990–2002; Founder and Chair. Forum 21 group of leaders who discuss Slovenian issues 2004–; mem. Club of Madrid. *Address:* c/o Office of the President, 1000 Ljubljana, Erjavčeva 17, Slovenia (office).

KUČERA, Jan; Czech scientist; Sr Researcher, Nuclear Physics Inst., Acad. of Sciences of Czech Repub., Řež; mem. Nuclear Analytical Methods in the Life Sciences Int. Cttee, Chair. 2002–, Gen. Chair. Fifth Int. Conf., Prague 1993; Hevesy Medal 2006. *Publications:* Nuclear Analytical Methods in the Life Sciences (co-ed.) 1994; numerous scientific papers in professional journals. *Address:* Nuclear Physics Institute, Academy of Sciences of the Czech Republic, 250 68 Řež, Czech Republic (office). *Telephone:* (2) 66172268 (office). *Fax:* (2) 20941130 (office). *E-mail:* kucera@ujf.cas.cz (office). *Website:* www.ujf.cas.cz (office).

KUCHERENA, Anatoly G., Dr Jur; Russian barrister; *Chairman, Institute of Democracy and Cooperation;* b. 23 Aug. 1961; ed Moscow Inst. of Law; Prof., Chair. Moscow Acad. of Law; f. one of the first Bureaux of Barristers' Argument 1995–; currently Chair. Inst. of Democracy and Cooperation; mem. Moscow Collegium of Barristers, Public Chamber; Head, Civil Soc.(NGO). *Publications include:* Ball of Lawlessness, Diagnosis of a Barrister, Who Profits, One Cannot Do Without Blood; contrib. numerous publications to the press on legal problems. *Address:* Bureau of Barristers' Argument, Prechistenka str. 33/19, Moscow 119031, Russia (office). *Telephone:* (495) 105-05-21 (office).

KUCHMA, Leonid Maksimovych, CTechSc; Ukrainian politician and manager; b. 1938, Chatikine, Chernihiv Oblast; m. Ludmyla Mykolayovna Kuchma; one d.; ed Dnipropetrovsk Nat. Univ.; mem. CPSU 1960–91; engineer, constructor, Chief Constructor Research-Production Yuzmash eng plant 1960–75, Sec. Party Cttee 1975–82, Deputy Dir-Gen. 1982–86, Dir-Gen. 1986–92; mem. Cen. Cttee CP Ukrainian SSR 1981–91; People's Deputy of Ukraine 1991–94; Prime Minister of Ukraine 1992–93 (resgnd); Chair. Ukrainian Union of Industrialists and Entrepreneurs 1993–94; Pres. of Ukraine 1994–2005; Order of St Volodymyr (Gold) 1999; Lenin Prize 1981, State Prize 1993. *Address:* Ukrainian Presidential Fund of Leonid Kuchma

Charity Organisation, 01024 Kyiv, vul. P. Orlyka 1/15, Ukraine (office). *Telephone:* (44) 465-93-77 (office). *Fax:* (44) 465-93-78 (office). *E-mail:* press@ldk-fund.org.ua (office). *Website:* www.kuchma.org.ua (office).

KUCZYNSKI, Pedro Pablo, BA, MA, MPA; Peruvian economist and politician; b. 1939, Lima; ed Oxford Univ., UK, Princeton Univ., USA; Loan Officer and Economist Latin America and New Zealand, World Bank 1961–66; Deputy Dir Peruvian Central Bank 1967–69; Sr Economist IMF 1973–75; Chief Economist Northern Latin America, World Bank 1971–72, Head Planning Div. 1972–73; Vice-Pres. Kuhn, Loeb & Co. Int. 1973–75; Chief Economist Int. Finance Corpn 1975–77; Pres. Halco Mining Co. 1977–80; Minister of Energy and Mines 1980–82; Man. Dir First Boston Corpn then Pres. First Boston Int. 1982–92; Pres. Westfield Capital 1992–94; Pres. and CEO Latin America Enterprise Fund 1994–; Minister of Economy and Finance 2001–02, 2004–2005; Prime Minister 2005–06; fmr mem. Bd Tenaris SA, Southern Peru Copper Corpn, current mem. Comm. on Growth and Devt. *Publications:* Peruvian Democracy under Economic Stress 1977. *Address:* c/o Secretariat of the Commission on Growth and Development, c/o Dorota A. Nowak, 1818 H Street NW, MSN- MC-4-401, Washington, DC 20433, USA (office).

KUDELKA, James Alexander, OC; Canadian choreographer, dancer and fmr ballet company artistic director; b. 10 Sept. 1955, Newmarket, Ont.; s. of John Kudelka and Kathleen Mary Kudelka (née Kellington); ed Nat. Ballet School of Canada; dancer, Nat. Ballet of Canada 1972–81, Artist in Residence 1992–96, Artistic Dir 1996–2005, Resident Choreographer 2005–07; Prin. Dancer, Grand Ballets Canadiens 1981–84, Resident Choreographer 1984–90; Isadora Duncan Dance Award 1988, Dora Mavor Moore Award (for Fifteen Heterosexual Duets) 1991–92, (for The Nutcracker) 1995–96, Jean A. Chalmers Choreographic Award 1993, numerous Canada Council Grants. *Major works:* (for Nat. Ballet of Canada) Washington Square 1977, Pastorale 1990, Musings 1991, The Miraculous Mandarin 1993, Spring Awakening 1994, The Actress 1994, The Nutcracker 1995, The Four Seasons 1997, Swan Lake 1999, The Firebird 2000, The Contract (The Pied Piper) 2002, Chacony 2004, Cinderella 2004, An Italian Straw Hat 2005; (for Grand Ballets Canadiens) In Paradisum 1983, Désir 1991; (for Toronto Dance Theatre) Fifteen Heterosexual Duets 1991; (for Birmingham Royal Ballet, UK) Le Baiser de la fée 1996; (for American Ballet Theater) Cruel World 1994, States of Grace 1995; (for San Francisco Ballet) The Comfort Zone 1989, The End 1992, Terra Firma 1995, Some Women and Men 1998; (for Joffrey Ballet) The Heart of the Matter 1986. *Address:* The Walter Carsen Centre for The National Ballet of Canada, 470 Queens Quay West, Toronto, ON M5V 3K4, Canada (office). *Telephone:* (416) 345-9686 (office). *Fax:* (416) 345-8323 (office). *E-mail:* info@national.ballet.ca (office). *Website:* www.national.ballet.ca (office).

KUDLOW, Lawrence A., BA; American economist, broadcaster and fmr government official; *CEO, Kudlow and Company, LLC;* b. 20 Aug. 1947, Englewood, NJ; s. of Irving Howard and Ruth Kudlow (née Grodnick); m. 1st Susan Cullman 1981, one d.; m. 2nd Judith Pond 1987; ed Univ. of Rochester, Woodrow Wilson School of Public and Int. Affairs, Princeton Univ.; economist, Fed. Reserve Bank of New York 1973–75; Chief Economist and Corporate Vice-Pres. Paine, Webber, Jackson and Curtis, New York 1975–79; Chief Economist and Partner, Bear, Stearns and Co., New York 1979–81; Asst Dir for Econ. Policy, Office of Man. and Budget, Washington, DC 1981–82, Assoc. Dir for Econs and Planning 1982–83; Pres. and CEO Lawrence Kudlow and Assocs, Washington, DC 1983–84; Pres. and CEO Rodman & Renshaw Economics Inc. 1984–86; Chief Economist and Man. Dir Rodman and Renshaw Capital Group Inc. 1984–86; Chief Economist, Bear, Stearns & Co. 1986–94; currently CEO Kudlow and Co. LLC, New York; host, Kudlow and Co. (daily TV current affairs program on CNBC) and Larry Kudlow Show (weekly radio show); columnist and econs Ed. National Review magazine. *Publication:* American Abundance: The New Economic and Moral Prosperity 1998. *Leisure interests:* tennis, golf. *Address:* Kudlow and Company LLC, 1375 Kings Highway East, Suite 260, Fairfield, CT 06824, USA (office). *Telephone:* (203) 228-5050 (office). *Fax:* (203) 228-5040 (office). *E-mail:* svarga@kudlow.com (office). *Website:* www.kudlow.com (office).

KUDRIN, Aleksei Leonidovich, CandEcon; Russian politician; *Deputy Chairman and Minister of Finance;* b. 12 Oct. 1960, Dobele, Latvian SSR; m. Irina Kudrina; one d.; ed Leningrad (now St Petersburg) State Univ., Inst. of Econs, USSR Acad. of Sciences; on staff Inst. of Social-Econ. Problems Acad. of Sciences 1983–90; Deputy Chair. Cttee on Econ. Reform Leningrad City Exec. Bd 1990–91; Chair. Cttee on Finance St Petersburg Mayor's Office 1992–94; First Deputy Mayor of St Petersburg, Head Dept of Finance Mayor's Office, St Petersburg 1994–96; Deputy Head of Admin., Head Controlling Dept at Russian Presidency 1996–97; First Deputy Minister of Finance Russian Fed. 1997–99, concurrently Deputy Man. BRD 1997–99; First Deputy Chair. Unified Power Grids of Russia (state co.) 1999–2000; Deputy Chair. of the Govt 2000–04, 2007–, Minister of Finance 2000–. *Leisure interests:* tennis, swimming. *Address:* Ministry of Finance, 109097 Moscow, ul. Ilyinka 9, Russia (office). *Telephone:* (495) 298-91-01 (office). *Fax:* (495) 925-08-89 (office). *Website:* www.minfin.ru (office).

KUDROW, Lisa, BSc; American actress; b. 30 July 1963, Encino, Calif.; m. Michael Stern; one c.; ed Vassar Coll., Poughkeepsie, New York. *Television includes:* To the Moon Alice 1990, Murder in High Places 1991, Bob (series) 1992, Friends (series) 1994–2004, The Comeback (series) 2005. *Films include:* L.A. on $5 a Day 1989, Dance with Death 1991, The Unborn 1991, In the Heat of Passion 1992, In the Heat of Passion II: Unfaithful 1994, The Crazysitter 1995, Mother 1996, Romy and Michelle's High School Reunion 1997, Clockwatchers 1997, The Opposite of Sex 1998, Analyze This 1999, Hanging Up 2000, Lucky Numbers 2000, All Over the Guy 2001, Dr. Dolittle 2 (voice) 2001, Analyze That 2002, Bark 2002, Marci X 2003, Happy Endings 2005, Kabluey 2007, P.S. I Love You 2007. *Address:* c/o PMK/HBH, 700 San Vicente Boulevard, Suite G 910, West Hollywood, CA 90069; POB 36849, Los Angeles, CA 90036-0849, USA (office).

KUDRYAVTSEV, Vladimir Nikolaevich; Russian jurist; b. 10 April 1923, Moscow; m. Dodonova Yevgenia Nikolaevna 1945; two s.; ed Mil. Law. Acad.; on staff of Acad. 1950–56; teacher at Lenin Mil.-Political Acad. 1956–60; served in Soviet Army 1941–45; mem. CPSU 1945–91; on staff of Mil. Coll. of USSR Supreme Court 1960–63; Deputy Dir of All-Union Inst. for Crime Prevention 1963–69, Dir 1969–73; Dir of USSR Inst. of State and Law of Acad. of Sciences 1973–89, Hon. Dir 1989–; corresp. mem. USSR (now Russian) Acad. of Sciences 1974–84, mem. 1984–, Vice-Pres. 1988–; Foreign mem. Bulgarian, Hungarian Acads of Science; Vice-Pres. Int. Asscn of Democratic Lawyers 1984–90; People's Deputy of the USSR 1989–91; State Prize 1984. *Publications:* over 200 works on criminology and criminal law, including What Sort of State Are We Building? 1991, Social Deformations 1992, (ed.) The Manual of International Law (7 Vols) 1993–. *Leisure interests:* theatre, music, cinema, reading. *Address:* Russian Academy of Sciences, Leninski pr. 14, 17901 Moscow, Russia. *Telephone:* (495) 237-68-08. *Fax:* (495) 237-44-21.

KUEHN, Ronald L., Jr; American energy industry executive; *Chairman, El Paso Corporation;* b. 1935; Pres. and CEO Sonat Inc. 1984–99, also Chair. 1986–99; Chair. (non-exec.), El Paso Corpn 1999–2000, Lead Dir 2002–03, Chair. 2003–, also CEO March-Sept. 2003; business consultant 2001–03; mem. Bd of Dirs AmSouth Bancorporation, Praxair Inc., Dun & Bradstreet Corpn. *Address:* El Paso Corporation, 1001 Louisiana Street, Houston, TX 77002, USA. *Telephone:* (713) 420–2600 (office). *Fax:* (713) 420–6030 (office). *Website:* www.elpaso.com (office).

KUFUOR, John Kofi Agyekum, MA; Ghanaian lawyer, business executive and fmr head of state; b. 8 Dec. 1938, Kumasi, Ashanti Region; m. Theresa Kufuor; five c.; ed Osei Tutu Boarding School, Prempeh Coll., Kumasi, Lincoln's Inn, London and Exeter Coll., Oxford, UK; called to Bar, Lincoln's Inn 1961; Clerk of Kumasi City Council; Council Rep., Constituent Ass. 1968–69; mem. Parl.; founding mem. Progress Party (PP) 1969, Popular Front Party (PFP) 1979, PFP Spokesman on Foreign Affairs 1979–82, founding mem. New Patriotic Party (NPP) 1992–; Deputy Minister of Foreign Affairs 1969–72; arrested after mil. coup and imprisoned for 15 months 1972–73; Sec. for Local Govt 1982; returned to law practice; presidential cand. for New Patriotic Party 1996; Pres. of Ghana and C-in-C of Armed Forces 2001–09 (re-elected 2004); Chair. African Union Ass. 2007–08; Grand Cordon of The Most Venerable Order of the Kts of the Pioneers (Liberia) 2008. *Leisure interests:* table tennis, reading, soccer, films. *Address:* New Patriotic Party (NPP), C912/2 Duade Street, Kokomlemle, POB 3456, Accra-North, Ghana (office). *Telephone:* (21) 227951 (office). *Fax:* (21) 224418 (office). *E-mail:* npp@africanonline.com.gh (office).

KUHN, Gustav, DPhil; Austrian conductor, director, producer and composer; b. 28 Aug. 1945, Salzburg; s. of Friedrich Kuhn and Hilde Kuhn; m. Andrea Kuhn 1971; one s. one d.; ed Acads of Salzburg and Vienna and Univs of Salzburg and Vienna; advanced conducting studies under Bruno Maderna and Herbert von Karajan; professional conductor in Istanbul (three years), Enschede (Netherlands), Dortmund (prin. conductor) and Vienna; début at Vienna State Opera (Elektra) 1977, Munich Nat. Theatre (Così fan tutte) 1978, Covent Garden, London 1979, Glyndebourne, Munich Opera Festival and Salzburg Festival 1980, Chicago (Fidelio) 1981, Paris Opéra 1982, La Scala, Milan 1984, Arena di Verona (Masked Ball) 1986, Rossini Opera Festival, Pesaro 1987; Gen. Music Dir in Berne, Bonn and Rome; production début in Trieste (Fliegender Holländer) 1986; other projects include Parsifal, Naples 1988, Salome, Rome 1988, Don Carlos (French version) and Don Carlo (Italian) for 250th anniversary Teatro Reggio, Turin 1990; Artistic Dir Neue Stimmen (New Voices), Bertelsmann Foundation 1987–, Macerata Festival, Italy (productions of Così fan tutte and Don Giovanni) 1990/91, Marchigiana Philharmonic Orchestra (Dir-Gen. 2003–), Haydn Orchestra 2003–, Conservatorio di Milano Philharmonic Orchestra 2004; Founder and Pres. Accad. di Montegral 1992, Tyrolean Festival, Erl, Austria 1997–; Producer and Conductor Complete Ring Cycle of Richard Wagner, Tyrolean Festival, Erl 2003, 2004, 2005, 2007; First Prize, Int. Conducting Contest of Austrian TV and Broadcasting Corpn (ORF) 1969, Lilly Lehmann Medal (Mozarteum Foundation), Max Reinhardt Medal (Salzburg), Senator of Honour Award 'Lorenzo il Magnifico' (Florence) 1988. *Publication:* Aus Liebe zur Musik 1993. *Leisure interests:* sailing, motorcycling. *Address:* Winkl 25, 6343 Erl, Austria (office). *Telephone:* (5373) 8181. *Website:* www.tiroler-festspiele.at; www.gustavkuhn.at.

KUHN, Michael, LLB; film producer; ed Univ. of Cambridge; solicitor, Supreme Court 1974; lawyer, Denton, Hall and Burgin, London; legal adviser, Polygram UK, London 1974–78, Dir 1978–83, Gen. Counsel, Polygram Int., London 1983–87, Sr Vice-Pres. 1987–93, Pres. Polygram Filmed Entertainment, Beverly Hills, Calif. 1991–93, fmr Exec. Vice-Pres. Polygram Holding Inc., New York, mem. Man. Bd Polygram NV, Pres. and CEO Polygram Filmed Entertainment, Beverly Hills; f. Qwerty Films, London. *Films produced include:* Red Rock West 1993, Being John Malkovich 1999, Wonderous Oblivion 2003, The Order 2003, Stage Beauty 2004, Kinsey 2004, I Heart Huckabees 2004, The Moguls 2005, Alien Autopsy 2006, Severance 2006, The Duchess 2008. *Address:* Qwerty Films, 42–44 Beak Street, London, W1F 9RH, England (office). *Telephone:* (20) 7440-5920 (office). *Fax:* (20) 7440-5959 (office).

KÜHNE, Gunther Albert Hermann, DrIur, LLM; German legal scholar and academic; *Director, Institute for German and International Mining and Energy Law, Technical University, Clausthal;* b. 25 Aug. 1939, Gelsenkirchen; s. of Friedrich Kühne and Gertrud Kühne (née Belgard); m. Elvira Schulz

1992; ed Univ. of Cologne and Columbia Univ., New York; part-time legal adviser to German mining cos 1963–68; Research Asst Bochum Univ. Law School 1967–70; Sr Govt official, Ministry of Econs, Bonn 1971–74; Sr official German del. OECD, Paris 1972–73; Sr Govt official, Ministry of Justice, Bonn 1974–78; Lecturer Private Law, Private Int. and Comparative Law, Bochum Univ. 1971–79; Prof. of Mining and Energy Law, Dir Inst. for German and Int. Mining and Energy Law, Tech. Univ. Clausthal 1978–; Visiting Prof. Bergakademie Freiberg 1992, Tel-Aviv Univ. 1993–, Nanjing Univ. 2004; Ordinary mem. Braunschweig Soc. of Sciences 1994; Hon. Prof. of Law, Univ. of Göttingen 1986–. *Publications:* numerous books and articles on aspects of law, including Die Parteiautonomie im internationalen Erbrecht 1973, IPR-Gesetz-Entwurf (Private Int. Law Reform Draft) 1980, Memorandum on the State and Reform of German International Family Law 1980, Wandel und Beharren im Bergrecht (jtly) 1992, Rechtsfragen der Aufsuchung und Gewinnung von in Steinkohleflözen beisitzendem Methangas 1994, Gegenwartsprobleme des Bergrechts (jtly) 1995, Wettbewerb, Bestandsschutz, Umweltschutz (jtly) 1997, Bestandsschutz alten Bergwerkseigentums unter besonderer Berücksichtigung des Art. 14 Grundgesetz 1998, Braunkohlenplanung und bergrechtliche Zulassungsverfahren 1999, Das deutsche Berg- und Energierecht auf dem Wege nach Europa (jtly) 2002, Das neue Energierecht in der Bewährung (co-ed.) 2002, Berg- und Energierecht im Zugriff europäischer Regulierungstendenzen (ed.) 2004. *Address:* Arnold-Sommerfeld-Strasse 6, 38678 Clausthal-Zellerfeld, Germany. *Telephone:* (5323) 723025. *Fax:* (5323) 722507. *E-mail:* gunther.kuehne@iber.tu-clausthal.de (office). *Website:* www.iber.tu-clausthal.de (office).

KÜHNL, Karel, Jr, DIur; Czech politician; b. 12 Sept. 1954, Prague; m. Daniela Kühnlová; one s. one d.; ed Charles Univ., Prague; freelance journalist in Australia 1978–87; ed. Radio Free Europe, Munich 1987–91; Econ. Adviser to Premier 1991–92, to Minister of Economics 1992–93; Amb. to UK 1993–97; MP for Freedom Union Party 1998–, Chair. 1999–2002; Minister of Industry and Trade 1997–98, of Defence 2004–06; Chair. of Freedom Union Club 1999–; Leader, Coalition Freedom Union Party–DEU, KDU–ČSL, ODA (after merger of Freedom Union Party and DEU Dec. 2001). *Leisure interests:* cycling, tennis. *Address:* c/o Ministry of Defence, Tychonova 1, 160 01 Prague 6, Czech Republic (office).

KUHNT, Dietmar, PhD; German business executive; b. 16 Nov. 1937, Wrocław (Breslau); m. 1966; two c.; ed Univs of Cologne and Freiburg; perm. legal adviser, Rheinisch-Westfälisches Elektrizitätswerk AG 1968; mem. Bd Man. RWE Energie AG 1989, Chair. 1992–94; mem. Bd Man. RWE AG 1992–94, Chair. 1995–2003; mem. Supervisory Bd TUI AG, Allianz Versicherungs-AG, BDO Deutsche, Warentreuhand AG, Dresdner Bank AG, GEA Group AG, Hapag-Lloyd AG, Hochtief AG; mem. Bd of Dirs COMSTAR-United, TeleSystems. *Address:* c/o Supervisory Board, TUI AG, Karl-Wiechert-Allee 4, 30625 Hannover, Germany.

KUI, Gen. Fulin; Chinese army officer; b. Feb. 1938, Xinbin Co., Liaoning Prov.; joined CCP 1961; joined PLA Infantry School, Qiqihar 1956; served in combat units of Shenyang Mil. Region, successively promoted from platoon commdr to div. chief-of-staff; studied at PLA Mil. Acad. 1982; served as div. commdr then corps chief-of-staff; Deputy Dir and Dir Operation Dept, PLA Gen. Staff HQ 1985, Asst to Chief of Gen. Staff 1992–95, Deputy Chief PLA Gen. Staff 1995; mem. 15th CCP Cen. Cttee 1997–2002; rank of Gen. 2000. *Address:* c/o Ministry of National Defence, Jingshanqian Jie, Beijing, People's Republic of China.

KUJAT, Gen. Harald; German air force officer (retd); b. 1 March 1942, Mielke; m. Sabine Kujat (née Becker); three c.; ed Armed Forces and Command College Hamburg, NATO Defence Coll. Rome, Italy; Instructor in Non-commissioned Officer Training, Fed. Armed Forces, then Platoon Leader, Co. Exec. Officer and Personnel Officer 1959–72; with Fed. Ministry of Defence, positions included ADC to Minister 1972–75, Mil. Asst 1977–78, Armed Forces Staff Asst Br. Chief (Operational Doctrines, AF) 1978–80, Br. Chief (Nuclear and Global Arms Control) 1990–92, Deputy Chief of Staff (Mil. Policy and Strategy) 1995, Dir Policy and Advisory Staff to Minister 1998–2000; 20th Gen. Staff Course (AF), Bundeswehr Command and Staff Coll. 1975–77; Section Chief (A3a), AF Support Command N 1977; Commdr Second Bn AF Training Regt 1985–88; Section Chief, Staff German Mil. Rep., NATO Mil. Cttee, Brussels 1988–90, Dir of Staff and Deputy Mil. Rep. 1992–95, Asst Dir Int. Mil. Staff (Plans and Policy) and Deputy Dir IMS, NATO 1996–98, Chair. NATO Mil. Cttee 2002–05; Dir IFOR Co-ordination Centre (ICC), Supreme HQ Allied Powers in Europe (SHAPE), Belgium 1996; Chief of Staff, Fed. Armed Forces 2000–02; rank of Lt 1968, First Lt 1968, Capt. 1971, Maj. 1974, Lt-Col 1979, Col 1988, Brig.-Gen. 1992, Maj.-Gen. 1995, Lt-Gen. 1998, Gen. 2000; Gold Cross of Honour of the Bundeswehr, Commdr's Cross of the Order of Merit of the FRG, Commdr Ordre Nat. de la Légion d'honneur France, Commdr's Cross of Merit Poland, Order of the Cross of the Eagle 1st class Estonia; Tidal Flood Memorial Medal 1962. *Publications:* numerous works on int. security and military policy. *Leisure interests:* photography, horse riding. *Address:* c/o Federal Ministry of Defence, Stauffenbergstr. 18, 10785 Berlin, Germany.

KUKAN, Eduard, LLD; Slovak politician and diplomatist; b. 26 Dec. 1939, Trnovec nad Váhom, W Slovakia; m.; one s. one d.; ed Moscow Inst. of Int. Relations, Charles Univ., Prague; joined Czechoslovakian Foreign Service 1964, mem. Africa Dept 1964–68, various posts at Embassy in Zambia 1968–73, mem. Secr. of Minister for Foreign Affairs 1973–77, Minister Counsellor, Embassy in USA 1977–81, Head Dept of Sub-Saharan Africa 1981–85, Amb. to Ethiopia 1985–88, Perm. Rep. of Czechoslovakia to UN, New York 1990–93, of Slovakia 1993–94; Deputy to Nat. Council of Slovak Repub. (Parl.) 1994–, Minister of Foreign Affairs March–Dec. 1994, mem. Foreign Relations Cttee 1994–; mem. Exec. Cttee Democratic Union of Slovakia 1994–, Chair. 1997–98; Vice-Chair. Slovak Democratic Coalition (SDK) 1998–; Minister of Foreign Affairs 1998–2006; UN Special Envoy for the Balkans 1999–2001; Rep. to Parl. Ass., Council of Europe 2006–; mem. Advisory Bd Global Panel; Hon. LLD (Upsala Coll., NJ, USA) 1993. *Leisure interests:* tennis, theatre. *Address:* National Council of the Slovak Republic, 812 80 Bratislava, Namestie A. Dubceka 1, Slovakia (office). *Telephone:* (2) 5972-2501 (office). *E-mail:* eduard_kukan@nrsr.sk (office). *Website:* www.nrsr.sk (office).

KUKES, Simon G., MSc; American (b. Russian) business executive; *CEO, ZAO Samara-Nafta;* b. 1946, Moscow; ed Moscow Chemical-Tech. Inst. (Mendeleyev Inst.), Rice Univ., Houston, Tex.; engineer, Titan Production Co. 1969–70; mem. of staff USSR Acad. of Sciences 1970–77; emigrated from USSR to Tex., USA 1977; Tech. Dir Philips Petroleum 1980s; Tech. Dir then Vice-Pres. in charge of devt in Commonwealth of Ind. States, Amoco 1991–96; Dir Planning and Devt, Yukos (largest oil refinery in Russia) 1996–98, Chair. and CEO Tyumen Oil Co. (TNK), Russia 1998–2003, helped engineer merger between TNK and BP 2002; Chair. and CEO Yukos Corpn 2003–04; CEO ZAO Samara-Nafta (exploration and production co. in Volga-Urals) 2005–; mem. Bd of Dirs Amarin Corpn plc 2005–; mem. Council of Energy, Marine Transportation and Public Policy, Columbia Univ. *Address:* ZAO Samara-Nafta, 4, Smolensky Bulvar, Moscow 119034, Russia (office). *Telephone:* (495) 974-8431.

KULAKOV, Anatoly Vasilyevich, DPhys MathSci; Russian scientist; b. 15 July 1938; m.; one s.; ed Leningrad Polytech. Inst.; researcher, Sr engineer., Deputy Dean, Leningrad Polytech. Inst. 1962–79; Scientific Sec., Deputy Chair., First Deputy Chair., Council on Science and Tech., USSR Council of Ministers 1979–90; Dir-Gen. Russian Industrialists and Entrepreneurs Union 1991–; Vice-Pres. Moscow Econ. Union 1997–; mem. Bd Russian Bank of Reconstruction and Devt 1998–; Corresp. mem. USSR (now Russian) Acad. of Sciences 1984; main research in theory of electromagnetic interactions in systems of charged particles, plasma and solids. *Address:* Russian Academy of Sciences, Leninsky prosp. 32A, 117995 Moscow, Russia. *Telephone:* (495) 205-12-25 (office).

KUŁAKOWSKI, Jan Jerzy, DIur; Polish trade union official, diplomatist and politician; b. 25 Aug. 1930, Myszków; s. of Konrad Kułakowski and Elodie Claessens; m. Zofia Kułakowska; three d.; ed Catholic Univ. of Leuven, Belgium; participated in Warsaw Uprising; left Poland for Belgium 1944; organized groups of young Polish workers in Belgium 1947–54; mem. Gen. Secr. Int. Fed. of Christian Trade Unions (IFCTU) 1954, Gen. Sec. European Org. of IFCTU 1962–74; Sec. European Trade Union Confed. 1974–76; Gen. Sec. World Confed. of Labour 1976–89; Amb. of Poland to the EU 1990–96; adviser to Polish Govt Plenipotentiary for European Integration and Foreign Assistance 1996; mem. Cttee for European Integration 1996; Sec. of State in the Chancellery of the Prime Minister 1998; Minister Plenipotentiary and Chief Negotiator for Poland's negotiations on accession to the EU 1998–2001; mem. European Parl. representing Wielkopolska region 2004–; Vice-Pres. Asscn France-Pologne pour l'Europe 2002–, Supervisory Bd Polish Robert Schuman Foundation; Hon. mem. NSZZ 'Solidarność'; Commdr's Cross with Star, Order of Polonia Restituta 1995, Officer, Leopold II (Belgium) 1999, White Eagle Order 2002, Chevalier, Légion d'honneur 2007, Chevalier, Ordre nat. du Mérite 2007; Foreign Minister Special Diploma for outstanding merit in promotion of Poland abroad 2007. *Publications:* numerous reports, documents and dossiers on int. trade unions and EU–Poland relations, including Bagatela Encounters (co-author), The Accession Story – The EU from 15 to 25 Countries (co-author). *Leisure interests:* social and devt policies. *Address:* Bâtiment Altiero Spinelli, 08G252, 60 Rue Wiertz, 1047 Brussels, Belgium (office); Stary Rynek 27/28, 61-772 Poznań, Poland (office). *Telephone:* (2) 284-58-48 (Brussels) (office); (61) 8513239 (Poznań) (office). *Fax:* (2) 284-98-48 (Brussels) (office); (61) 8513239 (Poznań) (office). *E-mail:* jan.kulakowski-assistant@europarl.europa.eu (office). *Website:* www.europarl.europa.eu (office); www.jankulakowski.pl (home).

KULCZYK, Jan, DJur; Polish business executive; *President of the Supervisory Board, Kulczyk Holding SA;* b. 6 June 1950, Bydgoszcz; m. Grazyna Kulczyk; two c.; ed Adam Mickiewicz Univ., Poznań, Acad. of Economy, Poznań; researcher Western Studies Inst., Polish Acad. of Sciences (PAN) 1974–; employee in family business Kulczyk Aussenhandelgesellschaft, Germany; Founder Interkulpol co. and other cos. 1981–91, merged into Kulczyk Holding SA 1991, currently Pres. Supervisory Bd; also Pres. Supervisory Bd Telekomunikacja Polska SA, Towarzystwo Ubezpieczeń i Reasekuracji Warta SA, Autostrada Wielkopolska SA, Euro Agro Centrum SA, Kompania Piwowarska SA, Skoda Auto Polska SA; mem. Supervisory Bd Polenergia SA; Pres. Polish Council of Business 1995–97, Vice-Pres. 1997–; co-f. and Pres. Polish-German Chamber of Industry and Commerce 1995–98, Vice-Pres. 1998–2002, Pres. 2002–; Pres. Adam Mickiewicz Univ. Council, Poznań; mem. Nat. Museum Council, Church Commercial Council, Int. Govs. Council, Peres Centre for Peace 2000–; Order of Polonia Restituta, Order of Saint Stanisław, Order of Saint Bridget; Golden Medal of Saint Paul Fathers, Kisiel Award. *Address:* Kulczyk Holding SA, ul. Krucza 24/26, 00-526 Warsaw, Poland (office). *Telephone:* (22) 5223200 (office); (22) 5223120 (office). *Website:* www.kulczykholding.pl (office).

KULHÁNEK, Vratislav; Czech economist and engineer; *Chairman of the Supervisory Board, Škoda Auto AS;* b. 20 Nov. 1943, Plzeň; m. Marie Kulhánek 1944; ed Univs of Prague and Pardubice; Dir Motor Jirkov, České Budějovice 1991–92, Robert Bosch, České Budějovice; Chair. Bd Škoda Auto Mladá Boleslav 1998–, Chair. Supervisory Bd 2004–; Pres. Asscn of Car Industry; Chair. ICC 2001–, CIOD; Dr hc Ing.; Prize of Czech–German Understanding, Germany 2000, Man. for the 21st Century 2000. *Leisure interests:* tennis, cars, golf. *Address:* Škoda Auto A.S., Representative Offices, Masarykovo Nabrezi 28, Prague, 1 (office); Srubec 346, 370 06 České

Budějovice, Czech Republic (home). *Telephone:* 221907262 (office). *Fax:* 221907297 (office). *E-mail:* vratislav.kulhanek@skoda-auto.cz (office); kulhanek.cb@volny.cz (home). *Website:* www.skoda-auto.cz (office).

KULICHKOV, Alyaksandr N.; Belarusian politician; fmr Minister of Trade; Head of Property Man. Directorate, Office of the Pres. 2005–. *Address:* c/o Office of the President, vul. K. Marksa 38, Dom Urada, 220016 Minsk, Belarus (office).

KULIK, Gennady Vasilyevich; Russian politician; b. 20 Jan. 1935, Zhekomskoye, Pskov region; m.; one s.; ed Leningrad State Univ.; researcher, Head of Dept, Siberian Div. of All-Union Inst. of Agricultural Econ. 1957–65; First Deputy Head, Novosibirsk Regional Dept of Agric. 1965; Deputy Head, Chief Dept of Planning and Econs, Ministry of Agric. RSFSR 1965–86; First Deputy Chair., RSFSR State Cttee of Agric. and Industry 1986–90; First Deputy Chair., RSFSR Council of Ministers, Minister of Agric. and Food 1990–91; USSR Peoples' Deputy 1990–92; adviser to Dir, Inex-Interexport (Moscow) 1993; mem. Exec. Bd Russian Agrarian Party, Deputy Chair. Russian Agrarian Union; mem. State Duma; Deputy Chair. Cttee on Budget, Taxes, Banks and Finance 1993–98; Deputy Chair. Govt of Russian Fed. 1998–99; mem. State Duma (Parl.) (Otechestvo-All Russia faction, Yedinaya Rossiya faction) 1999–2003, re-elected 2003–, mem. Cttee on Budget and Taxes; Merited Economist of Russia. *Address:* State Duma, Okhotny ryad 1, 103265 Moscow, Russia. *Telephone:* (495) 292-62-23 (office). *Fax:* (495) 292-69-66 (office).

KULIKOV, Army Gen. Anatoly Sergeyevich, DEconSc; Russian politician and military officer; *Deputy Chairman, Committee on Security, State Duma;* b. 4 Sept. 1946, Aigursky Apanasenkovsky, Stavropol Region; m.; two s. one d.; ed Vladikavkaz Mil. Command School, USSR Ministry of Internal Affairs, M. Frunze Mil. Acad., Mil. Acad. of Gen. Staff; numerous mil. postings including Commdr of Internal Troops 1992–95; Head United Grouping of Fed. Troops in Chechen Repub. Jan.–July 1995; Minister of Internal Affairs 1995–98; Deputy Chair. of Russian Govt 1996–98; mem. Security Council of Russian Fed. 1995–98; mem. State Duma (Parl.) 1999–, Deputy Chair., Cttee on Security 2004–; Chair. Cen. Council Ratniki Otechestva (Warriors of the Fatherland) Movt; Chair. Council on Econ. Security, Russian Acad. of Social Sciences; Chair. World Anticriminal and Antiterrorism Forum –2001; mem. Acad. of Mil. Sciences, Acad. of Natural Sciences; Order for Services to the Fatherland (Third Degree), Order for Personal Courage, Order for Service to the Motherland in the Armed Forces of the USSR, 3rd Class, Order of Honour; more than 30 medals. *Publications:* Chechen Node 2000, Heavy Stars 2002; numerous articles in journals and newspapers. *Leisure interests:* hunting, fishing, shooting, woodworking. *Address:* 1 Okhotny ryad, 103265 Moscow, Russia (office). *Telephone:* (495) 692-97-45 (office); (495) 202-15-65 (office); (495) 290-15-66 (office). *Fax:* (495) 692-74-32 (office); (495) 290-46-28 (office). *E-mail:* askulikov@duma.gov.ru (office).

KULIKOV, Marshal Viktor Georgiyevich; Russian politician and army officer (retd); b. 5 July 1921; ed Frunze Military Acad., Acad. of General Staff; joined Soviet Army 1938; Commdr of Platoon 1940, Chief of Staff tank battalion, Regt, brigade 1941–45; various command posts in tank detachments 1945–48; Frunze Mil. Acad. 1948–53; Commdr tank Regt, Chief of Staff tank div., Deputy Commdr of Army, Commdr of Army 1953–67; Commdr Kiev Mil. Area 1967–69; C-in-C Soviet Forces in Germany 1969–71; mem. CPSU 1942–; mem. Cen. Cttee of CPSU 1971–89; Chief of Gen. Staff and First Deputy Minister of Defence 1971–77; Marshal of the Soviet Union 1977; C-in-C of Armed Forces of Warsaw Pact 1977–89; Gen. Insp., Ministry of Defence Inspectorate 1989–91; State Mil. Adviser 1992; USSR People's Deputy 1989–91; mem. State Duma (Parl.) (Otechestvo-All Russia faction) 1999–, Chair. Cttee on War Veterans; Hero of the Soviet Union and other decorations. *Address:* State Duma, Okhotny ryad 1, 103265 Moscow, Russia. *Telephone:* (495) 292-02-91. *Fax:* (495) 292-02-91.

KULIYEV, Eldar Gulam oglu; Azerbaijani diplomatist and organization official; *Executive Director, Congress of Russian Azerbaijanis;* b. 29 Aug. 1939, Baku; m.; two c.; ed Azerbaijani State Univ., Baku, Diplomatic Acad., Moscow; interpreter Project Aswan-Cairo, Egypt 1963–65; Second Sec., First Sec. Ministry of Foreign Affairs, Baku 1965–69; Vice-Consul, USSR Consulate, Aswan 1969–71, Consul 1971–73; First Sec. Soviet Embassy, Cairo 1973–76; Consul, USSR Consulate-Gen., Istanbul 1978–83; advanced studies at Diplomatic Acad., Moscow 1983–84; Counsellor Div. of Cultural Relations with Foreign Countries, Ministry of Foreign Affairs, Moscow 1983–85, Expert 1985–86; Expert Dept of Humanitarian and Cultural Relations, Ministry of Foreign Affairs, Moscow 1986–88; Minister-Counsellor USSR Embassy, Aden 1988–90; Deputy Consul-Gen. USSR Consulate-Gen., Aden 1990–91; Expert Legal Dept, Ministry of Foreign Affairs, Moscow 1991–92; Sr Counsellor Dept of Int. Orgs and Global Affairs, Ministry of Foreign Affairs, Moscow; Sr Counsellor Analysis and Research Dept 1993–94; Perm. Rep. to UN, New York 1994–2001; fmr adviser to Pres. Congress of Russian Azerbaijanis, currently Exec. Dir. *Address:* c/o Ministry of Foreign Affairs, Ghanjlar meydani 3, 370004 Baku, Azerbaijan (office).

KULIYEV, Vilayat Mukhtar oglu; Azerbaijani politician; b. 1952; mem. New Azerbaijan Party (NAP) 1992–; Minister of Foreign Affairs 1999–2004. *Address:* c/o Ministry of Foreign Affairs, Ghanjlar meydani 3, 370004 Baku, Azerbaijan (office).

KULKA, Konstanty Andrzej; Polish violinist; *Professor, Warsaw Academy of Music;* b. 5 March 1947, Gdańsk; m.; two d.; ed Higher State School of Music, Gdańsk; Prof., Acad. of Music, Warsaw 1994–; participant in two music competitions: Paganini Competition, Genoa 1964, Diploma and Special Prize; Music Competition, Munich 1966 (1st Prize); many gramophone, radio and TV recordings; soloist with Nat. Philharmonic Orchestra, Warsaw 1984–; Gold

Cross of Merit, Commdr's Cross, Order of Polonia Restituta; Minister of Culture and Arts Prize 1969, 1973, Minister of Foreign Affairs Prize 1977, Pres. of Radio and TV Cttee Prize 1978, Prize Winner, 33rd Grand Prix du Disque Int. Sound Festival, Paris 1981. *Performances:* since 1967 has given some 1,500 concerts all over the world and participates in many int. festivals including Lucerne, Prague, Bordeaux, Berlin, Granada, Barcelona, Brighton; concerts with Berlin Philharmonic Orchestra, Chicago Symphony Orchestra, Minneapolis Orchestra, London Symphony Orchestra, Konzertgebouw Amsterdam Orchestra, English Chamber Orchestra and others. *Recordings include:* Antonio Vivaldi Cztery pory roku (The Four Seasons), Szymanowski: Violin Concertos Nos. 1 & 2 1997, Mozart: Best Of 2000, Karlowicz: Tone Poems/Violin Concerto 2002, Paderewski: Violin & Piano Works 2003, Penderecki: Violin Concertos Nos. 1 & 2 2003. *Leisure interests:* collecting gramophone records, bridge, collecting interesting kitchen recipes. *Address:* Filharmonia Narodowa, ul. Jasna 5, 00-950 Warsaw, Poland. *Telephone:* (605) 194753; (22) 5517203. *E-mail:* konstanty.kulka@wp.pl (office).

KULLMAN, Ellen, BSc, MBA; American business executive; *Executive Vice-President, Safety and Protection, Coatings and Color, Marketing and Sales, and Safety and Sustainability, E. I. du Pont de Nemours and Co.;* m. Michael; two s. one d.; ed Tufts and Northwestern Univs; fmrly with General Electric; Marketing Man. medical imaging business, DuPont 1988, later Business Dir x-ray film business, Global Business Dir electronic imaging, Printing & Publishing, Global Business Dir White Pigment & Mineral Products 1994, Vice-Pres. and Gen. Man. 1995, Head DuPont Safety Resources 1998, Bio-Based Materials 1999, Group Vice-Pres. and Gen. Man. 2000, Head DuPont Flooring Systems and DuPont Surfaces 2001, Group Vice-Pres. Safety & Protection 2002–06, Exec. Vice-Pres. Safety & Protection, Coatings and Color, Marketing and Sales, and Safety and Sustainability 2006–; mem. Bd of Dirs General Motors Corpn, Nat. Safety Council; mem. Bd of Overseers Tufts Univ. School of Eng; mem. Cttee of 200; Aiming High Award 2004, ranked by Fortune magazine amongst 50 Most Powerful Women in Business in the US (46th) 2005, (21st) 2006, (25th) 2007, ranked by Forbes magazine amongst 100 Most Powerful Women (86th) 2008. *Address:* E. I. du Pont de Nemours and Co., 1007 Market Street, Wilmington, DE 19898, USA (office). *Telephone:* (302) 774-1000 (office). *Website:* www.dupont.com (office).

KULLMANN FIVE, Karin Cecilie (Kaci) (see FIVE, Karin Cecilie (Kaci) Kullmann).

KULONGOSKI, Ted; American lawyer, judge and state official; *Governor of Oregon;* b. 5 Nov. 1940, Mo.; m. Mary Kulongoski; three c.; ed Univ. of Mo.; served in US Marine Corps; fmr truck driver and steelworker; f. law firm, Eugene, Ore.; mem. Ore. House of Reps 1974–78, Ore. State Senate 1978–87; apptd Ore. Insurance Commr 1987–92; elected Ore. Attorney-Gen. 1992–96; elected Ore. Supreme Court 1996–2001; Gov. of Ore. 2003–; Democrat. *Address:* Office of the Governor, 160 Capitol Building, 900 Court Street, NE, Salem, OR 97301-4047, USA (office). *Telephone:* (503) 378-4582. *Fax:* (503) 378-6827. *Website:* www.governor.state.or.us.

KULOV, Feliks Sharshenbayevich; Kyrgyzstani politician; *Chairman, Dignity (Ar-Namys);* b. 29 Oct. 1948, Frunze (now Bishkek); ed Osh Univ.; began career with Ministry of Internal Affairs, held positions successively as Insp., Chief Insp., Head of Criminal Dept; apptd Vice-Chief, Internal Affairs Admin, Talas Duban 1978, later Vice-Minister of Internal Affairs, then Minister of Internal Affairs; resgnd party membership following coup attempt in Moscow 1991; Vice-Pres. of the Repub. 1992–93; investigated on charges of corruption 1993; resgnd following scandals surrounding Seabeco Affair 1993; Gov. of Chui Region 1993–97; Minister of Nat. Security 1997–98; Mayor of Bishkek 1998–99; Founding Chair. Dignity (Ar-Namys) Party 1999–; cand. in parl. elections 2000; charged with abuse of office during term as Minister of Nat. Security and sent to closed mil. trial June 2000, acquitted by court Aug., sent to retrial Sept., sentenced to seven years' imprisonment Jan. 2001; apptd Head of People's Congress (alliance among all opposition parties) Nov. 2001; sentenced to further 10 years' imprisonment on embezzlement charges May 2002, charges overturned 2005, temporarily in charge of armed forces and law enforcement April–July 2005; Prime Minister 2005–19 Dec. 2006 (resgnd), re-apptd Acting Prime Minister 19 Dec. 2006–29 Jan. 2007; Co-founder and Chair. United Front For A Worthy Future For Kyrgyzstan Feb. 2007–. *Address:* Dignity (Ar-Namys), 720033 Bishkek, Togolok Moldo 60A, Kyrgyzstan (office). *Telephone:* (312) 32-52-89 (office). *E-mail:* ar-namys@mail.kg (office). *Website:* www.ar-namys.org (office).

KULUKUNDIS, Sir Eddie, Kt, OBE, FRSA; British business executive and theatre director; b. 20 April 1932; s. of late George Elias Kulukundis and of Eugenie Diacakis; m. Susan Hampshire (q.v.) 1981; ed Collegiate School, New York, Salisbury School, Conn. and Yale Univ.; mem. Baltic Exchange 1959–; mem. Lloyds 1964–95, mem. Council 1983–89; Dir Rethymnis & Kulukundis Ltd 1964–, London & Overseas Freighters 1980–85, 1989–97; Chair. Knightsbridge Theatrical Productions Ltd 1970–; Chair. Ambassadors Theatre Group 1992–; Trustee Sports Aid Trust 1986–; mem. Exec. Cttee Royal Shakespeare Theatre 1977–2003, Royal Shakespeare Theatre Trust 1969 (Vice-Chair. 1983–); Gov. Royal Shakespeare Theatre 1977–2003; Vice-Pres. Traverse Theatre Club; Dir Hampstead Theatre Ltd 1969–2004; Bd of Management Soc. of London Theatre 1973–2003, Hon. Vice-President Soc. of London Theatre 2003–, Vice-President UK Athletics 1998–2003. *London productions include:* (some jtly) Enemy 1969, The Happy Apple, Poor Horace, The Friends, How the Other Half Loves, Tea Party and the Basement (double bill), The Wild Duck 1970, After Haggerty, Hamlet, Charley's Aunt, Straight Up 1971, London Assurance, Journey's End 1972; Small Craft Warnings, A Private Matter, Dandy Dick 1973, The Waltz of the Toreadors, Life Class, Pygmalion, Play Mas, The Gentle Hook 1974, A Little Night Music, Entertaining Mr Sloane, The Gay Lord Quex, What the Butler Saw,

Travesties, Lies, The Seagull, A Month in the Country, A Room with a View, Too True to be Good, The Bed Before Yesterday 1975, Dimetos, Banana Ridge, Wild Oats 1976, Candida, Man and Superman, Once a Catholic 1977, Privates on Parade, Gloo Joo 1978, Bent, Outside Edge, Last of the Red Hot Lovers 1979, Beecham, Born in the Gardens 1980, Tonight at 8.30, Steaming, Arms and the Man 1981, Steafel's Variations 1982, Messiah, Pack of Lies 1983, Of Mice and Men, The Secret Diary of Adrian Mole Aged 13³/⁴1984, Camille 1985, The Cocktail Party 1986, Curtains 1987, Separation, South Pacific, Married Love, Over My Dead Body 1989, Never the Sinner 1990, The King and I, Carmen Jones 1991, Noel & Gertie, Slip of the Tongue, Shades, Annie Get Your Gun, Making it Better 1992, The Prime of Miss Jean Brodie 1994, Neville's Island 1994, The Killing of Sister George 1995. *New York productions include:* (jtly): How the Other Half Loves 1971, Sherlock Holmes, London Assurance 1974, Travesties 1975, The Merchant 1977, Once a Catholic 1979.

KUMA, Kengo; Japanese architect and academic; *Principal, Kengo Kuma and Associates;* b. 8 Aug. 1954, Kanagawa; s. of Hiroko Kuma and Toma Kuma; m.; one s.; ed Univ. of Tokyo; Visiting Scholar, Columbia Univ., USA 1985–86; f. Spatial Design Studio 1987; f. Kengo Kuma & Assocs 1990; Visiting Prof. Keio Univ. 1998, Prof. 2001–; AIA Benedictus Award 1997, Architectural Inst. of Japan Award 1997, Int. Stone Architecture Award 2001. *Publications:* 10 Houses 1990, Introduction to Architecture – History and Ideology 1994, Catastrophe of Architectural Desire 1994, Anti Object 2000. *Address:* Kengo Kuma and Associates, 2-12-12-9F, Minamiaoyama, Minato-ku, Tokyo 107-0062 (office); 37-7-301 Yaraicho Shinjuku-ku, Tokyo 162-0805, Japan (home). *Telephone:* (3) 3401-7721 (office); (3) 3235-7784 (home). *Fax:* (3) 3401-7778 (office); (3) 3268-0928 (home). *E-mail:* kuma@ba2.so-net.ne.jp (office). *Website:* www02.so-net.ne.jp/~kuma (office).

KUMAKURA, Sadatake; Japanese pharmaceuticals distribution executive; *Representative Director, President and CEO, Mediceo Paltac Holdings Company Ltd;* fmr Pres. and CEO Kuraya Sanseido Inc.; Rep. Dir, Pres. and CEO Mediceo Paltac Holdings Co. Ltd 2004–. *Address:* Mediceo Paltac Holdings Co. Ltd, 7-15, Yaesu 2-chome, Chuo-ku, Tokyo 104-8464, Japan (office). *Telephone:* (3) 3517-5800 (office). *Fax:* (3) 3517-5011 (office). *E-mail:* info@mediceo-paltac.co.jp (office). *Website:* www.mediceo-paltac.co.jp (office).

KUMALO, Dumisana Shadrack, MA; South African diplomatist and journalist; *Permanent Representative, United Nations;* b. 16 Sept. 1947; m. (divorced); one s.; ed Univ. of South Africa, Indiana Univ., USA; reporter for Golden City Post 1967–79; feature writer Drum magazine 1969–70; political reporter Sunday Times, Johannesburg 1970–76; Marketing Exec. Officer, Total Oil Co. 1976–77; in exile 1977; Int. Educ. Program Co-ordinator, Phelps Stokes Fund, New York 1978–80; Projects Dir Africa Fund and American Cttee on Africa 1980–97; Dir of US Desk, Dept of Foreign Affairs 1997–99; Perm. Rep. to UN, New York 1999–. *Address:* Permanent Mission of South Africa to the United Nations, 333 East 38th Street, 9th Floor, New York, NY 10016, USA (office). *Telephone:* (212) 213-5583 (office). *Fax:* (212) 692-2498 (office). *E-mail:* soafun@worldnet.att.net (office). *Website:* www.southafrica-newyork.net/pmun (office).

KUMAR, Naveen; Indian television administrator; mem. Indian Admin. Service 1975–; Dir-Gen. Doordarshan (nat. broadcaster) 2004–06. *Address:* c/o Doordarshan, Mandi House, Doordarshan Bhawan, Copernicus Marg, New Delhi 110 001, India (office).

KUMAR, Nitish, BSc (Eng); Indian engineer and politician; *Chief Minister of Bihar;* b. 1 March 1951, Bakhtiarpur, Patna, Bihar; s. of the late Shri Kaviraj Ram Lakhan Singh and Smt. Parmeshwari Devi; m. Smt. Manju Kumari Sinha 1973; one s.; ed Bihar Coll. of Eng, Patna; involved in JP Movt led by Jayaprakash Narayan 1974–77, detained under the Maintenance of Internal Security Act 1974, and also during Emergency 1975; mem. Bihar Legis. Ass. 1985–89, mem. Cttee on Petitions 1986–87, Cttee on Public Undertakings 1987–89; Pres. Yuva Lok Dal 1987–88; elected to Lok Sabha 1989–, mem. Janata Dal (United) party, Sec.-Gen. Janata Dal, Bihar 1989, Gen. Sec. 1991–93, Deputy Leader of Janata Dal in Parl. 1991–93, Leader 2004–; mem. House Cttee 1989–90 (resgnd), mem. Railway Convention Cttee 1991–96, Chair. Cttee on Agric. 1993–96, mem. Cttee on Estimates 1996, Gen. Purposes Cttee 1996, 2004, Jt Cttee on the Constitution 1996 (Eighty-first Amendment Bill 1996), Cttee on Defence 1998, Cttee on Coal and Steel 2004, Cttee of Privileges 2004, Union Minister of State, Agriculture and Co-operation April–Nov. 1990, Union Minister for Railways and for Surface Transport 1998–99, resgnd following railway accident at Gaisal in NE India Aug. 1999; Union Minister for Surface Transport Oct.–Nov. 1999, for Agric. Nov. 1999–March 2000; Union Minister for Agric. 2000–01, with additional charge of Railways March–July 2001, Union Minister for Railways 2001–04; led Nat. Democratic Alliance to victory in Bihar Ass. elections Nov. 2005; Chief Minister of Bihar 3 March 2000, resgnd seven days later, Chief Minister of Bihar 2005–; Founder-mem. Samata Party Movt. *Address:* Office of the Chief Minister, Patna, Bihar (office); Vill. Hakikatpur, PO Bakhtiarpur, Distt. Patna 800 001, Bihar, India (home). *Telephone:* (612) 2223886 (office); (98) 68180490 (mobile); (612) 2222079 (home). *E-mail:* cmbihar@nic.in (office). *Website:* gov.bih.nic.in (office).

KUMAR, Rajendra; Indian government official; joined Indian Admin. Service; fmr Dir (Educ.) Govt of Nat. Capital Territory of Delhi; Commr-cum-Sec. (Health/Finance), Union Territory of Andaman and Nicobar Islands –2006; Admin. of Lakshadweep 2006; Chair. Lakshadweep Devt Corpn, SPORTS (Soc. for Promotion of Recreational Tourism and Sports); ex-officio Insp. Gen. of Police. *Address:* c/o Office of the Administrator, Kavaratti 682555, Lakshadweep, India (office).

KUMAR, Sanjay; American (b. Sri Lankan) fmr software industry executive; b. 1962, Colombo, Sri Lanka; emigrated from Sri Lanka to USA 1976; joined Computer Assocs Int., Inc. (CA) 1987, various sr positions in devt, strategic planning and operations, Pres. and COO 1994–2000, Pres. and CEO 2000–02, Chair. and CEO 2002–2004 (resgnd), Chief Software Architect 2004; charged with fraud related to CA accounting practices 2004, pleaded guilty to charges April 2006, sentenced to 12 years in prison Nov. 2006.

KUMARASWAMY, Haradanahalli Deve Gowda, BSc; Indian politician; b. 19 Dec. 1959, Haradana Halli, Hassan Dist, Karnataka; s. of Shri H. D. Deve 'Mannina Maga' Gowda and Smt. Chennamma Gowda; m. Anita; one s.; began career as distributor of Kannada films in Mysore, Mandya, Hassan and Coorg dists 1990–; began political career 1994, mem. Lok Sabha (Parl.) for Kanakapura (Bangalore Rural Dist) 1996–98, for Ramanagaram 2004–06, 2008–; organized Daridra Narayana rally to fight for rights of the urban and rural poor 2004; Chief Minister of Karnataka 2006–07 (resgnd); Pres. Karnataka Cinema Theatre Owners Asscn 2002–; Founder and Pres. Film Producers Asscn 2003–. *Address:* c/o Office of the Chief Minister, Government of Karnataka, Vidhana Soudha, Bangalore 560001, India.

KUMARATUNGA, Chandrika Bandaranaike, BSc, PhD; Sri Lankan politician and fmr head of state; b. 29 June 1945, Colombo; d. of the late S. W. R. D. Bandaranaike (f. Sri Lanka Freedom Party (SLFP) and fmr Prime Minister 1956–59, assassinated 1959) and Sirimavo R. D. Bandaranaike (first elected woman Prime Minister in the world in 1960–65, 1970–77, 1994–2000, died 2000); m. Vijaya Kumaratunga 1978 (assassinated 1988); one s. one d.; ed St Bridget's Convent, Colombo, Univ. of Paris (Sciences Po), France; mem. Exec. Cttee Women's League of SLFP 1974, Exec. Cttee and Working Cttee 1980, Cen. Cttee 1992, Deputy Leader of SLFP; Chair., Man. Dir Dinakara Sinhala (daily newspaper) 1977–85; Vice-Pres. Sri Lanka Mahajana (People's) Party (SLMP) 1984, Pres. 1986; Leader SLMP and People's Alliance; Chief Minister, Minister of Law and Order, Finance and Planning, Educ., Employment and Cultural Affairs of the Western Prov. Council 1993–94; Prime Minister Aug.–Nov. 1994, also held posts of Minister of Finance and Planning, Ethnic Affairs and Nat. Integration, of Defence, of Buddha Sasana; Pres. of Sri Lanka 1994–2005; fmrly also Minister of Defence, of Constitutional Affairs, of Educ. and of Public Security, Law and Order; Pres. Sri Lanka Freedom Party 2000–06; Additional Prin. Dir Land Reform Comm. 1972–75; Chair. Janawasa Comm. 1975–77; Expert Consultant, FAO 1977–80; Research Fellow, Univ. of London, UK 1988–91; Guest Lecturer, Univ. of Bradford, UK 1989, Jawaharlal Nehru Univ., India 1991; adviser on poverty alleviation to Clinton Global Initiatiative; mem. Club de Madrid; guest lecturer and keynote speaker at int. events and confs; ranked by Forbes magazine amongst 100 Most Powerful Women (44th) 2004, (25th) 2005. *Publications:* several research papers on land reform and food policies. *Leisure interests:* swimming, Kandyan (nat.) dance, music, reading, art and sculpture, drama, cinema. *Address:* Office of the Former President, # 27 Independence Avenue, Colombo 10, Sri Lanka (office). *Telephone:* (11) 269-437-2 (office). *Fax:* (11) 267-415-9 (office). *E-mail:* cbk_office@yahoo.co.uk (office). *Website:* www.presidentcbk.org (office).

KUMBLE, Anil; Indian cricketer; b. 17 Oct. 1970, Bangalore, Karnataka; leg-break and googly bowler; right-handed lower order batsman; teams played for Karnataka, Northants., Leics., Surrey, India; test debut versus England at Manchester 1990, one-day int. debut versus Sri Lanka at Sharjah, United Arab Emirates 1990; took 444 wickets in 92 tests (average 27.86); 323 wickets in 260 one-day ints (average 30.73); 902 wickets in 192 first-class matches; India's highest-ever wicket-taker in tests and joint-fifth highest wicket taker in tests internationally; became second player to capture all 10 wickets in a test match on 7 Nov. 1999 (for India versus Pakistan); Padma Shri 2005. *Address:* c/o Board of Control for Cricket in India, 'Kairali', GHS Lane, Manacaud, Trivandrum 695 009, India.

KUMIN, Maxine Winokur, MA; American writer and poet; b. 6 June 1925, Philadelphia; d. of Peter Winokur and Doll Simon; m. Victor M. Kumin 1946; one s. two d.; ed Radcliffe Coll; consultant in poetry, Library of Congress 1981–82; Fellow, Acad. of American Poets, Chancellor 1995–; Visiting Prof., MIT 1984, Univ. of Miami 1995, Pitzer Coll. 1996; McGee Prof. of Writing, Davidson Coll. 1997; Writer-in-Residence, Fla Int. Univ. 1998; Poet Laureate, State of New Hampshire 1989; Nat. Endowment for the Arts Grant 1966, Nat. Council on the Arts Fellowship 1967, Acad. of American Poets Fellowship 1985; mem. Poetry Soc. of America, PEN America, Authors' Guild, Writers' Union; various hon. doctorates; Lowell Mason Palmer Award 1960, William Marion Reedy Award 1968, Eunice Tietjens Memorial Prize 1972, Pulitzer Prize for Poetry 1973, American Acad. of Arts and Letters Award 1980, Poetry magazine Levinson Award 1987, American Acad. and Inst. of Arts Award 1989, Sarah Josepha Hale Award 1992, The Poet's Prize 1994, Aiken Taylor Poetry Prize 1995, Harvard Grad. School of Arts and Sciences Centennial Award 1996, Ruth Lilly Poetry Prize 1999. *Publications:* poetry: Halfway 1961, The Privilege 1965, The Nightmare Factory 1970, Up Country: Poems of New England, New and Selected 1972, House, Bridge, Fountain, Gate 1975, The Retrieval System 1978, Our Ground Time Here Will Be Brief 1982, Closing the Ring 1984, The Long Approach 1985, Nurture 1989, Looking for Luck 1992, Connecting the Dots 1996, Selected Poems 1960–1990 1997, The Long Marriage 2001, Bringing Together: Uncollected Early Poems 2003; fiction: Through Dooms of Love 1965, The Passions of Uxport 1968, The Abduction 1971, The Designated Heir 1974, Why Can't We Live Together Like Civilised Human Beings? 1982; other: In Deep: Country Essays 1987, To Make a Prairie: Essays on Poets, Poetry, and Country Living 1989, Women, Animals, and Vegetables: Essays and Stories 1994, Quit Monks or Die! 1999, Inside the Halo and Beyond (memoir) 2000, Always Beginning (essays) 2000; also short stories, children's books and poetry contribs to nat. magazines. *Leisure interest:* breeding horses. *Address:* Giles Anderson, The Giles Anderson Agency, 435 Convent Avenue, Suite 5, New York, NY 10031, USA (office). *Telephone:* (212) 234-0692 (office). *Fax:* (212) 234-0693 (office). *E-mail:* gilesa@rcn.com (office). *Website:* www.maxinekumin.com (office).

KUNADZE, Georgy Fridrikhovich, CHisSc; Russian diplomatist and academic; *Ambassador-at-Large and Chief Scientific Researcher, Institute of World Economy and International Relations (IMEMO), Russian Academy of Sciences;* b. 21 Dec. 1948, Moscow; m.; one s.; ed Moscow Inst. of Oriental Languages; researcher Inst. of Oriental Studies USSR Acad. of Sciences 1971–83; diplomatic service 1983–, scientific attaché Embassy in Japan 1982–87, head of sector, Chief of Div. Inst. of World Econs and Int. Relations 1987–91; Deputy Minister of Foreign Affairs of Russia 1991–93; Amb. to Repub. of Korea 1993–96, Amb.-at-Large 1996–; Deputy Dir Inst. of USA and Canada, Russian Acad. of Sciences 1997–99, Chief Scientific Researcher Inst. of Int. Econ. and Int. Relations (IMEMO), Russian Acad. of Sciences 1999–. *Publications:* numerous articles. *Address:* IMEMO, Profsoyuznaya str. 23, 117859 Moscow, Russia (office). *Telephone:* (495) 128-81-09 (office); (495) 128-25-18 (office). *Fax:* (495) 310-70-27 (office). *E-mail:* imemoran@imemo.ru (office). *Website:* www.imemo.ru/eng (office).

KÜNAST, Renate; German lawyer and politician; b. 15 Dec. 1955, Recklinghausen, North-Rhine/Westphalia; ed Düsseldorf Polytechnic, Freie Universität Berlin; social worker at youth correctional facililty in Berlin-Tegel 1977–79; Co-founder and mem. West Berlin Alternative List 1979, now Bündnis 90/Die Grünen MdB (Alliance 90/Greens), Chair. 1990–93, 1998–2000 (Deputy Chair. 1995–98), Chair. Nat. Exec. Cttee 2000–01; mem. Berlin Senate 1985–87, 1989–2000; mem. Parl. 2002–, Co-Chair. Green Parl. party 2005–; Fed. Minister for Consumer Protection, Food and Agric. 2001–05; mem. Women's Business Club 2003; Rachel Carson Prize 2001, German-British Forum Award 2001. *Publication:* Klasse statt Masse 2002, Die Dickmacher 2004. *Address:* Bündnis 90/Die Grünen MdB, Deutscher Bundestag, Platz der Republik 1, 11011 Berlin, Germany (office). *Website:* bundestag.de/mdb/bio/K/kuenare0.html (office); www.renate-kuenast.de.

KUNCZE, Gábor, BSc, PhD; Hungarian politician; b. 4 Nov. 1950, Pápa; m.; ed Ybl Miklós Coll. of Tech., Budapest, Karl Marx Univ. of Econs, Budapest; fmr economist and engineer, various industrial man. roles –1983; dept head then div. chief, Industrial Mechanisation Co. 1983–85; Deputy Dir ÉPGÉPTERV Co. 1985–90; mem. Parl. 1990–; joined Alliance of Free Democrats (Szabad Democraták Szövetsége—SzDSz) 1992, mem. Nat. Council 1992, leader of Parl. group 1993–94, 1998–2000, 2002–07, mem. Nat. Governing Cttee 1994–97, Pres. SzDSz 1997–98, 2001–07; mem. Council of Elders 1993–94, 1998–2000, 2002–; apptd Minister of the Interior and Deputy Prime Minister after his party signed coalition agreement with HSP (Magyar Szocialista Párt—MSZP) 1994–98. *Address:* Hungarian National Assembly, 1357 Budapest, Kossuth tér 1–3, Hungary (office). *Telephone:* (1) 441-5000 (office); (1) 441-5820 (office). *Fax:* (1) 441-5952 (office). *Website:* www.parlament.hu (office).

KUNDA, George, LLB; Zambian lawyer and politician; *Vice-President;* b. 26 Feb. 1956, Luanshya; s. of Njanamo Kunda and Eginala Mwelwa; m. Irene Kunda; six c.; ed Univ. of Zambia; admitted to Bar 1982; fmr solicitor and advocate, Luanshya Municipal Council; fmr attorney ND Patel and Co., Cave Malik and Co., Ndlola; Pnr, George Kunda and Co., Lusaka (law firm) 1990–; Chair. Law Asscn of Zambia 1996–2000; mem. Parl. for Muchinga 2002–; Attorney-Gen. and Minister of Justice 2005–08; Vice-Pres. 2008–; mem. Petroleum Cttee 2007–. *Address:* Office of the President, POB 30135, Lusaka, Zambia (office). *Telephone:* (21) 1266147 (office). *Fax:* (21) 1266092 (office). *Website:* www.statehouse.gov.zm (office).

KUNDERA, Milan; Czech/French novelist; b. 1 April 1929, Brno; s. of Dr Ludvik Kundera and Milada Kunderová-Janosikova; m. Věra Hrabánková 1967; ed Film Faculty, Acad. of Music and Dramatic Arts, Prague; Asst, later Asst Prof., Film Faculty, Acad. of Music and Dramatic Arts, Prague 1958–69; Prof., Univ. of Rennes 1975–80; Prof., Ecole des hautes études en sciences sociales, Paris 1980–94; mem. Union of Czechoslovak Writers 1963–69; mem. Editorial Bd Literární noviny 1963–67, 1968; Dr hc (Michigan) 1983; Commonwealth Award 1981, Prix Europa-Littérature 1982, Jerusalem Prize 1985, Prix de la critique de l'Acad. française 1987, Nelly Sachs Preis 1987, Österreichische Staatspreis für Europäische Literatur 1988, Jaroslav-Seifert Prize (Czech Repub.) 1994, Medal of Merit (Czech Repub.) 1995, J. G. Herder Prize (Austria) 2000, Grand Prize Acad. française (for novels Slowness, Identity and Ignorance) 2001. *Publications:* drama: Jacques and his master, an homage to Diderot 1971–81; short stories: Laughable Loves (Czechoslovak Writers' Publishing House Prize) 1970; novels: The Joke (Union of Czechoslovak Writers' Prize 1968) 1967, Life is Elsewhere (Prix Médicis) 1973, La Valse aux adieux (The Farewell Waltz) (Premio letterario Mondello 1978) 1976, Livre du rire et de l'oubli (The Book of Laughter and Forgetting) 1979, The Unbearable Lightness of Being (Los Angeles Times Prize) 1984, Immortality (The Independent Prize, UK 1991) 1989, Slowness 1995, L'Identità (Identity) 1997, La Ignorancia (Ignorance) 2000; essays: The Art of the Novel 1987, Les Testaments trahis (Aujourd'hui Prize, France) 1993, The Curtain 2005. *Website:* www.faber.co.uk (office).

KUNERT, Günter; German writer; *President, PEN Centre of German-speaking Writers Abroad;* b. 6 March 1929, Berlin; s. of Adolf Kunert and Edith Warschauer; m. Marianne Todten 1951; ed Basic-School, Berlin; Visiting Assoc. Prof., Univ. of Texas at Austin, USA 1972; Writer-in-Residence, Univ. of Warwick, UK 1975; mem. Akad. der Künste (Hamburg and Mannheim), Akad. für Sprache und Dichtung, Darmstadt; Pres. PEN Centre of German-speaking Writers Abroad 2005–; Bundesverdienstkreuz (First Class); Dr hc (Allegheny Coll., Pa) 1988, (Juniata Coll.), (Univ. of Turin); Heinrich Mann Prize, Akad. der Künste (East Berlin) 1962, Becher Prize for Poetry 1973, Heinrich Heine Prize (City of Düsseldorf) 1985, Hölderlin Prize 1991, E.R. Curtius Prize 1991, Georg-Trakl-Preis (Austria). *Film:* Abschied and others. *Play:* The Time Machine (based on the novel by H. G. Wells). *TV screenplays include:* King Arthur 1990, An Obituary of the Wall 1991, Endstation: Harembar 1991 and 13 others. *Radio:* 10 radio plays. *Publications:* 60 volumes of poetry, prose, satire, essays, novels, short stories and lectures. *Leisure interests:* travel, collecting tin toys. *Address:* Schulstrasse 7, 25560 Kaisborstel, Germany (home). *Telephone:* (4892) 1414 (home). *Fax:* (4892) 8403 (home).

KUNEVA, Meglena Shtilianova, LLM; Bulgarian lawyer and politician; *Commissioner for Consumer Affairs, European Commission;* b. 22 June 1957, Sofia; m. Andrey Pramov; one s.; ed St Kliment Ohridski Univ. of Sofia; Ed. and presenter, Bulgarian Nat. Radio 1987–91; Asst Prof., Faculty of Law St Kliment Ohridski Univ. of Sofia 1988–89; Sr Legal Advisor Council of Ministers 1990–2001; legal consultant 1992–98; Lecturer, Free Univ. of Burgas and New Bulgarian Univ. 1992–94; legal specialist, Human Rights Inst. Turku, Finland 1993 and in Int. Relations and Environmental Law, Georgetown Univ. 1995, 1999–2000, and Environmental Law at Oxford Univ. 1996; mem. Bulgarian Del. to 4th session of UN Comm. on Sustainable Devt 1995; mem. Nat. Ass. 2001–07, Deputy Minister, Ministry of Foreign Affairs and chief negotiator with EU 2001–02, Minister of European Affairs 2002–07, Special Rep. at Convention for Future of Europe 2002; Commr for Consumer Affairs, EC 2007–; mem. Berlin Conference on European Cultural Policy; mem. Nat. Movement Simeon II, Atlantic Club, Union of Bulgarian Jurists, UN Int. Council of Environmental Law, Advisory Bd Time Eco-projects Foundation; Order for Civil Merit, Spain 2002, Légion d'honneur 2003, Order Prince Enrique, Portugal 2004, Order of the Star of Italian Solidarity 2005, Gold Distinction of the Atlantic Club, Bulgaria 2005; Face of Bulgaria Award, Politika (newspaper) 2006. *Address:* Health and Consumer Protection Directorate-General, European Commission, 1049 Brussels, Belgium (office). *Telephone:* (2) 299-11-11 (office). *Fax:* (2) 296-62-98 (office). *E-mail:* sanco-mailbox@cec.eu.int (office). *Website:* ec.europa.eu/commission_barroso/kuneva/index_en.htm; ec.europa.eu/dgs/health_consumer/index_en.htm (office).

KÜNG, Hans, DTheol; Swiss theologian and academic; *President, Foundation for a Global Ethic;* b. 19 March 1928, Sursee, Lucerne; ed Gregorian Univ., Rome, Italy, Inst. Catholique and Univ. of the Sorbonne, Paris, France; ordained priest 1954; mem. practical ministry, Lucerne Cathedral 1957–59; Scientific Asst for Dogmatic Catholic Theol., Univ. of Münster Westfalen 1959–60; Prof. of Fundamental Theology, Univ. of Tübingen 1960–63; Prof. of Dogmatic and Ecumenical Theology and Dir, Inst. Ecumenical Research 1963–80, Prof. of Ecumenical Theology, Dir Inst. of Ecumenical Research (under direct responsibility of Pres. and Senate Univ. of Tübingen) 1980–96, Prof. Emer. 1996–; Guest Prof., Univ. of Chicago 1981, of Mich. 1983, of Toronto 1985, of Rice Univ., Houston 1987; numerous guest lectures at univs worldwide; mem. PEN; Pres. Foundation Global Ethic, Germany 1995–, Switzerland 1997–; Co-Pres. World Conf. on Religion and Peace, New York; Founding mem. Int. Review of Theology, Concilium; Hon. Citizen City of Syracuse, Italy 2002, Tübingen, Germany 2002, Mozart Hon. Chair, European Acad. of Yuste, Spain 2004; Grosses Bundesverdienstkreuz mit Stern 2003; numerous hon. doctorates including Hon. DD (Univ. of Wales) 1998, (Florida Int. Univ.) 2002, (Ecumenical Theological Seminary, Detroit) 2003, Hon. LHD (Ramapo Coll., NY) 1999, (Hebrew Union Coll., Cincinnati) 2000, Hon. DPhil (Univ. of Genova) 2004; Ludwig-Thoma Medal 1975, Oskar Pfister Award, American Psychiatric Asscn 1986, Karl Barth Prize, Evangelische Kirche der Union, Berlin 1992, Hirt Prize, Zürich 1993, Prize for Zivilcourage Zürich 1995, Univ. of Tübingen 1996, Theodor Heuss Prize, Stuttgart 1998, Interfaith Gold Medallion of the Int. Council of Christians and Jews 1998, Martin Luther Towns Prize 1999, Ernst-Robert-Curtius Literary Award Bonn 2001, Göttingen Peace Award 2002, Juliet Hollister Award of the Temple of Understanding 2004, Niwano Peace Prize 2005. *Publications:* The Council: Reform and Reunion 1961, That the World May Believe 1963, The Council in Action 1963, Justification: The Doctrine of Karl Barth and a Catholic Reflection 1964, (with new introductory chapter and response of Karl Barth) 1981, Structures of the Church 1964, (with new preface) 1982, Freedom Today 1966, The Church 1967, Truthfulness 1968, Menschwerdung Gottes 1970, Infallible? – An Inquiry 1971, Why Priests? 1972, Fehlbar? – Eine Bilanz 1973, On being a Christian 1976, Signposts for the Future 1978, The Christian Challenge 1979, Freud and the Problem of God 1979, Does God Exist? 1980, The Church – Maintained in Truth 1980, Eternal Life? 1984, Christianity and the World Religions: Paths to Dialogue with Islam, Hinduism and Buddhism (with others) 1986, The Incarnation of God 1986, Church and Change: The Irish Experience 1986, Why I am still a Christian 1987, Theology for the Third Millennium: An Ecumenical View 1988, Christianity and Chinese Religions (with Julia Ching) 1989, Paradigm Change in Theology: A Symposium for the future 1989, Reforming the Church Today 1990, Global Responsibility: In Search of a New World Ethic 1991, Judaism 1992, Credo: The Apostles' Creed Explained for Today 1993, Great Christian Thinkers 1994, Christianity 1995, A Dignified Dying: a plea for personal responsibility (with Walter Jens) 1995, Yes to a Global Ethic (ed.) 1996, A Global Ethic for Global Politics and Economics 1997, Breaking Through (with others) 1998, The Catholic Church: A Short History 2001, Women in Christianity 2001, Tracing the Way: Spiritual Dimensions of the World Religions 2002, My Struggle for Freedom (memoirs) 2003, Islam: Past, Present and Future 2006; ed. Journal of Ecumenical Studies, Revue Internationale de Théologie Concilium, Theological Meditations, Ökumenische Theologie. *Leisure interests:* water sports, skiing, classical music. *Address:* Waldhäuserstrasse 23, 72076 Tübingen, Germany. *Telephone:* 62646. *Fax:* 610140. *E-mail:* office@weltehos.org (office).

KUNIN, Madeleine May, MA, MS; American journalist, diplomatist, academic and fmr politician; *Chairman, Institute for Sustainable Communities;*

b. 28 Sept. 1933, Zürich, Switzerland; d. of Ferdinand May and Renee Bloch; m. Arthur S. Kunin 1959 (divorced 1995); three s. one d.; ed Univ. of Massachusetts, Columbia Univ. and Univ. of Vermont; came to USA in 1940; reporter, Burlington Free Press, Vt 1957–58; Asst Producer, WCAX-TV, Burlington 1960–61; freelance writer and instructor in English, Trinity Coll., Burlington 1969–70; mem. Vermont House of Reps 1973–78; Lt.-Gov. of Vermont 1979–82, Gov. of Vermont 1985–91; Deputy Sec., US Dept of Educ., Washington, DC 1993–96; Fellow, Inst. of Politics, Kennedy School of Govt, Harvard Univ. 1983–93; Amb. to Switzerland 1996–99; Lecturer, Middlebury Coll., also fmr Scholar-in-Residence 1999–2002; Distinguised Visiting Prof., Univ. of Vermont and St Michael's Coll. 2003–, James Marsh Scholar Prof.-at-Large, Univ. of Vermont 2007–; Founder and Chair. Inst. for Sustainable Communities 1991–; Fellow, Bunting Inst., Radcliffe Coll., Cambridge, Mass. 1991–92; Democrat; more than 15 hon. degrees. *Publications:* The Big Green Book (with M. Stout) 1976, Living a Political Life 1995, Pearls, Politics, and Power: How Women Can Win and Lead 2008; articles in professional journals, magazines and newspapers. *Address:* Institute for Sustainable Communities, 535 Stone Cutters Way, Montpelier, VT 05602 (office); 9 Harbor Watch Road, Burlington, VT 05401, USA (home). *Telephone:* (802) 229-2900 (office). *Fax:* (802) 229-2919 (office). *E-mail:* isc@iscvt.org (office). *Website:* www.iscvt.org (office); www.madeleinekunin.org.

KUNITZSCH, Paul Horst Robert, DPhil; German professor of Arabic Studies (retd); b. 14 July 1930, Neu-Krüssow; ed Free Univ. of West Berlin; Lecturer in Arabic, Univ. of Göttingen 1956–57; taught German, Cairo 1957–60; lecturer, Goethe Inst., FRG 1960–63; Special Adviser, Radio Deutsche Welle, Cologne 1963–68; Research Fellow, Deutsche Forschungsgemeinschaft 1969–75; Lecturer in Arabic, Univ. of Munich 1975–77, Prof. of Arabic Studies 1977–95; mem. Bavarian Acad. of Sciences, Acad. Int. d'Histoire des Sciences, Paris; Corresp. mem. Acad. of Arabic Language, Cairo; Göttingen Acad. of Sciences Prize 1974. *Publications:* Arab. Sternnamen in Europa 1959, Der Almagest 1974, The Arabs and the Stars 1989, Stars and Numbers 2004, C. Ptolemäus, Der Sternkatalog (ed.; three vols) 1986–91. *Address:* Davidstr. 17, 81927 Munich, Germany (home). *Telephone:* (89) 916280 (home). *Fax:* (89) 218073932 (office).

KÜNSCH, Hans Rudolf, PhD; Swiss mathematician and academic; *Professor, Seminar für Statistik, Eidgenössische Technische Hochschule Zürich (ETH Zürich);* b. 17 Oct. 1951; ed Eidgenössische Technische Hochschule Zürich; fmr Research Student, Univ. of Tokyo, Japan; joined faculty of Eidgenössische Technische Hochschule Zürich (ETH Zürich) 1983 as Prof. of Math., Seminar für Statistik 1983–, Chair., Dept of Math. 2007–; Co-Ed. Annals of Statistics 1998–2000; mem. Council Inst. of Math. Statistics 2003–06. *Address:* Seminar für Statistik, ETH Zürich, LEO D1, Leonhardstr. 27, 8092 Zürich, Switzerland (office). *Telephone:* 446323416 (office). *Fax:* 446321228 (office). *E-mail:* kuensch@stat.math.ethz.ch (office). *Website:* www.ethz.ch (office); www.stat.math.ethz.ch/~kuensch (office).

KUNTJORO-JAKTI, Dorodjatun, PhD; Indonesian politician, diplomatist and business executive; *Chairman, PT Bank Tabungan Pensiunan Nasional (BTPN);* b. 1939, Rangkasbitung; ed Univ. of Indonesia and Univ. of Calif., Berkeley, USA; Lecturer and fmr Dean of Econs, Univ. of Indonesia; Amb. to USA 2000–01; Co-ordinating Minister for the Economy, Finance and Industry 2001–04; apptd Co-Chair. Panel 45 to formulate Indonesia's position with regard to UN reforms 2005; Chair. PT Bank Tabungan Pensiunan Nasional (BTPN); mem. Bd of Govs Nat. Resilience Inst. (LEMHANNAS); Ind. Comm. American Int. Assurance/American Int. Group, Inc. (AIA/AIG), PT Hero Supermarket; Dr hc (Univ. Tech. Malaysia). *Address:* PT Bank BTPN KC Kebayoran Baru, Jl Petogogan II, No 6-8, Blok A, Kebayoran Baru, Indonesia.

KUNZE, Reiner; German writer; b. 16 Aug. 1933, Oelsnitz/Erzgeb.; s. of Ernst Kunze and Martha Kunze (née Friedrich); m. Dr Elisabeth Mifka 1961; one s. one d.; ed Univ. of Leipzig; mem. Bavarian Acad. of Fine Arts, Acad. of Arts, West Berlin 1975–92, German Acad. for Languages and Literature, Darmstadt, Free Acad. of Arts Mannheim, Sächsische Akad. der Künste, Dresden; Hon. mem. Collegium Europaeum Jenense of Friedrich-Schiller-Universität Jena; Dr hc; numerous awards and prizes including Literary Prize of Bavarian Acad. of Fine Arts 1973, Georg Trakl Prize (Austria) 1977, Andreas Gryphius Prize 1977, Georg Büchner Prize 1977, Bavarian Film Prize 1979, Eichendorff Literature Prize 1984, Weilheimer Literaturpreis 1997, Europapreis für Poesie, Serbia 1998, Friedrich Hölderlin-Preis 1999; Hans Sahl Prize 2001; Bayerischer Verdienstorden 1988, Grosses Verdienstkreuz der BRD 1993; Bayerischer Maximiliansorden für Wissenschaft und Kunst 2001, Kunstpreis zur Deutsch-tschechischen Verständigung 2002, Ján Smrek Preis 2003, STAB Preis 2004, Übersetzer Preis 'Premia Bohemica' 2004. *Publications:* Sensible Wege 1969, Der Löwe Leopold 1970, Zimmerlautstärke 1972, Brief mit blauem Siegel 1973, Die wunderbaren Jahre 1976, Auf eigene Hoffnung 1981, Eines jeden einziges Leben 1986, Das weisse Gedicht 1989, Deckname 'Lyrik' 1990, Wohin der Schlaf sich schlafen legt 1991, Mensch ohne Macht 1991, Am Sonnenhang 1993, Wo Freiheit ist... 1994, Steine und Lieder 1996, Der Dichter Jan Skácel 1996, Bindewort 'deutsch' 1997, Ein Tag auf dieser Erde 1998, Die Aura der Wörter 2002, Der Kuss der Koi 2002, Wo wir zu Hause das salz haben 2003, Die Chausseen der Dichter (with Mireille Gansel) 2004, Bleibt nur die eigne stirn 2005. *Address:* Am Sonnenhang 19, 94130 Obernzell, Germany.

KUNZRU, Hari Mohan Nath, BA, MA; British writer and journalist; b. 1969, Woodford Green, Essex, England; s. of Krishna Mohan Nath Kunzru and Hilary Ann David; ed Wadham Coll., Oxford and Univ. of Warwick; fmr journalist, Music Ed. Wallpaper magazine, Assoc. Ed. Wired magazine, Contrib. Ed. Mute magazine; Somerset Maugham Award 2003, John Llewellyn Rhys Prize 2003, Granta Best of Young British Novelists 2003, Lire 50 Écrivains Pour Demain 2005, British Book Award for Decibel Writer of the Year 2005. *Publications:* novels: The Impressionist (Observer Young Travel Writer of the Year 1999, Betty Trask Prize 2002) 2002, Transmission 2004, My Revolutions 2007; other: short stories, journalism; contrib. to Wired, London Review of Books, Guardian, Observer, New York Times, Daily Telegraph, BBC Midnight Review. *Leisure interest:* staring out of the window. *Address:* Curtis Brown, Haymarket House, 28–29 Haymarket, London, SW1 4SP, England (office). *Telephone:* (20) 7396-6600 (office). *Website:* www.harikunzru.com (office).

KUOK, Khoon Hong, BBA; Singaporean (b. Malaysian) business executive; *Chairman and CEO, Wilmar International Limited;* nephew of Robert Kuok; m.; four c.; ed Univ. of Singapore; joined uncle's palm oil business PPB Oil Palms, Malaysia 1973; Gen. Man. Federal Flour Mills Bhd 1986–91; Man. Dir Kuok Oils & Grains Pte Ltd 1989–91; Co-founder, Chair. and CEO Wilmar International Ltd (palm oil producer) 1991, merged with uncle's business and head of combined group 2007–. *Address:* Wilmar International Ltd, 56 Neil Road, Singapore 088830 (office). *Telephone:* 6216-0244 (office). *Fax:* 6223-6635 (office). *E-mail:* info@wilmar.com.sg (office). *Website:* www.wilmar-international.com (office).

KUOK, Robert; Malaysian business executive; b. (Kuok Hock Nien), 6 Oct. 1923, Johor Bahru, Johor; m. twice; eight c.; ed Raffles Coll., Singapore; father arrived in Malaya from Fujian, China early 20th century; worked in grains dept of Mitsubishi 1942–45; worked for father's food distribution co. (supplying produce for Japanese POWs in British Malaya) 1945–48, Co-founder (with other family mems) Kuok Brothers Co. (now Kuok Group) 1948, moved business to Singapore and began sugar trade 1953, built first sugar refinery in Singapore, also trading in sugar futures, palm oil, merged with Wilmar International and combined group now headed by nephew Kuok Khoon Hong 2007; built first of chain of Shangri-La hotels in Singapore early 1970s; acquired real estate in Malaysia, Singapore and China throughout the 1970s and 1980s; Head, Kerry Group (Hong Kong) –1993 (retd) with holdings in South-East Asia, People's Repub. of China, Australia and Canada; acquired holding in TV Broadcasts Ltd (Hong Kong) 1988, majority shareholding in Coca-Cola plant in China 1993, controlling share of South China Morning Post newspaper 1993 (Chair. South China Morning Post Publrs 1993–97); also owns significant shareholding in Citic Pacific, Chinese Govt's overseas conglomerate; currently Head, Kuok (Singapore) Ltd (investment holding co.), Transmile Group (air cargo outfit); est. several charitable foundations; majority of day-to-day businesses operations now handled by his son. *Address:* Kuok (Singapore) Ltd, No. 1 Kim Seng Promenade, #07-01 Great World City, Singapore 237994 (office). *Telephone:* 67333600 (office). *Fax:* 67389300 (home). *E-mail:* corporate@kuokgroup.com.sg (office). *Website:* www.kuokgroup.com.sg (office).

KURATA, Hiroyuki; Japanese politician; fmr Parl. Vice-Minister of Int. Trade and Industry; Minister of Home Affairs Jan.–Oct. 1996; mem. House of Councillors, Pres. 2002–04; mem. advisory panel to LDP drafting cttee for new Japanese constitution 2005 LDP. *Address:* c/o Liberal-Democratic Party—LDP (Jiyu-Minshuto), 1-11-23, Nagata-cho, Chiyoda-ku, Tokyo 100-8910, Japan.

KURBI, Abu Bakr al-; Yemeni politician; currently Minister of Foreign Affairs. *Address:* Ministry of Foreign Affairs, PO Box 1994, San'a, Yemen (office). *Telephone:* (1) 276612 (office). *Fax:* (1) 286618 (office). *E-mail:* mofa1@mofa.gov.ye (office). *Website:* www.mofa.gov.ye (office).

KUREISHI, Hanif, CBE, BA; British writer and dramatist; b. 5 Dec. 1954, Bromley; m. Tracey Scoffield; three c.; ed King's Coll., London; worked as typist at Riverside Studios; Writer-in-Residence, Royal Court Theatre, London 1981, 1985–86; Chevalier, Ordre des Arts et Lettres 2002; George Devine Award 1981. *Stage plays:* Soaking the Heat 1976, The Mother Country (Thames TV Playwright Award) 1980, The King and Me 1980, Outskirts (RSC) 1981, Cinders (after the play by Janusz Glowacki) 1981, Borderline (Royal Court) 1981, Artists and Admirers (after a play by Ostrovsky, with David Leveaux) 1981, Birds of Passage (Hampstead Theatre) 1983, Mother Courage (adaptation of a play by Brecht, RSC) 1984, Sleep With Me (Nat. Theatre) 1999, When the Night Begins (Hampstead Theatre) 2004. *Screenplays:* My Beautiful Laundrette (Evening Standard Best Film Award 1986, New York Critics' Best Screenplay Award 1987) 1986, Sammy and Rosie Get Laid 1988, London Kills Me (also directed) 1991, My Son The Fanatic 1997, The Mother 2002. *Television:* The Buddha of Suburbia (BBC) 1993. *Publications:* fiction: The Buddha of Suburbia (Whitbread Award for Best First Novel) 1990, The Black Album 1995, Love in a Blue Time (short stories) 1997, Intimacy 1998, Midnight All Day (short stories) 1999, Gabriel's Gift 2000, The Body 2002, Telling Tales (contrib. to charity anthology) 2004, Something to Tell You 2008; non-fiction: The Rainbow Sign (autobiog.) 1986, Eight Arms to Hold You (essay) 1991, Dreaming and Scheming: Reflections on Writing and Politics (essays) 2002, My Ear at his Heart (autobiog.) (Prix France Culture littérature étrangère, France 2005) 2004, The Word and The Bomb (essays) 2005; ed.: The Faber Book of Pop (co-ed.) 1995; stories in Granta, Harpers (USA), London Review of Books and The Atlantic; regular contrib. to New Statesman and Society. *Leisure interests:* jazz, cricket. *Address:* c/o Rogers, Coleridge & White Ltd, 20 Powis Mews, London, W11 1JN, England (office).

KURIHARA, Harumi; Japanese business executive, cook, cookery writer and broadcaster; b. Shimoda; m.; two s.; celebrity cook and homemaker; head of publishing, design and retail business; author of several multi-million-selling cookbooks; designer of tableware, gardening tools and bedlinen; launched Harumi K range of luxury brands; owns Yutori no Kuukan restaurant, Tokyo. *Television:* numerous appearances on TV talk shows. *Publications:* . *Address:* c/o Yutori no Kuukan, Sendagaya 3-16-5, Tokyo, Japan (office). *Telephone:* (3) 5410-8845 (office).

KŪRIS, Egidijus, DJur; Lithuanian judge and professor of law; *President of Constitutional Court;* b. 26 Oct. 1961, Vilnius; s. of Pranas Kūris and Vanda Kūrienė; m. Andronė Kūrienė; two s. one d.; ed Univ. of Vilnius, Moscow State Univ., Russia; Lecturer and Assoc. Prof., Faculty of Law, Univ. of Vilnius 1984–94, Assoc. Prof. then Prof., Inst. of Int. Relations and Political Science 1992–, Dir of Inst. 1992–99; Justice of Constitutional Court 1999–, Pres. 2002–; Great Cross of Commdr Order of Gediminas from the Grand Duke of Lithuania 2003, Grand Croix Ordre de Leopold II (Belgium) 2006, A Magyar Köztársasági Érdemrend Középkeresztje a Csillagal (Hungary) 2006, Grosse Verdienstkreuz des Verdienstordens (Germany) 2006, Ordinus Nat. 'Servinius Credencios' in gradul de Mare Cruce (Romania) 2007; Medal of Ministry of Foreign Affairs 2004, Gold Medal, Yerevan Univ. (Armenia) 2005. *Publications include:* Self-Government, Democracy and Law, Lithuania's National Interest and Her Political System (ed.), Democracy in Lithuania: Elite and Masses (ed.), Lithuania and Her Neighbours (ed.), Lithuanian Political Parties and Party System (Vols 1–2) (ed.), Interest Groups, Power and Politics (ed.), Lithuanian Constitutional Law (co-author); Constitutional Justice in Lithuania (co-author, English language); On Stability of the Constitution: Sources of Constitutional Law and Ostensible Omnipotence of Constitutional Courts (Russian language); over 50 articles in Lithuanian, Russian, English, French, Polish. *Address:* Constitutional Court, Gedimino pr. 36, 01104 Vilnius, Lithuania (office). *Telephone:* (5) 2126398 (office). *Fax:* (5) 2127975 (office). *E-mail:* mailbox@lrkt.lt (office). *Website:* www.lrkt.lt (office).

KURODA, Haruhiko, BA, MPhil; Japanese international banking official; *Chairman and President, Asian Development Bank;* b. 25 Oct. 1944; m. Kumiko Kuroda; two s.; ed Univ. of Tokyo, Univ. of Oxford, UK; joined Ministry of Finance 1967; secondment to IMF, Washington, DC 1975–78; Dir Int. Orgs Div., Int. Finance Bureau 1987–88; Sec. to Minister of Finance 1988–89; Dir of several divs, Tax Bureau 1989–92; Deputy Vice Minister of Finance for Int. Affairs 1992–93; Commr Osaka Regional Taxation Bureau 1993–94; Deputy Dir-Gen., Int. Finance Bureau 1994–96, Dir-Gen. 1997–99; Pres. Inst. of Fiscal and Monetary Policy 1996–97; Vice Minister of Finance for Int. Affairs 1999–2003; Special Adviser to Cabinet 2003–05; Chair. Bd of Dirs and Pres. Asian Devt Bank 2005–; Prof., Grad. School of Econs, Hitotsubashi Univ. 2003–05. *Publications:* several books on monetary policy, exchange rates, int. finance policy, int. taxation and int. negotiations. *Address:* Asian Development Bank, 6 ADB Avenue, Mandaluyong City 0401 Metro Manila (office); PO Box 789, 0980 Manila Philippines. *Telephone:* (632) 632-4444 (office). *Fax:* (632) 6362444 (office). *E-mail:* information@adb.org (office). *Website:* www.adb.org (office).

KUROKAWA, Hiroaki, LLB; Japanese computer and electronics industry executive; *Senior Executive Advisor, Fujitsu Limited;* ed Tokyo Univ.; joined Fujitsu 1967, various posts in Services, Software and Systems Engineering Depts, mem. Bd 1999–, Group Pres., Network Services Group, later Corp. Sr Vice-Pres. and Group Pres. of Software and Services Business Promotion Group 2002, Corp. Sr Exec. Vice-Pres. April–June 2003, Pres. and Rep. Dir June 2003–08, Sr Exec. Advisor 2008–, Pres. and Rep. Dir PT Fujitsu Indonesia. *Leisure interests:* mountaineering, trekking, soccer, nature, Japanese history. *Address:* Fujitsu Headquarters, Shiodome City Center, 1-5-2 Higashi-Shimbashi, Minato-ku, Tokyo 105-7123, Japan (office). *Telephone:* (3) 6252-2220 (office). *Fax:* (3) 6252-2783 (office). *E-mail:* info@fujitsu.com (office). *Website:* www.fujitsu.com (office).

KUROYANAGI, Nobuo; Japanese financial services industry executive; *President and CEO, Mitsubishi UFJ Financial Group, Inc.;* b. 1941; Dir Bank of Tokyo-Mitsubishi 1992–96, Man.-Dir 1996–2002, Deputy Pres. 2002–04, Pres. 2004–; Dir Mitsubishi Tokyo Financial Group Inc. 2003–, Pres. and CEO 2004–05, Pres. and CEO Mitsubishi UFJ Financial Group, Inc. (after merger with UFJ Holdings) 2005–, Pres. Bank of Tokyo-Mitsubishi UFJ Ltd 2006–, Chair. 2008–. *Address:* Mitsubishi UFJ Financial Group, Inc., 7-1 Marunouchi 2-Chome, Chiyoda-ku, Tokyo 100-8330, Japan (office). *Telephone:* (3) 3240-8111 (office). *Fax:* (3) 3240-8203 (office). *E-mail:* info@mufg.jp (office). *Website:* www.mufg.jp (office).

KUROYANAGI, Tetsuko, BA; Japanese actress; b. 9 Aug. 1933, Tokyo; d. of Moritsuna Kuroyanagi and Cho Kuroyanagi; ed Tokyo Coll. of Music; theatrical training at Bungakuza Theatre, Tokyo and Mary Tarcai Studio, New York; TV debut with Japan Broadcasting Corpn (NHK) 1954; host, Tetsuko's Room (TV talk show), Asahi Nat. Broadcasting Co. 1976–; regular guest, Discover Wonders of the World (quiz show), Tokyo Broadcasting System 1987–; numerous stage appearances throughout Japan; founder and Pres. Totto Foundation (for training of deaf actors) 1981–; Councillor, World Wide Fund for Nature, Japan 1977–; UNICEF Goodwill Amb. 1984–; Dir Chihiro Iwasaki Art Museum of Picture Books 1995–; Order of the Sacred Treasure, Gold Rays with Neck Ribbon; Minister of Foreign Affairs Award. *Publications:* From New York With Love 1972, Totto-chan: The Little Girl at the Window 1981, Animal Theatre (photographic essay) 1983, Totto-channel 1984, My Friends 1986, Totto-chan's Children: A Goodwill Journey to the Children of the World. *Leisure interests:* travel, calligraphy, study of giant pandas. *Address:* Yoshida Naomi Office, No. 2 Tanizawa Building, 4th Floor, 3-2-11 Nishi-Azabu, Minato-ku, Tokyo 106-0031, Japan. *Telephone:* 3403-9296 (office). *Fax:* 3403-5322 (office).

KUROYEDOV, Adm. Vladimir Ivanovich; Russian naval officer; b. 5 Oct. 1944, Bamburovo, Primorsk Territory, Russia; m.; one s.; ed Pacific Higher S.O. Makarov Navy School, Navy Mil. Acad. of Gen. Staff; service in Pacific Ocean Fleet 1967–93; Head of Staff Pacific Fleet, Commdr 1996–97; First Deputy Commdr Baltic Fleet 1993–96; First Deputy Commdr Russian Navy 1997, Commdr Nov. 1997–2005; Corresp. mem. Russian Acad. of Rocket and Artillery; several decorations. *Publications:* numerous publications on mil. sciences and political problems. *Address:* c/o General Staff of Russian Navy, Bolshoi Kozlovski per. 6, 103175 Moscow, Russia (office).

KURTÁG, György; Hungarian composer; b. 19 Feb. 1926, Lugos (Lugoj, Romania); ed Franz Liszt Music Acad., Budapest and in Paris with Marianne Stein; Repetiteur, Bela Bartok Music Secondary School, Budapest 1958–63, Nat. Philharmonic 1960–68; Asst to Pal Kadosa, Franz Liszt Acad. of Music, Budapest 1967, Prof. of Chamber Music 1967–86; Composer in Residence, Wissenschaftskolleg zu Berlin 1993–95, Wiener Konzerthaus, Vienna 1995–96; mem. Bayerische Akad. der Schönen Künste, Munich 1987, Akad. der Künste, Berlin 1987; Merited Artist of Hungarian People's Repub. 1980, Outstanding Artist 1984, Officier des Arts et Lettres 1985; Erkel Prize 1954, 1956, 1969, Kossuth Prize 1973, Bartok-Pasztory Award 1984, Herder Prize, Freiherr vom Stein, Hamburg 1993, Feltrinelli Prize, Accad. dei Lincei, Italy 1993, Austrian State Award for European Composers 1994, Denis de Rougemont Prize 1994, Kossuth Prize 1996, Ernst von Siemens Music Prize, Munich 1998. *Compositions include:* Viola Concerto 1954, String Quartet, Op. 1 1959, Wind Quintet 1959, The Sayings of Péter Bornemissza 1963–68, Hommage à Mihály András 1977, Bagatelles 1981, Scenes from a Novel 1981–82, Three Old Inscriptions 1967–86, Kafka-Fragmente 1985–87, Requiem for the Beloved 1982–87, Officium breve in memoriam Andreae Szervánszky 1988–89, Ligatura–Message to Frances-Marie 1989, Hommage à R. Sch. 1990, Transcriptions from Machaut to Bach 1974–91, Attila József Fragments 1981, Three in memoriam 1988–90, Games, two series, Beads 1994, Omaggio a Luigi Nono 1979, eight Choruses 1981–82, Songs of Despondency and Grief 1980–94, Inscriptions on a Grave in Cornwall 1994, Rückblick (Altes und Neues für vier Spieler, Hommage à Stockhausen) 1986, Three Songs to poems by János Pilinszky 1986, Mémoire de Laïka 1990, Curriculum Vitae 1992, Messages of the late Miss R. V. Troussova, Grabstein für Stephan for guitar and Instrumentengruppen, Op. 15c (Prix de Composition Musicale, Fondation Prince Pierre de Monaco 1993) 1989, ...quasi una fantasia..., Double Concerto for piano, cello and 2 chamber ensembles Op. 27.2 (Prix de Composition Musicale, Fondation Prince Pierre de Monaco 1993) 1989–90, Ligature e Versetti for organ 1990, Layka- Emlèk for synthesizer and real sounds (co-composition with his son) 1990, Samuel Beckett: What is the Word for solo voice, voices and chamber ensemble Op. 30b 1991. *Address:* Lihegő v.3, 2621 Verőce; Liszt Ferenc tér 9.I.6, 1061 Budapest, Hungary. *Telephone:* (1) 2735-0177; (91) 121-3994.

KURTZER, Daniel C., BA, PhD; American diplomatist and academic; *Lecturer and S. Daniel Abraham Visiting Professor in Middle East Policy Studies, Woodrow Wilson School of Public and International Affairs, Princeton University;* m. Sheila Kurtzer; three s.; ed Yeshiva Univ., Columbia Univ.; joined Foreign Service 1976; Dean, Yeshiva Coll. 1977–79; political officer, Bureau of Int. Organizational Affairs, embassies in Cairo and Tel-Aviv; Deputy Dir Office of Egyptian Affairs 1996; on Policy Planning Staff 1987; Deputy Asst Sec. for Near Eastern Affairs 1989; Prin. Deputy Asst Sec. for Intelligence and Research 1994, then Acting Asst Sec.; Amb. to Egypt 1997–2001, to Israel 2001–05; Lecturer and S. Daniel Abraham Visiting Prof. in Middle East Policy Studies, Woodrow Wilson School of Public and Int. Affairs, Princeton Univ. 2005–; Commr Israel Baseball League; Pres.'s Distinguished Service Award, Henrietta Szold Award by Hadassah 2005, Dir-Gen. of Foreign Service Award for Reporting. *Address:* 418 Robertson Hall, Woodrow Wilson School, Princeton University, Princeton, NJ 08544-1013, USA (office). *Telephone:* (609) 258-9859 (office). *E-mail:* dkurtzer@princeton.edu (office). *Website:* www.wws.princeton.edu (office); www.israelbaseballleague.com.

KURZWEIL, Raymond (Ray) C., BS; American computer scientist and business executive; *Chairman and CEO, Kurzweil Technologies;* b. 12 Feb. 1948, Queens, NY; m. Sonya R. Kurzweil; ed Massachusetts Inst. of Tech.; aspired to become an inventor from age of five; built and programmed his own computer to compose original melodies aged 15; founder and fmr CEO Kurzweil Computer Products, Inc. 1974–80, Kurzweil Music Systems, Inc. 1982–90, Kurzweil Applied Intelligence, Inc. 1982–97, Kurzweil Educational Systems, Inc. 1996; Chair. Strategy and Tech. Cttee Bd Dirs, Wang Laboratories, Inc. 1993–98; Founder, Chair. and CEO Kurzweil Technologies, Inc. 1995–, FAT KAT, Inc. 1999–, Kurzweil Cyber Art Technologies, Inc. 2000–; Founder, Pres. and CEO Medical Learning Co., Inc. and FamilyPractice.com 1997; Founder, CEO and Ed.-in-Chief www.KurzweilAI.net 2001–; Co-Founder, Chair. and Co-CEO Ray & Terry's Longevity Products, Inc. 2003; mem. Bd Dirs Medical Manager Corpn 1997–2000, Inforte 1999–, United Therapeutics 2002–; Chair. and Founder The Kurzweil Foundation; Chair. Robots and Beyond: The Age of Intelligent Machines (exhbn on Artificial Intelligence presented at eight leading science museums) 1987–90; Dir Massachusetts Computer Software Council; fmr Dir Boston Computer Soc.; Incorporator, Boston Museum of Science; mem. MIT Corpn Visiting Cttee, MIT School of Humanities, MIT School of Music, Bd of Overseers, New England Conservatory of Music; fmr mem. Tech. Advisory Cttee, Nat. Center on Adult Literacy, Univ. of Pennsylvania; wrote 'The Futurecast' (monthly column in Library Journal 1991–93); developed first computerized Four-Way Analysis of Variance (statistical program) 1964, first computer-based Expert System for College Selection 1967, first Text-to-Speech speech synthesis 1975, first CCD Flatbed Scanner 1975, first Print-to-Speech Reading Machine for the Blind (Kurzweil Reading Machine) 1976, first Omni-Font (any-type font) Optical Character Recognition (now Xerox TextBridge) 1976, first Computer Music Keyboard capable of accurately reproducing sounds of the grand piano and other orchestral instruments (Kurzweil 250) 1984, first Knowledge Base System for Creating Medical Reports (Kurzweil VoiceMED) 1985, first commercially marketed Large Vocabulary Speech Recognition (Kurzweil Voice Report) 1987, first Speech Recognition Dictation System for Windows (Kurzweil Voice for Windows) 1994, first Continuous Speech Natural

Language Command and Control Software (Kurzweil VoiceCommands) 1997, first Print-to-Speech Reading System for Persons with Reading Disabilities that Reads from a Displayed Image of the Page (Kurzweil 3000), first Virtual Performing and Recording Artist (Ramona) to perform in front of a live audience with a live band 2001, first 'host/hostess' Avatar on the Web to combine lifelike photo-realistic, moving and speaking facial image with a conversational engine 2001; Hon. Chair. for Innovation, White House Conf. on Small Business 1986; Hon. DHumLitt (Hofstra Univ.) 1982, (Misericordia Coll.) 1989, (Landmark Coll.) 2002, Worcester Polytechnic Inst. 2005; Hon. DMus (Berklee Coll. of Music) 1987; Hon. DSc (Northeastern Univ.) 1988, (Rensselaer Polytechnic Inst.) 1988, (New Jersey Inst. of Tech.) 1990, (City Univ. of New York) 1991, (Dominican Coll.) 1993; Hon. DEng (Merrimack Coll.) 1989; Dr hc in Science and Humanities (Michigan State Univ.) 2000; First Prize, Int. Science Fair in Electronics and Communications 1965, Mass's Gov.'s Award 1977, Grace Murray Hopper Award, Asscn for Computing Machinery (ACM) 1978, Nat. Award, Johns Hopkins Univ. 1981, admitted to Computer Industry Hall of Fame 1982, Pres.'s Computer Science Award 1982, Francis Joseph Campbell Award, American Library Asscn 1983, Best of the New Generation Award, Esquire Magazine 1984, Distinguished Inventor Award, Intellectual Property Owners 1986, The White House Award for Entrepreneurial Excellence 1986, Inventor of the Year Award, awarded by MIT, Boston Museum of Science and Boston Patent Law Asscn 1988, MIT Founders Award 1989, Engineer of the Year Award, Design News magazine 1990, Louis Braille Award, Associated Services for the Blind 1991, Massachusetts Quincentennial Award for Innovation and Discovery 1992, ACM Fellow Award 1993, Gordon Winston Award, Canadian Nat. Inst. for the Blind 1994, Dickson Prize, Carnegie Mellon Univ. 1994, Access Prize, American Foundation for the Blind 1995, Software Industry Achievement Award, Massachusetts Software Council 1996, Pres.'s Award, Asscn on Higher Educ. and Disability 1997, Stevie Wonder/SAP Vision Award for Product of the Year (for the Kurzweil 1000) 1998, Nat. Medal of Tech. 1999, Lemelson-MIT Prize 2000, Second Annual American Composers' Orchestra Award for the Advancement of New Music in America 2001, inducted into Nat. Inventors' Hall of Fame, US Patent Office 2002. *Film:* The Age of Intelligent Machines (The Chris Plaque, Columbus Int. Film Festival 1987, Creative Excellence Award, US Industrial Film and Video Festival 1987, Gold Medal – Science Educ., Int. Film and TV Festival of New York 1987, CINE Golden Eagle Award 1987, Tech. Culture Award, Int. Festival of Scientific Films, Belgrade 1988, Prize of the President of the Festival, Int. Film Festival of Czechoslovakia 1988) 1987. *Publications:* The Age of Intelligent Machines (MIT Press Best Seller 1991, Silicon Valley Best Seller 1991, Most Outstanding Computer Science Book of 1990 Award, Asscn of American Publishers 1991) 1990, The 10% Solution for a Healthy Life (Regional Best Seller 1993) 1993, The Age of Spiritual Machines, When Computers Exceed Human Intelligence (Nat. and Regional Best Sellers 1999, 2000, Literary Lights Prize, Boston Public Library 1999) 1999, Are We Spiritual Machines, Ray Kurzweil versus the Critics of Strong AI 2002, Fantastic Voyage: Live Long Enough to Live Forever (co-author) 2004, The Singularity is Near, When Humans Transcend Biology 2005. *Address:* Kurzweil Technologies, Inc., PMB 193 733, Turnpike Street, North Andover, MA 01845 (office); Kurzweil Technologies, Inc., 15 Walnut Street, Wellesley Hills, MA 02481, USA (office). *Telephone:* (718) 263-0000 (office). *Fax:* (718) 263-9999 (office). *E-mail:* raymond@kurzweiltech.com (office). *Website:* www.KurzweilTech.com (office); www.KurzweilAI.net (office).

KUSAKARI, Takao, BA; Japanese transport industry executive; *Chairman, Nippon Yusen Kabushiki Kaisha (NYK Line);* b. 1940; ed Keio Univ.; joined Nippon Yusen Kabushiki Kaisha (NYK Line) 1964, Gen. Man. of Cen./S America, Africa and Specialized Cargo Div. 1990, Dir 1994–97, Man. Dir 1997–99, Sr Man. Dir 1999, Pres. 1999–2004, Chair. 2004–; Pres. Japanese Shipowners' Asscn; Chair. Council for the Promotion of Regulatory Reform, Cabinet Office 2007–; Dir Japan Productivity Center for Socio-Econ. Devt; Chair. Shipping Econs Review Cttee, Asian Shipowners' Forum; mem. Int. Advisory Council, PSA Corpn; Official Commendation by Minister of Land, Infrastructure and Transport 2004, Medal with Blue Ribbon by Japanese Govt 2005. *Address:* Nippon Yusen Kabushiki Kaisha, 3-2, Marunouchi 2-chome, Chiyoda-ku, Tokyo 100-0005, Japan (office). *Telephone:* (3) 3284-5151 (office). *Fax:* (3) 3284-6359 (office). *E-mail:* info@nyk.com (office). *Website:* www.nyk.com (office).

KUSAMA, Saburo, BEng; Japanese manufacturing executive; *CEO, Seiko Epson Corporation;* b. 12 Oct. 1939, Aichi; m. Mizue Kusama; two s.; ed Univ. of Shizuoka; began work in Crystal Devices and Circuits Div., Seiko Epson Corpn 1963, various man. positions in Clocks and Tech. Design Divs, Gen. Man. Semiconductors Div. 1986, CEO Semiconductors Div. 1990, mem. Exec. Council 1990–, CEO Display and Liquid Crystals Div. 1994, Pres. Seiko Epson Corpn 2001–2005, CEO 2005–; Medal with Blue Ribbon 2006. *Leisure interests:* golf, classical music, museums. *Address:* Seiko Epson Corporation, 3-3-5 Owa Suwa, Nagano 392-8502, Japan (office). *Telephone:* (266) 52–3131 (office). *Fax:* (266) 53–4844 (office). *Website:* www.epson.com (office).

KUSHAKOV, Andrei Anatolyevich; Russian diplomatist; b. 1952; ed Moscow State Inst. of Int. Relations; mem. staff, Ministry of Foreign Affairs 1974–93; Adviser to Counsellor, Russian Embassy, South Africa 1993–97; Deputy Dir-Gen. Secr. of Ministry of Foreign Affairs, then Deputy Sec.-Gen. 1998–2000; Amb. to South Africa and Kingdom of Lesotho 2001–06. *Address:* c/o Ministry of Foreign Affairs, 119200 Moscow, Smolenskaya-Sennaya pl. 32/34, Russian Federation (office). *Website:* www.mid.ru (office).

KUSHERBAYEV, Krymbek Ye.; Kazakhstani diplomatist; fmr Amb. to Russian Fed.; currently Gov. Mangystau Oblast Administration. *Address:* Mangystau Oblast Administration, 133000 Mangystau obl., Aktau, 14 mikroraion, Kazakhstan (office). *Telephone:* (7292) 33-42-15 (office). *Fax:* (7292) 43-45-52 (office). *E-mail:* akimmangistau@mail.kz (office). *Website:* www.mangystau.kz (office).

KUSHNER, Aleksandr Semyonovich; Russian poet; b. 14 Sept. 1936, Leningrad; s. of Semyon Semyonovich Kushner and Asya Aleksandrovna Kushner; m. Elena Vsevolodovna Nevzglyadova 1981; one s.; ed Leningrad Pedagogical Inst.; lecturer in literature 1959–69; Northern Palmira Award 1995, Russian Fed. State Award 1995, German Pushkin Award, Alfred Toepfer Foundation 1999, Russian Fed. Alexander Pushkin Award 2001, Nat. 'The Poet' Award 2005. *Publications include:* First Impression 1962, Night Watch 1966, Omens 1969, Letter 1974, Direct Speech 1975, Voice 1978, Canvas 1981, The Tavrichesky Garden 1984, Daydreams 1986, Poems 1986 (Selected Poems), The Hedgerow 1988, A Night Melody 1991, Apollo in the Snow (selected essays on Russian literature of the nineteenth and twentieth centuries and personal memoirs) 1991, Apollo in the Snow (selected poems trans. into English) 1991, On the Gloomy Star (State Prize) 1995, Selected Poetry 1997, The Fifth Element 1999, The Bush 2002, Cold Month of May 2005, Selected Poems 2005, Apollo in the Grass (essays on poetry) 2005, In the New Century 2006, The Time is Not to Be Chosen 2007; essays in literary journals. *Leisure interests:* reading, world painting. *Address:* Kaluzhsky pereulok No. 9, Apt 48, 193015 St Petersburg, Russia (home). *Telephone:* (812) 577-32-56 (home). *E-mail:* kushner@mail.lanck.net (home).

KUSHNER, Eva, OC, PhD, FRSC; Canadian academic; *Mary Russell Jackman and Mary Coyne Rowell Professor, Victoria University, University of Toronto;* b. 18 June 1929, Prague, Czechoslovakia; d. of late Josef Dubsky and Anna Dubsky-Cahill (née Kafka); m. 1st Donn J. Kushner 1949 (deceased); three s.; m. 2nd Rev. Canon Bruce Mutch 2005; ed McGill Univ., Montreal; Prof., Carleton Univ. 1961–76; Prof., McGill Univ. 1976–87, Chair. French Dept 1976–80; Prof., Pres. Vic. Univ. at Univ. of Toronto 1987–94, Dir Comparative Literature, Univ. of Toronto 1994–95, Mary Rowell Jackman and Mary Coyne Rowell Prof., Victoria Univ. 2001–; Vice-Pres. Int. Fed. for Modern Languages and Literatures 1987–93, Pres. 1996–99; Vice-Pres. RSC 1980–82, Conseil Int. de la Philosophie et des Sciences Humaines 2006–; Visiting Prof., Princeton Univ. 2000; Hon. LitD (Acadia Univ.) 1988; Hon. DD (United Theological Coll., Montreal) 1992; Hon. DLitt (Univ. of St Michael's Coll.) 1993, (Univ. of Western Ont.) 1996; Dr hc (Szeged) 1997; Hon. Dr of Sacred Letters (Victoria Univ., Toronto) 2006; Lifetime Achievement Award, Canadian Soc. for Renaissance Studies 2002. *Publications:* Patrice de la Tour du Pin 1961, Le Mythe d'Orphée dans la littérature française contemporaine 1961, Chants de Bohême 1963, Rina Lasnier (two edns) 1964, 1969, Saint-Denys Garneau 1967, François Mauriac 1972, L'avènement de l'esprit nouveau 1400–80 (co-author) 1988, Théorie littéraire: problèmes et perspectives (co-author) 1989, Le problématique du sujet chez Montaigne (co-author) 1995, Histoire des poétiques (co-author) 1997, Crises et essors nouveaux 1560–1610 (co-author) 2000, Pontus de Tyard et son œuvre poétique 2001, The Living Prism: Itineraries in Comparative Literature 2001, Le Dialogue à la Renaissance: Histoire et Poétique 2004. *Leisure interests:* reading, swimming, travel, writing. *Address:* Victoria University, University of Toronto, 73 Queen's Park, Toronto, ON M5S 1K7 (office); 63 Albany Avenue, Toronto, ON M5R 3C2, Canada (home). *Telephone:* (416) 585-4592 (office); (416) 538-0173 (home). *Fax:* (416) 585-4459 (office). *E-mail:* eva.kushner@utoronto.ca (office). *Website:* www.vicu.utoronto.ca (office).

KUSHNER, Robert Ellis, BA; American artist; b. 19 Aug. 1949, Pasadena, Calif.; s. of Joseph Kushner and Dorothy Browdy; m. Ellen Saltonstall 1978; two s. one d.; ed Univ. of Calif., San Diego; has participated in numerous group shows at Whitney Museum and Museum of Modern Art, New York etc.; Venice Biennale 1980, 1984; works represented in maj. permanent collections in USA, Tate Gallery, London etc. *Address:* c/o Shark's Ink, 550 Blue Mountain Road, Lyons, CO 80540; c/o DC Moore Gallery, 724 Fifth Avenue, New York, NY 10019, USA. *E-mail:* rzkushner@asan.com (office).

KUSHNER, Tony, BA, MFA; American playwright; b. 16 July 1956, New York, NY; ed Columbia Univ., New York Univ.; Playwright-in-Residence, Juilliard School, New York 1990–92; Tony Award 1993, 1994, Critics' Circle Award, London Evening Standard Award. *Publications:* Yes, Yes, No, No 1985, Actors on Acting 1986, Stella 1987, A Bright Room Called Day 1987, Hydriotaphia 1987, The Illusion 1988, The Persistence of Prejudice 1989, Widows (with Ariel Dorfman) 1991, Angels in America: A Gay Fantasia on National Themes, Part One: Millennium Approaches (Pulitzer Prize 1993) 1991, Part Two: Perestroika 1992, Slavs! 1994, Holocaust and the Liberal Imagination 1994, Thinking About the Longstanding Problems of Virtue and Happiness 1995, Homebody/Kabul 2001, Caroline, or Change (Best New Musical, Laurence Olivier Awards 2007) 2006. *Address:* Steven Barclay Agency, 12 Western Avenue, Petaluma, CA 94952, USA (office). *Telephone:* (707) 773-0654 (office). *Fax:* (707) 778-1868 (office). *Website:* www.barclayagency.com (office).

KUSSA, Mussa; Libyan government official; *Secretary of the People's Committee for Foreign Liaison and International Co-operation;* Amb. to UK 1980; Deputy Sec. for Foreign Affairs 1992–94; Head of Libyan Intelligence Agency 1994–2009; Sec. of the People's Cttee for Foreign Liaison and Int. Co-operation 2009–. *Address:* Secretariat of the People's Committee for Foreign Liaison and International Co-operation, El-Shat Street, Tripoli, Libya.

KUSTURICA, Emir; Bosnia and Herzegovina film director and musician (guitar); b. 24 Nov. 1954, Sarajevo; ed FAMU School, Prague, Czechoslovakia; teacher, Columbia Univ., New York, USA; mem. rock and roll band, No Smoking Orchestra 1986–; lives abroad; Chair. of Jury, Cannes Film Festival 2005. *Films:* Do You Remember Dolly Bell? (Golden Lion Award, Venice) 1981, When Father Was Away On Business (Palme d'Or, Cannes 1984) 1984, Time of the Gypsies (Best Dir, Cannes) 1988, Arizona Dream (Special Jury Prize, Berlin) 1993, Underground (Palme d'Or, Cannes) 1995, Black Cat White Cat 1998, La Veuve de Saint-Pierre 2000, Super Eight Stories 2001, Life is a Miracle 2004, Maradona (documentary) 2008. *Recordings include:* albums with No Smoking Orchestra: Das ist Walter 1984, Dok cekaš sabah sa šejtanom 1985, Pozdrav iz zemlje Safari (Greetings from Safari Land) 1987, Male price o velikoj ljubavi (A Little Story of a Great Love) 1989, Ja nisam odavle 1997, Black Cat White Cat 1998, Unza Unza Time 2000, La Vie est un miracle (soundtrack to film) 2004. *Address:* c/o Rasta Films, Belgrade, Serbia (office). *Telephone:* (11) 308-64-60 (office). *Fax:* (11) 308-64-61 (office). *E-mail:* marie-christine.malbert@libertysurf.fr (office). *Website:* www.emirkusturica-nosmoking.com (office).

KUSUMAATMADJA, Mochtar, LLD; Indonesian politician; b. Feb. 1929, Jakarta; ed Univ. of Indonesia, Yale and Harvard Law Schools and Univ. of Chicago Law School, USA; Minister of Justice 1974–77; Acting Foreign Minister 1977–78, then Minister of Foreign Affairs 1978–88, fmr Head of UN Comm. responsible for the demarcation of the Iraq–Kuwait Border, resgnd 1992; Indonesian Rep. at Law of the Sea Conf., Geneva and at Seabed Cttee sessions, New York; involvement in numerous int. orgs. *Address:* c/o Ministry of Foreign Affairs, Jalan Taman Pejambon 6, Jakarta, Indonesia.

KUSZNIEREWICZ, Mateusz Andrzej; Polish yachtsman; b. 29 April 1975, Warsaw; s. of Zbigniew Kusznierewicz and Irena Kusznierewicz; m. Agnieszka Kusznierewicz; ed Acad. of Physical Educ., Warsaw; began sailing aged nine, competed in Club Championship, Zalew Zegrzynski 1984; won first event Puchar Spojnii, Zalew Zegrzynski 1985; Polish Youth Champion, OK-Dinghy Class 1989; European Champion, OK-Dinghy Class 1991; Olympic Champion, Finn Class, Atlanta 1996, Bronze Medal, Athens 2004; World Champion, Finn Class 1998, 2000; European Champion, Finn Class 2000; mem. Yacht Klub Polski, Warsaw; Kt's Cross of Order of Polonia Restituta 1999; Int. Sailing Fed. Sailor of the Year (Int. Sailing Fed.) 1999, Most Popular Sportsman in Poland 1999. *Leisure interests:* electromechanics, other sports (especially golf, tennis and skiing). *Address:* No Limit Kusznierewicz Events, ul. Ostrobramska 75C, 04-175 Warsaw, Poland (office). *Telephone:* (22) 6117272 (office). *Fax:* (22) 6117273 (office). *E-mail:* mkusznierewicz@akademia.org.pl (office). *Website:* www.kusznierewicz.pl (office).

KUTAFIN, Oleg Ye., Dr Jur.; Russian lawyer; *Rector, Moscow State Academy of Law;* b. 26 June 1937; m.; two c.; ed Moscow State Univ.; Asst Prof., then Prof. Moscow All-Union Extra-Mural Law Inst. 1964–71; Prof. Moscow State Univ. 1971–, Deputy Chair. Acad. of Law 1971–87, Chair. and Rector Acad. of Law 1987–; mem. Presidium Russian Acad. of Sciences 2003–, Supreme Scientific Qualification Bd, Higher Qualification Bd of Judges; Chair. Comm. on Citizenship; Co-Chair. Asscn of Russian Lawyers; mem. Presidential consultative bodies; mem. editorial bds of leading Russian law journals; merited worker of science and of justice, Hon. worker of higher education and procuracy, Hon. mem. Russian Acad. of Educ., Hon. Attorney; Orders of Merit to Motherland of II, III and IV degrees, other govt awards; Presidential Prize in the field of education. *Publications include:* Municipal Law of Russia, Constitutional Law of Russia; more than 300 scientific works, including Russian Citizenship, Immunity in the Constitutional Law of the Russian Federation, Russian Autonomy, Subjects of Constitutional Law of Russian Federation as Legal and Equated to them Persons; textbooks, manuals and articles on constitutional and municipal law. *Leisure interests:* classical music, literature, history. *Address:* Moscow State Law Academy, Sadovo-Kudrinskaya str. 9, Moscow 123995, Russia (office). *Telephone:* (495) 254-99-72 (office). *E-mail:* msal@msal.ru. *Website:* www.msal.ru.

KUTARAGI, Ken, BE; Japanese computer entertainment executive (retd) and game console designer; b. 8 Aug. 1950, Tokyo; ed Denki Tsushin Univ.; joined Sony Corpn 1975, various positions in eng and digital research labs 1980s, worked on liquid crystal displays and digital camera projects; designed PlayStation game console 1989 and persuaded Sony to produce it after initiation of jt venture with Nintendo failed, headed team to create Sony PlayStation, released in 1994, began work on PlayStation 2 1996, released 2000, Playstation 3 released 2006; apptd Chair. US Div. 1997, Pres. and CEO Sony Computer Entertainment Int. 1999–Dec. 2006, Chair. and CEO Dec. 2006–June 2007 (retd); fmr mem. Bd of Dirs Sony Corpn. *Address:* c/o Sony Computer Entertainment International, 2-6-21 Minami-aoyama, Minato-ku, Tokyo 107-0062, Japan (office).

KUTELIA, Batu, PhD; Georgian politician and diplomatist; *Ambassador to USA;* b. 16 Jan. 1974, Tbilisi; m.; one s.; ed Georgian Tech. Univ., Georgian Inst. of Public Affairs, NATO Defence Coll.; Deputy Head of Mil. Cooperation Div., Mil.-Political Dept, Ministry of Foreign Affairs 1997–98, Head of Div. 1998–2000, Deputy Dir Mil.-Political Dept 2000–03; Deputy Head of Mission, Embassy in London 2003–04; Dir Political Security Dept, Nat. Security Council May–June 2004; Head of Foreign Intelligence Dept, Ministry of State Security June–Oct. 2004, Deputy Minister of State Security Oct.–Dec. 2004; Head of Foreign Intelligence Special Service 2006; Deputy Minister of Defence 2006–08; Amb. to USA 2008–; Soros Foundation Scholarship 1994, 1995, 1996, 1997, Pres. of Georgia Scholarship 1998, NATO Defence Coll. Scholarship 2000. *Address:* Embassy of Georgia, 2209 Massachusetts Avenue, Washington, DC 20008, USA (office). *Telephone:* (202) 387-2390 (office). *Fax:* (202) 387-0864 (office). *E-mail:* embgeorgiausa@yahoo.com (office); consulate@georgiaemb.org (office). *Website:* embassy.mfa.gov.ge (office).

KUTESA, Sam; Ugandan lawyer and politician; *Minister of Foreign Affairs;* b. 1 Feb. 1949; in pvt law practice with Kutesa and Co. Advocates 1973–2001; Attorney Gen. 1985–86; mem. Parl. representing Mawogola Co 1996–; fmr Minister of State for Investment, Ministry of Finance, Planning and Econ. Devt 2001–05; Minister of Foreign Affairs 2005–. *Address:* Ministry of Foreign Affairs, Embassy House, POB 7048, Kampala, Uganda (office). *Telephone:* (41) 2345661 (office). *Fax:* (41) 2258722 (office). *E-mail:* info@mofa.go.ug (office). *Website:* www.mofa.go.ug (home).

KUTI, Femi Anikulapo; Nigerian musician (saxophone), singer and songwriter; b. 1962, Lagos; s. of the late Fela Kuti; m. Funke; one s.; musician in his father's band, The Egypt 80, specializing in Afrobeat music; performed at the Hollywood Bowl (as substitute for his father) 1985; formed own group Positive Force 1987; numerous concerts, TV and radio appearances; est. New Shrine open-air nightclub 2000; Kora Awards for Best Male Artist and Best West African Artist 1999, World Music Award for Best Selling African Artist 2000. *Recordings include:* albums: No Cause for Alarm? (with the Positive Force) 1989, M.Y.O.B. 1991, Femi Kuti 1995, Wonder Wonder 1995, Shoki Shoki 1998, Fight to Win 2001, Africa Shrine 2004, Day by Day 2008. *Publication:* AIDS in Africa (essay published by UNICEF in its Progress of Nations report) 2000. *Address:* c/o Wrasse Records, Wrasse House, The Drive, Tyrells Wood, Leatherhead, KT22 8QW, England. *Website:* www.wrasserecords.com.

KUTSUKAKE, Tetsuo; Japanese politician; b. 12 Sept. 1929; ed Univ. of Tokyo; joined Ministry of Construction 1953; Dir for Policy Planning, Minister's Secr. 1971; Dir Nat. Expressway Div., Road Bureau 1977, Dir-Gen. Road Bureau 1982; Vice-Minister for Eng 1984; elected mem. House of Councillors (Ishikawa Pref.) 1986, 1992, 2000, 2001, Chair. Deliberative Council on Political Ethics and Election System 2002–05, Liberal Democratic Party Policy Deliberation Comm. 2004; Parl. Vice-Minister of Int. Trade and Industry 1991; Sr Parl. Vice-Minister in charge of the Environment Agency 2000; Parl. Vice-Minister of Environment 2001; Chair. Nat. Public Safety Comm., Minister of State for Disaster Man., for Nat. Emergency Legislation 2005–06. *Address:* c/o Liberal-Democratic Party—LDP (Jiyu-Minshuto) 1-11-23, Nagata-cho, Chiyoda-ku, Tokyo 100-8910, Japan.

KUTZ, Kazimierz; Polish film and theatre director and politician; b. 16 Feb. 1929, Szopienice, nr Katowice; m.; two s. two d.; ed State Higher School of Film, Television and Theatre, Łódź 1953; film and theatre dir 1959–; Dir Gen. Katowice Regional Television 1976–81; Lecturer, Dept of Radio and TV, Univ. of Silesia 1979–82; Co-Founder and Pres. Silesian Film Soc. 1981–; Chair. Solidarity Alliance of Creative Communities of the Silesian Region 1981; teacher, Directing Dept, State Higher School of Theatre, Kraków 1986–91; Man. Dir Krakow Regional Television 1990–91; mem. Soc. of Authors ZAiKS; Senator (Unia Wolnosci—Freedom Union) 1997–; Vice-Marshal of Senate 2001–; Dr hc (Univ. of Opole) 1997; Officer's Cross, Order of Polonia Restituta; State Prize (First Class) 1970, Award of the Minister of Culture and Art (1st Class) 1981, Award of the Chairman of State Radio and Television 1987, Nat. Cultural Award of Merit 1989, Solidarity – 1989 Award of the Independent Culture Cttee 1990, Teatr monthly Konrad Swinarski Award for Lifetime Achievement in Television 1993, (Asscn of Stage Artists and Composers) Hon. Distinction for Outstanding Creative Achievement 1993, Warsaw Mermaid Polish Film Critics' Award 1994, Silesian Cultural Award, Govt of Lower Saxony 1995, Korfanty Award for Lifetime Artistic Achievement 1995, Hon. Crown of Casimir the Great 1997, Grand Prix, 5th Talia Comedy Festival, Tarnow 2001, Hon. 'Jancio Wodnik', Prowincjonalia Festival, Wrzesnia 2002. *Films include:* Krzyż Walecznych (Cross of Valour) 1959, Nikt nie woła (Nobody's Calling) 1960, Ludzie pociągu (Night Train) 1961, Tarpany (Wild Horses) 1962, Mil czenie (Silence) 1963, Upal (Heat) 1964, Ktokol wiek wie... (Whoever May Know) 1966, Skok (The Leap) 1967, Sól ziemi czarnej (Salt of the Black Earth) 1970, Perła w koronie (Pearl in the Crown) 1972, Linia (The Line) 1974, Znikad donikad (From Nowhere to Nowhere) 1975, Paciorki jednego różańca (The Beads of One Rosary) (Golden Lion, Gdansk Film Festival 1981) 1980, Linie 1975, Na straży swej stać będę (I Shall Always Stand Guard) 1983, Wkrotce nadejda bracia (The Brothers Will Come Soon) 1985, Straszny sen dzidziusia Gorkiewicza (The Terrible Dream of Babyface Gorkiewicz) (TV) 1993, Zawrocony (The Convert) (TV) (Golden Lion, Gdansk 1994, Special Prize, Prix Europa Festival, Berlin 1994, Golden Grapes, Lubushan Film Summer, Zielona Gora 1994, Golden Calf for Best European Film, Int. Film Festival, Utrecht 1995, Int. Jury Diploma, Int. Film Festival, Moscow 1995) 1994, Śmierć jak kromka chleba (Death Like a Slice of Bread) 1994, Zawrócony 1994, Pułkownik Kwiatkowski (Colonel Kwiatkowski) (Silver Grapes, 26th Lubushan Film Summer, Lagow 1996, Golden Duck for the Best Polish Film of 1996 1997) 1995, Slawa i chwala (Fame and Glory) (TV) 1997. *Screenplays:* Sól ziemi czarnej, Perła koronie, Paciorki jednego różańca. *Plays:* Do piachu (Down to Sand), Kartoteka roznucona (The Card Index Scattered), Kartoteka (The Card Index), Na czworakach (On All Fours), Spaghetti i miecz (Spaghetti and the Sword), Damy i huzary (Ladies and Hussar) 2001. *Address:* 40-079 Katowice, ul. Gliwicka 1; Senate, ul. Wiejska 6, 00-902 Warsaw (office); ul. Marconich 5 m. 6, 02-954 Warsaw, Poland. *Telephone:* (32) 2068803; (22) 8589259. *E-mail:* biuro@kazimierzkutz.pl; kutz@nw.senat.gov.pl (office). *Website:* www.senat.gov.pl (office); www.kazimierzkutz.pl.

KUUGONGELWA-AMADHILA, Saara, MSc; Namibian politician; *Minister of Finance;* ed Univ. of London, UK, Univ. of Namibia; Dir-Gen. Nat. Planning Comm. 1997–2003; fmr Gov. African Devt Bank; Minister of Finance 2003–. *Address:* Ministry of Finance, Fiscus Building, John Meinert Street, PMB 13295, Windhoek, Namibia (office). *Telephone:* (61) 2099111 (office). *Fax:* (61) 230179 (office). *E-mail:* skuugongelwa-amadhila@mof.gov.na (office).

KUWAIZ, Abdullah Ibrahim el-, MA, MBA, PhD; Saudi Arabian banker, politician and diplomatist; *Ambassador to Bahrain;* b. 21 Aug. 1939, Dawadmi; two s. two d.; ed King Saud Univ. Saudi Arabia, Pacific Lutheran Univ. and St Louis Univ., USA; accountant, Pensions Dept, Ministry of Finance and Nat. Economy 1959–67, economist, 1967–81 (adviser 1977–81); Exec. Dir Arab Monetary Fund, Abu Dhabi 1977–80; Co-Chair. Financial Co-operation Cttee, Euro-Arab Dialogue 1978–83; Asst Under-Sec. for Econ.

Affairs 1981–87; Deputy Minister of Finance and Nat. Economy, Saudi Arabia 1987–2001; Dir-Gen. and Chair. of Bd Arab Monetary Fund, Abu Dhabi 1987–89; Chair. of Bd, Saudi-Kuwait Cement Co., Saudi Arabia 1991–93; Asst Sec.-Gen. for Econ. Affairs, Co-operation Council for the Arab States of the Gulf 1981–95; mem. of Bd and mem. Exec. Cttee, Gulf Int. Bank, Bahrain 1977–90; mem. of Bd Gulf Co-operation Council's Org. for Measures and Standards 1984–95, Oxford Energy Inst., Oxford, UK 1985–, Int. Maritime Bureau, London 1985–88, Econ. Forum, Cairo 1994–2001, Islamic Devt Bank, Jeddah 1997–2003, Arab Fund for Econ. Devt, Kuwait 1998–2000; Gen. Man. Gulf Int. Bank, Bahrain 1997–2001; Chair. of Bd Bosna Bank Int. Sarajevo 2000; Amb. to Bahrain 2002–; Medal of Merit for Accomplishment in Global Climate Coalition (GCC) from King Fahd Ibn Abdulaziz 1989, Lifetime Accomplishment Award Arab Bankers Association of North America (ABANA) 2003. *Publications:* numerous papers relating to banking, oil, finance and econ. devt and integration delivered at symposia in N America, Europe and the Middle East. *Leisure Interests:* hiking, swimming, reading, debating and writing. *Address:* Royal Embassy of Saudi Arabia, PO Box 1085, Bldg 82, Rd 1702, Block 317, Diplomatic Area, Manama, Bahrain (office); PO Box 10866, Riyadh 11443, Saudi Arabia (home). *Telephone:* (1) 753-7722 (office); (1) 488-0882 (home). *Fax:* (1) 753-3261 (office); (1) 480-2190 (home). *E-mail:* kuwaiz@hotmail.com (home).

KUX, Barbara, MBA; Swiss business executive; *Chief Procurement Office and Member, Group Management Committee, Royal Philips Electronics NV;* b. 1954, Zürich; d. of Prof. Dr Ernst Kux; m.; ed Institut Européen d'Admin des Affaires (INSEAD), Paris; Marketing Man., Nestlé SA, Germany 1979–84, Vice-Pres. Cen. and Eastern Europe Region, responsible for building up market leading business in Poland and Russia 1993–99; Man. Consultant, McKinsey & Co., Germany 1984–89; Vice-Pres. Asea Brown Boveri AG (ABB) responsible for entry into Cen. and Eastern Europe 1989–92, Pres. ABB Power Ventures 1989–92; Exec. Dir Ford Europe 1999–2003; Chief Procurement Office and mem. Group Man. Cttee, Royal Philips Electronics NV 2003–; mem. Bd Dirs INSEAD 2003–; MBA with Distinction (third best student), ranked by Fortune magazine amongst 50 Most Powerful Women in Business outside the US (12th) 2003, (26th) 2004, (24th) 2005, (21st) 2006, (19th) 2007, elected Global Leader for Tomorrow, World Econ. Forum. *Leisure interests:* cultural activities, sports, spending time with friends and family. *Address:* Royal Philips Electronics NV, Breitner Centre, Amstelplein 2, 1096 BC Amsterdam, Netherlands (office). *Telephone:* (40) 2789930 (office). *Fax:* (40) 2782450 (office). *E-mail:* barbara.kux@philips.com (office). *Website:* www.philips.com (office).

KUZMANOVIĆ, Rajko, PhD; Bosnia and Herzegovina judge, academic, politician and head of state; *President of Republika Srpska;* b. 1 Dec. 1931, Čelinac; ed High School, Bosanska Gradiška, Teaching High School, Banja Luka, Faculties of Law and Philosophy, Univ. of Zagreb; fmr head of educ. service in municipality of Čelinac; fmr Speaker of Ass. in Čelinac; fmr Prin. of School of Politics, Banja Luka; fmr Head of Secr. of Educ., Science and Culture, Banja Luka; fmr mem. Exec. Bd Municipality of Banja Luka; teacher, Faculty of Law, Univ. of Banja Luka 1975–, External Collaborator-Asst 1975–77, Docent 1977–81, Assoc. Prof. 1981–85, Prof. of Constitutional Law 1985–, Head of Constitutional Science, Faculty of Law for 25 years, lectured on Parallel Political Systems for 15 years, on Philosophy of Management 1988–94, Deputy Dean 1979–81, a Dean of Faculty of Law 1983–85, 1996–2000, a Dean of Faculty of Business Economy, Deputy Rector Univ. of Banja Luka 1986–88, Rector 1988–92, Head of Bd of Univ. of Banja Luka Foundation, Pres. Council of the Univ., Educational and Scientific Council of the Univ., Council of Faculty of Law; fmr Deputy Rector Slavic Univ. Magen, Moscow; part-time Prof., Faculties of Law, Mostar and Priština, Faculty of Philosophy, Banja Luka, Coll. of Interior, Faculty of Business Economy, Banja Luka, Pan-European University 'Apeiron', Banja Luka; fmr Pres. Scientific Council Inst. for Int. Law and Int. Business Cooperation, Banja Luka, Scientific Council Centre for Political Studies and Research 'Veselin Masleša', Banja Luka, Council of History Inst., Asscn of Univ. Teachers and Scientific Cadre (Bosnia and Herzegovina), Community of Univs in Bosnia and Herzegovina, Community of Univs of Yugoslavia, Asscn of Lawyers in Republika of Srpska; mem. Council of Educational and Pedagogy Inst. (Bosnia and Herzegovina), Council of Museums of Bosnian Krajina, Council of Radio and TV in Serbian Repub. of Bosnia and Herzegovina; mem. Parl., Ass. of Serbian Repub. of Bosnia and Herzegovina 1961–65; mem. Comm. for Constitutional Issues of Fed. Nat. Ass. of Serbian Fed. Repub. of Yugoslavia 1974, Comm. for Creating the Constitution of Serbian Fed. Repub. of Yugoslavia 1974, Constitutional Comm. for Revision of the Constitution of Serbian Repub. Bosnia and Herzegovina 1990, Comm. for Constitutional Issues, Nat. Ass. of Republika Srpska 1995–2000, Comm. for Creating and Altering the Constitution of Republika Srpska, Council of Law in the Govt of Republika Srpska; Vice-Pres. Council of Balkanian centre for research of local self-govt; del. at numerous congresses in SSRN Yugoslavia 1960, congress of Asscn of Trade Unions of Bosnia and Herzegovina; mem. Communist Asscn of Bosnia and Herzegovina, Cen. Cttee of Communist Asscns of Bosnia and Herzegovina, Republican Conf. of SSRN of Bosnia and Herzegovina; judge 1994–98, Pres. Constitutional Court of Republika Srpska 1998–2002, mem. High Prosecutor's Council; mem. Alliance of Ind. Social Democrats; Pres. of Republika Srpska Dec. 2007–; fmr Pres. Editorial Bd for the creation of The Encyclopedia of the Republic of Srpska; Pres. Acad. of Arts and Science 2004– (Sec. Social Science Bd); Corresp. mem. Acad. of Science and Arts 1997, mem. 2004; mem. Int. Princedom's Acad. of Humanitarian and Natural Science (Mage), Moscow 2001–, Balkan Acad. of Science and Arts (WAAS), San Francisco, USA 2006–; Order for Work, Order for Mil. Merits, Order for Merits for People, Pres. of Serbian Fed. Repub. of Yugoslavia, Order of Honour Golden Rays; Pres. of Republika Srpska Award, Medallion and Charter, Univ.

of Banja Luka, Konji (Turkey), Katovica (Poland), Ostrava (Czech Repub.), Charter and Gold Coat of Arms of City of Banja Luka, Gold Medallion of Čelinac, Gold Medallion of Faculty of Law, Banja Luka, Medallion for scientific work 'Veselin Masleša', charters of several other cities. *Publications:* 21 textbooks, including Constitutional Law, Science of Managing Bases, Parallel Political Systems, Constitution and Civil Rights (co-author); more than 200 articles in scientific and professional journals on constitutional law and political systems, state man. and governing, educ. and schooling, and on numerous other gen. and social subjects. *Address:* Office of the President of Republika Srpska, 78000 Banja Luka, Bana Milosavljevića 4, Bosnia and Herzegovina (office). *Telephone:* (51) 211178 (office). *Fax:* (51) 212018 (office). *E-mail:* info@predsjednikrs.net (office). *Website:* www.predsjednikrs.net (office).

KUZMIN, Alexander Viktorovich; Russian architect; *Chief Architect of Moscow;* b. 12 July 1951, Moscow; s. of Victor Alexandrovich Kuzmin and Antonina Alexeevna Kuzmin; m. 1996; one s. one d.; ed Moscow Inst. of Architecture; researcher Research and Project Inst. of the Master Plan of Moscow, Dir 1987–; Deputy Head, Chief Moscow Dept of Architecture 1991, First Deputy Chair. Moscow Cttee of Architecture; elected Chief Architect of Moscow 1996–, Chair. Architectural and City Planning Cttee., Moscow; mem. Russian Acad. of Architecture and Building Sciences 1998; chief architect of reconstruction of Moscow streets, cen. region of Moscow, building of Olympic village. *Leisure interest:* collecting old medals. *Address:* Moscow Committee of Architecture and City Planning, Triumphalnaya pl.1, 125047 Moscow, Russia (office). *Telephone:* (495) 250-55-20 (office). *Fax:* (495) 250-20-51 (office).

KUZ'MUK, Col-Gen. Oleksander Ivanovich; Ukrainian military officer and politician; b. 17 April 1954, Dyatilivka, Khmelnitsk Region, Ukraine; m.; two c.; ed Kharkov Guards' Higher Tank School, Moscow Mil. Acad. of Armoured Forces; commdr tank platoon, Bn; Deputy Commdr Regt, Group of Soviet Troops in Germany 1975–83; Commdg posts in Leningrad, Carpathian, Odessa Mil. commands 1983–95; Commdr Nat. Guards of Ukraine 1995–96; Minister of Defence 1996–2001, 2004–05; Deputy Prime Minister 2006–07. *Address:* c/o Ministry of Defence, Bankova str. 6, 252005 Kiev, Ukraine (office).

KUZNETSOV, Anatoly Borisovich; Russian actor; b. 31 Dec. 1930, Moscow; s. of Boris Sergeyevich Kuznetsov and Maria Davydovna Kuznetsova; ed Moscow Art Theatre School; mem. Union of Cinematographers, Union of Theatre Workers; People's Artist of Russia. *Films include:* Dangerous Routes 1954, A Guest from Kuban 1955, A Trip to Youth 1956, On War Roads 1958, Fortune 1959, Wait for the Letters 1960, My Friend Kolka 1961, Morning Trains 1963, Conscience 1965, Spring on Oder 1967, White Sun of the Desert 1969, Stolen Train 1971, Freedom 1971, Hot Snow 1972, The Single Road 1974, In the Zone of Particular Attention 1977, Incognito from Petersburg 1977, Kids Like Kids 1978, Second Spring 1979, His Holidays 1981, Copper Angel 1984, Battle for Moscow 1985, Without Sun 1987. *Address:* Glinishchevsky per. 5/7, Apt. 88, 103009 Moscow, Russia (home). *Telephone:* (495) 200-58-47 (home).

KUZNETSOV, Boris Avramovich; Russian barrister; b. 19 March 1944, Kirov; s. of Avram Mikhailovich Kuznetsov and Nina Aleksandrovna Ukhanova; m. 2nd Nadezhda Georgiyevna Chernaya; two c.; ed Moscow Juridical Acad., Research Inst. USSR Ministry of Internal Affairs; on staff Criminal Investigation Dept St Petersburg and Magadan Region 1962–82; mem. Magadan Regional Bd of Lawyers 1982–85, twice expelled for disagreement with party officials; Head of Lab. Inst. of Biology Problems of the N br. USSR Acad. of Sciences, Magadan 1985–89; adviser to mems Inter-regional people's deputy 1989–91; mem. St Petersburg Bd of Lawyers 1991–95; mem. Lawyers' Interrepub. Bd 1995–; Head Boris Kuznetsov and Pnrs Lawyer's Agency; Golden Sign for Defence of Russian-Speaking People and Intellectuals Outside Russia, 1998, Anatoli Koni's Medal 2001, Award Hanger from the Navy of the Russian Fed. *Leisure interests:* pre-Revolutionary juridical literature and literature on the navy, sailing models construction. *Address:* Boris Kuznetsov and Partners, Novy Arbat str. 19, Office 2205-2207, 103025 Moscow (office); Frigate House, Koop 'Forest', Shoulgino Village, Moscow Region, Russia (home). *Telephone:* (495) 203-43-40 (office). *Fax:* (495) 203-44-71 (office).

KUZNETSOV, Fedor Andreyevich; Russian chemist; b. 12 July 1932; m.; two c.; ed Leningrad State Univ.; army engineer 1955–58; researcher, head of lab., Deputy Dir, Inst. of Inorganic Chem., Siberian br. USSR (now Russian) Acad. of Sciences 1961–83, Dir 1983, now Adviser to Russian Acad. of Sciences; corresp. mem., USSR (now Russian) Acad. of Sciences 1984, mem. 1987–; main research in synthesis and studies of inorganic materials; Foreign mem. American Electro-Chemical Soc.; Vice-Pres. Int. Council for Science, Cttee on Data for Science and Tech. 2000–02;; USSR State Prize 1981; N. Kurnakov Medal. *Address:* Siberian Branch of Russian Academy of Sciences, Institute of Inorganic Chemistry, Prospekt Akademika Lavrentieva, 3, 630090 Novosibirsk, Russia (office). *Telephone:* (3832) 34-44-90 (office). *Fax:* (3832) 34-44-89 (office). *E-mail:* fk@che.nsk.su (office). *Website:* www.che.nsk.su (office).

KUZNETSOV, Nikolai Aleksandrovich; Russian cybernetician; *Counsellor, Institute of Radioengineering and Electronics, Russian Academy of Sciences;* b. 9 March 1939; m.; two c.; ed Moscow Inst. of Physics and Tech.; Jr, Sr Researcher, Deputy Dir Inst. of Problems of Man. 1965–88; Dir Gen. of Research Production Union Moskva 1988–89; Dir Inst. for Information Transmission Problems (IPPI) 1990–2006; Counsellor, Inst. of Radioengineering and Electronics, Russian Acad. of Sciences 2006–; Corresp. mem. USSR (now Russian) Acad. of Sciences 1987, mem. 1994; mem. IEEE; research in theory of automatic man. and informatics; USSR State Prize. *Publications include:* Management of Observations in Automatic Systems 1961, Synthesis of Algorithms at Variable Criterion of Optimality 1966, Methods of Study of Stability of Dissynchronized Pulse Systems 1991. *Leisure interests:* mountain skiing, singing. *Address:* Institute for Information Transmission Problems (IPPI), Russian Academy of Sciences, Bolshoi Karetny per. 19, 127994 Moscow, Russia (office). *Telephone:* (495) 629-30-05 (office). *Fax:* (495) 629-30-05 (office). *E-mail:* kuznetsov@cplire.ru (office).

KUZNETSOV, Nikolai Vasilyevich; Russian mathematician; b. 24 June 1939, Hachmas, Azerbaijan; s. of Vasilii Kuznetsov and Evdokia Gureutieva; m. Galina Pavlovna Kuznetsova 1975; two c.; ed Moscow Inst. of Physics and Tech.; jr researcher, Inst. of Math., USSR Acad. of Sciences 1965–69; jr, sr researcher, Moscow V. Lenin Pedagogical Inst. 1969–70; Head of Div., Head of Dept, Cen. Research Inst. of Information and Tech.-Econ. Studies 1970–71; Head of Div., Research Inst. of Systems of Man. and Econs 1972–73; Sr Researcher, Head of Lab. Khabarovsk Research Inst. of Complex Studies 1973–81; Deputy Dir Computer's Cen., Far East br. USSR Acad. of Sciences 1989–91; Deputy Dir Inst. of Applied Math. 1991–92; Corresp. mem. USSR (now Russian) Acad. of Sciences 1987; research in spectral theory, theory of modular and automorphic functions in math. physics. *Publications:* On Eigenfunctions of One Integral Equation 1970, Poincaré Series and Extended Lemer Hypothesis 1985; numerous articles in scientific journals. *Leisure interest:* chess. *Address:* Institute of Applied Mathematics, Far East Branch of Russian Academy of Sciences, Radio str. 7, 690041 Vladivostok, Russia (office). *Telephone:* (4232) 31-19-07 (Vladivostok) (office); (4212) 33-46-76 (Khabarovsk) (office); (4212) 22-76-36 (home).

KUZNETSOV, Oleg Leonidovich, DTech; Russian geophysicist; *President, Russian Academy of Natural Sciences;* b. 1938; m.; two c.; ed Moscow S. Ordzhonikidze Inst. of Geological Research, Moscow State Univ.; researcher, Inst. of Oil, USSR (now Russian) Acad. of Sciences 1962–70; Head of lab., All-Union Inst. of Nuclear Geophysics and Geochemistry, USSR Ministry of Geology (now State Scientific Centre of All-Russian Inst. of Geosystems) 1970–79, Dir 1979–; Prof. Moscow State Univ. 1986–; Vice-Pres. Russian Acad. of Nat. Sciences 1990, Pres. 1993–; f. and Rector, Int. Univ. of Nature, Soc. and Man., Dubna 1994–; main research in geophysical processes, seismoacoustics, non-linear geophysics, geoinformatics and information tech.; mem. New York Acad. of Sciences 1994, Int. Acad. of Sciences on Nature and Soc. 1993, Int. Acad. of Higher Schooling 1995, Oriental Acad. of Oil and Gas 1994; Gen. Constructor, Global Information System GEOS 1985–1991; Hon. mem. Hungarian Soc. of Geophysics, Euro-Asian Geophysical Soc., Hon. Worker of Science and Eng of Russian Fed.; USSR State Prize 1982, Prize of German Econ. Club 1996, A. Chizhevsky Prize 1997, Golden ROSING-2002. *Publications:* over 280 scientific works including 11 monographs, 4 reference books, 67 inventions, over 60 patents. *Address:* Russian Academy of Natural Sciences, Varshavskoye shosse 8, 117105 Moscow, Russia (office). *Telephone:* (495) 954-53-50 (office). *Fax:* (495) 958-37-11 (office). *E-mail:* info@raen.ru (office). *Website:* www.raen.ru (office).

KUZNETSOVA, Svetlana; Russian professional tennis player; b. 27 June 1985, St Petersburg; d. of Alexandr Kuznetsov and Galina Tsareva; won Junior US Open doubles; turned professional 2000; Int. Tennis Fed. Girls Singles Champion 2001; Women's Tennis Asscn (WTA) singles titles Helsinki 2002, Bali 2002, 2004, 2006, Eastbourne, UK 2004, US Open 2004, Miami, Fla 2006, Beijing 2006, New Haven, Conn. 2007; WTA doubles titles Princess Cup 2002 (with Arantxa Sanchez-Vicario), Helsinki 2002, Sopot 2002, Koto, Japan 2002, Gold Coast, Australia 2002, 2004, Dubai 2002, Rome 2003, Toronto 2002, Leipzig 2003, Doha 2004, Australian Open 2005, Miami, Fla 2005, Eastbourne, UK 2006; highest WTA ranking fourth (2008); mem. Russian Olympic team 2004, 2008, Russian Fed. Cup team 2004 (won first-ever title in 2004); WTA Tour Newcomer of the Year 2002. *Leisure interest:* music. *Address:* c/o Women's Tennis Association, 1 Progress Plaza, Suite 1500, St. Petersburg, FL 33701, USA. *Website:* www.svetlanakuznetsovasite.com.

KVAMME, E. Floyd, BS, MSE; American computer scientist and government official; *Co-Chairman, President's Council of Advisors on Science and Technology (PCAST);* ed Univ. of California, Berkeley and Syracuse Univ.; Founder-mem. Nat. Semiconductor 1967, Gen. Man. Semiconductor Operations, Pres. Nat. Advanced Systems (subsidiary); Exec. Vice-Pres. of Sales and Marketing, Apple Computer 1982; Pnr, Kleiner Perkins Caufield & Byers 1984, now Pnr Emer.; Chair. Electronic Commerce Advisory Council for the State of Calif. 1998; Co-Chair. President's Council of Advisors on Science Tech (PCAST), Washington, DC 2001–; Chair. Empower America; mem. Bd of Dirs Brio Tech., Gemfire, Harmonic Lightwaves, Triquint Semiconductor, Photon Dynamics, Power Integrations; mem. of Advisory Bd Markkula Center for Applied Ethics, Santa Clara Univ., Nat. Venture Capital Asscn; mem. Exec. Cttee of The Tech. Network; fmr mem. Finance Cttee, Fong for Senate Campaign, High Tech. Advisory Cttee, Nat. Finance Cttee of the Bush for President Campaign. *Address:* President's Council of Advisors on Science and Technology (PCAST), Office of Science and Technology Policy, Executive Office of the President, Washington, DC 20502, USA (office). *Website:* www .ostp.gov/PCAST/pcast.html (office).

KVAPIL, Radoslav; Czech pianist; b. 15 March 1934, Brno; s. of Karel Kvapil and Marie Kvapilová; m. Eva Mašlaňová 1960 (died 1993); one s.; ed Gymnasium Dr. Kudely, Brno and Janáček Acad. of Musical Arts; first piano recital Brno 1954; 1st prize Janáček Competition 1958, Int. Competition, Czechoslovak Radio 1968; Prof. of Piano, Prague Conservatory 1963–73; concerts in countries throughout Europe, in USA and Japan 1963–; performed world premiere of Dvořák's Cypresses 1983; Dir South Bohemia Music Festival 1991–; Pres. Yehudi Menuhin Soc., Prague 1990–, Dvořák Soc., Prague 1997–, Czech Soc. for Music and Arts 1990–; Hon. Vice-Pres. Dvořák Soc., London; Chevalier des Arts et des Lettres 2002; Janáček Medal (Cultural Ministry). *Recordings include:* complete piano works of Dvořák and Martinů,

complete piano and chamber music of Janáček, complete piano works of Jan Hugo Voříšek 1973–74, complete polka cycles of Smetana, Czech contemporary piano music, Piano Concerto by A. Rejcha (first ever recording), Anthology of Czech piano music (for Unicorn-Kanchana label), eight vols, works of Dvořák performed on the composer's piano 1999, Ullman's Sonatas 5–7 2002. *Leisure interest:* chess. *Address:* c/o Margaret Murphy Management, 7 Grove Park, Wanstead, London E11 2DN, England (office); Hradecká 5, 13000 Prague 3, Czech Republic. *Telephone:* (20) 8530-1305 (office); (2) 67312430. *E-mail:* info@margaretmurphy.com (office); r.kvapil@ecn.cz (office). *Website:* www.margaretmurphy.com (office). *Fax:* (2) 67312430 (home).

KVASHA, Igor Vladimirovich; Russian actor and stage director; b. 4 Feb. 1933, Moscow; m. Tatyana Semenovna Putiyevskaya; one s.; ed Moscow Art Theatre; with Moscow Art Theatre 1955–57; cco-founder and leading actor Theatre Sovremennik 1956–; presenter Wait for Me (tv programme); regularly appears on TV and radio, reciting prose and poems; People's Artist of Russia, Kumir Prize 1999; prizes of many film and theatre festivals for performing Russian repertoire including plays by A. Chekhov. *Films:* roles in over 80 films by dirs Roshal, Room, Klimov, Bondarchuk, Daneliya and others 1960–. *Theatre:* (actor) theatre roles in classical and contemporary plays, including Cyrano de Bergerac (Cyrano de Bergerac by Rostand), Jimmy Porter (Look Back in Anger by Osborne), Luka (The Lower Depths by Gorky), Balalaikin (Balalaikin and Co. by Saltykov-Shchedrin), Gayev (Cherry Orchard by Chekhov), Chebutykin (Three Sisters by Chekhov), Dr. Stockman (Dr. Stockman by Ibsen), Lester (play by Schiller). *Theatre:* (director) staged productions include Days of the Turbins, The Hypocrites' Servitude by Bulgakov, The Average Downy Home Cat by Voinovich and G. Gorin, Cyrano de Bergerac (together with Yefremov), Molière by Bulgakov. *Radio:* many programmes including classical prose and poetry. *Television:* Wait For Me (Tefi Prize) 2001, Transformation, One Man and One Woman. *Leisure interest:* painting. *Address:* Chistoprudniy blv. 19, Moscow (office); Glinishchevsky per. 5/7, Apt. 90, 103009 Moscow, Russia (home). *Telephone:* (495) 921-25-43 (office); (495) 209-61-08 (home). *Fax:* (495) 921-66-29 (office).

KVASHNIN, Col-Gen. Anatoly Vassilyevich; Russian politician; *Representative of Russian President to Siberian Federal District;* b. 15 Aug. 1946, Ufa; ed Kurgan Machine Construction Inst., Acad. of Armoured Units, Acad. of Gen. Staff; army service, Commdr of regiment, div., army 1969–; Deputy, First Deputy Head Main Operation Dept 1993–95; Commdr Allied Group of armed forces in Chechnya 1994–95; Commdr Armed Forces of N Caucasian Command 1995–97; Acting Head, Head Gen. Staff of Armed Forces of Russian Fed. 1997–2004; First Deputy Minister of Defence, Russian Fed. 1997–2004; Rep. of Russian Pres. to Siberian Fed. Dist 2004–; Legion d'honneur 2004, Order of Honour 2006. *Leisure interests:* painting, sports. *Address:* Krasnyi pr. 62, 630091 Novosibirsk, Russia (office). *Telephone:* (383) 217-35-17 (office); (383) 220-17-80 (office). *E-mail:* sibokrug@atlas-nsk.ru (office). *Website:* www .sfo.nsk.su (office).

KVITSINSKY, Yuliy Aleksandrovich, CandJur; Russian politician and diplomatist; b. 28 Sept. 1936, Rzev; s. of Aleksander Kvitsinsky and Maria Orlova; m. Inga Kuznetsova 1955; two d.; ed Moscow Inst. of Int. Relations; served in Embassy in GDR 1959–65, in FRG 1978–81; head of Soviet del., negotiations on medium-range nuclear weapons until latter broken off 1983; subsequently responsible for negotiations on Strategic Defence Initiative (SDI) Geneva talks 1985; Amb. to FRG 1986–90; Deputy Foreign Minister 1990–91, First Deputy Foreign Minister May–Sept. 1991; Chief Adviser, Dept of Planning 1991–92; Vice-Pres. Foreign Policy Asscn 1992–; Adviser to Pres., Council of Russian Fed. (Upper Chamber) 1996–97; Amb. to Norway 1997–2003; cand. mem. CPSU Cen. Cttee 1986–89, mem. 1989–91; elected State Duma (Parl.) (Communist Party) 2003–; Honoured Diplomat of Russian Fed. 2002; Order of Red Banner 1971, Order of Friendship Among People 1981, Order of October Revolution 1986. *Publications:* Vor dem Sturm 1993, Judas Ischariot 1996, General Vlassov 1997, Apostate 2002. *Leisure interest:* fishing. *Address:* State Duma, Okhotnyi ryad 1, 103265 Moscow, Russia (office). *Telephone:* (495) 982-24-12 (office). *Fax:* (495) 692-98-25 (office). *E-mail:* www@duma.ru (office). *Website:* www.duma.ru (office).

KWANKWASO, Rabiu; Nigerian politician; Exec. Gov. Kano state 1999–2003; Minister of Defence 2003–07; Special Presidential Envoy to Somalia and Darfur 2007; currently Leader People's Democratic Party in Kano. *Address:* c/o People's Democratic Party, Wadata Plaza, Michael Okpara Way, Zone 5, Wuse, Abuja, Nigeria (office).

KWAPONG, Alex. A., PhD; Ghanaian professor and government official; b. 8 March 1927, Akropong, Akwapim; s. of E. A. and Theophilia Kwapong; m. Evelyn Teiko Caesar 1956; six d.; ed Achimota Coll. and King's Coll., Cambridge; Visiting Prof., Princeton Univ. 1962; fmr Pro Vice-Chancellor and Head of Classics Dept, Ghana Univ., Vice-Chancellor 1966–75; Vice-Rector for Institutional Planning and Resource Devt UN Univ. 1976–88; Lester B. Pearson Chair. in Devt Studies, Dalhousie Univ. 1988–91; Dir of African Programmes, Teacher Educ., Research and Evaluation, The Commonwealth of Learning 1991–93; mem. Council of State 2000–04, Chair. 2002–04; Chair. ARB Apex Bank Ltd.; mem. Political and Educ. Cttees., Nat. Liberation Council 1966; mem. Bd Aspen Inst. Berlin 1975–, Harold Macmillan Trust 1986–, Int. Council for Educ. Devt, Int. Foundation for Educ. and Self-help 1988–; Fellow, Ghana Acad. of Arts and Sciences; Order of Volta (Ghana); Hon. DLitt (Warwick, Ife, Ghana, Univ. of Ghana); Hon. LLD (Princeton) 1974. *Publications:* Higher Education and Development in Africa Today: A Reappraisal 1979; Under-development and the Challenges of the 1980s: The Role of Knowledge 1980, The Relevance of the African Universities to the Development Needs of Africa 1980, Medical Education and National Development 1987, Culture, Development and African Unity 1988, African Scientific and Technical Institution Building and the Role of International

Co-operation 1988, The Challenge of Education in Africa 1988, Some Reflections on International Education in the 90s in the Role of Service Learning in International Education 1989, Capacity Building and Human Resource Development in Africa (co-ed. with B. Lesser) 1990, Meeting the Challenge, The African Capacity Building Initiative (co-ed. with B. Lesser) 1992. *Leisure interests:* music, learning Japanese, tennis, billiards. *Address:* c/o Ghana Academy of Arts and Sciences, Lberation Link, Airport Residential Area, Accra, Ghana (office).

KWAŚNIEWSKA, Jolanta; Polish organization executive, lawyer and charity worker; b. 3 June 1955, Gdansk; d. of Julian Konty and Anna Konty; m. Aleksander Kwaśniewski (Pres. of Poland 1995–2005) 1979; one d.; ed Faculty of Law, Univ. of Gdansk; began career as lawyer 1984; est. real estate agency 1991, co-dir with husband until his assumption of Presidency of Poland 1995; est. Communication without Barriers Foundation (org. to help disabled people and cr. medical centre for children) 1997, Let's Open the World Programme (provides funds for Polish orphans to visit European countries), Help the Talented Youth Foundation; Patron Polish UNICEF, Nat. Coalition for Breast Cancer, Adults for Children Foundation; mem. UN Comité des Sages; mem. Hon. Bd Int. Centre for Missing and Exploited Children; Order of the Smile 1998, Grand Ribbon of the Order of Leopold (Belgium) 1999, Grand Cross of the Order of Isabella the Catholic (Spain) 2001, Grand Cross of the Order of Merit (Germany) 2002, Grand Cross with the Ribbon of Terra Mariana (Estonia) 2002, Grand Ribbon of the Order of the Precious Crown (Japan) 2002, Order of Merit and Companion of Honour (Malta) 2002, Grand Cross Royal Norwegian Order of Merit 2003; Woman of the Year and Warsaw Lady of the Year 1998, Holy Brother Albert–Adam Chmielowski Prize for Charitable Activities 1998, Dr Henryk Jordan Medal for Assistance to Children 1999, American Centre of Polish Culture in Washington Medal 1999, Big Golden Heart Award, St Stanislaw Kostka Foundation 2000, Medal of Merit for the Mining Industry for Aid Given to Orphaned Mining Families, TV Personality of the Year 2001, For The Future of Children of Europe Award of Hungarian Asscn, Future of Europe Asscn 2002. *Leisure interests:* literature, theatre, music, fine arts, spending time with her family, travel, skiing, tennis. *Address:* ul. Boicciarellego 4, 00-591 Warsaw, Poland (office). *Telephone:* (22) 849-9662 (office). *Fax:* (22) 695-1933 (office). *Website:* www.j .kwasniewska.aid.org.pl.

KWAŚNIEWSKI, Aleksander; Polish journalist, fmr politician and fmr head of state; b. 15 Nov. 1954, Białogard, Koszalin Prov.; s. of Zdzisław Kwaśniewski and Aleksandra Kwaśniewska; m. Jolanta Konty 1979; one d.; ed Gdańsk Univ.; fmr leader of youth movt, including Chair. Univ. Council of Polish Socialist Students' Union (SZSP) at Gdańsk Univ., Head of Culture Dept of SZSP Gen. Bd 1979–80, mem. Exec. Cttee of SZSP Chief Council 1980–81; Ed.-in-Chief Itd (student weekly newspaper), Warsaw 1981–84; Ed.-in-Chief of daily Sztandar Młodych (Banner of Youth), Warsaw 1984–85; mem. Council of Ministers 1985–89; Head, Socio-Political Cttee 1988–89; Minister for Youth Affairs 1985–87; Chair. Cttee for Youth and Physical Culture 1987–90; mem. Polish United Workers' Party (PZPR) 1977–90; mem. Social Democracy of Repub. of Poland Party (SDRP) 1990–95, Chair. 1990–95; participant in Round Table plenary debates, Co-Chair. team for trade union pluralism, mem. team for political reforms and group for asscns and territorial self-govt 1989; Co-f. Democratic Left Alliance 1991; Chair. Polish Olympic Cttee 1988–91; Deputy in Sejm (Parl.) 1991–95; Chair. Constitutional Cttee 1993–95; Supreme Commdr of Armed Forces 1995–2005; Pres. of Poland 1995–2005; Kt, Order of White Eagle and numerous int. honours and awards including Grand Croix, Légion d'honneur, Kt Grand Cross, Order of Bath, Kt Grand Cross, Order of St Michael and St George (GB), Grand Cross, Order of Merit (Italy) 1996, Order of Duke Gedyminas, First Class (Lithuania), Order of Leopold (Belgium), Golden Olympic Order, Int. Olympic Cttee 1998, Golden Order of Merit, Int. Amateur Athletic Fed. 1999, Order of Merit, European Olympic Cttee 2000, Order of the Repub. (Turkey) 2000, Great Order of King Tamislav with Ribbon and Great Star (Croatia) 2001, Order of Catholic Isabella with Chain (Spain) 2001, Nat. Order of Southern Cross (Brazil) 2002, Special Grand Cross of Merit (Peru) 2002, Grand Ribbon of the Great Order of Chrysanthemum (Japan) 2002; Common Wealth 2007 Award of Distinguished Service 2007. *Leisure interests:* sport, literature, films. *Address:* Aleja Przyjaciół 8/1, 00-565 Warsaw, Poland (office). *Telephone:* (22) 8487385. *Fax:* (22) 6294816. *E-mail:* biuro@kwasniewskialeksander.pl. *Website:* www .kwasniewskialeksander.pl.

KWEI-ARMAH, Kwame; British actor, playwright and singer; b. (Ian Roberts), 1967, London; m.; four c.; ed Barbara Speake Stage School; writer-in-residence, Bristol Old Vic 1999–01; currently writer on attachment to the Nat. Theatre Studio; took part in Celebrity Fame Acad. (BBC) 2003; Evening Standard Charles Wintour Award for Most Promising Playwright 2003. *Plays as writer:* Big Nose (adaptation of Rostand's Cyrano De Bergerac, Belgrade Theatre, Coventry) 1999, Blues Brother Soul Sister (musical, Bristol Old Vic) 2000, A Bitter Herb (Peggy Ramsey Bursary, Bristol Old Vic) 2001, Hold On (Durham Theatre Royal) 2002, Elmina's Kitchen (Royal Nat. Theatre, Charles Wintour Award for Most Promising Playwright, Evening Standard Theatre Awards 2004) 2003, Fix Up (Royal Nat. Theatre) 2004, Statement of Regret (Royal Nat. Theatre) 2007, Let There be Love (Tricycle Theatre) 2008. *Plays as actor:* Mozart and Salieri (Crucible, Sheffield). *Films:* Cutthroat Island 1995. *Television:* as actor: Between The Lines 1994, Casualty 1999–2004, Holby City 2000, Pride 2004, Fade to Black 2006, Robin Hood 2006, Lewis 2008, Hotel Babylon 2008. *Recordings:* album: Kwame 2003. *Address:* c/o A & C Black Publishing Ltd., 38 Soho Square, London, W1D 3HB, England (office); 19c Beaconsfield Road, London, N1 3AA, England. *Telephone:* (20) 7758-0200 (office). *Fax:* (20) 7758-0222 (office). *Website:* www.acblack.com (office).

KWEK, Leng Beng; Singaporean business executive; *Executive Chairman, Hong Leong Group Singapore;* s. of the late Kwek Hong Png; m.; two c.; father left Fujian Prov., China for Singapore and subsequently f. Hong Leong Group; joined family business in 1960s; Exec. Chair. Hong Leong Group Singapore 1990–; Chair. City Developments Ltd, Millennium & Copthorne (M&C) Hotels; mem. Bd Trustees Singapore Management Univ.; Hon. DUniv (Oxford Brookes Univ.); Hotelier of the Decade, Asia Pacific Hotel Investment Conference 2000. *Address:* Hong Leong Group Singapore, 9 Raffles Place, #36-00, Republic Plaza, Singapore 048619 (office). *Telephone:* 6438-0880 (office). *Fax:* 6534-3060 (office). *E-mail:* gerry@cdl.com.sg (office). *Website:* www.hongleong.com.sg (office).

KWIATKOWSKI, Marek; Polish professor of history of art; *Curator and Director, Royal Łazienki Palace and Park;* b. 25 April 1930, Caen, France; m.; ed Warsaw Univ.; Curator Royal Łazienki Palace and Park for over 50 years, currently Dir, has organized numerous exhbns and displays; mem. numerous asscns including Friends of Animals Asscn; Homo Varsoviensis, Commdr's Cross, Order of Polonia Restituta; Klio Award. *Publications:* 22 books on art including Szymon Bogumił Zug 1971, Stanisław August – król architekt 1983, Architektura mieszkaniowa Warszawy XVII-XIX W 1986, Historia Warszawy XVI-XX wieku. Zabytki mówią 1999. *Leisure interests:* paintings, own museum in Sucha village. *Address:* Royal Łazienki, ul. Agrykoli 1, 00-460 Warsaw, Poland (office). *Telephone:* (22) 6218212 (office). *Fax:* (22) 6296945 (office). *Website:* www.lazienki-krolewskie.pl (office).

KWIATKOWSKI, Michał; Polish business executive; *President, Management Board, EuRoPol GAZ;* b. 1947; m.; one c.; ed Silesian Tech. Univ., Gliwice; engineer, promoted to Chief Engineer KWK Sosnica coalmine 1971–90; Deputy Dir Knurów Coalmine 1990–91, Dir 1991–93; Pres. Gliwice Coal Co. 1993–98, Weglokoks Co. 1998–2001, Polish Oil and Gas Co. (PGNiG) SA 2001–03, Man. Bd EuRoPol GAZ 2003–. *Address:* EuRoPol GAZ Transit Gas Pipeline System, Al. St. Zjednoczonych 61, 04-028 Warsaw, Poland (office). *Telephone:* (22) 517-40-00 (office). *Fax:* (22) 517-40-40 (office). *E-mail:* info@europolgaz.com.pl (office). *Website:* www.europolgaz.com.pl (office).

KWOK, Raymond, MA (Cantab.), MBA, JP; Hong Kong business executive; *Vice-Chairman and Managing Director, Sun Hung Kai Properties Ltd;* b. (Kwok Ping-luen), 1952, Hong Kong; s. of Kwok Tak-seng and Kwong Siu-hing; younger brother of Walter Kwok and Thomas Kwok; ed Jesus Coll., Cambridge, UK, Harvard Univ., USA; family originated from Zhongshan, Guangdong Prov., China; with Sun Hung Kai Properties Ltd (largest property developer in Hong Kong) 1979–, currently Vice-Chair. and Man. Dir; Chair. SUNeVision Holdings Ltd, SmarTone Telecommunications Holdings Ltd; has interest in city bus operator KMB; Dir (non-exec.) Transport International Holdings Ltd, USI Holdings Ltd; Ind. Dir (non-exec.) Standard Chartered Bank (Hong Kong) Ltd; mem. Bd of Dirs Real Estate Developers Asscn of Hong Kong; mem. Gen. Cttee of Hong Kong Gen. Chamber of Commerce, Hong Kong Port Devt Council; Vice-Chair. Council of Chinese Univ. of Hong Kong; Hon. DBA (Open Univ. of Hong Kong); Hon. LLD (Chinese Univ. of Hong Kong). *Address:* Sun Hung Kai Properties Ltd, 45th Floor, Sun Hung Kai Centre, 30 Harbour Road, Wanchai, Hong Kong Special Administrative Region, People's Republic of China (office). *Telephone:* 2827-8111 (office). *Fax:* 2827-2862 (office). *E-mail:* shkp@shkp.com (office). *Website:* www.shkp.com (office).

KWOK, Thomas, BEng (Civil), MBA, JP; Hong Kong business executive; *Vice-Chairman and Managing Director, Sun Hung Kai Properties Ltd;* b. (Kwok Ping-kwong), 1951, Hong Kong; s. of Kwok Tak-seng and Kwong Siu-hing; brother of Walter Kwok and Raymond Kwok; ed London Business School and Imperial Coll., Univ. of London, UK; family originated from Zhongshan, Guangdong Prov., China; with Sun Hung Kai Properties Ltd (largest property developer in Hong Kong) 1982–, currently Vice-Chair. and Man. Dir; Chair. Route 3 (CPS) Co. Ltd; Jt Chair. IFC Development Ltd; Exec. Dir SUNeVision Holdings Ltd; Ind. Dir (non-exec.) Bank of East Asia Ltd; Exec. Vice-Pres. Real Estate Developers Asscn of Hong Kong; Govt apptd mem. Provisional Construction Industry Co-ordination Bd, Council for Sustainable Devt; fmr Chair. Property Man. Cttee Building Contractors' Asscn; fmr mem. Business Advisory Group, Land & Building Advisory Cttee, Registered Contractors' Disciplinary Bd, Gen. Chamber of Commerce Industrial Affairs Cttee, Council of Hong Kong Construction Asscn, Bd Community Chest of Hong Kong, Social Welfare Policies and Services Cttee, Council of The Open Univ. of Hong Kong; mem. Standing Cttee Ninth CPPCC Shanghai Cttee; Hon. Citizen of Guangzhou. *Address:* Sun Hung Kai Properties Ltd, 45th Floor, Sun Hung Kai Centre, 30 Harbour Road, Wanchai, Hong Kong Special Administrative Region, People's Republic of China (office). *Telephone:* 2827-8111 (office). *Fax:* 2827-2862 (office). *E-mail:* shkp@shkp.com (office). *Website:* www.shkp.com (office).

KWOK, Walter; Hong Kong business executive; *Chairman and CEO, Sun Hung Kai Properties Ltd;* b. (Kwok Ping-sheung), 1950, Hong Kong; s. of Kwok Tak-seng and Kwong Siu-hing; brother of Raymond Kwok and Thomas Kwok; m. 1st Lydia Ku 1982 (divorced 1982); m. 2nd Wendy Lee; family originated from Zhongshan, Guangdong Prov., China; Chair. and CEO Sun Hung Kai Properties Ltd (largest property developer in Hong Kong) 1990–, handed over exec. duties of SHKP to brothers while retaining title of Chair. and CEO, temporary leave of absence to visit USA and Beijing and other large cities announced 18 Feb. 2008, brought lawsuit against his brothers May 2008. *Address:* Sun Hung Kai Properties Ltd, 45th Floor, Sun Hung Kai Centre, 30 Harbour Road, Wanchai, Hong Kong Special Administrative Region, People's Republic of China (office). *Telephone:* 2827-8111 (office). *Fax:* 2827-2862 (office). *E-mail:* shkp@shkp.com (office). *Website:* www.shkp.com (office).

KWON, O-kyu, PhD; South Korean politician; b. 1952, Gangneung, Gangwon Prov.; ed Seoul Nat. Univ., Univ. of Minnesota, USA, Chung-Ang Univ., Seoul;

joined Ministry of Finance 1974, held various positions at now-defunct Econ. Planning Bd and at Ministry of Finance and Economy 1975–94; researcher, World Bank 1985, 1987; Presidential Sec. 1993–98; Alt. Exec. Dir to IMF 1997–99; Dir-Gen. Econ. Policy Bureau and Deputy Minister of Finance and Economy 1999–2001; Admin. Public Procurement Service 2002; Sr Presidential Sec. for Nat. Policy 2002–04; Perm. Rep. to OECD 2004–06; Chief Econ. Policy Adviser to the Pres. 2006; Deputy Prime Minister and Minister of Finance and Economy 2006–08. *Address:* c/o Ministry of Finance and Economy, Government Complex II, 88 Gwanmoonro, Gwacheon City, Gyeonggi Province, 427-725, South Korea (office).

KWONG, Most Rev. Peter K. K., MTh, DD, DSc; Hong Kong ecclesiastic; *Archbishop Emeritus of Hong Kong Sheng Kung Hui;* b. 28 Feb. 1936, Hong Kong; s. of Kwok-Kuen Kwong and Ching-lan Chan; m. Emily Ha; one s. two d.; ed Chung Chi Coll., Kenyon Coll. and Bexley Hall, Colgate Rochester; ordained priest, Anglican Church in Hong Kong 1966; Priest-in-Charge, Crown of Thorns Church, Hong Kong 1965–66; Vicar, St James's Church, Hong Kong 1967–70; Curate, St Paul's Church, Hong Kong 1971–72; mem. teaching staff, Chinese Univ. of Hong Kong 1972–79; Diocesan Gen. Sec. Anglican Diocese of Hong Kong and Macao 1979–81; Bishop of Hong Kong and Macao 1981–98, Archbishop and Primate of Hong Kong Sheng Kung Hui 1998–2006 (retd), now Archbishop Emer., Bishop of Diocese of Hong Kong Island 1998–2006, now Bishop Emer.; Sr Adviser Community Chest of Hong Kong 1999–; mem. Exec. Cttee, Consultative Cttee for Basic Law of Hong Kong 1985–90, Chair. Finance Cttee 1987–90; Adviser on Hong Kong Affairs, State Dept of People's Repub. of China 1992–97; mem. Preparatory Cttee for Special Admin. Region 1996–97, Selection Cttee 1996–97, CPPCC 1998–; Hon. Treas. Council of the Church of East Asia 1981–83, Chair. 1999–; Hon. Dir Chinese Christian Churches Union 1981–; mem. Court, Hong Kong Univ. 1981–; Vice-Pres. Church Mission Soc. 1995–; numerous appointments in health, educ., social welfare, youth orgs etc.; Gold Bauhinia Star. *Address:* Bishop's House, 1 Lower Albert Road, Hong Kong Special Administrative Region, People's Republic of China (office). *Telephone:* 25265355 (office). *Fax:* 25212199 (office). *E-mail:* office1@hkskh.org (office).

KY, Air Vice-Marshal Nguyen Cao; Vietnamese fmr politician and fmr air force officer; b. 8 Sept. 1930; ed High School, Hanoi and Officers' Training School, Hanoi; Flight Training, Marrakesh until 1954; commanded Transport Squadron 1954, later Commdr Tan Son Nhât Air Force Base, Repub. of Viet Nam; spent six months at U.S. Air Command and Staff Coll., Maxwell Field, Ala, USA; later Commdr Air Force, Repub. of Viet Nam; Prime Minister 1965–67; Vice-Pres. Repub. of Viet Nam 1967–71; went to USA April 1975; returned to Viet Nam 2004. *Publication:* Twenty Years and Twenty Days 1977, How We Lost the Vietnam War 1984, Buddha's Child: My Fight to Save Vietnam 2002.

KYDLAND, Finn K., BS, PhD; American (b. Norwegian) economist and academic; *Jeff Henley Chair in Economics, University of California, Santa Barbara;* b. 1943; m. Judy Henley; ed Norwegian School of Econs and Business Admin, Carnegie Mellon Univ., USA; Prof. of Econs, Carnegie Mellon Univ., Tepper School of Business, Pittsburgh, Pa –2004, now Richard P. Simmons Distinguished Prof. and and Univ. Prof. of Econs; Jeff Henley Chair in Econs, Univ. of Calif., Santa Barbara 2004–; Research Assoc., Fed. Reserve Banks of Cleveland and Dallas; mem. Editorial Bd Macroeconomic Dynamics 1996–; John Stauffer Nat. Fellowship, Hoover Inst. 1982–83, Fellow, Econometric Soc. 1992–; Research Assoc., Fed. Reserve Bank of Dallas, Fed. Reserve Bank of Cleveland; Alexander Henderson Award, Carnegie Mellon Univ. 1973, Nobel Prize in Econs (jtly with Edward C. Prescott) 2004. *Publications:* author or co-author of numerous articles in professional journals. *Address:* 2127 North Hall, University of California, Santa Barbara, CA 93106, USA (office). *Telephone:* (805) 893-5464 (office). *Fax:* (805) 893-8830 (office). *E-mail:* kydland@econ.ucsb.edu (office); kydland@andrew.cmu.edu (office). *Website:* www.econ.ucsb.edu (office).

KYEREMANTEN, Alan, BEcons, LLB; Ghanaian economist, politician, diplomatist and business executive; ed Univ. of Ghana; sr corp. exec. with subsidiary of Unilever Int., Ghana; Prin. Consultant to Man. Devt Productivity Inst.; est. Empretec Programme (promoting pvt. sector devt) 1990, expanding to 11 other countries in Africa; Amb. to USA 2001–03; Minister of Trade, Industry and Presidential Initiatives 2003–05, of Trade and Industry 2005–07; cand. for Pres. of Ghana (New Patriotic Party—NPP) 2007; fmr Hubert Humphrey Fellow, Univ. of Minnesota School of Man., USA; One of Top 100 Global Leaders for a New Millennium, Time magazine 1994. *Address:* c/o New Patriotic Party (NPP), C912/2 Duade Street, Kokomlemle, POB 3456, Accra-North, Ghana. *Telephone:* (21) 227951. *Fax:* (21) 224418. *E-mail:* npp@africanonline.com.gh. *Website:* www.nppghana.org.

KYL, Jon Llewellyn, BA, LLB; American lawyer and politician; *Senator from Arizona;* b. 25 April 1942, Oakland, Neb.; s. of John H. Kyl and Arlene Griffith; m. Caryll Collins 1964; one s. one d.; ed Univ. of Arizona; lawyer, Jennings, Strouss & Salmon, Phoenix, Ariz. 1966–86; legal counsel, Ariz. State Republican Party 1970–75; mem. US House of Reps 1986–94; Senator from Arizona 1994–. *Address:* 724 Senate Hart Building, Washington, DC 20515, USA (office). *Telephone:* (202) 224-4521 (office). *Fax:* (202) 224-2207 (office). *Website:* kyl.senate.gov (office).

KYMLICKA, Will, BA, DPhil; Canadian academic; *Canada Research Chair in Political Philosophy, Queen's University;* ed Queen's Univ., Kingston, Ont., Univ. of Oxford, UK; Lecturer, Dept of Philosophy, Queen's Univ. 1986–87, Queen's Nat. Scholar 1998–2003, Canada Research Chair in Political Philosophy 2003–; Lecturer, Dept of Philosophy, Princeton Univ., NJ 1987–88; Lecturer, Dept of Philosophy, Univ. of Toronto 1988–89, Asst Prof. 1989–90; Sr Policy Analyst, Royal Comm. on New Reproductive Technologies 1990–91; Research Dir Canadian Centre for Philosophy and Public Policy, Univ. of Ottawa 1994–98; Visiting Prof., Univ. of Ottawa 1991–93, Carleton Univ. 1994–98, Inst. for Advanced Studies, Vienna, Austria 1997, Nationalism Studies Program, Cen. European Univ., Budapest, Hungary 1998–, Univ. Pompeu Fabra, Barcelona, Spain 1998, 2003, Sciences-Po, Paris 2007; Visiting Fellow, European Forum, European Univ. Inst., Florence, Italy 1996; Pres. American Soc. for Political and Legal Philosophy 2004–06; mem. several editorial and advisory bds; Guiseppe Acerbi Prize 2001, Excellence in Research Prize, Queen's Univ. 2002, RSC Award 2003, Killam Prize in Social Sciences, Canada Council 2004; several fellowships. *Publications:* Liberalism, Community and Culture 1989, Contemporary Political Philosophy 1990, Justice in Political Philosophy (ed.) 1992, Multicultural Citizenship: A Liberal Theory of Minority Rights (Macpherson Prize, Canadian Political Science Asscn 1996, Bunche Award, American Political Science Asscn 1996) 1995, The Rights of Minority Cultures 1995, Ethnicity and Group Rights (co-ed.) 1997, States, Nations and Cultures: Spinoza Lectures 1997, Finding Our Way: Rethinking Ethnocultural Relations in Canada 1998, Citizenship in Diverse Societies (co-ed.) 2000, Politics in the Vernacular: Nationalism, Multiculturalism and Citizenship 2001, Alternative Conceptions of Civil Society (co-ed.) 2001, Can Liberal Pluralism be Exported? (co-ed.) 2001, Language Rights and Political Theory (co-ed.) 2003, Ethnicity and Democracy in Africa (co-ed.) 2004, Multiculturalism in Asia (co-ed.) 2005, Multiculturalism and the Welfare State (co-ed.) 2006, The Globalization of Ethics (co-ed.) 2007, Multicultural Odysseys: Navigating the New International Politics of Diversity 2007; numerous book chapters and articles in professional journals. *Address:* Department of Philosophy, Watson Hall 313, Queen's University, Kingston, ON K7L 3N6, Canada (office). *Telephone:* (613) 533-2182 (office); (613) 533-6000 (ext. 77043) (office). *Fax:* (613) 533-6545 (office). *E-mail:* kymlicka@queensu.ca (office). *Website:* post.queensu.ca/~kymlicka (office).

KYNASTON, Nicolas, ARCM, FRCO; British concert organist; *Organ Professor, Royal Academy of Music;* b. 10 Dec. 1941, Morebath, Devon; s. of the late Roger Tewkesbury Kynaston and of Jessie Dearn Caecilia Kynaston (née Parkes); m. 1st Judith Felicity Heron 1961 (divorced 1989); two s. two d.; m. 2nd Susan Harwood Styles 1989; ed Westminster Cathedral Choir School, Downside, Accademia Musicale Chigiana, Siena, Conservatorio Santa Cecilia, Rome, Royal Coll. of Music; Westminster Cathedral Organist 1961–71; debut recital, Royal Festival Hall 1966; recording debut 1968; concert career 1971–, travelling throughout Europe, N America, Asia and Africa; Artistic Dir J. W. Walker & Sons Ltd 1978–82, Consultant 1982–83; organist, Athens Concert Hall 1995–; Organ Prof., RAM 2002–; Jury mem. Grand Prix de Chartres 1971, St Albans Int. Organ Festival 1975; Pres. Inc. Asscn of Organists 1983–85; Chair. Nat. Organ Teachers Encouragement Scheme 1993–96; mem. Westminster Abbey Fabric Comm. 2000–05; consultant for various new organ projects; recordings include six nominated Critic's Choice, The Gramophone 1996 (also Ed.'s Choice); Hon. FRCO 1976; EMI/CFP Sales Award 1974; Deutscher Schallplattenpreis 1978. *Publication:* Transcriptions for Organ 1997. *Leisure interests:* walking, church architecture. *Address:* 28 High Park Road, Kew, Richmond-upon-Thames, Surrey, TW9 4BH, England. *Telephone:* (20) 8878-4455. *Fax:* (20) 8392-9314.

KYPRIANOU, Markos, MA; Cypriot politician; *Minister of Foreign Affairs;* b. 22 Jan. 1960, Limassol; ed Univ. of Athens, Greece, Univ. of Cambridge, UK, Harvard Law School, USA; Assoc., Antis Triantafyllides & Sons 1985–91; Pnr, Kyprianou & Boyiadjis 1991–95, George L. Savvides & Co. (following merger) 1995–2003; Municipal Councillor, Nicosia 1986–91; mem. Parl. for Nicosia 1991–2003, fmr Deputy Chair. Cttee on Foreign and European Affairs, fmr mem. Cttee on Legal Affairs, Chair. House Cttee on Financial and Budgetary Affairs 1999–2003; mem. and Chair. House of Reps Del. to Parl. Ass. of OSCE; fmr Parl. Leader Democratic Party; Minister of Finance 2003–04; EU Commr without Portfolio 2004, for Health and Consumer Protection 2004–06, for Health 2006–08; Minister of Foreign Affairs 2008–; Assoc. mem. ABA. *Address:* Ministry of Foreign Affairs, Presidential Palace Avenue, 1447 Nicosia, Cyprus (office). *Telephone:* 22401200 (office). *Fax:* 22663649 (office). *E-mail:* minforeign1@mfa.gov.cy (office). *Website:* www.mfa.gov.cy (office).

KYRIAKOU, Minos, BA; Greek shipowner and business executive; b. 1946, Athens; s. of Xenophon Kyriakou and Athina Revidies; m. (divorced); two s. one d.; ed in France and Switzerland and Columbia Univ., New York; Owner Athenian Tankers Inc. 1965–; est. Bacoil Int. and Athenian Oil Trading Inc. (oil trading corpns) 1978; Founder and Pres. Aegean Foundation 1985–; f. Antenna FM (pvt. radio station) 1987; Chair. and CEO Antenna 1988–; est. Antenna TV network 1989, through Antenna Satellite Inc. Antenna began broadcasting to whole American continent, Australia and Cyprus 1992; mem. Bd Govs Singapore Port Authority 1988; Chair. of UN org. for civil, linguistic and religious rights of nat. minorities 1989; Head, Panellinios A.C. 1997–; mem. Council of IAAF 2003–05, Hon. Life Pres. Prize 2005; Pres.Hellenic Olympic Cttee –2006, Pres. Int. Olympic Acad. 2006–; Chair. Hellenic-Kuwait Friendship Org. in Greece 1992–, Torch Relay Comm.; Founder Mediterranean Affairs Inc. (non-profit org.) publishing Mediterranean Quarterly, Washington, DC 1990–; Hon. Consul-Gen. of Singapore in Greece 1988–, Hon. Consul of Poland in Thessaloniki 1994–; Gold Medal, Legion of Honour of Poland 1984, Golden Cross of the Order of St. George 1986, Golden Medal of Honor, Repub. of Cyprus 1988, Golden Sword of Kuwait 1992. *Publications:* The Aegean Crisis (First Prize in literary competition 1987) 1986, Siesta on a Volcano 1988. *Leisure interests:* reading (especially of history), collecting paintings and sculpture. *Address:* c/o Office of the President, International Olympic Academy, 270 65 Ancient Olympia, Athens; 10–12 Kifisias Avenue, 15125 Marousi, Greece. *E-mail:* info@ioa.gr. *Website:* www.ioa.org.gr.

KYRILL, Metropolitan of Smolensk and Kaliningrad, DTheol; Russian ecclesiastic; b. (Vladimir Mikhailovich Gundyaev), 20 Nov. 1946, Leningrad; ed Leningrad Theological Acad.; took monastic vows, deacon, celibate priest 1969; personal sec. of Metropolitan of Leningrad 1970–71; ordained as archimandrite 1971; Rep. of Moscow Patriarchate to WCC, Switzerland 1971–74; mem. Cen. and Exec. Cttees., WCC 1975–79; Rector Leningrad Theological Acad. 1974–84; consecrated Bishop of Vyborg, Vicar of Leningrad Diocese 1976; Archbishop of Vyborg 1977–84, of Smolensk and Vyazma 1984–89, of Smolensk and Kaliningrad 1989–91; Metropolitan of Smolensk and Kaliningrad 1991–; Chair. Dept of External Church Relations of Moscow Patriarchate, mem. Holy Synod 1989–; Admin. Patriarchal parishes in Finland 1990–; TV broadcaster, Word of Pastor 1995–; Dr hc (Theological Acad., Budapest). *Address:* Moscow Patriarchate, Danilov Monastery, Danilovsky val. 22, 113191 Moscow, Russia. *Telephone:* (495) 230-22-50. *Fax:* (495) 230-26-19.

KYUMA, Fumio; Japanese politician; b. 4 Dec. 1940; ed Tokyo Univ.; mem. Nagasaki Prefectural Ass. 1971–80; mem. House of Reps 1980–, Parl. Vice-Minister of Transport 1987, Minister of State for Defence 1996–98, Dir-Gen. Defence Agency (State Minister) 1996–99; Chair. LDP Panel on Security Issues 2000, Chair. (acting) LDP Policy Research Council 2001, Acting LDP Sec.-Gen. 2002, Chair. LDP Gen. Council 2004, Minister of State for Defence 2006–07, Minister of Defence Jan.–July 2007. *Address:* c/o Ministry of Defence, 5-1 Ichigaya, Honmura-cho, Shinjuku-ku, Tokyo 162-8801, Japan (office).

KYUNG-WHA CHUNG (see Chung, Kyung-Wha).

L

LA FOREST, Gerard V., BCL, MA, LLD, JSD, DCL, FRSC; Canadian lawyer; *Distinguished Legal Scholar in Residence, University of New Brunswick;* b. 1 April 1926, Grand Falls, NB; s. of J. Alfred La Forest and Philomene Lajoie; m. Marie Warner 1952; five d.; ed St Francis Xavier Univ., Univ. of New Brunswick, St John's Coll. Oxford, UK and Yale Univ., USA; called to Bar, New Brunswick 1949; QC 1968; practising lawyer, Grand Falls 1951–52; Advisory Counsel, Dept of Justice, Ottawa 1952–55; Legal Adviser, Irving Oil and assoc. cos 1955–56; Assoc. Prof. of Law, Univ. of New Brunswick 1956–63, Prof. 1963–68; Dean of Law, Univ. of Alberta 1968–70; Asst Deputy Attorney-Gen. of Canada (Research and Planning) 1970–74; Commr Law Reform Comm. of Canada 1974–79; Prof. and Dir Legis. Drafting Program, Faculty of Law (Common Law Section), Univ. of Ottawa 1979–81; Judge, Court of Appeal of New Brunswick 1981; Judge, Supreme Court of Canada 1985–97; Counsel, Stewart McKelvie Stirling Scales 1998–; Distinguished Legal Scholar in Residence, Univ. of NB 1998–; consultant to fed. and provincial govts; mem. numerous cttees, public bodies etc.; Fellow, World Acad. of Art and Science; numerous hon. degrees and other distinctions. *Publications:* Disallowance and Reservation of Provincial Legislation 1955, Extradition to and from Canada 1961, The Allocation of Taxing Power Under the Canadian Constitution 1967, Natural Resources and Public Property Under the Canadian Constitution 1969, Water Law in Canada 1973. *Address:* Stewart McKelvie Stirling Scales, Suite 600, Frederick Square, POB 730, Fredericton, NB E3B 5B4 (office); 320 University Avenue, Fredericton, NB E3B 4J1, Canada (home).

LA PLANTE, Lynda, CBE; British television dramatist and novelist; *Chairman, La Plante Productions Ltd;* b. 15 March 1946, Formby; m. Richard La Plante (divorced); ed Royal Coll. of Dramatic Art; fmr actress; appeared in The Gentle Touch, Out, Minder; founder and Chair. La Plante Productions 1994–. *Television includes:* Prime Suspect 1991, 1993, 1995, Civvies, Framed, Seekers, Widows (series), Comics (two-part drama) 1993, Cold Shoulder 2 1996, Cold Blood, Bella Mafia 1997, Trial and Retribution 1997–, Killer Net 1998, Mind Games 2000, The Warden 2001, Framed 2002, Widows (mini-series) 2002, The Commander 2003. *Publications include:* The Widows 1983, The Widows II 1985, The Talisman 1987, Bella Mafia 1991, Framed 1992, Civvies 1992, Prime Suspect 1992, Seekers 1993, Entwined 1993, Prime Suspect 2 1993, Lifeboat 1994, Cold Shoulder 1994, Prime Suspect 3 1994, She's Out 1995, The Governor 1996, Cold Blood 1996, Trial and Retribution 1997, Cold Heart 1998, Trial and Retribution 2 1998, Trial and Retribution 3 1999, Trial and Retribution 4 2000, Sleeping Cruelty 2000, Trial and Retribution 5 2002, Trial and Retribution 6 2002, Royal Flush 2002, Like a Charm (short stories) 2004, Above Suspicion (novel) 2004, The Red Dahlia 2006, Clean Cut 2007. *Address:* La Plante Productions Ltd, Paramount House, 162–170 Wardour Street, London, W1F 8ZX, England (office). *Telephone:* (20) 7734-6767. *Fax:* (20) 7734-7878. *Website:* www.laplanteproductions.com.

LA RIVIÈRE, Jan Willem Maurits, PhD; Dutch environmental biologist and academic; *Professor Emeritus, UNESCO-IHE Institute for Water Education;* b. 24 Dec. 1923, Rotterdam; m. Louise A. Kleijn 1958; one s. two d.; ed Erasmus Gymnasium, Rotterdam and Delft Univ. of Tech.; Postdoctoral Rockefeller Fellowship, Stanford Univ., USA; mem. scientific staff, Microbiology Dept, Delft Univ. of Tech. 1953–63; Prof. of Environmental Microbiology and Deputy Dir, Int. Inst. for Infrastructural, Hydraulic and Environmental Eng (now UNESCO-IHE Inst. for Water Educ.), Delft 1963–88, Prof. Emer. and Hon. Fellow 1996–; Visiting Prof., Harvard Univ. 1967–68; Sec.-Gen. ICSU 1988–93; mem. numerous int. and nat. cttees, del. to UN confs, adviser, lecturer etc.; Fellow, World Acad. of Art and Science; Hon. mem. Council, Int. Cell Research Org.; Hon. Fellow, UNESCO-IHE Inst. for Water Educ.; Kt, Order of Lion of Netherlands 1988. *Publications:* Microbiology of Liquid Waste Treatment 1977, Biotechnology in Development Cooperation 1983, Water Quality: Present Status, Future Trends 1987, Threats to the World's Water 1989, Co-operation between Natural and Social Scientists in Global Change Research: Imperatives, Realities, Opportunities 1991, The Delft School of Microbiology in Historical Perspective 1996; some 80 publs in fields of microbiology, environment, water quality and int. scientific co-operation. *Leisure interests:* gardening, travel. *Address:* UNESCO-IHE, Westvest 7, 2611 AX Delft, Netherlands (office); 107 Veenweg, 2493 ZC The Hague, Netherlands (home). *Telephone:* (70) 3205825 (home). *E-mail:* lark@worldonline.nl (home). *Website:* www.unesco-ihe.org (office).

LA RUSSA, Ignazio; Italian lawyer and politician; *Minister of Defence;* b. 18 July 1947, Paternò; s. of Anthony La Russa; three s.; ed St Gallen, Switzerland, Univ. of Pavia; served in Italian mil.; early career in pvt. law practice; Regional Councillor, Lombardy 1985; mem. Camera dei Deputati (Parl.) for Liguria 1992–, Deputy Speaker 1994, Chair. Cttee on Parl. Immunity 1996–2001; Minister of Defence 2008–; mem. Italian Socialist Movt 1992–95, Alleanza Nazionale 1995–2008, Chair. AN Parl. Group in Chamber of Deputies 2001, 2004–05, AN – The People of Liberty 2008–. *Address:* Ministry of Defence, Palazzo Baracchini, Via XX Settembre 8, 00187 Rome, Italy (office). *Telephone:* (06) 46911 (office). *E-mail:* pi@smd.difesa.it (office); larussa_i@camera.it (office). *Website:* www.difesa.it (home); www.ignaziolarussa.it (office).

LA TOURETTE, John Ernest, BA, MA, PhD; American economist; *President and Professor Emeritus, Northern Illinois University;* b. 5 Nov. 1932, Perth Amboy, NJ; s. of John C. La Tourette and Charlotte R. Jones; m. Lillie (Lili) M. Drum 1957; one s. one d.; ed Rutgers Univ.; served in USAF, rank of Capt. 1955–58; Instructor in Econs, Rutgers Univ. 1960–61; Asst Prof., Assoc. Prof., Prof., State Univ. of New York, Binghamton 1961–76, Chair. Dept of Econs 1967–75, Provost for Grad. Studies 1975–76; Vice-Provost for Research and Dean, Grad. School, Bowling Green State Univ., Ohio 1976–79; Vice-Pres. and Provost, Northern Illinois Univ. 1979–86, Pres. 1986–2000, Pres. and Prof. Emer. 2000–; Ford Foundation Fellowship 1963; Brookings Inst. Research Professorship 1966–67; Univ. Research Fellowship, State Univ. of NY 1970; mem. Yavapai Coll. Foundation Bd, West Yavapai Guidance Clinic, Prescott, Ariz. *Publications:* contribs to journals of econs and to studies of Bearnais Protestantism (France), articles in the Bulletin du Centre d'Etude du Protestantisme Bearnais. *Leisure interests:* genealogy, history of Protestantism in Bearn, France, travel, distance educ. *Address:* 218 S Deerview Circle, Prescott, AZ 86303, USA (home). *Telephone:* (928) 443-1151 (home). *E-mail:* jlatour7@commspeed.net (home).

LAAGE, Gerhart, DiplIng; German architect and town planner; b. 19 April 1925, Hamburg; s. of Richard Laage and Valerie Laage (née Pitzner); m. Ursula Gebert 1959; one s. two d.; ed Technische Hochschule, Brunswick; freelance architect 1954–; Prof. of Theory of Architectural Planning, Univ. of Hanover 1963–92, Pro-Rector and Rector 1973–75, Dean 1983–84; Adviser to Fed. Govt on Planning for City of Bonn 1977–82; Pres. Fed. Architects Assen 1990–92. *Publications:* Wohnungen von heute für Ansprüche von Morgen 1971, Planung und Mitbestimmung 1973, Planungstheorie für Architekten 1976, Wohnen beginnt auf der Strasse 1977, Handbuch für Architekturplanung 1978, Weder Traum noch Trauma 1978, Das Stadthaus–mehr als eine Bauform 1980, Kosten- und flächensparendes Bauen 1984, Warum wird nicht immer so gebaut 1985, Von Architecten, Bossen und Banausen 1989, Architektur ist Glücksache 1997, Die emotionale stadt 2005. *Address:* Bei den Mühren 70, 20457 Hamburg, Germany (office). *Telephone:* (40) 431950 (office). *Fax:* (40) 4319599 (office). *Website:* www.ppl-hh.de (office).

LAANEOTS, Lt-Gen. Ants; Estonian military officer; *Chief of Defence;* b. 16 Jan. 1948, Kilingi-Nõmme; m.; two c.; ed Higher Mil. School, Ukraine, Malinovsky Armoured and Mechanized Forces Acad., Moscow, NATO Defence Coll., Rome, Finnish Nat. Defence Coll.; Platoon Leader, then Co. Commdr, then Battalion Commdr, 300th Tank Regt for Soviet Army in Ukraine 1970–78; posted to Soviet-Chinese border in Eastern Kazakhstan 1981–87, Exec. Officer, 96th Tank Regt 1981–83, Commdr 180th Tank Regt 1983–85, Deputy Commdr Chief of Staff, 78th Armoured Div. 1985–87; deployment to Ethiopia 1987–89, mil. advisor to infantry div. Commdr 1987, mil. advisor to Army Corps Gen. 1988–89; Chief of Regional Dept of Defence, Tartu, Estonia 1989–91; Chief of Gen. Staff 1991–94, 1997–99; Insp. Gen. of Defence Forces 1997–2000; promoted to Maj. Gen. 1998; Head of Baltic Defence Research Centre 2000–01; Commdt, Estonian Nat. Defence Coll. 2001–06; Chief of Defence 2006–; promoted to Lt Gen. 2008; Order of the Cross of the Eagle. *Address:* Ministry of Defence, Sakala 1, Tallinn 15094, Estonia (office). *Telephone:* 717-0022 (office). *Fax:* 717-0001 (office). *E-mail:* info@kmin.ee (office). *Website:* www.mod.gov.ee (office).

LAAR, Mart, MA; Estonian politician and historian; b. 22 April 1960, Viljandi; s. of Tõnis Laar and Aime Laar; m. Katrin Kask 1982; one s. one d.; ed Tartu State Univ.; history teacher, schools of Tallinn 1983–85; Head of Dept, Ministry of Culture of Estonia 1987–90; Deputy of Christian Democratic Party, Supreme Soviet of Estonia 1989–92; mem. Constitutional Ass. 1991–92, mem. Riigikogu (Estonian Parl.) 1992–; Founder and Chair. Pro Patria Union (Isamaaliit) Party 1992–95; Prime Minister of Estonia 1992–94, 1999–2002; apptd mem. ISTAL by European Comm.; mem. Advisory Bd Springfellow 2003–; fmr Pres. Council of Historians of the Foundation of the Estonia Inheritance, Soc. for the Preservation of Estonia History, Soc. of Univ. Students of Estonia; Estonian Order of the Nat. Coat of Arms (Second Class); Cavaliere di Gran Groce dei Santi Maurizio e Lazzaro; Das Grosskreuz des Verdienstorderns des Bundesrepublic Deutschland; Nat. Order of Merit, Malta; Grand Cross, Ordre nat. du Mérite, France; Young Politician of the World (Jr Chamber Int.) 1993; European Tax Payer Assen Year Prize 2001, European Bull, Davastoeconomic Forum, Global Link Award 2001, Adam Smith Award 2002. *Publications:* June 14 1941, Estonian History, War in the Woods, Little Country That Could, Back to the Future, Ten Years of Freedom in the CEE, and a number of scientific papers. *Leisure interests:* tennis, squash, history. *Address:* Estonian Parliament Riigikogu, Lossi plats 1A, 15161 Tallinn, Estonia (office). *Telephone:* 631-6612 (office). *Fax:* 631-6604 (office). *E-mail:* mart.laar@riigikogu.ee (office). *Website:* www.riigikogu.ee (office).

LABARDAKIS, Augoustinos; Greek ecclesiastic; *Greek Orthodox Metropolitan of Germany and Exarch of Central Europe;* b. (Georges Labardakis), 7 Feb. 1938, Voukoulies-Chania, Crete; s. of Emmanouil Labardakis and Eurydike Labardakis; ed theological schools in Chalki, Turkey, Salzburg, Austria, and Münster and West Berlin, Germany; ordained as priest, Greek Orthodox Church, FRG 1964; worked as priest, West Berlin 1964–72; elected Bishop of Elaia 1972; auxiliary bishop, Greek Orthodox Metropolitanate of Germany 1972–80; elected Greek Orthodox Metropolitan of Germany and Exarch of Cen. Europe 1980–; Chair. Comm. of Orthodox Church in Germany 2006–; Great Fed. Cross of Merit (Germany), Order of Merit of the Fed. State of North Rhine-Westphalia, Grand Commdr, Order of Honour of the Hellenic Repub.; Hon. DTheol (Bonn) 2006. *Address:* Greek Orthodox Metropolitanate of Germany, Dietrich-Bonhoeffer-Strasse 2, 53227 Bonn (office); PO Box 300555, 53185 Bonn, Germany (office). *Telephone:* (228) 9737840 (office). *Fax:* (228) 97378424 (office). *E-mail:* metropolit@orthodoxie.net (office). *Website:* www.orthodoxie.net (office).

LABIS; French ballet dancer, academic, choreographer and writer; b. 5 Sept. 1936, Vincennes; s. of Umberto Labis and Renée Labis (née Cousin); m. Christiane Vlassi 1959; two s.; ed Ecole de danse académique de l'Opéra, Paris; mem. Corps de Ballet at the Paris Opera 1952, Premier Danseur 1959, Premier Danseur Etoile Chorégraphe 1960–65, Maître de Ballet 1965–, Prof. of Dance; Prof. of Dance, Ecole de Danse; Prof. d'Adage et de Repertoire; Guest Dancer in London, Paris, Washington, Tokyo, Moscow, Kiev, Leningrad, Rome, Milan, Berlin, Munich, Stuttgart, Rio de Janeiro, Hong Kong, Singapore and Sydney; Chief Choreographer at the Paris Opera; World Amb. for l'Ecole Française; devised choreography for productions including Rencontre (TV) 1961, Arcades 1964, Romeo and Juliet 1967, Spartacus 1973, Raymonda 1973; has created and interpreted numerous ballets including Giselle, Sleeping Beauty, Swan Lake, Don Quixote, Pas de Dieux (Gene Kelly), Marines (Georges Skibine), Icare (Serge Lifar), Pas de danse (music by Gluck), Schéhérazade, Coppélia, Sarabande, Casse-Noisette, Etudes (Harold Lander), Spartacus, Arcades, Romeo et Juliette, Raymonda, Spartacus, Romeo and Juliette, Arcades (Berlioz), Sarabande (Rossini); Chevalier des Arts et Lettres; Chevalier, Légion d'honneur 2002; Prix Vaslaw Nijinsky. *Address:* Opéra de Paris, 8 rue Scribe, 75009 Paris (office); 13 Avenue Rubens, 78400 Chatou, France. *Telephone:* 1-30-53-48-07 (Paris) (home); 66-3781398 (mobile). *Fax:* 1-30-53-57-80 (Paris) (home). *E-mail:* attilio.labis.choregraphe@wanadoo.fr (home). *Website:* www.opera-de-paris.fr (office).

LABRIE, Fernand, OC, BA, MD, PhD, FRCP, FRSC; Canadian endocrinologist, physician and academic; *Professor of Physiology and Director, Laboratory of Molecular Endocrinology, Laval University;* b. 28 June 1937, Québec; m. Nicole Cantin; two s. three d.; ed Séminaire de Québec, Laval Univ.; residency in Internal Medicine, L'Hôtel-Dieu de Québec 1962–63; Post-doctoral research, Dept of Biochemistry, Univs of Cambridge and Sussex, UK 1966–68, Lab. of Molecular Biology, Univ. of Cambridge; Dir Lab. of Molecular Endocrinology, Laval Univ. 1969–2009, Dir Medical Research Group in Molecular Endocrinology 1973–2008, Prof., Dept of Physiology 1974–, Head, Dept of Physiology and Anatomy 1990–2002; full-time physician, Dept of Medicine, Le Centre Hospitalier de l'Université Laval (CHUL) 1972–, Head, Dept of Physiology and Anatomy 1990–2002, Dir of Research, CHUL Research Centre 1982–2008; Pres. Le Fonds de la recherche en santé du Québec 1992–95, Canadian Soc. of Endocrinology and Metabolism 1978–79; mem. Medical Advisory Bd The Gairdner Foundation, Toronto 1979–1985; Consultant, Study Section, Centre for Population Research, NICHD, NIH, Bethesda, Md 1976, 1977, 1979, 1980, 1983, 1984; mem. Exec. Int. Soc. of Endocrinology 1980–88; Invited Expert, WHO Task Force on the Regulation of Male Fertility 1981; Pres. Canadian Soc. for Clinical Investigation 1981–82; mem. Science Council of Canada 1983–87; Vice-Pres. Int. Soc. of Neuroendocrinology 1992–96; Founding Bd mem. Soc. Innovatech Québec et Chaudière-Appalaches, Pres. 2008–10, High Tech. Investment Fund 1994–, Pôle Québec-Chaudière-Appalaches 2002–; mem. Life Sciences Cttee La Caisse de Dépôt du Québec 2005–; Co-Pres. Pôle Québec Chaudière-Appalaches 2005–08, Pres. 2008–; Pres. Int. Cttee Int. Congress on Hormonal Steroids and Homones & Cancer 2008–10; Chair. Organizing Cttees of ten Congresses held in Québec City, including 7th Int. Congress of Endocrinology 1984 and mem. Scientific or Programme Cttees of 61 congresses held worldwide; Pres. 13th Int. Congress on Hormonal Steroids and Hormones & Cancer, Québec City 2008; Assoc. Ed. Journal of Molecular and Cellular Endocrinol 1973–81; Corresp. Ed. Journal of Steroid Biochemistry and Molecular Biology 1987–95; mem. Editorial Bd Journal of Cyclic Nucleotide Research 1974–80, Endocrinology 1977–81, Endocrine-Related Cancer 1994–98, Journal of Steroid Biochemistry and Molecular Biology 1995–; mem. 53 orgs, including Canadian Soc. of Endocrinology and Metabolism, Endocrine Soc. (USA), Canadian Soc. for Clinical Investigation, American Soc. of Clinical Oncology, American Asscn for Cancer Research, American Urological Asscn, Soc. for Endocrinology (UK), Biochemical Soc. (GB), American Soc. for Biochemistry and Molecular Biology, American Soc. of Physiology, la Soc. Française d'Endocrinologie, Canadian Fertility and Andrology Soc., World Fed. of Scientists, Soc. for Investigative Dermatology, Canadian Acad. of Health Sciences 2005; Officer, Ordre nat. du Québec 1991; Dr hc (Université de Caen, France) 1996, (Univ. of Athens) 2006; Prince of Wales Award 1957, Medal of Gov. Gen. of Canada 1957, Award of Coll. of Physicians and Surgeons of Prov. of Quebec 1959, Grant Medal 1960, Centennial Fellow, MRC of Canada 1966–69, Scholar of MRC of Canada 1969–73, Assoc. of MRC of Canada 1973–96, Assoc. of Royal Coll. of Physicians and Surgeons of Canada 1973–, Vincent Medal, Asscn Canadienne-Française pour l'Avancement des Sciences 1976, Medal of City of Nice 1977, Research Award, Soc. for the Study of Reproduction 1980, Award of Fondation de recherche en hormonologie, Paris 1981, MDS Health Group Award 1981, Medal of Collège de France, Paris 1984, Canada Award for Excellence in Business 1985, Award 'Fidéides' of Chamber of Commerce of Sainte-Foy 1985, 1990, (high-tech) 1997, Certificate of Merit Celebration of Govt of Canada 1988, French Canadian Scientist of the Year 1989, Magazine 'Aujourd'hui la Science' of CBC 1989, Michel Sarrazin Award, Canadian Physiological Soc. 1990, Michel Sarrazin Award, Club de recherches cliniques du Québec 1990, Canada Award for Excellence in Business 1990, Gloire de l'Escolle, Asscn des Diplômés de l'Université Laval 1991, Grand Québécois, Chambre de commerce et d'industrie du Québec métropolitain 1991, Antoni Nalecz Award, Canadian Soc. of Endocrinology and Metabolism 1990, 1993, Recognition Prize, Séminaire de Québec 1993, Mur des Célébrités, Québec 1994, MRC Distinguished Scientist 1996, Exceptional Merit Award, Canadian Soc. of Endocrinology and Metabolism 1998, The Izaak-Walton-Killam Memorial Prize, Canada Council for the Arts 1998, Award of Int. Acad. of Human Reproduction, 10th World Congress of Human Reproduction, Bahia 1999, Golden Spatula, Quebec Alpine Ski Fed., Career involvement in devt of Alpine Skiing 1999, Grand Bâtisseur Québécois 2000, Commdr, Laval Univ., Rector's Circle 2000–, The Queen's Golden Jubilee Medal (Canadian Govs Gen.) 2002,

mem. Excelcia Circle of Bioquebec, The Quebec Bio-Industries Network 2003, Personality — Special Issue of Business Plus Oct. 2003, chosen as one of the "101 Québécois au sommet de l'action" for Entreprendre magazine 2004, Mentor Scientifique Award, Club de recherches cliniques du Québec 2004, chosen among the celebrated grads of Laval Univ. 2004, chosen by public as First Entrepreneur of the Year, Chambre de Commerce des Entrepreneurs de Québec 2005, recognized as one of top five men and women of influence in Quebec City (Le Soleil) 2005, Armand-Frappier Prize (highest distinction from Govt Quebec) 2006, Reconnaissance Prize, Le Petit Séminaire de Québec 2006, Economy Leader of Quebec City area, Le Soleil and Radio-Canada 2006, King Faisal Int. Prize in Medicine, King Faisal Foundation (co-recipient) 2007, Scientific Career Award, Asscn des Médecins de Langue Française du Canada 2007, Grad. of Influence, Laval Univ. 2008, Career Award, Int. Soc. of Endocrinological Gynecology 2009. *Publications:* Proceedings of the 12th International Congress on Hormonal Steroïds and Hormones & Cancer (ed.) 2007, Endocrinology and the Prostate, Best Practice and Research, Clinical Endocrinology and Metabolism, Vol. 22, No. 2, (Guest Ed.) 2008; 1205 publs with over 40,000 citations (most-cited Canadian scientist (all disciplines) in world literature). *Address:* Laboratory of Molecular Endocrinology and Oncology, Le Centre hospitalier de l'Université Laval, 2705 boulevard Laurier, Québec, PQ G1V 4G2 (office); 2989 de la Promenade, Ste-Foy, PQ G1W 2J5, Canada (home). *Telephone:* (418) 654-2704 (office). *Fax:* (418) 654-2735 (office). *E-mail:* fernand.labrie@crchul.ulaval.ca (office). *Website:* www .crchul.ulaval.ca (office); www.fernandlabrie.com.

LABRO, Philippe; French screenwriter, director and actor; b. 1936, Menthon-Saint-Bernard, Haute-Savoie; ed Washington and Lee Univ., Va, USA; worked as radio and newspaper reporter; soldier in Algeria early 1960s; began writing for French TV on short films. *Films include:* as actor: Le chat et la souris 1975; as writer: Tout peut arriver (aka Don't Be Blue) 1969, Sans mobile apparent (Without Apparent Motive) (also actor, uncredited) 1971, L'héritier (The Inheritor, adaption) (also actor, uncredited) 1973, Le hasard et la violence (Chance and Violence) 1974, L'alpagueur (aka Hunter Will Get You, USA) 1976, La crime (aka Cover Up) 1983, Rive droite, rive gauche (Right Bank, Left Bank) 1984; as writer and dir: Des feux mal éteints (Poorly Extinguished Fires) 1994, Foreign Student 1994. *Television:* Les deux D: Marie Dubois, Françoise Dorléac (dir) 1966. *Address:* c/o Editions Gallimard, 5 rue Sébastien-Bottin, 75328 Paris Cedex 07, France.

LABUDA, Gerard, PhD; Polish historian and academic; *Professor, University of Poznań;* b. 28 Dec. 1916, Nowahuta, Kartuzy Dist; s. of Stanisław Labuda and Anastazja Baranowska; m. Countess Alberta Wielopolska 1943 (died 1999); four s. one d.; ed Clandestine Univ. of Western Lands, Warsaw; Docent 1945–50, Extraordinary Prof. 1950–56, Prof. Univ. of Poznań 1956–; Rector, Adam Mickiewicz Univ., Poznań 1962–65; Sec.-Gen. Poznań Soc. of Friends of Learning 1961–72, Pres. 1972–75; Ed. Roczniki Historyczne (Annals of History) 1969–85; Corresp. mem. Polish Acad. of Sciences 1964–69, mem. 1969–, mem. Presidium 1972–94, Vice-Pres. 1984–86, 1987–89; mem. Consultative Council attached to Chair. of State Council 1986–89; Chair. Cttee for Research on Poles Living Abroad, Polish Acad. of Sciences 1973–80; fmr Chair. Poznań Br. of Polish Acad. of Sciences; Pres. Polish Acad. of Sciences and Letters, Kraków 1989–94; mem. European Soc. of Culture 1963–; Fellow Wissenschaftskoll. zu Berlin, Inst. for Advanced Studies 1981–82; mem. New York Acad. of Sciences 1995; Kt's Cross, Order of Polonia Restituta 1954, Officer's Cross 1960, Commdr's Cross 1976; Commdr's Cross with Star 1986, Great Cross 1996 and others; Dr hc (Gdańsk) 1986, (Toruń) 1993, (Jagiellon Univ. Kraków) 1995, (Warsaw) 1997, (Wrocław) 1999; State Prizes (3rd class) 1949, 1951, (2nd class) 1970; Palacki Medal (Czechoslovakia) 1968, Johannes Gottfried Herder Preis, Vienna 1991. *Publications:* Pierwsze państwo słowiańskie—państwo Samona (First Slavonic State–Samon's State) 1949, Fragmenty dziejów Słowiańszczyzny Zachodniej (Fragments of History of the West Slavs) Vols I–III 1960–74, Polska granica zachodnia: Tysiąc lat dziejów politycznych (The Western Frontier of Poland: A Thousand Years of Political History) 1971–1974, co-author, Słownik Starożytności Słowiańskich (Dictionary of Slavonic Antiquities), Historia Pomorza (History of Pomerania), Historia dyplomacji polskiej (Średniowiecze) (History of Polish Medieval Diplomacy) 1981, Dzieje Zakonu Krzyżackiego w Prusach (History of the Order of the Teutonic Knights in Prussia) 1986, Studia nad początkami państwa polskiego (Studies of the Origin of the Polish State Vols I and II) 1987–88, Mieszko II, King of Poland (1025–1034) 1992, Kashubian and their History 1995, Polsko-niemieckie rozmowy o przeszłości (Polish and German Talks About the Past) 1996, Kaszubskie, pomorskie i morskie (Kashubian, Pomeranian and Sea) 2000, Święty Wojciech, biskup-męczennik 2000, Mieszko I 2002, Szkice historyuzne X i XI wieku 2004. *Leisure interests:* sociology, linguistics. *Address:* ul. Kanclerska 8, 60-327 Poznań, Poland. *Telephone:* (61) 8673585. *Fax:* (61) 8687600 (home).

LABUS, Miroljub, MSc, PhD; Serbian politician, lawyer and economist; b. 27 Feb. 1947, Mala Krsna; s. of Zdravko Labus and Draginja Labus (née Pavlovic); m. Olivera Labus (née Grabic); two d.; ed Belgrade Univ.; attorney-at-law, Belgrade 1970–71; Lecturer in Law, Belgrade Univ. 1971, Prof. of Econs 1971–; Fulbright Lecturer, Cornell Univ., USA 1983, Visiting Asst Prof. 1984; Sr Adviser, Fed. Statistics Office 1986–94; mem. Bd Ekonomska Misl i Ekonomske Analize journals; Fellow, Econ. Inst. 1993–99; Deputy Prime Minister and Minister of Foreign Econ. Relations, Fed. Repub. of Yugoslavia 1987–91, Deputy Prime Minister, with responsibility for econ. relations with the int. community 2001–03; presidential cand. 2002; Deputy Prime Minister in charge of European Integration, Repub. of Serbia 2004–06; mem. Fed. Parl. and Cttee on Monetary Policy; Vice-Pres. Democratic Party 1994–97; mem. Standing Cttee on Econ. Affairs, UNDPM Sarajevo 1996; with UNDP 1996–97; joined IBRD 1997; Ed. The Economic Trends, Fed. Statistics Office, Belgrade, The Economic Barometer, Econ. Inst., Belgrade 2000–; Pres.

Admin. Bd G17 Plus movt (later G17 Plus party) 1999–2000, Pres. G17 Plus 2003–. *Publications:* Social and Collective Property Rights 1987, General Equilibrium Modelling (co-author) 1990, Contemporary Political Economy 1991, Foundations of Political Economy 1992, Foundations of Economics 1995, other books and numerous articles on econ. problems. *Leisure interests:* woodwork, skiing. *Address:* c/o Office of the Prime Minister, Nemanjina 11, 11000 Belgrade (office); Gospodar Jevremova str. 13, Belgrade, Serbia (home).

LaBUTE, Neil; American playwright, film writer and director; b. 19 March 1963, Detroit, Mich.; m.; two c.; ed Brigham Young Univ., Univ. of Kan., New York Univ. *Films include:* In the Company of Men (writer, dir) (Sundance Film Festival Filmmakers' Trophy, Soc. of Tex. Film Critics Best Original Screenplay Award, New York Film Critics' Circle Best First Film) 1997, Your Friends and Neighbors (writer, dir) 1998, Tumble (writer) 2000, Nurse Betty (dir) 2000, Possession (screenplay writer, dir) 2002, The Shape of Things (writer, dir) 2003, The Wicker Man 2006, Lakeview Terrace 2008. *Theatre productions include:* Woyzeck, Dracula, Sangguinarians & Sycophants, Ravages, Rounder, Lepers, Filthy Talk For Troubled Times, In the Company of Men (Asscn for Mormon Letters Award for Drama 1993) 1992, Bash: Latterday Plays 2000, The Shape of Things 2001, The Distance From Here (Almeida, London) 2002, The Mercy Seat 2002, Merge 2003, Wrecks (Everyman Palace, Cork) 2005, This is How it Goes (New York, and Donmar Warehouse London) 2005, Some Girl(s) 2005, Land of the Dead/Helter Skelter 2007, Reasons to be Pretty 2008. *Television includes:* Bash: Latter-Day Plays 2001. *Publications include:* In the Company of Men 1998, Your Friends and Neighbors 1999, Bash: Latterday Plays 2000, The Shape of Things 2001, The Distance from Here 2003, The Mercy Seat 2003, Seconds of Pleasure (short stories) 2004. *Address:* William Morris Agency, One William Morris Place, Beverly Hills, CA 90212, USA (office). *Telephone:* (310) 859-4000 (office). *Fax:* (310) 859-4462 (office). *Website:* www.wma.com (office).

LACALLE HERRERA, Luis Alberto; Uruguayan fmr head of state, farmer and lawyer; b. 13 July 1941, Montevideo; s. of Carlos Lacalle and María Hortensia de Herrera Uriarte; m. María Julia Pou Brito del Pino 1970; two s. one d.; ed Universidad de la República Oriental del Uruguay; journalist, Clarín daily newspaper 1961; currently contributor to El Debate of Montevideo; columnist, Correo de los Viernes, La Patria de Montevideo, Spanish newspaper ABC; joined Partido Nacional (Blanco) 1958; Deputy to Legis. Ass. 1971–73; elected Senator 1984, mem. Cttee for Public Funds, for Transportation, for Public Works; cand. for Pres. for Blanco Party 1989; Pres. of Uruguay 1990–95; presidential cand. 2004; Leader Nationalist sector, Herrerismo, and is part of Party's Directorate; Co-founder MERCOSUR 1991; mem. Club de Madrid; Gran Collar de la Orden Nacional del Mérito del Ecuador 1990, Gran Collar de la Orden al Mérito de Chile 1991, Collar de la Orden del Libertador Gral. San Martín de Argentina 1991, Gran Collar del Cóndor de los Andes de Bolivia 1991, Gran Cruz de la Orden Cruzeiro do Sul de Brasil 1991, Grand Cross of the Most Distinguished Order of St Michael and St George; Dr hc (Universidad Complutense de Madrid) 1992, (Hebrew Univ. of Jerusalem) 1992, (Autonomous Univ. of Guadalajara, Mexico) 1993, (Nat. Univ. of Paraguay) 1993; Gold Medal of the Xunta de Galicia (Spain) 1994, Jerusalem Award 1995. *Address:* c/o Oficina del Presidente, Casa de Gobierno, Edif. Libertad, Avda Luis Alberto de Herrera 3350, Montevideo, Uruguay.

LACARTE-MURÓ, Julio; Uruguayan international civil servant and diplomat (retd); b. 29 March 1918, Montevideo; s. of Antonio Lacarte and Julieta Muró de Lacarte; m. Ivy E. O'Hara de Lacarte 1940; three c.; Deputy Exec. Sec. GATT 1947–48, Amb. to GATT, Chair. (Governing Council and the Contracting Parties), has participated in all eight GATT rounds 1947, 1949, 1951, 1956, 1960–61, 1964–67, 1973–79, 1986–93 (Uruguay round), as Perm. Rep. for Uruguay 1961–66, 1982–92; mem., later Chair. Appellate Body WTO 1995–; fmr Minister of Industry and Trade; fmr Amb. to numerous countries, including EC, India, Japan, USA and Thailand; fmr Deputy Dir Int. Trade and Balance-of-Payments Div., UN; fmr Dir Econ. Cooperation Among Developing Countries, UNCTAD; lecturer and int. consultant; decorations from Ecuador, Bolivia, Argentina and Germany. *Publications:* The Globalisation of World Trade 1994 and other books on int. trade. *Leisure interests:* tennis, golf, chess, history. *Address:* c/o GATT, Centre William Rappard, 154 rue de Lausanne, 1211 Geneva 21, Switzerland.

LACEY, Richard Westgarth, MD, PhD, FRCPath; British microbiologist and academic; *Professor Emeritus of Medicial Microbiology, University of Leeds;* b. 11 Oct. 1940, London; s. of Jack Lacey and Sybil Lacey; m. Fionna Margaret Lacey 1972; two d.; ed Felsted School, Essex, Jesus Coll., Cambridge, London Hosp.; house officer, London Hosp. 1964–66, St Mary's Hosp., Eastbourne 1966; Sr House Officer, Registrar in Pathology, Bristol Royal Infirmary 1966–68; Lecturer, Reader in Clinical Microbiology, Univ. of Bristol 1968–74; Consultant in Chemical Pathology, Queen Elizabeth Hosp., King's Lynn 1975–83; Consultant in Infectious Diseases, East Anglian Regional Health Authority 1974–83, Leeds Health Authority 1983–98; Prof. of Medical Microbiology, Univ. of Leeds 1983–98, Prof. Emer. 1998–; consultant, WHO 1983–; Dick Memorial Lecture, Edin. Veterinary School 1990; Evian Health Award Winner 1989, Caroline Walker Award 1989, Campaign for Freedom of Information Award 1990. *Publications:* Safe Shopping, Safe Cooking, Safe Eating 1989, Unfit for Human Consumption 1991, Hard to Swallow 1994, Mad Cow Disease: the History of B.S.E. in Britain 1994, Poison on a Plate 1998 and over 200 papers and articles for journals. *Leisure interests:* gardening, painting, antique restoration (intermittently). *Address:* Department of Biochemistry and Microbiology, University of Leeds, Leeds, LS2 9JT; Carlton Manor, Nr Yeadon, Leeds, LS19 7BE, England (home). *Telephone:* (113) 233 5596. *Website:* www.bmb.leeds.ac.uk (office).

LACHAPELLE, David; American photographer; b. 1969, NC; ed Art Student's League, School of Visual Arts NC; began career by creating fine art images for Interview Magazine; photographer advertising campaigns for Keds, Estee Lauder, Prescriptives, Volvo, MasCosmetics, Diesel Jeans; widely published in fashion, music and entertainment magazines; photography prints and TV for clients including Jean Paul Gaultier, Giorgio Armani, MTV, Pepsi and Levis; fashion portraits of celebrities include Debbie Harry, Britney Spears, Madonna, David Bowie and Elton John; Best New Photographer of the Year, French Photo Magazine 1995, American Photo Magazine 1995; Photographer of the Year, VH1 Fashion Awards 1996; Infinity Award, Int. Centre of Photography 1997. *Film:* Rize (dir) 2005. *Publication:* LaChapelle Land (vol. of photographic images) 1997. *Address:* c/o Barbican Gallery, Barbican Centre, Silk Street, London, EC2Y 8DS, England (office).

LACHMANN, Henri; French business executive; *Chairman, Supervisory Board, Schneider Electric SA;* b. 13 Sept. 1938; m.; two c.; ed Ecole des Hautes Etudes Commerciales (HEC); with Arthur Andersen 1963; joined Pompey steel co. (later Strafor Facom) 1970, Chair. Strafor Facom 1981; Dir Schneider Electric SA 1996–, Chair. and CEO 1999–2006, Chair. Supervisory Bd 2006–; mem. Bd of Dirs AXA Group; mem. Man. Cttee AXA Millésimes (SAS), Comité d'Orientation of Institut de l'Entreprise; Chair. Centre Chirurgical Marie Lannelongue. *Address:* Schneider Electric SA, 43–45 boulevard Franklin-Roosevelt, 92500 Rueil-Malmaison, France (office). *Telephone:* 1-41-29-70-00 (office). *Fax:* 1-41-29-71-00 (office). *Website:* www.schneider-electric.com (office).

LACHMANN, Sir Peter Julius, Kt, ScD, FRS, FRCP, FRCPath, FMedSci; British immunologist; *Sheila Joan Professor Emeritus of Immunology, University of Cambridge;* b. 23 Dec. 1931, Berlin, Germany; s. of Heinz Lachmann and Thea Heller; m. Sylvia Stephenson 1962; two s. one d.; ed Trinity Coll., Univ. of Cambridge and Univ. Coll. Hosp., London; Research Student, Dept of Pathology, Univ. of Cambridge 1958–60, Research Fellow, Empire Rheumatism Council 1962–64, Asst Dir of Research, Immunology Div. 1964–71; Prof. of Immunology, Royal Postgraduate Medical School, Univ. of London 1971–75; Hon. Consultant Pathologist, Hammersmith Hosp. 1971–75; Dir MRC Research Group on serum complement 1971–75; Sheila Joan Smith Prof. of Immunology, Univ. of Cambridge 1977–99, Prof. Emer. 1999–; Hon. Dir, MRC Molecular Immunopathology Unit 1980–97; Hon. Consultant Clinical Immunologist, Cambridge Health Dist 1976–99; Pres. Royal Coll. of Pathologists 1990–93, Acad. of Medical Sciences 1998–2002; Biological Sec. and Vice-Pres. The Royal Soc. 1993–98; Visiting Investigator Rockefeller Univ., New York 1960–61, Scripps Clinic and Research Foundation, La Jolla, Calif. 1966, 1975, 1980, 1986, Basel Inst. for Immunology 1971; Meyerhof Visiting Prof., Weizmann Inst., Rehovot 1989; Visiting Prof., Collège de France 1993; Fellow, Christ's Coll., Univ. of Cambridge 1962–71, 1976–, Royal Postgraduate Medical School 1995, Imperial Coll. London 2001; Foreign Fellow Indian Nat. Acad. of Science 1997; mem. Medical Advisory Cttee, British Council 1983–97, Scientific Advisory Bd SmithKline Beecham 1995–2000; Chair. Science Cttee Asscn Medical Research Charities 1988–92, Medical Research Cttee Muscular Dystrophy Group 1986–90, Research Cttee, CORE (Digestive Disorders Foundation) 2003–; Pres. Fed. of European Acads of Medicine 2004–05 (Pres. Emer. 2005–07), Henry Kunkel Soc. 2003–05; Trustee Arthritis Research Campaign 2000–06; Hon. Fellow, Trinity Coll. 2007; Hon. DSc (Leicester) 2005; Gold Medal, European Complement Network 1997, Medicine and Europe Senior Prize, Inst. des Sciences de la Santé 2003; Foundation Lecturer, Royal Coll. of Pathologists 1983, Langdon Brown Lecturer, Royal Coll. of Physicians 1986, Heberden Orator, British Soc. of Rheumatology 1986, Charnock Bradley Memorial Lecturer 1992, Plenary Lecturer, Vienna 1993, Congress Lecturer, BSI 1993, Frank May Lecturer, Leicester 1994, Vanguard Medical Lecture, Univ. of Surrey 1998, Lloyd Roberts Lecturer, Medical Soc. of London 1999, Jean Shanks Lecturer, Acad. of Medical Sciences, London 2001. *Publications:* Jt Ed. Clinical Aspects of Immunology 1975, 1982, 1993. *Leisure interests:* keeping bees, walking in mountains. *Address:* Department of Veterinary Medicine, Madingley Road, Cambridge, CB3 0ES (office); 36 Conduit Head Road, Cambridge, CB3 0EY, England (home). *Telephone:* (1223) 766242 (office); (1223) 354433 (home). *Fax:* (1223) 766244 (office); (1223) 300169 (home). *E-mail:* pjl1000@cam.ac.uk (office). *Website:* www.christs.cam.ac.uk/college-life/people/fellows-list/display.php?id=72 (office).

LACHOUT, Karel, MusD; Czech composer, musicologist, writer, pianist and teacher; b. 30 April 1929, Prague; s. of Karel Lachout and Marie Lachoutová; m. (divorced); ed Charles Univ., Prague, Acad. of Musical Arts, Prague; teacher of music and English (approbation for grammar schools) 1952; Ed. Music Dept. Radio Prague 1953–79; freelance artist, composer and musicologist with specialization in Spanish and Latin American folk music; recognition from Pres. Eduardo Frei of Chile for promotion of Chilean music in Prague 1999. *Compositions include:* Such is Cuba orchestral suite 1962, Symphonietta for grand orchestra, America Latina orchestral suite (including 'Mar del Plata'), string quartets, piano pieces. *Radio:* scripts for music programmes on Radio Prague of authentic music from Latin America, Spain and other countries, including Music From Cristóbal Colón's Land series 1974. *Publications:* The World Sings (Czech Music Fund Prize) 1957, Music of Chile 1976, Music of Cuba (honoured by invitation from UNEAC to Music Festival, Havana 1986) 1979, Folk Music of Latin America (edn to commemorate 500th anniversary of discovery of S America, with two LPs and booklet) 1992, Folk Music of Spain (double LP and booklet) 1993. *Leisure interests:* languages (German, English, Spanish, Latin), travelling to explore origins of authentic folk music, relaxing in Spain at Costa Brava, philosophy of deeper sense of human life and belief in higher justice. *Address:* Viklefova 11, 130 00 Prague 3, Czech Republic (home). *Telephone:* (2) 71770347 (home).

LACHOWSKI, Sławomir, BEcons, PhD; Polish banking executive; *President of the Board of Management and CEO, BRE Bank SA;* b. 1958; ed Univ. of Planning and Statistics, Warsaw (now Warsaw School of Econs), Gutenberg Univ., Mainz, Germany, Univ. of Zurich, Switzerland, Stanford Univ., USA, INSEAD, France; fmr Researcher, Inst. of Econ. Devt; fmr Deputy Pres., PKO BP and First Deputy Pres., PBG SA; mem. Bd of Man. and Deputy Pres. in charge of retail banking, BRE Bank SA –2001, Pres., Bd of Man. 2004–, also CEO. *Address:* BRE Bank SA, Str. Senatorska 18, 00-950 Warsaw, Poland (office). *Telephone:* (22) 8290000 (office). *Fax:* (22) 8290010 (office). *E-mail:* info@brebank.pl (office). *Website:* www.brebank.pl (office).

LACINA, Ferdinand, MA; Austrian politician; b. 31 Dec. 1942, Vienna; s. of Anna and Ferdinand Lacina; m. Monika Lacina 1966; one s. one d.; ed Hochschule für Welthandel, Vienna; various posts in Kammer für Arbeiter und Angestellte, Vienna 1964; Beirat für Wirtschafts- und Sozialfragen 1974; Dir Dept of Financial Planning, Österreichische Industrieverwaltungs AG 1978; Dir Pvt. Office of Fed. Chancellor Kreisky 1980; Sec. of State, Fed. Chancellery 1982; Fed. Minister of Transport 1984–85, of Public Economy and Transport 1985–86, of Finance 1986–95; consultant, Montana AG, Vienna 1995–, Erste Bank AG 1996–, Bank Austria Creditanstalt AG 2001–; Chair. Man. Bd GiroCredit AG 1996–; Pres. WISE Forum, Vienna; mem. Vienna Chapter, American-Austrian Foundation, Inc. *Publications:* Auslandskapital in Österreich (with O. Grünwald); articles in trade union newspapers and political and econ. journals. *Leisure interests:* literature, walking. *Address:* Erste Bank, Graben 21, 1010 Vienna, Austria (office). *Telephone:* (50) 100-10100 (office).

LACK, Andrew, BFA; American media industry executive; b. 16 May 1947, New York, NY; m. Betsy Kenny Lack; two s. one d.; ed Sorbonne, France, Boston Univ.; joined CBS News division 1976, producer 60 Minutes 1977, Exec. Producer West 57th 1985–89, Sr Exec. Producer CBS Reports 1978–85, produced various documentaries, left CBS 1993; Pres. NBC News 1993–2001, Pres. and COO NBC 2001–03; Chair. and CEO Sony Music Entertainment Inc. 2003–04, CEO Sony BMG (following merger with Bertelsmann's BMG) 2004–06; Chair. Sony BMG Music Entertainment 2006; CEO Bloomberg multimedia group 2008–. *Address:* Bloomberg LLP, 731 Lexington Avenue, New York, NY 10022, USA (office). *E-mail:* bloomberg@bloomberg.net (office). *Website:* www.bloomberg.com (office).

LACLOTTE, Michel René; French museum director; b. 27 Oct. 1929, Saint-Malo; s. of Pierre Laclotte and Huguette de Kermabon; ed Lycée Pasteur, Neuilly, Inst. d'art et d'archéologie de l'Univ. de Paris and Ecole du Louvre; Insp. Inspectorate of Provincial Museums 1955–66; Chief Curator of Paintings, Musée du Louvre 1966–87, of collection Musée d'Orsay 1978–86, Dir Musée du Louvre 1987–92, Pres. de l'Etablissement Public (Musée du Louvre) 1992–94; Pres. Mission de préfiguration, Institut Nat. d'Histoire de L'Art 1994–98; Commdr, Légion d'honneur, Ordre nat. du Mérite, des Arts et des Lettres; Grand prix nat. des Musées 1993; Hon. CBE 1994. *Publications:* various works on history of art, catalogues and articles in reviews mainly on Italian and French painting (14th to 15th centuries) and the Louvre Museum. *Address:* 10 bis rue du Pré-aux-Clercs, 75007 Paris, France (home).

LACOSTE, Paul, OC, PhD; Canadian university administrator; b. 24 April 1923, Montréal; s. of Emile and Juliette (née Boucher) Lacoste; m. 1st Louise Mackay (divorced), 2nd Louise Marcil 1973 (died 1995); one s. two d.; ed Montréal, Chicago, Paris Univs; Vice-Pres., Montréal Univ. 1966–75; Prof., Dept of Philosophy, Montréal Univ. 1948–86; lawyer 1960–; Pres. Asscn des universités partiellement ou entièrement de langue française 1978–81, Fonds Int. de coopération universitaire 1978–81, Asscn of Univs and Colls of Canada 1978-79, Conf. of Rectors and Prins of Québec Univs 1977–80, mem. Bd Asscn of Commonwealth Univs 1977–80, Ecole polytechnique Montréal 1975–85, Clinical Research Inst. of Montréal 1975–, Ecole des hautes commerciales de Montréal 1982–85; Pres., Univ. of Montréal 1975–85; Chair. Comm. and Cttees of the Fed. Environmental Assessment Review to the Great-Whale Hydroelectric Project 1991–98; Chevalier, Légion d'Honneur 1985; Hon. LLD (McGill Univ.) 1975, (Univ. of Toronto) 1978; Dr hc (Laval Univ.). *Publications:* Justice et paix scolaire 1962, A Place of Liberty 1964, Le Canada au seuil du siècle de l'abondance 1969, Principes de gestion universitaire 1970, Education permanente et potentiel universitaire 1977. *Leisure interests:* reading, music, travel. *Address:* Universite de Montréal, CP 6128, Pavillion 2910, Bureau 127, Montréal, Québec H3C 3J7 (office); 802–60 Willowdale Avenue, Montréal, Québec H3T 1H5, Canada (home). *Telephone:* (514) 343-7727 (office); (514) 342-6150 (home). *Fax:* (514) 343-5744 (office).

LACOTTE, Urs; Swiss international organization executive; *Director-General, International Olympic Committee;* ed Univ. of Berne, Univ. of Bayreuth, Germany; fmr tech. official for ski competitions in Switzerland; worked with Electrowatt Eng Co. in Asia and with forerunner to Swiss Sports Asscn; fmr planner, Ministry of Defence; Dir-Gen. IOC 2003–. *Address:* International Olympic Committee, Château de Vidy, 1007 Lausanne, Switzerland (office). *Telephone:* (21) 621 6111 (office). *Fax:* (21) 621 6216 (office). *Website:* www.olympic.org (office).

LACROIX, Christian Marie Marc; French fashion designer; b. 16 May 1951, Arles; s. of Maxime Lacroix and Jeannette Bergier; m. Françoise Roesenstiehl 1989; ed Lycée Frédéric Mistral, Arles, Univ. Paul Valéry, Montpellier, Univ. Paris-Sorbonne and Ecole du Louvre; Asst Hermès 1978–79, Guy Paulin 1980–81; Artistic Dir Jean Patou 1981–87, Christian Lacroix Feb. 1987–, Emilio Pucci 2002–; design for Carmen, Nîmes, France 1988, for L'as-tu revue? 1991, for Les Caprices de Marianne 1994, for Phèdre, Comédie Française 1995; created costumes for Joyaux, Opera Garnier 2000; decorated the TGV Méditerranée 2001; decorated Petit Moulin Hotel, Paris; Creative Dir Emilio Gucci 2002; Commdr, Ordre des Arts et Lettres 1996; Chevalier, Légion d'honneur 2002; Dés d'or 1986, 1988, Council of Fashion Designers of America 1987, Prix Balzac 1989, Goldene Spinnrad Award (Germany) 1990, Prix Molière (for costumes in Phèdre) 1996. *Dance:* Costumes for Opera Garnier (Paris), Stadt Oper (Vienna) and several ballets. *Plays:* costumes for Phèdre, Comédie Française (Paris). *Publication:* Pieces of a Pattern 1992, illustrations for albums Styles d'aujourd'hui 1995, Journal d'une collection 1996. *Address:* 73 rue du Faubourg Saint Honoré, 75008 Paris, France. *Telephone:* 1-42-68-79-00 (office); 1-42-65-79-08. *Fax:* 1-42-68-79-57 (office). *E-mail:* fquere@christian.lacroix.fr.

LACROIX, Hubert T., LLB, MBA; Canadian lawyer and broadcasting executive; *President and CEO, Canadian Broadcasting Corporation (CBC)/ Radio-Canada;* b. 13 July 1955, Montréal; ed Collège Jean-de-Brébeuf, Montréal, McGill Univ.; admitted to Quebec Bar 1977; lawyer with O'Brien, Hall, Saunders 1977–84; Pnr McCarthy Tétrault 1984–2000; Exec. Chair. Telemedia Corpn 2000–03, Sr Adviser Telemedia Ventures Inc. 2003–05; Sr Adviser Stikeman Elliott LLP 2003–07; Pres. and CEO CBC/Radio-Canada 2008–; Adjunct Prof., Faculty of Law, Univ. of Montréal; basketball commentator Télévision de Radio-Canada during Summer Olympics 1984, 1988, 1996; fmr weekly contrib. to Hebdo-sports show, Radio Canada; mem. Bd of Dirs Zarlink Semiconductor Inc. 1992–, Transcontinental Inc., ITS Investments Ltd Partnership; Chair. SFK Pulp Fund; Dir Montréal Gen. Hosp. Foundation; fmr Dir Donohue Inc., Circo Craft Co. Inc., Adventure Electronics Inc., Cambior Inc., Secor Inc., Michelin Canada Inc.; Trustee Lucie and André Chagnon Foundation, Martlet Foundation (McGill Univ.). *Address:* Canadian Broadcasting Corporation, 181 Queen Street, Ottawa, ON K1P 1K9, Canada (office). *Telephone:* (613) 288-6000 (office). *E-mail:* liaison@cbc.ca (office). *Website:* www.cbc.ca (office).

LACSON, Panfilo Morena 'Ping', BS (Eng), BS, MA; Philippine politician; *Senator;* b. 1 June 1948, Imus, Cavite; adopted s. of Cebu Lacson; m. Alice Perio de Lacson; three s.; ed High School, Imus Inst., Lyceum of the Philippines, Philippine Mil. Acad., Pamantasan ng Lungsod ng Maynila; joined Philippine Constabulary 1971, with Metrocom Intelligence and Security Group 1971–86, PC-INP Anti-Carnapping Task Force 1986–88; Prov. Commdr Prov. of Isabela 1988–89; Commdr Cebu Metrodiscom 1989–92; Prov. Dir Prov. of Laguna Feb.–July 1992; Chief, Presidential Anti-Crime Comm., Task Force Habagat 1992–95; Project Officer, Special Project Alpha 1996; Chief, Presidential Anti-Organized Crime Task Force 1998–2001; Chief, Philippine Nat. Police 1999–2001; mem. Laban ng Demokratikong Pilipino (LDP) Party; senatorial cand. Feb. 2001; elected Senator May 2001–, Asst Minority Floor Leader 2001– (mem. cttees: Accountability of Public Officers and Investigations (Blue Ribbon), Cultural Communities, Environment and Natural Resources, Finance, Games, Amusement and Sports, Justice and Human Rights, Labor, Employment and Human Resources Devt, Local Govt, Nat. Defense and Security, Public Order and Illegal Drugs, Science and Tech., Social Justice, Welfare and Rural Devt, Trade and Commerce, Ways and Means); presidential cand. 2004; One of Ten Outstanding Policemen of the Philippines 1988, Philippine Mil. Acad. Alumni Achievement Award 1988, Philippine Constabulary Metrodiscom Officer of the Year 1992, two Outstanding Achievement Medals, five Bronze Cross Medals, 17 Military Merit Medals, three Medalya ng Kadakilaan, three Medalya ng Kagalingan Awards. *Address:* Room 523, 5th Floor, Senate of the Philippines, GSIS Financial Center, Pasay City, The Philippines (office). *Telephone:* (2) 552-6601 (office). *Fax:* (2) 552-6743 (office). *E-mail:* costaff@pinglacson.ph (office); senlacson@pinglacson.ph (home).

LACY, Alan J., BS, MBA; American business executive and financial analyst; *Vice-Chairman and CEO, Sears Holding Corporation;* ed Georgia Inst. of Tech., Emory Univ.; began career with Kraft Foods Inc., various sr financial positions at Dart and Kraft Inc., Sr Vice-Pres. Finance and Strategy Kraft General Foods; fmr Vice-Pres. Financial Services and Systems, Philip Morris Cos Inc.; fmr Pres. Philip Morris Capital Corpn; Sr Vice-Pres. Finance, Sears Roebuck and Co. 1994–95, Exec. Vice-Pres. and Chief Financial Officer 1995–97, Pres. Credit 1997–98, Pres. Credit and Chief Financial Officer 1998–99, Pres. Services 1999–2000, Chair. and CEO 2000–05, Vice-Chair. and CEO Sears Holding Corpn (formed after merger of Sears and KMart Holding Corpn) 2005–; mem. Bd Dirs The Econ. Club of Chicago, Lyric Opera of Chicago, Nat. Retail Fed.; mem. Civic Cttee Commercial Club of Chicago; mem. Bd Trustees Field Museum of Natural History. *Address:* Sears Holding Corporation, 3333 Beverly Road, Hoffman Estates, IL 60179, USA (office). *Telephone:* (847) 268-2500 (office). *Fax:* (847) 286-7829 (office). *Website:* www .searshc.com (office).

ŁĄCZKOWSKI, Paweł Julian, DSoc; Polish politician; *Head of Political Council, Alliance of Polish Christian Democrats;* b. 31 July 1942, Kielce; m. Maria Łączkowska; one s. three d.; ed Adam Mickiewicz Univ., Poznań; fmr scientific worker, Adam Mickiewicz Univ., Poznań 1966–90 1994–; mem. Solidarity Ind. Self-governing Trade Union 1980–; Deputy to Sejm (Parl.) 1989–93, 1997–2001, Deputy Chair. Civic Parl. Club 1989–90, Chair. Sejm Circle of Christian Democrats 1990–91, Chair. Parl. Club of Christian Democrats' Party (PChD) 1991–93, Parl. Comm. for Regulations and Deputies 1997–2001, mem. Solidarity Election Action Parl. Caucus 1997–2001; Co-Founder Christian Democrats' Party (PChD) 1990, Leader 1992–99, merged with two other parties to form Alliance of Polish Christian Democrats 1999, currently Head of Political Council; fmr Deputy Prime Minister; Deputy Chair. Presidium Nat. Bd Solidarity Election Action 1999–2001; mem. Coordination Team Solidarity Election Action (AWS) 1996–99; Deputy Chair. Council of Ministers 1992–93. *Publications:* Circumstances for Stabilizing Worker Staff in Industrialized Districts 1977; numerous articles. *Leisure interest:* gardening. *Address:* Porozumienie Polskich Chrzescijanskich

Demokratów, Sejm, ul. Wiejska 4/6, 00-902 Warsaw, Poland (office). *Telephone:* (61) 8520120 (home).

LADER, Malcolm Harold, OBE, PhD, MD, DSc, FRCPsych, FMedSci; British professor of clinical psychopharmacology; *Professor Emeritus, Institute of Psychiatry, King's College London;* b. 27 Feb. 1936, Liverpool; s. of Abe Lader and Minnie Lader; m. Susan Packer 1961; three d.; ed Liverpool Inst. High School and Liverpool and London Univs; external mem. of scientific staff of MRC 1966–2001; Reader, King's Coll., Univ. of London 1973–78, Prof. 1978, now Prof. Emer.; Consultant Psychiatrist, Bethlem Royal and Maudsley Hosps 1970–2001; mem. various UK Govt advisory bodies; Trustee, Psychiatry Research Trust 2002–; Hon. Fellow American Coll. of Psychiatrists 1994, British Asscn for Psychopharmacology 1994, Soc. for the Study of Addiction 1998; Heinz Karger Memorial Foundation Prize 1974, Taylor Manor Award 1989. *Publications:* Psychiatry on Trial 1977, Biological Treatments in Psychiatry 1990, Anxiety Panic and Phobias 1997; numerous articles on psychopharmacology. *Leisure interests:* antiques, paintings. *Address:* P 056, Institute of Psychiatry, De Crespigny Park, Denmark Hill, London, SE5 8AF, England (office). *Telephone:* (20) 7848-0372 (office). *Fax:* (20) 8650-0366 (office). *E-mail:* m.lader@iop.kcl.ac.uk (office). *Website:* www.iop.kcl.ac.uk (office).

LADER, Philip, BA, MA, JD; American diplomatist, government official, business executive and lawyer; *Senior Adviser, Morgan Stanley International;* b. 17 March 1946, Jackson Heights, NY; m. Linda LeSourd 1980; two d.; ed Duke Univ., Univ. of Michigan, Oxford and Harvard Univs; Pres. Sea Pines Co. 1979–83, Winthrop Univ., SC 1983–85, Bond Univ., Gold Coast, Australia 1991–93, Business Execs for Nat. Security, 1991; Exec. Vice-Pres. Sir James Goldsmith's US Holdings; Deputy Dir for Man., Office of Man. and Budget, Exec. Office of the Pres. 1993; Chair. Pres.'s Council for Integrity and Efficiency 1993, Pres.'s Man. Council, Policy Cttee, Nat. Performance Review 1993; Deputy Chief of Staff and Asst to Pres., White House 1993–94; Admin., US Small Business Admin. and mem. Pres.'s Cabinet 1995–97; Amb. to UK 1997–2001; Chair. WPP 2001–; Sr Adviser, Morgan Stanley Int. 2001–; mem. Bd of Dirs AES, WPP, Marathon Oil and RAND Corpns; mem. Council of Lloyds 2003–, Council on Foreign Relations; mem. Chief Execs Org., Prince of Wales' Trust Advisory Bd; Trustee British Museum, 21st Century Foundation, Windsor Leadership Trust, St Paul's Cathedral Foundation; 14 hon. doctorates; RSA Benjamin Franklin Medal 2001. *Leisure interests:* reading, tennis, walking. *Address:* 25 Cabot Square, Canary Wharf, London, E14 4QA, England (office); 41 East Battery, Charleston, SC 29401, USA (home). *Telephone:* (20) 7425-6524 (office).

LADREIT DE LACHARRIÈRE, Marc; French business executive; b. 6 Nov. 1940, Nice; s. of Pierre Ladreit de Lacharrière and Hélène Mora; m. Sibylle Lucet 1967; one s. three d.; ed Ecole Nat. d'Admin; Asst Man. Banque de Suez et de l'Union des Mines 1970, Asst Dir 1971, Deputy Dir 1973; Vice-Pres. Masson Belfond Armand Colin 1974–95; Vice-Dir Banque de l'Indochine et de Suez 1975, Corp. Affairs Dir 1976; Financial Dir L'Oréal 1976, Man. Dir Admin. and Finance 1977, Vice-Pres. Man. Cttee 1978, mem. Strategic Cttee, Dir and Exec. Vice-Pres. 1984–91, Pres. of Finances 1987–91, mem. Bd Dirs L'Oréal Finance 1984–; Pres. La Revue des deux Mondes 1990–, Financière Marc de Lacharrière (Fimalac) 1991–, Council Banque de la Mutuelle industrielle 1988; Vice-Pres. Sofres 1992–97; fmr Vice-Pres. Centenaire Blanzy, Pres. 1994–98; Pres. Financière Sofres 1992–97, Lille Bonnières & Colombe et Alspi 1993–96, Comptoir Lyon Allemand Louyot 1995–96; Chair. Geral, USA, Fitch Ratings, Inc.; Man. Dir Regefi and Holdilux, Luxembourg; Vice-Chair. L'Oréal (GB), Editions Masson; Dir Collection de l'Institut de l'Entreprise, France Télécom 1995–98, Air France 1996–97, Canal+ 1998–, Flo Group 1998–, Louvre Museum 1999–, Renault 2002–, Casino, Cassina; mem. Int. Council Renault Nissan 2000–; mem. Consultative Cttee, Banque de France; mem. Bd Conseil Arstistique des Musées Nationaux, Fondation Bettencourt Schueller, Soc. des Amis du Musée du Quai Branly, Fondation Nationale des Sciences Politiques, Musée du Louvre, Le Siècle, Strategic Cttee for French Econ. Attractiveness; Lecturer, Inst. d'Etudes Politiques, Paris 1971, then Prof.; Adviser, Foreign Trade of France; Hon. Pres. Inst. of Research and Study for Corp. Security (IERSE); Officier, Légion d'honneur, Ordre Nat. du Mérite, Officier des Arts et Lettres. *Leisure interests:* tennis, skiing. *Address:* Fimalac, 97 rue de Lille, 75001 Paris, France.

LAERMANN, Karl-Hans, DrIng; German politician and academic; *Professor Emeritus of Statics, Bergische Universität Wuppertal;* b. 26 Dec. 1929, Kaulhausen; s. of Johann Laermann and Elisabeth Laermann; m. Hilde Woestemeyer 1955; three s. one d.; ed Rhenish-Westphalian Coll. of Advanced Tech., Aachen; Lecturer in Experimental Statics, Rhenish-Westphalian Coll. of Advanced Tech. 1966–74; Prof. of Statics, Bergische Univ. G.H. Wuppertal, Head Lab. for Experimental Stress Analysis and Measurement 1974–, now Emer.; mem. FDP 1968–, mem. Fed. Exec. Cttee 1980–90, N Rhine-Westphalian Exec. Cttee 1978–94, Chair. Fed. Cttee on Research and Tech. of FDP 1981–96; mem. Bundestag (Parl.) 1974–98; Deputy Chair. working group of FDP Parl. Group on Educ. and Science, Research and Tech. 1980–94; Fed. Minister of Educ. and Science Feb.–Nov. 1994; mem. Bd Trustees Volkswagen Foundation 1984–94, Friedrich Naumann Foundation 1984–, Anglo-German Foundation for the Study of Industrial Society 1989–99; mem. Admin. Bd Inter Nationes 1995–99; Extraordinary mem. Goethe Institut 1995–98; Hon. mem. VDI (Verein Deutscher Ingenieure, Asscn of German Engineers); Hon. CBE (UK) 1978, Commdr Order of Orange-Nassau (Netherlands) 1982, Great Cross with Star of Order of FRG 1996; Hon. DrIng (Magdeburg); Dr hc (Tech. Univ. Prague, Transilvania Univ. Braşov, Romania, Tech. Univ. Košice, Slovakia); Gold Medal of Honour, VDI 1999. *Publications:* Konstruktiver Ingenieurbau (Ed.) 1967, Experimentelle Plattenuntersuchungen-Theoretische Grundlagen 1971, Experimentelle Spannungsanalyse I, II 1972, 1977, Perspektiven – Ein Wissenschaftler in der Politik 1984, Optical Methods in Experimental Solid Mechanics (ed.) 2000, Inverse Problems in Experimental Structural Analysis 2008; about 238 publs on science and politics in int. journals. *Leisure interests:* painting, sailing. *Address:* Bergische Universität Wuppertal, FBD, Pauluskirche str. 7, 42285 Wuppertal (office). *Telephone:* (202) 4394077 (office). *Fax:* (202) 4394078 (office). *E-mail:* laermann@uni-wuppertal.de (office). *Website:* www.uni-wuppertal.de (office).

LAFER, Celso; Brazilian politician and professor of law; b. 7 Aug. 1941, São Paulo; Prof. of Law, Univ. of São Paulo; Minister of Foreign Affairs 1992, 2001–03; Amb. to WTO and Head WTO Gen. Council and Dispute Settlement Comm. 1995–98; Minister of Industry and Commerce 1999; Pres. Fiesp 2000; mem. Brazilian Acad. of Letters 2006; Grand Cross (Brazil) 2002, Grand Officer, Légion d'honneur 2002; Dr hc (Buenos Aires Univ.) 2001, (Cordoba Univ.) 2002. *Address:* Avenida Brigadeiro Faria Lima 1306, Jardim Paulistano, 01451-914 São Paulo, Brazil (office). *E-mail:* c_lafer@uol.com.br (home).

LAFFAN, Brigid, PhD, MRIA; Irish political scientist and academic; *Principal, College of Human Sciences, University College Dublin;* b. (Brigid Burns), 6 Jan. 1955, Co. Kerry; d. of Con Burns and Aileen Burns; m. Michael Laffan 1979; one s. two d.; ed Univ. of Limerick, Coll. of Europe, Bruges, Trinity Coll. Dublin; researcher, European Cultural Foundation 1977–78; Lecturer, Coll. of Humanities, Univ. of Limerick 1979–86; Lecturer, Inst. of Public Admin 1986–89; Newman Scholar, Univ. Coll. Dublin (UCD) 1989–90, Lecturer, Dept of Politics 1990–91, Jean Monnet Prof. of European Politics 1991–, Research Dir Dublin European Inst., UCD, Prin., Coll. of Human Sciences 2005–; Visiting Prof., Coll. of Europe, Bruges 1992–2004; adviser on EU enlargement, Oireachtas (Parl.) Foreign Affairs Cttee; mem. Council, Inst. of European Affairs, Dublin; mem. Irish Govt Asia Strategy Group 2005–. *Publications:* Ireland and South Africa 1988, Integration and Co-operation in Europe 1992, Constitution Building in the European Union (ed.) 1996, The Finances of the European Union 1997, Europe's Experimental Union: Re-thinking Integration (co-author) 1999, Renovation or Revolution: New Territorial Politics in Ireland and the United Kingdom (contributing co-ed. with J. Coakley and J. Todd) 2005, Ireland in the European Union (with Jane O'Mahoney) 2008; numerous articles on Irish foreign policy, EC budgetary policy, insts, governance and political union. *Leisure interests:* theatre, reading, swimming. *Address:* College of Human Sciences, University College, Belfield, Dublin 4 (office); 4 Willowbank, The Slopes, Monkstown, Co. Dublin, Ireland (home). *Telephone:* (1) 7168344 (office); (1) 2862617 (home). *Fax:* (1) 7161171 (office); (1) 2845331 (home). *E-mail:* brigid.laffan@ucd.ie (office). *Website:* www.ucd.ie/humansciences (office).

LAFFITTE, Pierre Paul; French engineer and politician; *President, Rassemblement Democratique et Social Europeen;* b. 1 Jan. 1925, St Paul, Alpes Maritimes; s. of Jean Laffitte and Lucie Fink; m. 1st Sophie Glikman-Toumarkine (deceased); m. 2nd Anita Garcia; ed Lycée de Nice, Ecole Polytechnique, Ecole des Mines de Paris; Dir Office of Geological, Geophysical and Mining Research 1953; Asst Dir-Gen. Office of Geological and Mining Research 1959–62, Deputy Dir 1963, Dir 1973–84; Gen. Engineer Mines 1973–; Pres. Conseil de Perfectionnement, Ecole Nat. Supérieure des Mines, Paris 1984–91; Founder Pres. Sophia-Antipolis 1969; Pres. Franco-German Asscn for Science and Tech., AFAST (German-French Asscn for Science and Tech.); Senator from Alpes Maritimes 1985–; Pres. Rassemblement Democratique et Social Europeen 2007–; Officier, Légion d'honneur; Officier, Ordre nat. du Mérite; Commdr, Order of Polar Star (Sweden); Commdr, Order of Merit (Germany); Hon. PhD (Colorado School of Mines, USA) 1984, (Open Univ., England) 1990; De Gaulle-Adenauer Prize 1994. *Publications:* works on mining and geology, science parks, the information age, local development. *Leisure interest:* gardening. *Address:* Sophia Antipolis, place Sophie Laffitte, 06560 Valbonne (office); Palais du Luxembourg, 75291 Paris Cedex 06; Ecole des Mines, 60 boulevard Saint Michel, 75006 Paris, France. *Telephone:* (4) 92-96-78-00 (office); (4) 93-32-85-90 (home). *Fax:* (4) 93-32-95-26 (home). *E-mail:* p.laffitte@senat.fr (office). *Website:* www.sophia-antipolis.com (office).

LAFFONT, Robert Raoul, LenD; French publishing executive; b. 30 Nov. 1916, Marseille; s. of Raymond Laffont and Nathalie Périer; m. Hélène Furterer 1987; three s. two d. (from previous marriages); ed Lycée Périer, Marseille and Ecole des Hautes Etudes Commerciales, Paris; Lt 94th Regt of Artillery, Montagne; f. Editions Robert Laffont, Marseille 1941, transferred to Paris 1945, Pres. 1959–86, Hon. Pres. 2002–; Fondateur du Pont-Royal; Chevalier, Légion d'Honneur, Officier, Ordre Nat. du Mérite. *Publication:* Robert Laffont, éditeur 1974, Léger étonnement avant le saut 1995. *Leisure interest:* football. *Address:* Editions Robert Laffont, 24 avenue Marceau, 75008 Paris (office); 11 rue Pierre Nicole, Paris 75005, France (home). *Telephone:* 1-43-29-12-33 (office); 1-43-26-02-41 (home). *Website:* www.laffont.fr (office).

LAFFORGUE, Laurent, DèsSc; French mathematician and academic; *Permanent Professor of Mathematics, Institut des Hautes Etudes Scientifiques;* b. 6 Nov. 1966, Antony, Hauts-de-Seine; ed Ecole Normale Supérieure, Paris and Université de Paris-Sud XI; taught at École Spéciale Militaire, Saint-Cyr-Coëtquidan 1991–92; Research Fellow, CNRS 1990–2000, Research Dir 2000; Perm. Prof. of Math., Institut des Hautes Etudes Scientifiques, Bures-sur-Yvette 2000–; mem. Acad. des Sciences 2003–; mem. editorial cttee for Math. Publs, Institut des Hautes Etudes Scientifiques, editorial cttee Moscow Mathematical Journal; Chevalier de la Légion d'Honneur; Prix Peccot and Cours Peccot, Collège de France 1996, Invited Lecturer, Int. Congress of Mathematicians, Berlin 1998, Bronze Medal, CNRS 1998, Clay Research Award 2 2000, Jacques Herbrand Prize in Math., Acad. des sciences, Paris 2001, Fields Medal, 24th Int. Congress of Mathematicians, Beijing (jtly) 2002. *Publications:* Chtoucas de Drinfeld et conjecture de Ramanujan-Petersson

Astérisque 243 1997, Une compactification des champs classifiant les chtoucas de Drinfeld JAMS 1998, Chtoucas de Drinfeld et correspondance de Langlands Inventiones 147 2002, Chirurgie des Grassmanniennes CRM Monograph Series 19 2003, numerous articles in math. journals on number theory and analysis. *Address:* Institut des Hautes Etudes Scientifiques, Le Bois-Marie 35, route de Chartres, 91440 Bures-sur-Yvette, France (office). *Telephone:* 1-60-92-66-00 (office). *Fax:* 1-60-92-66-09 (office). *E-mail:* laurent@ihes.fr (office). *Website:* www.ihes.fr (office).

LAFLEY, Alan G., AB, MBA; American business executive; *Chairman and CEO, Procter & Gamble Company;* b. 13 June 1947, Keene, NH; ed Hamilton Coll., Harvard Business School; served with USN 1970–75; brand asst, Joy, Procter & Gamble Co. 1977–78, sales training, Denver Sales Dist 1978–80, Asst Brand Man. Tide 1978–80, Brand Man. Dawn & Ivory Snow 1980–81, Ivory Snow 1981–82, Cheer 1982–83, Assoc. Advertising Man. PS & D Div. 1983–86, Advertising Man. 1986–88, Gen. Man. Laundry Products PS & D Div. 1988–91, Vice-Pres. Laundry and Cleaning Products 1991–92, Group Vice-Pres., Pres. Laundry and Cleaning Products 1992–94, Group Vice-Pres. Far East Div. 1994–95, Exec. Vice-Pres., Pres. Asia Div. 1995–98, Exec. Vice-Pres. North American Div. 1998–99, Pres. Global Beauty Care and North America 1999–2000, Pres. and CEO Procter & Gamble Co. 2000–02, Chair., Pres. and CEO 2002–07, Chair. and CEO 2007–; Chair. Cincinnati Center City Devt Corpn (3CDC); mem. Bd Dirs General Electric Co., Dell, Inc., Grocery Mfrs of America, United Negro Coll. Fund; fmr mem. Bd Dirs General Motors Corpn; mem. The Business Council, The Business Roundtable, McKinsey Advisory Council, The Lauder Inst. Bd of Govs (Wharton School of Arts and Sciences), Harvard Business School Bd of Dean's Advisors; mem. American Soc. of Corp. Execs; fmr mem. American Chamber of Commerce in Japan, G100 (fmrly The M&A Group); Trustee, Hamilton Coll., US Council for Int. Business; fmr Trustee, Cincinnati Fine Arts Fund, Cincinnati Playhouse in the Park, Cincinnati Symphony Orchestra, Medical Center Fund of Cincinnati, The Seven Hills School, Xavier Univ. *Address:* The Proctor & Gamble Co., 1 Procter & Gamble Plaza, Cincinnati, OH 43202-3315, USA (office). *Telephone:* (513) 983-1100 (office). *Fax:* (513) 983-9369 (office). *E-mail:* info@pg.com (office). *Website:* www.pg.com (office).

LAFON, Jean-Pierre; French international organization official and fmr diplomatist; *President, Bureau International des Expositions;* ed Lycée Condorcet, Institut d'Etudes Politiques, Ecole Nationale d'Administation; mil. service in Germany 1964; Lecturer, Ecole Nationale d'Administation, Côte d'Ivoire 1964–66; joined Ministry of Foreign Affairs 1968, Second then First Sec., Embassy in London 1971–74, mem. del. to Conf. on Security and Co-operation in Europe, Geneva 1973–74; with Econ. Affairs Div., Ministry of Foreign Affairs 1974–76; Adviser, Embassy in Iran 1977–79; Inspector of Foreign Affairs 1980–83, Head of Méthodes-Formation-Informatique Div. 1983–84; Consul in Arlit, Niger 1984–85; Adviser to Cabinet of Jacques Chirac 1986–88; Dir UN Div., Ministry of Foreign Affairs 1989–94; Amb. to Lebanon 1994–97; Pres. French Council for Protection of Refugees 1997–2002; Amb. to China 2002–04; Sec.-Gen. of Foreign Affairs 2004–06; Pres. Bureau international des expositions, Paris 2007–; Chevalier de la Légion d'Honneur 1991, Officier de l'Ordre National du Mérite 2003. *Address:* Bureau International des Expositions, 34, Avenue d'Iéna, Paris 75116, France (office). *Telephone:* 1-45-00-38-63 (office). *Fax:* 1-45-00-96-15 (office). *E-mail:* info@bie-paris.org (office). *Website:* www.bie-paris.org (office).

LAFONT, Bernadette Paule Anne; French actress; b. 28 Oct. 1938, Nîmes; d. of Roger Lafont and Simone Illaire; m. György Medveczky (divorced); one s. two d. (one deceased); ed Lycée de Nîmes; Pres. Assoc. Acas 1990–; Chevalier, Légion d'honneur; Commdr des Arts et Lettres, Officier de l'Ordre Nat. du Mérite 2005; Triomphe du cinéma 1973, César for Best Supporting Actress 1985, Prix d'interprétation Lucarno 1993, Swann du coup de foudre de l'année, Festival of Romantic Film 1998, César d'honneur Life Achievement Award 2003. *Films include:* Les Mistons 1957, L'Eau à la bouche 1959, Les Bonnes femmes 1959, Compartiment tueurs 1965, Le Voleur 1966, La Fiancée du pirate 1969, Out One 1971, La Maman et la putain 1972, Une belle fille comme moi 1972, Zig-Zig 1974, Retour en force 1979, La Bête noire 1983, Le Pactole 1984, L'Effrontée 1985, Masques 1987, Prisonnières 1988, L'Air de rien 1990, Ville à vendre 1992, Personne ne m'aime 1994, Pourquoi partir? 1996, Rien sur Robert 1999, Recto! Verso 1999, Les Amants du Nil 2001, Les petites couleurs 2001, Super Ripoux 2003, Les petites vacances 2006, Prête-moi ta main 2006, Le Prestige de la mort 2006, Broken English 2007, 48 heures par jour 2008, Mes amis, mes amours 2008, Nos 18 ans 2008, La Première étoile 2009. *Plays include:* Bathory la Comtesse sanglante 1978, La Tour de la défense 1981, Désiré 1984, Barrio Chino 1987, Le Baladin du monde occidental 1988, Les Joyeuses et horrifiques farces du père Lalande 1989, La Frousse 1993, La Marguerite 1993, La Traversée 1996, L'Arlésienne 1997, Une table pour six 1998, Le faucon 1998, Monsieur Anédée 1999, Léo 2002, Monologues du vagin 2002–03, Un beau salaud 2002, Ecrits d'amour 2004. *Radio:* Le feu au lac, Festival d'Avignon 1999, Les bonnes, France Culture 2000. *Television:* Les pigeons de Notre Dame 1964, Le malheur de Maloo 1982, Sautes de velours 1987,Paul et ses femmes 2008, Ma soeur est moi 2008. *Publications:* La Fiancée du cinéma 1978, Mes Enfants de la balle 1988, Le Roman de ma vie 1997 (autobiog.). *Address:* c/o Adequat, 80, rue d'Amsterdam, 75009 Paris, France (office). *Telephone:* 1-42-80-00-42.

LAFONT, Bruno; French business executive; *Chairman and CEO, Lafarge SA;* b. 1956; ed Hautes Etudes Commerciales, Ecole Nationale d'Admin; joined Lafarge SA as internal auditor in Finance Dept 1983, Chief Financial Officer Sanitaryware Div., Germany 1984, Chief Div. Finance Dept 1986–88, Int. Devt Dept 1988–89, Vice Pres. Lafarge Cement and Aggregates and Concrete operations, Turkey 1990–94, Group Exec. Vice-Pres., Finance and mem. Exec. Cttee 1994–98, Exec. Vice-Pres. Gypsum Div. 1998–2003, COO Lafarge SA 2003–06, mem. Bd of Dirs 2005–, CEO 2006–, Chair. 2007–; mem. Bd of Dirs EDF 2008–. *Address:* Lafarge SA, 61 rue des Belles Feuilles, BP 40, 75782 Paris Cedex 16, France (office). *Telephone:* 1-44-34-11-11 (office). *Fax:* 1-44-34-12-00 (office). *E-mail:* info@lafarge.com (office). *Website:* www.lafarge.com (office).

LAFONTAINE, Oskar; German politician; b. 16 Sept. 1943, Saarlouis; m. Doris Vartan 1984; one step-d.; ed Univs of Bonn and Saarbrücken; Mayor of Saarbrücken 1976–85; mem. Saarland Landtag (Regional Parl.), Minister-Pres. 1985–98; Chair. SPD Regional Asscn, Saar 1977–96; mem. SPD Cen. Cttee; Vice-Chair. SPD 1987–96; Cand. for Chancellorship 1990; Leader SPD 1995–99 (resgnd); Minister of Finance 1998–99 (resgnd). *Publications:* Angst vor den Freunden 1983, Der andere Fortschritt 1985, Die Gesellschaft der Zukunft 1988, Das Lied vom Teilen 1989, Deutsche Wahrheiten 1990, Keine Angst vor der Globalisierung (jtly) 1998, Das Herz schlägt links (autobiog.) 2000. *Address:* c/o Ministry of Finance, Wilhelmstrasse 97, 10117 Berlin, Germany.

LAFORTE, Conrad, DèsSc, FRSC; Canadian archivist and academic; b. 10 Nov. 1921, Kenogami, PQ; s. of Philippe Laforte and Marie-Mathilda Dallaire; m. Hélène Gauthier 1957; one d.; ed Montréal Univ. and Laval Univ.; librarian and archivist, Folklore Archives, Laval Univ. 1951–75; Instructor CELAT, Laval Univ. 1965–67, Asst Prof. 1967–73, Assoc. Prof. 1973–77, Prof. 1977–81, Titular Prof., Dept of History and CELAT 1981–88; mem. Royal Soc. of Canada 1982; Fellow Emer. CELAT, Laval Univ. 1984; Distinguished Perm. mem. Folklore Studies Asscn of Canada 1988; Dr hc (Sudbury, Ont.) 2000; Grand Prix, Soc. du patrimoine d'expression du Québec 1999, Médaille Luc Lacourcière 1981, Marius Barbeau Medal, Folklore Studies Asscn of Canada 1999 and other awards for folklore research. *Publications:* La chanson folklorique et les écrivains du XIX[e]siècle 1973, Poétiques de la chanson traditionnelle française 1976, Catalogue de la chanson folklorique française (six vols) 1977–87, Menteries drôles et merveilleuses 1978, Survivances médiévales dans la chanson folklorique 1981, Chansons folkloriques à sujet religieux 1988, La chanson de tradition orale, une découverte des écrivains du XIXe siècle (en France et au Québec) 1995, Vision d'une société par les chansons de tradition orale à caractère épique et tragique 1997, Chansons de facture médiévale retrouvées dans la tradition orale (two vols) 1997. *Address:* 949 rue Gatineau, Ste-Foy, PQ, G1V 3A2, Canada.

LAGARDE, Christine; French lawyer and government official; *Minister of Economy, Finance and Industry;* b. 1956; m. (divorced); two s.; ed Univ. of Aix-en-Provence, Political Science Inst., Paris Law School, Paris Univ.; started career as lecturer at Paris X Univ.; joined Baker & McKenzie LLP (law firm) 1981, Partner 1987–, Man. Partner 1991–95, elected to Global Exec. Cttee 1995, Chair. European Regional Council and Professional Devt Cttee 1995–98, Chair. Exec. Cttee 1999–2004, Chair. Global Policy Cttee 2004–05; Minister for Foreign Trade 2005–07, of Agric. 2007, of Economy, Finance and Industry 2007–; mem. Supervisory Bd ING Group 2005–; mem. Int. Advisory Bd Escuela Superior de Administración y Dirección de Empresas; mem. Int. Bd of Overseers, Ill. Inst. of Tech.; mem. Bd and Sec., Execs Club of Chicago; mem. Strategic Council on Attractivity of France; co-Chair. US-Europe-Poland Action Comm., Center for Strategic and Int. Studies; mem. Int. Business Advisory Bd, Mayor of Beijing; Chevalier de la Légion d'honneur; Jaume Cordelles Award from ESADE 2004, ranked by Forbes magazine amongst 100 Most Powerful Women (76th) 2004, (88th) 2005, (30th) 2006, (12th) 2007, (14th) 2008. *Address:* Ministry of the Economy, Finance and Industry, 139 rue de Bercy, 75572 Paris Cedex 12, France (office). *Telephone:* 1-40-04-04-04 (office). *Fax:* 1-43-43-75-97 (office). *Website:* www.minefi.gouv.fr (office).

LAGARDE, Paul, DenD; French academic; *Professor Emeritus of Law, University of Paris I;* b. 3 March 1934, Rennes; s. of Gaston Lagarde and Charlotte Béquignon; m. Bernadette Lamberts 1962; two s. one d.; ed Paris Univ.; Prof., Faculty of Law, Nancy 1961–69, Nanterre 1969–71; Prof. of Private Int. Law, Univ. of Paris I 1971–2001, now Prof. Emer.; Gen. Sec. Revue critique de droit international privé 1962, Ed.-in-Chief 1976, Dir 1990; Pres. Comité Français de droit int. privé 1987–90; Conseiller d'Etat en service extraordinaire 1996–2001; mem. Inst. of Int. Law; Gen. Sec. Comm. Int. de l'Etat Civil 2000–; Chevalier, Légion d'honneur; Dr hc (Freiburg i.Br.); Prize of Foundation Alexander von Humboldt 1992; Le droit international privé: esprit et méthodes : Mélanges en l'honneur de Paul Lagarde (Publ. in his honour) 2005. *Publications:* Recherches sur l'ordre public en droit international privé 1959, La réciprocité en droit international privé 1977, Le principe de proximité dans le droit international privé contemporain 1987, Traité de droit international privé (with Henri Batiffol) 1993, La nationalité française 1997. *Address:* 2 Rue Henri Bocquillon, 75015 Paris, France (home). *Telephone:* 1-45-58-30-89 (home). *E-mail:* paul.lagarde@orange.fr (home).

LAGARDÈRE, Arnaud; French media executive; *Chairman and CEO, Lagardère Media;* b. 18 March 1961, Boulogne-Billancourt; s. of Jean-Luc Lagardère; ed Univ. of Paris IX – Dauphine; fmr Deputy Chair., Supervisory Bd ARJIL bank; Chair. Grolier Inc., USA 1994–98; fmr Head, Dept of Emerging Activities and Electronic Media, Matra; fmr Man. Dir, Lagardère SAS, becoming Chair. Lagardère Group, Chair. and CEO Lagardère Media 1999–, Gen. and Man. Pnr, Lagardère SCA, Pres., Lagardère Active, Chair. and CEO Lagardère Active Broadcast 2001–, also Chair. Lagardère Capital & Management; Chair. EADS (European Aeronautic Defence and Space) NV 2003–; mem. Supervisory Bd, DaimlerChrysler AG 2005–; Chair. Jean-Luc Lagardère Foundation. *Address:* Lagardère SCA, 4 rue de Presbourg, 75116 Paris, France (office). *Telephone:* 1-40-69-16-00 (office). *Fax:* 1-40-69-18-35 (office). *Website:* www.lagardere.com (office).

LAGAYETTE, Philippe Ernest Georges; French government official and business executive; *President, JP Morgan et Compagnie SA;* b. 16 June 1943, Tulle (Corrèze); s. of Elie Lagayette and Renée Portier; m. Marie-Louise Antoni 1979; two s. two d.; ed Ecole Polytechnique and Ecole Nat. d'Admin; Eng Génie Maritime 1965; Insp. des Finances 1970; Deputy Dir Treasury Man., Ministry of Economy, Finance and Budget 1980; Dir Cabinet of Minister of Economy, Finance and Budget 1981–84; Deputy Gov. Banque de France 1984, First Deputy Gov. 1990; Insp.-Gen. des Finances 1988–; Dir-Gen. Caisse des Dépôts et Consignations 1992–97; Pres. JP Morgan et Cie SA 1998–; Chair. Institut des Hautes Etudes Scientifiques 1995–, French American Foundation 2003–; Bd mem. Comm. des Operations de Bourse (French Stock Market Regulator) 1989–92, Eurotunnel 1993–2004; Officier, Légion d'honneur, Commdr Ordre nat. du Mérite. *Leisure interests:* hunting, tennis, skiing, cinema. *Address:* JP Morgan, 14 Place Vendôme, 75001 Paris, France (office). *Telephone:* 1-40-15-49-88 (office). *Fax:* 1-40-15-41-36 (office). *E-mail:* philippe .lagayette@jpmorgan.com (office). *Website:* www.jpmorgan.com (office).

LAGE DÁVILA, Carlos, MD; Cuban politician; *Vice-President and Executive Secretary, Council of Ministers;* b. 15 Oct. 1951, Havana; ed Univ. of Havana; trained as pediatrician 1970s; apptd Pres. Fed. of Univ. Students 1975; worked as physician at Hosp. Pediátrico d La Habana; sent to Ethiopia in charge of medical mission; apptd First Sec., UJOTAC 1981; mem. Grupo de Coordinación y Apoyo del Comandante en Jefe (Fidel Castro's inner staff) 1986; mem. Politburo; currently Vice-Pres. and Exec. Sec., Council of Ministers. *Address:* c/o Council of Ministers, Havana, Cuba.

LAGERFELD, Karl-Otto; German fashion designer; b. 1938, Hamburg; ed privately and at art school, Hamburg; fashion apprentice with Balmain and Patou 1959; freelance designer associated with Fendi, Rome 1963–, Chloe, Paris 1964–83, Isetan, Japan; Creative Dir, Chanel, Paris 1982–, designer Karl Lagerfeld's Women's Wear, Karl Lagerfeld France Inc. 1983–; first collection under his own name 1984; Hon. Teacher, Vienna 1983; costume design for film Comédie d'Amour 1989; awarded Golden Thimble 1986. *Publications:* Lagerfeld's Sketchbook (with Anna Piaggi), Helmut Newton 1990, Karl Lagerfeld – Off the Record 1995, The Karl Lagerfeld Diet. *Address:* Karl Lagerfeld France Inc., 75008 Paris, France (office); Chanel, 135 avenue Charles de Gaulle, Neuilly-sur-Seine, Paris, France (office). *Website:* www .karllagerfeld.com (office); www.chanel.com (office).

LAGHDAF, Moulaye Ould Mohamed, DèsSc; Mauritanian diplomatist and politician; *Prime Minister;* b. 1957, Nema; m.; four c.; ed Univ. of Liège, Univ. of Louvain; expert on Africa, The Caribbean and The Pacific, Centre for Industrial Devt 1991–97; Co-ordinator of devt project for Hodh Chargui region 2000–06; Amb. to Belgium and EU 2006–08, Prime Minister 2008–. *Publications:* Enrichissement des minerais d'oxyde de cuivre 1983, Utilisation des schistes bitumineux en tant que matière minérale et organique en cimenterie 1984, Combustion des gaz dans un lit fluidisé 1992, Lutte contre les émissions d'oxyde d'azote 1992. *Address:* Office of the Prime Minister, BP 237, Nouakchott, Mauritania (office). *Telephone:* 525-33-37 (office).

LAGOS ESCOBAR, Ricardo, PhD; Chilean politician; *President, Club de Madrid;* b. 2 March 1938, Santiago; m. Luisa Durán; five c.; ed Univ. of Chile, Duke Univ., N Carolina; Prof. Univ. of Chile 1963–72, fmr Head School of Political and Admin. Sciences, fmr Dir Inst. of Econs, Gen. Sec. 1971; Visiting Prof. Univ. of N Carolina, Chapel Hill 1974–75; Chair. Alianza Democrática (AD) 1983–84; Chair. Partido por la Democracia (PPD) 1987–90; Minister of Educ. 1990–92, of Public Works 1994; Pres. of Chile 2000–06; Founder and Pres. Fundación Democracia y Desarrollo (Foundation for Democracy and Development) 2006–; Pres. Club de Madrid 2006–; UN Sec.-Gen.'s Special Envoy on Climate Change 2007–. *Publications:* Población, Pobreza y Mercado de Trabajo en América Latina 1997, numerous books and articles on econs and politics. *Address:* Club de Madrid, Casa Goya 5-7, Pasaje 2ª, 28001 Madrid, Spain (office). *Telephone:* (91) 1548230 (office). *Fax:* (91) 1548240 (office). *E-mail:* clubmadrid@clubmadrid.org (office). *Website:* www.clubmadrid.org (office).

LAGRAVENESE, Richard, BFA; American screenwriter, director and producer; b. 30 Oct. 1959, Brooklyn, New York; s. of Patrick LaGravenese and Lucille LaGravenese; m. Ann Weiss LaGravenese 1986; one d.; ed Lafayette High School, Emerson Coll. and New York Univ.; Ind. Film Project Writer of the Year, Best Original Screenplay 2000. *Films include:* Rude Awakening 1989, The Fisher King (also actor) 1991, The Ref (also producer) 1994, A Little Princess 1995, The Bridges of Madison County 1995, Unstrung Heroes 1995, The Mirror Has Two Faces 1996, The Horse Whisperer 1998, Living Out Loud (also dir) 1998, Beloved 1998, The Legend of Bagger Vance 1999, Erin Brockovich (uncredited co-writer) 2000, Blow (actor) 2001, The Defective Detective 2002, A Decade Under the Influence (also producer and dir) 2003, Monster-in-Law 2005, Paris, je t'aime (dir) 2006, Freedom Writers (dir) 2007, P.S. I Love You 2007. *Leisure interests:* theatre, books, family. *Address:* c/o Kirsten Bonelli, 8383 Wilshire Boulevard, Suite 340, Beverly Hills, CA 90211, USA.

LAGU, Lt-Gen. Joseph; Sudanese politician, army officer and diplomatist; b. 21 Nov. 1931, Moli; s. of Yakobo Yanga and Marini Kaluma; ed Rumbek Secondary School, Mil. Acad. Omdurman; served in Sudanese Army 1960–63; joined South Sudan Liberation Movt 1963, Leader SSLM 1969; signed peace agreement with Govt of Sudan March 1972; Vice-Pres. of Sudan 1978–80, 1982–85; Pres. Supreme Exec. Council for the South 1978–80; fmr Perm. Rep. to UN; moved with his family to UK; Order of the Two Niles 1972. *Publication:* The Anya-Nya – What We Fight For 1972. *Address:* c/o Ministry of Foreign Affairs, Khartoum, Sudan.

LAGUMDŽIJA, Zlatko, MSc, PhD; Bosnia and Herzegovina politician; b. 26 Dec. 1955, Sarajevo; m.; two c.; ed Univ. of Sarajevo, Harvard Univ., USA; Visiting Prof., Arizona Univ. 1988–89; Prof. of Econ. and Electrical Eng, Univ. of Sarajevo 1989–, Dir Centre for Man. and Computer Tech. 1995; co-f. Social and Democratic Party of Bosnia and Herzegovina (Socijaldemokratska Partija —SDP BiH) 1990, Chair. 1997–; mem. House of Reps of Parl. Ass. 1996–; Prime Minister, Minister of Foreign Affairs and Treasurer of the Insts of Bosnia and Herzegovina 2001; Minister of Foreign Affairs 2001–03. *Address:* Socijaldemokratska Partija BiH, Alipašina 41, 71000 Sarajevo, Bosnia and Herzegovina (office). *Telephone:* (33) 664044 (office). *Fax:* (33) 644042 (office). *E-mail:* generalni.sekretar@sdp-bih.org.ba (office). *Website:* www.sdp-bih.org .ba (office).

LAHHAM, Duraid, BSc; Syrian actor, comedian and director; b. 1934, Damascus; m. 1st May al-Husayni two c.; m. 2nd Hala Bitar; one d.; ed Damascus Univ.; Instructor, Chem. Dept, Univ. of Damascus 1955–60; stage roles 1960–; starred in mini-series Sahret Dimashq (Damascus Evening) on Syrian TV with Nihad Qali 1960, cr. duo called Duraid & Nihad, achieved dramatic success in Arab World until Qali retired from acting due to illness in 1976; Pres. of the Syrian Assoc. of Artists 1967; UNICEF representative in Syria for children's affairs 1990, UNICEF Ambassador for Childhood in the Middle East and North Africa 1999–2004; Medal of the Syrian Repub. (Excellence Class) 1976, Medal of the Tunisian Repub. 1979, Medal of the Libyan Repub. 1991, Order of Merit of the Lebanese Repub. 2000. *Theatre includes:* Ukd al-Lulu (The Pearl Necklace) 1966, Masrah al-Shawk (The Thorn Theatre) 1968, Qadiyyah wa Haramiyya (A Cause and Thieves) 1972, Day'at Tishreen (October Village) 1974, Ghorba (Alienation) 1976, Kasak ya Watan (Cheers to the Homeland) 1978, Shaka'ik al-Nu'man (Anemones) 1987, Sani' al-Matar (The Rainmaker) 1992, Al-Asfura al-Sa'ida (The Happy Bird) 1992. *Films include:* Ghawar La'eb al-Kura (Ghawar the Football Player), Ukd al-Lulu (The Pearl Necklace) 1965, Al-Lus al-Zarif (The Nice Thief), Al-Sa'alik (The Crooks) 1968, Al-Sadikan (The Two Friends), Al-Sheridan (The Two Homeless Men), Al-Millionera (The Millionaire), Gharam fi Istanbul (Love Affair in Istanbul) 1967, Maqlab min al-Maksik (A Prank from Mexico), Lika' fi Tadmur (Rendezvous in Palmyra), Al-Rajul al-Munasib (The Right Man), Fundok al-Ahlam (The Dream Hotel) 1966, Khayyat lil Sayyidat (A Seamstress for Women) 1969, Wahid Za'ed Wahid (One plus One), Al-Nassaben al-Thalatha (The Three Crooks), Misk wa Anbar (Misk and Anbar), Al-Muzayafun (The Imposters), Al-Tha'lab (The Fox), Zawjati min al-Hippez (My Hippie Wife), Ana Antar (I am Antar), Imra'a Taskun Wahdiha (A Women Lives on Her Own), Sah al-Nawm (Good Morning), Abd al-Latiff Fathi, Ghawar James Bond, Indama Taghib al-Zawjat (When Wives are Absent), Samak bala Hasak (Fish with no Skeleton), Imbaratoriyyat Ghawar (The Empire of Ghawar), Al-Hudud (The Border), Al-Takrir (The Report), Kafroun. *Television includes:* Al-Ijaza al-Sa'ida (The Happy Holiday) 1960, Sahret Dimashq: (Damascus Evening) 1960, Maqalib Ghawar (Ghawar's Pranks) 1966, Hammam al-Hana (Pleasant Bath) 1968, Sah al-Nawm (Good Morning) 1971, Sah al-Nawm (Part 2) 1972, Melh wa Sukkar (Salt and Sugar) 1972, Wayn al-Ghalat (Where is the Error?) 1980, Wadi al-Misk (Misk Valley) 1982, Al-Doghri (The Doghri) 1991, Ahlam Abu al-Hana (The Dreams of Abu al-Hana) 1994, Awdet Ghawar (The Return of Ghawar) 1999, A'ilati wa Ana (My Family and I) 2001, Ala Mas'uliyati (On My Responsibility) 2002, Alam Doreid (Doreid's World, Doreid haza al-Mas'a (Doreid this Evening). *Publications:* author of several comedies. *Leisure interest:* accordionist. *Address:* c/o Syrian Broadcasting Corporation, Omayya Square, Damascus, Syria. *Website:* www .duraidlahham.com.

LAHLAIDI, Abdelhafid, PhD; Moroccan professor of medicine and cardiovascular specialist; *Chief, Department of Morphology, Université Mohammed V;* b. 20 May 1942; m.; three c.; ed Univ. of Paris, France, Univ. of Geneva, Switzerland; Professorial Asst, Faculty of Medicine, Univ. of Geneva, Switzerland 1973; Prof., Faculty of Medicine, Université Mohammed V 1973–, Chief, Dept of Morphology; Fellow, Islamic Acad. of Sciences 1990–; Fellow Académie Islamique des Sciences; mem. New York Acad. of Sciences; Grand Prix Scientifique, Morocco 1986, Prix Scientifique du Président de la République Tunisienne 1987, Prix Scientifique du Président de la République Algérienne 1989, Médaille d'or de l'Académie Nationale Française de Médecine 1990, Médaille de l'Académie des Sciences, Jordan 1991. *Publications:* Anatomie topographique, Applications, Anatom-Chirurgicles (five vols) 1986. *Leisure interests:* painting, writing. *Address:* Université Mohammed V, BP 6203, Rabat Institute, Rabat (office); Temara – Les Vieux Marocains, Allée 3, Maison 121, Rabat, Morocco (home). *Telephone:* (37) 77-04-21 (office); (37) 74-10-27 (home). *Fax:* (37) 77-37-01 (office); (37) 67-30-56 (home). *E-mail:* LAHLAIDI@online.fr (office); lahlaidi@gmail.com (home). *Website:* www.emi .ac.ma (office).

LAHNSTEIN, Manfred; German politician, civil servant and academic; b. 20 Dec. 1937, Erkrath, Rhineland; m. Sonja Lahnstein; two c.; ed Univ. of Cologne; joined SPD 1959; at European Comm., Brussels, latterly as Chef de Cabinet to Commr Wilhelm Haferkamp 1967–73; econ. adviser, Chancellery 1973; moved to Finance Ministry 1974, successively Div. Head and State Sec. in charge of Financial and Monetary Policy 1974–80; Chancellor's Chief Civil Servant 1980–82; Minister of Finance April–Oct. 1982; mem. Bd Dirs Bertelsmann AG and Pres. Electronic Media Group 1983–94, mem. Supervisory Bd 1994–98, Special Rep. of the Bd 1998–2004; mem. Trilateral Comm.; mem. Supervisory or Advisory Bds Hansa Treuhand, Korn/Ferry Europe, Thalia Theater Hamburg; Prof. of Cultural Man., Univ. for Music and Theatre, Hamburg; Chair. Bd Govs Univ. of Haifa, Israel 2001–; Chair. Bd Trustees Ebelin and Gerd Bucerius ZEIT Foundation, Germany; Pres. German-Israel Soc. *Publications:* three books and numerous articles. *Leisure interests:* music, smoking cigars. *Address:* ZEIT-Stiftung, Feldbrunnenstrasse 56, 20148 Hamburg (office). *Telephone:* (40) 413366 (office). *Fax:* (40) 41336700 (office). *E-mail:* zeit-stiftung@zeit-stiftung.de (office). *Website:* www.zeit -stiftung.de (office).

LaHOOD, Raymond (Ray) H., BS; American politician and government official; *Secretary of Transportation;* b. 6 Dec. 1945, Peoria, Ill.; m. Kathleen LaHood; two s. two d.; ed Canton Jr Coll., Bradley Univ.; began career as teacher 1971–77; Dist Admin. Asst to US Congressman Tom Railsback 1977–82; mem. Ill. State House of Reps 1982; Chief of Staff to US Congressman and House Minority Leader Bob Michels, Washington, DC 1982–94; mem. US House of Reps from 18th Ill. Dist 1995–2009; US Sec. of Transportation, Washington, DC 2009–; Republican; Dr hc (Lincoln Coll.) 2000, (Eureka Coll.) 2002, (Tri-State Univ.) 2004, (MacMurray Coll.) 2006. *Address:* Department of Transportation, 1200 New Jersey Ave, SE, Washington, DC 20590, USA (office). *Telephone:* (202) 366-4000 (office). *Fax:* (202) 366-7202 (office). *E-mail:* dot.comments@dot.gov (office). *Website:* www.dot.gov (office).

LAHOTI, Ramesh Chandra; Indian judge; b. 1940, Guna, Madhya Pradesh; Dist. and Sessions Judge 1977–78; joined Madhya Pradesh High Court 1978, Additional Judge 1988–89, Perm. Judge 1989–94; with Delhi High Court 1994–98; Judge, Supreme Court 1998–05, Chief Justice 2004–05 (retd). *Address:* c/o Supreme Court, New Delhi, India (office).

LAHOUD, Gen. Emile; Lebanese politician, naval officer and fmr head of state; b. 1936, Baabdat; s. of Gen. Jamil Lahoud and Adrinée Badjakian; m. Andrée Amadouni; two s. one d.; ed Brumana High School, also attended various courses at Naval Acads in UK and USA 1958–80; joined Mil. Acad. as cadet officer 1956, promoted to Sub.-Lt 1959, Lt 1962, Lt-Commdr 1969, Commdr 1974, Cap. 1980, Rear-Adm. 1985, Vice-Adm. 1989; Commdr of Second Fleet 1966–68, of First Fleet 1968–70; Staff of Army Fourth Bureau 1970–72; Chief of Personal Staff of Gen. Commdr of Armed Forces 1973–79; Dir of Personnel, Army HQ 1980–83; Head of Mil. Office, Ministry of Defence 1983–89; Commdr-in-Chief of Armed Forces 1989; Pres. of the Repub. of the Lebanon 1998–2007; Lebanese Medal of Merit Gen. Officer 1989; Medal of Merit and Honour, Haiti 1974; War Medals 1991, 1992; Dawn of the South Medal 1993; Nat. Unity Medal 1993; Medal of Esteem 1994; Grand Cordon Order of the Cedar 1993; Commdr Légion d'Honneur 1993; Grand Cross (Argentina) 1998; Order of Merit Sr Officer Level (Italy) 1997; Order of Hussein ibn Ali (Jordan) 1999, Order of St Misrope Mashtos (Armenia) 2000, King Abdul-Aziz Collar (Saudi Arabia) 2000, Great Collar of the Union (UAE) 2000, Great Collar of Mubarak (Kuwait) 2000, Great Collar of the Nile (Egypt) 2000, Great Collar of Independence (Qatar) 2000, Great Collar of the Khalifite Order (Bahrein) 2000, Order of the White Double Cross 1st Class (Slovakia) 2001, Star of Romania Collar 1999, 2001, Great Cross Légion d'honneur (France) 2001, Al Muhammadi Decoration Extraordinary Grade (Morocco) 2001, Order of November 7th (Tunisia) 2001, Great Cross Order of the Grimaldis (Monaco) 2001, Great Cross Order of the Redeemer (Greece) 2001, Grand Cordon Nat. Order of Oumaya (Syria) 2002, Badge Order of Prince Yaroslav the Wise 1st class (Ukraine) 2002, Grand Collar Order of Makarios III (Cyprus) 2002, Nat. Order of Merit Al-Athir (Algeria) 2002, Order of the Repub. (Yemen) 2002, Order Stara Planina (Bulgaria) 2003, Nat. Order of the South Cross (Brazil) 2004, Grand Cross of the Ipiranga Order (Brazil) 2004, Grand Cross with Chain Order of Merit (Hungary) 2004, Knight Grand Cross of Merit with Gold Star of the Sacred Military Constantinian Order of St George 2004, Grand Cross of Order of Merit (Poland) 2004, Knight Grand Cross of Merit with Gold Plate of the Sacred Military Constantinian Order of St George 2005. *Publication:* Method and Style, Promise and Fulfilment. *Leisure interests:* diving, swimming, reading, music. *Address:* c/o Presidential Palace, Baabda, Lebanon (office).

LAI, Jimmy; Hong Kong business executive, journalist and publisher; *Proprietor, Next Media;* Propr Giordano (retail clothing chain) 1980–, Chair. 1980–94; Propr Next Magazine 1990–, Apple Daily 1995–, Sharp Daily 2006–. *Address:* Apple Daily, 6/F Garment Centre, 576–586 Castle Peak Road, Cheung Sha Wan (office). *Telephone:* 29908388 (office). *Fax:* 27410830 (office). *E-mail:* adnews@appledaily.com (office). *Website:* appledaily.atnext.com (office).

LAI, Shin-yuan, MA, MPhil, DPhil; Taiwanese politician; *Minister of Mainland Affairs Council;* ed London School of Econs and Univ. of Sussex, UK; Dir and Research Fellow, Div. of Int. Affairs, Taiwan Inst. of Econ. Research 1996–2000; Dir-Gen. Chinese Taipei Pacific Basin Econ. Cttee 1996–2000; Founder and Dir Chinese Taipei APEC Study Center 1997–2000; Adjunct Assoc. Prof., Grad. School for Social Transformation Studies, Shih Hsin Univ. 1997–98; Adjunct Assoc. Prof., Dept of Int. Business Man., Tamkang Univ. 1997–2008; Dir-Gen., Confed. of Asia-Pacific Chambers of Commerce and Industry 1999–2000; Sec.-Treasurer, Asian Bankers Asscn 1999–2000; Sr Adviser, Nat. Security Council 2000–04; chief negotiator for Taiwan's accession to WTO 2001; adviser to Taiwan WTO Centre, Chung-Hua Inst. for Econ. Research 2004; mem. Legis. Yuan 2005–08; Minister, Mainland Affairs Council, Exec. Yuan 2008–. *Address:* Mainland Affairs Council, 15/F, 2-2 Chi Nan Road, Sec. 1, Taipei 10054, Taiwan (office). *Telephone:* (2) 23975589 (office). *Fax:* (2) 23975300 (office). *E-mail:* macst@mac.gov.tw (office). *Website:* www.mac.gov.tw (office).

LAIDLAW, Sir Christophor Charles Fraser, Kt; British business executive; b. 9 Aug. 1922; s. of the late Hugh Alexander Lyon Laidlaw and Sarah Georgina Fraser; m. Nina Mary Prichard 1952; one s. three d.; ed Rugby School and St John's Coll. Cambridge; served War of 1939–45, Europe and Far East, Maj. on Gen. Staff; joined British Petroleum Co. Ltd (BP) 1948, BP rep. in Hamburg 1959–61, Gen. Man. Marketing Dept 1963–67, Dir BP Trading 1967, Pres. BP Belgium 1967–71, Dir (Operations) 1971–72, Chair. BP Germany 1972–83, Man. Dir BP Co. Ltd 1972–81, Deputy Chair. 1980–81; Chair. BP Oil 1977–81, BP Oil Int. 1981, ICL 1981–84; Pres. ICL France 1983; Dir Commercial Union Assurance Co. 1978–83, Barclays Bank Int. Ltd 1980–87, Barclays Bank 1981–88, Amerada Hess Corpn 1983–94, Dalgety 1984–92, Redland 1984–92, Barclays Merchant Bank 1984–87, Amerada Ltd 1985–98, Mercedes-Benz (UK) 1986–93, Daimler Benz (UK) Ltd 1994–99, Daimler Chrysler UK Holding 1999–2000; Chair. Boving & Co. 1984–85, Bridon PLC 1985–90; Dir INSEAD 1987–94 (Chair. UK Advisory Bd 1984–91); Master Tallow Chandlers Co. 1988–89; Pres. German Chamber of Industry and Commerce 1983–86; Vice-Pres. British-German Soc. 1996–2002; Hon. Fellow St John's Coll., Cambridge 1996. *Leisure interests:* fishing, shooting, opera. *Address:* 49 Chelsea Square, London, SW3 6LH, England (home). *Telephone:* (20) 7352-6942 (home). *Fax:* (20) 7376-3182 (home).

LAIDLAW, (William) Samuel (Sam) Hugh, MBA, FRSA; British solicitor and energy industry executive; *Chief Executive, Centrica plc;* b. 3 Jan. 1956, London; m.; four c.; ed Univ. of Cambridge, Institut Européen d'Admin des Affaires (INSEAD); solicitor, Macfarlanes, London, 1977–79; Corp. Planner, Société Françaises Pétroles BP, Paris, 1979–80; Man. of Corp. Planning Amerada Hess Corpn, New York City, USA 1981–83, Vice-Pres. Amerada Hess Ltd, London 1983–85, Man. Dir 1986–1995, Chair. 1995, Exec. Vice-Pres. Amerada Hess Corpn 1993–95, Pres. and COO, London 1995–2001; CEO Enterprise Oil 2001–03; Exec. Vice-Pres. Chevron Corpn 2003–06; Chief Exec. Centrica plc 2006–, Chair. Exec. Cttee, Disclosure Cttee; Dir (non-exec.) Hanson plc 2003–07 (also Chair. Nomination Cttee), HSBC Holdings plc 2008–; mem. Bd of Dirs Business Council for Int. Understanding; Trustee, RAFT (medical charity); mem. UK Council of INSEAD; fmr Pres. UK Offshore Operators Asscn; fmr Chair. Petroleum Science and Tech. Inst.; fmr mem. UK Energy Advisory Panel. *Address:* Centrica plc, Millstream, Maidenhead Road, Windsor, Berks., SL4 5GD, England (office). *Telephone:* (1753) 494000 (office). *Fax:* (1753) 494001 (office). *E-mail:* info@centrica.co.uk (office). *Website:* www.centrica.co.uk (office).

LAIDLER, David Ernest William, PhD, FRSC; Canadian/British economist and academic; *Fellow-in-Residence, C. D. Howe Institute;* b. 12 Aug. 1938, Tynemouth, UK; s. of John Alphonse Laidler and Leonora Laidler (née Gosman); m. Antje Charlotte Breitwisch 1965; one d.; ed Tynemouth School, London School of Econs, Univs of Syracuse and Chicago, USA; Asst Lecturer, LSE 1961–62; Asst Prof., Univ. of Calif., Berkeley 1963–66; Lecturer, Univ. of Essex 1966–69; Prof., Univ. of Manchester 1969–75; Prof. of Econs, Univ. of Western Ont. 1975–2004, Bank of Montreal Prof. 2000–05, now Prof. Emer., Dept Chair. 1981–84; Special Adviser, Bank of Canada 1998–99; Fellow-in-Residence, CD Howe Inst., Toronto 1990–; Visiting Economist, Reserve Bank of Australia 1977; Assoc. Ed. Journal of Money, Credit and Banking 1979–; mem. Editorial Bd Pakistan Devt Review 1987–, European Journal of the History of Econ. Thought 1993–; fmr mem. editorial Bd several other journals; Co-Founder and mem. Exec. Cttee Money Study Group 1970–75; mem. Econs Cttee, CNAA, GB 1971–75, Econs Cttee, SSRC, GB 1972–75, Consortium on Macroeconomic Modelling and Forecasting, ESRC, GB 1981–88, Econ. Advisory Panel to Minister of Finance, Canada 1982–84; Co-ordinator Research Advisory Group on Econ. Ideas and Social Issues, Royal Comm. on the Econ. Union and Devt Prospects for Canada (Macdonald Comm.) 1984–85; Dir Philip Allan Publrs Ltd 1972–99; Pres. Canadian Econs Asscn 1987–88; BAAS Lister Lecturer 1972; Canadian Econs Asscn Douglas Purvis Prize 1994, Hellmuth Prize, Univ. of Western Ontario 1999, Donner Prize 2004. *Publications:* The Demand for Money 1969, Essays on Money and Inflation 1975, Monetarist Perspectives 1982, Taking Money Seriously 1990, The Golden Age of the Quantity Theory 1991, The Great Canadian Disinflation (with W. P. B. Robson) 1993, Money and Macroeconomics: Selected Essays 1998, Fabricating the Keynesian Revolution 1999, Two Percent Target (with W. P. B. Robson) 2004, Macroeconomics in Retrospect: Selected Essays 2004. *Leisure interests:* going to concerts, opera and theatre. *Address:* C.D. Howe Institute, 67 Yonge Street, Suite 300, Toronto, Ont. M5E 1J8 (office); Department of Economics, Room 4024, SSC, University of Western Ontario, London, Ont., N6A 5C2 (office); 45–124 North Centre Road, London, Ont., N5X 4R3, Canada (home). *Telephone:* (416) 865-1904 (C.D. Howe) (office); (519) 661-3400 (office); (519) 673-3014 (home). *Fax:* (416) 865-1866 (C.D. Howe) (office); (519) 661-3666 (office). *E-mail:* laidler@uwo.ca (office); cdhowe@cdhowe.org (office). *Website:* www.ssc.uwo.ca/economics/faculty/Laidler (office); www.cdhowe.org (office).

LAINE, Dame Clementina (Cleo) Dinah, DBE; British singer; b. 28 Oct. 1927, Southall, Middx; m. 1st George Langridge 1947 (dissolved 1957), one s.; m. 2nd John Philip William Dankworth (q.v.) 1958, one s. one d.; joined Dankworth Orchestra 1953; lead role in Seven Deadly Sins, Edinburgh Festival and Sadler's Wells 1961; acting roles in Edinburgh Festival 1966, 1967; f. Wavendon Stables Performing Arts Centre (with John Dankworth) 1970; many appearances with symphony orchestras performing Façade (Walton) and other compositions; Julie in Show Boat, Adelphi Theatre 1971; title role in Colette, Comedy Theatre 1980; Desiree in A Little Night Music, Mich. Opera House, USA 1983; The Mystery of Edwin Drood, Broadway, NY 1986; Into the Woods (US Nat. Tour) 1989; frequent tours and TV appearances, Europe, Australia and USA; Freedom of Worshipful Co. of Musicians 2002; Hon. MA (Open Univ.) 1975, Hon. DMus (Berklee School of Music) 1982, (York) 1993, (Cambridge) 2004, Hon. DA (Luton) 1994; Melody Maker and New Musical Express Top Girl Singer Awards 1956; Moscow Arts Theatre Award for acting role in Flesh to a Tiger 1958; top place in Int. Critics' Poll of American Jazz magazine Downbeat 1965; Woman of the Year (9th annual Golden Feather Awards) 1973; Edison Award 1974; Variety Club of GB Show Business Personality Award (with John Dankworth) 1977; TV Times Viewers' Award for Most Exciting Female Singer on TV 1978; Grammy Award for Best Jazz Vocalist-Female 1985; Best Actress in a Musical (Edwin Drood) 1986; Theatre World Award for Edwin Drood 1986, Nat. Asscn of Recording Merchandisers (NARM) Presidential Lifetime Achievement Award 1990, Vocalist of the Year (British Jazz Awards) 1990, Lifetime Achievement Award (USA) 1991, ISPA Distinguished Artists Award 1999, Back Stage Bob

Harrington Lifetime Achievement Award (with John Dankworth) 2001, BBC British Jazz Awards Lifetime Achievement Award (with John Dankworth) 2002. *Film:* Last of the Blonde Bombshells 2000. *Recordings include:* albums: Smilin' Through (with Dudley Moore) 2005, I Hear Music 2007. *Publications:* Cleo: An Autobiography 1994, You Can Sing If You Want To 1997. *Leisure interest:* painting. *Address:* The Old Rectory, Wavendon, Milton Keynes, MK17 8LT, England (home). *Fax:* (1908) 584414 (home). *Website:* www.quarternotes.com (office).

LAINE, Jermu Tapani, LLM; Finnish politician, lawyer and author; b. 1931, Turku; m. 1954; three d.; ed Univ. of Helsinki, Univ. of Pennsylvania, USA; functionary, Ministry of Trade and Industry 1955–65; Lecturer in Commercial Studies, Valkeakoski 1965–69; Rector, Commercial Inst., Mänttä 1969–; municipal positions in Valkeakoski and Mänttä 1968–; Political Sec. to Prime Minister Sorsa 1972–73; Minister for Foreign Trade 1973–75; mem. Parl. 1975–; Minister, Ministry of Finance 1982–83; Minister for Foreign Trade 1983–87; Chair. Supervisory Bd Valmet Og 1987–88; Dir-Gen. Finnish Customs Bd 1988–94; Chair. Finnish Nat. Theatres; mem. Social Democratic Party. *Plays:* Paniikkihäiriö 2001, Marie Curie. *Publications:* Autobiography 1991, Alexis de Toqueville 1999, Finland in 1906 2006, Finnish Foreign Trade towards the West 2006. *Leisure interests:* literature, theatre, cinema.

LAÍNEZ RIVAS, Francisco Esteban, MA, MBA; Salvadorean business executive and politician; b. 23 March 1961, San Salvador; m. Monica Miccolo; three c.; ed Univ. of Texas and MIT Sloan School of Business, USA, Univ. Francisco Marroquin, Guatemala; began career serving in several exec. positions in family business Laboratorios Laínez; mem. Republican Nationalist Alliance Party (ARENA), positions included mem. Business Sector, Sec. of Int. Relations, Dir of Communications and Transport and Vice-Pres. of Org., Del. to Union of Latin American Parties (UPLA); fmr Presidential Commr for Cen. American Integration; Minister of Foreign Affairs 2004–08; Dir Centre of Political Studies, FUNTER, Salvadorean Asscn of Industries, Young Entrepreneurs Org (YEO), Sani Mi Corazón Foundation; fmr Dir and Pres. INQUIFAR; fmr mem. Exec. Cttee Teleton. *Address:* Alianza Reoublicana Nacionalista, Prolongación Calle Arce 2423, entre 45 y 47 Avda Norte, San Salvador, El Salvador (office). *Telephone:* 2260-4400 (office). *Fax:* 2260-5918 (office). *Website:* www.arena.com.sv (office).

LAING, Jennifer Charlina Ellsworth; British advertising executive; b. 1947, Southampton; d. of the late James Ellsworth Laing and of Mary McKane (née Taylor); m. (divorced); joined Garland Compton 1969, firm subsequently taken over by Saatchi & Saatchi, Dir Saatchi & Saatchi Garland Compton 1977, Jt Chair. 1987–88, Chair. Saatchi & Saatchi Advertising 1995–96, Chief Exec. N American Operations, New York 1997–2000; Chair. and CEO Aspect Hill Holliday 1988; f. Laing Henry Ltd 1990 (acquired by Saatchi & Saatchi 1995); Assoc. Dean, External Relations, London Business School 2002–07; mem. Bd of Dirs (non-exec.) Hudson Highland Group, Inc. 2003–, Intercontinental Hotels Group 2005–, Great Ormond Street Hosp. for Children NHS Trust 1994–96; fmr Dir Remploy; Fellow, Marketing Soc., Inst. of Practitioners in Advertising; mem. Exec. Bd Saatchi & Saatchi Advertising Worldwide 1996–2000. *Leisure interests:* racing, ballet, opera, theatre, race-horse owner. *Address:* 20 Gloucester Crescent, London, NW1 7DS, England (home).

LAING, (John) Stuart, MA; British diplomatist; *Ambassador to Kuwait;* b. 22 July 1948, Limpsfield, Surrey; s. of Denys Laing and Judy Dods; m. Sibella Dorman 1971; one s. two d.; ed Rugby School, Corpus Christi Coll., Cambridge; joined HM Diplomatic Service in 1970, served in Jedda 1973–75, 1992–95, Brussels 1975–78, Cairo 1983–87, Prague 1989–92 and Riyadh, High Commr in Brunei 1999–2002, Amb. to Oman 2002–05, to Kuwait 2005–. *Leisure interests:* playing chamber music, hill-walking, desert travel. *Address:* British Embassy, PO Box 2, Safat, 13001, Kuwait (office). *Telephone:* 2403334 (office). *Fax:* 2426799 (office). *E-mail:* stuart.laing@fco.gov.uk (office); britemb@qualitynet.net (office). *Website:* www.britishembassy.gov.uk/kuwait (office).

LAING, R(obert) Stanley, BS (MechEng), MBA; American business executive; b. 1 Nov. 1918, Seattle; s. of Robert Vardy Laing and Marie Laing (née Scott); m. 1st Janet Emmott Orr 1947 (died 1986), one s. four d.; m. 2nd Eva Nofke 1986 (died 1988); m. 3rd Mary Wilshire 1988; ed Univ. of Washington and Harvard Business School; with Nat. Cash Register Co., Dayton, Ohio 1947–72, Special Asst in Exec. Office 1947–49, Asst to Comptroller 1949, Gen. Auditor 1950–53, Asst Comptroller 1953–54, Comptroller 1954–60, Vice-Pres. (Finance) 1960–62, Exec. Vice-Pres. 1962–64, Pres. 1964–72; Dir and Chair. Business Equipment Mfg Asscn 1963–64; fmr Chair. Denison Univ. Bd of Trustees; fmr Dir Gen. Mills Inc., Mead Corpn, NCR Corpn, Cincinnati Milacron Inc., B. F. Goodrich Co., Armco Corpn, Amdahl Corpn, Sinclair Community Coll. Foundation; consultant to Fujitsu Ltd, Japan 1977–95; Order of Lateran Cross (Vatican). *Address:* 3430 South Dixie, Dayton, OH 45439 (office); 650 West David Road, Dayton, OH 45429, USA (home). *Telephone:* (513) 298-0884 (office).

LAING OF DUNPHAIL, Baron (Life Peer), cr. 1991, of Dunphail in the District of Moray; **Hector Laing;** British business executive (retd); b. 12 May 1923, Edinburgh; s. of Hector Laing and Margaret Norris Grant; m. Marian Clare Laurie 1950; three s.; ed Loretto School, Musselborough and Jesus Coll., Cambridge; joined McVitie & Price Ltd as a Dir 1947, Chair. 1963–64; Dir of United Biscuits Ltd 1953–64, Man. Dir 1964–85, Chair. United Biscuits (Holdings) PLC 1972–90; Council mem. Inst. of Dirs 1969–75; mem. Intervention Bd for Agric. Produce 1972–75; Dir Royal Insurance Co. 1970–78, Court of Bank of England 1973–91, Allied-Lyons 1979–82, Exxon Corpn (USA) 1984–94; Chair. Food & Drink Industries Council 1977–79, Scottish Business in the Community 1982–90, Business in the Community 1987–91; Pres. Inst. of Business Ethics 1991–94, Trident Trust 1992–94; mem. Advisory Council, London Enterprise Agency 1981; Jt Treas. Conservative Party 1988–93; Dr hc (Stirling) 1985, Hon. DLitt (Herriot Watt) 1986; Bronze Star (USA), Hambro Award 1979; Businessman of the Year 1979; Nat. Free Enterprise Award 1980. *Leisure interests:* gardening, walking. *Address:* High Meadows, Windsor Road, Gerrards Cross, Bucks., SL9 8ST, England. *Telephone:* (1753) 882437 (home). *Fax:* (1753) 885106 (home).

LAIRD, Sir Gavin Harry, Kt, CBE; British fmr trade union official; b. 14 March 1933, Clydebank, Scotland; s. of James Laird and Frances Laird; m. Catherine Gillies Campbell 1956; one d.; shop stewards' convener, Singer, Clydebank for seven years; Regional Officer, Amalgamated Eng Union (fmrly Amalgamated Union of Eng Workers) 1972–75, Exec. Councillor for Scotland and NW England 1975–82, Gen. Sec. (AEU Section) 1992–95; Chair. Greater Manchester Buses North 1994–97; fmr Chair. Murray Johnstone Venture Capital Trust 4; mem. Murray Johnston Private Acquisition Partnership Advisory Cttee 1999–; mem. Scottish TUC Gen. Council 1973–75; mem. TUC Gen. Council 1979–82; part-time Dir Highlands and Islands Devt Bd 1974–75; mem. Industrial Devt Advisory Bd 1979–86, Arts Council 1983–86, part-time Dir BNOC 1976–86; Chair. The Foundries EDC 1982–85; Dir Bank of England 1986–94; Dir (non-exec.) Scottish TV (Media Group) PLC 1986–99, Britannia Life 1988–2000, Britannia Investment Mans Ltd, Britannia Fund Mans (now Britannic Asset Mans) Ltd 1996–2000, GEC Scotland 1991–99, Edinburgh Investment Trust Ltd; fmr Pres. Kent Active Retirement Asscn; fmr Vice-Pres. Pre-Retirement Asscn of GB and NI; fmr Trustee Anglo-German Foundation 1994–2000, John Smith Memorial Trust; fmr mem. Editorial Bd European Business Journal; mem. Advisory Bd Know-How Fund for Poland 1990–95; mem. Armed Forces Pay Review Body 1995–98, Employment Appeal Tribunal; Fellow Paisley Coll. of Tech. 1991; Hon. DLitt (Keele Univ.), (Heriot Watt Univ.) 1994. *Leisure interests:* music, hill-walking, reading. *Address:* 9 Clevedon House, Holmbury Park, Bromley, BR1 2WG, England (home). *Telephone:* (20) 8460-8998 (home). *Fax:* (20) 8460-8998 (home). *E-mail:* laird.gavin@btopenworld.com (home).

LAIRD, Melvin Robert, BA; American fmr government official; *Senior Counsellor, National and International Affairs, The Reader's Digest Association, Inc.;* b. 1 Sept. 1922, Omaha, Neb.; s. of Melvin and Helen Laird (née Connor); m. 1st Barbara Masters 1945 (died 1992); two s. one d.; m. 2nd Carole Fleischman 1993; ed Carleton Coll., Northfield, Minn.; served with Task Force 38 and 58, US Navy Pacific Fleet 1942–46; mem. Wisconsin Senate 1946–52, Chair. Wisconsin Legis. Council; mem. US House of Reps 1952–69, served on Appropriations Cttee, Chair. House of Republican Minority, mem. Republican Coordinating Council, Vice-Chair. Republican Nat. Platform Council 1960, Chair. 1964; US Sec. of Defense 1968–73; Counsellor to Pres. for Domestic Affairs 1973–74; Senior Counsellor for Nat. and Int. Affairs, Readers' Digest Asscn 1974–, now Vice-Pres.; Chair. COMSAT Corpn 1992–96; fmr mem. Bd the Kennedy Center, George Washington Univ., Airlie Foundation; mem. Bd Nat. Defense and Energy Projects of American Enterprise Inst., Thomas Jefferson Center Foundation of Univ. of Virginia, World Rehabilitation Fund; fmr Dir The Reader's Digest Asscn Inc., Metropolitan Life Insurance Co., Northwest Airlines, IDS Mutual Funds Group, Communications Satellite Corpn (Chair. 1992–96), Martin Marietta Corpn, Science Application Int. Corpn, Dir Public Oversight Bd; fmr Trustee, DeWitt and Lila Wallace-Reader's Digest Funds; Republican; over 300 awards and hon. degrees, including Albert Lasker Public Service Award, Statesman in Medicine Award (Airlie Foundation), The Harry S. Truman Award for distinguished service in defense; Presidential Medal of Freedom (USA), Order of Merit (1st Class) (Fed. Repub. of Germany), Commdr Légion d'honneur (France). *Publications include:* A House Divided: America's Strategy Gap 1962, The Conservative Papers (Ed.) 1964, Republican Papers (Ed.) 1968. *Address:* c/o The Reader's Digest Association, Inc.,Reader's Digest Road, Pleasantville, NY 10570-7000; 1730 Rhode Island Avenue, NW, Suite 212, Washington, DC 20036, USA (office).

LAJČÁK, Miroslav; Slovak diplomatist and politician; *Minister of Foreign Affairs;* b. 20 March 1963, Poprad; m.; two d.; ed Comenius Univ., Bratislava, State Inst. of Int. Relations, Moscow, Russia and George C. Marshall European Center for Security Studies, Germany; joined Ministry of Foreign Affairs in 1988; served in Embassy in Moscow 1991–93; Dir Cabinet of Minister of Foreign Affairs 1993–94, 1998–2001; Dir Cabinet of Prime Minister of Slovakia 1993–94; Amb. to Japan 1994–98, to Fed. Repub. of Yugoslavia (also accred to Albania and FYR Macedonia) 2001–05; Special Asst to UN Sec.-Gen.'s Special Envoy to the Balkans 1999–2001; Dir-Gen. of Political Affairs, Ministry of Foreign Affairs 2005–07; Special Rep. of EU for Common Foreign and Security Policy, Montenegro 2006; High Rep. of Int. Community and Special Rep. of EU, Mission in Bosnia and Herzegovina 2007–09; Minister of Foreign Affairs 2009–. *Address:* Ministry of Foreign Affairs, Hlboká 2, 833 36 Bratislava, Slovakia (office). *Telephone:* (2) 5978-3001 (office). *Fax:* (2) 5978-3009 (office). *E-mail:* miroslav.lajcak@mzv.sk (office). *Website:* www.mzv.sk (office).

LAJOLO, HE Cardinal Giovanni, BCL; Italian ecclesiastic and diplomatist; *President, Governatorate of Vatican City State;* b. 3 Jan. 1935, Novara; ordained priest of Novara 1960; entered Vatican diplomatic service 1970, served at Vatican Nunciature in Germany and in Secr. of State; Titular Archbishop of Caesariana and Sec. of Admin of Patrimony of the Apostolic See 1988–95; Apostolic Nuncio to Germany 1995–2003; Sec. for Relations with States 2003–06; Pres. Governatorate of Vatican City State 2006–, Pontifical Comm. for Vatican City State 2006–; cr. Cardinal 2007, apptd Cardinal-Deacon of S. Maria Liberatrice a Monte Testaccio 2007. *Address:* Governatorate of Vatican City State, Palazzo Apostolico Vaticano, Città del Vaticano 00120, Italy (office). *E-mail:* info@vatican.va (office). *Website:* www.vatican.va/vatican_city_state (office).

LAJUNEN, Samppa; Finnish professional skier; b. 23 April 1979, Turku; entered his first cross-country race aged two; was skiing 300 miles a year by age five; added ski jumping to pursuits aged nine; won overall World Cup title in Nordic combined 1997; Silver Medals, Individual and Team events, Winter Olympics, Nagano, Japan 1998; Gold Medals, Nordic Combined, Sprint and Team events, Winter Olympics, Salt Lake City, USA 2002; First Place, Individual Discipline, World Cup, Nayoro, Japan 2004; Second Place, Sprint Discipline, World Cup, Reit im Winkl, Germany 2004, Seefeld, Austria 2004, Individual Mass Start, Sapporo, Japan 2004, Sprint, Oslo, Norway 2004, Individual Discipline, Oslo 2004; Third Place, Individual Discipline, World Cup, Kuusamo, Finland 2003; mem. Jyvaeskylaen Hiihtoseura Ski Club; now (retd. *Address:* c/o Finnish Ski Association, Radiokatu 20, 00240 Helsinki, Finland. *Telephone:* (9) 348121. *Fax:* (9) 34812484. *E-mail:* samppa.lajunen@hiihtoliitto.fi. *Website:* www.hiihtoliitto.fi.

LAKATANI, Sani; Niuean politician; Prime Minister of Niue March 1999–2001; Minister for External Affairs, Finance, Customs and Revenue, Econ. and Planning Devt and Statistics, Business and Pvt. Sector Devt, Civil Aviation, Tourism, Int. Business Co. and Offshore Banking, Niue Devt Bank March 1999–2001; fmr Leader Niue People's Party (NPP); Chancellor Univ. of the South Pacific, Fiji 2000–03; Deputy Premier and Minister for Planning, Econ. Devt and Statistics, the Niue Devt Bank, Post, Telecommunications and Information Computer Tech. Devt, Philatelic Bureau and Numismatics, Shipping, Investment and Trade, Civil Aviation and Police, Immigration and Disaster Man. 2002. *Address:* c/o Office of the Prime Minister, Alofi, Niue (office).

LAKE, Anthony, PhD; American fmr government official and academic; *Distinguished Professor in Practice of Diplomacy, Edmund A. Walsh School of Foreign Service, Georgetown University;* b. 1939, New York; m.; three c.; ed Harvard Univ., Cambridge Univ., UK, Woodrow Wilson School of Public and Int. Affairs, Princeton Univ.; joined Foreign Service 1962, Special Asst to Amb. Henry Cabot Lodge, Viet Nam; aide to Nat. Security Adviser Henry Kissinger 1969–70; Head State Dept's policy planning operation –1981; Prof., Amherst Coll., Mass. 1981–84, Mount Holyoke Coll. 1984–92; currently Distinguished Prof. in Practice of Diplomacy, Edmund A. Walsh School of Foreign Service, Georgetown Univ.; co-f. journal Foreign Policy; foreign policy adviser to fmr Pres. Clinton during presidential campaign 1992; Nat. Security Adviser 1993–96. *Publications:* The 'Tar Baby' Option: American Policy Toward Southern Rhodesia 1976, Third World Radical Regimes: US Policy under Carter and Reagan 1985, Somoza Falling: A Case Study of Washington at Work 1990, Six Nightmares 2001. *Address:* Edmund A. Walsh School of Foreign Service, Georgetown University, 37th and O Street, NW, Washington, DC 20057, USA. *Telephone:* (202) 687-6083. *Fax:* (202) 687-1427. *E-mail:* lakea@georgetown.edu. *Website:* www.georgetown.edu/sfs (office).

LAKE-TACK, Louise Agnetha; Antigua and Barbuda nurse, magistrate and government official; *Governor-General;* b. 26 July 1944, Long Lake Estate, Parish of St Phillips, Antiqua; ed Antigua Girls High School, Charing Cross Hosp., UK; worked as nurse at Nat. Heart Hosp. and Harley Street Clinic, UK; magistrate Marylebone and Horseferry Magistrate Courts 1995, also sat at Pocock Street Crown Court; Gov.-Gen. of Antigua and Barbuda (first woman) 2007–; mem. Antigua and Barbuda Nat. Asscn. *Address:* Office of the Governor-General, St John's, Antigua and Barbuda (office). *Website:* www.antigua.gov.ag (office).

LAKER, John, BEcon (Hons), MSc, PhD; Australian business executive; *Chairman, Australian Prudential Regulation Authority;* ed Univ. of Sydney, Univ. of London, UK; worked in Commonwealth Treasury and IMF before joining Int. Dept of Reserve Bank of Australia (RBA) in 1982, held sr positions in econ., bank supervision and int. areas before becoming RBA's Chief Rep. in Europe, based in London 1991–93, Asst Gov. (Corp. Services) 1993–98, Asst Gov. (Financial System) 1998–2003; mem. Bd of Dirs Australian Prudential Regulation Authority (APRA) and Deputy Chair. Payments System Bd 1998–2003, Chair. APRA 2003–, APRA's rep. on Payments System Board of RBA and APRA's rep. on Council of Financial Regulators. *Address:* Australian Prudential Regulation Authority, GPO Box 9836, Sydney, NSW 2000, Australia (office). *Telephone:* (2) 9210-3000 (office). *Fax:* (2) 9210-3411 (office). *E-mail:* J.Laker@apra.gov.au (office). *Website:* www.apra.gov.au (office).

LAKHANI, Amin Mohammed, BSc, MBA; Pakistani industrialist; *Managing Director, Lakson Group of Companies;* ed Stanford Univ., Wharton School of Business, Univ. of Pennsylvania, USA; currently Man. Dir Lakson Group, conglomerate with interests in computer software, cosmetics, insurance, fast food and textiles; CEO McDonald's Pakistan; Founding mem. Pakistan Chapter, Young Press' Org.; Hon. Consul-Gen. of Repub. of Singapore in Pakistan; Public Service Star, Govt of Singapore. *Address:* Lakson Group of Companies, Lakson Square Building No. 2, Sarwar Shaheed Road, Karachi, Pakistan (office). *Telephone:* (21) 5688243 (office). *Fax:* (21) 5680093 (office). *E-mail:* amin@cyber.net.pk (office). *Website:* www.lakson.com.pk (office).

LAKHDAR, Zohra Ben, PhD; Tunisian physicist and academic; *Professor of Physics, University of Tunis;* ed Univ. of Tunis, Univ. of Paris VI; fmr Head Spectroscopy Lab., Supervisor, postgraduate students for Tunisian DEA Diploma, Co.-Chair. Molecular Spectroscopy Group for Master's Degree and PhD courses; Prof. of Physics, Univ. of Tunis 1978–; Founder mem. Tunisian Physics Soc., Tunisian Astronomy Soc.; Founding mem. and Pres. Tunisian Optical Soc.; mem. Islamic Acad. of Sciences 1994–; Sr Assoc. Abdus Salam Int. Centre for Theoretical Physics 2001–; L'Oréal-UNESCO Women in Science Award 2005. *Publications:* numerous papers in scientific journals and contribs to textbooks. *Address:* Faculté des Sciences de Tunis Département de Physique, Campus Universitaire, Tunis 1060, Tunisia (office). *Telephone:* 873-366 (office). *Fax:* 872-055 (office).

LAKHERA, Lt-Gen. Madan Mohan, MSc; Indian army officer (retd) and government administrator; *Governor of Mizoram;* b. 21 Oct. 1937, Jakhand village, UP (now in Uttaranchal); s. of the late Jaya Nand Lakhera and Smt. Kalawati; m. Pushpa Lakhera; four d.; ed Rashtriya Indian Mil. Coll., Dehra Dun, Nat. Defence Acad., Pune, Defence Services Staff Coll., Wellington, School of Artillery, Devlali, Coll. of Defence Man., Secundrabad; commissioned in Indian Army 1958; took part in Goa operation 1961, in Indo-Pakistan war, Jammu and Kashmir 1965, 1971; instructor, School of Artillery 1967–81; commanded 4th Bn Kumaon Regt, Jammu and Kashmir 1975–78; Deputy Commdr brigade in Manipur 1981–82; rank of Brig. 1982; Commdr brigade in Kanpur 1984–85; Sub-Area Commdr in Kashmir valley 1985–90; rank of Maj.-Gen. 1990; Chief of Staff Kashmir valley-based Corps HQ 1990–92; rank of Lt-Gen. of Indian Army 1993; apptd Chief of Staff, Cen. Command HQ 1992, later Chief of Staff, Northern Command HQ; Adjutant Gen. of Indian Army 1993, Chair. Prin. Personnel Staff Officers' Cttee of three services; Col Commdt Kumaon Regt; following retirement, joined Indian Nat. Congress party, Chair. All India Congress Cttee Ex-Servicemen's Cell; Lt-Gov. of Pondicherry 2004–06, of Andaman and Nicobar Islands Feb.–Dec. 2006; Gov. of Mizoram 2006–; Chief of Army Staff Commendation Card (twice) 1985, Vishisht Seva Medal 1990, Ati Vashisht Seva Medal 1991, Param Vishisht Seva Medal 1995. *Leisure interests:* golf, reading. *Address:* Raj Bhavan, Aizawl 796001, Mizoram, India (office). *Telephone:* (389) 2322262 (office). *Fax:* (389) 2323344 (office). *E-mail:* rbaizawl@sancharnet.in (office). *Website:* mizoram.nic.in (office).

LAKHOVA, Yekaterina Filippovna; Russian paediatrician and politician; b. 26 May 1948; m.; one d.; ed Sverdlovsk State Medical Inst.; Deputy Head of Div., Sverdlovsk (now Yekaterinburg) City Dept of Public Health, Deputy Head of Main Dept of Public Health, Sverdlovsk Regional Exec. Cttee 1972–90; RSFSR Peoples' Deputy, mem. Council of Repub. RSFSR Supreme Soviet, Chair. Cttee on Problems of Women, Motherhood and Childhood 1990–93; State Adviser on Problems of Family, Protection of Motherhood and Childhood 1992–; adviser to Russian Pres. on Problems of Family, Protection of Motherhood and Childhood 1992–94; Chair. Cttee on Problems of Women, Family and Demography of Russian Presidency 1992–; Founder and Chair. Women of Russia (political movt) 1993; mem. State Duma 1993–, head of State Duma Cttee on Women, Families and Children's Affairs; mem. Socialist Party of Russia 1996, Otechestvo (Homeland) political movt 1998–2000, Yedinaya Rossiya 2000–. *Address:* Committee on Women, Families and Children's Affairs, State Duma, 103265 Moscow, Okhotny ryad 1, Russia. *Telephone:* (495) 292-19-00 (office). *Fax:* (495) 292-94-64 (office). *E-mail:* www@duma.ru (office). *Website:* www.duma.ru (office).

LAL, Deepak Kumar, MA, BPhil; British academic; *James S. Coleman Professor of International Development Studies, Department of Economics, University of California, Los Angeles;* b. 3 Jan. 1940, Lahore, India; s. of the late Nand Lal and of Shanti Devi; m. Barbara Ballis 1971; one s. one d.; ed Doon School, Dehra Dun, St Stephen's Coll., Delhi, India, Jesus Coll., Oxford; Indian Foreign Service 1963–65; Lecturer, Christ Church, Oxford 1966–68; Research Fellow, Nuffield Coll., Oxford 1968–70; Lecturer, Univ. Coll. London 1970–79, Reader 1979–84, Prof. of Political Economy, Univ. of London 1984–93, Prof. Emer. 1993–; James S. Coleman Prof. of Int. Devt Studies, UCLA 1991–; Consultant, Indian Planning Comm. 1973–74; Research Admin., World Bank, Washington, DC 1983–87; Dir Trade Policy Unit, Centre for Policy Studies 1993–96, Trade and Devt Unit, Inst. of Econ. Affairs 1997–2002; Pres. Mont Pelerin Soc. 2008–; consultancy assignments ILO, UNCTAD, OECD, IBRD Ministry of Planning, Sri Lanka, Repub. of Korea 1970–2002; Int. Freedom Award for Econs, Società Liberia (Italy) 2007. *Publications:* Wells and Welfare 1972, Methods of Project Analysis 1974, Appraising Foreign Investment in Developing Countries 1975, Unemployment and Wage Inflation in Industrial Economies 1977, Men or Machines 1978, Prices for Planning 1980, The Poverty of "Development Economics" 1983, Labour and Poverty in Kenya (with P. Collier) 1986, Stagflation, Savings and the State (co-ed. with M. Wolf) 1986, The Hindu Equilibrium (two vols) 1988, 1989, Public Policy and Economic Development (co-ed. with M. Scott) 1990, Development Economics (four vols) (ed.) 1991, The Repressed Economy 1993, Against Dirigisme 1994, The Political Economy of Poverty, Equity and Growth (with H. Myint) 1996, Unintended Consequences 1998, Unfinished Business 1999, Trade, Development and Political Economy (co-ed. with R. Snape) 2001, In Praise of Empires 2004, The Hindu Equilibrium 2005, Reviving the Invisible Hand: The Case for Classical Liberalism in the 21st Century 2006. *Leisure interests:* opera, theatre, tennis, bridge. *Address:* Department of Economics, 8369 Bunche Hall, UCLA, Box 951477, Los Angeles, CA 90095-1477, USA (office); A30 Nizamuddin West, New Delhi 110013, India (home); 2 Erskine Hill, London, NW11 6HB, England (home). *Telephone:* (310) 825-4521 (office); (310) 206-2382 (office); (20) 8458-3713 (London) (home); (11) 462-9465 (New Delhi) (home). *Fax:* (310) 825-9528 (office). *Website:* econweb.sscnet.ucla.edu (office).

LAL, Devendra, MSc, PhD, FRS; Indian scientist and academic; *Professor, Scripps Institute of Oceanography, University of California, San Diego;* b. 14 Feb. 1929, Varanasi (Banaras); s. of the late Dr Radhekrishna Lal and of Sita Devi; m. Aruna Damany 1955 (died 1993); ed Harish Chandra High School, Banaras Hindu Univ., Varanasi and Bombay Univ.; Assoc. Prof., Tata Inst. of Fundamental Research, Bombay 1960–63, Prof. 1963–70, Sr Prof. 1970–72, Fellow 1996–; Visiting Prof., Univ. of Calif. 1965–66, Prof., Scripps Inst. of Oceanography, Univ. of Calif. 1967–; Dir Physical Research Lab., Ahmedabad, 1972–83, Sr Prof. 1983–89, Fellow 1989–; Chair. working group on River Inputs to Ocean System 1977–81; Vice-Pres. Indian Acad. of Sciences, Bangalore 1978–82; Pres. Int. Asscn for Physical Sciences of the Ocean 1979–82, Int. Union of Geodesy and Geophysics 1983–87, Indian Geophysical Union 1980–82; Foreign Sec. Indian Nat. Science Acad., New Delhi 1981–84;

mem. Scientific Advisory Cttee to the Cabinet 1979–83; mem. Jt Scientific Cttee of WMO 1979–83; mem. Group of Experts on Scientific Aspects of Marine Pollution, UNESCO, 1979–81; mem. Advisory Cttee on Environment, ICSU 1990–94; Foreign Assoc., NAS; Fellow, Indian Acad. of Sciences, Bangalore 1964, Indian Nat. Science Acad., New Delhi 1971, Meteoritical Soc. 1975, Indian Geophysical Union 1963, Centre of the Earth Sciences Studies, Cochin 1983, Nat. Acad. Sciences, Allahabad 1988, Physical Research Laboratory, Ahmedabad 1990, Physical Research Laboratory, Ahmedabad 1991, Geological Soc. of India 1992, Geochemical Soc. (USA) 1997, AAAS 1997, American Geophysical Union 2005; Founding mem. Third World Acad. of Sciences, Italy 1983; Assoc. Royal Astronomical Soc. 1984; mem. Int. Acad. of Astronautics 1985; Hon. DSc (Banaras Univ., Varanasi) 1981; Krishnan Medal for Geochemistry and Geophysics 1965, Shanti Swarup Bhatnagar Award for Physical Sciences, Council of Scientific and Industrial Research 1967, Repub. Day Nat. Award, Padma Shri 1971, Fed. of Indian Chambers of Commerce and Industry Award in Science and Tech. 1974, Outstanding Scientist 1974, NASA Special Recognition Award for Principal Investigators, Lunar Program 1979, K.S. Krishnan Memorial Lectureship 1981, NASA Group Achievement Award (Skylab III) 1986, Pandit Jawaharlal Nehru Award for Science 1986, H. Burr Steinbach Visiting Scholar, Woods Hole Oceanographic Institution 1988. Sir C.V. Raman Birth Centenary Award 1996–7. K.R. Ramanathan Memorial Lecture 1997 Goldschmidt Medal 1997. *Publications:* over 300 articles in scientific journals; Early Solar System Processes and the Present Solar System (ed.), Biogeochemistry of the Arabian Sea (ed.),. *Leisure interests:* photography, painting, mathematical puzzles, chess. *Address:* Scripps Institution of Oceanography, GRD/0244, University of California, San Diego, La Jolla, CA 92093-0244 (office); 4445 Via Precipicio, San Diego, CA 92122, USA (home); No. 20, Jayantilal Park, Amli Bopal Road, Village Makarba, Ahmedabad 380058, India (home). *Telephone:* (858) 534-2134 (office); (858) 587-1535 (USA) (home); 79-6741451 (India) (home). *E-mail:* dlal@ucsd.edu (office). *Website:* sio.ucsd.edu (office).

LAL, Mahesh B., BS; Indian oil industry executive (retd); b. 1947; ed Indian Inst. of Tech., Kanpur, Indian Inst. of Man., Ahmedabad; trained as chemical engineer; fmr Adviser on Refineries, Ministry of Petroleum and Natural Gas; fmr Dir of Operations, Madras Refineries Ltd; Dir of Refineries, Bharat Petroleum Corpn Ltd –2002; Chair. and Man. Dir Hindustan Petroleum Corpn Ltd 2002–07; Adviser to Tech. Mission on Cotton 2003; Technical mem. (Petroleum and Natural Gas) Appellate Tribunal for Electricity 2007–; fmr mem. Bd of Dirs Cochin Refineries, IBP Co. Ltd, Numaligarh Refineries Ltd. *Address:* c/o Hindustan Petroleum Corpn Ltd, Petroleum House, 17 Jamshedji Tata Road, Mumbai 400 020; Appellate Tribunal for Electricity, 7th Floor, CORE-4, Scope Complex, Lodhi Road, New Delhi 110 003, India. *Telephone:* (22) 2202-6151 (Mumbai); (11) 2436 8477 (New Delhi). *Fax:* (11) 2436 8479 (New Delhi). *E-mail:* registrar-aptel@nic.in. *Website:* aptel.gov.in.

LALIBERTÉ, Guy, OQ, OC; Canadian entertainment industry executive; *Founder and CEO, Cirque du Soleil Inc.;* b. 2 Sept. 1959, Quebec City; began career as musician and street performer; joined stiltwalker troupe Les Echassiers De Baie-Saint-Paul; est. summer festival La Fête Foriane, Baie-Saint-Paul 1982; created govt-sponsored event Le Grand Tour du Cirque Du Soleil 1984, show toured Canada for several years, began touring USA 1987, grew into major int. org. producing multiple shows worldwide as Cirque du Soleil, to date over 20 differently themed shows have been produced across five continents combining traditional circus skills with various other artistic and cultural elements, currently CEO; finished fourth, Season Five World Poker Tour championship 2007; Great Montrealer, Académie des Grands Montréalais 2001, named one of the 100 most influential people in the world, Time magazine 2004, Ernst & Young Entrepreneur of the Year 2006. *Address:* Cirque du Soleil, 8400 2nd Avenue, Montreal, PQ H1Z 4M6, Canada (office). *Telephone:* (514) 722-2324 (office). *Fax:* (514) 722-3692 (office). *E-mail:* mediainfo@cirquedusoleil.com (office). *Website:* www.cirquedusoleil.com (office).

LALIVE d'EPINAY, Pierre, BA, PhD, LicJur, LicLitt; Swiss lawyer; b. 8 Oct. 1923, La Chaux-de-Fonds; s. of Auguste Lalive and Mme Lalive; m.; ed Geneva Univ. and Univ. of Cambridge, UK; called to Geneva Bar; Prof. of Law, Geneva Univ. 1955, Dir Dept of Pvt. Law, Dean of Law School 1967–69; Prof. of Int. Business Law, Graduate Inst. of Int. Studies 1962–86, Hon. Prof. 1986–; Sr Partner, Lalive and Partners; Pres. ICC Inst. of Int. Business Law and Practice, Swiss Arbitration Asscn; Visiting Prof., Columbia, Brussels and Cambridge Univs; Pres. Inst. of Int. Law, numerous Swiss Fed. comms and dels; Chair. of numerous int. arbitration tribunals; Hon. DJur (Lyon, Paris, Brussels, Rome); Balzan Prize 1990. *Publications:* more than 150 publns on int. law (public, pvt.), arbitration, contracts and family law. *Leisure interests:* tennis, music (opera), literature, book collecting. *Address:* Geneva University, Faculty of Law, 24 rue Général-Dufour, 1211 Geneva 4; c/o Lalive & Partners, 6 Athénée, 1205 Geneva (office); Plateau de Champel 16, Geneva, Switzerland (home). *Telephone:* (22) 3198700 (office); (22) 7890312 (home). *Fax:* (22) 3198760 (office); (22) 3198762. *E-mail:* pr.lalive@lalive.ch (office).

LALLA AÏCHA, HRH Princess; Moroccan diplomatist; b. 17 June 1930, Rabat; eldest d. of the late King Mohammed V; eldest sister of the late King Hassan II of Morocco; m. 2nd Prince Moulay al-Hasan 1972; Amb. to UK 1965–69, to Italy 1969–73 (also accred to Greece); Pres. Moroccan Red Crescent –1967, Nat. Mutual Aid Soc.; Grand Cordon of Order of the Throne. *Address:* c/o Ministry of Foreign Affairs, avenue Franklin Roosevelt, Rabat, Morocco.

LALONDE, Brice; French politician and environmental consultant; *Chairman, Round Table on Sustainable Development, Organisation for Economic Co-operation and Development;* b. 10 Feb. 1946, Neuilly-sur-Seine; s. of Alain-Gauthier Lévy Lalonde and Fiona Lalonde (née Forbes); first cousin of US Senator John Kerry; m. Patricia Raynaud 1986; two s. (one deceased) two d.; one s. one d. from previous marriage; ed Univ. of the Sorbonne, Paris; Pres. Union nationale des étudiants de france 1968; Chair. Friends of the Earth 1972, French br. 1978; cand. for Green Party, French presidential election 1981; Admin. European Environment Bureau 1983; Dir Paris Office Inst. for European Environmental Policy 1987; Sec. of State for the Environment 1988–89, for the Environment and the Prevention of Tech. and Natural Disasters 1989–90, Minister Del. 1990–91, Minister of the Environment 1991–92; Pres. Génération Ecologie (political movt) 1990–2002, Hon. Pres. 2002–; Mayor of Saint-Briac-sur-Mer 1995–; Chair. Cttee to Free Alexandr Nikitin 1996–; mem. Conseil Régional, Brittany 1998, Comité nat. de l'eau 1998–; Chair. Round Table on Sustainable Development, OECD 2007–. *Publication:* L'écologie en bleu. *Address:* Round Table on Sustainable Development, 2 rue André Pascal, 75016 Paris (office); 65 boulevard Arago, 75013 Paris (home); Mairie, 18 rue de la Mairie, 35800 Saint-Briac-sur-Mer, France. *Telephone:* 1-45-24-90-82 (office). *Fax:* 1-45-24-84-08 (office). *E-mail:* webmaster@oecd.org (office). *Website:* www.oecd.org (office).

LALOR, Patrick Joseph; Irish politician; b. 21 July 1926, Dublin; s. of Joseph Lalor and Frances Lalor; m. Myra Murphy 1952; one s. three d.; ed in Abbeyleix and at Knockbeg Coll., Carlow; fmr mem. Laois Co. Council and fmr exec. mem. Retail Grocery, Dairy and Allied Trades Asscn (RGDATA); mem. Dáil Eireann 1961–81; Parl. Sec. to Minister of Agric. and Fisheries 1965–66, to Minister for Transport, Power, Posts and Telegraphs 1966–69; Minister of Posts and Telegraphs 1969–70, for Industry and Commerce 1970–73; mem. Fianna Fáil, Chief Whip Parl. Party 1973–77; Parl. Sec. to the Taoiseach (Prime Minister) and to Minister of Defence Jan.–Dec. 1977, Minister of State at Depts of the Taoiseach and of Defence 1979 (resgnd); MEP 1979–94, Leader of Fianna Fail Party in European Parl. 1979, Vice-Pres. Group of European Progressive Democrats 1979–84; Quaestor 1979–82; Vice-Pres. of European Parl. 1982–87; Vice-Pres. European Renewal and Democratic Alliance Group 1986, European Democratic Alliance Group 1988; Quaestor of European Parl. 1989–94; mem. European Parl. Cttees on Transport and Tourism, Rules of Procedure, Political Affairs, Bureau and Enlarged Bureau 1989–94; Grand Officier du Ouissam Alaouite (Morocco) 1981. *Leisure interests:* hurling, Gaelic football, golf, drama. *Address:* Main Street, Abbeyleix, Portlaoise, Co. Laois, Ireland. *Telephone:* (502) 31206.

LALUMIÈRE, Catherine; French politician; b. 3 Aug. 1935, Rennes; m. Pierre Lalumière (deceased); specialist in public law; Lecturer, Univ. of Paris; mem. Steering Cttee, Parti Socialiste 1979; mem. Nat. Ass. for Gironde 1986–89; Adviser to Pres. on civil service; Sec. of State for the Civil Service and Admin. Reforms May–June 1981, Minister for Consumer Affairs 1981–83, Sec. of State 1983–84, Minister for European Affairs 1984–86; Sec.-Gen. Council of Europe 1989–94; Urban Community Councillor, Bordeaux 1989–; Municipal Councillor, Talence 1989–95; MEP 1994–2004, Vice-Pres. 2001–04; Deputy Pres. Radical France 1996 (now Radical Socialist Party); Pres. European Radical Alliance 1994–; Hon. DCL (Durham) 1995.

LAM, Barry, BEng, MEng; Taiwanese electronics industry executive; *Chairman, Quanta Computer Inc.;* b. Shanghai; m.; two c.; ed Nat. Taiwan Univ.; Co-founder Kimpo (handheld calculator mfr) 1973; f. Quanta Computer Inc. (computer and components mfr) 1988, currently Chair.; Chair. Quanta Culture and Educ. Foundation; mem. Bd of Dirs Cloud Gate Theatre Group; Business Week's 50 Stars of Asia 1999, 2002, Business Week's 25 Managers of the Year 2002. *Address:* Quanta Computer Inc., 211 Wen Hwa Second Road, Kui Shan Hsiang, Taoyuan, Taiwan (office). *Telephone:* (3) 327-2345 (office). *Fax:* (3) 327-1511 (office). *E-mail:* campus@quantatw.com (office). *Website:* www.quantatw.com (office).

LAMB, Allan Joseph; South African fmr professional cricketer; b. 20 June 1954, Langebaanweg, Cape Province; s. of Michael Lamb and Joan Lamb; m. Lindsay Lamb 1979; one s. one d.; ed Wynberg Boys' High School and Abbotts Coll.; middle-order right-hand batsman; teams: Western Province 1972–82 and 1992–93, OFS 1987–88, Northants. 1978–95 (Capt. 1989–95); qualified for England 1982 and played in 79 Tests 1982–92 (three as Capt.), scoring 4,656 runs (average 36.0) including 14 hundreds; toured Australia 1982–83, 1986–87, 1990–91; scored 32,502 first-class runs (89 hundreds); scored 1,000 runs in a season on 15 occasions; 122 limited-overs ints; Dir Lamb Assocs Event Man. Co., Grenada Sports Ltd; contrib. to Sky Sports Cricket; Wisden Cricketer of the year 1981. *Play:* Beef and Lamb in a stew (roadshow with Ian Botham) 1994–95. *Publication:* Silence of the Lamb (autobiog.) 1995. *Leisure interests:* tennis, golf, cycling, rugby, horse racing, fly-fishing, shooting. *Address:* Lamb Associates Ltd, First Floor, 4 St Giles Street, Northampton, NN1 1JB, England. *Telephone:* (1604) 231222 (office). *Fax:* (1604) 239930 (office).

LAMBECK, Kurt, DPhil, DSc, FRS, FAA; Australian (b. Dutch) geophysicist and academic; *Professor of Geophysics, Research School of Earth Sciences, Australian National University; President, Australian Academy of Science;* b. 20 Sept. 1941; ed Univ. of NSW, Univ. of Oxford, UK; Geodesist, Smithsonian Astrophysical Observatory 1967–70; Dir of Research, Paris Observatory 1970–73; Prof. of Geophysics, Univ. of Paris 1973–77; Prof. of Geophysics, Research School of Earth Sciences, ANU 1977–; Fellow, Australian Acad. of Science 1984–, Pres. 2006–; Foreign Mem. Royal Netherlands Acad. of Arts and Sciences 1993, Norwegian Acad. of Science and Letters 1998, Academie des Sciences, France 2005; Hon. mem. European Geophysics Soc. 1988–; Hon. DEng (Nat. Tech. Univ. of Greece), Hon. DSc (Univ. NSW); Macelwane Award, American Geophysical Union 1976, Whitten Medal, American Geophysical Union 1993, Jaeger Medal, Australian Acad. of Science 1995, Alfred Wegener Medal, European Union of Geosciences 1996. *Publications:* The Earth's Variable Rotation 1980, Geophysical Geodesy 1988; numerous papers on geodesy and geophysics. *Address:* Research School of

Earth Sciences, Mills Road, Australian National University, Canberra, ACT 0200 (office). *Telephone:* (2) 61255161 (office). *E-mail:* Kurt.Lambeck@anu.edu.au (office). *Website:* www.rses.anu.edu.au/geodynamics/lambeck/index.htm (office).

LAMBERT, Christopher; American actor; b. (Christophe Guy Dénis Lambert), 29 March 1957, Manhasset, New York; ed L'Ecole Roche, Int. School, Lycée d'Annemasse, Coll. Floriment, Geneva, Florent School, Paris and Paris Conservatoire; mil. service with Alpine Corps, Grenoble; trainee, Barclay's Bank, London 1976. *Films include:* Le Bar du téléphone 1980, Asphalte 1981, Une sale affaire 1981, Putain d'histoire d'amour 1981, Légitime violence 1982, Greystoke: the Story of Tarzan, Lord of the Apes 1983, Paroles et Musiques 1984, Subway 1985, Highlander 1986, I Love You 1986, The Sicilian 1987, Love Dream 1988, To Kill A Priest 1988, Why Me? 1990, Highlander II: The Quickening 1991, Knight Moves 1992, Max & Jeremie 1992, Fortress 1993, Gunmen 1994, Road Killers 1994, Highlander III: The Sorcerer 1994, The Hunted 1995, Mortal Kombat 1995, Tashunga 1996, Adrenalin: Fear the Rush 1996, Hercule et Sherlock 1996, Nirvana 1997, Arlette 1997, Mean Guns 1997, Fortress 2 1999, Operation Splitsville 1999, Beowulf 1999, Resurrection 1999, Gideon 1999, Highlander: Endgame 2000, Aparté 2001, Vercingétorix 2001, The Point Men 2001, The Piano Player 2002, Absolon 2003, Janis et John 2003, À ton image 2004, Metamorphosis 2006, Day of Wrath 2006. *Television includes:* Douchka 1981, La Dame de coeur 1982, King of Bandit Jing (miniseries) 2002, Dalida (miniseries) 2005. *Website:* www.christopherlambert.org.

LAMBERT, Phyllis, CC, GOQ, CAL, BA, MS (Arch), FRSC; Canadian architect and museum director; *Founding Director and Chair of the Board of Trustees, Centre Canadien d'Architecture / Canadian Centre for Architecture, Montréal;* b. 24 Jan. 1927, Montréal, Québec; d. of Samuel Bronfman and Saidye Bronfman (née Rosner); ed The Study, Montréal, Vassar Coll., New York, Illinois Inst. of Tech., Chicago; Adjunct Prof., School of Architecture, McGill Univ. 1986–; Assoc. Prof., Faculté de l'aménagement, École d'architecture, Université de Montréal 1989–; Bd Chair. and Prin., Ridgway Ltd, Architects/Developers, Los Angeles 1972–84; Founding Dir and Chair. Bd of Trustees, Centre Canadien d'Architecture (CCA), Montréal 1979–, Consulting Architect and Client CCA 1984–89; cr. Fonds d'investissement de Montréal, pvt. fund for revitalization of Montréal neighbourhoods 1996; est. Int. Foundation for the Canadian Centre for Architecture Prize for Design of Cities 1999; jury mem. several cttees for architectural and urban design projects; numerous exhbns; mem. Bd of Trustees Inst. of Fine Arts, New York Univ. 1973-, Bd of Advisors Temple Hoyne Buell Center for the Study of American Architecture, Columbia Univ., New York 1984– (Founding Chair. 1984–89), Advisory Council School of Architecture, Princeton Univ. 1990–2003, 2006–, Bd Acquisitions Cttee Nat. Gallery of Canada 1991–, Provost's Advisory Bd Faculty of Architecture, Univ. of Toronto 1992–2004, Visiting Cttee Grad. School of Design, Harvard Univ. 1993–2005, and several other bodies; Founding mem. Bd Int. Confed. of Architectural Museums 1984– (Pres. 1984–87); fmr mem. Bd of Overseers, Coll. of Architecture and Planning, Ill. Inst. of Tech.; frequent guest lecturer at univs and professional orgs in N America and abroad; Academician, RCA 1977; Life mem. Council of the Ontario Asscn of Architects 2003–; Fellow, Royal Architectural Inst. of Canada (RAIC) 1983; Foreign Hon. mem. American Acad. of Arts and Sciences 1995; Hon. FRIBA 2001; Hon. FAIA 2003; Chevalier, Ordre de la Pléiade, Assemblée parlementaire de la Francophonie 1998, Grand Oficier, Ordre nat. du Québec 2005, Commdr, Ordre des Arts et des Lettres 2006; 27 hon. degrees from univs in N America and Europe; numerous awards and prizes, including Médaille de l'Acad. d'Architecture de France 1988, Gabrielle Léger Medal, Heritage Canada Foundation 1988, Prix d'excellence en architecture, Ordre des Architectes du Québec (for CCA) 1989, Médaille d'Honneur, Soc. Historique de Montréal 1990, RAIC Gold Medal 1991, AIA Honor Award (for CCA) 1992, AIA Inst. Honor (for CCA) 1992, Lescarbot Award, Govt of Canada 1992, Prix Gérard-Morisset, Gov. of Québec 1994, Hadrian Award, World Monuments Fund 1997, Montblanc Int. Arts Patronage Award 2001, Prix Meilleur(e) Ami(e) des Musées Montréalais, Soc. des directeurs des musées montréalais 2002, Chrysler Design Award (as Design Champion) 2002, Prix Blanche Lemco van Ginkel, Ordre des Urbanistes du Québec 2003, Award of Excellence, Advocate for Architecture, RAIC 2005, Vincent J. Scully Prize, Nat. Building Museum 2006, Prix d'excellence de l'Opération patrimoine architectural de Montréal, Ville de Montréal et Héritage Montréal 2007, Pillar of New York Award, Preservation League of New York State 2007, Woodrow Wilson Award for Public Service, Canada Inst. of the Woodrow Wilson Int. Centre for Scholars 2007. *Projects include:* Seagram Bldg, New York (Dir of Planning) (AIA 25-Year Award 1984, New York Landmarks Conservancy Award 1989) 1954–58, Toronto-Dominion Centre, Toronto (consultant) 1962, Saidye Bronfman Centre, YM-YWHA, Montréal (architect) (RAIC Massey Medal 1970) 1963–68, Les Promenades St-Bruno Shopping Centre, St Bruno, Québec (consultant) 1974, Jane Tate House renovation, Montréal (architect) 1974–76, Biltmore Hotel renovation, Los Angeles (architect and developer) (AIA Award of Honor 1978) 1976, renovation of housing units, St-Hubert Street, Montréal (developer) 1978, 700-unit co-operative housing renovation project, Milton Park, Montréal (Pres.) 1979–85, Ben Ezra Synagogue Restoration Project, Cairo, Egypt (Dir) 1981–94. *Publications:* Court House: A Photographic Document 1978, Photography and Architecture: 1839–1939 1982, Architecture and its Image 1989, Canadian Centre for Architecture: Building and Gardens 1989, Opening the Gates of Eighteenth-Century Montréal (ed.) 1992, Fortifications and the Synagogue: The Fortress of Babylon and the Ben Ezra Synagogue, Cairo (ed.) 1994, Viewing Olmsted: Photographs by Robert Burley, Lee Friedlander and Geoffrey James (ed.) 1996, Autonomy and Ideology: Positioning an Avant-Garde in America 1997, Mies in America (ed.) 2001; numerous essays in architectural periodicals. *Address:* Centre Canadien d'Architecture, 1920 rue Baile, Montréal, PQ H3H 2S6, Canada (office). *Telephone:* (514) 939-7025 (office). *Fax:* (514) 939-7032 (office). *E-mail:* plambert@cca.qc.ca (office). *Website:* www.cca.qc.ca (office).

LAMBERT, Richard Peter, BA; British journalist and organization official; *Director-General, Confederation of British Industry (CBI);* b. 23 Sept. 1944; s. of Peter Lambert and Mary Lambert; m. Harriet Murray-Browne 1973; one s. one d.; ed Fettes Coll. and Balliol Coll. Oxford; mem. staff, Financial Times 1966–2001, Lex Column 1972, Financial Ed. 1978, New York Corresp. 1982, Deputy Ed. 1983, Ed. Financial Times 1991–2001; lecturer and contrib. to The Times 2001–; external mem. Bank of England Monetary Policy Cttee (MPC) 2003–06; Dir-Gen. Confederation of British Industry (CBI), London 2006–; Dir (non-exec.) London Int. Financial Futures Exchange (LIFFE), AXA Investment Mans, Int. Rescue Cttee UK; Chair. Visiting Arts; Gov. Royal Shakespeare Co.; UK Chair. Franco-British Colloque; mem. UK–India Round Table; mem. Int. Advisory Bd, British-American Business Inc.; Hon. DLitt (City Univ. London) 2000; Princess of Wales Amb. Award 2001, World Leadership Forum Business Journalist Decade of Excellence Award 2001. *Address:* CBI, Centre Point, 103 New Oxford Street, London, WC1A 1DU, England (office). *Telephone:* (20) 7395-8001 (office). *Website:* www.cbi.org.uk (office).

LAMBERT, Yves Maurice; French international organization official and engineer; b. 4 June 1936, Nancy, Meurthe-et-Moselle; s. of André Arthur Lambert and Paulette Franck; m. Odile Revillon 1959; three s. two d.; ed Ecole Polytechnique, Paris, Nat. Civil Aviation School, Centre de Préparation à l'Admin des Entreprises; Dir Org. de Gestion et de Sécurité de l'Algérie (OGSA), Algeria 1965–68; Tech. Adviser to Minister of Transport, France 1969–72; Rep. of France to ICAO Council 1972–76; Sec.-Gen. ICAO Aug. 1976–88, Dir of Air Navigation, Ministry of Equipment and Housing, Transport and the Sea 1989–93; Dir-Gen. Eurocontrol 1994–2001; Fellow Royal Aeronautical Soc. (UK); mem. Acad. Nat. de l'Air et de l'Espace; Officier, Légion d'honneur, Ordre nat. du Mérite; Médaille de l'Aéronautique, Glen Gilbert Award, Air Traffic Control Asscn 1997. *Address:* c/o Eurocontrol, 96 rue de la Fusée, 1130 Brussels, Belgium.

LAMBO, (Thomas) Adeoye, OBE, MB, ChB, MD, FRCPE, FRCPsy; Nigerian neuro-psychiatrist; *Executive Director, Lambo Foundation;* b. 29 March 1923, Abeokuta; s. of the late Chief David Basil Lambo and Felicia Lambo; m. Dinah V. Adams 1945; three s.; ed Baptist Boys' High School, Abeokuta, Univ. of Birmingham and Inst. of Psychiatry, Univ. of London, UK; Medical Officer, Nigerian Medical Services 1950–56; Govt Specialist-in-charge, Aro Hospital for Nervous Diseases; Consultant Physician, Univ. Coll., Ibadan 1956–63; Prof. and Head of Dept of Psychiatry and Neurology, Univ. of Ibadan 1963–71, Dean of Medical Faculty 1966–68; Vice-Chancellor, 1968–71; Asst Dir-Gen. WHO 1971–73, Deputy Dir-Gen. 1973–88; mem. Exec. Comm. World Fed. for Mental Health 1964–; Exec. Dir Lambo Foundation 1988–; Chair. Scientific Council for Africa, UN Advisory Cttee for Prevention of Crime and Treatment of Offenders, Co-ordinating Bd African Chairs of Tech. in Food Processing, Biotechnology, Nutrition and Health; Vice-Pres. World Asscn of Social Psychiatry; mem. of numerous asscns including Advisory Cttee for Mental Health, WHO, Exec. Cttee Council for Int. Org. for Medical Sciences, UNESCO, Expert Advisory Panel on Mental Health, WHO, Advisory Cttee for Health Research, WHO (Geneva), Royal Medico-Psychological Asscn, UK, Pontifical Acad. of Sciences Int. Epidemiological Asscn, Int. Hosp. Fed., Nigerian Medical Council; Founding mem. African Acad. of Sciences; Assoc. mem. Int. Asscn For Child Psychiatry and Allied Professions; Patron Asscn of Gen. and Pvt. Medical Practitioners of Nigeria 1999–; Hon. mem. Swiss Acad. of Medical Sciences, Third World Acad. of Sciences (Founding mem.); Commdr Order of the Niger 1979; Nigerian Nat. Order of Merit 1979; Hon. DSc (Ahmadu Bello) 1967, (Long Island) 1975, (McGill) 1978, (Jos) 1979, (Nskukka) 1979, (Hacettepe) 1980, (Hahnemann) 1984; Hon. LLD (Kent State) 1969, (Birmingham) 1971, (Pennsylvania) 1985; Dr hc (Benin) 1973, (Aix-Marseille) 1974, (Catholic Univ. of Louvain) 1976, (Debrecen) 1987; Haile Selassie African Research Award 1970, Leader of Psychiatry Award, World Psychiatric Asscn 1999. *Publications:* Psychiatric Disorder among the Yorubas (co-author) 1963 and numerous articles in various medical journals. *Leisure interests:* collection of ethnographic material on Africa, of art of traditional and tribal religions, of ancient books on the history of medicine and on literature and philosophy. *Address:* Lambo Foundation, 11 Olatunbosun Street, Shonibare Estate, Maryland, PO Box 702, Ikeja, Lagos State, Nigeria (office); 15 Olatunbosan Street, Shonibare Estate, Maryland, Ikeja, Lagos, Nigeria (home). *Telephone:* (1) 4976110 (office); (1) 4976110 (home). *Fax:* (1) 4976110 (office); (1) 4976110 (home). *E-mail:* talambo@beta.linkserve.com.

LAMBRAKIS, Christos D.; Greek newspaper proprietor and journalist; b. 24 Feb. 1934; s. of the late Dimitrios Ch. Lambrakis; ed LSE; Publr and Ed. weekly Tachydromos (Courier) 1955–, now Chair.; succeeded father as propr of dailies To Vima (Tribune), Ta Nea (News) and the weeklies Economicos Tachydromos (Economic Courier) 1957, Omada (The Team) 1958; Publr monthly Epoches 1963; Pres. Greek Section, Int. Press Inst.; imprisoned (Folegandros Prison Island) Nov. 1967; Chair. Lambrakis Research Foundation. *Address:* c/o Lambrakis Press SA, Michalakopoulou str., 80, 115 28 Athens, Greece. *Telephone:* (21) 3657000. *Fax:* (21) 3686445. *E-mail:* info@in.gr. *Website:* www.dol.gr.

LAMBRON, Marc; French journalist and writer; b. 4 Feb. 1957, Lyon; s. of Paul Lambron and Jacqueline Lambron (née Denis); m. Sophie Missoffe 1983; one s. two d.; ed Ecole normale supérieure, Institut d'etudes politiques, Ecole nationale d'admin; columnist, Point 1986–, Madame Figaro; mem. Conseil d'Etat 1985–; Chevalier, Ordre des Arts et des Lettres, Chevalier, Légion d'honneur 2004; Prix des Deux Magots 1989, Prix Colette 1991, Prix Fémina 1993. *Publications:* L'Impromptu de Madrid 1988, La nuit des masques 1990,

Carnet de bal 1992, L'oeil du silence 1993, 1941 1997, Etrangers dans la nuit 2001, Carnet de bal II 2003, Les Menteurs 2004, Une saison sur la terre 2006. *Leisure interests:* music, cinema. *Address:* 17 rue Lagrange, 75005 Paris, France. *Telephone:* 1-40-51-02-12. *Fax:* 1-46-33-43-18.

LAMBSDORFF, Otto Graf Friedrich Wilhelm von der Wenge, DIur; German politician, government official and fmr company executive; b. 20 Dec. 1926, Aachen; ed Univs of Bonn and Cologne; mil. service, prisoner of war, seriously wounded 1944–46; admitted to Bar at local and Dist courts of Düsseldorf 1960; activities in credit business, rising to power of attorney for a private bank 1955–71; mem. bd of dirs of an insurance co. 1971–77; mem. Bundestag 1972–; Fed. Minister of Econs 1977–84; Chair. Free Democratic Party (FDP) 1988–93, European Chair. Trilateral Comm. 1991–; Chair. Bd Friedrich Naumann Foundation 1995–; Pres. Liberal Int. 1993–96; Rep. of Fed. Chancellor for the Foundation Initiative for German Industry 1999–2002; Dr hc 1980. *Publications:* Zielsetzungen-Aufgaben und Chancen der Marktwirtschaft 1978, Bewährung-Wirtschaftspolitik in Krisenzeiten 1980. *Address:* Strässchensweg 7, 53113 Bonn, Germany (office). *Telephone:* (228) 236061 (office). *Fax:* (228) 236069 (office). *E-mail:* o.lambsdorff@t-online.de (office).

LAMEDA, Guaicaipuro, MA; Venezuelan business executive, army officer and engineer; b. 6 Aug. 1954, Barquisimeto, Estada Lara; ed Mil. Acad. of Venezuela, Pacific Univ., USA, Inst. of Advanced Studies of Nat. Defense, Gen. Staff and Command School, USA; numerous managerial and educational posts in Venezuelan army and govt, including Chief Planning Officer, Venezuelan Co. of Mil. Industries (CAVIM) 1992, Dir of Budget Office, Ministry of Defence 1996, Dir Govt Cen. Budget Office 1998; Chair. Petróleos de Venezuela SA (PDVSA) 2000–02; Pres. of the Repub. Award, Nat. School for Advanced Defense Studies; 15 nat. and foreign distinctions; 3 mil. merit badges, 23 mil. honour awards. *Address:* c/o Edif. Petróleos de Venezuela, Torre Est, Avda Libertador, La Campina, Apdo 169, Caracas 1010-A, Venezuela.

LAMFALUSSY, Baron Alexandre, LèsSc (Econ), DPhil; Belgian banker and academic; b. 26 April 1929, Kapuvar, Hungary; m. Anne-Marie Cochard 1957; two s. two d.; ed Catholic Univ. of Louvain and Nuffield Coll., Oxford, UK; economist, then econ. adviser, Banque de Bruxelles 1955–65; Visiting Lecturer, Yale Univ., USA 1961–62; Exec. Dir and Chair. Exec. Bd Banque de Bruxelles 1965–75; Exec. Dir Banque Bruxelles Lambert 1975; Econ. Adviser, Head of Monetary and Econ. Dept BIS 1976–81, Asst Gen. Man. 1981–85, Gen. Man. 1985–93; Pres. of the European Monetary Inst. 1994–97; Chair. Cttee of Wise Men on the Regulation of European Securities Markets, European Council 2000–01; currently teaching and involved in research at Institut d'études européennes, Catholic Univ. of Louvain. *Publications include:* Investment and Growth in Mature Economies: The Case of Belgium 1961, The UK and the Six: An Essay on Growth in Western Europe 1963, Les marchés financiers en Europe 1968, Financial Crises in Emerging Markets: An Essay on Financial Globalization and Fragility 2000. *Address:* Institut d'études européennes, Université catholique de Louvain, Ottignies-Louvain-la-Neuve, Louvain, Belgium (office); Postfach 102031, 60020 Frankfurt, Germany. *Telephone:* (69) 272270. *Fax:* (69) 27227227.

LAMINE LOUM, Mamadou; Senegalese politician; fmr Minister of Econ., Finance and Planning; Prime Minister of Senegal 1998–99; mem. Parti Socialiste (PS). *Address:* c/o Office of the Prime Minister, ave. Léopold Sedar Senghor, Dakar, Senegal. *Telephone:* 823-10-88. *Fax:* 822-55-78.

LAMIZANA, Mariam, MA; Burkinabè politician and organization official; *Honorary President, Inter-African Cttee (IAC) on Traditional Practices;* b. 26 July 1951, Bobo-Dioulasso; m.; four c.; ed Univ. of Paris X–Nanterre and Institut de Service Social et de Recherches Sociales, Montrouge, France; Attaché d'Etudes, Soc. of African Studies and Devt, Ouagadougou 1976; Social Asst Bureau of Social Aid 1979–90; Prof. of Sociology, Institut Nat. d'Educ. 1981–84; Prov. Dir of Family Expansion and Nat. Solidarity, Houet—Bobo-Dioulasso 1984–86; Sec.-Gen. Ministry of Family Expansion and Nat. Solidarity 1986–88; Tech. Adviser to Minister of Social Action and the Family 1988–97; Pres. Inter-African Cttee (IAC) on Traditional Practices, Nat. Cttee of the Struggle against Circumcision (CNLPE) 1988–97, Perm. Sec. 1997–2000, now Hon. Pres.; mem. House of Reps 1996–99; Regional Councillor for Francophone Africa, RAINBO (Research, Action and Information Network for Bodily Integrity of Women), New York, USA 1997–2000; Dir-Gen. of Nat. Solidarity, Ministry of Social Action and Nat. Solidarity 2001, Minister for Social Action and Nat. Solidarity 2002–05; Pres. Voice of Women Asscn, Burkina Faso 2000; mem. Ind. Nat. Election Cttee 2001; chair. numerous govt cttees; del. to int. org. including UN, UNICEF, OAU, Inter-African Cttee; Chevalier Ordre du Mérite (Burkina Faso); Nathalie Masse Int. Prize, Centre Int. de l'Enfant 1995. *Publications include:* Développement Communautaire au Burkina Faso, Mémoire de Maîtrise 1980. *Address:* CNLPE (Comité national de lutte contre la pratique de l'excision), BP 515/01, Ouagadougou 01, Burkina Faso. *Telephone:* 26-30-79-15.

LAMJAV, Banzrachiin; Mongolian fmr politician; b. 1920; ed Higher School for Party Cadres, Ulaanbaatar and Higher Party School of the CPSU Cen. Cttee; Instructor at Prov. Cttee of the Mongolian Revolutionary Youth League; served in army as private, elected as Bureau secretary of the Youth League Cttee, worked as asst and deputy chief of political dept of regt, then a brigade; Head of Section, Political Directorate, Mongolian People's Army (MPRP), then Deputy Chief of Dept; Deputy Chair. Party Cen. Cttee of MPRP Cen. Cttee 1954–56; First Sec. Party Cttee of Zavkhan Aimak (Prov.) 1956–58; Instructor at the MPRP Cen. Cttee 1958–62; Head of Personnel Dept MPRP Cen. Cttee 1962–86; concurrently First Deputy Chair. Party Control Cttee of MPRP Cen. Cttee 1979–86; Alt. mem. Political Bureau of MPRP Cen. Cttee 1986–87, mem. 1987–90 and Chair. Party Control Cttee MPRP Cen. Cttee 1986–90 (resgnd); fmr Deputy to the Great People's Hural; mem. of Presidium of Great People's Hural 1976–86.

LAMM, Donald Stephen, BA; American publisher; *Literary Agent, Carlisle & Company;* b. 31 May 1931, New York; s. of Lawrence W. Lamm and Aleen A. Lassner; m. Jean S. Nicol 1958; two s. one d.; ed Fieldston School, Yale Univ. and Univs of Oxford, UK; Counter-intelligence Corps, US Army 1953–55; joined W. W. Norton & Co. Inc. 1956, college rep. 1956–59, Ed. 1959–2000, Dir 1964–2000, Vice-Pres. 1968–76, Chair. 1984–2000; Pres. Yale Univ. Press 1984–2000; currently Literary Agent, Fletcher & Parry; mem. Editorial Bd The American Scholar; Regents Lecturer, Univ. of Calif., Berkeley 1997–99; mem. Advisory Council Inst. of Early American History and Culture 1979–82; mem. Council on Foreign Relations 1978–; mem. Council, Woodrow Wilson Center, Int. Advisory Bd, Logos; Guest Fellow, Yale Univ. 1980, 1985; Trustee, The Roper Center 1984–; Fellow, Branford Coll. Yale Univ. 1985–2000, Center for Advanced Study in Behavioral Sciences 1998–99; Guest Fellow Woodrow Wilson Center 1996; Pres. Bd of Govs Yale Univ. 1986–; Ida H. Beam Distinguished Visiting Prof. Univ. of Iowa 1987–88; mem. American Acad. of Arts and Sciences (first book publisher elected in AAAS history); Vice-Pres. Phi Beta Kappa Soc. 2003–; Trustee Univ. of Calif. Press. *Publications:* Economics and the Common Reader 1989, Beyond Literacy 1990, Book Publishing in the United States Today 1997, Perception, Cognition and Language 2000. *Leisure interests:* wilderness canoeing, skiing. *Address:* Fletcher & Parry, 78 Fifth Avenue, Co., 24 East 64th Street, New York, NY 10011, USA (office).

LAMM, Richard D., LLB, JD, CPA; American fmr politician, lawyer and academic; *University Professor, Co-Director of the Institute for Public Policy Studies and Executive Director of the Center for Public Policy and Contemporary Issues, University of Denver;* b. 8 Aug. 1935, Madison, Wis.; s. of A. E. Lamm; m. Dottie Lamm; one s. one d.; ed Univ. of Wis. and Univ. of Calif., Berkeley; Certified Public Accountant, Ernst & Ernst, Denver 1961–62; lawyer, Colo Anti-Discrimination Comm. 1962–63; lawyer, Jones, Meiklejohn, Kilroy, Kehl & Lyons 1963–65; pvt. practice 1965–74; mem. Colo House of Reps 1966–74; Assoc. Prof. of Law, Univ. of Denver 1969–74; Gov. of Colo 1975–87 (three terms); Univ. Prof., Co-Dir Inst. for Public Policy Studies and Exec. Dir Center for Public Policy and Contemporary Issues, Univ. of Denver 1987–; founding mem. Colo Trail Foundation; mem. Bd of Advisors, Foundation for Defense of Democracies. *Publications:* The Angry West (with Michael McCarthy) 1982, 1988 (with Arnie Grossman) 1985, Megatraumas 1985, The Immigration Time Bomb 1985, A California Conspiracy (with Arnold Grossman) 1988. *Leisure interests:* mountain climbing, reading, bicycling. *Address:* Institute for Public Policy Studies, University of Denver, Mary Reed Building 107, 2199 South University Blvd., Denver, CO 80208, USA (office). *Telephone:* (303) 871-2468 (office). *Fax:* (303) 871-3066 (office). *E-mail:* ipps@du.edu (office). *Website:* www.du.edu/ipps (office).

LAMM, Vanda Éva, PhD, DSc; Hungarian professor of international law and international legal official; *Director, Institute for Legal Studies, Hungarian Academy of Sciences;* b. 26 March 1945, Budapest; d. of Robert T. Lamm and Hedvig Lamm (née Vandel); ed Univ. of Budapest, Faculté int. pour l'enseignement du droit comparé, Strasbourg, France, Hague Acad. of Int. Law, Netherlands, Columbia Univ., USA; Research Fellow, Inst. for Legal Studies, Hungarian Acad. of Sciences, Dir 1991–; Prof. of Int. Law Univ. of Miskolc 1998, Univ. of Budapest-Győr; Head, Dept of Int. Law, Széchenyi István Univ.; mem. Perm. Court of Arbitration 1999–; Deputy mem. Court of Arbitration of OSCE; mem. UN CEDAW Cttee monitoring implementation of 1979 Convention on Elimination of Discrimination against Women; Pres. Int. Nuclear Law Asscn 2000–01, Hon. Pres. and mem. Bd of Man. 2004–05; Sec.-Gen. Hungarian Br., Int. Law Asscn; Vice-Chair. Group of Governmental Experts on Third Party Liability, OECD-NEA; Assoc. mem. Inst. of Int. Law 2001–; Ed.-in-Chief Állam-és Jogtudomány; Ed. Acta Juridica Hungarica. *Publications:* numerous publs on nuclear law and int. law. *Address:* Institute for Legal Studies, Hungarian Academy of Sciences, PO Box 25, I. Országház u. 30, 1250 Budapest (office); Department of International Law, Széchenyi István University, Egyetem tér 1, 9026 Győr, Hungary. *Telephone:* (1) 355-7384 (office); (96) 503-478. *Fax:* (1) 375-7858 (office); (96) 503-400/3535. *E-mail:* lamm@jog.mta.hu (office); lammv@mail.sze.hu.

LAMO DE ESPINOSA Y MICHELS DE CHAMPOURCÍN, Jaime; Spanish politician and agronomic engineer; b. 4 April 1941, Madrid; s. of Emilio Lamo de Espinosa and María Luisa Michels de Champourcín; m. Carmen Rocamora 1965; four d.; ed Colegio de Nuestra Señora del Pilar, Escuela Técnica Superior de Ingenieros Agrónomos, Univ. of Madrid; Asst Engineer, Study Group, Servicio Nacional de Concentración Parcelaria 1964–69; Tech. Dir Fondo de Ordenación y Regulación de Productos y Precios Agrarios (FORPPA) 1969–73; Sub-commissar for Devt Plan 1973; Dir of Tech. Cttee, Ministry of Agric. 1974; Dir-Gen. Food Industries 1974–76; Under-Sec. of Agric. 1976; Asst to Third Vice-Pres. of Govt 1977–78; Minister of Agric. and Fisheries 1978–81; Minister Asst to Pres. Council of Ministers 1981–82; mem. Congress of Deputies for Castellón 1979–; mem. Unión de Centro Democrático (UCD); Chief UCD spokesman in Congress 1981–82; Pres. 20th FAO World Conf. 1979–81; Pres. Conf. of OECD Ministers of Agric. 1980; Prof., Int. Centre for Advanced Mediterranean Agronomic Studies, Montpellier, France (OECD) 1980; Gran Cruz del Mérito Agrícola; Gran Cruz del Mérito Civil; Encomienda del Mérito Agrícola; Cross of Merit (FRG); Croix du Mérite Civil (France). *Publications:* Agricultura a tiempo parcial y minifundios, Reflexiones sobre la política de precios y su armonización con la política general agraria, Los latifundios y el desarrollo agrario, Interrelación de las políticas de precio y de estructura en la agricultura, La agricultura en una sociedad democrática.

Leisure interests: reading, music, painting. *Address:* José Abascal 46, Madrid, Spain. *Telephone:* 4413415.

LAMONT, Donald Alexander, MA; British diplomatist; *CEO, Wilton Park;* b. 13 Jan. 1947; s. of Alexander Lamont and Alexa Lee Will; m. Lynda Margaret Campbell 1981; one s. one d.; ed Univ. of Aberdeen; with British Leyland Motor Corpn 1970; Second Sec., then First Sec. FCO 1974; First Sec. UNIDO/IAEA, Vienna 1977; First Sec. (Commercial) Moscow 1980; First Sec. FCO 1982; Counsellor on secondment to IISS 1988; Political Adviser and Head of Chancery, British Mil. Govt, Berlin 1988–91; Amb. to Uruguay 1991–94; Head of Repub. of Ireland Dept, FCO 1994–97; Chief of Staff and Deputy High Rep., Sarajevo 1997–99; Gov. of Falkland Islands and Commr for S Georgia and S Sandwich Islands 1999–2002; Amb. to Venezuela 2003–07; CEO Wilton Park (FCO conference unit) 2007–. *Address:* Wilton Park Conferences, Wiston House, Steyning, West Sussex, BN44 3DZ, England (office). *Telephone:* (1903) 817766 (office). *Fax:* (1903) 879647 (office). *E-mail:* admin@wiltonpark.org.uk (office). *Website:* www.wiltonpark.org.uk (office).

LAMONT OF LERWICK, Baron (Life Peer), cr. 1998, of Lerwick in the Shetland Islands; **Rt Hon. Norman Stewart Hughson Lamont,** PC; British politician and writer; b. 8 May 1942, Lerwick, Shetland; s. of the late Daniel Lamont and of Helen Irene Hughson; m. Alice Rosemary White 1971 (separated 1999); one s. one d.; ed Loretto School, Fitzwilliam Coll., Cambridge; personal Asst to Rt Hon Duncan Sandys MP 1965; mem. staff Conservative Research Dept 1966–68; MP for Kingston upon Thames 1972–97; Merchant Banker with NM Rothschild & Sons 1968–79, Dir Rothschild Asset Man.; Parl. Pvt. Sec. to Norman St John Stevas (Lord St John of Fawsley) 1974; Opposition Spokesman on Prices and Consumer Affairs 1975–76, on Industry 1976–79; Parl. Under-Sec. of State, Dept of Energy 1979–81; Minister of State, Dept of Trade and Industry 1981–85, of Defence Procurement 1985–86; Financial Sec. to Treasury 1986–89, Chief Sec. 1989–90; Chancellor of the Exchequer 1990–93; Chair. Conservatives Against a Fed. Europe 1998–99; Chair. East European Food Fund 1995–; Chair. Bruges Group 2003–; mem. House of Lords Select Cttee on EU 2001–03; Dir (non-exec.) N. M. Rothschild & Sons Ltd 1993–95; Dir Balli Group, Scottish Re Group, RAB Capital; Adviser, Rotch Property Group; Chair. Cambridge Univ. Conservative Asscn 1963; Pres. Cambridge Union 1964. *Publication:* Sovereign Britain 1995, In Office 1999. *Leisure interests:* ornithology, theatre, literature. *Address:* House of Lords, London, SW7A 0PW (office); c/o Balli Group PLC, 5 Stanhope Gate, London, W1Y 5LA, England. *Telephone:* (20) 7306-2138 (office). *E-mail:* catherinep@balli.co.uk (office).

LAMOUR, Jean-François; French government official and fmr fencer; b. 2 Feb. 1956; fmr sabre fencer; Silver Medal (team), Gold Medal (individual) LA Olympics 1984; Gold Medal (individual) Seoul Olympics 1988; Bronze Medal (team) Barcelona Olympics 1992; World Champion Lausanne 1987; Adviser on Youth and Sports, Office of the Mayor of Paris 1993–95, to the Presidency 1995; Minister of Youth, Sports and Social Asscns –2007. *Address:* c/o Ministry of Youth, Sports and Social Associations, 95 ave de France, 75650 Paris Cédex 13, France (office).

LAMPERT, Edward (Eddie) S., BEcons; American retail executive; *Chairman, Sears Holding Corporation;* b. 1963, Greenwich, Conn.; m. Kinga Lampert 2001; one d.; ed Yale Univ.; sales and training internship Goldman Sachs & Co. 1984, held positions in Risk Arbitrage Dept 1985–88; Founding Chair. and CEO ESL Investments Inc. (pvt. investment fund), Greenwich, Conn. 1988–; Chair. Kmart Holding Corpn 2003–, then Sears Holding Corpn (after merger of KMart Holding and Sears, Roebuck 2005); mem. Bd of Dirs AutoNation Inc., AutoZone Inc. *Address:* Sears Holding Corpn, 3333 Beverly Road, Hoffman Estates, IL 60179 (office); ESL Investments, 200 Greenwich Avenue, Greenwich, CT 06830, USA. *Telephone:* (847) 286-2500 (office). *Fax:* (847) 286-7829 (office). *E-mail:* info@searshc.com (office). *Website:* www .searshc.com (office).

LAMRANI, Mohammed Karim (see KARIM-LAMRANI, Mohammed).

LAMY, Pascal Lucien Fernand, MBA; French civil servant and international organization official; *Director-General, World Trade Organization;* b. 8 April 1947, Levallois-Perret (Seine); s. of Jacques Lamy and Denise Dujardin; m. Geneviève Luchaire 1972; three s.; ed Lycée Carnot, Paris, Ecole des Hautes Etudes Commerciales, Paris, Inst. d'Etudes Politiques, Ecole Nationale d'Admin, Paris; Lt-Commdr (navy); served in Inspection Générale des Finances 1975–79; Sec.-Gen. Mayoux Cttee 1979; Deputy Sec.-Gen., then Sec.-Gen. Interministerial Cttee for the Remodelling of Industrial Structures (CIASI) Treasury Dept 1979–81; Tech. Adviser, then Deputy Dir Office of the Minister for Econ. and Financial Affairs 1981–82; Deputy Dir Office of the Prime Minister (Pierre Mauroy) 1983–84; Chef de Cabinet to Pres. of Comm. of EC (Jacques Delors) 1984–94; Dir Gen. and mem. Exec. Cttee Crédit Lyonnais 1994–99; Commr for Trade, European Comm. 1999–2004; Pres. Asscn 'Notre Europe' 2004–; Assoc. Prof. Institut d'Etudes Politiques, Paris 2004–; Dir Gen. WTO 2005–; Officier, Légion d'honneur 1990, Kt Commdr's Cross (Badge and Star) of the Order of Merit (Germany) 1991, Commdr Order of Merit (Luxembourg) 1995, Officer of the Order of Merit (Gabon) 2000, Order of the Aztec Eagle (Mexico) 2003, Order of Merit (Chile) 2004; Dr hc (Louvain) 2003. *Publications:* Report on Welfare Assistance for Children (co-author) 1979, Report on "Monde-Europe" (XI Plan of the Commissariat Général au Plan) 1993, L'Europe en première ligne 2002, L'Europe de nos volontés (co-author) 2002, La démocratie monde 2004. *Leisure interests:* Nordic skiing, jogging, marathon running. *Address:* Office of the Director-General, World Trade Organization, Centre William Rappard, rue de Lausanne 154, 1211 Geneva, Switzerland (office). *Telephone:* (22) 739-51-00 (office). *Fax:* (22) 739-54-60 (office). *E-mail:* enquiries@wto.org (office). *Website:* www.wto.org (office).

LANCASTER, (Christopher Ronald) Mark, BA; British artist; b. 14 May 1938, Holmfirth; s. of Charles Ronald Lancaster and Muriel Roebuck; ed Holme Valley Grammar School, Bootham School, York, Univ. of Newcastle-upon-Tyne; asst to Andy Warhol, New York 1964; Lecturer, Univ. of Newcastle 1965–66, Bath Acad. of Art 1966–68; Artist in Residence, King's Coll., Cambridge 1968–70; Pvt. Sec. to Jasper Johns, New York 1972–83; Prin. Designer and Artistic Adviser Merce Cunningham Dance Co., New York 1980–84; New York Dance and Performance Award 1989. *Address:* c/o Robert Rogal, Rogallery.com, 47-15 36th Street, Long Island City, NY 11101, USA. *Telephone:* (718) 937-0901. *Fax:* (718) 937-1206. *E-mail:* art@rogallery.com. *Website:* www.rogallery.com.

LANCE, James Waldo, AO, CBE, MD, FRCP, FRACP, FAA; Australian neurologist and academic; *Professor Emeritus of Neurology, University of New South Wales;* b. 29 Oct. 1926, Wollongong, NSW; s. of Waldo Lance and Jessie Lance (née Stewart); m. Judith L. Logan 1957; one s. four d.; ed Geelong Grammar School, The King's School, Parramatta and Univ. of Sydney; Chair. Div. of Neurology, Prince Henry and Prince of Wales Hosps, Sydney 1961–91; Prof. of Neurology, Univ. of NSW 1975–91, Prof. Emer. 1992–; Pres. Australian Asscn of Neurologists 1978–81, Int. Headache Soc. 1987–89; Vice-Pres. Australian Acad. of Sciences 1984–85, World Fed. of Neurology 1991–93; Hon. DSc 1991; Harold G. Wolff Award of American Asscn for Study of Headache 1967, 1983. *Publications:* Headache 1975, The Golden Trout 1978, A Physiological Approach to Clinical Neurology (with J. G. McLeod 1981), Introductory Neurology (with J. G. McLeod) 1995, The Mechanism and Management of Headache with P. J. Goadsby 1998, Migraine and Other Headaches (2nd edn) 2000. *Leisure interests:* swimming, trout fishing, travel. *Address:* Medicolegal Opinions, Level 8, 179 Elizabeth Street, Sydney, NSW 2000 (office); 54 Queen Street, Woollahra, NSW 2025, Australia (home). *Telephone:* (2) 9264-5422 (office); (2) 9362-1876 (home). *Fax:* (2) 9362-9782 (home). *E-mail:* jimlance@bigpond.com (home).

LANCELOT, Alain, DèsSc et LHum; French political scientist and academic; *Professor Emeritus, Institut d'Etudes Politiques, Paris;* b. 12 Jan. 1937, Chêne-Bougeries, Geneva, Switzerland; s. of Elisée Lancelot and Suzanne Perrin-Lancelot; m. Marie Thé Merlet 1958; one s. one d.; ed Inst. d'Etudes Politiques, Paris and Univ. of Paris-Sorbonne; Asst French Political Science Asscn 1959–62, Sec.-Gen. 1970–75; naval service 1962–63; Researcher, CNRS 1963–67; Prof. Inst. d'Etudes Politiques, Paris 1967–99, Prof. Emer. 1999–; Dir Centre for Study of French Political Life 1975–86; Dir Inst. d'Etudes Politiques de Paris and Exec. Officer Fondation Nat. des Sciences Politiques 1987–96, mem. Bd 2001–; Pres. Observatoire Interrégional du Politique; mem. Conseil Constitutionnel 1996–2001, Council for Democratic Elections 2002–, Bd Fondation Robert Schuman 2003–; substitute mem. Venice Comm. for Democracy Through Law 2002–; Grand Officier, Légion d'honneur, Officier Ordre Nat. du Mérite, des Arts et des Lettres, des Palmes Académiques; decorations from Germany and Italy. *Publications:* L'abstentionnisme électoral en France 1968, La vie politique en France depuis 1940 1975, Les élections sous la cinquième république 1983. *Leisure interest:* sailing. *Address:* Fondation Nationale des Sciences Politiques, 27 rue Saint-Guillaume, 75007 Paris (office); 4 ter rue du Cherche-Midi, 75006 Paris, France (home). *Telephone:* 1-45-49-50-50 (office). *Website:* www.sciences-po.fr (office).

LANCI, Gianfranco; Italian business executive; *President, Acer Inc.;* b. 1954, Turin; m.; several c.; ed Politecnico of Turin; joined Texas Instruments (TI) Italia in 1981, Country Man. for Portable Computers and Printers Div. in Italy, Middle East and Africa 1991–96, Pres. Europe, Middle East, Africa (EMEA) for TI's Personal Productivity Products Div. 1996–97, Man. Dir Acer Italy (following merger of TI's portable PC business with Acer in 1997) 1997–2000, Pres. Acer Europe 2000–02, Pres. Acer EMEA 2002–03, Pres. Acer's Int. Operations Business Group 2003–04, Pres. Acer Inc. 2004–. *Leisure interests:* reading, playing tennis. *Address:* Acer Inc., 9F, 88 Hsin Tai Wu Road, Sec 1, Hsichih, Taipei, 221, Taiwan (office). *Telephone:* (2) 696-1234 (office). *Fax:* (2) 696-3535 (office). *Website:* www.acer.com (office).

LANCRY, Yehuda; Israeli diplomatist; b. 25 Sept. 1947, Bujad, Morocco; s. of Amram Lancry and Rouhama Lancry; m.; two s.; ed Univ. of Haifa, Univ. of Nice, France; served in Israel Defense Forces 1966–70, airplane mechanic in Israel Air Force; Head, Documentary and Film Publs Dept, Authority for Defence Tech. 1980–83; Mayor of Shlomi 1983–92; Guest Lecturer in French Literature, Haifa Univ. 1988–92; Head, Public Council, Israel TV and Radio (Channel Two) 1991; Amb. to France 1992–95; mem. Knesset (Parl.) 1996–99; Perm. Rep. to UN, New York 1999–2002; Co-Chair. High-level France-Israel Group, Ministry of Foreign Affairs 2003–; Commdr, Légion d'honneur. *Publications:* Michel Butor ou la résistance 1994, Trêves et rêves (with Michel Butor and Henri Maccheroni) 1996. *Address:* c/o Ministry of Foreign Affairs, Hakirya, Romema, Jerusalem 91950, Israel. *Telephone:* 2-5303111. *Fax:* 2-5303367. *E-mail:* feedback@mfa.gov.il. *Website:* www.mfa.gov.il.

LAND, Michael Francis, MA, PhD, FRS; British neurobiologist and academic; *Professor of Neurobiology, University of Sussex;* b. 12 April 1942, Dartmouth; s. of the late Prof. F. W. Land and of Mrs N. B. Land; m. 1st Judith Drinkwater 1966 (divorced 1980), one s.; m. 2nd Rosemary Roper 1980; two d.; ed Birkenhead School, Jesus Coll. Cambridge, Univ. Coll. London and Univ. of Calif., Berkeley (Miller Fellowship); Asst Prof., Univ. of California, Berkeley 1969–71; Lecturer, School of Biological Sciences, Univ. of Sussex 1971–77, Reader 1977–84, Prof. of Neurobiology 1984–; Fellow, Univ. Coll. London 1998; Visiting Prof., Univ. of Ore. 1980; Sr Visiting Fellow, ANU, Canberra 1982–84; Foreign mem. Royal Physiographical Soc., Lund, Sweden 1995; Frank Smart Prize in Zoology, Cambridge 1963, ALCON Prize for Vision Research 1996, Rank Prize for Opto-electronics 1998; Frink Medal, Zoological Soc. of London 1994. *Publications:* Animal Eyes (with D. E. Nilsson) 2002; 170 articles and papers on aspects of vision in animals from visual optics to behaviour. *Leisure interests:* gardening, music. *Address:* Department of Biology and Environmental Science, University of Sussex, Brighton, BN1 9QG (office); White House, Cuilfail, Lewes, Sussex, BN7 2BE, England (home). *Telephone:* (1273) 678505 (office); (1273) 476780 (home). *Fax:* (1273) 678433 (office). *E-mail:* m.f.land@sussex.ac.uk (office). *Website:* www.sussex .ac.uk/biology (office).

LANDABURU ILLARRAMENDI, Eneko; Spanish international organization official; *Director-General for External Relations, European Commission;* b. 11 March 1948, Paris; s. of Francisco Javier Nicolas Landaburu and Prudencia Francisca Constantina Illarramendi; m. Dominique Rambaud 1971; two s. one d.; ed Univ. of Paris, France; mem. staff Admin. and Financial Man. Dept, Société Labaz, Paris 1971–73, Asst to Man. Belgian subsidiary SA Labaz NV, Brussels 1973–75; Head of Study and Lecture Programmes, Centre Européen d'Etudes et d'Information sur les Sociétés Multinationales (CEEIM), Brussels 1975–79; PSOE Deputy, Spanish Basque Regional Parl. 1980–81; Adviser to Latin American Dept, Nestlé, Vevey, Switzerland 1981–82; Dir Institut de Recherche sur les Multinationales (IRM), Geneva, Switzerland 1983–86; Dir-Gen. for Regional Politics, EC Comm., Brussels 1986–2000, for Enlargement (later External Relations) 2000–; Lecturer, Institut d'Etudes Européennes, Free Univ. of Brussels 1990–94; Alt. mem. Bd of Dirs of EIB 1993–; mem. Supervisory Bd European Investment Fund FEI-EIF 1994–; mem. Bd of Dirs Fondation 'Notre Europe' 1996–. *Address:* Office Char 15/119, 1049 Brussels (office); Avenue Brugmann 125, 1190 Brussels, Belgium (home). *Telephone:* (2) 295-19-68 (office). *Fax:* (2) 299–32–19 (office). *E-mail:* eneko.landaburu@cec.eu.int (office).

LANDAU, Igor, MBA; French business executive; b. 13 July 1944, Saint-Flour, Cantal; ed Hautes Etudes Commerciales, Institut Européen d'Admin des Affaires (INSEAD); Pres. La Compagnie du Roneo (German subsidiary), Frankfurt 1968–70; consultant, McKinsey Co., Paris 1971–75; Deputy to Pres. of Health Div., Rhône-Poulenc Inc. 1975, Exec. Vice-Pres. of Div. 1977–80, Chair. Health Sector 1987, mem. Exec. Cttee 1987, Group Pres. 1992, mem. Bd of Dirs 1998; mem. Man. Bd Aventis 1999–2002, Chair. Man. Bd 2000–, Chair. Supervisory Bd Aventis Pharma AG 1999–2002, mem. Bd of Dirs Sanofi-Aventis 2004–; Pres. Supervisory Bd Centre Européen d'Educ. Perm.; mem. Institut pour le Développement Industrial; mem. Bd Dirs Essilor. *Address:* Sanofi-Aventis, 174 avenue de France, 75013 Paris, France (office). *Telephone:* 1-53-77-44-50 (office). *Fax:* 1-53-77-46-22 (office). *Website:* www .sanofi-aventis.com (office).

LANDAU, Jean-Pierre; French economist; *Second Deputy Governor, Banque de France;* b. 7 Nov. 1946, Paris; s. of André Landau and Andrée Pestre; m. Evelyne Dova 1979; ed Inst. d'études politiques de Paris, Ecole nat. d'admin; served in Ministry of Health and Social Security 1978–79; Asst Sec. for Trade Policy, Direction des Relations Économiques Extérieures 1986–89, various other positions in Ministry of Econ. and Finance; Exec. Dir IMF 1989–93; Dir Relations Economiques Extérieures (DREE) 1993–96; Dir-Gen. French Asscn of Banks 1999–2000; Financial Counsellor, French Embassy in UK 2001–06; Dir EBRD 2001–06; Second Deputy Gov. and mem. Gen. Council Banque de France 2006–, Chair. Credit Insts and Investment Firms Cttee, Supervisory Bd Institut d'émission des départements d'Outre-Mer, mem. Supervisory Bd Caisse des dépots et consignations; fmr Teacher of Econs, Inst. d'études politiques; fmr mem. of Bd, Renault. *Address:* Banque de France, 31 rue Croix des Petits Champs, 75001 Paris (office); 13 rue de l'Odéon, 75006 Paris, France. *Telephone:* 1-42-92-42-92 (office). *E-mail:* infos@banque-france .fr (office). *Website:* www.banque-france.fr (office).

LANDAU, Moshe, LLB; Israeli judge (retd); b. 29 April 1912, Danzig, Germany (now Gdańsk, Poland); s. of Dr Isaac Landau and Betty (née Eisenstädt); m. Leah Doukhan 1937; three d.; ed London Univ.; went to Israel 1933; called to Palestine Bar 1937; Magistrate of Haifa 1940, Dist Court Judge, Haifa 1948; Justice, Supreme Court, Jerusalem 1953–82, (Presiding Judge, Eichmann Trial), Deputy Pres. 1976–80, Pres. 1980–82; Israel Prize 1991. *Leisure interest:* piano. *Address:* 10 Alharizi Street, Jerusalem, Israel. *Telephone:* 2-5632757.

LANDAU, Peter, DJur; German professor of law; *President, Stephan Kuttner Institute of Medival Canon Law;* b. 26 Feb. 1935, Berlin; m. Angelika Linnemann 1971; one s. one d.; ed Univs of Berlin, Freiburg, Bonn and Yale Univ., USA; Prof. Univ. of Regensburg 1968–87; Prof. of Law, Univ. of Munich 1987–2003; mem. Bayerische Akad. der Wissenschaften; mem. Inst. for Advanced Study, Princeton, USA 1990–91; currently Pres. Stephan Kuttner Inst. of Medieval Canon Law; mem. Medieval Acad. of America; Hon. DrIur (Basel) 1981; Dr hc (Munich) 1997, (Paris) 2001. *Publications:* Die Entstehung des kanonischen Infamiebegriffs von Gratian bis zur Glossa ordinaria 1966, Ius patronatus 1975, Strafrecht, Strafprozess und Rezeption (Jt Ed.) 1984, Officium und Libertas christiana 1991, Kanones und Dekretalen 1997. *Leisure interest:* art. *Address:* Leopold-Wenger-Institut für Rechtsgeschichte, Professor-Huber-Platz 2, 80539 Munich (office); Sperberstr. 21c, 81827 Munich, Germany (home). *Telephone:* (89) 21803263 (office); (89) 4300121 (home). *Fax:* (89) 21803081 (office). *E-mail:* peter.landau@jura.uni-muenchen .de (office). *Website:* www.lrz-muenchen.de/~SKIMCL/mitarbeiter_pl_english (office).

LANDAU, Uzi, PhD; Israeli politician and systems analyst; b. 1943, Haifa; m.; three c.; ed Haifa Technion, Mass. Inst. of Tech., USA; served as a paratrooper officer during mil. service; mem. Knesset (Likud Party) 1984–, Chair. Foreign Affairs and Defense Cttee, State Control Cttee; Knesset Observer at the European Council; mem. Israeli Del. to Madrid Peace Conf.; Observer at the European Council; Minister of Public Security 2001–03; fmr Minister in charge of overseeing the intelligence services and the US–Israel strategic dialogue in the Prime Minister's Office; Dir-Gen. Ministry of Transport;

Lecturer, Technion, Israel Inst. of Tech., Haifa; mem. Bd El-Al Airlines, Israel Port Authority, Israel Airport Authority, Soc. for the Protection of Nature, Si'ah Vasig (Israel Debating Soc.). *Publications:* articles in professional journals on transport planning, articles in the press on foreign policy, strategic and security affairs. *Address:* The Knesset, Jerusalem 91181, Israel (office). *Telephone:* (2) 6753868 (office). *E-mail:* klandau@knesset.gov.il (office). *Website:* www.knesset.gov.il (office).

LANDEL, Michel; French business executive; *Group CEO, Sodexho Alliance;* b. 1951; m.; three c.; ed European Business School, Paris; Gen. Man. Poliet Group 1980–84; Chief Operating Man. for E and N Africa, Sodexho 1984–86, Pres. Group Remote Site Operations, Africa 1986–89, Head of N American Operations 1989–99, CEO Sodexho Inc. 1989–2000, Vice-Chair. Exec. Cttee, Sodexho Alliance 2000–03, COO Sodexho Alliance 2003–05, Group CEO 2005–, Pres. Group Exec. Cttee, Pres. Sodexo STOP Hunger Asscn; Golden Chain Award for Multi-Unit Food Service Operators 1997, Ivy Award for Restaurant & Institutions 1998, Penn State Hotel and Restaurant Soc. Hospitality Exec. of the Year 2002, Diversity Best Practice CEO Leadership Award, Asian Enterprise CEO Advocate of the Year 2004. *Leisure interests:* travel, relaxing in the kitchen preparing delicious and unique dishes for family and friends. *Address:* Sodexho Alliance, Parc des Activités du Pas-du-Lac, 3 avenue Newton, 78180 Montigny-le-Bretonneu, France (office). *Telephone:* 1-30-85-75-00 (office). *Fax:* 1-30-43-09-58 (office). *E-mail:* info@sodexho .com (office). *Website:* www.sodexho.com (office).

LANDER, Eric S., DPhil; American biologist and academic; *Director, The Broad Institute;* b. 1957, Brooklyn, NY; ed Princeton Univ. and Univ. of Oxford, UK; taught econs to business students at Harvard Univ.; Fellow, Whitehead Inst. for Biomedical Research MIT 1985–89, f. Center for Genome Research at MIT 1990, fmr Assoc. Prof. of Biology, now Prof. of Biology and Dir Whitehead Inst. for Biomedical Research/MIT Center for Genome Research, Dir The Broad Inst. 2003–; serves on numerous govt advisory cttees; Founder and Dir Millennium Pharmaceuticals; fmr Chair. Jt Steering Cttee for Public Policy; Rhodes Scholar, Univ. of Oxford, J. Allyn Taylor Int. Prize in Medicine, John P. Robarts Research Inst. (co-recipient) 2001. *Publications:* numerous articles in scientific journals; led group of bioinformatics specialists who produced an analysis of draft human genome for publication in Nature 2001. *Address:* Office of the Provost, NE125-2246, The Broad Institute, 320 Charles Street, Cambridge, MA 02141-2023, USA (office). *Telephone:* (617) 252-1906 (office); (617) 258-5192 (Whitehead Inst.) (office). *Fax:* (617) 258-0903 (office). *E-mail:* lander@broad.mit.edu (office); lander@genome.wi.mit.edu (office). *Website:* web.mit.edu/biology/www (office); www.broad.mit.edu (office).

LANDER, Sir Stephen James, Kt, KCB, CB, MA, PhD; British public servant; *Independent Commissioner, The Law Society;* m. Felicity Lander 1972; one s. (died 2002) one d.; ed Bishop's Stortford Coll., Herts., Queens' Coll., Cambridge Univ.; with Inst. of Historical Research, London Univ. 1972–5; joined Security Service 1975–, Dir 1992–96, Dir-Gen. 1996–2002; Ind. Commr (overseeing complaints against solicitors) The Law Soc. 2002–; Dir (non exec.) HM Customs and Excise 2002–, Northgate Information Solutions 2004–; Chair. Serious and Organised Crime Agency (SOCA) 2004–. *Address:* The Law Society, 113 Chancery Lane, London, WC2A 1PL, England (office). *Telephone:* (1926) 822057 (office). *Fax:* (1926) 823140 (office). *Website:* www.lawsociety .org.uk (office).

LANDES, David S., PhD; American economist and academic; *Professor Emeritus, Department of Economics, Harvard University;* b. 29 April 1924, New York; s. of Harry Landes and Sylvia Landes; m. Sonia Tarnopol 1943; one s. two d.; ed City Coll., New York, Harvard Univ.; Jr Fellow, Soc. of Fellows, Harvard Univ. 1950–53; Asst Prof. of Econs, Columbia Univ., New York 1952–55, Assoc. Prof. 1955–58; Fellow, Center for Advanced Study in Behavioral Sciences, Stanford, Calif. 1957–58; Prof. of History and Econs, Univ. of Calif., Berkeley 1958–64; Prof. of History, Harvard Univ. 1964–72, LeRoy B. Williams Prof. of History and Political Science 1972–75, Robert Walton Goelet Prof. of French History 1975–81, Prof. of Econs 1977–98, Coolidge Prof. of History 1981, now Prof. Emer.; Chair. Faculty Cttee on Social Studies 1981; Pres. Council on Research in Econ. History 1963–66; Dir Center for Middle Eastern Studies, Harvard Univ. 1966–68; Acting Dir Center for West European Studies, Harvard Univ. 1969–70; Pres. Econ. History Asscn 1976–77; Ellen McArthur Lecturer, Univ. of Cambridge 1964; Visiting Prof., Univ. of Paris IV 1972–73, Univ. of Zürich and Eidgenössische Technisch Hochschule, Zürich 1978; Richards Lectures, Univ. of Virginia 1978, Janeway Lectures, Princeton Univ. 1983; mem. Bd of Eds, various journals of history; Fellow, NAS, American Acad. of Arts and Sciences, American Philosophical Soc., British Acad., Royal Historical Soc.; Overseas Fellow, Churchill Coll., Cambridge 1968–69; Visiting Fellow, All Souls, Oxford 1985; mem. American Historical Asscn, Econ. History Asscn (also Trustee), Econ. History Soc., Soc. for French Historical Studies, Soc. d'Histoire Moderne and others; Assoc. mem. Fondation Royaumont pour le Progrès des Sciences de l'Homme; Dr hc (Lille) 1973. *Publications:* Bankers and Pashas 1958, The Unbound Prometheus 1968, Revolution in Time: Clocks and the Making of the Modern World 1983, The Wealth and Poverty of Nations: Why Some Are So Rich and Some So Poor 1998, Dynasties: Fortune & Misfortune in the World's Greatest Family Businesses 2007, and other books and articles on econ. and social history. *Leisure interests:* antiquarian horology, squash, tennis. *Address:* 24 Highland Street, Cambridge, MA 02138, USA (home). *Telephone:* (617) 354-6308 (office); (617) 354-6308 (home). *Fax:* (617) 354-5335 (home). *E-mail:* soniatl@aol.com (home). *Website:* www.economics.harvard.edu (office).

LANDON, Howard Chandler Robbins, BMus; American writer, musicologist and academic; *John Bird Professor of Music, University College Cardiff;* b. 6 March 1926, Boston, Mass; s. of William G. Landon and Dorothea LeB. Robbins; m. 1st Christa Landon; m. 2nd Else Radant 1977; ed Lenox School,

Mass., Swarthmore Coll. and Boston Univ.; corresp. The Times 1958–61; Hon. Professorial Fellow, Univ. Coll. Cardiff 1971–78, John Bird Prof. of Music 1978–; Prof. of the Humanities, Middlebury Coll., Vt 1980–83; Verdienstkreuz für Kunst und Wissenschaft (Austria); Hon. DMus (Boston) 1969, (Belfast) 1974, (Bristol) 1982, (Toulouse) 1991; Siemens Prize (Germany) 1992. *Publications:* The Symphonies of Joseph Haydn 1955, The Mozart Companion (ed. with Donald Mitchell) 1956, The Collected Correspondence and London Notebooks of Joseph Haydn 1959, Essays on the Viennese Classical Style: Gluck, Haydn, Mozart, Beethoven 1970, Beethoven: A Documentary Study 1970, Joseph Haydn: Chronicle and Works (five vols) 1976–80, Haydn: A Documentary Study 1981, Mozart & the Masons 1983, Handel and his World 1984, 1791: Mozart's Last Year 1987, Haydn: his Life and Music (with D. Jones) 1988, Mozart: The Golden Years 1989, The Mozart Compendium (ed.) 1990, Mozart and Vienna 1991, Five Centuries of Music in Venice (with John Julius Norwich) 1991, Vivaldi: Voice of the Baroque 1992, Une Journée particulière de Mozart 1993, The Mozart Essays 1995, Horns in High C (memoirs) 1999. *Leisure interests:* walking, swimming, cooking. *Address:* Château de Foncoussières, 81800 Rabastens (Tarn), France (home). *Telephone:* 5-63-40-61-45 (home). *Fax:* 5-63-40-62-61 (home). *E-mail:* foncous@aol.com (home).

LANDRIEU, Mary L., BA; American politician; *Senator from Louisiana;* b. 23 Nov. 1955, Arlington, Va; d. Moon Landrieu; m. E. Frank Snellings; two c.; ed Ursuline Academy, New Orleans and Louisiana State Univ., Baton Rouge; Louisiana State Rep., Dist 90 1980–88, State Treas. 1986–96; Del. Democratic Nat. Convention 1980; cand. for Democratic gubernatorial nomination 1995; Senator from Louisiana 1997–; mem. Women Execs in State Govt, Fed. of Democratic Women. *Address:* 328 Hart Senate Office Building, Washington, DC 20510, USA (office). *Telephone:* (202) 224-5824 (office). *Fax:* (202) 224-9735 (office). *Website:* landrieu.senate.gov (office); www.marylandrieu.com.

LANDRY, Donald W., BS, MD, PhD; American professor of medicine; *Chair, Department of Medicine, Columbia University College of Physicians and Surgeons;* b. 1954, Jersey City, NJ; m. Maureen O'Reilly-Landry; two s.; ed Lafayette Coll., Harvard Univ., Columbia Univ.; Resident in Medicine, Harvard Medical School, Mass Gen. Hosp., Boston 1983–85; Dir Div. of Clinical Pharmacology and Experimental Therapeutics, Columbia Univ. Coll. of Physicians and Surgeons 1998–, Dir of Nephrology 2001–, Chair. Dept of Medicine 2008–; mem. ACS, NY Acad. of Sciences, American Soc. for Clinical Investigation, Asscn of American Physicians, Practitioners Soc. of NY, American Soc. for Pharmacology and Experimental Therapeutics; Presidential Citizens Medal 2009. *Publications include:* more than 160 articles in learned journals. *Address:* Columbia University College of Physicians and Surgeons, Presbyterian Hospital, Room 8 East, 105 622 West 168th Street, New York, NY 10032, USA (office). *Telephone:* (212) 305-5839 (office). *E-mail:* dwl1@columbia.edu (office). *Website:* asp.cpmc.columbia.edu (office).

LANDSBERGIS, Vytautas, (Jonas Zemkalnis); Lithuanian politician, musicologist, pianist and fmr head of state; b. 18 Oct. 1932, Kaunas; s. of Vytautas Landsbergis-Zemkalnis and Ona Jablonskytė-Landsbergienė; m. Grazina Ručyte; one s. two d.; ed J. Gruodis School of Music, Kaunas, Aušra Gymnasium, Kaunas, Lithuanian Acad. of Music, Vilnius; teacher of piano and Prof. of Musicology, Vilnius Conservatoire, Vilnius Pedagogical Inst.; fmr mem. Exec. Council and Secr. Composers' Union; Pres. M.K. Čiurlionis Soc.; mem. various arts and science bodies; elected to Initiative Group, Sajūdis Reform Movt, then to Sajūdis Seimas (Ass.) and Council 1988, Pres. Sajūdis Seimas Council 1988–90, Hon. Pres. Sajūdis Dec. 1991–; f. Lithuanian Conservative Party, Chair. 1993–2003; elected Deputy to USSR Congress of People's Deputies 1989–90; elected to Supreme Council of Lithuania Feb. 1990, Pres. Supreme Council (Head of State) 1990–91; mem. Seimas (Parl.) 1992–2004, Leader of Parl. Opposition 1992–96, Pres. Seimas 1996–2000; cand. for presidential elections 1997; mem. European Parl. 2004–; Paul Harris Fellow (Rotary) 1991; Academician, Lithuanian Catholic Acad. 1997; gave concert at Moscow Conservatoire with Russian Nat. Acad. Symphonic Orchestra 1999; piano recitals in Calw, Hanover, Helsinki, Guangzhou, Moscow, New York, Paris, Tokyo, Trieste, Uznam, Vilnius, Warsaw, etc.; Hon. Fellow, Univ. of Cardiff, UK 2000; Hon. Citizen of Turin, Italy 2007; Grand Officer, European St Sebastian's Order of Kts 1995, Chevalier, Légion d'Honneur 1997, Order of Grand Duke Vytautas, First Class (Lithuania) 1998, Grand Cross, Royal Norwegian Order of Merit 1998, Grand Cross Order of the Repub. (Poland) 1999, Order of Merit (Grand Cross), Order of Malta 1999, Grand Cross, Order of Honour (Greece) 1999, Pléiade Ordre de la Francophonie (France) 2000, Three Stars Order (Second Class) (Latvia) 2001, Order of the Cross of St Mary's Land (First Class) (Estonia) 2002, Kt Grand Cross, Order of Orange-Nassau (Netherlands) 2008; Hon. LLD (Loyola Univ., Chicago) 1991; Hon. PhD (Vytautas the Great Univ., Kaunas) 1992, (Klaipėda Univ., Lithuania) 1997; Hon. HD (Weber Univ., USA) 1992; Hon. DIur (Lithuanian Acad. of Law) 2000; Dr hc (Helsinki) 2000, (Sorbonne) 2001, (Lithuanian Acad. of Art) 2003, (St Lucas Acad., Netherlands-Germany) 2004; Lithuanian State Award (for monograph on M. K. Čiurlionis) 1975; Norwegian People's Peace Prize (for role in restoration of Lithuanian independence; has used prize to establish Landsbergis Foundation to help disabled children and young musicians) 1991, Award of France Fund of Future 1991, Hermann-Ehlers Prize 1992, Catalan Ramon Llull IX Int. Prize 1994, Vibo Valentia Testimony Prize (Italy) 1998, Truman-Reagan Freedom Award (USA) 1999, Constitutional Medallion of Saxonian Parl. (Germany) 2003, Lithuanian Foundation Award 2004, Aschaffenburger Mutig-Preis, Germany 2004, Robert Schuman Medal, European Parl. 2005, Mérite Européen Medal (Luxembourg) 2006. *Recording:* Čiurlionis, Born of the Human Soul (works for solo piano) 1998. *Publications:* 24 books on musicology, art and music history (especially on artist and composer M. K. Čiurlionis) and politics, including M. K. Čiurlionis – Time and Content 1992, Lithuania Independent Again 2000; numerous edns of scores (mostly of works by M. K. Čiurlionis); M. K. Čiurlionis – Thoughts, Pictures, Music (film script) 1965; poetry collections: Intermezzo 1991, Intermezzo non finito 2004, Who Are We? (under pseudonym Jonas Zemkalnis) 2004, Glimmers of History 2006, It's Serious, Children (poems) 2006, memoirs, essays, Un peuple sort de prison 2007, Crossroad of Europe 2008. *Leisure interests:* history, poetry. *Address:* Traidenio Street 34–15, Vilnius 08116, Lithuania (office); European Parliament, Bâtiment Altiero Spinelli, 11E157, 60 rue Wiertz, 1047 Brussels, Belgium (office). *Telephone:* (52) 663676 (office); (52) 724466 (home); (2) 284-55-50 (Brussels) (home). *Fax:* (52) 663675 (office); (52) 790505 (home); (2) 284-95-50 (Brussels) (home). *E-mail:* vyland@lrs.lt (office); vytautas.landsbergis@europarl.europa.eu (office). *Website:* www.landsbergis.lt (office); www.europarl.europa.eu (office).

LANE, Sir David Philip, Kt, PhD, FRS, FRSE, FRCPath, FRCSE, FMedSci; British academic; *Professor of Molecular Oncology, University of Dundee;* b. 1 July 1952; s. of John Wallace Lane and Cecelia Frances Evelyn Wright; m. Ellen Birgitte Muldal 1975; one s. one d.; ed Univ. Coll. London; Research Fellow Imperial Cancer Research Fund 1976–77, Staff Scientist 1985–90; lecturer Imperial Coll., London 1977–85; Prof. of Molecular Oncology, Univ. of Dundee 1990–, Dir Transformation Research Group, Cancer Research Campaign 1990–; Visiting Fellow Cold Spring Harbor Labs, NY 1978–80; Gibb Fellow Cancer Research UK; mem. European Molecular Biology Org. 1990; Co-Founder FMedSci 1998; Hon. DSc (Abertay, Dundee) 1999, (Stirling) 2000, (Aberdeen) 2002, (Birmingham) 2002; Charles Rodolphe Brubacher Foundation Prize 1993, Joseph Steiner Foundation Prize 1993, Yvette Mayent Prize, Inst. Curie 1994, Swedish Soc. of Oncology Medal 1994, Meyenberg Foundation Prize 1995, Silvanus Thompson Medal, British Inst. of Radiology 1996, Henry Dryerre Prize 1996, Paul Ehrlich Prize 1998, Tom Conors Prize 1998, Bruce Preller Prize 1998, Soc. of Chemical Industry Medal 2003, Royal Soc. Buchanan Medal 2004, Biochemistry Soc. Award 2004. *Address:* Cancer Research UK Laboratories, Department of Surgery and Molecular Oncology, University of Dundee, Dundee, DD1 9SY, Scotland (office). *Telephone:* (1382) 496362 (office). *Fax:* (1382) 496363 (office). *Website:* www.dundee.ac.uk/surgery.

LANE, Nathan; American actor and producer; b. (Joseph Lane), 3 Feb. 1956, Jersey City, NJ; ed St Peter's Preparatory High School, Jersey City; co-hosted Tony Awards 1995, 1996. *Plays include:* Lips Together, Teeth Apart 1991. *Musicals include:* Guys and Dolls, Broadway 1992, The Producers, Broadway (Tony Award) and Theatre Royal, London 2004, A Funny Thing Happened on the Way to the Forum (Tony Award). *Films include:* Ironweed 1987, Joe Versus the Volcano 1990, The Lemon Sisters 1990, He Said, She Said 1991, Frankie and Johnny 1991, Life with Mikey (aka Give Me a Break) 1993, Addams Family Values 1993, The Lion King (voice) 1994, Stand by Me 1995, Jeffrey 1995, The Birdcage 1996, Timon and Pumbaa's Wild Adventure: Live and Learn (video, voice) 1997, Mousehunt 1997, Merry Christmas, George Bailey 1997, The Lion King II: Simba's Pride (video, voice) 1998, The Best Man 1999, At First Sight 1999, Stuart Little (voice) 1999, Isn't She Great 2000, Love's Labour's Lost 2000, Titan A.E. (voice) 2000, Trixie 2000, Stuart Little 2 (voice) 2002, Austin Powers in Goldmember 2002, Nicholas Nickleby 2002, Teacher's Pet (voice) 2004, Win a Date with Tad Hamilton! 2004, The Lion King $1\frac{1}{2}$ (video, voice) 2004, Behind the Legend: Timon (video, voice) (uncredited) 2004, The Producers 2005. *Television includes:* Jacqueline Susann's Valley of the Dolls (aka Valley of the Dolls) 1981, One of the Boys (series) 1982, Alice in Wonderland 1983, The Last Mile 1992, The Wizard of Oz in Concert: Dreams Come True 1995, Timon and Pumbaa (series) 1995, The Boys Next Door 1996, Encore! Encore! (series) 1998, George and Martha (series) 1999, The Man Who Came to Dinner 2000, Teacher's Pet (series) (voice) 2000–02, One Saturday Morning (series) (voice) 2000, Laughter on the 23rd Floor 2001, Charlie Lawrence (series) (also producer) 2003. *Address:* c/o Scott Bankston, Propaganda Management, 940 N. Mansfield Avenue, Hollywood, CA 90038, USA (office); c/o Bryan Lourd, Creative Artists Agency, 9830 Wilshire Blvd, Beverly Hills, CA 90212-1825, USA. *Telephone:* (310) 288-4545. *Fax:* (310) 288-4800. *Website:* www.caa.com.

LANE, Neal Francis, MS, PhD, FAAS; American physicist and academic; *Malcom Gillis University Professor and Senior Fellow in Science and Technology, James A. Baker III Institute for Public Policy, Rice University;* b. 22 Aug. 1938, Oklahoma; s. of Walter Lane and Harietta Hollander; m. Joni Williams 1960; one s. one d.; ed Univ. of Oklahoma; NSF Post-doctoral Fellow 1964–65; Asst Prof. of Physics, Rice Univ. Houston 1966–69, Assoc. Prof. 1969–72, Prof. 1972–84, 1986–93, Prof. of Space Physics and Astronomy 1972–84, Chair. Dept of Physics 1977–82, Provost 1986–93; Dir Div. of Physics, NSF, Washington, DC 1979–80, Dir NSF 1993–98; Chancellor, Univ. of Colo at Colorado Springs 1984–86; Asst to Pres. for Science and Tech., Dir Office of Science and Tech. Policy, Washington 1998–2001; Univ. Prof. and Sr Fellow in Science and Tech and Gillis Univ. Prof., James A. Baker III Inst. of Public Policy, Rice Univ. 2001–; Visiting Fellow, Jt Inst. for Lab. Astrophysics, Univ. of Colo at Boulder 1965–66, 1975–76, non-resident Fellow 1984–93; Distinguished Visiting Scientist, Ky Univ., Lexington 1980; mem. Comm. on Physics, Science, Math. and Applications, Nat. Research Council 1989–93, Bd Overseers Superconducting Super Collider (SSC), Univs Research Asscn 1985–93, Advisory Cttee, Math. and Physical Sciences, NSF 1992–93; other professional appointments; Fellow, American Physics Soc., American Acad. of Arts and Sciences; mem. American Inst. of Physics; Alfred P. Sloan Foundation Fellow 1967–71; Hon. DHL (Okla, Marymount Univs 1995, (Ill. Inst. of Tech.) 1999; Hon. DSc (Univ. of Ala) 1994, (Mich. State Univ.) 1995, (Ohio State Univ.) 1996, (Washington Coll.) 1998, (Colorado) 1999, (Illinois Inst. of Tech.) 1999, (Queen's Univ. Belfast) 2000, (N Carolina State Univ.) 2001, (Mt Sinai School of Medicine, State Univ. of New York) 2002; Philip Hauge Abelson Award, American Asscn for the Advancement of Science 2000,

William D. Carey Award, American Asscn for the Advancement of Science 2001. *Publications:* Quantum States of Atoms, Molecules and Solids, Understanding More Quantum Physics, articles in professional journals. *Leisure interests:* tennis, squash. *Address:* Department of Physics and Astronomy, MS 108, Rice University, P.O. Box 1892, Houston, TX 77251 (office); James A. Baker III Institute for Public Policy, MS 40, 6100 Main Street, Rice University, Baker Hall, Suite 120, Houston, TX 77005, USA (office). *Telephone:* (713) 348-2925 (office). *Fax:* (713) 348-5143 (office). *E-mail:* neal@rice.edu (office). *Website:* bakerinstitute.org/Persons/bio_nlane.htm (office).

LANE, (Alan) Piers, BMus, ARCM; British/Australian pianist, broadcaster and artistic director; *Professor, Royal Academy of Music;* b. 8 Jan. 1958, London; s. of Peter Alan Lane and Enid Muriel Hitchcock; ed Queensland Conservatorium of Music, Royal Coll. of Music, London; broadcaster for BBC Radio 3; critic CD Review; has appeared with numerous orchestras, including London Philharmonic, Philharmonia, Royal Philharmonic, all BBC orchestras, City of Birmingham Symphony, Halle, Australian Chamber Orchestra, New Zealand Symphony Orchestra, Auckland Philharmonic, Orchestra Ensemble Kanazawa (Japan), Orchestre National de France, American Symphony Orchestra, Warsaw Philharmonic; has toured extensively in Australia, Africa, Europe, India, Japan, New Zealand, Scandinavia, S America, USA; has appeared at festivals, including Aldeburgh, BBC Promenade Concerts, Royal Albert Hall, Huntington, Husum Festival of Piano Rarities, Germany, Blair Atholl, Speedside, Toronto, Singapore Piano Festival, Newport Festival, Rhode Island, Duznicki Chopin Festival, Poland, Ruhr Piano Festival, Bergen Festival, Bridgewater Piano Festival, Manchester 2003, Bagatelles Chopin Festival, Paris; La Roque d'Anthéron; Int. Adjudicator Tbilisi and Sydney Int. Piano Competitions; Prof., RAM 1989–; Dir Myra Hess Day Nat. Gallery 2006–, Australian Festival of Chamber Music 2007–; Dir and Trustee The Hattori Foundation; Patron, European Piano Teachers' Asscn, The Old Granary Studio, Queensland Music Teachers' Asscn, Accompanists' Guild of Queensland, Youth Music Foundation of Australia; Hon. mem. RAM 1994; Dr hc (Griffith Univ.) 2007; Special Prize Bartok–Liszt Int. Competition, Budapest 1976, Best Australian Pianist, Sydney Int. Piano Competition 1977. *Recordings include:* Moskowski, Paderewski Concertos 1990, Complete Etudes of Scriabin 1992, Piano Quintet by Brahms (New Budapest Quartet) 1992, Violin Virtuoso (with Tasmin Little) 1992, Cello Sonatas (with Alexander Baillie) by Shostakovich, Prokofiev, Schnittke and Rachmaninoff, d'Albert Concertos 1994, Vaughan-Williams and Delius Concertos plus Finzi Eclogue 1994, Elgar Piano Quintet (with Vellinger String Quartet) 1994, Delius Violin Sonatas (with Tasmin Little) (Diapason d'Or) 1997, d'Albert Solo Piano Works 1997, Saint-Saëns Complete Etudes 1998, Kullak & Dreyschock Concertos (with Niklas Willen) 1999, Complete Scriabin Preludes 2000, Grainger Piano Transcriptions 2001, Bach Transcriptions 2002, Moscheles Etudes 2003, Henselt Etudes 2004, Stanford Quintet (with Vanburgh Quartet) 2004, Delius and Ireland Piano Concertos 2005, Alnaes and Sinding Concertos 2005, Bloch Piano Quintets (with Goldner String Quartet) 2008, Bridge Piano Quintet (with Golder String Quartet) 2008. *Address:* Hazard Chase, 25 City Road, Cambridge CB1 1DP, England (office). *Telephone:* (1223) 312400 (office). *Fax:* (1223) 460827 (office). *E-mail:* sibylle.jackson@hazardchase.co.uk (office). *Website:* www.hazardchase.co.uk (office); www.pierslane.com.

LANE, Robert W., MBA; American business executive; *Chairman, President and CEO, Deere & Company;* b. 14 Nov. 1949, Washington, DC; m. Patricia Lane; three c.; ed Wheaton Coll., Ill., Univ. of Chicago Grad. School of Business; began career in corp. banking; joined Deere & Co. 1982, various positions in Worldwide Construction Equipment Div., Pres. and COO Deere Credit Inc., Sr Vice-Pres. World Agric. Equipment Div., Sr Vice-Pres. and Chief Financial Officer Deere & Co. 1996–97, Sr Vice-Pres. and Man. Dir for Operations Europe, Middle E, India and fmr USSR 1997–98, Pres. Worldwide Agric. Equipment Div. 1998–2000, Pres. and COO Jan.–Aug. 2000, Chair., Pres. and CEO Aug. 2000–; mem. The Business Roundtable, Business Council; mem. Bd of Dirs General Electric Co., Verizon Communications Inc., Deerfoot Lodge, NY Wilderness Camp, Lyric Opera of Chicago; Co-Chair. Capital Campaign Cttee, Davenport (IA) Museum of Art Foundation; mem. Bd Trustees Cttee for Devt; Hon. Dir, Lincoln Park Zoo. *Address:* Deere & Co. World Headquarters, One John Deere Place, Moline, IL 61265, USA (office). *Telephone:* (309) 765-8000 (office). *Fax:* (309) 765-5671 (office). *E-mail:* info@deere.com (office). *Website:* www.deere.com (office).

LANE FOX, Martha, BA; British business executive; b. 10 Feb. 1973; ed Oxford High School, Westminster School, Magdalen Coll., Oxford; business analyst, Spectrum Strategy Consultants 1994–96, Assoc. 1996–97; Business Devt Dir Carlton Communications 1997–98; Co-Founder (with Brent Hoberman q.v.) and COO lastminute.com 1998–2003; co-f. Lucky Voice Private Karaoke 2005; Founder and Chair. Antigone (charity trust) 2008–; Dir (non-exec.) Channel 4 2005–, Marks and Spencer 2007–, Mydeco.com 2008–; Advisor Twitter Partners 2009–; Patron and Trustee, Reprieve. *Address:* Antigone, 27-28 Eastcastle Street, London, W1W 8DH, England (office). *Telephone:* (20) 7907-7738 (office). *Website:* www.antigone.org.uk (office).

LANG, Brian Andrew, MA, PhD, FRSE; British university vice-chancellor and management consultant; *Principal Emeritus, University of St Andrews;* b. 2 Dec. 1945, Edinburgh; s. of Andrew Lang and Mary Lang; m. 1st 1975 (divorced 1982); m. 2nd 1983 (divorced 2000); two s. one d.; m. 3rd 2002; ed Royal High School, Edinburgh and Univ. of Edinburgh; social anthropological field research, Kenya 1969–70; Lecturer in Social Anthropology, Århus Univ., Denmark 1971–75; mem. scientific staff, Social Science Research Council 1976–79; Sec., Historic Building Br., Scottish Office 1979–80; Sec. Nat. Heritage Memorial Fund 1980–87, Deputy Chair. 2005–; Dir of Public Affairs, Nat. Trust 1987–91; Chief Exec. and Deputy Chair. British Library 1991–2000; Prin. and Vice-Chancellor Univ. of St Andrews 2001–08, now Prin. Emer.; Visiting Prof., Napier Univ., Edin. 1999–; Visiting Scholar, Getty Inst., Calif. 2000; Chair. European Nat. Libraries Forum 1993–2000, Heritage Lottery Fund Cttee for Scotland 2005–, Royal Scottish Nat. Orchestra 2008–; Pres. Inst. of Information Scientists 1993–94; mem. Council, Nat. Trust for Scotland 2001–04, Council, St Leonard's School, St Andrews 2001–08, Bd Scottish Enterprise, Fife 2003–08, Scottish Exec. Cultural Cttee 2004–05; Trustee, Hopeton House Preservation Trust 2001–05, Newbattle Abbey Coll. 2004–08; Hon. LLD (St Andrews), Hon. Dr (Edinburgh) Hon. Fellow, The Library Asscn 1997. *Leisure interests:* reading, music, museums, galleries, pottering. *Address:* 10 Wiltshire House, Maidstone Building Mews, Borough High Street, London, SE1 1GH, England (home); 10 Carlton Terrace, Edinburgh, EH7 5DD, Scotland (home). *Telephone:* (20) 7207-3236 (London) (home); (131) 558-8455 (Edinburgh) (home). *E-mail:* brian@lang-uk.com (office). *Website:* www.lang-uk.com (office).

LANG, David, PhD; American composer; b. 1 Aug. 1957, LA; m.; three c.; ed Stanford Univ., Univ. of Iowa, Yale School of Music; studied with Jacob Druckman, Hans Werner Henze (q.v.) and Martin Bresnick; Jr Composer-in-Residence, Horizons Summer Festival 1980s; commissioned by Boston Symphony Orchestra, Cleveland Orchestra, St Paul Chamber Orchestra, BBC Singers, American Composers Orchestra and Santa Fe Opera and Settembre Musica Festival, Turin; co-f. (with Michael Gordon and Julia Wolfe) New York annual music festival Bang on a Can 1987–; composed albums Cheating, Lying, Stealing 1996 and Brian Eno: Music for Airports 1998 for group Bang on a Can All-Stars; Rome Prize, American Acad., Rome; BMW Prize, Munich Biennale for New Music Theatre; Friedheim Award, Kennedy Center; Revson Fellowship with New York Philharmonic; grants from Guggenheim Foundation, New York Foundation of Arts and Nat. Endowment for the Arts. *Compositions include:* chamber music: Frag 1984, Dance/Drop 1987, Burn Notice 1989, Music for Gracious Living 1992, Cheating, Lying, Stealing 1993, Face so Pale 1992, Wreck/Wed 1995, Slip 1996, Follow 1996, Little Eye 1999, My Very Empty Mouth 1999, Sweet Air 1999, Short Fall 2000, Birds of Minnesota 2000; for chorus: By Fire 1984, Hecuba 1995, This Condition 2000, I Lie 2001, Again (After Ecclesiastes) 2005, Evening Morning Day 2007, The Little Match Girl Passion (Pulitzer Prize for Music 2008) 2007; opera: Judith and Holofernes 1989, Music for Gracious Living 1992, Modern Painters 1995, The Carbon Copy Building 1999, The Difficulty of Crossing a Field 2000, Lost Objects 2001; orchestral and large ensemble: Hammer Amour 1978, Eating Living Monkeys 1985, Spud 1986, Are You Experienced? 1987–89, Bonehead 1990, International Business Machine 1990, Fire and Forget 1992, My Evil Twin 1992, Slow Movement 1993, Under Orpheus 1994, Grind to a Halt 1996, The Passing Measures 1998, I Fought the Law 1998, Ariel's Version 1998, Haircut 2000, How to Pray 2002, Fur 2004, Loud Love Songs 2004, Pierced 2007, Every Ounce of Strength 2007. *Address:* Red Poppy Music, 222 East Fifth Street, No. 12, New York, NY 10003, USA (office). *Telephone:* (646) 498-8822 (office). *Fax:* (212) 388-1727 (office). *E-mail:* info@redpoppymusic.com (office). *Website:* www.redpoppymusic.com (office).

LANG, Helmut; Austrian fashion designer; b. 10 March 1956, Vienna; est. own studio in Vienna 1977; made-to-measure shop opened in Vienna 1979; development of ready-to-wear collections 1984–86; presented Helmut Lang women's wear, Paris fashion week 1986–, menswear 1987–; began licence business 1988; Helmut Lang Underwear 1994; Helmut Lang Protective Eyewear 1995; Prof. of Masterclass of Fashion, Univ. of Applied Arts, Vienna 1993–; Council of American Fashion Designers of the Year Award 1996. *Address:* c/o Michele Montagne, 184 rue St Maur, 75010 Paris, France. *Telephone:* 1-42-03-91-00. *Fax:* 1-42-01-12-22.

LÁNG, István; Hungarian agrochemist; b. 26 Dec. 1931, Mohács; s. of József Láng and Anna Világi; m. Etelka Sorosinszki; one d.; ed Agricultural Univ. of Ivanovo, USSR; Fellow, Research Inst. for Soil Sciences and Agricultural Chem., Budapest 1955–63; Exec. Sec. Section of Biological Sciences, Hungarian Acad. of Sciences 1963–70, Deputy Sec.-Gen. 1970–85, Sec.-Gen. 1985–93, Science Policy Adviser 1993–; Chair. Advisory Bd, Ministry of Environmental and Regional Policy 1994–96, Vice-Chair. 1998–; Chair. Hungarian Research Fund 1986–90; Chair. Local Preparatory Cttee for the World Conf. on Science 1998; mem. World Comm. on Environment and Devt (Brundtland Comm.), Advisory Cttee on Environment, Int. Council for Science, Selection Panel for Global Environment Leadership Award 1999; mem. World Science Forum. *Publications include:* Agricultural Production and Global Environment Protection 2003. *Leisure interests:* philately, bird watching. *Address:* c/o Hungarian Academy of Sciences, 1051 Budapest, Roosevelt tér 9, Hungary. *Telephone:* (1) 2692656. *Fax:* (1) 2692655. *E-mail:* ilang@office.mta.hu (office).

LANG, Jack, DenD; French politician; b. 2 Sept. 1939, Mirecourt; s. of Roger Lang and Marie-Luce Bouchet; m. Monique Buczynski 1961; two d.; ed Lycée Henri-Poincaré, Nancy, Inst. of Political Studies, Paris; Founder and Dir World Festival of Univ. Theatre, Nancy 1963–77; Dir Théâtre du palais de Chaillot 1972–74; Prof. of Int. Law 1976–; Dir Educ. and Research Unit for econ. and legal sciences, Nancy 1977; Councillor, Paris 1977–81; Deputy Nat. Ass. 1986; Special Adviser to First Sec., Parti Socialiste (PS) 1978–81, PS Nat. Del. for Culture 1979–81, Nat. Sec. 2005–07; Minister of Culture and Communications 1981–83, 1984–86, May–June 1988, 1991–92, of Educ. and Culture 1992–93, also Minister for Major Public Works and Bicentenary 1988–89, of Educ. 2000–02; Govt spokesman 1991; Mayor of Blois 1989–2001; mem. European Parl. 1994–97; Socialist Deputy from Loir-et-Cher March—Dec. 1993, 1997–; Pres. Foreign Affairs Cttee, Nat. Ass.; Chevalier, Légion d'honneur; Hon. DLitt (Nottingham) 1990, Dr hc (Royal Coll. of Art) 1993; Prix

Antonio de Sancha (Spain) 1997, Prix Wartburg (Germany) 1998. *Publications:* Demain les femmes 1995, Lettre à Malraux 1996, François Premier 1997, Une école élitaire pour tous 2003, Un nouveau regime politique pour la France 2004, Nelson Mandela: une leçon de vie pour l'Avemir 2005. *Address:* Assemblée nationale, 126 rue de l'Université, 75355 Paris 07 SP, France (office). *Telephone:* 1-40-63-60-00 (office). *Fax:* 1-45-55-75-23 (office). *E-mail:* jlang@assemblee-nationale.fr (office). *Website:* www.assemblee-nationale.fr (office).

LANG, Kathryn Dawn (k.d.); Canadian singer and songwriter; b. 2 Nov. 1961, Consort, Alberta; d. of Adam Lang and Audrey L. Lang; began playing guitar aged 10; formed band The Reclines in early 1980s, played N American clubs 1982–87; performed at closing ceremony, Winter Olympics, Calgary 1988; performed with Sting, Bruce Springsteen, Peter Gabriel and Tracy Chapman in Amnesty Int. tour 1988; headline US tour 1992; played at Royal Albert Hall, London 1992; Earth Day benefit concert, Hollywood Bowl 1993; sang with Andy Bell, BRIT Awards 1993; Canadian Country Music Asscn Awards for Best Entertainer of Year 1989, Best Album of Year 1990, Grammy Awards for Best Female Country Vocal Performance 1990, Best Pop Vocal 1993, American Music Awards, Favourite New Artist 1993, Songwriter of the Year (with Ben Mink) 1993, BRIT Award for Best Int. Female 1995. *Film appearances:* Salmonberries 1991, Teresa's Tattoo 1994, The Last Don 1997, Eye of the Beholder 1999; features on soundtrack to Dick Tracy. *Recordings include:* albums: A Truly Western Experience 1984, Angel With A Lariat 1987, Shadowland 1988, Absolute Torch And Twang 1989, Ingénue (Album of the Year 1993) 1992, Even Cowgirls Get The Blues (film soundtrack) 1993, All You Can Eat 1995, Drag 1997, Australian Tour 1997, Invincible Summer 2000, Live By Request 2001, A Wonderful World (with Tony Bennett; Grammy Award for Best Traditional Pop Vocal Album 2004) 2003, Hymns of the 49th Parallel 2004, Reintarnation 2006, Watershed 2008. *Address:* Direct Management Group, 947 North La Cienega Blvd, Suite G, Los Angeles, CA 90069, USA (office); Asgard Promotions Ltd, 125 Parkway, London, NW1 7PS, England (office). *Website:* www.kdlang.com (office).

LANG, Larry H. P., BA, MA, PhD; Taiwanese economist and academic; *Chair Professor of Finance, Chinese University of Hong Kong;* ed Tunghai Univ., Nat. Taiwan Univ., Wharton School of Business, Univ. of Pennsylvania, USA; fmr Lecturer, Wharton School of Business; fmr Prof. of Finance, Grad. School of Business, Michigan State Univ., Coll. of Business, Ohio State Univ., Stern School of Business, New York Univ.; fmr Visiting Prof. of Finance, Grad. School of Business, Univ. of Chicago; currently Chair Prof. of Finance, Faculty of Business Admin, Chinese Univ. of Hong Kong; Pnr, GITIC-Lehman Infrastructure Fund, Lehman Brothers 1994–96; Consultant on Corp. Governance Projects to World Bank, Washington, DC 1998–2000, on WTO/Banking Issues to OECD 2000, on Corp. Governance to China Shenzhen Stock Exchange, Hong Kong Govt; presenter, half-hour talk show, Larry Lang Live 2004–06, show cancelled following criticism of Chinese Politburo. *Publications:* numerous articles and research papers in professional journals. *Address:* Room 225, Leung Kau Kui Building, Department of Finance, Chinese University of Hong Kong, Shatin, New Territories, Hong Kong Special Administrative Region, People's Republic of China (office). *Telephone:* 2609-7761 (office). *Fax:* 2603-6586 (office). *E-mail:* llang@baf.msmail.cuhk.edu.hk (office). *Website:* www.cuhk.edu.hk (office).

LANG, Hon. Otto, PC, OC, QC, BA, LLB, BCL, LLD; Canadian lawyer, politician, business executive and consultant; b. 14 May 1932, Handel, Sask.; s. of Otto T. Lang and Maria Theresa Wurm; m. 1st Adrian Ann Merchant 1963 (divorced 1988); three s. four d.; m. 2nd Deborah J. McCawley 1989; one step-s. one step-d.; ed Univ. of Sask. and Oxford Univ., UK; admitted to Sask. Bar 1956, to Ont., Yukon and NWT Bars 1972, Manitoba Bar 1988; Asst Prof., Univ. of Sask., Faculty of Law 1956, Assoc. Prof. 1957, Prof. 1961, Dean of Law School 1961–68; MP for Saskatoon-Humboldt 1968–79; Minister without Portfolio 1968, with responsibility for Energy and Water Resources 1969, with responsibility for Canadian Wheat Bd 1969–79; Minister of Manpower & Immigration 1970–72, of Justice 1972–75, of Transport 1975–79, of Justice and Attorney-Gen. Aug.–Nov. 1978; Pres. Asscn of Canadian Law Teachers 1962–63; Vice-Pres. Sask. Liberal Asscn 1956–63; Fed. Campaign Chair. Liberal Party 1963–64; Past Pres. Saskatoon Social Planning Council; Exec. Vice-Pres. Pioneer Grain Co. Ltd 1979–88; mem. Bd of Dirs Investor Group Trust Co. 1985–; Chair. Transport Inst., Univ. of Manitoba 1988–93; Pres. and CEO Central Gas Manitoba Inc. 1993–99; consultant with GPC 2000–; Vice-Chair. of Bd, Winnipeg Airports Authority 1995–; Campaign Chair. Winnipeg United Way 1983; Chair. Royal Winnipeg Ballet Capital Campaign 1996–2000; Rhodes Scholar 1953; QC for Ont. 1972, for Sask. 1972; Hon. Consul-Gen. of Japan 1992–97. *Publication:* Contemporary Problems of Public Law in Canada (ed.) 1968. *Leisure interests:* curling, bridge, golf. *Address:* 6 Liss Road, St Andrews, Manitoba, R1A 2XZ (office); Twin Oaks, 292 River Road, St Andrews, Manitoba, R1A 2X2, Canada (home). *Telephone:* (204) 338-7242 (office); (204) 334-9476 (home). *Fax:* (204) 338-1524 (office). *E-mail:* olang@mb.sympatico.ca (office).

LANG, Rein, LLM; Estonian politician; *Minister of Justice;* b. 4 July 1957, Tartu; s. of Ants Lang and Ulve Lang; one d.; ed Tartu State Univ.; previous positions include Deputy Man. Linnahall arena, Deputy Dir Muusik club, Chair., then Head Supervisory Council, Trio media co.; apptd Deputy Mayor of Tallinn 2001; mem. Tallinn City Council 2002; founding mem. Reform Party; mem. Parl. 2003–, First Deputy Speaker –2005; Minister of Foreign Affairs 2005, of Justice 2005–; mem. Rotary Club of Tallinn; Commdr Ordre Nat. (France) 2004, Order of the White Star (2nd class) 2006; Estonian Police Award (2nd class) 2003. *Address:* Ministry of Justice, Tõnismägi 5a, Tallinn 15191, Estonia (office). *Telephone:* 620-8100 (office). *Fax:* 620-8109 (office). *E-mail:* rein.lan@just.ee (office); rein@kuku.ee (home). *Website:* www.just.ee (office); www.lang.ee (home).

LANG OF MONKTON, Baron (Life Peer), cr. 1997, of Merrick and the Rhinns of Kells in Dumfries and Galloway; **Ian (Bruce) Lang,** OStJ, BA; British politician; b. 27 June 1940; s. of the late James F. Lang, DSC and of Maude Stewart; m. Sandra Montgomerie 1971; two d.; ed Lathallan School, Kincardineshire, Rugby School and Sidney Sussex Coll. Cambridge; MP for Galloway 1979–83, for Galloway and Upper Nithsdale 1983–97; Asst Govt Whip 1981–83; a Lord Commr of HM Treasury 1983–86; Parl. Under-Sec. of State, Dept of Employment 1986, Scottish Office 1986–87; Minister of State, Scottish Office 1987–90; Sec. of State for Scotland and Lord Keeper of the Great Seal of Scotland 1990–95; Pres. Bd of Trade 1995–97; mem. House of Lords Select Cttee on the Constitution 2001–05; Chair. Thistle Mining Inc. 1998–, US Special Opportunities Trust PLC; Dir Marsh & McLennan Inc. 1997–, Lithgows Ltd 1997–, Charlemagne Capital Ltd 2006–; Gov. Rugby School 1997–2007; mem. Queen's Bodyguard for Scotland (Royal Co. of Archers) 1974–; DL Ayrshire and Arran 1998; mem. Conservative Party; Hon. Pres. St Columba's School, Renfrewshire 1999–. *Publication:* Blue Remembered Years 2002. *Address:* House of Lords, London, SW1A 0PW, England.

LANGAT, Nancy Jebet; Kenyan athlete; b. 22 Aug. 1981; middle-distance runner; Gold Medal, 1,500m, Olympic Games, Beijing 2008. *Address:* c/o Kenya Athletics Federation, PO Box 46722, Aerodrome Road, Riadha House, 00100 Nairobi West, Kenya. *Telephone:* (2) 605021. *Fax:* (2) 605020. *E-mail:* athleticskenya@gt.co.ke. *Website:* www.athleticskenya.org.

LÅNGBACKA, Ralf Runar, MA; Finnish theatre director and professor of theatre science; b. 20 Nov. 1932, Närpes; s. of Runar Emanuel Långbacka and Hulda Emilia Långbacka (née Backlund); m. Runa Birgitta Danielsson 1961; two s. one d.; ed Åbo Akademi, Munich Univ. and Freie Univ., Berlin; Ed. Finnish Radio literary programmes 1956; Asst and Dir Lilla Teatern, Helsinki 1958–60; Man. and Artistic Dir Swedish Theatre, Turku 1960–63; Dir Finnish Nat. Theatre 1963–65; Artistic Dir Swedish Theatre, Helsinki 1965–67; Dir Municipal Theatre, Gothenburg, Sweden; mem. Finnish State Comm. of Dramatic Art 1967–70; Artistic Dir Municipal Theatre, Turku 1971–77; Head Finnish Dirs Asscn 1978–82; Artistic and Man. Dir Municipal Theatre, Helsinki 1983–87, Artistic Prof. 1979–83, 1988–93; Prof. of Theatre Science, Åbo Akademi, Turku 1994–97; Pres. Finnish Centre, Int. Theatre Inst. (ITI) 1983–96, mem. Bd (Excom) of ITI 1991–95; Corresp. mem. Akad. der Künste, Berlin 1979; freelance dir in Finland, Sweden, Denmark, Germany, Norway, Russia, USA, Chile 1960–2004; Academician, Finnish Acad. 2004–; The Critics Spurs 1963, Pro Finlandia 1973, Henrik-Steffens Award (Germany) 1994, Finland Prize, Swedish Acad., Sweden 1999, Finland Prize for Theatre 2001. *Film:* Puntila 1979. *Music:* directed operas: Wozzeck (Berg) 1967, 2001, Carmen (Bizet) 1969, Don Giovanni (Mozart) 1973, 1984, Macbeth (Verdi) 1980, 1993, Don Carlos (Verdi) 1995, Rigoletto (Verdi) 2000, 2001. *Plays:* directed over 100 performances of plays, including Shakespeare, Chekhov, Brecht and Büchner. *Television:* Premiär (four-part feature) 1992. *Publications:* Teatterikirja (The Theatre Book) (with Kalle Holmberg) 1977, Bland annat om Brecht (On Brecht and Others) 1981, Möten med Tjechov (Meetings with Chekhov) 1986, Denna långa dag, detta korta liv (This long day, This short life: poems) 1988, Krocketspelaren (The Croquet Player, play) 1990, Olga, Irina och jag (Olga, Irina and I, play) 1991, Brecht og det realistiske teater (Brecht and the Realistic Theatre) 1998 and articles. *Leisure interests:* music, mushrooms, sailing. *Address:* Hopeasalmenranta 1B, 00570 Helsinki 57, Finland (home). *Telephone:* (9) 6849508 (home); (40) 7323323 (home). *Fax:* (9) 6849508 (home). *E-mail:* ralf.langbacka@kolumbus.fi (home).

LANGBO, Arnold G.; Canadian business executive; b. 13 April 1937, Richmond, BC; s. of Osbjourn Langbo and Laura Marie Langbo (née Hagen); m. Martha M. Miller 1959; eight c.; ed Univ. of British Columbia, Vancouver; Sales Rep. Kellogg Canada Inc. 1956–67, Int. Div. 1967–69, Admin. Asst to Kellogg Co., Pres. 1969–70, Exec. Vice-Pres. 1970–71, Vice-Pres. of Kellogg Canada 1971–76, Salada Foods Ltd 1971–76, Pres., CEO Kellogg Salada Canada Ltd Inc. 1976–78, Pres. U.S. Food Products Div. of Kellogg Co. 1978–79, Corp. Vice-Pres. 1979–81, Exec. Vice-Pres. 1981–83, Group Exec. Vice-Pres. Kellogg Co. 1983–86, Pres. Kellogg Int. 1986–90, Pres., COO, Dir Kellogg Co. 1990–91, Chair., CEO 1992–2000 (retd); mem. Bd of Dirs Johnson and Johnson, Weyerhaeuser Co., Whirlpool Corpn, Int. Youth Foundation; fmr mem. Bd of Dirs Grocery Mfrs of America; mem. Advisory Bd J. L. Kellogg Grad. School of Man., Northwestern Univ.; Adrian Trimpe Distinguished Service Award, Haworth Coll. of Business, Western Mich. Univ. 2000. *Address:* c/o Board of Directors, Johnson & Johnson, 1 Johnson & Johnson Plaza, New Brunswick, NJ 08933; 7614 La Corniche Circle, Boca Raton, FL 33433, USA (home).

LANGE, Andrew E., BA, PhD; American cosmologist and academic; *Marvin L. Goldberger Professor of Physics, California Institute of Technology;* ed Princeton Univ., Univ. of California; Visiting Assoc., Calif. Inst. of Tech. 1993–94, Prof. 1994–2001, Marvin L. Goldberger Prof. of Physics 2001–; Calif. Scientist of the Year (jtly) 2003, Gordon and Betty Moore Foundation Award 2006, Balzan Prize for Observational Astronomy and Astrophysics (co-winner) 2006. *Publications:* numerous scientific papers in professional journals on the Cosmic Background Radiation. *Address:* Caltech Observational Cosmology Group, MC 59-33, Pasadena, CA 91125, USA (office). *Telephone:* (626) 395-4318 (office). *Fax:* (626) 584-9929 (office). *E-mail:* ael@astro.caltech.edu (office). *Website:* www.astro.caltech.edu/%7Elgg (office).

LANGE, Hartmut; German author and dramatist; b. 31 March 1937, Berlin; s. of Johanna Lange and Karl Lange; m. Ulrike Ritter 1971; ed Babelsberg Film School; playwright at Deutsches Theater, Berlin 1961–65; freelance writer, W Berlin 1965–; Gerhart-Hauptmann-Preis 1968, Literatur Preis der

Adenauer Stiftung 1998, Ehrengabe der Schiller-Stiftung von 1859 2000, Italo Svevo Preis 2003, Preis der LiteraTour Nord 2004. *Publications:* Die Revolution als Geisterschiff 1974, Die Selbstverbrennung 1982, Deutsche Empfindungen 1983, Die Waldsteinsonate 1984, Das Konzert 1986, Die Ermüdung 1988, Vom Werden der Vernunft 1988, Gesammelte Theaterstücke (Collected Plays) 1988, Die Wattwanderung 1990, Die Reise nach Triest 1991, Die Stechpalme 1993, Schnitzlers Würgeengel 1995, Der Herr im Café 1996, Italienische Novellen 1998, Eine andere Form des Glücks 1999, Die Bildungsreise 2000, Das Streichquartett 2001, Irrtum als Erkenntnis 2002, Leptis Magna 2003, Der Wanderer 2005, Der Therapeut 2007. *Leisure interest:* chess. *Address:* Hohenzollerndamm 197, 10717 Berlin, Germany; 06010 Niccone, Perugia, Italy.

LANGE, Hermann, DJur; German professor of law; *Professor Emeritus, University of Tübingen;* b. 24 Jan. 1922, Dresden; s. of Arno Lange and Käthe (née Braun) Lange; m. Ulrike Moser 1960; one s. one d.; ed Kreuzgymnasium, Dresden and Univs of Leipzig, Munich and Freiburg/Breisgau; Asst Inst. of Legal History, Univ. of Freiburg/Breisgau 1949–53; Privatdozent, Freiburg/Breisgau 1953–55; Extraordinary Prof. Univ. of Innsbrück 1955–57; Prof. Univ. of Kiel 1957–62, Univ. of Mainz 1962–66, Univ. of Tübingen 1966– (now Emer.); mem. Akad. der Wissenschaften und Literatur, Mainz. *Publications:* Schadensersatz und Privatstrafe in der mittelalterlichen Rechtstheorie 1955, Familienrecht (Kommentar) 1962, 1989 (12), Die Consilien des Baldus de Ubaldis 1974, Schadensersatzrecht 1979, Wandlungen des Schadenersatzrechts 1987, 2003 (3) Die Anfänge der modernen Rechtswissenschaft 1993, Römisches Recht im Mittelalter I 1997, 100 Jahre Bürgerliches Gesetzbuch 2001, Die Universitäten des Mittelalters und das Römische Recht 2006, Römisches Recht im Mittelalter II 2007. *Address:* Ferdinand-Christian-Baur-Strasse 3, 72076 Tübingen, Germany. *Telephone:* (7071) 61216.

LANGE, Jessica; American actress; b. 20 April 1949, Cloquet, Minn.; d. of Al Lange and Dorothy Lange; m. Paco Grande 1970 (divorced 1982); one d. (with Mikhail Baryshnikov); one s. one d. (with Sam Shepard); ed Univ. of Minnesota; student of mime with Etienne DeCroux, Paris; Dancer Opéra Comique, Paris; model, Wilhelmina Agency, New York; Star Showtime TV production Cat On A Hot Tin Roof 1984; in Summer stock production Angel On My Shoulder, NC 1980; play: A Streetcar Named Desire, London (Theatre World Award, Golden Globe for TV performance) 1996. *Films include:* King Kong 1976, All That Jazz 1979, How to Beat the High Cost of Living 1980, The Postman Always Rings Twice 1981, Frances 1982, Tootsie 1982 (Acad. Award for Best Supporting Actress 1982), Country (also producer) 1984, Sweet Dreams 1985, Crimes of the Heart 1986, Everybody's All American 1989, Far North 1989, Music Box 1989, Men Don't Leave 1989, Blue Sky 1990, Cape Fear 1991, Far North 1991, Night and the City 1993, Losing Isaiah, Rob Roy 1994, Blue Sky (Acad. Award for Best Actress 1995) 1994, A Thousand Acres 1997, Hush 1998, Cousin Bette 1998, Titus 1999, Prozac Nation 2003, Normal 2003, Masked and Anonymous 2003, Great Performances 2003, Big Fish 2003, Don't Come Knockin' 2005, Broken Flowers 2005, Neverwas 2005, Bonneville 2006. *Plays:* Long Day's Journey into Night 2000, A Glass Menagerie 2005, 2007. *Address:* 9401 Wilshire Blvd, Beverly Hills, CA 90212; c/o Toni Howard, ICM, 8942 Wilshire Boulevard, Beverly Hills, CA 90211, USA.

LANGE, Otto Ludwig, Dr rer. nat; German professor of botany (retd); *Professor Emeritus, Julius-von-Sachs-Institut für Biowissenschaften, Universität Würzburg;* b. 21 Aug. 1927, Dortmund; s. of Otto Lange and Marie (née Pralle) Lange; m. Rose Wilhelm 1959; two d.; ed Univs of Göttingen and Freiburg; Asst Prof., Univ. of Göttingen 1953–61; Dozent, Technische Hochschule Darmstadt 1961–63; Prof. of Forest Botany, Univ. Göttingen 1963–67; Prof. of Botany, Univ. of Würzburg 1967–92, Prof. Emer. 1992–; Visiting Scientist, Utah State Univ. 1973, 1985, ANU, Canberra 1978–79; Dir Botanical Garden, Univ. of Würzburg 1967–92; Co-Ed. scientific journal Flora; mem. Deutsche Akad. der Naturforscher Leopoldina, Bayerische Akad. der Wissenschaften, Academia Europaea, Acad. Scientiarum et Artium Europaea; Corresp. mem. Akad. der Wissenschaften, Göttingen; Foreign Hon. mem. American Acad. of Arts and Sciences 1994; Bundesverdienstkreuz (1st Class) 1985; Dr hc (Bayreuth) 1995, (Tech. Univ., Lisbon) 1996, (Darmstadt) 2001; Antarctic Service Medal, US Govt 1974, Gottfried-Wilhem-Leibniz Prize, Deutsche Forschungsgemeinschaft 1986, Balzan Prize 1988, Adalbert Seifriz Prize 1990, Bayerische Maximiliansorden for Science and Art 1991, Acharius Medal, Int. Asscn of Lichenology 1992. *Publications:* ed. (with others) four vols of Physiological Plant Ecology in Encyclopedia of Plant Physiology 1981–83; books on water and plant life, plant response to stress, forest decline, air pollution and biological soil crusts; book series Ecological Studies; 360 scientific papers. *Address:* Julius-von-Sachs-Institut für Biowissenschaften der Universität Würzburg, Julius-von-Sachs-Platz 3, 97082 Würzburg (office); Leitengraben 37, 97084 Würzburg, Germany (home). *Telephone:* (931) 888-6205 (office); (931) 65249 (home). *Fax:* (931) 6193178 (home). *E-mail:* ollange@botanik.uni-wuerzburg.de (office). *Website:* www.botanik.uni-wuerzburg.de.

LANGELLA, Frank, BA; American actor; b. 1 Jan. 1940, Bayonne, NJ; s. of Frank A. Langella, Sr; m. Ruth Weil 1977 (divorced); ed Syracuse Univ. *Plays include:* numerous stage appearances on Broadway and elsewhere including Seascape (Tony Award for Best Featured Actor in a Play) 1975, Fortune's Fool (Tony Award for Best Featured Actor in a Play) 2002, Sherlock's Last Case 1987, Frost/Nixon (Tony Award for Best Leading Actor in a Play) 2007, A Man for All Seasons 2008. *Films include:* Diary of a Mad Housewife 1970,The Twelve Chairs 1970, The Wrath of God 1972, The Mark of Zorro 1974, Dracula 1979, And God Created Woman 1988, Body of Evidence 1993, The Beast 2001, Now You See It 2005, Good Night and Good Luck 2005, Starting Out in the Evening (Boston Soc. of Film Critics Award) 2007, Frost/Nixon 2008, The Box 2009. *Television:* Sherlock Holmes 1981. *Address:* CESD Talent Agency NY, 257 Park Avenue South, Suite 900, New York, NY 10010, USA (office). *Telephone:* (212) 477-1666 (office). *Fax:* (212) 979-2011 (office). *Website:* www.cesdtalent.com (office).

LANGER, Ivan, MD, MCL; Czech politician; *Minister of the Interior;* b. 1 Jan. 1967, Olomouc; m. Markéta Vobořilová; one s. one d.; ed Univ. of Palacký, Charles Univ., Prague; Secr. Ministry for Justice of Czech Repub. 1993–96; mem. Council Olomouc 1994; mem. of Civic Democratic Party (ODS), Vice-Chair. 1998–2002, 2004–; mem. Parl. 1996–; Shadow Minister of the Interior 1999–2002; Vice-Chair. Chamber of Deputies (Parl.) 1998–2006; Minister of the Interior June–Oct. 2006 (resgnd), reinstated Jan. 2007–, of Information 2007; Hon. mem. Maltese Order of Help 1994–. *Publications:* Rational Anti-drug Policy, After the Velvet Revolution. *Leisure interests:* tennis, music, theatre, film, golf. *Address:* Ministry of the Interior, Nad štolou 3, Prague 7, 170 34 Czech Republic (office). *Telephone:* 974811111 (office). *Fax:* 261433552 (office). *E-mail:* langer@psp.cz (office); posta@mvcr.cz (office). *Website:* www.langer.cz; www.mvcr.cz (office).

LANGER, Robert S., ScD, BS; American chemical engineer and academic; *Institute Professor, Massachusetts Institute of Technology;* b. 29 Aug. 1948, Albany, NY; m. Laura Langer; three c.; ed Cornell Univ. and MIT; Postdoctoral Fellow, Children's Hosp., Boston 1974; Germeshausen Prof. of Chemical and Biomedical Eng, MIT 1990–2005, Inst. Prof. 2005–; mem. SCIENCE Bd, US Food and Drug Admin 1995–2002, Chair. 1999–2002; mem. Bd Dir or Scientific Advisory Bd Wyeth, Alkermes, Mitsubishi Pharmaceuticals, Warner-Lambert, Momenta Pharmaceuticals; mem. Inst. of Medicine (NAS) 1989, NAS, Nat. Acad. of Eng (NAE) 1992 (one of few people ever elected to all three US Nat. Acads and the youngest in history at age 43); Dr hc (ETH Switzerland), (Technion Univ. Israel), (Hebrew Univ. of Jerusalem), (Université Catholique de Louvain, Belgium), (Univ. of Liverpool, UK), (Univ. of Nottingham, UK), (Albany Medical Coll.), (Pennsylvania State Univ.), (Uppsala Univ., Sweden), (Yale Univ.), (Northwestern Univ.); more than 170 major awards, including ACS Award for Applied Polymer Science (Phillips Award) 1992, Gairdner Foundation Int. Award 1996, AIChE William Walker Award 1996, Lemelson-MIT Prize for Invention and Innovation 1998, ACS Award in Polymer Chem. 1999, ACS (Delaware Section) Wallace Carothers Award 2000, NAE Charles Stark Draper Prize 2002, Dickson Prize for Science 2002, Heinz Award for Tech., Economy and Employment 2003, Harvey Prize 2003, John Fritz Award 2003, General Motors Kettering Prize for Cancer Research 2004, Dan David Prize in Materials Science 2005, Albany Medical Center Prize in Medicine and Biomedical Research 2005, Nat. Medal of Science 2006, Millennium Technology Prize 2008, Max Planck Research Award 2008, Prince of Asturias Award for Technical and Scientific Research 2008; inducted into Nat. Inventors Hall of Fame 2006; named by Bio World as one of 25 most important individuals in biotechnology in the world 1990, by Forbes Magazine 1999, named by Time Magazine and CNN as one of the 100 most important people in America and one of the 18 top people in science or medicine in America 2001, named by Discover Magazine as one of the 20 most important people in this area 2002, selected by Forbes Magazine as one of the 15 innovators worldwide who will re-invent our future 2002, selected by Parade Magazine as one of six "Heroes whose research may save your life" 2004. *Publications:* more than 1,000 articles in scientific journals on drug delivery, biomaterials, tissue engineering, biotechnology, immobilized enzymes, biomedical engineering, and more than 600 issued or pending patents worldwide. *Address:* Massachusetts Institute of Technology, Room E25-342, 77 Massachusetts Avenue, Cambridge, MA 02139-4307, USA (office). *Telephone:* (617) 253-3107 (office). *Fax:* (617) 258-8827 (office). *E-mail:* rlanger@mit.edu (office); langeroffice@mit.edu (office). *Website:* web.mit.edu/langerlab (office).

LANGHOFF, Stephanie R., BS, MBA, PhD; American chemist; *Chief Scientist, NASA Ames Research Center;* ed Colorado Coll., Univ. of Washington, Massachusetts Inst. of Tech.; Post-Doctoral Fellow, Battelle Memorial Inst., Columbus, OH 1973–76; Nat. Research Council Fellow, NASA Ames Research Center 1976–78, Research Scientist, Computational Chem. Br. 1978–92, Br. Chief 1992–97, Chief Scientist 1998–, Chair. NASA Ames Basic Research Council 1999–2002; Sloan Fellow, MIT 1997–98; mem. American Physical Soc.; mem. US Dept of Energy Panel on Combustion Research, Panel on Innovative Concepts in Nuclear Propulsion. *Address:* NASA Ames Research Center, MS 230–3, Moffett Field, CA 94035, USA (office). *Telephone:* (650) 604-6213 (office). *Fax:* (650) 604-0350 (office). *E-mail:* stephanie.r.langhoff@nasa.gov (office). *Website:* www.nasa.gov/centers/ames (office).

LANGHOLM, Sivert; Norwegian historian and academic; b. 19 May 1927, Haugesund; s. of Karl Johan Langholm and Anna Langholm; m. Eva Synnøve Bakkom 1959; one s. one d.; ed Univ. of Oslo; Lecturer in History, Univ. of Oslo 1961–71, research (project) leader 1971–74, Reader in History 1974–76, Prof. 1976–94, Dean, Faculty of Humanities 1985–90; mem. Det Norske Videnskaps Akademi; Hon. mem. Int. Comm. for the History of Univs. *Publications:* Stillingsretten 1966, Historisk Rekonstruksjon og Begrunnelse 1967, Elitenes Valg 1984. *Address:* Universitetet i Oslo, Avdeling for Historie, Postboks 1008, Blindern 0315, Oslo (office); Parkgt. 12, 3513 Hønefoss, Norway (home). *Telephone:* 22-85-68-09 (office); 32-12-14-48 (home). *Website:* www.hf.uio.no/hi/english (office).

LANGLANDS, Sir (Robert) Alan, Kt, BSc, FCGI, CIMgt; British university principal and healthcare administrator; *Principal and Vice-Chancellor, University of Dundee;* b. 29 May 1952; s. of James Langlands and May (née Rankin) Langlands; m. Elizabeth McDonald 1977; one s. one d.; ed Allan Glen's School, Univ. of Glasgow; grad. trainee Nat. Health Service Scotland 1974–76; with Argyll and Clyde Health Bd 1976–78; with Simpson Memorial Maternity Pavilion, Elsie Inglis Hosp. 1978–81; Unit Admin. Middx and Univ. Coll. Hosps and Hosp. for Women, Soho 1981–85; Dist Gen. Man. Harrow Health Authority 1985–89; Practice Leader Health Care, Towers Perrin

1989–91; Gen. Man. NW Thames Regional Health Authority 1991–92; Deputy Chief Exec. Nat. Health Service 1993–94, Chief Exec. 1994–2000; mem. Central Research and Devt Cttee Nat. Health Service 1991–92; mem. Inst. of Health Services Man., Nat. Forum for Research and Devt 1994–2000; mem. Advisory Bd Centre for Corp. Strategy and Change, Univ. of Warwick 1995–2000; Prin. and Vice-Chancellor Univ. of Dundee 2000–; mem. Nat. Advisory Bd, Healthcare Advisory Bd Institut Européen d'Admin des Affaires (INSEAD) 1998–; Hon. Prof., Warwick Business School 1996, Johns Hopkins Univ. 2000–; Hon. FFPHM 1994; Hon. FIA 1999; Hon. FCGI 2000; Hon. CCMI CIMgt 2000; Hon. Fellow, Royal Coll. of Gen. Practitioners 2001; Hon. FRCP 2001; Hon. FRCSE 2001; Hon. FRCPSGlas 2002; Hon. DUniv Glasgow 2001. *Leisure interests:* walking in Yorkshire and Scotland. *Address:* University of Dundee, Dundee, DD1 4HN, Scotland (office).

LANGLANDS, Robert Phelan, MA, PhD, FRS; Canadian mathematician and academic; *Hermann Weyl Professor, School of Mathematics, Institute for Advanced Study, Princeton;* b. 6 Oct. 1936, New Westminster; s. of Robert Langlands and Kathleen J. Phelan; m. Charlotte Cheverie 1956; two s. two d.; ed Univ. of British Columbia, Yale Univ., USA; Instructor, Assoc. Prof. Princeton Univ. 1960–67; Prof. Yale Univ. 1968–72; Hermann Weyl Prof. Inst. for Advanced Study, Princeton 1972–; mem. NAS, American Math. Soc.; Wolf Prize for Mathematics 1995/96, Frederic Esser Nemmers Prize in Math. 2006. *Publications:* Automorphic Forms on GL(2) (with H. Jacquet) 1970, Euler Products 1971, On the Functional Equations Satisfied by Eisenstein Series 1976, Base Change for GL (2) 1980, Les Débuts d'une Formule des Traces Stable 1983. *Leisure interests:* reading, travel. *Address:* School of Mathematics, Fuld Hall 115, Institute for Advanced Study, Einstein Drive, Princeton, NJ 08540 (office); 60 Battle Road, Princeton, NJ 08540, USA (home). *Telephone:* (609) 734-8117 (office); (609) 921-7222 (home). *E-mail:* rpl@ias.edu (office). *Website:* www.sunsite.ubc.ca/DigitalMathArchive/Langlands/intro.html (office).

LANGSLET, Lars Roar, MA; Norwegian writer and politician; *Chairman, National Ibsen Committee;* b. 5 March 1936, Nesbyen; s. of Knut Langslet and Alma Langslet; ed Univ. of Oslo; Assoc. Prof. 1969–89; MP 1969–89; Minister of Culture and Science 1981–86; writer Aftenposten newspaper 1990–97; Ed. Ordet 1997–; State Scholarship 1997–99; Pres. of Norwegian Acad. for Language and Literature 1995–; Chair., Nat. Ibsen Cttee; Commdr Order of St Olav, Dannebrog, Order of Gregory the Great, etc. . *Publications:* Karl Marx 1963, Conservatism 1965, (biogs of) John Lyng 1989, King Olav V 1995, St Olav 1995, King Christian IV 1997, King Christian VIII 1998–99, Ludvig Holberg 2001. *Address:* Ibsen.net, c/o The National Library of Norway, PO Box 2674 Solli, 0203 Oslo, Norway (office). *Telephone:* 23-27-60-15 (office). *Fax:* 23-27-60-10 (office). *Website:* www.ibsen.net (office).

LANGUETIN, Pierre; Swiss diplomatist and central banker; b. 30 April 1923, Lausanne; m. Florentina Lobo 1951; one s. one d.; ed Univ. de Lausanne and LSE, UK; diplomatic career 1949–; in Div. of Exchange, OEEC, Paris; in Div. of Commerce, Fed. Dept of Public Economy 1955–76, Head of Secr. 1957–61, Chief of Section IA 1961–63; Chief of Subdiv. 1963; has been concerned with problems of European econ. co-operation; Asst Head of Bureau of Integration, Fed. Political Dept and Dept of Public Economy 1961; Swiss Del. to Trade Cttee, OECD, Paris 1961–76, Vice-Pres. 1963–76; mem. Swiss Del. to UNCTAD, Geneva 1964, New Delhi 1968; Swiss Rep. at various int. orgs 1965–66; Del. of Fed. Council for Trade Negotiations, title of Minister Plenipotentiary 1966–68; Head of Swiss Del. to EFTA Geneva 1967–76, title of Amb. 1968–76; Deputy Head of Swiss Negotiating Team with EEC 1970–72; Head of Swiss Del. to Exec. Cttee in special session OECD 1972–76; Head of Swiss Del. for accession negotiations to Int. Energy Agency 1974, Rep. for Switzerland to Governing Bd 1974–76; mem. Governing Bd of Swiss Nat. Bank 1976–81, Vice-Chair. 1981–84, Chair. 1985–88; mem. Bd of Dirs BIS 1985–88; Chair. Inst. for Public Admin. Studies, Lausanne 1988–97, Inst. for Bank and Financial Man., Lausanne 1990–96; Vice-Chair. Sandoz SA 1988–95; Chair. Rosbank (fmrly Unexim), Switzerland 1995–; mem. Bd of Dirs Ludwig Inst. 1987–2007, Swiss Reinsurance Co. 1988–93, Pargesa Holding SA 1988–2002, Paribas (Suisse) 1989–96 (Vice-Chair. 1992), Renault Finance 1989–99, Fin. Cpy Tradition 1995–; mem. Advisory Bd American Int. Group 1989–97, Arthur Andersen (Switzerland) 1991–97; mem. Bd of Dirs Chase Manhattan Pvt. Bank (Switzerland) 1991–2001, Dryden Bank (formerly Prumerica Pvt. Bank) (Switzerland) 2002–05; mem. Int. Red Cross Cttee 1988–93; Dr hc (Lausanne) 1979. *Address:* 37 Muelinenstrasse, 3006 Bern, Switzerland. *Telephone:* (31) 3526613. *Fax:* (31) 3526613.

LANKESTER, Sir Timothy Patrick, Kt, KCB, MA; British government and university administrator; *President, Corpus Christi College, University of Oxford;* b. 15 April 1942, Cairo, Egypt; s. of the late Robin P. A. Lankester and of Jean D. Gilliat; m. Patricia Cockcroft 1968; three d.; ed Monkton Combe School, St John's Coll. Cambridge and Jonathan Edwards Coll., Yale; teacher St Michael's Coll., Belize 1960–61; Feraday Fellow, St John's Coll. Oxford 1965–66; Economist IBRD, Washington, DC 1966–69, New Delhi 1970–73; HM Treasury 1973–78, Under-Sec. 1983–85, Deputy Sec. 1988–89; Pvt. Sec. to Prime Minister Callaghan 1978–79, to Prime Minister Thatcher 1979–81; seconded to S. G. Warburg & Co. 1981–83; Econ. Minister, Washington, DC and UK Exec. Dir IMF and IBRD 1985–88; Perm. Sec. Overseas Devt Admin., FCO 1989–93, Dept for Educ. 1994–95; Dir SOAS, Univ. of London 1996–2000; Pres. Corpus Christi Coll. Oxford 2001–; Dir European Investment Bank 1988–89, Smith and Nephew 1996–2003, London Metal 1997–2001, Mitchells and Butler plc 2003–, Actis 2004–; Gov. Asia-Europe Foundation 1997–; Deputy Chair. British Council 1998–2003. *Address:* Corpus Christi College, Merton Street, Oxford OX1 4JF, England (office). *Telephone:* (1865) 276740 (office). *Fax:* (1865) 276769 (office). *E-mail:* tim.lankester@ccc.ox.ac.uk (office).

LANKHORST, Gertjan, AB; Dutch energy industry executive; *CEO, GasTerra BV;* b. 22 Dec. 1957, Amsterdam; ed Amsterdam Free Univ.; held teaching position at Amsterdam Free Univ. 1982–86; joined Gen. Econ. Policy Dept, Ministry of Econ. Affairs 1986, becoming Dir of Oil and Gas 1996–99, Competition Dir 1999–2003, Dir-Gen. for Energy 2004–05; CEO GasTerra BV (fmrly Gasunie Trade & Supply BV) 2006–. *Address:* GasTerra BV, PO Box 477, 9700 AL Groningen; GasTerra BV, Rozenburglaan 11, 9727 DL Groningen, Netherlands (office). *Telephone:* (50) 364-86-48 (office). *Fax:* (50) 364-86-00 (office). *E-mail:* communicatie@gasterra.nl (office). *Website:* www.gasterra.com (office).

LANOTTE, Johan Vande, MA, PhD; Belgian politician; *Deputy Prime Minister and Minister for the Budget and Public Enterprise;* b. 6 July 1955, Poperinge; ed Sint-Stanislascollege, Univ. of Antwerpen (UIA), Rijksuniversiteit Gent (RUG); Asst Dept of Political and Social Sciences, UIA 1982–83; Asst Special Admin. Law, RUG 1983–87; Head of Office for Minister of the Interior 1988–91; Minister of the Interior and the Civil Service 1994–95; Deputy Prime Minister and Minister of the Home Dept 1995–98; Deputy Prime Minister and Minister of the Budget, Social Integration and Social Economy 1999; currently Deputy Prime Minister and Minister for the Budget and Public Enterprise; Chair. Sociaal Progressief Alternatief (Socialist Party—Flemish wing). *Publications:* Krachtlijnen van een vernieuwd gemeentebeleid 1983, Wonen in België. Mythen en werkelijkheid (co-author) 1985, Petitierecht 1987, De noodzakelijke decentralisatie 1988, De recente evolutie en de knelpunten in de ruimtelijke ordening en de stedebouw (co-author) 1988, De geschiedenis van de Provinciewet (co-author) 1990, De nieuwe gemeentelijke comptabiliteit (co-author) 1990, Inleiding tot het publiek recht 1994, Overzicht van het Belgisch Administratief Recht (co-author) 1996, Het Europees verdrag tot bescherming van de Rechten van de Mens: In Hoofdlijnen (co-author), 1997, België voor beginners: Wegwijs in het Belgisch labyrint (co-author) 1998, Handboek Europees Verdrag voor de Rechten van de Mens (co-author) 2004. *Leisure interest:* basketball. *Address:* Ministry of the Budget and Public Enterprise, 180 rue Royale, 1000 Brussels, Belgium (office). *Telephone:* (2) 210-19-11 (office). *Fax:* (2) 217-33-28 (office). *E-mail:* info@johanvandelanotte.be (office). *Website:* www.begroting.be (office).

LANOVOY, Vasiliy Semenovich; Russian actor; b. 16 Jan. 1934, Moscow; s. of Semion Petrovich Lanovoy and Agafia Ivanovna Yakubenko; m. Irina Petrovna Kupchenko 1972; two s.; ed Shchukin Theatre School; actor with Vakhtangov Theatre 1957–; also works as narrator; Prof., Faculty of Artistic Speech, Shchukin's Theatre School, Moscow 1995–; mem. CPSU 1968–90; Lenin Prize 1980, People's Artist of USSR 1985. *Theatrical roles include:* Ognev in Korneichuk's Front, Prince Calaf in Gozzi's Princess Turandot, Caesar in Shaw's Antony and Cleopatra, Sagadeev in Abdullin's Thirteenth President, Don Juan in Pushkin's The Stone Guest, Trotsky in M. Shatrov's Peace of Brest, Oscar in La Bize's Murder at Lursin Street, Astrov in Uncle Vanya, J.B. Shaw in I. Kiltye's Dear Liar, King Henry in The Lion in Winter. *Films include:* War and Peace, Anna Karenina, The Strange Woman, Going in a Thunderstorm, The Picture, The Scarlet Sails, The Officers, Unknown War, The Colleges, Strategy for Victory, The Trifles of Life, Barin's Daughter. *Leisure interests:* volleyball, badminton, hunting, skiing, dogs. *Address:* 121002 Moscow, Starokonyushenny per. 39, Apt 18, Russia. *Telephone:* (495) 203-94-03.

LANSBURY, Angela, CBE; British actress; b. 16 Oct. 1925, London; d. of Edgar Lansbury and Moyna Macgill (Charlotte Lillian McIldowie); m. 1st Richard Cromwell 1945 (divorced 1946); m. 2nd Peter Shaw 1949 (died 2003); one s. one d. one step-s.; ed Webber Douglas School of Singing and Dramatic Art, Kensington, Feagin School of Drama and Radio, NY; film debut in Gaslight 1944; numerous appearances on London and New York stages and on TV; Hon. DHumLitt (Boston) 1990; Silver Mask for Lifetime Achievement BAFTA 1991, Lifetime Achievement Award, Screen Actors' Guild 1997, numerous other awards. *Films include:* Manchurian Candidate, In the Cool of the Day, Harlow, Moll Flanders, Bedknobs and Broomsticks, Death on the Nile, The Lady Vanishes 1980, The Mirror Cracked 1980, The Pirates of Penzance 1982, Company of Wolves 1983, Beauty and the Beast 1991, Anastasia (voice) 1997, Nanny McPhee 2005. *Television includes:* Murder She Wrote 1984–96 (with special episodes thereafter), The Shell Seekers 1989, South by Southwest 1997, A Story to Die For 2000, The Blackwater Lightship 2004. *Stage appearances include:* Hotel Paradiso 1957, Dear World 1969 (Tony Award), The King and I 1978, A Little Family Business 1983, Deuce 2007. *Publication:* Angela Lansbury's Positive Moves (with Mimi Avins) 1990. *Address:* Corymore Productions, Building 426, 100 Universal City Plaza, Universal City, CA 91608, USA; c/o William Morris (UK) Ltd, 31–32 Soho Square, London, W1V 6HH, England. *Telephone:* (20) 7534-6800 (London). *Fax:* (20) 7437-0238 (London).

LANSING, Sherry, BS; American film producer and business executive; *CEO, Sherry Lansing Foundation;* b. (Sherry Lee Heimann), 31 July 1944, Chicago, Ill.; d. of Norton Lansing and Margot Lansing; m. 2nd William Friedkin (q.v.) 1991; ed Northwestern Univ., Evanston, Ill.; math. and English teacher, Public High Schools, LA, Calif. 1966–69; model, TV commercials, Max Factor Co. and Alberto-Culver 1969–70; appeared in films Loving and Rio Lobo 1970; Exec. Story Ed., Wagner Int. 1970–73; Vice-Pres. for Production, Heyday Productions 1973–75; Exec. Story Ed., then Vice-Pres. for Creative Affairs, MGM Studios 1975–77; Vice-Pres., then Sr Vice-Pres. for Production, Columbia Pictures 1977–80; Pres. 20th Century-Fox Productions 1980–83; Founder Jaffe-Lansing Productions, LA 1982–; Chair. Paramount Pictures 1992–2005; Founder and CEO Sherry Lansing Foundation 2005–; mem. Bd of Regents Univ. of Calif. 1999–; mem. Bd of Dirs Teach for America, American Film Inst., The Carter Center, DonorsChoose, American Assn for Cancer

Research, Friends of Cancer Research; Trustee Calif. Museum for History, Women and the Arts; Dr hc (American Film Inst.); Woodrow Wilson Award for Corporate Citizenship, Milestone Award from Producers Guild of America, Overcoming Obstacles Achievement Award for Business, YWCA Silver Achievement Award, Outstanding Woman in Business Award frome Women's Equity Action League, Distinguished Community Service Award from Brandeis Univ., Alfred P. Sloan, Jr. Memorial Award, Pioneer of the Year by Foundation of Motion Picture Pioneers 1996, first woman studio head to receive a star on Hollywood Walk of Fame 1996, named on Power 100 List in Women in Entertainment Report, The Hollywood Reporter No. 1 2002, No. 4 2003, ranked by Fortune magazine amongst 50 Most Powerful Women in Business in the US (19th) 2002, (20th) 2003, (27th) 2004, ranked 71st by Forbes magazine amongst 100 Most Powerful Women 2004, Exemplary Leadership in Management Award, UCLA Anderson School of Man. 2005, Jean Hersholt Humanitarian Award 2007. *Films produced include:* Racing with the Moon 1984, Firstborn 1984 (exec. producer), When the Time Comes (TV) (exec. producer), Fatal Attraction 1987, The Accused 1988, Black Rain 1989, School Ties 1992, Indecent Proposal 1993, The Untouchables: Capone Rising 2006. *Address:* Sherry Lansing Foundation, 2121 Avenue of the Stars, Suite 2020, Los Angeles, CA 90067, USA (office). *Telephone:* (310) 788-0057 (office). *Website:* www.sherrylansingfoundation.org (office).

LANTIGUA, José Rafael, BEd; Dominican Republic writer and politician; *Secretary of State for Culture;* b. 17 Sept. 1949, Moca; ed Pedro Henríquez Ureña Nat. Univ.; Ed. Literary Section, Ultima Hora (newspaper) 1985–2000; Chair. Nat. Book Fair Standing Cttee 1996–2000; Sec. of State for Culture 2004–; mem. Dominican Acad. of Language 2008–; Nat. Essay Prize 1976, Nat. Prize for Journalism 1988, Caonabo de Oro Prize 1999. *Publications:* poetry: Sobre un tiempo de esperanza 1982, Semblanzas del corazón 1985; essays: Domingo Moreno Jimenes: biografía de un poeta 1976, Hacia una revalorización del ideal duartiano 1985, La conjura del tiempo 1994, El oficio de la palabra 1995; anthology: del cuento cubano y dominicano 1999. *Address:* Secretariat of State for Culture, Centro de Eventos y Exposiciones, Avda George Washington, esq. Presidente Vicini Burgos, Santo Domingo, Dominican Republic (office). *Telephone:* 221-4141 (office). *Fax:* 221-3342 (office). *E-mail:* contacto@cultura.gov.do (office). *Website:* www.cultura.gov.do (office).

LANXADE, Adm. Jacques; French naval officer; *Chairman, Fondation Mediterranéenne des Etudes stratgiques;* b. 8 Sept. 1934, Toulon; m. Loïse Rostan d'Ancezune 1959; one s. three d.; ed Ecole Navale, Institut d'Admin des Affaires (Université Dauphiné); Commdr destroyers Le Champenois 1970–72, La Galissonnière 1976–77, frigate Duguay-Trouin 1980–81; rank of Rear-Adm. 1984; Commdr Indian Ocean maritime zone 1984–86; Commdr French fleet in the Indian Ocean 1986; rank of Vice-Adm. 1987; Chef du Cabinet Militaire to Minister of Defence 1988–89; Chief of Staff, Elysée Palace 1989; Chief of Staff of French Armed Forces 1991–95; Amb. to Tunisia 1995–99; mem. Atomic Energy Cttee 1991–95; mem. Initiative for a Renewed Transatlantic Partnership, Center for Strategic and Int. Studies 2003–; Chair. Fondation Mediterranéenne des Etudes stratgiques; Grand Officier Légion d'honneur, Officier, Ordre nat. du Mérite, Croix de la Valeur Militaire. *Publications:* Quand le monde a basculé 2001, Organizer la politique européenne et internationale de la France (report) 2002. *Leisure interests:* tennis, skiing. *Address:* Center for Strategic and International Studies, 1800 K Street, NW, Washington, DC 20006, USA (office); 41 rue Saint-André des Arts, 75006 Paris, France (home). *Telephone:* (202) 775-3149 (Washington, DC) (office); 1-43-25-60-15 (Paris) (office); 1-46-33-39-05 (home). *Fax:* 1-43-25-60-15 (Paris) (office). *E-mail:* jacqueslanxade@noos.fr (office). *Website:* www.csis.org/europe/initiative (office).

LANYON, Lance Edward, CBE, PhD, DSc, FMedSci, MRCVS; British professor of veterinary anatomy and university administrator; b. 4 Jan. 1944; s. of the late Henry Lanyon and Heather Gordon (née Tyrrell); m. Mary Kear (divorced 1997); one s. one d.; ed Christ's Hosp., Univ. of Bristol; Lecturer, Univ. of Bristol 1967, Reader in Veterinary Anatomy 1967–79; Assoc. Prof., Tufts School of Veterinary Medicine, Boston, USA 1980–83, Prof. 1983–84; Prof. of Veterinary Anatomy, Royal Veterinary Coll., Univ. of London 1984–89, personal title 1989–, Head of Dept of Veterinary Anatomy 1984–87, of Veterinary Basic Sciences 1987–88; Prin. Royal Veterinary Coll. 1989–2004 (retd); Pro-Vice-Chancellor Univ. of London 1997–99. *Publications include:* numerous articles in professional journals; chapters in books on osteoporosis, orthopaedics and athletic training. *Leisure interests:* building, home improvements, sailing. *Address:* c/o Royal Veterinary College, Royal College Street, London, NW1 0UT, England (office). *Telephone:* (20) 7387-2898 (office). *Website:* www.rvc.ac.uk (office).

LANZMANN, Claude; French filmmaker and director; *Professor of Documentary Film, European Graduate School, Saas-Fee, Switzerland;* b. 27 Nov. 1925, Paris; ed studied philosophy in Univ. of Tübingen, Germany and in Paris where he graduated with a Diplomé d'Etudes Supérieures de Philosophie; fmr Lecturer in French Literature and Philosophy, Free Univ. of Berlin; Dir journal Les Temps Modernes; Prof. of Documentary Film, European Grad. School, Saas-Fee, Switzerland, where he teaches an Intensive Summer Seminar; Hon. PhD (European Grad. School) 2004. *Films:* Élise ou la vraie vie (writer) 1970, Pourquoi Israel (Israel, Why) 1974, Shoah (Special Award, Los Angeles Film Critics' Asscn 1985, Caligari Film Award, FIPRESCI Prize, Forum of New Cinema and OCIC Award – Honorable Mention, Berlin Int. Film Festival 1986, Hon. César 1986, IDA Award, Int. Documentary Asscn 1986, Rotterdam Award for Best Documentary 1986, Rotterdam Int. Film Festical 1986, BAFTA Flaherty Documentary Award and Flaherty Documentary Award (TV) 1987) 1985, Tsahal (also writer) (1994, Un vivant qui passe (A Visitor from the Living) (also producer) 1997, Sobibór, 14 octobre 1943, 16 heures (Sobibor, Oct. 14, 1943, 4 p.m.) (also writer) (Reader Jury of the 'Standard' Award, Viennale Film Festival 2001) 2001. *Publication:* The Complete Text of the Acclaimed Holocaust Film Shoah. *Address:* European Graduate School, Media & Communications Division, Ringacker, 3953 Leuk-Stadt, Switzerland (office). *Telephone:* (27) 474-9917 (office). *Fax:* (27) 474-9969 (office). *E-mail:* info@egs.edu (office). *Website:* www.egs.edu (office).

LAO, Chongpin; Chinese artist; b. 3 Nov. 1936, Xinxing City, Guangdong Prov.; s. of Lao Xiangguang and Chen Ermei; m. Luo Yuzing 1956; two s. one d.; ed Fine Arts Dept, Cen. China Teachers' Coll.; has painted more than 1000 landscapes and human figures in Japan, Canada, France, Egypt, Yugoslavia, Democratic People's Repub. of Korea, Pakistan, Burma, Jordan, Hungary, USSR, Albania 1973–; Dir Poetry Inst. 1987–; mem. staff Chinese Exhbn Agency, Ministry of Culture; mem. Chinese Artists' Asscn, Advisory Cttee, Beijing Children's Fine Arts Research Acad., Chinese Poetry Asscn, Int. Biographical Asscn; Hon. Dir Hanlin Forest of Steles, Kaifeng, China Shaolin Research Inst. of Painting and Calligraphy 1989. *Major works:* Harvest Time, Spring Ploughing, Harbour, Riverside, Arashiyama in Rain, Mosque in Lahore, Golden Pagoda of Rangoon, Pyramid and Sphinx, Autumn in Amman, Morning Glory on Seine River, Niagara Falls; group exhbns include Seven Star Cliff, Japan 1979, Scenery on Xinghu Lake, Mexico 1980, Drum Beaters, Hong Kong 1982, Panda, Wulongtang Waterfall, Belgium 1982, Scenery on Huangshan Mountain, Jordan 1983, Light Boats on the Yangtze River (Nat. Arts Museum, Romania) 1986, Scenes of Petra (Sact City Museum, Jordan) 1987, Waterfall of Lushan Mountain (Zacheta Art Museum, Poland) 1987; one-man exhbns in many Chinese cities and provs 1979–, Hong Kong 1988, Philippines 1989, Jordan 1990, Singapore 1995, India 1996; Sixth Asian Art Biennale, Bangladesh 1993. *Publication:* An Album of Sketches of Life in Foreign Countries 1986. *Leisure interests:* travel, music. *Address:* 1-301 Building No. 43, Xidahe Dongli, Chaoyang Qu, Beijing 100028, People's Republic of China. *Telephone:* (10) 64672946.

LAOKPESSI, Col Pitalouna-Ani; Togolese government official and military officer; *Minister of Security;* fmr Commdr, fmr Asst Chief of Army Staff; Minister of Security 2005–. *Address:* Ministry of Security, rue Albert Sarraut, Lomé, Togo (office). *Telephone:* 222-57-12 (office). *Fax:* 222-61-50 (office). *E-mail:* info@republicoftogo.com (office).

LAOUROU, Grégoire; Benin politician; Pres. Council of Ministers, W African Econ. and Monetary Union (UEMOA); Minister of Finance and the Economy 2003–05. *Address:* c/o Ministry of Finance and the Economy, BP 302, Cotonou, Benin (office).

LAPANG, D. Dethwelson, BA; Indian politician; b. 10 April 1934; s. of Donwa War; m. Amethyst Lynda Jomes Blah 1958; one s. one d.; ed Shillong High School, St Anthony's Coll., Shillong; Minister of State for Co-operation, Jails, Education and Civil Defence 1978–79; Minister of Health and Family Welfare, Labour, Information and Public Relations 1979–83; Minister of Planning, Finance, Home, Revenue, Food & Civil Supply 1983–85; Minister of Finance, Planning, Evaluation, Home and Revenue 1985–87; Minister of Planning and Programme Implementation 1987–88; Minister of Home, Revenue and Excise 1987–88; Deputy Minister of Internal Affairs 1988–90; Chief Minister of Meghalaya 1992–93, 2003–06, 2007–08 (resgnd); Deputy Chief Minister 1998–2003; Chair. State Planning Board 1993–95, Comm. on Resources Mobilization 1995–97; Pres. Meghalaya State Council of Indo-Soviet Cultural Soc. 1979, Meghalaya State Indo-GDR Friendship Asscn; f. Bhoi Student Asscn, Meghalaya State Basketball Asscn, Meghalaya Eds and Publrs Asscn, Affiliated State Olympic Asscn. *Address:* Jaiaw Main Road, Shillong, Meghalaya, India (office).

LAPHAM, Lewis H., BA; American writer and editor; *Editor Emeritus, Harper's Magazine;* b. 8 Jan. 1935, San Francisco; m.; three c.; ed Yale Univ., Univ. of Cambridge, UK; reporter San Francisco Examiner newspaper 1957–59, New York Herald Tribune 1960–62; Ed. Harper's Magazine 1976–81, 1983–2005, Ed. Emer. and columnist 2005–; syndicated newspaper columnist 1981–87; univ. lecturer; appearances on American and British TV, broadcasts on nat. public radio; Nat. Magazine Award for Essays 1995, Thomas Paine Journalism Award 2002. *Publications:* Fortune's Child (essays) 1980, Money and Class in America 1988, Imperial Masquerade 1990, Hotel America: Scenes in the Lobby of the Fin-de-Siècle 1995, Waiting for the Barbarians 1997, The Agony of Mammon 1999, Lapham's Rules of Influence 1999, Theater of War 2002, 30 Satires 2003, Gag Rule 2004, Pretensions to Empire: Notes on the Criminal Folly of the Bush Administration 2007; contrib. 'Notebook' monthly essay Harper's Magazine; also contrib. to Commentary, Nat. Review, Yale Literary Magazine, Elle, Fortune, Forbes, American Spectator, Vanity Fair, Parade, Channels, Maclean's, London Observer, New York Times, Wall Street Journal. *Address:* c/o Harper's Magazine, 666 Broadway, New York, NY 10012, USA (office). *E-mail:* ann@harpers.org (office). *Website:* www.harpers.org.

LAPHEN, Michael W., MBA; American information technology executive; *President and Chief Operating Officer, Computer Sciences Corporation;* m.; ed Pa State Univ., Wharton School, Univ. of Pa; served in USAF and Pa Air Nat. Guard; joined Computer Sciences Corpn 1977, has held numerous man. positions including Vice-Pres. Finance and Admin, Pres. Integrated Systems Div. 1992–98, Pres. Fed. Sector Civil Group 1998–2000, Pres. European Group 2000–03, Pres. and COO 2003–; mem. Information Technology Asscn of America, Armed Forces Communications and Electronics Asscn, Nat. Defense Industrial Asscn. *Address:* Computer Sciences Corporation, 2100 East Grand Avenue, El Segundo, CA 90245, USA (office). *Telephone:* (310) 615-0311 (office). *Fax:* (310) 322-9768 (office). *Website:* www.csc.com (office).

ŁAPICKI, Andrzej; Polish actor and director; b. 11 Nov. 1924, Riga, Latvia; s. of Borys Łapicki and Zofia Łapicka; m. Zofia Chrząszczewska 1947; one s. one d.; ed Underground Inst. of Theatrical Art, Warsaw; Actor in Łódź: Polish

Army Theatre 1945–48, Kameralny (Chamber) Theatre 1948–49; in Warsaw: Współczesny (Contemporary) Theatre 1949–64, 1966–72, Dramatyczny (Dramatic) Theatre 1964–66, 1982–83, Narodowy (Nat.) Theatre 1972–81, Polski Theatre, Warsaw 1983–89; Artistic Dir Polski Theatre 1995–98; Lecturer Higher State School of Drama, Warsaw 1953–, Asst Prof. 1970–79, Extraordinary Prof. 1979–87, Ordinary Prof. 1987–, Dean Actors' Faculty 1971–81, Rector 1981–87, 1993–96; mem. SPATiF-ZASP (Asscn of Polish Theatre and Film Actors) until 1982, 1989–96, (Vice-Pres. 1976–79), Pres. 1989–96; mem. Int. Theatre Inst. (ITI) 1983–, mem. Gen. Bd 1983–91, Pres. 1989–96; Deputy to Sejm (Parl.) 1989–91 (Solidarity); Chair. Parl. Comm. of Culture and Mass Media 1989–91; Commdr's Cross with Star, Order of Polonia Restituta, Gold Cross of Merit and other distinctions; Minister of Culture and Art Prize (1st Class), Pres. of Radio and TV Cttee Prize (five times), Gold Medal Gloria Artis 2005. *Stage appearances:* about 100 roles, including The Respectable Prostitute, The Night of the Iguana, L'Ecole des femmes, Ring Round the Moon, Biedermann und die Brandstifter, Way of Life. *Film appearances:* about 30 roles, including Dolle 1968, Everything for Sale 1969, Pilatus und Andere 1972, How Far from Here, How Near 1972, The Wedding 1973, Jealousy and Medicine 1973, Lava 1989; also some 50 TV roles; Dir of about 50 TV and 30 theatre plays. *Publication:* To Keep One's Distance 1999, The Property 2004. *Address:* ul. Kartowicza 1/7 m. 50, 02-501 Warsaw, Poland.

LAPIERRE, Dominique; French journalist, writer and philanthropist; b. 30 July 1931, Châtelaillon, Charente-Maritime; s. of Jean Lapierre and Luce Lapierre (née Andreotti); m. 2nd Dominique Conchon 1980; one d. (by first m.); ed Lycée Condorcet, Paris and LaFayette Univ., Easton, USA; Ed. Paris Match Magazine 1954–67; founder and Pres. Action Aid for Lepers' Children of Calcutta; Citizen of Honour of the City of Calcutta; Chevalier, Légion d'honneur 2000; Commdr, Confrérie du Tastevin 1990; Grand Cross of the Order of Social Solidarity (Spain) 2002; Dr hc (Lafayette Univ.) 1982; Christopher Book Award 1986, 2002, Gold Medal of Calcutta, Int. Rainbow Prize, UN 2000, Vatican Prize for Peace 2000, Gold Medal of the City of Milan 2006. *Publications:* Un dollar les mille kilomètres 1949, Honeymoon around the World 1953, En liberté sur les routes d'U.R.S.S. 1957, Russie portes ouvertes 1957, Les Caïds de New York 1958, Chessman m'a dit 1960, The City of Joy 1985, Beyond Love 1991, A Thousand Suns 1998, Five Past Midnight in Bhopal 2002, It Was Once the USSR 2006, Un Arc-en-Ciel dans la Nuit 2008; with Larry Collins: Is Paris Burning? 1964, ...Or I'll Dress You In Mourning 1967, O Jerusalem 1971, Freedom at Midnight 1975, The Fifth Horseman 1980, Is New York Burning? 2004. *Leisure interests:* riding, tennis, collecting antiques, vintage cars. *Address:* 37 Rue Charles-Laffitte, 92200 Neuilly; Les Bignoles, Val de Rian, 83350 Ramatuelle, France. *Telephone:* 1-46-37-34-34 (Neuilly); (4) 94-97-17-31 (Ramatuelle). *Fax:* (4) 94-97-38-05. *E-mail:* D.Lapierre@wanadoo.fr (home). *Website:* cityofjoyaid.org (office).

LAPIS, Károly, PhD, DSci; Hungarian pathologist, clinical oncologist and cytopathologist; *Professor Emeritus, Semmelweis University of Budapest;* b. 14 April 1926, Túrkeve; s. of Károly Lapis and Eszter Földesi; m. Ibolya Keresztes 1955; one s. one d.; ed Lóránd Eötvös Univ. Budapest; trainee, First Inst. of Pathology and Experimental Cancer Research, Eötvös Loránd Univ., Budapest 1950–51; Asst, Inst. of Pathology Medical Univ., Debrecen 1951–54; Scientific worker Oncopathological Research Inst. 1954–63; Prof. Postgraduate Medical School, Budapest 1963–68; Prof. 1st Inst. of Pathology and Experimental Cancer Research, Semmelweis Univ. of Budapest 1968–96, Prof. Emer. 1998– (Dir 1968–93); Gordon Jacob Fellow Chester Beatty Research Inst., London 1959–60; Eleanor Roosevelt Fellow, Paris 1963–64; Visiting Prof., Duke Univ. Medical School, Durham, NC 1972; Fogarty Scholar, Nat. Cancer Inst., Bethesda 1984–85; Corresp. mem. Hungarian Acad. of Sciences 1970, mem. 1979–; Foreign mem. Medical Acad. of the USSR (now Acad. of Medical Sciences of Russia) 1987, Serbian Acad. of Sciences and Arts 1989; Pres. 14th Int. Cancer Congress of the UICC, Budapest 1986; Vice-Pres. European Assoc. for Cancer Research 1979–85; mem. Exec. Cttee European Soc. of Pathology 1989–93, French Electron Microscope Soc., German Soc. of Pathology, Int. Gastro-Surgical Club, Hungarian Cancer Soc. (Pres. 1974–84), Hungarian Soc. of Gastroenterology, Hungarian Soc. of Pathologists, Int. Acad. of Pathology (Hungarian section); Corresp. mem. American Asscn for Cancer Research; Dir Metastasis Research Soc. 1986–90; Chief Ed. Acta Morphologica Hungarica 1985–94; Hon. Citizen of Mezotur 1997; Labour Order of Merit 1978, 4th of April Order of Merit 1986; Genersich Prize 1994, Széchényi Prize 1996, George Weber Foundation Prize 1997; Krompecher Memorial Medal 1985, Semmelweis Memorial Medal 1987, Baló József Memorial Medal 1987, Hetényi Géza Memorial Medal 1990, 'Pro Optimo Merito in Gastroenterologia' Memorial Medal 1992. *Publications:* Lymphknotengeschwülste (co-author) 1966, The Liver 1979, Sejtosztodas Szabalyozasa es Befolyasolasa (co-author) 1981, Mediastinal Tumors and Pseudotumors (co-author) 1984, Liver Carcinogenesis (co-ed.) 1979, Ultrastructure of Tumours in Man 1981, Regulation and Control of Cell Proliferation (co-author) 1984, Tumour Progression and Markers 1982, Models, Mechanisms and Etiology of Tumour Promotion 1984, Biochemistry and Molecular Genetics of Cancer Metastasis (co-author) 1986, Abstracts of Lectures, Symposia, and Free Communications (co-author) 1986, Lectures and Symposia of the 14th International Cancer Congress (co-author) 1987, Molecular Biology and Differentiation of Cancer Cells (Oncogenes, Growth Factors, Receptors) (co-author) 1987, Carcinogenesis and Tumour Progression (co-author) 1987, Radiotherapy, Paediatric Oncology, Neurooncology (co-author) 1987, Biological Response Modifiers, Leukaemias and Lymphomas (co-author) 1987, Medical Oncology (co-author) 1987, Morphological Diagnosis of Liver Diseases (in Russian) 1989, Pathology (textbook in Hungarian) 1989, Sincerely About Cancer for Men and Women (in Hungarian) 2001. *Leisure interests:* tennis, gardening. *Address:* First Institute of Pathology and Experimental Cancer Research, Semmelweis University, Üllői út 26, 1085 Budapest (office); Lónyay u. 25, 1093 Budapest, Hungary (home). *Telephone:* (1) 266-1912 (office); (1) 217-9699 (home). *Fax:* (1) 317-1074 (office). *E-mail:* klapis@korb1.sote.hu (office); lapkar@t-online.hu (home).

LAPLI, Father Sir John Ini, Kt, DipLicTheol; Solomon Islands government official and Anglican priest; b. June 1955; s. of Christian Mekope and Ellen Lauai; m. Helen Lapli 1985; three s. one d.; ed Selwyn Coll., Guadalcanal, St John's Theological Coll., Auckland, New Zealand; tutor Theological Coll., Auckland 1982–83; teacher Catechist School, Rural Training Centre 1985; Parish Priest 1986; Bible Translator 1987–88; Premier of Temotu Prov. 1988–99; Gov.-Gen. of Solomon Is July 1999–2004; Order of St Michael and St George; Order of Propitious Clouds with Special Grand Cordon (ROC). *Leisure interest:* gardening, research and writing on oral local tradition and culture. *Address:* Luepe Village, Graciosa Bay, c/o Lata Post Office, Temotu Province, Solomon Islands (home). *Telephone:* 53111 (home).

LAPPERT, Michael F., PhD, DSc, FRCS, FRS; British chemist and academic; *Research Professor Emeritus of Chemistry and Associate Research Professor, University of Sussex;* b. 31 Dec. 1928, Brno, Czechoslovakia; s. of Julius and Kornelie (née Beran) Lappert; m. Lorna McKenzie 1980; ed Wilson's Grammar School and Northern Polytechnic, London; Asst Lecturer, Northern Polytechnic, London 1952–53, Lecturer 1953–55, Sr Lecturer 1955–59; Lecturer, UMIST 1959–61, Sr Lecturer 1961–64; Reader, Univ. of Sussex 1964–69, Prof. of Chem. 1969–97, Research Prof. Emer. and Assoc. Research Prof. 1997–; Science and Eng Research Council Sr Research Fellow 1980–85; Pres. Dalton Div., Royal Soc. of Chem. (RSC) 1989–91; Hon. Prof., Shanxi Univ., China 2000; Hon. Dr rer. nat (Munich) 1989; Chem. Soc. Award in Main Group Metal Chem. 1970, RSC Tilden Lecturer 1972–73, Chem. Soc. Award in Organometallic Chem. 1978, ACS F.S. Kipping Award 1976, RSC Nyholm Lecturer 1994, RSC Sir Edward Frankland Lecturer 1999, Alfred Stock Prize, German Chemical Soc. 2008. *Publications:* Metal and Metalloid Amides (jtly) 1980, Chemistry of Organo-Zirconum and Hafnium Compounds (jtly) 1986 and more than 750 papers in scientific journals. *Leisure interests:* theatre, opera, art, travel, walking, tennis. *Address:* Department of Chemistry, School of Life Sciences, University of Sussex, Brighton, E Sussex, BN1 9QJ (office); 4 Varndean Gardens, Brighton, BN1 6WL (home); John Dalton Cottage, Eaglesfield, Cockermouth, Cumbria, CA13 0SD, England (home). *Telephone:* (1273) 678316 (office); (1273) 503661 (home). *Fax:* (1273) 876687 (office). *E-mail:* m.f.lappert@sussex.ac.uk (office). *Website:* www.sussex.ac.uk/chemistry/profile1552.html (office).

LAPTEV, Ivan Dmitrievich, DPhilSc; Russian editor and journalist; b. 15 Oct. 1934, Sladkoye, Omsk Dist; m. Tatyana Kareva 1966; one d.; ed Siberian Road Transport Inst., Acad. of Social Sciences; worked for CPSU Cen. Cttee; mem. CPSU 1960–91; worked at Omsk River Port 1952–60; teacher 1960–61; instructor, Soviet Army Sports Club 1961–64, literary collaborator and special corresp. Sovietskaya Rossiya 1964–67; Consultant for Kommunist (later named Free Thought) 1967–73; work with CPSU Cen. Cttee 1973–78; Section Ed. Pravda 1978–82, Deputy Ed. 1982–84; Chief Ed. Izvestiya 1984–90; mem. USSR Supreme Soviet 1989–91; People's Deputy of the USSR 1989–91; Chair. Council of Union 1990–91; Gen. Man. Izvestiya Publrs 1991–94; Deputy Chair. Fed. Press Cttee 1994–95, Chair. 1995–99; Head of Sector Professional Acad. of State Service to Russian Presidency 1995–; mem. Int. Acad. of Information 1993; Pres. Asscn of Chief Eds and Publrs 1993–. *Publications:* Ecological Problems 1978, The World of People in the World of Nature 1986; over 100 scientific articles on ecological problems. *Leisure interests:* reading, automobile engineering, cycle racing. *Address:* Academy of State Service, Vernadskogo prosp. 84, 117606 Moscow, Russia. *Telephone:* (495) 436-99-07.

LAPTEV, Vladimir Viktorovich, DJur; Russian jurist; *Chief Scientific Researcher, Institute of State and Law, Russian Academy of Sciences; Head of Chair of Entrepreneurial Law, Academic Law University, Moscow;* b. 28 April 1924, Moscow; s. of V. I. Laptev and V. A. Lapteva; m. 1950; two s.; ed Law Dept, Moscow Inst. for Foreign Trade; mem. staff, Inst. of State and Law, Russian Acad. of Sciences, Moscow 1955, Head Section, Econ. Law 1959, Head Centre of Entrepreneurial and Econ. Law 1992–97, Chief Scientific Researcher 1997–; Head, Chair of Entrepreneurial Law, Academic Law Univ., Moscow 1997–; Visiting Prof., Emory Univ., Atlanta, Ga, USA 1992–93; Corresp. mem. USSR (now Russian) Acad. of Science 1979–87, mem. 1987–; Honoured Scientist of Russian Fed. 1977. *Publications:* more than 350 books and articles on econ. law, including Legal Status of Enterprises in Russia 1993, Introduction to Entrepreneurial Law 1994, Entrepreneurial Law: Notion and Subjects 1997, Joint Stock Company Law 1999, Subjects of Entrepreneurial Law 2003. *Address:* Institute of State and Law, Znamenka Str. 10, 119992, Moscow, Russia (office). *Telephone:* (495) 291-86-03 (office); (495) 331-32-24 (home). *Fax:* (495) 291-85-74 (office).

LAPTHORNE, Richard D., CBE; British business executive; *Chairman, Cable & Wireless PLC;* Group Financial Controller Courtaulds PLC –1986, Finance Dir 1986–92; Finance Dir British Aerospace PLC 1992–98, Vice-Chair. 1998–99; Dir (non-exec.) Amersham International PLC 1998, later Chair. Amersham PLC 1999; Chair. and Dir (non-exec.) Cable & Wireless PLC 2003–; Chair. (non-exec.) Morse PLC, Avecia PLC Tunstall Holdings Ltd, TI Automotive, Oasis International Leasing Co. P.J.S.C. (Abu Dhabi); Vice-Chair. JP Morgan Investment Bank. *Address:* Cable & Wireless PLC, 7th Floor, The Point, 37 North Wharf Road, Paddington Basin, London, W2 1LA, England (office). *Telephone:* (20) 7315-4000 (office). *Website:* www.cw.com (office).

LAQUEUR, Walter; American historian, academic, editor and political commentator; *Academic Director, Center for Strategic and International Studies;* b. 26 May 1921, Breslau, Germany (now Wrocław, Poland); s. of Fritz Laqueur and Else Berliner; m. 1st Barbara Koch 1941 (deceased); m. 2nd C. S.

Wichmann; two d.; Ed. Survey 1955–65; Dir Inst. of Contemporary History and Wiener Library, London 1964–91; Founding Ed. Journal of Contemporary History 1965–; Prof. of History Brandeis Univ. 1967–72; Prof. of History, Tel-Aviv Univ. 1970–87; Prof. of Govt Georgetown Univ. 1977–90; Chair. Int. Research Council, Center for Strategic and Int. Studies, Washington DC 1973–2001, currently Academic Dir; Ed. Washington Papers 1973–2001, Washington Quarterly 1978–2001; Visiting Prof. of History, Harvard Univ. 1977; Rockefeller Fellow, Guggenheim Fellow; several hon. degrees. *Publications:* Young Germany 1962, The Road to War 1967 1968, Europe Since Hitler 1970, A History of Zionism 1972, Confrontation 1974, Weimar 1974, Guerrilla 1976, Terrorism 1977, A Continent Astray: Europe 1970–78 1979, The Missing Years (novel) 1980, The Terrible Secret 1981, Farewell to Europe (novel) 1981, Germany Today 1985, A World of Secrets 1985, Breaking the Silence 1986, The Age of Terrorism 1987, The Long Road to Freedom 1989, Stalin 1990, Thursday's Child has Far to Go (autobiog.) 1993, Black Hundred 1993, The Dream That Failed 1994, Fascism 1997, Generation Exodus 2001, Yale Encyclopedia of the Holocaust (Ed.) 2001, No End to War 2003. *Leisure interest:* swimming. *Address:* Center for Strategic and International Studies, 1800 K Street, NW, Suite 400, Washington, DC 20006, USA (office); c/o Journal of Contemporary History, 4 Devonshire Street, London, W1N 2BH, England. *Telephone:* (202) 887-0217 (office). *Fax:* (202) 775-3199 (office). *E-mail:* wlaqueur@csis.org (office); walter@laqueur.net (home). *Website:* www.csis.org (office).

LARA, Brian Charles; Trinidadian professional cricketer (retd); b. 2 May 1969, Santa Cruz; s. of Banty Lara and Pearl Lara; ed San Juan Secondary, Fatima Coll., Port of Spain; started playing cricket aged six; played football for Trinidad Under-14; played cricket for West Indies Under-19; captained a West Indies Youth XI against India, scoring 186; left-hand batsman; teams: Trinidad and Tobago 1987– (Capt. 1993–), Warwicks. 1994, 1998 (Capt.), making world record first-class score of 501 not out, including most runs in a day (390) and most boundaries in an innings (72) v. Durham, Edgbaston, 3–4 June 1994; 112 Tests for West Indies 1990– (37 as Capt.), scoring 10,094 runs (average 52.84) including 26 hundreds, highest score 400 not out (world record vs England, St John's, Antigua 10–12 April 2004); has scored 19,835 first-class runs (55 hundreds), including 2,066 off 2,262 balls for Warwicks. 1994, with six hundreds in his first seven innings; 246 One Day Ints, scoring 9,031 runs (average 42.39); retd from int. cricket April 2007; Wisden Cricketer of the Year 1995, Fed. of Int. Cricketers' Asscns Int. Cricketer of the Year 1999. *Publication:* Beating the Field (autobiog.) 1995. *Leisure interests:* golf, horse racing. *Address:* c/o West Indies Cricket Board, PO Box 616, St John's, Antigua.

LARA BOSCH, José Manuel; Spanish media executive; *President, Grupo Planeta;* b. Barcelona; s. of the late José Manuel Lara Hernández and María Teresa Bosch Carbonell; m.; four c.; CEO Grupo Planeta (owns TV and radio stations, publishing imprints, chain of bookshops, newspapers and real estate firms) 1998–2003, Pres. 2003–; Pres. Antena 3; fmr Pres. Quiero TV, UTECA; Chair. Inst. of Family Businesses 2000–03, Fundación José Manuel Lara; Pres. Círculo de Economía 2005–08. *Address:* Grupo Planeta SA, Edifici Planeta, Diagonal 662–664, 08034 Barcelona, Spain (office). *Telephone:* (93) 4928999 (office). *Fax:* (93) 4928562 (office). *E-mail:* direccion@planeta.es (office).

LARA CASTRO, Jorge, MA; Paraguayan diplomatist and social scientist; b. 5 Aug. 1945, Asunción; s. of Mariano Lara Castro and Carmen Casco; m.; ed Catholic Univ., Asunción, Latin American Faculty of Social Sciences, Mexico City; Prof., Autonomous Nat. Univ. of Mexico 1979–81; Prof., Catholic Univ., Asunción 1974–75; Prof., Centre for Econ. Research and Teaching, Mexico City 1980–91; Prof., Faculty of Philosophy and Human Sciences, Catholic Univ. of Asunción, Paraguay 1992–98, Dir Dept of Sociology 1997–99; Pres. Inst. of San Martín, Paraguay; Perm. Rep. to UN, New York 2000–01. *Publications:* numerous publs on capitalism in Brazil, the birth of campesino movt, Latin American political systems and educ. and human rights in Paraguay. *Address:* c/o Ministry of Foreign Affairs, Juan E. O'Leary y Presidente Franco, Asunción, Paraguay (office). *Telephone:* 687-3490 (office). *Fax:* 818-1282 (office).

LARAKI, Azeddine, PhD; Moroccan politician; b. 1929, Fez; ed Faculty of Medicine, Paris, France; Cabinet Dir, Ministry of Nat. Educ. 1958, of Public Health 1959; Dir Avicenne Hosp., Head of Respiratory Surgery and Pneumology 1960–, Prof. of Medicine 1967–; fmr mem. Exec. Cttee Istiqlal –1984; Minister of Nat. Educ. 1977–86; Prime Minister of Morocco 1986–92; Sec.-Gen. Org. of the Islamic Conf. 1996–2000; mem. Royal Acad. of Morocco. *Address:* c/o Organization of the Islamic Conference, Kilo 6, Mecca Road, PO Box 178, Jeddah 21411, Saudi Arabia.

LARAKI, Moulay Ahmed; Moroccan politician, physician and diplomatist; b. 15 Oct. 1931, Casablanca; ed Univ. de Paris, France; with Ministry of Foreign Affairs 1956–57; Perm. Rep. to UN 1957–59; Head of Hosp. Services, Casablanca 1956–61; Amb. to Spain 1962–65, to Switzerland 1965–66, to USA and concurrently accred to Mexico, Canada and Venezuela 1966–67; Minister of Foreign Affairs 1967–69; Prime Minister 1969–71; Minister of Medical Affairs 1971–74; Minister of State for Foreign Affairs 1974–77; Minister of the Environment *c.* 1998; Pres. Soc. marocaine des sciences médicales. *Address:* c/o Office of the Prime Minister, Rabat, Morocco.

LARCOMBE, Brian, BCom; British business executive; b. 27 Aug. 1953; s. of John George Larcombe and Joyce Lucile Larcombe; m. Catherine Bullen 1983; ed Bromley Grammar School, Univ. of Birmingham; joined 3i Group PLC 1974, Local Dir 1982–88, Regional Dir 1988–92, Finance Dir and mem. Exec. Cttee 1992–2004, CEO 1997–2004; Dir (non-exec.) NXD Smith & Nephew PLC, F & C Asset Management plc 2005–, also mem. Remuneration Cttee. *Address:* c/o F & C Asset Management plc, Exchange House, Primrose Street, London EC2A 2NY, England. *Telephone:* (20) 7628-8000 (office). *Fax:* (20) 7628-8188 (office). *E-mail:* enquiries@fandc.com (office).

LARDY, Henry (Hank) Arnold, PhD, DSC; American biochemist and academic; *Vilas Professor Emeritus of Biological Sciences, University of Wisconsin;* b. 19 Aug. 1917, SDak; s. of Nick Lardy and Elizabeth Lardy; m. Annrita Dresselhuys 1943; three s. one d.; ed S Dakota State Univ. and Univs of Wis. and Toronto, Canada; Asst Prof., Univ. of Wis. 1945–47, Assoc. Prof. 1947–50, Prof. 1950–66, Co-Dir Inst. for Enzyme Research 1950–88, Vilas Prof. of Biological Sciences 1966–88, Vilas Prof. Emer. 1988–; Pres. Citizens vs. McCarthy 1952; mem. Nat. Acad. of Sciences, American Acad. of Arts and Sciences, American Philosophical Soc., American Soc. Biological Chemists (Pres. 1964), The Endocrine Soc., Harvey Soc.; Hon. mem. Japanese Biochemical Soc.; Hon. DSc (S Dakota State Univ.) 1978; ACS Paul Lewis Award in Enzyme Chem. 1949, Neuberg Medal, American Soc. of European Chemists 1956, Wolf Foundation Prize in Agric. 1981, Nat. Award for Agricultural Excellence 1981, Amory Award, American Acad. of Arts and Sciences 1984, Carl Hartman Award, Soc. for the Study of Reproduction 1984, W. C. Rose Award American Soc. of Bio chem. and Molecular Biology 1988, Hilldale Award, Univ. of Wis. 1988. *Publications:* The Enzymes (co-ed.), 8 vols 1958–63 and 465 research papers in biochemistry in scientific journals; two short stories. *Leisure interests:* tennis, riding, retriever field trials. *Address:* Institute for Enzyme Research, Room 303, University of Wisconsin-Madison, 1710 University Avenue, Madison, WI 53726 (office); Thorstrand Road, Madison, WI 53705, USA (home). *Telephone:* (608) 262-3372 (office); (608) 233-1584 (home). *Fax:* (608) 265-2904 (office). *Website:* www.biochem.wisc.edu (office).

LARGE, Sir Andrew Mcleod Brooks, Kt, MA (Econ.), MBA; British banker; b. 7 Aug. 1942, Goudhurst, Kent; s. of the late Maj.-Gen. Stanley Large and of Janet Brooks Large; m. Susan Melville 1967; two s. one d.; ed Winchester Coll., Univ. of Cambridge, Institut Européen d'Admin des Affaires (INSEAD), Fontainebleau; British Petroleum 1964–71; Orion Bank Ltd 1971–79; Swiss Bank Corpn 1980–89, Man. Dir SBCI London 1980–83, Chief Exec. and Deputy Chair. SBCI London 1983–87, Group Chief Exec. SBCI London 1987–88, mem. Bd SBC 1988–90; Chair. Large, Smith & Walter 1990–92; Chair. Securities & Investments Bd (SIB) 1992–97; Deputy Chair. Barclays Bank 1998–2002, Dir 1998–2002; Chair. Euroclear 1998–2000; mem. Bd on Banking Supervision, Bank of England 1996–97, Deputy Gov. 2002–06. *Leisure interests:* skiing, walking, gardening, apples, photography, music. *Address:* Marshall Wace, 13th Floor, The Adelphi, 1-11 John Adam Street, London, WC2N 6HT, England (office). *Telephone:* (20) 7925-4826 (office). *Fax:* (20) 7316-2281 (office).

LARGE, David Clay, PhD; American historian, academic and writer; *Professor of European History, Montana State University;* b. 13 Aug. 1945, Scott Field, Ill.; s. of H. R. Large, Jr; m. 1st Jacque Hambly 1968 (divorced 1977); one s.; m. 2nd Margaret Wheeler 1980; one d.; ed Univ. of Washington, Univ. of California, Berkeley; taught Modern European History, Smith Coll. 1973–78, Yale Univ. 1978–83, Dean, Pierson Coll. 1981–83; Prof. of European History, Mont. State Univ. 1983–; Contrib. Ed. Military History Quarterly 1989; Woodrow Wilson Fellowship, Morse Fellowship (Yale), Nat. Endowment for the Humanities Fellowship, German Marshall Fund Fellowship. *Publications:* The Politics of Law and Order: A History of the Bavarian Einwohnerwehr 1980, Wagnerism in European Culture and Politics 1984, Between Two Fires: Europe's Path in the 1930s 1990, Contending with Hitler: Varieties of German Resistance in the Third Reich 1991, Germans to the Front: West German Rearmament in the Adenauer Era 1996, Where Ghosts Walked: Munich's Road to the Third Reich 1997, Berlin 2000, And the World Closed Its Doors: One Family Abandoned to the Holocaust 2008. *Leisure interests:* running, skiing, music, hiking. *Address:* Department of History and Philosophy, Montana State University, 2-162 Wilson Hall, Bozeman, MT 59717-2320 (office); 721 W Koch, Bozeman, MT 59715, USA (home). *Telephone:* (406) 994-5203 (office); (406) 522-8630 (home). *E-mail:* davidclay@imt.net (office). *Website:* www.montana.edu/~wwwhi (office).

LARIJANI, Ali Ardashir, BSc, MS, PhD; Iranian politician; *Speaker, Majlis-e-Shura-e Islami (Parliament);* b. 1958, Najaf, Iraq; s. of Ayatollah Mirza-Hashem Amoli; ed Sharif Univ., Tehran Univ.; began career after 1979 revolution as dir of state TV; served in sr positions at Ministry of Revolutionary Guards, including Deputy Minister; Minister of Culture and Islamic Guidance 1992–94; Head Islamic Repub. of Iran Broadcasting 1994–2004; Sec. Shura-ye Ali-ye Amniyyat-e Melli (Supreme Nat. Security Council) (one of two reps of Supreme Leader of Iran, Ayatollah Khamenei) 2005–07 (resgnd), roles included chief nuclear negotiator; Speaker Majilis-e-Shura-e Islami (Parliament) 2008–; presidential cand. 2005. *Address:* Office of the Speaker, Majlis-e-Shura-e Islami (Parliament), Tehran, Iran. *E-mail:* info@abadgaran.ir (office). *Website:* www.abadgaran.ir (office).

LARKINS, Richard, AO; Australian university administrator, endocrinologist and academic; b. 17 May 1943; James Stewart Chair of Medicine, Royal Melbourne Hosp. 1984–97; Dean of Medicine, Dentistry and Health Sciences, Melbourne Univ. 1998–2003; Vice-Chancellor and Pres. Monash Univ. 2003–08 (retd); Chair. Nat. Health and Medical Research Council of Australia 1997–2000; Pres. Endocrine Soc. of Australia 1982–84, Royal Australasian Coll. of Physicians 2000–02; Chair. Accreditation Cttee, Australian Medical Council 1991–95; mem. Nat. Aboriginal and Torres Strait Islander Health Council 1997–2000; Eric Susman Prize 1982, Sir William Upjohn Medal 2002. *Address:* c/o Office of the Vice-Chancellor, Monash University, Wellington Road, Clayton, Vic. 3800, Australia (office).

LARMORE, Jennifer May, BMus; American singer (mezzo-soprano); b. 21 June 1958, Atlanta, GA; d. of William C. Larmore and Eloise O. Larmore; m. William Powers 1980; ed Sprayberry High School, Marietta, Ga, Westminster Choir Coll., Princeton, NJ; operatic debut with L'Opéra de Nice, France 1985, debut with Metropolitan Opera, New York 1995, Salzburg Festival debut 1993, Tanglewood Festival debut 1998; specializes in music of the Bel Canto and Baroque periods; Spokesperson and Fundraiser, US Fund for UNICEF 1998–; Chevalier, Ordre des Artes et des Lettres 2002; William M. Sullivan Fellowship 1983, Maria Callas Vocal Competition, Barcelona 1984, McAllister Vocal Competition, Indianapolis 1986, Alumni Merit Award, Westminster Choir Coll. 1991, Gramophone Award for Best Baroque Album 1992, Richard Tucker Foundation Award, New York 1994. *Music:* over 40 recordings of operatic and solo repertoire; operatic appearances with most of the world's leading cos; recital appearances include Carnegie Hall, New York, Wigmore Hall, London, Musik Verein, Vienna, Concertgebauw, Amsterdam, Palais Garnier, Paris, L. G. Arts Center, Seoul, Teatro Colón, Buenos Aires, Teatro Liceo, Barcelona, Teatro Monnaie, Brussels, Arts Centre, Melbourne, etc. *Television:* appearances include Star Trek 30th Anniversary broadcast, live Christmas Eve service from St Patrick's Cathedral, numerous live broadcasts from the Metropolitan Opera, etc. *Achievements:* selected by the US Olympic Cttee to sing the Olympic Hymn for the closing of the Atlanta Olympic Summer Games 1996. *Leisure interests:* playing with pet dog, relaxing poolside, shopping. *Address:* IMG Artists, The Light Box, 111 Power Road, London W4 5PY, England (office). *Telephone:* (20) 7957-5800 (office). *Fax:* (212) 7957-5801 (office). *E-mail:* salmansi@imgartists.com (office); jenniferlarmore@aol.com (home). *Website:* www.imgartists.com (office); www.jenniferlarmoremezzo.com.

LAROCCO, James A., MA; American diplomatist; *Director General, Sinai Multinational Force and Observers;* b. Chicago, Ill.; m. Janet Larocco; three c.; ed Univ. of Portland, Johns Hopkins School of Advanced Int. Studies; entered Foreign Service 1973; staff Asst Office of Congressional Relations, State Dept; Commercial Attaché, Jeddah 1975–77; Econ. Officer, Cairo 1978–81; Econ. Section Chief Kuwait 1981–83; Deputy Dir, Office of Pakistan, Afghanistan and Bangladesh Affairs, Near East Asia Bureau 1984; Minister-Counsellor for Econ. Affairs, Beijing; Kuwait Task Force Co-ordinator, State Operations Center, Operation Desert Storm 1990; Deputy Dir American Inst. in Taiwan 1991; Deputy Chief of Mission, Tel-Aviv 1993; Amb. to Kuwait 1996–2001; Prin. Deputy Asst Sec. Bureau of Near Eastern Affairs, Dept of State 2001–; Dir Gen. Sinai Multinational Force and Observers (ind. (non-UN) peacekeeping mission) 2004–; Congressional Fellowship 1983;*Fax:* (2) 4156796. *E-mail:* Email@mfo.org. *Website:* www.mfo.org.

LAROQUE, Michèle; French actress; b. 15 June 1960, Nice; d. of Claude Laroque and Doïna Trandabur; m. Dominique Deschamps (divorced); one d.; ed Univ. of Nice; f. own production co. PBOF (Please Buy Our Films); Chevalier des Arts et Lettres. *Films include:* Suivez cet avion 1989, The Hairdresser's Husband 1990, Une époque formidable 1991, Max & Jeremie 1992, La Crise 1992, Paranoïa 1993, Tango 1993, Louis, enfant roi 1993, Chacun pour toi 1994, Personne ne m'aime 1994, Aux petits bonheurs 1994, Le Fabuleux destin de Madame Petlet 1995, Nelly & Monsieur Arnaud 1995, Pédale Douce 1995, Les Aveux de l'innocent 1996, Passage à l'acte 1996, Fallait pas! 1996, Le Plus Beau Métier du Monde 1996, Ma Vie en Rose 1996, Serial Lover 1997, Doggy Bag 1999, Epouse-moi 2000, Le Placard 2001, Malabar Princess 2003, Pedale Dure 2004, L'Anniversaire 2005, Comme t'y es belle! 2006, La Maison du bonheur 2006, L'Entente cordiale 2006, Enfin veuve 2007, The Neighbor 2007. *Theatre:* Silence en coulisses, Ornifle 1991, La Face cachée d'Orion, Une Folie 1993, Ils s'aiment 1996, Ils se sont aimés 2001. *Television includes:* Vivement lundi 1988, Le Retour d'Arsène Lupin 1989, La Télé des inconnus 1990, Imogène 1990, Bébé express 1991, C'est quoi ce petit boulot? 1992, Les Cravates léopards 1992, Navarro 1993, B comme Bolo 1994, Quatre pour un loyer 1995, Une femme dans mon coeur 1995, Le Nid tombé de l'oiseau 1995, Mouton noir 1995, Elvis Aziz 1996, Week-end 1998, Le Mur 1998, Une femme neuve 2000, L'Oiseau rare 2001, La Chose publique 2003, Mon voisin du dessus 2003, Petits secrets et gros mensonges 2006, En marge des jours 2007, Faisons un rêve 2007. *Leisure interests:* tennis, skiing, riding, golf. *Address:* c/o Agent associés Guy Bonnet, 201 rue du fbg Saint-Honoré, 75008 Paris, France (office). *Website:* www.michelelaroque.com.

LAROSIÈRE DE CHAMPFEU, Jacques Martin Henri Marie de; French international civil servant; *Senior Adviser, BNP Paribas;* b. 12 Nov. 1929, Paris; s. of Robert de Larosière and Hugayte de Larosière (née de Champfeu); m. France du Bos 1960; one s. one d.; ed Lycée Louis-le-Grand, Paris Univ. and Ecole nat. d'Admin; Insp. adjoint 1958, Insp. des Finances 1960; Chargé de Mission in Inspectorate-Gen. of Finance 1961, External Finance Office 1963, Treasury 1965; Asst Dir Treasury 1967; Deputy Dir then Head of Dept, Ministry of Econs and Finance 1971; Prin. Pvt. Sec. to Valéry Giscard d'Estaing (then Minister of Econs and Finance) 1974; Under-Sec. of Treas. 1974–78; Pres. Group of Ten 1976–78; Dir-Gen. IMF 1978–87; Gov. Banque de France 1987–93, Hon. Gov. 1993–; Chair. Cttee of Govs, Group of Ten 1990–93; Pres. EBRD 1993–98; Sr Adviser BNP Paribas 1998–; Chair. Strategic Cttee, French Treasury; Insp. Gen. des Finances 1981; mem. Bd of Dirs Dir Renault 1971–74, Banque nat. de Paris 1973–78, Air France and Soc. nat. de chemins de fer français (SNCF) 1974–78, Soc. nat. industrielle aérospatiale 1976–78, Power Corpn 1998–2001; Alstom 1998–2001, France Télécom 1998–, Stichting NYSE Euronext (the Dutch Foundation) 2007–; mem. AIG Int. Advisory Bd; Trustee Reuters 1999–; Censeur Banque de France 1974–78, Crédit nat. 1974–78, Comptoir des Entrepreneurs 1973–75, Crédit foncier de France 1975–78; mem. Bd of Dirs France Telecom 1998–; Vice-Pres. Caisse nat. des Télécommunications 1974–78; mem. Acad. of Moral and Political Sciences 1993; Hon. mem. Soc. des Cincinnati de France; Commdr, Légion d'honneur; Chevalier, Ordre nat. du Mérite; Hon. KBE; numerous awards. *Address:* BNP Paribas, 3 rue d'Antin, 75078 Paris Cedex 02 (office); 5 rue de Beaujolais, 75001 Paris, France (home). *Telephone:* 1-42-98-24-28 (office). *Fax:* 1-42-98-22-37 (office). *E-mail:* jacques.delarosiere@bnpparibas.com (office). *Website:* www.bnpparibas.net (office).

LARQUIÉ, André Olivier, LenD; French civil servant; *President, Palais Multisports Paris-Bercy;* b. 26 June 1938, Nay; s. of Henri Larquié and Simone Tauziède; ed Lycée Louis-le-Grand, Univ. of Paris and Ecole nat. d'Admin.; Deputy Dir Musique Art lyrique et Danse, Ministry of Culture and Communications 1978–79, Official Rep. 1981–83, 1987; Govt Commr Centre nat. d'art et de Culture Georges Pompidou 1981–84; Pres. Paris Opera 1983–87; Tech. Adviser to the Prime Minister May 1988–89; Pres. Théâtre Contemporain de la Danse, Asscn pour le Dialogue entre les Cultures 1985; Pres. Radio France Int. 1989–95; Pres. Cité de la Musique, Paris –2002, Ballet de Nancy et Lorraine, Théâtre du Chatelet, Paris; Departmental Head, Gen. Inspectorate, Ministry of Culture and Communication 2001; Pres. Communication Cttee, French Comm. for UNESCO; Pres. Palais Multisports Paris-Bercy 2004–; Commdr des Arts et Lettres 1983 Officier, Légion d'honneur 1996 Chevalier dans l'Ordre de la Pléïade 1997 Officier Ordre du Mérite agricole 1998 Commdr Ordre nat. du Mérite 2000 Commdr des Palmes académiques 2002–. *Publications:* official reports. *Leisure interests:* song and dance. *Address:* 8 blvd de Bercy, 75012 Paris (office); 26 blvd Raspail, 75007 Paris, France (home). *Telephone:* 1-40-02-60-28 (office). *Fax:* 1-40-02-60-29 (office); 1-45-48-48-30 (home). *E-mail:* alarquie@bercy.fr (office). *Website:* www.alarquie-chatelet-theatre.com.

LARRAIN, Juan, BA; Chilean diplomatist; *Expert Adviser, United Nations Security Council Counter Terrorism Committee Executive Directorate;* b. 29 Aug. 1941, Santiago; m. Mariel Cruchaga Belaunde; four c.; ed German School and Mil. Acad., Chile, Univ. of Chile, Diplomatic Acad., Ministry of Foreign Affairs; Asst Prof. School of Journalism, Catholic Univ. of Chile 1964–65; Prof. of Contemporary History Diplomatic Acad., Ministry of Foreign Affairs and Ed. Diplomacia (publ. of Acad.) 1978–79; Deputy Chief of Mission, OAS 1983–87, London 1988–90, Head First Commercial Mission to Ireland 1991, Deputy Dir Multilateral Econ. Affairs 1991–92, Consul-Gen. New York 1992–94, Deputy Perm. Rep. to UN 1994–99, Perm. Rep. 1999–2001, also Deputy Perm. Rep. to UN Security Council 1996–97; fmr Head Monitoring Mechanism for Angola; Expert Adviser UN Security Council Counter Terrorism Cttee Exec. Directorate 2003–. *Leisure Interests:* history, classical music, reading, golf. *Address:* United Nations, 405 Lexington Avenue, Room 5075, New York, NY 10174 (office); 66 Mallard Drive, Greenwich, CT 06830, USA (home). *Telephone:* (212) 457-1078 (office); (203) 629-6075 (home). *Fax:* (212) 457-4041 (office); (203) 629-2855 (home). *E-mail:* larrain@un.org (office); december79@aol.com (home).

LARSEN, Kai, BA, MSc; Danish botanist and academic; *Professor Emeritus of Botany, University of Århus;* b. 15 Nov. 1926, Hillerød; s. of Axel G. Larsen and Elisabeth Hansen; m. Supee Saksuwan 1971; one s. three d.; ed Univ. of Copenhagen; Asst Scientist, Botany Dept Univ. of Copenhagen 1952–55; Asst Prof. Royal Danish School of Pharmacy 1955–62, Assoc. Prof. 1962–63; Prof. of Botany, Århus Univ. 1963–96, Prof. Emer. 1996–; Founder Botanical Inst. and Herbarium Jutlandicum, Århus; Ed.-in-Chief Nordic Journal of Botany and Opera Botanica 1979–2001; Ed. Flora of Thailand; Danish Ed. Flora Nordica; mem. Exec. Cttee Flora Malesiana Foundation (Leiden, Netherlands); adviser to Flora of China; led 13 botanical expeditions to Thailand 1958–95; Consultant, Queen Sirikit Botanical Gardens, Thailand 1996–; botanical consultant, Danish Nat. Encyclopedia; Visiting lecturer, Russian Acad. of Sciences, Acad. Sinica; Pres. Int. Asscn of Botanic Gardens 1981–87; mem. Royal Danish Acad. and Royal Norwegian Acad. of Science and Corresp. mem. of other int. socs; Kt Order of Dannebrog, First Class; Officer, Crown of Thailand; Hon. DSc (Prince of Songkla Univ., Thailand) 1994. *Publications:* about 250 scientific books and articles on tropical botany, nature conservation. *Leisure interests:* classical music (playing piano). *Address:* Department of Systematic Botany, Institute of Biological Sciences, University of Århus, Nordlandsvej 68, 8240 Risskov (office); Graastenvej 6, Søften, 8382 Hinnerup, Denmark (home). *Telephone:* 89-42-47-08 (office); 86-98-59-82 (home). *Fax:* 89-42-47-47 (office). *E-mail:* kai.larsen@biology.au.dk (office). *Website:* herb140.bio.au.dk/botany/home/index.html (office).

LARSEN, Ralph Stanley, BA; American business executive; b. 19 Nov. 1938, Brooklyn, NY; s. of Andrew Larsen and Gurine (née Henningsen) Larsen; m. Dorothy M. Zeitfuss 1961; one s. two d.; ed Hofstra Univ.; served in USN 1956–58; manufacturing trainee, then supervisor of Production and Dir Marketing, Johnson & Johnson, New Brunswick, NJ 1962–77, Vice-Pres. Operations and Marketing, McNeil Consumer Products Co. Div. 1977–81, Pres. Chicopee Div. 1982–83, Co. Group Chair. 1985–86, Vice-Chair. Exec. Cttee, Bd of Dirs 1986–89, Chair. and CEO 1989–2002, also Pres.; Pres. Becton Dickenson Consumer Products, Paramus, NJ 1981–83; mem. Bd of Dirs Xerox, GE; Trustee Robert Wood Johnson Foundation. *Leisure interests:* skiing, boating, art. *Address:* c/o Johnson & Johnson, 1 Johnson & Johnson Plaza, New Brunswick, NJ 08933, USA.

LARSON, Alan P., PhD; American economist; *Senior Advisor, Covington & Burling LLC;* ed Univ. of Iowa; joined State Dept 1973, serving in sr positions covering econs, trade, finance, energy, sanctions, transport, telecommunications; Amb. to OECD 1990–93; served in econ. sections of Embassies in Jamaica, Zaire, Sierra Leone; Under Sec. of State for Econ., Business and Agric. Affairs 1999–2005; Sr Advisor, Covington & Burling LLC 2005–; Distinguished Fellow, Council on Competitiveness; consultant, World Econ. Forum; Chair. Bd of Dirs Transparency Int. (US chapter); mem. Bd of Dirs Bread for the World; Univ. of Iowa Distinguished Alumnus Award 2003. *Address:* Covington & Burling LLP, 1201 Pennsylvania Avenue, NW, Washington, DC 20004-2401, USA (office). *Telephone:* (202) 662-5756 (office).

E-mail: alarson@cov.com (office). *Website:* www.cov.com/lawyers/alarson/biography.html (office).

LARSON, Gary, BA; American cartoonist; b. 14 Aug. 1950, Tacoma, Wash.; s. of Vern Larson and Doris Larson; m. Toni Carmichael 1988; ed Washington State Univ.; performed in jazz duo 1972–75; worked in a music store; sold first cartoons to Pacific Search magazine; subsequently sold cartoons to Seattle Times, San Francisco Chronicle, Chronicle Features Syndicate; f. FarWorks Inc.; announced retirement Oct. 1994; Nat. Cartoonists Soc. Award for best syndicated panel of 1985; Outstanding Cartoonist of the Year Award 1991, 1994; Max and Moritz Prize for Best Int. Cartoon 1993; insect named after him: Strigiphilus garylarsoni (biting louse), also butterfly Serratoterga larsoni. *Films:* Gary Larson's Tales From The Far Side 1994 (Grand Prix, Annecy Film Festival 1995), Gary Larson's Tales From The Far Side II 1997. *Publications:* The Far Side, Beyond The Far Side, In Search of The Far Side, Bride of The Far Side, Valley of The Far Side, It Came From The Far Side, Hound of The Far Side, The Far Side Observer, Night of the Crash-test Dummies, Wildlife Preserve, Wiener Dog Art, Unnatural Selections, Cows of Our Planet, The Chickens Are Restless, The Curse of Madame "C", Last Chapter and Worse 1996; Anthologies: The Far Side Gallery 1, 2, 3, 4 and 5, The PreHistory of The Far Side, There's A Hair in my Dirt! A Worm's Story 1998. *Leisure interests:* jazz guitar, pickup basketball. *Address:* c/o Andrews McMell Publishing, 4520 Main Street, Suite 700, Kansas City, MO 64111; Creators Syndicated International, 5777 West Century Boulevard, Suite 700, Los Angeles, CA 90045, USA (office). *Website:* www.thefarside.com.

LARSSON, Commr Freda; British Salvation Army officer (retd); b. (Freda Turner), 1939, Scotland; m. Gen. John Larsson 1969; two s.; officer, Upper Kingston-upon-Thames Corps, Salvation Army 1965, served as Corps Officer, Area Youth Officer, Area Sec. 1965–1969, Corps Officer, Territorial Guide Organiser in Scotland, Asst Youth Dept, Nat. HQ 1969–1980; S America W Territorial Home League Sec. 1980–84; Coll. Librarian, Int. Training Coll. 1984; Coordinator of Married Women Officers, Int. HQ 1988–90; UK Territorial Pres. of Women's Org. 1990; served in NZ and Fiji Territory 1993–96, Sweden and Latvia Territory 1996–99; World Sec. for Women's Ministries and World Pres. Boy Scouts, Guides and Guards, Int. HQ 1999–2003, World Pres. of Women's Ministries 2003–06 (retd). *Address:* c/o Salvation Army HQ, 101 Newington Causeway, London, SE1 6BN, England.

LARSSON, John, BD; Swedish Salvation Army officer (retd); b. 2 April 1938; s. of Sture Larsson and Flora Larsson; m. Freda Turner 1969; two s.; ed Univ. of London, UK; commissioned as Officer, Upper Norwood Corps, The Salvation Army 1957; various appointments in UK including Corps Officer, Trainer, Territorial Youth Sec. for Scotland, British Territory Nat. Youth Sec.; apptd Chief. Sec., S America W 1980–84; Prin. William Booth Memorial Training Coll., London 1984–88; Asst Admin. Planning to Chief of Staff for UK 1988–90; Territorial Commdr of UK and Repub. of Ireland Territory 1990–93, of NZ and Fiji Territory 1993–96, of Sweden and Latvia Territory 1996–99; Chief of Staff of the Salvation Army 1999–2002, 17th Gen. of the Salvation Army 2002–06 (retd). *Music includes:* co-author with Gen. John Gowans (retd) of 10 full-length musicals, Take-Over Bid 1967, Hosea 1969, Jesus Folk 1972, Spirit 1973, Glory 1975, White Rose 1977, The Blood of the Lamb 1978, Son of Man 1983, Man Mark II 1985, and The Meeting 1990. *Publications include:* Doctrine Without Tears 1974, Spiritual Breakthrough 1983, The Man Perfectly Filled with the Spirit 1986, How Your Corps Can Grow 1988. *Leisure interests:* music, walking.

LARSSON, Per; Swedish business executive; *CEO, Borse Dubai;* b. Feb. 1961, Harnosand; m.; four c.; ed Uppsala Univ.; fmr broker, Föreningssparbanken; Chief Exec. OM Group (Swedish trading tech. firm) 1985–2003 (resgnd after OM merger with HEX exchange); CEO Dubai Int. Financial Exchange (DIFX) 2006–07, CEO Borse Dubai 2007–; Global Leader for Tomorrow, World Econ. Forum 2001. *Leisure interests:* sport, spending time at second home in France, tennis. *Address:* Borse Dubai, PO Box 506690, Dubai, United Arab Emirates (office). *Telephone:* (4) 3612222 (office). *Fax:* (4) 3612130 (office). *E-mail:* info@dubaigroup.com (office). *Website:* www.borsedubai.ae (office).

LASICA, Milan, AM; Slovak actor, dramatist and scriptwriter; b. 3 Feb. 1940, Zvolen; s. of Vojtech Lasica and Edita Šmáliková; m. Magdalena Vašáryová; two d.; ed Univ. of Musical Arts, Bratislava; dramatist Slovak TV 1964–67; actor with theatres Divadlo na Korze 1967–71, Divaldo Večerní Brno 1971–72, Nová scéna 1972–89; f. Štúdio S-Bratislava 1989, Dir 1989–; co-operation as actor, dramatist and scriptwriter with Slovak and Czech TV, radio and theatres Semafor, Divadlo bez zábradlí and Labyrint; TV Prize Monte Carlo Festival. *Films include:* Sladké hry minulého léta (TV) 1969, Srdečný pozdrav ze zeměkoule (also screenwriter) 1982, Tři veteráni (Three Veterans) 1983, Vážení přátelé 1989, Tajomstvo alchymistu Storitza 1991, Vystrel na Bonaparta (TV) 1992, O psíckovi a macicke 1993, Mimozemštané, Saturnin 1994, Výchova dívek v Čechách (Bringing Up Girls in Bohemia) 1997, Pasti, pasti, pasticky (Traps) 1998, Hanele 1999, Talár a ptači zob 2003, Konečná stanica 2005, Obsluhoval jsem anglického krále 2006. *Films directed include:* Úlet (TV) 2002. *Plays include:* Cyrano, Don Juan, Mrtvé duše. *Leisure interest:* golf. *Address:* Stúdio Lasica-Satinský, Nám 1 Mája 5, Bratislava, Slovakia (office). *Telephone:* (2) 5292-1584 (office). *Fax:* (2) 5292-5082 (office).

LASKAWY, Philip A.; American management consultant (retd); *Chairman, Fannie Mae (Federal National Mortgage Association);* b. 1941; m.; two s.; Partner, Ernst & Whinney 1978–81, Man. Partner 1981–85; Vice-Chair., Regional Man. Partner Ernst & Young (formed from merged cos Ernst & Whinney and Arthur Young) 1985–93, Deputy Chair. 1993, Chair. and CEO 1994–2001, Chair. Ernst & Young Int. 1997–2001; Chair. Fannie Mae (Fed. Nat. Mortgage Asscn) 2008–; mem. Bd Dirs Cap Gemini, Ernst & Young, General Motors Corpn, Heidrick & Struggles Int., Inc., Henry Schein, Inc., Loews Corpn 2003–, The Progressive Corpn; Chair. of Trustees, Int. Accounting Standards Bd 2006–08; mem. Constitution Cttee, Int. Accounting Standards Cttee Foundation Trustee Cttee (Chair. 2006–07); mem. Bd Dirs General Motors Corpn, Henry Schein, Inc., Lazard Ltd, Loews Corpn, Discover Financial Services; mem. Bd Dance Theater Foundation (Alvin Ailey American Dance Theater), Educational Broadcasting Corpn (Thirteen WNET/New York), The Philharmonic Symphony Soc. of New York, Inc. *Address:* Fannie Mae, 3900 Wisconsin Avenue, NW, Washington, DC 20016-2892, USA (office). *Telephone:* (202) 752-7000 (office). *E-mail:* headquarters@fanniemae.com (office). *Website:* www.fanniemae.com (office).

LASKEY, Ronald Alfred, MA, DPhil, FRS, FMedSci; British professor of molecular biology and embryology; *Honorary Director, Cancer Cell Unit, Hutchison/Medical Research Council Research Centre, University of Cambridge;* b. 26 Jan. 1945, High Wycombe; s. of Thomas Leslie Laskey and Bessie Laskey; m. Margaret Anne Page 1971; one s. one d.; ed High Wycombe Royal Grammar School, Queen's Coll., Oxford; scientific staff mem., Imperial Cancer Research Fund 1970–73, Lab. of Molecular Biology, MRC 1973–83; Co-Dir Molecular Embryology Group, Cancer Research Campaign (CRC) 1983–91; Dir CRC, Wellcome CRC Inst. 1991–; Charles Darwin Prof. of Animal Embryology, Darwin Coll., Cambridge 1983–, Fellow 1982–; Hon. Dir MRC Cancer Cell Unit, Hutchison/MRC Research Centre, Cambridge 2001–; Distinguished Visitor, Agency for Science, Tech. and Research (A*STAR), Singapore 2002; mem. Scientific Advisory Cttee, European Molecular Biology Lab., Heidelberg; Assoc. Ed. Cell; Pres. British Soc. of Cell Biology 1996–99; Vice-Pres. Acad. of Medical Sciences 2007–; Trustee Strangeways Research Lab. 1993–, Inst. of Cancer Research 2007–; mem. Academia Europaea 1989; Coleworth Medal, Biochemical Soc. 1979, CIBA Medal, Biochemical Soc. 1997, Feldberg Foundation Prize 1998, Louis Jeantet Prize for Medicine, Jeantet Foundation, Geneva 1998, Univ. Medal of Charles Univ., Prague 1999, BBC Tomorrow's World Health Innovation Award for devt of new screening test for cancer 2000; his research papers have been listed amongst the 100 most highly cited papers in scientific literature, and two research papers were distinguished with the Citation Classics Honour 1983. *Publications include:* Songs for Cynical Scientists, More Songs for Cynical Scientists; articles on cell biology in professional journals. *Leisure interests:* music, mountains. *Address:* MRC Cancer Cell Unit, Hutchison/MRC Research Centre, Hills Road, Cambridge, CB2 2XZ, England (office). *Telephone:* (1223) 334106/7 (office). *Fax:* (1223) 763293 (office). *E-mail:* ral19@mole.bio.cam.ac.uk (office). *Website:* www.dar.cam.ac.uk (office); www.hutchison-mrc.cam.ac.uk (office).

LASORDA, Thomas (Tom) W., BA, MBA; Canadian automobile industry executive; *President and Vice Chairman, Chrysler LLC;* b. 24 July 1954, Windsor, Ont.; ed Univ. of Windsor; with General Motors Corpn 1977–2000; Sr Vice-Pres. Powertrain Manufacturing, Chrysler Group, DaimlerChrysler Corpn 2000–02, Sr Vice-Pres. Production 2002–04, COO DaimlerChrysler Corpn, Auburn Hills, Mich. 2004–06, Pres. and CEO 2006–07, Pres. and CEO Chrysler LLC (after acquisition of Chrysler group by Cerberus Capital Man. LP) –Aug. 2007, Pres. and Vice Chair. Aug. 2007–; Deputy mem. Bd of Man. DaimlerChrysler AG 2004–05, mem. 2005–07. *Address:* Chrysler LLC, 1000 Chrysler Drive, Auburn Hills, MI 48326-2766, USA (office). *Telephone:* (248) 576-5741 (office). *Fax:* (248) 576-4742 (office). *Website:* www.chrysler.com (office).

LASSALLE, Jacques Louis Bernard; French theatre director, actor and writer; b. 6 July 1936, Clermont-Ferrand; s. of Antoine Lassalle and Louise Lassalle (née Courbouleix); m. Françoise Marty 1958; three s.; ed Sorbonne, Paris, Conservatoire National Supérieur d'Art Dramatique de Paris; Asst Teacher, Institut d'Etudes Théâtrales 1969–77; f. Studio Théâtre de Vitry 1970; Teacher Conservatoire Nat. Supérieur de Paris 1981–83, 1994–2001; Dir-Gen. Théâtre Nat. de Strasbourg 1983–90; Administrateur Général, Comédie Française 1990–93; Dir Compagnie pour Mémoire; Chevalier, Ordre nat. du Mérite 1988, Officier, Légion d'honneur 1992, Commdr des Arts et des Lettres 1996; Grand prix nat. du théâtre 1998. *Film:* Après 2002. *Plays:* Dir about 100 plays, particularly by Molière, Corneille, Racine, Euripides, Marivaux, Goldoni, Shakespeare, Labiche, Pirandello, Chekhov, Ibsen, Svevo, Lessing, Büchner, Hofmannsthal, Kundera, Sarraute, Brecht, Hare and Vinaver, also operas; recent productions include: La vie de Galilée 2000, Médée 2000, Le malin plaisir 2000, L'Ecole de danse 2000, Un jour d'été 2000, L'Ecole de femmes 2001, The Aspern Papers 2002, Don Juan 2002, Iphigénie en Tauride, La douleur, Platonov, Le Danse de Mort, Le Béte dans la Jungle, Le Jeu de l'Amour et du Hasard. *Television:* Ferveur Jacques Lassalle, Medée (Festival d'Avignon) 2000, Don Juan 2002. *Publications:* Jonathan des années 30, Un couple pour l'hiver, Pauses 1991, Conversations sur Don Juan 1994, L'amour d'Alceste 2000, Après 2002, Nathalie Sarraute ou l'obscur commencement de la parole 2002, Conversations sur la Formation de l'Acteur, La Madone des poubelles (play) 2004; numerous articles. *Leisure interests:* walking, swimming, reading, music, pre-1970 American films. *Address:* 47 boulevard Voltaire, 75011 Paris, France (home). *Telephone:* 1-47-00-32-78 (home). *Fax:* 1-47-00-32-78 (home). *E-mail:* lassalle.fra@wanadoo.fr (home).

LASSERRE, Bruno Marie André, MPL; French public servant; *Chairman, Conseil de la Concurrence;* b. 4 Jan. 1954, Talence, Gironde; s. of Jacques Lasserre and Marie Garrigou-Lagrange de David de Lastours; m. Marie-Laure Sergent 1988; two d.; ed Bordeaux Faculty of Law, Inst. of Political Studies, Bordeaux, Ecole Nat. d'Admin, Paris; mem. Conseil d'Etat 1978–, Maître des Requêtes 1983–; Chair.-Del. Nat. Comm. on right of reply on radio and TV 1980–82, Nat. Comm. on Freedom of Information 1982–86; Commissaire du gouvernement, Litigation Section of Conseil d'Etat 1984–86; Legal Counsel, France Telecom 1986–89; Head Regulatory Directorate for Posts and Telecommunications 1989–93; Dir-Gen. of Posts and

Telecommunications 1993–97; consultant to Ministers for Industry and Foreign Affairs on Int. Telecommunications (1997–98); Pres. comité de sélection des inspecteurs des finances au tour extérieur 1998–2000; mem. Conseil de la concurrence 1998–, Chair. 2004–; Supervisor of Privatization of Société française de production (SFP) 2001; Pres. Fonds de modernisation de la presse 1999; mem. comité de selection des banques-conseils d'Etat 1997; Deputy Pres. Litigation section of conseil d'Etat 2001–; Chevalier, Légion d'Honneur; Officier Ordre nat. du Mérite. *Publication:* Open Government 1987. *Address:* Conseil de la concurrence, 11 rue de l'Echelle, 75001 Paris (office); 14 avenue de Breteuil, 75007 Paris, France (home). *Telephone:* 1-55-04-00-00 (office). *Fax:* 1-55-04-02-35 (office). *E-mail:* communication@conseil-concurrence.fr (office). *Website:* www.conseil-concurrence.fr (office).

LASSETER, John A., BFA; American animator and film industry executive; *Chief Creative Officer, Pixar and Disney Animation Studios;* b. 12 Jan. 1957, Hollywood, Calif.; m. Nancy Lasseter; five s.; ed California Inst. of the Arts; joined The Walt Disney Company as Jungle Cruise skipper at Disneyland, Anaheim, Calif., later animator at Walt Disney Feature Animation 1979–84; worked as 'interface designer' at Lucasfilm Computer Graphics Group 1984–86, worked on project that resulted in his first computer–animated short The Adventures of André and Wally B, later made first computer–animated feature Toy Story; Founding mem. and Exec. Producer, Pixar 1986 (bought by Disney 2006), Chief Creative Officer of both Pixar and Disney Animation Studios 2006–, Prin. Creative Advisor, Walt Disney Imagineering 2006–; Fellow, American Acad. of Arts and Sciences; Contribution to Cinematic Imagery Award, Art Dirs Guild 2003, Lifetime Achievement Award, Venice Film Festival 2009. *Films include:* as dir: Lady and the Lamp 1979, Luxo Jr. 1986, Red's Dream 1987, Tin Toy (Academy Award for Animated Short Film) 1988, Knick Knack 1989, Toy Story (Special Achievement Academy Award) 1995, A Bug's Life 1998, Toy Story 2 1999, Who Is Bud Luckey? 2004, Cars 2006, Mater and the Ghostlight 2006; as exec. producer: Geri's Game 1997, It's Tough to Be a Bug 1998, For the Birds 2000, Monsters, Inc. 2001, Sen to Chihiro no kamikakushi (aka Spirited Away) 2001, Finding Nemo 2003, Boundin' 2003, The Incredibles 2004, Hauru no ugoku shiro (aka Howl's Moving Castle) 2004, One Man Band 2005, Mater and the Ghostlight 2006, Lifted 2006, Meet the Robinsons 2007, Ratatouille 2007, How to Hook Up Your Home Theater 2007, Presto 2008, Glago's Guest 2008, Bolt 2008, Wall-E 2008. *Address:* Pixar Animation Studios, 1200 Park Avenue, Emeryville, CA 94608 (office); Walt Disney Feature Animation, 500 South Buena Vista Street, Burbank, CA 91521, USA (office). *Telephone:* (510) 922-3000 (Emeryville) (office); (818) 560-1000 (Burbank) (office). *Fax:* (510) 922-3151 (Emeryville) (office); (818) 560-1930 (Burbank) (office). *E-mail:* info@pixar.com (office). *Website:* www.pixar.com (office); www.disneyanimation.com (office); corporate.disney.go.com/careers/who_imagineering.html (office); disney.go.com/disneypictures (office).

LASSEZ, Jean-Louis, MSc, DEA, PhD; French computer scientist and academic; *Professor and Chairman, Department of Computer Science, Coastal Carolina University;* b. 24 Dec. 1944; Lecturer, Acad. Commerciale Inte 1968–70, Dept of Mathematics, Sherbrooke Univ., Canada 1970–72; Research Fellow and Asst Prof., Dept of Computer Science, Purdue Univ., USA 1972–73; Adjunct Prof., Dept of Math., Univ. of Moncton, Canada 1974–79; Reader, Dept of Computer Science, Univ. of Melbourne, Australia 1976–85; Researcher, IBM T. J. Watson Research Center, Yorktown Heights, NY 1985–96; Prof., New York Univ. 1993–96; Prof. of Computer Science, New Mexico Inst. of Tech. 1996–2002; Prof. and Chair. Dept of Computer Science, Coastal Carolina Univ., SC 2002–. *Publications:* Logic Programming: The 4th International Conference (ed.) 1987, Computational Logic – Essays in Honor of Alan Robinson (co-ed.) 1991; numerous articles in scientific journals. *Address:* Coastal Carolina University, Coastal Science Center 111, Conway, SC 29528-6054, USA (office). *Telephone:* (843) 349-2359 (office). *E-mail:* jlassez@coastal.edu (office). *Website:* www.coastal.edu (office).

LÁSZLÓ, Géza, BEcons, PhD; Hungarian business executive; *CEO, Antenna Hungária;* b. 1963; ed Univ. of Econ. Sciences, Budapest, Princeton Univ., USA; Man., Budapest Bank Rt. 1992–93; Sr Economist, Investel Rt. 1993–96; Strategic and Business Devt Dir, MATÁV Rt. 1996–98; Chair. Antenna Hungária 1998–2002, CEO 1999–; mem. Hungarian Acad. of Sciences 1996. *Address:* Petzvál József u. 31–33, 1119 Budapest, Hungary (office). *Telephone:* (1) 203–6060 (office). *Fax:* (1) 464–2525 (office). *E-mail:* antennah@ahrt.hu (office). *Website:* www.antenna.hu (office).

LATASI, Kamuta; Tuvaluan politician; fmr Minister of Health, Educ. and Community Services; Prime Minister of Tuvalu 1993–97, Minister of Foreign Affairs and Econ. Planning 1993–97. *Address:* c/o Office of the Prime Minister, Vaiaku, Funafuti, Tuvalu.

LATHAM, Mark, BEc; Australian politician; b. 28 Feb. 1961, Sydney; s. of Donald Charles Latham and Lorraine Lillian Latham; ed Sydney Univ.; Councillor, Liverpool Council 1987–94; mem. Fed. Parl. (Australian Labour Party) for Werriwa 1994–; Shadow Minister for Urban Devt and Housing 2001–02; Shadow Minister for Econ. Ownership and Community Security 2002–03; Fed. Parl. Leader Australian Labor Party 2003–Jan. 2005 (resgnd due to ill health). *Publications:* Reviving Labor's Agenda 1990, Social Capital 1998, Civilising Global Capital 1998, What Did You Learn Today? 2001, The Enabling State (co-Ed.) 2001. *Address:* c/o Australian Labor Party, Centenary House, 19 National Circuit, Barton, ACT 2600, Australia (office). *Website:* www.alp.org.au (office); www.marklatham.com.au.

LATHEEF, Mohamed; Maldivian politician; *Spokesperson, Maldivian Democratic Party;* one d.; fmr mem. Parl.; fmr Vice-Pres. Maldives Nat. Chamber of Commerce; Co-Founder Maldivian Democratic Party (banned opposition group), currently Spokesperson. *Address:* Maldivian Democratic Party (MDP), 1st Floor, M. Gloryge, Fareedhee Magu, Malé, The Maldives (office). *Telephone:* 3340044 (office). *Fax:* 3322960 (office). *E-mail:* secretariat@mdp.org.mv (office). *Website:* www.mdp.org.mv (office).

LATHEEF, Mohamed, MA, PhD; Maldivian diplomatist, politician and civil servant; m.; three c.; ed Univ. of Wales, UK, postgraduate studies in Cardiff Univ., Wales; mem. and Deputy Speaker People's Special Majlis (Ass.) 1979–97; Dir-Gen. Maldives Centre for Man. and Admin 1992–93; Nat. Dir Project for Public Admin. Reform 1992–93; Deputy Minister, Ministry of Atolls Admin 1993; Minister of Educ. 1993–2002; Vice-Chair. Nat. Educ. Council 1993–2002; mem. Parl. 2000–02; held posts at Ministry of Foreign Affairs and Embassy in Sri Lanka; Amb. to USA Feb. 2002–; Chargé d'affaires a.i., Perm. Mission of Maldives to UN Sept.–Nov. 2002, Perm. Rep. to UN Nov. 2002–08. *Address:* c/o Ministry of Foreign Affairs, Boduthakurufaanu Magu, Malé 20-307, Maldives (office).

LATORTUE, Gerald; Haitian academic, business consultant and politician; b. Gonaives; ed Inst. of Political Sciences and Inst. of Econ. and Social Devt, Paris; returned to Haiti to work as lawyer and law school Prof. 1960; flees Haiti 1963, lives in Jamaica, Washington DC, Puerto Rico working as econs teacher; joined UNO for Industrial Devt, living in Togo, Ivory Coast, and Vienna; returns to Haiti and named Minister of Foreign Affairs 1988; after coup four months later returns to UN; int. business consultant and radio show host Fla 1994; Host of Haitian TV Network of America talk shows Revue de la semaine and L'inviter 2003; Interim Prime Minister of Haiti March 2004–06. *Address:* c/o Office of the Prime Minister, Villa d'Accueil, Delmas 60, Musseau, Port-au-Prince, Haiti (office).

LATOUR-ADRIEN, Hon. Sir (Jean François) Maurice, Kt, LLB; Mauritian judge; b. 4 March 1915, Vacoas; s. of the late Louis C. E. Adrien and Maria E. Latour; ed Royal Coll., Mauritius, Univ. Coll., London and Middle Temple, London; called to the Bar, Middle Temple 1940 and in Mauritius 1946; District Magistrate 1947–48; Crown Counsel 1948–60; Asst Attorney-Gen. 1960–61; Solicitor-Gen. 1961–64; Dir of Public Prosecutions 1964–66; Puisne Judge 1966–70; Chief Justice of the Supreme Court of Mauritius 1970–77; Acting Gov.-Gen. Feb. 1973, July–Aug. 1974, Jan.–Feb. 1975, June–Aug. 1975, July–Sept. 1976; Pres. Mauritius Red Cross Soc. 1978–; Vice-Pres. Mauritius Mental Health Assn 1978–85, Pres. 1986–; Dir Mauritius Union Assurance Co. Ltd 1978–82, Chair. 1982–2005; Dir Mauritius Commercial Bank Ltd 1980–83, 1984–87, 1988–91, 1992–95, 1996–99, 2000–02; Legal Consultant 1983–, Dir 1992–95, 1996–99, 2000–02, Vice-Pres. 1993, Pres. 1994, Vice-Pres. 1996–97; Legal Consultant, Fincorp Investment Ltd (fmrly Mauritius Commercial Bank Finance Corpn) 1991–, Caudan Devt Co. Ltd 1991–, Mauritius Commercial Bank Registry and Securities Ltd 1991–, Promotion and Devt Co. Ltd 1985–; Dir Union and Policy Investment Ltd 1998–, Union and Policy Offshore Ltd 1998–, MUA Leasing Ltd 1998–; Co-Ed. Mauritius Law Reports 1970–77; mem. War Memorial Bd of Trustees 1978–84, Vice-Pres. 1985–; mem. Institut de Droit d'Expression Française; Kt Order of St Lazarus of Jerusalem 1969. *Leisure interests:* music, reading. *Address:* Vacoas, Mauritius (home). *Telephone:* 686-0389 (home).

LATTÈS, Robert; French business executive; b. 13 Dec. 1927, Paris; s. of Sadi Lattès and Renée Levi; m. Monique Lang 1949; two d.; ed Ecole Normale Supérieure; researcher in Pure Math., CNRS 1953–56; worked in math. physics and computers, French Atomic Energy Agency, Saclay 1956–59; joined Metra Group 1959, f. SIA (Société d'Informatique Appliquée) within Metra 1962, with SIA until 1974; Adviser to Chair. and Pres., then Exec. Vice-Pres. Paribas 1975–87; Pres. Pallas Venture 1988–95, Parindev 1988–95; Founding Chair., then Hon. Chair. Transgène 1980–87; Vice-Pres. Conseil supérieur du mercenat culturel, of Hemera Harfang Managers 1988–2000, of Pallas-Finance 1990–95, of Electra Fleming and Assocs 1994–96; Dir Expand SA, European Venture Capital Assn, Orchestre de Paris, Inst. des Vaisseaux et du Sang 1995–2000, Institut Pasteur, Lille 1995–2000; mem. Nat. Council on Cultural Devt 1971–73, Accounts and Budget Comm. 1976–81; mem. Bd of Dirs L'Institut Lumière; mem. Conseil des applications de l'Acad. des Sciences 2000, Conseil nat. des incubateurs et capital d'amorçage 1999–; mem. Acad. des Technologies; Officier, Légion d'honneur; Commdr, Ordre nat. du Mérite. *Achievements include:* winner of World Bridge Championship 1956. *Publications:* Méthode de Quasi-Réversibilité et Applications (with J.-L. Lions; trans. in English and other languages) 1967, Quelques problèmes aux limites de la Physique Mathématique 1967, Mille Milliards de dollars 1969, Matière grise année zero 1970, Pour une autre croissance 1973, La Fortune des Français 1977, L'Apprenti et le Sorcier (Les défis de l'innovation) 1988, Le Risque et la fortune 1990. *Leisure interests:* books, symphonic music, opera, art, cinema. *Address:* Académie des technologies, Grand Palais des Champs Elysées, Porte C, Avenue Franklin D. Roosevelt, 75008 Paris (office); 74 rue Raynouard, 75016 Paris, France (home). *Telephone:* 1-53-85-44-44 (office); 1-42-88-17-05 (home). *Fax:* 1-53-85-44-45 (office); 1-42-88-85-55 (home). *E-mail:* robert.lattes@academie-technologies.fr (office). *Website:* www.academie-technologies.fr (office).

LATTRE, André Marie Joseph de; French banker; b. 26 April 1923, Paris; m. Colette Petit 1947; three s. two d.; ed Univs de Paris à la Sorbonne and Grenoble and Ecole Libre des Sciences Politiques; Insp. of Finance 1946; with Ministry of Finance 1948–; Dept of External Finance 1949–54, Deputy Dir 1955–58; Alt. Exec. Dir IMF 1954; Prof. Inst. d'Etudes Politiques, Paris 1958–83; Financial Adviser to Pres. of the Repub. 1958–60; Perm. Sec. Ministry of Finance 1960–61; Dir of External Finance 1961; Censor, Bank of France 1962, Vice-Gov. 1966–74; Mission to India for Pres. IBRD 1965; Alt. Dir BIS 1973; Pres. Crédit National 1974–82; World Bank Special Rep. to IDA 1983; Man. Dir Inst. of Int. Finance, Washington 1983–86; Chair. Banque Française Standard-Chartered 1987–89; Chair. Banque Française de Service et de Crédit 1990–97; Commdr, Légion d'honneur and foreign awards.

Publications: Les Finances extérieures de la France 1959, Politique économique de la France depuis 1945 1967, Servir aux Finances 1999. *Leisure interests:* skiing, tennis. *Address:* 69 rue Perronet, 92200 Neuilly, France (home). *Telephone:* 1-46-24-79-00 (home).

LATYPAW, Ural Ramdrakovich, LLD; Belarusian (b. Bashkir) politician; *Head of Presidential Administration;* b. 28 Feb. 1951, Katayevo, Bashkir ASSR; m.; one s. one d.; ed Kazan State Univ., State and Law Inst., USSR Acad. of Sciences, Higher KGB courses in Minsk; researcher for KGB, involvement in anti-terrorist measures, latterly Deputy Chief, Educational and Research Centre, Minsk 1974–98; retd from mil. (rank of Col) 1993; Jt Founder, Head, Deputy Head for Research and Science, Research Inst. for Devt and Security, Repub. of Belarus 1993–94; Asst on int. affairs to Belarus Pres. 1994–95, Chief Asst to Pres. 1995–98; Minister of Foreign Affairs 1998–99; Deputy Prime Minister and Minister of Foreign Affairs 1999–2000; State Sec. Feb.–Sept. 2001; Head of Presidential Admin Sept. 2001–; mem. Belarus and Russian Asscns of Int. Law. *Publications:* Legislative Problems in Combating Terrorism; articles on legislative, nat. and int. security issues. *Address:* Office of the President, vul. K. Marksa 38, Dom Urada, 220016 Minsk, Belarus. *Telephone:* (17) 222-60-06.

LAU, Joseph, BSc; Hong Kong real estate executive; *Chairman and CEO, Chinese Estates Holdings Limited;* b. (Lau Luen-hung), Hong Kong; m. (divorced); three c.; ed Univ. of Windsor, Canada; family originated in Chaozhou, Guangdong Prov., China; has over 32 years' experience in corp. finance, manufacturing and property investment and devt; joined Chinese Estates Holdings Ltd 1989, currently Chair. and CEO; Dir (non-exec.) Lifestyle International Holdings Ltd. *Leisure interest:* collecting art. *Address:* Chinese Estates Holdings Ltd, 26/F, MassMutual Tower, 38 Gloucester Road, Wanchai, Hong Kong Special Administrative Region, People's Republic of China (office). *Telephone:* 2866-6999 (office). *Fax:* 2866-2822 (office). *E-mail:* corpcomm@chineseestates.com (office). *Website:* www.chineseestates.com (office).

LAU, Lawrence J., BS, MA, PhD, JP; Chinese economist, university administrator and academic; *President (Vice-Chancellor) and Ralph and Claire Landau Professor of Economics, Chinese University of Hong Kong;* ed Stanford Univ. and Univ. of California, Berkeley, USA; Acting Asst Prof. of Econs, Stanford Univ., USA 1966–67, Asst Prof. of Econs 1967–73, Assoc. Prof. of Econs 1973–76, Prof. of Econs 1976–2006, Kwoh-Ting Li Prof. of Econ. Devt 1992–2006, Kwoh-Ting Li Prof. of Econ. Devt Emer. 2006–, Vice-Chair. Dept of Econs 1990–92, Co-Dir Asia/Pacific Research Center 1992–96, Dir Stanford Inst. for Econ. Policy Research 1997–99, Sr Fellow, Inst. for Int. Studies 1992–2004, Sr Fellow, Hoover Inst. on War, Revolution and Peace 1997–2004, Sr Fellow, Stanford Inst. for Econ. Policy Research 1997–2007; Visiting Asst Research Economist, Univ. of California, Berkeley 1968–69; Visiting Prof. of Econs, Harvard Univ. 1978–79; Prof. of Econs, Chinese Univ. of Hong Kong 2004–, Ralph and Claire Landau Prof. of Econs 2007–, also Pres. (Vice-Chancellor) 2004–; JP, Hong Kong Special Admin. Region (SAR) 2007–; Non-official mem., Exec. Council, Govt of Hong Kong SAR 2009–; mem. 11th Nat. Cttee, CPPCC, People's Repub. of China 2008–; mem. editorial bds of several journals; Academician, Academia Sinica, Taipei 1982, Int. Eurasian Acad. of Sciences 1999; mem. American Econ. Asscn; Fellow, Econometric Soc.; Trustee, Hong Kong/Stanford Univ. Charitable Trust 1994–; Hon. Prof., Coll. of Man., Qing Hua Univ., Beijing 1987–, People's Univ. of China 1994–, Shantou Univ., 1994–, Inst. of Systems Science, Chinese Acad. of Sciences, Beijing 1996–, Nankai Univ., Tianjin 1998–, Nanjing Univ. 2000–, Southeast Univ., Nanjing 2000–; Hon. Research Fellow, Inst. of Quantitative and Tech. Econs, Chinese Acad. of Social Sciences, Beijing 1989–, Shanghai Acad. of Social Sciences 1998–; Hon. Mem. Chinese Acad. of Social Sciences, Beijing, 1997, Bd of Trustees, San Yuan Yu You-Ren Memorial Museum, San Yuan, Shaanxi, China 1997–; Hon DScS (Hong Kong Univ. of Science and Tech.) 1999; Hon. LLD (Waseda Univ.) 2007; Dr hc (Soka Univ.) 2007. *Publications:* Farmer Education and Farm Efficiency (co-author) 1982, Models of Development: A Comparative Study of Economic Growth in South Korea and Taiwan (ed. and contrib.) 1986, Econometrics and the Cost of Capital: Essays in Honor of Dale W. Jorgenson (ed. and contrib.) 2000, North Korea in Transition: Prospects for Economic and Social Reform (co-ed. and contrib.) 2001, US Direct Investment in China (co-author) 2002; more than 160 articles and notes in professional journals. *Address:* Office of the President and Vice-Chancellor, Room 101, 1/F, University Administration Building, Chinese University of Hong Kong, Shatin, New Territories, Hong Kong Special Administrative Region, People's Republic of China (office). *Telephone:* 2609-8600 (office). *Fax:* 2603-5230 (office). *E-mail:* lawrencelau@cuhk.edu.hk (office). *Website:* www.cuhk.edu.hk/v6/en/cuhk/officers/vc_biography.html (office).

LAU, Siu-Kai, JP, PhD; Chinese academic and political adviser; *Head, Central Policy Unit, Hong Kong Special Administrative Region;* b. 7 June 1947, Hong Kong; s. of Keng-por Lau and Wai-sin Fong; m. Sophie Lai-mui Kwok 1972; one s.; ed Univ. of Hong Kong, Univ. of Minnesota, USA; Assoc. Dir Hong Kong Inst. of Asia-Pacific Studies, Chinese Univ. of Hong Kong 1990–2002, Prof. of Sociology 1990–, Chair. Dept of Sociology 1994–2002; mem., Preparatory Cttee for Hong Kong Special Admin. Region 1996–97; Head, Central Policy Unit, Hong Kong Special Admin. Region 2002–; mem. CPPCC 2003–08; political commentator on Hong Kong issues on TV, radio and in newspapers and magazines. *Publications:* Society and Politics in Hong Kong 1982, The Ethos of the Hong Kong Chinese 1988. *Leisure interests:* reading, walking. *Address:* Room 507, Esther Lee Building, Hong Kong Institute of Asia-Pacific Studies, Chinese University of Hong Kong Shatin, NT, Hong Kong Special Administrative Region (office); Flat B3, 8/F Cloudview Mansion, 8 Lok Fung Path, Fotan, NT, Hong Kong Special Administrative Region, People's Republic of China (home). *Telephone:* 26098778 (office); 26096618 (office); 26036438 (home). *Fax:* 26035215 (office); 26035213 (office); 26036438 (home). *E-mail:* siukailau@cuhk.edu.hk (office). *Website:* www.cuhk.edu.hk/hkiaps (office); www.cuhk.edu.hk/soc/homepage.htm (office); www.info.gov.hk/cpu/ (office).

LAUDA, Andreas-Nikolaus (Niki); Austrian fmr racing driver; b. 22 Feb. 1949, Vienna; s. of Ernst Peter Lauda and Elisabeth Lauda; m. Marlene Knaus 1976; two s.; competed in hill climbs 1968, later in Formula 3, Formula 2 and sports car racing; winner 1972 John Player British Formula 2 Championship; started Formula 1 racing in 1971; World Champion 1975, 1977, 1984, runner-up 1976; retd 1979; returned to racing 1981, won US Formula 1 Grand Prix, British Grand Prix 1982, Dutch Grand Prix 1985; retd again 1985; f. LaudaAir 1979, Chair. –2000; CEO Ford Motor Co. Premier Performance Div. 2001–02; Head Jaguar Racing Team 2001–02; f. FlyNiki airline 2003; winner of Victoria Sporting Club's Int. Award for Valour in 1977, following recovery from near-fatal crash in 1976 German Grand Prix at Nürburgring. *Grand Prix wins:* 1974 Spanish (Ferrari), 1974 Dutch (Ferrari), 1975 Monaco (Ferrari), 1975 Belgian (Ferrari), 1975 Swedish (Ferrari), 1975 French (Ferrari), 1975 United States (Ferrari), 1976 Brazilian (Ferrari), 1976 South African (Ferrari), 1976 Belgian (Ferrari), 1976 British (Ferrari), 1977 South African (Ferrari), 1977 German (Ferrari), 1977 Dutch (Ferrari), 1978 Swedish (Brabham-Alfa Romeo); 1978 Italian (Brabham-Alfa Romeo). *Leisure interests:* music, skiing. *Website:* www.flyniki.com.

LAUDER, Evelyn; American (b. Austrian) business executive and photographer; b. (Evelyn Hausner), Vienna, Austria; d.-in-law of Estée Lauder (née Mentzer); m. Leonard A. Lauder (q.v.) 1959; two s.; ed Hunter Coll.; following her marriage joined family co. Estée Lauder, Head of Fragrance Devt Worldwide and Sr Corp. Vice-Pres. The Estée Lauder Companies, Inc.; Dir The Lauder Foundation; mem. Bd Central Park Conservancy and The Parks Council, New York; prominent campaigner in promoting breast cancer awareness and originator of pink ribbon symbol and Breast Self Exam 1992–; Founder Estée Lauder Companies' Breast Cancer Awareness Program; mem. Bd of Overseers, Memorial Sloan-Kettering's Cancer Center, built Evelyn H. Lauder Breast Center, New York 1992; f. The Breast Cancer Research Foundation 1993; heath-care activist and philanthropist; Hon. DH (Muhlenberg Coll., Pa) 1996; Chevalier, Légion d'honneur 2002; Greater New York Chapter of the Nat. Soc. of Fund Raising Execs' Philanthropists of the Year Award (jtly with her husband) 1993, Int. Woman's Forum New York Forum's Woman Who Has Made A Difference 1994, Soc. of Memorial Sloan-Kettering's Award for Excellence in Philanthropy 2001, Nat. Ethnic Coalition of Orgs Ellis Island Medal of Honor 2001, Council of Fashion Designer's of America Humanitarian Award 2002, Cosmetic Executive Women Lifetime Achievement Award 2004, FIFI Hall of Fame Lifetime Achievement Award, The Fragrance Foundation 2006, Partners in Progress Award, American Soc. of Clinical Oncology 2007. *Publication:* The Seasons Observed 1994, An Eye for Beauty 2002. *Leisure interests:* sports, travel, photography. *Address:* c/o The Estée Lauder Companies, Inc., 767 Fifth Avenue, New York, NY 10153, USA.

LAUDER, Leonard Alan; American business executive; *Chairman, Estée Lauder Companies Inc.;* b. 19 March 1933, New York; s. of the late Joseph Lauder and Estée Lauder (née Mentzer); m. Evelyn Hausner (q.v.) 1959; two s.; ed Wharton School, Univ. of Pennsylvania; with Estée Lauder Inc. (cosmetics and fragrance co.) New York 1958–, Exec. Vice-Pres. 1962–72, Pres. 1972–82, Pres. and CEO 1982–, now Chair.; Gov. Joseph H. Lauder Inst. of Man. and Int. Studies 1983–; Trustee Aspen Inst. for Humanistic Studies 1978–, Univ. of Pennsylvania 1977–; Pres. Whitney Museum of American Art 1977–. *Address:* Estée Lauder Inc., 767 Fifth Avenue, New York, NY 10153, USA (office). *Telephone:* (212) 572-4200 (office). *Fax:* (212) 572-6633 (office). *Website:* www.elcompanies.com (office).

LAUDER, Ronald Stephen, BS; American business executive and diplomatist; *President, World Jewish Congress;* b. 26 Feb. 1944, New York; s. of the late Joseph Lauder and Estée Lauder (née Mentzer); m. Jo Carole Knopf 1967; two d.; ed Bronx High School of Science, Wharton School of the Univ. of Pennsylvania, Univ. of Paris (Sorbonne), Univ. of Brussels; Estée Lauder NV Belgium 1965–67, Estée Lauder SA France 1967, Estée Lauder Sales Promotion Dir 1968–69, Vice-Pres. Sales Promotion, Clinique 1969–72, Exec. Vice-Pres., Gen. Man. Clinique, Inc. 1972–75, Exec. Vice-Pres. Estée Lauder Int. 1975–78, Exec. Vice-Pres. Estée Lauder Inc., Chair. Estée Lauder Int. 1978–83; Deputy Asst Sec. of Defense for European and NATO Policy 1983–86; Amb. to Austria 1986–87, pvt. investment man. New York 1987–, now E and Cen. Europe; Trustee, Museum of Modern Art 1975– (Chair. 1995–), Mt. Sinai Medical Center 1981–; Chair. and Pres. Lauder Investments; Chair. (non-exec.) Cen. European Devt Corpn (now Cen. European Media Enterprises Ltd); Pres. Jewish Nat. Fund 1997–; Pres. Ronald S. Lauder Foundation; Pres. World Jewish Congress 2007–; mem. NY Landmarks Conservancy's Advisory Bd, Bd of Govs Joseph H. Lauder Inst. of Man. and Int. Studies at Univ. of Pennsylvania, Visiting Cttee Wharton School, Int. Bd of Govs Tel-Aviv Museum, Chair. Bd Trustees Sakharov Archive at Brandeis Univ., US Holocaust Memorial Council, Bd Dirs Jewish Theological Seminary, Bd Dirs American Jt Jewish Distribution Cttee, Bd Trustees Anti-Defamation League Foundation, Bd Trustees Abraham Fund; Chevalier, Ordre nat. du Mérite; Great Cross of the Order of Aeronautical Merit with White Ribbon (Spain); Dept of Defense Medal for Distinguished Public Service; ranked 12 on ArtReview magazine's Power 100 list 2005. *Address:* World Jewish Congress, PO Box 90400, Washington, DC 20090, USA (office); Lauder Investments Inc., 767 Fifth Avenue, Suite 4200, New York, NY 10153. *Telephone:* (212) 755-5770 (office). *Fax:* (212) 755-5883 (office). *E-mail:* info@worldjewishcongress.org (home). *Website:* www.worldjewishcongress.org (office).

www.worldwhoswho.com

LAUDER, William P.; American business executive; *President and CEO, The Estée Lauder Companies Inc.;* grandson of co. founder Estée Lauder; m.; several c.; ed Wharton School, Univ. of Pennsylvania and Univ. of Grenoble, France; completed Macy's exec. training program, New York, later Assoc. Merchandising Man. New York Div./Dallas 1985; Regional Marketing Dir Clinique USA, The Estée Lauder Companies 1986, Vice-Pres./Gen. Man., later Pres. of Origins Natural Resources Inc. 1990–98, Pres. Clinique Laboratories 1998–2001, Pres. Clinique Worldwide and Group Pres. The Estée Lauder Companies 2001–03, COO The Estée Lauder Companies Inc. 2003–04, Pres., CEO and mem. Bd of Dirs 2004–; mem. Bd of Dirs Univ. of Pennsylvania, The Fresh Air Fund, The 92nd Street Y; mem. Bd of Trustees The Trinity School. *Leisure interests:* golf, skiing, tennis, hiking. *Address:* The Estée Lauder Companies Inc., 767 Fifth Avenue, New York, NY 10153-0023, USA (office). *Telephone:* (212) 572-4200 (office). *Fax:* (212) 572-6633 (office). *Website:* www.elcompanies.com (office).

LAUER, Reinhard, DPhil; German academic; *Professor Emeritus of Slavonic Philology, University of Göttingen;* b. 15 March 1935, Bad Frankenhausen; s. of Erich Lauer and Rose Fischer; m. Stanka Ibler 1962; one d.; ed Univs of Marburg, Belgrade and Frankfurt and Freie Univ. Berlin; reader in German Language, Univ. of Zagreb 1960–62; Research Fellow, Univ. of Frankfurt 1962–69; Prof. of Slavonic Philology and Head of Dept of Slavonic Philology, Univ. of Göttingen 1969–, now Prof. Emer.; mem. Göttingen Acad., Serbian Acad., Croatian Acad., Austrian Acad. of Sciences, Slovenian Acad.; Hon. mem. Bulgarian Philology Soc.; Valjavec Prize 1961, Yugoslav Flag with Golden Garland 1989. *Publications:* Heine in Serbien 1961, Gedichtform zwischen Schema und Verfall 1975, Europäischer Realismus (ed.) 1980, M. Krleža und der deutsche Expressionismus 1984, Sprachen und Literaturen Jugoslaviens (ed.) 1985, Poetika i ideologija 1987, Sprache, Literatur und Folklore bei Vuk St Karadžić (ed.) 1989, Kulturelle Traditionen in Bulgarien (co-ed.) 1989, Künstlerische Dialektik und Identitätssuche (ed.) 1990, Die Moderne in den Literaturen Südosteuropas (ed.) 1991, Höfische Kultur in Südosteuropa (co-ed.) 1994, Serbokroatische Autoren in deutscher Übersetzung (ed.) 1995, Slavica Gottingensia (ed.) 1995, Die Kultur Griechenlands in Mittelalter und Neuzeit (co-ed.) 1996, Die russische Seele 1997, Geschichte der russischen Literatur 2000, Deutsche und Slovakische Literatur (ed.) 2000, A. S. Puškins Werk und Wirkung (co-ed.) 2000, Philologie in Göttingen (ed.) 2001, Die literarische Avantgarde in Südosteurope und ihr politische und gesellschaftliche Bedeutung (ed.) 2001, Studije i rasprave 2002, Kleine Geshichte der russischen Literatur 2005. *Leisure interests:* music, painting, ornithology. *Address:* Seminar für Slavische Philologie der Universität Göttingen, Humboldt-Allee 19, 3400 Göttingen (office); Allensteiner Weg 32, 37120 Bovenden, Germany. *Telephone:* (551) 394702 (office); (551) 81375 (home). *E-mail:* slavist@gwdg.de (office). *Website:* wwwuser.gwdg.de/~slavist (office).

LAUGERUD GARCÍA, Gen. Kjell Eugenio; Guatemalan former head of state and army officer; b. 24 Jan. 1930, Guatemala City; s. of Pedro E. Laugerud and Catalina García; m. Helen Losi 1951; three s. two d.; Minister of Defence, Chief of Gen. Staff of Army 1970–74; presidential cand. of Movimiento de Liberación Nacional/Partido Institucional Democrático (MLN/PID) March 1974; Pres. of Guatemala 1974–78; mem. Asociación de Veteranos Militares de Guatemala (AVEMILGUA/AVMG) 1995–; numerous decorations, including Legion of Merit (USA) 1971, Gran Collar Orden del Quetzal (Guatemala) 1974, Gran Cruz Brillantes Orden de El Sol (Peru), Orden del Mérito (Chile) 1978. *Leisure interests:* horseback riding, collecting small arms, military history. *Address:* c/o Movimiento de Liberación Nacional (MLN), Of. 10a, Condiminio Reforma, Avda Reforma 10-00, Zona 9, Guatemala City, Guatemala.

LAUGHLIN, Robert B., AB, PhD; American physicist, academic and university administrator; *President, Korea Advanced Institute of Science and Technology (KAIST);* b. 1 Nov. 1950, Visalia, Calif.; m. Anita Rhona Perry 1979; two s.; ed Univ. of Calif. Berkeley, MIT; Postdoctoral Fellow Bell Telephone Labs 1979–81, Lawrence Livermore Nat. Lab. 1981–82; Assoc. Prof. of Physics, Stanford Univ. 1985–89, Prof. of Physics 1989, Robert M. and Anne Bass Professor of Physics –2004; Pres. Korea Advanced Inst. of Science and Tech. (KAIST), Taejon 2004–; Fellow, AAAS, American Physics Soc., American Acad. of Arts and Sciences, mem. Nat. Acad. of Sciences; E.O. Lawrence Award for Physics 1985, Oliver E. Buckley Prize 1986, Franklin Inst. Medal 1998, Nobel Prize in Physics (for discovery of a new form of quantum fluid with fractionally charged excitations) 1998. *Publications:* A Different Universe 2005; contrib. numerous papers in scientific journals. *Address:* Korea Advanced Institute of Science and Technology (KAIST), 373-1 Kusong-dong, Yusong-ku, Taejon 305-701, Republic of Korea (office). *Telephone:* (42) 869-2114 (office). *Fax:* (42) 869-2260 (office). *E-mail:* oir@sorak.kaist.ac.kr (office). *Website:* www.kaist.ac.kr (home).

LAUGHTON, Sir Anthony Seymour, Kt, PhD, FRS; British oceanographic scientist; b. 29 April 1927; s. of Sydney T. Laughton and Dorothy (Chamberlain) Laughton; m. 1st Juliet A. Chapman 1957 (dissolved 1962), one s.; m. 2nd Barbara C. Bosanquet 1973, two d.; ed Marlborough Coll. and King's Coll. Cambridge; RNVR 1945–48; John Murray Student, Columbia Univ., New York 1954–55; Nat. Inst. of Oceanography, later Inst. of Oceanographic Sciences 1955–88, fmr Dir; mem. Jt IOC/IHO Guiding Cttee GEBCO (ocean charts) 1974–2003, Chair. 1986–2003; mem. Council, Univ. Coll. London 1983–93; mem. Co-ordinating Cttee for Marine Science and Tech. 1987–91; Pres. Challenger Soc. for Marine Science 1988–90, Soc. Underwater Tech. 1995–97, Hydrographic Soc. 1997–99; mem. Governing Body Charterhouse School 1981–2000, Chair. 1995–2000; Trustee Natural History Museum 1990–95; Royal Soc. of Arts Silver Medal 1958, Prince Albert 1er Monaco Gold Medal 1980, Founders Medal, Royal Geographical Soc. 1987, Murchison Medal, Geological Soc. 1989. *Publications:* papers on marine geophysics. *Leisure interests:* music, gardening, sailing, woodwork. *Address:* Okelands, Pickhurst Road, Chiddingfold, Surrey, GU8 4TS, England (home). *Telephone:* (1428) 683941 (home). *E-mail:* asl@soc.soton.ac.uk (home).

LAUNDER, Brian Edward, ScD, DSc (Eng), DEng, FRS, FREng, FCGI, FIMechE, FRAeS; British engineer, academic and editor; *Research Professor, University of Manchester;* b. 20 July 1939, London; s. of Harry Edward Launder and Elizabeth Ann Launder (née Ayers); m. Dagny Simonsen 1968; one s. one d.; ed Enfield Grammar School, Imperial Coll., London, MIT, Cambridge, USA; Lecturer, then Reader, Mechanical Eng Dept, Imperial Coll., London 1964–76; Prof. of Mechanical Eng, Univ. of California, Davis 1976; Prof. of Mechanical Eng, UMIST (now Univ. of Manchester) 1980–98, Head, Mechanical Eng Dept 1983–85, 1993–95, Research Prof. 1998–; Dir Environmental Strategy Group 1998–2004; Regional Dir Tyndall Centre for Climate Change Research 2001–06; Ed.-in-Chief Int. Journal of Heat and Fluid Flow 1987–; mem. Scientific Advisory Bd CERFACS, Toulouse 1992–; assessor, Center for Turbulence Research, Stanford Univ., Calif. 1996–2004; Hon. Prof., Nanjing Aerospace Inst. 1993; Dr hc (Inst. Nat. Polytechnique, Toulouse) 1999, (Aristotle Univ., Thessaloniki, Greece) 2005, (Univ. Paul Cézanne, Aix-en-Provence) 2008; Busk Prize, Royal Aeronautical Soc. 1995, Computational Mechanics Award, Japan Soc. of Mechanical Engineers 1995, Daniel and Florence Guggenheim Award, Int. Council of Aeronautical Sciences 2000. *Publications include:* Mathematical Models of Turbulence 1972, Turbulent Shear Flows, Vols 1–9 (ed.), Computational Strategies for Turbulent and Transitional Flows (ed.) 2002 and over 250 papers on measurement and modelling of turbulent flow. *Leisure interests:* French culture and cuisine, bicycling and walking, photography. *Address:* School of Mechanical, Aerospace and Civil Engineering, University of Manchester, PO Box 88, Manchester, M60 1QD, England (office). *Telephone:* (161) 306-3801 (office). *Fax:* (161) 306-3723 (office). *E-mail:* brian.launder@manchester.ac.uk (office). *Website:* www.manchester.ac.uk (office).

LAURA, Ernesto Guido; Italian film festival director; b. 4 May 1932, Villafranca, Veronese; s. of the late Manuel Laura and of Pia Romei Laura; m. Anna Maria Vercellotti 1958; two s.; ed Dept of Law, Catholic Univ., Milan; Co-Nat. Sec. Centri Universitari Cinematografici 1953–54; Admin. Nat. Sec. Federazione Italiana Circoli del Cinema 1954–55; Chief Ed. Bianco e Nero 1956–58, Filmlexicon 1968; Film Critic, Il Veltro 1958–; mem. Editorial Bd Rivista del Cinematografo 1967–; Pres. Immagine, Centro Studi Iconografici 1968–; Dir Venice Film Festival 1969–; has directed various film documentaries including Diario di Una Dama Veneziana 1958, Riscoperta di un Maestro 1960, Alla Ricerca di Franz Kafka 1964, Spielberg 1964, Don Minzoni (Special Award) 1967. *Publications:* Il Film Cecoslovacco 1960, La Censura Cinematografica 1961, Ladri di Biciclette 1969.

LAUREDO, Luis J., BA; American diplomatist, lawyer and business executive; m. Maria Regina Lauredo; two d.; ed Columbia Univ., Univ. of Madrid, Spain and Georgetown Univ.; Commr, Fla Public Service Comm. 1992–94; Exec. Dir Summit of the Americas 1994; Pres. Greenberg Taurig Consulting Inc.; Perm. Rep. to OAS 1999–2001; consultant Hunton & Williams law firm 2001–; mem. Presidential Advisory Cttee for Trade Promotion Negotiations 2003–; Exec. Dir FTAA Ministerial and American Business Forum 2003; Sr Vice-Pres., Export-Import Bank of the United States; Trustee Pan-American Devt Foundation; Chair. Miami Int. Press Center; mem. Bd Hispanic Council on Foreign Affairs. *Address:* Hunton & Williams, 1111 Brickell Avenue, Suite 2500, Miami, FL 33131, USA (office). *Telephone:* (305) 810-2500 (office). *Fax:* (305) 810-2460 (office). *Website:* www.hunton.com/offices/miami.html (office).

LAUREL, Salvador Hidalgo, AB, LLD; Philippine politician; b. 18 Nov. 1928, Manila; s. of José P. Laurel; m. Celia Franco Diaz Laurel; eight c.; ed Univ. of the Philippines and Yale Univ., USA; senator 1967–73 until imposition of martial law; Prof. of Law and Jurisprudence; f. Legal Aid Soc. of the Philippines; mem. interim Nat. Ass. 1978; active in opposition politics 1982–; Leader, United Nationalist Democratic Org. 1981–91, Union for Nat. Action 1988–91; Vice-Pres. of Philippines 1986; Prime Minister Feb.–March 1986; Minister of Foreign Affairs 1986–87, Pres. Nacionalista Party 1989.

LAUREN, Ralph; American couturier; b. 14 Oct. 1939, Bronx, NY; s. of Frank Lifschitz and Frida Lifschitz; m. Ricky Low-Beer 1964; two s. one d.; ed DeWitt Clinton High School, the Bronx, NY and City Coll. of New York; changed name from Lifschitz to Lauren aged 16; served in US Army 1962–64; salesman, Bloomingdale's, New York, Brooks Bros New York (cr. Polo label for them); Asst Buyer, Allied Stores, New York; Rep. Rivetz Necktie Mfrs New York; neckwear designer, Polo Div., Beau Brummel, New York 1967–69; est. Polo Menswear Co., New York 1968–, Ralph Lauren's Women's Wear, New York 1971–, Polo Leathergoods 1978–, Polo Ralph Lauren Luggage 1982–, Ralph Lauren Home Collection 1983–; Chair. Polo Ralph Lauren Corpn (66 stores in USA, over 140 world-wide); cr. other brands, including Chaps, Club Monaco, Purple Label, Polo Jeans Co., Ralph Lauren Rugby 2004; recipient of many fashion awards including American Fashion Award 1975, Council of Fashion Designers of America Award 1981, CFDA Lifetime Achievement Award 1992, CFDA American Fashion Legend Award 2007. *Publication:* Ralph Lauren 2007. *Leisure interest:* collecting and showing classic automobiles. *Address:* Polo Ralph Lauren Corporation, 650 Madison Avenue, New York, NY 10022, USA (office). *Telephone:* (212) 318-7000 (office). *Fax:* (212) 888-5780 (office). *Website:* www.polo.com (office).

LAURÉN, Reidunn, DIur; Swedish lawyer and politician; m.; three c.; fmr Judge Admin. Court of Appeal, Stockholm; fmr Deputy Sec. Parl. Standing Cttee on Social Affairs; Legal Adviser Ministry of Labour; Perm. Under-Sec. Ministry of Housing and Physical Planning; Justice of the Supreme Admin.

Court; Chair. Labour Court; Chair. Equal Opportunities Tribunal; Minister for Constitutional and Civil Law 1991–93; Pres. Admin. Court of Appeal 1994–97; Chair. Queen Sophia's Hosp. 1995–2002; King's Medal for distinguished legal service 2000. *Publications:* Equal Opportunities at Work for Women and Men; numerous articles on legal matters. *Address:* Administrative Court of Appeal, Box 2302, 103 17 Stockholm, Sweden. *Telephone:* 700-3801.

LAURENS, André Antoine; French journalist; *Vice-President and Director-General, L'Indépendant;* b. 7 Dec. 1934, Montpellier (Hérault); s. of André Laurens and Mme Laurens (née Raymonde Balle); ed Lycée de Montpellier; journalist, L'Eclaireur Meridional (fortnightly), Montpellier 1953–54, Agence centrale de Presse, Paris 1958–62; mem. political staff, Le Monde 1963–69, Asst to head of political Dept 1969–82; Dir Le Monde 1982–84, Chief writer 1986–, Ombudsman 1994–; Vice-Pres. Soc. des Rédacteurs; Vice-Pres. and Dir-Gen. L'Indépendant 2000–. *Publications:* Les nouveaux communistes 1972, D'une France à l'autre 1974, Le Métier politique ou la conquête du pouvoir 1980. *Address:* L'Independant, Mas de la Garrigue, 2 avenue Alfred Sauvy, BP 105, 66605 Rivesaltes (office); 58 rue de la Roquette, Paris 75011 (home); 1 Espace Mediterraneé, Perpignan 66605 , France (home). *Telephone:* 4-68-64-88-88 (office). *Fax:* 4-68-64-88-49 (office). *Website:* www.lindependant.com (office).

LAURENT, Jean, MSc, CE; French banking executive and administrator; *Chairman, Board of Directors, Calyon;* b. 31 July 1944, Mazamet; m.; five c.; ed École Nat. Supérieure d'Aéronautique, Wichita State Univ., USA; Dir AMACAM Co. 1994–, Indocam 1996–, Indosuez Bank of Pvt. Man. 1998–, Crédit Lyonnais Oct. 1999–; Chair. Bd Segespar May 1999– (Dir 1994–), Union of Studies and Investments June 1999–, (Dir 1996–); fmr CEO Crédit Agricole SA; Vice-Pres. Banca Intesa and Bank Espirito Santo 1999–, Bd of Trustees Crédit Agricole Indosuez 2000–; Pres. Fédération Bancaire Française, A.F.E.C.E.I. 2001–; currently Chair. Bd of Dirs Calyon; Chevalier, Légion d'honneur, Officier, Ordre du Mérite agricole. *Address:* Calyon, 9 Quai du President Paul Dourner, 9290 La Défense cedex, Paris, France (office). *Telephone:* 1-41-89-00-00 (office). *Fax:* 1-57-87-04-23 (office). *Website:* www.calyon.com (office).

LAURENT, Torvard Claude, MD, PhD; Swedish biochemist and academic; *Professor Emeritus of Medical and Physiological Chemistry, University of Uppsala;* b. 5 Dec. 1930, Stockholm; s. of Torbern Laurent and Bertha Svensson; m. Ulla B. G. Hellsing 1953; one s. two d.; ed Karolinska Inst., Stockholm; Instructor Karolinska Inst. 1949–52, 1954–58; Research Fellow and Research Assoc. Retina Foundation, Boston, USA 1953–54, 1959–61; Assoc. Prof. in Medical Chem., Univ. of Uppsala 1961–66, Prof. of Medical and Physiological Chem. 1966–96, Prof. Emer. 1996–; mem. Swedish Natural Science Research Council 1968–70, Swedish Medical Research Council 1970–77; Chair. Swedish Biochemical Soc. 1973–76; Visiting Prof. Monash Univ. 1979–80; Pres. Swedish Royal Acad. of Sciences 1991–94; mem. Nobel Cttee of Chem. 1992–2000; Science Sec., Wenner-Gren Foundation 1993–2002; Officier, Ordre nat. du Mérite 2000; Hon. MD (Turku) 1993, (Bergen) 2000; Hon. PharmD (Bologna) 1994; Anders Jahre Prize, Univ. of Oslo 1968, Pharmacia Award 1986, Eric Fernström Nordic Prize in Medicine, Lund Univ. 1989, Björkén Prize, Univ. of Uppsala 1990, King Carl XVI Gustaf's Gold Medal 1994, Rudbeck Award, Univ. of Uppsala 2006. *Publications:* approx. 230 scientific papers. *Address:* Department of Medical Biochemistry and Microbiology, University of Uppsala BMC, Box 582, 751 23 Uppsala (office); Hävelvägen 9, 756 47 Uppsala, Sweden (home). *Telephone:* (18) 471-41-55 (office); (18) 30-96-12 (home). *Fax:* (18) 471-46-73 (office). *E-mail:* Torvard.Laurent@imbim.uu.se.

LAURENTS, Arthur, BA; American playwright; b. 14 July 1917, New York; s. of Irving Laurents and Ada Robbins; ed Cornell Univ.; radio scriptwriter 1939–40; mem. Screenwriters Guild, Acad. Motion Picture Arts and Sciences; Dir La Cage aux Folles (Tony Award) 1983, Sydney (Best Dir Award) 1985, London 1986, Birds of Paradise 1987; screenwriter, co-producer film The Turning Point 1977; writer and Dir of several Broadway plays including The Enclave 1973, Gypsy 1974, 1989; mem. Acad. of Motion Picture Arts and Sciences, Authors League, Dramatists Guild, PEN, Screenwriters Guild, Theatre Hall of Fame; Tony Award 1967, 1984, Drama Desk Award 1974, William Inge Festival Award 2004. *Publications:* novels: The Way We Were 1972, The Turning Point 1977; memoirs: Original Story By 2000, Mainly on Directing: Gypsy, West Side Story and Other Musicals 2009; screenplays: The Snake Pit 1948, Rope 1948, Caught 1948, Anna Lucasta 1949, Anastasia 1956, Bonjour Tristesse 1958, The Way We Were 1972, The Turning Point (Writers Guild of America Award, Screenwriters' Guild Award and Golden Globe Award) 1978; plays: Home of the Brave (American Acad. of Arts and Letters Award) 1946, The Bird Cage 1950, The Time of the Cuckoo 1952, A Clearing in the Woods 1956, Invitation to a March 1960, The Enclave 1973, Scream 1978, Jolson Sings Again 1995, The Radical Mystique 1995, My Good Name 1997, Big Potato 2000, Venecia (also dir) 2001, Claude Lazlo 2001, The Vibrator 2002, Closing Bell 2002, Attacks on the Heart 2003, Two Lives 2003, Collected Plays 2004; musical plays: West Side Story 1957, Gypsy 1959, Anyone Can Whistle 1964, Do I Hear a Waltz? 1964, Hallelulah Baby 1967, Nick and Nora 1991. *Leisure Interest:* skiing. *Address:* William Morris Agency, 1325 Avenue of the Americas, New York, NY 10019, USA (office). *Website:* www.wma.com (office).

LAURIE, (James) Hugh Callum, OBE; British actor and writer; b. 11 June 1959; s. of the late (William George) Ranald (Mundell) Laurie; m. Jo Laurie 1989; two s. one d.; ed Eton Coll., Univ. of Cambridge; fmr Pres. Footlights, Univ. of Cambridge. *Television appearances:* Santa's Last Christmas, Alfresco (series, also writer) 1983, The Crystal Cube (also writer) 1983, Mrs Capper's Birthday 1985, Saturday Live (writer) 1986, A Bit of Fry and Laurie (series,

also writer) 1986–91, The Laughing Prisoner (also writer) 1987, Blackadder the Third (series) 1987, Up Line 1987, Blackadder: The Cavalier Years 1988, Les Girls (series) 1988, Blackadder's Christmas Carol 1988, Blackadder Goes Forth (series) 1989, Hysteria 2! 1989, Jeeves and Wooster (series) 1990–92, Treasure Island (series) 1993, All or Nothing at All 1993, Look at the State We're In! (series, also dir) 1995, The Adventures of Mole 1995, The Best of Tracey Takes On… 1996, The Place of Lions 1997, Blackadder Back & Forth 1999, Little Grey Rabbit (series) 2000, Preston Pig (series) 2000, Life with Judy Garland: My and My Shadows 2001, Second Star to the Left 2001, Spooks (series) 2002, Stuart Little (series) 2003, Fortysomething (series, also dir) 2003, The Young Visiters [sic] 2003, House (Golden Globe Award for Best Performance in a Drama TV Series 2006, Golden Globe Award for Best Actor in a Drama TV Series 2007, Screen Actors' Guild Award for Outstanding Performance by a Male Actor in a Drama Series 2007) 2004–. *Films:* Plenty 1985, Strapless 1989, Peter's Friends 1992, A Pin for the Butterfly 1994, Sense and Sensibility 1995, 101 Dalmatians 1996, The Snow Queen's Revenge 1996, The Borrowers 1997, Spice World 1997, The Ugly Duckling 1997, The Man in the Iron Mask 1998, Cousin Bette 1998, Stuart Little 1999, Carnivale 2000, Maybe Baby 2000, Lounge Act 2000, The Piano Tuner 2001, Chica de Río 2001, Stuart Little 2 2002, Flight of the Phoenix 2004, Street Kings 2008. *Publications:* Fry and Laurie 4 (with Stephen Fry) 1994, The Gun Seller 1996, The Paper Soldier 2009. *Address:* c/o Lorraine Hodell, Hamilton Hodell Ltd, 5th Floor, 66–68 Margaret Street, London, W1W 8SR, England (office). *Telephone:* (20) 7636-1221 (office). *Fax:* (20) 7636-1226 (office). *E-mail:* info@hamiltonhodell.co.uk (office). *Website:* www.hamiltonhodell.co.uk (office).

LAURIE, Robert Stephen, AM, BA; Australian diplomatist (retd); b. 5 Nov. 1936, Sydney; s. of the late W. R. Laurie; m. Diana V. M. Doyne 1969; one s. one d.; ed Knox Grammar School and Univ. of Sydney; joined Dept of External Affairs (now Dept of Foreign Affairs and Trade) 1958; served Colombo 1960, Moscow 1960–63; First Sec. Washington 1965–68; Counsellor, Hong Kong 1968–69; Deputy High Commr in India 1969–71; Amb. to Burma 1975–77, to Poland 1977–80; High Commr in Canada 1985–89, in New Zealand 1989–92; First Asst Sec., South Pacific, Middle East and Africa Divs, Dept of Foreign Affairs and Trade 1993–97; High Commr in India 1997–2001. *Leisure interests:* tennis, cricket, golf, music. *Address:* c/o Department of Foreign Affairs and Trade, Canberra, ACT 2600; 31 Arthur Circle, Manuka, ACT 2603, Australia.

LAURISTIN, Marju, PhD; Estonian politician, sociologist and academic; *Professor Emerita of Social Communication, Tartu University;* b. 7 April 1940, Tallinn; d. of Johannes Lauristin and Olga Lauristin; m. Peeter Vihalemm 1978; two d.; ed Tartu Univ.; sociologist and Head of Dept of Journalism, Tartu Univ. –1989, Prof. 1993, Prof. of Social Communication 2003, now Prof. Emer.; mem. CPSU –1990; f. Popular Front of Estonia 1988–92; Chair. Estonia Social-Democratic Party 1990–94; USSR People's Deputy 1989–90; Deputy Speaker of Estonian Supreme Soviet (now Parl.) 1990–92; mem. Estonian Parl. 1992–95, 1999–2003; Minister of Social Affairs 1992–94; mem. Advisory Cttee for the Protection of Nat. Minorities, Council of Europe 2004–; mem. Bd European Sociological Asscn 2007–; mem. United Nations Univ. Council 2004–; Order of Nat. Coat of Arms, Third Class 1998, Second Class 2003, Kt, Order of the White Rose, First Class, Finland 2003; Dr hc (Univ. of Helsinki) 2006; Democracy and Civil Soc. Award, USA and EU 1998. *Publication:* Return to the Western World: Cultural and Political Perspectives on the Estonian Post-Communist Transition (ed. with P. Vihalemm), The Challenge of the Russian Minority: Emerging Multicultural Democracy in Estonia (jt ed.) 2002. *Leisure interest:* literature. *Address:* Siili 6, Apt 35, Tartu 50104 (home); Ülikooli 18, Tartu 50090, Estonia (office). *Telephone:* (7) 375-188 (office); (7) 471-532 (home). *Fax:* (7) 376-355 (office). *E-mail:* marju.lauristin@ut.ee (home). *Website:* www.jrnl.ut.ee (office).

LAUTENBERG, Frank R., BS, DHL; American politician and business executive; *Senator from New Jersey;* b. 23 Jan. 1924, Paterson, NJ; s. of Samuel and Mollie Lautenberg; m.; one s. three d.; ed Columbia Univ.; f. Automatic Data Processing Inc., Clifton, NJ 1953, Exec. Vice-Pres. Admin. 1961–69, Pres. 1969–75, Chair. and CEO 1975–82; Senator from NJ 1982–2001, 2003–; Nat. Pres. American Friends of Hebrew Univ. 1973–74; Gen. Chair. and Pres. Nat. United Jewish Appeal 1975–77; Commr Port Authority, New York; mem. Int. Bd of Govs Hebrew Univ., Jerusalem; mem. Pres.'s Comm. on the Holocaust; f. Lautenberg Center for Gen. and Tumor Immunology, Medical School, Hebrew Univ., Jerusalem 1971; fmr Pres. Asscn of Data Processing Service Orgs; mem. Advisory Council, Columbia Univ. School of Business; mem. Bd Dirs eSpeed Inc. 2002; Hon. DHL (Hebrew Union Coll., Cincinnati and New York) 1977; Hon. PhD (Hebrew Univ., Jerusalem) 1978; Torch of Learning Award, American Friends of Hebrew Univ. 1971; Scopus Award 1975. *Address:* Hart Senate Office Building, Suite 324, Washington, DC 20510 (office); 405 Route 3, Clifton, NJ 07015, USA (home). *Telephone:* (202) 224-3224 (office). *Fax:* (202) 228-4054 (office). *Website:* lautenberg.senate.gov (office).

LAUTI, Rt Hon. Toaripi, PC; Tuvaluan politician; b. 28 Nov. 1928, Papua New Guinea; m.; three s. two d.; ed Queen Victoria School, Fiji, Wesley Coll., Paerata, NZ, St Andrew's Coll., Christchurch, Christchurch Teachers' Coll.; teacher in Tarawa, Gilbert Is (now Kiribati) 1953–62; Labour Relations and Training Officer for Nauru and Ocean Is Phosphate Comm. 1962–74; returned to Ellice Is (now Tuvalu) 1974; Chief Minister of Tuvalu 1975–78, Prime Minister 1978–81 (replaced as a result of his alleged involvement in investment scandal); Leader of the Opposition 1981–90; Gov. Gen. of Tuvalu 1990–93; also fmr Minister of Finance and Foreign Affairs. *Address:* PO Box 84, Funafuti, Tuvalu.

LAUTMANN, Rüdiger, DPhil, DJur; German sociologist and academic; *Professor, Department of Sociology, University of Bremen;* b. 22 Dec. 1935,

Koblenz; s. of Kurt Lautmann and Sibylle Lautmann; Research Asst, Univ. of Bielefeld and Dortmund 1968–71; Prof. of Sociology, Law School, Univ. of Bremen 1971–82, Dept of Sociology 1982–; Pres. Inst. of Research in Security and Prevention, Hamburg. *Publications:* Wert und Norm 1969, Die Funktion des Rechts in der modernen Gesellschaft (co-ed.) 1970, Die Polizei (co-ed.) 1971, Soziologie vor den Toren der Jurisprudenz 1971, Justiz–die stille Gewalt 1972, Seminar Gesellschaft und Homosexualität 1977, Rechtssoziologie–Examinatorium (co-ed.) 1980, Der Zwang zur Tugend 1984, Die Gleichheit der Geschlechter und die Wirklichkeit des Rechts 1990, Das pornographierte Begehren (co-author) 1990, Männerliebe im alten Deutschland (co-ed.) 1992, Homosexualität (ed.) 1993, Vom Guten, das noch stets das Böse schafft (co-ed.) 1993, Die Lust am Kind 1994, Der Homosexuelle und sein Publikum 1997, Ausgrenzung macht krank (co-author) 2000, Soziologie der Sexualität 2002, NS–Terror gegen Homosexuelle (co-ed.) 2002, Punitivität (co-ed.) 2004, Lexikon zur Soziologie (co-ed.) 2007. *Leisure interest:* theatre. *Address:* University of Bremen, Fachbereich 8, Bremen 28334 (office); Holzdamm 41, 20099 Hamburg, Germany (home). *Telephone:* (40) 2802503. *Fax:* (40) 2802509. *E-mail:* lautmannhh@aol.com (home). *Website:* www.lautmann.de (office).

LAUTNER, Georges Charles; French film director; b. 24 Jan. 1926, Nice; s. of Charles Lautner and Marie-Louise Vittoré; m. Caroline Ragon 1950; one s. one d.; ed Lycée Janson-de-Sailly, Ecole Montcel, Paris, Ecole Libre des Sciences Politiques and Faculté de Droit, Paris; Commdr des Arts et Lettres, Chevalier, Légion d'honneur; Prix de l'Amicale des cadres de l'industrie cinématographique. *Films include:* Goubbiah, mon amour (actor) 1956, La môme aux boutons 1958, Marche ou crève 1960, Arrêtez les tambours 1960, Le monocle noir 1961, En plein cirage 1961, Le septième juré 1962, L'oeil du monocle 1962, Les tontons flinguers 1963, Des pissenlits par la racine 1964, Le monocle rit jaune 1964, Les barbouzes 1964, Les bons vivants 1965, Galia (aslo actor) 1966, Ne nous fâchons pas 1966, La grande sauterelle 1967, Fleur d'oseille 1968, Le pacha 1968, La route de Salina 1971, Laisse aller... c'est une valse 1971, Il était une fois un flic... 1971, Quelques messieurs trop tranquilles 1973, La valise 1973, Les seins de glace 1974, Pas de problème! 1975, On aura tout vu 1976, Mort d'un pourri 1977, Ils sont fous ces sorciers 1978, Flic ou voyou 1979, Le guingolo 1980, Est-ce bien raisonnable? 1981, Le professionnel 1981, Attention! Une femme peut en cacher une autre (also actor) 1983, Joyeuses Pâques 1984, Le cowboy 1984, La cage aux folles III 1985, La vie dissolue de Gérard Floque 1987, La maison assassinée 1988, L'invitée surprise 1989, Présumé dangereux 1990, Triplex 1991, Room Service 1992, L'inconnu dans la maison 1992, Scénario sur la drogue (segment Le bistrot) 2000, Scénarios sur la drogue: Le bistrot 2000. *Television includes:* Le Gorille (series) 1990, Prêcheur en eaux troubles 1992, L'homme de mes rêves 1994, Le comédien 1996, Les redoubtables (series) 2001, La trilogie des 'Monocle' (writer) 2003. *Publications:* Fontu Fourbi 2000, On aura tout vu 2005. *Address:* 1 boulevard Richard Wallace, 92200 Neuilly-sur-Seine (home); 9 chemin des Basses Ribes, 06130 Grasse, France. *Telephone:* (4) 93-36-30-06 (office); 1-47-22-09-63 (home). *Fax:* (4) 93-36-00-10 (office). *E-mail:* glautner@wanadoo.fr (office).

LAUVERGEON, Anne Alice Marie; French government official and business executive; *Chairman of the Executive Board, Areva Group;* b. 2 Aug. 1959, Dijon; d. of Gérard Lauvergeon and Solange Martellière; m. Jean-Eric Molinard 1986; ed Lycées Lakanal, Sceaux, Lycée Voltaire, Orléans, Ecole Normale Supérieure and Ecole Nat. Supérieure des Mines, Paris; began her professional career in iron and steel industry, first in Canada, then with Usinor 1983–84; Eng Inst. for Protection and Nuclear Safety, Centre d'Energie Atomique and Head of Div. Direction Régionale de l'Industrie et de la Recherche, Ile-de-France 1985–88; Asst to Head of Service of Conseil-Général des Mines 1988–89; Adviser on int. econ. and foreign trade, Presidency of Repub. 1990; Deputy Sec.-Gen. Presidency of Repub. 1990–95; Partner and Man. Lazard Frères & Cie 1995–98; Deputy Dir-Gen. Alcatel Alsthom 1997–, mem. Exec. Cttee Alcatel Group 1998; Pres., Dir-Gen. Compagnie générale des matières nucléaires (Cogema) 1999–, Chair. Exec. Bd Areva Group (formed by merger of Cogema, CEA-Industrie, Framatome) 2001–; Vice-Pres. Bd of Dirs Société d'applications générales d'électricité et de mécanique (Sagem) 2000–; mem. Strategy, Ethics and Environment Cttees, Suez Lyonnaise Group 2000; Dir Total Fina Elf 2000–; mem. Bd Pechiney 1996–, Framatome 1998; ranked by Fortune magazine amongst 50 Most Powerful Women in Business outside the US (second) 2001, (third) 2002, (third) 2003, (first) 2004, (first) 2005, (second) 2006, (second 2007), ranked by Forbes magazine amongst 100 Most Powerful Women (53rd) 2004, (11th) 2005, (eighth) 2006, (14th) 2007, (ninth) 2008, ranked by the Financial Times amongst Top 25 Businesswomen in Europe (second) 2005, (second) 2006, (first) 2007. *Publication:* Sur les traces des dirigeants ou la vie du chef dans les grandes entreprises (co-author) 1988. *Address:* Areva Group, 27–29 rue Le Peletier, 75009 Paris Cedex 9 (office); Cogema, 2 rue Paul Dautier, BP 4, 78141 Vélizy-Villacoublay (office); Sagem, 6 avenue d'Iéna, 75116 Paris, France (office). *Telephone:* 1-44-83-71-00 (Areva) (office). *Fax:* 1-44-83-25-00 (Areva) (office). *Website:* www.arevagroup.com (office).

LAUZANNE, Bernard, LèsL; French journalist; b. 22 June 1916, Paris; s. of Gaston Lauzanne and Sylvia Scarognino; m. Lucie Gambini 1949; two d.; ed Lycée Condorcet and Univ. of Paris; war service and prisoner of war in Germany 1939–45; joined Radiodiffusion Française (RTF) and worked on programme 'Paris vous parle' 1945–59; Chief Sub-Ed., Le Monde 1945–59, News Ed. 1959–69, Asst Ed. 1969–74, Ed. 1974–78, Man. Ed. 1978–83; Directeur de Collection Éditions Denoël 1983–; Pres. France-Japan Asscn, Comité d'histoire de la radiodiffusion 1991–; Lauréat de l'Acad. française 1987; Chevalier, Légion d'honneur, Croix de guerre, Commdr of Sacred Treasure, Japan. *Leisure interests:* music, theatre, painting. *Address:* Éditions Denoël, 9 rue du Cherche-Midi, 75278 Paris Cedex 06 (office); 5 rue Jean-Bart, 75006 Paris, France (home). *Telephone:* 1-42-84-01-74.

LAVADOS MONTES, Hugo, MA; Chilean politician; *Minister of the Economy, Economic Promotion and Reconstruction;* b. Aug. 1949, Talca; m.; two c.; ed Univ. of Chile, Boston Univ., USA; Gen. Man. Manpower Chile 1983–90; Supervisor, Valores y Seguros 1990–94; Gen. Man. Banco BHIF 1994–98; Dir ProChile (govt agency to promote exports) 2003–06; Minister of the Economy, Econ. Promotion and Reconstruction 2008–; mem. Anti-Trust Comm. 1990–94; Prof. of Econs, Univ. of Chile; fmr consultant to World Bank and Inter-American Devt Bank. *Address:* Ministry of the Economy, Economic Promotion and Reconstruction, Teatinos 120, 10°, Santiago, Chile (office). *Telephone:* (2) 672-5522 (office). *Fax:* (2) 696-6305 (office). *E-mail:* economia@economia.cl (office). *Website:* www.economia.cl (office).

LAVAGNA, Roberto; Argentine politician and economist; b. 24 March 1942, Buenos Aires; ed Univ. of Buenos Aires and Univ. of Brussels, Belgium; fmr mem. Radical Party; Sec. of Industry and Foreign Trade –1987; mem. Justicialist Party; Visiting Researcher, Center for Int. Affairs, Harvard Univ., USA 1995; fmr Prof., Univ. of Buenos Aires; Dir Ecolatina consulting firm 1995; Amb. to EU 2000–02; Minister of Economy 2002–05. *Address:* c/o Ministry of the Economy, Hipólito Yrigoyen 250, 1310 Buenos Aires, Argentina (office).

LAVANT, Denis; French actor; b. 17 June 1961, Neuilly-sur-Seine, Hauts-de-Seine. *Films include:* Les Misérables 1982, Paris ficelle 1983, Coup de foudre 1983, L'homme blessé (The Wounded Man) 1983, Viva la vie! (Long Live Life) 1984, Boy Meets Girl 1984, Partir, revenir (Going and Coming Back) 1985, Mauvais sang (Bad Blood) 1986, L'étendu 1987, Un tour de manège (Roundabout) 1989, Mona et moi (Mona and I) 1989, C'est merveilleux 1991, Les amants du Pont-Neuf (The Lovers on the Bridge, USA) 1991, Drôle d'immeuble 1992, Fuis la nuit 1993, De force avec d'autres (Forced to Be with Others) 1993, La partie d'échecs (The Chess Game) 1994, L'ennemi 1995, Visiblement je vous aime (Obviously I Need You) 1995, Yasaeng dongmul bohoguyeog (Wild Animals) 1996, Don Juan 1998, Le monde à l'envers 1998, Cantique de la racaille (Melody for a Hustler, USA) 1998, Beau travail (Good Work) 1999, Tuvalu 1999, Promenons-nous dans les bois (Deep in the Woods) 2000, La squale (The Squale) 2000, Married/Unmarried 2001, Affaire Libinski 2001, La merveilleuse odyssée de l'idiot Toboggan (voice) 2002, Luminal 2004, Un long dimanche de fiançailles (A Very Long Engagement) 2004, Camping sauvage 2005, Mister Lonely 2006. *Television includes:* L'ombre sur la plage 1982, Hôtel du siècle (series) 1985, Oscar et Valentin 1986.

LAVAUDANT, Georges; French theatre director; *Director, Odéon-Théâtre de l'Europe;* b. 18 Feb. 1947, Grenoble (Isère); first production Lorenzaccio by Musset, Théâtre Partisan, Grenoble 1975; Co-Dir Centre Dramatique Nat. des Alpes 1976–, Maison de la Culture de Grenoble 1981, Théâtre nat. populaire de Villeurbanne (Rhône) 1986–96; Dir Odéon-Théâtre de l'Europe, Paris 1996–. *Productions include:* Le Régent by Jean-Christophe Bailly 1987, texts of Denis Roche (Louve basse), Pierre Bourgeade (Palazzo Mentale), Jean-Christophe Bailly (Les Céphéides and Pandora), Michel Deutsch (Féroé, la nuit...), Le Clézio (Pawana), Veracruz, Les Iris, Terra Incognita, Ulysse/Matériaux, interspersed with productions of works by Musset, Shakespeare, Chekhov, Brecht, Labiche, Pirandello, Genet and others; Comédie Française: Lorenzaccio, Le Balcon, Hamlet; Opéra de Paris: Roméo et Juliette by Gounod; Opéra de Lyon: L'enlèvement au sérail by Mozart, Malcolm by Gérard Maimone, Rodrigue et Chimène by Debussy; in Mexico City: Le Balcon, Pawana; in Montevideo: Isidore Ducasse/Fragments; in Bhopal: Phèdre; in Hanoi: Woyzeck; in St Petersburg: Reflets, Lumières (I) 'Près des ruines' 1995, Lumières (II) 'Sous les arbres' 1996, Théâtre Maly de St Petersburg in Russian adapation of Lumières: Reflets 1997, Prova d'orchestra by Giorgio Battistelli, Opéra du Rhin 1997; Odéon-Théâtre de l'Europe: Le Roi Lear by Shakespeare 1996, Bienvenue by Lavaudant 1996, Reflets by Jean-Christophe Bailly 1997, Ajax et Philoctête by Sophocle (Petit Odéon) 1997, Histoires de France (in collaboration with Michel Deutsch) 1997, Un chapeau de paille d'Italie by Eugène Labiche 1997, La dernière nuit by Lavaudant (Petit Odéon) 1997, Pawana by Jean-Marie Le Clézio 1997, La noce chez les petits bourgeois et Tambours dans la nuit by Bertolt Brecht 1998, L'Orestie by Aeschylus 1999, Les Géants de la Montagne by Pirandello (in Catalan) 1999, Fanfares 2000, Un fil à la patte by Feydeau 2001, La mort de Danton by Büchner 2002, El Pelele by Jean-Christophe Bailly 2003, The Cherry Orchard by Chekhov 2004, La rose et la hache 2004, Les Cenci 2007; Ateliers Berthier, Paris: Cassandre 2006; Centre dramatique nat. de Montreuil: Troïlus et Cressida 2007. *Address:* Odéon-Théâtre de l'Europe, Place de l'Odéon, 75006 Paris, France (office). *Telephone:* 1-44-85-40-40 (office).

LAVE, Lester B., BA, PhD; American economist and academic; *Harry B. and James H. Higgins Professor of Economics and University Professor, Tepper School of Business, Carnegie-Mellon University;* b. 5 Aug. 1939, Philadelphia, Pa; m. Judith Rice 1965; one s. one d.; ed Reed Coll., MIT and Harvard Univ.; Prof. of Econs, Carnegie-Mellon Univ. 1963–, Harry B. and James H. Higgins Prof. of Econs 1984, 1992–, also Univ. Prof., also currently Dir, Carnegie Mellon Green Design Initiative, Co-Dir, Carnegie Mellon Electricity Industry Center; Sr Fellow, Brookings Inst. 1978–82; Visiting Asst Prof., Northwestern Univ. 1965–66; consultant, Gen. Motors Research Labs, US Depts of Justice, Defense, Transportation, Health and Welfare, Environmental Protection Agency, Nuclear Regulatory Comm., NSF, Office of Tech. Assessment; Pres. Soc. for Risk Analysis 1985–86; George Leland Bach Teaching Award 1987. *Publications:* Technological Change 1966, Air Pollution and Human Health 1977, The Strategy of Social Regulation 1981, Scientific Basis of Health & Safety Regulation 1981, Clearing the Air 1981, Quantitative Risk Assessment 1982, Toxic Chemicals, Health and the Environment (with A. Upton) 1987; more than 200 scientific articles. *Leisure interests:* swimming, skiing. *Address:*

Graduate School of Industrial Administration, Carnegie-Mellon University, 5000 Forbes Avenue, Pittsburgh, PA 15213, USA (office). *Telephone:* (412) 268-2000 (office). *Fax:* (412) 268-7838 (office). *E-mail:* LL01@andrew.cmu.edu (office). *Website:* public.tepper.cmu.edu (office).

LAVELLI, Jorge; French theatre and opera director; b. Buenos Aires, Argentina; ed Ecole Charles Dullin et Jacques Lecoq, Paris, Université du Théâtre des Nations; Dir Théâtre Nat. de la Colline 1987–96; fmr Pres. Centre français de l'Institut Int. du Théâtre (UNESCO); Chevalier de la Légion d'honneur; Chevalier, Ordre nat. du Mérite, Commdr, Ordre des Arts et Lettres; Cross of Commdr Order of Merit, Poland. *Plays include:* Le Mariage, Paris 1963, Berlin Festival 1964 (Grand Prix at Concours nat. des jeunes compagnies), Jeux de Massacre, Paris 1970 (Prix de la Critique), Le Roi se meurt, Paris 1976 (Prix Dominique de la mise en scène, Prix de la Critique), Doña Rosita La Soltera, Madrid, Jerusalem and Caracas Festivals and Paris 1980; at Théâtre Nat. de la Colline: Une Visite inopportune by Copi 1988 (Prix de la meilleure création française, Syndicat de la Critique), Réveille-toi Philadelphie 1988 (Prix de la meilleure création d'une pièce française, Syndicat de la Critique), La Veillée 1989, Greek 1990 (Molière Prize for best production), La Nonna 1990, Heldenplatz 1991, 1992, Le Désarroi de Monsieur Peters 2002, La Hija del aire 2004, Merlin ou la terre dévastée 2005, Himmelweg 2007. *Operas include:* The Trial (by Von Einem), Vienna State Opera 1970, Idomeneo, Angers 1975, Faust, Opéra de Paris 1975, L'Heure Espagnole and L'Enfant et les Sortilèges, La Scala Milan 1975, La Traviata, Aix-en-Provence Festival 1976, Faust, Metropolitan Opera, New York, Kennedy Center, Washington 1976, Pelléas et Mélisande, Opéra de Paris 1977, Fidelio, Toulouse 1977, Madame Butterfly, La Scala, Milan and Opéra de Paris 1978, Alcina, Aix-en-Provence Festival 1978, Carmen, Strasbourg, Brussels 1978, Oedipus Rex, Opéra de Paris 1979, Le Nozze di Figaro, Aix-en-Provence Festival, Liège 1979, Dardanus (by Rameau), Opéra de Paris 1980, Les Arts Florissants (by Charpentier), Versailles 1982, Norma, Bonn 1983, Salome, Zürich 1986, La Clemenza di Tito, Hamburg 1986, The Makropoulos Affair, Buenos Aires 1986, Die Zauberflöte, Aix-en-Provence Festival 1989, Die Entführung aus dem Serail, Aix-en-Provence Festival 1990, Cecilia 2000, Siroe 2000, Ariodante 2001, Medea 2001–02, L'Enfant et les sortilèges 2002–03, Faust 2003; several opera productions for TV. *Address:* c/o Théâtre National de la Colline, 15 rue Malte Brun, 75020 Paris, France.

LAVENTHOL, David, MA; American publisher; b. 15 July 1933, Philadelphia; s. of Jesse Laventhol and Clare Horwald; m. Esther Coons 1958; one s. one d.; ed Yale Univ. and Univ. of Minnesota; reporter, later News Ed., St Petersburg Times 1957–63; City Ed. New York Herald Tribune 1963–66; Asst Man. Ed. The Washington Post 1966–69; Assoc. Ed. Newsday 1969, Exec. Ed. 1969–70, Ed. 1970–78, Publr and CEO 1978–86, Chair. 1986–87; Group Vice-Pres. Times Mirror 1981–86, Sr Vice-Pres. 1986, Pres. 1987–93; CEO and Publr LA Times 1989–93; Ed.-at-Large Times Mirror Co., LA 1994–98, Consultant Ed. 1998–99; Ed. and Publr Columbia Journalism Review 1999–2003; Chair. Pulitzer Prize Bd 1988–89; Vice-Chair. Int. Press Inst. 1985–92, Chair. 1992–95; Chair. Museum of Contemporary Art, LA 1993–97, Cttee to Protect Journalists –2005; Dir Newspaper Advertising Bureau, American Press Inst. 1988–, LA Times Washington Post/News Service, Times Mirror Foundation, United Negro Coll. Fund; mem. Bd Dirs Assoc. Press 1993–96, Columbia Journalism School 1995–, Nat. Parkinson Foundation 1995–, Saratoga Performing Arts Center 1993–96; mem. American Soc. of Newspaper Eds Writing Awards Bd, American Newspaper Publr Asscn, Century Asscn, Council on Foreign Relations. *Address:* c/o Columbia Journalism Review, Columbia University, 2950 Broadway, New York, NY 10027, USA (office).

LAVER, Rod(ney) George, MBE; Australian fmr tennis player; b. 9 Aug. 1938, Rockhampton, Queensland; s. of R. S. Laver; m. Mary Benson 1966; one s.; ed Rockhampton Grammar and High Schools; turned professional 1963; Australian Champion 1960, 1962, 1969; Wimbledon Champion 1961, 1962, 1968, 1969; USA Champion 1962, 1969; French Champion 1962, 1969; only player to win two Grand Slams 1962, 1969; played Davis Cup for Australia 1958, 1959, 1960, 1961, 1962 and 1973 (first open Davis Cup); in a 23-year career won 47 professional titles; Int. Tennis Hall of Fame 1981; Melbourne Park centre court renamed Rod Laver Arena in his honour 2000. *Publications:* How to Play Winning Tennis 1964, Education of a Tennis Player 1971. *Leisure interests:* golf, fishing, skiing. *Address:* c/o Tennis Australia, Private Bag 6060, Richmond South, Vic. 3121, Australia.

LAVER, William Graeme, PhD, FRS; Australian biochemist and academic; b. 3 June 1929; s. of Lawrence Laver and Madge Laver; m. Judith Garrard Cahn 1954; one s. two d.; ed Univ. of Melbourne, Univ. of London; Tech. Asst Walter and Eliza Hall Inst. of Medical Research 1947–52; Research Asst Dept of Biochemistry, Univ. of Melbourne 1954–55; Research Fellow, John Curtin School of Medical Research, ANU 1958–62, Fellow 1962–64, Sr Fellow 1964–; Head, Influenza Research Unit, ANU 1983–2001; Australia Prize (jtly) 1996. *Publications:* numerous papers on the structure of influenza viruses, devt of anti-viral drugs and on the origin and control of pandemic influenza. *Leisure interests:* climbing volcanoes, raising beef cattle, viticulture. *Address:* Barton Highway, Murrumbateman, NSW 2582, Australia. *Telephone:* (2) 6227-0061 (office). *Fax:* (2) 6227-0062 (office). *E-mail:* graeme.laver@bigpond.com (office); wgraemelaver@hotmail.com (home).

LAVEROV, Nikolai Pavlovich, DGeol Mineral Sc; Russian geologist; *Vice-President, Russian Academy of Sciences;* b. 12 Jan. 1930, Pozharishche, Archangel Region; s. of Pavel Nikolavich Laverov and Klavdia Savvateevna Laverova; m.; two d.; ed Moscow Inst. of Nonferrous Metals; mem. CPSU 1959–91; participated in geological expeditions, Jr researcher, scientific sec. on geological stations of Inst. of Geology, Ore Deposits, Mineralogy and Chemistry 1958–66; Deputy Chief Dept of research orgs., USSR Ministry of

Geology 1966–68, Chief 1968–72; Scientific Leader on research of Resources of Urals Project 1972–87; Corresp. mem. USSR (now Russian) Acad. of Sciences 1979, mem. 1987, Vice-Pres. 1988–; Prof., Prorector, Head of Chair of Ecology and rational use of natural resources, Acad. of Nat. Econs, USSR Council of Ministers 1983–87; Pres. Acad. of Sciences of Kirghiz SSR 1987–89; Vice-Chair. USSR Council of Ministers, Chair. Cttee on Science and Tech. 1989–91; mem. Cen. CPSU Cttee 1990–91; Head of Comms of Acad. of Sciences investigating consequences of earthquake in Armenia 1988–; Chair. USSR Nat. Cttee of Geologists 1990–91; Pres. Lomonosov Fund 1992–; Head Comm. on problem of safe burial of radioactive waste; Ed.-in-Chief Geology of Ore Deposits. *Publications:* works on geology of uranium deposits, continental volcanism, econs of mineral products. *Address:* Presidium of Russian Academy of Sciences, Leninsky prospekt 12, 117901 Moscow, Russia (office). *Telephone:* (495) 954-29-68 (office).

LAVIER, Bertrand; French artist; b. 14 June 1949, Châtillon-sur-Seine; s. of Jean Lavier and Geneviève Duteil; m. Gloria Friedmann 1989; ed Ecole Nat. Supérieure d'Horticulture; landscape artist and town planner, Marne Lavallée New Town 1971–72; at Centre de Recherches et d'Etudes sur le Paysage, Paris 1973–75; artist 1974–; First Prize (Sculpture), Biennale, Budapest 1984, Grand Prix Nat. de la Sculpture 1994. *Publication:* Bertrand Lavier présente la peinture des Martin de 1603 à 1984 1984. *Leisure interests:* hunting, motor-racing, tennis. *Address:* Galerie Durand-Dessert, 28 rue de Lappe, 75011 Paris (office); rue La Demoiselle, 21510 Aignay-le-Duc, France (home).

LAVIN, Franklin L., BSc, MSc, MA, MBA; American business executive, fmr government official and fmr diplomatist; *Managing Director and Chief Operating Officer, Cushman & Wakefield Investors Asia;* b. OH; m.; three c.; ed Georgetown Univ., Johns Hopkins Univ., Univ. of Pennsylvania; served as Deputy Exec. Sec., Nat. Security Council and Dir Office of Political Affairs during Reagan Admin; Deputy Asst Sec. of Commerce for Asia and Pacific during George H. W. Bush Admin; sr man. positions Citibank and Bank of America in Hong Kong and Singapore 1996–2001; Amb. to Singapore 2001–05; Under-Sec. of Commerce for Int. Trade, Int Trade Admin 2005–07; Man. Dir and COO Cushman & Wakefield Investors Asia, Hong Kong 2007–; fmr Lt Commdr in USNR; fmr mem. Council on Foreign Relations, IISS. *Address:* Cushman & Wakefield Investors Asia, 6th Floor, Henley Bldg, 5 Queen's Road, Central Hong Kong Special Administrative Region, People's Republic of China (office). *Telephone:* 29563888 (office). *Website:* www.cushwake.com (office).

LAVÍN, Joaquín; Chilean politician and economist; *Mayor of Santiago;* b. (Joaquín José Lavín Infante), 23 Oct. 1953, Santiago; s. of Joaquín Lavín Pradenas and Carmen Infante Vial; m. María Estela León Ruiz; seven c.; ed Pontificia Univ. Católica de Chile, Univ. of Chicago; econ. adviser, ODEPLAN (Ministry for Planning) 1975–77, Dean Faculty of Econ. and Admin. Sciences, Concepción Univ. 1979–81; Econ. Ed. El Mercurio 1986–88; fmr Sec.-Gen. UDI (Ind. Democratic Union); Dean Faculty of Econs and Business, Univ. del Desarrollo 1996–98; Mayor Las Condes 1992–96, 1996–2000; presidential cand. 1999, 2005; Mayor of Santiago 2000–; Founder La Vaca (NGO); mem. Opus Dei. *Publications:* Miguel Kast: Pasión de Vivir 1986, Chile Revolución Silenciosa 1987. *Address:* Partido Unión Demócrata Independiente, Suecia 286, Santiago, Chile (office). *E-mail:* joaquin@joaquinlavin.cl (office). *Website:* www.joaquinlavin.cl (office).

LAVIZZO-MOUREY, Risa, MBA, MD; American physician and foundation executive; *President and CEO, The Robert Wood Johnson Foundation;* b. Seattle, Wash.; m.; two c.; ed Harvard Medical School and Wharton School, Univ. of Pennsylvania; residency in internal medicine, Brigham and Women's Hosp., Boston, Mass; fmr Robert Wood Johnson Clinical Scholar, Univ. of Pennsylvania; fmr Deputy Admin. Agency for Health Care Policy and Research (now Agency for Health Care Research and Quality), Dept of Health and Human Services; fmr Co-Chair. Working Group on Quality of Care, White House Task Force on Health Care Reform; Sylvan Eisman Prof. of Medicine and Health Care Systems and Dir Inst. on Aging, Univ. of Pennsylvania –2001; Sr Vice-Pres. and Dir Health Care Group, The Robert Wood Johnson Foundation 2001–03, Pres. and CEO The Robert Wood Johnson Foundation 2003–; mem. several cttees, including Nat. Cttee for Vital and Health Statistics (Chair. Sub-cttee on Minority Populations), Pres.'s Advisory Comm. on Consumer Protection and Quality in the Health Care Industry, Bd of Dirs American Bd of Internal Medicine, Bd of Regents American Coll. of Medicine; Co-Dir Inst. of Medicine study on racial disparities in health care, resulting in the publication of Unequal Treatment, Confronting Racial and Ethnic Disparities in Health Care 2004; mem. Inst. of Medicine (NAS); two hon. doctorates; numerous awards, including those from Harvard School of Public Health, Dept of Health and Human Services, NAS, American Coll. of Physicians, Nat. Library of Medicine, American Medical Women's Asscn, Nat. Medical Asscn, Univ. of Pennsylvania, ranked by Forbes magazine amongst 100 Most Powerful Women (22nd) 2008. *Publications:* several books and numerous articles. *Address:* The Robert Wood Johnson Foundation, PO Box 2316, College Road East and Route 1, Princeton, NJ 08543, USA (office). *Telephone:* (888) 631-9989 (office). *Website:* www.rwjf.org (office).

LAVRENTYEV, Mikhail Mikhailovich; Russian mathematician; *Director, S.L. Sobolev Institute of Mathematics, Russian Academy of Sciences;* b. 21 July 1932, Krasny Liman, Ukraine; m.; three c.; ed Moscow State Univ.; jr, then sr researcher, then Head of Lab. S. L. Sobolev Inst. of Math., Siberian Br. USSR (now Russian) Acad. of Sciences 1957–64, Dir 1986–, Head of Lab., then Deputy Dir Computation Centre 1964–86; mem. Russian Acad. of Sciences 1981; Lenin Prize 1962, USSR State Prize 1987. *Address:* S.L. Sobolev Institute of Mathematics, Universitetsky prosp. 4, 630090 Novosibirsk, Russia (office). *Telephone:* (3832) 35-44-50 (office).

LAVROV, Sergei Viktorovich; Russian diplomatist and politician; *Minister of Foreign Affairs;* b. 21 March 1950, Moscow; m. Mariya Lavrova; one d.; ed Moscow State Inst. of Int. Relations; has served in diplomatic service since 1972; attaché, USSR Embassy in Sri Lanka 1972–76, Sec., Dept of Int. Econ. Orgs, Ministry of Foreign Affairs 1976–81, Sec. and Counsellor, Perm. Mission of USSR to UN, New York 1981–88; Deputy Chair., then Chair. Dept of Int. Econ. Relations, Ministry of Foreign Affairs 1988–90; Dir Dept of Int. Orgs and Global Problems, Ministry of Foreign Affairs 1990–92, Deputy Minister of Foreign Affairs 1992–94, Perm. Rep. to UN, New York 1994–2004, Minister of Foreign Affairs 2004–; Order of Honour 1996, Order of Service to the Nation 1997. *Leisure interest:* white-water rafting. *Address:* Ministry of Foreign Affairs, 119200 Moscow, Smolenskaya-Sennaya pl. 32/34, Russia (office). *Telephone:* (495) 244-16-06 (office). *Fax:* (495) 230-21-30 (office). *E-mail:* ministry@mid.ru (office). *Website:* www.mid.ru (office).

LAVROVSKY, Mikhail Leonidovich; Russian ballet dancer, choreographer and academic; *Artistic Director, Stanislavsky and Nemirovitch-Danchenko State Theatre, Moscow;* b. 29 Oct. 1941, Tbilisi, Georgia; s. of Leonid Lavrovsky and Yelena Chikvaidze; m. Dolores García Ordonyez 1986; one s.; ed Moscow Coll. of Choreography, Moscow State Inst. of Theatre Art; soloist Bolshoi Theatre 1963–88, coach Bolshoi Theatre 1992–; Prof. Moscow Coll. of Choreography 1988–94; Prof. of Choreography, Moscow Sate Inst. of Theatre Art 2002–; Artistic Dir Stanislavsky and Nemirovitch-Danchenko State Theatre, Moscow 2005–; prize winner, Int. Competition in Varna, Bulgaria 1965, Lenin Prize 1970, Nizhinsky Prize, Paris Acad. of Dance 1972, USSR People's Artist 1976, USSR State Prize 1977. *Repertoire includes:* Giselle, Flames of Paris, Cinderella, Legend about Love, Don Quixote, Romeo and Juliet, Nutcracker, Angara, Paganini, Ivan the Terrible, Anyuta, Spartacus, Swan Lake, Bayadère. *Choreography:* Mtsiri (ballet film) (First Prize New York Film Festival 1978) 1977, Prometheus (ballet film) 1981, Porgy and Bess 1983, Novella (Bach and Liszt) 1986, Bach Suite No. 2 for Flute 1987, Plastic Ballet Revelations (Kikta), Fantasy on the Theme of Casanova (Mozart) 1987, 1993, The Dreamer 1989, Revelations 1991, Jazz Café 1992, More powerful than Gold and Death 1996, Giselle (with Leonid Lavrovsky), Richard III 2000, Diaghilev in Nijinsky 2000, Matador 2001. *Films include:* choreography and lead role Ali Baba and the Forty Thieves (Dir Kakhagadze), Fantasior (Dir Bunin). *Publication:* From Myself to My Friends. *Leisure interests:* sport, fencing, reading, painting, philosophy, drama, cinema. *Address:* Bolshoi Theatre, Teatralnaya pl. 1, Moscow (office); Voznesensky per. 16/4, Apt. 7, 125009 Moscow, Russia (home). *Telephone:* (495) 991-31-16 (office); (495) 629-27-71 (office); (495) 629-65-49 (home). *E-mail:* cbasgarcia@condenast.ru (office); lavrovsky@mail.ru (office). *Fax:* (495) 629-94-42 (home). *Website:* www.lavrovsky.com (office).

LAW, HE Cardinal Bernard F., BA; American ecclesiastic; b. 4 Nov. 1931, Torreón; s. of Bernard A. Law and Helen Stubblefield; ed Harvard Univ.; ordained 1961; Bishop of Springfield-Cape Girardeau 1973; Archbishop of Boston 1984–2002 (resgnd); cr. Cardinal by Pope John Paul II 1985 and maintains that rank despite resignation. *Address:* c/o Cardinal's Residence, 2101 Commonwealth Avenue, Brighton, MA 02135, USA.

LAW, Jude; British actor; b. 29 Dec. 1972, London; s. of Peter Law and Maggie Law; m. Sadie Frost 1997 (divorced 2003); one step-s. two s. one d.; fmrly with Nat. Youth Music Theatre; co-f. Natural Nylon (production co.), Dir 2000–03; Chevalier, Ordre des Arts et des Lettres 2007; Hon. César Award 2007. *Stage appearances include:* Joseph and the Amazing Technicolor Dreamcoat, Les Parents Terribles 1994, Ior 1995, Tis A Pity She's A Whore 1999, Doctor Faustus 2002. *Film appearances include:* Shopping 1994, I Love You I Love You Not 1996, Wilde 1997, Gattaca 1997, Midnight in the Garden of Good and Evil 1997, Bent, Music From Another Room 1998, Final Cut 1998, The Wisdom of Crocodiles 1998, eXistenZ 1999, The Talented Mr Ripley (BAFTA Award for Best Supporting Actor) 1999, Enemy at the Gates 2000, Love Honour and Obey 2000, AI: Artificial Intelligence 2001, Road to Perdition 2002, Cold Mountain 2003, Sky Captain and the World of Tomorrow 2004, Alfie 2004, I Heart Huckabees 2004, The Aviator 2004, Lemony Snicket's A Series of Unfortunate Events (voice) 2004, Breaking and Entering 2006, All the King's Men 2006, The Holiday 2006, My Blueberry Nights 2007, Sleuth 2007. *Address:* c/o Julian Belfrage Associates, 46 Albemarle Street, London, W1S 4DF, England. *Website:* www.jude-law.net (office).

LAW, Phillip Garth, AC, CBE, MSc, FTSE, FAA, FRSV, FAIP, FANZAAS, FRGS; Australian scientist, Antarctic explorer and educationist; b. 21 April 1912, Tallangatta, Vic.; s. of the late Arthur James Law and Lillie Law; m. Nel Allan 1941; ed Ballarat Teachers' Coll. and Univ. of Melbourne; Science master in secondary schools 1933–38; Tutor in Physics Newman Coll., Melbourne Univ. 1940–45 and Lecturer in Physics 1943–47; Research Physicist and Asst Sec. Scientific Instrument and Optical Panel, Ministry of Munitions 1940–45; Scientific Mission to New Guinea battle areas for the Australian Army 1944; Sr Scientific Officer Aust. Nat. Antarctic Research Expeditions 1947–48, Leader 1949–66; Dir Antarctic Div., Dept of External Affairs 1949–66; Australian Observer Norwegian-British-Swedish Antarctic Expedition 1950; led expeditions to establish first perm. Australian research station at Mawson, MacRobertson Land 1954, stations at Davis, Princess Elizabeth Land 1957 and at Casey 1965; exploration of coast of Australian Antarctica 1954–66; mem. gov. council Melbourne Univ. 1959–78, La Trobe Univ. 1964–74; Exec. Vice-Pres. Victoria Inst. of Colls 1966–77; Chair. Australian Nat. Cttee on Antarctic Research 1966–80, Royal Melbourne Inst. of Tech. Foundation 1994–99; mem. Council of Science Museum of Vic. 1968–83; Pres. Royal Soc. of Vic. 1967, 1968, Graduate Union, Univ. of Melbourne 1972–77, Victorian Inst. of Marine Sciences 1978–80, Australia and NZ Scientific Exploring Soc. 1976–81, Patron 1982–; Fellow Royal Soc. of Vic., Australian Acad. of Technological Sciences and Eng, Australian Acad. of Science; Hon. Fellow

Royal Melbourne Inst. of Tech.; several hon. degrees including Hon. DAppSci (Melbourne), Hon. DSc (La Trobe), Hon. DEd (Vic. Inst. of Colls); Award of Merit Commonwealth Professional Officers Asscn 1957, Clive Lord Memorial Medal Royal Soc. of Tasmania 1958, Founder's Medal Royal Geographical Soc. 1960, John Lewis Gold Medal Royal Geographical Soc. of Australia 1962, Vocational Service Award Melbourne Rotary Club 1970, James Cook Medal of the Royal Soc. of NSW 1988, Gold Medal Australian Geographic Soc. 1988, Pres.'s Award, Australian Scouts Asscn 1996, Clunies Ross Nat. Award for Lifetime Contribs to Science and Tech. 2001. *Publications:* ANARE (with Bechervaise) 1957, Antarctic Odyssey 1983, The Antarctic Voyage of H.M.A.S. Wyatt Earp 1995, You Have to be Lucky 1995, also numerous articles on Antarctic exploration and research and papers on cosmic rays, thermal conductivity, optics and education. *Leisure interests:* writing, music, tennis, skiing, swimming. *Address:* 3 Balwyn Manor, 23 Maleela Avenue, Balwyn, Vic. 3103, Australia (home).

LAWLER, James Ronald, MA, DUP; Australian academic; *Professor Emeritus, Department of Romance Languages and Literatures, University of Chicago;* b. 15 Aug. 1929, Melbourne; m. Christiane Labossière 1954 (died 2004); one s. one d.; ed Univs of Melbourne and Paris, France; lecturer in French, Univ. of Queensland 1955–56; Sr Lecturer, Univ. of Melbourne 1956–62; Prof. of French, Head of Dept, Univ. of Western Australia 1963–71; mem., Australian Research Grants Cttee 1969–72; Prof. of French, Chair., Univ. of Calif., Los Angeles 1971–74; McCulloch Prof. of French, Dalhousie Univ. 1974–79; Prof. of Romance Languages, Univ. of Chicago 1979, Edward Carson Waller Distinguished Service Prof. 1983–97, Prof. Emer. 1998–; Visiting Prof. Collège de France 1985; Pres. Asscn Int. des Etudes Françaises 1998–2002; Pres. Soc. des Amis de Rimbaud 2006–; Ed. Rimbaud Vivant 2006–; Carnegie Fellowship 1961–62; Myer Fellow, Australian Acad. of the Humanities; Commonwealth Interchange Visitor 1967; Foundation Fellow, Australian Acad. of the Humanities 1969; Guggenheim Fellowship 1974; Nat. Endowment of Humanities Fellowship 1984–85; Prix Int. des Amitiés Françaises 1986, Prix du Rayonnement de la Langue Française, Acad. Française 1999; Officier, Ordre des Palmes académiques. *Publications:* Form and Meaning in Valéry's Le Cimetière Marin 1959, An Anthology of French Poetry 1960, Lecture de Valéry: Une Etude de Charmes 1963, The Language of French Symbolism 1969, The Poet as Analyst: Essays on Paul Valéry 1974, Paul Valéry: An Anthology 1976, René Char: The Myth and the Poem 1978, Edgar Poe et les Poètes français 1989, Paul Valéry (ed.) 1991, Rimbaud's Theatre of the Self 1992, Poetry and Moral Dialectic: Baudelaire's Les Fleurs du Mal 1997, Paul Claudel: Knowing the East 2004, Edgar Allan Poe (with others) 2006; Founding Ed.: Essays in French Literature 1964, Dalhousie French Studies 1979. *Address:* c/o Department of Romance Languages and Literatures, 1050 East 59th Street, Chicago, IL 60637, USA (office); 72 bis rue Michel Ange, 75016 Paris, France (home). *Telephone:* (312) 702-8481 (office). *Fax:* (1) 46 51 45 57 (home).

LAWRENCE, Carmen Mary, PhD; Australian politician and fmr psychologist; b. 2 March 1948, Morawa, WA; d. of Ern Lawrence and Mary Lawrence; m. 1979; one s.; ed Santa Maria Coll., Perth and Univ. of Western Australia; Sr Tutor, Dept of Psychiatry and Behavioural Science, Univ. of Western Australia 1979, Lecturer and Course Controller in Behavioural Science applied to Medicine 1980–83; Lecturer and Tutor, Curtin Univ., Univ. of Melbourne; Research Psychologist in Research and Evaluation Unit, Psychiatric Services, Health Dept of WA 1983–86; mem. (for Subiaco) Western Australia State Ass. 1986–89, Glendalough 1989, apptd Minister for Educ. 1988, fmr Minister for Educ. and Aboriginal Affairs, Premier of WA 1990–93, also Treas., Minister for the Family and for Women's Interests; Leader of the Opposition, Shadow Treas., Shadow Minister for Employment, for Fed. Affairs 1993–94; Fed. Shadow Minister of Health 1994–96, on Status of Women and on Environment and the Arts 1996–97; mem. Fed. Parl. for Fremantle 1994–2007 (retd); Minister for Human Services and Health and Minister Assisting the Prime Minister for the Status of Women 1994–97; Shadow Minister for the Environment, the Arts and Asst to the Leader of the Opposition on the Status of Women 1996–97; Shadow Minister for Industry, Innovation and Tech. 2000, for the Status of Women 2000–02, for Reconciliation, Aboriginal and Torres Strait Islander Affairs 2000–02; Professorial Fellow, Univ. of Western Australia 2008, currently mem. Faculty Advisory Bd Faculty of Arts, Humanities and Social Sciences; Benjamin Rosenstamm Prize in Econs, British Psychological Soc. Prize for Psychology, Australian Psychological Soc. Prize for Psychology, H. I. Fowler Prize for Research in Psychology, J.A. Wood Memorial Prize and other awards and prizes. *Publications:* several academic papers on psychology. *Leisure interests:* reading, theatre, classical music, cooking. *Address:* Faculty of Arts, Humanities and Social Sciences, University of Western Australia, 35 Stirling Highway, Crawley, Perth, WA 6009; Unit 7, Queensgate Mall, William Street, Fremantle WA 6160, Australia (office).

LAWRENCE, Peter Anthony, PhD, FRS; British biologist; *Scientist Emeritus, Medical Research Council Laboratory of Molecular Biology;* b. 23 June 1941, Longridge; s. of Ivor D. Lawrence and Joy Liebert; m. Birgitta Haraldson 1971; ed Univ. of Cambridge; Commonwealth Fellowship, USA 1965–67; Dept of Genetics, Univ. of Cambridge 1967–69, Staff Scientist, MRC Lab. of Molecular Biology, Zoology Dept 1969–2007, Jt Head, Cell Biology Div. 1984–87, Scientist Emer. 2007–; Foreign mem. Swedish Royal Acad. of Sciences 2000; Medal of Zoological Soc. of London 1977, Darwin Medal, Royal Soc. 1994, Prize Vinci d'Excellence Moët et Chandon, Paris 1996, Waddington Medal, British Soc. of Developmental Biology 2006, Prince of Asturias Award for Scientific and Tech. Research, Oviedo (co-recipient) 2007. *Publications:* The Making of a Fly 1992; numerous scientific papers. *Leisure interests:* garden, golf, trees, fungi, ascalaphidae, theatre. *Address:* 9 Temple End, Great Wilbraham, Cambridge, CB1 5JF (home); Department of Zoology,

University of Cambridge, Downing Street, Cambridge, CB2 3EJ (office); MRC Laboratory of Molecular Biology, Hills Road, Cambridge, CB2 0QH, England (office). *Telephone:* (1223) 769015 (office); (1223) 880505 (home). *E-mail:* pal@mrc-lmb.cam.ac.uk (office). *Website:* www.mrc-lmb.cam.ac.uk (office).

LAWRENCE, Robert Swan; American physician and academic; *Director, Center for a Livable Future, Bloomberg School of Public Health, Johns Hopkins University;* b. 6 Feb. 1938, Philadelphia, Pa; s. of Thomas George Lawrence and Catherine Swan Lawrence; m. Cynthia Starr Cole 1960; three s. two d.; ed Harvard Coll. and Medical School; Internal Medicine Residency, Mass Gen. Hosp. 1964–66, 1969–70; Medical Epidemiologist, Center for Disease Control, US Public Health Service, Atlanta 1966–69; Asst to Assoc. Prof. of Medicine, Dir Div. of Community Medicine, NC Univ. School of Medicine 1970–74; Dir Div. of Primary Care, Asst to Assoc. Prof. of Medicine, Harvard Medical School 1974–91, Charles Davidson Assoc. Prof. of Medicine 1981–91; Assoc. Chief of Medicine, Cambridge Hosp. 1974–77, Chief of Medicine, Dir Dept of Medicine 1980–91; Dir Health Sciences, Rockefeller Foundation 1991–95; Adjunct Prof. of Medicine, New York Univ. 1991–95; Prof. of Health Policy, Assoc. Dean for Professional Educ. and Dir Center for a Livable Future, Bloomberg School of Public Health, Johns Hopkins Univ., 1995–2006, Prof. of Medicine, Johns Hopkins School of Medicine 1996–, Edyth Schoenrich Prof. of Preventive Medicine 2000–06, Prof. of Environmental Health Sciences 2006–, inaugural Center for a Livable Future Prof. 2008–; Chair. US Preventive Services Task Force, Dept of Health and Human Services, US Govt 1984–89, mem. 1990–95; Ed. American Journal of Preventive Medicine 1990–92; mem. Inst. of Medicine, NAS 1978; Duncan Clark Lecture (Asscn of Teachers of Preventive Medicine) 1993; Pres. Physicians for Human Rights 1998–2002, Chair. Bd Trustees 2007–; Trustee, Teachers' Coll., Columbia Univ. 1991–97; Maimonides Prize 1964, John Atkinson Ferrell Prize, UNC 1998, Special Recognition Award, American Coll. of Preventive Medicine 1988, Leadership Award, Soc. for Gen. Internal Medicine 1996, Albert Schweitzer Humanitarian Award 2002. *Publications:* Co-Ed. Preventing Disease: Beyond the Rhetoric 1990, Health Promotion and Disease Prevention in Clinical Practice 1996, International Perspectives on Environment, Development and Health 1997; 80 articles in scientific journals. *Address:* Johns Hopkins Bloomberg School of Public Health, 615 N Wolfe Street, Baltimore, MD 21205 (office); Highfield House 1112, 4000 N Charles Street, Baltimore, MD 21218-1737, USA (home). *Telephone:* (410) 614-4590 (office); (410) 235-5474 (home). *Fax:* (410) 502-7579 (office). *E-mail:* rlawrenc@jhsph.edu (office). *Website:* www.jhsph.edu/Environment (office).

LAWRENCE, Walter Nicholas Murray, MA; British underwriting agent; b. 8 Feb. 1935, London; s. of Henry Walter Neville Lawrence and Sarah Schuyler Lawrence (née Butler); m. Sally Louise O'Dwyer 1961; two d.; ed Winchester Coll., Trinity Coll., Oxford; with C. T. Bowring and Co. Ltd 1957–62, 1976–84, Treaty Dept 1957–62, Dir 1976–84; with Harvey Bowring and Others 1962–84, Asst Underwriter 1962–70, Underwriter 1970–84; Dir C. T. Bowring (Underwriting Agencies) Ltd 1973–84; Chair. Fairway Underwriting Agencies Ltd 1979–85; mem. Lloyd's Underwriter's Non-Marine Asscn, Deputy Chair. 1977, Chair. 1978; served Cttee of Lloyd's 1979–82, 1991, Deputy Chair. 1982, mem. Council of Lloyd's 1984–91, Deputy Chair. 1984–87, Chair. 1988–90; Dir, Chair. Murray Lawrence Holdings Ltd 1988–94, Murray Lawrence Members Agency Ltd 1988–92, Murray Lawrence & Partners Ltd (now Amlin Underwriting Ltd) 1989–93. *Leisure interests:* golf, opera, travel. *Address:* c/o Amlin Underwriting Limited, St Helen's, One Undershaft, London, EC3A 8ND, England. *Telephone:* (20) 7746-1000.

LAWRENSON, Peter John, DSc, FIEEE, FREng, FRS; British electrical engineer and business executive; b. 12 March 1933, Prescot; s. of John Lawrenson and Emily Houghton; m. Shirley H. Foster 1958; one s. three d.; ed Prescot Grammar School and Manchester Univ.; research Eng General Electric Co., Ltd 1956–61; Lecturer, Univ. of Leeds 1961–65, Reader 1965–66, Prof. of Electrical Eng 1966–91, Head, Dept of Electrical and Electronic Eng 1974–84, Chair. Faculty of Science and Applied Science 1978–80; Chair. Switched Reluctance Drives Ltd 1981–97, Dir 1997–2002; Consultant Rolls-Royce 2000–02; Pres. IEE 1992–93; James Alfred Ewing Medal 1983, Royal Soc. Esso Medal 1985, Faraday Medal (IEE) 1990, RAE Sir Franck Whittle Medal 2005, IEEE (NY) Thomas Edison Medal 2005, and other awards. *Publications:* The Analytical and Numerical Solution of Electromagnetic Field Problems 1992, other books and over 160 articles and patents in the field of electrical eng, particularly electromagnetics and electromechanics. *Leisure interests:* squash, lawn tennis, bridge, chess, jewellery making. *Address:* Hard Gap, Main Street, Linton, Wetherby, Yorks., LS22 4HT; Switched Reluctance Drives Ltd, East Park House, Otley Road, Harrogate, HG3 1PR, England (office). *Telephone:* (1423) 845200 (office). *Fax:* (1423) 845201 (office); (1937) 588801 (home).

LAWS, Richard Maitland, CBE, ScD, FRS, FIBiol; British scientist; b. 23 April 1926, Whitley Bay; s. of Percy Malcolm Laws and Florence May Heslop; m. Maureen Isobel Holmes 1954; three s.; ed Dame Allan's School, Newcastle and St Catharine's Coll., Cambridge; Biologist and Base Leader, Falkland Islands Dependencies Survey 1947–53; Whaling Insp., F/F Balaena 1953–54; Prin. Scientific Officer, Nat. Inst. of Oceanography, Godalming 1954–61; Dir, Nuffield Unit of Tropical Animal Ecology, Uganda 1961–67; Dir, Tsavo Research Project, Kenya 1967–68; Head, Life Sciences Div., British Antarctic Survey 1969–73; Dir, British Antarctic Survey, Cambridge 1973–87; Dir Sea Mammal Research Unit, Cambridge 1977–87; Master, St Edmund's Coll. Cambridge 1985–96; Sec. Zoological Soc. of London 1984–88; mem. Council of the Senate, Univ. of Cambridge 1989–92, Financial Bd 1988–91; Pres. Scientific Cttee for Antarctic Research 1990–94, Hon. mem. 1996; Foreign mem. Norwegian Acad. of Science and Letters 1998; 36th Annual Lecture, Ciba Foundation 1984, 2nd Cranbrook Memorial Lecture, Mammal Soc. 1987, 4th Annual Dice Lecture, Univ. of Kent 1997; Hon. mem. Soc. for Marine Mammalogy 1994; Hon. Warden, Uganda Nat. Parks 1996; Hon. Fellow St Catharine's Coll. 1982, St Edmund's Coll. 1996; Hon. DSc (Bath) 1991; Bruce Medal 1954, Scientific Medal, Zoological Soc., London 1965, Polar Medal 1976 and Second Clasp 2001. *Publications:* The Elephant Seal: Growth and Age 1953, The Elephant Seal: General Social and Reproductive Behaviour 1956, The Elephant Seal: The Physiology of Reproduction 1956, Reproduction, Growth and Age of Southern Fin Whales 1961, Elephants and Their Habitats (co-author) 1975, Scientific Research in Antarctica (ed.) 1977, Antarctic Ecology (ed.) 1984, Antarctic Nutrient Cycles and Food Webs (co-ed.) 1985, Antarctica: The Last Frontier 1989, Life at Low Temperatures (co-ed.) 1990, Antarctica and Environmental Change (co-ed.) 1992, Antarctic Seals: Research Methods and Techniques (ed.) 1993, Elephant Seals: Population Ecology, Behaviour and Physiology (co-ed.) 1994. *Leisure interests:* writing, gardening, photography, painting. *Address:* 3 The Footpath, Coton, Cambs., CB3 7PX, England. *Telephone:* (1954) 210567.

LAWSON, Hon. Dominic Ralph Campden, BA, FRSA; British journalist and editor; b. 17 Dec. 1956, London; s. of Nigel Lawson, now Lord Lawson of Blaby (q.v.) and the late Lady (Vanessa) Ayer; m. 1st Jane Fiona Wastell Whytehead 1982 (divorced 1991); m. 2nd Hon. Rosamond Monckton 1991; two d.; ed Westminster School, Christ Church, Oxford; mem. staff World Tonight and The Financial World Tonight, BBC 1979–81; mem. staff Financial Times (Energy Corresp. and Lex column) 1981–87; Deputy Ed. The Spectator 1987–90, Ed. 1990–95; Ed. The Sunday Telegraph 1995–2005; columnist, Sunday Corresp. 1990, The Financial Times 1991–94, Daily Telegraph 1994–95, The Independent 2006–, The Sunday Times 2008–; Harold Wincott Prize for Financial Journalism, Ed. of the Year, Soc. of Magazine Eds. 1990. *Publications:* Korchnoi, Kasparov 1983, Britain in the Eighties (jtly) 1989; ed. The Spectator Annual 1992, 1993, 1994, The Inner Game 1993. *Leisure interests:* chess, cricket. *Address:* The Sunday Times, 1 Pennington Street, London, E98 1ST, England (home). *Telephone:* (20) 7782-5000 (office). *Fax:* (20) 7782-5658 (office). *Website:* www.sunday-times.co.uk (home).

LAWSON, Lesley (Twiggy); British model, singer and actress; b. 19 Sept. 1949, London; d. of William Hornby and Helen Hornby (née Reeman); m. 1st Michael Whitney Armstrong 1977 (died 1983); one d.; m. 2nd Leigh Lawson 1988; ed Brondesbury and Kilburn Grammar School; model 1966–70; Man. and Dir Twiggy Enterprises Ltd 1966–; f. Twiggy & Co. 1998–; launched Twiggy skin care range 2001; own British TV series; has made several LP records; two Golden Globe Awards 1970. *Films include:* The Boy Friend 1971, W, There Goes the Bride 1979, Blues Brothers 1981, The Doctor and the Devils 1986, Club Paradise 1986, Harem Hotel, Istanbul 1988, Young Charlie Chaplin (TV) 1989, Madame Sousatzka 1989, Woundings 1998. *Plays:* Cinderella 1976, Captain Beaky 1982, My One and Only 1983–84, Blithe Spirit, Chichester 1997, Noel and Gertie, USA 1998, If Love Were All, New York 1999, Blithe Spirit, New York 2002, Play What I Wrote 2002, Mrs Warren's Profession 2003. *Television:* own musical series 1975–76; has appeared in numerous TV dramas in UK and USA; chat shows: Twiggy's People 1998, Take Time with Twiggy 2001, This Morning 2001. *Publications:* Twiggy: An Autobiography 1975, An Open Look 1985, Twiggy in Black and White 1997. *Leisure interests:* music, design. *E-mail:* info@twiggylawson.co.uk (office). *Website:* www.twiggylawson.co.uk.

LAWSON, Sonia, MA, RA, RWS; British artist; b. 2 June 1934, Darlington, Co. Durham; d. of the late Frederick Lawson and Muriel Metcalfe; m. Charles William Congo 1969; one d.; ed Royal Coll. of Art, London; travelling scholarship to France 1956–60; one of four young artists for John Schlesinger's BBC TV documentary 1960; Visiting Lecturer, Royal Acad. Schools 1985–; Lorne Scholarship, Univ. of London 1986–87; works in collections including Arts Council, Great Britain, Belfast Art Gallery, Bolton Art Gallery, Carlisle Art Gallery, Cartwright Hall, Bradford, Chatsworth Collection, Graves Art Gallery, Sheffield, Harrogate Art Gallery, Huddersfield Art Gallery, Imperial War Museum, Leeds Univ., Middlesbrough Art Gallery, Nuffield Collection, Rochdale Art Gallery, RCA Collection, Royal Acad. of Arts Collection, Univ. of Birmingham, The Vatican, Rome, Wakefield Art Gallery; works commissioned by Imperial War Museum, BAOR 1984, Lambeth Palace for the Pope 1989, drawings for Look at it This Way! (collection of poems) by James Kirkup 1993, two related works for Univ. Centre, Birmingham 1994, New Year's Eve (short story) by Fay Weldon 1995, Barclays Capital Paris 1998; Rowney Drawing Prize 1984, Eastern Arts Drawing Prize 1984, 1989, Lorne Award 1987, Eastern Art Drawing Prize 1990. *Address:* c/o Royal Academy of Arts, Burlington House, Piccadilly, London, W1V 0DS, England. *Telephone:* (20) 7300-5680 (Academicians' Affairs Office). *Fax:* (20) 7300-5812. *E-mail:* art@sonialawson.co.uk (home). *Website:* www.sonialawson.co.uk.

LAWSON OF BLABY, Baron (Life Peer), cr. 1992, of Newnham in the County of Northamptonshire; **Nigel Lawson,** MA, PC; British politician and business executive; *Chairman, Central Europe Trust Co. Ltd;* b. 11 March 1932, London; s. of Ralph Lawson and Joan Lawson (née Davis); m. 1st Vanessa Salmon (divorced 1980, died 1985); m. 2nd Thérèse Mary Maclear 1980; two s. four d. (one deceased); ed Westminster School and Christ Church, Oxford; Sub Lt, RNVR 1954–56; mem. editorial staff, Financial Times 1956–60; City Ed. Sunday Telegraph 1961–63; Special Asst to Prime Minister 1963–64; Financial Times columnist and BBC broadcaster 1965; Ed. The Spectator 1966–70; regular contributor to Sunday Times and Evening Standard 1970–71, The Times 1971–72; Fellow, Nuffield Coll. Oxford 1972–73; Special Political Adviser, Conservative Party HQ 1973–74; MP for Blaby, Leics. 1974–92; Opposition Whip 1976–77; Opposition spokesman on Treasury and Econ. Affairs 1977–79; Financial Sec. to the Treasury 1979–81; Sec. of State for Energy 1981–83, Chancellor of the Exchequer 1983–89; mem. House of Lords 1992–, House of Lords Econ. Affairs Cttee 1992–; Dir (non-exec.) Barclays Bank 1990–98; Chair. Cen. Europe Trust Co. Ltd 1990–, CAIB Emerging Russia Fund 1997–98; Adviser BZW 1990–91; Dir (non-exec.) and Consultant Guinness Peat Aviation (GPA) 1990–93; Dir Inst. for Int. Econs, Wash. 1991–2001; mem. Int. Advisory Bd Creditanstalt Bankverein 1991–99, TOTAL SA 1994–99, Advisory Council Prince's Youth Business Trust 1994–2001; mem. Governing Body, Westminster School 1999–2005, Fellow 2005–; Pres. British Inst. of Energy Econs 1995–2004; Hon. Student Christ Church, Oxford 1996; Finance Minister of the Year, Euromoney Magazine 1988. *Publications:* The Power Game (with Jock Bruce-Gardyne) 1976, The View from No. 11: Memoirs of a Tory Radical 1992, The Nigel Lawson Diet Book (with Thérèse Lawson) 1996, An Appeal to Reason: A Cool Look at Global Warming 2008, and various pamphlets. *Address:* House of Lords, London, SW1A 0PW, England.

LAWTON, Sir John Hartley, Kt, CBE, PhD, FRS; British ecologist and academic; *Chairman, Royal Commission on Environmental Pollution;* b. 24 Sept. 1943, Preston, Lancs.; s. of Frank Hartley and Mary Lawton; m. Dot (Lady Dorothy) Lawton; one s. one d.; ed Univ. of Durham; Lecturer in Zoology, St Anne's and Lincoln Coll., Univ. of Oxford 1968–71; Lecturer, Sr Lecturer, Reader then Prof. of Biology, York Univ. 1972–89; Founding Dir Centre for Population Biology, Natural Environment Research Council (NERC), Imperial Coll. London, Silwood Park 1989–99, Chief Exec. Natural Environment Research Council 1999–2005; Adviser to Royal Comm. on Environmental Pollution 1986–89, mem. 1990–96, Chair. 2005–08; Chair. Royal Soc. for the Protection of Birds 1993–98, currently Vice-Pres.; Pres. Council of British Ecological Soc. 2005–; Vice-Pres. British Trust for Ornithology; Trustee, WWF-UK; Scientific Adviser and Presenter, The 300 Million Years War, BBC 1985 and The State of the Plant, Soc. 2000; Hon. Fellow, Royal Entomological Soc. 2001; Hon. DSc (Lancaster) 1993, (Birmingham, East Anglia, York, Aberdeen, Imperial Coll.); Pres.'s Gold Medal, British Ecological Soc. 1987, Frink Medal, Zoological Soc. of London 1998, La Roe Award, Soc. for Conservation Biology 2002, Japan Prize for Science and Tech. for Conservation of Biodiversity 2004. *Publications:* author or ed. of five books and more than 320 papers, articles and book chapters. *Leisure interests:* bird watching, gardening, natural history, walking, cooking, playing with his grandchildren. *Address:* Royal Commission on Environmental Pollution, Third Floor, 5–8 The Sanctuary, Westminster, London, SW1P 3JS, England (office). *Telephone:* (20) 7799-8984 (office). *Fax:* (20) 7799-8971 (office). *E-mail:* chairman@rcep.org.uk (office). *Website:* www.rcep.org.uk (office).

LAWZI, Ahmed Abdel Kareem al-; Jordanian politician; b. 1925, Jubeiha, nr Amman; m.; ed Teachers' Training Coll., Baghdad, Iraq; teacher 1950–53; Asst to Chief of Royal Protocol 1953–56; Head of Ceremonies, Ministry of Foreign Affairs 1957; mem. Parl. 1961–62, 1962–63; Asst to Chief of Royal Court 1963–64; Minister of State, Prime Minister's Office 1964–65; mem. Senate 1965, 1967; Minister of the Interior for Municipal and Rural Affairs April–Oct. 1967; Minister of Finance 1970–71; Prime Minister 1971–73; Pres. Nat. Consultative Council 1978–79; various Jordanian and foreign decorations. *Address:* c/o Ministry of Foreign Affairs, PO Box 35217, Amman 11180, Jordan.

LAX, Peter D., AB, PhD; American mathematician and academic; *Professor Emeritus of Mathematics, Courant Institute of Mathematics, New York University;* b. 1 May 1926, Budapest, Hungary; s. of Henry Lax and Klara Kornfeld; m. Anneli Cahn 1948 (died 1999); two s.; ed New York Univ.; with Los Alamos Scientific Lab., Manhattan Project 1945–46; Asst Prof., New York Univ. 1951, Prof. 1957–99, Prof. Emer. 1999–, Dir AEC Computing and Applied Math. Center 1964–72, Courant Inst. of Math. Sciences 1972–80, Courant Math. and Computing Lab. 1980–; Fulbright Lecturer in Germany 1958; Visiting Lecturer, Univ. of Oxford 1969; Vice-Pres. American Math. Soc. 1969–71, Pres. 1978–80; mem. Nat. Science Bd 1980–86; mem. American Acad. of Arts and Sciences 1982, NAS 1982, American Philosophical Soc. 1996, Moscow Math. Soc. 1995; Foreign Assoc. French Acad. of Sciences 1982, Academia Sinica 1993, Hungarian Acad. of Sciences 1993; Foreign mem. Soviet (now Russian) Acad. of Sciences 1989; Hon. Life Mem. New York Acad. of Sciences 1982; Dr hc (Kent State) 1975, (Paris) 1979, (Tech. Univ. of Aachen) 1988, (Heriot Watt) 1990, (Tel-Aviv) 1992, (Univ. of Maryland, Baltimore) 1993, (Brown) 1993, (Beijing) 1993, (Texas A&M) 2000; Lester R. Ford Award 1966, 1973, Von Neumann Lecturer, S.I.A.M. 1969, Hermann Weyl Lecturer 1972, Hedrick Lecturer 1973, Chauvenet Prize, Math. Asscn of America 1974, Norbert Wiener Prize, American Math. Soc. and Soc. of Industrial and Applied Math. 1975, NAS Award in Applied Math. and Numerical Sciences 1983, Nat. Medal of Science 1986, Wolf Prize 1987, Steele Prize, American Math. Soc. (co-winner) 1992, Distinguished Teaching Award, New York Univ. 1995, Abel Prize, Norwegian Acad. of Arts and Letters 2005. *Publications:* numerous papers in learned journals. *Address:* Courant Institute of Mathematics, New York University, Room 912, 251 Mercer Street, New York, NY 10012, USA (office). *Telephone:* (212) 998-3232 (office). *Fax:* (212) 995-4121 (office). *E-mail:* lax@cims.nyu.edu (office). *Website:* www.math.nyu.edu (office).

LAYARD, Baron (Life Peer), cr. 2000, of Highgate in the London Borough of Haringey; **Peter Richard Grenville Layard,** BA, MSc; British economist and academic; *Co-Director, Centre for Economic Performance, London School of Economics;* b. 15 March 1934, Welwyn Garden City; s. of John Willoughby Layard and Doris Layard; m. Molly Meacher 1991; ed Univ. of Cambridge, London School of Econs; school teacher, London Co. Council 1959–61; Sr Research Officer, Robbins Cttee on Higher Educ. 1961–64; Deputy Dir Higher Educ. Research Unit, LSE 1964–74, Lecturer, LSE 1968–75, Reader 1975–80, Prof. of Econs 1980–99, Co-Dir Centre for Econ. Performance 1990–, Head, Centre for Labour Econ. 1974–90; Consultant, Centre for European Policy Studies, Brussels 1982–86; mem. Univ. Grants Cttee 1985–89; Chair.

Employment Inst. 1987–92; Co-Chair., World Economy Group of the World Inst. for Devt Econs Research 1989–93; Econ. Adviser to Russian Govt 1991–97; Fellow Econometric Soc. *Publications:* Cost Benefit Analysis 1973, Causes of Poverty (with D. Piachaud and M. Stewart) 1978, Microeconomic Theory (with A. A. Walters) 1978, More Jobs, Less Inflation 1982, The Causes of Unemployment (Co-Ed. with C. Greenhalgh and A. Oswald) 1984, The Rise in Unemployment (Co-Ed. with C. Bean and S. Nickell) 1986, How to Beat Unemployment 1986, Handbook of Labor Economics (Co-Ed. with Orley C. Ashenfelter) 1987, The Performance of the British Economy (jtly) 1988, Unemployment: Macroeconomic Performance and the Labour Market (jtly) 1991, East-West Migration: the alternatives (jtly) 1992, Post-Communist Reform: Pain and Progress 1993 (jtly), Macroeconomics: a Text for Russia 1994, The Coming Russian Boom 1996 (jtly), What Labour Can Do 1997, Tackling Unemployment 1999, Tackling Inequality 1999, What the Future Holds (Co-Ed. with R. Cooper), Happiness: Lessons from a New Science 2005. *Leisure interests:* walking, tennis. *Address:* Centre for Economic Performance, London School of Economics, Houghton Street, London, WC2A 2AE (office); 45 Cholmeley Park, London, N6 5EL, England (home). *Telephone:* (20) 7955-7281 (office). *Fax:* (20) 7955-7595 (office). *E-mail:* r.layard@lse.ac.uk (office). *Website:* cep.lse.ac.uk/layard (office).

LAYNE, Kingsley, BA; Saint Vincent and the Grenadines civil servant and diplomatist; b. 1949; ed Univ. of the West Indies, Univ. of British Columbia, Inst. for Applied Behavioural Sciences; economist, Ministry of Trade, Agric. and Tourism 1973–74; Sr Official, Econ. Affairs Secr., Org. of Eastern Caribbean States, St John's, Antigua 1982–86; Perm. Sec., Ministry of Trade, Agric. and Industry 1986–87, Tourism, Aviation and Culture 1987–89, Trade and Tourism 1989–90; Perm. Rep. of Saint Vincent and the Grenadines to UN, New York 1990–94; Amb. to USA 1991–2000; Perm. Rep. to OAS, Vice-Chair. –1999; mem. New Democratic Party. *Publications:* several publs on staff devt and man. training. *Address:* c/o New Democratic Party (NDP), Murray Road, POB 1300, Kingstown, Saint Vincent and the Grenadines. *Telephone:* 457-2647.

LAYNIE, Tamrat; Ethiopian politician; mem. Ethiopian People's Revolutionary Democratic Front (EPRDF); Prime Minister of Ethiopia 1991–95; sentenced to 18 years' imprisonment for corruption, embezzlement and abuse of office 2000. *Address:* c/o Office of the Prime Minister, PO Box 1013, Addis Ababa, Ethiopia.

LAZAR, Philippe; French scientist and administrator; b. 21 April 1936, Paris; s. of Maximilien Lazar and Françoise Lazar; m. Monique Lazar 1960; one s. one d.; ed Ecole Polytechnique, Paris; researcher, Nat. Inst. of Hygiene 1960, Dir of Research Institut Nat. de la Santé et de la Recherche Médicale (INSERM) 1964, Dir Environmental Health Research Unit 1977, Chair. Scientific Council 1981, Dir-Gen. INSERM 1982–96; Chair. European Medical Research Councils (EMRC) 1994–96; Chair. Bd Research Inst. for Devt (IRD) 1997–2001; with Cour des Comptes 2001–05; Visiting Prof. Harvard School of Public Health 1975; Commdr, Ordre nat. du Mérite; Officier, Légion d'honneur; Chevalier, Ordre des Arts et des Lettres. *Publications:* Eléments de probabilités et statistiques 1967, Méthodes statistiques en expérimentation biologique 1974, Les explorateurs de la santé 1989, L'éthique biomédicale en question 1995, La République a-t-elle besoin de savants? 1998, Autrement dit laïque 2003, Court traité de l'âme 2008. *Leisure interests:* arts, literature. *Address:* 9, rue Friant, 75014 Paris, France (office). *Telephone:* (6) 81-11-80-67 (office). *E-mail:* philippe.lazar@orange.fr (office).

LAZARAN, Frank, BSc; American retail executive; *President, CEO and Director Winn-Dixie Stores Inc.;* b. 1957; ed Calif. State Univ. at Long Beach, Univ. of Southern Calif.; joined Ralphs Grocery Co., Compton, CA 1974, various positions including Group Vice-Pres. of Sales, Advertising and Merchandising –1997; Sr Vice-Pres. of Sales, Merchandising and Logistics, Randalls Food Market Inc., Houston, TX 1997–99, Pres. 1999–2002; Exec. Vice-Pres. and COO Winn-Dixie Stores Inc., Jacksonville, FL 2002–03, Pres., CEO and Dir 2003–. *Address:* Winn-Dixie Stores Inc., 5050 Edgewood Court, Jacksonville, FL 32254-3699, USA (office). *Telephone:* (904) 783-5000 (office). *Fax:* (904) 783-5294 (office). *Website:* www.winn-dixie.com (office).

LAZARENKO, Pavlo Ivanovych, DEconSc; Ukrainian politician; b. 23 Jan. 1953, Karpivka, Dniepropetrovsk Region; m. Tamara Ivanivna Lazarenko; one s. two d.; ed Dniepropetrovsk Inst. of Agric.; worked as agronomist 1972–79, Chair. of Kolkhoz 1979–84, Head Dist Dept of Agric. Man.; First Deputy Chair. Dist Exec. Cttee; Chair. Council of Agro-Industrial Complex Dniepropetrovsk Region, First Deputy Chair. Regional Exec. Cttee; People's Deputy 1990–; Rep. of Pres. of Ukraine in Dniepropetrovsk Region 1992–95, concurrently Chair. Dniepropetrovsk Regional State Admin.; elected deputy of Verkhivna Rada (Ukrainian legislature) 1994; First Vice-Prime Minister of Ukraine 1995–96, Prime Minister of Ukraine 1996–97; elected to lead Unity faction in legislature 1997; Head Hromada (political movt); charged with corruption 1999, arrested in USA 2000, charges lifted by Parl. of Ukraine 2002, convicted by US jury of money-laundering and extortion June 2004. *Address:* c/o Hromada, Laboratornyi provylok 1, 01133, Kyiv, Ukraine (office).

LAZAREV, Alexander Nikolayevich; Russian conductor; *Principal Conductor, Japan Philharmonic Orchestra;* b. 5 July 1945; m. Tamara Lazarev; one d.; ed Leningrad and Moscow Conservatoires; conducting debut at Bolshoi Theatre 1973, conducted numerous ballets and operas of the Bolshoi Theatre's European and Russian repertoires, founder and conductor Ensemble of Soloists of the Bolshoi Theatre 1978–89, Chief Conductor, Artistic Dir, Bolshoi Theatre 1987–95; Chief Conductor Duisburg Symphony Orchestra 1988–93; has conducted numerous orchestras including Berlin Philharmonic, Munich Philharmonic, Orchestra Sinfonica del Teatro alla Scala di Milano, Orchestre Nat. de France and others; UK debut with Royal Liverpool Philharmonic

Orchestra 1987; subsequently performed with the City of Birmingham Symphony Orchestra, the Royal Scottish Nat. Orchestra, etc.; Prin. Guest Conductor BBC Symphony Orchestra, 1992–95, Royal Scottish Nat. Orchestra 1994–97, Prin. Conductor 1997–2005, Conductor Emer. 2005–; Prin. Conductor, Japan Philharmonic Orchestra 2007–; Hon. Prof., Univ. of Glasgow 2005 First Prize USSR Nat. Competition 1971, First Prize and Gold Medal Karajan Competition (Berlin) 1972. *Address:* c/o Tennant Artists, Unit 2, 39 Tadema Road, London, SW10 0PZ, England (office). *Telephone:* (20) 7376-3758 (office). *Fax:* (20) 7351-0679 (office). *E-mail:* info@tennantartists .com (office). *Website:* www.tennantartists.com (office).

LAZARIDIS, Mike; Canadian engineer, inventor and business executive; *President and Co-CEO, Research in Motion Ltd;* b. Istanbul, Turkey; s. of Nick Lazaridis and Dorothy Lazaridis; m. Celia Lazaridis; one s. one d.; ed Univ. of Waterloo; emigrated to Canada with family aged five 1966; awarded industrial automation contract by General Motors in 1984; Founder, Pres. and Co-CEO Research in Motion Ltd (designer and manufacturer of wireless electronic products)1984–; est. Perimeter Inst. for Theoretical Physics, Univ. of Waterloo 2000; Chancellor Univ. of Waterloo 2003–; inventor of BlackBerry wireless e-mail pager device 1991; Hon. DEng (Waterloo); numerous industry and community awards for innovations for wireless radio tech. and software, including Academy Award for Tech. Achievement for invention of digital barcode reader for film editing 1999; named by readers of newspaper The Globe and Mail 'Canada's Nation Builder of the Year 2002'. *Publications:* more than 30 patents. *Leisure interests:* cinema, cars. *Address:* Research in Motion Ltd, 295 Phillip Street, Waterloo, ON N2L 3W87, Canada (office). *Telephone:* (519) 888-7465 (office). *Fax:* (519) 888-7884 (office). *Website:* www.rim.net (office).

LAZARUS, Rochelle (Shelly), BA, MBA; American advertising executive; *Chairman and CEO, Ogilvy & Mather Worldwide;* b. 1 Sept. 1947, New York; m. George Lazarus; three c.; ed Smith Coll., Columbia Univ. Business School; with Clairol 1970; with Ogilvy & Mather 1971–74, 1976–, Pres. Ogilvy & Mather Direct US 1989–91, Pres. Ogilvy & Mather Advertising, New York 1991–94, Pres. Ogilvy N America 1994–95, Pres. and COO Ogilvy & Mather Worldwide 1995–96, CEO 1996–, Chair. 1997–; mem. Bd of Dirs General Electric, New York Presbyterian Hosp., American Museum of Natural History, World Wildlife Fund, Merck & Co. 2004–; mem. Bd Overseers Columbia Business School, Advertising Educ. Foundation, Cttee to Encourage Corp. Philanthropy; mem. Council on Foreign Relations, Business Council, Advertising Women of New York, Cttee of 200, Women's Forum, American Asscn of Advertising Agencies' Advisory Council, Yale Pres.'s Council on Int. Activities, Advisory Bd Judge Inst. of Man. Studies, Cambridge Univ. (UK); fmr Chair. American Asscn of Advertising Agencies, Bd Trustees Smith Coll.; ranked by Fortune magazine amongst 50 Most Powerful Women in Business in the US 1998–2001, (14th) 2002, (16th) 2003, (26th) 2004, (26th) 2005, (30th) 2006, (34th) 2007, ranked by Forbes magazine amongst 100 Most Powerful Women (93rd) 2004, (78th) 2005, (87th) 2006, (96th) 2007, Distinguished Leadership Award in Business, Columbia Business School (first woman recipient), numerous advertising, communications, and business leadership awards. *Address:* Ogilvy & Mather Worldwide, Worldwide Plaza, 309 West 49th Street, New York, NY 10019, USA (office). *Telephone:* (212) 237-4000 (office). *Fax:* (212) 237-5123 (office). *Website:* www.ogilvy.com (office).

LAZENBY, Alec, AO, ScD, FTSE, FIBiol, FAIAST; Australian/British agronomist and university administrator; b. 4 March 1927, UK; s. of G. Lazenby and E. Lazenby; m. Ann J. Hayward 1957; one s. two d.; ed Univ. Coll. of Wales and Univ. of Cambridge, UK; Scientific Officer, Welsh Plant Breeding Station 1949–53; Demonstrator, Agricultural Botany, Univ. of Cambridge 1953–58, Lecturer in Agricultural Botany 1958–65, Fellow and Asst Tutor, Fitzwilliam Coll. 1962–65; Foundation Prof. of Agronomy, Univ. of New England, NSW 1965–70, Vice-Chancellor 1970–77; Dir Grassland Research Inst. 1977–82; Visiting Prof. Reading Univ. 1978–82; Hon. Professorial Fellow, Univ. of Wales 1979–82; Vice-Chancellor, Univ. of Tasmania 1982–91; consultant in higher educ. and agricultural research and man. 1991–; Hon. Prof., Vic. Univ. of Tech. 1992; Hon. DRurSci (New England) 1981; Hon. LLD (Tasmania) 1992; Centenary Medal for Contrib. to Rural Science and Tech. 2003. *Publications:* Intensive Pasture Production (co-ed.) 1972, Australian Field Crops (co-ed.), Vol I 1975, Vol. II 1979, Australia's Plant Breeding Needs 1986, The Grass Crop (co-ed.) 1988, The Story of IDP 1999, Competition and Succession in Pastures (co-ed.) 2001; papers on pasture plant breeding, agronomy and weed ecology in various scientific journals. *Leisure interests:* golf, gardening and current affairs. *Address:* 16/99 Groom Street, Hughes, ACT 2605, Australia (home). *Telephone:* (2) 6281-2898 (home). *Fax:* (2) 6281-0451 (home). *E-mail:* alazenby@netspeed.com.au (home).

LAZIO, Enrico (Rick) A., AB, JD; American lawyer, business executive and fmr politician; *Executive Vice President of Global Government Affairs and Public Policy, J.P. Morgan Chase & Company;* b. 13 March 1958, Amityville, NY; s. of Anthony Lazio and Olive E. (Christensen) Lazio; ed Vassar Coll., American Univ.; called to New York Bar 1984; Asst Dist Attorney Suffolk Co. Rackets Bureau, Hauppage, NY 1983–88, Exec. Asst Dist Attorney Suffolk Co. 1987–88, Village Attorney, Village of Lindenhurst, NY 1988–93; Man. Partner Glass, Lazio and Glass, Babylon, NY 1989–93; mem. Suffolk Co. Legis. from 11th Dist, NY 1989–93, mem. House of Reps, Deputy Majority Whip, then Asst Majority Leader 1993–2000; cand. for Senate, New York State 2000; Pres. and CEO Financial Services Forum 2001–05; Exec. Vice Pres. of Global Government Affairs and Public Policy, JP Morgan Chase and Co., also mem. Exec. Cttee; mem. Bd of Dirs Polaroid Corpn, TB Woods Corpn, World Rehabilitation Fund, Audubon New York; mem. Advisory Cttee The Ad Council; mem. Suffolk Co. Bar Asscn. *Leisure interests:* numismatics, guitar. *Address:* JPMorgan Chase & Company, 270 Park Avenue, New York, NY 10017, USA

(office). *Telephone:* (212) 270-6000 (office). *Fax:* (212) 270-1648 (office). *Website:* www.jpmorganchase.com (office).

LAZORTHES, Guy Aman Félix, MD, DèsSc; French doctor and academic; b. 4 July 1910, Toulouse (Haute-Garonne); s. of Léonce Lazorthes; m. 1st Paulette Lazorthes (née Lahary); three s.; m. 2nd Annick Bouvy 1986; ed Lycée et Facultés de médecine et des sciences de Toulouse, Faculté des sciences de Paris; Prof. of Anatomy, Faculty of Medicine and Pharmacy of Toulouse 1948–63, Prof. of Clinical Neurosurgery 1963–79, Doyen of the Faculty 1958–70; Pres. Soc. de neurochirurgie de langue française 1958; Corresp. mem. Nat. Acad. of Medicine 1960, mem. 1970; Corresp. mem. Institut de France (Acad. des sciences) 1972, mem. 1975; participated in official missions to USA 1945–46, UK 1948, Latin America 1956, 1957, 1961, 1964, 1967, 1972, 1978, Denmark 1958, Turkey 1964, Far East 1967; Grand-croix, Légion d'honneur 2003, Grand-croix, Ordre nat. du Mérite, Commdr des Palmes académiques, Officier du Mérite agricole; Dr hc (Lima, Peru), (Santiago, Chile), (Bonn, Germany), (Barcelona, Spain). *Publications include:* Le Sympathique du membre inférieur 1938, Le Sympathique des membres 1941, Le Nerf terminal 1944, Le Système neurovasculaire (Prix Chaussier, Acad. des sciences 1951) 1949, Les Hémorragies intracraniennes 1952, Le Système nerveux périphérique (3rd edn) 1981, L'Hémorragie cérébrale vue par le neurochirurgien 1956, Vascularisation et Circulation cérébrales 1961, Le Système nerveux central (3rd edn) 1983, Vascularisation et Circulation de la moelle épinière 1973, Vascularisation et Circulation de l'encéphale, Vol. 1 1975, Vol. 2 1977, Le Cerveau et l'esprit 1982, L'Ouvrage des sens, fenêtres étroites sur le réel 1986, Le Cerveau et l'ordinateur 1988, Croyance et raison 1991, L'Homme, la médecine et le médecin 1992, L'Homme, la société et la médecine 1995, Sciences humaines et sociales 1996, Les Hallucinations (Prix La Bruyère, Acad. française 1997) 1996, L'Imagination: source d'irrationnel et d'irréel, puissance créatrice 1999, L'Histoire du cerveau: genèse, organisation, devenir 1999, Carnets d'un médecin universitaire 2001, les Hallucinés célèbres 2001; numerous contribs to publs on neurosurgery and anatomy. *Address:* Institut de France, 23 quai Conti, 75006 Paris (office). Résidence Garonne La Belle, 5 avenue Charles Malpel, bât. A – Appt 19, 31500 Toulouse, France (home).

LAZOVIĆ, Vujica, PhD; Montenegrin economist, academic and politician; *Deputy Prime Minister, responsible for Economic Policy;* b. 10 March 1963; ed Univ. of Podgorica; fmr mem. Faculty of Econs, Univ. of Montenegro; currently Prof. of Econs and Dean of Faculty of Econs, Univ. of Podgorica; Deputy Prime Minister, responsible for Econ. Policy 2007–. *Publications:* numerous books and articles on economics. *Address:* Ministry of Economic Development, 81000 Podgorica, Rimski trg 46, Montenegro (office). *Telephone:* (81) 234156 (office). *Fax:* (81) 234131 (office). *E-mail:* vujicalazovic@mn.yu (office). *Website:* www.gom.cg.yu (office).

LAZUTKIN, Valentin Valentinovich, CandPhil; Russian politician and journalist; b. 10 Jan. 1945, Kraskovo, Moscow Region; m.; one s. one d.; ed Moscow State Univ., Acad. of Social Sciences Cen. Cttee CPSU; Head Div. of Press and Information Cttee of Youth Orgs 1967–73; Deputy Head, Head Dept of Int. Relations, mem. Exec. Bd, Deputy Chair. USSR State Cttee on Radio and TV 1974–91; First Deputy Chair. 1991, Deputy Chair., Dir-Gen. of Int. Relations, Russian State TV-Radio Broadcasting Co. Ostankino 1991–93; First Deputy Chair. Feb.–Dec. 1993, First Deputy Head Russian Fed. Service on TV and Radio Broadcasting, concurrently Dir-Gen. Russian State TV-Radio Broadcasting Co. Ostankino 1993–95; Head Russian Fed. Service on TV and Radio Broadcasting 1995–98; Rector Humanitarian Inst. of TV and Radio 1998–; Chair. Interstate TV Service, Union of Russia and Belarus 1998–, Coordinating Bd Soyuz (Union) Media Group 2001–, Moscow TV Center Channel –2005; Deputy Head Exec. Cttee Union of Russia and Belarus 2000–; Dir Nat. TV Broadcasters Asscn, Russian CATV Asscn; mem. Bd Dirs Moscow CableCom 2004–; mem. Russian TV Acad., Int. TV Acad., Russia Acad. of Natural Sciences; Officier des Arts et Lettres, Peter the Great Prize and other decorations. *Leisure interests:* history, military heraldry. *Address:* Humanitarian Institute of TV and Radio Broadcasting, Brodnikov per. 3, 109180 Moscow, Russia (office). *Telephone:* (495) 238-49-75 (office).

LE, Jingyi; Chinese fmr swimmer; b. March 1975, Shanghai; entered Chinese Women's Swimming Team 1991; fmr world record-holder at 50m and 100m freestyle; broke Olympic record for women's 100m freestyle and won gold medal at 26th Olympics, Atlanta 1996; affected by illness in the build-up to 27th Olympics, Sydney 2000; United Press Int. Athlete of the Year 1994, World Pacific Rim Swimmer of the Year 1996, State Physical Culture and Sports Comm. Nat. Sports Medal of Honour and First Prize 1996. *Address:* c/o State General Bureau for Physical Culture and Sports, 9 Tiyuguan Road, Chongwen District, Beijing, People's Republic of China.

LE BLANC, Bart, PhD; Dutch banker; *Professor of Political Economy, University of Tilburg;* b. 4 Nov. 1946, Bois-le-Duc; s. of Christian Le Blanc and Johanna Bogaerts; m. Gérardine van Lanschot; one s. two d.; ed Leiden and Tilburg Univs; Special Adviser, Prime Minister's Office, Deputy Sec. to Cabinet 1973–79; Deputy Dir-Gen. for Civil Service at Home Office 1979–80; Dir-Gen. for Budget at Treasury 1980–83; Deputy Chair. Man. Bd F. van Lanschot Bankiers NV, 's-Hertogenbosch 1983–91; Sec.-Gen. EBRD, London 1991–94, Vice-Pres., Finance 1994–98; Dir Int. Finance, Caisse des Dépôts et Consignations, Paris 1998–; Prof. of Political Economy Univ. of Tilburg 1991–; Hon. Prof. Tilburg Univ. 1991–; Kt, Order of Netherlands Lion. *Publications:* books and contribs on econ. and fiscal policy to nat. and int. journals. *Leisure interest:* farming in France. *Address:* University of Tilburg, Warandelaan 2, PO Box 90153, 5000 LE Tilburg, Netherlands.

LE BRIS, Raymond-François; French professor of law and university administrator; b. 18 Sept. 1935, Gouesnou; s. of François Le Bris and

Bernadette Le Bris (née Lunven); m. Jacqueline Pareau 1964; one s. two d.; ed Coll. Notre-Dame-de-Bon-Secours, Brest, Univ. of Rennes; Asst Lecturer, Law Faculty, Univ. of Rennes 1958–63, Lecturer 1963–65; Prof., Univ. of Bordeaux 1965–68; Asst Dir Institut Henry-Vizioz des Antilles-Guyanne 1966; Prof., Univ. of Bretagne Occidentale 1969, 1976–77, Pres. 1971; Dir Institut de droit et des sciences économiques, Brest 1969; Deputy Dir for higher educ. and research, Ministry of Nat. Educ. 1972, Dir-Gen. 1972–74; Dir de Cabinet of Sec. of State for Univs 1974–76; Préfet, L'Ariège 1977–79, L'Ain 1979–81, Seine-Saint-Denis 1986–90; Prof. Univ. of Paris IX – Dauphiné 1981–86; Sec.-Gen. Conseil pour l'avenir de la France 1982–86; Dir-Gen. Chambre de commerce et d'industrie de Paris 1990–95; Dir Ecole Nat. d'Admin 1995–2000; expert consultant to Tekelec Airtronic, Sociovision CoFremca, NN France, Tilder Associates; mem. Bd MIT France, Bd of Trustees, Int. Council for Educational Devt; Préfet Honoraire; Officier, Légion d'Honneur; Commdr, Ordre Nat. du Mérite; Commdr des Palmes Académiques; Grand Officier, Ordre de Castello Branco (Brazil). *Publications:* La relation de travail entre epoux 1965, Les universités à la loupe 1986, L'Etat quand même 2005, Réflexion et propositions sur l'organisation et le fonctionnement des services de l'Etat à l'étranger 2005. *Leisure interest:* cross-country and marathon running. *Address:* Tekelec Airtronic, 5 rue Carle Vernet, Sèvres 92 (office); CoFremca, 16 rue d'Athènes, 75009, Paris (office); 34 rue des Vignes, 75007 Paris, France (home); Tilder Associates, 57 boulevard de Montmorency, 75026, Paris. *Telephone:* 1-46-90-23-50 (office); 1-59-70-60-00 (office); 1-45-25-14-32 (home). *Fax:* 1-46-90-23-92 (office). *E-mail:* raymond-francois.lebris@temex.fr (office).

LE BROCQUY, Louis, PhD, FRSA, FSIAD; Irish artist; b. 10 Nov. 1916, Dublin; s. of the late Albert le Brocquy and Sybil de Lacy Staunton; m. 1st Jean Atkinson Stoney 1938; one d.; m. 2nd Anne Madden-Simpson 1958; two s.; ed St Gerard's School, Wicklow; Founder-mem. Irish Exhbn of Living Art 1943; Visiting Instructor, Cen. School of Arts and Crafts, London 1947–54; Visiting Tutor, RCA, London 1955–58; mem. Irish Council of Design 1963–65; Dir Kilkenny Design Workshops 1965–77; Dir Irish Museum of Modern Art 1989–94; works in public collections, including Albright Knox Museum, Buffalo, Carnegie Inst., Pittsburgh, Detroit Inst., Hirshhorn Museum and Sculpture Garden, Smithsonian Inst., Washington, DC, Kunsthaus, Zürich, Guggenheim Museum, New York, Musée Picasso, Antibes, Uffizi Gallery, Florence, Columbus Museum, Ohio, San Diego Museum, Tate Gallery, London, Fondation Maeght, Saint Paul, Hugh Lane Municipal Gallery of Modern Art, Dublin, Irish Museum of Modern Art, Dublin, Ulster Museum, Belfast, Musée d'Art Moderne de la Ville de Paris, Nat. Gallery of Ireland, Dublin, Calouste Gulbenkian Foundation, Lisbon; Hon. Council mem. Royal Hibernian Acad.; Hon. Assoc. Nat. Coll. of Art and Design, Dublin 2006; Hon. Freeman of the City of Dublin 2007; Chevalier, Légion d'honneur 1975; Officier des Arts et des Lettres 1996, Ordre de la Couronne Belge 2001; Commdr du Bontemps de Médoc et des Graves 1969; Hon. DLitt (Dublin) 1962; Hon. LLD (Univ. Coll. Dublin) 1988; Hon. PhD (Dublin City Univ.) 1999; Hon. DUniv (Queen's Univ., Belfast) 2002; Hon. DPhil (Dublin Inst. of Tech.) 2004; Premio Acquisto, Venice Biennale 1956, elected Saoi, Aosdána (Irish affiliation of distinguished artists) 1992, Glen Dimplex Prize 1998, IMMA/Glen Dimplex Award for Sustained Contribution to the Visual Arts in Ireland. *Commissions include:* large-scale tapestries: Massing of the Armies, RTE Dublin, Triumph of Cuchulainn, Nat. Gallery of Ireland; paintings: Image of Bono, Nat. Gallery of Ireland 2003. *Theatre design:* Scarecrow over the Corn, Gate Theatre, Dublin 1941, Amphitryon 38, Olympia Theatre, Dublin 1942, Waiting for Godot, Gate Theatre, Dublin 1988, Lincoln Center, New York 1996, Dublin 2003. *Television:* An Other Way of Knowing, 1 hour documentary, M. Garvey, RTE 1986. *Illustrator:* Legends of Ireland (J. J. Campbell) 1955, The Tain (trans. Kinsella) 1969, The Playboy of the Western World (Synge) 1970, The Gododdin (trans. O'Grady) 1978, Ugolino (Seamus Heaney) 1979, Eight Irish Writers, A. Carpenter 1981, Dubliners (Joyce) 1986, Stirrings Still (Samuel Beckett) 1988, An Anthology for Shakespeare (Ted Hughes) 1988, Poems 1930–1989 (Samuel Beckett) 2002. *Publications:* subject of four monographs and a biog. (Louis le Brocquy – A Painter Seeing His Way, Anne Madden le Brocquy) 1993. *Address:* c/o Gimpel Fils, 30 Davies Street, London, W1Y 1LG, England. *E-mail:* pierre.le.brocquy@wanadoo.fr (home). *Website:* www.lebrocquy.com (home).

LE BRUN, Christopher Mark, MA, DFA, RA; British artist; b. 20 Dec. 1951, Portsmouth; s. of John Le Brun, BEM and Eileen B. Le Brun (née Miles); m. Charlotte Verity 1979; two s. one d.; ed Portsmouth Southern Grammar School, Slade School of Fine Art and Chelsea School of Art; Visiting Lecturer, Brighton Polytechnic 1975–82, Slade School of Fine Art 1978–83, Wimbledon School of Art 1981–83; Prof. of Drawing RA 2000–02; mem. Advisory Cttee, Prince of Wales's Drawing Studio 2000–; Chair. Educ. Cttee RA 2000–; work in numerous public collections including Tate Gallery, London and Museum of Modern Art, New York; Trustee Tate Gallery 1990–95, Nat. Gallery 1996–2003, Dulwich Picture Gallery 2000–; major comms include Liverpool Anglican Cathedral 1996; Chair. Academic Advisory Bd, Prince of Wales Drawing School 2004–; Trustee, Princes' Drawing School 2004–; Gulbenkian Printmakers Award 1983, DAAD Award, W Berlin 1987–88 and other prizes. *Publication:* Christopher Le Brun 2001, Booth-Clibborn Edns. *Address:* c/o The Royal Academy of Arts, Burlington House, Piccadilly, London W1V 0DS, England.

Le CARRÉ, John (see Cornwell, David John Moore).

LE CLÉZIO, Jean Marie Gustave; British/French writer; b. 13 April 1940, Nice; s. of Raoul Le Clézio and Simone Le Clézio; m. 1st Rosalie Piquemal 1961; one d.; m. 2nd Jemia Jean 1975; ed Bristol Univ., Univ. de Nice, Univ. de Provence, Univ. de Perpginan; lived in Nigeria as a child 1948–50; has taught at univs in Bangkok, Mexico City, Boston, Austin, Albuquerque; Chevalier des

Arts et Lettres, Légion d'honneur; Prix Renaudot 1963, Prix Larbaud 1972, Grand Prix Paul Morand (Acad. française) 1980, Grand Prix Jean Giono 1997, Prix Prince de Monaco 1998, Stig Dagermanpriset 2008, Nobel Prize for Literature 2008. *Publications:* Le procès-verbal (The Interrogation) 1963, Le jour où Beaumont fit connaissance avec sa douleur 1964, La fièvre (Fever) 1965, Le procès 1965, Le déluge 1966, L'extase matérielle 1967, Terra amata 1967, Le livre des fuites 1969, La guerre 1970, Haï 1971, Conversations 1971, Les géants 1973, Mydriase 1973, Voyages de l'autre côté 1975, Mondo et autres histoires 1978, L'inconnu sur la terre 1978, Vers les Icebergs 1978, Voyages au pays des arbres 1978, Désert 1980, Trois villes saintes 1980, Lullaby 1980, Celui qui n'avait vu la mer suivi de la Montagne du dieu vivant 1982, La ronde et autres faits divers 1982, Journal du chercheur d'or 1985, Balaabilou 1985, Villa Aurore 1985, Voyage à Rodrigues 1986, Le rêve mexicain ou la pensée interrompue 1988, Printemps et autres saisons 1989, La Grande Vie 1990, Sirandanes, Suivi de Petit lexique de la langue créole et des oiseaux (jtly) 1990, Onitsha 1991, Étoile errante 1992, Pawana 1992, Diego et Frida 1993, La Quarantaine 1995, Le Poisson d'or 1997, La Fête chantée 1997, Hasard et Angoli Mala 1999, Coeur brûlé et autres romances 2000, Révolutions 2003, L'Africain 2004, Ourania 2005, Raga: approche du continent invisible 2006, Ballaciner 2007, Ritornelle de la faim 2008. *Address:* c/o Editions Gallimard, 5 rue Sébastien-Bottin, 75328 Paris, France (office). *Website:* www.gallimard.fr (office).

LE COZ, Martine; French novelist; b. Sept. 1955, *Publications include:* Gilles de Raiz ou La confession imaginaire 1989, Le pharaon qui n'avait pas d'ombre 1992, Hypnose et graphologie 1993, La palette du jeune Turner 1993, Le journal de l'autre 1995, Gilles de Rais ignoble et chrétien 1995, Les confins du jour 1996, Léo la nuit 1997, Le Briquet 1997, Le chagrin du zèbre 1998, Le nègre et la Méduse 1999, Catherine d'Alexandrie ou la philosophie défaite par la foi 1999, La beauté 2000, Le rire de l'arbre au milieu du jardin 2000, Céleste (Prix Renaudot) 2001, Gilles de Rais ou la confession imaginaire 2002, Nos lointains et nos proches 2004, La reine écarlate 2007. *Address:* c/o Editions du Rocher, 6 place Saint-Sulpice, 75006 Paris, France (office).

LE FLOCH-PRIGENT, Loïk; French business executive; b. 21 Sept. 1943, Brest; s. of Gérard Le Floch and Gabrielle Julienne; m.; one s. two d.; ed Institut Nat. Polytechnique, Grenoble and Univ. of Missouri, USA; scientific and tech. research, DGRST 1969–81; Dir of Cabinet of Industry Minister, Pierre Dreyfus 1981–82; Chair. and CEO Rhône-Poulenc 1982–86, Elf Aquitaine 1989–93, SNCF 1995–96; Chair. Gaz de France 1993–95, Asscn Europe et Entreprises 1994–, Club des présidents d'université et entreprise, Ecole Nat. Supérieure de Création Industrielle 1992–95; Dir Crédit Nat. 1985–97, Compagnie Gén. des Eaux 1990–96, Banco Cen. Hispano Americano 1990–94, Pallas 1991–, Pinault Printemps Redoute 1991–, Entrepose-Montalev 1994–; imprisoned for involvement in Elf Affair (financial scandal) May 2001, sentenced to five years in prison Nov. 2003, released in April 2004 for health reasons, ordered to return to prison June 2007 to serve remainder of his sentence; Officier, Légion d'honneur, Ordre nat. du Mérite.

LE FUR, Gérard; French physician and pharmaceuticals industry executive; b. 1950; trained as doctor of pharmacy and science with specialisation in area of cen. nervous system disorders; Head of Lab., Dept of Pharmacological Biochemistry, Pharmuca 1973–82; Dir of Biology Dept, Rhône-Poulenc 1982–86; Assoc. Dir of Research and Devt, Sanofi 1986–95, Dir of Research and Devt 1995–98, Man.-Dir in charge of Scientific Depts 1998, Dir of Research, Sanofi-Synthélabo (following merger of Sanofi and Synthélabo 1998) 1999–2002, Group Man.-Dir 2002–04; Chair. Man. Bd Aventis 2004–06, CEO Sanofi-Aventis SA (following merger of Sanofi-Synthélabo and Aventis) 2006–08, consultant 2008–; mem. Acad. des Sciences 1999–2003, Corresp. mem. 2003–04; Galien Prize 1983, 2000. *Publications:* more than 300 scientific papers in int. publs. *Address:* Sanofi-Aventis SA, 174 Avenue de France, 75013 Paris, France (office). *Telephone:* 1-53-77-42-23 (office). *Fax:* 1-53-77-42-65 (office). *E-mail:* info@sanofi-aventis.com (office). *Website:* www.sanofi-aventis.com (office).

LE GENDRE, Bertrand; French journalist; b. 25 Feb. 1948, Neuilly-sur-Seine; s. of Bernard Le Gendre and Catherine Chassaing de Borredon; m. 1st Jacqueline de Linares 1987 (divorced 1995); one s.; m. 2nd Nadia du Luc-Baccouche 1995; one s.; ed Collège Sainte-Croix-de-Neuilly, Univ. of Paris X, Institut d'études politiques, Paris, Institut des hautes études de défense nationale; joined Le Monde as journalist 1974, in charge of judicial desk 1983, Reporter 1987, Ed.-in-Chief 1993–2000; Visiting Assoc. Prof., Univ. de Paris II 2000–; Sub-Ed. Gallimard 1986–89; Prix de la Fondation Mumm pour la presse écrite 1986. *Address:* Le Monde, 80 Boulevard Auguste-Blanqui, 75707 Paris Cedex 13 (office); 16 rue de la Glacière, 75013 Paris, France (home). *Telephone:* 1-57-28-26-14 (office). *E-mail:* legendre@lemonde.fr (office).

LE GOFF, Jacques Louis; French historian and academic; b. 1 Jan. 1924, Toulon; s. of Jean Le Goff and Germaine Ansaldi; m. Anna Dunin-Wasowicz 1962; one s. one d.; ed Lycées, Toulon, Marseilles and Louis-le-Grand, Paris, Ecole normale supérieure, Paris; history teacher 1950; Fellow of Lincoln Coll., Oxford 1951–52; mem. Ecole française de Rome 1953–54; Asst at Univ. of Lille 1954–59; Prof., then Dir of Studies, 6th Section, Ecole des hautes études (EHE) 1960–72; Pres. Ecole des hautes études en sciences sociales (fmr 6th Section of EHE) 1972–77; mem. Comité nat. de la recherche scientifique 1962–70, Comité des travaux historiques 1972, Conseil supérieur de la Recherche 1985–87; Co-dir reviews Annales-Economies, sociétés, civilisations and Ethnologie Française 1972; Pres. commission scientifique Ecole Nationale du Patrimoine; mem. Acad. Culturelles des Cultures 1990; Grand Prix Nat. 1987, Gold Medal, CNRS 1991, Grand Prix Gobert 1996, Grand Prix d'Histoire 1997, Prix d'Histoire Heineken 2004, Dan David Prize 2007. *Publications:* Marchands et banquiers du Moyen Age 1956, Les Intellectuels au Moyen Age 1957, Le Moyen Age 1962, La Civilisation de l'occident médiéval 1964, Pour un autre Moyen Age (trans. as Time, Work and Culture in the Middle Ages) 1978, La Naissance du purgatoire 1981, L'Apogée de la chrétienté 1982, L'Imaginaire médiéval (trans. as The Medieval Imagination) 1985, La Bourse et la vie 1986, Histoire de la France religeuse (co-author) 1988, L'Homme médiéval (trans. as Medieval Callings) 1989, L'Etat et les pouvoirs 1989, St Louis 1996, Une Vie pour l'histoire 1996, L'Europe racontée aux jeunes 1996, Un Autre Moyen Age 1999, Saint François d'Assise 1999, Dictionnaire raisonné de l'Occident médiéval 1999, La Vieille Europe et la nôtre 2000, Le Moyen Age en images 2001, A la recherche du Moyen Age 2002, Dieu au Moyen Age 2003, Héros du Moyen Age: le Saint et le Roi 2004, Vu long Moyen Age 2004, Héros et Merveilles du Moyen Age 2004, Le Moyen Age expliqué aux enfants 2006. *Leisure interests:* gastronomy and lecture. *Address:* c/o Ecole des Hautes, Etudes en Sciences Sociales, 54 Boulevard Raspail, 75006 Paris (office); 5 rue de Thionville, 75019 Paris, France (home).

LE GOY, Raymond Edgar Michel, MA; British civil servant; b. 1919, London; s. of J. Goy and May Callan; m. Silvia Ernestine Burnett 1960; two s.; ed William Ellis School, London, Gonville and Caius Coll. Cambridge; British Army 1940–46; entered Civil Service 1947, Road Transport and Establishments Divs, Ministry of Transport 1947–48; UK Shipping Adviser in Japan, Far East and SE Asia 1948–52; various posts in shipping and highway divs, Ministry of Transport and Civil Aviation 1952–57; Dir Goeland Co. 1953; Asst Sec. Railways and Inland Waterways Div., Ministry of Transport and Civil Aviation 1958; Asst Sec. Finance and Supply Ground Services and Aerodrome Management, Ministry of Aviation 1959–61, Dir of Admin. Navigational Services 1961–62; Asst Sec. Aviation Overseas Policy, Ministry of Aviation and Bd of Trade 1962–67; Under-Sec. of Civil Aviation 1968–73; Head Del. to European Civil Aviation Conf.; Dir-Gen. of Transport Comm. of EEC 1973–81, of Comm. of EU 1981–. *Publication:* The Victorian Burletta 1953. *Leisure interests:* theatre, music, race relations. *Address:* c/o Fortis Banque, Agence Schuman, Rond Point Schuman 10, 1040 Brussels, Belgium.

LE GREW, Daryl John, MArch; Australian university administrator and professor of architecture; *Vice-Chancellor and President, University of Tasmania;* b. 17 Sept. 1945, Melbourne, Vic.; s. of A. J. Le Grew; m. Josephine Le Grew 1971; one s. two d.; ed Trinity Grammar School, Kew and Univ. of Melbourne; Lecturer, Dept of Town and Regional Planning, Univ. of Melbourne 1969–73, Lecturer and Sr Lecturer, Dept of Architecture and Building 1973–85; Prof. of Architecture, Deakin Univ. 1986–98, Dean Faculty of Design and Tech. 1992–93, Chair. Academic Bd 1992–98, Pro-Vice-Chancellor (Academic) 1993–94, Deputy Vice-Chancellor and Vice-Pres. (Academic) 1994–98; Vice-Chancellor Univ. of Canterbury, NZ 1998–2002; Vice-Chancellor and Pres. Univ. of Tasmania 2003–; Visiting Fellow, Bartlett School of Architecture and Planning, Univ. Coll. London; consultant, UK Science Research Council Training Programme; architectural consultant and Adviser to Dir and Trustees of Nat. Gallery of Victoria, Melbourne for re devt of gallery site, to Dir and Council Museum of Victoria, Melbourne for its re devt, mem. Council; several sr appointments in business and higher educ.; Life Fellow, Museum of Vic. 1997. *Leisure interests:* swimming, music, poetry, philosophy. *Address:* University of Tasmania, Private Bag 51, Hobart, Tasmania 7001, Australia (office). *Telephone:* (3) 6226-2003 (office). *Fax:* (3) 6226-2001 (office). *E-mail:* Vice.Chancellor@utas.edu.au (office). *Website:* www.utas.edu.au (office).

LE GUIN, Ursula Kroeber, BA, MA; American writer and poet; b. 21 Oct. 1929, Berkeley, Calif.; d. of Alfred L. Kroeber and Theodora K. Kroeber; m. Charles A. Le Guin 1953; one s. two d.; ed Radcliffe Coll., Columbia Univ.; taught French, Mercer Univ., Univ. of Ida 1954–56; teacher, resident writer or visiting lecturer at numerous univs, including Bennington Coll., Portland State Univ., Pacific Univ., Reading Univ., Univ. of Calif. at San Diego, Indiana Writers' Conf., Kenyon Coll., Clarion West Writers' Workshop, First Australian Workshop in Speculative Fiction, Beloit, Haystack, Flight of the Mind, Stanford, etc. 1971–; Mellon Prof., Tulane Univ. 1986; mem. Science Fiction Research Asscn, Authors' League, Writers' Guild W, PEN; Fellow, Columbia Univ. 1952, Fulbright Fellow 1953; Arbuthnot Lecturer, American Library Asscn 2004; Hon. DLitt (Bucknell Univ., Lawrence Univ.); Hon. DHumLitt (Lewis and Clark Coll., Occidental Coll., Emory Univ., Univ. of Ore., Western Ore. State, Kenyon, Portland State); Hugo Awards 1969, 1974, 1975, Jupiter Awards 1975, 1976, Nebula Awards 1969, 1975, 1990, 1996, 2008, Gandalf Award 1979, Lewis Carroll Shelf Award 1979, Prix Lectures-Jeunesse 1987, American Acad. and Inst. of Arts and Letters Harold Vursell Award 1991, Pushcart Prize 1991, Hubbub annual poetry award 1995, Asimov's Reader's award 1995, Theodore Sturgeon Award 1995, James Tiptree Jr Retrospective Award 1996, Locus Award 1973, 1984, 1995, 1996, 2001, 2002, 2003, Bumbershoot Arts Award, Seattle, WA 1998, LA Times Robert Kirsch Lifetime Achievement Award 2000, Pacific NW Booksellers' Asscn Lifetime Achievement Award 2001, Willamette Writers' Lifetime Achievement Award 2002, PEN/Malamud Award for Short Fiction 2002, World Fantasy Award 2002, SFWA Grand Master 2003, YALSA Margaret A. Edwards Award for Lifetime Achievement 2004, PEN Center USA Award for Children's Literature 2005, Maxine Cushing Gray Award for Literary Achievement 2006, ICON Gallun Award 2007. *Films:* King Dog (screenplay) 1985. *Television:* The Lathe of Heaven. *Publications:* fiction: Rocannon's World 1966, Planet of Exile 1966, City of Illusion 1967, A Wizard of Earthsea (Earthsea series) (Boston Globe-Horn Award) 1968, The Left Hand of Darkness (Nebula Award, Hugo Award) 1969, The Tombs of Atuan (Earthsea series) (Newbery Silver Medal 1972) 1970, The Lathe of Heaven (Locus Award 1973) 1971, The Farthest Shore (Earthsea series) (Nat. Book Award) 1972, The Dispossessed: An Ambiguous Utopia (Hugo Award, Nebula Award) 1974, The Wind's Twelve Quarters (short stories) 1975, The Word for World is Forest 1976, Very Far Away from Anywhere Else 1976, Orsinian Tales (short stories) 1976, Malafrena 1979, The Beginning Place 1980, The Compass Rose (short stories)

(Locus Award 1984) 1982, The Eye of the Heron 1983, Always Coming Home (Kafka Award 1986) 1985, Buffalo Gals (short stories) (Hugo Award 1988, Int. Fantasy Award 1988) 1987, Tehanu (Earthsea series) (Nebula Award) 1990, Searoad (short stories) (H. L. Davis Award 1992) 1991, A Fisherman of the Inland Sea (short stories) 1994, Four Ways to Forgiveness (short stories) (Locus Award) 1995, Unlocking the Air (short stories) 1996, The Telling (Locus Award, Endeavor Award) 2000, Tales from Earthsea (Earthsea series) (Locus Award, Endeavor Award) 2001, The Other Wind (Earthsea series) 2001, The Birthday of the World (short stories) (Locus Readers' Award) 2002, Changing Planes (short stories) 2003, Kalpa Imperial (translation) 2003, Gifts 2004, Voices 2006, Powers 2007, Lavinia 2008; juvenile fiction: Leese Webster 1979, Cobbler's Rune 1983, Solomon Leviathan 1988, Catwings 1988, A Visit from Dr Katz 1988, Fire and Stone 1989, Catwings Return 1989, Fish Soup 1992, A Ride on the Red Mare's Back 1992, Wonderful Alexander and the Catwings 1994, Jane on her Own 1999, Tom Mouse 2002; poetry: Wild Angels 1974, Walking in Cornwall (chapbook) 1976, Tillai and Tylissos (chapbook, with Theodora Kroeber) 1979, Hard Words 1981, In the Red Zone (chapbook, with Henk Pander) 1983, Wild Oats and Fireweed 1988, No Boats (chapbook) 1992, Blue Moon over Thurman Street (with Roger Dorband) 1993, Going out with Peacocks 1994, Sixty Odd 1999, Selected Poems of Gabriela Mistral (translation) 2003, Incredible Good Fortune 2006; non-fiction: Dancing at the Edge of the World (criticism) 1989, The Language of the Night (criticism) 1992, A Winter Solstice Ritual for the Pacific Northwest (chapbook, with Vonda N. McIntyre) 1991, Findings (chapbook) 1992, The Art of Bunditsu (chapbook) 1993, Lao Tzu: Tao Te Ching: A Book About the Way and the Power of the Way (trans.) 1997, The Twins, The Dream/Las Gemelas, El Sueño (trans. with Diana Bellessi) 1997, Steering the Craft (criticism) 1998, The Wave in the Mind (criticism) 2004, Cheek by Jowl: Talks and Essays on How and Why Fantasy Matters 2009; contrib. to periodicals, including New Yorker, Omni, Redbook, Fantasy and Science Fiction, Fantastic, Amazing, Playboy, Playgirl, Tri-Quarterly, Kenyon Review, Calyx, Milkweed, Mr Cogito, Seattle Review, NW Review, Open Places, Backbone, Orion, Parabola, Paradoxa, Yale Review, Antaeus Foundation, SF Studies, Critical Inquiry. *Address:* Virginia Kidd Agency, PO Box 278, Milford, PA 18337, USA (office). *E-mail:* vkagency@ptd.net (office). *Website:* www.ursulakleguin.com.

LE PEN, Jean-Marie, LenD; French politician; *President, Front National;* b. 20 June 1928, La Trinité-sur-Mer, Morbihan; s. of Jean Le Pen and Anne-Marie Hervé; m. 1st Pierrette Lalanne, 1960 (divorced); three d.; m. 2nd Jeanne-Marie Paschos 1991; ed Coll. des Jésuites Saint-François-Xavier, Vannes, Lycée de Lorient, Univ. de Paris; Pres. Corpn des étudiants en droit de Paris 1949–51; Sub-Lt 1st foreign Bn of paratroopers, Indochina 1954–55; Political Ed. Caravelle 1955, Nat. Del. for Union de défense de la jeunesse française, then Deputy 1st Sector, La Seine; mem. Groupe d'union et de fraternité at Nat. Ass., independent Deputy for la Seine 1958–62; Gen. Sec. Front Nat. Combattant 1956, of Tixier Vignancour Cttee 1964–65; Dir Soc. d'études et de relations publiques 1963–; Pres. Front Nat. 1972–(2011), Front Nat. Provence-Alpes-Côte d'Azur 1992–2000; mem. Nat. Ass. 1986–88; mem. European Parl. 1984–2000, Pres. groupe des droites européennes 1984–2000; presidential cand. 1988, 2002, 2007; guilty of physical assault and banned from holding or seeking public office for two years, given three-month suspended prison sentence April 1998; sentence on appeal: immunity removed by European Parl. Oct. 1998; Croix de la Valeur militaire. *Publications:* Les Français d'abord 1984, La France est de retour 1985, L'Espoir 1986, J'ai vu juste 1998. *Address:* Serp, 6 rue de Beaune, 75007 Paris (office); 8 parc de Montretout, 92210 St-Cloud, France (home).

LE PENSEC, Louis; French politician; *Senator;* b. 8 Jan. 1937, Mellac; s. of Jean Le Pensec and Marie-Anne Hervé; m. Colette Le Guilcher 1963; one s.; Personnel Officer, Soc. nationale d'étude et de construction de moteurs d'aviation 1963–66, Soc. anonyme de véhicules industriels et d'équipements mécaniques 1966–69; Teacher of Personnel Man., Legal Sciences Teaching and Research Unit, Univ. of Rennes 1970–73; Mayor of Mellac 1971–97; Deputy (Finistère) to Nat. Ass. 1973–81, 1983–88, 1993; Councillor for Finistère 1976–, Senator 1998–; mem. Steering Cttee, Parti Socialiste 1977, Exec. Bureau 1979; Minister for the Sea 1981–83, 1988, of Overseas Depts and Territories 1988–93; Govt Spokesperson 1989–91; Vice-Pres. for Europe, Council of European Communities 1983–; Minister of Agric. and Fisheries 1997–98; Vice-Pres. County Council (Finistère) 1998–; Head ASEAN Mission for External Trade; mem. Senate Del. for EU 1999–; Vice-Pres. Council of European Municipalities and Regions 2007–; Commdr du Mérite maritime, du Mérite agricole; Order du Mérite (Côte d'Ivoire); Grand-croix du Royaume (Thailand). *Publication:* Ministre à Babord 1997. *Leisure interest:* golf. *Address:* Hôtel du département, 32 quai Dupleix, 29196 Quimper Cedex (office); Sénat, 75291 Paris (office); Kerviguennou, 29300 Mellac, France (home). *Telephone:* (2) 98-76-20-24 (office); (2) 98-35-08-00 (home). *Fax:* (2) 98-76-21-96 (office); (2) 98-35-08-09 (home). *E-mail:* louis.le-pensec@wanadoo.fr (office).

LE PICHON, Xavier; French geologist and academic; *Professor and Chair of Geodynamics, Collège de France;* b. 18 June 1937, Quinhon, Viet Nam; s. of Jean-Louis Le Pichon and Hélène Tyl; m. Brigitte Barthélemy 1962; five c.; ed Sciences Physiques, Strasbourg; Research Asst Columbia Univ., New York 1963; Scientific Adviser, Centre Nat. pour l'Exploitation des Océans 1968, 1973; Head, Dept of Oceanography, Centre Océanologique de Bretagne, Brest 1969; Prof. Univ. P. & M. Curie, Paris 1978; Dir Dept of Geology, Ecole Normale Supérieure, Paris 1984–91, Dir Lab. of Geology 1984–2000; Prof. and Chair. of Geodynamics, Collège de France 1987–; Pres. Ifremer Scientific Council 1991–2000, Sr Jury Inst. Universitaire de France 1997; Visiting Prof. Oxford Univ. 1994, Univ. of Tokyo 1995, Rice Univ. Houston 2002; mem. Acad. des Sciences; Founder mem. Acad. Europaea 1988, NAS, USA 1995; Chevalier Légion d'Honneur, Commdr Ordre Nat. du Mérite; Dr hc (Dalhousie Univ.)

1989, (ETH, Zürich) 1992; Maurice Ewing Medal, American Geophysical Union 1984, Huntsman Award (Canada) 1987, Japan Prize 1990, Wollaston Medal (Geological Soc. of London) 1991, Balzan Prize 2002, Wagener Medal 2003. *Publications:* Plate Tectonics (with others) 1973, Expédition Famous, à 3000m sous l'Atlantique (with C. Riffaud) 1976, Kaiko, voyage aux extrémités de la mer 1986, Aux racines de l'homme, De la Mort à l'Amour 1997, La Mort, Desclée de Brouwer 1999. *Address:* Chaire de Géodynamique, Collège de France, BP 80, 13545, Aix-en-Provence, Cedex 04, France (office). *Telephone:* 4-42-50-74-02 (office). *Fax:* 4-42-50-74-01 (office). *E-mail:* lepichon@cdf.u-3mrs.fr. *Website:* www.cdf.u-3mrs.fr (office).

LE PORS, Anicet; French politician, economist and jurist; *Section President, National Court of Asylum;* b. 28 April 1931, Paris; s. of François Le Pors and Gabrielle Croguennec; m. Claudine Carteret 1959; one s. two d.; ed Collège Arago, Paris, Ecole de la Météorologie, Univ. of Paris, Centre d'étude des programmes économiques; Meteorological Eng, Marrakesh, Morocco 1953, Paris 1957–65; trade union official (CGT) 1955–77; Consultant, World Meteorological Org., Léopoldville, Congo (now Kinshasa, Democratic Repub. of Congo) 1960; Sec. Communist section of Metropolitan Office 1962; Head of Dept, Ministry of Economy and Finance 1965; Sec. Cttee of Cen. Admin., Parti Communiste Français (PCF) 1976–77, Head of Nationalizations, Industrial Policy and Insts Dept, then of Int. Dept, PCF 1978, mem. Cen. Cttee 1979; Head of Interministerial Comm., Univ. of Paris XIII 1976–77 and Ecole supérieure des Sciences Economiques et Commerciales 1978; Senator (Hauts-de-Seine) 1977–81; Minister-Del. for the Civil Service and Admin. Reforms, attached to Prime Minister 1981–83; Sec. of State in charge of Public and Admin. Reform 1983–84; Sr mem. Council of State 1985–; mem. Higher Council for Integration; Councillor-Gen. from Hauts-de-Seine 1985–98; Vice-Pres. Nat. Council of Tourism 2000–; Chair. Youth Employment Programme, Cttee de pilotage pour l'égal accès des femmes et des hommes (cttee for equal rights for men and women); Section Pres. Comm. de recours des réfugiés (now Cour nationale du droit d'asile, Nat. Court of Asylum) 2000–; Officier, Légion d'honneur; Officier, Ordre nat. du mérite. *Publications:* Les transferts Etats-industries en France et dans les pays occidentaux 1976, Les béquilles du capital 1977, Marianne à l'encan 1980, Contradictions 1984, L'état efficace 1985, Pendant la mue, le serpent est aveugle 1993, Le Nouvel Age de la citoyenneté 1997, La Citoyenneté 1999, Eloge de l'échec 2001, le droit d'asile 2005. *Leisure interests:* swimming, sailing. *Address:* Conseil d'Etat, place du Palais-Royal, 75001 Paris (office); 189 boulevard de la République, 92210 St-Cloud, France (home). *Telephone:* (6) 80-20-81-67 (office). *E-mail:* anicetlp@club-internet.fr (office).

LE PORTZ, Yves; French financial executive; b. 30 Aug. 1920, Hennebont; s. of Joseph Le Portz and Yvonne Le Doussal; m. Bernadette Champetier de Ribes 1946; five c.; ed Univ. de Paris à la Sorbonne, Ecole des Hautes Etudes Commerciales and Ecole Libre des Sciences Politiques; attached to Gen. Inspectorate of Finances 1943, Dir Adjoint du Cabinet, Président du Conseil 1948–49, Sous-Dir, Chef de Service, Ministry of Finance and Econ. Affairs 1951; Chief of Staff to Sec. of State for Finance and Econ. Affairs 1951–52; Chief of Staff to Minister for Posts, Telegraphs and Telephones 1952–55; Chief of Staff to Minister for Reconstruction and Housing 1955–57; French Del. to Econ. and Social Council of UN 1957–58; Dir-Gen. of Finance for Algeria 1958–62; Dir-Gen. Bank for Devt of Algeria 1959–62; Vice-Pres. and Vice-Chair. Bd Dirs European Investment Bank (EIB) 1962–70, Pres. and Chair. 1970–84, Hon. Pres. 1984; Pres. Supervisory Cttee, Bourse (Stock Exchange) Aug. 1984–88; Pres. Supervisory Cttee Investment Cos and Funds, Principality of Monaco 1988–; Insp.-Gen. of Finances 1971–84; Pres. Comité de déontologie de l'indépendance (CDI) des Commissaires aux comptes des sociétés faisant appel public à l'épargne 1999–; Commdr, Légion d'honneur 1978, Grand Officier, Ordre nat. de Mérite. *Address:* 127 avenue de Wagram, 75017 Paris, France (home). *Telephone:* 1-42-27-76-88.

LE ROY, Alain; French diplomatist and UN official; *Under-Secretary-General for Peacekeeping Operations, United Nations;* b. 5 Feb. 1953; m.; one s.; ed Ecole nationale supérieure des Mines, Paris, Paris 1 (Sorbonne) Univ.; early career as petroleum engineer for Total; with Sous-préfet d'Avallon 1991–92; Cabinet Chief, Ministry of Agric. 1992–93; Counsellor Cour des comptes 1993–95, 1995–99; Deputy to UN Special Co-ordinator for Sarajevo and Dir of Operations for restoration of essential public services March-Sept. 1995; UN Regional Admin. in Kosovo (W Region) 1999–2000; Nat. Co-ordinator for Stability Pact for South-East Europe, Ministry of Foreign Affairs 2000; fmr EU Special Rep. in the Fmr Yugoslav Repub. of Macedonia; fmr Asst Sec. for Econ. and Financial Affairs, Ministry for Foreign Affairs; fmr Amb. to Madagascar; Conseiller Maître, Cour des comptes and Amb. in charge of Union for Mediterranean Initiative 2007–08; UN Under-Sec.-Gen. for Peacekeeping Operations 2008–. *Address:* Department of Peacekeeping Operations, United Nations, New York, NY 10017, USA (office). *Telephone:* (212) 963-1234 (office). *Fax:* (212) 963-4879 (office). *Website:* www.un.org/Depts/dpko/dpko (office).

LE ROY LADURIE, Emmanuel, DèsSc; French historian and academic; *Professor of History of Modern Civilization, Collège de France;* b. 19 July 1929, Les Moutiers en Cinglais; s. of Jacques Le Roy Ladurie and Léontine Dauger; m. Madeleine Pupponi 1956; one s. one d.; ed Ecole Normale Supérieure; taught Lycée de Montpellier 1955–57; research attaché, CNRS 1957–60; Asst Faculté des Letters, Montpellier 1960–63; Asst lecturer, Dir of Studies Ecole des Hautes Etudes 1963; lecturer, the Sorbonne 1970–71, University of Paris VII 1971–73; Prof. of History of Modern Civilization, Collège de France 1973–; Gen. Admin. Bibliothèque Nat. 1987–94, Pres. Scientific Council 1994–; mem. Conseil scientifique de l'Ecole Normale Supérieure 1998–; mem. Acad. des Sciences morales et politiques; Foreign Hon. mem. Acad. des Sciences américaines 1984; Commdr Légion d'honneur, Ordre des Arts et Lettres; 15 hon. degrees; Medal of Center for French Civilization and Culture, New York Univ. 1985. *Publications include:* Les paysans de Languedoc 1966, Histoire du climat depuis l'an mil 1967, Le territoire de l'historien Vol. I 1973, Vol. II 1978, Montaillou, village occitan de 1294 à 1324 1975, Le carnaval de Romans 1579–80 1980, L'argent, l'amour et la mort en pays d'oc 1980, Histoire de la France urbaine, Vol. III 1981, Paris-Montpellier PC-PSU 1945-1963 1982, La Sorcière de Jasmin 1983, Parmi les historiens 1983, The French Peasantry 1450–1680, Pierre Prion, scribe 1987, Monarchies 1987, L'Histoire de France de: L'Etat Royal 1460–1610 (jtly) 1987, L'Ancien Régime 1610–1770 (jtly) 1991, The Royal French State 1460–1610 1994, Le Siècle des Plaeter (1499–1628) 1995, The Ancien Régime: A History of France 1610–1774 1996, Mémoires 1902–1945 1997, L'Historien, le chiffre et le texte 1997, Saint-Simon, le système de la Cour 1997, Le Voyage de Thomas Plaeter 2000, Histoire de France des Régions 2001, Histoire des paysans français de la Peste Noire à la Revolution 2002. *Leisure interests:* cycling, swimming. *Address:* Collège de France, 11 Place Marcelin-Berthelot, 75005 Paris; 88 rue d'Alleray, 75015 Paris, France (home). *Telephone:* 1-44-27-10-38 (office); 1-48-42-01-27. *Fax:* 1-44-27-12-40 (office). *E-mail:* e.m.ladurie@wanadoo.fr (home).

LEA, Ruth Jane, BA, MSc, FRSA, FSS; British economist; *Economic Adviser and non-Executive Director, Arbuthnot Banking Group;* b. 22 Sept. 1947, Cheshire, England; d. of Thomas Lea and of the late Jane Lea (née Brown); ed Lymm Grammar School, Univs of York and Bristol; asst statistician, Sr Econ. Asst, HM Treasury 1970–73, statistician 1977–78; Lecturer in Econs, Thames Polytechnic 1973–74; statistician, Civil Service Coll. 1974–77, Cen. Statistics Office 1978–84; briefing and policy posts, Dept of Trade and Industry 1984–88; with Mitsubishi Bank 1988–93, Chief Economist 1990–93; Chief UK Economist, Lehman Brothers 1993–94; Econs Ed. Ind. TV News 1994–95; Head of Policy Unit, Inst. of Dirs 1995–2003; Dir Centre for Policy Studies 2004–07; mem. Bd Dirs Arbuthnot Banking Group 2005–, Econ. Adviser 2007–; Dir Global Vision 2007–; mem. Retail Prices Advisory Cttee 1992–94, Nat. Consumer Council 1993–96, Rowntree Foundation Income and Wealth Inquiry Group 1993–94, Nurses' Pay Review Body 1994–98, Research Centres Bd ESRC 1996, Research Priorities Bd 1996–97, Statistics Advisory Cttee Office of Nat. Statistics 1996–97; Trustee, New Europe Research Trust 1999–2005; Council mem. Univ. of London 2001–06; Gov. LSE 2003–08; Hon. DBA (Greenwich) 1997. *Publications:* various publs on business and econ. topics and the EU. *Leisure interests:* music, philately, natural history and countryside, heritage. *Address:* Arbuthnot Banking Group, Arbuthnot House, 20 Ropemaker Street, London, EC2Y 9AR (office); 25 Redbourne Avenue, Finchley, London, N3 2BP, England (home). *Telephone:* (7800) 608-674 (office); (20) 8346-3482 (home). *E-mail:* ruthlea@arbuthnot.co.uk (office); ruth.lea@btinternet.com (home). *Website:* www.arbuthnotgroup.com (office).

LEACH, Adm. of the Fleet Sir Henry (Conyers), GCB, DL; British naval officer; b. 18 Nov. 1923; s. of Capt. John Catterall Leach and Evelyn Burrell Lee; m. Mary Jean McCall 1958 (died 1991); two d.; ed St Peter's Court, Broadstairs, Royal Naval Coll., Dartmouth; served cruiser Mauritius, S Atlantic and Indian Ocean 1941–42; battleship Duke of York (involved in Scharnhorst action) 1943–45, destroyers, Mediterranean 1945–46, gunnery 1947; gunnery appointments 1948–51; Gunnery Officer, cruiser Newcastle, Far East 1953–55; staff appointments 1955–59; commanded destroyer Dunkirk 1959–61; frigate Galatea (Capt. (D) 27th Escort Squadron and Mediterranean) 1965–67; Dir of Naval Plans 1968–70; commanded Commando Ship Albion 1970; Asst Chief of Naval Staff (Policy) 1971–73; Flag Officer First Flotilla 1974–75; Vice-Chief of Defence Staff 1976–77; C-in-C Fleet and Allied C-in-C, Channel and Eastern Atlantic 1977–79; Chief of Naval Staff and First Sea Lord 1979–82; First and Prin. Naval ADC to the Queen 1979–82; Pres. RN Benevolent Soc., Sea Cadet Assen 1984–93; Pres. Royal Bath & West of England Soc. 1993, Vice-Pres. 1994–; Chair. St Dunstan's 1983–98, Hon. Vice-Pres. 1999–; Chair. Council, King Edward VII Hosp. 1987–98, Hon. Vice-Pres. 1998–; Gov. Cranleigh School 1983–93, St Catherine's 1987–93; Patron Meridian Trust Asscn, Hampshire Royal British Legion 1994–; Hon. Freeman Merchant Taylors, Shipwrights, City of London. *Publication:* Endure No Makeshifts (autobiog.) 1993, Anecdotage (miscellany) 1996. *Leisure interests:* fishing, shooting, gardening, antique furniture repair. *Address:* Wonston Lea, Wonston, Winchester, Hants., SO21 3LS, England. *Telephone:* (1962) 760344 (home). *Fax:* (1962) 760344 (home).

LEAF, Alexander, MD; American physician and academic; *Jackson Professor of Clinical Medicine, Emeritus, Harvard Medical School;* b. 10 April 1920, Yokohama, Japan; s. of Dr Aaron L. Leaf and Dora Hural Leaf; m. Barbara L. Kincaid 1943; three d.; ed Univs of Washington and Michigan; Intern, Massachusetts Gen. Hosp. 1943–44, mem. staff 1949–, Physician-in-Chief 1966–81, Physician 1981–; Resident, Mayo Foundation, Rochester, Minn. 1944–45; Research Fellow, Univ. of Mich. 1947–49; mem. Faculty, Medical School, Harvard Univ. 1949–, Jackson Prof. of Clinical Medicine 1966–81, Ridley Watts Prof. of Preventive Medicine 1980–90, Jackson Prof. of Clinical Medicine Emer. 1990–; Visiting Fellow, Balliol Coll. Oxford 1971–72; Distinguished Physician, Brockton/West Roxbury Medical Center, Va 1992–97; mem. NAS, AAAS, American Acad. of Arts and Sciences, American Coll. of Physicians, The Biochemical Soc. (UK), Inst. of Medicine 1978, etc.; Kober Medal, Asscn of American Physicians 1995, A. M. Richards Award, Int. Soc. of Nephrology 1997. *Publications:* Significance of the Body Fluids in Clinical Medicine, Youth in Old Age, Renal Pathophysiology; 357 articles in professional journals. *Leisure interests:* music (flautist), jogging. *Address:* Massachusetts General Hospital, East, Building 149, 13th Street, Charlestown, MA 02129 (office); 5 Sussex Road, Winchester, MA 01890-3846, USA (home). *Telephone:* (617) 726-5908 (office); (781) 729-5852 (home). *Fax:* (617) 726-6144 (office). *E-mail:* aleaf@partners.org (office).

LEAHY, Sir John H. G., KCMG, MA; British diplomatist (retd); b. 7 Feb. 1928, Worthing, Sussex; s. of the late William H. G. Leahy and Ethel Leahy; m. Elizabeth Anne Pitchford 1954; two s. two d.; ed Tonbridge School, Clare Coll. Cambridge, Yale Univ., USA; joined diplomatic service 1951, Third Sec., Singapore 1955–57; Second Sec., then First Sec., Paris 1958–62; First Sec., Tehran 1965–68; Counsellor, Paris 1973–75; attached to Northern Ireland Office, Belfast 1975–76; Amb. to South Africa 1979–82; Deputy Under-Sec. (Africa and the Middle East), FCO 1982–84; High Commr to Australia 1984–88; Dir Observer newspaper 1989–92; Dir (non-exec.) Lonrho PLC 1993–98, Chair. 1994–97; Master, Skinners' Co. 1993–94; Chair. Britain-Australia Soc. 1994–97; mem. Franco-British Council (Chair. 1989–93); Chair. Govs' Cttee Tonbridge School 1994–99; Pro-Chancellor City Univ. 1991–97; Officier, Légion d'honneur; Hon. DCL (City Univ.) 1997. *Publication:* A Life of Spice 2006. *Address:* 16 Ripley Chase, The Goffs, Eastbourne, E Sussex, BN21 1HB, England (home). *Telephone:* (1323) 725368 (home). *Fax:* (1323) 720437 (home). *E-mail:* johnleahy@dsl.pipex.com (home).

LEAHY, Patrick Joseph, JD; American politician and lawyer; *Senator from Vermont;* b. 31 March 1940, Montpelier, Vt; s. of Howard Leahy and Alba Leahy (née Zambon); m. Marcelle Pomerleau Leahy 1962; two s. one d.; ed St Michael's Coll., Winooski, Vt and Georgetown Univ. Law Center, Washington, DC; admitted to practise law, State of Vermont 1964, US Supreme Court, Second Circuit Court of Appeals, New York, US Fed. Dist Court of Vt; Senator from Vermont 1975–; Vice-Chair. Senate Intelligence Cttee 1985–86; Chair. Judiciary Cttee 2001, 2007–, sr mem. Agric. Cttee and Appropriations Cttee; mem. Vt Bar Asscn 1964–; Vice-Pres. Nat. Dist Attorneys' Asscn 1971–74; Distinguished Service Award of Nat. Dist Attorneys' Asscn 1974, Harry S. Truman Award, Nat. Guard Asscn 2003. *Leisure interests:* photography, reading, hiking, cross-country skiing. *Address:* 433 Russell Senate Office Building, Washington, DC 20510, USA (office). *Telephone:* (202) 224-4242 (office). *Website:* leahy.senate.gov (office).

m**LEAHY, Sir Terence Patrick,** Kt, BSc; British business executive; *Chief Executive, Tesco PLC;* b. 28 Feb. 1956, Liverpool; m. Alison Leahy; two s. one d.; ed St Edward's Coll., Liverpool, Univ. of Manchester Inst. of Science and Tech.; mem. of staff Co-op supermarket group 1977–79; joined Tesco PLC 1979, Marketing Dir 1992–95, Deputy Man. Dir 1995–97, Chief Exec. 1997–; Co-Chancellor Manchester Univ.; Special Adviser Everton Football Club 2004–. *Leisure interests:* sport, reading, theatre, architecture. *Address:* Tesco PLC, Tesco House, PO Box 18, Delamare Road, Cheshunt, Herts. EN8 9SL, England (office). *Telephone:* (1992) 632222 (office). *Fax:* (1992) 644962 (office). *E-mail:* terry.leahy@tesco.com (office). *Website:* www.tesco.com (office).

LEAKEY, Louise N., BS, PhD; palaeontologist; *Head, Koobi Fora Research Project;* b. 1972, Kenya; d. of Richard Leakey and Meave Leakey (née Epps); grand-d. of the late Louis Leakey; m.; ed Univ. of Bristol, Univ. of London; worked with parents from early age in Turkana Basin, Kenya; currently Head, Koobi Fora Research Project, East Turkana; named (with mother) Nat. Geographic Soc. Explorer-in-Residence 2002. *Achievements include:* discovery of Kenyanthropus platyops, a new human species that extended diversity in hominid family record back to 3.5 million years. *Address:* Koobi Fora Research Project, Lake Turkana, Kenya; c/o The Leakey Foundation, POB 29346, 1002A O'Reilly Avenue, San Francisco, CA 94129, USA. *Telephone:* (415) 561-4646 (USA). *Fax:* (415) 561-4647 (USA). *Website:* www.kfrp.com; www.leakey.com.

LEAKEY, Richard Erskine Frere, FRAI; Kenyan politician, palaeontologist and conservationist; b. 19 Dec. 1944, Nairobi; s. of the late Louis Leakey and Mary Leakey; m. 1st Margaret Cropper 1965; m. 2nd Meave Gillian Epps 1970; three d.; ed Duke of York School (later known as Lenana School), Nairobi; trapper of primates for research 1961–65; co-leader of research expeditions to Lake Natron 1963–64, Omo River 1967; Dir Root & Leakey Safaris (tour co.) 1965–68; archaeological excavation, Lake Baringo 1966; Admin. Dir Nat. Museums of Kenya 1968–74, Dir and Chief Exec. 1974–89; research in Nakali/Suguta Valley 1978; leader of research projects, Koobi Fora 1979–81, W Turkana 1981–82, 1984–89, Buluk 1983; Dir Wildlife Conservation and Man. Dept 1989–90; Dir Kenya Wildlife Service 1990–94, 1998–99; Man. Dir Richard Leakey & Assocs Ltd 1994–98; Co-Founder and Gen.-Sec. Safina Party 1995–98; nominated MP Nat. Ass. –1999; Perm. Sec., Sec. to the Cabinet, Head of the Public Service, Office of the Pres., Rep. of Kenya 1999–2001; interim Chair. Transparency International (Kenya br.) 2007; numerous hon. positions including Chair. Wildlife Clubs of Kenya 1969–80 (Trustee 1980–), Foundation for Research into the Origins of Man (USA) 1971–85, Kenya Nat. Cttee of the United World Colls 1982–, E African Wildlife Soc. 1984–89, SAIDIA 1989–; Chair. Bd of Trustees, Nat. Museums of Kenya 1989–94; Co-founder and mem. Bd Dirs Wildlife Direct 2004–; Life Trustee, L.S.B. Leakey Foundation; Trustee, Nat. Fund for Disabled in Kenya 1980–95, Agricultural Research Foundation, Kenya 1986–; has given more than 750 public and scholarly Lectures; Foreign Hon. mem. American Acad. of Arts and Sciences 1998; Order of the Burning Spear, Kenya 1993; nine hon. degrees; numerous awards and honours, including James Smithsonian Medal, USA 1990, Gold Medal, Royal Geographical Soc., UK 1990, World Ecology Medal, Int. Centre for Tropical Ecology, USA 1997. *TV documentaries:* Bones of Contention, Survival Anglia 1975, The Making of Mankind, BBC 1981, Earth Journal (presenter), NBC 1992. *Publications:* numerous articles on finds in the field of palaeontology in scientific journals, including Nature, Journal of World History, Science, American Journal of Physical Anthropology, etc.; contrib. to General History of Africa (Vol. I), Perspective on Human Evolution and Fossil Vertebrates of Africa; Origins (book, with R. Lewin) 1977, People of the Lake: Man, His Origins, Nature and Future (book, with R. Lewin) 1978, The Making of Mankind 1981, Human Origins 1982, One Life 1983, Origins Reconsidered (with R. Lewin) 1992, Origins of Humankind (with R. Lewin) 1995, The Sixth Extinction (with R. Lewin) 1995, Wildlife Wars: My Fight to Save Africa's Natural Treasures (with V. Morrell) 2001. *Leisure interests:* sailing and cooking. *Address:* Africa Conservation Fund, PO Box 24926, Karen 00502, Nairobi, Kenya (office). *Telephone:* (3) 865120 (office). *E-mail:* info@wildlifedirect.org (office); leakey@wananchi.com (home). *Website:* www.leakey.com; www.leakeyfoundation.org; richardleakey.wildlifedirect.org.

LEAL, Guilherme Peirão; Brazilian business executive; *Chairman, Natura Cosméticos SA;* b. 1950; five c.; ed Univ. of São Paulo, Harvard Business School, USA; joined Natura Cosméticos SA 1979, mem. Bd of Dirs 1998–, Co-Chair. 2001–; f. Instituto Ethos 1998, currently Pres. and mem. Admin. Council; mem. Superior Council on Social Responsibility, (FIESP), Nat. Council on Food Security; mem. Bd of Dirs Brazilian Fund for Biodiversity; mem. Admin. Council, Grupo 'O Estado de São Paulo', WWF Brasil; Citizen of the State of Rio de Janeiro 2004. *Address:* Natura Cosméticos SA, Rodavia Régis Bittencourt, s/nº, km 293, Potuverá, 06882-700 Itapecerica da Serra, São Paulo, Brazil (office). *Telephone:* (11) 3074-1504 (office). *E-mail:* guilhermeleal@natura.net (office). *Website:* www.natura.net (office).

LEAPE, James P.; American lawyer and international organization official; *Director-General, WWF International;* b. 1956; ed Harvard Coll. and Harvard Law School; has worked in nature conservation for more than 30 years; began his career as an environmental lawyer, working on environmental protection cases in USA, advising UNEP, Nairobi, Kenya and co-authoring a text on environmental law; joined WWF-US 1989, Exec. Vice-Pres. of its worldwide conservation programmes 1991–2001, Dir-Gen. WWF International 2005–; Dir conservation and science initiatives, David and Lucile Packard Foundation 2001–05. *Address:* WWF International, Avenue du Mont-Blanc 27, 1196 Gland, Switzerland (office). *Telephone:* (22) 364-91-11 (office). *Fax:* (22) 364-88-36 (office). *E-mail:* cdoole@wwfint.org (office). *Website:* www.wwfint.org (office); www.panda.org (office).

LEAR, Evelyn; American singer (soprano); b. 8 Jan. 1926, Brooklyn, New York; d. of Nina Quartin; m. 2nd Thomas Stewart (deceased); one s. one d. by previous marriage; ed New York Univ., Hunter Coll., Juilliard School, Lincoln Teachers Coll.; won Fulbright Scholarship for study in Germany 1957; joined Berlin Opera, debut in Ariadne auf Naxos 1959; debut in UK in Four Last Songs with London Symphony Orchestra 1957; debut at Metropolitan Opera in Mourning Becomes Electra 1967; debut at La Scala, Milan, in Wozzeck 1971; regular performances with leading opera cos and orchestras in Europe and USA; guest appearances with Berlin Opera and Vienna State Opera; soloist with the leading American orchestras including New York Philharmonic, Chicago Symphony, Philadelphia Orchestra, Boston Symphony, San Francisco Symphony and Los Angeles Philharmonic; has given many recitals and orchestral concerts and operatic performances with Thomas Stewart; Concert Artists Guild Award 1955, Grammy Award for Best Operatic Performance 1965. *Film:* Buffalo Bill 1976. *Major roles include:* Marie in Wozzeck, Marschallin in Der Rosenkavalier, Countess in The Marriage of Figaro, Fiordiligi in Così fan tutte, Desdemona, Mimi, Dido in The Trojans, Donna Elvira in Don Giovanni, Marina in Boris Godunov, Tatiana in Eugene Onegin, Lavinia in Mourning Becomes Electra, title role in Lulu. *Recordings include:* Wozzeck, Lulu, The Flying Dutchman, The Magic Flute, Boris Godunov, Eugene Onegin, Bach's St John Passion, Pergolesi's Stabat Mater, Der Rosenkavalier. *Leisure interests:* reading, teaching, golf. *Address:* c/o Alex D. Fletcher, Neil Funkhouser Artists Management, 105 Arden Street, #5G, New York, NY 10040, USA (office). *E-mail:* Alex@funkhouserartists.com (office). *Website:* www.evelynlear.com (office).

LÉAUD, Jean-Pierre; French actor; b. 28 May 1944, Paris; s. of Pierre Léaud and Jacqueline Pierreux; debut as Antoine Doinel in Truffaut's The 400 Blows 1959, first of a series of Doinel films directed by Truffaut over 20 years. *Films include:* Les quatre cents coups (The Four Hundred Blows) 1959, La Tour, prends garde! (aka Killer Spy) 1960, Boulevard 1960, Le testament d'Orphée, ou ne me demandez pas pourquoi! (The Testament of Orpheus) (uncredited) 1962, L'amour à vingt ans (Love at Twenty) 1962, Les mauvaises fréquentations (Bad Company) 1963, La peau douce (The Soft Skin) (asst dir; uncredited) 1964, L' amour à la mer (Love at Sea) 1963, Une femme mariée: Suite de fragments d'un film tourné en 1964 (asst dir) 1964, Mata-Hari (also asst dir; uncredited) 1964, Alphaville, une étrange aventure de Lemmy Caution (Alphaville, a Strange Case of Lemmy Caution) (also asst dir; uncredited) 1965, Pierrot le fou (also asst dir; uncredited) 1965, Le Père Noël a les yeux bleus (Santa Claus Has Blue Eyes) 1966, Masculin, féminin: 15 faits précis 1966, Made in U.S.A. (also asst dir) 1966, Le plus vieux métier du monde (The Oldest Profession in the World) (uncredited) 1967, Le départ 1967, La chinoise 1967, Week End 1967, Dialóg 20-40-60 1968, La Concentration 1968, Baisers volés (Stolen Kisses) 1968, Paul 1969, Der Leone have sept cabeças (The Lion Has Seven Heads) 1969, Le gai savoir (Joy of Learning) 1969, Porcile (Pigsty) 1969, Domicile conjugal (Bed & Board) 1970, Os herdeiros (The Heirs) 1970, Une aventure de Billy le Kid (aka A Girl Is a Gun, USA) 1971, Out 1, noli me tangere 1971, Les deux anglaises et le continent (Two English Girls and the Continent) 1971, Out 1: Spectre 1972, Last Tango in Paris 1972, La nuit américaine (aka Day for Night) 1973, La maman et la putain (The Mother and the Whore) 1973, De quoi s'agit-il? (dir) 1974, Umarmungen und andere Sachen 1975, Les lolos de Lola 1976, L'amour en fuite (Love on the Run) 1979, Parano 1980, La cassure 1981, Aiutami a sognare (Help Me Dream) 1981, Rebelote 1983, Paris vu par… vingt ans après (Paris Seen By… 20 Years After) 1984, Treasure Island 1985, Csak egy mozi 1985, Détective 1985, Boran – Zeit zum Zielen 1986, Corps et biens (Lost with All Hands) 1986, Ossegg oder Die Wahrheit über Hänsel und Gretel 1987, Jane B. par Agnès V. 1987, Les keufs (Lady Cops) 1987, 36 fillette (Junior Size 36) 1988, La couleur du vent (The Colour of the Wind) 1988, Bunker Palace

Hôtel 1989, I Hired a Contract Killer 1990, Paris s'éveille (Paris Awakens) 1991, C'est la vie 1991, La vie de bohème (Bohemian Life) 1992, La naissance de l'amour (The Birth of Love) 1993, Personne ne m'aime (Nobody Loves Me) 1994, Les cent et une nuits de Simon Cinéma (A Hundred and One Nights of Simon Cinema) 1995, Mon homme (My Man) 1996, Le journal du séducteur (Diary of a Seducer) 1996, Irma Vep 1996, Pour rire! 1996, Elizabeth (uncredited) 1998, Innocent 1999, Une affaire de goût (A Question of Taste) 2000, L'affaire Marcorelle (The Marcorelle Affair) 2000, Ni neibian jidian (What Time Is It There?) 2001, Le Pornographe (The Pornographer) 2001, La guerre à Paris (The War in Paris) 2002, Folle embellie 2004, Léaud de Hurledents (writer) 2004, J'ai vu tuer Ben Barka 2005. *Television includes:* L'éducation sentimentale (mini-series) 1973, Le petit pommier 1981, Mersonne ne m'aime 1982, Le tueur assis 1985, L'herbe rouge 1985, Néo Polar (series; episode Des choses qui arrivent) 1985, Grandeur et décadence 1986, Sei delitti per padre Brown (mini-series) 1988, Femme de papier (Front Woman) 1989.

LEAVER, Sir Christopher, Kt, GBE, KStJ, JP; British business executive; b. 3 Nov. 1937, London; s. of Dr Robert Leaver and Audrey Kerpen; m. Helen Mireille Molyneux Benton 1975; one s. two d.; ed Eastbourne Coll.; commissioned Royal Army Ordnance Corps 1956–58; mem. Retail Food Trades Wages Council 1963–64; JP, Inner London 1970–83, City 1974–93; mem. Council, Royal Borough of Kensington and Chelsea 1970–73; Court of Common Council (Ward of Dowgate), City of London 1973, Sheriff, City of London 1979–80; Lord Mayor of London 1981–82; Chair. London Tourist Bd Ltd 1983–89; Deputy Chair. Thames Water PLC 1989–93, Chair. 1993–94, Vice-Chair. 1994–2000; Bd of Brixton Prison 1975–78; Adviser to Sec. of State on Royal Parks 1993–96; Bd of Govs, City Univ. 1978–; Gov. Christ's Hospital School 1975, City of London Girls' School 1975–78; Chair. Young Musicians' Symphony Orchestra Trust 1979–81, Eastbourne Coll.; Trustee, London Symphony Orchestra 1983–91; Chancellor, City Univ. 1981–82; Vice-Pres. Nat. Playing Fields Assen 1983–99; Church Commr 1982–93, 1996–99; Dir (non-exec.) Unionamerica Holdings 1994–97; Trustee, Chichester Festival Theatre 1982–97; Chair. Pathfinder Properties PLC 1997; Hon. Col 151 Regt RCT(V) 1983–89; Hon. Col Commdt RCT 1988–91; Hon. Liveryman, Farmers' Co. 1980, Water Conservators' Co. 2000; Freeman Co. of Watermen and Lightermen; Order of Oman. *Leisure interests:* gardening, music, travel.

LEAVER, Christopher John, CBE, BSc, MA, PhD, DIC, ARCS, FRS, FRSE; British scientist and academic; *Emeritus Professor of Plant Sciences, University of Oxford;* b. 31 May 1942, Bristol; s. of Douglas P. Leaver and Elizabeth C. Leaver; m. Anne Huggins 1971; one s. one d.; ed Imperial Coll. of Science, London, Univ. of Oxford; Fulbright Scholar, Purdue Univ., Ind., USA 1966–68; Scientific Officer, ARC Unit of Plant Physiology, Imperial Coll. London 1968–69; Lecturer, Univ. of Edinburgh 1969–80, Reader 1980–86, Science and Eng Research Council Sr Research Fellow, 1985–89, Prof. of Plant Molecular Biology 1986–89; Sibthorpian Prof. of Plant Sciences, Univ. of Oxford 1990–2007, now Prof. Emer., Head of Dept of Plant Sciences 1991–2007; Nuffield Commonwealth Bursary, Sr Visiting Fellowship (SERC), CSIRO Div. of Plant Industry, Canberra 1975; European Molecular Biology Org. Long-term Fellowship, Biozentrum, Basle 1980; Trustee and mem. Governing Council, John Innes Centre, Norwich 1984–; Trustee, Nat. History Museum, London 1997–2006; mem. Council, Agric. and Food Research Council 1990–93; mem. Ministry of Agric., Fisheries and Food Priorities Bd 1990–93; mem. Royal Soc. Council 1992–94; mem. European Molecular Biology Org. (Council mem. 1992–97, Chair. 1996–97), Advisory Council on Science and Tech. 1992–93, Council Biochemical Soc. (Chair. NA & MB Group) (Vice-Chair. Exec. Cttee 2002–04, Chair. 2005–07); Dir Isis Innovation Ltd, Univ. of Oxford 1996–2002; Visiting Prof. Univ. of Western Australia 2002–; Del. Oxford Univ. Press 2002–07; mem. Individual Merit Promotion Panel, Biotechnology and Biological Sciences Research Council (BBSRC) 1996–2005 (mem. BBSRC Council 2000–03); Chair. External Scientific Advisory Bd, Inst. of Molecular and Cell Biology, Univ. of Oporto; mem. Scientific Advisory Bd, Inst. of Molecular and Cellular Biology, Singapore, Int. Advisory Panel, A*Star Graduate Acad., Singapore, ITQB Advisory Cttee, Univ. of Lisbon; mem. Academia Europaea; corresponding mem., American Soc. of Plant Biologists 2003; Emer. Fellow, St John's Coll. Oxford; Huxley Gold Medal, Imperial Coll. 1970; Tate & Lyle Award, Phytochemical Soc. of Europe 1984, Humboldt Prize 1997. *Publications:* ed. several books; numerous papers in int. scientific journals. *Leisure interests:* walking and talking in Upper Coquetdale. *E-mail:* chris.leaver@plants.ox.ac.uk (office).

LEAVER, Peter Lawrence Oppenheim, QC; British lawyer; b. 28 Nov. 1944; s. of Marcus Isaac Leaver and Lena Leaver (née Oppenheim); m. Jane Rachel Pearl 1969; three s. one d.; ed Aldenham School, Elstree, Trinity Coll., Dublin; called to Bar Lincoln's Inn 1967, Recorder 1994–, Bencher 1995; Chief Exec. Football Assen Premier League 1997–99; Chair. Bar Cttee 1989, Int. Practice Cttee 1990; mem. Cttee on Future of the Legal Profession 1986–88, Council of Legal Ed. 1986–91, Gen. Council of the Bar 1987–90; Dir Investment Man. Regulatory Org. 1994–2000; Deputy High Court Judge; Deputy Chair. FSA Regulatory Decisions Cttee; mem. Chartered Inst. of Arbitrators, Soc. of Legal Scholars; mem. Dispute Resolution Panel for Winter Olympics, Salt Lake City 2002; recent work includes acting in large-scale arbitration in Dubai (validity of termination of man. contract governed by Middle Eastern law), acting in Grupo Torras litigation (Court of Appeal), appearing for firm of stockbrokers in MGNPT Ltd v. Invesco, acting in Girozentrale and Bank der Österreichischen Sparkassen AG v. TOSG Fund Ltd litigation, appearing for 47 banks in Walker v. Standard Chartered Bank and Jasaro SA v. Standard Chartered Bank litigation, acting in Dimskal Shipping Co. SA v. ITWF The Evia Luck case (House of Lords), appearing in Agip (Africa) Ltd v. Jackson litigation (Court of Appeal), acting in MacLaine Watson v. Dept of Trade and Industry and Int. Tin Council case. *Publication:* Pre-Trial and Pre-Hearing Procedures Worldwide (contrib.) 1990. *Leisure interests:* sport, theatre, wine, opera. *Address:* Chambers of Lord Grabiner QC, 1 Essex Court, Temple, London, EC4Y 9AR (office); 5 Hamilton Terrace, London, NW8 9RE, England (home). *Telephone:* (20) 7583-2000 (office); (20) 7286-0208 (home). *Fax:* (20) 7583-0118 (office). *E-mail:* pleaver@oeclaw.co.uk (office).

LEAVEY, Thomas Edward, MA, PhD; American international postal official (retd); b. 10 Nov. 1934, Kansas City, Mo.; m. Anne Roland 1968; ed Josephinum Coll., Columbus, Ohio, Inst. Catholique, Paris and Princeton Univ.; Prof. Farleigh Dickinson Univ. Teaneck, NJ and George Washington Univ., Washington, DC 1968–70; various man. and exec. positions in US Postal Services, Los Angeles, Chicago and Washington DC 1970–87; Asst Postmaster-Gen. Int. Postal Affairs, USPS HQ 1987–94; Chair. Exec. Council, Universal Postal Union (UPU) 1989–94, Dir-Gen. Int. Bureau of UPU 1995–2004; John Wanamaker Award 1991, Heinrich von Stephan Medal. *Leisure interests:* golf, tennis.

LEAVITT, Michael Okerlund; American politician, insurance industry executive and fmr government official; b. 11 Feb. 1951, Cedar City, Utah; s. of Dixie Leavitt and Anne Okerlund; m. Jacalyn Smith; four s. one d.; ed S Utah Univ.; Sales Rep. Leavitt Group, Cedar City 1972–74, Account Exec. 1974–76; Man. Underwriting, Salt Lake City 1976–82, COO 1982–84, Pres. and CEO 1984–92; mem. Bd of Dirs Pacificorp, Portland, Ore., Utah Power and Light Co., Salt Lake City, Great Western Thrift & Loan, Salt Lake City; mem. staff, Reagan–Bush '84; Gov. of Utah 1993–2003; Admin. US Environmental Protection Agency, Washington, DC 2003–05; US Sec. of Health and Human Services 2005–09. *Leisure interest:* golf. *Address:* c/o Department of Health and Human Services, 200 Independence Avenue, SW, Washington, DC 20201, USA.

LEBED, Aleksey Ivanovich; Russian politician; *Head of Government, Republic of Khakassia;* b. 14 April 1955, Novocherkassk, Rostov Region; m.; one s. one d.; ed Ryazan Higher School of Airborne Troops, Frunze Mil. Acad., St Petersburg State Univ.; mil. service in Afghanistan 1982; participated in mil. operations in different parts of USSR 1980–92; Regt Commdr, 14th Army in Chişinău 1992, resgnd 1995; mem. State Duma 1995–96; Head of Govt Repub. of Khakassia 1996–; mem. Council of Fed. 1996–2001; mem. Congress of Russian Communities; Order of the Red Star; Dr hc (Khakassia Katanov State Univ.); Hon. Diploma (Supreme Council, Repub. of Khakassia); Medal for Courage, Peter the Great Prize 2001. *Publication:* article on regional econ. devt. *Leisure interests:* football, table tennis, billiards, downhill skiing. *Address:* House of Government, prosp. Lenina 67, 655019 Abakan, Republic of Khakassia, Russia. *Telephone:* (39022) 9-91-02 (office). *Fax:* (39022) 6-50-96 (office). *E-mail:* pressa@khakasnet.ru (office). *Website:* www.gov.khakassia.ru.

LEBEDEV, Aleksander Aleksandrovich, CandHist; Russian diplomatist; *President, National Investment Council;* b. 3 June 1938, Voronezh; m.; ed Moscow Inst. of Int. Relations; Head of Sector, USSR Cttee of Youth Orgs –1964, First Deputy Chair. 1969–70; Rep., Vice-Pres. Int. Union of Students in Prague, Czechoslovakia 1964–69; Head of Div. Cen. Komsomol Cttee 1970–71; mem. Exec. Bd, Head of Dept All-Union Copyright Agency (VAAP) 1973–76; Rep. to World Peace Council, Helsinki, Finland 1976–79; Head of Div. World Econs and Int. Relations journal 1979–80, Deputy Ed.-in-Chief 1985–86; Head of Div. Int. Life journal 1980–85, New Time journal 1986–87; consultant and Head of Sector, Cen. CPSU Cttee 1987–90, counsellor-envoy 1990–91; Amb. to Czechoslovakia 1991–93, to Czech Repub. 1993–97, of Special Missions, Ministry of Foreign Affairs 1998, to Turkey 1998–2002; Founder and Pres. Nat. Reserve Bank 1995–2000 (Chair. 2000–05), Nat. Investment Council 2000–; mem. Motherland party, left 2003; cand. for Mayor of Moscow 2003; mem. State Duma 2003–, Deputy Chair. CIS Cttee; mem. Bd of Dirs RAO UES of Russia; mem. Russian Acad. of Sciences; Order, Sign of Hon. *Address:* National Investment Council, Ul. B. Kommunisticheskaya, d. 5, str. 2, 109004 Moscow, Russian Federation (office). *Telephone:* (495) 730-1409 (office). *Fax:* (495) 956-3230 (office). *E-mail:* mail@rnic.ru (office). *Website:* www.rnic.ru (office).

LEBEDEV, Aleksander Yevgenyevich; Russian banker; *President, National Reserve Bank;* b. 16 Dec. 1960; m.; one s.; ed Moscow Inst. of Int. Relations; staff mem. Inst. mem. of Econs of World Socialist System, USSR Acad. of Sciences 1982–83; staff mem. Ministry of Foreign Affairs 1983–; First, then Second Sec. Embassy to UK 1987–92; Rep. Swiss Bank in Russia 1992–93; Founder and Chair. of Bd Russian Investment Finance Co. 1993–; Pres. Nat. Reserve Bank 1995–; Chair. Nat. Investment Bd 1999–. *Address:* National Reserve Bank, N. Barmannaya str. 37A, 107066 Moscow, Russia (office). *Telephone:* (495) 956-32-30 (office). *Fax:* (495) 596-32-30 (office).

LEBEDEV, Col-Gen. Sergei Nikolayevich; Russian international organization official and fmr intelligence officer; *Executive Secretary, Commonwealth of Independent States;* b. 9 April 1948, Jizzax, Uzbek SSR; m. Vera Mikhailovna; two s.; ed Kyiv Polytechnic Inst., Diplomatic Acad. of USSR; staff mem., Chernihiv br., Kyiv Polytechnic Inst. 1970; army service 1971–72; with state security bodies 1973–75, Foreign Intelligence Service 1975–78; Rep. of Foreign Intelligence Service to USA 1998–2000; Dir Fed. Foreign Intelligence Service (SVR) 2000–07; Exec. Sec. CIS 2007–; numerous state awards. *Leisure interests:* travelling, Greco-Roman wrestling, shooting. *Address:* Office of the Executive Secretary, Commonwealth of Independent States, 220000 Minsk, vul. Kirova 17, Belarus (office). *Telephone:* (17) 222-35-17 (office). *Fax:* (17) 227-23-39 (office). *E-mail:* anna@cis.minsk.by (office). *Website:* www.cis.minsk.by (office).

LEBEDEVA, Tatyana Romanovna; Russian athlete; b. 21 July 1976, Sterlitamak, Volgograd; m.; one d.; specialises in triple jump and long jump; set two world records at 2004 World Indoor Championships in Budapest, finished with leap of 15.36m; produced best-ever series of triple jumps prior to 2000 Olympic Games, of 15.14m, 15.32m, 15.15m, 15.16m, 14.86m; personal best of 7.33m in long jump, Tula 2004; winner Gold Medal for triple jump, European Cup, Gateshead 2000, Bremen 2001, European Indoor Championships, Ghent 2000, Goodwill Games, Brisbane 2001, World Championships, Edmonton 2001, World Championships, Paris 2003, Russian Indoor Championships 2003, World Indoor Championships, Budapest 2004, European Championships, Gothenburg 2006; winner Gold Medal for long jump, World Indoor Championships, Budapest 2004, Olympic Games, Athens 2004, World Championships, Osaka 2007; winner Silver Medal for triple jump, Int. Asscn of Athletics Feds (IAAF) World Cup, Johannesburg 1998, Goodwill Games, NY 1998, Olympic Games, Sydney 2000, World Indoor Championships, Lisbon 2001, World Championships, Osaka 2007, Olympic Games, Beijing 2008; winner Silver Medal for long jump, Olympic Games, Beijing 2008; winner Bronze Medal for triple jump, World Jr Championships 1994, Olympic Games, Athens 2004; only athlete to record six wins in six Golden Leagues, winning Golden League jackpot 2005; mem. Volgograd Army Club, RUS. *Address:* c/o All-Russia Athletic Federation, 8, Luzhnetskaya nab., Moscow 119871, Russia. *Website:* www.lebedeva.ru.

LEBEGUE, Daniel Simon Georges, BL; French banker; *Chairman, Institut Français des Administrateurs;* b. 4 May 1943, Lyon; s. of Robert Lebègue and Denise Lebègue (née Flachet); m. Chantal Biron 1970; one s. one d.; ed Univ. of Lyons, Inst. for Political Sciences and Nat. School for Admin., Paris; civil servant, Ministry of Economy and Finance 1969–73; Financial Adviser, Embassy in Japan 1974–76; Head of Balance of Payments Section, Treasury 1976–79, Head of Monetary Funds Section 1979–80; Deputy Dir of Savings and Financial Market 1980–81; Counsellor in charge of Economy and Finance, Prime Minister's Office 1981–83; Head of Dept of Financial and Monetary Affairs at Treasury 1983–84, Head of Treasury 1984–87; Pres. and COO Banque Nat. de Paris 1987–96, Vice-Chair. 1996–97; Pres. and CEO Caisse des dépôts et consignations (CDC) 1997–2002, Chair. CDC Ixis (formed after merger of CDC and CNCE) 2001–02, Dir CDC Ixis Capital Markets; Dir Gaz de France, Thales, Areva; Chair. Institut Français des Administrateurs 2003–; Chevalier, Légion d'honneur, Ordre nat. du Mérite. *Publications:* Le Trésor et la politique financière 1988, La fiscalité de l'épargne dans le marché unique européen 1988. *Leisure interests:* opera, cinema, hiking. *Address:* Institut Français des Administrateurs, 27 avenue de Friedland, 75382 Paris Cedex 08, France (office). *Telephone:* 1-55-65-81-32 (office). *Fax:* 1-55-65-75-99 (office). *E-mail:* president@ifa-asso.com (office). *Website:* www.ifa-asso.com (office).

LEBEL, Jean-Jacques; French artist and art critic; b. 1936, Neuilly-sur-Seine; ed Accad. delle Belle Arti, Florence, Italy; first one-man show Galleria Numero, Florence 1955; has exhibited in many galleries and museums in Europe, USA and Japan; ran Front Unique (poetry, art and politics magazine); worked with American Happening artists, Claes Oldenburg 1962 and Allan Kaprow 1963; involved in NO!art and took part in Involvement Show and Doom Show 1960–61, March Gallery, New York; has produced more than 80 Happenings (Direct Poetry actions or performances worldwide); set up Festival de la Libre Expression, American Center in Paris (an int. exchange of experimental arts); directed Picasso's Desire Caught by the Tail 1967; has participated in most major int. poetry festivals and art shows since 1960s; co-ed. series of re-edns of historical anarchist texts for Belfond publishing house, Paris; has curated 20 int. art shows, including shows by Erro, Paysages (Musee d'Art Moderne de la Ville de Paris 1985), Victor Hugo, peintre (Galleria d'Arte Moderna, Ca' Pesaro, Venice 1993), Disegno del nostro secolo (Fondazione Antonio Mazzotta, Milano 1994), Picabia, Maquinas y Espanolas (IVAM, Valencia, Fuindacio Tapies, Barcelona 1995), Picabia, 1922 (Musee National d'Art Moderne, Centre Georges Pompidou, Paris 1996), Juegos Surrealistas (Museo Thyssen-Bornemisza, Madrid 1996), Victor Hugo, du Chaos dans le pinceau (Museo Thyssen-Bornemisza, Madrid and Maison de Victor Hugo, Paris 2000), Picasso erotique (Musee des Beaux Arts, Montreal 2001). *Works include:* 8m high Monument to Felix Guattari (open-ended motorized multi-media desiring machine, including live performances and videos by poets, philosophers, musicians, anti-psychiatrists and artists close to Guattari and Lebel), Off Limits Exhbn, Centre Georges Pompidou, Paris 1994, large installation entitled Reliquaire pour un Culte de Venus. *Publications:* Happening (The Burial of Tinguely's Chose) 1960; has published 10 books of essays on culture and politics, including Poesie Directe, Happenings and Interventions, Paris 1994; trans of Ginsberg, Corso, Burroughs, Ferlinghetti were the first to appear in French. *Address:* c/o Berliner Kunstprojekt, Gneisenaustr. 33, Berlin -Kreuzberg, Germany (office).

LeBLANC, Matt; American actor; b. 25 July 1967, Newton, Mass; m. Melissa McKnight 2003; ed Newton North High School; trained as a carpenter; appeared in TV commercials for a variety of products, New York 1987; began formal acting training 1988. *Television includes:* series: TV 101 (as Chuck Bender) 1988, Top of the Heap 1991, Vinnie & Bobby 1992, Red Shoe Diaries, Rebel Highway, Friends (as Joey Tribbiani) 1994–2004, Joey 2004–06; films: Anything to Survive 1990, Reform School Girl 1994. *Films include:* Killing Box 1993, Lookin' Italian 1994, Ed 1996, Lost in Space 1998, Charlie's Angels 2000, All the Queen's Men 2001, Charlie's Angels: Full Throttle 2003. *Leisure interest:* landscape photography. *Address:* c/o United Talent Agency, 9560 Wilshire Boulevard, Suite 500, Beverly Hills, CA 90212, USA (office).

LEBLANC, Rt Hon. Roméo A., PC, CC, CMM, CD; Canadian fmr Governor-General; b. 18 Dec. 1927, L'Anse-aux-Cormier, Memramcook, NB; s. of Philias LeBlanc and Lucie LeBlanc; m. Diana Fowler; four c.; ed St-Joseph and Paris Univs; teacher, Drummond High School, NB 1951–53, NB Teachers' Coll., Fredericton 1955–59; corresp., Radio-Canada, Ottawa 1960–62, UK 1962–65, USA 1965–67; Press Sec. to Prime Minister Lester Pearson 1967–68, to Prime Minister Pierre Trudeau 1968–71; Asst to Pres. and Dir of Public Relations, Université de Moncton 1971–72; MP for Westmorland-Kent 1972–84; Minister of Fisheries 1974–76, of Fisheries and the Environment 1976–79, of Fisheries and Oceans 1980–82, of Public Works 1982–84; Senator, Beauséjour, NB 1984–95, Speaker 1993–95; Gov.-Gen. of Canada and C-in-C 1995–99; Visiting Scholar, Inst. of Canadian Studies, Carleton Univ., Ottawa 1985–86; Founding Pres. CBC/Radio-Canada Corresps' Asscn 1965; mem. Canada–France Parl. Asscn; 8 hon. degrees 1979–96. *Address:* PO Box 5254, Shediac, NB, E4P 8T9, Canada.

LEBOUDER, Jean-Pierre; Central African Republic politician; b. 1944; ed Ecole nationale supérieure agronomique, Toulouse, France; Dir Research Centre, Union cotonnière centrafricaine 1971–72, Dir-Gen. 1974–76; Minister of Rural Devt 1976, of Planning, Statistics and Int. Co-operation 1978–80; Prime Minister 1980–81; Minister of State, responsible for Planning, the Economy, Finance, the Budget and Int. Co-operation Dec. 2003–05.

LEBOWITZ, Joel L., MS, PhD; American mathematician and academic; *Professor, Department of Mathematics, Rutgers University;* b. 10 May 1930, Taceva, Czechoslovakia; m. 1st Estelle Mandelbaum 1953 (died 1996); 2nd Ann K. Beneduce 1999; ed Brooklyn Coll. and Syracuse Univ.; Nat. Science Foundation Postdoctoral Fellow, Yale Univ. 1956–57; Asst Prof. Stevens Inst. of Tech. 1957–59; Asst Prof. Belfer Grad. School of Science, Yeshiva Univ. 1959–60, Assoc. Prof. 1960–65, Prof. of Physics 1965–77, Chair. Dept of Physics 1968–76; Dir Center for Mathematical Sciences Research and Prof. of Math. and Physics, Rutgers Univ. 1977–; mem. NAS, AAAS, New York Acad. of Sciences, American Physical Soc.; Dr hc (Ecole Polytechnique Fédérale, Lausanne, Clark Univ.) 1999; Henri Poincaré Prize, IAMP 2000, Boltzmann Medal 1992, Max Planck Research Award 1993, Delmar S. Fahrney Medal, Franklin Inst. 1994, AAAS Scientific Freedom and Responsibility Award 1999 and other distinctions. *Publications:* 450 scientific papers. *Address:* Room 612, Hill Center, Building For The Mathematical Sciences, Busch Campus, Rutgers University, New Brunswick, NJ 08903, USA (office). *Telephone:* (732) 932-3117 (office). *Fax:* (732) 445-4936 (office). *E-mail:* lebowitz@math.rutgers.edu (office). *Website:* www.math.rutgers.edu/~lebowitz (office).

LEBRANCHU, Marylise; French politician and academic; b. 25 April 1947, Loudéac (Côtes-d'Armor); d. of Adolphe Perrault Lebranchu and Marie Epert; m. Jean Lebranchu 1970; three c.; responsible for research, Nord-Finistère Semi-public Co. 1973–78; joined Parti Socialiste Unifié (PSU) 1972, Parti Socialiste (PS) 1977; Parl. Asst to Marie Jacq 1978–93; municipal councillor, Morlaix (Finistère) 1983, Mayor 1995–97; regional councillor 1986–; Nat. Ass. Deputy for Morlaix Constituency 1997–; Minister of State attached to Minister for the Economy, Finance and Industry, with responsibility for small and medium-sized enterprises, trade and artisan activities 1997–2000, Minister of Justice and Keeper of the Seals 2000–02; Jr Lecturer in Econs applied to town and country planning, Univ. of Brest 1990–; Trombinoscope Politician of the Year Award 2000. *Publication:* Etre Juste, Justement. *Leisure interest:* music. *Address:* 6, place Emile Souvestre, 29600 Morlaix (office); Assemblée nationale, 126 rue de l'Université, 75355 Paris 07 SP, France. *Fax:* 1-40-63-77-65 (office). *E-mail:* mlebranchu@assemblee-nationale.fr; permanence.lebranchu@wanadoo.fr. *Website:* www.lebranchu.fr.

LEBRAT, Jean Marcel Hubert; French engineer; b. 21 Jan. 1933, Levallois/Seine; s. of Marcel Lebrat and Simone Landré; m. Andrée Blaize 1956; two s.; ed Coll. de Mirecourt, Lycée Henri Poincaré, Nancy and Ecole spéciale des travaux publics; head of office of studies of navigation service of Saint-Quentin 1956–59; head of office of studies of construction service of canal from the North to Compiègne 1959–63; Eng Etablissement Public pour l'Aménagement de La Défense (Epad) 1963–68, asst to head of highway div. Epad 1968–70; divisional eng 1970; Asst Tech. Dir Soc. d'Aménagement des Halles (Semah) 1970–79, Tech. Dir 1979–83, Dir 1984–89; Dir Etablissement public du Grand Louvre 1983–98, Pres. 1989–98; Engineer of bridges and roads 1995, Engineer-Gen. 1995–; Pres. Asscn Concordium Musée de la Fraternité 1998–; Admin. Musée des Arts Décoratifs; Hon. Pres. Cuba Co-operation; Hon. Sr Engineer, Ponts et Chaussées; Chevalier, Légion d'honneur, Commdr, Ordre nat. du Mérite. *Publication:* The Grand Louvre: A Museum Transfigured 1981-1993 (co-author) 1990. *Leisure interests:* drawing, tennis, water sports. *Address:* 56 boulevard Saint-Denis, 92400 Courbevoie, France (office). *Telephone:* 1-47-88-03-29 (office). *E-mail:* lebrat.jean@wanadoo.fr (office).

LeBRETON, Marjory; Canadian politician; *Leader of the Government in the Senate and Secretary of State for Seniors;* b. 1940, Nepean, Ont.; m. Douglas LeBreton; one d. (deceased); one s.; ed Ottawa Business Coll.; worked for Progressive Conservative Party of Canada (PC) nat. campaign group 1962, 1963 general elections; worked in office of John G. Diefenbaker 1963–67, in office of Robert L. Stanfield 1967–75, office of Joe Clark 1976–79; mem. Senate 1993–, fmr Chief Opposition Whip, fmr mem. several Standing Cttees including Social Affairs, Human Rights, Forestry and Agric., Internal Economy, Banking, currently Co-Chair Senate Standing Cttee on Health, Leader of the Govt in the Senate 2006–, Sec. of State for Seniors 2007–; Chair. Bd of Dirs Mothers Against Drunk Drivers, Canada. *Address:* Senate of Canada, Ottawa, ON K1A 0A4, Canada (office). *Telephone:* (613) 992-4793 (office). *E-mail:* lebrem@sen.parl.gc.ca (office). *Website:* www.parl.gc.ca (office).

LECAT, Jean-Philippe; French politician and lawyer; *Consultant for Public Affairs;* b. 29 July 1935, Dijon; s. of Jean Lecat and Madeleine Bouchard; m. Nadine Irène Romm 1965; two d.; ed Ecole Nat. d'Admin.; mem. Council of State 1963–66, 1974, Auditor 1963–; Chargé de Mission, Prime Minister's

Office 1966–68; Deputy to the Nat. Ass., Beaune 1968–72, 1973, 1978–81; Nat. Del. for Cultural Affairs, Union des Démocrates pour la République 1970–71, Asst Sec.-Gen. for Cultural Affairs and Information 1971–72; Spokesman of the Govt 1972–73; Sec. of State for Econ. 1973–74; Minister of Information 1973–74, of Culture and Communication 1978–81; mem. Bourgogne Regional Council 1973–; Del. to Natural Resources Conservation Conf. 1975; Chargé de Mission, Pres. of Repub. 1976–78 and Spokesman of the Pres. 1976–81, Conseiller d'Etat 1988; Pres. Amis de Mozart Asscn 1987, Comm. du Château de Vincennes 1988–, Admin. Council Ecole Nat. du Patrimoine 1990–99, Admin. Council Acad. de France in Rome (Villa Medici) 1996; Special Adviser to Pres. Thomson Consumer Electronics 1991 (later Thomson Multimedia 1994–97); Pres. Acad. de France, Rome 1996–99; Consultant for Public Affairs, Paris 2003–; Officier, Légion d'honneur, Commdr, Ordre nat. du Mérite, Commdr, Arts et Lettres; Grand Prix Nat. awarded by Minister of Culture 1996, Croix de la Valeur Militaire. *Television:* L'Europe de la Toison d'or. *Publications:* Quand flamboyait la Toison d'or 1982, Beaune 1983, La Bourgogne 1985, Le siècle de la Toison d'or 1986, Bourgogne 1989, L'Ardeur et le tourment 1989. *Leisure interest:* Elizabethan theatre. *Address:* 131 boulevard du Général Koenig, 92200 Neuilly-sur-Seine, France (home). *Telephone:* 1-47-22-37-79 (home). *E-mail:* jplecat@aol.com (home).

LECHLEITER, John C., BSc, MSc, PhD; American pharmaceutical industry executive; *President and CEO, Eli Lilly and Company;* m. Sarah Leckleiter; two s. one d.; ed Xavier Univ., Cincinnati, OH, Harvard Univ., Mass (NSF Fellow); joined Eli Lilly as sr organic chemist in process research and devt 1979, Pharmaceutical Product Devt Dir, Lilly Research Center, UK 1983–86, Man. European Research and Devt, USA 1986–88, Dir Devt Projects Man. 1988–91, Exec. Dir Pharmaceutical Product Devt 1991–93, Vice-Pres. 1993, Vice-Pres. Regulatory Affairs 1994–96, Vice-Pres. Lilly Research Labs 1996–98, Sr Vice-Pres. Pharmaceutical Products 1998–2001, Exec. Vice-Pres. Pharmaceutical Products and Corporate Devt 2001–04, Exec. Vice-Pres. Pharmaceutical Operations 2004–05, mem. Bd Dirs, Pres. and COO 2005–08, Pres. and CEO 2008–; mem. Bd of Dirs United Way of Cen. Indiana, Fairbanks Inst. (also mem. Exec. Cttee), Cincinnati, Indianapolis Downtown, Inc.; mem. Exec. Cttee of Bd of Dirs Pharmaceutical Research and Mfrs of America (PhRMA); mem. Business Roundtable, Business Council; mem. Visiting Cttee, Harvard Business School 2004–, Health Policy and Man. Council, Harvard School of Public Health 2004–, Dean's Advisory Bd, Indiana Univ. School of Medicine; Distinguished Advisor, The Children's Museum of Indianapolis; mem. Bd of Trustees Xavier Univ.; mem. ACS; Hon. DBA (Marian Coll., Indianapolis).

LECLANT, Jean, DèsSc; French professor of Egyptology; *Permanent Secretary, Académie des Inscriptions et Belles Lettres;* b. 8 Aug. 1920, Paris; s. of René Leclant and Laure Pannier; m. Marie-Françoise Alexandre-Hatvany 1988; ed Ecole Normale Supérieure, Paris and Inst. Français d'Archéologie Orientale, Cairo; Prof. Univ. of Strasbourg 1953–63, Sorbonne 1963–79, Coll. de France (Chair. of Egyptology) 1979–90 (Hon. Prof. 1990–); Dir of Studies, Ecole Pratique des Hautes Etudes (Vème Section) 1963–90; Perm. Sec. Acad. des Inscriptions et Belles Lettres (Inst. de France) 1983–; annual excavations Egypt, especially Karnak 1948–, Saqqarah 1963–; mem. Inst. Français in Cairo 1948–52; led archaeological expedition, Ethiopia 1952–56; Pres. Soc. Française d'Egyptologie, High Cttee of Nat. Celebrations 1998–; mem. Acad. des Sciences d'Outre-Mer, and many other learned socs in France and abroad; Grand Officier, Légion d'honneur; Grand Officier, Ordre du Mérite; Commdr, Ordre des Palmes Académiques; Commdr des Arts et Lettres; Chevalier, Mérite Militaire; Imperial Order of Menelik (Ethiopia); Grand Officier, Ordre de la Répub. d'Egypte, Ordre des Deux-Nils (Sudan), Répub. Italienne; Dr hc (Leuven, Bologna); Prix Balsan, Prix Int. Cino del Duca. *Publications:* Karnak-Nord IV (jtly) 1954, Dans les Pas des Pharaons 1958, Montouemhat, Prince de la Ville 1963, Soleb I, Soleb II (jt ed.) 1966, 1971, Kition II (jtly) 1976, La culture des chasseurs du Nil et du Sahara, 2 vols (with P. Huard) 1980, Répertoire d'Epigraphique Méroïtique, 3 vols (jtly) 2000, Les Textes de la Pyramide de Pépy Ier 2001 and about 1,000 articles and notes. *Address:* Académie des Inscriptions et Belles-Lettres, 23 quai Conti, 75006 Paris (office); 25 quai Conti, 75006 Paris, France (home). *Telephone:* 1-44-41-43-10 (office). *Fax:* 1-44-41-43-11 (office). *E-mail:* j.leclant.aibl@dial.oleane.com (office). *Website:* www.aibl.fr (office).

LECLERC, Edouard; French business executive; b. 20 Nov. 1926, Landerneau; s. of Eugène Leclerc and Marie Kerouanton; m. Hélène Diquélou 1950; one s. two d.; ed seminaries in Paris, Uriage-les-Bains and Saint-Cirgues; pioneer of Leclerc supermarket chain (first opened Landerneau) 1949–, more than 600 brs; Pres. Asscn nat. des centres Leclerc 1960–; Chevalier, Ordre nat. du Mérite. *Publications:* Ma vie pour un combat, La part du bonheur 1976, Combat pour la distribution, Le soleil de l'Ouest. *Leisure interests:* archaeology, writing. *Address:* 11 rue Bélerit, 29800 Landerneau (office); La Haye-Saint-Divy, PO Box 733, 29800 Landerneau, France (home).

LECLERCQ, Patrick; French diplomatist; b. 2 Aug. 1938, Lille; m. 2nd Marie-Alice Berard; two s.; one s. from previous m.; ed Institut d'Etudes Politiques, Paris, Ecole Nat. d'Admin; joined Diplomatic Service 1966; Consul-Gen. Montréal, Canada 1982–85; Amb. to Jordan 1985–89, to Egypt 1991–96, to Spain 1996–99; Minister of State and Dir of External Relations for Monaco 2000–05; Officier, Légion d'honneur, Ordre nat. du Mérite; several foreign decorations including Orden del Merito and Isabel la Católica, Spain, Ordre de Saint-Charles, Monaco. *Address:* c/o Office of the Minister of State, Ministry of State, Place de la Visitation, 98000 Monaco (office).

LECONTE, Patrice; French film director; b. 12 Nov. 1947, Tours; ed Institut des Hautes Etudes Cinématographiques. *Films include:* L'Espace vital 1969, Le Laboratoire de l'angoisse 1971, La Famille heureuse (Famille Gazul) 1973, Les Vécés étaient fermés de l'interieur 1976, Les Bronzés 1978, Les Bronzés

font du ski 1979, Viens chez moi, j'habite chez une copine 1981, Ma femme s'appelle reviens 1982, Circulez y'a rien à voir 1983, Les Spécialistes 1985, Tandem 1987), Monsieur Hire 1989, Le Mari de la coiffeuse 1990, Contre l'oubli 1991, Le Batteur du boléro 1992, Tango 1993, Le Parfum d'Yvonne 1994, Lumière et compagnie 1996, Les Grands ducs 1996, Ridicule 1996, Une chance sur deux 1998, La Fille sur le pont 1999, La Veuve de Saint-Pierre 2000, Félix et Lola 2001, Rue des plaisirs 2002, L'Homme du train 2002, Confidences trop intimes 2004, Dogora-Ouvrons les yeux 2004, Les Bronzés 3: amis pour la vie 2006, Mon meilleur ami 2006.

LEDER, Philip, MD, FAAS; American biologist and academic; *John Emory Andrus Professor of Genetics and Head, Department of Genetics, Harvard Medical School;* b. 19 Nov. 1934, Washington, DC; ed Harvard Coll. and Harvard Medical School; Intern and Resident in Medicine, Univ. of Minnesota Hosps 1960–62; Research Assoc., Biochemical Genetics, NIH Nat. Heart Inst., Bethesda, Md 1962, joined lab. of Marshall Nirenberg 1963, Research Medical Officer, Biosynthesis, Lab. of Biochemistry, Nat. Cancer Inst. 1966–69; Chair. Dept of Biochemistry, Grad. Program of Foundation for Advanced Educ. in the Sciences 1968–73, mem. Bd of Dirs 1968–74 (Vice-Pres. Foundation 1970–71, Pres. 1973); Head, Section on Molecular Genetics, Lab. of Molecular Genetics, Nat. Inst. of Child Health and Human Devt 1969–71, Dir Lab. for Molecular Genetics 1972–80; John Emory Andrus Prof. of Genetics and Head Dept of Genetics, Harvard Medical School 1980–, Dir Harvard Inst. of Human Genetics 1995–; Sr Investigator, Howard Hughes Medical Inst. 1986–; Visiting Scientist, Weizmann Inst., Rehovot, Israel 1965–66; Dir Pharmacia (fmrly Monsanto Co.) 1990–, Genome Therapeutics, Inc. 1994–, Schering-Plough Corpn 2003–; mem. NAS 1979–, American Acad. of Arts and Sciences 1981–, Inst. of Medicine 1982–; Trustee and Chair. Bd Charles A. Revson Foundation; Trustee Foundation for Advanced Educ. in the Sciences, Hadassah Medical Org. 1996–; Hon. Trustee Massachusetts Gen. Hosp.; Hon. DSc (Yale Univ.) 1984, (Mount Sinai Medical Center) 1985, (Univ. of Guelph) 1986, (Hebrew University of Jerusalem) 1996; Detur Award for Academic Excellence 1954, NIH Director's Award 1976, Drew Award in Biomedical Research, CIBA-Geigy Ltd 1978, Award in Biological and Medical Sciences, New York Acad. of Sciences 1978, Warren Triennial Prize, Massachusetts Gen. Hosp. 1980, Dickson Prize, Univ. of Pittsburgh School of Medicine 1980, NAS Richard Lounsberry Award 1981, Harvey Prize in Human Health, Technion-Israel Inst. of Tech. 1983, Award for Distinguished Research in the Biomedical Sciences, American Asscn of Medical Colls 1983, Steven C. Beering Award for Advancement of Biomedical Science, Indiana Univ. School of Medicine 1984, Bristol-Meyers Award for Distinguished Achievement in Cancer Research (co-recipient) 1985, Giovanni Lorenzini Foundation Prize for Basic Biomedical Research 1987, Albert Lasker Basic Medical Research Award 1987, Cancer Research Award in Basic Sciences Milken Family Medical Foundation 1988, V. D. Mattia Award, Roche Inst. of Molecular Biology 1988, Nat. Medal of Science 1989, Dr H. P. Heinekin Prize for Biochemistry, Royal Netherlands Acad. of Arts and Sciences 1990, Lee Kuan Yew Distinguished Visitorship, Repub. of Singapore 1990, Ernst W. Bertner Award, Univ. of Texas M. D. Anderson Cancer Center 1991, City of Medicine Award, City of Durham, NC 1991, American Coll. of Physicians Award 1991, Distinguished Alumnus Award, NIH Nat. Inst. of Child Health and Human Devt 1994, William Allan Award for Exceptional Contributions in the Field of Human Genetics, American Soc. of Human Genetics 1997, Albert Einstein Lecturer, Israel Acad. of Sciences and Humanities 2000. *Publications:* more than 240 articles in scientific journals. *Address:* Harvard Medical School, New Research Building, Room 356e, 77 Avenue Louis Pasteur, Boston, MA 02115, USA (office). *Telephone:* (617) 432-7667 (office). *Fax:* (617) 432-7944 (office). *E-mail:* leder@rascal.med.harvard.edu (office). *Website:* www .hms.harvard.edu (office); www.hhmi.org (office).

LEDERMAN, Leon M., PhD; American physicist and academic; *Pritzker Professor of Science, Department of Biology, Chemistry and Physical Sciences, Illinois Institute of Technology;* b. 15 July 1922, New York City; s. of the late Morris Lederman; m. 1st Florence Gordon; two d. one s.; m. 2nd Ellen Lederman; ed City Coll. of New York, Columbia Univ., New York; entered US Army 1943, rank of 2nd Lt Signal Corps 1946; grad. research involved building a Wilson Cloud Chamber for Cyclotron Project, Columbia Univ. 1948–51, Asst Prof. of Physics 1951–58, Prof. of Physics 1958–79; organised g-2 experiment, CERN 1958; Dir Nevis Labs 1961–78; Dir Fermi Nat. Accelerator Laboratory 1979–89, Dir Emer. 1989–; Prof. of Physics, Univ. of Chicago 1989–; currently Pritzker Prof. of Science, Illinois Inst. of Tech.; apptd Science Adviser to Gov. of Illinois 1989; Pres. American Asscn for the Advancement of Science 1991–; Resident Scholar IMSA Great Minds Program 1998; Founding mem. High Energy Physics Advisory Panel, Int. Cttee on Future Accelerators; Co-Founder and mem. Bd Trustees Illinois Math. and Science Acad.; mem. American, Finnish and Argentine Nat. Acads of Science; serves on 13 bds of dirs of museums, schools, science orgs and govt agencies; recipient of fellowships from Ford, Guggenheim, Ernest Kepton Adams and Nat. Science Foundations; Hon. DSc (City Coll. of New York, Univ. of Chicago, Illinois Inst. of Tech., Northern Illinois Univ., Lake Forest Coll., Carnegie Mellon Univ., Univ. of Pisa, Univ. of Guanajuarto); Nat. Medal of Science 1965, Elliot Cresson Medal, Franklin Inst. 1976, Wolf Prize for Physics 1982, Nobel Prize for Physics 1988, Enrico Fermi Prize. *Publications include:* Nuclear and Particle Physics (with J. Weneser) 1969, From Quarks to the Cosmos: Tools of Discovery (with David N. Schramm) 1989, Portraits of Great American Scientists 2001, Symmetry and the Beautiful Universe (with Christopher T. Hill) 2004; numerous scientific articles. *Leisure interest:* horse-riding. *Address:* Illinois Institute of Technology, LS 106, 3300 South Federal Street, Chicago, IL 60616-3793 (office); Fermilab, PO Box 500, Batavia, IL 60510-0500, USA (office). *Telephone:* (312) 567-8920 (office); (630) 840-3000 (Fermilab) (office). *Fax:* (630) 840-4343 (Fermilab) (office). *E-mail:* lederman@

LED THE INTERNATIONAL WHO'S WHO 2010 LEE

iit.edu (office); lederman@fnal.gov (office). *Website:* www.iit.edu (office); www.fnal.gov (office).

LEDGER, Sir Philip Stevens, Kt, CBE, MA, DMus, LLD, FRCM, FRNCM, FRCO; British conductor, organist, pianist/harpsichordist and academy principal; b. 12 Dec. 1937, Bexhill-on-Sea, Sussex; s. of the late Walter Stephen Ledger and Winifred Kathleen Ledger (née Stevens); m. Mary Erryl Wells 1963; one s. one d.; ed Bexhill Grammar School, King's Coll. Cambridge; Master of the Music, Chelmsford Cathedral 1962–65; Dir of Music, Univ. of East Anglia 1965–73, Dean of School of Fine Arts and Music 1968–71; an Artistic Dir Aldeburgh Festival of Music and Arts 1968–89, Vice-Pres. 1989–; Conductor, Cambridge Univ. Musical Soc. 1973–82; Dir of Music and Organist, King's Coll. Cambridge 1974–82; Prin. Royal Scottish Acad. of Music and Drama 1982–2001; John Stewart of Rannoch Scholar in Sacred Music; Pres. Royal Coll. of Organists 1992–94; Pres. Inc. Soc. of Musicians 1994–95; Chair. Cttee of Prins of Conservatoires 1994–98; Hon. Prof. Univ. of Glasgow 1993–98; Hon. mem. RAM, Guildhall School of Music; Hon. LLD (Strathclyde) 1987, Hon. DUniv (Central England) 1998, Hon. DMus (St Andrews, Glasgow and RSAMD) 2001; Silver Medal of Worshipful Company of Musicians. *Compositions include:* Requiem (A Thanksgiving for Life) 2007. *Publications:* (Ed.) Anthems for Choirs 2 and 3 1973, Oxford Book of English Madrigals 1978, edns of Byrd, Handel and Purcell and carol arrangements. *Leisure interests:* swimming, theatre, membership of Sette of Odd Volumes. *Address:* 2 Lancaster Drive, Upper Rissington, Cheltenham, Glos., GL54 2QZ, England (home).

LEDINGHAM, John Gerard Garvin, MA, DM, FRCP; British medical scientist and academic; *Professor Emeritus of Clinical Medicine, University of Oxford;* b. 19 Oct. 1929, London; s. of John Ledingham and Una C. Garvin; grandson of J. L. Garvin; m. Dr Elaine Maliphant 1962; four d.; ed Rugby School, New Coll. Oxford and Middlesex Hosp. London; Registrar, Middlesex Hosp. 1960–62; Sr Registrar in Medicine, Westminster Hosp. 1962–64; Visiting Fellow, Columbia Univ., New York 1965–66; Consultant Physician, United Oxford Hosps 1966–74; May Reader in Medicine, Univ. of Oxford 1974–95, Prof. of Clinical Medicine 1989–95, Prof. Emer. 1995–, Dir of Clinical Studies 1977–81, 1990–95; Fellow, New Coll. Oxford 1974–95, Emer. Fellow 1995–, Hon. Fellow 2001–, Sub-Warden 1994–95; Hon. Clinical Dir Biochemical and Clinical NMR Unit, Medical Research Council 1988–95; mem. Nuffield Council on Bioethics 2001–03; Trustee, Nuffield Trust 1978–2002, Beit Trust 1988–2008; Hon. Fellow, New Coll., Oxford; Osler Memorial Medal 2000. *Publications:* Oxford Textbook of Medicine (co-ed.) 1983, Concise Oxford Textbook of Medicine 2000; contribs to medical journals. *Leisure interests:* music, reading, golf. *Address:* 124 Oxford Road, Cumnor, Oxford, OX2 9PQ, England (home). *Telephone:* (1865) 865806 (home). *Fax:* (1865) 865806 (home). *E-mail:* jeled@btopenworld.com (home).

LEE, Allen Peng-Fei, CBE, OBE, BS, JP; Chinese business executive; b. 24 April 1940, Chefoo; m. Maria Choi Yuen Ha; two s. one d.; ed Univ. of Mich., USA; joined Lockheed Aircraft Ltd 1966, Test Eng Supervisor 1966–67, Test Eng Man. 1968–70; Eng Operations Man. Fabri-Teck Ltd 1967; Test Man., Ampex Ferrotec Ltd 1970–72, Man. Dir 1974–79; Gen. Man. Dataproducts Hong Kong Ltd 1972–74; Man. Dir Ampex World Operations SA 1979–83, Ampex Far East Operations 1983–; Dir, consultant Elec & Eltek Co. Ltd 1984; Chair. Hong Kong Productivity Council 1982; Chair. Hong Kong Liberal Party 1994–98; Deputy NPC 1997–2004; Chair. Pacific Dimensions Consultants Ltd; Dir Sam Woo Holdings Ltd 2003–; mem. Industry Devt Bd 1983, Hong Kong Gen. Chamber of Commerce (Cttee and Council mem.), Fed. of Hong Kong Industries, Broadcasting Review Bd 1984, Political Section of Preparatory Cttee for Hong Kong Special Admin. Region; Outstanding Young Persons of Hong Kong Award 1977. *Leisure interests:* fishing, swimming, tennis. *Address:* c/o Liberal Party, Shun Ho Tower, 2/F, 24–30 Ice House Street, Central Energy Plaza, Tsimshatsui East, Kowloon, Hong Kong Special Administrative Region, People's Republic of China (office).

LEE, Ang; Taiwanese film director; b. 1954, Taipei; m. Jane Lin; ed New York Univ.; moved to USA 1978; winner of nat. script-writing contest (Taiwanese Govt) 1990. *Films:* Pushing Hands 1992, The Wedding Banquet 1993, Eat Drink Man Woman 1995, Sense and Sensibility 1996, The Ice Storm 1998, Ride with the Devil 1998, Crouching Tiger, Hidden Dragon (Acad. Award for Best Foreign Film, David Lean Award for Best Dir, BAFTA Award 2001, Golden Globe for Best Dir 2001) 1999, Chosen 2001, Hulk 2003, Brokeback Mountain (Venice Film Festival Golden Lion, Critics' Choice Award for Best Film and Best Dir, Golden Globe for Best Dir and Best Drama, Dirs Guild of America Best Dir 2006, BAFTA David Lean Award for Achievement in Direction 2006, Acad. Award for Best Dir 2006) 2005, Se jie (Lust, Caution; Golden Lion, Venice Film Festival 2007) 2007. *Address:* c/o Creative Artists Agency, Inc., 9830 Wilshire Blvd., Beverly Hills, CA 90212-1825, USA.

LEE, C. Y., MArch; Taiwanese architect; *Principal, C. Y. Lee Architect;* ed Columbia Univ., Univ. of Ill., USA, Han Yang Univ.; Prin. C. Y. Lee Architect, Toronto, Canada; Architect Taipei 101, world's tallest building 2003; Ont. Asscn of Architects (OAA) Design Award, Archifest Scholarship Award. *Address:* 204–200 Finch Avenue West, Toronto, Ont. M2R 3W4, Canada (office). *Telephone:* (416) 223-6400 (office). *Fax:* (416) 223-0100 (office). *E-mail:* info@cyleearchitect.com (office). *Website:* www.cyleearchitect.com (office).

LEE, Christopher Frank Carandini, CBE; British actor, author and singer; b. 27 May 1922, London; s. of the late Lt-Col Geoffrey Trollope Lee and of Contessa Estelle Marie Carandini; m. Birgit Kroencke 1961; one d.; ed Summer Fields Preparatory School, Wellington Coll.; served RAF and Special Forces 1941–46; mentioned in despatches 1944; film industry 1947–; appeared in over 250 motion pictures and TV films; Officier des Arts, Sciences et des Lettres 1973; Officier des Arts et Lettres 2002; Commdr St John of Jerusalem 1997; Life Achievement Award, Evening Standard Film Awards 2002, Life Achievement Award, Empire Magazine, World Award for Lifetime Achievement, Vienna 2002, German Video Award for Lifetime Achievement 2002. *Films include:* Moulin Rouge 1953, The Curse of Frankenstein 1956, Tale of Two Cities 1957, Dracula 1958, The Hound of the Baskervilles 1959, The Mummy 1959, Rasputin the Mad Monk 1965, The Wicker Man 1973, The Three Musketeers 1973, The Private Life of Sherlock Holmes 1973, The Four Musketeers 1975, The Man With the Golden Gun 1975, To the Devil a Daughter 1976, Airport 77 1977, Return from Witch Mountain, 1977, How the West Was Won 1977, Caravans 1977, The Silent Flute 1977, The Passage 1978, 1941 1978, Bear Island 1978, The Serial 1979, The Salamander 1980, An Eye for an Eye, Goliath Awaits, Charles and Diana, The Last Unicorn, The Far Pavilions, The House of the Long Shadows, The Return of Captain Invincible, The Howling Z, Behind the Mask, Roadstrip, Shaka Zulu, Mio my Mio, The Girl, Un Métier du Seigneur, Casanova, The Disputation (TV), Murder Story, Round The World in 80 Days (TV), For Better, For Worse, Return of the Musketeers, Outlaws, Gremlins II 1989, Sherlock Holmes (US TV), Rainbow Thief, L'Avaro (Italy), Wahre Wunder (German TV) 1990, Young Indy (TV) 1991, Cybereden 1991, Death Train 1992, The Funny Man 1993, Police Academy–Mission to Moscow 1993, A Feast at Midnight 1994, The Stupids 1995, Moses (TV) 1995, Jinnah 1997, Sleepy Hollow 1999, The Lord of the Rings: The Fellowship of the Ring 2000, Star Wars: Episode II–Attack of the Clones 2000, The Lord of the Rings: The Two Towers 2002, The Lord of the Rings: The Return of the King 2003, Rivières Pourpres II: Les anges de l'apocalypse 2004, Star Wars Episode III: The Revenge of the Sith 2005, Charlie and the Chocolate Factory 2005, The Corpse Bride (voice) 2005, Pope John Paul II (TV) 2006, The Golden Compass 2007, The Heavy 2007, The Stone of Destiny 2007, The Colour of Magic 2007, Monstermania (animation) 2007, Boogie Woogie 2007. *Music:* The King of Elfland's Daughter, Peter and the Wolf, The Soldier's Tale, The King and I, Wandering Star, It's Now or Never, Christopher Lee Sings Rogues, Devils, and Other Villains—From Broadway to Bayreuth, The Dark Secret by Rhapsody featuring Christopher Lee 2005, 'Revelation' 2007. *Television appearances include:* Gormenghast 2000. *Publications:* Christopher Lee's Treasury of Terror, Christopher Lee's Archives of Evil 1975, Christopher Lee's The Great Villains 1977, Tall, Dark and Gruesome (autobiog.) 1977, (updated) 1997, (updated) 2003 as Lord of Misrule. *Leisure interests:* music, travel, golf. *Address:* ICM, Oxford House, 76 Oxford Street, London W1D 1BS, England (office). *Telephone:* (20) 7636-6565 (office). *Fax:* (20) 7323-0101 (office). *E-mail:* webmaster@christopherleeweb.com (office).

LEE, David Morris, PhD; American physicist and academic; *Professor of Low Temperature Physics, Cornell University;* b. 20 Jan. 1931, Rye, NY; s. of Marvin Lee and Annette Lee (née Franks); m. Dana Thorangkul 1960; two s.; ed Harvard Univ., Univ. of Connecticut, Yale Univ.; served in US Army 1952–54; Instructor in Physics, Cornell Univ., Ithaca, NY 1959–60, Asst Prof. 1960–63, Assoc. Prof. 1963–68, Prof. 1968–97; James Gilbert White Distinguished Prof. of Physical Sciences 1997–; Visiting Scientist Brookhaven Nat. Lab., Upton, NY 1966–67; Visiting Prof., Univ. of Fla, Gainesville 1974–75, 1994, Univ. of Calif., San Diego, La Jolla 1988; Visiting Lecturer, Peking Univ., Beijing, China 1981; Chair. Joseph Fourier Univ., Grenoble, France 1994; co-discoverer superfluid 3He, tricritical point of 3He-4He mixtures; co-observation of spin waves in spin polarized hydrogen gas; Fellow AAAS; mem. American Acad. of Arts and Sciences, NAS; John Simon Guggenheim Fellow 1966–67, 1974–75; Japan Soc. for Promotion of Sciences Fellow 1977; Sir Francis Simon Memorial Prize, British Inst. of Physics 1976, Oliver Buckley Prize, American Physical Soc. 1981, shared Nobel Prize for Physics 1996, Wilber Cross Medal, Yale Univ. 1998. *Address:* 610 Clark Hall, Laboratory of Atomic and Solid Physics, Cornell University, Ithaca, NY 14853-2501, USA (office). *Telephone:* (607) 255-5286 (office). *Fax:* (607) 255-6428 (office). *E-mail:* dml20@cornell.edu (office). *Website:* www.lassp.cornell.edu/lassp_data/dmlee (office).

LEE, David Tawei, PhD; Taiwanese government official; b. 15 Oct. 1949, Taipei; m.; one s. one d.; ed Nat. Taiwan Univ., Univ. of Virginia, USA; Man. Ed. Asia and the World Forum 1976–77; staff consultant, Co-ordination Council for North American Affairs, Washington, DC 1982–88; Prin. Asst to Minister of Foreign Affairs 1988–89; Adjunct Assoc. Prof. of Int. Politics, Grad. School of Social Science, Nat. Taiwan Normal Univ. 1988–93; Deputy Dir Dept of Int. Information Services, Govt Information Office 1989–90; Deputy Dir Dept of N American Affairs, Ministry of Foreign Affairs 1990–93, Dir 1996, Deputy Minister 1998–2001; Assoc. in Research, Fairbank Center for E Asian Research, Harvard Univ. 1993–96; Dir-Gen. Taipei Econ. and Cultural Office, Boston 1993–96; Deputy Dir-Gen. Govt Information Office, Exec. Yuan 1996–97; Dir-Gen. Govt Information Office, Exec. Yuan and Govt Spokesman 1997–2000; Rep. to Belgium, Luxembourg and EU 2001, currently Rep. to USA, Taipei Econ. and Cultural Rep. Office. *Address:* Taipei Economic and Cultural Representative Office, 4201 Wisconsin Avenue, NW, Washington, DC 20016, USA. *Telephone:* (202) 895-1800 (office).

LEE, Edward Graham, QC, LLM; Canadian diplomatist and lawyer; b. 21 Nov. 1931, Vancouver, BC; s. of William C. Lee and Dorothy F. Graham; m. Beverly J. Saul 1955; three d.; ed Univ. of British Columbia and Harvard Univ., USA; joined Canadian Dept of External Affairs 1956; Second Sec. Djakarta 1959–61; Counsellor, London 1965–69; Dir of Personnel, Dept of External Affairs 1969–72, Legal Adviser 1973–75; Amb. to Israel 1975–79, to S Africa 1982–86; Asst Under-Sec. for USA Affairs 1979–82; Legal Adviser and Asst Deputy Minister for Legal, Consular and Immigration, Dept of External Affairs 1986–90; Amb. to Austria and Perm. Rep. to UN, Vienna 1990–93; Gov. IAEA 1990–93; Adjunct Prof. of Int. Law, Univ. of Ottawa 1993–; UN Observer, S African Elections 1994; Lecturer, S African Ministry of Foreign Affairs 1994; Pres. Canadian Council on Int. Law 1994–96. *Publications:*

1266 www.worldwhoswho.com

numerous articles in Canadian legal journals. *Leisure interests:* golf, walking, reading, gardening. *Address:* 703 Chapman Boulevard, Ottawa, Ont., K1G 1T5, Canada.

LEE, Hae-chan; South Korean politician; fmr Vice Mayor of Seoul; fmr chief policy-maker for Millennium Democratic Party; Minister for Educ. 1998–99; Prime Minister 2004–06 (resgnd). *Address:* c/o Office of the Prime Minister, 77 Sejong-no, Jongno-gu, Seoul, Republic of Korea (office).

LEE, Han-dong, BA; South Korean politician; b. 5 Dec. 1934, Gyeonggi-do; m. Nam Sook Cho; one s. two d.; ed Kyungbok High School, Seoul Nat. Univ.; Mil. Prosecutor, Rep. of Korea Army 1959, Staff Judge Advocate with 5th Corps 1961; Judge, Seoul Dist Court 1963, Prosecutor 1969, Prosecutor, Seoul High Prosecutor's Office and Deputy Dir of Legal Affairs Training, Ministry of Justice 1974; Sr Prosecutor, Daejeon Dist Prosecutor's Office 1975, Pusan Dist Prosecutor's Office 1977, Seoul Dist Prosecutor's Office 1980; mem. Nat. Ass. 1981–, Vice-Speaker 1995; Deputy Floor Leader for Democratic Justice Party (DJP) 1981, Chief Sec. to Party Pres. 1982, DJP Sec. Gen. 1984, Floor Leader 1986, mem. Cen. Exec. Council 1990; Minister of Home Affairs 1988; Floor Leader for Democratic Liberal Party (DLP) 1993, Sr Adviser to Party Pres. 1996; Chief Exec., Chair. New Korea Party 1997, Grand Nat. Party 1997, Vice-Pres. 1998, Acting Pres. 1998; Acting Pres. United Liberal Democrats 2000, Pres. 2000–; Prime Minister of Repub. of Korea 2000–02; presidential cand. 2002; Service Merit Medal 1976. *Address:* c/o Office of the Prime Minister, 77, Sejong-no, Jongno-gu, Seoul, Republic of Korea (office).

LEE, (Nelle) Harper; American writer; b. 28 April 1926, Monroeville, Ala; d. of Amasa Coleman Lee and Frances Finch Cunningham Lee; ed Huntingdon Coll., Univ. of Ala and Univ. of Oxford, UK; worked as airline reservation clerk for Eastern Airlines and BOAC (NY) 1950s; accompanied Truman Capote to Holcombe, Kan., as research asst for his novel In Cold Blood; mem. Nat. Council of Arts 1966–71; Hon. DHumLitt (Spring Coll., Ala) 1997, (Notre Dame) 2006; Alabama Library Asscn Award 1961, Nat. Conference of Christians and Jews Brotherhood Award 1961, Los Angeles Public Library Literary Award 2005, Presidential Medal of Freedom 2007. *Publications:* fiction: To Kill A Mockingbird (Pulitzer Prize for Fiction 1961, Best Sellers' Paperback of the Year Award 1962) 1960; essays: Love: In Other Words (essay in Vogue) 1961, Christmas to Me (essay in McCalls) 1961, When Children Discover America (essay in McCalls) 1965, High Romance and Adventure (essay, part of Ala History and Heritage Festival) 1983; contribs to numerous magazines. *Leisure interest:* golf. *Address:* PO Box 278, Monroeville, AL 36461, USA.

LEE, Hermione, CBE, MA, MPhil, FRSL, FBA; British academic, writer and broadcaster; *Goldsmiths' Professor of English Literature, University of Oxford;* b. 29 Feb. 1948, Winchester; d. of Dr Benjamin Lee and Josephine Lee; m. John Barnard 1991; ed Univ. of Oxford; Instructor, Coll. of William and Mary, Williamsburg, Va 1970–71; Lecturer, Dept of English, Univ. of Liverpool 1971–77; Lecturer, Dept of English, Univ. of York 1977–87, Sr Lecturer 1987–90, Reader 1990–93, Prof. 1993–98; Goldsmiths' Chair of English Literature and Fellow of New Coll., Oxford 1998–2008; Pres. Wolfson Coll. Oxford 2008–; presenter of Book Four on Channel Four TV (UK) 1982–86; Chair. judges Man Booker Prize for Fiction 2006; Mel and Lois Tukman Fellow, Dorothy and Lewis B. Cullman Center for Scholars and Writers, New York Public Library 2004–05; Foreign Hon. mem. American Acad. of Arts and Sciences; Hon. Fellow, St Hilda's Coll. Oxford 1998, St Cross Coll. Oxford 1998; Hon. DLitt (Liverpool) 2002, (York) 2007. *Publications:* The Novels of Virginia Woolf 1977, Elizabeth Bowen 1981 (2nd. ed. 1999), Philip Roth 1982, The Secret Self I 1985 and II 1987, The Mulberry Tree: Writings of Elizabeth Bowen 1986, Willa Cather: A Life Saved Up 1989, Virginia Woolf 1996, Virginia Woolf: Moments of Being (ed.) 2002, Body Parts: Essays on Life-Writing 2005, Virginia Woolf's Nose 2005, Edith Wharton (biog.) 2007. *Leisure interests:* reading, music, countryside. *Address:* New College, Oxford, OX1 3BN, England (office). *Telephone:* (1865) 279482 (office). *E-mail:* hermione .lee@new.ox.ac.uk (office). *Website:* www.new.ox.ac.uk (office); www .hermionelee.com.

LEE, Hoi-chang, BA; South Korean politician; b. 2 June 1935, Sohung, Hwanghae Prov.; m.; two s. one d.; ed Kyonggi High School, Seoul Nat. Univ., Harvard Univ., USA; service in AF, attained rank of Capt.; Judge, Incheon and Seoul Dist Court 1960–65; apptd Judge, Seoul High Court 1965, Sr Judge 1977; Prof., Judicial Research and Training Inst. 1971; Dir Planning and Co-ordination Office, Ministry of Court Admin 1980; Justice, Supreme Court 1981–86, 1988–93; practised law 1986–88, 1994–; Head of Nat. Election Comm. 1988–93; Head of Bd of Audit and Inspection 1993; Prime Minister of Repub. of Korea 1993; cand. of ruling New Korea Party in presidential elections 1997; Pres. Grand Nat. Party (GNP) 2000–02; cand. of GNP in presidential elections 2002, ind. cand. 2007. *Leisure interest:* listening to classical music. *Address:* 10-1401 Asia Seonsuchon Apt, Jamsil-7-dong, Songpa-gu, Seoul, Republic of Korea (home). *Telephone:* (2) 3432-2030 (home).

LEE, Hong-koo, PhD; South Korean politician and political scientist; *President, Seoul Forum for International Affairs;* b. 9 May 1934, Seoul; m.; one s. two d.; ed Seoul Nat. Univ., Emory and Yale Univs, USA; Asst Prof., Emory Univ. 1963–64, Case Western Reserve Univ. 1964–67; Asst Prof., Assoc. Prof., Prof. of Political Science, Seoul Nat. Univ. 1968–88, Dir Inst. of Social Sciences 1979–82; Fellow Woodrow Wilson Int. Center for Scholars, Smithsonian Inst. 1973–74, Harvard Law School 1974–75; Minister of Nat. Unification 1988–90; Special Asst to Pres. 1990–91; Amb. to UK 1991–93; Sr Vice-Chair. Advisory Council for Unification; Chair. Seoul 21st Century Cttee, The World Cup 2002 Bidding Cttee 1993–94; Deputy Prime Minister and Minister of Nat. Unification April–Dec. 1994, Prime Minister 1994–95; mem. Comm. on Global Governance 1991–95; Chair. New Korea Party May 1996;

Amb. to USA 1998–2001; currently Pres. Seoul Forum for Int. Affairs; Sheth Distinguished Int. Alumni Award from Emory Univ. 2002. *Publications:* An Introduction to Political Science, One Hundred Years of Marxism, Modernization. *Address:* c/o Ministry of Foreign Affairs and Trade, 77 1-ga, Sejong-no, Jongno-gu, Seoul, Republic of Korea (office).

LEE, Gen. Honkon; South Korean diplomatist and army officer; b. 11 Dec. 1920, Kongjoo, Chungcheong Nan-do; s. of Kidong Lee and Jinsil Ahn; m. Kwiran Lee 1946; two s. four d.; ed Japanese Imperial Mil. Acad., Japanese Field Artillery School and U.S. Infantry School; Supt Korean Mil. Acad. 1946–48; Mil. Attaché, Washington 1949; Commdg Gen., Eighth Repub. of Korea Army Div. 1949–50, Third Army Corps 1950–51, First Army Corps 1952–54; UN Command Del. to Korean Armistice 1951–52; Chair. Jt Chiefs of Staff 1954–56, Chief of Staff 1956–58; Nat. Pres. Korean Veterans Asscn 1958–61; Amb. to Philippines 1961–62, to UK 1962–67 (also to Scandinavian countries, Iceland, Malta and African countries concurrently); Amb. at large 1967–69; Chair. President's Advisory Comm. on Govt Admin. 1969; Chair. Korea Anti-Communist League 1976–; Chair. Korea-British Soc. 1978–; decorations from Republic of Korea, USA, France, UK, Greece and Vatican. *Publications:* Nation's Destination 1950, Free Opinion (monthly publ.) 1976–. *Leisure interests:* horse riding, reading, music appreciation.

LEE, Brig.-Gen. Hsien Loong, (BG Lee); Singaporean politician and fmr military officer; *Prime Minister;* b. 10 Feb. 1952; s. of Lee Kuan Yew (q.v.) and Kwa Geok Choo; m. 1st (deceased 1982), one s. one d.; m. 2nd Ho Ching 1985; two s.; ed Catholic High School, Nat. Jr Coll., Cambridge Univ., UK, Kennedy School of Govt Harvard Univ., USA; nat. service 1971; Sr Army course at Fort Leavenworth, USA; Asst Chief of Gen. Staff (Operations) 1981–82, Chief of Staff (Gen. Staff) Singapore Army 1982–84; resgnd as Brig.-Gen. Aug. 1984, Nat. Reserves –2002; Political Sec. to Minister of Defence; MP for Teck Ghee 1984–; Chair. Comm. for Restructuring of the Economy 1985; Minister of State for Defence and for Trade and Industry 1985–86, for Trade and Industry 1986–93; Deputy Prime Minister 1990–2004, also Minister of Finance, Minister of Defence 1993–95, Second Minister of Defence (Services), Head Monetary Authority of Singapore; Prime Minister of Singapore and Minister of Finance 2004–07, Prime Minister 2007–; Second Asst Sec.-Gen. People's Action Party 1989–. *Leisure interests:* swimming, reading, jogging, computers. *Address:* Office of the Prime Minister, Orchard Road, Istana Annexe, Istana, Singapore 238823 (office). *Telephone:* 2358577 (office). *Fax:* 7324627 (office). *Website:* www.pmo.gov.sg (office).

LEE, Huan, MA; Taiwanese politician; b. 8 Feb. 1917, Hankow City; m.; two s. two d.; ed Nat. Chengchi Univ. and Columbia Univ., New York, USA; Dir Shenyang Daily News 1946–48; Chief Sec., Deputy Dir-Gen. and Dir-Gen. China Youth Corps 1952–77; Prof. Nat. Chengchi Univ. 1962–79; Chair. Comm. for Youth Assistance and Guidance, Exec. Yuan 1967–72; Exec. Officer, Alumni Asscn of Nat. Chengchi Univ. 1977–80; Pres. Nat. Sun Yat-sen Univ. 1979–84; Minister of Educ. 1984–87; Prime Minister of Taiwan 1989–90; Sec.-Gen. Cen. Cttee Kuo-Min-Ta-Hui 1987–; Hon. PhD (Tan Kok) 1978; Hon. LLD (Sun Kyun Kwan) 1981. *Address:* c/o Kuomintang (KMT) (Nationalist Party of China), 11 Jongshan South Road, Taipei 100, Taiwan.

LEE, Hun-jai, MA; South Korean government official and financial analyst; b. 17 April 1944, Shanghai, China; ed Seoul Nat. Univ., IMF Inst., Boston Univ. and Harvard Business School, Mass, USA; Dir Financial Policy Div., Ministry of Finance 1974–78, Deputy Dir-Gen. Office of Public Finance and Monetary Policy 1978–79; Exec. Man. Dir and CEO Daewoo Semiconductor Co. Ltd 1984–85; Pres. and CEO Korea Investors Service Co., Ltd 1985–1991; Head of Secr. to Jt Presidential Cttee for Econ. Policy 1997–98; Chair. Financial Supervisory Comm. 1998–2000; Minister of Finance and Economy 2000; Chair. Korean Inst. of Dirs 2002–04; Deputy Prime Minister and Minister of Finance and the Economy 2004–05 (resgnd); Chair. Bd of Govs, Asian Devt Bank; mem. Advisory Bd, Cen. Cttee of Agric. Cooperative Union 1993–97; mem. Citizens Advisory Cttee, City of Seoul 1995–97. *Publications:* Development of the Credit Rating System in Korea 1988. *Address:* c/o Ministry of Finance and the Economy, 1 Jungang-dong, Gwacheon City, Gyeonggi Province, Republic of Korea (office).

LEE, Hyung-koo; South Korean banker; b. 30 Aug. 1940; m. 1969; ed Seoul Nat. Univ.; Deputy Dir Planning and Man. Office, Budget Bureau, Econ. Planning Bd (EPB) 1964; Sec. for Econ. Affairs, Presidential Secr. 1969–70; Dir and Dir-Gen. EPB 1971–81; Parvin Fellow, Woodrow Wilson School of Public Admin., Princeton Univ. 1978–79; Asst Minister, Ministry of Finance 1982; Vice-Minister, Ministry of Construction 1986, Ministry of Finance 1988, EPB 1988; Gov. Korea Devt Bank 1990–96. *Publications:* Economic Development in Korea, The Korean Economy, The Korean Economy Looks to the 21st Century. *Leisure interests:* golf, tennis. *Address:* 10-2, Gwancheol-dong, Jongno-gu, CPO Box 28, Seoul, 110-111, Republic of Korea. *Telephone:* (2) 398-6114.

LEE, In-ho, BA; South Korean banking executive; *President and CEO, Shinhan Financial Group Co. Ltd;* b. 2 Nov. 1943; ed Yonsei Univ.; joined Shinhan Bank as incorporator 1982, later Pres. and CEO Shinhan Bank, Dir (non-exec.) Shinhan Financial Group Co. Ltd, Pres. and CEO 2005–. *Address:* Shinhan Financial Group Co. Ltd, 120 Taepyung-ro 2-ga, Jung-gu, Seoul 100-102, South Korea (office). *Telephone:* (822) 6360-3072 (office). *E-mail:* info@ shinhangroup.com (office). *Website:* www.shinhangroup.com (office).

LEE, Jae-joung; South Korean academic and politician; b. 1944, Jincheon, N Chungcheong prov.; m.; one d.; ed Korea Univ. and Univ. of Manitoba and Trinity Coll., Canada; ordained Anglican priest 1972; teacher then Pres. Sung Kong Hoe Univ., Seoul 1994–2000; mem. Nat. Ass. 2000–04; Chief Campaign Man. for Pres. Roh during 2002 presidential campaign; co-f. Uri Party, now Adviser; worked at House of Shalom (shelter for migrant workers) 2004; Sr

Vice Chair. Nat. Unification Advisory Council and presidential advisor on N Korea policy 2004–06; Minister of Unification 2006–08; arrested for accepting illegal political funds during the 2002 presidential campaign 2004, sentenced to a fine, received presidential pardon 2006. *Address:* c/o Ministry of Unification, 77-6, Sejong-no, Jongno-gu, Seoul 110-760, Republic of Korea (office).

LEE, Jang-moo, BSc, PhD; South Korean engineer, university administrator and academic; *President, Seoul National University;* b. Seoul; ed Seoul Nat. Univ., Iowa State Univ., USA; Prof., Coll. of Eng, Seoul Nat. Univ. 1976–, Dean Coll. of Eng 1997–2002, Pres. Seoul Nat. Univ. 2006–; Visiting Scholar, MIT, USA 1982–83; Chair. Univ. Educ. Section Cttee, Educational Policy Council, Korean Ministry of Educ. 1998–2000, Industrial Tech. Evaluation Inst., Korean Ministry of Industry and Resources 1999–2005, Founding Cttee for the Nat. Science Museum 2001–06; Pres. Korean Soc. for Precision Eng 1996–99, Nat. Asscn of Deans of Eng Colls 1998–2000, Korean Soc. of Mechanical Engineers 2000, Korean Soc. for New and Renewable Energy 2004–06; Vice-Pres. Asscn of Korean Socs of Science and Tech. 2005–; mem. Nat. Presidential Advisory Cttee on Science and Tech. 1998–99, Nat. Cttee for Innovation of Science and Tech. 2004–06; Fellow, American Soc. of Mechanical Engineers, Int. Acad. of Production Research, Korean Acad. of Science and Tech.; mem. Korean Acad. of Eng; Korean Acad. of Science Award. *Address:* Office of the President, Seoul National University, San 56-1, Sillim-dong Gwanak-gu, Seoul 151-742, South Korea (office). *Telephone:* (2) 880-5001 (office). *Fax:* (2) 889-7515 (office). *E-mail:* leejm@snu.ac.kr (office). *Website:* www.useoul.edu (office).

LEE, John Joseph, MA, MRIA; Irish historian and academic; *Glucksman Professor of Irish Studies and Director, Glucksman Ireland House, New York University;* b. 9 July 1942, Tralee, Co. Kerry; s. of Thomas P. Lee and Catherine Burke; m. Anne Marie Mitchell 1969; one s. two d.; ed Franciscan Coll. Gormanston, Univ. Coll. Dublin, Inst. for European History, Mainz, Germany, Peterhouse Coll., Cambridge, UK; Admin. Officer, Dept of Finance, Dublin 1963; Asst in History, Univ. Coll. Dublin 1963–68; Research Fellow, Peterhouse Coll., Univ. of Cambridge 1968–70, Official Fellow, Lecturer, Tutor 1970–74; Prof. of Modern History, Univ. Coll. Cork (UCC) 1974–93, Prof. of History 1993–2007, Dean Faculty of Arts 1976–79, Vice-Pres. UCC 1982–85; Visiting Mellon Prof., Univ. of Pittsburgh, USA 1979, European Univ. Inst., Florence, Italy 1981; Guest Fellow, Austrian Acad. 1989; Eisenhower Fellow, USA 1989, Distinguished Visiting Prof. of World Peace, L.B.J. School, Univ. of Texas 1989–90; Visiting Prof. of Govt, Colby Coll. 1991; Visiting Sr Parnell Fellow, Magdalene Coll., Cambridge 1992–93, Visiting Arbuthnot Fellow, Univ. of Edin. 1997; Visiting Prof. of Irish Studies, New York Univ. 1999–2000, now Glucksman Prof. of Irish Studies, Prof. of History and Dir Glucksman Ireland House; Distinguished Visiting Fellow, Queen Mary, Univ. of London 2007; columnist, Sunday Tribune 1996–2002; Chair. Irish Scholarships Exchange Bd 1980–92, Irish Fulbright Comm. 1992–96; mem. Irish Senate 1993–97; mem. British-Irish Parl. Body 1993–97; Hon. DLitt (Nat. Univ. of Ireland) 2006; Irish Life/Sunday Independent Arts Award 1991, Aer Lingus/Irish Times Prize for Literature 1992, Donnelly Prize for History and Social Sciences, American Conf. for Irish Studies 1992. *Publications:* The Modernization of Irish Society 1848–1918 1973, 1989, Labour in German Industrialisation, in Cambridge Economic History of Europe, VII 1978, Ireland 1912–1985: Politics and Society 1989, Europe and America in the 1990s (co-ed.) 1991, The Shifting Balance of Power, Exploring the 20th Century 2000, Making the Irish American (co-ed.) 2006. *Leisure interests:* sport, reading. *Address:* Glucksman Ireland House, One Washington Mews, New York, NY 10003, USA (office). *Telephone:* (212) 998-3950 (office). *Fax:* (212) 995-4373 (office). *E-mail:* jl91@nyu.edu (office). *Website:* (office).

LEE, Jye; Taiwanese naval officer; b. 6 June 1940, Tianjin City; m.; three d.; ed ROC Naval Acad., Navy Command and Staff Coll., Naval War Coll., USA; served as Submarine Commdg Officer, Submarine Squadron Commdr, Antisubmarine Warfare Commdr, Taiwan Navy 1992–94, Chief of Staff Navy Gen. HQ 1994–95, Commdg Gen. of Fleet Command 1995–96, Deputy Commdr-in-Chief Navy Gen. HQ 1996–97, Commdr-in-Chief Navy Gen. HQ 1999–2002; Vice Chief of Gen. Staff, Ministry of Nat. Defence Taiwan 1997–99, Chief of Gen. Staff 2002–04, Minister of Nat. Defence 2004–05, 2006–07; mem. Kuomintang (KMT, Nationalist Party of China) –2007. *Address:* c/o Ministry of National Defence, 2/F, 164 Po Ai Road, Taipei, Taiwan (office).

LEE, Ki-taek, BSc; South Korean politician; b. 25 July 1937, Pohang; s. of the late Lee Dong-Sup and of Kim Nam-Chool; m. Lee Kyung-Ui 1968; one s. three d.; ed Korea Univ., Seoul, Univ. of Pennsylvania; involved in politics as student; mem. Korean Nat. Ass. 1967–; Chair. Special Cttee on Investigation of Political Corruption of the 5th Repub. 1988 and of Special Investigation Cttee of the 5th Repub. 1990; Chair. Pusan City Charter, New Democratic Party 1972, Sec. Gen. 1976, Vice-Pres. 1979; Chair. Inst. of Democratic Thoughts 1979; Vice-Pres. New Korea Democratic Party 1984, 1986; Vice-Pres. Reunification Democratic Party 1988–89, Floor Leader 1989; Chair. Democratic Party of Korea 1990, 1993, Co-Chair. 1991, Adviser 1995–96, Pres. 1995, 1996–98 (merged with New Korea Party to form Grand Nat. Party 1997); Hon. Prof. Yonbyun Univ., China 1995; Nat. Foundation Medal 1963. *Publications:* The Bridge of No Return 1978, History of Minority Parties in Korea 1987. *Leisure interest:* calligraphy. *Address:* 51-5, Yong Kang-dong, Mapo-gu, Seoul (office); 187-12, Ahyun-dong, Seodaemun-gu, Seoul, Republic of Korea (home). *Telephone:* (2) 711-3301 (office); (2) 313-8551 (home). *Fax:* (2) 711-3326 (office); (2) 313-5219 (home).

LEE, Ku-taek, BE; South Korean business executive; *Chairman and CEO, POSCO;* b. 1946; ed Kyunggi High School, Seoul, Seoul Nat. Univ.; joined POSCO 1969, various positions including steel specialist Pohang Works, Gen. Man. Export Dept, Gen. Man. Corp. Strategic Planning Dept, Sr Exec. Vice-Pres. 1996–98, Pres. 1998–2003, Chair. and CEO POSCO 2003–; fmr Pres. Korea Iron and Steel Asscn; mem. Exec. Cttee, Int. Iron and Steel Inst. (IISI) 2004–, Vice-Chair. 2005–07, Chair. 2007–; sr positions, Korea-US Econ. Council (KUSEC), Korea Inst. of Tech. (KITECH). *Address:* POSCO, POSCO Centre, 892 Daechi-4-dong, Gangnam-ku, Seoul, Republic of Korea (office). *Telephone:* (2) 3457-0114 (office). *Fax:* (54) 220-6000 (office). *E-mail:* info@posco.com (office). *Website:* www.posco.com (office); www.posco.co.kr (office).

LEE, Kuan Yew, MA; Singaporean politician and barrister; *Minister Mentor;* b. 16 Sept. 1923, Singapore; s. of the late Lee Chin Koon and Chua Jim Neo; m. Kwa Geok Choo 1950; two s. one d.; ed Raffles Coll., Singapore, Fitzwilliam Coll. Cambridge, UK; called to Bar, Middle Temple, London 1950, Hon. Bencher 1969; Advocate and Solicitor, Singapore 1951; a founder of People's Action Party 1954, Sec.-Gen. 1954–92; mem. Legis. Ass. 1955–; first Prime Minister Repub. of Singapore 1959, re-elected 1963, 1968, 1972, 1976, 1980, 1984, 1988; resgnd as Prime Minister Nov. 1990; Sr Minister in the Prime Minister's Office 1990–2004; Minister Mentor 2004–; mem. Singapore Internal Security Council 1959–; MP Fed. Parl. of Malaysia 1963–65; Chair. Singapore Investment Corpn 1981–; Fellow, Inst. of Politics, Harvard Univ. 1968; Hoyt Fellow, Berkeley Coll., Yale Univ. 1970; Hon. Fellow, Fitzwilliam Coll. Cambridge 1969, Royal Australasian Coll. of Surgeons 1973, RACP 1974; Hon. LLD (Royal Univ. of Cambodia) 1965, (Hong Kong) 1970, (Liverpool) 1971, (Sheffield) 1971; Hon. CH 1970; Hon. GCMG 1972; Bintang Republik Indonesia Adi Pradana 1973, Order of Sikatuna (Philippines) 1974, Most Hon. Order of Crown of Johore (First Class), 1984, Hon. Freeman, City of London 1982, numerous other distinctions. *Publications:* The Singapore Story – Memoirs of Lee Kuan Yew (Vol. 1), From Third World to First: The Singapore Story 1965–2000 (Vol. 2). *Leisure interests:* jogging, swimming, golf. *Address:* c/o Prime Minister's Office, Istana Annexe, 238823 Singapore.

LEE, Kun-hee, MBA; South Korean business executive; b. 9 Jan. 1942, Utryung, Gyeongnam; s. of Lee Byung-Chull and Park Doo-Eul; m. Ra Hee-ong 1967; one s. three d.; ed Waseda Univ. Tokyo and George Washington Univ., USA; Exec. Dir Joong-Ang Daily News, Seoul 1968–78, Tong-Yang Broadcasting Corpn Seoul 1968–78; Vice-Chair. Samsung Group, Seoul 1978–87, Chair. 1987–98, Chair. and CEO Samsung Group 1998–2008 (resgnd); Vice-Chair. Korea-Japan Econ. Comm., Seoul 1981–, Fed. of Korean Industries 1987–; Chair. Korea Welfare Promotion Asscn for Disabled 1998–; Pres. Korean Amateur Wrestling Fed. 1982–96, now Hon. Pres.; Vice-Pres. Korean Olympic Cttee 1993–96, now Hon. Pres.; found guilty of bribery and sentenced to two years' imprisonment, suspended for three years Aug. 1996; indicted for breach of trust in connection with plan to transfer control of co. to his son and tax evasion April 2008; Order of Sport Merit, Maengho Medal 1984, Order of Sport Merit, Cheongryong Medal 1986, Olympic Order, IOC 1996; Hon. DBA (Seoul Nat. Univ.) 2000. *Publication:* Samsung New Management 1993. *Leisure interests:* horse-riding, golf, vintage car collection. *Address:* 740-10 Hannam-dong, Yongsan-gu, Seoul 100-742, Republic of Korea (home).

LEE, Kyung-shik; South Korean politician and banker; ed Korea Univ.; joined Bank of Korea; Econ. Planning Bd 1961–72; served in Office of Pres. 1972–74; later Vice-Minister of Communications and mem. Monetary Bd of Korea; Pres. Daewoo Motor Co. 1988–93, Korea Gas Corpn until 1993; Deputy Prime Minister and Minister of Econ. Planning 1993; Gov. Bank of Korea 1995–98. *Address:* c/o Bank of Korea, 110, 3-ga, Namdaemun-no, Jung-gu, Seoul 100-794, Republic of Korea.

LEE, Martin Chu Ming, QC, JP, BA; Hong Kong barrister; b. 8 June 1938, Hong Kong; m. Amelia Lee 1969; one s.; ed Univ. of Hong Kong; Chair. Hong Kong Bar Asscn 1980–83; mem. Hong Kong Legis. Council 1985–2008, Hong Kong Law Reform Comm. 1985–91, Basic Law Drafting Cttee 1985–90 (expelled for criticism of People's Repub. of China); Chair. Hong Kong Consumer Council 1988–91; formed United Democrats of Hong Kong, party opposed to Chinese mil. suppression of Tiananmen Square demonstrators in 1989, Leader 1990–94 (merged with Meeting Point party to become Democratic Party of Hong Kong), Chair. 1994–2002; Goodman Fellow, Univ. of Toronto 2000; Bencher, Hon. Soc. of Lincoln's Inn 2000; Hon. LLD (Holy Cross Coll.) 1997, (Amherst Coll., USA) 1997, (Warwick Univ.) 2006; Prize for Freedom, Liberal Int. 1996, Int. Human Rights Award (American Bar Asscn) 1995, Democracy Award, Nat. Endowment for Democracy, USA 1997, Statesmanship Award, Claremont Inst., USA 1998, Schuman Medal, European Parl. 2000, Rutgers Coll. Brennan Human Rights Award 2004. *Publication:* The Basic Law: some basic flaws (with Szeto Wah) 1988. *Address:* Admiralty Centre, Room 704A, Tower I, 18 Harcourt Road, Hong Kong Special Administrative Region, People's Republic of China (office). *Telephone:* 25290864 (office). *Fax:* 28612829 (office). *E-mail:* oml@martinlee.org.hk (office). *Website:* www.martinlee.org.hk (office).

LEE, Myung-bak, BA; South Korean business executive, politician and head of state; *President;* b. 19 Dec. 1941, then-Korean residential dist of Nakakawachi-gun, Osaka Pref., Japan (now Hirano-ku, Osaka City); s. of Lee Cheung-u and Chae Taewon; m. Kim Yun-ok; one s. three d.; ed Korea Univ., Seoul Nat. Univ., Yonsei Univ.; worked for Hyundai Group 1977–92, fmr Pres. Hyundai Construction; Assemblyman, 16th Nat. Ass. 1996–2001; Mayor of Seoul City 2002–06; Founder and Exec. Chair. Anguk Forum 2006; Pres. of S Korea 2008–; Chair., Korea Atomic Industry Forum Inc. 1980; Chair. Int. Contractors Asscn of Korea 1980; Pres. Korea Amateur Swimming Fed. 1981–92; Exec. mem. Korean Olympic Cttee 1982–92; Chief, Construction Div., Econ. Cooperation Cttee in SE Asian Countries 1982; Deputy Chair. Korea Chamber of Commerce 1982; Vice Pres., Korea Man. Asscn 1983; Bureau mem. FINA 1984; Deputy Chair., Korea-USSR Econ. Asscn 1989; Exec. Dir, Korea Electric Asscn 1990; mem. NE Asia Econ. Cttee 1991; Vice-

Chair., World Fed. of Korean Asscn of Commerce 1993; Founder East Asia Foundation, Chair. 1994–2002; Pres. Asian Pacific Foundation, Korea 2000–02; Commr, Sub-cttee on Future Competitiveness, Nat. Cttee, Grand Nat. Party 2001–02; Advisor, Overseas Korean Traders Asscn 2001–07; Econ. Advisor to Hun Sen, Prime Minister of Kingdom of Cambodia 2000–07; Hon. Consul Gen. of Kingdom of Bhutan to Korea 1986–99; Hon. Amb. of Arkansas State 1992–2007; Hon. Instructor, Undergraduate School of Business Admin, Korea Univ. 1993–; Hon. Instructor, Grad. School of Political Science, Kookmin Univ. 1995–, Hon. Instructor, Grad. School of Business Admin, Korea Univ. 1997–; Order of Civil Merit 1984, Order of Industrial Service Merit, Gold Tower 1985; Hon. DSc (Korea Nat. Univ. of Physical Educ.) 1998; Hon. DBA (Sogang Univ.) 2004; Hon. DEcon (Nat. Univ. of Mongolia) 2005, (Mokpo Nat. Univ.) 2005; Dr hc (Eurasia Univ., Astana, Kazakhstan) 2004; Excellent Enterprise Award by Pres. 1979, Excellent Enterprise Award, Business Admin Center, Korea Univ. 1983, selected as one of top 50 business leaders contributing to Nat. Devt, Daily Chosun 1998, selected as one of the top 30 business leaders in Korea in 20th century, Daily Maekyung and Fed. of Korean Industries 1999, Personality of the year 2005 awarded by fDi Magazine, affiliate magazine of the Financial Times 2005, Time magazine Hero of the Environment 2007. *Publications:* History of June 3rd Student Movement 1994, There Is No Such Thing as a Myth 1995, See Hope When Everyone Else Talks of Despair 2002, Cheonggyecheon Flows to the Future 2005, Unwavering Promise 2007, My Mother 2007. *Leisure interests:* tennis, swimming. *Address:* Office of the President, Chong Wa Dae (The Blue House), 1, Sejong-no, Jongno-gu, Seoul, South Korea (office). *Telephone:* (2) 770-0055 (office). *Fax:* (2) 770-0344 (office). *E-mail:* president@cwd.go.kr (office). *Website:* english.president.go.kr (office); www.bluehouse.go.kr (office).

LEE, Pal-seung, BL, MBA; South Korean business executive; *Chairman and CEO, Woori Finance Holdings Co. Ltd;* ed Korea Univ.; CEO Woori Investment & Securities and Exec. Man. Dir Hanil Bank –2008, Chair. and CEO Woori Finance Holdings Co. Ltd 2008–. *Address:* Woori Finance Holdings Co. Ltd, 20F 203 Hoehyon-dong 1-ga, Chung-gu, Seoul 100-792, South Korea (office). *Telephone:* (2) 2125-2000 (office). *Fax:* (2) 2125-2191 (office). *E-mail:* woorifg@woorifg.com (office). *Website:* www.woorifg.com (office).

LEE, Patrick A., PhD; American physicist and academic; *William and Emma Rogers Professor of Physics and Division Head, Atomic, Biological, Condensed Matter and Plasma Physics, Massachusetts Institute of Technology;* b. 8 Sept. 1946; ed MIT; Gibbs Instructor, Yale Univ. 1970–72; mem. tech. staff, Theoretical Physics Dept, Bell Labs 1972–73, 1974–81, Head, Theoretical Physics Dept 1981–82; Prof. of Physics, MIT 1982–, William and Emma Rogers Prof. of Physics and Div. Head, Atomic, Biological, Condensed Matter and Plasma Physics 1990–, affiliated with Quantum-Effects Devices Group of Research Lab. of Electronics; Asst Prof., Univ. of Washington 1973–74; Co-Chair. Gordon Research Conf. 1984; Guest Ed. Special Issue on Disordered Solids, Physics Today 1988; mem. Editorial Bd Chinese Physics 1980–85; mem. Proposal Review Bd Stanford Synchrotron Radiation Lab. 1977–80, Bd of Trustees Aspen Center for Physics 1981–87, Advisory Bd Inst. for Theoretical Physics 1992–95; mem. NAS, American Acad. of Arts and Sciences, Academia Sinica (Taiwan); Fellow, American Physical Soc.; Oliver Buckley Prize, American Physical Soc. 1990, Dirac Medal, Int. Centre for Theoretical Physics 2005. *Publications:* numerous articles in scientific journals. *Address:* Department of Physics, NE25-4101, Massachusetts Institute of Technology, 77 Massachusetts Avenue, Cambridge, MA 02139-4307, USA (office). *Telephone:* (617) 253-8325 (office). *Fax:* (617) 253-2562 (office). *E-mail:* palee@mit.edu (office). *Website:* web.mit.edu/physics (office).

LEE, Sang-dae; South Korean business executive; *President and CEO, Samsung C&T Corporation;* ed Korea Univ.; has held numerous sr man. positions with Samsung Corpn including Exec. Vice-Pres. Samsung Training Inst., Exec. Vice-Pres. Planning and Man. Office, Pres. and CEO Housing Devt Div., Pres. and CEO Construction and Devt Div., currently Pres. and CEO Samsung C&T Corpn, also Pres. and CEO Construction Group, Housing Group, Exec. Vice-Pres. Office of Strategic Planning, Exec. Dir and Vice-Pres. Samsung Human Resources Devt Centre, Man. Dir HQ for Planning and Man., Samsung E&C Ltd. *Address:* Samsung C&T Corpn, 310 Taepyeong-Ro 1 Ga, Jung-Gu, Seoul, Republic of Korea (office). *Telephone:* (2) 2145-2114 (office). *Fax:* (2) 2145-3114 (office). *E-mail:* info@samsungcorp.com (office). *Website:* www.samsungcorp.com (office).

LEE, Gen. Sang-hee; South Korean army officer (retd) and politician; *Minister of National Defense;* b. 12 Aug. 1945, Wonju, Gangwon Prov.; m. Kim Sun Young; one s. one d.; ed Kyung-Gi High School, Seoul, Repub. of Korea (ROK) Mil. Acad., Coll. of Liberal Arts and Science, Seoul Nat. Univ., Center for Int. Security Studies, Univ. of Maryland, USA; Commdr 29th Regt, 9th Infantry Div. 1989–91, Chief of Mil. Strategy, J-5 Directorate, Jt Chiefs of Staff 1991–92, Advisor to the Pres. for Nat. Defense Policy, Office of the Presidential Secr. 1992–94, Chief of Force Planning, G-5 Directorate, ROK Army HQ 1995–96, Commanding Gen., 30th Infantry Div. (Mechanized) 1996–98, Dir Policy Planning Bureau, Ministry of Nat. Defense 1998–99, Commanding Gen. 5th Corps 1999–2001, Chief Dir, Strategy and Plans (J5), Jt Chiefs of Staff 2001–02, Chief Dir, Operations (J3), Jt Chiefs of Staff 2002–03, promoted to four-star Gen. and Commanding Gen., Third ROK Army 2003, 32nd Chair. Jt Chiefs of Staff 2005–06 (retd); Minister of Nat. Defense 2008–; Visiting Fellow, Brookings Inst., Washington, DC 2007; Presidential Citation, Order of Nat. Security 'Samil' Medal, Order of Nat. Security 'Chonsu' Medal, Order of Nat. Security 'Gukson' Medal, Armed Forces Merit Award (Turkey), Legion of Merit, Commdr and Officer Grade, (USA). *Address:* Ministry of National Defense, 1, 3-ga, Yeongsan-dong, Yeongsan-gu, Seoul 140-701, South Korea (office). *Telephone:* (2) 795-0071 (office). *Fax:* (2) 703-3109 (office). *E-mail:* cyber@mnd.go.kr (office). *Website:* www.mnd.go.kr (office).

LEE, Seng Wee, MBA; Singaporean business executive; b. 1930; m.; ed Univs of Toronto and Western Ontario, Canada; mem. Bd of Dirs Oversea-Chinese Banking Corpn (Singapore's third-largest bank) 1966–, Chair. 1995–2003, mem. Bd Exec. Cttee, Bd Nominating Exec. 2003–; mem. Bd of Dirs Great Eastern Holdings Ltd, GIC Real Estate Pte Ltd, Lee Rubber Group of Cos, Lee Foundation; Chair. Temasek Trust. *Address:* Oversea-Chinese Banking Corporation, 65 Chulia Street, #29-02, OCBC Centre, Singapore 049513 (office). *Telephone:* 6318-7222 (office). *Fax:* 6533-7955 (office). *E-mail:* info@ocbc.com (office). *Website:* www.ocbc.com (office).

LEE, Seong-tae, BA, MA; South Korean central banker; *Governor, Bank of Korea;* ed Seoul Nat. Univ., Univ. of Illinois, USA; joined Bank of Korea 1968, Chief of Monetary Policy Dept 1981–83, Chief of Research Dept 1983–86, Deputy Dir Research Dept 1986–89, Deputy Gen. Man. Pusan Br. 1989–91, Deputy Dir Monetary Policy Dept 1991–94, Gen. Man. Changwon Br. 1994–95, Dir Public Information Dept 1995–96, Dir Support Services and Properties Dept 1996–97, Dir Budget and Man. Dept 1997–98, Dir Research Dept 1998–2000, Deputy Gov. 2000–03, Sr Deputy Gov. 2003–04, Sr Deputy Gov. and mem. Monetary Policy Cttee 2004–06, Gov. Bank of Korea 2006–. *Address:* Bank of Korea, 110, 3-ga, Namdaemun-no, Jung-gu, Seoul 100-794, South Korea (office). *Telephone:* (2) 759-4114 (office). *Fax:* (2) 759-4139 (office). *E-mail:* bokdplp@bok.or.kr (office). *Website:* www.bok.or.kr (office).

LEE, Shau Kee; Hong Kong real estate executive; *Chairman and Managing Director, Henderson Land Development Company Limited;* b. Guangdong; m. (divorced); five c.; Founder Henderson Land Development Co. Ltd, Chair. and Man. Dir 1976–; Founder, Chair. and Man. Dir Henderson Investment Ltd; Chair. Henderson Cyber Ltd; Exec. Dir Henderson China Holdings Ltd; Chair. Hong Kong and China Gas Co. Ltd; Vice-Chair. Sun Hung Kai Properties Ltd; Dir Hong Kong Ferry (Holdings) Co. Ltd, The Bank of East Asia Ltd, Miramar Hotel and Investment Co. Ltd, Rimmer (Cayman) Ltd, Riddick (Cayman) Ltd, Hopkins (Cayman) Ltd, Henderson Development Ltd, Believegood Ltd, Cameron Enterprise Inc.; nicknamed "Asia's Warren Buffet"; Grand Bauhinia Medal 2007; Hon. DBA; Hon. DSSc; Hon. LLD. *Address:* Henderson Land Development Co. Ltd, 6th Floor, World-Wide House, 19 Des Voeux Road, Central, Hong Kong (office). *Telephone:* 29088888 (office). *Fax:* 29088838 (office). *E-mail:* corpcomm@hld.com (office). *Website:* www.hld.com (office).

LEE, Tan Sri Dato' Shin Cheng; Malaysian business executive and real estate executive; *Executive Chairman and CEO, IOI Group;* m.; two s. four d.; became field supervisor at palm oil co. aged 22; controlled small co. by 1981, bought Industrial Oxygen Inc. 1981, changed name to IOI 1995, currently Exec. Chair. and CEO IOI Group (operator of palm oil plantations, refineries and related mfg activities); mem. Council Malaysian Palm Oil Asscn, Malaysia-China Business Council; Adviser to KL & Selangor Chinese Chamber of Commerce and Industry; mem. Bd Universiti Putra Malaysia; Hon. Pres. Asscn of Eng Choon Socs of Malaysia, Fed. of Hokkien Asscn of Malaysia; Hon. Doctorate in Agric. (Universiti Putra Malaysia) 2002; FIABCI Malaysia Property Man of the Year Award 2001. *Address:* IOI Corporation Berhad, 2 IOI Square, IOI Resort, 62502 Putrajaya, Malaysia (office). *Telephone:* (3) 8947-8888 (office). *Fax:* (3) 8943-2266 (office). *E-mail:* corp@ioigroup.com (office). *Website:* www.ioigroup.com (office).

LEE, Si-Chen, BS, MS, PhD; Taiwanese engineer, university administrator and academic; *President, National Taiwan University;* b. 13 Aug. 1952, Gon-Shan; ed Nat. Taiwan Univ., Stanford Univ., USA; Researcher, Energy Conversion Devices, Inc., Troy, Mich., USA 1980–82; Visiting Assoc. Prof., Dept of Electrical Eng, Nat. Taiwan Univ. 1982–85, Prof. of Electrical Eng, Coll. of Electrical Eng and Computer Science 1985–, Chair. Dept of Electrical Eng 1988–92, Dean of Academic Affairs 1996–2002, Pres. Nat. Taiwan Univ. 2005–; Asst to Minister of Nat. Defence 1993–94; Chair. University Mobility in Asia and the Pacific 2005–; Pres. Asscn of Nat. Univs of Taiwan 2006–; Leader Bioenergy Field Group, Biology Dept, Nat. Science Council 1992–98, Microelectronics Group, Eng Dept 1988–93; mem. Directorate, Asscn of Chinese Electrical Engineers 1992–94; consultant, Electronics Research and Service Org., Industrial Tech. Research Inst. 1986–89, 1991–92; mem. Directorate, Chinese Asscn of Electromagnetism in Life Science 1999–2004; Assoc. Ed. Materials Chemistry and Physics 1992–2004, Journal of Chinese Engineers 1996–2000; Fellow, IEEE 2002 (mem. Vice-Directorate, IEEE Taipei section 2001–02); mem. Chinese Inst. of Electrical Eng, Asia-Pacific Acad. of Materials 1997; Dr hc (Kansai Univ.) 2005; five consecutive Outstanding Research Awards from Nat. Science Council 1986–96, Sun Yat-San Academic Award (Eng) 1987, Young Distinguished Engineer, Chinese Engineer Asscn 1987, Special Contracted Researcher, Nat. Science Council 1996–2002, IEEE Third Millennium Medal 2000, Annual Medal, Chinese Asscn of Electrical Engineers 2002, 47th Academic Award, Ministry of Educ. 2003. *Publications:* numerous scientific papers in professional journals. *Address:* Office of the President, 1 Roosevelt Road, Section 4, Taipei 106, Taiwan (office). *Telephone:* (2) 3366-2000 (office). *Fax:* (2) 2362-1877 (office). *E-mail:* sclee@cc.ee.ntu.edu.tw (office). *Website:* www.ntu.edu.tw (office).

LEE, Soo-chang; South Korean insurance executive; *President and CEO, Samsung Life Insurance Co. Ltd;* b. 1949, Yecheon, Gyeongsangbuk-do; m. three c.; ed Daechang High School, Coll. of Veterinary Medicine, Seoul Nat. Univ.; joined Samsung Life Insurance Co. Ltd 1973, Dir Cheil Jedang (subsidiary co.) 1990, Dir Shipbuilding Dept, Samsung Heavy Industries 1990–92, Dir Heavy Machinery Dept, Samsung Heavy Industries Jan.–Dec. 1993, Man. Dir Samsung Life Insurance Co. 1993–95, Man. Dir Samsung Fire 1995–95, Sr Man. Dir 1996–98, Vice-Pres. 1998–99, Vice-Pres. and CEO 1999–2001, Pres. and CEO 2001–06, Pres. and CEO Samsung Life Insurance

Co. Ltd 2006–; Iron Tower Order of Industrial Service 2000; 1st Nat. Country Love-Leader Award 2006, Forbes Korea Excellence in Leadership Award 2007. *Leisure interests:* reading, go, golf. *Address:* Samsung Life Insurance Co. Ltd, 150 Taepyung-ro 2-ga, Jung-gu, Seoul 100-716, Republic of Korea (office). *Telephone:* (2) 1588-3114 (office). *Fax:* (2) 751-8021 (office). *E-mail:* info@samsunglife.com (office). *Website:* www.samsunglife.com (office).

LEE, Soo-ho, BA; South Korean business executive; *President, Korean Gas Corporation;* b. 8 Feb. 1944, Jinju, Kyungnam Prov.; m. Young-Sook Park; one s. one d.; ed Jinju High School, Yonsei Univ.; began career with trading co. 1968–78; joined Bando Int. (renamed LG Int.) 1978, Sr Man. Gen. Merchandise Dept 1980–81, with Br. Office, Jakarta, Indonesia 1981–84, Overseas Man. Div./Resources 1985–88, Br. Offices, Singapore and Hong Kong 1988–92, Man. Dir Sales Group/Support 1992–95, Sr Man. Dir Support 1995–96, Vice-Pres. Business Operations 1996–97, CEO LG Int. Corpn 1997–2003; Pres. Korean Gas Corpn (KOGAS) 2005–; Order of Merit for Industrial Service 1997. *Address:* Korea Gas Corporation, 215 Jeongja-dong, Bundang-gu, Seongnam, Gyeonggi-do, 463-754, Republic of Korea (office). *Telephone:* (31) 710-0114 (office). *Fax:* (31) 710-0117 (office). *E-mail:* kogasmaster@kogas.or.kr (office). *Website:* www.kogas.or.kr (office).

LEE, Soo-sung; South Korean politician and academic; *President, National Council of Saemaul-Undong Movement;* fmr Pres. Seoul Nat. Univ.; Prime Minister of Repub. of Korea 1995–97; currently Pres. Nat. Council of Saemaul-Undong Movement; Head, Screening Cttee, Asscn for Enhancing and Practicing the Spirit of Manhae. *Address:* National Council of Saemaul-Undong Movement, 1008-4 Daichi-dong Kangnam-Ku, Seoul, Republic of Korea (office). *Telephone:* (2) 699-8888 (office). *Fax:* (2) 260-03618 (office). *E-mail:* aaa@polcom.com (office). *Website:* www.saemaul.or.kr (office).

LEE, Spike; American filmmaker and actor; b. (Shelton Jackson Lee), 20 March 1957, Atlanta; s. of Bill Lee and Jacquelyn Shelton; m. Tonya Lewis 1993; one d.; ed Morehouse Coll., Atlanta and New York Univ. Inst. of Film and Television; wrote scripts for Black Coll.: The Talented Tenth, Last Hustle in Brooklyn; produced, wrote, Dir Joe's Bed-Stuy Barbershop: We Cut Heads; has directed music videos, TV commercials and other short projects; f. Forty Acres and a Mule Filmworks; Commdr des Arts et des Lettres 2003; Dr hc (New York Univ.) 1998; Cannes Film Festival Best New Dir 1986, LA Film Critics' Asscn Awards 1986, 1989, Chicago Film Festival Critics' Awards 1990, 1992, Golden Satellite Best Documentary 1997; inducted into Nat. Asscn for the Advancement of Colored People (NAACP) Hall of Fame 2003. *Films include:* She's Gotta Have It 1985 (Cannes Film Festival Prize for Best New Film), School Daze 1988, Do the Right Thing 1989, Love Supreme 1990, Mo' Better Blues 1990, Jungle Fever 1991, Malcolm X 1992, Crooklyn, Girl 6, Clockers 1995, Get on the Bus, He Got Game 1998, Summer of Sam 1999, Tales from the Hood 1995 (exec. producer), Bamboozled 2000, The Original Kings of Comedy 2000, Lisa Picard is Famous 2001, A Huey P. Newton Story 2001, The 25th Hour 2003, CSA: Confederate States of America (exec. producer) 2004, She Hate Me 2004, Inside Man 2006. *Television:* Sucker Free City 2004. *Documentaries:* Four Little Girls 1997, When the Levees Broke 2006. *Publications:* Spike Lee's Gotta Have It: Inside Guerrilla Filmmaking 1987, Uplift the Race 1988, The Trials and Tribulations of the Making of Malcolm X 1992, Girl 6 1996, Get on the Bus 1996. *Leisure interest:* basketball. *Address:* William Morris Agency, One William Morris Place, Beverly Hills, CA 90212, USA (office); Forty Acres and a Mule Filmworks, 124 De Kalb Avenue, Suite 2, Brooklyn, New York, NY 11217, USA. *Telephone:* (310) 859-4000 (office); (718) 624-3703. *Fax:* (310) 859-4462 (office); (718) 624-2008. *Website:* www.wma.com (office).

LEE, Stan; American comic book writer and film producer; *Chairman Emeritus, Marvel Comics;* b. (Stanley Martin Lieber), 28 Dec. 1922, New York, NY; s. of Jack Lieber and Celia Lieber; m. Joan Lee 1947; two c.; ed De Witt Clinton High School; fmr Asst Ed., Ed. Timely Comics Group (later known as Marvel Comics), first comic book script appeared in Captain America 1941, fmr positions at Marvel Comics include Head Writer, Art Dir, Publisher, Ed.-in-Chief, Pres. and Chair., currently Chair. Emer.; comic book creations (together with illustrators) include Fantastic Four, Hulk, Spider-Man, X-Men, The Avengers, Iron Man, Daredevil, Silver Surfer; f. Pow! Entertainment Inc. 2005; Nat. Medal of Arts 2008. *Films include:* Exec. Producer: Captain America 1991, Generation X 1996, Nick Fury: Agent of Shield 1998, Blade 1998, X-Men 2000, Blade II 2002, Spider-Man 2002, Daredevil 2003, X2 2003, Hulk 2003, The Punisher 2004, Spider-Man II 2004, Blade: Trinity 2004, Elektra 2005, Man-Thing 2005, Fantastic Four 2005. *Publication:* Excelsior! The Amazing Life of Stan Lee (autobiography) 2002. *Address:* c/o Marvel Entertainment Inc., 417 Fifth Avenue, New York, NY 10016, USA (office). *Telephone:* (212) 576-4000 (office). *Fax:* (212) 576-8517 (office). *Website:* www.marvel.com (office); www.powentertainment.com (office); www.stanleeweb.com.

LEE, Tsung-Dao, PhD; Chinese physicist; *Professor of Physics, Columbia University;* b. 25 Nov. 1926, Shanghai; s. of Tsing-Kong Lee and Ming-Chang Chang; m. Jeanette H. C. Chin 1950 (died 1995); two s.; ed Nat. Chekiang Univ., Nat. Southwest Univ., China and Univ. of Chicago, USA; Research Assoc. in Astronomy, Univ. of Chicago 1950; Research Assoc. and Lecturer in Physics, Univ. of California 1950–51; mem. Inst. for Advanced Study, Princeton, NJ 1951–53; Asst Prof. of Physics, Columbia Univ., New York 1953–55, Assoc. Prof. 1955–56, Prof. 1956–60, 1963, Enrico Fermi Prof. of Physics 1964–, Univ. Prof. 1984–; Prof. Princeton Inst. for Advanced Study 1960–63; mem. NAS; shared Nobel Prize for Physics 1957 with Prof. Yang Chen-ning for work on elementary particles; Albert Einstein Award in Science 1957; numerous other awards including New York Acad. of Science Award 2000, Order of the Rising Sun, Gold and Silver Star (Japan) 2007. *Publications:* articles in physical journals. *Address:* Department of Physics, Columbia

University, Building 538, Morningside Heights, W 120th Street, New York, NY 10027 (office); 25 Claremont Avenue, New York, NY 10027, USA (home). *Telephone:* (212) 854-1759 (office). *Fax:* (212) 932-0418 (office). *E-mail:* tdl@phys.columbia.edu (office). *Website:* www.columbia.edu (office).

LEE, Teng-Hui, PhD; Taiwanese politician; b. 15 Jan. 1923, Taiwan; m. Tseng Wen-fui; two d.; ed Kyoto Imperial Univ., Japan, Nat. Taiwan Univ., Iowa State and Cornell Univs, USA; Asst Prof. Nat. Taiwan Univ. 1949–55, Assoc. Prof. 1956–58; Research Fellow, Taiwan Co-operative Bank 1953; Specialist and Econ. Analyst, Dept of Agric. and Forestry, Taiwan Prov. Govt 1954–57; Specialist, Joint Comm. on Rural Reconstruction (JCRR) 1957–61, Sr Specialist and Consultant 1961–70, Chief, Rural Economy Div. 1970–72; Prof. Nat. Chengchi Univ. 1958–78; Minister without Portfolio 1972–78; Mayor of Taipei City 1978–81; Gov. Taiwan Province 1981–84; Vice-Pres. of Repub. of China (Taiwan) 1984–88, Pres. 1988–2000; co-f. Taiwan Solidarity Union 2001; expelled from KMT (Kuomingtang) Party 2001; Hon. LLD (Southern Methodist Univ., USA) 1994; Int. Distinguished Achievement Citation, Iowa State Univ., USA and other awards. *Publications:* several works on agricultural development in Taiwan. *Leisure interests:* art, music and sport. *Address:* c/o Office of the President, 122 Chungking South Road, Sec. 1, Taipei 100, Taiwan.

LEE, Gen. Tien-yu; Taiwanese military official; b. 1946, Nanjing; served in Tactical Fighter Wing, Armed Forces of Taiwan 1990–92, Commdr Combat Air Command 1998–2001, Commdr of Air Force 2002–04, Chief of Gen. Staff 2004–2007; Strategic Adviser to Pres. Chen Shui-bian Feb.–May 2007; Minister of Nat. Defense 2007–08 (resgnd); Order of Blue Sky and White Sun with Grand Cordon 2007. *Address:* c/o Ministry of National Defense, 2/F, 164 Po Ai Road, Taipei, 10048, Taiwan (office).

LEE, Ufan; South Korean painter; b. 1936, Gyeonsang Nam-do; ed Seoul Nat. Univ. and Nihon Univ., Tokyo; mem. Mono-Ha group (Japanese avant-garde art movt) late 1960s; Prof. Tama Art Univ., Tokyo 1973–93; Prof. Ecole Nat. Supérieure des Beaux-Arts, Paris 1997–98; prize for critical writing 1969, Praemium Imperiale Award, Japan Art Asscn 2001; Cultural Decoration 1990, Chevalier des Arts et des Lettres 1991. *Address:* c/o Ecole Nationale Supérieure des Beaux-Arts, 14 rue Bonaparte, 75006 Paris, France (office).

LEE, Won-gul; South Korean business executive; *President and CEO, Korea Electric Power Corporation (KEPCO);* fmr Dir Aerospace Industry Div., Basic Industry Bureau, Ministry of Trade; Vice-Minister of Commerce, Industry and Energy –2006; Pres. and CEO Korea Electric Power Corpn (KEPCO) 2006–. *Address:* Korea Electric Power Corpn, 411 Yeongdong-daero, Gangnam-gu, Seoul 135-791, Republic of Korea (office). *Telephone:* (2) 3456-3114 (office). *Fax:* (2) 556-3694 (office). *E-mail:* info@kepco.co.kr (office). *Website:* www.kepco.co.kr (office).

LEE, Yeh Kwong Charles, LLM, ACIS; Chinese lawyer; *Non-Official Member, Executive Council of Hong Kong;* b. 16 July 1936, Shanghai; m. Nancy Lee 1960; one s. one d.; ed London School of Econs, UK; audit asst, Li Kwan Hung 1954–57, Peat Marwick Mitchell & Co., Hong Kong 1957–60; Asst Registrar, Registrar-Gen.'s Dept 1960–65; articled clerk, Nigel, Wallis & Apfel, Solicitors, UK 1965–68; solicitor, Registrar-Gen.'s Dept 1968–70, Johnson Stokes & Master 1970–72, Partner 1972–73; Partner Charles Lee & Stephen Lo 1973, Woo Kwan Lee & Lo 1973–; non-official mem., Exec. Council of Hong Kong 2005–; mem. Council, Stock Exchange of Hong Kong Ltd 1988–, Chair. 1991; Dir several listed cos; Fellow Chartered Asscn of Certified Accountants; Hon. DBA (Hong Kong Polytechnic Univ.) 2001. *Leisure interests:* boating, scuba diving. *Address:* Woo Kwan Lee & Lo, 26/Fl. Jardine House, 1 Connaught Place, Hong Kong Special Administrative Region, People's Republic of China (office). *Telephone:* 8477823 (office). *Fax:* 8450239 (office).

LEE, Yock Suan, BSc; Singaporean politician; b. 30 Sept. 1946, Singapore; m.; one s. one d.; ed Queenstown Secondary Technical School, Raffles Institution, Imperial Coll., Univ. of London, UK, Univ. of Singapore; Div. Dir (Projects), Econ. Devt Bd 1969–80; MP 1980–; Deputy Man. Dir Petrochemical Corpn of Singapore (Pte.) Ltd Jan.–Sept. 1981; Minister of State (Nat. Devt) 1981–83, (Finance) 1983–84, Sr Minister of State and Acting Minister for Labour 1985–86, Minister for Labour 1987–91, Second Minister of Educ. 1991–92, Minister of Educ. 1992–97, of Trade and Industry 1998–99, for Information and the Arts 1999–2001, of Environment 1999–2000, Minister in Prime Minister's Office and Second Minister of Foreign Affairs 2001–04; Deputy Chair. People's Asscn 1984–91. *Leisure interest:* badminton. *Address:* 9 Bishopsgate, Singapore249988. *Telephone:* 62381600. *E-mail:* leeyocksuan2004@yahoo.com.sg. *Website:* www.parliament.gov.sg.

LEE, Yong-kyung, MSc, PhD; South Korean telecommunications executive; ed Seoul Nat. Univ., Univ. of Okla, Univ. of Calif. at Berkeley, USA; Asst Prof. of Information Eng, Univ. of Ill., Chicago 1975–77; scientist Exxon Enterprises 1977–79; mem. Tech. Staff AT&T Bell Labs 1979–91; Vice-Pres. Outside Plant T Lab., Korea Telecom 1991–94, Vice-Pres. Telecommunication Systems Lab. and Software Lab. 1994–95, Vice-Pres. Wireless Tech. Lab. 1995–96, Exec. Vice-Pres. Research and Devt Group 1996–2000; CEO KT Freetel Co. 2000–02, Pres. and CEO KT Corpn (telecommunications service provider) 2002–05. *Address:* c/o KT Corporation, 206 Jungja-dong, Bundang-gu, Sungnam, Kyonggi 463-711, Republic of Korea (office).

LEE, Yuan-Tseh, PhD; Taiwanese scientist and academic; b. 19 Nov. 1936, Hsinchu; s. of Tse Fan Lee and Pei Tasi; m. Bernice Wu 1963; two s. one d.; ed Nat. Taiwan Univ., Univ. of California, Berkeley, USA; Asst Prof., James Franck Inst. and Dept of Chem., Univ. of Chicago 1968–71, Assoc. Prof. 1971–72, Prof. of Chem. 1973–74; Prof. of Chem., Univ. of California, Berkeley 1974–94, Prof. Emer. 1994–, also Prin. Investigator, Lawrence Berkeley Lab. 1974–97; Distinguished Research Fellow, Inst. of Atomic and Molecular

Sciences, Academia Sinica, Taiwan 1994–, Pres. 1994–2006; Sloan Fellow 1969; Guggenheim Fellow 1976; Miller Professorship 1981–82; mem. Int. Council for Science 1993–, mem. Standing Cttee on Freedom in the Conduct of Science 1996–2005, elected Pres. 2008 to take up office 2010; mem. American Acad. of Arts and Sciences, NAS, American Physical Soc. and numerous other scholarly socs; Hon. Prof., Inst. of Chem., Chinese Acad. of Sciences, Beijing 1980–, Hon. Foreign Mem. Indian Nat. Science Acad. 1997, Hon. Mem. Chemical Soc. of Japan 2002–; E. O. Lawrence Award (US Dept of Energy) 1981, Harrison Howe Award, Rochester Section, ACS, 1983, Nobel Prize for Chem. (jtly) 1986, Nat. Medal of Science 1986, Peter Debye Award of Physical Chem., ACS 1986, Faraday Medal, Royal Soc. of Chem., UK 1992, Clark Kerr Award, Univ. of California, Berkeley 1999, Jawaharlal Nehru Centenary Medal, Indian Nat. Science Acad. 2004, and many other awards and prizes. *Publications:* articles in professional journals. *Address:* c/o Academia Sinica, 128 Academia Road, Section 2, Nanking, Taipei 11529, Taiwan (office). *Telephone:* (2) 27899400 (office). *Fax:* (2) 27853852 (office). *E-mail:* ytlee@gate .sinica.edu.tw (office). *Website:* www.sinica.edu.tw (office).

LEE, Yung-San, MA, PhD; Taiwanese politician, economist and banking executive; b. 7 Dec. 1938; m.; three d.; ed Nat. Taiwan Univ., Univ. of Wisconsin, Madison, USA; joined as Asst, Inst. of Econs, Academia Sinica, served successively as Asst Research Fellow, Assoc. Research Fellow, Research Fellow 1962–70, Deputy Dir 1985–87, Dir 1988–90; Prof. of Econs, Nat. Taiwan Univ. 1973–94; Visiting Scholar, Harvard Univ., USA 1976–77; Dir Econ. Research Dept, Cen. Bank of China 1977–85; Pres. Chiao Tung Bank 1990–94; Chair. Farmers Bank of China 1994–98, Int. Commercial Bank of China 1998–2002, Bankers Asscn of Taiwan 2000–02, Asian Bankers Asscn 2000–02; Minister of Finance 2002. *Address:* c/o Ministry of Finance, 2 I-Kuo West Road, Taipei, Taiwan (office).

LEE-CHIN, Michael; Canadian/Jamaican investment industry executive; *Chairman, AIC Limited;* b. 1951, Port Antonio, Jamaica; m. Adrian Chin 1974 (separated 1997); three c.; pnr Sonya Hamilton; two c.; ed McMaster Univ.; began career in financial services in 1977, positions included Financial Advisor, Investors Group and Regional Br Man., Regal Capital Planning; est. Berkshire Group (financial services co.) 1985; purchased Advantage Investment Council 1987 (renamed AIC) and developedit into an investment co. with funds over C$12 billion, CEO –2006, currently Chair., AIC acquired 75 per cent of Nat. Commercial Bank of Jamaica 2002, established AIC Caribbean Fund 2004; Dr hc (McMaster Univ.) 2003; Hon. LLD, Univ. of Toronto 2007; Harry Jerome Award for Business Leader of the Decade 2002, one of Time magazine's 'Canada's Heroes' 2004. *Address:* AIC Limited, 1375 Kerns Road, Burlington, ON L7R 4X8, Canada (office). *Telephone:* (905) 331-4242 (office). *E-mail:* info@aic.com (office). *Website:* www.aic.com (office).

LEE HANG, Niko; Samoan accountant and politician; *Minister of Finance;* fmr Public Trustee; elected to one of the two parl. seats reserved for Individual Voters March 2006; nominated to cabinet post by the Prime Minister; Minister of Finance 2007–. *Address:* Ministry of Finance, Private Bag, 2–4th Floors, Central Bank Building, Matafele, Apia, Samoa (office). *Telephone:* 34333 (office). *Fax:* 21312 (office). *E-mail:* treasury@samoa.ws (office); information@ mof.gov.ws (office). *Website:* www.mof.gov.ws (office).

LEE-VERCOE, Sandra Rose Te Hakamatua; New Zealand diplomatist and former politician; b. 8 Aug. 1952, Wellington; two d.; co-f. Mana Motuhake party 1979, Pres. 1991–94, Leader 1994–2001; elected mem. Waiheke County Council 1983–89, Chair. 1989; Councillor Auckland City Council 1989–94; Founding mem. Alliance coalition 1991, Political Leader 1994, Leader 1994–95; mem. Parl. 1993–96, 1996–2002; Minister of Local Govt and of Conservation and Assoc. Minister of Maori Affairs 1999–2002; High Commr to Niue 2003–05; mem. Bd of Dirs Housing NZ 2006–, Museum of New Zealand Te Papa Tongarewa 2007–; fmr mem. Ministry for the Environment Working Group on Climate Change, on Waste Man.; Founding mem. Hauraki Gulf Islands Br., Forest and Bird Soc.; fmr mem. Hauraki Gulf Maritime Park Bd, Auckland Domestic Violence Centre Bd, Auckland Dist Maori Council, Council of the Auckland Inst. and Museum. *Address:* c/o Board of Directors, Museum of New Zealand Te Papa Tongarewa, 55 Cable Street, PO Box 467, Wellington, New Zealand. *Telephone:* (4) 381-7000. *E-mail:* mail@tepapa.govt .nz. *Website:* www.tepapa.govt.nz.

LEEBRON, David W., JD; American lawyer and university administrator; *President, Rice University;* b. 1956, Philadelphia; s. of Norman D. Leebron; m. Y. Ping Sun; one s. one d.; ed Harvard Coll., Harvard Law School; began career as clerk, US Ninth Circuit Court of Appeals; Assoc., Cleary, Gottlieb, Steen & Hamilton (law firm), New York 1981–83; Prof. of Law, New York Univ. (NYU) 1983, also Dir NYU Int. Legal Studies Program 1983–89; joined faculty, Columbia Univ. Law School 1989, Dean of Law School 1996; Pres. Rice Univ. 2004–; mem. NY State Bar; mem. American Law Inst., Council on Foreign Relations, American Soc. of Int. Law; mem. Bd of Dirs IMAX Corpn; mem. Editorial Bd Foundation Press; Commandeur de l'Ordre Nat. du Mérite 2006. *Address:* Office of the President, Rice University, PO Box 1892, Houston, TX 77251-1892, USA (office). *E-mail:* info@rice.edu (office). *Website:* www .professor.rice.edu/professor/Office_of_the_President.asp (office).

LEENHARDT, Jacques; French sociologist and academic; *Director of Studies, École des Hautes Études en Sciences Sociales;* b. 17 April 1942, Geneva, Switzerland; s. of Franz J. Leenhardt and Antoinette Chenevière; m. 1st Françoise Warnod 1964 (divorced 1970); one s.; m. 2nd Sabine Wespieser 2006; contrib. to Le Journal de Genève 1963–98, to Le Temps 1998–; Fellow, Inst. for Advanced Study, Princeton, NJ 1979–80; Visiting Prof. to Univs in Brazil, Chile, Germany, Mexico, Portugal, Puerto Rico, USA 1974–; now Dir of Studies, School of Advanced Studies in Social Sciences, Paris; Pres. French Art Critics Asscn 1981–90, Crestet Centre d'Art 1987–2002, Int. Art Critics

Asscn 1990–96, Art in Nature 1991–; mem. European Acad. of Arts and Sciences 1992–; Chevalier des Arts et des Lettres 1983, Ordre nat. du Mérite 1987; Oficial Ordem Nacional do Cruzeiro do Sul (Brazil) 1998; Edra-Place Award 2000. *Publications include:* Lecture politique du roman 1973, Lire la lecture 1982, La force des mots 1982, Au Jardin des Malentendus 1990, Les Amériques latines en France 1992, Dans les jardins de Roberto Burle Marx 1994, Villette-Amazone 1996, Bienal do Mercosur 1998, Michel Corajoud, Paysagiste 2000, Erico Veríssimo. O romance da História 2001, Conscience du paysage: Le passant de Montreuil 2002, Reinventar o Brasil: Gilberto Freyre entre historia e ficçao 2006. *Address:* École des Hautes Études en Sciences Sociales, 10 rue Monsieur le Prince, 75006 Paris, France (office). *Telephone:* 1-53-10-54-74 (office). *Fax:* 1-53-10-54-76 (office). *E-mail:* jacques.leenhardt@ ehess.fr (office). *Website:* cral.ehess.fr (office).

LEES, Sir David (Bryan), Kt, CBIM, FCA, FRSA; British business executive; *Chairman, Tate & Lyle PLC;* b. 23 Nov. 1936, Aberdeen; s. of the late Rear-Admiral D. M. Lees, CB, DSO, and of C. D. M. Lees; m. Edith M. Bernard 1961; two s. one d.; ed Charterhouse; articled clerk, Binder Hamlyn & Co. (Chartered Accountants) 1957–62, Sr Audit Clerk 1962–63; Chief Accountant, Handley Page Ltd 1964–68; Financial Dir Handley Page Aircraft Ltd 1969; Chief Accountant, GKN Sankey Ltd 1970–72, Deputy Controller 1972–73, Dir, Sec., Controller 1973–76; Group Finance Exec. GKN Ltd 1976–77, Gen. Man. Finance 1977–82; Finance Dir GKN PLC 1982–87, Group Man. Dir 1987–88, CEO 1988–96, Chair. 1988–2004; Chair. Courtaulds 1996–98 (Dir 1991–98); Deputy Chair. Brambles Industries Ltd and Brambles Industries PLC 2001–; Dir Bank of England 1991–99, Royal Opera House 1998–; Chair. Tate & Lyle PLC 1998–; Pres. Eng Employers' Fed. (EEF) 1990–92, Soc. of Business Economists 1994–99; mem. CBI Council 1988–, Chair. CBI Econ. Affairs Cttee 1988–94, mem. CBI Pres.'s Cttee 1988–96; Commr, Audit Comm. 1983–90; Gov. Shrewsbury School 1986–, Chair. 2004; mem. Listed Cos Advisory Cttee 1990–97, Nat. Defence Industries Council 1995–2004, European Round Table 1995–2002, Panel on Takeovers and Mergers 2001– and other bodies; Gov. Sutton's Hosp. in Charterhouse 1995–; Officer's Cross, Order of Merit (Germany) 1996; ICAEW Award for Outstanding Achievement 1999. *Leisure interests:* walking, golf, opera, music. *Address:* Tate & Lyle PLC, Sugar Quay, Lower Thames Street, London, EC3R 6DQ, England (office). *Website:* www .tateandlyle.co.uk (office).

LEES, Martin, BMechEng; British engineer, international official and university administrator; *Rector Emeritus, United Nations University for Peace;* b. 1941; m.; four c.; ed Fettes Coll., Edinburgh, Univ. of Cambridge, Coll. of Europe, Belgium; joined OECD 1971; Special Adviser to Bradford Morse, Admin. UNDP 1978, Exec. Dir UN Financing System for Science and Tech. for Devt 1979–84, Asst Sec.-Gen. UN 1984; Exec. Dir InterAction Council of Former Heads of State and Govt 1983; Founder mem. Toyota Int. Advisory Bd 1996; Rector and CEO UN Univ. for Peace 2001–05, Rector Emer. 2005–. *Address:* United Nations University for Peace, Apartado 138, 6100 San José, Costa Rica (office). *Telephone:* 205-9000 (office). *Fax:* 249-1929 (office). *E-mail:* info@upeace.org (office). *Website:* www.upeace.org (office).

LEEVES, Jane; British actress; b. 18 April 1963, Ilford, Essex; d. of Colin Leeves and Ruth Leeves; m. Marshall Cohen 1996; one d.; co-f. (with Frasier co-star Peri Gilpin) Bristol Cities Production Co. 1998. *Films:* Monty Python's The Meaning of Life 1983, To Live and Die in LA 1985, The Hunger 1983, Mr Write 1994, Miracle on 34th Street 1994, James and the Giant Peach (voice) 1996, Hercules (voice) 1998, Don't Go Breaking My Heart 1998, Music of the Heart 1999, The Adventures of Tom Thumb and Thumbelina (voice) 2000, The Event 2003, Garfield: A Tail of Two Kitties (voice) 2006, Endless Bummer 2008. *Television:* The Benny Hill Show 1969, Double Trouble 1984, Throb 1986, Murphy Brown 1988, Seinfeld, Red Dwarf 1992, Just Deserts 1992, 1999, Frasier 1993–2004, Pandora's Clock 1996, The Great War and the Shaping of the 20th Century (voice) 1996. *Theatre:* Cabaret, Broadway 2002. *Leisure interests:* reading, cooking, sports, dance classes. *Address:* Bristol Cities Productions, c/o Paramount Productions, 5555 Melrose Avenue, Los Angeles, CA 90038, USA (office). *Telephone:* (323) 956-3513 (office). *E-mail:* BrstlCty@aol.com (office).

LEFEBVRE, Georges; French postal service executive; *CEO, La Poste Group;* ed Ecole Nationale Supérieure des PTT; joined La Poste 1970, becoming Man. Human Resources and Employee Relations 1990, CEO La Poste Group 2002–, also mem. council various subsidiary cos including Sofipost, Geopost, Banque postale, Poste Immo. *Address:* La Poste Group, 44 boulevard de Vaugirard, 75757 Paris Cedex, France (office). *Telephone:* 1-55-44-00-00 (office). *Fax:* 1-55-44-33-00 (office). *E-mail:* info@laposte.fr (office). *Website:* www.laposte.fr (office).

LEFKOWITZ, Robert J., BA, MD; American biologist/biochemist and academic; *James B. Duke Professor of Medicine and Professor of Biochemistry, Duke University Medical Center;* b. 15 April 1943, New York, NY; ed Columbia Univ.; Intern, Dept of Medicine, Columbia-Presbyterian Medical Center, NY 1966–67, Asst Resident 1967–68; Clinical and Research Assoc., US Public Health Service, NIH, Bethesda, Md 1968–70; Sr Resident, Dept of Medicine, Mass Gen. Hosp., Boston 1970–71, Clinical and Research Fellow, Dept of Cardiology 1971–73; Teaching Fellow, Harvard Medical School, Dept of Medicine, Boston 1971–73; Assoc. Prof. of Medicine, Duke Univ. Medical Center Durham, NC 1973–77, Asst Prof. of Biochemistry 1973–85, Prof. of Medicine 1977–82, James B. Duke Prof. of Medicine 1982–, Prof. of Biochemistry 1985–, Investigator, Howard Hughes Medical Inst. 1976–; George Thorn Visiting Prof., Brigham and Women's Hosp. 1984; Sterling Drug Visiting Prof. of Pharmacology, Univ. of Mich. Medical School 1986; Sterling Drug-Maurice L. Tainter Professorship, Stanford Univ. School of Medicine 1988; Bulfinch Visiting Prof., Mass Gen. Hosp. 1999; Sec./Treasurer American Fed. for Clinical Research 1980–83; Pres. American Soc. for Clinical Investigation

1987–88; Treasurer Asscn of American Physicians 1989–94, Vice-Pres. 1999–2000, Pres. 2000–01; mem. American Fed. for Clinical Research, American Soc. of Biological Chemists, American Soc. for Clinical Investigation, American Heart Asscn Councils on Basic Science, Clinical Cardiology and Hypertension, American Soc. for Pharmacology and Experimental Therapeutics, Endocrine Soc., Asscn of American Physicians, American Physiological Soc.; mem. Editorial Bd Journal of Clinical Investigation 1990–, Proceedings of the Asscn of American Physicians 1995–, Molecular Biology of the Cell 1996–, Physiological Genomics 1999–, Molecular Interventions 2000–, Circulation 2000–, Fellowship, Int. Acad. of Cardiovascular Sciences 2002; Hon. mem. Japanese Biochemical Soc. 1990; Hon. DSc (Medical Univ. of South Carolina) 2004, (Mount Sinai School of Medicine, New York Univ.) 2004; Roche Prize for Excellence in Medical Studies 1962, Janeway Prize 1966, John J. Abel Award in Pharmacology, American Soc. for Pharmacology and Experimental Therapeutics 1978, George W. Thorn Award for Scientific Excellence, Howard Hughes Medical Inst. 1979, Gordon Wilson Lecture and Award, American Clinical and Climatological Asscn 1982, Ernst Oppenheimer Memorial Award, Endocrine Soc. 1982, Award for Outstanding Research, Int. Soc. for Heart Research 1985, Steven C. Beering Award for Outstanding Achievement in Biomedical Science, Indiana Univ. School of Medicine 1986, H.B. van Dyke Award for Excellence in Medical Research, Columbia Univ. Coll. of Physicians and Surgeons 1986, Goodman and Gilman Award, American Soc. for Pharmacology and Experimental Therapeutics 1986, North Carolina Award for Science 1987, Gairdner Foundation Int. Award 1988, American Heart Asscn Basic Research Prize (co-recipient) 1990, Asscn of American Medical Colls Biomedical Research Award 1990, Novo Nordisk Biotechnology Award 1990, City of Medicine Award (co-recipient) 1991, Giovanni Lorenzini Prize for Basic Biomedical Research 1992, Bristol-Myers Squibb Award for Distinguished Achievement in Cardiovascular Research 1992, Columbia Univ. Coll. of Physicians and Surgeons Alumnus Award for Distinguished Achievements in Medicine 1992, Joseph Mather Smith Prize, Columbia Univ. Coll. of Physicians and Surgeons 1993, Ciba Award for Hypertension Research 1996, Miami 1996 Bio/Technology Winter Symposia Feodor Lynen Award 1996, Glorney-Raisbeck Award in Cardiology, The New York Acad. of Medicine 1997, F.E. Shideman-Sterling Award 2000, Novartis/Drew Award in Biomedical Research 2000, Francis Gilman Blake Award, Asscn of American Physicians 2001, Peter Harris Distinguished Scientist Award, Int. Soc. for Heart Research 2001, NAS Jessie Stevenson Kovalenko Medal 2001, Fred Conrad Koch Award, The Endocrine Soc. 2001, Louis and Artur Lucian Award for Research in Circulatory Disease 2001, Pasarow Cardiovascular Research Award 2002, Medal of Merit, Int. Acad. of Cardiovascular Sciences 2003, IPSEN Endrocrinology Prize, France 2003, Grand Prix for Science, Fondation Lefloulon-Delalande, Instituit de France 2003, Founding Distinguished Scientist Award, American Heart Asscn, Herbert Tabor Lecture Award, First American Soc. of Biological Chemistry and Molecular Biology 2004, Distinguished Faculty Award, Duke Univ. Medical Center 2004, Eugene Braunwald Academic Mentorship Award, American Heart Asscn 2006, Albany Medical Center Prize in Medicine and Biomedical Research 2007, The Shaw Prize in Life Science and Medicine 2007, Distinguished Lecture Award in Basic Science, Heart Failure Soc. of America 2007, Nat. Medal of Science 2007. *Publications:* more than 800 articles in scientific and medical journals. *Address:* Department of Medicine, Howard Hughes Medical Institute, Duke University Medical Center, Box 3821, Durham, NC 27710, USA (office). *Telephone:* (919) 684-2974 (office). *Fax:* (919) 684-8875 (office). *E-mail:* lefko001@receptor-biol.duke.edu (office). *Website:* www.lefkolab.org (office).

LEFRANÇOIS, Jacques Roger; Belgian accountant; *Secretary-General, Conseil mondial de crise;* b. 1 March 1929, Eu, Seine Maritime, France; s. of Roger Lefrançois and Simone Boussy; m. Rosa Van Laer Londerzeel 1952; one s. one d.; ed Coll. d'Eu, Inst. Nat. de Comptabilité; second accountant (Sogeco mar) 1948–52; publicity agent (Publi-Buro) 1952–68; confidential employee 1966–78; mem. Congress of European People (EFB-MFE) 1961–65; World Citizen for Peace through Human Rights 1965; proposed UN Day for World Peace and the Environment 1970; mem. Professional Union of Int. School of Detective Experts 1950–75, Belgium Comm. World Political Union, The Hague 1978–; First Sec. Universal Charter for Survival (UFOS) 1975; Pres. Group 'L'Homme Planétaire' 1970–98; Founder and Sec.-Gen. Conseil mondial de crise 1998–; mem. Flemish Asscn of Journalists of Periodical Press 1970–97; Ed. L'Indépendant Schaerbeek 1964–, Het Watervlietje 1975–2001; Sec. Flemish Regions, Parti Progressiste Belge 1989–93, Pres. 1985–89; Belgian Ombudsman/Médiateur Belge 1986–88; Pres. Flemish Progressive Party, European Flemish Programme 1989–92; Vice-Pres. European Progressive Party; Hon. Pres. and Public Relations Ombudsman Parti Mondial du Coeur 1993–97; mem. Assemblée consultative du congrès des peuples; Prize for Action to Promote European Federalism 1967. *Address:* 9 Rue Leo Baekelandstraat, 2030 Antwerp, Belgium. *Telephone:* (3) 542-04-58.

LEGGESE, Addiso; Ethiopian politician; Pres. Amhara Nat. Regional State 1992–2000; mem. Parl. for Belessa 2005–; Deputy Prime Minister of Ethiopia 2005–, Minister of Agric. and Rural Devt 2005–08; Chair. Population Census Comm. 2006–. *Address:* c/o Office of the Prime Minister, POB 1013, Addis Ababa, Ethiopia (office). *Telephone:* (1) 552044 (office).

LEGGETT, Anthony J., PhD, FRS; British/American physicist and academic; *John D. and Catherine T. MacArthur Professor of Physics and Professor, Center for Advanced Study, University of Illinois at Urbana-Champaign;* ed Balliol, Merton and Magdalen Colls, Oxford; Postdoctoral Research Assoc., Univ. of Illinois, USA 1964–65, Visiting Research Assoc. 1967; Lecturer in Physics, Univ. of Sussex 1967–71, Reader 1971–78, Prof. 1978–83; Fellow, Magdalene Coll. Oxford 1965–67; John D. and Catherine T. MacArthur Prof. of Physics and Prof., Center for Advanced Study, Univ. of Illinois at Urbana-Champaign 1983–; mem. American Philosophical Soc. 1991–, American Acad. of Arts and Sciences 1996–; Foreign Assoc. NAS 1997–; Foreign mem. Russian Acad. of Sciences 1999–; Fellow, American Physical Soc., American Inst. of Physics; Hon. FInstP 1999–; Prize Fellowship, Magdalene Coll., Oxford 1963–64; Inst. of Physics (UK) Maxwell Medal and Prize 1975, Inst. of Physics Simon Memorial Prize 1981, Fritz London Memorial Award 1981, Inst. of Physics Paul Dirac Medal and Prize 1992, John Bardeen Prize (jt recipient) 1994, Wolf Prize (jt recipient) 2003, Nobel Prize in Physics (shared with Alexei Abrikosov and Vitaly Ginzburg) 2003. *Publications:* The Problems of Physics 1986; numerous articles on superconductivity, superfluidity and theoretical condensed matter physics in scientific journals. *Address:* Department of Physics, University of Illinois at Urbana-Champaign, 1110 West Green Street, Urbana, IL 61801-3080, USA (office). *Telephone:* (217) 333-2077 (office). *Fax:* (217) 333-9819 (office). *E-mail:* aleggett@uiuc.edu (office). *Website:* www.physics.uiuc.edu/People/Faculty/profiles/Leggett (office).

LEGHARI, Farooq Ahmed Khan; Pakistani politician and fmr head of state; *Chairman, Millat Party;* b. 29 May 1940, Dera Ghazi Khan; s. of Nawabzada Sardar Mohammad Khan Leghari; m. 1965; two s. two d.; ed Punjab Univ. and Univ. of Oxford, UK; joined Pakistan People's Party 1973; Chief Baluchi Leghari Tribe; Pakistan Civil Service 1964–73; elected to Senate 1975, to Nat. Ass. 1977; Minister for Production 1977; periods of imprisonment for opposition to Govt 1977–88; Sec.-Gen. Pakistan People's Party and mem. Exec. Cttee 1978; elected mem. Nat. Ass. and Prov. Ass. 1988–, Leader of Opposition, Prov. Ass. 1988; Minister for Water and Power 1988–90; Deputy Leader of Opposition 1990–93; Minister of Finance 1993, of Foreign Affairs Oct.–Nov. 1993; Pres. of Pakistan 1993–97; dismissed Govt of Benazir Bhutto 1996; Organizer and Founder Millat Party 1998, currently Chair. *Leisure interests:* hunting, horse riding. *Address:* Millat Party, 21-E/3, Gulberg, Lahore (office); Village Choti, District Dera Ghazikhan, Punjab, Pakistan (home). *Telephone:* (42) 5757805 (office); (42) 5756718 (home). *E-mail:* millat@lhr.comsats.net.pk (office).

LEGORRETA VILCHIS, Ricardo; Mexican architect; *General Director, Legorreta + Legorreta;* b. 7 May 1931, México, DF; s. of Luis Legorreta and Guadalupe Vilchis; m. María Luisa Hernández 1956; three s. three d.; ed Univ. Autonoma de Mexico; draftsman and Chief Designer with José Villagran García 1948–55, Partner 1955–60; Prof. of Design, Univ. of Mexico 1959–62, Head of Experimental Group 1962–64; pvt. practice 1961–63; f. Legorreta Arquitectos with Noe Castro and Carlos Vargas 1963, Dir 1963–, currently Gen. Dir, Legorreta + Legorreta; f. Legorreta Arquitectos Diseños 1977, Pres. 1977–; mem. Int. Cttee, Museum of Modern Art, New York 1970; mem. Bd of Judges, AIA 1977; Emer. Fellow, Colegio de Arquitectos de México 1978, mem. Bd of Judges 1980; mem. Pritzker Prize Jury 1984; mem. IAA (Sofia) 1989; Hon. mem. American Inst. of Architects. *Main works:* Camino Real Hotel, Mexico City, Hotel Regina, Cancún, Solana Project, Dallas, USA, Cathedral in Managua, Nicaragua. *Publication:* Los muros de México (with Celanese Mexicana). *Leisure interests:* tennis, music. *Address:* Palacio de Versalles 285-A, Col Lomas Reforma, Código Postal 11020, México 10, DF, Mexico (office). *Telephone:* (55) 5552519698 (office). *E-mail:* info@lmasl.com.mx (office). *Website:* www.legorretalegorreta.com (office).

LEGQOG; Chinese politician; *Chairman, Standing Committee, Tibet Autonomous Regional People's Congress;* b. Oct. 1944, Gyangze Co., Tibet; ed CCP Cen. Cttee Cen. Party School; teacher, Gyangze Co., Tibet Autonomous Region 1964–71; Political Cadre, Gyangze Co., Tibet Autonomous Region 1971–73; joined CCP 1972; Sec. Gyangze Co. Autonomous Co. Cttee, CCP Communist Youth League 1973–75; mem. Standing Cttee CCP Communist Youth League Autonomous Prefectural Cttee, Xigaze Prefecture, Tibet Autonomous Region 1973–75; Sec. Org. Dept (Supervisory and Org. Divs) CCP Tibet Autonomous Regional Cttee 1975–80, Deputy Head Org. Dept and Deputy Chief Org. Div. 1980–86, Exec. Deputy Head Org. Dept 1986–91, mem. Standing Cttee CCP Tibet Autonomous Regional Cttee 1991–, Deputy Sec. CCP Tibet Autonomous Regional Cttee 1994–; Sec. CCP Lhasa City Cttee 1991–94; Vice-Chair. Tibet Autonomous Region People's Govt 1995–98, Chair. 1998–2004; Chair. Standing Cttee Tibet Autonomous Regional People's Congress 2003–; Alt. mem. CCP 15th Cen. Cttee 1997–2002, mem. CCP 16th Cen. Cttee 2002–07, mem. CCP 17th Cen. Cttee 2007–. *Address:* c/o People's Government of Tibetan Autonomous Region, Lhasa, Tibet, People's Republic of China.

LEGRAS, Guy; French diplomatist and international organization official; b. 19 July 1938, Angers; s. of René Legras and Pauline Legras; m. Borka Oreb 1971; one s. one d.; ed Faculté de Droit, Paris, Inst. d'Etudes Politiques, Paris and Ecole Nat. d'Admin; joined Ministry of Foreign Affairs 1967; Cabinet of Sec. of State for Foreign Affairs 1968–71; Sec.-Gen. of Interministerial Cttee (SGCI) for European Affairs (Prime Minister) 1971–74; Cabinet of Sec.-Gen. of OECD 1974–77; Counsellor, Perm. Rep. of France at European Communities, Brussels 1977–80; Asst Sec.-Gen. SGCI 1980-82; Head, Dept of Econ. Affairs, Ministry of Foreign Affairs 1982–85; Dir-Gen. for Agricultural Comm. of European Communities (now EC), Brussels 1985–99, for External Affairs 1999–2003 (retd); currently Adviser to Croatia for EU accession talks; Minister Plenipotentiary 1988; Officier, Ordre nat. du Mérite; Chevalier, Légion d'honneur. *Leisure interest:* tennis. *Address:* c/o Ministry of Foreign Affairs, 37 quai d'Orsay, 75351 Paris cedex 07, France (office).

LEGRIS, Manuel Christophe; French ballet dancer; *Danseur Etoile, Opéra de Paris;* b. 19 Oct. 1964, Paris; s. of Michel Legris and Raymonde Gazave; ed Paris Opera School of Dancing; mem. corps de ballet, Opéra de Paris 1980, 'Danseur Etoile' 1986–; major roles at Paris Opéra include Arepo (Béjart) 1986, In the Middle Somewhat Elevated (Forsythe) 1987, Magnificat (Neumeier) 1987, Rules of the Game (Twyla Tharp) 1989, The Sleeping Beauty (Nureyev) 1989, Manon (MacMillan) 1990, Dances at the Gathering (Robbins) 1993, Variations sur Carmen (Roland Petit) 2003, Phrases de

Quatuor (Maurice Béjart) 2003; in Hamburg created Cinderella Story and Spring and Fall (Neumeier); has also appeared at Bolshoi Ballet, Moscow, La Scala, Milan, Royal Ballet, London, New York City Ballet, Tokyo Ballet, Stuttgart Ballet and others; Chevalier des Arts et Lettres 1993, Officier 1998, Chevalier dans l'Ordre nat. du Mérite 2002; Gold Medal, Osaka Competition 1984, Prix du Cercle Carpeaux 1986, Nijinsky Prize 1988, Benois de la danse Prize 1998, Nijinsky Award 2000, Prix Léonide Massine 2001, Prix Danza & Danza 2002. *Film appearances include:* Romeo and Juliet, Le Spectre de la Rose, Notre Dame de Paris, L'Arlésienne, The Sleeping Beauty, Don Quixote. *Address:* Théâtre national de l'Opéra de Paris, 8 rue Scribe, 75009 Paris, France (office). *E-mail:* manuel.legris@manuel-legris.com (office). *Website:* www.manuel-legris.com (office).

LEGWAILA, Legwaila Joseph, MA; Botswana diplomatist; *Secretary General's Special Adviser on Africa, United Nations;* b. 2 Feb. 1937, Mathathane; s. of Madume Legwaila and Morongwa Legwaila; m. Pholile Matsebula 1975; three d.; ed Bobonong School, Brussels School, SA, Serowe Teacher Training Coll., Univs of Calgary and Alberta, Canada; Asst Prin. External Affairs, Govt of Botswana 1973–74, Sr Pvt. Sec. to Pres. of Botswana 1974–80; apptd Perm. Rep. to UN 1980, High Commr in Guyana 1981, in Jamaica 1982, Amb. to Cuba 1983; Deputy Special Rep. of the UN Sec.-Gen. for Namibia 1989–90, Head of UN Mission in Ethiopia and Eritrea (UNMEE) 2000–06, Sec.-Gen.'s Special Adviser on Africa 2006–. *Publication:* Safari to Serowe (co-author) 1970. *Leisure interests:* music, cycling. *Address:* Office of Special Adviser on Africa, c/o Office of the Secretary General, United Nations, New York, NY 10017, USA (office). *Telephone:* (212) 963-1858 (office). *Fax:* (212) 963-4879 (office). *E-mail:* wrightd@un.org (office). *Website:* www.un.org/africa/osaa (office).

LEHMAN, Ronald Frank, II, PhD; American security expert and government official; *Director, Center for Global Security Research, Lawrence Livermore National Laboratory;* b. 25 March 1946, Napa, Calif.; s. of Ronald Lehman and Esther Suhr; m. Susan Young 1979; ed Claremont Men's Coll. and Claremont Grad. School; army service, Viet Nam 1969–71; Legis. Asst US Senate 1976–78; mem. professional staff, US Senate Armed Services Cttee 1978–82; Deputy Asst Sec. of Defense, Office of Int. Security Policy 1982–83; Sr Dir Defense Programs and Arms Control, Nat. Security Council 1983–86; Deputy US Negotiator for Strategic Nuclear Arms, Dept of State, Washington, DC 1985–86, Chief US Negotiator Geneva 1986–88; Deputy Asst to Pres. for Nat. Security Affairs 1986; Asst Sec. Dept of Defense 1988–89; Dir Arms Control and Disarmament Agency, Washington, DC 1989–93; Asst to Dir Lawrence Livermore Nat. Lab. 1993–, Dir Center for Global Security Research 1996–; mem. Presidential Advisory Bd on Arms Proliferation Policy 1995–96; Adjunct Prof. Georgetown Univ. 1982–89; mem. Bd Dirs US Inst. of Peace 1988–93, Keck Center for Int. and Strategic Studies (now Chair.), Claremont McKenna Coll.; mem. Int. Advisory Bd Inst. of Global Conflict and Cooperation, Univ. of Calif. San Diego 1994–; mem. IISS, Council on Foreign Relations, Atlantic Council. *Address:* Center for Global Security Research, Lawrence Livermore National Laboratory, PO Box 808, L-1, Livermore, CA 94551 (office); 693 Encina Grande Drive, Palo Alto, CA 94306, USA (home). *Telephone:* (925) 422-6141. *Fax:* (925) 422-5252. *E-mail:* lehman3@llnl.gov. *Website:* cgsr.llnl.gov.

LEHMANN, Erich Leo, PhD; American academic; *Professor Emeritus of Statistics, University of California, Berkeley;* b. 20 Nov. 1917, Strasbourg, France; s. of Julius Lehmann and Alma Schuster; m. Juliet Popper Shaffer; one s. two d.; ed High School, Zurich, Switzerland, Univ. of Cambridge, Univ. of Calif., Berkeley; mem. Dept of Math. Univ. of Calif., Berkeley 1946–55, Dept of Statistics 1955–88, Prof. Emer. 1988–, Chair. Dept of Statistics 1973–76; Visiting Assoc. Prof. Columbia Univ. 1950, Stanford Univ. 1951–52, Visiting Lecturer Princeton Univ. 1951, Guggenheim Fellow 1955, 1966, 1979, Miller Research Prof. 1967, 1972; Sr Scholar, Educ. Testing Service 1995–; mem. NAS, American Acad. of Art and Sciences; fmr Pres. Inst. Math. Statistics; Dr hc (Leiden) 1985, (Chicago) 1991; American Statistical Asscn Samuel S. Wilks Memorial Award 1996. *Publications:* Testing Statistical Hypotheses 1959, Basic Concepts of Probability and Statistics (with J. L. Hodges, Jr) 1964, Nonparametrics: Statistical Methods based on Ranks 1975, Elements of Large Sample Theory 1998, Theory of Point Estimation (with George Casella) 1998, Ed. Annals of Mathematical Statistics 1953–55. *Leisure interests:* music, reading, hiking. *Address:* Department of Statistics, 445 Evans Hall, University of California, Berkeley, CA 94270-3860, USA. *Telephone:* (510) 642-2781 (office). *Fax:* (510) 642-7892 (office). *E-mail:* lehmann@stat.Berkeley.edu (office); shaffer@stat.berkeley.edu (office). *Website:* stat-www.berkeley.edu (office).

LEHMANN, HE Cardinal Karl, DPhil, DTheol; German ecclesiastic; *Chairman of the German Bishops' Conference;* b. 16 May 1936, Sigmaringen; ed in Freiburg, Rome, Munich, Münster; ordained priest 1963; asst. to Karl Rahner, Munich and Münster 1964–67; consecrated Bishop of Mainz 1983; Pres. of Conf. of German Bishops 1987–; cr. Cardinal 2001; Prof. of Theology, Univ. of Mainz 1968–71, Univ. of Freiburg 1971–83; Hon. Citizen of Mainz 2001; Dr hc (Innsbruck, Washington, Maynooth, Warsaw, Graz, Opole (Poland)); FrieKarl Barth Prize, Evangelical Union of Churches 1994, 'Golden Flower from Rheydt' of the town Mönchengladbach 1995, Bundesverdienstkreuz 2000. *Publications:* ed. of numerous religious journals. *Address:* Bischofsplatz 2A, 55116 Mainz, Germany (office). *Telephone:* (6131) 253101 (office). *Fax:* (6131) 229337 (office). *E-mail:* bischof.lehmann@bistum-mainz.de (office). *Website:* www.bistum-mainz.de.

LEHMANN, Klaus-Dieter; German librarian; *President, The Goethe Institute;* b. 29 Feb. 1940, Breslau (today Wrocław, Poland); ed Max-Planck-Institut für Chemie, Mainz; trained as a librarian, graduated in Library Science 1970; worked at Municipal Library and Univ. Library, Frankfurt am Main 1973–88, Man. Dir 1978–88; Dir-Gen. Univ. Library, Frankfurt 1988–98; following re-unification, led two Nat. Libraries in Frankfurt and Leipzig (Die Deutsche Bibliothek—German Nat. Library); Pres. Prussian Cultural Heritage Foundation, Berlin 1998–2008; Vice-Pres. Goethe Inst. 2002–08, Pres. and mem. Bd of Trustees 2008–; mem. Bd of Trustees, Bertelsmann Foundation, Acad. of Sciences and Literature, Mainz, Peace Prize of German Publrs and Booksellers; Hon. Prof., Univ. of Frankfurt am Main, Humboldt Univ., Berlin; Ordre des Palmes académiques, Bundesverdienstkreuz (First Class), Order of Merit of the Land Berlin 2006, Austrian Honorary Cross for Science and Art (First Class) 2007, Culture of the German Cultural Council groschen 2008; Dr hc (Ludwig-Maximilians Univ., Munich). *Publications:* Treasures of the World Cultures in the Collections of the Stiftung Preussischer Kulturbesitz 2004, Digital Resources from Cultural Institutions for Use in Teaching and Learning 2005, Science and Culture in Libraries, Museums and Archives 2005, Phoenix Bird 2007, Picture Book and Archetypes 2008. *Address:* Goethe-Institut, Head Office, Dachauer Strasse 122, 80637 Munich, Germany (office). *Telephone:* (89) 15921-0 (office). *Fax:* (89) 15921-450 (office). *E-mail:* praesident@goethe.de (office). *Website:* www.goethe.de (office).

LEHMBERG, Stanford Eugene, PhD, LittD, FRHistS, FSA; American historian and academic; *Professor Emeritus of History, University of Minnesota;* b. 23 Sept. 1931, McPherson, Kan.; s. of W. E. Lehmberg and Helen Lehmberg; m. Phyllis Barton 1962; one s.; ed Univ. of Kansas, Univ. of Cambridge, UK; mem. History Faculty, Univ. of Tex. at Austin 1956–69; Prof. of History, Univ. of Minn. 1967–98, now Prof. Emer.; Organist and Choirmaster, St Clement's Episcopal Church, St Paul, Minn. 1970–98; Fulbright Scholarship 1954–56, Guggenheim Fellow 1955–56, 1985–86. *Publications:* Sir Thomas Elyot, Tudor Humanist 1960, Sir Walter Mildmay and Tudor Government 1966, The Reformation Parliament, 1529–1536 1970, The Later Parliaments of Henry VIII 1977, The Reformation of Cathedrals 1988, The Peoples of the British Isles from Prehistoric Times to 1688 1991, Cathedrals Under Siege 1996, The University of Minnesota 1945–2001 2001, Holy Faith of Santa Fe 2004, English Cathedrals: a History 2005, Churches for the Southwest 2005; Ed. Sir Thomas Elyot, The Book Named the Governor 1962; articles, reviews. *Leisure interests:* music, the arts. *Address:* 1005 Calle Largo, Santa Fe, NM 87501, USA (home). *Telephone:* (505) 986-5074 (home). *Fax:* (505) 986-1724 (home). *E-mail:* lehmberg@earthlink.net (home).

LEHN, Jacques André, LèsL; French business executive; b. 15 July 1944, Lausanne, Switzerland; s. of François-Xavier Lehn and Geneviève Jaeger; ed lycées in Rabat, Morocco and Sceaux, Sorbonne, Paris, Inst. d'Etudes Politiques, Paris and Ecole des Hautes Etudes Commerciales; Man. Consultant, Arthur Andersen 1969–76; Finance Dir Warner Lambert France 1976–79; Dir-Gen. Adams' France 1979–80; Dir Matra, Médias Br. 1980–81; Dir Hachette Group 1981–84, Deputy Dir-Gen. 1984–90, Dir-Gen. 1990; Dir-Gen. Matra-Hachette 1993–; Vice-Pres. Europe I Communication 1986–94, Deputy Pres. 1994–99; Pres., Dir-Gen. Europe développement int. 1996–; Pres. Supervisory Bd Europa Plus, France 1996–, Holpa 1996–; Chair. and CEO Go Mass Media, Go Outdoor Holdings Systems 1999–; Chair. Supervisory Bd Giraudy 1999–; Founding mem. ORMA (Ocean Racing Multihull Asscn) 1993–, Pres. 1993–2004; Vice-Chair. Oceanic Sub-cttee, Int. Sailing Fed. 2005–; numerous other business affiliations; Chevalier, Ordre nat. du Mérite, Chevalier, Légion d'honneur. *Leisure interest:* yachting. *Address:* ORMA, 9 rue Royale, 75008 Paris (office); ISAF UK (Ltd), Ariadne House, Town Quay, Southampton, Hants., SO14 2AQ, England; 47 blvd Lannes, 75116 Paris, France (home). *Telephone:* 1-53-30-86-07 (office); (23) 8063-5111. *Fax:* (23) 8063-5789; 1-47-42-32-14 (office). *E-mail:* jacques.lehn@libertysurf.fr (office); secretariat@isaf.co.uk. *Website:* www.sailing.org.

LEHN, Jean-Marie Pierre, DèsSc, PhD; French chemist and academic; *Director, Institut de Science et d'Ingénierie Supramoléculaires, Université Louis Pasteur;* b. 30 Sept. 1939, Rosheim, Bas-Rhin; s. of Pierre and Marie (née Salomon) Lehn; m. Sylvie Lederer 1965; two s.; ed Univ. of Strasbourg; various posts, CNRS 1960–66; post-doctoral Research Assoc. with Prof. R. B. Woodward, Harvard Univ., USA 1963–64; Asst Prof., Univ. of Strasbourg 1966–70, Assoc. Prof. 1970, Prof. 1970–79; currently Dir Institut de Science et d'Ingénierie Supramoléculaires,Université Louis Pasteur; Visiting Prof. of Chem., Harvard Univ. 1972, 1974, ETH, Zurich 1977, Univ. of Cambridge 1984, Barcelona Univ. 1985; Prof., Collège de France, Paris 1979–; Pres. Scientific Council of Rhône-Poulenc 1992–, of Ministry of Nat. Educ., Youth and Sport 1989–93; mem. Research Strategy Cttee 1995, Inst. de France, Deutsche Akad. der Naturforscher Leopoldina, Accad. Nazionale dei Lincei; Foreign assoc. NAS; Foreign mem. Royal Netherlands Acad. of Arts and Sciences, Royal Soc. and many others; Foreign Hon. mem. American Acad. of Arts and Sciences; Commdr, Légion d'honneur, Officier, Ordre nat. du Mérite, mem. Order 'Pour le Mérite' 1990, Ostereischihes Ehrenkreuz für Wissenschaft und Kunst, Erste Klasse 2001; shared Nobel Prize in Chem. 1987; Gold, Silver and Bronze Medals of CNRS; Gold Medal, Pontifical Acad. of Sciences 1981; Paracelsus Prize, Swiss Chemical Soc. 1982, von Humboldt Prize 1983, Karl Ziegler Prize (German Chemical Soc.) 1989, Davy Medal (Royal Soc.) 1997, Lavoisier Medal 1997, A. R. Day Award 1998. *Publications:* about 700 scientific publs. *Leisure interest:* music. *Address:* Chemistry laboratory Supramoléculaire, ISIS/ULP, Allée Gaspard Monge 8, LP 70028, 67083 Strasbourg Cedex (office); Collège de France, 11 place Marcellin Berthelot, 75005 Paris (office); 6 rue des Pontonniers, 67000 Strasbourg, France (home). *Telephone:* 3-90-24-51-45 (office); 1-44-27-13-60 (office); (88) 37-06-42 (home). *Fax:* 3-90-24-51-40 (office); 1-44-27-13-56 (office). *E-mail:* lehn@isis.u-strasbg.fr (office); lehn@chimie.u-strasbg.fi (office). *Website:* www-isis.u-strasbg.fr/supra/.

LEHNER, Ulrich; business executive; b. 1 May 1946, Düsseldorf; m. Johanna Ewers 1970; three c.; mem. Bd of Man., Henkel KGaA 1995–2000, Chair. Exec. Bd, Pres. and CEO 2000–08, mem. Shareholders' Cttee 2008–; Chair. Supervisory Bd Dial Corpn, Deutsche Telekom AG; mem. Supervisory Bd E.ON AG, HSBC Trinkaus & Burkhardt KGaA, Ecolab Inc., Novartis AG. *Address:* Henkel KGaA, Henkelstrasse 67, 40191 Düsseldorf, Germany (office). *Telephone:* (211) 7970 (office). *Fax:* (211) 7982484 (office). *E-mail:* info@henkel.com (office). *Website:* www.henkel.com (office).

LEHOHLA, Archibald Lesao, BSc, BA, MA; Lesotho politician; *Deputy Prime Minister and Minister of Home Affairs, Public Safety and of Parliamentary Affairs;* b. 28 July 1946, Mafeteng; m.; two s. one d.; ed Mafeteng Secondary School, Basutoland High School, Univ. of Botswana, Lesotho and Swaziland, Roma, Univ. of Oxford, UK; Teaching Asst in Math., Univ. of Botswana, Lesotho and Swaziland 1971–72; Asst Teacher, Bereng High School 1975–76, Headmaster 1977–93; mem. Parl. for Mafeteng 1993–; Minister of Home Affairs (Local Govt, Rural and Urban Devt) 1993–95, of Transport, Posts and Telecommunications 1995–96, of Educ. and Manpower Devt 1996–2004, of Home Affairs and Public Safety 2004–, and of Parl. Affairs 2007–; Deputy Prime Minister 2003–; Chair. Scott Hosp. Comm. of Inquiry 1990; fmr Chair. Mafeteng Tractor Owners' Cooperative; Church Elder and mem. Mafeteng LEC consistory; fmr mem. Lesotho Headmasters' and Headmistresses' Asscn, Lesotho Evangelical Church Law Review Comm., LEC Educational Sec.'s Advisory Cttee on Educ.; rep. Lesotho at Commonwealth Seminar on Educational Admin and Supervision, Univ. of Nairobi, Kenya 1977; UNESCO Fellowship to Univ. of Oxford 1975. *Leisure interests:* gardening, singing, crop farming. *Address:* Ministry of Home Affairs and Public Safety, POB 174 Maseru 100, Lesotho (office). *Telephone:* 323771 (office). *Website:* www.lesotho.gov.ls (office).

LEHR, Ursula M., PhD; German government official, psychologist and academic; *Founding Director and Senior Consultant, Deutsches Zentrum für Alternsforschung (DZFA);* b. 5 June 1930, Frankfurt am Main; d. of Georg-Josef Leipold and Gertrud Jendorff; m. 1st Helmut Lehr 1950 (died 1994); two s.; m. 2nd Hans Thomas 1998 (died 2001); Research Asst, Univ. of Bonn 1955–60, Research and Teaching Asst, Inst. of Psychology 1960–68, mem. perm. staff 1968–69, Additional Prof. and Head Dept of Developmental Psychology 1969–72, Chair. Dept of Psychology and Dir Inst. of Psychology 1976–86, Hon. Prof. 1987–; Chair. of Pedagogics and Pedagogical Psychology, Albertus Magnus Univ., Cologne 1972; Dir Inst. of Gerontology, Ruprecht Karls Univ., Heidelberg 1986–88, 1991–96; Founding Dir and Sr Consultant Deutsches Zentrum für Alternsforschung (DZFA) (German Centre for Research on Aging), Heidelberg 1996–; Fed. Minister of Youth, Families, Women and Health 1988–91; mem. Families Advisory Bd, Fed. Ministry of Youth, Families and Health 1972–80, WHO Expert Advisory Panel on Health of Elderly Persons 1983–87; mem. Parl. 1990–94; Pres. Asscn of Fmr Mems of the German and European Parliament 2002–; Vice-Pres. German Gerontological Soc. 1973–78, 1980–84, Pres. 1997–99; Founder mem. Acad. of Sciences, Berlin 1987–91; Corresp. mem. Acad. of Sciences, Austria 1994–, Sächsische Akad. der Wissenschaften 1998–; mem. European Acad. of Yuste, Spain 2000–; Hon. mem. Socs of Gerontology of Switzerland, Spain, Mexico; Grosses Bundesverdienstkreuz 1996; Hon. PhD (Fribourg, Switzerland); Landesverdienstmedaille Baden-Württemberg 1999, Lifetime award Bund Deutscher Psychologen 2003. *Publications:* more than 700 scientific texts. *Leisure interests:* art (paintings of the Middle Ages), history of art. *Address:* Am Büchel 53B, 53173 Bonn, Germany (home). *Telephone:* (228) 352849 (home). *Fax:* (228) 352741 (home). *E-mail:* ursula.lehr@t-online.de (home). *Website:* www.dzfa.uni-heidelberg.de/english_version/index.html (office).

LEHRER, James (Jim) Charles, AA, BJ; American broadcast journalist and writer; *Executive Editor and Anchor, The News Hour with Jim Lehrer;* b. 19 May 1934, Wichita, Kan.; m. Kate Lehrer (née Staples); three d.; ed Victoria Coll., Tex., Univ. of Missouri; served as infantry officer US Marine Corps 1956-58; reporter, Dallas Morning News (daily newspaper) 1959–61; reporter and columnist Dallas Times-Herald 1961–70; Exec. Dir of Public Affairs, on-air host, and Ed., nightly news program KERA–TV, Dallas 1970–72; Public Affairs Coordinator, Public Broadcasting Service (PBS), Washington, DC 1972–73, also mem. Journalism Advisory Bd and Fellow, Corpn for Public Broadcasting; correspondent Nat. Public Affairs Center for TV (NPACT) 1973–, co-hosted coverage of US Senate Watergate hearings and US House Judiciary Cttee Nixon impeachment inquiry, Washington correspondent, Robert MacNeil Report 1975, co-anchor MacNeil/Lehrer Report 1975–83, co-anchor MacNeil/Lehrer NewsHour 1983–96, Exec. Ed. and Anchor, The News Hour with Jim Lehrer 1996–; Fellow, American Acad. of Arts and Sciences; numerous awards for journalism including two Emmys, Fred Friendly First Admendment Award, George Foster Peabody Broadcast Award, William Allen White Foundation Award for Journalistic Merit, Medal of Honor, Univ. of Missouri School of Journalism; Nat. Humanities Medal 1999; inducted (with Robert MacNeil) TV Hall of Fame, Silver Circle of Washington, DC Chapter of Nat. Acad. of TV Arts and Sciences. *Plays:* Chili Queen 1987, Church Key Charlie Blue 1988, The Will and Bart Show 1992. *Publications include:* We Were Dreamers 1975, Kick the Can 1988, Crown Oklahoma 1989, The Sooner Spy 1990, Lost and Found 1991, Short List 1992, A Bus of My Own 1992, Blue Hearts 1993, Fine Lines 1994, The Last Debate 1995, White Widow 1997, Purple Dots 1998, The Special Prisoner 2000, No Certain Rest 2002, Flying Crows 2004, The Franklin Affair 2005, The Phony Marine 2006. *Address:* The NewsHour with Jim Lehrer, 3620 S 27th Street, Arlington, VA 22206, USA (office). *Telephone:* (703) 998-2813 (office). *E-mail:* newshour@pbs.org (office). *Website:* www.pbs.org/newshour/aboutus/bio_lehrer.html (office).

LEHTO, Olli Erkki, PhD; Finnish mathematician and academic; b. 30 May 1925, Helsinki; s. of P. V. Lauri Lehto and Hilma Autio; m. Eva G. Ekholm 1954; one s. two d.; ed Univ. of Helsinki; Docent, Univ. of Helsinki 1951–56, Assoc. Prof. 1956–61, Prof. of Math. 1961–88, Dean, Faculty of Science 1978–83, Rector 1983–88, Chancellor 1988–93; Pres. Finnish Math. Soc. 1962–85, Finnish Acads of Science and Letters 1979–98; mem. Exec. Cttee Int. Math. Union 1975–90, Sec.-Gen. 1982–90; mem. Gen. Cttee Int. Council of Scientific Unions 1982–90; mem. Admin. Bd Int. Asscn of Univs 1985–95, Vice-Pres. 1990–95; Visiting Prof. at numerous univs in Europe, N America and Asia; Hon. Pres. Finnish Cultural Foundation 1998–; Grand Cross, Order of the Finnish Lion 1989; Hon. PhD (Turku) 1980, (Moscow) 1989, (Åbo) 1993, (Bucharest) 1996, (Joensuu) 1999. *Publications:* History of the International Mathematical Union, biography of Rolf Nevanlinna, memoirs, four monographs and 60 papers in math. journals. *Leisure interest:* butterflies. *Address:* Ritarikatu 3 A 7, 00170 Helsinki, Finland (home). *Telephone:* (3589) 662526 (home). *E-mail:* olli.lehto@helsinki.fi (home).

LEHTO, Sakari Tapani, BLL, BSc(Econ); Finnish business executive and writer; b. 26 Dec. 1923, Turku; s. of Reino Lehto and Hildi Lehto; m. Karin Hildén 1950; three d.; ed Helsinki School of Econs and Business Admin., Helsinki Univ. and MIT Sloan School; Chief Legal Counsellor and Dir Foreign Activities, United Paper Mills Ltd 1952–64; Man. Dir and Pres. Fed. of Finnish Industries 1964–71; Pres. and CEO Partek Corpn 1972–87, Vice-Chair. 1987–95; Chair. Insurance Ltd Sampo 1976–89, Insurance Co. Kaleva 1978–91, Tamfelt Oy Ab 1982–94, Keskus-Sato Oy 1984–91, Pensions Sampo 1985–90; Kuratorium Pro Baltica Forum 1993–98; Minister of Foreign Trade 1975–76; mem. Finland Defence Bd 1976–92; Fellow World Innovation Foundation; Hon. mem. Finnish Soc. for Futures Studies; Commdr Order of Liberty, First Class (Finland); Commdr Order of White Rose, First Class (Finland); Commdr Order of the Polar Star, First Class (Sweden); Commdr Order of the Lion of Finland; Hon. TechD; Hon. Econ.D. . *Publications:* Managing Change – Strategies and Thoughts, Experiences Within Finnish Industry, With Luck? How Next? – Challenges to the Management; numerous articles in the areas of commercial law, trade and industrial policy. *Leisure interests:* golf, boating, skiing, literature, languages. *Address:* Puistokatu 9A5, 00140 Helsinki, Finland (Office/Home). *Telephone:* (9) 653447 (office); (9) 660349 (home). *Fax:* (9) 653447. *E-mail:* sakari.t.lehto@kolumbus.fi (office).

LEHTOMÄKI, Paula Ilona, MSc; Finnish politician; *Minister of the Environment;* b. 29 Nov. 1972, Kuhmo; m.; one c.; acting sr teacher 1995; research asst 1998; mem. Kuhmo Town Council 1997; mem. Parl. (Centre Party) 1999–; mem. Finnish Del. to Nordic Council 1999–2003, to Council of Europe 2003; Minister for Foreign Trade and Devt and Minister at the Prime Minister's Office 2003–07, of the Environment 2007–; mem. Supervisory Bd VR-Group Ltd 2000–03, Bd Audiator Oy 2000–03, Exec. Cttee Lasten Keskus Publishing House 2000–01, Cttee Finnish 4H Fed. 2001–03, Bd Finland-Russia Soc. 2000–03. *Leisure interest:* fitness training. *Address:* Ministry of the Environment, Kasarmikatu 25, POB 35, 00023 Helsinki, Finland (office). *Telephone:* (9) 16039300 (office). *Fax:* (9) 16039307 (office). *E-mail:* paula.lehtomaki@ymparisto.fi (office). *Website:* www.environment.fi (office).

LEI, Jieqiong, MA; Chinese politician and jurist; b. 1905, Guangzhou, Guangdong Prov.; d. of Lei Zichang and Li Peizhi; m. Yan Jingyao 1941; ed in USA; Prof., Yenching Univ., 1931–52; Vice-Dean Inst. of Politics and Law 1953–73; mem. Cttee for Implementation Campaign of Marriage Laws 1953; Deputy Dir, Bureau of Foreign Experts Admin. under State Council 1956–66, Prof. Beijing Univ. 1973–; Vice-Mayor of Beijing 1979–83; Chair. China Asscn for Promoting Democracy 1987–97; mem. Standing Cttee, 5th CPPCC 1978–83, Vice-Chair. Nat. Cttee, 6th CPPCC 1983–88; mem. Standing Cttee 6th NPC and Vice-Chair. of Law Cttee 1983–88; Vice-Chair. 6th NPC 1986–88; Vice-Chair. 7th NPC 1988–93; Vice-Chair. Standing Cttee 8th NPC 1994–98; numerous other appointments and hon. positions; Hon. Pres. China Asscn of Women Judges, Asscn for Int. Understanding of China, Western Returned Students' Asscn, China Social Workers' Asscn. *Address:* c/o 19 Xi Jiaomen Xiang, Xicheng District, Beijing, People's Republic of China.

LEI, Lt-Gen. Mingqiu; Chinese army officer; *Political Commissar, Nanjing Military Region, People's Liberation Army;* b. March 1942, Jiangjiaqiao, Qidong Co., Hengyang City, Hunan Prov.; ed Zhuzhou Aeronautical Acad. Hunan and PLA Political Acad.; joined PLA 1962, CCP 1964; platoon leader and Deputy Political Instructor, Mortar Bn 1965–69; Deputy Section Chief of Org., Div. Political Dept 1969–71, Dir Div. Political Dept 1982–83; clerk and Deputy Chief (later Chief) of Youth Affairs Section, Political Dept, Guangzhou City, PLA Guangzhou Mil. Region 1971–80; Deputy Political Commissar, 42nd Army, Army (or Ground Force), PLA Services and Arms 1983–85, Political Commissar 1985–92; Dir Political Dept, Guangzhou Mil. Region 1992–94; Deputy Political Commissar, Nanjing Mil. Region 1994–2000 (Sec. Comm. for Discipline Inspection, CCP Party Cttee 1994–99), Political Commissar 2000–; mem. 13th CCP Cen. Cttee 1987–92, 14th CCP Cen. Cttee 1992–97, 15th CCP Cen. Cttee 1997–2002, 16th CCP Cen. Cttee 2002–07. *Address:* Office of the Political Commissar, Nanjing Military Region, People's Republic of China.

LEI, Zuhua; Chinese banker; fmr Vice-Pres. Bank of China, Vice-Chair. Bd of Dirs 1993–; Pres. Import and Export Bank of China 1994–99; Sr Adviser, Dayue Consulting Co. Ltd. *Address:* c/o Import and Export Bank of China, 1 Dingandongli, Yongdingmenwai, Beijing, People's Republic of China.

LEIBINGER, Berthold; German business executive; *Owner and CEO, TRUMPF GmbH & Company KG;* joined TRUMPF as engineer 1950, now owner and Chief Exec.; mem. Advisory Bd Deutsche Bank, BASF. *Address:* TRUMPF GmbH & Co. KG, Johann-Maus-Strasse 2, 71254 Ditzingen, Germany. *Telephone:* (7156) 303230. *E-mail:* berthold.leibinger@de.trumpf.com (office). *Website:* www.trumpf.com.

LEIBLER, Kenneth Robert, BA; American business executive; *Chairman, Boston Options Exchange (BOX);* b. 21 Feb. 1949, New York; s. of Max Leibler and Martha (née Dales) Leibler; m. Marcia Kate Reiss 1973; one s. one d.; ed Syracuse Univ. and Univ. of Pennsylvania; Options Man. Lehman Bros. 1972–75; Vice-Pres. Options American Stock Exchange, NY 1975–79, Sr Vice-Pres. Admin. and Finance 1979–81, Exec. Vice-Pres. Admin. and Finance 1981–85, Sr Exec. Vice-Pres. 1985–86, Pres. 1986–90; Pres. Liberty Financial Cos. 1990–2000; Chair. CEO Boston Stock Exchange 2000–04; founder pnr and Chair. Boston Options Exchange (BOX) 2004–; Instructor NY Inst. of Finance; Dir Securities Industry Automation Corpn; mem. Finance Execs Inst. of Securities Industry Asscn American Stock Exchange Clearing Corpn. *Publication:* (contrib.) Handbook of Financial Markets: Securities, Options, Futures 1981. *Address:* Boston Options Exchange, c/o Boston Stock Exchange, 100 Franklin Street, Boston, MA 02110, USA (office). *Telephone:* (617) 416-2429 (office). *Website:* www.bostonoptions.com (office).

LEIBOVITZ, Annie; American photographer; b. 2 Oct. 1949, Westport, Conn.; ed San Francisco Art Inst. and studies with photographer Ralph Gibson; lived on a kibbutz in Israel and participated in archaeological dig at site of King Solomon's temple 1969; photographed rock 'n' roll stars and other celebrities for Rolling Stone magazine 1970–83; served as concert-tour photographer for The Rolling Stones band 1975; Chief Photographer, Vanity Fair 1983–; Propr Annie Leibovitz Studio, New York; official photographer Olympic Games, Atlanta 1996; advertising campaigns for American Express 2005, Disney 2007; celebrity portraits include John Lennon, Mick Jagger, Bette Midler, Louis Armstrong, Ella Fitzgerald, Jessye Norman, Mikhail Baryshnikov, Arnold Schwarzenegger, Tom Wolfe 1991, HM Queen Elizabeth II 2007; Photographer of the Year Award, American Soc. of Magazine Photographers 1984, Innovation in Photography Award, American Soc. of Magazine Photographers 1987, Clio Award 1987, Campaign of the Decade Award, Advertising Age magazine 1987, Infinity Award for applied photography, Int. Center for Photography 1990. *Film:* Annie Leibovitz Life through a Lens 2006. *Publications:* Photographs 1970–90 1992, Women (with Susan Sontag) 2000, A Photographer's Life 1990–2005 2006, Annie Leibovitz at Work 2008. *Address:* Annie Leibovitz Studio, 443 West 18th Street, Suite 4, New York, NY 10011-3817 (office); c/o Jim Moffat, Art and Commerce, 755 Washington Street, New York, NY 10014, USA. *Telephone:* (212) 594-3817 (office). *E-mail:* als@leibovitzstudio.com (office). *Website:* www.leibovitzstudio.com (office).

LEIFERKUS, Sergey Petrovich; Russian singer (baritone); b. 4 April 1946, Leningrad; ed Leningrad Conservatory with Barsov and Shaposhnikov; stage debut in Leningrad Theatre of Musical Comedy 1972; soloist Maly Theatre of Opera and Ballet 1972–78, sang in Eugene Onegin, Iolanta, Il Barbiere di Siviglia and Don Giovanni; Kirov (now Mariinsky) Theatre of Opera and Ballet 1977–85, sang Prince Andrei in War and Peace by Prokofiev; Wexford Festival 1982–86, in Griséledis and Le Jongleur de Notre Dame by Massenet, Hans Heiling by Marschner and Königskinder by Humperdinck; Scottish Opera from 1985, as Don Giovanni, Germont and Eugene Onegin 1988; Covent Garden 1987, as Eugene Onegin and Tomsky in The Queen of Spades, with the Kirov Company; ENO 1987, as Zurga in Les Pêcheurs de Perles; US debut 1987, in Symphony No. 13 by Shostakovich, with the Boston Symphony; Wigmore Hall debut recital, sang Luna in a new production of Il Trovatore at Covent Garden and appeared in a concert performance of Giovanna d'Arco at the Festival Hall 1989; concert performance of Mlada by Rimsky-Korsakov, Barbican Hall; US opera debut at San Francisco, as Telramund in Lohengrin, and the title role in Prince Igor at Covent Garden 1989–90; sang Rangoni in Boris Godunov at the Kirov Theatre, St Petersburg 1990; Luna at the Teatro Colón, Buenos Aires, Mazeppa at the Bregenz Festival and Netherlands Opera, Amsterdam, Ruprecht in Prokofiev's Fiery Angel at the BBC Promenade Concerts, London; Tomsky in The Queen of Spades in Boston and New York with the Boston Symphony; Onegin in Montreal, Ruprecht in St Petersburg, Tomsky at Glyndebourne and Vienna State Opera, Rangoni at San Francisco, Iago at Covent Garden and at the Metropolitan 1992; sang Carlo in La Forza del Destino for VARA Radio at the Amsterdam Concertgebouw, Shostakovich 13th Symphony with the New York Philharmonic, Scarpia, Amonasro, Escamillo and Luna 1993; debut at La Scala in The Fiery Angel, further performances as Iago at the Metropolitan, New York, Scarpia at Opéra Bastille, Paris, sang Mephistopheles in La Damnation de Faust with Ozawa and the Berlin Philharmonic in Berlin, the title role in Nabucco at the Bregenz Festival, sang Ruprecht in San Francisco and gave recitals across America, Escamillo at the Teatro Colón, Buenos Aires and Prokofiev's Ivan the Terrible at La Scala 1994; sang Iago at Covent Garden, Mazeppa at Netherlands Opera, Amsterdam, Shostakovich 13th Symphony in Leipzig with the Gewandhaus Orchestra, Gryaznoy in The Tsar's Bride for Opera Orchestra of New York in Carnegie Hall, Escamillo in a gala performance of Carmen in Stuttgart, Iago at the Vienna State Opera, recitals at Cologne and Graz, Amonasro at the Berlin State Opera under Mehta, Scarpia at the Ravinia Festival 1995; Boccanegra in the original version of Verdi's opera and Telramund in Lohengrin at Covent Garden 1997; Klingsor in Parsifal with the Royal Opera, RFH 1998; Klingsor at the Royal Albert Hall (concert), Simon Boccanegra at Melbourne and Prince Igor in Houston 2000–01; season 2001–02 in Pique Dame in Los Angeles and Washington, DC, Simon Boccanegra in Dallas, Aida in Berlin, Lohengrin in Munich, Tosca in London and Munich, solo recitals in Paris and London; season 2002–03 in Otello in Japan (tour), London and San Francisco, Pique Dame in Munich, Fidelio in Dallas, Tosca in Munich, Shostakovich Symphony No. 13 in Prague and Lohengrin in London. *Address:* Askonas Holt Ltd, Lincoln House, 300 High Holborn, London, WC1V 7JH, England (office). *Telephone:* (20) 7400-1700 (office). *Fax:* (20) 7400-1799 (office). *E-mail:* info@askonasholt.co.uk (office). *Website:* www.askonasholt.co.uk (office).

LEIFLAND, Leif, LLB; Swedish diplomatist; b. 30 Dec. 1925, Stockholm; s. of Sigfrid Leifland and Elna Leifland; m. Karin Abard 1954 (died 1999); one s. two d.; ed Univ. of Lund; joined Ministry of Foreign Affairs 1952; served Athens 1953, Bonn 1955, Washington 1961, 1970; Sec. Foreign Relations Cttee, Swedish Parl. 1966–70; Under-Sec. for Political Affairs 1975–77; Perm. Under-Sec. of State for Foreign Affairs 1977–82; Amb. to UK 1982–91; Chair. Bd, Swedish Inst. of Int. Affairs 1991–2002; Hon. GCVO. *Publications:* The Blacklisting of Axel Wenner-Gren 1989, General Böhme's Choice 1992, The Year of the Frost 1997; various articles on foreign policy and national security questions. *Address:* Nybrogatan 77, 114 40 Stockholm, Sweden. *Telephone:* 86-61-46-12.

LEIGH, Irene May, BSc, MBBS, MD, DSc (Med), FRCP, FMedSci; British dermatologist, cell biologist and academic; *Vice Principal and Head of the College of Medicine, Dentistry and Nursing, University of Dundee;* b. 25 April 1947, Liverpool; d. of A. Allen and M. L. Allen; m. 1st Nigel Leigh 1969 (divorced 1999); one s. three d.; m. 2nd J. E. Kernthaler 2000; two step-s. one step-d.; ed Merchant Taylors' Girls' School, London Hosp. Medical Coll.; Dir Cancer Research UK (fmrly Imperial Cancer Research Fund) Skin Tumour Lab. 1989–98; Prof. of Dermatology, Barts and London School of Medicine and Dentistry (BLSMD) 1992–98, Research Dean 1996–2001, Prof. of Cellular and Molecular Medicine 1998–2006; Vice Prin. and Head of the Coll. of Medicine, Dentistry and Nursing, Univ. of Dundee 2006–; Jt Research Dir Barts and London NHS Trust and BLSMD 2002. *Publications:* more than 60 peer-reviewed publs in biomedical literature. *Leisure interests:* baroque music, opera, theatre, cinema, children, grandchildren. *Address:* College of Medicine, Dentistry and Nursing, University of Dundee, Dundee DD1 4HN, Scotland; 14 Oakeshott Avenue, London, N6 6NS, England (home). *Telephone:* (1382) 632763 (office); (20) 8340-4761 (home). *Fax:* (1382) 644267 (office). *E-mail:* i.m.leigh@dundee.ac.uk (office). *Website:* secure.dundee.ac.uk/medden (office).

LEIGH, Jennifer Jason; American actress; b. 5 Feb. 1962, Los Angeles, Calif.; d. of the late Vic Morrow and of Barbara Turner; ed Palisades High School; appeared in Walt Disney TV movie The Young Runaways aged 15; other TV films include The Killing of Randy Webster 1981, The Best Little Girl in the World 1981. *Films include:* Eyes of a Stranger 1981, Fast Times at Ridgemont High 1982, Grandview, USA 1984, Flesh and Blood 1985, The Hitcher 1986, The Men's Club 1986, Heart of Midnight 1989, The Big Picture 1989, Miami Blues 1990, Last Exit to Brooklyn 1990, Crooked Hearts 1991, Backdraft 1991, Rush 1992, Single White Female 1992, Short Cuts 1993, The Hudsucker Proxy 1994, Mrs Parker and the Vicious Circle 1994, Georgia 1995, Kansas City 1996, Washington Square 1997, eXistenZ 1999, The King is Alive 2000, The Anniversary Party 2001, Crossed Over 2002, Road to Perdition 2002, In the Cut 2003, The Machinist 2004, Childstar 2004, The Jacket 2005, Palindromes 2005, Rag Tale 2005, Margot at the Wedding 2007, Synecdoche, New York 2008. *Stage appearances include:* Sunshine, Off-Broadway 1989. *Address:* c/o Tracey Jacobs, 8942 Wilshire Boulevard, Beverly Hills, CA 90211 (office); c/o Elaine Rich, 2400 Whitman Place, Los Angeles, CA 90068, USA.

LEIGH, Mike, OBE; British dramatist and film and theatre director; b. 20 Feb. 1943, Salford, Lancs.; s. of the late A. A. Leigh and the late P. P. Leigh (née Cousin); m. Alison Steadman (q.v.) 1973 (divorced 2001); two s.; ed Royal Acad. of Dramatic Art, Camberwell School of Arts and Crafts, Cen. School of Art and Design, London Film School; Chair. Govs London Film School 2001–; Officier des Arts et des Lettres; Hon. MA (Salford) 1991, (Northampton) 2000; Hon. DLitt (Staffs.) 2000, (Essex) 2002. *Plays:* The Box Play 1965, My Parents Have Gone to Carlisle, The Last Crusade of the Five Little Nuns 1966, Nenaa 1967, Individual Fruit Pies, Down Here and Up There, Big Basil 1968, Epilogue, Glum Victoria and the Lad with Specs 1969, Bleak Moments 1970, A Rancid Pong 1971, Wholesome Glory, The Jaws of Death, Dick Whittington and His Cat 1973, Babies Grow Old, The Silent Majority 1974, Abigail's Party 1977 (also TV play), Ecstasy 1979, Goose-Pimples (London Evening Standard and London Drama Critics' Choice Best Comedy Awards 1981) 1981, Smelling A Rat 1988, Greek Tragedy 1989 (in Australia), 1990 (in UK), It's a Great Big Shame! 1993, Two Thousand Years (Cottlesloe Theatre, London) 2005. *Television films:* A Mug's Game 1972, Hard Labour 1973, The Permissive Society, The Birth of the 2001 F.A. Cup Final Goalie, Old Chums, Probation, A Light Snack, Afternoon 1975, Nuts in May, Knock for Knock 1976, The Kiss of Death 1977, Abigail's Party 1977, Who's Who 1978, Grown-Ups 1980, Home Sweet Home 1981, Meantime 1983, Four Days in July 1984, The Short and Curlies 1987. *Feature films:* Bleak Moments (Golden Leopard, Locarno Film Festival, Golden Hugo, Chicago Film Festival 1972) 1971, High Hopes (Int. Critics' Prize, Venice Film Festival 1989, London Evening Standard Peter Sellers Best Comedy Film Award 1990) 1989, Life is Sweet 1991, Naked (Best Dir Cannes Film Festival 1993) 1993, Secrets and Lies (winner Palme d'Or) 1996, (Alexander Korda Award, BAFTA 1997), Career Girls 1997, Topsy-Turvy 1999 (London Evening Standard Best Film 1999, Los Angeles Film Critics' Circle Best Film 1999, New York Film Critics' Circle Best Film 1999), All or Nothing 2002, Vera Drake (Best British Ind. Film, Best Dir, British Ind. Film Awards, Best Film, Evening Standard British Film Awards 2005, David Lean Award for Achievement in Direction, BAFTA Awards 2005) 2004, Happy-Go-Lucky 2008. *Radio play:* Too Much of a Good Thing 1979. *Publications:* Abigail's Party and Goose-Pimples 1982, Ecstasy and Smelling a Rat 1989, Naked and other Screenplays 1995, Secrets and Lies 1997, Career Girls 1997, Topsy-Turvy 1999, All or Nothing 2002, Two Thousand Years 2006, Vera Drake 2008, Mike Leigh on Mike Leigh 2008. *Address:* United Agents, 12–26 Lexington Street, London W1F 0LE, England (office). *Telephone:* (20) 3214-0800 (office). *Fax:* (20) 3214-0801 (office). *E-mail:* info@unitedagents.co.uk (office). *Website:* unitedagents.co.uk (office).

LEIGH-PEMBERTON, Rt Hon. Robert (Robin) (see KINGSDOWN, Baron).

LEIGHTON, Allan Leslie; British business executive; *Chairman, Royal Mail Holdings PLC;* b. 12 April 1953; m.; two s. one d.; ed Magdalen Coll. School, North Oxon. Polytechnic, A.M.P. Harvard; with Mars Confectionery 1974–91, rising to Business Sector Man. UK Grocery Div.; Sales Dir Pedigree Petfoods 1991–92; joined ASDA Stores Ltd as Group Marketing Dir 1992, then successively Retail Dir, Deputy Chief Exec.; Chief Exec. 1996; Pres. and CEO Wal-Mart Europe 1999–2000; Dir (non-exec.) Wilson Connolly Holdings PLC 1995 (Deputy Chair. 2000, interim CEO 2001–02); Dir (non-exec.) BSkyB PLC 1999–, Dyson Ltd –2004, Cannons –2004, Scottish Power PLC 2001, George Weston Ltd 2001 (currently Deputy Chair.), Consignia PLC 2001; Chair. (non-exec.) lastminute.com 2000–04, Cannons Group Ltd 2001; Dir (non-exec.) Royal Mail Holdings PLC 2001–, Chair. 2002–; Chair. Race for Opportunity 2000, BHS Ltd 2000–; Deputy Chair. (non-exec.) Leeds Sporting PLC 1998, Loblaw Companies Ltd, Selfridges & Co. *Publication:* On Leadership 2007. *Address:* Royal Mail Holdings PLC, 148 Old Street, London, EC1V 9HQ, England (office). *Telephone:* (20) 7250-2888 (office). *Fax:* (20) 7659-4948 (office). *E-mail:* info@royalmailgroup.com (office). *Website:* www .royalmailgroup.com (office).

LEIGHTON, John; British art historian and museum director; *Director-General, National Galleries of Scotland;* b. 1959, Belfast; ed Univ. of Edinburgh, Edinburgh Coll. of Art, Courtauld Inst. of Art; trained as art historian and taught art history at Univ. of Edinburgh; Curator for 19th Century Paintings, Nat. Gallery, London 1987–97; Dir Van Gogh Museum, Amsterdam 1997–2005, organized exhbn 'Van Gogh and Gauguin' in conjunction with Chicago Art Inst. 1997–2002; Dir-Gen. Nat. Galleries of Scotland 2006–. *Address:* National Gallery of Scotland, The Mound, Edinburgh, EH2 2EL, Scotland (office). *Telephone:* (131) 624-6200 (office). *E-mail:* enquiries@nationalgalleries.org (office). *Website:* www .nationalgalleries.org (office).

LEIJONHUFVUD, Baron Axel Stig Bengt, PhD; Swedish professor of economics; *Professor of Monetary Economics, University of Trento;* b. 9 June 1933, Stockholm; s. of Erik G. Leijonhufvud and Helene A. Neovius; m. 1st Marta E. Ising 1955 (divorced 1977), 2nd Earlene J. Craver 1977; one s. two d.; ed Univs of Lund, Pittsburgh and Northwestern Univ.; Acting Asst Prof. of Econs, UCLA 1964–67, Assoc. Prof. 1967–71, Prof. of Econs 1971–94, Chair. Dept of Econs 1980–83, 1990–92, Dir Center for Computable Econs 1991–97; Prof. of Monetary Econs, Univ. of Trento 1995–; Dir Computable and Experimental Econs Lab. 1996–; Visiting Prof., Stockholm School of Econ. and Commerce 1979–80, 1986, 1987, 1996, Inst. for Advanced Studies, Vienna 1976, 1987, Inst. for Advanced Studies, Jerusalem 1987, Nihon Univ. Tokyo 1980, European Univ. Inst., Florence 1982, 1986–87, 1989, Istituto Torcuato di Tella, Buenos Aires 1989, 1995; Ständiger Gastprofessor Univ. of Konstanz 1982–85; mem. Econ. Export Cttee of Pres. of Kazakhstan 1991; other professional appointments, Cttee memberships etc.; Brookings Inst. Fellow 1963–64; Marshall Lecturer, Univ. of Cambridge 1974; Overseas Fellow, Churchill Coll. Cambridge 1974; Inst. for Advanced Study Fellow 1983–84; Dr hc (Lund) 1983, (Nice, Sophia Antipolis) 1995. *Publications:* On Keynesian Economics and the Economics of Keynes: A Study in Monetary Theory 1968, Keynes and the Classics: Two Lectures 1969, Information and Coordination: Essays in Macroeconomic Theory 1981, High Inflation (jtly) 1995, Macroeconomic Instability and Coordination 2000, Monetary Theory as a Basis for Monetary Policy (ed.) 2001, Monetary Theory and Policy Experience (ed.) 2001; contribs to professional journals. *Address:* Department of Economics, University of Trento, Via Inama 5, 38100 Trento, Italy. *Telephone:* (0461) 882279. *E-mail:* axel@ucla.edu (office). *Website:* www.ceel.economia.unitn.it.

LEINONEN, Tatu Einari, MSc, DTech; Finnish engineer and academic; *Professor of Machine Design, University of Oulu;* b. 21 Sept. 1938, Kajaani; s. of Aate Leinonen and Aili Leinonen (née Nieminen); m. Tuula Tuovinen 1968; one s. two d.; Lecturer, Tech. Inst. of Helsinki 1963; Researcher, Tech. Research Centre of Finland 1965; Design Engineer, State Railway Co. 1966; Prof. of Machine Design, Univ. of Oulu 1968–; Visiting Prof., Univ. of Vt, USA 1976, Mich. Tech. Univ., USA 1977, 1981–82, 1991, Univ. of Fla, USA 1991, Lakehead Univ., Canada 1991, 2000, Toin Univ. of Yokohama, Japan 1994, Yanshan Univ., China 2000; fmr Sec.-Gen IFToMM. *Publications:* more than 300 papers and books 1966–. *Leisure interests:* cross-country skiing, golf. *Address:* Department of Mechanical Engineering, PO Box 4900, University of Oulu, 9014 Oulu (office); Matemaatikontie 6, 90570 Oulu, Finland (home). *Telephone:* (8) 5532050. *Fax:* (8) 5532026. *E-mail:* tatu@me.oulu.fi (office). *Website:* www.oulu.fi (office).

LEIPOLD, Gerd, PhD; German environmentalist; *Executive Director, Greenpeace International;* b. 1 Jan. 1951, Rot an der Rot; two c.; ed Max Planck Inst. for Meteorology, Hamburg; trained as scientist; joined Greenpeace Germany as volunteer 1980, joined full-time 1983, later mem. Exec. Cttee and Trustee, Int. Co-ordinator Nuclear Free Seas Campaign 1987, fmr Chair. Bd Green Peace Nordic, mem. Bd Greenpeace USSR, Dir Greenpeace Nuclear Disarmament Campaign, London, Acting Int. Exec. Dir Greenpeace International Feb.–June 2001, Int. Exec. Dir June 2001–; set up own consultancy, GEM Partners Ltd, London to advise NGOs on strategy and communications 1993, Dir 1993–2001. *Leisure interests:* playing piano, literature, soccer, history. *Address:* Greenpeace International, Ottho Heldringstraat 5, Amsterdam 1066 AZ, Netherlands (office); c/o Im Hebsack 4, 88430 Rot, Germany (home). *Telephone:* (20) 718-2081 (office). *Fax:* (20) 718-2578 (office). *E-mail:* gerd .leipold@int.greenpeace.org (office). *Website:* www.greenpeace.org (office).

LEIRNER, Sheila Anne; Brazilian journalist, art critic, curator and writer; b. (Sheila Anne Klinger), 25 Sept. 1948, São Paulo; d. of Abraham L. Klinger and Giselda Leirner Klinger; m. 1st Décio Tozzi 1970 (divorced 1972); one s.; m. 2nd Gustavo Halbreich 1974 (divorced 1988); one s.; m. 3rd Jean-Louis Andral 1991 (divorced 2000); m. 4th Patrick Corneau 2007; ed Univ. of Vincennes, Ecole Pratique des Hautes Etudes, Sorbonne, Paris; art critic, O Estado de São Paulo 1975–90; Gen. Curator, 18th and 19th São Paulo Biennial 1985, 1987; curator of various exhbns in Brazil and abroad; now ind. curator and art critic; apptd to Île-de-France regional comm. to examine projects of the "1% artistic", French Ministries of the Interior and Educ.; mem. French and Brazilian sections, Int. Asscn of Art Critics; mem. juries and invited lecturer in Latin America, Africa, USA, Asia and Europe; corresp. for nat. and foreign publs; lives and works in Paris; Chevalier, Ordre des Arts et des Lettres; Critic of the Year Award, Brazilian Asscn of Art Critics and Sec. of Culture of the State of São Paulo, Artistic Personality of the Year in Latin America, Argentine Asscn of Art Critics. *Publications:* selected works of art criticism, anthologies and monographies, including Leopoldo Nóvoa, Art as Measure 1982, Art and Its Time 1991, Ars in Natura 1996, Lateinamerikanische Kunst 1993, Sky Above – A Tombeau for Haroldo de Campos 2005, The Surrealism (with J. Guinsburg) 2008. *Leisure interests:* literature, music, collecting miniatures and dolls houses. *Address:* c/o Editora Perspectiva, Avenida Brigadeiro Luis Antônio, 3025-3035, 01401-000 São Paulo, Brazil (office). *E-mail:* sheila.leirner@gmail.com (home). *Website:* perso.wanadoo.fr/sheila .leirner (home); sheilaleirner.blogspot.com (home).

LEITE, Arcangelo; Timor-Leste politician; *Minister of Internal Administration;* has held several govt posts including Dir Nat. Directorate for State Admin, Acting Dir (Territories), Ministry of State Admin; Minister of Internal Admin 2007–. *Address:* Ministry of Internal Administration, Dili, Timor-Leste (office).

LEITER, Michael E., BA, JD; American naval officer, lawyer and government official; *Director, National Counterterrorism Center;* ed Columbia Univ., Harvard Law School; Naval Flight Officer, USN 1991–97, served on US, NATO and UN missions in fmr Yugoslavia and Iraq; fmr Harvard Law School Human Rights Fellow, Int. Criminal Tribunal for the Fmr Yugoslavia, The Hague; fmr law clerk to Assoc. Justice Stephen G. Breyer of US Supreme Court and to Chief Judge Michael Boudin of US Court of Appeals for the First Circuit; Asst US Attorney, Eastern Dist of Va, US Dept of Justice 2002–05; Deputy Gen. Counsel and Asst Dir, Pres.'s Comm. on Intelligence Capabilities of US Regarding Weapons of Mass Destruction (Robb-Silberman Comm.) 2005; Deputy Chief of Staff, Office of Dir of Nat. Intelligence 2005–07; Prin. Deputy Dir Nat. Counterterrorism Center Feb.–Nov. 2007, Acting Dir 2007–08, Dir 2008–. *Address:* United States National Counterterrorism Center, c/o Director of National Intelligence, Washington, DC 20511, USA (office). *Telephone:* (703) 733-8600 (office). *Website:* www.nctc.gov (office).

LEITH, Prudence Margaret (Prue), OBE, FRSA; British caterer and author; b. 18 Feb. 1940, Cape Town, South Africa; d. of late Stewart Leith and of Margaret Inglis; m. Rayne Kruger (died 2002); one s. one d.; ed Haywards Heath, Sussex, St Mary's, Johannesburg, Cape Town Univ., Sorbonne, Paris and Cordon Bleu School, London; started Leith's Good Food (commercial catering co.) 1965, Leith's restaurant 1969; cookery corresp. Daily Mail 1969–73; Man. Dir Prudence Leith Ltd 1972–94, Chair. Leith's Ltd 1994–96; opened Leith's School of Food and Wine 1975; added Leith's Farm 1976; cookery corresp. Daily Express 1976–80; Cookery Ed. The Guardian 1980–85, columnist 1986–90; subject of TV documentaries by BBC and Channel 4; presented series Tricks of the Trade, BBC 1; Vice-Pres. Restaurateurs' Asscn of GB; Gov. Nat. Inst. of Econ. and Social Research; Vice-Patron Women in Finance and Banking; Chair. UK Cttee New Era Schools' Trust 1994–2000, Royal Soc. of Arts 1995–97 (Deputy Chair. 1997–2000), The British Food Heritage Trust 1997–, Forum for the Future 2000; Dir (non-exec.) Halifax PLC 1992–99, Whitbread PLC 1995–, Argyll Group 1989–96, Woolworths 2001–; Hon. Fellow Univ. Salford 1992; Visiting Prof., Univ. of N London 1993–; Chair. School Food Trust 2006–; mem. Nat. Council for Vocational Qualifications and UK Skills, Stamp Cttee 1997–; Gov. Kingsmead City Tech. Coll., Ashridge Man. Coll.; Reader for Queen's Anniversary Prizes; Patron Prue Leith Coll. of Food and Wine, Johannesburg 1997–; Chair. 3Es Enterprises 1998–, King's Coll. 1998; Trustee Forum for the Future 1998–; Training for Life 1999–, Places for People 1999–; Patron Prue Leith Group; DL Greater London 1998; Fellow, Univ. of Salford; Freeman, City of London 1994; Dr hc (Open Univ.) 1997; Hon. DUniv (Oxford Brookes) 2000; Business Woman of the Year 1990. *Publications include:* Leith's All-Party Cook Book 1969, Parkinson's Pie 1972, Cooking for Friends 1978, The Best of Prue Leith 1979, Leith's Cookery Course (with J. B. Reynaud) 1979–80, The Cook's Handbook 1981, Prue Leith's Pocket Book of Dinner Parties 1983, Dinner Parties 1984, Leith's Cook Book 1985, Leith's Cookery School (with Caroline Waldegrave) 1985, Entertaining with Style (with P. Tyrer) 1986, Confident Cooking (part-work) 1989–90, Leith's Cookery Bible (with Caroline Waldegrave) 1991, Leith's Complete Christmas 1992, Sunday Times Slim Plan: The 21-Day Diet for Slimming Safely 1992, Leith's Baking (with Caroline Waldegrave) 1993, Leith's Vegetarian Cookery 1993, Leith's Step by Step Cookery 1993, Salads 1993, Chicken Dishes 1993, Starters 1993, Fruit 1993, Quick and Easy 1993, Leith's Contemporary Cooking (with Caroline Yates and Alison Cavaliero) 1994, Leith's Guide to Wine (with Richard Harvey) 1995, Leaving Patrick (novel) 1999, Sisters (novel) 2001, A Lovesome Thing (novel) 2004, Choral Society (novel) 2009. *Leisure interests:* walking, fishing, gardening, tennis, old cookbooks, kitchen antiques, Trollope. *Address:* 94 Kensington Park Road, London, W11 2PN, England. *Telephone:* (20) 7221-5282. *Fax:* (20) 7221-1846. *E-mail:* pmleith@dial.pipex.com (office).

LEJEUNE, Michael L.; American international finance official; b. 22 March 1918, Manchester, UK; s. of F. Arnold Lejeune and Gladys Lejeune (née Brown); m. Margaret Werden Wilson 1947; two s. one d.; ed Cate School, Carpinteria, Calif., Yale Univ. and Yale Univ. Grad. School; Teacher St Paul's School, Concord, New Hampshire 1941; Volunteer in King's Royal Rifle Corps in British Army 1942–46; joined staff of IBRD (World Bank) 1946, Personnel

Officer 1948–50, Asst to Loan Dir and Sec. Staff Loan Cttee, Loan Dept 1950–52, Chief of Div., Europe, Africa and Australasia Dept 1952–57, Asst Dir of Operations, Europe, Africa and Australasia 1957–63, Asst Dir of Operations, Far East 1963–64; Dir of Admin., IBRD, IDA and IFC 1964–67, Dir, Middle East and North Africa Dept 1967–68, Dir, Europe, Middle East and North Africa Dept 1968–69, Dir, Eastern Africa Dept 1970–74, Exec. Sec., Consultative Group on Int. Agric. Research 1974–83, Sr Adviser to Vice-Pres. Operations Policy 1983; Consultant 1983–; Trustee, Santa Barbara Foundation 1991–99, Vice-Pres. 1999. *Publication:* Partners Against Hunger: The Consultative Group on International Agricultural Research (with Warren C. Baum) 1986. *Address:* 1024A Senda Verde, Santa Barbara, CA 93105, USA (home). *Telephone:* (805) 569-1350 (home).

LEKHANYA, Maj.-Gen. Justin Metsing; Lesotho politician and army officer; *Leader, Basotho National Party;* b. 7 April 1938, Thaba-Tseka; Commdr of Lesotho Army; overthrew Prime Minister Leabua Jonathan in a mil. coup 1986; Head Mil. Council and Council of Ministers 1986–91, Minister of Defence and Internal Security 1986–91, also Minister of Public Service, Youth and Women's Affairs, Food Man. Units and Cabinet Office; deposed King of Lesotho in mil. coup 1990, later restored; Lekhanya ousted in coup 1991; now Leader Basotho Nat. Party. *Address:* Basotho National Party, PO Box 124, Maseru 100, Lesotho.

LEKISHVILI, Niko Mikhailovich; Georgian politician; b. 20 April 1947, Tbilisi; m.; two d.; ed Tbilisi Polytech. Inst., Moscow Acad. of Nat. Econ.; Sr Lab. Asst Georgian Polytech. Inst. 1971–72; Komsomol functionary 1972–77; Second Sec., Chair. Dist Exec. Cttee, First Sec. Pervomay Dist CP Cttee, Tbilisi 1977–89; Second Sec., First Sec. Tbilisi City CP Cttee 1989–90; Chair. Tbilisi City Soviet 1990; Deputy Supreme Soviet Georgian SSR 1990–91; Chief State Counsellor Georgian Cabinet of Ministers Jan.–Nov. 1992; mem. Parl. Repub. of Georgia 1992–95, 1999–; Deputy Prime Minister Sept.–Oct. 1993; Mayor of Tbilisi 1993–95; State Minister of Georgia 1995–98; Chair. Union of Tax-Payers. *Leisure interests:* music, football, travel. *Address:* Kargareteli Str. 3a, 380064 Tblisi, Georgia (home); Ingorokva str. 7, 380034, Tbilisi, Georgia.

LEKOTA, Mosiuoa Patrick (Terror); South African politician; *President, Congress of the People (COPE);* b. 13 Aug. 1948, Senekal, Orange Free State; s. of the late Mapiloko Lekota and Mamosiuoa Lekota; m. Cynthia Lekota 1975; two s. two d. (deceased); ed Univ. of the North (Turfloop); perm. organizer, South African Students' Org. (SASO) 1972–74; charged under Terrorism Act 1974; tried and imprisoned on Robben Island 1976–82; Nat. Publicity Sec. United Democratic Front (UDF) 1983–91; fmrly with African Nat. Congress (ANC) in Natal; organizer for ANC in Northern Free States 1990; mem. ANC Working Cttee 1991–, Nat. Chair. ANC Nat. Exec. Cttee 1991–, Chair. Southern OFS of Nat. Exec. Comm. 1991, Sec. Elections Comm. 1992–94; Nat. Chair. ANC 1997–2007, detained 1983, 1984, 1985; on trial with 21 others charged with treason and murder in Delmas case 1986, convicted 1988, sentenced to 12 years imprisonment after being held in custody for four years; conviction overturned by Appeal Court 1989; in exile, returned to S Africa 1990; Premier Free State Prov. Legislature 1994; Chair. Nat. Council of Provinces 1997–99; Minister of Defence 1999–2008 (resgnd); Co-founder and Pres. Congress of the People party 2008–. *Leisure interests:* cycling, reading, soccer, rugby and studying wildlife. *Website:* www.congressofthepeople.org.za.

LELONG, Pierre; Haitian diplomatist and engineer; b. 5 Jan. 1936, Jeremie; m.; two c.; ed Nat. Autonomous Univ. of Mexico; joined Ministry of the Navy, Mexico, Officer-in-Charge of Structural Studies, Directorate-Gen. of Maritime Projects 1962–72, Asst Dir-Gen. for Computer Science 1972–82, Dir of works and structural safety, Fed. Dist 1989; Amb. to Mexico 1991–96; fmr del. to many regional orgs, del. to Second Int. Conf. of New or Restored Democracies, Managua 1994, Conf. on the Situation of Haitian Refugees, Tegucigalpa 1994 and Conf. of OAS, Managua 1994; Perm. Rep. to UN 1996–2001; Chair. Sixth Cttee (Legal), UN Gen. Ass. 2001–03; Lecturer, Faculty of Eng, Nat. Autonomous Univ. of Mexico 1975–90. *Address:* c/o Ministry of Foreign Affairs and Religion, blvd Harry S Truman, Cité de l'Exposition, Port-au-Prince, Haiti (office).

LELONG, Pierre Alexandre; French administrative official; *President, Commission des Marchés Publics de l'Etat;* b. 22 May 1931, Paris; s. of Prof. Marcel Lelong; m. Catherine Demargne 1958; four s. one d.; ed Coll. Stanislas, Paris, Univ. of Paris and Ecole Nat. d'Admin.; Ministry of Finance and Econ. Affairs 1958–62; Econ. Adviser to Prime Minister Pompidou 1962–67; Gen. Man. Fonds d'Orientation et de Régularisation des Marchés Agricoles (FORMA) 1967–68; MP for Finistère 1968–74; Sec. of State for Posts and Telecommunications 1974–75; Judge, Court of Accounts 1975–77; mem. European Court of Auditors 1977–84, Pres. 1981–84; Pres. of Section (Defence) at Court of Accounts 1990–94, Pres. of Chamber (European Affairs) 1994–97; Pres. Interministerial Cttee for Mil., Aeronautic and Mechanical State Procurements 1997–2004; Pres. Consultative Cttee on Secret Defence Affairs 1999–2005; Pres. Commission des Marchés Publics de l'Etat 2005–; Commdr, Légion d'Honneur, Officier, Ordre du Mérite; Grand Cross, Ordre de la Couronne de Chêne (Luxembourg). *Address:* Ministere de l'Economie et des Finances, 6 rue Louise Wein, 75013 Paris (office); 130 rue de Rennes, 75006 Paris, France (home). *Telephone:* 1-42-75-75-00 (office); 1-45-44-12-49 (home). *Fax:* 1-42-75-75-97 (office); 1-45-44-12-49 (home). *E-mail:* pierre.lelong@pm.gouv.fr (office); lelongdemargne@noos.fr (home).

LELONG, Pierre Jacques, DèsSc; French academic; *Professor Emeritus, University of Paris V;* b. 14 March 1912, Paris; s. of Charles Lelong and Marguerite Lelong (née Bronner); m. 1st Jacqueline Ferrand 1947, two s. two d.; m. 2nd France Fages 1976; ed Ecole Normale Supérieure and Ecole des Sciences Politiques; Prof., Science Faculty, Grenoble 1942–44; Prof., Science Faculty, Lille 1944–54, Université de Paris VI 1954–81, now Prof. Emer.; Research Counsellor for Pres. De Gaulle 1959–62; Pres. du Comité Consultatif de la Recherche et de la Comm. du Plan 1961–63; Pres. Comm. mathématique CNRS 1962–66; mem. Section (Plan), Conseil Economique et Social 1992–96; mem. Acad. des Sciences 1986–; Commdr Légion d'Honneur, Commdr du Soleil (Peru), Commdr de l'Etoile Noire. *Publications:* Fonctions plurisoush-armoniques 1942, Integration and Positivity in Complex Analysis 1958, Entire functions of several complex variables 1986, Le Général de Gaulle et la Recherche Scientifique et Technique, numerous research papers on complex analysis and articles on politics, the economy and scientific research. *Address:* 9 place de Rungis, 75013 Paris, France. *Telephone:* 1-45-81-51-45 (home).

LELOUCH, Claude; French film director, producer and writer; b. 30 Oct. 1937, Paris; s. of Simon Lelouch and Charlotte Abeilard; m. Christine Cochet 1968 (divorced); m. 2nd Marie-Sophie Pochat; four c., three c. from previous relationships; m. 3rd Alessandra Martines 1995; Pres. and Dir-Gen. Société Les Films 13, 1966–; Chevalier, Ordre nat. du Mérite, Officier des Arts et des Lettres, Grand Prix Nationaux 1993; Dr hc (UMIST) 1996; Palme d'or, Cannes 1966, Acad. Award 1966. *Films include:* L'amour des si… (In the Affirmative) 1962, La femme-spectacle (Night Women) 1964, Une fille et des fusils 1964, Les grands moments 1965, …pour un maillot jaune (For a Yellow Jersey) 1965, Jean-Paul Belmondo 1965, Un homme et une femme (A Man and a Women) (uncredited) 1966, Loin du Vietnam (Far from Vietnam) 1967, Vivre pour vivre (Live for Life) 1967, 13 jours en France (aka Challenge in the Snow) 1968, Un homme qui me plaît (A Man I Like) 1969, La vie, l'amour, la mort (Life Love Death) 1969, Le voyou (The Crook) 1970, Smic Smac Smoc 1971, L'Aventure c'est l'aventure (aka Money Money Money) 1972, La bonne année (Happy New Year) 1973, Visions of Eight (also co-dir) 1973, Toute une vie (also producer, dir, author) 1974, Mariage 1974, Le chat et la souris (Cat and Mouse) 1975, C'était un rendez-vous 1976, Le bon et les méchants (The Good Guys and the Bad Guys) 1976, Si c'était à refaire (If I Had to Do It All Over Again) 1976, Un autre homme, une autre chance (Another Man, Another Chance) 1977, Robert et Robert 1978, A nous deux (Us Two) 1979, Les uns et les autres (aka Within Memory) 1981, Edith et Marcel 1983, Viva la vie! 1984, Partir, revenir (Going and Coming Back) 1985, Un homme et une femme, 20 ans déjàs (A Man and a Woman: 20 Years Later) 1986, Attention bandits 1986, Itinéraire d'un enfant gâté 1988, Il y a des jours… et de lunes 1990, La belle histoire (The Beautiful Story) 1992, Tout ça… pour ça! (All That… for This?!) 1993, Les Misérables (Golden Globe 1996, Ephèbe d'or 1996) 1995, Lumière et compagnie 1996, Hommes, Femmes, mode d'emploi (Men, Women: A User's Manual) 1996, Hasards ou coïncidences 1998, Une pour toutes (One 4 All) 1999, And Now… Ladies and Gentlemen… 2002, 11'09"01 – September 11 2002, Le genre humain – 1ère partie: Les parisiens 2004, Le courage d'aimer 2005. *Television includes:* Les uns et les autres (mini-series) 1983. *Publication:* Itinéraire d'un enfant très gâté (autobiog.) 2000. *Address:* 15 avenue Hoche, 75008 Paris, France. *Telephone:* 42-25-00-89.

LELYVELD, Joseph Salem; American journalist; b. 5 April 1937, Cincinnati; s. of Arthur Joseph Lelyveld and Toby Bookholz; m. Carolyn Fox 1958; two d.; ed Columbia Univ., New York; reporter, Ed. New York Times 1963–, Foreign Corresp. Johannesburg, New Delhi, Hong Kong, London 1965–86, columnist, staff writer 1977, 1984–85, Foreign Ed. 1987–89, Deputy Man. Ed. 1989–90, Man. Ed. 1990–94, Exec. Ed. 1994–2001, Interim Exec. Ed. 2003; George Polk Memorial Award 1972, 1984. *Publication:* Move Your Shadow (Pulitzer Prize) 1985, Omaha Blues: A Memory Loop 2005. *Address:* c/o New York Times, 229 W 43rd Street, New York, NY 10036, USA.

LEMAN, Alexander B., FRAIC, FRSA; Canadian urban analyst and planner; b. 5 May 1926, Belgrade, Yugoslavia; s. of Boris E. Leman and Nataly Leman; m. 1st Catherine B. Leman 1950 (deceased); m. 2nd N. Bella Leman 1968; two s. two d.; ed Univ. of Belgrade; Prin. Partner, The Leman Partnership, Architects 1956–; Pres. Leman Group Inc., Consultants on Human Settlements and Devt 1971–; Chair. and CEO Urbanitas, Inc., Planners and Builders of Urban Communities; Chair. of Bd Royal Architectural Inst. of Canada Research Corpn 1982–86; Co-Chair. UNESCO Int. Conf. on Culture and Devt 1985; Chair. World Congress on Conservation of Natural and Built Environments 1989; Dir Devt of Bangkok Regional Plan 1992–95; Adviser to Ont. Ministry of Housing on New Town Devt 1994–95; Founding mem. and Dir Shelter for the Homeless Foundation; Progressive Architecture Award 1973, UN Habitat Award 1990. *Publications:* Great Lakes Megalopolis: From Civilization to Ecumenization 1976 and articles on human settlements, environment and urban planning and analysis in professional journals. *Leisure interests:* writing, travel, community activities. *Address:* Leman Group Inc., The Hudson's Bay Centre, 2 Bloor Street East, 28th Floor, Toronto, Ont., M4W 1A8 (office); 44 Charles Street W, Suite 4203, Toronto, Ont., M4Y 1R8, Canada (home). *Telephone:* (416) 964-1865 (office). *Fax:* (416) 964-6065 (office). *E-mail:* lemanab@aol.com (office).

LEMANN, Jorge Paulo; Brazilian business executive; b. 26 Aug. 1939, Rio de Janeiro; m. Susanna Lemann; five c.; ed Harvard Univ., USA; f. Banco de Investimentos Garantia 1971, Sr Pnr 1971–98; CEO Brahma 1990–99, mem. Bd of Dirs Companhia de Bebidas das Américas/Ambev (formed after merger of Brahma and Antarctica) 1999–2004, mem. Admin. Council InBev NV/SA (after merger of Interbrew and Ambev) 2004–; mem. Admin. Council Gillette Corpn 1998–2005; mem. Advisory Cttee New York Stock Exchange 1998–2005; mem. Int. Advisory Bd DaimlerChrysler AG; mem. Advisory Council Fundação Estudar; mem. Bd of Deans Advisors, Harvard Business School; est. Lemann Scholarships 2005. *Sporting achievements:* Swiss nat. tennis champion 1963. *Leisure interests:* tennis. *Address:* Companhia de Bebidas das Américas/Ambev, Rua Renato Paes de Barros, 1017, 4° andar, 04530-001 São Paulo, Brazil (office). *Telephone:* (11) 2122-1200 (office). *Fax:* (11) 2122-1526 (office). *Website:* www.ambev.com.br (office).

LEMANN, Nicholas Berthelot, BA; American journalist and academic; *Dean and Henry R. Luce Professor, Graduate School of Journalism, Columbia University;* b. 11 Aug. 1954, New Orleans, La; m. 1st Dominique Alice Browning 1983; two s.; m. 2nd Judith Anne Shulevitz 1999; one s. one d.; ed Harvard Coll.; Assoc. Ed. and Man. Ed., Washington Monthly magazine 1976–78; Assoc. Ed. and Exec. Ed. Texas Monthly magazine 1978–79, Exec. Ed. 1981–83; Nat. Staff Reporter, Washington Post 1979–81; Nat. Corresp. The Atlantic Monthly magazine 1983–99; staff writer, The New Yorker magazine 1999–, Washington Corresp. 2000–03, currently Contrib.; Henry R. Luce Prof., Grad. School of Journalism, Columbia Univ. 2003–, Dean Grad. School of Journalism 2003–; fmr contrib. to numerous publs including New York Times, New York Review of Books, New Republic, Slate, American Heritage; mem. Bd of Dirs Authors Guild, Center for Humanities, CUNY Grad. Center, Soc. of American Historians; mem. New York Inst. for Humanities. *Television:* documentary projects for Blackside Inc., Frontline, Discovery Channel, BBC. *Publications:* The Fast Track: Texans and Other Survivors 1981, Out of the Forties 1983, The Promised Land: The Great Black Migration and How It Changed America 1991, The Big Test: The Secret History of the American Meritocracy 1999 (Washington Monthly Political Book Award), Redemption: The Last Battle of the Civil War 2006. *Address:* Columbia University Graduate School of Journalism, 2950 Broadway, New York, NY 10027, USA (office). *Telephone:* (212) 854-6056 (office). *E-mail:* lemann@columbia.edu (office). *Website:* www.journalism.columbia.edu (office).

LEMIERRE, Jean; French international civil servant; b. 6 June 1950, Sainte Adresse; m.; three c.; ed Institut d'Etudes Politiques de Paris, Ecole Nationale d'Admin; Inspection Générale des Finances 1976; various positions, Tax Policy Admin 1980–87, Head 1987–89; Directeur Général des Impôts 1989–95; Directeur de Cabinet, French Pvt. Office, Minister of Economy and Finance, Paris 1995; Head of Treasury 1995–2000; mem. European Monetary Cttee 1995–98; Chair. European Econ. and Finance Cttee 1999–2000, Paris Club 1999–2000; Pres. EBRD 2000–08. *Address:* c/o European Bank for Reconstruction and Development, One Exchange Square, 175 Bishopgate, London, EC2A 2JN, England (office).

LEMIEUX, Joseph Henry, BS; American business executive; b. 2 March 1931, Providence, RI; s. of Joseph C. Lemieux and Mildred L. Lemieux; m. Frances J. Schmidt 1956; three s. two d.; ed Stonehill Coll., Univ. of Rhode Island, Bryant Coll., Providence; joined Glass Container Div., Owens-Illinois as trainee 1957, numerous posts include Plant Comptroller 1961, Admin. Man. 1964, Plant Man. 1965–72, Vice-Pres. 1972–78, Group Vice-Pres. 1979–84, Exec. Vice-Pres. and Pres. Packaging Operations 1984–86, Pres and COO 1986–90, CEO 1990–2003, Chair. 1991–2004; Chair. Bd of Dirs Health Care and Retirement Corpn of America 1986; mem. Bd of Dirs Manor Care, Inc –2004; Dr hc Business Admin. (Bryant Coll.) 1994; Outstanding Young Man of America, US Jr Chamber of Commerce 1965, Ellis Island Medal of Honor 2001. *Leisure interests:* golf, tennis. *Address:* c/o Owens-Illinois Inc., One Sea Gate, Toledo, OH 43666, USA.

LEMIEUX, Mario; Canadian ice hockey executive and fmr ice hockey player; *Chairman and CEO, Pittsburgh Penguins;* b. 5 Oct. 1965, Montreal; m. Nathalie Asselin; four c.; picked first overall in 1984 Nat. Hockey League (NHL) Entry Draft by Pittsburgh Penguins; winner of Stanley Cup 1991, 1992, retd 1997; led group that acquired Penguins 1999, returned as player 2000, retd 2006; currently Chair., CEO; played for Canadian nat. team in Canadian Cup 1988, Olympics 2002; est. Mario Lemieux Foundation 1993; Calder Memorial Trophy 1985, Lester B. Pearson Award 1986, 1988, 1993, 1996, Second All-Star Team Centre 1986, 1987, 1992, 2001, Art Ross Trophy 1988, 1989, 1992, 1993, 1996, 1997, First All-Star Team Centre 1988, 1989, 1993, 1996, 1997, Hart Memorial Trophy 1988, 1993, 1996, Conn Smythe Trophy 1991, 1992, Bill Masterton Memorial Trophy 1993. *Leisure interest:* golf. *Address:* Pittsburgh Penguins, 1 Chatham Center, Suite 400, Pittsburgh, PA 15219-3447, USA (office). *Telephone:* (412) 642-1300 (office). *Fax:* (412) 642-1859 (office). *Website:* www.pittsburghpenguins.com (office).

LEMINE, Mohamed Mahmoud Ould Mohamed, DEcon; Mauritanian politician; *Minister of National Defence;* b. 1952, Hodh El Gharbi; m.; ed studied in Cairo, Egypt; fmr Prof. of Econs, Univ. of Nouakchott –1996; Dir-Gen. Ecole Nationale de l'Administration (ENA), Nouakchott 1996–2007; Minister of Nat. Defence 2007–. *Address:* Ministry of National Defence, Nouakchott, Mauritania (office). *Telephone:* 525-41-42 (office).

LEMINE, Mohamed Saleck Ould Mohamed; Mauritanian diplomatist and government official; b. 1963, Kiffa; m.; four c.; ed Ecole Nationale d'Administration; joined Ministry of Foreign Affairs and Co-operation 1984; Head, UN Dept 1987–92; First Counsellor, Perm. Mission to UN 1992–96; Amb. to Switzerland 1996–2007; Consul-Gen. Canary Islands 1997; Perm. Rep. to UN and Int. Orgs, Geneva 1997–2007, mem. UNCTAD Trade and Devt Bd 1998–2007 (Vice-Pres. 2003, Pres. 2006–07), Pres. Africa Cttee 2001, Vice-Pres. Comm. on Human Rights 2005; Minister of Foreign Affairs and Co-operation 2007–08. *Address:* c/o Ministry of Foreign Affairs and Co-operation, BP 230, Nouakchott, Mauritania (office).

LEMOND, Greg; American motor racing driver and fmr professional cyclist; b. 26 June 1961, Los Angeles; m. Kathy LeMond; two s. one d.; began professional competitive cycling career 1980; won Coors Classic stage race 1981, 1985; won Tour de France 1986, 1989, 1990; three World Champion titles; retd from cycling due to injury 1994; currently designer of bicycles; also leads cycling tours; now engaged in auto racing, professional series debut 1997 (with U.S. F2000); Sports Illustrated Sportsman of the Year 1989, ABC Wide World of Sports Athlete of the Year 1989, 1990, Jesse Owens Int. Trophy Awards—World's Most Outstanding Athlete 1991; two times winner of the Pernod Trophy (for best cyclist in the world); mem. Cycling Hall of Fame. *Address:* c/o Trek Travel, 801 West Madison, Waterloo, WI 53594, USA. *Website:* www.lemondbikes.com (office).

LEMOS, Nikolas Spyridon; Greek business executive; b. 8 Sept. 1933, Oinoussai, Chios; s. of Spyros A. Lemos and Irene N. Pateras; m. Irini Doxiadis 1976; three s. three d.; ed Univ. School of Navigation, Southampton, Edinburgh Univ.; officer, Capt. on various types of merchant ships; port capt. several shipyards in numerous countries; Man. Dir Lemos & Pateras 1966–83; Founder and Chair. NS Lemos & Co. Ltd (Shipbrokers) 1983–99; Pres. Maritime Museum Oinoussai; mem. Council Det Norske Veritas; Trustee Thyateira and St Nicholas Trust; Actuarius of Ecumenical Patriarche Constantinopoleos. *Leisure interests:* fishing, sailing, scuba diving, skiing, swimming. *Address:* 23A Vas Sofias Avenue, 10674 Athens, Greece (office). *Telephone:* (1) 07260500 (office). *Fax:* (1) 07260552 (office).

LEMOS SIMMONDS, Carlos, DrIur; Colombian politician; b. Popayán, Cauca; m. Martha Blanco Guake; four c.; ed Lycée of Cauca Univ. and Cauca Univ.; Prof. of Colombian Political History, Universidad Javeriana; Prof. of Colombian Econ. History, Free Univ. of Colombia; Dir of Consigna magazine 1982–87; mem. of Bogotá Council 1972–74, 1986–88; mem. House of Reps 1974–78; Gov. of Cauca Prov. 1976–77; Sec.-Gen. of the Presidency 1978–79; Senator 1978–81; Minister of Foreign Affairs 1981–82; Amb. to the OAS 1987–89; Minister of Communications Feb.–Oct. 1989; Minister of Government (Interior) 1989–90; Del. to Nat. Constitutional Ass. 1990–91; Chair of Bogotá Council 1992; cand. for Pres. of Colombia 1992; Amb. to Austria 1995, to UK 1995; Vice-Pres. of Colombia 1996–98; Orders of Boyacá, San Carlos, Civil Merit (Spain), Independence (Equatorial Guinea), Merit (Italy, Chile and Ecuador), Sol (Peru) and Balboa (Panama), Commdr Order of Isabel la Católica. *Publications include:* Francisco de Paula Santander, An Iconography, The Pre-Columbian Economy. *Address:* Palacio de Nariño, Carrera 8A, 7–26, Bogotá, DC, Colombia.

LEMPER, Ute; German singer, dancer and actress; b. 4 July 1963, Münster; pnr Todd Turkisher; two s. one d.; ed Dance Acad., Cologne, Max Reinhardt Seminary for Dramatic Art, Vienna; leading role in Viennese production of Cats 1983; appeared in Peter Pan, Berlin, Cabaret, Düsseldorf and Paris (recipient of Molière Award 1987), Chicago (Laurence Olivier Award) 1997–99 (London and New York), Life's a Swindle tour 1999, Punishing Kiss tour 2000, The Last Tango in Berlin tour 2009; Die sieben Todsünden (Weill) at Covent Garden Festival, London 2000; collaborations with Michael Nyman; French Culture Prize 1993. *Recordings include:* Life is a Cabaret 1987, Ute Lemper Sings Kurt Weill 1988, (Vol. 2) 1993, Threepenny Opera 1988, Mahagonny Songspiel 1989, Crimes of the Heart 1989, The Threepenny Opera 1990, The Seven Deadly Sins 1990, Songbook (with Michael Nyman) 1992, Illusions 1992, Espace Indécent 1993, Portrait of Ute Lemper 1995, City of Strangers 1995, Berlin Cabaret Songs 1996, Nuits Étranges 1997, All that Jazz/The Best of Ute Lemper 1998, Punishing Kiss 2000, But One Day 2002, Blood and Feathers 2006, Between Yesterday and Tomorrow 2008. *Television appearances include:* L'Affaire Dreyfus (Arte), Tales from the Crypt (HBO), Illusions (Granada) and The Look of Love (Gillian Lynn). *Film appearances include:* L'Autrichienne 1989, Moscou Parade 1992, Coupable d'Innocence 1993, Prêt à Porter 1995, Bogus 1996, Combat de Fauves, A River Made to Drown In, Appetite 1997. *Address:* c/o Delphine Beroske, 40 rue de la Folie Régnault, 75011 Paris, France (office). *Telephone:* 1-44-93-02-02 (office). *Fax:* 1-44-93-04-40 (office). *E-mail:* dberoske@visiteursdusoir.com (office). *Website:* www.visiteursdusoir.com (office); www.utelemper.com.

LENAERTS, Baron; **Koen,** Lic.iuris, LLM, MPA, PhD; Belgian judge; *Judge, Court of Justice of the European Communities;* b. (Koenraad Lenaerts), 20 Dec. 1954, Mortsel; m. Kris Grimonprez; six d.; ed Univs of Namur and Leuven, Belgium and Harvard Univ., USA; Asst Prof., Leuven Univ. 1979–82, Assoc. Prof. 1982–83, Prof. of EC Law 1983–; Prof. of European Insts, Coll. of Europe, Bruges 1984–89; law clerk to Judge R. Joliet, Court of Justice of the European Communities 1984–85; mem. Brussels Bar 1986–89; Judge, Court of First Instance of the European Communities, Luxembourg 1989–2003, Court of Justice of the European Communities 2003–; Visiting Prof. of Law, Univ. of Burundi 1983, 1986, Univ. of Strasbourg 1986–89, Harvard Univ. 1988–89; numerous academic distinctions, fellowships and prizes. *Publications:* 'The Negative Implications' of the Commerce Clause and 'Preemption' Doctrines as Federalism Related Limitations on State Power: a Historical Review 1978, Constitutie en rechter 1983, International privaatrecht (with G. Van Hecke) 1986, Le juge et la constitution aux Etats-Unis d'Amérique et dans l'ordre juridique européen 1988, Two Hundred Years of U.S. Constitution and Thirty Years of EEC Treaty: Outlook for a Comparison 1988, Constitutional Law of the European Union (with P. Van Nuffel) 1999 (revised second edn 2005), Procedural Law of the European Union (with D. Arts and I. Maselis) 1999 (revised second edn 2006), articles and contribs to reviews etc. *Address:* Court of Justice of the European Communities, blvd Konrad Adenauer, 2925 Luxembourg (office). *Telephone:* 4303-3553 (office). *Fax:* 4303-3541 (office). *E-mail:* koen.lenaerts@curia.europa.eu (office). *Website:* www.curia.europa.eu (office).

LENDL, Ivan; American (b. Czech) fmr professional tennis player; b. 7 March 1960, Ostrava; s. of Jiri Lendl and Olga Lendlova; m. Samantha Frankel 1989; five d.; Davis Cup player 1978–85, winner 1980; winner, Italian Jr Singles 1978, French Jr Singles 1978, Wimbledon Jr Singles 1978, Spanish Open Singles 1980, 1981, S. American Open Singles 1981, Canadian Open Singles 1980, 1981, WCT Tournament of Champion Singles 1982, WCT Masters Singles 1982, WCT Finals Singles 1982, Masters Champion 1985, 1986, French Open Champion 1984, 1986, 1987, US Open Champion 1985, 1986, 1987, US Clay Court Champion 1985, Italian Open Champion 1986, Australian Open Champion 1989, 1990; finalist Wimbledon 1986; held World No. One

www.worldwhoswho.com

ranking for a record 270 weeks 1985–87, 1989; won 94 singles titles and six doubles; named World Champion (Int. Tennis Fed.) 1985, 1986, 1990; retd Dec. 1994; granted US citizenship 1992; ATP Player of the Year 1985, 1986, 1987, inducted Int. Tennis Hall of Fame 2001, mem. Laureus World Sports Acad. *Publication:* Ivan Lendl's Power Tennis. *Leisure interests:* golf, collecting art. *Address:* c/o Laureus World Sports Academy, 15 Hill Street, London, W1 5QT, England. *Telephone:* (20) 7514-2700.

LENDLEIN, Andreas, Dr. sc. nat. (Habil.); German scientist and academic; *Director, Institute of Polymer Research, GKSS Research Centre;* ed Univ. of Technology (RWTH), Aachen; Postdoctoral Fellow, Dept for Material Science, ETH, Zurich, Switzerland 1996–97; Visiting Scientist, Dept of Chemical Eng, MIT, USA 1997–98; Head of Dept, Devt and Eng of Biocompatible Polymer Systems, German Wool Research Inst., Univ. of Technology (RWTH), Aachen 1997–2002; Man. Dir Nemoscience GmbH, Aachen 1998–2003; Dir Inst. for Tech. and Devt, Medical Devices (ITEMP), RWTH 2004–06; Prof., Medical Faculty, RWTH 2004–06; Vice-Dir and Co-ordinator of Research Field 'Bio-Engineering', Berlin-Brandenburg Centre for Regenerative Therapies, Virchow Charité, Berlin 2003–, mem. Medical Faculty Bd; Speaker, Research Programme 'Regenerative Medicine', Helmholtz Asscn of German Research Centres 2002–; Dir Inst. of Polymer Research, GKSS Research Centre, Teltow 2006–; Prof., Materials in Life Sciences, Faculty of Math. and Natural Sciences, Univ. of Potsdam 2006–; World Tech. Award in Health and Medicine, The World Tech. Network 2005. *Publications:* numerous scientific papers in professional journals on biomaterials for clinical applications in regenerative medicine. *Address:* Institute of Polymer Research, Kantstraße 55, 14513 Teltow-Seehof, Germany (office). *Telephone:* (3328) 352450 (office). *Fax:* (3328) 352452 (office). *E-mail:* andreas.lendlein@gkss.de (office). *Website:* www.gkss.de/institute/polymer_research/head/lendlein/index.php.en (office).

LENG, James (Jim) W.; British steel industry executive and mining industry executive; *Chairman, Rio Tinto Group PLC;* b. 1945; CEO Low & Bonar PLC –1995; CEO Laporte PLC 1995–2001; apptd Dir (non-exec.) Corus Group PLC (fmrly British Steel) 2001, Deputy Chair. and Sr Ind. Dir 2002–03, Chair. 2003–09; Chair. Rio Tinto Group PLC 2009–; mem. Bd of Dirs Alstom 2003–, Pilkington PLC –2006, IMI PLC –2005, JP Morgan Fleming Mid Cap Investment Trust PLC –2004, Hanson PLC 2004–07; Gov. Nat. Inst. of Econ. and Social Research. *Address:* Rio Tinto Group PLC, 6 St James's Square, London, SW1Y 4LD, England (office). *Telephone:* (20) 7930-2399 (office). *Fax:* (20) 7930-3429 (office). *Website:* www.riotinto.com (office).

LENG, Rongquan, MSc; Chinese telecommunications executive; *Vice-President, China Telecommunications Corporation;* b. 1949, Liaoning Prov.; ed Beijing Inst. of Posts and Telecommunications; Chief Engineer, Beijing Long Distance Telephone Bureau 1989–94, Deputy Chief Engineer, Telecommunications Bureau, Ministry of Posts and Telecommunications 1994–99, Deputy Dir Gen. 1999–2000, Exec. Dir 2004–, China Telecommunications Corpn 2004–, Pres. and COO 2004–08, Vice-Pres. 2008–, also Deputy Gen. Man., China Network Communications Group Corpn –2004, Vice-Chair. China Netcom Group Corpn (HK) Ltd –2004. *Address:* China Telecommunications Corporation, 31 Jinrong Street, Xicheng District, Beijing 100032, People's Republic of China (office). *Telephone:* (10) 58501800 (office). *Fax:* (10) 66010728 (office). *Website:* en.chinatelecom.com.cn (office).

LENIHAN, Brian Joseph, BA, LLB; Irish lawyer and politician; *Minister for Finance;* b. 21 May 1959, Dublin; s. of Brian Lenihan; m. Patricia Ryan; one s. one d.; ed Belvedere Coll., Trinity Coll. Dublin, Univ. of Cambridge, King's Inns Dublin; Lecturer in Law, Trinity Coll. Dublin 1984; called to the Bar, Dublin 1984; mem. Criminal Injuries Compensation Tribunal and Garda Síochána Complaints Appeal Bd 1992–95; elected TD (mem. Parl.) for Dublin West in by-election 1996, re-elected in gen. election 1997, Chair. All-Party Oireachtas Cttee on Constitution 1997–2002, mem. Cttee on Procedure and Privileges 1997–2002, Minister of State (with special responsibility for children) 2002–07, Minister for Justice 2007–08, Minister for Finance 2008–; mem. Fianna Fail; mem. Inc. Council of Law Reporting. *Address:* Department of Finance, Government Buildings, Upper Merrion Street, Dublin 2 (office); Laurel Lodge Shopping Centre, Dublin 15, Ireland. *Telephone:* (1) 6767571 (office); (1) 8220970 (constituency) (office). *Fax:* (1) 6789936 (office); (1) 8220972 (constituency) (office). *E-mail:* webmaster@finance.irlgov.ie (office); brianlenihantd@gmail.com (office). *Website:* www.finance.gov.ie (office); www.brianlenihan.ie (office).

LENK, Hans Albert Paul, PhD; German academic; *Professor Emeritus of Philosophy, Karlsruhe University;* b. 23 March 1935, Berlin; s. of Albert Lenk and Annemarie Lenk; m. Ulrike Reincke; two s. one d.; ed Lauenburgische Gelehrtenschule, Ratzeburg, Freiburg and Kiel Univs, Tech. Univ. of Berlin; Asst Prof., Tech. Univ. of Berlin 1962, Assoc. Prof. 1966, Prof. (Wissenschaftlicher Rat und Prof.) 1969; Chair. and Prof. of Philosophy, Karlsruhe Univ. 1969, now Prof. Emer., Dean, Coll. of Humanities and Social Sciences 1973–75; Dean and Prof. Philosophy of Social Sciences and Theory of Planning, European Faculty of Land Use and Devt, Strasbourg 1983–2006; Visiting Prof. numerous foreign univs; Hon. Prof. Tech. Univ., Budapest 1992; Green Honors Prof., Tex. Christian Univ., Fort Worth 1987; Pres. Int. Philosophic Soc. for Study of Sport 1980–81, Int. Olympic Union 1980–90, European Forum, Baden 1980–; Vice-Pres. European Acad. of Sciences and Philosophy of Law 1986–; Pres. Gen. Soc. for Philosophy in Germany 1991–93; Pres. Argentine-German Soc. of Philosophy 1992–, German-Hungarian Soc. of Philosophy 1993–2005, Chilean-German Soc. of Philosophy 1995–, German-Romanian Soc. of Philosophy 2000–, German-Russian Soc. for the Philosophy of Science and Technology 2002–, Int. Inst. of Philosophy (World Acad.) 2005–; Vice-Pres. Féd. Int. des Sociétés de Philosophie 1998–2003; mem. American Acad. of Kinesiology and Physical Educ., Nat. Olympic Cttee for Germany –1992, German UNESCO Comm. –1992, Inst. Int. de Philosophie 1994 (mem. Bd 1996–2000), Int. Acad. of Philosophy of Science 1995–; Hon. mem. Int. Olympic Acad., Romanian Acad. of Science, Dept of Philosophy 2001; Dr hc (Deutsche Sporthochschule, Cologne) 1986, (Córdoba) twice 1992, (Tech. Univ. Budapest) 1993, (Univ. Pécs) 1994, Moscow (Univ. of Humanistic Studies) 1995, (Int. Ind. Univ. for Ecology and Politology) 2001, Rostov 2002; four German, two European and one Olympic title for rowing, Silver Leaf of Fed. Pres. 1959, 1960, Scientific Diem Plaque 1962, Sievert Award (Olympian Int.) 1973, Noel Baker Prize (UNESCO) 1978, Outstanding Academic Book Award (USA) 1979, Outstanding Intellectual and Outstanding Scholar of the 20th Century (IBC), Man of the Year 2000 (ABI), American 'Hall of Fame' (ABI) 2002, mem. Russian Acad. of Science 2003, Lifetime Achievement Award (IBC) 2003, Fed. Pres. of Germany's Great Merit Cross 2005, World Achievement Award (ABI) 2008. *Achievements include:* Olympic Champion, Eight Oar Crew 1960, two European championships in rowing, Amateur Coach World Champion Eight Oar Crew 1966. *Publications:* more than 125 books, including Kritik der logischen Konstanten 1968, Team Dynamics 1977, Pragmatische Vernunft 1979, Social Philosophy of Athletics 1979, Zur Sozialphilosophie der Technik 1982, Eigenleistung 1983, Zwischen Wissenschaftstheorie und Sozialwissenschaft 1985, Zwischen Sozialpsychologie und Sozialphilosophie 1987, Kritik der kleinen Vernunft 1987, Das Prinzip Fairness 1989, Tagebuch einer Rückreise 1991, Prometheisches Philosophieren zwischen Praxis und Paradox 1991, Zwischen Wissenschaft und Ethik 1992, Philosophie und Interpretation 1993, Interpretationskonstrukte 1993, Macht und Machtbarkeit der Technik 1994, Schemaspiele 1995, Interpretation und Realität 1995, Einführung in die angewandte Ethik 1997, Einführung in die Erkenntnistheorie 1998, Konkrete Humanität 1998, Praxisnahes Philosophieren 1999, Erfassung der Wirklichkeit 2000, Kreative Aufstiege 2000, Albert Schweitzer – Ethik als Konkrate Humanität 2000, Advances and Problems in the Philosophy of Technology (ed.) 2001, Das Denken und sein Gehalt 2001, Kleine Philosophie des Gehirns 2001, Denken und Handlungsbindung 2001, Erfolg oder Fairness? 2002, Natur-Umwelt-Ethik 2003, Grasping Reality 2003, Bewurstein als Schema interpretation 2004, Wittgenstein y el giro pragmatico en la Filosofía 2005, Veranwortung und Gewissen des Forschers 2006, Das Gefass 2006, Ethics Facing Globalization (co-ed.) 2006, Kant Today (chief ed.) 2006, Bewusstsein Kreativität und Leistung 2007, Global Technoscience and Responsibility 2007, Humanitätsforschung als interdisziplinäre Anthropologie 2008; more than 1,200 articles. *Address:* Universität (TH) Karlsruhe, Institut für Philosophie, Kollegium am Schloss, Bau 2, 76128 Karlsruhe (office); Neubrunnenschlag 15, 76337 Waldbronn, Germany (home). *Telephone:* (721) 6082149 (office); (7243) 67971 (home). *Fax:* (721) 6083084 (office); (7243) 980120 (home). *E-mail:* sekretariat@rz.uni-karlsruhe.de (office); hans.lenk@philosophie.uni-karlsruhe.de (home). *Website:* www.rz.uni-karlsruhe.de/~philosophie/lenk.html (office).

LENK, Thomas; German sculptor and graphic artist; b. 15 June 1933, Berlin; s. of Franz Lenk and Anneliese Lenk (née Hoernecke); m. Maria Bendig 1959; two d.; Guest Prof., Heluwan Univ., Cairo 1978; mem. Humboldt-Gesellschaft 1992; Hon. Life mem., Art Gallery of Ont., Toronto 1988; Carnegie Int. Purchase Award 1967, Third Prize, Socha Piestanskych Parkov, Bratislava 1969, Prize of 2nd Norwegian Graphics Biennale 1974, Verleihung des Professorentitels 1989. *Address:* Hübscher Weg 2017, 74523 Schwäbisch Hall, Germany. *Telephone:* (791) 9566490.

LENNINGS, Manfred, DrIng; German industrialist; b. 23 Feb. 1934, Oberhausen; s. of Wilhelm Lennings and Amanda Albert; m. Renate Stelbrink 1961; one s. one d.; ed Gymnasium Geislingen/Steige, Univ. of Munich and Bergakademie Clausthal; Chair. German Student Org. 1959–60; Asst of Man. Bd, Gutehoffnungshütte Aktienverein 1964–67, Deputy mem. 1969, Chair. 1975–83; mem. Man. Bd, Deutsche Werft AG 1968–69; Chair. Man. Bd Howaldtswerke-Deutsche Werft AG 1970–74; Consultant, Westdeutsche Landesbank 1984–99; Consultant 1999–; Chair. Supervisory Bd Gildemeister AG, Heitkamp-Deilmann-Haniel GmbH; fmr Chair. Supervisory Bd Fried Krupp AG Hoesch-Krupp; mem. Supervisory Bd Thyssen Krupp AG, Deutsche Post AG, IVG Immobilien AG, Bayer AG –2002. *Leisure interests:* modern painting and literature, swimming. *Address:* Schmachtenbergstrasse 142, 45219 Essen, Germany. *Telephone:* (2054) 12020. *Fax:* (2054) 120222.

LENNKH, Georg, LLD; Austrian diplomatist; *Special Envoy for Africa for the Austrian Presidency, European Union;* b. 8 Dec. 1939, Graz; s. of Friedrich Lennkh and Elisabeth Lennkh; m. Annie Lechevalier 1966; one s. one d.; ed Univ. of Graz, Johns Hopkins School of Advanced Informational Studies, Bologna and Univ. of Chapel Hill, NC, USA; entered Fed. Ministry for Foreign Affairs 1965; served Tokyo 1968–72, Austrian Mission to UN, New York 1972–76, Dept for Int. Orgs, Ministry of Foreign Affairs 1976–78; served Cabinet Office of Fed. Chancellor Kreisky, with responsibility for foreign relations 1978–82; Perm. Rep. to OECD 1982–93; Dir Gen. Dept for Devt Cooperation, Fed. Ministry of Foreign Affairs 1993, currently Special Envoy for Africa for the Austrian Presidency, EU; Pres. Global Forum on Sustainable Energy. *Leisure interest:* skiing. *Address:* Ministry for Foreign Affairs, Ballhausplatz 2, 1014 Vienna, Austria. *Telephone:* (1) 531-15-0. *Fax:* (1) 535-45-30. *E-mail:* georg.lennkh@aon.at; georg.lennkh@bmaa.gv.at (office). *Website:* www.bmaa.gv.at (office).

LENNOX, Annie, ARAM; British rock singer and lyricist; b. 25 Dec. 1954, Aberdeen, Scotland; d. of late Thomas A. Lennox and of Dorothy Lennox (née Ferguson); m. 1st Rahda Raman 1984 (divorced); m. 2nd Uri Fruchtmann; one s. two d.; ed Aberdeen High School for Girls, Royal Acad. of Music; Founder-mem. (with Dave Stewart q.v.) The Catch 1977, renamed The Tourists 1979–80, Eurythmics 1980–89, 1999–; numerous Eurythmics tours worldwide; solo artist 1988–; Dr hc (Royal Scottish Acad. of Music and Drama, Glasgow) 2006; American Soc. of Composers Award, BPI Award for Best

Female Vocalist 1982/83, 1987/88, 1989/90, 1992/93, Grammy Award for Best Female Performance (for Sweet Dreams) 1983, Ivor Novello Award for Best Pop Song (for Sweet Dreams, with Dave Stewart) 1983, MTV Music Award for Best New Artist Video (for Sweet Dreams (Are Made Of This)) 1984, Ivor Novello Award for Best Song (for It's Alright (Baby's Coming Back, with Dave Stewart) 1987, Ivor Novello Award for Best Song (for Why) 1992, BRIT Award for Best Female Solo Artist 1996, Grammy Award for Best Female Pop Vocals (for No More I Love You) 1996, BRIT Award for Outstanding Contrib. to Music 1999, Tartan Cleff Award 2001, Acad. Award for Best Song (for Into the West and Use Well the Days, from the film Lord of the Rings: The Two Towers) 2004, ASCAP Founders Award 2006. *Film:* Revolution 1985. *Recordings include:* albums: with The Tourists: The Tourists 1979, Reality Affect 1980, Luminous Basement 1980; with Eurythmics: In The Garden 1981, Sweet Dreams (Are Made of This) (Grammy Award for Best Video Album) 1982, Touch 1983, 1984 (For The Love of Big Brother) 1984, Be Yourself Tonight 1985, Revenge 1986, Savage 1987, We Too Are One 1989, Peace 1999, The Ultimate Collection 2005; solo: Diva (BPI Award for Best Album) 1992, Medusa 1995, Train In Vain 1995, Bare 2003, Songs of Mass Destruction 2007. *Address:* 19 Management, 33 Ransomes Dock, 35–37 Parkgate Road, London, SW11 4NP, England (office). *Telephone:* (20) 7801-1919 (office). *Fax:* (20) 7801-1920 (office). *Website:* www.annielennox.co.uk; www.eurythmics.com.

LENNOX-BOYD, Simon Ronald Rupert (see BOYD OF MERTON, 2nd Viscount).

LENO, Jay, BA; American comedian; *Host, The Tonight Show;* b. (James Douglas Muir Leno), 28 April 1950, New Rochelle, NY; m. Mavis Nicholson; ed Emerson Coll., Boston, Mass; started career as stand-up comedian and comedy writer in 1970s; named one of several guest hosts Tonight Show (NBC) 1986, exclusive guest host 1987–92, Host 1992–; Emmy Award 1995. *Films include:* American Hot Wax 1978, Silver Bears 1978, Americathon 1979, What's Up, Hideous Sun Demon (voice) 1983, Collision Course 1989, We're Back! A Dinosaur's Story (voice) 1993, The Flintstones 1994, Robots (voice) 2005, Ice Age: The Meltdown (voice) 2006, Cars (voice) 2006, Ice Age 2: The Meltdown (voice) 2006, The Astronaut Farmer 2007. *Leisure interests:* classic cars and motorcycles. *Address:* The Tonight Show with Jay Leno, 3000 West Alameda Avenue, Burbank, CA 91523 (office); c/o ICM, 8942 Wilshire Boulevard, Beverly Hills, CA 90211, USA. *Website:* www.nbc.com/The_Tonight_Show_with_Jay_Leno/index.shtml.

LENZ, Carl Otto, DJur; German lawyer; b. 5 June 1930, Berlin; s. of the late Dr Otto Lenz and of Marieliese Pohl; m. Ursula Heinrich 1960; two s. three d.; ed schools in Germany and Switzerland, Univs of Bonn, Freiburg and Munich, Germany, Univ. of Fribourg, Switzerland, and Harvard and Cornell Univs, USA; Sec.-Gen. Christian Democratic Group, European Parl. 1956–66; mem. Bundestag 1965–84; Advocate-Gen. European Court of Justice 1984–97; Hon. Prof. of European Law, Saarland Univ. 1990–; Grosses Bundesverdienstkreuz 1976, Grosseskreuz des Verdienstordens (Grand Duchy of Luxembourg) 1998 and numerous other honours. *Publications:* Die Notverstandsverfassung des GG 1971, EG Handbuch Recht im Binnenmarkt 1994, EG-Vortrag Kommentar 1994. *Address:* Baker & McKenzie LLP, Bethmannstrasse 50-54, 60311 Frankfurt am Main (office); Rodensteinstrasse 22, 64625 Bensheim, Germany. *Telephone:* (69) 29908-189 (office). *Fax:* (69) 29908-108 (office). *E-mail:* otto.c.lenz@bakernet.com (office). *Website:* www.bakernet.com/BakerNet/Locations/Europe%20Middle%20East/Offices/Germany/default.htm.

LENZ, Guy; Luxembourg army officer; b. 28 Jan. 1946, Pétange; s. of Louis Lenz and Hélène Ludovicy; m. Liliane Wetz; two d.; ed Belgian Infantry School, Armed Forces Staff Coll., Norfolk, Va; rank of Lt 1973, Capt. 1976, Maj. 1982, Lt-Col 1986, Col 1998; Chief of Staff of the Luxembourg Army 1998–; served as Head of Operations and Training, Deputy Commdr of the Mil. Training Centre; Head of GIVO at HQ, Mil. Councillor at NATO; Mil. Rep. at SHAPE; Perm. Rep. to NATO Mil. Cttee; Mil. Del. WEU Perm. Council; Commdr, Ordre de Mérite, Cross for 25 years service; Kt Order of Civilian and Mil. 'Mérite de Adolphe de Nassau', Meritorious Service Medal (USA), Commdr Ordre de la Couronne de Chêne (Belgium); Kt, Ordre d'Orange Nassau (Netherlands). *Address:* Headquarters of the Armed Forces, 38–44 rue Goethe, BP 873, 1018 Luxembourg (office); 50 rue um Böchel, 9017 Ettelbruck, Luxembourg (home). *Telephone:* 488836 (office); 819680 (home). *Fax:* 402605 (office); 819680 (home). *E-mail:* burcema@pt.lu (office).

LENZ, Siegfried; German writer; b. 17 March 1926, Lyck, East Prussia; m. Liselotte Lenz; ed High School, Samter and Univ. of Hamburg; Cultural Ed. Die Welt 1949–51; freelance writer 1952–; Hon. Citizen of Hamburg 2001–; Gerhart Hauptmann Prize 1961, Bremer Literaturpreis 1962, German Freemasons' Literary Prize 1970, Kulturpreis, Goslar 1978, Bayern Literary Prize 1995, Goethe Prize 1999, Lev Kopelev Prize for Peace and Human Rights 2009. *Publications:* include: Es waren Habichte in der Luft 1951, Duell mit dem Schatten 1953, So zärtlich was Suleyken 1955, Das schönste Fest der Welt 1956, Das Kabinett der Konterbande 1956, Der Mann im Strom 1957, 1958, Jäger des Spotts 1958, Lukas, sanftmütiger Knecht 1958, Brot und Spiele 1959, Das Feuerschiff 1960, Zait der Schuldlosen 1961, Stimmungen der See 1962, Stadtgespräche 1963, Das Gesicht 1964, Lehmanns Erzählungen 1964, Der Spielverderber 1965, Haussuchung 1967, Deutschstunde 1968, Leute von Hamburg 1968, Die Augenbinde 1970, Das Vorbild 1973, Wie bei Gogol 1973, Einstein überquert die Elbe bei Hamburg 1975, Heimatmuseum 1978, Drei Stücke 1980, Der Verlust 1981, Ein Kriegsende 1984, Das serbische Mädchen 1987, Die Auflehnung 1994, Ludmilla 1996, Arnes Nachlass 1999, Fundbüro 2003, Zaungast 2004, Die Erzählungen 2006, Ein Freund der Regierung 2006, Schweigeminute 2008, Kummer mit jütländischen Kaffeetafeln 2008, Der Anfang von etwas 2009; stories: So zärtlich war Suleyken 1955, Jäger des Spotts 1958, Das Feuerschiff 1960, Der Spielverderber 1965, Einstein überquert die Elbe bei Hamburg 1975; plays: Zeit der Schuldlosen 1961, Das Gesicht 1963, Haussuchung (radio plays) 1967. *Address:* c/o Hoffman und Campe Verlag, Harvestehuder Weg 42, 20149 Hamburg, Germany (office). *E-mail:* email@hoca.de (office). *Website:* www.hoca.de (office).

LEÓN PORTILLA, Miguel, PhD; Mexican anthropologist and historian; b. 22 Feb. 1926, Mexico City; s. of Miguel León Ortiz and Luisa Portilla Nájera; m. Ascensión Hernández Triviño 1965; one d.; ed Loyola Univ. of Los Angeles and Nat. Univ. of Mexico; Sec.-Gen. Inter-American Indian Inst. 1955–59, Asst Dir 1959–60, Dir 1960–66; Asst Dir Seminar for Náhuatl Culture, Nat. Univ. of Mexico 1956, Dir Inst. of Historical Research 1963–78, Prof. Emer. 1988–; Dir América Indígena 1960; Adviser, Int. Inst. of Different Civilisations 1960; Perm. Rep. of Mexico to UNESCO, Paris 1987; mem. Bd Govs Nat. Univ. Mexico 1976; mem. American Anthropological Asscn 1960–, Mexican Acad. of Language 1962–, Société des Américanistes de Paris 1966–, Mexican Acad. of History 1969–, Nat. Coll. of Mexico 1971–; Corresp. mem. Royal Spanish Acad. of History 1969–; Guggenheim Fellow 1969; Fellow, Portuguese Acad. of History, Lisbon 1995, NAS 1995; Hon. mem. American Historical Asscn 1991, NAS 1995; Commendatore Repub. Italiana 1977, Great Cross of Alfonso X el sabio (Spain) 1998, Ordre des Palmes académiques 2000, Orden del Mérito Civico (en grado de Gran Cruz) (Spain) 2003; Hon. PhD (Southern Methodist Univ., Dallas, Tex.) 1980, (California) 1986, (Tel-Aviv) 1987, (Toulouse) 1990, (Colima) 1993, (San Andrés, Bolivia) 1994, (Brown Univ.) 1996, (Carolina Univ., Prague) 2000; Fifth Distinguished Lecturer, American Anthropological Asscn 1974, Serra Award 1978, Nat. Prize in the Social Sciences (Mexico) 1981, Manuel Gamio Anthropological Award 1983, Nat. Univ. of Mexico Prize 1994, Belisario Domínguez Medal (Mexico) 1997, Bartolomé de las Casas Prize (Spain) 2001, Investigador Nacional de Excelencia (Mexico) 2002, Presea 'Estado de Mexico 2001' 2002, Universidad Latinoamericana Prize, 2003, Veracruz Prize 2003, Medalla Ignacio de la Llave 2003, recognized for his historical investigations over 46 years by UNAM 2003, Toltecáyod Prize, Universidad de Tula Hidalgo 2005, Tlamatili Prize, Universidad Iberoamericana, Mexico 2005, Fundación México Unido Prize 2005, Chiapas Prize 2006. *Publications:* La Filosofía Náhuatl 1956, Visión des los Vencidos 1959, Los Antiguos Mexicanos 1961, The Broken Spears, Aztec Account of the Conquest of Mexico 1962, Rückkehr der Götter 1962, Aztec Thought and Culture 1963, Literaturas Precolombinas de México 1964, Imagen del México Antiguo 1964, Le Crépuscule des Aztèques 1965, Trece Poetas del Mundo Azteca 1967, Pre-Columbian Literatures of Mexico 1968, Tiempo y Realidad en el Pensamiento Maya 1968, Testimonios Sudcalifornianos 1970, De Teotihuacan a los Aztecas 1971, The Norteño Variety of Mexican Culture 1972, The Voyages of Francisco de Ortega to California 1632–1636 1972, Time and Reality in the Thought of the Maya 1973, Historia Natural y Crónica de la Antigua California 1973, Il Rovescio della Conquista, Testimonianze Asteche, Maya e Inca 1974, Aztecs and Navajos 1975, Endangered Cultures: The Indian in Latin America 1975, Indian Place Names of Baja California 1977, L'Envers de la conquête 1977, Los Manifestos en Náhuatl de Emiliano Zapata 1978, Toltecayotl, Aspectos de la Cultura Náhuatl 1980, Mesoamerican Spirituality 1980, Middle America 1981, Literaturas de Anahuac y del Imcario 1982, Mesoamerica before 1519 1984, Codex Fejerváry-Mayer, a Book of the Merchants, 1985, La Pensée Aztèque 1985, Libro de los Coloquios 1986, Das Alte Mexiko: Religion 1986, Huehuehtlahtolli, Testimonies of the Ancient Word 1988, Mesoamerica in 1492 and on the eve of 1992, 1988, Poésie Náhuatl d'amour et d'amitié 1991, Fifteen Poets of the Aztec World 1992, The Aztec Image of Self and Society 1992, Raíces indígenas, presencia hispánica 1993, La flecha en el blanco 1995, Bernardino de Sahagún: Pionero de la antropología 1999, Tonantzin Guadalupe 2000, La Visión de los Vencidos (published in English as The Broken Spear), La Filosofía Náhuatl (published as Aztec Thought and Culture), Motivos de la Antropología Americanista, Indagación en la Diferencia 2001, In the Language of Kings – An Anthology of Mesoamerican Literature Pre-Columbian to the Present 2001, México an 1554, Tres Diálogos Latinos de Francisco Cervantes de Salazr 2001, Los hombres que disperso la danza 2002, Ordenanzas de Tema Indígena en Castella y náhuatl – Expedidas par Maximiliano de Habsburgo 2003, Codices – Los antiguos libros del Nuevo Mundo 2003, Obras de Miguel León-Portillo, Pueblos Indígenas de México – Autonomía y Diferencia Cultural 2003, Obras de Miguel León-Portillo – En torno a la Historia de Mesoamérica 2004, Aztecas-Mexicas – Desarrollo de una civilización originaria 2005. *Leisure interests:* scouting and gardening. *Address:* Instituto de Investigaciones Históricas, Circuitro Mtro. Maria de la Cueva, Zona Cultural, Ciudad Universitaria, UNAM, 04510 México, DF (office); Alberto Zamora 131 antes 103, Col. Coyoacán, 04520 Delegación, México, DF, Mexico (home). *Telephone:* (5) 665-44-17 (office); (55) 54-08-02 (home). *Fax:* (5) 665-0070 (office). *E-mail:* portilla@servidor.unam.mx (office).

LEONARD, Brian Edmund, PhD, DSc, MRIA; Irish pharmacologist and academic; *Professor Emeritus of Pharmacology, National University of Ireland, Galway;* b. 30 May 1936, Winchester, Hants., England; s. of Harold E. Leonard and Dorothy Coley; m. Helga F. Mühlpfordt 1959; two d.; ed Univ. of Birmingham; Dept of Medical Biochemistry, Univ. of Birmingham 1956–62; Lecturer in Pharmacology, Univ. of Nottingham 1962–68; Tech. Officer, CNS Research, ICI Pharmaceuticals Div. Alderley Park, Cheshire 1968–71; Group Leader, CNS Pharmacology, Organon International BV, Oss, Netherlands 1971–74; Prof. of Pharmacology, Univ. Coll. (now Nat. Univ. of Ireland) Galway 1974–, Prof. Emer. 1999–; Councillor, CINP 1996–2000, Treas. 1992–96, Pres. Elect 2002–04, Pres. 2004–06; Visiting Prof., Brain and Behaviour Research Inst., Maastricht Univ.; Pres. British Asscn Psychopharmacology 1988–90; Past Pres. Int. Soc. for the Investigation of Stress; Assoc. mem. Royal Coll. of Psychiatrists; Foreign Corresp. mem. American Coll. Neuropsychopharmacology; Visiting Fellow, Magdalen Coll. Oxford 1990–91; Hon. Prof., Faculty of Medicine, Queen's Univ. Belfast, NI, Dept of Psychiatry,

www.worldwhoswho.com

Univ. of Hong Kong 2004–06; Hon. mem. S African Asscn of Psychiatrists; Silver Medal, Royal Irish Acad. 1996. *Publications:* Fundamentals of Psychopharmacology 1992, Fundamentals of Psychoimmunology 2000; over 400 articles in int. scientific journals. *Leisure interests:* entomology, classical music, political science. *Address:* Pharmacology Department, National University of Ireland, University Road, Galway (office); Currabhaitia, Tullykyne, Moycullen, Co. Galway, Ireland (home). *Telephone:* (91) 524411 (ext. 3837) (office); (91) 555292 (home). *Fax:* (91) 525700 (office). *E-mail:* belucg@iol.ie (home). *Website:* www.nuigalway.ie/pharmacology (office).

LEONARD, Elmore, PhB; American novelist and screenwriter; b. 11 Oct. 1925, New Orleans; s. of Elmore John and Flora Amelia Leonard (née Rivé); m. 1st Beverly Claire Cline 1949 (divorced 1977); three s. two d.; m. 2nd Joan Leanne Lancaster 1979 (died 1993); m. 3rd Christine Kent 1993; ed Univ. of Detroit; mem. Writers' Guild of America, Authors' Guild, MWA, Western Writers of America, PEN; Hon. DLitt (Florida Atlantic Univ.) 1995, (Univ. of Detroit Mercy) 1997; MWA Edgar Allan Poe Award 1984, MWA Grand Master Award 1992, Mich. Foundation for the Arts Award for Literature 1985, Cartier Diamond Dagger Award 2006. *Publications:* novels: The Bounty Hunters 1953, The Law at Randado 1954, Escape from Five Shadows 1956, Last Stand at Saber River 1959, Hombre 1961, The Big Bounce 1969, The Moonshine War 1969, Valdez is Coming 1970, Forty Lashes Less One 1972, Mr Majestyk 1974, Fifty-Two Pickup 1974, Swag 1976, Unknown Man # 89 1977, The Hunted 1977, The Switch 1978, Gold Coast 1980, Gun Sights 1979, City Primeval 1980, Split Images 1981, Cat Chaser 1982, Stick 1983, La Brava 1983, Glitz 1985, Bandits 1986, Touch 1987, Freaky Deaky 1988, Killshot 1989, Get Shorty 1990, Maximum Bob 1991, Rum Punch 1992, Pronto 1993, Riding the Rap 1995, Out of Sight 1996, Jackie Brown 1997, Cuba Libre (also film screenplay) 1998, Be Cool (also film screenplay) 1999, Pagan Babies 2000, Tishomingo Blues 2002, When the Women Come Out to Dance 2002, A Coyote's in the House (juvenile) 2004, Mr Paradise 2004, The Hot Kid 2005, Comfort to the Enemy 2005, Up In Honey's Room 2007, Road Dogs 2009; short story collections: Dutch Treat 1985, Double Dutch Treat 1986, The Tonto Woman and Other Stories 1998, The Complete Western Stories 2006. *Address:* c/o Michael Siegel, 9150 Wilshire Blvd, Suite 350, Beverly Hills, CA 90212, USA. *Website:* www.elmoreleonard.com.

LEONARD, Rt Rev. Monsignor and Rt Hon. Graham Douglas, KCVO, PC, MA, DD, STD; British ecclesiastic; b. 8 May 1921, Greenwich; s. of the late Rev. Douglas Leonard; m. Vivien Priscilla Swann 1943; two s.; ed Monkton Combe School, Balliol Coll. Oxford, Westcott House, Cambridge; Capt. Oxon. and Bucks. Light Infantry 1941–45, Army Operational Research Group 1944–45; ordained Deacon 1947, Priest 1948; Curacies 1948–52; Vicar of Ardleigh 1952–55; Dir Religious Educ., Diocese of St Albans, Canon, St Albans Cathedral 1955–58; Gen. Sec. Nat. Soc. and Gen. Sec. Church of England Schools Council 1958–62; Archdeacon of Hampstead, Rector of St Andrew Undershaft and St Mary Axe 1962–64; Bishop of Willesden 1964–73, of Truro 1973–81, of London 1981–91; received into Roman Catholic Church and ordained conditionally as a priest April 1994; mem. Anglican/Orthodox Joint Doctrinal Comm. 1974–81; Superior Gen. Soc. of Mary 1973–94 (Vice-Pres. 1994–); Chair. Church of England Bd for Social Responsibility 1976–83, Churches Main Cttee 1981–91, BBC and IBA Cen. Religious Advisory Cttee 1984–89, Bd of Educ. 1983–88; Pres. Path to Rome Int. Convention 1998–2001; mem. Polytechnics and Colls Funding Council 1989–93; Dean of HM Chapels Royal 1981–91, Prelate of Order of British Empire 1981–91, Prelate Imperial Soc. of Kts Bachelor 1986–91; Episcopal Canon of Jerusalem 1981–91; John Findlay Green Foundation Lecture, Fulton 1987; Hensley Henson Lecturer, Oxford Univ. 1991–92; Hon. Fellow Balliol Coll. Oxford 1986; Hon. Bencher, Middle Temple 1981; Prelate of Honour of His Holiness 2000; Hon. DD (Episcopal Theological Seminary, Kentucky) 1974; Hon. DCnL (Nashotah House) 1983; Hon. STD (Siena Coll.) 1994; Hon. LLD (Simon Greenleaf School of Law) 1987; Hon. DD (Westminster Coll. Fulton) 1987; Hon. DLitt (CNAA) 1989. *Publications:* The Gospel is for Everyone 1971, God Alive: Priorities in Pastoral Theology 1981, Firmly I Believe and Truly 1985, Life in Christ 1986, Path to Rome (contrib.) 1999; contribs to several theological works. *Leisure interests:* music, reading. *Address:* 25 Woodlands Road, Witney, Oxon., OX28 2DR, England.

LEONARD, Hugh Terence; New Zealand broadcasting executive; b. 20 July 1938, Greymouth; s. of Michael James Leonard and Elizabeth Leonard (née Storey); m. Pauline Lobendahn 1965; one s. two d.; joined NZ Broadcasting Service 1956, Fiji Broadcasting Comm. 1960, Gen. Man. 1973–85; Sec.-Gen. Asia-Pacific Broadcasting Union 1985–2002, Special Adviser to the Pres. 2002–03 (retd); Fiji Independence Medal 1970. *Leisure interests:* classic motorcycles, remote-controlled model aircraft, computers. *Address:* c/o Asia-Pacific Broadcasting Union, PO Box 1164, 59700 Kuala Lumpur, Malaysia. *Telephone:* (3) 22823592.

LEONARD, Jason, MBE; British professional rugby football player (rugby union); b. 14 Aug. 1968, Barking, Essex; s. of Frank Leonard and Maria Leonard; two s. one d.; ed Warren Comprehensive, Chadwell Heath, Essex; prop forward (usually loose-head); teams: Barking, Saracens, Harlequins 1990– (264 appearances, five tries), England Under-21, England A (2 caps), England 1990– (debut versus Argentina); 114 Tests (world record) for England (2 as Capt.), one try, to 31 March 2004; mem. Grand Slam winning squads 1991, 1992, 1995, 2003, Five Nations Championship winners 1999, Six Nations Championship winners 2000, 2001, World Cup winning squad 2003, runners-up 1991, 4th place 1995; mem. British Lions' team, New Zealand (2 Tests) 1993, South Africa (1 Test), 1997 Australia (2 Tests) 2001; Freeman, City of Greater London. *Address:* c/o Harlequins Football Club, Stoop Memorial Ground, Craneford Way, Twickenham, Middx, TW2 7SQ, England

(office). *Telephone:* (20) 8410-6000 (office). *Fax:* (20) 8410-6001 (office). *E-mail:* kerries@quins.co.uk (office). *Website:* www.harlequins.co.uk (office).

LEONARD, Ray Charles ("Sugar Ray"); American fmr professional boxer; b. 17 May 1956, Wilmington, NC; s. of Cicero Leonard and Getha Leonard; m. 1st Juanita Wilkinson 1980 (divorced 1990); two s.; m. 2nd Bernadette Robi 1993; one s. one d.; ed Palmer Park High School, Md; amateur boxer 1970–77; won 140 of 145 amateur fights; world amateur champion 1974, US Amateur Athletic Union champion 1974, Pan-American Games gold medallist 1975, Olympic gold medallist 1976; guaranteed record purse of US $25,000 for first professional fight Feb. 1977; won North American welterweight title from Pete Ranzany August 1979; won World Boxing Council version of world welterweight title from Wilfred Benitez Nov. 1979; retained title against Dave Green March 1980, lost it to Roberto Durán (q.v.), Montréal, June 1980, regained it from Durán, New Orleans, Nov. 1980; world jr middleweight title, World Boxing Asscn (WBA) June 1981; won WBA world welterweight title from Tommy Hearns to become undisputed world champion Sept. 1981, drew rematch June 1989; 36 professional fights, 33 wins, lost two, drawn one; retd from boxing Nov. 1982; returned to the ring April 1987; won World middleweight title, lost to Terry Norris 1991, retd from boxing 1991; returned to ring March 1997; lost Int. Boxing Council middleweight title fight to Hector Camacho 1997; boxing promoter (Sugar Ray Leonard Boxing); commentator for Home Box Office TV Co.; motivational speaker; Ring magazine's Fighter of the Decade for the 1980s. *Television:* The Contender 2005. *Address:* Suite 206-B, 4401 East West Highway, Bethesda, MD 20814, USA. *Telephone:* (310) 471-3100 (office). *Website:* www.srlboxing.com (office).

LEONG, Alan, LLB, LLM; Chinese barrister and politician; *Member, Legislative Council of Hong Kong;* b. 22 Feb. 1958, Hong Kong; m.; three c.; ed Wah Yan Coll., Kowloon, Univ. of Hong Kong, Univ. of Cambridge, UK; called to Hong Kong Bar 1983, to Inner Bar 1998 (first to be apptd after establishment of Hong Kong Special Admin. Region; mem. Legis. Council (Civic Party) representing Kowloon East 2004– (nominated as Civic Party cand. for 2007 election for Chief Exec.); Chair. Special Cttee on Mainland Practice and Relations; Chair. Asscn of Heads of Secondary Schools of Tsuen Wan, Kwai Chung and Tsing Yi Dist 1998–; Chair. Water Pollution Control Appeal Bd 2001–; Dir Applied Research Council 2000–; mem. Criminal and Law Enforcement Injuries Compensation Bd 2000–, Ind. Police Complaints Council 2000–, Hong Kong Bar Asscn 2000– (Chair. 2001–03), Professional Services Advisory Cttee Hong Kong Trade Devt Council 2002–, Chief Justice's Steering Cttee on Implementation of Use of Chinese in the Courts 1996–2003, Task Group on Promotion of English Standards in the Workplace, Standing Cttee on Language Educ. and Research 1999–2000, Cen. Policy Unit Panel on Social Cohesion 2002–03, Cttee of Bilingual Legal System in Hong Kong 1998–2004; Pres. Kwai Tsing Lions Club 1998–99; Chair. Task Force on Accreditation re Internship, Advisory Cttee on Teacher Educ. and Qualification 2003; Bar's Rep. on the Working Group on Review of Legal Educ. and Training 1999–2002; Hon. Lecturer, Dept of Professional Legal Educ., Univ. of Hong Kong 2002–. *Address:* Room 601D, Citibank Tower, 3 Garden Road, Central, Hong Kong Special Administrative Region, People's Republic of China (office). *Telephone:* 25093116 (office). *Fax:* 25093101 (office). *E-mail:* al@alanleong.net (office); contact@alanleong.net (office). *Website:* www.alanleong.net (office).

LEONG, Lampo, MFA, PhD; American (b. Chinese) artist and academic; *Associate Professor of Art and Chair, Art Department, University of Missouri-Columbia;* b. (Liang Lanbo), 3 July 1961, Guangzhou; ed Central Acad. of Fine Arts, Guangzhou, Acad. of Fine Arts and California Coll. of Arts & Crafts, Oakland, USA; Instructor, Calif. Coll. of Arts and Crafts 1986–87; Lecturer, San Francisco State Univ., Calif. 1988–96, Visiting Asst Prof. 1996–2001; Assoc. Prof. of Art, Univ. of Missouri-Columbia 2001–, also Chair., Art Dept; Instructor, Univ. of Calif., Berkeley 1989, Art Studio 1990–; Instructor Chabot Coll., Hayward, Calif. 1989–94, Diablo Valley Coll., Pleasant Hill, Calif. 1998–; Guest Speaker Asian Art Museum of San Francisco 1985, 1990, 1992, 1994, 1996–2001, Univ. of Calif., Berkeley, Dept of Art History 1997, 1998, 2001, 2006, Stanford Univ. Inst. for Int. Studies 1999, 2000, Univ. of Minnesota 2005, 2006; over 55 solo exhbns and 250 group exhbns Japan, China, Macao, Hong Kong, Taiwan, Canada, USA, England, France, Spain 1981–; works in 20 museums and many public collections world-wide including Japan, China, Hong Kong, Macao, Taiwan, Indonesia, Canada, USA, Germany; Vice-Pres. Oriental Art Asscn, USA; Co-Founder, Dir Chinese–American Culture Exchange Asscn, USA; mem. Nat. Modern Meticulous Painting Soc., China, Macao Soc. of Social Sciences; Gold Medal Award, 15th Macao Painting Exhbn 1998, Mayoral Proclamation: Lampo Leong Day (Nov. 19th), City of San Francisco 1999, Macao, Winner Tulane Review Art Contest 2002, Juror's Award, Ninth Great Plains Nat. Art Exhbn 2003, Best of Show, 42nd Annual Exhbn, Sumi-e Soc. of America 2005, Diploma of Excellence, Medial 1.Art Biennial, Medial Museum, London 2005, Top Ten Award, Exposição Annual de Artes Visuais, Instituto Cultural do Governo da Macao 2007, Faculty-Alumni Awards, Univ. of Missouri-Columbia 2007, Cover Award, New Art International, NewYork 2009. *Publications:* contributor to numerous art books and journals, including 37 essays and over 810 reviews and publications internationally. *Leisure interests:* photography, film, travel, ballroom dancing. *Address:* Department of Art, A129 Fine Arts, University of Missouri-Columbia, Columbia, MO 65211, USA (office). *Telephone:* (573) 882-3761 (office); (573) 874-7931 (home). *Fax:* (573) 884-6807 (office). *E-mail:* leongl@missouri.edu (office). *Website:* www.LampoLeong.com (office).

LEONI, Téa; American actress; b. 25 Feb. 1966; m. 1st Neil Tardio; m. 2nd David Duchovny (q.v.) 1997; two c. *Films:* Switch 1991, A League of Their Own 1992, Wyatt Earp 1994, Bad Boys 1995, Flirting with Disaster 1996, Deep

Impact 1998, There's No Fish Food in Heaven 1999, Life in the Fast Lane 1999, The Family Man 2000, Jurassic Park III 2001, Hollywood Ending 2002, People I Know 2003, House of D 2004, Spanglish 2004, Fun with Dick and Jane 2005, You Kill Me 2007, Ghost Town 2008. *Television:* (sitcoms) Naked Truth, Flying Blind 1995. *Address:* ICM, 8942 Wilshire Boulevard, Beverly Hills, CA 90211, USA (office).

LEONOV, Maj.-Gen. Aleksey Arkhipovich; Russian cosmonaut; *Vice-President, Alfa Bank;* b. 30 May 1934, Listvianka, Kamerovo Region; s. of Arkhip Leonov and Yevdokia Leonova; m. Svetlana Leonova; two d.; ed Kremenchug Air Force School for Pilots, Chuguevsky Air Force School for Pilots and Zhukovsky Air Force Engineering Academy; Pilot 1956–59; mem. CPSU 1957–91; cosmonaut training 1960; first man to walk in space 1965: took part in flight of space-ship Voskhod 2 and moved 5 metres into space outside space-ship; Pilot-Cosmonaut of USSR; Deputy Commdr Gagarin Cosmonauts Training Centre 1971; took part in joint flight Soyuz 19–Apollo 1975; Maj.-Gen. 1975; Chair. Council of Founders of Novosti Press Agency 1969–90; Deputy Head, Centre of Cosmonaut Training 1975–92, Commdr of Cosmonauts 1976–92; Dir Cheteck-Cosmos Co. 1981–92, Pres. Investment Fund Alfa-Capital 1993–; Vice-Pres. Alfa Bank 1998–; Co-Chair. Bd Int. Asscn of Cosmonauts; mem. Int. Acad. of Astronauts, Soviet Artists Union; Acting Mem. and Academician, Russian Acad. of Arts; Acting Mem. New York Acad. of Arts; hon. citizen of cities in Russia and USA; Order of Red Star 1961, Hero of the Soviet Union 1965, 1975, Yuri Gagarin Gold Medal 1965, Hero of Bulgaria 1965, Hero of Vietnam 1965, Master of Sports 1965, Order of Lenin 1965, 1975, Lenin Komsomol State Prize 1980, USSR State Prize 1981; Hon. DrScEng 1981. *Publications:* numerous books, papers and articles, notably on the psychological activity of cosmonauts; Two Sides of the Moon (with David Scott) 2004. *Leisure interests:* painting, shooting movies. *Address:* Alfa-Capital, Mashi Poryvayevoy str. 9, 107078 Moscow, Russia. *Telephone:* (495) 755-58-42 (office). *Fax:* (495) 786-45-01 (office). *E-mail:* saltayaz@alfabank.ru (office). *Website:* www.alfabank.ru (office).

LEONTYEV, Leopold Igorevich, DrTechSci; Russian metallurgist; b. 1 Dec. 1934, Sverdlovsk (now Yekaterinburg); m.; two s.; ed Urals Polytechnic Inst.; researcher, Head of Lab., then Deputy Dir Inst. of Metallurgy, Ural br. of USSR (now Russian) Acad. of Sciences 1957–93, Deputy Chair. 1993, currently mem. Presidium, also mem. Russian Acad. of Sciences 1997, mem. Presidium 2000; First Deputy Minister of Science and Tech. 1993–96, 1997–2000; First Deputy Chair. State Cttee on Science and Tech. 1996–97. *Publications:* numerous scientific publs on the devt of physical and chem. fundamentals and processes of complex use of metallurgic raw materials. *Address:* Presidium of Ural Branch of Russian Academy of Sciences, Yekaterinburg, Pervomayskaya str. 91, 620219 Yekaterinburg, Russia Federation (office). *Telephone:* (495) 237-39-31 (Moscow) (office); (3432) 74-53-85 (Yekaterinburg) (office).

LEONTYEV, Mikhail Vladimirovich; Russian journalist; b. 12 Oct. 1958, Moscow; m.; two c.; ed Moscow Plekhanov Inst. of Nat. Econs; political reviewer Kommersant (newspaper) 1987–90; on staff newspaper Atmoda (Riga) and Experimental Creative Cen. in Moscow 1989–91; Ed. Div. of Politics Nezavisimaya Gazeta (newspaper) 1990–92; First Deputy Ed.-in-Chief Business MN (daily) 1992–93; First Deputy Ed.-in-Chief Segodnya (newspaper) 1993–97; political reviewer TV-Cen. Channel 1997–98, ORT Channel 1999–; Ed.-in-Chief journal Fas 2000–. *Address:* Obshchestvennoye Rossiyskoe Televideniye (ORT), Akademika Koroleva str. 12, 127000 Moscow, Russia (office). *Telephone:* (495) 217 94-72 (office); (495) 217-94-73 (office).

LEOPHAIRATANA, Prachai, MSEE; Thai business executive; *CEO, Thai Petrochemical Industry Public Co. Ltd;* b. 28 Aug. 1944; s. of Phorn Leophairatana and Boonsri Leophairatana; m. Orapin Leophairatana 1974; ed Canterbury Univ., New Zealand, Univ. of California, Berkeley, USA; CEO Thai Petrochemical Industry Public Co. Ltd (PCL) 1988–, TPI Polene PCL, TPI Group of Cos 1988–; Man. Dir Hong Yiah Seng Co. Ltd 1986–; mem. Senate; Chair. Bd Dirs United Grain Industry Co. Ltd 1986–, Bangkok Union Insurance PCL 1986–, Thai Industrial Estate Corp. Ltd 1988–, Exec. Bd Thai Caprolactam PCL 1989–, Uhde (Thailand) Co. Ltd 1990–, Thai Int. Tankers Co. Ltd 1994–; Vice-Chair. Bd Dirs Thai Alliance Textile Co. Ltd 1986–; Dir Rice Export Asscns, Thai–Chinese Friendship Asscn, Thai–Chinese Promotion of Investment and Trade Asscn, Bd of Trade of Thailand; Sec.-Gen. Environment for Better Life Foundation; Kt Grand Cross Most Noble Order of the Crown of Thailand, Kt Grand Cross (1st Class) Exalted Order of the White Elephant, Kt Grand Cordon (Special Class) Most Noble Order of the Crown of Thailand, Companion (4th Class) Most Admirable Order of the Direkgunabhom. *Address:* Thai Petrochemical Industry PCL, TPI Tower, 26/56 Thanen Chan Tat Mai, Thungmahamek Sathorn, Bangkok 10210, Thailand (office). *Telephone:* (2) 6785000 (office). *Fax:* (2) 6785001–5 (office). *E-mail:* prachai@prachai.com (office). *Website:* www.tpigroup.co.th (office); www.prachai.com (office).

LEOS, Raúl Muñoz; Mexican business executive and chemical engineer; b. 14 Oct. 1939, México; ed Nat. Univ. of Mexico (UNAM); joined Du Pont SA 1964, various sr positions in production, sales, market research, planning and admin, Exec. Vice-Pres. Du Pont Mexico –1988, Pres. (first Mexican to head co.) 1988–2000; Dir-Gen. Pemex (Petróleos Mexicanos) 2000–04; mem. Bd of Dirs Química Flúor SA, Nylon de México, Sears Roebuck and Co., Mexican Foundation for Rural Devt, Mexican Health Foundation; Nat. Vice-Pres. COPARMEX; Pres. Grupo Diálogo Inversión; fmr Pres. Mexican Inst. of Chemical Engineers; mem. Edit. Bd El Economista; mem. Diálogo México, American Chamber of Commerce of Mexico; Trustee UNAM Faculty of Chemistry, Museum of the City of Mexico, Antiguo Colegio de San Ildefonso. *Address:* c/o Petróleos Mexicanos (Pemex), Avenida Marina Nacional 329, Colonia Huasteca, 11311 México, DF, Mexico (office).

LÉOTARD, François Gérard Marie; French politician, diplomatist and civil servant; b. 26 March 1942, Cannes; s. of André Léotard and Antoinette Tomasi; m. 1st France Reynier 1976; m. 2nd Ysabel Duret 1992; one s. one d.; ed Lycées Charlemagne and Henri IV, Paris, Faculté de Droit and Inst. d'Etudes Politiques, Paris and Ecole Nat. d'Admin; Sec. of Chancellery, Ministry of Foreign Affairs 1968–71; Admin. Town Planning 1973–75; Sous-préfet 1974–77; Mayor of Fréjus 1977–92, 1993–97, Municipal Councillor 1992; Deputy to Nat. Ass. (UDF-PR) 1978–86, 1988–92; Conseiller-Gen., Var 1980–88; Sec.-Gen. Parti Républicain 1982–88, Pres. 1988–90, 1995–97, Hon. Pres. 1990–95; Vice-Pres. Union pour la Démocratie Française (UDF) 1983–84, Pres. 1996–98; Minister of Culture and Communications 1986–88, of Nat. Defence (oversaw peace-keeping operations in Bosnia) 1993–95; Deputy for Var 1988–92, 1995–97, 1997–2002; apptd EU Special Envoy to Macedonia 2001; Insp. Gen. des Finances pour l'extérieur 2001; convicted of money-laundering and illegal party funding, received ten month suspended sentence Feb. 2004; Chevalier, Ordre nat. du Mérite. *Publications:* A Mots Decouverts 1987, Culture: Les Chemins de Printemps 1988, La Ville aimée: mes chemins de Fréjus 1989, Pendant la Crise, le spectacle continue 1989, Adresse au Président des Républiques françaises 1991, Place de la République 1992, Ma Liberté 1995, Pour l'honneur 1997, Je vous hais tous avec douceur 2000, Paroles d'immortels 2001, La Couleur des Femmes 2002, À mon frère qui n'est pas mort 2003, Ça va mal finir 2008. *Leisure interests:* running, tennis, parachuting. *Address:* c/o Assemblée Nationale, 75355 Paris, France.

LEPAGE, Corinne Dominique Marguerite; French lawyer and politician; *Leader, CAP 21-Citoyenneté Action Participation pour le 21è siècle;* b. 11 May 1951, Boulogne-Billancourt; d. of Philippe Lepage and Jacqueline Schulmann; m. 1st Christian Jessua, one d.; m. 2nd Christian Huglo, one s.; ed Lycée Molière, Univ. of Paris II and Inst. d'Etudes Politiques, Paris; in legal partnership 1971–76; barrister, Paris 1978–; Dir of Studies, Univ. of Paris II 1974–77; Dir of Educ. Univ. of Metz 1978–80; Mayor adjoint of Cabourg 1989–2001; Maître de conférences, Inst. d'Etudes Politiques, Paris 1979–87, 1989–1994; Course Dir Univ. of Paris II 1982–86, Univ. of Paris XII 1987–92; mem. Bar Council 1987–89; Vice-Pres. then Pres. Asscn of Admin. Law Advocates 1989–95; Minister of the Environment 1995–97; Pres. Asscn nationale des docteurs en droit 1998–2003; Vice-Pres. Environnement sans frontières 1998–, Modem; Pres. Comité de Recherche Indépendante et d'Information sur le Génie Génétique (CRII-GEN); Leader CAP 21-Citoyenneté Action Participation pour le 21è siècle, presidential cand. 2002; Prof., Inst. d'Etudes Politiques de Paris 1994–; Pres. Observatoire de vigilance et d'alerte écologique; Chevalier, Légion d'Honneur. *Publications:* Code annoté des procédures administratives contentieuses 1990, Les audits de l'environnement 1992, On ne peut rien faire, Madame le ministre 1998, Bien gérer l'environnement, une chance pour l'entreprise 1999, La Politique de Précaution 2001, Oser l'Espérance, Robert Jauze 2002, De l'Écologie, Hors de l'Imposture et l'Opportunisme 2003, Santé et Environnement, l'Abécédaire 2005, Ecoresp I et II, Et si c'était elle? 2006; numerous articles in La Gazette du Palais. *Leisure interests:* cinema, reading, tennis, skiing, swimming. *Address:* CAP 21, 40 rue de Monceau, 75008 Paris, France (office). *Telephone:* 1-56-59-29-59 (office). *Fax:* 1-56-59-29-39 (office). *E-mail:* corinne.lepage@huglo-lepage.com (home). *Website:* www.cap21.net (office); www.huglo-lepage.com (home).

LEPAGE, Robert; French-Canadian actor and theatre and film director; *Artistic Director, Ex Machina;* b. 1957, Québec City; ed Conservatoire d'Art Dramatique Québec, Canada; Artistic Co-Dir Théatre Repère 1986–89; Founder and Pres. Robert LePage Inc. 1988–; Artistic Dir Nat. Arts Centre Ottawa, Canada 1989–93; Artistic Dir Ex Machina 1994–; Founder, Pres. and Artistic Dir In Extremis Inc. 1995–2004; Founder La Caserne Dalhousie 1997–; Hon. PhD (Laval) 1994; Hon. DLitt (Toronto, McGill) 1997; Hon. LLD (Concordia) 1999; Evening Standard Award for Best Play 2001, Europe Theatre Prize 2007 and various other awards. *Films:* (scriptwriter, dir): The Confessional 1995, The Polygraph 1996, Nô 1998, Possible Worlds 2000, The Far Side of the Moon 2003. *Operas:* (dir): Bluebeard's Castle 1992, Erwartung 1992, The Damnation of Faust 1999, The Rake's Progress 2007. *Productions include:* Dragon's Trilogy (co-writer, dir and actor) 1984, Vinci (writer, dir and actor) 1986, Tectonic Plates (co-writer, dir and actor) 1988, A Midsummer Night's Dream (dir) 1992, The Geometry of Miracles (co-writer, dir) 1998, The Far Side of the Moon (writer, dir and actor) 2000, The Andersens' Project 2005, Lipsynch 2007. *Publications:* Connecting Flights 1995; (in French): La Trilogie des Dragons 2005, Le Projet Andersen 2007, La Face cachée de la Lune 2007, Chantiers d'écriture scénique 2007. *Address:* 103 Dalhousie, Québec City, PQ G1K 4B9, Canada (office). *Telephone:* (418) 692-0055 (home). *Fax:* (418) 692-5400 (office). *E-mail:* rli@exmachina.qc.ca (office). *Website:* lacaserne.net (office).

LEPPARD, Raymond John, CBE, MA; British conductor and composer; b. 11 Aug. 1927, London; s. of A. V. Leppard and B. M. Beck; ed Trinity Coll. Cambridge; Fellow of Trinity Coll., Univ. Lecturer in Music 1958–68; Music Dir, BBC Philharmonic (fmrly BBC Northern Symphony) Orchestra 1973–80; Prin. Guest Conductor, St Louis Symphony Orchestra 1984–93; Music Dir Indianapolis Symphony Orchestra 1987–2001, Conductor Laureate 2001–; has also conducted New York Philharmonic, Chicago Symphony, Philadelphia and Pittsburgh Symphony Orchestras and Royal Opera, Covent Garden, English Nat. Opera, Metropolitan Opera, New York, New York City Opera and San Francisco Opera; realizations of Monteverdi's L'Incoronazione di Poppea, Il Ritorno d'Ulisse and L'Orfeo and Cavalli's L'Ormindo, L'Egisto, La Calisto and L'Orione; Commendatore della Republica Italiana; Dr hc (Purdue Univ.). *Publication:* Authenticity in Music 1989. *Leisure interests:* friends, theatre, reading. *Address:* Schmidt Artists International, Inc., 59 Easr 54th Street, Suite 83, New York, NY 10022, USA (office); Orchard House, 5040 Buttonwood Crescent, Indianapolis, IN 46228-2323 (home). *Telephone:* (212)

421-8500 (office); (317) 259-0916 (home). *Fax:* (212) 421-8583 (office). *E-mail:* info@schmidtart.com (office). *Website:* www.schmidtart.com (office).

LEPPER, Andrzej; Polish politician and trade union official; *Leader, Self-Defence Party of the Republic of Poland;* b. 13 June 1954, Stowięcin; s. of Jan Lepper and Anna Lepper; m. Irena Lepper; one s. two d.; ed Tech. School of Agric., Sypniewo; worked in public and co-operative sector 1976–80; farmer 1980–; Founder and Pres. Trade Union of Farmers (Samoobrona) 1991–; mem. Nat. Council of Agric. Chambers 1998–; Councillor, Local Parl. of the Western Pomeranian Voivodship 1998–2001; Deputy to Sejm (Parl.) 2001–, Vice-Marshal of Sejm 2001–02; Leader, Self-Defence Party of the Repub. of Poland 2001–; Deputy Prime Minister and Minister for Agriculture and Rural Devt 2006–07, Deputy Speaker of Sejm, mem. cttees on Legal Affairs and Human Rights, Parl. Ass. of the Council of Europe; faced more than 130 criminal charges for accusations of slander and corruption against ministers and deputies 2002; Dr hc (Int. Personnel Acad., Kiev); Medal of Hope of Pope John Paul II 1995, Medal of Albert Schweitzer 2001. *Publications include:* Samoobrona—dlaczego, przed czym? (Self Defence—Why and Against What?) 1993, Kazdy kij ma dwa konce (Every Stick Has Two Ends) 2001, Lista Leppera (The List of Lepper) 2002. *Leisure interests:* horse riding, swimming, boxing. *Address:* Self-Defence Party of the Republic of Poland (Partia Samoobrona Rzeczpospolitej Polskiej), 00-204 Warsaw, Al. Jerozolimskie 30, Poland (office). *Telephone:* (22) 6250472 (office). *Fax:* (22) 6250477 (office). *E-mail:* samoobrona@samoobrona.org.pl (office). *Website:* www .samoobrona.org.pl (office).

LEPPING, Sir George, GCMG, MBE; Solomon Islands politician and government official; *President, People's Alliance Party;* b. 22 Nov. 1947; s. of Chief Dionisio Tanutanu and Regina Suluki; m. Margaret Kwalea Teioli 1972; two s. five d.; ed King George VI Secondary School, Agric. Coll., Vudal, Univ. of Reading, UK; field officer, Dept of Agric. and Rural Econ. 1968, Pres. Solomon Is. Amateur Athletics Union 1970–73, 1981–82; Sr Field Officer then Under-Sec. (Agric.), Ministry of Agric. 1979–80; Perm. Sec. Ministry of Home Affairs and Nat. Devt 1981–84; Project Dir Rural Services Project 1984–87; Minister of Finance 1988; Gov.-Gen. 1988–94; Leader, then Pres. People's Alliance Party 1996–; Perm. Sec., Policy Evaluation Unit 2002–; fmr mem., Dir or Chair. various govt bodies. *Leisure interests:* reading, swimming, lawn tennis, snooker, snorkelling, high-speed boat driving, fishing; first Solomon Islands athlete to win int. sports medals; KStJ 1991. *Address:* PO Box 1431, Honiara; People's Alliance Party, PO Box 722, Honiara, Solomon Islands.

LERACH, Wiliam S., BA, JD; American lawyer; *Chairman and Partner, Lerach Coughlin Stoia Geller Rudman & Robbins LLP;* m. (divorced) three times; three c.; partner Michelle Ciccarelli; ed Univ. of Pittsburgh; pnr Reed Smith Shaw & McClay, Pittsburgh, then opened West Coast office of Milberg Weiss 1976, served as Co-Chair.; Chair. and Pnr, Lerach Coughlin Stoia Geller Rudman & Robbins LLP (fmrly Milberg Weiss Bershad Hynes & Lerach LLP) 2004–; frequent commentator and lecturer on securities and corp. law, class and derivative actions, accountants' liability and attorneys' fees; mem. ABA's Litigation Section's Cttee on Class Actions and Derivative Skills, American Law Inst. Faculty on Fed. and State Class Action Litigation; Master American Inns of Court; fmr Pres. Nat. Asscn of Securities and Commercial Lawyers; mem. Editorial Bd Class Action Reports; Guest Lecturer at Stanford Univ., UCLA, Univ. of Calif. at San Diego, San Diego State Univ., Univ. of Pittsburgh, Council of Institutional Investors, Int. Corp. Governance Network; mem. United States Holocaust Memorial Council. *Address:* Lerach Coughlin Stoia Geller Rudman & Robbins LLP, 401 B Street, Suite 1700, San Diego, CA 92101, USA (office). *Telephone:* (619) 231-1058 (office). *Fax:* (619) 231-7423 (office). *Website:* www.lerachlaw.com (office).

LERCHE, Peter Fritz Franz, DJur; German legal scholar and academic; *Professor of Public Law, University of Munich;* b. 12 Jan. 1928, Leitmeritz; s. of Dr Fritz Lerche and Karoline Lerche (née Artmann); m. Dr Ilse Lerche (née Peschek) 1955; two s.; ed Univ. of Munich; Prof. Freie Universität Berlin 1960; Prof. of Public Law, Univ. of Munich 1965–; mem. Bavarian Acad. of Sciences; fmr mem. Council of Science; First Pres. Union of German Lecturers in Public Law 1982; fmr mem. numerous govt comms and attorney in governmental lawsuits, etc.; Bavarian Order of Merit, Maximiliansorden; Hon. DJur; numerous other awards. *Publications:* Ordentlicher Rechtsweg und Verwaltungsrechtsweg 1953, Übermass und Verfassungsrecht 1961, Werbung und Verfassung 1967, Rundfunkmonopol 1970, Verfassungsrechtliche Fragen zur Pressekonzentration 1971, Verfassungsrechtliche Aspekte der 'inneren Pressefreiheit' 1974, Kernkraft und rechtlicher Wandel 1981, Städte und Kabelkommunikation 1982, Mitarbeit an Maunz/Dürig, Kommentar zum Grundgesetz, Verfassungsgerichtsbarkeit in besonderen Situationen 2001. *Leisure interest:* study of the hippopotamus. *Address:* Junkersstrasse 13, 82131 Gauting, Germany (home). *Telephone:* (89) 8502088 (home).

LERNER, Gerda, MA, PhD; American (b. Austrian) historian and academic; *Robinson-Edwards Professor Emerita of History, University of Wisconsin;* b. 1920, Vienna, Austria; d. of Robert Kronstein and Ilona Kronstein; m. 2nd Carl Lerner (died 1973); one s. one d.; ed New School for Social Research (now New School Univ.) and Columbia Univ.; involved in underground resistance movt against Nazi rise to power, later imprisoned and subsequently forced into exile with her family; moved to USA 1938, naturalized citizen 1943; worked to create an interracial civil rights movt, for better schools in New York, for peace and social justice and against McCarthyism; taught first post-war coll. course in women's history at New School for Social Research 1963; teacher Long Island Univ., Brooklyn, NY 1965–68, Sarah Lawrence Coll., Bronxville, NY 1968–72, Prof. of History 1972–80, Dir Grad. Program in Women's History 1972–80; Robinson-Edwards Prof. of History, Univ. of Wisconsin, Madison 1980–1991, now Prof. Emer.; Pres. Org. of American Historians 1981–82 (first woman in 50 years); mem. American Acad. Arts and Sciences 1998 and numerous other professional orgs; Fellow, Endowment for the Humanities, Ford Foundation, Lilly Foundation and Guggenheim Inst.; 17 hon. degrees; Bruce Catton Prize for Lifetime Achievement in Historical Writing, AHA Lifetime Achievement Award 1992, Austrian Cross of Honor for Science and Art 1996, Distinguished Service Award, Org. of American History 2002, Soc. of American Historians (first woman recipient) 2002, Wis. Alumni Research Foundaton, Sr Distinguished Research Prof. 1984–91. *Publications include:* No Farewell (novel) 1955, Black Like Me (screenplay, with Carl Lerner) 1964, The Grimke Sisters from South Carolina: Rebels Against Slavery 1967, The Woman in American History (textbook) 1971, Black Women in White America: A Documentary History 1972, Women Are History: A Bibliography in the History of American Women 1975, The Female Experience: An American Documentary (Ed.) 1976, A Death of One's Own 1978, The Majority Finds Its Past: Placing Women in History 1979, Teaching Women's History 1981, Women and History, Vol. 1: The Creation of Patriarchy 1986, Vol. 2: The Creation of a Feminist Consciousness, From the Middle Ages to 1870 1993, Why History Matters: Life and Thought 1997, Fireweed: A Political Autobiography 2002. *Address:* University of Wisconsin-Madison, 4108 Mosse Humanities Building, Mailbox 5049, 455 North Park Street, Madison, WI 53706 (office); c/o Temple University Press, 1601 North Broad Street, 306 USB, Philadelphia, PA 19122, USA (office). *E-mail:* glerner@wisc .edu (office). *Website:* history.wisc.edu (office).

LERNER, Randolph D., LLB; American lawyer and business executive; *Chairman, MBNA Corporation;* b. 1962; s. of the late Alfred Lerner; ed Columbia Coll., Clare Coll. Cambridge, UK, Columbia Univ. Law School; mem. NY and DC Bar Asscns; began career as Investment Analyst, Progressive Corpn; Founder and Man.-Dir Securities Advisors Inc. 1991–2001; apptd Dir MBNA Corpn 1993, Chair. 2002–, also Dir MBNA America Bank 1993–; Chair. NY Acad. of Arts 1998–2003; Owner Cleveland Browns Football Club, Nat. Football League (NFL) 2002–, mem. NFL Business Ventures Cttee; Trustee Hosp. for Special Surgery, NY City 1996–; fmr Trustee Corcoran Museum, Washington DC. *Address:* MBNA Corporation, 1100 North King Street, Wilmington, DE 19884-0131, USA (office). *Telephone:* (302) 453-9930 (office). *Fax:* (302) 432-3614 (office). *Website:* www .mbna.com (office); www.clevelandbrowns.com.

LERNER, Richard A., MD, PhD; American chemist and academic; *Lita Annenberg Hazen Professor of Immunochemistry, Cecil H. and Ida M. Green Chair in Chemistry, and President, Scripps Research Institute;* ed Northwestern Univ., Stanford Medical School; fmr intern, Palo Alto Stanford Hosp.; Postdoctoral Research Fellow, Scripps Clinic and Research Foundation, later Chair., Dept of Molecular Biology, Scripps Research Inst. 1982–86, Pres. Scripps Research Inst. 1986–, also Lita Annenberg Hazen Prof. of Immunochemistry and Cecil H. and Ida M. Green Chair. in Chem.; Staff mem., Wistar Inst., Phila 1970–; mem. Scientific Advisory Bd, Dyadic Group 2004–; Senomyx; mem. Editorial Bd Journal of Virology, Molecular Biology and Medicine, Vaccine, In Vivo, Peptide Research, Bioorganic and Medicinal Chem. Letters, Drug Targeting and Delivery; Sr Contributing Ed. PNAS, Chem. and Biology, Bioorganic and Medicinal Chem., Molecular Medicine, Catalysis Technology, Angewandte Chemie; mem. Scientific Policy Advisory Cttee, Uppsala Univ., Sweden 1991; mem. Scientific Advisory Bd, Econ. Devt Bd, Singapore 1991; Trustee, Neurosciences Research Foundation, Inc. 1992–; mem. Advisory Bd Chemical & Engineering News 1994–; mem. ETH Inst. of Biotechnology Advisory Bd, Zurich, Switzerland 1994; mem., Stanford Linear Accelerator Center Scientific Policy Cttee, Stanford, CA 1995–98; mem., Center for Nanoscale Science and Tech. Scientific Advisory Bd 1996; mem. Bd of Dirs, Calif. Council on Science and Tech. 1996–97; mem., Advisory Steering Group for Chem., Calif. State Univ. 1996; mem., Academic Cttee, Bd of Govs, Technion Israel Inst. of Tech., Haifa, Israel 1998; mem. NAS 1991–, American Soc. for Experimental Pathology, American Soc. of Microbiology, New York Acad. of Sciences, Biophysical Soc., Pluto Soc.; foreign mem. Royal Swedish Acad. of Sciences 1985–; Hon. DSc (Technion Israel Inst. of Tech.) 2001 Parke Davis Award 1978, John A. Muntz Memorial Prize 1990, San Marino Prize 1990, Arthur C. Cope Scholar Award 1991, Jeanette Piperno Memorial Award 1991, CIBA-GEIGY Drew Award in Biomedical Research 1992, Humboldt Research Award 1994, Wolf Prize in Chem. 1994, Calif. Scientist of the Year Award 1996, Coley Award for Distinguished Research in Basic and Tumor Immunology 1999, Univ. of Calif. Presidential Medal 2002, Paul Ehrlich and Ludwig Darmstaedter Prize, Frankfurt, Germany, 2003. *Address:* Scripps Research Institute, 10550 North Torrey Pines Road, La Jolla CA 92037, USA (office). *Telephone:* (858) 784-8265 (office). *Fax:* (858) 784-9899 (office). *E-mail:* rlerner@scripps.edu (office). *Website:* www.scripps.edu (office).

LERNMARK, Åke, PhD; Swedish medical scientist, biologist and academic; *R. H. Williams Professor of Medicine and Adjunct Professor of Immunology, University of Washington School of Medicine;* fmr Principal investigator, Swegene (The Postgenomic Research and Tech. Programme in South Western Sweden), Dept of Medicine, Surgery and Orthopaedics, Malmö; currently R. H. Williams Prof. of Medicine and Adjunct Prof. of Immunology, Univ. of Washington School of Medicine, USA; mem. Pacific Northwest Research Inst. Bd of Trustees and Chair. Scientific Advisory Cttee; Consultant, Beta Cell Transplant Project, Brussels, Belgium 1994–; mem. Scientific and Medical Advisory Bd Diamyd Medical; mem. American Soc. for Clinical Investigation 1989–; J. Allyn Taylor Int. Prize for Medicine (co-recipient) 2002, Terry and Louise Gregg Diabetes in Pregnancy Research Award, American Diabetes Asscn Research Foundation 2004–06. *Publications:* numerous articles in medical journals on genetic causes of diabetes. *Address:* University of Washington, Department of Medicine, Room K165, Box 357710, Seattle, WA 98195-7710, USA (office). *Telephone:* (206) 543-5316 (office). *Fax:* (206) 543-3169 (office). *E-mail:* ake@u.washington.edu (office). *Website:* depts .washington.edu/mcb (office).

LEROI, Armand Marie, BSc, PhD; Dutch evolutionary biologist; *Reader in Evolutionary Developmental Biology, Imperial College London;* b. 16 July 1964, Wellington, New Zealand; ed Dalhousie Univ., Halifax, Canada, Univ. of California at Irvine, USA; postdoctoral work at the Albert Einstein Coll. of Medicine, New York; Lecturer Imperial Coll. London 1996–2001, Reader in Evolutionary Developmental Biology 2001–. *Television:* Mutants (three-part series, Channel 4) 2004. *Publications:* Mutants: On the Form, Varieties and Errors of the Human Body (Guardian First Book Award 2004) 2003; contrib. to London Review of Books; numerous research papers. *Address:* Department of Biological Sciences, Silwood Park Campus, Imperial College London, Ascot, Berkshire SL5 7PY, England (office). *Telephone:* (20) 7594-2396 (office). *Fax:* (20) 7594-2339 (office). *E-mail:* a.leroi@imperial.ac.uk (office). *Website:* www.armandleroi.com.

LESAR, David J., BS, MBA; American business executive; *Chairman, President and CEO, Halliburton Company;* b. 1955; ed Univ. of Wisconsin; Pnr and Commercial Group Dir, Arthur Anderson Co., Dallas, Tex. –1993; Exec. Vice-Pres. Finance and Admin, Halliburton Energy Services 1993–95, Exec. Vice-Pres. and Chief Financial Officer Halliburton 1995–96, Pres. and CEO 1997–2000, Chair., Pres. and CEO 2000–; Pres. and CEO Brown & Root Inc. 1996–97; mem. Bd of Dirs Lyondell Chemical Co., Mirant Corpn; mem. Upstream Cttee, American Petroleum Inst. *Address:* Halliburton Company, 5 Houston Center, 1401 McKinney, Suite 2400, Houston, TX 77010-4008, USA (office). *Telephone:* (713) 759-2600 (office). *Fax:* (713) 759-2635 (office). *Website:* www.halliburton.com (office).

LESCHLY, Jan; Danish business executive; m. Lotte Enngelbred 1963; four s.; ed Coll. of Pharmacy, School of Econ. and Business Administration Copenhagen, Princeton Univ., USA; Novo Industries A/S 1972–1979; Vice-Pres. Commercial Devt, Squibb Corpn 1979, US Pres. 1981, Group Vice-Pres. and Dir 1984, Exec. Vice-Pres. 1986; Pres. and COO 1988; Chair. SmithKline Beecham Pharmaceuticals 1990, CEO 1994–2000; Chair. and CEO Care Capital LLC 2000–; mem. pharmaceutical assocs and educational bodies. *Address:* Care Capital LLC, Princeton Overlook I, 100 Overlook Center and Route 1, Princeton, NJ 08540, USA.

LESCURE, Pierre François Amar; French business executive and actor; b. 2 July 1945, Paris; s. of François Lescure and Paulette Baudoin; m. Frédérique Fayles-Bernstein 1996; ed Lycée Turgot, Paris, Centre de formation des journalistes; reporter and newsreader Radio Télé Luxembourg 1965–68; with Radio Caroline and Radio Monte Carlo 1968–72; newsreader and presenter Office de radiodiffusion télévision française (ORTF) 1973–77, Deputy Ed., weekend programmes 1977–80, Dir Programmes Europe 1 1980–81; Ed.-in-Chief Antenne 2 1982–84, Head of Programmes 1984–86; Dir-Gen. Canal+ 1986–94, Chair. and Man. Dir 1994–2000, Chair. Bd Dirs 2000–02; Chair. Canal Jimmy 1991–2002; Chair. and Man. Dir Paris Saint-Germain Football SA 1991–, Le Studio Canal+ 1991–2002, Le Monde Presse 1994–; Chair. UGCDA (audiovisual rights co.) 1997–, CanalPro 1997–2002, Multithématiques 2001–; Deputy Chair. Exec. Cttee Havas 1997–; Co-CEO Vivendi Universal 2000–02; Dir and mem. Strategic Cttee Havas Group 1993–; mem. Advisory Bd Lagardère Group 2000–; mem. Bd Dirs Kudelski Group 2004–; Chevalier, Ordre nat. du Mérite, Officier des Arts et Lettres; Homme de la décennie de la télévision, CB News 1996, Man. de l'année, le Nouvel économiste 1996 and other awards. *Films include:* 5% de risques (voice) 1980, Le quart d'heure américain 1982, Mon petit doigt m'a dit... 2005. *Television includes:* Graffiti 60 (mini-series) (screenplay) 2005. *Publication:* A nous la radio. *Address:* c/o Paris Saint-Germain Football, 30 avenue du Parc des Princes, 75016 Paris, France.

LESIN, Mikhail Yuryevich; Russian politician and journalist; b. 11 July 1958; m.; one s.; ed Moscow Inst. of Eng and Construction; fmr eng constructor; f. Igrotechnika (later Intelleks) Co-operative 1989–91; Founder and Chair. Bd of Dirs Videoint. (advertising co.) 1991–94; mem. of staff RIA Novosti, Dir-Gen. Novosti-TV Co. 1993–96; Head of Dept of Public Relations, Russian Presidency 1996–97 (resgnd); First Deputy Chair. All-Russian State TV Co. 1997–99; Minister of Press, TV, Broadcasting and Telecommunications (subsequently the Press, Broadcasting and Mass Media) 1999–2004; Adviser to the Pres. 2004–08; mem. Bd of Dirs Pervyi Kanal 2004–. *Address:* c/o Office of the President, Kremlin, 103073 Moscow, Russia (office).

LESOURNE, Jacques François; French newspaper editor, economist and academic; *President, Futuribles International;* b. 26 Dec. 1928, La Rochelle; s. of André Lesourne and Simone Lesourne (née Guille); m. Odile Melin, 1961; one s. two d.; ed Lycée Montaigne, Bordeaux, École Polytechnique, École Nationale Supérieure des Mines de Paris; Head Econ. Service of French Collieries 1954–57; Dir Gen., later Pres. METRA Int. and SEMA 1958–75; Prof. of Econs École des Mines de Saint-Étienne 1958–61; Prof. of Industrial Econs École Nationale Supérieure de la Statistique 1960–63; Pres. Asscn Française d'Informatique et de Recherche Operationnelle 1966–67; mem. Council Int. Inst. of Applied Systems Analysis, Vienna 1973–79, Inst. of Man. Science 1976–79; Prof. Conservatoire Nat. des Arts et Métiers 1974–; Dir Projet Interfuturs OECD 1976–79; Dir of Studies, Inst. Auguste Comte 1979–81; Pres. Comm. on Employment and Social Relations of 8th Plan 1979–81; mem. Comm. du Bilan 1981, Council European Econ. Asscn 1984–89; Pres. Asscn Française de Science Économique 1981–83, Int. Federation of Operational Research Socs 1986–89; Dir and Man. Ed. Le Monde 1991–94; Pres. Futuribles Int. 1993–, Centre for Study and Research on Qualifications 1996–; Bd mem. Acad. des Technologies; Officier, Légion d'honneur 1993, Commdr 2009, Commdr, Ordre nat. du Mérite, Officier des Palmes Académiques. *Publications:* Economic Technique and Industrial Management 1958, Du bon usage de l'étude économique dans l'entreprise 1966, Les systèmes du destin 1976, L'entreprise et ses futurs 1985, Éducation et société, L'après-Communisme, de l'Atlantique à l'Oural 1990, The Economics of Order and Disorder 1991, Vérités et mensonges sur le chômage 1995, Le Modèle français: Grandeur et Décadence 1998, Un Homme de notre Siècle 2000, Ces Avenirs qui n'ont pas eu lieu 2001, Leçons de Microéconomie évolutionniste (with A. Orléan and B. Wallises) 2002, Democratie: Marché et Gouvernance, Quels Avenirs? 2004, Evolutionary Microeconomics (with André Orléan and Bernard Walliser) 2006, La recherche et l'innovation en France (with Denis Radet) 2007. *Leisure interest:* piano. *Address:* 52 rue de Vaugirard, 75006 Paris, France (home). *Telephone:* 1-43-25-66-05 (home). *Fax:* 1-56-24-47-98. *E-mail:* jolesourne@wanadoo.fr. *Website:* www.futuribles.com (office).

LESSARD, Claude; Canadian business executive; *President and CEO, Groupe Cossette Communication;* b. 29 July 1949, Notre Dame du Portage; s. of Carmen Cerat and Jean-Luc Lessard; m. Marie Lortie 1971; three s.; ed Univ. Laval, Québec; joined Groupe Cossette Communication 1972, Pres. and CEO 1980–; Dir Canam-Manac, Inst. de cardiologie de Québec, Opéra de Québec, Faculté des Sciences de l'Admin, Univ. Laval, Fondation Communautaire du Grand Québec, DiagnoCure Inc., Ronald McDonald Children's Charities of Canada, Faculté des sciences de l'admin at l'Université Laval; Co.-Chair. Canadian Congress of Advertising 1995; Hermes Prize (Univ. of Laval) 1984, Dimensions Prize 1987, 'Spiess' Bessies Award 1993, ACA Gold Medal 1994. *Leisure interests:* golf, skiing, riding. *Address:* Groupe Cossette Communication, 801 chemin Saint-Louist, Québec, PQ, G1S 1C1, Canada (office). *Telephone:* (418) 647-2727 (office). *Fax:* (418) 647-2564 (office). *Website:* www.cossette.com (office).

LESSELS, Norman, CBE, CA; British chartered accountant; b. 2 Sept. 1938, Edinburgh, Scotland; s. of John Clark Lessels and Gertrude Margaret Ellen Lessels (née Jack); m. 1st Gillian Durward Clark 1960 (died 1979); one s. (and one s. one d. deceased); m. 2nd Christine Stevenson Hitchman 1981; ed Melville Coll., Edin., Edin. Acad.; apprentice with Graham Smart & Annan, Edin. 1955–60, with Thomson McLintock & Co., London 1960–61; Pnr, Wallace & Somerville, Edin., subsequently merged with Whinney Murray & Co., latterly Ernst & Whinney 1962–80; Pnr, Chiene & Tait, CA 1980–93, Sr Pnr 1993–98; Dir (non-exec.) The Standard Life Assurance Co. 1978–2002 (Chair. 1988–98), Cairn Energy PLC 1988–2002, Bank of Scotland 1988–97, General Surety & Guarantee Co. Ltd 1988–97, Havelock Europa PLC –1998 (Chair. 1993–98), NWS Bank PLC 1989–97, Robert Wiseman Dairies PLC 1994–2003, Martin Currie Portfolio Investment Trust PLC 1999–2001; Pres. Inst. of Chartered Accountants of Scotland 1987–88; Chair. Tilney & Co. 1993–98. *Leisure interests:* golf, bridge, music. *Address:* 17 India Street, Edinburgh, EH3 6HE, Scotland (home).

LESSING, Doris May, CH, CLit; British writer; b. 22 Oct. 1919, Kermanshah, Persia; d. of Alfred Cook Tayler and Emily Maude Tayler (née McVeagh); m. 1st F. A. C. Wisdom 1939–43; m. 2nd Gottfried Anton Nicolai Lessing 1944 (divorced 1949; two s. (one deceased) one d.; ed Roman Catholic Convent and Girls' High School, Salisbury, Southern Rhodesia; Assoc. mem. American Acad. of Arts and Letters 1974; Nat. Inst. of Arts and Letters (USA) 1974; mem. Inst. for Cultural Research 1974; Pres. Book Trust 1996–; Hon. Fellow, MLA (US) 1974, Companion of Honour 1999; D.Fellow in Literature (East Anglia) 1991; Hon. DLitt (Princeton) 1989, Durham (1990), (Warwick) 1994, (Bard Coll. New York State) 1994, (Harvard) 1995, (Oxford) 1996; Somerset Maugham Award 1954, Soc. of Authors 1954–, Austrian State Prize for European Literature 1981, Shakespeare Prize, Hamburg 1982, Grinzane Cavour Award, Italy 1989, Woman of the Year, Norway 1995, Premio Internacional Cataluña, Spain 1999, David Cohen Literary Prize 2001, Príncipe de Asturias Prize, Spain 2001, PEN Award 2002, Nobel Prize in Literature 2007. *Publications:* novels: The Grass is Singing 1950, Children of Violence (Martha Quest 1952, A Proper Marriage 1954, A Ripple from the Storm 1965, The Four-Gated City 1969), Retreat to Innocence 1956, The Golden Notebook (Prix Médicis for French trans., Carnet d'Or 1976) 1962, Landlocked 1965, Briefing for a Descent into Hell 1971, The Summer Before the Dark 1973, The Memoirs of a Survivor 1974, Canopus in Argos series (Re: Colonised Planet 5, Shikasta 1979, The Marriages between Zones Three, Four and Five 1980, The Sirian Experiments 1981, The Making of the Representative for Planet 8 1982, The Sentimental Agents in the Volyen Empire 1983), The Diary of a Good Neighbour (as Jane Somers) 1983, If the Old Could (as Jane Somers) 1984, The Diaries of Jane Somers 1984, The Good Terrorist (WHSmith Literary Award 1986, Palermo Prize and Premio Internazionale Mondello 1987) 1985, The Fifth Child 1988, Love, Again 1996, Playing the Game 1996, Mara and Dann: an Adventure 1999, Ben, in the World 2000, The Old Age of El Magnifico 2000, The Sweetest Dream 2001, The Story of General Dann and Mara's Daughter, Griot and the Snow Dog 2005, The Cleft 2007; short stories: Collected African Stories: Vol. 1, This Was the Old Chief's Country 1951, Vol. 2, The Sun Between Their Feet 1973, Five 1953, The Habit of Loving 1957, A Man and Two Women 1963, African Stories 1964, Winter in July 1966, The Black Madonna 1966, The Story of a Non-Marrying Man and Other Stories 1972, A Sunrise on the Veld 1975, A Mild Attack of the Locusts 1977, Collected Stories: Vol. 1, To Room Nineteen 1978, Vol. 2, The Temptation of Jack Orkney 1978, London Observed: Stories and Sketches 1992, The Grandmothers 2003; non-fiction includes: Going Home 1957 (revised edn 1968), In Pursuit of the English 1960, Particularly Cats 1967, Particularly Cats and More Cats 1989, African Laughter: Four Visits to Zimbabwe 1992, Under My Skin: Volume One of My Autobiography to 1949 (Los Angeles Times Book Prize 1995, James Tait Memorial Prize 1995) 1994, Walking in the Shade: Volume Two of My Autobiography 1949–62 1997, Time Bites 2004, Alfred and Emily 2008; plays: Each His Own Wilderness 1958, Play with a Tiger 1962, The Singing Door 1973; other: Fourteen Poems 1959, A Small Personal Voice 1974, Doris Lessing Reader 1990. *Leisure interests:* theatre, gardening. *Address:* c/o Jonathan Clowes Ltd, 10 Iron Bridge House,

www.worldwhoswho.com

Bridge Approach, London, NW1 8BD, England. *Telephone:* (20) 7722-7624 (office). *Fax:* (20) 7794-0985 (home). *E-mail:* jonathanclowes@aol.com.

LESTER, Adrian (Anthony); British actor; b. 14 Aug. 1968, Birmingham; m. Lolita Chakrabarti; two d.; ed Royal Acad. of Dramatic Art; mem. Amnesty Int., Greenpeace, Council Royal Acad. of Dramatic Art, Artistic Bd Royal Nat. Theatre; Time Out Award 1992, Olivier Award 1996, Carlton Theatre Award 2001. *Theatre appearances include:* Cory in Fences, Garrick 1990, Paul Poitier in Six Degrees of Separation (Time Out Award), Royal Court and Comedy Theatre 1992, Anthony Hope in Sweeney Todd, Royal Nat. Theatre 1994, Rosalind in As You Like It (Time Out Award), Albery and Bouffes du Nord 1995, Company (Olivier Award), Albery and Donmar 1996, Hamlet, Bouffes du Nord and Young Vic 2001, Henry V, Royal Nat. Theatre 2003. *Films include:* Les Soeurs Soleil 1997, Primary Colors 1997, Storm Damage, Love's Labour's Lost 2000, Best 2000, Maybe Baby 2000, Born Romantic 2000, Dust 2001, The Final Curtain 2002, The Day After Tomorrow 2004, As You Like It 2006, Scenes of a Sexual Nature 2006, Starting Out in the Evening 2007, Case 39 2007, Doomsday 2008. *Television includes:* The Affair 1995, Company 1996, Storm Damage 1998, Jason and the Argonauts 2000, The Tragedy of Hamlet 2002, Girlfriends (episodes) 2002–03, Hustle (as Mickey Stone) 2003–, Afterlife (episode) 2005, The Ghost Squad (episode) 2005, Beyond 2006, Empire's Children 2007, Bonekickers 2008, Hustle 2009, Sleep With Me 2009. *Radio:* The Making Of Slavery (BBC Radio 4) 2007. *Leisure interests:* martial arts, music, scuba diving, dance. *Address:* c/o Tina Price Consultants, 88 Satchell Lane, Hamble Hampshire, SO31 4HL (office); c/o Artists Rights Group (ARG), 4 Great Portland Street, London, W1W 8PA, England (office). *Telephone:* (23) 8045-4570 (Tina Price) (office); (20) 7436-6400 (ARG) (office). *Fax:* (23) 8045-4574 (Tina Price) (office); (20) 7436-6700 (ARG) (office). *E-mail:* tina@tinapriceconsultants.com (office); latimer@argtalent.com (office). *Website:* www.argtalent.com (office).

LESTER, Richard; American film director; b. 19 Jan. 1932, Philadelphia; s. of Elliott Lester and Ella Young; m. Deirdre V. Smith 1956; one s. one d.; ed William Penn Charter School, Univ. of Pennsylvania; TV Dir, CBS 1952–54, ITV 1955–59; composer 1954–57; film director 1959–; Grand Prix, Cannes Festival 1965; Best Dir, Rio de Janeiro Festival 1966; Gandhi Peace Prize, Berlin Festival 1969; Best Dir, Tehran Festival 1974. *Films directed:* The Running, Jumping and Standing Still Film 1959, It's Trad, Dad 1962, The Mouse on the Moon 1963, A Hard Day's Night 1963 (re-release 2000), The Knack 1965, Help! 1965, A Funny Thing Happened on the Way to the Forum 1966, How I Won the War 1967, Petulia 1969, The Bed Sitting Room 1969, The Three Musketeers 1973, Juggernaut 1974, The Four Musketeers 1974, Royal Flash 1975, Robin and Marian 1976, The Ritz 1976, Butch and Sundance: The Early Days 1979, Cuba 1979, Superman II 1980, Superman III 1983, Finders Keepers 1984, The Return of the Musketeers 1989, Get Back 1991. *Leisure interests:* tennis, music. *Address:* c/o Creative Artists Agency, 9830 Wilshire Boulevard, Beverly Hills, CA 90212, USA.

LESTER OF HERNE HILL, Baron (Life Peer), cr. 1993, of Herne Hill in the London Borough of Southwark; **Anthony Paul Lester,** QC, BA, LLM; British barrister; b. 3 July 1936, London; s. of Harry Lester and Kate Lester; m. Catherine Elizabeth Debora Wassey 1971; one s. one d.; ed City of London School, Trinity Coll. Cambridge, Harvard Law School; called to Bar, Lincoln's Inn 1963, Bencher 1985; Special Adviser to Home Sec. 1974–76; QC 1975; Special Adviser to Northern Ireland Standing Advisory Comm. on Human Rights 1975–77; Recorder, South-Eastern Circuit 1987–93; Hon. Visiting Prof., Univ. Coll. London 1983–; mem. Bd of Dirs Salzburg Seminar 1996–2000; mem. Bd of Overseers, Univ. of Pa Law School 1977–90, Council of Justice; mem. Court of Govs, LSE 1980–94; Pres. Interights 1983–; UK legal expert EEC Comm. Network Cttee on Equal Pay and Sex Discrimination 1983–93; mem. House of Lords Select Cttee on European Communities Sub cttee E (Law and Insts) 2000–Jan. 2004, rejoined Dec. 2004, Sub cttee on 1996 Inter-Governmental Conf., Sub cttee F (Social Affairs, Educ. and Home Affairs) 1996–2000; Co-Chair. of Bd European Roma Rights Centre, Budapest 1999–2001; Gov. British Inst. of Human Rights; Chair. Bd of Govs, James Allen's Girls' School 1987–93; Chair. Runnymede Trust 1990–93; mem. Advisory Cttee Centre for Public Law, Univ. of Cambridge 1999–, Int. Advisory Bd, Open Soc. Inst. Justice Initiative 2000–, Parl. Jt Human Rights Comm. 2001–04, 2005–; Ind. Adviser to Justice Sec. on Constitutional Reform 2007–; Foreign Hon. mem. American Acad. of Arts and Sciences 2002, Foreign mem. American Philosophical Soc. 2003; Hon. Adjunct Prof. of Law, Univ. Coll. London 2007; hon. degrees/fellowships from Open Univ., Univ. Coll., London Univ., Ulster Univ., South Bank Univ., Stirling Univ.; Liberty Human Rights Lawyer of the Year 1997, Liberty and Justice Judges Award for Lifetime Achievement 2007. *Publications:* Justice in the American South (Amnesty Int.) 1964, Race and Law (co-author) 1972; Ed.-in-Chief Butterworths Human Rights Cases; Consultant Ed. and Contrib. Halsbury's Laws of England Title Constitutional Law and Human Rights (4th Edn 1996), Human Rights Law and Practice (co-ed.) 1999, 2nd edn 2004, and articles on race relations, public affairs and int. law. *Leisure interests:* painting, walking. *Address:* Blackstone Chambers, Blackstone House, Temple, London, EC4Y 9BW, England. *Telephone:* (20) 7583-1770. *E-mail:* anthony.lester@blackstonechambers.com. *Website:* www.blackstonechambers.com.

L'ESTRANGE, Michael, MA; Australian diplomatist and civil servant; *Secretary, Department of Foreign Affairs and Trade;* b. 12 Oct. 1952, Sydney; s. of James Michael L'Estrange and Iris Corrigan; m. Jane Allen 1982; five s.; ed St Aloysius Coll. (Milson's Point), Sydney Univ., Univ. of Oxford, UK; mem. staff Dept of Prime Minister and Cabinet 1981–87; Visiting Fellow, Georgetown Univ., Washington, DC 1987–88, Univ. of California at Berkeley, USA 1988–89; Sr Policy Adviser Office of Fed. Leader of Opposition 1989–94; Exec. Dir Menzies Research Centre 1995–96; Sec. to Cabinet and Head of Cabinet Policy Unit, Canberra 1996–2000; High Commr in UK 2000–05; Sec. Dept of Foreign Affairs and Trade 2005–; Hon. Fellow, Worcester Coll. Oxford; Harkness Fellowship 1986, Rhodes Scholar, Univ. of Oxford 1975. *Leisure interests:* cricket, rugby, golf. *Address:* Department of Foreign Affairs and Trade, John McEwen Crescent, Barton, ACT 0221, Australia (office). *Telephone:* (2) 6261-2214 (office). *Fax:* (2) 6273-2081 (office). *Website:* www.dfat.gov.au (office).

LETERME, Yves Camille Désiré, LLB, BSc, LLM, MPA; Belgian politician; b. 6 Oct. 1960, Wervik, West Flanders; m. Sofie Haesen; ed Catholic Univ. of Leuven, Ghent Univ.; served as auditor at Court of Audit (Rekenhof/Cour des Comptes); Adjunct, then Nat. Sec. CVP, resigned to become civil servant with EU, indefinite leave 1997, apptd mem. Belgian Parl. (House of Reps) 1997–, elected 1999, 2003; mem. City Council of Ypres 1995–2001, Alderman of Ypres 1995–2001; Chair. Christen-Democratisch en Vlaams (Christian Democratic and Flemish party—CD&V) 2003–04; Minister-Pres. of Flanders 2004–07; fmr Flemish Minister of Agric. and Fisheries; fmr Deputy Prime Minister and Minister of Budget, Institutional Reforms, Transport and the North Sea in Belgian Fed. Govt; Prime Minister of Belgium 2008. *Address:* Christian Democratic and Flemish Party, Wetstraat 89, 1040 Brussels (office); Diksmuidsestraat 58, 8900 Iepre, Belgium. *Telephone:* (2) 238-38-11 (office); (57) 20-63-61. *Fax:* (2) 238-38-71 (office); (57) 20-08-14. *E-mail:* info@cdenv.be (office); info@leterme.fed.be. *Website:* www.cdenv.be (office); leterme.cdenv.be.

LETH, Jørgen; Danish filmmaker; b. 14 June 1937, Århus; has also written, produced, edited, filmed, designed production for and acted in many of his own films; cycling commentator, Tour de France on Danish TV2. *Films include:* as Dir (English titles): Stop for Bud 1963, Look Forward to a Time of Security 1964, The Perfect Human 1967, Ophelia's Flowers 1968, Near Heaven, Near Earth, 1968, Jens Otto Krag 1969, The Deer Garden 1969, without Kin 1970, Teatret i de grønne bjerge 1970, Motional Picture 1970, The Search 1970, Life in Denmark 1971, Chinese Ping-Pong 1972, Eddy Merckx in the Vicinity of a Cup of Coffee (TV) 1973, The Impossible Hour 1974, Stars and the Water Carriers 1974, Klaus Rifbjerg 1974, The Good and the Bad 1975, Sunday in Hell 1976, Peter Martins: A Dancer 1978, A Midsummer's Play (TV) 1979, Kalule 1979, At danse Bournonville 1979, Step on Silence 1982, 66 Scenes from America 1982, Haiti Express 1983, Pelota 1984, Notebook from China 1986, Moments of Play 1986, Composer Meets Quarter 1987, Notes on Love 1989, Dansk litteratur 1989, Traberg 1992, Michael Laudrup: A Football Player 1993, Haiti, Untitled 1996, I Am Alive 1999, Dreamers 2002, New Scenes from America 2003, The Five Obstructions 2003. *Address:* c/o Zentropa Production, Filmbyen 22, 2650 Hvidovre (home); c/o Danish Film Institute, Gothersgade 55, 1123 Copenhagen K, Denmark (office).

LETOKHOV, Vladilen Stepanovich, PhD, DSc; Russian physicist; *Head, Laser Spectroscopy Department, Institute of Spectroscopy, Russian Academy of Sciences;* b. 10 Nov. 1939, Irkutsk; s. of Stepan G. Letokhov and Anna V. Letokhova (née Sevastianova); m. 1st Maria Letokhova 1965 (divorced 1973); m. 2nd Tina Karu 1979; one d.; ed Moscow Physical Tech. Inst., P.N. Lebedev Physical Inst.; researcher, P. N. Lebedev Physical Inst. 1966–70; Head Laser Spectroscopy Dept, Inst. of Spectroscopy, USSR (now Russian) Acad. of Sciences 1970–, Vice-Dir for Research 1970–89; Prof., Moscow Physical-Tech. Inst. 1973–; Dir Laser Lab., Soviet (now Russian) Branch of World Lab. 1990–; Fellow American Optical Soc.; mem. New York Acad. of Sciences, Max Planck Soc., Germany, European Acad. of Arts and Science, Academia Europaea; Lenin Prize for Science and Tech. 1978, Jubilee Medal of 600th Anniversary of Heidelberg Union 1985, European Physics Soc. Prize for Quantum Electronics 1998, State Prize for Science and Tech. 2002. *Publications:* Nonlinear Laser Spectroscopy 1977, Nonlinear Laser Chemistry 1987, Photoionization Laser Spectroscopy 1987, Laser Control of Atoms and Molecules 2007, Dalla Siberia alla Scienza del Laser 2008, Astrophysical Lasers 2009, 10 other scientific books and more than 900 publs in scientific journals. *Leisure interests:* music, swimming, house design. *Address:* Institute of Spectroscopy of the Russian Academy of Sciences, Troitsk, 142190 Moscow Region (office); Puchkovo-66, Troitsk, Moscow Region, Russia (home). *Telephone:* (496) 751-05-78 (office). *Fax:* (496) 751-08-86 (office). *E-mail:* letokhov@isan.troitsk.ru (office). *Website:* www.isan.troitsk.ru (office).

ŁĘTOWSKA, Ewa Anna, MA, LLD; Polish lawyer and judge; b. 22 March 1940, Warsaw; m. Janusz Łętowski (deceased); ed Faculty of Law, Warsaw Univ.; scientific worker, Inst. of Legal Sciences, Polish Acad. of Sciences, Warsaw 1962–; Lecturer, Dept of Law, Warsaw Univ. 1963–83; first Commr for Civil Rights Protection 1987–92; lecturer and author of educational material, Helsinki Foundation for Human Rights, Warsaw 1992–99; mem. Expert Cttee, ILO 1993–2002; Judge, Supreme Administrative Court 1999–2002; Judge, Polish Constitutional Tribunal 2002–; mem. Int. Comm. of Jurists 1995–, mem. Exec. Cttee 1995–98, Vice-Pres. 1998–2001; fmr mem. Bd of Stichting European Human Rights Foundation, Legis. Council at Chair. of Council of Ministers, Codifying Comm. for the Reform of Civil Law; Corresp. mem. Polish Acad. of Arts and Sciences, Kraków and Acad. of Comparative Law, Paris; mem. Polish Helsinki Cttee 1991–; Kt's Cross, Order of Polonia Restituta; Friedrich Ebert Stiftung Award; recipient of many scientific awards. *Publications:* 19 books on civil law, consumer protection and constitutional law; co-author of three books about music; introductions to theatre programmes, concerts and opera reviews; over 30 articles. *Leisure interests:* classical music, vocalism. *Address:* Biuro Trybunału Konstytucyjnego, ul. J. Ch. Szucha 12A, 00-918 Warsaw (office); Instytut Nauk Prawnych PAN, ul. Nowy Świat 72, 00-330 Warsaw, Poland (office). *Telephone:* (22) 8267853 (Institute) (office). *Website:* www.trybunal.gov.pl (office).

LETSIE III, King of Lesotho, BLL; b. 17 July 1963, Morija; s. of the late King Moshoeshoe II and Queen Mamohato Berenc Seeiso; m. Anna Karabo

Mots'oeneng (now Queen 'Masenate Mohato Seeiso) 2000; two d.; ed Nat. Univ. of Lesotho, Univs of Bristol, Cambridge and London; Prin. Chief of Matsieng 1989; installed as King Nov. 1990, abdicated Jan. 1995, reinstated following his father's death Feb. 1996–; Patron of Prince Mohato Award (Khau Ea Khosana Mohato). *Leisure interests:* classical and traditional music, horse riding, rugby, squash, tennis. *Address:* Royal Palace, Maseru, Lesotho.

LETTA, Enrico, PhD; Italian politician; b. 20 Aug. 1966, Pisa; m. Gianna Letta; two s.; ed Univ. of Pisa, Sant'Anna School of Advanced Studies; researcher, Agency for Research and Legislation, Rome 1991–94, Sec.-Gen. 1994–; Chair. European Young Christian Democrats 1991–95; Head of Secr. of Foreign Minister Beniamino Andreatta 1993–94; Sec.-Gen. Cttee for the Euro, Ministry of the Treasury, the Budget and Econ. Planning 1996–97; Deputy Sec. Italian People's Party 1997–98; Minister for Community Policies 1998–99, for Industry, Trade and Crafts Jan.–April 2000, for Industry and Foreign Trade 2000–01; nat. official of Margherita party responsible for the economy 2001–07; mem. Chamber of Deputies 2001–04, 2006– (Olive Tree coalition); mem. Partito Democratico 2007–; mem. European Parl. for NE Italy 2004–06, part of Alliance of Liberals and Democrats for Europe, mem. Cttee on Econ. and Monetary Affairs, mem. Del. for relations with the Maghreb countries and the Arab Maghreb Union (including Libya); Under-Sec. of State to the Presidency of the Council of Ministers 2006–08; Vice-Pres. Aspen Inst. Italy 2004–; Shadow Minister for Welfare 2008–; Prof. under contract, Libera Università Cattaneo 2001–03, la Scuola superiore S. Anna di Pisa 2003, Haute école de commerce, Paris 2004, 2005; mem. Trilateral Comm. *Publications:* Passaggio a Nord-Est 1994, Euro sì – Morire per Maastricht 1997, La Comunità competitiva 2001, Dialogo intorno all'Europa (with L. Caracciolo) 2002, L'allargamento dell'Unione europea 2003, Viaggio nell'economia italiana (with P. Bersani) 2004), L'Europa a Venticinque 2005. *Address:* Partito Democratico, Piazza Saint'Anastasia 7, 00186 Rome, Italy (office). *Telephone:* (06) 675471 (office). *Fax:* (06) 67547319 (office). *E-mail:* info@partitodemocratico.it (office). *Website:* www.partitodemocratico.it (office).

LETTE, Kathy; Australian author and playwright; b. 11 Nov. 1958, Sydney; d. of Mervyn Lette and Val Lette; m. Geoffrey Robertson (q.v.) 1990; one s. one d.; fmr columnist, Sydney and NY; fmr satirical news writer and presenter Willasee Show, Channel 9; fmr TV sitcom writer Columbia Pictures, LA; fmr guest presenter This Morning with Richard and Judy, ITV; writer-in-residence, The Savoy, London 2003; Australian Literature Board Grant 1982. *Plays include:* Wet Dreams 1985, Perfect Mismatch 1985, Grommits 1986, I'm So Happy For You, I Really Am 1991. *Films:* Puberty Blues 1982, Mad Cow 2001. *Publications:* Puberty Blues (with G. Carey) 1979, Hit and Ms 1984, Girls' Night Out 1987, The Llama Parlour 1991, Foetal Attraction 1993, Mad Cows 1996, She Done Him Wrong (essays), The Constant Sinner by Mae West (introduction) 1995, Altar Ego 1998, Nip 'n Tuck 2001, Dead Sexy 2003, How to Kill Your Husband 2005, A Stitch in Time 2005; contribs to Sydney Morning Herald, The Bulletin, Cleo Magazine. *Leisure interests:* scuba diving, opera, feminism. *Address:* c/o Pan Macmillan, 25 Eccleston Place, London, SW1W 9NF (office); c/o Ed Victor, 6 Bayley Street, London, WC1B 3HB, England. *Telephone:* (20) 7304-4100 (office). *Fax:* (20) 7304-4111 (office). *E-mail:* kathy.lette@virgin.net (office). *Website:* www.kathylette.com (office).

LETTERMAN, David; American comedian, talk show host and producer; *Host, Late Show with David Letterman;* b. 12 April 1947, Indianapolis; s. of Joseph Letterman and Dorothy Letterman; m. 1st Michelle Cook 1969 (divorced 1977); m. 2nd Regina Lasko 2009; one s.; ed Ball State Univ.; radio and TV announcer in Indianapolis 1970–75; performer, The Comedy Store, LA 1975; frequent guest host on The Tonight Show; host, David Letterman Show 1980, Late Night with David Letterman (NBC) 1982–93; Late Show with David Letterman (CBS, also writer and producer) 1993–; Founder and Chair. Worldwide Pants Inc. (production co.) 1993–; TV scriptwriter including Bob Hope Special, Good Times, Paul Lynde Comedy Hour, John Denver Special; co-owner Rahal Letterman Racing 1996–; recipient of six Emmy Awards. *Publications include:* The Late Night with David Letterman Book of Top Ten Lists 1990, An Altogether New Book of Top Ten Lists, 1991, David Letterman's Book of Top Ten Lists 1996. *Leisure interests:* baseball, basketball, running, auto racing. *Address:* Late Show with David Letterman, Ed Sullivan Theater, 1697 Broadway, New York, NY 10019 (office); Worldwide Pants Inc., 1697 Broadway, Suite 805, New York, NY 10019, USA. *Telephone:* (212) 975-5300 (Worldwide Pants). *Fax:* (212) 975-4780 (Worldwide Pants). *Website:* www.cbs.com/latenight/lateshow (office); www.rahal.com.

LETTINGA, Gatze, DrIr; Dutch chemical engineer and academic; *Advisor to the Board, Lettinga Associates Foundation;* b. 4 Jan. 1936, Dongjum, Friesland; ed RHBS High School, Harlingen, Tech. Univ., Delft, Inter Univ. Reactor Inst., Delft; began his work on devt and implementation of anaerobic treatment systems in 1971, developed Upflow Anaerobic Sludge Bed Reactor system 1972, succeeded in implementing it in sugar beet industry for treatment of wastewater; joined Dept of Environmental Tech., Wageningen Agricultural Univ. 1970, Prof. in Environmental Tech. 1988–2001 (retd); currently Consultant and mem. Bd of Dirs Lettinga Associates Foundation (LeAF— fmrly Environmental Protection and Resources Conservations Foundation, Chair. 1997–2002); has served on organizing or scientific cttees of several nat. and int. confs, including Second Int. AD-Symposium 1981, Third Int. AD-Symposium, Boston 1983; organized yearly int. courses on Anaerobic Digestion for developing countries; fmr mem. Editorial Bd Agricultural Wastes (now Bioresources Technology), Re/Views in Environmental Science and Bio/Technology, Journal of Environmental Science and Health; mem. Dutch Asscn of Water Pollution Control (NVA), Dutch Asscn of Biotechnology (NBV), Int. Water Asscn; Dr hc (Univ. of Valladolid, Spain) 2001; NVA Prize, Dutch Asscn on Wastewater Treatment 1979, Medaille d'argent de la Ville de Paris 1981, Karl Imhoff Award, Int. Asscn of Water Pollution Research Control 1992, Royal Shell Prize for Sustainable Devt and Energy 2001, Tyler Prize for Environmental Achievement 2007. *Achievements include:* was involved in more than 15 eng projects on anaerobic wastewater treatment plants in developing countries, including Cuba, Brazil, Indonesia, India and Viet Nam 1980s, Morocco present day. *Publications:* more than 500 scientific papers in professional journals on anaerobic digestion and treatment of solid and liquid wastewater in modern high-rate treatment systems under psychrophilic, mesophilic and thermophilic conditions for remediation and energy production. *Address:* Lettinga Associates Foundation, PO Box 500, 6700 AM Wageningen, Netherlands (office). *Telephone:* (317) 482023 (office). *Fax:* (317) 482108 (office). *E-mail:* gatze.lettinga@wur.nl (office). *Website:* www.lettinga-associates.wur.nl (office).

LETWIN, Rt Hon. Oliver, MA, PhD, FRSA; British politician; *Chairman of the Policy Review and Chairman of the Conservative Research Department;* b. 19 May 1956; s. of the late W. Letwin and Shirley R. Letwin; m. Isabel Grace 1984; one s. one d.; ed Eton, Trinity Coll. Cambridge, London Business School; visiting research fellow Princeton Univ. 1980–81; research fellow Darwin Coll. Cambridge 1981–82; special adviser Dept of Educ. and Science 1982–83; mem. Prime Minister's Policy Unit 1983–86; Dir N.M. Rothschild and Sons Ltd 1991–; MP (Conservative) Dorset W 1997–2003; Opposition Front Bench Spokesperson on Constitutional Affairs 1998–99; Shadow Financial Sec. to Treasury 2000–01; Shadow Chief Sec. to Treasury 2000–01; Shadow Sec. of State for Home Affairs 2001–02; Privy Councillor 2002; Shadow Sec. of State for Econ. Affairs and Shadow Chancellor of the Exchequer 2003– May 2005; Shadow Sec. of State for Environment, Food and Rural Affairs May-Dec. 2005; Chair. of Policy Review and Chair. of Conservative Research Dept 2005–; Fellow, Darwin Coll., Cambridge 1981–83. *Publications include:* Ethics, Emotion and the Unity of Self 1984, Privatising the World 1987, Aims of Schooling 1988, Drift to Union 1990, The Purpose of Politics 1999; numerous articles in professional and popular journals. *Leisure interests:* philosophy, walking, skiing, tennis. *Address:* House of Commons, London, SW1A 0AA (office); Conservative Party, 32 Smith Square, London, SW1P 3HH, England (office). *Telephone:* (1308) 456891 (office). *Fax:* (1308) 456891 (office). *E-mail:* letwino@parliament.uk (office). *Website:* www.dorsetwestconservatives.com (office); www.conservatives.com (office).

LEUENBERGER, Moritz; Swiss politician and lawyer; *Head, Federal Department of Transport, Energy and Communications;* b. 21 Sept. 1946, Biel/Bienne; s. of Robert Leuenberger and Ruth Leuenberger; m. Gret Loewensberg 2003; two s.; ed Univ. of Zürich; pvt. practice as lawyer 1972–91; joined Social Democratic Party (SP) 1969, Leader Zürich SP 1972–80; mem. Zürich City Council 1974–83; Pres. Swiss Tenants' Asscn 1986–91; elected to Nat. Council 1979; elected to Zürich Cantonal Council 1991, Dir of Justice and Internal Affairs 1991–95; Fed. Councillor 1995–; Minister, Fed. Dept of Transport, Communications and Energy 1995–, Head of Fed. Dept of Environment, Transport, Energy and Communications (subsequently Transport, Energy and Communications) 2001–; Vice-Pres. Swiss Confed. 2000, 2005, Pres. 2001, 2006. *Address:* Federal Department of Transport, Energy and Communications, Bundeshaus-Nord, 3003 Berne, Switzerland (office). *Telephone:* (31) 3225511 (office). *Fax:* (31) 3225976 (office). *E-mail:* webmaster@gs-uvek.admin.ch (office). *Website:* www.uvek.admin.ch (office).

LEUNG, C. C., BSc; Taiwanese business executive; *Vice-Chairman and President, Quanta Computer Inc.;* ed Nat. Taiwan Univ.; co-f. Quanta Computer Inc. 1988, Pres. 1993–2006, 2007–, also Vice-Chair. and Chief Research and Devt Officer; Pres. Quanta Research Inst. *Address:* Quanta Computer Inc., 211 Wen Hwa Second Road, Kui Shan Hsiang, Taoyuan, Taiwan (office). *Telephone:* (3) 327-2345 (office). *Fax:* (3) 327-1511 (office). *E-mail:* campus@quantatw.com (office). *Website:* www.quantatw.com (office).

LEUNG, Chun-Ying, JP; Chinese civil servant; *Non-Official Member, Executive Council of Hong Kong;* b. 1954, Hong Kong; m. Regina Tong Ching Yee; three c.; ed Bristol Polytechnic and King's Coll. London, UK; fmr Sec. Gen. Basic Law Consultative Cttee; Vice-Chair. Preparatory Cttee, Hong Kong Special Admin. Region; Convenor Exec. Council, Non-Official Mem. 1997–; Chair. DTZ Debenham Tie Leung Ltd, One Country Two Systems Research Inst. Ltd; Fellow Hong Kong Inst. of Surveyors; Gold Bauhinia Star; Hon. DBA. *Leisure interests:* gardening, sports. *Address:* 10th Floor, Jardine House, Central, Hong Kong Special Administrative Region, People's Republic of China (office). *Telephone:* (852) 25070503 (office). *Fax:* (852) 25301555 (office). *E-mail:* leungcy@dtz.com.hk (office).

LEUNG, Oi Sie (Elsie), LLM, JP; Chinese politician and legal official (retd); b. 24 April 1939, Hong Kong; ed Univ. of Hong Kong; admitted as solicitor of Hong Kong 1968, as overseas solicitor, UK Supreme Court 1976; Notary Public 1978; admitted as solicitor and barrister of Victoria, Australia 1982; founding mem. Hong Kong Fed. of Women Lawyers 1975, Hong Kong Fed. of Women 1993; Pres. Int. Fed. of Women Lawyers 1994; del. 7th People's Congress of Guangdong Prov. 1989–93, 8th Nat. People's Congress, People's Repub. of China 1993–97; Sec. for Justice of Hong Kong Special Admin. Region 1997–2005, also Chief Legal Adviser and Ex-Officio Mem. Exec. Council of Hong Kong 1997–2005; Fellow Int. Acad. of Matrimonial Lawyers 1994; Hon. LLD (China Univ. of Political Science and Law) 2004, (Warwick) 2005; Grand Bauhinia Medal (Hong Kong) 2002. *Address:* c/o Department of Justice, Secretary for Justice's Office, 4th Floor, High Block, Queensway Government Offices, 66 Queensway, Hong Kong Special Administrative Region, People's Republic of China (office).

LEUNG, Tony Chiu Wai; Hong Kong actor; b. 27 June 1962, Hong Kong. *Films:* Feng kuang ba san (Mad Mad 83) 1983, Qing chun chai guan (Young Cops) 1985, Din lo jing juen (The Lunatics) 1986, Deiha tsing (Love Unto

Waste) 1986, Yan man ying hung (The People's Hero) 1987, Sha shou hu die meng (My Heart is that Eternal Rose) 1987, Kai xin kuai huo ren (Happy Go Lucky) 1987, Tie jia wu di Ma Li A (I Love Maria) 1988, Beiqing chengshi (City of Sadness) 1989, Zhong yi qun ying (Seven Warriors) 1989, Liang ge you qi jiang (Two Painters) 1989, Die xue jie tou (Bullet in the Head) 1990, A Fei jing juen (Days of Being Wild) 1991, Hoyat gwan tsoi loi (Au revoir mon amour) 1991, Sinnui yauman III (Chinese Ghost Story 3) 1991, Zhong huan ying xiong (Don't Fool Me) 1991, Wu hu jiang zhi jue lie (The Tigers) 1991, Sha Tan-Zi yu Zhou Shih-Nai (Royal Scoundrel) 1991, Qian Wang (The Great Pretenders) 1991, Haomen yeyan (The Banquet) 1991, Lashou shentan (Hard Boiled) 1992, Ge ge de qing ren (Three Summers) 1993, Ya Fei yu Ya Ji (The Days of Being Dumb) 1992, Ti dao bao (Lucky Encounter) 1992, Fan dou ma liu (Come Fly the Dragon) 1992, Yi yu zhi mo lu ying xiong (End Of The Road) 1993, Xin xian hao shen zhen (The Magic Crane) 1993, Xin nan xiong nan di (He Ain't Heavy, He's My Father) 1993, Xin liu xing hu die jian (Butterfly and Sword) 1993, Wei Xiao Bao zhi feng zhi gou nu (Hero Beyond The Boundary Of Time) 1993, Seidu yinghung tsun tsi dung sing sai tsau (The Eagle Shooting Heroes) 1993, Mo hua qing (Fantasy Romance) 1993, Feng chen san xia (Tom, Dick, and Hairy) 1993, Chong qing sen lin (Chungking Express) 1994, Dung che sai duk (Ashes of Time) 1994, Shen long du sheng zhi qi kai de sheng (Always Be the Winners) 1994, Dun jeuk nai guay loy (The Returning) 1994, Xich lo (Cyclo) 1995, Ming yat tin aai (Tomorrow) 1995, Liu mang yi sheng (Dr Mack) 1995, Jushi shengun (Heaven Can't Wait) 1995, Tou tou ai ni (Blind Romance) 1996, Hong xing zi zhi jiang hu da feng bao (War of the Underworld) 1996, Cheun gwong tsa sit (Happy Together) 1997, Zui jia pai dang zhi zui jie pai dang (97 Aces Go Places) 1997, Aau dut (The Longest Nite) 1998, Hai shang hua (Flowers of Shanghai) 1998, Mooi tin oi lei siu shut (Your Place or Mine) 1998, Hei yu duan chang ge zhi qi sheng zhu rou (Chinese Midnight Express) 1998, Chiu si hung yiu oi (Timeless Romance) 1998, Bor lei jun (Gorgeous) 1999, Dong jing gong lue (Tokyo Raiders) 2000, Fa yeung nin wa (In the Mood for Love) (Best Actor Cannes Film Festival) 2000, Tung gui mat yau (Fighting for Love) 2001, Hap gwat yan sam (Healing Hearts) 2001, Yau ching yam shui baau (Love Me, Love My Money) 2001, Tian xia wu shuang (Chinese Odyssey 2002) 2002, Ying xiong (Hero) 2002, Wu jian dao (Infernal Affairs) 2002, Xing yun chao ren (My Lucky Star) 2003, Wu jian Dao 3 (Infernal Affairs III) 2003, Dei gwong tit 2003, Di xia tie 2003, 2046 (Best Actor Hong Kong Film Critics' Society 2005) 2004. *Address:* c/o Jet Tone Productions Limited, Flat E, 3/F, Kalam Court 9, Grampion Road, Kowloon, Hong Kong Special Administrative Region, People's Republic of China (office).

LEUNG KAM CHUNG, Antony, BSc; Hong Kong banker and government official; b. 29 Jan. 1952, Hong Kong; m. 1st Sophie Leung; m. 2nd Fu Mingxia (q.v.) 2002; one d.; ed Univ. of Hong Kong, Harvard Business School, USA; Man. Dir and Regional Man. for Greater China and the Philippines, Chase Manhattan Bank; Chair. Univ. Grants Cttee 1993–98; Dir Hong Kong Futures Exchange 1987–90, Hong Kong Policy Research Inst. 1996–; Trustee Queen Mary Hosp. Charitable Trust 1993–, Hong Kong Centre for Econ. Research 1995–98; Hong Kong Affairs Adviser 1994–97; Arbitrator China Int. Econ. and Trade Arbitration Comm. 1994–; mem. Industrial Devt Bd 1985, Univ. and Polytechnic Grants Cttee 1990–93, Bd Provisional Airport Authority 1990–95, Bd Airport Authority 1995–99, Cen. Policy Unit 1992–93, Bd Hong Kong Community Chest 1992–94, Educ. Comm. 1993–98 (Chair. 1998), Standing Council Chinese Soc. of Macroeconomics, State Planning Comm. 1994–, Exchange Fund Advisory Cttee 1993–, Prep. Cttee of Hong Kong Special Admin. Region 1996–97, Exec. Council Hong Kong Special Admin. Region 1997–; Financial Sec. Exec. Council 2001–03 (resgnd). *Leisure interest:* golf.

LEUTHARD, Doris; Swiss politician; *Vice President of the Federal Council and Head of the Federal Department of Economic Affairs;* b. 10 April 1963; m. Roland Hausin; ed Zürich Univ.; mem. Swiss Nat. Council 1999–2006; Grossrätin, Aragau Canton 1997–2000; Vice-Pres. Christian Democratic Party 2001–04, Pres. 2004–06; mem. Fed. Council and Head of Fed. Dept of Econ. Affairs 2006–, also responsible for Agric., Veterinary Affairs, Consumer Affairs, Housing, Vocational Training, European Integration, Vice-Pres. Fed. Council 2009–. *Address:* Federal Department of Economic Affairs, Bundeshaus Ost, 3003 Bern, Switzerland (office). *Telephone:* 313222007 (office). *Fax:* 313222194 (office). *E-mail:* info@gs-evd.admin.ch (office). *Website:* www.evd.admin.ch (office); www.doris-leuthard.ch.

LEVADA, HE Cardinal William Joseph, STD; American ecclesiastic; *Prefect, Congregation for the Doctrine of the Faith;* b. 15 June 1936, Long Beach, Calif.; s. of Joseph Levada, Jr and Lorraine Nunez Levada; ed St Anthony's High School, Long Beach, Our Lady Queen of Angels Seminary, San Fernando, St John's Seminary, Camarillo, North American Coll. and Pontifical Gregorian Univ., Rome, Italy; ordained priest 1961; Assoc. Pastor, St Louis of France Parish, San Gabriel Valley community of La Puente 1962; Assoc. Pastor, St Monica's Church, Santa Monica 1963–67, where he served as high school religion teacher and chaplain of local Community Coll. Newman Center; taught theology at St John's Seminary School of Theology, Los Angeles 1970–76; served as first Dir Continuing Educ. for the Clergy, Archdiocese of Los Angeles 1973; Pres. Senate of Priests 1975–76; official of Congregation for the Doctrine of the Faith, Vatican City 1976–82; part-time Instructor, Pontifical Gregorian Univ. 1976–82; Exec. Dir California Catholic Conf. of Bishops, Sacramento 1982–84; Auxiliary Bishop of Los Angeles (Titular Bishop of Capri) 1983–86; Episcopal Vicar for Santa Barbara Co. 1984–86; Chancellor and Moderator of the Curia 1986; Archbishop of Portland, Ore. 1986–95; Coadjutor Archbishop of San Francisco Aug.–Dec. 1995, Archbishop of San Francisco 1995–2005; Apostolic Admin. Diocese of Santa Rosa 1999–2000; Bishop Co-Chair. Anglican–Roman Catholic Dialogue in the US 2000–05; mem. Congregation for the Doctrine of the Faith 2000–05, Prefect 2005–; cr. Cardinal 2006; Chair. US Conf. of Catholic Bishops' Cttee on Doctrine 2003–05. *Address:* Congregation for the Doctrine of the Faith, Palazzo del Sant'Uffizio, Piazza del S. Uffizio 11, 00193 Rome, Italy (office). *Telephone:* (06) 69883357 (office). *Fax:* (06) 69883409 (office). *E-mail:* cdf@cfaith.va (office). *Website:* www.vatican.va/roman_curia/congregations/cfaith (office).

LEVEAUX, David; British theatre director; b. 13 Dec. 1957; s. of Michael Leveaux and Eve Powell; ed Univ. of Manchester; Assoc. Dir Riverside Studios 1981–85; Artistic Dir Theatre Project Tokyo 1993– has directed productions for Nat. Theatre, RSC, ENO. *Productions include:* A Moon for the Misbegotten 1984, No Man's Land 1992, Anna Christie (Tony Award 1993), Moonlight, The Turn of the Screw, Salome, The Real Thing, Nine 1996, Electra 1998. *Address:* c/o Simpson Fox Associates Ltd, 52 Shaftesbury Avenue, London, W1V 7DE, England (office). *Telephone:* (20) 7434-9167 (office). *Fax:* (20) 7494-2887 (office). *E-mail:* cary@simpson-fox.demon.co.uk (office).

LEVELT, Willem J. M. (Pim), PhD; Dutch psychologist, psycholinguist and academic; *Director Emeritus, Max-Planck-Institute for Psycholinguistics;* b. 17 May 1938, Amsterdam; s. of Dr W. H. Levelt and J. Levelt-Berger; m. Elisabeth C. M. Jacobs 1963; two s. one d.; ed Leiden Univ.; staff. mem. Inst. for Perception, Soesterberg 1962–65; Research Fellow Center for Cognitive Studies, Harvard Univ. 1965–66; Visiting Asst Prof. Univ. of Illinois 1966–67; Prof. of Experimental Psychology, Groningen Univ. 1967–70, Nijmegen Univ. 1971–79, Hon. Prof. of Psycholinguistics 1980–; Leader Max-Planck Project Group for Psycholinguistics, Nijmegen 1976–79; Dir Max-Planck-Inst. for Psycholinguistics, Nijmegen 1980–2005, now Dir Emer. 2005–; Visiting Prof. Louvain Univ. 1967–70; mem. Inst. for Advanced Study, Princeton 1971–72; mem. Royal Netherlands Acad. of Sciences, Pres. 2002–05; mem. Academia Europaea, American Philospohical Soc., NAS, Leopoldina and other acads; Hon. dgress from Univs of Maastricht, Antwerp, Louvain, Padua. *Publications:* On binocular rivalry 1968, Formal grammars in linguistics and psycholinguistics, 3 Vols 1974, Speaking: From intention to articulation 1989. *Leisure interest:* playing the traverso. *Address:* Max-Planck-Institute for Psycholinguistics, Wundtlaan 1, 6525 XD Nijmegen, Netherlands (office). *Telephone:* (24) 352-1317 (office). *Fax:* (24) 352-1213 (office). *E-mail:* PIM@mpi.nl (office). *Website:* www.mpi.nl/world/persons/profession/pim.html (office).

LEVELT SENGERS, Johanna Maria Henrica, (Anneke), PhD; American (b. Dutch) physicist; *Scientist Emerita, National Institute of Standards and Technology;* b. 3 March 1929, Amsterdam; d. of Wilhelmus Levelt and Josephine Berger; m. Jan V. Sengers 1963; two s. two d.; ed Univ. of Amsterdam; joined Nat. Bureau of Standards (now Nat. Inst. of Standards and Tech.) 1963, Group Leader Chemical Science and Tech. Lab. (Physical and Chemical Properties Div.) 1978–87, Sr Fellow 1984, Scientist Emer. 1995–; Fellow American Physical Soc., AAAS, Int. Asscn for the Properties of Water and Steam (IAPWS); mem. NAS, Nat. Acad. of Eng; Corresp. mem. Royal Netherlands Acad. of Arts and Sciences; fmr Pres. IAPWS and US nat. rep. to IAPWS on behalf of ASME; Jt Organizer first NATO Summer School on Supercritical Fluids 1994; Dr hc (Tech. Univ. of Delft, Netherlands); Dept of Commerce Gold Medal 1978, N American recipient of L'Oréal-UNESCO Women in Science Award 2003, Yeram S. Touloukian Award 2006. *Publications include:* How Fluids Unmix 2002; numerous papers and reviews on thermodynamics and properties of fluids and fluid mixtures near their critical points, 14 book chapters. *Leisure interests:* swimming, hiking, travelling, reading. *Address:* Physical and Chemical Properties Division, Chemical Science and Technology Laboratory, National Institute of Standards and Technology, Gaithersburg, MD 20899-8380 (office); 110 N. Van Buren Street, Rockville, MD 20850, USA (home). *Telephone:* (301) 975-2463 (office). *Fax:* (301) 869-4020 (office). *E-mail:* johanna.sengers@nist.gov (office). *Website:* www.cstl.nist.gov (office).

LEVENE, Ben, RA; British painter; b. 23 Dec. 1938, London; s. of Charlotte Levene (née Leapman) and Mark Levene; m. Susan Margaret Williams 1978; one s. two d.; ed Slade School of Fine Art, Boise Scholarship to paint in Spain; as Visiting Lecturer taught painting and drawing at Camberwell School of Art 1963–89; Visiting Tutor RA Schools 1980–95, City and Guilds 1990–95; Curator Royal Acad. Schools 1995–98; elected Assoc. of Royal Acad. 1975. *Publication:* contrib. to Oils Masterclass 1996. *Leisure interest:* gardening. *Address:* c/o Edith Devaney, The Royal Academy of Arts, Piccadilly, London W1V 0DS; c/o Browse & Darby, 19 Cork Street, London W1X 2LP, England. *Telephone:* (20) 7734-7984 (Gallery); (20) 7439-7438 (Royal Academy).

LEVENE OF PORTSOKEN, Baron (Life Peer), cr. 1997, of Portsoken in the City of London; **Peter Keith Levene,** KBE, BA, JP, FCIT, CIMgt; British business executive; *Chairman, Lloyd's;* b. 8 Dec. 1941, Pinner, Middx; s. of the late Maurice Levene and Rose Levene; m. Wendy Ann Levene 1966; two s. one d.; ed City of London School and Univ. of Manchester; joined United Scientific Holdings 1963, Man. Dir 1968, Chair. 1982; Personal Adviser to Sec. of State for Defence 1984; Chief of Defence Procurement, Ministry of Defence 1985–91; mem. SE Asia Trade Advisory Group 1979–83, Council, Defence Mfrs Asscn 1982–85, Vice-Chair. 1983–84, Chair. 1984–85; Chair. European NATO Nat. Armaments Dirs 1990–91, Docklands Light Railway Ltd 1991–94; Special Adviser to Sec. of State for the Environment 1991–92; Adviser to Prime Minister on Efficiency 1992–97; Special Adviser to Pres. of the Bd of Trade 1992–95; Chair. Public Competition and Purchasing Unit, HM Treasury 1991–92; Deputy Chair. Wasserstein Perella & Co. Ltd 1991–94; Chair. and CEO Canary Wharf Ltd 1993–96; Sr Adviser Morgan Stanley & Co. Ltd 1996–98; Chair. Bankers Trust Int. 1998–99, Investment Banking Europe, Deutsche Bank AG 1999–2001 (Vice-Chair. Deutsche Bank UK 2001–02), General Dynamics UK Ltd 2001–, Lloyd's 2002–; mem. Bd Dirs Haymarket Group Ltd 1997–, J. Sainsbury PLC 2001–04, China Construction Bank 2006–; mem. Supervisory Bd Deutsche Boerse AG 2004–05; Alderman, City of London 1984–, Sheriff 1995–96, Lord Mayor of London 1998–99; Fellow, Queen Mary and Westfield Coll., Univ. of London 1995; Hon. Col Commdt,

Royal Corps of Transport 1991–93, Royal Logistics Corps 1993–; Master, Worshipful Co. of Carmen 1992–93; KStJ 1998; Commdr, Order nat. du Mérite 1996; Kt Commdr, Order of Merit (Germany) 1998, Middle Cross Order of Merit (Hungary) 1999; Hon. DSc (City Univ.) 1998, (Univ. of London) 2005. *Leisure interests:* skiing, travel, watching Association football. *Address:* Lloyd's, One Lime Street, London, EC3M 7HA, England (office). *Telephone:* (20) 7327-6556 (office). *Fax:* (20) 7327-5926 (office). *E-mail:* peter.levene@lloyds.com (office). *Website:* www.lloyds.com (office).

LEVENS, Marie E.; Suriname politician and international organization official; *Director, Department of Human Development, Organization of American States;* b. 1950; fmr Sr Policy Adviser, Higher Educ. Devt Scholarship and Exchange Programs, Ministry of Educ. and Community Devt; Consultant, Inter-American Devt Bank 1998; Minister of Foreign Affairs 2000–05; mem. Suriname Nat. Party (NPS-Nationale Partij Suriname); currently Dir Dept of Human Devt, OAS, Washington, DC. *Address:* Organization of American States, General Secretariat Building (GSB), Office 760, 1889 F Street, NW, Washington, DC 20006, USA (office). *Telephone:* (202) 458-6166 (office). *Website:* www.oas.org (office).

LEVENTAL, Valery Yakovlevich; Russian artist and stage designer; b. 17 Aug. 1942, Moscow; ed All-Union State Cinematography Inst.; with Bolshoi Theatre 1965–95, Chief designer 1988–95; Chief designer Moscow A. P. Chekhov Arts Theatre 2001–; corresp. mem. USSR (now Russian) Acad. of Arts 1988; People's Artist of the USSR 1989; designs and sets for Cinderella, Romeo and Juliet, Anna Karenina, Khovanshchina, Prince Igor (Vilnius and Sofia), Tosca, Così fan tutte, Madame Butterfly, Otello, Till Eulenspiegel, Icarus, décor for experimental ballets of Maiya Plisetskaya (q.v.) and Vladimir V. Vasiliyev; also for Love for Three Oranges (Berlin), War and Peace, Dead Souls (Bolshoi). *Theatrical designs:* Woe from Wit, The Bedbug, The Wedding (Gogol), The Marriage of Figaro, The Duenna, Macbeth (1979), The Seagull (1979), Boris Godunov. *Film designs:* Romeo and Juliet, Phèdre. *Address:* Sadovaya-Spasskaya Street 19, Apartment 88, 107078 Moscow, Russia. *Telephone:* (495) 975-14-94.

LÉVÊQUE, Jean André Eugène; French aeronautical engineer; b. 30 April 1929, Béthune; s. of André and Elise (Forêt) Lévêque; m. Geneviève Cauwet 1953; two s.; ed Ecole Polytechnique, Paris, Ecole Nationale Aviation Civile; with Air Navigation Directorate of Ministry of Public Works and Transport 1954–60, Eng in Air Traffic Bureau 1954, Head of Airports Bureau 1956–60; Civil Aviation Tech. Adviser to Minister of Public Works and Transport 1960–63; Head of Div. in European Org. for the Safety of Air Navigation (EUROCONTROL), Brussels 1964–67; with Secr.-Gen. for Civil Aviation, Paris 1968–78, Tech. Adviser to Sec.-Gen. 1968–70, Acting Sec.-Gen., then Dir of Air Navigation 1971–78; Dir-Gen. EUROCONTROL 1978–83, now mem.; Head of Gen. Inspection for Civil Aviation 1983; Chair. Conseil Supérieur Infrastructure and Air Navigation 1989–94; Pres. Admin. Council Ecole Nationale de l'Aviation Civile 1990–97; Vice-Pres. Admin. Bd Météo-France; Officier, Légion d'honneur; Commdr de l'Ordre nat. du Mérite; Médaille de l'Aéronautique. *Leisure interests:* skiing, table tennis. *Address:* 13 rue Gambetta, 92100 Boulogne-Billancourt, France (home). *Telephone:* 1-48-25-50-66 (home). *E-mail:* jean.leveque7@wanadoo.fr (home).

LÉVÊQUE, Jean-Maxime; French banker; b. 9 Sept. 1923, Paris; s. of Pierre Lévêque and Marthe Tisserand; m. Anne Charles-Laurent 1947; one s. two d. (one d. deceased); ed Lycée Buffon, Faculté de Droit, Paris, Ecole libre des sciences politiques and Ecole Nat. d'Admin; Inspector of Finances 1950; external finance official 1950–56; temporary appointment, IMF and IBRD 1956–58; Dir European Investment Bank 1958–60; Adviser, Sec.-Gen. of Presidency of Repub. 1960–64; Sec.-Gen. Conseil Nat. du Crédit 1960–64; Dir-Gen. Crédit Commercial de France 1964, Chief Exec. 1966, Vice-Pres. 1971, Pres. 1976, then Hon. Pres.; Pres. Union des Banques pour l'Equipement 1965, Vice-Pres. 1976–82; Pres., Dir-Gen. Crédit Lyonnais 1986–88, Hon. Pres. 1988; Pres. Banque de l'Union Maritime et Financière 1989–97, Euro-Clinvest 1988–94, Financière Galliéra 1990–94; numerous other directorships and professional appointments; Officier, Légion d'honneur, Commdr Ordre nat. du Mérite, Croix de guerre; Prix Renaissance 1983. *Publications:* Dénationalisations: mode d'emploi 1985, En première ligne 1986. *Address:* c/o Editions Albin Michel, 22 rue Huyghens, 75014 Paris (office); 16 rue de Bièvre, 75005 Paris, France.

LÉVÊQUE, Michel, LenD; French diplomatist; b. 19 July 1933, Algiers, Algeria; s. of Raymond Lévèque and Suzanne Lévèque (née Lucchini); m. Georgette Vandekerchove 1956; one s. two d.; ed Lycée Henri-IV, Faculté de Droit, Paris Univ.; adviser to Minister of Finance and Planning, Abidjan 1960–63; adviser on Atomic Affairs, Ministry of Foreign Affairs, Paris 1963–64, First. Sec., American Section 1968–69, Second Adviser, Personnel Dept 1972–73, Asst Dir of African and Malagasy Affairs 1982–85, Dir 1989–91; First Embassy Sec., Moscow 1965–67, Second Adviser, Sofia 1970–71, Cultural and Co-operation Adviser, Tunis 1974–78; Political Adviser, NATO Int. Secr. 1978–82; Amb. to Libya 1985–89, to Morocco 1991–93, to Brazil 1993–94, to Algeria 1995–97, Minister of State for the Principality of Monaco 1997–2000; Commdr, Légion d'Honneu, Officier, Ordre nat. du Mérite, Croix de la Valeur Militaire. *Address:* 57 rue de l'Université, 75007 Paris, France.

LEVER, Sir Jeremy Frederick, Kt, KCMG, MA, QC, FRSA; British lawyer; b. 23 June 1933, London; s. of the late Arnold Lever and of Elizabeth Cramer (née Nathan); ed Bradfield Coll., Berks., University Coll. Oxford, Nuffield Coll., Oxford; Fellow, All Souls Coll. Oxford 1957–, Sub-Warden 1982–84, Sr Dean 1988–; QC (England and Wales) 1972, (Northern Ireland) 1988; Bencher, Gray's Inn 1986–; Dir (non-exec.) Dunlop Holdings Ltd 1973–80, The Wellcome Foundation 1983–94; mem. arbitral tribunal, US/UK Arbitration concerning Heathrow Airport user charges 1989–94, Univ. of Portsmouth Ind. Inquiry 1995; Chair. Oftel Advisory Body on Fair Trading in Telecommunications 1996–2000, Performing Rights Soc. Appeals Panel 1997–2001; Visiting Prof. Wissenschaftszentrum Berlin für Sozialforschung Jan.–March 1999; Pres. Oxford Union Soc. 1957; mem. Council British Inst. of Int. and Comparative Law 1987–2005; Africa Gen. Service Medal 1953. *Publications:* The Law of Restrictive Trading Agreements 1964, Comparative Law Casebook, Torts (with W. van Gerven) and other legal works. *Leisure interests:* porcelain, music. *Address:* All Souls College, Oxford, OX1 4AL; Monckton Chambers, 1–2 Raymond Buildings, Gray's Inn, London, WC1R 5NR, England (office). *Telephone:* (1865) 279379 (Oxford); (20) 7405-7211 (office). *Fax:* (1865) 279299 (Oxford); (20) 7405-2084 (office). *E-mail:* chambers@monckton.co.uk (office). *Website:* www.monckton.co.uk (office).

LEVER, Sir Paul, KCMG, MA; British diplomatist (retd) and business executive; *Global Development Director, RWE Thames Water PLC;* b. 31 March 1944; s. of John Morrison Lever and Doris Grace Lever (née Battey); m. Patricia Anne Ramsey 1990; ed St Paul's School, Queen's Coll., Oxford; Third Sec. FCO 1966–67; Third then Second Sec., Embassy Helsinki 1967–71; Second then First Sec., UK Del. to NATO 1971–73; with FCO, London 1973–81; Asst Pvt. Sec. to Sec. of State for Foreign and Commonwealth Affairs 1978–81; Chef de Cabinet to Vice-Pres. of EEC 1981–85; Head UN Dept, FCO 1985–86, Head Defence Dept 1986–87, Security Policy Dept 1987–90; Amb. and Head UK Del. to Conventional Arms Control Negotiations, Vienna 1990–92; Asst Under-Sec. of State, FCO 1992–94, Deputy Sec. Cabinet Office and Chair. Jt Intelligence Cttee 1994–96; Deputy Under-Sec. of State (Dir for EU and Econ. Affairs), FCO 1996–97; Amb. to Germany 1998–2003; currently Global Devt Dir RWE Thames Water PLC; mem. Bd of Dirs Königswinter 2003–; Chair. Royal United Services Inst. 2004–; Hon. LLD (Birmingham) 2001. *Leisure interests:* walking, art deco pottery, the music of Sandy Denny. *Address:* RWE Thames Water PLC, 14 Cavendish Place, London, W1G 9NU (office); Royal United Services Institute, Whitehall, London, SW1, England. *Telephone:* (20) 7833-6144 (office). *Fax:* (20) 7833-6134 (office). *E-mail:* paul.lever@rwethameswater.com (office).

LEVETT, Michael John (Mike), BComm, FIA, FFA; South African insurance executive; b. 6 June 1939, Cape Town; m. Mary Gillian Aston 1966; two s. one d.; ed Christian Brothers Coll., Cape Town, Univ. of Cape Town; joined Old Mutual Life Assurance Soc. 1959, Gen. Man. 1981–85, Man. Dir 1985–, Chair. 1990–2005, CEO –2001; Deputy Chair. Mutual & Federal; Dir Barlows, Cen. Africa Bldg Soc., South African Breweries (now SABMiller) 1984–2004, Nedcor; Hon. DEconSc; Businessman of the Year, Sunday Times Business Times Top 100 Companies 1999. *Leisure interests:* skiing, tennis. *Address:* c/o Old Mutual PLC, 3rd Floor, Lansdowne House, 57 Berkeley Square, London, W1J 6ER, England. *Telephone:* (20) 7569-0100. *E-mail:* michael.levett@omg.co.uk (office).

LEVEY, Gerald Saul, AB, MD; American physician and academic; *Dean, David Geffen School of Medicine, University of California, Los Angeles;* b. 9 Jan. 1937, Jersey City, NJ; m. Barbara Ann Levey (née Cohen) 1961; two c.; ed Univ. of Medicine and Dentistry of New Jersey; intern, Jersey City Medical Center 1961–62, resident 1962–63; Postdoctoral Fellow, Dept of Biological Chem., Harvard Univ. Medical School 1963–65; Medical Resident, Mass Gen. Hosp., Boston 1965–66; Clinical Assoc., Clinical Endocrinology Br., Nat. Inst. of Arthritis and Metabolic Diseases, NIH, Bethesda, Md 1966–68; Clinical Assoc., Nat. Heart and Lung Inst. 1968–69, Sr Investigator 1969–70; Assoc. Prof. of Medicine, Univ. of Miami School of Medicine 1970–73, Prof. of Medicine 1973–79, also Howard Hughes Medical Inst. Investigator; Prof. and Chair. Dept of Medicine, Univ. of Pittsburgh School of Medicine 1979–91, also Physician-in-Chief, Presbyterian Univ. Hosp.; Sr Vice-Pres. for Medical and Scientific Affairs, Merck and Co. 1991–94; Prof. and Vice Chancellor, Medical Sciences, David Geffen School of Medicine, UCLA 1994–, also Provost of Medical Sciences and Dean; Co-Chair. Nat. Study of Internal Medicine Manpower; Fellow, ACP; fmr Pres. Asscn of Profs of Medicine; mem. Bd of Govs American Bd of Internal Medicine; mem. American Medical Asscn, Asscn of American Physicians, Soc. of Gen. and Internal Medicine, Southern Soc. for Clinical Investigation, Endocrine Soc., American Soc. for Clinical Investigation, American Fed. for Clinical Research, American Thyroid Asscn. *Address:* Office of the Dean, David Geffen School of Medicine, 12-138 CHS, Los Angeles, CA 90095-1722, USA. *Telephone:* (310) 825-5687 (office). *Fax:* (310) 206-2142 (office). *E-mail:* glevey@mednet.ucla.edu (office). *Website:* dgsom.healthsciences.ucla.edu/deans-site/levey (office).

LEVI, Arrigo, PhD; Italian journalist and political writer; b. 17 July 1926, Modena; s. of Enzo Levi and Ida Levi (née Donati); m. Carmela Lenci 1952; one d.; ed Univs of Buenos Aires and Bologna; refugee in Argentina 1942–46; Negev Brigade, Israeli Army 1948–49; BBC European Services 1951–53; London Corresp. Gazzetta del Popolo and Corriere d'Informazione 1952–59; Moscow Corresp. Corriere della Sera 1960–62; news anchorman on Italian State Television 1966–68; special corresp. La Stampa 1969–73, Ed. in Chief 1973–78, Special Corresp. 1978–; columnist on int. affairs, The Times 1979–83; Leader Writer, Corriere della Sera 1988–; Premio Trento 1987, Premio Luigi Barzini 1995, Premio Ischia Internazionale di Giornalismo 2001. *Publications:* L'economia degli Stati Uniti oggi 1966, Il potere in Russia 1965, La televisione all'italiana 1969, Viaggio fra gli economisti 1970, PCI, la lunga marcia verso il potere 1971, Un'idea dell'Italia 1983, La Democrazia nell'Italia che cambia 1984, Intervista sulla Dc 1986, Noi: gli italiani 1988, Tra Est e Ovest 1990, Yitzhak Rabin 1996, Le due fedi 1996, La vecchiaia può attendere 1997, Rapporto sul Medio Oriente 1998, Russia del '900 1999, Dialoghi di fine Millennio 1999, Dialoghi sulla fede 1999, America Latina 2004, Cinque discorsi tra due secoli 2004.

LEVI, Isaac, PhD; American philosopher and academic; *John Dewey Professor Emeritus of Philosophy, Columbia University;* b. 30 June 1930, New York; s. of Eliezer Asher Levi and Eva Lunenfeld; m. Judith R. Levi 1951; two s.; ed New York and Columbia Univs; Asst Prof. of Philosophy, Case Western Reserve Univ. 1957–62, The City Coll. of New York 1962–64; Assoc. Prof. then Full Prof. of Philosophy, Case Western Reserve Univ. 1964–67, Chair. Dept 1968–70; Prof. of Philosophy, Columbia Univ. 1970–, Chair. Dept 1973–76, 1989–91, John Dewey Prof. of Philosophy 1992–, now Emer.; Visiting Fellow Corpus Christi Coll. Cambridge, UK 1973, Darwin Coll. 1989, All Souls Coll. Oxford, UK 1988, Inst. of Advanced Study, Princeton, Hebrew Univ. of Jerusalem 1994, Wolfson Coll. Cambridge, UK 1997; mem. American Acad. of Arts and Sciences; Dr hc (Lund) 1988; Guggenheim Fellow, Fulbright Scholar; Univ. of Helsinki Medal and other awards. *Publications:* For the Sake of the Argument 1966, 1996, Gambling with Truth 1967, Enterprise of Knowledge 1980, Decisions and Revisions 1984, Hard Choices 1986, The Fixation of Belief and its Undoing 1991, For the Sake of the Argument 1996, The Covenant of Reason 1997, Mild Contradiction 2004. *Address:* 25 Claremont Avenue, New York, NY 10027, USA (home). *Telephone:* (212) 864-3615 (home). *E-mail:* levi@columbia.edu (office). *Website:* www.columbia.edu/cu/philosophy/fac-bios/levi/faculty.html (office); www.columbia.edu/~levi (office).

LEVI, Noel, CBE, BA; Papua New Guinea politician and diplomatist; b. (Wasangula Noel Levi), 6 Feb. 1942, Nonopai, Kavieng; m. Josepha Muna Levi; two s. two d.; ed Scots Coll., Queensland, Papua New Guinea Admin. Coll., Cromwell Coll. Univ. of Queensland and Univ. of Papua New Guinea; patrol officer Dept of Dist Admin., Papua New Guinea 1967, later Asst Dist Commr; Asst Sec. Dept of Chief Minister 1973; Sec. Dept of Defence 1974; Minister of Foreign Affairs 1980; Amb. to People's Repub. of China 1987; High Commr to UK (also accred to Israel, Zimbabwe and Egypt) 1991; Sec. Dept of the Prime Minister and Nat. Exec. Council 1995; Sec.-Gen. Pacific Islands Forum Secr. 1998–2003. *Leisure interests:* reading, walking, watching rugby. *Address:* c/o Pacific Islands Forum Secretariat, Private Mail Bag, Suva (office); House No. 4, Forum Secretariat Compound, Ratu Sukuna Road, Suva, Fiji (home). *Telephone:* (679) 3306535 (home).

LEVI, Yoel, MA; Romanian/American conductor; *Principal Conductor, Orchestre national d'Ile de France;* b. 16 Aug. 1950, Romania; m.; ed Tel-Aviv and Jerusalem Acads of Music, Guildhall School of Music, London; grew up in Israel; studied under Mendi Rodan, Franco Ferrara, Kiril Kondrashin; won First Prize Conductors' Int. Competition Besançon, France 1978; Asst to Lorin Maazel Cleveland Orchestra for six years, Resident Conductor 1980–84; Music Dir Atlanta Symphony Orchestra (ASO) 1988–2000, extensive European tour 1991, Music Dir Emer. 2000–; Principal Guest Conductor Israel Philharmonic Orchestra, US tour 2004; Music Adviser to Flemish Radio Orchestra; Principal Conductor Orchestre Nat. d'Ile de France 2005–; frequent guest conductor of orchestras throughout N America, Europe and the Far East; conducted Stockholm Philharmonic at Nobel Prize Ceremony 1991; performed at Opening Ceremonies of Centennial Olympic Games 1996; apptd first Music Adviser to Israel Festival for 1997/98 seasons; opera conducting debut La Fanciulla del West at Teatro Comunale, Florence 1997; has also conducted Carmen at Lyric Opera of Chicago, Makropoulus Case by Janacek in Prague, Puccini's Edgar with Orchestra Nat. de France (released as live performance on CD by Radio France), with ASO: Mozart's Magic Flute, The Abduction from the Seraglio, Bartok's Bluebeard's Castle; Distinguished Visiting Prof., Univ. of Georgia School of Music; Chevalier des Arts et des Lettres 2001; Hon. DFA (Oglethorpe Univ., Atlanta) 1997; Best Orchestra of the Year (awarded to ASO), Int. Classical Music Awards 1991–92. *Recordings:* more than 40 recordings on different labels with various orchestras, including Cleveland Orchestra, London Philharmonic, Philharmonia Orchestra, Atlanta Symphony Orchestra, of music by Barber, Beethoven, Brahms, Copland, Dohnanyi, Dvorak, Hindemith, Kodaly, Mahler, Mendelssohn, Mussorgsky, Neilsen, Prokofiev, Puccini, Ravel, Rossini, Saint-Saens, Schoenberg, Shostakovich, Sibelius, Stravinsky and Tchaikovsky. *Address:* La maison de l'Orchestre national d'Ile de France, 19 rue des Ecoles, 94140 Alfortville, France (office). *Telephone:* 1-43-68-76-00 (office). *Fax:* 1-41-79-03-50 (office). *E-mail:* courrier@orchestre-ile.com (office). *Website:* www.orchestre-ile.com (office).

LEVI-MONTALCINI, Rita; Italian research scientist; b. 22 April 1909, Turin; d. of Adamo Levi and Adele Montalcini; ed Turin Univ. Medical School; engaged in neurological research in Turin and Brussels 1936–41, in a country-cottage in Piemonte 1941–43; in hiding in Florence during German occupation 1943–44; medical doctor working among war refugees in Florence 1944–45; resumed academic positions at Univ. of Turin 1945; worked in St Louis, USA with Prof. Viktor Hamburger from 1947, Assoc. Prof. 1956, Prof. 1958–77; Dir Inst. of Cell Biology of Italian Nat. Council of Research, Rome 1969–78, Guest Prof. 1979–89, Guest Prof. Inst. of Neurobiology 1989; Pres. European Brain Research Inst.; f. Rita Levi-Montalcini Onlus Foundation; Pres. Inst. della Enciclopedia Italiana Treccani 1993–98; mem. Accademia Nazionale dei Lincei, l'Accademia Pontificia,'Accademia delle Scienze, NAS (USA), Royal Soc.; Nobel Prize for Medicine 1986 (with Stanley Cohen) for work on chemical growth factors which control growth and devt in humans and animals; Nat. Medal of Science 1987; apptd Senator for Life 2001. *Publication:* In Praise of Imperfection: My Life and Work 1988, Ninety Years in the Galaxy of the Mind 1999. *Address:* European Brain Research Institute, Via del Fosso di Fiorano 64, 00143 Rome, Italy (office). *Telephone:* (06) 501703024 (office). *Fax:* (06) 501703335 (office). *E-mail:* scientific.assist@ebri.it (office). *Website:* www.ebri.it (office).

LÉVI-STRAUSS, Claude; French anthropologist, academic and writer; *Honorary Professor, Collège de France;* b. 28 Nov. 1908, Brussels, Belgium; s. of Raymond Lévi-Strauss and Emma Lévy; m. 1st Dina Dreyfus 1932; m. 2nd Rose Marie Ullmo 1946, one s.; m. 3rd Monique Roman 1954; one s.; ed Lycée Janson de Sailly, Paris and Univ. de Paris à la Sorbonne; Prof. Univ. of São Paulo, Brazil 1935–39; Visiting Prof. New School for Social Research, New York 1942–45; Cultural Counsellor, French Embassy to USA 1946–47; Assoc. Dir Musée de l'Homme, Paris 1949–50; Dir of Studies, Ecole Pratique des Hautes Etudes, Paris 1950–74; Prof. Collège de France 1959–82, Hon. Prof. 1983–; mem. Acad. Française; Foreign mem. Royal Acad. of the Netherlands, Norwegian Acad. of Sciences and Letters, American Acad. of Arts and Sciences, American Acad. and Inst. of Arts and Letters, British Acad.; Foreign Assoc. US NAS; Hon. mem. Royal Anthropological Inst., American Philosophical Soc. and London School of Oriental and African Studies; Grand-Croix, Légion d'Honneur, Commdr Ordre Nat. du Mérite, des Palmes académiques, des Arts et des Lettres; Dr hc (Brussels, Harvard, Yale, Chicago, Columbia, Oxford, Stirling, Zaire, Mexico, Uppsala, Johns Hopkins, Montréal, Québec, Visva-Bharati Univ., India); Prix Paul Pelliot 1949; Huxley Memorial Medal 1965, Viking Fund Gold Medal 1966, Gold Medal CNRS 1967; Erasmus Prize 1973, Aby M. Warburg Prize 1996, Int. Prize, Catalunya 2002. *Publications:* La vie familiale et sociale des indiens Nambikwara 1948, Les structures élémentaires de la parenté 1949, Tristes tropiques 1955, Anthropologie structurale 1958, Le totémisme aujourd'hui 1962, La pensée sauvage 1962, Le cru et le cuit 1964, Du miel aux cendres 1967, L'origine des manières de table 1968, L'homme nu 1971, Anthropologie structurale deux 1973, La voie des masques 1975, 1979, Le regard éloigné 1983, Paroles données 1984, La potière jalouse 1985, De près et de loin (with Didier Eribon) 1988, Histoire de Lynx 1991, Regarder, écouter, lire 1993, Saudades do Brasil 1994. *Leisure interest:* country life. *Address:* Laboratoire d'Anthropologie Sociale, Collège de France, 52 rue du Cardinal Lemoine, 75005 Paris (office); 2 rue des Marronniers, 75016 Paris, France (home). *Telephone:* 1-44-27-17-31 (office); 1-42-88-34-71 (home). *Fax:* 1-44-27-17-66 (office). *E-mail:* eva-kempinski@college-de-france.fr (office). *Website:* www.ehess.fr/centres/las (office).

LEVIE, Simon Hijman; Dutch art historian (retd); b. 17 Jan. 1925, Rheden; m. Mary Levie-Lion 1955; one s. two d.; ed Univ. of Basel, Switzerland; Keeper, Central Museum, Utrecht; Dir, Historical Museum, Amsterdam; Dir-Gen. Rijksmuseum Amsterdam; Dir Simart Art Consultancy, Amsterdam 1990–. *Address:* Minervalaan 70 II, 1077 PG Amsterdam, Netherlands (home). *Telephone:* (20) 6718895 (home). *E-mail:* simart@hetnet.nl (home).

LEVIN, Carl, JD; American politician; *Senator from Michigan;* b. 28 June 1934, Detroit, Mich.; s. of Saul R. Levin and Bess Levin (née Levinson); m. Barbara Halpern 1961; three d.; ed Detroit Central High School, Swarthmore Coll., Pa and Harvard Law School; Mich. Asst Attorney Gen. and Gen. Counsel for Mich. Civil Rights Comm. 1964–67; Special Asst Attorney Gen. and Chief Appellate Attorney for Defender's Office of Legal Aid and Defender Assoc. of Detroit 1968–69; elected to Detroit City Council 1969, re-elected as City Council Pres. 1973; US Senator from Michigan 1979–; Chair. Armed Services Cttee 2001–03, 2007–; mem. Governmental Affairs Cttee; Democrat; Christian A. Herter Award, WorldBoston 2002, Distinguished Public Service Award, Sec. of the Navy 2003, Harry S. Truman Award, Nat. Guard Asscn 2004. *Address:* 269 Russell Senate Office Building, Washington, DC 20510, USA (office). *Telephone:* (202) 224-6221 (office). *Fax:* (202) 224-1388 (office). *Website:* levin.senate.gov (office).

LEVIN, Gerald Manuel, BA, LLB; American fmr media executive; *Presiding Director, Moonview Sanctuary;* b. 6 May 1939, Philadelphia, Pa; s. of David Levin and Pauline Schantzer; m. 1st Carol S. Needlemam 1959 (divorced 1970), two s. (one s. deceased), one d.; m. 2nd Barbara Riley 1970, one s. one d.; m. 3rd Laurie Perlman 2005; ed Haverford Coll. and Univ. of Pa; Assoc. Simpson, Thatcher & Bartlett, New York 1963–67; Gen. Man., COO Devt and Resources Corpn New York 1967–71; Rep. Int. Basic Economy Corpn Tehran 1971–72; Vice-Pres. Programming, Home Box Office, New York 1972–73, Pres., CEO 1973–76, Chair., CEO 1976–79; Group Vice-Pres. (Video), Time Inc. New York 1979–84, Exec. Vice-Pres. 1984–88, Vice-Chair., Dir 1988–90; Vice-Chair., Dir Time-Warner Inc. 1990–92, Jt CEO 1992–93, CEO and Chair. 1992–2001, CEO AOL Time Warner (created after merger of Time Warner and American Online 2000) 2001–02 (retd); currently Presiding Dir Moonview Sanctuary (spiritual healing firm); Hon. LLD (Texas Coll.) 1985, (Middlebury Coll.) 1994, Hon. LHD (Univ. of Denver) 1995; Media Person of the Year Award, Cannes Lions Int. Advertising Festival 2001. *Leisure interests:* reading, jogging. *Address:* Moonview Sanctuary, PO Box 1518, Santa Monica, CA 90406, USA (office). *Telephone:* (866) 601-0601 (office). *E-mail:* glevin@moonviewsanctuary.com (office). *Website:* www.moonviewsanctuary.com (office).

LEVIN, Richard Charles, PhD; American economist, academic and university administrator; *President, Yale University;* b. 7 April 1947, San Francisco; s. of Derek Levin and Phylys Goldstein; m. Jane Aries 1968; two s. two d.; ed Stanford and Yale Univs and Merton Coll. Oxford; Asst Prof. of Econs Yale Univ. 1974–79, Assoc. Prof. 1979–82, Prof. of Econs and Man. 1982–92, Dir Grad. Studies in Econs 1984–86, Chair. Dept of Econs 1987–92, Frederick William Beinecke Prof. of Econs 1992–, Dean, Grad. School 1992–93, Pres. Yale Univ. 1993–; Trustee Hewlett Foundation, Univs Research Asscn 1994–99; Fellow Merton Coll. Oxford 1996; Fellow American Acad. of Arts and Sciences; mem. Yale-New Haven Hosp. Bd of Trustees 1993–, Yale-New Haven Health Services Corpn Inc. 1993–; mem. American Econ. Asscn, Econometric Soc.; mem. Bd of Dirs Hewlett Foundation, Lucent Technologies, Satmetrix; Hon. LLD (Princeton) 1993, (Harvard) 1994; Hon. DCL (Oxford) 1998. *Publication:* The Work of the University 2003. *Address:* Office of the President, Yale University, 105 Wall Street, New Haven, CT 06511, USA (office). *Telephone:* (203) 432-1333 (office). *Website:* www.yale.edu/opa/president (office).

LEVIN, Richard I., BS, MD; American physician, academic and university administrator; *Dean, Faculty of Medicine, McGill University;* b. 28 July 1948, Long Branch, NJ; m. Jane Levin (née Bressman 1970; three c.; ed Yale Univ., New York Univ. School of Medicine; Postdoctoral Fellowship, Cornell Univ. Medical Coll. 1979–83; Founder, Vice-Pres. and Medical Dir Q-Med, Inc., Eatontown, NJ 1983–; practised and taught medicine for 25 years at Bellevue Hospital Center, New York City; Prof. of Medicine, New York Univ. (NYU) 1996–2006, also Vice-Dean for Educ., Faculty and Academic Affairs, NYU School of Medicine; Vice-Prin. (Health Affairs), McGill Univ., Montréal, also Dean, Faculty of Medicine 2006–; consultant to Lipsome Co., Princeton 1988–; Fellow, American Coll. of Physicians, American Coll. of Cardiology; mem. American Fed. for Clinical Research (Councilor 1986–88), Harvey Society, NY Heart Asscn. *Address:* Office of the Dean, Faculty of Medicine, McGill University, McIntyre Building, 3655 Promenade Sir William Osler, Montréal, PQ H3G 1Y6, Canada (office). *Telephone:* (514) 398-3524 (office). *Fax:* (514) 398-4423 (office). *E-mail:* richard.levin@mcgill.ca (office). *Website:* www.medicine.mcgill.ca/dean (office).

LEVIN, Simon Asher, PhD; American mathematician, ecologist and academic; *George M. Moffett Professor of Biology, Department of Ecology and Evolutionary Biology and Director, The Center for BioComplexity, Princeton University;* b. 22 April 1941, Baltimore, Md; s. of Theodore S. Levin and Clara G. Levin; m. Carole Lotte Leiffer; one s. one d.; ed Johns Hopkins Univ., Baltimore, Univ. of Maryland, College Park; Asst Prof., Cornell Univ., Ithaca, NY 1965–70, Assoc. Prof. 1971–77, Chair. Section of Ecology and Systematics, Div. of Biological Sciences 1974–79, Prof. of Applied Math. and Ecology 1977–92, Charles A. Alexander Prof. of Biological Sciences 1985–92, Adjunct Prof. 1992–, Dir Ecosystems Research Center 1980–87, Dir Center for Environmental Research 1987–90, Dir Program on Theoretical and Computational Biology 1990–92; Associated Faculty, Program in Applied and Computational Math., Princeton Univ. 1992–, George M. Moffett Prof. of Biology 1992–, Associated Faculty, Princeton Environmental Inst. 1993–, Dir Princeton Environmental Inst. 1992–98, Dir The Center for BioComplexity 2001–; numerous visiting positions including Univ. of Maryland, College Park 1968, Univ. of British Columbia, Vancouver 1979–80, Weizmann Inst., Rehovot, Israel 1977, 1980, Univ. of Kyoto, Japan 1983–84, Colorado State Univ. (Visiting Distinguished Ecologist) 1987, Stanford Univ., Calif. 1988, All Souls Coll., Oxford, UK (Visiting Fellow) 1988, Inst. for Advanced Study, Princeton 1999, 2008–09, Univ. of Miami 2004–05, Univ. of California, Irvine 2007, 2009; Visiting Miller Research Prof., Univ. of California, Berkeley 2003, Univ. of Miami 2004–05, Univ. of California, Irvine 2007, 2009; Chair. Council Int. Inst. for Applied Systems Analysis (IIASA), Laxenburg, Austria 2003–08, (Vice-Chair. 2009–), US Nat. Cttee for IIASA, The Nat. Academies 2003–; Vice-Chair. (Math.) The Committee of Concerned Scientists 1979–; mem. Steering Cttee Ecological Econs Programme, Int. Centre for Theoretical Physics, Fondazione Eni Enrico Mattei and Beijer Inst. 2003–; mem. numerous advisory bds including Biodiversity Science and Educ. Initiative (BSEI), Smithsonian Inst. 2005–, DIMACS, Rutgers Univ. 2008–(11), Center for Social and Econ. Dynamics, Brookings Inst. 2008–, Int. Network of Research on Coupled Human and Natural Systems (CHANS-Net) 2009–, Miller Inst. for Basic Research in Science, Univ. of California, Berkeley 2009–(12); mem. Science Bd Inst. for Medical BioMathematics, Bene Ataroth, Israel 1999–, Santa Fe Inst., NM 1991–99, 2001–; Ed.-in-Chief Encyclopedia of Biodiversity, Online Edn 2005–; Co-Ed.-in-Chief Princeton Series in Theoretical and Computational Biology 2000–; Co-Man. Ed. Monographs in Population Biology 1992–, Complexity Series 1992–; mem. Editorial Bd numerous journals including Evolutionary Theory 1976–, Mathematical and Computer Modelling 1979–, Applied Mathematics Letters 1987–, Mathematical Biosciences 1987–, Conservation Ecology 1995–, Issues in Ecology 1995–, Journal of Biomathematics (China) 1999–, Journal of Mathematical Biology 1995–; mem. Advisory Bd Journal of Theoretical Biology 1977–2008, Journal of Environmental and Ecological Statistics 1992–, Ecological Research 1996–, Ecological Complexity 2004–, Mathematical Biosciences and Engineering 2004–; Fellow, American Acad. of Arts and Sciences 1992, AAAS 1992; mem. American Inst. of Biological Sciences, American Soc. of Naturalists, British Ecological Soc., Ecological Soc. of America (Pres. 1990–91), Sigma Xi Soc. for Conservation Biology, Soc. for Industrial and Applied Math., Soc. for Math. Biology (Pres. 1987–89, Past Pres. and Vice-Pres. 1989–91), Soc. for the Study of Evolution, NAS 2000, American Philosophical Soc. 2003; Foreign mem. Istituto Veneto di Scienze, Lettere ed Arti, Venice 2008; Beijer Fellow 2007; Resources for the Future Univ. Fellow 2008–(11); Hon. Ed. Bulletin of Mathematical Biology 1996–; Hon. mem. Lund (Sweden) Ecological Soc. 1999, Eastern Europe Soc. of Math. Ecology 1995, Asian Math. Ecology Soc. 1995, World Innovation Foundation 2003; Hon. DSc (Eastern Michigan Univ.) 1990; Hon. DHumLitt (Whittier Coll.) 2004; MacArthur Award, Ecological Soc. of America 1988, Biology Colloquium Award, Honor Soc. of Phi Kappa Phi 1991, Distinguished Statistical Ecologist Award, Int. Asscn for Ecology 1994, Distinguished Service Citation, Ecological Soc. of America 1998, First Okubo Lifetime Achievement Award, Soc. for Math. Biology and Japanese Soc. for Theoretical Biology 2001, "Most cited paper in the field of Ecology and Environment for the 1990s", Inst. for Scientific Information 2002, Distinguished Landscape Ecologist Award, US Regional Asscn of Int. Asscn for Landscape Ecology 2003, Medallion of Université de Montpellier 2004, Dr A. H. Heineken Prize for Environmental Sciences, Royal Netherlands Acad. of Arts and Sciences 2004, Kyoto Prize in Basic Sciences, Inamori Foundation, Japan 2005, SIAM I.E. Block Community Lecture Award 2006, Distinguished Scientist Award, American Inst. of Biological Sciences 2007, Stelson Lecturer, Georgia Inst. of Tech. 2008. *Publications:* numerous publs on modelling of ecological systems, dynamics of populations and communities, spatial heterogeneity and problem of scale, evolutionary, math. and theoretical ecology. *Address:* Department of Ecology and Evolutionary Biology, 203 Eno Hall, Princeton University, Princeton, NJ 08544-1003, USA (office). *Telephone:* (609) 258-6880 (office). *Fax:* (609) 258-6819 (office). *E-mail:* slevin@princeton.edu (office). *Website:* www.eeb.princeton.edu/~slevin (office).

LEVINE, Alan J., BS, JD; American lawyer and entertainment industry executive; b. 8 March 1947, Los Angeles; s. of Phil Levine and Shirley Lauber; m. Judy Birnbaum 1973; two c.; ed Univ. of Southern Calif.; called to Bar, Calif. 1972, US Dist Court (South Dist), Calif. 1972; Pnr, Pacht, Ross, Warne, Bernhard & Sears, LA 1971–78, Schiff, Hirsch & Schreiber, Beverly Hills, Calif. 1978–80, Armstrong, Hirsch & Levine, LA 1980–89; Pres. and COO SONY Pictures Entertainment Inc., Culver City, Calif. 1989–96, Chair. 1994–96, entertainment and media consultant 1996–99; Of Counsel, Ziffren, Brittenham, Branca & Fischer (now Ziffren, Brittenham, Branca, Fischer, Gilbert-Lurie, Stiffleman & Cook LLP), LA 1999–; mem. Board of Councilors, School of Cinema-TV, Univ. of Southern Calif. *Address:* Ziffren, Brittenham, Branca, Fischer, Gilbert-Lurie, Stiffleman & Cook LLP, 1801 Century Park West, Los Angeles, CA 90067, USA. *Telephone:* (310) 275-2611. *Fax:* (310) 275-7305.

LEVINE, David, BFA, BS; American artist; b. 20 Dec. 1926, Brooklyn; s. of Harry Levine and Lena Levine; m. Kathy Hayes Levine; one s. one d.; ed Temple Univ. and Hans Hoffman School of Painting; served in US Army 1945–46; mem. American Acad. of Arts and Letters; Guggenheim Fellow 1967; Gold Medal for Graphic Art, American Acad. of Arts and Letters, Tiffany, Polk Award, Soc. of Illustrators Hall of Fame and other awards. *Publication:* Aesop (The Fables of) 1975, The Arts of David Levine 1978. *Leisure interest:* tennis. *Address:* 161 Henry Street, New York, NY 11201 (home); c/o Forum Gallery, 745 5th Avenue, New York, NY 10151, USA; c/o Galerie Claude Bernard, 9 rue des Beaux-Arts, Paris 6ème, France. *Telephone:* (718) 522-1808. *Website:* www.davidlevineart.com.

LEVINE, Jack; American artist; b. 3 Jan. 1915, Boston, Mass; s. of Samuel Levine and Mary Levine (née Grinker); m. Ruth Gikow 1946 (died 1982); one d.; ed studied with Dr Denman W. Ross and H. K. Zimmerman; social realist painter; was employed by Works Progress Admin; mem., fmr Pres., fmr Chancellor American Acad. of Arts and Letter; fmr Pres. Inst. of Arts and Letters; Hon. DFA (Colby Coll., Maine). *Publication:* Jack Levine by Jack Levine 1989. *Address:* c/o DC Moore Gallery, 724 Fifth Avenue, 8th Floor, New York, NY 10019, USA. *Telephone:* (212) 247-2111. *Fax:* (212) 247-2119. *E-mail:* dcmooregal@earthlink.net. *Website:* www.artnet.com/dcmoore.html.

LEVINE, James; American musician, conductor and pianist; *Music Director, Metropolitan Opera;* b. 23 June 1943, Cincinnati, OH; s. of Lawrence M. Levine and Helen Levine (née Goldstein); ed Walnut Hills High School, Cincinnati, The Juilliard School, New York; Asst Conductor, Cleveland Orchestra 1964–70; Prin. Conductor, Metropolitan Opera, New York 1973–, Music Dir 1976–, Artistic Dir 1986–2004; Music Dir Ravinia Festival 1973–93, Cincinnati May Festival 1974–78; Chief Conductor, Munich Philharmonic 1999–2004; Music Dir UBS Verbier Festival Youth Orchestra 2000–04; Music Dir Boston Symphony Orchestra 2004–; Artistic Dir Metropolitan Opera Lindemann Young Artist Devt Program in partnership with the Juilliard School (2010–); regular appearances as conductor and pianist in Europe and the USA with orchestras including Vienna Philharmonic, Berlin Philharmonic, Chicago Symphony, Philadelphia Orchestra, Philharmonia, Dresden Staatskapelle, Boston Symphony, New York Philharmonic, Israel Philharmonic, Salzburg and Bayreuth Festivals; conducted Metropolitan Opera premieres of I Vespri Siciliani, Stiffelio, I Lombardi (Verdi), The Rise and Fall of the City of Mahagonny (Weill), Lulu (Berg), Porgy and Bess (Gershwin), Oedipus Rex (Stravinsky), Idomeneo, La Clemenza di Tito (Mozart), Erwartung, Moses und Aron (Schönberg), La Cenerentola (Rossini), Benvenuto Cellini (Berlioz), The Ghosts of Versailles (Corigliano) (world premiere), The Great Gatsby (Harbison) (world premiere); conductor Salzburg Festival premieres of Offenbach's Les contes d'Hoffmann 1980 and Schönberg's Moses und Aron 1987; conducted Munich Philharmonic Orchestra at the London Proms 2002, Benvenuto Cellini at the Met 2003; Dr hc (Univ. of Cincinnati, New England Conservatory, Northwestern Univ., State Univ. of New York, The Juilliard School); Grammy Awards for recordings of Orff's Carmina Burana, Mahler's Symphony No. 7, Brahms' A German Requiem, Verdi's La Traviata, Wagner's Das Rheingold, Die Walküre, Götterdämmerung, Strauss' Ariadne auf Naxos; Cultural Award of New York City 1980, Smetana Medal 1987, Musical America's Musician of the Year Award, Gold Medal, Nat. Inst. of Social Sciences 1996, Nat. Medal of Arts 1997, Anton Seidl Award 1997, Lotus Award 1997, Kennedy Center Honors 2002, World Econs Forum Crystal Award 2003, Metropolitan Opera Guild Opera News Award 2006, Nat. Endowment for the Arts Opera Award 2008. *Recordings:* over 100 albums of symphonic works, chamber music, lieder and song recitals, solo piano music and 36 complete operas. *Address:* Metropolitan Opera, Lincoln Center, New York, NY 10023, USA. *Telephone:* (212) 799-3100 (office). *Website:* www.metopera.org (office); www.bso.org (office); www.verbierorchestra.com (office).

LEVINE, Seymour, PhD; American psychiatrist and academic; *Adjunct Professor, Department of Psychiatry, University of California, Davis;* b. 23 Jan. 1925, Brooklyn, NY; s. of Joseph Levine and Rose Reines; m. Barbara Lou McWilliams 1950; one s. two d.; ed Univ. of Denver, New York Univ.; Asst Prof., Div. of Research, Boston Univ. 1952–53; Postdoctoral Fellow, Michael Reese Hosp., Chicago 1953–55, Research Assoc. 1955–56; Asst Prof., Dept of Psychiatry, Ohio State Univ. 1956–60; Postdoctoral Fellow, Maudsley Hosp., London, UK 1960–62; Assoc. Prof., Dept of Psychiatry, Stanford Univ. 1962–69, Prof. 1969–96, fmr Dir Stanford Primate Facility; Dir Biological Sciences Research Training Program 1971, Prof. Emer. 1995–; Research Prof., Dept of Psychology, Univ. of Delaware and Dir Neuroscience Program 1995–2000; Adjunct Prof., Dept of Psychiatry, Univ. of California, Davis

www.worldwhoswho.com

1999–; Consultant, Foundation of Human Devt, Univ. Coll. Dublin, Ireland 1973–; Pres. Int. Soc. of Developmental Psychobiology 1975–76; Pres. Int. Soc. of Psychoneuroendocrinology; Hoffheimer Research Award 1961, Research Career Devt Award 1962, Research Scientist Award 1967. *Publications:* Stress, arousal and the pituitary-adrenal system (co-author) 1979, chapters and articles on stress in animals and humans. *Leisure interests:* music, art, sports. *Address:* University of California, Davis, Department of Psychiatry, 2230 Stockton Boulevard, Sacramento, CA 95817-1419, USA (office). *Telephone:* (530) 752-1887 (office). *E-mail:* slevine@ucdavis.edu (office). *Website:* neuroscience.ucdavis.edu/psychiatry/faculty/levine_seymour (office).

LEVINGSTON, Gen. Roberto Marcelo; Argentine politician and army officer; b. 10 Jan. 1920, San Luis; s. of Guillermo Levingston and Carmen Laborda; m. Betty Nelly Andrés 1943; two s. (one deceased) one d.; ed Pius IX Coll., Nat. Mil. Coll., Army Intelligence School, Escuela Superior de Guerra and Center for High Mil. Studies; entered army as cadet, Nat. Mil. Coll. 1938, Sub-Lt 1941, Brig.-Gen. 1966; Army Information Officer 1947–50; mem. Gen. Staff 1951–57; Prof., Escuela Superior de Guerra 1958–62; Head of Army Information Services 1963–64; Dir-Gen. Lemos School of Logistics 1965–66; Head of Intelligence of Jt Chiefs of Staff 1967–68; Mil. Attaché Army Del. to Interamerican Defense Bd and Pres. Special Comm. on Acquisitions in USA 1969–70; Pres. and Prime Minister of Argentina 1970–71; Pres. Circle of Studies of Nat. Argentine Movt. *Publications:* political and military works. *Leisure interests:* reading of all kinds, particularly on politics, economics and military subjects, music and sport. *Address:* 11 de Septiembre 1735-17 A, Buenos Aires, Argentina. *Telephone:* 782-4433 (home).

LEVINSON, Barry; American screenwriter, film director and producer; b. 6 April 1942, Baltimore, Md; m. 1st Valerie Curtin 1975 (divorced); m. 2nd Diana Rhodes; ed American Univ.; fmrly wrote and acted on TV comedy show in LA; later worked on network TV; wrote and appeared, The Carol Burnett Show; worked on film scripts for Silent Movie and High Anxiety (with Mel Brooks q.v.); f. Baltimore Pictures, Inc. and The Levinson/Fontana Co. (Exec. Producer); Hon. DFA (American Univ.) 1999; ShoWest Director of the Year Award 1998, named one of Variety Winners 'Billion Dollar Directors' 1998, Creative Achievement Award, 13th Annual American Comedy Awards 1999, ACE Golden Eddie Filmmaker of the Year Award 2002. *Actor:* High Anxiety 1977, Rain Man 1988, Quiz Show 1994, Bee Movie (voice) 2007. *Writer:* Diner, Tin Men, Avalon; co-wrote screenplays (with Valerie Curtin) for And Justice for All, Inside Moves, Best Friends, Unfaithfully Yours, Toys, Liberty Heights. *Films directed:* Diner 1982, The Natural 1984, Young Sherlock Holmes 1985, Tin Men 1987, Good Morning Vietnam 1987, Rain Man (Academy Award for Best Picture 1988, Academy Award for Best Dir 1988, Directors Guild Award for Best Dir 1988) 1988, Disclosure 1994; directed and produced Avalon (Writers Guild Award for Best Screenplay 1989) 1990, Bugsy (Golden Globe Award for Best Picture 1991) 1991, Toys 1992, Jimmy Hollywood (dir, writer) 1994, Sleepers 1996, Wag the Dog 1997, Sphere 1998, Liberty Heights 2000, An Everlasting Piece 2001, Bandits 2001, Envy 2004, Man of the Year 2006, What Just Happened? 2008. *Television includes:* writer for Tim Conway Comedy Hour, The Marty Feldman Comedy Machine, The Carol Burnett Show (Emmy Awards for TV Comedy Writing 1974, 1975); exec. producer: Harry, 30 Minutes of Investigative Ticking, Diner, Homicide: Life on the Street (series) (Emmy Award for Best Dir 1993, Peabody Award 1993, 1995, 1997, Writers Guild Award 1994, 1995, The Nancy Susan Reynolds Award for Outstanding Portrayal of Sexual Responsibility in a Dramatic Series 1996, The Prism Commendation from the Nat. Inst. Inst. on Drug Use and The Entertainment Industries Council 1997, DGA Award for Outstanding Directorial Achievement for Dramatic Series 1998, TCA Award for Program of the Year and Drama of the Year 1998, Emmy Award for Best Male Actor in a Drama Series 1998, Emmy Award for Best Casting in a Drama Series 1998, Humanitas Award 1999), Oz, The Beat 2000, Shot in the Heart 2001, Baseball Wives 2002, Possession 2002, Analyze That 2002, Deliver Us from Eva 2003, Strip Search 2004, Envy 2004, The Jury (series) 2004, The Bedford Diaries (series) 2006. *Publications:* Levinson on Levinson 1992, Sixty-Six (novel) 2003. *Address:* Baltimore Pictures, Inc., 8306 Wilshire Boulevard, PMB 1012, Beverly Hills, CA 90211, USA (office). *Website:* www.levinson.com (office).

LEVITIN, Igor Yevgenyevich; Russian politician; *Minister of Transport;* b. 1952; m.; one d.; ed Mil. Acad. of Rear Services and Transportation; mil. service 1970–94; Head of Transport Dept, Phoenix-Trans Co. 1995–98; Head of Railway Dept, Deputy Dir Severstaltrans Co. 1994–2004; Minister of Transport 2004–. *Address:* Ministry of Transport, ul. Rozhdestvenka 1/1, 109012 Moscow, Russia (office). *Telephone:* (495) 926-97-97 (office). *Fax:* (495) 926-93-35 (office). *E-mail:* KSO@mintrans.ru (office). *Website:* www.mintrans.ru (office).

LEVITIN, Mikhail Zakharovich; Russian stage director and writer; *Artistic Director, Hermitage Theatre;* b. 27 Dec. 1945, Odessa, Ukraine; m.; one d. one s.; ed Moscow Inst. of Theatre Arts; Founder and Artistic Dir Moscow Hermitage Theatre 1981–. *Stage productions include:* Wanderings of Pilgrim Billy, Faryatyev's Fantasies in Moscow Theatre of Soviet Army, Alice Behind the Mirror, Moscow Theatre of Young Spectators, Harm! Harms! Shardam! or Clowns' School 1981, Pauper or Zanda's Death 1986, Evening in a Lunatic Asylum 1991, Maria, Hermitage Theatre 1996, New Year Tree at Ivanovs', Omsk Drama Theatre 1996; Hermitage Theatre: Suyer-Viyer 2005, Rescue Cantata 2005, Dissecting Room of Engineer Evno Azef 2005, A Feast in the Time of Plague 2005–06, Erendira and Her Grandmother 2006, Under the Bed 2006. *Publications:* Other Man's Spectacle, My Friend Believes, Bolero, Sheer Indecency, Plutodrama, Dog's Shit, Dissecting Room of Engineer Evno Azef. *Address:* Moscow Hermitage Theatre, Karentny Ryad 3, 103006 Moscow, Russia (office). *Telephone:* (495) 209-20-76 (office).

LEVITIS, Yefim Zavelyevich; Russian religious leader; b. 29 Nov. 1930; m.; one s.; ed Moscow Inst. of Aviation, Jewish seminary at Moscow Choral Synagogue, Higher Rabbis' School, Budapest; Scientific Sec. Moscow Jewish community 1975–80; Rabbi, St Petersburg 1980–91; Chief Rabbi, Great Choral Synagogue 1991–; Deputy Chief Rabbi of Russia responsible for co-operation with non-Jewish orgs; mem. Jewish Conf. of Rabbis; mem. Working Group, Consultative Council of Confession Heads, St Petersburg. *Address:* Great Choral Synagogue, 2nd Lermontovsky pr., St Petersburg, Russia (office). *Telephone:* (812) 114-00-78 (office).

LEVITT, Arthur, Jr; American business executive and fmr government official; *Senior Advisor, The Carlyle Group;* b. 3 Feb. 1931, Brooklyn; s. of Arthur Levitt and Dorothy Wolff; m. Marylin Blauner 1955; one s. one d.; ed Williams Coll.; Asst Promotion Dir Time Inc. New York 1954–59; Exec. Vice-Pres., Dir Oppenheimer Industries Inc. Kansas City 1959–62; with Shearson Hayden Stone Inc. (now Shearson Lehman Bros Inc.), New York 1962–78, Pres. 1969–78; Chair., CEO, Dir American Stock Exchange, New York 1978–89; Chair. Levitt Media Co. New York 1989–93, New York City Econ. Devt Corpn 1990–93; Chair. SEC 1993–2001; Sr Advisor, The Carlyle Group 2001–; Hon. LLD (Williams Coll.) 1980, (Pace) 1980, (Hamilton Coll.) 1981, (Long Island) 1984, (Hofstra) 1985. *Address:* The Carlyle Group, 520 Madison Avenue, New York, NY 10022, USA (office). *Telephone:* (212) 381-4900 (office). *Fax:* (212) 381-4901 (office). *Website:* www.thecarlylegroup.com (office).

LEVITTE, Jean-David, LLB; French diplomatist and civil servant; b. 14 June 1946, Moissac; s. of Georges Levitte and Doreen Levitte (née Duggan); m. Marie-Cécile Levitte 1970; two d.; ed Inst. of Political Science, Nat. School of Oriental Languages; joined Ministry of Foreign Affairs 1970, positions included Man. Econ. Affairs 1974–75, Asst Dir Dept for W Africa 1984–86, Adjunct Dir of Cabinet 1986–88, Dir Dept for Asia and Oceania 1990–93, Dir-Gen. of Cultural, Scientific and Tech. Relations 1993–95; Vice-Consul in Hong Kong 1971; Third Sec., Embassy in Beijing, People's Repub. of China 1972–74; Counsellor, Perm. Mission to UN, New York 1981–84, Perm. Rep. to UN, Geneva 1988–90, New York 2000–02; Amb. to USA 2002–07; Diplomatic Adviser to Pres. 1995–2000, 2007–; Chargé de Mission, Secr.-Gen. of Presidency 1975–81; Officier, Légion d'honneur. *Address:* c/o Office of the President, Palais de l'Elysée, 55–57 rue du Faubourg Saint Honoré, 75008 Paris, France. *Telephone:* 1-42-92-81-00. *Fax:* 1-47-42-24-65. *Website:* www.elysee.fr.

LEVITZKI, Alexander, PhD; Israeli biochemist and academic; *Wolfson Family Professor of Biochemistry and Director, Institute for Advanced Studies, Hebrew University of Jerusalem;* ed Hebrew Univ. of Jerusalem, Weizmann Inst. of Science, Rehovot and Univ. of Calif., Berkeley, USA; Fulbright-Hayes Fellow 1968–71; Sr Scientist, Dept of Biophysics, Weizmann Inst. of Science 1970, Assoc. Prof. 1974–76; Assoc. Prof., Hebrew Univ. of Jerusalem 1974, Prof. 1976–, Wolfson Family Prof. of Biochemistry 1985–, Dir Inst. for Advanced Studies 1998–2001, currently with Dept of Biological Chem., Alexander Silberman Inst. of Life Sciences; Visiting Prof. of Chem. and Research Assoc., Inst. of Molecular Biology, Univ. of Ore. Eugene 1974; Visiting Prof. of Biochemistry, Univ. of Calif., Berkeley 1974; Visiting Scientist, Nat. Cancer Inst., Nat. Insts of Health, Bethesda, Md 1979–80; Fogarty Scholar-in-Residence, NIH, Bethesda, Md 1984–85; Visiting Scholar, Stanford Univ., Calif. 1993–94; Visiting Prof., Comprehensive Cancer Center, Univ. of Calif., San Francisco 2001–03; Edward Rotan Visiting Prof., The MD Anderson Cancer Center, Houston, Tex. 2002–; Sr Consultant, Biotechnology Research Consultants, Tel-Aviv 1982–86, Rorer Biotechnology, King of Prussia, Pa, USA 1987–92; consultant and mem. Bd of Dirs Int. Diagnostic Labs, Jerusalem 1984–88; consultant, Eldan-Tech 1987–91; mem. Scientific Advisory Bd SUGEN, Inc., Redwood City, Calif. 1993–97, Vice-Pres. Research 1993–94; Chief Scientific Advisor and mem. Scientific Advisory Bd Peptor Ltd 1997–2003; co-founder TK Signal, Israel 2000, UnResto 2001; founder Algen Biopharmaceuticals, Israel and USA 2001; mem. Scientific Advisory Bd ProteoLogics, Rehovot 2002; founder NovoTyr Pharmaceuticals 2005; Vice-Pres. Fed. of Israeli Socs of Experimental Biology 1999, Pres. 2002–05; Ed. Current Topics in Cellular Regulation 1987–91; Assoc. Ed. Cellular Signalling 1987–; mem. Editorial Bd European Journal of Biochemistry 1975–81, Molecular Physiology 1982–85, Journal of Cyclic Nucleotide Research 1982–94, Pharmacology 1991–, Science 1993–96, Anti-cancer Drug Design 1995–, Molecular Biology Research Communications 1998–2001, European Journal of Chemical Biology (ChemBiochem) 2000–, Journal of Biological Chemistry 2002, Oncology Research 2002, Current Signal Transduction Therapy 2006; mem. European Molecular Biology Org. 1978, Israel Acad. of Sciences 1999– (Chair. Div. of Natural Sciences 2004); Hon. mem. American Soc. of Biological Chemists 1985; Bi-Annual Shlomo Hestrin Prize, Israel Biochemical Soc. 1975, Bronze Medal for Biochemistry, Free Univ. of Brussels 1983, Israel Prize in Biochemistry 1990, Rothschild Prize in Biology 1990, Lectureship Award, Fed. of European Biochemical Socs 1991, Schender Prize for Pharmacology and Drug Research 1998, Lichtenstein Memorial Lecturer 1998, Hamilton-Fairley Award, European Soc. of Medical Oncology 2002, Medal of the Univ., Univ. of Helsinki 2003, Al Wolf Lectureship (IRSC), Australia 2003, Wolf Prize for Medicine 2005 (jt winner). *Publications:* numerous articles in scientific journals on developing techniques for targeted destruction of cancer cells through biochemical means. *Address:* The Levitzki Lab, Unit of Cellular Signalling, Department of Biological Chemistry, The Alexander Silberman Institute of Life Sciences, The Hebrew University of Jerusalem, 91904 Jerusalem, Israel (office). *Telephone:* (2) 6585404 (office). *Fax:* (2) 6512958 (office). *E-mail:* levitzki@vms.huji.ac.il (office). *Website:* biolchem.huji.ac.il/levitzki/levitzki.html (office).

LEVY, Alain M., MBA; French record company executive; b. 19 Dec. 1946; ed Ecole des Mines and Univ. of Pennsylvania, USA; Asst to the Pres. CBS Int.,

New York 1972–73, Vice-Pres. Marketing for Europe, Paris 1973, Vice-Pres. of Creative Operations for Europe, also Man. CBS Italy 1978; Man. Dir CBS Disques, France 1979, CEO PolyGram France 1984, Exec. Vice-Pres. PolyGram Group, France and FRG 1988, Man. US Operations PolyGram Group 1990–98, Pres., CEO, mem. Bd Man. PolyGram USA 1991–98; mem. Group Man. Cttee Philips Electronics, majority shareholder PolyGram USA 1991–98; Chair. Bd EMI Group PLC 2001–07, Chair. and CEO EMI Recorded Music 2001–07; mem. advisory bd Film Business Academy 2006–. *Address:* c/o Film Business Academy, Cass Business School, 106 Bunhill Row, London, EC1Y 8TZ, England.

LEVY, Andrea, BA; British writer; b. 7 March 1956, London; d. of Winston Levy and Amy Levy; m. Bill Mayblin; two step-d.; ed Highbury Hill High School, London and Middlesex Polytechnic; fmr graphic designer; Dr hc (Middlesex) Arts Council Award 1998. *Publications:* Every Light in the House Burnin' 1994, Never Far from Nowhere 1996, Fruit of the Lemon 1999, Small Island (Orange Prize 2004, Whitbread Novel of the Year and Whitbread Prize 2005, Commonwealth Writers Prize 2005, Orange Prize for Fiction tenth anniversary award 2005) 2004. *Leisure interests:* reading, films, TV and swimming. *Address:* David Grossman Literary Agency, 118B Holland Park Avenue, London, W11 4VA, England (office); c/o Review Press, Hodder Headline, 338 Euston Road, London, NW1, England. *Telephone:* (20) 7221-2770 (office). *Fax:* (20) 7221-1445 (office).

LÉVY, Bernard-Henri; French writer and philosopher; b. 5 Nov. 1948, Beni-Saf, Algeria; s. of André Lévy and Ginette Lévy; m. 1st Sylvie Bouscasse 1980; one s. one d.; m. 2nd Arielle Sonnery 1993; ed Ecole Normale Supérieure (rue d'Ulm), Paris; War Corresp. for Combat 1971–72; Lecturer in Epistemology, Univ. of Strasbourg, in Philosophy, Ecole Normale Supérieure 1973; mem. François Mitterrand's Group of Experts 1973–76; joined Editions Grasset as Ed. 'nouvelle philosophie' series 1973; Ed. Idées section, Quotidien de Paris; Contrib. to Nouvel Observateur and Temps Modernes 1974; co-founder Action Int. contre la Faim 1980, Radio Free Kabul 1981, SOS Racisme; f. and Dir Règle du jeu 1990–; Pres. Supervisory Council Sept-Arte 1993–; seconded by French Govt to Kabul, Afghanistan 2002. *Film directed:* Le Jour la Nuit 1997. *Publications:* Bangladesh: Nationalisme dans la révolution 1973, Les Indes rouges 1973, La barbarie à visage humain 1977 (Prix d'honneur 1977), Le testament de Dieu 1979, L'idéologie française 1981, Questions de principe 1983, Le diable en tête (Prix Médicis) 1984, Impressions d'Asie 1985, Questions de principe II 1986, Eloge des intellectuels 1987, Les derniers jours de Charles Baudelaire (Prix Interallié) 1988, Questions de principe III 1990, Frank Stella: Les années 80 1990, Les bronzes de César 1991, Les aventures de la liberté 1991, Piet Mondrian 1992, Piero Della Francesca 1992, Le jugement dernier (play) 1992, Questions de principe IV 1992, Les hommes et les femmes (jtly) 1993, Un jour dans la mort de Sarajevo (screenplay, jtly) 1993, Bosna! (screenplay, jtly) 1994, La pureté dangereuse 1995, Questions de principe V 1995, Le lys et la cendre 1996, Comédie 1997, The Rules of the Game 1998 (revised edn What Good Are Intellectuals?: 44 Writers Share Their Thoughts 2000), Le siècle de Sartre 2000, Réflexion sur la guerre, Le mal et la fin de l'histoire 2001, Mémoire vive 2001, Qui a tué Daniel Pearl? 2003, American Vertigo 2006, Ce grand cadavre à la renverse 2007, Ennemis publics (with Michel Houellebecq) 2008. *Leisure interests:* skiing, judo, water-skiing. *Address:* c/o Editions Grasset et Fasquelle, 61 rue des Saint-Pères, 75006 Paris, France (office). *Telephone:* 1-44-39-22-00 (office). *Fax:* 1-42-22-64-18 (office). *Website:* www.grasset.fr (office).

LEVY, David; Israeli politician; *Leader, Gesher party;* b. 1938, Morocco; emigrated to Israel 1957; construction worker; joined Histadrut; elected to Knesset (Parl.), representing Herut (Freedom) group of Gahal 1969– (subsequently of Likud Bloc); Likud cand. for Sec.-Gen. of Histadrut 1977, 1981; Minister of Immigrant Absorption 1977–78, of Construction and Housing 1978–90, of Foreign Affairs 1990–92, 1996–97, 1999–2000, Deputy Prime Minister 1981–84, 1988–92, Minister without portfolio –2002; f. Gesher Party 1996, currently Leader. *Address:* c/o Gesher, Jerusalem, Israel. *Website:* www.gesher.org.il.

LEVY, Itzhak; politician and rabbi; b. 1947, Morocco; m.; five c.; ed Kerem B'Yavne and Yeshivat Hakotel; emigrated to Israel in 1957; ordained rabbi; served in Israeli Defence Forces, to rank of Maj.; Nat. Religious Party mem. Knesset (Parl.) 1988–, mem. Knesset House Cttee, Cttees on Finance, on Constitution, Law and Justice, on Labour and Social Welfare 1988–92, on Knesset House Cttee and Cttee on Constitution, Law and Justice 1992–96; Minister of Transport 1996–98, later of Housing, Minister without Portfolio; mem. Bnei Akiva Exec. and World Secr.; Leader Nat. Religious Party; Chair. Israel–Argentina Parl. Friendship League. *Address:* National Religious Party, Jerusalem, Israel. *Telephone:* 2-377277. *Fax:* 2-377757.

LÉVY, Jacques Bernard, DèsSc; French metallurgist; *President, Fondation Industries Minerales, Minières et Metallurgiques;* b. Jan. 1937, Constantine, Algeria; s. of Gilbert Lévy and Renée Cassin; m. Marianne Neuburger 1964; two s. one d.; ed Ecole Polytechnique, Ecole des Mines de Paris, Univ. de Paris VI; Prof. of Metallurgy, Ecole des Mines de St-Etienne 1962, Dir Dept of Metallurgy 1974; Post-doctoral Fellow, Univ. of Waterloo, Ont., Canada 1968; Scientific Dir Ecole des Mines de Paris 1976, Dir 1984–2001; Ingénieur général du corps des mines 1983; Chair. (Research Comm.) Conf. des Grandes Ecoles 1984; mem. Royal Swedish Acad. of Eng Sciences 1989; Pres. Conf. of European Schools for Advanced Eng Educ. and Research 1990; Pres. Conf. des Grandes Ecoles 1993, Fondation Industries Minerales, Minières et Metallurgiques 2001–; mem. Conseil pour les Applications de l'Académie des Sciences 1999, Acad. des Technologies 2000–; Officier, Légion d'honneur, Commdr, Ordre nat. du mérite, Commdr, Ordre des Palmes académiques; Dr hc (Catholic Univ. of Louvain) 1996; Prix Jean Rist (Soc. Française de Métallurgie) 1972. *Publications:* about 30 publs on physical metallurgy (grain boundaries and interfaces, structure and properties of metals and alloys), official reports on materials science and eng higher educ. *Leisure interests:* skiing, tennis. *Address:* Ecole Nationale Supérieure des Mines, 60 boulevard Saint-Michel, 75272 Paris Cedex 06, France. *Telephone:* 1-40-51-90-18. *Fax:* 1-40-51-90-25. *E-mail:* jacques.levy@ensmp.fr (office). *Website:* www.ensmp.fr (office).

LÉVY, Jean-Bernard; French media and telecommunications executive; *Chairman of the Management Board and CEO, Vivendi;* b. 18 March 1955; ed École Polytechnique, École nationale supérieure des télécommunications; engineer with France Telecom 1978–86; Tech. Adviser to Minister for Postal Services and Telecommunications 1986–88; Gen. Man. Communication Satellites, Matra Marconi Space 1988–93; Chief of Staff to Minister for Industry, Postal Services, Telecommunications and Foreign Trade 1993–94; Chair. and CEO Matra Communication (Lagardère Group) 1995–98; Man. Partner, Corp. Finance, Oddo Pinatton (equities broker) 1998–2002; COO Vivendi Universal (now Vivendi) 2002–05, Chair. Man. Bd and CEO 2005–, mem. Bd of Dirs Vivendi Games, Inc.; Chair. Supervisory Bd Canal+ France, Viroxis; Vice-Chair. Supervisory Bd Groupe Canal+, Maroc Telecom; mem. Supervisory Bd Canal+ Group; mem. Bd of Dirs NBC Universal Inc., SFR, Vinci, Institut Pasteur. *Address:* Vivendi, 42 avenue de Friedland, 75380 Paris Cedex 08, France (office). *Telephone:* 1-71-71-10-00 (office). *Fax:* 1-71-71-10-01 (office). *E-mail:* info@vivendi.com (office). *Website:* www.vivendi.com (office).

LÉVY, Maurice; French advertising executive; *Group Chairman and CEO, Publicis Groupe SA;* b. 18 Feb. 1942, Oudja, Morocco; m.; three s.; joined Publicis Groupe SA and given responsibility for data processing and information tech. systems 1971, apptd Corp. Sec. 1973, Man. Dir 1976, Chair and CEO of Publicis Conseil 1981, Vice Chair Publicis Groupe 1986, Vice Chair of Man. Bd 1988, Chair. and CEO of Man. Bd 1987, Group Chair. and CEO 1988–; mem. Foundation Bd World Econ. Forum; mem. Advisory Cttee Banque de France; Pres. Palais de Tokyo (arts centre), Paris; French Pres. French-American Business Council; Dir Musée des Arts Décoratifs, Paris, Council on Foreign Relations, NY; Commdr, Légion d'Honneur, Ordre Nat. du Mérite. *Address:* Publicis Groupe SA, 133 Avenue des Champs Elysées, 75380 Paris, France (office). *Telephone:* 1-44-43-73-00 (office). *Fax:* 1-44-43-75-25 (office). *Website:* www.publicisgroupe.com (office).

LEVY, Baron (Life Peer), cr. 1997, of Mill Hill in the London Borough of Barnet; **Michael Abraham Levy,** FCA, CA; British consultant; b. 11 July 1944, London; s. of Samuel Levy and Annie Levy; m. Gilda Levy (née Altbach) 1967; one s. one d.; ed Hackney Downs Grammar School; chartered accountant Lubbock Fine 1961–66; Prin. M. Levy & Co. 1966–69; Pnr Wagner, Prager, Levy & Partners 1969–73; Chair. Magnet Group of Cos 1973–88, D & J Securities Ltd 1988–92, M & G Records 1992–97; Vice-Chair. Phonographic Performance Ltd 1979–84, British Phonographic Industry Ltd 1984–87; Chair. British Music Industry Awards Cttee 1992–95, Patron 1995–; Nat. Campaign Chair. United Jt Israel Appeal 1982–85, Hon. Vice-Pres. 1994–2000, Hon. Pres. 2000–; Special Envoy of Prime Minister and Adviser on Middle East, South America and Kazakhstan 1997–2007; Chair. Jewish Care 1992–97, Pres. 1998–; fmr Chair. Jewish Care Community Foundation, Foundation for Educ.; Vice-Chair. Cen. Council for Jewish Community Services 1994–, Chair. Chief Rabbinate Awards for Excellence 1992–2007; mem. Jewish Agency World Bd of Govs 1990–95, World Chair. Youth Aliyah Cttee 1991–95; mem. Keren Hayesod World Bd of Govs 1991–95, World Comm. on Israel–Diaspora Relations 1995–, Int. Bd Govs Peres Centre for Peace 1997–, Advisory Council Foreign Policy Centre 1997–, Nat. Council Voluntary Orgs Advisory Cttee 1998–, Community Legal Service Champions Panel 1999–, Hon. Cttee Israel, Britain and the Commonwealth Asscn 2000–; Pres. CSV (Community Service Volunteers) 1998–; Trustee Holocaust Educ. Trust 1998–2007; Gov. Jewish Free School 1990–95, Hon. Pres. 2001–; Chair. Wireart Ltd and Chase Music Ltd (fmrly M & G Music Ltd) 1992–2008; Chair. Bd of Trustees New Policy Network Foundation 2000–07; Chair. International Standard Asset Management 2008–; mem. Devt Bd British Library 2008–; mem. Exec. Cttee Chai-Lifeline 2001–02; Patron Prostate Cancer Charitable Trust 1997–, Friends of Israel Educ. Trust 1998–, Save a Child's Heart Foundation 2000–, Simon Mark's Jewish Primary School Trust 2002–; Hon. Patron, Cambridge Univ. Jewish Soc. 2002–; Hon. PhD (Middlesex Univ.) 1999; B'nai B'rith First Lodge Award 1994, Scopus Award Hebrew Univ. of Jerusalem 1998, Israel Policy Forum Special Recognition Award (USA) 2003. *Publication:* A Question of Honour (memoir) 2008. *Leisure interest:* tennis, swimming. *Address:* House of Lords, Westminster, London, SW1A 0PW, England (office). *Telephone:* (20) 7487-5174 (office). *Fax:* (20) 7486-7919 (office). *E-mail:* ml@lmalvy.demon.co.uk (office).

LÉVY, Thierry; French lawyer and writer; b. 13 Jan. 1945, Nice (Alpes-Maritimes); s. of Paul Lévy; admitted to the Bar, Paris 1969, assigned to defend Claude Buffet who was later executed by guillotine 1972, won acquittal of Roger Knobelspiess 1986; Chair. Int. Observatory of Prisons 2000–04. *Publications:* Convaincre, Dialogue sur l'éloquence (with Jean-Denis Bredin) 1997, Éloge de la barbarie judiciaire 2004, Nos têtes sont plus dures que les murs des prisons 2006, Lévy oblige 2008; numerous legal articles. *Address:* c/o Éditions Grasset & Fasquelle, 61 rue des Saints-Pères, 75006 Paris, France. *Telephone:* 1-44-39-22-00. *Fax:* 1-42-22-64-18. *E-mail:* info@grasset.fr. *Website:* www.grasset.fr.

LEWANDOWSKI, Janusz Antoni, MA, DEcon; Polish politician and economist; b. 13 June 1951, Lublin; s. of Karol Lewandowski and Halina Lewandowska; m. Lidia Talewska Lewandowska 1997; one d.; ed Gdańsk Univ.; Lecturer, Gdańsk Univ. 1974–84 (dismissed); econ. adviser, Solidarity Trade Union, Gdańsk 1980–81; Lecturer, Harvard Univ., USA; with Polish Ocean Lines, then consulting firm 1984–85; Assoc., journal Przegląd

Polityczny (pen-name Jędrzej Branecki) 1984–89; Co-Founder pvt. Gdańsk Inst. of Market Econs 1989–, Chair. Programme Bd 1993–94; Minister of Proprietary Transformations 1991–93; Co-Founder and Pres. Liberal-Democratic Congress 1990–94; Deputy to Sejm (Parl.) 1991–93, 1997–2004, Vice-Chair. Parl. Cttee for Treasury, Affranchisement and Privatization 1997–2004, Parl. Cttee on Europe 2001–04; mem. Freedom Union (UW) 1994–2001, Citizens' Platform (Platforma Obywatelska—PO) 2001–; Observer to European Parl. 2003–04; mem. European Parl. (Group of the European People's Party—Christian Democrats and European Democrats) 2004–, mem. Bureau 2004–, Chair. Cttee on Econ. and Monetary Affairs 2004–, Conf. of Cttee Chairmen 2004–, Cttee on Budgets 2004–, Substitute mem. Temporary Cttee on Policy Challenges and Budgetary Means of the Enlarged Union 2007–2013 2004–, mem. Del. for Relations with Japan; Chair. Athletics Club of Sopot 2000–. *Publication:* Samorząd w dobie 'Solidarności' 1984, Neoliberałowie wobec współczesności 1989, Strategia rozwoju województwa gdańskiego (jtly) 1997. *Leisure interests:* sport, mountain hiking. *Address:* European Parliament, Bâtiment Altiero Spinelli, 05F365, 60 rue Wiertz, 1047 Brussels, Belgium (office); Biuro Poselskie w Gdyni, ul. Świetojawska 60/2, 81-393 Gdynia, Poland. *Telephone:* (2) 284-5742 (office); (58) 699-36-00. *Fax:* (2) 284-9742 (office). *E-mail:* jlewandowski-a@europarl.eu.int (office); janusz.lewandowski@januszlewandowski.pl (office). *Website:* www.januszlewandowski.pl (office).

LEWENT, Judy C., MS; American business executive; ed Goucher Coll., Baltimore, Massachusetts Inst. of Tech. Sloan School of Management; Assoc., Corp. Finance, E.F. Hutton 1972–74; Asst Vice-Pres. Bankers Trust 1974–75; Sr Financial Analyst, Norton Simon 1975–76; Man. Business Devt, Pfizer Medical Systems 1976–77; Controller, Pfizer Diagnostic Products 1977–78; Dir Acquisitions and Capital Analysis, Merck & Co. Inc. 1980–83, Asst Controller MRL 1983–85, Exec. Dir Financial Evaluation and Analysis 1985–87, Vice-Pres. and Treasurer 1987–90, Vice-Pres. Finance and Chief Financial Officer 1990–92, Sr Vice-Pres. and Chief Financial Officer 1992–2001, Exec. Vice-Pres. and Chief Financial Officer 2001–02, mem. Man. Cttee, Exec. Vice-Pres., Chief Financial Officer and Pres. Human Health Asia, Merck & Co. Inc. 2003–07 (retd); mem. Bd of Dirs Johnson & Johnson, Merck Consumer Pharmaceuticals Co., Merck/Schering-Plough Partnership, Merial Ltd, Motorola Inc. 1995–, Nat. Bureau of Econ. Research, Dell Inc. 2001–, Thermo Fisher Scientific Inc., 2008–; Life mem. MIT Corpn; mem. American Acad. of Arts and Sciences; Officers' Conf. Group; mem. Bd Trustees Univ. of Pennsylvania Health System; Trustee Rockefeller Family Trust; ranked by Fortune magazine amongst 50 Most Powerful Women in Business in the US (21st) 2002, (23rd) 2003, (35th) 2004. *Address:* c/o Board of Directors, Thermo Fisher Scientific Inc., 81 Wyman Street, Waltham, MA 02454, USA.

LEWINTON, Sir Christopher, Kt, CEng, FEng, FIMechE,; British/American engineer and business adviser; *Chairman, J. F. Lehman & Company Europe;* b. 6 Jan. 1932, London; s. of Joseph Lewinton and Elizabeth Lewinton; m. 1st Jennifer Alcock (divorced); two s.; m. 2nd Louise Head 1979; two step-s.; ed Acton Tech. Coll.; commissioned army service in REME; Pres. Wilkinson Sword, N America 1959–71, CEO Wilkinson Sword Group 1970–85; Pres. Int. Group, Allegheny Int. 1978–85; Chief Exec. TI Group 1986–99, Chair. and CEO 1989–2000; Dir Reed Elsevier 1993–99, Messier-Dowty 1994–1998, Y&R/WPP 1996–2003; mem. Supervisory Bd Mannesmann AG 1995–99; Chair. J. F. Lehman Europe 2000–; Adviser to Booz Allen Hamilton Inc. 2000–, to Morgan Stanley Capital Pnrs (now Metalmark Capital) 2000–, Compass Advisers 2004–, Compass Pnrs Int. 2006–; Hon. FRAeS 1993; Hon. DTech (Brunel) 1997. *Leisure interests:* golf, tennis, travel, reading. *Address:* J. F. Lehman & Co., 4 Grosvenor Place, London, SW1X 7HJ, England (office). *Telephone:* (20) 7201-5490 (office). *Fax:* (20) 7201-5499 (office). *E-mail:* clewinton@cl-partners.co.uk (office).

LEWIS, Anthony, AB; American journalist and academic; *James Madison Visiting Professor, Columbia University;* b. 27 March 1927, New York, NY; m. 1st Linda Rannells 1951 (divorced); one s. two d.; m. 2nd Margaret H. Marshall 1984; ed Harvard Univ.; deskman, Sunday Dept 1948–52, reporter, Washington Bureau 1955–64, Chief London Bureau 1965–72, editorial columnist 1969–2001, New York Times; reporter, Washington Daily News 1952–55; Lecturer on Law, Harvard Univ. 1974–89; James Madison Visiting Prof., Columbia Univ. 1983–; mem. American Acad. of Arts and Sciences; Hon. DLitt (Adelphi Univ.) 1964, (Rutgers Univ.) 1973, (Williams Coll.) 1978, (Clark Univ.) 1982, Hon. LLD (Syracuse Univ.) 1979, (Colby Coll.) 1983, (Northeastern Univ.) 1987; Heywood Broun Award 1955, Pulitzer Prizes for Nat. Reporting 1955, 1963, Nieman Fellow 1956–57, MWA Best Fact-Crime Book Award 1964, Presidential Citizen's Medal 2001. *Publications:* Gideon's Trumpet 1964, Portrait of a Decade: The Second American Revolution 1964, Make No Law: The Sullivan Case and the First Amendment 1991, Written into History: Pulitzer Prize Reporting of the Twentieth Century from the New York Times (ed.) 2001, Freedom for the Thought that We Hate: A Biography of the First Amendment 2008; contrib. to professional journals. *Address:* 1010 Memorial Drive, Cambridge, MA 02138, USA (home). *Telephone:* (617) 354-2229 (office). *Fax:* (617) 354-2458 (office); (617) 876-3641 (home).

LEWIS, Aylwin B., BA, MBA; American retail executive; ed Univ. of Houston; started career as Dist Man. of Operations Jack in the Box restaurants in Tex.; held various exec. positions at food retailers including KFC Corpn, COO Pizza Hut 1996–2000, Exec. Vice Pres. of Operations and New Business Devt Tricon Global Restaurants Inc. then Pres., Chief Multibranding and Operating Officer YUM! Brands Inc. (fmrly Tricon) 2000–03; Pres. and CEO Kmart Holdings Corpn 2004, Pres. and CEO Sears Holding Corpn (after merger of Kmart and Sears, Roebuck) 2005–08, also mem. Bd of Dirs; mem. Bd of Dirs Halliburton Co., Walt Disney Co. *Address:* c/o Sears Holding Corporation, 3333 Beverly Road, Hoffman Estates, IL 60179, USA (office).

LEWIS, Bernard, PhD, FBA, FRHistS; American writer and academic; *Cleveland E. Dodge Professor Emeritus of Near Eastern Studies, Princeton University;* b. 31 May 1916, London, England; m. Ruth Hélène Oppenhejm 1947 (divorced 1974); one s. one d.; ed Univs of London and Paris; Lecturer in Islamic History, School of Oriental Studies, Univ. of London 1938; served in RAC and Intelligence Corps 1940–41; attached to Foreign Office 1941–45; Prof. of History of the Near and Middle East, Univ. of London 1949–74; Cleveland E. Dodge Prof. of Near Eastern Studies, Princeton Univ. 1974–86, Prof. Emer. 1986–; Dir Annenberg Research Inst., Philadelphia 1986–90; Visiting Prof. of History, Univ. of Calif. at LA 1955–56, Columbia Univ. 1960, Ind. Univ. 1963, Princeton Univ. 1964, Univ. of Calif. at Berkeley 1965, Coll. de France 1980, École des Hautes Études en Sciences Sociales, Paris 1983, 1988, Univ. of Chicago 1985; Visiting mem. Inst. for Advanced Study, Princeton Univ. 1969, mem. 1974–86; A. D. White Prof.-at-Large, Cornell Univ. 1984–90; mem. Bd of Dirs, Institut für die Wissenschaften von Menschen, Vienna 1988; Jefferson Lecturer in the Humanities, US Nat. Endowment for the Humanities 1990; Tanner Lecturer, Brasenose Coll., Oxford 1990; Henry M. Jackson Memorial Lecturer (Seattle) 1992; mem. British Acad., American Philosophical Soc. 1973, American Acad. of Arts and Sciences 1983; American Oriental Soc., Corresp. mem. Inst. d'Egypte, Cairo 1969–, Inst. de France 1994–; Fellow, Univ. Coll., London 1976; Hon. mem. Turkish Historical Soc., Société Asiatique, Paris, Atatürk Acad. of History, Language and Culture, Ankara, Turkish Acad. of Sciences; Hon. Fellow SOAS, London 1986; 15 hon. doctorates including (Hebrew Univ., Jerusalem) 1974, (Tel-Aviv) 1979, (State Univ. of NY Binghamton, Univ. of Penn., Hebrew Union Coll., Cincinnati) 1987, (Univ. of Haifa, Yeshiva Univ., New York) 1991, (Bar-Ilan Univ.) 1992, (Brandeis) 1993, (Ben-Gurion, Ankara) 1996, (Princeton Univ.) 2002; Citation of Honour, Turkish Ministry of Culture 1973, Harvey Prize, Technion-Israel Inst. of Tech. 1978, Educ. Award for Outstanding Achievement in Promotion of American-Turkish Studies 1985, Atatürk Peace Prize 1998, Golden Plate Award, Acad. of Achievement, Washington DC 2004, Nat. Endowment for the Humanities 2007, Irving Kristol Award 2007. *Publications:* The Origins of Ismā'ilism: A Study of the Historical Background of the Fatimid Caliphate 1940, Turkey Today 1940, British Contributions to Arabic Studies 1941, Handbook of Diplomatic and Political Arabic 1947, Land of Enchanters (ed.) 1948, The Arabs in History 1950, Notes and Documents from the Turkish Archives: A Contribution to the History of the Jews in the Ottoman Empire 1952, Encyclopedia of Islam (co-ed.) 1956–86, The Emergence of Modern Turkey 1961, The Kingly Crown 1961, Historians of the Middle East (co-ed. with P. M. Holt) 1962, Istanbul and the Civilization of the Ottoman Empire 1963, The Middle East and the West 1964, The Assassins: A Radical Sect in Islam 1967, The Cambridge History of Islam (ed. with P. M. Holt and Ann K. S. Lambton, two vols) 1970, Race and Colour in Islam 1971, Islam in History: Ideas, Men and Events in the Middle East 1973, Islamic Civilization (ed.) 1974, Islam from the Prophet Muhammad to the Capture of Constantinople (ed. and trans., two vols) 1974, History: Remembered, Recovered, Invented 1975, Studies in Classical and Ottoman Islam: Seventh to Sixteenth Centuries 1976, The World of Islam: Faith, People, Culture (ed.) 1976, Population and Revenue in the Towns of Palestine in the Sixteenth Century (with Amnon Cohen) 1978, The Muslim Discovery of Europe 1982, Christians and Jews in the Ottoman Empire (two vols) 1982, The Jews of Islam 1984, Semites and Anti-Semites: An Inquiry into Conflict and Prejudice 1986, As Others See Us (co-ed.) 1986, The Political Language of Islam 1988, Race and Slavery in the Middle East: A Historical Enquiry 1990, Islam and the West 1993, The Shaping of the Modern Middle East 1994, Cultures in Conflict: Christians, Muslims and Jews in the Age of Discovery 1995, The Middle East: Two Thousand Years of History from the Rise of Christianity to the Present Day 1995, The Future of the Middle East 1997, The Multiple Identities of the Middle East 1998, A Middle East Mosaic: Fragments of Life, Letters and History 2000, Music of a Distant Drum, Classical Arabic, Persian, Turkish and Hebrew Poems 2001, What Went Wrong? Western Impact and Middle Eastern Response 2002, The Crisis of Islam: Holy War and Unholy Terror 2003, From Babel to Dragomans: Interpreting the Middle East 2004, Political Words and Ideas in Islam 2008, Islam: The Religion and The People (co-author) 2008; numerous contribs to professional journals. *Address:* c/o Department of Near Eastern Studies, 110 Jones Hall, Princeton University, Princeton, NJ 08544, USA. *Telephone:* (609) 258-4280.

LEWIS, Carl (Frederick Carlton); American fmr professional athlete; b. 1 July 1961, Birmingham, Ala; s. of the late William Lewis and of Evelyn Lawler Lewis; ed Univ. of Houston; bronze medal for long jump, Pan-American Games 1979; won World Cup competition 1981, first World Championships (with 8.55m); achieved world record 8.79m jump 1983; gold medals at Olympic Games 1984 for 100m, 200m., long jump and 4×100m; athlete in fields of sprints and long jump; silver medal for 200m, gold medal for 100m, Olympic Games 1988; jumped 8.64m New York 1991; world record for 100m 9.86 seconds Aug. 1991 (surpassed 1994); gold medal, long jump Olympic Games 1992; gold medal for long jump (8.50m), Olympic Games 1996; retd 1997; has won a total of nine Olympic gold medals; revealed in 2003 to have failed a drugs test at Olympics 1988, he was disqualified at the time, but the case was dismissed after an appeal; f. Carl Lewis Fund to help disadvantaged youths; appeared in several TV and film projects produced by the Carl Lewis Entertainment Group; Hon. Chair. Negro Coll. Fund; Track and Field News Athlete of the Decade 1980–89, World Athlete of the Year 1982, 1983, 1984, IAAF Athlete of the Century 1999. *Address:* c/o Carl Lewis Foundation, 15332 Antioch Street, Suite 728, Pacific Palisades, CA 90272-3628, USA. *Telephone:* (310) 578-1885. *Website:* www.carllewis.com (office).

LEWIS, Charles Edwin; American professor of medicine; *Professor of Health Services, Medicine, and Nursing, School of Public Health and Director, Center for Health Promotion and Disease Prevention, UCLA;* b. 28 Dec. 1928, Kansas City, Mo.; s. of Claude Herbert Lewis and Maudie Friels (née Holaday); m. Mary Ann Gurera 1963; three s. one d.; ed Univs of Kansas and Cincinatti and Harvard Medical School; USAF 1955–56; Fellow, The Kettering Lab. 1956–59; Asst Prof. Epidemiology, Baylor Univ. 1959–61; Assoc. Prof. of Medicine, Univ. of Kansas 1962–64, Prof. and Chair. Dept of Community Medicine 1964–69; Prof. and Head of Div. of Health Services and Prof. of Medicine, UCLA 1970–72, Chief, Div. of Gen. Internal Medicine 1972–90, Prof. of Nursing, School of Nursing 1973–, Dir UCLA Center for Health Promotion and Disease Prevention 1991–, Head Div. of Preventive and Occupational Medicine 1991–93, Dir Health Services Research Center 1991–93, Chair. Academic Senate 1995–96; Regent, ACP 1989; Master American Coll. of Physicians; mem. Inst. of Medicine (NAS); Ginsberg Prize, Univ. of Kan., Rosenthal Award (ACP) 1980. *Publications:* more than 120 research publs in journals and 15 chapters in books. *Leisure interests:* music, travel. *Address:* UCLA School of Public Health, Box 951772, Los Angeles, CA 90095-1772 (office); 221 Burlingame Avenue, Los Angeles, CA 90049, USA (home). *Telephone:* (310) 206-6322 (office); (310) 825-6709 (office). *Fax:* (310) 206-5717 (office); (310) 394-8929 (home). *E-mail:* Lewis@ph.ucla.edu (office). *Website:* www.ph.ucla.edu (office).

LEWIS, Dan, PhD, DSc, FRS; British geneticist; *Professor Emeritus of Botany, University College London;* b. 30 Dec. 1910, Stoke on Trent; s. of Ernest Albert Lewis and Edith Jane Lewis; m. Mary P. E. Burry 1933 (died 2003); one d.; ed High School, Newcastle under Lyme and Univs of Reading and London; student gardener 1929–31; plant breeder, John Innes Inst. 1935, Head Dept of Genetics 1947; Rockefeller Fellowship, Calif. Inst. of Tech. 1955–56; Quain Prof. of Botany, Univ. Coll. London 1957–78, Prof. Emer. 1978–; Hon. Research Fellow, Univ. Coll. London 1978–; Visiting Prof. of Genetics, Univ. of California, Berkeley 1961, Delhi 1965, Singapore 1970; Visiting Prof., Queen Mary Coll., London 1978–; Pres. Genetical Soc. 1968–71; mem. Univ. Grants Cttee 1968–74; Freedom Chelsea Physic Garden 1977; Hon. Life Mem. City Univ. 1999. *Publications:* Sexual Incompatibility in Plants and articles on genetics; Ed. Science Progress. *Leisure interests:* music. *Address:* Flat 2, 56/57 Myddelton Square, London, EC1R 1YA, England (home). *Telephone:* (20) 7278-6948 (home).

LEWIS, Denise, OBE; British professional athlete; b. 27 Aug. 1972, West Bromwich; d. of Joan Lewis; partner Patrick Stevens; one d.; specializes in heptathlon; club: Birchfield Harriers; Commonwealth heptathlon record-holder (6,736 points) 1997; fifth European Jr Championships 1991; gold medal Commonwealth Games 1994; gold medal European Cup 1995; bronze medal Olympic Games 1996; silver medal World Championships 1997; gold medal European Championships 1998; gold medal Commonwealth Championships 1998; silver medal World Championships 1999; new Commonwealth Record (6,831 points) 2000; gold medal, Olympic Games 2000; finished 5th World Championships 2002; British Athletics Writers Female Athlete of the Year 1998, 2000, Sports Writers Asscn Sportswoman of the year 2000. *Publication:* Denise Lewis: Faster, Higher, Stronger (autobiog.) 2001. *Address:* c/o MTC (UK) Ltd, 20 York Street, London, W1U 6PU, England. *Telephone:* (20) 7935-8000. *Fax:* (20) 7935-8066. *E-mail:* info@mtc-uk.com (office). *Website:* www.mtc-uk.com (office).

LEWIS, Douglas (Doug) Grinslade, PC, LLB, FCA, QC; Canadian fmr politician; b. 17 April 1938, Toronto, Ont.; s. of Horace Grinslade and Brenda Hazeldine Lewis (née Reynolds); m. Linda Diane Haggans 1962; two s. three d.; ed Univ. of Toronto, Osgoode Hall Law School; Progressive Conservative MP for Simcoe N 1979–93; Parl. Sec. to Minister of Supply and Services 1979; Deputy Opposition House Leader 1981, Opposition House Leader 1983; Parl. Sec. to Pres. of Treasury Bd 1984, to Pres. of Privy Council 1985, to Deputy Prime Minister and Pres. of Queen's Privy Council for Canada 1986–87; Minister of State (Deputy House Leader) and Minister of State (Treasury Bd) 1987–88; Acting Pres. Treasury Bd 1988; Minister of Justice, Attorney-Gen. and Govt House Leader 1989–90; Minister of Transport 1990–91; Solicitor-Gen. 1991–93. *Address:* Box 535, Orillia, Ont., L3V 6K2, Canada.

LEWIS, Geoffrey David, MA, FSA; British museum director and university teacher; b. 13 April 1933, Brighton, Sussex; s. of David Lewis and Esther Lewis; m. Frances May Wilderspin 1956; three d.; ed Varndean Grammar School, Brighton, Univ. of Liverpool; Asst Curator, Worthing Museum and Art Gallery 1950–60; Deputy Dir (and Keeper of Antiquities) Sheffield City Museum 1960–65; Dir Sheffield City Museums 1966–72, Liverpool City Museums 1972–74, Merseyside Co. Museums 1974–77; Dir of Museum Studies, Univ. of Leicester 1977–89, Assoc. Teacher 1989–92; Fellow, Museums Asscn London 1966, Pres. 1980–81, Pres. Int. Council of Museums 1983–89, Chair. Advisory Cttee 1974–80, Chair. Ethics Cttee 1996–2004; currently a museum consultant; mem. Bd of Trustees Royal Armouries 1990–99, Chair. Design Cttee 1995–99; Chair. Printing Matters (Bude) Ltd 1991–96; Deputy Chair. The Genesis Agendum 1996–2008; Gov. Wolvey School 1993–2003, Chair. of Govs 1998–2003; Hon. Lecturer in British Prehistory, Univ. of Sheffield 1965–72; Hon. Fellow, Museums Asscn 1989; Hon. Mem. Int. Council of Museums 2004. *Publications:* The South Yorkshire Glass Industry 1964, Prehistoric and Roman Times in the Sheffield Area (co-author) 1968, For Instruction and Recreation: A Centenary History of the Museums Association 1989, Manual of Curatorship (co-ed.) 1984, 1992; contrib. to Encyclopaedia Britannica and Britannica Online 2007; many articles relating to archaeology and museums. *Leisure interests:* walking, computing. *Address:* 4 Orchard Close, Wolvey, Hinckley, Warwicks., LE10 3LR, England. *Telephone:* (1455) 220708; (560) 230-6257. *E-mail:* iww@geoffreylewis.co.uk. *Website:* www.geoffreylewis.co.uk.

LEWIS, Gwyneth, MA, DPhil, FRSL; British poet and writer; b. 1959, Cardiff, Wales; m. Leighton; ed Girton Coll., Cambridge, Univ. of Harvard, USA, Columbia Univ., USA, Balliol Coll., Oxford; fmr freelance journalist in New York, USA and documentary prod. and dir, BBC Wales; composed the bilingual inscription on the front of Cardiff's Wales Millennium Centre, opened in 2004; Nat. Poet of Wales 2005–06; Hon. Fellow, Univ. of Cardiff 2005; Harkness Fellow 1982–84, Eric Gregory Award 1987, Nat. Endowment for Science, Technology and the Arts Fellowship 2002–07, Wellcome Trust Sciart Award. *Radio:* Sunbathing in the Rain (BBC Radio 4), Stardust: A Love Story (BBC Radio 4). *Television:* Zero Gravity (BBC 2). *Publications:* Llwybrau bywyd (poems) 1977, Ar y groesffordd (poems) 1978, Sonedau Redsa a Cherddi Eraill 1990, Parables and Faxes (poems) (Aldeburgh Poetry Festival Prize) 1995, Cyfrif Un ac Un yn Dri (poems) 1996, Zero Gravity (poems) 1998, Y Llofrudd Iaith (poems) (Welsh Arts Council Book of the Year) 2000, Sunbathing in the Rain: A Cheerful Book About Depression (non-fiction) 2002, Keeping Mum (poems) 2003, Redflight/Barcud (libretto) 2005, The Most Beautiful Man from the Sea (oratorio) 2005, Two in a Boat: A Marital Voyage 2005, Tair mewn Un (poems) 2005, Chaotic Angels (poems) 2005, Dolffin (libretto) 2006. *Address:* c/o Zoe Waldie, Rogers, Coleridge & White Literary Agency, 20 Powis Mews, London, W11 1JN, England (office). *Telephone:* (20) 7221-9084 (office); (20) 7792-3485 (office). *Fax:* (20) 7229-9084 (office). *Website:* www.rcwlitagency.co.uk (office); www.gwynethlewis.com (office). *E-mail:* gl@gwynethlewis.com (office).

LEWIS, Baron (Life Peer), cr. 1989, of Newnham; **Jack Lewis,** Kt, PhD, FRSC, FRS; British chemist and academic; *Professor Emeritus of Chemistry, University of Cambridge;* b. 13 Feb. 1928, Barrow; m. Elfreida M. Lamb 1951; one s. one d.; ed Barrow Grammar School and Univs of London and Nottingham; Lecturer, Univ. of Sheffield 1954–56, Imperial Coll. London 1956–57; Lecturer-Reader, Univ. Coll. London 1957–61; Prof. of Chem., Univ. of Manchester 1961–67, Univ. Coll. London 1967–70, Univ. of Cambridge 1970–95, now Emer.; Warden, Robinson Coll. Cambridge 1975–2001; mem. numerous cttees etc.; Foreign Assoc. NAS; Foreign mem. American Philosophical Soc. 1994, Accad. Naz. dei Lincei 1995; Hon. FRSC; Hon. Fellow Sidney Sussex Coll. Cambridge (Fellow 1970–77); Chevalier, Ordre des Palmes Académiques, Commdr Cross of the Order of Merit (Poland) and other distinctions; 22 hon. degrees; Davy Medal, Royal Soc. 1985, Royal Medal 2004, and other awards. *Publications:* papers in scientific journals. *Address:* Robinson College, Grange Road, Cambridge, CB3 9AN, England (office). *Telephone:* (1223) 339198 (office); (1223) 360222 (home).

LEWIS, Jerry; American comedian, writer, director, producer and actor; b. (Joseph Levitch), 16 March 1926, Newark, NJ; s. of Danny Lewis and Rachael Lewis; m. 1st Patti Palmer 1944 (divorced); five s.; m. 2nd SanDee Pitnick 1983; one d.; performed in nightclubs as a comedian before teaming with Dean Martin in 1946 at the 500 Club, Atlantic City, NJ; Nat. Chair. Muscular Dystrophy Asscn of America 1951–; Prof. of Cinema at Univ. of Southern Calif.; mem. Screen Directors Guild; Chevalier, Légion d'honneur 1984; Commdr des Arts et Lettres 1984; Hon. DHumLitt (Mercy Coll., Westchester, NY) 1987, (Emerson Coll., Boston, Mass) 1993; N. Neal Pike Prize for Service to the Handicapped, Boston Univ. School of Law 1984; numerous awards and honours including Best Dir of the Year Award (8 times), Lifetime Achievement Award, American Medical Asscn 1996, Golden Lion Award, Venice Int. Film 1999. *Films:* made film début with Dean Martin in My Friend Irma 1949; other films (many also as producer and/or Dir) include: My Friend Irma Goes West 1950, That's My Boy 1951, The Caddy 1952, Sailor Beware 1952, Jumping Jacks 1953, The Stooge 1953, Scared Stiff 1953, Living it Up 1954, Three Ring Circus 1954, You're Never Too Young 1955, Partners 1956, Hollywood or Bust 1956, The Delicate Delinquent 1957, The Sad Sack 1958, Rock a Bye Baby 1958, The Geisha Boy 1958, Visit to a Small Planet 1959, The Bellboy 1960, Cinderfella 1960, It's Only Money 1961, The Errand Boy 1962, The Patsy 1964, The Disorderly Orderly 1964, The Family Jewels 1965, Boeing-Boeing 1965, Three On a Couch 1965, Way Way Out 1966, The Big Mouth 1967, Don't Raise the Bridge, Lower the River 1968, One More Time 1969, Hook, Line and Sinker 1969, Which Way to the Front? 1970, The Day the Clown Cried 1972, Hardly Working 1979, King of Comedy 1981, Slapstick of Another Kind 1982, Smorgasbord 1983, How Did You Get In? 1985, Mr Saturday Night 1992, Funny Bones 1995. *Play:* Damn Yankees 1995, on tour 1995–97. *Television appearances include:* Startime, The Ed Sullivan Show and the Jazz Singer, Martin & Lewis – Colgate Comedy Hour. *Publications:* The Total Film-Maker 1971, Jerry Lewis in Person 1982, Dean and Me (memoir, with James Kaplan) 2006. *Leisure interests:* golf, sailing. *Address:* Jerry Lewis Films Inc., 3180 W Sahara Avenue, C-16, Las Vegas, NV 89102; c/o William Morris Agency Inc., 1 William Morris Place, Beverly Hills, CA 90212, USA. *Telephone:* (702) 362-9730 (office). *Fax:* (702) 362-9015 (office). *Website:* www.jerrylewiscomedy.com (office).

LEWIS, Jerry Lee; American rock singer and musician (piano); b. 29 Sept. 1935, Ferriday, LA; m. m. 6th Kerrie Lynn McCarver Lewis 1984 (divorced 2005); two s. (one deceased); one d.; ed Waxahachie Bible Inst., Texas; numerous concert tours, festival appearances. *Films include:* Jamboree 1957, High School Confidential 1958, Be My Guest 1965. *Theatre includes:* Iago in Catch My Soul. *Recordings include:* albums: Jerry Lee Lewis 1957, Jerry Lee's Greatest 1961, Live At The Star Club 1965, The Greatest Live Show On Earth 1965, The Return Of Rock 1965, Whole Lotta Shakin' Goin' On 1965, Country Songs For City Folks 1965, By Request – More Greatest Live Show On Earth 1967, Breathless 1967, Together (with Linda Gail Lewis) 1970, Rockin' Rhythm And Blues 1971, Sunday Down South (with Johnny Cash) 1972, The Session (with Peter Frampton and Rory Gallagher) 1973, Jerry Lee Lewis 1979, When Two Worlds Collide 1980, My Fingers Do The Talking 1983, I Am What I Am 1984, Keep Your Hands Off It 1987, Don't Drop It 1988, Great Balls of Fire! (film soundtrack) 1989, Rocket 1990, Young Blood 1995, Keep Your

Eyes Off Of It 2000, By Invitation Only 2000, Last Man Standing 2006. *Address:* Al Embry International, PO Box 23162, Nashville, TN 37202, USA (office); The Lewis Ranch, Box 384, Nesbit, MS 38651, USA.

LEWIS, Joseph C. (Joe); British business executive; b. London; s. of the late Charles Lewis; m.; one d.; joined father's small catering business; with father ran Hanover Grand chain of banqueting suites, London 1970s; moved to New Providence, Bahamas 1979; Founder and Owner Tavistock Group of financial services, property and retail businesses; shareholder Rapallo Ltd, London, English Nat. Investment Corpn, Tamarind Int., Hong Kong, auction house Christie's, London. *Address:* PO Box N7776, Lyford Cay, New Providence, Bahamas.

LEWIS, Juliette; American film actress and musician; b. 21 June 1973, Los Angeles, Calif.; d. of Geoffrey Lewis and Glenis Batley Lewis; m. Steve Berra 1999; f. band Juliette & The Licks 2003; Chicago Film Critics' Asscn Most Promising Actress 1991, NATO/ShoNest Female Star of Tomorrow 1993, Venice Film Festival Pasinetti Prize 1994. *Films include:* My Stepmother is an Alien 1988, Meet the Hollowheads 1989, National Lampoons Christmas Vacation 1989, Cape Fear 1991, Crooked Hearts 1991, Husbands and Wives 1992, Kalifornia 1993, One Hot Summer, That Night 1993, What's Eating Gilbert Grape 1993, Romeo is Bleeding 1994, Natural Born Killers 1994, Mixed Nuts 1994, The Basketball Diaries 1995, Strange Days 1995, From Dusk Till Dawn 1996, The Evening Star 1996, The Audition, Full Tilt Boogie 1997, The Other Sister 1999, The 4th Floor 1999, Way of the Gun 2000, My Louisiana Sky 2002, Hysterical Blindness 2002, Enough 2002, Gaudi Afternoon 2003, Old School 2003, Cold Creek Manor 2003, Blueberry 2004, Starsky and Hutch 2004, Aurora Borealis 2005, Daltry Calhoun 2005, Lightfield's Home Videos 2006, The Darwin Awards 2006, Grilled 2006, Catch and Release 2006. *Television appearances include:* Homefires (mini-series), I Married Dora 1988, Too Young To Die (movie) 1989, A Family For Joe 1990. *Theatre:* Fool for Love (Apollo Theatre, London) 2006. *Recordings include:* albums: You're Speaking My Language 2005, Four on the Floor 2006. *Address:* c/o Norman Brokaw, William Morris Agency, 1 William Morris Place, Beverly Hills, CA 90212, USA (office). *Website:* www.julietteandthelicks.com (office).

LEWIS, Kenneth D., BA; American banking executive; *President and CEO, Bank of America Corporation;* b. 9 April 1947, Meridian, Miss.; ed Georgia State Univ., Stanford Univ.; credit analyst, North Carolina Nat. Bank (NCNB, predecessor to NationsBank and Bank of America), Charlotte, NC 1969–77, Man. NCNB Int. Banking Corpn, NY 1977–79, Sr Vice-Pres. and Man. US Dept 1979–83, Middle Market Group Exec. (following creation of Bank of America group) 1983–86, Pres. Fla Div. 1986–88, Pres. Tex. Div. 1988–90, Pres. Consumer and Commercial Banking 1990–99, Pres. and COO Bank of America Corpn 1999–2001, Pres. and CEO 2001–, Chair. 2001–09; mem. Bd of Dirs Health Man. Assocs Inc., Homeownership Educ. and Counseling Inst., Lowe's Cos Inc., Presbyterian Hosp. Foundation (fmr Chair.); fmr Chair. Nat. Urban League; Vice-Chair. Corp. Fund Bd of The John F. Kennedy Center for the Performing Arts; mem. Financial Services Roundtable, Financial Services Forum, Cttee to Encourage Corporate Philanthropy; Fifth Dist's Rep. on Fed. Advisory Cttee; mem. Bd, Exec. Cttee and past Chair. United Way of Central Carolinas, Inc.; mem. Bd Dirs Homeownership Educ. and Counseling Inst.; Banker of the Year, American Banker 2002, Top CEO, US Banker 2002, named by Time Magazine to The Time 100 List 2007. *Address:* Bank of America Corporate Center, 100 North Tryon Street, Charlotte, NC 28255, USA (office). *Telephone:* (704) 386-1845 (office). *Fax:* (704) 386-6699 (office). *E-mail:* info@bankofamerica.com (office). *Website:* www.bankofamerica.com (office).

LEWIS, Lennox, CBE; British professional boxer; b. 2 Sept. 1965, London; s. of Violet Blake; defeated Jean Chanet to win European heavyweight title, Crystal Palace 1990; defeated Gary Mason to win British heavyweight title, Wembley 1991; Commonwealth heavyweight; WBC heavyweight 1992; defeated Frank Bruno (q.v.) 1993; WBC world champion 1993–94, 1997–; defended WBC title and challenged for World Boxing Asscn (WBA) and Int. Boxing Fed. (IBF) titles against Evander Holyfield (q.v.) March 1999, bout declared a draw; undisputed world heavyweight champion 1999–2001 (lost WBC and IBF titles when defeated by Hasim Rahman April 2001); regained title of world heavyweight champion from Hasim Rahman Nov. 2001; retained title of undisputed world heavyweight champion June 2002 (after beating Mike Tyson q.v.) and June 2003 (after beating Vitali Klitschko); 41 professional wins (two defeats, one draw, 31 knock-outs); announced retirement Feb. 2004; f. Lennox Lewis Coll., Hackney 1994; Dr hc (Univ. of London) 1999. *Film:* Ocean's Eleven 2002. *Publications:* Lennox Lewis (autobiog.) 1993, Lennox 2002. *Leisure interests:* action movie watching, urban music, cross training, golf, chess. *Address:* Office of Lennox Lewis, Suite 206, Gainsborough House, 81 Oxford Street, London, W1D 2EU, England (office). *Telephone:* (20) 7903-5074 (office). *Fax:* (20) 7903-5075 (office). *E-mail:* rose@lennoxlewis.com (office); roseobianwu@lennoxlewis.com (office). *Website:* www.lennoxlewis.com (office).

LEWIS, Neville Brice, MP; Jamaican politician; b. 19 May 1936, Middle Quarters, St Elizabeth; s. of Neville C. and Marie Lewis; m. Jasmin Lewis; one s. one d.; ed Munro Coll., St Elizabeth and Lincoln's Inn, London; accounting clerk, McCaulay's Motor Service, Kingston 1959–61; legal studies in London 1961; later worked in property man. in London; returned to Jamaica 1976; MP for NW St Elizabeth 1976–; Minister of Social Security 1980–83, of Local Govt 1983–89; mem. Jamaica Labour Party (Deputy Leader 1983). *Address:* c/o Jamaica Labour Party, 20 Belmont Road, Kingston 5, Jamaica.

LEWIS, Patrick Albert, PhD; Antigua and Barbuda diplomatist and historian; b. 27 Nov. 1938, St John's; m.; two c.; ed Hampton Inst. and Univ. of Cincinnati; Asst Prof. Univ. of Cincinnati 1971–73, Asst Prof., Assoc. Prof., Prof. of History, Hampton Univ. 1973–84; Adviser to Deputy Prime Minister of Antigua and Barbuda 1984–87, Minister-Counsellor, Perm. Mission to the UN 1987–91, apptd Amb. to UN 1995, to Brazil 1999. *Leisure interests:* cricket, movies, theatre, music. *Address:* c/o Ministry of Foreign Affairs, Queen Elizabeth Highway, St John's, Antigua and Barbuda (office).

LEWIS, Peter B.; American business executive; *Chairman, The Progressive Corporation;* b. 11 Nov. 1933; ed Princeton Univ.; joined The Progressive Corpn as underwriting trainee 1955, Chair., Pres. and CEO 1965–2001, Chair. 2001–, Chair., Pres. and CEO Progressive Casualty Insurance Co. –2000; Trustee Solomon R. Guggenheim Foundation 1993–, mem. Exec. and Finance Cttee 1996–98, Chair. Bd of Trustees 1998–2005; Trustee Cleveland Museum of Art, Princeton Univ., Cleveland Center for Contemporary Art, Cleveland Inst. of Art. *Address:* The Progressive Corporation, 6300 Wilson Mills Road, Mayfield Village, OH 44143, USA (office). *Telephone:* (440) 461-5000 (office). *Fax:* (440) 603-4420 (office). *Website:* www.progressive.com (office).

LEWIS, Roger Charles, BMus, FRWCMD; British broadcasting executive; *Managing Director, ITV Wales;* b. 24 Aug. 1954; s. of the late Griffith Charles Job Lewis and Dorothy Lewis (née Russ); m. Christine Trollope 1980; two s.; ed Cynffig Comprehensive School, Bridgend, Univ. of Nottingham; freelance musician 1976–80; Music Officer Darlington Arts Centre 1980–82; presenter Radio Tees 1981–84; producer Capital Radio 1984–85; BBC Radio 1 1985–87, Head of Music Radio 1 1987–90; Dir Classical Div. EMI Records 1990–95, Man. Dir 1995, Man. Dir EMI Premier 1995–97; Pres. Decca Record Co. 1997–98; Man. Dir and Programme Controller Classic FM 1998–2004; Dir GWR PLC 1998–2004, The Radio Corpn Ltd 1999–2004; Man. Dir ITV Wales 2004–; Dir HTV Ltd, HTV Group 2004–; Dir Wales Millennium Centre 2004–; Deputy Chair. Boosey & Hawkes 2004–; Chair. Classic FM Charitable Trust 1998–2004, Music and Dance Scheme Advisory Group, Dept for Educ. and Skills 2000–04, Barchester Group 2001–; Trustee Masterprize (Int. Composers' Competition) 1995–, Masterclass Charitable Trust 2000–04; Chair. Trustees Ogmore Centre 1996–; Pres. Bromley Youth Music Trust 2000–05; mem. British Phonographic Inst. (Classical Cttee 1990–98, Chair. 1996–98), WNO (Devt Circle 2001–); Dir Digital One 2003–04; Dir Liverpool Capital of Culture 2008 (mem. of bd Liverpool Culture Co.); Chair. Royal Liverpool Philharmonic 2003; Vice-Pres. London Welsh Male Voice Choir 2004–; Hon. Fellow Royal Welsh Coll. of Music and Drama, hon. mem. Royal Coll. of Music; Sony Radio Award 1987, 1988, 1989, Grand Award Winner and Gold Medal, New York Radio Festival 1987, One World Broadcasting Trust Award 1989, NTL Commercial Radio Programmer of the Year 2002. *Leisure interests:* rugby, walking, skiing. *Address:* ITV Wales, Television Centre, Culverhouse Cross, Cardiff CF5 6XJ, Wales (office). *Telephone:* (2920) 590191 (office). *E-mail:* roger.lewis@itvwales.com (office). *Website:* www.itv1wales.com (office).

LEWIS, Russell T., BA, JD; American newspaper executive; b. 1948; ed State Univ. of New York at Stony Brook, Brooklyn Law School; joined New York Times as a copy boy, while attending coll. 1966; litigation assoc. Cahill, Gordon and Reindel 1973; staff attorney New York Times legal dept 1977; Pres., Gen. Man. The New York Times, New York 1993–97, Pres., CEO 1997–2004 (retd); Acad. of Man. Distinguished Exec. of the Year 2002, American Lung Asscn of NY Life & Breath Award 2002, Nat. Human Relations Award, American Jewish Cttee 2003. *Leisure interests:* fitness, running, golf. *Address:* c/o The New York Times, 229 West 43rd Street, New York, NY 10036, USA (office).

LEWIS, Hon. Samuel Winfield, MA; American diplomatist; *Senior Adviser, Israel Policy Forum;* b. 1 Oct. 1930, Houston, Tex.; s. of Samuel W. Lewis and Sue Roselle Hurley Lewis; m. Sallie S. Smoot 1953; one s. one d.; ed Yale and Johns Hopkins Univs; Exec. Asst American Trucking Asscn, Washington 1953–54; entered Foreign Service 1954; with Consulate, Naples 1954–55; Consul, Florence 1955–59; Officer-in-Charge Italian Affairs, Dept of State 1959–61; Special Asst to Under-Sec. of State 1961–63; Deputy Asst Dir US AID Mission to Brazil 1964–66; Deputy Dir Office for Brazil Affairs, Dept of State 1967–68; sr staff mem. for Latin American Affairs, Nat. Security Council, White House 1968–69; Special Asst for Policy Planning, Bureau of Inter-American Affairs 1969, to Dir-Gen. Foreign Service 1969–71; Deputy Chief of Mission and Counsellor, US Embassy, Kabul 1971–74; Deputy Dir Policy Planning Staff, Dept of State 1974–75, Asst Sec. of State for Int. Orgs 1975–77; Amb. to Israel 1977–85; Pres. US Inst. of Peace 1987–93; Dir Policy Planning Staff, Dept of State 1993–94; Visiting Fellow, Princeton Univ. 1963–64; Diplomat-in-Residence, Johns Hopkins Foreign Policy Inst. 1985–87; Guest Scholar, The Brookings Inst., Washington, DC 1987; Visiting Prof., Hamilton Coll. 1995, 1997, 2008; Counselor, Washington Inst. for Near East Policy 1995–98; Adjunct Prof. Georgetown Univ. 1996; mem. Council on Foreign Relations, Vice-Chair. Center for Preventive Action 1995–97; Vice-Chair. American Acad. of Diplomacy 1995–99; mem. The Middle East Inst., Cousteau Soc.; mem. Bd of Dirs Inst. for the Study of Diplomacy, Georgetown Univ. 1994–, Asscn for Diplomatic Studies and Training 1994–2005, Pnrs for Democratic Change 2004–; Sr Adviser Israel Policy Forum 1998–; Chair. Bd of Overseers, Harry S. Truman Inst. for Advancement of Peace, Hebrew Univ. of Jerusalem 1986–91; Sr Int. Fellow, Dayan Centre for Middle Eastern and African Affairs, Tel-Aviv Univ. 1986–87; Professorial Lecturer, School of Advanced Int. Studies, Johns Hopkins Univ. 2005; Chair. Advisory Cttee Search for Common Ground in the Middle East 2005–; Dr hc, Hon. DHumLitt; William A. Jump Award 1967, Meritorious Honor Award (Dept of State, AID) 1967, Presidential Man. Improvement Award 1970, Distinguished Honor Awards 1977, 1985, Wilbur J. Carr Award 1985. *Publications:* Soviet and American Attitudes toward the Arab-Israeli Peace Process, in Super Power Rivalry in the Middle East 1987, The United States and Israel 1977–1988, in The Middle East: Ten Years after Camp David 1988, Making Peace among Arabs and Israelis 1991, The United States and Israel: Evolution of an

Unwritten Alliance 1999; numerous articles. *Leisure interests:* golf, tennis, scuba diving, nature photography, travel, painting. *Address:* 6232 Nelway Drive, McLean, VA 22101, USA (home). *Telephone:* (703) 448-1997 (home). *Fax:* (703) 448-1997 (home). *E-mail:* sixtymeter@aol.com (home).

LEWIS, Stephen, CC; Canadian international advocate and academic; *Co-Director, AIDS-Free World;* b. 11 Nov. 1937, Ottawa; s. of David and Sophie Lewis; m. Michele Landsberg 1963; three c.; ed Univ. of Toronto, Univ. of British Columbia; spent one year teaching and travelling in Africa; Prov. Leader, New Democratic Party (NDP) 1970–77; MP for Scarborough W, Ont. Legis. 1963–78; Canadian Amb. to UN 1984–88; Special Adviser to UN Sec.-Gen. on Africa 1986–91; Special Rep. to UNICEF 1990, Deputy Exec. Dir 1995–99; mem. Int. Panel of Eminent Personalities to investigate genocide in Rwanda 1998; UN Special Envoy for HIV/AIDS in Africa 2001–06; Co-Dir AIDS-Free World 2007–; Prof., McMaster Univ. 2007–; Founder and Chair. Stephen Lewis Foundation 2003–; Hon. LLD from 28 univs; Gordon Sinclair ACTRA Award 1982, Maclean's Magazine Canadian of the Year 2003, listed by TIME magazine as one of 100 most influential people in the world 2005. *Publications:* Art Out of Agony 1983, Race Against Time 2005. *Address:* c/o Stephen Lewis Foundation, 260 Spadina Avenue, Suite 501, Toronto, ON M5T 2E4, Canada. *Telephone:* (416) 533-9292 (office). *Fax:* (416) 850-4910 (office). *E-mail:* info@stephenlewisfoundation.org (office); info@aids-freeworld.org. *Website:* www.stephenlewisfoundation.org (office); www.aids-freeworld.org (office).

LEWIS, Tony (Anthony Robert), CBE, DL, MA; British sports commentator, journalist, writer and fmr cricketer; *Director, Welsh National Opera;* b. 6 July 1938, Swansea, Wales; s. of Wilfrid Lewis and Florence Lewis (née Flower); m. Joan Pritchard 1962; two d.; ed Neath Grammar School, Christ's Coll. Cambridge; right-hand batsman; teams: Glamorgan, Cambridge Univ.; double blue and debut at int. level; led Glamorgan to their second Co. Championship title 1969; played in nine Tests (eight as Capt.) scoring 457 runs (average 32.64); 20,495 first-class runs (average 32.4) including 30 hundreds; retd 1974; became cricket commentator and journalist; Pres. Marylebone Cricket Club (MCC) 1998–2000, secured admission of women into MCC Club, Trustee 2002–; fmr Chair. Glamorgan Co. Cricket Club (CCC), Pres. 1987–93, 2003–; Chair. Welsh Tourist Bd 1992–2000; led successful Welsh campaign to host 2010 Ryder Cup; Chair. (non-exec.) World Snooker Ltd 2003–; Dir Welsh Nat. Opera 2003–; Hon. Fellow, St David's Univ. Coll., Lampeter 1993, Univ. of Glamorgan 1995, Univ. of Wales, Swansea 1996, Univ. of Cardiff 1999. *Publications:* A Summer of Cricket 1976, Playing Days 1985, Double Century 1987, Cricket in Many Lands 1991, MCC Masterclass 1994, Taking Fresh Guard 2003. *Leisure interests:* classical music, golf. *Address:* Castellau, Near Llantrisant, Mid Glamorgan CF72 8LP, Wales (home); c/o Angie Bainbridge Management, 3 New Cottages, The Holt, Washington, West Sussex, RH20 4AW, England (office). *Telephone:* (1903) 8933748 (office). *Fax:* (1903) 891320 (office). *E-mail:* angie.bainbridge@btopenworld.com (office).

LEWIS, Vaughan Allen, PhD, CBE; Saint Lucia politician and academic; *Professor of International Relations, University of the West Indies;* b. 17 May 1940; m. Shirley May Lewis; two d.; ed Univ. of Manchester, UK; temporary Asst Lecturer, Dept of Political Theory, Univ. Coll. Swansea, Wales 1963–64; Asst Lecturer, Dept of Politics, Univ. of Liverpool 1964–66; Research Fellow Dept of Govt, Univ. of Manchester 1966–68; Lecturer, Dept of Govt, Univ. of the West Indies, Mona, Jamaica 1968–72, Part-time Lecturer, Inst. of Int. Relations, Univ. of the West Indies, St Augustine, Trinidad 1974–80, Acting Dir Inst. of Social and Econ. Research, Univ. of the West Indies 1974, Dir (rank of Full Prof.) 1977–82; Dir-Gen. Org. of Eastern Caribbean States, Castries, St Lucia 1982–95; Prime Minister of Saint Lucia 1996–97; Prof. of Int. Relations, Inst. of Int. Relations, Univ. of the West Indies 1999–; Visiting Prof. Fla Int. Univ. 1980, Ford Foundation Visiting Fellow Yale Univ. 1981. *Publications:* numerous books, papers and articles on int. relations, particularly concerning the Caribbean. *Address:* Institute of International Relations, University of the West Indies, St Augustine Campus, St Augustine, Trinidad and Tobago. *E-mail:* lewisv@diplomacy.edu (office); lewisv@candw.lc (home).

LEWIS, William; British journalist and newspaper editor; *Editor-in-Chief, Daily Telegraph and Sunday Telegraph;* b. 2 April 1969; m. Rebecca Lewis; three c.; worked on financial section of Mail on Sunday (UK) 1991–94; Global News Ed., later Mergers and Acquisitions Ed. (based in New York), later Investment Corresp., Financial Times 1994–2002; Business Ed. Sunday Times 2002–05; Jt Deputy Ed. Daily Telegraph 2005–06, Man. Dir (Editorial) 2006, Ed. 2006–07, Ed.-in-Chief 2007–, also of Sunday Telegraph 2007–; several awards, including Wincott Young Financial Journalist of the Year. *Address:* Telegraph Media Group, 111 Buckingham Palace Road, London, SW1W 0DT, England (office). *Website:* www.telegraph.co.uk (office).

LEY, Steven, BSc, PhD, FRS, FRSC, CBE; British chemist and academic; *BP (1702) Professor of Organic Chemistry, University of Cambridge;* b. 10 Dec. 1945, Stamford, Lincs.; ed Loughborough Univ.; Post Doctoral Fellow, Ohio State Univ., USA 1972–74; Post Doctoral Fellow, Imperial Coll., London 1974–75, Probationary Lecturer 1975–76, Lecturer 1976–83, Prof. of Organic Chem. 1983–92, Head of Dept 1989–92, Fellow 2001–; BP (1702) Prof. of Organic Chem., Univ. of Cambridge 1992–, Head of Organic Chem. 1992–, Fellow, Trinity Coll. 1993–; numerous hon. lectureships including at univs in USA, Canada, Japan, Australia; Pres. Royal Soc. of Chem. 2002–03; Hon. Fellow, Chemical Research Soc. of India 2001; Hon. DSc (Loughborough Univ.) 1994, (Univ. of Salamanca, Spain) 2000, (Univ. of Huddersfield) 2003; 29 major prizes and awards, including Gesellschaft Deutscher Chemiker August-Wilhelm-von Hofmann Medal 2001, Royal Soc. Davy Medal 2000, Wolfson Merit Award 2003, ACS Ernest Guenther Award in the Chem. of Natural Products 2003, oChemE Award for Innovation in Applied Catalysis

2004, Alexander-von-Humboldt Award 2004, Yamada-Koga Prize 2005, Royal Soc. of Chem. Robert Robinson Award and Medal 2006. *Publications:* 560 papers in scientific journals. *Address:* Department of Chemistry, University of Cambridge, Lensfield Road, Cambridge, CB2 1EW, England (office). *Telephone:* (1223) 336398 (office). *E-mail:* svl1000@cam.ac.uk (office). *Website:* leygroup.ch.cam.ac.uk (office).

LEYE, Jean-Marie; Ni-Vanuatu fmr head of state; Pres. of Vanuatu 1994–99. *Address:* c/o Office of the President, Port Vila, Vanuatu.

L'HEUREUX-DUBÉ, The Hon. Madame Justice Claire, CC, BA, LLL; Canadian judge (retd); b. 7 Sept. 1927, Québec City; d. of Paul L'Heureux and Marguerite Dion; m. Dr Arthur Dubé 1957 (died 1978); one s. (died 1994) one d.; ed Monastère des Ursulines, Rimouski, Coll. Notre-Dame de Bellevue, Québec, Laval Univ.; called to Québec Bar 1952; practised with Bard, L'Heureux & Philippon (known as L'Heureux, Philippon, Garneau, Tourigny, St Arnaud & Assocs. from 1969) 1952–73; Counsellor of the Québec Bar 1968–70, Del. at Gen. Council 1968–70; QC 1969; Lecturer in Family Law, Cours de formation professionnelle du Barreau du Québec 1970–73; Royal Comm. of Inquiries in matters relating to the Dept of Manpower and Immigration 1973–76; Judge, Superior Court of Québec 1973, Québec Court of Appeal 1979; Judge, Supreme Court of Canada 1987–2002; Vice-Pres. Canadian Consumers' Council 1970–73, Vanier Inst. of the Family 1972–73, Int. Soc. on Family Law 1982–88; mem. Canadian Bar Asscn, Canadian Inst. for Admin of Justice; Pres. Family Law Cttee and Family Court Cttee, Québec Civil Code Revision Office 1972–76, Int. Comm. of Jurists (Canadian Section) 1981–83, Vice-Pres. 1992–98, Pres. 1998–2002; mem. Nat. Council, Canadian Human Rights Foundation 1980–84, Québec Asscn of Comparative Law (Pres. 1984–90); Chair. Editorial Bd The Canadian Bar Review 1985; Assoc. mem. Int. Acad. of Comparative Law 1992–; mem. American Law Inst. 1995–; numerous other professional appointments and affiliations; Hon. Lt Col Helicopter Squadron 430 1994 (retd 1996); Hon. mem. American Coll. of Trial Lawyers 1995, Grand Officer, National Order of Quebec 2004; Hon. LLD (Dalhousie) 1981, (Montréal) 1983, (Laval) 1984, (Ottawa) 1988, (Québec à Rimouski) 1989, (Toronto) 1994, (Queen's) 1995, (Gonzaga) 1996, (Windsor) 2000, (York) 2001, (Concordia) 2001, (Law Soc. of Upper Canada) 2002; Medal of Québec Bar 1987, 1995, Montréal Bar 1994; Int. Year of the Family Medal (Québec) 1994, Canadian Award, Canadian Hadassah-WIZO 1996, Prix de la Justice, Canadian Inst. for the Administration of Justice 1997, Margaret Brent Women Lawyers of Achievement Award, ABA 1998, Int. Acad. of Law and Mental Health Yves Pélicier Award 2002. *Address:* Université Laval, rue des Sciences Humaines, Pavillon de Koninck, Bureau #3107, Québec City, G1K 7P4, Canada (office).

LHO, Shin-yong; South Korean politician and diplomatist; b. 28 Feb. 1930, S. Pyongyang Prov.; ed Law Coll. of Seoul Nat. Univ., Kentucky State Univ.; joined diplomatic service 1956, Dir Planning and Man. Office, Ministry of Foreign Affairs 1967; Consul-Gen., LA, USA 1969–72; Amb. to India 1973, to Geneva 1976; Vice-Foreign Minister 1974, Foreign Minister 1980–82, Prime Minister 1985–87; Head, Agency of Nat. Security Planning 1982–85; mem. Democratic Justice Party (later New Korea Party to be merged with Democratic Party to form Grand Nat. Party).

LI, Arthur K.C., GBS, BChir, MA, MD, JP; British surgeon and academic; *Secretary for Education and Manpower, Hong Kong Special Administrative Region;* b. 23 June 1945, Hong Kong; ed St Paul's Co-educational Coll., King's Coll., Cambridge, Middlesex Hosp. Medical School, Harvard Medical School, USA; house physician, Addenbrooke's Hosp., Cambridge 1969–70, Rotational Sr House Officer 1970–71; house surgeon, Middx Hosp., London 1970; Rotational Surgical Registrar, Queen Elisabeth II Hosp. 1971-71, Hillingdon Hosp., Uxbridge 1972–73; Surgical Registrar, St Mary's Hosp., London 1973–75; Lecturer in Surgery and Sr Surgical Registrar, Royal Free Hosp., London 1975–77, Chair. Div. of Jr Hosp. Doctors 1975–77, Consultant Surgeon and Sr Lecturer in Surgery 1980–82; Stanley Thomas Johnson Foundation Research Fellow, Harvard Medical School, Massachusetts Gen. Hosp. and Shriners Burns Inst., Boston 1977–78, Clinical and Research Fellow 1978–79, Surgical Staff and Instructor in Surgery 1979–80; Foundation Prof. of Surgery and Chair. of Surgical Services, Chinese Univ. of Hong Kong and the Prince of Wales Hosp. 1982–95, Assoc. Dean, Faculty of Medicine 1986–92, Dean 1992–96, Prof. of Surgery 1995, Vice-Chancellor (Pres.) and mem. Univ. Council 1996–2002; Chair. Hosp. Gov. Cttee, United Christian Hosp. 1987–97; mem. Exec. Council and Sec. for Educ. and Manpower, Hong Kong Special Admin. Region 2002–; Visiting Prof., Royal Australian Coll. of Surgeons 1984, 1986, Nat. Univ. of Singapore 1986, Yale Univ. 1989; Pearce Gould Visiting Prof. in Surgery, Univ. Coll. London and Middlesex School of Medicine 1993; Edward Tooth Prof., Royal Brisbane Hosp. 1995; mem. Bd United Christian Medical Services 1987–; fmr mem. Bd Dirs Hong Kong Science and Tech. Parks Corpn, Hong Kong Applied Science and Tech. Research Inst.; mem. Int. Advisory Panel Ministry of Health, UAE 1993–; fmr Vice-Pres. Asscn of Univ. Pres of China; Hon. Prof. of Surgery, Sun Yat-sen Univ. of Medical Sciences, Guangzhou 1986, People's Hosp., Beijing Medical Univ. 1987, Mil. Postgraduate Medical School and Chinese PLA Gen. Hosp., Beijing 1994; Hon. Prof., Peking Union Medical Coll. 1996, Shanghai Medical Univ.; Hon. Fellow, Sidney Sussex Coll. Cambridge, Philippines Coll. of Surgeons 1994, Asscn of Surgeons of GB and Ireland 1998; Hon. FRCS (Glasgow) 1995; Hon. FRCS (Ireland); Hon. FRSM 1997; Hon. FACS 2000; Hon. FRCP; Hon. DSc (Hull) 1999; Hon. DLitt (Hong Kong Univ. of Science and Tech.) 1999; Dr hc (Soka Univ., Tokyo) 1999; European Soc. for Surgical Research Prize 1980, Moynihan Medal 1982, Royal Coll. of Surgeons Gordon Watson Medal 1987, Stanford Cade Memorial Medal 1988, Royal Marsden Surgical Soc. Ernest Miles Memorial Medal 1990, Edward Hallaran Bennett Lecturer, Trinity Coll. Dublin 1995, Pres.'s Gold Medal Royal Coll. of

Surgeons of Edin. 1996, Sir Edward Dunlop Memorial Lecturer, Royal Australian Coll. of Surgeons 2000, Gold Bauhinia Star, Govt of Hong Kong Special Admin. Region 2000, Shaw Prize 2004. *Publications:* numerous research papers in learned journals. *Leisure interests:* reading, skiing, scuba diving. *Address:* Education and Manpower Bureau, 15/F, Wu Chung House, 213 Queen's Road East, Wan Chai, Hong Kong Special Administrative Region, People's Republic of China (office). *Telephone:* (852) 28910088 (office). *Fax:* (852) 28930858 (office). *E-mail:* embinfo@emb.gov.hk (office). *Website:* www .emb.gov.hk (office).

LI, Baotian; Chinese actor; b. Dec. 1946, Xuzhou, Jiangsu Prov.; ed Cen. Acad. of Drama; teacher, Cen. Acad. of Drama 1981–; acted in Judou, Shanghai Triad, Prime Minister Hunchback Liu (TV series); Best Supporting Actor, 8th Golden Rooster Awards. *Films include:* Ju Dou 1990, Shanghai Triad 1995, Keep Cool 1997. *Address:* Central Academy of Drama, Beijing, People's Republic of China.

LI, Boyong; Chinese state official and engineer; b. 1932, Tianjin City; ed Air Force Inst. of Mil. Eng, fmr USSR; Vice-Minister, Labour and Personnel 1986–93; mem. 14th CCP Cen. Cttee 1992–97; Minister of Labour 1993–98; Vice-Chair. Legal Affairs Cttee of 9th NPC 1998–2003. *Address:* c/o Standing Committee of National People's Congress, Beijing 100716, People's Republic of China.

LI, Chang'an; Chinese party and state official; b. 1935, Tai'an Co., Liaoning Prov.; ed Shandong Tech. Coll.; joined CCP 1961; Alt. mem. 12th CCP Cen. Cttee 1982, mem. 1985; Deputy Sec. CCP Cttee, Shandong Prov. 1983–88; Gov. of Shandong 1985–88; Deputy Sec.-Gen. CCP State Council 1987; Deputy Head State Flood Control HQ 1988, Cen. Forest Fire Prevention 1987; Deputy Head Leading Group for Comprehensive Agricultural Devt 1990–; Vice-Chair. State Tourism Cttee 1988. *Address:* c/o State Council, Zhong Nan Hai, Beijing, People's Republic of China.

LI, Changchun; Chinese party and government official; b. Feb. 1944, Dalian City, Liaoning Prov.; m. Zhang Shurong; ed Harbin Inst. of Tech.; joined CCP 1965; at Harbin Inst. of Tech. 1966–68; technician, Shenyang Switchgear Plant, Liaoning Prov. 1968–75; Deputy Man. later Man. Shenyang Electrical Equipment Co. 1975–80 (Vice-Chair. CCP Revolutionary Cttee, mem. Standing Cttee and Deputy Sec. CCP Party Cttee 1975–80); Deputy Dir Bureau of Mechanical and Electrical Industry, Shenyang City 1980–81 (Deputy Sec. CCP Party Cttee 1980–81); Deputy Sec.-Gen. CCP Municipal Cttee, Shenyang City 1981–82; Vice-Mayor Shenyang City 1982–83, Mayor 1983–85; Sec. Shenyang Municipal CCP Cttee 1983–86 (Chair. Econ. Cttee 1982–83); Deputy Sec. Liaoning Prov. CCP Cttee 1985–90; Vice-Gov. (also Acting Gov.) of Liaoning Prov. 1986–87, Gov. 1987–90; Vice-Gov. (also Acting Gov.) of Henan Prov. 1990–91, Gov. 1991–92; Sec. CCP 5th Henan Prov. Cttee 1992–98; Chair. Standing Cttee Henan Prov. People's Congress 1993–98; Alt. mem. 12th CCP Cen. Cttee 1981–82, mem. 13th CCP Cen. Cttee 1987–92, 14th CCP Cen. Cttee 1992–97, 15th CCP Cen. Cttee 1997–2002, Politburo 15th CCP Cen. Cttee 1997–2002, 16th CCP Cen. Cttee 2002–07, Politburo 16th CCP Cen. Cttee 2002–07, Standing Cttee Politburo 16th CCP Cen. Cttee 2002–07, 17th CCP Cen. Cttee 2007–, Standing Cttee Politburo 17th CCP Cen. Cttee 2007–; Sec. CCP Guangdong Prov. Cttee 1998–2002. *Address:* Standing Committee of the Politburo, Chinese Communist Party Central Committee, Beijing, People's Republic of China (office).

LI, Changjin, MEng; Chinese railway industry executive; *President and Executive Director, China Railway Group Ltd;* ed Changsha Railway Inst., Southwest Jiaotong Univ.; Vice-Pres. The Fourth Survey and Design Inst., MOR Jan.–Dec. 1995, Deputy Dir and Sr Engineer, The Second Eng Bureau of MOR (predecessor of China Railway No. 2 Eng Group Co. Ltd) 1996–98, Vice-Chair. and Gen. Man. China Railway No. 2 Eng Group Co. Ltd 1998–2002, also Chair. and Sec. to CCP Cttee, Deputy Gen. Man. China Railway Eng Corpn (CRECG) 2002–06, mem. Bd of Dirs 2006–, Pres. and Exec. Dir China Railway Group Ltd, Chair. Safety, Health and Environmental Protection Cttee, mem. Nomination Cttee, Strategy Cttee; recognized as prof.-level sr engineer by Ministry of Personnel 2003. *Address:* China Railway Group Ltd, 26 Lianhuachi Nanli, Beijing 100055, People's Republic of China (office). *E-mail:* info@crecg.com (office). *Website:* www.crecg.com (office).

LI, Chunting; Chinese provincial governor; b. Oct. 1936, Luotang village, Zhaili, Qixia Co., Shandong Prov.; joined CCP 1958; worked as farmer; assumed leading posts at village, township, co., prefectural and city level; fmr Deputy Sec. CCP Qixia Co. Cttee, Deputy Sec. CCP Yantai Prefectural Cttee, Head Prov. Metallurgical Dept; Vice-Gov. Shandong Prov. 1988–95, Gov. 1995–97; Deputy Sec. CCP Shandong Prov. Cttee 1992–2001; mem. 15th CCP Cen. Cttee 1997–2002; Vice-Chair. NPC Agric. and Rural Affairs Cttee 2001–. *Address:* National People's Congress, Tiananmen, Beijing, People's Republic of China.

LI, Dadong; Chinese engineer; b. 24 Feb. 1938, Beijing; ed Peking Univ.; joined Research Inst. of Petroleum Processing (RIPP) 1962, becoming Group Leader, Dir, Research Dept, Deputy Chief Engineer 1987–88, Vice-Pres. 1988–91, Pres. 1991–2003, Dir Science Cttee 2004–; Fellow Chinese Acad. of Eng 1994–, Chair. Standing Cttee of Chemical Eng, Metallurgy and Material Eng Dept; many nat., prov. and ministerial prizes. *Publications:* published 70 research papers. *Address:* Petrochemical Science Research Institute, 18 Xueyuan Road, Beijing 100083, People's Republic of China (office). *Telephone:* (10) 62310757 (office). *Fax:* (10) 62311290 (office). *E-mail:* ripp@mimi.cnc.ac.cn (office).

LI, Daoyu; Chinese diplomatist; *President, Chinese International Public Relations Association;* b. 7 Aug. 1932, Shanghai; m. Ye Zhao Lie 1956; two s.; ed Univ. of Shanghai; joined Foreign Service 1952; held various posts Dept of Int. Orgs and Confs; Deputy Perm. Rep. to UN at Geneva 1983–84; Dir Dept of Int. Orgs, Foreign Ministry 1984–88; Asst Foreign Minister 1988–90; Perm. Rep. to UN, New York 1990–93, Amb. to USA 1993–98; led Chinese Del. to ESCAP session 1989; fmr Vice-Chair. Chinese Nat. Comm., UNESCO, Nat. Cttee for Pacific Econ. Co-operation, Preparatory Cttee of China for Int. Space Year 1992, Nat. Cttee for Int. Decade for Natural Disaster Reduction; fmr rep. of China on Comm. on Human Rights, ECOSOC and UNCTAD; Vice-Chair. Overseas Chinese Affairs Cttee of 9th NPC 1998; mem. Standing Cttee NPC 1998–2003; Prof. School of Int. Studies, Beijing Univ., Inst. of Int. Studies, Tsinghua Univ., Foreign Affairs Coll., Center for American Studies, Fudan Univ., Pacific Inst., Tongji Univ.; Pres. China Int. Public Relations Asscn 1999–, Chinese Asscn of Arms Control and Disarmament 2001–; Vice-Pres. China Int. Friendship Exchange Asscn, China Women Devt Fund; mem. Council Chinese People's Inst. of Foreign Affairs; Sr Adviser China Inst. of Int. Strategic Studies; Adviser China Int. Law Soc., Centre for Across-the-Straits Relationship Studies, Shanghai WTO Affairs Consulting Centre. *Address:* China International Public Relations Association, Room 918, 7 Fuchengmen-wai Street, Beijing, 100037, People's Republic of China (office). *Telephone:* (10) 68095777 (office). *Fax:* (10) 68095775 (office). *E-mail:* info@cipra.org.cn (office). *Website:* www.cipra.org.cn (office).

LI, Gen. Desheng; Chinese army officer (retd); b. 1916, Xinxian Co., Henan Prov.; joined Red Army 1930, CCP 1932; Commdr, Red 4th Front Army on Long March 1934–36; Div. Commdr 2nd Field Army, People's Liberation Army 1949; Maj.-Gen. PLA 1955, Gen. 1988; Commdr Anhui Mil. Dist, PLA 1967; Chair. Anhui Revolutionary Cttee 1968; Alt. mem. Politburo, 9th Cen. Cttee of CCP 1969; Dir, Gen. Political Dept, PLA 1969–74; First Sec. CCP Anhui 1971–73; mem. Standing Cttee of Politburo and Vice-Chair. 10th Cen. Cttee of CCP 1973–75; mem. Politburo 11th Cen. Cttee of CCP 1977; mem. Politburo 12th Cen. Cttee of CCP 1982–85; Commdr Shenyang Mil. Region, PLA 1974–85, Head, Leading Group for the Prevention and Treatment of Endemic Disease in N China, Cen. Cttee 1977; First Sec. CCP Cttee, PLA Shenyang Mil. Region 1978–85; mem. Standing Cttee, Cen. Advisory Comm. 1985–92; Political Commissar, Leading Group of All-Army Financial and Econ. Discipline Inspection 1985–, PLA Nat. Defence Univ.; mem. Standing Comm. CCP Cen. Advisory Comm. 1985, 1987; Hon. Pres. Beijing Inst. of Modernization Admin Aug. 1986–; Sr Adviser China Soc. of Mil. Sciences 1991–; Pres. Chinese Patriotic Programs Fed. 1995–; Hon. Pres. Wushi (Martial Arts) Asscn 1988–; mem. Presidium 14th CCP Nat. Congress Oct. 1992. *Address:* c/o Shenyang Military Region, People's Republic of China (office).

LI, Dezhu, (Li Dek Su); Chinese party and government official; b. 1943, Wangqing Co., Jilin Prov.; ed Yanbian Univ.; joined CCP 1965; Vice-Gov. of Jilin Prov. 1988–93; Deputy Head United Front Work Dept 1992; Pres. Chinese Asscn of Ethnic Minorities for External Exchanges 1992–98; Minister State Comm. of Ethnic Affairs 1998–2008; mem. 14th CCP Cen. Cttee 1992–97, 15th CCP Cen. Cttee 1997–2002, 16th CCP Cen. Cttee 2002–07. *Address:* c/o State Ethnic Affairs Commission, 252 Teipingqiao Street, Beijing 100800, People's Republic of China.

LI, Dongsheng; Chinese electronics industry executive; *Chairman, TCL–Thomson Electronics Company Limited (TTE);* b. July 1957; ed Huanan Tech. Inst.; started career as technician with TTK Home Appliances Co. Ltd 1982, later Deputy Workshop Dir, Business Man.; Gen. Man. TCL Communication Equipment Co. 1985–93, Gen. Man. TCL Corpn 1993–96, Chair. and Pres. 1996–2004, Chair. TCL–Thomson Electronics Co. Ltd (TTE) 2004–; mem. 16th CPPCC 2002–07; Special Contributor to China Household Appliance Industry 1994, Nat. Excellent Young Entrepreneur 1995, Nat. Model Worker 2000. *Address:* TCL Corporation, East Yunshan Road, Jiangbei Huizhou, Guangdong 516003, China (office). *Telephone:* (752) 2803898 (office). *Fax:* (752) 2803188 (office). *Website:* (office).

LI, Fang, BA, LLB; Chinese political scientist (retd); b. 7 March 1925, Changde City, Hunan Prov.; s. of Li Xin Zhai and Wang Fu Ying; m. Zhang Cun Li 1954; one s. one d.; ed Nanjing Univ. and Beijing Foreign Studies Univ.; Prof. and Research Fellow, Beijing Inst. of Political Science, Chinese Acad. of Social Sciences 1980–89; fmr Dir Research Dept of Public Admin, Inst. of Political Science; fmr Prof., Beijing Univ., Nanjing Univ., Lanzhou Univ.; fmr Perm. Council mem. Chinese Soc. of Public Admin; fmr Council mem. Asscn for Political Reform of China; fmr Visiting Scholar and Research Fellow, Erasmus Univ., Netherlands, Univ. of Newcastle, UK, Tokyo Univ., Japan, City Coll. of New York, Columbia Univ., USA, Murdoch Univ., WA, Albert Einstein Inst., USA; fmr Deputy Ed.-in-Chief The Volume of Public Administration of the Encyclopaedia of China; mem. Asscn of Political Science of America, American Soc. of Public Admin; Fellowship, Ford Foundation 1989–90, Albert Einstein Inst. 1993–94. *Publications:* Selections from Chinese literature (two vols) 1980, Outline of Public Administration, 1985, Elements of Public Administration 1989, Nonviolent Struggle 1997; numerous articles on science and literature. *Leisure interests:* carpentry, Chinese opera. *Address:* 9th Building, 905 Furongli, Wanquanhelu, Haidian, Beijing 100080; c/o Institute of Political Science, 5 Jian Nei Da Jie, Beijing 100732, People's Republic of China. *Telephone:* (10) 62569305. *E-mail:* bj-hd-lifang@sohu.com (home).

LI, Fanghua; Chinese physicist; *Professor of Condensed Matter Physics, Institute of Physics, Chinese Academy of Sciences;* b. Jan. 1932, Hong Kong; m. Haifu Fan 1960; one d. one s.; ed Beijing Furen High School, Lingnan and Zhongshan Univs, Guangzhou, Wuhan Univ., Hubei Prov., Leningrad (now St Petersburg) Univ., USSR; internship Inst. of Physics, Chinese Acad. of Sciences 1956, Academician 1993, currently Prof. of Condensed Matter Physics; Academician Third World Acad. of Science 1998; Asia-Pacific recipient l'Oréal-UNESCO For Women in Science Award (first Chinese woman) 2003. *Publications include:* numerous articles in scientific journals.

Leisure interests: singing, T'ai ji boxing. *Address:* Institute of Physics, 8 Nanran Road, Zhong-guan-cun, Beijing, 100080, People's Republic of China (office). *Telephone:* (10) 82649170 (office). *Fax:* (10) 82649531 (office). *E-mail:* lifh@aphy.iphy.ac.cn (office). *Website:* www.iphy.ac.cn (office).

LI, Furong; Chinese sports administrator; b. 1942, Shanghai City; Deputy, 5th NPC 1978–83; Deputy Dir Training Bureau under the Comm. for Physical Culture and Sports 1983, Dir 1986–; Vice-Chair. Youth Fed. 1983; Vice-Minister of the Physical Culture and Sports Comm. 1987; Sec.-Gen. Chinese Olympic Team, Seoul 1988; Vice-Pres. Chinese Olympic Cttee 1989–; apptd Vice-Minister in charge of State Gen. Admin for Sports 1999; Pres. Asian Table Tennis Union 2001–; Head of Chinese Delegation, World Univ. Games 2008. *Address:* 9 Tiyuguan Road, Beijing 100763, People's Republic of China.

LI, Fushan; Chinese artist and engraver; b. June 1940, Quinhuangdao, Hebei; s. of Li Yinchang and Wang Lihui; m. Lei Suoxia 1961; one s. two d.; worked at Quinhuangdao Cultural Centre 1959–62, at Shanhaiguan Cultural Centre 1962–, deputy researcher 1994–; his works are in pvt. collections in Canada, USA, Italy, NZ and countries in SE Asia; Dir Quinhuangdao Arts Asscn; mem. Hebei Br. China Arts Asscn, Hebei Prov. Research Asscn of Etched Plates. *Leisure interests:* classical literature, photography. *Address:* Shanhaiguan Cultural Centre, Quinhuangdao, Hebei Province, People's Republic of China. *Telephone:* 5051418; 3069987.

LI, Genshen, DSc; Chinese party official and engineer; b. 1 July 1930, Huzhou City, Zhejiang Prov.; s. of Li Xin-pei and Zhang Zhu-bao; m. Xu Ying; one s. two d.; ed Jiaotong Univ., Shanghai and in USSR; Dir and Chief Engineer, No. 3 Research Inst., No. 7 Research Acad., China Shipbuilding Industrial Corpn; Chair. Bd Harbin Power Equipment Co. 1993–97, Dir (non-exec.) 1997–; mem. Standing Cttee Heilongjiang Prov. CCP Cttee 1983–92, Sec.-Gen. 1984, Deputy Sec. 1985–86; Vice-Chair. Heilongjiang Prov. 8th People's Congress 1993–96; Sec. Harbin Mun. CCP Cttee 1985, Chair. 1983–; Standing Cttee CCP Heilongjiang Prov. Cttee 1988; mem. 13th CCP Cen. Cttee 1987–92; mem. Standing Cttee 1988. *Publication:* Principles, Design and Testing of Marine Steam and Gas Turbines. *Leisure interest:* reading. *Address:* 1 Guomin Street, Nangang District, Harbin 150001, Heilongjiang Province, People's Republic of China (office). *Telephone:* (451) 3624054 (office); (451) 53660615 (home). *Fax:* (451) 2135700 (office).

LI, Gong; Chinese actress; b. 31 Dec. 1965, Shenyang, Liaoning; m. Ooi Hoe-Seong 1996. *Films include:* Red Sorghum 1987, Evil Empress 1988, Operation Cougar 1988 (Hundred Flowers Award for Best Supporting Actress 1989), The Terracotta Warrior 1989, Ju Dou 1990, The Banquet 1991, God of Gamblers II: Back to Shanghai 1991, Raise the Red Lantern 1991 (Hundred Flowers Award for Best Actress 1993), The Story of Qiu Ju 1991 (Golden Rooster Awards for Best Actress, 1993, Venice Film Festival Volpi Cup for Best Actress), Mary from Beijing 1992, Farewell, My Concubine 1993 (New York Film Critics Circle Award 1993), Flirting Scholar 1993, To Live 1994, La Peintre 1994, The Great Conqueror's Concubine 1994, Semi-Gods and Semi-Devils 1994, Shanghai Triad 1995, Temptress Moon 1996, The Empress and the Assassin 1997, Chinese Box 1998, Breaking the Silence 1999 (Golden Rooster Awards for Best Actress 2000, Montreal World Film Festival for Best Actress 2000), Zhou Yu's Train 2002, Eros 2004, 2046 2004, Miami Vice 2006, Man cheng jin dai huang jin jia (Curse of the Golden Flower) 2006 (Hong Kong Film Awards for Best Actress, 2007), Hannibal Rising 2007, Shanghai 2008.

LI, Gui Rong; Chinese brewery executive; *Chairman, Tsingtao Brewery Co;* fmr Deputy Dir, then Dir Qingdao Municipal Planning Comm.; Chair. Tsingtao Brewery Co. Ltd 1996–. *Address:* Tsingtao Beer Tower, May Fourth Square, Hong Kong Road, Central Qingdao, Shandong 266071, People's Republic of China (office). *Telephone:* (532) 5711119 (office). *Fax:* (532) 5714719 (office). *Website:* www.tsingtaobeer.com.cn (office).

LI, Guixian; Chinese party official; *Vice-Chairman, 10th National Committee, Chinese People's Political Consultative Conference;* b. 1938, Gaixian Co., Liaoning Prov.; ed Chinese Univ. of Science and Tech., Mendeleyev Chemical Tech. Inst., Moscow, USSR; joined CCP 1962; worker, Research Inst., Ministry of Public Security 1966–67; technician, later Workshop Dir, later Deputy Dir, later Chief Engineer, No. 777 Factory 1967–77 (Deputy Sec. CCP Party Cttee 1967–77); Deputy Dir, Chief Engineer Jinzhou City Bureau of Electronics Industry 1977–79; Deputy Dir Liaoning Provincial Bureau of Electronics Industry 1979–82 (Deputy Sec. CCP Leading Party Group 1979–82); Vice-Gov. Liaoning Prov. 1982–85; Chair. Science and Tech. Comm. CCP Liaoning Prov. Cttee, CCP Leading Party Group 1982–83; Sec. CCP Cttee, Liaoning Prov. 1985–86, Anhui Prov. 1986–87; Gov. People's Bank of China 1988–93 (resgnd); State Councillor 1988–98; mem. 12th CCP Cen. Cttee 1982–87, 13th CCP Cen. Cttee 1987–92, 14th CCP Cen. Cttee 1992–97, 15th CCP Cen. Cttee 1997–2002, 16th CCP Cen. Cttee 2002–07; Vice-Chair. Nat. Cttee of 9th CPPCC 1998–2003, Nat. Cttee of 10th CPPCC 2003–; Pres. Chinese Asscn for Int. Understanding 1999–; fmr Dir China Cttee of Int. Decade for Natural Disaster Reduction. *Address:* National Committee of Chinese People's Political Consultative Conference, 23 Taipingqiao Street, Beijing, People's Republic of China. *Website:* www.cafiu.org.cn.

LI, Guoguang; Chinese judge; Vice-Pres., mem. judicial Cttee Supreme People's Court 1995. *Address:* Supreme People's Court, Beijing, People's Republic of China.

LI, Guorui; Chinese engineer and business executive; *Chairman and General Manager, China Railway Construction Corporation Ltd;* b. 1950; ed Southwest Jiaotong Univ.; Sec. to CCP Cttee, China Railway Engineering Corpn 1996–97; joined China Railway Construction Corpn (CRCC) Ltd 1997, Sec. to CRCC CCP Cttee 1997–2007, Deputy Gen. Man. CRCC 2002–05, Chair. 2005–, also Gen. Man. 2007–; Chair. Nanjing Changjiang Tunnel Co. Ltd; mem. 17th CCP Congress. *Address:* China Railway Construction Corpn Ltd, 40 Fuxing Road, Beijing 100855, People's Republic of China (office). *Telephone:* (10) 51888114 (office). *Fax:* (10) 68217382 (office). *E-mail:* info@crcc.cn (office). *Website:* www.crcc.cn (office).

LI, Hao; Chinese politician; b. Dec. 1926, Dianbai Co., Guangdong Prov.; s. of Li Hansan and Cheng Li; m. Cheng Huizheng 1943; one s. two d.; ed Zhongshan Univ., Guangzhou; joined CCP 1949; Deputy Sec.-Gen. of State Council, Beijing 1983–85; Vice-Gov. Guangdong Prov. 1985–88; Mayor, Shenzhen City, Sec. of CCP Shenzhen Cttee 1985–93; mem. and Vice-Chair. Financial and Econ. Cttee 8th NPC 1993–98; part-time Prof., Beijing Univ. and People's Univ. of China. *Address:* Shenzhen People's Government, Guangdong, People's Republic of China. *Telephone:* (755) 2239440.

LI, Hongzhi; Chinese spiritual leader; b. 13 May 1951, Jilin Prov.; m.; one d.; fmr stud farm worker, trumpeter in police band and grain clerk; Leader, Falun Gong spiritual movt 1992–; lives in exile in New York, USA. *Publication:* Zhuan Falun (Law of the Wheel) 1996. *Address:* c/o The Universe Publishing, PO Box 193, Gillette, NJ 07933, USA (office). *Telephone:* (888) 353-2288 (office). *Fax:* (888) 214-2172 (office).

LI, Huaji; Chinese artist; b. 16 Feb. 1931, Beijing; s. of Li Jue-Tian and Zhang Yun-Zheng; m. Quan Zhenghuan 1959; two d.; mem. Acad. Cttee and Dir Mural Painting Dept, Cen. Acad. of Fine Arts; Vice-Dir Mural Painting Cttee, Artists' Asscn of China; mem. Oil Painting Research Asscn 1988–; important murals include Hunting (Harbin Swan Hotel), 5,000 Years of Culture (Beijing Nat. Library). *Leisure interests:* classical music, Beijing opera. *Address:* 6/F Hongmiao Beili, 100025 Beijing 3-601, People's Republic of China. *Telephone:* (1) 552213.

LI, Jet; Chinese actor, producer and martial artist; b. 26 April 1963, Beijing; m. 1st Qiuyan Huang 1987 (divorced 1990); two d.; m. 2nd Nina Li Chi 1999; two d.; began training at Wu Shu (martial arts) Acad., Beijing aged nine; winner of five gold medals in Chinese Wu Shu Championships aged 11; world Wu Shu champion on several occasions; became Wu Shu nat. coach age 20; film debut in Shao Lin tzu (The Shaolin Temple) 1979. *Films include:* Shao Lin tzu 1979, Shao Lin xiao zi 1983, Zhong hua ying xiong 1986, Nan bei Shao Lin 1986, Long zai tian ya 1988, Once upon a Time in China 1991, The Legend (also producer) 1993, Lord of the Wu Tang (also producer) 1993, Claws of Steel (also producer) 1993, Tai-Chi (also producer) 1993, The Legend 2 (also producer) 1993, The Defender (also producer) 1994, High Risk 1995, The Enforcer 1995, Adventure King 1996, Lethal Weapon 4 1998, Romeo Must Die 2000, Kiss of the Dragon (also producer) 2001, The One 2001, Ying xiong 2002, The Contract Killer 2002, Legend of the Red Dragon (also producer) 2002, Legend of the Swordsman 2002, Rise to Honor 2003, Danny the Dog 2005, Huo Yuan Jia 2006, War 2007, The Warlords 2007, The Forbidden Kingdom 2008, The Mummy: Tomb of the Dragon Emperor 2008, The Warlords 2008. *Website:* www.jetli.com.

LI, Jianguo; Chinese politician; *Vice-Chairman, 11th NPC Standing Committee;* b. April 1946, Juanchen Co., Shandong Prov.; ed Shandong Univ., joined CCP 1971; joined CCP 1971; worker, Culture and Educ. Bureau, Ninghe Co., Shandong Prov., Publicity Dept, CCP Co. Cttee, Ninghe Co., Publicity Div., Agricultural Cttee, Tianjin Municipality, Gen. Office CCP Tianjin Municipal Cttee (Deputy Office Dir 1981, Dir 1983, Deputy Sec.-Gen. CCP Tianjin Municipal Cttee 1988, Sec.-Gen. 1989, Deputy Sec. 1992–97); Sec. CCP Heping Dist Cttee, Tianjin 1991–92; Vice-Sec. CCP Tianjin Mun. Cttee 1992;; apptd Sec. CCP Shaanxi Prov. Cttee 1997–98, elected Sec. 1998–2002, Chair. Standing Cttee of Shaanxi Prov. People's Congress 1998–; Alt. mem. 14th CCP Cen. Cttee 1992–97, mem. 15th CCP Cen. Cttee 1997–2002, 16th CCP Cen. Cttee 2002–07, 17th CCP Cen. Cttee 2007–; Sec.-Gen. and Vice-Chair. 11th NPC Standing Cttee 2008–. *Address:* c/o Chinese Communist Party Shaanxi Provincial Committee, Xian City, Shaanxi Province, People's Republic of China.

LI, Jiating; Chinese politician; b. April 1944, Shiping, Yunnan Prov.; ed Tsinghua Univ.; joined CCP 1964; cadre CCP Heilongjiang Prov. Cttee; Vice-Dir Office of Heilongjiang Prov. Econ. Comm. then Vice-Dir of Comm.; Vice-Mayor then Mayor of Harbin; Asst Gov. of Heilongjiang Prov. 1968–93; Vice-Gov. Yunnan Prov. 1993–98, Gov. 1998–2001; Alt. mem. CCP 14th and 15th Cen. Cttees 1992–2002; arrested and detained pending trial on corruption charges 2002, convicted of corruption, received suspended death sentence 2003. *Address:* c/o Yunnan Provincial People's Government, Kunming, People's Republic of China.

LI, Ji'nai; Chinese army officer; b. July 1942, Tengzhou City, Shandong Prov.; ed Harbin Acad. of Mil. Eng; joined CCP 1965; joined PLA 1967; various posts, 2nd Artillery; Dir Cadre Dept PLA Gen. Political Dept 1987–90, Deputy Dir 1990–92; Deputy Political Commissar, State Comm. of Science, Tech. and Industry for Nat. Defence 1992–95, Political Commissar 1995, PLA Gen. Equipment Dept 1998–2002; rank of Maj.-Gen. 1988, Lt-Gen. 1993, Gen. 2000; Alt. mem. 14th CCP Cen. Cttee 1992–97, mem. 15th CCP Cen. Cttee 1997–2002, 16th CCP Cen. Cttee 2002–07; mem. 16th CCP Cen. Cttee Cen. Military Comm. 2002–07, 17th CCP Cen. Cttee Cen. Military Comm. 2007–. *Address:* State Commission of Science, Technology and Industry for National Defence, Jingshanqian Jie, Beijing, People's Republic of China. *Telephone:* (1) 6370000.

LI, Adm. Jing; Chinese naval officer and party official; b. 1930; ed Air Force Aviation Acad. of China; joined PLA 1946, CCP 1949; Deputy Chief PLA Navy Staff 1973–80; Deputy Commdr Naval Air Force 1980–82; Deputy Commdr PLA Navy 1982–92 and concurrently Commdr Naval Air Force 1985–90; Deputy Chief of PLA Gen. Staff HQ 1992–95; rank of Vice-Adm. 1988, Adm. 1994; mem. 7th NPC 1987–92; mem. 14th CCP Cen. Cttee 1992–97; mem.

www.worldwhoswho.com

Standing Cttee, Vice-Chair. Foreign Affairs Cttee, 9th Nat. Cttee of CPPCC 1998–2003; mem. Standing Cttee 9th NPC 1998–2008; Sr Adviser Int. Strategy Soc. 1998–. *Address:* c/o National Committee of Chinese People's Political Consultative Conference, 23 Taipingqiao Street, Beijing, People's Republic of China (office).

LI, Jinhua; Chinese politician; *Vice-Chairman, 11th CPPCC National Commitee;* b. 1943, Rudong Co., Jiangsu Prov.; ed Cen. Inst. of Finance and Banking, CCP Cen. Cttee Cen. Party School; joined CCP 1965; fmr teacher, Northwest China Inst. of Finance and Banking, Shaanxi Prov.; fmr Deputy Dir later Dir Factory, Ministry of Aeronautics Industry (Deputy Sec. CCP Party Cttee); Dir Econ. and Trade Dept of Shaanxi Prov. 1985; Deputy Auditor Gen. Nat. Audit Office 1985–98, Auditor-Gen. 1998–2007; mem. 14th CCP Cen. Cttee for Discipline Inspection 1992–97, 15th CCP Cen. Cttee 1997–2002, 16th CCP Cen. Cttee 2002–07; Vice-Chair. 11th CPPCC Nat. Cttee 2008–; Chair. Environmental Auditing Cttee (and mem. Governing Bd), Asian Org. of Supreme Audit Insts; Hon. Prof. Peking Univ., Nankai Univ., Cen. Univ. of Finance and Banking, Nanjing Audit Inst. *Leisure interests:* calligraphy, bridge, swimming, climbing. *Address:* Chinese People's Political Consultative Conference, No. 23, Taipingqiao Street, Beijing 100811, People's Republic of China (office). *Website:* www.cppcc.gov.cn (office).

LI, Jinyuan, MBA; Chinese business executive; *Chairman and President, Tiens Group;* b. June 1958, Changzhou, Hebei Prov.; ed Nankai Univ.; left school at 14 and worked in oil field and plastics factory for seven years before starting own business in 1985, set up printing co., flour mill and fodder factory; Chair. and Pres. Tiens Group 1995–; named as one of Most Popular Personages in Daily Chemical Industry in China 2004, elected as one of Top Ten Men of the Year, Forum for Contemporary Chinese Celebrities 2004, honoured with title of Patriotic Entrepreneur by Patriotic Chinese Businessmen New Year Gathering and Forum of Econ. and Business Cooperation 2005, named as one of Top Ten Philanthropists in Mainland China 2005, honoured with title of State Advanced Individual in Nat. Unity 2005, named as one Top 10 Econ. Talents in China 2005, named China's Top Business Education Leader 2008. *Address:* Tiens Group, F20 No. 1 Building, Henderson Center, No. 18, JianGuoMen Nei Street, Beijing 100005, People's Republic of China (office). *Telephone:* (10) 65186239 (office). *E-mail:* support.china@tiens.com.cn (office). *Website:* www.tiens.com/tiens/group/en (office).

LI, Ka-Shing, CBE, JP; Chinese entrepreneur and business executive; *Chairman, Cheung Kong (Holdings) Ltd;* b. 1928, Chaozhou; m. Chong Yuet-ming (deceased); two s.; moved with family from mainland to Hong Kong 1940; worked in watch-strap co. 1943; salesman, later Man. then Gen. Man., for toy mfg co. 1945–47; est. Cheung Kong Plastics Factory 1950; first real estate venture 1958; est. Cheung Kong Real Estate Co. Ltd 1971; listed Cheung Kong (Holdings) Ltd in Hong Kong 1972, now Chair.; acquired Hutchison Whampoa Ltd 1979, Chair. 1981–; est. Li Ka Shing Foundation Ltd 1980; f. Shantou Univ. 1981; acquired Hong Kong Electric Holdings Ltd 1985, Cheung Kong Infrastructure Holdings Ltd spun off in listing 1996, CK Life Sciences International (Holdings) Inc. listed on GEM Stock Exchange 2000; has investments in numerous countries; mem. Drafting Cttee for Basic Law of Hong Kong Special Admin. Region (HKSAR) 1985–90; Hong Kong Affairs Adviser 1992–97; mem. Preparatory Cttee for the HKSAR 1995–97, mem. Selection Cttee of Govt of HKSAR 1996; mem. Int. Business Advisory Council of the UK 2006; Hon. citizen of eight cities in People's Repub. of China (PRC); Grand Officer, Order Vasco Nuñez de Balboa (Panama) 1982, Commdr, Order of the Crown (Belgium) 1986, Hon. KBE 2000, Commdr, Order of Leopold (Belgium) 2000, Commdr, Légion d'honneur 2005; Hon. LLD (Univ. of Hong Kong) 1986, (Univ. of Calgary, Canada) 1989, (Chinese Univ. of Hong Kong) 1997, (Univ. of Cambridge, UK) 1999; Hon. DScS (Hong Kong Univ. of Science and Tech.) 1995, (City Univ. of Hong Kong) 1998, (Open Univ. of Hong Kong) 1999; Dr hc (Peking) 1992; Entrepreneur of the Millennium Award, The Times newspaper and Ernst & Young, UK 1999, Int. Distinguished Entrepreneur Award (Univ. of Manitoba, Canada) 2000, Grand Bauhinia Medal of the HKSAR 2001, Malcolm S. Forbes Lifetime Achievement Award 2006, Special Hon. for Econ. Contrib., China Central Television 2007, Lifetime Achievement Award for Philanthropy, PRC Ministry of Civil Affairs 2007, Presidential Award, Teachers of English to Speakers of Other Languages, Inc. 2007. *Address:* 70/F, Cheung Kong Center, 2 Queen's Road, Central, Hong Kong Special Administrative Region, People's Republic of China (office). *Telephone:* (852) 21288888 (office). *Fax:* (852) 21288348 (office). *E-mail:* contactckh@ckh .com.hk (office). *Website:* www.ckh.com.hk (office).

LI, Keqiang, MA, PhD; Chinese politician; *Vice Premier, State Council;* b. 1955, Dingyuan Co., Anhui Prov.; ed Beijing Univ.; sent to do manual labour, Dongling Production Brigade, Damiao Commune early 1970s (Sec. CCP Party Br. 1976–78); joined CCP 1976; Head, Beijing Univ. Students' Fed. 1978–82; Sec. Communist Youth League, Beijing Univ. 1978–82; fmr Deputy Dir Dept of Schools and Colls of Communist Youth League Cen. Cttee; Sec.-Gen. All-China Students' Fed. 1982, Vice-Chair. 1990; Sec. Secr. of Communist Youth League Cen. Cttee 1982–93, First Sec. 1993–98; Pres. China Youth Political Coll. 1993; Deputy Sec. CCP Henan Prov. Cttee 1998–2002 (mem. Standing Cttee 2001–), Sec. 2002–04; Deputy Gov. Henan Prov. 1998, Acting Gov. 1998–99, Gov. 1999–2003; Chair. Standing Cttee Henan Prov. People's Congress 2003–04, Standing Cttee Liaoning Prov. People's Congress 2004–07; Sec. CCP Liaoning Prov. Cttee 2004–07; mem. Standing Cttee of NPC 1993–98, Cttee for Internal and Judicial Affairs of NPC 1993–98, Credentials Cttee of NPC 1993–98; mem. 15th CCP Cen. Cttee 1997–2002, 16th CCP Cen. Cttee 2002–07, Standing Cttee Politburo 17th CCP Cen. Cttee 2007–; Vice-Premier of State Council 2008–. *Address:* Office of the Vice-Premier, Great Hall of the People, West Edge, Tiananmen Square, Beijing, People's Republic of China (office). *Website:* english.gov.cn (office).

LI, Keyu; Chinese fashion and costume designer; b. 15 May 1929, Shanghai; m. Yuan Mao 1955; ed Cen. Acad. of Fine Arts; Chief Costume Designer of Cen. Ballet; Deputy Dir Chinese Soc. of Stage Design; mem. Bd All-China Artists' Asscn, Chinese Dancers' Asscn; Deputy Dir China Export Garments Research Centre; Sr consultant, Beijing Inst. of Fashion Tech.; has designed costumes for many works, including Swan Lake, Le Corsaire, The Maid of the Sea, The Fountain of Bakhchisarai, La Esmeralda, The Red Detachment of Women, The East is Red, The New Year Sacrifice (Ministry of Culture costume design prize), Zigeunerweisen (Ministry of Culture costume design prize), Othello (for Peking Opera, Beijing's costume design prize), Tang Music and Dance, Zheng Ban Qiao (Houston Ballet), Fu (Hongkong Ballet), La Péri (Houston Ballet); winner sole costume design prize, 4th Japan World Ballet Competition, Osaka 1984. *Publications:* two vols of sketches. *Address:* 21 Gong-jian Hutong, Di An-Men, Beijing 100009, People's Republic of China. *Telephone:* 4035474.

LI, Hon. Kwok Nang Andrew, CBE, MA, LLM, QC, JP; Chinese judge; *Chief Justice, Court of Final Appeal, Hong Kong Special Administrative Region;* b. 12 Dec. 1948, Hong Kong; s. of Li Fook Kow and of the late Edith Kwong Li; m. Judy Mo Ying Li; two d.; ed St Paul's Co-Educational Coll., Hong Kong, Repton School, Univ. of Cambridge, UK; called to the Bar, Middle Temple 1970, Hong Kong 1973; practised at Hong Kong Bar 1973–97; QC 1988, Chief Justice, Court of Final Appeal Hong Kong 1997–; Grand Bauhinia Medal 2008; Hon. Bencher Middle Temple 1997; Hon. Fellow, Fitzwilliam Coll. Cambridge 1999; hon. degrees (Hong Kong Univ. of Science and Tech.) 1993, (Baptist Univ.) 1994, (Open Univ. of Hong Kong) 1997, (Univ. of Hong Kong), (The Griffith Univ.) 2001, (Univ. of NSW) 2002, (Univ. of Tech., Sydney) 2005, (Chinese Univ. of Hong Kong) 2006. *Leisure interests:* reading, tennis, hiking. *Address:* Court of Final Appeal, No. 1 Battery Path, Central, Hong Kong Special Administrative Region (office); Chief Justice's House, 18 Gough Hill Road, The Peak, Hong Kong Special Administrative Region, People's Republic of China (home). *Telephone:* 21230011 (office); 28497169 (home). *Fax:* 21210310 (office); 28492191 (home). *E-mail:* andrewknli@judiciary.gov.hk (office). *Website:* www .judiciary.gov.hk (office).

LI, Gen. Laizhu; Chinese army officer and party official; b. 1932, Shen Co., Shandong Prov.; ed PLA Mil. and Political Acad.; joined PLA 1947, CCP 1948; Deputy Commdr of Beijing Mil. Area Command 1985; rank of Lt-Gen., PLA 1988; Commdr Beijing Mil. Region 1994–97; Gen. mem. 14th CCP Cen. Cttee 1992–97; rank of Gen. 1994–. *Address:* Beijing Military Area Command, People's Liberation Army, Beijing, People's Republic of China.

LI, Lanqing; Chinese government and party official; b. May 1932, Zhengjiang Co., Jiangsu Prov.; ed Fudan Univ., Shanghai; joined CCP 1952; worker, No. 1 Automobile Works, Changchun City Jilin Prov. 1952, Chief of Planning Section 1957–59; trainee, Liharchev and Gorky Automobile Factories, USSR 1956–57; worker, First Ministry of Machine-Building Industry 1959–81, State Econ. Comm. 1959–81, No. 2 Automobile Works 1959–81, No. 3 Automobile Factory 1959–81; Chief, Govt Loan Office, State Admin Comm. on Import and Export Affairs 1981–82; Dir Foreign Investment Admin. Bureau, Ministry of Foreign Econ. Relations and Trade 1982; Vice-Mayor Tianjin 1983–85; Vice-Minister of Foreign Econ. Relations and Trade 1986–90, Minister 1990–92; Vice-Premier State Council 1993–2002; Head Nat. Leading Group for Foreign Investments (State Council) 1994–; Deputy Head Cen. Leading Group for Party Bldg Work 1994–; Chair. Academic Degrees Cttee 1995–; Dir Nat. Cttee for the Patriotic Public Health Campaign 1998–; Deputy Head, State Steering Group of Science, Tech. and Educ. 1998–; mem. 8th NPC 1993–98; Alt. mem. 13th CCP Cen. Cttee 1987–92, mem. 14th CCP Cen. Cttee 1992–97 (mem. Politburo 1992–97), 15th CCP Cen. Cttee 1997–2002 (mem. Standing Cttee of Politburo 1997–2002). *Address:* c/o Zhongguo Gongchan Dang (Chinese Communist Party), Zhongnanhai, Beijing, People's Republic of China (office).

LI, Ligong; Chinese party official; b. 20 Feb. 1925, Jiaocheng, Shanxi; s. of Li Zhengliang and Li Shi; m. Xie Bin; two s. three d.; Sec. CCP County Cttee, Sec. CCP Pref. Cttee, Sec. Communist Youth League of Shanxi Prov., mem. Cen. Cttee Communist Youth League 1953–65; Sec. Communist Youth League, Beijing Municipal Cttee 1966; Vice-Dir Beijing Municipal Revolutionary Cttee 1977; Sec. CCP Beijing Municipal Cttee 1978–81; Exec. Sec. CCP Shanxi Prov. Cttee 1981–83, Sec. 1983–91; Dir CCP Shanxi Advisory Cttee 1991–92; mem. CCP Cen. Comm. for Inspecting Discipline 1979–82; mem. 12th Cen. Cttee CCP 1982–87, 13th Cen. Cttee 1987–92; mem. Standing Cttee 8th NPC 1992–98, mem. 9th NPC 1998–2003. *Publication:* Shanxi in Contemporary China (Chief Ed.). *Leisure interests:* swimming, fencing, tennis, hiking. *Address:* General Office of the Chinese Communist Party Shanxi Provincial Committee, 369 Yingze Street, Taiyuan, Shanxi, People's Republic of China (office). *Telephone:* 4045093 (office).

LI, Lihui, DEcon; Chinese banker; *Vice-Chairman and President, Bank of China;* b. 1952, Fujian prov.; ed Xiamen Univ., Guanghua School of Man. at Peking Univ.; with People's Bank of China, Fujian Br. 1977–84; joined Industrial and Commercial Bank, Fujian Br. 1984, served in several positions 1989–94, including Deputy Gen. Man. Fujian Br., Chief Rep. of Singapore Rep. Office and Gen. Man. Int. Business Dept, Exec. Vice-Pres. Industrial and Commercial Bank 1994–2002; Deputy Gov. Hainan Prov. 2002–04; Vice-Chair. and Pres. Bank of China 2004–; Chair. BOCI 2005–; Chair. Bohai Industry Investment Management Ltd 2006–.

LI, Lin; Chinese physicist; b. 31 Oct. 1923, Beijing; d. of J.S. Lee and Lin Hsu; m. Zou Chenglu 1949 (died 2006); one d.; ed Birmingham Univ., Cambridge Univ., UK; returned to China 1951; researcher, Mechanics Lab., Academia Sinica 1951–57; Research Fellow, Beijing Atomic Energy Inst. 1958–; Research Fellow, Inst. of Physics, Academia Sinica 1978–; mem. Dept of Math. and Physics, Academia Sinica 1980–; mem. Chinese Acad. of Sciences;

First Prize Nat. Science and Tech. Awards; winner of several collective prizes. *Leisure interest:* music. *Address:* Institute of Physics, Chinese Acad. of Sciences, P.O. Box 603, Beijing 100080, People's Republic of China. *Telephone:* (10) 82649175 (office); (10) 68422342 (home). *Fax:* (10) 82649531 (office). *E-mail:* lilin@aphy.iphy.ac.cn (office); annalee@yeah.com (home).

LI, Ling; Chinese musician; b. 28 Dec. 1913, Taishan Co., Guangdong Prov.; s. of Li Daoxi and Wu Lianzhu; m. Chen Yunfeng; one s. three d.; ed Yan'an Lu Xun Art Coll.; joined CCP 1941; Art Dir, Cen. Song and Dance Ensemble 1952–56; Dir Cen. Philharmonic Soc. 1956–66; in disgrace during Cultural Revolution 1966–77; Vice-Chair. Chinese Musicians' Asscn 1979–; Sec. Fed. Literary and Art Circles of China 1981–; Dir China Musical Coll. 1980–86; Vice-Chair. Standing Cttee, 8th Guizhou Prov. Peoples' Congress 1994–. *Leisure interest:* painting. *Address:* Chinese Musicians Association, Beijing, People's Republic of China (office). *Telephone:* (1) 5029308 (office).

LI, Lingwei; Chinese fmr badminton player; b. 1964; won women's singles title at 3rd World Badminton Championships, Copenhagen 1982; elected 7th in list of 10 best Chinese athletes 1984; won women's singles and women's doubles (co-player Wu Dixi) at 5th ALBA World Cup, Jakarta 1985; won women's singles, at World Badminton Grand Prix finals, Tokyo 1985, at Dunhill China Open Badminton Championships, Nanjing 1987, at Malaysian Badminton Open, Kuala Lumpur 1987, at World Grand Prix, Hong Kong 1988, at China Badminton Open 1988, at Danish Badminton Open, Odense 1988, at All-England Badminton Championships 1989, at 6th World Badminton Championships, Jakarta; coached Chinese women's singles players; took part in Olympic Torch Relay as flame bearer, Hangzhou 2008 mem. Int. Badminton Fed. (IBF) Events and Devt Cttee; IBF Hall of Fame 1998; Int. Olympic Cttee Women and Sport Trophy for Asia 2008. *Address:* China Sports Federation, Beijing, People's Republic of China.

LI, Luye; Chinese diplomatist (retd); b. 1925, Beijing; Dir Dept of Int. Orgs of Foreign Ministry 1980; Pres. of Chinese People's Asscn for Friendship with Foreign Countries 199–, Dir Chinese Int. Studies Centre 199–, Vice-Chair. Foreign Affairs Cttee; Pres. China Nat. Cttee for Pacific Econ. Co-operation 1991; mem. Standing Cttee of 8th NPC 1993–98. *Address:* c/o Chinese People's Association for Friendship with Foreign Countries, Taijichang, Beijing 100002, People's Republic of China.

LI, Moran; Chinese actor; b. (Li Shaocheng), 28 Nov. 1927, Shangzhi, Heilongjiang Prov.; joined Qingwen Drama Soc. 1945; joined the Arts Troupe affiliated to Northeast Arts Workers' Asscn in Harbin 1947; actor, Vice-Pres., Pres. Liaoning People's Arts Theatre 1954–; Chair. Chinese Dramatists' Asscn. *Films include:* Jiawu Fengyun (The Navel Battle of 1894) 1962. *Address:* 52 Dongsi Ba Tiao, Beijing 100007, People's Republic of China (office). *Telephone:* (10) 64042457 (office).

LI, Peigen, BSc, MSc, PhD; Chinese engineer, academic and university administrator; *President, Huazhong University of Science and Technology;* ed Shanghai Textile Inst. of Tech., Huazhong Univ. of Science and Tech., Univ. of Wisconsin, USA; Dean, School of Mechanical Science and Eng, Huazhong Univ. of Science and Tech. (HUST) 1995–2002, Vice Pres. HUST 2002–05, Pres. 2005–; mem. Chinese Acad. of Eng 2003–; Govt of Hubei Prov. Outstanding Professionals Award 2001. *Publications:* three books and over 100 papers. *Address:* Office of the President, Huazhong University of Science and Technology, 1037 Luoyu Road, Wuchang, Wuhan, People's Republic of China (office). *Telephone:* (27) 87544088 (office). *Website:* www.hust.edu.cn/english (office).

LI, Peng; Chinese politician; b. Oct. 1928, Chengdu City, Sichuan Prov.; s. of the late Li Shuoxun and of Zhao Juntao; m. Zhu Lin 1958; two s. one d.; ed Yan'an Inst. of Natural Sciences, Zhangjiakou Vocational School of Industry, Moscow Power Inst., USSR; joined CCP 1945; technician, Shanxi-Chahar-Hebei Power Co. 1946–48; Asst Man. Harbin Grease Co. 1946–48 (Sec. CCP Party Cttee 1946–48); Chief Engineer and Deputy Dir Fengman Hydroelectric Power Plant, Jilin Prov. 1955; fmr Deputy Chief Engineer, Northeast China Power Admin, later Dir Electricity Dispatch Dept; fmr Dir Fuxin Power Plant, Liaoning Prov. (Deputy Sec. CCP Party Cttee); Acting Sec. Beijing Power Supply Bureau, CCP Party Cttee 1966–76 (Chair. CCP Revolutionary Cttee 1966–76); Deputy Sec. Power Admin, CCP Party Cttee, Beijing 1966–76; Chair. Power Admin, CCP Revolutionary Cttee, Beijing 1966–76; Dir Power Admin, Beijing 1966–76 (Sec. CCP Leading Party Group 1966–76); Vice-Minister of Electric Power Industry 1979–81, Minister 1981–82; Vice-Minister of Water Conservancy and Electric Power 1982–83 (Deputy Sec. CCP Leading Party Group); Vice-Premier of State Council 1983–87; Minister in Charge of State Educ. Comm. 1985–88; Acting Premier, State Council 1987–88, Premier 1988–98; Minister, State Comm. for Restructuring the Economy 1988–90; Chair. Standing Cttee 9th NPC 1998–2003; mem. 12th Cen. Cttee of CCP 1982–87, 13th CCP Cen. Cttee 1987–92, 14th CCP Cen. Cttee 1992–97, 15th CCP Cen. Cttee 1997–2002; mem. Political Bureau 1985–2002, Standing Cttee 1987–2002; mem. Secr. CCP Cen. Cttee 1985–87; announced retirement 2003. *Address:* c/o Zhongguo Gongchan Dang (Chinese Communist Party), Zhongnanhai, Beijing, People's Republic of China (office).

LI, Qi; Chinese artist; b. Sept. 1928, Pingyao, Shanxi Prov.; ed North China United Univ.; Lecturer then Prof. of Chinese Painting, Cen. Acad. of Fine Art 1950–. *Works include:* several portraits of Chinese leaders including Portrait of Mao Zedong 1960. *Publication:* Portraits by Li Qui. *Address:* Central Academy of Fine Art, 5 Xiaowei Hutong, East District, Beijing 100730, People's Republic of China.

LI, Lt-Gen. Qianyuan; Chinese army officer; *Commander, Lanzhou Military Region;* b. March 1942, Linzhou, Henan Prov.; ed Zhengzhou Textile Machinery Inst., Mil. Acad. of the Chinese PLA; joined PLA 1961; joined CCP 1963; Regimental Commdr, PLA 1976; Div. Chief of Staff, PLA 1982–83, Deputy Chief of Staff 1st Army, Army (or Ground Force), PLA Services and Arms 1983–85, Army Commdr Group Army, PLA Services and Arms 1985–90 (Deputy Sec. CCP Party Cttee 1985–90); Deputy Chief of Staff, Guangzhou Mil. Command 1990–94; rank of Maj.-Gen. 1997, Lt-Gen. 1996; Chief of Staff, Lanzhou Mil. Region 1994–99, Commdr 1999–; Alt. mem. 14th CCP Cen. Cttee 1992–97, 15th CCP Cen. Cttee 1997–2002, mem. 16th CCP Cen. Cttee 2002–07. *Address:* Headquarters, Lanzhou Military Region, Lanzhou, Gansu Province, People's Republic of China (office).

LI, Qingkui, PhD; Chinese biologist, soil scientist and administrator; b. 1912, Ningpo Co., Zhejiang Prov.; ed Univ. of Illinois, USA; elected one of first mems of Academic Cttee, Chinese Acad. of Sciences 1955; Chair. Soc. of Pedology 1962; Deputy Dir Nanjing Inst. of Soil Science, Chinese Acad. of Sciences 1965, fmr Hon. Pres.; Pres. China Soc. of Pedology 1978; Vice-Chair. Jiangsu Prov. CP 1983; mem. Dept of Biology, Academia Sinica 1985; fmr 4th Vice Chair. Int. Soc. of Soil Science; Holeung Ho Lee Foundation Agronomy Prize 2001. *Publications include:* The Analysis Method of Soil, China's Red Soil. *Address:* Nanjing Institute of Soil Science, No. 71 East Beijing Road, Nanjing, Jiangsu Province, People's Republic of China. *E-mail:* iss@issas.ac.cn. *Website:* www.issas.ac.cn.

LI, Renchen; Chinese journalist; b. Oct. 1941, Changyi County, Shandong Prov.; ed Fudan Univ.; mem. CCP 1975–; Features and Photos Service, Comm. for Cultural Relations with Foreign Countries 1964–66; Ed. Huizhou Bao, Anhui Prov., Ed. People's Daily and Deputy Dir Commentary Dept People's Daily 1983–86; Deputy Ed.-in-Chief, then Ed.-in-Chief, Renmin Ribao (People's Daily) 1986; writes under pen name Chen Ping; Sr Visiting Prof. Tsinghua Univ.; Standing mem. CPPCC Nat. Cttee; Vice-Chair. CPPCC Learning and Historical & Cultural Data Cttee. *Address:* c/o Renmin Ribao, 2 Jin Tai Xi Lu, Choo Yong Men Nai, Beijing 100733, People's Republic of China. *Telephone:* (1) 65092121. *Fax:* (1) 65091982.

LI, Richard; Hong Kong computer engineer and business executive; *Chairman and CEO, Pacific Century CyberWorks Ltd;* b. (Li Tzar Kai), 1966; s. of Li Ka-shing; ed Stanford Univ., USA; cr. Star TV (first satellite cable TV network in Asia) 1992; Founder, Chair. and CEO Pacific Century Group (PCG—internet co.) 1993–, Pacific Century CyberWorks (PCCW) Ltd 1999– (PCCW merged with Cable & Wireless HKT 2000), PCCW Japan 2000–; Chair. Pacific Century Regional Devts Ltd, Singapore, Pacific Century Premium Devts Ltd; cr. Network of the World (NOW—internet and digital TV content service) 2000, NOW Japan 2001; Gov. World Econ. Forum for Information Technologies and Telecommunications; mem. Int. Councillors' Group, Center for Strategic and Int. Studies, Washington, DC, Global Information Infrastructure Comm., Panel of Advisors to UN Information and Communication Technologies Task Force. *Address:* Pacific Century CyberWorks Ltd, Floor 39, PCCW Tower, Taikoo Place, 979 Kings Road, Quarry Bay 070, Hong Kong Special Administrative Region, People's Republic of China (office). *Telephone:* 28882888 (office). *Fax:* 28778877 (office). *Website:* www.pccw.com (office).

LI, Robin, MSc, BSc; Chinese business executive; *Founder, Chairman and CEO, Baidu.com, Inc.;* b. (Li Yanhong), 1968, Yangquan, Shanxi prov.; ed Beijing Univ., State Univ. of New York, Buffalo; joined Dow Jones & Company, New Jersey 1994, served as sr consultant for IDD Information Services, USA 1994–97; staff engineer Infoseek 1997–99; Founder Baidu.com Inc. (internet search engine) 2000, Chair. 2000–, CEO 2004–. *Address:* Baidu.com, Inc., 12/F Lixiang International Mansion, No 58, Beisihuan West Road, Beijing, People's Republic of China (office). *E-mail:* ir@baidu.com (office). *Website:* (office).

LI, Rongrong; Chinese economist and state official; *Chairman, State-Owned Assets Supervision and Administration Commission (SASAC);* b. Dec. 1944, Suzhou, Jiangsu Prov.; ed Tianjin Univ.; workshop chief, Wuxi Oil Pump and Oil Throttle Factory, Deputy Dir, then Dir 1968–86; Vice-Chair. Wuxi Municipal Econ. Comm. 1986, later Dir Wuxi Municipal Light Industry Bureau and Chair. Wuxi Municipal Planning Comm.; Vice-Chair. Jiangsu Prov. Planning and Econ. Comm. 1986–91; Production Planning Bureau, State Council Production Office 1992; Deputy Dir-Gen., Foreign Econ. Cooperation Dept, State Council Econ. and Trade Office 1992, later Dir-Gen., Technical Renovation Dept and Sec.-Gen., State Econ. and Trade Comm. (SETC), becoming Vice-Chair. and Deputy Party Sec., Chair. 2001–; Vice-Chair., State Devt and Planning Comm. (SDPC) 1998–; Chair. State-Owned Assets Supervision and Admin Comm. (SASAC) 2003–; joined CCP 1983, mem. 16th CCP Cen. Cttee 2002–07, 17th CCP Cen. Cttee 2007–. *Address:* Office of the Chairman, State-Owned Assets Supervision and Administration Commission (SASAC), 26 Xuanxumen Xidajie, Beijing 100053, People's Republic of China (office). *Telephone:* (10) 63193615 (office). *Fax:* (10) 63193571 (office). *E-mail:* iecc@sasac.gov.cn (office). *Website:* (office).

LI, Rui; Chinese party official; b. 1917, Pingjiang Co., Hunan Prov.; ed Wuhan Univ.; joined CCP 1937; cadre in Hunan 1950; Asst Minister of Water Conservancy and Electrical Power 1955–58; in political disgrace 1967–79; fmr Sec. to Mao Zedong; Vice-Minister, 4th Ministry of Machine Building 1979–82; Vice-Minister, Power Industry 1979–82; Dir State Bureau of Computers 1980; mem. 12th Cen. Cttee CCP 1982–87; mem. Cen. Advisory Comm. 1987; Deputy Dir State Bureau of Tech. Supervision 1991; Deputy Head Org. Dept CCP 1983. *Publications:* The Early Revolutionary Activities of Comrade Mao Zedong, Some Fundamental Problems Concerning the Total Utilization Plan for the Yellow River. *Address:* Central Committee of the Chinese Communist Party, Beijing, People's Republic of China (office).

LI, Ruihuan; Chinese party and government official; b. Sept. 1934, Baodi Co., Tianjing; ed part-time studies at an architecture eng inst.; construction worker, Beijing No. 3 Construction Co. 1951–65; Joined CCP 1959; Deputy

Sec. Beijing Building Materials Co. CCP Party Cen. 1965–66; Vice-Chair. Beijing Municipal Trade Union Fed. 1971; Vice-Chair. All-China Youth Fed. 1971–80; Dir-Gen. Work Site for Mao Zedong Memorial Hall, Beijing 1977; Deputy for Beijing, 5th NPC 1978; Sec. Communist Youth League 1979–81; mem. Standing Cttee, 5th NPC 1978–83; Deputy Mayor Tianjin 1981, Acting Mayor 1982, Mayor Tianjin 1982–89; Sec. CCP Municpal Cttee, Tianjin 1982–84; mem. 12th CCP Cen. Cttee 1982–87, 13th CCP Cen. Cttee 1987–92, 14th CCP Cen. Cttee 1992–97, 15th CCP Cen. Cttee 1997–2002; mem. Politburo 1987–2002, Standing Cttee Politburo 1989, Perm. mem. Politburo 1992–2002; Chair. 8th Nat. Cttee CPPCC 1993–98, 9th Nat. Cttee CPPCC 1998–2003; Hon. Pres. Chinese Fed. for the Disabled 1993–; Hon Pres. Chinese Table Tennis Asscn 1990–; named Nat. Model Worker 1979. *Address:* c/o National Committee of the Chinese People's Political Consultative Conference, No.23, Taipingqiao Street, Beijing 100811; Zhongguo Gongchan Dang (Chinese Communist Party), Zhongnanhai, Beijing, People's Republic of China (office).

LI, Sanli, DSc; Chinese computer scientist; b. 1935, Shanghai; ed Tsinghua Univ., Acad. of Sciences, USSR; Co-Chair. Accreditation Cttee Computer Discipline of State Academic Comm. of the State Council; Deputy Chief Ed. China Computer Encyclopaedia; Exec. Dir of China Computer Fed.; Pres. IEEE in China; Dir EUROMICRO Europe 1984–97; Dir Research Inst. of Computer Sciences and Eng, Tsinghua Univ.; Jt Dean Coll. of Computer Eng and Science, Shanghai Univ.; mem. Chinese Acad. of Engineering; many awards including First Grade Award (govt of Shanghai) 2001. *Publications:* 11 books including RISC – Single and Multiple Issue Architecture and more than 100 research papers. *Address:* Research Institute of Computer Sciences and Engineering, Tsinghua University, 1 Qinghuayuan, Beijing 100084, People's Republic of China (office). *Telephone:* 62561144 (office). *Fax:* 62562768 (office). *Website:* www.tsinghua.edu.cn (office).

LI, Shenglin; Chinese politician; *Minister of Transport;* b. Nov. 1946, Nantong Co., Jiangsu Prov.; ed Zhejiang Coll. of Agricultural Machinery 1970; joined CCP 1973; fmr Planner, Tools Workshop, Tianjin Tractor Plant (Clerical Sec., later Deputy Sec., later Sec. CCP Communist League, later Sec. CCP Party Br.); fmr Deputy Man. Chemical Industry Machinery Co., Tianjin, later Deputy Office Dir; fmr Deputy Section Chief, Tractor Industry Co., Tianjin; fmr Cadre, Planning Div., People's Govt, Tianjin Municipality, later Deputy Sec.-Gen. People's Govt; fmr Dir CCP Party Cttee, Tianjin Municipality; fmr Dir Textile Industry Bureau, Tianjin Municipality (Deputy Sec. CCP Party Cttee); Dir Planning Cttee, Tianjin Municipality 1983; Deputy Sec. Work Cttee, CCP Tianjin Municipal Cttee 1983, Deputy Sec. Municipal Cttee 1993–98, mem. Standing Cttee of Municipal Cttee 2002–; apptd Vice-Mayor of Tianjin 1991–93, elected Mayor 1993–98; Vice-Sec. CCP Tianjin Mun. Cttee 1993–; mem. 15th CCP Cen. Cttee 1997–2002, 16th CCP Cen. Cttee 2002–07, 17th CCP Cen. Cttee 2007–; Minister of Transport 2008–; Deputy, 9th NPC 1998–2003. *Address:* Ministry of Transport, Beijing, People's Republic of China (office).

LI, Shiji; Chinese opera singer; b. May 1933, Suzhou Co., Jiangsu Prov.; Head First Troupe, Beijing Opera Theatre 1989–; mem. 7th CPPCC 1988–93, 8th 1993–98; Vice-Chair. China Fed. of Literary and Art Circles 2001. *Repertoire includes:* Tears in the Wild Mountain, The Unicorn Purse, Snow in Midsummer, The Story of Su San, Chen Sanliang Appeals at Court. *Beijing operas include:* Wenji's Return to the Hans, Concubine Mei, A Green Jade Hairpin, Wedding on the Execution Ground. *Address:* Beijing Opera Theatre, 11 Hufang Road, Xuanwu District, Beijing 100052, People's Republic of China (office).

LI, Simon Fook-sean, LLB; Chinese judge (retd); b. 19 April 1922, Hong Kong; m. Maria Veronica Lillian; four s. one d.; ed King's Coll., Hong Kong, Univ. of Hong Kong, Nat. Kwangsi Univ., Univ. Coll. London, Lincoln's Inn, London; Crown Counsel, Attorney-Gen.'s Chambers 1953–65, Hong Kong Govt Dist Judge 1966–71, High Court Judge 1971–80, Justice of Appeal 1980–84, Vice-Pres. Court of Appeal 1984–87; Hong Kong Affairs Adviser, People's Repub. of China 1992–97; Deputy Dir Preparatory Cttee for Hong Kong Special Admin. Region 1995–97; Dir Bank of E Asia, Hong Kong 1987–2006; Fellow, Univ. Coll. London 1991; Hon. Fellow, Chinese Univ. of Hong Kong 2002; Hon. LLD (Chinese Univ. of Hong Kong) 1986; Grand Bauhinia Medal, HKSAR 1997. *Address:* 3/F Shun Pont Commercial Building, 5–11 Thomson Road, Hong Kong Special Administrative Region, People's Republic of China (office). *Telephone:* 2866 8680 (office). *Fax:* 25202016 (office); 25776490 (home).

LI, Sush-der, BBA, MBA; Taiwanese government official; *Minister of Finance;* b. 29 Nov. 1951, Taipei; ed Tamkang Univ., Mankato State Univ., USA; Section Chief and Sr Specialist, Nat. Treasury Agency, Ministry of Finance 1980–88, Chief Sec., Nat. Treasury Agency 1988–91, Chief Sec., Taipei Nat. Tax Admin 1991–93, Deputy Dir Nat. Tax Admin of N Taiwan Prov. 1993–94, Deputy Dir-Gen. Nat. Treasury Agency 1994–96, Dir-Gen. Kaohsiung Nat. Tax Admin. 1996–98; Commr Dept of Finance, Taipei City Govt 1998–2006; Sec.-Gen. Taipei City Govt 2006–08; Minister of Finance 2008–. *Address:* Ministry of Finance, 2 Ai Kuo West Road, Taipei 10066, Taiwan (office). *Telephone:* (2) 23228000 (office). *Fax:* (2) 23965829 (office). *E-mail:* root@mof .gov.tw (office). *Website:* www.mof.gov.tw (office).

LI, Tieying; Chinese state official; *Vice-Chairman, 10th Standing Committee, National People's Congress;* b. Sept. 1936, Changsha City, Hunan Prov.; s. of the late Li Weihan; m. Qin Xinhua; ed Charles Univ., Czechoslovakia; joined CCP 1955; worker, Research Inst., Ministry of Electronics Industry 1961, Chief Engineer and Dir 1976; Deputy Dir Science and Tech. Cttee, Shenyang City, Liaoning Prov. 1976; Sec. CCP Shenyang City Cttee 1981–83, CCP Liaoning Prov. Cttee 1983–86; Minister of Electronics Industry 1985–88;

Minister in charge of State Comm. for Econ. Restructuring 1987–88, 1993–98, of State Educ. Comm. 1988–93; Chair. Cen. Patriotic Public Health Campaign Cttee; State Councillor 1988–98; Head Leading Group for the Reform of the Housing System 1991–; Deputy Head Nat. Leading Group for Anti-Disaster and Relief Work 1991–; Dir Nat. Cttee for the Patriotic Public Health Campaign; Vice-Chair. NPC 10th Standing Cttee 2003–; Pres. Chinese Acad. of Social Sciences 1998–2003; Del., World Conf. on Educ., Bangkok 1990, visited India, Laos 1992; Alt. mem. 12th CCP Cen. Cttee 1982, mem. 1985, mem. 13th CCP Cen. Cttee 1987–92, 14th CCP Cen. Cttee 1992–97, 15th CCP Cen. Cttee 1997–2002, mem. Politburo of CCP 1992–2002; Hon. Pres. Mao Zedong Acad. of the Arts 1997–, Athletics Asscn, Soc. of Nat. Conditions; Nat Nat. ional Science Conf. Prize 1978. *Address:* Zhongguo Gongchan Dang, Beijing (office); Chinese Academy of Social Sciences, 5 Jianguomen Nei Da Jie, Beijing 100732, People's Republic of China (office). *Telephone:* (10) 65137744 (office).

LI, Tingye, PhD; American (b. Chinese) communications engineer (retd); b. 7 July 1931, Nanjing, China; m. Edith Hsiu-hwei Wu; two d.; ed Univ. of Witwatersrand, SA, Northwestern Univ., Evanston, Ill., USA; joined AT&T Bell Labs, Red Bank, NJ 1957, mem. Tech. Staff 1957–67, Head, Lightwave Systems Research Dept 1967–96, Div. Man., Communications Infrastructure Research Lab. 1996–98; ind. consultant in the field of lightwave communications 1998–; Fellow, Optical Soc. of America (OSA) (Vice-Pres. 1993, Pres. 1995), IEEE, AAAS, Photonic Soc. of Chinese-Americans, Int. Eng Consortium; mem. Nat. Acad. of Eng 1980–, Academia Sinica (Taiwan), Chinese Acad. of Eng 1996–; Hon. Prof. at several univs in People's Repub. of China including Tsinghua Univ., Shanghai Jiaotong Univ., Beijing Univ. of Posts and Telecommunications, Northern Jiaotong Univ., Fudan Univ., Nankai Univ., Tianjin Univ., Univ. of Electronic Science and Tech. of China, Qufu Normal Univ., Hon. DEng (Nat. Chiao Tung Univ., Taiwan); numerous awards including IEEE W. R. G. Baker Prize 1975, IEEE David Sarnoff Award 1979, OSA/IEEE John Tyndall Award 1995, OSA Frederic Ives Medal/Jarus Quinn Endowment 1997, AT&T Science and Tech. Medal 1997, Northwestern Univ. Alumni Merit Award 1981, IEEE Photonics Award 2004. *Achievements:* holder of 15 patents. *Publications:* more than 100 journal papers, patents, books and book chapters. *Address:* c/o AT&T Laboratories-Research, 100 Schultz Drive, Red Bank, NJ 07701, USA.

LI, Weikang; Chinese opera singer; b. Feb. 1947, Beijing; ed China Acad. of Traditional Operas; Dir Troupe No. 2, China Peking Opera Co., performer Beijing Peking Opera Co. 1987–; Plum Blossom Award 1984, Gold Album Award for Lead Role at Nat. Theatrical Performance Ass., Gold Prize at Nat. Mei Lanfang Grand Competition, Gold Eagle Award for Best Actress. *Recordings include:* Selected Arias of Li Weikang 1995, Battle on the Plain, Unicorn Trapping Purse. *Address:* c/o Beijing Opera Company, Beijing, People's Republic of China (office).

LI, Xiaolin, ME; Chinese business executive; *CEO and Chairman China Power International Development Ltd;* b. 1961; d. of Li Peng, fmr Premier, People's Repub. of China; ed Tsinghua Univ.; worked as engineer at Equipment Introduction Office, Beijing Power Supply Bureau; fmr Assoc. Dir Int. Econ. and Trade Dept, Ministry of Energy; fmr Dir Int. Econ. and Trade Dept, Ministry of Electric Power; joined China Power Int. Devt Ltd (CPI) as Gen. Man. 1996, CEO, Vice-Chair. and mem. Exec. Bd 2004, currently CEO and Chair., also serves as Vice-Pres. CPI Group and mem. Exec. Bd CPI Holding; mem. Bd of Dirs Companhia de Electricidade de Macau. *Address:* China Power International Development Ltd, Suite 6301, 63rd Floor, Central Plaza, Wanchai, Kowloon, Hong Kong Special Administrative Region, People's Republic of China (office). *Telephone:* 28023861 (office). *Fax:* 28023922 (office). *Website:* www.chinapower.hk (office).

LI, Gen. Xinliang; Chinese army officer and party official; b. 1936, Laiyang Co., Shandong Prov.; joined PLA 1953, CCP 1956; Commdr Autonomous Region Mil. Dist, Guangxi Prov. 1983–88; Party Cttee Sec. PLA Guangxi Mil. Area Command 1986–89; mem. 13th CCP Cen. Cttee 1987–92; Deputy Commdr Guangzhou Mil. Region 1989–94; Political Commissar Shenyang Mil. Region 1994–95, Commdr Shenyang Mil. Area Command 1995–97; Commdr Beijing Mil. Area Command 1997; mem. 15th CCP Cen. Cttee 1997–2002; rank of Lt-Gen. 1993–98, Gen. 1998–. *Address:* Commander's Office, Beijing Military Area Command, Beijing, People's Republic of China.

LI, Xu'e; Chinese politician and aerospace industry executive; b. 1928, Hanyang, Hubei Prov.; ed Tsinghua Univ.; joined CCP 1955; Vice-Minister of Space Industry 1982–85; Minister of Astronautics (Space) Industry 1985–88; Vice-Minister State Science and Tech. Comm. 1988–93; Chair. Bd of Dirs China Science and Tech. Consultant Corpn 1983–; Vice-Chair. Environmental Protection Cttee 1988–; a Deputy Head Co-ordination Group for Weather Change 1990–; a Vice-Chair. China Cttee of Int. Decade for Nat. Disaster Reduction 1991–; Pres. Soc. of Social Devt Science 1992–, of China Soc. of Geographic Information System 1994; mem. 12th CCP Cen. Cttee 1982–87, 8th NPC 1993–98, 9th NPC 1998–2003; Vice-Chair. Educ., Science, Culture and Public Health Cttee; Head Dels to Poland, Finland, India. *Address:* Standing Committee of National People's Congress, Beijing, People's Republic of China.

LI, Yining; Chinese economist; *Dean, Guanghua School of Management, Peking University;* b. Nov. 1930, Yizheng City, Jiangsu Prov.; ed Beijing Univ.; Prof., Dean Economy Admin. Dept, Beijing Univ. 1955–; joined CCP 1984; Vice-Chair. 8th Chinese Democratic League Cen. Cttee 1997–; mem. Standing Cttee 7th NPC, 8th NPC; Vice-Chair. Finance and Econ. Cttee of 9th NPC 1998–; Dean Guanghua School of Man. 1993–. *Address:* Guanghua School of Management, Peking University, 5 Yiheyuan Road, Hai Diau, Beijing 100871,

People's Republic of China (office). *Telephone:* 62752114 (office). *Fax:* 627517207 (office). *Website:* www.pku.edu.cn (office).

LI, Yiyi; Chinese metallurgist; b. 20 Oct. 1933, Suzhou, Jiangsu Prov.; ed Beijing Univ. of Iron and Steel Tech.; China's first female workshop chief in charge of a blast furnace late 1950s; researcher, Metal Research Inst., Chinese Acad. of Sciences 1962–, Vice-Dir 1986, Dir 1990–98; mem. Chinese Acad. of Sciences 1993–, mem. Fourth Presidium 2000–; Vice-Pres. Chinese Soc. for Metals, Chinese Materials Research Soc.; mem. Third World Acad. of Sciences 1999–; mem. Bd Int. Cryogenic Materials Conf. 1985–; mem. Editorial Bd, Modelling of Simulation in Materials Science and Eng 2002–; developed five series of hydrogen-resistant steels and alloys; Nat. Science and Tech. Advancement Award (five times), Chinese Acad. of Sciences Award for Advancement in Science and Tech. (seven times). *Publications:* more than 200 research papers. *Address:* Metal Research Institute, Chinese Academy of Sciences, 72 Wenhua Road, Shenyang 110016, People's Republic of China (office). *Telephone:* (24) 23881881 (office). *Fax:* (24) 23891320 (office). *E-mail:* yyli@imr.ac.cn (office).

LI, Yuanchao, MS, PhD; Chinese politician; *Secretary, Jiangsu Provincial Party Committee, CPC;* b. 1950, Lianshui Co., Jiangsu Prov.; ed Shanghai Fudan Univ., Beijing Univ., Central Party School; joined CPC 1978; Sec. Shanghai Municipal Cttee Communist Youth League 1983; mem. Sec. Youth League Central Cttee 1983–90; Dir Nat. Cttee for Young Pioneers' work 1984; Vice-Chair. Nat. Youth Fed. 1986–96; Dir First Bureau, Int. Publicity Leading Group 1990–93, Vice-Minister Int. Publicity Office under CCP Central Cttee 1993–96, Vice-Minister of Culture 1996–2000; Deputy Sec. CCP Jiangsu Prov. Party Cttee 2000–02, Sec. 2002–07, Chair. Standing Cttee 2003–07; Sec. CCP Party Cttee Nanjing City 2001–03; Vice-Chair. Women and Youth Sub-Cttee, CPPCC; mem. CPPCC 7th Nat. Cttee 1988–93, 8th Nat. Cttee 1993–98, 9th Nat. Cttee 1998–2003; Alt. mem. 16th CPC Cen. Cttee 2002–07; mem. 17th Cen. Cttee 2007–; mem. Political Bureau and Secr. Cen. Cttee, Ministry of Org. Dept 2007–. *Address:* Organization Department, Central Committee of the Communist Party of China, People's Republic of China (office).

LI, Zehou; Chinese philosopher; b. 1930, Changsha, Hunan Prov.; ed Hu'an No. 1 Prov. Normal School, Peking Univ.; Asst Research Fellow, Assoc. Research Fellow then Research Fellow Philosophy Inst., Chinese Acad. of Sciences 1955–; Vice-Chair. Aesthetics Soc. of China; mem. Exec. Council Chinese Writers Asscn and Soc. of Sun Yat-sen Studies. *Publications:* Critique of Critical Philosophy, The Course of Beauty, History of Chinese Aesthetics, Essays on China's Ancient Intellectual History. *Address:* Institute of Philosophy, Chinese Academy of Social Sciences, Beijing, People's Republic of China (office).

LI, Zemin; Chinese party official; *Chairman, Standing Committee, Zhejiang Provincial People's Congress;* b. 1934, Cangxi Co., Sichuan Prov.; ed People's Univ. of China; joined PLA 1950, soldier in Korean War 1952; joined CCP 1954; Deputy Dir Marxism-Leninism Teaching and Research Centre, Shenyang Agricultural Coll., Liaoning Prov. 1973–78 (Sec. CCP Party Br. 1973–78); Deputy Sec. Shenyang Mun. CCP Cttee, Liaoning Prov. 1983–85, Sec. 1986–88; Deputy Sec. Liaoning Prov. CCP Cttee 1985–86; First Sec. CCP Party Cttee, Zhejiang Mil. Dist, PLA Nanjing Mil. Region 1988; Sec. CCP Zhejiang Prov. Cttee 1988–98; Chair. Standing Cttee of Zhejiang Prov. People's Congress 1993–; mem. 13th CCP Cen. Cttee 1987–92, 15th CCP Cen. Cttee 1997–2002; Deputy, 8th NPC 1993–98. *Address:* Standing Committee of Zhejiang Provincial People's Congress, Hangzhou, Zhejiang Province, People's Republic of China (office).

LI, Zhaoxing, MA; Chinese politician and diplomatist; b. Oct. 1940, Jiaonan, Shandong Prov.; m.; one s.; ed Beijing Univ., Beijing Foreign Languages Inst.; joined CCP 1965; on staff, Chinese People's Inst. of Foreign Affairs 1967–70; attaché, Embassy, Nairobi, Kenya 1970–77; Third Sec., later Second Sec., later Deputy Div. Chief, Information Dept, Ministry of Foreign Affairs 1977–83, Deputy Dir-Gen., later Dir-Gen. 1985–90 (also Spokesman, Ministry of Foreign Affairs 1985–90), Asst to Vice-Minister of Foreign Affairs 1990–93; First Sec. Embassy, Maseru, Lesotho 1983–85; Chinese Rep. and Amb. to UN 1993–95; Vice-Minister of Foreign Affairs 1995–98; Amb. to USA 1998–2001; Vice-Minister of Foreign Affairs in charge of American and Latin American Affairs 2001–03, Minister of Foreign Affairs 2003–07; Alt. mem. 15th CCP Cen. Cttee 1997–2002, mem. 16th CCP Cen. Cttee 2002–07. *Address:* c/o Ministry of Foreign Affairs, 225 Chaoyangmen Nan Dajie, Chaoyang Qu, Beijing 100701, People's Republic of China (office).

LI, Zhaozhuo; Chinese politician; *Chairman, People's Government of Guangxi Zhuang Autonomous Region;* b. Sept. 1944, Pingguo, Guangxi Zhuang Autonomous Region; ed Guangxi Univ., Nanning, CCP Guangxi Zhuang Autonomous Regional Cttee Party School, CCP Cen. Cttee Cen. Party School; sent to do manual labour, Army Farms, Guangxi Zhuang Autonomous Region and Hunan Prov. 1968–70; technician, Du'an Commune, Debao Co., Guangxi Zhuang Autonomous Region 1970–74; joined CCP 1974; technician, Sec., later Deputy Dir Debao Co. Hydroelectric Power Bureau, Guangxi 1975–80; Deputy Dir Capital Construction Bureau, Debao Co., Guangxi Zhuang Autonomous Region 1980–83, Deputy Dir Planning Cttee 1980–83; Dir Econ. Cttee, CCP Autonomous Co. Cttee, Debao Co., Guangxi Zhuang Autonomous Region 1983–84 (also mem. Standing Cttee), Sec. CCP Autonomous Co. Cttee 1984–85; Deputy Sec. CCP Autonomous Prefectural Cttee, Bose Prefecture, Guangxi Zhuang Autonomous Region 1985–92 (Sec. 1992–93), Commr, Prefectural Admin. Office 1985–93; Sec. CCP Fangchenggang Autonomous City Cttee, Guangxi Zhuang Autonomous Region 1993–95, Chair. Autonomous Regional People's Congress 1993–95; Sec. Nanning Autonomous City Cttee, Guangxi Zhuang Autonomous Region 1994–96; Deputy Sec. Guangxi Zhuang Autonomous Regional Cttee 1996–2002 (mem.

Standing Cttee 1996–2002); Chair. People's Govt of Guangxi Zhuang Autonomous Region 1997–; mem. 15th CCP Cen. Cttee 1997–2002, 16th CCP Cen. Cttee 2002–07, 17th CCP Cen. Cttee 2007–; Vice-Chair. 10th CPPCC Nat. Cttee 2003–08, 11th CPPCC Nat. Cttee 2008–. *Address:* People's Government of Guangxi Zhuang Autonomous Region, 1 Minle Road, Nanning 530012, Guangxi, People's Republic of China (office). *Telephone:* (771) 284114 (office). *E-mail:* gov@gxi.gov.cn (office). *Website:* www.gxi.gov.cn (office).

LI, Zhengwu; Chinese physicist; *Honorary Director, Southwestern Institute of Physics;* b. Nov. 1916; Pres. Soc. of Nuclear Fusion and Plasma 1980–; mem. Chinese Acad. of Sciences 1980–; mem. Nat. Cttee 7th CPPCC 1988–93; Hon. Dir Southwestern Inst. of Physics; mem. Ed. Bd Plasma Science and Technology (journal). *Address:* Southwestern Institute of Physics, Chengdu 610041, People's Republic of China (office). *Website:* www.swip.ac.cn (office).

LI, Zhensheng; Chinese geneticist; *Senior Research Fellow, Institute of Genetics and Developmental Biology;* b. 1931, Zibo, Shandong Prov.; ed Shandong Agricultural Coll.; Dir Northwest Botanical Research Inst.; Vice-Chair. China Science and Tech. Asscn; currently Sr Research Fellow Inst. of Genetics and Developmental Biology, Chinese Acad. of Sciences; mem. 4th Presidium, Chinese Acad. of Sciences 2000–; Fellow, Chinese Acad. of Sciences, fmr Vice-Pres.; mem. Third World Acad. of Sciences 1990–; bred super wheat varieties Xiaoyan Nos. 4, 5 and 6; created the blue-grained wheat monosomic system (BGM); pioneered 'the nullisomic backcrossing method' for fast breeding alien substitution lines of wheat and laid a foundation for wheat chromosome eng breeding; awarded title of Nat. Model Worker 1980, Nat. Supreme Scientific and Technological Award 2006. *Publications:* Outline of Distant Hybridisation of Plants, Distant Hybridisation of Wheat. *Address:* Institute of Genetics and Developmental Biology, Datun Road, Andingmenwai, Beijing 100101, People's Republic of China (office). *Telephone:* (10) 64889331 (office). *Fax:* (10) 64856610 (office). *E-mail:* zsli@genetics.ac.cn (office). *Website:* www.genetics.ac.cn (office).

LI SHAN, Rev. Joseph; Chinese ecclesiastic; *Bishop of Beijing;* b. 1965; ed Chinese Catholic Acad. of Theology and Philosophy, Beijing Theological Seminary; among first priests ordained after Cultural Revolution 1989; taught the Bible at Beijing Theological Seminary; Vice-Chair. Beijing Church Affairs Cttee; Deputy to Beijing Municipal People's Congress (local parl.); selected for appointment as bishop by mems of Patriotic Catholic Asscn, consecrated Bishop of Beijing in pvt. ceremony 2007. *Address:* Catholic Diocese of Beijing, Beijing, People's Republic of China (office).

LI YAN, (Zhuang Bei) Chinese painter; *Professor, Academy of Arts, Tsinghua University;* b. Nov. 1943, Beijing; s. of Li Ku Chan and Li Hui Wen; m. Sun Yan Hua 1972; one d.; Prof., Cen. Inst. of Arts and Crafts and of Shandong; fmr Vice-Pres. Li Ku Chan Museum; mem. Chinese Artists' Asscn; currently Prof., Acad. of Arts, Tsinghua Univ.; Deputy Dir of Li Kuchan Memorial; Vice-Pres. Int. Soc. Yi Jing, Research Fellow Research Soc. Yi Jing; Specialist, Appraising Cttee of Chinese Arts of Calligraphy and Painting; specializes in painting figures, animals and mountains and water scenes and in calligraphy; over 10,000 sketches and paintings from life, 3,000 exercises in Chinese painting 1956–; mem. 9th CPPCC 1998–2003, 10th CPPCC 2003–; mem. Beijing PCCC; works have been exhibited in Sweden, USA, Canada, Japan, Singapore, Philippines, Hong Kong, Tanzania; gave lectures at Hong Kong Univ. 1980; held lectures and exhbn in India 1989, in Malaysia 1991, in Indonesia 1993; subject of TV films by Shen Zhen TV 1986 and Swedish TV 1986, presenter of CCTV's The Wind of China 1995; important works include Chinese Emperor, Zhou Wen Emperor, Lao Zi, Confucian Worry about Taoism, Lao Zi and Einstein, Five-Colour Earth, Start Sailing, A Swarm of Monkeys, Cat and Chrysanthemum, Tiger Cub. *Publications:* Yi Jing Album 1993; several magazine articles on art. *Leisure interests:* writing poetry, Qigong, The Book of Changes. *Address:* No. 2-1, Building 15, Nan sha Go, San Li He, Xi Cheng District, Beijing, People's Republic of China. *Telephone:* (10) 68534056 (office). *Fax:* (10) 68512920 (office). *E-mail:* sumantar@hotmail.com (office).

LIAN, Hans Jacob Biörn; Norwegian diplomatist; b. 31 March 1942, Oslo; ed Univ. of Neuchâtel, Switzerland; Political Dir 1992–94, Amb. and Perm. Rep. to UN, New York 1994–98, to NATO 1998–2002. *Address:* c/o North Atlantic Treaty Organization, blvd Léopold III, 1110 Brussels (office); 2, clos Henri Vaes, Brussels, Belgium (home). *Telephone:* (2) 731-86-62 (home).

LIANG, Congjie; Chinese environmentalist, historian and academic; *President, Friends of Nature;* b. 1932; ed studies in history; worked in educ., culture and publishing fields; joined Acad. of Chinese Culture 1988, currently Prof. of History and Vice-Pres.; Founder and Pres. Friends of Nature (first pvt. entity in China dedicated to protecting the environment) 1994–; Ramon Magsaysay Award 2000. *Address:* Friends of Nature, Room 301, Wanbo Office Building, 53 Ganyu Street, Eastern Dictrict, Beijing 100006, People's Republic of China (office). *Telephone:* (10) 65232040 (office). *Fax:* (10) 65286069 (office). *E-mail:* office@fon.org.cn (office). *Website:* www.fon.org.cn (office).

LIANG, Dongcai, PhD; Chinese molecular biophysicist and protein crystallographer; b. 29 May 1932, Guangzhou, Guangdong Prov.; ed Zhongshan Univ., Inst. of Organo-Element Compounds, USSR Acad. of Sciences, Royal Inst., UK, Univ. of Oxford, UK; Prof., Inst. of Biophysics, Chinese Acad. of Sciences (Dir 1983–86); mem. Chinese Acad. of Sciences 1980–, Dir Biology Div.; Vice-Chair. Nat. Natural Science Foundation of China 1986–95, adviser 1995–98, Chair. Inspection Cttee 1998–2001; mem. Cttee on Biomacromolecule Crystallography of Int. Soc. of Crystallography 1981–84; mem. Council of Int. Soc. of Biophysics 1993–99, 4th Presidium of Depts, Chinese Acad. of Sciences 2000–; Pres. Chinese Biophysics Soc. 1983–86, 1990–98; Vice-Pres. Chinese Biochemistry Soc. 1987–90; Fellow, Third World Acad. of Sciences 1985–; Alt. mem. 12th CCP Cen. Cttee 1982–87; mem. 13th CCP Cen. Cttee

1987–92; Chinese Nat. Scientific Prize (2nd Rank) 1982, 1989, Scientific Prize (2nd Rank), Chinese Acad. of Sciences 1986, 1992, Scientific Prize (1st Rank), Chinese Acad. of Sciences 1987. *Publications:* more than 140 papers in scientific journals. *Address:* Institute of Biophysics, Chinese Academy of Sciences, Beijing 100101, People's Republic of China (office). *Telephone:* (10) 64888506 (office). *Fax:* (10) 64889867 (office).

LIANG, Gen. Guanglie; Chinese army officer and government official; *Minister of National Defence;* b. Dec. 1940, Santai Co., Sichuan Prov.; ed Xinyang Infantry Acad. 1963, PLA Mil. Acad., Nat. Defence Univ.; joined CCP 1958, PLA 1959; Vice-Div. Commdr and then Div. Commdr 1979–82; Vice-Army Commdr then Army Commdr, Vice-Commdr PLA Beijing Mil. Area Command 1983–97; rank of Lt-Gen. 1995, Gen. 2002; Commdr PLA Shenyang Mil. Area Command 1997–2000; Commdr PLA Nanjing Mil. Area Command 2000–03; Alt. mem. 13th CCP Cen. Cttee 1982–87, 14th CCP Cen. Cttee 1987–92, mem. 15th CCP Cen. Cttee 1997–2002, 16th CCP Cen. Cttee 2002–07, 17th CCP Cen. Cttee 2007– (mem. Cen. Mil. Comm. 2002–); Chief, HQ of Gen. Staff, PLA 2002–07; Minister of Nat. Defence 2008–; State Councillor 2008–. *Address:* Ministry of National Defence, 20 Jingshanqian Jie, Beijing 100009, People's Republic of China (office). *Telephone:* (10) 66730000 (office). *Fax:* (10) 65962146 (office).

LIANG, Shoupan, MS; Chinese rocket engineer; b. 13 April 1916, Fuzhou City, Fujian Prov.; s. of Ching Tung Liang and Yun Jiao Lin; m. He Fu 1942; one s.; ed Tsinghua Univ., Mass. Inst. of Tech., USA; Deputy Dir Rocket Research Inst. 1965–81; Deputy Dir of Science and Tech., Ministry of Astronautics 1982–88; Sr Technical Adviser, Ministry of Aeronautics and Astronautics Industry 1999–; Chief designer 'Silkworm' and other anti-ship missile projects; Sr Tech. Adviser, China Aerospace Science and Tech. Corpn 1999–, China Aerospace Machinery and Electronics Corpn 1999–; mem. Chinese Acad. of Sciences 1980–, Dept of Tech. Sciences, Academia Sinica 1981–; Hon. Special Prize of Nat. Tech. 1988. *Leisure interests:* Chinese history, novels, Chinese chess. *Address:* Ministry of Aeronautics and Astronautics Industry, PO Box 849, Beijing, People's Republic of China (office). *Telephone:* 68371539 (office). *Fax:* 68370849 (office).

LIANG, Xiaosheng; Chinese writer; b. Sept. 1949, Harbin; worker on land reclamation project; local newspaper reporter; Chinese language student, Fudan Univ. 1975; mem. Chinese Writers' Asscn, Chinese Filmmakers' Asscn; mem. and official of Chinese Film Scriptwriters' Asscn; Film Script Ed., Beijing Film Studio. *Publications:* four anthologies of short stories, an anthology of medium-length novels and two novels, most of which have been adapted as films or TV plays; works include: This is a Strange Land, Father, Literary Accomplishments, Blizzard at Midnight (all of which have won All-China Short Novel Prizes), For the Harvest, TV play based on Blizzard at Midnight (awarded All-China TV Playscript Grand Prize), Floating City 1992, Panic 2002, Deaf 2002, Growth Rings (TV series), Snow City, Bitter Love, Broken Heart Bar. *Address:* Editorial Department, 'Creative Cinema', 19 Beihuan Xilu Street, Beijing, People's Republic of China.

LIAO, Hui; Chinese government official; b. 1942, Huiyang Dist, Guangdong Prov.; s. of the late Liao Chengzhi and Jing Puchum; ed Mil. Eng Inst. of Chinese PLA; joined CCP 1965; fmr technician, Air Force, PLA Services and Arms (Rep. in charge of Mil. Inspection); fmr Staff Officer, HQ of the Gen. Staff, PLA Beijing Mil. Region; Dir Overseas Chinese Affairs Office, State Council 1984–, Dir Leading Party Group 1984–87, Sec. Leading Party Group 1984–97; Dir Hong Kong and Macao Affairs Office of the State Council 1997–; Vice-Chair. Macao Special Admin. Region Preparatory Cttee 1998–99; Vice-Chair. 10th CPPCC Nat. Cttee 2003–08, 11th CPPCC Nat. Cttee 2008–; mem. 12th CCP Cen. Cttee 1982–87, 13th CCP Cen. Cttee 1987–92, 14th CCP Cen. Cttee 1992–97, 15th CCP Cen. Cttee 1997–2002, 16th CCP Cen. Cttee 2002–07, 17th CCP Cen. Cttee 2007–; Deputy Pres. China Overseas Exchanges Asscn 1991–; mem. 21st Century Comm. for Sino-Japanese Friendship 1985–; Hon. Vice-Chair. Zhonghai Inst. of Agricultural Tech. 1987–. *Address:* c/o State Council, Zhong Nan Hai, Beijing, People's Republic of China.

LIAO, Gen. Xilong; Chinese army officer; *Director, Logistics Department, People's Liberation Army;* b. June 1940, Sinan Co., Guizhou Prov.; ed Mil. Acad. of Chinese PLA; joined PLA 1959, CCP 1963; served as Platoon Commdr 1966–67, Co. Commdr 1969–71, Deputy Chief of a regimental combat training section 1971–73, Deputy Chief of a div. mil. affairs section 1973–78, Deputy Regt Commdr 1978–79, Regt Commdr 1979–80, Deputy Div. Commdr 1981–83, Div. Commdr 1983, Army Commdr 1984–85, Deputy Commdr Chengdu Mil. Region 1985–95, Commdr 1995–2003; rank of Maj.-Gen. 1988–93, Lt-Gen. 1993–2000, Gen. 2000–; Dir Logistics Dept, PLA 2002–; mem. 15th CCP Cen. Cttee 1997–2002, 16th CCP Cen. Cttee 2002–07, 17th CCP Cen. Cttee 2007– (mem. Cen. Mil. Comm. 2002–). *Address:* People's Liberation Army, c/o Ministry of National Defence, 20 Jingshanqian Jie, Beijing 100009, People's Republic of China.

LIBAI, David, LLD; Israeli politician and lawyer; b. 1934, Tel-Aviv; ed Chicago Univ., USA; Head Israel Bar Asscn; Deputy Attorney-Gen.; Dir Inst. of Criminology and Criminal Law, Tel-Aviv Univ., Dean of Students; Chair. Labour Party Constitution Cttee; Chair. Israel–Britain Parl. Friendship Asscn; Chair. Public Audit (Control) Cttee 1984–92; Spokesman Ministry of Justice, Minister of Justice 1992–96; fmr mem. Nat. Comm. of Inquiry on Prison Conditions, Press Council, Knesset (Parl.) 1984–, served on various cttees; mem. Israel Labour Party. *Publications:* numerous articles on legal issues. *Address:* Israel Labour Party, PO Box 62033, Tel-Aviv, 61620 (office); Knesset, Jerusalem, Israel. *Telephone:* (3) 6899444 (office). *Fax:* (3) 6899420 (office). *E-mail:* avoda@inter.net.il (office).

LIBANIO CHRISTO, Carlos Alberto (Frei Betto); Brazilian Dominican friar and writer; b. 25 Aug. 1944, Belo Horizonte, Minas Gerais; s. of Antônio Carlos Vieira Christo and Maria Stella Libanio Christo; ed Univ. of Brazil, Escola Dominicana de Teologia and Seminário São Leopoldo; Vice-Pres. High School Municipal Union of Belo Horizonte 1961; Nat. Leader Catholic Young Students 1961–64; political prisoner 1964; newspaper and magazine ed. 1966–69; political prisoner held in São Paulo, accused of carrying out subversive activities 1969–73; organizer of basic Church communities 1973–79; teacher, popular educ. 1977–; writer and teacher with Workers' Pastoral 1979–; was sued, under the Media Law, by São Paulo Mil. Police for denouncing the violent acts of some its mems 1992, absolved by court 1993; Dir América Libre (magazine) 1993–2003; mem. Council Swedish Foundation for Human Rights 1991–96, Inst. for Critical Research, Amsterdam, Cajamar Inst., São Paulo, 'Sedes Sapientiae' Centre for Popular Educ., São Paulo; Consultant, Movimento dos Trabalhadores Rurais Sem Terra (MST); mem. and consultant Inst. Cidadania –2003; consultant to Itau Cultural Inst.; Special Assessor of the Presidency of the Repub., acting as Co-ordinator of Social Mobilization for the Zero Hunger Programme 2003–04; mem. Strategic Bd Faca Parte (Join In); assisted the Popular Movts Cen. Bd Workers Pastoral in the ABC area, São Paulo, Centre of Popular Movts, Ecclesiastical Base Communities; Co-ordinator ANAMPOS (Nat. Articulation for Popular and Union Movts Sindicais); consultant to Rural Landless Workers Movt; fmr Dir America Libre magazine; has lectured and given pastoral courses in Brazil and overseas; Intellectual of the Year Prize, Brazilian Writers' Union 1985, Human Rights Prize, Bruno Kreisky Foundation, Vienna 1987, Human Rights Prize, Bruno Kreisky Foundation 1988, Crea de Meio Ambiente Prize, Conselho Regional de Engenharia e Arquitetura, Rio de Janeiro, Paolo E. Borsellino Award (Italy) for work in human rights 1998, Award of Rio de Janeiro Regional Council for Architecture and Eng 1998, Chico Mendes de Resistência Medal, Grupo Tortura Nunca Mais, Rio de Janeiro 1998, Solidarity Medal (Cuba) 2000, Prêmio Abogados de Atocha (Spain), Paulo Freire Trophy for Social Commitment, Brazilian Psycology Council 2000. *Publications:* Cartas da Prisão (Letters from the Prison) 1974, Das Catacumbas 1976, Oração na Ação (Prayers in the Action) 1977, Natal, a ameaça de um menino pobre (Christmas, a Threat of a Poor Boy) 1978, A Semente e o Fruto, Igreja e Comunidade (The Seed, the Fruit, Church and the Community) 1981, Diário de Puebla (Diary of Puebla) 1979, A Vida Suspeita do Subversivo Paul Parelo (The Suspect Life of Paul Parelo - short stories) 1979 (re-published with the title O Aquária Negro—The Black Fishbowl) 1986), Puebla para o Povo (Puebla for the People) 1979, Nicarágua Livre, o Primeiro Passo (Nicaragua Free, First Step) 1980, O que é Comunidade Eclesial de Base (What is an Ecclesiastical Base Community) 1981, O Fermento na Massa (The Baking Powder in the Dough) 1981, CEBs, Rumo à Nova Sociedade (EBC – A Step to a New Society) 1981, Fogãozinho, culinária em histórias infantis (Cooking in Children's Stories) (with Maria Stella Libanio Christo) 1984, Fidel e a Religião, Conversas com Frei Betto (Fidel and Religion – Talks with Frei Betto) 1985, Batismo de Sangue, Os dominicanos e a morte de Carlos Marighella (Blood Baptism, The Dominican Friars and the Death of Carlos Marighella) (Jabuti Prize, Brazilian Book Asscn 1983) 1982, OSPB, Introdução à Politica Brasileira (Social and Political Organization of Brazil - Introduction to Brazilian Politics) 1985, O Dia de Angelo (Angelo's Day) (romance) 1987, Cristianismo & Marxismo (Christianity and Marxism) 1988, Sinal de contradição (Sign of Contradiction) (with Afonso Borges Filho) 1988, Essa escola chamada vida (A School Called Life) (with Paulo Freire and Ricardo Kotscho) 1988, A Proposta de Jesus (Jesus' Proposal) (Popular Catechism, Vol. I) 1989, A Comunidade de Fé (The Faith Community) (Popular Cathecism, Vol. II) 1989, Militantes do Reino (Militants of the Kingdom) (Popular Catechism, Vol. III) 1990, Viver em Comunhão de Amor (Living in a Communion of Love) (Popular Catechism, Vol. IV) 1990, Popular Catechism (condensed version) 1992, Lula – Biografia Politica de um Operário (Lula - Political Biography of a Worker) 1989, A Menina e o Elefante (The Girl and the Elephant) (teenage book) 1990, Fome de Pão e de Beleza (Hunger of Bread and Beauty) 1990, Uala, o Amor (Uala and Love) (teenage literature) 1991, Sinfonia Universal, a cosmovisão de Teilhard de Chardin (Universal Symphony – The Cosmovision of Teilhard de Chardin) 1997, Alucinado Som de Tuba (Allucinated Sound of Tuba) (romance) 1993, Por que Eleger Lula Presidente da República (Why Elect Lula President of the Republic?) 1994, Mistica e espiritualidade (Mystic and Spirituality) (with Leonardo Boff) 1994, O Paraiso Perdido – nos bastidores do socialismo (The Lost Paradise – In the Backstage of Socialism) 1993, Cotidiano & Mistério (Everyday Stories and Mystery) 1996, O Desafio Ético (The Ethical Challenge) (with Eugenio Barba and Jurandir Freire Costa) 1995, A Obra do Artista – uma visão holistica do Universo (The Artist's Work – A Holistic Vision of the Universe) 1995, Comer como um frade – divinas receitas para quem sabe por que temos um céu na boca (Eating like a Fries – Divine Recipes) 1996, O Vencedor (The Winner) (romance) 1996, Entre todos os homens (Amongst All Men) (novel) 1997, Talita abre a porta dos evangelhos (Talita Opens the Doors of the Gospels) 1998, A noite em que Jesus nasceu (The Night when Jesus was Born) (Best Young Readers' Book, Art Critics Asscn of São Paulo 1998) 1998, Hotel Brasil (detective story) 1999, Mysterium Creationes – Um olhar interdisciplinar sobre o Universo (Jabuti Prize 2000) 2000, Brasil 500 Anos: trajetórias, identidades e destinos (Brazil 500 Years: Routes, Identities and Destinies) 2000, O Decálogo (The Commandments) (short stories in partnership with Moacyr Scliar, Luiz Vilela, Ivan Angelo, José Roberto Torero and others) 2000, A mula de Balaão (Balaao's Mule) 2001, Os dois irmãos (The Two Brothers) 2001, A mulher Samaritana (The Samaritan) 2001, Alfabetto – Autobiografia Escolar (Alfabetto – An Educational Self-Biography) 2002, Gosto de Uva – Textos selecionados (Taste of Grapes – Selected Articles) 2003, Típicos Tipos – Coletânea de Perfis Literários (Typical Types – Collective of Literary Profiles) 2004, Uma saborosa viagem pelo Brasil – Limonada e sua turma em historias e receitas a bordo do Fogãozinho (A Tasteful Journey in Brazil – Lemonade and his Gang with Their Stories and Recipes on Board a Cooker) 2004, Treze contos diabólicos e um angélico 2005, A Mosca Azul 2006; numerous articles in Brazilian newspapers and magazines, including Diário Popular, O Globo, Folha de S. Paulo, O Estado de Minas, Correio Braziliense, O Dia, Caros Amigos, Brasileira, Chronica Brasil. *Leisure interests:* cooking, swimming. *Address:* Rua Atibaia 420, 01235-010 São Paulo, SP, Brazil. *Telephone:* (11) 38640844 (R. 224); (11) 38651473. *Fax:* (11) 38656941. *E-mail:* fbetto@uol.com.br.

LIBBRECHT, Kenneth G., BS, PhD; American physicist and academic; *Professor of Physics, California Institute of Technology;* b. 9 June 1958, Fargo, ND; m. Rachel Wing; two c.; ed Calif. Inst. of Tech., Princeton Univ.; Asst Prof. of Astrophysics, Calif. Inst. of Tech. 1984–89, Assoc. Prof. 1989–95, Prof. of Physics 1995–, Exec. Officer for Physics Dept 1997–; Fellow AAAS 1996–; Calif. Inst. of Tech. Fisher Prize for Physics 1979, NSF Presidential Young Investigator Award 1987, American Astronomical Soc. Newton Lacy Pierce Prize in Astrophysics 1991. *Publications:* The Snowflake: Winter's Secret Beauty 2003 (Benjamin Franklin Book Award 2004, Nat. Outdoor Book Award 2004); numerous research papers and articles in learned journals. *Address:* Physics Department, California Institute of Technology, Caltech 264–33, Pasadena, CA 91125, USA (office). *Telephone:* (626) 395-3722 (office). *Fax:* (626) 395-3814 (office). *E-mail:* kgl@caltech.edu (office). *Website:* www.its.caltech.edu (office).

LIBERADZKI, Bogusław Marian, DEcon; Polish politician and economist; b. 12 Sept. 1948, Sochaczew; m.; two s.; ed Main School of Planning and Statistics, Warsaw and Univ. of Illinois, USA; Scientist, Main School of Planning and Statistics (now Warsaw School of Econs) Warsaw 1971–75, Asst 1971–75, Tutor 1975–82, Asst Prof. 1982–99, Prof. of Econs 1999–, Head, Dept of Transport; Dir Transport Econs Research Centre, Warsaw 1986–89; Prof., Maritime Univ., Szcecin 1998–; Deputy Minister of Transport 1989–93; mem. Transport Comm., Polish Acad. of Sciences 1988–96, European Rail Congress Council, Brussels; Chair. Supervisory Bd Polish LOT Airways –1993; Minister of Transport and Maritime Economy 1993–97; mem. Democratic Left Alliance (Sojusz Lewicy Demokratycznej-Unia Pracy—SLD-UP) Parl. Club; Deputy to Sejm (Parl.) 1997–2004, Vice-Chair. Infrastructure Cttee 2001–04, European Cttee 2003–04, Polish-Nordic Group 2001–04, Chair. Perm. Sub-cttee on Transport 2001–04, Perm. Sub-cttee for Monitoring the Utilization of EU Funds 2001–04; Observer to European Parl. 2003–04; mem. European Parl. (Socialist Group) 2004–, Cttee on Transport and Tourism 2004–, Substitute mem. Cttee on the Internal Market and Consumer Protection 2004–, mem. Del. to the EU-Russia Parl. Cooperation Cttee 2004–, Substitute mem. Del. for Relations with the United States 2004–; Golden Medal of Merit 1978; Medal of the National Education Committee, Fulbright Scholarship 1986. *Publications:* Economics of Railways 1980, Supply of Railroad Services 1981, Transport: Demand, Supply, Equilibrium 1999. *Leisure interests* biographies, gardening. *Address:* European Parliament, 07H141, 60 rue Wiertz, 1047 Brussels, Belgium (office); Biuro Poselskie, ul. Garncarska 5, 70-402 Szczecin, Poland. *Telephone:* (91) 4341918. *Fax:* (2) 284-9423 (office). *Website:* www.europarl.eu.int (office).

LIBERIA-PETERS, Maria; Netherlands Antilles politician; b. 20 May 1941, Willemstad, Curaçao; m.; two adopted c.; fmr kindergarten teacher; mem. Curaçao Island Council 1975–82; elected mem. Staten (legislature) 1982–; Minister of Economic Affairs 1982–84; mem. Nat. Volkspartij (Nat. People's Party), fmr Pres.; Prime Minister of Netherlands Antilles 1984–86, 1988–94; Leader of the Opposition 1986–88, 1994–; mem. Council of Women World Leaders. *Address:* Partido Nashonal di Pueblo, Winston Churchillweg 133, Willemstad, Curaçao, Netherlands Antilles (office). *Telephone:* (9) 869-6777 (office). *Fax:* (9) 869-6688 (office).

LIBESKIND, Daniel, BArch, MA; American architect; *Owner and Architect, Studio Daniel Libeskind;* b. 1946, Łódź, Poland; s. of Nachman Libeskind and Dora Blaustein; m. Nina Lewis 1969; two s. one d.; ed Cooper Union School of Architecture, New York, Univ. of Essex, UK; fmr Head, Dept of Architecture, Cranbrook Acad. of Art; fmr Sr Scholar, John Paul Getty Centre; fmr Visiting Prof., Harvard Univ.; fmr Bannister Fletcher Prof., Univ. of London; fmr holder Davenport Chair, Yale Univ.; architectural practice Berlin 1989–; apptd lead architect for rebuilding of World Trade Center site 2003; Prof., Hochschule für Gestaltung, Karlsruhe; holder of Creative Chair, Univ. of Pa, USA; mem. Akad. der Kunst 1990–, European Acad. of Arts and Letters, American Acad. of Arts and Letters; Hon. RA 2002; Dr hc (Humboldt Univ.) 1997, (Univ. of Essex) 1999, (Technion, Israel); DHumLitt hc (De Paul Univ.) 2002, (Brandeis) 2007; DScS hc (Edinburgh) 2002; LLD hc (Toronto) 2004; Commander's Cross, Order of Merit (Germany); numerous awards including Lion d'Or, Venice Biennale 1985, Berlin Cultural Prize 1996, Award for Architecture, American Acad. of Arts and Letters 1996, Goethe Medallion 2000, Hiroshima Art Prize 2001, Holocaust Educational Trust Award, Leo Baeck Inst. Award, Trebbia European Award, Prague 2006, Gold Medal Award for Architecture, Genoa, Italy, Nat. Arts Club Gold Medal for Architecture 2007, Penn State IAH Medal for Distinguished Contribution to Public Advancement of Arts and Humanities, Yivo Inst. for Jewish Research "Lifetime Achievement" Award, New York City. *Opera:* stage sets: Tristan und Isolde (also costume design), Saarbrücken, Germany 2001, Saint Francis of Assisi, Berlin, Germany 2002. *Projects include:* (architectural) Felix-Nussbaum-Haus, Osnabrück, Germany 1998, Jewish Museum, Berlin 1999 (German Architecture Prize 1999, Art Forum Int. Best of 1998), Imperial War Museum North, Manchester 2001 (RIBA Award 2004, British Construction Industry Building of the Year), Eighteen Turns (summer pavilion) Serpentine Gallery, London 2001, Weil Gallery, Majorca 2001, Jewish Museum, Copenhagen 2002, CUBE Bar and Restaurant, Manchester 2002, London

Metropolitan Univ. Graduate Centre 2004 (RIBA Award), Wohl Centre, Bar-Ilan Univ., Israel 2005 (RIBA Int. Award), Denver Art Museum Residences 2006 (American Inst. of Architects Award of Honor 2008, CNBC Americas Property Awards 2008), Royal Ontario Museum, Canada 2007 (Award of Merit for innovative steel design), Ascent at Roebling's Bridge, Ky 2008 (CNBC Americas Property Awards 2008), Jewish Museum, San Francisco 2008; projects in progress include: new faculty for JVC Univ. Guadalajara, Mexico, Creative Media Centre, Hong Kong, Złota 44 (apartment tower), Warsaw, Poland, Reflections at Keppel Bay, Singapore. *Publications:* Radix—Matrix: Architecture and Writings 1997, The Space of Encounter 2001, Breaking Ground (with Sarah Crichton) 2004, Counterpoint: Daniel Libeskind in Conversation with Paul Goldberger 2008. *Address:* Architect Daniel Libeskind AG, Walchestrasse 9, 8006 Zürich, Switzerland (office). *Telephone:* (44) 540-4700 (office). *Fax:* (44) 540-4760 (office). *E-mail:* info@daniel-libeskind.com (office). *Website:* www.daniel-libeskind.com.

LICK, Dale Wesley, BS, MS, PhD; American mathematician, academic and university administrator; *University Professor, Florida State University;* b. 7 Jan. 1938, Marlette, Mich.; s. of John R. Lick and Florence May Lick (née Baxter); m. Marilyn Kay Foster 1956; one s. three d.; ed Michigan State Univ., Univ. of California, Riverside; Instructor and Chair. Dept of Math., Port Huron Jr Coll. (later St Clair Co. Community Coll.), Port Huron, Mich. 1959–60; Asst to Comptroller, Line and Staff Man., Michigan Bell Telephone Co., Detroit, Mich. 1961; Instructor of Math., Univ. of Redlands, Calif. 1961–63; Teaching Asst in Math., Univ. of Calif., Riverside, Calif., 1964–65; Asst Prof. of Math., Univ. of Tenn. 1965–67, Assoc. Prof. 1968–69; textbook and manuscript reviewer for several publrs 1966–; Visiting Research Mathematician, Applied Math. Dept, Brookhaven Nat. Lab., Upton, New York 1967–68; Consultant, Computing Tech. Center, Union Carbide Corpn, Oak Ridge, Tenn., under auspices of US Atomic Energy Comm. 1966–71; Adjunct Assoc. Prof., Dept of Pharmacology (Biomathematics), Temple Medical School, Temple Univ. 1969–72; Head and Assoc. Prof., Dept of Math., Drexel Univ., Philadelphia, Pa 1969–72; Vice-Pres. for Academic Affairs, Russell Sage Coll., Troy, New York 1972–74; Dean, School of Sciences and Health Professions and Prof. of Math. and Computing Sciences, Old Dominion Univ., Norfolk, Va 1974–78; Pres. and Prof. of Math. and Computer Sciences, Georgia Southern Coll., Statesboro, Ga 1978–86; Pres. and Prof. of Math., Univ. of Maine 1986–91; Prof. of Math., Florida State Univ., Tallahassee 1991–93, Univ. Prof., Learning Systems Inst. and Dept of Educ. Leadership 1993–; mem. Editorial Bd Innovate (journal), International Journal for the Scholarship of Teaching and Learning; mem. American Asscn of Univ. Admins, American Asscn of Univ. Profs, American Math. Soc., Math. Asscn of America, Asscn Study of Higher Educ., Nat. Staff Devt Council, American Educ. Research Asscn; Pres.'s Award, US Baseball Fed. 1985, Man of the Year Award, Rotary Club of Statesboro 1985, Certificate of Appreciation, US Dept of Educ. 1985, Silver Beaver Award, Coastal Empire Council of Boy Scouts of America 1986, Medallion of Merit, US Govt Printing Office 1988, Athletic Hall of Fame, Georgia Southern Univ. 1990, Renaissance Award for Leadership and Enlightenment, Southeast Georgia, Black Image Steering Cttee 1993, honoured as one of Forty Alumni Who Make a Difference, Univ. of California, Riverside 1994, Circle of Gold, Florida State Univ. Alumni Asscn, Rosa Parks Servant Leader Award, Florida State Univ. 1996, Distinguished Alumni Award, Michigan State Univ. 2006, named by Univ. of California, Riverside "One of 40 Alumni Who Make a Difference" 2006. *Publications:* Fundamentals of Algebra 1970, Whole-Faculty Study Groups: A Powerful Way to Change School and Enhance Learning (co-author) 1998, New Directions in Mentoring: Creating a Culture of Synergy (co-author) 1999, Whole-Faculty Study Groups: Creating Student-Based Professional Development (co-author) 2001, Whole-Faculty Study Groups: Creating Professional Learning Communities That Target Student Learning (co-author) 2005, The Whole-Faculty Study Group Fieldbook: Improving Schools and Enhancing Student Learning (co-author) 2005, The Whole-Faculty Study Groups Fieldbook: Lessons Learned and Best Practices from Classrooms, Districts, and Schools (with Murphy) 2007, Schoolwide Action Research for Professional Learning Communities: Improving Student Learning Through the Whole-Faculty Study Groups Approach (with Clauset and Murphy) 2008; numerous book chapters, papers and articles in learned journals and around 300 newspaper columns. *Leisure interests:* sports, reading, writing, the arts, church work. *Address:* University Center C-4600, Florida State University, Tallahassee, FL 32306-2540 (office); 348 Remington Run Loop, Tallahassee, FL 32312-1402, USA (home). *Telephone:* (850) 284-3219 (office); (850) 553-4080 (home). *Fax:* (850) 553-4081 (office). *E-mail:* dlick@lsi.fsu.edu (office); dwlick@comcast.net (home). *Website:* www.fsu.edu/~elps/he/faculty_lick.htm (office).

LIDDELL, Rt Hon. Helen Lawrie, PC; British politician, diplomatist and economist; *High Commissioner to Australia;* b. 6 Dec. 1950; d. of Hugh Reilly and the late Bridget Lawrie Reilly; m. Alistair Henderson Liddell 1972; one s. one d.; ed St Patrick's High School, Coatbridge, Univ. of Strathclyde; Head, Econ. Dept Scottish TUC 1971–75, Asst Sec. 1975–76; Econ. Corresp. BBC Scotland 1976–77; Scottish Sec. Labour Party 1977–88; Dir Personnel and Public Affairs, Scottish Daily Record and Sunday Mail Ltd 1988–92; Chief Exec. Business Venture Programme 1993–94; MP for Monklands E 1994–97, for Airdrie and Shotts 1997–, Opposition spokeswoman on Scotland 1995–97; Econ. Sec. HM Treasury 1997–98, Minister of State Scottish Office 1998–99; Minister of Transport 1999, Minister for Energy and Competitiveness in Europe 1999–2001; Sec. of State for Scotland 2001–03; High Commr to Australia 2005–; Hon. LLD (Strathclyde). *Publication:* Elite (novel) 1990. *Leisure interests:* cooking, hill-walking, music, writing. *Address:* British High Commission, Commonwealth Avenue, Canberra, ACT 2600, Australia (office). *Telephone:* (2) 6270-6666 (office). *Fax:* (2) 6273-3236 (office). *E-mail:* bhc.canberra@britaus.net (office). *Website:* bhc.britaus.net (office).

LIDDY, Edward M., MBA; American business executive; b. New Brunswick, NJ; ed Catholic Univ. of America, George Washington Univ.; joined G.D. Searle & Co. 1979, Sr Vice-Pres. and COO –1986; Exec. Vice-Pres. ADT 1986–88; sr financial and operation positions Sears, Roebuck & Co. 1988–91, Chief Financial Officer 1991–94; Pres. and COO The Allstate Corpn 1994–99, Chair. 1999–2008, also Pres. and CEO 1999–2005, CEO 1999–2006; mem. Bd of Dirs The Kroger Co., 3M, Insurance Information Inst., Insurance Inst. for Highway Safety, Northwestern Memorial Hosp., United Way/Crusade of Mercy, The Boeing Co. 2007–; Chair. and Nat. Gov. Boys & Girls Clubs of America (BGCA); mem. Civic Cttee Commercial Club, Financial Services Forum, Business Roundtable, Catalyst; Trustee Northwestern Univ. *Address:* c/o The Allstate Corporation, 2775 Sanders Road, Northbrook, IL 60062, USA (office).

LIEBENBERG, Christo Ferro, MPA, PMD; South African politician and banker retd ; b. 2 Oct. 1934, Touwsriver; s. of Christiaan Liebenberg and Helene Griessel; m. Elly Liebenberg 1959; two s.; ed Worcester Boys' High School, Harvard Univ., USA, Institut Européen d'Admin des Affaires, Paris and Cranfield Polytechnic, UK; joined Nedbank, Cape Town 1952; Man. Dir Nedbank, Johannesburg 1988–90; CEO Nedcor 1990–94; fmr Chair. Credit Guarantee Insurance Corpn of Africa Ltd, Syfrets Ltd, Cape Town; fmr Deputy Chair. NedPerm Bank; Pres. Inst. of Bankers in S Africa 1991; Minister of Finance 1994–96; Dir various financial insts. *Leisure interests:* music, photography, theatre, ballet, reading, golf. *Address:* c/o Ministry of Finance, 240 Vermeulen Street, Pretoria 0002, South Africa.

LIEBER, Charles Michael, BA, PhD; American chemist and academic; *Mark Hyman Professor of Chemistry, Harvard University;* b. 9 April 1959, Philadelphia, Pa; s. of Robert and Marlene Lieber; m. Jennifer Karas Lieber; one s. one d.; ed Franklin and Marshall Coll., Stanford Univ., California California Inst. of Tech.; Asst Prof. of Chem., Columbia Univ., New York 1987–90, Assoc. Prof. 1990–91; Prof. of Chem., Harvard Univ. 1991–99, holds jt appointment in Dept of Chem. and Chemical Biology, as Mark Hyman Prof. of Chem., and School of Eng and Applied Sciences 1999–; Co-Ed. Nano Letters; Consulting Ed. International Journal of Biomedical Nanoscience and Nanotechnology; mem. Editorial Bd Advances in Nanoscale Materials and Nanotechnology, Applied Physics Letters, Chemical and Engineering News, Current Nanoscience, Dictionary of Nanoscience and Nanotechnology, e-Journal of Surface Science and NanoTechnology, Encyclopedia of Nanoscience and Nanotechnology, Frontiers of Physics; Fullerenes, Nanotubes and Carbon Nanostructures, Journal of Applied Physics, Journal of Computational and Theoretical Nanoscience, Journal of Nanoscience and Nanotechnology, Journal of Nanotechnology, Journal of Physical Chemistry, Journal of Physics: Condensed Matter, Journal of Scanning Probe Microscopy, Nano Research, Nano Today, Nanomedicine, Nanotech Briefs, Nanotechnology Opportunity Report(TM), Recent Patents on Material Science, Research Letters in Nanotechnology; Small; Virtual Journal of Nanoscale Science and Technology; mem. Tech. Advisory Cttee, Samsung Electronics; has been active in commercializing nanotechnology; f. Nanosys, Inc. 2001, Vista Therapeutics 2007; mem. NAS 2004–, Optical Soc. of America, SPIE; Fellow, American Physical Soc. 1996–, AAAS 1996–, IUPAC 2001–, World Tech. Network 2002–, American Acad. of Arts and Sciences 2002–, Inst. of Physics 2007–, Materials Research Soc. 2008–; Hon. Prof., Zhejiang Univ. 2002, Fudan Univ. 2002, Univ. of Science and Tech. of China 2002, Peking Univ. 2008; ACS Award in Pure Chem. 1992, NSF Creativity Award 1996, Feynman Prize in Nanotechnology 2001, MRS Medal 2002, Harrison Howe Award, Univ. of Rochester 2002, American Physical Soc. McGroddy Prize for New Materials 2003, New York Intellectual Property Law Assn Inventor of the Year 2003, Scientific American 50 Award in Nanotechnology and Molecular Electronics 2003, World Tech. Award in Materials, The World Tech. Network 2003, 2004, ACS Award in the Chem. of Materials 2004, Nanotech Briefs Nano 50 Award 2005, NBIC Research Excellence Award, Univ. of Pennsylvania 2007, Einstein Award, Chinese Acad. of Sciences 2008, NIH Pioneer Award 2008. *Publications:* more than 290 papers in peer-reviewed journals on the synthesis of a broad range of nanoscale materials, the characterization of the unique physical properties of these materials and the development of methods of hierarchical assembly of nanoscale wires, together with the demonstration of applications of these materials in nanoelectronics, nanocomputing, biological and chemical sensing, neurobiology and nanophotonics; prin. inventor on more than 30 patents. *Address:* Department of Chemistry and Chemical Biology, Harvard University, 12 Oxford Street, Cambridge, MA 02138, USA (office). *Telephone:* (617) 496-3169 (office). *Fax:* (617) 496-5442 (office). *E-mail:* cml@cmliris.harvard.edu (office). *Website:* http://cmliris.harvard.edu (office).

LIEBERMAN, Avigdor, BA; Israeli politician; *Deputy Prime Minister and Minister of Foreign Affairs;* b. 5 June 1958, USSR; m.; three c.; ed Hebrew Univ.; rank of corporal during mil. service; mem. Knesset (Israel Beytenu Party, Ihud Leumi-Israel Beytenu Party) 1999–, Founder and Chair. Israel Beytenu Party 1999–, mem. Foreign Affairs and Defence Cttee; Minister of Nat. Infrastructure 2001–02, of Transport 2003–04; Deputy Prime Minister and Minister of Strategic Affairs 2006–08, Deputy Prime Minister and Minister of Foreign Affairs 2009–; Sec. Nat. Workers' Union; Chair. Bd of Dirs of Information Industries; Dir of Econ. Corpn of Jerusalem 1983–88; Dir Likud Movt 1993–96; Dir Prime Minister's Office 1996–97; f. Zionist Forum. *Leisure interests:* football, tennis. *Address:* Ministry of Foreign Affairs, 9 Yitzhak Rabin Blvd, Kiryat Ben-Gurion, Jerusalem 91035 (office); Israel Beytenu (Israel Is Our Home) (Nash dom Izrail), 78 Yirmeyahu Street, Jerusalem 94467, Israel (office). *Telephone:* 2-5303111 (Ministry) (office); 2-5012999 (office). *Fax:* 2-5303367 (Ministry) (office); 2-5377188 (office). *E-mail:* pniot@mfa.gov.il (office); gdv7191@hotmail.com (office). *Website:* www.mfa.gov.il (office); www.beytenu.org.il (office).

LIEBERMAN, Joseph I., BA, JD; American politician; *Senator from Connecticut;* b. 24 Feb. 1942, Stamford, Conn.; s. of Henry and Marcia (née Manger) Lieberman; m. Hadassah Freilich 1983; two s. two d.; ed Yale Univ.; called to Bar, Conn. 1967; mem. Conn. Senate 1971–81, Senate Majority Leader 1975–81; Pnr, Lieberman, Segaloff & Wolfson, New Haven 1972–83; Attorney Gen. State of Conn., Hartford 1983–88, Senator for Conn. 1989–; Chair. Democratic Leadership Council 1995–; Vice-Pres. Cand. for Democratic Party 2000; sought Democratic Party presidential candidacy 2004; mem. Governmental Affairs Cttee, Small Business Cttee, Trustee Wadsworth Atheneum, Univ. of Bridgeport; Democrat –2006, Ind. Democrat 2007–. *Publications:* The Power Broker 1966, The Scorpion and the Tarantula 1970, The Legacy 1981, Child Support in America 1986. *Address:* 706 Hart Senate Office Building, Washington, DC 20510, USA (office). *Telephone:* (202) 224-4041 (office). *Fax:* (202) 224-9750 (office). *Website:* lieberman.senate.gov (office).

LIEBERMAN, Seymour, PhD; American biochemist and academic; *Professor Emeritus of Biochemistry, College of Physicians and Surgeons, Columbia University;* b. 1 Dec. 1916, New York; s. of Samuel D. Lieberman and Sadie Levin; m. Sandra Spar 1944; one s.; ed Brooklyn Coll., New York, Univ. of Illinois and Stanford Univ., Calif.; Prof. of Biochem., Coll. of Physicians and Surgeons, Columbia Univ. 1962–87, Prof. Emer. 1987–, Assoc. Dean 1984–90, Vice-Provost 1988–89, Assoc. Dir Office of Science and Tech. 1991–99; Program Officer The Ford Foundation 1974–75; Pres. St Luke's-Roosevelt Inst. for Health Sciences 1981–97; mem. NAS 1977–; Ciba Award 1952, Koch Award 1970, Roussel Prize (France) 1984, Dale Medal 1986, Dist Service Award (Columbia Univ.) 1991. *Publications:* A Heuristic Proposal for Understanding Steroidogenic Processes 1984, Detection in Bovine Brain of Sulfate Esters of Cholesterol and Sitosterol 1985 and more than 150 other publs. *Leisure interest:* tennis. *Address:* 515 East 72nd Street, New York, NY 10021 (home); 432 W. 58th Street, New York, NY 10019, USA (office). *Telephone:* (212) 523-7148 (office); (212) 744-8772 (home). *Fax:* (212) 523-7442 (office). *E-mail:* sl22@columbia.edu (office). *Website:* cpmcnet.columbia.edu/dept/ps (office).

LIEDTKE, Kurt W., LLD; German lawyer and business executive; *President, Chairman and CEO, Robert Bosch Corporation;* b. 23 March 1943, Darmstadt; m.; three c.; ed Univ. of Frankfurt am Main; began career as lawyer specialising in tax law, Frankfurt 1972–74; Gen. Counsel, Laufenberg Power Station, Switzerland 1974–77; Sr Consultant, Corp. Law and Contracts Dept, Robert Bosch GmbH, Stuttgart 1977–81, various positions, Marketing Dept, Fàbrica Española Magnetos SA, Spain 1981–82, Man.-Dir Robert Bosch Comercial Española Magnetos SA, Spain 1982–89, Man.-Dir Robert Bosch Ltd, London, UK 1989–96, Pres. Robert Bosch Australia Pty Ltd, Melbourne 1996–2001, Assoc. mem. Bd of Man. Robert Bosch GmbH 2001–02, mem. 2002–, Pres., Chair. and CEO Robert Bosch Corpn, USA 2001–. *Address:* Robert Bosch Corporation, 2800 South 25th Avenue, Broadview, IL 60155, USA (office). *Telephone:* (708) 865-5200 (office). *Fax:* (708) 865-6430 (office). *Website:* www.boschusa.com (office).

LIEM SIOE LIONG; Indonesian business executive; *Chairman, Salim Group;* b. 16 July 1916, Haikou, Fuqing Dist, Fujian, S China; m.; three s. one d.; emigrated to cen. Java 1938; began own coffee powder business during World War II, establishing himself as provisions supplier for rebel army fighting for independence from the Dutch; began to build own business empire in late 1940s, now has substantial shareholdings in 192 cos involved in trade, finance, food, chemicals, pharmaceuticals, textiles; majority shareholder in First Pacific Group (Hong Kong-based banking, trading and property co.); major shareholdings in Bank of Cen. Asia (Indonesia's largest pvt. bank), Indocement and Bogasari Flour Mills; Chair. Salim Group; Econ. Advisor to Indonesian Govt; ranked 25th by Forbes magazine amongst Southeast Asia's Richest 2004. *Address:* PT Perkasa Indonesia Cement Enterprise, Level 13, Wisma Indocement Kav. 70–71, Jalan Jenderal Sudirman, Jakarta, Indonesia (office).

LIEN, Chan, MSc, PhD; Taiwanese politician; *Chairman, Kuomintang (KMT);* b. 27 Aug. 1936, Sian, Shansi; s. of Chen Tung Lien and Chao Lan-Kun Lien; m. Yui Fang; two s. two d.; ed Nat. Taiwan Univ. and Univ. of Chicago, USA; Assoc. Prof. Nat. Taiwan Univ. 1968–69, Prof. and Chair. Dept of Political Science and Dir Graduate Inst. of Political Science 1969–75; Amb. to El Salvador 1975–76; Dir Dept of Youth Affairs, Cen. Cttee Kuomintang 1976–78; Deputy Sec.-Gen. Cen. Cttee Kuomintang 1978, mem. Cen. Standing Cttee 1983–, Chair. 2000–; Chair. Nat. Youth Comm., Exec. Yuan 1978–81; Minister of Communications 1981–87; Vice-Premier 1987–88; Minister of Foreign Affairs 1989–90; Gov. Taiwan Provincial Govt 1990–93; Premier of Taiwan 1993–97; Vice-Pres. of Taiwan 1997–2000; Presidential Cand. 2000; Pres. Chinese Assn of Political Science 1979–82. *Publications:* The Foundation of Democracy, Taiwan in China's External Relations, Western Political Thought. *Leisure interests:* golf, swimming, music. *Address:* Kuomintang, 11 Chung Shan South Road, Taipei 100, Taiwan (office). *Telephone:* (2) 23121472 (office). *Fax:* (2) 2343524 (office). *Website:* www.kmt.org.tw (office).

LIEN, Siaou-Sze, MSc; Singaporean business executive; *Senior Executive Coach, Mobley Group Pacific Ltd;* b. Singapore; one d.; ed Nanyang Univ., Imperial Coll. of Science and Tech., Univ. of London, UK; joined Hewlett-Packard as systems engineer 1978, later Vice-Pres. and Man. Dir HP Asia Pacific, Sr Vice-Pres. HP Services Asia Pacific (following merger with Compaq; first woman vice-pres. in region) 2002–06 (retd); Sr Exec. Coach, Mobley Group Pacific Ltd 2006–; mem. Bd of Dirs Luvata Ltd, Huhtamäki Oyj 2009–; Deputy Chair. Bd Govs Republic Polytechnic (Chair. Admin. Cttee); fmr Dir PSA (Port of Singapore Authority) Int.; fmr adviser, Gov. of Guangdong Prov., People's Repub. of China; Trustee Nanyang Technological Univ.; ranked by Fortune magazine amongst 50 Most Powerful Women in Business outside the

US (fifth) 2001, (eighth) 2002, (eighth) 2003, (19th) 2004, (22nd) 2005, (31st) 2006. *Leisure interests:* sports, jogging, dancing, hot-air ballooning. *Address:* Mobley Group Pacific Ltd, Room 2006-2007, 20/F, One Corporate Avenue, 222 Hu Bin Road, Shanghai 200021, People's Republic of China (office). *Telephone:* (21) 63406222 (office). *Fax:* (21) 63406226 (office). *Website:* www .mobleygrouppacific.com (office).

LIENDO, Maj.-Gen. Horacio Tomás; Argentine politician and army officer; b. 17 Dec. 1924, Córdoba; ed Mil. Coll.; first post with 4th Bn, Communications; with 6th Motorized Bn, Communications; as Capt., entered Army War Coll. 1954, later Gen. Staff Officer; served in Communications Inspection, Army Gen. Staff, and, as Second-in-Command, 4th Bn, Communications; rank of Maj. 1959; 61st Communications Command; under orders of Mil. Attaché, USA 1962; rank of Lt-Col 1965, Col 1970, Gen. 1980; Minister of Labour 1976–79; Chief of Staff, Armed Forces 1979–81; Minister of the Interior March–Nov. 1981; Pres. of Argentina (a.i.) Nov.–Dec. 1981.

LIEPA, Andris; Russian/Latvian ballet dancer and choreographer; b. 6 Jan. 1962, Moscow; s. of the late Marius Liepa and of Margarita Zhigunova; brother of Ilze Liepa (q.v.); m. Yekaterina Liepa; one d.; ed Moscow Choreographic School of Bolshoi Theatre; with Bolshoi Ballet 1980–87; prize-winner int. competitions Moscow 1985, Jackson, USA (Grand Prix) 1986; lived in the West 1987–; appeared with New York City Ballet, subsequently with American Ballet Theater; danced in Raymonda Variations, Swan Lake (Baryshnikov), Romeo and Juliet (Macmillan), Violin Concerto (Balanchine); worked with Nina Ananiashvili, Carla Fracci and other partners; choreographer 1993–; has adapted Fokine ballets for film, including Return to the Firebird; guest artist with Kirov (now Mariinsky) Ballet, London tour 1990; works in USA, Russia and Latvia. *Address:* Bryusov per. 17, Apt 13, 103009 Moscow, Russia. *Telephone:* (095) 241-81-37.

LIEPA, Ilze; Russian/Latvian ballerina; b. 22 Nov. 1963; d. of the late Maris Liepa and of Margarita Zhigunova; sister of Andris Liepa (q.v.); m. 1st Sergey Stadler (divorced); m. 2nd Vladislovas A. Paulius; ed Russa Academic Choreography Coll. (studied with N. V. Zolotariova), Pedagogic Faculty of Moscow Theatre Art Acad.; with Bolshoi ballet 1982–, currently First Soloist; danced on various stages of Europe and America performing parts of classic repertoire, including Legend about Love, Romeo and Juliet, Firebird, Don Quixote, Corsair, Raimonda, Prince Igor; début in England concert Stars of World Ballet, Covent Garden (Firebird), tours with Bolshoi Theatre in most countries of Europe and America, independently toured in Argentina, Greece, Taiwan, Japan; Artistic Dir Golden Age Asscn 1994–98; f. Maris Liepa Foundation; Prize of Russian Trade Unions, Hon. Artist of Russian Fed. 1996, People's Artist of Russia 2002, Gold Mask (Best Female Ballet Role) 2003. *Films include:* The Shining World 1983, Bambi's Childhood 1984, Lermontov 1985, Lomononov 1987, Return of the Firebird 1994. *Plays include:* Your Sister and Captive 1999, The Empress's Dream 2000. *Publication:* Circle of the Sun (play) 2000. *Address:* Bolshoi Theatre, 1 Thetral'nyy proyezd, Moscow; Bryusov per. 17, Apt 12, 103009 Moscow, Russia. *Telephone:* (495) 229-23-88. *Fax:* (495) 229-23-88. *E-mail:* vpaulius@stk.mmtel.ru. *Website:* www.bolshoi.ru.

LIESEN, Klaus, DJur; German business executive; b. 15 April 1931; fmr Chair. Exec. Bd E.ON Ruhrgas AG, Chair. Supervisory Bd 1996–2003; Chair. Supervisory Bd Volkswagen AG, Allianz AG 1996–2003; mem. Supervisory Bd TUI AG 2005–(also mem. Presiding Cttee), Otto Wolff Industrieberatung und Beteiligungen GmbH; other directorships in steel, energy, banking and insurance cos; Hon. Dr rer. pol. *Address:* E.ON Ruhrgas AG, Huttropstrasse 60, 45117 Essen, Germany (office). *Telephone:* 20118400 (office).

LIEW, Datuk Vui Keong, LLB, JP; Malaysian lawyer and politician; *President, Liberal Democratic Party;* b. 18 Jan. 1960, Kota Belud, Sabah; s. of the late Ping-Hon Liew and Yet Liew Wong; m. Dr Lindai Lee; four c.; ed Diploma in Business and Finance, Univ. of North London, Lincoln's Inn, London, UK; active legal practitioner in criminal law and jurisdiction in Malaysia; called to Malayan Bar 1990, Borneo Bar 1992; est. own legal practice 1997; legal adviser to the Sabah United Chinese Chamber of Commerce, United Sabah Sze Yip Asscn, Sabah Motion Picture & Entertainment Asscn, Sabah Sze Yip Asscn (West Coast), Sabah Women Asscn, Kota Belud Chinese Chamber of Commerce, Kota Kinabalu Journalists Asscn, Sabah Law Asscn; joined Liberal Democratic Party (LDP) 1994, Head, Usukan Div., Kota Belud 1994–2004, Kapayan Div. 2004–, Asst Sec.-Gen. LDP 1999–2004, Sec.-Gen. 2005–06, Pres. 2006–; Vice-Pres. Barisan Nasional, Malaysia. *Leisure interests:* swimming, reading. *Address:* Messrs V. K. Liew & Partners, Lots 905-911B, 9th Floor, Wisma Merdeka Phase 2, Jalan Tun Abdul Razak, 88000 Kota Kinabalu, Sabah (office); Liberal Democratic Party, Tingkat 1, No. 33, Karamunsing Warehouse, PO Box 16033, 88868 Kota Kinabalu, Sabah, Malaysia. *Telephone:* (88) 248986 (office); (88) 246896 (office); (88) 218985; (88) 256352 (office). *Fax:* (88) 240698 (office); (88) 240598. *E-mail:* vkliew26@gmail.com (office); ldpkk@tm.net.my (office). *Website:* www .ldpsabah.com (office).

LIGACHEV, Yegor Kuzmich; Russian politician; b. 29 Sept. 1920; m.; one s.; ed Moscow Inst. of Aviation and CPSU Higher Party School; Engineer 1943–49; joined CPSU 1944; Party and Local Govt Official Novosibirsk 1949–55; Vice-Chair. Novosibirsk Regional Soviet of Working People's Deputies 1955–58; Sec. Novosibirsk Regional Cttee CPSU 1959–61, mem. Cen. Cttee CPSU 1961–65; First Sec. Tomsk Regional Cttee CPSU 1965–83; Cand. mem. Cen. Cttee CPSU 1966–76, mem. 1976–90, mem. Politburo 1985–90; Deputy to Supreme Soviet 1966–89; Sec. Cen. Cttee in Charge of Personnel and Ideology 1983–88; in Charge of Agric. 1988–90; People's Deputy of the USSR 1989–91; active in Russian nat. and communist movt; Vice-Chair. Union of Communist Parties of fmr USSR 1995–; mem. State Duma (Parl.)

1999–2003. *Publication:* Inside Gorbachev's Kremlin 1993. *Address:* Communist Party of Russian Federation, per. M. Sukharevskii 3/1, 103051 Moscow, Russia (home). *Telephone:* (495) 928-71-29 (office). *Fax:* (495) 292-90-50 (office). *E-mail:* cprf2000@mail.ru (office). *Website:* www.kprf.ru (office).

LIGHT, Jay, BA, PhD; American academic and university administrator; *Dwight P. Robinson, Jr. Professor of Business Administration and Dean, Harvard Business School;* b. Ohio; m. Judy Light; two c.; ed Cornell Univ., Harvard Univ.; early career in data communications and satellite guidance at Jet Propulsion Lab. –1970; mem. of Faculty, Harvard Business School 1970–, Dwight P. Robinson, Jr. Prof. of Business Admin 1979–, held various sr positions including Chair. Finance Area 1985–88, Sr Assoc. Dean and Dir of Faculty Planning 1988–92, Sr Assoc. Dean and Dir of Planning and Devt 1998–2005, Interim Dean, Harvard Business School 2005–06, Dean 2006–; took leave of absence from Harvard to serve as Dir of Investment and Financial Policies, Ford Foundation 1977–79; mem. Bd of Dirs Harvard Man. Co., Pnrs HealthCare, also Chair., Investment Cttee; Trustee Groton School. *Publications:* The Financial System (with W.L. White) 1979; numerous articles in professional journals and more than 50 cases and notes. *Address:* Office of the Dean, Harvard Business School, Soldiers Field, Boston, MA 02163, USA. *Telephone:* (617) 495-6000. *Website:* www.hbs.edu.

LIGHTFOOT, Edwin N., BS, PhD; American scientist and academic; *Hilldale Professor Emeritus of Chemical and Biological Engineering, University of Wisconsin;* m.; five c.; ed Cornell Univ., New York; joined faculty of Univ. of Wisconsin-Madison 1953, became one of the country's first profs in biochemical eng, now Hilldale Prof. Emer. of Chemical and Biological Eng; mem. Nat. Acad. of Eng 1979, Royal Norwegian Soc. of Sciences and Letters 1985, NAS 1995; Hon. DrTech (Tech. Univ. of Norway) 1985; Fulbright Research Scholar, Tech. Univ. of Norway 1962, AIChE William H. Walker Award 1975, AIChE Warren K. Lewis Award 1991, Nat. Medal of Science (jt recipient) 2004. *Publications:* Transport Phenomena 1960, Transport Phenomena and Living Systems: Biomedical Aspects of Momentum and Mass Transport 1974; numerous scientific papers in professional journals. *Address:* Department of Chemical and Biological Engineering, 3018 Engineering Hall, 1415 Engineering Drive, Madison, WI 53706, USA (office). *Telephone:* (608) 262-6934 (office). *Fax:* (608) 262-5434 (office). *E-mail:* lightfoot@engr.wisc.edu (office). *Website:* www.engr.wisc.edu (office).

LIGHTING, Jane; British television executive; *CEO, Channel 5 Broadcasting Ltd.;* began career with Crown Cassette Communications 1976; fmr marketing exec. for Video Arts (training film co.), then with its sister co., later worked in int. sales and distribution; f. and Man. Dir, Minotaur International (distribution co.) 1995, acquired by Flextech (part of UK cable group Telewest) 1999; Man. Dir of Broadcast and TV, Flextech, oversaw five TV channels: Bravo, Living, Trouble, Challenge and Freeview entertainment channel FTN as well as 10-channel jt venture with BBC, including UK Gold and UK History 1999–2002, CEO Flextech 2002–03; CEO Channel 5 2003–; Fellow, Royal TV Soc. 2006–, Chair. 2006–; Dir (non-exec.) Trinity Mirror PLC 2008–; Olswang Business Award, Carlton Women in Film and TV Awards 2001. *Address:* Channel Five Broadcasting Ltd, 22 Long Acre, London, WC2E 9LY, England (office). *Telephone:* (20) 7550-5555 (office). *Website:* www.five.tv (office).

LIGHTMAN, Alan Paige, AB, PhD; American physicist, writer and academic; *Adjunct Professor of Humanities, Creative Writing, Physics, Massachusetts Institute of Technology;* b. 28 Nov. 1948, Memphis, Tenn.; m. Jean Greenblatt 1976; two d.; ed Princeton Univ., California Inst. of Technology; Postdoctoral Fellow, Cornell Univ. 1974–76; Asst Prof., Harvard Univ. 1976–79; staff scientist Smithsonian Astrophysical Observatory, Cambridge 1979–88; Prof. of Science and Writing, MIT 1988–2002, John E. Burchard Chair 1995–2001, f. Grad. Program in Science Writing 2001, Adjunct Prof. of Humanities, Creative Writing, Physics 2002–; Fellow, American Acad. of Arts and Sciences, American Physical Soc.; mem. American Astronomical Soc.; Asscn of American Publishers Most Outstanding Science Book in the Physical Sciences Award 1990, Boston Globe Winship Book Prize 1993, American Inst. of Physics Andrew Gemant Award 1996, Nat. Public Radio Book of the Month 1998, Distinguished Alumnus Award Calif. Inst. of Tech. 2003. *Publications:* fiction: Einstein's Dreams 1993, Good Benito 1994, The Diagnosis 2000, Reunion 2003; non-fiction: Problem Book in Relativity and Gravitation 1974, Radiative Process in Astrophysics (with George B. Rybicki) 1976, Time Travel and Papa Joe's Pipe 1984, A Modern Day Yankee in a Connecticut Court and Other Essays on Science 1986, Origins: The Lives and Worlds of Modern Cosmologists (with Roberta Brawer) 1990, Ancient Light: Our Changing View of the Universe (adapted from Origins) 1991, Great Ideas in Physics 1992, Time for the Stars: Astronomy in the 1990s 1992, The World is Too Much with Me: Finding Private Space in the Wired World 1992, Dance for Two: Selected Essays 1996, A Sense of the Mysterious: Science and the Human Spirit 2005; editor: Revealing the Universe: Prediction and Proof in Astronomy (with James Cornell) 1982, The Best American Essays 2000; contrib. to professional journals and literary magazines. *Address:* Massachusetts Institute of Technology, Room 14E-303, 77 Massachusetts Avenue, Cambridge, MA 02139, USA (office). *Telephone:* (617) 253-2308 (office). *Website:* web.mit.edu/humanistic/www/faculty/lightman.html (office).

LIGI, Jürgen, BA, MBA; Estonian economist and politician; b. 16 July 1959, Tartu; m.; two s.; ed Tartu Secondary School, Univ. of Tartu, Estonian Business School; Economist, Estonian SSR Planning Inst. 1982–89; Chief Specialist, Saaremaa Agro-Industrial Asscn 1989–90; Head, Saaremaa Dept, Chamber of Commerce and Industry 1990–91; consultant on entrepreneurial activities 1991–92; Econ. Adviser, Kaarma Rural Municipal Govt 1992–93; Head of Br. Office, EVEA Bank, Kuressaare 1993–95; joined Reform Party 1994; elected MP for Harju and Rapla Dist 1995–2005; Minister of Defence 2005–07; Chair. Compensation Fund Supervisory Bd; mem. Estonian Athletic

Asscn; Trustee Tallinn Tech. Univ. *Publications:* articles in newspapers. *Address:* c/o Ministry of Defence, Sakala 1, Tallinn 15094, Estonia (office).

LIGRESTI, Giulia Maria; Italian business executive; *Chairman and CEO, Premafin Finanziaria SpA;* Chair. and CEO Premafin Finanziaria SpA 2002–, Chair. and Man. Dir Premafin Finanziaria Holding di Partecipazioni SpA; Deputy Chair. Fondiaria SAI SpA, mem. Bd of Dirs several subidiary cos; Chair. Gilli Srl, Fondazione FON-SAI; Man. Dir SAI Holding Italia SpA; mem. Bd of Dirs Finadin SpA, Milano Assicurazioni SpA, Sailux SA, Sainternational SA, Saifin SpA, Filarmonica della Scala, Helm Finance SGR SpA, ATA Hotels SpA, Istituto Europeo di Oncologia Srl. *Address:* Premafin Finanziaria SpA, Via Daniele Manin 37, Milan 20121, Italy (office). *Telephone:* (02) 667041 (office). *E-mail:* info@primafin.it (office). *Website:* www.premafin.it (office).

LIGRESTI, Jonella, BEcons; Italian insurance industry executive; *Chairwoman, Fondiaria-SAI SpA;* b. 23 March 1967, Milan; d. of Salvatore Ligresti; m. Omar Bonomelli; two c.; ed Bocconi Univ. of Milan; joined Bd of Società Assicuratrice Industriale SpA 1995, later Deputy Chair., Chair. 2001–02, Chair. Fondiaria-SAI SpA (following merger with La Fondiaria SpA 2002) 2002–; Chair. Jena Presbourg SA, Nuova Maa Assicurazioni SpA, Sim Etoile SA, Sinergia Terza SpA; Vice-Chair. Athotels SpA, Premafin Finanziaria SpA Hdp 1997–2001 (Chair. of its SAI unit 2001–); mem. Bd Mediobanca SpA 2007–; strategic consultant to Salvatore Ligresti, Finadin SpA, ItalResidence SpA, Sim Defense SA. *Leisure interests:* dachshunds, horse-riding (Italian Amazon Champion 2001), Japanese cuisine, water-skiing, sailing, surfing. *Address:* Fondiaria-SAI SpA, Piazza della Libertà, 6, 50129 Florence, Italy (office). *Telephone:* (055) 47941 (office). *Fax:* (055) 476026 (office). *E-mail:* fondiaria-sai@fondiaria-sai.it (office). *Website:* www.fondiaria-sai.it (office).

LIIKANEN, Erkki Antero, MPolSc; Finnish politician and central banker; *Governor, Bank of Finland;* b. 19 Sept. 1950, Mikkeli; m. Hanna-Liisa Issakainen 1971; ed Univ. of Helsinki; mem. Parl. 1972–; Minister of Finance 1987–90; mem. Social Democratic Party (SDP) Cttee 1978–, Gen. Sec. 1981–87; Amb. to EU 1990–95; EC Commr for Budget, Personnel and Admin 1995–99, for Industry and Information (subsequently Enterprise, Competitiveness, Innovation and the Information Society) 1999–2004; Gov. Bank of Finland 2004–, also mem. Governing Council, European Cen. Bank 2004, IMF Gov. for Finland 2004–; Hon. DSc (Tech.) (Univ. of Tech.). *Address:* Bank of Finland, Snellmaninaukio, PO Box 160, 00101 Helsinki, Finland (office). *Telephone:* (10) 8312001 (office). *Fax:* (10) 8312022 (office). *E-mail:* erkki.liikanen@bof.fi (office). *Website:* www.bof.fi (office).

LIKENS, Gene Elden, PhD; American ecologist, academic and research institute director; *Distinguished Senior Scientist, Ecologist, Founding Director and President Emeritus, Institute of Ecosystem Studies;* b. 6 Jan. 1935; ed Univ. of Wisconsin, Madison; joined faculty of Dartmouth Coll. 1961; Co-founder Hubbard Brook Ecosystem Study at Hubbard Brook Experimental Forest, White Mountains of NH; Founder Inst. of Ecosystem Studies, Millbrook, NY (part of New York Botanical Garden) 1983, inst. became ind. 1993, Dir and Pres. 1993–2007, Distinguished Sr Scientist, Ecologist, Founding Dir and Pres. Emer. 2007–; held faculty positions at Yale, Cornell, Rutgers Univs, State Univ. of NY, Albany and Univ. of Connecticut; fmr Pres. Int. Soc. of Theoretical and Applied Limnology, American Inst. of Biological Sciences, Ecological Soc. of America, American Soc. of Limnology and Oceanography; mem. American Acad. of Arts and Sciences 1979, NAS 1981, American Philosophical Soc. 2006; Foreign mem. Royal Swedish Acad. of Sciences 1988, Royal Danish Acad. of Sciences and Letters 1994, Austrian Acad. of Sciences 2000; Flagship Fellowship in Water for a Healthy Country Flagship, CSIRO, Australia 2007–08; Hon. mem. British Ecological Soc.; nine hon. doctorate degrees; Guggenheim Fellowship 1972, Tyler Prize, The World Prize for Environmental Achievement (with F. H. Bormann) 1993, Australia Prize for Science and Tech. 1994, Naumann-Thienemann Medal, Societas Internationalis Limnologiae 1995, Eminent Ecologist Award, Ecological Soc. of America 1995, Nat. Medal of Science 2001, Blue Planet Prize (with F. H. Bormann) ("Nobel Prize of Ecology"), Asahi Glass Foundation 2003, Miegunyah Fellowship, Melbourne, Australia 2004. *Achievements include:* best known for his discovery of acid rain in N America. *Publications:* author, co-author or ed. 17 books, including Pattern and Process in a Forested Ecosystem (co-author) 1979, Limnological Analyses (co-author) 1979, Biogeochemistry of a Forested Ecosystem (co-author) 1995, The Ecosystem Approach: Its Use and Abuse. Excellence in Ecology, Vol. 3 1992, Dynamics of Lake, Watershed and Atmospheric Linkages (co-ed.) 2008; more than 490 scientific papers in professional journals. *Address:* Cary Institute of Ecosystem Studies, PO Box AB, Millbrook, NY 12545-0129, USA (office). *Telephone:* (845) 677-5343 (office). *Fax:* (845) 677-5976 (office). *E-mail:* likensg@ecostudies.org (office). *Website:* www.ecostudies.org (office).

LIKHACHEV, Vasily Nikolayevich, DJur; Russian politician and diplomatist; *Representative of the Legislature of the Republic of Ingushetiya in the Federation Council;* b. 5 Jan. 1952, Gorky; s. of Nina F. Likhacheva; m. Nailya Imatovna Taktasheva; two d.; ed Kazan State Univ.; Asst, then Docent Chair of State Law, Kazan State Univ. 1978–82, 1983–87; teacher, Nat. School of Law Guinea-Bissau 1982–83; Prof., Univ. of Madagascar 1987–88; Head, Div. of State Law Tatar Regional CPSU Cttee 1988–90; Chair. Cttee of Constitutional Control Tatar SSR 1990–91; elected Vice-Pres. Repub. of Tatarstan 1991–95, Chair. State Council of Tatarstan 1995–; Deputy Chair. Council of Fed. of Russian Parl. 1996–98; Amb. and Perm. Rep. of Russian Fed. to EU 1998–2003; Rep. of Legislature of Repub. of Ingushetiya in the Fed. Council 2004–; Deputy Chair. Int. Affairs Cttee, Fed. Council. *Publications:* nine books; more than 400 articles on questions of int. and state law. *Leisure interests:* music, art, sailing. *Address:* Federation Council, ul. B.Dmitrovka 26, 103426 Moscow (office); ul. Akademika Zelinskogo 6–10, 119334 Moscow, Russia (home). *Telephone:* (495) 986-60-36 (office); (495) 692-13-42 (office);

(495) 135-74-93 (home). *E-mail:* VNLikhachev@council.gov.ru (office). *Website:* www.council.gov.ru (office).

LILIĆ, Zoran; Serbian politician; *Vice-President, Socialist Party of Serbia;* b. 27 Aug. 1953, Brza Palanka, Serbia; s. of Sokol Lilić and Dobrila Lilić; m. Ljubica Brković-Lilić 1980; one s.; ed Belgrade Univ.; several posts as grad. engineer, then man., with state-owned Rekord enterprise, Belgrade; fmr Pres. Exec. Bd Yugoslav Tyre Makers Business Asscn, mem. Presidency of Belgrade Chamber of Economy, Pres. Man. Bd of Belgrade Airport, mem. Council of Faculty of Tech.; mem. Serbian League of Communists, subsequently Socialist Party of Serbia (SPS); Deputy to Nat. Ass. of Repub. of Serbia 1990, Chair. Cttee on Industry, Energy, Mining and Construction, Chief of Group of SPS Deputies; re-elected Deputy and also Pres. of Nat. Ass. 1992; Pres. of Fed. Repub. of Yugoslavia 1993–97; Vice-Prime Minister of Yugoslavia 1997–2000; Vice-Pres. Socialist Party of Serbia (SPS) 1995–; testified against successor Slobodan Milosevic at Int. Criminal Tribunal for Fmr Yugoslavia, The Hague, Netherlands July 2002. *Leisure interests:* fishing, football, chess. *Address:* Socijalistička partija Srbije, bul. Lenjina 6, 11000 Belgrade, Serbia (office). *Telephone:* (11) 634291 (office). *Fax:* (11) 628642 (office). *Website:* www.sps.org .yu (office).

LILIUS, Mikael, BBA; Finnish business executive; *President and CEO, Fortum;* b. 1949, Helsinki; m.; three c.; ed Helsinki School of Econs; Marketing Dir Huhtamäki Oy Polarpak, Helsinki 1981–84, Pres. 1984–85, Pres. Packing Div. 1985–89; Pres. and CEO KF Industri AB (Nordico), Stockholm 1989–90; Pres. and CEO Incentive AB, Stockholm 1990–98; Pres. and CEO Gambro AB (medical supply co.), Stockholm 1998–2000; Pres. and CEO Fortum (Finnish state-owned energy co.), Espoo 2000–; Dir Gambro AB, Sweden-Japan Foundation, Huhtamäki Van Leer Oyj, Instrumentarium Oy, Perlos Oy, A. Ahlstrom Corpn; mem. EQT Advisory Bd. *Address:* Fortum Corporation, Keilaniemi, 00048 Espoo, Finland (office). *Telephone:* (358) 10-45-11 (office). *Fax:* (358) 10-45-24447 (office). *E-mail:* communications@fortum.com (office). *Website:* www.fortum.com (office).

LILL, John Richard, CBE, FRCM, FLCM, FTCM; British pianist; b. 17 March 1944, London; s. of George Lill and the late Margery (née Young) Lill; m. Jacqueline Clifton Smith; ed Leyton County High School and Royal Coll. of Music; London debut at Royal Festival Hall 1963; plays regularly in European capitals, the USA and the Far East, as recitalist and as soloist with most prin. orchestras; recognized as leading interpreter of Beethoven; Prof., Royal Coll. of Music; Hon. DSc (Univ. of Aston), Hon. DMus (Exeter Univ.);Hon. FTCL, FLCM; first prize Royal Overseas League Competition 1963, first prize Int. Tchaikovsky Competition, Moscow 1970, Dinu Lipatti Medal, Chappel Gold Medal. *Recordings include:* complete Beethoven piano sonatas, concertos and bagatelles, complete piano works of Rachmaninov (with BBC Nat. Orchestra of Wales/Otaka), Brahms piano concertos, Tchaikovsky Piano Concerto No. 1 (with London Symphony Orchestra), complete Prokofiev sonatas 1991. *Leisure interests:* chess, amateur radio, walking. *Address:* c/o Askonas Holt Ltd, Lincoln House, 300 High Holborn, London, WC1V 7JH, England (office). *Telephone:* (20) 7400-1700 (office). *Fax:* (20) 7400-1799 (office). *E-mail:* info@askonasholt.co.uk (office). *Website:* www.askonasholt.co.uk (office).

LILLEE, Dennis Keith, MBE; Australian fmr professional cricketer; b. 18 July 1949, Perth; s. of K. Lillee; m. Helen Lillee 1970; two s.; ed Belmay State School, Belmont High School; right-arm fast bowler, lower-order right-hand batsman; played for WA 1969–84, Tasmania 1987–88, Northants 1988; 70 Tests for Australia 1970–84, taking then world record 355 wickets (average 23.9), including record 167 wickets in 29 Tests against England; toured England 1972, 1975, 1980, 1981, 1983 (World Cup), took 882 first-class wickets (average 23.5); Coach Western Australian Cricket Asscn 2000; coaching fast bowlers, MRF Pace Foundation, Chennai, India 2001, Dennis Lillee Fast Bowling Acad. (est. June 2002) 2002–; continued playing cricket, bowling for the Australian Cricket Bd Chair.'s XI –2000; Wisden Cricketer of the Year 1973, named mem. of Australia's Team of the Century. *Publications:* Back to the Mark 1974, The Art of Fast Bowling 1977, Dennis Lillee's Book of Family Fitness 1980, My Life in Cricket 1982, Over and Out 1984. *Leisure Interests:* music, philately. *Address:* c/o Swan Sport, P.O. Box 158, Byron Bay, NSW 2481, Australia.

LILLEY, James Roderick, BA, MA; American diplomat, scholar and intelligence officer; b. 15 Jan. 1928, Tsingtao, China; s. of late Frank W Lilley and Inez Bush; m. Sally Booth 1954; three s.; ed Phillips Exeter Acad., Yale Univ. and George Washington Univ.; Adjunct Prof., School of Advanced Int. Studies, Johns Hopkins Univ. 1978–80; Consultant, Hunt Oil, Dallas, Tex. 1979–81; East Asian Dir Nat. Security Council, White House, Washington, DC Jan.–Nov. 1981; Dir American Inst. in Taiwan, Taipei 1982–84; Consultant, Otis Elevator Co., Farmington, Conn. 1984–85; Deputy Asst Sec. of State, East Asian and Pacific Affairs, Dept of State 1985–86; Amb. to Republic of Korea 1986–89, to People's Repub. of China 1989–91; Asst Sec., US Defense Dept 1991–93; Sr Fellow, American Enterprise Inst., Washington 1993–2006; Distinguished Intelligence Medal, Kang Hwa Medal, Rep. of Korea. *Publications:* Beyond MFN 1994, Chinese Military Modernization 1996, Crisis in the Taiwan Strait 1997, China's Military Faces the Future 1999, China Hands 2004. *Leisure interests:* swimming, bicycling, reading history. *Address:* 2801 New Mexico Avenue, NW, Apt 407, Washington, DC 20815, USA (home). *Telephone:* (301) 337-0534 (home). *Fax:* (301) 337-5980 (home). *E-mail:* jlilley@aei.org (office).

LILLEY, Rt Hon. Peter Bruce, PC, MA; British politician; b. 23 Aug. 1943, Kent; s. of S. Arnold Lilley and Lilian Lilley (née Elliott); m. Gail Ansell 1979; ed Dulwich Coll., Clare Coll., Cambridge; Chair. Bow Group 1973; MP for St Albans 1983–97, for Hitchin and Harpenden 1997–; Econ. Sec. to Treasury 1987–89, Financial Sec. 1989–90; Sec. of State for Trade and Industry

1990–92, for Social Security 1992–97; Opposition Front Bench Spokesman for Treasury 1997–98; Deputy Leader of the Opposition 1998–99; fmr Dir Greenwell Montagu (Oil Analyst); Dir (non-exec.) JP Morgan Fleming Claverhouse Investment 1997–, IDOX PLC 2002–, Melchior Japan Investment Trust 2006–, Tethys Petroleum Ltd 2006–. *Publications:* The Delusion of Incomes Policy (with Samuel Brittan) 1977, The End of the Keynesian Era 1980, Thatcherism: The Next Generation 1990, Winning the Welfare Debate 1996, Patient Power 2000, Common Sense on Cannabis 2001, Taking Liberties 2002, Save Our Pensions 2003, The Case Against ID Cards 2004, Too Much of a Good Thing? 2005, All in it Together (Report of Global Poverty Group) 2007. *Leisure interest:* France (and most things French). *Address:* House of Commons, Westminster, London, SW1A 0AA, England (office). *Website:* www.peterlilley.co.uk (office).

LILLIKAS, Yiorgos, MA; Cypriot politician; b. 1 June 1960, Pafos; m. Barbara Petropoulou; one s.; ed Inst. of Political Science, Lyon, France, Inst. of Political Science, Grenoble, Switzerland; mem. Historic Politology Research Team, Nat. Scientific Research Centre of France 1985–87; Special Advisor to Pres. of Repub. of Cyprus 1988–90; Gen.-Sec. Secr. for the New Generation 1990–93; Man. Dir of public relations, strategic marketing and advertising co. 1993–96; mem. House of Reps from Nicosia electoral district 1996–; Minister of Commerce, Industry and Tourism 2003–06, of Foreign Affairs 2006–07; fmr mem. Parl. Cttees on Finance, Foreign and European Affairs, Educ., Trade, fmr Chair. Environment Cttee; fmr Head, Del. to Parl. Ass. of OSCE; Vice-Pres., OSCE Political Affairs and Security Cttee Jan.-June 2006; mem. AKEL party (Progressive Party of the Working People); active in asscns and orgs involved in the anti-drug movement and social integration of children with special needs. *Address:* AKEL Progressive Party of the Working People (Anorthotiko Komma Ergazomenou Laou), POB 21827, 4 E. Papaioannou Street, 1513 Nicosia, Cyprus (office). *Telephone:* 22761121 (office). *Fax:* 22761574 (office). *E-mail:* k.e.akel@cytanet.com.cy (office). *Website:* www .akel.org.cy (office).

LILOV, Alexander Vassilev, PhD; Bulgarian politician and scientist; b. 31 Aug. 1933, Granichak, Vidin; s. of Vassil Lilov and Kamenka Petrovski; m. Anna Lilova 1962; one s. two d.; ed Sofia Univ.; leading mem. Young Communist League 1951–63; Deputy Head Propaganda Dept, Head Arts and Culture Dept, Bulgarian CP (BCP) Cen. Cttee; mem. BCP Cen. Cttee 1971–, Sec. 1972–83, 1989–, mem. Politburo 1974–83, 1989–; Dir Inst. for Contemporary Sciences 1983–90; Chair. Higher Council Bulgarian Socialist Party 1990–91, mem. 1991–; Dir Inst. for Strategic Investigations 1991–; fmr mem. State Council; mem. Nat. Ass. 1990–; Corresp. mem. Bulgarian Acad. of Sciences. *Publications:* The Nature of Works of Art 1979, Imagination and Creative Work 1986, Europe: To Be or Not to Be 1988 (co-author), Europe: Dialogue and Co-operation 1989. *Leisure interests:* art, skiing. *Address:* Higher Council of the Bulgarian Socialist Party, PO Box 382, 20 Positano Street, Sofia (office); 12 Veliko Tirnovo Str., 1504 Sofia, Bulgaria (home). *Telephone:* 87-34-64 (office); 44-60-33 (home).

LIM, Chwen Jeng, AA Dip; British architect and academic; *Director, Studio 8 Architects;* b. 1964, Ipoh, Malaysia; s. of Kar Sun Lim and Yoke Kheng Leong; ed St Michael's Inst., Ipoh, Malaysia, Ashville Coll., Harrogate, Architectural Asscn School of Architecture, London; Prof. of Architecture and Cultural Design, Bartlett School of Architecture, Univ. Coll. London (UCL) 1993–, UCL Pro-Provost of N America 2008–, Dir Bartlett Architecture Research Lab. 1999–; Sr Lecturer Univ. of E London 1990–93, Univ. of N London 1991–99; Dir Studio 8 Architects, London 1994–; Visiting Prof. Curtin Univ., Perth, Australia 1996, Stadelschule, Frankfurt 1997–98, 2000–01, Technological Univ., Lund, Sweden 2001, MacKintosh School of Architecture, Glasgow 2001–, School of Architecture, Århus, Denmark 2002, Chiba Inst. of Tech., Japan 2004; RIBA External Examiner 2000–; numerous exhbns Europe, Japan, Canada, USA, Australia; RIBA Pres.'s Medals for Academic Contrib. in Architecture 1997, 1998, 1999; several prizes for architectural research projects including First Prize Bldg Centre Trust Competition 'Housing: a demonstration project' 1987, UCL Cultural Centre Int. Competition 1996, Cen. Glass Int. Competition Japan: Glasshouse 2001, 2nd Prize Japanese/NCE Competition: an image of the bridge of the future 1987, Concept House 2000 (Int.) Ideal Home Exhbn 1999, Tangshan Earthquake Memorial Landscape China 2007, NanYu Shopping Park China 2008. *Achievements:* represented UK at the Venice Biennale 2004. *Publications:* 441/10... We'll Reconfigure the Space When You're Ready 1996, Sins + Other Spatial Relatives 2000, Realms of Impossibility: Water 2002, Realms of Impossibility: Ground 2002, Realms of Impossibility: Air 2002, How Green is Your Garden? 2003, Museums (Work in Process) 2004, Devices 2005, Neoarchitecture 2005, Virtually Venice 2006, New Trend of Architecture in Europe Asia-Pacific 2008-2010. *Address:* Studio 8 Architects, 95 Greencroft Gardens, London, NW6 3PG, England (office). *Telephone:* (20) 7679-4842 (office). *E-mail:* mail@cjlim-studio8.com (office). *Website:* www.cjlim-studio8.com (office).

LIM, Dong-won; South Korean politician and diplomatist; *Chairman, Sejong Foundation;* b. 25 July 1934; ed Korea Mil. Acad., Seoul Nat. Univ.; Asst Prof. Korean Mil. Acad. 1964–69; with Armed Forces, attained rank of Maj.-Gen. 1980, now retd; apptd Amb. to Nigeria 1981, to Australia 1984; Chancellor Inst. of Foreign Affairs and Nat. Security, Ministry of Foreign Affairs 1988–92; Chair. Presidential Comm. on Arms Control 1990; Del. South–North High-Level Talks 1990–92; apptd Chair. Asscn for Nat. Unification of Korea 1993; mem. Unification Policy Evaluation Cttee 1993; Sec.-Gen. Kim Dae Jung Peace Foundation for the Asia-Pacific 1995; Sr Sec. for Nat. Security and Foreign Affairs, Pres. Sec. 1998; Minister for Unification (involved in reconciliatory Sunshine Policy towards North Korea) 1999–2001; Dir-Gen. Nat. Intelligence Service 1999–2001; Special Envoy to North Korea April 2002; fmr staff mem. Sejong Inst., Chair. Sejong Foundation 2004–. *Address:*

c/o Sejong Institute, Shihung-dong 230, Sujeong-gu, Seongnam-shi, Kyonggi-do, Seoul 461-370, Republic of Korea (office). *E-mail:* public@sejong.org (office). *Website:* www.sejong.org/foundation/eng/main01.htm (office).

LIM, Hng Kiang, BSc, MPA; Singaporean government official; *Minister of Trade and Industry;* b. 9 April 1954; m. Lee Ai Boon; two s.; ed Raffles Inst., Univ. of Cambridge, UK, Kennedy School, Harvard Univ., USA; with Singapore Armed Forces 1976–85, Ministry of Defence 1986; Deputy Sec. Ministry of Nat. Devt 1987; CEO Housing and Devt Bd 1991; mem. Parl. 1991–; Minister of State for Nat. Devt 1991–94, Acting Minister for Nat. Devt and Sr Minister of State for Foreign Affairs 1994–95, Minister for Nat. Devt 1995–99, Second Minister for Foreign Affairs 1995–98, Second Minister for Finance 1998–2004, Minister of Health 1999–2003, Minister, Prime Minister's Office 2003–04, Minister of Trade and Industry 2004–, also Deputy Chair. Monetary Authority of Singapore; mem. Bd of Dirs Govt of Singapore Investment Corpn. *Leisure interests:* swimming, golf. *Address:* Ministry of Trade and Industry, 100 High Street, 09-01 The Treasury, 179434 Singapore (office). *Telephone:* 62259911 (office). *Fax:* 63327260 (office). *E-mail:* mti_email@mti.gov.sg (office). *Website:* www.mti.gov.sg (office).

LIM, Datuk Seri Keng Yaik, MB, BCh; Malaysian politician; *Party Adviser, Parti Gerakan Rakyat Malaysia Barisan Nasional;* b. 8 April 1939, Tapah, Perak; m. Wong Yoon Chuan; three c.; ed Queen's Univ., Belfast; Senator 1972–78; Minister with Special Functions 1972–73, of Primary Industries 1986–2004, of Energy, Water and Communications 2004–07; mem. State Exec. Council, Perak 1978–86; mem. Parl. 1986–; Co-founder and Pres. Gerakan 1980–2007, Party Adviser 2007–. *Address:* Parti Gerakan Rakyat MalaysiaBarisan Nasional, Tingkat 5, Menara PGRM, 8 Jalan Pudu Ulu, Cheras, 56100 Kuala Lumpur, Malaysia. *Telephone:* (3) 22747511 (office). *Fax:* (3) 22745014 (office). *E-mail:* gerakan@gerakan.org.my (office). *Website:* www .gerakan.org.my (office).

LIM, Pin, MA, MD, FRCP, FRCPE, FRACP, FACP; Singaporean medical scientist, endocrinologist and academic; *Professor of Medicine and Senior Consultant Endocrinologist, National University Hospital, Singapore;* b. 12 Jan. 1936, Penang, Malaysia; m. Shirley Loo Ngai Seong 1964; two s. one d.; ed Raffles Inst., Singapore and Cambridge Univ.; Registrar, King's Coll. Hosp., London 1965; Medical Officer, Ministry of Health, Singapore 1965–66; Lecturer in Medicine, Nat. Univ. of Singapore 1966–70; Sr Lecturer 1971–73, Assoc. Prof. of Medicine 1974–77, Prof. and Head of Dept 1978–81, Deputy Vice-Chancellor 1979–81, Vice-Chancellor 1981–2000; Prof. of Medicine Nat. Univ. of Singapore 2000–, Prof. of Medicine and Sr Consultant Endocrinologist, Nat. Univ. Hosp. 2000–; Commonwealth Medical Fellow, The Royal Infirmary, Edin. 1970; Chair. Nat. Wages Council, Bio-ethics Advisory Cttee, Tropical Marine Science Inst., Nat. Longevity Insurance Cttee 2007–, Singapore-MIT Alliance for Research & Tech. 2007–, Special Needs Trust Co. 2008–, Singapore Millennium Foundation Ltd 2008–; Dir United Overseas Bank; mem. Chinese Heritage Council 1995–; Patron Mensa Singapore, Eisenhower Fellow 1982, Dir Raffles Medical Group; Hon. Fellow, Coll. of General Practitioners, Singapore 1982, Royal Australian Coll. of Obstetricians and Gynaecologists 1992, Royal Coll. of Physicians and Surgeons of Glasgow 1997, Royal Coll. of Surgeons of Edin. 1997, Int. Coll. of Dentists, USA 1999 (Dental Surgery), Royal Coll. of Surgeons of Edin. 1999; Officier, Ordre des Palmes académiques 1988, Singapore Distinguished Service Order 2000; Hon. DSc (Univ. of Hull) 1999; Rep. of Singapore Public Admin. Medal (Gold) 1984, Meritorious Service Medal 1990, Friend of Labour Award, NTUC 1995, Gordon Arthur Ransome Orator 2000, Lee Foundation–NHG Lifetime Achievement Award 2002, Nat. Univ. of Singapore Outstanding Service Award 2003. *Publications:* numerous articles in medical journals. *Leisure Interest:* swimming. *Address:* Department of Medicine, National University of Singapore/National University Hospital, 5 Lower Kent Ridge Road, 119074 Singapore (office). *Telephone:* 67724976 (office). *Fax:* 67735627 (office). *Website:* www.nus.edu.sg (office).

LIMA, Cassio Casseb, BE; Brazilian banking executive; b. 8 Aug. 1955; m.; two c.; ed Univ. of São Paulo; began career with Leading and Credit Dept, Bank Boston 1976–79; Account Officer, Chief Financial Officer then Commercial Officer NW Region, Banco Francês & Brasileiro (Credit Lyonnaise) 1979–88; Chief Financial Officer then Exec. Vice-Pres. Banco Mantrust SRL 1988–92; Coordinator Industrial Restructuring Vila Romana Group 1992–93; Vice-Pres. Finance (Treasurer) Citibank 1993–97; Pres. Credicard SA 1997–99; apptd Head Industrial Strategy Vichuna Textil, Fibra Dupont, Fibrasil, Companhia Siderúrgica Nacional, Vale do Rio Doce, Maxitel, Banco Fibra 1999; Pres. Banco do Brasil 2003–05; mem. Bd Nat. Asscn Open Market Insts. (ANDIMA), Brazilian Banking Science Inst. (IBCB) 1993–97; mem. Bd Dirs Vicunha, Banco Fibra, Solpart 1999; Man. Inst. Reciclar; mem. Superior Econ. Council, Fed. of Industry for São Paulo (FIESP) 2006–. *Address:* c/o FIESP, Avenida Paulista, 1313, 01311-923 São Paulo, Brazil (office).

LIMONOV, Eduard; Russian/French writer and poet; b. (Eduard Veniaminovich Savenko), 22 Feb. 1943, Dzerzhinsk, Gorky Dist (now Nizhny Novgorod); m. 1st Yelena Limonova Shchapova 1971 (divorced); m. 2nd Natalia Medvedeva (divorced); m. 6th Ekaterina Volkova 2006; one s.; first wrote poetry at age of 15; in Kharkov 1965–67, moved to Moscow in 1967, worked as a tailor; left USSR 1974; settled in New York, USA 1975; moved to Paris, France 1982; participant in Russian nationalist movt 1990–; returned to Russia 1991; Chair. Nat. Radical Party 1992–93; Chair. Nat. Bolshevik Party 1994–; arrested on terrorism and conspiracy charges 2001, sentenced by Saratov Oblast Court to four years' imprisonment for illegal acquisition and possession of arms April 2003, released June 2003; f. Russia without Putin movt Jan. 2004. *Publications include:* verse and prose in Kontinent, Ekho, Kovcheg, Apollon –1977 (in trans. in England, USA, Austria and Switzerland); over 40 books including It's Me – Eddie (novel) 1979, Russian (Russkoye) (verse) 1979, Diary of a Failure 1982, Teenager Savenko: Memoir of a Russian Punk 1983, The Young Scoundrel (memoir) 1986, The Death of Contemporary Heroes 1993, The Murder of the Sentry 1993, Selected Works (3 vols) 1999, The Exile (with Mark Ames and Matt Taibbi) 2000, My Political Biography; articles in Russian Communist and Nationalist newspapers 1989–. *E-mail:* nbpinfo@gmail.com (office). *Website:* www.nbp-info.com (office).

LIN, Chia-Chiao, MA, PhD, LLD; American mathematician and academic; *Institute Professor and Professor Emeritus of Applied Mathematics, Massachusetts Institute of Technology;* b. 7 July 1916, Fukien, China; s. of Kai and Y. T. Lin; m. Shou-Ying Liang 1946; one d.; ed Nat. Tsing Hua Univ., Univ. of Toronto, Calif. Inst. of Technology; Asst Prof. of Applied Math., Brown Univ. 1945–46, Assoc. Prof. 1946–47; Assoc. Prof. of Math., MIT 1947–53, Prof. 1953–66, Inst. Prof. of Applied Math., 1966–87, Prof. Emer. of Applied Math. 1987–; Guggenheim Fellow 1954–55, 1960; Pres. Soc. for Industrial and Applied Math. 1973; mem. NAS; John von Neumann Lecturer, Soc. for Industrial and Applied Math. 1967. *Publications:* The Theory of Hydrodynamic Stability 1955, Turbulent Flow, Theoretical Aspects 1963. *Leisure interest:* astronomy. *Address:* Department of Mathematics, Room 2-330, Massachusetts Institute of Technology, Cambridge, MA 02139, USA (office). *Telephone:* (617) 253-1796 (office). *E-mail:* cclin@math.mit.edu (office). *Website:* www-math.mit.edu (office).

LIN, Chin-Sheng, BL; Taiwanese government official; b. 4 Aug. 1916; ed Law Coll., Tokyo Imperial Univ.; Magistrate, Chiayi Co. Govt 1951–54; Chair. Yunlin Co. HQ, Kuomintang (Nationalist Party of China) 1954–57; Magistrate, Yunlin Co. Govt 1957–64; Dir Cheng-Ching Lake Industrial Waterworks 1964–67; Commr Taiwan Prov. Govt 1966–70; Sec.-Gen. Taiwan Provincial HQ, Kuomintang 1967–68, Chair. Taipei Municipal HQ 1969–70, Deputy Sec.-Gen. Cen. Cttee 1970–72, mem. Standing Cttee of Cen. Cttee 1976–; Minister of the Interior 1972–76, of Communications 1976–81, without Portfolio 1981–84; Vice-Pres. Examination Yuan 1984–93; Sr Adviser to Pres. of Taiwan 1993; mem. Standing Cttee of Kuomintang Cen. Cttee 1976–; Order of the Brilliant Star. *Address:* c/o Kuomintang, 11 Chung Shan South Road, Taipei 100, Taiwan.

LIN, Cho-Liang, BMus; American violinist; b. 29 Jan. 1960, Taiwan; s. of Kuo-Jing Lin and Kuo-Ling Yu; m. Deborah Lin; ed Juilliard School, New York, Sydney Conservatoire; concert tours worldwide; over 100 performances a year; soloist with leading orchestras including London Symphony Orchestra, Philharmonia, Concertgebouw, Orchestre de Paris, Chicago Symphony Orchestra, Philadelphia Orchestra and Boston Symphony Orchestra; played Tchaikovsky's Concerto at London Proms 1999; 20 solo albums; Founder, Dir Taipei Int. Music Festival; mem. Faculty Juilliard School 1991–; Gramophone Record Award 1989, Musical American's Instrumentalist of the Year 2000. *Leisure interests:* tennis, wine. *Address:* Opus 3 Artists, 470 Park Avenue South, 9th Floor North, New York, NY 10016, USA (office). *Telephone:* (212) 584-7500 (office). *Fax:* (646) 300-8200 (office). *E-mail:* info@opus3artists.com (office). *Website:* www.opus3artists.com (office).

LIN, Chuan, PhD; Taiwanese politician; b. 13 Dec. 1951; m.; two d.; ed Fu Jen Catholic Univ., Nat. Chengchi Univ., Univ. of Ill., USA; Assoc. Research Fellow, Chung Hua Inst. for Econ. Research 1994–89; Assoc. Prof., Dept of Public Finance, Nat. Chengchi Univ. 1989–90, Prof. 1990–95, 1998–2000; Dir Bureau of Finance, Taipei City Govt 1995–98; Dir-Gen. Directorate-Gen. of Budget, Accounting and Statistics 2000–02; Minister of Finance 2002–05. *Address:* Ministry of Finance, 2 Ai Kuo West Road, Taipei, Taiwan (office).

LIN, Hsin-i, BSc; Taiwanese politician and business executive; b. 2 Dec. 1946; m.; three c.; ed Nat. Cheng Kung Univ.; engineer, China Motor Corpn, later Deputy Man. Eng Div. 1972–76, Deputy Man. Marketing Div. 1976–79, Man. Yangmei Plant 1980–82, Vice-Pres. 1982–87, Exec. Vice-Pres. 1987–90, Pres. 1991–96, Vice-Chair. 1997–2000; Chair. Sino Diamond Motors Ltd 1993–2000, Automotive Research and Testing Centre 1996–2000, Newa Insurance Co. Ltd 1999–2000; Minister of Econ. Affairs 2000–02; Vice-Premier and Chair. Council of Econ. Planning and Devt 2002–04 (resgnd). *Address:* c/o Council for Economic Planning and Development, 9th Floor, 87 Nanking East Road, Section 2, Taipei, Taiwan (office).

LIN, Lin; Chinese writer; b. 27 Sept. 1910, Zhao'an Co., Fujian Prov.; s. of the late Lin Hede and of Zhen Yilian; m. 1st Wu Lanjiao 1930 (deceased); m. 2nd Chen Ling 1950; two s. two d.; ed Zhao'an middle school, Chinese Univ., Beijing, Waseda Univ. Tokyo, Japan; joined Left-Wing Movt in Literature, 1934–36; returned to Shanghai 1936; Ed., Jiuwang Daily, Shanghai 1937, Guangzhou 1938, Guilin 1939–41; Chief Ed. of Huaqiao Guide, Manila, Philippines 1941–47; Prof., Dept of Chinese Literature, Dade Coll., Hong Kong 1947–49; Cultural Counsellor, Embassy, New Delhi, India 1955–58; Vice-Pres. of the China-Japan Friendship Asscn 1965–; Vice-Pres. Chinese People's Asscn for Friendship with Foreign Countries 1973–86; Pres. China Soc. for Study of Japanese Literature 1980–94, Hon. Pres. 1994–; mem. 5th, 6th and 7th Nat. Cttees CPPCC 1978–93; Hon. mem. Nat. Cttee, Chinese Writers' Asscn 2002–; Yakushi Inoue Cultural Exchange Award 1996. *Publications:* Poems of India 1958, Essays about Japan 1982, A Selection of Japanese Classical Haiku 1983, The Sea and the Ship (essays) 1987, A Selection of Japanese Modern Haiku 1990, Amaranthus (poems) 1991, Cutting Clouds (Chinese haiku) 1994, Continued Essays About Japan 1994, Memoirs of My First 88 Years 2002. *Address:* Room 402, Building 22, Congwenmen Dongdajie Street, Beijing 100062, People's Republic of China (home).

LIN, Liyun; Chinese state official; b. 1933, Taizhong, Taiwan; ed Minatogawa High School, Kyoga Prefecture, Japan, Beijing Univ.; teacher, Chinese School, Kobe, Japan 1952; Bureau Chief, CCP Cen. Cttee Int. Dept 1953–78; joined CCP 1963; council mem. Sino-Japanese Friendship Asscn 1973–; mem. Standing Cttee 4th NPC 1975–78, Standing Cttee 5th NPC 1978–83, Standing Cttee 6th NPC 1983–88 (mem. Presidium 6th NPC 1986–88, mem. Credentials Cttee NPC 1984–88), Standing Cttee 7th NPC 1988–93, Standing Cttee 8th NPC 1993–98; Deputy for Taiwan to 5th NPC 1978, 6th NPC 1983; Deputy Sec. CCP Langfang Prefectural Cttee, Hebei Prov. 1981; Vice-Chair. Exec. Cttee All-China Women's Fed. 1978 (mem. Secr. and Leading Party Group 1978); Vice-Chair. All-China Sports Asscn 1979; Pres. All-China Fed. of Taiwan Compatriots 1981–; mem. Overseas Chinese Affairs Cttee NPC 1988–98 (now Vice-Chair.); mem. Working Group for Unification of the Motherland 1984–; Vice-Pres. China Int. Cultural Exchange Centre 1984–; adviser Asscn for the Promotion of the Peaceful Reunification of China 1988–; Vice-Pres. All China Fed. of Returned Overseas Chinese 1994–; adviser, Asscn for Relations Across the Taiwan Straits; mem. 10th CCP Cen. Cttee 1972–77, 11th CCP Cen. Cttee 1977–82, 12th CCP Cen. Cttee 1982–87, 13th CCP Cen. Cttee 1987–92, 14th CCP Cen. Cttee 1992–97, 15th CCP Cen. Cttee 1997–2002. *Address:* Chinese Communist Party Central Committee, Beijing, People's Republic of China.

LIN, Maya, PhD; American architect and sculptor; b. 5 Oct. 1959, Athens, OH; d. of Prof. Henry H. Lin and Prof. Julia Lin (née Chang); m. Daniel Wolf; two c.; ed Yale Univ.; architectural designer, Pers Forbes & Assocs, New York 1986–87; pvt. practice, New York 1987–; mem. Batey & Mack, San Francisco 1983, Fumihiko Maki Assoc., Tokyo 1985; f. Maya Lin Studio, New York 1986; William A. Bernoudy Resident in Architcture, American Acad., Rome, Italy 1998–99; artwork rep. by Gagosian Gallery; mem. Bd Nat. Resources Defense Council; subject of Acad. Award-winning documentary Maya Lin: A Strong Clear Vision 1995; American Acad. of Arts and Letters Award in Architecture, Finn Juhl Architecture Award 2003. *Major projects include:* Vietnam Veterans' Memorial, Washington, DC 1982; Peace Chapel, Juniata Coll., Pennsylvania; Langston Hughes Library, Clinton, Tennessee; Civil Rights Memorial, Montgomery, AL 1989; The Women's Table, Yale Univ., CT 1993; Groundswell, Wexner Center for the Arts, Columbus, OH 1993, Museum for African Art, New York 1993, Eclipsed Time, Pennsylvania Station, New York 1994, The Wave Field, Univ. of Michigan Coll. of Eng, Ann Arbor 1995, Langston Hughes Library, Clinton, Tenn. 1999, Federal Courthouse, Manhattan, New York, Ecliptic, Grand Rapids, Mich. 2000, the character of a hill, under glass, American Express Financial Advisors, Minneapolis, Minn., Aveda HQ, Manhattan 2002. *Publications:* Maya Lin: Public/Private 1994, Boundaries 2000. *Address:* 52 East 78th Street, New York, NY 10075-1810, USA (office). *Website:* www.mayalin.com.

LIN, Rong-San; Taiwanese publisher and business executive; *Owner, Liberty Times;* b. 27 May 1939, Lujhou, Taipei; brother of Lin Yu-Lin; m.; four c.; began in business growing vegetables and selling rice, began developing property late 1960s; fmr Publr of Liberty Times (daily newspaper), Taipei Times (daily newspaper) 1999–; Founder Union Bank of Taiwan (still retains holding); fmr Taiwan legislator and nat. policy adviser to two past presidents; Founder and Chair. Lin Rong San Foundation of Culture and Social Welfare. *Address:* Liberty Times, 399 Rueiguang Road, Nei-Hu District, Taipei 11492, Taiwan (office). *Telephone:* (2) 26562828 (office). *Fax:* (2) 26561034 (office). *E-mail:* newstips@libertytimes.com.tw (office). *Website:* www.libertytimes.com.tw (office); www.taipeitimes.com.

LIN, Ruo; Chinese party official; b. 1924, Chaoan, Guangdong Prov.; ed Zhongshan Univ.; joined CCP 1945; First Deputy Sec. Zhanjiang Pref. 1966–, Deputy Dir Nanfang Daily 1971–, Sec. CCP Cttee Zhanjiang Pref. 1977–; Dir Nanfang Ribao 1980; Sec. CCP Cttee, Guangdong Prov. 1983–93; Chair. People's Congress of Guangdong Prov. 1990–96; mem. 12th CCP Cen. Cttee 1982–87, 13th CCP Cen. Cttee 1987–92; Del. 7th NPC 1988–92. *Address:* c/o Guangdong Provincial Chinese Communist Party, Guangzhou, Guangdong, People's Republic of China.

LIN, See-Yan, MA, MPA, PhD, CStat, FIB, FRSS, FIBM; Malaysian banker, financial consultant and university chancellor; *Pro-Chancellor, Universiti Sains Malaysia;* b. 3 Nov. 1939, Ipoh; ed Univ. of Malaya in Singapore, Harvard Univ., USA; Tutor in Econs, Univ. of Malaya 1961–63, Harvard Univ. 1970–72, 1976–77; Statistician, Dept of Statistics 1961–63; Econ. Adviser, Minister of Finance 1966–69; Dir Malaysian Rubber Exchange and Licensing Bd 1974–85; mem. Council on Malaysian Invisible Trade 1981–85, Econ. Panel of the Prime Minister 1982–87, Capital Issues Cttee 1985–86; Chief Economist, Bank Negara Malaysia (Cen. Bank of Malaysia) 1973–77, Econ. Adviser 1977–80, Deputy Gov. 1980–94; Chair., Pres. and CEO Pacific Bank Group 1994–98; Chair. Credit Guarantee Corpn Malaysia Berhad, Malaysian Insurance Inst.; Deputy Chair. Industrial Bank of Malaysia Berhad (Bank Industri); Dir Malaysia Export Credit Insurance Berhad, Govt Officers Housing Corpn, Seacen Research and Training Centre, Malaysian Wildlife Conservation Foundation; mem. Malaysia Program Advisory Council, US-ASIAN Centre for Tech. Exchange, Commonwealth Group of Experts on the Debt Crisis 1984, IMF Working Party on Statistical Discrepancy in World Currency Imbalances 1985–87, IMF Cttee of Balance of Payments Compilers 1987; Pres. Malaysian Econ. Asscn; mem. Nat. Econ. Action Council Working Group, Asian Financial Regulatory Shadow Committee, USA; Econ. Advisor, Associated Chinese Chambers of Commerce and Industry of Malaysia; Trustee Malaysia Univ. for Science and Tech.; mem. Bd Dirs Monash Univ. (Sunway Campus) Malaysia; Gov. Asian Inst. of Man., Manila; mem. bds several publicly listed and pvt. cos in Malaysia, Singapore and Indonesia; Chair. Harvard Grad. School Alumni Asscn Council, Harvard Univ., Regional Dir for Asia, Harvard Alumni Asscn, mem. Visiting Cttee for Asian Studies; Pres. Harvard Club of Malaysia; Pro-Chancellor Universiti Sains Malaysia; Adjunct Prof. of Econs, Universiti Utara Malaysia; Trustee Tun Ismail Ali Foundation (PNB), Harvard Club of Malaysia Foundation, Malaysian Econ. Asscn Foundation, MAKNA (Nat. Cancer Council); Eisenhower Fellow 1986, mem. Eisenhower Fellowships' International Advisory Council, Phila, USA; Distinguished Fellow, Inst. of Strategic and Int. Studies; Fellow, Inst. of Statisticians, Malaysian Inst. of Man., Malaysian Econ. Asscn; Hon. PhD (Universiti Utara Malaysia); Hon. Fellow, Malaysian Insurance Inst. *Publications:* numerous articles in academic, banking and business journals. *Address:* Office of the Pro-Chancellor, Universiti Sains Malaysia, Kuala Lumpur, Malaysia (office). *Website:* www.usm.my (office).

LIN, Yang-kang, (alias Chih-Hung), BA; Taiwanese politician; b. 10 June 1927, Nantou Co.; s. of Lin Chih-Chang and Lin Chen Ruan; m. Chen Ho 1945; one s. three d.; ed Nat. Taiwan Univ.; Chair. Yunlin Co. HQ, Kuomintang 1964–67; Magistrate, Nantou Co. 1967–72; Commr Dept of Reconstruction, Taiwan Provincial Govt 1972–76; Mayor of Taipei 1976–78; Gov. Taiwan Prov. 1978–81; Minister of Interior 1981–84; Vice-Premier of Taiwan 1984–87; Pres. Judicial Yuan 1987–94; Sr Advisor to Pres. 1994–95 (party membership suspended 1995); stood as ind. Presidential cand. March 1996; Order of Diplomatic Service Merit, Korea 1977. *Leisure interests:* hiking, reading and studying, music, films. *Address:* 124 Chungking South Road, Section 1, Taipei, Taiwan.

LIN, Yu-Lin; Taiwanese real estate executive; *Chairman, Hung Tai Group;* brother of Lin Rong-San; m.; seven c.; Chair. Hung Tai Group (property devt co.), Owner Hung Tai Center and Exchange Square (office bldgs); owns stakes in Hung Sheng Construction and Capital Securities. *Address:* Hung Tai Center, 168 Tun Hwa North Road, Taipei 105, Taiwan (office).

LIN, Zhaohua, BA; Chinese theatre director; *Senior Director, Beijing People's Art Theatre;* b. 1 July 1936, Tianjin; s. of Lin Baogui and Zhang Shuzhen; m. He Binzhu 1964; one s. one d.; ed Cen. Acad. of Drama, Beijing; Vice-Pres. and Dir Beijing People's Art Theatre 1984–, Chair. Art Cttee 1984–; Artistic Dir Lin Zhaohua Drama Studio 1990–; mem. Standing Cttee, China Theatre Asscn 1984–; Chair. Peking Univ. Theatre Research Inst. 2005–. *Theatre productions include:* The Red Heart 1978, Just Opinion 1980, Absolute Signal 1982, Bus Stop 1983, Festivities of Marriage and Funeral 1984, Wildman 1985, Schweyk in the Second World War 1986, Uncle Doggie's Nirvana 1986, Peace Lake 1988, Filed. . .Filed 1989, Peking Man 1989, Chinese Orphan 1990, Hamlet 1990, Countryside Anecdote 1990, A Report from Hu-Tuo River 1991, Birdman, Romulus the Great 1992, Ruan Lingyu 1994, Faust 1994, Chessman 1995, Fisherman 1997, The Three Sisters Waiting For Godot (adapted from Chekhov's Three Sisters and Beckett's Waiting for Godot) 1998, The Teahouse 1999, Boundless Love 2000, A Parody 2000, Richard III 2001, Cai Wen Ji (Anhui Opera) 2002, Zhao's Orphan 2003, Toilet 2004, The Cherry Orchard 2004, The Dream Play 2005, Bird People, Antiques, Tea House, Frameless Wind and Moon, Beijingers, The Assassin 2008;. *Beijing Opera productions include:* Mountain Flower 1991, Turandot, The Humpbacked Prime Minister Liu 2000, The Minister Liu Luoguo I 2000, The Minister Liu Luoguo II 2001, The Minister Liu Luoguo III 2002, The Bravest and Cleverest Soldier Sun Wu 2002, Farewell My Concubine 2003, The Very Best Zhangxie 2003. *Videos:* The Ape and His Six Roars – An Anthology of Lin Zhaohua Drama 2003, The Anthology of Lin Zhaohua Drama Studio (eight dramas and interview with Lin Zhaohua) 2004. *Publications:* Stage Art of Absolute Signal (ed.) 1985, Stage Art of Marriage and Funeral 1997, Lin Zhaohua on Theatrical Directing 1992. *Leisure interests:* Chinese yoga, swimming, music, playing the erhu. *Address:* Beijing People's Art Theatre, 22 Wangfujing Street, Beijing (office); 3-7-503, East Block, Ditan Beili, Heping li, Beijing, People's Republic of China (home). *Telephone:* (10) 65254346 (office); (10) 84043339 (home). *Fax:* (10) 62753253 (office). *E-mail:* lzh@linzhaohua.org (office); linzhaohua1936@hotmail.com (home). *Website:* www.linzhaohua.org (home).

LINACRE, Sir (John) Gordon Seymour, Kt, CBE, AFC, DFM, CCMI; British newspaper executive; b. 23 Sept. 1920, Sheffield; s. of John J. Linacre and Beatrice B. Linacre; m. Irene A. Gordon 1943; two d.; ed Firth Park Grammar School, Sheffield; served RAF, rank of Squadron Leader 1939–46; journalistic appointments Sheffield Telegraph/Star 1937–47; Kemsley News Service 1947–50; Deputy Ed. Newcastle Journal 1950–56, Newcastle Evening Chronicle 1956–57; Ed. Sheffield Star 1958–61; Asst Gen. Man. Sheffield Newspapers Ltd 1961–63; Exec. Dir Thomson Regional Newspapers Ltd, London 1963–65; Man. Dir Yorkshire Post Newspapers Ltd 1965–83, Deputy Chair. 1981–83, Chair. 1983–90, Pres. 1990–; Dir United Newspapers PLC 1969–91, Deputy Chair. 1981–91, Chief Exec. 1983–88; Deputy Chair. Express Newspapers PLC 1985–88; also fmr Chair. United Provincial Newspapers Ltd, Sheffield Newspapers Ltd, Lancashire Evening Post Ltd, Northampton Mercury Co. Ltd, East Yorkshire Printers Ltd etc.; Dir Yorkshire TV 1969–90; Chair. Leeds Univ. Foundation 1989–2000; Chair. Chameleon TV Ltd 1994–; Chair. Opera North Ltd 1978–98, Pres. 1998–; many other professional and public appointments; Commendatore, Ordine al Merito della Repubblica Italiana 1973, Grand Ufficiale 1987; Kt Order of the White Rose, Finland 1987; Hon. LLD (Leeds) 1991. *Leisure interests:* fly-fishing, hill-walking, golf, music, theatre. *Address:* White Windows, Staircase Lane, Bramhope, Leeds, LS16 9JD, England.

LINAKER, Lawrence Edward (Paddy); British business executive; b. 22 July 1934, Hants.; s. of late Lawrence Wignall and Rose Linaker; m. Elizabeth Susan Elam 1963; one s.; ed Malvern Coll.; with Esso Petroleum 1957–63; joined M & G Group 1963, Deputy Chair. and Chief Exec. 1987–94; Chair. M & G Investment Man. 1987–94; Dir Securities Inst. 1992–94; Chair. Fleming Geared Growth Investment Trust PLC 1997–, Fleming Geared Income and Investment Trust PLC 1997–2001; fmr Chair. Marling Industries PLC, Fisons; mem. Bd Lloyds TSB Group PLC, Fleming Mercantile Investment Trust 1994–, Wolverhampton & Dudley Breweries PLC 1996–; mem. Council, Royal Postgrad. Medical School 1977–88, Gov. Body, Soc. for the Promotion of Christian Knowledge 1976–94, Council, Malvern Coll. 1989–; Chair. Institutional Fund Man.'s Asscn 1992–94; YMCA Nat. Coll. 1992–2000; Trustee TSB

Foundation for England and Wales. *Leisure interests:* music, wine, gardening. *Address:* Swyre Farm, Aldsworth, Nr Cheltenham, Glos., England.

LINCOLN, Blanche Lambert, BA; American politician; *Senator from Arkansas;* b. 30 Sept. 1960, Helena, Ark.; ed Randolph-Macon Woman's Coll.; mem. US House of Reps 1992–96; Senator from Arkansas 1999–; mem. Senate Finance Cttee 2001–, also mem. Agric., Nutrition and Forestry Cttee, Special Cttee on Aging, Select Cttee on Ethics, Social Security Task Force, Rural Health Caucus; Democrat. *Address:* 355 Dirksen Senate Office Building, Washington, DC 20510-0404, USA (office). *Telephone:* (202) 224-4843 (office). *Fax:* (202) 228-1371 (office). *Website:* lincoln.senate.gov (office).

LINDAHL, George, III, BSc; American petroleum industry executive; *Managing Partner, Sandefer Capital Partners;* ed Univ. of Alabama, Tulane Univ., Harvard Univ.; began career as geologist and Man. Amoco Production Co.; Exec. Vice-Pres., Dir and Partner Walker Energy Partners of Houston –1987; joined Union Pacific Resources (UPR) Group, Inc. Jan. 1987, Pres. and COO 1996–99, Chair., Pres. and CEO 1999–2001; Dir Anadarko Petroleum Corpn, Vice-Chair. –2001; currently Man. Pnr, Sandefer Capital Pnrs; mem. Advisory Bd NAPE (fmrly North American Prospect Expo); mem. Pres.'s Council, Univ. of Ala; mem. visiting Cttee Petroleum and Geosystems Engineering Dept, Univ. of Tex. at Austin; mem. Texas Hall of Fame Foundation; fmr Pres. Fort Worth Petroleum Club; mem. All-American Wildcatters 1999. *Address:* Sandefer Capital Partners, 515 Congress Avenue, Suite 1875, Austin, TX 78701-3518, USA (office). *Telephone:* (512) 495-9925.

LINDAHL, Tomas, MD, FRS; Swedish scientist; *Researcher, Mutagenesis Laboratory, London Research Institute, Cancer Research UK;* b. 28 Jan. 1938, Stockholm; ed Karolinska Inst., Stockholm; joined Cancer Research 1981, Deputy Dir of Research, Cancer Research UK London Research Inst., now Researcher, Mutagenesis Lab.; INSERM (French Nat. Inst. for Health and Medical Research) Prix Etranger 2007, Royal Soc. Medal 2007. *Address:* Mutagenesis Laboratory, London Research Institute, Clare Hall Laboratories, Blanche Lane, South Mimms, Herts., EN6 3LD, England (office). *Telephone:* (1707) 625993 (office). *Fax:* (1707) 625803 (office). *E-mail:* Tomas.Lindahl@cancer.org.uk (office). *Website:* science.cancerresearchuk.org/research/loc/london/lifch/lindahlt (office).

LINDBÆK, Jannik; Norwegian petroleum industry executive; *Chairman, Statoil ASA;* b. 1939; ed Norwegian School of Economics and Business Admin, Bergen; Pres. and CEO Storebrand Group 1976–85; Pres. and CEO Nordiska Investeringsbanken (Nordic Investment Bank), Helsinki 1986–94; Exec. Vice Pres. Int. Finance Corpn (World Bank Group), Washington, DC 1994–99; Chair. Statoil ASA 2003–; Chair. Bergen Int. Festival, Transparency Int. Norge, Plan Int. Norge, Gearbulk; fmr Chair. Gaz de France Norge, Saga Petroleum, Den Norske Bank; mem. Bd of Dirs Kristian Gerhard Jebsen Skipsrederi (shipping co.); Fulbright Scholar, Univ. of Kan. 1961–62. *Address:* Statoil ASA, Forusbeen 50, Stavenger 4035, Norway (office). *Telephone:* 51-99-00-00 (office). *Fax:* 51-99-00-50 (office). *Website:* www.statoil.com (office).

LINDBECK, Assar, PhD; Swedish economist and academic; *Professor of International Economics, University of Stockholm;* b. 26 Jan. 1930, Umeå; s. of Carl Lindbeck and Eugenia Lindbeck (née Sundelin); m. Dorothy Nordlund 1953; one s. one d.; ed Univs of Uppsala and Stockholm; Asst Prof., Univ. of Michigan, USA 1958; with Swedish Treasury 1953–56; Asst Prof. of Econs, Univ. of Stockholm 1962–63, Prof., Stockholm School of Economics 1964–71, Prof. of Int. Econs 1971–, Dir Inst. of Int. Econs 1971–94; Visiting Prof., Columbia Univ., USA 1968–69, Univ. of California, Berkeley 1969, ANU 1970, Yale Univ. 1976, Stanford Univ. 1977; Consultant, World Bank 1986–87; mem. Nobel Prize Cttee on Econs 1969–94 (Chair. 1980–94); Frank Siedman Distinguished Award in Political Economy 1996, Bernard Harms Prize in Int. Econs 1996, Great Gold Medal of the Royal Swedish Acad. of Eng Sciences 2001. *Music:* Sonata for Clarinet and piano: Fantasi i folkton 1948, performed in City Hall, Luleå 1948. *Publications:* A Study in Monetary Analysis 1963, The Political Economy of the New Left 1971, Economics of the Agricultural Sector 1973, Swedish Economic Policy 1975, The Insider-Outsider Theory (with Dennis Snower) 1988, Unemployment and Macroeconomics 1993, The Swedish Experiment 1997. *Leisure interest:* painting. *Address:* Institute for International Economic Studies, Stockholm University, 106 91 Stockholm (office); Karlavägen 78, 114 59 Stockholm, Sweden (home). *Telephone:* (8) 16-30-78 (office); (8) 21-23-37 (home). *Fax:* (8) 16-29-46 (office); (8) 21-23-37 (home). *E-mail:* assar@iies.su.se (office). *Website:* www.iies.su.se/~assar (office).

LINDBLOM, Seppo Olavi, LicPolSc; Finnish bank executive and politician; b. 9 Aug. 1935, Helsinki; s. of Olavi and Aura (née Sammal) Lindblom; m. Anneli Johanson 1958; four d.; ed Univ. of Helsinki; Man. br. office, Finnish Workers' Savings Bank 1958–60; Economist, Bank of Finland 1960–68; Sec. to Prime Minister 1968–70; Head, Labour Inst. for Econ. Research 1970–72; Minister in Ministry of Trade and Industry 1972; Head, Dept of Nat. Econ. Ministry of Finance 1973–74; Nat. Conciliator for Incomes Policy 1973–74; Dir Bank of Finland 1974–82, mem. Bd of Man. 1982–87; Minister of Trade and Industry 1983–87; Chair. and Chief Exec. Postipankki Ltd 1988–96. *Leisure interests:* music, chess.

LINDEGAARD, Jørgen; Danish airline executive; *President and CEO, SAS AB;* b. 1948; worked as exec. in telecommunications eng; fmr Pres. Fyns Telefon A/S, Københavns Telefon A/S; fmr mem. Exec. Bd Tele Danmark; Pres. and CEO GN Store Nord 1997–; Pres. and CEO SAS Group 2001–. *Address:* SAS AB, Frösundaviks Allé 1, Solna, 195 87 Stockholm, Sweden (office). *Telephone:* (8) 797-00-00 (office). *Fax:* (8) 797-12-10 (office). *Website:* www.scandinavian.net (office).

LINDEMAN, Fredrik Otto, DPhil; Norwegian academic; *Professor Emeritus of Indo-European Linguistics, University of Oslo;* b. 3 March 1936, Oslo; s. of Carl Fredrik Lindeman and Agnes Augusta Lindeman; m. Bente Konow Taranger 1960; one s. one d.; ed Univ. of Oslo, Sorbonne, Paris; Prof. of Indo-European Linguistics, Univ. of Copenhagen 1970–76; Prof. of Indo-European Linguistics, Univ. of Oslo 1976–2005, now Emer.; Visiting Prof., Dublin Inst. for Advanced Studies, School of Celtic Studies 1982–83; Dals Prize for Outstanding Achievement, Univ. of Oslo 1997. *Publications:* Les Origines Indo-Européennes de la 'Verschärfung' Germanique 1964, Einführung in die Laryngaltheorie 1970, The Triple Representation of Schwa in Greek and some related problems of Indo-European Phonology 1982, Studies in Comparative Indo-European Linguistics 1996, Introduction to the 'Laryngeal Theory' 1997, Våre Arveord Etymologisk Ordbok (with Harald Bjorvand) 2000, (enlarged and revised edn) 2007. *Leisure interest:* music. *Address:* Henrik Wergelands hus, Niels Henrik Abels vei, 0313 Oslo, Norway (office); Abbedikollen 13, 0280 Oslo 2 (home); c/o Institutt for lingvistiske fag, Universitetet i Oslo, PB 1102 Blindern, 0317 Oslo, Norway (office). *Telephone:* 22-50-92-78 (home). *E-mail:* bente.lindeman@c2i.net (home).

LINDENSTRAUSS, Joram, PhD; Israeli mathematician and academic; *Professor Emeritus, Einstein Institute of Mathematics, Hebrew University of Jerusalem;* b. 28 Oct. 1936, Tel-Aviv; m. Naomi Salinger 1962; one s. three d.; ed Hebrew Univ., Jerusalem; Sr Lecturer in Math., Hebrew Univ. 1965, Assoc. Prof. 1967, Prof. 1970–2007, Prof. Emer. 2007–; Visiting Prof., Yale Univ., Univs of Washington, California and Texas, Texas A&M Univ., Inst. Mittag Leffler, Inst. for Advanced Study, Princeton; mem. Israel Acad. of Science and Humanities; Foreign mem. Austrian Acad. of Sciences; Dr hc (Kent State Univ., Ohio); Israel Prize in Math. 1981, Banach Medal, Polish Acad. of Sciences. *Publications:* Classical Banach Spaces, Vols I–II, 1977, 1979, Geometric Non Linear Functional Analysis, Vol. I (co-author) 2000, Handbook of the Geometry of Banach Spaces, Vol. I (co-ed.) 2001. *Address:* Einstein Institute of Mathematics, Edmond J. Safra Campus, Givat Ram, Manchester House 101, Hebrew University of Jerusalem, Jerusalem 91904, Israel (office); 36 Habanai Str., Jerusalem, Israel. *Telephone:* (2) 6522762 (home). *Fax:* (2) 6537266 (office). *E-mail:* joram@math.huji.ac.il (office). *Website:* www.math.huji.ac.il (office).

LINDERBERG, Jan Erik, FD; Danish chemist and academic; *Professor Emeritus of Theoretical Chemistry, Århus University;* b. 27 Oct. 1934, Karlskoga, Sweden; s. of David Linderberg and Sara Bäckström; m. Gunnel Björstam 1957; two s.; ed Uppsala Univ.; Docent, Uppsala Univ. 1964–68; Prof. of Theoretical Chem., Århus Univ. 1968–, now Prof. Emer.; Adjunct Prof. of Chem., Univ. Florida, Gainesville, Univ. of Utah; mem. Royal Danish Soc. of Sciences and Letters, Int. Acad. of Quantum Molecular Science, Royal Soc. of Science (Uppsala). *Publications:* Role of Correlation in Electronic Systems 1964, Propagators in Quantum Chemistry (co-author), Quantum Science (with others) 1976; more than 100 papers in refereed journals. *Leisure interest:* orienteering. *Address:* Århus University, Department of Chemistry, Langelandsgade 140, 8000 Århus C (office); Janus la Cours gade 20, 8000 Århus C, Denmark (home). *Telephone:* 89-42-38-33 (office); 86-12-02-41 (home). *Fax:* 86-19-61-99 (office). *E-mail:* jan@chem.au.dk (office). *Website:* www.chem.au.dk/~teo/mainmenu/Staff/Jan (office).

LINDNER, Carl Henry, Jr; American business executive; *Chairman and CEO, American Financial Group Inc.;* b. 22 April 1919, Dayton, Ohio; s. of Carl Henry Lindner and Clara Lindner (née Serrer); m. Edith Bailey 1953; three s.; Co-Founder United Dairy Farmers 1940; Pres. American Finance Corpn, Cincinnati 1959–84, Chair. 1959–, CEO 1984–; Chair., CEO and Chair. Exec. Cttee United Brands Co. (now Chiquita Brands Int. Inc.), NY 1984–; Chair. Penn Cen. Corpn (now American Premier Underwriters), Greenwich, Conn. 1983–, CEO 1987–94; Chair. and CEO Great American Communications Co. 1987–; now Chair. and CEO American Financial Group (insurance co.), Cincinnati; mem. Bd of Dirs Mission Inst., Bd of Advisers Business Admin. Coll., Univ. of Cincinnati; owner, CEO Cincinnati Reds (baseball team) 1999–2005; cr. Carl H. and Martha S. Lindner Center for Art History, Univ. of Virginia 2004; ranked 133rd by Forbes magazine among The 400 Richest Americans 2005. *Leisure interest:* working. *Address:* American Financial Group Inc., 1 East 4th Street, Cincinnati, OH 45202, USA (office). *Telephone:* (513) 579-2121 (office). *Fax:* (513) 579-2113. *Website:* www.amfnl.com (office).

LINDSAY, Most Rev. and Hon. Orland Ugham, OD, OJ, BD; Jamaican/Antiguan ecclesiastic (retd); b. 24 March 1928, Jamaica; s. of Hubert Lindsay and Ida Lindsay; m. Olga Daphne Wright 1959; three s.; ed Mayfield Govt School, Southfield, Jamaica, Culham Coll. Oxford, England, St Peter's Theological Coll., Jamaica, Montréal Diocesan Theological Coll. at McGill Univ., Canada; served in RAF 1944–49; teacher Franklin Town Govt School 1949–52; Asst Master Kingston Coll. 1952–53, 1958–63; ordained Deacon, Jamaica 1956; Asst Curate St Peter's Vere Cure 1956–57; ordained Priest 1957; Chaplain Kingston Coll. 1958–63; Asst Curate in charge of Manchioneal Cure 1960–63; Sec. Jamaica Diocesan Synod 1962–70; Chaplain Jamaica Defence Force 1963–67; Prin. Church Teachers' Coll., Mandeville, Jamaica 1967–70; Bishop of Antigua, latterly of NE Caribbean and Aruba 1970–98; Archbishop of the West Indies 1986–98; Order of Distinction (Antigua) 1996, Order of Jamaica 1997; Hon. DD (Berkeley Divinity School, Yale Univ.) 1978, (St Paul's Coll., S Va) 1998; Hon. STD (Diocesan Theological Coll., Montréal) 1997. *Leisure interests:* swimming, listening to music, reading, photography. *Address:* Crosbies, PO Box 3456, Antigua (home). *Telephone:* 560-1724 (home). *Fax:* 462-2090 (home). *E-mail:* orland@candw.ag (home).

LINDSAY, Robert; British actor; b. (Robert Lindsay Stevenson), 13 Dec. 1949, Ilkeston, Derbyshire; s. of Norman Stevenson and the late Joyce Stevenson; m. 1st Cheryl Hall (divorced); m. 2nd Rosemarie Ford; two s.; one d. by actress Diana Weston; ed Royal Acad. of Dramatic Art; began career as dialect coach with repertory company in Exeter, later joined regional theatre group, then moved on to West End and to television roles; first became household name in UK as Wolfie in sitcom Citizen Smith 1977; stage career commenced at Manchester Royal Exchange; Patron of New Arts Course, NCN (fmrly Clarendon Coll.) – Robert Lindsay Theatre; Hon. Fellow, Univ. of Manchester; Dr hc (Nottingham, Derby). *Theatre includes:* Hamlet, Royal Exchange, Manchester (then tour of UK) 1983, Bill Snibson in Me and My Girl, Adelphi Theatre, London, Broadway and LA (Laurence Olivier Award for Outstanding Performance by an Actor in a Musical, Tony Award for Best Actor in a Musical, Drama Desk Best Actor Award, Outer Critics' Best Actor Award, Fred Astaire Award for Best Dancer on Broadway) 1985–87, Henry II in Anouilh's Beckett, West End, London (Variety Club Best Theatre Actor) 1991, Cyrano de Bergerac, Theatre Royal, London 1992, Oliver! (Laurence Olivier Award for Best Actor), Beaux Stratagem/Philoctetes, Royal Exchange, Manchester (Manchester Evening News Award), Richard III, tour by RSC then at Stratford-upon-Avon then at Savoy Theatre, London 1998, The Changeling, Riverside Studios, London, The Cherry Orchard, The Roundhouse, London, Godspell, Wyndhams Theatre, How I Got That Story, Hampstead Theatre, Octavius in Julius Caesar, Royal Exchange, Manchester, Leaping Ginger, Royal Exchange, Manchester, Lower Depths, The Roundhouse, London, Power, Royal Nat. Theatre, London, D'Artagnan in Three Musketeers, Royal Exchange, Manchester, Trelawny of The Wells, Old Vic, London, The Entertainer, Old Vic, London. *Films include:* That'll Be the Day 1973, Three for All 1974, Adventures of a Taxi Driver 1976, Bert Rigby, You're a Fool 1989, Strike It Rich (aka Loser Takes All; Money Talks) 1990, Goodbye My Love 1996, Fierce Creatures 1997, Remember Me? 1997, The Canterbury Tales (voice) 1998, Divorcing Jack 1998, Wimbledon 2004; training videos: The Dreaded Appraisal, The Helping Hand, I Wasn't Prepared For That, Meeting Breaks – Bosses From Hell, From 'No' To 'Yes', Sell It To Me!. *Radio includes:* Puttin' On The Style (BBC Radio 2), Peer Gynt (BBC Radio 4) (Sony Award), Oedipus (Radio 4), Frankenstein (BBC World Service), Nineteen Ninety Four, (Radio 4) Nobody Will Laugh (Milan R3), as Iago with Robert Stephens as Othello (Prince's Trust CD); audiobooks: Pinocchio, Fortysomething, Falling, Tom Jones, Virgin And The Gypsy, Sherlock Holmes, Mary Shelley's 'Frankenstein', Can't You Sleep Little Bear?. *Television includes:* Get Some In! (series) 1975–77, Wolfie in Citizen Smith (series) 1977, Twelfth Night 1980, Seconds Out (series) 1981, All's Well That Ends Well 1981, A Midsummer Night's Dream 1981, Cymbeline 1982, Give us a Break (series) 1983, Edmund in King Lear (Granada) 1984, Much Ado About Nothing 1984, Confessional 1989, Nightingales (series) 1990, Michael in GBH (mini-series; Channel 4) (BAFTA Award for Best Actor, Royal Television Soc. Award for Best Actor) 1991, Genghis Cohn 1993, The Wimbledon Poisoner (mini-series) 1994, Jake's Progress (mini-series) 1995, The Office 1996, Brazen Hussies 1996, In Your Dreams (series; voice) 1998, Capt. Pellew in Hornblower: The Even Chance (aka Horatio Hornblower: The Duel, USA) 1998, Hornblower: The Examination for Lieutenant (Horatio Hornblower: The Fire Ship, USA) 1998, Hornblower: The Duchess and the Devil (Horatio Hornblower: The Duchess and the Devil, USA) 1999, Hornblower: The Frogs and the Lobsters (Horatio Hornblower: The Wrong War, USA) 1999, Oliver Twist (mini-series) 1999, My Family (series) 2000, Hawk (aka Hawkins, UK) (mini-series) 2001, The Heat Is On (series) 2001, Hornblower: Mutiny 2001, Hornblower: Retribution (aka Horatio Hornblower: Retribution, USA) 2001, Don't Eat the Neighbours (series) 2001, Out of Eden (voice) 2002, Hornblower: Duty 2003, Hornblower: Loyalty (aka Horatio Hornblower 3, USA) 2003, Friends and Crocodiles 2005, A Very Social Secretary 2005, Jericho (series) 2005, Space Race (BBC series) (narrator) 2005, Friends and Crocodiles 2006, Gideon's Daughter 2006, The Trial of Tony Blair 2007, Extras (Series 2; as himself) 2007; guest appearances in Absolutely Fabulous (BBC), Whodunnit! (episode 'Pop Goes The Weasels'), The Good Life (episode 'Our Speaker Today') (BBC), Tales From The Crypt (episode 'Ear Today... Gone Tomorrow'), Victoria Wood With All The Trimmings (BBC), The Parkinson Show (ITV) 2005. *Address:* c/o Lorraine Hamilton, Hamilton Hodell Ltd, 5th Floor, 66–68 Margaret Street, London, W1W 8SR, England (office). *Telephone:* (20) 7636-1221 (office). *Fax:* (20) 7636-1226 (office). *E-mail:* lorraine@hamiltonhodell.co.uk (office). *Website:* www.hamiltonhodell.co.uk (office); www.robertlindsay.net.

LINDSEY, Lawrence B., AB, MA, PhD; American economist and fmr government official; *President and CEO, Lindsey Group;* b. 18 July 1954, Peekskill, NY; s. of Merritt Lindsey and Helen Hissam; m. Susan Lindsey 1982; three c.; ed Bowdoin Coll., Harvard Univ.; on staff of Pres. Reagan's Council of Econ. Advisers; Special Asst for Policy Devt to Pres. Bush; fmr Prof. of Econs, Harvard Univ.; mem. Bd of Govs Fed. Reserve System 1991–97; Man. Dir Econ. Strategies Inc. 1997–2001; Econ. Adviser to Pres. 2001–02; Dir Nat. Econ. Council 2001–02; Pres. and CEO Lindsey Group 2003–; Chair. Bd Neighborhood Reinvestment Corpn 1993–97; Resident Scholar and holder Arthur C. Burns Chair., American Enterprise Inst. 1997–2001, now Visiting Scholar; Hon. JuD (Bowdoin Coll.) 1993; Distinguished Public Service Award, Boston Bar Assn 1994. *Publications:* The Growth Experiment: How the New Tax Policy is Transforming the US Economy 1990, Econ. Puppermasters: Lessons From the Halls of Power 1999; numerous articles in professional publs. *Address:* The Lindsey Group, 11320 Random Hills Road, Suite 310, Fairfax, VA 22030; American Enterprise Institute, 1150 17th Street, NW, Washington, DC 20036, USA (office). *Telephone:* (703) 621-1170 (office). *Fax:* (703) 218-3956 (office). *E-mail:* info@thelindseygroup.com (office); LLindsey@aei.org (office). *Website:* www.thelindseygroup.com (office).

LINDSKOG, Martin B.; Swedish broadcasting executive; b. 5 April 1953, Stockholm; s. of Bjorn Lindskog and Britt-Marie Lindskog; m. Joan Estes; one s.; ed Stockholm School of Econs; with Esselte Group 1977–90; CEO Filmnet

Int. Holdings 1990–93; joined SBS 1993, Pres. 1996–2001; mem. Bd Dirs MTV Produktion. *Address:* MTV Produktion, Kungsgatan 84, 112 27 Stockholm, Sweden (office). *Telephone:* (8) 52-72-70-00 (office). *Website:* www.mtv.se (office).

LINDSTEN, Jan Eric, PhD, MD; Swedish geneticist and academic; *Professor Emeritus of Medical Genetics, Karolinska Institute;* b. 23 Jan. 1935, Stockholm; s. of Carl-Eric Lindsten and Lisa M. Hallberg; m. Marianne E. Östling 1960; two s. one d.; ed Uppsala Univ. and Karolinska Inst. Stockholm; Prof. of Human Genetics, Århus 1968–70; Prof. of Medical Genetics, Karolinska Inst. 1969–2000, Prof. Emer. 2000–, Head, Dept of Clinical Genetics 1970–90; Chief Medical Officer, Karolinska Hosp. 1987–90, Man. Dir 1990–94; Man. Dir Nat. Univ. Hosp. Copenhagen 1994–96; Dean Medical Faculty, Karolinska Inst. 1996–98; Sec. Nobel Ass. and Medical Nobel Cttee Karolinska Inst. 1979–90; mem. Royal Swedish Acad. of Sciences, Pres. 2003–. *Publications:* 300 publs in the field of medical genetics, especially clinical genetics. *Address:* Council of Cultural Affairs, Karolinska Institutet, 17177 Stockholm, Sweden (office). *Telephone:* (8) 52-48-39-29 (office). *Fax:* (8) 316774 (office). *E-mail:* jan.lindsten@ki.se (office).

LINEKER, Gary Winston, OBE; British television presenter, journalist and fmr professional footballer; b. 30 Nov. 1960, Leicester; s. of Barry Lineker and Margaret Patricia Morris Lineker (née Abbs); m. Michelle Denise Cockayne 1986 (divorced 2006); four s.; ed City of Leicester Boys' Grammar School; debut as professional footballer, Leicester City 1978; transferred to Everton 1985; mem. England team 1984–92, scoring 48 goals in 80 appearances, rep. England 1986 World Cup, Mexico, 1990 World Cup, Italy, Capt. of England 1990–92; FC Barcelona 1986–89; transferred to Tottenham Hotspur 1989–92; Grampus Eight, Japan 1994; never booked in 16-year career; Freeman City of Leicester 1995; Hon. MA (Leicester) 1992, (Loughborough) 1992; Football Writers' Asscn Player of the Year 1986, 1992, Professional Footballers' Asscn Footballer of the Year 1986, FIFA Fair Play Award 1990; only English player to win Golden Boot Award for scoring most goals in a World Cup 1986. *Television includes:* presenter Match of the Day, BBC TV 1995–; team capt. They Think It's All Over (quiz show) 1995–2003. *Leisure interests:* cricket, golf, snooker. *Address:* c/o Diana van Bunnens, Jon Holmes Media Ltd, 5th Floor, Holborn Gate, Southampton Buildings, London, WC2A 1PQ, England (office). *Telephone:* (20) 7861-2550 (office). *Fax:* (20) 7861-3067 (office). *E-mail:* diana@jonholmesmedia.com (office). *Website:* www.jonholmesmedia.com (office).

LING, Jiefang, (Er Yuehe); Chinese writer; b. Oct. 1945, Xiyang, Shanxi Prov.; Chair. Nanyang Literary and Art Circles 1985–; Vice-Chair. He'nan Prov. Asscn of Writers 1996–; Deputy, 11th NPC 2008; Nat. Achievement by Self-Study Medal 1996, Nat. Wuyi Labour Medal 1998. *Publications:* The Great Emperor Kangwi (four vols), Emperor Yongzheng (three vols, Nat. Excellent Novel 1997), Emperor Qianlong (six vols). *Leisure interests:* chess, card games. *Address:* 13 South Square Street, Nanyang 473000, He'nan Province (office); Literary and Art Circles of Wolong District, Nanyang 473000, He'nan Province, People's Republic of China (home). *Telephone:* (377) 3161798 (office); (377) 3219098 (home). *Fax:* (377) 3219098 (home).

LING, Sergei Stepanovich; Belarusian politician, diplomatist and agronomist; *Chairman, State Committee on Economics and Planning;* b. 7 May 1937; m.; three c.; ed Belarus Agricultural Acad., Higher CPSU School, CPSU Cen. Cttee; agronomist sovkhoz, Lesnoye Kopylsk Dist, Chief Agronomist Sovkhoz, Krynitsa Kopylsk Dist, Chief Agronomist, Deputy Dir Lyuban Production Co., Chief Soligorsk Production Agric. Admin; Deputy Chair. then Chair. Slutsk Dist Exec. Cttee, Sec. Smolevichi Dist CPSU Cttee 1960–72; Chief Agric. Div., Sec. Minsk Regional Belarus CP Cttee 1972–82; First Deputy Chair. then Chair. Exec. Cttee Minsk Regional Soviet 1982–86; Chair. Belarus State Cttee on Prices, Deputy Chair. State Planning Cttee 1986–90; Head Agric. Div., Sec. Cen. Cttee Belarus CP 1990–91; Deputy Chair. Belarus Council of Ministers; Chair. State Cttee on Econs and Planning 1991–; Deputy Prime Minister of Belarus 1994–96, Acting Prime Minister 1996–97, Prime Minister 1997–2000; Perm. Rep. to UN 2000–02.

LING LIONG SIK, Dato' Seri, MB, BS; Malaysian politician; b. 18 Sept. 1943, Kuala Kangsar, Perak; m. Datin Ee Nah Ong 1968; two c.; ed King Edward VII School, Royal Mil. Coll. and Univ. of Singapore; Parl. Sec. Ministry of Local Govt and Fed. Territory 1976–77; Deputy Minister of Information 1978–82, of Finance 1982–84, of Educ. 1985–86; fmr Minister of Transport; Deputy Pres. Malaysian Chinese Asscn 1985–87, Pres. 1987–2003. *Leisure interests:* reading, golf. *Address:* c/o Malaysian Chinese Association, 8th Floor, Wisma MCA, 163, Jalan Ampang, 50450 Kuala Lumpur, Malaysia (office).

LINGHU, An; Chinese politician; *Deputy Auditor-General, National Audit Office;* b. Oct. 1946, Pinglu Co., Shanxi Prov.; ed Beijing Eng Inst.; joined CCP 1965; fmr Deputy Dir City Machin-Building Industry Bureau, Dalian City, Liaoning Prov., City Instrument, Meter and Electronics Bureau, Dalian City (later Deputy Gen. Man.); fmr Deputy Sec. CCP Dalian City Cttee; fmr Chair. Dalian Fed. of Trade Unions; fmr Vice-Chair. Comm. for Restructuring the Economy, Dalian City; Exec. Vice-Mayor Dalian City 1988; fmr mem. CCP Standing Cttee, Dalian City Cttee; fmr Dir Gen. Office, People's Govt, Dalian City; fmr Dir Retired Cadres Bureau, Ministry of Labour; Vice-Minister of Labour 1989–93; Deputy Sec. CCP Yunnan Prov. Cttee 1993–97, Sec. 1997–2001; Chair. Yunnan Prov. People's Political Consultative Conf. 1998–2001; Deputy Auditor-Gen. Nat. Audit Office 2001–; mem. 15th CCP Cen. Cttee 1997–2002; Del., 14th CCP Nat. Congress 1992–97. *Address:* National Audit Office of China, 1 Beiluyuan, Zhanlan Road, Beijing, 100830 People's Republic of China. *Telephone:* (10) 68301520 (office). *E-mail:* cnao@audit.gov.cn (office).

LINGLE, Linda; American state official; *Governor of Hawaii;* b. 4 June 1953, St. Louis, Mo.; ed Birmingham High, Calif., California State Univ., Northridge; fmr public information officer Hawaii Teamsters and Hotel Workers' Union; f. Moloka'i Free Press; mem. Maui Co. Council 1980–90; Mayor of Maui Co. 1990–98; unsuccessful bid for Gov.'s office 1998; adviser to Guam and Pohnpei on performance-based budgeting; Republican Party Chair, Hawaii 1999–; Gov. of Hawaii 2002–; mem. Bd Girl Scout Council; Evelyn McPhail Award 2000. *Address:* Office of the Governor, State Capitol, Honolulu, HI 96813, USA (office). *Telephone:* (808) 586-0034 (office). *Fax:* (808) 586-0006 (office). *Website:* gov.state.hi.us (office).

LINI, Ham; Ni-Vanuatu politician; *Minister for Public Works and Utilities;* mem. Nat. United Party (NUP), Pres. 1999–; Deputy Prime Minister 2003–04, also Minister of Home Affairs, of Infrastructure and Public Utilities, of Civil Aviation; Prime Minister of Vanuatu 2004–08; Minister of Public Works and Utilities 2008–. *Address:* Ministry of Public Works and Utilities, Port Vila, Vanuatu (office).

LINK, Christoph, DJur; German/Austrian legal scholar and academic; *Professor Emeritus of State Administration and Church Law, University of Erlangen;* b. 13 June 1933, Dresden; s. of late Hellmuth Link and of Gerda Link; m. 1st Eva Link 1957; m. 2nd Sibylle Obermayer 1991; two s. one d.; ed Kreuzschule, Dresden and Univs of Marburg, Cologne and Munich; Prof. Vienna 1971–77, Salzburg 1977–79, Hon. Prof. 1979–, Göttingen 1979–86; Prof. of State Admin and Church Law, Univ. of Erlangen 1986, now Prof. Emer.; Dir Hans-Liermann-Inst. für Kirchenrecht 1986–2001; mem. Akad. der Wissenschaften, Göttingen; DTheol hc (Vienna), (Tübingen) Österreichisches Ehrenkreuz für Wissenschaft und Kunst, 1st Klasse 2004. *Publications:* Die Grundlagen der Kirchenverfassung im lutherischen Konfessionalismus des 19ten Jahrhunderts 1966, Herrschaftsordnung und bürgerliche Freiheit 1979, Hugo Grotius als Staatsdenker 1983, Kirchen und privater Rundfunk (with A. Pahlke) 1985, Staat und Kirche in der neueren deutschen Geschichte 2000. *Address:* Hans-Liermann-Institut für Kirchenrecht, 91054 Erlangen, Hindenburgstrasse 34 (office); Ruehlstrasse 35, 91054 Erlangen, Germany (home). *Telephone:* (9131) 8522242 (office); (9131) 209335 (home). *Fax:* (9131) 8524064 (office); (9131) 534566 (home). *E-mail:* hli@jura.uni-erlangen.de (office); linkerta@aol.com (home). *Website:* www.jura.uni-erlangen.de (office).

LINKEVIČIUS, Linas Antanas; Lithuanian politician and diplomatist; *Permanent Representative, NATO;* b. 6 Jan. 1961, Vilnius; m. 1982; two d.; ed Kaunas Polytechnical Inst.; worked in technical insts 1983–92; reviewer, newspaper Tiesa 1992–93; mem. Democratic Labour Party 1990–95; elected to Seimas (Parl.) 1992; Chair. Parl. delegation to N Atlantic Ass. 1992–93; Deputy Chair. Parl. Comm. on Foreign Affairs 1992–93; Minister of Nat. Defence 1993–96, 2000–04; Amb. and Head of Lithuanian Mission to NATO and to WEU 1997–99; Amb. for special missions, Ministry of Foreign Affairs 2004–05; Perm. Rep. of Lithuania to NATO 2005–. *Address:* NATO Headquarters, Blvd Leopold III, 1110 Brussels, Belgium (office). *Telephone:* (2) 707-28-49 (office). *Fax:* (2) 707-28-50 (office). *E-mail:* delagation@ltunato.org (office). *Website:* amb.urm.lt/nato (office).

LINKLATER, Richard; American film director; b. 1967; f. Detour Films, Austin, Tex.; founder and Artistic Dir Austin Film Soc. *Films:* Slacker 1991, Dazed and Confused 1993, Before Sunrise (Berlin Film Festival Silver Bear) 1995, Suburbia 1997, The Newton Boys 1998, Waking Life 2001, Tape 2001, Live from Shiva's Dance Floor 2003, School of Rock 2003, Before Sunset 2004, Bad News Bears 2005, A Scanner Darkly 2006, Fast Food Nation 2006. *Address:* c/o Creative Artists Agency, Inc., 9830 Wilshire Blvd., Beverly Hills, CA 90212-1825, USA.

LINNANE, Anthony William, AM, DSc, PhD, FRS, FAA, FTSE; Australian biochemist and academic; *Managing Director, Centre for Molecular Biology and Medicine;* b. 17 July 1930, Sydney; s. of late W P. Linnane; m. 1st Judith Neil 1956 (dissolved 1979); one s. one d.; m. 2nd Daryl Woods 1980; one s. one d.; ed Sydney Univ., Univ. of Wisconsin, USA; Postdoctoral Fellow, Univ. of Wis. 1956–58; Lecturer, then Sr Lecturer, Sydney Univ. 1958–62; Reader, Monash Univ. 1962–65, Prof. of Biochem. 1965–95, Emer. Prof. 1996–; Dir Centre for Molecular Biology and Medicine 1984–, Man. Dir 1996–; Man. Dir Magral Ltd 2002–; Ed.-in-Chief Biochemistry and Molecular Biology Int. 1980–98; Visiting Prof., Univ. of Wis. 1967–68; Hon. Prof., Melbourne Univ. 1996–; Pres. Australian Biochemical Soc. 1974–76, Fed. of Asian and Oceanic Biochemical Socs 1975–77, 12th Int. Congress of Biochem., Perth 1982; Foundation Pres. Australian Soc. for Cellular and Molecular Gerontology 2000; Treas., Int. Union of Biochemistry and Molecular Biology 1988–97; Distinguished Service Award, Int. Union of Biochem. and Molecular Biology 2000, Centenary Medal of Australia 2003. *Publications:* over 300 scientific publs. *Leisure interests:* golf, reading, horseracing. *Address:* 24 Myrtle Road, Canterbury, Vic. 3126 (home); Centre for Molecular Biology and Medicine, 185–187 Hoddle Street, Richmond, Vic. 3121, Australia (office). *Telephone:* (3) 9888-6526 (home); (3) 9426-4200 (office). *Fax:* (3) 9830-5415 (home); (3) 9426-4201 (office). *E-mail:* tlinnane@cmbm.com.au (office). *Website:* www.cmbm.com.au (office).

LINNER, Carl Sture, MA, PhD; Swedish international civil servant and writer; b. 15 June 1917, Stockholm; s. of Carl W. Linner and Hanna Hellstedt; m. Clio Tambakopoulou 1944; two s.; ed Stockholm and Uppsala Univs; Assoc. Prof. of Greek, Uppsala Univ. 1943; Del. to Int. Red Cross, Greece 1943–45; Dir AB Electrolux, Stockholm 1945–50; Dir Swedish Employers' Confed. 1950–51; Exec. Vice-Pres. AB Bahco, Stockholm 1951–57; Pres. Swedish Lamco Syndicate 1957; Exec. Vice.-Pres. and Gen. Man. Liberian-American-Swedish Minerals Co., Monrovia 1958–60; Chief UN Civilian Operations, later UN Mission, in the Congo 1960–61; Special Rep. of UN Sec.-Gen. in

www.worldwhoswho.com

Brussels and London 1962; UN Rep. in Greece, Israel and Cyprus 1962–65, in London 1965–68, in Tunis 1968–71, UNDP, New York 1971–73; Resident Rep. UNDP in Egypt 1973–77; Sr Consultant, FAO 1977–87; mem. Royal Swedish Acad. of Letters, History and Antiquities, Royal Acad. of Arts and Sciences, Uppsala, Societas Litterarum Humaniorum Regiae Upsaliensis; Hon. Prof. (Uppsala) 1992, Amb. of Hellenism (Gov. of Athens); Star of Africa, Commdr Order of Phoenix, Commdr Order of Honour (Greece); Hon. DPhil (Cyprus) 1998; Prince Carl Medal, Royal Award, Swedish Acad., Letterstedts Award, Royal Acad. of Science, Cultural Award, Natur & Kultur, Bonniers Award, City of Athens Award, Ax:son Johnsons Stiftelse Award. *Publications:* Syntaktische und lexikalische Studien zur Historia Lausiaca des Palladios 1943, Giorgos Seferis 1963, Roms Konungahävder 1964, Fredrika Bremer i Grekland 1965, W. H. Humphreys' First Journal of the Greek War of Independence 1967, Thucydides 1978, Min odyssé 1982, Bysantinska porträtt 1984, Homeros 1985, Bistånd till Afrika 1985, Disaster Relief for Development 1986, Hellenika 1986, En värld utan gränser 1988, Den gyllene lyran: Archilochos, Sapfo, Pindaros 1989, Europas födelse 1991, Lans och bage: Aischylos Perserna 1992, Anna Komnenas värld 1993, Bysantinsk Kulturhistoria 1994, Ensamhet och gemenskap 1995, Mulåsnan på Akropolis 1996, Pol Pot och Kambodja 1997, Ökenfäderna 1998, Hellenskt och romerskt 1998, Sicilien 1999, Tidevarv komma, tidevarv försvinna 2000, Europas ungtid 2002. *Leisure interests:* poetry, sports. *Address:* 24 Phokylidou, 10673 Athens, Greece. *Telephone:* (1) 3611780.

LINNEY, Laura, BFA; American actress; b. 5 Feb. 1964, New York, NY; m. David Adkins 1995 (divorced 2000); ed Northfield Mount Hermon School, Northwestern Univ., Brown Univ., Juilliard School; Theatre World Award 1992, Calloway Award 1994, Best Actress, Toronto Film Critics Asscn 2000, Best Actress, Nat. Soc. Film Critics 2000, Best Actress, NY Film Critics Circle 2000, Best Actress, Boston Soc. Film Critics 2000, Emmy Award, Outstanding Lead Actress 2002, Best Supporting Actress, Nat. Bd of Review 2004, Desert Palm Award for Best Actress, Palm Springs Int. Film Festival 2004, Emmy Award, Best Guest Actress in a Comedy Series 2004, Special Civil Rights Award, Pride Awards 2004, Best Supporting Actress, Broadcast Film Critics Asscn 2004. *Plays include:* The Seagull, Six Degrees of Separation, Sight Unseen, Hedda Gabler, Holiday 1995, Honour 1998. *Films include:* Lorenzo's Oil 1992, Dave 1993, Blind Spot 1993, Searching for Bobby Fischer 1993, A Simple Twist of Fate 1994, Congo 1995, Primal Fear 1996, Absolute Power 1997, The Truman Show 1998, You Can Count on Me 2000, The House of Mirth 2000, Lush 2000, Maze 2000, Running Mates 2000, The Laramie Project 2001, The Mothman Prophecies 2002, The Life of David Gale 2003, Mystic River 2003, Love, Actually 2003, P.S. 2004, Kinsey 2004, The Squid and the Whale 2005, The Exorcism of Emily Rose 2005, Driving Lessons 2006, Jindabyne 2006, The Hottest State 2006, Man of the Year 2006, The Savages 2007, Breach 2007, The Nanny Diaries 2007, The City of Your Final Destination 2007, The Other Man 2008. *Television includes:* Armistead Maupin's Tales of the City 1993, Class of '61 1993, More Tales of the City 1998, Love Letters 1999, Wild Iris 2001, Further Tales of the City 2002, Frasier (series) 2003–04, John Adams (series, HBO) (Golden Globe Award for Best Performance by an Actress in a Mini-Series 2009) 2008–. *Address:* c/o Toni Howard, ICM, 8942 Wilshire Blvd, Beverly Hills, CA 90211, USA.

LINSKENS, Hansferdinand, (Ingenrieth), DrPhil; German botanist and academic (retd); b. 22 May 1921, Lahr; s. of the late Albert W. Linskens and Maria E. Bayer; m. Ingrid M. Rast 1954; two s. two d.; ed Univs of Berlin, Cologne and Bonn, Eidgenössische Tech. Hochschule, Zürich; Battelle Memorial Fellow, ETH, Zürich 1952–53; Privat Dozent, Univ. of Cologne 1954–56; Prof. of Botany, Univ. of Nijmegen, Netherlands 1957–86, Dean, Faculty of Science 1980–85; Prof. of Geobotany, Univ. of Eichstätt 1986–2002; Adjunct Prof. Univ. of Mass. 1988–2001; Prof. a Contratto, Univ. of Siena 1987–2002; mem. Royal Dutch Acad., Deutsche Akad. der Naturforscher Leopoldina, Linnean Soc. of London, Royal Belgian Acad., New York Acad. of Science, Accad. dei Fisiocritici, Siena; NATO stipendiary, Lisbon 1960; Visiting Prof. Marine Biological Lab., Woods Hole, Mass. 1966, 1968; Man. Ed. Sexual Plant Reproduction 1988–93, Theoretical and Applied Genetics 1975–85; Hon. mem. Royal Dutch Botanical Soc. 1980, Leopoldina (Germany); Dr hc (Lille) 1982, (Siena) 1985; Hon. DrPhil (Dresen); K. Heyer Prize for Allergy Research 1984. *Publications:* Papierchromatographie in der Botanik 1958, Pollen Physiology and Fertilization 1964, Fertilization in Higher Plants 1974, Pollen Biology Biochemistry 1974, Cellular Interaction (with J. Heslop-Harrison) 1985; Modern Methods in Plant Analysis (series) 1966–99, Monographs in Theoretical and Applied Genetics (series) 1975–1999, Sexual Plant Reproduction 1988–. *Leisure interests:* history of science, collecting autographs. *Address:* Oosterbergweg 5, 6573 EE Beek, Netherlands; Goldberglein 7, 91056 Erlangen, Germany. *Telephone:* (246) 841652 (Beek); (9131) 440517 (Erlangen). *Fax:* (24) 652409 (Nijmegen). *E-mail:* joseb@sci.kun.nl (office); ProfhfLinskens@aol.com (home); blblinskens@hotmail.com (home).

LINTOTAWELA, Vivien; Sri Lankan business executive; Dir John Keells Holdings Ltd 1986–, Deputy Chair. 1997–2000, Chair. 2000–05; Chair. Ceylon Cold Stores (subsidiary of John Keells Holdings Ltd); Vice-Chair. Employers' Fed. of Sri Lanka. *Address:* c/o John Keells Holdings Ltd, 130 Glennie Street, PO Box 76, Colombo 2, Sri Lanka.

LIONS, Pierre-Louis, DèsSc; French mathematician and academic; *Professor of Mathematics, Collège de France;* b. 11 Aug. 1956, Grasse, Alpes-Maritime; s. of Jacques-Louis Lions and Andrée Olivier; m. Lila Laurenti 1979; one s.; ed Lycée Pasteur and Lycée Louis-le-Grand, Paris, Ecole Normale Supérieure, Paris, Univ. of Paris VI; Researcher, CNRS 1979–81, Dir of Research 1995–; Prof. of Math., Univ. of Paris-Dauphine 1981–2002; Prof. of Applied Math., Ecole Polytechnique, Palaiseau 1992–; Prof., Collège de France 2002–; mem Acad. des sciences, Paris, Naples Acad., Academia Europaea; mem. Editorial Bd 25 int. journals; Chevalier, Légion d'honneur; Dr hc (Heriot-Watt Univ., Edinburgh, UK, Univ. of Hong Kong); Doistau-Blutet Foundation Prize, Acad. des sciences 1986, IBM Prize 1987, Philip Morris Prize 1991, Ampère Prize, Acad. des sciences 1992, Fields Medal, Int. Congress of Mathematicians, Zürich 1994, Prix d'équipe Institut de Finance Europlace 2003, Thomson Prize 2004. *Publications:* numerous articles in math. journals on theory of nonlinear partial differential equations. *Leisure interests:* cinema, reading, rugby, swimming. *Address:* (office); Collège de France, 11 place Marcelin Berthelot, 75005 Paris, France (office). *Telephone:* 1-44-27-12-11 (office). *Fax:* 1-44-05-49-08 (office). *E-mail:* lions@dmi.ens.fr (office). *Website:* www.college-de-france.fr (office).

LIOTTA, Ray, BFA; American actor; b. 18 Dec. 1955, Newark, NJ; s. of Alfred Liotta and Mary Liotta; m. Michelle Grace 1997; one d.; ed Univ. of Miami. *Films:* The Lonely Lady 1983, Something Wild 1986, Arena Brains 1987, Dominick and Eugene 1988, Field of Dreams 1989, Goodfellas 1990, Article 99 1992, Unlawful Entry 1992, No Escape 1994, Corrina, Corrina 1994, Operation Dumbo Drop 1995, Unforgettable 1996, Turbulence 1997, Phoenix 1997, Copland 1997, The Rat Pack 1998, Forever Mine 1999, Muppets From Space 1999, Blow 2001, Heartbreakers 2001, Hannibal 2001, John Q. 2002, A Rumor of Angels 2002, Narc 2002, Identity 2003, Last Shot 2004, Control 2004, Happy Endings 2005, Slow Burn 2005, Revolver 2005, Take the Lead 2006, Even Money 2006, Local Color 2006, Comeback Season 2006, Smokin' Aces 2006, Wild Hogs 2007, Battle in Seattle 2007, Bee Movie (voice) 2007, Crossing Over 2007. *Television appearances include:* Another World, NBC 1978–80, Hardhat & Legs (CBS movie) 1980, Crazy Times (ABC pilot) 1981, Casablanca, NBC 1983, Our Family Honor, NBC 1985–86, Women & Men 2–In Love There Are No Rules 1991, The Rat Pack 1998, Point of Origin 2002, Smith (series) 2006. *Address:* c/o Endeavor Talent Agency, 9701 Wilshire Boulevard, 10th Floor, Beverly Hills, CA 90212, USA.

LIPENGA, Ken, BEd, PhB; Malawi journalist, editor and politician; *Minister of Economic Planning and Development;* b. 14 Feb. 1952; ed Univ. of Malawi, Univ. of New Brunswick; Ed.-in-Chief Blantyre Newspapers Ltd and Gen. Man. Blantyre Printing and Publishing Co. 1986–92; Founding Ed.-in-Chief The Malawi Nation 1993–95; Minister of Educ., Sports and Culture 1999–2004, of Labour and Vocational Training 2005–06, Deputy Minister of Finance 2006–08, Minister of Econ. Planning and Devt 2008–; mem. Parl. for Phalombe East 2004–; mem. Democratic Progressive Party. *Address:* Ministry of Economic Planning and Development, POB 30136, Capital City, Lilongwe, Malawi (office). *Telephone:* 1788390 (office). *Fax:* 1788131 (office). *E-mail:* epd@malawi.net (office).

LIPIČ, Maj.-Gen. Ladislav, BSc; Slovenian army officer; b. 30 Nov. 1951, Murska Sobota; ed Univ. of Ljubljana; Asst for Organizational and Mobilization Affairs, Murska Sobota Municipal Territorial Defence HQ 1987–90; Chief of Logistics, Territorial Defence Regional Command (Vzhodna Štajerska Region) 1990–94, Commdr 1994–97; Chief of Logistics, Slovenian Armed Forces Gen. Staff 1997–2000, Deputy Chief of Gen. Staff 2000–01, Chief of Gen. Staff 2001–06; Co-Dir CAE 98 Exercise (jt NATO and PfP member countries exercise), Slovenia 1998; apptd Brig. 1998, Maj.-Gen. 2003; guest lecturer, Faculty of Social Sciences, Univ. of Ljubljana. *Address:* c/o Ministry of Defence, General Staff, Kardeljeva ploščad 25, 1000 Ljubljana, Slovenia (office).

LIPMAN, David J., BA, MD; American biologist/biochemist and academic; *Director, Genomics and Genetics Section, National Center for Biotechnology Information, National Institutes of Health;* ed Brown Univ., Providence, RI, Univ. of New York, Buffalo; currently Dir Genomics and Genetics Section, Nat. Center for Biotechnology Information, Nat. Library of Medicine, NIH, Bethesda, Md; Fellow, American Coll. of Medical Informatics 2001–; mem. NAS 2003–. *Publications:* numerous articles in scientific journals on sequence comparison methods, comparative genomics and molecular evolution. *Address:* National Center for Biotechnology Information, Building 38A, Room 8N807, 8600 Rockville Pike, Bethesda, MD 20894, USA (office). *Telephone:* (301) 496-2475 (office). *Fax:* (301) 480-9241 (office). *E-mail:* lipman@ncbi.nlm.nih.gov (office). *Website:* www.ncbi.nlm.nih.gov (office).

LIPOVSEK, Marjana; Slovenian singer (contralto); b. 3 Dec. 1946, Ljubljana; ed in Ljubljana and Graz Music Acad., Austria; joined Vienna State Opera, then Hamburg State Opera, FRG; operatic roles include Oktavian in Der Rosenkavalier, Dorabella in Così fan tutte, Marina in Boris Godunov, Ulrica in Un ballo in maschera, Mistress Quickly in Falstaff, Orfeo, Azucena in Il trovatore, Amneris in Aida, Brangäne in Tristan und Isolde, Eboli in Don Carlo, Fricka, Marfa in Khovanshchina, Marina in Boris Godunov, Marie in Wozzeck, Klytemnestra in Elektra, and Amme in Die Frau ohne Schatten; has sung in the leading European opera houses including Berlin, Madrid, Frankfurt, La Scala, Vienna State Opera and Bavarian State Opera, Munich; int. debut as recitalist, Salzburg Festival 1985; Grand Prix du Disque for Frank Martin's Cornet, Prix Spécial du Jury Nouvelle Académie du Disque Français; Gustav Mahler Gold Medal (Bavaria) 1993, (Vienna) 1996. *Recordings include:* the Bach Passions, Gluck's Orfeo, Handel's Messiah, Beethoven's Choral Symphony, Wagner's Das Rheingold, Johann Strauss's Die Fledermaus and Frank Martin's Cornet, Marina in Boris Godunov under Claudio Abbado, Mahler's Kindertotenlieder, recital discs of Brahms Lieder and Schumann Lieder. *Television includes:* various concerts and recitals, Carmen, Samson and Delila, Der Ring des Nibelungen, Die Frau ohne Schatten, Tristan und Isolde. *Address:* Künstleragentur Dr. Raab & Dr. Böhm, Plankengasse 7, 1010 Vienna, Austria (office). *Telephone:* (1) 512-05-01 (office). *Fax:* (1) 512-77-43 (office). *E-mail:* office@rbartists.at (office). *Website:* www.rbartists.at (office).

LIPP, Robert I., MBA, JD; American insurance industry executive; *Chairman, The St Paul Travelers Companies Inc.;* m. 1st Bari Lipp (deceased); m. 2nd Martha Berman; five c.; ed Williams Coll., Harvard Univ., NY Univ.; various positions with Chemical NY Corpn (now JPMorgan Chase & Co.) 1963–86; joined Citigroup 1986, Chair. and CEO CitiFinancial Credit Co. 1991–93, Co-Chair. Citigroup Inc. 1998–99, Vice-Chair. and mem. Office of Chair. 2000, Chair. and CEO Global Consumer Business 1999–2000; Vice-Chair. and Dir Travelers Group Inc. 1991–98; Chair. and CEO Travelers Insurance Group Inc. 1993–2000; CEO and Pres. Travelers Insurance Group Holdings Inc. 1996–98, Chair. 1996–2000, 2001; Chair. and CEO Travelers Property Casualty Corpn 2001–04; Chair. The St Paul Travelers Cos Inc. (following merger of The St Paul Co. and Travelers Insurance Group 2004) 2004–; mem. Bd Dirs JPMorgan Chase & Co., Bank One Corpn, Accenture Ltd 2001–; Pres. NY City Ballet; Chair. Bd Trustees, Williams Coll.; Founder Bari Lipp Foundation; Treasurer Mass Museum of Contemporary Art; Trustee Carnegie Hall. *Address:* The St Paul Travelers Companies Inc., 385 Washington Street, St Paul, MN 55102, USA (office). *Telephone:* (651) 310-7911 (office). *Fax:* (651) 310-3386 (office). *Website:* www.stpaultravelers.com (office).

LIPPARD, Stephen J., BA, PhD; American chemist and academic; *Arthur Amos Noyes Professor of Chemistry, Massachusetts Institute of Technology;* b. 12 Oct. 1940, Pittsburgh, PA; ed Haverford Coll., Haverford, PA, MIT; Asst Prof. of Chemistry, Columbia Univ. 1966–69, Assoc. Prof. 1969–72, Prof. 1972–82; Prof. of Chemistry, MIT 1983–89, Arthur Amos Noyes Prof. of Chemistry 1989–, Head Dept of Chemistry 1995–; mem. NAS 1989–, Nat. Inst. of Medicine 1993–; Scientific Mem. Max-Planck-Gesellschaft 1996–; Fellow Alfred P. Sloan Foundation 1968–70, John Simon Guggenheim Foundation 1972–, John E. Fogarty Int. Center 1979–, AAAS 1980–, American Acad. of Arts and Sciences 1986–; Hon. Fellow Woodrow Wilson Foundation 1962, Hon. Mem. Italian Chemical Soc. 1996; Hon. DSc (Texas A&M Univ.) 1995; Int. Precious Metals Inst. Henry J. Albert Award 1985, American Chemical Soc. Award in Inorganic Chemistry 1987, Remsen Award 1987, Univ. of Ill. John S. Bailar Jr Award 1993, American Chemical Soc. Award for Distinguished Service in Inorganic Chemistry 1994, William H. Nichols Medal 1995, Nat. Medal of Science 2006. *Address:* Department of Chemistry, Massachusetts Institute of Technology, Room 18-590, Cambridge, MA 02139, USA (office). *Telephone:* (617) 253-1892 (office). *Fax:* (617) 258-8150 (office). *E-mail:* lippard@lippard.mit.edu (office). *Website:* web.mit.edu/chemistry/www/faculty/lippard.html (office).

LIPPE, Stefan, PhD; German insurance industry executive; *CEO, Swiss Reinsurance Company;* b. 1955; ed Univ. of Mannheim; joined Bavarian Re 1983, Head of Non-proportional Underwriting Dept 1986, Deputy Mem. Bd of Dirs 1988–91, Full Mem. Bd of Dirs 1991–93, Chair. Bd of Man. 1993, mem. Exec. Cttee Swiss Re Co. (as Head of Bavarian Re Group) 1995–, Head of Property and Casualty Business Group, Swiss Re Co. 2001–05, Head of Reinsurance Products 2005–08, COO and Deputy CEO 2008–09, CEO 2009–; Kurt Hamann foundation prize f. *Address:* Swiss Reinsurance Company, Mythenquai 50/60, 8022 Zürich, Switzerland (office). *Telephone:* 432852121 (office). *Fax:* 432852999 (office). *E-mail:* stefan_lippe@swissre.com (office). *Website:* www.swissre.com (office).

LIPPENS, Count Maurice, MBA, LLD; Belgian business executive; b. 9 May 1943; m.; four c.; ed Univ. Libre de Bruxelles (ULB), Harvard Business School, USA; Dir Scienta 1967–80; mem. Supervisory Bd Groupe AG 1981–83, Dir 1983–88, Chair. 1988–90; Co-Founder Fortis 1990, Chair. Exec. Cttee 1990–2000, Chair. Bd of Dirs 2000–08; Chair. Het Zoute, Compagnie Immobilière d'Hardelot, Hazegras, CDC United Network; Vice-Pres. Soc. Gen. de Belgique, Royal Belgo-British Union; Dir Groupe Bruxelles Lambert (GBL), Finasucre, Groupe Sucrier, Village No. 1; mem. Bd of Dirs Harvard Business School, Trilateral Comm., Belgium Council INSEAD; Dir and Treasurer Musée des enfants; Grand Officer Order of Léopold II (Belgium) 2004. *Address:* c/o Fortis, Rue Royale 20, 1000 Brussels, Belgium (office).

LIPPONEN, Paavo Tapio; Finnish politician; *Speaker of the Parliament;* b. 23 April 1941, Turtola (now Pello); m. Päivi Lipponen 1998; three d.; ed Univ. of Helsinki, Dartmouth Coll., USA; journalist 1963–67; Research and Int. Affairs Sec. and Head Political Section Finnish Social Democratic Party (SDP) 1967–79; Pvt. Sec. (Special Political Adviser) to Prime Minister 1979–82; Political Sec. to Minister of Labour 1983; Man. Dir Viestintä Teema Oy 1988–95; Head Finnish Inst. of Int. Affairs 1989–91; Chair. Supervisory Bd Outokumpu Oy 1989–90; mem. Helsinki City Council 1985–95; MP 1983–87, 1991–; mem. SDP Party Cttee 1987–90, Chair. SDP Helsinki Dist 1985–92, Chair. of SDP 1993–2005; Speaker of Parl. March–April 1995, 2003–; Prime Minister of Finland 1995–2003; Dr hc (Dartmouth Coll., USA) 1997, (Finlandia Univ.) 2000. *Publications:* Muutoksen suunta 1986, Kohti Eurooppaa 2001. *Leisure interests:* architecture, swimming. *Address:* Parliament of Finland, 00102, Helsinki, Finland (office). *Telephone:* (9) 4323101 (office). *Fax:* (9) 4322705 (office). *E-mail:* paavo.lipponen@parliament.fi (office). *Website:* www.eduskunta.fi (home).

LIPŠIC, Daniel; Slovak politician and lawyer; *Deputy Prime Minister and Minister of Justice;* b. 8 July 1973, Bratislava; ed Comenius Univ., Harvard Law School, USA; Chair. Civil Democratic Youth 1991–95; Project Leader Advisory Centre for Slovak Businesses and Banks 1996–97; with Dist Mil. Prosecutor, Prešov 1997–98, Ernest Valko legal firm 1998; Head Office of Ministry of Justice 1998–2002; currently Deputy Prime Minister and Minister of Justice; Deputy Chair. for Internal Policy, Christian Democratic Movement; mem. Council of Experts, Inst. of Bankruptcy Law 1997–. *Address:* Ministry of Justice, Župné nám. 13, 813 11 Bratislava, Slovakia (office). *Telephone:* (2) 5935-3499 (office). *Fax:* (2) 5935-3605 (office). *E-mail:* terezia.sabova@justice.sk (office). *Website:* www.justice.gov.sk (office).

LIPSKA, Ewa; Polish poet; b. 8 Oct. 1945, Kraków; ed Acad. of Fine Arts, Kraków; Co-Ed. Pismo 1981–83; mem. editorial Bd Dekada Literacka 1990–92; First Sec. Polish Embassy, Vienna 1991–95, Adviser 1995–97; Deputy Dir Polish Inst., Vienna 1991–95, Dir 1995–97; mem. Asscn of Polish Writers, Polish and Austrian PEN Club; Koscielscy Foundation Award (Switzerland) 1973, Robert Graves PEN Club Award 1979, Ind. Foundation of Supporting of Polish Culture—Polcul Foundation Award 1990, PEN Club Award 1992, Alfred Jurzykowski Foundation Award (USA) 1993, City of Kraków Award 1995, Andrzej Bursa Award 1997, Literary Laurel 2002. *Publications include:* Wiersze (Poems) 1967, Drugi zbiór wierszy (Second Vol. of Poems) 1970, Trzeci zbiór wierszy (Third Vol. of Poems) 1972, Czwarty zbiór wierszy (Fourth Vol. of Poems) 1974, Piaty zbiór wierszy (Fifth Vol. of Poems) 1978, Zywa smierc (Living Death) 1979, Dom Spokojnej Mlodosci (House of the Quiet Youth) 1979, Nie o smierc tutaj chodzi, lecz o bialy kordonek 1982, Utwory wybrane (Selected Poems) 1986, Przechowalnia ciemnosci 1985, Strefa ograniczonego postoju 1990, Wakacje Mizantropa (Misantrope's Holidays) 1993, Stypendyscі czasu 1994, Wspólnicy zielonego wiatraczka 1996, Ludzie dla poczatkujacych (People for Beginners) 1997, Zycie zastepcze (Substitute Life) (Polish-German edition 1998), Godziny poza godzinami (After-hours Hours) 1999, Biale truskawki (White Strawberries) 2000, Sklepy zoologiczne (Pet Shops) 2001, Uwaga stopien 2002; selections of poems translated include Versei (Hungary) 1979, Vernisaz (Czechoslovakia) 1979, Such Times (Canada) 1981, Huis voor een vredige jeugd 1982, Auf den Dächern der Mausoleen (Germany) 1983, En misantrops ferie (Denmark) 1990, Meine Zeit. Mein Leib. Mein Leben (Austria) 1990, Poet? Criminal? Madman? (UK) 1991, Wakancitie na mizantropa (Bulgaria) 1994, Zon (Sweden) 1997, Stipiendisti Wremiena (Yugoslavia) 1998, Mennesker for Begyndere (Denmark) 1999, Mesohu me vdekjen (Albania) 2000, Menseen voor beginners (Netherlands) 2000, Sedemnast cervenych vevericiek (Slovakia) 2001, Selection of Poems (Israel) 2001, Fresas Blancas (Spain) 2001, Pet Shops (UK) 2002, Uwaga 2002, Ja 2003, Wiersze do Piosenek. Serca na rowerach 2004, Gdzie indziej 2005, Drzazga 2006. *Address:* c/o Wydawnictwo Literackie (Literary Publishing House), 31-147 Kraków, ul. Długa 1, Poland (office). *E-mail:* redakcja@wl.net.pl (office). *Website:* www.wl.net.pl (office); lipska.wydawnictwoliterackie.pl.

LIPSKY, John, BA, MA, PhD; American international organization official; *First Deputy Managing Director, International Monetary Fund;* ed Wesleyan and Stanford Univs; spent a decade at IMF, where he helped manage exchange rate surveillance procedure and analysed devts in int. capital market, also participated in negotiations with several mem. countries and served as IMF Resident Rep. in Chile 1978–80, Chair. Financial Sector Review Group 2000, First Deputy Man. Dir IMF 2006–; joined Saloman Brothers Inc. 1984, directed European Econ. and Market Analysis Group, London, UK 1989–92, Chief Economist 1992–97; Chief Economist and Dir of Research, Chase Manhattan Bank 1997; fmr Chief Economist, JPMorgan, later Vice-Chair. JPMorgan Investment Bank; mem. Bd of Dirs Nat. Bureau of Econ. Research and several corpns and non-profit orgs. *Address:* International Monetary Fund, 700 19th Street, NW, Washington, DC 20431, USA (office). *Telephone:* (202) 623-7000 (office). *Fax:* (202) 623-4661 (office). *E-mail:* webmaster@imf.org (office). *Website:* www.imf.org (office).

LIPSTOK, Andres; Estonian central banker; *Governor, Bank of Estonia;* b. 6 Feb. 1957, Haapsalu; m.; one s. one d.; ed Haapsalu Secondary School No. 1, Univ. of Tartu; Deputy Head 1980–83, Head 1983–86, Finance Dept of the Exec. Cttee of Haapsalu District; Chair. Planning Comm. 1986–89; Deputy Minister of Finance of Estonian SSR 1989; Gov. Lääne-Viru County 1989–94; Minister of Finance 1994–95; Minister of Econ. Affairs 1995–96; MP 1995–2005; Gov. Eesti Bank (Bank of Estonia) 2005–; mem. Council of Lääne-Viru Co. 1989–93, Estonian Liberal Democratic Party 1993–94, Estonian Reform Party 1994–2005, Congress of Estonia, Lions Club 1992; IV Class Order of the Nat. Coat of Arms. *Address:* Bank of Estonia, Estonia pst. 13, Tallinn 15095, Estonia (office). *Telephone:* 668-0810 (office). *Fax:* 668-0836 (office). *E-mail:* info@epbe.ee (office). *Website:* www.eestipank.info (office).

LIPTON, Stuart A., MD, PhD; American neuroscientist and academic; *Professor and Scientific Director, Del E. Webb Center for Neuroscience and Aging, The Burnham Institute;* b. 11 Jan. 1950, Danbury, Conn.; ed Cornell and Harvard Univs, Univ. of Pennsylvania; Intern in Medicine, Beth Israel Hosp., Boston, Mass 1977–78, Chief Resident in Neurology 1980, Asst in Neurology 1981–86, Assoc. in Neurology 1986–93, Sr Assoc. in Neurology, Beth Israel Deaconess Medical Center 1993–99; Jr and Sr Asst Resident, Longwood Area Neurology Program, Harvard Medical School, Boston 1978–80, Instructor in Neurology 1981–83, Asst Prof. of Neurology (Neuroscience) 1983–87, Assoc. Prof. of Neurology (Neuroscience) 1987–97, Assoc. Prof. of Neuroscience (Neurosurgery) 1997–2001; Chief Resident in Neurology, Children's Hosp. 1980, Asst in Neurology 1981–88, Dir Lab. of Cellular and Molecular Neuroscience 1987–97, Assoc. in Neurology 1988–97; Chief Resident in Neurology, Brigham and Women's Hosp. 1980, Assoc. in Neurology 1988–97, Chief, CNS Research Inst. 1997–99; Clinical Asst in Neurology, Massachusetts Gen. Hosp. Boston 1991–92, Clinical Assoc. in Neurology 1992–97; Prof. and Scientific Dir, Center for Neuroscience and Aging, The Burnham Inst., La Jolla, Calif. 1999–; Attending Neurologist, Medical Center, Univ. of California, San Diego, La Jolla 1999–, Adjunct Prof., Depts of Neurosciences and Psychiatry 1999–; Adjunct Prof., Dept of Neuropharmacology and Molecular and Experimental Medicine, Scripps Research Inst., La Jolla 1999–; Adjunct Prof. of Neuroscience, Salk Inst., La Jolla 2002–; Established Investigator, American Heart Asscn 1988–93; Chair. Neurobiology of Disease Workshops, Soc. for Neuroscience 1998–; mem. Asscn for Research in Vision and Ophthalmology 1974–, American Acad. of Neurology 1979–98, AAAS 1980–, Soc. for Neuroscience 1982–, Biophysical Soc. 1986–;

mem. Scientific Advisory Bd, HIV Neurobehavioral Research Center, School of Medicine, Univ. of California, San Diego 1995–99, Center for Neurovirology and Neurodegenerative Disorders, Univ. of Nebraska and Creighton Univ. 1997–, AIDS Research Center, Scripps Research Inst. 1997–; Assoc. Ed. Neuron 1995–; Reviewing Ed. Cell Death and Differentiation 2000–; mem. Editorial Bd CNS Meeting Reports 1994–99, CNS Drug Reviews 1994–, Frontiers in Bioscience 1995–, Journal of NeuroVirology 1995–, European Journal of Pharmacology (Molecular Pharmacology Section) 1995–, Journal of Molecular Neuroscience 2000–, Neurobiology of Disease 2000–, NeuroMolecular Medicine 2001–; Grant Referee, NSF 1982–; Stroke Council Fellow, American Heart Asscn 1992–; Fellow, American Acad. of Neurology 1998–; Hon. mem. British Brain Research Association 1982–, European Brain and Behaviour Soc. 1982–; Ford Foundation Scholarship 1968–72, NIH MD-PhD Fellowship 1972–77, Mary Ellis Bell Prize for Research, Univ. of Pennsylvania School of Medicine 1973, Baluin-Lucke Memorial Prize for Research 1976, Von L. Meyer Research Award, Children's Hosp., Boston 1979, Hartford Foundation Fellowship 1981–84, NIH Teacher-Investigator Development Award 1984–89, Pattison Award in Neuroscience, Research Inst. for Child Devt Research, Inc. 1989, Nobel Foundation Lectureship, Karolinska Institutet, Stockholm 1994, Grass Foundation Lectureship 1995, San Diego Health Hero Award, American Parkinson's Disease Asscn 2002, Ernst Jung Prize for Medicine 2004. *Publications:* more than 520 articles in scientific and medical journals. *Address:* Center for Neuroscience and Aging, The Burnham Institute, 10901 Torrey Pines Road, La Jolla, CA 92037, USA (office). *Telephone:* (858) 713-6261 (office). *Fax:* (858) 713-6262 (office). *E-mail:* slipton@burnham.org (office). *Website:* www.burnham.org (office).

LIPTON, Sir Stuart Anthony, Kt; British property developer; *Deputy Chairman, Chelsfield Partners LLP;* b. 9 Nov. 1942; s. of Bertram Green and Jeanette Lipton; m. Ruth Marks 1966; two s. one d.; ed Berkhamsted School; Dir Sterling Land Co. 1971–73, First Palace Securities Ltd 1973–76; Man. Dir Greycoat PLC 1976–83; Founder and Chair. Stanhope Properties PLC 1983–95, Stanhope PLC 1995–2006; Deputy Chair. Chelsfield Partners LLP 2006–; Chair. Comm. for Architecture and the Built Environment 1999–2005; adviser, new Glyndebourne Opera House 1988–94; Dir Nat. Gallery Trust Foundation 1998–; mem. Bd Royal Nat. Theatre 1988–98, Royal Opera House 1998–2006; mem. Governing Body Imperial Coll. 1987–2000, Royal Fine Art Comm. 1988–99, LSE 2000–06; Trustee, Whitechapel Art Gallery 1987–94, Architecture Foundation 1991–, Urban Land Inst.; Hon. FRIBA; Hon. Fellow, Imperial Coll.; Hon. LLD (Bath) 2005. *Address:* Chelsfield Partners LLP, 53 Grosvenor Street, London, W1K 3HU, England (office). *Telephone:* (20) 7290-2388 (office). *Fax:* (20) 7493-7667 (office). *E-mail:* slipton@chelsfield.com (office).

LIPWORTH, Sir (Maurice) Sydney, Kt, BCom, LLB; British barrister and business executive; b. 13 May 1931, Johannesburg, South Africa; s. of Isidore Lipworth and Rae Lipworth; m. Rosa Liwarek 1957; two s.; ed King Edward VII School, Johannesburg, Univ. of Witwatersrand; practising barrister, Johannesburg 1956–64; Dir (non-exec.) Liberty Life Asscn of Africa Ltd 1956–64; Exec. Pvt. Trading Cos. 1964–67; Exec. Dir Abbey Life Assurance PLC 1968–70; Vice-Pres. and Dir Abbey Int. Corpn Inc. 1968–70; one of co-founders and Dir Allied Dunbar Assurance PLC 1970–88, Deputy Man. Dir 1977–79, Jt Man. Dir 1979–84, Deputy Chair. 1984–88; Dir J. Rothschild Holdings PLC 1984–87, BAT Industries PLC 1985–88; Deputy Chair., Dir (non-exec.) Nat. Westminster Bank 1993–2000; Chair., Dir (non-exec.) Zeneca Group PLC 1995–99 (Dir 1994–99); Dir (non-exec.) Carlton Communications PLC 1993–, Centrica PLC 1999–2002; Chair. Monopolies and Mergers Comm. 1988–92, Bar Asscn for Commerce, Finance and Industry 1991–92, Financial Reporting Council 1993–2001; Arbitrator/Mediator, One Essex Court (The Chambers of Lord Grabiner QC) 2004–; mem. Sr Salaries Review Body 1994–, Panel of Conciliators and of Arbitrators, Int. Centre for Settlement of Investment Disputes, Int. Advisory Bd, SOAS 2004–; Vice-Chair. Trustees Philharmonia Orchestra 1986–93, Chair. 1993–; Trustee South Bank Ltd 1996–; mem. Constitution Committee, Int. Accounting Standards Cttee Foundation Trust 2000–; mem. European Policy Forum; Hon. QC 1993. *Publications:* The Monopolies and Mergers Yearbook: March 1989–December 1990 Vol. 1 1991, Major Issues in Regulation: Regulation Lectures (co-author) 1992. *Leisure interests:* music, theatre, tennis. *Address:* One Essex Court, Temple, London, EC4Y 9AR (office); International Accounting Standards Board, 30 Cannon Street, EC4M 6XH, England. *Telephone:* (20) 7583-2000 (office); (20) 7726-1000. *Fax:* (20) 7583-0118 (office); (20) 7726-1038. *E-mail:* clerks@oeclaw.co.uk (office). *Website:* www.oeclaw.co.uk (office); www.iasb.org.

LISITSYN, Aleksander Petrovich; Russian marine geologist, geophysicist and geochemist; *Head of Department, P.P. Shirshov Institute of Oceanology, Russian Academy of Sciences;* b. 3 July 1923; m.; two c.; ed Moscow Geological Prospecting Inst.; Jr, Sr Researcher, Head of Lab., Head of Div., P.P. Shirshov Inst. of Oceanology, USSR (now Russian) Acad. of Sciences 1953–81, Head of Dept 1981–; Corresp. mem. USSR (now Russian) Acad. of Sciences 1974, mem. 1994–; research in marine geology, geophysics and geochemistry of seas and oceans; USSR State Prize, F. Shepard Award. *Publications include:* Sedimentation in the World Ocean 1972, Processes of Oceanic Sedimentation 1978, Geological History of Oceans 1980, Biogeochemistry of Oceans 1983, Avalanche Sedimentation and Gapes in Sedimentation in Seas and Oceans 1988, Marine Glacial and Marine Ice Sedimentation 1994, Oceanic Sedimentation, Lithography and Geochemistry 1996, Litology of Lithospheric Plates 2001, Sea-Ice and Iceberg Sedimentation in the Ocean 2002; numerous journal contribs. *Address:* P.P. Shirshov Institute of Oceanology, Russian Academy of Sciences, Nachimovsky Prospect 36, 117851 Moscow (office); Ivanovskaya 8A, 1 127434 Moscow, Russia (home). *Telephone:* (495) 124-85-28 (office); (495) 977-97-02 (home). *Fax:* (495) 124-85-28 (office). *Website:* www.ocean.ru (office).

LISITSYN, Anatoly Ivanovich; Russian politician; *Governor of Yaroslavl Region;* b. 26 June 1947, Bolshiye Smenki, Kalinin Region; m.; one c.; ed Leningrad Acad. of Forest Tech.; Rybinsk furniture factory 1987, also Chair., Rybinsk City Dist Exec. Cttee 1987–90; Chair. Rybinsk City Exec. Cttee 1990–91; Deputy Head, Head, Yaroslavl Regional Admin 1991–92; mem. Council of Fed. 1993–; mem. Movt Our Home is Russia (resgnd); mem. People's Democratic Party 1995; Gov. Yaroslavl Region 1995–; Chair. Interregional Asscn Cen. Russia; mem. Council of Russian Fed. 1996–2000; mem. Bd Union of Russian Govs. *Address:* Office of the Governor, Sovetskaya pl. 3, 150000 Yaroslavl, Russia (office). *Telephone:* (852) 72-81-28 (office). *Fax:* (852) 32-84-14 (office). *E-mail:* gubern@adm.yar.ru (office). *Website:* www.adm.yar.ru (office).

LIŠKA, Juraj; Slovak politician; b. 29 Nov. 1964, Trenčin; m.; two c.; ed Slovak Tech. Univ., Univ. of Transport, Žilina; employed in State Forest 1982–84; TOS Trenčin 1989–91; entrepreneur in wood production, Finnish saunas 1991–; Chair. Regional Asscn, Slovak Democratic Christian Union 2000; elected mem. Národná rada Slovenskej republiky (Parl.) 2002–, mem. Finances, Budget and Currency Cttee, Standing Del. to Parl. EU Cttee; apptd Mayor of Trenčin 2002; Minister of Defence 2003–06 (resgnd); resgnd as Deputy Chair. Slovak Democratic and Christian Uniion (SDKÚ) 2008. *Address:* Národná rada Slovenskej republiky (National Council of the Slovak Republic), nám. Alexandra Dubčeka 1 1, 812 80 Bratislava, Slovakia (office). *Telephone:* (2) 5972-1111 (office). *Fax:* (2) 5441-9529 (office). *E-mail:* info@nrsr.sk (office). *Website:* www.nrsr.sk (office).

LISNYANSKAYA, Inna Lvovna; Russian writer and poet; b. 24 June 1928, Baku; m. Semen I. Lipkin (died 2003); one d.; began writing poetry at age 10; first works published 1948; poems published in Moscow literary journal Novyi mir (New World) and Iunost (Youth) 1957–; in internal exile 1979–89, following contribs to literary almanac Metropole; resgnd from Union of Writers 1980 (membership restored 1989); mem. Russian PEN Centre. *Publications include:* This Happened to Me 1957, Faithfulness 1958, Not Simply Love 1963, At First Hand 1966, Grape Light 1978, Rains and Mirrors 1983, Verse 1970–83, 1984, On the Edge of Sleep 1984, The Circle 1985, Airy Layer 1990, Poetry 1991, The Music of Akhmatova's 'Poem without a Hero' 1991, After Everything 1994, The Lonely Gift 1995, The Box with a Triple Bottom (Study on Akhmatova's Poem Without the Hero) 1995, Selected Poetry 2000, Without You 2003; contribs to literary journals including Novyi mir, Oktiabr, Znamia. *Address:* c/o Russian PEN Centre, 107031 Moscow, st. Neglinnaya, 18 / 1, p. 2; 125315 Moscow, Usievicha Street 8, Apt 16, Russia. *Telephone:* (495) 155-75-98. *E-mail:* penrussian@mail.ru.

LISOV, Yevgeny Kuzmich; Russian politician and lawyer; b. 1940, Ivanovo Region; ed Saratov State Univ.; investigator, Dist Prosecutor's Office, Kursk Region, Sr Investigator, Head of Div., Deputy Head, Investigation Dept, RSFSR Prosecutor's Office; Deputy Gen. Prosecutor of Russian Fed. 1991–93; investigated coup d'état 1991; Deputy Prosecutor of Moscow 1993–95; attorney, Moscow Regional Coll. of Barristers; expert, magazine Ogonyok 1995–98; Deputy Head, Admin of Russian Presidency, Head, Main Control Dept, Admin of Russian Presidency 1998–2004. *Publications:* Kremlin Conspiracy (with V. G. Stepankov q.v.); articles in magazines and newspapers. *Address:* c/o Administration of the President, Staraya pl. 4, 103132 Moscow, Russia. *Telephone:* (495) 206-48-51.

LISSAKERS, Karin Margareta, MA; American economist and fmr government official; *Director, Revenue Watch Institute;* b. 16 Aug. 1944; m.; two c.; ed Ohio State Univ. and Johns Hopkins Univ.; mem. staff, Cttee on Foreign Relations, US Senate, Washington, DC 1972–78; Deputy Dir Econ. Policy Planning Staff, US Dept of State 1978–80; Sr Assoc. Carnegie Endowment for Int. Peace, New York 1981–83; Lecturer in int. banking, Dir int. business and banking programme, School of Int. Public Affairs, Columbia Univ. 1985–93; US Exec. Dir IMF 1993–2001; mem. Council on Foreign Relations; Chief Adviser to George Soros on globalization issues, Soros Fund Management LLC 2001–06; Dir Revenue Watch Inst. 2006–. *Publications:* Banks, Borrowers and the Establishment 1991; articles in professional journals. *Address:* Revenue Watch Institute, 400 West 59th Street, New York, NY 10019, USA (office). *Telephone:* (212) 548-0696 (office). *E-mail:* klissakers@revenuewatch.org (office). *Website:* www.revenuewatch.org (office).

LISSNER, Stéphane Michel; French theatre director; *Artistic Director, Teatro alla Scala;* b. 23 Jan. 1953, Paris; s. of Georges Lissner and Elisabeth Landenbaum; two s. one d.; ed Coll. Stanislas and Lycée Henri IV, Paris; Sec.-Gen. Centre dramatique, Aubervilliers 1977–78; Co-Dir Centre dramatique, Nice 1978–83; Dir-Gen. Orchestre de Paris 1994–96; Artistic Dir Teatro Real de Paris 1996–97; Dir Aix-en-Provence Festival 1996–2007; Co-Dir Théâtre des Bouffes du Nord, Paris 1998–; currently Dir Théâtre de la Madeleine, Paris, and Music Dir Vienna Festival; Superintendent and Artistic Dir Teatro alla Scala 2005–(13). *Publication:* Métro Chapelle 2000. *Address:* c/o Théâtre de la Madeleine, 19 rue de Surène, 75008 Paris, France; c/o Teatro alla Scala, Via Filodrammatici 2, Milan 20121, Italy. *Website:* www.theatremadeleine.com; www.festwochen.at; www.teatroallascala.org; www.bouffesdunord.com.

LISSOUBA, Pascal, DèsSc; Republic of the Congo fmr head of state; b. 15 Nov. 1931, Tsinguidi, Congo (Brazzaville); s. of Albert Lissouba and Marie Bouanga; m. 2nd Jocelyne Pierrot 1967; one s. six d.; ed secondary education in Nice, France and Ecole Supérieure d'Agric., Tunis, Tunisia; fmr agricultural specialist; Prime Minister of Congo (Brazzaville) 1963–66, concurrently Minister of Trade and Industry and Agric.; Prof. of Genetics, Brazzaville 1966–71, concurrently Minister of Planning 1968, Minister of Agric., Waterways and Forests 1969; Dir Ecole Supérieure des Sciences, Brazzaville 1970; sentenced to life imprisonment for complicity in assassination of Pres. Ngouabi 1977, subsequently released and exiled; Dir African Bureau for

Science and Tech., Nairobi 1981–; Leader Union panafricaine pour la Démocratie sociale (UPADS); Pres. Repub. of the Congo 1992–97; in exile, Burkina Faso. *Leisure interests:* geology, music.

LIST, Roland, DrScNat, CCM, FRSC; Canadian physicist and international official; *Secretary-General, International Association of Meteorology and Atmospheric Sciences;* b. 21 Feb. 1929, Frauenfeld, Thurgau, Switzerland; s. of August Joseph List and Anna Kaufmann; m. Gertrud K. Egli 1956 (died 1996); two c.; ed Swiss Fed. Inst. of Tech., Zürich; Head, Hail Section, Swiss Fed. Inst. for Snow and Avalanche Research, Davos 1952–63; Prof. of Physics (Meteorology), Dept of Physics, Univ. of Toronto 1963–82, 1984–94, Prof. Emer. 1994–, Assoc. Chair. Dept of Physics 1969–73; Deputy Sec.-Gen. WMO 1982–84; Chair. Exec. Cttee Panel of Experts on Weather Modification, WMO, Geneva 1969–82; Dir Univ. Corpn for Atmospheric Research, Boulder, Colo 1974–77; mem. Science Council, Space Shuttle Program (NASA) 1978–80; Chair. Italian Scientific Cttee for Rain Enhancement 1990–98; Sec.-Gen. Int. Asscn of Meteorology and Atmospheric Sciences 1995–; Rep. of Int. Union for Geodesy and Geophysics with WMO and World Climate Research Program 1995–; mem. and Chair. Planned and Inadvertent Weather Modification Cttee, American Meteorological Soc. 1996–2003; mem. or chair. many int., Canadian, US and Swiss cttees; consultant to UN, UNEP, World Bank, Inco and many other orgs; Visiting Prof., Swiss Fed. Inst. of Tech., Zürich 1974, 1998; Pres. Rotary Club of Toronto–Don Mills 1995–96; mem. Canadian and Swiss Acads of Sciences, Canadian Meteorological and Oceanic Soc., American Meteorological Soc., American Geophysical Union, Royal Meteorological Soc., American and Swiss Physical Socs, etc.; Hon. Prof., Chinese Acad. of Meteorological Sciences 2005; Sesquicentennial Medal, Univ. of Leningrad 1970, Patterson Medal, Canadian Meteorological Service, Plaque of Recognition, Thailand, Paul Harris Fellow, Rotary International, Golden Cumulonimbus Award, Spanish Inst. of Meteorology 2005, Weather Modification Trophy (UAE) 2005. *Publications:* more than 260 papers and many reports in the field of cloud physics, cloud dynamics, weather modification, classical physics, heat and mass transfer and aerodynamics. *Address:* Department of Physics, University of Toronto, Toronto, ON, M5S 1A7 (office); Ph-8, 1555 Finch Avenue E, North York, ON, M2J 4X9, Canada (home). *Telephone:* (416) 978-2982 (office); (416) 494-3621 (home). *Fax:* (416) 978-8905 (office). *E-mail:* list@atmosp.physics.utoronto.ca (office); roland.list@sympatico.ca (home).

LISTER, Gwen, BA; Namibian journalist; *Editor, The Namibian;* b. 5 Dec. 1953, East London, S Africa; one s. one d.; ed Univ. of Cape Town; began career as journalist with Windhoek Advertiser 1975; Co-founder (with Hannes Smith) Windhoek Observer 1978, Political Ed. 1978–84 (S African authorities banned newspaper during coverage of independence talks 1984, ban defeated, resgnd because of accusations by newspaper sr staff 1984); Founder The Namibian newspaper 1985, Ed. 1985– (copies confiscated by authorities, advertising boycott by business community, office bldg burned down 1988, prohibition of govt advertising in newspaper 2001); Co-founder Media Inst. of Southern Africa, fmr Chair. Governing Council and mem. Trust Funds Bd; mem. UNESCO Press Freedom Council, African Advisory Bd Int. Women's Media Foundation, Advisory Bd Int. Consortium of Investigative Journalists; Inter Press Service Int. Journalism Award 1988, S African Soc. of Journalists Pringle Prize for Journalism 1988, Cttee to Protect Journalists Int. Journalism Award 1991, Nieman Fellowship, Harvard Univ. 1995–96, Media Inst. of S Africa Press Freedom Award 1997, named Int. Press Inst. Press Freedom Hero 2000, Int. Women's Media Foundation Courage in Journalism Award 2004. *Address:* The Namibian, POB 20783, 42 John Meinert Street, Windhoek, Namibia (office). *Telephone:* (61) 279600 (office). *Fax:* (61) 279602 (office). *E-mail:* gwen@namibian.com.na (office). *Website:* www.namibian.com.na (office).

LITAVRIN, Gennady Grigoryevich; Russian historian; b. 6 Oct. 1925; m.; two c.; ed Moscow State Univ.; Teacher Moscow State Univ. 1954–55; Sr Ed. Ministry of Public Educ. 1955; Jr, Sr Researcher Inst. of History USSR Acad. of Sciences 1955–68; Sr, Leading Researcher Inst. of Slavonic Studies USSR Acad. of Sciences 1968–87, Head of Div. 1987–; corresp. mem. USSR (now Russian) Acad. of Sciences 1987, mem. 1994; research in history of Bulgaria, processes of formation of feudal regime, agrarian relations and social struggle in Byzantium, of Russian-Byzantine relations, problems of Balkan ethnogenesis; mem. Comm. on Studies and Promotion of Slavic Cultures, on Studies of Treasures of Aphone Monasteries. *Publications include:* Byzantine Society and State in the X–XI Centuries 1977. *Address:* Institute of Slavonic Studies, Russian Academy of Sciences, Leninsky pr. 32, 117334 Moscow, Russia. *Telephone:* (495) 938-57-85 (office); (495) 938-17-80; (495) 211-88-87 (home).

LITHERLAND, Albert Edward, PhD, FRS, FRSC; Canadian physicist and academic; *University Professor Emeritus, University of Toronto;* b. 12 March 1928, Wallasey, England; s. of Albert Litherland and Ethel Clement; m. Anne Allen 1956; two d.; ed Wallasey Grammar School and Liverpool Univ.; Scientific Officer, Atomic Energy of Canada 1955–66; Prof. of Physics, Univ. of Toronto 1966–79, Univ. Prof. 1979–93, Univ. Prof. Emer. 1993–, Dir Isotrace Lab. 1982–; Guggenheim Fellow 1986; Hon. DSc (Toronto) 1998; Gold Medal, Canadian Asscn of Physicists 1971, Rutherford Medal and Prize, Inst. of Physics 1974, Henry Marshall Tory Gold Medal, Royal Soc. of Canada 1993. *Publications:* numerous scientific papers. *Leisure interests:* reading, travel. *Address:* Apartment 801, 120 Rosedale Valley Road, Toronto, ON M4W 1P8, Canada (home). *Telephone:* (416) 978-3785 (office); (416) 923-5616 (home). *Fax:* (416) 923-4711 (office). *E-mail:* ted.litherland@utoronto.ca.

LITTELL, Robert; American writer; b. 1935, New York, NY; journalist Newsweek 1964; writer of Cold War espionage fiction. *Publications include:* Read America First 1968, If Israel Lost the War (with Richard Z. Cheznoff and Edward Klein) 1969, The Czech Black Book 1969, The Defection of A. J. Lewinter 1973, Sweet Reason 1974, The October Circle 1976, Mother Russia 1978, The Debriefing 1979, The Amateur 1981, The Sisters 1985, The Revolutionist 1988, The Once and Future Spy 1990, An Agent in Place 1991, The Visiting Professor 1994, Walking Back the Cat 1996, For the Future of Israel (with Shimon Peres) 1998, The Company 2002, Legends: A Novel of Dissimulation 2005, Vicious Circles 2007, The Stalin Epigram 2009. *Address:* c/o Author Mail, Simon and Schuster, 1230 Avenue of the Americas, 11th Floor, New York, NY 10020, USA (office). *Website:* www.simonandschuster.com (office).

LITTLE, Ian Malcolm David, AFC, CBE, DPhil, FBA; British economist and academic; b. 18 Dec. 1918, Rugby; s. of Brig.-Gen. M. O. Little and Iris H. Little (née Brassey); m. 1st Doreen Hennessey 1946 (died 1984); one s. one d.; m. 2nd Lydia Segrave 1991; ed Eton Coll. and New Coll. Oxford; RAF Officer 1939–46; Fellow, All Souls Coll. Oxford 1948–50, Trinity Coll. Oxford 1950–52, Nuffield Coll. Oxford 1952–76, Prof. Econs of Underdeveloped Countries 1971–76, Fellow Emer. 1976–; Deputy Dir Econ. Section, HM Treasury 1953–55; mem. MIT Center for Int. Studies, India 1958–59, 1965; Vice-Pres. OECD Devt Centre, Paris 1965–67; mem. Bd British Airports Authority 1969–74; Special Adviser, IBRD, Washington, DC 1976–78, Consultant 1984–85; Project Dir Twentieth Century Fund, New York 1978–81; Hon. DSc (Edin.). *Publications:* A Critique of Welfare Economics 1950, The Price of Fuel 1952, Aid to Africa 1964, Economic Development, Theory, Policy and International Relations 1982, Collection and Recollections 1999, Ethics, Economics, and Politics 2002; jt author of several other books. *Address:* Hedgerows, Pyrton, Watlington, 0X49 5AP, England (home). *Telephone:* (1491) 613703 (home). *E-mail:* lydiasegrave@hotmail.com (office).

LITTLE, Robert Alastair, MA; British restaurateur and chef; b. 25 June 1950, Colne, Lancs.; s. of R. G. Little and M. I. Little; m. 1st Kirsten Pedersen 1981; one s. one d.; m. 2nd Sharon Jacob 2000; ed Downing Coll., Cambridge; Chef, Old Compton Wine Bar 1974–77, L'Escargot 1981–82, 192 Kensington Park Road 1982–83; Chef, Propr Le Routier 1977–79, Simpsons 1979–81, Alastair Little 1985–; food columnist, Daily Mail 1993–. *Publications:* Keep it Simple 1993, Mediterranean Redefined (with Richard Whittington) 1995, Alastair Little's Italian Kitchen 1996, Soho Cooking 2000. *Leisure interests:* jigsaws, trashy novels, travel, wine. *Address:* Alastair Little, 49 Frith Street, London, W1D 4SQ, England (office). *Telephone:* (20) 7734-5183 (office). *Fax:* (20) 7734-5206 (office).

LITTLE, Tasmin E., ARCM, FGSM; British violinist; b. 13 May 1965, London; d. of George Little and Gillian Little; one s. one d.; ed Yehudi Menuhin School, Guildhall School of Music; studied privately with Lorand Fenyves in Canada; performed with New York Philharmonic, Leipzig Gewandhaus, Berlin Symphony, London Symphony, Philharmonia, Royal Philharmonic, Royal Liverpool Philharmonic, European Community Chamber, Royal Danish and Stavanger Symphony orchestras; has played in orchestras conducted by Kurt Masur, Vladimir Ashkenazy, Leonard Slatkin, Tadaaki Otaka, Sir Charles Groves, Andrew Davis, Jerzy Maksymiuk, Vernon Handley, Yan Pascal Tortelier, Sir Edward Downes, Yehudi Menuhin and Sir Simon Rattle; played at the Proms since 1990; concerto and recital performances in UK, Europe, Scandinavia, South America, Hong Kong, Oman, Zimbabwe, Australia, NZ, USA and Japan; numerous TV appearances including BBC Last Night of the Proms 1995, 1998; Hon. DLitt (Bradford) 1996; Hon. DMus (Leicester) 2002, Hon. DArts (Hertfordshire) 2007, (City Univ.) 2008. *Recordings include:* concertos of Bruch, Dvořák, Brahms, Sibelius, Delius, Rubbra, Saxton, George Lloyd, Ravel, Debussy, Poulenc, Delius, Elgar, Bax, Finzi; Dohnanyi violin sonatas, Bruch Scottish Fantasy, Lalo Symphonie Espagnole, Pärt Spiegel im Spiegel and Fratres, The Naked Violin (Gramophone/Classic FM Award for Innovation 2008) 2007. *Publication:* paper on Delius' violin concerto. *Leisure interests:* theatre, cinema, swimming, languages. *Address:* 67 Teignmouth Road, London, NW2 4EA, England (office). *Telephone:* (20) 8208-2480 (office). *Fax:* (20) 8208-2490 (office). *E-mail:* d.kantor.kcm@btinternet.com (office). *Website:* www.tasminlittle.net.

LITTLE RICHARD; American rock singer and songwriter; b. (Richard Wayne Penniman), 5 Dec. 1932, Macon, Ga; adopted s. of Enotris Johnson and Ann Johnson; R&B singer in various bands, including own band The Upsetters; gospel singer 1960–62; worldwide tours and concerts; announced retirement 2002; Grammy Lifetime Achievement Award 1993. *Recordings include:* albums: Cast A Long Shadow 1956, Little Richard Vol. 1 1957, Little Richard Vol. 2 1957, Little Richard Vol. 3 1957, Here's Little Richard 1957, The Fabulous Little Richard 1959, Clap Your Hands 1960, Pray Along With Little Richard Vol. 1 1960, Pray Along With Little Richard Vol. 2 1960, King Of The Gospel Singers 1962, Sings Spirituals 1963, Sings the Gospel 1964, Little Richard Is Back 1965, The Wild and Frantic Little Richard 1965, The Explosive Little Richard 1967, Rock 'n' Roll Forever 1967, Good Golly Miss Molly 1969, Little Richard 1969, Right Now 1970, Rock Hard Rock Heavy 1970, Little Richard 1970, Well Alright! 1970, Mr Big 1971, The Rill Thing 1971, The Second Coming 1971, Dollars 1972, The Original 1972, You Can't Keep A Good Man Down 1972, Rip It Up 1973, Talkin' 'Bout Soul 1974, Recorded Live 1974, Keep A Knockin' 1975, Sings 1976, Little Richard Live 1976, Now 1977, Lucille 1988, Shake It All About 1992, Shag On Down By The Union Hall 1996. *Films include:* Don't Knock the Rock 1956, Mr Rock 'n' Roll 1957, The Girl Can't Help It 1957, Keep On Rockin' 1970, Down and Out in Beverly Hills 1986, Mother Goose Rock 'n' Rhyme (Disney Channel) 1989. *Address:* Richard de la Font Agency Inc., 4845 South Sheridan Road, Suite 505, Tulsa, OK 74145-5719, USA (office).

LITTLECHILD, Stephen Charles, PhD; British economist and public servant; b. 27 Aug. 1943, Wisbech; s. of Sidney F. Littlechild and Joyce M. Littlechild; m. Kate Crombie 1974 (died 1982); two s. one d.; ed Wisbech Grammar School, Univ. of Birmingham, Univ. of Texas, USA; Harkness Fellow 1965–67; Sr Research Lecturer in Econs, Graduate Centre for Man.

Studies, Birmingham 1970–72; Prof. of Applied Econs and Head of Econs, Econometrics, Statistics and Marketing Subject Group, Aston Man. Centre, Birmingham 1972–75; Prof. of Commerce, Univ. of Birmingham 1975–94, Head, Dept of Industrial Econs and Business Studies 1975–89, Hon. Prof. 1994–2004, Prof. Emer. 2004–; Visiting Scholar, Dept of Econs, UCLA, USA 1975; Visiting Prof., New York, Stanford and Chicago Univs and Virginia Polytechnic 1979–80; mem. Monopolies and Mergers Comm. 1983–89, Sec. of State for Energy's Advisory Council on Research and Devt 1987–89; Dir-Gen. of Electricity Supply 1989–98; Prin. Research Fellow, Judge Business School, Univ. of Cambridge 2000–04, Sr Research Assoc. 2004–; mem. Postcomm 2006–; Hon. DSc (Birmingham) 2001; Hon. DCL (East Anglia) 2004. *Publications:* Operational Research for Managers 1977, (with M. F. Shutler) 1991, The Fallacy of the Mixed Economy 1978, 1986, Elements of Telecommunications Economics 1979, Energy Strategies for the UK (with K. G. Vaidya) 1982, Regulation of British Telecommunications' Profitability 1983, Economic Regulation of Privatised Water Authorities 1986. *Leisure interest:* family history. *Address:* White House, The Green, Tanworth-in-Arden, Solihull, West Midlands, B94 5AL, England (home). *E-mail:* sclittlechild@tanworth.mercianet.co.uk (office).

LITTLEWOOD, Peter Brent, BA, PhD; British physicist and academic; *Head of Cavendish Laboratory, University of Cambridge;* b. 1955; ed Cavendish Lab., Univ. of Cambridge,; worked at Bell Labs, Murray Hill, NJ, USA 1980–97, Head of Theoretical Physics Research Dept 1992–97; Prof. of Physics, Cavendish Lab., Univ. of Cambridge 1997–2005, Head of Theory of Condensed Matter Group, Cavendish Lab. 1997–2005, Head of Dept of Physics, Cavendish Lab. 2005–, Head of Cavendish Lab. 2005–; Fellow, Inst. of Physics, American Physical Soc., Trinity Coll., Cambridge; mem. Royal Soc. 2008–. *Address:* Cavendish Laboratory, Department of Physics, J.J. Thomson Avenue, Cambridge, CB3 0HE, England (office). *Telephone:* (1223) 337429 (office). *E-mail:* hod@phy.cam.ac.uk (office). *Website:* www.phy.cam.ac.uk (office).

LITTMAN, Mark, QC; British barrister-at-law and business executive; b. 4 Sept. 1920, London; s. of Jack Littman and Lilian Littman; m. Marguerite Lamkin 1965; ed Owen's School, LSE and Queens Coll. Oxford; Lt, RNVR 1941–46; called to Bar, Middle Temple 1947; Dir Rio Tinto-Zinc Corpn 1968–91; Pres. Bar Asscn for Commerce, Finance and Industry 1974–80; mem. Bar Council 1973–75, mem. of Senate of the Inns of Court and the Bar 1974–75; Deputy Chair. British Steel Corpn 1970–79; Dir Commercial Union Assurance Co. Ltd 1970–81, Granada Group Ltd 1977–93, British Enkalon Ltd 1972–80; Amerada Hess Corpn 1973–86, Envirotech Corpn 1974–78, Burton Group PLC 1983–93; Treas. Middle Temple 1988; Bencher of the Middle Temple 1970; mem. Royal Comm. on Legal Services 1976; mem. Int. Council for Commercial Arbitration 1978–; mem. Court of Govs, LSE 1980–; Vice-Chair. London Int. Arbitration Trust 1980–. *Address:* 79 Chester Square, London, SW1W 9DU, England. *Telephone:* (20) 7730-2973.

LITTON, Andrew, MM; American conductor and pianist; *Music Director, Bergen Philharmonic Orchestra;* b. 16 May 1959, New York; ed Fieldston High School, New York, Mozarteum, Juilliard School; Asst Conductor La Scala, Milan 1980–81; Exxon/Arts Endowment Asst Conductor, then Assoc. Conductor, Nat. Symphony Orchestra, Washington, DC 1982–86; Prin. Guest Conductor Bournemouth Symphony Orchestra 1986–88, Prin. Conductor and Artistic Adviser 1988–94, Conductor Laureate 1994–; Prin. Conductor and Music Dir Dallas Symphony Orchestra 1994–2006, Music Dir Emeritus 2006–; guest conductor many leading orchestras worldwide, including Chicago Symphony, Philadelphia, Los Angeles Philharmonic, Pittsburgh Symphony, Toronto Symphony, Montréal Symphony, Vancouver Symphony, London Philharmonic, Royal Philharmonic, London Symphony, English Chamber Orchestra, Leipzig Gewandhaus, Moscow State Symphony, Stockholm Philharmonic, RSO Berlin, RAI Milan, Orchestre Nat. de France, Suisse Romande, Tokyo Philharmonic, Melbourne Symphony and Sydney Symphony orchestras; debut at Metropolitan Opera, New York with Eugene Onegin 1989; also conducted at St Louis Opera, LA Opera, Royal Opera House, Covent Garden and ENO; music consultant to film The Chosen; Prin. Conductor Bergen Philharmonic Orchestra 2002–(11), Music Dir 2005–; Artistic Dir Minnesota Orchestra's Sommerfest –(2011); winner Bruno Walter Conducting Fellowship 1981, Hon. DMus (Bournemouth) 1992; winner William Kapell Memorial US Nat. Piano Competition 1978, BBC/Rupert Foundation Int. Conductors Competition 1982, Yale Univ. Sanford Medal. *Recordings include:* Mahler Symphony No. 1 and Songs of a Wayfarer, Elgar Enigma Variations, complete Tchaikovsky symphony cycle, complete Rachmaninov symphony cycle, Shostakovich Symphony No. 10, Gershwin Rhapsody in Blue, Concerto in F and Ravel Concerto in G (as piano soloist and conductor), Bernstein Symphony No. 2, Brahms Symphony No. 1, Walton's Belshazzar's Feast (with Bryn Terfel and Bournemouth Symphony) (Grammy Award), Rachmaninov Piano Concertos (with Stephen Hough and Dallas Symphony Orchestra) (Classical BRIT Critics' Award 2005) 2004. *Address:* c/o Columbia Artists Management, 1790 Broadway, New York, NY 10019-1412, USA (office). *Telephone:* (212) 841-9500 (office). *Fax:* (212) 841-9744 (office). *E-mail:* info@cami.com (office). *Website:* www.cami.com (office); www.filharmonien.no; www.andrewlitton.com.

LITVAK KING, Jaime, MA, PhD; Mexican archaeologist; *Professor Emeritus, University of Mexico;* b. 10 Dec. 1933, Mexico City; s. of Abraham Litvak and Eugenia King; m. 1st Elena Kaminski 1954 (divorced 1968); one d.; m. 2nd Carmen Aguilera 1972 (divorced 1978); ed Univ. Nacional Autónoma de México (UNAM), Asst, Dept of Prehistory, Inst. Nacional de Antropología e Historia 1960–63, Researcher 1963–66; Lecturer, Escuela Nacional de Antropología e Historia 1963–74; Head, Sección de Máquinas Electrónicas, Museo Nacional de Antropología 1966–68; Asst Research Fellow, Anthropo-

logical Section, UNAM 1968–72, Full Research Fellow 1972–74, Head of Section 1973, Dir Inst. for Anthropological Research 1973–85, Dir-Gen. for Academic Projects 1985–86, Prof. Emer. 1998–, Nat. Researcher System 1998–; Chair. Anthropology, Univ. of the Americas 1987–89; Jt Chair. Archaeology Dept, Escuela Nacional de Antropología 1966–67, Chair. 1969–71; Nat. Researcher, Mexican Scientific Research Acad. 1984; Visiting Prof., Univ. of Minnesota 1981, Univ. of New Mexico 1985–86; Mellon Prof. of Humanities, Tulane Univ., USA 1988; Coordinator Library of the Inst. of Anthropological Research 1993–; Gen. Sec. Mexican Anthropological Soc. 1970–76, 1981–83; mem. Publs Cttee, Instituto de Geografía, UNAM 1985–; mem. Mexican Scientific Research Acad. 1972–, Consultative Council (Archaeology) El Colegio de México, Diccionario del Español en México 1974–83, Nat. Researcher, Class III, Mexico; mem. Bd Dirs Museum Computer Network 1982–88; mem. Scientific Cttee Arqueologia Mexicana 1995–98; Assoc. Research Ed. for Mesoamerica, American Antiquity, Soc. for American Archaeology 1971–76, 1984–85; Ed. Antropología Matemática 1966–68, Jt-Ed. 1968–76; Research Ed. American Antiquity 1971–74; Advisory Ed. Abstracts in Anthropology 1975–77; Ed. Humanidades 1990–; Jt-Ed. Revista Mexicana de Estudios Antropologicos 1997–98; mem. Editorial Comm. Reimpresos 1975–85, Ciencia y Desarrollo 1988–94; mem. Editorial Council Ciencia 1979–82, Pantoc (Publicaciones sobre Antropología de Occidente) 1981–, ¿Como ves? 1999; mem. Editorial Bd Advances in Computer Archaeology 1981–90, Latin America Antiquity 1989, HRAF Collection of Archaeology 1997; mem. Editorial Cttee Monografias Mesoamericanas series, Universidad de las Americas 1992, Universidad Autonoma Metropolitana 1995–, Investigaciones religiosas 1998, Revista Digital Universitaria 1999; Consultant for Anthropology, Editorial Alhambra 1981–84; Editorial Consultant, Cuadernos de Arquitectura Mesoamericana 1983–, Review Bd Trabajos de Prehistoria 1997, Revista Auriga 1998; Reviewer, Boletin. Investigaciones Geograficas 1998, Arqueologia Industrial 1999, Fronteras en Movimiento: Expansion en territorios septentrionales 1999; Life mem. Sociedad Mexicana de Antropología 2000; Fray Bernardino de Sahagún (Mexican Nat. Award for Anthropology) 1970, "Huésped Distinguido", Veracruz 1978, Maestro Distinguido, Universidad Autónoma da Guadalajara 1980, Visitante distinguido de Honduras, El Instituto Hondureno de Turismo 1983, "Valor heróico" 1986, Diploma al "Merito Universitario", UNAM 1987, 1992, 1997, 2002, Diploma, Universidad Juarez de Durango 1992, Prize in Humanities Research, UNAM 1996, Diploma, 60th Anniversary of Radio Universidad, UNAM 1997, "Reflejo Politico Internacional, Universidad de las Americas-Puebla 1998, Honoured by Consejo Estatal para la Cultura y las Artes de Hidalgo 2001, Honoured by Sociedad Mexicana de Antropología 2001, "Huésped distinguido", Gov. of Zacatecas 2002, Lifetime Achievement Award, Soc. for American Archaeology 2002, "Al Mérito Universitario", UNAM 2002, Honoured by Periodico Humanidades de la Coordinacion de Humanidades, UNAM 2004. *Radio:* Espacio Universitario, Radio UNAM 1985–2001, La Música en la vida, Radio Unam 1996–. *Television:* Introducción a la Universidad 1977–79, Videocosmos, Antropología e Informática 1987–88. *Publications:* El Valle de Xochicalco 1970, Religión en Mesoamerica, XII Mesa Redonda (co-ed. with Noemi Castillo) 1972, Cihuatlán y Tepecoacuilco 1971, Xochicalco: Un Asentamiento Urbano Prehispánico 1974, Balance y perspectiva de la antropología de Mesoamérica y el Norte de México (five vols) (co-ed. with Noemi Castillo) 1975, Las fronteras de Mesoamerica, XIV Mesa Redonda (two vols) (co-ed. with Paul Schmidt) 1976, Arqueología y derecho en México (co-ed. with Luis González R. and María del Refugio González) 1980, Interacción cultural en México Central (co-ed. with Evelyn Rattray and Clara Diaz) 1981, Ancient Mexico 1985, Todas las piedras tienen 2000 años 1985, History of the Cultural Development of Mankind Vols III–IV (co-ed.) 1997, History of Humanity Vol. IV (co-ed. with Paul Schmidt and Paul Gendrop) 1998 and others. *Address:* Instituto de Investigaciones Antropológicas, Universidad Nacional Autónoma de México, Ciudad Universitaria, 04510 México, DF (office); Teruel 402, Pedregal 2, Contreras, México, DF CP 10720, Mexico (home). *Telephone:* (5) 622-9659 (office); (5) 568-6176 (home). *Fax:* (5) 622-9660 (office). *E-mail:* litvak@servidor.unam.mx (home).

LITVINOV, Boris Vasilyevich; Russian physicist and engineer; b. 12 Nov. 1929; m.; three c.; ed Moscow Inst. of Mech.; lab. engineer, Sr Engineer, Sr Researcher, Deputy Head of Div., Research Inst. of Experimental Physics 1952–61; Chief Constructor, All-Union Inst. of Tech. Physics, USSR (now Russian) Ministry of Medium Machine Bldg (now Ministry of Atomic Energy) 1961–77; First Deputy Scientific Dir 1978–97, Deputy Scientific Dir 1997–; Corresp. mem. USSR (now Russian) Acad. of Sciences 1991, mem. 1997–; main research in applied physics, devt of new constructions of exploding devices; Labour Banner 1956, Order of Lenin 1962, 1977, 1981, Order of October Revolution 1971; Lenin Prize 1966, Hero of Socialist Labour 1981, Merit to Motherland (3rd Class) 1995. *Publications:* Metals and Minerals Research in Spherical Shockwaves, Power Engineering of Deuterium Explosion, Basic Engineering Activity. *Leisure interest:* carving. *Address:* Institute of Technical Physics, PO Box 245, 456770 Chelyabinsk, Russia. *E-mail:* lit@kbone.ch70.chel.su (office); litvinov@snezhinsk.zu (home).

LITVINOVA, Renata Muratovna; Russian actress and scriptwriter; b. 11 Jan. 1968, Moscow; d. of Murat Vergazov and Alissa Litvinova; m. Mikhail Dobrovsky; ed All-Union State Inst. of Cinematography; mem. Union of Theatre Workers. *Films include:* The Border–Taiga Romance, Dve strely. Detektiv kamennogo veka (Two Arrows: The Crime Story from the Stone Age) 1989, Uvlecheniya (Passions) 1994, Tri istorii (Three Stories) 1997, 8½ $ (voice) 1999, Aprel (April) 1992, Nebo. Samolyot. Devushka. (Sky. Plane. Girl.) (also writer and producer) 2002, Net smerti dlya menya (There is No Death for Me) (dir) 2002, The Tulse Luper Suitcases, Part 3: From Sark to the Finish 2003, Nastroyshchik (The Tuner) 2004, Boginya: kak ya polyubila (Goddess: How I Felt in Love) (also writer and dir and producer) 2004, Zhmurki 2005,

Vokaldy paralelder 2005, Zhest 2006, Mne ne bolno 2006, Dva v odnom 2007, Zhestokost 2007, Wow! (Generation P) 2009. *Scriptwriter for films:* Leningrad, November, Nelyubov (No Love) 1991, Traktoristy (Tractor Drivers) 1992, Muzhskiye otkroveniya (Revelations of Men) 1995, Principal and Compassionate Eye, Tri istorii (Three Stories) 1997, Strana glukhikh (The Country of Deaf People) 1998. *Television includes:* Granitsa. Tayozhnyy roman (miniseries) 2001, Diversant (mini-series) 2004. *Publications:* Prize of Film Festival Centaurs for Passions. *Leisure interests:* antiques, cats. *Address:* Menzhinskogo str. 38. korp. 1, Apt 104, Moscow, Russia (home). *Telephone:* (495) 470-35-52 (home).

LIU, Benren; Chinese engineer and business executive; *Chairman, China Metallurgical Group Corporation;* b. 1942; ed Wuhan Iron and Steel Univ., Training Dept of Party School of CCP; fmr Man. Wuhan Hot Rolling Plant, later Vice-Chief Engineer, later Vice-Gen. Man. and Party Cttee mem. Wuhan Iron and Steel Plant Gen. Man., also Party Cttee mem. and Vice-Sec. Party Cttee Wuhan Iron and Steel Group Corpn (WISCO) 1993–2004; Chair. and External Dir China Metallurgical Group Corpn 2004–; mem. Nat. Cttee CPPCC. *Address:* China Metallurgical Group Corpn, 11 Gaoliangqiao Xiejie, Haidian, Beijing 100081, People's Republic of China (office). *Telephone:* (10) 82169999 (office). *Fax:* (10) 82169988 (office). *E-mail:* mcc@mcc.com.cn (office). *Website:* www.mcc.com.cn (office).

LIU, Bingsen; Chinese calligrapher; b. Aug. 1937, Shanghai; ed Beijing Acad. of Arts; asst technician, Asst Research Fellow, Assoc. Research Fellow, Research Fellow, Nat. Palace Museum, Taipei, Taiwan 1962–86; mem. Nat. Cttee 7th, 8th and 9th CPPCC 1988–2003; Vice-Chair. and mem. Exec. Council Chinese Calligraphers' Asscn; Vice-Chair. China Fed. of Literary and Art Circles 2001; Exec. mem. All-China Youth Fed.; Fushi Fine Arts Award (Japan) 1990. *Publications:* Travel Notes of Past Dynasties; Purple Wall and Autumn Grass. *Address:* Chinese Calligraphers Association, No.10, Nanli, Nong Zhanguan (Agricultural Exhibition Hall), Beijing 100026, People's Republic of China (office).

LIU, Bosu; Chinese professor of fine art; b. Nov. 1935, Nanchang City, Jiangxi Prov.; ed Cen. Inst. of Fine Arts 1955; Assoc. Prof. Cen. Inst. of Fine Arts 1981–83, Prof. 1983–, Vice Dir 1986–; Dir Chinese Painting Acad. 1993–; mem. 7th CPPCC 1988–93, 8th CPPCC 1993–98. *Address:* c/o Central Academy of Fine Arts, No.2 West Wanhong Street, Jiuxianqiao, Beijing 100015, People's Republic of China.

LIU, Chao-shiuan, BS, MS, PhD; Taiwanese politician; *Premier;* b. 10 May 1943; ed Nat. Taiwan Univ., Univ. de Sherbrooke and Univ. of Toronto, Canada; Assoc. Prof., Nat. Tsing Hua Univ. 1971–75, Prof. 1975–79, Dean, Coll. of Science 1982–84, Pres., Nat. Tsing Hua Univ. 1987–93, Chair Prof. 2000; Dir-Gen. Dept of Planning and Evaluation, Nat. Science Council, Exec. Yuan 1979–82, Deputy Minister 1984–87, Minister 1996–97; Minister of Transportation and Communications 1993–96; Vice Premier 1997–2000, Premier 2008–; Pres. Soochow Univ. 2004–08; Pres. Asscn of Pvt. Univs and Colls 2006–08; Vice-Chair. Nat. Policy Foundation 2000–04; Chair. Monte Jade Science and Tech. Asscn of Taiwan 2001–05, K.T. Li Foundation for Devt of Science and Tech. 2000–08; Pres. Chemical Soc. 1986–87. *Address:* Government Information Office, 2 Tientsin Street, Taipei 10051, Taiwan (office). *Telephone:* (2) 33568888 (office). *Fax:* (2) 23568733 (office). *E-mail:* service@mail.gio.gov.tw (office). *Website:* www.gio.gov.tw (office).

LIU, Chiu-Te; Taiwanese insurance industry executive; Pres. Cathay Life Insurance Co. Ltd 1998–2008; Dir The Life Assurance Asscn of the Repub. of China, Cathay Financial Holding Co. *Address:* c/o Cathay Life Insurance Co. Ltd, 296 Jen Ai Road, Section 4, Taipei 10639, Taiwan. *Telephone:* (2) 2755-1399.

LIU, Chuanzhi; Chinese computer scientist and business executive; *Chairman and President, Legend Holdings Group;* b. 29 April 1944, Zhenjiang, Jiangsu Prov.; ed Xi'an Mil. Telecommunications Inst.; researcher, Research Inst. No. 10 of State Science and Tech. Comm., Chengdu 1967–70; researcher, Computational Science Research Inst. of Chinese Acad. of Sciences 1970–83, later Dir; Cadre, Cadre Bureau, Chinese Acad. of Sciences 1983; Founder and Pres. Computational Science Research Inst. Inc. 1984; Founder, Pres. and Chair. Bd Legend Holdings Group Inc., Hong Kong Special Admin. Region 1989– (largest computer co. in China), also Pres. and Chair. Lenovo Group 1994–2005; Deputy 10th NPC 2003–; Vice-Chair. Exec. Cttee All-China Fed. of Industry and Commerce; elected one of China's Top Ten Econ. Figures 2000. *Address:* Legend Holdings Group, 23rd Floor, Lincoln House, Taikoo Place, 979 King's Road, Hong Kong Special Administrative Region (office); 10 Kexueyuan Nan Lu, Beijing 100080, People's Republic of China (office). *Telephone:* 25900228 (Hong Kong) (office); (10) 62572078 (office). *Fax:* 25165384 (Hong Kong) (office). *Website:* www.lenovo.com (office).

LIU, Chunhong; Chinese weightlifter; b. 29 Jan. 1985, Yantai, Shandong Prov.; ed Yantai Sports School; switched from judo to weightlifting at Sports School 1996; mem. Shandong Prov. Weightlifting Team 1998–; mem. nat. team 2002–; competes in 63–69kg weight div.; silver medal at clean and jerk World Championships, Warsaw 2002; gold medals at snatch (with world record weight of 120kg), clean and jerk (world record 150kg) and combined (world record 270kg) World Championships, Vancouver 2003; gold medal, Olympic Games, Athens 2004, broke world records at snatch (122.5kg), clean and jerk (152.5kg), combined (275kg); gold medal, Olympic Games, Beijing 2008, broke world records at snatch (128kg), clean and jerk (158kg), combined (286kg); has set 27 world records (12 jr, 15 sr) throughout career. *Address:* 9 Tiyuguan Road, Beijing, 100763, China. *Telephone:* (10) 67116669. *Fax:* (10) 67115858. *E-mail:* coc@olympic.cn. *Website:* www.olympic.cn.

LIU, Danzhai; Chinese traditional artist; b. 4 March 1931, Wenzhou, Zhejiang; s. of Liu Xiuqing and Liu Chenshi; m. Wang Weilin 1953; one s. one d.; also known as Liu Xiaosu, Liu Hun and Hai Yun Sheng; noted for "ren wu hua" (figure painting); teacher Wenzhou Westlake Elementary School 1949–51; Painter, Shanghai Books Publs 1951–56; Art Ed. Shanghai Educational Publishing House 1956–72; Painter, Shanghai People's Fine Arts Publishing House 1972–83; Prof. Shanghai Teachers' Univ. 1985–; Visiting Prof., Wenzhou Univ. 1985–; Artist, Shanghai Acad. of Chinese Arts 1956–; Art Counsellor, Shanghai Jiaotong Univ. 1981–; Head of Fine Arts Faculty, Shanghai Teacher's Univ. 1987–; mem. Chinese Artists' Asscn 1953–, mem. Bd of Dirs, Shanghai Br. 1953–; Nat. First Award for Prints 1981; First Award for Chinese Prints (Japan) 1981; Hon. Prize for Chinese Sport Art (Chinese Olympic Cttee) 1985. *Publications:* Images of a Dream of Red Mansions 1979, The 12 Beauties of Jinling from A Dream of Red Mansions (prints) 1981, Album of Chinese Poets 1983, Liu Danzhai: One Hundred Illustrations for 'Strange Studio' 1985, A Dream of Red Mansions 1985, Liu Danzhai (monograph) 1987, Liu Danzhai: Selections from Picture-Story Book 1987, Album of Liu Danzhai's Paintings 1988, Calendar of Paintings 1993; monographs on paintings and calligraphy by Liu Danzhai Shanghai, Hong Kong, Taiwan 1996. *Leisure interests:* poetry, travel, stone collecting. *Address:* 43 An Ting Road, Apt. 6, Shanghai, 200031, People's Republic of China. *Telephone:* 64720332.

LIU, Dehai; Chinese musician and university professor; b. May 1937, Cangxian Co., Hebei Prov.; ed Centre Music Inst.; began learning Pipa and other traditional Chinese instruments (including Erhu and Sanxian) at age 13; toured extensively abroad and performed with many famous orchestras including Boston Symphony Orchestra, Berlin Symphony Orchestra; Prof., Centre Music Inst. 1984–; mem. 7th CPPCC Nat. Cttee 1988–93, 8th 1993–98. *Address:* c/o CRC Jianian, Inc., No. 18, Jianguo Mennei Street, Rm 1706-1708, Henderson Center, Dongcheng District, Beijing 100005, People's Republic of China.

LIU, Deshu, BEng, EMBA; Chinese petrochemical industry executive; *President, Sinochem Corporation;* b. Nov. 1952; ed Tsinghua Univ., China-Europe Int. Business School; active in foreign trade for more than 20 years; Pres. China Nat. Machinery Import and Export Corpn –1998; Pres. Sinochem 1998–; mem. 10th CPPCC; Del. 16th CCP Nat. Cttee 2002–07, 17th CCP Nat. Cttee 2007–; mem. Int. Acad. of Man. 2003–. *Address:* Sinochem Tower A2, 28 Fuxingmenwai Dajie, 100031 Beijing, People's Republic of China (office). *Telephone:* (10) 8807-8898 (office). *Fax:* (10) 8807-8890 (office). *E-mail:* info@sinochem.com (office). *Website:* www.sinochem.com (office).

LIU, Lt-Gen. Dongdong; Chinese army officer; *Political Commissar, Jinan Military Region, People's Liberation Army;* b. Oct. 1945, Wuhan, Hubei Prov.; ed PLA Political Acad., Beijing; joined PLA 1961, CCP 1963; soldier, later staff mem., later Head of Propaganda Dept, later Deputy Political Commissar Artillery Regt, later Dir Artillery Regt (Political Section), later Section Head Org. Section (Army Political Dept), later Dir Political Dept, later Deputy Political Commissar, later Political Commissar, 139th Div.Div., 47th Group Army, PLA Services and Arms, later Dir Political Dept, 47th Group Army, later Deputy Political Commissar 47th Group Army; Dir Political Dept, PLA Lanzhou Mil. Region, Gansu Prov. –2000, Political Commissar 2000–03; Political Commissar PLA Jinan Mil. Region, Shandong Prov. 2003–; rank of Maj.-Gen. 1992, Lt-Gen. 1999; mem. 16th CCP Cen. Cttee 2002–07, 17th CCP Cen. Cttee 2007–. *Address:* People's Liberation Army Lanzhou Military Area Command, Lanzhou, Gansu Province, People's Republic of China (office).

LIU, Fangren; Chinese party official; *Chairman of Standing Committee, Guizhou Provincial People's Congress;* b. 1936, Wugong, Shaanxi Prov.; ed Shenyang Building Materials Eng Coll.; joined CCP 1954; worker, later technician, later Deputy Workshop Head, later Deputy Chief Engineer, later Deputy Factory Dir, Ministry of Ordnance Industry; fmr Deputy Sec., later Sec. CCP Jiujiang City Cttee, Jiangxi Prov.; Deputy Sec. Jiangxi Prov. CCP Cttee 1985–93; First Sec. CCP Party Cttee Guizhou Mil. Dist, PLA Chengdu Mil. Region 1993; Sec. CCP 7th Guizhou Prov. Cttee 1993–2001; Chair. Standing Cttee Guizhou Prov. People's Congress 1998–; Alt. mem. 13th CCP Cen. Cttee 1987–92, 14th CCP Cen. Cttee 1992–97, mem. 15th CCP Cen. Cttee 1997–2002; Deputy, 8th NPC 1993–98, 9th NPC 1998–2003 (Vice-Chair. Agriculture and Rural Affairs Cttee 1998–2003). *Address:* Standing Committee of Guizhou Provincial People's Congress, Guiyang, Guizhou Province, People's Republic of China.

LIU, Fuchun; Chinese business executive; b. 1949; ed Univ. of Int. Business and Econs, Beijing; several years' work experience in N America and Europe; Exec. Dir and Man. Dir China Nat. Cereals, Oils & Foodstuffs Import and Export Corpn (COFCO) 2000–07, also Pres. and Vice-Chair. 2000, Man. Dir COFCO HK; Dir China Aviation Oil (Singapore) Corpn Ltd 2006–, DaChan Food (Asia) Ltd 2007–. *Address:* c/o China National Cereals, Oils & Foodstuffs Import and Export Corporation (COFCO), 11th Floor, COFCO Plaza, 8 Jian Gou Men Nei Avenue, Beijing 100005, China (office).

LIU, Gang; Chinese dissident; ed Columbia Univ., USA; leader of Tiananmen Square pro-democracy demonstrations 1989; imprisoned 1989–95; fled China; granted temporary asylum in USA 1996.

LIU, Guoguang; Chinese economist; *Special Invited Consultant, Chinese Academy of Social Sciences;* b. 23 Nov. 1923, Nanjing; s. of Liu Zhihe and Zhiang Shulang; m. Liu Guoshiang 1948; two s. one d.; ed Southwest China United Univ., Kunming and Moscow State Inst. of Econs, USSR; joined CCP 1961; Deputy Dir-Gen. Nat. Bureau of Statistics 1980–82; Dir Inst. of Econs, Chinese Acad. of Social Sciences 1982–85, Vice-Pres. Chinese Acad. of Social Sciences 1982–93, Special Invited Consultant 1993–; Prof., Beijing Univ.; Alt. mem. 12th Cen. Cttee, CCP 1982–87, 13th Cen. Cttee 1987–92; mem. 8th NPC

Standing Cttee 1993–98, mem. Financial and Econ. Cttee; mem. State Academic Degree Comm. 1988–95; mem. State Council Project Review Cttee for Three Gorges Project 1990–93; China Econs Award 2005. *Publications include:* The Problem Concerning the Reform of the Management System of the National Economy, Problems Concerning China's Strategy of Economic Readjustment, Economic Reform and Economic Readjustment, Developing Marxist Theory in the Practice of Reform, Reform, Stability and Development: Macroeconomic Management under the Dual-Track System, New Stage of China's Economic Reform and Development, Two Fundamental Transformations in China's Economy. *Leisure interest:* music. *Address:* Chinese Academy of Social Sciences, Beijing, People's Republic of China (office). *Telephone:* (10) 85195012 (office); (10) 87752681 (home). *Fax:* (10) 65137435 (office); (10) 87752680 (home). *E-mail:* liugg2005@yahoo.com.cn (home).

LIU, Hanzhang; Chinese business executive; b. 1936, Gongxian, Henan Prov.; ed Taiyuan School of Metallurgical Industry; worker Anshan Iron and Steel Co. 1956–58; technician, workshop dir, subsidiary factory dir, gen. factory dir, then Chair. and Gen. Man. Handan Iron and Steel Co. 1958–. *Address:* Handan Iron and Steel Company, Handan, Henan, People's Republic of China (office).

LIU, Hongliang; Chinese scientist; b. 20 June 1932, Dalian, Liaoning Prov.; ed Tsinghua Univ.; Fellow, Chinese Acad. of Eng 1994–; Pres. and Prof., Chinese Environmental Science Research Inst. 1982–; Chair. Agric., Textile and Environment Eng Div., Chinese Acad. of Eng. *Publications:* over 20 research papers and a number of monographs. *Address:* Chinese Environmental Science Research Institute, Dayangfang, Beiyuan, Andingmen Wai, Beijing 100012, People's Republic of China (office). *Telephone:* (10) 64232542 (office). *Fax:* (10) 64232542 (office). *E-mail:* engach@mail.cae.ac.cn (office).

LIU, Hongru; Chinese business executive; b. 1930, Yushu, Jilin; ed Northeast Mil. Coll., Chinese People's Univ., Moscow Univ., Moscow Financial Coll., USSR; joined CCP 1948; Vice-Gov. Agricultural Bank of China 1979–80; Vice-Gov. People's Bank of China 1981–89, Vice-Pres. Council People's Bank of China 1980; Vice-Minister State Comm. for Restructuring the Economy 1988–93; Vice-Gov. People's Bank of China 1981–89; Vice-Chair. Securities Comm. of the State Council 1992–95; Part-time Prof., Beijing, Qinghua and Nankai Univs; Pres. Financial and Banking Inst. of China, China Monetary Coll. 1989–, China Finance and Economics Univ.; Deputy Head Leading Group for the Reform of the Housing System 1991–; Chair. China Securities Regulatory Comm. 1992–95; Alt. mem. 13th CCP Cen. Cttee 1987–92; Vice-Chair. Econ. Sub-cttee 8th and 9th Nat. Cttees. of CPPCC 1993–2003; Ind. Supervisor PetroChina 1999–2002, Ind. Dir (non-exec.) 2002–; Hon. Pres. Securities and Futures Coll., Univ. of Hanzhou 1995–. *Publications include:* Questions on Socialist China's Currency and Banking, Questions on Socialist Credit. *Address:* National Committee of Chinese People's Political Consultative Conference, 23 Taipingqiao Street, Beijing, People's Republic of China.

LIU, Huan; Chinese singer; b. Aug. 1963, Tianjin; ed Beijing Int. Relations Inst.; solo artist; univ. teacher; performed official theme song "You and Me" at Summer Olympic Games Opening Ceremony, Beijing, August 2008. *Stage production:* Sister Liu (opera) 2003. *Compositions include:* themes to TV dramas: Plainclothes Cop 1986, The Water Margin, A Native of Beijing in New York, Snow City, Sun Rises in the East and Rain Drops in the West; songs: Asking Myself a Thousand Times for That, Helpless Love. *Address:* c/o Beijing International Relations Institute, Beijing, People's Republic of China (office).

LIU, Huanzhang; Chinese sculptor; b. 30 Dec. 1930, Balihan, Inner Mongolia; m. Shen Chaohui 1968; one d.; ed Beijing Yuying Pvt. School, Beijing Cen. Acad. of Fine Arts; Assoc. Prof., Sculpture Studio, Beijing Cen. Acad. of Fine Arts 1956–; works at Tangshan No. 1 Middle School, Chen Jinlun Middle School, Beijing, Meixian, Guangdong Prov., Lanzhou Inst., Gansu Prov. *Publications:* Liu Huanzhang Carre Works Selection 1984, Sculpture Works Selection 1985, Seals Selection 1988. *Leisure interests:* sports, growing flowers. *Address:* Building No. 3, 1-102, Hong Miao Beili Chao Yang, Beijing, People's Republic of China.

LIU, Gen. Huaqing; Chinese naval officer (retd); b. Oct. 1916, Dawu Co., Hubei Prov.; m. Xu Hongxin; joined Red Army 1931, CCP 1935; Head, Political Dept, 11th Corps, 2nd Field Army 1949; transferred to Navy 1950; Maj.-Gen. PLA 1955; Rear-Admiral, PLA, Luda (Port Arthur and Dairen) 1958; Vice-Chair. Scientific and Technological Comm. for Nat. Defence 1967, First Vice-Chair. 1968; mem. Cultural Revolution Group, PLA 1967; disappeared during Cultural Revolution; Vice-Minister, State Scientific and Technological Comm., State Council 1978–80; Asst to Chief of PLA Gen. Staff 1979–80; Deputy Chief of Staff, PLA 1980–88, Commdr PLA Navy 1982–88; Vice-Chair. CCP Cen. Mil. Comm. 1990–97; mem. 12th CCP Cen. Cttee 1982–85, 14th CCP Cen. Cttee 1992–97; mem. Cen. Advisory Cttee 1985–92; Gen., PLA 1988–; Vice-Chair. Cen. Mil. Comm. 1989–97; standing mem. CCP Politburo 1992–97; Vice-Chair. Cen. Mil. Comm. of PRC 1994; Hon. Pres. Chinese Soc. of Mil. Sciences 1991–, Yachting Asscn. *Address:* c/o People's Liberation Army, Central Military Commission of the People's Republic of China, Beijing, People's Republic of China (office).

LIU, Huaqiu; Chinese diplomatist; *Director of Foreign Affairs Office, State Council;* b. Nov. 1939, Wuchuan Co., Guangdong Prov.; ed Foreign Affairs Inst., Beijing; joined CCP 1965; Second Sec., Embassy, Accra, Ghana 1973–81; Clerk, Gen. Office of State Council 1981; Counsellor then Minister, Embassy, Sydney, Australia 1984–86; Dir Dept of Affairs of the Americas and Oceania, Ministry of Foreign Affairs 1986–87; Asst Minister of Foreign Affairs 1987–89; Vice-Minister of Foreign Affairs 1989–98; Dir Foreign Affairs Office, State Council 1994–; Alt. mem. 14th CCP Cen. Cttee 1992–97, mem. 15th CCP Cen. Cttee 1997–2002, 16th CCP Cen. Cttee 2002–07; Dir Cen. Foreign Affairs Office, CCP Cen. Cttee 1998–; fmr Deputy Dir China Cttee of the Int. Decade for Natural Disaster Reduction; fmr Vice-Chair. Chinese Preparatory Committee, UN World Summit on Social Devt. *Address:* c/o Ministry of Foreign Affairs, 225 Chaoyangmen Nan Dajie, Chaoyang Qu, Beijing 100701, People's Republic of China. *Telephone:* (10) 65961114. *Fax:* (10) 65962146. *E-mail:* webmaster@mfa.gov.cn. *Website:* .

LIU, Jianfeng; Chinese politician and government official; *Director, Civil Aviation Administration of China;* b. 1936, Ninghe Co., Hebei Prov.; ed Kiev Eng Coll., USSR; joined CCP 1956; Deputy Dir, later Dir No. 1425 Research Inst., 4th Ministry of Machine-Building Industry 1968–84 (Acting Sec. CCP Party Cttee 1968–84); Vice-Minister of Electronics Industry 1984–88; Sec. Work Cttee, CCP Hainan Prov. Cttee 1988; Deputy Sec. CCP Hainan Prov. Cttee 1988–93; Gov. Hainan Prov. 1989–93; Vice-Minister of Electronics Industry 1993–98; Vice-Minister of Information Industry 1998–2003; Dir, Gen. Admin, Civil Aviation Admin of China 1998–; mem. 14th CCP Cen. Cttee 1992–97, 15th CCP Cen. Cttee 1997–2002, 16th CCP Cen. Cttee 2002–07; Del., 13th CCP Nat. Congress 1987–92; Pres. Electronics Br., China Council for the Promotion of Int. Trade. *Address:* Civil Aviation Administration of China, 155 Four East West Main Streets, Dongcheng District, Beijing, People's Republic of China (office). *Website:* www.caac.gov.cn (office).

LIU, Jiang; Chinese government official; *Vice-Chairman, National Development and Reform Commission;* b. 1940, Beijing; m.; two d.; ed Shihezi Agricultural Coll., Xinjiang Uygur Autonomous Region, CCP Cen. Cttee Cen. Party School; technician, later Chief, Mil. Farm, Tibet Autonomous Region; Farm Head, later Dir Animal Husbandry Bureau, Beijing 1972–84 (Sec. CCP Party Cttee 1972–84); joined CCP 1978; Vice-Minister of Agric., Animal Husbandry and Fishery 1986–90; Vice-Chair. State Planning Comm. 1990–93; Minister of Agric. 1993–98; Chair. Beijing Greening Cttee 1997; Vice-Chair. Nat. Devt and Reform Comm. 1998–; Deputy Head State Working Group for Comprehensive Agricultural Devt, Leading Group, Aid-the-Poor Projects 1998–; mem. 15th CCP Cen. Cttee 1997–2002; Vice-Chair. China Council for Int. Cooperation on Environment and Devt Development (CCICED). *Address:* National Development and Reform Commission, 38 Yuetan Nan Jie, Xicheng Qu, Beijing, People's Republic of China.

LIU, Jibin; Chinese politician; b. Dec. 1938, Longkou, Shandong Prov.; ed Beijing Aeronautics Inst.; joined CCP 1966; engineer, Section Dir then Vice-Man. Shenyang Songling Machinery Factory 1981–85; Deputy Chief Engineer, Ministry of Aeronautics Industry 1985; Minister of Aeronautics Industry 1985–88; Dir State Admin of State Property 1985–88; Vice-Minister of Finance 1988–98; Minister in Charge of Comm. of Science, Tech. and Industry for Nat. Defence 1998–2003; Del., 14th CCP Nat. Congress 1992–97; mem. Cen. Comm. for Discipline Inspection, CCP Cen. Cttee 1992–2002, Nat. Narcotics Control Comm. 1993, State Academic Degrees Cttee 1995–97, Hong Kong Special Admin. Region Preparatory Cttee 1995–97 (mem. Govt Del., Hong Kong Hand-Over Ceremony 1997), State Steering Group of Science, Tech. and Educ. 1998–. *Address:* c/o Zhongguo Gongchan Dang (Chinese Communist Party), 1 Zhongnanhai, Beijing, People's Republic of China (office).

LIU, Jie; Chinese business executive; b. Nov. 1943, Shucheng, Anhui Prov.; ed Wuhan Iron and Steel Inst., E.M. Beijing Iron and Steel Inst.; technician, Wuhan Iron and Steel Co. 1968; Chair. and Gen. Man., Anshan Iron and Steel Group Inc. 1994–2007 (retd); Alt. mem. 15th CCP Cen. Cttee 1997–02, 16th CCP Cen. Cttee 2002–07; Fellow, Chinese Acad. of Eng 1996–. *Address:* c/o Anshan Iron and Steel Group Inc., Huangang hu, Tiexi Qu, Anshan 114021, People's Republic of China (office).

LIU, Jingsheng; Chinese writer and dissident; b. 1954, Beijing; m. Jin Yanming; one c.; ed Middle School; factory worker; pro-democracy campaigner; Co-founder and fmr Co-ed. Tansuo (Explorations) journal late 1970s; joined Democracy Wall movt 1978, this involvement leading to theft charge and arrest for producing and distributing the journal; released from prison and resumed job as bus driver; helped establish China Freedom and Democracy Party after Tiananmen Square incident 1989; detained incommunicado for two years in 1992, trial July 1994, found guilty of membership in counter-revolutionary orgs, most notably Chinese Progressive Alliance, Liberal Democratic Party of China, and Free Labour Union of China; sentenced to eight years' imprisonment in Beijing Prison No. 2 for "organising and leading a counter-revolutionary organisation" and a further eight years for "inciting counter-revolutionary subversion" 1994; these were combined into 15-year prison sentence and four years' deprivation of political rights, sentence reduced by one year and three months in 2000 and 2001 for "good behaviour"; released early from prison 27 Nov. 2004; est. Bei jing Huaxia Gongwei Consultation Center April 2005, forcefully locked out by govt; est. Jingsheng Work House Sept. 2005; Hon. mem. UK, German, NZ, Netherlands and Swedish PEN Centres; PEN/Barbara Goldsmith Freedom to Write Award 1998. *Address:* Zhongguan Village A21-203, Haidan District, Beijing 100080, People's Republic of China (home). *Telephone:* (10) 82591379 (home); 13718766884 (mobile). *E-mail:* ljs6454@hotmail.com (home). *Website:* www .chinesepen.org.

LIU, Gen. Jingsong; Chinese army officer; b. 1933, Shishou, Hubei Prov.; ed PLA 7th Infantry Acad.; joined CCP 1954; platoon leader, Training Bn, First Mechanized Div., PLA Services and Arms, later Commdr Artillery Gun Co., Tank Regt; Regimental Staff Officer, Operations and Training Dept, PLA Regimental Office, later Div. Staff Officer; Deputy Commdr, later Chief of Staff, Artillery Gun Regt, PLA Services and Arms; Div. Commdr, later Div. Chief of Staff, later Army Commdr, PLA; Commdr, Shenyang Mil. Region, PLA 1985–; rank of Lt-Gen., PLA 1988, Gen. 1994; Commdr Lanzhou Mil. Region 1992–97; Pres. PLA Acad. of Mil. Sciences 1997–99; mem. 12th CCP Cen. Cttee 1985–87, 13th CCP Cen. Cttee 1987–92, 14th CCP Cen. Cttee

1992–97, 15th CCP Cen. Cttee 1997–2002. *Address:* c/o PLA Academy of Military Sciences, Beijing, People's Republic of China (office).

LIU, Jiyuan; Chinese aeronautical engineer; *General Manager, China Aerospace Science and Technology Corporation;* b. 1933, Xing Co., Shanxi Prov.; ed higher industrial inst. Moscow, USSR; joined CCP 1952; technician, No. 5 Research Acad. Ministry of Nat. Defence 1960–64; Dir and Sr Engineer No. 12 Research Inst. of No. 1 Research Acad. under 7th Ministry of Machine-Bldg Industry 1980–83; Deputy Dir No. 1 Research Acad. under Ministry of Astronautics Industry 1983–84; Vice-Minister of Astronautics Industry 1984–88; Vice-Minister of Aeronautics and Astronautics Industry 1988–93; Dir China Nat. Aerospace Admin 1993–98; Gen. Man. China Aerospace Science and Tech. Corpn 1993–; mem. 14th CCP Cen. Cttee 1992–97, 15th CCP Cen. Cttee 1997–2002; mem. 9th Standing Cttee of NPC 1998–2003; Pres. China Astronautics Soc.; mem. Russian Acad. of Navigation 1997. *Address:* China Aerospace Science and Technology Corporation, No 9 Fuchenglu, Haidian District, Beijing 100830, People's Republic of China (office).

LIU, Liying; Chinese civil servant; b. 1932, Dongping, Shandong Prov.; ed Harbin Public Security Bureau Cadre School; joined CCP 1949; fmrly Deputy Chief and then Chief Cadre Section, Dir Political Dept, Deputy Chief Constable of Shenyang Public Security Bureau; Deputy Dir Discipline Inspection Dept, Discipline Inspection Cttee of CCP Cen. Cttee, mem. Standing Cttee 1983–; Deputy Sec. Discipline Inspection Cttee of CCP Cen. Cttee 1997–; Del., 13th CCP Nat. Congress 1987–92, 14th CCP Nat. Congress 1992–97; mem. Exec. Cttee, All-China Women's Fed.; headed the investigation into several major corruption cases; given title Nat. Bearer of March 8th Red-Banner 1979. *Address:* Discipline Inspection Committee of Chinese Communist Party Central Committee, Beijing, People's Republic of China.

LIU, Lucy; American actress and artist; b. 2 Dec. 1968, Jackson Heights, Queens, NY; ed Brooklyn Technical High School, Stuyvesant High School, NY Univ., Univ. of Mich.; currently serving as UNICEF Amb. *Films include:* Bang 1995, Jerry Maguire 1996, Payback 1999, Play it to the Bone 1999, Shanghai Noon 2000, Charlie's Angels 2000, Cypher 2002, Chicago 2002, Charlie's Angels: Full Throttle 2003, Kill Bill Vol. 1 2003, Domino 2005, Lucky Number Slevin 2005, 3 Needles 2005, Rise 2005, The Year of Getting to Know Us 2007, Code Name: The Cleaner 2007, Rise: Blood Hunter 2007, Watching the Detectives 2007, Kung Fu Panda (voice) 2008; as producer: Freedom's Fury 2005. *Television:* Beverly Hills 90210 1991, L.A. Law 1993, Coach 1994, Home Improvement 1995, ER 1995, Pearl 1996, The X-Files 1996, Nash Bridges 1996, NYPD Blue 1997, Ally McBeal (series) 1998–2002, Futurama (voice) 2001–02, Joey 2004–05, Ugly Betty 2007. *Address:* c/o Framework Entertainment, 9057 Nemo Street, Suite C, West Hollywood, CA 90069; c/o Creative Artists Agency, 9830 Wilshire Boulevard, Beverly Hills, CA 90212-1825, USA (office). *Telephone:* (310) 288-4545 (CAA) (office). *Fax:* (310) 288-4800 (CAA) (office). *Website:* www.caa.com (office).

LIU, Mingkang, MBA; Chinese banker and public servant; *Chairman, China Banking Regulatory Commission;* b. 1946, Fuzhou, Fujian Prov.; m.; two s.; ed City Univ., London, UK; Vice-Pres. Bank of China Fujan Branch 1988–92, Pres. 1992–93, Chair. and Pres. Bank of China 2000–03; Deputy Gov. Fujian Prov. 1993–94; Deputy Gov. State Devt Bank of China 1994–98; First Deputy Gov. People's Bank of China and Vice-Chair. Monetary Policy Cttee 1998–99; Chair. China Everbright Group, Hong Kong 1999–2000; Chair. China Banking Regulatory Comm. 2003–; Alt. mem. 16th CCP Cen. Cttee 2002–07, mem. 17th CCP Cen. Cttee 2007–; mem. Bd of Dirs Int. Centre for Leadership in Finance, Bank Negara Malaysia; mem. Consultant Cttee for Chair. of Financial Stability Forum, BIS; mem. Int. Advisory Council, Faculty of Business Admin, Chinese Univ. of Hong Kong; Hon. Dir Fudan Univ. Int. Financial Centre, Hon. Prof. Chinese Univ. of Hong Kong. *Leisure interests:* jogging, swimming. *Address:* General Office of the China Banking Regulatory Commission, Jia No. 15, Financial Street, Xiacheng District, Beijing 100800, People's Republic of China (office). *Telephone:* (10) 66279977 (office). *Fax:* (10) 66299077 (office). *E-mail:* songhongmou@cbrc.gov.cn (office). *Website:* www.cbrc.gov.cn (office).

LIU, Mingzu; Chinese political official; *Chairman, Agriculture and Rural Affairs Committee, National People's Congress;* b. 1936, Weihai City, Shandong Prov.; joined CCP 1959; fmr Deputy Dir Office of CCP Weihai City Cttee, later Deputy Sec. then Sec. Weihai City Cttee; fmr Sec. CCP Rushan Co. Cttee, Shandong Prov.; fmr Deputy Sec. CCP Yantai Prefectural Cttee, Shandong Prov.; fmr Sec. CCP Linyi Prefectural Cttee, Shandong Prov.; Chair. Guangxi Regional People's Congress 1993–94; Deputy Sec., Standing Cttee and mem. CCP Guangxi Regional Cttee 1988–94; mem., Standing Cttee, mem. and Sec. CCP Inner Mongolia Autonomous Region Cttee 1994–2000; Chair. Inner Mongolia Regional People's Congress 1997–99; Alt. mem. 14th CCP Cen. Cttee 1992–97, mem. 15th CCP Cen. Cttee 1997–2002; Deputy, 8th NPC 1993–98, 9th NPC 1998–2003, Vice-Chair. Ethnic Affairs Cttee 2002, Chair. Agric. and Rural Affairs Cttee 2003–; Del., 12th CCP Nat. Congress 1982–87, 13th CCP Nat. Congress 1987–92. *Address:* Agriculture and Rural Affairs Committee, National People's Congress, Beijing, People's Republic of China (office).

LIU, Nianqu; Chinese composer; b. 24 Nov. 1945, Shanghai; s. of Liu Jin Chuang and Wang Yun Cong; m. Cai Lu 1973; one d.; Art Inspector Gen. Shanghai Int. Arts Festival 1987; Art Dir Shanghai Creation Centre; Vice Sec.-Gen. Org. Cttee 1990, Shanghai Art Festival; Vice-Chair. Exec. Cttee 1991, Shanghai Spring Arts Festival; Vice-Chair. Shanghai Musicians' Asscn; Councillor China Musicians' Asscn. *Compositions include:* Phoenix Singing at Qi San Mountain (dance drama) 1983, 1989, Spring of Life and Universe (oratorio) 1989 (1st Prize Shanghai Art Festival). *Leisure interests:* table tennis, football. *Address:* Shanghai Municipal Bureau of Culture, 709 Ju Lu Road, Shanghai, People's Republic of China (office).

LIU, Qi; Chinese government official; *Secretary of Beijing Municipal Committee;* b. 1942, Wujin Co., Jiangsu Prov.; ed Beijing Inst. of Iron and Steel Eng; joined CCP 1975; gas controller, furnaceman and founder, No. 2 Blast Furnace, Steel Works, Wuhan Iron and Steel Co. 1968–78, technician and Deputy Head, No. 3 Blast Furnace 1978–83, Deputy Dir Steel Works and Head Production Dept 1983–85, First Deputy Man. Wuhan Iron and Steel Co. 1985–90 (mem. Standing Cttee CCP Party Cttee 1985–93), Man. 1990–93; Minister of Metallurgical Industry 1993–98 (Sec. CCP Leading Party Group at Ministry 1993–98); Deputy Sec. CCP Beijing Municipal Cttee 1998–2002, Sec. 2002–; Vice-Mayor of Beijing 1998–99, Mayor of Beijing 1999–2002; Alt. mem. 14th CCP Cen. Cttee 1992–97, mem. 15th CCP Cen. Cttee 1997–2002, 16th CCP Cen. Cttee 2002–07 (mem. Politburo 2002–07), 17th CCP Cen. Cttee 2007– (mem. Politburo 2007–); Chair. Chinese Olympic Cttee, Beijing Municipality 2007–. *Address:* Beijing, People's Republic of China (office).

LIU, Shahe; Chinese poet; b. (Wu Xuntan), 11 Nov. 1931, Chengdu, Sichuan Prov.; m. 1st 1966; one s. one d.; m. 2nd 1992; ed Sichuan Univ.; mem. editorial staff The Stars (poetry magazine) –1957 and 1979–; satirical poem Verses of Plants (1957) led to condemnation as 'bourgeois rightist'; in labour camp during Cultural Revolution 1966–77, rehabilitated 1979. *Publications include:* Night on the Farm 1956, Farewell to Mars 1957, Liu Shahe Poetic Works 1982, Travelling Trace 1983, Farewell to my Home 1983, Sing Alone 1989, Selected Poems of Seven Chinese Poets 1993, Random Notes by Liu Shahe 1995, River of Quicksand (poetry) 1995, River of Quicksand (short texts) 2001. *Leisure interest:* UFOs. *Address:* 30 Dacisi Road, Chengdu City, Sichuan Province, People's Republic of China. *Telephone:* (28) 6781738 (home).

LIU, Shao Yong; Chinese airline executive; *President, China Southern Air Holding Company;* b. Nov. 1958; ed Civil Aviation Flight Univ. of China, Tianjin Univ. of Finance and Econs; Pres. China Eastern Airlines Co. Ltd (state-owned airline) 2000–02; Vice-Minister Civil Aviation Admin of China 2002–04; Pres. China Southern Air Holding Co. 2004–, Chair. China Southern Airlines Co. Ltd 2004–. *Address:* China Southern Air Holding Co., 278 Airport Road, Guangzhou 510405, Guangdong, People's Republic of China (office). *Telephone:* (20) 86130870 (office); (20) 86130873 (office). *E-mail:* webmaster@cs-air.com (office). *Website:* (office).

LIU, Shaohui; Chinese artist; b. 27 Aug. 1940, Szechuan; s. of Liu Veizheng and Xiong Wenying; m. Yang Yijing 1968; one s. one d.; ed Cen. Inst. of Applied Arts, Beijing; fmr Dir Art Layout Office, Yunnan People's Publishing House; Assoc. Prof., Pedagogical Inst., Guilin Pref.; mem. Chinese Artists Asscn; Assoc. Pres. Guilin Chinese Painting Acad. 1995–; engaged in design and research; exhbns in USA, Japan, Bulgaria, Hong Kong, Italy, Taiwan; works at Guilin Arts Garden; main designer for film Fire Boy (1st Prize, Int. Animated Film Festival, Japan 1984); Prize of Nat. Art Works of Excellence 1981, 1983, Japanese Int. Fine Arts Exhbn Prize of the Highest Honour. *Works include:* Zhaoshutun – Legend of a Dai Prince, An Elementary Theory on Binding and Layout of Books, The Candlewick Fairy 1985, Cowrie and a Little Girl 1986, Fine Arts Collection 1989. *Publications:* Yunnan School – A Renaissance in Chinese Painting 1988, Selected Paintings by Liu Shaohui 1989, The Third Sister Liu 1993, Selected Paintings of Guilin Chinese Painting Academy 1995. *Leisure interests:* music, travel, table-tennis. *Address:* Pedagogical Institute, Guilin Prefecture, 45 Xing Yi Road, Guilin, People's Republic of China (office).

LIU, Gen. Shunyao; Chinese air force officer; ed PLA Nat. Defence Univ.; fmrly Deputy Commdr, then Commdr Air Force, Lanzhou Mil. Region; Deputy Commdr, later Commdr PLA Air Force 1996–2002 (retd); rank of Lt-Gen. 1994, Commdr 1996, Gen. 2000–; mem. 15th CCP Cen. Cttee 1997–2002. *Address:* c/o Ministry of National Defence, Jingshangian Jie, Beijing, People's Republic of China (office). *Telephone:* (10) 66370000 (office).

LIU, Lt-Gen. Shutian; Chinese army officer; *Political Commissar, Guangzhou Military Region, People's Liberation Army;* b. 1940, Tengzhou Co., Shandong Prov.; ed Nanjing Political Coll. of the Chinese PLA; joined PLA 1958, CCP 1960; platoon leader, later staff mem., later Deputy Section Head, later Section Head, Cadre Section, Div. Political Dept; Political Commissar, Regt 1983; Political Commissar, 8th Div., Artillery Force, PLA Services and Arms 1983–86; Dir 26th Army (Political Dept), Army (or Ground Force), PLA Services and Arms 1986–88, Political Commissar 26th Army 1988–92; Deputy Political Commissar, Guangzhou Mil. Area Region 1994–98 (Sec. Comm. for Discipline Inspection, CCP Party Cttee 1994–98), Political Commissar 1998–; mem. 15th CCP Cen. Cttee 1997–2002, 16th CCP Cen. Cttee 2002–07. *Address:* Guangzhou Military Area Command Headquarters, Guangzhou, People's Republic of China (office).

LIU, Ts'un-yan, AO, PhD, DLit; Australian professor of Chinese; *Professor Emeritus, China and Korea Centre, Australian National University;* b. 11 Aug. 1917, Peking, China; s. of the late Tsung-ch'üan Liu and of Huang Yü-shu Liu; m. Chiang Szuyung 1940; one s. one d.; ed Univs of Peking, London and Hong Kong; Chair. Chinese Panel, Queen's Coll., Hong Kong 1952–59; lecturer Northcote Training Coll., Hong Kong 1959–62; Sr Lecturer Govt Evening School, Hong Kong 1959–62; Sr Lecturer, Reader in Chinese, ANU 1962–66, Prof. and Head of Dept of Chinese 1966–82, Dean Faculty of Asian Studies 1970–72, 1973–75, Prof. Emer. 1983–, Univ. Fellow 1983–; Visiting Prof. Columbia Univ. 1966, Harvard-Yenching Inst. 1969, Hawaii Univ. 1969, Univ. of Paris (Vincennes) 1973, Univ. of Malaya 1976, Chinese Univ. of Hong Kong 1976–77, Waseda Univ. 1981, Nat. Univ. of Singapore 1984–85; Fellow, Royal Asiatic Soc. 1957; Foundation Fellow, Australian Acad. of the Humanities 1969; Hon. D. Litt. (Yeungnam Univ., South Korea) 1972, (Hong Kong) 1988,

(Murdoch) 1989, (ANU) 1997. *Publications:* Buddhist and Taoist Influences on Chinese Novels 1962, Chinese Popular Fiction in Two London Libraries 1967, Selected Papers from the Hall of Harmonious Wind 1976, Chinese Middlebrow Fiction from the Ch'ing and Early Republican Era 1984, New Excursions from the Hall of Harmonious Wind 1984, Hofengtang Wenji (selected papers in Chinese) 1992, Ta Tu, The Grand Capital 1996, Hofentang Xinwenji 1997, Daojia yii daoshu 2000. *Leisure interests:* singing, Beijing opera. *Address:* China and Korea Centre, Level 3, Baldessin Precinct Building, Australian National University, Canberra, ACT 0200, Australia. *Telephone:* (2) 6125-3165 (office). *Website:* www.anu.edu.au/asianstudies/chkocen (office).

LIU, Xiang; Chinese athlete; b. 13 July 1983, Shanghai; ed Jr Sports School, Putuo District, Shanghai, East China Normal Univ., Shanghai; began competitive athletics career as a high jumper, switched to 110m. hurdles in 1998; set world jr and Asian records for 110m. hurdles Lausanne, 2001; won titles at World Univ. Games, Asian Games and Asian Championships in 2001–02; bronze medal 110m. World Indoor Championships, Birmingham, UK 2003; silver medal 110m. World Indoor Championships, Budapest 2004; bronze medal 110m. hurdles World Championships, Paris 2003; three Grand Prix victories in 2004; gold medal 110 m. hurdles Olympic Games, Athens 2004 in world-record equalling time of 12.91 seconds; set world-record time of 12.88 seconds, Lausanne 2006; first Chinese man to win Olympic track and field gold medal; 1st place, 60m. hurdles, IAAF World Indoor Championships, Valencia 2008; forced to withdraw from Beijing Olympics due to injury 2008; Male Athlete of the Year 2003 by Chinese Sports Journalists. *Leisure interests:* music, video games, karaoke. *Address:* c/o Beijing Organizing Committee for the Games of the XXIX Olympiad (BOCOG), 24 Dongsi Shitiao Street, Beijing, 100007, China. *Website:* http://liuxiang.sports.cn.

LIU, Xiaoqing; Chinese actress and business executive; b. 30 Oct. 1955, Chengdu City, Sichuan Prov.; d. of Ran Changru and Liu Huihua; m. Chen Guojun (divorced 1991); ed Sichuan Music Coll. Affiliated High; joined Chengdu's Army Performing Group 1973; head of business empire ranging from film production to real estate (45th richest person in China), including Xiaoqing Cultural Arts Ltd, Beijing; detained, convicted of tax-dodging and imprisoned 2002; also sued for defamation, Nanjing 2002. *Films include:* Great Wall of South China Sea 1976, Spring Song 1978, Wedding 1978, Little Flower 1979, Look at this Family (3rd Hundred Flowers (Baihua) Best Actress Award) 1980, Burning Down Yuan Ming Yuan 1983, Furong Zhen (Lotus Town) (10th Hundred Flowers Best Actress Award, 7th Golden Cock Best Actress Award 1986) 1986, Loveless Lover 1986, Hibiscus Town 1986, Yuanye (11th Hundred Flowers Best Actress Award) 1988, A Woman For Two 1988, Evil Empress 1988, Dream of Red Mansion 1, 1988, 2 1988, 3, 1989, 4 1989, 5 1989, 6 1989, Chuntao (12th Hundred Flowers Best Actress Award) 1989, Li Lianying, the Imperial Eunuch 1991, Town of Furong (Baihua Best Actress Award), Plastic Flowers 2004. *Television includes:* Wu Ze Tian 1995, Huo Shao E Pang Gong 1998, Tian Gui Hua 2000, Huo Feng Huang 2001, Lotus Lantern 2005,. *Plays:* The Last Night of Taipan Chin, Taipei 2008. *Publication:* My Way, My Eight Years, From a Movie Star to Billionaire. *Address:* PO Box 38, Asia Sport Village, Beijing, People's Republic of China. *Telephone:* (10) 4915988. *Fax:* (10) 4915899.

LIU, Xinwu; Chinese writer; b. 4 June 1942, Chengdu, Sichuan Prov.; s. of Liu Tianyan and Wang Yuntao; m. Lu Xiaoge 1970; one s.; ed Beijing Teachers' Coll.; school teacher 1961–76; with Beijing Publishing House 1976–80; lived in Beijing 1950–; Ed.-in-Chief People's Literature 1987–89; professional writer 1980–; mem. Standing Cttee, China All Nation Youth Fed. –1992; mem. Council, Chinese Writers' Asscn. *Publications:* short stories: Class Counsellor (Nationwide Short Story Prize) 1977, The Position of Love 1978, I Love Every Piece of Green Leaves (Nationwide Short Story Prize) 1979, Black Walls 1982, A Scanning over the May 19th Accident 1985; novels: Ruyi (As You Wish) 1980, Overpass 1981, Drum Tower (Mao Dun Literature Prize) 1984; Liu Xinwu Collected Works (eight vols) 1993, A Small Block of Wood, Four Decorated Archways, Wind Passing through the Ear; non-fiction: Construction and Environment in My Eyes 1998, The Beauty of Material 2004. *Leisure interests:* reading, travelling, painting, stamp collecting, music, gardening, football. *Address:* 8 Building No. 1404, Anding Menwai Dongheyan, Beijing 100011, People's Republic of China. *Telephone:* 4213965 (home).

LIU, Yandong; Chinese politician; *State Councillor;* b. 1944, Nantong City, Jiangsu Prov.; ed Jilin Univ.; joined CCP 1964; Sec. Org. Dept, CCP Beijing Municipal Cttee 1980–81; Deputy Sec. CCP Chaoyang Dist Cttee, Beijing 1980–81; mem. Secr. CCP Communist Youth League of China 1982–87; Vice-Pres. All-China Youth Fed. 1982, later Pres.; mem. Standing Cttee, CPPCC Nat Cttee 1983–2003; fmr Deputy Dir Youth Ideological Educ. Research Centre; Deputy Head United Front Work Dept 1991–2002; Alt. mem. 15th CCP Cen. Cttee 1997–2002, mem. 16th CCP Cen. Cttee 2002–07, 17th CCP Cen. Cttee 2007– (mem. Politburo 2007–); Vice-Chair. 10th CPPCC Nat. Cttee 2003–08; State Councillor 2008–; fmr Pres., later Sec.-Gen. China Youth Devt Foundation; fmr Vice-Pres. China Inventors' Asscn; mem. Sino-Japanese Friendship Asscn. *Address:* State Council, 22 Xi'anmen Avenue, Beijing, People's Republic of China (office). *Telephone:* (10) 66036884 (office).

LIU, Yonghao; Chinese business executive; *President, New Hope Group;* b. 1951, Xinjin, Sichuan Prov; brother of Liu Yongxing; fmr Lecturer, Cadres' Inst., Sichuan Machinery Ministry; co-f. New Hope Group 1982, co. restructured in 1995, currently Pres. New Hope Group; Vice-Chair. Chinese Minsheng Bank Co. Ltd 1996–2003; Deputy Pres. Chinese Feed Industry Asscn, Chinese Dairy Industry Asscn, Chinese Glory Undertaking Enhance Asscn; mem. 9th CPPCC Standing Cttee 1998–2003, Deputy Dir Econ. Cttee 2003–; named as one of Top Ten Private Entrepreneurs of China, Man of China's Reform, Top Ten Poverty-fighters, The Most Outstanding Enterprise Admin Talent, Man of China Real Estate and Star of Asia (Business Weekly)

2000. *Address:* New Hope Group, 4th Floor, Block B, Waltz Plaza #7, Hangkong Road, Chengdu 610041, Sichuan, People's Republic of China (office). *Website:* www.newhopegroup.com (office).

LIU, Yongxing, BS; Chinese business executive; *Chairman, East Hope Group;* b. 1948, Xinjin, Sichuan Prov.; brother of Liu Yonghao; started family business called Hope Group raising quail and chickens in Sichuan with his three brothers 1982, grew into second largest animal feed producer in China, co. later restructured into four entities each owned by one of the brothers, East Hope Group relocated from Sichuan to Shanghai 1999; currently Chair. East Hope Group; maintains portfolio interests in MinSheng Bank, MinSheng Insurance, Bright Dairy; recognized by Forbes magazine as one of most successful entrepreneurs in mainland China 2001, 2002, honoured by CCTV as one of Top 10 Economic People of 2001, by Sohu.com as one of Top 10 Financial People of 2001, recognized by Asia Week magazine as one of the Most Influential Entrepreneurs in China in the 21st Century. *Address:* East Hope Group, 57 Songlin Road, Pudong, Shanghai 200120, People's Republic of China (office). *Telephone:* (21) 5831-2099 (office). *Fax:* (21) 6876-8702 (office). *Website:* (office).

LIU, Lt-Gen. Yuan; Chinese government official; b. 1951, Beijing; s. of the late Liu Shaoqi and Wang Guangmei; joined CCP 1982; Vice-Mayor Henan Prov. City 1985–88, Vice-Gov. Henan 1988–92; Second Political Commissar, PRC Police Force 1992–98; rank of Lt-Gen. 2003; Deputy Political Commissar, PLA Gen. Logistics Dept 2003–05; Political Commissar, Acad. of Military Sciences 2005–; mem. 17th CCP Cen. Cttee 2007–. *Address:* People's Liberation Army Academy of Military Sciences, Beijing, People's Republic of China.

LIU, Yunshan; Chinese politician; b. July 1947, Xinzhou, Shanxi Prov.; ed Jining Normal School, Inner Mongolia, CCP Cen. Cttee Cen. Party School; teacher, Baishi School, Inner Mongolia 1968; sent to do manual labour, Sobugai People's Commune, Inner Mongolia 1968–69; clerk, Publicity Dept, CCP Inner Mongolia Autonomous Prefectural Cttee 1969–75; joined CCP 1971; reporter, Div. Head, Xinhua News Agency, Inner Mongolia Autonomous Region 1975–82; Deputy Sec. Communist Youth League Inner Mongolia Autonomous Regional Cttee 1982–84; Deputy Head Publicity Dept CCP Inner Mongolia Autonomous Regional Cttee 1984–86, Head 1986–87 (mem. Standing Cttee 1986–92), Sec.-Gen. CCP Inner Mongolia Autonomous Regional Cttee 1987–91 (Sec. Insts of Higher Learning Work Cttee 1987–91), Deputy Sec. 1992–93; Sec. CCP Chifeng Municipal Cttee, Inner Mongolia Autonomous Region 1991–93; Sec. CCP Inner Mongolia Autonomous Regional Cttee; Vice-Dir Propaganda Dept of CCP Cen. Cttee 1993; Alt. mem. 12th CCP Cen. Cttee 1987–92, 14th CCP Cen. Cttee 1992–97, mem. 15th CCP Cen. Cttee 1997–2002, 16th CCP Cen. Cttee 2002–07 (mem. Politburo 2002–07, Secr. of Politburo 2002–07), 17th CCP Cen. Cttee 2007– (mem. Politburo 2007–); Deputy Head, Publicity Dept CCP Cen. Cttee 1993–97, Head 1997–2002; Head, Office of Spiritual Civilization Steering Cttee, Offices Under Cen. Cttee CCP Cen. Cttee 2002–07. *Address:* Chinese Communist Party Central Committee, Beijing, People's Republic of China (office).

LIU, Zhengwei; Chinese party official; b. 1930, Xinzheng, Henan; joined CCP 1952; mem. 12th CCP Cen. Cttee 1982; Sec. CCP Cttee, Nanyang Pref., Henan 1982–83; Sec. CCP Cttee, Henan Prov. 1983, Deputy Sec. 1983; Deputy Sec. CCP Guizhou Prov. Cttee 1987, Sec. 1988–93; mem. 13th CCP Cen. Cttee 1987–92, 14th CCP Cen. Cttee 1992–97; Chair. Standing Cttee of People's Congress, Guizhou 1993; Deputy Sec. Work Cttee for Cen. Govt Organs 1993–94, Sec. 1994. *Address:* c/o Guizhou Provincial Chinese Communist Party, Guiyang, Guizhou, People's Republic of China.

LIU, Lt-Gen. Zhenwu; Chinese army officer; *Commander, Guangzhou Military Region, People's Liberation Army;* b. 1944, Nanxian Co., Hunan Prov.; joined PLA 1961; squad leader, later platoon leader, 42nd Army (124 Div., 370 Regt, 4th Co.), Army (or Ground Force), PLA Services and Arms, Deputy Army Commdr and Chief of Staff 42nd Army 1983–92, Army Commdr 1992–94; Commdr PLA Hong Kong Garrison 1994–99; fmr staff mem., later Head, Regimental Combat Training Br., PLA Guangzhou Mil. Region, Guangdong Prov., later Section Head, Combat Training Dept, later Deputy Dir Mil. Training Dept, Deputy Commdr PLA Guangzhou Mil. Region 1999–2002, Commdr 2002–; Alt. mem. 15th CCP Cen. Cttee 1997–2002, 16th CCP Cen. Cttee 2002–07; rank of Maj.-Gen. 1990–97, Lt-Gen. 1997–. *Address:* Ministry of National Defence, Jingshanqian Jie, Beijing, People's Republic of China (office).

LIU, Zhenya; Chinese energy industry executive; *President and CEO, State Grid Corporation of China;* b. 1052, Shandong Prov.; ed Electric Power Dept, Shandong Eng and Tech. Inst.; several positions at Shandong Linyi Power Supply Utility 1984–91 including Section Chief, then Vice-Dir, then Dir; Vice-Pres. then Pres. Shandong Electric Power Bureau 1997–2004, renamed State Grid Corpn of China, Man. State Grid Corpn of China 1997–2004, Pres. and CEO 2004–; joined CCP 1984; Alt. mem. 17th CCP Cen. Cttee 2007–. *Address:* State Grid Corporation of China, Number 86, West Chang'an Street, Western City District, Beijing 100031, People's Republic of China (office). *Telephone:* (10) 66598583 (office). *Fax:* (10) 66598794 (office). *E-mail:* sgcc-info@sgcc.com.cn (office). *Website:* www.sgcc.com.cn (office).

LIU, Zhongde; Chinese administrator; *Chairman, Sub-committee for Education, Science, Culture, Health and Sports, Chinese People's Political Consultative Conference;* b. 1933, Ji'an Co., Jilin Prov.; ed Northeast PLA Flying School, Mudanjiang City, Heilongjiang Prov., Harbin Technological Univ., Heilongjiang Prov.; joined Northeast Democratic Youth League 1948; fmr Deputy Sec. Gen. Br., CCP Communist Youth League, Harbin Technological Univ.; joined CCP 1958; worked in Harbin Civil Eng Inst.; Lecturer, later Assoc. Prof., Nanjing Eng Inst. 1962 (also Chief, Teaching and Research

Office and Sec. CCP Party Cttee); fmr mem. CCP Jiangsu Prov. Cttee; Vice-Minister, State Educ. Comm. 1985; Deputy Sec.-Gen. of State Council 1988–92; Deputy Head, Propaganda Dept CCP Cen. Cttee 1990–98; mem. Cen. Group for Propaganda and Thought; Vice-Minister of Culture 1992–93 (also Acting Minister), Minister 1993–98; mem. Nat. Cttee of 7th CPPCC 1988–93, Standing Cttee of Nat. Cttee of 9th CPPCC 1998–2003, Chair. Sub-cttee for Educ., Science, Culture, Health and Sports 1998–; Pres. Asscn for Artists of Ministry of Culture 1993–; Vice-Pres. Party Bldg Research Soc.; Del., 13th CCP Nat. Congress 1987–92; mem. 14th CCP Cen. Cttee 1992–97, 15th CCP Cen. Cttee 1997–2002; mem. Govt Del., Hong Kong Hand-Over Ceremony, Hong Kong Special Admin. Region Preparatory Cttee 1997. *Address:* A 83 Beiheyan Street, Beijing 100722, People's Republic of China.

LIU, Zhongli; Chinese state official; b. 1934, Ningbo City, Zhejiang Prov.; joined CCP 1954; Deputy Div. Chief, Vice-Chair., Chair. Heilongjiang Prov. Planning Comm. 1973–84, Chair. Planning and Econ. Comm. 1984–95; Vice-Gov. Heilongjiang Prov. 1985–88; Vice-Chair. State Cttee for Enterprise Man. 1988; Vice-Minister of Finance 1988–92, Minister 1992–98; Deputy Sec.-Gen. State Council 1990, Dir Econ. System Reform Office of State Council 1998–2000; Dir State Gen. Admin. of Taxation 1994–98; Deputy Head Cen. Financial and Econ. Leading Group; mem. 14th CCP Cen. Cttee 1992–97, 15th CCP Cen. Cttee 1997–2002; Pres. Nat. Social Security Fund Council 2000–04; Chair. CPPCC Sub-Cttee of Economy 2003–. *Address:* Chinese Communist Party, Beijing, People's Republic of China (office).

LIU, Zhongyi; Chinese administrator; b. 1930, Wuchang City, Hubei Prov.; ed Zhongyuan Univ., Hainan Prov.; squad leader, Sub-Regional Training Unit, PLA Cen. China Mil. Command 1949; joined CCP 1954; fmr Dir Agriculture, Forestry and Water Conservancy Planning Bureau, State Devt and Reform Comm.; Vice-Minister, State Planning and Reform Comm. 1985–90; Minister of Agric. 1990–93; Research Fellow and Deputy Dir Environmental Protection Cttee of the State Council 1992; Deputy Dir-Gen. Devt Research Centre of the State Council 1993–98; State Leading Group for Comprehensive Agricultural Devt 1990; mem. 14th CCP Cen. Cttee 1992–97; Del., 15th CCP Nat. Congress 1997–2002; mem. Standing Cttee 9th NPC 1998–2003, Vice-Chair. Agric. and Rural Affairs Cttee 1998–2003; Chair. Sino-Finnish Friendship Asscn. *Address:* c/o Standing Committee of National People's Congress, Beijing, People's Republic of China.

LIVADIOTTI, Massimo; Italian painter; b. 20 Nov. 1959, Zavia, Libya; s. of Mario Livadiotti and Giovanna Mattera; ed Accad. di Belle Arti, Rome; major shows Rome 1987, 1989, 1994, 2000, Milan 1990, 1992, Bologna 1994; retrospectives Petöfi Museum, Budapest 1997, Sociedade Nacional de Belas Artes, Lisbon 2000; numerous group exhbns; work inspired by San Filippo Neri acquired by the Vatican 1995; Triennale Int. di Arte Sacra, Celano 2007. *Publications:* Monograph 1987, Anthology Monographs to accompany exhbns at Centro Ausoni, Rome, Petöfi Museum, Budapest, Sociedade Nacional de Belas Artes, Lisbon 2001, Kalós Arte Contemporanea 2001. *Leisure interests:* gardening and light exercise. *Address:* Piazza Vittorio Emanuele II, N 31, 00185 Rome, Italy. *Telephone:* (06) 4468302; (06) 77590553 (home). *Fax:* (06) 7726 1541.

LIVELY, Penelope Margaret, OBE, CBE, FRSL; British writer; b. 17 March 1933, Cairo, Egypt; d. of Roger Low and Vera Greer; m. Jack Lively 1957; one s. one d.; ed St Anne's Coll. Oxford; mem. Bd British Library 1993–99, Bd British Council 1998–; mem. Soc. of Authors, PEN; Hon. Fellow Swansea Univ. 2002, St Anne's Coll. Oxford 2007; Hon. DLitt (Tufts Univ.) 1993, (Warwick) 1998. *Publications:* juvenile fiction: Astercote 1970, The Whispering Knights 1971, The Wild Hunt of Hagworthy 1971, The Driftway 1972, Going Back 1973, The Ghost of Thomas Kempe (Carnegie Medal) 1973, The House in Norham Gardens 1974, Boy Without a Name 1975, Fanny's Sister 1976, The Stained Glass Window 1976, A Stitch in Time (Whitbread Award) 1976, Fanny and the Monsters 1978, The Voyage of QV66 1978, Fanny and the Battle of Potter's Piece 1980, The Revenge of Samuel Stokes 1981, Uninvited Ghosts and Other Stories 1984, Dragon Trouble, Debbie and the Little Devil 1984, A House Inside Out 1987, The Cat, the Crow and the Banyan Tree 1994, Heatwave 1996, Beyond the Blue Mountains: Stories 1997, Spiderweb 1998, In Search of a Homeland: The Story of the Aeneid 2001; fiction: The Road to Lichfield 1977, Nothing Missing but the Samovar and Other Stories (Southern Arts Literature Prize) 1978, Treasures of Time (Nat. Book Award) 1979, Judgement Day 1980, Next to Nature, Art 1982, Perfect Happiness 1983, Corruption and Other Stories 1984, According to Mark 1984, Moon Tiger (Booker-McConnell Prize) 1986, Pack of Cards: Stories 1978–86 1986, Passing On 1989, City of the Mind 1991, Cleopatra's Sister 1993, The Photograph 2003, Making It Up 2005; non-fiction: The Presence of the Past: An Introduction to Landscape History 1976, Oleander, Jacaranda (autobiog.) 1994, A House Unlocked (memoir) 2001, Consequences 2007; television and radio scripts; contrib. to numerous journals and magazines. *Leisure interests:* gardening, landscape history, talking, listening. *Address:* David Higham Associates, 5–8 Lower John Street, Golden Square, London, W1F 4HA, England (office). *Telephone:* (20) 7434-5900 (office). *Fax:* (20) 7437-1072 (office).

LIVERIS, Andrew N., BSc; Australian chemical industry executive; *Chairman, President and CEO, Dow Chemical Company;* b. Darwin; m. Paula Liveris; three c.; ed Univ. of Queensland; joined Dow Chemical Co. 1976, Gen. Man. Thailand 1989–92, Group Business Dir Midland, Mich. 1992–93, Gen. Man. 1993–94, Vice-Pres. 1994–95, Pres. Dow Chemical Pacific Hong Kong 1995–98, Vice-Pres. Specialty Chemicals, Midland 1998–2000, Business Group Pres. 2000–04, Pres. Dow Chemical 2003–, COO 2003–04, mem. Bd of Dirs and CEO 2004–, Chair. 2006–, mem. Bd of Dirs Dow Corning Corpn; mem. Bd of Dirs Citigroup; Chair. US-China Business Council; Vice-Chair. US Business Council; mem. American Chem. Council, Int. Council of Chemical

Asscns, United States Climate Action Partnership, American Australian Asscn, Business Roundtable, Detroit Econ. Club, Nat. Petroleum Council, Soc. de Chimie Industrielle; Trustee, Tufts Univ., Herbert H. and Grace A. Dow Foundation. *Leisure interests:* science, maths, astronomy, sports. *Address:* Dow Chemical Co., 2030 Dow Center, Midland, MI 48674, USA (office). *Telephone:* (989) 636-1000 (office). *Fax:* (989) 636-3518 (office). *E-mail:* info@dow.com (office). *Website:* www.dow.com (office).

LIVERMORE, Ann Martinelli, BA, MBA; American computer company executive; *Executive Vice-President, Technology Solutions Group, Hewlett-Packard Company;* b. 23 Aug. 1958, Greensboro, N Carolina; ed Univ. of N Carolina at Chapel Hill and Stanford Univ., Calif.; joined Hewlett-Packard in 1982, held several man. positions in Marketing, Sales, Research and Devt, Business Man. before being elected a Corp. Vice-Pres. in 1995, CEO Enterprise Computing Solutions Org. 1996, Exec. Vice-Pres. HP Services 2001–04, Exec. Vice-Pres. Tech Solutions Group 2004–; mem. Bd Dirs United Parcel Service Inc. 1997–; mem. Bd of Visitors Kenan-Flagler Business School at Univ. of N Carolina at Chapel Hill, Bd of Advisors at Stanford Business School; ranked by Fortune magazine amongst 50 Most Powerful Women in Business in the US (23rd) 2002, (24th) 2003, (22nd) 2004, (18th) 2005, (14th) 2006, (13th) 2007, ranked by Forbes magazine amongst 100 Most Powerful Women (20th) 2005, (19th) 2006, (36th) 2007, (33rd) 2008. *Address:* HP Technology Solutions Group, 3000 Hanover Street, Palo Alto, CA 94304-1185, USA (office). *Telephone:* (650) 857-1501 (office). *Fax:* (650) 857-5518 (office). *Website:* www.hp.com (office).

LIVERPOOL, Nicholas Joseph Orville, LLD; Dominican head of state; *President;* b. 9 Sept. 1934; ed Sheffield Univ. (UK); called to the Bar, Inner Temple, London 1961; lawyer and legal consultant 1970s; prepared new criminal code for Belize 1980; Justice of Appeal for Belize 1990–92; Law Review Commr 1992; Judge, Eastern Caribbean Court of Appeal 1993–95; fmr Judge Court of Appeal, Grenada, Bahamas and High Court of Antigua and Montserrat; Chair. Constitution Review Comm. for Grenada 2002; Pres. of Dominica 2003–; fmr Prof. of Law, Univ. of the West Indies, Barbados; fmr Amb. of Dominica to the UN; fmr Project Dir Caribbean Justice Improvement Project; Dominica Award of Honour (DAH) 2003. *Address:* Office of the President, Morne Bruce, Roseau (office); 37 Margaret's Gap, Goodwill, Roseau (home); POB 233, Roseau, Dominica. *Telephone:* 4482054 (office); 4488968 (home). *Fax:* 4498366 (office). *E-mail:* presidentoffice@cwdom.dm (office).

LIVINGSTON, Ian P., BA; British chartered accountant and business executive; *CEO, BT Group plc;* ed Univ. of Manchester; held sr man. positions at 3i Group and Bank of America International; joined Dixons in 1991, held several operational and financial roles, both in UK and abroad, Group Finance Dir Dixons Group 1997–2002; Group Finance Dir BT Group plc 2002–05, CEO BT Retail 2005–08, CEO BT Group plc 2008–; mem. Bd of Dirs Freeserve; Dir (non-exec.) Celtic plc. *Address:* BT Group plc, BT Centre, 81 Newgate Street, London, EC1A 7AJ, England (office). *Telephone:* (20) 7356-5000 (office). *Fax:* (20) 7356-5520 (office). *E-mail:* info@btplc.com (office). *Website:* www.btplc.com (office).

LIVINGSTONE, Kenneth (Ken) Robert; British politician; b. 17 June 1945, London; s. of Robert Moffat Livingstone and Ethel Ada Kennard; m. Christine Pamela Chapman 1973 (divorced 1982); ed Tulse Hill Comprehensive School, Phillipa Fawcett Coll. of Educ.; technician, Cancer Research Unit, Royal Marsden Hosp. 1962–70; Councillor, Borough of Lambeth 1971–78, of Camden 1978–82, of Greater London Council 1973–86 (Leader 1981–86); MP for Brent East 1987–2001; Mayor of London 2000–08; joined Labour Party 1969, mem. Regional Exec. 1974–86, Nat. Exec. Cttee 1987–89, 1997–98, NI Select Cttee 1997–99; consultant to Venezuelan Pres., Hugo Chavez 2008; mem. Council, Zoological Soc. of London 1994–2000 (Vice-Pres. 1996–98). *Publications:* If Voting Changed Anything They'd Abolish It 1987, Livingstone's Labour 1989. *Leisure interests:* science fiction, cinema, natural history, thinking while gardening. *Address:* c/o Labour Party, 39 Victoria Street, London, SW1H 0HA, England (office).

LIVINGSTONE, Marco Eduardo, MA; American/British art historian, writer and curator; b. 17 March 1952, Detroit; s. of Leon Livingstone and Alicia Arce Fernández; partner, Stephen Stuart-Smith; ed Univ. of Toronto, Courtauld Inst. of Fine Art, Univ. of London; Asst Keeper of British Art, Walker Art Gallery, Liverpool 1976–82; Deputy Dir Museum of Modern Art, Oxford 1982–86; Area Ed. for 20th Century The Dictionary of Art 1986–91, Deputy Ed. for 19th and 20th Centuries 1987–91; UK adviser to Art Life, Tokyo 1989–98; freelance writer and exhbn organizer 1991–. *Publications include:* Sheer Magic by Allen Jones 1979, Allen Jones Retrospective 1979, David Hockney 1981, Patrick Caulfield 1981, Peter Phillips Retrovision 1982, Duane Michals 1984, Stephen Buckley: Many Angles 1985, Arthur Tress: Talisman 1986, Stephen Farthing: Mute Accomplices 1987, David Hockney: Faces 1987, Michael Sandle 1988, Pop Art: A Continuing History 1990, Tim Head 1992, Tom Wesselmann 1993, Duane Hanson 1994, David Hockney in California 1994, Jim Dine: Flowers and Plants 1994, Allen Jones Prints 1995, Jim Dine: The Body and its Metaphors 1996, George Segal 1997, The Pop '60s: Transatlantic Crossing 1997, The Essential Duane Michals 1997, R. B. Kitaj: An American in Europe 1998, Jim Dine: The Alchemy of Images 1998, David Hockney: Space and Line 1999, Signature Pieces: Contemporary British Prints and Multiples 1999, Patrick Caulfield 1999, Photographics 2000, Jim Dine: Subjects 2000, Encounters: New Art from Old (contrib.) 2000, Kienholz Tableau Drawings 2001, Callum Innes: Exposed Paintings 2001, Langlands & Bell: The Language of Places 2002, David Hockney: Egyptian Journeys 2002, Clive Barker Sculpture (with Ann Fermon) 2002, Maurice Cockrill (with Nicholas Alfrey) 2002, Blast to Freeze (contrib.) 2002, Tony Bevan: Paintings 2000–2003 2003, David Hockney's Portraits and People (with Kay Heymer) (Sir Bannister Fletcher Award for Best Book on the Arts 2004) 2003, Pop Art

UK: British Pop Art 1956–1972 2004, R. B. Kitaj: Portrait of a Hispanist 2004, Patrick Caulfield: Paintings 2005, British Pop 2005, Tom Wesselmann (contrib.) 2005, British Pop 2005, Richard Woods 2006, Tilson 2007, Tony Bevan Monotypes 2007, Gary Hume: Prints 2007, Tony Bevan (contrib.) 2007, Seeing Double: The Poetic Focus of Claes Oldenburg and Coosje van Bruggen 2007. Gilbert & George: Major Exhibition (contrib.) 2007, Peter Blake: A Retrospective (contrib.) 2007, Paula Rego 2007, Antony Donaldson: French Paintings 2008, John Wesley: Works on Paper & Paintings 2008, Paula Rego: Human Cargo 2008, Colin Self: Art in the Nuclear Age (contrib.) 2008, Jim Dine: Talking about Aldo 2008. *Leisure interests:* music, languages, travel, collecting art. *Address:* 1 Empire Square, London, N7 6JN, England (office); 36 St George's Avenue, London, N7 0HD (home). *Telephone:* (20) 7272-8727 (office); (20) 7607-0282 (home). *E-mail:* marcolivingstone@aol.com (office).

LIVNAT, Limor, BA; Israeli politician; b. 22 Sept. 1950, Haifa; m.; two c.; ed Tel-Aviv Univ.; in Israel Defense Forces, served in Educ. and Social Welfare Unit; worked in advertising and public relations; mem. Knesset (Parl.) 1992–, mem. Knesset Educ. and Culture Cttee, Labour and Social Affairs Cttee 1991–96, Chair. Knesset Cttee for Advancement of Status of Women 1993–94, Sub-Cttee on Women's Representation, Parl. Comm. of Inquiry into domestic violence 1995; Chair. of Likud and of Benjamin Netanyahu's election campaign 1996; Minister of Communications 1996–99, of Educ. 2001–06 (resgnd), Minister of Culture and Sports 2002–06 (resgnd); fmr Vice-Chair. World Likud Movt, fmr mem. Educ. and Cultural Cttee, Labour and Social Affairs Cttee, Cttee for Commercial TV. *Address:* Knesset, Kiryat Ben-Gurion, Jerusalem 91950, Israel (office). *Telephone:* 2-6408032 (office). *Fax:* 2-6496406 (office). *E-mail:* llivnat@knesset.gov.il (office). *Website:* www.knesset.gov.il (office).

LIVNI, Tzipi, LLB; Israeli politician and lawyer; *Leader, Kadima Party;* b. 5 July 1958; d. of Eitan Livni; m.; two c.; ed Bar-Ilan Univ.; with Mossad 1980–84; practised law in pvt. firm for ten years before entering public life; Gen. Man. Govt Cos Authority 1996–99; mem. Likud Party –2005, Co-founder and mem. Kadima Party 2005–, Leader 2008–; mem. Knesset 1999–, served as mem. Constitution, Law and Justice Cttee, Cttee on the Status of Women, Chair. Sub-cttee responsible for legislation of the Prevention of Money Laundering Law; Minister of Regional Co-operation –2001, without Portfolio 2001–02, of Agric. and Rural Devt 2002, of Immigrant Absorption; Acting Minister of Housing and Construction 2004, Minister of Housing and Construction 2004–05; Acting Minister of Justice 2004–05, 2006–07, Minister of Justice 2005–06; Minister of Foreign Affairs 2006–09, Vice-Premier May 2006–09; Champion of Good Govt Award 2004, ranked by Forbes magazine amongst 100 Most Powerful Women (40th) 2006, (39th) 2007, (52nd) 2008. *Address:* c/o Kadima, Petach Tikva, Tel-Aviv, Israel (office). *Telephone:* 3-9788000 (office). *Fax:* 3-9788020 (office). *Website:* www.kadima.org.il (office).

LIVSHITZ, Aleksander Yakovlevich, DEcon; Russian economist; *Adviser to Prime Minister;* b. 6 Sept. 1946, Berlin, Germany; s. of Yakov Livshitz and Liya Livshitz; m. Galina Markina 1966; two d.; ed G. Plekhanov Inst. of Nat. Econ.; teacher, Chair, Prof. Moscow Machine Tool Instrumentation Inst. 1974–; Deputy Chief Analytical Centre, Admin. of Pres. 1992–94; Head of Pres.'s Advisers 1994; Asst to Pres. on problems of economy 1994–96; Deputy Prime Minister and Minister of Finance 1996–97; Deputy Head of Pres. Admin. 1997–98; Head Econ. Policy Fund 1998–; Pres. Rep. for relations with G7 countries 1999; Adviser to Prime Minister 2000–; Deputy Dir-Gen. Russian Aluminium Co. 2001–; mem. UN Comm. on Financing of Devt 2001. *Publications:* Introduction to Market Economy 1991, Economic Reform in Russia and its Price 1994, more than 150 works on econ. problems of Russia, econ. situation in USA in 1980s. *Address:* Russkiy Aluminiy, Nikoloyamskaya str. 13, Bldg 1, 109240 Moscow, Russia. *Telephone:* (495) 720-51-70.

LJUNGGREN, Olof, LLB; Swedish publisher and business executive; b. 5 Jan. 1933, Eskilstuna; s. of Lars Ljunggren and Elisabeth Ljunggren; m. 1st Lena Carlsöö; m. 2nd Margreth Bäcklund; three s.; ed Univ. of Stockholm; Sec. Tidningarnas Arbetsgivareförening (Swedish Newspaper Employers' Asscn) 1959–62, Pres. and CEO 1962–66; Deputy Pres. and CEO Allers Förlag AB 1967–72, Pres. and CEO 1972–74; Pres. and CEO Svenska Dagbladet 1974–78; Pres. and CEO Svenska Arbetsgivareföreningen (Swedish Employers' Confed.) 1978–89; Chair. of Bd Askild & Kärnekull Förlag AB 1971–74, Nord Artel AB 1971–78, Centralförbundet Folk och Försvar (Vice-Chair. 1978–83) 1983–86, Richard Hägglöf Fondkommission AB 1984–87, Svenska Dagbladet 1989–91, Liber AB 1990–98 (Vice-Chair. 1998–), Intentia AB 1994–, AMF 1995–, AFA 1995–2001, Addum AB 1996–99, Consolis AB Oy 1997–; mem. Bd, SPP 1978–93, Investor 1989–92, Providentia 1989–92, Alfa Laval 1989–92, Trygg Hansa 1990–95, and numerous other bds; Kt Commdr Order of the White Rose of Finland 1982, The King's Medal of the 12th Dimension with the Ribbon of the Order of the Seraphim 1987, Kommendörskorset av Den Kgl. Norske Fortjenstorden; Hon. MD. *Leisure interests:* shooting, golf, classical music, playing the piano. *Address:* Skeppargatan 7, 114 52 Stockholm, Sweden. *Telephone:* (707) 472346 (office); (8) 6678785 (home). *Fax:* (8) 6678785 (home). *E-mail:* olof.ljunggren2@comhem.se (home).

LJUNGQVIST, Bengt, BA; Swedish business executive and lawyer; b. 13 Aug. 1937, Stockholm; s. of Gunnar Ljungqvist and Solveig Ljungqvist; m. 1st Sylvia Elmstedt 1961 (divorced 1977); m. 2nd Christina (née Hedén) Ljungqvist 1978; two s. two d.; ed Stockholm Univ.; joined Malmström and Malmenfelt Advokatbyrå, Stockholm 1967, Partner 1971–; Solicitor-Royal 1995–; Pres. Bd of City Planning, Danderyd 1976–85, Chair. City Council, Danderyd 1986–; mem. Council, Swedish Bar Asscn 1983–, Vice-Pres. 1985–; Pres. Swedish Bar Asscn 1989–92; mem. Council Int. Bar Asscn 1984–90; Pres. JP-Bank Stockholm, Swedish Real Property Owners Asscn 1991–96; Vice-Pres. Union Int. de la Propriété Immobilière 1993–96; mem. Bd, Länsförsäkringar-Stockholm 1993–, Pres. 1995–. *Address:* Midgårdsvägen 1, 182 61 Djursholm, Sweden (home). *Telephone:* (8) 679-69-50 (office); (8) 755-31-96 (home).

LLEWELLYN, John; American scientist and academic; *Director, Academic Computing Technologies, University of South Florida;* b. 22 April 1933, Cardiff, UK; s. of John Llewellyn and Morella (née Roberts); m. Valerie Davies-Jones; one s. two d.; ed Univ. Coll., Cardiff, Wales; Research Fellow, Nat. Research Council of Canada 1958–60; Assoc. Prof. School of Eng Science, Florida State Univ. 1964–72; selected by NASA as scientist-astronaut 1967; Dean, School of Eng Science, Florida State Univ. 1970–72; Prof. Depts of Chemical and Mechanical Eng, Coll. of Eng, Univ. of South Fla, Tampa 1973–, Dir Eng Computing 1986–, Dir Academic Computing Techs 1993–; Co-ordinator, Scientist in the Sea Project 1973; aquanaut Nat. Oceanographic Atmospheric Admin; Scientific consultant on marine environment, energy and industrial computer applications; mem. Royal Inst. of Chem., AIAA, Radiation Research Soc., Computer Soc., Asscn for Computing Machinery. *Publications:* Principles and Applications of Digital Devices 1983, Basic Elements of Digital Systems 1983. *Leisure interests:* sailing, underwater exploration. *Address:* Academic Computing Technologies (ACT), University of South Florida, 4202 E Fowler Avenue, L1B 618, Tampa, FL 33620-5452 (office); 141 140th Avenue, Madeira Beach, FL 33708, USA (home). *Telephone:* (813) 974-1780 (office). *Fax:* (813) 974-1799. *E-mail:* tony@usf.edu (office). *Website:* www.acomp.usf.edu (office).

LLEWELLYN SMITH, Sir Chris(topher) Hubert, Kt, DPhil, FRS; British theoretical physicist; b. 19 Nov. 1942, Giggleswick, W. Yorks.; s. of the late John Clare Llewellyn Smith and of Margaret Emily Frances Crawford; m. Virginia Grey 1966; one s. one d.; ed Wellington Coll. and New Coll. Oxford; Royal Soc. Exchange Fellow, Lebedev Inst., Moscow 1967–68; Fellow, CERN, Geneva 1968–70, Staff mem. 1972–74, Chair. Scientific Policy Cttee 1990–92, Dir-Gen. CERN European Lab. for Particle Physics 1994–98; Research Assoc., Stanford Linear Accelerator Center (SLAC), Calif., USA 1970–72; Univ. Lecturer in Theoretical Physics, Univ. of Oxford and Fellow St John's Coll. 1974–98, Reader in Theoretical Physics 1980–87, Prof. 1987–98 (on leave of absence 1994–98), Chair. of Physics 1987–92, Sr Research Fellow in Theoretical Physics 2002–03; Visiting Prof. 2004–; Pres. and Provost Univ. Coll. London 1999–2002; mem. various advisory bodies for SLAC, CERN, DESY (Deutsches Elektronen-Synchrotron, Hamburg), SERC (Science and Eng Research Council), CCLRC, Princeton Plasma Physics Lab., Max Planck Inst. for Plasma Physics, Forschung Zentrum Karlsruhe, Saclay; mem. Advisory Council on Science and Tech. 1989–92; Dir United Kingdom Atomic Energy Authority (UKAEA) Culham Division 2003–08; Chair. Consultative Cttee for Euratom on Fusion 2004–, Council of Int. Tokamak Experimental Reactor (ITER) 2007–; Pres. Council of Synchrotron-light for Experimental Science and its Apllications in the Middle East (SESAME) 2008–; mem. Academia Europaea 1989; Fellow, American Physical Soc. 1994; Foreign Fellow, Indian Nat. Science Acad. 1998; Hon. Fellow, Univ. of Wales 1998, St John's Coll. Oxford 2000, New Coll. Oxford 2002; Hon. DSc (Bristol, Shandong, Granada); Maxwell Medal 1979, US Dept of Energy Distinguished Assoc. Award 1998, US NSF Distinguished Service Award 1998, Medal of Japanese Assoc. of Medical Sciences 1997, Gold Medal, Slovak Acad. of Science 1998, Glazebrook Medal, Inst. of Physics 1999. *Publications:* numerous articles in scientific journals including Nuclear Physics, Physics Letters, Physical Review. *Leisure interests:* books, travel, opera. *Address:* Theoretical Physics, 1 Keble Road, Oxford, OX1 3NP, England (office). *Telephone:* (1235) 466531 (office). *Fax:* (1235) 466209 (office). *E-mail:* c.llewellyn-smith@physics.ox.ac.uk (office).

LLEWELLYN SMITH, Elizabeth, CB, BA, MA; British public servant and college principal (retd); b. 17 Aug. 1934, Upshire; d. of the late John Clare Llewellyn Smith and of Margaret Emily Frances Crawford; sister of Sir Michael John Llewellyn Smith (q.v.) and Sir Chris Llewellyn Smith; ed Christ's Hosp., Univ. of Cambridge and Royal Coll. of Defence Studies; fmr civil servant; Deputy Dir-Gen. of Fair Trading 1982–87; Deputy Sec. Dept of Trade and Industry 1987–90; Dir European Investment Bank 1987–90; Prin. St Hilda's Coll. Oxford 1990–2001; mem. Accountancy Investigation and Disciplinary Bd 2003–, Council Which? (Consumers' Asscn) 2002–; Hon. Fellow, Girton Coll., Cambridge 1994, St Mary's Coll., Univ. of Durham 1999, St Hilda's Coll., Oxford 2001. *Leisure interests:* travel, books, entertaining. *Address:* Brook Cottage, Taston, nr Charlbury, Oxon., OX7 3JL, England (home). *Telephone:* (1608) 811874 (home). *E-mail:* e.llewellynsmith@btopenworld.com (home).

LLEWELLYN SMITH, Sir Michael John, Kt, KCVO, CMG, MA, DPhil; British diplomatist (retd) and writer; b. 25 April 1939; s. of the late John Clare Llewellyn Smith and of Margaret Emily Frances Crawford; brother of Elizabeth Llewellyn Smith (q.v.) and Sir Chris Llewellyn Smith; m. Colette Gaulier 1967; one s. one d.; ed New Coll. Oxford, St Antony's Coll. Oxford; at Embassy, Moscow 1973–75, at Embassy, Paris 1976–78; at Royal Coll. of Defence Studies 1979; at Embassy, Athens 1980–83; Head, Western European Dept, FCO 1984–85, Head of Soviet Dept 1985–88; Minister, Embassy, Paris 1988–91; Amb. to Poland 1991–96, to Greece 1996–99; Vice-Chair. Cathedrals Fabric Comm. for England 1999–2006; Dir (non-exec.) Coca-Cola HBC SA 2000–; Hon. Fellow St Antony's Coll. Oxford 2007; John D. Criticos Prize 1999. *Publications:* The Great Island: A Study of Crete 1965, Ionian Vision: Greece in Asia Minor 1919–22 1973, The British Embassy Athens 1998, Olympics in Athens 1896: The Invention of the Modern Olympic Games 2004, Athens: a Cultural and Literary History 2004. *Leisure Interests:* music, walking in Greek mountains. *Address:* c/o United Oxford and Cambridge University Club, 71 Pall Mall, London, SW1Y 5HD. *Website:* www.michaellewellynsmith.co.uk (home).

LLORENTI SOLIS, Sacha Sergio; Bolivian lawyer and diplomatist; *Deputy Minister for Coordination of Social Movements and Civil Society;* Pres.

Asamblea Permanente de Derechos Humanos de Bolivia (Human Rights Permanent Nat. Ass. of Bolivia) –2005; mem. Nat. Council for the Constituent's Ass.; Amb. to USA 2006–07; Deputy Minister for Coordination of Social Movts and Civil Soc.,Ministry of the Presidency 2007–. *Publications:* numerous articles and books on the defence of human rights in Bolivia. *Address:* Ministry of the Presidency, Palacio de Gobierno, Plaza Murillo, La Paz, Bolivia (office). *Telephone:* (2) 237-1082 (office). *Fax:* (2) 237-1388 (office).

LLOWARCH, Martin Edge, CBIM, FCA, FICA; British business executive; b. 28 Dec. 1935; s. of Wilfred Llowarch and Olga Llowarch; m. Ann Marion Buchanan 1965; one s. two d.; ed Stowe School; with Buckingham, Coopers & Lybrand 1962–68; with British Steel PLC (fmrly British Steel Corpn) 1968–, Head of Special Projects 1968, Man. Dir (SA) 1971, Dir Finance and Admin. (Int.) 1973, Finance Dir Tubes Div. 1975, Financial Controller Strip Products Group 1980, Man. Dir for Finance 1983, Dir 1984–91, Deputy CEO 1986, CEO 1986–91; Chair. (part-time) Transport Devt Group PLC 1992–2000; Deputy Chair. (non-exec.) Firth Rixson (fmrly Johnson and Firth Brown PLC) 1992–93, Chair. 1993–2001; Dir (non-exec.) Abbey Nat. PLC 1989–99 (Deputy Chair. 1994–99), Hickson Int. PLC 1992–99; mem. Accounting Standards Cttee 1985–87. *Leisure interests:* sport, music, gardening, reading.

LLOYD, Chris(tine) Marie Evert (see EVERT, Chris(tine) Marie).

LLOYD, Christopher; American actor; b. 22 Oct. 1938, Stamford, Conn.; ed Neighborhood Playhouse, New York. *Plays:* Red White & Madox, Possessed, Midsummer Night's Dream, Kaspar (Drama Desk and Obie Awards 1973), Unexpected Man 2002, Mornings at 7 (Broadway) 2002, Twelfth Night (Shakespeare in the Park) 2002. *Films include:* One Flew Over the Cuckoo's Nest 1975, Three Warriors 1978, Goin' South 1978, Butch and Sundance: The Early Days 1979, The Onion Field 1979, The Black Marble 1980, The Legend of the Lone Ranger 1981, Mr Mom 1983, To Be or Not To Be 1983, Star Trek III: The Search for Spock 1984, The Adventures of Buckaroo Banzai Across the 8th Dimension 1984, Back to the Future 1985, Clue 1985, Walk Like a Man 1987, Who Framed Roger Rabbit? 1988, Track 29 1988, Eight Men Out 1988, The Dream Team 1989, The Real Blonde, Back to the Future Part II 1989, Why Me? 1990, Back to the Future Part III 1990, The Addams Family 1991, Twenty Bucks (Independent Spirit Award for Best Dramatic Actor) 1993, Dennis the Menace 1993, Addams Family Values 1993, Angels in the Outfield 1994, The Pagemaster 1994, Camp Nowhere 1994, Radioland Murders 1994, Things To Do in Denver When You're Dead 1995, Cadillac Ranch 1996, Changing Habits 1997, Anastasia 1997, Dinner at Fred's 1999, Baby Geniuses 1999, My Favorite Martian 1999, Man on the Moon 1999, Wish You Were Dead 2002, Interstate 60 2002, Hey Arnold! The Movie (voice) 2002, Haunted Lighthouse 2003, Merry Christmas Space Case (voice) 2003, Admissions 2004, A Fate Totally Worse Than Death 2005, Enfants terribles 2005, Flakes 2007, Fly Me to the Moon (voice) 2007. *Television includes:* Lacy and the Mississippi Queen 1978, The Word (mini-series) 1978, The Fantastic Seven 1979, Barney Miller 1978, 1979, Taxi (series) (two Emmy Awards including Best Supporting Actor) 1978-83, Visions 1980, Best of the West (series) 1981, Pilgrim, Farewell 1982, Money on the Side 1982, September Gun 1983, Cheers 1984, Old Friends 1984, The Cowboy and the Ballerina 1984, Street Hawk 1985, Amazing Stories 1986, Tales from the Hollywood Hills: Pat Hobby Teamed with Genius 1987, Back to the Future (series) 1991, Road to Avonlea (Emmy Award for Best Supporting Actor) 1992, T Bone N Weasel 1992, Dead Ahead: The Exxon Valdez Disaster 1992, Fallen Angels 1993, Mrs. Piggle-Wiggle (series) 1994, In Search of Dr. Seuss 1994, Deadly Games (series) 1995, Rent-a-Kid 1995, The Right to Remain Silent 1996, Quicksilver Highway 1997, Angels in the Endzone 1997, The Ransom of Red Chief 1998, Spin City - Back to the Future IV - Judgment Day 1999, Alice in Wonderland 1999, It Came from the Sky 1999, On the Edge 2001, The Tick 2001, Chasing Destiny 2001, The Big Time 2001, When Good Ghouls Go Bad 2001, Cyberchase (series; voice) 2002, Malcolm in the Middle 2002, Ed 2003, Tremors (episodes) 2003, Grim & Evil (voice) 2004, I Dream (series) 2004, Clubhouse (series) 2004, King of the Hill (voice) 2005, The West Wing (episode The Wake Up Call) 2005, Stacked (series) 2005, Detective 2005, Here Comes Peter Cottontail: The Movie (voice) 2005, Stacked (series) 2005–06, A Perfect Day 2006. *Address:* c/o The Gersh Agency, 252 North Canon Drive, Beverly Hills, CA 90210 (office); c/o Andy Freedman, 20 Ironsides Street, Suite 18, Marina Del Ray, CA 90292, USA (office).

LLOYD, Clive Hubert, AO CBE; Guyanese fmr professional cricketer; b. 31 Aug. 1944, Georgetown, British Guiana (now Guyana); s. of the late Arthur Christopher Lloyd and Sylvia Thelma Lloyd; cousin of Lance Gibbs; m. Waveney Benjamin 1971; one s. two d.; ed Chatham High School, Georgetown; left-hand batsman, right-arm medium-paced bowler; played for British Guiana/Guyana 1963–83, Lancashire 1968–86 (Capt. 1981–83, 1986); 110 Tests for W Indies 1966–1985, record 74 as Capt., scoring 7,515 runs (average 46.6) including 19 hundreds; scored 31,232 first-class runs including 79 hundreds; W Indies Team Man. 1988–89 and 1996–99; Int. Cricket Council (ICC) Referee 1992–95, Match Referee 2002–; Exec. Promotions Officer, Project Fullemploy 1987–; Dir Red Rose Radio PLC 1981; Patron Nat. Lottery Charities Bd; Hon. Fellow Manchester Polytechnic, Lancs. Polytechnic 1986; Hon. MA (Manchester, Hull); Hon. DLitt (Univ. of W Indies, Jamaica); Golden Arrow of Achievement (Guyana) 1975, Wisden Cricketer of the Year 1971. *Publications:* Living for Cricket (with Tony Cozier) 1980, Winning Captaincy (with Mihir Bose) 1995. *Address:* c/o Harefield, Harefield Drive, Wilmslow, Cheshire, SK9 1NJ, England.

LLOYD, David Robert, MA, PhD, ScD, MRIA, FInstP; British chemist and academic; *Fellow Emeritus, Department of Chemistry, Trinity College Dublin;* b. 19 May 1937, Derby, England; s. of George Lloyd and Effie Lloyd; m. Heidi Hoffman 1964; one s. one d.; ed Halesowen Grammar School, Worcs. and Selwyn Coll., Cambridge; temporary Lecturer, Chem. Dept, Northwestern Univ., Evanston, USA 1963–65; Lecturer in Chem., Univ. of Birmingham 1965–78; Prof. of Chem., Trinity Coll. Dublin, Ireland 1978–2000, now Fellow Emer., Head of Chem. Dept 1978–85, 1992–94; A. von Humboldt Fellowship 1962–63; Fellow, Trinity Coll. Dublin. *Publications:* approx. 118 papers on aspects of chemistry and physics, three on Plato's view of the elements. *Leisure interests:* music, hill walking, domestic chores, theology, classical Greek. *Address:* Department of Chemistry, University of Dublin, Trinity College, Dublin 2, Ireland (office). *Telephone:* (1) 6081726 (office). *E-mail:* chemdept@tcd.ie (office). *Website:* www.tcd.ie/Chemistry (office).

LLOYD, Sir Geoffrey Ernest Richard, Kt, PhD, FBA; British academic; *Emeritus Professor of Ancient Philosophy and Science, University of Cambridge;* b. 25 Jan. 1933, London; s. of William Ernest Lloyd and Olive Irene Neville Lloyd; m. Janet Elizabeth Lloyd 1956; three s.; ed Charterhouse and King's Coll. Cambridge; Asst Lecturer in Classics, Cambridge Univ. 1965–67, Lecturer 1967–74, Reader in Ancient Philosophy and Science 1974–83, Prof. 1983–2000, Emer. Prof. 2000–; Master, Darwin Coll., Cambridge 1989–2000, Hon. Fellow 2000–; Fellow King's Coll. 1957–89, Hon. Fellow 1990–; A. D. White Prof.-at-Large, Cornell Univ. 1990–96; Chair. East Asian History of Science Trust 1992–2002; mem. Japan Soc. for the Promotion of Science, Int. Acad. of the History of Science; Zhu Kezhen Visiting Prof., Inst. for the History of Natural Science, Beijing 2002; Foreign Hon. mem. American Acad. of Arts and Sciences 1995; Hon. LittD (Athens) 2003; Sarton Medal 1987, Kenyon Medal 2007. *Publications:* Polarity and Analogy 1966, Aristotle, the Growth and Structure of his Thought 1968, Early Greek Science: Thales to Aristotle 1970, Greek Science after Aristotle 1973, Hippocratic Writings (ed.) 1978, Aristotle on Mind and the Senses (ed., with G. E. L. Owen) 1978, Magic, Reason and Experience 1979, Science, Folklore and Ideology 1983, Science and Morality in Greco-Roman Antiquity 1985, The Revolutions of Wisdom 1987, Demystifying Mentalities 1990, Methods and Problems in Greek Science 1991, Adversaries and Authorities 1996, Aristotelian Explorations 1996, Greek Thought (ed.) 2000, The Ambitions of Curiosity 2002, The Way and the Word (with N. Sivin) 2002, In the Grip of Disease, Studies in the Greek Imagination 2003, Ancient Worlds, Modern Reflections 2004, The Delusions of Invulnerability 2005, Principles and Practices in Ancient Greek and Chinese Science 2006, Cognitive Variations, Reflections on the Unity and Diversity of the Human Mind 2007. *Leisure interest:* travel. *Address:* Needham Research Institute, 8 Sylvester Road, Cambridge, CB3 9AF (office); 2 Prospect Row, Cambridge, CB1 1DU, England (home). *Telephone:* (1223) 311545 (office); (1223) 355970 (home). *E-mail:* eahost1@hotmail.com (office); gel20@cam.ac.uk (office).

LLOYD, John Nicol Fortune, MA; British journalist; *Contributing Editor, Financial Times;* b. 15 April 1946; s. of Christopher Lloyd and Joan A. Fortune; m. 1st Judith Ferguson 1974 (divorced 1979); m. 2nd Marcia Levy 1983 (divorced 1997); one s.; ed Waid Comprehensive School and Univ. of Edinburgh; Ed. Time Out 1972–73; reporter, London Programme 1974–76; Producer, Weekend World 1976–77; industrial reporter, labour corresp., industrial and labour ed., Financial Times 1977–86; Ed. New Statesman 1986–87, Assoc. Ed. 1996–2003; with Financial Times 1987–, posts include East Europe Ed., Financial Times Magazine Ed., Moscow Corresp. 1991–95, currently Contributing Ed.; freelance journalist 1996–; Dir East-West Trust, New York 1997–, Foreign Policy Centre 1999–; Journalist of the Year, Granada Awards 1984, Specialist Writer of the Year, IPC Awards 1985; Rio Tinto David Watt Memorial Prize 1997. *Publications:* The Politics of Industrial Change (with Ian Benson) 1982, The Miners' Strike: Loss without Limit (with Martin Adeney) 1986, In Search of Work (with Charles Leadbeater) 1987, Counterblasts (contrib.) 1989, Rebirth of a Nation: an Anatomy of Russia 1998, Re-engaging Russia 2000, The Protest Ethic 2001, What the Media are Doing to Our Politics 2004, The Republic of Entertainment 2005. *Leisure interests:* opera, hill walking, squash. *Address:* Financial Times, One Southwark Bridge, London, SE1 9HL, England (office). *Telephone:* (20) 7873-3000 (office). *E-mail:* john.lloyd@ft.com (office). *Website:* www.ft.com (office).

LLOYD, Robert Andrew, CBE, MA; British singer (bass); *Senior Artist, Royal Opera House;* b. 2 March 1940, Southend; s. of William Edward Lloyd and May Lloyd (née Waples); m. 1st Sandra D. Watkins 1964 (divorced 1990); one s. three d.; m. 2nd Lynda A. Hazell (née Powell) 1992; ed Southend High School for Boys, Keble Coll. Oxford, London Opera Centre; served as Lt in Royal Navy 1963–66; Lecturer, Bramshill Police Coll. 1966–68; Prin. Bass, Sadler's Wells Opera 1969–72, Royal Opera House 1972–83, Sr Artist, Royal Opera House 2004–; freelance singer with all maj. opera houses and orchestras world-wide, frequent broadcasts as presenter, BBC radio and TV 1983–; film appearances: Parsifal, Bluebeard's Castle; performed title role in Tarkovsky production of Boris Godunov at Kirov Opera, Leningrad 1990; created role of Tyrone in Tower by Alun Hoddinott; Visiting Prof. Royal Coll. of Music, London 1996–; Pres. British Youth Opera 1988–94, Southend Choral Soc. 1996–; mem. Exec. Cttee Musicians' Benevolent Fund 1989–92; mem. Conservatoires Advisory Group 1993–99; Pres. Inc. Soc. of Musicians 2006; Hon. Fellow Keble Coll. 1990; Patron Carl Rosa Trust 1994–; Hon. mem. Royal Acad. of Music; Artist of the Year, Teatro Colón, Buenos Aires 1996, Charles Santley Award 1997, Chaliapin Commemoration Medal (St Petersburg) 1998. *Radio:* regular presenter for BBC Radio 3. *Television:* wrote and presented documentary Six Foot Cinderella 1990, subject of BBC documentary Bob the Bass. *Publications:* numerous contribs to magazines. *Leisure interests:* sailing, hill walking, history. *Address:* Askonas Holt Ltd, Lincoln House, 300 High Holborn, London, WC1v 7JH, England (office). *Telephone:* (20) 7400-1700 (office). *Fax:* (20) 7400-1799 (office). *E-mail:* info@askonasholt.co.uk (office). *Website:* www.askonasholt.co.uk (office).

LLOYD-JONES, David Mathias, BA; British musician and conductor; b. 19 Nov. 1934, London; s. of the late Sir Vincent Lloyd-Jones and Margaret Alwena Mathias; m. Anne Carolyn Whitehead 1964; two s. one d.; ed Westminster School, Magdalen Coll. Oxford; Repetiteur, Royal Opera 1959–61; Chorus Master, New Opera Co. 1961–64; conducted at Bath Festival 1966, City of London Festival 1966, Wexford Festival 1967–70, Scottish Opera 1968, Welsh Nat. Opera 1968, Royal Opera, Covent Garden 1971, Sadler's Wells Opera Co. (now ENO) 1969; Asst Music Dir ENO 1972–78; Artistic Dir Opera North 1978–90; also conductor for TV operas (Eugene Onegin, The Flying Dutchman, Hansel and Gretel) and has appeared with most British symphony orchestras and conducted worldwide; Chair. Delius Trust 1997–, Gen. Ed. William Walton Edn 1996–; Hon. mem. Royal Philharmonic Soc. 2007; Hon. DMus (Leeds) 1986. *Music:* many acclaimed recordings of British and Russian music; has edited works by composers, including Mussorgsky, Bizet, Walton, Berlioz, Elgar and Sullivan. *Publications:* Boris Godunov–Translation, Vocal Score, Eugene Onegin–Translation, Vocal Score, Boris Godunov–Critical Edition of Original Full Score, numerous contribs to publs including Grove's Dictionary of Music and Musicians, Musik in Geschichte und Gegenwart, Music and Letters, The Listener. *Leisure interests:* theatre, French cuisine, rose growing. *Address:* c/o Allied Artists, 42 Montpelier Square, London SW7 1JZ, England (office); 94 Whitelands House, Cheltenham Terrace, London, SW3 4RA, England (home). *Telephone:* (20) 7589-6243 (office); (20) 7730-8695. *Fax:* (20) 7581-5269 (office); (20) 7730-8695. *E-mail:* info@alliedartists.co.uk (office). *Website:* www.alliedartists.co.uk (office).

LLOYD-JONES, Sir (Peter) Hugh (Jefferd), Kt, MA, FBA; British classical scholar; *Regius Professor of Greek Emeritus, University of Oxford;* b. 21 Sept. 1922, St Peter Port, Guernsey; s. of Brevet-Major W. Lloyd-Jones, DSO and Norah Leila Jefferd; m. 1st Frances Elisabeth Hedley 1953 (divorced 1981); two s. one d.; m. 2nd Mary R. Lefkowitz 1982; ed Lycée Français du Royaume-Uni (London), Westminster School and Christ Church, Oxford; served in Indian Intelligence Corps 1942–46; Fellow, Jesus Coll. Cambridge 1948–54; Fellow and E.P. Warren Praelector in Classics, Corpus Christi Coll. Oxford 1954–60, Regius Prof. of Greek and Student of Christ Church 1960–89, Prof. Emer. 1989–; J. H. Gray Lecturer, Cambridge 1961; Visiting Prof. Yale Univ. 1964–65, 1967–68; Sather Prof. of Classical Literature, Univ. of Calif. at Berkeley 1969–70; Alexander White Visiting Prof. Univ. of Chicago 1972; Visiting Prof., Harvard Univ. 1976–77; mem. British Acad., Acad. of Athens; Corresp. mem. American Acad. of Arts and Sciences, Nordrhein-Westfälische Akad. der Wissenschaften, Accad. di Archeologia, Lettere e belle Arti di Napoli, Bayerische Akad. der Wissenschaften, American Philosophical Soc.; Hon. DHumLitt (Chicago) 1970; Hon. DPhil (Tel Aviv) 1984; Hon. PhD (Thessaloniki) 1999, (Göttingen) 2002; Chancellor's Prize for Latin Prose, Ireland and Craven Scholarships 1947. *Publications:* Appendix to Aeschylus (Loeb Classical Library) 1957, Menandri Dyscolus (Oxford Classical Texts) 1960; The Justice of Zeus 1971, (ed.) Maurice Bowra: a Celebration 1974, Females of the Species 1975, Myths of the Zodiac 1978, Mythical Beasts 1980, Blood for the Ghosts 1982, Classical Survivals 1982, Supplementum Hellenisticum (with P. J. Parsons) 1983, Supplementum Supplementi 2005; translated Paul Maas, Greek Metre 1962, Aeschylus Agamemnon, The Libation-Bearers and The Eumenides 1970, Sophoclea (with N. G. Wilson) 1990, Academic Papers (2 Vols) 1990, Vol. III 2005, Sophoclis Fabulae (with N. G. Wilson) 1990, Greek in a Cold Climate 1991, Sophocles (Loeb Classical Library, 3 Vols) 1994–96, Sophocles: Second Thoughts (with N. G. Wilson) 1997; edited The Greeks 1962, Tacitus 1964; articles and reviews in periodicals. *Leisure interests:* cats, remembering old cricket. *Address:* 15 West Riding, Wellesley, MA 02482, USA. *Telephone:* (781) 237-2212. *Fax:* (781) 237-2246. *E-mail:* mlefkowitz@wellesley.educ (home).

LLOYD WEBBER, Baron (Life Peer), cr. 1997, of Sydmonton in the County of Hampshire; **Andrew Lloyd Webber,** FRCM; British composer; *Chairman, The Really Useful Group Ltd;* b. 22 March 1948; s. of the late William Southcombe Lloyd Webber and Jean Hermione Johnstone; brother of Julian Lloyd Webber (q.v.); m. 1st Sarah Jane Tudor (née Hugill) 1971 (divorced 1983); one s. one d.; m. 2nd Sarah Brightman 1984 (divorced 1990); m. 3rd Madeleine Astrid Gurdon 1991; two s. one d.; ed Westminster School, Magdalen Coll. Oxford, Royal Coll. of Music; Chair. The Really Useful Group Ltd; owner of eight London theatres including the Palace Theatre, Theatre Royal Drury Lane, The London Palladium; seven Tony Awards, four Drama Desk Awards, six Laurence Olivier Awards, Triple Play Awards 1996, ASCAP 1988, Praemium Imperiale Award 1995, three Grammy Awards, Golden Globe Award, Academy Award 1996, Richard Rodgers Award for Excellence in Musical Theatre 1996, Kennedy Center Honor 2006; Commander's Cross of the Order of Merit, Hungary 2005. *Works:* musicals: Joseph and the Amazing Technicolor Dreamcoat (lyrics by Tim Rice) 1968 (revised 1973, 1991), Jesus Christ Superstar (lyrics by Tim Rice) 1970 (revised 1996), Jeeves (lyrics by Alan Ayckbourn) 1975 (revised as By Jeeves 1996), Evita (lyrics by Tim Rice) 1976 (stage version 1978), Tell Me on a Sunday (lyrics by Don Black) 1980, revised 2003, Cats (based on T. S. Eliot's Old Possum's Book of Practical Cats) (Tony Awards for Best Score and Best Musical 1983) 1981, Song and Dance (lyrics by Don Black) 1982, Starlight Express (lyrics by Richard Stilgoe) 1984, The Phantom of the Opera (Tony Award for Best Musical 1988) (lyrics by Richard Stilgoe and Charles Hart) 1986, Aspects of Love (lyrics by Don Black and Charles Hart) 1989, Sunset Boulevard (Tony Awards for Best Score and Best Musical 1995) (lyrics by Christopher Hampton and Don Black) 1993, Whistle Down the Wind (lyrics by Jim Steinman) 1996, The Beautiful Game (with lyrics by Ben Elton) (London Critics' Circle Best Musical 2000) 2000; other compositions: Variations (based on A minor Caprice No. 24 by Paganini) 1977 (symphonic version 1986), Requiem Mass 1985, Amigos Para Siempre (official theme for 1992 Olympic Games), The Woman in White; film scores: Gumshoe 1971, The Odessa File 1974. *Producer:* Joseph and the Amazing Technicolor Dreamcoat 1973, 1974, 1978, 1980, 1991, Jeeves Takes Charge 1975, Cats 1981, Song & Dance 1982, Daisy Pulls it Off 1983, The Hired Man 1984, Starlight Express 1984, On Your Toes 1984, The Phantom of the Opera 1986, Café Puccini 1986, The Resistible Rise of Arturo Ui 1987, Lend Me a Tenor 1988, Aspects of Love 1989, Shirley Valentine (Broadway) 1989, La Bête 1992, Sunset Boulevard 1993, By Jeeves 1996, Whistle Down the Wind 1996, 1998, Jesus Christ Superstar 1996, 1998, The Beautiful Game 2000, Bombay Dreams 2002, Tell Me On A Sunday, 2003, The Woman in White 2004, The Sound of Music 2006 and others. *Film:* The Phantom of the Opera (Dir by Joel Schumacher) 2004. *Publications:* Evita (with Tim Rice) 1978, Cats: the book of the musical 1981, Joseph and the Amazing Technicolor Dreamcoat (with Tim Rice) 1982, The Complete Phantom of the Opera 1987, The Complete Aspects of Love 1989, Sunset Boulevard: from movie to musical 1993; food critic Daily Telegraph 1999–. *Leisure interests:* architecture, art. *Address:* The Really Useful Group Ltd, 22 Tower Street, London, WC2H 9TW, England (office). *Telephone:* (20) 7240-0880 (office). *Fax:* (20) 7240-1204 (office). *Website:* www.reallyuseful.com (office).

LLOYD WEBBER, Julian, FRCM; British cellist and writer; b. 14 April 1951, London; s. of the late William Southcombe Lloyd Webber and of Jean Hermione Johnstone; brother of Lord Lloyd Webber (q.v.); m. 1st Celia M. Ballantyne 1974 (divorced 1989); m. 2nd Zohra Mahmoud Ghazi 1989 (divorced 1999); one s.; m. 3rd Kheira Bourahla 2001 (divorced 2007); ed Univ. Coll. School, Royal Coll. of Music, also studied with Pierre Fournier; debut at Queen Elizabeth Hall 1972; debut with Berlin Philharmonic Orchestra 1984; appears at major int. concert halls and has undertaken concert tours throughout Europe, N and S America, S Africa, Australasia, Singapore, Japan, China, Hong Kong and Korea; numerous television appearances and broadcasts in UK, Netherlands, Africa, Germany, Scandinavia, France, Belgium, Spain, Australasia and USA; patron Jacqueline du Pré Charity Concerts 2006–; Chair., UK Govt's In Harmony initiative 2009–; Hon. Doctorate (Univ. of Hull) 2003, (Thames Valley Univ.) 2004; Suggia Gift 1968, Seymour Whinyates Award 1971, Percy Buck Award 1972, Brit Award for Elgar Cello Concerto recording 1987, Crystal Award, World Economic Forum (Switzerland) 1998, Classic FM Red Award for outstanding services to music (2003). *Recordings:* world premiere recordings of Britten's 3rd Suite for Solo Cello, Bridge's Oration, Rodrigo's Cello Concerto (Spanish Ministry of Culture Award for world premiere recording 1982), Holst's Invocation, Gavin Bryar's Cello Concerto, Michael Nyman's Cello and Saxophone Concerto, Sullivan's Cello Concerto, Vaughan Williams' Fantasia on Sussex Folk Tunes, Andrew Lloyd Webber's Variations (Gold disc 1978), Elgar's Cello Concerto (British Phonographic Industry Award for Best Classical Recording 1986), Dvořák Concerto, Saint-Saëns Concerto, Lalo Concerto, Walton Concerto, Britten Cello Symphony; Philip Glass Cello Concerto. *Radio:* numerous broadcasts worldwide. *Publications:* Classical Cello 1980, Romantic Cello 1981, French Cello 1981, Frank Bridge, Six Pieces 1982, Young Cellist's Repertoire (three vols) 1984, Holst's Invocation 1984, Travels with my Cello 1984, Song of the Birds 1985, Recital Repertoire for Cellists (four vols) 1986, Short Sharp Shocks 1990, The Great Cello Solos 1992, The Essential Cello 1997, Cello Moods 1999, String Quartets, 2003; Made in England 2003; columnist, Daily Telegraph 2003–; contribs to: The Times, The Sunday Times, USA Today. *Leisure interests:* topography (especially British), football (Leyton Orient), turtles. *Address:* IMG Artists Europe, The Light Box, 111 Power Road, London, W4 5PY, England (office). *Telephone:* (20) 8233-5800 (office). *Fax:* (20) 8233-5801 (office). *E-mail:* labrahams@imgartists.com (office). *Website:* www.imgartists.com (office); www.julianlloydwebber.com (office).

LÔ, Ismaël; Senegalese musician; b. Aug. 1956; m.; ed Institut des arts de Dakar; singer and composer of African folk songs in Wolof and French. *Recordings:* 21 albums including Iso 1995, Jammu Africa 1996, Dabah 2001. *Leisure interests:* painting, farming.

LO, Vincent Hong Sui; Chinese business executive; *Chairman and Chief Executive, Shui On Group;* b. 18 April 1948, Hong Kong; m. Jean Lo 1981; one s. one d.; ed Univ. of New South Wales, Australia; f. Shui On Group 1971, now Chair. and Chief Exec.; Chair. Hong Kong Gen. Chamber of Commerce 1991–92; mem. Exec. Cttee Basic Law Consultative Cttee 1985–90; mem. Bd Land Devt Corpn 1988–90; mem. Hong Kong Trade Devt Council 1991–92, Hong Kong Baptist Coll. 1987–89; mem. Standing Cttee on Judicial Salaries & Conditions of Service 1988–94, Standing Cttee on Directorate Salaries & Conditions of Service 1988–94; mem. Council, Exec. Cttee Hong Kong Man. Assen 1984–94; Pres. Business and Professionals Fed. of Hong Kong; mem. Preparatory Cttee for the Hong Kong Special Admin. Region 1996–97; Hong Kong Affairs Adviser, People's Repub. of China State Council's Office of Hong Kong and Macao Affairs/Xinhua News Agency, Hong Kong Br. 1994–97; Adviser China Soc. of Macroeconomics, Peking Univ. China Centre for Econ. Research; mem. Gov.'s Business Council 1992–97, Airport Authority 1990–99, Hong Kong/United States Econ. Co-operation Cttee; Dir The Real Estate Developers Assen of Hong Kong, The Community Chest of Hong Kong 1990–95, Great Eagle Holdings Ltd; Dir (non-exec.) Hang Seng Bank Ltd, New World China Land Ltd; Chair. Council Hong Kong Univ. of Science and Tech.; JP 1999; Advisory Professorship (Shanghai Tongji Univ.) 1996, (Shanghai Univ.) 1998; Hon. Citizen of Shanghai 1998; Gold Bauhinia Star 1998; Hon. DBA (Hong Kong Univ. of Science and Tech.) 1996. *Address:* 34/F Shui On Centre, 6–8 Harbour Road, Hong Kong Special Administrative Region, People's Republic of China. *Website:* www.shuion.com (office).

LOACH, Kenneth, BA; British film director; b. 17 June 1936, Nuneaton; s. of the late John Loach and of Vivien Loach (née Hamlin); m. Lesley Ashton 1962; three s. (one deceased) two d.; ed King Edward VI School, Nuneaton, St Peter's Hall (now Coll.), Oxford; BBC trainee, Drama Dept 1963; freelance film dir 1963–; Léopard d'honneur for Lifetime Achievement, Locarno Film Festival

2003; Hon. DLitt (St Andrews), (Staffs. Univ., Bristol); Dr hc (Royal Coll. of Art) 1998; Hon. Fellow, St Peter's Coll. Oxford; Praemium Imperiale 2003, London Film Critics' Circle Award for Outstanding Contrib. to Cinema 2005. *Films:* Poor Cow 1967, Kes 1969, In Black and White 1970, Family Life 1971, Black Jack 1979, Looks and Smiles 1981, Fatherland 1986, Hidden Agenda 1990, Riff-Raff 1991, Raining Stones 1993, Ladybird, Ladybird 1994, Land and Freedom 1995, Carla's Song 1996, My Name is Joe 1998, Bread and Roses 2000, The Navigators 2001, 11.09.01 UK Segment 2002, Sweet Sixteen 2003, A Fond Kiss 2004, Tickets (with others) 2005, The Wind That Shakes the Barley (Palme d'Or, Cannes Film Festival 2006, Best Film, Irish Film and Television Awards 2007) 2006, It's a Free World 2007. *Television:* Diary of a Young Man 1964, Three Clear Sundays 1965, The End of Arthur's Marriage 1965, Up the Junction 1965, Coming Out Party 1965, Cathy Come Home 1966, In Two Minds 1966, The Golden Vision 1969, The Big Flame 1970, After a Lifetime 1971, The Rank and File 1972, Days of Hope (four films) 1975, The Price of Coal 1977, The Gamekeeper 1979, Auditions 1980, A Question of Leadership 1980, The Red and the Blue 1983, Questions of Leadership 1983, Which Side are You on? 1984, The View from the Woodpile 1988, Time to Go 1989, Dispatches: Arthur Scargill 1991, The Flickering Flame 1996, Another City 1998. *Address:* c/o Sixteen Films, 2nd Floor, 187 Wardour Street, London, W1F 8ZB, England.

LOADER, Danyon Joseph, ONZ; New Zealand fmr swimmer; b. 21 April 1975, Timaru; s. of Peter Loader and Daphne Loader; ed Berkeley Univ., San Francisco, USA; world short-course record in 200m butterfly 1991; silver medallist Olympic Games 1992; gold, silver (three times) and bronze medallist Commonwealth Games 1994; gold medallist 200m and 400m freestyle Olympic Games 1996; est. over 40 NZ records; retd 2000; motivational speaker with Speakers New Zealand; NZ Sportsman of the Decade (1990s), Lonsdale Cup, NZ Olympic Cttee. *Leisure interests:* reading, films, surfing, scuba diving, socializing. *Address:* 9 Prince Albert Road, St Kilda, Dunedin, New Zealand (home). *Telephone:* (3) 455-2486 (home).

LOAYZA MARIACA, Armando; Bolivian government official; b. 8 Dec. 1943, La Paz; m. Teresita Keel de Loaiza; one s.; ed Univ. of Montevideo, Uruguay; Undersec. of Econ. Integration 1980; Gen. Adviser of the Chancellery 1991; Undersec. of Bilateral Policy 1993; diplomatic postings in Montevideo, Caracas, Geneva, Brussels; Dir Academia Diplomática Boliviana Rafael Bustillo 1993, 1998–2003; Consul-Gen. in Santiago 1993; Amb. to Santa Sede (Vatican) 1994–98; Amb. to Uruguay and Perm. Rep. to ALADI 2003; Minister of Foreign Affairs and Worship –2006. *Address:* c/o Ministry of Foreign Affairs and Worship, Calle Ingavi, esq. Junín, La Paz, Bolivia (office).

LOBASHEV, Vladimir Mikhailovich; Russian nuclear physicist; b. 29 July 1934, Leningrad (now St Petersburg); s. of Mikhail Yefimovich Lobashev and Nina Vladimirovna Yevropeitseva; m. Muza Romanovna Lobasheva; two s. one d.; ed Leningrad Univ.; mem. CPSU 1970–91; mem. of staff of Physical-Tech. Inst. 1957–72; Scientific Leader, Moscow Meson Factory Programme; Head, Experimental Physics Div. of Inst. for Nuclear Research at USSR (now Russian) Acad. of Sciences 1972–; Leader, Lab. for Weak Interaction Study, Leningrad (now St Petersburg) Inst. for Nuclear Physics 1972–; Corresp. mem. USSR (now Russian) Acad. of Sciences 1970–2003, Academician, Russian Acad. of Sciences 2003–; Bruno Pontecorvo Prize, Jt Inst. for Nuclear Research, Dubna 1998, Markov Prize 2004. *Leisure interest:* tennis. *Address:* Institute for Nuclear Research, Academy of Sciences, 142190 Troitsk, Moscow Region (office); Institute for Nuclear Research, Academy of Sciences, Prospect 60 Let Oktyabrya 7A, 117312 Troitsk, Moscow Region, Russia (office). *Telephone:* (495) 334-01-90 (office); (495) 334-03-18 (home). *E-mail:* lobashev@al20.inr.troitsk.ru (office). *Website:* www.inr.troitsk.ru (office).

LOBATO, Edson, MS; Brazilian agronomist and administrator; b. 1940; ed Nat. School of Agronomy (now Coll. of Agricultural Sciences), Southern Illinois Univ., USA; began career in soil fertility research through programme sponsored by IRI Research Inst., USAID and Brazilian Ministry of Agric. 1964; received USAID fellowship to study soil fertility in USA 1972–73; hired as researcher, Brazilian Corpn of Agricultural Research (EMBRAPA) 1973, responsible for coordinating several programmes, including outlining plan for Cerrado Agricultural Research Centre, served in variety of positions at EMBRAPA Cerrado Centre, including Tech. Dir 1975–2004; World Food Prize (co-recipient) 2006. *Publications:* Cerrado: Soil Correction and Fertilization; more than 80 publs in professional journals. *Address:* c/o Embrapa, Parque Estação Biológica - PqEB s/nº, Brasília, DF - 70770-901, Brazil. *Telephone:* (61) 3448-4433. *Fax:* (61) 3347-1041. *E-mail:* sac@embrapa.br. *Website:* www .embrapa.br.

LOBKOWICZ, Michal; Czech business executive and fmr politician; *Partner, Corsum Group;* b. 20 July 1964, Prague; m.; one s.; ed Charles Univ., Prague; mem. Parl. for Civic Democratic Party (ODS) 1992–98, for Freedom Union (FU) 1998–2002; Chef de Cabinet for Minister of Foreign Affairs 1993–96; Minister of Defence Jan.–July 1998; mem. Cttee for European Integration 1998–2002, Cttee for Defence and Security 1998–2002; left parl. functions following elections in 2002; Partner, Corsum Group 2002–; mem. Supervisory Bd Massag Bílovec, SK Slavia Prague soccer club. *Address:* Corsum Group s.r.o. Opatovická 4, 110 00 Prague 1, Czech Republic (office). *Telephone:* (2) 24934707 (office). *Fax:* (2) 24934701 (office). *E-mail:* corsum@corsum.cz (office). *Website:* www.corsum.cz (office).

LOBKOWICZ, Nicholas, DPhil; American academic; *Director, Institute of Central and Eastern European Studies, Catholic University of Eichstätt;* b. 9 July 1931, Prague, Czechoslovakia (now Czech Repub.); s. of Prince Jan Lobkowicz and Countess Marie Czernin; m. 1st Countess Josephine Waldburg-Zeil 1953; three s. two d.; m. 2nd Aleksandra N. Cieślińska 1999; ed Collegium Maria Hilf, Switzerland, Univs of Erlangen and Fribourg; Assoc. Prof. of Philosophy, Univ. of Notre Dame, Ind. 1960–67; Prof. of Political Theory and Philosophy, Univ. of Munich 1967–90, Dean School of Arts and Letters 1970–71, Rector Magnificus 1971–76, Pres. Univ. of Munich 1976–82; Pres. Catholic Univ. of Eichstätt 1984–96, Dir Inst. of Cen. and Eastern European Studies 1994–; mem. Bd of Dirs Fed. Inst. of Int. and E European Studies, Cologne 1972–75, Senate, West German Rectors' Conf. 1976–82, Perm. Cttee European Rectors' Conf. 1979–84, Council Int. Fed. of Catholic Univs 1984–91; founding mem. Int. Metaphysical Asscn; mem. Cen. Cttee of German Catholics 1980–84; mem. Ukrainian Acad. of Arts and Science (USA) 1979–; mem. W Europe Advisory Cttee to Radio Free Europe/Radio Liberty 1980–2002, Chair. 1994–2002; Founder mem., Vice-Pres. European Acad. of Sciences and Arts 1990–; Pres. Freier Deutscher Autorenverband 1985–91; mem. Pontifical Council for Culture 1982–93; Pres. Czechoslovak Christian Acad. in Rome 1983–90; Administrator of Faculty of Catholic Theology, Charles Univ. Prague 2002–03; ; Hon. Citizen Dallas, Tex.; Hon. DHL (Wayne State Univ.); Hon. DLL (Univ. of Notre Dame); Hon. DrPhil (Seoul and Ukrainian Univ., Munich, Catholic Univ. of America); Hon. DTheol (Charles Univ., Prague). *Publications:* Theory and Practice 1967, Ende aller Religion? 1976, Marxismus und Machtergreifung 1978, Wortmeldung zu Staat, Kirche, Universität 1981, Irrwege der Angst 1983, Das europäische Erbe 1984, Das Konzil 1986, Zeitwende 1993, Czas przelomu 1996, Rationalität und Innerlichkeit 1997, Duše Evropy 2001. *Address:* Oskar-von-Hiller-Strasse 20, 82319 Starnberg (home); Katholische Universität, 85071 Eichstätt, Germany. *Telephone:* (8421) 931717 (office). *Fax:* (8421) 931780 (office). *E-mail:* 05299@ku-eichstaett.de (office); nikolaus.lobkowicz@nexgo.de (home). *Website:* www.zimos/KUE.de (office).

LOBO, José Carlos; Mozambican politician and fmr teacher; b. 14 Sept. 1942, Quelimane; s. of Carlos Lobo Chibaia and Catarina Carlos Ernesto; m. Iveth Venichand Lobo 1978; two c.; ed California State Univ., USA; joined Mozambique Liberation Front (FRELIMO) in Tanzania 1964; Teacher and Dean of Students at Mozambique Inst., Dar es Salaam 1965–66; studied at Calif. State Univ., USA until 1973; Headmaster, FRELIMO Secondary School, Bagamoyo, Tanzania 1974–75; Headmaster, FRELIMO Secondary School, Ribaue, Mozambique 1975; Dir of Int. Orgs and Confs Dept, Ministry of Foreign Affairs 1975–76; Perm. Rep. to UN 1976–83; mem. Cen. Cttee FRELIMO 1983–; Minister of Mineral Resources 1983–84; mem. of People's Ass. 1983–; Vice-Minister of Foreign Affairs 1984–; FRELIMO 20th Anniversary Medallion. *Address:* c/o Ministry of Foreign Affairs and Co-operation, Avda Julius Nyerere 4, Maputo, Mozambique.

LOBO ANTUNES, António, MD; Portuguese novelist; b. 1 Sept. 1942, Lisbon; s. of João Alfredo Lobo Antunes and Maria Margarida Almeida Lima; three d.; ed higher educ. in Portugal; fmr doctor and psychiatrist; now full-time writer (his experience of the Portuguese colonial war in Angola being a major influence); French Culture Prize 1996, 1997, Prix du Meilleur Livre Etranger, Rosália de Castro Prize 1999, European Literature Prize of Austria 2000, Latin Union Int. Prize 2003, Jerusalem Prize 2005, Premio Camões 2007. *Publications include:* novels: Memória de Elefante 1979, Os Cus de Judas 1979, Conhecimento do Inferno 1980, Explicação dos Pássaros 1981, Fado Alexandrino 1983, Auto dos Danados 1985, As Naus 1988, Tratado das Paixões da Alma 1990, A Ordem Natural das Coisas 1992, A Morta de Carlos Gardek 1994, O Manual dos Inquisidores 1996, O Esplendor de Portugal 1997, Livro de Crónicas 1998, Exortação aos Crocodilos 1999, Não Entres Tão Depressa Ness Noite Excura 2000, Que Farei Quando Tudo Arde? 2001, Segundo Livro de Crónicas 2002, Boa Tarde ás Coisas Aqui em Baixo 2003, Eu Hei-de Amar Uma Pedra 2004, Terceiro Livro de Crónicas 2006, Ontem Não Te Vi em Babilónia 2006, O Meu Nome é Legião 2007, O Arquipélago da Insónia 2008; short stories: A História do Hidroavião 1994–2005 2005, The Fat Man and Infinity and Other Writings (in trans.) 2009; other: Letrinhas de Cantigas 2002, Apontar com o dedo o centro da terra 2002, D'este Viver Aqui Neste Papel Descripto 2005, Quem me assassinou para que eu seja tão doce? 2008. *Address:* c/o Publicações Dom Quixote, Rua Cidade de Códova 2, 2610-038 Alfragide, Portugal (office). *Website:* www.dquixote.pt (office).

LOBO SOSA, Porfirio (Pepe); Honduran politician and lawyer; *President, Partido Nacional;* b. 1947, Trujillo; ed Univ. of Miami, Coral Gables; Deputy Nat. Congress 1990; Head Honduran Corpn for Forestry Devt 1990–94; presidential candidate 2005; currently Pres. Partido Nacional. *Address:* c/o Partido Nacional, Paseo el Obelisco, Comayagüela, Tegucigalpa, Honduras (office). *Telephone:* 237-6300 (office). *Fax:* 237-6299 (office). *E-mail:* partidonacional@partidonacional.hn (office); pepeloboo1@hotmail.com (office).

LOC, Nguyen Van, LLM; Vietnamese politician, lawyer and writer; b. 24 Aug. 1922, Vinh-Long; s. of Nguyen Van Hanh and Tran Thi Ngo; m. Nguyen Thi Mong Hoa; two s.; ed Univ. of Montpellier and Paris, France; lawyer, Saigon Court of Appeal 1955; Lecturer, Nat. Inst. of Admin 1965; Chair. People's and Armed Forces Council 1966, People's and Armed Forces Council Political Cttee 1966; Vice-Chair. Constituent Ass. Electoral Law Preparation Cttee; mem. Barristers Fraternity 1961–67; Del. in charge of campaigning, Cttee for Aid to War Victims (Viet Nam Red Cross); Counsellor, Viet Nam Asscn for Protection of Human and People's Rights; Sec.-Gen., Inter-Schools Asscn 1965–67; Prime Minister of Repub. of Viet Nam 1967–68; Prof. Univ. of Hóa-Hao 1970; founder and Rector, Cao-Dai Univ. 1971–75; escaped to Singapore 1983. *Publications:* Uprising (novel) 1946, Rank 1948, New Recruits (novel) 1948, Poems on Liberation (collection) 1949, Recollections of the Green Years 1960, Free Tribune (collection) 1966, Poisonous Water (novel) 1971.

LOCHHEAD, Liz; British poet, playwright, screenwriter and teacher; b. 26 Dec. 1947, Motherwell; fmr art school teacher, Glasgow and Bristol; Lecturer, Univ. of Glasgow; Dr hc (Edinburgh) 2000; BBC Scotland Prize 1971, Scottish Arts Council Award 1972. *Television includes:* Damages (BBC). *Publications* *include:* poetry: Memo for Spring 1972, The Grimm Sisters 1981, Dreaming of Frankenstein and Collected Poems 1984, True Confessions and True Clichés 1985, Bagpipe Muzak 1991, Cuba/Dog House (with Gina Moxley) 2000, The Colour of Black and White: Poems 1984–2003 2003; plays: Blood and Ice 1982, Silver Service 1984, Dracula (adaptation) 1989, Mary Queen of Scots Got Her Head Chopped Off 1989, Molière's Tartuffe (Scots trans. in rhyming couplets), Perfect Days 1998, Medea (adaptation) 2000, Misery Guts (adaptation) 2002, Thebans 2003, Good Things 2006; screenplay: Now and Then 1972; anthology contribs: Penguin Modern Poets Vols 3 and 4, Shouting It Out 1995. *Address:* 57 Productions, 57 Effingham Green, Lea Green, London, SE12 8NT, England (office). *Telephone:* (20) 8463-0866 (office). *E-mail:* paul@57productions.com (office). *Website:* www.57productions.com (office).

LOCHTE, Karin, MSc, PhD (Habil.); German oceanographer, environmental scientist, academic and research institute director; *Director, Alfred Wegener Institute for Polar and Marine Research;* b. 20 Sept. 1952, Hanover; ed Tech. Univ., Hanover, Marine Science Labs, Menai Bridge, Univ. Coll. of N Wales, Bangor, UK, Univ. of Bremen; Post-doctoral researcher, Inst. of Oceanography, Kiel 1985–90; mem. Scientific Staff, Alfred Wegener Inst. for Polar and Marine Research, Bremerhaven, Germany 1990–94, Scientific Advisor 1999–2003, Dir 2007–; Head of Section, Biological Oceanography and Prof. of Biological Oceanography, Inst. for Baltic Sea Research, Univ. of Rostock 1995–2000; Prof. of Biological Oceanography, Leibniz Inst. for Marine Sciences, Christian-Albrechts Univ., Kiel 2000–07; Project Co-ordinator for ADEPD (Atlantic Data Base for Exchange Processes at the Deep Sea Floor—EU-funded marine research project) 1998–2000; Chair. Governing Bd Jacobs Univ., Bremen 2007–; mem. ECOPS Working Group 'Deep Sea Floor Instrumentation Development' 1991–92, Scientific Steering Cttee Jt Global Ocean Flux Studies 1995–2001, Bd of Trustees Terramare Research Centre, Wilhelmshaven 1996–98, Nat. Cttee for Global Change Research (Co-Chair. 2000–05), Scientific Cttee Int. Geosphere-Biosphere Programme (Vice-Chair. 2001-06), DFG Fachkollegiums 313 'Atmosphären- und Meeresforschung' 2004–05, Senate Cttee Deutsche Forschungsgemeinschaft for Oceanography 1995– (Chair. 2004–), Jury for Science Prize of WGL 'Society Needs Science' 2002–, Science Council 2004 (Chair. Scientific Comm. 2006–), Grant Cttee of Excellence Initiative 2005–, Exec. Cttee Acad. of Sciences, Hamburg 2005–; Scientific Advisor, Royal Netherlands Inst. for Sea Research (NIOZ), Texel 1998–2004, Instituts Chemie und Biologie des Meeres, Universität Oldenburg 1998–2006 (Chair. 2003–), Potsdam Instituts für Klimafolgenforschung 2002–05, Max Plank Inst. for Marine Microbiology, Bremen 2006–; Consultant, Third World Aid Programme to S America, Deutscher Akademischer Austausch Dienst 2003–; Mentor, Advancement Programme for Young Scientists, Univ. of Bremen 2005–07. *Publications:* numerous scientific papers in professional journals. *Address:* Alfred Wegener Institute, Building E-3226, Am Handelshafen 12, 27570 Bremerhaven, Germany (office). *Telephone:* (471) 4831-1101 (office). *E-mail:* karin.lochte@awi.de (office). *Website:* www.awi.de (office).

LOCK, Margaret, PhD, FRSC; Canadian anthropologist and academic; *Marjorie Bronfman Professor in Social Studies in Medicine, McGill University;* m.; one s. one d.; ed Univ. of California, Berkeley; at McGill Univ., Montréal 1977–, currently Marjorie Bronfman Prof. in Social Studies in Medicine, affiliated with Dept of Social Studies of Medicine and Dept of Anthropology; mem. Canadian Inst. of Advanced Research, Population Programme 1993–2002; Officier, Ordre nat. du Québec; Canada Council Killam Fellowship 1993–95, Prix du Québec, domaine Sciences Humaines 1997, Molson Prize, Canada Council for the Arts 2002, Robert B. Textor Prize 2003, Killam Prize, Canada Council for the Arts 2005, Trudeau Foundation Fellowship 2005, named a Grande Montréalaise, Secteur Social 2005. *Publications:* East Asian Medicine in Urban Japan: Varieties of Medical Experience 1980, Health and Medical Care in Japan: Cultural and Social Dimensions (co-ed.) 1987, Biomedicine Examined (co-ed.) 1988, La santé mentale et ses visages: Un Québec pluriethnique au quotidien (co-author) 1992, Knowledge, Power and Practice: The Anthropology of Medicine and Everyday Life (co-ed.) 1993, Encounters With Aging: Mythologies of Menopause in Japan and North America (six prizes, including Staley Prize, School of American Research, Canada-Japan Book Prize, Wellcome Medal, Royal Anthropological Soc. of GB 1997) 1993, Social Suffering (co-ed.) 1997, Pragmatic Women and Body Politics (co-ed.) 1998, Living and Working with the New Medical Technologies: Intersections of Inquiry (co-ed.) 2000, Remaking a World: Violence, Social Suffering, and Recovery (co-ed.) 2001, Twice Dead: Organ Transplants and the Reinvention of Death (several awards) 2002, New Horizons in Medical Anthropology: A Festschrift in Honor of Charles Leslie (co-ed.) 2002, Remaking Life and Death: Towards an Anthropology of the Biosciences (co-ed.) 2003; more than 170 scholarly articles. *Address:* Department of Social Studies of Medicine, Room 207, 3647 Peel Street, Montréal, PQ H3A 1X1, Canada (office). *Telephone:* (514) 398-6033 (office). *Fax:* (514) 398-1498 (office). *Website:* www.mcgill.ca/ssom (office); www.mcgill.ca/anthropology (office).

LOCK, Thomas Graham, BSc, CEng, CBIM, FIMMM; British business executive; b. 19 Oct. 1931, Cardiff; s. of Robert H. Lock and Morfydd Lock (née Thomas); m. 1st Janice O B. Jones 1954 (divorced 1992, died 1995); two d.; m. 2nd Judith Elizabeth Lucy 2004; ed Whitchurch Grammar School, Univ. Coll. of S. Wales, Monmouthshire Coll. of Advanced Tech. (Aston) and Harvard Business School, USA; Instructor Lt RN 1953–56; joined Lucas Industries Ltd 1956; Production Foreman, Lucas Electrical Ltd 1957–59, Factory Man. 1959–61; Dir Girling Bremsen GmbH 1961–66; Overseas Operations Dir Girling Ltd 1966–73; Gen. Man. and Dir Lucas Service Overseas Ltd 1973–79; Man. Dir Industrial Div. Amalgamated Metal Corpn PLC 1979–83, Chief Exec. 1983–91; Dir (non-exec.) Evode Group PLC 1985–91, Marshalls Universal PLC 1983–86; Liveryman Co. of Gold and Silver Wyre Drawers 1988–; Freeman, City of London. *Leisure interests:* sailing, music, skiing. *Address:* Parolas Villa, 4520 Pareklisia, nr Limassol, Cyprus (home). *Telephone:* (25) 634965 (home). *Fax:* (25) 634965 (home). *E-mail:* brython@cytanet.com.cy (home).

LOCKE, Gary, BA, JD; American lawyer and fmr state official; *Partner, Davis Wright Tremaine LLP;* b. 21 Jan. 1950; s. of James Locke and Julie Locke; m. Mona Lee Locke 1994; three c.; ed Yale Univ., Boston Univ.; Deputy Prosecuting Attorney, State of Washington, King Co.; mem. State House of Reps 1982–93; Chief Exec. King Co. 1994–97; Gov. of Washington 1996–2005; Pnr, Davis Wright Tremaine LLP (law firm), Seattle 2005–; nominated for US Sec. of Commerce 2009; mem. Bd of Dirs Digital Learning Commons, 2003–, Pacific Health Summit Sr Advisory Group 2004–, Fred Hutchinson Cancer Research Center 2005, Safeco, Inc. 2005–. *Address:* Davis Wright Tremaine LLP, 2600 Century Square, 1501 Fourth Avenue, Seattle, WA 98101-1688, USA (office). *Telephone:* (206) 622-3150 (office). *Fax:* (206) 628-7699 (office). *E-mail:* garylocke@dwt.com (office). *Website:* www.dwt.com (office).

LOCKHART, James, BMus, FRCM, FRCO (CHM); British conductor and music director; b. 16 Oct. 1930, Edinburgh; s. of Archibald C. Lockhart and Mary B. Lawrence; m. Sheila Grogan 1954; two s. one d.; ed George Watson's Coll., Edin., Univ. of Edin. and Royal Coll. of Music; Asst Conductor, Yorkshire Symphony Orchestra 1954–55; Repetiteur and Asst Conductor, Städtische Bühnen Münster 1955–56, Bayerische Staatsoper, Munich 1956–57, Glyndebourne Festival Opera 1957–59; Dir Opera Workshop, Univ. of Texas 1957–59; Repetiteur and Asst Conductor, Royal Opera House, Covent Garden 1959–60, Conductor 1962–68; Asst Conductor, BBC Scottish Orchestra 1960–61; Conductor, Sadler's Wells Opera 1961–62; Prof. Royal Coll. of Music 1962–72; Musical Dir Welsh Nat. Opera 1968–73; Generalmusikdirektor, Staatstheater Kassel 1972–80, Koblenz and Theater der Stadt, Koblenz 1981–88, Rheinische Philharmonie 1981–91; Prin. Guest Conductor, BBC Concert Orchestra 1982–87; Dir of Opera, Royal Coll. of Music 1986–92, London Royal Schools' Vocal Faculty 1992–96, Opera Consultant 1996–98; Guest Prof. of Conducting, Tokyo Nat. Univ. of Fine Arts and Music (Tokyo Geidai) 1998–2001, Prof. Emer. 2001–; freelance conductor 2001–; Hon. RAM 1993. *Leisure interests:* travel, swimming, hill-walking. *Address:* 105 Woodcock Hill, Harrow, Middx, HA3 0JJ, England (home). *Telephone:* (20) 8907-2112 (home). *Fax:* (20) 8907-2112 (home). *E-mail:* Lockgrog@aol.com (home).

LOCKWOOD, David, CBE, PhD, FBA; British academic; *Professor Emeritus of Sociology, University of Essex;* b. 9 April 1929, Holmfirth, Yorks.; s. of Herbert Lockwood and Edith Annie Lockwood (née Lockwood); m. Leonore Davidoff 1954; three s.; ed Honley Grammar School, London School of Econs; trainee, Victoria Textiles, Honley, Yorks. 1944–47; Nat. Service, Intelligence Corps, Austria 1947–49; Univ. of London Postgraduate Studentship in Econs 1952–53; Asst Lecturer and Lecturer in Sociology, LSE 1953–60; Rockefeller Fellow, Univ. of Calif., Berkeley, USA 1958–59; Univ. Lecturer, Faculty of Econs and Fellow of St John's Coll. Cambridge 1960–68; Visiting Prof., Dept of Sociology, Columbia Univ., USA 1966–67; Prof., Dept of Sociology, Univ. of Essex 1968–2001, Prof. Emer. 2001–, Pro-Vice-Chancellor 1989–92; Visiting Prof., Delhi School of Econs 1975, Stockholm Univ. 1989; Visiting Fellow, RSSS ANU 1993; mem. Social Science Research Council (Chair. Sociology and Social Admin. Cttee 1973–76), Academia Europaea 1990; Chair. Econ. and Social Research Council Review of Govt Social Classifications 1994–98; Hon. DUniv (Essex) 2001, Hon. LittD (Cambridge) 2004. *Publications:* The Affluent Worker in the Class Structure (three vols) (jtly) 1968–69, The Blackcoated Worker 1958, (revised edn 1989), Solidarity and Schism 1992; numerous articles in journals and symposia. *Address:* 82 High Street, Wivenhoe, Essex CO7 9AB, England (home). *Telephone:* (1206) 823530 (home). *E-mail:* lockd@essex.ac.uk (office).

LOCKYER, Darren; Australian rugby football player (rugby league); *Captain, Brisabane Broncos, Queensland & Australia;* b. 24 March 1977, Brisbane, Queensland; s. of David and Sharon Lockyer; m. Loren Lockyer; ed ed Wandoan State School, Roma, Queensland; player for Brisbane Broncos 1995–, Queensland 1998–, Australia 1998–; 292 appearances by 2009 for Brisbane Broncos (111 tries, 1,143 points), 27 appearances for Queensland in State of Origin games, 40 tests for Australia (22 as Capt.); mem. Australian World Cup winning team 2000; mem. Australian Tri-Nations winning team 2004, 2006; Brisbane Broncos Rookie of the Year 1995, Clive Churchill Medal 2000, Brisbane Broncos Player of the Year 2002, 2003, Rugby League World Golden Boot Award 2003, 2006. *Address:* c/o Brisbane Broncos, Fulcher Road, Red Hill, Queensland 4059, Australia (office). *E-mail:* media@broncos.com.au (office). *Website:* www.broncos.com.au (office).

LODDER, Celsius Antônio, MSc; Brazilian international administrator and economist; b. 28 May 1944, Nova Lima, Minas Gerais; s. of Ary Lodder and Maria van Krimpen Lodder; three d.; ed Fed. Univ. of Minas Gerais, Belo Horizonte, Getúlio Vargas Foundation, Rio de Janeiro and Inst. of Social Studies, The Hague; researcher, Applied Econs Research Inst. Ministry of Econ., Finance and Planning 1970–80; subsequently held appointments with State of Minas Gerais and Fed. Govt of Brazil; Sec. for Commercial Policy, Ministry of Finance, later at Ministry of Industry, Commerce and Tourism; Supt Nat. Supply Authority, Ministry of Finance; Chief Adviser, State Bank of Minas Gerais 1983–84; Co-ordinator, Intergovernmental Relations Office, Civil Cabinet of Pres. of Brazil; Lecturer in Econs at various Brazilian univs; Exec. Dir Int. Coffee Org. 1994–2002. *Publications:* books and reports on matters related to regional planning and devt. *Leisure interests:* reading, walking. *Address:* c/o International Coffee Organization, 22 Berners Street, London, W1P 4DD, England.

LODGE, David John, CBE, PhD, FRSL; British writer and academic; *Professor Emeritus of English Literature, University of Birmingham;* b. 28 Jan. 1935,

London; s. of William F. Lodge and Rosalie M. Lodge (née Murphy); m. Mary Frances Jacob 1959; two s. one d.; ed St Joseph's Acad., Blackheath and Univ. Coll., London; asst, British Council, London 1959–60; Asst Lecturer in English, Univ. of Birmingham 1960–62, Lecturer 1963–71, Sr Lecturer 1971–73, Reader 1973–76, Prof. of English Literature 1976–87, Hon. Prof. 1987–2000, Prof. Emer. 2001–; Chair. Booker Prize Cttee 1989; Harkness Commonwealth Fellow, 1964–65; Visiting Assoc. Prof. Univ. of Calif. at Berkeley 1969; Henfield Writing Fellow, Univ. of E Anglia 1977; Fellow, Univ. Coll. London 1982, Goldsmith's Coll. 1992; Chevalier, Ordre des Arts et des Lettres 1997; Yorkshire Post Fiction Prize 1975, Hawthornden Prize 1976, RTS Award for Best Drama Serial 1990. *Publications:* fiction: The Picture-goers 1960, Ginger, You're Barmy 1962, The British Museum is Falling Down 1965, Out of the Shelter 1970, Changing Places: A Tale of Two Campuses 1975, How Far Can You Go? (aka Souls and Bodies) (Whitbread Book of Year Award) 1980, Small World: An Academic Romance 1984, Nice Work (Sunday Express Book of the Year Award) 1988, The Writing Game (play) 1991, Paradise News 1991, Therapy 1995, Home Truths (novella) 1999, Thinks... (novel) 2001, Author, Author 2004, Deaf Sentence (novel) 2008; non-fiction: Language of Fiction 1966, Graham Greene 1966, The Novelist at the Crossroads and Other Essays on Fiction and Criticism 1971, Evelyn Waugh 1971, Twentieth-Century Literary Criticism: A Reader (ed.) 1972, The Modes of Modern Writing: Metaphor, Metonymy and the Typology of Modern Literature 1977, Working with Structuralism: Essays and Reviews on Nineteenth- and Twentieth Century Literature 1981, Write On: Occasional Essays 1986, Modern Criticism and Theory: A Reader (ed.) 1988, After Bakhtin: Essays on Fiction and Criticism 1990, The Art of Fiction: Illustrated from Classic and Modern Texts 1992, The Practice of Writing: Essays, Lectures, Reviews, and a Diary 1996, Consciousness and the Novel 2002, The Year of Henry James 2006. *Leisure interests:* tennis, television, cinema. *Address:* c/o Department of English, University of Birmingham, Birmingham, B15 2TT, England (office). *Telephone:* (121) 414-5670 (office). *Fax:* (121) 414-5668 (office). *E-mail:* english@bham.ac.uk (office). *Website:* www.english.bham.ac.uk (office).

LODHI, Maleeha, BSc, PhD; Pakistani diplomatist, journalist and academic; b. Lahore; m. (divorced); one s.; ed Univ. of Oxford and London School of Econs, UK; Lecturer in Politics and Sociology, LSE 1980–85; fmr Lecturer, Dept of Public Admin, Quaid-i-Azam Univ., Islamabad; Ed. The Muslim; Ed. and Co-founder The News (daily newspaper) 1985–93, 1997–2000; Amb. to USA 1993–97, (with rank of Minister of State) 1999–2002, High Commr to UK 2003–08; mem. UN Sec.-Gen.'s Advisory Bd on Disarmament; Fellow, Pakistan Inst. of Devt Econs; award from All Pakistan Newspaper Soc. 1994, named by Time Magazine as one of 100 global pacesetters and leaders who would define the 21st century 1994, Hilal-e-Imtiaz Presidential Award for public service 2002. *Publications:* Pakistan's Encounter with Democracy, The External Dimension 1994; numerous contribs to int. journals. *Address:* Ministry of Foreign Affairs, Constitution Avenue, Islamabad, Pakistan (office). *Telephone:* (51) 9210335 (office). *Fax:* (51) 9207600 (office). *E-mail:* sadiq@mofa.gov.pk (office). *Website:* www.mofa.gov.pk (office).

LODIN, Azizullah, BA, PhD; Afghan politician and government official; *President, Independent Election Commission of Afghanistan;* b. 1939, Herat; ed high school in Kabul, Kabul Univ., Univ. of Köln, Germany; Lecturer, Faculty of Econs, Kabul Univ. 1976–78; held as political prisoner and put in Pule-Charkhi for involvement with Anti-Communist activist group in Kabul 1978–80; joined mujahidin movt as political adviser to leadership of Harakat Inqlab Islami Afghanistan, Peshawar, Pakistan 1980; fmr Vice-Chair. Political Dept, Islamic Unity of Afghanistan, mem. Supreme Council 1983–85; worked on Afghan refugee affairs and liaisons with Govt of Pakistan and Int. Orgs; Founder Afghan's Doctor Union outside the country (first Afghan non-governmental org. in Pakistan); Founder Nahid-e-Shahid High School for Afghan refugee girls, Peshawar 1983; Chair. Afghan del. at Tribunal de peuple, Sorbonne, Paris, France 1981; Dir Political Dept, Islamic Revolutionary Party of Afghan mujahidin, Peshawar 1985–89; Econ. and Political Adviser to Pres. of Afghan Interim Govt chaired by Prof. Mujadidy; fmr mem. Bd of Dirs Reconstruction Authority for Afghanistan; fmr Pres. Task Force Cttee for Emergency Assistance Inside Afghanistan; Head of Afghan Consulting GmbH, Herat 1992–95; served as Pres. Afghan Econ. Council, SW Prov.; attached to resistance org. against Taliban in Iran 1995–2001; Founder Cyprus Peace Conf.; fmr Head of Political Affairs, Cyprus Del. to Bonn Conf. and a signing mem. of Bonn Agreement; Adviser to Pres. Karzai in SW Prov., Herat 2003; Pres. Gen. Admin of Anti-Bribery and Corruption, with rank of Minister 2003–04; Gen. Sec. Secr. of Nat. Ass. of Afghanistan 2004–07; Pres. Ind. Election Comm. of Afghanistan 2007–. *Address:* Independent Election Commission, PO Box 979, IEC compound, Jalalabad Road, Paktia Kot, Kabul, Afghanistan (office). *Telephone:* (752) 035203 (mobile) (office). *E-mail:* info@iec.org.af (office). *Website:* www.iec.org.af (office).

LOEHNIS, Anthony David, CMG, MA; British banker; b. 12 March 1936, London; s. of Sir Clive Loehnis and Rosemary Loehnis (née Ryder); m. Jennifer Forsyth Anderson 1965; three s.; ed Eton Coll., New Coll. Oxford, Harvard School of Public Admin; in Diplomatic Service 1960–66; with J. Henry Schroder Wagg and Co. Ltd 1967–80 (seconded to Bank of England 1977–79); Assoc. Dir Bank of England 1980–81, Exec. Dir (Overseas Affairs) 1981–89; Group Exec. Dir, Vice-Chair. S. G. Warburg and Co. 1989–92; Exec. Dir UK–Japan 21st Century Group 1999–2002; Dir (non-exec.) St James's Place Capital PLC 1993–, St James's Place Int. PLC 1995–, Alpha Bank London PLC 1994–, Tokyo-Mitsubishi Int. PLC 1996–, AGCO Corpn (USA) 1997–; Chair. Public Works Loan Bd 1997–. *Address:* 2nd Floor, 14–16 Regent Street, London, SW1Y 4PH; 11 Cranleigh, 139 Ladbroke Road, London, W11 3PX, England. *Telephone:* (20) 7925-1144 (office). *Fax:* (20) 7930-0931 (office).

LÖFFELHOLZ, Thomas, DrJur; German journalist and editor; Chair. German Press Asscn, Bonn 1982–83; Chief Ed. Stuttgarter Zeitung 1983–95; Ed., then Chief Ed. Die Welt 1995–98, re-apptd. Ed.-in-Chief 2001–08; Chevalier Ordre de la Couronne (Belgium); Karl Bräuer Prize 1981, Ludwig Erhard Prize 1984, Franz Karl Maier Prize 1992, Theodor Wolff Prize 1972, 1998, Bundesverdienstkreuz (First Class) 1999. *Address:* c/o Die Welt, Axel-Springer-Strasse 65, 10888 Berlin, Germany.

LÖFGREN, Lars, PhD; Swedish theatre, film and television director, playwright and poet; *Lord Chamberlain;* b. 6 Sept. 1935, The Arctic Circle; m. Anna-Karin Gillberg 1963; one s. two d.; ed Gustavus Adolphus Coll., USA, Stanford Univ., USA, Sorbonne, France, Uppsala Univ., Sweden; Dir Royal Dramatic Theatre of Sweden 1985–97, Nordic Museum 1997–2001; Lord Chamberlain 1999–; Lord-in-Waiting to His Majesty the King; Commdr, Légion d'honneur 2001; Royal Prize of Swedish Acad. 1996. *Publications:* various plays, filmscripts, TV scripts, poetry, novels, Svensk Teater — Artistry of the Swedish Theater 2003. *Address:* The Office of the Marshal of the Court of the Royal Palace, 11130 Stockholm (office); Sjötullsbacken 27, 11525 Stockholm, Sweden (home). *Telephone:* (8) 402-6000 (office); (8) 855822 (home). *E-mail:* lars.lofgren@pof.se (home).

LOGAN, Malcolm Ian, AC, DipEd, PhD; Australian university vice-chancellor; b. 3 June 1931, Inverell, NSW; s. of the late A. J. Logan; m. Antoinette Lalich 1954; one d.; ed Tamworth High School, New England Univ. Coll., Sydney Teachers' Coll., Sydney Univ.; Lecturer in Geography, Sydney Teachers' Coll. 1956–58, Univ. of Sydney 1959–64, Sr Lecturer 1965–67; Prof. of Geography and Urban and Regional Planning, Univ. of Wisconsin, Madison, USA 1967–71; Prof. of Geography, Monash Univ. 1971–86, Pro-Vice-Chancellor 1982–85, Deputy Vice-Chancellor 1986, Vice-Chancellor 1987–96, also fmr Pres.; Deputy Chair. Int. Devt Program of Australian Univs 1991–93; Chair. Australian Centre for Contemporary Art 1990, Open Learning Agency of Australia 1993–96, Monash Int. Pty Ltd 1994–96 TENTAS Pty Ltd 1998–, Australia Educ. Gateway Pty Ltd 1998–; Dir Australia Communications Computing Inst. 1998–, Job Scene Pty Ltd 2000–; Chair. and Dir Pinnacle Pty Ltd 2000–; mem. Comm. for the Future 1995–; Visiting Prof., Univ. of Ibadan, Nigeria 1970–71, LSE, London, UK 1973, Nanyang Univ., Singapore 1979. *Publications:* co-author: Studies in Australian Geography 1968, New Viewpoints in Urban and Industrial Geography 1971, Urban and Regional Australia 1975, Urbanisation, The Australian Experience 1980, The Brittle Rim 1989, Reconstructing Asia: The Economic Miracle That Never Was, The Future That Is 1998. *Leisure interests:* golf, reading. *Address:* 1/50 Bourke Street, Melbourne, Vic. 3000; c/o Monash University, Wellington Road, Clayton, Vic. 3168, Australia.

LOGUE, Christopher John, CBE; British writer and poet; b. 23 Nov. 1926, Southsea; s. of John Logue and Molly Logue (née Chapman); m. Rosemary Hill 1985; ed Prior Park Coll., Bath and Portsmouth Grammar School; First Wilfred Owen Award for Poetry 1998, Civil List Pension for Services to Literature 2002. *Screenplays:* The End of Arthur's Marriage 1965, Savage Messiah 1972, Crusoe (based on Defoe's novel, with Walon Green) 1989. *Recordings:* Red Bird (poetry and jazz, with Tony Kinsey and Bill Le Sage) 1960, Songs from the Establishment 1962, The Death of Patroclus 1963, Audiologue (recordings 1958–98) 2001. *Film roles:* Swinburne in Ken Russell's Dante's Inferno 1966, John Ball in John Irvin's The Peasant's Revolt 1969, Cardinal Richelieu in Ken Russell's The Devils 1970; also TV and stage roles. *Publications:* poetry: Wand & Quadrant 1953, Devil, Maggot & Son 1954, The Weakdream Sonnets 1955, The Man Who Told His Love: 20 Poems Based on P. Neruda's 'Los Cantos d'amores' 1958, Songs 1959, Songs from 'The Lily-White Boys' 1960, Patrocleia 1962, Pax 1967, The Establishment Songs 1966, The Girls 1969, New Numbers 1969, Abecedary 1977, Ode to the Dodo 1981, War Music 1981, Fluff 1984, Kings 1991, The Husbands 1994, Selected Poems 1996, Prince Charming: A Memoir 1999, Logue's Homer: War Music 2001, All Day Permanent Red 2003; plays: The Trial of Cob & Leach 1959, The Lily-White Boys (with Harry Cookson) 1959, Antigone 1961, The Seven Deadly Sins 1986; other: Lust, by Count Plamiro Vicarion (ed.) 1955, Count Palmiro Vicarion's Book of Limericks (ed.) 1959, The Arrival of the Poet in the City: A Treatment for a Film 1964, True Stories 1966, The Children's Book of Comic Verse (ed.) 1979, The Bumper Book of True Stories 1980, London in Verse (ed.) 1982, Sweet & Sour: An Anthology of Comic Verse (ed.) 1983, The Oxford Book of Pseuds (ed.) 1983, The Children's Book of Children's Rhymes (ed.) 1986, Cold Calls: War Music Continued (Whitbread Prize for Poetry) 2005; contrib. to Private Eye, The Times, Sunday Times. *Address:* 41 Camberwell Grove, London, SE5 8JA, England.

LOGUNOV, Anatoly Alekseyevich; Russian theoretical physicist; *Research Head, Institute for High Energy Research (IHEP);* b. 30 Dec. 1926, Obsharovka, Samara Region; s. of Aleksei Ivanovich Logunov and Agrippina Kuzminichna Logunova; m. Anna Nikolayevna Eshliman 1951 (died 1997); one s. (deceased) one d.; ed Moscow State Univ.; mem. CPSU 1960–91; mem. faculty staff Moscow State Univ. 1951–56; Deputy Dir for Research, Theoretical Physics Lab., Jt Inst. for Nuclear Research, Dubna 1956–63, Prof. 1961; Dir of Serpukhov Inst. for High Energy Physics (IHEP), Protvino, Moscow 1963–74, IHEP Research Head 1974–, Dir State Research Centre IHEP 1993–2003; Rector Moscow State Univ. 1977–92; mem. USSR (now Russian) Acad. of Sciences 1972–, Vice-Pres. 1974–91; Head, State Scientific-Tech. Programme of High Energy Physics 1987–91; mem. Acad. of Creative Endeavours 1992–; Full Prof., Inst. of Fundamental Research, Molise, Italy; mem. Editorial Bd Asia-Pacific Peace Forum 1995–; Chief Ed. annual publ. Science and Humankind 1977–91, journal Theoretical and Mathematical Physics 1989–; main research on quantum field theory, elementary particle physics, gravitation and relativity theory; Cand. mem. Cen. Cttee CPSU 1981–86, mem. 1986–90; Deputy, USSR Supreme Soviet 1978–89; four Orders of Lenin, Order of Honour, Order of Pole Star (Mongolia), Order of Yugoslavian Banner with Ribbon, Commdr Cross of Order of Merit (Poland), Order for Service to the Motherland (third and second classes) 1995, 2002; Dr hc (Belgrade, Berlin, Bratislava, Havana, Helsinki, Prague, Sofia Univs, several Japanese Univs; Lenin Prize 1970, USSR State Prizes 1973, 1984, Lyapunov Medal, Gibbs Medal, Hero of Socialist Labour 1980, Gold Medal Czech Acad. of Sciences. *Publications include:* The Updated Analysis of the Problem 1987, On Henri Poincaret's work On the Dynamics of the Electron 1988, The Third Irisated Bridge 1988, Relativistic Theory of Gravitation 1989, Principles of Quantum Field Theory 1990, Lectures in Relativity and Gravitation: A Modern Look 1991, Gravitational Field Theory 2000, The Theory of Gravity 2001, Poincaré and Relativity Theory 2005, Henri Poincaret's Relativistic Theory of Gravitation 2006; more than 350 contribs to scientific journals on high energy and elementary particle physics and on latest ideas about space-time and gravitation. *Address:* State Research Centre Institute for High Energy Physics, 142281 Protvino, Moscow Region, Russia (office). *Telephone:* (4967) 74-25-79 (office). *Fax:* (4967) 74-49-37 (office). *E-mail:* Anatoly.Logunov@ihep.ru (office).

LOHANI, Prakash Chandra, PhD; Nepalese politician; b. 1944; ed Univ. of Calif., USA; fmr Lecturer, Univ. of Calif.; fmr Minister of Foreign Affairs and of Finance; Minister of Finance, Interim Govt 2003–04; currently Joint Gen.-Sec. Rashtriya Jana Shakti Party (National People's Power Party). *Address:* Rashtriya Jana Shakti Party (National People's Power Party), Ramalphokhari, Kathmandu, Nepal (office). *Telephone:* (1) 4437063 (office). *Fax:* (1) 4437064 (office). *E-mail:* rjpnepal@info.com.np (office). *Website:* www.rjpnepal.org (office).

LOHIA, Ashok Kumar; Nepalese business executive; f. Mahashakti Soap and Chemical Industries Pvt. Ltd 1970, currently Chair. *Address:* Mahashakti Soap and Chemical Industries Pvt. Ltd, 534 Exhibition Road, Kathmandu, Nepal (office). *Telephone:* (1) 4226638 (office). *Fax:* (1) 4225178 (office). *E-mail:* puja@msci.wlink.com.np (office).

LOHIA, Renagi Renagi, CBE, MA; Papua New Guinea broadcasting executive and fmr diplomatist; b. 15 Oct. 1945, Tubesereia; s. of Lohia and Koborei Lohia; m. Patty Lohia 1969; three s. two d.; ed Univ. of Papua New Guinea and Univ. of London, UK; Research Asst, Univ. of Papua New Guinea 1970–73; Sr Tutor 1973, Lecturer in Educ. 1974–82, Pro-Vice-Chancellor 1976, Deputy Vice-Chancellor 1977, Vice-Chancellor 1977–82, Chair. Educational Planning Cttee 1974–75, Educ. Faculty Rep. Jt Cttee on Teacher Educ. 1975–76; Chair. Public Services Comm. 1982–83; Amb. to USA and Mexico and High Commr in Canada 1983–89; Perm. Rep. to UN 1983–94; Chair. UN Decolonization Cttee; Special Asst Dept of Foreign Affairs 1986–87; Chief of Staff, Office of Prime Minister 1994–95; Chair. and CEO Nat. Broadcasting Comm. 1995–99; High Commr to Australia –2005. *Leisure interest:* sports. *Address:* c/o Department of Foreign Affairs, Central Government Offices, Kumul Ave, Post Office, Wards Strip, Waigani, NCD, Papua New Guinea.

LOHSE, Eduard, DTheol; German ecclesiastic; b. 19 Feb. 1924, Hamburg; s. of Dr Walther Lohse and Dr Wilhelmine Lohse (née Barrelet); m. Roswitha Flitner 1952; two s. one d.; ed Bethel/Bielefeld and Göttingen; Pastor, Hamburg 1952; Privatdozent, Faculty of Protestant Theology, Mainz 1953; Prof. of New Testament, Kiel 1956, Göttingen 1964; Bishop of Hanover 1971–88; Pres. of the Council of the Evangelical Church in Germany 1979–85; mem. Göttingen Akad. der Wissenschaften; Hon. DTheol (Mainz) 1961, (Glasgow) 1983. *Publications:* Märtyrer und Gottesknecht 1955, Die Offenbarung des Johannes 1960, Die Texte aus Qumran 1964, Die Geschichte des Leidens und Sterbens Jesu Christi 1964, Die Briefe an die Kolosser und an Philemon 1968, Umwelt des Neuen Testaments 1971, Entstehung des Neuen Testaments 1972, Die Einheit des Neuen Testaments 1973, Grundriss der neutestamentlichen Theologie 1974, Die Urkunde der Christen 1979, Die Vielfalt des Neuen Testaments 1982, Die Ethik der Bergpredigt 1984, Kleine Evangelische Pastoralethik 1985, Theologische Ethik des Neuen Testaments 1988, Erneuern und Bewahren Evangelische Kirche 1970–90 1993, Paulus – eine Biographie 1996, Der Brief an die Römar 2003. *Leisure interest:* music. *Address:* Ernst-Curtius-Weg 7, 37075 Göttingen, Germany. *Telephone:* (551) 42424 (home).

LOHSE, Martin J., DrMed; German pharmacologist and academic; *Head of Institute for Pharmacology and Toxicology, Julius Maximilians University of Würzburg;* b. 26 Aug. 1956, Mainz; s. of Prof. Eduard Lohse and Roswitha Lohse; m. Friederike Lohse; three s.; ed Univ. of Göttingen, Univ. of London, UK and Univ. of Paris, France; worked at Pharmacological Insts in Bonn and Heidelberg; Asst Prof. Duke Univ., Durham, NC, USA 1988–90; Leader, GeneCenter, Max-Planck Inst. for Biochemistry, Martinsried 1990–93; Head of Inst. for Pharmacology and Toxicology, Julius Maximilians Univ. of Würzburg 1993–, Chair. Graduate School 2003–; Chair. Rudolf-Virchow-DFG Research Center for Experimental Biomedicine 2001–; project man. several European research programmes; mem. Bavarian Acad. of Science 1998, Leopoldina German Acad. of Science 2000, Northrhine-Westfalia Acad. of Science 2004; mem. Editorial Bd Nature, Science, The EMBO Journal; mem. Advisory Bd numerous scientific foundations; Fed. Order of Merit (1st class) 2002, Bavarian Order of Merit 2006; Gerhard Hess Prize, FRG 1990, Research Prize, Fed. Dept of Health 1991, William Vaillant Prize 1996, Gottfried Wilhelm Leibniz Prize, Deutschen Forschungsgemeinschaft 1999, Ernst Jung Prize in Medicine 2000, Research Achievement Award, Int. Soc. of Heart Research 2007. *Publications:* numerous articles in scientific journals. *Address:* Julius-Maximilians-Universität Würzburg, Institut für Pharmakologie und Toxikologie, Versbacher Straße 9, 97078 Würzburg, Germany (office). *Telephone:* (931) 201-48400 (office). *Fax:* (931) 201-48411 (office). *E-mail:* lohse@toxi.uni-wuerzburg.de (office). *Website:* www.pharmakologie.uni-wuerzburg.de (office).

LOKOLOKO, Sir Tore, GCMG, OBE; Papua New Guinea politician; b. 21 Sept. 1930, Iokea, Gulf Province; s. of Paramount Chief Lokoloko Tore and Kevau-Sarufa; m. Lalahaia Meakoro 1950; four s. six d.; elected to House of Ass. (now Nat. Parl.) as Opposition mem. for Kerema (Gulf Prov.); Gov.-Gen. of Papua New Guinea 1977–83; Chair. Indosuez Niugine Bank 1983–89; KStJ. *Leisure interests:* golf, fishing. *Address:* PO Box 5622, Boroko, NCD, Papua New Guinea.

LOKUBANDARA, W(ijesinghe) J(ayaweera) M(udiyanselage); Sri Lankan attorney and politician; *Speaker of the Parliament;* b. 5 Aug. 1941; m.; mem. Parl. (United Nat. Party) for Badulla, currently Speaker of the Parl., mem. Cttee of Selection, House Cttee, Cttee on Standing Orders, Cttee on Parl. Business; fmr Minister for Justice, Law Reform and Nat. Integration and Minister for Buddha Sasana. *Address:* Office of the Speaker, Parliament of Sri Lanka, Sri Jayewardenepura Kotte, Colombo (office); No. 14, Samagi Mawatha, Gangodawila, Nugegoda, Colombo, Sri Lanka (home). *Telephone:* (11) 2777100 (office). *Fax:* (11) 2777564 (office). *E-mail:* webmaster@parliament.lk (office). *Website:* www.parliament.lk (office).

LOLLOBRIGIDA, Gina; Italian actress, photographer and sculptor; b. 4 July 1927, Sibiaco; d. of Giovanni Mercuri and Giuseppina Mercuri; m. 1st Milko Skofic 1949; one s.; ed Liceo Artistico, Rome; fmr model; first screen role in Pagliacci 1947; currently photographer and sculptor. *Films include:* Campane a Martello 1948, Cuori senza Frontiere 1949, Achtung, Banditi! 1951, Enrico Caruso 1951, Fanfan la Tulipe 1951, Altri Tempi 1952, The Wayward Wife 1952, Les belles de la nuit 1952, Pane, amore e fantasia 1953, La Provinciale 1953, Pane, amore e gelosia, La Romana 1954, Il Grande Gioco 1954, La Donna più bella del Mondo 1955, Trapeze 1956, Notre Dame de Paris 1956, Solomon and Sheba 1959, Never So Few 1960, Go Naked in the World 1961, She Got What She Asked For 1963, Woman of Straw 1964, Le Bambole 1965, Hotel Paradiso 1966, Les Sultans 1966, Le Piacevoli Notti 1966, Cervantes 1966, La Morte Fatto L'uovo (A Curious Way to Love) and (Death Laid an Egg) 1967, Stuntman 1968, Buona Sera Mrs Campbell 1968, Un Bellissimo Novembre (That Splendid November) 1968, The Private Navy of Sgt O'Farrell 1968, Peccato Mortale (Mortal Sin also known as The Lonely Woman also known as Roses and Green Peppers) 1972, King, Queen, Knave 1972, Le Avventure Di Pinocchio 1972, Bad Man's River 1972, Falcon Crest TV Series 1984, Deceptions 1985, (TV film) 1985, The Bocce Showdown 1990, Les Cent et Une Nuits (A Hundred and One Nights) 1995, Plucked, XXL 1997. *Publications:* Italia Mia (photography) 1974, The Philippines. *Leisure interest:* photography. *Address:* Via Appia Antica 223, 00178 Rome, Italy.

LOM, Herbert; British actor; b. 11 Sept. 1917, Prague, Bohemia, Austria-Hungary (now Czech Repub.); s. of Charles Lom and Olga Lom; m. (divorced); two s. one d.; ed Prague Univ., Westminster School and Old Vic, London; theatre work in Prague before coming to England in 1939; joined the Old Vic theatre school; entered films 1940; worked with BBC European Section 1940–46; Artis Bohemiae Amicis, Czech Ministry of Culture Medal 2002. *Films include:* Zena pod krízem 1937, Bozí mlýny (God's Mills) 1938, The Young Mr. Pitt 1942, Secret Mission 1942, Tomorrow We Live 1943, The Dark Tower 1943, Hotel Reserve 1944, The Seventh Veil 1945, Dual Alibi 1946, Night Boat to Dublin 1946, Appointment With Crime 1946, Portrait from Life 1948, Brass Monkey 1948, Snowbound 1948, Good Time Girl 1948, Night and the City 1950, State Secret 1950, Golden Salamander 1950, The Black Rose 1950, Cage of Gold 1950, Whispering Smith Hits London 1951, Hell is Sold Out 1951, Two on the Tiles 1952, Mr. Denning Drives North 1952, The Ringer 1952, Star of India 1953, The Net 1953, The Man Who Watched the Trains Go By 1953, Rough Shoot 1953, The Love Lottery 1954, Beautiful Stranger 1954, The Wrong Widget 1955, The Ladykillers 1955, War and Peace 1956, Chase a Crooked Shadow 1957, Fire Down Below 1957, Hell Drivers 1957, Action of the Tiger 1957, Passport to Shame 1958, No Trees in the Street 1958, I Accuse! 1958, The Roots of Heaven 1958, Intent to Kill 1958, North-West Frontier 1959, The Big Fisherman 1959, Third Man on the Mountain 1959, Wernher von Braun 1960, Spartacus 1960, Mr. Topaze 1961, The Frightened City 1961, Mysterious Island 1961, El Cid 1961, The Phantom of the Opera 1962, Tiara Tahiti 1962, Der Schatz im Silbersee (Treasure of Silver Lake) 1962, A Shot in the Dark 1964, Onkel Toms Hütte (Uncle Tom's Cabin) 1965, Return from the Ashes 1965, Our Man in Marrakesh 1966, Gambit 1966, Die Nibelungen, Teil 2: Kriemhilds Rache 1967, The Karate Killers 1967, Villa Rides 1968, The Face of Eve 1968, Assignment to Kill 1968, 99 mujeres (99 Women) 1969, Doppelgänger 1969, Hexen bis aufs Blut gequält 1970, Count Dracula 1970, The Picture of Dorian Gray 1970, Murders in the Rue Morgue 1971, Asylum 1972, Dark Places 1973, And Now the Screaming Starts! 1973, And Then There Were None 1974, The Return of the Pink Panther 1975, The Pink Panther Strikes Again 1976, Charleston 1976, Revenge of the Pink Panther 1977, The Lady Vanishes 1979, The Man with Bogart's Face 1980, Hopscotch 1980, Trail of the Pink Panther 1982, Curse of the Pink Panther 1983, The Dead Zone 1983, Memed My Hawk 1984, King Solomon's Mines 1985, Whoops Apocalypse 1986, Scoop 1987, Skeleton Coast 1987, The Crystal Eye 1988, Going Bananas 1988, Master of Dragonard Hill 1989, Ten Little Indians 1989, River of Death 1989, Masque of the Red Death 1990, The Pope Must Die 1991, The Sect 1991, Son of the Pink Panther 1993. *Television includes:* Errol Flynn Theater (series) 1957, The Horse Without a Head 1963, The Human Jungle (series) 1963, The Man from U.N.C.L.E. 1967, Mister Jerico 1970, Hawaii Five-O 1971, Peter and Paul 1981, Lace 1984, Scoop 1987, Marple: The Murder at the Vicarage 2005. *Plays include:* The King and I, Theatre Royal, Drury Lane, London 1951–53. *Publications:* Enter a Spy, The Double Life of Christopher Marlowe 1978, Dr Guillotine 1992. *Leisure interest:* books. *Address:* c/o Jean Diamond Management, 3 Percy Street, London, W1T 2DD, England (office).

LOMAIA, Alexander, PhD; Georgian engineer and government official; *Minister of Education and Science;* b. 1963, Tblisi; m.; two c.; ed Georgian Tech. Univ.; Moscow Construction Engineering Inst.; engineer, Tbilhihroproekti Inst. 1985–87; fmr Ed., Argumenti Newspaper; mem., Georgian Community Hall, Moscow 1989–92; Deputy Rep. of Govt of Georgia to Moscow 1991, later acting Rep.; Co-ordinator, Eurasia Fund Civil Public and Media Program 1995–2000; Dir, Georgia Representation to Eurasia Fund 2000–02; Regional Dir Democracy Coalition in post-Soviet states 2002–03; Exec. Dir Open Society Georgia 2003–; active in 'rose revolution' of 2003; Minister of Education and Sciences 2004–. *Address:* Ministry of Education and Science, 0102 Tbilisi, Uznadze 52, Georgia (office). *Telephone:* (32) 95-70-10 (office). *Fax:* (32) 91-04-47 (office). *E-mail:* pr@mes.gov.ge (office). *Website:* www.mes.gov.ge (office).

LOMAX, (Janis) Rachel, MA, MSc; British civil servant and economist; b. 15 July 1945; d. of William Salmon and Dilys Salmon; m. Michael Acworth Lomax 1967 (divorced 1990); two s.; ed Cheltenham Lady's Coll., Girton Coll., Cambridge, London School of Econs; Econ. Asst, HM Treasury 1968, Econ. Adviser 1972, Sr Econ. Adviser 1978, Prin. Pvt. Sec. to Chancellor of the Exchequer 1985–86, Under-Sec. 1986–90, Deputy Chief Econ. Adviser 1990–92, Deputy Sec. Financial Insts and Markets 1992–94, Deputy Sec. Cabinet Office 1994–95; Vice-Pres. and Chief of Staff, IBRD 1995–96; Perm. Sec. Welsh Office 1996–99, Dept of Social Security, then Dept for Work and Pensions 1999–2002; Perm. Sec. Dept for Transport 2002–; Deputy Gov. (responsible for monetary policy) Bank of England July 2003–08; Chair. UK Selection Cttee, Harkness Fellowships 1995–97; mem. Council Royal Econ. Soc. 1989–94; Gov. De Montfort Univ. 1997–2007, Henley Coll. of Man. 2000–03, LSE 2003–; Dir Royal Nat. Theatre 2002–; Pres. Inst. of Fiscal Studies 2007–. *Address:* Bank of England, Threadneedle Street, London, EC2R 8AH, England (office). *Telephone:* (20) 7601-4444 (office). *Fax:* (20) 7601-3047 (office). *Website:* www.bankofengland.co.uk (office).

LOMBARD, Didier; French telecommunications executive; *Chairman and CEO, France Telecom SA;* b. 1942; m.; three s.; ed École Polytechnique, École Nationale Supérieure des Télécommunications; with CNET (now Research and Devt Div., France Telecom) 1967; Scientific and Tech. Dir, Ministry of Research and Tech. 1988–90; Gen. Man. of Industrial Strategy, Ministry of Economy 1991–98; Founder, Chair. and Deputy Amb. for Int. Investment, Agency for Int. Investment 1999–2003; Exec. Vice-Pres., in charge of Technologies, Strategic Partnerships and New Usages, France Telecom SA 2003–, Chair. and CEO 2005–; mem. Bd Dirs Thomson, Thales; mem. Supervisory Bd Radiall, ST Microelectronics. *Address:* France Telecom SA, 6 place d'Alleray, 75505 Paris Cedex 15, France (office). *Telephone:* 1-44-44-22-22 (office). *Fax:* 1-44-44-95-95 (office). *E-mail:* info@francetelecom.com (office). *Website:* www.francetelecom.com (office).

LOMBARD, Marie-Christine, MBA; French business executive; *Group Managing Director, TNT Express;* b. 1958, Paris; m.; two c.; ed ESSEC Business School, Paris; began career at Lord & Taylor, New York, USA; fmr banker with Chemical Bank, Paris, Paribas Bank, Lyon; Chief Financial Officer Jet Services, France 1993–97, Man. Dir 1997–99, co. acquired by TNT Express (Dutch postal and logistics group) in 1999, Chair. and Man. Dir TNT Express France 1999–2004, Group Man. Dir TNT Express and mem. Bd of Man. 2004–; mem. Supervisory Bd Royal Wessanen NV, Metro Group; Chevalier Légion d'honneur 2005; ranked by the Financial Times amongst Top 25 Businesswomen in Europe (23rd) 2005, (23rd) 2006, (23rd) 2007. *Address:* TNT NV Group Head Office, Neptunus straat 41–63, 2132 JA Hoofddorp, PO Box 13000, 1100 KG Amsterdam, Netherlands (office). *Telephone:* (20) 500-6000 (office). *Fax:* (20) 500-7000 (office). *Website:* www.tnt.com (office); group.tnt.com (office).

LOMU, Jonah; New Zealand rugby union player; b. 12 May 1975, Auckland; m. Tanya Rutter 1996 (divorced); pnr Teina Stace; ed Wesley Coll., Auckland; bank officer ASB Bank of NZ; youngest ever capped All Black (at 19 years and 45 days); wing; int. debut NZ versus France 1994; semi-finalist at World Cup, 1995 and 1999; out of action for a year during 1996–97 with a rare kidney disorder, returned to int. side for All Blacks' UK tour end of 1997; gold medal rugby sevens, Kuala Lumpur Commonwealth Games 1998; missed World Cup of 2003 after kidney disorder recurred; 63 caps (185 Test points including 37 tries); ran 100m in 10.8 seconds;*Website:* www.jonahlomu.com (office).

LONDOÑO PAREDES, Julio; Colombian politician and diplomatist; *Ambassador to Cuba;* b. 10 June 1938, Bogotá; m.; ed San Isidro Hermanos Maristas School, El Carmen Inst. and Mil. Cadet School, Bogotá; Prof. of Int. Politics, Univ. of Jorge Tadeo Lozano, Bogotá; Prof. of Int. Public Law, Univ. of El Rosario, Bogotá; served in army, retd 1981 with rank of Lt-Col; Head of Frontier Div., Ministry of Foreign Affairs 1968–79, Sec.-Gen. 1979–82, Vice-Minister 1982–83, Minister 1986–90; Amb. to Panama 1983–86; Perm. Rep. to UN 1994–99; currently Amb. to Cuba. *Publications:* History of the Colombo-Peruvian Conflict of 1932, Colombian Territorial Law, Colombian Border Issues. *Address:* Embassy of Colombia, Calle 14, No 515, entre 5 y 7, Miramar, Havana, Cuba (office). *Telephone:* (7) 24-1246 (office). *Fax:* (7) 24-1249 (office). *E-mail:* embacub@cancilleria.gov.co (office).

LONFERNINI, Giovanni; San Marino government official; *Co-Captain-Regent;* Co-Capt.-Regent of San Marino 2003–; Sec.-Gen. San Marino Christian Democrat Party (Partito Democratico Cristiano Sammarinese). *Address:* Partito Democratico Cristiano Sammarinese (PDCS), Via delle Scalette 6, 47890 San Marino (office). *Telephone:* 0549 991193 (office). *Fax:* 0549 992694 (office).

LONG, Malcolm William, LLB; Australian broadcasting executive; b. 13 April 1948, Fremantle, WA; s. of William Long and Dorothy Long; m. Helen Trotter 1973; two d.; ed Univ. of Western Australia; Dir Radio Talks and Documentaries, ABC 1978–82; Man. (Radio) Victorian ABC 1982–84; Dir ABC Radio 1985–92; Deputy Man. Dir Australian Broadcasting Corpn 1992–93; Dir PAN TV Ltd 1996–; Man. Dir SBS Corpn 1993–97; Man. Dir Malcolm Long Assocs Pty Ltd 1997–2003; Pres. Australian Museum Trust 1995–2000; Dir Macquarie Communications Infrastructure Group 2001–, Australian Film Television and Radio School 2003–07; fmr Chair. Exec. Cttee Int. Inst. of Communications; mem. Australian Broadcasting Authority 2000–05, Australian Communications and Media Authority 2005–. *Publications:* Marx & Beyond 1973, Beyond the Mechanical Mind (with P. Fry) 1977; numerous articles on broadcasting policy and culture. *Leisure interests:* music, reading, running. *Address:* Australian Communications and Media Authority, PO Box Q500, Queen Victoria Building, NSW 1230, Australia (office). *Telephone:* (2) 9334-7700 (office). *Fax:* (2) 9334-7799 (office). *E-mail:* ml@mlongdigital.com (office). *Website:* www.acma.gov.au (office).

LONG, Marceau, LèsL, LenD; French civil servant; *President, Institut français des relations internationales;* b. 22 April 1926, Aix-en-Provence, Bouches-du-Rhône; s. of Lucien Long and Marcelle Seymard; m. Josette Niel 1949; two s. three d.; ed Lycée Mignet, Univ. of Aix-en-Provence, École nat. d'admin; Lecturer, Ecole nat. d'admin 1953–56, Inst. d'Etudes politiques 1953–56; seminars Ecole nat. d'admin 1963–68; at Council of State 1952–57, 1975–, Vice-Pres. 1987–95, apptd auditor 1952, master of petitions 1957, Sec.-Gen. to Govt 1975–82, Counsellor of State on long-term secondment 1976; apptd to Govt Comm. 1957, Tech. Counsellor to Cabinet, Sec. of State on Tunisian and Moroccan Affairs, then Foreign Affairs, then Judicial Counsellor to French Embassy, Morocco 1958, Dir-Gen. Admin. and Public Offices 1961–67, Sec. Gen. Admin, Ministry of Armies 1967–73, mem. Atomic Energy Cttee 1975–82; Chair. Organisation de la radio et de la télévision françaises (ORTF) 1973–74; Chair. Cie Air-Inter 1982–84; Chair. Cie Air France 1984–87; Chair. Cttee Inquiry on Law of Nationality 1987, Council of Admin. Tribunals and Courts of Appeal 1988–95; Lecturer Inst. d'études politiques de Paris, Ecole nat. d'admin 1963–68 (Chair. Bd of Govs 1987); Dir Crédit industriel et banque commericale 1982–87, Soc. de Gestion de participations aéronautiques 1985; Vice-Pres. Conseil d'Etat 1987–95; apptd Pres. Admin. Council, Ecole nat. d'admin, Institut int. d'admin publique 1987, Inst. français des relations int. 1998–; Pres. Franco-American Foundation 1989–92, Hon. Pres. 1993–; Pres. Haut conseil à l'intégration 1989–93, 1994–95, Inst. des hautes études de la justice 1995–97, Inst. de la gestion déléguée 1996–2001; mem. Court of Arbitration, The Hague 1991–; mem. numerous admin. councils and cttees; Grand Officier, Légion d'honneur; Commdr Ordre nat. du Mérite; Officier des Palmes académiques. *Publications:* L'Economie de la Fonction Publique 1967, Les Services de Premier Ministre 1981, Les Grands Arrêts de la Jurisprudence Administrative (co-author) 1984, Etre Français aujourd'hui et demain, Rapport de la Commission de la Nationalité 1988, L'Esprit de justice: Portalis 1997, Les grands arrêts de la jurisprudence administrative (jtly 2005 and numerous contribs to magazines and books on public office and law. *Address:* Institut français des relations internationales, 27 rue de la Procession, 75015 Paris (office).

LONG, Richard, RA; British artist; b. 2 June 1945, Bristol; s. of Maurice Long and Frances Carpenter; m. Denise Johnston 1969 (divorced 1999); two d.; pnr Denise Hooker; ed West of England Coll. of Art, Bristol and St Martin's School of Art, London; has exhibited widely since mid-1960s; work exhibited Städtisches Museum, Mönchengladbach 1970, Museum of Modern Art, New York 1972, Stedelijk Museum, Amsterdam 1973, Scottish Museum of Modern Art, Edin. 1974, Kunsthalle, Berne 1977, Nat. Gallery of Canada, Ottawa 1982, Solomon R. Guggenheim Museum, New York 1986, Tate Gallery 1990, Hayward Gallery, London (retrospective) 1991, ARC, Paris 1993, Palazzo delle Esposizioni, Rome 1994, São Paulo Bienal 1994, Nat. Modern Art Museum of Kyoto 1996, Kunstverein Hanover 1999, Guggenheim, Bilbao 2000, Museum Kurhaus Kleve 2001, Tate St Ives 2002, Galleria Lorcan O'Neill Roma 2003; Chevalier des Arts et des Lettres 1990; Hon. DLit (Bristol) 1995; Turner Prize 1989, Wilhelm Lembruck Prize 1995. *Publications include:* South America 1972, River Avon Book 1979, Twelve Works 1981, Countless Stones 1983, Stone Water Miles 1987, Old World New World 1988, Nile 1990, Walking in Circles 1991, Mountains and Waters 1992, River to River 1993, Mirage 1997, A Walk Across Across England 1997, From Time to time 1997, Every Grain of Sand 1999, Midday 2001, A Moving World 2002, Walking the Line 2002. *Address:* c/o Haunch of Venison, 6 Haunch of Venison Yard, London, W1K 5ES, England. *Website:* www.richardlong.org.

LONGO, Jeannie Michèle Alice; French cyclist; b. 31 Oct. 1958, Annecy; d. of Jean Longo and Yvette Longo; m. Patrice Ciprelli 1985; ed Inst. d'Etudes Commerciales (Grenoble), Univ. of Limoges; French cycling champion 1979–86; winner of 13 world titles including world champion (road) 1979–89, 1992, 1995, 1998, 1999, 2000, runner up 1981, world champion (track) 1984, 1985, world champion (pursuit) 1986, 1988, 1989, world champion (against the clock) Spain 1997; winner Tour of Colorado 1986, 1987, Tour of Colombia 1987, 1988, Tour of Norway 1987, Tour de France 1987; silver medal World Track Race 1984, 1985, 1987; holder of several world records including world record for three km covered track, Grenoble 1992, five km uncovered track 1989; winner French Cycle Racing Championship 1992; silver medallist Olympic Games, Barcelona 1992, gold and silver medallist Road Race, Olympic Games, Atlanta 1996, bronze medallist, Olympic Games, Sydney 2000; still competing in 2005 having amassed over 700 career wins, more than any other cyclist in history, setting 37 world records; Consultant France Télévision 1999–; Officier, Légion d'Honneur, Commdr Ordre National du Mérite, Officer, Sovereign Order of Malta; Médaille d'Or, La Jeunesse et les Sports, Médaille d'Or, Acad. des Sports, Médaille du mérite et dévouement Français 2002. *Address:* Fédération Française de Cyclisme, 5 rue de Rome, 93561 Rosny-sous-Bois, France. *E-mail:* jeannielongo@free.fr (home). *Website:* www.jeannielongo.com (home).

LONGRIGG, Anthony James, CMG; British diplomatist; b. 21 April 1944; m. Jane Rosa Cowlin 1968; three d.; joined FCO 1972, with Research Unit 1973; First Sec. Chancery, Moscow 1975–78; with E African Dept FCO 1978–80, Conf. for Security and Co-operation in Europe, FCO 1980–81; First Sec., Brasilia 1981–85; with Soviet Dept FCO 1985–87; Counsellor, Moscow 1987–91; Counsellor Econ./EU Affairs, Madrid 1991–95; Head S Atlantic/Antarctic Dept FCO 1995–97; Minister and Deputy Head of Mission, Moscow 1997–2000; Gov. of Montserrat 2001–04 (retd). *Address:* c/o Foreign and Commonwealth Office, King Charles Street, London, SW1A 2AH, England (office).

LONGUET, Gérard Edmond Jacques; French politician; b. 24 Feb. 1946, Neuilly-sur-Seine; s. of Jacques Longuet and Marie-Antoinette Laurent; m. Brigitte Fossorier 1967; four d.; ed Paris Univ., Ecole Nationale d'Administration; Pvt. Sec. to Prefect of Eure's Office 1973–74, to Prefect of Somme's Office 1974–76, to Sec. of State (attached to Prime Minister's Office) 1977–78; Deputy of Meuse 1978–81, 1988–93, Vice-Pres. Gen. Councillor's Office 1982–92; Gen. Councillor Seuil d'Argonne 1979–92, Town Councillor 1983; mem. European Parl. 1984–86; Sec. of State March–Aug. 1986, then Minister at Ministry of Industry 1986–88, Minister of Industry, Posts and Telecommunications and Foreign Trade 1993–94; Sec.-Gen. Union pour la Démocratie Française (UDF) 1989; Pres. Republican Party 1990–95, Regional Council of Lorraine 1992–; Senateur de la Meuse 2001–; Collection Dir France Empire publrs; Pres. Sokrates Group; Pres. ETD 2003; Pres. Asscn des Régions de France. *Publications:* L'Epreuve de vérité 1995, L'Espoir industriel 1995. *Leisure interest:* skiing. *Address:* Conseil Regional de Lorraine, Place Gabriel Hocquard, B.P. 1004, 57036 Metz cedex 1; Palais du Luxembourg, 15 rue de Vaugirard, 75006, Paris; Sokrates Group, 119 rue de Paris, 92 100 Boulogne-Billancourt, France (office). *Telephone:* 3-87-33-60-01 (Metz); 1-42-34-39-71 (Senate). *Fax:* 3-87-33-61-01 (Metz); 1-42-34-43-14 (Senate). *E-mail:* glonguet@c-lorraine.fr (office); g.longuet@senat.fr (office).

LONGUET-HIGGINS, Michael Selwyn, MA, PhD, FRS; British physicist and academic; *Senior Research Physicist Emeritus, Institute for Nonlinear Science, University of California, San Diego;* b. 8 Dec. 1925, Lenham, Kent; s. of the late Henry H. L. Longuet-Higgins and Albinia Cecil Bazeley; brother of Hugh Christopher Longuet-Higgins; m. Joan R. Tattersall 1958; two s. two d.; ed Winchester Coll., Trinity Coll., Cambridge Univ.; Research Fellow, Trinity Coll. Cambridge 1951–55, Commonwealth Fund Fellow, Scripps Inst., La Jolla, 1951–52; Research Scientist, Nat. Inst. of Oceanography 1954–67; Visiting Prof., MIT 1958, Inst. of Geophysics, Univ. of California 1961–62, Univ. of Adelaide 1963–64; Prof. of Oceanography, Oregon State Univ., Corvallis 1967–69; Royal Soc. Research Prof., Univ. of Cambridge (jt appointment with Inst. of Oceanographic Sciences) 1969–89; Sr Research Physicist, Inst. for Nonlinear Science, Univ. of California, San Diego 1989–, now Sr Research Physicist Emer.; Fellow, Trinity Coll. Cambridge 1969–; Foreign Assoc. NAS 1979; Hon. LLD (Glasgow) 1979; Hon. DTech (Tech. Univ. of Denmark) 1979; Sverdrup Gold Medal of American Meteorological Soc. 1983; Int. Coastal Eng Award, American Soc. of Civil Engineers 1984. *Publications:* contribs to scientific journals on physics and math. of the sea, especially ocean waves and currents. *Leisure interests:* music, gardening, mathematical toys. *Address:* Gage Farm, Comberton, Cambridge, CB3 7DH, England (home); Institute for Nonlinear Science, University of California San Diego, La Jolla, CA 92093, USA (office). *Telephone:* (858) 534-3936 (office); (1223) 262346 (home). *E-mail:* mlonguet@ucsd.edu (office). *Website:* inls.ucsd.edu (office).

LØNNING, Inge Johan, DTheol; Norwegian politician and theologian; *President, Lagtinget;* b. 20 Feb. 1938, Bergen; s. of the late Per Lønning and of Anna (née Strømø) Lønning; m. Kari Andersen 1962 (died 2008); two s. two d.; ed Univs of Bergen and Oslo and Pastoral Seminary of Church of Norway, Univ. of Tübingen, Germany; Naval Chaplain 1964–65; Asst Prof. Univ. of Oslo 1965–70; Research Fellow, Univ. of Tübingen 1967; Prof. of Systematic Theology, Univ. of Oslo 1971–, Dean, Faculty of Theology 1977–81, Rector, Univ. of Oslo 1985–92; mem. Oslo City Council 1972–76; Chair. Bd Norwegian Research Council for Science and Humanities 1980–84; Pres. Norsemen's Fed. 1989–2000, Nat. Rectors' Conf. 1989–92; Leader, European Movt in Norway 1993–95; mem. Parl. 1997–, Vice-Pres. Stortinget (Parl.) 2001–05, Pres. Lagtinget (Parl. of Åland) 2005–; Vice-Pres. Høyre 1997–2002; Pres. Nordic Council 2003; Ed. Kirke og Kultur journal 1968–; mem. Norwegian Acad. of Science and Letters, Royal Norwegian Soc., Royal Soc. of Letters, Sweden; Commdr, Royal Norwegian Order of St Olav; Commdr with Star, Order of Merit of FRG; Hon. DD (Luther Coll. Decorah, USA, Åbo Acad., Finland). *Publications:* Kanon im Kanon. Zum Dogmatischen Grundlagenproblem des Neutestamentlichen Kanons 1972, Martin Luther: Selected Writings (six vols, ed.) 1978–83, Fellesskap og frihet. Tid for idepolitikk 1997. *Leisure interests:* fishing, skiing. *Address:* Stortinget, Karl Johans Gate, 0026 Oslo (office); Skullerudstubben 22, 1188 Oslo, Norway (home). *Telephone:* 23-31-30-04 (office); 22-28-95-12 (home). *Fax:* 23-31-38-38 (office). *E-mail:* inge.lonning@stortinget.no (office). *Website:* www.stortinget.no (office).

LONSDALE, Anne M., CBE, BA LitHum, BA Or.Stud.; British university administrator (retd); b. 16 Feb. 1941, Huddersfield, Yorks.; d. of A. C. G. Menzies and Molly Menzies; m. 1st Geoffrey Griffin 1962 (died 1962); m. 2nd Roger Lonsdale 1964 (divorced 1994); one s. one d.; ed St Anne's Coll., Oxford; Lecturer in Classical Chinese, St Anne's Coll. Oxford 1965–73; Univ. Admin. 1973–86; Dir External Relations Office, Univ. of Oxford 1986–93; Sec.-Gen. Cen. European Univ. 1993–96; Pres. New Hall Cambridge 1996–2008, Pro-Vice-Chancellor, Univ. of Cambridge 1998–2004, Deputy Vice-Chancellor 2004–08, mem. Council of Senate 1997–2004; mem. Commonwealth Scholarship Comm. 1996–2003; Trustee, Moscow School of Social and Econ. Sciences, LEAD Int. UK, European Humanities Univ., Vilnius/Minsk; Hon. Sec. CARA (Cttee for Assistance to Refugee Academics); Chair. CAMFED Int; Cavaliere del'Ordine al Merito della Repubblica Italiana 1992, Officier des Palmes académiques 2003; Dr hc (Tashkent Oriental Studies Univ., Uzbekistan) 2001. *Publications:* publs on Chinese literature and univ. admin. *Leisure interests:* travel, film, contemporary art. *E-mail:* al213@cam.ac.uk (office).

LOONE, Eero; Estonian philosopher; *Professor of Political Theory, Tallinn University of Technology;* b. 26 May 1935, Tartu; s. of Nikolai Loone and Leida Loone (née Rebane); m. 1st Halliki Uibo 1965; m. 2nd Leiki Sikk 1971; two d.; ed Moscow Univ. and Acad. of Sciences, Moscow; mem. CPSU 1965–90; teacher, Univ. of Tartu 1963–, Prof. 1985–2000, Head, Dept of Philosophy 1986–89, 1993–94, 1998–2000, Head, Dept of Philosophy and Political Science 1989–93, Prof. Emer. 2000–; Prof. of Political Theory, Tallinn Univ. of Tech. 2008–; Visiting Prof., British Acad. 1993, Ashby Lecturer 1994; Founding mem. ind. Estonian Union of Scientists 1989–, Estonia Foreign Policy Inst. 1991, Estonian Political Science Asscn 1993–; mem. Int. Political Science Asscn 1994–; NATO Democratic Insts Fellow 1993–94; Life mem. Clare Hall (Cambridge) 1990–; Fulbright Scholar, Columbia Univ. 1997. *Publications include:* Contemporary Philosophy of History 1980 (trans. into English as Soviet Marxism and Analytical Philosophies of History 1990). *Leisure interest:* science fiction. *Address:* Department of Philosophy, University of Tartu, Ulikooli 18, 50090 Tartu (office); Vabaduse pst. 168-5, 10917 Tartu, Estonia (home). *Telephone:* (7) 375314 (office); (6) 778685 (home). *Fax:* (7) 375345 (office). *E-mail:* eero.loone@ut.ee (office).

LOPARDO, Frank; American singer (tenor); b. 23 Dec. 1957, New York; m. Carolyn J. Montalbano 1982; two s.; ed Queen's Coll. New York and Juilliard School of Music; studied with Dr Robert White Jr; professional debut as Tamino in The Magic Flute, St Louis 1984; debut at La Scala, Milan 1987, Glyndebourne Festival 1987, Metropolitan Opera as Almaviva in Il Barbiere di Siviglia 1989–90; now appears regularly at leading opera houses and music festivals around the world; roles include Alfredo in La Traviata, Lensky in Eugene Onegin, Edgardo in Lucia di Lammermoor, The Duke in Rigoletto, Ferrando in Così fan tutte, Don Giovanni, Lenski in Eugene Onegin, Rodolfo in La Bohème; also appears as soloist with leading orchestras and in recordings of such works as Mozart's Requiem, Carl Orff's Carmina Burana, Mozart's Don Giovanni and Così fan tutte, Verdi's Falstaff and La Traviata, as well as Rossini's Il Barbiere di Siviglia, Semiramide and L'Italiana in Algeri; Hon. DMus (Aaron Copland School of Music). *Leisure interest:* golf. *Address:* Columbia Artists Management Inc. 1790 Broadway, New York, NY 10019-1412, USA (office). *Telephone:* (212) 841 9500 (office). *Fax:* (212) 841 9744 (office). *E-mail:* info@cami.com (office); mail@franklopardo.com (office). *Website:* www.cami.com (office); www.franklopardo.com.

LOPATKIN, Nikolai Alekseyevich, DMed; Russian urologist; *Director, Research Institute of Urology;* b. 18 Feb. 1924; ed Second Moscow Medical Inst.; intern, Docent, Second Moscow Medical Inst. 1950–62; Prof., Head of Chair of Urology and Operative Nephrology 1963; Main Urologist of USSR Ministry of Public Health 1978–83; Dir and Prof., Research Inst. of Urology 1983–; Chair. All-Union Soc. of Urologists 1972–91; mem. Russian Acad. of Medical Sciences 1974; Chair. Scientific Council on Urology and Operative Nephrology, Russian Acad. of Sciences 1991; Ed.-in-Chief Urology and Nephrology; Hero of Socialist Labour and other decorations; USSR State Prize (three times). *Publications:* more than 250 works on urology, diagnostics and treatment of kidney insufficiency and kidney transplantation. *Address:* Research Institute of Urology, 3 Parkovaya ul. 51, 105483 Moscow, Russia (office). *Telephone:* (495) 164-66-20 (office).

LOPATKINA, Ulyana Vyacheslavovna; Russian ballerina; b. 23 Oct. 1973, Kerch, Ukraine; ed Vaganova Acad. of Russian Ballet (studied with Natalya Dudinskaya); soloist, Kirov Ballet/Mariinsky Theatre 1991–95, Prin. Dancer 1995–; winner Int. Vaganova-prix Competition, St Petersburg 1991, Golden Sofit 1995, Golden Mask 1997, Baltika Prize 1997, 2001, State Prize of Russian Fed. 1999, Honoured Artist of Russia 2000, Peoplés Artist of Russia 2006. *Repertoire includes:* leading roles in Giselle, Sleeping Beauty, Anna Karenina, Fountain of Bakhchisarai, Raimonda, Sheherazade, Swan Lake, Bayadera, Le Corsaire; performs in Goya-Divertissement; tours with Mariinsky Theatre in Europe, N and S America. *Address:* Mariinsky Theatre, Teatralnaya pl. 1, St Petersburg, Russia (office). *Telephone:* (812) 315-57-24 (office). *Website:* www.mariinsky.ru/en/company/ballet (office).

LOPES, António Simões, PhD; Portuguese academic and economist; *President, Ordem dos Economistas;* b. 3 Feb. 1934, Colmeal, Góis; s. of António Lopes de Oliveira and Emília Simões; m. Maria Helena Simões 1960; ed Instituto Superior de Ciências Económicas e Financeiras, Universidade Técnica de Lisboa, Brasenose Coll., Oxford Univ., UK; Asst Prof. 1962–68; researcher, Gulbenkian Inst. for Science 1964–72; Consultant, Gulbenkian Foundation 1972–74; Prof., Tech. Univ. of Lisbon 1973, Vice-Rector 1982–85, Acting Rector 1985–87, Rector 1987; mem. Bd, Univ. of Evora 1974–77; Prof., Portuguese Catholic Univ. 1979–81; mem. Scientific Bd, Faculty of Econs, Univ. of Coimbra 1979–; Chair. Portuguese Council of Rectors 1985–87, Portuguese Asscn for Regional Devt 1985–90, Asscn of Univs of Portuguese-Speaking Countries 1986–89; Pres. Ordem dos Economistas 2005–; Hon. Prof. Univ. of Maranhão, Brazil; Chevalier, Ordre Nat. du Mérite, France, Grã-Cruz, Ordem da Instrucção Pública, Portugal; Hon. DCL (Kent) 1992. *Publications:* Estrutura da População Activa Portuguesa 1967, As Funções Económicas dos Pequenos Centros 1971, Desenvolvimento Regional (3rd edn) 1989 and other books; various articles. *Address:* Ordem dos Economistas, Rua da Estrela 8, 1200–669, Lisbon (office); R. Abade Baçal 21, Mercês, 2725 Mem Martins; Alameda Sto António Capuchos 1, 1100 Lisbon, Portugal. *Telephone:* (21) 3929470 (office). *Fax:* (21) 3961428 (office). *E-mail:* ordemeconomistas@mail.telepac.pt (office). *Website:* www.ordemeconomistas.pt (office).

LOPES, Henri Marie Joseph; Republic of the Congo author, politician and diplomatist; *Ambassador to France, Portugal, Spain, UK and Holy See (Vatican);* b. 12 Sept. 1937, Léopoldville, Belgian Congo (now Kinshasa, Democratic Repub. of the Congo); s. of Jean-Marie Lopes and Micheline Vulturi; m. Nirva Pasbeau 1961; one s. three d.; ed France; Minister of Nat. Educ. 1968–71, of Foreign Affairs 1971–73; mem. Political Bureau, Congolese Labour Party 1973; Prime Minister and Minister of Planning 1973–75, of Finance 1977–80; UNESCO Asst Dir-Gen. for Programme Support 1982–86, UNESCO Asst Dir-Gen. for Culture and Communication 1986–90, for Culture 1990–94, for Foreign Affairs 1994–95, Deputy Dir-Gen. 1996–98; Amb. to France (also accred to Portugal, Spain, UK and Holy See (Vatican)) 1998–; mem. Haut Conseil de la Francophonie; Chevalier, Légion d'honneur, Commdr du Mérite Congolais, etc.; Prix littéraire de l'Afrique noire 1972, Prix SIMBA de littérature 1978, Prix de littérature du Président (Congo), Prix de l'Acad. de Bretagne et des Pays de la Loire 1990, Grand Prix de la Francophonie de l'Acad. française 1993. *Publications:* Tribaliques (short stories), La Nouvelle Romance (novel), Learning to be (with others), Sans tam-tam (novel) 1977, Le Pleurer Rire (novel) 1982, Le Chercheur d'Afriques (novel) 1990, Sur l'autre Rive (novel) 1992, Le Lys et le flamboyant (novel) 1997. *Address:* Embassy of the Republic of the Congo, 37 bis rue Paul Valéry, 75116 Paris, France (office). *Telephone:* 1-45-00-60-57 (home). *Fax:* 1-40-67-17-33 (office). *E-mail:* ambacongo_france@yahoo.fr (office). *Website:* www.ambacongo.org (office).

LOPEZ, Jennifer, (J.Lo); American actress and singer; b. 24 July 1970, Bronx, NY; m. 1st Ojani Noa 1997 (divorced); m. 2nd Chris Judd 2001 (divorced 2002); m. 3rd Marc Anthony 2004; one s. one d.; collaborations with Ja Rule, Big Pun, Fat Joe; established clothing and lingerie lines and a perfume range; Golden Globe 1998, MTV Movie Award 1999, Billboard Latin Award for Hot Latin Track of the Year 2000, MTV Video Music Award for Best Dance Video 2000, VH1/Vogue Fashion Versace Award 2000, MTV Europe Music Award for Best Female Act 2001, MTV Award for Best Female 2002, American Music Award for Favorite Latin Artist 2007. *Films:* My Little Girl 1986, My Family, Mi Familia 1995, Money Train 1995, Jack 1996, Blood and Wine 1996, Selena 1997, Anaconda 1997, U Turn 1997, Out of Sight 1998, Antz (voice) 1998, The Cell 2000, The Wedding Planner 2001, Angel Eyes 2001, Enough 2002, Maid in Manhattan 2002, Gigli 2003, Jersey Girl 2004, Shall We Dance? 2004, Monster-in-Law 2005, An Unfinished Life 2006, El Cantante 2006, Bordertown (Artists for Amnesty Prize 2007) 2007. *Television includes:* Nurses on the Line: The Crash of Flight 7 1993, In Living Color 1990, Second Chances (series) 1993, South Central (series) 1994, Hotel Malibu (series) 1994. *Recordings include:* albums: On The 6 1999, J.Lo 2001, J To Tha L-O! (remixes) 2002, This Is Me... Then 2002, Rebirth 2005, Como Ama una Mujer 2007, Brave 2007. *Address:* c/o William Morris Agency, One William Morris Place, Beverly Hills, CA 90212, USA (office). *Website:* www.jenniferlopez.com (office).

LÓPEZ, Patxi; Spanish politician; *Lehendakari (President) of Basque Government;* b. 4 Oct. 1959, Portugalete; joined Young Basque Socialists 1975, Sec.-Gen. 1985–88; mem. Basque Socialist Party-Basque Left (PSE-EE/PSOE) 1977–, mem. Exec. Cttee 1988–, Sec. PSE-EE/PSOE 1991–95, Sec.-Gen. 1997–; mem. Basque Parl. 1991–; Lehendakari (Pres.) of Basque Govt 2009–. *Address:* Palacio de Ajuria-Enea, Paseo Fray Francisco 5, 01007 Vitoria-Gasteiz, Spain (office). *E-mail:* patxilopez@socialistasvascos.com. *Website:* www.patxilopez.com.

LÓPEZ ARELLANO, Gen. Oswaldo; Honduran former head of state and air force officer; b. 30 June 1921, Danlí; s. of Enrique Lopez and Carlota Arellano; ed American School, Tegucigalpa, School of Mil. Aviation and Flight Training, USA; joined armed forces 1939, Lt 1947, Col 1958, later Gen.; Chief of Armed Forces 1956–75; mem. Mil. Junta, Chief of Mil. Govt of Honduras, Minister of Nat. Defence, Minister of Public Security 1963–66; Pres. of Honduras 1963–71 (took office when he seized power in a mil. coup 10 days before presidential elections were due, later allowed further elections to take place April 1971), 1972–75 (again seized power until he handed over to Juan Alberto Melgar Castro); now Pres. Servicio Aéreo de Honduras SA; several decorations. *Address:* Servicio Aéreo de Honduras SA, Apdo 129, Tegucigalpa, DC, Honduras (office).

LÓPEZ-COBOS, Jesús, DPhil; Spanish conductor; *Music Director, Teatro Real, Madrid;* b. 25 Feb. 1940, Toro; s. of Lorenzo López and Gregoria Cobos; ed Madrid Univ. (philosophy), Madrid Conservatory (composition) and Vienna Acad. (conducting); worked with major orchestras including London Symphony, Royal Philharmonic, Philharmonia, Concertgebouw, Vienna Philharmonic, Vienna Symphony, Berlin Philharmonic, Hamburg NDR, Munich Philharmonic, Cleveland, Chicago Symphony, New York Philharmonic, Philadelphia, Pittsburgh Symphony; conducted new opera productions at La Scala, Milan, Covent Garden, London and Metropolitan Opera, New York; Gen. Musikdirektor, Deutsche Oper, Berlin 1981–90; Prin. Guest Conductor London Philharmonic Orchestra 1981–86; Prin. Conductor and Artistic Dir, Spanish Nat. Orchestra 1984–89; Music Dir, Cincinnati Symphony Orchestra 1986–2001 (now Music Dir Emer.), Music Dir Lausanne Chamber Orchestra 1990–2000, Orchestre Français des Jeunes 1998–2001, Teatro Real, Madrid 2002–; Cross of Merit (1st Class) (FRG) 1989; Officier des Arts et des Lettres 2001; Dr hc (Arts Univ. Cincinatti); First Prize, Besançon Int. Conductors' Competition 1969, Prince of Asturias Award (Spanish Govt) 1981, Founders Award, American Soc. of Composers, Authors and Publrs 1988, Fine Arts Medal (Spain) 2001. *Recordings include:* Bruckner symphonies, Haydn symphonies; Donizetti's Lucia di Lammermoor, Rossini's Otello and recital discs with José Carreras; works by Mahler, Respighi, Franck, de Falla, Villa-Lobos and Richard Strauss; Rossini's Il Barbiere di Siviglia and L'Italiana in Algeri; Il Comte Ory, Manon, Les Contes d'Hoffmann, Il Viaggio a Reims. *Address:* c/o Terry Harrison Artists Management, The Orchard, Market Street, Charlbury, Oxon. OX7 3PJ, England (office); 8 Chemin de Bellerive, 1007 Lausanne, Switzerland. *Telephone:* (1608) 810330 (office). *Fax:* (1608) 811331 (office); (21) 6010852 (office). *E-mail:* artists@terryharrison.force9.co.uk (office). *Website:* www.terryharrison.force9.co.uk (office); www.teatro-real.com (office).

LOPEZ COLOMÉ, Ana Maria, PhD; Mexican neuroscientist, biochemist and academic; *Professor of Neuroscience and Biochemistry, Institute of Cellular Physiology, National Autonomous University (UNAM);* widow; one s. one d.; ed UNAM; fmr Lecturer, Faculty of Sciences, UNAM, Mexico City, currently Prof. of Neuroscience and Biochemistry, Inst. of Cellular Physiology; Univ. Councilor, UNAM; mem. Soc. for Neuroscience, Int. Soc. for Neurochemistry, American Soc. for Neurochemistry, ISDN, Mexican Soc. for Biochemistry, Mexican Soc. for Physiological Sciences, Academia de la Investigación Científica; Regional Ed. Molecules; mem. Editorial Bd Journal of Neuroscience Research; L'Oreal-UNESCO For Women in Science Award 2002. *Publications:* numerous articles in scientific journals. *Address:* Instituto de Fisiología Celular, UNAM, Departamento de Neurociencias, Apartado postal 70-253, 04510 Mexico, DF, Mexico (office). *Telephone:* (525) 622-5617 (office). *Fax:* (525) 622-5607 (office). *E-mail:* acolome@ifc.unam.mx (office). *Website:* www.ifisiol.unam.mx (office).

LÓPEZ GARCÍA, Antonio; Spanish painter, draughtsman and sculptor; b. 6 Jan. 1936, Tomelloso, La Mancha; m. María Moreno 1961; two d.; ed Escuela de Bellas Artes de San Fernando, Madrid; his art evolved from primitivist and Surrealist influences to a strict realism; gave classes at Escuela de Bellas Artes de San Fernando 1964–69; works in public collections including Museum of Fine Arts, Boston, Reina Sofía Nat. Museum, Madrid; Prize of Diputación de Jaén 1957, Prize of Fundación Rodríguez Acosta 1958, Molino de Oro Prize of Exposición Regional de Valdepeñas 1959, Darmstadt Prize 1974, Medalla de Oro, Castilla-La Mancha 1986, Medalla de Oro, Comunidad de Madrid 1990. *Film:* El Sol del Membrillo (The Quince Tree Sun) 1992. *Address:* c/o Galería Marlborough SA, Orfila 5, 28010 Madrid (office); Poniente 3, 28036 Madrid, Spain (home). *Telephone:* (91) 3191414 (office). *Fax:* (91) 3084345 (office). *E-mail:* info@galeriamarlborough.com (office). *Website:* www.galeriamarlborough.com (office).

LÓPEZ-IBOR, Juan José, MD, PhD; Spanish physician, psychiatrist and academic; *Director, Institute of Psychiatry and Mental Health, San Carlos Clinical Hospital and Professor of Psychiatry, Madrid Complutense University;* b. 17 Dec. 1941, Madrid; s. of Juan J. López-Ibor Sr and Socorro Alino; four c.; ed Madrid and Frankfurt Univs and St Bartholomew's Hosp., London; Asst Prof. of Psychiatry, Madrid Univ. 1962–72; Head Prof. of Psychiatry, Oviedo Univ. 1972–73, Salamanca Univ. 1973–77, Alcalá de Henares Univ. 1982–; Head, Psychiatric Unit, Ramón y Cajal Hosp. 1977–; currently Dir Inst. of Psychiatry and Mental Health, San Carlos Clinical Hosp. and Prof. of Psychiatry, Madrid Complutense Univ.; Pres. Spanish Psychiatry Soc. 1978–80, Int. Coll. of Psychosomatic Medicine 1985, World Psychiatric Asscn 1999–2002; Temporary Adviser WHO 1984; Fellow, Royal Nat. Acad. of Medicine, Hon. mem. World Psychiatric Asscn. *Publications:* Los Equivalentes Depresivos 1972, 1978, El Cuerpo y la Corporalidad 1974, Las Depresiones 1976, Tratado de Psiquiatría 1982, 1984. *Leisure interests:* skiing, water skiing. *Address:* Avenida Nueva Zelanda 44, 28035 Madrid, Spain. *Telephone:* (91) 3739199. *Fax:* (91) 3162749. *E-mail:* jli@lopez-ibor.com.

LÓPEZ OBRADOR, Andrés Manuel; Mexican politician; b. 1953, Tepetitán, Tabasco; m. Rocio Beltran (died 2003); three s.; ed Universidad Nacional Autónoma de México; Dir Instituto Indigenista de Tabasco 1984; Dir of Social Promotion, Instituto Nacional del Consumidor 1985; joined Corriente Democrática 1986; joined Frente Democrático Nacional and stood for Gov. of Tabasco; joined Partido de la Revolución Democrática 1989 and led party in Tabasco, stood for Gov. and lost 1994; Pres. Partido de la Revolucíon Democrática 1996–99; Mayor of Mexico City 2000–July 2005 (resgnd to work on his unsuccessful 2006 campaign for Pres.). *Address:* Partido de la Revolucíon Democrática (PRD), Col. Roma, Monterrey 50, 06700 Mexico (office). *Telephone:* (55) 5525-6059 (office). *Fax:* (55) 5208-7833 (office). *Website:* www.prd.org.mx (office).

LÓPEZ RODRIGUEZ, HE Cardinal Nicolás de Jesús, DScS; Dominican Republic ecclesiastic; *Archbishop of Santo Domingo;* b. 31 Oct. 1936, Barrancas; ed Pontifical Seminary 'Santo Tomas de Aquino', Santo Domingo, Int. Center for the Sociological Formation of the Clergy, Rome, Italy, Pontifical St Thomas Univ. and Pontifical Gregorian Univ., Rome; ordained priest 1961; pastoral work in diocese of La Vega 1961–64, 1966–68; Diocesan Counsellor, La Vega, 1969–78; Ecclesiastical Assessor Christian Family Movt and Cursillo Movt; Diocesan Vicar, later Pro-Vicar General, Gen. later Vicar Gen.; Bishop of San Francisco de Macoris 1978; Rector Nordestana di San Francisco de Macorís Univ. 1979–84; Metropolitan and Primate of Santo Domingo 1981; Grand Chancellor Catholic Univ. of Santo Domingo 1982; Mil. Ordinary for the Dominican Repub. 1982; Del. to Dominican Bishops' Conf. 1979–81, Pres. Bishops' Justice and Peace Comm., mem. (currently Pres.) Permanent Comm., Nat. Chaplain to the Christian Renewal of the Holy Spirit, Pres. Dominican Bishops' Conf. 1984–2002; attended Sixth Ordinary Ass. World Synod of Bishops, Vatican City 1983, Second Extraordinary Ass. World Synod of Bishops, Vatican City 1985; Pres. Latin American Episcopal Council 1991; cr. Cardinal Priest of S Pio X alla Balduina 1991; Grand Cross of Isabella the Catholic (Spain) 1989; hon. degrees from Univ. of Santo Domingo and Creighton Univ., Neb., USA. *Address:* Calle Pellerano Alfau 1, Ciudad Colonial, Santo Domingo, Dominican Republic (office). *Telephone:* 221-8430 (office). *Fax:* 685-0227 (office).

LÓPEZ SUÁREZ, Guillermo; Salvadorean politician and banker; *Secretary for Commercial Affairs and International Finance;* ed Inst. of Tech. and Higher Studies, Monterrey, Mexico, N Dakota State School of Science, USA; Asst to Dir-Gen., Empresa Cocotera and Empresa Cafetalera Sol Mollet 1978–81; Head of Finance, Granjero and Sello de Oro 1983–84; Dir-Gen. Grupo Lotisa, Maquilishuat, and Cumbres de Cuscatlán 1984–97; Financial Dir Grupo Avicola Salvadoreña and Grupo La Sultana 1987–95, Dir-Gen. 1995–; Dir-Gen. Grupo Pollo Campero 1994–2004; Minister of the Treasury 2004–06; Sec. for Commercial Affairs and Int. Finance 2006–; Adviser to Nat. Asscn of Pvt. Commerce, Asscn of Poultry Farmers of El Salvador, Fed. of Poultry Farmers of Cen. America and the Caribbean; mem. Bd of Govs World Bank, IBRD, Int. Finance Corpn, IDA. *Address:* Office of the Secretary for Commercial Affairs and International Finance, Ministry for the Presidency, Avenida Cuba, Calle Darío González 806, Barrio San Jacinto, San Salvador, El Salvador (office). *Telephone:* 2248-9000 (office). *Fax:* 2248-9370 (office). *E-mail:* casapres@casapres.gob.sv (office). *Website:* www.casapres.gob.sv (office).

LORAN, Oleg Borisovich, DrMed; Russian surgeon and urologist; b. 24 June 1943, Moscow; s. of Boris Yulievich Loran and Irina Donatovna Loran; m. Irina Petrovna Grebennikova; one s. two d.; ed Moscow Sechenov Inst. of Medicine; surgeon Salda City Hosp. Sverdlovsk Region 1966–69; intern, urologist Moscow Botkin Hosp. of Urgent Medicine 1969–72; Asst, Head Div. of Urology, Prof. Moscow Medical Inst. of Stomatology (now Moscow State Medical and Stomatological Univ.) 1972–; Chief Urologist Ministry of Public Health of Russian Fed.; Chief Scientific Sec. Russian Soc. of Urologists 1978; mem. European Asscn of Urologists 1992; mem. Exec. Bd E European Soc. of Urologists; mem. Editorial Bd journals Urology and Nephrology, Annals of Surgery; mem. Higher Attestation Comm. of Russian Fed.; Diplomas of American Asscn of Urologists and American Urological Foundation. *Publications:* more than 230 scientific works including nine books on problems of urology, ten patents. *Leisure interests:* music, theatre. *Address:* Moscow State Medical Stomatological Institute, Delegatskaya str. 20/1, 103473 Moscow, Russia (office). *Telephone:* (495) 281-65-13 (office).

LORD, Hon. Bernard, BA; Canadian politician; b. 27 Sept. 1965; m. Diane Lord; two c.; ed Université de Moncton; Leader, Progressive Conservative Party of NB 1997; MLA for Moncton East (becoming Leader of the Official Opposition) 1998; Premier of NB 1999–2006, also Pres. of Exec. Council, Minister of Intergovernmental Affairs, Minister responsible for NB Advisory Council on Youth, Minister responsible for Premier's Council on Status of Disabled Persons; Grand Officier de l'Ordre de la Pléiade, Int. Asscn of Francophone Parliamentarians; Dr hc (Univ. of NB), (Université de Moncton); Alumni of the Year from the Université de Moncton. *Address:* c/o Office of the Premier, Centennial Building, POB 6000, Fredericton, NB E3B 5H1, Canada.

LORD, Winston, BA, MA; American civil servant and diplomatist; b. 14 Aug. 1937, New York; s. of Oswald Bates Lord and Mary Lord (née Pillsbury); m. Bette Bao 1963; one s. one d.; ed Yale Univ., Fletcher School of Law and Diplomacy; mem. Staff Congressional Relations, Politico-mil. and Econ. Affairs, US Dept of State, Washington 1961–65, Geneva 1965–67; mem. staff Int. Affairs, US Dept of Defense, Washington 1967–69; mem. staff Nat. Security Council, Washington 1969–73, Special Asst to Asst to Pres. on Security Affairs 1970–73; Dir Policy Planning Staff, US Dept of State, Washington 1973–77; Pres. Council on Foreign Relations 1977–85; Amb. to People's Repub. of China 1985–89; freelance lecturer, writer New York 1989–93; Asst Sec. of State for East Asian and Pacific Affairs 1993; Chair. Carnegie Endowment Nat. Comm. on America and the New World 1991–92, Nat. Endowment for Democracy 1992–93; Vice-Chair. Int. Rescue Cttee 1991–93, Co-Chair. 1997–2005, Chair. Emer. 2005–; fmr mem. Bd of Dirs Fletcher School of Law and Diplomacy, Int. Rescue Cttee, Nat. Cttee on US–China Relations, Nat. Endowment for Democracy, US–Japan Foundation; several hon. degrees. *Leisure interests:* sports, literature, arts. *Address:* c/o Board of Directors, International Rescue Committee, 122 East 42nd Street, New York, NY 10168, USA.

LORDKIPANIDZE, Vazha Giorgevich, DEcon; Georgian politician, sociologist and demographer; *Head of Demography Department, Tbilisi State University;* b. 29 Nov. 1949, Tbilisi; m. Irina Khomeriki; two d.; ed Tbilisi State Univ., Moscow Acad. of Social Sciences; Teacher Tbilisi State Univ. 1975–, Head Demography Dept 2000–; Sec., Second, First Secr. Cen. Comsomol Cttee of Georgia 1980–86; First Sec. Tbilisi Dist CP Cttee 1986–88; Head Dept of Culture and Ideology Cen. Cttee, CP of Georgia 1988–90; Sr Researcher Inst. of Demography and Sociology, Georgian Acad. of Sciences 1991–92; Chief State Counsellor State Council of Georgia 1992; Head of Personnel Eduard Shevardnadze Admin. 1992–95; Amb. to Russia 1995–98; Minister of State 1998–2000; mem. Parl. 2000–; Pres. Demographers' Asscn of Georgia 2000–; Vice-Pres. Int. Research Centre for East–West Relationships 2000–; mem. Georgian Acad. of Econs 1996–, UN Int. Acad. of Informatics; Pres. Special Olympic Cttee 2001; Head Christian Democrat Party of Georgia 2002–. *Publications:* various scientific articles, monographs and books. *Leisure Interest:* football. *Address:* Tbilisi State University, 1 Chavchavadze Avenue, 380079 Tbilisi (office); 5 Larsi Street, Flat 9, Tbilisi, Georgia (home). *Telephone:* (32) 25-12-38 (office); (32) 23-20-70 (home). *Fax:* (32) 25-12-39 (office); (32) 233259 (office); (32) 99-05-13 (home). *E-mail:* ikhomeriki@hotmail .com.

LOREN, Sophia; Italian actress; b. (Sofia Villani Scicolone), 20 Sept. 1934, Rome; d. of Riccardo Scicolone and Romilda Villani; m. 1st the late Carlo Ponti 1957 (marriage annulled 1962; m. 2nd 1966, died 2007); two s.; ed Scuole Magistrali Superiori; first screen appearance as an extra in Quo Vadis; has appeared in many Italian and other films including E Arrivato l'Accordatore 1951, Africa sotto i Mari (first leading role), La Tratta delle Bianche, La Favorita 1952, Aida 1953, Il Paese dei Campanelli, Miseria e Nobiltà, Il Segno di Venere 1953, Tempi Nostri 1953, Carosello Napoletano 1953, L'Oro di Napoli 1954, Attila 1954, Peccato che sia una canaglia, La Bella Mugnaia, La Donna del Fiume 1955, Boccaccio 1970, Matrimonio All'Italiana; and in the following American films: The Pride and the Passion 1955, Boy on a Dolphin, Legend of the Lost 1956, Desire Under the Elms 1957, That Kind of Woman 1958, Houseboat 1958, The Key 1958, The Black Orchid (Venice Festival Award 1958) 1958, It Started in Naples, Heller in Pink Tights 1960, The Millionairess 1961, Two Women (Cannes Film Festival Award for Best Actress 1961) 1961, El Cid 1961, Madame Sans Gêne 1962, Yesterday, Today and Tomorrow 1963, The Fall of the Roman Empire 1964, Lady L 1965, Operation Crossbow 1965, Judith 1965, A Countess from Hong Kong 1965, Arabesque 1966, More than a Miracle 1967, The Priest's Wife 1970, Sunflower 1970, Hot Autumn 1971, Man of La Mancha 1972, Brief Encounter (TV) 1974, The Verdict 1974, The Voyage 1974, The Cassandra Crossing 1977, A Special Day 1977, Firepower 1978, Brass Target 1979, Blood Feud 1981, Mother Courage 1986, Two Women 1989, Prêt à Porter 1994, Grumpier Old Men 1995, Between Strangers 2002, Peperoni ripieni e pesci in faccia 2004; Chair. Nat. Alliance for Prevention and Treatment of Child Abuse and Maltreatment; Goodwill Amb. for Refugees 1992; Chevalier Légion d'honneur; numerous awards including Hon. Acad. Award for Lifetime Achievement 1990. *Publications:* Eat with Me 1972, Sophia Loren on Women and Beauty 1984. *Address:* Case Postale 430, 1211 Geneva 12, Switzerland; William Morris Agency, 1 William Morris Place, Beverly Hills, CA 90212, USA.

LORENTZ, Francis; French business executive; *Chairman, Institut de l'Audiovisuel et des Télécommunications en Europe (IDATE);* b. 22 May 1942, Mulhouse; s. of Paul Lorentz and Lucienne Lorentz (née Biechy); m. Laure Doumenc; three c.; ed Lycée Kléber, Strasbourg, Ecole des Hautes Etudes Commerciales, Ecole Nat. d'Admin; with Ministry of Economy 1970–80; Exec. Vice-Pres. Société Lyonnaise des Eaux 1980–82; joined Honeywell-Bull as CEO 1982, Chair. and CEO Groupe Bull 1987–92; Chair. Dir-Gen. Régie autonome des transports parisiens (RATP) 1992–94; Prof., Univ. of Paris-Dauphine 1994–2000; Chair. Etablissement public de financement et de restructuration (EPFR) 1996–2000; Head of French Nat. e-Business Task Force 1997–2000; Dir Gen. Laser (groupe Galeries Lafayette) 2000–04; CEO e-LaSer and LaSer Informatique 2000–04; Chair. Institut de l'audiovisuel et des télécommunications en Europe (IDATE) 2000–; Exec. Chair. Lorentz, Deschamps et Associés (LD&A) 2004–; Chevalier du mérite nat., Chevalier, légion d'honneur. *Publications:* several publs on devt admin, state-owned cos, industrial policy and future of e-commerce. *Leisure interests:* skiing, mountaineering, contemporary art, diving, tennis. *Address:* Lorentz, Deschamps et Associés, 8 rue Halévy, 75009 Paris, France (office). *Telephone:* 1-58-18-39-00 (office). *Fax:* 1-53-43-09-76 (office). *E-mail:* florentz@ldaglobal.com (office). *Website:* www.idate.org (office); www.ldaglobal.com (office).

LORENZ, Hans-Walter, Dr rer. pol; German economist; b. 3 Aug. 1951, Bielefeld; s. of Walter Lorenz and Lieselotte Lorenz; m. Karin Hottmann 1987; ed Univ. of Göttingen; Research Asst, Univ. of Göttingen 1977–82, Asst Prof. 1984–91, Privatdozent 1991–94; Prof. of Econs, Univ. of Jena 1994–; Visiting Scholar, Univ. of Calif., Berkeley 1982–83; Visiting Prof., Univ. of Tech., Sydney, Australia 1999. *Publications:* Business Cycle Theory (with G. Gabisch) 1987, Nonlinear Dynamical Economics and Chaotic Motion 1989, Determinismus, nicht-lineare Dynamik und wirtschaftliche Evolution 1991. *Address:* Wirtschaftswissenschaftliche Fakultät, Friedrich-Schiller-Univerität, 07740 Jena; Hermann-Föge-Weg 1A, 37073 Göttingen, Germany. *Telephone:* (3641) 943210 (office); (551) 44317 (home). *Fax:* (3641) 943212; (551) 44974 (home). *E-mail:* H.W.Lorenz@wiwi.uni-jena.de (office).

LORIMER, George Huntly, PhD, FRS; British scientist; b. 14 Oct. 1942; s. of the late Gordon Lorimer and of Ellen Lorimer; m. Freia Schulz-Baldes 1970; one s. one d.; ed George Watson's Coll., Edinburgh, Univ. of St Andrews and Univ. of Illinois and Michigan State Univ., USA; scientist, Max-Planck Soc., Berlin, 1972–74; Research Fellow, Inst. for Advanced Studies, Canberra 1974–77; Prin. Investigator, then Research Leader Cen. Research Dept, E.I. Du Pont de Nemours & Co. 1978–91, Dupont Fellow 1991–97; scientist, Soc. for Environmental Research, Munich 1977; mem. NAS 1997, Editorial Bd Journal of Biological Chem. 1998; Research Award, Alexander von Humboldt Foundation 1997. *Leisure interests:* philately, music. *Address:* 7705 Lake Glen Drive, Glen Dale, MD 20769, USA.

LORING, Jeanne, BS, PhD; American biologist and academic; *Director, Center for Regenerative Medicine, Scripps Research Institute;* ed Univ. of Washington, Univ. of Oregon; Asst Prof. of Embryology, Univ. of Calif., Davis 1982–87; Sr Staff Scientist, Parkinson's Disease Research Program, Hana-Biologics Inc. 1987–89; Sr Scientist, GenPharm International Inc. 1989–95; Sr Research Fellow, Molecular Dynamics Inc. 1995–97; Sr Dir (Transgenics and Neurobiology), Incyte Genomics Inc. 1997–2001; Founder and Chief Scientific Officer, Arcos BioScience Inc. 1997–2004; Adjunct Prof. of Stem Cells and Regenerative Medicine and Co-Dir NIH Exploratory Center for Human Embryonic Stem Cell Research, Burnham Inst. for Medical Research 2004–, also Dir Human Embryonic Stem Cell Training Course 2004–; Prof. of Developmental Neurobiology, Scripps Research Inst. 2007–, Dir Center for Regenerative Medicine 2008–; mem. numerous scientific advisory bds. *Publications:* Human Stem Cell Manual: A Laboratory Guide 2007; numerous scientific papers. *Address:* Scripps Research Institute, 10550 North Torrey Pines Road, La Jolla, CA 92037, USA (office). *Telephone:* (858) 784-1000 (office). *E-mail:* jloring@scripps.edu (office). *Website:* www.scripps.edu (office).

LORING, John Robbins, BA; American artist, designer and author; *Design Director, Tiffany & Co.;* b. 23 Nov. 1939, Chicago; s. of Edward D'Arcy and China Robbins Loring (née Logeman); ed Yale Univ., Ecole des Beaux Arts, Paris; Distinguished Visiting Prof., Univ. of Calif., Davis 1977; Bureau Chief

Architectural Digest magazine, New York 1977–78; Design Dir Tiffany and Co., New York 1979–, Exec. Vice-Pres., 1981–84, Sr Vice-Pres. Design and Merchandising 1984–; mem. acquisitions comm. Dept of prints and illustrated books, Museum of Modern Art, New York 1990–; Contributing Ed. Arts magazine 1973–; work in perm. collections Museum of Modern Art, New York, Whitney Museum of American Art, Chicago Art Inst., Boston Museum of Fine Arts, RI School of Design, Baltimore Museum of Art, Yale Univ. Art Gallery, NY Historical Soc.; works commissioned by US Customhouse, New York, Prudential Insurance Co., Woodbridge, NJ, City of Scranton, Pa; Hon. DrArts (Pratt Inst.) 1996; Edith Wharton Award, Design and Art Soc. 1988, Pratt Inst. Legends Award 2002, Dallas Fashion Award 2004, Lifetime Achievement Award, Museum of Art and Design 2005. *Publications:* The New Tiffany Table Settings 1981, Tiffany Taste 1986, Tiffany's 150 Years 1987, The Tiffany Wedding 1988, Tiffany Parties 1989, The Tiffany Gourmet 1992, A Tiffany Christmas 1996, Tiffany's 20th Century 1997, Tiffany Jewels 1999, Paulding Farnham, Tiffany's Last Genius 2000, Magnificent Tiffany Silver 2001, Louis Comfort Tiffany at Tiffany & Co. 2002, Tiffany in Fashion 2003, Greetings from Andy Warhol 2004, Tiffany's Palm Beach 2005, Tiffany Diamonds 2005, Tiffany Colored Gems 2007, Tivoli Gardens 2007. *Leisure interests:* collecting 20th-century decorative arts, writing on design and lifestyle. *Address:* Tiffany & Co., 600 Madison Avenue, New York, NY 10022 (office); 621 Avon Road, West Palm Beach, FL 33401, USA (home). *Telephone:* (212) 230-5339 (office); (561) 659-3452 (home). *Fax:* (212) 230-5341 (office); (561) 651-7009 (home). *Website:* www.tiffany.com (office).

LORIOD, Yvonne; French pianist; b. 20 Jan. 1924, Houilles; d. of Gaston Loriod and Simone Loriod (née Bilhaut); m. Olivier Messiaen 1961 (died 1992); Prof. of Piano, Conservatoire National de Musique, Paris; specializes in interpretation of complete works including Bach's Well-Tempered Klavier, Beethoven sonatas, Mozart piano concertos, works of Chopin and Debussy and complete works of Olivier Messiaen; first performances in Paris of Bartok's 1st and 2nd concertos, Schoenberg concerto and works by Messiaen, Jolivet, Boulez and other contemporary composers; Commdr Légion d'honneur, Officier des Arts et Lettres, Grand Officier du Mérite; 7 Grand Prix du Disque, Grand Prix de la Sacem 1986. *Address:* c/o Bureau de concerts Lorentz, 3 rue La Boétie, 75008 Paris, France (office).

LORIUS, Claude, LèsSc, DèsSc; French glaciologist, academic and research institute director; *Director Emeritus of Research, Centre National de la Recherche Scientifique (CNRS);* b. 25 02, Besançon; ed Univ. of Besançon; joined CNRS, Grenoble 1953, Asst Dir Laboratoire de glaciologie et geophysique de l'environnement 1979–83, Dir 1983–88, currently Dir Emer. of Research, CNRS; responsibilities at Ministries of Research and the Environment, French Nat. Cttee on Antarctic Research 1987–94, French Inst. for Polar Research and Tech. (f. 1992); took part in 22 polar expeditions, mostly to Antarctica, led several French polar expeditions 1984–87; mem. World Climate Research Programme (OMM-ICSU) 1980–84, Exec. Cttee Past Global Changes (IGBP) 1989–98, European Cttee on Oceanography and Polar Sciences (European Science Foundation (ESF) and EC) 1989–97, Exec. Cttee Greenland Ice Core Project 1989–93; contributed to work of Scientific Cttee on Antarctic Research, Int. Council for Science (Pres. 1986–90), Int. Arctic Science Cttee 1991–98; led a working group on glaciology, ESF 1985–93; presided over European Program for Ice Coring in Antarctica project 1993–95; has helped organize many int. collaborations, notably the Vostok ice core; Corresp. mem. Acad. des Sciences (mem. 1994), Acad. des Technologies 2000; Foreign mem. Russian Acad. of Sciences 1994; mem. Academia Europaea 1989; Fellow, European Geophysical Soc. 1999; Officier, Légion d'honneur 1998; Humbold Prize 1989, Belgica Medal 1989, Italgas Prize 1994, Tyler Prize for Environmental Achievement 1996, Balzan Prize for climatology (jtly with Jean Jouzel) 2001, Medaille d'or du CNRS 2002, Vernadsky Medal, European Geosciences Union 2006, Blue Planet Prize, Asahi Glass Foundation (co-recipient) 2008. *Achievements include:* was instrumental in discovery and interpretation of palaeo-atmosphere information within ice cores. *Publications:* Glaces de l'Antarctique: une mémoire, des passions 1991, L'Antarctique (with R. Gendrin) 1997; more than 100 scientific papers in professional journals. *Address:* CNRS, Campus Gérard Mégie, rue Michel-Ange, 16th arrondissement, Paris, France (office). *E-mail:* webcnrs@cnrs-dir.fr (office). *Website:* www.cnrs.fr (office).

LÖSCHER, Peter, MA, MBA; Austrian business executive; *President and CEO, Siemens AG;* b. 17 Sept. 1957, Villach; ed Vienna Univ., Chinese Univ. of Hong Kong and Harvard Business School, USA; began career at Kienbaum and Pnr (man. consultants), Germany 1985; mem. Strategic Planning Man. Team, Hoechst AG 1988–89, Dir Business Devt 1989–91, Man. Dir Hoechst Roussel Veterinaria AIE, Spain 1991–94, Vice-Pres. 1994–95, Project Leader 1996–97, Pres. and CEO Hoechst Marion Roussel Ltd, UK 1999; Chair., Pres. and CEO Aventis Pharma Ltd, Japan 2000–02; Pres. Amersham Health (life sciences co.), UK 2002–04, COO 2004; CEO General Electric Healthcare Bio-Sciences and mem. Corp. Exec. Council 2004–05; Pres. Global Human Health Div. and mem. Exec. Cttee, Merck and Co. Inc. 2006–07; Pres. and CEO Siemens AG 2007–, also Head of Corp. Devt. *Address:* Siemens AG, Wittelsbacherplatz 2, 80333 Munich, Germany (office). *Telephone:* (89) 63600 (office). *Fax:* (89) 63652000 (office). *E-mail:* contact@siemens.com (office). *Website:* www.siemens.com (office).

LÖSCHNAK, Franz, DJur; Austrian politician; b. 4 March 1940, Vienna; m.; one s.; ed Univ. of Vienna; employed with Vienna City Council 1959–77, Dir of Personnel Affairs and Admin. Org. 1977; Under-Sec. Fed. Chancellery 1977; Minister, Fed. Chancellery 1985–87; Minister of Health and the Civil Service 1987–89; Minister of the Interior 1989–95.

LOSHAK, Victor Grigoryevich; Russian journalist; *Editor-in-Chief, Ogoniok;* b. 20 April 1952, Zaporozhye, Ukraine; s. of Grigory Abramovich Loshak and Anna Davydovna Loshak; m. Marina Devovna Loshak; one d.; ed Odessa State Univ.; corresp. for various Odessa newspapers 1973–83; special corresp. Izvestia 1983–86; political observer Moskovskye Novosti 1986–91, First Deputy Ed. 1991–92, Ed.-in-Chief 1992–2003; Ed.-in-Chief Ogoniok (periodical) 2003–; broadcaster for Kultura (TV channel); mem. Int. Inst. of Press (Vice-Pres. Russian br.); Prize of Journalists' Union of Moscow, Order of Honour. *Address:* Ogoniok, Krasnokazarmennaya str. pb. 14, 111250 Moscow, Russia (office). *Telephone:* (495) 540-47-10 (office). *Fax:* (495) 775-41-06 (office). *E-mail:* pochta@ovarpress.ru (office). *Website:* www.ogoniok.com (office).

LOSHCHININ, Valery Vassilyevich; Russian diplomatist; *Permanent Representative, United Nations, Geneva;* b. 11 Sept. 1940, Gomel Region, Byelorussia; m.; two s. two d.; ed Belarus State Univ., Diplomatic Acad. of USSR Ministry of Foreign Affairs; with Ministry of Foreign Affairs Belarus SSR, then USSR Ministry of Foreign Affairs 1965–77; with Perm. Mission to Russia 1977–89; Deputy Perm. Rep. to int. orgs, Geneva 1989–95, Perm. Rep. 2006–; Dir Second European Dept, Russian Ministry of Foreign Affairs 1995–96; Amb. to Belarus 1996–99; Perm. Rep. to int. orgs, Vienna 1999–2001; Deputy Minister of Foreign Affairs (responsible for relations with CIS countries) 2001–2002, First Deputy Minister of Foreign Affairs 2002–05. *Address:* Permanent Mission of the Russian Federation, 15 Avenue de la Paix, 1211 Geneva 20, Switzerland (office). *Telephone:* (22) 7331870 (office). *Fax:* (22) 7344044 (office). *E-mail:* mission.russian@vtxnet.ch (office). *Website:* www.geneva.mid.ru (office).

LOSYUKOV, Alexander Prokhorovich; Russian diplomatist; b. 15 Nov. 1943; m.; two d.; ed Moscow State Inst. of Int. Relations; Intern, USSR Embassy, Afghanistan 1968–70, Attaché, 1970–72; Attaché, Third Sec., then Second Sec. Secr. of the First Deputy Minister of Foreign Affairs 1972–78; Second Sec., then First Sec. USSR Embassy, USA 1978–81; First Sec., Gen. Secr., Ministry of Foreign Affairs 1981–82; Asst to Deputy Minister of Foreign Affairs 1982–85; Minister-Counsellor, USSR Embassy, The Philippines 1985–90; Head, Directorate of Pacific and SE Asia countries, Ministry of Foreign Affairs 1990, 1992, Head, Directorate of Gen. Problems of Asian-Pacific Ocean region 1990–92; Amb. to New Zealand (concurrently Kingdom of Tonga, Western Samoa) 1992–94, to Australia (concurrently Fiji, Vanuatu and Nauru) 1994–97; Dir Second Dept of Asia 1997–99, Ministry of Foreign Affairs, Sec.-Gen. 1999–2000, Deputy Minister of Foreign Affairs 2000–04; Amb. to Japan 2004–07. *Address:* c/o Ministry of Foreign Affairs, 119200 Moscow Smolenskaya-Sennaya pl. 32/34, Russia (office). *Website:* www.mid.ru (office).

LOTHE, Jens, DPhil; Norwegian physicist and academic; *Professor Emeritus of Physics, University of Oslo;* b. 25 Nov. 1931, Oslo; s. of Jakob Lothe and Borghild Lothe; m. Solveig E. Seeberg 1960; two s. one d.; ed Univ. of Oslo; lecturer, Univ. of Oslo 1959–63, Assoc. Prof. 1963–72, Prof. of Physics 1972–now Emer.; mem. Norwegian Acad. of Science and Letters. *Publications:* The Theory of Dislocations (with J. P. Hirth) 1967; numerous papers on elastic waves. *Address:* Department of Physics, University of Oslo, Blindern 0316 Oslo (office); Nedre Ringvolls 5, 1339 Voyenenga, Norway. *Telephone:* 22856491 (office); 67133076. *E-mail:* lothe@fys.uio.no (office). *Website:* www.fys.uio.no/english (office).

LOTON, Brian Thorley, AC, B.MET.E.; Australian business executive; b. 17 May 1929, Perth; s. of the late Sir Thorley Loton; m. Joan Kemelfield 1956; two s. two d.; ed Hale School, Perth, Trinity Coll., Melbourne Univ.; started as Cadet, Broken Hill Pty Co. Ltd 1954, Tech. Asst to Production Superintendent 1959, Asst Chief Engineer 1961, Gen. Man. Planning and Devt 1969, Man. Dir 1982–91, CEO 1985–91, Deputy Chair. 1991–92, Chair. 1992–97; Chair. Business Council of Australia 1989–90, Pres. 1990–92; Pres. Australian Mining Industry Council 1983–84; Chair. Int. Iron and Steel Inst. 1991–92; Jt Vice-Chair. Nat. Australia Bank 1992–99 (Dir 1988–99); Dir Amcor 1992–99; Chair. Atlas Copco Australia Pty Ltd 1996–2001; mem. Faculty of Eng, Melbourne Univ. 1980–83; Int. Counsellor, The Conf. Bd 1984–96; Dept of Immigration and Ethnic Affairs Advisory Cttee 1980–82; Australasian Inst. of Mining and Metallurgy, Australian Science and Tech. Council 1977–80; Fellow, Australian Inst. of Co. Dirs, Australian Acad. of Tech. Sciences and Eng, Trinity Coll. (Univ. of Melbourne) 1990; Hon. Fellow, Inst. of Engineers Australia. *Address:* P.O. Box 86A, Melbourne, Vic. 3001, Australia. *Telephone:* (3) 9609-3945. *Fax:* (3) 9609-3946.

LOTT, Dame Felicity Ann Emwhyla, CBE, DBE, BA, LRAM, FRAM; British singer (soprano); b. 8 May 1947, Cheltenham; d. of John A. Lott and Whyla Lott (née Williams); m. 1st Robin Golding 1973 (divorced); m. 2nd Gabriel Woolf 1984; one d.; ed Pate's Grammar School for Girls, Cheltenham, Royal Holloway Coll., Univ. of London and Royal Acad. of Music; debut with ENO as Pamina in Die Zauberflöte 1975; prin. roles at Glyndebourne, Covent Garden, ENO, WNO, New York Metropolitan Opera, Vienna, La Scala, Paris Opéra, Brussels, Hamburg, Munich, Chicago, San Francisco, Dresden; wide recital repertoire; founder mem. Songmakers' Almanac; mem. Equity, Incorporated Soc. of Musicians; Hon. Fellow Royal Holloway Coll., Hon. FRCM; Officier des Arts et des Lettres 2000, Chevalier Légion d'honneur 2001; Dr hc (Sussex) 1990; Hon. DLitt (Loughborough) 1996; Hon. DMus (London) 1997, (Royal Scottish Acad. of Music and Drama) 1998, (Oxford) 2001; Kammersängerin, Bayerische Staatsoper, Munich 2003. *Roles include:* Countess in Le Nozze de Figaro; Ellen Orford in Peter Grimes; Fiordiligi in Così fan Tutti; Elvira in Don Giovanni; Xiphares in Mitridate; Marschallin in Der Rosenkavalier; Countess in Capriccio (Richard Strauss); many recitals with Graham Johnson and duets with Ann Murray; DVD of Offenbach's Hélène in La Belle Hélène and La Grande Duchesse. *Leisure interests:* reading, gardening. *Address:* Askonas Holt Ltd, Lincoln House, 300 High Holborn, London, WC1V 7JH, England (office). *Telephone:* (20) 7400-1700 (office). *Fax:* (20) 7400-0799 (office). *E-mail:* info@askonasholt.co.uk (office); mail@felicitylott.de (office). *Website:* www.askonasholt.co.uk (office); www.felicitylott.de (home).

LOTT, (Chester) Trent, BPA, JD; American fmr politician; b. 9 Oct. 1941, Grenada, Miss.; s. of Chester P. Lott and Iona Lott (née Watson); m. Patricia E. Thompson 1964; one s. one d.; ed Univ. of Mississippi; called to Miss. Bar 1967; Assoc. Bryan & Gordon, Pascagoula, Miss. 1967; Admin. Asst to Congressman Colmer 1968–73; mem. 93rd–100th Congresses from 5th Dist Miss., Repub. Whip 97th and 98th Congresses; Senator from Miss. 1989–2007 (resgnd); Senate Majority Leader 1996–2001, Nov.–Dec. 2002, Minority Leader 2001–02; named as observer from House to Geneva Arms Control talks; mem. Senate Republican Policy Cttee; mem. American Bar Asscn; Republican; Golden Bulldog Award, Guardian of Small Business Award. *Address:* c/o 487 Russell Senate Building, Washington, DC 20510, USA.

LOUA, Alexandre Cécé, LenD; Guinean diplomatist and politician; *Minister of Foreign Affairs and Guineans Abroad;* b. 1956, N'zérèkorè; ed Conakry Univ.; Asst Lecturer, Faculty of Law, Conakry Univ. 1982–87; attaché to State Prosecutor, Conakry Regional Court 1982–84; Judge, Court of First Instance, Conakry 1984–86; Head of Legal Affairs Div., Ministry of Foreign Affairs 1986–94, Dir Legal and Consular Affairs 1994–96; Amb. to fmr Yugoslavia (also accred to Bulgaria) 1996–98, to South Africa (also accred to Angola, Botswana, Mozambique, Namibia, Madagascar and Zimbabwe) 2007, to Germany 2007–09; Minister of Foreign Affairs and Guineans Abroad 2009–. *Address:* Ministry of Foreign Affairs and Guineans Abroad, face au Port, ex-Primature, BP 2519 Conakry Guinea (office). *Telephone:* 30-45-12-70 (office). *Fax:* 30-41-16-21 (office). *Website:* www.mae.gov.gn (office).

LOUCKS, Vernon R., Jr, MBA; American business executive; *Chairman, The Athena Group LLC;* b. 24 Oct. 1934, Evanston, Ill.; s. of Vernon Reece Loucks and Sue Burton; m. Linda Olson; six c.; ed Yale Univ. and Harvard Graduate School of Business Admin.; served as First Lt US Marine Corps; fmr Sr man. consultant, George Fry & Assocs; joined Baxter Int. Inc. 1966, mem. Bd of Dirs 1975, Pres. and COO 1976, CEO 1987–98, Chair. 1987; currently Chair. The Athena Group (pvt. equity group) 2001–; mem. Advisory Bd PAX Scientific, Inc; fmr Special Advisor US NIH; mem. Bd of Dirs Emerson Electric Co., Inc., Anheuser-Busch Cos, Affymetrix, Inc., Edwards Lifesciences Corpn; fmr mem. Bd of Dirs The Dun & Bradstreet Corpn, Quaker Oats Co.; several awards including Chicago Inst. of Medicine Citizen Fellowship Award 1982, Yale Medal 1997. *Address:* The Athena Group LLC, 712 Fifth Avenue, 8th Floor, New York, NY 10019, USA. *Telephone:* (212) 459-0200. *Website:* www .theathenagroup.com.

LOUDON, Aarnout Alexander, LLM; Dutch business executive; b. 10 Dec. 1936, The Hague; m. Talitha Adine Charlotte Boon 1962; two s.; ed Univ. of Utrecht; joined Bank Mees & Hope 1964, Head, New Issues Dept 1967; joined Akzo Group 1969, Dir Financial Affairs Akzo, Arnhem 1971; Finance Dir Akzo Coatings, France 1972; Pres. Akzo, Brazil 1975–77; mem. Man. Bd Akzo NV 1977, Deputy Chair. 1978, Chair. Bd 1982–94; Chair. Supervisory Bd Akzo Nobel NV 1994–96; Chair. Supervisory Bd ABN AMRO Holding NV 1994–96; mem. Supervisory Bd Royal Dutch Petroleum Co. 1997–2007; Sr Adviser Cinven PLC; mem. Senate, Dutch Parl. 1995–99. *Leisure interest:* horse riding. *Address:* Houtweg 73, 2514 BN The Hague, Netherlands (home). *Telephone:* (70) 3608147 (office); (70) 3463260 (home). *Fax:* (70) 3603825 (office). *E-mail:* aarnout@loudon.nl.

LOUDON, Rodney, DPhil, FRS; British theoretical physicist; b. 25 July 1934, Manchester; s. of Albert Loudon and Doris Helen Loudon (née Blane); m. Mary A. Philips 1960; one s. one d.; ed Bury Grammar School, Oxford Univ., Univ. of California at Berkeley, USA; Scientific Civil Servant, RRE, Malvern 1960–65; mem. Tech. Staff, Bell Laboratories, Murray Hill, NJ, USA 1965–66, 1970, RCA, Zürich, Switzerland 1975, British Telecom Research Labs 1984, 1989–95; Prof. of Theoretical Physics, Essex Univ. 1967–2007; Visiting Prof. Yale Univ. 1975, Univ. of Calif. Irvine 1980, Ecole Polytechnique, Lausanne 1985, Univ. of Rome 1987, 1996; Fellow Optical Soc. of America 1994; Thomas Young Medal and Prize (Inst. of Physics) 1987, Max Born Award (Optical Soc. of America) 1992, Humboldt Award 1998. *Publications:* The Quantum Theory of Light 1973, 1983, 2000, Scattering of Light by Crystals (with W. Hayes) 1978, 2004, Surface Excitations (Ed. with V.M. Agranovich) 1984, An Introduction to the Properties of Condensed Matter (with D. Barber) 1989. *Leisure interest:* classical music. *Address:* 3 Gaston Street, East Bergholt, Colchester, Essex, CO7 6SD, England. *Telephone:* (1206) 298550.

LOUEKOSKI, Matti Kalevi; Finnish politician, business executive and lawyer; *Deputy Governor, Bank of Finland;* b. 14 April 1941, Oulu; m. Pirjo Hiltunen 1969; one s. one d.; Sec.-Gen. Union of Finnish Student Corpns 1967–69; official at Ministry of Finance and Ministry of Interior 1969–70; Counsellor of Higher Educ. 1970–72; Special Adviser, Office of the Council of State 1975–76; established own law firm 1978; Dir Finnish Workers' Savings Bank 1979–83; mem. Parl. 1976–79, 1983–96; Minister of Educ. 1971–72; Minister without Portfolio Feb.–Sept. 1972; Minister of Justice 1972–75, of Justice and Nordic Co-operation 1987–90, of Finance 1990–91; Vice-Speaker of Parl. 1985–87, 1995–96; mem. Bd Bank of Finland 1996–2000, Deputy Gov. 2001–; mem. Social Democratic Party. *Address:* Bank of Finland, P.O. Box 160, 00101 Helsinki, Finland. *Telephone:* 1831. *Fax:* 661676. *E-mail:* info@bof .fi. *Website:* www.bof.fi.

LOUEMBE, Blaise; Gabonese government official; *Minister of Economy, Finance, Budget and Privatization;* m.; six c.; ed Université des Sciences sociales de Grenoble, Switzerland; served in several positions at Treasury including Head of Customs Directorate 1988–90, Deputy Dir 1990–92, Gen-Man. Disbursement Services; Treasurer Paymaster Gen., Ministry of Economy, Finance, Budget and Privatization 2000–08, Minister of Economy, Finance, Budget and Privatization 2008–. *Address:* Ministry of Economic Affairs, Finance, the Budget and Privatization, BP 165, Libreville, Gabon (office). *Telephone:* 76-12-10 (office). *Fax:* 76-59-74 (office).

LOUËT, Philippe Marie Alexandre Gabriel, LenD; French diplomatist; b. 7 July 1933, Paris; s. of Michel Louet and Marguerite Louet (née Perrin); m. 1st Hélène Delorme; one s.; m. 2nd Penelope Wilkinson 1974; two s. one step-s.; ed Coll. Saint-Martin, Pontoise, Lycée Janson-de-Sailly, Inst. d'études politiques de Paris, Ecole nat. d'admin; with Dept of Political Affairs, Ministry of Foreign Affairs 1962–66; Second, later First Sec. to Perm. Rep. of France to the EEC 1966–71; Tech. Adviser, Ministry of Industrial and Scientific Devt 1971–74, Ministry of Foreign Affairs 1974, Deputy Dir for Scientific Affairs and Dir for Spatial and Atomic Matters 1976–81; Deputy Perm. Rep. to the UN 1981–86; Amb. to Turkey 1986–88; Perm. Rep. to the EEC, Brussels 1988–89; Amb. to Sweden 1989–92; Diplomatic Adviser to the Govt 1992–; Officier, Légion d'honneur, Officier, Ordre nat. du Mérite, Grand Officier, Ordre de l'Etoile Polaire (Sweden). *Leisure interest:* sailing. *Address:* Conseiller diplomatique du gouvernement, 19 avenue Kléber, 75116 Paris (office); 2 avenue de Camoëns, 75116 Paris, France (home). *Telephone:* 1-43-17-77-66 (office). *Fax:* 1-43-17-77-73 (office).

LOUGHRAN, James, FRNCM, FRSAMD; British conductor; b. 30 June 1931, Glasgow; s. of James Loughran and Agnes (née Fox) Loughran; m. 1st Nancy Coggon 1961 (divorced 1983, died 1996); two s.; m. 2nd Ludmila Navratil 1985; ed Glasgow, Bonn, Amsterdam and Milan; Assoc. Conductor, Bournemouth Symphony Orchestra 1962–65; debut Royal Opera House, Covent Garden 1964; Prin. Conductor BBC Scottish Symphony Orchestra 1965–71; Prin. Conductor and Musical Adviser, Hallé Orchestra 1971–83, Conductor Laureate 1983–91; debut New York Philharmonic with Westminster Choir 1972; Prin. Conductor Bamberg Symphony Orchestra 1979–83; Chief Guest Conductor BBC Welsh Symphony Orchestra 1987–90; Guest Conductor of prin. orchestras of Europe, America, Australia and Japan, Guest Perm. Conductor, Japan Philharmonic Symphony Orchestra 1993; Chief Conductor Århus Symphony Orchestra, Denmark 1996–2003; BBC Proms 1965–89 including The Last Night 5 times 1977–85; recorded complete Beethoven Symphonies with London Symphony Orchestra as contribution to European Broadcasting Union Beethoven Bicentenary Celebrations 1969–70; recordings with Hallé, London Philharmonic, Philharmonia, BBC Symphony, Århus Symphony and Scottish Chamber Orchestras; Liveryman, Worshipful Co. of Musicians 1992; Hon. DMus (Sheffield) 1983, (RSAMD) 2005; First Prize, Philharmonia Orchestra Conducting Competition 1961, Mancunian of the Year 1981, Gold Disc EMI 1983. *Leisure interest:* unwinding, golf. *Address:* 18 Hatfield Drive, Glasgow, G12 0YA, Scotland (home). *Telephone:* (141) 337-2091 (home). *Fax:* (141) 357-0643 (home). *E-mail:* jamesloughran@btinternet.com (home).

LOUIS, Jean-Victor, DenD; Belgian lawyer and academic; *Professor Emeritus, Université Libre de Bruxelles;* b. 10 Jan. 1938, Uccle; m. Maria Rosa Moya Benavent 1963; three s.; ed Univ. Libre de Bruxelles; Sec. Inst. d'Etudes Européennes, Univ. Libre de Bruxelles 1967–71, Dir 1971–72, Dir of Research 1977–80, Pres. 1980–92; Lecturer, Univ. Libre de Bruxelles 1970–73, Prof. 1973–2003, Prof. Emer. 2003–; Prof. European Univ. Inst. 1998–2002; Adviser, Nat. Bank of Belgium 1972–80, Head, Legal Dept 1980–97, Adviser to Bd of Dirs 1990–97; Pres. Belgian Asscn for European Law 1983–85; legal expert, Institutional Cttee European Parl. 1992–94; Pres. Initiative Cttee 96, Int. European Movt 1995–98; mem., Monetary Cttee of Int. Law Asscn; Ed. Cahiers de Droit Européen 1977–; Exec. Dir Philippe Wiener-Maurice Anspach Foundation 1971–2002, Pres. 2002–; mem. European Constitutional Law Network (ECLN); mem. Bd and Acting Sec.-Gen. Trans-European Policy Studies Asscn (TEPSA); Francqui Chair 2007–08; Dr hc (Univ. Paris 2) 2001; Commdr, Order of Belgian Crown; Emile Bernheim Prize 1969, P.H. Spaak Prize 1979. *Publications:* Les règlements de la Communauté économique européenne 1969, Le Droit de la Communauté économique européenne (dir and co-author), 15 vols 1970–, The European Community Legal Order 1979, Implementing the Tokyo Round (with J. Jackson and M. Matsushita) 1984, Vers un Système européen de banques centrales (ed.) 1989, From the EMS to the Monetary Union 1990, Banking Supervision in the EC (ed.) 1995, L'Union européenne et l'avenir de ses institutions 1996, The Euro and European Integration (ed.) 1999, The Euro in the National Context (ed.) 2002, The Euro: Law, Politics, Economics (ed. with A. Komninos), L'Ordre juridique de l'Union européenne (with T. Ronse) 2005; many articles on EC law, especially in field of monetary cooperation and integration. *Address:* 524 avenue Louise, Boîte 9, 1050 Brussels, Belgium (home).

LOUIS-DREYFUS, Robert Louis Maurice, MBA; French business executive; *Chairman and CEO, Louis Dreyfus SAS;* b. 14 June 1946, Paris; s. of Jean Louis-Dreyfus and Jeanne Depierre; m. 1st Sarah Oberholzer; m. 2nd Margarita Bogdanova; three s.; ed Lycée Marcel Roby, Saint-Germain-en-Laye and Harvard Business School, USA; Dir Louis-Dreyfus, SA 1973–81, Sr Exec. Vice-Pres. and COO 1982–83; Pres. and CEO IMS Int. 1984–89; Gen. Man. Saatchi & Saatchi 1989–93, CEO 1990–93, Dir (non-exec.) 1993; Pres. Adidas (now Adidas-Salomon) AG 1993–2001, Pres. L'Olympique de Marseille 1996–, Louis Dreyfus Communication (Now Neuf Telecom) 2000–04, Chair. and CEO Louis Dreyfus SAS 2006–; Chair. Bd Dirs Tag Heuer à Mariu 1997–99; mem. Bd of Dirs Neuf Cegetal 2004–. *Address:* Louis Dreyfus SAS, 87 avenue de la Grande Armee, 75782, France (office); Ortstrasse 4, 7270 Davos-platz, Switzerland (home). *Telephone:* 1-47-77-17-00 (office). *Fax:* 1-47-77-17-01 (office). *E-mail:* DRH-Paris@louisdreyfus.fr (office). *Website:* www .louisdreyfus.com (office).

LOUISY, Rt Hon. Allan (Fitzgerald Laurent), PC, CBE; Saint Lucia politician; fmr Judge Supreme Court of Grenada; Leader of Saint Lucia Labour Party 1974–82; Prime Minister of Saint Lucia, Minister of Finance, Home Affairs, Information and Tourism 1979–81, Minister without Portfolio 1981–82, Minister of Legal Affairs Jan.–May 1982.

LOUISY, Dame Calliopa Pearlette, GCMG, GCSL, DStJ, BA, MA, PhD; Saint Lucia government official and academic; *Governor-General;* b. 8 June 1946, Laborie, Saint Lucia; d. of Rita Louisy; ed St Joseph's Convent Secondary School, Univ. of the West Indies, Université Laval, Québec, Canada, Univ. of Bristol, UK; grad. teacher, St Joseph's Convent 1969–72, 1975–76; tutor, Saint Lucia 'A' Level Coll. 1976–1981, Prin. 1981–86; Dean Sir Arthur Lewis Community Coll. 1986–94, Vice-Prin. 1994–95, Prin. 1996–97; Gov.-Gen. of Saint Lucia 1997–; Commonwealth Scholar 1972; Hon. Distinguished Fellow, Univ. of the West Indies 2003; Grand Cross, Order of St Lucia 1997, Dame of the Equestrian Order of St Gregory the Great 2002; Hon. LLD (Bristol) 1999, (Sheffield) 2003; Int. Woman of the Year 1998, 2001, Paul Harris Fellow, Rotary Int. 2001, Caribbean Luminary 2007. *Publications:* A Guide to the Writing of Creole 1985, The Changing Role of the Small State in Higher Education 1993, Dilemmas of Insider Research in a Small Country Setting 1997, Higher Education in the Caribbean: Issues and Strategies 1999, Expanding the Horizons of Creole Research 1999, Globalisation and Comparative Education: A Caribbean Perspective 2001, Nation Languages and National Development in the Caribbean 2002, Whose Context for What Quality? – Informing Educational Strategies for the Caribbean 2004, Global Trends in Education – The Cultural Dimension 2007. *Leisure interests:* the performing arts, culture, gardening. *Address:* Government House, Morne Fortune, Castries, Saint Lucia, West Indies (office). *Telephone:* (758) 452-2481 (office). *Fax:* (758) 453-2731 (office). *E-mail:* govgenslu@candw.lc (office). *Website:* www.stluciagovernmenthouse.com (office).

LOULY, Lt-Col Mohamed Mahmoud Ould Ahmed; Mauritanian politician and army officer; b. 1943; Minister for Control and Investigation July 1978–Jan. 1979, in charge of the Perm. Secr. of the Mil. Cttee for Nat. Recovery (CMRN) Jan.–March 1979, for the Civil Service and Higher, Tech. and Vocational Training March–May 1979; Pres. of Mauritania 1979–80. *Address:* c/o Office du Président, Comité de Redressement National, Nouackchott, Mauritania.

LOURDUSAMY, HE Cardinal Simon, DCL; Indian ecclesiastic; *Prefect Emeritus, Congregation for the Eastern Churches;* b. 5 Feb. 1924, Kalleri, Pondicherry; ed Loyola Coll. of Madras, Pontifical Urban Univ. of Rome, Italy; ordained priest 1951; diocesan chancellor and sec. to Archbishop of Pondicherry; Ed. weekly Catholic magazine Sava Viaby; Dir Catholic Doctors' Guild, Catholic Medical Students' Guild, Newman Asscns, catholic univ. students' union and of other ecclesiastical orgs; apptd Auxiliary Bishop of Bangalore, India 1962, Coadjutor Archbishop 1964, Archbishop 1968–71; consecrated Bishop (Titular Church of Sozusa, Libya) 1962; Titular Archbishop of Philippi 1964; Adjunct Sec. Congregation for the Evangelization of Peoples 1971–73, Sec. 1973–85; Pres. Pontifical Missionary Works 1973; Vice-Grand Chancellor Pontifical Urban Univ. 1973; cr. Cardinal-Deacon of S. Maria delle Grazie alle Fornaci fuori Porta Cavalleggeri (Deaconry raised pro hac vice) 1985, Cardinal-Priest 1996; Prefect Congregation for the Eastern Churches 1985–91, Prefect Emer. 1991–; fmr Pres. Nat. Liturgical Comm. for India; Founder National Nat. and Catechetical Centre, Bangalore; fmr mem. Bishops' Catechetics Comm.; del. to first ordinary ass. of Synod of Bishops 1967; Rep. of Bishops of India at Pan-Asiatic Catechetical-Liturgical Conf., Manila, Philippines 1967 (Vice-Pres. and Pres. Liturgy Section). *Address:* Congregation for the Eastern Churches, Palazzo del Bramante, Via della Conciliazione 34, 00193 Rome (office); Palazzo dei Convertendi, Via dei Corridori 64, 00193 Rome, Italy (home). *Telephone:* (06) 69884282 (office); (06) 69884796 (home). *Fax:* (06) 69884300 (office).

LOUSTEAU, Martin, BSc, MSc; Argentine economist, banker and government official; b. 8 Dec. 1970; ed Univ. of San Andres, LSE; worked at Ministry of Economy and Public Works 1996–97; Chief Economist and Dir, APL Economia (business consulting firm) 1997–2002; Adviser to Pres. of Cen. Bank and mem. Cttee on Inflation Targets 2003–04; Chief of Staff, Ministry of Production 2004–05, Minister of Production for Buenos Aires Prov. 2005; Pres. Banco de la Provincia de Buenos Aires 2005–07; Minister of the Economy 2007–08 (resgnd). *Address:* c/o Ministry of Economy and Production, Hipólito Yrigoyen 250, C1086AAB Buenos Aires, Argentina (office).

LOUTFY, Aly, PhD; Egyptian fmr politician and professor of economics; b. 6 Oct. 1935, Cairo; s. of Mahmoud Loutfy; m. Eglal Mabrouk 1966; one s.; ed Ain Shams and Louzan Univs; joined staff, Faculty of Commerce Ain Shams Univ. 1957, Prof. and Chair. Dept of Econs 1980; Prof. High Inst. of Co-operative and Admin. Studies; Part-time Prof. Inst. of Arab Research and Studies, Cairo; mem. Bd of Dirs Bank of Alexandria 1977–78, Bank of Commerce and Devt (Cairo) 1981–; mem. Legis., Political Science and Econ. Asscn 1977, Delta Sugar Co. 1978, Bank of Commerce and Devt 1980; Minister of Finance 1978–80; Prime Minister of Egypt 1985–86; Speaker of the Shoura Council 1985–89; Ideal Prof. Award, Egyptian Univs 1974, Gold Mercury Int. Award 1979. *Publications:* Economic Evolution, Economic Development, Economic Planning, Studies on Mathematical Economics and Econometrics, Financing Problems in Developing Countries, Industrialization Problems in Under-Developed Countries; 30 research papers in economics in Arabic, French and English. *Leisure interests:* tennis, reading, travel. *Address:* 29 Ahmed Heshmat Street, Zamalek, Cairo, Egypt (home). *Telephone:* 7366068.

LOUVIER, Alain; French composer and conductor; b. 13 Sept. 1945, Paris; s. of René Louvier and Marthe Louvier (née Fournier); one s. one d.; ed Centre Nat. de Télé-Enseignement, Conservatoire Nat. Supérieur de Musique, Paris; Dir Conservatoire Nat. de Région, Boulogne-Billancourt 1972–86; Dir Conservatoire Nat. Supérieur de Musique, Paris 1986–91, Prof. of Musical Analysis 1991–; Prix de Rome 1968, Arthur Honegger Award 1975, Paul Gilson Award 1981. *Works include:* Chant des limbes (for orchestra) 1969, 3 Atmosphères (for clarinet and orchestra) 1974, Le Clavecin non tempéré 1978, Messe des Apôtres 1978, Casta Diva (with Maurice Béjart) 1980, Poèmes de Ronsard (for voice ensemble and chamber orchestra) 1984, Envol d'écailles (for flute, viola and harp) 1986, Chant des aires (for 25 flutes) 1988, L'Isola dei Numeri 1992, Itinéraires d'outre-rêve 1994, Un gamelan à Paris 1995, Concerto for alto 1996, Météores (for two pianos and orchestra) 1998, String Quartet 1999, Eclipse (for flute and string trio) 2000, Une cloche de feu rose dans les nuages (for piano and 11 voices) 2000, Nuit de feu, Rumeur d'espace 2001, Heptagone 2004, Solstices 2005, Archimède 2006, Etuder pur Agresseurs (6 livres pour piano, clavecin, orgue) 1964–82. *Publications:* L'Orchestre 1997, Louvier, Les claviers de lumière, par P.A. Castanet 2002. *Leisure interests:* botany and entomology. *Address:* CNSMDP, 209 avenue Jean Jaurès, 75019 Paris (office); 53 avenue Victor Hugo, 92100 Boulogne-Billancourt, France (home). *Telephone:* 1-48-25-14-68 (home). *Fax:* 1-48-25-10-92 (home). *E-mail:* alainlouvier@yahoo.fr (home). *Website:* www.cnsmdp.fr (office).

LOUVRIER, Franck; French public relations officer and civil servant; *Director of Communications, Office of the President;* b. 1968; Chief of Staff to Mayor of Neuilly, Nicolas Sarkozy 1999–2002; press and communications adviser to Sarkozy at Interior Ministry 2002–04, 2005–07, Finance Ministry 2004; Dir of Communications, Union pour un mouvement populaire (UMP) 2004–, presidential campaign of Nicolas Sarkozy 2005–06, Office of the Pres. of the Repub. 2007–. *Address:* Palais de l'Elysée, 55 rue du faubourg Saint-Honoré, 75008 Paris, France (office). *Telephone:* 1-42-92-81-00 (office). *Website:* www.elysee.fr (office).

LOUW, Eugene, BA, LLB; South African politician and lawyer; *Chairman and Senior Partner, Louw & Coetzee;* b. 15 July 1931, Cape Town; s. of Anath Louw and Johanna de Jager; m. Hantie Phyfer 1964; three s. one d.; ed Bellville High School and Univ. of Stellenbosch; Chair. Students' Council, Univ. of Stellenbosch 1957; attorney, pvt. practice, Durbanville 1964–79, 1993–; Mayor of Durbanville 1967–72; mem. Parl. for Durbanville 1974–79, Malmesbury 1972–74, Paarl 1989–94; Admin. of Cape Prov. 1979–89; Minister of Home Affairs 1989–92, of Defence and Public Works 1992–93; Chair. and Sr Partner Louw and Coetzee 1994–; Chair. Nat. Huguenot Tercentenary Festival Cttee 1988, Capab 1982–88, Nat. Dias Quincentenary Festival Cttee 1988, Constitutional Investigation Cttee into Regional Local Govt; Patron Western Prov. Rugby Union 1979–89; Abe Bailey Travel Bursary Holder; Alumnus of the Year Award (Stellenbosch Univ.) 1993; recipient of seven hon. citizenships; four public buildings named after him. *Leisure interests:* politics, legal profession, sport. *Address:* Louw & Coetzee, 35 Main Road, 7550 Durbanville (office); 10 Watsonia Close, Plattekloof, 7500 Parow (home); PO Box 15432, 7506 Panorama, South Africa. *Telephone:* (21) 9763180 (office); (21) 9305620 (home); (21) 9305620. *Fax:* (21) 9764288 (office); (21) 9305621 (home). *E-mail:* elouw@louwcoet.co.za (office). *Website:* www.louwcoet.co.za (office).

LOUW, Michael James Minnaar, BA; South African civil servant; b. 9 Nov. 1939; m.; three c.; ed Orange Free State Univ.; with Dept of Labour; with Directorate for Mil. Intelligence, South African Defence Force 1964–69; joined Bureau for State Security (became Nat. Intelligence Service) 1969, Special Adviser to Dir-Gen., Deputy Dir-Gen. 1988–92, Dir-Gen. 1992–94, Chief 1994–. *Address:* Private Bag X3, Hatfield 0028, South Africa.

LOUW, Raymond; South African publishing executive; *Editor and Publisher, Southern Africa Report;* b. 13 Oct. 1926, Cape Town; s. of George K. E. Louw and Helen K. Louw (née Finlay); m. Jean Ramsay Byres 1950; two s. one d.; ed Parktown High School, Johannesburg; reporter on Rand Daily Mail 1946–50, Worthing Herald 1951–52, North-Western Evening Mail 1953–54, Westminster Press Provincial Newspapers (London) 1955–56; Night News Ed. Rand Daily Mail 1958–59, News Ed. 1960–65, Ed. 1966–77; News Ed. Sunday Times 1959–60; Chair. SA Morning Newspaper Group 1975–77; Gen. Man. SA Associated Newspapers 1977–82; Ed. and Publr Southern Africa Report 1982–; Chair. Media Defence Fund 1989–94, Campaign for Open Media 1985–94 (now merged as Freedom of Expression Inst., Chair. 1994–96); New Era Schools Trust; Africa Consultant, World Press Freedom Cttee 2003–; mem. Task Group on Govt Communications 1996; mem. Exec. Bd, Int. Press Inst., London, 1979–87, Fellow 1994; mem. Independent Media Comm. 1994; chosen by Int. Press Inst. to travel to Cameroon to make plea for release from jail of Pius Njawe (Ed. of Le Messager) 1998; mem. IPI delegations to the Pres. of Indonesia 2000, Zimbabwean Govt 2001, Israeli Govt 2003, Ethiopian Govt 2004 on media freedom issues; Pringle Medal for services to journalism 1976, 1992. *Publications:* Four Days in Lusaka – Whites from 'Home' in talks with the ANC 1989, Report on the media situation in South Africa (for UNESCO) 1994; narrative for Nelson Mandela Pictorial Biography by Peter Magubane 1996; Undue Restriction: Laws Impacting on Media Freedom in the SADC (ed.); numerous papers and articles on the media and press freedom. *Leisure interests:* sailing, walking, travel, wildlife. *Address:* Southern Africa Report, PO Box 261579, Excom, Johannesburg 2023 (office); 23 Duncombe Road, Forest Town, Johannesburg 2193, South Africa (home). *Telephone:* (11) 646-8790 (office). *Fax:* (11) 646-6085 (office). *E-mail:* rlouw@sn.apc.org (office). *Website:* www.sareport.co.za (office).

LOVASZ, László, PhD; Hungarian/American mathematician and computer scientist; *Senior Researcher, Theory Group, Microsoft Research;* b. 9 March 1948, Budapest; ed Eötvös Loránd Univ., Budapest; William K. Lanman Prof. of Computer Science and Math., Yale Univ., New Haven, Conn. 1993; currently Sr Researcher, Theory Group, Microsoft Research, Redmond, WA; Ed.-in-Chief Combinatorica; Ed. 12 other journals; mem. Hungarian Acad. of Sciences; affiliated with Budapest Semesters in Math. (programme in English for American and Canadian undergraduates); Hungarian Nat. Order of Merit 1998; George Polya Prize, Soc. for Industrial and Applied Math. 1979, Best Information Theory Paper Award, IEEE 1981, Ray D. Fulkerson Prize, American Math. Soc.-Math. Programming Soc. 1982, Hungarian State Prize

1985, Tibor Szele Medal, Bolyai Soc. 1992, Brouwer Medal, Dutch Math. Soc. 1993, Bolzano Medal, Czech Math. Soc. 1998, Wolf Prize (Israel) 1999, Knuth Prize, Asscn for Computing Machinery 1999, Corvin Chain Award (Hungary) 2001, Goedel Prize, Asscn for Computing Machinery-European Asscn for Theoretical Computer Science 2001, John von Neumann Medal 2003. *Publications:* Combinatorial Problems and Exercises 1979, Algorithmic Theory of Numbers, Graphs, and Convexity 1986, Geometric Algorithms and Combinatorial Optimization 1993, Combinatorial Optimization: Papers from the Dimacs Special Year (co-author) 1995, Graph Theory and Combinatorial Biology (co-author) 1999, Computation Complexity (co-author) 2002, Discrete Mathematics: Elementary and Beyond (co-author) 2003, Handbook of Combinatorics (co-author) 2003, Discrete Mathematics and Computation 2004; more than 200 articles in math. journals and four monographs on discrete math., theory of computing and combinatorial optimization. *Address:* Microsoft Research, One Microsoft Way, Redmond, WA 98052-6399, USA (office). *Telephone:* (425) 882-8080 (office). *Fax:* (425) 936-7329 (office). *E-mail:* lovasz@microsoft.com (office). *Website:* research .microsoft.com/~lovasz/ (office).

LOVE, Courtney; American rock musician, singer and actress; b. (Love Michelle Harrison), 9 July 1964, San Francisco; d. of Hank Harrison and Linda Carroll; m. 1st James Moreland; m. 2nd Kurt Cobain (deceased); one s. one d.; began career as a stripper, occasional actress and mem. of bands Faith No More and Babes in Toyland; f., singer and guitarist, rock band Hole 1989–2002; solo artist 2003–. *Films:* Sid and Nancy 1986, Straight To Hell 1987, Tapeheads 1988, Basquiat 1996, Feeling Minnesota 1996, The People vs Larry Flynt 1996, 200 Cigarettes 1999, Man on the Moon 1999, Beat 2000, Julie Johnson 2001, Trapped 2002. *Recordings include:* albums: with Hole: Retard Girl 1990, Pretty On The Inside 1991, Live Through This 1994, Celebrity Skin 1998; solo: America's Sweetheart 2004; singles: with Hole: Beautiful Son 1993, Doll Parts 1994, Ask for It 1995, Celebrity Skin 1998, Malibu 1998, Awful 1999; solo: Mono 2004, Nobody's Daughter 2009. *Publication:* Dirty Blonde (autobiog.) 2006. *Address:* Q-Prime Inc, 729 Seventh Avenue, 14th Floor, New York, NY 10019, USA (office); c/o David Geffen Co., 9130 W Sunset Boulevard, Los Angeles, CA 90069, USA (office). *Website:* www.courtneylove.com.

LOVE, Mike; American singer and songwriter; b. 15 March 1941, Baldwin Hills, Calif.; mem. Beach Boys 1961–; mem. own band, Endless Summer 1981; numerous tours, concerts and festival appearances; band est. Brother Records label 1967–; American Music Awards Special Award of Merit 1988, Grammy Lifetime Achievement Award 2001. *Recordings include:* albums: with The Beach Boys: Surfin' Safari 1962, Surfer Girl 1963, Little Deuce Coupe 1963, Shut Down Vol. 2, All Summer Long 1964, Christmas Album 1964, The Beach Boys Today! 1965, Summer Days (and Summer Nights) 1965, Beach Boys Party 1966, Pet Sounds 1966, Smiley Smile 1967, Wild Honey 1968, Friends 1968, 20/20 1969, Sunflower 1970, Surf's Up 1971, Carl and the Passions – So Tough 1972, Holland 1973, The Beach Boys in Concert 1973, Endless Summer 1974, 15 Big Ones 1976, The Beach Boys Love You 1977, M.I.U. 1978, LA (Light Album) 1979, Keepin' The Summer Alive 1980, The Beach Boys 1985, Still Cruisin' 1989, Two Rooms 1991, Summer in Paradise 1992, The Sounds of Summer – The Very Best of The Beach Boys 2003; solo: Looking Back With Love 1981. *Address:* c/o Elliott Lott, Boulder Creek Entertainment Corporation, 4860 San Jacinto Circle West, Fallbrook, CA 92028, USA (office); c/o Capitol Records, 1750 North Vine Street, Hollywood, CA 90028, USA. *Website:* www.thebeachboys.com.

LØVEID, Cecilie Meyer; Norwegian playwright and poet; b. 21 Aug. 1951, Mysen; d. of Erik Løveid and Ingrid Meyer; m. Bjørn H. Ianke 1978; one s. two d.; ed arts and crafts school in Bergen and studies in graphic design, theatre history and drama; mem. editorial staff, Profil (magazine) 1969; Sec. Norsk Forfattersentrum, Vestlandsardelingen 1974; Teacher, Writing Arts Centre, Bergen 1986; mem. Literary Council, Den norske Fordatterforening 1987; Prix Italia 1982; Aschehons Prize; Donblans Prize. *Publications:* Most (novel) 1972, Sug (novel) 1979, Måkespisere (radio play) 1982, Balansedame (play) 1986, Maria Q. (play) 1991, Rhindøtrene (play) 1996, Osterrike (play) 1998. *Leisure interests:* old wooden toys, walking in the mountains, swimming.

LOVEJOY, Thomas Eugene, III, BS, PhD; American biologist, conservationist and academic; *Biodiversity Chair, H. John Heinz III Center for Science, Economics and the Environment;* b. 22 Aug. 1941, New York City; m. Charlotte Seymour 1966 (divorced 1978); three d.; ed Yale Univ.; has worked in Brazilian Amazon since 1965; directed conservation programme at World Wildlife Fund-US 1973–87; Asst Sec. for Environmental and External Affairs, Smithsonian Inst., Washington, DC 1987–98; apptd Counsellor to Sec. for Biodiversity and Environmental Affairs 1994; Chief Biodiversity Advisor to Pres. World Bank and Lead Specialist for Environment for Latin America and the Caribbean –2002; Sr Adviser to Pres. UN Foundation –2002; Pres. H. John Heinz III Center for Science, Econs, and the Environment 2002–08, Biodiversity Chair 2008–; Chair. Yale Inst. for Biospheric Studies; fmr Chair. US Man and Biosphere Program; Past Pres. American Inst. of Biological Sciences, Soc. for Conservation Biology; conceived idea for Minimum Critical Size of Ecosystems project (jt project between Smithsonian Inst. and Brazil's Instituto Nacional de Pesquisas da Amazônia); Fellow, AAAS, American Acad. of Arts and Sciences, American Philosophical Soc., Linnaean Soc. of London, American Ornithologists' Union; Order of Rio Branco (Brazil), Grand Cross of the Order of Scientific Merit (Brazil); Tyler Prize for Environmental Achievement 2001, Lindbergh Award 2002, BBVA Foundation Frontiers of Knowledge Award in the Ecology and Conservation Biology category (co-recipient) 2008. *Achievements include:* developed 'debt-for-nature swaps' for purchase of biologically sensitive tracts of land in debtor nations for purposes of environmental protection; has also supported Forests Now Declaration, calling for new market-based mechanisms to protect tropical forests; played key role in establishing conservation biology through First Int. Conf. on Research in Conservation Biology, La Jolla, Calif. Sept. 1978, introduced terms 'conservation biology' and 'biological diversity' to scientific community; serves on numerous scientific and conservation bds and advisory groups; drew up first projections of global extinction rates for Global 2000 Report to the President, predicted in 1980 extinction of 10–20 per cent of all species by 2020. *Television:* started public TV series Nature. *Publications:* numerous books and articles. *Address:* H. John Heinz III Center for Science, Economics and the Environment, 900 17th Street NW, Suite 700, Washington, DC 20006, USA (office). *Telephone:* (202) 737-6307 (office). *Fax:* (202) 737-6410 (office). *E-mail:* lovejoy@heinzctr.org (office). *Website:* www.heinzctr.org (office).

LOVELL, Sir (Alfred Charles) Bernard, Kt, OBE, PhD, MSc, FRS; British radio astronomer; b. 31 Aug. 1913, Oldland Common, Glos.; s. of Gilbert Lovell and Emily Laura Lovell (née Adams); m. Mary Joyce Chesterman 1937 (died 1993); two s. three d.; ed Bristol Univ.; Asst Lecturer in Physics, Univ. of Manchester 1936–39, Lecturer 1945–47, Sr Lecturer 1947–49, Reader 1949–51, Prof. of Radio Astronomy 1951–81, Emer. Prof. 1981–; with Telecommunications Research Est. 1939–45; Founder and Dir Nuffield Radio Astronomy Labs, Jodrell Bank 1945–81; Fellow, Royal Soc. 1955; Pres. Royal Astronomical Soc. 1969–71, British Asscn 1974–75; Vice-Pres. Int. Astronomical Union 1970–76; mem. Aeronautical Research Council 1955–58, Science Research Council 1965–70; Pres. Guild of Church Musicians 1976–89; Master Worshipful Co. of Musicians 1986–87; Hon. Foreign mem. American Acad. of Arts and Sciences 1955; Hon. mem. New York Acad. of Sciences 1960, Royal Northern Coll. of Music; Hon. Fellow Royal Swedish Acad. 1962, Inst. of Electrical Engineers 1967, Inst. of Physics 1975; Hon. Freeman City of Manchester 1977; Ordre du Mérite pour la Recherche et l'Invention 1962; Polish Order of Merit 1975; Hon. LLD (Edin.) 1961, (Calgary) 1966, (Liverpool) 1999; Hon. DSc (Leicester) 1961, (Leeds) 1966, (Bath, London) 1967, (Bristol) 1970; Hon. DUniv (Stirling) 1974, (Surrey) 1975; Royal Medal of Royal Soc. 1960, Daniel and Florence Guggenheim Int. Astronautics Award 1961. Maitland Silver Medal, Inst. of Structural Engineers 1964, Churchill Gold Medal, Soc. of Engineers 1964, Benjamin Franklin Medal, Royal Soc. of Arts 1980, Gold Medal, Royal Astronomical Soc. 1981. *Publications:* Science and Civilisation 1939, World Power Resources and Social Development 1945, Radio Astronomy 1952, Meteor Astronomy 1954, The Exploration of Space by Radio 1957, The Individual and the Universe (The Reith Lectures 1958), The Exploration of Outer Space 1962, Discovering the Universe 1963, Our Present Knowledge of the Universe 1967; Ed. (with Tom Margerison) The Explosion of Science: The Physical Universe 1967, The Story of Jodrell Bank 1968, The Origins and International Economics of Space Exploration 1973, Out of the Zenith: Jodrell Bank 1957–1970 1973, Man's Relation to the Universe 1975, P. M. S. Blackett – A Biographical Memoir 1976, In the Centre of Immensities 1978, Emerging Cosmology 1981, The Jodrell Bank Telescopes 1985, Voice of the Universe 1987, Pathways to the Universe (with Sir Francis Graham-Smith) 1988, Astronomer by Chance 1990, Echoes of War 1991. *Leisure interests:* music, gardening, cricket. *Address:* The Quinta, Swettenham, nr Congleton, Cheshire, CW12 2LD, England (home). *Telephone:* (1477) 571254. *Fax:* (1477) 571954.

LOVELL, Harold Earl Edmund, Jr, BA, MJ; Antiguan politician and barrister; *Minister of Finance, the Economy and Public Administration;* b. 27 Sept. 1955, St John's; ed Antigua Grammar School, Univ. of the West Indies, Thames Valley Univ., Middle Temple and Univ. of Birmingham, UK; fmr teacher, Antigua Grammar School, Antigua State Coll.; Minister of Foreign Affairs, Tourism, Int. Travel and Trade 2004–05, of Tourism, Civil Aviation, Culture and the Environment 2005–09, of Finance, the Economy and Public Admin 2009–; fmr Vice-Pres. Guild of Undergraduates, Univ. of the West Indies; fmr Gen. Sec., then Vice-Chair. Antigua Caribbean Liberation Movement; fmr Gen. Sec. Antigua and Barbuda Union of Teachers; Vice-Chair. United Progressive Party; mem. BBC Advisory Council for Leicestershire 1990–92. *Address:* Ministry of Finance and Economy, Government Office Complex, Parliament Drive, St John's, Antigua and Barbuda (office). *Telephone:* 462-5015 (office). *Fax:* 462-4860 (office). *E-mail:* minfinance@ antigua.gov.ag (office).

LOVELOCK, James Ephraim, CH, CBE, PhD, DSc, FRS; British scientist, inventor, writer and academic; *Honorary Visiting Fellow, Green College, Oxford;* b. 26 July 1919, Letchworth Garden City, Herts.; s. of Tom Arthur Lovelock and Nellie Ann Elizabeth Lovelock (née March); m. 1st Helen Mary Hyslop 1942 (died 1989); two s. two d.; m. 2nd Sandra Jean Orchard 1991; ed Strand School, Univ. of Manchester, London School of Hygiene and Tropical Medicine; staff scientist, Nat. Inst. for Medical Research, London 1941–61; Prof. of Chem., Baylor Univ. Coll. of Medicine, Tex., USA 1961–64; ind. scientist 1964–; Hon. Visiting Fellow, Green Coll., Oxford 2004–; Rockefeller Travelling Fellowship in Medicine, Harvard Univ., USA 1954; Visiting Scientist, Yale Univ. Medical School 1958–59; Visiting Prof., Univ. of Reading 1967–90; Pres. Marine Biology Asscn 1986–90; mem. Environmentalists for Nuclear Energy; Hon. DSc (Univ. of East Anglia) 1982, (Plymouth Polytechnic) 1988, (Univ. of Exeter) 1988, (Stockholm Univ.) 1991, (Univ. of Edinburgh) 1993, (Univ. of Kent) 1996, (Univ. of East London) 1996, (Univ. of Colorado) 1997; CIBA Foundation Award for Research in Ageing 1955, three NASA Certificates of Recognition for: Gas Chromatograph Interface System and Method, Vapor Phase Detectors, Combined Carrier Gas Separator and Generator for Gas Chromatographic Systems 1972, Tswett Medal for Chromatography 1975, ACS Chromatography Award 1980, Stephen Dal Nogare Award 1985, Norbert Gerbier Prize, Silver Medal and Prize, Plymouth Marine Lab. 1986, World Meteorological Asscn 1988, Dr A.H. Heineken Prize for the Environment, Royal Netherlands Acad. of Arts and Sciences 1990, Rosenstiel Award in Oceanographic Science 1990, Nonino Prize 1996, Volvo

Environment Prize 1996, The Blue Planet Prize 1997, Goi Peace Prize 2000, Discovery Lifetime Award, Royal Geographical Soc. 2001, Wollaston Medal, Geological Soc. 2006. *Achievements:* inventor of the electron capture detector (which made possible the detection of CFCs and other atmospheric nano-pollutants) and of the microwave oven; originator of the 'Gaia hypothesis' during 1960s as a result of work for NASA concerned with detecting life on Mars; hypothesis proposes that living and non-living parts of the Earth form a complex interacting system that can be thought of as a single organism; named after Greek goddess Gaia, hypothesis postulates that biosphere has a regulatory effect on the Earth's environment that acts to sustain life. *Publications:* Gaia: A New Look at Life on Earth 1979, The Great Extinction (co-author) 1983, The Greening of Mars (co-author) 1984; The Ages of Gaia 1988, Gaia: The Practical Science of Planetary Medicine 1991, Homage to Gaia: The Life of an Independent Scientist 2000, Gaia: Medicine for an Ailing Planet 2005, The Revenge of Gaia: Why the Earth Is Fighting Back – And How We Can Still Save Humanity 2006, The Vanishing Face of Gaia 2009. *Leisure interests:* walking, reading novels, music. *Address:* Coombe Mill, St Giles on the Heath, Launceston, Cornwall, PL15 9RY, England. *Website:* www.jameslovelock.org.

LOVINS, Amory B., MA, PhD, FRSA; American physicist, environmentalist and academic; *Chairman and Chief Scientist, Rocky Mountain Institute;* b. 13 Nov. 1947, Washington, DC; m. Hunter Lovins; ed Harvard Univ., Univ. of Oxford, UK; spent two years at Harvard Univ.; transferred to Univ. of Oxford; fmr spokesman for Friends of the Earth (UK); has been Regents' Lecturer in Energy and Resources and in Econs at Univ. of California; Grauer Lecturer, Univ. of British Columbia; Luce Visiting Prof., Dartmouth Coll.; Distinguished Visiting Prof., Univ. of Colorado; Oikos Visiting Prof., Business School, Univ. of St Gallen; an Eng Visiting Prof., Peking Univ.; MAP/Ming Prof., Stanford Univ. 2007; Co-founder (with his wife), Rocky Mountain Inst. (non-profit applied research centre), currently Chair. and Chief Scientist; co-f. and sold (to Financial Times Group 1999) E SOURCE (information source on advanced electric efficiency); Founder and Chair. RMI's fourth spinoff, Fiberforge, Inc. (eng firm); has briefed 19 heads of state and given expert testimony in eight countries and more than 20 states; served on US Dept of Energy's Sr Advisory Bd 1980–81, Defense Science Bd task force on mil. energy strategy 1999–2001, 2006–07; occasional adviser to Nat. Assn of Regulatory Utility Commrs, World Business Council for Sustainable Devt, Kleiner Perkins Caufield & Byers; Fellow, AAAS 1984, World Acad. of Arts and Sciences 1988, World Business Acad. 2001; Hon. Mem. AIA 2007; Hon. Sr Fellow, Design Futures Council; 10 hon. doctorates; shared with Hunter Lovins: Mitchell Prize 1982, Right Livelihood ("Alternative Nobel") Award 1983, Lindbergh Award 1999, Time magazine's Heroes for the Planet 2000; winner of first DELPHI Prize, Onassis Foundation 1989, MacArthur Fellowship 1993, Blue Planet Award, Shingo Prize, Jean Meyer Prize, Nissan Prize 1993, Heinz Award 1997, World Tech. Award (Environment) 1999, Happold Medal, Construction Industry Council (UK) 2000, Benjamin Franklin Medal, Royal Soc. of Arts 2005, named by The Wall Street Journal one of 39 people world-wide "most likely to change the course of business in the '90s", honoured by Newsweek as "one of the Western world's most influential energy thinkers"; ranked by Car magazine as the 22nd most powerful person in the global automotive industry, Volvo Environment Prize, Volvo Environment Foundation 2007. *Publications:* 29 books, including Soft Energy Paths: Towards a Durable Peace 1977, Non-Nuclear Futures: The Case for an Ethical Energy Strategy 1980, A Golden Thread: 2500 Years of Solar Architecture & Technology 1980, Energy/War, Breaking the Nuclear Link 1981, Least-Cost Energy: Solving the CO 2 Problem 1982, Brittle Power: Energy Strategy for National Security 1982, 2001, Energy Unbound: A Fable for America's Future 1986, Consumer Guide to Home Energy Savings 1991, Reinventing Electric Utilities: Competition, Citizen Action, and Clean Power 1996, Factor Four: Doubling Wealth – Halving Resource Use: A Report to the Club of Rome 1997, Natural Capitalism: Creating the Next Industrial Revolution 2000, Small is Profitable: The Hidden Economic Benefits of Making Electrical Resources the Right Size 2003, Winning the Oil Endgame: Innovation for Profit, Jobs and Security 2005; several hundred papers in professional journals as well as poetry, landscape photography, music (fmr pianist and composer) and an electronics patent. *Address:* Rocky Mountain Institute, 2317 Snowmass Creek Road, Snowmass, CO 81654 (office); Rocky Mountain Institute, 1820 Folsom Street, Boulder, CO 80302, USA (office). *Telephone:* (970) 927-3851 (Snowmass) (office); (303) 245-1003 (Boulder) (office). *E-mail:* info@rmi.org (office). *Website:* www.rmi.org (office); www.fiberforge.com (office).

LOVRIN, Ana, LLB; Croatian lawyer and politician; b. 2 Dec. 1953, Zagreb; m. Miodrag Lovrin; four d.; ed Faculty of Law, Univ. of Zagreb; legal officer in Tankerska plovidba, Zadar 1978–80; Man. Legal Dept, Zadar Airport 1980; mem. Zadar City Council, Zadar 1993; mem. Croatian Democratic Union (Hrvatska demokratska zajednica—HDZ) 1993–, Vice-Pres. 1999–2001, Pres. 2003–05, mem. Cen. Cttee 2003–; State Sec. of Zadar, in charge of legal affairs 1993–2001; Deputy Mayor of Zadar 2001–04, Mayor 2004–05; mem. Zadar local govt in charge of property rights and local govt matters 2005–06; Deputy in Sabor (Ass.) 2005–, Chair. Legislation Cttee, mem. Cttee for the Constitution, Rules of Procedure and Political System, Cttee for Tourism; Minister of Justice 2006–08. *Leisure interests:* reading, classical music. *Address:* Croatian Democratic Union, 10000 Zagreb, trg Žrtava fašizma 4, Croatia (office). *Telephone:* (1) 4553000 (office). *Fax:* (1) 4552600 (office). *E-mail:* hdz@hdz.hr (office). *Website:* www.hdz.hr (office).

LOW, Frank James, BS, MA, PhD; American physicist, astronomer and academic; *Regents Professor Emeritus, University of Arizona;* b. 23 Nov. 1933, Mobile, Ala; m. Edith Low (née Morgan) 1956; one s. two d.; ed Yale Univ., Rice Univ.; mem. tech. staff Texas Instruments, Inc., Dallas 1959–62; Assoc.

Scientist Nat. Radio Astronomy Observatory, West Va. 1962–65; Research Prof., Univ. of Arizona 1965–, Regents Prof. 1988, now Regents Prof. Emer.; Founder and Pres. Infrared Laboratories, Inc., Tucson 1967, now Tech. Advisor; Prof. of Space Science, Rice Univ. 1966–71, Adjunct Prof. 1971–79; developed instrumentation for Spitzer Space Telescope; mem. NAS, American Astronomical Soc., American Physical Soc., Astronomical Soc. of the Pacific, American Acad. of Arts and Sciences; Helen Warner Prize, American Astronomical Soc. 1968, Rumford Prize, American Acad. of Arts and Sciences 1986, Joseph Weber Award, American Astronomical Soc. 2003, Jansky Lectureship, Nat. Radio Astronomy Observatory 2006, Bruce Medal, Astronomical Soc. of the Pacific 2006. *Achievements include:* invented low temperature bolometer and has made numerous other discoveries in the field of infrared astronomy; proposed, co-designed and built Infrared Astronomy Satellite (IRAS), which made first survey of infrared sky from space in 1983;. *Publications:* numerous articles in professional journals. *Address:* Steward 258, Department of Astronomy/Steward Observatory, 933 North Cherry Avenue, Tucson, AZ 85721-0065, USA (office). *Telephone:* (520) 621-2779 (office); (520) 621-2727 (office). *Fax:* (520) 621-1532 (office). *E-mail:* flow@as.arizona.edu (office). *Website:* www.as.arizona.edu (office); www.irlabs.com.

LOWASSA, Hon. Edward, MSc; Tanzanian politician; b. 1953; ed Univ. of Bath; Minister for Environment and Poverty 1988–2000; Man. Dir Arusha Int. Conference Centre 1989–90; Minister for Judiciary and Parliamentary Affairs 1990–93; Minister of Lands and Human Settlement Devt 1993–95; Minister of Water and Livestock Devt 2000–05; Prime Minister 2005–08 (resgnd). *Address:* c/o Office of the Prime Minister, POB 980, Dodoma, Tanzania (office).

LOWE, Douglas Ackley, AM; Australian fmr politician and administrator; b. 15 May 1942, Hobart; s. of Ackley Reginald Lowe and Dulcie Mary Lowe; m. Pamela June Grant 1963; two s. two d.; ed St Virgil's Coll.; worked as electrical fitter, Electrolytic Co.; State Sec. Tasmanian Section, Australian Labour Party 1965–69, State Pres. 1974–75; mem. Tasmania House of Ass. for Franklin 1969–81, Independent 1981–86; Minister for Housing 1972–74; Chief Sec. 1974–76; Deputy Premier 1975–77; Minister for Planning and Reorganization 1975–76, for Industrial Relations 1976–79, for Planning and Environment 1976, for Health 1976–77; Premier of Tasmania 1977–81; Minister for Manpower Planning 1977–79, for Econ. Planning and Devt 1979–80, for Energy 1979, Treas. 1980–81; mem. Tasmanian Legis. Council 1986–92; Deputy Govt Leader Tasmanian Legis. Council 1989–92; Exec. Officer, Tasmanian Br., Australian Medical Assn 1992–; Del. to Australian Constitutional Convention; Queen's Silver Jubilee Medal 1977; State Pres., Tasmanian Swimming Inc. 1991–98, Life mem. 2000–; Australian Sports Medal 2000, Centenary Medal 2000. *Publication:* The Price of Power 1984. *Leisure interests:* swimming, tennis, fishing, football. *Address:* Australian Medical Association (Tasmanian Branch), 2 Gore Street, South Hobart, Tasmania 7004 (office); 1 Michele Court, Berriedale, Tasmania 7010, Australia (home). *Telephone:* (362) 232-047 (office). *Fax:* (362) 236-469.

LOWE, Sir Frank Budge, Kt, FRSA; British business executive; b. 23 Aug. 1941; s. of Stephen Lowe and Marion Lowe; m. Dawn Lowe 1991; two s. one d.; ed Westminster School; Man. Dir Collett Dickenson Pearce 1972–79; Founder and Chair. Lowe Agency 1981–2003 (retd), Emer. Chair. 2003–; Founder and Chair. Octagon 1997–2003; Dir Interpublic 1990–2003; Founder and Chair. The Red Brick Road 2006–; Visiting Prof., Univ. Coll. London 1990–; The President's Award, Design and Art Dirs Assen of London 1985. *Leisure interests:* tennis, skiing, shooting. *Address:* The Red Brick Road, 50-54 Beak Street, London, W1F 9RN, England (office). *Telephone:* (20) 7575-7654 (office). *Website:* www.theredbrickroad.co.uk (office).

LOWRY, Glenn David, MA, PhD; American museum director; *Director, Museum of Modern Art;* b. New York; s. of Warren Lowry and Laure Lowry (née Lynn); m. Susan Chambers 1974; three s.; ed Williams Coll., Harvard Univ.; Asst Curator Fogg Art Museum, Harvard Univ. 1978–80; research asst in archaeological survey, Amalfi, Italy 1980; Curator (Oriental art) Museum of Art, Providence, RI 1981–82; Dir Joseph and Margaret Muscarelle Museum of Art, Williamsburg, Va 1982–84; Curator (Near Eastern Art) Freer Gallery, Smithsonian Inst., Washington 1984–90, Curatorial Co-ordinator 1987–89; Dir Art Gallery of Ont., Toronto 1990–95; Dir Museum of Modern Art, New York 1995–. *Publications include:* Fatehpur-Sikri: A Source Book 1985, From Concept to Context: Approaches to Asian and Islamic Calligraphy 1986, A Jeweler's Eye 1988, Timur and the Princely Vision: Persian Art and Culture in the Fifteenth Century 1989, Europe and the Arts of Islam: The Politics of Taste 1991. *Address:* Museum of Modern Art, 11 West 53rd Street, New York, NY 10019-5498, USA (office). *Website:* www.moma.org (office).

LOWY, Frank, AC; Australian business executive; *Chairman, Westfield Group;* b. 22 Oct. 1930, Czechoslovakia; m.; three s.; spent World War II years in Budapest, then moved to Palestine where he fought in underground Zionist army Haganah; immigrated to Australia 1952; Co-founder and Exec. Chair. Westfield Group (shopping centre co.) 1959–; Founder and Chair. Lowy Inst. for Int. Policy; mem. Int. Advisory Council, Brookings Inst.; Chair. Football Fed. Australia; fmr Pres. Art Gallery of New South Wales; fmr mem. Bd of Dirs Reserve Bank of Australia; Dir Daily Mail and General Trust, UK; Dr hc (Univ. of New South Wales), (Tel-Aviv Univ.); Australian Grad. School of Man. Financial Times Global Business Leader Award 2005, Woodrow Wilson Award for Corp. Citizenship, Woodrow Wilson Int. Center for Scholars 2005, Henni Friedlander Award for the Common Good, Bowdoin Coll., Brunswick, Me 2007. *Address:* Westfield Group, Westfield Towers, 100 William Street, Sydney 2011, Australia (office). *Telephone:* (2) 9358-7000 (office). *Fax:* (2) 9358-7079 (office). *Website:* www.westfield.com (office).

LOZANCIĆ, Niko; Bosnia and Herzegovina politician and lawyer; b. 1957, Kakanj; mem. Croatian Democratic Union (HDZ), Leader 2001, Vice-Pres. 2001–; fmr municipal councillor, mem. House of Peoples and state-level House of Reps; Pres. Fed. of Bosnia and Herzegovina 2003–07. *Address:* c/o Office of the President, 71000 Sarajevo, Bosnia and Herzegovina (office).

LOZI, Salem al-; Sudanese international organization executive; *Director-General, Arab Organization for Agricultural Development;* fmr Dir-Gen. Agricultural Marketing Org.; currently Dir-Gen. Arab Org. for Agricultural Devt, Khartoum, Sudan. *Address:* Arab Organization for Agricultural Development, 7 al-Amarat Street, PO Box 474, Khartoum 11111, Sudan (office). *Telephone:* (1) 83472176 (office). *Fax:* (1) 83471402 (office). *E-mail:* info@aoad.org (office). *Website:* www.aoad.org (office).

LOZOYA-SOLIS, Jesús; Mexican paediatric surgeon; b. 3 March 1910, Parral, Chihuahua; s. of the late Leodegario Lozoya and Josefa Solis; m. 1st Susana Thalmann 1937 (divorced 1958); m. 2nd Margarita Prieto de Lozoya 1959; four s. one d.; ed Mil. Medical School of Mexico, Western Reserve Univ. Hosp., Cleveland, Ohio, Harvard Univ. Children's Hosp.; founder of paediatric surgery in Mexico 1940–52; Hosp. Infantil of Mexico 1940–52; Asst Prof. Pediatrics and Surgical Pediatrics 1940; Pres. Mexican Soc. of Pediatrics 1948–50; Pres. Mexican br. American Acad. of Pediatrics 1944–46; Pres. Laboratorios Infan of Mexico 1949–; Pres. Mexican Soc. Pediatric Surgery 1958–60; Founder and first Pres. Pan-American Pediatric Surgery Asscn 1966–68, World Symposium Pediatric Surgery 1965–68, World Fed. Pediatric Surgeons 1974; Founder of Dept of Pediatrics of Armed Forces of Mexico 1940 (Prof. Emer. Mexico Mil. Medical School), Nat. Inst. for the Protection of Children 1958; Senator of the Repub. 1952–55; Gov. of Chihuahua 1955–56; Gen. of Mexican Army 1949 (retd 1977); Guest Prof. of Pediatric Surgery at numerous univs; mem. American Acad. of Pediatrics 1944, American Coll. of Surgeons 1945, American Mil. Surgeons Asscn, Mediterranean Acad.; Pres. organizing Cttee World Fed. of Pediatric Surgery Asscns 1972–74; Pediatric Surgery Adviser to Int. Pediatric Asscn 1980–83; Hon. mem. American Pediatric Surgical Asscn, Pacific; Asscn of Pediatric Surgeons and many other pediatric surgery asscns awards; Chevalier, Hospitalare of Malta 1976, Medical Benefactor 1976. *Publications:* Paediatría Quirúrgica 1959, México ayer y hoy, visto por un pedíatra mexicano 1965, La escuela médico militar de México 1977 and numerous articles. *Leisure interests:* history, philosophy, anthropology, writing, lecturing, gardening, travelling, riding. *Address:* Calzada Tlalpan 4515, México 22, DF, Mexico. *Telephone:* 5730094.

LU, (Hsiu-lien) Annette; Taiwanese politician; b. 7 June 1944, Taoyuan; ed Taiwan Prov. Taipei First Girls' High School, Nat. Taiwan Univ., Univ. of Illinois and Harvard Univ., USA; fmr Sr Specialist, Section Chief Exec. Law and Regulations Cttee of Exec. Yuan; participated in street demonstrations; sentenced to twelve years' imprisonment 1979, released after five years and four months on medical parole; f. N American Taiwanese Women's Asscn, Clean Election Coalition 1985–90; organized and led Alliance for the Promotion of UN Membership for Taiwan 1991; mem. Legis. Yuan for Taoyuan (Democratic Progressive Party), mem. Foreign Affairs Cttee 1992–95; Nat. Policy Adviser to Pres. 1996; Magistrate for Taoyuan Co. 1996–99; Vice-Pres. of Taiwan 2000–08; Chair. Third Global Summit of Women, Taiwan 1994; f. Centre for Women's and Children's Safety; World Peace Prize 2001. *Publications:* novels: These Three Women, Empathy; non-fiction: New Feminism, I Love Taiwan, Viewing Taiwan from Abroad, Retrying the Formosa Case. *Address:* c/o Democratic Progressive Party, 10/F, 30 Beiping East Rd, Taipei 10051, Taiwan.

LU, Daopei; Chinese medical scientist; b. Oct. 1931, Shanghai; ed Tongji Medical Coll.; doctor, Doctor-in-Charge, Chief Doctor, Prof. and Dir of Internal Medicine, People's Hosp. of Beijing Medical Coll. 1955–; Dir Blood Disease Research Inst., Beijing Medical Univ. of China; joined Chinese Peasants and Workers Democratic Party 1992, Chair. Beijing Municipal Cttee 1992–; Vice-Chair. CPPCC Beijing Municipal Cttee 1998–, mem. Standing Cttee 9th CPPCC Nat. Cttee 1998–2003; f. Daopei Hospitals Group; Vice-Chair. Chinese Medical Soc.; mem. Int. Bd of Marrow Transplantation Registration 1995–; Fellow, Chinese Acad. of Eng 1996–; initiator of bone-marrow transplants in China; Scientific and Technological Progress Award, Ho Leung Ho Lee Foundation 1997, Chen Jia-gen Prize for Promotion in Medicine & Pharmacy 1997. *Address:* Beijing Medical University, 42 Bei Lishi Lu, Beijing 100044, People's Republic of China (office). *Telephone:* (10) 68314422 (office).

LU, Gongxun; Chinese party official; *Chairman, Standing Committee, Shanxi Provincial People's Congress;* b. 1933, Shuozhou City, Shanxi Prov.; joined CCP 1950; worker, Org. Dept, CCP Yanbei Prefectural Cttee, Shanxi Prov. 1956–57; Deputy Dir, Rural Work Dept, Shuoxian Co., Shanxi Prov. 1957–65; Deputy Sec. CCP Youyu Co. Cttee, Shanxi Prov. 1965–70; Deputy Sec. CCP Zuoyun Co. Cttee, Shanxi Prov. 1970–82, Sec. 1982–83; Head, Org. Dept, CCP Shanxi Prov. Cttee 1983–89; mem. Standing Cttee, CCP Shuozhou City Cttee, Shanxi Prov. 1983–89, Deputy Sec. 1988–93; Pres. Party School, CCP Shanxi Prov. Committee 1988–93; Chair. Standing Cttee of People's Congress, Shanxi Prov. 1993–; Alt. mem. 12th CCP Cen. Cttee 1982–87, 13th Cen. Cttee 1987–92; Del., 14th CCP Nat. Congress 1992–97, 15th CCP Nat. Congress 1997–2002; Deputy, 8th NPC 1993–98, 9th NPC 1998–2003. *Address:* Shanxi Provincial Chinese Communist Party, Taiyuan, Shanxi, People's Republic of China (office).

LU, Guanqiu; Chinese business executive; *Chairman, Wanxiang Group;* b. Dec. 1944, Xiaoshan, Zhejiang Prov.; Founder, Ningwei Commune Farm Machinery Plant 1969; Founder and Pres. Hangzhou Wanxiang Group (producer and exporter of cardan joints) –2003, currently Chair.; Del., 13th CCP Nat. Congress 1987–92, 14th CCP Nat. Congress 1992–97, Deputy 9th NPC 1998–2003. *Address:* Wanxiang Group, Wang Xiang Road, Xiao Shan District, Hangzhou, Zhejiang Province, 311215, People's Republic of China (office). *Telephone:* (571) 82832999 (office). *Fax:* (571) 82602132 (office). *Website:* www.wanxiang.com (office).

LU, Hao; Chinese politician; *Governor of Gansu Province;* b. April 1947, Changli, Hebei Prov.; ed Shenyang School of Chemical Eng, Dalian Eng Coll., Lanzhou Univ.; technician, Research Inst., Group Army, PLA Services and Arms 1968–71; technician, No. 5266 Factory 1971–78, Personnel Sec. 1971–75; joined CCP 1981; teaching asst, political tutor, Lanzhou Univ. 1982; Deputy Dir then Dir, Gen. Office of CCP Gansu Prov. Cttee (Sec. Div.) 1982–85; Deputy Dir then Dir Org. Dept of CCP Gansu Prov. 1985–96; Sec. CCP Lanzhou City Cttee, Gansu Prov. 1996–2000; Gov. Gansu Prov. 2001–; Deputy Sec. CCP Gansu Prov. Cttee 2002–; Alt. mem. 15th CCP Cen. Cttee 1997–2002, mem. 16th CCP Cen. Cttee 2002–07, 17th CCP Cen. Cttee 2007–. *Address:* Office of the Governor, Gansu Provincial People's Government, Lanzhou, Gansu Province, People's Republic of China (office).

LU, Jianxun; Chinese telecommunications engineer; b. 11 Sept. 1929, Beijing; ed Tsinghua Univ.; fmrly Pres. China Ships Research Inst.; Chair. Standing Cttee Information and Electronic Eng Dept, Chinese Acad. of Eng; Fellow Chinese Acad. of Eng; Vice-Chair. China Shipbuilding Eng Soc.; presided over research and devt of communications system on submarines, pioneered research on long-wave communications and developed a range of communications equipment and systems for testing intercontinental ballistic missiles. *Address:* 2A Shuangquanbao, Deshengmen Wai, Beijing 100085, People's Republic of China (office). *Telephone:* (10) 64876644 (office). *Fax:* (10) 64881612 (office). *E-mail:* ljx@public.bta.net.cn (office).

LU, Lay Sreng; Cambodian politician; *Deputy Prime Minister and Minister of Rural Development;* b. 10 March 1937; ed California State Univ., Long Beach, USA; mem. resistance movt against Vietnamese occupation of Cambodia 1982–91; Minister of Information 1993–2003, Deputy Prime Minister and Minister of Rural Devt 2003–; First Vice-Pres. United Nat. Front for an Ind., Neutral, Peaceful and Co-operative Cambodia Party (Funcinpec). *Address:* Ministry of Rural Development, Jok Dimitrov, cnr rue 169, Phnom-Penh, Cambodia (office). *Telephone:* (23) 880007 (office). *E-mail:* mrd@cambodia.gov.kh (office). *Website:* www.mrd.gov.kh (office).

LU, Liangshu; Chinese agronomist; b. 3 Nov. 1924, Shanghai; s. of Lu Zezhi and Hu Lian; m. Yin Xueli 1950; three s.; deputy to 3rd NPC 1965, 5th NPC 1978; Deputy to 13th CCP 1988; Deputy Dir Science and Tech. Committee, Ministry of Agric. 1983; Pres. Chinese Acad. of Agricultural Sciences 1982–87; Pres. Chinese Asscn of Agricultural Science Socs 1982–92, now Hon. Pres.; mem. Chinese Acad. of Eng (Vice-Pres. 1994). *Publications:* Food Composition and Development Strategy in China, Compilation on China's Agricultural Devt Strategy and the Progress of Science and Tech. *Leisure interests:* swimming, music. *Address:* Chinese Academy of Agricultural Sciences, 30 Baishiqiao Road, Beijing 100081, People's Republic of China (office). *Telephone:* (10) 68975516 (office). *Fax:* (10) 62174142 (office). *E-mail:* xujm@mail.caas.net.cn (office).

LU, Peijian; Chinese banking executive; *Chairman, Board of Supervisors, China Development Bank;* b. Aug. 1928, Hongze Co., Jiangsu Prov.; m. Sheng Lixia 1985; three c.; joined CCP 1944, New 4th Army 1944; accountant, Cen. China and E China Mil. Commands 1944–49; Section Chief, later Div. Chief, later Deputy Dir Gen. Office, Ministry of Finance 1949–78, Vice-Minister of Finance 1978–82; Pres. People's Bank of China 1982–85; Auditor-Gen. Nat. Audit Office of China 1985–94; Chair. Governing Bd ASOSAI (Asian Org. of Supreme Audit Insts) 1991–94; Chair. Bd of Supervisors, China Devt Bank 1994–; mem. 12th CCP Cen. Cttee 1982–87, 13th CCP Cen. Cttee 1987–92, 14th CCP Cen. Cttee 1992–97; mem. Standing Cttee 9th CPPCC Nat. Cttee 1998–2003. *Address:* China Development Bank, No. 29 Fuchengmenwai Street, Xicheng District, Beijing 100037, People's Republic of China (office). *Telephone:* (10) 68306532 (office).

LU, Ping; Chinese civil servant; *Vice-Chairman, China Welfare Institute;* b. 7 Oct. 1927, Shanghai; m. Xi Liang 1949; one s. one d.; ed St John's Univ., Shanghai; Deputy Dir of Hong Kong and Macao Affairs Office, State Council 1987–90, Dir 1990–97; mem. 14th CCP Cen. Cttee 1992–97; Del. 15th CCP Nat. Congress; Vice-Chair. Preparatory Working Cttee for the Hong Kong Special Admin. Region 1993–95, Sec.-Gen. 1995; Dir Hong Kong Govt Admin. Dept 1994–97; Vice-Chair. China Welfare Inst. 1998–. *Address:* China Welfare Institute, Beijing, People's Republic of China (office).

LU, Qihui; Chinese sculptor; *Professor, Shanghai Oil Painting and Sculpture Institute;* b. 8 April 1936, Shanghai; d. of Ren Jin; m. Fang Zengxian 1960; one s. one d.; ed Sculpture Dept, Cen. Art Acad., E China Branch 1955–61; teacher, Shanghai Art College 1961–65; professional sculptor, Shanghai Oil Painting and Sculpture Inst. 1965–, Prof. 1988–; mem. Chinese Artists' Asscn. *Works include:* Transplanting rice seedlings, workers group statues, Nat. Industrial Exhibition 1960, Statue of Child Labourers 1974, Sculpture for Chairman Mao Memorial Hall 1977, Statue of Lu Xun 1979, Angrily Seeking Verses against Reign of Terror 1980, Plateau in the Morning Sun 1986, Bada, an ancient Chinese Artist 1987 (exhibited New York in Contemporary Oil Painting from the PRC), The Emotion at Plateau 1989, Zhang Zhong-Jingi a Pioneer of Chinese Medical Science 1990 (bronze), Song Jie-Cai Rang of a Tibetan 1990 (stone), Hawk-dancing 1991 (statue), Wang Ge-Ji memorial (bronze) 1992, Magic painter Mar-Lang (bronze) 1993, Wu Chan-Shu memorial (bronze), one for Shanghai Memorial Hall 1994, one for Japanese Fakuoka 1995, Xia-Qiu-Son (bronze) 1995, Balzac Memorial (bronze), Garden of Famous People, Shanghai 1996, Sampan (bronze), for Shanghai Stadium 1997, Wu Fu-Zhi memorial (bronze) 1998, The Sound of Spring (forging) 2001, Liu Kai-Qu memorial (bronze) 2004. *Leisure interests:* Chinese painting, sport. *Address:*

278, 333 Alley, Chang-Dong Road, Xin-Qiao Town, Song Jiang, Shanghai, People's Republic of China (home). *Telephone:* (21) 67644032 (home).

LU, Qikeng; Chinese mathematician; b. 17 May 1927, Fushan City, Guangdong Prov.; m. Mulan Zhang 1962; one s. one d.; ed Zhongshan Univ.; Research Fellow, Math. Inst. Academia Sinica 1978–; Deputy Dir of Math. Inst. 1981–83; Research Prof., Shantou Univ. 1994–; mem. Dept Math. and Physics, Academia Sinica 1980–92, Chinese Math. Soc. 1952–, Chinese Acad. of Sciences 1980–, American Math Soc. 1992–, AAAS 1996–, New York Acad. of Sciences 1997–; Hua Loo Keng Prize 1992. *Publications:* Introduction to Several Complex Variables 1961, Differential Geometry and its Application to Physics 1983, The Classical Manifolds and Classical Domains 1994, New Results of Classical Manifolds and Classical Domains 1997. *Leisure interest:* classical music. *Address:* Institute of Mathematics, Shantou University, Beijing 515063, People's Republic of China (office). *Telephone:* (10) 6254-1841 (office); (10) 6255-5142 (home). *Fax:* (10) 6256-8356.

LU, Rongjing; Chinese politician; b. 1933, Lujiang Co., Anhui Prov.; joined CCP 1954; Dir Tongguanshan Mine, Anhui Prov. 1968–76 (Sec. CCP Party Cttee 1968–76); fmr Deputy Sec. CCP Tongling City Cttee and Ma'anshan City Cttee, Anhui Prov.; Deputy Dir Industrial and Communications Office, Anhui Prov. 1978, Prov. Econ. Cttee 1979; Head, Org. Dept, CCP Anhui Prov. Cttee 1983–84, Deputy Sec. CCP Anhui Prov. Cttee 1985–88, Sec. 1988–98; Vice-Gov. Anhui Prov. 1987, Acting Gov. 1987–93; Chair. CPPCC Anhui Prov. Cttee 1996; mem. 13th CCP Cen. Cttee 1987–92, 14th CCP Cen. Cttee 1992–97, 15th CCP Cen. Cttee 1997–2002. *Address:* c/o Anhui Provincial Government, 1 Changjang Road, Hefei City, Anhui Province, People's Republic of China (office).

LU, Ruihua, MA; Chinese politician; *Governor of Guangdong Province;* b. Nov. 1938, Chaozhou City, Guangdong Prov.; ed Zhongshan Univ., Guangdong Prov.; joined CCP 1972; fmrly engineer, Deputy Dir, Dir Foshan Analytical Instrument Factory; fmrly Mayor of Foshan, Vice-Chair. Foshan City Econ. Cttee, mem. Standing Cttee CCP Guangdong Prov. Cttee, mem. then Deputy Sec. Standing Cttee CCP Foshan City Cttee; Vice-Gov. Guangdong Prov. 1991–96, Gov. 1996–; Deputy Sec. CCP Guangdong Prov. Cttee 1996– (mem. Standing Cttee 2002–); Alt. mem. 14th CCP Cen. Cttee 1992–97, mem. 15th CCP Cen. Cttee 1997–2002; Deputy 7th NPC 1988–93, 8th NPC 1993–98, 9th NPC 1998–2003. *Address:* People's Government of Guangdong, Guangzhou, Guangdong Province, People's Republic of China (office).

LU, Shengrong; Chinese sports official; b. 1940, Beijing; ed Beijing Foreign Languages Inst.; Vice-Pres. Int. Badminton Fed. 1984–93, Pres. 1993–2001; Chair. Int. Badminton Council; mem. IOC 1996–. *Address:* c/o State General Bureau for Physical Culture and Sports, 9 Tiyuguan Road, Chongwen District, Beijing, People's Republic of China (office).

LU, Shengzhong, MA; Chinese artist; b. 4 Jan. 1952, Pingdu Co., Shandong Prov.; s. of Lu Wanjin and Jiang Yongzhen; m. Liu Guangjun 1980; one s.; ed Cen. Acad. of Fine Arts; specializes in Chinese folk arts; Instructor at Cen. Acad. of Fine Arts; Deputy Sec.-Gen. Chinese Asscn of Fine Artists. *Works include:* When Heaven and Earth are in Harmony, All Living Things, Thrive, Life, Solitary Walking, Magic and Acrobatics. *Publications include:* Chinese Folk Papercut, Chinese Folk New Year Paintings, Arts from My Mother, Solitary Walk on the Holy Road, Outline of Chinese Folk Woodcut Print, Words of Calling the Souls. *Address:* Central Academy of Fine Arts, No.8 Hua Jia Di Nan St., Chao Yang District, Beijing 100102, People's Republic of China (office). *Website:* www.cafa.edu.cn (office).

LU, Shih-Peng, BA; Taiwanese historian and academic; b. 16 Sept. 1928, Kao-yu, Chiang Su; s. of the late Lu Chun-tai and Lu Chia Chu-yin; m. Julia Wei-chun; one s. one d.; ed Nat. Taiwan Univ., Taipei, Harvard Univ., USA; Teaching Asst, Nat. Taiwan Univ., Taipei 1953–55; Research Asst, Academia Sinica, Taipei 1955–58; Lecturer, Tunghai Univ., Taichung 1958–63, Assoc. Prof. 1963–67, Prof. of History 1967–, Dir Evening School 1972–81, Chair. Dept of History 1981–87, Dean Coll. of Arts 1988–94; Visiting Scholar, Harvard Univ. 1961–63; Outstanding Youth, China Youth Corps 1952; Outstanding Prof., Ministry of Educ. 1992. *Publications:* Vietnam during the period of Chinese Rule 1964, The Modern History of China 1979, The Contemporary History of China 1992. *Address:* Tunghai University, 181 Tunghai harbour Road, Sec. 3, Taichung, Taiwan (office). *Telephone:* (4) 3590121 (office). *Fax:* (4) 3590361 (office). *E-mail:* kpwang@mail.thu.edu.tw (office).

LU, Shumin; Chinese diplomatist; *Commissioner, Ministry of Foreign Affairs, Macao Special Administrative Region;* b. 24 Feb. 1950, Xi'an, Shanxi Province; m. Gao Shuqing; one d.; staff mem. Dept of N American and Oceanian Affairs, Ministry of Foreign Affairs 1976–77, Embassy in Canada 1977–79, Diplomatic Personnel Services Bureau, Beijing 1979–85; Third Sec., Embassy in Australia 1985; Second Sec. –1989; various staff positions at Ministry of Foreign Affairs including Deputy Div. Chief, Div. Chief, Counsellor –1993, Deputy Dir-Gen 1993–94, Counsellor, Embassy in USA 1994, Minister Counsellor –1998; Dir-Gen 1998–2002; Amb. to Indonesia 2002–05, to Canada 2005–08; Commr of Ministry of Foreign Affairs, Macao Special Admin. Region 2008–. *Address:* Office of the Commissioner of the Ministry of Foreign Affairs of the People's Republic of China, Macao Special Administrative Region, People's Republic of China (office). *E-mail:* fmco_mo@mfa.gov.cn (office). *Website:* www.fmcoprc.gov.mo (office).

LU, Xueyi; Chinese economist; b. 1933, Wuxi, Jiangsu Prov.; ed Beijing Univ. Inst. of Philosophy, Chinese Acad. of Social Sciences; Vice-Dir Rural Devt Research Inst., Vice-Dir then Dir Inst. of Sociology, Chinese Acad. of Social Sciences 1985–, currently Prof. and Sr Researcher. *Publications:* A Golden

Time for Agricultural Development, Contemporary Chinese Countryside, Contemporary Chinese Peasants. *Address:* Institute of Sociology, Chinese Academy of Social Sciences, Beijing, People's Republic of China (office). *Website:* www.sociology.cass.cn (office).

LU, Yongxiang; Chinese university professor and government official; *President, Chinese Academy of Sciences;* b. 28 April 1942, Ningbo City, Zhejiang Prov.; s. of Lu Zhau and Lee Feng; m. Diao Linlin 1966; one s. one d.; ed Zhejiang Univ., Tech. Univ. of Aachen, Germany; Asst Lecturer, Dept of Mechanical Eng, Zhejiang Univ. 1964–79, Assoc. Prof. 1981–83, Full Prof., Dir Inst. of Fluid Power Transmission and Control 1981–, Vice-Pres. Inst. of Science and Tech. 1985–88, Pres. and Deputy Dir 1988–95; Academician, Chinese Acad. of Sciences 1991, Vice-Pres. 1993–97, Pres. 1997–, mem. 4th Presidium of Depts 2000–; Vice-Chair. China Asscn for Science and Tech. 1986–96; mem. Academic Degrees Comm. of State Council 1986– (Vice-Chair. 1999), State Steering Group of Science, Tech. and Educ. 1998; mem. Third World Acad. of Sciences 1990 (Vice-Pres. 1998–), Chinese Acad. of Eng 1993, Nat. Natural Sciences Foundation of China; Del. NPC 1983–91; joined CCP 1964; mem. 14th CCP Cen. Cttee 1992–97, 15th CCP Cen. Cttee 1997–2002, 16th CCP Cen. Cttee 2002–07, 17th CCP Cen. Cttee 2007–; Vice-Chair. 10th NPC Standing Cttee 2003–08; Vice-Pres. First Council, China Overseas Friendship Asscn 1997; Foreign mem. German Acad. of Natural Scientists Leopoldina 2005, Russian Acad. of Sciences 2006; Hon. DEng (The Hong Kong Univ. of Science and Tech.) 1996; Second Prize for Nat. Invention 1988, Third Prize 1989, Higher Eng Educ. Prize of Nation 1989, Gao Hua Super Prize 1993, Rudolf Diesel Gold Medal (Germany) 1997, Abdus Salam Medal, Acad. of Sciences for the Developing World 2006, Max-Planck-Gesellschaft Harnack-Medaille (Germany) 2006, and many other awards and prizes. *Publications:* Electrohydraulic Proportional Technique 1988; more than 160 published papers and over 20 patents. *Leisure interests:* model aeroplanes, playing football. *Address:* Chinese Academy of Sciences, 52 Sanlihe Road, Beijing 100864, People's Republic of China (office). *Telephone:* (10) 68597289 (office). *Fax:* (10) 68512458 (office). *E-mail:* engach@mail.cae.ac.cn (office). *Website:* english.cas.ac.cn (office).

LU, Youmei; Chinese engineer; *Chairman, Chinese National Committee on Large Dams;* b. 1934, Taicang Co., Jiangsu Prov.; ed Dept of River Structure and Hydropower Station Construction of E China Inst. of Water Conservancy; mem. CCP 1956–; engineer Bureau for Construction of Liujia Gorge Hydro-power Station of Yellow River –1970; posts in various bureaux of Ministry of Water Conservancy and Electric Power 1978–84; Vice-Minister of Water Conservancy and Electric Power 1984–88; Vice-Minister, Ministry of Energy Resources 1988–93; Pres. China Yangtze Three Gorges Project Construction; Vice Chair. Three Gorges Project Construction Cttee 1993–; currently Chair. Chinese Nat. Cttee on Large Dams (CHINCOLD); mem. Chinese Acad. of Engineering 2003–. *Address:* Chinese National Committee on Large Dams, No. 20 West Chegongzhuang Road, POB 366, Beijing 100044, People's Republic of China (office). *E-mail:* chincold@iwhr.com (office). *Website:* www.chincold.org.cn (office).

LUBBERS, Ruud (Rudolphus) Frans Marie; Dutch politician and international organization official; b. 7 May 1939, Rotterdam; s. of Paulus J. Lubbers and Wilhelmine K. Van Laack; m. Maria E. J. Hoogeweegen 1962; two s. one d.; ed Erasmus Univ., Rotterdam; Sec. to Man. Bd, Lubbers Hollandia Eng Works 1963–65, Co-Dir 1965; mem. Bd Netherlands Christian Employers' Fed., Fed. of Mechanical and Electrical Eng Industries; mem. Programmes Advisory Council of Catholic Broadcasting Asscn; Minister of Econ. Affairs 1973–77; mem. Christian Democratic Appeal 1977, Parl. Leader 1978; mem. Second Chamber of States-Gen. (Parl.) 1977–2000; Prime Minister of the Netherlands 1982–94; Hon. Minister of State; taught Globalization Studies at Tilburg Univ. and John F. Kennedy School of Govt, Harvard Univ., USA 1995–2000; Chair. Globus, the Inst. for Globalization and Devt, Tilburg 1995–2000; Vice-Chair. Ind. World Comm. on the Oceans 1995–2000; UN High Commr for Refugees 2000–05 (resgnd); Dr hc (Radboud Univ., Nijmegen) 2004. *Address:* c/o United Nations High Commissioner for Refugees, CP 2500, 1211 Geneva 2 dépôt, Switzerland (office).

LUBCHENCO, Jane, BA, MS, PhD; American environmental scientist, academic and government official; *Under-Secretary of Commerce for Oceans and Atmosphere and Administrator, National Oceanic and Atmospheric Administration;* b. 4 Dec. 1947, Denver; m.; two c.; ed Colorado Coll., Univ. of Washington, Harvard Univ.; Asst Prof. of Ecology, Harvard Univ. 1975–77; Research Assoc. Smithsonian Inst. 1978–84; Asst Prof., Oregon State Univ. 1977–82, Assoc. Prof. 1982–88, Prof. of Zoology 1988–, Distinguished Prof. of Zoology 1993–, Wayne and Gladys Valley Prof. of Marine Biology 1995–2008; US Under-Sec. of Commerce for Oceans and Atmosphere and Admin. Nat. Oceanic and Atmospheric Admin, Washington, DC 2009–; Fellow, AAAS, Pres. 1997–98, Ed.-in-Chief Science 1999–2000; Pres. Ecological Soc. of America 1992–94; mem. Bd of Trustees David and Lucile Packard Foundation, Environmental Defense, Monterey Bay Aquarium 2001–04, Trustee Emer. 2004–; Commr Pew Oceans Comm.; mem. Bd of Dirs Royal Swedish Acad. of Sciences' Beijer Inst. of Environmental Econs; mem. NAS 1996–, American Acad. of Arts and Sciences, American Philosophical Soc., Nat. Science Bd; MacArthur Fellow and Pew Scholar in Conservation and the Environment; Pres. ICSU 2001–05; Founder and Co-Chair. Aldo Leopold Leadership Program; Dr hc (Drexel Univ.) 1992, (Colorado Coll.) 1993, (Bates Coll.) 1997, (Unity Coll.) 1998, (Southampton Coll.) 1999, (Long Island Univ.) 1999, (Princeton Univ.) 2001, (Plymouth State Coll.) 2002, (Michigan State Univ.) 2003; numerous awards, including Scientist of the Year, Oregon Acad. of Sciences and American Philosophical Asscn 1994, David B. Stone Award 1999, Golden Plate Award 2001, Howard Vollun Award 2001, Heinz Award in the Environment 2002, Ed Ricketts Memorial Award, Monterey Bay Nat. Marine

Sanctuary 2002, Nierenberg Prize for Science in the Public Interest, Scripps Inst. of Oceanography 2003, Distinguished Service Award, Soc. for Conservation Biology 2003, Distinguished Scientist Award, American Inst. of Biological Sciences 2004, Environmental Law Inst. Award 2004. *Publications include:* 50 publs on ecology, biodiversity, climate change, sustainability science and the state of the oceans. *Address:* National Oceanic and Atmospheric Administration, 1401 Constitution Avenue, NW, Room 6217, Washington, DC 20230, USA (office). *Telephone:* (202) 482-6090 (office). *Fax:* (202) 482-3154 (office). *Website:* www.noaa.gov (office).

LUBIMOV, Alexey Borisovich; Russian pianist and academic; *Professor, Moscow Conservatory;* b. 16 Sept. 1944, Moscow; m. Aza Lubimova; one d.; ed Moscow State Conservatory; soloist, chamber musician, pianist, harpsichordist, organist; organizer and artistic dir of chamber ensembles and festivals of experimental character; well-known performer on historical keyboard instruments 1980–; teacher Moscow Conservatory 1968–75, Prof. 1997–; Prof. Univ. Mozarteum, Salzburg 1999–; winner, int. competitions in Rio de Janeiro 1965 (First Prize) and Montreal 1968; Honoured Artist of Russia 2003. *Recordings:* more than 40 CDs (classical, Baroque and contemporary music) 1990–2004, Silvestrov: Metamusik 2003, Pärt's Lamentate 2005. *Leisure interests:* collecting ancient keyboard instruments. *Address:* Mr. Helge R. Augstein, Munich, Germany (office); Klimentovskiy per. 9, Apt 12, Moscow, Russia (home). *Telephone:* (89) 26024333 (office); (495) 951-62-51 (home). *Fax:* (89) 26024344 (office); (495) 629-51-45 (office); (495) 951-62-51 (home). *E-mail:* mail@augstein.info (office); alexeilubimov@mail.ru (home). *Website:* www.augstein.info (office).

LUBIN, Steven, BA, MS, PhD; American pianist; *Adjunct Professor, School of the Arts, Purchase College, State University of New York;* b. 22 Feb. 1942, New York; s. of Jack Lubin and Sophie Lubin; m. Wendy Lubin 1974; two s.; ed Harvard Univ., Juilliard School, New York Univ.; piano studies with Lisa Grad, Nadia Reisenberg, Seymour Lipkin, Rosina Lhevinne, Beveridge Webster; recital and concert tours in USA, Canada, Mexico, UK, France, Netherlands, Spain, Italy, Germany, Austria, Finland, Australia and Ukraine; f. The Mozartean Players 1978–; mem. Faculty Juilliard School 1964–65, Aspen Music School 1967, Vassar Coll. 1970–71, Cornell Univ. 1971–75; Adjunct Prof., School of the Arts, State Univ. of New York, Purchase, NY 1975–; Martha Baird Rockefeller Grant 1968, Stereo Review Recording of the Year Award 1988, Kempner Distinguished Professor Award, State Univ. of New York, Purchase, NY 1999–2001. *Recordings:* complete Beethoven Piano Concertos, Mozart and Schubert Trios, Six Mozart Concertos as soloist and conductor and other solo and chamber music. *Publications:* articles in The New York Times, Keynote, Ovation, Keyboard Classics and Historical Performance, Brahms Soc. Newsletter 1999; contrib. to The Complete Schwanengesang 2000. *Leisure interests:* reading about relativity and quantum mechanics. *Address:* Hunstein Artist Services, 65 West 90th Street, Suite 13F, New York, NY 10024, USA (office); Conservatory of Music, School of the Arts, State University of New York, Purchase, NY 10577, USA (office). *Telephone:* (212) 724-2693 (office); (914) 251-6715 (office). *Fax:* (212) 724-9393 (office). *E-mail:* DAH@hunsteinartists.com (office). *Website:* www.hunsteinartists.com (office); www.stevenlubin.com.

LUBOVITCH, Lar; American choreographer; *Artistic Director, Lar Lubovitch Dance Company;* b. 9 April 1943, Chicago, Ill.; ed Univ. of Iowa, Juilliard School; danced in numerous modern, ballet and jazz cos; Founder and Artistic Dir Lar Lubovitch Dance Co. 1968–; has choreographed more than 100 dances for the co.; his works are included in repertoires of most major int. dance cos including New York City Ballet, American Ballet Theater, Paris Opera Ballet, Royal Danish Ballet, Stuttgart Ballet, White Oak Dance Project and Netherlands Dance Theatre; has created dances for ice-skaters including John Curry; Guggenheim Fellowship 1971, Astaire Award 1994, Elan Award 2004. *Dances created include:* Whirligogs (music by Luciano Berio) 1969, The Time Before the Time After (After the Time Before) (Stravinsky) 1971, Les Noces (Stravinsky) 1976, Marimba (Steve Reich) 1976, Exultate, Jubilate (Mozart) 1977, Scriabin Dances (Scriabin) 1977, North Star (Philip Glass) 1978, Cavalcade (Reich) 1980, Beau Danube (Strauss) 1981, Big Shoulders (no music) 1983, A Brahms Symphony 1985, Concerto Six Twenty-Two (Mozart) 1986, Sleeping Beauty (Tchaikovsky; full-length televised ice-dancing version starring Robin Cousins and Rosalynn Sumners) 1987, Into the Woods (Sondheim) 1987, Musette (Poulenc) 1988, Rhapsody in Blue (Gershwin) 1988, Fandango (Ravel) 1989, Waiting for the Sunrise (Les Paul and Mary Ford) 1991, American Gesture (Charles Ives) 1992, The Red Shoes (Jule Styne; Astaire Award, Theater Devt Fund 1994) 1993, The Planets (Holst) (Emmy Award 1995, Grammy Award 1995) 1994, Oklahoma! (Rodgers and Hammerstein) 1994, The King and I (Rodgers and Hammerstein) 1996, Adagio (Bach) 1996, Othello (Goldenthal) 1997, Meadow (Schubert, etc.) 1999, The Hunchback of Notre Dame (Menken) 1999, Men's Stories (Marshall) 2000, My Funny Valentine (Rodgers) 2001, Smile With My Heart (Laird) 2002, Artemis (Chris Theofanidis) 2003, Pentimento (Richard Woodbury) 2004, Love Stories (Kurt Elling) 2005, Elemental Brubeck (Brubeck) 2005, Recordare (Goldenthal) 2005, Little Rhapsodies (Schumann; solo version) 2006, (trio version) 2007, Serenade (Dvorak) 2007, Cryptoglyph (Monk) 2007. *Film:* The Company (Robert Altman) 2003. *Television:* The Sleeping Beauty 1987, Concerto Six Twenty-Two and North Star/Dancemaker 1988, Fandango/Pictures From the Edge 1989, The Planets 1995, Othello 2003. *Address:* Lar Lubovitch Dance Company, 229 West 42nd Street, 8th Floor, New York, NY 10036, USA (office). *Telephone:* (212) 221-7909 (office). *Fax:* (212) 221-7938 (office). *E-mail:* lubovitch@aol.com (office). *Website:* www.lubovitch.org (office).

LUBRANI, Uri; Israeli diplomatist; *Adviser, Ministry of Defence;* b. 7 Oct. 1926, Haifa; s. of Ahron Lubrani and Rose Lubrani; m. Sarah Levi 1953; four d.; ed Univ. of London, UK; fmr Head of Chancery, Office of Foreign Minister, Office of Prime Minister, Adviser to Prime Minister on Arab Affairs; later Amb. to Uganda, Rwanda, Burundi, Ethiopia and Iran; now Govt Co-ordinator for Lebanese Affairs; in charge of airlift of 18,000 Ethiopian Jews (Falashas) to Israel 1991; head Israeli team, negotiations on release of Israeli hostages in Lebanon and Shia Muslim prisoners in Israel; head Israeli del. to bilateral peace talks with Lebanon, Washington, DC 1992; now Adviser to the Minister of Defence; Hon. DPhil (Ben-Gurion Univ.) 1991, (Beer) 1991; Jabotinsky Annual Award for Services to the Jewish People 1991, David Ben-Gurion Award. *Address:* Office of the Adviser to the Minister of Defence, Ministry of Defence, Hakirya, Tel-Aviv (office); Shamgar Street 34, Tzahala, Tel-Aviv, Israel (home). *Telephone:* (3) 6975157 (office); (3) 6474919 (home). *Fax:* (3) 6977358 (office); (3) 6493084 (home). *E-mail:* liban@mod.gov.il (office).

LUCAS, Sir Colin Renshaw, Kt, MA, DPhil, FRHistS; British academic; *Warden, Rhodes House Oxford;* b. 25 Aug. 1940; s. of the late Frank Renshaw Lucas and of Janine Charpentier; m. 1st Christiane Berchon de Fontaine Goubert 1964 (divorced 1975); one s.; m. 2nd Mary Louise Hume 1990; ed Sherborne School, Lincoln Coll., Oxford; Asst Lecturer, then Lecturer Sheffield Univ. 1965–69; Visiting Asst Prof., Indiana Univ., USA 1969–70; Lecturer, Univ. of Manchester 1970–73; Fellow, Balliol Coll. Oxford and Lecturer in Modern History, Univ. of Oxford 1973–90; Prof., Chicago Univ., USA 1990–94, Dean Div. of Social Sciences 1993–94; Master Balliol Coll. 1994–2001; Pro-Vice-Chancellor Univ. of Oxford 1995–97, Vice-Chancellor 1997–2004; Warden Rhodes House, Oxford 2004–; Chair. British Library 2006–; Officier des Arts et des Lettres 1990; Chevalier, Ordre nat. du Mérite 1994, Officier 2005; Chevalier, Légion d'honneur 1998; Hon. DLitt (Lyon) 1989, (Sheffield) 2000, (Univ. of WA) 2000, (Glasgow) 2001, (Princeton) 2002, (Beijing) 2002, (Francis Xavier) 2003, (Oxford) 2003, (Oxford Brookes) 2004, (Warwick) 2006. *Publications:* The Structure of the Terror 1973, Beyond the Terror (with G. Lewis) 1983, The Political Culture of the French Revolution (ed.) 1988; contribs to academic journals. *Address:* Rhodes House, South Parks Road, Oxford, OX1 3RG, England. *Telephone:* (1865) 270902 (office). *Fax:* (1865) 270914 (office). *E-mail:* warden@rhodeshouse.ox.ac.uk (office).

LUCAS, Cornel, FRPS, FBIPP; British photographer; b. 12 Sept. 1920, London; s. of the late John Thomas Lucas and of Mary Elizabeth Lucas; m. Jennifer Susan Linden Travers 1960; three s. one d.; ed Westminster Univ.; RAF Photographic School 1941–46; mem. staff Two Cities Films, Denham, Pinewood Studios, Columbia Pictures, Universal Int. Films 1947–59; opened own studios No. 2, Chelsea Manor Studios, London 1959, Man. Dir 1959–; work in perm. collections of Nat. Portrait Gallery, Nat. Museum of Photography, Museum of Photography, Bradford, Royal Photographic Soc., Bath, Jersey Museum of Photography; Hon. mem. BAFTA; BAFTA Award for outstanding contrib. to British Film Industry. *Publication:* Heads and Tales 1988, Shooting Stars 2005. *Leisure interests:* painting, music, gardening, golf. *Address:* 57 Addison Road, London, W14 8JJ, England. *Telephone:* (20) 7602-3219.

LUCAS, Craig, BFA; American playwright and screenwriter; b. 30 April 1951, Atlanta, Ga; s. of Charles Samuel Lucas and Eleanore Alltmont Lucas; ed Boston Univ.; Rockefeller and Guggenheim Fellowships; mem. Dramatists' Guild, PEN, Writers' Guild of America; Sundance Audience Award, Obie and Outer Critics' Award, Los Angeles Drama Critics' Award, two Tony nominations. *Plays:* Missing Persons 1980, Reckless 1983, Blue Window 1984, Prelude to a Kiss 1987 and The Scare 1989, God's Heart 1994, The Dying Gaul 1996, Savage Light (with David Schulner) 1996. *Musicals:* Marry Me a Little (anthology of songs by Stephen Sondheim) 1981, Three Postcards (music and lyrics by Craig Carnelia) 1987, The Light in the Piazza 2004. *Films:* Blue Window 1987, Longtime Companion 1990, Prelude to a Kiss 1991, Reckless 1995, Secret Lives of Dentists 2002, The Dying Gaul 2005. *Address:* c/o Peter Franklin, William Morris Agency, 1325 Aveue of the Americas, New York, NY 10019, USA. *E-mail:* craig.lucas@mac.com (home).

LUCAS, George W., Jr., BA; American screenwriter and film director and producer; *Chairman and CEO, Lucasfilm Ltd.;* b. 14 May 1944, Modesto, Calif.; ed Univ. of Southern Calif. School of Cinema-TV; apprenticeship at Warner Brothers Studios; co-founder (with Francis Ford Coppola) American Zoetrope (film production co.) 1969; f. Lucasfilm Ltd 1971, now includes Lucasfilm Animation Ltd, Lucas Digital (Industrial Light & Magic and Skywalker Sound), LucasArts Entertainment Co., Lucas Licensing; founder and Chair. George Lucas Educational Foundation; mem. Bd of Councilors Univ. of Southern Calif. School of Cinema-TV; Dr hc (Univ. of Southern Calif.) 1994; Irving Thalberg Award 1992, American Film Inst. Lifetime Achievement Award 2005, Inaugural Filmmaker's Award from Motion Picture Sound Editors 2005. *Films include:* writer and dir: Look at Life 1965, Herbie 1966, Freiheit 1966, The Emperor 1967, Anyone Lived in a Pretty How Town 1967, Filmmaker 1968, American Graffiti 1973; producer: Kagemusha 1980, Body Heat 1981, Twice Upon a Time 1983, Howard the Duck 1986; writer and producer: Star Wars Episode V: The Empire Strikes Back 1980, Raiders of the Lost Ark 1981, Star Wars Episode VI: Return of the Jedi 1983, Indiana Jones and the Temple of Doom 1984, Captain Eo 1986, Willow 1988, Indiana Jones and the Last Crusade 1989, Radioland Murders 1994; writer, producer and dir: THX 1138 1971, Star Wars Episode IV: A New Hope 1977, Star Wars Episode I: The Phantom Menace 1999, Star Wars Episode II: Attack of the Clones 2002, Star Wars Episode III: Revenge of the Sith 2005. *Address:* Lucasfilm Ltd, 5858 Lucas Valley Road, Nicasio, CA 94946 (office); George Lucas Educational Foundation, POB 3494, San Rafael, CA 94912, USA. *Telephone:* (415) 662-1800 (office). *Fax:* (415) 448-2495 (office). *E-mail:* george.lucas@lucasfilm.com (office). *Website:* www.lucasfilm.com (office); www.edutopia.org.

LUCAS, Michel; French banking executive; *President and Chairman of the Management Board, CIC Crédit Industriel & Commercial SA;* joined Confédération Nationale du Crédit Mutuel 1971, has held several exec. positions, currently CEO; Gen. Man. Banque Federative du Crédit Mutuel, Caisse Centrale du Crédit Mutuel, Crédit Mutuel Centre Est Europe; Pres. and Chair. Man. Bd CIC Crédit Industriel & Commercial SA 1998–; Pres. Assurances du Crédit Mutuel; Pres. Europay France SA –2004, Vice-Pres. 2004–; Dir Regional Bd MasterCard Europe 1992–, Vice-Chair. 2002–, Dir MasterCard International Inc. 2004–; mem. Bd of Dirs Banque de Luxembourg, Banque de Tunisie, Banque Marocaine du Commerce Extérieur, Caisses Desjardins, Banque Transatlantique. *Address:* CIC Crédit Industriel & Commercial SA, 6 avenue de Provence, 75452 Paris 9, France (office). *Telephone:* 1-45-96-96-96 (office). *Fax:* 1-45-96-96-66 (office). *E-mail:* filbass@cic.fr (office). *Website:* www.cic.fr/en (office).

LUCAS, Robert Emerson, BA, PhD; American economist and academic; *John Dewey Distinguished Service Professor, Department of Economics, University of Chicago;* b. 15 Sept. 1937, Yakima, Wash.; Asst Prof. of Econs, Carnegie Inst. of Tech. 1963–67; Assoc. Prof. Carnegie-Mellon Univ. 1967–70, Prof. 1970–74; Prof. Univ. of Chicago 1975–80, John Dewey Distinguished Service Prof. 1980–; Assoc. Ed. Journal of Monetary Econs 1977–; Ed. Journal of Political Economy 1988–; Fellow AAAS; mem. NAS; Dr hc (Université Paris-Dauphine) 1992, (Athens Univ. of Econs and Business) 1994, (Univ. of Montreal) 1998; Nobel Prize for Econs 1995. *Publications:* Studies in Business-Cycle Theory 1981, Lectures in Economic Growth 2001. *Address:* Department of Economics, University of Chicago, 1126 E 59th Street, Chicago, IL 60637, USA (office). *E-mail:* relucas@uchicago.edu (office). *Website:* home.uchicago.edu/~sogrodow (office); economics.uchicago.edu.

LUCAS, Sarah, BA; British artist; b. 1962, London; d. of Irene Lucas; ed Working Men's Coll., London, London Coll. of Printmaking, Goldsmiths Coll., London; emerged as one of the major Young British Artists during the 1990s; works with a variety of materials and media, including photographs, sculpture and installations that use humour and visual puns to explore gender. *Dance:* Before and After: The Fall, The Michael Clark Co. (set design for a new work performed on tour) 2001. *Television:* Two Melons and a Stinking Fish (Illuminations for BBC TV/Arts Council) 1996, This Is Modern Art (Channel 4 six-part series) 1999, The History of Britart (BBC) 2001. *Address:* c/o Sadie Coles HQ, 69 South Audley Street, London W1K 2QZ, England. *Telephone:* (20) 7493-8611. *Fax:* (20) 7499-4878. *E-mail:* info@sadiecoles.com (office). *Website:* www.sadiecoles.com (office).

LUCE, Baron (Life Peer), cr. 2000, of Adur in the County of West Sussex; **Richard Napier Luce,** Kt, PC, GCVO, DL; British politician; b. 14 Oct. 1936, London; s. of the late Sir William Luce, GBE, KCMG and of Lady Luce (née Margaret Napier); m. Rose Helen Nicholson 1961; two s.; ed Wellington Coll. and Christ's Coll., Cambridge, Wadham Coll. Oxford; Subaltern, Wilts. Regiment, Nat. Service 1955–57; Dist Officer, Kenya 1961–63; Marketing Man. Gallaher Ltd 1963–65; Marketing Man. Spirella Co. of GB 1965–67; Dir Nat. Innovation Centre 1967–71; mem. European Advisory Bd Corning Glass Int. 1976–79; Dir (non-exec.) Booker Tate 1991–96, Meridian Broadcasting 1991–97; MP for Arundel and Shoreham 1971–74, for Shoreham 1974–92; Opposition Whip 1974–75; Opposition Spokesman, Foreign and Commonwealth Affairs 1977–79; Parl. Under-Sec. of State 1979–81; Minister of State, FCO 1981–82, 1983–85; Minister of State (Minister for the Arts) and Minister of State for Civil Service, Privy Council Office 1985–90; Gov. and C-in-C Gibraltar 1997–2000; Lord Chamberlain of her Majesty's Household 2000–06; Vice-Chancellor Univ. of Buckingham 1992–96; Chair. Atlantic Council of UK 1991–96, Commonwealth Foundation 1992–96; mem. Royal Mint Advisory Cttee, Bd Trustees, Royal Collection Trust; Pres. Voluntary Arts Network, Royal Overseas League, King George V Fund for Actors and Actresses; Vice-Pres. Friends of the Commonwealth Foundation; Trustee Geographers' Map Trustees Ltd (A–Z); Trustee Emer. Royal Acad. of Arts; Vice-Patron Harambee and Langalanga Trusts; Parl. Crossbencher (Independent) in the House of Lords; Hon. Vice-Pres. Overseas Pensioners' Asscn; Hon. Fellow, Christ's Coll. Cambridge; Hon. Fellow, Atlantic Council of the UK; KStJ. *Publications:* Ringing the Changes: A Memoir 2007. *Leisure interests:* walking, swimming, painting, reading, piano. *Address:* c/o House of Lords, Westminster, London, SW1A 0PW, England.

LUCE, R(obert) Duncan, PhD; American mathematical psychologist and academic; *Distinguished Professor Emeritus, School of Social Sciences, University of California, Irvine;* b. 16 May 1925, Scranton, Pa; s. of Robert R. Luce and Ruth Downer Luce; m. 1st Gay Gaer 1950; m. 2nd Cynthia Newby 1967; one d.; m. 3rd Carolyn A. Scheer 1988; ed Massachusetts Inst. of Tech.; mem. staff, Research Lab. of Electronics, MIT 1950–53; Asst Prof. of Sociology and Math. Statistics, Columbia Univ., New York 1954–57; Fellow, Center for Advanced Study in the Behavioral Sciences 1954–55, 1966–67, 1987–88; Lecturer in Social Relations, Harvard Univ. 1957–59, Prof. of Psychology 1976–83, Victor S. Thomas Prof. of Psychology 1984–88, Prof. Emer. 1988–; Prof. of Psychology, Univ. of Pennsylvania 1959–68, Benjamin Franklin Prof. 1968–69; Prof. of Social Science, Univ. of California, Irvine 1972–75, Distinguished Prof. of Cognitive Sciences 1988–94, Dir Irvine Research Unit in Math. Behavioral Science 1988–92, Dir Inst. for Math. Behavioral Sciences 1992–98, Distinguished Research Prof. of Cognitive Sciences and Research Prof. of Econs 1994–, now Distinguished Prof. Emer.; Visiting Prof., Inst. for Advanced Study, Princeton, NJ 1969–72; mem. NAS, American Acad. of Arts and Sciences, American Philosophical Soc., Soc. of Experimental Psychologists; American Psychological Asscn Distinguished Scientific Contrib. Award 1972, American Psychological Foundation Gold Medal for Life Achievement 2001, Univ. of Calif. Irvine Award 2001, Daniel G. Aldrich, Jr Distinguished Univ. Service Award 2003, Frank P. Ramsey Medal, Decision Analysis Soc. 2003, Nat. Medal of Science 2003, Norman Anderson Lifetime Contrib. Award, Soc. of Experimental Psychologists 2004. *Publications:* Games and Decisions (with H. Raiffa), Individual Choice Behavior, Handbook of Mathematical Psychology (co-ed.), Contemporary Developments in Mathematical Psychology (co-ed.), Foundations of Measurement Vols I, II, III (with D. H. Krantz, P. Suppes and A. Tversky) 1971, 1989, 1990, Response Times, Stevens' Handbook of Experimental Psychology (co-ed.), Sound & Hearing, Utility of Gains and Losses: Measurement – Theoretical and Experimental Approaches 2000; more than 218 articles in scientific journals. *Leisure interests:* art, gardening. *Address:* 2133 Social Sciences Plaza A, University of California, Irvine, CA 92697-5100 (office); 20 Whitman Court, Irvine, CA 92612-4057, USA (home). *Telephone:* (949) 824-6239 (office); (949) 854 8203 (home). *Fax:* (949) 824-3733 (office). *E-mail:* rdluce@uci.edu (office). *Website:* www.imbs.uci.edu/personnel/luce/luce.html (office).

LUCIE-SMITH, (John) Edward (McKenzie), MA, FRSL; British art critic and poet; b. 27 Feb. 1933, Kingston, Jamaica; s. of John Dudley Lucie-Smith and Mary Lushington; ed King's School, Canterbury, Merton Coll. Oxford; officer RAF 1954–56; fmrly worked in advertising and as freelance journalist and broadcaster; contributes to The Times, Sunday Times, Independent, Mail-on-Sunday, Spectator, New Statesman, Evening Standard, Encounter, London Magazine, Illustrated London News; mem. Acad. de Poésie Européenne. *Publications as sole author include:* A Tropical Childhood and Other Poems 1961, Confessions and Histories 1964, What is a Painting? 1966, Thinking About Art 1968, Towards Silence 1968, Movements in Art Since 1945 1969, Art in Britain 69–70 1970, A Concise History of French Painting 1971, Symbolist Art 1972, Eroticism in Western Art 1972, The First London Catalogue 1974, The Well Wishers 1974, The Burnt Child (autobiog.) 1975, The Invented Eye (early photography) 1975, World of the Makers 1975, Joan of Arc 1976, Fantin-Latour 1977, The Dark Pageant (novel) 1977, Art Today 1977, A Concise History of Furniture 1979, Super Realism 1979, Cultural Calendar of the Twentieth Century 1979, Art in the Seventies 1980, The Story of Craft 1981, The Body 1981, A History of Industrial Design 1983, Art Terms: An Illustrated Dictionary 1984, Art in the Thirties 1985, American Art Now 1985, Lives of the Great Twentieth Century Artists 1986, Sculpture Since 1945 1987, Art in the Eighties 1990, Art Deco Painting 1990, Fletcher Benton 1990, Jean Rustin 1991, Harry Holland 1992, Art and Civilisation 1992, Andres Nagel 1992, Wendy Taylor 1992, Alexander 1992, British Art Now 1993, Race, Sex and Gender: Issues in Contemporary Art 1994, American Realism 1994, Art Today 1995, Visual Arts in the Twentieth Century 1996, Arts Erotica: an Arousing History of Erotic Art 1997, Adam 1998, Stone 1998, Zoo 1998, Judy Chicago: an American Vision 2000, Flesh and Stone 2000, Changing Shape (poems) 2002, Censoring the Body 2008; has edited numerous anthologies. *Leisure interest:* the Internet. *Address:* c/o Pat White, Rogers, Coleridge and White, 20 Powis Mews, London, W11 1JN, England (office). *Telephone:* (20) 7221-3717 (office). *Fax:* (20) 7229-9084 (office). *E-mail:* info@rcwlitagency.com (office); edward@edwardlucie-smith.co.uk (office). *Website:* www.rcwlitagency.com (office); www.edwardlucie-smith.co.uk.

LUCINSCHI, Petru, CandPhilSc, PhD; Moldovan fmr head of state and politician; *Head, Foundation for Strategic Studies and Development of International Relations;* b. 27 Jan. 1940, Floreşti; s. of Chiril Lucinschi and Parascovia Lucinschi; m. Antonina Georgievna Lucinschi 1965; two s.; ed Kishinev (Chişinău) Univ. and CPSU Cen. Cttee Higher Party School; served in Soviet Army 1962–63; Komsomol work for Cen. Cttee of Moldavian CP 1963–71; mem. CPSU 1964–91; First Sec. of Bălti City Komsomol Cttee 1964–65; Head of Section, Second Sec., First Sec. of Cen. Cttee of Moldavian Komsomol 1965–71; Sec. of Cen. Cttee of Moldavian CP 1971–76, First Sec. Nov. 1989–91; First Sec. of Kishinev City Cttee 1976–78; Deputy Head, Propaganda Dept of CPSU Cen. Cttee 1978–86; Second Sec. of Cen. Cttee of Tadzhik CP 1986–89; Cand. mem. of CPSU Cen. Cttee 1986–89, mem. 1989–91, Sec. 1990–91; Deputy to USSR Supreme Soviet 1986–89; USSR People's Deputy 1989–91; mem. CPSU Politburo, 1990–91; Moldovan Amb. to Russia 1992–93; fmr Leader Agrarian Democratic Party; Chair. Moldovan Parl. 1993–2001; Pres. of Moldova 1996–2000; Head, Foundation for Strategic Studies and Devt of Int. Relations 2001–; mem., Russian Fed. Social Sciences Acad.; Chevalier, Légion d'honneur 1998, Order of Repub. of Moldova; Dr hc (Minsk, Baku); numerous awards, including Int. Pilgrim of Peace Award, Assisi (Italy). *Publications:* The Last Days of the USSR 1998, The Life and Death 2003, Moldova and Moldavians 2007. *Leisure interests:* sports, travelling, reading, theatre, hunting. *Address:* 76 Bucuresti str., Chişinău, Moldova (home). *Telephone:* (22) 237979 (office). *Fax:* (22) 237981 (office). *E-mail:* office@ipa.dnt.md (office).

ŁUCZAK, Aleksander Piotr, PhD; Polish politician and historian; *Vice-President, National Broadcasting Council;* b. 10 Sept. 1943, Legionowo; m. Janina Zakrzewska; one d.; ed Warsaw Univ. and Adam Mickiewicz Univ., Poznań; mem. United Peasants' Party (ZLS) 1966–91; mem. Polish Peasants' Party (PSL) 1991–; lecturer, Dept of History of the Peasant Movt Cen. Cttee ZSL until 1976; mem. Faculty, Univ. of Warsaw 1976–, Asst Prof. 1983–91, Prof. 1991; Adviser to Pres. of Cen. Cttee ZSL 1976–79; Head, Dept of Ideology, Press and Propaganda, Cen. Cttee PSL 1986, Vice-Chair., Head Council PSL 1991–97; Deputy Minister of Nat. Educ. 1986–87; Head, Office of Council of Ministers June–Oct. 1992; Deputy Prime Minister and Minister of Educ. 1993–94; Deputy Prime Minister, Minister and Head of Scientific Research Cttee 1994–96; Minister and Head of Scientific Research Cttee 1996–97; Deputy to Sejm (Parl.) 1989–2001; Chair. Polish Asscn of Adult Educ. 1995–2001; Pres. World Scout Parl. Union 1997–2000; mem. Nat. Broadcasting Council (KRRiT) 2001–, Vice-Pres. 2003–. *Publications:* more than 30 publs on recent history of Poland and the peasant movt. *Leisure interest:* tennis. *Address:* National Broadcasting Council, ul. Sobieskiego 101,

00-763 Warsaw, Poland (office). *Telephone:* (22) 8402379 (office). *E-mail:* luczak@krrit.gov.pl (office).

LUDER, Owen (Harold), CBE, FRSA, PP RIBA; British architect, planner, environmentalist and writer; b. 7 Aug. 1928, London; s. of the late Edward Charles Luder and of Ellen Clara Luder; m. 1st Rose Dorothy (Doris) Broadstock 1951 (divorced 1988); one s. (deceased) four d.; m. 2nd Jacqueline Ollerton 1989; ed Brixton School of Building, Regent St Polytechnic Evening School of Architecture (now Univ. of Westminster), Brixton School of Architecture; f. Owen Luder Partnership 1957, Sr Partner until 1978 (when partnership became unlimited co.), Chair. and Man. Dir 1978–87; f. Owen Luder Consultancy Communication in Construction 1988–2003; Dir (non-exec.) Jarvis PLC 1995–2003; Council mem. RIBA 1967–97, Hon. Treas. 1975–78, Pres. 1981–83, Sr Vice-Pres. 1994–95, Pres. 1995–97, Architect mem. Architects' Registration Bd and Vice-Chair. 1997–2002, Chair. 2002–03; Pres. Norwood Soc. 1982–92; Sec.-Treas. Commonwealth Asscn of Architects 1985–87; Pres. UIA Congress 1986; Vice-Pres. Membership Communications 1989–90; Dir Communication in Construction Ltd 1990; Consultant to Nat. Coal Bd for environmental, architectural and planning issues on Vale of Belvoir Coal Mining Project, UK 1975–87; Architect/Planner for revitalization schemes for British Rail Eng Works at Shildon, Co. Durham and Swindon; consultant for many commercial devt schemes, architectural consultant and qualified mediator; mem. Acad. of Experts 1992–, Vice-Chair. 1997–98; RIBA Architecture Bronze Medal 1963, Town Planning and Housing Council Silver Jubilee Award 'Housing in the 80s', Business Consultant of the Year 1985, and various other architectural, design and civic trust awards and commendations. *Publications:* Adventure in Architecture – A Portrait of the Owen Luder Partnership 1976, Promotion and Marketing for Building Professionals 1988, Sports Stadia After Hillsborough 1990, Keeping Out of Trouble 1999; frequent contribs to nat. and tech. publs. *Leisure interests:* photography, writing, Arsenal Football Club, swimming. *Address:* Owen Luder Consultancy Ltd, Apartment 702, Romney House, 47 Marsham Street, London, SW1P 3DS, England (office). *Telephone:* (20) 7222-0198 (office). *E-mail:* owen.luder@dial.pipex.com (office).

LUDEWIG, Johannes, PhD; German civil servant and business executive; *Executive Director, Community of European Railways and Infrastructure Companies;* b. 6 July 1945, Hamburg; m.; three c.; ed Univ. of Hamburg, Stanford Univ., USA, Ecole Nat. d'Admin., Paris, France; worked on energy, econ. and business policy, Fed. Ministry of Econs 1975–83; joined Office of the Fed. Chancellor 1983, Ministerial Dir, Dept of Econ. and Financial Policy 1991–94; fmr State Sec., Fed. Ministry of Econs; fmr Commr of Fed. Govt for New German Fed. States; mem. Exec. Bd Deutsche Bahn AG 1997–99, Chair. 1997–99; currently Exec. Dir Community of European Railways and Infrastructure Cos (CER). *Address:* CER, 53 Avenue des Arts, 1000 Brussels, Belgium (office). *Telephone:* (2) 213-08-71 (office). *Fax:* (2) 512-64-32 (office). *E-mail:* johannes.ludewig@cer.be (office). *Website:* www.cer.be (office).

LUDFORD, Baroness (Life Peer), cr. 1997, of Clerkenwell in the London Borough of Islington; **Sarah Ludford,** MSc; British politician; b. 14 March 1951; d. of Joseph Campbell Ludford and Valerie Kathleen Ludford (née Skinner); m. Steve Hitchins; ed Portsmouth High School for Girls, London School of Econs; barrister, called to the Bar Gray's Inn 1979; official, Secr.-Gen. and Directorate Gen. Competition, EC 1979–85; European and UK policy adviser, Lloyds of London 1985–87; Vice-Pres. Corp. External Affairs, American Express European 1987–90; freelance Euro consultant 1990–99; mem. Liberal Democrat Party; Councillor (Liberal Democrat) Islington Borough Council 1991–99; Vice-Chair. Liberal Democrat Federal Policy Cttee 1991–98; Vice-Pres. Gay and Lesbian Lib Dems (DELGA); MEP (Liberal Democrat) for London 1999–; mem. Council European Liberal Democrat and Reform (ELDR) Party; mem. Cttee on Citizens' Freedoms and Rights, Justice and Home Affairs, Foreign Affairs, Human Rights, Common Security and Defence Policy; mem. Inter-Parl. dels: Cyprus, South-East Europe (also Vice-Pres.); ELDR spokeswoman on Justice and Home Affairs; rapporteur on Anti-Racism, European Parl. 2000, on Legal Rights for EU-resident foreign nationals 2001–02; Vice-Pres. European Parl. Inter-Group on Anti-Racism, co-ordinating European Parl. Kurdish Network; mem. Royal Inst. of Int. Affairs, European Movt. *Publications include:* The EU: From Economic Community to Human Rights Community (article); contrib. to To the Power of Ten 2000. *Leisure interests:* theatre, ballet, gardening. *Address:* European Parliament, Office 10-G-65, Rue Wiertz, 1047 Brussels, Belgium (office); Constituency Office, 36 St Peter's Street, London, N1 8JT (office); House of Lords, Westminster, London, SW1A 0PW, England. *Telephone:* (2) 284-71-04 (Belgium) (office); (20) 7288-2526 (office); (20) 7219-5353 (House of Lords). *Fax:* (2) 284-91-04 (office); (20) 7288-2581 (office). *E-mail:* sludford@europarl.eu.int (office); sludfordmep@cix.co.uk (office). *Website:* www.sarahludfordmep.org.uk (office).

LUDWIG, Christa; Austrian/French singer (mezzo-soprano); b. 16 March 1928, Berlin, Germany; d. of Anton Ludwig and Eugenie Besalla-Ludwig; m. 1st Walter Berry 1957 (divorced 1970, died 2000); one s.; m. 2nd Paul-Emile Deiber 1972; opera debut at 18, guest appearance at the Athens Festival in Epidauros 1965; joined Vienna State Opera 1955, Hon. mem. 1981; appearances at Festivals in Salzburg, Bayreuth, Lucerne, Holland, Prague, Saratoga, Stockholm; guest appearances in season in Vienna, New York, Chicago, Buenos Aires, Milan, Berlin, Munich; numerous recitals and soloist in concerts; Hon. mem. Vienna Konzerthaus, Vienna Philharmonic; Hon. Prof.; Commdr des Arts et des Lettres 1989; Chevalier, Légion d'honneur 1989; Grosses Ehrenzeichen 1994; Commdr, Ordre pour le Mérite (France) 1997; Officier de la Légion d'honneur 2003; winner of Bach-Concours, record award for Fricka in Walküre and Des Knaben Wunderhorn, awarded title of Kammersängerin by Austrian Govt 1962, Prix des Affaires Culturelles for recording of Venus in Tannhäuser, Paris 1972, Silver Rose (Vienna Philharmonic) 1980, Golden Ring (Staatsoper, Vienna) 1980, Golden Gustav Mahler Medal 1980, Hugo Wolf Medal 1980, Gold Medal (City of Vienna) 1988, Midem Classical Lifetime Achievement Award 2008. *Recordings include:* Lieder and complete operas including Norma (with Maria Callas), Lohengrin, Così fan tutte, Der Rosenkavalier, Carmen, Götterdämmerung, Die Walküre, Bluebeard's Castle, Don Giovanni, Die Zauberflöte, Le Nozze di Figaro, Capriccio, Fidelio. *Publication:* In My Own Voice (biog.) 1994. *Leisure interests:* music, archaeology, reading, home movie making, cooking, sewing, fashion, shopping, weaving, rug knitting and travelling. *Address:* 1458 Ter, Chemin des Colles, 06740 Châteauneuf de Grasse, France; c/o Heidrun Artmüller, Goethegasse 1, 1010 Vienna, Austria. *Telephone:* (4) 97010531 (home). *Fax:* (4) 97010529 (home).

LUEDERITZ, Alexander, DrIur; German professor of law; b. 19 March 1932, Göttingen; s. of Heinrich Luederitz and Gertrud Luederitz; m. Renate (née Wessling) Luederitz 1960; one s. one d.; ed Cologne School of Law and Lausanne School of Law, Switzerland; mem. of the Bar 1961–65; Prof. of Law, Frankfurt Univ. 1966–70, Dean, Faculty of Law 1969–70; Prof. of Law and Dir Inst. for Int. and Foreign Pvt. Law, Univ. of Cologne 1971–, Dean, Faculty of Law 1979–80; Visiting Prof. Univ. of Calif., Berkeley 1982, Univ. d'Auvergne 1989, 1991, Univ. of Ill., Urbana 1995, Univ. of Toulouse 1995, 1996; Fellow, American Council of Learned Socs. *Publications:* Auslegung von Rechtsgeschäften 1966, International Sales 1991, International Privatrecht 1992, Commentary on German Conflicts Law (Corporation, Agency, Torts) 1996, Family Law 1997; articles in learned journals. *Leisure interests:* hiking, stamp collecting. *Address:* Kellerhardtsweg 12, 51503 Roesrath, Germany. *Telephone:* (221) 470-2288; (2205) 3124. *Fax:* (221) 470 5129; (2205) 3124.

LUERS, William Henry, MA, FAAS; American diplomatist and museum president; *President and CEO, United Nations Association of the USA;* b. 15 May 1929, Springfield, Ill.; s. of Carl U. Luers and Ann L. Luers; m. Wendy Woods Turnbull 1979; three s. one d. by previous marriage and two step-d.; ed Hamilton Coll., Columbia and Northwestern Univs; Foreign Service Officer Dept of State 1957; Vice-Consul, Naples, Italy 1957–60; Second Sec. Embassy, Moscow 1963–65; Political Counsellor, Caracas, Venezuela 1969–73; Deputy Exec. Sec., Dept of State 1973–75; Deputy Asst Sec. for Inter-American Affairs, Washington 1975–77, Deputy Asst Sec. for Europe 1977–78; Amb. to Venezuela 1978–82, to Czechoslovakia 1983–86; Pres. Metropolitan Museum of Art, New York 1986–99; Pres. and CEO UN Asscn of USA 1999–; mem. Bd Rockefeller Brothers Fund, AOL-Latin America, Scudder Funds, Wickes Corpn; mem. Council on Foreign Relations, American Acad. of Arts and Sciences, American Acad. of Diplomacy; Hon. LLD (Hamilton Coll.) 1982; American Foreign Service Cup 1988. *Address:* UNA-USA, 801 Second Avenue, New York, NY 10017 (office); 419 East 57th Street, Apt 14A, New York, NY 10022, USA (home). *Telephone:* (212) 907-1313 (office); (212) 593-0586 (home). *Fax:* (212) 972-3585 (office). *E-mail:* wluers@unausa.org (office). *Website:* www.unausa.org (office).

LUGANSKY, Nikolai L.; Russian pianist; b. 26 April 1972, Moscow; s. of Lev Borisovich Lugansky and Anna Nikolayevna Luganskaya; m. Lada Borisovna Luganskaya; one s. one d.; ed Moscow State Conservatory; wide repertoire comprises over 40 piano concertos and music from Bach to modern composers; ensemblist and interpreter of chamber music; performances in Russia and abroad in Australia, Austria, Belgium, Brazil, Canada, England, France, Germany Italy, Japan and elsewhere, including at the Royal Festival Hall and Wigmore Hall in London, the Gaveau and Louvre in Paris, Conservatoria Verdi in Milan, Gasteig in Munich, Concertgebouw in Amsterdam, Alte Oper in Frankfurt; first prize All-Union students' competition Tbilisi Georgia 1988, silver medal Bach Int. Competition, Leipzig, Germany 1988, second prize Rachmaninov Competition, Moscow 1990, first prize Tchaikovsky Int. Competition, Moscow 1994, Terence Judd award for the most promising pianist of a generation 1995. *Recordings include:* some 25 albums. *Leisure interests:* chess, table tennis, reading. *Address:* Opus 3 Artists, 470 Park Avenue South, 9th Floor North, New York, NY 10016, USA (office); Kosygina str. 2, apt 2, Moscow 119334, Russia (home). *Telephone:* (212) 584-7500 (office); (495) 137-18-36 (home). *Fax:* (646) 300-8200 (office). *E-mail:* info@opus3artists.com (office). *Website:* www.opus3artists.com (office).

LUGAR, Richard Green, MA; American politician; *Senator from Indiana;* b. 4 April 1932, Indianapolis, Ind.; s. of Marvin L. Lugar and Bertha Green Lugar; m. Charlene Smeltzer 1956; four s.; ed Shortridge High School, Denison Univ., Ohio, Pembroke Coll., Oxford Univ.; Rhodes Scholar, Pembroke Coll. Oxford 1956; served USN 1957–60; Vice-Pres. and Treas. Thomas Green & Co. Inc. 1960–67, Sec.-Treas. 1968; Treas. Lugar Stock Farms Inc. 1960; mem. Bd of Trustees, Denison Univ. 1966, Advisory Bd, Ind. Univ., Purdue Univ. at Indianapolis 1969–75, Bd of Trustees of Ind. Cen. Univ. 1970; Vice-Chair. 1975, Visiting Prof. of Political Science, Dir of Public Affairs 1975–76; mem. Visiting Cttee of Harvard–MIT Jt Centre for Urban Studies 1973; mem. Bd of Dirs, Indianapolis Centre for Advanced Research 1973–76; mem. Indianapolis Bd of School Commrs 1964–67, Vice-Pres. 1965; Mayor of Indianapolis 1968–75; del. and keynote speaker, Ind. Republican Convention 1968, del. 1972; del. mem. Platform Cttee, Repub. Nat. Convention 1968, del., keynote speaker and mem. Platform Cttee 1972; Candidate for US Senate 1974, Senator from Indiana 1977–; mem. Advisory Comm. on Intergovernmental Relations 1969–75, Vice-Chair. 1970–75; mem. Advisory Bd of US Conf. of Mayors 1969–75; mem. Pres. Model Cities Advisory Task Force 1969–70, State and Local Govt Advisory Cttee of Office of Econ. Opportunity 1969–73, Nat. Advisory Comm. on Criminal Justice Standards and Goals 1971–73; Pres. of Advisory Council, Nat. League of Cities 1971, mem. Council 1972–75; Chair. Nat. Republican Senatorial Cttee 1983–84; Chair. Foreign Relations Cttee 1985–87, 2003–, Cttee on Agric. 1995–2001;

mem. Bd of Dirs Westview Osteopathic Hosp. 1969–76, Indianapolis Symphony Orch., Nat. Endowment for Democracy; mem. Nat. Acad. of Public Admin, Rotary Club of Indianapolis and other civic orgs; Trustee Denison Univ., Indianapolis Univ.; Hon. Doctorates from 20 colls and univs in USA 1970–78; Exceptional Service Award, Office of Econ. Opportunity 1972, Fiorello La Guardia Award, New School of Social Research 1975. *Publication:* Letters to the Next President 1988. *Leisure interests:* music, reading, running, golf, tennis. *Address:* 306 Hart Senate Office Building, Washington, DC 20510, USA (office). *Telephone:* (202) 224-4814 (office). *E-mail:* senator_luga@lugar.senate.gov (office). *Website:* lugar.senate.gov (office).

LUGO MÉNDEZ, Fernando Armindo; Paraguayan politician, fmr bishop and head of state; *President;* b. 30 May 1951, San Solano; one s.; ed Catholic Univ. of Our Lady of the Assumption, Pontifical Gregorian Univ., Rome; ordained priest of Soc. of the Divine Word 1977; moved to Ecuador as missionary in Bolivar prov., then studied in Rome; returned to Paraguay, appted Bishop of San Pedro 1994–2005 (resgnd), resgnd from priesthood 2006; Leader, Movimiento Popular Tekojoja; Pres. of Paraguay 2008–. *Address:* Palacio de López, Asunción (office); Movimiento Popular Tekojoja, Asunción, Paraguay. *Telephone:* (21) 4140200 (office). *E-mail:* joaquinbonett@gmail.com. *Website:* www.presidencia.gov.py (office).

LUHRMANN, Bazmark (Baz) Anthony; Australian film and theatre director; b. 17 Sept. 1962, NSW; s. of Leonard and Barbara Luhrmann; m. Catherine Martin 1997; one d.; ed Narrabeen High School, Sydney; theatre work with Peter Brook (q.v.); owns Bazmark Inq. production co., Sydney; acting roles in films The Winter of Our Dreams 1982, The Dark Room 1984; directed advertisement for Chanel No. 5 2004. *Recording:* Something for Everybody (concept album, including track Everybody's Free To Wear Sunscreen) (Platinum Album, Australia, Gold Album, USA). *Films:* Strictly Ballroom 1992 (Cannes Film Festival Prix de la Jeunesse, Toronto Film Festival People's Choice Award, Chicago Film Festival Award for Best Feature Film), La Bohème (TV) 1993, Romeo + Juliet 1996, Moulin Rouge 2001 (numerous awards including Golden Globe, Producers' Guild of America Film of the Year, Hollywood Film Festival Best Movie). *Plays:* Strictly Ballroom, Haircut. *Operas directed:* La Bohème, Sydney 1990, New York 2002–03, San Francisco 2002, A Midsummer Night's Dream, Sydney 1993. *Television includes:* A Country Practice (actor) 1981–82. *Screenplays written:* Strictly Ballroom 1992, Romeo + Juliet 1996, Moulin Rouge (also story) 2001. *Address:* Bazmark Inq, PO Box 430, Kings Cross, NSW 1340, Australia (office); c/o Robert Newman, The Endeavor Agency, 9601 Wilshire Blvd., 10th Floor, Beverly Hills, CA 90212, USA (office). *Telephone:* (2) 9361-6668 (office). *Fax:* (2) 9361-6667 (office). *Website:* www.bazmark.com (office).

LUHRMANN, Reinhard; German biochemist and academic; *Director, Department of Cellular Biochemistry, Max Planck Institute of Biophysical Chemistry;* fmrly with Institut für Molekularbiologie und Tumorforschung, Marburg; currently Dir Dept of Cellular Biochemistry, Max-Planck-Institut für biophysikalische Chemie, Göttingen; Feldberg Foundation Prize Lecturer 2002. *Publications:* numerous articles in scientific journals. *Address:* Max-Planck-Institut für biophysikalische Chemie, Abteilung Zelluläre Biochemie, Am Faßberg 11, 37077 Göttingen, Germany (office). *Telephone:* (551) 201-1405 (office). *Fax:* (551) 201-1197 (office). *E-mail:* reinhard.luehrmann@mpi-bpc.mpg.de (office). *Website:* www.mpibpc.gwdg.de/abteilungen/index_en.html (office).

LUI, Frank Fakaotimanava; Niuean politician; Premier of Niue 1993–99, also Minister for External Relations, Niueans Overseas, Police and Immigration, Civil Aviation and Public Service Comm. *Address:* c/o Office of the Premier, Alofi, Niue.

LUIK, Jüri; Estonian diplomatist, politician and journalist; *Permanent Representative, NATO;* b. 17 Aug. 1966, Tallinn; m. one s.; ed Tallinn 7th High School, Tartu Univ. and postgraduate research, Carnegie, USA; Political Ed. Vikerkaar (monthly) 1988–90, Ed. 1990; specialist on Anglo-Saxon Countries, Estonian Inst. 1989–91; mem. Pro Patria (Isamaaliit) Party 1989–; attaché, Embassy of Estonia, UK 1991; Head, Political Dept, Ministry of Foreign Affairs 1991–92; mem. Riigikogu (Parl.) 1992–95; Minister without portfolio responsible for Estonian-Russian Negotiations 1992–93; Minister of Defence 1993–94, 1999–2002, of Foreign Affairs 1994–95; Sr Research Fellow, Carnegie Foundation 1995–96; Amb. to NATO and Benelux States, Brussels 1996–99; head of govt del. for accession talks with NATO 2002–03; Amb. to USA (also accred to Canada) 2003–07, Perm. Rep. to NATO, Brussels 2007–. *Leisure interests:* theatre, films, tennis. *Address:* Office of the Permanent Representative of Estonia, Blvd Léopold III, 1110 Brussels, Belgium (office). *Telephone:* (2) 707-41-11 (home). *Fax:* (2) 707-45-79 (office). *E-mail:* natodoc@hq.nato.int (office). *Website:* www.nato.int (office).

LUKAS, D. Wayne, EdM; American race horse trainer; b. 2 Sept. 1935, Antigo, Wis.; s. of Ted Lukas and Bea Lukas; m. Laura Lukas; one s.; ed Univ. of Wisconsin; began career as Asst Basketball Coach, Univ. of Wisconsin, then Head Basketball Coach, LaCrosse High School; later spent more than ten years training quarter horses, with a record 150 wins; switched to training thoroughbreds 1978; six consecutive Triple Crown race wins: Tabasco Cat–Preakness 1994, Belmont 1994, Thunder Gulch–Derby 1995, Belmont 1995, Timber Country–Preakness 1995, Grindstone–Kentucky Derby 1996; total of 16 Breeder's Cup wins; all-time leading money winner (over US $200 million); now makes guest appearances as motivational speaker; four-time Eclipse Award winner–Trainer of the Year, Nat . Museum of Racing's Hall of Fame 1999. *Address:* c/o Program Resources Professional Speakers Bureau, P.O. Box 22307, Louisville, KY 40252, USA (office).

LUKASHENKA, Alyaksandr Rygorovich; Belarusian politician, economist and head of state; *President;* b. 30 Aug. 1954, Kopys; m. Halyna Rodionovna Lukashenko (estranged); two s.; ed Mogilev State Univ. and Belarus Agric. Acad.; served in Soviet Army 1975–77, 1980–82; Sec. Komsomol Cttee, Shklov, instructor Political Div. Komsomol Cttee W Border Dist 1975–77; Sec. Komsomol Cttee Mogilev City Food Dept; instructor regional Exec. Cttee 1977–80; Deputy Commdr of Co. 1980–82; Deputy Chair. Udarnik collective farm 1982–83; Deputy Dir Enterprise of Construction Materials 1983–85; Sec. CP Cttee Collective Farm of V.I. Lenin, Shklov Dist 1985–87; Dir Gorodets state farm 1987–94; elected Deputy of Supreme Council of Belarus SSR 1990–94; Chair. Parl. Comm. on Struggle against Corruption 1993–94; elected Pres. of Belarus 1994–; C-in-C Armed Forces of Belarus 1994–; Chair. Higher Council of Belarus and Russia Union 1997–; Chair. Supreme State Council of the Union State of Belarus and Russia 2000–; Hon. Academician, Russian Acad. of Sciences 1995; Order of the Holy Cross of the Kts of the Holy Sepulchre 2000, Order of St Vladimir (First Class), Russian Orthodox Church 2007; M. Sholokhov Int. Award 1997. *Address:* Office of the President, 220016 Minsk, vul. K. Marksa 38, Dom Urada, Belarus (office). *Telephone:* (17) 222-35-03 (office). *Fax:* (17) 222-30-20 (office). *E-mail:* press@president.gov.by (office). *Website:* www.president.gov.by (office).

LUKE, Hon. Justice Desmond Edgar Fashole, BL, MA; Sierra Leonean chief justice (retd), diplomatist and politician; b. 6 Oct. 1935, Freetown; s. of Sir Emile Fashole-Luke and Lady Christina Fashole-Luke; one s. one d.; ed Prince of Wales School, Freetown, King's Coll., Taunton, UK, Keble Coll., Oxford, UK, Magdalene Coll., Cambridge, UK, Georgetown Univ., Washington, DC, USA; admitted to Bar of England and Wales 1962, of Sierra Leone 1963; in pvt. practice, barrister and solicitor 1963–69; Legal Adviser to Mobil Oil, British Petrol, Bata Shoe Co., Barclays Bank, Diamond Corpn, Allen & Elliot (SL) Ltd, Singer Sewing Machine Co. Ltd, Trade Marks Owners' Asscn, Adams and Adams Patent Attorneys and other industrial and commercial cos 1963–69; UN Human Rights Fellow, India 1964; Amb. to FRG (also accred to Netherlands, Belgium and Luxembourg 1970–73) 1969–73, to France, Italy and Perm. Rep. to EEC 1971–73; Deputy Leader Del. to Heads of State Summit of OAU, Addis Ababa, Non-Aligned Summit, Algeria 1969, Commonwealth Prime Minister's Conf., Ottawa 1973, Abidjan Peace Talks 1996, ECOWAS Conf., Abuja 1997, UN Gen. Ass., NY 1997; Leader Del. to IAEA Conf., Vienna 1970, to African Econ. Conf., Milan 1971, to Council of Ministers of OAU, Addis Ababa 1973–75, to UN Gen. Ass., NY 1973–74; Minister of Foreign Affairs 1973–75 (resgnd), of Health 1977–78; Man. Dir Africa Int. Ltd 1975; Chair. Comm. for Consolidation of Peace 1996–97; Chief Justice of Sierra Leone 1998–2002; Special Envoy of Pres. Kabbah to Pres. Kuffour of Ghana 2002; Grand Cross Order of Merit (FRG) 1973, Grand Cordon of Order of Menelik II (Ethiopia) 1973; Oxford Blues Athletic Awards 1955–58, finalist (long jump) Commonwealth Games, Cardiff 1958, Oxford and Cambridge Freshman's Champion and Record Holder (high jump) 1954; Men in Action Certificate of Merit for Contrib. to Restoration of Democracy in Sierra Leone 1999, Jarwlee Lewis Meritorious Award for Services to State 2001. *Publications include:* Republican Constitution: What Form?. *Leisure interests:* sports, art, music. *Address:* c/o Office of the Chief Justice, Supreme Court, Freetown (office); Luke House, PO Box 214, Freetown, Sierra Leone (home). *Telephone:* (22) 231863 (office). *Fax:* (22) 225670 (office). *E-mail:* fasholeluke@yahoo.com (home).

LUKIANENKO, Levko (Hryhorovych); Ukrainian politician and lawyer; b. 24 Aug. 1928, Chrypivka, Chernigiv Region; s. of Hryzko Lukianenko and Natalka Lukianenko; m. Nadia Oleyandrivna Lukianenko; two d.; ed Moscow M.V. Lomonosov State Univ.; mem. CPSU 1953–61; served in Soviet Army 1944–53; legal adviser, Lvov CPSU Regional Cttee 1958–59; barrister 1959–61; sentenced to death 1961 for formation of Ukrainian Workers' and Peasants' League, but sentence commuted to 15 years' imprisonment, released 1976; Co-Founder, on release, of Ukrainian Helsinki Group 1976, again arrested, sentenced to 10 years' imprisonment and 5 years' exile, returned to Ukraine 1989; mem. Verkhovna Rada (Parl.) 1990–92, 1994–98, 2002–06; Chair. Ukrainian Republican Party 1990–92, 2000–02, 2005–, Hon. Chair. 1992–; Presidential Cand. Ukrainian elections 1991; Amb. to Canada 1992–93; Chair. Ukrainian Asscn of Researchers into Famine in Ukraine; Academician Acad. of Higher School of Ukraine 2002; Hero of Ukraine 2005; Hon. LLD (Alberta); Merit of Honour of Ukrainian Pres. *Publications:* Confession from the Condemned Cell 1991, For Ukraine 1991, I Believe in God and Ukraine 1991, I Do Not Permit Ukraine to Perish 1994, The Birth of a New Era 1997, In the Land of the Maple Leaf 1998, National Idea and National Will 2003, Indestructibility 2004, From the Time of Imprisonment 2005. *Leisure interests:* music, gardening. *Address:* 5 Hrushevsky Street, 01008, Kiev (office); 20 Sadova Street, v. khotiv, Kyivo-Sviatosh District, 08171 Kiev, Ukraine (home). *Telephone:* (44) 255-34-08 (office); (44) 255-16-84 (home). *Fax:* (44) 489-05-27 (office); (44) 989-33-25 (home).

LUKIN, Vladimir Petrovich, PhD, DSc; Russian politician and diplomatist; *Commissioner for Human Rights (Federal Ombudsman);* b. 13 June 1937, Omsk; m.; two s.; ed Moscow State Pedagogical Inst., USSR Acad. of Sciences; researcher, Museum of Revolution, Inst. of World Econs and Int. Relations, USSR Acad. of Sciences 1959–65; on staff of journal World Review, Prague until Aug. 1968 when he was recalled to USSR for protesting against Soviet invasion of Czechoslovakia; Research Fellow, Inst. of US and Canadian Studies, USSR Acad. of Sciences 1969–87; Deputy Dir Dept of Assessment and Planning of the USSR Ministry of Foreign Affairs 1987–90; People's Deputy of RSFSR (now Russia) 1990–93; Chair. Foreign Affairs Cttee of the Russian Supreme Soviet 1990–92; Amb. to USA 1992–93; Co-Founder and Leader, pre-election bloc (later political movt) Yabloko (with G. Javlinsky) 1993, currently Deputy Chair.; mem. State Duma (Parl.) 1993–2003, Chair. Cttee for Foreign Affairs 1994–99; Deputy Chair. State Duma 2000–02; Commr for Human Rights of Russian Fed. (Fed. Ombudsman) 2004–; two decorative orders, one medal. *Publications include:* Centres of Power: Conceptions and Reality,

China's Place in US Global Policy, With Concern and Hope: Russia and the West. *Leisure interests:* sport. *Address:* Office of the Commissioner for Human Rights in the Russian Federation, Myasnitskaya str. 47, 103084 Moscow (office); c/o Yabloko Party, Novy Arbat str. 21, 18th Floor, 121019 Moscow, Russia (office). *Telephone:* (495) 207-39-69 (office). *Fax:* (495) 207-39-77 (office). *E-mail:* lukin@rodnet.ru (office). *Website:* www.ombudsman.gov.ru (office).

LUKMAN, Rilwanu, BSc, CEng; Nigerian international civil servant, business executive and engineer; b. 26 Aug. 1938, Zaria, Kaduna State; s. of Qadi Lukman and Hajia Ramatu Lukman; m. 1966; two s. one d.; ed Govt Coll. Zaria (now Barewa), Nigerian Coll. of Arts, Science and Tech. (now Ahmadu Bello Univ.), Royal School of Mines, Imperial Coll. of Science and Tech., Univ. of London, Inst. of Prospecting and Mineral Deposits, Univ. of Mining and Metallurgy, Leoben, Austria, McGill Univ., Montreal, Canada; Asst Mining Engineer, A.G. Statagruvor, Sweden 1962–64; Inspector of Mines and Sr Inspector of Mines, Ministry of Mines and Power, Jos 1964–67, Acting Asst Chief Inspector of Mines 1968–70; Gen. Man. Cement Co. of Northern Nigeria Ltd, Sokoto 1970–74; Gen. Man. and Chief Exec. Nigerian Mining Corpn, Jos 1974–84; Fed. Minister of Mines, Power and Steel, Lagos 1984–85, of Petroleum Resources, Lagos 1986–89, of Foreign Affairs 1989–90; Pres. OPEC Conf. 1986–89, Sec.-Gen. OPEC 1995–2000, Head Del. from Nigeria 2001, Alt. Pres. 2001–02; Fellow and Hon. Fellow Inst. of Mining and Metallurgy; Fellow Imperial Coll. London, Nigerian Mining and Geoscience Soc.; Past Vice-Pres. Asscn of Geoscientists for Int. Devt; mem. Soc. of Mining Engineers of AIME; Hon. KBE 1989; Officier Légion d'honneur 1990; Order of Liberator, First Class, Venezuela 1990; Hon. PhD (Bologna) 1988; Hon. DSc (Maiduguri) 1989, (Ahmadu Bello) 1991; Dr hc (Moore House Coll. Atlanta) 1989. *Leisure interests:* reading, walking. *Address:* c/o OPEC, Obere Donaustrasse 93, 1020 Vienna, Austria.

LUKOJI, Mulumba; Democratic Republic of the Congo politician and university professor; First State Commr March–July 1991.

LUKŠIĆ, Igor, MA, PhD; Montenegrin politician; *Minister of Finance;* b. 1976, Bar; ed Univ. of Montenegro, Podgorica; twice elected Deputy of Parl. of Repub. of Montenegro; fmr Sec. of Ministry of Foreign Affairs; Deputy Minister of Foreign Affairs of Serbia and Montenegro 2003; adviser to Prime Minister of Montenegro 2003; Minister of Finance 2004–06 (resgnd), Nov. 2006–; mem. Democratic Socialist Party of Montenegro. *Publications include:* several academic works as well as poetry. *Address:* Ministry of Finance, 81000 Podgorica, Stanka Dragojevića 2, Montenegro (office). *Telephone:* (81) 224609 (office). *Fax:* (81) 224450 (office). *E-mail:* mf@mn.yu (office). *Website:* www .vlada.cg.yu/minfin (office).

LUKYANOV, Anatoliy Ivanovich, DJurSc; Russian politician and poet; b. 7 May 1930; m.; one d.; ed Moscow Univ.; mem. CPSU 1955–91; mem. CP of Russian Fed. 1992–; Chief Consultant on Legal Comm. of USSR Council of Ministers 1956–61; Deputy Head of Dept of Presidium of USSR Supreme Soviet 1969–76, Head of Secr. 1977–83; mem. of editorial staff of Sovietskoe Gosudarstvo i Pravo 1978; mem. Cen. Auditing Comm. CPSU 1981–86, 1986–89; Deputy of RSFSR Supreme Soviet 1984–91; Head of Gen. Dept of Cen. Cttee CPSU 1985–87, Sec. of Cen. Cttee 1987–88; Cand. mem. Political Bureau 1988–90; First Vice-Chair. of Presidium, USSR Supreme Soviet 1988–90, Chair. 1990–91; Chief Adviser on Legal Reform in USSR 1986–89; mem. Cen. Cttee CPSU 1986–91; People's Deputy of USSR 1989–91; arrested 1991 following failed coup d'état; charged with conspiracy Jan. 1992; released on bail Dec. 1992, on trial 1993–94; mem. State Duma (Parl.) 1993–2003, mem. Cttee for Legis. and Judicial Reform 1994, Chair. 1996–99; Chair. Cttee for State Org. 2000–2002; mem. Presidium, Cen. Exec. Cttee CP of Russian Fed. *Publications include:* many articles and books on Soviet legal system and Soviet constitution, three vols of poetry (under pseudonym A. Osenev). *Address:* c/o Communist Party of the Russian Federation, per. M. Sukharevskii 3/1, 103051 Moscow, Russia. *Telephone:* (495) 928–71–29. *Fax:* (495) 292-90-50.

LULA DA SILVA, Luis Inácio; Brazilian trade union official, politician and head of state; *President;* b. 27 Oct. 1945, Garanhuns, Pernambuco; s. of Aristides Inácio da Silva and Eurídice Ferreira de Mello; m. Marisa Leticia 1974; five c.; qualified as mechanic; started working at Indústrias Villares steelworks 1966; Assoc. mem. Exec. Cttee, São Bernardo do Campo and Diadema Metalworkers' Union 1969–72, First Sec. (responsible for social security) 1972–75, Pres. 1975–80; led steelworkers' strikes 1978, 1979; Pres. Partido dos Trabalhadores (Labour Party) 1980–87, 1993; a leader of the 'Elections Now' campaign for direct presidential elections 1984; a leader of campaign to impeach Pres. Collor de Mello 1992; Fed. Deputy 1986–; Presidential cand. 1989, 1994, 2002; f. a 'Parallel Govt' (to prepare an alternative set of policies for the country) 1990; Councilor, Citizenship Inst. 1992–; Pres. of Brazil 2003–. *Address:* Office of the President, Palácio do Planalto, Praça dos Três Poderes, 70150-900, Brasília, DF, Brazil (office). *Telephone:* (61) 3411-1225 (office). *E-mail:* protocolo@planalto.gov.br (office). *Website:* www.presidencia.gov.br (office).

LULLA, Kishore, BA; Indian film industry executive; *Chairman and CEO, Eros International;* ed Mumbai Univ.; est. UK office of family-owned film distribution co. Eros Int. 1988, currently Chair. and CEO, has expanded co's operations into film production and financing; mem. BAFTA, Young Pres.'s Org.; BDO Stoy Hayward Business of the Year, Eastern Eye Asian Business Awards 2007, India Splendour Awards 2007. *Address:* Eros International Ltd, Unit 23, Sovereign Park, Coronation Road, London NW10 7QP, England (office). *Telephone:* (20) 8963-8700 (office). *Fax:* (20) 8963-0154 (office). *E-mail:* UK-business@erosintl.co.uk (office). *Website:* www.erosplc.com (office).

LUMET, Sidney; American film director; b. 25 June 1924, Philadelphia; s. of Baruch Lumet and Eugenia Wemus; m. 1st Rita Gam (divorced); m. 2nd Gloria Vanderbilt 1956 (divorced 1963); m. 3rd Gail Jones 1963 (divorced 1978); m. 4th Mary Gimbel 1980; two d.; ed Columbia Univ.; started as a child actor, later theatrical dir and teacher; Assoc. Dir CBS 1950, Dir 1951–57; Hon. Life Mem. Dirs Guild of America; D. W. Griffith Lifetime Achievement Award 1993, Lifetime Achievement Award, Acad. Awards 2005. *Films include:* Twelve Angry Men 1957, Stage Struck 1958, That Kind of Woman 1959, The Fugitive Kind 1960, A View from the Bridge 1961, Long Day's Journey into Night 1962, The Pawnbroker 1965, Fail Safe 1964, The Hill 1965, The Group 1965, The Deadly Affair 1966, Bye, Bye Braverman 1968, The Seagull 1968, The Appointment 1969, Blood Kin 1969, The Anderson Tapes 1971, The Offence 1972, Child's Play 1973, Serpico 1973, Lovin' Molly 1974, Murder on the Orient Express 1974, Dog Day Afternoon 1975, Network 1976, Equus 1977, The Wiz 1978, Just Tell Me What You Want 1980, Prince of the City 1981, Deathtrap 1982, The Verdict 1982, Daniel 1983, Garbo Talks 1984, Power 1986, The Morning After 1986, Running on Empty 1988, Family Business 1989, Close to Eden 1992, A Stranger Among Us 1992, Guilty as Sin 1993, Night Falls on Manhattan 1997, Critical Care 1997, Q & A 1998, Gloria 1999, Rachel, quand du seigneur 2004, Find Me Guilty 2006, Before the Devil Knows You're Dead 2007. *Television includes:* 100 Centre Street (series) 2001–02. *Play:* Caligula 1960. *Publication:* Making Movies 1995. *Address:* c/o ICM, 8942 Wilshire Boulevard, Suite 219, Beverly Hills, CA 90211, USA.

LUMLEY, Joanna Lamond, OBE, FRGS; British actress; b. 1 May 1946, Kashmir; d. of James Rutherford Lumley and Thyra Beatrice Rose Lumley; m. 1st Jeremy Lloyd (divorced); m. 2nd Stephen Barlow 1986; one s.; ed Army School, Kuala Lumpur, Mickledene Kent, St Mary's St Leonards on Sea; Hon. DLitt (Kent) 1994; Hon. DUniv (Oxford Brookes) 2000; BAFTA Award 1992, 1994, Special BAFTA 2000. *Films include:* Some Girls Do, Tam Lin, The Breaking of Bumbo, Games That Lovers Play, Don't Just Lie There Say Something, The Plank, On Her Majesty's Secret Service, Trail of the Pink Panther, Curse of the Pink Panther, Satanic Rites of Dracula 1978, Shirley Valentine, Innocent Lies 1995, James and the Giant Peach 1996, Cold Comfort Farm 1996, Prince Valiant 1997, Parting Shots 1998, The Tale of Sweeney Todd 1998, Mad Cows 1999, Maybe Baby 1999, Ella Enchanted 2002, The Cat's Meow 2000, EuroTrip 2004, Ella Enchanted 2004, The Magic Roundabout (voice) 2005, Corpse Bride (voice) 2005, Stories of Lost Souls 2006, Dolls 2006. *Stage appearances include:* Noël Coward's Blithe Spirit 1986, Vanilla 1990, Revengers Comedies 1991, The Letter 1995, Hedda Gabler, Private Lives, An Ideal Husband, The Cherry Orchard 2007. *Television appearances include:* Release, Mark II Wife, Comedy Playhouse, It's Awfully Bad for Your Eyes Darling, Coronation Street, The Protectors, General Hospital 1974–75, The New Avengers 1976–77, Steptoe & Son, Are You Being Served?, The Cuckoo Waltz, Up The Workers, That was Tori, Sapphire and Steel 1978, Absolutely Fabulous (TV series) 1992–94, Class Act 1994, Girl Friday (documentary) 1994, White Rajahs of Sarawak (documentary), Joanna Lumley in the Kingdom of the Thunder Dragon (documentary) 1997, Coming Home 1998, A Rather English Marriage 1998, Nancherrow, Dr Willoughby, MD, Mirrorball 1999, Absolutely Fabulous (series 4) 2001, Giraffes on the Move (documentary) 2001, Up in Town 2002, Absolutely Fabulous Special 2002, Marple 2004, Sensitive Skin 2005–07, Jam & Jerusalem 2006–08; co-producer The Cazalets (BBC 1) 2001. *Publications:* Stare Back and Smile (autobiog.) 1989, Forces' Sweethearts 1993, Girl Friday 1994, Joanna Lumley in the Kingdom of the Thunder Dragon 1997, No Room for Secrets (autobiog.) 2004. *Leisure interests:* walking, gardening, collecting things, painting, music, travelling. *Address:* c/o Conway van Gelder, 3rd Floor, 18–21 Jermyn Street, London, SW1 6HP, England.

LUMSDEN, Andrew Gino Sita, PhD, FRS, FMedSci; British neurobiologist and academic; *Professor of Developmental Neurobiology, King's College London;* b. 22 Jan. 1947, Beaconsfield; m. (divorced); two d.; ed Kingswood School, Bath, St Catharine's Coll. Cambridge, Yale Univ., USA, London Univ.; Lecturer in Anatomy, Sr Lecturer, then Reader, Guy's Hosp. Medical School; Prof. of Developmental Neurobiology, King's Coll., London 1989–; Visiting Prof., Univ. of California, Berkeley 1994; Howard Hughes Int. Research Scholar 1993–98; Fulbright Scholar. *Publications:* The Developing Brain (co-author) 2001, more than 150 scientific publs. *Leisure interests:* mechanical eng, natural history. *Address:* Medical Research Council Centre for Developmental Neurobiology, King's College London, New Hunts House, Guy's Campus, London, SE1 1UL (office); 16 Elephant Lane, London, SE16 4JD, England (home). *Telephone:* (20) 7848-6520 (office); (20) 7640-0187 (home). *Fax:* (20) 7848-6550 (office); (20) 7640-0189 (home). *E-mail:* andrew.lumsden@ kcl.ac.uk (office).

LUMSDEN, Sir David James, Kt, MusB, MA, DPhil; British musician; b. 19 March 1928, Newcastle-upon-Tyne; s. of Albert Lumsden and Vera May Lumsden (née Tate); m. Sheila Daniels 1951; two s. two d.; ed Dame Allan's School, Newcastle-upon-Tyne, Selwyn Coll., Cambridge (Organ Scholar); Asst Organist, St John's Coll. Cambridge 1951–53; Organist and Choirmaster St Mary's, Nottingham and Univ. Organist 1954–56; Founder and Conductor Nottingham Bach Soc. 1954–59; Rector Chori Southwell Minster 1956–59; Dir of Music, Keele 1958–59; Prof. of Harmony, RAM 1959–61; Fellow and Organist, New Coll. Oxford and Lecturer, Faculty of Music, Univ. of Oxford 1959–76; Prin. Royal Scottish Acad. of Music and Drama, Glasgow 1976–82, RAM 1982–93; Conductor Oxford Harmonic Soc. 1961–63; Organist, Sheldonian Theatre 1964–76; Harpsichordist to the London Virtuosi 1972–75; Pres. Inc. Asscn of Organists 1966–68; Visiting Prof., Yale Univ., USA 1974–75; Conductor Oxford Sinfonia 1967–70; Choragus, Univ. of Oxford 1968–72; Pres. Inc. Soc. of Musicians 1984–85, Royal Coll. of Organists 1986–88; Chair. Nat. Youth Orchestra 1985–94, Nat. Early Music Asscn 1986–89; mem. Bd Scottish Opera 1978–83, ENO 1984–89; Hon. Fellow, Selwyn Coll. Cambridge,

New Coll. Oxford, King's Coll., London; Hon. RAM; Hon. FRCO; Hon. GSMD; Hon. FRCM; Hon. FRSAMD; Hon. FRNCM; Hon. FTCL; Hon. FLCM; Hon. FRSCM; Hon. FGCM 2005; Hon. DLitt (Reading) 1989. *Music:* recordings of organ, choral and chamber music. *Publications:* An Anthology of English Lute Music 1954, Thomas Robinson's Schoole of Musicke 1603 1971, Music for the Lute (Gen. Ed.) 1965–82. *Leisure interests:* reading, walking, theatre, photography, travel. *Address:* 26 Wyke Mark, Dean Lane, Winchester, SO22 5DJ, England (home). *Telephone:* (1963) 877807 (home). *Fax:* (1963) 877891 (home). *E-mail:* lumsdendj@aol.com (home).

LUNA, Bigas; Spanish film director; m . *Films:* Jamoń, Jamoń, Huevos de Oro (Golden Balls) 1994, The Tit and the Moon 1994, Bambola 1996, La Femme de Chambre du Titanic 1997, Volvérunt 1999, Son de Mar 2001. *Website:* www.bigasluna.com.

LUNA MENDOZA, Ricardo V., AB, MIA; Peruvian diplomatist; *Ambassador to UK;* b. 19 Nov. 1940, Lima; s. of Ricardo Luna and Victoria Mendoza de Luna; m. Margarita Proaño 1969; one d.; ed Princeton Univ., NJ and Columbia Univ., USA, Diplomatic Acad. of Peru; joined Diplomatic Service 1967, posts held include Third Sec., Div. of Econ. Affairs, Foreign Ministry 1967, Third Sec., Embassy in UK 1968–70, Second Sec., Embassy in Israel 1970–71, First Sec., Perm. Mission of Peru to UN Office at Geneva, Head, UN Dept, Foreign Ministry 1975–77, Counsellor, Washington, DC 1978, Chef du Cabinet of Minister for Foreign Affairs 1979, Minister Counsellor, Mission of Peru to UNESCO 1980, Quito 1987, Minister, Perm. Mission to UN 1984, Under-Sec. for Multilateral Policy, Ministry of Foreign Affairs 1987–89, Perm. Rep. to UN 1989–92, Amb. to USA 1992–99, to UK 2006–; Fellow, Center for Int. Affairs, Harvard Univ., USA 1980–81; Adjunct Prof. of Latin American Affairs, The Fletcher School, Tufts Univ. 1999–2006; fmr Lecturer, Woodrow Wilson School of Public and Int. Affairs, Princeton Univ.; Founding mem. Peruvian Centre for Int. Studies; mem. Peruvian Soc. of Int. Law; Order de Mayo (Argentina), Order Río Branco (Brazil), Panamerican Foundation Pan American Order. *Leisure interests:* art, art history, jazz, cinema, mountain climbing, hiking. *Address:* Embassy of Peru, 52 Sloane Street, London, SW1X 9SP, England (office). *Telephone:* (20) 7235-1917 (office). *Fax:* (20) 7235-4463 (office). *E-mail:* postmaster@peruembassy-uk.com (office). *Website:* www .peruembassy-uk.com (office).

LUND, Helge, MBA; Norwegian oil industry executive; *President and CEO, StatoilHydro;* b. 16 Oct. 1962; m.; two c.; ed Norwegian School of Econs and Business Admin (NHH), Bergen, Institut Européen d'Admin des Affaires (INSEAD), Fontainebleu, France; fmr Political Adviser to Conservative Parl. (Storting) Group; consultant with McKinsey & Co. –1993; joined Hafslund Nycomed 1993, Deputy Man.-Dir Nycomed Pharma AS 1997–99; Deputy Chief Exec. and COO Aker RGI Holding ASA 1999–2002; Deputy Chair. Aker Martitime 2001; apptd mem. Bd Kværner ASA 2001, Pres. and CEO Aker Kværner ASA (following merger between Aker and Kværner) 2002–04; Pres. and CEO Statoil ASA (renamed StatoilHydro in 2007 following merger between Statoil and Norsk Hydro's oil and gas business) 2004–. *Address:* StatoilHydro, Forusbeen 50, 4035 Stavanger, Norway (office). *Telephone:* 51-99-00-00 (office). *Fax:* 51-99-00-50 (office). *E-mail:* statoil@statoilhydro.com (office). *Website:* www.statoilhydro.com (office).

LUND, Henning, DrPhil; Danish scientist and academic; *Professor Emeritus of Chemistry, University of Århus;* b. 15 Sept. 1929, Copenhagen; s. of Prof. Hakon Lund and Bergljot I. G. Lund (née Dahl); m. Else Margrethe Thorup 1953; one s. three d.; ed Århus Katedralskole and Tech. Univ. of Copenhagen; Research Chemist, Leo Pharmaceutical Products 1952–60; Research Fellow, Harvard Univ. 1954–55; Asst Prof. of Chem., Univ. of Århus 1960, Prof. 1964–99, Prof. Emer. 1999–; Visiting Prof., Japan 1976, France 1981; Chair. UNESCO workshop for European Co-operation in Organic Electrochemistry 1976–81; Section Co-Chair. Int. Soc. of Electrochemistry 1973–78, 1986–90, Nat. Sec. 1986–90; Pres. Learned Soc., Univ. of Århus 1973–79; mem. Danish Research Council for Tech. Sciences 1977–82, Vice-Chair. 1980–82; mem. Royal Danish Acad. of Sciences and Letters 1979; Dr hc (Rennes) 1998; Bjerrums Gold Medal 1969, M. M. Baizer Award (Electrochemical Soc.) 1996. *Publications:* Elektrodereaktioner i Organisk Polarografi og Voltammetri 1961, Encyclopaedia of Electrochemistry of the Elements, Vols 11–15 (co-ed.) 1978–84, Organic Electrochemistry (ed.) 1983, 1991, 2000. *Leisure interests:* music, literature, jogging. *Address:* Department of Chemistry, University of Århus, 8000 Århus (office); Vinkelvej 8A, 8240 Risskov, Denmark (home). *Telephone:* (45) 89-42-39-05 (office); (45) 86-17-90-27 (home). *Fax:* (45) 86-19-61-99 (office). *E-mail:* hlund@chem.au.dk (office). *Website:* www.chem.au.dk (office).

LUND, Peter Anthony; American broadcasting executive; *Chairman, EOS International Inc.;* b. 12 Jan. 1941, Minneapolis; s. of Arthur H. Lund and Elizabeth Rohan; m. Theresa M. Kessel 1960; two s.; ed St Thomas Coll.; announcer, sales rep., Station KCCR, Pierce, SD 1961–62; sales rep., Station KELO TV, Sioux Falls, SD 1962–64; sales rep., sales man., Station WTTC, Minneapolis 1964–66; Gen. Sales Man. Westinghouse Broadcasting Co. 1966–71; Vice-Pres., Man. Station KSDO, San Diego, Calif. 1972–75, Station WTOP, Washington, DC 1976–77; Vice-Pres. CBS-owned AM Stations, New York 1977–80; Vice-Pres., Gen. Man. WBBM-TV, Chicago 1980–83, WCBS-TV, New York 1983–84; Exec. Vice-Pres. CBS Sports, New York 1984–85, Pres. 1985–87; Pres. Multimedia Entertainment 1987–90; Exec. Vice-Pres., Pres. Marketing, CBS 1990–94; Broadcast Group Pres. CBS Pres. 1995–97, Exec. Vice-Pres. CBS TV Network 1994–95, CEO CBS 1995–97, Pres. CEO CBS TV and Cable 1997; mem. Bd of Dirs DIRECTV Group Inc. 2000–, Crown Media Holdings, Inc., Emmis Communications Corpn; currently Chair. EOS Int. Inc. *Address:* EOS International Inc., 73 Turning Mill Lane, New Canaan, CT 06840, USA (office). *Telephone:* (203) 966-6708 (office).

LUNDBERG, Bo Klas Oskar, FRAeS; Swedish aeronautical scientist; b. 1 Dec. 1907, Karlskoga; s. of Ehrenfried Lundberg and Fanny Lundberg; m. Svea Maria Johansson 1935; two s. two d.; ed Hudiksvalls Läroverk and Royal Inst. of Tech., Stockholm; Dr in Aeronautics; Designer Test Pilot, AB Svenska Järnvägsverkstäderna, Aeroplanavdelningen, Linköping 1931–35, Sparmanns flygplanverkstad, Stockholm 1935–37; Asst Insp. at the Bd of Civil Aviation, Stockholm 1937–38; Chief, Aeronautical Dept, Götaverken, Gothenburg 1939; Chief Designer J-22 Fighter, Royal Air Bd 1940–44; Chief, Structures Dept, Aeronautical Research Inst. of Sweden 1944–47, Dir-Gen. 1947–67, Aviation Consultant 1967–; Fellow Royal Swedish Acad. of Eng Sciences, Canadian Aeronautics and Space Inst., Socio Onorario, Istituto Internazionale delle Comunicazioni; mem. AAAS; Hon. Fellow AIAA; Thulin Medal, Silver 1948, Gold 1955, Flight Safety Foundation Air Safety Award 1960, Sherman Fairchild Certificate of Merit 1963, Monsanto Aviation Safety Award 1963, Carl August Wicander Gold Medal 1966. *Publications include:* Fatigue Life of Airplane Structures (18th Wright Brothers Lecture) 1954, Should Supersonic Airliners be Permitted? 1961, Some Special Problems Connected with Supersonic Transport 1961, Speed and Safety in Civil Aviation (3rd Daniel and Florence Guggenheim Memorial Lecture) 1962, The Allotment of Probability Shares (APS) Method, A Guidance for Flight Safety Measures 1966, Economic and Social Aspects of Commercial Aviation at Supersonic Speeds 1972, Why the SST Should Be Stopped Once and For All 1973; numerous articles and papers mainly on the problems of aircraft safety and supersonic transport. *Leisure interests:* golf, tennis.

LUNDGREEN-NIELSEN, Flemming Torkild Jacob, DPhil; Danish academic; b. 24 Jan. 1937, Hellerup; s. of Otto Nielsen and Edith Mortensen; ed Frederiksborg Statsskole and Univ. of Copenhagen; teaching posts at Univ. of Copenhagen 1965–2007, Lecturer 1972–88, Prof., DIS Study Div. 1970–90, Docent 1988–2007; mem. Danish Soc. of Language and Literature, Royal Acad. of Sciences and Letters. *Publications:* Grundtvig. Skaebne og forsyn 1965, Den nordiske fortaelling i det 18. årh. 1968, Det handlende ord I-II 1980, CC Lyschanders digtning I-II 1989, Jens Bielke: Relation om Grønland 1990, Grundtvig og danskhed, in Dansk identitetshistorie 3 1992, På sporet af dansk identitet 1992, København laest og påskrevet 1997, Svøbt i mår. Dansk Folkevisekultur 1550–1700 I–IV (Ed. and Contrib.) 1999–2002; articles on Danish and Scandinavian literary subjects. *Address:* Upsalagade 22, 2100 Copenhagen Ø, Denmark (home). *E-mail:* fln@privat.tele.dk (home); fln@ royalacademy.dk (home).

LUNDGREN, Dolph, MA; American (b. Swedish) actor; b. 3 Nov. 1959, Stockholm, Sweden; m. Anette Lundgren 1994; two d.; ed Washington State Univ., Mass. Inst. of Tech. and Royal Inst. of Tech. Stockholm; f. Thor Pictures (production co.) 1992. *Films include:* A View to a Kill 1985, Rocky IV 1985, Masters of the Universe 1987, Red Scorpion 1989, The Punisher 1989, Dark Angel 1990, Cover Up 1991, Showdown in Little Tokyo 1991, Universal Soldier 1992, The Joshua Tree 1993, Pentathlon 1994, Men of War 1994, Johnny Mnemonic 1995, The Shooter 1995, Silent Trigger 1996, The Peacekeeper 1997, The Minion 1998, Sweepers 1998, Storm Catcher 1999, Bridge of Dragons 1999, Jill the Ripper 2000, The Last Patrol 2000, Agent Red 2000, Hidden Agenda 2001, Detention 2003, Direct Action 2004, Fat Slags 2004, Retrograde 2004, The Defender 2004, The Mechanik 2005, The Inquiry 2006. *Address:* c/o Jack Gilardi, ICM, 8942 Wilshire Boulevard, Beverly Hills, CA 90211, USA. *Telephone:* (310) 550-4135. *E-mail:* jgilardi@icmtalent.com. *Website:* www.dolphlundgren.com.

LUNDGREN, Terry J., BA; American retail executive; *Chairman, President and CEO, Macy's, Inc.;* b. 1953, Long Beach, Calif.; m. Nancy Lundgren; two c.; ed Univ. of Arizona; joined Bullock Div., Federated Dept Stores Inc. (FDSI), LA 1975, Pres. Bullock Wilshire Security Operations –1988, Chair. and CEO Neiman Marcus 1988–94, Head, Federated Merchandising Group, New York 1994–95, COO and Chief Merchandising Officer, FDSI (renamed Macy's, Inc. 2007) 1997–2003, Pres. 1997–, CEO 2003–, Chair. 2004–. *Address:* Macy's Inc., 7 West Seventh Street, Cincinnati, OH 45202, USA (office). *Telephone:* (513) 579-7000 (office). *Fax:* (513) 579-7555 (office). *E-mail:* info@macysinc .com (office); info@fds.com (office). *Website:* www.macysinc.com (office); www .fds.com (office).

LUNDY, Victor Alfred, MArch, FAIA; American architect; b. 1 Feb. 1923, New York; s. of Alfred Henry Lundy and Rachel Lundy; m. 1st Shirley Corwin 1947 (divorced 1959); one s. one d.; m. 2nd Anstis Manton Burwell 1960; one s.; ed New York Univ. Coll. of Architecture, Harvard Univ.; mil. service 1943–46; pvt. practice, Sarasota, Fla 1951–59, New York 1960–75, projects include St Paul's Lutheran Church, Sarasota 1959, US Tax Court Bldg and Plaza, Washington, DC, US Embassy in Colombo, Sri Lanka, Recreation Shelters for Smithsonian Inst., travelling air-supported Exhbn Bldg and exhibit for US Atomic Energy Comm. and commercial, religious and govt bldgs throughout the USA and overseas; pvt. practice, Houston, Tex. 1976–87, Design Prin. and Vice-Pres. HKS Inc., Dallas, Tex. 1984–90, visiting professorships and lectureships, Harvard, Yale, Columbia, Calif. (Berkeley) and Houston Univs and Rome Univ., Italy; work included in many exhbns including São Paulo Int. Biennial Exhbn of Architecture 1957, America Builds, Berlin 1957, Fifth Congress Union Internationale des Architectes, Moscow 1958, Expo '70, Osaka, Japan 1970; Purple Heart Medal, US Combat Infantry Badge; numerous prizes and awards. *Projects include:* GTE Telephone Operations World HQ, Irving, Tex., Greyhound Corp. (now Dial Corp.) Center, Phoenix, Ariz., Mack Center II, Tampa, Fla, Walnut Glen Tower (now Dr Pepper Bldg), Dallas, Tex. Austin Centre-Radisson Hotel and One Congress Plaza, Austin, Tex. *Address:* HKS Inc., 1111 Plaza of the Americas North, Suite LB 307, Dallas, TX 75201 (office); 701 Mulberry Lane, Bellaire, TX 77401, USA (home). *Telephone:* (214) 969-3396.

LUNENFELD, Bruno, MD, FRCOG; Israeli endocrinologist; *President, International Society for the Study of the Aging Male;* b. 11 Feb. 1927, Vienna, Austria; s. of David Lunenfeld and Ernestine Lunenfeld; m. Pnina Buyanover 1996; two s.; ed British Inst. of Eng Tech., Medical School, Univ. of Geneva, Switzerland; Acting Chief, Endocrine Research and Devt, Tel-Hashomer 1962–64; Scientist, Weizman Inst. of Science 1961–66; Assoc. Prof. and Head Dept of Biology, Bar-Ilan Univ. 1964–69, Prof. Ordinarius and Head Dept of Life Sciences 1969–71, Prof. of Life Sciences 1971; Dir Inst. of Endocrinology, Sheba Medical Centre 1964–92, Chair. Div. of Labs 1977–81, Chair. Research and Ethical Cttee 1977–81; mem. Expert Cttee on Biological Standardization, WHO 1967–87; Counsellor External Relations to Minister of Health and Head Dept of Int. Relations, Ministry of Health 1981–85; Acting Chief Scientist, Ministry of Health 1984–86; mem. Nat. Council for Research and Devt 1985–87; Visiting Prof., Yale School of Medicine, USA 1986–87; mem. Nat. Council for Health and Social Affairs 1985–87; Pres. Israel Fertility Asscn 1979–83, Israel Endocrine Soc. 1992–95; Founder and Pres., Int. Soc. for the Study of the Aging Male (ISSAM) 1997–; Medical Dir Int. Fertility Inst., Ranana 1996–99; Vice-Pres. Scientific Council of Israel Medical Asscn; mem. Exec. Bd Scientific Council, Exec. Council of Int. Cttee for Research in Reproduction, Exec. Council Medical Examination Bd, Exec. Council of Int. Andrology Soc., Exec. Council of Int. Soc. of Gynaecological Endocrinology (and Treas. 1992–96); Ed.-in-Chief The Aging Male 1997–; Hon. mem. Int. Fed. of Fertility Socs, European Soc. of Human Reproduction and Embryology; Hon. Fellow American Coll. of Obstetricians and Gynecologists; Verdienstkreuz First Class (Germany) 1995; Pliskin Prize, Israel Trade Union Sick Fund 1962, Yaffeh Prize, Ministry of Health 1963, US Public Health Service Special Recognition Award 1983, Jacob Henle Medal (Georg Augustus Univ., Göttingen) 1993. *Achievement:* discovered the clinical use of Human Menopausal Gonadotropin for the treatment of female and male infertility; pioneer in the study of gender-specific aging. *Publications:* 21 books including, Infertility, Diagnosis and Treatment of Functional Infertility 1978, Ovulation Induction 1982, Diagnosis and Management of Male Infertility 1984, Ovulation Induction and In Vitro Fertilization 1986, Infertility in Male and Female 1986, 1993, Textbook of Men's Health 2002; 25 chapters in books; 495 papers in scientific journals; 120 published lectures and abstracts. *Leisure interest:* walking, opera, sociology, photography. *Address:* 7 Rav Ashi Street, 69395 Tel-Aviv, Israel (home). *Telephone:* 3-6425434 (home). *Fax:* 3-6424454 (home). *E-mail:* blunert@attglobal.net (office). *Website:* www.issam.ch.

LUNGIN, Pavel Semenovich; Russian scriptwriter and director; b. 12 July 1949, Moscow; m. Yelena Lungina; ed Moscow State Univ.; debut as scriptwriter 1976, film director 1990; Special Prize, Cannes Film Festival. *Films include:* The Problem is Brother 1976, The End of Taiga Emperor 1978, Invincible 1983, Fellow Traveller 1987, Oriental Romance 1992; Dir: Taxi-Blues 1990, Luna Park 1992, Line of Life 1996, Wedding 1999, Oligarch 2001. *Address:* Novy Arbat str. 31, apt 8, 121009 Moscow, Russia (home). *Telephone:* (495) 205-04-32 (home).

LUNN, Gary, BL; Canadian politician; *Secretary of State for Sport;* b. 1957; m. Alexandra; two c.; ed Univ. of Victoria; fmr carpenter; fmr safety officer Crestbrook Forest Industries; lawyer 1995–97; mem. Parl. 1997–, fmr Vice-Chair. Standing Cttee on Fisheries and Oceans; fmr Critic for Northern Devt, for Métis and Non-Status Indians, for Human Resources Devt, for Int. Trade, for Nat. Revenue and for Fisheries and Oceans, for Public Works and Govt Services and for the Privy Council; Minister of Natural Resources 2006–08; Sec. of State for Sport 2008–; mem. BC Law Soc. *Address:* Sport Canada, Canadian Heritage, 15 rue Eddy, Gatineau, QC K1A 0M5, Canada (office). *Telephone:* (819) 997-0055 (office). *Fax:* (819) 953-5382 (office). *Website:* www.pch.gc.ca (office).

LUO, Gan, DipEng; Chinese state official, party official (retd) and engineer; b. 14 July 1935, Jinan, Shandong Prov.; m. He Zuozhi 1965; one s. one d.; ed Beijing Inst. of Iron and Steel Eng, Karl Marx Univ. and Freiburg Inst. of Mining and Metallurgy, Leipzig, GDR, May 7th Cadre School; worker, Leipzig Iron and Steel Plant and Leipzig Metal Casting Plant 1955–56; joined CCP 1960; Project Group Leader and Technician, Mechanical Eng Research Inst., First Ministry of Machine-Building Industry, Zhengzhou City, Henan Prov. 1962–69, Deputy Dir, later Dir Luohe Preparatory Office 1970–80; Chair. Science and Tech. Cttee, Henan Prov. 1980–81; Vice-Gov. Henan Prov. 1981–83; Sec. CCP Henan Prov. Cttee 1981–83; Minister of Labour and Social Services 1988; Sec.-Gen. of State Council 1988–98, State Councillor 1993–2003, Vice-Premier of State Council 1998–2003; Sec. Work Cttee for Cen. Govt Organs 1989–; Alt. mem. 12th CCP Cen. Cttee 1982–87, mem. 13th Cen. Cttee 1987–92, 14th Cen. Cttee 1992–97, 15th CCP Cen. Cttee 1997–2002, 16th CCP Cen. Cttee 2002–07; mem. CCP Politburo, Sec. Secr. CCP Cen. Cttee 1997–2002; mem. Standing Cttee, CCP Politburo 2002–07; Deputy Sec. Political and Legis. Affairs Cttee, Offices Under Cen. Cttee, 14th CCP Cen. Cttee 1993–98, Sec. 1998–07; mem. Secr. and Vice-Pres. All-China Fed. of Trade Unions 1983–88 (Deputy Sec. CCP Leading Party Group 1983–88). *Address:* c/o State Council, Zhong Nan Hai, Beijing, People's Republic of China (office).

LUO, Haocai; Chinese judge and politician; *President, Chinese Society for Human Rights Studies (CSHRS);* b. March 1934, Anxi Co., Fujian Prov.; ed Beijing Univ.; teaching asst, Lecturer, Assoc. Prof., Prof., Dept of Law, Beijing Univ. 1960–86; Vice-Pres. Beijing Univ. 1986–95; joined China Zhi Gong Party (Public Interest Party) 1992, Vice-Chair. Cen. Cttee 1992–97, Chair. Cen. Cttee 1997–2002; mem. Standing Cttee and Deputy Sec.-Gen. CPPCC 8th Nat. Cttee 1993–98, Vice-Chair. 9th Nat. Cttee 1998–2003, 10th Nat. Cttee 2003–; Chair. Beijing Fed. of Returned Overseas Chinese, Vice-Chair. All-China Fed. of Returned Overseas Chinese; adviser, Chinese Asscn for Int. Understanding 1999; fmr Vice-Chair. China Law Soc., Vice-Pres. 1986; Vice-

Pres. and mem. Judicial Cttee Supreme People's Court 1995–2000; Pres. Chinese Soc. for Human Rights Studies (CSHRS) 2007–; mem. Exec. Council China Admin. Man. Asscn; mem. Govt Del., Macao Hand-Over Ceremony, Macao Special Admin. Region Preparatory Cttee 1999. *Address:* Chinese Society for Human Rights Studies, No. 22 Building, An Yuan Bei Li, Beijing 100029, Peoples Republic of China (office). *Website:* www.humanrights-china.org (office).

LUO, Pingan; Chinese artist; b. 12 April 1945, Xian; s. of Luo Deyu and Tian Cuilan; m. Qi Juyan 1969; two s.; ed Xian Acad. of Fine Arts; mem. China Artists' Asscn, Shaanxi Br.; Artist of Shaanxi Imperial Art Gallery (traditional Chinese painting); Vice-Pres. Changan Imperial Art Acad.; Dir Artistic Cttee of China Artistic Asscn, Shaanxi br.; Excellent Works Prize, Beijing 1988, Copper Medal of 7th Nat. Artistic Works-Exhbn 1989, Tabei City, Taiwan. *Publications:* The Collection of Luo Pingan's Painting, Collected Landscapes by Luo Pingan. *Leisure interests:* literature, folk art, countryside and music. *Address:* 32 North Street, Xian, Shaanxi Province, People's Republic of China. *Telephone:* 25333; 7251984 (home).

LUO, Xuejuan; Chinese swimmer; b. 24 Jan. 1984, Hangzhou; specialises in breaststroke; began swimming competitively in Hangzhou 1991; coached by Yadong Zhang 1996–; debut for China Team, World Championships, Fukuoka 2001; winner Gold Medal for 50m. breaststroke, World Championships, Fukuoka 2001, World Cup SC, Shanghai 2000, 2002, Melbourne 2000, NY 2001, Edmonton 2001, Barcelona 2003, Olympic Games, Athens 2004; winner Gold Medal for 100m. breaststroke, World Championships, Fukuoka 2001, Barcelona 2003, World Cup, Shanghai 2000, Melbourne 2000, Edmonton 2001, NY 2001, Shanghai 2001; winner Gold Medal for 400m. medley relay, World Championships, Barcelona 2003; winner Silver Medal for 50m. breaststroke, World Championships SC, Moscow 2002, World Cup, Imperia 2002; winner Bronze Medal for 200m. breaststroke, World Championships, Fukuoka 2001, World Cup SC, Shanghai 2002; winner Bronze Medal for 100m. breaststroke, Pan Pacific Games 2002, World Championships SC, Moscow 2002; mem. Zhejiang Club, CHN; retired 2007; first Chinese torchbearer, Summer Olympics torch relay, Olympia, Greece 2008. *Leisure interest:* listening to pop music. *Address:* c/o International Association of Athletics Federations (IAAF), 17 rue Princesse Florestine, BP 359, MC98007, Monaco. *Website:* en.olympic.cn/coc.

LUO, Yuanzheng, PhD; Chinese university professor; b. 14 Feb. 1924, Chengdu, Sichuan Prov.; s. of Zhungi Luo and Suqing You; m. Lida Feng 1947; one s. one d.; ed West Union Univ. Chengdu, Univ. of Calif., St Olife Coll., USA and Univ. of Leningrad, Russia; Sec. Econ. Dept Scientific Planning Cttee State Council 1956–57; Dir Co-ordination Office for Econ. Affairs, State Planning Comm. 1978–80; Deputy Dir and Research Fellow, Inst. of World Econs and Politics, Chinese Acad. of Social Sciences 1978–83; mem. Econ. Research Centre, State Council 1980–84; Exec. Chair. Sec. and Founder, All-China Union of Asscns for Econ. Studies 1981–84; Visiting Prof. Australian Nat. Univ. 1981; Prof., Beijing Univ. (and a dozen other Chinese univs) 1981–; sr adviser to several provs and municipalities 1981–; Pres. Chinese Correspondence Univ. of Econ. Sciences 1984–88; Prof., European Man. School, Paris 1988; other professional appointments, editorships etc.; Vice-Pres. Int. Econ. Asscn 1989–92; Pres. China Int. Cultural Educ. Inst. 1992–; Chair. Econ. Forum of Hong Kong 1992; mem. Academic Advisory Bd Int. Centre for Econ. Growth 1992–; mem. CPPCC 1986–, mem. Econ. Cttee 1986–; Gen. Adviser to China Chamber of Commerce; Dir Asia Pacific Bd of Lucas; recipient of awards of State Council, Ministry of Higher Educ. etc. *Publications include:* On an Economic Community in the Pacific Region 1981, Impact of Socio-Economic Model on Education, Science and Culture 1983, Internationalization of Economic Life and China's Policy of Opening to the Outside World 1984, World Economy and China, On the Developmental Strategy Problems of an Economic Society 1986, Structural Reform and Economic Development in China 1989, Selected Works of Luo Yuangheng, The New Phase of China's Economic Development and Prospects for the New Century; papers on China's economy, world econ. devt etc. *Leisure interests:* music, Chinese classical poetry and verse. *Address:* 10-7-41 Xibianmenwai Dajei, 100045 Beijing, People's Republic of China. *Telephone:* 8523152 (office); 8312308 (home). *Fax:* 8534865 (office).

LUONG, Tran Duc; Vietnamese head of state, politician and fmr mining engineer; b. 1937; apptd a Vice-Prime Minister 1992; Pres. of Viet Nam 1997–2006; mem. Dang Cong san Viet Nam (Communist Party of Viet Nam) Politburo 1996–97. *Address:* c/o Dang Cong san Viet Nam, 1 Hoang Van Thu, Hanoi, Viet Nam.

LUPERTZ, Markus; German artist and professor; b. 25 April 1941, Liberec, Bohemia; ed Werkkunstschule, Krefeld, Kunstakademie, Düsseldorf, Villa Romana, Florence; Prof. State Acad. of Fine Arts, Karlsruhe 1976, Prof. and Dir Acad. of Art, Düsseldorf 1986–; numerous exhbns; Villa Romana Prize 1970, Prize of Deutschen Kritikerverband, Esslingen Artists' Guild 1990. *Publications:* Selected Poems 1961–83. *Address:* c/o Galerie Michael Werner, Gertrudenstrasse 24-28, 5000 Cologne 1, Germany. *Telephone:* (221) 925462.

LUPOLIANSKI, Uri; Israeli politician; s. of Jacob Lupolianski and of the late Sarah Lupolianski; m.; twelve c.; school teacher, Jerusalem 1970s; Founder and Chair. Yad Sarah (charitable foundation) 1976–; Deputy Mayor of Jerusalem –2003, Acting Mayor, then Mayor 2003–08; mem. United Torah Judaism; The Israel Prize 1994. *Address:* Yad Sarah, 124 Herzl Boulevard, 96187 Jerusalem, Israel (office). *Telephone:* (2) 2644401/2/3 (office); (2) 6297997 (office). *Fax:* (2) 6444498 (office); (2) 6296014 (office). *E-mail:* UriL@yadsarah.org.il (office); LPUri@Jerusalem.muni.il (office). *Website:* www.yadsarah.org.il (office).

LUPU, Radu, MA; Romanian pianist; b. 30 Nov. 1945, Galaţi; s. of Meyer Lupu and Ana Gabor; ed High School, Braşov, Moscow Conservatoire, USSR; first piano lessons 1951; won scholarship to Moscow 1961; entered Moscow Conservatoire 1963, graduated 1969; First Prize, Van Cliburn Competition 1966, Enescu Int. Competition, Bucharest 1967, Leeds Int. Competition 1969; a leading interpreter of the German classical composers; appears frequently with all the major orchestras; has toured Eastern Europe with London Symphony Orchestra; American debut 1972; gave world première of André Tchaikowsky Piano Concerto, London 1975; Grammy Award for Best Instrumental Record of Year (for Schubert record) 1995, Edison Award for Best Instrumental Record of Year (for Schumann record) 1995. *Recordings include:* complete Beethoven cycle (with Israel Philharmonic and Zubin Mehta), complete Mozart sonatas for violin and piano with Szymon Goldberg), Brahms piano concerto No. 1 (with Edo de Waart and London Philharmonic Orchestra), Mozart piano concerto K467 (with Uri Segal and English Chamber Orchestra), various Beethoven and Schubert sonatas, Mozart and Beethoven wind quintets in E flat, Mozart concerto for 2 pianos and concerto for 3 pianos transcribed for 2 pianos (with Murray Perahia and English Chamber Orchestra), Schubert Fantasie in F minor and Mozart sonata in D for 2 pianos (with Murray Perahia), Schubert Lieder (with Barbara Hendricks), Schubert Piano Duets (with Daniel Barenboim). *Leisure interests:* history, chess, bridge. *Address:* Opus 3 Artists, 470 Park Avenue South, 9th Floor North, New York, NY 10016, USA (office). *Telephone:* (212) 584-7500 (office). *Fax:* (646) 300-8200 (office). *E-mail:* info@opus3artists.com (office). *Website:* www.opus3artists.com (office).

LUQMAN, Ahmad Mohammad; Egyptian international organization executive; Dir-Gen. Arab Labour Org. (ALO). *Address:* Arab Labour Organization, PO Box 814, Cairo, Egypt (office). *Telephone:* (2) 3362721 (office). *Fax:* (2) 3484902 (office). *E-mail:* info@alolabor.org (office). *Website:* www.alolabor.org (office).

LURIE, Alison, AB; American novelist and academic; *Frederic J. Whiton Professor of American Literature Emerita, Cornell University;* b. 3 Sept. 1926, Chicago; d. of Harry Lawrence Lurie and Bernice Stewart Lurie; m. 1st Jonathon Peale Bishop 1948 (divorced 1985); three s.; m. 2nd Edward Hower 1996; ed Radcliffe Coll., Mass; Editorial Asst, Oxford University Press 1946; worked as receptionist and sec.; Lecturer in English, Cornell Univ. 1969–73, Adjunct Assoc. Prof. 1973–76, Assoc. Prof. 1976–79, Frederic J. Whiton Prof. of American Literature 1979, now Prof. Emer.; Yaddo Foundation Fellow 1963, 1964, 1966, 1984, Guggenheim Fellow 1965, Rockefeller Foundation Fellow 1967; New York State Cultural Council Foundation Grant 1972; American Acad. of Arts and Letters Literature Award 1978, Prix Femina Étranger 1989, Parents' Choice Foundation Award 1996. *Publications:* V. R. Lang: a Memoir 1959, Love and Friendship 1962, The Nowhere City 1965, Imaginary Friends 1967, Real People 1969, The War Between the Tates 1974, Only Children 1979, Clever Gretchen and Other Forgotten Folktales (juvenile) 1980, The Heavenly Zoo (juvenile) 1980, Fabulous Beasts (juvenile) 1981, Foreign Affairs 1984 (Pulitzer Prize in Fiction 1985), The Man with a Shattered World 1987, The Truth about Lorin Jones 1988, Women and Ghosts 1994, The Last Resort 1998, Familiar Spirits 2001, Truth and Consequences 2005; non-fiction: The Language of Clothes 1981, Don't Tell the Grown Ups, Subversive Children's Literature (essays) 1990, Boys and Girls Forever: Reflections on Children's Classics (essays) 2003. *Address:* Department of English, 263 Goldwin Smith Hall, Cornell University, Ithaca, New York, NY 14853-3201, USA (office). *Telephone:* (607) 255-4235 (office). *E-mail:* al28@cornell.edu (office). *Website:* www.writers.cornell.edu/entirelist/#lurie (office).

LURIE, Ranan Raymond; American political cartoonist; b. 26 May 1932, Port Said, Egypt; s. of Joseph Lurie and Rose Lurie (née Sam) (parents Israeli citizens); m. Tamar Fletcher 1958; two s. two d.; ed Herzelia Coll., Tel Aviv and Jerusalem Art Coll.; Corresp. Maariv Daily 1950–52; Features Ed. Hador Daily 1953–54; Ed.-in-Chief Tavel (weekly magazine) 1954–55; staff political cartoonist Yedioth Aharonot Daily 1955–66, Honolulu Advertiser 1979; went to USA (invited by Life Magazine) 1968, naturalized 1974; political cartoonist, Life Magazine, New York 1968–73; political cartoonist interviewer Die Welt, Bonn 1980–81; Contrib. New York Times 1970–; Contrib. Ed. and political cartoonist, Newsweek Int. 1974–76; Ed., political cartoonist, Vision Magazine of S America 1974–76; syndicated United Features Syndicate 1971–73; syndicated nationally by Los Angeles Times and internationally by New York Times to over 260 newspapers 1973–75; syndicated nationally by King Features Syndicate, internationally by Editors Press Syndicate (345 newspapers) 1975–83, in USA by Universal Press Syndicate 1982–86; Lecturer, Univ. of Hawaii, American Program Bureau, Boston; political cartoonist, The Times, London 1981–83; Sr Political Analyst and cartoonist, The Asahi Shimbun, Tokyo 1983–84; Sr Analyst and political cartoonist, US News and World Report, Washington 1984–85; political cartoonist Time Magazine 1994–97; Ed.-in-Chief Cartoon News 1996–; Chief Editorial Dir Editors' Press Service 1985; inventor of first animated electronic television news cartoon; joined MacNeil/Lehrer News Hour as daily political cartoonist/analyst, appearing on 275 TV stations; Nightline (ABC TV network programme) and ZDF (German nat. TV); launched TV cartoon nationally; creator of Taiwan's official new nat. cartoon symbol 'Cousin Lee'; cr. Japan's nat. cartoon symbol 'Taro San'; TV Cartoon launched by ABC (USA) and ZDF (Germany); fine arts shows in Israel, Canada, USA 1960–75, including Expo 1967, Canada, Dominion Gallery, Montréal, Canada, Lim Gallery, Tel-Aviv 1965, Overseas Press Club, New York 1962, 1964, 1975, US Senate, Washington 1973, Honolulu Acad. Fine Arts 1979; exhibited in numerous group shows including Smithsonian Inst. 1972; trained as Parachute Officer, French Foreign Legion 1955, British Paratroopers 1956, US 101 Airborn Div. 1962, served as Combat Paratroop Maj., Israeli Army Reserve 1950–67; Sr Adjunct Fellow with The Center for Strategic and Int. Studies, Washington, DC; mem. Asscn of Editorial Cartoonists, Nat. Cartoonists' Soc. of America; mem. MENSA; Nat. Fed. of Hispanic-owned Papers est. Ranan R. Lurie Political Cartoon Award 1994; syndicated internationally to 1,098 papers in 104 countries; listed in Guinness Book of World Records as most widely syndicated political cartoonist in the world (Certificate of Merit for 20 years as consecutive title holder); Chief Judge Seoul Int. Cartoon Competition 1996; the UN established an Annual Int. Award in his honour (LurieUNaward.com) 1999; Hon. Assoc. mem. Asahi Shimbun; recipient highest Israeli journalism award 1954; U.S. Headliners Award 1972; named Outstanding Editorial Cartoonist of Nat. Cartoonist Soc. 1972–78; Salon Award, Montréal Cartoon 1971; New York Front Page Award 1972, 1974, 1977, Certificate of Merit of US Publication Designers 1974, Hon. Mention, Overseas Press Club 1979, winner of John Fischetti Political Cartoon Award 1982, Toastmasters' Int. and Leadership Award 1985, UN Soc. of Writers Award for Excellence 1995, Hubert H. Humphrey First Amendment Freedoms Prize 1996, Cartoon Award, UN 2000. *Publications:* Among the Suns 1952, Lurie's Best Cartoons (Israel) 1961, Nixon Rated Cartoons (New York Times) 1973, Pardon Me, Mr President (New York Times) 1974, Lurie's Worlds (USA) 1980, So sieht es Lurie (Germany) 1981, Lurie's Almanac (UK) 1982, (USA) 1983, Taro's International Politics, Taro-San No Kokusai Seijigaku (Japan) 1984, Lurie's Middle East 1986, Lurie's Mideast Almanac (Israel) 1986, Lurie's Far East Views (China) 1987, The Cartoonist's Mask (novel) 2004; creator The Expandable Painting 1969. *Leisure interests:* Tamar (wife), Rod, Barak (sons), Daphne, Danielle (daughters). *Address:* Cartoonews International, 375 Park Avenue, Suite 1301, New York, NY 10152, USA. *Telephone:* (212) 980-0855 (office). *Fax:* (212) 980-1664 (office). *Website:* cartoonews.com.

LUSCOMBE, David Edward, LittD, FBA, FSA, FRHistS; British historian and academic; *Research Professor Emeritus of Medieval History, University of Sheffield;* b. 22 July 1938, London; s. of Edward Dominic Luscombe and Nora Luscombe; m. Megan Phillips 1960; three s. one d.; ed St Michael's Convent School, Finchley Catholic Grammar School, London and King's Coll. Cambridge; Fellow, King's Coll. 1962–64, Churchill Coll. Cambridge 1964–72; Prof. of Medieval History, Univ. of Sheffield 1972–95, Leverhulme Personal Research Prof. of Medieval History 1995–2000, Research Prof. of Medieval History 2000–03, Research Prof. Emer. of Medieval History 2003–, Dean of Faculty of Arts 1985–87, Pro-Vice-Chancellor 1990–94, Chair. Humanities Research Inst. 1992–2003, Dir for Research in the Humanities Div. of Grad. School 1994–2003; mem. Governing Body, later the Asscn of St Edmund's House, Cambridge 1971–84; Visiting Prof., Royal Soc. of Canada 1991, Univ. of Conn. at Storrs 1993; Visiting Fellow, All Souls Coll. Oxford 1994; Raleigh Lecturer, British Acad. 1988; British Acad. Exchange Visitor to Japan Acad. 1996; mem. Council, British Acad. 1989–97, Chair. Medieval Texts Editorial Cttee 1991–2004; mem. Cttee, Soc. for Study of Medieval Languages and Literature 1991–96, Council, Royal Historical Soc. 1981–85, Cttee, Ecclesiastical History Soc. 1976–79, Supervisory Cttee British Acad./Oxford Univ. Press for New Dictionary of Nat. Biography 1992–99, Assoc. Ed. 1993–; Vice-Pres. Soc. int. pour l'étude de la philosophie médiévale 1987–97, Pres. 1997–2002; mem. Commonwealth Scholarships Comm. in UK 1994–2000; Auditor, Higher Educ. Quality Council, Div. of Quality Audit 1994–97; mem. Council Worksop Coll. and Ranby House School 1996–; Fellow, Woodward Corpn 2000–08, Hon. Fellow 2008–. *Publications:* The School of Peter Abelard, Peter Abelard's Ethics, Church and Government in the Middle Ages (co-ed.) 1976, Petrus Abaelardus (1079–1142): Person, Werk, und Wirkung (co-ed.) 1980, The Evolution of Medieval Thought by David Knowles (ed. revised edn with C. Brooke) 1988, David Knowles Remembered (co-author) 1991, Anselm, Aosta, Bec and Canterbury (co-ed.) 1996, Medieval Thought 1997; Cambridge Studies in Medieval Life and Thought, 4th series (Advisory Ed.) 1983–88, (Gen. Ed.) 1988–2004; The New Cambridge Medieval History, IV, 1–2 (co-Ed.) 2004; articles in learned journals. *Leisure interests:* children and grandchildren, using libraries, walking. *Address:* Department of History, University of Sheffield, Jessop West, 1 Upper Hanover Street, Sheffield, S3 7RA (office); 28 Endcliffe Hall Avenue, Sheffield, S10 3EL, England (home). *Telephone:* (114) 222-2559 (office). *Fax:* (114) 222-2576 (office). *E-mail:* D.Luscombe@sheffield.ac.uk (office). *Website:* www.shef.ac.uk/history (office).

LUSCOMBE, Michael Gerard, BEc; Australian retail executive; *CEO and Group Managing Director, Woolworths Ltd;* m. Karen Luscombe; three c.; ed Monash Univ., Monash Mount Eliza Business School; joined Woolworths in Vic. as trainee 1978, Store Man. 1980–94, Category Man., Buying and Marketing Dept 1994, later Merchandise Man., Operations Man., Vic. 1995–98, Nat. Man. Banking Dept, Sydney 1998–99, Gen. Man. Supply Chain 1999–2004, Dir of Supermarkets 2004–06, COO and Dir Woolworths Ltd 2006–, also CEO 2006–; Chair. ALH Group; Chair. Australian Nat. Retailers Asscn; mem. Bd Dirs CIES – The Food Business Forum; Williamson Fellow, Vic. Community Leadership Program 1992. *Address:* Woolworths Ltd, PO Box 8000, Baulkham Hills, NSW 2153 (office); Woolworths Ltd, 1 Woolworths Way, Bella Vista, NSW 2153, Australia (office). *Telephone:* (2) 8885-0000 (office). *E-mail:* info@woolworthslimited.com.au (office). *Website:* www.woolworthslimited.com.au (office).

LUSINCHI, Jaime; Venezuelan politician and paediatrician; b. 27 May 1924, Clarines, Anzoátegui; m. Gladys Castillo (divorced 1988); five c.; ed Univ. del Oriente, Univ. Central; active mem. Acción Democrática (AD) Party 1941–; Pres. Legis. Ass. for Anzoátegui and regional Gen. Sec. 1948–52; arrested during presidency of Gen. Marcos Pérez Jiménez; in exile in Argentina, Chile and USA 1952–58; returned to Venezuela 1958; mem Rómulo Betancourt's electoral comm. 1958, mem. Nat. Exec. Cttee of AD 1958, Dir Int. Affairs 1958–61, Deputy for Anzoátegui 1959–67, Pres. Parl. Group 1968–78, Senator for Anzoátegui 1979–83, Presidential Cand. 1977, Sec.-Gen. AD 1980–83, Party Leader 1980–84; Pres. of Venezuela 1984–89; Senator 1989; sought refuge in Costa Rica from legal proceedings 1995; Paediatrician, Lincoln

Hosp., Bellevue Medical Centre, New York 1958; mem. American Acad. of Pediatrics.

LÜST, Reimar, Dr rer. nat; German physicist; *Professor of Physics, University of Hamburg;* b. 25 March 1923, Barmen; s. of Hero Lüst and Grete Lüst (née Strunck); m. 1st Dr Rhea Kulka 1953; two s.; 2nd Nina Grunenberg 1986; ed Univs of Frankfurt am Main and Göttingen; Research Physicist, Max Planck Insts (MPIs), Göttingen and Munich 1950–60, Enrico Fermi Inst., Univ. of Chicago 1955–56, Princeton Univ. 1956; Head, Dept for Extraterrestrial Physics, MPI for Physics and Astrophysics 1960, Dir Inst. of Extraterrestrial Physics 1963–72, later Scientific Mem. for Extraterrestrial Physics, MPI; Visiting Prof., Univ. of New York 1959, MIT 1961, Calif. Inst. of Tech. 1962, 1966; Chair. German Research Council 1969–72, Deutsche Gesellschaft für Luft- und Raumfahrt 1968–72; Pres. Max-Planck-Gesellschaft 1972–84; Dir-Gen. European Space Agency 1984–90; Prof. of Physics, Univ. of Hamburg 1992–; Pres. Alexander von Humboldt Foundation 1989–99, Hon. Pres. 1999; Chair. Bd Int. Univ. Bremen 1999–2004, Hon. Chair. 2005–; mem. Int. Acad. of Astronautics, Royal Astronomical Soc., Bavarian Acad. Sciences; Corresp. mem. Real Acad. de Ciencias Exactas, Físicas y Naturales de Madrid; Fellow, Imperial Coll. of Science and Tech., London; Hon. Prof., Inst. for Theoretical Physics, Chinese Acad. of Sciences, Beijing 1997, Beijing Univ. 1997; Hon. Foreign mem. American Acad. of Arts and Sciences, Austrian Acad. of Sciences; Hon. mem. Heidelberg Acad. of Sciences, Senat Max-Planck-Gesellschaft, Deutsche Gesellschaft für Luft- und Raumfahrt; Hon. Citizen of State of Texas 1999; Hon. Citizen of Freie Hansestadt Bremen 2001; Officier, Ordre des Palmes Académiques; Officier, Légion d'honneur; Bayerischer Maximiliansorden für Wissenschaft und Kunst; Grosses Verdienstkreuz mit Stern und Schulterband; Distinguished Service Cross (Poland) 1997; Dr hc (Sofia) 1991, (Birmingham) 1993, (Slovak Acad. of Sciences) 1995 and several other hon. degrees from int. univs; Planet 4386 named Lüst 1991; Daniel and Florence Guggenheim Int. Astronautics Award, Personality of the Year 1986, Tsiolkowsky Medal (USSR Fed. of Cosmonauts) 1987, Harnack Medal of Max Planck Soc. 1993 and numerous other awards; shared Adenauer-de Gaulle Prize 1994. *Publications:* articles on space research, astrophysics and plasmaphysics. *Leisure interests:* history, tennis, skiing. *Address:* Max-Planck-Institut für Meteorologie, Bundesstrasse 53, 20146 Hamburg (office); Bellevue 49, 22301 Hamburg, Germany. *Telephone:* (40) 41173300. *Fax:* (40) 41173390; (40) 41173390 (office). *E-mail:* sengbusch@dkrz.de.

LUSTIG, Arnošt; American (b. Czech) writer and academic; *Professor Emeritus of Literature, American University;* b. 21 Dec. 1926, Prague; s. of Emil Lustig and Terezie Lustig (née Löwy); m. Věra Weislitz 1949; one s. one d.; ed Coll. of Political and Social Sciences, Prague; in concentration camps at Terezín (Theresienstadt), Auschwitz-Birkenau and Buchenwald, Second World War; Radio Prague corresp. in Arab-Israeli war 1948, 1949; Radio Prague reporter 1948–58; Ed. Mladý svět (weekly) 1958–59, screenplay writer for Studio Barandov 1960–68, for Jadran-Film Yugoslavia 1969–70; naturalized American citizen 1979; mem. Cen. Cttee Union of Czechoslovak Writers 1963–69, mem. Presidium 1963–69; mem. Int. Writing Program 1970–71; Visiting Lecturer, Univ. of Iowa 1971–72; Visiting Prof., Drake Univ., Iowa 1972–73; Prof. of Literature, American Univ., Washington, DC 1973–2005, Prof. Emer. 2005–; Visiting Prof. in Cooperation with Charles Univ., Prague, Univs of New Orleans and Michigan, summer courses 1993; Lecturer, J. Škvorecký Literary Acad. 2000–; Hon. Pres. Franz Kafka Soc., Prague 1990–; Hon. mem. Club of Czech Writers 1999–; Hon. DHL (Spertus Coll. of Judaica, Chicago) 1986; Klement Gottwald State Prize 1967, B'nai B'rith Prize 1974, Nat. Jewish Book Award 1980, 1986, Emmy Award, The Nat. Acad. of Television Arts and Sciences 1986, Publishers Weekly Literary Prize, USA 1991, Karel Čapek Literary Prize, Prague PEN Club Int. 1996, Medal of Merit, Czech Repub. 2000, American Acad. of Arts and Letters 2004, Franz Kafka Prize 2008. *Screenplays:* Names for which there are no people (Prague) 1960, Theresienstadt (Prague) 1965, Stolen Childhood (Italy) 1966, Triumph of Memory (PBS) 1984, Precious Legacy (USA) 1984, Fighter (USA) 2000, Tanga (Prague) 2002. *Films:* Europa (co-author; autobiographical documentary) 1998, Fighter (autobiographical documentary) 2000. *Publications:* fiction: Démanty noci (short stories, trans. as Diamonds of the Night) 1958, Blue Day (story) 1960, Night and Hope (short stories) 1958, Modlitba za Kateřinu Horovitzovou (novel, translated as A Prayer for Katerina Horovitzova) 1965, Dita Saxova (novel) 1962, The Street of Lost Brothers (short stories) 1962, Prague Crossroads 1964, The Man the Size of a Stamp (radio plays) 1965, Nobody will be Humiliated (stories) 1965, The White Birches in Autumn (novel) 1966, Bitter Smell of Almonds (novel) (translated as Indecent Dreams) 1968, Darling (novel) 1969, Darkness Casts No Shadow (novel) 1976, Children of the Holocaust (three vols, collected stories) 1977–78, The Holocaust and the Film Arts (essay with Josef Lustig) 1980, The Precious Legacy (screenplay for documentary) 1984, The Unloved (from the diary of 17-year-old Pearl Sch., novel) 1985, Indecent Dreams (collection of novellas) 1988, Street of Lost Brothers (short stories) 1990, Colette, Girl from Antwerp (novel) 1993, Tanga, Girl from Hamburg (novel) 1993, Leah, Girl from Antwerp (translated as Waiting for Leah 2005), Porges (novel) 1995, Friends (novel) 1995, House of the Echo Returned (novel) 1995, Chasm (novel) 1996, Beautiful Green Eyes 1997, Fire on the Water (three novellas) 1998, Initiation 2001, Bitter Smell of Almonds (three vols of collected stories) 2001, Collected Works (eight vols) 1992–2002, Lustig ist Gott, Gott ist Lustig 2001, House of Returned Echo 2002; non-fiction: text for symphonic poem Night and Hope (with Otmar Macha) 1963, The Beadle of Prague (text for a cantata) 1983; Answers (two interviews) 2002, Essays 2002, 3×18, portraits and observations (interviews) 2002, Confession (four CD autobiog.) 2005. *Leisure interests:* swimming, travelling, skiing, soccer. *Address:* 4000 Tunlaw Road, NW, Apartment 825, Washington, DC 20007, USA (home). *Telephone:* (202) 885-2984 (office); (202) 338-5357 (home); (420) 736227001 (mobile). *Fax:* (202) 885-2938 (office).

LUSZTIG, George, MA, PhD, FRS; American academic; *Norbert Wiener Professor of Mathematics, Massachusetts Institute of Technology;* b. 20 May 1946, Timişoara, Romania; m. Michal-Nina Abraham 1972 (divorced 2000); two d.; ed Univ. of Bucharest and Princeton Univ.; Visiting mem. Inst. for Advanced Study, Princeton, NJ 1969–71; Research Fellow, Dept of Math., Univ. of Warwick 1971–72, Lecturer 1972-74, Prof. 1974-78; Prof. of Math., MIT 1978–, now Norbert Wiener Prof.; mem. NAS; Guggenheim Fellowship 1982; Cole Prize in Algebra (American Math. Soc.) 1985, Brouwer Medal (Dutch Math. Soc.) 1999, Steele Prize for Lifetime Achievement (American Math. Soc.) 2008. *Publications:* The Discrete Series of GLn over a Finite Field, 1974, Characters of Reductive Groups over a Finite Field 1984, Introduction to Quantum Groups 1993. *Leisure interest:* yoga. *Address:* Department of Mathematics, Massachusetts Institute of Technology, Room 2-276, 77 Massachusetts Avenue, Cambridge, MA 02139, USA (office). *Telephone:* (617) 253-4398 (office). *Fax:* (617) 253-4358 (office). *E-mail:* gyuri@math.mit.edu (office). *Website:* www-math.mit.edu/~gyuri (office).

LUTE, Jane Holl, PhD, JD; American UN official and fmr army officer; m. Lt. Gen. Douglas Lute; two d.; ed Stanford Univ., Georgetown Univ.; career Officer, US Army (retd 1994); fmr teacher of Political Science, West Point Mil. Acad.; served in Europe, Persian Gulf during Operation Desert Storm 1991; mem. of Staff, Nat. Security Council, Dir of European Affairs 1991–94; Head of Carnegie Comm. on Preventing Deadly Conflict 1994–99; Sr Public Policy Fellow, Woodrow Wilson Centre for Int. Scholars 1994–99; Exec. Dir Asscn of US Army Project on role of American mil. power 2000; Exec. Vice-Pres. and COO UN Foundation and Better World Fund 2000–03; Asst Sec.-Gen. for Mission Support, UN Dept Peace-keeping Operations 2003–09; nominated as Deputy Sec. US Dept of Homeland Security, Washington, DC 2009; mem. of Va Bar.

LÜTKESTRATKÖTTER, Herbert, Dr-Ing; German business executive; *Chairman of the Executive Board, HOCHTIEF AG;* b. 1950; ed Aachen Tech Univ. and its Inst. of Hydraulic Eng and Water Resources Man.; held planning and man. roles at Lahmeyer International 1978–99, becoming Man. Dir and also mem. Exec. Bd, Lahmeyer AG; Int. Business Man. Philipp Holzmann AG 1999, Labour Relations Dir 2000; fmr Chair. Exec. Bd Dussmann AG & Co. KGaA; joined HOCHTIEF AG 2003, mem. Exec. Bd 2003–, Deputy Chair. 2006–07, Chair. 2007–, responsible for the Americas and Europe divs, for Corp. Devt, Corp. Communications and Corp. Governance; mem. Bd of Dirs Aecon Group Inc. 2005–; mem. Supervisory Bd ThyssenKrupp Elevator AG; Alt. Dir (non-exec.) Leighton Holdings Ltd 2004–07, Dir 2007–.

LUTON, Jean-Marie; French engineer; *Honourary President, Starsem;* b. 4 Aug. 1942, Chamalières; s. of Pierre Luton and Marie Luton; m. Cécile Robine 1967; three s.; ed Lycée Blaise Pascal, Clermont-Ferrand, Lycée St Louis, Paris, Faculté des Sciences, Paris and Ecole Polytechnique; with CNRS 1964–71; Ministry of Industrial and Scientific Devt 1971–73; Head of Research, Centre Nat. d'Etudes Spatiales 1974–75, Head of Planning 1975–78, Dir of Programmes and Planning 1978–84, Deputy Dir-Gen. 1984–87, Dir-Gen. 1989–90; Dir of Space Programmes, Aérospatiale 1987–89; Dir-Gen. European Space Agency 1990–97; Pres., Dir-Gen., then Chair. Arianespace 1997–2006; Chair. and CEO Starsem 2002–06, Hon. Pres. 2006–; Chevalier, Légion d'honneur, Officier, Ordre nat. du Mérite; Prix de l'Astronautique; Prix de l'Innovateur industriel, Society of Satellite Professionals (USA) 1998. *Leisure interests:* tennis, sailing. *Address:* Starsem, 2 rue François Truffaut, 91042 EVRY Cedex, France (office). *Telephone:* 1-69-87-01-10 (office). *Fax:* 1-60-78-31-99 (office). *E-mail:* communication@starsem.com (office). *Website:* www.starsem.com (office).

LUTSENKO, Yuriy Vitaliyovych; Ukrainian engineer and politician; *Minister of Internal Affairs;* b. 14 Dec. 1964, Rivne; s. of the late Vitaliy Ivanovych Lutsenko and Vira Mikhailivna Lutsenko; m.; three s.; ed Lviv Polytechnical Inst.; mil. service in army 1984–86; Chief Constructor and Head, Tech. Workshop, Gazotron, Rivne 1989–94; Deputy Head, Rivne Oblast Council of People's Deputies 1994–96; Head, Rivne Oblast Admin Econs Cttee 1996–97; Deputy Minister of Science and Tech. 1997–98; adviser to Prime Minister 1998–99; adviser to Leader of Socialist Party of Ukraine 1999–2002; Deputy, Verkhovna Rada (Parl.) 2002–; Minister of Internal Affairs 2005–06, 2007–; mem. Socialist Party of Ukraine, Sec., Political Council 1996, later held number of sr positions; mem. Construction, Transportation, Communal Services and Communications Cttee; active in Ukraine Without Kuchma! (UBK) campaign and 'Orange Revolution' of 2004. *Address:* Ministry of Internal Affairs, 01024 Kyiv, vul. Ak. Bohomoltsya 10, Ukraine (office). *Telephone:* (44) 256-03-33 (office). *Fax:* (44) 256-16-33 (office). *E-mail:* mail@centrmia.gov.ua (office). *Website:* mvs.gov.ua (office).

LUTTER, Marcus Michael, PhD; German professor of law; *Professor Emeritus and Dean, Zentrum für Europäisches Wirtschaftsrecht, University of Bonn;* b. 11 Dec. 1930, Munich; s. of Michael Lutter; m. Rebecca Garbe 1957; one s. two d.; ed Univs of Munich, Paris and Freiburg; notary, Rockenhausen 1957–60; research scholarship, Deutsche Forschungsgesellschaft, Brussels, Strasbourg, Paris, Rome, Utrecht 1961–63; notary, Rockenhausen and external lecturer, Univ. of Mainz 1964–65; Prof. Inst. for Civil Law, German and European Trade and Econ. Law, Univ. of Bochum 1966–79; fmr Prof. and Dir Inst. for Trade and Econ. Law, Univ. of Bonn, now Prof. Emer. and Dean of the Centre for European Econ. Law; Visiting Prof., Univ. of California, Berkeley 1972, Techno Univ., Tokyo 1982, Univ. of Oxford 1997; Pres. German Lawyers' Asscn 1982–88; Hon. PhD (Vienna, Warsaw, Jena). *Publications:* Information and Confidentiality in the Supervisory Board 1984, 2006, European Company Law 1996, The Letter of Intent 1998, Duties and Rights of Board Members 2002; various monographs and treatises especially on participation, jt stock cos and supervisory bds; Publr Zeitschrift für Unternehmens-und Gesellschaftsrecht. *Address:* Zentrum für Europäisches Wirtschaftsrecht der Universität Bonn, Adenauerallee 24–42, 53113 Bonn (office); Auf der Steige 6, 53129 Bonn, Germany (home). *Telephone:* (228) 739559 (office); (228) 231722 (home). *Fax:* (228) 737078 (office). *E-mail:* marcus.lutter@jura.uni-bonn.de (office). *Website:* www.jura.uni-bonn.de (office).

LUTTWAK, Edward Nicolae, PhD; American academic, international consultant and writer; *Senior Fellow, Center for Strategic and International Studies;* b. 4 Nov. 1942, Arad, Romania; s. of Joseph Luttwak and Clara Baruch; m. Dalya Iaari 1970; one s. one d.; ed elementary schools in Palermo and Milan, Carmel Coll., Wallingford, UK, London School of Econs and Johns Hopkins Univ.; Lecturer, Univ. of Bath, UK 1965–67; Consultant, Walter J. Levy SA (London) 1967–68; Visiting Prof., Johns Hopkins Univ. 1974–76; Sr Fellow, Center for Strategic and Int. Studies 1977–87, Burke Chair. of Strategy 1987–92, Sr Fellow 1992–; Consultant to Office of Sec. of Defense 1975, to Policy Planning Council, Dept of State 1981, Nat. Security Council 1987, Dept of Defense 1987, to Govts of Italy, Korea, Spain; Prin., Edward N. Luttwak Inc. Int. Consultants 1981–; Pres. Servicios Agricolas Tupinamba, Bolivia; Int. Assoc. Inst. of Fiscal and Monetary Policy, Japan Ministry of Finance (Okurasho); mem. editorial Bd of The American Scholar, Journal of Strategic Studies, The National Interest, Géopolitique, The Washington Quarterly, Orbis; Nimitz Lectureship, Univ. of Calif. 1987, Tanner Lecturer, Yale Univ. 1989, Rosenstiel Lecturer, Grinner Coll. 1992, Hon. LLD (Bath) 2007. *Publications:* Coup d'Etat 1968, Dictionary of Modern War 1972, The Israeli Army 1975, The Political Uses of Sea Power 1976, The Grand Strategy of the Roman Empire 1978, Strategy and Politics: Collected Essays 1979, The Grand Strategy of the Soviet Union 1983, The Pentagon and the Art of War 1985, Strategy and History: collected essays 1985, International Security Yearbook 1984/85 (with Barry M. Brechman) 1985, On the Meaning of Victory 1986, Strategy: The Logic of War and Peace 1987, The Dictionary of Modern War (with Stuart Koehl) 1991, The Endangered American Dream 1993, Il Fantasma della Povertà (co-author) 1996, Cose è davvero la Democrazia 1996, La Renaissance de la puissance aérienne stratégique 1998, Turbo-Capitalism 1999, Il Libro della Libertà 2000, Strategy: The Logic of War and Peace (ed.) 2002; his books have been translated into 14 languages. *Leisure interest:* ranching in the Amazon. *Address:* Center for Strategic and International Studies, 1800 K Street, NW, Washington, DC 20006, USA. *Telephone:* (301) 656-1972 (office); (202) 775-3145. *Fax:* (202) 775-3199. *Website:* www.csis.org.

LUTZ, Robert (Bob) A., BS, MBA; American automotive industry executive; *Vice-Chairman and Senior Advisor to the CEO, General Motors Corporation;* b. 12 Feb. 1932, Zürich, Switzerland; s. of Robert H. Lutz and Marguerite Lutz; m. 1st Betty D. Lutz 1956 (divorced 1979); m. 2nd Heide-Marie Schmid 1980 (divorced 1993); m. 3rd Denise Ford 1994; four d. from 1st marriage; ed Univ. of California, Berkeley; Capt. US Marine Corps 1954–59; Research Assoc. IMEDE, Lausanne 1962–63; Sr Analyst, Forward Planning, General Motors Corpn (GM), New York 1963–65, Staff Asst, Man. Dir's Staff, Adam Opel AG (GM) 1965–66, various man. positions at GM France 1966–69, Asst Domestic Gen. Sales Man., Merchandising, Adam Opel AG 1969, Dir of Sales and mem. Man. Bd 1969–70; Vice-Pres. (Sales) and mem. Man. Bd, BMW AG 1970–74; Gen. Man. Ford of Germany 1974–76, Vice-Pres. (Truck Operations), Ford of Europe 1976–77; Pres. Ford of Europe 1977–79, Vice-Pres. Ford Motor Co. and Chair. of Bd Ford of Europe 1979–82; Exec. Vice-Pres. Ford Int. Automotive Operations, Dearborn, Mich. 1982–86, Exec. Vice-Pres. N American Truck Operations 1986; Head, Int. Operations, Pres. and COO Chrysler Corpn 1988–96, Vice-Chair. 1996–98; Chair., CEO and Pres. Exide Corpn 1998–2001, Chair. 2001–02; Vice-Chair. of Product Devt, General Motors (GM) 2001–09, Chair. GM N America 2001–09, Vice Chair. and Sr Adviser to CEO 2009–; Chair. Bd Dirs Silicon Graphics, ASCOM, Switzerland. *Publication:* Guts. *Address:* General Motors Corporation, 300 Renaissance Center, Detroit, MI 48265-3000, USA (office). *Telephone:* (313) 556-5000 (office). *Fax:* (248) 696-7300 (office). *Website:* www.gm.com (office).

LUXON, Benjamin Matthew, CBE, FGSM; British singer (baritone); b. 24 March 1937, Redruth, Cornwall; s. of Maxwell Luxon and Lucille Grigg; m. Sheila Amit 1969; two s. one d.; ed Truro School, Westminster Training Coll., Guildhall School of Music and Drama; always a freelance artist; sang with English Opera Group 1963–70; has sung with Royal Opera House, Covent Garden and Glyndebourne Festival Opera 1971–96, Boston Symphony Orchestra 1975–96, Netherlands Opera 1976–96, Frankfurt Opera House 1977–96, Paris Opéra 1980, La Scala, Milan 1986; roles include Monteverdi's Ulisse, Janáček's Forester, Mozart's Don Giovanni and Papageno, Tchaikovsky's Onegin, Verdi's Posa and Falstaff, Wagner's Wolfram, Alban Berg's Wozzeck, Count Almaviva and Sherasmin in Oberon; performs as recitalist with piano accompanist David Willison; folk-singing partnership with Bill Grofut 1976–96; has recorded for all major record cos; retd from professional singing due to severe hearing loss 1996; vocal coach at Tanglewood, USA 1996; Hon. mem. RAM; Bard of Cornish Gorseth; Hon. DMus (Exeter), (RSA of Music and Drama) 1996, (Canterbury Christ Church Coll.) 1997. *Recordings include:* Mahler's 8th Symphony, Schubert's Song Cycles. *Leisure interests:* most sports, English watercolours of 18th and 19th centuries.

LUXTON, John, BAgrSc; New Zealand politician; *Spokesman for Tourism, Communications and Inward Investment, National Party;* m.; three c.; ed Massey Univ.; Nat. Party MP for Matamata 1987–96, for Karapiro 1996–99; Minister of Housing and Energy, Assoc. Minister of Educ. 1990–93, Assoc. Minister of Maori Affairs 1991–97; Minister of Maori Affairs, Police and Assoc. Minister of Educ. 1993–97, Minister of Commerce, Fisheries, Lands and Biosecurity, for Industry and Assoc. Minister for Agric. 1997–98; Minister of

Food, Fibre, Biosecurity and Border Control, Assoc. Minister of Immigration and Assoc. Minister for Int. Trade 1998–99; Nat. Party Spokesperson on Int. Trade Negotiations and Inward Investment and Regional Devt, Assoc. Foreign Affairs 2000–01; Nat. Party Spokesman for Tourism, Communications, Inward Investment 2001–; fmr Chair. Tatua Industry Co-operative Dairy Co. Ltd, Deputy Chair. Wallford Meats Ltd; Dir Wallace Corpn Ltd, Tatua Co-operative Dairy Co., Asia 2000 Foundation; int. agric. consultant and farmer; AC Cameron Memorial Award 1987. *Address:* Parliament Buildings, Wellington, New Zealand. *Telephone:* (4) 471-9509 (office). *Fax:* (4) 473-0469 (office). *E-mail:* john.luxton@parliament.govt.nz (office).

LUZHKOV, Yurii Mikhailovich; Russian politician; *Mayor of Moscow;* b. 21 Sept. 1936, Moscow; m. Marina Bashilova 1958 (died 1989); two s.; m. 2nd Yelena Baturina 1991; two d.; ed Gubkin Inst. of Oil and Gas, Moscow; researcher, Research Inst. of Plastic Materials 1958–64; Head of Div. Ministry of Chemical Industry 1964–87; First Deputy Chair. Exec. Cttee, Moscow City Council and Chair. Moscow Agric. Industry Dept 1987–90; Chair. Exec. Cttee, Moscow City Council 1990–91; Vice-Mayor of Moscow and Premier, Moscow City Govt 1991–92, Mayor and Head of City Govt 1992–, re-elected 1996, 1999, 2003, apptd 2007–; mem. Russian Council of Fed. 1996–2001; Founder and Co-Chair. Fatherland (Otechestvo) Movt 1998–2001, formed alliance with All Russia party in 1999, subsequently merged with pro-Putin Unity party to create Unity and Fatherland-United Russia party (UF-UR) 2001, later simply United Russia (Yedinaya Rossiya); Co-Chair. Supreme Council, UF-UR; Chair. Int. Fund Assistance to Free Enterprise; Pres. Moscow Int. Business Asscn 2002–; Hon. Prof., Acad. of Labour and Social Relations; Lenin Order, Red Banner Order, Order in the Name of Russia 2004; Hon. DSc Lomonosov State Univ. Moscow; Golden Mask Prize for support of the arts. *Publications:* 72 Hours of Agony 1991, The Quietist Negotiations 1994, We Are Your Children, Moscow 1996. *Leisure interests:* football, tennis, skiing, equestrian sport, fishing, bee-keeping. *Address:* Office of the Mayor and Prime Minister of the Government of Moscow City, 125032 Moscow, ul. Tverskaya 13, Russia (office). *Telephone:* (495) 777-77-77 (office). *Fax:* (495) 234-32-97 (office). *E-mail:* mayor@mos.ru (office). *Website:* www.mos.ru (office); www.luzhkov.ru (office).

LUZÓN LÓPEZ, Francisco; Spanish banker; b. 1 Jan. 1948, Cañavate, Cuenca; trainee, Banco de Vizcaya 1972, Regional Man. Seville 1974, Man. of Planning and Man. Control, Bilbao 1975–78, Int. Div. Madrid 1978–80, Man. London 1980–81; mem. Bd and Gen. Man. Banco de Crédito Comercial 1981–82; mem. Bd and Gen. Man. Banco Occidental 1982–85; Gen. Man. Commercial Banking Network 1985–87; mem. Bd and Gen. Man. Banco de Vizcaya 1987–88, Banco Bilbao-Vizcaya 1988; Chair. Banco Exterior de España 1988–99; Vice-Pres. Banco Atlántico and mem. Bd Teneo 1991–94; Chair. Argentaria 1991, Caja Postal SA 1991–, Banco de Crédito Local 1994–99, Banco Hipotecario de España 1994–, Corporación Bancaria de España SA; Dir Banco Santander Central Hispano (BNC) 1997–. *Address:* Banco Santander Central Hispano, Sede Operativa Plaza de Canalejas 1, 28014 Madrid (office); Paseo de Recoletos 10, 28001 Madrid, Spain. *Telephone:* (91) 5581111 (office); (91) 5377000. *Fax:* (91) 5378034. *Website:* www .gruposantander.com (office).

LUZZATTO, Lucio, FRCPath, FRCP; Italian geneticist and haematologist; *Professor of Haematology, Institute of Cancer Research, Genoa;* b. 28 Sept. 1936, Genoa; s. of the late Aldo Luzzatto and of Anna Luzzatto Gabrielli; m. Paola Caboara 1963; one s. one d.; ed Liceo D'Oria, Genoa, Univ. of Genoa Medical School, Univ. of Pavia; Sr Lecturer in charge of Sub-Dept of Haematology, Univ. of Ibadan, Nigeria 1967–68; Prof. of Haematology 1968–74, Consultant Haematologist, Univ. Coll. Hosp. Ibadan, Nigeria 1967–68; Dir Int. Inst. of Genetics and Biophysics, CNR, Naples 1974–81; Prof. of Haematology (Univ. of London) and Dir of Haematology Dept Royal Postgrad. Medical School, Consultant Haematologist Hammersmith Hosp., London, UK 1981–94, Hon. Dir MRC/LRF Leukaemia Unit, London 1987–93; Chair. Dept of Human Genetics, Courtney Steel Chair., Attending Physician in Genetics and Haematology, mem. Cell Biology Program, Memorial Sloan-Kettering Cancer Center, New York, Prof. of Medicine and Human Genetics, Cornell Univ. Medical Coll., New York 1994–2000; Scientific Dir Nat. Inst. of Cancer Research (IST), Genoa, Italy 2000–04, personal Chair of Haematology 2002–; Founding Pres. Nigerian Soc. for Haematology; fmr Pres. Italian Asscn of Genetics; fmr Chair. Ethics Cttee American Soc. for Gene Therapy; mem. European Molecular Biology Org. 1979–, Human Genome Org. (HUGO) 1990–, American Asscn of Physicians; Foreign mem. American Acad. of Arts and Sciences 2004–; Hon. mem. American Soc. of Hematology; Hon. DSc (Ibadan) 1998; Dr hc of Pharmacy (Urbino) 1990; William Dameshek Medal 1975, Pius XI Medal 1976, Sanremo Int. Prize for Human Genetics 1982, Int. Chiron Award for Biomedical Research 1995, Premio Napoli 1995, Jose Carreras Medal 2002. *Publications:* more than 330 articles in scientific journals and scientific and medical textbooks. *Address:* Istituto Nazionale Ricerca sul Cancro (IST), Largo R. Benzi 10, Genoa, Italy (office). *Telephone:* (10) 352776 (office). *Fax:* (10) 355573 (office). *E-mail:* lucio.luzzatto@istge.it (office).

LVOV, Dmitry Semenovich, DEconSc; Russian economist; b. 2 Feb. 1930, Moscow; m.; two c.; ed Moscow S. Ordzhonikidze Inst. of Eng and Econ.; Sr Researcher, Head of Lab., Head of Div., Prof., Moscow Inst. of Eng and Econ., later Inst. of Econ. USSR Acad. of Sciences; Deputy Dir Cen. Inst. of Math. and Econ.; Corresp. mem. USSR (now Russian) Acad. of Sciences 1987, mem. 1994, Deputy Chair. Council on Econ. Man. 1995–, Acad.-Sec. Dept of Econs 1996–2002; author of alternative econ. reform project Oct. 1998–; Pres. Int. Cen. for studies of econ. reforms; Ed.-in-Chief Econ. Science of Contemporary Russia. *Publications include:* 14 books including Effective Management of Technical Development 1990; more than 250 works on econ. efficiency of capital investments and new tech., pricing, prognosis of tech. processes. *Leisure interest:* poetry. *Address:* Central Institute of Mathematics and Economics, Krasikov str. 32, 117418 Moscow, Russia (office). *Telephone:* (495) 129-08-22 (office); (495) 129-16-44 (office).

LYAKHOV, Vladimir Afanasyevich; Russian cosmonaut (retd); b. 20 July 1941, Antratsit, Voroshilovgrad Oblast, Ukrainian SSR; m.; two c.; ed Kharkov Aviation School for Pilots, Chuguyev, Kharkov Oblast, Gagarin Mil. Acad.; mem. CPSU 1963–91; served in fmr Soviet Air Force 1964–; mem. Cosmonaut team 1967–94; Commdr of space-ship Soyuz-32 1979 and Soyuz T-9 which connected up with orbital station Salyut-7; Commdr Soyuz TM-6 1988; space-walked 1983; worked in Yuri Gagarin Centre 1995–99; Hero of Soviet Union (twice); K. Tsiolkovski Gold Medal. *Leisure interest:* hockey. *Address:* Yuri Gagarin Centre, Zvezdny Gorodok, Moscow Region, Russia (office). *Telephone:* (495) 971-86-16 (office).

LYAKISHEV, Nikolai Pavlovich, DTechSc; Russian metallurgist; *Research Manager, Baikov Institute of Metallurgy and Material Science;* b. 5 Oct. 1929; m.; two d.; ed Moscow Inst. of Steel and Alloys; Researcher, then Head of Lab., Deputy Dir Bardin Cen. Research Inst. of Ferrous Metallurgy 1954–87, Dir 1977–87; Dir Baikov Inst. of Metallurgy and Material Science, USSR (now Russian) Acad. of Sciences 1987–2004, Research Man. 2004–; Corresp. mem. USSR (now Russian) Acad. of Sciences 1981, mem. 1987, mem. Presidium 1991–2001; Foreign mem. Eng Acad. of Science, China, Nat. Acad. of Science, Ukraine; mem. Bd Novolipetsk Steel 2005–; Lenin Prize, USSR State Prize. *Publications include:* main works in the field of steelmaking and ferroalloys, structural materials, including Niobium in Steel and Alloys 1971, Metallurgy of Chromium 1977, Aluminothermics 1978, Theory and Practice of Ferroalloys Production 1999, Metallic Single Crystals 2002. *Leisure interest:* chess. *Address:* Baikov Institute of Metallurgy and Material Science, Leninsky Prospect 49, 119911 Moscow, Russia (office). *Telephone:* (495) 135-20-60 (office). *Fax:* (495) 135-86-80 (office).

LYALL, John Adrian, RIBA, FRSA; British architect; b. 12 Dec. 1949, Daws Heath, Essex; s. of Keith Lyall and Phyllis Lyall (née Sharps); m. Sallie Jean Davies 1991; one s. one d.; ed Southend High School for Boys, Essex, Architectural Asscn School of Architecture; worked for Cedric Price, Piano & Rogers, Bahr, Vermeer & Haecker, Rock Townsend 1996–79; Founder Multimatch Design Group 1970–73; in practice with Will Alsop as Alsop & Lyall, later Alsop, Lyall & Störmer 1980–91; Man. Dir John Lyall Architects 1991–; RIBA Vice-Pres. of Cultural Affairs 1997, of Future Studies 1999–2000, Chair. of Validation Task Force, RIBA 2001; Bannister Fletcher Prof. Univ. Coll. London 1998; design teaching and lecturing at Architectural Asscn and Bartlett Schools, London and univs in USA, UK, Russia, Chile, Colombia and Ecuador; design adviser to Cardiff Bay Devt Corpn and English Partnerships; apptd as enabler for CABE 2001 and Chair. of RIBA's Educ. Validation Task Force 2001–02. *Television:* contrib. to Masterclass – Denys Lasdun; panel mem. BBC Knowledge 2000–01. *Dance:* design collaborator with Rosemary Butcher Dance Co. on various performances 1990–96. *Music:* production designer for Opera 80 travelling opera 1980–83. *Achievements:* award-winning bldgs include: The Corn Exchange, Leeds (Ironbridge Award, British Archaeological Soc. 1990, 1998, Leeds Award for Architecture 1990, Europa Nostra Award, 1991, RIBA National Award, 1991, RIBA White Rose Award 1991, Civic Trust Commendation 1991, British Council of Shopping Centres Award 1991, Design Week Award 1991, Royal Inst. of Chartered Surveyors Urban Renewal Award 1995) 1991, White Cloth Hall, Leeds (Leeds Award for Architecture 1992, The Minerva Award 1993) 1992, Tottenham Hale Overground Station, London (Aluminium Imagination Award 1993) 1992 (Tottenham Hale London Underground Station and Station Forecourt 1999), Harry Ramsden's Restaurant, Cardiff Bay 1996, North Greenwich Jubilee Line Station, London (RIBA Regional Award 1999, RIBA Nat. Category Award 1999, Civic Trust Commendation 2000) 1999, Crystal Palace Park, London 2003, Silver House, Carnaby Street, London 2003–04, Regeneration of Cranfields Mills, Ipswich 2004–, Hammersmith Pumping Station (residential conversion and new-build affordable housing block) 2004–, Wellington Court, Covent Garden. *Publications:* John Lyall: Contexts and Catalysts 1999; contrib. to A Guide to Recent Architecture: London 1993, A Guide to Recent Architecture: England 1995, Context – New Buildings in Historic Settings 1998. *Leisure interest:* choral singing. *Address:* John Lyall Architects, 13–19 Curtain Road, London, EC2A 3LT (office); Newlands, Gandish Road, East Bergholt, Suffolk, CO7 6TP, England (home). *Telephone:* (20) 7375-3324 (office); (1206) 298368 (home). *Fax:* (20) 7375-3325 (office). *E-mail:* john@johnlyallarchitects.com (office); john.lyall4@virgin.net (home). *Website:* www.johnlyallarchitects.com (office).

LYELL, Sir Nicholas (Walter), Kt, PC, QC; British politician and lawyer; *Chairman, Society for Conservative Lawyers;* b. 6 Dec. 1938; s. of the late Sir Maurice Legat Lyell and of Veronica Mary Lyell; m. Susanna Mary Fletcher 1967; two s. two d.; ed Stowe School, Christ Church, Oxford; nat. service RA 1957–59; Walter Runciman & Co. 1962–64; called to the Bar, Inner Temple 1965, Bencher 1986; pvt. practice London (Commercial, Industrial and Public Law) 1965–86, 1997–, a Recorder 1985–2001; Jt Sec. Constitutional Cttee 1979; MP for Hemel Hempstead 1979–83, for Mid Bedfordshire 1983–97, for Bedfordshire North East 1997–2001; Parl. Pvt. Sec. to Attorney-Gen. 1979–86; Parl. Under-Sec. of State (Social Security) DHSS 1986–87; Solicitor-Gen. 1987–92, Attorney-Gen. 1992–97; Shadow Attorney-Gen. 1997–99; Chair. Soc. for Conservative Lawyers 2001–; Vice-Chair. British Field Sports Soc. 1983–86; Gov. Stowe School 1990–, Chair. 2001–. *Leisure interests:* gardening, shooting, drawing. *Address:* Monckton Chambers, 4 Raymond Buildings, Grays Inn, London, WC1R 5BP (office); Society for Conservative Lawyers, 30 Bronsart Road, London, SW6 6AA, England (office). *Telephone:* (20) 7405-7211 (office). *Website:* www.conservativelawyers.com (office).

LYGO, Adm. Sir Raymond Derek, KCB, FRSA, CBIM; British business executive; b. 15 March 1924, Ilford, Essex; s. of the late Edwin Lygo and of Ada E. Lygo; m. Pepper van Osten 1950 (died 2004); two s. one d.; ed Ilford County High School and Clarkes Coll., Bromley; The Times 1940; naval airman, RN 1942; served in VUSN 1949–51; CO 759 Squadron 1951–53, 800 Squadron 1954–56, HMS Lowestoft 1959–61, HMS Juno 1967–69, CO HMS Ark Royal 1969–71; Vice-Chief of Naval Staff 1975–77, Chief of Naval Staff 1977–78; joined British Aerospace 1978, Man. Dir Hatfield/Lostock Div. 1978–80, Chair. and Chief Exec. Dynamics Group 1980–82; Man. Dir British Aerospace PLC 1983–86, mem. Bd 1980–89, Chief Exec. 1985–89; Chair. British Aerospace Enterprises Ltd, British Aerospace (space systems) Ltd and British Aerospace Holdings Inc. 1988–89, Rutland Trust PLC 1992–99, TNT Express (UK) 1992–97, TNT Europe Ltd 1992–97, River and Mercantile First UK Investment Trust (now Liontrust) 1997–2004; Dir James Capel Corporate Finance 1990–92; Chair. Royal Ordnance PLC 1987; Pres. Soc. of British Aerospace Cos 1984–85; Patron Youth Sports Trust 1996–; Liveryman, Coachmakers, Shipwrights; Pres. HMS St Vincent Asscn; Pres. Fleet Air Arm Officers' Asscn 2008; Freeman City of London; Hon. FRAeS. *Publications:* Collision Course (autobiog.). *Leisure interests:* building, gardening, joinery, flying. *Address:* c/o Fleet Air Arm Officers' Association, 4 St James's Square, London, SW1Y 4JU, England (office).

LYKKETOFT, Mogens; Danish politician; *Spokesman on Foreign Affairs, Social Democratic Party;* b. 9 Jan. 1946, Copenhagen; s. of Axel and Martha Lykketoft; m. Mette Holm; two d.; ed Univ. of Copenhagen; worked at Econ. Council of the Labour Movt 1966–81, Head of Dept 1975–81; mem. Folketing (Parl.) 1981–, Political Spokesman for Social Democratic Party 1991–93, 2001–02, Leader 2002–05, Spokesman on Foreign Affairs 2005–; Minister for Inland Revenue 1981–82; Minister of Finance 1993–2000, of Foreign Affairs 2000–01. *Publications:* ed. of several books and numerous articles in magazines, periodicals and newspapers. *Address:* Folketinget, Christiansberg, 1240 Copenhagen (office); Odensegade 17, 1, 2100 Copenhagen, Denmark (home). *Telephone:* 33-37-40-34 (office). *Fax:* 33-89-40-34 (office). *E-mail:* smoly@ft.dk (office). *Website:* www.socialdemokratiet.dk (office); www.kykketoft.dk (home).

LYMAN, Princeton, PhD; American diplomatist; *Adjunct Senior Fellow for African Policy, Council on Foreign Relations;* b. 20 Nov. 1935, San Francisco, Calif.; s. of Arthur Lyman and Gertrude Lyman; m. Helen Ermann 1957; three d.; ed Univ. of Calif. at Berkeley and Harvard Univ.; joined US Govt service 1961; Agency for Int. Devt 1961–80; Dir USAID, Addis Ababa 1976–78; Dept of State 1980–; Deputy Asst Sec. for Africa 1981–86; Amb. to Nigeria 1986–89, to South Africa 1992–95; Dir Bureau of Refugee Programs 1989–92; Asst Sec. of State for Int. Org. Affairs 1996–98; fmr Exec. Dir Global Interdependence Initiative, Aspen Inst.; fmr Ralph Bunche Sr Fellow for African Policy, Council on Foreign Relations, currently Adjunct Sr Fellow; mem. Bd of Dirs Acad. of Diplomacy; Dept of State Superior Honor Award, Pres.'s Distinguished Service Award. *Publications:* Korean Development: The Interplay of Politics and Economics 1971. *Leisure interests:* tennis, photography, piano. *Address:* Council on Foreign Relations, 19779 Massachusetts Avenue, NW, Washington, DC 20036, USA (office). *Telephone:* (202) 518-3469 (office). *Fax:* (202) 986-2984 (office). *E-mail:* plyman@cfr.org (office). *Website:* www.cfr.org (office).

LYNAM, Desmond (Des) Michael, OBE, ACII; British sports broadcaster; b. 17 Sept. 1942, Ennis, Repub. of Ireland; s. of Edward Lynam and Gertrude Veronica Malone; m. Susan Eleanor Skinner (divorced 1974); one s.; ed Varndean Grammar School, Brighton, Brighton Business Coll.; career in insurance –1967; freelance journalist and reporter local radio 1967–69; reporter, presenter and commentator BBC Radio 1969–78; presenter and commentator BBC TV Sport 1978–99 (including Grandstand, Sportsnight, Match of the Day, Commonwealth and Olympic Games and World Cup coverage); presenter Holiday (BBC) 1988–89, How Do They Do That? (BBC) 1994–96; presenter, The Des Lynam Show (BBC Radio) 1998–99, ITV Sport 1999–2004, BAFTA TV Awards (ITV) 2000, The Premiership (ITV) 2001–04, Des Meets 2004, Countdown (Channel 4) 2005–06, Britain's Favourite View (ITV) 2007, Setanta Sports (Setanta) 2007–; TV Sports Presenter of the Year, TRIC 1985, 1987, 1988, 1993, 1997, Radio Times Male TV Personality 1989, RTS Sports Presenter of the Year 1994, 1998, Richard Dimbleby Award, BAFTA 1994, Variety Club of GB Media Award 1997. *Publications:* Guide to the Commonwealth Games 1986, The 1988 Olympics 1988, The 1992 Olympics 1992, Sport Crazy 1998, I Should Have Been At Work! (autobiog.) 2005. *Leisure interests:* golf, tennis, Brighton and Hove Albion, reading, theatre. *Address:* c/o Jane Morgan Management, Thames Wharf Studios, Rainville Road, London, W6 9HA, England. *Telephone:* (20) 7386-5345 (office). *Fax:* (20) 7386-0338 (office). *E-mail:* enquiries@janemorganmgt.com (office). *Website:* www.janemorganmgt.com (office).

LYNCH, David; American film director; b. 20 Jan. 1946, Missoula, Mont.; m. 1st Peggy Reavey 1967 (divorced); one d.; m. 2nd Mary Fisk 1977 (divorced); one s.; m. 3rd Mary Sweeney 2006 (divorced); one s.; ed Hammond High School, Alexandria, Corcoran School of Art, Washington, DC, School of Museum of Fine Arts, Boston and Pennsylvania Acad. of Fine Arts, Philadelphia; Fellow, Center for Advanced Film Studies, American Film Inst., LA 1970; Officier, Légion d'Honneur 2007; Dr hc (Royal Coll. of Art) 1991; Stockholm Int. Film Festival Lifetime Achievement Award 2003, Venice Film Festival Golden Lion 2006. *Films include:* The Grandmother 1970, Eraserhead 1977, The Elephant Man 1980, Dune 1984, Blue Velvet 1986 (Golden Palm, Cannes), Wild at Heart 1990 (Golden Palm, Cannes 1990), Storyville 1991, Twin Peaks: Fire Walk With Me 1992, Lost Highway 1997, Crumb (presenter), The Straight Stay 1999, Mullholland Drive (Best Dir, Cannes Film Festival) 2001, Darkened Room 2002, Rabbits 2002, Inland Empire 2006. *Television includes:* Twin Peaks 1990, Mulholland Drive 2000.

Address: c/o Endeavor Agency, 9701 Wilshire Boulevard, 10th Floor, Beverly Hills, CA 90212, USA (office).

LYNCH, John, BA, BL, MBA; American politician and business executive; *Governor of New Hampshire;* b. 25 Nov. 1952, Waltham, Mass; s. of William Lynch and Margaret Lynch; m. Susan Lynch 1977; one s. two d.; ed Univ. of New Hampshire, Harvard Business School, Georgetown Univ. Law Center; fmr Dir Admisssions, Harvard Business School; fmr Pres. and CEO Knoll, Inc.; apptd to Univ. System of New Hampshire's Bd of Trustees 2000, Chair. 2001–04; Pres. The Lynch Group; Gov. of New Hamphsire 2005–; fmr Pres. Univ. of New Hampshire Alumni Asscn; mem. Bd Catholic Medical Center 1997–2003, Citizens' Bank of New Hampshire, Capitol Center for the Arts; Democrat. *Address:* Office of the Governor, State House, 25 Capitol Street, Concord, NH 03301, USA (office). *Telephone:* (603) 271-2121 (office). *Fax:* (603) 271-8788 (office). *Website:* www.state.nh.us/governor (office).

LYNCH, Michael Francis, AM, CBE; Australian arts administrator; *Chief Executive, South Bank Centre, London;* b. 6 Dec. 1950, Sydney; s. of Wilfred Brian Lynch and Joan Margaret Lynch; m. 1st Jane Scott 1967 (divorced 1987); one d.; m. 2nd Irene Hannan; two step s.; m. 3rd Christine Josephine Lynch; ed Marcellin Coll., Randwick, Univ. of Sydney; began career with Australian Council for the Arts 1973; fmr Gen. Man. King O'Malley Theatre Co., Australian Theatre for Young People; Admin. Australian Nat. Playwrights Conf.; Gen. Man. Nimrod Theatre 1976–78; Casting Dir and Man. Partner Forcast Pty Ltd 1981–89; Gen. Man. Sydney Theatre Co. 1989–94, Australia Council 1994–98; Chief Exec. Sydney Opera House 1998–2002; Chief Exec. South Bank Centre, London 2002–09; fmr Chair. Australia Asia Pacific Performing Arts Centres (AAPPAC); fmr mem. Performing Arts Centres Consortium (PACC) of N America. *Films:* Crocodile Dundee (Casting Dir) 1986, Raw Nerve (producer) 1988,Crocodile Dundee in Los Angeles (Casting Dir) 2001. *Leisure interests:* film, theatre, racing, beach. *Address:* South Bank Centre, South Bank, London, SE1 8XX, England (office). *Website:* www.sbc.org.uk (office).

LYNCH, Peter; American investor; *Vice Chairman, Fidelity Management and Research Company;* b. 19 Jan. 1944; m. Carolyn Lynch; three d.; intern Fidelity Investments 1966; Man. Fidelity Magellan Fund, Boston 1977–90; Trustee Fidelity Investments 1990–; currently Vice-Chair. Fidelity Man. and Research Co.; Chair. Inner-City Scholarship Fund; f. Lynch Foundation; Pres. Catholic Schools Foundation; mem. Univ. Bd of Trustees Boston Coll.; 14 hon. degrees; Hon. Chair. Boston Coll. Ever to Excel campaign; Mother Seton Award, Interfaith Relations Award. *Publication:* One Up on Wall Street 1989, Beating the Street 1993, Learn to Earn 1996 (all with John Rothchild). *Address:* Fidelity Investments Institutional Services Company Inc., 82 Devonshire Street, Boston, MA 02109, USA. *Telephone:* (617) 563-7000. *Fax:* (617) 476-3876. *Website:* www.401k.com.

LYNCH, Philip, CBE; business executive; fmr Man. Dir Lehman Brothers; fmr Chair. Int. Petroleum Exchange; Chief Exec. Exchange Clearing House (ECHO) 1996–97, COO mem. Bd Dirs CLS Services Ltd (after acquisition of ECHO) 1997–2000 (retd).

LYNDEN-BELL, Donald, CBE, MA, PhD, FRS; British astrophysicist and academic; *Professor of Astrophysics, Institute of Astronomy, University of Cambridge;* b. 5 April 1935, Dover; s. of the late Lt-Col L. A. Lynden-Bell and of M. R. Lynden-Bell; m. Ruth M. Truscott 1961; one s. one d.; ed Marlborough Coll. and Clare Coll. Cambridge; Harkness Fellow, Calif. Inst. of Tech. and Hale Observatories 1960–62, Visiting Assoc. 1969–70, Research Fellow, then Fellow and Dir of Studies in Math., Clare Coll. Cambridge 1960–65; Asst Lecturer in Applied Math. Univ. of Cambridge 1962–65; Prin. Scientific Officer, later Sr Prin. Scientific Officer, Royal Greenwich Observatory, Herstmonceux 1965–72; Prof. of Astrophysics, Univ. of Cambridge 1972–2001; Dir Inst. of Astronomy, Cambridge 1972–77, 1982–87, 1992–94, now Prof.; Visiting Professorial Fellow, Queen's Univ. Belfast 1996–; Pres. Royal Astronomical Soc. 1985–87; Foreign Assoc., NAS 1993; Hon. mem. American Astronomical Soc. 2001; Hon. DSc (Sussex) 1987; Eddington Medal 1984, Gold Medal (Royal Astronomical Soc.) 1993, (Royal Soc. of SA), Catherine Wolf Bruce Medal of the Astronomical Soc. of the Pacific 1998, J. J. Carty Award, NAS 2000, Russell Lecturer, American Astronomical Soc. 2000, Kavli Prize 2008. *Publications:* article in journal Nature 1969 gave the theory of quasars predicting giant black holes in galactic nuclei (found 1995); contribs to Monthly Notices of Royal Astronomical Soc. *Leisure interest:* hill-walking. *Address:* Institute of Astronomy, OBS O13, The Observatories, Madingley Road, Cambridge, CB3 0HA, England. *Telephone:* (1223) 337525 (office). *E-mail:* dlb@ast.cam.ac.uk (office). *Website:* www.cirs.net/researchers/Astronomy/Lynden-Bell (office).

LYNE, Adrian; British film director; b. Peterborough; m. Samantha Lyne; one d.; ed Highgate School; joined J. Walter Thompson (advertising agency) in post room, later became asst producer of commercials; with two pnrs est. Jennie & Lyne 1971; dir of commercials; Palme d'Or, Cannes Commercial Film Festival 1976, 1978. *Films include:* Mr. Smith 1976, Foxes 1980, Flashdance 1983, 9½ Weeks 1986, Fatal Attraction 1987, Jacob's Ladder (also co-writer) 1990, Indecent Proposal 1993, Lolita 1997, Unfaithful 2002. *Address:* c/o ICM, Oxford House, 76 Oxford Street, London, W1D 1BS, England. *Telephone:* (20) 7636-6565. *Fax:* (20) 7323-0101. *E-mail:* directors@icmlondon.co.uk.

LYNE, Sir Roderic Michael John, KBE, CMG, BA; British diplomatist (retd) and business consultant; *Special Adviser, BP plc;* b. 31 March 1948; s. of the late Air Vice-Marshal Michael Lyne and Avril Joy Buckley; m. Amanda Mary Smith 1969; two s. one d.; ed Eton Coll., Univ. of Leeds; joined Diplomatic Service 1970, British Embassy, Moscow 1972–74, British Embassy, Senegal 1974–76; Eastern Europe and Soviet Dept, FCO 1976–78, Rhodesia Dept 1979, Asst Pvt. Sec. to Foreign and Commonwealth Sec. 1979–82; Perm. Mission to UN, New York 1982–86; Visiting Research Fellow, Royal Inst. of Int. Affairs (Chatham House) 1986–87, mem. Council 2008–; Head of Chancery and Political Section, Embassy, Moscow 1987–90; Head of Soviet Dept, FCO 1990–91, of Eastern Dept 1992–93; Pvt. Sec. to Prime Minister 1993–96; Dir of Policy Devt for CIS, Middle East and Africa, British Gas PLC 1996; Perm. Rep. to UN, Geneva 1997–2000; Amb. to Russia 2000–04; Special Adviser, BP plc, HSBC Bank plc 2004–07; Chair. Int. Advisory Bd Altimo 2006–07; mem. Bd of Dirs Aricom 2006–, Accor 2006–, Russo-British Chamber of Commerce 2006–; Sr Adviser, JPMorgan Chase Bank 2007–; Visiting Prof., Kingston Univ. Business School 2005–, mem. Bd Govs Kingston Univ. 2007–; Hon. Prof., Moscow Higher School of Social and Econ. Studies 2001; Hon. PhD (Leeds) 2002; Hon. DBA (Kingston) 2004; Hon. DLitt (Heriot-Watt) 2004. *Publication:* Engaging with Russia: The Next Phase – Report to the Trilateral Commission (co-author) 2006 (updated edns in Japanese and Russian) 2007. *Leisure interests:* sport, grandchildren. *Address:* 39 Richmond Park Road, London, SW14 8JU, England (home). *E-mail:* Roderic.Lyne@btinternet.com (office).

LYNGSTAD, Anni-Frid (Frida); Norwegian singer; b. 15 Nov. 1945, Ballangen, Narvik, Norway; m. Benny Andersson 1978 (divorced 1981); one s. one d. (from previous relationship); leader of own dance band Anni-Frid Four; mem. pop group ABBA 1973–82; winner, Eurovision Song Contest 1974; world-wide tours; concerts include Royal Performance, Stockholm 1976, Royal Albert Hall, London 1977, UNICEF concert, New York 1979, Wembley Arena 1979; reunion with ABBA, Swedish TV This Is Your Life 1986; solo artist 1983–; World Music Award, Best Selling Swedish Artist 1993. *Film:* ABBA: The Movie 1977. *Recordings:* albums: with ABBA: Waterloo 1974, ABBA 1976, Greatest Hits 1976, Arrival 1977, The Album 1978, Voulez-Vous 1979, Greatest Hits Vol. 2 1979, Super Trouper 1980, The Visitors 1981, The Singles: The First Ten Years 1982, Thank You For The Music 1983, Absolute ABBA 1988, ABBA Gold 1992, More ABBA Gold 1993, Forever Gold 1998, The Definitive Collection 2001; solo: Frida Alone 1976, Something's Going On 1982, Shine 1983, Djupa Andetag 1996, Frida 1967–72 1998, Frida: The Mixes 1998, Svenska Popfavoriter 1998; singles include: with ABBA: Ring Ring 1973, Waterloo 1974, Mamma Mia 1975, Dancing Queen 1976, Fernando 1976, Money Money Money 1976, Knowing Me Knowing You 1977, The Name Of The Game 1977, Take A Chance On Me 1978, Summer Night City 1978, Chiquitita 1979, Does Your Mother Know? 1979, Angel Eyes/Voulez-Vous 1979, Gimme Gimme Gimme (A Man After Midnight) 1979, I Have A Dream 1979, The Winner Takes It All 1980, Super Trouper 1980, On And On And On 1981, Lay All Your Love On Me 1981, One Of Us 1981, When All Is Said And Done 1982, Head Over Heels 1982, The Day Before You Came 1982, Under Attack 1982, Thank You For The Music 1983; solo: Time (duet with B. A. Robertson). *Website:* www.abbasite.com.

LYNN, Dame Vera, DBE; British singer; b. (Vera Margaret Welch), 20 March 1917; d. of Bertram Welch and Ann Welch; m. Harry Lewis 1939; one d.; ed Brampton Road School, East Ham; began singing aged seven; adopted her grandmother's maiden name Lynn as her stage name; joined singing troupe 1928; ran dancing school 1932; broadcast with Joe Loss and joined Charlie Kunz band 1935; singer with Ambrose Orchestra 1937–40, then went solo; voted most popular singer in Daily Express competition 1939; own radio show Sincerely Yours 1941–47; sang to troops abroad during World War II, named 'Forces' Sweetheart'; appeared in Applesauce, London 1941; post-war radio and TV shows and numerous appearances abroad including Denmark, Canada, South Africa and Australia; most successful record Auf Wiederseh'n; Pres. Printers' Charitable Corpn 1980; Hon. Citizen Winnipeg 1974; Freedom of City of London 1978; Commdr Order of Orange-Nassau (Holland), Burma Star Medal and War Medal 1985; Variety Club Int. Humanitarian Award, European Woman of Achievement Award 1994. *Publications:* Vocal Refrain (autobiog.) 1975, We'll Meet Again (with Robin Cross) 1989, The Woman Who Won the War (with Robin Cross and Jenny de Gex) 1990, Unsung Heroines 1990. *Leisure interests:* gardening, painting, sewing, swimming. *Address:* c/o David Higham Associates, 5-8 Lower John Street, Golden Square, London, W1F 9HA, England.

LYNTON, Michael, MBA; American business executive; *Chairman and CEO, Sony Pictures Entertainment;* b. 1 Jan. 1960, London, UK; s. of Mark O. L. Lynton and Marion Sonnenberg; m. Elizabeth Jane Alter; two d.; ed Harvard Coll., Harvard Business School; Assoc., The First Boston Corpn 1982–85; Sr Vice-Pres. Disney Publishing Group 1987–93, Pres. Hollywood Pictures, The Walt Disney Co. 1993–96; Chair. and CEO The Penguin Group 1996–2000; Pres. AOL Int. 2000–03, also Pres. for Int. Efforts and Exec. Vice-Pres. AOL Time Warner Inc. 2002–03; Chair. and CEO Sony Pictures Entertainment 2004–. *Address:* Sony Pictures Entertainment, 10202 West Washington Boulevard, Culver City, CA 90232, USA. *Telephone:* (310) 244-4000 (office). *Fax:* (310) 244-2626 (office). *Website:* www.sonypictures.com (office).

LYON, Mary Frances, BA, PhD, ScD, FRS, FIBiol; British geneticist; b. 15 May 1925, Norwich; d. of Clifford James Lyon and Louise Frances Lyon (née Kirby); ed Woking Grammar School, Girton Coll. Cambridge; on Medical Research Council (MRC) Scientific Staff, Inst. of Animal Genetics Edin. 1950–55; Scientific Staff MRC Radiobiology Unit, Harwell 1955–90, Head of Genetics Section 1962–87; Clothworkers Visiting Research Fellow, Girton Coll. Cambridge 1970–71; Foreign Assoc. NAS 1979; Foreign Hon. mem. American Acad. of Arts and Sciences 1980; Francis Amory Prize, American Acad. of Arts and Sciences 1977, Royal Medal, Royal Soc. 1984, San Remo Int. Prize for Genetics 1985, Gairdner Int. Award 1985, William Allan Award, American Soc. of Human Genetics 1986, Wolf Prize in Medicine 1997, Mendel Medal, Genetics Soc. 2003, March of Dimes Prize in Developmental Biology 2004, Pearl Meisler Greengard Award 2006, Rosenstiel Award, Brandeis Univ. 2007. *Publications:* papers on genetics in scientific journals. *Address:*

Medical Research Council Mammalian Genetics Unit, Harwell, Didcot, Oxon., OX11 0RD, England. *Telephone:* (1235) 841000. *Fax:* (1235) 841200. *E-mail:* m.lyon@har.mrc.ac.uk (office).

LYONS, Sir John, Kt, LittD, PhD, FBA; British academic; *Visiting Professor of Linguistics, University of Sussex;* b. 23 May 1932, Manchester; s. of Michael Austin Lyons and Mary Bridget O'Sullivan; m. Danielle Jacqueline Simonet 1959; two d.; ed St Bede's Coll. Manchester and Christ's Coll. Cambridge; Lecturer in Comparative Linguistics, SOAS, Univ. of London 1957–61; Lecturer in Linguistics and Fellow of Christ's Coll., Univ. of Cambridge 1961; Prof. of Gen. Linguistics, Univ. of Edin. 1964–76; Prof. of Linguistics, Univ. of Sussex 1976–84, Dean, School of Social Sciences 1979–81, Pro-Vice-Chancellor 1981–84, Visiting Prof. of Linguistics 1984–; Master of Trinity Hall, Cambridge 1984–2000; Hon. Fellow Christ's Coll. Cambridge 1985; Hon. mem. Linguistic Soc. of America; Dr hc (Univ. Catholique, Louvain) 1980; Hon. DLitt (Reading) 1986, (Edin.) 1988, (Sussex) 1990, (Antwerp) 1992. *Publications:* Structural Semantics 1963, Introduction to Theoretical Linguistics 1968, Chomsky 1970, 1977, 1991, New Horizons in Linguistics 1970, Semantics 1 and 2 1977, Language and Linguistics 1980, Language, Meaning and Context 1981, Natural Language and Universal Grammar 1991, Linguistic Semantics 1995.

LYONS, Sir Michael, Kt, KBE, PhD; British economist, politician and television industry executive; *Chairman, BBC Trust;* b. 1950; m.; three c.; ed Stratford Grammar School, Middlesex Univ. and Queen Mary Coll., Univ. of London; worked as part-time street trader at Bell Street Market, London to fund higher educ.; furthered career as economist in public sector; fmr Lecturer in Econs, Univ. of Nottingham, Wallbrook Coll., London; mem. (Labour) Birmingham City Council 1980–83; Chief Exec. Wolverhampton Borough Council 1985–90, Notts. County Council 1990–94, Birmingham City Council 1994–2001; Prof. of Public Policy, Birmingham Univ. 2001–06; responsible for Lyons Inquiry into Local Govt, commissioned by Deputy Prime Minister and Chancellor of the Exchequer 2004–07; Chair. BBC Trust 2007–; Chair. English Cities Fund 2002–, City of Birmingham Symphony Orchestra 2001–07, Regional Advisory Council, ITV –2006; Deputy Chair. and Acting Chair. The Audit Comm. 2003–06; Dir (non-exec.) Central Television 2003–06, MouchelParkman PLC, Wragge and Co., SQW Ltd. *Address:* BBC Trust Unit, Room 211, 35 Marylebone High Street, London, W1U 4AA, England (office). *Telephone:* (870) 010-3100 (office). *E-mail:* trust.enquiries@bbc.co.uk (office). *Website:* www.bbc.co.uk/bbctrust (office).

LYONS, Richard Kent, BS, PhD; American economist, academic and university administrator; *Bank of America Dean, Haas School of Business, University of California, Berkeley;* b. 10 Feb. 1961, Palo Alto, Calif.; m.; two c.; ed Univ. of California, Berkeley, Massachusetts Inst. of Tech.; Research Analyst, Financial Industries Div., SRI Int., Menlo Park, Calif. 1983–84; Assoc. and Asst Prof., School of Business and School of Int. Affairs, Columbia Univ. 1987–93; Asst Prof. of Int. Business, Haas School of Business, Univ. of California, Berkeley 1993–96, Assoc. Prof. 1996–2000, Prof. 2000–04, Acting Dean 2004–05, Exec. Assoc. Dean 2005–06, Bank of America Dean 2008–, S.K. and Angela Chan Chair. in Global Man., Faculty Dir Blum Center for Developing Economies; Chief Learning Officer, Goldman Sachs, New York 2006–08; Assoc. Ed. California Management Review; consultant to IMF, World Bank, US Fed. Reserve System, EC, UN, Citibank; mem. Council on Foreign Relations; fmr Chair., Bd of Dirs Matthews Asian Funds; fmr mem., Bd of Dirs iShares; NSF Grad. Fellowship 1984–87, Int. Affairs Fellowship, Council on Foreign Relations 1993, Schwabacher Fellowship, Univ. of California, Berkeley 1994, Nat. Science Foundation Grants 1994–97, 1997–2000, 2000–03; Distinguished Teaching Award, Univ. of Calif., Berkeley 1998. *Publications:* The Microstructure Approach to Exchange Rates 2001; numerous articles and papers. *Address:* Office of the Dean, Haas School of Business, University of California, Berkeley, CA 94720-1900, USA (office). *Telephone:* (510) 643-2027 (office). *Fax:* (510) 643-1420 (office). *E-mail:* lyons@haas.berkeley.edu (office). *Website:* faculty.haas.berkeley.edu/lyons (office).

LYSSARIDES, Vassos, MD; Cypriot politician; b. 13 May 1920, Lefkara; s. of Michael Lyssarides and Eleni Lyssanides; m. Barbara Cornwall 1963; ed Univ. of Athens; mem. House of Reps 1960–, Pres. 1985–91; Pres. Socialist Party of Cyprus (EDEK) (now Movt of Social Democrats (KISOS)) 1969–2002, Hon. Pres. 2002–; Sec.-Gen. Int. Cttee of Solidarity with the Struggle of the Peoples of Southern Africa; Vice-Pres. Presidium, Afro-Asian Peoples' Solidarity Org.; Hon. Pres. Nicosia Medical Assen Hippocrates. *Leisure interests:* poetry, painting. *Address:* PO Box 21064, 1096 Nicosia, Cyprus. *Telephone:* 22-666763 (office); 22-665385 (home). *Fax:* 22-666762 (office). *E-mail:* info@kisos.org (office). *Website:* www.kisos.org (office); www.lyssarides.com (home).

LYTH, Ragnar Vilhelm, BA; Swedish theatre director and academic; *Head of Theatre Directing, Swedish Dramatic Institute;* b. 2 April 1944, Karlstad; s. of Arne Lyth and Reidunn Eleonore; m. 1st Karin Falk 1967; m. 2nd Kerstin Österlin 1996; two s.; ed Nat. Film School, Swedish Dramatic Inst.; theatre and TV dir in Sweden, Norway and Denmark; represented Sweden at int. TV festival 'INPUT', Philadelphia, Banff, Montreal 1985, 1989, 1993; Head of Stage Dirs, Swedish Dramatic Inst. 1984–86, currently Head of Theatre Directing; Chair. Swedish Dirs' Union; Head, Vestmanlands Theatre; Prof. of Theatre Direction; Sweden Art Award. *Plays directed include:* The Wild Duck 1997, Hedda Gabler 1998, Faust (I and II) 1999, Temperance 2000, The General Inspector 2001, Twelfth Night 2002, The Visit 2003, Endgame 2004, Tartuffe 2005. *Television:* Death Dance 1981, Hamlet 1985, Don Juan 1988, Maclean 1991. *Publications:* Theatre Life 2003. *Leisure interest:* nature. *Address:* Sjöbjörnsvägen 25, 11767 Stockholm, Sweden. *Telephone:* (8) 19-88-93. *E-mail:* ragnar.lyth@draminst.se (office); lyth@chello.se (home).

LYTVYN, Volodymyr Mykhaylovych, DrHis; Ukrainian academic and politician; *Chairman, Verkhovna Rada (Parliament);* b. 28 April 1956, Sloboda, Zhytomyr Oblast; s. of Mykhaylo Lytvyn and Olga Lytvyn; m. Tetyana Lytvyn; one s. one d.; ed Kyiv T. Shevchenko State (now Nat.) Univ.; researcher, Docent, Vice-Rector Kyiv State Univ. 1978–86; Head of Dept Ukrainian Ministry of Higher Educ. 1986–89; Lecturer, consultant, Asst to Sec., Cen. Cttee of Ukrainian Komsomol 1989–91; Docent and Prof., Kyiv State Univ. 1991–94; Adviser to Ukrainian Pres. 1994–2002, Deputy Head, Admin. to the Pres. 1995–96, Head Admin. 1999–2002; apptd to Nat. Security and Defence Council 1999; mem. Co-ordination Cttee on Problems of Foreign Policy 1996–; elected to Verkovna Rada (Parl.) 2002, Chair. 2002–06 2008–; currently Leader, People's Party (Narodna Partiya); Corresp. mem. Ukrainian Acad. of Sciences. *Publications include:* Political Arena of Ukraine 1995; more than 200 articles on contemporary politics. *Address:* Office of the Chairman, Verkhovna Rada, 01008 Kyiv, vul. M. Hrushevskoho 5 (office); People's Party (Narodna Partiya), 01034 Kyiv, vul. Reitarska 6a, Ukraine (office). *Telephone:* (44) 255-21-15 (Verkhovna Rada) (office); (44) 270-61-86 (Narodna Partiya (office). *Fax:* (44) 253-32-17 (Verkhovna Rada) (office); (44) 270-65-91 (Narodna Partiya (office). *E-mail:* umz@rada.gov.ua (office); info@narodna.org.ua (office). *Website:* www.rada.gov.ua (office); www.narodna.org.ua (office).

LYU, Joseph Jye-Cherng; Taiwanese government official and banker; ed Nat. Chengchi Univ., Kellogg Grad. School of Man., Northwestern Univ., USA; fmr Assoc. Prof. Nat. Chengchi Univ.; fmr Vice-Pres. Bank of New York, Taipei Br. and New York Head Office, Banque Nationale de Paris, Taiwan; Pres. Land Bank of Taiwan –2004; Chair. Bank of Taiwan 2004–06; Minister of Finance 2006; Minister without Portfolio 2006–; fmr Chair. Bankers Asscn of Taiwan; fmr Man. Dir Bd Trust Asscn; fmr Dir Mega Financial Holding Co., Financial Information Service Co. Ltd, Taiwan Futures Exchange. *Address:* c/o Ministry of Finance, 2 Ai Kuo West Road, Taipei 100, Taiwan (office).

LYUBIMOV, Yuri Petrovich; Russian/Israeli/Hungarian theatrical director and actor; *Artistic Director, Moscow Taganka Theatre;* b. 30 Sept. 1917, Yaroslavl'; m. Katalin Koncz; one s.; ed Vakhtangov Theatre Studio; served in Soviet Army 1939–47; Teacher and Dir, Shukin Drama School (Vakhtangov Theatre) 1953–64; Founder and Artistic Dir, Moscow Theatre of Drama and Comedy (Taganka) 1964–84, 1989–; deprived of Soviet citizenship 1983, left Soviet Union 1984, acquired Israeli citizenship 1987, returned 1988, citizenship restored 1989, acquired Hungarian citizenship 1999; numerous decorations including Medal for the Defence of Leningrad 1943, for the Defence of Moscow 1944, State Prizes 1952, 1997, Order of the Labour Red Banner 1977, State Prize of Russia 1991, Order of the Great Patriotic War 1996, Services to the Motherland, 1st Class 1997, Golden Medal of Honour of the Pres. of Hungary 1997, Triumph Premium 1998, Nat. Order of the Repub. of Hungary 2002, Kt Commdr of Arts and Literature (France) 2002, Star of Italian Solidarity 2003, Estonian Order of the Cross of Terra Mariana 2003, Royal Order of the Polar Star (Sweden) 2004, Chevalier Cross Order of Honour of Poland 2004; numerous awards including Honoured Artist of the RSFSR 1954, Grand Prix, Int. Theatre Festival, Bonn 1998, Grand Prix, Int. Theatre Festival, Thessalonika 1999, Golden Mask Theatre Prize 2000, Diploma of American Acad. of Arts 2001, K. Stanislavsky Fund Prize 2003. *Roles include:* Oleg Koshevoy (The Young Guard, by Fadeyev), Shubin (On the Eve, by Turgenev), Chris (All My Sons, by Arthur Miller), Benedict (Much Ado About Nothing), Mozart (The Little Tragedies, by Pushkin); prominent in Soviet films 1947–, including Busy Stock, Robinson Crusoe, Cuban Cossacks. *Theatre productions include:* The Good Man from Szechuan 1963, Ten Days that Shook the World 1965, Mother (Gorky) 1969, Hamlet 1972, Boris Godunov (Moscow) 1982, Crime and Punishment (London) 1983, The Devils (London, Paris) 1985, Hamlet (London) 1987, Self-Murderer (Moscow) 1990, Electra (Moscow) 1992, Zhivago (Vienna) 1993, The Seagull (Athens) 1993, Creditors (Athens) 1994, Medea (Athens) 1995, The Brothers Karamazov (Moscow) 1997, Marat-Sade (Moscow) 1998, Sharashka (Moscow) 1998, Chronicles (Moscow) 2000, Eugene Onegin (Moscow) 2000, Theatrical Novel (Moscow) 2000, Socrates (Moscow) 2001, Faust (Moscow) 2002, Before and After 2003, Go and Stop the Progress (Moscow) 2004 and others (total of 104). *Opera productions include:* Al gran sole carico d'amore (La Scala) 1975, Boris Godunov (La Scala) 1981, Lulu (Turin, Chicago) 1983, Rigoletto (Florence) 1984, Hovancshina (La Scala) 1985, St Matthew's Passion (La Scala) 1985, Jenufa (London) 1986, Eugene Onegin (Bonn) 1987, The Queen of Spades (Karlsruhe), 1990, Lady Macbeth of Mtsensk (Hamburg) 1990, Nabucco (Bonn) 1997, Love for Three Oranges (Munich) 1991 and others. *Publications:* Le Feu Sacré 1985, Zapiski starego trepacha (Notes from an old Blabbermouth) 2000; several articles in the field of theatre. *Leisure interests:* music, cinema, gardening, poetry. *Address:* Taganka Theatre, Zemlanoy val 76, Moscow 109004 Russia (office). *Telephone:* (095) 915-10-37 (office); (095) 290-19-34 (home). *Fax:* (495) 764-92-24 (office); (095) 290-19-34 (home). *E-mail:* taganka-theatre@mtu-net.ru (office). *Website:* www.taganka-theatre.ru (office).

LYUBSHIN, Stanislav Andreyevich; Russian actor; b. 6 April 1933; m.; two s.; ed Shchepkin Theatre School; worked with various Moscow theatres: Sovremennik, Taganka, Yermolova, Malaya Bronnaya 1959–80; one of prin. actors with Moscow Arts Theatre 1980–, Anton Chekhov Arts Theatre 1987–; film debut 1959; RSFSR People's Artist 1981. *Films include:* Segodnya uvolneniya ne budet (There Will Be No Leave Today) 1959, Tretya raketa (The Third Missile) 1963, Esli ty prav... 1963, Mne dvadtsat let (I am Twenty) 1964, Kakoe ono, more? 1964, Bolshaya ruda (The Big Ore) 1964, Alpiyskaya ballada 1965, Shchit i mech (The Shield and the Sword) 1968, Krasnaya ploshchad (Red Square) 1970, Pechki-lavochki (Happy Go Lucky, aka The Ship Crowd) 1972, Moya zhizn 1972, Monolog 1972, Slovo dlia zashchity (Speech for the Defence) 1976, Sentimentalnyy roman (Sentimental Romance)

1976, Pozovi menya v dal' svetluyu (Call Me from Afar) 1976, Step (The Steppe) 1977, Vstrecha (The Meeting) 1979, Tema (The Theme) 1979, Pyat vecherov (Five Evenings) 1979, My vesely, schastlivy, talantlivy! (We Are Cheerful, Happy, Talented!) 1986, Kin-Dza-Dza 1986, Zabavy molodykh (Joys of the Youth) 1987, Chyornyy monakh (The Black Monk) 1988, Vechnyy muzh 1989, Kanuvshee vremya 1989, Shkura (Skin) 1991, Nelyubov (No Love) 1991, Uvidet Parizh i umeret (To See Paris and Die) 1992, Bolshoy kapkan, ili solo dlya koshki pri polnoy lune (Big Trap, or Solo for Cat Under Full Moon) 1992, Tsar Ivan Groznyy (Tsar Ivan the Terrible) 1993, Mechty idiota (Idiot Dreams) 1993, Terra incognita 1994, Tsarevich Aleksei 1996, Kino pro kino 2002. *Television includes:* Pervaya lyubov (First Love) 1968, Ne strelyayte v belykh lebedey 1980, Dym (mini-series) 1992. *Address:* Vernadskogo prosp. 123, Apt 171, 117571 Moscow, Russia. *Telephone:* (495) 433-35-14.

LŽICAR, Josef, DIur; Czech lawyer; b. 6 June 1944, Švábenice; s. of Josef Lžicar and Anna Lžicar; m. Zdenka; one s.; ed Charles Univ., Prague; lawyer and advocate 1967–; Chief of Office of Pres. of Czechoslovak Repub. 1989–1990; mem. Czech Chamber of Advocates 1990–, Czech Helsinki Cttee 1990–. *Leisure interest:* ornithology. *Address:* c/o Czech Helsinki Committee, Ostrovského 3, 150 00 Prague 5; Sokolovská 24–37, 18600 Prague 8, Czech Republic (office). *Telephone:* (2) 22325334 (office). *E-mail:* sekr@helcom.cz.

M

MA, Chung-Ch'en (see MA, Zhongchen).

MA, Feng, (Ma Shuming); Chinese writer; b. 1922, Xiaoyi Co., Shanxi Prov.; ed Lu Xun Acad. of Literature and Art, Yan'an; joined 8th Route Army and CCP 1938; first short story (First Reconnaissance) published 1942; mem. China-Britain Friendship Asscn 1983–; Vice-Chair. CPPCC Prov. Cttee, Shanxi 1986–; Pres. Soc. of Chinese Folk Literature 1987–; Exec. Vice-Chair. Nat. Cttee China Fed. of Literary and Art Circles 1988–; Vice-Chair. Chinese Writers' Asscn 1990–; mem. Foreign Affairs Cttee. *Publications include:* Heroes of Lüliang (with Xi Rong), Liu Hulan (novel), The Young People of One Village (film script) and numerous short stories, including The Marriage Ceremony (Nat. Short Story Award Winner 1980). *Address:* China Federation of Literary and Art Circles, 10 Nong Zhan Guan Nanli, Beijing 100026, People's Republic of China (office). *Telephone:* 5005588.

MA, Fucai, BEng; Chinese oil industry executive; *Vice Director, State Energy Office;* b. 1947; ed Beijing Petroleum Inst.; Deputy Dir, later Dir Shengli Petroleum Admin Bureau 1990–96; Asst to Pres., China Nat. Petroleum Corpn (CNPC) Nov.-Dec. 1996, Vice-Pres. 1996–98, Pres. 1998–2004 (resgnd) Chair. PetroChina 1999–2004; Vice-Dir State Energy Office 2005–; Dir Daqing Petroleum Admin Bureau 1997–98; Alt. mem. 16th CCP Cen. Cttee 2002–07. *Address:* State Energy Office, Beijing, People's Republic of China (office).

MA, Jack, BA; Chinese business executive; *Chairman and CEO, Alibaba Group;* b. Nov. 1964, Hangzhou, Zhejiang Prov.; ed Hangzhou Teacher's Institute; began as English teacher, Hangzhou Electronics and Eng Inst.; f. China Pages (chinapages.com), regarded to be China's first internet-based co. 1995; Head, Information Dept China Int. Electronic Commerce Center (CIECC) 1998–99; f. Alibaba Group (China's largest e-commerce co.), Hangzhou, Chair. and CEO 1999–; chosen by World Econ. Forum as one of Young Global Leaders; named one of the "25 Most Powerful Businesspeople in Asia" by Fortune Magazine 2005, a "Businessperson of the Year" by BusinessWeek Magazine 2007, one of the 30 "World's Best CEOs" by Barron's 2008. *Address:* Alibaba.com, 6th Floor Chuangye Mansion, East Software Park, No. 99 Huaxing Road, Hangzou, Zhejiang Province, 310012 (office); Alibaba.com Technology Corpn Ltd, Room 408, Fanli Building, 22 Chaoyangwai Street, Chaoyang District, Beijing, 100020, People's Republic of China (office). *Telephone:* (571) 85022088 (Hangzhou) (office); (10) 6588-9698 (office). *Fax:* (571) 88157866 (Hangzhou) (office); (10) 6588-9699 (office). *Website:* www .alibaba.com (office).

MA, Kai; Chinese politician; *Secretary-General, State Council;* b. 1946, Shanghai, Jinshan; ed People's Univ. of China; fmr Deputy Dir State Comm. of Reform for Econ. Systems; Deputy Dir State Planning Comm. 1995–98; Vice-Sec.-Gen. State Council 1998–2003, Sec.-Gen. 2008–; Minister of Nat. Devt and Reform Comm. (f. as State Planning Comm. 1952, renamed State Devt Planning Comm. 1998, merged with State Council Office for Restructuring the Econ. System and several offices under State Econ. and Trade Comm., renamed Nat. Devt and Reform Comm. 2003) 2003–08; mem. 16th CCP Cen. Cttee 2002–07, mem. 17th CCP Cen. Cttee 2007–; Pres. Nat. School of Admin 2007–. *Address:* State Council, Great Hall of the People, West Edge, Tiananmen Square, Beijing, People's Republic of China (office). *Website:* english.gov.cn (office).

MA, Mary, BA; Chinese business executive; *Non Executive Vice-Chair, Lenovo Group Holdings;* b. (Ma Xuezheng), Tianjin; ed Capital Normal Univ. and King's Coll., London, UK; began career as English trans. at Chinese Acad. of Sciences; Exec. Dir and Sr Vice-Pres. Legend Holdings Ltd (name changed to Lenovo Group Holdings 2003), Chief Financial Officer 2000–07, Non-Exec. Vice-Chair. 2007–; ind. Dir (non-exec.) Standard Chartered Bank (Hong Kong) Ltd, Sohu.com Inc. 2000–; mem. Hong Kong Dirs' Soc.; ranked by Fortune magazine amongst 50 Most Powerful Women in Business outside the US (3rd) 2001, (fifth) 2002, (fifth) 2003, (14th) 2004, (ninth) 2005, (10th) 2006, ranked by Forbes magazine amongst 100 Most Powerful Women (80th) 2004, (57th) 2005. *Address:* Lenovo Group Holdings, No. 6 Chuang Ye Road, Shangdi Information Industry Base, Haidan District, Beijing 100085, People's Republic of China (office). *Telephone:* (10) 58868888 (office). *E-mail:* cmk@ lenovo.com (office). *Website:* www.lenovo.com (office).

MA, Mingzhe, PhD; Chinese business executive; *Chairman and CEO, China Ping An Insurance Corporation;* b. 1960; ed Zhongnan Univ. of Econs and Law; fmr Deputy Man. China Merchants Shekou Industrial Zone Social Insurance Co.; f. Shekou Ping An Insurance Co. (precursor to Ping An Insurance Group Co.) 1988, Chair. China Ping An Insurance Co. Ltd 1994–, also CEO 2001–; mem. 10th CPPCC Nat. Cttee. *Address:* China Ping An Insurance Corpn, Ping An Building, Bagua No. 3 Road, Shenzhen 518029, Guangdong (office); Ping An Insurance (Hong Kong) Co. Ltd, 11th Floor, Dah Sing Financial Centre, 108 Gloucester Road, Wanchai, Hong Kong Special Administrative Region, People's Republic of China (office). *Telephone:* (755) 82262888 (Shenzhen) (office); 28271883 (Hong Kong) (office). *Fax:* (755) 82414817 (Shenzhen) (office); 28020018 (Hong Kong) (office). *E-mail:* IR@paic .com.cn (office). *Website:* www.pingan.com.cn (office).

MA, Qingyun, MArch; Chinese architect and academic; *Dean, School of Architecture, University of Southern California;* b. 1965, Xi'an; ed Tsinghua Univ., Grad. School of Fine Arts, Univ. of Pennsylvania, USA; Architect, Kohn Pederson and Fox, New York 1991–95; Kling Lindquist 1997–99; Assoc. Prof. and Asst Dean of Architecture, Shenzhen Univ. 1995–96; f. MADA s.p.a.m., New York 1995–, Beijing and Shanghai 1999–; Lecturer, Architecture Dept,

Univ. of Pennsylvania 1997–2000; Visiting Lecturer, Tongji Univ., Shanghai 2001–, Nanjing Univ. 2002–, Berlage Inst., Netherlands 2003, ETH 2004, Tech. Univ., Berlin 2004; Dean, School of Architecture, Univ. of Southern California 2007–, Della and Harry MacDonald's Dean Chair. in Architecture 2007–; fmr Visiting Prof., Harvard Univ., Columbia Univ., Universität Karlsruhe, École Speciale d'Architecture, Paris; Frank Miles Day Memorial Prize, Design Vanguard Award, Architectural Record, Phaidon's Emerging Design Talents designation, New Trends of Architecture designation, Euro-Asia Foundation. *Buildings designed include:* Longyang Residential Complex, Shanghai, Silk Tower, Xi'an, Qingpu Community Island, Shanghai, Centennial TV and Radio Center, Xi'an, Tianyi City Plaza, Ningpo. *Address:* Dean's Office, School of Architecture, University of Southern California, Watt Hall, Suite 204, Los Angeles, CA 90089-0291, USA (office). *Telephone:* (213) 740-2723 (office). *Fax:* (213) 740-8884 (office). *E-mail:* archdean@usc.edu (office). *Website:* arch.usc.edu (office).

MA, Qizhi; Chinese politician; *Chairman, Ningxia Hui Autonomous Regional People's Government;* b. Nov. 1943, Jingyuan, Ningxia Hui Autonomous Region; ed Cen. Univ. for Nationalities; joined CCP 1972; teacher, Yucheng Middle School, Anshan Iron and Steel Works, Yinchuan City No. 2 Middle School, Ningxia Hui Autonomous Region; cadre of Communist Youth League, Ningxia Hui Autonomous Region Cttee; Vice-Sec. CCP Guyuan Pref. Cttee; Cttee Vice-Sec., now Dir-Gen. CCP Yinnan Pref.; Dir Propaganda Dept of CCP Ningxia Hui Autonomous Region Cttee 1969–93, Vice-Sec. 1993–98; Vice-Chair. Ningxia Hui Autonomous Regional People's Govt 1995–96, Chair. 1996–; Alt. mem. 14th CCP Cen. Cttee 1992–97, 15th CCP Cen. Cttee 1997–2002, mem. 16th CCP Cen. Cttee 2002–07. *Address:* c/o People's Government of Ningxia Hui Autonomous Region, Yinchuan, Ningxia, People's Republic of China.

MA, Wanfan, (Mayi); Chinese business executive; b. 1930, Longkou Co., Shandong Prov.; Chair. China Nat. Chemicals Corpn 1989; mem. 7th CPPCC Nat. Cttee 1987–92, 8th Nat. Cttee 1993–98, 9th Nat. Cttee 1998–2003. *Address:* c/o China National Chemicals Corporation, 16 Hepingli 7 District, Beijing 100013, People's Republic of China (office).

MA, Wanqi; Chinese politician; b. 1919, Nanhai Co., Guandong Prov.; mem. 5th Nat. Cttee CPPCC 1978–82, Perm. mem. 6th Nat. Cttee CPPCC 1983–88, Vice-Chair. 8th Nat. Cttee CPPCC 1993–98, 9th Nat. Cttee 1998–2003; mem. 6th Standing Cttee NPC 1986–88, 7th Standing Cttee 1988–92; Vice-Pres. All-China Sports Fed. *Address:* c/o National Committee of Chinese People's Political Consultative Conference, 23 Taiping Qiao Street, Beijing, People's Republic of China (office).

MA, Ying-jeou, LLM, SJD; Taiwanese politician, academic and head of state; *President;* b. 13 July 1950, Hong Kong; m. Chow Mei-ching; two d.; ed Nat. Taiwan Univ., New York Univ. Law School, Harvard Univ. Law School, USA; with Marine Corps, Navy 1972–74; Legal Consultant First Nat. Bank of Boston, USA 1980–81; Research Consultant Univ. of Maryland Law School 1981; Assoc. Cole and Deitz Law School, New York 1981; Deputy Dir First Bureau, Office of the Pres. of Taiwan 1981–88; Adjunct Assoc. Prof., Graduate School of Law, Nat. Chengchi Univ. 1981, Assoc. Prof. of Law, Nat. Chengchi Univ. Law School 1997–98; Deputy Sec.-Gen. Cen. Cttee, Kuomintang (KMT) 1984–88, Chair. 2005–07 (resgnd); Chair. Research, Devt and Evaluation Comm., Exec. Yuan 1988–91; Sr Vice-Chair. Mainland Affairs Council 1991–93; Minister of Justice 1993–96; Minister of State without Portfolio 1996–97; Mayor of Taipei 1998–2006; Pres. 2008–. *Publications:* Legal Problems of Seabed Boundary Delimitation in the East China Sea 1984, The Diauyutai (Senkaku) Islets and the Maritime Boundary Problems in the East China Sea (Chinese) 1986, Cross-Straits Relations at a Crossroad: Impasse of Breakthrough 2001; 17 academic papers. *Leisure interests:* jogging, music, charity. *Address:* Office of the President, 122 Chungking South Rd, Sec. 1, 10048 Taipei (office); Kuomintang, 232 Sec. 2, Bade Rd, Taipei 10492, Taiwan (office). *Telephone:* (2) 23113731 (office); (2) 87711234 (office). *Fax:* (2) 23311604 (office); (2) 23434561 (office). *E-mail:* public@mail.oop.gov.tw (office). *Website:* www.president.gov.tw (office); www.kmt.org.tw (office).

MA, Yo-Yo, BA; American cellist; b. 7 Oct. 1955, Paris, France; of Chinese parentage; m. Jill A. Hornor 1978; one s. one d.; ed Harvard Univ. and cello studies with his father, with Leonard Rose and at Juilliard School of Music, New York; first public recital at age of five; performed under many distinguished conductors with all the maj. orchestras of the world, including Berlin Philharmonic, Boston Symphony, Chicago Symphony, Israel Philharmonic, London Symphony and New York Philharmonic; regularly participates in festivals of Tanglewood, Ravinia, Blossom, Salzburg and Edinburgh; also appears in chamber music ensembles with artists such as Isaac Stern, Emanuel Ax, Leonard Rose, Pinchas Zukerman, Gidon Kremer and fmrly Yehudi Menuhin; premiered the Concerto by H. K. Gruber, Tanglewood 1989; recital tour with Emanuel Ax celebrating 20th anniversary of their partnership 1995–96; Bach's suites for solo cello at the Barbican Hall, London 1995; established The Silk Road Project to promote study of cultural, artistic and intellectual traditions of the route 2001; Smithsonian Folklife Festival 2002; apptd messenger of peace by UN Sec.-Gen. 2006; Dr hc (Northeastern) 1985 and from other colls or univs, including Harvard, Yale, Tufts and Juilliard, Chinese Univ. of Hong Kong; Avery Fisher Prize 1978, Glenn Gould Prize 1999, Nat. Medal of the Arts 2001, Dan David Prize 2006, Sonning Prize 2006, 15 Grammy Awards, two Emmy Awards, 19 Canadian Gemini Awards, Musical America Award for Musician of the Year 2009. *Recordings include:* Portrait of Yo-Yo Ma 1989, The Japanese Album 1989, A Cocktail Party 1990,

Hush 1992, Made in America 1993, The New York Album 1994, King Gesar 1996, From Ordinary Things 1997, Seven Years in Tibet 1997, Liberty! 1997, Piazzolla: Soul of the Tango 1997, The Protecting Veil and Wake Up...and Die 1998, John Williams Greatest Hits 1969–1999 1999, My First 79 Years 1999, Solo 1999, Brahms: Piano Concerto No.2, Cello Sonata Op.78 1999, Lulie the Iceberg 1999, Songs and Dances 1999, Franz Joseph Haydn 1999, Simply Baroque 1999, Crouching Tiger, Hidden Dragon (film soundtrack) 2000, Corigliano: Phantasmagoria 2000, Simply Baroque II 2000, Appalachian Journey 2000, Dvorak: Piano Quartet No. 2, Sonatina in G, Romantic Pieces 2000, Classic Yo-Yo 2001, Classical Hits 2001, Heartland: An Appalachian Anthology 2001, Yo-Yo Ma Plays Bach 2002, Isaac Stern: In Tribute and Celebration 2002, Mozrt: Piano Quartets 2002, Naqoyqatsi (film soundtrack) 2002, Yo-Yo Ma Plays the Music of John Williams 2002, Silk Road Journeys—When Strangers Meet 2002, Obrigado Brazil 2003, Classics for a New Century 2003, Paris—La Belle Époque 2003, Vivaldi's Cello 2004, The Dvorák Album 2004, Silk Road Journeys—Beyond the Horizon 2005, Essential Yo-Yo Ma 2005, R. Strauss: Don Quixote 2005, Memoirs of a Geisha (film soundtrack) 2005, Yo-Yo Ma plays Ennio Morricone 2006, Bach: Unaccompanied Piano Suites 2006, Appassionato 2007, Songs of Joy and Peace 2008. *Address:* Opus 3 Artists, 470 Park Avenue South, 9th Floor North, New York, NY 10016, USA (office). *Telephone:* (212) 584-7500 (office). *Fax:* (646) 300-8200 (office). *E-mail:* info@opus3artists.com (office). *Website:* www.opus3artists.com (office); www.yo-yoma.com.

MA, Yongwei; Chinese banker; b. 1942, Rongcheng, Shandong Prov.; ed Liaoning Inst. of Finance and Econs; joined CCP 1965; fmr Gov. Agric. Bank of China (Sec. CCP Leading Party Group); Exec. mem. and Vice-Chair. Int. Confed. for Agricultural Credit 1993–98; mem. Monetary Policy Comm., People's Bank of China 2000; Chair., Pres. People's Insurance Co. of China 1994–95, Chair. and Pres. China Insurance Group Co. 1995–98; Chair. China Insurance Regulatory Comm. 1998–2003; Dir China Life Insurance Co. 2006–; Del., 13th CCP Nat. Congress 1987–92, 14th CCP Nat. Congress 1992–97, 15th CCP Nat. Congress 1997–2002. *Address:* China Life Insurance Company Limited, 16 Chaowai Ave., 23rd Fl. Chinalife Building, Chaoyang District, Beijing 100020, People's Republic of China (office).

MA, Yuan; Chinese judge; b. 30 June 1930, Xinmin Co., Liaoning Prov.; two s.; ed Chinese People's Univ., Beijing; joined CCP 1953; teacher Dept of Law, Beijing Univ. and part-time lawyer 1955–62, part-time Prof. 1990–; Asst Judge, Judge Supreme People's Court 1963–82, Deputy Dir Civil Dept 1982–85, Vice-Pres. Supreme People's Court 1985–98; mem. Standing Cttee All China Women's Fed.; Vice-Pres. China Marriage and Family Research Inst. 1983–; Pres. Chinese Asscn of Women Judges 1994–; Asst Sec.-Gen. Civil and Econ. Law Cttee, China Law Soc. 1983–; Hon. Prof. Renmin Univ. School of Law. *Address:* c/o The School of Law, Renmin University of China, 59 Zhongguancun Ave, Beijing 100872, People's Republic of China (office).

MA, Yuzhen; Chinese diplomatist; b. 26 Sept. 1934, Beijing; s. of Ma Zhiqiang and Li Jinhui; m. Zou Jichun 1961; one s. one d.; ed Beijing Inst. of Foreign Languages; served in Information Dept, Ministry of Foreign Affairs 1954–63, Deputy Div. Chief, then Div. Chief 1969–80, Dir 1984–88; Attaché, Third Sec. Embassy, Burma 1963–69, First Sec., Counsellor Embassy, Ghana 1980–84, Consul-Gen. (ambassadorial rank) LA 1988–91, Amb. to UK 1991–95; Deputy Dir State Council's Information Office 1995–97; Foreign Ministry Commr for China, Hong Kong 1997–2001, Amb., Ministry of Foreign Affairs 2001–04; mem. 9th CPPCC Nat. Cttee 1998–2003. *Leisure interests:* reading, music, Beijing Opera. *Address:* c/o Ministry of Foreign Affairs, Beijing 100701 (office); Room 501, No. 30, Dongjiaominxiang, Beijing 100006, People's Republic of China (home).

MA, Zhengang; Chinese diplomatist; *President, China Institute of International Studies;* b. 9 Nov. 1940, Shandong; m. Chen Xiaodong; one s.; ed Beijing Foreign Languages Univ., Ealing Tech. Coll., London, LSE; staff mem., Attaché, Embassy in Yugoslavia 1970–74; Attaché N American and Oceanic Affairs Dept, Ministry of Foreign Affairs, Beijing 1974–81, Deputy Dir, then Dir N American and Oceanic Affairs Dept 1985–90, Deputy Dir-Gen., then Dir-Gen. N American and Oceanic Affairs Dept 1991–95; Vice-Consul, Consul, Consulate-Gen., Vancouver 1981–85; Counsellor, Embassy in Washington, DC 1990–91; Vice-Minister of Foreign Affairs 1995–97; Amb. to UK 1997–2002; Vice-Chair. 10th CPPCC Nat. Cttee 2003–; Amb., Ministry of Foreign Affairs 2002–04; Pres. China Inst. of Int. Studies (CIIS) 2004–, Chair. China Nat. Cttee, Council for Security Cooperation in Asia Pacific (CSCAP), Chair. editorial bd International Studies, Chair. of Academic Cttee. *Leisure interests:* literature, bridge, table tennis. *Address:* China Institute of International Studies, No.3, Toutiao, Taijichang, Beijing 100005, People's Republic of China (office). *Website:* www.ciis.org.cn (office).

MA, Zhongchen; Chinese party official; b. 1936, Tai'an, Shandong Prov.; joined CCP 1956; Deputy Sec. CCP Tai'an Co. Cttee, Shandong Prov. 1966–76, Sec. 1978–83; Sec. CCP Zhangqiu Co. Cttee, Shandong Prov. 1976–78; Sec. CCP Tai'an City Cttee, Shandong Prov. 1983–86; Vice-Gov. Shandong Prov. 1986–88; Sec.-Gen. People's Govt, Shandong Prov. 1986–88; Deputy Sec.-Gen. State Council 1987; Deputy Sec. CCP Shandong Prov. Cttee 1988–90; Vice-Minister of Agric. 1990–92; Vice-Gov. Henan Prov. 1992, Acting Gov. 1992–93, Gov. 1993–98; Deputy Sec. CCP Henan Prov. Cttee 1995–98, Sec. 1998–2000; Alt. mem. 12th CCP Cen. Cttee 1982–87, 13th Cen. Cttee 1987–92, 14th Cen. Cttee CCP 1992–97, mem. 15th CCP Cen. Cttee 1997–2002. *Address:* c/o Office of the Governor, Zhengzhou City, Henan Province, People's Republic of China.

MA SI-HANG, Frederick, BA; Hong Kong government official; *Secretary for Financial Services and the Treasury;* b. 1952, Hong Kong; ed Univ. of Hong Kong; fmrly with J. P. Morgan Private Bank, Chase Manhattan Bank, Kumagai Gumi (HK) Ltd, RBC Dominion Securities Ltd, Hong Kong Exchanges and Clearing Ltd, Hong Kong Securities and Futures Comm.; Group Chief Financial Officer, Exec. Dir, mem. Exec. Cttee PCCW Ltd –2002; Sec. for Financial Services and the Treasury, Hong Kong Special Admin. Region 2002–. *Address:* c/o Government Secretariat, Central Government Offices, Lower Albert Road, Central, Hong Kong Special Administrative Region, People's Republic of China (office). *Telephone:* 28102900 (office). *Fax:* 28457895 (office). *Website:* www.fstb.gov.hk (office).

MAAFO, Yaw Osafo; Ghanaian politician; Minister of Finance and Econ. Planning –2005. *Address:* c/o Ministry of Finance and Economic Planning, POB M40, Accra, Ghana (office).

MAALIM, Mahboub, BSc, MSc; Kenyan engineer and international organization official; *Executive Secretary, Intergovernmental Authority on Development (IGAD);* b. Garissa; ed Univ. of Texas, USA; Dist Water Engineer, Ministry of Water 1985–94; Nat. Coordinator Arid Lands Resource Man. Project 1996–2004; Perm. Sec. Ministry of Water and Irrigation 2006–08; Exec. Sec. Intergovernmental Authority on Devt (IGAD) 2008–; Assoc. mem. American Soc. of Civil Engineers. *Address:* Office of the Executive Secretary, Intergovernmental Authority on Development, Avenue Georges Clemenceau, PO Box 2653, Djibouti (office). *Telephone:* 356452 (office). *Fax:* 353520 (office). *E-mail:* igad@igad.org (office). *Website:* www.igad.org (office).

MAALOUF, Amin, Maîtrise en Sociologie; Lebanese/French writer; b. 25 Feb. 1949, Beirut; s. of the late Ruchdi Maalouf and of Odette Ghossein; m. Andrée Abouchdid 1971; three c.; ed Univ. Saint-Joseph, Beirut, Univ. de Lyon; journalist, an-Nahar 1971–76, Economia 1976–77; Ed. Jeune Afrique 1978–79, 1982–84; Commdr, Ordre du Cèdre (Lebanon), Officier, Ordre nat. du Mérite, Chevalier, Légion d'honneur; hon. degrees from Univ. Catholique de Louvain, Belgium, American Univ. of Beirut, Lebanon, Tarragona Univ., Spain, Evora Univ., Portugal; Prix France-Liban 1986, Grand Prix de l'Unicef 1991, Prix Goncourt 1993, Premio Nonino 1997, Premio Elio Vittorini 1997, Prix européen de l'essai 1998, Premio Grinzane Cavour 2001, Premio Antonio de Sancha 2003, Prix Méditerranée 2004. *Publications:* Les Croisades vues par les Arabes 1983, Léon l'Africain 1986, Samarcande 1988, Les Jardins de lumière 1991, Le Premier siècle après Béatrice 1992, Le Rocher de Tanios 1993, Les Echelles du Levant 1996, Les Identités meurtrières 1998, Le Périple de Baldassare 2000, L'Amour de Loin (opera libretto) 2001, Origines 2004, Adriana Mater (opera libretto) 2006, Le Dérèglement du monde 2009. *Address:* c/o Editions Grasset, 61 rue des Saints-Pères, 75006 Paris, France.

MAATHAI, Wangari Muta, BS, MS, PhD; Kenyan ecologist, organization official and politician; *Goodwill Ambassador, Congo Basin Forest Initiative;* b. 1 April 1940, Ihithe village, Tetu Div., Nyeri Dist; d. of Muta Njugi and Wanjiru Kibicho; m. Mwangi Maathai 1969 (divorced 1980); three c.; ed Loreto Convent Secondary School, Limuru, studied biology in USA and Germany, Mount St Scholastica (now Benedictine Coll.), Univ. of Pittsburgh, Univ. of Nairobi; Dean of Faculty and Chair. Dept of Veterinary Anatomy, Univ. of Nairobi 1976, apptd Assoc. Prof. of Veterinary Anatomy 1977; f. Maendeleo Ya Wanawake (Nat. Council of Women of Kenya) 1964; Dir Kenya Red Cross 1973–80; Founder and Co-ordinator Kenya Green Belt Movt 1977–2002, Founding Chair. Green Belt Movt Int. 2005–; Founding mem. GROOTS Int. 1985; violently attacked and imprisoned several times during regime of Daniel Arap Moi for demanding multi-party elections and an end to political corruption and tribal politics; fmr mem. Forum for Restoration of Democracy; presidential cand. 1997; MP (Nat. Rainbow Coalition) for Tetu Constituency 2002–07; Asst Minister for Environment, Natural Resources and Wildlife 2003–05; f. Mazingira Green Party of Kenya 2003; first Presiding Officer Econ., Social and Cultural Council of the African Union (ECOSOCC) 2005–07; cand. in Parl. elections Dec. 2007; mem. Advisory Bd Clinton Global Initiative, UN Sec.-Gen.'s Advisory Bd on Disarmament Matters, UN Comm. on Global Governance, advisory bd Democracy Coalition Project, Earth Charter Comm., Selection Cttee Sasakawa Environmental Prize, UNEP, Kenya; mem. Bd of Dirs Women's and Environment Devt Org., World Learning, Green Cross Int., Environment Liaison Centre Int., Kenya, WorldWIDE Network of Women in Environmental Work, Nat. Council of Women of Kenya; Montgomery Fellow, Dartmouth Coll., USA 2001; Dorothy McCluskey Visiting Fellow for Conservation, Global Inst. for Sustainable Forestry, Yale Univ. 2002; Goodwill Amb., Congo Basin Forest Initiative 2005–; Paul Harris Fellow, Rotary Int; Hon. FRIBA 2008; Order of the Golden Ark (The Netherlands) 1994, Elder of the Burning Spear (Kenya) 2003, Chevalier, Légion d'honneur 2006; Hon. LLD (Williams Coll.) 1990, (Yale Univ.) 2004; Hon. DSc (Hobart Coll.) 1994, (William Smith Coll.) 1994, (Aoyama Gakuin Univ.) 2004, (Soka Univ.) 2004, (Univ. of Nairobi) 2005, (Willamette Univ.) 2005, (Ochanomizu Univ.) 2005, (Morehouse Coll.) 2006, (Egerton Univ.) 2007; Hon. DAgric (Univ. of Norway) 1997; Hon. DHumLitt (Connecticut Coll.) 2006; Hon. Dr Public Service (Univ. of Pittsburg) 2006; Woman of the Year Award 1983, Right Livelihood Award (Sweden) 1984, Better World Society Award 1986, Windstar Foundation Award for the Environment 1988, WomenAid Women of the World Award (UK) 1989, Benedictine Coll. Offeramus Medal 1990, Goldman Foundation Environmental Prize 1991, UN Hunger Project Africa Prize for Leadership (co-recipient) 1991, MRC Edinburgh Medal 1993, Jane Addams Conf. Leadership Award 1993, Endowed Chair in Gender and Women's Studies named 'Fuller-Maathai', Connecticut Coll. 2000, Temple of Understanding Juliet Hollister Award (USA) 2001, Kenyan Community Abroad Excellence Award (USA) 2001, Bridges to Community Outstanding Vision and Commitment Award (USA) 2002, World Asscn of Non-Governmental Orgs (WANGO) Environment Award 2003, Columbia Univ. Center for Environmental Research and Conservation Scientist Award 2004, Arbor Day Foundation J. Sterling Morton Award 2004, Heinrich Boell Foundation Petra Kelly Environment Prize 2004, Sophie Foundation Prize 2004, Nobel Peace Prize (Norway) 2004, New York Women's Foundation Century Award 2005, Disney

Wildlife Conservation Fund Award 2006, Int. Asscn for Impact Assessment (IAIA) Global Environment Award 2006, Indira Gandhi Int. Award for Peace, Disarmament and Devt 2006, World Citizenship Award 2007, Cross of the Order of St Benedict, Benedictine Coll., Kan. 2007, Jawaharlal Nehru Award for Int. Understanding 2007, Nelson Mandela Award for Health and Human Rights 2007, NAACP Image Award (Chair.'s Award; co-recipient) 2008. *Achievement:* one of the eight flag bearers at Winter Olympics Opening Ceremony, Turin, Italy 2006. *Publications:* Bottom is Heavy Too: Edinburgh Medal Lecture 1994, The Canopy of Hope: My Life Campaigning for Africa, Women and the Environment 2002, The Greenbelt Movement: Sharing the Approach and the Experience 2003, Unbowed: A Memoir 2007. *Leisure interests:* swimming, reading. *Address:* c/o Economic Social and Cultural Council of the African Union (ECOSOCC), First Floor, Hughes Building, Kenya Avenue Wing, Muindi Mbingu Street, Nairobi, Kenya. *Telephone:* (202) 11842. *E-mail:* jkaruga@greenbeltmovement.org (office). *Website:* www .greenbeltmovement.org (office).

MAAZEL, Lorin, FRCM; American conductor and musician; *Music Director, Palau de les Arts Reina Sofía;* b. 6 March 1930, Neuilly, France; s. of Lincoln Maazel and Marie Varencove Maazel; m. 1st Israela Margalit; four c.; m. 2nd Dietlinde Turban 1986; one s.; ed under Vladimir Bakaleinikoff and at Univ. of Pittsburgh; début as conductor 1938; Conductor, American Symphony Orchestras 1938–; violin recitalist; European début 1953; festivals include Bayreuth, Salzburg, Edin.; tours include S America, Australia, USSR and Japan; Artistic Dir, Deutsche Oper Berlin 1965–71; Musical Dir Radio Symphony Orchestra, Berlin 1965–75; Assoc. Prin. Conductor, New Philharmonia Orchestra, London 1970–72; Dir Cleveland Orchestra 1971–82, Conductor Emer. 1982–86; Prin. Guest Conductor London Philharmonia 1976–80; Dir Vienna State Opera 1982–84, Music Dir Pittsburgh Symphony Orchestra 1988–96; Music Dir Bavarian Radio Symphony Orchestra 1993–2001, NY Philharmonic 2002–09, Palau de les Arts Reina Sofía, Valencia 2005–; Music Dir Orchestre Nat. de France 1988–90; Officier, Légion d'honneur 1981, Finnish Commdr of the Lion, Portuguese Commdr, Bundesverdienstkreuz (Germany); Hon. DMus (Pittsburgh) 1968, (Royal Coll. of Music) 1984; Hon. DHumLitt (Beaver Coll.) 1973; Hon. DCL (Univ. of S Sewanee) 1988; Dr hc (Ind.) 1988. *Composition:* 1984 (premiere Royal Opera House, London) 2005. *Leisure interests:* swimming, tennis, reading. *Address:* Palau de les Arts Reina Sofía, Autopista del Saler 1, 46013 Valencia, Spain (office). *Telephone:* (96) 1975800 (office). *Fax:* (96) 3952201 (office). *E-mail:* info@lesarts.com (office). *Website:* www.lesarts.com (office); maestromaazel .com.

MABILANGAN, Felipe H., MA; Philippine diplomatist and international organization official; *Senior Foreign Affairs Adviser;* m. Ada Kalaw Ledesma; three c.; ed Univs of Oxford, UK and Geneva, Switzerland; various positions, Dept of Foreign Affairs 1971–79, Dir-Gen. for European Affairs 1988; Amb. to France (also accred to Portugal) 1979–87, to China (also accred to Mongolia) 1989–95; Perm. Rep. to UN 1995–2001; currently Sr Foreign Affairs Adviser, Dept of Foreign Affairs; mem. UN Advisory Cttee on Admin. and Budgetary Questions 2001–04; del. to numerous int. confs; Chevalier Ordre nat. du Mérit (France), Gawad Mabini (Philippines). *Leisure interests:* golf, tennis. *Address:* Department of Foreign Affairs, DFA Building, 2330 Pasay City, Metro Manila, Philippines (office). *Telephone:* (2) 8189449 (office).

MABUS, Raymond Edwin, Jr, MA, JD; American fmr politician, lawyer and consultant; b. 11 Oct. 1948, Starkville, Miss.; s. of Raymond Edwin Mabus, Sr and Lucille C. Mabus; m. (divorced); two d.; ed Univ. of Mississippi, Johns Hopkins Univ., Harvard Univ.; called to Texas Bar 1976, Washington, DC 1978, Miss. 1982; Law Clerk US Circuit Court of Appeals, Montgomery, Ala 1976–77; Legal Counsel to House of Reps, DC 1977–78; Assoc. Fried, Frank et al., Washington, DC 1979–80; Gov.'s Legislative Aide, State of Miss., Jackson 1980–83; State Auditor, State of Miss. 1984–88; Gov. of Miss. 1988–92; Amb. to Saudi Arabia 1994–96; Counsel, Baker Donaldson Bearman & Caldwell 1996–; fmr Chair. Southern Govs' Asscn, Southern Regional Educ. Bd; Woodrow Wilson Scholarship, Johns Hopkins Univ. 1969; Democrat; King Abdul Aziz Award, Saudi Arabia 1996, Distinguished Public Service Award, US Dept of Defense. *Leisure interests:* spectator sports, walking, reading, photography, scuba diving. *Address:* 345 Richardson Road, Ridgelands, MS 39157 (office); 345 Richardson Road, Ridgelands, MS 39157, USA (home). *Telephone:* (601) 605-9400 (office); (601) 605-7400 (home). *Fax:* (601) 607-7104 (office); (601) 607-7104 (home).

McALEESE, Mary Patricia, LLB, MA, FRSA, MRIA; Irish academic, journalist and head of state; *President;* b. 27 June 1951, Belfast, Northern Ireland; d. of Patrick J. Leneghan and Claire McManus; m. Dr Martin McAleese 1976; one s. two d.; ed Queen's Univ. Belfast, Inn of Court of Northern Ireland, King's Inns, Dublin and Trinity Coll., Dublin; called to Northern Ireland Bar 1974; Reid Prof. of Criminal Law, Criminology and Penology, Trinity Coll., Dublin 1975–79, 1981–87; current affairs journalist and presenter, Radio Telefís Éireann 1979–85; Dir Inst. of Professional Legal Studies 1987–97; Pro-Vice-Chancellor, Queen's Univ., Belfast 1994–97; Pres. of Ireland 1997– (re-elected 2004); Dir (non-exec.) Northern Ireland Electricity 1992–97, Channel 4 TV 1993–97; fmr Dir Royal Group of Hosps Trust; Founder mem. Irish Comm. for Prisoners Overseas; mem. Catholic Church Episcopal Del. to the New Ireland Forum 1984, Catholic Church Del. to the North Comm. on Contentious Parades 1996; Del. to White House Conf. on Trade and Investment in Ireland 1995, and to the follow-up Pittsburg Conf. 1996; Hon. Fellow Trinity Coll. Dublin, Inst. of Engineers of Ireland, Royal Coll. of Surgeons, Coll. of Anaesthetists, Liverpool John Moore's Univ., Royal Coll. of Physicians and Surgeons, Glasgow; Hon. Bencher, King's Inns, Inn of Court of Northern Ireland; Hon. LLD (Nat. Univ. of Ireland, Vic. Univ. of Tech., Australia, Saint Mary's Univ., Canada, Loyola Law School, LA, Univ. of Aberdeen, Univ. of

Surrey, Queen's, Belfast), (Nottingham) 1998, (Trinity Coll. Dublin, Metropolitan Univ., Manchester, Univ. of Delaware, Univ. of Bristol); Hon. DHumLitt (Rochester Inst. of Tech., NY, USA); Hon. DLitt (Univ. of Ulster); Silver Jubilee Commemoration Medal, Charles Univ., Prague, Great Gold Medal, Comenius Univ., Bratislava, ranked by Forbes magazine amongst 100 Most Powerful Women (33rd) 2004, (21st) 2005, (55th) 2006, (58th) 2007, (74th) 2008. *Publications:* The Irish Martyrs 1995, Reconciled Being 1997. *Leisure interests:* hillwalking, theology. *Address:* Áras an Uachtaráin, Phoenix Park, Dublin 8, Ireland (office). *Telephone:* (1) 617-1000. *Fax:* (1) 617-1001. *E-mail:* webmaster@president.ie (office). *Website:* www.president.ie (office).

McALLISTER, Sir Ian, Kt, CBE, BSc; British transport industry executive; *Chairman, Network Rail Ltd;* b. 17 Aug. 1943, Glasgow; m. Susan Mitchell; three s. one d.; ed Thornleigh Salesian Coll., Bolton, Univ. Coll. London; grad. economist, Ford Motor Co. Ltd 1964, responsible for German Operations 1980s, Man. Dir Ford of Britain 1991, Chair. 1992–2002; Chair. (non-exec.) Network Rail Ltd 2002–; Chair. Carbon Trust 2001–; Chair. Greater Essex Prosperity Forum 2007–; Dir (non-exec.) Scottish & Newcastle, Energy Saving Trust 2001–; Dir UCL Business 2007–. *Leisure interest:* Manchester United football club. *Address:* Network Rail Ltd, 40 Melton Street, London, NW1 2EE, England (office). *Telephone:* (20) 7557-8000 (office). *Fax:* (20) 7557-9000 (office). *Website:* www.networkrail.co.uk (office).

MACAN, Tom, BA; British diplomatist (retd); b. 14 Nov. 1946, Manchester; s. of Dr Thomas Townley Macan and Zaida Bindloss Macan (née Boddington); one s. one d.; ed Shrewsbury School, Univ. of Sussex; joined HM Diplomatic Service 1969, served in Bonn, Brasília and FCO; Press Sec. Embassy at Bonn 1981; Head Commonwealth Co-ordination Dept, FCO 1986–88, Head Training Dept 1988–90; Deputy Head of Mission at Lisbon 1990–95; Amb. to Lithuania 1995–98; seconded to BOC Group 1998–99; Minister at New Delhi 1999–2002; Gov. of the Virgin Islands 2002–06; mem. Inst. of Linguists. *Leisure interests:* sailing, steamboats, church architecture. *Address:* Stevney, Outgate, Ambleside, Cumbira LA22 0NH, England (home). *Telephone:* (1539) 436978 (office). *E-mail:* ttm@mailcan.com (office).

McANUFF, Des; American/Canadian producer, director and writer; *Artistic Director, Stratford Shakespeare Festival;* b. 19 June 1952, Princeton, Ill.; m. Susan Berman 1984; one d.; ed Woburn Collegiate; trained under drama coach Basya Hunter, Toronto; raised in Scarborough, Toronto; worked with Toronto Free Theatre as dir of several plays; moved to New York City, where he co-f. Dodger Theatre Co. 1978, directed first production, Gimme Shelter; directed for American Repertory Theatre at Harvard, also Yale Rep; fmr faculty mem. Juilliard School; Artistic Dir La Jolla Playhouse (revived 1983) –2007, directed Romeo and Juliet, A Mad World, My Masters, Big River, As You Like It, The Sea Gull, The Matchmaker, A Walk in the Woods, Two Rooms, 80 Days, Macbeth, A Funny Thing Happened on the Way to the Forum, Twelfth Night, Three Sisters, Elmer Gantry, Much Ado About Nothing, The Who's Tommy and How to Succeed in Business Without Really Trying; Co-Artistic Dir Stratford Shakespeare Festival 2006–08, Artistic Dir 2008–; also produced Tony award-winning revivals of Broadway classics, including Guys and Dolls, The Music Man, Into the Woods, 42nd Street, The King and I, and many others. *Productions include:* Big River (Tony Award for Best Dir (Musical) 1985) 1985, A Walk in the Woods 1988, The Gospel at Colonus 1988, Dangerous Games 1989, The Grapes of Wrath 1990, Prelude to a Kiss 1990, The Who's Tommy (Tony Award for Best Dir (Musical) 1993, Laurence Olivier Theatre Award for Best Dir of 1996 at Shaftesbury Theatre 1997) 1993, How to Succeed in Business Without Really Trying 1995, I Am My Own Wife 2003, Dracula, The Musical 2004, 700 Sundays 2004, Good Vibrations 2005, Jersey Boys 2005, The Farnsworth Invention 2007, Cry-Baby 2008. *Films:* Cousin Bette 1998, The Iron Giant (producer) 1999, The Adventures of Rocky and Bullwinkle 2000, Quills (exec. producer) 2000. *Address:* Stratford Shakespeare Festival, PO Box 520, 55 Queen Street, Stratford, ON N5A 6V2, Canada (office). *Telephone:* (519) 271-4040 (office). *Fax:* (519) 271-1126 (office). *E-mail:* info@stratfordshakespearefestival.com (office). *Website:* www .stratfordshakespearefestival.com (office).

MACAPAGAL ARROYO, Gloria, PhD; Philippine politician, economist, journalist and head of state; *President;* b. 5 April 1947, San Juan; d. of the late Diosdado Pangan Macapagal (fmr Pres. of the Philippines) and Dr Evangelina Macaraeg Macapagal; m. Jose Miguel Tuason Arroyo 1968; two s. one d.; ed Assumption Convent, Georgetown Univ., Assumption Coll., Ateneo de Manila Univ., Univ. of the Philippines; Asst Prof., Ateneo de Manila Univ. 1977–87; Chair. Econs Dept, Assumption Coll. 1984–87; Prof., Univ. of the Philippines School of Econs 1977–87; Prof., Mary Knoll Coll., St Scholastica's Coll.; Asst Sec., Dept of Trade and Industry 1987–89, Under-Sec. 1989–92; Exec. Dir Garments and Textile Export Bd 1988–90; Senator 1992–98; Sec. Dept of Social Welfare and Devt 1998–2000; Vice-Pres. of Repub. 1998–2001, Pres. of the Philippines 2001– (re-elected 2004); Chair. and Pres. Univ. of the Philippines Health Maintenance Org. 1989–98; Exec. Dir Philippine Center for Econ. Devt 1994–98; Chair. Univ. of the Philippines Econ. Foundation 1994–98; mem. Presidential Task Force on Tax and Tariff Reforms 1994–98, Tech. Working Group of the Philippine Nat. Devt Plan for the 21st Century (Cttee on Nat. Framework for Regional Devt and Macroeconomics Framework for Devt Financing); mem. or fmr mem. Asscn for Philippines-China Understanding, Philippine Econs Soc., Georgetown Club of the Philippines, Concerned Women of the Philippines; Hon. LLD (La Trobe Univ.) 2000, (Waseda Univ.) 2002, (Fordham Univ.) 2003, (Old Dominion Univ.) 2003; Hon. DEcon (Tsinghua Univ.) 2001; Hon. DH (Mapua Inst. of Tech.) 2004; Hon. Community Coll. Assoc. Degree in Int. Relations (City Coll. of San Francisco) 2003; UPSE Fellowship 1970–71, Japan Foundation Grant 1976–77, Rockefeller Foundation Scholarship 1978–83, named Outstanding Senator and One of Asia's Most Powerful Women by Asiaweek, Woman of the Year by

Catholic Educ. Asscn of the Philippines, Ulirang Ina, Ulirang Ina Awards Cttee 2001, Most Distinguished Alumna, Univ. of the Philippines Alumni Asscn 2001, Making a Difference for Women – Women of Distinction Award, Soroptimist International of the Philippines Region 2003, ranked by Forbes magazine amongst 100 Most Powerful Women (ninth) 2004, (fourth) 2005, (45th) 2006, (51st) 2007, (41st) 2008. *Address:* Office of the President, New Executive Building, Malacañang Palace Compound, J. P. Laurel Street, San Miguel, Metro Manila, Philippines (office). *Telephone:* (2) 7356047 (office). *Fax:* (2) 7358006 (office). *E-mail:* gma@easy.net.ph (office). *Website:* www.kgma.org (office).

MACARA, Sir Alexander Wiseman, Kt, DPH, DSc, FRCP, FRCPE, FRCGP, FFPHM, FFOM, FMedSci; British physician; *President, National Heart Forum;* b. 4 May 1932, Irvine, Scotland; s. of the Rev. Alexander Macara and Marion Macara; m. Sylvia May Williams 1964; one s. one d.; ed Irvine Royal Acad., Univ. of Glasgow, London School of Hygiene and Tropical Medicine; Lecturer, then Consultant Sr Lecturer in Social Medicine, Univ. of Bristol 1964–97; Sec.-Gen. Asscn of Schools of Public Health in Europe 1975–89, World Fed. for Educ. and Research in Public Health 1988–97; Dir WHO Collaborating Centre in Environmental Health 1988–97; Chair. BMA 1993–98; Visiting Prof. of Health Studies, Univ. of York 1998–2002; Chair. Nat. Heart Forum (UK) 1998–2007, now Pres.; Chair., Programme Devt Groups for NICE (Nat. Inst. for Health and Clinical Excellence) 2006–; Hon. Dr of Hygiene (Athens School of Public Health) 1992; Hecht Prize, London School of Hygiene and Tropical Medicine 1960, Gold Medal, Italian Soc. of Hygiene and Preventive Medicine 1991, Médaille d'Or, Ordre de Médecine Français 1997, Gold Medal, British Medical Asscn 1999, Andrija Stampar Medal 2002. *Publications:* has published extensively on public health, ethics in medicine, health care and epidemiology. *Leisure interests:* music, gardening, human rights activities. *Address:* Elgon, 10 Cheyne Road, Stoke Bishop, Bristol, BS9 2DH, England (home). *Telephone:* (117) 968-2838 (home). *Fax:* (117) 968-4602 (home). *E-mail:* alexandermacara@yahoo.co.uk (home).

MACARRÓN JAIME, Ricardo; Spanish painter; b. 9 April 1926, Madrid; m. Alicia Macarrón Jaime 1951; two d.; ed Escuela Superior de Bellas Artes de San Fernando, Madrid and scholarship in Paris; Prof. of Drawing and Painting, Escuela Superior de Bellas Artes, Madrid; has painted many portraits of royalty and nobility; mem. Royal Soc. of Portrait Painters 1962; numerous solo exhbns in Spain and abroad including two in London and one in New York; represented at Museo de Arte Contemporáneo, Madrid, Univ. of Oslo and Fundación Güell, Barcelona, portraits at the Royal Soc. of Portrait Painters; numerous awards. *Leisure interests:* walking in the country, hunting, playing chess. *Address:* Agustín de Bethencourt No. 7, Madrid 3, Spain.

MacARTHUR, Dame Ellen Patricia, MBE, DBE; British yachtswoman; b. 8 July 1977, Whatstandwell, Derbyshire; d. of Ken and Avril MacArthur; ed Anthony Gell School, Wirksworth; circumnavigated UK single-handed (youngest person to pass Yachtmaster Offshore Qualification) 1995; took part in Mini Transat race 1997; Class Winner Route du Rhum race 1999, 2002; second place in Vendée Globe Race (94 days' solo sailing, youngest woman to circumnavigate the globe single-handedly) 2001; set non-stop round the world record of 71 days, 14 hours, 18 minutes and 33 seconds 2005; BT/YJA Young Sailor of the Year 1995, Sailing's Young Hope (France) 1998, BT/YJA Yachtsman of the Year 1999, Cable Industry Outstanding Achievement Award, Women of the Year Awards 2001, Royal Geographical Soc. Discovery Award 2001, Walpole Medal of Excellence 2001, Pride of Britain Award 2001, Royal Inst. of Navigation Award 2001, Times Sportswoman of the Year 2001, Runner-up Sports Personality of the Year 2001, Int. Sailing Fed. World Sailor of the Year 2001. *Publication:* Taking on the World 2002, Race Against Time 2005. *Address:* c/o OC Group, Cowes Waterfront, Venture Quays, Castle Street, East Cowes, Isle of Wight, PO31 6EZ, England. *Telephone:* (1983) 282797. *Website:* www.btteamellen.com.

McASLAN, John Renwick, MA, RIBA, FRSA, FRIAS; British architect; *Executive Chairman, John McAslan + Partners;* b. 16 Feb. 1954, Glasgow, Scotland; s. of Prof. T. Crawford and Jean Renwick McAslan; m. Dava Sagenkahn 1981; one s. two d.; ed Dunoon Grammar School, Dollar Acad., Univ. of Edin.; trained with Cambridge Seven Assocs, Boston, Mass. 1978–80; Richard Rogers and Partners, London 1980–84; Founding Pnr and Dir Troughton McAslan (later John McAslan + Partners) 1984–96, Exec. Chair. 1996–; extensive int. teaching experience at architectural schools including Glasgow, Belfast, Cardiff, Dublin, Beijing, London, Edin., Mexico City, Sydney, Helsinki, Seoul, Tokyo 1990–; Chair. of numerous architectural award juries in the UK 1990–; Visiting Prof., Univ. of Wales 1998–2001; Foundation Trustee, Whitechapel Art Gallery 1989–97; Founder, John McAslan Family Trust, London 1997; founder, Volubilis Foundation, Morocco 2001; founder, RIBA/ICE McAslan Bursary 2004; External Examiner, various univs; Assoc. Int. mem. AIA; mem. Architectural Inst. of Japan; Architect of the Year Award, Civic Trust Award, RIBA Award for Architecture, Int. Brunel Award, Structural Steel Design Award, Royal Acad. of Arts Award, European Heritage Award, Architectural Inst. of Japan Award, AIA Merit Award. *Completed and ongoing work includes:* Apple Computers Headquarters, London, Christopher Place School, London, De La Warr Pavilion, Bexhill-on-Sea, Derngate, Northampton, Florida Southern Coll., USA, Imperial Coll., London, King's Cross Station, London, Kobe Inst., Japan, Max Mara Headquarters, Italy, Manchester Metropolitan Univ., Royal Acad. of Music, London, Trinity Coll. of Music, Greenwich, Yapl Kredi Bank Operations Centre, Istanbul, Royal Welsh Coll. of Music and Drama, Cardiff, Roundhouse, London, Volubilis, Morocco, Univ. of Manchester, Birmingham New Street Station, Univ. of Kingston, numerous City acads. *Publications:* over 500 int. publs on architectural work, including monographs and profiles. *Leisure interests:* travel, sport, jazz, blues and opera, spending time with family. *Address:* John McAslan + Partners, 49 Princes Place, London, W11 4QA, England (office). *Telephone:* (20) 7727-2663 (office). *Fax:* (20) 7721-8835 (office). *E-mail:* j.mcaslan@mcaslan.co.uk (office). *Website:* www.mcaslan.co.uk (office).

McAULIFFE, Terry, JD; American politician and lawyer; b. Syracuse, New York; m. Dorothy Swann; five c.; ed Catholic Univ. of America, Georgetown Law Center; joined Carter-Mondale Re-election Cttee; mem. Democratic Party, served in various positions including Finance Dir Democratic Nat. Cttee (DNC), Finance Dir Democratic Congressional Campaign Cttee, Nat. Finance Chair. Presidential Campaign of Dick Gephardt 1988, Nat. Co-Chair. Presidential Campaign Clinton–Gore 1996, Co-Chair. Presidential Inaugural Cttee 1997, Chair. DNC Convention, LA 2000, Chair. DNC 2001–05, cr. Hispanic Project, Women's Vote Center, Voting Rights Inst.; est. many cos in fields of banking, insurance, marketing and real estate; practising attorney. *Publication:* What a Party! My Life Among Democrats 2007. *Address:* c/o Democratic National Committee, 430 South Capitol Street, SE, Washington, DC 20003, USA (office).

McAVOY, James; British actor; b. 21 April 1979, Glasgow; s. of James McAvoy and Elizabeth McAvoy; m. Anne Marie Duff 2006; ed Royal Scottish Acad. of Music and Drama; BAFTA Orange Rising Star Award 2006. *Films include:* Regeneration 1997, Bright Young Things 2003, Inside I'm Dancing 2004 (Edinburgh Int. Festival Audience Award), Wimbledon 2004, Strings 2004, The Chronicles of Narnia: The Lion, the Witch and the Wardrobe 2005, The Last King of Scotland 2006, Penelope 2006, Burns 2006, Starter for Ten 2006, Becoming Jane 2007, Atonement 2007, Penelope 2007, Wanted 2008. *TV includes:* An Angel Passes By 1997, The Bill 1997, Lorna Doone 2000, Murder in Mind 2001, Band of Brothers 2001, Payment in Blood 2002, White Teeth 2002, Foyle's War 2002, Bollywood Queen 2002, Children of Dune 2003, State of Play 2003, Early Doors 2003, Shameless 2005, Macbeth 2005. *Theatre includes:* The Reel of the Hanged Man, Edinburgh 2000, Out in the Open, Hampstead Theatre 2001, Privates On Parade, Donmar Warehouse 2001–02, Breathing Corpses, Royal Court Theatre 2005. *Address:* United Agents, 12–26 Lexington Street, London, W1F 0LE, England (office). *Telephone:* (20) 3214-0800 (office). *Fax:* (20) 3214-0801 (office). *E-mail:* info@unitedagents.co.uk (office). *Website:* unitedagents.co.uk (office).

McBRIDE, Christian; American jazz bass player; b. 31 May 1972, Philadelphia, Pa; s. of Lee Smith; ed High School for the Creative and Performing Arts, Philadelphia, Juilliard School, New York; began playing electric bass aged nine, followed by acoustic bass two years later; tour to Europe with Philadelphia Youth Orchestra 1989; travelling USA with classical jazz fusion group, Free Flight 1989; played with Bobby Watson, Freddie Hubbard 1990–93, Ray Brown and Jay Clayton 1991, Benny Green, Roy Hargrove, Joshua Redman, Diana Krall, Pat Metheny 1992, Joe Henderson, D'Angelo, Kathleen Battle, Herbie Hancock, Quincy Jones, Natalie Cole and Milt Jackson; signed to Verve Records 1994; joined George Duke's band 2002; f. own groups, including Christian McBride Band; soloist; Co-Dir The Jazz Museum, Harlem 2005–; Creative Chair for Los Angeles Philharmonic 2005–; Scholarship to Juilliard School, named by Rolling Stone magazine "Hot Jazz Artist" of 1992. *Commissions include:* Bluesin' in Alphabet City by Jazz at Lincoln Center, performed by Wynton Marsalis with Lincoln Center Jazz Orchestra, The Movement, Revisited by the Portland (ME) Arts Soc. and Nat. Endowment for the Arts, written and arranged for quartet and 30-piece gospel choir 1998. *Films include:* Café Society 1995, Kansas City 1996. *Recordings include:* albums: Ray Brown's Super Bass 1989, Roy Hargrove's Public Eye 1990, Kenny Kirkland 1991, Joshua Redman 1993, Fingerpainting: The Music of Herbie Hancock 1997, Introducing Joshua Redman 1999, Bobby Hutcherson's Skyline 1999, Don Braden's Fire Within 1999, Sting's All This Time (CD, DVD and tour) 2001, George Duke's Face the Music 2002; solo albums include: Gettin' To It 1994, Number Two Express 1996, A Family Affair 1998, Sci-Fi 2000, The Philadelphia Experiment 2001, Vertical Vision (with electrical quartet) 2003, Live at Tonic 2006. *Address:* c/o David Sholemson, Ted Kurland Associates, 173 Brighton Avenue, Boston, MA 02134, USA (office). *Telephone:* (617) 254-0007 (office). *Fax:* (617) 254-5491 (office). *E-mail:* davidsho@mac.com (office); info@christianmcbride.com. *Website:* www.tedkurland.com/pbuild/artist.cfm?code=CMB (office); www.christianmcbride.com.

McBRIDE, William Griffith, AO, CBE, MD, FRCOG, FRACOG, FRSM, MACT; Australian molecular biologist and medical practitioner; b. 25 May 1927, Sydney; s. of John McBride and Myrine Griffith; m. Patricia Glover 1957; two s. two d.; ed Canterbury Boys' High School, Sydney, Conservatorium of Music, Sydney, Univ. of London, Univ. of Sydney; Medical Officer, St George Hosp. 1950, Consultant Obstetrician and Gynaecologist 1958; Medical Officer, Launceston Gen. Hosp. 1951; Medical Officer, Women's Hosp., Sydney 1952–53, Medical Supt 1955–57, Consultant Obstetrician 1966–83; Consultant Gynaecologist, Bankstown Hosp., Sydney 1957–66; Consultant Obstetrician and Gynaecologist, Royal Hosp. for Women 1983–88; Consultant, L. B. Johnson Tropical Medicine Center, American Samoa 1998–, Govt of Solomon Islands Medical Services (for AUSAID) 1999–; Examiner in Obstetrics and Gynaecology, Univs of Sydney and NSW; Fellow of the Senate, Univ. of Sydney 1974–90, mem. Faculty of Medicine, Univ. of Sydney 1966–90; mem. WHO Cttee on Safety of Contraceptives 1971; Dir Foundation 41 Research Lab. 1972–93; discovered that thalidomide caused birth defects (Lancet 1961), that thalidomide is a mutagen (British Medical Journal 1994); showed that radioactive labelled thalidomide binds with DNA in rats 1997; allegations of scientific fraud relating to anti-nausea drug, Debendox in 1987, led to his being struck off 1993, charges of misconduct in his obstetrics practice were dismissed and he was reinstated 1998; Dir Australian Opera 1979–82, mem.

Australian Opera Council 1984–; Hereford cattle judge, W. Midlands Show 1988; mem. AAAS American Coll. of Toxicologists, Soc. for Risk Analysis, New York Acad. of Sciences; Australian of the Year 1962, Gold Medal and BP Prize, L'Institut de la Vie 1971. *Publications:* Killing the Messenger 1994, Pharmacology & Toxicology 1999; more than 100 papers in medical and scientific journals. *Leisure interests:* surfing, tennis, riding, golf, breeder of Hereford cattle. *Address:* 11 Waratah Street, Mona Vale 2103 (home); 95 Elizabeth Bay Road, Elizabeth Bay, NSW 2011, Australia. *Telephone:* (2) 9368-7808. *Fax:* (2) 9368-7807.

McBRIDE, William James (Willie-John), MBE; Irish business executive and fmr rugby union player; b. 6 June 1940, Toomebridge, Northern Ireland; s. of William James McBride and Irene Patterson; m. Penny Michael 1966; one s. one d.; ed Ballymena Acad.; first played rugby for Ireland against England 1962; six Lions tours, S. Africa 1962, NZ 1966, S. Africa 1968, NZ 1971, S. Africa 1974, Capt. unbeaten Lions 1974, Man. Lions 1983 NZ; holder of 63 int. caps; 17 Test appearances for Lions (record); toured Australia 1967 and Argentina 1970 for Ireland; fmr Asst Bank Man.; Pres. Ballymena RFC, Vice-Pres. Northern Ireland Riding for Disabled; Freeman Borough of Newtownabbey; Int. Rugby Hall of Fame 1997; Dr hc (Nat. Univ. of Ireland) 2004. *Leisure interests:* golf, gardening, after-dinner speaking. *Address:* Gorse Lodge, 105 Ballycorr Road, Ballyclare, Co. Antrim, BT39 9DE, Northern Ireland. *Telephone:* (28) 9335-2710. *Fax:* (28) 9335-2710.

McBRIEN, Rev. Richard Peter, MA, STD; American academic; *Crowley-O'Brien Professor of Theology, University of Notre Dame;* b. 19 Aug. 1936, Hartford, Conn.; s. of the late Thomas H. McBrien and Catherine Botticelli; ed St Thomas Seminary, Bloomfield, Conn., St John Seminary, Brighton, Mass. and Pontifical Gregorian Univ., Rome; Prof. of Theology and Dean of Studies Pope John XXIII Nat. Seminary, Weston, Mass. 1965–70; Prof. Boston Coll., Newton, Mass. 1970–80; Chair. Dept of Theology, Univ. of Notre Dame, Ind. 1980–91, Crowley-O'Brien Prof. of Theology 1980–; John Courtney Murray Award, Catholic Theology Soc. of America 1976. *Publications:* Do We Need the Church? 1969, Church: The Continuing Quest 1970, The Remaking of the Church 1973, Catholicism (2 vols) (Christopher Award 1981) 1980, Caesar's Coin: Religion and Politics in America 1987, Report on the Church: Catholicism since Vatican II 1992, Catholicism (new edn) 1994, The HarperCollins Encyclopedia of Catholicism (Gen. Ed.) 1995, Responses to 101 Questions on the Church 1996, Lives of the Popes: The Pontiffs from St Peter to John Paul II 1997, Lives of the Saints: From Mary and St Francis of Assisi to John XXIII and Mother Teresa 2001, The Church: The Evolution of Catholicism 2008. *Leisure interests:* reading, films. *Address:* Department of Theology, University of Notre Dame, 130 Malloy Hall, Notre Dame, IN 46556, USA. *Telephone:* (574) 631-5151. *E-mail:* rmcbrien@nd.edu (office). *Website:* www.nd.edu/~theo/faculty/mcbrien.html (office).

McCABE, Eamonn Patrick; British photographer; b. 28 July 1948; s. of James McCabe and Celia McCabe; m. 1st Ruth Calvert 1972 (divorced 1993); one s.; m. 2nd Rebecca Smithers 1997; one d.; ed Challoner School, Finchley and San Francisco State Coll., USA; began career as photographer with Physics Dept, Imperial Coll., London; fmr freelance photographer for local papers and The Guardian for one year; staff photographer, The Observer 1977–86, 1987–88; Official Photographer, Pope's Visit to Britain 1982; Picture Ed. Sportsweek 1986–87, The Guardian 1988–2001; freelance photographer 2001–; Dir Newscast 2001–; Fellow in Photography, Nat. Museum of Photography and TV, Bradford 1988; Hon. Prof., Thames Valley Univ. 1994; Sports Photographer of the Year, Royal Photographic Soc. and Sports Council 1978, 1979, 1981, 1984, News Photographer of the Year, British Press Awards 1985, Picture Ed. of the Year, Nikon Press Awards (six times from 1992). *Publications:* Sports Photographer 1981, Eamonn McCabe, Photographer 1987, Emerald Gems of Ireland 2001, Making of Great Photographs 2005, Artists and Their Studios 2008. *Leisure interests:* playing tennis, squash, cinema. *Address:* c/o The Guardian, 119 Farringdon Road, London, EC1R 3ER, England. *Telephone:* (20) 7278-2332.

McCABE, John, CBE, MusB, FRNCM, FLCM, FRCM, RAM, FTCL; British pianist and composer; b. 21 April 1939, Huyton, Lancs. (now Merseyside); s. of Frank McCabe and Elisabeth McCabe (née Herlitzius); m. 1st Hilary Tann 1968 (divorced 1974); m. 2nd Monica Smith 1974; ed Liverpool Inst. High School for Boys, Manchester Univ., Royal Manchester Coll. of Music, Staatliche Hochschule für Musik, Munich; pianist-in-residence, University Coll., Cardiff 1965–68; Pres. Inc. Soc. of Musicians 1983–84; Dir London Coll. of Music 1983–90; Chair. Asscn of Professional Composers 1985–86; travels world-wide as pianist-composer; Hon. DPhil (Thames Valley) 2001; Royal Manchester Inst. Medal 1962, Royal Philharmonic Prize 1962, Special Citation, Koussevitsky Recording Foundation 1974, Award for service to British music, Composers Guild 1975. *Compositions include:* The Chagall Windows, Variations on a theme of Hartmann, Notturni ed Alba, Concerto for Orchestra, Cloudcatcher Fells, Fire at Durilgai, Canyons, Edward II (ballet), Arthur, Part I: Arthur Pendragon, Arthur, Part II: Le Morte d'Arthur (ballets), plus other stage works, symphonies, concertos, much orchestral and chamber music, vocal works and keyboard music; numerous piano recordings including complete piano works of Haydn and Nielsen. *Publications:* Rachmaninov, Bartok's Orchestral Music, Haydn's Piano Sonatas, Alan Rawsthorne: Portrait of a Composer and numerous articles on music. *Leisure interests:* books, films, cricket, snooker. *Address:* c/o Novello and Co. Ltd, Music Sales, 8/9 Frith Street, London, W1V 5TZ, England (office). *Telephone:* (20) 7434-0066. *Fax:* (20) 7287-6329. *E-mail:* promotion@musicsales.co.uk.

McCABE, Patrick; Irish writer; b. 27 March 1955, Clones, Co. Monaghan; m. Margot Quinn 1981; two d.; ed St Patrick's Teacher Training Coll., Dublin; fmr teacher of disabled children; Irish Press Hennessy Award 1979, Sunday Independent Arts Award. *Play:* has written plays for BBC radio, Frank Pig Says Hello (stage play, based on novel The Butcher Boy). *Film screenplay:* The Butcher Boy (co-writer). *Publications:* The Adventures of Shay Mouse 1985, Music on Clinton Street 1986, Carn 1989, The Butcher Boy (Irish Times/Aer Lingus Fiction Prize) 1992, Frank Pig Says Hello (play based on The Butcher Boy) 1992, The Dead School 1995, Breakfast on Pluto 1997, Mondo Desperado 1998, Emerald Gems of Ireland 2000, Call Me the Breeze 2003, Winterwood (Hughes and Hughes/Irish Independent Irish Novel of the Year 2007) 2006, The Holy City 2009; contrib. to anthologies, periodicals. *Leisure interests:* cinema, music. *Address:* c/o Bloomsbury Publishing, 36 Soho Square, London, W1D 3QY, England (office). *Telephone:* (20) 7494-2111 (office). *Fax:* (20) 7434-0151 (office). *Website:* www.bloomsbury.com (office).

McCAFFREY, Gen. Barry R., MA; American army officer (retd), academic, news analyst and consultant; *President, BR McCaffrey Associates LLC;* b. 17 Nov. 1942, Taunton, Mass.; m. Jill Ann Faulkner 1964; one s. two d.; ed Phillips Acad., Mass, US Mil. Acad., American Univ., Harvard Univ., Western Behavioral Science Inst., Nat. Defense Univ., Command and Gen. Staff Coll., Army War Coll.; commissioned into US Army 1964; served in Viet Nam 1966–67, 1968–69; Asst Prof. of Social Sciences, Dept of Social Sciences, US Mil. Acad. 1972–75, currently Adjunct Prof. of Int. Affairs; 3rd Infantry Div., Germany 1979–83; Div. Chief of Staff 9th Infantry Div. 1982–86; Asst Commandant US Army Infantry School 1986–88; US Deputy Mil. Rep. to NATO 1988–89; Prin. Staff Asst to Chair. of Jt Chiefs of Staff, Chief of Strategic Planning 1989–90; 24th Infantry Div. 1990–92; led div. into Iraq in Operation Desert Storm 1991; fmr Commdr-in-Chief US Armed Forces Southern Command; at retirement youngest four-star Gen. in Army and most highly decorated combat officer; Dir White House Office of Nat. Drug Control Policy 1996–2001; fmr mem. prin. negotiation team START II Nuclear Arms Control Treaty; mem. Nat. Security Council, Council on Foreign Relations, Nat. Asscn for Advancement of Colored People; Pres. B. R. McCaffrey Associates; currently NBC News analyst on terrorism; decorations from France, Brazil, Argentina, Colombia, Peru, and Venezuela; Distinguished Service Cross (twice), Silver Star (twice), Distinguished Service Medal, Combat Infantry Badge, US Health and Human Services Lifetime Achievement Award For Extraordinary Achievement in the Field of Substance Abuse Prevention 2004, recognized as one of the 500 Most Influential People in American Foreign Policy by World Affairs Councils of America 2004, US Dept of State Superior Honor Award for the Strategic Arms Limitation Talks, CIA Great Seal Medallion, US Coast Guard Distinguished Public Service Award, NAACP Roy Wilkins Renown Service Award, Norman E. Zinberg Award of the Harvard Medical School, Fed. Law Enforcement Foundation Nat. Service Award, Community Anti-Drug Coalitions of America Lifetime Achievement Award, Nat. Leadership Award by Community Anti-Drug Coalitions of America 2007, Golden Eagle, Soc. of American Mil. Engineers (SAME) 2007, inducted into US Army Ranger Hall of Fame 2007, American Red Cross Lifetime of Achievement Award, Air Force Asscn W. Stuart Symington Award. *Television:* appeared in over 6,000 TV interviews; media coverage includes Meet the Press, This Week, Fox Sunday News, Nightline, Today, Good Morning America, John McLaughlin's One on One, numerous feature interviews on CBS Evening News, NBC Nightly News, on World News, on PBS, on CNN, Montel Williams, Charlie Rose, Diane Rehm on NPR, C-Span Washington Journal. *Publications:* Proceedings of the Twenty-Fifth Student Conference on United States Affairs 1973, We Are Soldiers All: An Analysis of Possible Roles for Women in the Army 1973, numerous articles on mil. subjects, drugs law enforcement and money laundering. *Leisure interests:* hunting, reading military history. *Address:* BR McCaffrey Associates LLC, 2900 South Quincy Street, Suite 300A, Arlington, VA 22206, USA (office). *Telephone:* (703) 824-5160 (office). *Fax:* (703) 671-6318 (office). *E-mail:* brm@mccaffreyassociates.com (office). *Website:* www.mccaffreyassociates.com (office).

McCAIN, John Sidney III, DFC; American politician and fmr naval officer; *Senator from Arizona;* b. 29 Aug. 1936, Panama Canal Zone, Panama; s. of John Sidney McCain and Roberta McCain (née Wright); m. 1st Carol Shepp 1965 (divorced 1980); one d.; m. 2nd Cindy Hensley 1980; two s. two d. one adopted d.; ed US Naval Acad. and Nat. War Coll.; served in USN 1958–81, prisoner of war in Vietnam 1967–73; promoted to Capt. 1977; Dir Navy Senate Liaison Office, Washington, DC 1977–81; mem. Bd of Dirs Community Assistance League, Phoenix 1981–82; mem. US House of Reps from 1st Ariz. Dist 1983–86; Senator from Arizona 1987–, mem. Armed Services Cttee, Science and Transport Cttee, Indian Affairs Cttee; unsuccessful campaign for Republican nomination for US Pres. 2000; unsuccessful Republican cand. for US Pres. 2008; f. Country First PAC 2009; Chair. Int. Republican Inst. 1993–; Dr hc (Johns Hopkins Univ.) 1999, (Colgate Univ.) 2000, (Univ. of Pennsylvania) 2001, (Wake Forest Univ.) 2002, (Univ. of Southern California) 2004; various decorations including Legion of Merit, Silver Star, Purple Heart, Vietnamese Legion of Honour. *Publication:* Faith of My Fathers (with Mark Salter) 1999, Worth the Fighting For: A Memoir 2002, Why Courage Matters: The Way to a Braver Life 2004, Character is Destiny 2005, Hard Call (with Mark Salter) 2007. *Address:* 241 Russell Senate Office Building, Washington, DC 20510, USA (office). *Telephone:* (202) 224-2235 (office). *Fax:* (202) 228-2862 (office). *Website:* mccain.senate.gov (office); www.countryfirstpac.com.

McCALL, Carolyn, OBE, BA, MA; British media executive; *Chief Executive, Guardian Media Group PLC;* b. 13 Sept. 1961; m.; three c.; ed Univ. of Kent, Univ. of London; teacher Holland Park School 1982–84; Risk Analyst, Costain Group PLC 1984–86; Planner, Guardian Newspapers Ltd (GNL) 1986–88, Advertisement Exec. 1988–89, Advertisement Man. 1989–91, Product Devt Man. 1991–92, Display Advertisement Man. 1992, Advertisement Dir Wired UK 1992–94, Deputy Advertisement Dir 1994–95, Advertisement Dir 1995–97, Commercial Dir 1997–98 (with responsibility for internet strategy

– launched Guardian Unlimited 1999), Deputy Man. Dir 1998–2000, CEO of GNL 2000–06, and mem. Bd of Dirs Guardian Media Group PLC (GMG) 2000–, Chief Exec. GMG 2006–; mem. Bd of Dirs New Look Group PLC 1999–2004, Tesco PLC 2005–; Chair. Opportunity Now (gender equality and diversity org.) 2005–; Trustee Tools for Schools (educ. charity) 2000–05. *Address:* Guardian Media Group PLC, Kings Place, 90 York Way, London N1 9GU, England (office). *Telephone:* (20) 3353-2000 (office). *E-mail:* ceoffice@gmgplc.co.uk (office). *Website:* www.gmgplc.co.uk (office).

McCALL SMITH, Alexander, CBE; British writer and academic; *Emeritus Professor of Medical Law, University of Edinburgh;* b. 1948, Southern Rhodesia (now Zimbabwe); m. Elizabeth; two d.; currently Emer. Prof. of Medical Law, Univ. of Edinburgh; fmr mem. Human Genetics Comm. (fmr Vice-Chair.), UNESCO Int. Bioethics Comm., British Medical Journal Ethics Cttee (fmr Chair.), Roslin Inst. Ethics Cttee (fmr Chair.); DIur hc (Univ. of Edinburgh) 2007; British Books Awards Author of the Year 2004, Booksellers Asscn Author of the Year 2004, Waterstone's Author of the Year 2004. *Publications:* fiction: The No. 1 Ladies' Detective Agency 1998, Tears of the Giraffe 2000, Morality for Beautiful Girls 2001, The Kalahari Typing School for Men 2002, The Full Cupboard of Life (Saga Award for Wit) 2003, At the Villa of Reduced Circumstances 2003, Portuguese Irregular Verbs 2003, In the Company of Cheerful Ladies 2004, 44 Scotland Street (serialized in The Scotsman) 2004, The Sunday Philosophy Club 2004, The 2½ Pillars of Wisdom 2004, Friends, Lovers, Chocolate 2005, Blue Shoes and Happiness 2006, Dream Angus: The Celtic God of Dreams 2006, Love Over Scotland 2007, The World According to Bertie 2007, The Right Attitude to Rain 2007, The Careful Use of Compliments 2007, The Miracle at Speedy Motors 2008, Corduroy Mansions 2008, Tea Time for the Traditionally Built 2009, The Unbearable Lightness of Scones 2009; non-fiction: Law and Medical Ethics (with J. K. Mason) 1983, The Duty to Rescue: The Jurisprudence of Aid (with Michael A. Menlowe) 1993, Forensic Aspects of Sleep (with C. Shapiro) 1997, Justice and the Prosecution of Old Crimes: Balancing Legal, Psychological, and Moral Concerns (with Daniel W. Shuman) 2000, The Criminal Law of Botswana; children's fiction includes: White Hippo 1980, The Perfect Hamburger 1982, Jeffrey's Joke Machine 1990, The Five Lost Aunts of Harriet Bean 1990, Marzipan Max 1991, Uncle Gangster 1991, The Spaghetti Tangle 1992, Harriet Bean and the League of Cheats 1991, The Ice-Cream Bicycle 1992, Akimbo and the Lions 1992, The Doughnut Ring 1992, Springy Jane 1992, The Princess Trick 1992, The Cowgirl Aunt of Harriet Bean 1993, My Chameleon Uncle 1993, The Muscle Machine 1993, Paddy and the Ratcatcher 1994, The Banana Machine 1994, Akimbo and the Crocodile Man 1995, Billy Rubbish 1995, The Watermelon Boys 1996, Calculator Annie 1996, The Bubblegum Tree 1996, Bursting Balloons Mystery 1997, The Popcorn Pirates 1999, Chocolate Money Mystery 1999; short story collections: Children of Wax: African Folk Tales 1991, Heavenly Date and Other Stories (revised edn as Heavenly Date: And Other Flirtations) 1995, The Girl Who Married a Lion (short stories) 2004, One City (contrib.) 2006. *Address:* David Higham Associates, 5–8 Lower John Street, Golden Square, London, W1F 9HA, England (office). *Website:* www.alexandermccallsmith.co.uk.

McCALLISTER, Michael (Mike) B., MA, MBA; American business executive; *President and CEO, Humana Incorporated;* ed Pepperdine Univ., Louisiana Tech. Univ.; joined Humana Inc. 1974, various positions including finance specialist, Vice-Pres. Health Plans and Hosps, Ariz. 1989–92, Vice-Pres. Health Plans and Hosps, Tex. 1992–96, Pres. Tex., Fla and Puerto Rico Div. 1996–97, Sr Vice-Pres. Health Plan Div. 1997–99, apptd to Office of the Chair. 1999–2000, Pres. and CEO 2000–; mem. Bd Greater Louisville Health Enterprises Network, Louisville Fund for the Arts, Business Roundtable, American Asscn of Health Plans; mem. Advisory Bd Coll. of Admin and Business, Louisiana Tech. Univ. *Address:* Humana Inc., 500 West Main Street, Louisville, KY 40202, USA (office). *Telephone:* (502) 580-1000 (office). *Fax:* (502) 580-3677 (office). *E-mail:* info@humana.com (office). *Website:* www.humana.com (office).

McCALLUM, Martin, FRSA; British theatre producer; b. 6 April 1950, Blackpool; s. of Raymond McCallum and Jessie McCallum; m. 1st Lesley Nunnerley 1971 (divorced); one s. one d.; m. 2nd Julie Edmett (divorced); one d.; m. 3rd Mary Ann Rolfe; two s.; ed Barfield School Surrey, Frensham Heights School Surrey; began career as student Asst Stage Man., Castle Theatre, Farnham Surrey 1967; worked as actor, stage man., lighting and sound technician; Production Man. Nat. Theatre at Old Vic (with Laurence Olivier) 1971–75, productions included Filumena, Evita, Sweeney Todd, CATS; Consultant to Glyndebourne Festival Opera, Arts Council's Regional Theatre Scheme; Man. Dir Cameron Mackintosh Ltd 1981–2000, Vice-Chair. 2000–03; Dir Donmar Warehouse Theatre 1992–, Chair. 1996–2004 (resgnd), currently Bd Dir; initiated Wyndham Report 1998; est. New Writing Symposium 1999; Pres. Soc. of London Theatre 1999–2002; initiated inaugural jt Theatre Conf. of SOLT/TMA/ITC Theatre 2001 Future Directions; mem. League of American Theatres and Producers 1988–, Drama Panel, Arts Council of England 1999–2004, Cultural Strategy Group London 2000–04; mem. V&A Theatre Museum Cttee; consultant on design projects including Old Fire Station Theatre, Oxford (new build), Prince Edward Theatre (restoration) 1993, Musical Hall, Stuttgart (new build) 1994, Capital Theatre, Sydney (restoration) 1995, Musical Theatre, Duisberg (new build) 1996, Theatre Royal, Sydney (restoration) 1998, Wales Millennium Centre, Lyric Theatre (new build) 1998, Auditorium Theatre, Chicago (restoration) 2001, Schaumburg Village Theatre, Illinois (new build) 2003, Fine Arts Building Theatre, Chicago (restoration study) 2003, Prince of Wales Theatre, London (restoration) 2003, Montecasino Theatre, Johannesburg, SA 2007; Co-Producer Matthew Bourne's new dance production of Edward Scissorhands, London 2005–; currently developing a new musical, Nightingale, based on the original Hans Christian Andersen story, with book and lyrics by Steven Sater

and composed by Duncan Sheik. *Leisure interests:* performing arts, music, art, gardens. *Address:* PO Box 630, Avalon, NSW, Australia (home). *Telephone:* (401) 279464 (office). *E-mail:* martin@sunriseroad.com (office).

McCANDLESS, Bruce, II; American astronaut (retd) and scientist; *Chief Scientist, Reusable Space Transportation Systems, Lockheed Martin Space Systems Company;* b. (Byron Willis McCandless), 8 June 1937, Boston, Mass.; s. of late Rear-Adm. Bruce McCandless and Sue W.B. McCandless Inman; m. Alfreda Bernice Doyle 1960; one s. one d.; ed US Naval Acad., Stanford Univ. and Univ. of Houston; flight training, Pensacola, Fla and Kingsville, Tex.; weapons system and carrier landing training, Key West, Fla 1960; carrier duty, Fighter Squadron 102 1960–64; instrument flight instructor, Attack Squadron 43, Naval Air Station, Apollo Soucek Field, Oceana, Va; graduate studies in electrical Eng, Stanford Univ. until 1966; selected by NASA as astronaut April 1966; Co-investigator Astronaut Manoeuvring Unit Experiment on Skylab 1968–74; back-up crew for first Skylab Mission 1973; Mission Specialist on STS-11, first flight of manned manoeuvring unit; Mission Specialist on STS-31, Hubble Space Telescope deployment; retd from Navy as Capt. Aug. 1990; Man. Payload Systems and Tech., Lockheed Martin Astronautics Group and Vice-Pres. Lockheed Martin Overseas Corpn 1990–; Prin. Staff Engineer Lockheed Martin Astronautics 1990–97; Chief. Scientist Reusable Space Transportation Systems 1997–; V. A. Prather Award, American Astronautical Soc. 1975, 1985, NASA Space Flight Medal 1984, 1991, Nat. Air and Space Museum Trophy 1985, Nat. Aeronautical Asscn Collier Trophy 1985, NASA Exceptional Eng Achievement Medal 1985, Defense Distinguished Service Medal 1985, Legion of Merit 1988, US Astronaut Hall of Fame 2005. *Leisure interests:* electronics, scuba diving, sailing, photography. *Address:* Lockheed Martin Space Systems Company, 12257 South Wadsworth Blvd., Littleton, CO 80125-8500 (office); Mail Stop DC 3005, Lockheed Martin Astronautics, P.O. Box 179, Denver, CO 80201 (office); 21852 Pleasant Park Road, Conifer, CO 80433-6802, USA (home). *Telephone:* (303) 971-6308 (office). *Fax:* (303) 971-7698 (office). *E-mail:* bruce .mccandless@lmco.com (office); brucemcc@logcabin.com (home). *Website:* www .lockheedmartin.com (office).

McCANN, Renetta, BS; American business executive; b. (Renetta E. Walker), 8 Dec. 1956, Chicago, Ill.; d. of Aditha Lorraine Collymore Walker; m.; two c.; ed Aquinas Dominican High School and Northwestern Univ.; joined Leo Burnett advertising agency as client service trainee 1978–79, Media Supervisor 1979–88, Vice-Pres. 1988–89, Media Dir 1989–95, Sr Vice-Pres. 1995–98, Man. Dir Starcom 1998, CEO Starcom MediaVest Group Americas (following merger with D'Arcy) –2005, CEO Starcom MediaVest Group Worldwide 2005–08, Head of Talent Devt Platform, VivaKi (subsidiary of Publicis Groupe) 2008–; mem. Bd Chicago United; winner of numerous Effies and Cannes Lions, chosen as 'Media Maven' by Advertising Age 1991, selected as one of Ebony magazine's 57 Most Intriguing Blacks, named by Black Enterprise as Executive of the Year 2002, selected by Women's Advertising Club of Chicago as Advertising Woman of the Year 2002, named by Essence magazine as one of 50 Women Who Are Changing The World, ranked by Forbes magazine amongst Most Powerful Women (27th) 2006, (41st) 2007. *Address:* c/o Publicis Groupe, 4 Herald Square, 950 6th Avenue, New York, NY 10001, USA. *Website:* www.vivaki.com (office).

McCARRICK, HE Cardinal Theodore Edgar, BA, MA, DD, PhD; American ecclesiastic; *Archbishop Emeritus of Washington;* b. 7 July 1930, New York; ed St. Joseph's Seminary, Yonkers, New York, Catholic University of America; ordained priest 1958; Auxiliary Bishop of New York 1977; Bishop of Metuchen 1981; Archbishop of Newark 1986–2000; Archbishop of Washington 2001–06, Archbishop Emer. 2006–; Cardinal Priest of the Titulus Ss. Nerei et Achillei 2001; Pres. Papal Foundation 1997–; Chancellor The Catholic Univ. of America 2001–06; Pres. Bd of Trustees, Basilica of the Nat. Shrine of the Immaculate Conception; mem. US Sec. of State's Advisory Cttee on Religious Freedom Abroad 1996–99, US Comm. for Int. Religious Freedom 1999–2001; Order of Cedars of Lebanon 2000, Eleanor Roosevelt Award for Human Rights 2000. *Address:* Archdiocese of Washington Pastoral Center, 5001 Eastern Avenue, PO Box 29260, Washington, DC 20017-0260, USA (office). *Telephone:* (301) 853-4500 (office). *Website:* www.adw.org (office).

McCARTHY, Sir Callum, PhD; British civil servant, economist and banker; *Chairman, Financial Services Authority;* b. 29 Feb. 1944, Brentwood, Essex; s. of Ralph McCarthy and Agnes Graham; m. Penelope Ann Gee 1966; two s. one d.; ed Univs of Oxford and Stirling, Business School, Stanford Univ.; econ. and operations researcher ICI 1965; Prin. Pvt. Sec. to Roy Hattersley (q.v.) and Norman Tebbit (q.v.), Dept of Trade and Industry 1972–85, also Under-Sec.; Dir of Corp. Finance, Kleinwort Benson 1985–89; Man. Dir, Head of Corp. Finance, BZW 1989–93; CEO Barclays Bank Group Japan and N America 1993–98; Dir-Gen. of UK Gas Supply 1998–2003; Dir-Gen. of UK Electricity Supply 1999–2003; Chair. Gas and Electricity Markets Authority 2000–03; Chief Exec. Ofgem 2000–03; Chair. Financial Services Authority (FSA) 2003– (08); Hon. Fellow Merton Coll., Oxford 2006, Freeman, City of London 2008; Dr hc (Stirling Univ.) 2004. *Publication:* Introduction to Technological Economics (with D. S. Davies) 1967. *Leisure interests:* walking, reading, bee-keeping. *Address:* The Financial Services Authority, 25 The North Colonnade, Canary Wharf, London, E14 5HS, England. *Telephone:* (20) 7066-1000 (office). *Website:* www.fsa.gov.uk (office).

McCARTHY, Cormac; American writer; b. 1933, Rhode Island; s. of Charles Joseph McCarthy and Gladys McGrail; m. 1st Lee Holleman 1961 (divorced); one s.; m. 2nd Annie DeLisle (divorced); m. 3rd Jennifer Winkley 1998; ed Univ. of Tennessee; USAF 1953–57; MacArthur Fellowship 1981; Guggenheim Fellowship; Rockefeller Fellowship; PEN/Saul Bellow Award for Lifetime Achievement 2009. *Play:* The Stonemason 1994. *Publications:* novels: The Orchard Keeper 1965, Outer Dark 1968, Child of God 1973, Suttree 1979,

Blood Meridian 1985, All the Pretty Horses (Vol. 1 of The Bouden Trilogy) 1992, The Crossing (Vol. 2 of The Bouden Trilogy) 1994, Cities of the Plain (Vol. 3 of The Bouden Trilogy) 1998, No Country for Old Men 2005, The Road (James Tait Black Memorial Prize for Fiction 2007, Pulitzer Prize for Fiction 2007, Quill Award for General Fiction 2007) 2006. *Address:* c/o Santa Fe Institute, 1399 Hyde Park Road, Santa Fe, NM 87501, USA.

McCARTHY, James J., BS, PhD; American oceanographer and academic; *Professor of Biological Oceanography and Alexander Agassiz Professor of Biological Oceanography, Harvard University;* ed Gonzaga Univ., Scripps Inst. of Oceanography; Dir Museum of Comparative Zoology, Harvard Univ. 1982–2002, Acting Curator Malacology Dept, currently Prof. of Biological Oceanography and Alexander Agassiz Prof. of Biological Oceanography, holds faculty appointments in Dept of Organismic and Evolutionary Biology and Dept of Earth and Planetary Sciences, Head Tutor for degrees in Environmental Science and Public Policy, Master of Pforzheimer House; Chair. int. cttee that establishes research priorities and oversees implementation of Int. Geosphere – Biosphere Program 1986–93; has served and serves on numerous nat. and int. planning cttees, advisory panels and comms relating to oceanography, polar science and study of climate and global change; involved in two int. assessments on climate impacts; Co-Chair. Intergovernmental Panel on Climate Change (IPCC), Working Group II, for Third IPCC Assessment 2001; a lead author on Arctic Climate Impact Assessment; Vice-Chair. Northeast Climate Impacts Assessment 2007; Founding Ed. American Geophysical Union's Global Biogeochemical Cycles; Fellow, AAAS, Pres.-elect 2008–09, Pres. 2009–; Fellow, American Acad. of Arts and Sciences; Foreign mem. Royal Swedish Acad. of Sciences; David B. Stone Award, New England Aquarium. *Publications:* numerous scientific papers in professional journals on the regulation of plankton productivity in the sea. *Address:* 524 MCZ Labs, Museum of Natural History, Harvard University, 26 Oxford Street, Cambridge, MA 02138, USA (office). *Telephone:* (617) 495-2330 (office). *E-mail:* jmccarthy@oeb.harvard.edu (office). *Website:* www.oeb.harvard.edu/faculty/mccarthy/mccarthy-oeb.html (office); www.oeb.harvard.edu/faculty/mccarthy/McCarthyLab.html (office).

McCARTHY, John Philip, AO, MA, LLB; Australian lawyer and diplomatist; *High Commissioner to India;* b. 29 Nov. 1942, Washington, DC, USA; s. of Edwin McCarthy and Marjorie McCarthy; two d.; ed Cambridge Univ.; practised as barrister, London 1965–66; with Shearman and Sterling (law firm), New York 1966–67; 1964; joined Dept of Foreign Affairs 1968; Second Sec. Vientiane 1969–72; First Sec. Washington 1973–75; Chargé d'affaires, Damascus 1977–78; Sr Pvt. Sec. to Minister for Foreign Affairs 1979–80; Amb. to Democratic Repub. of Viet Nam 1981–83, to Mexico 1985–87, to Thailand 1992–94, to USA 1995–97, to Indonesia 1997–2000, to Japan 2001–05; High Commr in India and Amb. to Bhutan 2005–; Deputy Sec. Dept of Foreign Affairs and Trade, Canberra 1994–95. *Leisure interests:* skiing, Asian art, walking, travel. *Address:* Embassy of Australia, 1/50-g Shanti Path, Chanakyapuri, New Delhi 110 021, India (office). *Telephone:* (11) 51399900 (office). *Fax:* (11) 26885199 (office). *Website:* www.ausgovindia.com (office).

McCARTHY, Paul; American artist; b. 1945, Salt Lake City; early work includes series of black paintings 1967–68; became known for visceral performances and film works 1970s; extended practice into stand-alone sculptural figures, installations and a series of large, inflatable sculptures 1990s; Tate Gallery Modern commissioned outdoor inflatable sculptures for North Landscape, London 2003. *Artistic Works include:* Blockhead, Tate Modern 2003, Daddies Bighead, Tate Modern 2003. *Recent Group Exhibitions include:* Stunt Videos, Tennis Palace City Art Museum, Helsinki (Finland) 2003, Spiritus, Magasin 3 Stockholm Konsthall (Sweden) 2003, Apparation, Kettle's Yard, Cambridge (UK) 2003, Spiritus, Douglas Hyde Gallery, Dublin (Ireland) 2003, Twilight, Gimpel Fils, London 2003, Sphere, Presentation House Gallery, Vancouver (Canada) 2003, From East to West, Gas Art Gallery, Torino (Italy) 2003,C'est arrive demain, Musée a'Art Contemporain, Lyon (France) 2004, Spiritus, Sundsvalls Museum, (Sweden) 2004, Partners, Haus der Kunst, Munich (Germany) 2004, Playlist, Palais de Tokyo, Paris (France) 2004, Point of View, Museum of Contemporary Art, NY 2004, Speaking with Hands, Guggenheim New York 2004, I am the Walrus, Chelm & Reid, NY 2004, Monument to Now, Deste Foundation Centre for Contemporary Art, Athina 2004. *Recent Solo Exhibitions include:* Retrospective, Museum of Contemporary Art, LA 2000, Retrospective, New Museum of Contemporary Art, NY 2001, Villa Arson (France) 2001, Tate Liverpool (UK) 2001, Stor retrospektiv, Museet for Samtidskunst, Oslo (Norway) 2003, Inaugural Show, Hauser & Wirth, London (UK) 2003, Painter 1995, Herzliya Museum of Art, Herzeliyya (Israel) 2004, Brain Box Dream Box, Stedelijk Van Abbemuseum (Netherlands) 2004. *Address:* c/o Luhring Augustine Gallery, 531 West 24th Street, New York, NY 10011, USA (office).

McCARTNEY, Rt Hon. Ian; British politician; *Minister for Trade, Foreign and Commonwealth Office and Department of Trade and Industry;* b. 25 April 1951; s. of Hugh McCartney; m. 1st (divorced); two d. one s. (deceased); m. 2nd Ann Parkes; joined Labour Party 1966, Labour Party Organizer 1973–87; Councillor for Wigan Borough 1982–87; MP (Labour) for Makerfield 1987–; Opposition Spokesperson on NHS (Nat. Health Service) 1992–94, on Employment 1994–96, Chief Spokesperson on Employment 1996–97; Minister of State Dept of Trade and Industry 1997–99, Cabinet Office 1999–2001; Minister for Pensions Dept for Work and Pensions 2001–03; Minister without Portfolio, Chair. Labour Party 2003–06; Minister for Trade, FCO and Dept of Trade and Industry 2006–; Minister to Watch, Spectator Awards 1999. *Leisure interests:* Rugby League (supports Wigan Warriors). *Address:* House of Commons, London, SW1A 0AA (office); The Labour Party, 16 Old Queen Street, London SW1H 9HP, England (office). *Telephone:* (20) 7219-4033

(office). *Fax:* (20) 7219-2771 (office). *E-mail:* IanMcCartney@1makerfield .freeserve.co.uk. *Website:* www.labour.org.uk (office).

McCARTNEY, Sir (James) Paul, Kt, MBE, FRCM; British singer, songwriter and musician (guitar, piano, organ); b. 18 June 1942, Liverpool; s. of James McCartney and Mary McCartney; m. 1st Linda Eastman 1969 (died 1998); one s. two d. one step-d.; m. 2nd Heather Mills 2002 (divorced 2008); one d.; ed Stockton Wood Road Primary School, Speke, Joseph Williams Primary School, Gateacre and Liverpool Inst.; wrote first song 1956, wrote numerous songs with John Lennon; joined pop group The Quarrymen 1956; appeared under various titles until formation of The Beatles 1960; appeared with The Beatles for performances in Hamburg 1960, 1961, 1962, The Cavern, Liverpool 1960, 1961; worldwide tours 1963–66; attended Transcendental Meditation Course at Maharishi's Acad., Rishikesh, India Feb. 1968; formed Apple Ltd, parent org. of The Beatles Group of Cos 1968; left The Beatles after collapse of Apple Corpn Ltd 1970; formed MPL Group of Cos 1970; first solo album McCartney 1970; formed own pop group Wings 1971–81, tours of Britain and Europe 1972–73, UK and Australia 1975, Europe and USA 1976, UK 1979, World Tour 1989–90; also records as The Fireman, dance music duo with Youth 1994–; solo performance at Party at the Palace, Buckingham Palace 2002; Fellow, British Acad. of Composers and Songwriters 2000; Hon. Fellow (Liverpool John Moores Univ.) 1998; Dr hc (Sussex) 1988, Hon. DMus (Yale) 2008; two Grammy Awards for Band on the Run (including Best Pop Vocal Performance) 1975, Ivor Novello Award for Best Selling British Record 1977–78 for single Mull of Kintyre, for Int. Hit of the Year 1982 for single Ebony and Ivory, for Outstanding Services to British Music 1989, Guinness Book of Records Triple Superlative Award (43 songs each selling more than 1m copies, holder of 60 gold discs, estimated sales of 100m albums and 100m singles) 1979, Lifetime Achievement Award 1990, Freeman of the City of Liverpool 1984, Lifetime Achievement Award People for the Ethical Treatment of Animals (with Linda McCartney) 1996, Polar Music Prize 1992, Radio Acad. lifetime achievement award 2007, Q Icon Award 2007, BRIT Award for Outstanding Contribution to Music 2008. *Recordings include:* albums: with The Beatles: Please Please Me 1963, A Hard Day's Night 1964, Beatles for Sale 1965, Help! 1965, Rubber Soul 1966, Revolver 1966, Sgt Pepper's Lonely Hearts Club Band 1967, Magical Mystery Tour 1967, The Beatles (White Album) 1968, Yellow Submarine 1969, Abbey Road 1969, Let It Be 1970, 1962–1966 (Red Album) 1973, 1967–1970 (Blue Album) 1973, Past Masters Vol. One 1988, Past Masters Vol. Two 1988, The Beatles Anthology: 1 1995, The Beatles Anthology: 2 1996, The Beatles Anthology: 3 1996, 1 2000; with Wings: Wild Life 1971, Red Rose Speedway 1973, Band On The Run 1973, Venus and Mars 1975, Wings at the Speed of Sound 1976, Wings Over America 1976, London Town 1978, Wings Greatest 1978, Back To The Egg 1979, Wingspan 2001; solo: McCartney 1970, Ram 1971, McCartney II 1980, Tug of War 1982, Pipes of Peace 1983, Give My Regards to Broad Street 1984, Press To Play 1986, All the Best! 1987, CHOBA B CCCP 1988, Flowers in the Dirt 1989, Tripping the Live Fantastic 1990, Unplugged: The Official Bootleg 1991, Paul McCartney's Liverpool Oratorio (with Carl Davis) 1991, Off the Ground 1993, Paul is Live 1993, Flaming Pie 1997, Standing Stone (symphonic work) 1997, Run Devil Run 1999, Working Classical 1999, A Garland for Linda (with eight other composers for a capella choir) 2000, Driving Rain 2001, Back in the US: Live 2002, Back in the World 2003, Chaos and Creation in the Back Yard 2005, Ecce Cor Meum (classical) (Classical BRIT Award for Best Album 2007) 2006, Memory Almost Full 2007; with The Fireman: Strawberries Oceans Ships Forest 1994, Rushes 1998, Electric Arguments 2008; film soundtracks: The Family Way 1966, James Paul McCartney 1973, Live and Let Die 1973, The Zoo Gang (TV series) 1973. *Radio:* (series) Routes of Rock (BBC) 1999. *Films:* A Hard Day's Night 1964, Help! 1965, Magical Mystery Tour (TV film) 1967, Yellow Submarine (animated colour cartoon film) 1968, Let it Be 1970, Wings Over the World (TV) 1979, Rockshow 1981, Give My Regards to Broad Street (wrote and directed) 1984, Rupert and the Frog Song (wrote and produced) (BAFTA Award Best Animated Film) 1985, Press to Play 1986, Get Back (concert film) 1991. *Publications:* Paintings 2000, The Beatles Anthology (with George Harrison and Ringo Starr) 2000, Sun Prints (with Linda McCartney) 2001, Many Years From Now (autobiog.) 2001, Blackbird Singing: Poems and Lyrics 1965–1999 2001, High in the Clouds (juvenile, with Philip Ardagh and Geoff Dunbar) 2005. *Address:* MPL Communications Ltd, 1 Soho Square, London, W1V 6BQ, England (office). *Website:* www.paulmccartney.com.

McCARTNEY, Stella, BA; British fashion designer; b. 13 Sept. 1971, London; d. of Sir Paul McCartney (q.v.) and the late Linda McCartney; m. Alasdhair Willis; two s. one d.; ed Cen. St Martin's Coll. of Art and Design; work with Christian Lacroix at age 15 and later with Betty Jackson; work experience in Fashion Dept, Vogue magazine; set up own clothing line, London 1995; Creative Dir Chloe, Paris 1997–2001; designed collection for Gucci 2001; established own fashion house, in partnership with Gucci Group 2001–; designed costumes for film Sky Captain and the World of Tomorrow 2004; designed sportswear ranges for Adidas 2007–; VH1/Vogue Fashion and Music Designer of the Year 2000, Woman of Courage Award 2003, Glamour Award for Best Designer of the Year 2004, Designer of the Year, British Fashion Awards 2007. *Address:* Peake House, 92 Golborne Road, London, W10 5PS, England (office). *Telephone:* (20) 7518-3111. *Fax:* (20) 7518-3112. *E-mail:* press@stellamccartney.com. *Website:* www.stellamccartney.com (office).

McCASKILL, Claire, BS; American lawyer and politician; *Senator from Missouri;* b. Rolla, Mo.; d. of William Y. McCaskill and Betty Anne McCaskill; m. 1st David Exposito (divorced 1995, died 2005); one s. two d.; m. 2nd Joseph Shepard 2002; four step-c.; ed Hickman High School, Columbia, Univ. of Missouri-Columbia; has worked in public sector continuously since 1978; spent one year as a law clerk on Mo. Court of Appeals for Western Dist, Kansas City; fmr Asst Prosecutor, Jackson Co. Prosecutor's office, specializing in arson cases; attorney in pvt. practice 1989–91; mem. Mo. House of Reps for Brookside neighbourhood of Kansas City 1983–88; elected to Jackson Co. Legislature 1990–92; Jackson Co. Prosecutor (first woman) 1993–98; State Auditor 1999–2006; defeated Gov. Bob Holden in Democratic primary race 2004 (first person to defeat an incumbent gov. in state history); Senator from Mo. 2007–, mem. Armed Services, Commerce, Homeland Security Cttee, Indian Affairs Cttee, Special Cttee on Aging; Democrat. *Address:* Hart Senate Office Building, SH-717, Washington, DC 20510, USA (office). *Telephone:* (202) 224-6154 (office). *Fax:* (202) 228-6326 (office). *Website:* mccaskill.senate .gov (office); www.claireonline.com (office).

McCLEAN, Maxine, BPA, MA, MBA; Barbadian management consultant and politician; *Minister of Foreign Affairs, Foreign Trade and International Business;* ed Univ. of the West Indies; fmr Lecturer in Man. Studies, Univ. of the West Indies; Founder Strategic Interventions Inc. (consultancy firm) 1991; mem. Senate 2008–; Leader of Govt Business and Minister in the Prime Minister's Office Jan.–Dec. 2008; Minister of Foreign Affairs, Foreign Trade and Int. Business 2008–; fmr Pres., Vice-Pres. and mem. Supervisory Cttee City of Bridgetown Cooperative Credit Union Ltd; currently Pres. Univ. of the West Indies Cave Hill Campus Alumni Asscn; fmr Chair. Bd of Dirs Bridgetown Cruise Terminals Inc., Need Trust Fund of the Pinelands Creative Workshop, Dir Goddards Enterprises Ltd, RBTT Bank Barbados Ltd, Barbados Stock Exchange Inc.; OAS Fellowship, Univ. of Ohio 1979, Fulbright Fellowship, Louisiana State Univ. 1986. *Address:* Ministry of Foreign Affairs, Foreign Trade and International Business, 1 Culloden Road, St Michael, Barbados (office). *Telephone:* 431-2200 (office). *Fax:* 429-6652 (office). *E-mail:* info@foreign.gov.bb (office). *Website:* www.foreign.gov.bb (office).

McCLELLAN, Scott; American business executive and fmr government official; *Senior Vice President for Corporate and Government Affairs, HHB Inc.;* b. 14 Feb. 1968, Austin, Tex.; s. of Carole Keeton Strayhorn; m. Jill Martinez 2003; ed Univ. of Tex.; Deputy Communications Dir for Gov. George W. Bush of Texas 1999; served as travelling press sec. during 2000 presidential campaign; Deputy Press Sec., The White House 2001–03, Press Sec. 2003–06; Sr Vice Pres. for Corp. and Govt Affairs, HHB Inc. 2006–; mem. APCO Worldwide Int. Advisory Council 2008–. *Publication:* What Happened: Inside the Bush White House and Washington's Culture of Deception 2008. *Address:* HHB Inc., 3666 University Avenue, 3rd Floor, Riverside, CA 92501, USA (office). *Telephone:* (951) 682-4445 (office). *Fax:* (619) 568-3114 (office). *E-mail:* info@hardhatbid.com (office). *Website:* www.hardhatbid.com (office).

McCLELLAND, Robert, LLM; Australian lawyer and politician; *Attorney-General;* b. 26 Jan. 1958, Sydney; s. of Douglas McClelland; m. Michelle McClelland; one s. three d.; ed Univ. of NSW, Univ. of Sydney; worked as assoc. to Hon. Justice Philip Evatt, Fed. Court of Australia 1980–82; Solicitor, Turner Freeman Solicitors 1982–88, Pnr 1988–96; MP (Austalia Labor Party) for Barton, NSW 1996–, Shadow Attorney-Gen. 1998–2001, Shadow Minister for Workplace Relations 2001–03, for Justice and Community Security 2003, for Homeland Security 2003, for Defence and Homeland Security 2004, for Defence 2005, for Foreign Affairs 2006–07, Attorney-Gen. 2007–. *Publications:* numerous legal essays. *Leisure interests:* Australian history, surfing, sailing, rugby league (St George). *Address:* Attorney General's Department, Central Office, Robert Garran Offices, National Circuit, Barton ACT 2600, Australia (office). *Telephone:* (2) 6250-6666 (office). *Fax:* (2) 6250-5900 (office). *Website:* www.ag.gov.au (office); www.alp.org.au/people/nsw/ mcclelland_robert.php.

McCLUNG, A(ndrew) Colin, BA, MS, PhD; American agronomist (retd); b. 1923; ed Univ. of West Virginia, Cornell Univ.; agronomy researcher, N Carolina State Coll. 1950–56; joined Int. Basic Econ. Corpn Research Inst. (later known as IRI Research Inst.) 1956, initiated research on soil degradation in central Brazil, including the 300 million-acre wasteland known as Cerrado, currently Washington Rep. of IRI Research Inst.; fmr mem. Rockefeller Foundation, Winrock International; World Food Prize (co-recipient) 2006, recognized by Soil Science Soc. of America 2006. *Address:* c/o IRI Research Institute, Matão, São Paulo, Brazil.

McCOLGAN, Ellyn, BA, MBA, LLD; American business executive; b. 16 Jan. 1954, Jersey City, NJ; ed Montclair State Coll., NJ; with Shearson Lehman Brothers, New York 1983, later with Bank of New England; joined Fidelity 1990, fmrly with Fidelity Accounting and Custody Services, Pres. Fidelity Investments Tax-Exempt Services Co. 1996–2000, Fidelity Investments Institutional Retirement Group 2000–01, Fidelity Financial Intermediary Services (FFIS) 2001–02, Fidelity Brokerage Co. 2002–07 (resgnd); Pres. and COO Global Wealth Man. Group, Morgan Stanley 2008–09, mem. Man. Cttee; mem. Bd of Dirs Decision Resources Inc.; Trustee Babson Coll.; mem. Boston Club; ranked by Fortune magazine amongst 50 Most Powerful Women in Business in the US (45th) 2005, (44th) 2006. *Address:* 91 Central Park West, 8A, New York, NY 10023-4600, USA.

McCOLL OF DULWICH, Baron (Life Peer), cr. 1989, of Bermondsey in the London Borough of Southwark; **Ian McColl**, CBE, MS, FRCS, FRCSE, FACS; British professor of surgery; *Part-Time Lecturer, Guy's Hospital;* b. 6 Jan. 1933; s. of the late Frederick George McColl and Winifred Edith McColl; m. Jean Lennox McNair 1960; one s. two d.; ed Hutchesons' Grammar School, Glasgow, St Paul's School, London, Guy's Hosp. Medical School, Univ. of London; Moynihan Fellowship, Asscn of Surgeons 1967; Reader in Surgery, St Bartholomew's Hosp., London 1967–71, Sub-Dean, St Bartholomew's Hosp. Medical Coll. 1969–71; Prof. of Surgery, Guy's Hosp., London 1971–98, Consultant Surgeon 1971–98, Dir of Surgery 1985–98, currently Part-time Lecturer; Chair. Dept of Surgery, United Medical and Dental Schools, St Thomas' Hosps 1985–92; Hon. Consultant to British Army 1976–98; Parl. Pvt.

Sec. (Lords) to Prime Minister 1994–97; Deputy Speaker House of Lords 1994–2002; Chair. Bd Govs Mildmay Mission Hosp. 1984–; Vice-Chair. Disablement Services Authority for England 1987–91; Chair. Bd Dirs, Vice-Chair. Int. Bd Mercy Ships 1998–; mem. Council, Royal Coll. of Surgeons 1986–94, Council, Imperial Cancer Research Fund 1986–94; Pres. Nat. Asscn of Limbless Disabled, Soc. of Minimally Invasive Surgery, Leprosy Mission; Vice-Pres. John Grooms Asscn for the Disabled; mem. Bd Govs American Coll. of Surgeons 1982–88; Fellow, King's Coll. London 2001; George and Thomas Hutcheson's Award 2000, Nat. Maritime Historical Soc. Award 2002, Great Scot Award 2002. *Eponymous lectures:* Arris and Gale (2), Erasmus Wilson, Haig Gudenian Memorial, Colles, Letsomian, Lord Cohen Memorial. *Publications:* Intestinal Absorption in Man 1976, NHS Data Book 1984, Govt Report on supply of artificial legs and wheelchairs for England; articles on colonic diseases, medical audit and amputations. *Leisure interest:* forestry. *Address:* House of Lords, Westminster, London, SW1A 0PW, England (office). *Telephone:* (20) 7219-5141 (office). *E-mail:* mccolli@parliament.uk (office).

McCOMB, Leonard William Joseph, RA, Dipl. Fine Art; British artist; b. 3 Aug. 1930, Glasgow, Scotland; s. of Archibald McComb and Delia McComb; m. 1st Elizabeth Henstock 1955 (divorced 1963); m. 2nd Joan Allwork 1966 (died 1967); m. 3rd Barbara Gittel 1973; ed Manchester Art School, Slade School of Fine Art, Univ. of London; teacher at art schools in Bristol, Oxford and London (RA schools, Slade, Goldsmiths', Sir John Cass) 1960–; Assoc. RA 1987, RA 1991, Keeper of the RA 1995–98; Judge, The Winsor & Newton Turner Watercolour Award 2005; Hon. mem. Royal Watercolour Soc. 1996, Royal Soc. of Printmakers 1996; Dr hc (Oxford Brookes Univ.) 2004; Jubilee Prize, RA 1986, Korn Ferry Award 1990, Times Watercolour Competition Prize 1992, 1993, Nordstern Printmaking Prize, RA 1992, Royal Watercolour Soc. Prize 1998, Sir Hugh Casson Drawing Prize, Royal Acad. Summer Exhbn 2005; Turner Medal, Royal Acad. Summer Exhbn 2006. *Works on display in public collections include:* Arts Council, British Council, ICA, Univ. of Cambridge, Tate Gallery, Victoria & Albert Museum, Ulster Museum, Cecil Higgins Art Gallery and Museum, Bedford, Birmingham City Art Gallery, British Museum, Manchester Art Gallery, National Portrait Gallery, Swindon Art Gallery, Towner Art Gallery, Eastbourne, Art Galleries of Worcester, Leicester and Belfast. *Radio:* Kaleidoscope (BBC Radio Four) 1984, Life's Little Luxuries (BBC Radio Four) 2001. *Television:* The South Bank Show – Royal Acad. Chat 1999. *Publication:* Leonard McComb: Drawings, Paintings and Sculptures 2004. *Leisure interests:* travelling, walking. *Address:* 4 Blenheim Studios, 29 Blenheim Gardens, London, SW2 5EU, England (home). *Telephone:* (20) 8671-5510 (home). *Fax:* (20) 8671-5510 (home). *E-mail:* membershipoffice@royalacademy.org.uk. *Website:* www .royalacademy.org.uk/?lid=201.

McCOMB, William L., BA (Econ), MBA; American business executive; *CEO, Liz Claiborne, Inc.;* b. Columbia, Mo.; m.; three c.; ed Miami Univ., Ohio, Univ. of Chicago Grad. School of Business; held several positions with Leo Burnett advertising firm in Chicago, working on advertising for The Procter & Gamble Co. –1992; Asst Product Dir for Johnson & Johnson Consumer Products Co. 1992–95, joined Johnson & Johnson-Merck as Group Product Dir 1995–99, Vice-Pres., Marketing, McNeil Consumer Products Co. 1999–2001, Pres. McNeil Consumer Healthcare, with additional responsibilities as Pres. McNeil Consumer & Specialty Pharmaceuticals and Ortho Women's Health & Urology 2004–05, Co. Group Chair. Johnson & Johnson, responsible for the DePuy business 2005–06, mem. Medical Devices & Diagnostics Group Operating Cttee; CEO and mem. Bd of Dirs Liz Claiborne, Inc. 2006–; Vice-Chair. on Exec. Cttee and mem. Bd of Dirs Consumer Healthcare Products Asscn 2001–05; mem. Bd GS1, OREF, INROADS of Philadelphia. *Address:* Liz Claiborne, Inc., 1441 Broadway, New York, NY 10018, USA (office). *Telephone:* (212) 626-5200 (office). *E-mail:* info@lizclaiborneinc.com (office). *Website:* www.lizclaiborneinc.com (office).

McCONAUGHEY, Matthew; American actor; b. 4 Nov. 1969, Ulvade, Tex.; ed Univ. of Texas at Austin. *Film appearances include:* Dazed and Confused, The Return of the Texas Chainsaw Massacre, Boys on the Side, My Boyfriend's Back 1993, Angels in the Outfield 1994, Scorpion Spring, Submission 1995, Glory Daze, Lone Star, A Time to Kill 1996, Larger Than Life 1997, Amistad, Contact, Making Sandwiches, Last Flight of the Raven, Newton Boys, South Beach, EdTV 1999, U-571 2000, The Wedding Planner 2001, Frailty 2001, Reign of Fire 2002, How to Lose a Guy in Ten Days 2003, Tiptoes 2003, Sahara 2005, Two for the Money 2005, Failure to Launch 2006, We Are Marshall 2006, Fool's Gold 2008, Tropic Thunder 2008. *Address:* Creative Artists Agency, Inc., 9830 Wilshire Blvd., Beverly Hills, CA 90212-1825; c/o J.K. Livin, POB 596, Zachary, LA 70791, USA. *Telephone:* (310) 288-4545. *Fax:* (310) 288-4800. *Website:* www.caa.com.

McCONNELL, Addison Mitchell (Mitch), Jr, BA, JD; American politician and lawyer; *Senator from Kentucky and Senate Minority Leader;* b. 20 Feb. 1942, Tuscumbia, Ala; s. of Addison Charles McConnell and Julia McConnell (née Shockley); m. Elaine Chao (q.v.) 1993; three d.; ed Univs of Louisville and Ky; admitted to Bar, Ky 1967; Chief Legis. Asst to Senator Marlow Cook, Washington 1968–70; est. legal practice, Louisville 1970; Deputy Asst US Attorney-Gen. 1974–75; judge, Jefferson Co., Louisville 1978–85; Senator from Ky 1985–, Majority Whip 2002–07, Minority Leader 2007–; Chair. Nat. Republican Senatorial Cttee, Rules and Admin Cttee, mem. Agric., Nutrition and Forestry Cttee, Appropriations Cttee, Chair. Jefferson Co. Republican Cttee 1973–74; Co-Chair. Nat. Child Tragedies Coalition 1981; Founding Chair. Ky Task Force on Exploited and Missing Children 1982; mem. Pres.'s Partnership on Child Safety; mem. Ky Asscn of Co. Judge Execs (Pres. 1982), Nat. Inst. of Justice (mem. Advisory Bd 1982–84); Commendation, Nat. Trust in Historical Preservation in the US 1982; Conservationist of the Year Award, League of Ky Sportsmen 1983; Certificate of Appreciation, American

Correctional Asscn 1985. *Leisure interests:* cooking, fishing. *Address:* 361-A Russell Senate Office Building, Washington, DC 20510, USA (office). *Telephone:* (202) 224-2541 (office). *Website:* www.mcconnell.senate.gov (office).

McCONNELL, David John, PhD, MRIA; Irish geneticist and academic; *Professor of Genetics, Trinity College Dublin;* b. 15 May 1944, Dublin; s. of John J. McConnell and Joan Warwick; m. Janet Overend 1966; two s.; ed Zion Nat. Schools, Rathgar, Dublin, Sandford Park School, Ranelagh, Dublin, Trinity Coll. Dublin and Calif. Inst. of Tech.; Lecturer in Genetics, Trinity Coll. Dublin 1970–85, Fellow 1978, Assoc. Prof. of Genetics 1985–90, Head, Dept of Genetics 1987–, Prof. of Genetics 1990–; Eleanor Roosevelt Fellow, Int. Union Against Cancer, Lab. of Prof. Wally Gilbert, Dept of Biochem. and Molecular Biology Harvard Univ. 1976–77; Visiting Prof. Univ. of Calif. (Davis) 1979; consultant in genetic eng and biotech. UNIDO 1982–; UNDP Star consultant, Beijing Agric. Univ. 1987; Chair. Adelaide Hosp. 1988–94, Pres. 1995–2001; Pres. Royal Zoological Soc. of Ireland 1992–96, Fellow; other professional appts; mem. European Molecular Biological Org. (EMBO); Vice-Provost for Quatercentenary Affairs, Trinity Coll. Dublin 1991–92; Vice-Provost Trinity Coll. Dublin 1999–2001; Chair. Irish Times Trust 2001–; Co-Vice Chair., European Action on Global Life Sciences (EAGLES) 2004–; mem. Irish Council for Science, Tech. and Innovation 1997–2003; mem. Exec. Bd European Fed. of Biotechnology 2004–. *Publications:* more than 100 papers in scientific journals. *Leisure interests:* windsurfing, Kerry, gardening. *Address:* Department of Genetics, Smurfit Institute of Genetics, Trinity College, Dublin 2, Ireland (office). *Telephone:* (1) 702-2008 (office); (1) 702-1140 (office). *Fax:* (1) 671-4968 (office). *E-mail:* david.mcconnell@tcd.ie (office). *Website:* www.tcd.ie/Genetics (office).

McCONNELL, Harden M., PhD; American chemist and academic; *Professor Emeritus, Department of Chemistry, Stanford University;* b. 18 July 1927, Richmond, Va; s. of Harry R. McConnell and Frances McConnell (née Coffee); m. Sofia Glogovac 1956; two s. one d.; ed George Washington Univ., California Inst. of Tech. and Univ. of Chicago; with Dept of Physics, Univ. of Chicago, Nat. Research Fellow 1950–52; Shell Devt Co., Emeryville, Calif. 1952–56; Asst Prof. of Chem., Calif. Inst. of Tech. 1956–58, Assoc. Prof. of Chem. 1958–59, Prof. of Chem. 1959–63, Prof. of Chem. and Physics 1963–64; Prof. of Chem., Stanford Univ. 1964–79, Robert Eckles Swain Prof. of Chem. 1979–, now Prof. Emer., Chair. Dept of Chem. 1989–92; mem. several bds, Neuroscience Research Program, MIT; f. Molecular Devices Corpn 1983; Pres., Foundation for Basic Research in Chemistry 1990–96; Fellow, AAAS 1982, American Physical Soc., Biophysical Soc. 1999, American Soc. of Biological Chemists; mem. ACS, NAS, Int. Acad. of Quantum Molecular Science; Foreign mem. Serbian Acad. of Sciences and Arts; Harkins Lecturer, Univ. of Chicago 1967, Falk-Plaut Lecturer, Columbia Univ. 1967, Renaud Foundation Lecturer 1971, Peter Debye Lecturer, Cornell Univ. 1973, Harvey Lecturer, Rockefeller Univ. 1977, A. L. Patterson Lecturer, Inst. for Cancer Research, Philadelphia 1978, Pauling Lecturer, Stanford Univ. 1981, Remsen Memorial Lecturer, Maryland Section ACS 1982, Prof. du Collège de France 1986, Le Bel Lecturer, Strasbourg 1986, Swift Lecturer, Calif. Inst. of Tech. 1986, Venable Lecturer, Univ. of N. Carolina 1987, Linus Pauling Distinguished Lecturer, Oregon State Univ. 1987, Davis Lecturer, Univ. of New Orleans 1994; Calif. Section Award of ACS 1961, Nat. ACS Award in Pure Chem. 1962, Harrison Howe Award 1968, Irving Langmuir Award in Chemical Physics 1971, Alumni Achievement Award (George Washington Univ.) 1971, Dickson Prize for Science (Carnegie-Mellon Univ.) 1982, Distinguished Alumni Award (Calif. Inst. of Tech.) 1982, Wolf Prize in Chemistry 1983–84, ISCO Award 1984, Pauling Medal, Puget Sound and Oregon ACS Sections 1987, Wheland Medal, Univ. of Chicago 1988, NAS Award in Chemical Sciences 1988, Sherman Fairchild Distinguished Scholar, Calif. Inst. of Tech. 1988, Nat. Medal of Science 1989, Peter Debeye Award, Physical Chemistry, American Chemistry Society 1990, Bruker Prize, Royal Soc. of Chem. 1995, ACS Award in Surface Science 1997, Gold Medal of Int. ESR Soc. 1997, Zavoisky Award 2000, Welch Award 2002. *Publications:* more than 400 scientific publs in the field of chem., chemical physics, biophysics and immunology. *Leisure interest:* mathematics. *Address:* Department of Chemistry, Stanford University, Stanford, CA 94305, USA (office). *Telephone:* (415) 723-4571 (office). *Website:* www.stanford.edu/dept/chemistry (office).

McCONNELL, Rt Hon. Jack Wilson, BSc, DipEd, MSP, PC; British politician, diplomatist and teacher; *Prime Minister's Special Representative on Conflict Resolution Mechanisms;* b. 30 June 1960, Irvine, Ayrshire; s. of William Wilson McConnell and Elizabeth McEwan McConnell; m. Bridget Mary McLuckie 1990; one s. one d.; ed Arran High School, Isle of Arran, Stirling Univ.; math. teacher, Alloa 1983–92; Labour mem. Stirling Dist Council 1984–92, Treas. 1988–92, Leader 1990–92; Gen. Sec. Scottish Labour Party (SLP) 1992–98, Leader 2001–07 (resgnd); co-ordinated Labour's Yes Yes Referendum Campaign 1997; mem. Scottish Constitutional Convention 1989–98; currently MSP for Motherwell and Wishaw; Minister for Finance, Scottish Exec. 1999–2000, for Educ. and External Affairs 2000–01; First Minister of Scotland 2001–07; Head, Clinton Hunter Devt Initiative on developing educ. in Malawi and Rwanda; apptd Prime Minister's Special Rep. on Conflict Resolution Mechanisms 2008; mem. Convention of Scottish Local Authorities (COSLA) 1988–92; mem. Amnesty Int; Hon. DUniv (Stirling) 2008. *Leisure interests:* golf, music, watching football. *Address:* Scottish Parliament, Edinburgh, EH99 1SP (office); Constituency Office, 265 Main Street, Wishaw, Lanarkshire, ML2 7NE, Scotland (office). *Telephone:* (131) 348 5831 (Parl.) (office); (1698) 303040 (office). *Fax:* (131) 348 6833 (Parl.) (office); (1698) 303060 (office). *E-mail:* Jack.Mcconnell.msp@scottish.parliament.uk (office). *Website:* www.jackmcconnell.org (office).

McCONNELL, Vice Adm. John Michael (Mike); American consultant and naval officer (retd) and fmr government official; *Senior Vice-President, Booz Allen Hamilton Inc.;* b. 26 July 1943, Greenville, South Carolina; m. Terry McConnell; two c. two step-c.; ed Furman Univ.; commissioned as line officer in USN in 1967, served a tour in Vietnam and became intelligence officer, served as intelligence officer for Jt Chiefs Chair. Colin Powell during first Gulf War; Dir Nat. Security Agency 1992–96; Sr Vice-Pres. Booz Allen Hamilton Inc., McLean, Va 1996–2007, 2009–; Dir of Nat. Intelligence, Washington, DC 2007–09 (resgnd); mem. Pres.'s Intelligence Advisory Bd 2009–; mem. Bd of Dirs CompuDyne Corpn 2004–07. *Address:* Booz Allen Hamilton Inc., 8283 Greensboro Drive, McLean, VA 22102, USA (office). *Telephone:* (703) 902-5000 (office). *E-mail:* communications@bah.com (office). *Website:* www.boozallen.com (office).

McCONNELL, Will (see SNODGRASS, W. D.).

McCORKINDALE, Douglas H.; American business executive; *Chairman, President and CEO, Gannett Co. Inc.;* b. 14 June 1939, New York; ed Columbia Coll. and Law School; Harlan Fiske Stone Scholar, Columbia Law School; joined Gannett as gen. counsel in 1971, Sr Vice-Pres. Finance and Law and mem. Bd Dirs 1977, Chief Financial and Admin. Officer 1983–97, Vice-Chair. 1985–2001, Pres. 1997–, CEO 2001–, Chair. 2001–; Dir Continental Airlines Inc., Associated Press, Lockheed Martin Corpn; dir or trustee of numerous mutual funds in Prudential Group. *Address:* Gannett Co. Inc., 7950 Jones Branch Drive, McLean, VA 22107, USA (office). *Telephone:* (703) 854-6000 (office). *E-mail:* gcishare@info.gannett.com (office). *Website:* www.gannett.com (office).

MacCORMAC, Sir Richard Cornelius, Kt, CBE, P.P.R.I.B.A., FRSA, RA; British architect; *Chairman, MacCormac Jamieson Prichard Ltd.;* b. 3 Sept. 1938; s. of Henry MacCormac and Marion Maud Broomhall; m. Susan Karin Landen 1964 (separated); two s. (one deceased); ed Westminster School, Trinity Coll. Cambridge, Univ. Coll. London; served RN 1957–59; Project Architect, London Borough of Merton 1967–69; est. pvt. practice 1969; partner MacCormac, Jamieson, Prichard Architects 1972–, Chair. 2002–; taught in Dept of Architecture, Cambridge Univ. 1969–75, 1979–81, Univ. Lecturer 1976–79; Studio Tutor, LSE City Policy and Eng 1998; Pres. RIBA 1991–93; London Forum of Amenity and Civic Socs 1997–; Dir Spitalfields Workspace 1981–; mem. Royal Fine Art Comm. 1983–93, mem. Architecture Cttee, Chair. Royal Acad. 1998–, Exhbns Cttee 1999–; Visiting Prof. Univ. of Edin. 1982–85, Univ. of Hull 1998–99; Adviser British Council 1993–; Trustee Greenwich Foundation 1997–2002; Royal Fine Arts Comm. (RFAC)/Sunday Times Bldg of the Year Award 1994, Ind. on Sunday Bldg of the Year 1994, 1996, Brick Award Supreme Winner 1996, RIBA Regional Award 1997, Civic Trust Award 1997, RFAC/BSkyB Bldg of the Year, Univs. Winner 1998, Celebrating Construction Achievement, Regional Award for Greater London 2000, Millennium Bldg of the Year, RFAC Trust/BSkyB 2000, Royal Town Planning Inst. Planning Award, English Partnerships' Regeneration Award 2004. *Major works include:* Cable & Wireless Coll., Coventry; Garden Quadrangle, St John's Coll., Oxford; Bowra Bldg, Wadham Coll., Oxford; Burrell's Fields, Trinity Coll., Cambridge; Ruskin Library, Lancaster Univ.; Southwark Station, Jubilee Line extension, London; Wellcome Wing, Science Museum, London; Bldg 1 in Paternoster Square, adjacent to St Paul's Cathedral; Phoenix Initiative. *Leisure interests:* sailing, music, reading. *Address:* 9 Heneage Street, London, E1 5LJ, England (office). *Telephone:* (20) 7377-9262 (office). *Fax:* (20) 7247-7854 (office). *E-mail:* mjp@mjparchitects.co.uk (office). *Website:* www.mjparchitects.co.uk (office).

McCORMICK, Richard D.; American business executive; *Vice-Chairman, United States Council for International Business (USCIB);* engineer with AT&T 1961, Pres. Northwestern Bell 1982; Exec. Vice-Pres. US WEST (now part of Qwest Communications) 1985, Pres. and COO 1986, CEO 1991–98, Chair. 1992, Chair. (non-exec.) 1998–99, Chair. Emer. 1999–; fmr. Chair. U.S. Council for Int. Business; Vice-Pres. ICC 1998–2000, Pres. 2001–02; Chair. US Council for Int. Business 1995–2001, now Vice-Chair; mem. Bd United Airlines, Wells Fargo & Co., United Technologies, Concept Five Technologies, Health Trio, Inc.; mem. Bd Creighton Univ., Omaha; Trustee Denver Art Museum. *Address:* United States Council for International Business, 1212 Avenue of the Americas, New York, NY 10036, USA (office). *Telephone:* (212) 354-4480. *Fax:* (212) 575-0327 (office). *E-mail:* info@uscib.org (office). *Website:* www.uscib.org (office).

McCORMICK, Richard L., BA, PhD; American historian, university administrator and academic; *President, Rutgers University;* b. 26 Dec. 1947, New Brunswick, NJ; m. Joan Barry McCormick; one s. one d.; ed Piscataway Township High School, NJ, Amherst Coll., Yale Univ.; Asst Prof. of History, Rutgers Univ. 1976–81, Assoc. Prof. 1981–85, Prof. 1985–92, Chair. Dept of History 1987–89, Founding Dir Rutgers Center for Historical Analysis 1988–89, Dean Faculty of Arts and Sciences 1989–92, Pres. Rutgers Univ. 2002–; Exec. Vice-Chancellor, Provost and Vice-Chancellor for Academic Affairs, Univ. of N Carolina 1992–95; Pres. Univ. of Wash. 1995–2002; Gov. James E. McGreevey's Comm. on Jobs, Growth, and Econ. Devt 2003–04, James E. McGreevey's Review, Planning, and Implementation Steering Cttee 2003–04, James E. McGreevey's Comm. to Support and Enhance New Jersey Mil. and Coast Guard Installations 2004–; mem. Asscn of American Univs 1995–, Business-Higher Educ. Forum 1999–, Council of Presidents, Asscn of Governing Bds of Univs and Colls 2001–, Interdisciplinary Task Force of Asscn of American Univs 2002–, Capital Planning Task Force of Comm. on Higher Educ. 2005–; mem. Bd of Dirs New Jersey Tech. Council 2003–, Robert Wood Johnson Univ. Hosp., New Brunswick, NJ 2003–; mem. Bd Overseers Robert Wood Johnson Medical School, Univ. of Medicine and Dentistry of NJ 2003–; mem. Bd Trustees State Theatre, New Brunswick 2003–, New Jersey Network Foundation 2003–, New Jersey Historical Soc. 2005–; George

Washington Egleston Prize, Yale Univ. 1977, Visiting Fellowship, Shelby Cullom Davis Center for Historical Studies, Princeton Univ. 1981–82, John Simon Guggenheim Memorial Foundation Fellowship 1985, Woodrow Wilson Int. Center for Scholars Fellowship 1985. *Publications:* From Realignment to Reform: Political Change in New York State, 1893–1910 1981, Progressivism (co-author) 1983, The Party Period and Public Policy: American Politics from the Age of Jackson to the Progressive Era 1986; numerous articles. *Address:* Office of the President, Rutgers, The State University of New Jersey, Old Queen's, College Avenue Campus, 83 Somerset Street, New Brunswick, NJ 08901, USA (office). *Telephone:* (732) 932-7454 (office). *Fax:* (732) 932-8060 (office). *E-mail:* president@rutgers.edu (office). *Website:* www.president .rutgers.edu (office).

McCORMICK, Steven J., BS, JD; American conservationist and lawyer; *President and CEO, The Nature Conservancy;* ed Univ. of Calif., Berkeley, Univ. of Calif. Hastings Coll., Stanford Univ.; Western Regional Rep., The Nature Conservancy (TNC) 1977–80, Calif. Field Rep. 1980–94, Exec. Dir TNC Calif. 1984–2000, Western Div. Rep. 1998–2000, Pres. and CEO TNC 2001–; Partner, Resources Law Group LLP 2000–01; Silver Award, Dept of the Interior 1986, Conservation Award 1989, Edmund G. Pat Brown Award 1999. *Address:* The Nature Conservancy, 4245 North Fairfax Drive, Suite 100, Arlington, VA 22203-1606, USA (office). *Telephone:* (703) 841-5300 (office). *Website:* nature.org (office).

McCOURT, Frank; Irish writer; b. 1930, New York, USA; s. of Malachy McCourt and Angela McCourt; moved to Ireland in 1935; taught in New York City public schools for 27 years; with brother, Malachy, performed a two-person musical review based on their life as young men in Ireland. *Publications:* Angela's Ashes (Pulitzer Prize 1997, Nat. Book Critics' Circle Award 1997, Los Angeles Times Book Award 1997) 1996, 'Tis: A Memoir 1999, Teacher Man 2005, Angela and the Baby Jesus 2007. *Address:* c/o Simon and Schuster Publicity Department, Simon and Schuster, Inc., 1230 Avenue of the Americas, New York, NY 10020, USA (office). *Website:* www.simonsays.com (office).

McCOWEN, Alec, CBE; British actor; b. 26 May 1925, Tunbridge Wells; s. of Duncan McCowen and Mary Walkden; ed Skinners School, Tunbridge Wells and Royal Acad. of Dramatic Art; mem. Nat. Theatre; Variety Club Stage Actor 1970; Old Vic Theatre: played Touchstone, Ford, Richard II, Mercutio, Malvolio, Oberon 1959–60; with RSC: played Fool in King Lear 1964; Hadrian VII 1968, The Philanthropist 1970, The Misanthrope 1972, Dr Dysart in Equus 1972, Henry Higgins in Pygmalion 1974, Ben in The Family Dance 1976; with Prospect Co.: Antony in Antony and Cleopatra 1977; solo performance of St Mark's Gospel 1978, 1981; Frank in Tishoo 1979; Malvolio in Twelfth Night (TV) 1980; with Nat. Theatre: Crocker-Harris in The Browning Version, Arthur in Harlequinade; Capt. Corcoran in HMS Pinafore 1981, Adolf Hitler in The Portage to San Cristobal of AH 1982, solo performance in Kipling 1983, Reilly in The Cocktail Party 1986, Nicolai in Fathers and Sons 1987, Vladimir in Waiting for Godot 1987, Modern Love 1988, Dr Scoper in The Heiress 1989, Harry in Exclusive 1989, George in A Single Man 1990, Father Jack in Dancing at Lughnasa 1990, Caesar in Caesar and Cleopatra, Michael in Someone Who'll Watch Over Me 1992, Prospero in The Tempest 1993, Elgar in Elgar's Rondo, Gaev in The Cherry Orchard 1995, Clem in Tom and Clem 1997, Narrator in Peter Pan 1998; Dir: Definitely the Bahamas 1987; Evening Standard (now The Standard) Best Actor 1969, 1972, 1982. *Films:* Frenzy 1971, Travels with my Aunt 1973, Stevie 1978, The Assam Garden 1985, Personal Services 1986, Henry V 1989, Age of Innocence 1992, Gangs of New York 2000. *Television:* Private Lives 1976, Mr. Palfrey of Westminster 1984, Hunted Down 1989. *Publications:* Young Gemini 1979, Double Bill 1980 and Personal Mark 1984. *Leisure interests:* music and gardening. *Address:* c/o Jeremy Conway, Eagle House, 18–21 Jermyn Street, London, SW1Y 6HP, England.

McCOY, Tony; Irish jockey; b. 4 May 1974, Co. Antrim, NI; s. of Peadar McCoy; apprentice to Jim Bolger 1989; won first race riding Legal Steps at Thurles 1992; Champion Hurdle Winner, Make a Stand 1997; Cheltenham Gold Cup Winner, Mr Mulligan 1997; 1,000th winner Majadou, Cheltenham 1999; 1,500th winner Celtic Nave, Exeter 2001; 2,000th winner Magical Bailiwick, Wincanton 2004; champion jump jockey for nine successive seasons 1995–2004; greatest number of career winners by any jockey 2002; greatest number of winners in any season by any jockey (289) 2001/02 (broke 55-year old record). *Publication:* McCoy: The Autobiography 2002. *Address:* c/o Midas Public Relations, 7–8 Kendrick Mews, London, SW7 3HG, England (office).

McCREDIE, Andrew Dalgarno, AM, MA, DPhil, FAHA; Australian academic; b. 3 Sept. 1930, Sydney; s. of Harold A. McCredie and Marjorie C. McCredie (née Dalgarno); m. Xenia Rosner 1965; one d.; ed Univ. of Sydney, Royal Acad. of Music, London, Univs of Copenhagen, Stockholm, Hamburg; Sr Research Fellow, Univ. of Adelaide 1965–69, Sr Lecturer in Musicology 1970–73, Reader in Musicology 1974–77, Prof. 1978–94, Prof. Emer. 1994–; Adjunct Prof. Monash Univ. 1997–; Hon. Visiting Prof. Univ. of Queensland (Brisbane) 1997–; Visiting Lecturer, Univs of Amsterdam, Utrecht 1964, Western Australia 1970, City Univ. of New York 1974, Yale, Pennsylvania 1977, Ljubljana, Bologna, Marburg, Frankfurt, Kraków, Warsaw 1978, Copenhagen, Belfast (Queen's Univ.), Hamburg, Munich, Zentral Inst. für Musikforschung (Berlin), Berne, Basle, Zurich 1983, Melbourne, Stockholm, Tübingen 1986, Heidelberg, Saarbrücken, Queen's Univ., Kingston, Ont., Brandeis (Boston), City Univ. of New York, NSW (Sydney) 1987, Munich, Braunschweig 1988, Wolfenbüttel, Mainz, Edmonton, Calgary, Saskatoon, London (Ont.), Toronto 1989, Cardiff 1992, Cologne 1994, Zagreb 1994, Dresden (1994, 1996), Cologne Weimar (2001), Louvain (2002); mem. Council Int. Musicological Soc. 1977–87; Mem. Inst. for Advanced Musical Studies, King's Coll. Univ., London 1993; Adviser Musica Antiqua Europae Orientalis

1977–; Advisory Corresp.; appointments with Int. Review of Aesthetics and Sociology of Music 1981–, Current Musicology 1987–, Studies in Music 1980; Edward J. Dent Medal 1974, Paderewski Medal-Bydgoszcz Philharmonia 1982, Australian Centennial Medal 2004. *Publications:* Musical Composition in Australia (3 vols) 1969, Karl Amadeus Hartmann: Catalogue of all his works with biography 1981 (trans. German), Miscellanea Musicologica, Adelaide (ed.) 1966–94, Paperbacks on Musicology (Gen. Ed.) 1978–, From Colonel Light into the Footlights: The Performing Arts in South Australia from 1836 to the Present 1988, Clemens von Franckenstein 1991, Ludwig Thuille 1993, Karl Amadeus Hartmann 1995, Werner Egle 1997. *Leisure interests:* travel, books, art, antiques, walking. *Address:* Tintorettostrasse 1, 80638 Munich, Germany; 13/18 Lansell Road, Toorak, Vic. 3142, Australia (home). *Telephone:* (89) 178-2325 (Germany); (3) 9826-6348 (Australia) (home).

McCREEVY, Charlie, BComm, FCA; Irish politician; *Commissioner for Internal Market and Services, European Commission;* b. Sept. 1949, Sallins, Co. Kildare; m. (separated); three s. three d.; ed Univ. Coll. Dublin; partner, Tynan Dillon & Co. (chartered accountants), Dublin, Naas and Ballyhaunis; mem. Kildare Co. Council 1979–85; mem. Dáil 1977–; Minister for Social Welfare 1992–93, for Tourism and Trade 1993–94, for Finance 1997–2004; EU Commr for Internal Market and Services 2004–; fmr Fianna Fáil Spokesperson on Finance. *Address:* European Commission, 200 rue de la Loi, 1049 Brussels, Belgium (office); Hillview House, Kilcullen Ross, Naas, Co. Kildare, Ireland. *Telephone:* (2) 299-11-11 (office). *Fax:* (2) 295-01-38 (office). *E-mail:* charlie.mccreevy@cec.eu.int (office). *Website:* europa.eu (office).

McCRUM, (John) Robert, MA; British writer and newspaper editor; b. 7 July 1953; s. of Michael William McCrum and Christine Mary Kathleen fforde; m. 1st Olivia Timbs (divorced 1984); m. 2nd Sarah Lyall 1995; two d.; ed Sherborne School, Corpus Christi Coll., Cambridge and Univ. of Pennsylvania; house reader Chatto & Windus 1977–79; Editorial Dir Faber and Faber Ltd 1979–89, Ed.-in-Chief 1990–96; Literary Ed. Observer newspaper 1996–2008; scriptwriter and co-producer The Story of English TV series 1980–86; Tony Godwin Prize 1979, Peabody Award 1986, Emmy Award 1987. *Publications:* In the Secret State 1980, A Loss of Heart 1982, The Fabulous Englishman 1984, The Story of English 1986, The World is a Banana 1988, Mainland 1991, The Psychological Moment 1993, Suspicion 1996, My Year Off 1998, Wodehouse: A Life (biog.) 2004. *Leisure interest:* the works of P. G. Wodehouse. *Address:* c/o The Observer, 3–7 Herbal Hill, London, EC1R 5EJ, England (office).

McCULLAGH, Peter, PhD, FRS; British statistician; *Professor, University of Chicago;* b. 8 Jan. 1952, Plumbridge, Northern Ireland; s. of John A. McCullagh and Margaret B. McCullagh; m. Rosa Bogues 1977; one s. three d.; ed Univ. of Birmingham, Imperial Coll. London; Asst Prof., Univ. of Chicago 1977–79, Prof. 1985–; Lecturer, Imperial Coll. London 1979–85; Fellow American Acad. of Arts and Sciences 2002; Guy Medal (Bronze), Royal Statistical Soc. 1983, COPSS Award 1990. *Publications:* Tensor Methods 1987, Generalized Linear Models (jtly) 1989. *Address:* Department of Statistics, University of Chicago, 5734 University Avenue, Chicago, IL 60637 (office); 5039 Ellis Avenue, Chicago, IL 60615, USA (home). *Telephone:* (773) 702-8340 (office). *Fax:* (773) 702-9810 (office). *E-mail:* pmcc@galton.uchicago .edu (office). *Website:* www.stat.uchicago.edu/~pmcc (office).

McCULLIN, Donald (Don), CBE; British photographer; b. 9 Oct. 1935, London; s. of Frederick and Jessica McCullin; m. 1st Christine Dent 1959 (divorced 1987); two s. one d. and one s. by Laraine Ashton; m. 2nd Marilyn Bridges 1995 (divorced 2001); m. 3rd Catherine Fairweather 2002; one s.; ed Tollington Park Secondary Modern, Hammersmith Art and Crafts School; RAF Nat. Service; photographer with Observer for four years; photographer with Sunday Times, London for eighteen years; freelance 1980–; has covered eight wars–Viet Nam, Cambodia, Biafra, Congo, Israel, Cyprus, Chad, Lebanon–and many famine areas; has travelled to 64 countries; World Press Photographer 1964, Warsaw Gold Medal 1964, Granada TV Award 1967, 1969, Two Gold, One Silver Art Director Awards, UK, Cornell Capa Award 2006. *Publications:* The Destruction Business 1971, The Concerned Photographer II 1972, Is Anyone Taking Notice? 1973, Hearts of Darkness 1980, Battle Beirut–A City in Crisis 1983, Perspectives 1987, Skulduggery 1987, Open Skies 1989, Unreasonable Behaviour (autobiog.) 1990, Sleeping with Ghosts 1995; A Life's work in Photography 1995, India 1999, Don McCullin A Retrospective 2001, Don McCullin 2004, Don McCullin in Africa 2005, Don McCullin in England 2007. *Leisure interests:* walking, collecting Victorian children's books, antiques.

McCULLOCH, Ernest Armstrong, OC, MD, FRCPC; Canadian cellular biologist and academic; *Senior Scientist, Ontario Cancer Institute;* b. Toronto; ed Univ. of Toronto; began career as Researcher, Lister Inst., London, UK 1948; joined Ont. Cancer Inst. (OCI) 1957, currently Sr Scientist, Div. of Stem Cell and Developmental Biology, created first method to identify stem cells and pioneered research on blood cell devt with colleague James E. Till; fmr head Research Div., Inst. of Medical Science, Univ. of Toronto, currently Univ. Prof. Emer.; fmr Pres. Nat. Acad. of Science; apptd Fellow Royal Soc. of Canada 1974, Royal Soc. of London 1999; Gairdner Foundation Int. Award (with James E. Till) 1969, inducted into Canadian Medical Hall of Fame 2004. *Publications:* numerous articles in scientific journals on stem cell research. *Address:* Princess Margaret Hospital, 9th Floor, Room 112, 610 University Avenue, Toronto, Ont. M5G 2M9, Canada (office). *Telephone:* (416) 946-2957 (office). *Fax:* (416) 946-2065 (office). *E-mail:* mcculloc@uhnres.utoronto.ca. *Website:* www.uhnresearch.ca.

McCULLOUGH, Colleen; Australian author; b. 1 June 1937, Wellington, NSW; m. Ric Robinson 1984; ed Holy Cross Coll., Woollahra, Sydney Univ.,

Inst. of Child Health, London Univ.; trained as neuroscientist and worked in Sydney and English hospitals; researcher lecturer Dept of Neurology, Yale Univ. Medical School, USA 1967–77; moved to Norfolk Island, S Pacific 1979; mem. New York Acad. of Sciences, Bd of Visitors Int. Programs Center Dept of Political Science, Univ. of Oklahoma; Fellow American Asscn for the Advancement of Science; fmr Patron Gerontology Foundation of Australia; currently Patron Macular Degeneration Foundation of Australia; Hon. Founding Gov. Prince of Wales Medical Research Inst.; Hon. DLitt (Macquarie) 1993; designated one of Australia's Living National Treasures. *Publications:* novels: Tim 1974, The Thorn Birds 1977, An Indecent Obsession 1981, A Creed for the Third Millennium 1985, The Ladies of Missalonghi 1987, The First Man in Rome 1990, The Grass Crown 1991, Fortune's Favourites 1993, Caesar's Women 1996, Caesar 1997, The Song of Troy 1998, Morgan's Run 2000, The October Horse 2002, The Touch 2003, Angel Puss 2004, On, Off 2006; non-fiction: Cooking with Colleen McCullough and Jean Easthope 1982, Roden Cutler, VC – The Biography 1998 (aka The Courage and the Will 1999), Antony and Cleopatra 2007. *Address:* 'Out Yenna', Norfolk Island, Oceania (via Australia). *Fax:* (6723) 23313.

McCULLOUGH, David Gaub, BA; American historian and writer; b. 7 July 1933, Pittsburgh, PA; m. Rosalee Ingram Barnes 1954; three s. two d.; ed Yale Univ.; Ed., Time Inc., New York 1956–61, United States Information Agency, Washington, DC 1961–64, American Heritage Publishing Co., New York 1964–70; Scholar-in-Residence, Univ. of New Mexico 1979, Wesleyan Univ. 1982, 1983; Visiting Prof., Cornell Univ. 1989; Marian McFadden Memorial Lecturer, Indianapolis-Marion County Public Library 2002; mem. Jefferson Legacy Foundation, Nat. Trust for Historic Preservation, Soc. of American Historians, Harry S. Truman Library Inst.; various hon. doctorates; Nat. Book Award for History 1978, Samuel Eliot Morison Award 1978, Cornelius Ryan Award 1978, Francis Parkman Prize 1978, 1993, Los Angeles Times Prize for Biography 1981, American Book Award for Biography 1982, Pulitzer Prize in Biography 1993, 2002, Harry S. Truman Public Service Award 1993, Pennsylvania Governor's Award for Excellence 1993, St Louis Literary Award 1993, Pennsylvania Soc. Gold Medal Award 1994, Nat. Book Foundation Medal for Distinguished Contributions to American Letters 1995. *Television:* host, Smithsonian World 1984–88, The American Experience 1988– (both PBS). *Publications:* The Great Bridge 1972, The Path Between the Seas 1977, The Johnstown Flood 1978, Mornings on Horseback 1981, Brave Companions 1991, Truman 1992, John Adams 2001, 1776 2005, The Course of Human Events 2005. *Address:* Janklow & Nesbit Associates, 445 Park Avenue, New York, NY 10022, USA (office). *Website:* www.davidmccullough.com.

McCULLY, Murray, LLB; New Zealand politician; *Minister of Foreign Affairs, for Sport and Recreation and for the Rugby World Cup;* b. 19 Feb. 1953, Whangarei; MP for East Coast Bays 1987–99, 2002–, for Albany 1999–2002, mem. Māori Affairs Select Cttee 2002–03, Foreign Affairs, Defence and Trade Cttee 2005–08; Minister of Customs 1991–96, of Housing 1993–96, of Tourism 1996–99, for Sport, Fitness and Leisure 1996–99, for Accident Rehabilitation and Compensation Insurance 1997–99, for Housing Corpn 1998–99, for Housing New Zealand 1998–99, for Accident Insurance 1999, of Foreign Affairs, for Sport and Recreation and for the Rugby World Cup 2008–; Assoc. Minister of Tourism 1991–96, of Immigration 1998–99; Spokesman for Infrastructure 1999–2005, for Local Govt 1999–2002, for Sport, Fitness and Leisure 1999–2002, for Immigration 2002–03, for State Services 2002–05, for Conservation 2005–06; Parl. Asst to Leader of the Opposition 2003–05; mem. New Zealand Nat. Party. *Address:* Ministry of Foreign Affairs and Trade, Private Bag 18901, Wellington 5045, New Zealand (office). *Telephone:* (4) 439-8000 (office). *Fax:* (4) 472-9596 (office). *E-mail:* enquiries@mfat.govt.nz (office). *Website:* www.mfat.govt.nz (office).

McDAID, James, MB, BCh, BAO; Irish politician and medical doctor; *Minister of State at the Department of Transport;* b. 3 Oct. 1949, Termon, Co. Donegal; m. Marguerite McLoughlin (separated); three s. one d.; ed St Eunan's Coll., Letterkenny, Nat. Univ. of Ireland, Galway; Sr Surgical House Officer, Letterkenny Gen. Hosp. 1974–79; Gen. Practitioner, Letterkenny 1979; Founder, Pres. Donegal Hospice Movt 1988; mem. Dáil Éireann for Donegal NE 1989; Minister (desig.) for Defence 1991 (resgnd); mem. Dáil Cttee on Women's Rights 1992, Cttee of Public Accounts 1993, Cttee on Foreign Affairs and NI Sub-Cttee 1995; Spokesperson on North/South Devts 1995, for Equality and Law Reform 1996–97; Minister for Tourism, Sport and Recreation 1997–2002; Minister of State at the Dept of Transport (with special responsibility for road traffic including road haulage) 2002–. *Leisure interests:* football, horse racing, golf. *Address:* Department of Transport, 44 Kildare Street, Dublin 2 (office); Pearse Road, Letterkenny, Co. Donegal, Ireland (home). *Telephone:* (1) 6041089 (office); (74) 25132 (home). *Fax:* (1) 6041185 (office). *E-mail:* minister@transport.ie (office). *Website:* www .transport.ie (office).

McDIARMID, Ian, MA; British actor and artistic director; b. 11 Aug. 1944, Carnoustie, Scotland; s. of the late Frederick McDiarmid and Hilda Emslie; ed Univ. of St Andrews, Royal Scottish Acad. of Music and Dramatic Art, Glasgow; Actor; Assoc. Dir Royal Exchange, Manchester; Jt Artistic Dir (with Jonathan Kent) Almeida Theatre 1990–2002; Gold Medal Royal Scottish Acad. of Music and Dramatic Art 1968. *Films include:* The Awakening 1980, Dragonslayer 1981, Gorky Park 1983, Return of the Jedi 1983, Dirty Rotten Scoundrels 1988, Restoration 1995, Little Orphan Annie 1995, Star Wars: Episode I: The Phantom Menace 1999, Sleepy Hollow 2000, Star Wars Episode II: Attack of the Clones, Star Wars Episode III: Revenge of the Sith 2005. *Plays include:* Almeida Theatre: Volpone, Ivanov, Tartuffe, School for Wives, Creditors, Kurt Weill Concerts, Government Inspector, The Jew of Malta, The Tempest, Faith Healer (Olivier Award for Best Actor, Critics Circle Award for Best Actor 2001), RSC: Henry V, The Merchant of Venice, The

Party, Crimes in Hot Countries, The Castle; Royal Court: Hated Nightfall, Love of a Good Man, Insignificance; Barbican: The Soldier's Tale; Royal Exchange, Manchester: Edward II, The Country Wife; Aldwych: The Black Prince; Oxford Playhouse: Peer Gynt, Mephisto; Booth Theater, New York: Faith Healer (Tony Award for Best Featured Actor) 2006; Donmar Warehouse: Pirandello's Henry IV 2005, Ibsen's John Gabriel Borkman 2007. *Plays directed include:* Almeida Theatre: Scenes from an Execution, Venice Preserved, Siren Song, A Hard Heart, Lulu, The Possibilities, The Rehearsal; Royal Exchange: Don Juan; Donmar Warehouse: Pirandello's Henry IV, Be Near Me 2009; Chichester Festival/Gielgud Theatre: Six characters in search of an author 2008. *Television includes:* Richard's Things 1981, Chernobyl: The Final Warning 1991, Heart of Darkness 1994, Hillsborough 1996, Rebecca, Karaoke, Creditors, The Nation's Health, The Professionals, Great Expectations 1999, All the King's Men 1999, Crime and Punishment 2001, Charles II 2004, Elizabeth I 2005, Our Hidden Lives 2005, City of Vice 2008, Margaret 2009. *Radio:* numerous plays and readings, including Volpone (title role), The Cocktail Party (as The Uninvited Guest). *Appearances:* Aldeburgh Festival, Scottish Chamber Orchestra, London Symphony Orchestra (The Soldier's Tale), Royal Opera House, Covent Garden (The King goes forth to France). *Publications:* Be Near Me (adapted from the novel by Andrew O'Hagan) 2009. *Address:* c/o Independent, Oxford House, London, W1D 1BS, England (office).

McDONAGH, Edna; Irish theologian and academic; *Professor of Moral Theology, St Patrick's College;* b. 27 June 1930, Co. Mayo; s. of Patrick McDonagh and Mary Kelly; ed St Jarlath's Coll., Tuam, St Patrick's Coll., Maynooth, Gregorian Univ., Rome and Univ. of Munich; Prof. of Moral Theology (and Canon Law), St Patrick's Coll. 1958–, Dir Postgraduate Studies in Theology 1970–76, Dean of Faculty of Theology 1973–79; Lecturer in Irish School of Ecumenics, Dublin 1970–; Husking Prof. of Theology, Univ. of Notre Dame, USA 1979–81; McKeever Prof. of Theology, New York 1990–92; Chair. Governing Body, Univ. Coll. Cork 1999–2007; Leverhulme Research Fellow, Univ. of Cambridge, UK 1978; Hon. LLD (Nat. Univ. of Ireland) 2000; Hon. DD (Trinity Coll. Dublin) 2001; Ferguson Lecturer, Univ. of Manchester 1978. *Publications:* Roman Catholics and Unity 1963, Religious Freedom 1967, Invitation and Response: Essays in Christian Moral Theology 1972, Gift and Call: Towards a Christian Theology of Morality 1975, Social Ethics and the Christian: Towards Freedom in Communion 1979, Doing the Truth: The Quest for Moral Theology (co-author) 1979, Church and Politics: From Theology to a Case History of Zimbabwe 1980, The Making of Disciples: Tasks of Moral Theology 1982, Between Chaos and New Creation 1985, Between Chaos and New Creation: Doing Theology at the Fringe (Theology and Life Series, No. 19) 1987, Small Hours of Belief 1989, The Gracing of Society 1989, Survival or Salvation?: A Second Mayo Book of Theology 1994, Faith in Fragments 1997, Religion and Politics in Ireland at the Turn of the Millennium: Essays in Honour of Garret Fitzgerald on the Occasion of His Seventy-Fifth Birthday (co-author) 2004, Vulnerable To The Holy: In Faith, Morality And Art 2005; ed. and contrib. The Meaning of Christian Marriage 1963, Moral Theology Renewed 1965, Truth and Life 1968, Faith and the Hungry Grass 1989, The Gracing of Society 1990, Salvation or Survival 1993, Faith in Fragments 1995, Vulnerable to the Holy 2005, Immersed in Mystery 2007. *Leisure interests:* theatre, poetry and the visual arts. *Address:* St Patrick's College, Maynooth, Co. Kildare, Ireland (office). *Telephone:* (1) 285222 (office). *Website:* www.maynoothcollege.ie (office).

McDONALD, Donald Benjamin, AO, BCom; Australian business executive; *Chairman, Australian Broadcasting Corporation;* b. 1 Sept. 1938, Sydney; s. of Benjamin McDonald and Maida Hands; m. Janet Isabel McDonald AO 1964; one s. one d.; ed Fort Street Boys' High School and Univ. of New South Wales; Finance Dir Vogue Publs 1965–68; with Australian Opera 1968–72 (Gen. Man. 1987–96); Musica Viva Australia 1972–78; Gen. Man. Sydney Theatre Co. 1980–86; Dir Australian Tourist Comm. 1993–96; Chair. State Opera Ring Corpn, S Australia 1996–98, Australian Broadcasting Corpn 1996–, Constitutional Centenary Foundation 1997–2000, The Really Useful Company (Aust) Pty Ltd; Dir Festival, Perth 1998–, Univ. of NSW Foundation 1998–, Focus Publishing Pty Ltd 1999–2000; fmr Dir Sydney 2000 Olympic Bid Ltd, Chair. Sydney 2000 Bid Cultural Cttee; fmr mem. Bd Sydney Organising Cttee for the Olympic Games (SOCOG), Chair. SOCOG's Cultural Comm.; mem. Bd Welsh Nat. Opera, Cardiff, UK 1997–2000, Opera Australia Capital Fund, Perth Int. Festival; Visiting Fellow, Univ. of Edin., UK 1992; Fellow, Senate of Univ., Sydney 1994–97. *Publication:* The Boyer Collection (ed.) 2001. *Leisure interests:* reading, swimming. *Address:* Australian Broadcasting Corporation, 700 Harris Street, Ultimo, NSW 2007, Australia (office). *Telephone:* (2) 9333-1500 (Radio) (office). *Fax:* (2) 9333-2603 (Radio) (office). *Website:* www.abc.net.au (office).

MacDONALD, Hon. Donald Stovel, PC, CC, BA, LLM; Canadian politician and lawyer; b. 1 March 1932, Ottawa, Ont.; s. of Donald A. Macdonald and Marjorie I. Stovel; m. 1st Ruth Hutchison 1961 (died 1987); four d.; m. 2nd Adrian Merchant Lang 1988; three step-s. three step-d.; ed Ottawa public schools, Ashbury Coll., Ottawa, Univs of Toronto and Cambridge and Osgoode Hall and Harvard Law Schools; with McCarthy and McCarthy, Barristers, Toronto 1957–62; MP 1962–78; Parl. Sec. to Minister of Justice 1963–65, to Minister of Finance 1965, to Sec. of State for External Affairs 1966–68, to Minister of Industry 1968; Minister without Portfolio 1968; Pres. Privy Council and Govt House Leader 1968; Minister of Nat. Defence 1970–72, of Energy, Mines and Resources 1972–75, of Finance 1975–77; partner, firm McCarthy & McCarthy, Toronto 1977–88; Counsel, McCarthy Tétrault, Toronto 1991–2000; High Commr in the UK 1988–91; Chair. Royal Comm. on the Econ. Union and Devt Prospects for Canada 1982–85, Inst. for Research and Public Policy, Montreal 1991–97; Chair. and Dir Siemens Canada Ltd, Dir Aber Diamond Corpn, Alberta Energy Co. Ltd, Sun Life Assurance Co. of Canada, Trans-Canada Pipelines Ltd, Boise Cascade Corpn 1996–, Chair.

Atlantic Council of Canada, Special Advisory Cttee on competition in Ont.'s electricity system 1995–96, Design Exchange, Toronto 1993–96, Canadian Friends of Cambridge Univ. 1995–97; Sr Adviser UBS Bunting Warburg, Toronto 2000; Rowell Fellowship, Canadian Inst. of Int. Affairs 1956; Freeman City of London; Hon. Fellow, Trinity Hall, Cambridge, UK 1994; Hon. LLD (St Lawrence Univ., Univ. of New Brunswick), (Univ. of Toronto) 2000; Hon. DEng (Colo School of Mines). *Leisure interests:* cross-country skiing, tennis. *Address:* 27 Marlborough Avenue, Toronto, Ont., M5R 1X5, Canada (home). *Telephone:* (416) 964-6757 (home). *Fax:* (416) 964-8901 (home). *E-mail:* London@merchantmac.com.

MacDONALD, Hon. Flora Isabel, CC, PC; Canadian politician and consultant; *Secretary, Future Generations Canada;* b. 3 June 1926, North Sydney, NS; d. of George Frederick and Mary Isabel (née Royle) MacDonald; ed North Sydney High School, Empire Business Coll. and National Defence Coll., Kingston, Ont.; Exec. Dir Progressive Conservative HQ 1957–66; admin. officer and tutor, Dept of Political Studies, Queen's Univ. 1966–72; Nat. Sec. Progressive Conservative Asscn of Canada 1966–69; MP for Kingston and the Islands, Ont. 1972–88; Sec. of State for External Affairs 1979–80; Minister of Employment and Immigration 1984–86, of Communications 1986–88; host, weekly TV series North/South 1990–94; Chair. Int. Devt Research Centre 1992–97, Shastri Indo-Canada Advisory Council 1997–2004, HelpAge Int., London, UK 1997–2001; Co-Chair. Canadian Co-ordinating Cttee UN Year of Older Persons 1999; Pres. Future Generations, Franklin, W Va 1998–2007, Sec. Future Generations Canada 2007–, Partnership Africa-Canada 2002–04; mem. Carnegie Comm. on Preventing Deadly Conflict 1994–99; Visiting Fellow, Centre for Canadian Studies, Univ. of Edin. Sept.–Dec. 1989; Pres. Asscn of Canadian Clubs 1999–2003, World Federalist Movt —Canada (fmrly World Federalists of Canada) 2001–04, UNIFEM Canada; Patron, Commonwealth Human Rights Initiative; Hon. Patron for Canada of Nat. Museums of Scotland; Companion Order of Ont. 1995, Order of NS 2007; Padma Shri (India) 2004; 18 hon. degrees; Pearson Peace Medal, UN Asscn 2000, UNIFEM Canada Award 2002. *Leisure interests:* travel, reading, speedskating. *Address:* 1103 – 350 Queen Elizabeth Driveway, Ottawa, ON K1S 3N1, Canada (home). *Telephone:* (613) 238-1098 (home). *Fax:* (613) 238-6330 (home). *E-mail:* flora@intranet.ca (home).

McDONALD, Forrest, PhD; American academic; *Distinguished Research Professor, University of Alabama;* b. 7 Jan. 1927, Orange, Tex.; s. of John Forrest and Myra M. McGill; m. Ellen Shapiro 1963; five c.; ed Orange High School and Univ. of Tex. (Austin); State Historical Soc. of Wis. 1953–58; Assoc. Prof., Brown Univ. 1959–64, Prof. 1964–67; Prof., Wayne State Univ. 1967–76; Prof., Univ. of Ala 1976–87, Distinguished Research Prof. 1976, 1987–; J.P. Harrison Visiting Prof., Coll. of William and Mary 1986–87; Jefferson Lecturer Nat. Endowment for the Humanities 1987; Guggenheim Fellow 1962–63; mem. American Antiquarian Soc., Philadelphia Soc., The Historical Soc.; George Washington Medal (Freedom's Foundation) 1980, Frances Tavern Book Award 1980, American Revolution Round Table Book Award 1986, 16th Jefferson Lecturer in the Humanities (Nat. Endowment for the Humanities) 1987, Ingersoll Prize, Richard M. Weaver Award 1990, Salvatori Award for Academic Excellence 1992. *Publications:* We The People: The Economic Origins of the Constitution 1958, Insull 1962, E Pluribus Unum: The Formation of the American Republic 1965, Presidency of George Washington 1974, The Phaeton Ride 1974, Presidency of Thomas Jefferson 1976, Alexander Hamilton: A Biography 1980, A Constitutional History of the United States 1982, Novus Ordo Seclorum: The Intellectual Origins of the Constitution 1985, Requiem: Variations on Eighteenth-Century Themes 1988, The American Presidency: An Intellectual History 1994, States' Rights and the Union 2000, Recovering the Past: A Historian's Memoir 2004. *Leisure interests:* gardening, tennis. *Address:* P.O. Box 155, Coker, AL 35452, USA. *Telephone:* (205) 339-0317.

McDONALD, Gabrielle Kirk, LLB; American judge; *Judge, Iran–US Claims Tribunal;* b. 12 April 1942, St Paul, Minn.; d. of James G. Kirk and Frances R. Kirk; m. Mark T. McDonald; one s. one d.; ed Howard Univ.; fmr law professor; Fed. Judge, Houston, Tex. 1979–88; Pnr, Matthews Branscomb, Austin, Tex. (law firm) 1988–; Judge UN int. tribunal on war crimes in fmr Yugoslavia, The Hague 1993–99, Pres. 1997–99; Judge Iran–US Claims Tribunal, The Hague 2001–; mem. Bd of Dirs Freeport-McMoran Copper & Gold (mining co.), Special Counsel on Human Rights to Bd Chair.; mem. ABA, Nat. Bar Asscn; hon. degrees from Georgetown Univ., Univ. of Notre Dame, Amherst Coll.; American Bar Asscn Margaret Brent Women Lawyers of Achievement Award, Central E European Law Initiative Leadership Award 2003. *Address:* Iran-United States Claims Tribunal, Parkweg 13, 2585 JH The Hague, Netherlands (office). *Telephone:* (70) 352-0064 (office). *Fax:* (70) 350-2456 (office). *E-mail:* registry@iusct.org (office). *Website:* www.iusct.org (office).

MacDONALD, (Hugh) Ian, OC, BCom, BPhil, MA; Canadian economist, academic and university administrator; *President Emeritus and Professor Emeritus of Economics and Policy, York University;* b. 27 June 1929, Toronto; five c.; ed Univ. of Toronto, Univ. of Oxford, UK; Chief Economist, Govt of Ont. 1965–67, Deputy Treas. 1967–68, Deputy Minister of Treasury and Econs 1968–72, Deputy Minister of Treasury, Econs and Intergovernmental Affairs 1972–74; Pres. York Univ., Toronto 1974–84, Pres. Emer. 1984–, Dir York Int. 1984–94, Prof. of Econs and Public Policy 1984–, now Prof. Emer., Dir Master of Public Admin. Program 1994–; Chair. McGraw-Hill Ryerson 1985–; Chair. Commonwealth of Learning, Vancouver 1994–2003, Fellow 2004; mem. The AGF Funds 1979–; Hon. Life mem. Canadian Olympic Asscn 1997–; Kt of Grace, Order of St Lazarus of Jerusalem 1978; Gov.-Gen.'s Medal 1952, Centennial Medal 1967, Queen's Silver Jubilee Medal 1977, Canadian Confed. Medal for the 125th Anniversary 1992, Award of Merit, Canadian Bureau for Int. Educ. 1994, Vanier Medal 2000, Queen's Golden Jubilee Medal 2002; Hon.

LLD (Toronto) 1974, DUniv (Open Univ., UK) 1998, Hon. DLitt (Open Univ., Sri Lanka) 1999, (The B.R. Ambedkar Open Univ., Hyderabad, India) 2002. *Publications:* numerous articles, essays and contribs to books. *Leisure interests:* ice hockey and tennis. *Address:* York University, Room N207, Schulich School of Business, 4700 Keele Street, Toronto, Ont. M3J 1P3, Canada (office). *Telephone:* (416) 736-5632 (office). *Fax:* (416) 736-5643 (office). *E-mail:* yorkmpa@yorku.ca (office). *Website:* www.schulich.yorku.ca (office).

McDONALD, John W., AB, JD; American diplomatist, international organization executive and lawyer; *Chairman, Institute for Multi-Track Diplomacy;* b. 18 Feb. 1922, Koblenz, Germany; s. of John Warlick McDonald and Ethel Mae Raynor; m. 1st Barbara Jane Stewart 1943 (divorced); one s. three d.; m. 2nd Christel Meyer 1970; ed Univ. of Illinois, Nat. War Coll., Washington, DC; admitted to Ill. Supreme Court Bar 1946, to US Supreme Court 1951; Legal Div., US Office of Mil. Govt, Berlin 1947; Asst District Attorney, US Mil. Govt Courts, Frankfurt 1947–50; Sec. Law Cttee, Allied High Comm. 1950–52; mem. Mission to NATO and OECD, Paris 1952–54; Office of Exec. Sec. Dept of State 1954–55; Exec. Sec. to Dir of Int. Co-operation Admin. 1955–59; US Econ. Co-ordinator for CENTO Affairs, Ankara 1959–63; Chief, Econ. and Commercial Sections, Cairo 1963–66; Deputy Dir Office of Econ. and Social Affairs, Dept of State 1967–68, Dir 1968–71; Co-ordinator, UN Multilateral Devt Programmes, Dept of State 1971–74, Acting Deputy Asst Sec. for Econ. and Social Affairs 1971, 1973; Deputy Dir-Gen. ILO 1974–78; Pres. Int. Telecommunications Satellite Org. (INTELSAT) Conf. on Privileges and Immunities 1978; Amb. to UN Conf. on TCDC 1978; Sec.-Gen. 27th Colombo Plan Ministerial Meeting 1978; US Co-ordinator for UN Decade on Drinking Water and Sanitation 1979; rep. to UN Confs with rank of Amb. 1978–; Amb. to UNIDO III 1979–80; Chair. Fed. Cttee for UN Int. Year of Disabled Persons; Amb. to UN World Ass. on Ageing 1981–82; Co-ordinator for Multilateral Affairs, Center for the Study of Foreign Affairs, US Dept of State 1983–87; Pres. Iowa Peace Inst. 1988–92, People-to-People Cttee for the Handicapped, Countdown 2001, World Cttee: UN Decade of Disabled Persons; del. to many int. confs; Bd of Dirs Global Water; Chair. American Asscn for Int. Ageing 1983–; Professorial Lecturer in Law, The George Washington Univ. Nat. Law Center 1987–89; Adjunct Prof. of Political Science, Grinnell Coll. 1989–92; Distinguished Visiting Prof., George Mason Univ., Fairfax, Va 1992–93; Adjunct Prof., Union Inst. 1995–98, George Mason Univ. 1998–2000; Chair. and Co-founder Inst. for Multi-Track Diplomacy, Washington, DC 1992–; mem. Cosmos Club, American Foreign Service Asscn, US Asscn for the Club of Rome, DKE; Hon. PhD (Mount Mercy Coll.) 1989, (Teiko Mary Crest Univ.) 1991, (Salisbury State Univ.) 1993; Hon. LLD (St John's Univ.) 2007; Superior Honour Award, Dept of State 1972, Presidential Meritorial Service Award 1984. *Publications:* The North-South Dialogue and the United Nations 1982, How To Be a Delegate 1984, International Negotiations 1985, Perspectives on Negotiation: Four Case Studies 1986, Conflict Resolution: Track Two Diplomacy 1987, US-Soviet Summitry 1987, US Base Rights Negotiations 1989, Multi-Track Diplomacy 1991, Defining a US Negotiating Style 1996. *Leisure interests:* reading, tennis, fencing, skiing. *Address:* Institute for Multi-Track Diplomacy, 1901 North Fort Myer Drive, Suite 405, Arlington, VA 22209 (office); 3800 North Fairfax Drive, 1001 Washington, VA 22209, USA (home). *Telephone:* (703) 528-3863 (office); (703) 525-9755 (home). *Fax:* (703) 528-5776 (office). *E-mail:* jmcdonald@imtd.org (office). *Website:* www.imtd.org (office).

MacDONALD, Julien, OBE, MA; British fashion designer; b. 19 March 1972, Merthyr Tydfyl; ed Royal Coll. of Art; worked for Alexander McQueen and Koji Tatsuno as a student; knitwear designer for Chanel Ready-to-Wear, Chanel Couture and Karl Lagerfeld; has had four shows in his own right; Art Dir Max Factor Spring/Summer 1999 advertising campaign (including TV commercial); Chief Designer Givenchy 2001–04; consultant Boots PLC 2001–; London Fashion Award for Glamour. *Address:* First Floor Studio, 135–139 Curtain Road, London, EC2A 3BX; 20th Century Theatre, 291 Westbourne Grove, London, W11 2CA, England.

MacDONALD, Sir Ken, Kt, BA, QC; British barrister; *Director of Public Prosecutions and Head of Crown Prosecution Service;* ed St Edmund Hall, Oxford; called to the Bar 1978, QC 1997; part-time judge, Crown Court 2001–; Dir of Public Prosecutions and Head of Crown Prosecution Service 2003–; Chair. Criminal Bar Asscn; Founder-mem. Matrix Chambers; Bencher of the Inner Temple 2003–. *Leisure interests:* Arsenal Football Club, crime thrillers, film noir, 20th century history. *Address:* Crown Prosecution Service, 50 Ludgate Hill, London, EC4M 7EX, England (office). *Telephone:* (20) 7796-8000 (office). *Website:* www.cps.gov.uk (office).

MacDONALD, Roderick Alexander, BA, LLL, LLB, LLM, FRSC; Canadian professor of law; *F.R. Scott Professor of Constitutional and Public Law, Faculty of Law, McGill University;* b. 6 Aug. 1948, Markham, Ont.; ed Univ. of Toronto, Univ. of Ottawa, York Univ.; Asst Prof., Faculty of Law, Univ. of Windsor, Ont. 1975–77, Assoc. Prof. 1977–79; Assoc. Prof., Faculty of Law, McGill Univ. 1979–84, Prof. 1984–95, F. R. Scott Prof. of Constitutional and Public Law 1995–; visiting positions at Osgoode Hall Law School, Univ. of Toronto, Univ. of British Columbia, ANU, Univ. Blaise Pascal, Clermont-Ferrand, Univ. of Aix-Marseilles; Pres.-elect Royal Soc. of Canada 2008–09, Pres. 2009–; Dir, Law in Soc. Programme, Canadian Inst. for Advanced Research 1989–94; Pres. Law Comm. of Canada 1997–2000; consultant to World Bank, Ukraine 2002–04; Fellow, Trudeau Foundation 2004–; mem. Law Soc. of Upper Canada 1977–, Québec Bar 1983–, Int. Acad. of Comparative Law 2004–; Univ. of Ottawa Section Droit Civil Ordre du Mérite 2007; Royal Soc. of Canada Sir William Dawson Medal for Social Sciences 2007. *Publications:* more than 200 scholarly works. *Address:* Faculty of Law, 3674 Peel Street, Room 301, Montréal, PQ H3A 1W9, Canada (office). *Telephone:* (514) 398-8914 (office). *Fax:* (514) 398-3233 (office). *E-mail:* roderick

.macdonald@mcgill.ca (office). *Website:* people.mcgill.ca/roderick.macdonald (office).

MacDONALD, Rodney, BS; Canadian politician; *Premier of Nova Scotia;* b. 2 Jan. 1972, Inverness, Nova Scotia; s. of Alex Angus and Elizabeth Ann MacDonald; m. Lori-Ann MacDonald; one s.; ed St. Francis Xavier Univ.; taught for Strait Regional School Board –1999; elected to Legislative Ass. as MLA for Inverness 1999, re-elected 2003; Leader Nova Scotia Progressive Conservative Party 2006–; Premier of Nova Scotia 2006–; fmr Vice-Pres. GlennRod Music Inc. *Address:* Premier's Office, POB 726, Halifax, NS B3J 2T3, Canada (office). *Telephone:* (902) 424-6600 (office). *E-mail:* Premier@gov.ns.ca (office). *Website:* www.gov.ns.ca/premier (office).

McDONALD, Sir Trevor, Kt, OBE; British broadcast journalist; b. 16 Aug. 1939, Trinidad; m.; two s. one d.; worked on newspapers, radio and TV, Trinidad 1960–69; Producer BBC Caribbean Service and World Service, London 1969–73; reporter Ind. TV News 1973–78, sports corresp. 1978–80, diplomatic corresp. 1980–87, newscaster 1982–87, Diplomatic Ed. Channel Four News 1987–89, newscaster News at 5.40 1989–90, News at Ten 1990–99, ITV Evening News 1999–2000, ITV News at Ten 2001–04, 2008, News at 10.30 2004–05; Chair. Better English Campaign 1995–97, Nuffield Language Inquiry 1998–2000; Gov. English-Speaking Union of the Commonwealth 2000–; Pres. European Year of Languages 2000; Chancellor South Bank Univ. 1999–; Hon. Fellow, Liverpool John Moores Univ. 1998; Hon. DLitt (South Bank) 1994, (Plymouth) 1995, (Southampton Inst.) 1997, (Nottingham) 1997; Dr hc (Surrey) 1997, (Open Univ.) 1997; Hon. LLD (Univ. of West Indies) 1996; Newscaster of the Year TV and Radio Industries Club 1993, 1997, 1999; Gold Medal, Royal TV Soc. 1998, Richard Dimbleby Award for outstanding contrib. to TV, BAFTA 1999, Royal Television Soc. lifetime achievement award 2005. *Publications:* Clive Lloyd: A Biography 1985, Vivian Richards: A Biography 1987, Queen and Commonwealth 1989, Fortunate Circumstances (autobiog.) 1993, Favourite Poems 1997, World of Poetry 1999. *Leisure interests:* tennis, golf, cricket. *Address:* c/o ITN, 200 Gray's Inn Road, London, WC1X 8XZ, England. *Telephone:* (20) 7833-3000 (office). *Website:* www.itv.com/news (office).

McDONNELL, Sanford N., MS; American business executive; b. 12 Oct. 1922, Little Rock, Ark.; s. of William A. and Carolyn C. McDonnell; nephew of James S. McDonnell; m. Priscilla Robb 1946; one s. one d.; ed Princeton Univ., Univ. of Colorado and Washington Univ.; joined McDonnell Aircraft Co. 1948, Vice-Pres. (Project Man.) 1959, F4H Vice-Pres. and Gen. Man. 1961, mem. Bd of Dirs 1962–67, mem. Finance Cttee 1962, Exec. Cttee 1963; Vice-Pres. Aircraft Gen. Man. 1965, Pres. 1966; Dir McDonnell Douglas Corpn 1967, Vice-Pres. March 1971; Exec. Vice-Pres. McDonnell Aircraft Co. March 1971; Pres. McDonnell Douglas Corpn 1971–72, Pres. 1972–80, CEO 1972–88, Chair. 1980–88, Chair. Emer. 1988–97; mem. Bd of Govs Aerospace Industries Asscn Nov. 1974–; founder and Chair. CHARACTERplus, St. Louis; Fellow American Inst. of Aeronautics and Astronautics and of mem. many other professional orgs; mem. Bd of Dirs First Union Bank Corpn in St Louis; mem. Nat. Exec. Bd, Boy Scouts of America. *Address:* CHARACTERplus, 8225 Florissant Road, St. Louis, MO 63121, USA. *Telephone:* (800) 835-8282 (toll-free in US). *Fax:* (314) 692-9700. *E-mail:* characterplus@csd.org. *Website:* www.characterplus.org.

McDONOUGH, William Andrews; American architect and business executive; *Founding Principal, William McDonough + Partners;* b. 21 Feb. 1951, Tokyo, Japan; ed Dartmouth Coll., Yale Univ.; Founding Prin. William McDonough + Partners, New York City 1981– (moved to Charlottesville, Va 1994); first major comm. Environmental Defense Fund HQ 1985; Dean of School of Architecture, Univ. of Virginia 1994–99; several large corp. projects for The Gap, Nike and Herman Miller; commissioned in 1991 to write The Hannover Principles: Design for Sustainability as guidelines for the City of Hannover's EXPO 2000; commissioned for 20-year, US $2 billion environmental re-eng of Ford Motor Co.'s River Rouge Plant, Dearborn, Mich., including world's largest "living roof"; Co-founder and Prin., MBDC; Venture Pnr and Sr Advisor, VantagePoint Venture Partners; first and only individual recipient of Presidential Award for Sustainable Devt 1996, named by TIME magazine as a Hero for the Planet 1999, Nat. Design Award, Smithsonian Cooper-Hewitt Nat. Design Museum 2004, Presidential Green Chem. Challenge Award. *Projects include:* Herman Miller 'GreenHouse' Factory and Offices 1995, 901 Cherry, Offices for Gap Inc. 1997, Oberlin Coll.'s Adam Joseph Lewis Center for Environmental Studies 2000. *Publication:* Cradle to Cradle: Remaking the Way We Make Things (co-author) 2002. *Address:* William McDonough + Partners, 700 East Jefferson Street, Charlottesville, VA 22902, USA (office). *Telephone:* (434) 979-1111 (office). *Fax:* (434) 979-1112 (office). *E-mail:* info@mcdonoughpartners.com (office); media@mcdonough.com. *Website:* www.mcdonoughpartners.com (office); www.mcdonough.com.

McDONOUGH, William J., BS, MA; American banker; b. 21 April 1934, Chicago, Ill.; m. Suzanne Clarke 1985; three s. three d.; ed Holy Cross Coll., Worcester, Mass. and Georgetown Univ.; US Navy 1956–61; US State Dept 1961–67; First Nat. Bank of Chicago 1967–89, Vice-Chair. Bd and Dir holding co. 1986–89; subsequently served as adviser to IBRD and IFC; special adviser to Pres. of IDB; Chair. Ill. Comm. on Future of Public Service; Exec. Vice-Pres. and Head, Markets Group, Fed. Reserve Bank of New York and Man. Open Market Operations for Fed. Open Market Cttee 1992–93, Vice-Chair. Fed. Open Market Cttee; Pres. and CEO Fed. Reserve Bank of New York 1993–2003; Chair. Public Co. Accounting Oversight Bd 2003–05; mem. New York Philharmonic Orchestra, Inst. for Int. Econs; Yale Distinguished Leadership in Global Capital Markets Award 2001. *Address:* c/o Public Company Accounting Oversight Board, 1666 K Street, NW, Washington, DC 20006-2803, USA (office).

McDORMAND, Frances; American actress; b. 23 June 1957, Chicago, Ill.; d. of Veron McDormand and Noreen McDormand; m. Joel Coen (q.v.) 1994; one s.; ed Yale Univ. School of Drama; Screen Actors' Guild Award 1996, London Film Critics' Circle Award 1996, Ind. Spirit Award 1996, American Comedy Award 1997, LA Film Critics Award 2000. *Films include:* Blood Simple 1984, Raising Arizona 1987, Mississippi Burning 1988, Chattahoochee 1990, Darkman 1990, Miller's Crossing 1990, Hidden Agenda 1990, The Butcher's Wife 1991, Passed Away 1992, Short Cuts 1993, Beyond Rangoon 1995, Fargo 1996 (Acad. Award for Best Actress), Primal Fear 1996, Lone Star 1996, Paradise Road 1997, Johnny Skidmarks 1997, Madeline 1998, Talk of Angels 1998, Wonder Boys 1999, Almost Famous 2000, The Man Who Wasn't There 2001, Upheaval 2001, Laurel Canyon 2002, City By the Sea 2002, Something's Gotta Give 2003, North Country 2005, Miss Pettigrew Lives for a Day 2007, Burn After Reading 2008. *Stage appearances include:* Awake and Sing 1984, Painting Churches 1984, The Three Sisters 1985, All My Sons 1986, A Streetcar Named Desire 1988, Moon for the Misbegotten 1992, Sisters Rosensweig 1993, The Swan 1993. *Address:* The Endeavor Agency, 9701 Wilshire Blvd., Tenth Floor, Beverly Hills, CA 90212, USA.

McDOUGALL, Douglas; British business executive; *Chairman, Scottish Investment Trust PLC;* b. 1944; ed Univ. of Oxford; joined Baillie Gifford & Co. 1965, Pnr 1969–89, Jt Sr Pnr 1989–99; Chair. Scottish Investment Trust PLC 2003–; fmr Chair. Investment Man. Regulatory Org. Ltd (IMRO), Asscn of Investment Trust Cos, Institutional Fund Mans Asscn; currently Chair. Law Debenture Corpn PLC, 3i Bioscience Investment Trust PLC, Foreign & Colonial Eurotrust PLC, The Independent Investment Trust PLC, Pacific Horizon Investment Trust PLC; Dir The Herald Investment Trust PLC, The Monks Investment Trust PLC. *Address:* The Scottish Investment Trust, 6 Albyn Place, Edinburgh, EH2 4NL, Scotland (office). *Telephone:* (131) 225-7781 (office). *Fax:* (131) 226-3663 (office). *Website:* www.sit.co.uk (office).

MacDOWELL, Andie; American film actress; b. 21 April 1958, S. Carolina; d. of Marion MacDowell and the late Pauline MacDowell; m. 1st Paul Qualley; two d. one s.; m. 2nd Rhett DeCamp Hartzog 2001. *Television appearances include:* Secret of the Sahara 1987, Women and Men 2, In Love There Are No Rules 1991, Jo 2002, Riding the Bus with My Sister 2005, The Prince of Motor City 2008. *Films include:* Greystoke 1984, St Elmo's Fire 1985, Sex, Lies and Videotape 1989, Green Card 1990, Hudson Hawk 1991, The Object of Beauty 1991, The Player 1992, Ruby 1992, Groundhog Day 1993, Short Cuts 1993, Bad Girls 1994, Four Weddings and a Funeral 1994, Unstrung Heroes 1995, My Life and Me 1996, Multiplicity 1996, The End of Violence 1997, Town and Country 1998, Shadrack 1998, The Scalper 1998, Just the Ticket 1998, Muppets From Space 1999, The Music 2000, Town and Country 2001, Harrison's Flowers 2002, Crush 2002, Ginostra 2002, The Last Sign 2004, Beauty Shop 2005, Tara Road 2005, Barnyard (voice) 2006, Inconceivable 2008. *Address:* c/o ICM, 10250 Constellation Blvd, Los Angeles, CA 90067, USA.

McDOWELL, David Keith, MA; New Zealand diplomatist, conservationist and environmental consultant; b. 30 April 1937, Palmerston North; s. of Keith McDowell and Gwen McDowell; m. Jan Ingram 1960; one s. three d.; ed Victoria Univ. of Wellington; joined Ministry of Foreign Affairs 1959, Head, UN and African and Middle East Divs 1973, Dir of External Aid 1973–76, Head, Econ. Div. 1980–81, Special Asst to Sec. Gen., Commonwealth Secr., London 1969–72; High Commr in Fiji 1977–80, in India, Nepal and Bangladesh 1983–85; Asst Sec. of Foreign Affairs for Asia, Australia and the Americas 1981–85; First Sec., Perm. Mission to UN 1964–68, Perm. Rep. 1985–88; Dir-Gen. Dept of Conservation 1988–89; CEO Dept of Prime Minister and Cabinet 1989–91; Amb. to Japan 1992–94; Dir-Gen. Int. Union for Conservation of Nature (IUCN—World Conservation Union), Switzerland 1994–99; pvt. consultant 1999–. *Leisure interests:* fishing, boating, tennis, conservation, gardening, music. *Address:* 86 Waerenga Road, Otaki, New Zealand. *Telephone:* (6) 364-6296 (office). *Fax:* (6) 364-6205 (office). *E-mail:* jan.david.mcdowell@xtra.co.nz (office).

McDOWELL, John Henry, MA, FBA, FAAS; British academic; *University Professor, University of Pittsburgh;* b. 7 March 1942, Boksburg, South Africa; s. of Sir Henry McDowell and Norah (née Douthwaite) McDowell; m. Andrea Lehrke 1977; ed St John's Coll. Johannesburg, Univ. Coll. of Rhodesia and Nyasaland, New Coll., Oxford; Fellow, Praelector in Philosophy, Univ. Coll., Oxford 1966–86; Prof. of Philosophy, Univ. of Pittsburgh 1986–88, Univ. Prof. 1988–; Hon. DHumLitt (Chicago) 2008. *Publications:* Ed. (with Gareth Evans) Truth and Meaning, Ed. (with Philip Pettit) Subject, Thought and Context, Mind and World, Mind, Value and Reality, Meaning, Knowledge and Reality, Having the World in View, The Engaged Intellect; trans of Plato, Theaetetus. *Leisure interests:* gardening, reading. *Address:* Department of Philosophy, University of Pittsburgh, Pittsburgh, PA 15260, USA. *Telephone:* (412) 624-5792.

McDOWELL, Malcolm (Malcolm Taylor); British actor; b. 13 June 1943, Leeds; m. 1st Mary Steenburgen 1980; one s. one d.; m. 2nd Kelley Kuhr 1992; began career with the RSC at Stratford 1965–66; early television appearances in such series as Dixon of Dock Green, Z Cars. *Stage appearances:* RSC, Stratford 1965–66, Entertaining Mr. Sloane, Royal Court 1975, Look Back in Anger, New York 1980, In Celebration, New York 1984, Holiday Old Vic 1987, Another Time, Old Vic 1993. *Films include:* If... 1969, Figures in a Landscape 1970, The Raging Moon 1971, A Clockwork Orange 1971, O Lucky Man 1973, Royal Flash 1975, Aces High 1976, Voyage of the Damned 1977, Caligula 1977, The Passage 1978, Time After Time 1979, Cat People 1981, Blue Thunder 1983, Get Crazy 1983, Britannia Hospital 1984, Gulag 1985, The Caller 1987, Sunset 1987, Sunrise 1988, Class of 1999, Il Maestro 1989, Moon 44, Double Game, Class of 1999, Snake Eyes, Schweitzer, Assassin of the Tsar 1991, The Player, Chain of Desire, East Wind, Night Train to Venice, Star Trek:

Generations 1995, Tank Girl 1995, Kids of the Round Table, Where Truth Lies, Mr Magoo 1998, Gangster No 1 2000, Island of the Dead 2000, Just Visiting 2001, The Void 2001, Dorian 2001, The Barber 2001, Between Strangers 2002, Superman: Shadow of Apokolips 2002, I Spy 2002, I'll Sleep When I'm Dead 2003, Tempo 2003, Inhabited 2003, Red Roses and Petrol 2003, The Company 2003, Hidalgo 2004, Evilenko 2004, Bobby Jones, Stroke of Genius 2004, Tempesta 2004, Pinocchio 3000 (voice) 2004, Rag Tale 2005, Dinotopia: Quest for the Ruby Sunstone (voice) 2005, Cut Off 2006, Bye Bye Benjamin 2006, Exitz 2007, The List 2007, Halloween 2007, Doomsday 2008. *Television includes:* Our Friends in the North, Entourage, Heroes. *Address:* c/o Markham and Froggatt, 4 Windmill Street, London, W1P 1HF, England.

MacEACHEN, Hon. Allan J., OC, PC, MA; Canadian politician; b. 6 July 1921, Inverness, NS; s. of Angus MacEachen and Annie Gillies; ed St Francis Xavier Univ., Univs of Toronto and Chicago and MIT; Prof. of Econs, St Francis Xavier Univ. 1946–48, later Head, Dept of Econs and Social Sciences; mem. House of Commons 1953–58, 1962–84; MP for Cape Breton Highlands-Cans., NS 1953–84; Special Asst and Consultant on Econ. Affairs to Lester Pearson 1958; Minister of Labour 1963–65; Minister of Nat. Health and Welfare 1965–68, of Manpower and Immigration 1968–70, of Finance 1980–82; Pres. Privy Council and Govt House Leader 1970–74; Sec. of State for External Affairs 1974–76; Pres. Privy Council 1976–77 and Deputy Prime Minister 1977–79; Deputy Leader of Opposition and Opposition House Leader 1979; Deputy Prime Minister and Minister of Finance 1980–82; Deputy Prime Minister and Sec. of State for External Affairs 1982–84; mem. Senate 1984–96, Leader of Govt in Senate June–Oct. 1984, Leader of Opposition in Senate 1984–91; Chair. Int. IMF Group of Ten 1980–81, Interim Cttee of IMF, Conf. on Int. Econ. Co-operation, 1982 Ministerial Meeting of the GATT, Int. Advisory Council of Bank of Montreal 1986–91; Canadian Chair. Atlantik-Brücke Annual Symposium (Canada-Germany Conf.) 1984–; Chair. Advisory Council Int. Ocean Inst. 1996–; Bd Dirs North-South Inst. 1996–; Trustee Royal Ottawa Health Care Group 1987–95; mem. Bd of Govs St Francis Xavier Univ.; Order of Merit, Germany. *Address:* R.R.1, Whycocomagh, Nova Scotia B0E 3M0, Canada (home).

McENERY, Peter Robert; British actor; b. 21 Feb. 1940; s. of the late Charles McEnery and of Ada Mary Brinson; m. 1978; one d.; Founder-mem. and Assoc. Artist with RSC. *Theatre roles include:* Eugene in Look Homeward Angel 1962, Rudge in Next Time I'll Sing to You 1963, Konstantin in The Seagull 1964, Edward Gover in Made in Bangkok 1986, Trigorin in The Seagull 1975, Fredrick in A Little Night Music 1990, Torvald in A Doll's House 1994, Hector in Heartbreak House 1997, Claudius in Hamlet (Royal Nat. Theatre) 2000–01, Laertes, Clarence, Tybalt, Silvius, Patroclus, Bassanio, Orlando, Pericles, Brutus, Antipholus, Albie Sachs, Lorenzaccio (with RSC). *Plays directed:* Richard III 1971, The Wound 1972. *TV:* Clayhanger 1976, The Aphrodite Inheritance 1979, The Jail Diary of Albie Sachs 1980, Japanese Style 1982, The Collectors 1986, The Mistress 1986, Witchcraft 1991, Reach for the Moon 2000. *Films:* Tunes of Glory 1961, Victim 1961, The Moon-spinners 1963, Entertaining Mr Sloane 1970, La Curée, J'ai tué Raspoutine, Le Mur d'Atlantique, Le Montreur de Boxe. *Leisure interests:* steam railway preservation, skiing, American football. *Address:* Richard Stone Partnership, 2 Henrietta Street, London, C2E 8PS, England. *Telephone:* (20) 4497-0849. *Fax:* (20) 7323-0101.

McENROE, John Patrick; American professional tennis player; b. 16 Feb. 1959, Wiesbaden, then Fed. Repub. of Germany; s. of John P. McEnroe I and Katy McEnroe; brother of Patrick McEnroe, fmr professional tennis player; m. 1st Tatum O'Neal (q.v.) 1986; two s. one d.; 2nd Patty Smyth; two c.; one step-d.; ed Trinity High School, NJ and Stanford Univ., Calif.; amateur player 1976–78 (including NCAA singles championship 1978), professional 1978–93; winner of 77 singles titles during professional career, ranked world number one 1981–84; US Open Singles Champion 1979, 1980, 1981, 1984; US Open Doubles Champion 1979, 1981, 1989; Wimbledon Champion (doubles) 1979, 1981, 1983, 1984, 1992, (singles) 1981, 1983, 1984; WCT Champion 1979, 1981, 1983, 1984, 1989; Grand Prix Champion 1979, 1983, 1984; played Davis Cup for USA 1978–85, Capt. 1999–2000; only player to have reached the Wimbledon semi-finals as pre-tournament qualifier 1977; tennis sportscaster USA Network 1993–, CBS 1994–; mem. Men's Sr Tours Circuits 1994–, winner numerous titles including Quality Challenge 1997, 1998, 1999, Honda Challenge 2003; owner John McEnroe Gallery, NY; coach, British Lawn Tennis Asscn 2003–; Nat. Father of the Year Award 1996, Int. Tennis Hall of Fame 1999. *Television:* presenter The Chair (game show) 2002, McEnroe (talk show) CNBC 2004–. *Publications:* You Cannot Be Serious (autobiog. with James Kaplan) 2002. *Leisure interest:* music. *Address:* The John McEnroe Gallery, 41 Greene Street, New York, NY 10013, USA.

McENTEE, Andrew, BA, LLB; British lawyer; b. 2 July 1957, Glasgow, Scotland; s. of Shaun McEntee and Margaret McEntee (née O'Neill); ed Univ. of Stirling, Univ. of Wolverhampton, Univ. of N. London; case worker, Citizens' Advice Bureau 1982–83, Scottish Council for Civil Liberties (now Scottish Human Rights Centre) 1983–84; community care worker, Strath-clyde Social Work Dept 1985–86; Gen. Sec. Chile Cttee for Human Rights/South American Human Rights Coordination 1986–91; Gen. Sec. Cen. America Human Rights Cttee 1993–96; UK-apptd Chair. Amnesty Int. Lawyers Network 1994, Chair. Amnesty Int. UK 1998; Sr Consultant Atlantic Celtic Films Co. 1996–; UK Chair. Coalition for an Int. Criminal Court 1997–; adviser to Spanish and Chilean lawyers and victims and coordinator of Amnesty Int. case during extradition proceedings against Gen. Augusto Pinochet 1998–2000; writer and lecturer on human rights. *Leisure interests:* gardening, walking, 20th-century arts.

McEWAN, Angus David, BE, MEngSc, PhD, FAA, FTSE; Australian oceanographer; *Senior Scientific Adviser, Bureau of Meteorology;* b. 20 July 1937,

Alloa, Scotland; s. of David R. McEwan and Anne Marion McEwan; m. Juliana R. Britten 1961 (divorced 1982); two d.; ed Melbourne High School, Caulfield Tech. Coll., Melbourne Univ., Cambridge Univ.; engineer, Aeronautical Research Labs, Melbourne 1956–58, Research Scientist 1961–62, 1966–69; Research Scientist, Program Leader, Chief Research Scientist, Div. of Atmospheric Research, CSIRO, Aspendale, Vic. 1972–81, Foundation Chief, Div. of Oceanography, Hobart 1981–95; Sr Scientific Adviser (Oceanographer) to CSIRO and Bureau of Meteorology 1995–; Hon. Research Prof. Univ. of Tasmania 1988–; Chief Australian Nat. Del., Inter-governmental Oceanographic Comm. (IOC) 1995–; Chair. Intergovernmental Cttee for the Global Ocean Observing System 1997–2001; Nat. Del. Oceanic Research (SCOR); mem. numerous other nat. bodies and cttees concerning marine science; Queen Elizabeth Fellow 1969–71; Rossby Fellow (Woods Hole Oceanographic Inst.) 1975; Australian Centenary Medal 2003. *Publications:* scientific articles on geophysical fluid dynamics. *Leisure interests:* sailing, sketching, woodwork. *Address:* Bureau of Meteorology, Box 727, Hobart, Tasmania 7001 (office); 300 Sandy Bay Road, Sandy Bay, Tasmania 7005, Australia (home). *Telephone:* (3) 6221-2090. *Fax:* (3) 6221-2089. *E-mail:* amcewan@bom.gov.au (office); oceans@iprimus.com.au (home).

McEWAN, Geraldine; British actress; b. 9 May 1932, Old Windsor, Berks.; d. of Donald McKeown and Norah McKeown; m. Hugh Cruttwell 1953; one s. one d.; ed Windsor County Girls' School. *Stage appearances:* first engagement with Theatre Royal, Windsor 1949; London appearances in Who Goes There? 1951, Sweet Madness, For Better, For Worse, Summertime; Shakespeare Memorial Theatre, Stratford on Avon 1956, 1958, 1961 playing Princess of France (Love's Labours Lost), Olivia (Twelfth Night), Ophelia (Hamlet), Marina (Pericles), Beatrice (Much Ado about Nothing); played in School for Scandal, USA 1962, The Private Ear and The Public Eye, USA 1963; appearances as mem. Nat. Theatre 1965–71: Armstrong's Last Goodnight, Love for Love, A Flea in Her Ear, The Dance of Death, Edward II, Home and Beauty, Rites, The Way of the World, The White Devil, Amphitryon 38; other theatre appearances include: Dear Love 1973, Chez Nous 1974, The Little Hut 1974, Oh Coward! (musical) 1975, On Approval 1975, Look After Lulu 1978; with Nat. Theatre: The Browning Version 1980, Harlequinade 1980, The Provoked Wife 1980–81, The Rivals (Evening Standard Drama Award for Best Actress), You Can't Take It With You 1983–84; A Lie of the Mind (Royal Court) 1987, Lettice and Lovage (Globe Theatre) 1988–89, Hamlet (Riverside Studios) 1992, The Bird Sanctuary (Abbey Theatre) 1994, The Way of the World (Nat. Theatre; Evening Standard Drama Award for Best Actress) 1995, Grace Note (Old Vic) 1997, The Chairs (Royal Court) 1997, (Golden Theater, New York) 1998, Hay Fever (Savoy) 1999. *Films:* The Adventures of Tom Jones 1975, Escape from the Dark 1978, Foreign Body 1986, Henry V 1989, Robin Hood: Prince of Thieves 1991, Moses 1995, The Love Letter 1999, Titus 2000, Love's Labours Lost 2000, The Contaminated Man 2000, The Magdalene Sisters 2002, Food for Love 2002, Pure 2002, The Lazarus Child 2004, Vanity Fair 2004. *Radio:* Arrived 2002. *Television:* The Prime of Miss Jean Brodie (TV Critics Best Actress Award) 1978, L'Elégance 1982, The Barchester Chronicles 1982, Come Into the Garden, Maude 1982, Mapp and Lucia 1985–86, Oranges Are Not The Only Fruit 1990 (BAFTA Best Actress Award), Mulberry 1992–93, The Red Dwarf 1999, Thin Ice 2000, Victoria Wood's Christmas Special 2000, Carrie's War 2003, Agatha Christie's Marple (ITV) 2004, 2006. *Directed:* As You Like It 1988, Treats 1989, Waiting for Sir Larry 1990, Four Door Saloon 1991, Keyboard Skills 1993. *Address:* c/o ICM Oxford House, 76 Oxford Street, London, W1D 1BS, England.

McEWAN, Ian Russell, CBE, MA, FRSL; British writer; b. 21 June 1948, Aldershot, Hants.; s. of the late David McEwan and Rose Moore; m. 1st Penny Allen 1982 (divorced 1995); two s. and two step-d.; m. 2nd Annalena McAfee 1997; ed Woolverstone Hall, Univs of Sussex and E Anglia; Hon. Fellow American Acad. of Arts and Sciences 1997; Hon. DPhil (Sussex) 1989, (E Anglia) 1993, (London) 1998; Primo Letterario, Prato 1982, Shakespeare Prize, Germany 1999, British Book Award for Author of the Year 2008. *Screenplays:* The Imitation Game & Other Plays 1981, The Ploughman's Lunch 1985, Sour Sweet 1989. *Publications:* novels: The Cement Garden 1978, The Comfort of Strangers 1981, Rose Blanche (juvenile) 1985, The Child in Time (Whitbread Novel of the Year 1987, Prix Fémina Etranger 1993) 1987, The Innocent 1989, Black Dogs 1992, The Daydreamer (juvenile) 1994, Enduring Love 1997, Amsterdam (Booker Prize for Fiction 1998) 1998, Atonement (WHSmith Literary Award 2002, Nat. Book Critics Circle Fiction Award 2002, Los Angeles Times Prize for Fiction 2003, Santiago Prize for the European Novel 2004) 2001, Saturday (James Tait Black Memorial Prize 2006) 2005, On Chesil Beach (British Book Award for Book of the Year 2008) 2007; short stories: First Love, Last Rites (Somerset Maugham Award 1976) 1975, In Between the Sheets 1978; librettos: Or Shall We Die? (oratorio) 1983, For You (opera) 2008. *Leisure interest:* hiking. *Address:* c/o Jonathan Cape, Random Century House, 20 Vauxhall Bridge Road, London, SW1V 2SA, England. *Website:* www.ianmcewan.com.

McFADDEN, Daniel L., BS, PhD; American economist and academic; *Professor of Economics, University of California, Berkeley;* b. 29 July 1937, Raleigh, NC; m. Beverlee Tito Simboli McFadden; one d. two s.; ed Univ. of Minnesota; Asst Prof. of Econs Univ. of Pittsburgh 1962–63; Asst Prof. of Econs Univ. of Calif. at Berkeley 1963–66, 1966–68, Prof. of Econs 1968–79, 1990–, E. Morris Cox Chair 1990–, Dir Econometrics Lab. 1991–95, 1996–, Chair. Dept of Econs 1995–96; Visiting Assoc. Prof. Univ. of Chicago 1966–67; Irving Fisher Research Prof. Yale Univ. 1977–78; Prof. of Econs Mass Inst. of Tech. 1978–91, James R. Killian Chair, 1984–91, Dir Statistics Center 1986–88; Sherman Fairchild Distinguished Scholar Calif. Inst. of Tech. 1990; Pres.-Elect American Econ. Asscn 2004–; mem. American Acad. of Arts and Sciences, Nat. Acad. of Science; hon. degree (Univ. Coll. London) 2003; Econometrics Soc. Frisch Medal 1986, Nemmers Prize in Econs 2000, Nobel

Prize for Econs (jt recipient) 2000, Richard Stone Prize in Applied Econometrics 2000. *Publications include:* Lectures on Longitudinal Analysis (Underground Classics in Economics) (jt author), Handbook of Econometrics IV (with R. Engle) 1994. *Address:* Department of Economics, University of California, 549 Evans Hall #3880, Berkeley, CA 94720-3880, USA (office). *Telephone:* (510) 643-8428 (office). *Fax:* (510) 642-0638 (office). *E-mail:* mcfadden@econ.berkeley.edu (office). *Website:* emlab.berkeley.edu/users/mcfadden (office).

McFADDEN, Mary; American fashion designer; b. 1 Oct. 1938, New York; d. of Alexander Bloomfield McFadden and Mary Josephine Cutting; m. 1st Philip Harari 1964 (divorced); one d.; m. 2nd Frank McEwen 1968 (divorced); m. 3rd Armin Schmidt (divorced); m. 4th Kohle Yohannan (divorced); m. 5th Vasilios Calitsis 1996 (divorced); ed École Lubec, Paris, Sorbonne, Paris, Traphagen School of Design, New York and Columbia Univ., New York and New School for Social Research, New York; Dir of Public Relations, Christian Dior, New York 1962–64; Merchandising Ed. Vogue, SA 1964–65; political and travel columnist, Rand Daily Mail, SA 1965–68; Founder Vukutu Sculpture Workshop, Rhodesia 1968–70; freelance ed. My Fair Lady, Cape Town and French Vogue 1968–70; Special Projects Ed. American Vogue 1970–73; fashion and jewellery designer (noted for tunics made from African and Chinese silks), New York 1973–; Chair. Mary McFadden Inc. 1976–; Partner, MMcF Collection by Mary McFadden 1991–; fmr Pres. Council of Fashion Designers of America; adviser, Nat. Endowment for Arts; numerous awards, including Coty Award 1976, Neiman Marcus Award 1979, Best Dressed List Hall of Fame 1979, Coty American Fashion Critics' Hall of Fame Award 1979, Woman of the Year, Police Athletic League 1990, New York Landmarks Conservancy 1994, Designer of the Decade and Beyond, Fashion Group Int. and Philadelphia Breast Health Inst. 1997, Legends Award, Pratt Inst., Pres.'s Fellows Award, Rhode Island School of Design. *Films:* Zooni – The Last Chak Empress, Sufism in India. *Television:* QVC, Worldly Accessories. *Publications:* contribs to Vogue and House & Garden. *Leisure interests:* tennis, squash, travelling the world, lecturing. *Address:* 525 East 72nd Street, Apt 2A, New York, NY 10021 (home); Mary McFadden Inc., 240 West 35th Street, Floor 17, New York, NY 10001, USA (office). *Telephone:* (212) 736-4078 (office); (212) 772-1125 (home). *Fax:* (212) 239-7259 (office); (212) 239-7259. *E-mail:* mcfconture@aol.com (office). *Website:* www.marymcfadden.conture.com (office).

MACFADYEN, Air Marshal Ian David, CB, OBE, FRAeS,; British government official (retd) and air force officer (retd); *Honorary Inspector General, Royal Auxiliary Air Force;* b. 19 Feb. 1942, Maidenhead, Berks.; s. of Air Marshal Sir Douglas Macfadyen and Lady Macfadyen (now Rowan); m. Sally Harvey 1967; one s.; one d.; ed Marlborough, RAF Coll. Cranwell; joined RAF 1960, Cranwell cadet 1960–63, 19 Squadron 1965–68, HQ, RAF Strike Command 1969; Flying Instructor RAF Coll. Cranwell 1970–73, RAF Staff Coll. 1973, 111 Squadron 1974–75; Flight Commdr 43 Squadron 1976, HQ 2ATAF RAF Germany 1976–79, Command 29 Squadron 1980–83, 23 Squadron 1983; with Ministry of Defence 1983–85, 1989–90; with Command RAF Leuchars, Fife 1985–87, Royal Coll. of Defence Studies 1988; Chief of Staff then Commdr HQ British Forces Middle East, Riyadh 1990–91, Asst Chief of Defence Staff, Operational Requirements (Air Systems) 1991–94; Dir-Gen. Saudi Arabia Armed Forces Project 1994–98; retd 1999; Lt-Gov. Isle of Man 2000–05; Nat. Pres. The Royal British Legion 2006–09; Trustee RAF Museum 1999–2005; Hon. Inspector Gen. Royal Auxiliary Air Force 2009–; Liveryman Guild of Air Pilots and Navigators (GAPAN) 1999–; Trustee Bentley Priory Battle of Britain Trust 2006–; Sword of Honour, Cranwell 1963; Queen's Commendation for Valuable Service in the Air (QCVSA) 1973; Officer, Order of St John of Jerusalem 2001. *Publication:* Gulf War contrib. to Imperial War Museum Book of Modern Warfare 1945–2000 2002. *Leisure interests:* golf, shooting, watercolour painting, gliding, history. *Address:* Collyns Mead, Hawkesbury Upton, Badminton, S Glos., GL9 1BB, England (home). *Telephone:* (1454) 238544 (home). *E-mail:* poacher3@aol.com (home).

McFADYEN, Jock, MA; British artist; b. 18 Sept. 1950, Paisley, Scotland; s. of James Lachlan McFadyen and Margaret McFadyen; m. 1st Carol Hambleton 1972 (divorced 1987); one s.; m. 2nd Susie Honeyman 1991; one s. one d.; ed Chelsea School of Art; has made works about London, New York, Belfast, Berlin, Orkney and France; represented in 30 public collections and in numerous pvt. and corp. collections; artist in residence Nat. Gallery, London 1981; part-time Lecturer Slade School of Fine Art 1985–2004; designed sets and costumes for The Judas Tree, Royal Opera House, Covent Garden 1992; Arts Council Major Award 1979, Prize-winner John Moores Liverpool Exhbn 1991. *Publications:* several catalogues of exhibitions. *Leisure interests:* cycling, motorcycling, walking, swimming, children. *Telephone:* (7910) 359-087 (office). *E-mail:* info@jockmcfadyen.com (office). *Website:* www.jockmcfadyen.com (office).

MacFARLANE, Alan Donald James, DPhil, PhD, MA, FBA; British academic; *Professor of Anthropological Science, University of Cambridge;* b. 20 Dec. 1941, Assam, India; s. of Donald Macfarlane and Iris Macfarlane; m. 1st Gillian Ions 1965; m. 2nd Sarah Harrison 1981; one d.; ed Sedbergh School, Worcester Coll., Oxford, London School of Econs and School of Oriental & African Studies, London Univ.; Sr Research Fellow in History, King's Coll. Cambridge 1971–75; Lecturer in Social Anthropology, Univ. of Cambridge 1975–81, Reader in Historical Anthropology 1981–91; Prof. of Anthropological Science 1991–; Fellow, King's Coll., Cambridge 1981–; Radcliffe-Brown Memorial Lecture (British Acad.) 1992; Rivers Memorial Medal 1984. *TV series:* The Day the World Took Off (adviser and participant), Channel 4 2000. *Publications:* Witchcraft in Tudor and Stuart England 1970, Family Life of Ralph Josselin 1970, The Diary of Ralph Josselin (Ed.) 1976, Resources and Population 1976, The Origins of English Individualism 1977, The Justice and the Mare's Ale 1981, Marriage and Love in England 1986, The Culture of

Capitalism 1987, The Nagas: Hill Peoples of North India (co-author) 1990, The Cambridge Database System Manual 1990, The Savage Wars of Peace 1997, The Riddle of the Modern World: Of Liberty, Wealth and Equality 2000; Ed. and trans. (with Sarah Harrison) of Bernard Pignède, The Gurungs of Nepal 1993, The Making of the Modern World: Visions from West and East 2002, The Glass Bathyscaphe: How Glass Changed the World (with Gerry Martin) 2002, Green Gold: The Empire of Tea (with Iris Macfarlane) 2003, Letters to Lily: On How the World Works 2005, Japan through the Looking Glass 2007. *Leisure interests:* gardening, walking, music. *Address:* King's College, Cambridge, CB2 1ST, England (office). *Telephone:* (1223) 811976.

MacFARLANE, Alistair George James, Kt, CBE, DSc, PhD, ScD, FRS, FEng, FRSE; British professor of engineering and vice-chancellor (retd); b. 9 May 1931, Edinburgh; s. of George R. MacFarlane and Mary MacFarlane; m. Nora Williams 1954 (died 2005); one s.; m. Anwen Tudor Davies 2008; ed Hamilton Acad., Univ. of Glasgow, Univ. of London, Univ. of Manchester; with Metropolitan-Vickers, Manchester 1953–58; Lecturer, Queen Mary Coll., Univ. of London 1959–65, Reader 1965–66; Reader in Control Eng, UMIST 1966–69, Prof. 1969–74; Prof. of Eng, Univ. of Cambridge 1974–89; Fellow, Selwyn Coll., Cambridge 1974–89, Vice-Master 1980–88; Prin. and Vice-Chancellor, Heriot-Watt Univ., Edin. 1989–96, Emer. Research Fellow 1997–99; Chair. Cambridge Control Ltd 1985–89; mem. Council Science and Eng Research Council (SERC) 1981–85, Computer Bd 1983–88; Chair. Scottish Council for Research in Educ. 1992–98, Scottish Library and Information Council 1994–98, Advisory Body on High Performance Computing 1994–98, BT Advisory Forum 1997–2000; Academic Adviser Univ. of Highlands and Islands Project 1997–2001; Trustee Scottish Library and Information System Council 1994–98; mem. Royal Soc. Council 1997–99, Vice-President Educ. Cttee 1997–99, Chair. 2000–04; Hon. Fellow, Selwyn Coll. 1989–; Hon. DEng (Glasgow) 1995, Hon. DUniv (Heriot-Watt) 1997, (Paisley) 1997, Hon. DSc (Abertay Dundee) 1998, Hon. DLitt (Lincolnshire and Humberside) 1999. *Publications:* Engineering Systems Analysis 1964, Dynamical System Models 1970, (with I. Postlethwaite) A Complex Variable Approach to the Analysis of Linear Multivariable Feedback Systems 1979, Frequency-Response Methods in Control Systems (ed.) 1979, Complex Variable Methods for Linear Multivariable Feedback Systems (ed.) 1980, (with S. Hung) Multivariable Feedback: a quasi-classical approach 1982, (with G. K. H. Pang) An Expert Systems Approach to Computer-Aided Design of Multivariable Systems 1987. *Leisure interest:* computing. *Address:* Tregarth, 2 Marine Parade, Barmouth, Gwynedd LL42 1NA, Wales (home). *Telephone:* (1341) 280445 (home). *E-mail:* alistair.macfarlane@btinternet.com (home).

MacFARLANE, Ian J., AC; Australian central banker; b. 22 June 1946, Sydney; ed Monash Univ.; taught at Monash Univ.; with Inst. of Econs and Statistics, Oxford Univ., then in various positions at OECD, Paris 1973–78; joined Reserve Bank of Australia (Research Dept) 1979, Head of Research 1988, Asst Gov. (Econ.) 1990–92, Deputy Gov. 1992–96, Gov. 1996–2006 (retd); Hon. DSc, Hon. DLitt. *Address:* c/o Reserve Bank of Australia, GPO Box 3947, Sydney, NSW 2001, Australia (office).

McFARLANE, John, OBE, MA, MBA; British banking executive; b. June 1947, Dumfries, Scotland; ed Dumfries Acad., Univ. of Edinburgh, Cranfield School of Man., London Business School; with Ford Motor Co., UK 1969–74; various exec. positions with Citibank, 1975–93, including Man. Dir Citicorp Investment Bank Ltd 1987–90, Man. Dir Citicorp and Citibank UK 1990–93; Group Exec. Dir Standard Chartered Bank PLC 1993–97; CEO Australia and New Zealand Banking Group Ltd (ANZ) 1997–2007; Deputy Chair. Axiss Australia; mem. Financial Markets Foundation for Children; Chair. Council, Australian Bankers Asscn; Pres., Int. Monetary Conference; non-Exec. Dir, Australian Business Arts Foundation; fmr Dir London Stock Exchange 1989–91, Securities Asscn 1989–90, Auditing Practices Bd 1991–97, Cranfield School of Man. 1992–96, Financial Law Panel 1994–99, Capital Radio PLC 1995–98, Australian Graduate School of Man., Business Council of Australia; Fellow, Hong Kong Inst. of Bankers (FHKIB) 1995, The Australasian Inst. of Banking and Finance (FAIBF) 1997; Distinguished Alumnus Award, Cranfield 2003 MSI, The Securities Inst. (UK) 1993, Australian Centenary Medal 2003. *Leisure interests:* business education, personal computing, keeping fit, playing acoustic guitar, cinema, modern sculpture and painting. *Address:* c/o Australia and New Zealand Banking Group Ltd, 100 Queen Street, Melbourne 3000, Australia (office).

MacFARLANE, (Stephen) Neil, MA, DPhil; Canadian political scientist and academic; *Lester B. Pearson Professor of International Relations, St Anne's College, Oxford;* b. 7 March 1954; ed Dartmouth Coll., Oxford; Research Assoc., IISS, London 1981–82; Postdoctoral Fellow, Centre for Int. Affairs, Harvard Univ. 1982–83; Research Assoc., Inst. for Int. Relations, Univ. of British Columbia 1983–84; Asst Prof. of Govt and Foreign Affairs, Univ. of Virginia 1984–87, Assoc. Prof. of Govt and Foreign Affairs 1987–91, Grad. Co-ordinator 1987–89, Dir Centre for Russian and East European Studies 1989–91; Research Assoc., Center for Slavic and East European Studies, Univ. of California, Berkeley 1986–87; Prof. of Politics, Queen's Univ., Kingston, Ont. 1991–96, Co-ordinator, Post-Soviet Studies Program, Centre for Int. Relations 1992–97, Grad. Admissions Co-ordinator, Dept of Political Studies 1993–94, Chair. Skelton Clark Cttee for Visiting Scholars, Dept of Political Studies 1993–96, Dir Centre for Int. Relations 1995–96; Lester B. Pearson Prof. of Int. Relations, St Anne's Coll., Oxford 1996–, Dir Centre for Int. Studies 1997–, currently Head of Dept and Fellow, St Anne's Coll.; Adjunct Prof. of Political Science, Dalhousie Univ., Halifax, NS 1996–; Visiting Prof. in Int. Relations, Coll. of Europe, Bruges, Belgium 2007–08; Visiting Prof., S. Rajaratnam Prof. of Strategic Studies, Nanyang Technological Univ., Singapore 2008; mem. Bd Faculty of Social Studies, Univ. of Oxford 1997–, mem. Bd of Examiners for MPhil in Int. Relations 1998–2000 (Chair. 1999),

Co-ordinator MPhil Admissions in Int. Relations 1999; mem. Econ. and Social Research Council Research Grants Bd 2007–; Int. Fellow, Tbilisi State Univ., Georgia. *Publications:* Western Engagement in the Caucasus and Central Asia 1999, Politics and Humanitarian Action 2000, Humanitarian Action: The Conflict Connection 2001, Intervention in Contemporary World Politics 2002, US Hegemony and International Organizations (co-author) 2003, The UN and Human Security: A Critical History (co-author) 2006. *Address:* St Anne's College, University of Oxford, Oxford, OX2 6HS, England (office). *Telephone:* (1865) 274891 (office). *Fax:* (1865) 274899 (office). *E-mail:* neil.macfarlane@politics.ox.ac.uk (office). *Website:* www.politics.ox.ac.uk (office).

McFARLANE, Robert Carl (Bud), MS; American fmr government official; *Principal, Energy and Communications Solutions LLC;* b. 12 July 1937, Washington, DC; s. of William McFarlane and Alma Carl; m. Jonda Riley 1959; one s. two d.; ed US Naval Acad. and Inst des Hautes Etudes, Geneva; US Marine Corps, Second Lt rising to Lt-Col 1959–79; White House Fellow, Exec. Asst Council to Pres. for Legis. Affairs 1971–72; Mil. Asst to Henry Kissinger (q.v.) 1973–75; Exec. Asst to Asst to Pres. for Nat. Security Affairs 1975–76; Special Asst to Pres. 1976–77; Research Fellow Nat. Defense Univ., Washington, DC 1977–78; mem. Professional Staff Senate Comm. on Armed Services 1979–81; Counselor Dept of State 1981–82; Deputy Asst to Pres., Nat. Security Affairs 1982–83; Personal Rep. of US Pres. in Middle East July–Oct. 1983; Asst to Pres. for Nat. Security Affairs 1983–85; co-founder and fmr CEO Global Energy Investors; currently Prin. Energy and Communications Solutions LLC, Washington DC; mem. Bd of Dirs AEGIS; Chair. and CEO McFarlane Asscn 1986–; lobbyist for Macedonia 1992; Distinguished Service Medal and other medals and awards. *Publications:* At Sea Where We Belong 1971, Crisis Resolution (co-author) 1978, The Political Potential of Parity 1979. *Address:* Energy and Communications Solutions LLC, 2121 K Street, NW, Suite 830, Washington, DC 20037, USA (office). *Telephone:* (202) 223-2016 (office). *Fax:* (202) 457-0602 (office). *E-mail:* info@energyandcommunications.com (office). *Website:* www.energyandcommunications.com (office).

MACFARLANE OF BEARSDEN, Baron (Life Peer), cr. 1991, in the District of Bearsden and Milngavie; **Norman Somerville Macfarlane,** KT, FRSE; British business executive; *Honorary Life President, United Distillers PLC;* b. 5 March 1926; s. of Daniel Robertson Macfarlane and Jessie Lindsay Somerville; m. Marguerite Mary Campbell 1953; one s. four d.; ed Glasgow High School; f. N. S. Macfarlane and Co. Ltd 1949, Chair. Macfarlane Group (Clansman) PLC 1973–98, Man. Dir 1973–90; Chair. Scottish Industrialists Council 1975–; Dir Glasgow Chamber of Commerce 1976–79; Chair. The Fine Art Soc. PLC 1976–98 (Hon. Pres. 1998); Underwriting mem. of Lloyds 1978–97; Dir American Trust PLC 1980–97, Chair. 1984–97; Dir Clydesdale Bank PLC 1980–96, Deputy Chair. 1993–96; Dir Edin. Fund Mans PLC 1980–98; Dir Gen. Accident Fire and Life Assurance Corpn PLC 1984–96; Chair. Guinness Co. 1987–89, Jt Deputy Chair. 1989–92; Chair. United Distillers PLC 1987–96, Hon. Life Pres. 1996–; Chair. Arthur Bell Distillers 1989; mem. Council CBI Scotland 1975–81; mem. Bd Scottish Devt Agency 1979–87; Chair. Glasgow Devt Agency 1985–92; Vice-Chair. Scottish Ballet 1983–87, (Dir 1975–87), Pres. 2001–; Pres. Stationers' Asscn of GB and Ireland 1965, Co. of Stationers of Glasgow 1968–70, Glasgow High School Club 1970–72, Royal Glasgow Inst. of the Fine Arts 1976–87; Hon. Pres. Charles Rennie Mackintosh Soc. 1988–; Regent Royal Coll. of Surgeons, Edin. 1997–; Dir Scottish Nat. Orchestra 1977–82, Third Eye Centre 1978–81; Gov. Glasgow School of Art 1976–87; Scottish Patron, Nat. Art Collection Fund 1978–; Patron Scottish Licensed Trade Asscn 1992–; Chair. Govs, High School of Glasgow 1979–92, Hon. Pres. 1992–; mem. Royal Fine Art Comm. for Scotland 1980–82; Lord High Commr Gen. Ass., Church of Scotland 1992, 1993, 1997; mem. Court, Glasgow Univ. 1979–87; Trustee, Nat. Heritage Memorial Fund 1984–97, Nat. Galleries of Scotland 1986–97; DL Dunbartonshire 1993; Vice-Pres. Professional Golfers Asscn; f. Scotvec.; Hon. Patron, Queen's Park F.C.; Hon. FRIAS, FRCPS (Glas); Hon. Fellow, Glasgow School of Art 1993; Hon. Patron Queen's Park Football Club; Freeman Dumfries & Galloway 2006, City of Glasgow 2007; Hon. LLD (Strathclyde) 1986, (Glasgow) 1988, (Glasgow Caledonian) 1993, (Aberdeen) 1995; Hon. DUniv (Stirling) 1992; Dr hc (Edin.) 1992; St Mungo Award 2005, Goodman Award for Art and Business 2007. *Leisure interests:* golf, cricket, theatre, art. *Address:* Macfarlane Group PLC, Clansman House, 21 Newton Place, Glasgow, G3 7PY (office); 50 Manse Road, Bearsden, Glasgow, G61 3PN, Scotland. *Telephone:* (141) 333-9666 (office). *Fax:* (141) 333-1988 (office).

McGAUCHIE, Donald G., AO,; Australian telecommunications industry executive; *Chairman, Telstra Corporation Ltd;* Partner, C&E McGauchie-Terrick W Estate; Pres. Nat. Farmers' Fed. 1994–98; Chair. Woodstock Australia Ltd 1999–2002; apptd Dir Telstra Corpn Ltd 1998, Chair. 2004–; Chair. Rural Finance Corpn 2003–04, Advisory Bd Telstra Country Wide; Deputy Chair. Ridley Corpn Ltd 1998–2004; mem. Bd Dirs Reserve Bank of Australia, Nat. Foods Ltd 2000–05, James Hardie Industries NV, Nufarm Ltd, Sinclair Knight Merz (SKM) Consulting 2001–04; fmr mem. Foreign Affairs Council, Trade Policy Advisory Council; fmr Adviser to Prime Minister's Supermarket to Asia Council; fmr mem. Int. Policy Council on Agric., Food and Trade, Washington DC; Fellow, Australian Inst. of Co. Dirs. *Address:* Telstra Corporation Ltd, 242 Exhibition Street, Melbourne, Vic. 3000, Australia (office). *Telephone:* (3) 9634-6400 (office). *Fax:* (3) 9632-3215 (office). *E-mail:* info@telstra.com.au (office). *Website:* www.telstra.com.au (office).

MacGIBBON, Ross; British film director and fmr ballet dancer; ed Royal Ballet School; dancer with Royal Ballet 1973–86; started working in TV 1986. *Films:* dance film White Man Sleeps (Channel 4), Wyoming (1st Prize, IMZ DanceScreen competition) 1989; directed The Far End of The Garden 1991, Should Accidentally Fall (Special Jury Prize, 1994 Video-Dance Grand Prix, Vancouver), Echo 1996 (Special Jury Prize). *Television:* directed and produced Swinger (BBC 2) 1996, Peter and the Wolf (BBC 1), The Judas Tree (Channel 4), film on closure of the Royal Opera House (BBC 2).

McGILLIS, Kelly; American actress; b. 9 July 1957, Newport Beach, Calif.; m. 1st Boyd Black 1979 (divorced 1981); m. 2nd Fred Tillman 1988 (divorced 2002); two d.; ed Pacific School of Performing Arts and Juilliard School of Music, New York. *Films include:* Reuben, Reuben 1983, Witness 1985, Top Gun 1986, Ha-Holmim 1987, Made in Heaven 1987, The House on Carroll Street 1988, The Accused 1988, Winter People 1989, Cat Chaser 1989, Grand Isle 1991, The Babe 1992, North 1994, Painted Angels 1998, Ground Control 1998, The Settlement 1999, Morgan's Ferry 1999, At First Sight 1999, The Monkey's Mask 2000, No One Can Hear You 2001. *Television includes:* In the Best of Families: Marriage, Pride & Madness 1994, Dark Eyes (series) 1995, Remember Me 1995, We the Jury 1996, The Third Twin 1997, Perfect Prey 1998, Storm Chasers: Revenge of the Twister 1998, Cold Shoulder 2006, Black Widower 2006. *Plays include:* The Graduate 2004. *Address:* c/o Chuck James, The Gersh Agency, 232 North Canon Drive, Suite 201, Beverly Hills, CA 90210, USA.

McGINN, Colin, MA, BPhil; British academic; *Professor, Department of Philosophy, University of Miami;* b. 10 March 1950; s. of Joseph McGinn and June McGinn; one s.; ed Manchester and Oxford Univs; lecturer, Univ. Coll. London 1974–85; Wilde Reader in Mental Philosophy, Oxford Univ. 1985–90; Prof., Rutgers Univ., USA 1990–2005, Univ. of Miami 2005–; John Locke Prize 1973. *Publications:* The Character of Mind 1981, The Subjective View 1982, Wittgenstein on Meaning 1984, Mental Content 1989, The Problem of Consciousness 1991, The Space Trap 1992, Moral Literacy 1992, The Space Trap 1992, Problems in Philosophy 1993, Minds and Bodies: Philosophers and their Ideas 1997, Ethics, Evil and Fiction 1997, Knowledge and Reality 1998, The Mysterious Flame 1999, Logical Properties 2000, The Making of a Philosopher 2002, Consciousness and its Objects 2004, Mindsight: Image, Dream, Meaning 2004, The Power of Movies 2005, Shakespeare's Philosophy 2006, Mindfucking 2008. *Leisure interest:* fitness. *Address:* Department of Philosophy, University of Miami, PO Box 248054, Coral Gables, FL 33124-4670 (office); 270 West End Avenue, Apt 9E, New York, NY 10023, USA. *Telephone:* (305) 284-4757 (office). *E-mail:* cmcginn@mail.as.miami.edu (office). *Website:* www.as.miami.edu/phi (office); www.colinmcginnblog.com (home).

McGINN, Richard A., BA; American business executive; *General Partner, RRE Ventures LLC;* b. 1947; m.; one d.; ed Grinnell Coll., Iowa; with Ill. Bell 1969; exec. positions int. and computer systems groups AT&T 1978, CEO network systems; CEO, Pres. Lucent Technologies 1997–2000, Chair., CEO –2000; Gen. Pnr, RRE Ventures LLC (investment advisory and venture capital firm) 2001–; mem. Bd of Dirs American Express Co. 1998–, Mountain Top Foundation, Via Systems, Inc.; fmr mem. Bd of Dirs Lucent Technologies, Oracle Corpn; mem. Business Council. *Leisure interests:* adventure sports, deep-sea fishing. *Address:* RRE Ventures LLC, 126 East 56th Street, New York, NY 10022, USA (office). *Telephone:* (212) 418-5100 (office). *Website:* www.rre.com (office).

McGLADE, Jacqueline M., BSc, MA, PhD, FLS, FRSA; British/Canadian environmental scientist, academic and international organization official; *Executive Director, European Environment Agency;* b. 1955; ed Univ. Coll. of N Wales, Univ. of Guelpf, Canada, Univ. of Cambridge, UK; early career as Sr Research Scientist, Dept of Fisheries and Oceans, Canada; fmr academic positions include Prof. of Biological Sciences, Univ. of Warwick, England, Dir of Theoretical Ecology, Forschungszentrum Jülich, Germany, Prof. Aachen Univ., Germany, Adrian Fellow, Darwin Coll., Univ. of Cambridge, UK, Assoc. Prof., Int. Ecotechnology Research Centre, Cranfield Univ., UK; Dir NERC Centre for Coastal and Marine Sciences –2000; NERC Professorial Fellow in Environmental Informatics, Univ. Coll. London 2000–03. Prof. of Math. Biology 2003–; Exec. Dir, European Environment Agency 2003–; fmr Chair., The Earth Centre; Bd mem. Environment Agency 1998–2003; Trustee, Natural History Museum; mem. UK-China Forum; holds full diplomatic status in Denmark; Hon. DSc (Kent) 2004; Swedish Jubileum Award 1990, Minerva Prize 1993, Masaryk Gold Medal 2005, Brno Univ. Gold Medal. *Radio:* The Ocean Planet, BBC Radio 4 2000, King John's Treasure, BBC Radio 4 2001, Learning from Nature BBC Radio 4 2002. *Television:* The Next Big Thing BBC 2 2000. *Publications include:* Integrated Fisheries Management: Understanding the Limits to Marine Resource Exploitation 1989, Governance of Fisheries and Aquaculture 1993, Ecology, Thermodynamics and Odum's Conjectures (co-author) 1993, Multi-Disciplinary Modelling: An Overview and Practical Implications for the Governance of the Gulf Region 1993 (co-author), Advanced Ecological Theory (ed.) 1999, Gulf of Guinea Ecosystem (co-ed.) 2002, The European Environment: State and Outlook 2005, Millennium Ecosystem Assessment, Vol.: 2 Scenarios (co-ed.) 2005; more than 150 publs. *Address:* European Environment Agency, Kongens Nytorv 6, 1050 Copenhagen, Denmark (office). *Telephone:* 33367100 (office). *Fax:* 33367199 (office). *E-mail:* jacqueline.mcglade@eea.europa.eu (office). *Website:* www.eea.europa.eu (office).

McGOUGH, Roger Joseph, CBE, MA, DLitt, FRSL; British poet and children's writer; b. 9 Nov. 1937, Liverpool; s. of Roger McGough and Mary McGarry; m. 1st Thelma Monaghan 1970 (divorced 1980); m. 2nd Hilary Clough 1986; three s. one d.; ed St Mary's Coll., Liverpool, Hull Univ.; Poetry Fellow Univ. of Loughborough 1973–75; writer-in-residence Western Australia Coll. of Educ., Perth 1986, Univ. of Hamburg 1994; Vice-Pres. The Poetry Society 1996– (mem. Exec. Council 1989–93); Fellow John Moores Univ. 1999; Trustee Chelsea Arts Club 1987–, fmr Chair.; Freeman City of Liverpool 2001; Hon. Prof. Thames Valley Univ. 1993; Hon. MA (Nene Coll.) 1998, Hon. DLitt (Hull Univ.) 2004, (Univ. of Surrey) 2006; Signal Award 1984, 1998, BAFTA Awards

1984, 1992, Cholmondeley Award 1998, Centre for Literacy in Primary Educ. Award for Best Book of Poetry for Children 2004, 2005. *Music:* wrote and performed Top Twenty hits Lily the Pink and Thank U Very Much 1968–69. *Plays include:* The Sound Collector and My Dad's a Fire-eater (for children); wrote lyrics for Broadway production of The Wind in the Willows 1984. *Plays for radio include:* Summer with Monika, FX, Walking the Dog. *Television:* Kurt, Mungo, B. P. and Me (Thames Television) 1985, The Elements (Channel 4) (Royal Television Soc. Award) 1993. *Publications:* The Mersey Sound (with Brian Patten and Adrian Henri) 1967, Watchwords 1969, After the Merry-making 1971, Out of Sequence 1972, Gig 1972, Sporting Relations 1974, In the Glassroom 1976, Summer with Monika 1978, Holiday on Death Row 1979, Unlucky for Some 1981, Waving at Trains 1982, Melting into the Foreground 1986, Blazing Fruit: Selected Poems 1967–1987 1989, You at the Back 1991, Defying Gravity 1992, The Spotted Unicorn 1998, The Way Things Are 1999, Everyday Eclipses 2002, Collected Poems of Roger McGough 2003, Said and Done (memoir) 2005, Selected Poems 2006; for children: Mr Noselighter 1977, The Great Smile Robbery 1982, Sky in the Pie 1983, The Stowaways 1986, Noah's Ark 1986, Nailing the Shadow 1987, An Imaginary Menagerie 1988, Helen Highwater 1989, Counting by Numbers 1989, Pillow Talk 1990, The Lighthouse That Ran Away 1991, My Dad's a Fire-eater 1992, Another Custard Pie 1993, Lucky 1993, Stinkers Ahoy! 1995, The Magic Fountain 1995, The Kite and Caitlin 1996, Bad Bad Cats 1997, Until I Met Dudley 1998, Good Enough to Eat 2002, Moonthief 2002, The Bees' Knees 2002, Dotty Inventions 2002, What On Earth Can It Be? 2003; editor: Strictly Private 1981, The Kingfisher Book of Comic Verse 1986, The Kingfisher Books of Poems About Love 1997, The Ring of Words (anthology) 1998, Wicked Poems 2002, All the Best 2002, Sensational (anthology) 2004. *Address:* United Agents, 12–26 Lexington Street, London, W1F 0LE, England (office). *Telephone:* (20) 3214-0800 (office). *Fax:* (20) 3214-0801 (office). *E-mail:* info@unitedagents.co.uk (office); personal@rogermcgough.org.uk (office). *Website:* unitedagents.co.uk (office); www.rogermcgough.org.uk.

McGOVERN, George Stanley, PhD; American international organization official and fmr politician; *Global Ambassador on Hunger, United Nations Food and Agriculture Organization;* b. 19 July 1922, Avon, S Dak; s. of Rev. J. C. McGovern and Frances McLean McGovern; m. Eleanor Faye Stegeberg 1943; one s. four d.; ed Dakota Wesleyan Univ. and Northwestern Univ.; served USAF, Second World War; Teacher, Northwestern Univ. 1948–50; Prof. of History and Political Science, Dakota Wesleyan Univ. 1950–53; Exec. Sec. SDak Democratic Party 1953–56; mem. US House of Reps 1957–61, served Agricultural Cttee; Dir 'Food for Peace' Programme 1961–62; Senator from South Dakota 1963–81; Pnr, John Kornmeier Assocs, Washington, DC 1981; Lecturer, Northwestern Univ. 1981; Democratic cand. for US President 1972, 1984; Chair. Americans for Common Sense 1981–82; apptd Perm. Rep., FAO, Rome 1998, UN Global Amb. on Hunger 2001–; fmr Pres. Middle East Policy Council; fmr jt owner roadside inn, Stratford, Conn.; Presidential Medal of Freedom 2000, Food for Life Award, World Food Program 2000. *Publications:* The Colorado Coal Strike 1913–14 1953, War Against Want 1964, Agricultural Thought in the Twentieth Century 1967, A Time of War, a Time of Peace 1968, The Great Coalfield War (with Leonard Guttridge) 1972, An American Journey 1974, Grassroots (autobiog.) 1978, Terry: My Daughter's Life-and-Death Struggle with Alcoholism 1996. *Address:* PO Box 5591, Friendship Station, Washington, DC 20016, USA (home).

McGOWAN, Kieran, BComm; Irish business executive; *Chairman, CRH plc;* joined IDA Ireland ((Industrial Devt Agency) 1966, CEO 1990–98; mem. Bd of Dirs (non-exec.) CRH plc 1998–, Chair. 2007–; mem. Bd of Dirs Elan Corpn plc, Enterprise Ireland 1998–, Irish Life & Permanent plc, United Drug plc; Chair. Governing Authority Univ. Coll. Dublin 2004–; Founder mem. Inter Trade Ireland; fmr Chair. Irish Man. Inst., Dublin Molecular Medicine Centre. *Address:* CRH plc, Belgard Castle, Clondalkin, Dublin 22, Ireland (office). *Telephone:* (1) 404-1000 (office). *Fax:* (1) 404-1007 (office). *E-mail:* mail@crh.com (office). *Website:* www.crh.com (office).

McGRATH, Glenn Donald; Australian cricketer; b. 9 Feb. 1970, Dubbo, New South Wales; ed ed Narromine Primary School, Narromine High School, NSW; right-handed batsman, right-arm fast-medium bowler; teams: New South Wales 1993–, Australia 1993–2007 (retd), test debut Australia versus New Zealand at Perth; one-day international debut versus South Africa at Melbourne 1994; Worcestershire 2000, Middlesex 2004; 106 tests for Australia, scored 556 runs and took 481 wickets (average 21.43) with 25 five-wicket and three 10-wicket performances, best bowling 8-24 versus Pakistan at the WACA 2004; scored 892 runs and took 749 wickets (average 20.63) with 38 five-wicket and seven 10-wicket performances in first-class cricket; 196 one-day internationals, took 293 wickets (average 22.76), best bowling 7-15; test hat-trick versus West Indies at Perth 2001; 32 wickets in 2001 series versus England; 8th to pass 400 wickets in test cricket (2nd Australian); included in the New South Wales Team of the Millennium; first Australian fast bowler to play in 100 Test matches; highest score of 61 runs against New Zealand in 2005, the third highest score in history for a No. 11 batsman; Wisden Cricketer of the Year 1998, Wisden Australian Cricketer of the Year 1999, Allan Border Medal 2000. *Publications:* World Cup Diary: Glenn McGrath. *Leisure interests:* time with family, golf. *Address:* c/o Titan Management, PO Box 6832, Silverwater, BC NSW 2128, Australia (office). *Telephone:* (2) 9746-6355 (office). *Fax:* (2) 9746-6366 (office). *E-mail:* sports@titanmanagement.com.au (office). *Website:* www.nswblues.com.au (office).

McGRATH, John Brian, BSc, FRSA; British business executive; *Chairman, Cicely Saunders International;* b. 20 June 1938, Ruislip, Middlesex; m. Sandy Watson 1964; one s. one d.; ed Brunel Univ.; worked at UKAEA 1962–65; with NCB 1965–67; with Ford Motor Co. 1967–71; with Jaguar Cars 1971–75; with Stone-Platt 1976–82; Man. Dir Construction and Mining Div. and Chief Exec. Compair 1982–83; joined Grand Metropolitan PLC 1985, Group Dir Watney Mann & Truman Brewers Ltd 1985, Chair. and Man. Dir Grand Metropolitan Brewing 1986–88, Jt Man. Dir Int. Distillers & Vintners 1988–91, Man. Dir and COO 1991–92, Chief Exec. 1992–93, Chair. and Chief Exec. 1993–96, Group Chief Exec. Grand Metropolitan PLC 1996–97; Dir (non-exec.) Cookson Group 1993–; Chair. Scotch Whisky Asscn 1995–2000; Chair. Guinness Ltd (now Diageo PLC) 1997–2000, CEO 1997–2000; Chair. Boots Co. PLC 2000–03 (Dir 1998–2003); Dir Carlton Communications PLC 2003, ITV PLC (formed by merger of Carlton Communications and Granada) 2004–07; Chair. Cicely Saunders Int. 2002–; Gov. Brunel Univ. 2004–. *Address:* 63 Walnut Court, St Mary's Gate, Marloes Road, London, W8 5UB, England (home). *E-mail:* jbmcgrath99@yahoo.co.uk (home).

McGRATH, Judith (Judy), BA; American television executive; *Chairperson and CEO, MTV Networks Company;* b. 1952, Scranton, Pa; ed Cedar Crest Coll., Allentown, Pa; fmrly Copy Chief, Glamour Magazine, Sr Writer Mademoiselle Magazine, copywriter, Nat. Advertising, Phila; copywriter, Warner Amex Satellite Entertainment Co. (later MTV Networks Co.) 1981, subsequently Editorial Dir MTV, Exec. Vice-Pres., Creative Dir, then Co-Pres. and Creative Dir, Chair. and CEO MTV Networks 2004–; Pres. VH1, Networks, New York City Ballet, Rock the Vote; Hon. Chair. Cable Positive 2005; ranked by Fortune magazine amongst 50 Most Powerful Women in Business in the US 1998–2003, (11th) 2004, (10th) 2005, (12th) 2006, (18th) 2007, ranked by Forbes magazine amongst 100 Most Powerful Women (64th) 2004, (49th) 2005, (52nd) 2006, (31st) 2007, (60th) 2008. *Film:* Joe's Apartment (exec. producer). *Address:* MTV Networks Company, 1515 Broadway, New York, NY 10036, USA (office). *Telephone:* (212) 846-8712 (office). *Fax:* (212) 846-6361 (office). *E-mail:* judith.mcgrath@mtv.com (office); contact@mediavillage.com. *Website:* www.mtv.com (office).

McGRAW, Harold Whittlesey (Terry), III, BA, MBA; American publishing executive; *Chairman, President and CEO, The McGraw-Hill Companies, Inc.;* b. 30 Aug. 1948, Summit, NJ; s. of Harold W. McGraw, Jr; m. Nancy Goodrich 1973; one s. one d.; ed Tufts Univ., Univ. of Pennsylvania; fmr mem. financial man. staff GTE, GTE Man. Corp.; Asst Vice-Pres. Pension Investment McGraw-Hill Inc., New York 1980–83, Dir Corp. Planning Systems 1983–84, Vice-Pres. Corp. Planning, mem. Bd Dirs 1984–85; Group Vice-Pres. Public Transport Group, McGraw-Hill Publs Co., New York 1985–86, Group Vice-Pres. Public Transport, Aerospace and Defense Group 1986–98, Pres. 1987–88; Pres. McGraw-Hill Financial Services Co., New York 1988–89; mem. Bd Dirs The McGraw Hill Cos 1987–, Pres., COO 1993–98, Pres., CEO 1998–99, Chair., Pres., CEO 1998–; mem. Bd of Dirs United Techs Corpn, Hartley House (New York community settlement house) 1983–, Nat. Actors Theater, Nat. Acad. Foundation, Nat. Org. on Disability, Nat. Council on Econ. Educ., Wharton Graduate Exec. Bd,; Co-Chair. Carnegie Hall's Corp. Fund; mem. The Business Council, Business Roundtable; Chair. Emergency Cttee for American Trade; fmr Dir Bestfoods. *Address:* The McGraw Hill Companies, Suite C3A, Floor 49, 1221 Avenue of the Americas, New York, NY 10020, USA (office). *Telephone:* (212) 512-2000 (office). *Fax:* (212) 512-3840 (office). *Website:* www.mcgraw-hill.com (office).

McGREEVEY, James E., BA; American state official; b. 6 Aug. 1957, Jersey City; s. of John McGreevey and Veronica McGreevey; m. Dina Matos; two d.; ed St Joseph's High School, Columbia Univ., Georgetown Univ., Harvard Univ.; fmrly man. with Merck & Co.; fmr Asst Prosecutor for Middlesex Co., Exec. Dir of State Parole Bd; mem. State Ass., New Jersey 1990–91, State Senate 1994–97; Mayor of Woodbridge 1992–2002; Gov. of New Jersey 2002–04 (resgnd). *Address:* c/o Office of the Governor, POB 001, Trenton, NJ 08625, USA (office).

McGREGOR, Ewan; British actor; b. 31 March 1971, Perth, Scotland; s. of James McGregor and Carol McGregor; m. Eve Mavrakis; one adopted d.; ed Guildhall School of Music and Drama; began career with Perth Repertory Theatre; Hon. DLitt (Ulster Univ.). *Theatre includes:* What the Butler Saw, Little Malcolm and his Struggle against the Eunuchs (Hampstead Theatre Club) 1999 and Comedy Theatre, London, Guys and Dolls (Piccadilly Theatre, London) 2005, Othello (Donmar Warehouse, London) 2007. *Television includes:* Lipstick on Your Collar, Scarlet and Black, Kavanagh QC, Doggin' Around, Tales From the Crypt, ER, Long Way Round, Long Way Down. *Films include:* Being Human, Family Style, Shallow Grave (Best Actor Dinard Film Festival 1994), Blue Juice, The Pillow Book, Trainspotting, Emma, Brassed Off, Nightwatch, The Serpent's Kiss, A Life Less Ordinary, Velvet Goldmine, Star Wars Episode I: The Phantom Menace, Little Voice, Rogue Trader, Eye of the Beholder, Nora, Moulin Rouge (Best Actor, Berlin Film Festival, Empire Award, Variety Club Awards, Film Critics' Awards) 2001, Black Hawk Down 2002, Star Wars Episode II: Attack of the Clones 2002, Down with Love 2003, Young Adam (Scottish BAFTA Award for Best Actor 2004) 2003, Big Fish 2004, Stay 2004, Star Wars Episode III: Revenge of the Sith 2005, The Island 2005, Stay 2005, Stormbreaker 2006, Scenes of a Sexual Nature 2006, Miss Potter 2006, Cassandra's Dream 2007, Deception 2007, Incendiary 2008. *Publication:* Long Way Round (with Charley Boorman) 2005, Lond Way Down (with Charley Boorman) 2007. *Leisure interest:* motor bikes. *Address:* United Agents, 12–26 Lexington Street, London W1F 0LE, England (office); c/o Creative Artists Agency, 9830 Wilshire Boulevard, Beverly Hills, CA 90212-1825, USA (office). *Website:* unitedagents.co.uk (office); www.caa.com/ (office).

McGREGOR, Harvey, QC, MA, DCL, SJD; British barrister; b. 25 Feb. 1926, Aberdeen; s. of the late William G. R. McGregor and Agnes Reid; ed Inverurie Acad., Scarborough Boys' High School, Queen's Coll. Oxford and Harvard Univ.; Bigelow Teaching Fellow, Univ. of Chicago 1950–51; called to the Bar, Inner Temple, London 1955, Bencher 1985; Fellow, New Coll. Oxford 1972–85, Warden 1985–96, Hon. Fellow 1996; Privilegiate, St Hilda's Coll. Oxford 2001; consultant to Law Comm. 1966–73; Deputy Ind. Chair. London and the

Theatre Council 1971–92, Ind. Chair. 1992–; Visiting Prof., New York Univ. and Rutgers Univ. 1963–69; Fellow, Winchester Coll. 1985–96; mem. Editorial Bd Modern Law Review 1986–; mem. Acad. of European Pvt. Lawyers 1994–; Trustee Oxford Union 1977–2004 (Chair. 1994–2004); Trustee Migraine Trust 1999–; Assoc. mem. Soc. of Writers to the Signet 2002–; Founding Fellow Inst. of Contemporary Scotland 2002; Hon. Prof. Univ. of Edin. 1998–. *Publication:* A Contract Code 1993, McGregor on Damages (17th edn) 2003, European Contract Code (trans. from French) 2004. *Leisure interests:* music, theatre, travel. *Address:* Hailsham Chambers, 4 Paper Buildings, Temple, London, EC4Y 7EX (office); 29 Howard Place, Edinburgh, EH3 5JY, Scotland (home). *Telephone:* (20) 7643-5000 (office); (131) 556-8680 (home). *Fax:* (20) 7353-5778 (office); (131) 556-8686 (home). *E-mail:* harvey.mcgregor@hailshamchambers.com (office). *Website:* www.hailshamchambers.com (office).

MacGREGOR, Joanna Clare, BA, FRAM; British musician; *Artistic Director, Bath International Music Festival;* b. 16 July 1959, London; d. of Angela MacGregor and Alfred MacGregor; m. Richard Williams 1986 (divorced); one d. (deceased); ed South Hampstead High School for Girls, New Hall Coll. Cambridge, Royal Acad. of Music; Young Concert Artists Trust 1985–88; performances of classical, jazz and contemporary music in more than 70 countries; has performed with Rotterdam, Oslo and Netherlands Radio and Royal Philharmonic Orchestras, Sydney, Berlin, Chicago, BBC, RTE and London Symphony Orchestras, New York and Hong Kong Philharmonics, Philharmonia, London Mozart Players, Manchester Camerata, Royal Scottish, Royal Liverpool, Hallé, English and Irish Chamber Orchestras; has worked with Sir Harrison Birtwistle, Pierre Boulez, John Adams, Lou Harrison, Arvo Pärt and numerous jazz artists including Jason Yarde, Seb Rochford and Andy Sheppard; electronica artists and world music artists including Dhafer Youssef, Kuljit Bhamra and Sibongile Khumalo; numerous radio and TV appearances including Last Night of the Proms 1997; established own record label SoundCircus 1998; Prof. of Music, Gresham Coll. 1998–2002; Prof. of Performance, Liverpool Hope Univ., Visiting Prof. Royal Coll. of Art 2008–; mem. Arts Council of England 1998–2002; conducting debut on UK tour with Britten Sinfonia 2000, Assoc. Artistic Dir 2002–; created Cross Border, multimedia work touring China with Jin Xing's Dance Theatre of Shanghai 2003; Artistic Dir Bath Int. Music Festival 2005–; created On the Edge of Life examining social issues through music/multimedia 2006–; Hon. Fellow, Royal Acad. of Music, Trinity Coll. of Music, RSA, New Hall Coll. Cambridge; Dr hc (Open Univ.) 2005, (Bath Univ.) 2008; European Encouragement Prize for Music 1995, NFMS Sir Charles Grove Award 1998, South Bank Show Award for Classical Music 2000, Royal Philharmonic Soc. Audience Development Award. *Recordings:* American contemporary music (Ives, Monk, Nancarrow, Copland, Barber, Cage, Lou Harrison), Britten Concerto, Satie, Gershwin recordings with LSO, and music by Bach (The Art of Fugue, French Suites, Goldberg Variations), Scarlatti, Bartók, Debussy, Ravel and Messaien (Vingt Regards), Memoirs of an Amnesiac (radio play about Satie), Deep River (music of the Deep South, with Andy Sheppard) 2006, orchestral arrangements of Moondog Sidewalk Dances 2007, commissions and recordings of Harrison Birtwistle, Nitin Sawhney, Talvin Singh, Moses Molelekwa, Django Bates. *Compositions include:* Lute Songs (orchestra), Lullaby for M (percussion), arrangements of Piazzolla tangos and American songs and spirituals (Lost Highway). *Publications:* wrote series of children's books for Faber Music 2001; Piano World (five vols) 2001, Art Not Chance 2001, Unbeaten Tracks 2006. *Address:* c/o Ingpen & Williams, 7 St George's Court, 131 Putney Bridge Road, London, SW15 2PA, England (office). *Telephone:* (20) 8874-3222 (office). *Fax:* (20) 8877-3113 (office). *E-mail:* info@ingpen.co.uk (office). *Website:* www.ingpen.co.uk (office); www.soundcircus.com (office).

MacGREGOR, Baron (Life Peer), cr. 2001, of Pulham Market in the County of Norfolk; **John Roddick Russell MacGregor,** OBE, PC, MA, LLB; British politician and business executive; b. 14 Feb. 1937, Glasgow; s. of the late Dr. N. S. R. MacGregor; m. Jean Mary Elizabeth Dungey 1962; one s. two d.; ed Merchiston Castle School, Edin., St Andrews Univ., King's Coll., London; Univ. Admin. 1961–62; Editorial Staff, New Society 1962–63; Special Asst to Prime Minister, Sir Alec Douglas-Home 1963–64; Conservative Research Dept 1964–65; Head of Pvt. Office of Rt Hon. Edward Heath (Leader of Opposition) 1965–68; Conservative MP for South Norfolk 1974–2001; an Opposition Whip 1977–79; a Lord Commr of HM Treasury 1979–81, Parl. Under-Sec. of State, Dept of Industry 1981–83; Minister of State, Minister of Agric., Fisheries and Food 1983–85, 1987–89; Chief Sec. to HM Treasury 1985–87; Sec. of State for Educ. and Science 1989–90; Lord Pres. of the Council and Leader of the House of Commons 1990–92; Sec. of State for Transport 1992–94; with Hill Samuel & Co. Ltd 1968–79, Dir 1973–79, Deputy Chair. Hill Samuel Bank 1994–96, also Dir; Dir Slough Estates 1995–2006, Associated British Foods 1994–2007, Unigate (now Uniq) 1996–2005, London and Manchester Group 1997–98, Friends Provident 1998–, Supervisory Bd Daf Trucks NV 2000–07; Jt Chair. UK Food and Agriculture Advisory Bd, Rabobank International; Vice-Pres. Local Govt Asscn 1997–99; mem. Neill Cttee (now Wicks Cttee) on Standards in Public Life 1998–2003; Chair. Fed. of Univ. Conservative and Unionist Asscns 1959, Bow Group 1963–64; First Pres. Conservative and Christian Democratic Youth Community 1963–65; mem. Magic Circle 1989, Inner Magic Circle 1999; mem. Council King's Coll. London 1996–2002, Inst. of Dirs 1996–2007, Norwich Cathedral Council 2002–, High Steward and Chair. of Council 2007–; Deputy Chair., Asscn of Governing Bodies of Ind. Schools 2001–06; Hon. Fellow King's Coll. London 1990; Hon. LLD (Westminster) 1995. *Leisure interests:* music, reading, travelling, gardening, conjuring. *Address:* House of Lords, London, SW1A 0PW, England. *Telephone:* (20) 7219-4439 (office).

MacGREGOR, (Robert) Neil; British museum director; *Director, British Museum;* b. 16 June 1946; s. of Alexander MacGregor and Anna MacGregor (née Neil); ed Glasgow Acad., New Coll., Oxford, Univ. of Edinburgh, Courtauld Inst. of Art; Lecturer, Univ. of Reading 1976; Ed. The Burlington Magazine 1981–86; Dir Nat. Gallery 1987–2002; Dir British Museum 2002–; Trustee Pilgrim Trust 1990–, Raad van Toezicht, Rijksmuseum, Amsterdam; Chair. Conf. of UK Nat. Museum Dirs 1991–97; Curator Cen. Inst. for Art History, Munich 1992–; mem. Supervisory Bd Rijksmuseum 1995–; mem. Bd of Electors Ashmolean Museum, Fitzwilliam Museum; mem. UNESCO; mem. Advisory Bd of the Hermitage, St Petersburg 1997–; mem. Visiting Cttee J. Paul Getty Museum, Malibu, Calif., USA; fmr Chair. Nat. Museums Dirs' Conf.; mem. Courtauld Inst. of Art 2002–; Fellow, New Coll. Oxford, Birkbeck Coll. London 2004; mem. Faculty of Advocates, Edin. 1972; Hon. mem. Royal Scottish Acad. 1995; Hon. Fellow Ecole Normale Supérieure, Paris, British Acad. Dr hc (York) 1992, (Edin.) 1994, (Reading) 1997, (Leicester) 1997, (Glasgow) 1998, (Strathclyde) 1998, (Oxford) 1998, (Exeter) 1998, (London) 1999. *Radio:* contributor to numerous radio programmes. *Television:* has presented two major series on art. *Video:* Making Masterpieces (three-video set; writer and presenter). *Publications:* A Victim of Anonymity 1994, Seeing Salvation 2000, Britain's Paintings: the story of art through masterpieces in British Collections 2003; numerous articles in Apollo, The Burlington Magazine, Connoisseur, etc. *Address:* The British Museum, Great Russell Street, London, WC1B 3DG, England (office). *Telephone:* (20) 7323-8299 (office). *Website:* www.thebritishmuseum.ac.uk (office).

MacGREGOR, Susan (Sue) Katriona, CBE, FRSA; British broadcaster and journalist; b. 30 Aug. 1941, Oxford; d. of the late Dr James MacGregor and Margaret MacGregor; ed Herschel School, Cape, SA; announcer/producer South African Broadcasting Corpn 1962–67; BBC Radio reporter World at One, World This Weekend, PM 1967–72; Presenter (BBC Radio 4) Woman's Hour 1972–87, Tuesday Call, Conversation Piece, Today 1984–2002, A Good Read 2003–, The Reunion 2003–, (BBC TV) Around Westminster, Dateline London; Visiting Prof. of Journalism Nottingham Trent Univ. 1995–2003; mem. Royal Coll. of Physicians Cttee on Ethical Issues in Medicine 1985–2000; mem. Bd Royal Nat. Theatre 1998–2003; Trustee, John Ellerman Foundation 2002–; Trustee, UNICEF UK 2004–; Bd mem., Young Concert Artists' Trust 2003–; Hon. MRCP 1995; Hon. DLitt (Nottingham) 1996; Hon. LLD (Dundee) 1997; Hon. DLitt (Nottingham Trent) 2000, (Staffordshire) 2001, (N London) 2002. *Publication:* Woman of Today 2002. *Leisure interests:* theatre, cinema, skiing. *Address:* c/o Felicity Bryan, 2A North Parade, Oxford, OX2 6LX, England (office). *Telephone:* (1865) 513816 (office).

McGREGOR, Wayne; British choreographer; *Resident Choreographer, Royal Ballet;* b. 1970, Stockport; ed Univ. Coll. Bretton Hall and José Limon School, NY, USA; originally trained in contemporary dance; created works for The Royal Ballet, Skindex, Stuttgart Ballet, English Nat. Ballet, San Francisco Ballet and Rambert Dance Co.; other work includes choreography for film Harry Potter and The Goblet of Fire and for Channel 4 (UK), BBC TV, The Old Vic, Nat. Theatre, Royal Court Theatre, ENO and Peter Hall Co.; Founder Random Dance 1992, became Resident Co. of Sadler's Wells Theatre 2001–; Resident Choreographer Royal Ballet 2006–; Outstanding Achievement in Dance Award, Time Out Live Awards 2001, Outstanding Choreography Award, Time Out Live Awards 2002, IMZ Dance Screen Award 2002, Laurence Olivier Award 2004. *Dances include:* Chroma, Engram, Qualia, Symbiont(s), NDT1 for Royal Ballet, over thirty pieces for Random Dance. *Address:* Royal Opera House, Bow Street, Covent Garden, London, WC2E 9DD England. *Website:* info.royaloperahouse.org/ballet.

McGUFFIN, Peter, MB ChB, PhD, FRCP, FRCPsych, FMedSci; British psychiatrist and geneticist; *Dean and Head of School, Institute of Psychiatry, King's College London;* b. 4 Feb. 1949, Belfast; s. of Capt. William McGuffin and Melba M. Burnison; m. Prof. Anne Farmer 1972; one s. two d.; ed Univs of Leeds and London; MRC Fellow and Lecturer, Inst. of Psychiatry, London 1979–81; Visiting MRC Fellow, Washington Univ. Medical School, St Louis, Mo. 1981–82; MRC Sr Fellow, Hon. Consultant and Sr Lecturer, Inst. of Psychiatry, King's Coll. Hosp. London 1982–86; Prof. of Psychological Medicine, Univ. of Wales Coll. of Medicine 1987–98; Prof. of Psychiatric Genetics and Dir Social, Genetic and Developmental Psychiatry Research Centre, Inst. of Psychiatry, King's Coll. London 1998–2006, Dean and Head of School 2006–; Distinguished Fellow, Int. Soc. of Affective Disorders 2000; Fattorini Prize, Univ. of Leeds 1972, Foundation Fellow, Acad. of Medical Sciences (UK) 1998, Stromgren Medal, Danish Psychiatric Asscn 2004, Lifetime Achievement Award, Int. Soc. for Psychiatric Genetics 2007. *Publications include:* Scientific Principles of Psychopathology, The New Genetics of Mental Illness, Seminars on Psychiatric Genetics, Essentials of Postgraduate Psychiatry, Behavioural Genetics (4th edn), Measuring Psychopathology, Psychiatric Genetics and Genomics; many scientific papers and articles. *Leisure interests:* music (especially classical guitar), horse riding, running with my dogs. *Address:* Dean's Office, Institute of Psychiatry, Box P001, de Crespigny Park, London, SE5 8AF, England (office). *Telephone:* (20) 7848-0154 (office). *Fax:* (20) 7848-0866 (office). *E-mail:* p.mcguffin@iop.kcl.ac.uk (office). *Website:* www.iop.kcl.ac.uk/staff/profile/default.aspx?go=10199 (office).

McGUINNESS, Frank, MPhil; Irish playwright and academic; *Lecturer in English Literature, University College Dublin;* b. 29 July 1953, Buncrana, Donegal; s. of Patrick McGuinness and Celine McGuinness; ed University Coll. Dublin; Lecturer in English, Univ. of Ulster, Coleraine 1977–79, Univ. Coll. Dublin 1979–80, St Patrick's Coll., Maynooth 1984–97; Writer-in-Residence, School of English and Drama, Univ. Coll. Dublin 1997–; Dir Abbey Theatre, Dublin 1992–96; Officier des Arts et Lettres; Hon. DLitt (Ulster) 2000; Harvey's Award, Evening Standard Drama Award, Ewart-Biggs Peace Prize, Cheltenham Literary Prize, Fringe First, Irish American Literary Prize 1992, Independent on Sunday Best Play 1992, New York Drama Critics'

Award 1993, Writers' Guild Award 1993, Tony Award for Best Revival 1997. *Publications:* The Factory Girls 1982, Observe the Sons of Ulster Marching towards the Somme 1985, Baglady 1985, Innocence 1986, Rosmersholm, A Version 1987, Scout 1987, Yerma: A Version 1987, Carthaginians 1988, The Hen House 1989, Peer Gynt, A Version 1989, Mary and Lizzie 1989, Three Sisters, A Version 1990, The Bread Man 1990, The Threepenny Opera, A Version 1991, Someone Who'll Watch Over Me 1992, The Bird Sanctuary 1994, Hedda Gabler, A Version 1994, Uncle Vanya, A Version 1995, Booterstown: Poems 1995, Selected Plays: Vol. I 1996, The Dazzling Dark: Introduction 1996, A Doll's House: A Version 1996, The Caucasian Chalk Circle: A Version 1997, Electra: A Version 1997, Mutabilitie 1997, Dancing at Lughnasa: A Screenplay 1998, The Storm: A Version 1998, Dolly West's Kitchen 1999, The Sea With No Ships: Poems 1999, Miss Julie: A Version 2000, The Barbaric Comedies 2000, Gates of Gold 2002, The Stone Jug (poems) 2003, Hecuba 2004, Speaking Like Magpies 2005, Phaedra 2006, There Came a Gypsy Riding 2007, Ghosts (A Version) 2007, Supper With Judas 2007. *Leisure interests:* walking, painting, botany. *Address:* School of English and Drama, Department of Anglo-Irish Literature, University College Dublin, Belfield, Dublin 4, Ireland (office). *Telephone:* (1) 7168420 (office). *E-mail:* englishdramafilm@ucd.ie (office). *Website:* www.ucd.ie/englishanddrama (office).

McGUINNESS, Martin; Irish politician; *Deputy First Minister of Northern Ireland;* b. 23 May 1950, Derry; m.; four c.; took part in secret London talks between Sec. of State for NI and Irish Republican Army (IRA) July 1972; imprisoned for six months during 1973 in Irish Repub. after conviction for IRA membership; elected to NI Ass., refused seat; stood against John Hume (q.v.) in gen. elections of 1982, 1987, 1992; MP for Mid-Ulster, House of Commons 1997–; mem. Ulster-Mid, NI Ass. 1998–2000 (Ass. suspended Feb. 2000), 2000–02 (Ass. suspended Oct. 2002); Minister of Educ. 1999–2002; spokesman for Sinn Féin, also mem. Nat. Exec.; involved in peace negotiations with British Govt; Deputy First Minister of NI Ass. 2007–. *Leisure interest:* fly-fishing. *Address:* Office of the Deputy First Minister, Parliament Buildings, Stormont Estate, Belfast, BT4 3XX (office); Sinn Féin, 51–55 Falls Road, Belfast, BT12 4PD, Northern Ireland (office). *Telephone:* (28) 9022-3000. *E-mail:* sinnfein@iol.ie (office). *Website:* www.irlnet.com/sinnfein (office).

McGUINTY, Hon. Dalton, JD; Canadian politician; *Premier of Ontario;* b. 19 July 1955; s. of the late Dalton, Sr and Elizabeth McGuinty; ed Univ. of Ottawa, McMaster Univ.; practiced law Ottawa; mem. Ont. Legislature representing Ottawa South 1990–; Leader Ont. Liberal Party 1996–; Premier of Ont. 2003–, also Minister of Research and Innovation and Minister of Intergovernmental Affairs. *Address:* Office of the Premier, Legislative Building, Queen's Park, Toronto, ON M7A 1A1, Canada (office). *Fax:* (416) 325-3745 (office). *E-mail:* Dalton.McGuinty@premier.gov.on.ca (office). *Website:* www.premier.gov.on.ca (office).

McGUIRE, William W., MD; American business executive; practising physician specialising in cardiopulmonary medicine 1980–85; Pres. and CEO Peak Health Plan 1985–88; joined United HealthCare Corpn (renamed UnitedHealth Group) 1988, Pres. and COO 1989–91, CEO and Chair. 1991–2006; mem. Nat. Insts of Health Nat. Cancer Policy Bd; One of the 50 Best CEOs in America, Worth Magazine 2001. *Address:* c/o UnitedHealth Group, POB 1459, Minneapolis, MN 55440-1459, USA (office).

McGWIRE, Mark David; American fmr professional baseball player; b. 1 Oct. 1963, Pomona, Calif.; s. of John McGwire and Ginger McGwire; brother of Dan McGwire, fmr pro baseball player; m. Kathy McGwire (divorced); one s.; ed Univ. of Southern Calif.; with Oaklands Athletics 1984–97; St Louis Cardinals 1997–2001; mem U.S. Olympic baseball team 1984; player World Series 1988–90; on All-Star team 1987–92, 1995–96, 1999; scored record 70 home runs during 1997–98 season and a total of 583 throughout career; retd 2001; f. Mark McGwire Foundation for Children 1987; American League Rookie of the Year, Baseball Writers' Asscn of America 1987; Golden Glove Award 1990; Silver Slugger Award 1992; Sportsman of the Year (jtly with Sammy Sosa), Sports Illustrated 1998, Player of the Month 1999, Player of the Year, Assoc. Press 1999. *Publications:* Mark McGwire: Home Run Hero (biog.) by Rob Rains 1999. *Address:* Mark McGwire Foundation for Children, c/o Jim Milner, 6615 East Pacific Coast Highway, Suite 260, Long Beach, CA 90803, USA. *Website:* www.mcgwire.com.

MACH, David Stefan, MA, RA; British sculptor; *Professor of Sculpture, Royal Academy;* b. 18 March 1956, Methil, Fife; s. of Joseph Mach and Martha Cassidy; m. Lesley June White 1979; ed Buckhaven High School, Duncan of Jordanstone Coll. of Art, Dundee and Royal Coll. of Art; full-time sculptor 1982–; Prof. of Inspiration and Discovery, Univ. of Dundee 1994–; Visiting Prof., Edin. Coll. of Art 1999–; Prof. of Sculpture, Royal Acad. 2000–; sculptures exhibited at galleries in England, Scotland, New York, São Paulo Biennale, Venice Biennale; Hon. Prof., Sculpture Dept, Edin. Coll. of Art 1999; Pat Holmes Memorial Prize 1975, Duncan of Drumfork Travelling Scholarship 1976, SED Minor Travelling Scholarship 1977, SED Major Travelling Scholarship 1978, RCA Drawing Prize 1982, City of Glasgow Lord Provost Prize 1992. *Leisure interests:* gardening, tennis, travelling, driving, films, television. *Address:* 64 Canonbie Road, Forest Hill, London, SE23 3AG, England (home). *Telephone:* (20) 8649-7947 (office); (20) 8699-1668 (home). *Fax:* (20) 8699-1211 (home). *E-mail:* davidmach@davidmach.com (office). *Website:* www.davidmach.com (office).

MACHADO VENTURA, José Ramón; Cuban physician and politician; *First Vice-President, Council of State;* b. 26 Oct. 1930, San Antonio de las Vueltas, Las Villas; ed Universidad de La Habana; served as guerrilla in Sierra Maestra mountains and cared for mems of rebel army during Cuban Revolution against Batista govt; Asst to the President and Chief of Medical Services, City of Havana 1959; Minister of Health 1960–67; Politburo Del. to Matanzas Prov. 1968–71; First Sec. Havana Provincial Cttee, Partido Comunista de Cuba 1971–75, mem. Secr. of Cen. Cttee 1975–2008, mem. Politburo 1975–; Deputy, Asamblea Nacional del Poder Popular (Parl.) for Guantánamo 1976–2008; Vice-Pres and Secr. Political Bureau 1976–2008, First Vice-Pres. 2008–. *Address:* Oficina del Primer Vice-Presidente, Havana, Cuba.

MACHARSKI, HE Cardinal Franciszek, DTheol; Polish ecclesiastic; *Archbishop of Kraków;* b. 20 May 1927, Kraków; ed Jagiellonian Univ., Kraków, Fribourg Univ., Switzerland; ordained priest, Kraków 1950; engaged in pastoral work 1950–56; taught pastoral theology Pontifical Faculty of Theology, Kraków 1962–68; Rector, Kraków Seminary 1970–78; Archbishop of Kraków 1979–; High Chancellor, Pontifical Acad. of Theology, Kraków; cr. Cardinal (Cardinal-Priest of S. Giovanni a Porta Latina) 1979; mem. Sacred Congregation for the Clergy 1979–, Sacred Congregation for Catholic Educ. 1979–, Sacred Congregation for Bishops 1983–, Sacred Congregation for Insts of Consecrated Life and Socs of Apostolic Life 1989–, Council for Public Affairs 1984–88; mem. Council of Cardinals and Bishops 1988–; mem. Secr. for Non-Believers 1981–86, Congregatation for the Clergy 1999–, Congregation for the Evangelization of Peoples 1999–; Vice-Pres. Episcopate of Poland, Conf. 1979–94; mem. Main Council Episcopate of Poland 1996–, Episcopate Cttee for Gen. Ministry 1989–; Vice-Chair. Scientific Council of Episcopate of Poland, 1984–89, Episcopate Cttee for Ministry of Working People 1981; Chair. Episcopate Cttee for Laity 1979–91, Episcopate Cttee for Catholic Science 1981–94; mem. Episcopate Cttee for Ministry of Priesthood 1996–, Perm. Council of Episcopate of Poland 1996–2002; Chair. Second Ass. of Synod of Bishops of Europe 1999; Papal Legate to Int. Marian and Mariological Congress Kevelaer 1987, Nat. Eucharistic Congress, Bratislava 2000; hon. citizen of many Polish cities and towns; Order of Smile 1998; Dr hc (Fu Jen Catholic Univ., Taipei, Adamson Univ., Manila) 1989, (Acad. of Catholic Theology, Warsaw) 1992, (Pontifical Acad. of Theology, Kraków) 2000, (Jagiellonian Univ., Kraków) 2000. *Publications:* Collections: Sermons at the Calvary Shrine 1994, To Serve with Wisdom 1994, From the See of St Stanislaus 1995; more than 250 articles, sermons, speeches and pastoral letters. *Address:* Kuria Metropolitalna, ul. Franciszkańska 3, 31-004 Kraków, Poland (office). *Telephone:* (12) 6288100 (office); (12) 4294749 (office). *Fax:* (12) 4294405 (office). *E-mail:* kuria@diecezja.krakow.pl (office). *Website:* www .diecezja.krakow.pl (office).

MACHEL, Graça, DBE BA; Mozambican university chancellor and international organization official; *Chancellor, University of Cape Town;* b. 1945, southern Gaza Prov.; m. 1st Samora Machel 1975 (died 1986); two c.; m. 2nd Nelson Mandela (q.v.) 1998; ed Univ. of Lisbon; worked underground for Front for Liberation of Mozambique (Frelimo) movt during country's war of independence from Portugal, Deputy Dir Frelimo Secondary School in Tanzania 1974; Minister for Educ. 1975–86; mem. Int. Steering Cttee, World Conf. on Educ. for All 1990; f. Foundation for Community Devt 1990; Chair. UNICEF study 1994, currently UNICEF Goodwill Amb., Pres. UNESCO Mozambique Nat. Comm.; Chair. of Nat. Org. of Children of Mozambique; Chancellor Univ. of Cape Town 1999–; Hon. DBE (UK) 2007; hon. degree (Univ. of the Western Cape) 1992, (Univ. of Évora) 2008; Nansen Medal (for outstanding contrib. on behalf of refugee children) 1995, InterAction Humanitarian Award 1997, CARE Award, North-South Prize 1998. *Address:* Office of the Chancellor, University of Cape Town, Private Bag, Rondebosch 7701, South Africa (office). *Website:* www.uct.ac.za (office).

MACHEN, J. Bernard (Bernie), DDS, MS, PhD; American dental surgeon, educational psychologist and university administrator; *President, University of Florida;* b. Greenwood, Miss.; m. Chris Machen; two s. one d.; ed Vanderbilt Univ., St Louis Univ., Univ. of Iowa; Diplomate, American Bd of Pediatric Dentistry; veteran US Army Maj.; Prof. and Assoc. Dean, Univ. of N Carolina School of Dentistry 1983–89; Dean School of Dentistry, Univ. of Michigan 1989–95, Provost and Exec. Vice-Pres. for Academic Affairs, Univ. of Michigan 1995–97; Pres. Univ. of Utah 1997–2003; Pres. Univ. of Florida 2004–; mem. NAS Inst. of Medicine Cttee on Educating Dentists for the Future 1992–95; fmr Chief of Dept of Extension Services at US Army Inst. of Dental Research; Pres. American Asscn of Dental Schools 1987. *Address:* Office of the President, 226 Tigert Hall, PO Box 113150, Gainesville, FL 32611, USA (office). *Telephone:* (352) 392-1311 (office). *Fax:* (352) 392-9506 (office). *E-mail:* president@ufl.edu (office). *Website:* www.president.ufl.edu (office).

McHENRY, Donald F., MSc; American diplomatist and academic; *Professor of Diplomacy, Georgetown University;* b. 13 Oct. 1936, St Louis, Mo.; m. Mary Williamson (divorced 1978); one s. two d.; ed Illinois State Univ., Southern Illinois and Georgetown Univs; taught at Howard Univ., Washington 1959–62; joined Dept of State 1963, Head Dependent Areas Section, Office of UN Political Affairs 1965–68; Asst to US Sec. of State 1969; Special Asst to Dept Counselor 1969–71; lecturer, School of Foreign Service, Georgetown Univ., Guest Scholar, The Brookings Inst. and Int. Affairs Fellow, Council on Foreign Relations (on leave from State Dept) 1971–73; resgnd from State Dept 1973; Project Dir Humanitarian Policy Studies, Carnegie Endowment for Int. Peace, Washington 1973–76; served Pres. Carter's transition team 1976–77; Amb. and Deputy Perm. Rep. to UN 1977–79, Perm. Rep. 1979–81; Distinguished Prof. in the Practice of Diplomacy, School of Foreign Service, Georgetown Univ. 1981–; Pres. IRC Group; Dir Coca Cola Co., Inst. for Int. Econs, The American Ditchley Foundation, mem. Council on Foreign Relations (fmr Dir); mem. Editorial Bd Foreign Policy Magazine; fmr Trustee The Brookings Inst., fmr Trustee Johnson Foundation; Chair. Ford Foundation Int. Fellows Program; fmr Chair. Bd Africare; fmr Gov. Mayo Foundation, American Stock Exchange; fmr Dir GlaxoSmithKline PLC, Fleet Boston Financial, Fleet Boston Bank, AT&T, Int. Paper Co.; Fellow American Acad. of

Arts and Sciences; Superior Honor Award, Dept of State 1966. *Publication:* Micronesia: Trust Betrayed 1975. *Address:* School of Foreign Service, Georgetown University, ICC 301, Washington, DC 20057, USA (office). *Telephone:* (202) 687-6083 (office). *Fax:* (202) 687-1427 (office). *E-mail:* mchenryd@georgetown.edu. *Website:* www.georgetown.edu/sfs (office).

MACHI, Sueo, PhD; Japanese atomic energy scientist; *National Co-ordinator, Forum for Nuclear Cooperation in Asia;* b. 15 Jan. 1934; s. of Yosaku Machi and Kichi Machi; m. 1964; one s. one d.; ed Univs of Shizuoka and Kyoto; employed in Japanese petrochemical industry 1959–63; joined Takasaki Radiation Chem. Research Establishment (TRCRE) of Japan Atomic Energy Research Inst. (JAERI) 1963; Gen. Man. Process Lab. II, TRCRE 1972–78; Gen. Man. Radiation Eng Section, TRCRE 1978–80; Section Head, Industrial Applications and Chem. Section and Co-ordinator of Regional Co-operative Agreement for Asia and Pacific, IAEA; Deputy Dir Office of Planning, JAERI, Tokyo; Dir Dept of Research, TRCRE 1986, later Dir Dept of Devt; Dir-Gen. TRCRE 1989–91; apptd Deputy Dir-Gen. and Head of Dept of Research and Isotopes, IAEA 1991, later Deputy Dir-Gen. Dept of Nuclear Sciences; fmr Sr Man. Dir Japan Atomic Industrial Forum and Nat. Co-ordinator Forum for Nuclear Co-operation in Asia; Commr Atomic Energy Comm. of Japan; Dr hc (Bucharest) 1995; Japan Chemical Soc. Prize 1969, The Iwatani Prize 1990, Minister of Science and Tech. Prize 1990. *Address:* Forum for Nuclear Cooperation in Asia, 5-18-7 Shimbashi, Minato-ku, Tokyo, 105-0004, Japan. *Telephone:* (3) 5470-1983. *Fax:* (3) 5470-1991. *E-mail:* fnca@fnca.mext.go.jp.

MACHIDA, Akira; Japanese judge; *Chief Justice, Supreme Court;* b. 16 Oct. 1936; ed Univ. of Tokyo; legal apprentice 1959; Asst Judge Tokyo Dist Family Court 1961, Sapporo Dist Muroran Br. Family Court and Civil Affairs Bureau, Gen. Secr. of Supreme Court 1961; Judge Sapporo Dist Family Court 1971; Chief Budget Div., Financial Affairs Bureau, Gen. Secr. of Supreme Court 1973, Gen. Affairs Div. 1975; Counsellor Cabinet Legislation Bureau 1977; Judge Tokyo Dist Court, Presiding Judge of Div. 1983; Dir Sec./Public Information Div., Gen. Secr. of Supreme Court 1984, Dir Financial Affairs Bureau 1986; Chief Judge Kofu Dist Court and Kofu Family Court 1991, Chiba Dist Court 1993; Judge Tokyo High Court, Presiding Judge of Div. 1994; Pres. Fukuoka High Court 1998, Tokyo High Court 1999; Justice Supreme Court 2000, currently Chief Justice. *Address:* Supreme Court of Japan, 4-2 Hayabusa-cho, Chiyoda-ku, Tokyo 102-8651, Japan (office). *Telephone:* (3) 3264-8111 (office). *Website:* www.courts.go.jp (office).

MACHIDA, Katsuhiko; Japanese electronics industry executive; *Chairman and CEO, Sharp Corporation;* ed Kyoto Univ.; joined Sharp Corpn 1969, various positions in audio-visual and household appliance depts, with Dept of Int. Business 1992–97, Pres. and Chair. Man. Bd, Sharp Corpn 1998–2007, Chair. and CEO 2007–. *Address:* Sharp Corpn, 22 Nagaike-cho, Abeno-ku, Osaka 545-8522, Japan (office). *Telephone:* (6) 6621-1221 (office). *Fax:* (6) 6627-1759 (office). *E-mail:* info@sharp.co.jp (office). *Website:* www.sharp.co.jp (office); sharp-world.com (office).

MACHIMURA, Nobutaka; Japanese politician; b. 17 Oct. 1944; ed Faculty of Econs, Univ. of Tokyo, Wesleyan Univ., USA; joined Ministry of Int. Trade and Industry (MITI) 1969, seconded to Nat. Land Agency 1974, seconded to Japan External Trade Org., NY Trade Center 1979, Dir of Planning Div., Petroleum Dept, Agency of Natural Resources and Energy, MITI –1982; elected to House of Reps 1983–, Chair. Standing Cttee on Health and Welfare 1996–97; Parl. Vice-Minister, Ministry of Educ., Science, Sports and Culture 1989–90; Dir Cultural Affairs Div., Liberal Democratic Party (LDP) 1990–92, Dir Nat. Defence Div., Policy Research Council 1992, Acting Sec.-Gen. LDP 2001–02, Dir-Gen. Election Bureau 2002–04; Minister of Educ., Science, Sports and Culture 1997–98, 2000–01; State Sec. for Foreign Affairs 1998–2000; Special Adviser to Prime Minister 2000; Dir-Gen. Science and Tech. Agency 2000–01; Minister of Foreign Affairs 2004–05, 2007; Chief Cabinet Sec. and Minister of State for the Abduction Issue 2007–08 (resgnd). *Address:* Liberal-Democratic Party (LDP), 1-11-23, Nagata-cho, Chiyoda-ku, Tokyo 100-8910, Japan (office). *Telephone:* (3) 3581-6211 (office). *E-mail:* koho@ldp.jimin.or.jp (office). *Website:* www.jimin.jp (office).

MACHINEA, José Luis, PhD; Argentine international organization official; *Executive Secretary, United Nations Economic Commission for Latin America and the Caribbean;* ed Univ. of Minnesota, USA; fmr Prof. of Macroeconomics, Catholic Univ. of Argentina; fmr Chief of Public Finance Dept and Chief of Research Dept at Argentine Cen. Bank, later Pres. Argentine Cen. Bank; Under-Sec. of Political Economy and Under-Sec. of Planning 1980s; consultant to World Bank and Inter-American Devt Bank 1990s (currently Special Expert in Integration and Trade, Integration and Regional Dept and mem. External Advisory Group); Dir of Research, Industrial Devt Inst. of the Argentine Industrial Union 1992–97; Pres. consultancy firm 1995–99; Pres. Argentine Foundation for Devt with Equity 1998–99; Minister of Economy 1999–2001; Exec. Sec. ECLAC 2003–. *Publications:* numerous articles in books and journals on macroeconomics, monetary and financial issues. *Address:* Economic Commission for Latin America and the Caribbean, Casilla de Correo 179-D, Santiago de Chile, Chile (office). *Telephone:* (2) 471-2000 (office); (2) 210-2000 (office); (2) 208-5051 (office). *Fax:* (2) 208-0252 (office). *E-mail:* eseclac@eclac.cl (office). *Website:* www.eclac.cl (office).

MACHULSKI, Juliusz; Polish film director, screenwriter and producer; b. 10 March 1955, Olsztyn; s. of Jan Machulski and Halina Machulski; m. 1995; two c.; ed State Acad. of Film Television and Theatre, Łódź, California Inst. of Arts, Valencia, USA; CEO Studio Filmowe Zebra 1988–; acted in Personnel (Personel) by Krzysztof Kieslowski, The Index (Indeks) by Janusz Kijowski, and Kill Me, Cop (Zabij mnie, glino) by Jacek Bromski; lectured on film directing at Hunter Coll., New York 1993; producer of about 25 films; Wyspianski Award 1985, Chair. of the Cttee of Cinematography Award 1990, Ministry of Culture and Art Award 1998. *Films:* Direct Connection (TV) 1979, Vabank 1981, Sexmission 1983, Vabank II 1984, Kingsajz 1987, Déjà vu 1989, V.I.P. 1991, The Squadron 1993, Girl Guide 1995, Mothers, Wives and Mistresses (TV series) 1995–98, Kiler 1997, Two Kilers 1999, Money Isn't Everything 2001, Superproduction 2003, Vinci (Prize for Best Screenplay, Polish Film Festival, Gdynia 2004) 2004. *Television play:* The Jury 1995, Meridian 19 2003. *Publications:* Vabank 1 and 2 (scripts) 1986, V.I.P. (script) 1990, Kiler (script) 1998, Kiler 2 1999, Sexmission 2001. *Leisure interest:* reading. *Address:* Studio Filmowe Zebra, ul. Puławska 61, 02-595 Warsaw, Poland (office). *Telephone:* (22) 845 54 84 (office).

MACHUNGO, Mário Fernandes da Graça; Mozambican politician; *President, Seguradora Internacional de Moçambique;* b. 1 Dec. 1940, Chicuque-Maxixe, Inhambane Prov.; m. Maria Eugénia Paiva Cruz; two d.; ed Inst. for Higher Learning in Econ. and Financial Sciences (ISCEF), Portugal; became underground mem. Mozambique Liberation Front (FRELIMO) 1962; Pres. Students' Union, ISCEF 1964–65; subsequently expelled from ISCEF; completed studies 1969; returned to Mozambique, worked as economist with Nat. Devt Bank; apptd. Minister for Econ. Co-operation in transitional Govt 1974; Minister for Trade and Industry 1975–76, for Industry and Energy 1976–78, for Agric. 1978–80, for Agric. and Planning 1980–83, for Planning 1983–94, Prime Minister of Mozambique 1986–94; elected to Cen. Cttee and Political Bureau of FRELIMO Party 1977, re-elected 1983, elected to Secr. and fmr Sec. for Econ. Policy 1986; Chair. Banco Internacional de Moçambique 1995; currently Pres. Seguradora Internacional de Moçambique (insurance co.). *Address:* Seguradora Internacional de Moçambique, Av 25 Setembro 1800, Maputo, Mozambique (office). *Telephone:* 21430959 (office). *Fax:* 21430241 (office). *E-mail:* simseg@zebra.uem.mz (office).

MACINA, Stefano; San Marino politician; *Secretary of State for Finance, the Budget, Post and Relations with the Azienda Autonoma di Stato Filatelica e Numismatica (AASFN);* b. 23 Jan. 1956; m.; one d.; Sec. Fed. Industry, San Marino Labour Confed. –1980, Adjunct Gen. Sec. 1981–84, Gen. Sec. 1984–91; Sec. Partito Progressista Democratico Sammarinese (PPDS) 1992–96, mem. Grand and Gen. Council 1993, Pres. Group to advise PPDS-IM 1996; Sec. of State for Econ. Planning, Foreign Trade, Social Security, Labour and Co-operation 2000–01; Pres. Comm. on Foreign Policy, Emigration and Immigration, Information, Transport and Telecommunications, Security and Public Order 2002–03; Dir Centro Commerciale 'Azzurro' 2003–06; Sec. of State for Finance, the Budget, Post and Relations with the Azienda Autonoma di Stato Filatelica e Numismatica (AASFN) 2006–; mem. several orgs and institutional comms, including Inter-parl. Group and Council of the XII; mem. Secr. Partito dei Socialisti e dei Democratici; Pres. San Marino Baseball Club. *Address:* Secretariat of State for Finance, the Budget, Post and Relations with the Azienda Autonoma di Stato Filatelica e Numismatica (AASFN), Palazzo Begni, Contrada Omerelli, 47890 San Marino (office). *Telephone:* (0549) 882242 (office). *Fax:* (0549) 882244 (office). *E-mail:* segr.finanze@omniway.sm (office). *Website:* www.finanze.sm (office).

McINERNEY, Jay; American writer; b. 1955; m. 1st Linda Rossiter; m. 2nd Merry Raymond; m. 3rd Helen Bransford 1991; one s. one d.; ed Williams Univ. *Publications include:* Bright Lights, Big City 1984, Ransom 1986, Story of My Life 1988, Brightness Falls 1992, The Last of the Savages 1996, Model Behavior 1998, How It Ended 2000, The Good Life (novel) 2006, A Hedonist in the Cellar: Adventures in Wine 2006, The Last Bachelor 2009, How it Ended: New and Collected Stories 2009. *Address:* c/o Bloomsbury Publishing Plc, 36 Soho Square, London, W1D 3QY, England (office). *Website:* www.bloonsbury.com (office).

MacINNIS, Joseph Beverley, CM, MD; Canadian marine research scientist; b. 2 March 1937, Barrie, Ont.; s. of Allistair MacInnis and Beverly Saunders; m. Deborah J. Ferris 1971; one s. three d.; ed Univs of Toronto and Pennsylvania; Pres. Undersea Research Ltd and has held consulting contracts for U.S. Navy, Smithsonian Inst., IBM, Canadian Ministry of State for Science and Tech. and Canadian Dept of Environment; est. SUBLIMNOS, Canada's first underwater manned station programme 1969; led 14 scientific expeditions into Arctic 1970–79 and during third expedition, SUB-IGLOO, world's first polar dive station established under ice; co-ordinated diving programme for ICE Station LOREX 1979; led team which discovered remains of English barque Breadalbane, sunk in 1853, 700 miles north of Arctic Circle in 340 feet of water; host, The New Wave (CBC television series) 1975–76, The Newfoundlanders: Voices from the Sea 1978; scientific consultant, Mysteries of the Sea (ABC) 1979; co-ordinator, Shot Point 260 (Texaco Canada film), Breakthrough (Dome Petroleum film) 1979; consultant Titanic Project 1985; first Canadian to dive to the Titanic 1987; Co-leader IMAX-Titanic Expedition 1991; has lectured and shown his films in all parts of world including Israel, Germany, Australia, the Philippines, USSR and Singapore; Pres. Undersea Research Ltd; mem. Canadian Environmental Advisory Council, Canadian Council of Fitness and Health; Fellow, Royal Canadian Geographical Soc.; Hon. FRCP; Hon. LLD; Dr hc (Queen's) 1990. *Publications:* Underwater Images 1971,Underwater Man 1974, Coastline Canada 1982, Shipwreck Shores 1982, The Land that Devours Ships 1984, Titanic: In a New Light 1992, Saving the Oceans 1992 (Gen. Ed.), more than 30 scientific papers and articles in Scientific American, National Geographic Magazine etc. *Address:* 14 Dale Avenue, Toronto, Ont. M4W 1K4, Canada.

McINTOSH OF HUDNALL, Baroness (Life Peer), cr. 1999, of Hampstead in the London Borough of Camden; **Genista Mary McIntosh,** BA, FRSA; British arts consultant; b. 23 Sept. 1946, London; d. of Geoffrey Tandy and Maire Tandy; m. Neil Scott Wishart McIntosh 1971 (divorced 1990); one s. one d.; ed Hemel Hempstead Grammar School, Univ. of York; Casting Dir, RSC 1972–77, Planning Controller 1977–84, Sr Admin. 1986–90, Assoc. Producer

1990; Dir Marmont Man. Ltd 1984–86; Exec. Dir Royal Nat. Theatre 1990–96, 1997–2002; Chief Exec. Royal Opera House Jan.–May 1997; Prin. The Guildhall School of Music and Drama 2002–03; mem. Bd Theatres Trust, The Roundhouse Trust, Southbank Sinfonia, Foundation for Sport and the Arts, Nat. Opera Studio, Royal Acad. of Dramatic Art (RADA); Patron, Helena Kennedy Bursary Scheme; Hon. Fellow, Goldsmiths Coll. 2003; DUnivs (York) 1998, (Middx) 2002, (City) 2002. *Leisure interests:* music, gardening, reading. *Address:* House of Lords, Westminster, London, SW1A 0PW, England (office). *Telephone:* (20) 7219-8732 (office).

McINTYRE, Sir Donald Conroy, Kt, CBE, OBE; British singer (bass); b. 22 Oct. 1934, Auckland, NZ; s. of George Douglas and Hermyn McIntyre; m. Jill Redington 1961; three d.; ed Mt Albert Grammar School, Auckland, Auckland Teachers' Training Coll. and Guildhall School of Music, London; Prin. Bass, Sadler's Wells Opera 1960–67; with Royal Opera House, Covent Garden 1967–; annual appearances at Bayreuth Festival 1967–81; frequent int. guest appearances; Hon. DMus (Auckland) 1992; Fidelio Medal, AIDO 1989, NZ Award for Outstanding Contribs, Festival of the Arts 1990. *Roles include:* Wotan and Wanderer in Der Ring, Dutchman in Der Fliegende Holländer, Telramund in Lohengrin, Barak in Die Frau ohne Schatten, Pizzaro in Fidelio, Golaud in Pelléas et Mélisande, Kurwenal and King Marke in Tristan and Isolde, Gurnemanz, Klingsor and Amfortas in Parsifal, Heyst in Victory, Jochanaan in Salome, Macbeth, Scarpia in Tosca, the Count in Marriage of Figaro, Nick Shadow in The Rake's Progress, Hans Sachs in Die Meistersinger, Dr. Schöne in Woyzeck, Cardillac in Cardillac by Hindemith, Rocco in Fidelio, The Doctor in Der Freischütz, Prospero in Un Re In Asloto, Sarastro in The Magic Flute, Balstrode in Peter Grimes, Telramund in Lohengrin, Prus in The Makropoulos Case, Rheingold, The Ring (video). *Recordings include:* Pelléas et Mélisande, Oedipus Rex, Il Trovatore. *Leisure interests:* farm, tennis, walking. *Address:* Ingpen & Williams, 7 St George's Court, 131 Putney Bridge Road, London, SW15 2PA, England (office); Fox Hill Farm, Jackass Lane, Keston, Bromley, Kent BR2 6AN, England (home). *Telephone:* (1689) 855368 (home). *Fax:* (1689) 860724 (home).

MacINTYRE, Iain, MB, ChB, PhD, DSc, FRS, FRCP, FRCPath, FMedSci; British professor of chemical pathology; *Professor Emeritus and Research Director, William Harvey Research Institute and Foundation, Queen Mary's School of Medicine and Dentistry;* b. 30 Aug. 1924, Glasgow; s. of John MacIntyre and Margaret Fraser Shaw; m. Mabel Wilson Jamieson 1947; one d.; ed Jordanhill Coll. School, Univs of Glasgow and London; Asst Clinical Pathologist, United Sheffield Hosps and Hon. Demonstrator in Biochemistry, Univ. of Sheffield 1948–52; Registrar in Chemical Pathology, Royal Postgraduate Medical School, Hammersmith Hosp., London 1952–54, Sir Jack Drummond Memorial Fellow 1954–56, Asst Lecturer in Chemical Pathology 1956–59, Lecturer 1959–63, Reader 1963–67, Prof. of Endocrine Chem. 1967–82, Dir Endocrine Unit 1967–89, Chair. Academic Bd 1986–89; Prof. of Chemical Pathology, Univ. of London 1982–89, also Research Dir William Harvey Research Inst., St Bartholomew's and the Royal London School of Medicine and Dentistry, Queen Mary Coll., London, now Prof. Emer.; Visiting Scientist, NIH, Bethesda, Md, USA 1960–61; Visiting Prof. of Medicine, Univ. of Calif., San Francisco 1964, Univ. of Melbourne 1980; Visiting Lecturer, USSR Acad. of Sciences, Moscow 1978; Visiting Prof., St George's Hosp. Medical School 1989–; Vice-Pres. English Chess Asscn 1989–; Founder Fellow, Acad. of Medical Sciences 1998; Hon. mem. Asscn of American Physicians 1998; Hon. MD (Turin), (Sheffield) 2002; Gairdner Int. Award, Toronto 1967, A.J.S. McFadzean Lecture, Univ. of Hong Kong 1981, Transatlantic Lecture, American Endocrine Soc. 1987, Per Edman Memorial Lecturer, Melbourne 1990, Elsevier Int. Award 1992, Paget Foundation John B. Johnson Award 1995, Royal Soc. Buchanan Medal 2006. *Publications:* numerous articles on endocrinology. *Leisure interests:* tennis, chess, music. *Address:* Centre for Clinical Pharmacology, Barts and The London, Queen Mary's School of Medicine and Dentistry, John Vane Science Centre, Charterhouse Square, London, EC1M 6BQ (office); Great Broadhurst Farm, Broad Oak, Heathfield, East Sussex, TN21 8UX, England (home). *Telephone:* (20) 7882-6168 (office); (1435) 883515 (home). *Fax:* (20) 7882-3408 (office); (1435) 883611 (home). *E-mail:* i.macintyre@qmul.ac.uk (office). *Website:* www.qmul.ac.uk (office).

MACK, Connie, III; American banker and fmr politician; *Senior Policy Advisor, Government Advocacy and Public Policy Practice Group, King and Spalding LLP;* b. (Cornelius McGillicuddy, III), 29 Oct. 1940, Philadelphia; s. of Cornelius M. McGillicuddy and Susan McGillicuddy (née Sheppard); m. Ludie Priscilla 1960; one s. one d.; ed Univ. of Fla; Vice-Pres. Business Devt First Nat. Bank, Ft Myers, Fla 1968–71; Sr Vice-Pres., Dir Sun Bank, Cape Coral, Fla 1971–75; Pres., Dir Fla Nat. Bank, Cape Coral 1972–82; mem. US House of Reps 1983–89, Senator from Fla 1989–2000; Republican Conf. Chair. 105th Congress 1996; Sr Policy Advisor, Shaw Pittman 2001; currently Sr Policy Advisor Govt Advocacy and Public Policy Practice Group, King and Spalding LLP, Washington, DC; Chair. Lee Moffitt Cancer Center and Research Inst., Tampa; mem. Bd of Dirs Darden Restaurants, Exact Sciences Corpn, Genzyme Corpn, Moody's Corpn, Mutual of America Life Insurance Co., American Momentum Bank, Spirit Aerosystems; Trustee Emer. American Cancer Soc. Foundation; mem. Pres's Advisory Panel for Fed. Tax Reform 2005; Republican;; Hon. DJur (Tampa Univ.); Hon. DHumLitt (St Thomas Univ.); Hon. Dr of Public Service (Miami Univ.); American Cancer Soc. Courage Award 1992, Nat. Coalition for Cancer Research Lifetime Achievement Award 1999, Susan G. Komen Breast Cancer Foundation Betty Ford Award. *Address:* King and Spalding LLP, 1700 Pennsylvania Avenue, NW, Washington, DC 20006, USA (office). *Telephone:* (202) 661-7952 (office). *Fax:* (202) 626-3737 (office). *E-mail:* cmack@kslaw.com (office). *Website:* www.kslaw.com (office).

MACK, James F., BA; American diplomatist and international organization executive; *Executive Secretary, Inter-American Drug Abuse Control Commission (Comisión Interamericana para el Control del Abuso de Drogas—CICAD);* b. 1941, Norwalk, Conn.; m. Sheila Marvin; four c.; ed Cornell Univ., Ithaca, NY; raised in Rye, NY; served as Peace Corps volunteer in Honduras; joined US Foreign Service 1966, first diplomatic postings were as political officer in Saigon and Nha Trang, S Viet Nam, and as Political Advisor to US Commdr of I Corps in Danang, served as S Viet Nam analyst in Bureau of Intelligence and Research, Dept of State 1969, as Political/Labor Officer, San José, Costa Rica, as Labor Officer, São Paulo, Brazil, as Prin. Officer, Ponta Delgada, Azores, Portugal, subsequent positions included Guatemala/Belize Desk Officer, Chief of Office of Labor/Man. Relations, Dept of State, Political Counselor at Embassy in San Salvador, Deputy Chief of Mission, Embassy in Asuncion, Dir Office of Andean Affairs, Dept of State 1990, Deputy Chief of Mission, Embassy in Quito, where also served as Chargé d'affaires for two years, Deputy Chief of Mission, Embassy in Lima 1994–97, additionally, while posted to US Embassies in Ecuador, Paraguay and Peru, coordinated US anti-narcotics assistance to those countries, Amb. to Guyana 1997–2000, now retd career mem. Sr Foreign Service, US Dept of State, served as Prin. Deputy Asst Sec. in Bureau of Int. Narcotics and Law Enforcement Affairs; Co-ordinator Inter-American Observatory on Drugs, Inter-American Drug Abuse Control Comm. (Comisión Interamericana para el Control del Abuso de Drogas—CICAD), OAS 2002, Exec. Sec. CICAD 2004–; numerous State Dept awards for superior service. *Address:* Inter-American Drug Abuse Control Commission (CICAD), 1889 F Street, NW, Washington, DC 20006, USA (office). *Telephone:* (202) 458-3178 (office). *Fax:* (202) 458-3658 (office). *E-mail:* oidcicad@oas.org (office). *Website:* www.cicad.oas.org (office).

MACK, John J.; American financial services industry executive; *Chairman and CEO, Morgan Stanley;* b. 1944; ed Duke Univ.; joined Morgan Stanley 1972, positions in bond dept 1972–76, Vice-Pres. 1976–77, Prin. 1977–79, Man. Dir 1979–85, Head Worldwide Taxable Fixed Income Div. 1985–92, apptd Dir 1987, Chair. Operating Cttee 1992–93, Pres. Morgan Stanley 1993–97; Pres., COO and Dir Morgan Stanley Dean Witter & Co. (later Morgan Stanley) 1997–2001; CEO Credit Suisse First Boston 2001–04, Co-CEO Credit Suisse Group 2003–04; Chair. and CEO Morgan Stanley 2005–; mem. Bd of Dirs Catalyst Inc., Celiant Corpn, Cousins Properties Inc., NY Stock Exchange; fmr Dir CICC (first investment bank in China), India Business School; mem. Int. Advisory Panel, Monetary Authority of Singapore, Chair's Advisory Cttee Nat. Asscn of Securities Dealers (NASD); Vice-Chair. NYC 2012 (NY City bid for Olympic Games); Chair. Bd of Trustees NY Presbyterian Hosp., Columbia and Cornell Univ. Hosps; mem. Bd of Trustees Duke Univ.; Trustee, Doris Duke Charitable Foundation. *Address:* Morgan Stanley, 1585 Broadway, New York, NY 10036, USA (office). *Telephone:* (212) 761-4000 (home). *Fax:* (212) 762-0575 (office). *E-mail:* mediainquiries@morganstanley.com (office). *Website:* www.morganstanley.com (office).

MACK, Timothy (Tim), BA; American athlete; b. 15 Sept. 1972, Cleveland, OH; ed Univ. of Tenn.; career as personal trainer; coached by Jim Bemiller; winner Gold Medal for pole vault, Golden League, Oslo 2002, Grand Prix, Rio de Janeiro 2001, Palo Alto 2002, Osaka 2002, 2004, Olympic Games, Athens (with performance of 19' 6.3") 2004; winner Bronze Medal for pole vault, Golden League, Zurich 2002. *Leisure interest:* coaching Knoxville youth pole vaulters in spare time. *Address:* c/o USA Track & Field, 1 RCA Dome, Suite 140, Indianapolis, IN 46225, USA (office). *Website:* www.usatf.org (office).

MACK SMITH, Denis, CBE, MA, FBA; British author and fmr professor of history; b. 3 March 1920, London; s. of Wilfrid Mack Smith and Altiora Gauntlett; m. Catharine Stevenson; two d.; ed St Paul's Cathedral Choir School, Haileybury Coll., Peterhouse, Cambridge; Fellow, Tutor, Peterhouse, Cambridge 1947, now Hon. Fellow; Sr Research Fellow, All Souls Coll., Oxford 1962, Emer. Fellow 1987–; Extraordinary Fellow, Wolfson Coll., Oxford 1987–2000, Hon. Fellow 2000–; Chair. Asscn for the Study of Modern Italy 1988–; Grande Ufficiale, Italian Order of Merit, Hon. Citizen of Santa Margherita Ligure. *Publications:* Cavour and Garibaldi in 1860 1954, Garibaldi 1957, Medieval and Modern Sicily 1968, The Making of Italy 1796–1866 1968, Italy: A Modern History 1969, Victor Emanuel, Cavour and the Risorgimento 1971, Mussolini's Roman Empire 1976, Cento Anni di Vita Italiana attraverso il Corriere della Sera 1978, Mussolini 1981, Cavour 1985, Italy and its Monarchy 1989, Mazzini 1993, Modern Italy 1997, La Storia Manipolata 1998. *Leisure interests:* music, travel. *Address:* White Lodge, Osler Road, Headington, Oxford, OX3 9BJ, England. *Telephone:* (1865) 762878.

MACKAY, Charles Dorsey, MA, MBA; British business executive; *Chairman, TDG PLC;* b. 14 April 1940, Congleton; s. of the late Brig. Kenneth Mackay and Evelyn Ingram; m. Annmarie Joder-Pfeiffer 1964; two s. (one deceased) one d.; ed Cheltenham Coll., Queens' Coll. Cambridge, INSEAD, Fontainebleau; with BP Co. 1957–69, McKinsey & Co. 1969–76, Pakhoed Holding N.V. Rotterdam 1976–81; Dir Chloride Group PLC 1981–86, Chair. Overseas Div. 1981–85, Power Electronics Div. 1985–86; Dir Inchcape PLC 1986–96, Chair. and Chief Exec. Inchcape Pacific Ltd 1986–91, Chief Exec. 1991–96, Deputy Chair. 1995–96; mem. Bd of Dirs (non-exec.) Hongkong and Shanghai Banking Corpn Ltd 1986–92, HSBC Holdings 1992–98, Midland Bank 1992–93, British Airways 1993–96, Gucci Group NV 1997–2001, Johnson Matthey PLC (Sr Ind. Dir) 1999–, Eurotunnel Group 1997–2004 (Deputy Chair. 1999–2001, Chair. 2001–04); Deputy Chair. Thistle Hotels PLC 1996–2003; Chair. TDG PLC 2000–; mem. Bd INSEAD 2000–. *Leisure interests:* travel, fishing, tennis, skiing, classical music, opera, chess. *Address:* TDG PLC, Windsor House, 50 Victoria Street, London, SW1H 0NR, England (office). *Telephone:* (20) 7222-7411 (office). *E-mail:* mackayc@tdg.co.uk (office). *Website:* www.tdg.eu.com (office).

MACKAY, David, BBA; Australian business executive; *President and CEO, Kellogg Company;* b. 16 Aug. 1955, Hamilton, New Zealand; m. Michelle Mackay; two c.; ed Charles Sturt University, NSW; joined Kellogg Australia as Group Product Man. 1985–87, Category Dir for ready-to-eat cereals, Kellogg HQ, USA 1987–91, Marketing and Sales Dir, Australia 1991–92, Man. Dir Sara Lee Bakery, Australia 1992–98, Man. Dir Australia 1998, UK and Ireland 1998–2000, Sr Vice-Pres. Kellogg Co. and Pres. Kellogg USA 2000, Exec. Vice-Pres. Kellogg Co. 2000–03, Pres. and COO 2003–06, Pres. and CEO 2006–; mem. Bd of Dirs Fortune Brands, Inc., Kalamazoo Inst. of Arts. *Address:* Kellogg Company, 1 Kellogg Square, Battle Creek, MI 49016-3599, USA (office). *Telephone:* (269) 961-2000 (office). *Fax:* (269) 961-2871 (office). *Website:* www.kelloggcompany.com (office).

MacKAY, Sir Donald Iain, Kt, MA, FRSE, FRSGS; British economist; b. 27 Feb. 1937, Kobe, Japan; s. of William MacKay and Rhona MacKay; m. Diana Marjory Raffan 1961; one s. two d.; ed Dollar Acad., Aberdeen Univ.; with English Electric Co. 1959–62; Lecturer Aberdeen Univ. 1962–65, Prof. 1971–76; Lecturer Glasgow Univ. 1965–68, Sr Lecturer 1968–71; Consultant to Sec. of State for Scotland 1971–; Chair. Pieda PLC 1974–97; lecturer BAAS 1974; Lister Prof. Heriot-Watt Univ. 1976–82, Hon. Prof. 1990–; Chair. Scottish Enterprise 1993–97, Chair. DTZ Pieda Consulting 1997–, Scottish Science Trust 1997–99, Edin. Business School 1997–; Dir Grampian Holdings 1987–99, Chair. 1999–; mem. Scottish Econ. Council 1985–; Dr. hc (Stirling) 1994; Hon. DLitt (Aberdeen) 1994. *Publications:* Geographical Mobility and the Brain Drain 1969, Local Labour Markets and Wage Structures 1970, Labour Markets under Different Employment Conditions 1971, The Political Economy of North Sea Oil 1975, The Economics of Self-Government 1977; numerous articles in econ. and political journals. *Leisure interests:* bridge, golf, tennis. *Address:* Newfield, 14 Gamekeeper's Road, Edinburgh, EH4 6LU, Scotland. *Telephone:* (131) 336-1936.

MACKAY, Sir Francis H., Kt; British business executive; *Chairman, Carlton Partners LLP;* b. 24 Oct. 1944, London; m. Christine Mackay; one s., two d.; ed Bonaventure Grammar School; qualified as accountant, Appleby and Wood 1967; began career in financial positions with LCS Ltd, SGT PLC; fmr Finance Dir Global Ltd; Finance Dir Compass Group PLC 1986–91, CEO 1991–99, Chair. 1999–2006; Chair. (non-exec.) Kingfisher PLC 2001–06; Chair. Carlton Partners LLP 2006–; Chair. ISS (Denmark) 2006–08; f. Graysons Restaurants 2007. *Leisure interests:* flying, opera, golf, family. *Address:* Carlton Partners LLP, Berger House, 38 Berkeley Square, London, W1J 5AE, England (office). *Telephone:* (20) 7355-2211 (office). *Fax:* (20) 7355-4965 (office). *E-mail:* trishakeaveny@carltoncf.com (office). *Website:* www.carltonllp.com (office).

MACKAY, Graham, BSc (Eng), BCom; South African business executive; *Chief Executive, SABMiller plc;* joined South African Breweries (SAB) Ltd 1978, has held several sr positions in the group, including Exec. Chair. beer business in SA, Group Man. Dir 1997–99, Chief Exec. South African Breweries plc 1999– (now SABMiller plc following acquisition of American brewer Miller in 2002), mem. Corp. Accountability and Risk Assurance Cttee, Exec. Cttee, Vice-Chair. MillerCoors (formed from merger of US and Puerto Rico operations of respective subsidiaries of SABMiller plc and Molson Coors Brewing Co.) 2007–; Sr Dir (non-exec.) Reckitt Benckiser plc; Dir Philip Morris International Inc. 2008–; fmr mem. Bd of Dirs Amalgamated Beverage Industries Ltd, CRE Beverage Ltd (Hong Kong), several directorships with Standard Bank. *Address:* SABMiller plc, 1 Stanhope Gate, London, W1K 1AF, England (office). *Telephone:* (20) 7659-0100 (office). *Fax:* (20) 7659-0111 (office). *E-mail:* info@sabmiller.com (office). *Website:* www.sabmiller.com (office).

MacKAY, Peter Gordon; Canadian politician; *Minister of National Defence;* b. 27 Sept. 1965, New Glasgow, Nova Scotia; ed Acadia and Dalhousie Univs; called to the Bar, Nova Scotia 1991; Crown Attorney for Cen. Region, Nova Scotia 1993; mem. Parl. 1997–; Leader Progressive Conservative Party of Canada 2003–04, Deputy Leader Conservative Party of Canada 2004; fmr Critic for the Prime Minister, for the Solicitor Gen., for Public Security, for the Leader of the Govt in the House of Commons, for Justice, for Public Safety and Emergency Preparedness; fmr mem. Interim Cttee on Nat. Security and Intelligence; Minister of Foreign Affairs 2006–07, of Nat. Defence 2007–. *Leisure interests:* rugby, baseball, football, hockey. *Address:* Department of National Defence, National Defence Headquarters, Maj.-Gen. George R. Pearkes Building, 101 Colonel By Drive, Ottawa, ON K1A 0K2, Canada (office). *Telephone:* (613) 995-2534 (office). *Fax:* (613) 992-4739 (office). *Website:* www.forces.gc.ca (office).

MACKAY OF CLASHFERN, Baron (Life Peer), cr. 1979, of Eddrachillis in the District of Sutherland; **James Peter Hymers Mackay,** KT, PC, QC, LLB, MA, FRSE; British advocate; b. 2 July 1927, Scotland; s. of James Mackay and Janet Hymers; m. Elizabeth Gunn Hymers 1958; one s. two d.; ed George Heriot's School, Edin., Univ. of Edin., Trinity Coll., Cambridge; Lecturer in Math., Univ. of St Andrews 1948–50; Major Scholar, Trinity Coll., Cambridge 1947, Sr Scholar 1951; admitted to Faculty of Advocates 1955; QC 1965; Vice-Dean Faculty of Advocates 1973–76, Dean 1976–79, Lord Advocate 1979–84; Sheriff Prin., Renfrew and Argyll 1972–74; Commr Northern Lighthouses 1972–84; Dir Stenhouse Holdings Ltd 1976–78; Senator of Coll. of Justice in Scotland 1984–85; Lord of Appeal in Ordinary 1985–87; Lord Chancellor 1987–97; Chancellor Heriot-Watt Univ. 1991–; Ed.-in-Chief Halsbury's Laws of England 1998–; Part-time mem. Scottish Law Comm. 1976–79; mem. Insurance Brokers' Registration Council 1978–79; Fellow, Inst. of Taxation, American Coll. of Trial Lawyers, Int. Acad. of Trial Lawyers; Hon. FICE; Hon. FRCPE; Hon. FRCSE; Hon. FRCOG; Hon. Fellow Trinity Coll., Cambridge, Girton Coll., Cambridge; Hon. LLD (Edin., Dundee, Strathclyde, Aberdeen, St Andrews, Birmingham, Newcastle, Bath, Leicester, De Montfort, Glasgow, Cambridge, Robert Gordon Nat. Law School of India); Hon. DCL (Newcastle),

(Oxford) 1998. *Publication:* Armour on Valuation for Rating (Sr Ed.) 1961, 1971. *Leisure interests:* walking, travel. *Address:* House of Lords, Westminster, London, SW1A 0PW, England (office).

McKEE, J(ohn) Angus; Canadian business executive; b. 31 Aug. 1935, Toronto, Ont.; s. of John W. McKee and Margaret E. Phippen; m. Susan E. Harley 1970; one s. one d.; ed Trinity Coll. School, Port Hope, Ont. and Univ. of Toronto; joined the Patiño Mining Corpn 1962, Asst to Pres. 1963, Vice-Pres. (Corporate Devt) 1966; Man. Dir Consolidated Tin Smelters Ltd 1968–71; owner J. A. McKee and Assocs. Ltd 1971–83; Pres. and CEO Canadian Occidental Petroleum Ltd 1983–93; Chair., Pres., CEO Gulfstream Resources Canada 1993–2001; Dir Stone and Webster Canada Ltd, Stone and Webster Inc. (USA), Teradyne Canada Ltd, CVI Ltd and others; mem. Bd of Govs, Trinity Coll. School, Port Hope. *Leisure interests:* skiing, shooting.

MacKELLAR, Hon. Michael John Randal, B.SCI.AGR., MA; Australian agricultural scientist, politician and business executive; b. 27 Oct. 1938, Sydney; s. of Geoffrey Neil and Colleen Randal MacKellar; m. Robin Morey Smith 1969; two s. one d.; ed Sydney Church of England Grammar School, Sydney Univ., Balliol Coll., Oxford; New South Wales Dept of Agric. 1961–69; mem. for Warringah, NSW, House of Reps. 1969–94; Parl. Sec. to Leader of Opposition 1973–74; Shadow Minister for Immigration 1974–75; Minister for Immigration and Ethnic Affairs 1975–79, Minister Assisting the Treas. 1978–79, Minister for Health 1979–82, Minister Assisting the Prime Minister 1979–80, Minister for Home Affairs and Environment Feb.–March 1981; Shadow Minister for Foreign Affairs 1983–84, for Science and Special Minister of State 1984–85; Deputy Opposition Leader of the House 1985; Opposition Whip 1989; mem. numerous House of Reps Cttees 1970–90; Chair. House of Reps Standing Cttee on Environment and Conservation 1982–83; mem. first Australian Parl. del. to People's Repub. of China 1973, Leader del. to UN Habitat Conf. 1976; mem. NSW Advisory Cttee for Australian Broadcasting Comm. 1973–75; Advisory Council of CSIRO 1984, Council of Australian Nat. Univ. 1970–76; CEO Plastics and Chemicals Industries Asscn 1994–97; COO Baker Medical Research Inst. 1997–; Bd mem. Sydney Paralympic Games Organizing Cttee 1997–2000; Chair. Australia/N.Z. Food Authority 1998–, Franchising Policy Council of Australia 1998–, FAO Centre for Excellence, Monash Univ. 1999–; Liberal Party. *Leisure interests:* tennis, cricket, golf, reading, photography. *Address:* 19/158–160 Wattletree Road Malvern, Vic. 3144, Australia.

McKELLEN, Sir Ian Murray, Kt, CBE, CH, BA; British actor; b. 25 May 1939, Burnley, Lancs.; s. of Denis Murray McKellen and Margery (Sutcliffe) McKellen; ed Bolton School, St Catharine's Coll., Cambridge; council mem. British Actors' Equity 1970–71; Cameron Mackintosh Prof. of Contemporary Theatre, Oxford Univ. 1991; Hon. DLitt (Nottingham) 1989, (Oxford) 1991; Clarence Derwent Award 1964, Variety and Plays and Players awards 1966, Actor of the Year (Plays and Players) 1976, Soc. of West End Theatres Award for Best Actor in Revival 1977, for Best Comedy Performance 1978, for Best Actor in a New Play 1979, Tony Award 1981, Drama Desk 1981, Outer Critics Circle Award 1981, Royal TV Soc. Performer of the Year 1983, Laurence Olivier Award 1984, 1991, Evening Standard Best Actor Award 1984, 1989, Screen Actor's Guild Award for best supporting Actor 2000, British Ind. Film Awards, Variety UK Personality Award 2003. *Films include:* Alfred the Great 1969, The Promise 1969, A Touch of Love 1969, Priest of Love 1981, The Keep 1982, Plenty, Zina 1985, Scandal 1988, The Ballad of Little Jo 1992, I'll Do Anything 1992, Last Action Hero 1993, Six Degrees of Separation 1993, The Shadow 1994, Jack and Sarah 1994, Restoration 1994, Richard III 1995, Bent 1996, Swept from the Sea 1996, Apt Pupil 1997, Gods and Monsters 1998, X-Men 1999, Lord of the Rings: The Fellowship of the Ring 2001, Lord of the Rings: The Two Towers 2002, X-Men 2 2003, Emile 2003, Lord of the Rings: The Return of the King 2003, Asylum 2005, Neverwas 2005, Doogal (voice) 2006, The Da Vinci Code 2006, Flushed Away (voice) 2006, For the Love of God 2007, Stardust (voice) 2007, The Golden Compass 2007. *Stage appearances:* first stage appearance as Roper (A Man for All Seasons), Belgrade Theatre, Coventry 1961; numerous other parts include title-roles in Henry V, Luther, Ipswich 1962–63; Aufidius (Coriolanus), Arthur Seaton (Saturday Night and Sunday Morning), title-role in Sir Thomas More, Nottingham Playhouse 1963–64; London début as Godfrey (A Scent of Flowers), Duke of York's Theatre 1964; Claudio (Much Ado About Nothing), Protestant Evangelist (Last Goodnight), Capt. de Foenix (Trelawny of the Wells), Nat. Theatre Co. 1965; Alvin (A Lily in Little India), Hampstead and St Martin's 1965–66; Andrew Cobham (Their Very Own and Golden City), Royal Court 1966; title-part in O'Flaherty, VC and Bonaparte (The Man of Destiny), Mermaid 1966; Leonidik (The Promise), Oxford Playhouse, Fortune and Henry Miller (Broadway début) 1966–67; Tom (The White Liars), Harold Gorringe (Black Comedy), Lyric 1968; Richard II (Edin. Festival 1969), Edward II, Hamlet, Prospect Theatre Co. 1968–71, British tour, Mermaid and Piccadilly Theatres; Darkly (Billy's Last Stand), Theatre Upstairs 1970; Capt. Plume (The Recruiting Officer), Corporal Hill (Chips With Everything), Cambridge Theatre Co. 1970; Svetlovidov (Swan Song), Crucible, Sheffield 1971; founder-mem. Actors' Co., Edin. Festival 1972 and touring as Giovanni ('Tis Pity She's A Whore), Page-Boy (Ruling the Roost), Prince Yoremitsu (The Three Arrows), title-role in Michael, the Wood Demon, Footman (The Way of The World), then Knots, Shaw Theatre, Edgar (King Lear), Brooklyn Acad. and Giovanni, Wimbledon 1973–74; début with RSC as Dr Faustus (Edin. Festival) 1974; title-role in The Marquis of Keith, Philip the Bastard (King John), Aldwych 1974–75; Colin (Ashes), Young Vic. 1975; Aubrey Bagot (Too True to Be Good), also at Globe, Romeo, Macbeth, Bernick (Pillars of the Community), Face (The Alchemist) Stratford season 1976; Langevin (Days of the Commune) 1976–78; organized RSC British tour of Twelfth Night (Toby Belch) and Three Sisters (Andrei); Max (Bent), Royal Court and Criterion 1979, Amadeus (New York) 1980, Short List (Hampstead Theatre Club),

Cowardice (Ambassadors) 1983; int. tour of one-man show Acting Shakespeare (LA and Ritz Theatre, New York) 1984, (London) 1987; Assoc. Dir Nat. Theatre of Great Britain (also actor) 1984–86; Venice Preserv'd (Pierre), Coriolanus; Wild Honey (Platonov); McKellen/Petherbridge Nat. Theatre Group: Duchess of Malfi (Bosola), Real Inspector Hound (Hound), The Critic (Mr Puff), The Cherry Orchard (Lopakhin); Wild Honey (Va Theatre, New York), USA Shakespeare tour 1987; Henceforward (Vaudeville Theatre) 1988–89; Othello (Iago) RSC 1989; Royal Nat. Theatre: Bent (Max), King Lear (Kent), Richard III 1990–92 (World Tour then US Tour), Napoli Milionaria 1991, Uncle Vanya 1992, An Enemy of the People 1997, Peter Pan 1997; Present Laughter, The Tempest (W Yorks. Playhouse) 1998–99, Dance of Death: (Broadhurst Theatre, NY) 2001, (Wyndham's Theatre, London) 2003, (Sydney Festival) 2004, The Seagull (RSC) 2007, King Lear (RSC) 2007. *TV appearances include:* David Copperfield 1965, Ross 1969, Richard II, Edward II and Hamlet 1970, Hedda Gabler 1974, Macbeth, Every Good Boy Deserves Favour, Dying Day 1979, Acting Shakespeare 1981, Walter, The Scarlet Pimpernel 1982, Walter and June 1983, Countdown to War 1989, Othello 1990, Tales of the City 1993, Cold Comfort Farm 1995, Rasputin 1996, Coronation Street 2005. *Publication:* William Shakespeare's Richard III (jtly) 1996. *Address:* c/o ICM, 76 Oxford Street, London, W1N 0AX, England. *Telephone:* (20) 7636-6565. *Fax:* (20) 7323-0101. *Website:* www.mckellen.com.

McKENNA, Andrew J., Sr, BA, LLB; American business executive; *Chairman, McDonald's Corporation;* b. 1930; ed Univ. of Notre Dame, DePaul Univ. School of Law; Chair. Chicago White Sox professional baseball team 1975–81, Chicago Cubs 1981–84; currently Chair. Schwarz Paper Co.; mem. Bd of Dirs McDonald's Corpn 1991, Chair. (non-exec.) 2004–; mem. Bd of Dirs Ryan Group 1970–82, Dean Foods 1982–2000, Tribune Co. 1982–2002, Aon Corpn 1982–, Bank One 1991–99, Chicago Bears Football Club Inc., Click Commerce Inc., Skyline Corpn; Founding Chair. Chicago Metropolis 2020; fmr Chair. Econ. Club of Chicago, The Commercial Club of Chicago; Dir The American Ireland Fund, Children's Memorial Hosp. of Chicago, Lyric Opera, United Way of Metropolitan Chicago; Vice-Chair. Bd of Trustees, Univ. of Notre Dame 1986–92, Chair. 1992–2000, Chair. Emer. 2000–; Trustee and Chair. Emer., Museum of Science and Industry. *Address:* McDonald's Corporation, 2915 Jorie Blvd, Oak Brook, IL 60523, USA (office). *Telephone:* (630) 623-3000 (office). *Fax:* (630) 623-7056 (office). *Website:* www.mcdonalds.com (office).

McKENNA, Frank Joseph, LLB, PC, QC; Canadian diplomatist, politician, lawyer and business executive; *Deputy Chairman, Toronto-Dominion Bank;* b. 19 Jan. 1948, Apohaqui, Kings Co., NB; s. of Joseph McKenna and Olive Moody; m. Julie Friel 1972; two s. one d.; ed St Francis Xavier Univ., Queen's Univ. and Univ. of NB; Special Asst to Pres., Privy Council 1971; Research Asst Constitutional Law Unit, PMO 1973; Pnr, Martin, Lordon, McKenna, Martin & Bowes; Counsel, McInnes, Cooper 1998–; mem. NB Bar Asscn, Canadian Bar Asscn; mem. Legis. Ass. 1982–97; Leader, NB Liberal Party 1985–97; Premier, Prov. of NB 1987–97; Amb. to USA 2005–06; Deputy Chair. Toronto-Dominion Bank 2006–; Chair. Bd of Dirs CanWest Global Communications Corpn –2005, mem. Bd of Dirs Gen. Motors of Canada Ltd –2005, Bank of Montreal –2005; Hon. LLD (Univ. of NB) 1988, (Mount Allison) 1991, (St Francis Xavier) 1994, (St Thomas) 1996, (Ryerson Polytechnic) 1999, (Royal Mil. Coll.) 2000; Vanier Award 1988, Econ. Developer of the Year, Econ. Developers' Asscn of Canada 1993, Distinction Award, Canadian Advanced Tech. Asscn 1996. *Leisure interests:* reading, sports and current affairs. *Address:* Toronto-Dominion Bank, Toronto-Dominion Centre, King Street West and Bay Street, Toronto, ON M5K 1A2, Canada. *Telephone:* 416-982-8222. *Fax:* 416-982-5671. *Website:* www.td.com.

McKENNA, Thomas Patrick (T. P.); Irish actor; b. 7 Sept. 1931, Cavan; s. of Ralph McKenna and Mary McKenna; m. May White 1956; four s. one d.; joined Abbey Theatre Co., Dublin 1954, Hon. Life Mem. 1966. *Films include:* Siege of Sidney Street, Girl with Green Eyes, Ferry Cross the Mersey, Young Cassidy, Ulysses, Charge of the Light Brigade, Anne of the Thousand Days, Perfect Friday, Villain, Straw Dogs, Portrait of the Artist as a Young Man, A Child's Voice, Exposure, The Outsider, Silver Dream Racer, The Scarlet and the Black, To the Lighthouse, Mehmed my Hawk, Doctor and the Devils, Honour, Profit and Pleasure, Cat's Eyes, Anything Legal Considered, O.S.S., Strong Medicine, Pascali's Island, Red Scorpion, Valmont, Monarch, Kings in Grass Castles, The American 1998, Longitude 2000, The Great Céile War 2002, The Libertine 2004. *Television includes:* Jack the Ripper, Dr Who, Miss Marple, Shoot to Kill (TV film), Parnell and the Englishwoman, The Chief (series 2, 3, 4), Rumpole of the Bailey, Events at Drimaghleen (TV film), The Law Lords (TV film), Lovejoy, Casualty, Heartbeat, Stendhal's Scarlet and Black, Kavanagh QC, The Ambassador, Morse, Ballykissangel, Anytime Now, The Bill, Rockface, Fair City (RTE), Waking The Dead 2004, Raphael: A Mortal God 2004. *Stage:* Molly Sweeney by Brian Friel, world premiere, Gate Theatre, Dublin 1994 and Almeida Theatre, London, Hirst in No Man's Land, Pinter Festival at Gate Theatre 1997, Brian Friel's version of Uncle Vanya, world premiere, Gate Theatre 1998 and Lincoln Center Festival, New York 1999. *Radio:* more than 100 radio plays for BBC. *Leisure interests:* reading, sport, music. *Address:* 28 Claverley Grove, London, N3 2DH, England (home). *Telephone:* (20) 8346-4118 (home). *Fax:* (20) 8346-4118 (home).

McKENNA, Virginia, OBE; British actress and conservationist; *Founder and Trustee, Born Free Foundation;* b. 7 June 1931, London; d. of Terence McKenna and Anne Marie Dennis; m. Bill Travers (died 1994); three s. one d.; ed Herons Ghyll, Horsham, Sussex, Herschel, Cape Town, S Africa, Cen. School of Speech and Drama, London; f. Zoo Check Charitable Trust (now the Born Free Foundation) 1984; film debut in The Second Mrs Tanqueray 1951; speaker at numerous events; patron to numerous orgs; Belgian Prix Femina Award 1957, BAFTA SWET (Soc. of West End Theatres) Variety Club. *Stage appearances include:* The King and I 1979 (Soc. of West End Producers Award for Best Actress in a musical), Hamlet (RSC) 1985, Winnie 1988, A Little Night Music, The Devils (RSC), The Beggar's Opera (RSC), A Winter's Tale, As You Like It, The River Line, Penny for a Song, I Capture the Castle, A Personal Affair, The Bad Samaritan. *Films include:* Father's Doing Fine, The Cruel Sea 1953, Simba 1955, The Ship that Died of Shame, A Town Like Alice (BAFTA Best Actress Award) 1956, The Smallest Show on Earth 1957, The Barretts of Wimpole Street 1957, Carve Her Name With Pride (Prix Fémina Award, Belgium) 1957, Passionate Summer 1958, The Wreck of the Mary Deare 1959, Two Living, One Dead 1961, Born Free (Best Actress Award, Variety Club) 1966, Ring of Bright Water 1969, An Elephant Called Slowly 1969, Waterloo 1970, Swallows and Amazons 1974, The Disappearance 1977, Holocaust 2000 1977, Staggered 1994, Sliding Doors 1998, What Do You See? 2005. *Radio:* The Devils, The Flame Trees of Thika, A Town Like Alice, The Tempest. *TV includes:* Romeo and Juliet 1955 (BBC TV Best Actress Award), Play of the Month: A Passage to India 1965, Play of the Month: Girls in Uniform 1967, The Lion at World's End (documentary) 1971, Play of the Month: The Deep Blue Sea 1974, The Gathering Storm 1974, Shades of Greene (episode Cheap in August) 1975, Peter Pan 1976, Waters of the Moon 1983, Puccini 1984, Lovejoy 1991, The Camomile Lawn (mini-series) 1992, Ruth Rendell Mysteries (episode The Speaker of Mandarin: Part One) 1992, September (mini-series) 1996, The Scold's Bridle 1998, Kavanagh QC (episode Time of Need) 1999, The Whistleblower 2001, Marple: A Murder is Announced 2005. *Publications:* On Playing with Lions (with Bill Travers), Some Of My Friends Have Tails, Into the Blue 1992, Journey to Freedom 1997; Co-Ed. and Contrib.: Beyond the Bars, Headlines from the Jungle (verse) 1990, Back to the Blue 1997. *Leisure interests:* classical music, poetry, walking in the countryside, gardening. *Address:* c/o Aude Powell, Brunskill Management, The Courtyard, Edinhall, Penrith, Cumbria, CA11 8ST, England (office); Born Free Foundation, 3 Grove House, Foundry Lane, Horsham, West Sussex, RH13 5PL, England (office). *Telephone:* (1403) 240170 (office). *Fax:* (1403) 327838 (office). *E-mail:* virginia@bornfree.org.uk (office). *Website:* www.bornfree.org.uk (office).

McKENNON, Keith Robert, BS; American business executive; b. 25 Dec. 1933, Condon, Ore.; s. of Russell McKennon and Lois Edgerton; m. Patricia Dragon 1961; three s.; ed Pendleton High School, Golden Gate Coll. and Oregon State Univ.; joined Dow Chemical USA 1955; Dir Public Affairs, The Dow Chemical Co. 1978, Vice-Pres. 1980, Vice-Pres. Agricultural Products 1982; Vice-Pres. Product Dept Man. Dow Chemical USA Jan. 1983; Group Vice-Pres. Global Agricultural Products, Legal, Employee Relations and Public Affairs, The Dow Chemical Co. April 1983; mem. Bd of Dirs The Dow Chemical Co. 1983–92, 2003–, Group Vice-Pres. and Dir of Research and Devt 1985, Exec. Vice-Pres. 1987–92, Pres. Dow Chemical USA 1987–90; Chair., CEO Dow Corning Corpn 1992–94; Chair. Pacific Corpn 1994–99; Deputy Chair. Scottish Power PLC 1999–2001; Dir Chemical Bank and Trust Co., Chemical Financial Corpn, Dowell Schlumberger Inc., Dow Corning Corpn, Marion Merrill Dow, Pacific Corpn, Nat. Legal Center for the Public Interests etc; Gold Medal, Soc. of Chemical Industry 1994. *Leisure interests:* tennis, fishing, reading. *Address:* c/o Board of Directors, Dow Chemical Company, 2030 Dow Center, Midland, MI 48674; 6079 N. Paradise View Drive, Paradise Valley, AZ 85253, USA. *Telephone:* (602) 553-0141 (home); (503) 226-0225 (summer). *Fax:* (602) 553-0182 (home). *E-mail:* kmck96@aol.com (home).

McKENZIE, Dan Peter, MA, PhD, FRS; British geologist and academic; *Royal Society Research Professor, Department of Earth Sciences, University of Cambridge;* b. 21 Feb. 1942, Cheltenham; s. of W. S. and N. M. (née Fairbrother) McKenzie; m. Indira M. Misra 1971; one s.; ed Westminster School and King's Coll., Cambridge; Fellow, King's Coll. 1965–73, 1977–, Sr Asst in Research, Dept of Earth Sciences, Univ. of Cambridge 1969–73, Asst Dir of Research 1973–79, Reader in Tectonics 1979–85, Prof. of Earth Sciences 1985–96, Royal Soc. Research Prof. 1996–; Foreign Assoc. NAS; Balzan Prize 1981, Japan Prize 1990, Crafoord Prize 2002, Companion of Honour 2003. *Publications:* papers in professional journals. *Leisure interest:* gardening. *Address:* Bullard Laboratories, Madingley Rise, Madingley Road, Cambridge, CB3 0EZ, England (office). *Telephone:* (1223) 337177 (office). *Website:* www.esc.cam.ac.uk/new/v10/index_geophysics.html (office).

MACKENZIE, Gen. Sir Jeremy John George, Kt, GCB, OBE, DL; British army officer; *Senior Military Adviser, Fabbrica d'Armi Pietro Beretta S.p.A;* b. 11 Feb. 1941, Nairobi, Kenya; s. of the late Lt-Col John William Elliot Mackenzie and of Valerie Mackenzie (née Dawes); m. Elizabeth Lyon (née Wertenbaker) 1969; one s. one d.; ed Duke of York School, Nairobi, Kenya, Staff Coll., Camberley; commissioned Queen's Own Highlanders 1961; Canadian Forces Staff Coll. 1974; Brigade Maj. 24 Airportable Brigade 1975–76; CO 1 Queen's Own Highlanders, NI and Hong Kong 1979–82; Instructor Staff Coll. 1982–83; Col Army Staff Duties 2 1983–84; Commdr 12th Armoured Brigade 1984–86; Service Fellowship King's Coll., Univ. of London 1987; Deputy Commdt 1987–89; Commdt 1989, Staff Coll.; GOC 4th Armoured Div. BAOR 1989–91; Col Commdt WRAC 1990–92, AG Corps 1992–98, APTC 1997–; Col Highlanders 1994–2001; Commdr 1st (British) Corps 1991–92, NATO's ACE Rapid Reaction Corps (ARRC) 1992–94, Deputy Supreme Allied Commdr, Europe 1994–98, now consultant to NATO aspirant cos; ADC (Gen.) 1997–99; Gov. Royal Hosp. Chelsea 1999–2006; Sr Mil. Adviser, Fabbrica d'Armi Pietro Beretta S.p.A 2006–; Brig. Queen's Bodyguard of Scotland (RCA); mem. Bd of Dirs Sirva plc 2003–, Selex Communications 2003–; mem. Advisory Bd Blue Hackle Security 2006–; Commdr US Legion of Merit 1997 (second award 1999), Hungarian Presidential Order of Merit (1st Class) 1998, Czech Defence Minister's Order of Merit (1st Class) 1998, Bulgarian Order of the Madara Horseman (1st Class) 1999, Slovenian Gold Medal of the Armed Forces 2003. *Publication:* The British Army and the Operational Level of War 1989. *Leisure interests:* shooting, fishing, painting.

MacKENZIE, Kelvin; British media executive; b. 22 Oct. 1946; m. Jacqueline M. Holland 1969; two s. one d.; joined The Sun newspaper, London, as sub-editor 1972, subsequently Night Ed.; apptd Man. Ed. New York Post 1978; rejoined The Sun as Night Ed. 1980; Night Ed. Daily Express Feb. 1981; rejoined The Sun, Ed. 1981–94; Man. Dir BSkyB Jan.–Oct. 1994 (resgnd); Dir Mirror Group PLC 1994–98, Deputy Chief Exec. and Group Man. Dir 1997–98; Chair. and CEO Talk Radio UK 1998–2000; Chair. and CEO The Wireless Group –2005; Exec. Chair. Highbury House Communications PLC Sept.–Dec. 2005 (resgnd); columnist, The Sun 2006–. *Address:* The Sun, 1 Virginia Street, London, E98 1SN, England (office). *Telephone:* (20) 7782-4000 (office). *Fax:* (20) 7782-4108 (office). *Website:* www.thesun.co.uk (office).

McKENZIE, Kevin; American ballet dancer, choreographer and director; *Artistic Director, American Ballet Theater (ABT);* b. 29 April 1954, Burlington, Vt; s. of Raymond James McKenzie and Ruth Davison; ed Acad. of Washington School of Ballet; soloist with Nat. Ballet of Washington 1972–74; Prin. Dancer, Joffrey Ballet 1974–78; Prin. Dancer, American Ballet Theater (ABT) 1979–91, Artistic Dir 1992–; Perm. Guest Artist, Washington Ballet 1990–91, Artistic Assoc. 1991–92; Assoc. Dir New Amsterdam Ballet 1984–; Hon. PhD (St Michael's Coll.); Silver Medal, Sixth Int. Ballet Competition, Varna 1972. *Principle roles include:* leading roles in all the major full-length classics, including Solor in La Bayadère, Don Jose in Carmen, the Prince in Cinderella, Franz in Coppélia, Gentleman With Her in Dim Lustre, Basil and Espada in Don Quixote (Kitri's Wedding), Albrecht in Giselle, a leading role in The Garden of Villandry, Her Lover in Jardin aux Lilas, leading role in The Leaves Are Fading, the Friend in Pillar of Fire, leading role in Raymonda (Grand Pas Hongrois), featured role in Requiem, Champion Roper in Rodeo, Romeo and Mercutio in Romeo and Juliet, Prince Desire in The Sleeping Beauty, Prince Siegfried in Swan Lake, James in La Sylphide and leading roles in Other Dances, Paquita, Les Sylphides, Sylvia Pas de Deux and Theme and Variations; cr. role of Amnon in Martine van Hamel's Amnon V'Tamar and a leading role in Clark Tippet's S.P.E.B.S.Q.S.A. *Directed:* Groupo Zamboria (New Amsterdam Ballet—NAB) 1984, Liszt Études (now called Transcendental Études) (NAB) 1991, Lucy and the Count (The Washington Ballet) 1992, The Nutcracker 1993; (with Susan Jones): Don Quixote (ABT) 1995, Swan Lake (ABT) 2000. *Address:* American Ballet Theater, 890 Broadway, New York, NY 10003, USA (office). *Telephone:* (212) 477-3030 (office). *Fax:* (212) 254-5938 (office). *Website:* www.abt.org (office).

McKENZIE SMITH, Ian, CBE, PRSA, PPRSW, RGI, FMA, FRSA, FRSE, FSA Scot, FSS, HRA, HRHA, HRUA, HRWA; British artist; b. 3 Aug. 1935, Montrose, Angus; s. of James McKenzie Smith and Mary Benzie; m. Mary Rodge Fotheringham 1963; two s. one d.; ed Robert Gordon's Coll., Aberdeen, Gray's School of Art, Aberdeen, Hospitalfield Coll. of Art, Arbroath, Aberdeen Coll. of Educ.; teacher of art, Fife 1960–63; educ. officer, Council of Industrial Design, Scottish Cttee 1963–68; Dir Aberdeen Art Gallery and Museums 1968–89; City Arts and Recreation Officer, Aberdeen 1989–96, Sec. Aberdeen Highland Games 1989–96; Deputy Pres. and Treas. RSA 1990–91, Sec. 1991–98, Pres. 1998–2007; Trustee Nat. Galleries of Scotland 1999–; mem. Scottish Arts Council 1970–77 (Chair. Art Cttee 1975–77), Scottish Museums Council 1980–87 (Chair. Industrial Cttee 1985–87); mem. Advisory Council on Export of Works of Art 1991–, Museums and Galleries Comm. 1997–2000; mem. Bd Friends of RSA 1972–, RSA Enterprises 1972–; trustee of numerous funds; Hon. RA 1999; Hon. LLD (Aberdeen) 1991; Hon. DArt (The Robert Gordon Univ., Aberdeen) 2000; RSA Guthrie Award 1971, RSA Gillies Award 1980, May Marshall Brown Award, Royal Scottish Soc. of Painters in Watercolours 1980.

McKERNAN, James, BA, PhD; American mathematician and academic; *Professor of Mathematics, Massachusetts Institute of Technology;* ed Trinity Coll., Cambridge, UK, Harvard Univ.; apptd instructor at Univ. of Utah 1991, later at Univ. of Texas –1995; Visiting Asst Prof., Oklahoma State Univ. 1994–95; faculty appointments at Univ. of California, Santa Barbara 1995–2007; Prof. of Math., MIT 2007–; Clay Research Award, Clay Math. Inst. 2007. *Publications:* numerous papers in professional journals on algebraic geometry. *Address:* Room 2-274, Department of Mathematics, Massachusetts Institute of Technology, 77 Massachusetts Avenue, Cambridge, MA 02139-4307, USA (office). *Telephone:* (617) 253-4391 (office). *Fax:* (617) 253-4358 (office). *E-mail:* mckernan@math.mit.edu (office). *Website:* www-math.mit.edu (office).

MACKERRAS, Sir Charles, Kt, CH, AC, CBE; British/Australian conductor; b. 17 Nov. 1925, Schenectady, NY, USA of Australian parentage; s. of Alan and Catherine Mackerras; m. Judith Wilkins 1947; two d.; ed Sydney Grammar School, NSW Conservatoire and Prague Acad. of Music; Prin. Oboist Sydney Symphony Orchestra 1943–46; Staff Conductor Sadler's Wells Opera 1948–53; Prin. Conductor BBC Concert Orchestra 1954–56; guest opera conductor at Covent Garden, English Nat. Opera, Berlin State Opera, Hamburg State Opera, Vienna State Opera, etc. 1956–66; First Conductor, Hamburg State Opera 1966–69; Musical Dir, Sadler's Wells Opera, later English Nat. Opera 1970–77, Chief Guest Conductor, BBC Symphony Orchestra 1976–79; Chief Conductor Sydney Symphony Orchestra 1982–85; Prin. Guest Conductor Royal Liverpool Philharmonic Orchestra 1986–88; Musical Dir Welsh Nat. Opera 1987–92, Conductor Emer. 1993–; Prin. Guest Conductor Scottish Chamber Orchestra 1992–95, Conductor Laureate 1995–; Prin. Guest Conductor San Francisco Opera 1993–96 (Conductor Emer. 1996–), Royal Philharmonic Orchestra 1993–96, Czech Philharmonic Orchestra 1997–2003, Philharmonia Orchestra 2002–; Music Dir Orchestra of St Luke's 1998–2001, Music Dir Emer. 2001–; Pres. Trinity Coll. of Music 2000–; Conductor Laureate, Brno Philharmonic Orchestra 2007–; Conductor Emer., Orchestra of the Age of Enlightenment 2007–; guest conductor in Europe, USA, Canada and Australia; associated with the Royal Opera House, Covent Garden for many years and conducted very regularly at the San Francisco Opera and the Metropolitan Opera, New York; Hon. RAM 1969, FRCM 1987, FRNCM 1999, FTCL 1999, Hon. Fellow, St Peter's Coll. Oxford 1999, Univ. of Cardiff 2003; Hon. mem. GSMD 2007; Hon. Pres., Edinburgh Int. Festival 2008–; Hon. DMus (Hull) 1990, (Nottingham) 1991, (York, Masaryk, Czech Repub. and Griffith, Australia) 1994, (Oxford) 1997, (Prague Acad. of Music) 1999, (Napier) 2000 (Melbourne) 2003, (Sydney) 2003, (Janáček Acad. of Music, Brno) 2004, (London) 2005, (Royal Welsh Coll. of Music and Drama) 2005; Evening Standard Award for Most Outstanding Achievement in Opera 1977, Janáček Medal 1978, Gramophone Record of the Year 1977, 1980, 1999, Grammy Award for Best Opera 1981, 2007, Gramophone Best Opera Recording 1983, 1984, 1994, 1999, Medal of Merit, Czech Repub. 1996, Prix Caecilia 1999, Preis der Deutschen Schallplattenkritik 1999, Chopin Prize and Lifetime Achievement Award, Midem, Cannes 2000, Asscn of British Orchestras Award 2001, first recipient of Queen's Medal for Music 2005, Royal Philharmonic Soc. Gold Medal and BBC Radio 3 Listeners' Award 2005, first recipient of Classic FM Gramophone Award for Lifetime Achievement 2006, The Worshipful Co. of Musicians Silver Medal 2006, Australian of the Year in the UK 2007. *Arrangements:* Ballets: Pineapple Poll (Sullivan) 1951, The Lady and the Fool (Verdi) 1954, Melbourne Cup 1965; reconstruction of Arthur Sullivan's Lost Cello Concerto 1986. *Recordings:* numerous, notably Janáček, Handel, Mozart operas and symphonies, Brahms, Beethoven, Dvořák, Mahler and Schubert. *Publications:* contributed four appendices to Charles Mackerras: A Musician's Musician by Nancy Phelan 1987, musical articles in various magazines. *Leisure interests:* languages, yachting. *Address:* c/o Mr Robert Rattray, Askonas Holt Ltd, Lincoln House, 300 High Holborn, London, WC1V 7JH, England (office). *Telephone:* (20) 7400-1710 (office). *Fax:* (20) 7400-1799 (office). *E-mail:* info@askonasholt.co.uk (office). *Website:* www.askonasholt.co.uk (office).

MACKEY, James Patrick, BA, LPh, BD, STL, DD, PhD; Irish philosopher, theologian and academic; *Visiting Professor, Trinity College Dublin;* b. 9 Feb. 1934, Ireland; s. of Peter Mackey and Esther Morrissey; m. Noelle Quinlan 1973; one s. one d.; ed Mount St Joseph Coll., Nat. Univ. of Ireland, Pontifical Univ., Maynooth and Queen's Univ., Belfast; ordained priest 1958; Lecturer in Philosophy, Queen's Univ., Belfast 1960–66; Lecturer in Philosophy and Theology, St John's Coll., Waterford 1966–69; Assoc. Prof. of Philosophical and Systematic Theology, Univ. of San Francisco, USA 1969–73, Prof. 1973–79; Visiting Prof., Univ. of California, Berkeley, USA 1974–75; Thomas Chalmers Prof. of Theology, Univ. of Edin., UK 1979–99, Dean of Faculty of Divinity 1984–88, Dir Grad. School and Assoc. Dean 1995–98, Prof. Emer. 1999–, Fellow, Faculty of Divinity 1999–2002; Visiting Prof., Univ. of Dublin Trinity Coll. 2000–; curricular consultant, Univ. Coll., Cork 2000–04; Visiting Prof., Dartmouth Coll., NH, USA 1989, Univ. of San Francisco 1990; mem. Ind. Assessment Panel and jt author of Report on NI Policing Bd 2005; Dir Derry City Int. Conf. on the Cultures of Europe 1992; mem. Consultative Group on the Past of N Ireland 2007–09; Ed. Studies in World Christianity 1995–2001; British Acad. Research Scholarship 1964–65. *Television:* scripted and presented series The Hall of Mirrors 1984, The Gods of War 1986, Perspectives (on Northern Ireland) 1986, Perspectives II 1987. *Publications:* Life and Grace 1966, Morals, Law and Authority (ed.) 1969, The Problems of Religious Faith 1974, Jesus, The Man and the Myth 1979, The Christian Experience of God as Trinity 1983, Religious Imagination (ed.) 1986, Modern Theology 1987, An Introduction to Celtic Christianity 1989, Power and Christian Ethics 1994, The Cultures of Europe (ed.) 1994, The Critique of Theological Reason 2000, Religion and Politics in Ireland at the Turn of the Millennium (ed.) 2003, Christianity and Creation 2006, The Scientist and the Theologian 2007, Jesus of Nazareth 2008. *Leisure interest:* sailing. *Address:* School of Religions and Theology, Trinity College, Dublin 2 (office); 15 Glenville Park, Dunmore Road, Waterford, Ireland (home). *Telephone:* (1) 6081297 (office); (51) 844624 (home). *E-mail:* jpmackey_ie@yahoo.co.uk (home).

MACKI, Ahmad bin Abd an-Nabi; Omani government official; fmr Minister of Civil Service; currently Minister of Nat. Economy, Supervisor of Finance Ministry and Deputy Chair. Financial Affairs and Energy Resources Council. *Address:* Ministry of National Economy, POB 881, Muscat 100, Oman (office). *Telephone:* 24698900 (office). *Fax:* 24698467 (office). *E-mail:* mone@omantel.net.om (office). *Website:* www.moneoman.gov.om (office).

MACKIE, Robert (Bob) Gordon; American costume and fashion designer; b. 24 March 1940, Monterey Park, Calif.; s. of Charles Robert Smith and Mildred Agnes Mackie (née Smith); m. Marianne Wolford 1960 (divorced); one s.; ed Chouinard Art Inst.; mem. staff Edith Head 1962–63; designed costumes for film Divorce, American Style 1966; Co-Designer for films Divorce American Style 1967, Lady Sings the Blues 1972, Funny Lady 1975, The Villain 1979, Smokey and the Bandit II 1980, Encore! 1980, . . .All the Marbles 1981, Pennies from Heaven 1981, Fake-Out 1982, Butterfly 1982, Max Dugan Returns 1983, Staying Alive 1983, Brenda Starr 1989; designer for numerous TV shows including: Brigadoon 1966, Alice Through the Looking Glass 1966, Carousel 1967, Kismet 1967, Fred Astaire Show 1968, Diana Ross and The Supremes 1969, The Carol Burnett Show 1967–77, Sonny and Cher Comedy Hour 1971, Cher 1975, Donny and Marie 1976, Mitzi. . . Roarin' in the 20's 1976, The 48th Annual Academy Awards 1976, Diahann Carroll Summer Show 1976, Sonny and Cher Show 1976–77, An Evening with Diana Ross 1977, Mitzi. . . Zings Into Spring 1978, Mitzi. . . What's Hot, What's Not 1978, The Goldie Hawn Special 1978, The Grass Is Always Greener Over the Septic Tank 1978, The Star Wars Holiday Special 1978, The Captain & Tennille Songbook 1979, Goldie and Liza Together 1980, Ann-Margret: Hollywood Movie Girls 1980, Celebration 1981, The 54th Annual Academy Awards 1982, Fresno (mini-series) 1986, Plaza Suite 1987, Cher. . . at the Mirage 1990, The Carol Burnett Show (series) 1991, The Carol Burnett Show: A Reunion 1993,

Gypsy 1993, Men, Movies & Carol 1994, Golden Anniversary 1995, Mrs. Santa Claus 1996, Blue Suede Shoes: Ballet Rocks! 1997, Bernadette Peters in Concert 1998, Cher: Live in Concert from Las Vegas 1999, Putting It Together 2000, Cher: The Farewell Tour 2003; Co-Designer theatrical productions On The Town 1971, Lorelei 1972, The Best Little Whorehouse Goes Public 1994; launched first ready-to-wear collection in 1982, line grew rapidly to include fragrances, eyewear, furs and various fashion accessories, added a line of knitwear, eveningwear, suits, a new fragrance, men's ties, handbags, scarves, watches, jewellery and stationery 1990s, launched made-to-order couture collection 1999; often called "the sultan of sequins, the rajah of rhinestones"; Emmy Award 1967 (co-recipient), 1969, 1976, 1983, Costume Designers' Guild Award 1968. *Publication:* Dressing for Glamour 1969. *Address:* Bob Mackie Studio, 1412 Broadway, New York, NY 10018, USA (office). *Telephone:* (212) 302-8200.

McKILLOP, Sir Thomas (Tom) Fulton Wilson, Kt, BSc, PhD; British business executive and chemist; b. 19 March 1943, Dreghorn, nr Irvine, Ayrshire; s. of Hugh McKillop and Annie McKillop (née Wilson); m. Elizabeth Kettle 1966; one s. two d.; ed Irvine Royal Acad., Univ. of Glasgow, Centre de Mécanique Ondulatoire Appliquée, Paris; research scientist, ICI Corp. Lab. 1969–75; Head of Natural Products Research, ICI Pharmaceuticals Ltd 1975–78, Dir of Research, France 1978–80, Chem. Man. 1980–84, Gen. Man. of Research 1984–85, Gen. Man. Devt 1985–89, Tech. Dir 1989–94; CEO AstraZeneca (fmrly Zeneca) 1994–2005, Dir 1996–2005; Deputy Chair. Royal Bank of Scotland Group 2005, Chair. 2006–08 (retd); Dir (non-exec.) Amersham Int. PLC 1992–97, Nycomed Amersham PLC 1997–2000, Lloyds TSB PLC 1999–, BP 2004–09; Dir Almirall 2007–; Pres. European Fed. of Pharmaceutical Industries and Asscns (EFPIA) 2002–05, Science Council 2007–; Pro-Chancellor Univ. of Leicester 1998–2008; mem. Soc. for Drug Research, ACS, Royal Inst.; Trustee, Darwin Trust of Edin. 1995–, Council for Industry & Higher Educ.; Hon. Fellow, Univ. of Lancashire 2004, ICHEME 2006; Hon. LLD (Manchester) 1999, (Dundee) 2003; Hon. DSc (Glasgow) 2000, (Leicester) 2000, (Huddersfield) 2000, (Nottingham) 2001, (St Andrews) 2004, (Salford) 2004, (Manchester) 2005, (Lancaster) 2007; Dr hc (Middlesex) 2000, (Paisley) 2006; Hon. DLit (Heriot Watt) 2006. *Leisure interests:* carpentry, music, reading, walking. *Address:* c/o Royal Bank of Scotland Group, Gogarburn, Edinburgh, EH2 1HQ, Scotland.

MACKIN, Martin, MA; Irish politician; *General Secretary, Fianna Fáil Party;* b. 23 Dec. 1963, Drogheda, Co. Louth; s. of Thomas Mackin and Josephine Mackin; ed Univ. Coll. Dublin, Coll. of Commerce, Dublin, Nat. Univ. of Ireland; press officer, Fianna Fáil 1992–95, Dir Fianna Fáil European Office 1995–98, Gen. Sec. Fianna Fáil 1998–. *Leisure interests:* music, current affairs, reading. *Address:* c/o Áras De Valera, 65–66 Lower Mount Street, Dublin 2, Ireland (office). *Telephone:* (1) 676-1551. *Fax:* (1) 678-5960. *E-mail:* martin@fiannafail.ie (office). *Website:* www.fiannafail.ie (office).

McKINLEY, Brunson, BA, MA; American diplomatist and international organization official; b. 8 Feb. 1943, Fla; s. of Kenneth William McKinley and Lois Rebecca McKinley; m. Nancy McKinley (née Padlon); one s. one d.; ed Univ. of Chicago, Harvard Univ.; US Army 1965–70, with service in Viet Nam; joined diplomatic service, overseas postings include Italy, China, Vietnam, UK, Germany; Amb. to Haiti 1986–89, specialized in refugee and migration issues 1990–94, helped defuse Haitian-Cuban boat crisis 1994, developed trans-Atlantic dialogue on migration, successfully directed US participation in comprehensive action plan for Indo-Chinese refugees; US Bosnia Humanitarian Coordinator 1995–98; prin. compiler of refugee annex of Dayton Accords; Dir-Gen. Int. Org. for Migration, Geneva 1998–2008; Bronze Star, Air Medal, Award for Valor. *Publications:* numerous studies on migration subjects. *Address:* c/o International Organization for Migration, 17 route des Morillons, CP 71, 1211 Geneva 19 (office); 15 Grande Rue, 1260 Nyon, Switzerland (home).

McKINNELL, Henry A. (Hank), Jr, BA, MBA, PhD; American pharmaceutical company executive; ed Univ. of British Columbia, Canada, Stanford Univ. Grad. School of Business; joined Pfizer Inc., Tokyo 1971, served in various exec. positions including Pres. Pfizer Asia, Hong Kong, Pres. Medical Technology Group, Chief Financial Officer, Pres. Pharmaceutical Group 1997, Pres. and COO Pfizer Inc. 1999–2000, Pres. 1999–2001, CEO 2001–06, Chair. 2001–07; Dir Chamber of Commerce, Business Council, Royal Shakespeare Co. America, Japan Soc.; mem. Bd of Dirs Moody's Corpn, ExxonMobil Corpn, John Wiley & Sons Inc., Business Roundtable (now Chair.), Business-Higher Educ. Forum (B-HEF); Chair. Advisory Council, Stanford Univ. Grad. School of Business; mem. Presidential Advisory Council on HIV/AIDS (PACHA); Fellow, New York City Public Library, New York City Police Foundation, Channel Thirteen/WNET, J.F. Kennedy Center for the Performing Arts; Trustee Memorial-Sloan Kettering Cancer Center, New York City Public Library, New York City Police Foundation; Dr hc (Polytechnic Univ.); Sitara-i-Eisaar Award (Pakistan), Global Leadership Award, UN Asscn of the USA, Woodrow Wilson Inst. Corp. Service Award, Cleveland E. Dodge Medal for Distinguished Service to Educ., Columbia Univ. Teachers Coll., Stanford Univ. Grad. School of Business/Excellence in Leadership Award. *Address:* Pfizer Inc., 235 East 42nd Street, New York, NY 10017-5755, USA (office).

McKINNON, Rt Hon. Donald (Don) Charles, PC, ONZ; New Zealand politician and international organization official; b. 27 Feb. 1939; s. of Maj.-Gen. Walter McKinnon and Anna McKinnon (née Plimmer); m. 1st Patricia Maude Moore 1964 (divorced 1995); three s. one d.; m. 2nd Clare de Lore 1995; one s.; fmr estate agent and farm man. consultant; Nat. Party MP for Albany 1978–; fmr Jr and Sr Govt Whip, Opposition Spokesperson for Defence and Health; Sr Opposition Whip 1984–87; Deputy Prime Minister 1990–96; Leader of the House 1993–96; Minister of Foreign Affairs and Trade, of Pacific Island Affairs, 1990–99, for Disarmament and Arms Control 1996–99; Sec.-Gen. of the Commonwealth 2000–08; Hon. DComm (Lincoln, NZ); Dr hc (four Univs of Manchester) 2002, (Heriot-Watt Univ., Edinburgh). *Leisure interests:* rugby, cricket, jogging, tennis, reading, riding. *Address:* c/o Commonwealth Secretariat, Marlborough House, Pall Mall, London, SW1Y 5HX, England. *Telephone:* (20) 7747-6103.

McKINNON, Sir James, Kt, CA, FCMA; British public servant; b. 1929; ed Camphill School; Co. Sec. Macfarlane Lang & Co. Ltd, Glasgow 1955–65; Business Consultant, McLintock, Moores & Murray, Glasgow 1965–67; Finance Dir Imperial Group PLC, London 1967–86; Dir-Gen. Office of Gas Supply 1986–93; Chair. Ionica 1993–98; Chair. (non-exec.) Cowie Group 1994–, Trafficmaster plc –2004, Discovery Trust PLC 2004–05; Deputy Chair. (non-exec.) United Business Media plc –2000; mem. Bd Dirs Martin Currie Capital Return Trust plc (renamed F&C Private Equity Trust plc) 2005–; Pres. Inst. of Chartered Accountants of Scotland 1985–86; Dr hc (Paisley) 1995. *Publications:* articles in professional publs. *Leisure interest:* skiing. *Address:* F&C Asset Management plc, 80 George Street, Edinburgh, EH2 3BU, Scotland (office). *Telephone:* (131) 465-1000 (office). *E-mail:* enquiries@fandc.com (office). *Website:* www.fandc.com (office).

MacKINNON, Roderick, MD; American physician and biophysicist; *Professor and Head of Laboratory of Molecular Neurobiology and Biophysics, The Rockefeller University;* b. 1956, Mass; ed Brandeis Univ., Waltham, Mass, Tufts Univ. School of Medicine, Mass, Harvard Medical School; staff mem., Harvard Medical School 1989, later full Prof.; Prof. and Head Lab. of Molecular Neurobiology and Biophysics, The Rockefeller Univ. 1996–; apptd Investigator at Howard Hughes Medical Inst. 1997–; Visiting Researcher, Brookhaven Nat. Lab.; mem. NAS 2000; Hon. DSc (Tufts) 2002; Albert Lasker Basic Medical Research Award 1999, Rosenstiel Award 2000, Gairdner Award 2001, Nobel Prize in Chem. (shared) 2003. *Publications:* numerous articles in scientific journals. *Address:* The Rockefeller University, 1230 York Avenue, New York, NY 10021, USA (office). *Telephone:* (212) 327-8000 (office). *Website:* www.rockefeller.edu (office).

McKINSTRY, Nancy, BA, MBA; American publishing executive; *CEO and Chairman of the Executive Board, Wolters Kluwer NV;* b. 1959; m.; ed Univ. of Rhode Island, Kingston and Columbia Univ., New York; held man. positions with Booz Allen Hamilton (int. man.-consulting firm) 1980s; held a succession of man. positions with Wolters Kluwer cos in North America 1991–99, Vice-Pres. Product Man. and Sr Officer for CCH Inc. and Asst Vice-Pres. Electronic Products Div. for CCH –1996, Pres. and CEO CCH Legal Information Services 1996, CEO Wolters Kluwer's operations in North America –2001, mem. Exec. Bd Wolters Kluwer NV 2001–, Chair. Exec. Bd Wolters Kluwer NV, responsible for Wolters Kluwer's Divs, Business Devt, Strategy and Tech. 2001–03, CEO and Chair. Exec. Bd 2003–; CEO SCP Communications (medical information co.) 1999; mem. Bd of Dirs Ericsson 2004–; mem. Bd of Dirs American Chamber of Commerce in the Netherlands 2004–, TiasNimbas Business School; mem. Advisory Bd Univ. of Rhode Island, mem. University Club of New York City; Hon. LLD (Univ. of Rhode Island); ranked by Fortune magazine as one of 50 Most Powerful Women in Business outside the US (fourth) 2003, (fourth) 2004, (seventh) 2005, (eighth) 2006, (10th) 2007, (13th) 2008, ranked by Forbes magazine amongst 100 Most Powerful Women (69th) 2004, (45th) 2005, (67th) 2006, (53rd) 2007, (82nd) 2008, ranked by the Financial Times amongst Top 25 Businesswomen in Europe (eighth) 2006, (14th) 2007; included in Wall Street Journal's 50 Women to Watch 2007. *Address:* Wolters Kluwer NV, Apollolaan 153, PO Box 75248, 1070 AE, Amsterdam, The Netherlands (office). *Telephone:* (20) 6070400 (office). *Fax:* (20) 6070490 (office). *E-mail:* info@wolterskluwer.com (office). *Website:* www.wolterskluwer.com (office).

MACKINTOSH, Sir Cameron Anthony, Kt; British theatre producer; b. 17 Oct. 1946, Enfield; s. of the late Ian Mackintosh and of Diana Mackintosh; ed Prior Park Coll. Bath; stage hand then Asst Stage Man. Theatre Royal, Drury Lane; worked with Emile Littler 1966, with Robin Alexander 1967; producer 1969–; Chair. Cameron Mackintosh 1981–; Dir Delfont Mackintosh 1991–; owns seven theatres in London's West End (Prince of Wales, Prince Edward, Novello, Wyndham's, Noël Coward, Queen's and Gielgud); Pres. Royal Scottish Acad. of Music and Drama 2004–; Hon. Fellow St Catherine's Coll. Oxford 1990; Observer Award for Outstanding Achievement, Laurence Olivier Award 1991, Richard Rodgers Award 2002, Oscar Hammerstein Award 2002. *Productions:* Little Women 1967, Anything Goes 1969, Trelawny 1972, The Card 1973, Winnie the Pooh 1974, Owl and the Pussycat Went to See 1975, Godspell 1975, Side by Side by Sondheim 1976, Oliver! 1977, Diary of a Madam 1977, After Shave 1977, Gingerbread Man 1978, Out on a Limb 1978, My Fair Lady 1979, Oklahoma! 1980, Tomfoolery 1980, Jeeves Takes Charge 1981, Cats 1981, Song and Dance 1982, Blondel 1983, Little Shop of Horrors 1983, Abbacadabra 1983, The Boyfriend 1984, Les Misérables 1985, Café Puccini 1985, Phantom of the Opera 1986, Follies 1987, Miss Saigon 1989, Just So 1990, Five Guys Named Moe 1990, Moby Dick 1992, Putting it Together 1992, The Card 1992, Carousel 1993, Oliver! 1994, Martin Guerre 1996, The Fix 1997, Oklahoma! 1999, The Witches of Eastwick 2000, My Fair Lady 2001, Mary Poppins 2004, Avenue Q 2006. *Leisure interests:* cooking, taking holidays. *Address:* Cameron Mackintosh Ltd, 1 Bedford Square, London, WC1B 3RB, England. *Telephone:* (20) 7637-8866. *Fax:* (20) 7436-2683.

MACKINTOSH, Nicholas John, DPhil, FRS; British professor of experimental psychology; b. 9 July 1935; s. of Dr Ian Mackintosh and Daphne Mackintosh; m. 1st Janet Ann Scott 1960 (divorced 1978); one s. one d.; m. 2nd Bundy Wilson 1978 (divorced 1989); two s.; m. 3rd Leonora Caroline Brosan 1992; one s.; ed Winchester and Magdalen Coll., Oxford; lecturer, Univ. of Oxford 1964–67; Resident Prof., Dalhousie Univ. 1967–73; Prof.,

Univ. of Sussex 1973–81; Prof. of Experimental Psychology and Professorial Fellow of King's Coll., Cambridge 1981–2002; Resident Fellow, Lincoln Coll., Oxford 1966–67; Visiting Prof., Univ. of Pennsylvania 1965–66, Univ. of Hawaii 1972–73, Bryn Mawr Coll. 1977; Ed. Quality Journal of Experimental Psychology 1977–84. *Publications:* Fundamental Issues in Associative Learning (ed. with W. K. Honig) 1969, Mechanisms of Animal Discrimination Learning (with N. S. Sutherland) 1971, the Psychology of Animal Learning 1974, Conditioning and Associative Learning 1983, Animal Learning and Cognition 1994, Cyril Burt: Fraud or Framed? 1995, IQ and Human Intelligence 1998, papers in psychological journals. *Address:* c/o King's College, Cambridge, CB2 1ST, England. *Telephone:* (1223) 351386.

McKNIGHT, Hon. William Hunter, PC; Canadian politician; *Principal, McKnight & Associates;* b. 12 July 1940, Elrose, Sask.; m. Beverley Ogden; two s.; ed Wartime and Elrose, Sask.; fmr farmer and business exec.; MP for Kindersley-Lloydminster (Sask.) 1979–93, fmr Chair. House Standing Cttee on Agric., fmr mem. Transport Cttee, Man. and Mem.'s Services Cttee, Finance, Trade and Econ. Affairs Cttee, fmr Progressive Conservative Party spokesperson on Canadian Wheat Bd, on Int. Trade, fmr Deputy Opposition House Leader; Progressive Conservative Party Minister of Labour 1984–86, of Indian Affairs and Northern Devt 1986–89, of Defence 1989–91, of Agric. 1991–93, of Energy, Mines and Resources 1993; Chair. NAFTA Trade Consultants Inc. 1993; Founder, Dir and Chair. Anvil Range Mining Corpn 1994–; Prin., McKnight & Assocs (int. trade and financial consultancy); Dir Gamblers Restaurant Inc. 1995–, Marvas Developments Ltd 1995–, Mid-North Resources Ltd 1995–, R.E.S. Int. Inc. 1995, Sci-Tec Instruments Inc. 1995–, Diadem Resources Ltd 2002–; Hon. Consul, Ecuador 1995. *Address:* McKnight & Associates, Standard Life Tower, 4th Floor, 128 4th Avenue South, Saskatoon, Sask. S7K 1M8, Canada (office). *Telephone:* (306) 242-3147 (office); (306) 244-6779 (office). *Fax:* (306) 244-7171 (office). *Website:* www.mcknightandassociates.ca (office).

McKUEN, Rod; American writer and composer; b. 29 April 1933, Oakland, Calif.; has appeared in numerous films, concerts and on TV; composer of film scores and background music for TV shows; composer-lyricist of many songs; Pres. of numerous record and book cos; mem. Bd of Dirs American Nat. Theater of Ballet, Animal Concern; mem. Bd of Govs Nat. Acad. of Recording Arts and Sciences; mem. American Soc. of Composers, Authors and Publishers (ASCAP), Writers Guild, AFTRA, MPA, NARAS; Pres. of American Guild of Variety Artists (AGVA); mem. Bd of Dirs Calif. Music Theater; Grand Prix du Disque 1966, 1974, 1975, 1982, Golden Globe 1969, Motion Picture Daily Award 1969; LA Shrine Club Award 1975, Freedoms Foundation 1975, Horatio Alger Award 1976; Brandeis Univ. Literary Trust Award 1981, Freedoms Foundation Patriot Medal 1981, Salvation Army Man of the Year 1983, Rose d'Or, Cannes 1986, Myasthenia Gravis Community Service Award 1986. *Works include:* Symphony Number One, Concerto for Guitar and Orchestra, Concerto for Four Harpsichords, Seascapes for Piano and Orchestra, Adagio for Harp and Strings, Piano Variations, Concerto Number Three for Piano and Orchestra 1972, The Plains of My Country (ballet) 1972, The City (orchestral suite) 1973, Ballad of Distances (orchestral suite) 1973, Bicentennial Ballet 1975, Symphony Number Three 1975, over 200 record albums. *Film scores:* Joanna 1968, The Prime of Miss Jean Brodie 1969, Me, Natalie 1969, A Boy Named Charlie Brown 1970, Come to Your Senses 1971, Scandalous John 1971, Wildflowers 1971, The Borrowers 1973, Lisa Bright and Dark 1973, Awareness of Emily 1976, The Unknown War 1979, Man to Himself 1980, Portrait of Rod McKuen 1982, Death Rides this Trail 1983, The Living End 1983, The Beach 1984. *Publications:* And Autumn Came 1954, Stanyan Street and Other Sorrows 1966, Listen to the Warm 1967, Twelve Years of Christmas 1968, In Someone's Shadow 1969, With Love 1970, Caught in the Quiet 1970, Fields of Wonder 1971, The Carols of Christmas 1971, And to Each Season 1972, Beyond the Boardwalk 1972, Come to Me in Silence 1973, America–An Affirmation 1974, Seasons in the Sun 1974, Alone, Moment to Moment 1974, The McKuen Omnibus 1975, Celebrations of the Heart 1975, My Country 200 1975, I'm Strong but I Like Roses, Sleep Warm, Beyond the Boardwalk 1976, The Sea Around Me... The Hills Above 1976, Finding My Father (biographical) 1977, Coming Close to Earth 1977, Hand in Hand... 1977, Love's Been Good to Me 1979, We Touch the Sky 1979, Looking for a Friend 1980, An Outstretched Hand 1980, The Power Bright and Shining 1980, Too Many Midnights 1981, Rod McKuen's Book of Days 1981, The Beautiful Strangers 1981, The Works of Rod McKuen, Vol. 1, Poetry 1982, Watch for the Wind... 1982, Rod McKuen – 1984 Book of Days 1983, The Sound of Solitude 1983, Suspension Bridge 1984, Another Beautiful Day 1985, Valentines 1985, Intervals 1986. *Address:* PO Box 2783, Los Angeles, CA 90028, USA.

MacLACHLAN, Kyle, BFA; American actor; b. 22 Feb. 1959, Yakima, Wash.; m. Desiree Gruber; ed Univ. of Washington, Seattle; stage appearances in regional Shakespeare productions and off-Broadway in Palace of Amateurs. *Films include:* Dune 1984, Blue Velvet 1986, The Hidden 1988, Don't Tell Her It's Me 1990, The Doors 1991, Where the Day Takes You 1992, The Trial 1993, Twin Peaks: Fire Walk With Me 1992, Rich in Love 1993, Against the Wall 1994, The Flintstones 1994, Showgirls 1995, Trigger Effect 1996, Mad Dog Time 1996, One Night Stand 1997, X-Change 2000, Hamlet 2000, Timecode 2000, Perfume 2001, Me Without You 2001, Miranda 2002, Northfork 2003, Touch of Pink 2004, Free Jimmy (voice) 2006. *Plays:* Palace of Amateurs, Minetta Lane Theatre (off Broadway), New York, On An Average Day, Comedy Theatre, London 2002. *Television includes:* Twin Peaks (series) 1990–91, Roswell 1994, Moonshine Highway 1996, Windsor Protocol 1996, The Invisible Man 1998, Thunder Point 1998, Route 9 1998, The Spring 2000, Sex and the City 2000–02, Jo 2002, The Librarian: Quest for the Spear 2004, Mysterious Island 2005, In Justice (series) 2006, Desperate Housewives (series) 2006–07. *Address:* c/o Wolf/Kasteller, 132 South Rodeo Drive, Suite 300, Beverly Hills, CA 90212, USA.

McLACHLIN, Beverley, MPh; Canadian lawyer and judge; *Chief Justice of Canada;* b. 7 Sept. 1943, Pincher Creek, Alberta; d. of Ernest Gietz and Eleanora Kruschell; m. 1st Roderick McLachlin (died 1988); one s.; m. 2nd Frank McArdle 1992; ed Univ. of Alberta, Edmonton; practised law with Wood, Moir, Hyde & Ross, Edmonton 1968–71; called to the Bar of BC; practised law with Bull, Housser and Tupper, Vancouver 1972–75; Assoc. Prof., Univ. of British Columbia 1974–81; named to Co. Court of Vancouver 1981, Supreme Court of BC 1981–85, BC Court of Appeal 1985–88; Chief Justice of the Supreme Court of BC 1988; Justice, Supreme Court of Canada 1989–, Chief Justice of Canada (first woman) 2000–; Chair. Canadian Judicial Council, Advisory Council of the Order of Canada, Bd of Govs of Nat. Judicial Inst.; mem. Privy Council of Canada.; Hon. LLD (Toronto) 1995, (York) 1999, (Law Soc. Upper Canada) 2000, (Ottawa) 2000, (Calgary) 2000, (Brock Univ.) 2000, (Simon Fraser Univ.) 2000, (Victoria) 2000, (Alberta) 2000, (Lethbridge) 2001, (Bridgewater State Coll.) 2001, (Mount St Vincent Univ.) 2002, (PEI) 2002, (Montreal) 2003, (Manitoba) 2004, (Queen's Univ. Belfast) 2004, (Dalhousie) 2004, (Carleton) 2004, (Maine at Fort Kent) 2005. *Leisure interests:* hiking, swimming, cross-country skiing. *Address:* Supreme Court of Canada, Supreme Court Building, 301 Wellington Street, Ottawa, ON K1A 0J1, Canada (office). *Telephone:* (613) 992-6940 (office). *Fax:* (613) 952-3192 (office). *Website:* www.scc-csc.gc.ca (office).

McLAGLEN, Andrew V.; British film director; b. 28 July 1920, London; s. of Victor McLaglen; m. Veda Ann Borg 1946 (divorced 1958, died 1973); one s. one d.; ed Univ. of Virginia; acted in films Since You Went Away 1944, Paris Underground 1945; Unit Production Man. for Hondo 1953. *Films include:* as Asst Dir: Love, Honor and Goodbye 1945, Bullfighter and the Lady 1951, Wild Stallion (uncredited) 1952, Here Come the Marines 1952, The Quiet Man (second asst dir) 1952, Big Jim McLain 1952, Kansas Pacific 1953, Fort Vengeance 1953, Plunder of the Sun 1953, Island in the Sky 1953, The High and the Mighty 1954, Track of the Cat 1954, Blood Alley 1955; as Dir: Gun the Man Down 1956, Man in the Vault 1956, Seven Men from Now (producer) 1956, The Abductors 1957, Freckles 1960, The Little Shepherd of Kingdom Come 1961, McLintock! 1963, Shenandoah 1965, The Rare Breed 1966, Monkeys, Go Home! 1967, The Way West 1967, The Ballad of Josie 1968, The Devil's Brigade 1968, Bandolero! 1968, Hellfighters 1968, The Undefeated 1969, Chisum 1970, One More Train to Rob 1971, Something Big (also producer) 1971, Fools' Parade (also producer) 1971, Cahill, U.S. Marshal 1973, Mitchell 1975, The Last Hard Men 1976, Steiner – Das eiserne Kreuz, 2. Teil (aka Breakthrough) 1979, The Wild Geese 1978, North Sea Hijack 1980, The Sea Wolves: The Last Charge of the Calcutta Light Horse 1980, Deprisa, Deprisa 1981, Sweet Hours 1982, Antonieta 1982, Carmen 1983, Sahara 1983, Eye of the Widow 1989, Return from the River Kwai 1989. *Television includes:* Gunsmoke (series) 1956–65, Have Gun – Will Travel (series, 116 episodes) 1957, Perry Mason (series) 1957, Hotel de Paree (series) 1959, Rawhide (series) 1959, The Virginian (series) 1962, Banacek (series) 1972, Hec Ramsey (series) 1972, The Log of the Black Pearl 1975, Stowaway to the Moon 1975, Banjo Hackett: Roamin' Free 1976, Trail of Danger 1977, Code R (series) 1977, The Fantastic Journey (series) 1977, Murder at the World Series 1977, The Shadow Riders 1982, The Blue and the Gray (mini-series) 1982, Travis McGee 1983, The Dirty Dozen: The Next Mission 1985, On Wings of Eagles (mini-series) 1986.

MacLAINE, Shirley; American film actress, writer and film director; b. 24 April 1934, Richmond, Va; d. of Ira Beaty and Kathlyn MacLean; sister of Warren Bull Beatty (q.v.); m. Steve Parker 1954; one d.; ed grammar school and Lee High School, Washington; fmr chorus girl and dancer; Theater Owners of America Star of the Year Award 1967, Berlin Film Festival Lifetime Achievement Award 1999, Malibu Film Festival Life Achievement Award 2001. *Films include:* The Trouble With Harry, Artists and Models, Around The World in 80 Days, Hot Spell, The Matchmaker, Can-Can, Career, The Apartment, Two For The Seesaw, The Children's Hour, Irma La Douce, What A Way To Go, The Yellow Rolls-Royce, Gambit, Woman Times Seven, The Bliss of Mrs Blossom, Sweet Charity, Two Mules For Sister Sara, Desperate Characters (Best Actress Award, Berlin Film Festival 1971), The Possessions of Joel Delaney, The Turning Point 1977, Being There 1979, Loving Couples 1980, The Change of Seasons 1981, Slapstick 1981, Terms of Endearment (Acad. Award for Best Actress) 1984, Out on a Limb 1987, Madame Sousatzka (Golden Globe Award for Best Actress) 1989, Steel Magnolias 1989, Waiting for the Light 1990, Postcards from the Edge 1990, Used People 1993, Wrestling Ernest Hemingway 1994, Guarding Tess 1994, Mrs Westbourne 1995, Mrs Winterbourne 1996, The Celluloid Closet, The Evening Star 1996, Looking for Lulu, Bet Bruce, Bruno (also dir), Joan of Arc 1999, The Dress Code 2000, Rumor Has It... 2005, In Her Shoes 2005, Bewitched 2005, Rumor Has It 2005, Ant Bully 2006, Closing the Ring 2007. *Revues:* If My Friends Could See Me Now 1974, To London With Love 1976, London 1982, Out There Tonight 1990. *Television films:* The West Side Waltz 1994, Joan of Arc, These Old Broads 2001. *Video:* Shirley MacLaine's Inner Workout 1989. *Produced and co-directed:* The Other Half of the Sky – A China Memoir 1973. *Publications:* Don't Fall Off the Mountain 1971, The New Celebrity Cookbook 1973, You Can Get There From Here 1975 (Vols 1 and 2 of autobiog.), Out on a Limb (Vol. 3) 1983, Dancing in the Light 1985 (Vol. 4), It's All in the Playing (Vol. 5) 1987, Going Within (Vol. 6) 1989, Dance While You Can (Vol. 7) 1991, My Lucky Stars (Vol. 8) 1995, The Camino 2000, Out on a Leash 2003, Sage-ing While Age-ing 2007. *Address:* MacLaine Enterprises Inc., 25200 Malibu Road, Suite 101, Santa Monica, CA 90265, USA (office). *Telephone:* (310) 317-8500. *Fax:* (310) 317-8504. *E-mail:* info@shirleymaclaine.com. *Website:* shirleymaclaine.com.

MacLAREN, Hon. Roy, PC; Canadian politician and business executive; b. 26 Oct. 1934, Vancouver; s. of Wilbur MacLaren and Anne Bailey MacLaren; m. Alethea Mitchell 1959; two s. one d.; ed Univ. of British Columbia, Univ. of Cambridge, UK, Harvard Univ., USA, Univ. of Toronto; joined Dept of External Affairs 1957; served in Hanoi, Prague, Geneva, Ottawa, New York; Dir Public Affairs, Massey Ferguson Ltd 1969–73; Pres. Ogilvy and Mather (Canada) Ltd 1974–76; Chair. CB Media Ltd 1977–83, 1984–93; Dir Deutsche Bank (Canada), Royal LePage Ltd, London Insurance Group Inc.; elected Liberal MP for Etobicoke North 1979–96; Parl. Sec. to Minister of Energy, Mines & Resources 1980–82; Minister of State (Finance) 1983, Minister of Nat. Revenue 1984, for Int. Trade 1993–96; High Commr in UK 1996–2000; Commr Trilateral Comm.; Dir (non-exec.) Standard Life, Brascan, Patheon, Broadview Press, Pacific Safety Products, Amec N American Advisory Bd 2001–; Dir Canadian Opera Co.; Chair. Canada-India Business Council, Canadian Inst. of Int. Affairs, Canada-Europe Round Table; Hon. Col 7th Toronto Regt Royal Canadian Artillery; Hon. Dr Sacred Letters (Toronto); Hon. Dr Civil Letters (Univ. of N Alabama); Hon. LLD (Univ. of New Brunswick, Univ. of Prince Edward Island). *Publications:* Canadians in Russia, 1918–1919 1976, Canadians on the Nile, 1882–1898 1978, Canadians Behind Enemy Lines, 1939–1945 1981, Honourable Mentions 1986, African Exploits: The Diaries of William Grant Stairs 1997, Commissions High 2006. *Leisure interests:* skiing, cross-country walking. *Address:* 425 Russell Hill Road, Toronto, Ont. M5P 2S4, Canada (home). *Telephone:* (416) 932-9255 (home). *Fax:* (416) 932-3571 (home).

McLARTY, Thomas F. (Mack); American fmr politician and business executive; *President, Kissinger McLarty Associates;* b. 1946; m. Donna K. Cochran 1969; two s.; ed Univ. of Arkansas; worked in family automobile and transport business; elected to Ark. House of Reps 1969; Chair. Ark. State Democratic Party 1974–76; apptd mem. Bd Arkla Inc., La, subsequently joined staff, apptd Chair. 1983; Chief of Staff to Pres. Bill Clinton 1992–94, Presidential Counselor 1994–2001, Special Envoy for Americas 1997; currently Pres. Kissinger McLarty Assocs Washington DC and New York City and Chair. McLarty Cos, Little Rock, Ark.; Sr Advisor, The Carlyle Group; mem. Bd Council of Americas, Inter-American Dialogue; Sec. of State's Distinguished Service Medal, Order of Aztec Eagle (Mexico) and numerous other awards and honours. *Address:* c/o The Carlyle Group, 1001 Pennsylvania Avenue, NW, Washington, DC 20004-2505, USA. *Telephone:* (212) 759-7919 (NY); (202) 822-8182 (DC).

MacLAURIN OF KNEBWORTH, Baron (Life Peer), cr. 1996, of Knebworth in the County of Hertfordshire; **Ian Charter MacLaurin,** Kt, DL, FRSA; British business executive; *Chairman, Vodafone Group Foundation;* b. 30 March 1937, Blackheath; s. of Arthur and Evelina MacLaurin; m. 1st Ann Margaret Collar 1962 (died 1999); one s. two d.; m. 2nd Paula Elizabeth Brooke 2001; ed Malvern Coll., Worcs.; joined Tesco as a Trainee Man. 1959; Dir Tesco Stores (Holdings) Ltd 1970, Man. Dir 1974–83, Deputy Chair. 1983–85, Chair. 1985–97; Chair. Vodafone 1998–99, Deputy Chair. 1999–2000, Chair. 2000–06, Adviser 2006–, Chair. Vodafone Group Foundation 2006–; Chancellor, Univ. of Herts. 1996–; Chair. England and Wales Cricket Bd 1996–2002; Dir (non-exec.) Enterprise Oil 1984–91, Gleneagles Hotels PLC 1992–, Guinness PLC 1986–95, Nat. Westminster Bank PLC 1990–97, Whitbread PLC 1997–2001 (Deputy Chair. 1999–), Health Clinic 2001–02, Evolution 2004–; Pres. Inst. of Grocery Distribution 1989–92; Fellow Inst. of Marketing 1987; Freeman of City of London 1981; Chair. Malvern Coll. Council 2003–; mem. MCC; mem. Lords Taverners and Worshipful Co. of Carmen; Hon. Fellow (Wales Cardiff) 1996; Hon. DUniv (Stirling) 1986, Dr hc (Hertfordshire). *Publication:* Tiger by the Tail (memoirs) 1999. *Leisure interests:* cricket, golf. *Address:* Vodafone Group Foundation, Vodafone House, The Connection, Newbury, Berks., RG14 2FN (office); House of Lords, London, SW1A 0PW, England. *E-mail:* groupfoundation@vodafone.com (office). *Website:* www.vodafonefoundation.org (office).

MacLAVERTY, Bernard, BA, DipEd; Irish writer and dramatist; b. 14 Sept. 1942, Belfast; s. of John MacLaverty and Mary MacLaverty; m. Madeline McGuckin 1967; one s. three d.; ed Queen's Univ., Belfast; fmrly medical lab. technician, English teacher; fmr Writer-in-Residence, Univ. of Aberdeen; mem. Aosdána; NI and Scottish Arts Councils Awards, Irish Sunday Independent Award 1983, London Evening Standard Award for Screenplay 1984, Scottish Writer of the Year (jtly) 1988, Soc. of Authors Travelling Scholarship 1994, Saltire Scottish Book of the Year Award 1997, Stakis Scottish Writer of the Year, Whitbread Novel of the Year, Creative Scotland Award 2003, Best First Dir, BAFTA Scotland 2004. *Television:* plays: My Dear Palestrina 1980, Phonefun Limited 1982, The Daily Woman 1986, Sometime in August 1989; documentary: Hostages 1992; adaptation: The Real Charlotte, by Somerville and Ross 1989. *Screenplays:* Cal 1984, Lamb 1985, Bye-Child (short film, also dir) 2003. *Radio plays:* My Dear Palestrina 1980, Secrets 1981, No Joke 1983, The Break 1988, Some Surrender 1988, Lamb 1992, Grace Notes 2003, The Woman from the North 2007. *Publications:* novels: Lamb 1980, Cal 1983, Grace Notes 1997, The Anatomy School 2001; short story collections: Secrets and Other Stories 1977, A Time to Dance and Other Stories 1982, The Great Profundo and Other Stories 1987, Walking the Dog and Other Stories 1994, Matters of Life & Death and Other Stories 2006; juvenile fiction: A Man in Search of a Pet 1978, Andrew McAndrew 1988. *Address:* c/o Gill Coleridge, Rogers, Coleridge & White, 20 Powis Mews, London, W11 1JN, England (office). *Telephone:* (20) 7221-3717 (office). *Fax:* (20) 7229-9084 (office). *E-mail:* info@rcwlitagency.co.uk (office). *Website:* www.rcwlitagency.co.uk (office); www.bernardmaclaverty.com (home).

McLAY, James Kenneth (Jim), QSO, LLB; New Zealand politician, lawyer and business consultant; *Managing Director, J. K. McLay Ltd;* b. 21 Feb. 1945, Auckland; s. of the late Robert McLay and Joyce Evelyn Dee; m. Marcy Farden 1983; one s.; ed King's Coll. and Univ. of Auckland; officer, Territorial Force 1967–70; barrister 1968–; Man. Ed. Recent Law 1969–70; MP for Birkenhead 1975–87; Attorney-Gen. and Minister of Justice 1978–84; Deputy Prime Minister 1984; Leader of Opposition 1984–86; Man. Dir J.K. McLay Ltd 1987–; Deputy Chair. TrustBank Auckland Ltd 1988–93; Chair. Macquarie New Zealand Ltd (Subsidiary of Macquarie Bank, Australia) 1994–, Unichem Chemist Ltd 1999–; mem. 1990 Comm. 1988–91; mem. Ministerial Working Party on Accident Compensation 1991; Chair. Review of Defence Funding and Man. 1991, Wholesale Electricity Market Study 1991–92, Wholesale Electricity Market Devt Group 1993–94; NZ Commr to Int. Whaling Comm. 1994–2002; Chair. Roading Advisory Group 1997, Project Marukav Audit Group 1998–, Council for Infrastructure Devt; mem. Bd Evergreen Forests Ltd 1995–, MotorRace NZ Ltd 1996–99, Neurouz Ltd 2001–, Generator Bonds Ltd 2003–, Metlifecare Ltd 2005–; mem. Advisory Bd Westfield New Zealand Ltd 1998–; Adviser to Building Industry Authority on revision to earthquake codes 1997; Trustee Auckland Medical School Foundation 1993–99; Nat. Party; NZ Suffrage Centennial Model. *Publications:* numerous papers, articles, etc. on political, commercial and environmental issues. *Leisure interest:* trout fishing. *Address:* J.K. McLay Ltd, PO Box 8885, Symonds Street, Auckland 1, New Zealand (office). *Telephone:* (9) 377-0633 (office). *Fax:* (9) 309-6220 (office). *E-mail:* jmclay@mclay.co.nz (office).

McLEAN, Don; American singer, instrumentalist and composer; b. 2 Oct. 1945, New Rochelle, NY; s. of Donald McLean and Elizabeth Bucci; m. Patrisha Shnier 1987; one s. one d.; ed Iona Coll.; Pres. Benny Bird Publishing Corpn, Inc., Don McLean Music, Starry Night Music; mem. Hudson River Sloop Singers 1969; solo concert tours throughout USA, Canada, Australia, Europe, Far East etc.; numerous TV appearances; composer of film scores for Fraternity Row, Flight of Dragons; composer of over 200 songs including Prime Time, American Pie, Tapestry, Vincent (Starry, Starry Night), And I Love You So, Castles In the Air, etc.; mem. ASCAP, BMI, NARAS, AFTRA, Lotos Club, Coffee House NYC, Grouch Club, London; recipient of many gold discs in USA, Australia, UK and Ireland; Israel Cultural Award 1981. *Recordings include:* Tapestry 1970, American Pie 1971, Don McLean 1972, Playin' Favorites 1973, Homeless Brother 1974, Solo 1976, Prime Time 1977, Chain Lightning 1979, Believers 1982, Dominion 1983, Love Tracks 1988, Headroom 1991, Don McLean Christmas 1992, Favorites and Rarities (Box Set) 1993, The River of Love 1995, For the Memories Vols I and II 1996, Christmas Dreams 1997, Starry Starry Night 2000, Don McLean Sings Marty Robbins 2001, The Western Album 2003, You've Got to Share 2003, Christmastime! 2004, Rearview Mirror 2005; singles include: The Mountains of Mourne 1973, Wonderful Baby 1975, Crying 1980, Since I Don't Have You 1981; hit cover versions: And I Love You So (Perry Como) 1973, American Pie (Madonna) 2000; numerous compiliation packages, etc. *Publications:* Songs of Don McLean 1972, The Songs of Don McLean (Vol. II) 1974. *Leisure interests:* antique furniture, film history, western horsemanship (trail riding). *Address:* c/o Steve Martin, The Agency Group, 1775 Broadway, New York, NY 10019, USA (office). *Telephone:* (212) 581-3100 (office). *E-mail:* joshuadick@theagencygroup.com (office). *Website:* www.theagencygroup.com (office); www.don-mclean.com.

McLEAN, Hon. Rev. Walter Franklin, PC, LLD, MDiv, DD; Canadian politician, clergyman and business consultant; *Chairman, McLean and Associates;* b. 26 April 1936, Leamington, Ont.; s. of J.L.W. McLean; m. Barbara Scott 1961; four s.; ed Victoria Coll., Univ. of British Columbia, Knox Coll., Univ. of Toronto, Univ. of Edinburgh; Co-Founder CUSO (fmrly first Nigerian Co-ordinator); fmr Exec. Dir Man. Centennial Corpn; fmr Minister of Knox Presbyterian Church, Waterloo; Alderman for City of Waterloo 1976–79; MP 1979–93; fmr mem. Standing Cttee on Communications and Culture, on External Affairs, on Nat. Defence; fmr mem. Special Sub-Cttee on Latin America and Caribbean; Sec. of State of Canada 1984–85, Minister of State (Immigration) and Minister Responsible for the Status of Women 1984–86; mem. Canadian Del. to UN 1986–93; Prime Minister's Special Rep. on Southern Africa and Commonwealth Affairs 1989–93; Canadian Rep. at Southern Africa Devt Co-ordination Conf. (SADCC) 1987–93, at Commonwealth Foreign Ministers' Confs 1987, 1988, 1989, 1991; Chair. Parl. Sub-Cttee on Devt and Human Rights, 1990–93; Pres. Franklin Consulting Services Ltd 1994–; Prin. Osborne Group 2000–; Chair. McLean and Associates 2004–; fmr Pres. Int. Council of Parliamentarians for Global Action; Chair. Canadian UNA Human Rights Cttee, Criminal Compensation Bd of Ontario 2000–03; Dir TAB International, Calgary 2005–; mem. Advisory Bd, Royal Reads Univ., Victoria, BC 1995–, Bd Toronto School of Theology, Univ. of Toronto 2005–; Convenor Millennium Celebration, Presbyterian Church in Canada; Hon. Consul for Namibia in Canada 1995–; Hon. LLD (Wilfrid Laurier) 1995, Hon. DD (Knox Coll. Toronto); Paul Harris Fellow, Rotary International 1984, Canada's 125th Anniversary Medal 1992, Canadian Bureau for Int. Educ. Award of Merit 1994, Queen's 50th Anniversary Medal 2002, Distinguished Alumni Award (Univ. of Victoria) 2002. *Publication:* Canada, South Africa and the 1990s 1992. *Leisure interests:* golf, curling, music. *Address:* 122 Avondale Avenue S, Waterloo, Ont., N2L 2C3, Canada (office). *Telephone:* (519) 578-5932 (office). *Fax:* (519) 578-7799 (office). *E-mail:* walter@mcleanandassociates.ca (office). *Website:* www.mcleanandassociates.ca (office).

McLEISH, Rt Hon Henry, PC; British politician and academic; b. 15 June 1948, Methil, Fife; m. 1st (died 1995); one s. one d.; m. 2nd Julie McLeish 1998; ed Buckhaven High School, Methil, Heriot-Watt Univ.; fmr professional football for East Fife FC and Leeds United FC; began career as local govt research officer and planning officer; lecturer in Social Sciences, Heriot-Watt Univ. 1973–87; mem. Kirkcaldy Dist Council 1974–77; mem. Fife Regional Council 1978–87, Leader 1982–87; MSP for Fife Cen. 1999–2001, Opposition Spokesman on Social Security 1996–97; Minister for Enterprise and Lifelong

Learning 1997–2000; First Minister of Scotland 2000–01; Consultant on Govt and Political Relations, Halogen Communications 2005–; mem. Scottish Broadcasting Comm. 2007–; Visiting Prof. Univ. of Arkansas, USA. *Publications:* Scotland First: Truth and Consequences 2004, Global Scots: Voices from Afar (with Kenny MacAskill) 2006, Wherever the Saltire Flies (with Kenny MacAskill) 2006, Scotland: The Road Divides (with Tom Brown) (2007). *Leisure interests:* reading, history, life and work of Robert Burns. *Address:* Halogen Communications, 4 Queen Street, Edinburgh, EH2 1JE (office). *Telephone:* (131) 2020120 (office). *Fax:* (131) 2253757 (office). *E-mail:* info@halogencom.com (office). *Website:* www.halogencom.com (office).

McLELLAN, Rt Hon. Anne, BA, LLB, PC; Canadian politician; b. 31 Aug. 1950, Hants. County, NS; d. of Howard Gilmore McLellan and Joan Mary Pullan; ed Dalhousie Univ. and King's Coll. (London, UK); Asst Prof. of Law Univ. of New Brunswick 1976–80; Acting Assoc. Dean and Assoc. Prof. of Law Univ. of Alberta 1980–89, Assoc. Dean 1985–87, Prof. 1989–93, Acting Dean 1991–92; MP for Edmonton W. 1993–; Minister of Natural Resources and Fed. Interlocutor for Métis and Non-Status Indians 1993–97; Minister of Justice and Attorney-Gen. 1997–2002; Minister of Health 2002–03; Deputy Prime Minister and Minister of Public Safety and Emergency Preparedness 2003–06; Chair. Social Union Cttee 1997–; Vice Chair. Special Cttee of Council 1997–; mem. Econ. Union Cttee 1997–, Treasury Bd 1997–; fmr mem. Bd of Dirs Canadian Civil Liberties Asscn, Alberta Legal Aid; fmr Vice-Pres. Univ. of Alberta Faculty Asscn. *Address:* 1000 ATCO Centre, 10035 - 105 Street NW, Edmonton, AB T5J 3T2, Canada (office). *Telephone:* (780) 969-2648 (office). *Website:* www.annemclellan.ca.

MacLENNAN, Murdoch; British newspaper executive; *CEO, Telegraph Group Ltd;* started career as graduate trainee The Scotsman newspaper; Production Dir Scottish Daily Record and Sunday Mail 1982–84; Dir of Production Mirror Group 1984–85; Production and Tech. Dir Express Newspapers 1985–89, Man. Dir 1989–92; Group Operations Dir Mirror Group Newspapers and Man. Dir Scottish Daily Record and Sunday Mail 1992–94; Group Man. Dir Associated Newspapers 1994–2004; CEO Telegraph Group Ltd 2004–; fmr Pres. IFRA (newspaper publishers' asscn); Chair. Press Asscn Remuneration Cttee; Vice-Pres. and Appeals Chair. Newspaper Press Fund; Companion Inst. of Man.; Freeman of the City of London; Dr hc (Paisley). *Address:* Telegraph Group Ltd, 1 Canada Square, Canary Wharf, London, E14 5DT, England (office). *Telephone:* (20) 7538-5000 (office). *Fax:* (20) 7513-2512 (office). *Website:* www.pressoffice.telegraph.co.uk.

MACLENNAN OF ROGART, Baron (Life peer), cr. 2001, of Rogart Sutherland; **Rt Hon. Robert Adam Ross Maclennan,** PC, MA, LLB; British politician and barrister-at-law; *Liberal Democrats Spokesman on Scotland and the Cabinet, House of Lords;* b. 26 June 1936, Glasgow; s. of Sir Hector Maclennan and Lady Maclennan; m. Helen Cutter Noyes 1968; one s. one d. one step-s.; ed Glasgow Academy, Balliol Coll., Oxford, Trinity Coll., Cambridge, Columbia Univ., New York; MP for Caithness and Sutherland 1966–97, Caithness, Sutherland and Easter Ross 1997–2001; Parl. Pvt. Sec. to Sec. of State for Commonwealth Affairs and Minister without portfolio 1967–70, Parl. Under-Sec. of State for Prices and Consumer Protection 1974–79; Opposition Spokesman on Scottish Affairs 1970–71, on Defence 1971–72, on Foreign Affairs 1980–81; resgnd from Labour Party 1981; Founder mem. SDP 1981; SDP Spokesman on Agriculture 1981–87, on Home and Legal Affairs 1983–87, on Econ. Affairs 1987; Leader SDP 1987–88; Jt Leader SLD 1988; Liberal Democrat convenor on Home Affairs 1988–94, Legal Affairs 1988–94, Nat. Heritage 1992–94; mem. Public Accounts Cttee 1979–2001; Liberal Democrat 1994–98, Spokesperson on Constitutional Affairs, Culture and Media 1994–2001; mem. Convention on Future of Europe 2002–03; currently Liberal Democrats Lords Spokesman on Scotland and the Cabinet; Légion d'Honneur 2004. *Music:* wrote libretti of operas The Lie 1992 and Friend of the People 1999. *Leisure interests:* music, theatre and visual arts. *Address:* House of Lords, London, SW1A 0PW, England (office). *Telephone:* (20) 7219-4133 (office). *E-mail:* maclennanr@parliament.uk (office).

MACLEOD, Hugh Angus MacIntosh, BSc, DTech; American (b. British) professor of optical sciences and business executive; *President, Thin Film Center Inc.;* b. 20 June 1933, Glasgow, Scotland; s. of Dr John Macleod and Agnes Donaldson Macleod; m. Ann Turner 1957; four s. one d.; ed Lenzie Acad., Univ. of Glasgow; engineer, Sperry Gyroscope Co. Ltd 1954–60; Chief Engineer, Williamson Mfg Co. Ltd 1960–62; Sr Physicist, Mervyn Instruments Ltd 1963; Tech. Man. Sir Howard Grubb, Parsons and Co. Ltd 1963–70; Reader in Thin Film Physics, Newcastle upon Tyne Polytechnic 1971–79; Assoc. Prof., Univ. of Aix-Marseille III 1976, 1979; Prof. of Optical Sciences, Univ. of Arizona, USA 1979–95, Prof. Emer. of Optical Sciences 1995–; Dir-at-Large, Optical Soc. of America 1987–89; Pres. Thin Film Center Inc. 1992–; Dir OptoSigma Corpn 1995–98, Precision Optics Corpn 1997–2002; Dir Soc. of Vacuum Coaters 1998–2004, Vice-Pres. 2006–08, Pres. 2008–(10); Fellow, Int. Soc. for Optical Eng (SPIE), Optical Soc. of America, Inst. of Physics (London); Dr hc (Aix-Marseille); Gold Medal SPIE 1987, Esther Hoffman Beller Medal, Optical Soc. of America 1997, John Matteuci Award 2000, Nathaniel H. Sugerman Award 2002, Life for Thin Film Award, Workshop of European Vacuum Coaters, Anzio 2004, Senator Award, Workshop of European Vacuum Coaters, Anzio 2008. *Publications:* Thin-Film Optical Filters 1969, (3rd edn 2001); over 200 articles, papers and book chapters on optics of thin films. *Leisure interests:* piano, computing. *Address:* Thin Film Center, Inc., 2745 East Via Rotonda, Tucson, AZ 85716-5227, USA (office). *Telephone:* (520) 322-6171 (office); (520) 795-5019 (home). *Fax:* (520) 325-8721 (office). *E-mail:* angus@thinfilmcenter.com (office). *Website:* www.thinfilmcenter.com (office).

McLEOD, James Graham, AO, MB, DPhil, DSc, FRACP, FRCP, FAA, FTSE; Australian professor of neurology and medicine; *Professor Emeritus of Neurology, University of Sydney;* b. 18 Jan. 1932, Sydney; s. of Hector R. McLeod and Dorothy S. McLeod (née Craig); m. Robyn E. Rule 1962; two s. two d.; ed Univ. of Sydney, Univs of Oxford and London, UK, Harvard Univ., USA; Sr Lecturer, Univ. of Sydney 1967–69, Assoc. Prof. 1970–72, Bosch Prof. of Medicine 1972–97, Bushell Prof. of Neurology 1978–97, Prof. Emer. 1997–; Visiting Medical Officer, Royal Prince Alfred Hosp., Sydney 1965–, Head, Dept of Neurology 1978–94; mem. Bd Dirs Royal North Shore Hosp., Sydney (Vice-Chair.) 1978–86; Pres. Australian Asscn of Neurologists 1980–83; Rhodes Scholar 1953–56; Nuffield Travelling Fellow 1964–65; Sir Arthur Sims Travelling Prof. 1983–84; Commonwealth Sr Medical Fellowship 1989; mem. Australian Science and Tech. Council 1987–93; Fellow, Australian Acad. of Tech., Science and Eng, Australian Acad. of Science (Vice-Pres. 1987–88, Treas. 1993–97); Dr hc (Aix-Marseille) 1992; Rhodes Scholar 1953. *Publications:* A Physiological Approach to Clinical Neurology (with J.W. Lance q.v.), Introductory Neurology (with J.W. Lance q.v.) 1989, Peripheral Neuropathy in Childhood (with R.A. Ouvrier and J.D. Pollard) 1999, Inflammatory Neuropathies (ed.) 1994. *Leisure interests:* swimming, boating, music, literature. *Address:* 2 James Street, Woollahra, NSW 2025, Australia (home). *Telephone:* (2) 9362-8362 (home). *Fax:* (2) 9362-8348 (home). *E-mail:* jmcl7953@mail.usyd.edu.au (home).

MACLEOD, Sir (Nathaniel William) Hamish, Kt, KBE, MA; British civil servant (retd); b. 6 Jan. 1940; s. of George Henry Torquil Macleod and Ruth Natalie Wade; m. Fionna Mary Campbell 1970; one s. one d.; ed Strathallan School, Perthshire, St Andrews Univ., Univ. of Bristol; commercial trainee Stewarts and Lloyds, Birmingham 1958–62; Admin. Officer Hong Kong Govt 1966, Dir of Trade and Chief Trade Negotiator 1983–87, Sec. for Trade and Industry 1987–89, Sec. for the Treasury 1989–91, Financial Sec. 1991–95; JP (Hong Kong) 1979–95; mem. Bd Scottish Oriental Smaller Cos Trust 1995–. *Leisure interests:* walking, golf. *Address:* 20 York Road, Edinburgh, EH5 3EH, Scotland (home). *Telephone:* (131) 552-5058 (home). *E-mail:* macleodhamish@hotmail.com (home).

McMAHON, Sir Christopher William 'Kit', Kt, MA; British fmr banker; b. 10 July 1927, Melbourne, Australia; s. of the late Dr J.J. and Margaret McMahon; m. 1st Marion E. Kelso 1956; two s.; m. 2nd Alison Braimbridge 1982; ed Melbourne Grammar School, Univ. of Melbourne and Magdalen Coll., Oxford; Econ. Asst, HM Treasury 1953–57; Econ. Adviser, British Embassy, Washington, DC 1957–60; Fellow and Tutor in Econs, Magdalen Coll., Oxford 1960–64; Adviser, Bank of England 1964–66, Adviser to Govs 1966–70, Exec. Dir 1970–80, Deputy Gov. 1980–85; Deputy Chair. and Chair. (desig.) Midland Bank PLC 1986–87, Dir 1986–91, Chair. 1987–91; Chair. (non-exec.) Coutts Consulting Group PLC 1992–96; Deputy Chair. Taylor Woodrow 1997–2000; Dir Eurotunnel 1987–91, Midland Montagu Holdings 1987–91, Hong Kong and Shanghai Banking Corpn 1987–91, Thomas Cook 1989–91, Pentos 1991–95, Taylor Woodrow PLC 1991–2000, Angela Flowers 1992–, Aegis 1993–99, FI Group 1994–2000; Dir (non-exec.) HistoryWorld 2001–; Chair. Japan Festival Fund 1992; mem. Steering Cttee, Consultative Group on Int. Econ. and Monetary Affairs (Group of Thirty) 1978–84; mem. Court London Univ. 1984–86; Trustee, Whitechapel Art Gallery 1984–90; Trustee Royal Opera House Trust 1984–86, Bd Royal Opera House 1989–97; Gov. Birkbeck Coll. London 1991–, Fellow 2003; Chevalier, Légion d'honneur. *Publications:* Sterling in the Sixties 1964, Techniques of Economic Forecasting 1965. *Leisure interests:* gardening, walking. *Address:* The Old House, Burleigh, Stroud, Glos., GL5 2PQ, England (home).

McMANUS, Sean, BA; American broadcasting executive; *President, CBS News;* s. of Jim McKay; m.; c.; ed Duke Univ.; with ABC (American Broadcasting Corpn) Sports 1977–79, positions including Production Asst, Assoc. Producer; Assoc. Producer NBC Sports 1979, Vice-Pres. Program Planning and Devt 1982–87; joined Trans World Int. 1987, Sr Vice-Pres. US TV Sales and Programming –1996; Pres. CBS Sports 1996–2005, Exec. Producer Nat. Football League (NFL) coverage, Pres. CBS News 2005–. *Address:* CBS News, 524 West 57th Street, New York, NY 10019, USA (office). *Telephone:* (212) 975-4114 (office). *Website:* www.cbsnews.com (office).

McMASTER, Sir Brian John, Kt, CBE, LLB; British arts administrator; b. 9 May 1943, Hitchin, Hertfordshire; ed Wellington Coll., Bristol Univ.; with Int. Artists' Dept, EMI Ltd 1968–73; Controller of Opera Planning, English Nat. Opera 1973–76; Gen. Admin., subsequently Man. Dir Welsh Nat. Opera 1976–91; Artistic Dir Vancouver Opera 1984–89; Festival Dir and CEO Edin. Int. Festival 1991–2006.

McMILLAN, C. Steven, MBA; American business executive; *Chairman and CEO, Sara Lee Corporation;* ed Auburn Univ., AL, Harvard Business School; supply officer, USN 1970–73; man. consultant McKinsey & Co., Chicago 1973–78; joined Sara Lee Corpn 1978, Pres. and CEO Aqualux Water Processing Co. 1978–79, Pres. and CEO Electrolux Canada 1979–82, Pres. and CEO Electrolux Corpn 1982–86, Sr Vice-Pres. Strategy Devt Sara Lee Corpn 1986–90, Head of Packaged Meats, Bakery and Foodservices Businesses 1990–93, and Coffee & Grocery and Household & Bodycare Businesses 1993–97, Pres. and COO Sara Lee Corpn 1997–2000, Pres. and CEO 2000–01, Chair., Pres. and CEO 2001–04, Chair. and CEO 2004–; mem. Bd of Dirs Monsanto, Bank of America; mem. Advisory Bd J.L. Kellogg Grad. School of Man., Northwestern Univ.; mem. Bd Grocery Mfrs Asscn, Econ. Club of Chicago, Chicago Council on Foreign Relations, Catalyst; mem. Business Council, The Business Roundtable, G-100, Exec. Club of Chicago, Civic Cttee of Commercial Club of Chicago; serves on Bd of Steppenwolf Theatre Co.; Trustee Chicago Symphony Orchestra; Dir Sara Lee Foundation, Charlie Trotter's Culinary Educ. Foundation. *Address:* Sara Lee Corporation, Three First National Plaza, Chicago, IL 60602-4260, USA (office). *Telephone:* (312) 558-8727 (office). *Fax:* (312) 558-8653 (office). *Website:* www.saralee.com (office).

McMILLAN, David, BA; British civil servant and international organization executive; *Director General, EUROCONTROL;* ed Univ. of Edinburgh; began his career in FCO 1976, served in Morocco and Zimbabwe, also worked as Transport Sec.-Gen. at British Embassy in Washington, DC; held several posts in Dept of Transport (DfT), including Head of Information, Leader Div. responsible for air traffic control policy 1998–2001, DfT Dir of Rail Restructuring 2001–02, Dir of Strategy and Delivery, responsible for DfT's delivery agenda and for relations with the EU 2002–04, Dir-Gen. of Civil Aviation 2004–07; Dir Gen. EUROCONTROL (European Org. for the Safety of Air Navigation) 2008–; First Vice-Pres. European Civil Aviation Conf. and spokesman for Europe on aviation and environment at Int. Civil Aviation Org. 2005–07; participated in EU's High Level Group on the future of aviation regulation in Europe 2006, 2007. *Address:* c/o Ms Pauline Coady, Assistant to the Director General, EUROCONTROL, Rue de la Fusée 96, 1130 Brussels, Belgium (office). *Telephone:* (2) 729-35-01 (office). *Fax:* (2) 729-91-00 (office). *E-mail:* pauline.coady@eurocontrol.int (office). *Website:* www.eurocontrol.int (office).

MacMILLAN, Jake, PhD, DSc, FRS; British chemist and academic; *Professor Emeritus of Organic Chemistry and Senior Research Fellow, University of Bristol;* b. 13 Sept. 1924, Scotland; s. of John MacMillan and Barbara Lindsay; m. Anne Levy 1952; one s. two d.; ed Lanark Grammar School and Univ. of Glasgow; Assoc. Research Man., ICI 1962–63; Lecturer in Organic Chem., Bristol Univ. 1963–68, Reader 1968–78, Personal Chair. 1978–83, Head of Dept and Alfred Capper Pass Prof. of Organic Chem. 1983–90, Prof. Emer. 1990–, Sr Research Fellow 1996–; Foreign Assoc. NAS (USA) 1991–; Flintoff Medal 1978 and Hugo Muller Medal 1989, Royal Soc. of Chem., Research Medal, Int. Plant Growth Substance Asscn 1982, Charles Reid Barnes Award, American Soc. of Plant Physiology 1988, Pergamon Phytochemistry Prize 1995. *Publications:* over 290 papers and three books on organic chemistry and plant hormones. *Leisure interests:* gardening, theatre. *Address:* School of Chemistry, University of Bristol, Bristol, BS8 1TS (office); 7 Burrough Way, Winterbourne, S Glos., BS36 1LF, England (home). *Telephone:* (117) 3317162 (office); (1454) 775244 (home). *Fax:* (117) 9298611 (office). *E-mail:* jake.macmillan@bris.ac.uk (office). *Website:* (office).

MacMILLAN, Margaret Olwen, OC, BA, BPhil, DPhil, FRSL; Canadian university administrator, historian and writer; *Warden, St Antony's College Oxford;* b. Dec. 1943, Toronto, Ont.; ed Univ. of Toronto, St Antony's Coll., Oxford, UK; Prof. of History, Ryerson Univ., Toronto 1975–2002; Provost and Vice Chancellor, Trinity Coll., Univ. of Toronto 2002–07; Warden St Antony's Coll., Oxford 2007–; Ed. International Journal 1995–2003; Sr Fellow, Massey Coll., Univ. of Toronto; Hon. Fellow, St Antony's Coll. Oxford; Gov.-Gen.'s Literary Award 2003, BBC 4 Samuel Johnson Prize for Non-Fiction, Duff Cooper Award, Hessell-Tiltman Prize. *Publications:* Women of the Raj 1988, Canada and NATO: Uneasy Past, Uncertain Future 1990, Peacemakers: Six Months that Changed the World 2001, Paris 1919 2002, Parties Long Estranged: Canada and Australia in the 20th Century (co-ed.) 2003, Canada's House: Rideau Hall and the Invention of a Canadian Home (with Marjorie Harris and Anne L. Desjardins) 2004, Seize the Hour: When Nixon Met Mao 2006, Nixon and Mao 2007, Dangerous Games: The Uses and Abuses of History 2009. *Address:* Office of the Warden, St Antony's College, 62 Woodstock Road, Oxford, OX2 6JF, England (office). *Telephone:* (1865) 284717 (office). *Fax:* (1865) 274526 (office). *E-mail:* margaret.macmillan@sant.ox.ac.uk (office). *Website:* www.sant.ox.ac.uk (office).

McMURTRY, Larry Jeff; American writer; b. 3 June 1936, Wichita Falls, Tex.; s. of William Jefferson McMurtry and Hazel McIver; m. Josephine Ballard 1959 (divorced 1966); one s. *Television includes:* co-writer and co-producer with Diana Ossana of CBS mini-series Streets of Laredo and ABC mini-series Dead Man's Walk 1996. *Publications:* Horseman Pass By (aka Hud) 1961, Leaving Cheyenne 1963, The Last Picture Show 1966, In a Narrow Grave (essays) 1968, Moving On 1970, All My Friends Are Going to be Strangers 1972, It's Always We Rambled (essay) 1974, Terms of Endearment 1975, Somebody's Darling 1978, Cadillac Jack 1982, The Desert Rose 1983, Lonesome Dove 1985, Texasville 1987, Film Flam: Essay on Hollywood 1987, Anything for Billy 1988, Some Can Whistle 1989, Buffalo Girls 1990, The Evening Star 1992, Streets of Laredo 1993, Pretty Boy Floyd (with Diana Ossana) 1993, The Late Child 1995, Dead Man's Walk 1995, Zeke and Ned (novel, with Diana Ossana) 1996, Comanche Moon 1997, Duane's Depressed 1998, Walter Benjamin at the Dairy Queen 1999, Boone's Lick 2000, Sin Killer: The Berrybender Narratives, Book One 2002, The Wandering Hill: The Berrybender Narratives, Book Two 2003, Folly and Glory: The Berrybender Narratives, Book Three 2004, Loop Group 2004, When the Light Goes 2007, Books: A Memoir 2008. *Leisure interest:* antiquarian bookselling. *Address:* Saria Co. Inc., 2509 North Campbell Avenue, Suite 95, Tucson, AZ 85719, USA (office).

McNALLY, Derek, PhD; British astronomer (retd); b. 28 Oct. 1934, Belfast; s. of David McNally and Sarah McNally (née Long); m. Shirley Allen 1959; one s. one d.; ed Royal Belfast Acad. Inst., Queen's Univ., Belfast and Royal Holloway Coll., London; Sec. Royal Astronomical Soc. 1966–72, Vice-Pres. 1972–73, Treas. 1996–2001; Asst Dir Univ. of London Observatory 1966–88, Dir 1988–97; Sr Lecturer in Astronomy, Univ. Coll., London 1970–99; Asst Gen. Sec. Int. Astronomical Union 1985–88, Gen. Sec. 1988–91; Chair. ICSU Working Group on Adverse Environmental Impacts on Astronomy 1993–96; Hon. Research Fellow, Univ. of Hertfordshire 1999–2003; mem. Bd Dirs International Dark-Sky Asscn. *Publications:* Positional Astronomy 1974, The Vanishing Universe (ed.) 1994, New Trends in Astronomy Teaching (ed.) 1998; numerous articles in astronomical journals. *Leisure interests:* natural history, music, travel. *E-mail:* dmn@star.herts.ac.uk (office).

McNAMARA, Michael (Mike) M., BS, MBA; American electronics industry executive; *CEO, Flextronics International Limited;* ed Univ. of Cincinnati, Santa Clara Univ.; Prin., Pittiglio, Rabin, Todd & McGrath (consulting firm) 1987–92; Vice-Pres., Mfg Operations, Anthem Electronics 1992–93; Pres. and CEO Relevant Industries 1993–94, Vice-Pres. N America Operations, Flextronics Int. Ltd (after Flextronic acquisition of Relevant Industries) 1994–97, Pres. N America Operations 1997–2001, COO, Singapore 2002–05, mem. Bd of Dirs 2005–, CEO 2006–. *Address:* Flextronics International Ltd, 2 Changi South Lane, 486123, Singapore (office). *Telephone:* 6299-8888 (office). *Fax:* 6543-1888 (office). *E-mail:* board@flextronics.com (office). *Website:* www.flextronics.com (office).

McNAMARA, Pamela, BSc; American business executive; *President of US Operations, Cambridge Consultants Inc.;* b. 1958; ed Tufts Univ.; consultant, Arthur D. Little, Inc. 1980, Head of North America Man. Consulting, Leader, Global Health Care Practice, mem. Bd of Dirs 1998–2004, Acting CEO Feb.–Aug. 2001, CEO Aug. 2001–04; CEO CRF Inc. 2004–08; Pres. of US Operations, Cambridge Consultants Inc., Cambridge, Mass 2009–; mem. Bd of Dirs GTC Biopharmaceuticals 2002–, Omrix Biopharmaceuticals, HealthBanks; mem. Corpn of Woods Hole Oceanographic Inst. *Address:* Cambridge Consultants Inc., 101 Main Street, Cambridge, MA 02142, USA (office). *Telephone:* (617) 532-4700 (office). *Fax:* (617) 532-4747 (office). *E-mail:* info@cambridgeconsultants.com (office). *Website:* www.cambridgeconsultants.com (office).

McNAMARA, Robert Strange, LLD; American politician, international civil servant and business executive; b. 9 June 1916, San Francisco; s. of Robert James McNamara and Clara Nell Strange; m. 1st Margaret Craig McNamara 1940 (died 1981); one s. two d.; m. 2nd Diana Byfield 2004; ed Univ. of California and Harvard Univ.; Asst Prof. in Business Admin., Harvard Univ. 1940–43; served USAAF 1943–46; Exec. Ford Motor Co. 1946–61, Vice-Pres. 1955–60, Pres. 1960–61; US Sec. of Defense 1961–68; Pres. IBRD (World Bank) 1968–81; Dir Royal Dutch Shell 1981; Dir The Washington Post Co. 1981, Bank of America 1981, Corning Glass Works 1981, TWA 1981, Caspian Holdings 1995–; Chair. Overseas Devt Council 1982; Adviser Robeco Group 1982; mem. Steering Cttee on IBRD Reorganization 1987; mem. Ford Foundation, Brookings Inst., Calif. Inst. of Tech., Urban Inst.; mem. American Acad. of Arts and Sciences, Advisory Council, Int. Reporting Systems 1981–83, Barbara Ward Fund 1982; Hon. LLD (St Andrews) 1981; Hon. DCL (Oxford) 1987, (Harvard) 1997; U.S. Medal of Freedom (with distinction) 1968, Albert Einstein Peace Prize 1983, Franklin D. Roosevelt Freedom Medal 1983, Onassis Award 1988; Legion of Merit. *Publications:* The Essence of Security: Reflections in Office 1968, One Hundred Countries–Two Billion People 1973, The McNamara Years at the World Bank 1981, Blundering into Disaster, Out of the Cold: New Thinking for American Foreign and Defence Policy in the 21st Century 1990, In Retrospect: The Tragedy and Lessons of Vietnam 1995, Argument Without End: The Search for Answers to the Vietnam Tragedy 1999, Wilson's Ghost 2001. *Address:* 1350 I Street, NW, Suite 500, Washington, DC 20005, USA. *Telephone:* (202) 682-3132. *Fax:* (202) 682-3130.

MacNAUGHTON, Sir Malcolm Campbell, Kt, MD, LLD, FRCOG, FRCP, FRSE, FFFP; British fmr medical scientist and academic; *Professor Emeritus of Obstetrics and Gynaecology, University of Glasgow;* b. 4 April 1925, Glasgow; s. of James Hay MacNaughton and Mary Robieson Hogarth; m. Margaret-Ann Galt 1955; two s. three d.; ed Glasgow Acad. and Glasgow Univ.; Sr Lecturer, Obstetrics and Gynaecology, Dundee and St Andrews Univs 1961–70; Muirhead Prof. of Obstetrics and Gynaecology, Univ. of Glasgow 1970–90, Prof. Emer. 1990–; Pres. Royal Coll. of Obstetricians and Gynaecologists, London 1984–87; Chair. Working Party on Accident and Emergency Services in Scotland (Scotmeg); Vice-Pres. Royal Coll. of Midwives 1992–; mem. Academic Bd St George's Univ. Medical School, Grenada, West Indies; Hon. Fellow, Sri Lanka Coll. of Obstetricians and Gynaecologists, Royal Australian Coll. of Obstetricians and Gynaecologists, American Coll. of Obstetricians and Gynaecologists, Royal Coll. of Anaesthetists. *Publications:* Combined Textbook of Obstetrics and Gynaecology 1976, The Ovary 1976, Medical Gynaecology 1985. *Leisure interests:* walking, fishing. *Address:* 9 Glenburn Road, Bearsden, Glasgow, G61 4PT, Scotland (home). *Telephone:* (141) 942-1909 (home). *Fax:* (141) 942-1909 (home). *E-mail:* macnaughtonmalcolm@hotmail.com (home).

McNEALY, Scott Glenn, BA, MBA; American computer industry executive; *Chairman, Sun Microsystems, Inc.;* b. 13 Nov. 1954, Columbus, Ind.; s. of Raymond William McNealy and Marmaline McNealy; m. Susan McNealy (née Ingemanson) 1994; four s.; ed Harvard and Stanford Univs; sales engineer, Rockwell Int. Corpn, Troy, Mich. 1976–78; staff engineer, FMC Corpn, Chicago 1980–81; Dir Operations, Onyx Systems, San José, Calif. 1981–82; Co-founder Sun Microsystems Inc., Mountain View, Calif. 1982, Vice Pres. of Operations 1982–84, Pres. and COO 1984, Chair., Pres. and CEO 1984–99, Chair. and CEO 1999–2002, Chair., Pres., CEO 2002–04, Chair. and CEO 2004–06, Chair. 2006–, also currently Chair. Sun Federal, Inc. (subsidiary); Distinguished Fellowship Award, British Computer Soc. 2007. *Leisure interest:* ice hockey, golf. *Address:* Sun Microsystems Inc., 4150 Network Circle, Santa Clara, CA 95054, USA (office). *Telephone:* (650) 960-1300 (office). *Fax:* (408) 276-3804 (office). *Website:* www.sun.com (office).

McNEE, Sir David Blackstock, Kt, QPM, FBIM, FRSA; British fmr police officer; b. 23 March 1925, Glasgow; s. of John McNee and the late Mary McNee (née Blackstock); m. Isabella Clayton Hopkins 1952 (died 1997); one d.; ed Woodside Sr Secondary School, Glasgow; Deputy Chief Constable, Dunbartonshire Constabulary 1968–71; Chief Constable, City of Glasgow Police 1971–75; Chief Constable, Strathclyde Police 1975–77; Commr Metropolitan Police 1977–82; Dir Fleet Holdings 1983–86; Chair. (non-exec.) Scottish Express Newspapers 1983; Orr Pollock & Co. Ltd (Greenock Telegraph), Craig

M. Jeffrey Ltd (Helensburgh Advertiser), Integrated Security Services Ltd; Adviser Bd British Airways 1982–87; Dir (non-exec.) Clydesdale Bank PLC; Pres. Royal Life Saving Soc. 1982–90, Nat. Bible Soc. of Scotland 1983–96, Glasgow City Cttee, Cancer Relief 1987–93; CBIM 1980; Freeman City of London 1977; Hon. Col 32 (Scottish) Signal Regt (Volunteers) 1988–92; KStJ 1974, Commdr 1977. *Publication:* McNee's Law 1983. *Leisure interests:* fishing, golf, music.

McNEE, John, MA; Canadian diplomatist; *Permanent Representative, United Nations;* m. Susan; two c.; ed York and Cambridge Univs; joined Dept of External Affairs 1978, positions in Madrid, London, Tel Aviv; Amb. to Syria 1993–97, also accred to Lebanon 1993–95; positions with Policy Devt Secr., Canada–US Transboundary Div., Ottawa, fmr Dir Personnel Div., Dir Gen., Middle East, North Africa and Gulf States Bureau; fmr mem. Prime Minister Trudeau's Task Force on Int. Peace and Security, Privy Council Office; Asst Deputy Minister, Africa and Middle East, Foreign Affairs, Ottawa 2001; Amb. to Belgium, also accred to Luxembourg –2006; Perm. Rep. to UN 2006–. *Address:* Office of the Permanent Representative from Canada, 1 Dag Hammarskjöld Plaza, 885 Second Avenue, 14th Floor, New York, NY 10017, USA (office). *Telephone:* (212) 848-1100 (office). *Fax:* (212) 848-1195 (office). *E-mail:* canada@un.int (office). *Website:* www.un.int/canada (office).

MacNEIL, Cornell Hill; American singer (baritone); b. 24 Sept. 1922, Minneapolis, Minn.; s. of Walter Hill and Harriette Belle (née Cornell) MacNeil; m. 1st Margaret Gavan 1947 (divorced 1972); two s. three d.; m. 2nd Tania Rudensky 1972; ed Julius Hartt School of Music, Univ. of Hartford, West Hartford, Conn.; appeared on Broadway in Sweethearts 1947, Where's Charley 1949; operatic début as John Sorel in world premiere of The Consul (Menotti) 1950; début with New York City Opera as Germont in La Traviata 1953, at La Scala, Milan, as Charles V in Ernani 1959, at Metropolitan Opera, New York in title-role of Rigoletto 1959; has appeared in leading opera houses of Europe, USA, S America; Pres. American Guild of Musical Artists 1971–77, mem. 1971–; Hon. DMus (Hartford) 1986; Alumnus of Year, Hartt School of Music 1976; Grammy Award for best opera recording (La Traviata) 1984; Medal of Achievement, Acad. of Vocal Arts 1985. *Leisure interests:* cooking, woodwork, gardening.

McNEIL, General Dan K., BS; American military officer; *Commanding General, International Security Assistance Force, Afghanistan;* ed North Carolina State Univ., US Army Command and Gen. Staff Coll., Fort Leavenworth, Kan.; began mil. career 1968, command positions have included E Company, 2nd Bn (Airborne), 505th Infantry, 82nd Airborne Div. 1977–78, 1st Bn, 325th Infantry, 82nd Airborne Div. 1986–88, 3rd Brigade, 82nd Airborne Div. 1991–93, Asst Div. Commdr, 2nd Infantry Div., Eighth US Army, Korea 1995–96, Deputy Commanding Gen., I Corps and Fort Lewis 1997–98, Commanding Gen., 82nd Airborne Div. 1998–2000, Commanding Gen., XVIII Airborne Corps and Fort Bragg 2000–03, including duty as Commanding Gen., Combined Jt Task Force-180, Afghanistan, Deputy Commanding Gen./Chief of Staff, US Army Forces Command 2003–07, Commanding Gen., Int. Security Assistance Force, Afghanistan 2007–; Defense Distinguished Service Medal, Defense Superior Service Medal, Legion of Merit, Bronze Star Medal, Expert Infantryman Badge, Master Parachutist Badge (with Bronze Service Star), Army Aviator Badge, Special Forces Tab. *Address:* International Security Assistance Force, Afghanistan, NATO Headquarters, Blvd Leopold III, Brussels 1110, Belgium (office); c/o United States Army Forces Command, 1777 Hardee Avenue, Southwest, Fort McPherson, GA 30330-1062, USA (office). *E-mail:* moc.web@hq.nato.int (office).

MacNEILL, Brian F., BCom, CPA, CM; Canadian accountant and business executive; *Chairman, Petro Canada;* b. 1939, Calgary; m.; four c.; ed Montana State Univ.; began career as accounts clerk at oil and gas co., Calgary 1960; Accountant, Haskins & Sells, San Francisco 1967; Vice-Pres. and Treas. Hiram Walker Resources Ltd 1980–82; fmr Exec. Vice-Pres. and COO Enbridge Inc., becoming CEO 1990–2001; mem. Bd of Dirs Petro-Canada 1995–, currently Chair.; mem. Bd of Dirs Toronto Dominion Bank, Telus Corpn, West-Fraser Timber Co. Ltd; fmr mem. Bd of Dirs Dofasco Inc., Veritas DGC Inc., Legacy Hotels REIT, Sears Canada Inc., Western Oil Sands Inc.; Chair. Bd of Govs Univ. of Calgary; fmr Chair. United Way of Calgary; mem. Canadian Inst. of Chartered Accountants, Financial Execs Inst.; Fellow, Alberta Inst. of Chartered Accountants, Inst of Corp. Dirs. *Address:* Petro-Canada, 150 6th Avenue, SW, Calgary, Alberta, T2P 3E3, Canada (office). *Telephone:* (403) 296-8000 (office). *Fax:* (403) 296-3030 (office). *E-mail:* info@petro-canada.ca (office). *Website:* www.petro-canada.ca (office).

McNERNEY, W. James, Jr, BA, MBA; American business executive; *Chairman, President and CEO, The Boeing Company;* b. 22 Aug. 1949, Providence, RI; ed Yale and Harvard Univs; began career in brand man., Procter & Gamble; Sr Man. McKinsey & Co. –1982; Gen. Man. General Electric (GE) Mobile Communications 1982–86, Pres. GE Information Services 1988–89, Exec. Vice-Pres. GE Financial Services and GE Capital 1989–91, Pres. and CEO GE Electrical Distribution and Control 1991–92, Pres. GE Asia-Pacific, Hong Kong 1993–95, Pres. and CEO GE Lighting 1995–97, Pres. and CEO GE Aircraft Engines 1997–2000, Chair. and CEO 3M 2000–05; Chair., Pres. and CEO Boeing Co. 2005–, mem. Special Programs Cttee; mem. Bd Dirs Procter & Gamble; mem. various business and educational orgs. *Address:* The Boeing Co., 100 North Riverside Plaza, Chicago, IL 60606-1596, Cttee (office). *Telephone:* (312) 544-2000 (office). *Fax:* (312) 544-2082 (office). *E-mail:* info@boeing.com (office). *Website:* www.boeing.com (office).

McNICOL, Donald, PhD; Australian psychologist, academic and fmr university vice-chancellor; b. 18 April 1939, Adelaide; s. of Ian Robertson McNicol and Sadie Isabelle Williams; m. Kathleen Margaret Wells 1963; one s. two d.; ed Unley High School, Univ. of Adelaide, Cambridge Univ.; Lecturer in Psychology, Univ. of Adelaide 1967–71; Sr Lecturer in Psychology, Univ. of NSW 1971–74, Assoc. Prof. 1975–81; Prof. of Psychology, Univ. of Tasmania 1981–86; Commr for Univs and Chair. Univs Advisory Council of Commonwealth Tertiary Educ. Comm. 1986–88; Vice-Chancellor Univ. of New England 1988–90, Univ. of Sydney 1990–96, Univ. of Tasmania 1996–2003; Deputy Pres. Australian Vice-Chancellors' Cttee 1993–94, Pres. 1994–96; Pres. Asscn of Univs of S Asia and the Pacific (AUAP) 1998–99; Pres. Australian Higher Educ. Industrial Asscn 2000–; Fellow, Australian Psychological Soc. *Publication:* A Primer of Signal Detection Theory 1972. *Leisure interests:* walking, music, reading. *Address:* POB 1155, Sandy Bay, Tasmania 7006, Australia (home). *Telephone:* (3) 6225-3195 (home). *E-mail:* don.mcnicol@mcnicol.info (home).

McPEAK, Gen. Merrill Anthony, DSM, DFC, MS; American air force officer (retd), investor and company director; *Chairman, Ethicspoint, Inc.;* b. 9 Jan. 1936, Santa Rosa, Calif.; s. of Merrill Addison McPeak and Winifred Alice McPeak Bendall (née Stewart); m. Elynor Fay Moskowitz 1956; two s.; ed San Diego State Coll., Calif., George Washington Univ., Washington, DC; commissioned officer, USAF 1957, progressed through ranks to Gen. 1988; C-in-C Pacific Air Forces, Hickam, Hawaii 1988–90; Chief of Staff USAF 1990–94, consultant 1994–; Chair. ECC Int. Corpn 1997–2002, Ethicspoint, Inc.; Silver Star, Legion Of Merit. *Address:* 123 Furnace Street, Lake Oswego, OR 97034, USA (office). *Telephone:* (503) 699-2931 (office). *E-mail:* mamcpeak@comcast.net (office).

McPHEE, John Angus, AB; American academic and writer; *Ferris Professor of Journalism, Princeton University;* b. 8 March 1931, Princeton, NJ; m. 1st Pryde Brown 1957; four d.; m. 2nd Yolanda Whitman 1972; two step-s. two step-d.; ed Princeton Univ., Univ. of Cambridge; dramatist, Robert Montgomery Presents television programme 1955–57; Assoc. Ed., Time magazine, New York 1957–64; staff writer, The New Yorker magazine 1965–; Ferris Prof. of Journalism, Princeton Univ. 1975–; Fellow, Geological Soc. of America; mem. American Acad. of Arts and Letters; various hon. doctorates; American Acad. and Inst. of Arts and Letters Award 1977, Princeton Univ. Woodrow Wilson Award 1982, American Asscn of Petroleum Geologists Journalism Award 1982, 1986, United States Geological Survey John Wesley Powell Award 1988, American Geophysical Union Walter Sullivan Award 1993, Pulitzer Prize for Non-Fiction 1999, Geological Soc. of America Public Service Award 2002, Acad. of Natural Sciences Gold Medal for Distinction in Natural History Art 2005, George Polk Career Award 2008. *Publications:* A Sense of Where You Are 1965, The Headmaster 1966, Oranges 1967, The Pine Barrens 1968, A Roomful of Hovings 1969, The Crofter and the Laird 1969, Levels of the Game 1970, Encounters with the Archdruid 1972, Wimbledon: A Celebration 1972, The Deltoid Pumpkin Seed 1973, The Curve of Binding Energy 1974, Pieces of the Frame 1975, The Survival of the Bark Canoe 1975, The John McPhee Reader 1977, Coming into the Country 1977, Giving Good Weight 1979, Alaska: Images of the Country (with Galen Rowell) 1981, Basin and Range 1981, In Suspect Terrain 1983, La Place de la Concorde Suisse 1984, Table of Contents 1985, Rising from the Plains 1986, Outcroppings 1988, The Control of Nature 1989, Looking for a Ship 1990, Assembling California 1993, The Ransom of Russian Art 1994, The Second John McPhee Reader 1996, Irons in the Fire 1997, Annals of the Former World 1998, The Founding Fish 2002, Uncommon Carriers 2006, Silk Parachute 2010. *Address:* Joseph Henry House, Princeton University, Princeton, NJ 08544 (office); 475 Drake's Corner Road, Princeton, NJ 08540, USA (home).

McPHEE, Jonathan; American music director and conductor; b. Philadelphia; ed Royal Acad. of Music, London and Juilliard School of Music; affiliate Martha Graham Dance Co., New York 1979–89, Joffrey Ballet, Chicago 1980–86, Dance Theater of Harlem 1980–86; now Music Dir and Prin. Conductor Boston Ballet; has conducted for numerous dance cos including American Ballet Theater and New York City Ballet; has also conducted dance music, musical theatre, operetta and grand opera. *Radio:* Kids Classical Hour (Gabriel Award 1998), WCRB radio station. *Recordings include:* The Nutcracker, The Sleeping Beauty 2000 (both with Boston Ballet Orchestra). *Address:* c/o Boston Ballet, 19 Clarendon Street, Boston, MA 02116-6100, USA (office). *Telephone:* (617) 695-6950 (office). *Website:* www.bostonballet.org (office).

MacPHERSON, Elle; Australian model, actress and business executive; b. (Eleanor Nancy Gow), 29 March 1963, Cronulla, New South Wales; d. of Peter Gow and Frances Macpherson; m. Gilles Bensimon (divorced 1989); two s. by Arpad Busson; Founder and Chief Exec. Elle Macpherson Inc.; f. Elle Macpherson sportswear, Elle Macpherson Intimates, The Body (beauty product line).; Co-owner Fashion Cafe, New York; appeared in Sports Illustrated Swimsuit magazine edition 1986, 1987, 1988, 1989, 1990, 1991, 1992, 1993, 1994, 2004, 2006. *Films include:* Alice 1990, Sirens 1994, Jane Eyre 1996, If Lucy Fell 1996, The Mirror Has Two Faces 1996, Batman and Robin 1997, The Edge 1997, Beautopia 1998, With Friends Like These 1998, South Kensington 2001; video: Stretch and Strengthen, The Body Workout 1995. *Television includes:* H3O (series) 1995, Friends 1999–2000, 2004, A Girl Thing (mini-series) 2001. *Address:* Artist Management, Penn House, B414 East 52nd Street, New York, NY 10022, USA (office).

McPHERSON, Harry Cummings, Jr, BA, LLB; American government official and lawyer; *Partner, DLA Piper Rudnick Gray Carey LLP;* b. 22 Aug. 1929, Tyler, Tex.; s. of Harry Cummings and Nan (née Hight) McPherson; m. 1st Clayton Read 1952 (divorced 1981); two s.; m. 2nd Patricia DeGroot 1981; one s.; ed Tyler High School, Texas, Southern Methodist Univ., Dallas, Univ. of the South, Sewanee, Tenn., Columbia Univ. and Univ. of Texas Law School; USAF 1950–53; admitted to Texas Bar 1955; Asst Gen. Counsel, Dem. Policy Cttee, US Senate 1956–59, Assoc. Counsel 1959–61, Gen. Counsel 1961–63;

Deputy Under-Sec. for Int. Affairs, Dept of Army 1963–64; Asst Sec. of State for Educational and Cultural Affairs 1964–65; Special Asst and Counsel to Pres. Johnson 1965–69; Special Counsel to the Pres. 1966–69; Vice-Chair. John F. Kennedy Center for Performing Arts 1969–76, Gen. Counsel 1977–91; Chair. Task Force on Domestic Policy, Democratic Advisory Council of Elected Officials 1974; mem. Pres.'s Comm. on the Accident at Three Mile Island 1979; Pres. Federal City Council, Washington, DC 1983–88; Vice-Chair. US Int. Cultural and Trade Center Comm. 1988–93; Pres. Econ. Club of Washington 1992–99; currently Pnr, DLA Piper Rudnick Gray Carey LLP; mem. Defense Base Closure and Realignment Comm. 1993; Hon. DCL. *Publication:* A Political Education 1972, 1988, 1995. *Address:* 1200 19th Street, NW, Washington, DC 20036 (office); 10213 Montgomery Avenue, Kensington, MD 20895, USA (home). *Telephone:* (202) 861-6464 (office); (301) 942-4395 (home). *E-mail:* harry.mcpherson@dlapiperrudnick.com (office). *Website:* www.dlapiperrudnick.com (office).

McPHERSON, James Munro, PhD; American historian, academic and writer; *George Henry Davis '86 Professor Emeritus of History, Princeton University;* b. 11 Oct. 1936, Valley City, ND; s. of James M. McPherson and Miriam O. McPherson; m. Patricia Rasche 1957; one d.; ed Gustavus Adolphus Coll. and Johns Hopkins Univ.; Instructor Princeton Univ. 1962–65, Asst Prof. 1965–66, Assoc. Prof. 1966–72, Prof. of History 1972–82, Edwards Prof. of American History 1982–91, George Henry Davis '86 Prof. of American History 1991, now Prof. Emer.; Pres. Soc. of American Historians 2000–; Woodrow Wilson Fellow and Danforth Fellow 1958–62; Guggenheim Fellow 1967–68; Huntingdon Library-Nat. Endowment for the Humanities Fellowship 1977–78; Center for Advanced Study in the Behavioural Sciences Fellowship 1982–83; Huntington Seaver Fellow 1987–88; Jefferson Lecture 2000; Pres. American Historical Asscn 2003; Anisfield-Wolf Prize in Race Relations 1965, Pulitzer Prize in History 1989, Christopher Award 1989, Best Book Award, American Military Inst. 1989, Lincoln Prize 1998, Theodore and Franklin D. Roosevelt Prize in Naval History 1998, Pritzker Mil. Library Literature Award for lifetime achievement in mil. writing 2007. *Publications:* The Struggle for Equality: Abolitionists and the Negro in the Civil War and Reconstruction 1964, The Negro's Civil War 1965, Marching Toward Freedom 1968, The Anti-Slavery Crusade in America (co-ed, 59 vols) 1969, Blacks in America (essays) 1971, The Abolitionist Legacy 1975, Ordeal by Fire: The Civil War and Reconstruction 1982, Religion, Race and Reconstruction (essays, co-ed) 1982, Battle Cry of Freedom: The Civil War Era 1988, Battle Chronicles of the Civil War (ed, six vols) 1989, Abraham Lincoln and the Second American Revolution 1991, Images of the Civil War 1992, Gettysburg 1993, What They Fought For 1861–1865 1994, The Atlas of the Civil War 1994, What They Fought For 1861–1865 1994, Drawn With the Sword: Reflections on the American Civil War 1996, The American Heritage New History of the Civil War (ed) 1996, For Cause and Comrades: Why Men Fought in the Civil War 1997, Lamson of the Gettysburg: The Civil War Letters of Lt Roswell H. Lamson, US Navy 1997, Is Blood Thicker Than Water? Crises of Nationalism in the Modern World 1998, The Encyclopedia of Civil War Biographies (ed, three vols) 1999, To the Best of My Ability: The American Presidents (ed) 2000, Crossroads of Freedom: Antietam, The Battle That Changed the Course of the Civil War 2002, Hallowed Ground: A Walk at Gettysburg 2003, The Illustrated Battle Cry of Freedom 2003, Into the West (juvenile) 2006, Tried by War: Abraham Lincoln as Commander in Chief (Lincoln Prize, Gettysburg Coll. 2009) 2008; contrib. to reference works, scholarly books and professional journals. *Leisure interests:* tennis, bicycling, sailing. *Address:* Department of History, 226 Dickinson Hall, Princeton University, Princeton, NJ 08544 (office); 15 Randall Road, Princeton, NJ 08540, USA (home). *Telephone:* (609)258-4173 (office); (609) 924-9226 (home). *E-mail:* jmcphers@princeton.edu (office). *Website:* his.princeton.edu (office).

McPHERSON, M(elville) Peter, BA, MBA, JD; American government official, lawyer and academic administrator; *President, National Association of State Universities and Land-Grant Colleges (NASULGC);* b. 27 Oct. 1940, Lowell, Mich.; s. of Donald McPherson and Ellura E. (Frost) McPherson; m. Joanne Paddock McPherson 1989; four c.; Peace Corps volunteer, Peru 1964–65; with Internal Revenue Service, Washington 1969–75; Special Asst to Pres. and Deputy Dir Presidential Personnel White House, Washington 1975–77; partner Vorys, Sater, Seymour & Pease, Washington 1977–80; Acting Counsel to Pres., White House 1980–81; Admin. Agency for Int. Devt, Washington 1981–87; Deputy Sec., Dept of Treasury 1987–89; Group Exec. Vice-Pres. Bank of America 1989–93; Pres. Mich. State Univ. 1993–2004, Pres. Emer. 2004–; financial coordinator Office of Reconstruction and Humanitarian Assistance, Iraq 2003; founder and co-Chair. Partnership to Cut Hunger and Poverty in Africa 2005–; Pres. Nat. Asscn of State Univs and Land-Grant Coll. (NASULGC) 2006–; Exec. Vice-Pres. Bank of America 1988–93; mem. Bd for Int. Food and Agric. Devt 1977–80; mem. Michigan and DC Bar Asscn. *Address:* NASULGC, 1307 New York Avenue, NW, Suite 400, Washington, DC, 20005-4722; Partnership to Cut Hunger and Poverty in Africa, 499 South Capitol Street, SW, Suite 500B, Washington, DC 20003, USA. *Telephone:* (202) 478-6040 (office). *Fax:* (202) 478-6046 (office). *Website:* www.nasulgc.org (office).

McQUEEN, Alexander, CBE, MA; British fashion designer; *Chief Designer, Gucci;* b. London; ed St Martin's School of Art, London; left school aged 16, worked for London tailors Anderson & Shepherd, Gieves & Hawkes and theatrical costumiers Bermans & Nathans, designers Koji Tatsuno and Romeo Gigli in Rome; his final collection at St Martin's 1992 est. his reputation; subsequent shows include The Birds, Highland Rape, The Hunger, Dante, La Poupée, It's a Jungle Out There, Untitled; acquired Italian Mfg co. Onward Kashiyama; Chief Designer, Givenchy, Paris 1996–2000, Gucci Dec. 2000–; Designer of the Year, London Fashion Awards 1996, 2000, Jt winner (with John Galliano q.v.) 1997, Special Achievement Award, London Fashion

Awards 1998, British Designer of the Year, British Fashion Awards 2004. *Address:* c/o Gucci Group NV, Rembrandt Tower, 1 Amstelplein, 1096 MA Amsterdam, Netherlands; 1st Floor, 10 Amwell Street, London, EC1R 1UQ, England. *Telephone:* (20) 7278-4333. *Fax:* (20) 7278-3828. *Website:* www.gucci.com (office).

McQUEEN, Steve, OBE; British artist and film director; b. 1969, London; ed Chelsea School of Art, Goldsmith's Coll., Tish School of Arts, New York Univ.; has exhibited widely in Europe and USA; major solo exhbn Inst. of Contemporary Art (ICA), London; works primarily in corp. film, photography and sculpture, apptd Official War Artist in response to the Iraq conflict, Imperial War Museum, London 2003; ICA Futures Award 1996, DAAD artist's scholarship 1998, Turner Prize 1999. *Film:* Hunger (dir) (BAFTA Carl Foreman Award for Special Achievement by a British Dir 2009) 2008. *Address:* c/o Thomas Dane Associates, First Floor, 11 Duke Street, St James's, London, SW1Y 6BN, England; c/o Marian Goodman Gallery, 24 West 57th Street, New York, NY 10019, USA. *E-mail:* info@thomasdane.com. *Website:* www.thomasdane.com/mcqueen.php.

MACRI, Mauricio; Argentine politician; *Mayor of Buenos Aires;* b. 8 Feb. 1959, Tandil, Buenos Aires; divorced; three c.; ed Catholic Univ. of Argentina, Universidad del CEMA, Columbia Business School, Wharton Business School, USA; joined family business1985 and served in various man. positions in cos including Sideco, SOCMA and Sevel; Pres. Boca Juniors football club 1995–; defeated in second round of election for Head of Govt of the Autonomous City of Buenos Aires 2003; serves as deputy representing city of Buenos Aires in Lower House of Congress 2005–; with Ricardo López Murphy created Propuesta Republicana (PRO) electoral front 2005–; Mayor of the Autonomous City of Buenos Aires 2007–; mem. Compromiso para el Cambio (Commitment to Change). *Address:* Compromiso para el Cambio, Edif. Anexo de la Cámara de Diputados, Riobamba 25, C 1025 ABA, Buenos Aires, Argentina (office). *Telephone:* (11) 6310-7710 (office). *E-mail:* ccambio@hcdn.gov.ar (office). *Website:* cpcambio.org.ar (office); www.ciudadpro.com; www.buenosaires.gov.ar.

McROBBIE, Michael A., BSc, MSc; Australian computer scientist, academic and university administrator; *President, Indiana University;* b. 11 Oct. 1950; m. Laurie Burns; three c., three step-c.; ed Univ. of Queensland, Australian Nat. Univ.; Prof. of Information Tech., Inst. of Advanced Study, ANU, also CEO Co-operative Research Centre for Advanced Computational Systems; Vice-Pres. for Information Tech., Indiana Univ., Bloomington, USA 1997–2006, also Vice-Pres. for Research 2003–06, Interim Provost and Vice-Pres. for Academic Affairs 2006–07, Pres. 2007–; Hon. mem. Alliance of Distinguished and Titled Profs; Dr hc (Queensland) 2007. *Publications:* several books, papers, and technical reports. *Leisure interests:* travel, reading, collecting art, theatre, opera. *Address:* Office of the President, Indiana University, Bryan Hall 200, 107 South Indiana Avenue, Bloomington, IN 47405, USA (office). *Telephone:* (812) 855-4613 (office). *E-mail:* iupres@indiana.edu (office). *Website:* www.indiana.edu/~pres (office).

MacSHANE, Denis, MA, PhD; British politician; b. 21 May 1948; s. of the late Jan Matyjaszec and of Isobel MacShane; m. Nathalie Pham 1987; one s. four d.; ed Merton Coll., Oxford, Birkbeck Coll., London; reporter, BBC 1969–77; Pres. Nat. Union of Journalists 1978–79; Policy Dir Int. Metalworkers Fed. 1980–92; Dir European Policy Inst. 1992–94; MP for Rotherham (Labour Party) 1994–; Parl. Pvt. Sec. to Ministers of Foreign Affairs 1997–2001; Parl. Under-Sec. of State, FCO 2001–02; Minister of State for Europe 2002–05; Visiting Fellow St Antony's Coll., Oxford 1998–99; mem. Council Royal Inst. of Int. Affairs 1999–, Council of Europe Parl. Ass. 2005–, NATO Parl. Ass. 2005–. *Publications include:* Solidarity: Poland's Independent Trade Union 1981, François Mitterrand: A Political Odyssey 1982, Black Workers, Unions and the Struggle for Democracy in South Africa 1984, International Labour and the Origins of the Cold War 1992, Britain's Steel Industry in the 21st Century 1996, Globalising Hatred: The New Anti-Semitism 2008. *Address:* House of Commons, London, SW1A 0AA, England (office). *E-mail:* macshaned@parliament.uk (office).

McSHARRY, Deirdre Mary; Irish journalist, editor and curator; b. 4 April 1932, London, England; d. of the late Dr John McSharry and Mary O'Brien; m. Ian Coulter Smyth; ed Dominican Convent, Wicklow, Trinity Coll., Dublin Univ.; actress at Gate Theatre, Dublin 1953–55; freelance with The Irish Times 1953; mem. staff Evening Herald, Dublin 1955–56; with bookshop Metropolitan Museum of Art, New York 1956; Reporter Women's Wear Daily, New York 1956–58; mem. staff Woman's Own 1959–62; Fashion Ed. Evening News 1962; Woman's Ed. Daily Express 1963–66; Fashion Ed. The Sun 1967–71; Fashion Ed. Cosmopolitan 1972, Ed. 1973–85; Ed.-in-Chief Country Living 1986–89; Consultant Nat. Magazine Co. and Magazine Div. The Hearst Corpn 1990–92; Ed. Countryside magazine, New York 1991–92; Chair. Bath Friends of The American Museum in Britain, Bath; mem. Council of the American Museum, Council of the Bath Festivals Trust 2002; Trustee The American Museum (in Britain) 2002–04; Ed. of the Year (Periodical Publrs Asscn) 1981, 1987, Mark Boxer Award: Editor's Ed. 1991. *Publication:* Inspirations: The Textile Tradition Then and Now (American Museum Catalogue) 2001. *Leisure interests:* architecture, textiles, decorative arts, literature. *Address:* Southfield House, 16 High Street, Rode, BA11 6NZ, England. *Telephone:* (1373) 831263 (home). *Fax:* (1373) 831263 (home). *E-mail:* deirdre.mcsharry@btopenworld.com.

MacSHARRY, Ray; Irish politician; b. 29 April 1938, Sligo; s. of Patrick McSharry and Annie Clarke; m. Elaine Neilan 1960; three s. three d.; ed Summerhill Coll., Sligo; fmr haulier, auctioneer, farm-owner; joined Sligo Jr Chamber of Commerce 1966 (past Pres.); mem. Sligo County Council, Sligo Borough Council and Sligo Town Vocational Educ. Cttee 1967–78; mem. Dáil

1969–89; Minister of State, Dept of Finance and Public Service 1977–79; Minister for Agriculture 1979–81; Tanaiste and Minister for Finance March–Nov. 1982; MEP for Connaught/Ulster 1984–87; Minister for Finance 1987–88; EC Commr with responsibility for Agric. and Rural Devt 1989–93; pvt. business 1993–; Chair. London City Airport, Irish Equine Centre 1995; Dir Ryanair, Bank of Ireland Group 1993–2005; Gov. E.I.B. 1982; Fianna Fáil; Freeman Borough of Sligo 1993; Grand-Croix, Order of Leopold II 1993; Hon. DEconSci (Limerick) 1994; Hon. LLD (Nat. Univ. of Ireland) 1994; Business and Finance Man. of the Year 1988, Marcora Prize, Italy 1991, European of the Year 1992. *Leisure interest:* sport. *Address:* Alcantara, Pearse Road, Sligo, Ireland. *Telephone:* (71) 69902. *Fax:* (71) 69902.

McSWEENEY, Barry, BSc, MSc; Irish biochemist; *Research Coordinator, Department of Communications, Marine and Natural Resources;* b. Cork; ed Univ. Coll., Cork, Trinity Coll., Dublin; fmr Man. of European Product Devt, American Hosps Supply Corpn, Switzerland and Belgium; Dir of Medical Business, Biocon Biochemicals Ltd, Cork and Sees, France –1987; Founding Dir BioResearch Ireland 1987–95; Head of Unit, Research DG, EC, Brussels 1995–2000, Dir Inst. for Health and Consumer Protection, Jt Research Centre (JRC), Ispra, Italy 2000–01, Dir-Gen. JRC 2001–04; Chief Science Adviser to Irish Govt 2004–05; Research Coordinator, Dept of Communications, Marine and Natural Resources; Chair. OECD Working Party on Biotechnology 1994–95, Sr Industry Advisory Group on Biotechnology (SAGB); Co-Chair. World Tech. Forum 1990; mem. Advisory Cttee on Biotechnology, Science Foundation Ireland 2000; Great Gold Medal, Cornelius Univ., Bratislava 2003, Alumni Achievement Award, Univ. Coll. Cork 2004. *Leisure interest:* horse-racing. *Address:* Department of Communications, Marine and Natural Resources, 29–31 Adelaide Road, Dublin 2, Ireland (office). *Telephone:* (1) 6782000 (office). *Fax:* (1) 6782449 (office). *E-mail:* barry.mcsweeney@dcmnr.gov.ie (office). *Website:* www.dcmnr.gov.ie (office).

McTEER, Janet, OBE; British actress; b. 8 May 1961, Newcastle-upon-Tyne; d. of Alan McTeer and Jean McTeer; ed Royal Acad. of Dramatic Arts, London; Bancroft Gold Medal 1983. *Theatre includes:* Much Ado About Nothing, Uncle Vanya, Simpatico, Vivat! Vivat Regina, London 1995, A Doll's House, London (Tony Award 1997, Laurence Olivier Theatre Award for Best Actress 1997, London Critics' Circle Theatre Award for Best Actress 1997), New York 1996–97. *Films include:* Half Moon Street 1986, Hawks 1988, Sweet Nothing 1990, I Dreamt I Woke Up 1991, Prince 1991, Wuthering Heights 1992, Carrington 1995, Velvet Goldmine (voice) 1998, Populous: The Beginning (video game; voice) 1998, Tumbleweeds 1999, Waking the Dead 2000, Songcatcher 2000, The King is Alive 2000, The Intended (also co-writer) 2002, Romeo and Me 2004, Tideland 2005, As You Like It 2006. *Television appearances include:* Les Girls (series) 1988, Precious Bane 1989, Yellowbacks 1990, Portrait of a Marriage 1990, 102 Boulevard Haussmann 1990, The Black Velvet Gown 1991, A Masculine Ending 1992, Dead Romantic 1992, Don't Leave Me This Way 1993, The Governor (series) 1995, Marple: The Murder at the Vicarage 2004. *Leisure interests:* cooking, gardens. *Address:* c/o Michael Foster, ARG, 46 Maddox Street, London, W1S 1QA, England. *Telephone:* (20) 7436-6400.

McTIERNAN, John; American film director; b. 8 Jan. 1951, Albany, NY; m. Donna Dubrow; ed Juilliard School of Drama, State Univ. of New York, Old Westbury Filmmaking Coll. *Films include:* Nomads (also screenplay) 1986, Predator 1987, Die Hard 1988, The Hunt for Red October 1990, Medicine Man 1992, Last Action Hero (also exec. producer) 1993, Die Hard: With a Vengeance (also producer) 1995, Amanda (1996) (producer) 1996, The 13th Warrior (also producer) 1999, The Thomas Crown Affair 1999, Rollerball (also producer) 2002, Basic 2003. *Television includes:* Robin Hood (exec. producer) 1991, The Right to Remain Silent (producer) 1996, Quicksilver Highway (exec. producer) 1997.

McVIE, John Gordon, MD, DSc, FRCP, FRCPS, FRCPE, FRCSE, FMedSci; British doctor and cancer specialist; *Senior Consultant, Istituto Europea Oncologica, Milan;* b. 13 Jan. 1945, Glasgow; s. of John McVie and Lindsaye Mair; m. 1st Evelyn Strang 1966 (divorced 1996); three s.; m. 2nd Claudia Joan Burke; one step-s. one step-d.; ed Royal High School, Edin. and Univ. of Edin.; MRC Fellow, Univ. of Edin. 1970–71, lecturer in Therapeutics 1971–76; Sr Lecturer in Clinical Oncology, Univ. of Glasgow 1976–80; Head, Clinical Research Unit, Netherlands Cancer Inst. Amsterdam 1980–84, Clinical Research Dir 1984–89; Scientific Dir Cancer Research Campaign 1989–96; Dir Gen. Cancer Research UK 1996–2002; Sr Consultant Istituto Europea Oncologica, Milan 2004–; Visiting Prof. British Postgrad. Medical Fed. Univ. of London 1990–96; Pres. European Org. for Research and Treatment of Cancer 1994; European Ed. Journal of Nat. Cancer Inst. 1995–2001; Dir Cancer Intelligence 2002–; mem. numerous advisory cttees etc. *Publications:* Cancer Assessment and Monitoring 1979, Autologous Bone Marrow Transplantation and Solid Tumours 1984, Microspheres and Drug Therapy 1984, Clinical and Experimental Pathology and Biology of Lung Cancer 1985; 35 chapters in books; 159 articles in books and journals. *Leisure interests:* opera, theatre, cooking, Italian wine-tasting. *Address:* Istituto Europea Oncologica, Via Ripamonti 435, 20141 Milan, Italy (office). *Telephone:* (02574) 89946 (office). *Fax:* (02574) 89922 (office). *E-mail:* gordonmcvie@ieo.it (office); gordonmcvie@doctors.org.uk (home). *Website:* www.ieo.it (office); www.cancerintelligence.com (office).

McWHA, James Alexander, BSc, BAgr (Hons), PhD; Northern Irish/New Zealand university administrator and academic; *Vice-Chancellor and President, University of Adelaide;* b. 28 May 1947, Co. Down, Northern Ireland; s. of David McWha and Sarah Isabel Caughey; m. Jean Lindsay Ferries 1970; one s. two d.; ed Queen's Univ., Belfast, Univ. of Glasgow; Lecturer in Plant Physiology, Univ. of Canterbury, NZ 1973–79, Head of Dept of Plant and Microbial Sciences 1980–85; Prof. of Agricultural Botany, Queen's Univ. Belfast 1985–89; Deputy Chief Scientific Officer, Dept of Agric. for NI 1985–89; Dir Dept of Scientific and Industrial Research Fruit Trees (NZ) 1989–92; CEO Horticulture and Food Research Inst. (NZ) 1992–95; Sec.-Gen. Int. Asscn of Univ. Presidents 2002–05 (Sec.-Gen. Emer. 2005–); mem. S Australia Vice-Chancellors' Cttee 2002 (Chair. 2002, 2007–08); mem. NZ Vice-Chancellors' Cttee 1996–2001 (Chair. 2001–02), Council of Asscn of Commonwealth Univs (Australian Rep. 2006–09, Hon. Treas. 2007–09, NZ Rep. 2000–02); mem. Bd NZ Foundation for Research Science and Tech. 1992–95, NZ Dairy Research Inst. 1995–98, Industrial Research Ltd 1996–2001, American Chamber of Commerce in NZ 2000–02, Group of Eight Ltd 2002–, Australian Univs' Quality Agency 2003–, Council Nat. Inst. of Agricultural Botany; PhD (ad eundem gradum) (Adelaide) 2002; Hon. DSc (Massey Univ.) 2004; Centenary Medal for services to educ. 2003. *Leisure interests:* classic and vintage cars, rugby union. *Address:* Office of the Vice-Chancellor, University of Adelaide, Adelaide, SA 5005, Australia (office). *Telephone:* (8) 8303-5780 (office). *Fax:* (8) 8303-4343 (office). *E-mail:* vice-chancellor@adelaide.edu.au (office). *Website:* www.adelaide.edu.au (office).

McWHERTER, Ned R.; American politician; b. 15 Oct. 1930, Palmersville, Tenn.; s. of Harmon R. McWherter and Lucille Smith; m. Bette Jean Beck (deceased); one s. one d.; mem. Tenn. House of Reps 1968–87, Speaker 1973–87; Gov. of Tenn. 1987–95; Chair. Bd Eagle Distributors Inc., Volunteer Distribution Co., Weakley Co. Bank; Dir Coca-Cola Bottling Co., Consolidated, Piedmont Natural Gas Co., American Battle Monument Comm.; Gov. US Postal Service, Washington 1996; Democrat. *Address:* PO Box 30, Dresden, TN 38225, USA.

McWILLIAM, Candia Frances Juliet, BA; British writer; b. 1 July 1955, Edin.; d. of Colin McWilliam and Margaret McWilliam; m. 1st Quentin Gerard Carew Wallop (now Earl of Portsmouth) 1981; one s. one d.; m. 2nd Fram Dinshaw; one s.; ed Sherborne School, Dorset and Girton Coll., Cambridge. *Publications:* A Cast of Knives 1988, A Little Stranger 1989, Debatable Land 1994, Change of Use 1996, Wait till I Tell You 1997, Lady Rose and Mrs Memmary (with Ruby Ferguson) 2004. *Leisure interest:* reading. *Address:* Aitken Alexander Associates Ltd, 18–21 Cavaye Place, London, SW10 9PT, England (office). *Telephone:* (20) 7373-8672 (office). *Fax:* (20) 7373-6002 (office). *Website:* www.aitkenalexander.co.uk (office). *E-mail:* cleminol@hotmail.com.

McWILLIAMS, Sir Francis, GBE, BSc, FREng, FCGI; British lawyer and arbitrator and civil engineer; b. 8 Feb. 1926, Edin.; s. of John McWilliams and Mary McWilliams; m. Winifred Segger 1950; two s.; ed Holy Cross Acad., Edin., Univ. of Edin.; engineer with various local authorities and contractors in UK 1945–53; Town Engineer, Petaling Jaya Devt Corpn, Malaysia 1954–64; Consulting Civil and Structural Engineer, F. McWilliams & Assocs, Kuala Lumpur 1964–76; full-time student 1976–78; called to English bar at Lincoln's Inn 1978; pupil barrister 1978–79; Int. Arbitrator 1979–; magistrate City of London Bench 1980–96; Chair. Centre for Econs and Business Research 1992–2002; Vice-Pres. and Chair. British/Malaysian Soc. 1994–2001; mem. Panel of Arbitrators of Inst. of Civil Engineers and other bodies; Sheriff City of London 1988–89, Lord Mayor of London 1992–93; Bencher of Lincoln's Inn 1993; fmr mem. Court of Aldermen, City of London; Master Worshipful Co. of Engineers 1990–91, Worshipful Co. of Loriners 1995; Hon. FICE; KStJ, Kt of St Gregory, Kt, Dato Sri Selera (Malaysia); Hon. DCL (City Univ.) 1992, Hon. DEng (Kingston), Dr hc (Edin.); and several other hons. *Publication:* Urban Regeneration and Environmental Challenge, Pray Silence for 'Jock' Whittington (From Building Sewers to Suing Builders). *Leisure interests:* golf, skiing. *Address:* Flat 7, Whittingehame House, Whittingehame, E Lothian, EH41 4QA, Scotland (home). *Telephone:* (1368) 850619 (home). *Fax:* (1368) 850619 (home).

MACY, William H.; American actor; b. 13 March 1950, Miami, Fla; m. Felicity Huffman; ed Goddard Coll., Vermont; co-f. St Nicholas Theater Co., Atlantic Theater Co. *Stage appearances include:* The Man in 605 1980, Twelfth Night, Bureaucrat, A Call From the East, The Dining Room, Speakeasy, Wild Life, Flirtations, Baby With the Bathwater, The Nice and the Nasty, Bodies Rest and Motion, Oh Hell!, Prairie du Chien, The Shawl, An Evening With Dorothy Parker, The Dining Room, A Call From the Sea, The Beaver Coat, Life During Wartime, Mr Gogol and Mr Preen, Oleanna, Our Town. *Play directed:* Boy's Life. *Films include:* Without a Trace, The Last Dragon, Radio Days, Somewhere in Time, Hello Again, House of Games, Things Change, Homicide, Shadows and Fog, Benny and Joon, Searching for Bobby Fischer, The Client, Oleanna, The Silence of the Lambs, Murder in the First, Mr Holland's Opus, Down Periscope, Fargo, Ghosts of Mississippi, Air Force One, Wag the Dog, Pleasantville 1998, A Civil Action, Psycho 1998, Magnolia 1999, State and Maine 2000, Panic 2000, Focus 2001, Jurassic Park III 2001, Welcome to Collinwood 2002, The Cooler 2003, Stealing Sinatra 2003, Out of Order (TV mini series) 2003, Seabiscuit 2004, Spartan 2004, Cellular 2004, Sahara 2005, Edmond 2005, Thank You for Smoking 2005, Doogal (voice) 2006, Bobby 2006, Inland Empire 2006, Everyone's Hero (voice) 2006, Wild Hogs 2007, He was a Quiet Man 2007. *Film directed:* Lip Service (TV) 1988. *Television appearances include:* Chicago Hope (series), The Murder of Mary Phagan (mini-series), Texan, A Murderous Affair, The Water Engine, Heart of Justice, A Private Matter, The Con, A Slight Case of Murder, Reversible Errors 2004, The Wool Cap 2004, The Unit 2007. *Address:* c/o Creative Artists Agency, 9830 Wilshire Blvd, Beverly Hills, CA 90212-1825, USA.

MĄDALSKI, Wojciech, MSc, MEng; Polish business executive; *CEO and President of the Management Board, Netia Holdings SA;* b. 2 May 1956, Wrocław; s. of Jozef Madalski and Hanna Madalska (née Machowska); m. Kasia Swiatek 1980; one d.; ed Tech. Univ. Wrocław, McMaster Univ., Hamilton, Ont., Canada; Teaching/Research Asst, McMaster Univ., Hamilton, Ont., Canada 1980–82; Research Engineer, Tech. Devt Div., Polysar Ltd,

Sarnia, Ont. 1982–84, Marketing/Business Planning Analyst, Styrenics Div. 1984–86, Business Man., Adhesives and Sealants Div. 1986–88; Gen. Man., Silicone Business, Novacor Chemicals Inc., Akron, OH, USA 1988–91; Pres. and CEO, Shincor Silicones Inc. 1991–93; CEO, E. Wedel SA and Pres., PepsiCo Foods International (PFI), Poland 1993–95, Vice-Pres., PFI Europe Group, UK 1996–97, ECR Dir, Walkers Snack Foods Ltd 1998; CEO and Pres., Hortex Holding SA 1998–2001; Man. Dir, Carlsberg Breweries A/S, Poland 2002; CEO and Pres., Man. Bd, Netia Holdings SA 2002–. *Address:* Netia Holdings SA, ul. Poleczki 13, 02-822 Warsaw, Poland (office). *Telephone:* (22) 3302000 (office). *Fax:* (22) 3302323 (office). *E-mail:* info@netia.pl (office). *Website:* www.netia.pl (office).

MAĎARIČ, Marek; Slovak politician; *Minister of Culture;* b. 23 March 1966, Bratislava; m.; ed Acad. of Musical and Dramatic Arts; Script Ed., Office of Literary and Dramatic Broadcasting, Slovak TV 1990–93, Ed.-in-Chief 1996–97, Script Ed., Slovak TV 1997–99, Deputy Pres. of the Council 2002–04; freelance scriptwriter 1993–96; copywriter, Istropolitana D̓Arcy (advertising agency) 1999–2000; Head of Media and Press Dept, Social Democracy Party 2000–02, 2004–06; Minister of Culture 2006–. *Address:* Ministry of Culture, nám. SNP 33, 813 31 Bratislava, Slovakia (office). *Telephone:* (2) 5939-1155 (office). *Fax:* (2) 5939-1174 (office). *E-mail:* mksr@culture.gov.sk (office). *Website:* www.culture.gov.sk (office).

MADDEN, Sir David, KCMG, MA; British fmr diplomatist; b. 1946; m. Lady Penelope Anthea Madden; ed Univ. of Oxford, Courtauld Inst., London; joined British Diplomatic Service 1970; overseas assignments in Berlin, Moscow, Athens and Belgrade; various positions in FCO including Head of S European Dept –1994; High Commr to Cyprus 1994–99; Amb. to Greece 1999–2004 (retd); Political Adviser, EU Force in Bosnia and Herzegovina (EUFOR) 2004–05; Trustee The Brooke (equine welfare charity) 2008–. *Leisure interests:* music (especially opera), sport (especially tennis, cricket and rowing), reading, animal welfare. *Address:* c/o Board of Trustees, The Brooke, Broadmead House, 21 Panton Street, London, SW1Y 4DR, England.

MADDEN, Francis J.; American engineer; key contrib. responsible for design, testing and production of Corona cameras for aerial photography; adapted techniques from motion-picture film, fabrics and other industries; served as Chief Engineer, Itek Corpn's Corona camera programme until retirement in 1975, collaborated with Physical Research Lab. at Boston Univ.; recognized for work on Corona by Dir of CIA 1995, named a Pioneer of Nat. Reconnaissance by Nat. Reconnaissance Office 2000, Charles Stark Draper Prize, Nat. Acad. of Eng (co-recipient) 2005. *Address:* c/o National Academy of Engineering, 500 Fifth Street, NW, Washington, DC 20001, USA. *Telephone:* (202) 334-3200. *E-mail:* NAEMembershipOffice@nae.edu.

MADDEN, John; British film director; b. 8 April 1949, Portsmouth, Hants. *Films include:* Golden Gate 1994, Mrs. Brown 1997, Shakespeare in Love (Acad. Award for Best Film, BAFTA Award for Best Film) 1998, Captain Corelli's Mandolin 2001, Proof 2004, Killshot 2006. *Television includes:* Grown-Ups 1985, The Return of Sherlock Holmes (series; episode The Priory School) 1986, A Wreath of Roses 1987, Inspector Morse (series; episodes Dead on Time, The Infernal Serpent, Promised Land, The Way Through the Woods) 1987, After the War (mini-series) 1989, The Widowmaker 1990, The Storyteller: Greek Myths (mini-series; episode Theseus and the Minotaur) 1990, The Casebook of Sherlock Holmes (series; episode The Disappearance of Lady Frances Carfax) 1990, Ethan Frome 1993, Meat 1994, Prime Suspect 4: The Lost Child 1995, Truth or Dare 1996.

MADDY, Penelope Jo, PhD; American academic; *Professor of Logic and Philosophy of Science and of Mathematics, University of California, Irvine;* b. 4 July 1950, Tulsa, Okla; d. of the late Richard Parsons and of Suzanne Lorimer Parsons; ed Univ. of California, Berkeley, Princeton Univ.; Lecturer then Asst Prof. of Philosophy, Univ. of Notre Dame 1978–83; Assoc. Prof. of Philosophy, Univ. of Illinois, Chicago 1983–87; Assoc. Prof. of Philosophy and Math., Univ., of California, Irvine 1987–89, Prof. 1989–, Chair. Philosophy Dept 1991–95, Prof. of Logic and Philosophy of Science 1998–, Chair. Logic and Philosophy of Science 1998–2001; mem. American Acad. of Arts and Sciences; Westinghouse Science Scholarship 1968–72, Marshall Fellowship 1972–73, American Asscn of Univ. Women Fellowship 1982–83, NSF Fellowships 1986, 1988–89, 1990–91, 1994–95, Romanell Lecturer 2001. *Publications:* Realism in Mathematics 1990, Naturalism in Mathematics (Lakatos Prize 2002) 1997. *Address:* Department of Logic and Philosophy of Science, Office SST 759, School of Social Sciences, University of California, Irvine, CA 92697-5100, USA (office). *Telephone:* (949) 824-4133 (office). *E-mail:* pjmaddy@uci.edu (office). *Website:* www.lps.uci.edu/home/fac-staff/faculty/maddy (office).

MADE, Joseph; Zimbabwean politician; *Minister of State for Agricultural Engineering and Mechanisation;* mem. Zimbabwe African Nat. Union-Patriotic Front (ZANU-PF); Minister for Lands, Agric. and Rural Devt –2007, of State for Agricultural Eng and Mechanisation 2007–; mem. Pres. Robert Mugabe's 'Gang of Four' politicians. *Address:* c/o Ministry of Lands, Agriculture and Rural Development, Ngungunyana Building, 1 Borrowdale Road, Private Bag 7701, Causeway, Harare, Zimbabwe (office).

MADELIN, Alain, LenD; French politician and lawyer; b. 26 March 1946, Paris; three c.; lawyer, Paris office, Fed. nat. des Républicains indépendants (FNRI) 1968–; mem. Nat. Secr. FNRI 1977; elected Deputy to Nat. Ass. (Union pour la démocratie française— UDF) 1978–86, 1988–93, 1995–2002, 2002–07 (UMP); co-organizer UDF 1989–93; Vice-Pres. UDF 1991–96; Minister of Industry, Posts and Telecommunications and Tourism 1986–88, of Enterprise and Econ. Devt 1993–95, of Econ. and Finance May–Aug. 1995; Sec.-Gen. Republican Party 1988–89, Vice-Pres. 1989–96; Pres. France-Corée Asscn 1991–93; Vice-Pres. Regional Council of Brittany 1992–98; Mayor of Redon 1995–2000; mem. European Parl. 1989–2002; Pres. Inst. Euro 92 1988–97, f., Pres. Idées Action 1993–97; Leader Démocratie libérale 1997–2002; mem. UMP 2002–; presidential cand. 2002. *Publications:* Pour libérer l'école 1984, Chers compatriotes 1994, Quand les autruches relèveront la tête 1995, Aux Sources du modèle libéral français 1997, Le Droit du plus faible 1999. *Address:* c/o Union pour un Mouvement Populaire, 55 rue La Boétie, 75384 Paris Cedex 08, France (office).

MADFAI, Husham H. Fahmi al-, BSc; Iraqi engineering consultant and government official; b. 28 Oct. 1928, Baghdad; s. of Hassan Fahmi Al-Madfai and Wajiha Nouri Al-Madfai; m. 1st Suad A. Mohloom (died 1984); one s. one d.; m. 2nd Suha M. A. Bakri 1993; ed Cen. High School, Baghdad, Eng Coll., Univ. of Baghdad, Hammersmith School of Art & Design, London, Inst. of Structural Engineers, London; civil engineer, Basrah Petroleum Co. 1953–55; with Dept of Housing and Tourism Design and Policies, Devt Bd 1957–63; Head. Tech. Dept, Municipality of Baghdad 1963–68; own consulting firm (architects, planners and designers) 1968–80; Deputy Mayor (responsible for planning and man.), City of Baghdad 1980–88; own consulting firm (studies and eng) 1988–; Regional Consultant (feasibility, studies and design), Amman, Jordan 1994–; mem. Iraqi Asscn of Philosophers and Scientists 1994. *Publications include:* Health Aspects in Town Planning 1968, Low-cost Prefabricated Housing 1975, Housing Programme for Iraq until the year 2000 1976, Environmental Problems in Arab Cities 1995. *Leisure interests:* archaeology, studying ancient cities, music, paintings, reading biographies, swimming, long walks. *Address:* PO Box 941021, Shmesan 1, Amman 11194, Jordan; Maghrib Street, Adhamiya 22/14/302, Baghdad, Iraq. *Telephone:* (6) 5688470 (Jordan); (1) 4225021/2 (Iraq). *Fax:* (6) 5688498 (Jordan).

MADFAI, Ilham al-; Iraqi guitarist and singer; b. 1942, Baghdad; m.; two s.; ed studied architecture; f. The Twisters, known as Iraq's first rock band; following studies returned to Iraq, f. 13½ 1967; left Iraq 1979; performed across Arab world; returned to Iraq 1991; emigrated to Jordan 1994; based in USA in late 1990s before returning to Jordan. *Recordings:* albums: Ilham Al-Madfai 1999, Khuttar 1999, Baghdad 2003. *Address:* c/o EMI Music Arabia, POB 61003, Dubai, United Arab Emirates (office). *E-mail:* info@emimusicarabia.com (office). *Website:* ilhamalmadfai.iraqimusic.com (office).

MADFAI, Kahtan al, BArch, PhD; Iraqi architect, town planner and author; b. 15 April 1926, Baghdad; s. of late Hassan Fahmi al Madfai and of Wajiha Shaikh Noori Shirwai; m. Lily Vassiliki Vorré 1957; one d.; ed Univ. of Wales Inst. of Science and Tech., Cardiff, UK; practised as architect in public housing sector 1957, planning and design 1961; co-f. Architectural School of Baghdad 1961; lecturer on theory of design 1955–69; f. architectural firm Dar al Imara 1954–79; Asst Man. Gen. Housing Iraq Project 1973–2000; designer and consultant architect; Chair. Pan-Arab Jury for awarding prizes for Arab Town Projects 1985–87; delivered papers and seminars Istanbul 1985, Oxford 1986, Tunis 1987, 1989, Bahrain 1994, Baghdad 1994, Univ. of South Georgia, USA 1996, AIA, Atlanta, USA 1996, Amman 1996; co-f. Soc. of Iraqi Artists; mem. S.P. Group of Artists, Baghdad; works in Baghdad include Ministry of Finance 1968, Bunniyd Mosque 1972, Museum of Natural History 1973, Burj Rubaya apartment building Abu Dhabi 1990, Fatiha Halls project 2003; several first prizes in architectural competitions, including Rohoon Bank Bldg, Baghdad 1955, Baghdad Cen. Commercial Zone 1970, Cen. PO 1975, Mohammedia Touristic Project, Basra 1977, Great Mosque Competition 1984. *Publications:* several books on architecture and town planning including Development of the Iraqi House 1956, Criteria for Baghdad's New Master Plan 1965, A Manifesto for Arabic Architecture 1986, Architecture and Language 1987, Allah and the Architect 1997; poetry: Fulool 1965, Zem Zem Zeman 1972, Reconstruction of the Sumerian God Abu 1990. *Leisure interests:* modern art, modern poetry, modern philosophy. *Address:* 22 Vassileos Constantinou, 11635 Athens, Greece. *Telephone:* (210) 723-2836 (office); (210) 751-4120 (home). *Fax:* (210) 724-9920 (office).

MADI, Hamada ('Boléro'); Comoran politician; b. 1965, Moheli Island; obtained degree in constitutional law in Ukraine; fmr high school head teacher; fmr adviser to Pres., Sec.-Gen. Comoros Republican Party; Sec.-Gen. Presidency, responsible for Defence 1999–2000, Prime Minister of the Comoros 2000–02, Interim Pres. Jan.–May 2002, apptd Minister of Defence and Security 2002. *Address:* c/o Ministry of External Defence and Territorial Security, Moroni, Comoros (office).

MADIKIZELA-MANDELA, (Nomzano) Winnie; South African politician; b. (Nomzamo Winifred Zanyiwe Madikizela), 26 Sept. 1934, Bizana, Pondoland, Transkei; m. Nelson Mandela (q.v.) 1958 (divorced 1996); two d.; mem. of African Nat. Congress (ANC) until its banning in 1960; campaigned constantly on behalf of her husband gaoled for life for political activities 1964–90; held in solitary confinement 1969–70; named a "banned person" by S African authorities 1976; Head of ANC Social Welfare Operations 1990–92; sentenced to six years' imprisonment on four counts of kidnapping and of being an accessory to assault May 1991; sentence upheld on appeal, except charge of being an accessory to assault; prison term waived to suspended two-year term, fine imposed June 1993; suspended from ANC Women's League 1993, Head 1997; mem. ANC Nat. Exec. Cttee 1994, Deputy Minister for Arts, Culture, Science and Tech., Govt of Nat. Unity 1994–95; charged with fraud Oct. 2001, convicted of 43 counts of fraud and 25 of theft and sentenced to five years' imprisonment with one year suspended April 2003, Pretoria High Court overturned conviction for theft and upheld one for fraud and handed her a three years and six months suspended sentence; Third World Prize 1985. *Publication:* Part of My Soul Went with Him 1985.

MADKOUR, Al-Sharif Mohamed Abdel-Khalek, PhD; Egyptian business executive, university professor and consultant; b. 8 Jan. 1948, Giza; s. of Ibrahim Bayoumi Madkour and Bahia Abdel-Khalek Madkour; m. Afkar el

Kharadly 1970; two d.; ed Ecole des Hautes Etudes en Sciences Sociales, Univ. de la Sorbonne, Paris and Univ. of Cairo; Attaché, Industrial Devt Centre for Arab States, League of Arab States, Cairo 1969–78; Dir-Gen. Al-Ahram Org. 1978–85; mem. Bd Al-Ahram Investment Co. 1981–85; Sr Research Scientist, School of Information and Computer Sciences, Ga Inst. of Tech. Atlanta, Ga, USA 1980–83; Dir Egyptian Nat. Scientific and Tech. Information Network 1980–82; Prof. Faculty of Mass Communications, Univ. of Cairo 1982; Pres. Phoenix Int.-Madkour Assocs Inc., McLean, Va, USA 1986; Chair. and CEO Egyptian Co. for Tourism and Services, Cairo 1987; Chair. Cairo-Systems, SARL, Cairo 1990–, Multinational Multimedia Computing Inc. Cairo 1992–; Chair. and CEO Marketing Via Internet, Cairo 1997–. *Publications:* Information Services of Egypt 1981, Towards a National Information Policy for Egypt 1982, Information Systems in Egypt: New Trends, Latent Challenges 1984. *Leisure interests:* bridge, snooker, tennis, soccer. *Address:* 4 Gamal el Din Abu el Mahassen Square, Garden City, Cairo (office); 8 Nile Street, Giza, Cairo, Egypt (home). *Telephone:* (2) 7960581 (office); (2) 7962407 (home). *Fax:* (2) 7962407 (office); (2) 5703014 (home). *E-mail:* mvi-egypt@bigfoot.com (office); madkour@intouch.com (home). *Website:* shopegypt.com (office).

MADKOUR, Nazli, MA; Egyptian artist and painter; b. 25 Feb. 1949, Cairo; d. of Mokhtar Madkour and Malak Salem; m. Mohamed Salmawy 1970; one s. one d.; ed Cairo Univ., American Univ., Cairo; fmrly econ. expert for Industrial Devt Centre for Arab States; professional artist 1981–; numerous solo and collective exhbns; represented in public and pvt. collections in Egypt and internationally. *Publication:* Egyptian Women and Artistic Creativity 1989. *Leisure interests:* travel, reading, music. *Address:* #40 Street 13, Maadi, Cairo 11431, Egypt (home). *Telephone:* (2) 5197047 (office); (2) 3804446 (home). *Fax:* (2) 5197047 (office).

MÁDL, Ferenc, PhD; Hungarian fmr head of state and lawyer; b. 29 Jan. 1931, Bánd Co. Veszprém; s. of A. Mádl; m. Dalma Némethy 1955; one s.; ed Univ. of Pécs, Eötvös Loránd Univ., Budapest and Univ. of Strasbourg, France; worked as legal clerk and then as court sec. 1955; political and legal rapporteur, Hungarian Acad. of Sciences Cen. Office 1956–71, later promoted to head of dept and later to controlling supervisor; Docent, Dept of Civil Law, Budapest Univ. of Sciences 1971–73, Univ. Tutor 1973–, Dir Faculty of Pvt. Int. Law 1985–; mem. Inst. for Legal Sciences and State Admin, Hungarian Acad. of Sciences 1972–80; Dir Inst. of Civil Law Disciplines, Eötvös Univ., Budapest 1978–85; head Dept of the Law of Conflicts and Int. Economic Relations 1985; apptd cen. judge on Washington-based Int. Selected Court for States and Foreign Investors 1989; govt commr Bős-Nagymaros hydroelectric power plant project 1991; Minister without Portfolio 1990–93, of Culture and Educ. 1992–94; Chair. Bd Dirs State Property Agency 1990, Science Policy Cttee 1990; Supervisor State Bank Supervisory Authority 1992, Chair. Bank Supervisory Authority Cttee 1992–93; Controlling Supervisor Nat. Scientific Research Fund 1992; Chair. inter-portfolio cttee to research those works of art illegally taken to the fmr Soviet Union from Hungary during and after World War II 1992; Head, Human Resources Policy Cabinet 1992–93; Minister for Culture and Educ. 1993–94; Chair. Council for Higher Educ. and Science February–July 1994, Nat. Cultural Fund 1994; stood as opposition MDF-KDNP-Fidesz's presidential cand. 1995; Chair. Hungarian Civil Cooperation Asscn 1996–; mem. Scientific Advisory Body for the Viktor Orbán govt 1999; Pres. of Hungary 2000–05; Corresp. mem. Hungarian Acad. of Sciences 1987–93, mem. 1993–; mem. Int. Acad. of Commercial Law, Harvard 1985–, Governing Council Rome Int. Inst. (UNIDROIT) 1988–; mem. European Acad. of Sciences and Art 1989–, European Acad. of Sciences 1990–, Inst. of Int. Law 1991–; Chevalier de la Légion d'honneur 1999; Széchenyi Prize 1999. *Publications:* author of 20 books on law of int. econ. relations, int. investment law, EEC law, etc. and about 200 law review articles. *Address:* Egyetem tér 1-3, 1364 Budapest, Hungary. *Telephone:* (1) 266-6486.

MADONNA; American singer and actress; b. (Madonna Louise Veronica Ciccone), 16 Aug. 1958, Bay City, Mich.; d. of Sylvio Ciccone and Madonna Ciccone; m. 1st Sean Penn 1985 (divorced 1989); one d. by Carlos Leon; m. 2nd Guy Ritchie 2000 (divorced 2008); two s. (one adopted); ed Univ. of Mich., Alvin Ailey Dance School; moved to New York 1979, dancer 1979–, actress 1980–, solo singer 1983–; numerous world-wide concerts, tours, television appearances; f. Maverick record label 1992 (sold to Warner Music Group 2004); Vice-Pres. ICA, London; established children's clothing line, Sweet Hearts 2004–; numerous MTV Video Awards, including Vanguard Award 1986, American Music Awards for Favorite Female Video Artist 1987, Favorite Dance Single 1991, Acad. Award for Best Song 1991, Juno Award for Int. Song of the Year 1991, Grammy Award for Best Longform Music Video 1992, BRIT Award for Best Int. Female 2001, 2006, numerous awards from Billboard, Vogue and Rolling Stone magazines, Echo Award for Best Int. Female Artist, Germany 2006, Ivor Novello Award for Int. Hit of the Year (for Sorry) 2007. *Films:* Vision Quest 1985, Desperately Seeking Susan 1985, A Certain Sacrifice 1985, Shanghai Surprise 1986, Who's That Girl? 1987, Bloodhounds on Broadway 1989, Dick Tracy 1990, Shadows and Fog 1991, In Bed With Madonna (documentary) 1991, A League of Their Own 1992, Body of Evidence 1992, Dangerous Game 1993, Blue in the Face 1995, Four Rooms 1995, Girl 6 1996, Evita 1996, The Next Best Thing 2000, Star 2001, Swept Away 2002, Arthur and the Invisibles (voice) 2006, Filth and Wisdom (dir) 2008, I Am Because We Are (documentary) 2008. *Plays:* Speed-the-Plow (Broadway) 1988, Up for Grabs (Wyndhams Theatre, London) 2002. *Recordings include:* albums: Madonna 1983, Like A Virgin 1984, True Blue 1985, Who's That Girl? (film soundtrack) 1987, Like A Prayer 1989, I'm Breathless (soundtrack to film Dick Tracy) 1990, The Immaculate Collection 1990, Erotica 1992, Bedtime Stories 1994, Something To Remember 1995, Evita (film soundtrack) 1997, Ray Of Light (Grammy Award for Best Pop Album) 1998, Next Best Thing (film soundtrack) 2000, Music 2000, GHV2 2001, American Life 2003, Remixed and Revisited (EP) 2004, Confessions On A Dance Floor (Grammy Award for Best Electronic/Dance Album 2007) 2005, I'm Going to Tell You a Secret 2006, Hard Candy 2008. *Publications:* Sex 1992, The English Roses (juvenile) 2003, Mr Peabody's Apples (juvenile) 2003, Yakov and the Seven Thieves (juvenile) 2004, The Adventures of Abdi (juvenile) 2004, Lotsa de Casha (juvenile) 2005. *Address:* Live Nation Inc., 9348 Civic Center Drive, Beverly Hills, CA 90210; 8491 West Sunset Boulevard, Suite 485, West Hollywood, CA 90069, USA. *Website:* www .madonna.com.

MADRAZO PINTADO, Roberto, LLB; Mexican politician and lawyer; b. 30 July 1952; s. of Carlos Madrazo Becerra y la Profra and Graciela Pintado Jiménez; m. Isabel de la Parra Trillo; two s. three d.; ed Universidad Nacional Autónoma, Mexico; entered civil service 1971; legal asst to Alvaro Obregón 1971–72; worked in office of Chief Justice 1972, adviser on social affairs 1979–81; Deputy Sec.-Gen. for Youth, Partido Revolucionario Institucional (PRI) 1975, Sec.-Gen. Nat. Movt of Revolutionary Youth 1977, Sec. of Public Relations and Man. 1984–87, Sec. of Org. 1988–, Pres. PRI 2002–06; elected Fed. Deputy, State of Tabasco 1976, State Gov. 1988–91; mem. 55th legislature, Fed. Govt 1991–93; Founder and Pres. Escuela Nacional de Cuadros; apptd Sec. of the Great Comm., Palace of San Lazaro; unsuccessful cand. for Pres. of Mexico 2006. *Publications:* Urbanism, Services and Public Security; numerous articles on social affairs, int. relations and devt. *Address:* c/o Partido Revolucionario Institucional, Insurgentes Norte 59, Edif. 2, subsótano, Col Buenavista, 06359 México, DF, Mexico (office).

MADRID HURTADO, Miguel de la (see DE LA MADRID HURTADO, Miguel).

MADSEN, Ib Hennig, PhD; Danish mathematician and academic; *Professor of Mathematics, Århus University;* b. 12 April 1942, Copenhagen; s. of Hennig Madsen and Gudrun Madsen (née Davids-Thomsen); m. 1st Benedicte Rechnitzer 1963 (divorced 1982); m. 2nd Ulla Lykke Jorgensen 1984; two s.; ed Univ. of Copenhagen, Univ. of Chicago, USA; Research Stipend, Århus Univ. 1965–70; Research Instructor, Univ. of Chicago 1971–72; Assoc. Prof., Århus Univ. 1971–83, Prof. of Math. 1983–; Ed Acta Mathematica 1988–; mem. Royal Danish Acad. of Sciences 1978, Inst. for Advanced Study, Princeton 1986–87, Royal Swedish Acad. of Sciences 1998, Royal Norwegian Acad. 2002; Rigmor and Carl Holst-Knudsen Science Prize 1982, Humboldt Research Award 1992, Plenary Lecturer, Int. Congress of Mathematicians, Madrid 2006. *Publications:* The Classifying Spaces for Surgery and Cobordism of Manifolds (with R. J. Milgram) 1979, From Calculus to Cohomology (with J. Tornehave) 1997. *Address:* Department of Mathematics, Århus University, 8000 Århus C (office); Vestervang 2, 222, 8000 Århus C, Denmark (home). *Telephone:* 89-42-34-51 (office). *Fax:* 86-13-17-69 (office). *E-mail:* imadsen@imf .au.dk (office). *Website:* www.imf.au.dk (office).

MADSEN, Mette; Danish writer and fmr politician; b. 3 July 1924, Pandrup, North Jutland; d. of Holger Fruensgaard; professional writer, including collections of poetry, hymns, songs, schoolbooks, local history, satire, radio and television 1958–; Liberal MP 1971–87; mem. of Presidium Folketing 1981–84; Minister for Ecclesiastical Affairs 1988–; Chair. Supervisory Cttee Royal Theatre 1978–84, Cttee for Culture and Information, N Atlantic Council 1982–84; IF2 1980, FNF4 1982, Commdr of Dannebrog 1985. *Publications:* Hen på Eftermiddagen (poetry) 1973, Sommerens veje (poetry) 1982, Og så er der Kaffe (political memoirs) 1992, I Anledning Af. (songs and poetry) 1994, Husk Nu at Neje (memoirs) 1997, Tiden der Fulgte: 20 Top-Chefers Farvel til Magten (Goodbye to Power) 1998, Hvad skal du Være (memoirs) 2004, Bidrag til Lokalhistorie 2005, 2006, 2007. *Address:* Blegdalsparken 53, 9000 Ålborg, Denmark (home). *Telephone:* (98) 18-78-03 (home).

MADSEN, Michael; American actor; b. 25 Sept. 1958, Chicago, Ill.; brother of Virginia Madsen; m. Jeannine Bisignano; one s.; began acting career at Steppenwolf Theater, Chicago, appearing in plays including Of Mice and Men, A Streetcar Named Desire; appeared in Broadway production of A Streetcar Named Desire 1992. *Films include:* Against All Hope 1982, WarGames 1983, Racing with the Moon 1984, The Natural 1984, The Killing Time 1987, Shadows in the Storm 1988, Iguana 1988, Kill Me Again 1989, Blood Red 1989, The End of Innocence 1990, Fatal Instinct 1991, The Doors 1991, Thelma and Louise 1991, Beyond the Law 1992, Almost Blue 1992, Reservoir Dogs 1992, Straight Talk 1992, Inside Edge 1993, A House in the Hills 1993, Trouble Bound 1993, Free Willy 1993, Money for Nothing 1993, Dead Connection 1994, Season of Change 1994, The Getaway 1994, Wyatt Earp 1994, Species 1995, Free Willy 2: The Adventure Home 1995, Man with a Gun 1995, Mulholland Falls 1996, The Winner 1996, Red Line 1996, Papertrail 1997, Surface to Air 1997, The Last Days of Frankie the Fly 1997, Donnie Brasco 1997, The Girl Gets Moe 1997, The Maker 1997, Catherine's Grove 1997, Executive Target 1997, Flat Out 1998, The Thief and the Stripper 1998, Ballad of the Nightingale 1998, Rough Draft 1998, Species II 1998, The Sender 1998, Fait Accompli 1998, The Florentine 1999, Detour 1999, Fall 2000, Bad Guys 2000, Ides of March 2000, The Stray 2000, Luck of the Draw 2000, The Alternate 2000, The Price of Air 2000, Outlaw 2001, Pressure Point 2001, The Ghost 2001, Choke 2001, L.A.P.D.: To Protect and to Serve 2001, Extreme Honor 2001, Welcome to America 2002, Love.com 2002, Die Another Day 2002, The Real Deal 2002, Where's Angelo? 2003, My Boss's Daughter 2003, Kill Bill: Vol. 1 2003, Vampires Anonymous 2003, Blueberry 2004, Kill Bill: Vol. 2 2004, Jacked$ 2004, Hoboken Hollow 2005, Firedog (voice) 2005, Sin City 2005, Chasing Ghosts 2005, The Last Drop 2005, L.A. Dicks 2005, Muzhskoy sezon. Barkhatnaya revolutsiya 2005, BloodRayne 2005, Living and Dying 2006, All In 2006, Last Hour 2006, Scary Movie 4 2006, Canes 2006, UKM: The Ultimate Killing Machine 2006. *Television includes:* War and Remembrance (miniseries) 1988, Vengeance Unlimited (series) 1998, Big Apple (series) 2001, 44 Minutes: The North Hollywood Shoot-Out 2003, Frankenstein 2004, Tilt (series) 2005. *Address:* c/o Michael Manchal, CAA, 9830 Wilshire Boulevard, Beverly Hills, CA 90212, USA. *Website:* www.michaelmadsen.com.

MADUEKWE, Chief Ojo; Nigerian politician; *Minister of Foreign Affairs;* b. 6 May 1945, Abia State; ed Univ. of Nigeria; called to Nigerian Bar 1973; mem. House of Reps 1983, Constituent Ass. 1988; Adviser to Minister of Foreign Affairs 1993–95; mem. Nat. Constituent Conf. 1994–95; Tech. Adviser to Vision 2010 Cttee 1997; elected Senator 1998; Minister of Culture and Tourism 1999–2000, of Transport 2000–03; Legal Adviser to the Pres. 2003–05; Minister of Foreign Affairs 2007–; Nat. Sec. People's Democratic Party (PDP). *Address:* Ministry of Foreign Affairs, Maputo St, Zone 3, Wuse District, PMB 130, Abuja, Nigeria (office). *Telephone:* (9) 5230570 (office). *Website:* www.mfa.gov.ng (office).

MADUNA, Penuell Mpapa, LLD; South African politician and lawyer; b. 29 Dec. 1952; m. Nompumelelo Cheryl Maduna; three c.; ed Univ. of Zimbabwe, Univ. of Witwatersrand; worked in underground structures of ANC in 1970s, twice incarcerated and prosecuted; left SA 1980; fmr Regional Admin. Sec. Tanzania, Office of Treasurer-Gen. of ANC; fmr staff mem. and Legal Adviser, ANC HQ Lusaka, est. Dept of Legal and Constitutional Affairs 1985, founder mem. Constitutional Cttee, participated in meetings with South African Govt and officials in 1980s and early 1990s leading to establishment of Convention for a Democratic South Africa, mem. Negotiating Comm., now mem. Nat. Exec. Cttee; MP Nat. Ass.; Minister of Mineral and Energy Affairs 1996–99, of Justice and Constitutional Devt 1999–2004; Bd mem. Faculty of Law, Univ. of Witwatersrand 1996–. *Publication:* Fundamental Rights in the New Constitution 1994 (co-author). *Leisure interests:* soccer, reading, debating. *Address:* c/o Ministry of Justice and Constitutional Development, Presidia Building, 8th Floor, corner Pretorius and Paul Kruger Streets, Pretoria 0002, South Africa (office).

MADURO JOEST, Ricardo, BA; Honduran head of state and central banker; b. Panamá, Panama; m. Miriam Andreu; one s. (deceased) three d.; ed Stanford Univ., USA; mem. Partido Nacional (Nationalist Party), currently Chair. Cen. Cttee; Dir Rafael Callejas's election campaigns 1985, 1989; apptd Chair. Banco Cen. de Honduras 1990; fmr Co-ordinator of the Econ. Office; Pres. of Honduras 2002–05. *Address:* c/o Partido Nacional (PN), Paseo el Obelisco, Comayagüela, Tegucigalpa, Honduras (office).

MADURO MOROS, Nicolás; Venezuelan politician; *Minister of Foreign Affairs;* b. 23 Nov. 1961, Caracas; m. Cilia Flores; two c.; worker on Caracas metro and founder of trade union for Caracas metro workers 1980s; also mem. Movimiento Bolivariano Revolucionario 200 1980s, mem. Nat. Directorate 1994–97; Founding mem. Movimiento Quinta Republica 200 (MVR) 1997, elected to Asamblea Nacional 1998, Pres. of Citizens' Participation Cttee 1999, Co-ordinator of MVR parl. team 2000–01, Co-ordinator of majority bloc parl. team 2001–05, Pres. Asamblea Nacional 2005–06; Minister of Foreign Affairs 2006–. *Address:* Ministry of Foreign Affairs, Torre MRE, esq. Carmelitas, Avda Urdaneta, Caracas 1010, Venezuela (office). *Telephone:* (212) 862-1085 (office). *Fax:* (212) 864-3633 (office). *E-mail:* criptogr@mre.gov.ve (office). *Website:* www.mre.gov.ve (office).

MADY, Mohamed H. al-, BSc, MSc; Saudi Arabian business executive and chemical engineer; *Vice-Chairman and CEO, Saudi Basic Industries Corporation;* ed Univs of Colo and Wyo., USA; joined Saudi Basic Industries Corpn (SABIC) 1976, Dir-Gen. for Projects –1998, Vice-Chair. and CEO 1998–, Chair. R & T Exec. Cttee, SABIC EuroPetrochemicals Exec. Bd; Chair. Saudi Arabian Fertilizer Co., Gulf Petrochemicals and Chemicals Asscn; mem. Bd Aluminium-Bahrain (ALBA), US-Saudi Business Council; ranked by ICIS Chemical Business magazine in list of Top 40 Power Players in the field of chemicals worldwide 2006, 2007. *Address:* Saudi Basic Industries Corporation, PO Box 5101, Riyadh 11422, Saudi Arabia (office). *Telephone:* (1) 2258000 (office). *Fax:* (1) 2259000 (office). *E-mail:* info@sabic.com (office). *Website:* www.sabic.com (office).

MAE, Vanessa; British violinist; b. 27 Oct. 1978, Singapore; ed Cen. Conservatoire, Beijing, People's Repub. of China, Royal Coll. of Music, London, UK; studied with Lin Yao Ji and Felix Andrievsky; concerto debut aged ten, Philharmonic Orchestra 1989; first nat. tour of UK with Tchaikovsky Concerto 1990; first int. tour with London Mozart Players 1990; released three classical recordings with orchestra (youngest artist to record both Tchaikovsky and Beethoven Violin Concertos) 1990–92; over 400 live performances in the Middle East, South Africa, China, SE Asia, Russia, Europe, Baltic States, Cen. Asia, USA, Cen. and S America; The Classical Tour 1997, Int. Red Hot Tour 1995, Storm on World Tour 1998; performed at Hong Kong to China Reunification Ceremony 1996, exclusively for HM The Queen, Buckingham Palace 1998, at 50th Anniversary of Geneva Conventions 1999; opened Classical Brit Awards, Royal Albert Hall 2000; collaborated on soundtrack for Walt Disney film Mulan; catwalk debut with Jean-Paul Gaultier; frequent TV appearances and participant in 'crossover' concerts; involved in work with ICRC, participated in TV Campaign Even Wars Have Limits; BAMBI Top Int. Classical Artist Award, Echo Klassik Award for Bestselling Album of the Year 1995, World Music Award for Best Selling Classical Artist 1996. *Recordings include:* Tchaikovsky and Beethoven Concertos 1990, The Violin Player (quadruple platinum) 1994, The Classical Album I 1996, China Girl: The Classical Album II 1997, Storm 1997, The Original Four Seasons 2000, Vanessa Mae: The Classical Collection Part I 2000, Subject to Change 2001, Choreography 2004. *Film:* Arabian Nights 2000. *Leisure interests:* snow skiing, dining out, academic studies, water-skiing, reading. *E-mail:* info@merlinelite.co.uk (office). *Website:* www.merlinelite.co.uk (office); www.vanessa-mae.com.

MAEDA, Terunobu, LLB; Japanese business executive; *President and CEO, Mizuho Financial Group, Inc.;* b. 2 Jan. 1945; ed Univ. of Tokyo; joined Fuji Bank Ltd 1968, Dir and Gen. Man. Credit Planning Div. 1995–96, Dir and Gen. Man. Corp. Planning Div. 1996–97, Man. Dir 1997–98, Man. Dir and Head of Public and Financial Insts Group 1998–99, Man. Dir and Chief Financial Officer (CFO) 1999–2001, Deputy Pres. and CFO 2001–02; mem. Bd Dirs Mizuho Holdings, Inc. (present Mizuho Financial Strategy Co. Ltd) 2002–, Pres. and CEO Mizuho Financial Group 2002–07, Pres. and CEO Mizuho Financial Group, Inc. 2003–. *Address:* Mizuho Financial Group, Inc., Marunouchi 2-chome Building, 2-5-1, Marunouchi, Chiyoda-ku, Tokyo 100-8333, Japan (office). *Telephone:* (3) 5224-1111 (office). *Fax:* (3) 3215-4616 (office). *E-mail:* info@mizuho-fg.co.jp (office). *Website:* www.mizuho-fg.co.jp (office).

MAEENA, Khaled al-; Saudi Arabian journalist and public relations consultant; *Editor-in-Chief, Arab News;* served as diplomat in China and Russia; Ed.-in-Chief, Arab News 1982–93, 1998–; Pres. and CEO Saudi Public Relations Co. (SPRC) 1993–2000; sr columnist for Gulf News, Urdu News, Asharq Al-Awsat, Al-Iqtisadiah, Times of Oman, China Post; joined Saudi Arabian Airlines (Saudia) 1982, held a variety of posts including public relations advisor and Editor-in-Chief of Saudia World (magazine); has hosted news and talk shows on Saudi TV; has represented Saudi Arabian media at several important Arab summit meetings including in Baghdad and Morocco. *Address:* Arab News, POB 10452, SRP Bldg, Madinah Road, Jeddah 21433, Saudi Arabia (office). *Telephone:* (2) 639-1888 (office). *Fax:* (2) 639-3223 (office). *E-mail:* almaeena@arabnews.com (office). *Website:* www.arabnews.com (office).

MAEGAARD, Jan Carl Christian, DrPhil, RDI; Danish musicologist and composer; b. 14 April 1926, Copenhagen; s. of the late Johannes H. Maegaard and Gerda Glahnson; m. Kirsten Offer Andersen 1973 (divorced 1993); two d.; ed Royal Danish Conservatory and Univ. of Copenhagen; freelance musician 1949–56; music critic for various newspapers 1952–60; teacher of theory and music history, Royal Danish Conservatory 1953–58; Asst Prof. Univ. of Copenhagen 1959, Assoc. Prof. 1961–71, Prof. 1971–96; Visiting Prof. State Univ. of New York at Stony Brook 1974; Prof. of Music. UCLA 1978–81; consultant to music Dept Danish State Radio 1962–78, Chief Consultant 1982–96; Chair. Music Cttee State Endowment for the Arts 1968–71; mem. Bd Danish State Radio and Television 1970–74; mem. Danish and Norwegian Acads; Kt of Dannebrog I (First Class). *Compositions include:* Elegy of Equinox for voice, cello and organ, Five Preludes for solo violin, Trio Serenade for piano trio, Chamber Concerto No. 2, Due tempi for orchestra, Musica riservata I for string quartet, Musica riservata II for reed quartet, Musica riservata III for flute, oboe, cello and cembalo, Canon for three flutes, Labirinto I for viola, Labirinto II for guitar, Triptykon for violin, string orchestra, Jeu mosaïque for harp and chamber orchestra, Partita for organ, Concerto for cello and orchestra, Partita for cello, Orchestration of Arnold Schoenberg's Variations on a Recitative for organ, Completion of J. S. Bach's Die Kunst der Fuge for organ, Duo-Phantasy for two guitars, Pierrot in the Ballroom for two guitars, Kinderblicke for two guitars, Progressive Variations for violin and cello, Die Engel for bass and organ, Intermezzo for organ, Die Verlassenen Liebhaber for bass and organ, Elegia for viola and string orchestra, Fantasia I for organ, Fantasia II for organ, Orchestrations of works by Nielsen, P. Heise, Wagner, J. S. Bach, Schoenberg, Mahler. *Publications:* Musikalsk Modernisme 1964, Studien zur Entwicklung des dodekaphonen Statzes bei Arnold Schönberg I–III 1972, Praeludier til Musik af Schönberg 1976, Indføring i Romantisk Harmonik I-II (with Teresa Waskowska Larsen) 1980, 1986, Kuhlaus Kanons (with Gorm Busk) 1996, Begreber i musikhistorien indbil ca. 1600 1999; numerous articles. *Leisure interest:* playing the double bass. *Address:* Duevej 14, 6, 2000 Frederiksberg, Denmark (home). *Telephone:* 38-88-07-80 (home).

MAEHLER, Herwig Gustav Theodor, PhD, FBA; German papyrologist; *Professor Emeritus, University College London;* b. 29 April 1935, Berlin; s. of Ludwig Maehler and Lisa Maehler; m. Margaret Anderson 1963; two d.; ed Katharineum, Lübeck and Univs of Hamburg, Tübingen and Basle; British Council Scholarship, Oxford 1961–62; Research Asst, Dept of Classics, Univ. of Hamburg 1962–63, Dept of Manuscripts, Hamburg Univ. Library 1963–64; Keeper of Greek Papyri, Egyptian Museum, West Berlin 1964–79; Lecturer in Classics, Freie Universität Berlin 1975–79; Reader in Papyrology, Univ. Coll. London 1979–81, Prof. 1981–2000, Prof. Emer. 2000–; Visiting Fellow, Inst. for Advanced Studies in the Humanities, Edin. 1977; Visiting Prof., Univs of Urbino 1984, Bologna 1986, Bari 1988, Basle 1990, Budapest 1998, 2001, 2004, Rome 1999, Venice 2004, Florence 2005; Corresp. mem. German Archaeological Inst.; Fellow Accad. Nazionale dei Lincei, Rome; Dr hc (Helsinki) 2000, (Budapest) 2001, (Rome II Tor Vergata) 2003. *Publications:* Die Auffassung des Dichterberufs im frühen Griechentum bis zur Zeit Pindars 1963, Die Handschriften der S. Jacobi-Kirche Hamburg 1967, Urkunden römischer Zeit 1968, Papyri aus Hermoupolis 1974, Die Lieder des Bakchylides (2 vols) 1982, 1997, Greek Bookhands of the Early Byzantine Period (with G. Cavallo) 1987, Bacchylides: A Selection 2004, Urkunden aus Hermupolis 2005; editions of Bacchylides and Pindar. *Leisure interests:* chamber music (viola), horse riding (dressage). *Address:* 11 Oak Avenue, Priory Park, London, N8 8LJ, England. *Telephone:* (20) 8348-1375 (home). *Fax:* (20) 7679-7475 (office). *E-mail:* hgt.maehler@virgin.net (home).

MAEMA, Lebohang Fine, KC, LLM, LLB, BA; Lesotho diplomatist and lawyer; *Permanent Representative, United Nations;* b. 22 July 1957, Masery; three d.; ed Nat. Univ. of Lesotho, Univ. of Cambridge, England; fmr mem. of Bd Cen. Bank of Lesotho; fmr Pres. Matlama Football Club; worked at Nat. Univ. of Lesotho; Crown Counsel, Attorney-Gen.'s Chambers 1982–83; Lecturer-in-Law, Nat. Univ. of Lesotho 1984–87; Deputy Pvt. Sec. to King of Lesotho, Royal Palace 1987–89, Pvt. Sec. 1989–90; Prin. Sec., Ministry of Justice and Prisons 1990–93; Attorney-Gen. 1993–2005; Perm. Rep. to UN, New York

2005–; Commdr of the Most Meritorious Order of Mohlomi; Cambridge Livingstone Scholar 1983. *Leisure interests:* listening to music, watching TV, soccer and movies. *Address:* Office of the Permanent Representative of Lesotho to the United Nations, 204 East 39th Street, New York, NY 10016, USA (office). *Telephone:* (212) 661-1690 (office). *Fax:* (212) 682-4388 (office). *E-mail:* prlesotho@un.int (office). *Website:* www.un.int/lesotho (office).

MAESTRE CORTADELLA, Mireia; Andorran politician; b. 1971; Sec.-Gen. for Finance 1999–2001; Minister for Finance 2001–04; mem. Partit Liberal d'Andorra (Liberal Party of Andorra—PLA). *Address:* Partit Liberal d'Andorra, Carrer Babot Camp 13, 2°, Andorra la Vella, AD500, Andorra (office). *Telephone:* 807715 (office). *Fax:* 869728 (office). *E-mail:* pla@pla.ad (office). *Website:* www.partitliberal.ad (office).

MAFATLAL, Arvind N.; Indian industrialist; b. 27 Oct. 1923, Ahmedabad; s. of the late Navinchandra Mafatlal and of Vijayalaxmi N. Mafatlal; m. Sushila A. Mafatlal; two s. one d.; ed St Xavier's High School and Sydenham Coll. of Commerce and Econs, Mumbai; joined Mafatlal Group of Cos. 1941, Chair. 1955–; Dir Tata Eng and Locomotive Co. Ltd and others; Chair. Nat. Organic Chem. Industries Ltd, Shri Sadguru Seva Sangh Trust; Trustee Bharatiya Agro-Industries Foundation, Uruli Kanchan, Employers' Del. to 43rd Session, ILO Conf.; Durga Prasad Khaitan Memorial Gold Medal 1966, Business Leadership Award (Madras Man. Asscn) 1971, Sir Jehangir Ghandy Medal for Industrial Peace (Xavier Labour Relations Inst.) 1979. *Leisure interest:* golf. *Address:* Mafatlal House, Backbay Reclamation, Mumbai 400 020 (office); 10 Altamount Road, Mumbai 400 026, India (home); Mafatlal Centre, Nariman Point, Mumbai 400021. *Telephone:* (22) 202-6944 (office); (22) 386-8350 (home). *Fax:* (22) 202-7750.

MAFFIA, Dante; Italian poet and author; b. 17 Jan. 1946, Roseto Capo Spulico (Cosenza); ed graduated in Rome; Founder and Ed. Il Policordo and Poetica magazines; contrib. to books of RAI and many periodicals, including Nuova Antologia, Misure critiche, Belfagor, Otto/Novecento, Cartolaria, Il Bel Paese, Hortus, Lunarionuovo, Idea, Poiesis; Ed. Rivista di Italianistica (S Africa), Il Belli; Corresp., La Naciòn; currently working at Univ. of Salerno; Calliope Award for literary fiction 1995. *Publications:* poetry: Il leone non mangia l'erba (Premio Viareggio, Pino d'Oro) 1974, Le favole impudiche 1977, Passeggiate romane (Premio Trastevere) 1979, L'eredità infranta (Premio Brutium) 1981, Caro Baudelaire (Prizes: Tarquinia-Cardarelli, Martina Franca, Rhegium Julii) 1983, Il ritorno di Omero (Premio Alfonso Gatto) 1984, A vite i tutte i jùrne (Premio Acireale e Premio Lentini) 1987, U ddIje poverille (Premio Brutium del Presidente e Premio Lanciano) 1990, L'educazione permanente (with an intoructory essay by Giacinto Spagnoletti) (Premio Città di Cariati, Premio Calliope, Premio Circe-Sabaudia) 1992, La castità del male (Premio Montale, Premio Città di Venezia) 1993, Confessione (with an aquatint by Antonio Bobò) 1993, Racconto (with a recording by Giacomo Soffiantino; edited by Fabrizio Mugnaini) 1994, I rùspe cannarùte 1995; prose: Corradino, «La clessidra» 1990, La danza del adiós (in Spanish) 1991, La barriera semantica (written in dialect poetry of the 20th century) 1996, Le donne di Courbet racconti (with a note by Alberto Moravia and a preface by Alberto Bevilacqua) 1996, Il romanzo di Tommaso Campanella (preface by Norberto Bobbio) (Premio Cirò Marina, Premio Stresa, Premio Palmi) 1996; other: exhbn catalogues and monographs of important painters and sculptors; works have been translated into many languages; ed.: Poesie alla Calabria, La narrativa calabrese dell'Otto/Novecento, Una simpatia di Giulio Carcano, Torquato Tasso di Carlo Goldoni, Torquato Tasso di Francesco De Sanctis (anthology). *Address:* P. le Caduti della Montagnola 50, 00142 Rome, Italy. *Telephone:* (339) 6567133 (mobile). *E-mail:* dantemaffia@libero.it (office). *Website:* www.dantemaffia.com (office).

MAGANDE, Ng'andu Peter, BA, MSc; Zambian diplomatist, business executive and farmer; b. 5 July 1947, Namaila, Mazabuka; m.; two s. three d.; ed Univ. of Zambia, Makerere Univ., Uganda; joined Civil Service 1971; apptd Dir of Budget, Ministry of Finance 1981; Perm. Sec. in various govt depts 1983–94; Man. Dir Zambia Nat. Commercial Bank, Lima Bank; Exec. Dir Industrial Devt Corpn, Zambia Industrial and Mining Corpn 1986–94; technical assistance consultant to Govt 1994; Sec.-Gen. African, Caribbean and Pacific Secr. 1996; Minister of Finance and Nat. Planning 2003–08; mem. Movt for Multi-party Democracy; Commdr of the Order of the Repub. of Benin; Best Commercial Tobacco Farmer 1989. *Address:* c/o Movement for Multi-party Democracy, POB 30708, Lusaka, Zambia.

MAGARIÑOS, Carlos Alfredo, MBA; Argentine international civil servant; b. 16 Aug. 1962, Buenos Aires; ed Nat. Univ. of Buenos Aires, Int. Devt Law Inst., Italy, Wharton School, Univ. of Pennsylvania; analyst, Office of Strategic Planning and Foreign Trade, Banco Ciudad de Buenos Aires 1984–86; joined Ministry of Economy 1992, Under-Sec. of State for Industry 1992–93, Sec. of State for Mining and Industry 1993–96; Econ. and Trade Rep. of Argentina, Washington, DC, USA 1996–97; rank of Amb. 1996; Dir-Gen. UNIDO 1997–2005 (re-elected 2001); Order of San Carlos, Colombia 2000, Order of Quetzal, Guatemala 2001, Order of Merit, Gov. of Italy 2003, Order of Industrial Merit, Gov. of Colombia 2004; Dr hc (Lomonosov, Moscow) 1999, (Econ. Sciences and Public Admin., Budapest) 2000, (Social and Business Sciences, Buenos Aires) 2001, Doctor hc, Nat. Tech. University of Ukraine 2002; Trophée des performances de l'année 2000, Inst. Supérieur de Gestion, Paris 2000, Peter the Great Int. Award, Russian Fed. 2002, Prix de la Fondation 2002, Crans Montana Forum, Monte Carlo 2002, Kennedy Cross, John F. Kennedy Univ. Argentina 2004, Priyadarshni Acad. Award, India 2004. *Publications:* El Rol del Estado en la Política Industrial de los 90 1995, China in the WTO: The Birth of a New Catching-Up Strategy 2002; articles on econ. and industrial issues: Gearing Up for a New Development Agenda 2000, Reforming the UN System: UNIDO's Need-Driven Model 2001, Updating and Fleshing Out the Development Agenda 2003, Economic Development and UN Reform: Towards a Common Agenda for Action 2005. *Address:* c/o United Nations Industrial Development Organization (UNIDO), Vienna International Centre, PO Box 300, 1400 Vienna, Austria (office).

MAGAZINER, Henry Jonas, BArch, FAIA; American historical architect, architectural historian and writer; b. 13 Sept. 1911, Philadelphia; s. of Louis Magaziner and Selma Magaziner; m. Reba Henken 1938 (died 1997); one s. one d.; ed Univ. of Pennsylvania, Stevens Inst. of Tech.; fmrly Day and Zimmermann Inc., Albert Kahn, Wright Aeronautical Corpn, Louis Magaziner; has worked for numerous public, institutional and commercial orgs; Nat. Park Service Regional Historical Architect 1972–87; pvt. practice 1956–72, 1987–; fmr Architectural Advisor, Philadelphia Historical Comm.; Chair., Historical Comm.'s Architects' Cttee; spokesman to the US Congress, representing American Inst. of Architects; fmr Chair., Physical Facilities Cttee, United Way; fmr Vice-Pres. for City Planning, Germantown Community Council; mem. AIA Coll. of Fellows and Comm. on Historic Resources, Carpenters Company Philadelphia; Founder, Past Pres. Ebenezer Maxwell Mansion (Victorian Museum); fmr Bd mem. . Asscn for Preservation Tech., Philadelphia Chapter; mem., Heritage Preservation; mem. Editorial Bd Soc. of Architectural Historians 55-vol. Buildings of the United States 1992–98; Presidential Award for Good Design for the Govt 1987, Biddle Award for Historical Preservation Projects 1999, John Harbeson Award for Contribs to Architectural Profession 2000, Germantown Hall of Fame for Community Service. *Achievements:* responsible for historic buildings presentation clauses in the standard bldg codes; Public Bldgs Cooperative Use Act 1976 (co-author). *Publications:* The Golden Age of Ironwork 2000, Our Liberty Bell 2007, various articles for the architectural press. *Address:* 2 Franklin Town Boulevard, #2404, Philadelphia, PA 19103, USA (home). *Telephone:* (215) 575-9360 (home).

MAGEE, Bryan, MA; British author and broadcaster; b. 12 April 1930, London; s. of Frederick Magee and Sheila Lynch; m. Ingrid Söderlund 1954 (died 1986); one d.; ed Christ's Hosp., Lycée Hôche, Versailles, Keble Coll. Oxford and Yale Univ.; Army Intelligence Corps 1948–49; TV reporter This Week; music and theatre critic Musical Times and The Listener; Lecturer in Philosophy, Balliol Coll. Oxford 1970–71; Visiting Fellow, All Souls Coll. Oxford 1973–74; MP for Leyton 1974–83; Pres. Critics Circle of GB 1983–84; Hon. Sr Research Fellow, King's Coll. London 1984–94, Visiting Prof. 1994–2000; Hon. Fellow, Queen Mary Coll. London 1988–; Fellow, Queen Mary and Westfield Coll. London 1989–; Visiting Fellow Wolfson Coll. Oxford 1991–94, New Coll. Oxford 1995, Merton Coll. Oxford 1998, St. Catherine's Coll. Oxford 2000, Peterhouse Cambridge 2001, Clare Hall Cambridge (Life Mem.) 2004; Visiting Prof. Univ. of Otago, Dunedin, New Zealand 2006; also at Yale, Harvard, Sydney, LSE; newspaper columnist; mem. Arts Council of GB and Chair. Music Panel 1993–94; mem. Soc. of Authors; Hon. Fellow Keble Coll. Oxford 1994–; Hon. DLitt (Univ. of Leicester) 2005; Silver Medal, Royal TV Soc. 1978. *Television:* Men of Ideas 1978, The Great Philosophers 1987. *Publications:* Crucifixion and Other Poems 1951, Go West Young Man 1958, The New Radicalism 1962, The Democratic Revolution 1964, Towards 2000 1965, One in Twenty 1966, The Television Interviewer 1966, Aspects of Wagner 1968 (revised edn 1988), Modern British Philosophy 1971 (re-issued as Talking Philosophy 2001), Popper 1973, Facing Death 1977, Men of Ideas 1978, The Philosophy of Schopenhauer 1983, 1997, The Great Philosophers 1987, On Blindness 1995 (re-issued as Sight Unseen 1998), Confessions of a Philosopher 1997, The Story of Philosophy 1998, Wagner and Philosophy 2000, Clouds of Glory: A Hoxton Childhood (J. R. Ackerley Prize for autobiography 2004) 2003, Growing Up In a War 2007. *Leisure interests:* music, theatre. *Address:* Wolfson College, Oxford, OX2 6UD, England (office).

MAGEE, Jeff, MSc, PhD, CE; British computer scientist and academic; *Head of Computing Department, Imperial College London;* currently Prof. of Computing and Head of Computing Dept, Imperial Coll., London; Chair. Steering Cttee, Int. Conf. on Software Eng 2002–04; fmr Co-Ed. IEE Proceedings on Software Engineering; adviser or consultant to numerous cos, including BP, BT, NATS, Fujitsu, Barclays Capital, QinetiQ, Kodak, Philips; Chartered Fellow, British Computer Soc.; IEE Informatics Premium Prize 1999, British Computer Soc. Brendan Murphy Memorial Prize 1999, Asscn for Computing Machinery Outstanding Research Award 2005. *Publications:* over 100 refereed publs. *Address:* Distributed Software Engineering Section, Department of Computing, Imperial College London, Huxley Building, Room 572, 180 Queen's Gate, London, SW7 2BZ, England (office). *Telephone:* (20) 7594-8269 (office). *Fax:* (20) 7594-8024 (office). *E-mail:* j.magee@imperial.ac.uk (office). *Website:* www-dse.doc.ic.ac.uk/cgi-bin/moin.cgi/jnm (office).

MAGGI, Maurren Higa; Brazilian athlete; b. 25 June 1976, São Carlos; m. Antônio Pizzonia; one d.; sprinter, hurdler and long jumper; S American record holder at 100m hurdles and long jump, with 12.71 seconds and 7.26m, respectively; has also jumped 14.53m in triple jump; first Brazilian woman to win Olympic gold medal in an individual sport; 100m hurdles titles: Silver Medal, South American Championships 1997; Gold Medal, South American Championships 1999; Silver Medal, Pan American Games 1999; Gold Medal, South American Championships 2001; Silver Medal, Universiade 2001; long jump titles: Gold Medal, South American Championships 1997, 1999 2001; Bronze Medal, Universiade 1999; Gold Medal, Pan American Games 1999; Gold Medal, Universiade 2001; Silver Medal, Int. Asscn of Athletics Feds (IAAF) World Cup 2002; Gold Medal, Ibero-American Championships 2002; Bronze Medal, IAAF World Indoor Championships 2003; suspended for two years, missed 2003 Pan American Games, gained a revocation 2004, missed Athens Olympics due to pregnancy; Gold Medal, Pan American Games 2007; Silver Medal, IAAF World Indoor Championships 2008; Gold Medal, Olympic Games, Beijing 2008. *Address:* c/o Confederação Brasileira de Atletismo, 874 Av. Sete de Setembro, 69005-140 Manaus, Amazonas, Brazil. *Telephone:* 92

6335022. *Fax:* 92 6334933. *E-mail:* cbat@cbat.org.br. *Website:* www.cbat.org.br.

MAGIDOR, Menachem, BSc, MSc, PhD; Israeli mathematician, university administrator and academic; *Professor of Mathematics and President, Hebrew University of Jerusalem;* b. 24 Jan. 1946, Petah Tikva; m.; four d.; ed Hebrew Univ. of Jerusalem; served in Israeli Navy and reached rank of Lt Commdr; has conducted research in computer science, dealing with artificial intelligence and semantics of programming languages; Prof. of Math., Hebrew Univ. of Jerusalem 1982–, Dean Faculty of Science 1992–96, Pres. Hebrew Univ. of Jerusalem 1997–; Pres. Asscn of Symbolic Logic 1996–98. *Publications:* more than 50 papers on set theory and model theory. *Address:* Office of the President, Hebrew University of Jerusalem, Mount Scopus, 91905 Jerusalem, Israel (office). *Telephone:* (2) 6584143 (office); 5881905 (office). *Fax:* (2) 5322545 (office). *E-mail:* hupres@cc.huji.ac.il (office); menachem@math.huji.ac.il (office); Menachem.Magidor@huji.ac.il (office). *Website:* www.huji.ac.il (office).

MAGLOIRE, Paul Gustave; Haitian government official; fmr adviser to Prime Minister Gerard Latortue; Minister of the Interior and Nat. Security 2005. *Address:* c/o Ministry of the Interior and Local Government, Palais de Ministéres, Port-au-Prince, Haiti (office).

MAGNER, Marjorie, BS, MSIA; American banker and business executive; *Managing Partner, Brysam Global Partners;* b. 1949, Brooklyn, NY; one s.; ed Brooklyn Coll. and Krannert School of Man., Purdue Univ.; joined Chemical Bank 1973, Man. Dir Chemical Technologies Div. –1983, actuarial analyst, Equitable Life Insurance Co. 1983–87; with Commercial Credit (predecessor of Citigroup) 1987, COO Global Consumer Group, Citigroup Inc., New York 2002–03, Chair. and CEO 2003–05, mem. Man. Cttee and Global Consumer Planning Group, Citigroup 2003–05; Founding Mem. and Man. Pnr, Brysam Global Partners 2007–; mem. Bd of Dirs Accenture 2006–, Gannett Co., Inc. 2006–; Chair. Brooklyn Coll. Foundation; mem. Bd of Dirs Millennium Promise, Do Something; mem. Dean's Advisory Council, Krannert School of Man., Purdue Univ.; fmr mem. Bd of Dirs Welfare to Work Partnership, Dress for Success Worldwide, Port Discovery Children's Museum, Baltimore, Md Business Roundtable for Educ.; Trustee Brooklyn Coll.; Hon. DMan (Purdue) 2004; ranked by Fortune magazine amongst 50 Most Powerful Women in Business in the US 2001, (22nd) 2002, (fifth) 2003, (fifth) 2004, ranked by Forbes magazine amongst 100 Most Powerful Women (19th) 2004, (34th) 2005, ranked by US Banker magazine amongst The 25 Most Powerful Women in Banking (first) 2004, (third) 2005, amongst Top 25 Non-Bank Women in Finance (11th) 2008, Distinguished Alumni Medal, Brooklyn Coll. 2005, The Marjorie Magner Lifetime Achievement Award named in her honour 2005. *Address:* Brysam Global Partners, 277 Park Avenue, 35th Floor, New York, NY 10172, USA (office). *Telephone:* (212) 622-4378 (office). *E-mail:* bgp@brysam.com (office). *Website:* www.brysam.com (office).

MAGNO, Adaljíza Albertina Xavier Reis, (Ajiza Magno); Timor-Leste politician; b. 1975; mem. Parl. 2002–; Vice-Minister of Foreign Affairs and Cooperation 2005–, Acting Minister of Foreign Affairs 2007. *Address:* c/o Ministry of Foreign Affairs and Cooperation, GPA Building #1, Ground Floor, Rua Avenida Presidente Nicolau Lobato, PO Box 6, Dili, Timor-Leste (office). *Website:* www.parlamento.tl.

MAGNUSSON, Thor Eyfeld; Icelandic state antiquary (retd); b. 18 Nov. 1937, Hvammstangi; s. of Magnus Richardson and Sigridur Thordardóttir; m. Maria V. Heiddal 1964; two s. one d.; ed Univ. of Uppsala; Asst Curator, Nat. Museum 1964, State Antiquary 1968–2001. *Address:* c/o National Museum, Suðurgata 41, 101 Reykjavik; Bauganes 26, 101 Reykjavik, Iceland (home). *Telephone:* 530-2200.

MAGOMEDOV, Magomedali Magomedovich; Russian/Dagestan politician; b. 15 June 1930, Levashi, Dagestan Autonomous Repub.; m.; six c.; ed Dagestan State Pedagogical Inst., Dagestan Inst. of Agric.; teacher, Dir Levashi secondary school, then Head Levashi Dept of Nat. Educ. 1949–57; Chair. Levashi Kolkhoz 1957–66; Head Agric. Production unit Levashi Dist 1966–69; Chair. Levashi Dist Exec. Cttee 1969–70; First Sec. Levashi Dist CP Cttee 1970–75; Head Div. of Agric. Dagestan Regional CP Cttee 1975–79; Deputy Chair., Chair. Council of Ministers Dagestan Autonomous Repub. 1979–87; Chair. Presidium Supreme Soviet Dagestan Autonomous Repub. 1987–94; Chair. State Council (Head Repub. of Dagestan) 1994–2006 (resgnd); mem. Russian Council of Fed. 1993–2001. *Address:* c/o House of Government, Lenina pl., 167005 Makhachkala, Dagestan, Russia (office).

MAGOWAN, Peter Alden, MA; American business executive; *President and Managing General Partner, San Francisco Baseball Associates, L.P.;* b. 5 April 1942, New York; s. of Robert Anderson and Doris Merrill Magowan; m. 1st Jill Tarlau (divorced 1982); m. 2nd Deborah Johnston 1982; three d. from 1st marriage; ed Stanford Univ., Univ. of Oxford, UK and Johns Hopkins School of Advanced Int. Studies; store man., Washington, DC, Safeway Stores, 1968–70, Dist Man., Houston, Tex. 1970, Retail Operations Man., Phoenix, Ariz. 1971–72, Div. Man., Tulsa, Okla 1973–76, Man., Int. Div., Toronto, Canada 1976–78, Western Regional Man., San Francisco, Calif. 1978–79, Dir, Safeway Stores, Inc. 1979, Chair. of the Bd 1980–98, CEO 1980–93, Pres. and COO 1988, also Chair. Exec. Cttee, retd 2005; Pres., Man. Gen. Partner, San Francisco Giants professional baseball team 1993–; fmr Dir of US Chamber of Commerce, The Hudson Inst., Pacific Gas and Electric Co., Food Marketing Inst.; Dir Caterpillar, Chrysler Corpn; mem. Advisory Council, Johns Hopkins School of Advanced Int. Studies; Trustee, Johns Hopkins Univ.; Exec. of the year 2000, Sports Business Journal. *Address:* San Francisco Baseball Associates, L.P., Pacific Bell Park, 24 Willie Mays Plaza, San Francisco, CA 94107, USA (office). *Telephone:* (415) 972-2000 (office). *Fax:* (415) 947-2800 (office). *Website:* www.sfgiants.com (office).

MAGRIS, Claudio; Italian journalist, writer and academic; *Professor Emeritus of German Language and Literature, University of Trieste;* b. 10 April 1939, Trieste; s. of Duilio Magris and Pia de Grisogono Magris; m. Marisa Madieri 1964; two s.; ed Univ. of Turin; Lecturer in German Language and Literature, Univ. of Trieste 1968–70, Turin 1970–78, Trieste 1978–, now Prof. Emer.; mem. Deutsche Akad. für Sprache und Dichtung (Darmstadt), Österreichische Akad. der Wissenschaften, Accad. delle Scienze di Torino, Ateneo Veneto, Akad. der Wissenschaften (Göttingen); Debenedetti 1972, Val di Comino 1978, Goethe Medaille 1980, Aquileia 1983, Premiolino 1983, San Giusto d'Oro 1984, Musil Medaille der Stadt Klagenfurt 1984, Bagutta 1987, Accad. dei Lincei 1987, Marotta 1987, Città di Modena 1987, Antico Fattore 1988, Juan Carlos I 1989, Premio Strega 1997, Premio Chiara alla Carriera 1999, Premio Würth per la Cultura Europea 1999, Premio Grinzane Piemonte 1999, Medaglia d'Oro della Cultura della Scuola e dell' Arte 1999, Premio Sikken 2000, Premio Nietsche 2000, Premium Erasmianum 2001, Leipziger Buchpreis zur Europäischen Verständigung 2001, Osterreichisches Ehrenkreuz für Wissenschaft und Kunst (First Class), Premio Principe de Asturias for Literature 2004. *Plays:* Stadelmann 1988, Le Voci 1999, La Mostra 2001. *Publications include:* Il Mito absburgico nella letteratura austriaca moderna 1963, 1988, Wilhelm Heinse 1968, Tre studi su Hoffman 1969, Lontano da dove 1971, Joseph Roth e la tradizione ebraico-orientale 1971, Dietro le parole 1978, L'altra ragione. Tre saggi su Hoffman 1978, Dietro le parole 1978, Itaca e oltre 1982, Trieste. Un'identità di frontiera 1982, 1987, L'anello di Clarisse 1984, Illazioni su una sciabola 1984, Danubio 1986 (trans. in numerous languages), Stadelmann 1988, Un altro mare 1991, Microcosmi 1997, Utopia e disincanto 1999, Telling Tales (contrib. to charity anthology) 2004, Alla cieca 2005, L'infinito viaggiare 2005, Lei dunque capirà 2006, La storia non è finita 2006, Davanti alla legge. Due Saggi 2006; numerous essays and book reviews in Corriere della Sera and other European newspapers and periodicals; trans. Ibsen, Kleist, Schnitzler, Büchner. *Address:* Department of Anglo-German Literature, University of Trieste, Via Lazzaretto Vecchio 8, III Piano, Stanza 309, 34123 Trieste, Italy (office). *Telephone:* (040) 5587252 (office). *Fax:* (040) 6763093 (office).

MAGSI, Nawab Zulfikar Ali; Pakistani politician and government official; *Governor of Balochistan;* b. 14 Feb. 1954, Jhal Magsi, Balochistan; ed Aitchison Coll., Lahore; current Nawab (Chief) of Magsi Tribe; first came to politics in 1977, won seat in prov. ass. as ind. cand.; served in numerous prov. ministries, also worked in Home Ministry 1990s; mem. Pakistan People's Party; Chief Minister of Balochistan Prov. in Govt of Benazir Bhutto May–July 1993, Oct. 1993–96; stood as ind. cand. from his native PB-32 Jhal Magsi constituency and won without opposition Feb. 2008; Gov. of Balochistan 2008–. *Address:* Governor House, Quetta, Balochistan, Pakistan (office). *Telephone:* (81) 9202170 (office). *Fax:* (81) 9202178 (office). *E-mail:* info@balochistan.gov.pk (office). *Website:* www.balochistan.gov.pk (office).

MAGUIRE, Adrian Edward, BPhil, MA, FSA; Irish fmr professional jockey; b. 29 April 1971; s. of Joseph Maguire and of the late Philomena Maguire; m. Sabrina Maguire 1995; one d.; ed Kilmessan Nat. School, Trim Vocational School; champion pony race rider 1986, champion point-to-point rider 1990–91, champion conditional jockey 1991–92; wins include Cheltenham Gold Cup, Irish Grand Nat. (youngest ever winning jockey), Galway Plate, Imperial Cup, Greenalls Gold Cup, Queen Mother Champion Chase, King George VI Chase, Triumph Hurdle, Cathcart Chase 1994, Scottish National 1998, Whitbread Gold Cup 1998; holds records for most point-to-point winners in a season, most winners in a season for a conditional jockey (71) 1991–92; retd 2002 following neck injury, having won over 1,000 races. *Leisure interests:* squash, watching television. *Address:* c/o The Jockey Club (Jockey Section), 42 Portman Square, London, W1H 0EM; 17 Willes Close, Faringdon, Oxon. SN7 7DU, England (home).

MAGUIRE, Joanne M., BEng, MEng; American aerospace industry executive; *Executive Vice-President, Space Systems, Lockheed Martin Space Systems Company;* d. of Mike Maguire; ed Michigan State Univ., Univ. of California, Los Angeles, Exec. Program in Man. at UCLA's Anderson School of Man., Harvard Program for Sr Execs in Nat. and Int. Security; joined TRW Space & Electronics (S&E) (now Northrop Grumman Space Tech.) 1975, held succession of increasingly responsible tech. and man. positions, later Program Man. for Defense Support Program, later Deputy Gen. Man. Defense Systems Div., later Vice-Pres. and Gen. Man. Space & Tech. Div., later Vice-Pres. and Gen. Man. Space & Laser Programs Div., later Deputy and Vice-Pres. Business Devt –2003; Vice-Pres. Special Programs, Lockheed Martin Space Systems Co. 2003, Vice-Pres. and Deputy of Lockheed Martin Space Systems Co. 2003–06, mem. Bd Dirs 2004–, Exec. Vice-Pres. Lockheed Martin Space Systems Co. 2006–, also Chair. United Launch Alliance (Lockheed Martin jt venture); mem. Bd Dirs Space Foundation, INROADS, Inc.; mem. AIAA, Soc. of Women Engineers; Outstanding Leadership Award, Women in Aerospace 1999, ranked by Fortune magazine amongst 50 Most Powerful Women in Business in US (35th) 2006, (38th) 2007, named by Corporate Board Member magazine as one of Top 50 Women in Technology 2008. *Address:* Lockheed Martin Space Systems Company, 12257 South Wadsworth Blvd, Littleton, CO 80125-8500, USA (office). *Telephone:* (303) 977-3000 (office). *E-mail:* martha.a.hirschfield@lmco.com (office). *Website:* www.lockheedmartin.com (office).

MAGUIRE, Robert Francis, III, BA; American real estate executive; *Chairman and Co-CEO, Maguire Properties Inc.;* b. 18 April 1935, Portland, Ore.; s. of Robert Francis Maguire, Jr and Jean Maguire (née Shepard); ed UCLA; Vice-Pres. Security Pacific Nat. Bank, LA 1960–64; Chair. Maguire Thomas Partners 1965, now Chair. and Co-CEO Maguire Properties Inc.; mem. Exec. Bd Medical Sciences, UCLA; mem. Bd Dirs LA County Museum of Art, St John's Hosp., Santa Monica, Calif.; mem. Bd of Govs LA Music Center; Trustee UCLA Foundation, Bard Coll. *Address:* Maguire Properties Inc., 333

South Grand Avenue, Suite 400, Los Angeles, CA 90071, USA. *Telephone:* (213) 626-3300 (office). *Fax:* (213) 687-4758 (office). *E-mail:* robert.maguire@maguirepartners.com. *Website:* www.maguireproperties.com (office).

MAGUIRE, Tobey; American actor; b. 27 June 1975, Santa Monica, Calif.; s. of Vincent Maguire and Wendy Maguire; m. Jennifer Meyer 2007; one d.; began career acting in commercials. *Television includes:* sitcoms: Blossom 1991, Roseanne 1991, Jake and the Fatman, Great Scott! 1992, This Boy's Life 1993; films: Spoils of War 1994, A Child's Cry for Help 1994. *Films include:* S.F.W. 1994, Revenge of the Red Baron 1994, Duke of Groove 1995, Seduced by Madness 1996, Joyride 1996, Deconstructing Harry 1997, The Ice Storm 1997, Pleasantville 1998, Fear and Loathing in Las Vegas 1998, Don's Plum 1998, Ride With the Devil 1999, The Cider House Rules 1999, Wonderboys 2000, Spider-Man 2002, Seabiscuit 2003, Spider-Man 2 2004, The Good German 2006, Spider-Man 3 2007, Tropic Thunder 2008. *Leisure interests:* boardgames, basketball, backgammon, yoga. *Address:* Creative Artists Agency, 9830 Wilshire Boulevard, Beverly Hills, CA 90212-1825, USA (office). *Telephone:* (310) 288-4545 (office). *Fax:* (310) 288-4800 (office). *Website:* www.caa.com (office).

MAGYAR, Bálint; Hungarian sociologist and politician; *State Secretary for Development Policy, Prime Minister's Office;* b. 1952, Budapest; m. Róza Hodosán; one d.; ed Eötvös Loránd Univ. of Budapest; Research Fellow, Inst. of World Econ., Hungarian Acad. of Sciences 1977–81, Inst. of Co-operation 1982–88; Financial Research Ltd 1988–90; involved in dissident political activities from 1979; Founding mem. Alliance of Free Democrats (SZDSZ), Pres. 1998–2000; mem. Exec. Bd 2001–; mem. Parl. 1990–; Minister of Culture and Educ. 1996–98, of Educ. 2002–06; State Sec. for Devt Policy, Prime Minister's Office 2007–; János Neumann Prize 1998. *Film:* Dir Hungarian Stories (documentary) (Special Prize, Critics' Prize, Budapest Film Festival 1988). *Publication:* Dunaapáti 1944–1958 (sociography of a Hungarian village, three vols) (Ferenc Erdei Prize 1986). *Address:* National Development Agency, Mozsár u. 16, 1066 Budapest (office); SZDSZ, Gizella u. 36, 1143 Budapest, Hungary. *Telephone:* (1) 472-2930 (office). *Fax:* (1) 472-2932 (office). *E-mail:* magyar.balint@meh.hu (office). *Website:* www.meh.hu (office).

MAH, Bow Tan, MSc; Singaporean politician; *Minister of National Development;* b. 12 Sept. 1948; m. Sheryn Kaye Von Senden; two d. two s.; ed St Joseph's Inst., Univ. of New South Wales, Australia; joined Singapore Bus Services 1974, Gen. Man. –1983; CEO Singapore Monitor, Singapore News and Publs Ltd (SNPL), later Group Gen. Man. SNPL, Group Gen. Man. (Co-ordination) Singapore Press Holdings Ltd 1985–88; Chair. Bd of Dirs NTUC Comfort 1983–86, Bd of Trustees 1988–93; Chair. Nat. Productivity Bd, Nat. Productivity Council, Skills Redevelopment Fund Advisory Council 1986–91; mem. Parl. 1988–; Minister of State for Trade and Industry and Minister of State for Communications and Information 1988, Minister of State for Trade and Industry and Minister of State for Communications 1990, Minister for Communications 1991–99, concurrently Minister for the Environment 1993–95, Minister for Nat. Devt 1999–; Chair. Service Improvement Unit, Political Supervisory Cttee 1991; Chair. Bd of Govs, Singapore Inst. of Labour Studies 1990–2002; Chair. Nat. Youth Achievement Award Advisory Bd 1994–, Singapore Labour Foundation 2001–; Adviser Football Asscn of Singapore (FAS) Council 1991–99, Pres. FAS 1999–2004, Adviser 2004–; Hon. DSc (Univ. of New South Wales) 2001; Nat. Trades Union Congress Medal of Honour 1991, Univ. of New South Wales Alumni Award for Achievement 1996. *Leisure interests:* golf, travelling, reading, football. *Address:* Ministry of National Development, 5 Maxwell Road, 21/22-00, Tower Block, MND Complex, 069110 Singapore (office). *Telephone:* 62221211 (office). *Fax:* 63257254 (office). *E-mail:* mnd_hq@mnd.gov.sg (office). *Website:* www.mnd.gov.sg (office).

MAHA VAJIRALONGKORN, HRH Crown Prince, BA, LLB; Thai; b. 28 July 1952, Bangkok; s. of HM King Bhumibol Adulyadej and Queen Sirikit; m. 1st Mom Luang Soamsawali Kitiyakara 1977 (divorced); one d.; fmr pnr Yuvadhida Polpraserth; four s. one d.; m. 2nd Mom Srirasmi Mahidol na Ayudhya (HRH Princess Srirasmi, The Royal Consort) 2001; one s.; ed Royal Military Coll. Duntroon and Univ. of New South Wales, Australia, Royal Thai Army Command and Gen. Staff Coll., Sukhothai Thammatirat Univ., Bangkok, Royal Coll. of Defence Studies, UK; conferred title Somdech Phra Boroma Orasadhiraj Chao Fah Maha Vajiralongkorn Sayam Makutrajakuman (heir to the throne) 28 Dec. 1972; Staff Officer Directorate of Army Intelligence 1975–78, Exec. Officer King's Own Bodyguard 1978–80, Commdr 1980–84, Commanding Officer 1984–88, Commanding Gen. 1988–92, Commanding Gen. Royalty Security Command, Office of the Supreme Commander 1992–, Instructor Pilot F-5 E/F fighter 1994, holds ranks of Gen. of the Royal Thai Army, Adm. of the Royal Thai Navy, Air Chief Marshal of the Royal Thai Air Force. *Address:* c/o The Government Public Relations Department, Rama VI Road, Bangkok, Thailand (office). *Telephone:* 618-2373 (office). *Fax:* 618-2358 (office). *Website:* www.thaimain.org.

MAHAMA, Alhaji Aliu, BSc; Ghanaian politician; *Vice-President;* b. 3 March 1946, Yendi; ed Govt Secondary School, Tamale, Kwame Nkrumah Univ. of Science and Tech., Kumasi, Inst. in Project Planning and Man. and in Leadership; construction engineer, Bolgatanga Regional Office, State Construction Corpn 1972–75, Asst Regional Man., Koforidua Regional Office 1975–76, Regional Man. in charge of Northern Region 1976–82; Founder and Man. Dir LIDRA Ltd 1982–; Councillor, Yendi Dist Council 1978; mem. Tamale Municipal Assembly 1990; fmr Minister of Defence; Vice-Pres. of Ghana 2001–; Chair. Northern Regional Contractors' Asscn 1996–2000; fmr Chair. Econ. Devt Cttee, Tamale-Louisville Sister State Cttee; fmr Bd mem. several secondary schools in Northern Region including Tamale Polytechnic; alumnus, Ghana Inst. of Man. and Public Admin; Founding mem. Real Tamale United Football Club; Fellow Inst. of Surveyors, Fellow Inst. of

Administrators. *Leisure interests:* reading, football, badminton. *Address:* c/o Office of the President, POB 1627, Osu, Accra, Ghana (office). *Telephone:* 665415 (office). *Fax:* 663044 (office).

MAHANTA, Prafulla Kumar, BSc, LLB; Indian politician; b. 23 Dec. 1952, Rupnarayan Satra; s. of Deva Kanta and Lakshmi Prava; m. Joyasree Goswami; one s. one d.; f. Asom Gana Parishad (regional political party) 1985; Chief Minister of Assam 1985–90, 1996–2001. *Address:* Rupnarayan Satra, Kallabor, Nagaon District, Assam, India (home). *Telephone:* (361) 562222 (office); (361) 561291. *Fax:* (361) 562069 (office).

MAHARAJ, Mac (Sathyandranath Ragunanan), BA; South African politician and business executive; b. 27 April 1935, Newcastle; s. of N.R. Maharaj; m. Zarina Maharaj; two c.; ed St Oswald's High School and Univ. of Natal, Durban; Ed. New Age 1956; lived in UK where he worked as a teacher, rubbish collector and a canning factory and building site worker 1957–61, Founding mem. British Anti-Apartheid Movement; mem. Umkhonto Wesizwe (African Nat. Congress—ANC's armed wing) 1961, underwent mil. training in GDR 1961–62; returned to SA 1962; sentenced to 12 years' imprisonment Dec. 1964, served prison sentence on Robben Island 1965–76; left SA 1976; with ANC HQ, Lusaka, Zambia, Sec. Underground Section 1977; mem. Revolutionary Council 1978, Politico-Mil. Council 1985; mem. ANC Negotiation Cttee, Political Cttee 1984, Nat. Exec. Council 1985–90, 1991–, Nat. Working Cttee; Commdr Operation Vula, SA 1988–90; mem. Political Bureau and Cen. Cttee 1990; with Codesa Secr.; Jt Sec. Transitional Exec. Council 1994; Minister of Transport, Govt of Nat. Unity 1994–99; active in business 1999–. *Address:* c/o Private Bag X193, Pretoria 0001, South Africa.

MAHAREY, Steve, BA, MA; New Zealand fmr politician and academic; m. Liz Mackay; two step-s.; taught business admin.; Sr Lecturer in Sociology, Massey Univ.; mem. Palmerston North City Council 1986–89, Chair. Palmerston North Labour Electorate Cttee, mem. Policy Council; Labour MP for Palmerston North 1990–; Opposition Spokesperson on Social Welfare and Employment, Broadcasting and Communications and Labour Relations 1994–97; Assoc. Spokesperson on Educ. with specific responsibility for Tertiary Educ., Educ. and Employment 1990–93, served on the Social Services, Educ. and Science, Commerce, Justice and Law Reform and Broadcasting Parl. Select Cttees; Minister for Social Devt and Employment 1999–2005, Assoc. Minister of Educ. (Tertiary Educ.) 1999–2004, Minister responsible for Community and Voluntary Sector 1999–2002, Minister of Broadcasting 2002–07, of Housing 2003–04, of Youth Affairs 2004, of Research, Science and Tech. 2004–07, Minister for Crown Research Insts. 2004–07, Minister of Educ. 2005–07, Minister responsible for the Educ. Review Office –2007; fmr Chair. Cabinet Social Devt Cttee; fmr mem. Cttees for Cabinet Policy, Appointments and Honours, Econ. Devt and Legislation; retd from politics 2007. *Publications:* numerous articles on media and cultural studies and social change. *Leisure interests:* mountain biking, swimming, music, social and political theory, travel, spectator sports. *Address:* c/o New Zealand Labour Party, Fraser House, POB 784, Wellington, New Zealand (office).

MAHAT, Ram Sharan, MA, PhD; Nepalese politician; b. 1 Jan. 1951, Nuwakot; s. of Tol Kumari Mahat; m. Roshana Mahat; one s. one d.; ed Tribhuban Univ., Gokhale Inst. of Politics and Econs, Pune, India, School of Int. Service, American Univ.; Asst Resident Rep. UNDP, Islamabad 1989–90; econ. adviser to Prime Minister of Nepal 1991–92; Vice-Chair. Nat. Planning Comm. 1991–94; MP from Nuwakot Dist 1994–; Minister of Finance 1995–99, 2001, 2006–07, fmr Interim Minister of Finance; Minister of Foreign Affairs 1999. *Publications:* Industrial Financing in Nepal, numerous articles on nat. and int. econ. issues. *Leisure interests:* social service, reading books. *Address:* c/o Ministry of Finance, POB 12845, Kathmandu (office); Bansbari, Kathmandu, Nepal (home).

MAHATHIR BIN MOHAMAD; Malaysian politician (retd); b. 20 Dec. 1925, Alur Setar, Kedah; m. Dr Siti Hasmah binti Haji Mohd Ali 1956; three s. two d.; ed Sultan Abdul Hamid Coll. and Univ. of Malaya in Singapore; Medical Officer, Kedah, Langkawi and Perlis 1953–57; private practice 1957–64; mem. UMNO (now Umno Baru) Supreme Council 1965–69, 1972–2008 (Pres. 1981), mem. Supreme Council 1972–2008; mem. House of Reps. for Kota Setar Selatan 1964–69, for Kubang Pasu 1974–; mem. Senate 1973; Chair. Food Industries of Malaysia Sdn. Bhd. 1973; Minister of Educ. 1974–77, of Trade and Industry 1977–81, of Defence 1981–86, of Home Affairs 1986–99, of Justice 1987, of Natural and Rural Devt; Deputy Prime Minister 1976–81, Prime Minister of Malaysia 1981–2003; Advisor, Petronas, Proton 2003–. *Publication:* The Malay Dilemma 1969, The Way Forward 1998. *Address:* c/o Petroliam Nasional Berhad (PETRONAS), Tower 1, Petronas Twin Towers, Kuala Lumpur City Centre, 50088 Kuala Lumpur, Malaysia (office). *E-mail:* webmaster@petronas.com.my (office). *Website:* www.petronas.com.my (office).

MAHAVIR, Bhai, PhD, LLB; Indian politician; b. 30 Oct. 1922, Lahore, Pakistan; s. of Bhai Parmanand and Bhagya Sudhi; m. Krishna Bhai Mahavir; two d.; Lecturer in Econs, D.A.V. Coll., Lahore 1944; fmr Man. Dir Akashvani Prakashan Ltd; founder mem. and first Gen. Sec. Bharatiya Jana Sangh; Pres. Delhi Pradesh Jana Sangh 1968–69; mem. Rajya Sabha 1968–74, 1978–84; Chair. Cttee on Subordinate Legislation of Rajya Sabha 1982–84; detained during Emergency Period; Chair. Governing Body, Rajdhani Coll., New Delhi; Dir Bhai Parmanand Vidya Mandir; Sec. Bhai Parmanand Smarak Samiti; mem. Nat. Exec. Bharatiya Janata Party; Gov. of Madhya Pradesh 1998–2003. *Address:* c/o Raj Bhavan, Bhopal (office); 389 D/S, New Rajendra Nagar, New Delhi 60, India (home).

MAHAYNI, Mohammad Khaled al-, PhD; Syrian politician and economist; b. 30 May 1943, Damascus; s. of Salim al-Mahayni and Weedad Araman; m. Falak Sakkal 1966; two s. two d.; ed Damascus Univ.; various public financial and econ. appointments 1961–70; auditor 1970–77; Dir of Debt Fund and Information, Ministry of Finance 1979–80, of Public Enterprises 1981–84; Deputy Minister of Finance 1984–87, Minister 1987–2001; Gov. IBRD 1987–2001, Arab Bank for Econ. Devt in Africa 1989–; Prof. Damascus Univ. 1992–. *Publications:* Methodology of the General Budget of the State in the Syrian Arab Republic 1984, Supplementary Policies for Financial Planning 1995, Government Accounting 1996, Public Finance and Tax Legislation 1999. *Leisure interests:* reading and computing. *Address:* c/o Ministry of Finance, P.O. Box 13136, Jule Jamal Street, Damascus, Syria.

MAHBUBANI, Kishore; Singaporean diplomatist, university administrator and author; *Professor in the Practice of Public Policy and Dean, Lee Kuan School of Public Policy, National University of Singapore;* b. 24 Oct. 1948, Singapore; s. of Mohandas Mahbubani; m. Anne King Markey 1985; two s. one d.; ed Univ. of Singapore and Dalhousie Univ., Canada; joined Ministry of Foreign Affairs 1971, Deputy Dir 1979–82, Deputy Sec. 1989–93, Perm. Sec. 1993–; Chargé d'affaires to Cambodia 1973–74; Counsellor at Singapore Embassy in Malaysia 1976–79; mem. of Singapore dels to several sessions of UN Gen. Ass. and int. confs 1979–83; Deputy Chief at Washington, DC Embassy 1982–84; Perm. Rep. to UN, New York (concurrently High Commr in Canada and Amb. to Mexico) 1984–89, Perm. Rep. to UN 1998–2004; Dean, Civil Service Coll. 1993–96; Prof. in the Practice of Public Policy and Dean, Lee Kuan Yew School of Public Policy, Nat. Univ. of Singapore 2004–; Public Administration Medal (Gold), Singapore Govt 1998, Foreign Policy Asscn Medal 2004, Dr Jean Mayer Global Citizenship Award, Inst. for Global Leadership, Tufts Univ. 2003–04, ranked by Foreign Policy and Prospect magazines amongst Top 100 Public Intellectuals in the World 2005. *Publications:* Can Asians Think? 2002, Beyond The Age of Innocence: Rebuilding Trust between America and the World 2005; contrib. of articles to journals and newspapers, including Foreign Affairs, Foreign Policy, Washington Quarterly, Survival, American Interest, National Interest, Time, Newsweek and New York Times. *Leisure interests:* golf, jogging. *Address:* Lee Kuan Yew School of Public Policy, National University of Singapore, Oei Tiong Ham Building, 469C Bukit Timah Road, Singapore 259772 (office). *Telephone:* 65166134 (office). *Fax:* 67781020 (office). *E-mail:* sppdean@nus.edu.sg (office); Kishore.Mahbubani@mahbubani.net (home). *Website:* www.spp.nus.edu.sg (office); www.mahbubani.net (home).

MAHDI, Adil Abd al-, PhD; Iraqi politician and economist; *Vice-President;* b. 1942, Baghhad; m.; four c.; moved to France 1969, worked for several think tanks; has also lived in Lebanon and Iran; returned to Iraq; interim Minister of Finance –2005; Vice-Pres. of Iraq 2005–; mem. Supreme Council for the Islamic Revolution in Iraq. *Address:* c/o Office of the President, Baghdad, Iraq.

MAHDI, Sadiq Al, (since 1978 known as Sadiq Abdul Rahman); Sudanese politician; b. 1936, great grandson of Imam Abdul-Rahman El Mahdi, s. of late Siddik El Mahdi; ed Comboni Coll., Khartoum and St John's Coll., Oxford; Leader, Umma Mahdist (now New Nat. Umma) Party 1961; Prime Minister 1966–67, 1986–89, Minister of Defence 1986–89; arrested on a charge of high treason 1969; exiled April 1970; returned to Sudan and imprisoned Feb. 1972, released April 1974; exiled 1974–77; led unsuccessful coup against fmr Pres. Nimeri July 1976, returned to Sudan Sept 1977; reconciliation with Pres. Nimeri 1977; led mediation mission in US hostages in Iran Crisis Jan. 1980; returned to prison Sept. 1983, released Dec. 1984; overthrown in coup June 1989, arrested July 1989, released and put under house arrest Nov. 1989; granted amnesty May 1991; arrested on charges of conspiring against mil. govt June 1994; rearrested May 1995; escaped from house arrest Dec. 1996; in Eritrea 1996–2000, returned to Sudan Nov. 2000; mem. Cttee Sudanese Socialist Union (SSU) 1978–79; mem. Nat. Ass. 1986–89; Visiting Fellow St Antony's Coll., Oxford 1983. *Publication:* Problems of the South Sudan.

MAHDI, Salah al-, PhD; Tunisian flautist and composer; b. 9 Feb. 1925, Tunis; ed Rashidia Inst., Zituna Univ., Inst. of Admin. Tunis and Univ. of Poitiers; teacher of music, Rashidiyya Inst. 1943; Dir Rashidiyya Inst. 1949; Judge, Law Courts of Tunis 1951; fmr Dir Dept of Fine Arts, Ministry of Educ.; participated in setting-up of Nat. Acad. of Music, Dance and Dramatic Art; Head of Direction of Music and Folk Art, Ministry of Culture 1961; later Pres. Nat. Cultural Cttee and Pres. Nat. Cttee of Music; f. Nat. Troupe of Popular Arts 1962; set up Tunisian Symphony Orchestra 1962, Nat. Soc. for Preservation of Koran, Nat. School of Koranic Intoned Psalms; participant at numerous UNESCO and other int. congresses; Founding mem. Int. Inst. of Comparative Music, Berlin; Pres. World Org. of Folk Arts and Traditions, Vienna; has held many other int. musical and cultural appointments; mem. Soc. des Auteurs, Compositeurs et Editions de Musique (SACEM), now Hon. mem. *Works include:* more than 600 compositions including classical and folk songs, oriental and Western instrumental music, four nubas, several muwashahs, bashrafs, symphonic poems, chamber music and pieces for piano, flute, violin and harp; wrote the Tunisian nat. anthem. *Publications:* many musical, historical and literary works on Arab music including a compilation of Tunisian musical heritage; radio and stage plays. *Address:* 22 rue Brasil, Tunis, Tunisia.

MAHDI AL TAJIR, Mohamed; Bahraini diplomatist and business executive; b. 26 Dec. 1931, Bahrain; m. Zohra Al-Tajir 1956; five s. one d.; ed Bahrain Govt School and Preston Grammar School, Lancs., England; with Dept of Port and Customs, Govt of Bahrain, Dir 1955–63; Dir Dept of His Highness the Ruler's Affairs and Petroleum Affairs 1963–; Dir Nat. Bank of Dubai Ltd 1963–; Dir Dubai Petroleum Co. 1963–; Dir Dubai Nat. Air Travel Agency 1966–; Dir Qatar-Dubai Currency Bd 1965–73; Chair. South Eastern Dubai Drilling Co. 1968–; Dir Dubai Dry Dock Co. 1973–; Amb. of UAE to UK 1972–82, 1983–86, also accred to France 1972–77; Hon. Citizen of State of Texas, USA 1963. *Leisure interest:* collecting antique silver artifacts. *Address:* PO Box 207, Dubai, United Arab Emirates.

MAHELE BOKOUNGO LIEKO, Gen.; Democratic Republic of the Congo army officer; joined Zaïrean army, involved in numerous conflicts in Zaïre, also in Zaïrean action in Rwanda 1990; fmr Chief of Staff, Zaïre Armed Forces (FAZ), reappointed Dec. 1996; removed when Mobutu Govt overthrown May 1997.

MAHENDRA, Ranbir Singh; Indian sports organization administrator; *President, Indian Board of Control for Cricket (BCCI);* b. Haryana; s. of Bansi Lal; trained as lawyer; elected Jt Sec., Bd of Control for Cricket in India (BCCI), Kolkata 1980–85, Sec. 1985–89, mem. Finance Cttee, Pres. 2004–; conducted first cricket World Cup outside of England 1987; fmr Sec. Haryana Cricket Asscn; Man. of Indian Cricket Team, World Cup, Australia 1992; fmr Vice-Pres. Nat. Cricket Acad.; mem. Indian Nat. Congress. *Address:* Indian Board of Control for Cricket, Kairali, GHS Lane, Manacaud, Trivandrum, 695 009, Kerala, India (office). *E-mail:* secbcci@sify.com (office).

MAHER, Ali Mohammad; Pakistani politician; s. of Ghulam Mohammad Maher; Chief Minister of Sindh 2002–04 (resgnd); mem. nat. security council. *Address:* c/o Chief Minister's Office, Government of Sindh, Sindh Secretariat, Karachi, Pakistan.

MAHER, Terence Anthony, FCCA; British bookseller and publisher; *Chairman, Maher Booksellers Ltd;* b. 5 Dec. 1935, Manchester; s. of the late Herbert Maher and Lillian Maher; m. Barbara Grunbaum 1960; three s.; ed Xaverian Coll., Manchester; Controller, Carborundum Co. Ltd 1961–69; Dir Corp. Finance, First Nat. Finance Corpn 1969–72; f. Pentos PLC 1972, Chair., CEO –1993; Chair. and CEO Dillons Bookstores 1977–93; Athena Int. 1980–93, Ryman 1987–93; Chair. The Chalford Publishing Co. Ltd 1994–98, Maher Booksellers Ltd 1995–, Race Dynamics Ltd 1998–; Founder Trustee of Liberal Democrats 1988; mem. Advisory Council on Libraries 1997–98; Fellow, Chartered Asscn of Certified Accountants. *Achievement:* led successful campaign to abolish price control on books in UK. *Publications:* Counterblast (co-author) 1965, Effective Politics (co-author) 1966, Against My Better Judgement (autobiog.) 1994, Unfinished Business (fiction) 2003, Grumpy Old Liberal – A Political Rant 2005. *Leisure interests:* skiing, tennis, walking, reading, bridge. *Address:* 33 Montagu Square, London, W1H 2LJ (home); The Old House, Whichford, nr Shipston on Stour, Warwicks., CV36 5PG, England. *Telephone:* (20) 7723-4254 (London); (1608) 684-614 (Whichford).

MAHER ALI, Abdel Moneim, PhD; Egyptian biologist and business executive; *President, ARADIS Company SAE;* b. 9 March 1922, Dammanhour; s. of Ali Elsayed Shehata and Nagia M. Manaä; m. Fardous Abbas Abdelal 1948; two s.; ed Cairo Univ., Univ. Coll. London, UK and Ein Shams Univ.; Founder, Gen. Sec. Egyptian Youth Hostel Assoc. 1955–1970; Dir Cen. Agric. Pesticide Lab. UNDP Project 1963–69; Head Plant Protection Dept Assiut Univ. 1970, Emer. Prof. 1982–; Gen. Sec. Egyptian Zoological Soc., Egyptian Asscn for Conservation of Nature and Natural Resources, Egyptian Asscn for Environment Care, Egyptian Asscn for Medicinal Plants 1975–; Founder then Consultant, Wady Elassiuty Protected Area 1980–94; Pres. ARADIS Co. SAE, Arab Co. Environment Disinfection SAE Co. 1983–; now Chief Ed. Egyptian Journal for Natural Resources and Wildlife; Conservation Merit Award, World Wildlife Fund, Science and Arts 1st Class, Order of the Repub. 5th, 3rd and 2nd and other awards. *Publications include:* textbook on pest control, articles in scientific periodicals. *Leisure interests:* travel, sightseeing, archaeological tours. *Address:* 45 Jule Gamal Street, Agouza, Gizah (office); 50 Wizaret El Ziraä Street, 12th Floor, Dokki, Gizah (home); PO Box 318, Dokki Gizah, Egypt. *Telephone:* (2) 346-2029 (office); (2) 337-3988 (office); (2) 336-0846 (home). *Fax:* (2) 346-2029 (office). *E-mail:* medplantus@yahoo.com (office).

MAHER ES-SAYED, Ahmad, LLB; Egyptian politician; b. 14 Sept. 1935, Cairo; m.; ed Cairo Univ.; served in embassies in Cairo, Kinshasa, Paris, Zürich 1959–77; Amb. to Portugal 1980–82, to Belgium 1982–84, to USSR 1988–92, to USA 1992–99; Dir Arab Fund for Tech. Assistance to African States, League of Arab States 2000–01; Minister of Foreign Affairs 2001–04 (resgnd); Order of the Repub. First Class (Egypt), Order of Merit Commdr Class (France), Order of the Great Cross (Portugal). *Address:* c/o Ministry of Foreign Affairs, Corniche en-Nil, Cairo, Egypt (office).

MAHINDRA, Anand, MBA; Indian business executive; *Vice-Chairman and Managing Director, Mahindra & Mahindra Ltd;* m. Anuradha Mahindra; ed Harvard Coll., Harvard Business School, USA; Exec. Asst to Finance Dir, Mahindra Ugine Steel Co. Ltd 1981, Pres. and Deputy Man. Dir 1989–91, Deputy Man. Dir Mahindra & Mahindra Ltd 1991–97, Man. Dir 1997–, Vice-Chair. 2001–; co-founder Harvard Business School Asscn of India; Chair. Nat. Inst. of Industrial Eng, Mumbai; Dir Nat. Stock Exchange of India Ltd; mem. Confed. of Indian Industry (Pres. 2003–04); mem. Advisory Cttee Harvard Univ. Asia Centre, Exec. Cttee The Nehru Centre, Mumbai; mem. Advisory Council of Initiative on Corp. Governance, Harvard Business School; mem. Int. Council, Asia Soc., NY; mem. Nat. Council of Applied Econ. Research, Econ. Devt Bd of Rajasthan; mem. Bd of Govs Mahindra United World Coll. of India, Nat. Inst. of Bank Man., Pune; Trustee K. C. Mahindra Educ. Trust. *Address:* Mahindra & Mahindra Ltd, Gateway Building, Apollo Bunder, Mumbai 400 001, India (office). *Telephone:* (22) 2202-5158 (office). *Fax:* (22) 2490-0830 (office). *Website:* www.mahindra.com (office).

MAHINDRA, Keshub, BSc; Indian business executive; *Chairman, Mahindra & Mahindra Ltd;* b. 9 Oct. 1923, Simla; s. of the late Kailash Chandra Mahindra and Savitri Mahindra; m. Sudha Y. Varde 1956; three d.; ed Wharton Business School, Univ. of Pennsylvania, USA; joined Mahindra and Mahindra Ltd 1947, Chair. 1963–; Chair. Housing and Urban Devt Corpn Ltd 1971–75, Indian Inst. of Man., Ahmedabad 1975–85, India Nominating Cttee "Single Nation Programme", Eisenhower Exchange Fellowships, USA 1998–2005; Pres. Asscn of Indian Automobile Mfrs 1964–65, Bombay Chamber of Commerce and Industry 1966–67, Assoc. Chamber of Commerce and Industry 1969–70, MVIRDC, World Trade Center 1978–95, Employers' Fed. of India 1985–97, Indo-American Soc. 1991–92; mem. Bd Govs Mahindra United World Coll. of India; Dir Bombay Dyeing and Mfg Co. Ltd, Bombay Burmah Trading Corpn Ltd, Housing Devt Finance Corpn Ltd (now Vice-Chair.), United World Coll. Int. Ltd, UK, Mahindra Ugine Steel Co. Ltd (now Chair.), etc.; mem. Apex Advisory Council of Assoc. Chambers of Commerce and Industry of India, Int. Council Asia Soc. New York, USA 1983–97; Pres. Centre for Research in Rural and Industrial Devt, Chandigarh, Governing Council, Univ. of Pennsylvania Inst. for Advanced Study of India, New Delhi; Pres. Emer., Employers' Fed. of India; Vice-Pres. Nat. Soc. for Clean Cities; Chair. Mahindra Foundation, Bombay First, Health and Environment Cttee, Bd Trustees, Population First; Chair. and Trustee, K.C. Mahindra Educ. Trust; Founding mem., Indo-Hellenic Friendship League, Governing Council, Integrated Research and Action for Devt (IRADe), New Delhi; mem. Foundation Bd, Int. Man. Inst., Geneva 1984–89, Prime Minister's Council on Trade and Industry, Governing Body of HelpAge India 2000–04, Governing Body/Bd Govs of Bharat Shiksha Kosh 2002–05, Governing Bd United Way of Mumbai, Bombay First, Int. Advisory Bd Univ. of Pennsylvania Center for Advanced Study of India, Philadelphia; Hon. Fellow, All India Man. Asscn 1990; Hon. mem. Business Advisory Council, IFC, Washington 1986–96, Rotary Club of Bombay 1984; Chevalier, Légion d'honneur 1987; numerous awards including Giants Int. Business Leadership Award 1972–82, Madras Man. Asscn Business Leadership Award 1983, Business India Indian Businessman of the Year 1989, Rotary Award for Vocational Excellence 1992, Shiromani Award 1992, Vikas Jyoti Award 1993, Sir Jengahir Ghandy Medal for Industrial Peace, XLRI, Jemshedpur 1994, Rotary Vocational Excellence Award in the Field of Industry 1996, IMC Diamond Jubilee Endowment Trust Award 1998, Motorindia Automan Award 2000, Dadabhai Naoroji Int. Award for Excellence and Lifetime Achievement 2000, All India Man. Asscn Lifetime Achievement Award for Man. 2003, Inst of Company Secs of India Lifetime Achievement Award for Excellence in Corp. Governance 2004, Qimpro Platinum Standard 'Statesman for Quality' Business Award 2005, Lakshya Business Visionary Award, NITIE 2006, Indian Business School Kolkata Lifetime Achievement Award 2007, Ernst & Young Entrepreneur of the Year Lifetime Achievement Award 2007, Soc. of Indian Automobile Manufacturers Award for "Lifetime Contribution to the Automotive Industry 2008, CNBC TV18 India Business Leaders Lifetime Achievement Award 2008. *Leisure interests:* golf, tennis, photography, reading. *Address:* Mahindra & Mahindra Ltd, Gateway Building, Apollo Bunder, Mumbai 400 001 (office); St Helen's Court, Pedder Road, Mumbai 400 026, India (home). *Telephone:* (22)24984403 (office); (22) 23514206 (home). *Fax:* (22) 24978412 (office). *E-mail:* mahindra.keshub@mahindra.com (office). *Website:* www.mahindra.com (office).

MAHMOUD, Mohamed Kamel, DSc; Egyptian professor of chemistry and research administrator; b. 5 Sept. 1926; ed Univ. of Cairo; Demonstrator, Chem. Dept, Faculty of Sciences, Cairo Univ. 1948–54, Lecturer 1954–57; mem. Nat. Research Centre mission to Switzerland 1957–60; Asst Research Prof., Nat. Research Centre 1960–64, Research Prof. and Head, Textile Research Div. 1964–74, Pres. Nat. Research Centre 1974–84; Pres. Acad. of Scientific Research and Tech. 1984–86; Research Prof. Nat. Research Centre 1986–; mem. Inst. of Egypt, Scientific Council of Africa, Egyptian Chem. Soc., Bd Acad. of Scientific Research and Tech.; Fellow Islamic Acad. of Sciences, Vice-Pres. 1986–94; State Prize of Chem. 1965, Order of Merit, First Grade with Star (Germany) 1979; Order of Science and Art, First Grade 1981. *Address:* National Research Centre, Al-Tahrir Street, Dokki, Cairo, Egypt (office). *Telephone:* (2) 701010 (office). *Fax:* (2) 700931 (office).

MAHMUDI, Al-Baghdadi Ali al-; Libyan politician; *General Secretary, General People's Committee;* fmr Sec., Gen. People's Cttee for Health and Social Security; Deputy Prime Minister responsible for production –2006, Gen. Sec., Gen. People's Cttee (Prime Minister) 2006–. *Address:* General People's Committee, Tripoli, Libya.

MAHON, Sir (John) Denis, Kt, CH, CBE, MA, FBA; British art historian; b. 8 Nov. 1910; s. of the late John FitzGerald Mahon and Lady Alice Evelyn Browne; ed Eton and Christ Church, Oxford; Trustee of the Nat. Gallery 1957–64, 1966–73; mem. Advisory Panel, Nat. Art Collections Fund 1975–; specialist in 17th-Century Italian paintings and has notable collection, exhibited Nat. Gallery London 1997; mem. Cttee of the Biennial Exhbns, Bologna, Italy; Corresp. Fellow Accad. Raffaello, Urbino 1968, Ateneo Veneto 1987; Hon. Citizen, Cento 1982; Hon. DLitt (Newcastle) 1969, (Oxford) 1994, (La Sapienza, Rome) 1998, (Bologna) 2002; Medal for Benemeriti della Cultura for services to criticism and history of Italian art 1957, Archiginnasio d'Oro, City of Bologna 1968, Serena Medal for Italian Studies, British Acad. 1972. *Publications:* Studies in Seicento Art and Theory 1947, Poussiniana 1962, The Drawings of Guercino in the collection of HM The Queen at Windsor Castle (with N. Turner) 1989; various contribs to catalogues of art exhbns and numerous articles in publs on history of art. *Address:* 33 Cadogan Square, London, SW1X 0HU, England. *Telephone:* (20) 7235-7311 (home). *Fax:* (20) 7235-2530 (home).

MAHONEY, Rev. John Aloysius (Jack), SJ, MA, DTheol; British ecclesiastic and academic; *Member, Mount Street Jesuit Centre, London;* b. 14 Jan. 1931, Coatbridge, Scotland; s. of Patrick Mahoney and Margaret Doris; ed Our Lady's High School, Motherwell, St Aloysius Coll., Glasgow, Univ. of Glasgow and Gregorian Univ., Rome; Lecturer in Moral and Pastoral Theology, Heythrop Coll., Oxon. 1967–70; Lecturer in Moral and Pastoral Theology, Heythrop Hall Coll., Univ. of London 1970–86, Prin. 1976–81; F. D. Maurice Prof. of Moral and Social Theology, King's Coll. London 1986–93 Prof. Emer. 1999–; Founding Dir King's Coll. Business Ethics Research Centre 1987–93; Mercers' School Memorial Prof. of Commerce, Gresham Coll. City of London 1987–93; Dixons Prof. of Business Ethics and Social Responsibility, London Business School 1993–98; Founder and Dir Lauriston Centre for Contemporary Belief and Action, Edin. 1998–2005; Lecturer in Theology, St Andrews Univ. 2004; Sr Research Asst Dir, Heythrop Inst. for Religion, Ethics and Public Life 2005–; Companion, Chartered Man. Asscn 1996; currently mem., Mount Street Jesuit Centre, London; Hon. Fellow, Faculty of Divinity, Univ. of Edin. 1998–, Gresham Coll., London 1999–, St Mary's Univ. Coll. 1999–, Heythrop Coll., Univ. of London 2000–; Hon. Lecturer in Business Ethics, Glasgow Business School 2003–04; Hon. DD (Univ. of London) 2004; President's Medal, Georgetown Univ., Washington, DC 2003. *Publications:* Seeking the Spirit: Essays in Moral and Pastoral Theology 1981, Bioethics and Belief: Religion and Medicine in Dialogue 1984, The Making of Moral Theology: A Study of the Roman Catholic Tradition 1987, Teaching Business Ethics in the UK, Europe and the USA 1990, Business Ethics in a New Europe (ed.) 1992, The Challenge of Human Rights: Origin, Development and Significance 2007. *Address:* 114 Mount Street, London, W1K 3AH, England (home). *Telephone:* (20) 7529-4813 (office). *E-mail:* jmlaur@aol.com (office).

MAHONY, HE Cardinal Roger Michael, BA, STB; American ecclesiastic; *Archbishop of Los Angeles;* b. 27 Feb. 1936, Hollywood, Calif.; s. of the late Victor James Mahony and Loretta Marie Baron; ed St John's Seminary Coll., St John's Theologate, Calif., Catholic Univ. of America, Washington, DC; ordained RC Priest, Fresno, Calif. 1962; Bishop, Fresno, Calif. 1975; Bishop of Stockton, Calif. 1980; Archbishop of LA 1985; cr. Cardinal Priest 1991; Archbishop of LA 1985–; mem. numerous cttees of Nat. Confs of Catholic Bishops, USA 1976–; several Pontifical Councils, Vatican 1984–; Dr hc (Loyola Marymount, LA) 1986, (Portland, Ore.) 1988, (Notre Dame, Ind.) 1989, (St Patrick's Coll., Ireland) 1991, (Southern Calif.) 2002. *Address:* 3424 Wilshire Boulevard, Los Angeles, CA 90010, USA (office). *Telephone:* (213) 637-7288 (office). *Fax:* (213) 637-6510 (office).

MAHSOULI, Sadeq, BS, MA; Iranian business executive and government official; *Minister of the Interior;* b. 1959, Uroumieh; ed Univ. of Science and Technology, Tehran Univ.; served in Revolutionary Guards; built businesses in construction and oil trading; served as Gov. of Uroumiyeh and Deputy Gov.-Gen. of West Azerbaijan; adviser to Pres. Ahmadinejad –2008; Minister of the Interior 2008–. *Address:* Ministry of the Interior, Jahad Sq., Fatemi St, Tehran, Iran (office). *Telephone:* (21) 88967866 (office). *Fax:* (21) 88964678 (office). *E-mail:* entekhabat@moi.gov.ir (office). *Website:* www.moi.ir (office).

MAHUAD WITT, Jamil, PhD; Ecuadorean lawyer, politician and fmr head of state; b. 29 July 1949, Loja; s. of Jorge Antonio Mahuad Chalela and Rosa Witt García; m. Tatiana Calderón (divorced); one d.; ed Pontificia Universidad Católica del Ecuador, John F. Kennedy School of Govt, Harvard Univ., USA; legal assessor and dir of pvt. credit banks 1973–78; Pres. Federación de Estudiantes Universitarios Católicos del Ecuador 1974–75; Regional Sec. Federación de Estudiantes de las Universidades Católicas de América Latina 1975–81; mem. Democracia Popular 1981; Dir Empresa Nacional de Productos Vitales 1981–83; Minister of Labour 1981–83; Pres. Democracia Popular 1987–88, 1991–93; Vice-Pres. Demócrata Cristiano de América (ODCA), Andina Region 1991–97; Mayor of Quito 1992–98; Pres. of Ecuador 1998–2000 (deposed by armed forces). *Address:* c/o Democracia Popular, Calle Luis Saá 153 y Hnos Pazmiño, Casilla 17-01-2300, Quito, Ecuador.

MAIDA, HE Cardinal Adam Joseph, JD; American ecclesiastic; b. 18 March 1930, East Vandergrift, Pa; s. of Adam Maida and Sophie Maida (née Cieslak); ed Scott Township High School, St Mary's High School, Orchard Lake, Mich., St Vincent's Coll., Latrobe, Pa, St Mary's Univ., Baltimore, Md, Pontifical Lateran Univ., Rome, Italy, Duquesne Univ., Pittsburgh; admitted to practice law in Pa and before US Supreme Court; ordained priest 1956; further studies in Rome 1956–60; pastoral work in Diocese of Pittsburgh and as Asst Chancellor, Vice-Chancellor, Diocesan Gen. Consultor in the diocesan tribunal 1960–83; fmr Asst Prof. of Theology, La Roche Coll.; fmr Chaplain St Thomas More's Soc.; faculty mem. Duquesne Univ. 1971–83; consecrated Bishop of Green Bay, Wis. 1984; Archbishop of Detroit 1990–2008; cr. Cardinal (Cardinal Priest of SS Vitale, Valeria, Gervasio e Protasio) 1994; mem. Roman Curia Congregation for Catholic Educ., Congregation for the Clergy, Pontifical Council for the Interpretation of Legislative Texts, Pontifical Council for the Pastoral Care of Migrants and Itinerant Peoples, Cardinal Comm. for the Supervision of the Inst. for Works of Religion; served as Chair. US Conf. of Catholic Bishops Canonical Affairs Cttee, Washington, DC 1992, mem. Ad Hoc Cttee for Aid to the Church in Cen. and Eastern Europe, Bishops' Cttee on Evangelization, ex-officio mem. Int. Policy Cttee, Consultant to Cttee on Migration, Cttee on Pro-Life Activities, Episcopal Liaison Cttee for the Polish Apostolate; Chairman Bd of Trustees Mich. Catholic Conf., Sacred Heart Major Seminary, Detroit, SS Cyril and Methodius Seminary, Orchard Lake; Ecclesiastical Protector Int. Order of Alhambra; mem. Bd of Govs Ave Maria School of Law, Ann Arbor, Mich.; Episcopal Moderator and Pres. John Paul II Cultural Foundation, USA; Pres. Pope John Paul II Cultural Center, Washington, DC; mem. Bd of Trustees Catholic Univ. of America, Washington, DC, Basilica of the Nat. Shrine of the Immaculate Conception, Washington, DC, The Papal Foundation, Phila, Pa, John Paul II Cultural Foundation, Rome; mem. Bd of Dirs Nat. Catholic Bioethics Center, Phila; Ecclesial Advisor, Nat. Fellowship of Catholic Men, Gaithersburg, Md; Papal Legate to 19th Int. Marian Congress, Czestochowa, Poland 1996; attended Special Ass. for America of World Synod of Bishops, Vatican City 1997, Special Ass. for Europe of World Synod of Bishops, Vatican City 1999; Superior of Mission sui iuris of Cayman Islands 2000. *Publications:* The Tribunal Reporter: A Casebook and Commentary on the Grounds for Annulment in the Catholic Church, Vol. 1 (ed.) 1970, Ownership, Control and Sponsorship of Catholic Institutions 1975, Issues in the Labor-Management Dialogue:

Church Perspectives (ed.) 1982, Church Property, Church Finances and Church-Related Corporations, a Canon Law Handbook 1983. *Address:* c/o Archdiocese of Detroit, 305 Michigan Avenue, Detroit, MI 48226-2605, USA (office). *Telephone:* (313) 237-5800 (office). *E-mail:* infodesk@aod.org (office). *Website:* www.archdioceseofdetroit.org (office).

MAIDEN, Sir Colin James, Kt, MEng, DPhil; New Zealand university vice-chancellor (retd) and company director; b. 5 May 1933, Auckland; s. of Henry A. Maiden and Lorna Richardson; m. Jenefor Mary Rowe 1957; one s. three d.; ed Univs of New Zealand and Oxford, UK; Head, Hypersonic Physics Section, Canadian Armament Research and Devt Establishment, Québec City, Canada 1958–60; Sr lecturer in Mechanical Eng Univ. of Auckland 1960–61; Head, Material Sciences Lab. Gen. Motors Corpn Defence Research Labs Santa Barbara, Calif. 1961–66; Man. of Process Eng Gen. Motors Corpn Tech. Centre, Warren, Mich. 1966–70; Vice-Chancellor, Univ. of Auckland 1971–94; Chair. NZ Energy Research and Devt Cttee 1974–81, NZ Vice-Chancellor's Cttee 1977–78, 1991, Liquid Fuels Trust Bd 1978–86, NZ Synthetic Fuels Corpn Ltd 1980–90, Tower Insurance Co. Ltd 1988–2002, Fisher & Paykel Ltd 1978–2001, Independent Newspapers Ltd 1989–2003; Dir Mason Industries Ltd 1971–78, Farmers Trading Co. Ltd, 1973–86, Winstone Ltd 1978–88, Wilkins & Davies Ltd 1986–89, New Zealand Steel Ltd 1988–92, ANZ Banking Group (NZ) Ltd 1990–93, The NZ Refining Co. Ltd 1991–2007, Progressive Enterprises Ltd 1992–2000, DB Breweries Ltd 1994–, Sedgwick (NZ) Ltd 1994–98, Transpower New Zealand Ltd 1994–2004, Tower Ltd 1995–2003, Foodland Associated Ltd 2000–05, Fisher and Paykel Healthcare Corpn Ltd 2001–; various professional appointments; Hon. Treas. Asscn of Commonwealth Univs 1988–98; Hon. LLD (Auckland); Queen Elizabeth Silver Jubilee Medal 1977, Medal of Univ. of Bonn 1983, Thomson Medal, Royal Soc. of NZ 1986, Symons Award, Asscn of Commonwealth Univs 1999. *Publications:* numerous scientific and tech. papers. *Leisure interest:* tennis. *Address:* 7 Chatfield Place, Remuera, Auckland 5, New Zealand (home). *Telephone:* (9) 529-0380 (home). *Fax:* (9) 522-4374 (home). *E-mail:* colinmaiden@slingshot.co.nz (office).

MAIGA, Ousmane Issoufi; Malian politician; Minister of Finance 2002–03; Minister of Equipment and Transport 2003–04; Prime Minister of Mali 2004–07. *Address:* c/o Office of the Prime Minister, quartier du Fleuve, BP 790, Bamako, Mali (office).

MAILLOT, Jacques; French director, writer and actor; b. 12 April 1962, Besançon; ed Institut d'Etudes Politiques de Lyon; worked as a graphic designer; hired at Cinémathèque Française as a conscientious objector; began his film career by directing four short films 1990; acted in Mille bornes (Milestones) 1999. *Films:* Des fleurs coupées (Cut Flowers) 1993, Corps inflammables (Flammable Bodies) (Prix Tournage, Avignon Film Festival 1995) 1995, 75 centilitres de prière (aka A Bottle of Wishes, USA) (Special Jury Award, Nat. Competition, Clermont-Ferrand Int. Short Film Festival 1994, Prix Jean Vigo for Short Film 1994) 1995, Entre ciel et terre (Between Heaven and Earth) 1996, Nos vies heureuses (Our Happy Lives) (Prix Tournage, Avignon Film Festival 1999) 1999, Froid comme l'été (Cold as Summer) (Prix Italia 2003) 2002, Rivals 2007, Les liens du sang (Rivals) 2008. *Television:* Les prédateurs (screenplay) 2007. *Address:* c/o Catherine Meynial, VMA, 20 avenue Rapp, 75007 Paris, France. *Telephone:* 1-43-17-37-00. *Fax:* 1-47-20-15-86. *E-mail:* d.leprestre@vma.fr. *Website:* www.vma.fr.

MAINI, Sir Ravinder Nath, Kt, BA, MB, BChir, FRCP, FRCPE, FMedSci, FRS; British rheumatologist and academic; *Professor Emeritus of Rheumatology, Imperial College London;* b. 17 Nov. 1937, India; s. of Sir Amar (Nath) Maini and Saheli Maini (née Mehra); m. 1st Marianne Gorm 1963 (divorced 1986); one s. one d. (and one s. deceased); m. 2nd Geraldine Room 1987; two s.; ed Univ. of Cambridge; jr medical appointments at Guy's, Brompton and Charing Cross Hosps 1962–70; Consultant Physician, St Stephen's Hosp., London 1970–79, Rheumatology Dept, Charing Cross Hosp. 1970; Prof. of Immunology of Rheumatic Diseases, Charing Cross and Westminster Medical School 1981–89; Dir Kennedy Inst. of Rheumatology 1990–2000 (Head Clinical Immunology Div. 1979); Prof. of Rheumatology 1989–, Head Kennedy Inst. of Rheumatology Div., Imperial Coll. School of Medicine at Charing Cross Hosp. Campus (fmrly Charing Cross and Westminster Medical School), Univ. of London 2000–02, Emer. Prof. of Rheumatology, Imperial Coll. 2002–; Pres. British Soc. for Rheumatology 1989–90 (Heberden Orator 1988), British League Against Rheumatism 1985–89; Chair. Research Sub-Cttee 1980–85 and mem. Scientific Coordinating Cttee, Arthritis and Rheumatism Council 1985–95; Chair. Standing Cttee for Investigative Rheumatology, European League Against Rheumatism 1990–97; mem. Exec. Cttee, Asscn of Physicians of GB and Ireland 1989–91; Chair. Rheumatology Cttee, Royal Coll. of Physicians 1992–96 (Croonian Lecturer 1995, Lumleian Lecturer 1999); mem. European Union of Medical Specialists 1994– (Pres. Section of Rheumatology 1996–99, Chair. European Bd of Rheumatology 1996–99); Samuel Hyde Lecturer, Royal Soc. of Medicine 1998; mem. Scientific Advisory Bd Nicholas Piramal India Ltd 2003–08; mem. Bd of Dirs Domantis, Cambridge 2003–07; mem., Council Medical Protection Soc. 2001–; mem. Scientific Advisory Bd Rana Therapeutics Ltd, Australia (previously known as Peptech) 2003–, Piramal Life Sciences, India 2008–; mem. Advisory Bd F-Star Biotechnologische Forschungs und Entwicklungsgesellschaft 2007–; mem. Bd of Trustees, Kennedy Inst. of Rheumatology Trust, Beit Memorial Fellowship, Sir Jules Thorn Trust, Graham Dixon Trust; Hon. Consultant, Charing Cross Hosp., Hammersmith Hosps NHS Trust; Hon. mem. Australian Rheumatism Asscn 1977, Norwegian Soc. for Rheumatology 1988, American Coll. of Rheumatology 1988, Hellenic Rheumatology Soc. 1989, Hungarian Rheumatology Soc. 1990, Scandinavian Soc. for Immunology 1996, Mexican Soc. for Rheumatology 1996, Hon. Fellowship, Sidney Sussex Coll., Univ. of Cambridge 2004, Hon. Fellowship, Royal Soc. of Medicine 2004, Master, American Coll. of

Rheumatology 2004; Dr hc (Univ. René Descartes, Paris) 1994, Hon. DSc (Glasgow Univ.) 2004; Carol Nachman Prize for Rheumatology (jt recipient), City of Wiesbaden 1999, Distinguished Investigator Award, American Coll. of Rheumatology 1999, Crafoord Prize (jt recipient), Royal Swedish Acad. of Sciences 2000, Courtin-Clarins Prize (jt recipient), Asscn de Recherche sur la Polyarthrite 2000, Albert Lasker Award for Clinical Medical Research 2003, Fothergillian Medal, Medical Soc. of London 2004, Cameron Prize (jt recipient), Univ. of Edin. 2004, Ambuj Nath Bose Prize, Royal Coll. of Physicians 2005, EULAR Meritorious Service Award in Rheumatology (jt recipient) 2005, Langdon Brown Lecture, Royal Coll. of Physicians 2005, Galen Medal, The Worshipful Soc. of Apothcaries of London 2006, Japan Rheumatism Foundation Int. RA Award (jt recipient) 2007, Dr Paul Janssen Award for Biomedical Research (jt recipient) 2008. *Publications include:* Immunology of Rheumatic Diseases 1977, Modulation of Autoimmune Disease (ed.) 1981, Textbook of the Rheumatic Diseases, 6th edn (contrib.) 1986, T-Cell Activation in Health and Disease (ed.) 1989, Rheumatoid Arthritis (ed.) 1992, Oxford Textbook of Rheumatology (contrib.) 1993, Rheumatology (section ed.) 1993, Manual of Biological Markers of Disease (co-ed.: Section A, Methods of Autoantibody Detection 1993, Section B, Autoantigens 1994, Section C, Clinical Significance of Autoantibodies 1996), Oxford Textbook of Medicine (contrib.) 2001; 480 articles in scientific journals. *Leisure interests:* music appreciation, walking. *Address:* Kennedy Institute of Rheumatology, 65 Aspenlea Road, London, W6 8LH, England (office). *Telephone:* (20) 8383-4403 (office). *Fax:* (20) 8748-3293 (office). *E-mail:* r.maini@imperial.ac.uk (office). *Website:* wwwfom.sk.med.ic.ac.uk/medicine/about/divisions/kennedy/default.html (office).

MAIORESCU, Mircea, PhD; Romanian professor of medicine and fmr government official; *Professor, Marie Skłodowska Curie Children's Hospital;* b. 23 May 1926, Bucharest; s. of Octav Maiorescu and Elena Maiorescu; m. Zoe Maiorescuh; one s. one d.; ed Paediatrics Coll. of Bucharest; teacher, Carol Davila Univ., Bucharest 1956–, Prof. 1974–; Dir Mother and Child Protection Inst. 1978–84; currently Prof., Marie Skłodowska Curie Children's Hosp., Bucharest Univ. of Medicine; mem. European Asscn of Paediatric Cardiology 1983, Acad. of Medical Sciences of Romania 1991, New York Acad. of Sciences 1992; Minister of Health 1991–92; Vice-Pres. WHO Gen. Ass. 1992; mem. Cttee Romanian Soc. of Paediatrics, Romanian Soc. of Paediatric Cardiology; Visiting Prof., Louisville Univ., Ky, USA 1995; Award for Int. Medical Cooperation, Baylor Health Care Systems, Dallas, Tex. and Humana Foundation, Louisville, Ky, USA 1999. *Publications:* over 300 works. *Leisure interests:* classical music, essays., philosophy, poetry. *Address:* Marie Skłodowska Curie Children's Hospital, Bulevard Brâncoveanu 20, 75544 Bucharest (office); Str. Nicolae Filimon 31, 77728 Bucharest, Romania (home).

MAIRE, Edmond; French trade union official; *President, Société d'Investissement France Active;* b. 24 Jan. 1931, Epinay-sur-Seine; s. of Julien Maire and Marie-Thérèse Conchou; m. Raymonde Le Goff 1954; three c.; ed Conservatoire Nat. des Arts et Métiers; technician, chemical industry; Perm. Sec. Fed. of Chemical Industries of Confédération Française Démocratique du Travail (CFDT) 1958–70; mem. Exec. Cttee of CFDT, in charge of professional and social action; Sec.-Gen. of CFDT 1971–88; Pres. Villages-Vacances-Familles (VVF) 1989–99; Pres. de la Section Affaires Sociales du Conseil Nat. du Tourisme 1989–99; Pres. Société d'investissement France Active 1999–; mem. Conseil Economique et Social 1969–74. *Publications:* Demain l'autogestion 1976, Nouvelles frontières pour le syndicalisme 1987, L'Esprit libre 1999. *Address:* 37 rue Bergère, 75009 Paris (office); 145 rue Pelleport, 75020 Paris, France (home). *Telephone:* 1-53-24-26-26 (office). *Fax:* 1-53-24-26-63 (office). *E-mail:* edmondm@franceactive.org (home).

MAISENBERG, Oleg; Austrian pianist; b. 29 April 1945, Odessa, USSR (now Ukraine); s. of Adel and Josef Maisenberg; two c.; ed Moscow Gnessin Inst. of Music (pupil of A. Yokheles); winner Franz Schubert Competition in Vienna 1967, 20th Century Music Competition, Vienna 1967; performed Rachmaninov's 1st Piano Concerto with Nat. Orchestra of Moldavia; emigrated to Austria 1981; concert performances world-wide as soloist and chamber musician; recordings of Schubert, Schuman, Liszt, Scriabin, Berg, Stravinsky, R. Strauss, Dvořák, Milhaud, Weber, Schönberg, Bartok, Rachmaninov and Prokofiev; Prof. Stuttgart Conservatory and Vienna Acad. of Music, Hon. mem. Konzerthaus Gesellschaft, Vienna. *Address:* c/o Matthias Dirnbacher, Künstleragentur Dr Raab and Dr Bohm, Plankengasse 7, 1010 Vienna, Austria (office). *Telephone:* (1) 5120501 (office). *Fax:* (1) 5127743 (office). *E-mail:* dirnbacher@rbartists.at (office). *Website:* www.rbartists.at (office).

MAISKY, Mischa (Michael); Belgian cellist; b. 10 Jan. 1948, Riga, Latvia (b. USSR); m. Maryanne Kay Lipman 1983; one s. one d.; ed Moscow Conservatory with Mstislav Rostropovich, Univ. of Southern Calif.; debut with Leningrad Philharmonic Orchestra 1965; emigrated to Israel 1972; debut with Pittsburgh Symphony Orchestra at Carnegie Hall 1973; debut at Royal Festival Hall 1976; debut at Berlin Philharmonic Hall 1978; numerous TV, film and video appearances all over the world; played Walton Concerto, London Festival Hall 1993, Shostakovich Concerto, London Proms; All-Soviet prize-winner 1965, Int. Tchaikovsky Competition 1966, winner of Cassada Competition, Florence 1973 and Rostropovich Competition, Paris 1981, Grand Prix du Disque, Paris 1985, Record Acad. Prize, Tokyo 1985. *Recordings include:* Six Suites for Solo Cello (Bach), Three Sonatas for Cello and Piano (Bach), Concerto in A minor Op. 102 for Violin, Cello and Orchestra (Brahms), Concerto for Cello and Orchestra in A Minor (Schumann). *Leisure interests:* music, chess, computing. *Address:* c/o Intermusica Artists Management Ltd, 16 Duncan Terrace, London, N1 8BZ, England (office); 138 Meerlaan, 1900 Overijse, Belgium. *Telephone:* (20) 7278-5455 (office). *Fax:* (20) 7278-8434 (office). *E-mail:* mail@intermusica.co.uk (office). *Website:* www.intermusica.co.uk (office).

MAISONROUGE, Jacques (Gaston); French business executive and electronics engineer; b. 20 Sept. 1924, Cachan; s. of Paul Maisonrouge and Suzanne Maisonrouge (née Cazas); m. Françoise Féron 1948; one s. four d.; ed Lycée Saint-Louis, Paris, Ecole Centrale des Arts et Manufactures; joined IBM France as engineer 1948, Asst Sales Dir 1954, mem. Bd Dirs 1965–; Marketing Man. IBM World Trade Europe Corpn 1956, Regional Man. 1958, Asst Gen. Man. 1959, Vice-Pres. 1962, Pres. and CEO 1964; Pres. IBM World Trade Corpn 1967–81, Sr Vice-Pres. IBM Corpn 1972–84, Chair. IBM World Trade Europe-Africa 1974–81, IBM World Trade Corpn 1976–84, mem. Bd Dirs IBM Corpn 1983–84, IBM Europe-Africa-Middle East 1988–95; Vice-Chair. Bd Dirs Liquid Air Corpn 1984–86 (mem. Bd Dirs 1971–94); Dir-Gen. for Industry, Ministry of Industry and Tourism 1986–87; Pres. Saint-Honoré Europe 1989–92; Chair. Bd Dirs Ecole Centrale des Arts et Manufactures 1977–87, Centre Français du Commerce Extérieur 1987–89, Image de la France Comm. 1989–90; Chair. Bd of Govs American Hosp., Paris 1993–96, Asscn France–Etats-Unis 1994–2000; Chancellor Int. Acad. of Man. 1988–93; mem. Atomic Energy Cttee 1986–87; Grand Officier Légion d'honneur; Commdr Ordre Nat. du Mérite et des Palmes Académiques; Officier des Arts et Lettres and decorations from Austria, Malta, Italy, Belgium, Sweden and Vatican City. *Publication:* International Manager 1985. *Leisure interests:* walking in the mountains, spending time with his 10 grandchildren. *Address:* 3 boulevard Flandrin, 75116 Paris, France (home). *Telephone:* 1-40-72-76-96. *Fax:* 1-40-72-71-38 (home).

MAITLAND, Sir Donald James Dundas, Kt, GCMG, OBE, MA, FRSA; British diplomatist and civil servant (retd) and academic; *Director, Project Hope UK;* b. 16 Aug. 1922, Edin.; s. of Thomas D. Maitland and Wilhelmina S. Dundas; m. Jean Marie Young 1950; one s. one d.; ed George Watson's Coll. and Edin. Univ.; army service 1941–47; joined Diplomatic Service 1947; Consul, Amara 1950; British Embassy, Baghdad 1950–53; Private Sec. to Minister of State, Foreign Office 1954–56; Dir Middle East Centre for Arab Studies, Lebanon 1956–60; Foreign Office 1960–63; Counsellor, British Embassy, Cairo 1963–65; Head, News Dept, Foreign Office 1965–67; Prin. Private Sec. to Foreign and Commonwealth Sec. 1967–69; Amb. to Libya 1969–70; Chief Press Sec. to Prime Minister 1970–73; Perm. Rep. to UN 1973–74; Deputy Under-Sec., FCO 1974–75; mem. British Overseas Trade Bd 1974–75; UK mem. Commonwealth Group on Trade, Aid and Devt 1975; UK Perm. Rep. to European Communities 1975–79; Deputy Perm. Under-Sec. FCO 1979–80; Perm. Under-Sec. of State, Dept of Energy 1980–82; Chair. UK Cttee World Communications Year 1983; Chair. Ind. Comm. World-wide Telecommunications Devt (Maitland Comm.) 1983–85; Govt Dir Britoil 1983–85; Dir Slough Estates 1983–92, Northern Eng Industries 1986–89; Adviser, British Telecom 1985–86; Deputy Chair. Independent Broadcasting Authority (IBA) 1986–89; Chair. Health Educ. Authority 1989–94; Pro-Chancellor, Bath Univ. 1996–2000, Visiting Prof. 2000–; mem. Commonwealth War Graves Comm. 1983–87; Chair. Christians for Europe (later Charlemagne Inst.) 1984–93; Pres. Federal Trust for Educ. and Research 1987–; Chair. Govs Westminster Coll., Oxford 1994–97; Chair. Thinknet Comm. 1989–95; Dir Project Hope UK 1996–; Visiting Prof., Univ. of Bath 2000–; Hon. Fellow, Bath Spa Univ. Coll. 2000; Hon. LLD (Bath) 1995; Hon. DLitt (Univ. of West of England) 2000. *Publications:* Diverse Times, Sundry Places (autobiog.) 1996, Spring Blossom, Autumn Leaves (miscellany) 1998, The Boot and Other Stories 1999, The Running Tide 2000, Edinburgh – Seat of Learning 2002. *Leisure interests:* music. *Address:* 2 Rosemary Walk, Church Street, Bradford on Avon, BA15 1BP, England (home). *Telephone:* (1225) 863063 (home).

MAITLAND SMITH, Geoffrey, FCA; British business executive and accountant; b. 27 Feb. 1933, London; s. of the late Philip John Maitland Smith and of Kathleen Maitland Smith (née Goff); m. 3rd Lucinda Enid Whyte 1986; four s. two d.; ed Univ. Coll. School, London; Partner, Thornton Baker & Co., Chartered Accountants 1960–70; Dir Sears PLC (fmrly Sears Holdings PLC) 1971–95, Chief Exec. 1978–88, Jt Chair. 1984–85, Chair. 1985–95; Chair. British Shoe Corpn 1984–92, Mallet PLC 1986–89, Selfridges Ltd 1985–93, Garrard & Co. 1985–90, Mappin & Webb Ltd 1985–90, Hammerson PLC 1993– 99 (Dir 1990–99), W. and F.C. Bonham and Sons Ltd 1996–2000, Fiske plc (non-exec.) 2000–05; Pres. Intercontinental Group of Dept Stores 1990–95; Deputy Chair. Midland Bank 1992–96 (Dir 1986–96); Dir Asprey PLC 1980–93, Cen. Ind. Television 1983–85, Courtaulds PLC 1983–90, Imperial Group PLC 1984–86, HSBC Holdings PLC 1992–96; Hon. Vice-Pres. Inst. of Marketing 1987–94; mem. Bd Financial Reporting Council 1990–98; Chair. Council, Univ. Coll. School 1987–96. *Leisure interest:* opera. *Address:* Manor Barn, Fifield, Oxon., OX7 6HF, England. *Telephone:* (1993) 832441 (home). *Fax:* (1993) 832442 (home).

MAITLIS, Peter M., PhD, FRS, FRSC, FCIC; British chemist and academic; *Research Professor Emeritus, Department of Chemistry, University of Sheffield;* b. 15 Jan. 1933, Berlin; s. of Jacob Maitlis and Judith Maitlis; m. Marion Basco 1959; three d.; ed Univ. of Birmingham and Univ. of London; Asst Lecturer, Univ. of London 1956–60; Fulbright Fellow and Research Assoc., Harvard and Cornell Univs, USA, 1960–62; Asst Prof., Assoc. Prof. and Prof., McMaster Univ., Canada 1962–72; Prof. of Inorganic Chem., Sheffield Univ. 1972–94, Research Prof. 1994–2002, Research Prof. Emer. 2003–; Fellow, Alfred P. Sloan Foundation 1967–69; Chair. Chem. Cttee Science and Eng Research Council 1985–88; Pres. Dalton Div., Royal Soc. of Chem. (RSC) 1985–87; mem. Council Royal Soc. 1991–93; Foreign mem. Accad. dei Lincei (Italy) 1999; Steacie Prize in Natural Sciences 1970, RSC Medal 1981, Kurnakov Medal, Russian Acad. of Sciences 1998. *Lectures:* Sir Edward Frankland Lecturer, Royal Soc. of Chem. 1985, Tilden Lecturer 1979, Ludwig Mond Lecturer 1999, David Craig Lecturer, ANU 2000, Stone Lecturer, Univ. of Bristol 2001, Paolo Chini Lecturer, Italian Chemical Soc. 2001, Glenn T. Seaborg Memorial Lecturer, Univ. of California, Berkeley 2004–05. *Publications:* The Organic Chemistry of Palladium (two vols) 1971, Metal-catalysis in Industrial Organic Processes (with G P Chiusoli) 2006; numerous research publs in scientific journals. *Leisure interests:* music, travel, reading, discussing politics. *Address:* Department of Chemistry, Room C52, University of Sheffield, Sheffield, S3 7HF, England (office). *Telephone:* (114) 222-9320 (office). *Fax:* (114) 222-9346 (office). *E-mail:* p.maitlis@sheffield.ac.uk (office). *Website:* www.shef.ac.uk/chemistry/staff/profiles/maitlis.html (office).

MAJALI, Abdel Salam al-, MD, DLC, FACS, DhC; Jordanian politician, physician and university president; b. 18 Feb. 1925, Karak; s. of Attallah Majali and Khadeejeh Serougi; m. Joan M. Lachlan 1956; two s. one d.; ed Medical Coll., Syrian Univ., Damascus; Dir-Gen. and Ear, Nose and Throat Consultant, The Royal Medical Services, Jordanian Armed Forces, Amman 1960–69; Minister of Health 1969–71; Pres. Univ. of Jordan, Amman 1971–76, 1980–90; Minister of Educ. and Minister of State for Prime Ministry Affairs 1976–79; Prime Minister of Jordan 1993–95, 1997–99, Minister of Defence and Foreign Affairs 1993–95, Minister of Defence 1997–99; Chair. and mem. UN Univ. Council, Tokyo 1977–83; Fellow, American Coll. of Surgeons; Jordan Independence Medal; Medal of St John of Jerusalem and other decorations; Dr hc (Hacettepe Univ., Ankara) 1974.

MAJEED, Gen. Tariq, MA; Pakistani army officer; *Chairman, Joint Chiefs of Staff Committee;* b. Aug. 1950, Lahore; ed Command and Staff Coll., Quetta, Malaysian Armed Forces Staff Coll., Kuala Lumpur, Asia-Pacific Center for Security Studies, Honolulu, Hawaii, Nat. Defence Coll., Islamabad; commissioned in Pakistan Army (Infantry, Baloch Regt) 1971, has commanded Light Anti-Tank Unit and an Infantry Bn, two Infantry Brigades, Infantry Div., participated in Indo-Pakistan War 1971, took part, as GOC Lahore in absence of Corps Commdr, in counter-coup launched by army high command against then govt of Mian Nawaz Sharif Oct. 1999, also led mil. operation on Jamia Hafsa, Dir Gen. Mil. Intelligence 2001–03, promoted to Lt-Gen. Dec. 2003, Chief of Gen. Staff 2003–06, Commdr 10 Corps, Rawalpindi 2006–07, in charge of armed forces who took down armed militias stationed inside mosque at Lal Masjid Siege 2007, promoted to four-star Gen. Oct. 2007, Chair. Jt Chiefs of Staff Cttee Oct. 2007–; Hilal-e-Imtiaz (Mil.), Nishan-e-Imtiaz (Mil.). *Address:* Joint Chiefs of Staff Committee, Joint Staff Headquarters, Chaklala, Rawalpindi, Pakistan (office).

MAJEKODUNMI, Chief the Hon. Moses Adekoyejo, Chief Otun of Egbaland, Chief Maiyegun of Lagos, Chief Bashegun of Ede, Chief Agba-Akin of Oshogbo, Chief Kaiyero of Akure, Chief Maiyegun of Iwo, Chief Asipa of Iragbiji, CMG, CFR, LLD, MA, MD, FRCPI, FMCOG, FRCOG, MAO, DCH, LM; Nigerian administrator and physician; *Chancellor, Ogun State University;* b. 17 Aug. 1916, Abeokuta; s. of Chief J. B. Majekodun, Chief Otun of Egbaland and Alice Oladunni (Soetan); m. 1st Nola C. Maclaughlin 1943 (divorced 1963); five s. three d.; m. 2nd Katsina Saratu Atta 1964; ed Abeokuta Grammar School, St Gregory's Coll., Lagos, Trinity Coll., Dublin; House Physician, Nat. Children's Hosp., Dublin 1941–43; Medical Officer, Nigeria 1943–49; Consulting Obstetrician, Massey Street Maternity Hosp., Gen. Hosp. and Creek Hosp., Lagos 1949–60; Sr Specialist Obstetrician, Nigerian Fed. Gov. Medical Services 1949–60; Senator and Leader of Senate 1960; Minister of State for the Army 1960–61, Fed. Minister of Health 1961–66; Fed. Minister of Health and Information 1965; Admin. for W Nigeria 1962; Pres. 16th World Health Assembly 1963; Int. Vice-Pres., 3rd World Conf. on Medical Educ., New Delhi 1966; Chancellor Ogun State Univ. 1986–; Chair. Merchant Banking Corpn Nigeria Ltd, Westminster Dredging (Nigeria) Ltd 1990–; Chair. Bd Govs St Nicholas Hosp., Lagos 1967–; Chair. Bd Dirs Lion Bldgs Ltd; Dir Abbott Labs (Nigeria) Ltd, Swiss Nigeria Chemical Co., Johnson and Johnson (Nigeria) Ltd; Gov. St Gregory's Coll., Lagos; Trustee J.K. Randle Memorial Hall, Lagos; mem. Soc. of Gynaecology and Obstetrics, Nigeria; Hon. LLD (Trinity Coll., Dublin); Hon. DSc (Lagos), (Ogun State Univ.). *Publications:* Premature Infants: Management and Prognosis 1943, Behold the Key (play) 1944, Partial Atresia of the Cervix Complicating Pregnancy 1946, Sub-Acute Intussusception in Adolescents 1948, Thiopentone Sodium in Operative Obstetrics 1954, Rupture of the Uterus involving the Bladder 1955, Effects of Malnutrition in Pregnancy and Lactation 1957, Medical Education and the Health Services: A Critical Review of Priorities in a Developing Country 1966. *Leisure interests:* riding, squash, swimming. *Address:* Ogun State University, PMB 2002, Ago-Iwoye, Ogun State (office); 3 Kingsway, Ikoyi, Lagos, Nigeria (home). *Telephone:* (37) 390149 (office); 681660 (home).

MAJEWSKI, Tomasz; Polish athlete; b. 30 Aug. 1981, Nasielsk; winner Shot Put, Nat. Championships 2003, 2004, 2005, Nat. Indoor Championships 2004, 2005, 2006; fourth place, Shot Put, World Indoor Championships, Budapest 2004; Gold Medal, Shot Put, 23rd Summer Universiade, İzmir 2005; Bronze Medal, Shot Put, European Winter Throwing Cup, Tel-Aviv 2006, World Indoor Championships, Valencia 2008 (threw 20.93m); Gold Medal, Shot Put, Olympic Games, Beijing 2008 (achieved personal best throw of 21.51m during Olympic final on 15 Aug., Poland's first Olympic medal in shot put since 1972). *Address:* c/o Polish Athletics Federation (Polski Zwiazek Lekkiej Atletyki), 68/70 Ceglowska, 01-809 Warsaw, Poland. *Telephone:* (22) 6397015. *Fax:* (22) 6397016. *E-mail:* pzla@pzla.pl. *Website:* www.pzla.pl (office).

MAJKO, Pandeli Sotir, LLB; Albanian politician; b. 15 Nov. 1967; s. of Sotir and Janulla; m. Enkeleida Majko; one s., one d.; ed Univ. of Tirana; Rep. Dec. 1990 Movt; co-f. Democratic Party 1990, left party 1991; Jt Socialist Party of Albania 1991, Sec.-Gen. of Public Relations 1996–97, Sec. 1997–99, also leader of Parl. Group, Head of Del. to OSCE; Prime Minister of Albania 1998–99, Feb.–July 2002; Minister of Defence 2002–05; fmr Sec. Gen., Socialist Party of Albania; f. Forum of Euro-Socialist Youth 1991; Chair. Euro-Socialist Forum 1992–95; mem. Parl. 1992–; Torch of Democracy Award 1993. *Leisure interest:*

reading. *Telephone:* (4) 227409 (office); (42) 251299 (home). *Fax:* (4) 227417 (office). *E-mail:* pandelimajko@hotmail.com (home). *Website:* www.ps-al.org (office).

MAJOOR, Franciscus (Frank) Antonius Maria, MCL; Dutch diplomatist; *Permanent Representative, United Nations;* b. 1 April 1949; m.; two c.; ed Univ. of Leiden, Inst. for Int. Relations, The Hague; served in Dutch embassies in Dar es Salaam 1977–79, Bonn 1979–82; Head of Environmental Affairs Section, Econ. Cooperation Dept, Ministry of Foreign Affairs 1982–85; Asst to Dir Gen. of Political Affairs 1985–86; Special Advisor on Political Security Matters, Deputy Dir of Atlantic Cooperation and Security Affairs Dept 1992–93; Dir of Security Policy Dept 1993–97; Amb.-at-Large 1999–2000; Sec. Gen. 2000–05; First Sec. (Political Matters), Perm. Mission to UN, New York 1986–88, Minister Plenipotentiary (Econ. and Financial Matters) 1988–92; Amb. to Conf. on Disarmament, Geneva 1997–99; Perm. Rep. to UN, New York 2005–. *Address:* Office of the Permanent Representative of the Netherlands to the United Nations, 235 East 45th Street, 16th Floor, New York, NY 10017, USA (office). *Telephone:* (212) 519-9612 (office). *Fax:* (212) 370-1954 (office). *E-mail:* nyv@minbuza.nl (office). *Website:* www.pvnewyork.org (office).

MAJOR, Clarence, PhD; American novelist, poet, painter and academic; *Professor of English, University of California, Davis;* b. 31 Dec. 1936, Atlanta, Ga; s. of Clarence Major and Inez Huff; m. Pamela Ritter 1980; ed Union Graduate School, Yellow Springs and Cincinnati, Ohio, Univ. of the State of New York, Albany; Prof., Dept of English, Univ. of California, Davis 1989–; has given lectures in USA, Europe and in N and W Africa; Fulbright Fellowship, Pushcart Prize, Nat. Council on the Arts Award, Int. Writers' Hall of Fame, Gwendolyn Brooks Foundation Award, Chicago State Univ., Western States Book Award, Sister Circle Book Award. *Publications:* novels: All-Night Visitors 1969, NO 1973, Reflex and Bone Structure 1975, Emergency Exit 1979, My Amputations (Western States Book Award for Fiction) 1986, Such was the Season 1987, Painted Turtle: Woman with Guitar 1988; short stories: Fun and Games 1990, Calling the Wind: Twentieth Century African-American Short Stories 1993, Dirty Bird Blues 1996, All-Night Visitors (new version) 1998; poetry: Swallow the Lake 1970, Symptoms and Madness 1971, Private Line 1971, The Cotton Club 1972, The Syncopated Cakewalk 1974, Inside Diameter: The France Poems 1985, Surfaces and Masks 1987, Some Observations of a Stranger at Zuni in the Latter Part of the Century 1989, The Garden Thrives, Twentieth Century African-American Poetry 1995, Configurations: New and Selected Poems 1958–98, 1998, Waiting for Sweet Baby 2002; non-fiction: Dictionary of Afro-American Slang 1970, The Dark and Feeling: Black American Writers and their Work 1974, Juba to Jive: A Dictionary of African-American Slang 1994, Necessary Distance: Essays and Criticism 2001, Come by Here: My Mother's Life 2002, Conversations with Clarence Major, Clarence Major and His Art; numerous works in anthologies and periodicals. *Address:* Department of English, 281 Voorhies Hall, University of California, Davis, CA 95616, USA (office). *Telephone:* (916) 752-5677 (office). *E-mail:* clmajor@ucdavis.edu (office). *Website:* www.english.ucdavis.edu/faculty/cmajor/cmajor.htm (office); www.clarencemajor.com (home).

MAJOR, Air Chief Marshal Fali Homi; Indian air force officer; *Chief of the Air Staff;* b. 29 May 1947, Secunderabad; m. Zareen Major; one s. one d.; ed Wesley High School, Secunderabad, Nat. Defence Coll., Army War Coll.; commissioned in Indian Air Force (IAF) 1967, has flown over 7,000 hours on Sentinel, T-6G, Mi-4, Mi-8 and Mi-17 helicopters, as Wing Commdr, commanded IAF's first Mi-17 Squadron, which operated at Siachen Glacier (world's highest battlefield), as Group Capt., commanded another Mi-17 Squadron, leading it during operations of Indian Peace Keeping Force in Sri Lanka, as Station Commdr of Air Force Station Sarsawa, led rescue of 11 passengers from stranded cable car at resort in Himachal Pradesh, has held several important staff and field appointments, including Jt Dir (Helicopter Operations) and Dir Operations (Transport & Helicopter), Air Officer Commdg Leh (Ladakh) following Kargil conflict 1999, promoted to rank of Air Vice-Marshal 2002, Asst Chief of the Air Staff (Personnel Airmen & Civilians) at Air HQ 2002–04, promoted to rank of Air Marshal 2004, Deputy Chief of Integrated Defence Staff (Operations), HQ Integrated Defence Staff 2004–05, directed relief, rescue and rehabilitation operations of Indian Armed Forces in India and abroad in aftermath of tsunami of Dec. 2004, Air Officer C-in-C Eastern Air Command 2005–07, Chief of the Air Staff 2007–; Vayu Sena Medal (Gallantry), Shaurya Chakra for gallantry, Ati Vishist Seva Medal 2002, Param Vishisht Seva Medal 2006. *Leisure interests:* avid golfer and cricket fan. *Address:* Public Relations Officer, Indian Air Force, Directorate of Public Relations, Ministry of Defence, Room No. 91, South Block, New Delhi, 110 011, India (office). *Telephone:* (11) 23019745 (office); (11) 23010231 (ext. 6903) (office). *E-mail:* pro_iaf2006@yahoo.co.in (office). *Website:* indianairforce.nic.in (office).

MAJOR, Jean-Louis, LPh, MA, PhD, FRSC; Canadian author and academic; *Professor Emeritus, University of Ottawa;* b. 16 July 1937, Cornwall, Canada; s. of Joseph Major and Noella Daoust; m. Bibiane Landry 1960; one d.; ed Univ. of Ottawa and Ecole Pratique des Hautes Etudes; Lecturer, Dept of Philosophy, Univ. of Ottawa 1961–65, Prof. Dept des Lettres Françaises 1965, Titular Prof. 1971–99, Assoc. Dean (Research), Faculty of Arts 1991–97, Prof. Emer. 1999–; Visiting Prof. Dept of French, Univ. of Toronto 1970–71; Dir Corpus d'éditions critiques and Bibliothèque du nouveau monde 1981–; Chair. Academic Advisory Cttee of Ont. Council on Univ. Affairs 1991–93; mem. Acad. des Lettres et Sciences Humaines 1976; Lorne Pierce Medal, Royal Soc. of Canada 2000. *Publications include:* Saint-Exupéry, l'écriture et la pensée 1968, Anne Hébert et le miracle de la parole 1976, Le jeu en étoile 1978, Entre l'écriture et la parole 1984, a critical edn of Cocteau's Léone, Journal d'Henriette Dessaules 1989, Trente arpents de Ringuet 1991, Mailles à l'envers 1999, Québec Literature: From Collective Identity to Modernity and Back 1999, Contes par-ci par-là 2001, Antifables 2002. *Address:* Corpus d'Éditions Critiques, Département des Lettres Françaises, University of Ottawa, Ottawa, Ont., K1N 6N5 (office); PO Box 357, St Isidore, Ont., K0C 2B0, Canada (home). *Telephone:* (613) 562-5798. *Fax:* (613) 562-5207. *E-mail:* corpus@uottawa.ca (office). *Website:* www.uottawa.ca/publications/bnm (office).

MAJOR, The Rt Hon., Sir John, KG CH, AIB, FIB; British fmr politician and banker; b. 29 March 1943, Merton; s. of the late Thomas Major and Gwendolyn Major; m. Norma Christina Elizabeth Johnson 1970; one s. one d.; ed Rutlish Grammar School, Merton; mem. Lambeth Borough Council 1968–71, Chair. Housing Cttee 1970–71; Sr Exec. Standard Chartered Bank PLC, various exec. posts in UK and overseas 1965–79; MP for Huntingdon 1983–2001 (Huntingdonshire 1979–83); Jt Sec., Conservative Parl. Party Environment Cttee 1979–81; Parl. Pvt. Sec. to Home Office Minister 1981–83; Asst Govt Whip 1983–84; Lord Commr of HM Treasury 1984–85; Parl. Under-Sec. of State for Social Security 1985–86; Minister for Social Security and the Disabled 1986–87; Chief Sec. to Treasury 1987–89; Sec. of State for Foreign and Commonwealth Affairs July–Oct. 1989; Chancellor of the Exchequer 1989–90; Prime Minister, First Lord of the Treasury and Minister for the Civil Service 1990–97; Leader of the Conservative Party 1990–97; Pres. Eastern Area Young Conservatives 1983–85, mem., Int. Bd of Govs., Peres Center for Peace, Israel 1997–; mem. Baker Inst. 1998–; mem. InterAction Council, Tokyo 1998–; Pres. Surrey Co. Cricket Club 2000–02; Adviser to Carlyle Group 1998–2001, Chair. (European Bd) 2001–04; Chair. Ditchley Council 2000–; non-exec. Dir, Mayflower Corpn 2000–03; Sr Adviser Credit Suisse First Boston (CSFB) 2001–; mem. Main Cttee Marylebone Cricket Club (MCC) 2001–04; Norfolk Cricket Umpires and Scorers Asscn 2002–; mem. European Bd, Siebel Systems Inc. 2001–02; mem. Club de Madrid 2002–; pres. Asthma UK 1998–; Hon. Pres. Sight Savers Appeal 2001–; Vice-Pres. Macmillan Cancer Relief, Inst. of Sports Sponsorship 2001–; British and Commonwealth Cricket Charitable Trust 2002–; patron of Mercy Ships, Prostate Cancer Charity, Wavemakers, Support for Africa 2000, Atlantic Partnership 2001–, Foreign and Commonwealth Office Asscn 2001–, Professional Cricketers' Asscn 2001–, Deafblind UK 2002–, Consortium for Street Children 2002–, 21st Century Trust 2002–, Goodman Fund, Chicago 2002–, DEMAND 2004–, Future Island 2004–, Dickie Bird Foundation 2004–; Vice-Patron, The Atlantic Council of the UK; Hon. Master of the Bench of the Middle Temple 1992, Hon. Bencher 1997–; Hon. Freeman Merchant Taylors' Co. 2002–; Hon. Life Vice-Pres., Surrey Co. Cricket Club, Hon. FCIB. *Publications:* John Major: The Autobiography 1999, More Than A Game: The Story of Cricket's Early Years 2007. *Leisure interests:* reading, travel, theatre, music, football, cricket and other sports. *Address:* PO Box 38506, London, SW1P 1ZW, England.

MAJOR, Dame Malvina Lorraine, DBE, PCNZM; New Zealand operatic soprano; *Professor of Vocal Studies, University of Canterbury;* b. 28 Jan. 1943, Hamilton; d. of Vincent Major and Eva Major; m. Winston William Richard Fleming 1965 (died 1990); one s. two d.; ed Hamilton Tech. Coll. and London Opera Centre; debut as Rosina in The Barber of Seville, Salzburg Festival 1968; performances in Europe, UK, USA, Australia, Japan, Jordan, Egypt and NZ; concerts, opera and recording with NZ Symphony Orchestra, Auckland Philharmonia and Southern Symphony Orchestra; Founder Dame Malvina Major Foundation (for excellence in the performing arts) 1991; Amb. for the NZ Year of the Family 1994; Prof. of Vocal Studies, Univ. of Canterbury; Hon. life mem. NZ Horticultural Soc.; Patron Christchurch City Choir, Canterbury Opera, Nelson School of Music, Waikato Multiple Sclerosis; Dr hc (Waikato Univ.); Hon. DLitt (Massey Univ.); NZ winner Mobil Song Quest 1963, Kathleen Ferrier Competition winner 1966, Outstanding Achievements in Music Award 1988, NZ Medal 1990, Entertainer and Int. Performer of the Year 1992, NZ Music Award–Classical Disc 1993, 1994 and numerous other awards for services to music. *Leisure interests:* family, golf, sewing. *Address:* c/o James Bennett MNZM., 12 The Peninsula, Huntingdon, Hamilton, New Zealand (office). *Telephone:* (4) 855-8185 (office). *E-mail:* jimbennett@clear.net.nz (office). *Website:* www.damemalvinamajor.co.nz.

MAK, Tak Wah, OC, BSc, MSc, PhD, FRSC; Canadian (b. Chinese) immunologist, molecular biologist and academic; *Professor, Department of Medical Biophysics and Department of Immunology, University of Toronto;* b. 4 Oct. 1946, People's Republic of China; s. of Kent Mak and Shu-tak Chan; m. Shirley Suet-Wan Lau (died 1998); two c.; ed Univ. of Wisconsin, Univ. of Alberta; Sr Scientist, Div. of Stem Cell and Developmental Biology, Advanced Medical Discovery Inst., Ont. Cancer Inst. 1974–, Head of Div. of Cellular and Molecular Biology 1991–93, currently Dir Advanced Medical Discovery Inst.; mem. Inst. of Medical Science, Univ. of Toronto 1979–, Prof., Dept of Medical Biophysics and Dept of Immunology 1984–, Grad. Sec., Dept of Medical Biophysics 1995–2001; Dir Amgen Research Inst. 1993–2004; Dir Campbell Family Inst. for Breast Cancer Research, Princess Margaret Hosp., Toronto 2004–; Ed. or Assoc. Ed. The International Journal of Immunology, The Immunologist, Current Opinion in Immunology, Cancer Cell, Proceedings of the National Academy of Sciences, USA; mem. numerous advisory bds of scientific journals and medical centres; Hon. Prof., Dept of Pathology, Univ. of Hong Kong 2004–07; E. W. R. Steacie Award, Nat. Sciences and Eng Research Council 1984, Ayerst Award, Canadian Biochemical Soc. 1985, Merit Award, Fed. of Chinese Professionals of Canada 1985, Stacie Prize, Stacie Trust Foundation 1986, Canadian Asscn of Mfrs of Medical Devices Award 1988, Emil von Behring Prize, Phillips-Universität Marburg (FRG) 1988, Univ. of Alberta 75th Anniversary Distinguished Scientist Award 1989, Gairdner Int. Award, Gairdner Foundation 1989, RSC McLaughlin Medal 1990, Canadian Foundation for AIDS Research Award 1991, Cinader Award 1994, Royal Soc. of London 1994, Sloan Prize, General Motors Cancer Foundation 1994, King

Faisal Int. Prize for Medicine 1995, Izaak Walton Killam Prize 2003, Paul Ehrlich and Ludwig Darmstaedter Prize 2003. *Achievements include:* recognized world-wide for his discovery of T cell receptor (TCR), a key component of the immune system. *Publications:* more than 600 scientific papers in professional journals. *Leisure interests:* music, tennis, golf. *Address:* Prince Margaret Hospital, 7th Floor Room 706, 620 University Avenue, Toronto, ON M5G 2C1, Canada (office). *Telephone:* (416) 946-4501 exts 2234, 2997 (office). *E-mail:* tmak@uhnres.utoronto.ca (office). *Website:* medbio.utoronto.ca/faculty/mak.html (office).

MAKANIN, Vladimir Semenovich; Russian writer; b. 13 March 1937, Orsk, Orenburg Region; ed Moscow Univ., Higher Workshop for Scenario Writers and Film Dirs; started writing 1965; Russian Booker Prize 1993, Pushkin Prize 1998, Penne Prize, Italy 1999, Russian State Prize 2000. *Publications include:* Straight Line 1965, Air-Vent, Portrait and Around (novel) 1976, Story about an Old Settlement (collection of short stories) 1974, Voices 1982, River with a Fast Current 1983, Where the Skies Meet the Hills 1987, One and One 1987, Subject of Averaging 1992, The Loss: A Novella and Two Stories (Writings from an Unbound Europe), Baize-Covered Table with Decanter 1993, Quasi 1993, Captives 1996, Escape Hatch and The Long Road Ahead: Two Novellas 1998, Underground, or a Hero of Our Time 1998, Letter A 2000, A Good Love Story 2000. *Address:* Novinski Boulevard 16, Apartment 14, 121069 Moscow, Russia. *Telephone:* (495) 291-92-53. *Fax:* (495) 781-01-82. *E-mail:* vmakanin@hotmail.com.

MAKARCZYK, Jerzy, LLD; Polish judge and professor of law; *Professor of Legal Sciences, Polish Academy of Sciences;* b. 24 July 1938; s. of Zbigniew Makarczyk and Hanna Olszowska; ed Warsaw Univ. and Inst. of Legal Sciences, Polish Acad. of Sciences; Assoc. Prof. of Int. Public Law 1975, Prof. 1988; Deputy Dir Inst. of Legal Sciences, Polish Acad. of Sciences 1981–88, Prof. 1992–; Deputy Minister of Foreign Affairs 1989–90; Sec. of State, Ministry of Foreign Affairs 1990–92; in charge of negotiations with USSR and then Russia on withdrawal of troops from Polish territory 1990–2002; Judge, European Court of Human Rights 1992–; mem. ILO High Level Team to Myanmar 2001–; Adviser to Pres. of Repub. of Poland 2002–; Pres. Int. Law Asscn 1988–90; mem. Inst de Droit Int. 1993, Pres. 2003–; nominated cand.-judge to European Communities Court of Justice 2004; Commdr Légion d'honneur; Manfred Lachs Foundation Award 1998. *Publications:* Financing of Economic Development in the United Nations System 1974, Principles of a New International Economic Order 1988; ed. Collection of Essays in Honour of Judge Manfred Lachs 1984, Theory of International Law at the Threshold of the XXIst Century (ed.) 1996. *Leisure interests:* tennis, sailing. *Address:* Al. Przyjaciol 3 m. 14, 00-565 Warsaw, Poland. *Telephone:* (22) 6769135. *Fax:* (22) 6429540. *E-mail:* jmakarczyk@prezydent.pl.

MAKAREVICH, Andrei Vadimovich; Russian composer, singer and artist; b. 11 Dec. 1953, Moscow; one s.; ed Moscow Inst. of Architecture; founder, artistic dir, soloist, Time Machine (first professional rock group in Russia) 1969–; creator, presenter Smak (TV programme); Leader, Creol Tango Orchestra; drawings have been exhibited in Moscow, St Petersburg, Riga, Caserta (Italy); merited artist RSFSR, Order of Honour, Order of Contribution to the Motherland. *Recordings:* 26 albums, including music for nine films. *Publications:* nine books of poetry and prose. *Leisure interest:* underwater hunting. *Address:* ORT (Russian Public TV), Smak, Akademika Koroleva str. 12, 127000 Moscow, Russia (office). *Telephone:* (495) 217-79-88 (office); (495) 367-63-09 (office). *Website:* www.mashina.ru (office); www.makar.info.

MAKAROV, Andrey Mikhailovich, CJur; Russian barrister; b. 22 July 1954, Moscow; ed Moscow State Univ.; worked in Research Inst., USSR Ministry of Internal Affairs 1976–83; mem. Moscow City Bd of Lawyers 1983–, acted as the defence lawyer in numerous major trials, including trial of fmr Deputy Minister of Internal Affairs V. Churbanov; Chief of Dept supervising activities of Comm. of Security Council in struggle against crime and corruption July–Oct. 1993; mem. State Duma (Parl.) 1993–, Vice-Chair. Budget and Taxation Cttee; Exec. Dir Russian br. of SOROS Foundation; Pres. Chess Fed. of Russia 1994–97; mem. Exec. Cttee Int. Chess Fed. (FIDE); Head, Barristers co. A. Makarov and A. Tobak 1998–; Chair. Council of Experts on Improving Tax System, State Duma 2000–. *Address:* Andrey Makarov and Aleksandr Tobak Barristers Bureau, Leningradsky Prospect 39A, 125167 Moscow, Russia (office). *Telephone:* (495) 213-86-94 (office).

MAKAROV, Igor Mikhailovich, DSc; Russian scientist; b. 22 Oct. 1927, Saratov; s. of Mikhail Ilyich Makarov and Yelena Ivanovna Makarova; m. Praskovia Alexandrovna Makarova 1953; one s.; ed S Ordzhonikidze Moscow Aviation Inst.; scientific worker and chief of lab. 1949–72; Instructor, Deputy Chief, Dept of Science and Educ., C.P.S.U. 1962–75; Deputy Minister for Higher and Specialized Secondary Educ. of USSR 1975–88; Corresp. mem. USSR (now Russian) Acad. of Sciences 1974–87, mem. 1987–; Chief Scientific Sec. Presidium of USSR (now Russian) Acad. of Sciences 1988–92, Chief Scientific Sec. Russian Acad. of Sciences 1992–96, Adviser to Pres. 1996–; Chair. Dept of Cybernetics, Moscow Inst. of Radio-electronics and Automation 1978–; Russian Rep. to Int. Council of Scientific Unions; Chair. Scientific Council on Robotics and Flexible Mfg, Russian Acad. of Sciences; Deputy Chief Ed. Automatic Control; mem. Editorial Bd Future of Science, Science and Humanity; Chief Ed. Herald of the Russian Acad. of Sciences; Chief Ed. Series Cybernetics; Deputy Chief Ed. Automation and Telemechanics; USSR State Prize 1984, Russian State Prize 1995; Order of Red Banner of Labour. *Publications:* Linear Automatic Systems 1975, Theory of Automatic Control (2 Vols) 1977, Objective-oriented Complex Programs 1980, Theory of Choice and Decision-making 1982, Cybernetics Today: Achievements, Challenges, Prospects 1984, Cybernetics and Informatics 1986, Informatics and Progress in Science and Technology 1987, Time-Impulse Automatic Control System 1998, Logistical Differential Models of Technological Transfer 1999; numerous

scientific papers on man. and control, artificial intelligence, robotics, mfg tech., educ. *Leisure interests:* tennis, skiing, hunting. *Address:* Presidium of the Russian Academy of Sciences, 32A Leninsky Prospect, 119991 Moscow GSP-1, Russia. *Telephone:* (495) 938-19-06. *Fax:* (495) 938-53-68.

MAKAROV, Gen. Nikolai; Russian army officer and government official; *Chief of the General Staff, Russian Armed Forces;* b. 7 Oct. 1949, Glebovo, Ryazan Oblast, Russian SFSR; m.; two s.; ed Moscow Combined Arms Command School, Frunze Mil. Acad., Gen. Staff Acad.; assumed command over a platoon (later, co. and bn) with the Group of Soviet Forces in Germany, Deputy Regiment Commdr, later Deputy Div. Commdr, later Motorized Rifle Div. Commdr, fmr Baikal Mil. Dist 1979–93, apptd Chief of Staff, Russian Jt Force, Tajikistan 1993, later assigned to Volga Mil. Dist as Chief of Staff for an ind. army, Land and Seashore Force Commdr, Baltic Fleet 1998–99, First Deputy Commdr, Moscow Mil. Dist 1999–2002, Commdr Siberian Mil. Dist 2002–05, rank of Gen. of the Army 2005, Chief of the ?rmament for Russian Armed Forces and Deputy Minister of Defence 2007–08, Chief of the Gen. Staff and First Deputy Minister of Defence 2008–. *Address:* Ministry of Defence, 105175 Moscow, ul. Myasnitskaya 37, Russian Federation (office). *Telephone:* (495) 696-44-38 (office). *Fax:* (495) 696-84-37 (office). *E-mail:* info@mil.ru (office). *Website:* www.mil.ru (office).

MAKAROV, Gen. Nikolai; Russian army officer and government official; *Chief of the General Staff, Russian Armed Forces;* b. 7 Oct. 1949, Glebovo, Ryazan Oblast, Russian SFSR; m.; two s.; ed Moscow Combined Arms Command School, Frunze Mil. Acad., Gen. Staff Acad.; assumed command over a platoon (later, co. and bn) with the Group of Soviet Forces in Germany, Deputy Regiment Commdr, later Deputy Div. Commdr, later Motorized Rifle Div. Commdr, fmr Baikal Mil. Dist 1979–93, apptd Chief of Staff, Russian Jt Force, Tajikistan 1993, later assigned to Volga Mil. Dist as Chief of Staff for an ind. army, Land and Seashore Force Commdr, Baltic Fleet 1998–99, First Deputy Commdr, Moscow Mil. Dist 1999–2002, Commdr Siberian Mil. Dist 2002–05, rank of Gen. of the Army 2005, Chief of the ?rmament for Russian Armed Forces and Deputy Minister of Defence 2007–08, Chief of the Gen. Staff and First Deputy Minister of Defence 2008–. *Address:* Ministry of Defence, 105175 Moscow, ul. Myasnitskaya 37, Russian Federation (office). *Telephone:* (495) 696-44-38 (office). *Fax:* (495) 696-84-37 (office). *E-mail:* info@mil.ru (office). *Website:* www.mil.ru (office).

MAKAROV, Gen. Nikolai; Russian army officer and government official; *Chief of the General Staff, Russian Armed Forces;* b. 7 Oct. 1949, Glebovo, Ryazan Oblast, Russian SFSR; m.; two s.; ed Moscow Combined Arms Command School, Frunze Mil. Acad., Gen. Staff Acad.; assumed command over a platoon (later, co. and bn) with the Group of Soviet Forces in Germany, Deputy Regiment Commdr, later Deputy Div. Commdr, later Motorized Rifle Div. Commdr, fmr Baikal Mil. Dist 1979–93, apptd Chief of Staff, Russian Jt Force, Tajikistan 1993, later assigned to Volga Mil. Dist as Chief of Staff for an ind. army, Land and Seashore Force Commdr, Baltic Fleet 1998–99, First Deputy Commdr, Moscow Mil. Dist 1999–2002, Commdr Siberian Mil. Dist 2002–05, rank of Gen. of the Army 2005, Chief of the ?rmament for Russian Armed Forces and Deputy Minister of Defence 2007–08, Chief of the Gen. Staff and First Deputy Minister of Defence 2008–. *Address:* Ministry of Defence, 105175 Moscow, ul. Myasnitskaya 37, Russia (office). *Telephone:* (495) 696-44-38 (office). *Fax:* (495) 696-84-37 (office). *E-mail:* info@mil.ru (office). *Website:* www.mil.ru (office).

MAKAROV, Gen. Nikolai; Russian army officer and government official; *Chief of the General Staff, Russian Armed Forces;* b. 7 Oct. 1949, Glebovo, Ryazan Oblast, Russian SFSR; m.; two s.; ed Moscow Combined Arms Command School, Frunze Mil. Acad., Gen. Staff Acad.; assumed command over a platoon (later co. and bn) with the Group of Soviet Forces in Germany, Deputy Regiment Commdr, later Deputy Div. Commdr, later Motorized Rifle Div. Commdr, fmr Baikal Mil. Dist 1979–93, apptd Chief of Staff, Russian Joint Force, Tajikistan 1993, later assigned to Volga Mil. Dist as Chief of Staff for an ind. army, Land and Seashore Force Commdr, Baltic Fleet 1998–99, First Deputy Commdr, Moscow Mil. Dist 1999–2002, Commdr Siberian Mil. Dist 2002–05, rank of Gen. of the Army 2005, Chief of the Armament for Russian Armed Forces and Deputy Minister of Defence 2007–08, Chief of the Gen. Staff and First Deputy Minister of Defence 2008–. *Address:* Ministry of Defence, 105175 Moscow, ul. Myasnitskaya 37, Russia (office). *Telephone:* (495) 696-44-38 (office). *Fax:* (495) 696-84-37 (office). *E-mail:* info@mil.ru (office). *Website:* www.mil.ru (office).

MAKAROV, Valery Leonidovich, PhD; Russian economist; *Director, Central Economics and Mathematics Institute, Russian Academy of Sciences;* b. 25 May 1937, Novosibirsk; s. of Leonid Makarov and Dina Yershov; m. Irena Nikolaev 1961; one s. one d.; ed Moscow Econ. Inst.; scientific worker, Inst. of Math., Siberian Div. USSR Acad. of Sciences 1961–67, Lab. Chief 1967–73, Deputy Dir 1973–80, Gen. Sec. Siberian Div. 1980–83; Prof. of Mathematical Econs Novosibirsk Univ. 1970–83; Dir Nat. Inst. of Industrial Man., Moscow 1983–85; Dir Central Econs and Math. Inst. 1985–; Prof. at Moscow Univ.; Founder and Rector, New Econ. School, Moscow 1992–; Ed.-in-Chief, Journal of Math. and Econ. Methods.; mem. Ed. Bd Econs of Planning, Econs of Transition, Econ. Systems Research; mem. Exec. Cttee, Int. Econ. Asscn 1995–; mem. several govt comms; Corresp. mem. USSR (now Russian) Acad. of Science 1979, mem. 1990; Fellow Econometric Soc.; Kantorovich Award (for contrib. to econ. theory) 1995. *Publications:* Mathematical Theory of Economic Dynamics and Equilibria (with A. Rubinov) 1977, Models and Computers in Economics 1979, Computer Simulation in Analysis of Regional Problems 1987, Mathematical Economic Theory: Pure and Mixed Types of Economic Mechanisms (with A. Rubinov and M. Levin) 1994. *Leisure interests:* tennis, skiing. *Address:* Central Economics and Mathematics Institute, Russian Academy of

Sciences, Nakhimouski Prospect 47, 117418 Moscow, Russia. *Telephone:* (495) 129-10-11 (office); (495) 229-01-50 (home). *Fax:* (495) 310-70-15.

MAKAROVA, Inna Vladimirovna; Russian actress; b. 28 July 1926, Taiga, Kemerovo Dist; d. of Vladimir Makarov and Anna German; m. 1st S. Bondarchuk 1947; m. 2nd M. Perelman; one d.; ed All-Union Film Inst.; Order of Red Banner of Labour, Order of Merit RSFSR 1967; USSR State Prize 1949, People's Artist of USSR 1985. *Films include:* Molodaya gvardiya (The Young Guard) 1948, Selskiy vrach (The Village Doctor) 1951, Vozvrashcheniye Vasiliya Bortnikova (The Return of Vasili Bortnikov) 1952, Dimitrovgradtsy (People of Dimitrovgrad) 1956, Vysota (Height) 1957, Dorogoy moy chelovek (My Dear Fellow!) 1958, Nash korespondent 1959, Devchata (Girls) 1961, Bratya Komarovy 1961, Zhenitba Balzaminova (The Marriage of Balzaminov) 1964, Bolshaya ruda (The Big Ore) 1964, Zhenshchiny 1966, Malenkiy beglets (The Little Runaway) 1966, Urok literatury (A Literature Lesson) 1968, Novenkaya (The Rookie) 1968, Prestupleniye i nakazaniye (Crime and Punishment) 1969, Lyubov Yarovaya 1970, Russkoye pole (Russian Field) 1971, Neispravimyy lgun (Incorrigible Liar) 1973, Bezotvetnaya lyubov (Unanswered Love) 1979, Kontrolnaya po spetsialnosti 1981, Zhivaya raduga (Living Rainbow) 1982, Detstvo Bambi (Bambi's Childhood) 1985, Yunost Bambi (Bambi's Youth) 1986, Lermontov 1986, Ssuda na brak (Loan for a Marriage) 1987, Bolshaya lyubov 2006. *Television includes:* Vas vyzyvaet Taymyr (Taimyr Calls You) 1970, Harsnatsun hyusisits (A Bride from the North) 1975, Pechniki (Stove Builders) 1982, Myortvye dushi (Dead Souls) (mini-series) 1984, Maritsa 1985. *Leisure interest:* gardening. *Address:* 121059 Moscow, Ukrainian Blvd 11, Apt 14, Russia. *Telephone:* (495) 243-00-93.

MAKAROVA, Natalia Romanovna; Russian ballerina; b. 1940, Leningrad; m. 3rd Edward Karkar 1976; one s.; ed Vagonova Ballet School, Leningrad; mem. Kirov Ballet 1959–70; sought political asylum, London 1970; Prin. Dancer, American Ballet Theater 1970–92; appeared with Kirov Co. in London 1988, USSR 1989; f. Makarova and Co. 1980; Guest Artist, Royal Ballet 1972; Guest Artist, London Festival Ballet 1984; retd from dancing 1992; Dir Sleeping Beauty, Royal Ballet 2003; Honoured Artist of RSFSR, Carina Ari Medal 2006. *Television:* In a Class of Her Own, Assoluta, Natasha 1985, Makarova Returns 1989, Great Railway Journeys: St Petersburg to Tashkent 1994. *Plays:* On Your Toes (musical), Broadway, New York (Tony Award for Best Actress in a Musical), West End, London (Laurence Olivier Award) 1984, Tovarich, Chichester Festival then West End, London 1991, Two for the Seesaw, Moscow 1992. *Publications:* A Dance Autobiography 1979, On Your Toes 1984.

MAKHALINA, Yulia Victorovna; Russian ballet dancer; b. 23 June 1968, St Petersburg; ed Vaganova Acad. of Russian Ballet under Prof. Marina Vasilyeva; ballet dancer, Mariinsky Theatre 1985–89, Prin. Dancer 1989–; Gold Medal and Grand Prix, Fourth Int. Ballet Competition in Paris 1990, Prix de Lumière (Italy), Merited Artist of Russia 1995, Benois de la Dance Prize 1998. *Roles include:* Aurora and Lilac Fairy (Sleeping Beauty), Giselle and Myrtha (Giselle), Kitri (Don Quixote), Medora (Le Corsaire), Odette/Odile (Swan Lake), Nikiya and Gamzatti (La Bayadère), Mekhmene and Banu (Legend of Love), Raymonda (Raymonda), Sylphide (La Sylphide), Maria (Fountain of Bakhchisarai), Juliet (Romeo and Juliet), Zobeide (Sheherezade), Fire Bird (Firebird), Maria Taglioni (Pas de Quatre), (Dying Swan), Anna (Anna Karenina), Fairy (Cinderella), Carmen (Carmen), Duchess of Alba (Goya Divertissement), Terpsichore (Apollo), Second Movt (Symphony in C), Third Movt (In the Night), Manon (Manon), (Youth and Death), Soloist ("Paquita" Grand Pas), Soloist (Theme and Variations). *Address:* Mariinsky Theatre, Teatralnaya pl. 1, St Petersburg, Russia (office). *Telephone:* (812) 315-57-12 (office).

MAKHMALBAF, Mohsen; Iranian film director and novelist; b. 1957, Tehran; Ecumenical Jury Prize (for Kandahar), Cannes Int. Film Festival 2001. *Films:* Nasooh Repentance 1982, Two Sightless Eyes 1983, Seeking Sanctuary 1984, The Boycott 1985, The Pedlar 1987, The Cyclist 1988, Marriage of the Blessed 1989, Time of Love 1991, Nights of Zayandeh Rude 1991, Once Upon a Time...the Cinema 1992, The Actor 1993, A Selection of Images in Ghajar Dynasty 1993, Stone and Glass 1994, Salam Cinema 1994, Gabbeh 1996, A Moment of Innocence 1996, The Apple 1998, The Silence 1998, Kandahar 2001. *Appearances include:* Joy of Madness (documentary) 2004. *Address:* Green Film House, 98 Mirdamad Boulevard, PO Box 19395/4866, Tehran, Iran (office); c/o MK2 Diffusion, 55 rue Traversière, 75012 Paris, France (office). *Telephone:* (21) 2225960 (Iran) (office); 1-43-07-92-74 (France) (office). *Fax:* (21) 2270970 (Iran) (office); 1-43-41-32-30 (France) (office). *Website:* www.makhmalbaf.com (office).

MAKHMALBAF, Samira; Iranian film director; b. 1980, Tehran; d. of Mohsen Makhmalbaf. *Films include:* The Apple (Jury Prize, Cannes Film Festival) 1998, Takhte Siah (Blackboards) 2000, At Five in the Afternoon 2003, Two Legged Horse 2008. *Appearances include:* Joy of Madness (documentary) 2004. *Address:* c/o Hojatoleslam Sayed Muhammad Khatami, Office of the President, Pastor Avenue, Tehran, Iran.

MAKHMUDOV, Lt-Gen. Eldar Akhmed oğlu; Azerbaijani government official and politician; *Minister of National Security;* b. 1956, Baku; m.; three c.; ed D. Bunyatzade Inst. of Economy, Baku State Univ.; career in mil. service; served Organized Crime and Criminal Investigation Divs, Ministry of Interior 1980–2004, positions included Chief of Br, Drugs Suppression Unit 1993, Chief, Economic Crimes Dept, Chief of Branch, Drugs Suppression Dept 2004; Minister of Nat. Security 2004–; promoted to Maj.-Gen. 2004, to Lt-Gen. 2005. *Address:* Ministry of National Security, 1602 Baku, Parliament pr. 2, Azerbaijan (office). *Telephone:* (12) 493-76-22 (office). *Fax:* (12) 495-04-91 (office). *E-mail:* cpr@mns.gov.az (office). *Website:* www.mns.gov.az (office).

MAKHULU, Most Rev. Walter Paul Khotso, CMG; British ecclesiastic; b. 2 July 1935, Johannesburg, SA; s. of Paul Makhulu; m. Rosemary Makhulu 1966; one s. one d.; ed Pimville Govt School, Johannesburg, Khaiso Secondary School, Coll. of the Resurrection and St Peter, SA, St Andrew's Coll., Birmingham; Area Sec. for Eastern Africa and African Refugees, Comm. on Inter-Church Aid Refugee and World Service, World Council of Churches 1975–79; Bishop of Botswana 1979–2000; Archbishop of Cen. Africa 1980–2000, Archbishop Emer. 2000–; Pres. All Africa Conf. of Churches 1981–86; Pres. World Council of Churches 1983–91; Hon. Curate Holy Trinity, Geneva; Presidential Order of Honour (Botswana) 2002, Officier, l'Ordre des palmes académiques 1981; Hon. DD (Kent) 1988, (Gen. Theological Seminary, New York) 1990. *Leisure interests:* music, int. affairs. *Address:* Cheyne House, 10 Crondace Road, Fulham, London, SW6 4BB, England. *Telephone:* (20) 7371-9419 (office). *E-mail:* bishmak@makhulu.fsnet.co.uk (office).

MAKI, Fumihiko, MArch; Japanese architect; *Principal Partner, Maki and Associates;* b. 6 Sept. 1928, Tokyo; m.; two c.; ed Univ. of Tokyo, Cranbrook Acad. of Art, Mich., Harvard Univ. Grad. School of Design, USA; Assoc. Prof., Washington Univ. 1956–62, Harvard Univ. 1962–66; Lecturer, Dept of Urban Eng, Univ. of Tokyo 1964–79, Prof. of Architecture 1979–89; Prin. Pnr, Maki and Assocs 1964–; Hon. FAIA 1980, FRIBA; Hon. Fellow, German Inst. of Architects, French Acad. of Architecture, Czech Inst. of Architects, Mexican Inst. of Architects, Bund Deutscher Architekten, American Acad. of Arts & Sciences, Academia Scientiarum et Artium Europaea, Royal Australian Inst. of Architects, Royal Incorporation of Architects in Scotland, Taiwan Inst. of Architects; Officier, Ordre des Arts et Lettres 1998; Hon. Dr of Art and Architecture (Washington, USA); Wolf Foundation Prize in Arts 1988, Thomas Jefferson Medal for Architecture 1990, Int. Union of Architects (UIA) Gold Medal 1993, Pritzker Architecture Prize 1993, Prince of Wales Prize in Urban Design 1993, Arnold Brunner Memorial Prize in Architecture 1994, Praemium Imperiale 1999. *Major works include:* Toyoda Memorial Hall, Nagoya Univ. 1960, Nat. Aquarium, Okinawa 1975, Hillside Terrace Housing Complex 1978–98, Iwasaki Art Museum 1979, Keio Univ. Library, Mita Campus 1981, Spiral 1985 (Reynolds Memorial Award 1987), Nat. Museum of Modern Art, Kyoto 1985, Tepia 1989, Nippon Convention Centre (Makuhari Messe) Stage 1 1989, Stage 2 1998, Tokyo Metropolitan Gymnasium 1990, Keio Univ. Fujisawa Campus 1992, YKK Research and Devt Centre 1993, Center for Arts Yerba Buena Gardens 1993, Isar Buropark 1995, Kaze-No-Oka Crematorium 1996, TV Asahi HQ 2003, Toki Messe 2003, Nat. Inst. for Japanese Language Tachikawa, Tokyo 2004, Sam Fox School of Design and Visual Arts, Washington Univ. 2006, Shimane Museum of Ancient Izumo 2007, Mihara Performing Arts Center 2007, Repub. Polytechnic Singapore 2007, Toyoda Memorial Hall Renovation, Nagoya, Aichi 2007, Univ. of Pennsylvania Annenberg Public Policy Center 2008, Novartis Campus, Basel, Switzerland 2009, MIT Media Arts and Sciences Building, Massachusetts, USA 2009. *Publications include:* Investigations in Collective Form 1964, Movement Systems in the City 1965, Metabolism 1960, Structure in Art and Science (contrib.) 1965, Miegakuresuru Toshi: A Morphological Analysis of the City of Edo-Tokyo 1979, Kioku no Keisho: A Collection of Essays 1992, Selected Passages on the City and Architecture 2000, Nurturing Dreams: Collected Essays on Architecture and the City 2008. *Address:* 13-4, Hachiyama-cho, Shibuya-ku, Tokyo 150-0035 (office); 16-22, 5-chome Higashi-Gotanda, Shinagawa-ku, Tokyo 141-0022, Japan (home). *Telephone:* (3) 3780-3880 (office). *Fax:* (3) 3780-3881 (office). *E-mail:* fmaki@maki-and-associates.co.jp (office). *Website:* www.maki-and-associates.co.jp (office).

MAKIHARA, Minoru, BA; Japanese business executive; *Senior Corporate Advisor, Mitsubishi Corporation;* b. 12 Jan. 1930, Hampstead, England; m. Kikuko Makihara; ed in England, Japan, Harvard Univ.; joined Mitsubishi Corpn Marine Products Dept 1956–59, London Br. 1959–70, Rep. Mitsubishi Int. Seattle and Washington 1970–80, Gen. Man. Marine Products Dept, Tokyo 1980–87, Pres. Mitsubishi Int. New York 1987–90, Sr Man. Dir Mitsubishi Corpn, also Chair. Mitsubishi Int. 1990–92, apptd Pres. Mitsubishi Corpn 1992, Chair. 1998–2004, now Sr Corp. Advisor; mem. Chair.'s Council DaimlerChrysler AG 2001–; mem. Bd of Dirs IBM Corpn 1997–2003, 2004–; mem. Int. Advisory Council Coca-Cola Co., J.P. Morgan Chase & Co., Inc. *Address:* Mitsubishi Corporation, 6-3, Marunouchi 2-chome, Chiyoda-ku, Tokyo, 100-8086, Japan (office). *Telephone:* (3) 3210-2121 (office). *Fax:* (3) 3210-8583 (office). *Website:* www.mitsubishi.co.jp (office).

MAKINE, Andreï; French/Russian writer; b. 1957, Siberia; s. of Maria Stepanovna Dolina; worked as teacher of literature in Novgorod; emigrated from USSR to France 1987, writes in French; Priz de la Fondation Prince Pierre de Monaco 2005. *Play:* Le Monde selon Gabriel 2007. *Publications:* fiction: La Fille d'un Héros (trans. as A Hero's Daughter) 1990, Confession d'un Porte-Drapeau Déchu (trans. as Confessions of a Fallen Standard-Bearer) 1992, Au Temps du Fleuve Amour (trans. as Once Upon the River Love) 1994, Le Testament Français (trans. as Dreams of My Russian Summers; Prix Goncourt, Prix Médicis Étranger, Prix Goncourt des Lycéens, Eeva Joenpelto Prize, Finland) 1995, Le Crime d'Olga Arbelina (trans. as The Crime of Olga Arbelina 1998, Requiem pour l'Est (trans. as Requiem for a Lost Empire 2001, La Musique d'un Vie (trans. as A Life's Music; Prix RTL-Lire) 2001, La Terre et le ciel de Jacques Dorme (trans. as The Earth and Sky of Jacques Dorme) 2003, La Femme qui Attendait (trans. as The Woman Who Waited; Prix Lanterna Magica 2005) 2004, L'Amour Humain 2006; non-fiction: St Pétersbourg (with Ferrante Ferranti) 2002, Cette France qu'on oublie d'aimer 2006. *Address:* c/o Editions du Seuil, 27, rue Jacob, 75006 Paris, France (office). *Website:* www.editionsduseuil.fr (office).

MÄKINEN, Tommi; Finnish fmr racing driver; b. 26 June 1964, Puuppola, Jyväskylä; s. of Jukka Mäkinen; pnr Eliisa Järvelä; two s.; first competed on farm tractors, won jr Finnish nat. ploughing title 1982, 1985, sr title 1992;

began rally car racing career in Finnish Championships 1985; Group N Finnish Champion 1988; won Arctic Rally 1989; with Nissan Motorsports Europe Team 1992; with Mitsubishi Ralliart Europe Team 1995–2001 (World Rally Champion 1996, 1997, 1998, 1999), set record for most world championship rally race wins (24 victories 1994–2002); record four consecutive wins at the Monte Carlo Rally –2002; with Subaru World Rally Team 2002–03. *Leisure interests:* skiing, cycling, trial biking, hunting. *Address:* c/o Fédération internationale de l'automobile, 8 place de la Concorde, 75008 Paris, France. *Website:* www.tommimakinen.net (office).

MAKK, Károly; Hungarian film director; b. 22 Dec. 1925; s. of Kálmán Makk and Emma Szmolka; m. Hanna Reichel Dömötör; one s. one d.; ed Budapest Univ. of Sciences, Univ. of Dramatic and Cinematic Arts; asst lecturer 1953, lecturer 1959–; mem. Univ. Council; worked as assistant Dir MAFILM Studio 1946–53, Dir 1954–; Guest Lecturer Istituto Centro Sperimentale per Film, Rome 1976 and German Film Acad., Munich 1973–74; mem. Hungarian Acad. of Art 1992–; Merited Artist and Eminent Artist titles, Balázs Béla Prize 1959, Kossuth Prize 1973, Outstanding Artist Prize 1982, Lifetime Achievement Award, Figueira da Foz, Portugal 1986, Life Achievement Award, Hungarian Film Festival 1994, Life Achievement Award, Karlovy Vary 2000, Master of Motion Picture, Hungary 2004. *Films directed include:* Liliomfi (Cannes selection) 1954, Ház a sziklák alatt (House under the Rocks) 1957 (San Francisco Grand Prix 1959), 39-es dandár (The Brigade No. 39) 1959, Megszállottak (The Fanatics) 1962, Elveszett paradicsom (The Lost Paradise) 1963, Az utolsó előtti ember (The Last but One) 1963, Isten és ember előtti (Before God and Man) 1968, Szerelem (Love) 1970 (1971 Int. Journalist Fed. Award and Jury's Special Award of Cannes), Macskajáték (Catsplay, nominated for Acad. Award) 1974, Egy erkölcsös éjszaka (A very moral night) 1977, Két történet a félmúltból (Two stories from the Recent Past), A téglafal mögött (Behind the Brick Wall), Philemon and Baucis, 1981, Egymásra nézve (Another Way) 1981 (1982 Int. Critiques Award and Best Female Performance of Cannes), Játszani kell (Playing for Keeps) 1984, Az utolsó kézirat (The Last Manuscript) 1987, Magyar rekviem (Hungarian Requiem) 1990, Magyar Pizza 1995, Játékos (The Gambler) 1997 (1998 Best Film, Pescara), Egy Hèt Pesten Ès Budàn (A Long Weekend in Pest and Buda) 2003. *Plays directed:* Enigma Variations 1998, Rebecaa 1999, WIT 2001. *Leisure interests:* reading, writing, tennis, riding. *Address:* 1022 Budapest, Hankóczy Jenő utca 15, Hungary. *Telephone:* (1) 326-9314. *Fax:* (1) 326-9314 (home). *E-mail:* ggaleria@axelero.hu (office).

MAKKAWI, Khalil, PhD; Lebanese diplomatist; *President, Lebanese-Palestinian Dialogue Committee;* b. 15 Jan. 1930, Beirut; s. of Abdel Basset Makkawi and Rosa Makkawi; m. Zahira Sibaei 1958; one s. one d.; ed American Univ. of Beirut, Cairo Univ., Egypt, Columbia Univ., New York, USA; joined Foreign Ministry 1957, served in UN Section 1957–59, Deputy Perm. Rep. to UN, New York 1961–64, First Sec., Embassy in Washington, DC 1964–67, Chief of Int. Relations Dept, Foreign Ministry, Beirut 1967–70, Counsellor, Embassy in London 1970–71, Minister Plenipotentiary, London 1971–73, Amb. to GDR 1973–78, to UK and Repub. of Ireland 1978–83; Dir Political Dept, Foreign Ministry, Beirut, Chair. Preparatory Cttee of Lebanese Nat. Dialogue, mem. Lebanese Security Arrangement Cttee for South of Lebanon 1983–85, Amb. to Italy and Perm. Rep. to FAO 1985–90, Perm. Rep. to UN, New York 1990–94; Vice-Chair. Exec. Bd UNICEF 1993–95, Pres. 1995; Co-Chair. Int. Support Group for mine clearance in Lebanon (representing Ministry of Nat. Defence) 2002–05; Pres. Lebanese-Palestinian Dialogue Cttee, Presidency of the Council of Ministers; Pres. Worldwide Alumni Asscn of Univ. of Beirut 2007–; Chevalier, Nat. Order of the Cedar (Lebanon), Great Cross of Merit (Italy). *Leisure interests:* music, swimming, reading, walking. *Address:* Bldg Al-Nada, 9th Floor, John Kennedy Street, Ein Mareissi, Beirut, Lebanon (home). *Telephone:* (1) 362662 (home). *Fax:* (1) 372550 (home). *E-mail:* khalil30@inco.com.lb (home).

MAKKI, Mohammed Hassan, DEcon; Yemeni politician and diplomatist; b. 22 Dec. 1933; ed Univs of Bologna and Rome; adviser, Ministry of Econ. 1960–62, Deputy Minister 1962, Minister 1963–64; Minister of Foreign Affairs April–Sept. 1966, 1967–68; Amb. to Italy 1968–70, 1977–79, to FRG 1970–72; Deputy Prime Minister 1972–74; Prime Minister March–June 1974; Deputy Prime Minister for Econ. Affairs June–Oct. 1974, 1980–84; Perm. Rep. to UN 1974–76, in Vienna 2000, Amb. to USA (also accred to Canada) 1975–76; Deputy Prime Minister of Yemen Arab Repub. 1985–90; First Deputy Prime Minister of Repub. of Yemen 1990–93.

MAKLAKOVS, Brig.-Gen. Juris; Latvian military officer; *Commander, National Armed Forces;* b. 27 Oct. 1964, Ņukšu; m.; one s.; ed Mil. Aviation Eng School, US Army War Coll.; radio technician, Mil. Aviation Eng School 1985–87, Head of Radio Tech. Equipment Service Group 1987–88; Chief Engineer, Computer Centre, Nat. Defence Acad. 1993, Lecturer, Dept of Mil. Weapons and their Usage 1993–94, Dept of Eng 1994–95, Head of Dept of Eng 1995–97, Deputy Commdt in Academics 1997–2001, Commdt Nat. Defence Acad. 2001–04; Air Force Commdr 2004–06; Commdr Nat. Armed Forces 2006–; Button Award 1997, Honour Sign for contribs to devt of Latvian Nat. Armed Forces 2000, Honour Sign of Recognition Award 2001, Memorial Medal 2004. *Address:* Ministry of Defence, K. Valdemāra iela 10–12, Rīga 1473, Latvia (office). *Telephone:* 6721-0124 (office). *Fax:* 6721-2307 (office). *E-mail:* kanceleja@mod.gov.lv (office). *Website:* www.mod.gov.lv (office).

MAKOGON, Yuri Feodorovich, MSc, DSc; Ukrainian physicist and engineer; *Visiting Professor/Research Associate, Texas A&M University;* b. 15 May 1930, Kherson; s. of Feodor Ivanovich Makogon and Efrosinia Dmitrievna Shevchenko; m. Inna Aleksandrovna Makogon 1961; one s. one d.; ed Krasnodar Tech. School, Gubkin Petroleum Inst., Moscow; worked at Shebelinskoe Gas-condensate Field, Ukraine 1956–58; Asst then Asst Prof., Gubkin Oil and Gas, Moscow Inst. 1961–74; Prof., Indian School of Mines, Dhanbad 1965–67, Freiberg Mining Acad., FRG 1967–73; Head, Gas-hydrate Lab., Cen. Gas Research Inst. of the USSR 1974–87; Dir Gas-hydrate Lab., Oil and Gas Research Inst., Russian Acad. of Sciences 1987–93, Hydrocarbon and Environment Inst., Russian Acad. of Natural Sciences 1987–93; Co-founder Russian Acad. of Natural Sciences 1990, first Chair. Oil-Gas Consulate, Chair. Cttee on Data for Science and Tech. and Regional Sec. US Section; Co-founder and first Chair. Russian Section Int. Soc. of Petroleum Engineers (SPE) 1991–93; invited to join Texas A&M Univ. 1993, currently Visiting Prof./ Research Assoc. and Head of Gas-hydrate Lab., Petroleum Eng Dept; recorded as scientific discoverer of gas hydrates in nature, State Register of USSR 1969; Hon. Diploma (Mendeleev Union Society of Russia) 1982; Dr hc (Nikolayev Inst. of Inorganic Chem., Russian Acad. of Sciences) 2005; Winner's Diploma, Ukraine Republican Inventors' Competition 1958, First Prize, Young Petroleum Scientist Conf. of Russia 1965, First Prize, Chess Tournament of Indian School of Mines 1967, Diploma of the Scientific Discovery Natural Gas Hydrates 1969, Golden Jubilee Medal of Russia 1970, Honour Diploma of Mendeleev Union Soc. Russia 1982, Gubkin State Prize 1989, Golden L. Kapitca Medal for Scientific Discovery 1997, V. Vernadsky Medal of Honour 2000, Albert Einstein Medal of Honour, Russian Acad. of Natural Sciences (US Section) 2002, Distinguished Lecturer Merit of SPE 2002–03, Golden Peter the Great Medal 2004, Hon. Merit in Science and Econs, Russian Acad. of Natural Sciences 2005. *Publications:* eight monographs, 217 papers and 29 patents on gas hydrates. *Leisure interests:* painting, travelling, photography. *Address:* Harold Vance Department of Petroleum Engineering, 3116 TAMU - 721 Richardson Building, Texas A&M University, College Station, TX 77843-3116, USA (office); Vernadskogo prosp. 9, Apt 509, Moscow 117311, Russia (home). *Telephone:* (979) 845-4066 (office); (495) 131-02-09 (home). *E-mail:* yuri.makogon@pe.tamu.edu (office). *Website:* www.pe.tamu.edu (office).

MAKONI, Simba Herbert Stanley, BSc, PhD; Zimbabwean politician; b. 22 March 1950, Makoni; s. of Basil Kamunda and Clara Kamunda (née Matimba); m. Chipo Makoni (née Ususu) 1975; three s.; ed Univ. of Leeds and Leicester Polytechnic, UK; joined Zimbabwe African Nat. Union-Patriotic Front (ZANU-PF); ZANU Chief Rep. to W Europe 1977–80; mem. Nat. Ass. of Zimbabwe 1980–84; Deputy Minister of Agric. 1980; Minister of Industry and Energy Devt 1981–83, of Youth, Sport and Culture 1984, of Finance and Econ. Devt 2000–02; Exec. Sec., Southern African Devt Community 1984–93; Chief Exec. and Man. Dir Zimbabwe Newspapers Ltd, Zimpapers 1994–; Man. Pnr Makonsult Ltd; mem. UN Panel of Advisers on African Devt 1992–94, Inst. of Dirs, Zimbabwe 1994–, Zimbabwe Inst. of Man. 1994–, Council of Reps., South Centre 1994–, Nat. Blood Transfusion Service 1995–; mem. Nat. Council, Conf. of Zimbabwe Industries (CZI) 1996–, Chair. Econ. Affairs Cttee 1996–; mem. Nat. Econ. Consultative Forum 1998; Patron Nat. Council of Disabled Persons of Zimbabwe 1982–, Zimbabwe Inst. of Motor Industry 1995–; resgnd from ZANU-PF party 2008, ind. cand. for Pres. of Zimbabwe 2008. *Leisure interests:* gardening, reading, squash, health and fitness. *Address:* c/o Ministry of Finance and Economic Development, 2nd Floor, Munhumutapa Building, Samora Machel Avenue, Private Bag 7705, Causeway, Harare, Zimbabwe (office).

MAKOVECZ, Imre, DLA; Hungarian architect; b. 20 Nov. 1935, Budapest; m. Marianne Szabó; two s. one d.; ed Budapest Tech. Univ.; with Buváti (architectural planning inst.) 1959–62; held various positions at planning and architectural insts, Szövterv 1963–71, Váti 1971–77; planning architect, Pilis Forest Park State Farm 1977–83; Founder Makona Architectural Studio 1983; projects include churches at Paks 1987, Siófok 1989, Hungarian Pavilion, Int. Fair, Seville 1992, Mako Cultural Centre 1998, Eger swimming pool complex 2000, Piliscsaba Catholic Univ. 2001, Lendva Cultural Centre 2004, Csikszereda Church 2004; Prof., Applied Arts School; mem. Int. Architectural Acad. 1992–; Hon. Fellow, American, German and Scottish Architectural Asscns; Hon. FRIBA; Dr hc (Dundee); Ybl Miklós Prize 1969, Kossuth Prize (Middle Cross with Star) 1990, Grand Gold Medal of French Architectural Acad. 1997. *Address:* Makona, 1034 Budapest, Kecske u. 25, Hungary (office). *Telephone:* (1) 388-1701 (office); (1) 388-1702 (office). *Fax:* (1) 388-1702 (office). *E-mail:* info@makovecz.hu (office). *Website:* www.makovecz.hu (office).

MAKOVETSKY, Sergey Vasilievich; Russian actor; b. 13 June 1958, Kiev; ed Moscow Shchukin Theatre School; with Moscow Vakhtangov Theatre 1980–; with Roman Viktyuk Theatre 1990–; Golden Aries Prize for Actor of the Year 1993, Nika Acad. of Cinema Award 1993. *Plays include:* The Master's Lessons, Madame Butterfly, Loika's Flat, Zoya's Apartment (Moscow Theatre Spring Prize 1989). *Films include:* Ekipazh mashiny boevoy (Battle Vehicle Crew) 1983, Polosa prepyatstviy (aka Stripe of Obstacles) 1984, Zaveshchaniye (Testament) 1986, Topinambury (American Artichokes) 1988, Posvyashchyonnyy (Initiated) 1989, Sukiny deti (Sons of Bitches) 1990, Chernov/ Chernov 1990, Rebyonok k noyabryu (A Child by November) 1992, Patrioticheskaya komediya (Patriotic Comedy) 1992, Nash amerikanskiy Borya (Our American Borya) 1992, Prorva (Moscow Parade) 1992, Trotsky 1993, Malenkie chelovechki Bolshevistskogo pereulka, ili Khochu piva (Little People of the Bolshevik Lane, or I Want Beer) 1993, Makarov 1993, Khorovod (Round Dance) 1994, Pyesa dlya passazhira (A Play for a Passenger) 1995, Pribytiye poyezda (The Arrival of a Train) 1995, Letnie lyudi (Country Visitors) 1995, Chyornaya vual (The Black Veil) 1995, Le violon de Rothschild (Rothschild's Violin) 1996, Tri istorii (Three Stories) 1997, Sochineniye ko dnyu pobedy (Composition for Victory Day) 1998, Retro vtroyem 1998, Pro urodov i lyudey (Of Freaks and Men) 1998, Russkiy bunt (The Captain's Daughter) 2000, Brat 1 (The Brother 1) 2000, Brat 2 (The Brother 2) 2000, Mekhanicheskaya syuita 2001, Klyuch ot spalni 2003, Tretiy variant 2003, 72 metra (72 Meters) 2004, Alesha Popovich i Tugarin Zmey (voice) 2004, Zhmurki 2005. *Television includes:* Zhizn Klima Samgina (The Life of Klim Samgin) (series) 1986, Teatr imeni menya (voice) 1994, Operatsiya 'S novym godom' (Operation Happy New Year) 1996, Neudacha Poirot 2002, Gibel imperii (mini-series) 2005. *Address:* Vakhtangov Theatre, Arbat str. 26, 121007 Moscow, Russia (office). *Telephone:* (495) 241-01-28 (office).

MAKRAM-EBEID, Mona, PhD; Egyptian professor of political science, international organization official and fmr politician; *Chairman, Association for the Advancement of Education;* b. Cairo; grand-d. of Makram Ebeid Pasha; m.; one s.; ed Univ. of Cairo and American Univ. in Cairo, Harvard Univ., USA; Prof. of Political Science and Political Sociology, American Univ. in Cairo 1983–, currently Distinguished Lecturer, Dept of Political Science; mem. People's Ass. (Parl.) 1990–95, mem. Foreign Affairs and Educ. Cttees; Pres. Parliamentarians for Global Action 1990–95; Founder-mem. Arab Org. for Human Rights; Adviser to World Bank for the Middle East and North Africa Region 1992–96; Founder and Chair. Asscn for the Advancement of Educ., Cairo 1995–; apptd Expert to UN Cttee for Policy Devt 2000–03; mem. Bd of Dirs British Univ. In Egypt, Jordan German Univ., Amman, Center for Political and Futuristic Studies, Cairo, Citadel Investment, Talal Abu Ghazalah Org.; Consultant to Search for Common Ground, Initiative for Peace and Co-operation in the Middle East, Washington, DC; Exec. mem. Club of Rome, Ibn Khaldum Centre for Developmental Studies, Nat. Centre for Middle Eastern Studies; mem. Int. Consultative Group for the Middle East Center for Strategic and Int. Studies, Washington, DC 1991, UNICEF Women for Devt Cttee, Women for Foreign Policy Group, Washington, DC, The Arab Thought Forum, Amman; several articles on politics in journals and magazines published in English, Arabic and French; Fulbright Scholar 1981, 1983; Chevalier de la Légion d'Honneur 1994, Commdr de la Pléiade, AIPLF (Int. Asscn for French-speaking Parliamentarians) 1995; Woman of the Year, Civil Soc. Review 1994. *Leisure interests:* tennis, theatre, ballet, swimming. *Address:* Department of Political Science, The American University in Cairo, PO Box 74, New Cairo 11835; Apt 16, 4th Floor, 14 Guezira St, Zamalek, Cairo, Egypt (home). *Telephone:* (2) 3407603. *Fax:* (2) 2608288. *Website:* www.aucegypt.edu/ACADEMICS/DEPT/POLS.

MAKSAKOVA, Ludmila Vasilyevna; Russian actress; b. 26 Sept. 1941, Moscow; d. of Maria Maksakova; m.; one s. one d.; ed Moscow Shchukin Theatre School; leading actress, Moscow Vakhtangov Theatre 1961–; numerous film roles; Order for Service to Motherland; RSFSR Merited Artist 1971, RSFSR People's Artist 1980. *Theatre includes:* Princess Turandot in Adelma, Masha in Living Corpse, Nicol in The Prodigious Snob, Nastasha Filipovna in The Idiot, Anna Karenina, Duchess of Marlborough in Glass of Water, Korzinkina in Guilty without Guilt (State Prize of Russian Fed. 1995), the Countess in The Queen of Spades. *Films include:* Zhili-byli starik so starukhoy (There Was an Old Couple) 1967, Konets Saturna 1967, Nepodsuden (Not Under the Jurisdiction) 1969, Propazha zvidetelya 1971, Antratsit 1971, Boy posle pobedy 1972, Prikosnoveniye 1973, Plokhoy khoroshiy chelovek (The Duel) 1973, Osen (Autumn) 1974, Den priyoma po lichnym voprosam (Day of Admittance on Personal Matters) 1974, Otets Sergei (Father Sergius) 1978, Prokhindiada, ili beg na meste (A Rogue's Saga) 1984, Poyezdki na starom avtomobile (Trips on an Old Car) 1985, Tam, gde nas net 1986, Po glavnoy ulitse s orkestrom (Through Main Street with an Orchestra) 1986, Desyat negrityat (Ten Little Indians) 1987, Dni cheloveka (The Days of a Man) 1989, Mu-Mu 1998. *Television includes:* Na vsyakogo mudretsa dovolno prostoty (There Are Enough Common People for Every Wise Man) 1971, Teatr Klary Gazul (Theatre of Clara Gazul) 1977, Letuchaya mysh (The Bat) 1979, Pered samim soboy (Before Yourself) 1985. *Address:* 103009 Moscow, Bryusov per. 7, Apt 70, Russia. *Telephone:* (495) 229-94-98.

MAKSYMIUK, Jerzy; Polish conductor, composer and pianist; *Conductor Laureate, BBC Scottish Symphony Orchestra;* b. 9 April 1936, Grodno, Byelorussia (now Belarus); s. of Roman Maksymiuk and Bronisława Maksymiuk; m. Irena Kirjacka; ed Acad. of Music, Warsaw; Conductor, Great Theatre, Warsaw 1970–72; f. Polish Chamber Orchestra 1972–84; Prin. Conductor Polish Nat. Radio Symphony Orchestra, Katowice 1975–77; Prin. Conductor BBC Scottish Symphony Orchestra, Glasgow 1984–93, tours of Greece, Canada and Germany, Conductor Laureate 1993–; Guest Conductor Calgary Symphony, Nat. Arts Centre (Ottawa), BBC Welsh and Philharmonic Orchestras, English Chamber Orchestra, Scottish Chamber Orchestra, City of Birmingham Symphony, London Symphony, London Philharmonic, Philharmonia, Orchestre National de France, Rotterdam Philharmonic, Luxembourg Philharmonic, Hong Kong Philharmonic, Royal Liverpool Philharmonic, Bournemouth Sinfonietta, Ulster Orchestra, Tokyo Metropolitan Symphony, Israeli Chamber Orchestra, Los Angeles Chamber Orchestra, Staatskapelle, Sinfonia Varsovia and other orchestras; has toured Europe, USA, Canada, Japan, Israel and Australia with Polish Chamber Orchestra; collaborated with ENO (Mozart's Don Giovanni) 1990, (Johann Strauss' Die Fledermaus) 1993; regularly performs works of Penderecki, Lutoslawski, Gorecki, Szymanowski, as well as British composers including Peter Maxwell Davies and James MacMillan; Hon. DLitt (Strathclyde) 1990; First Prize, Paderewski Piano Competition 1964, Gold Medal, Elgar Society 1999. *Recordings include:* Paderewski: Symphony 'Polonia', The Romantic Piano Concerto, (Vols 1–4), Vivaldi Violin Concertos, Grieg: Pier Gynt Suites Nos. 1 & 2. *Address:* Gdańska 2 m. 14, 01-633 Warsaw, Poland (home). *Telephone:* (22) 8323021 (home).

MAKTOUM, Hamdan bin Muhammad al-; United Arab Emirates politician; *Crown Prince of Dubai;* b. 14 Nov. 1982; s. of Sheikh Muhammad bin Rashid al-Maktoum and Sheikha Hind bint Maktoum bin Juma al-Maktoum; ed Rashid Private School, Sandhurst Mil. Acad., UK, London School of Econs, UK, Dubai School of Govt; Chair. Dubai Exec. Council 2006–; named Crown Prince of Dubai 2008–; Head of Sheikh Muhammad bin Rashid Establishment for Young Business Leaders; Pres. Dubai Sports Council. *Achievement:* won gold medal in equestrian event, Asian Games, Doha 2006. *Leisure interests:* horse riding, poetry. *Address:* Dubai Executive Council, Emirates Towers Building, 37th Floor, Sheikh Zayed Road, POB 73311, Dubai, United Arab Emirates (office). *Telephone:* (4) 330-2111 (office). *Fax:* (4) 330-3636 (office). *Website:* www.fazza3.com.

MAKTOUM, Sheikh Hamdan bin Rashid al-; United Arab Emirates politician; *Deputy Ruler of Dubai and Minister of Finance and Industry;* b. 1945; s. of Rashid bin Said al-Maktoum; brother of the late Sheikh Maktoum Bin Rashid Al Maktoum; Deputy Prime Minister UAE 1971–73, Minister of Finance and Industry 1971–, also Jt Deputy Ruler of Dubai 1995–; Pres. Dubai Municipal Council. *Address:* Ministry of Finance and Industry, PO Box 433, Abu Dhabi, United Arab Emirates. *Telephone:* (2) 6726000 (office). *Fax:* (2) 66663088 (office). *E-mail:* mofi@uae.gov.ae (office).

MAKTOUM, Maktoum bin Muhammad al-, BSc; United Arab Emirates politician; *Joint Deputy Ruler of Dubai;* b. 24 Nov. 1983; s. of Sheikh Muhammad bin Rashid al-Maktoum; ed Rashid School, American Univ. of Dubai; Chair. Dubai Tech. and Media Free Zone Authority (TECOM Investments); Chair. Dubai Media Inc.; Jt Deputy Ruler of Dubai 2008–; Vice-Pres. Al-Ahli Club (football club). *Leisure interest:* horse riding. *Address:* Office of the Chairman, Dubai Media Inc., POB 835, Dubai, United Arab Emirates (office). *Telephone:* (4) 336-9999 (office).

MAKTOUM, HH Sheikh Muhammad bin Rashid al-, (Ruler of Dubai); United Arab Emirates race horse owner; *Vice-President and Prime Minister;* b. 1948; s. of the late Rashid bin Said al-Maktoum; m. 1st Sheikha Hind bint Maktoum bin Juma al-Maktoum 1979; m. 2nd Princess Haya bint al-Hussein 2004; ed Mons Officer Cadet Training Coll., Sandhurst Coll., Univ. of Cambridge, UK; trained in British army and RAF; Dir of Police and Public Security 1971; Minister of Defence 1972; Crown Prince of Dubai 1990–2006, succeeded his brother, Sheikh Maktoum bin Rashid al-Maktoum, as 6th Sheikh 2006, Vice-Pres. of Dubai 2006–, Prime Minister 2006–; with brothers the late Sheikh Maktoum al-Maktoum, Sheikh Hamdan al-Maktoum and Sheikh Ahmed al-Maktoum, has had racing interests in UK 1976–; first winner, Hatta, Goodwood 1977; with brothers owns studs, stables, country houses and sporting estates in Newmarket and elsewhere in UK; worldwide racing interests based at Dalham Hall Stud, Newmarket; horses trained in England, Ireland and France; founder and Dir Godolphin Racing, Dubai 1994; f. Racing Post (daily) 1986; owner, Balanchine, winner, Irish Derby 1994; winner, numerous classic races; leading owner 1985–89, 1991–93. *Publication:* My Vision: Challenges in the Race for Excellence 2006. *Address:* Ruler's Palace, Dubai (office); Office of the Prime Minister, POB 12848, Dubai, United Arab Emirates (office); c/o Warren Towers, Newmarket, Suffolk, England (office). *Telephone:* (4) 3534550 (office). *Fax:* (4) 3530111 (office). *Website:* www.sheikhmohammed.co.ae.

MAKUZA, Bernard; Rwandan politician and fmr diplomatist; *Prime Minister;* b. 1961; m.; fmr mem. Mouvement démocratique républicain; fmr Amb. to Burundi, Amb. to Germany –2000; Prime Minister of Rwanda 2000–. *Address:* Office of the Prime Minister, Kigali, Rwanda (office). *Telephone:* 585444 (office). *Fax:* 583714 (office). *E-mail:* primature@gov.rw (office). *Website:* www.primature.gov.rw (office).

MAKWETU, Clarence Mlamli; South African politician; b. 6 Dec. 1928, Hoyita, Cofimvaba Dist, Transkei; s. of Minah Makwetu and the late Gqongo Makwetu; m. Mandisa Makwetu; two s.; ed Hoyita Primary School, Keilands Mission School, Nkwanca Sr Secondary School and Lovedale School; joined African Nat. Congress (ANC) Youth League 1954; instrumental in formation of ANC 1959; detained several times 1960–63; then served five years on Robben Island; subsequently returned to Transkei, working in construction and insurance; detained again 1977, 1979; banished by Chief Kaiser Matanzima (q.v.) to Libido Dist 1979–84; returned home and continued farming 1984; detained 1986; First Pres. Pan-Africanist Movt 1989–90; Deputy Pres. Pan-Africanist Congress of Azania (PAC) March–Dec. 1990; Pres. PAC 1990, expelled from PAC for bringing party into disrepute May 1997; MP Nat. Ass. 1994–97; claims lodged against his farm in Gwatyu, Cofimvaba Dist Sept. 2001. *Address:* c/o PAC, PO Box 25245, Ferreirastown 2048, South Africa.

MALABO, Capt. Cristino Seriche Bioke (see BIOKE MALABO, Capt. Cristino Seriche).

MALAJ, Arben; Albanian politician and economist; b. 19 Sept. 1961; m.; one c.; ed Univ. of Tirana; began career with Nat. Commercial Bank of Albania, Vlora; Dir Foundation of SME-s, Tirana –1997; Assoc. Prof. of Econ. Sciences, Univ. of Tirana 1997–; Minister of Finance and Gov. of Albania to the World Bank 1997–98; Chief of Parl. Comm. for the Economy and Econ. Table of the Stability Pact 1998–2000; Chief of Parl. Group of the Socialist Party 2000–02; Minister of Economy 2002–04, of Finance 2004–05; currently mem. Parl. for Kelmendi Dist (Socialist Party); lecturer in numerous academic insts including Univ. of Bocconi, Italy, Univ. of Tetova, Macedonia, Univ. of Pristina, Kosova; mem. Int. Acad. of Emerging Markets, New York, USA. *Publications:* author or co-author of several publications and scientific articles. *Address:* c/o Ministria e Financave, Kuvendi i Shqiperise, Bulevardi Dëshmorët e Kombit, Nr. 4, Tirana, Albania (office).

MALAN, Pedro, PhD; Brazilian economist; *Chairman, Unibanco SA;* b. 19 Feb. 1943, Rio de Janeiro; s. of Elysio S. Malan and Regina S. Malan; m. 1st Ana María Toledo Piza Rudge; m. 2nd Catarina Gontijo Souza Lima 1980; two s. one d.; ed St Ignatius School, Rio de Janeiro, Polytechnic School of Catholic Univ. of Rio de Janeiro, School of Econs and Univ. of California, Berkeley; with Inst. of Applied Research, Brazilian Ministry of Planning 1966–69, 1973–83; Faculty of Econs, Catholic Univ. of Rio de Janeiro Jan.–Dec. 1979; Head Int. Trade and Finance Section, Inst. of Applied Econ. Research 1980–83; Dir Policy Analysis and Research Div. Centre of Transnat. Corpns, UN, New York

1983–84, Dept of Int. Econs and Social Affairs 1985–86; Exec. Dir World Bank, Washington, DC 1986–90; Exec. Dir Inter-American Devt Bank 1990–92; Pres. Cen. Bank of Brazil 1993–94; Minister of Finance 1994–2002; Vice-Chair. Bd of Dirs, Unibanco SA 2003–04, Chair. 2004–; Fed. of São Paulo Industries Prize for book External Economic Policy and Industrialization in Brazil 1980, Légion d'honneur 1996, Order of Mil. Merit 1998, Order of Naval Merit 1998. *Publications:* The Structure of Protection in Brazil (with J. Bergsman) 1971, The Brazilian Economy in the 1970s: Old and New Developments (with R. Bonelli) 1977, Brazilian External Debt and its Implications 1978, Structural Models of Inflation and Balance of Payments Disequilibria in Semi-Industrialized Economies (with John R. Wells) 1984, Financial Integration with the World Economy, The Brazilian Case 1983, Relações Econômicas Internacionais do Brasil no Período 1945–64 1984, Debt, Trade and Development: The Crucial Years Ahead 1985. *Leisure interests:* literature, classical music, diplomatic and financial history, swimming, tennis. *Address:* Unibanco Holdings SA, Avenida Eusébio Matoso 891, 22nd Floor, 05423-901 São Paolo, Brazil (office). *Telephone:* (11) 3047-1313 (office). *Fax:* (11) 3813-6182 (office). *Website:* www.unibanco.com.br (office).

MALAN, Wynand Charl, BA, LLB; South African politician, attorney, consultant and business executive; b. 25 May 1943, Port Elizabeth; s. of Dawid Johannes Malan and Annie Malan (née de Swardt); m. Judith Rousseau 1967; two s. one d.; ed Linden Hoërskool, Johannesburg and Univ. of Pretoria; attorney and Partner, van Wyk de Vries, Malan & Steyn, Johannesburg 1966–67, Leader Nat. Jeugbond, Transvaal 1972–74; mem. Rapportraad 1971–73, Nat. Chair. 1974–76; Randburg Town Councillor and Chair. Man. Cttee 1977; Nat. Party MP for Randburg 1977–87, Ind. MP for Randburg 1987–88, Democratic Party MP for Randburg 1989–90; fmr Leader Nat. Democratic Movt; fmr Co-Leader Democratic Party; mem. The Truth and Reconciliation Comm. 1995–2002; CEO Thebe Securities Ltd 2002–05; strategy consultant, pvt. practice 2006–; Eisenhower Fellowship 1980; ASPU Newsmaker of the Year Award 1987. *Leisure interests:* golf, chess, numismatics, clivia propagation. *Address:* PO Box 2075, Randburg 2125, South Africa (office). *Telephone:* (11) 7820119 (office). *Fax:* (11) 7820119 (office). *E-mail:* wcmalan@mweb.co.za (office).

MALASHENKO, Igor Yevgenyevich, CandPhilSc; Russian journalist; b. 2 Oct. 1954, Moscow; m. Yelena Pivovarova; two d.; ed Moscow State Univ.; jr, sr researcher, Inst. of USA and Canada USSR Acad. of Sciences 1980–89, research in problems of the concept of nuclear deterrence and public opinion; staff-mem. Int. Div. Cen. Cttee CPSU, admin. of Pres. Gorbachev March–Dec. 1991; political Dir TV & Radio Co. Ostankino 1992–93; Pres. and Dir-Gen. Ind. TV Co. NTV 1993–, Pres. NTV-Telemost Holding 1998; First Deputy Chair. Bd of Dirs Media-Most Co. 1998–2001; adviser to Pres. of Russia on public relations problems, mem. election campaign staff of Boris Yeltsin 1996; Prize of Russian Union of Journalists 1994. *Leisure interests:* golf, photography. *Address:* NTV-Telemost, Academica Koroleva str. 19, 127427 Moscow, Russia. *Telephone:* (495) 215-15-88 (office).

MALATESTA, Lamberto; Italian chemist and academic; b. 20 June 1912, Milan; s. of Dr Giuseppe Malatesta and Clara Tombolan Fava; m. Rachele Pizzotti 1947; one s. two d.; ed Milan Univ.; Asst to the Chair of Industrial Chem., Milan Univ. 1937, Reader 1940, Lecturer 1942, Chair. Prof. of Analytical Chem. 1948–51, of Gen. and Inorganic Chem. 1951–87, Dir Istituto di Chimica Generale 1951–82, Dir Dept Inorganic Chem. 1982–87, Prof. Emer. 1987– (retd); Dir of a Centre of Consiglio Nazionale delle Ricerche 1970–82; Dir Gazzetta Chimica Italiana 1971–84; Pres. Società Chimica Italiana 1971–73, 1981–83; Pres. of Div. of Inorganic Chem., IUPAC 1975–77, Pres. Chemical Sciences Cttee, Nat. Research Council (CNR) 1976–81; Fellow, Accad. Nazionale dei Lincei, Istituto Lombardo Accad. di Scienze e Lettere; Hon. Fellow, Chemical Soc. (London); Prize of the Pres. of Italian Repub. 1963; Gold Medal for Educ., Culture and Art 1974, Gold Medal for Lifetime Achievement 1998, Gold Medal Federchimica 1999. *Publications:* General Chemistry (in Italian) 1965, Inorganic Chemistry (in Italian) 1968; co-author: Isocyanide Compounds of Metals 1968, Zerovalent Compounds of Metals 1974; about 140 original papers in scientific journals. *Leisure interests:* swimming, playing bridge. *Address:* Via Carpaccio 2, 20133 Milan, Italy. *Telephone:* (02) 2360350.

MALAURIE, Jean, PhD; French anthropogeographer and writer; *Director Emeritus, Centre d'études arctiques (EHESS);* b. 22 Dec. 1922, Mainz, Germany; s. of Albert Malaurie and Isabelle (Regnault) Malaurie; m. Monique Laporte 1951; one s. one d.; ed Lycée Condorcet, Faculté des Lettres de Paris, Inst. of Geography Univ. of Paris; Attaché then Research Fellow, CNRS 1948–56; mem. Nat. Comm. on Geography 1955–67, 1980–82; Prof. of Arctic Geomorphology and Anthropogeography, Ecole des Hautes Etudes en Sciences Sociales (EHESS), Paris 1957–; Founder and Dir Centre for Arctic Studies, CNRS-EHESS 1957–; Dir Arctic Research, CNRS 1979–91, Dir Emer. 1992–; Pres. Fondation Française d'études nordiques 1964–75, Soc. Arctique Française 1981–90; Founder and Dir Terre Humaine anthropological book series 1955–; Founder, Dir Inter-Nord int. journal of Arctic studies 1961 (20 vols); Chair. and organizer 14 int. Arctic confs and seminars; has made 9 documentary films on the Inuit, including The Last Kings of Thule 1970, Inuit, from Siberia to Greenland 1980, Hainak-Inuit 1993; has led 31 Arctic scientific expeditions; the first French explorer to reach North geomagnetic pole by dog-sledge 29 May 1951; Chair. Cttee for the Defence of Arctic Minorities in Russia, Foundation for Culture, Moscow 1990–; Dir Acad. of Human Sciences of Russia 1997–; mem. Institut Jean Malaurie de Recherche avancée pour et avec les autochtones, St Petersburg 2006; Hon. Pres. Fonds Polaire Jean Malaurie, Bibliothèque centrale, Nat. Museum of Natural History, Paris 1992–, State Polar Acad., St Petersburg 1994–; Hon. Dean Northern People's State Univ. Herzen, St Petersburg 1992 (and Gold Medal); Hon. Prof. HEC,

Paris 2005; Commdr Légion d'honneur, Commdr Ordre nat. du mérite, Commdr Ordre des Arts et Lettres; Hon. PhD (State Univ., St Petersburg) 2001; Award of Acad. française 1968, Polar Medal, Soc. de Géographie, Paris 1953, 1961, Acad. des sciences Award 1967, Gold Medal, Soc. arctique française 1990, CNRS Medal 1992, Gold Medal, Soc. de Géographie Paris 1996, Grand Prix de la Ville de Paris 1999 Grand Prix Jules Verne 2000, Patron's Gold Medal, Royal Geographical Soc., London 2005, Mungo Park Medal, Royal Scottish Geographical Soc. 2005. *Films:* Les Derniers Rois de Thulé 1969, 2002, Inuit from Greenland to Siberia (seven films) 1980, Haïnak Inuit 1993. *Publications include:* Hoggar 1954, Les Derniers Rois de Thulé (translated into 22 languages) 1955, Thèmes de recherche géomorphologique dans le nord-ouest du Groenland 1968, Ultima Thulé 1990 (2nd edn), Hummocks 1999, L'appel du nord 2001, Anthropogéographie arctique I 2002, L'allée des baleines 2003, Ot Kaminya K Tcheloveky 2003, Enfant de Mayence a paraître 2006. *Address:* Centre d'études arctiques (EHESS), 105 boulevard Raspail, 75006 Paris, France (office). *Telephone:* 1-53-63-51-45 (office). *Fax:* 1-53-63-51-00 (office). *E-mail:* jeanmalaurie@ehess.fr (office).

MALAVOLTA, Eurípedes, DSc; Brazilian agricultural biochemist; b. 13 Aug. 1926, Araraquara, São Paulo; s. of Antônio Malavolta and Lucia Canassa Malavolta; m. Leila M. B. Malavolta 1953 (divorced 1988); two s. three d.; ed Escola Superior de Agricultura, Luiz de Queiroz (Univ. de São Paulo) and Univ. of California (Berkeley), USA; Instructor in Agricultural Chem., Univ. de São Paulo 1949, Docent, Escola Superior de Agricultura Luiz de Queiroz 1948–84, Prof. of Agricultural Biochemistry 1958–84, Dean, Escola Superior de Agricultura Luiz de Queiroz 1964–70, Dean, Inst. of Physics and Chem., São Carlos 1972–76; Research Assoc., Univ. of California 1952–53, Visiting Prof. 1959–60; State Council of Educ. 1980–84; mem. Brazilian Acad. of Sciences 2000, São Paulo Acad. of Sciences, Int. Cttee of Plant Analysis and Fertilizer Problems, Int. Cttee of Plant Nutrition, Int. Soc. Soil Science, Third World Acad. of Sciences; Fellow, Rockefeller Foundation, USA; Hon. mem. Brazilian Soil Science Soc., Colombian Soil Science Soc.; Commdr Nat. Order of Scientific Merit 1998; Medalha do Jubileu CNPq, Nat. Council of Scientific and Technological Devt 1981, Moinho Santista Prize (Agric. Sciences) 1982, Fernando Costa Medal 1991, Prudente de Moraes Medal 1991, Pesquisador homenageado, FUNDECITRUS 1997, IFA Prize, Int. Fertilizer Asscn 2005. *Achievement:* pioneer work on the use of nuclear energy in agricultural research in Latin America. *Publications:* Elements of Agricultural Chemistry 1954, Manual of Agricultural Chemistry 1959, On the Mineral Nutrition of Some Tropical Crops 1962, Manual of Agricultural Chemistry-Soil Fertility and Plant Nutrition 1976, ABC of Fertilization 1954, Elements of Plant Nutrition 1981, Evaluation of the Nutritional Status of Plants 1989, Nutritional Disorders in Cerrado Soils 1985, Nutrition and Fertilization of Citrus 1990, Nutrition and Fertilization of Coffee 1992, Fertilizers and Their Impact on the Environment: Myths and Facts 1994, Nutrient and Fertilizer Management in Sugarcane 1994, History of Coffee in Brazil 2000. *Leisure interests:* reading, music, stamp-collecting. *Address:* Centro de Energia Nuclear na Agricultura, Universidade de São Paulo, Piracicaba, 13416-000 São Paulo, SP (office); Travessa Portugal, 146 Piracicaba, 13400-970 São Paulo, SP, Brazil (home). *Telephone:* (19) 3429-4695 (office); (19) 3422-3948 (home). *Fax:* (19) 3429-4610 (office). *E-mail:* mala@cena.usp.br (office). *Website:* www.cena.usp.br/pesquisador/malavolta.htm (office).

MALCHÁREK, Jirko; Slovak politician; b. 28 June 1966, Jeseník; widowed; one s.; ed Secondary School of Mechanical Eng, Bratislava, Slovak Tech. Univ., Bratislava; Asst Dir Bratislava Transport Co. 1989–91; Office of Govt Commr for Automotive Industry and Conversion of Special Production 1991; Man. Dir, VSŽ Selecta Praha, Slovak branch 1993–98; Founder and head operational leasing co., Slovakia 1995–98; mem. Nat. Council of Slovak Repub. 1998–2005; Deputy Prime Minister and Minister of the Economy 2005–06. *Address:* c/o Ministry of the Economy, Mierová 19, 827 15 Bratislava, Slovakia (office).

MALCOLM, James Ian (Jim), OBE; British diplomatist (retd); b. 29 March 1946; s. of William Kenneth Malcolm and the late Jennie Malcolm; m. Sheila Nicholson Moore 1967; one s. one d.; ed Royal High School, Edinburgh; entered British Diplomatic Service in 1966, Attaché, UK Del. to NATO, Brussels 1969–72, Attaché, Embassy in Rangoon, Burma (Union of Myanmar) 1972–74, Third Sec., FCO, London 1974–77, Commercial Attaché, British High Comm., Nairobi, Kenya 1977–80, Consul, British Embassy, Damascus, Syria 1980–83, Second Sec. (Commercial), Embassy in Angola 1983–85, First Sec., FCO (dealing with Counter-Terrorism issues) 1985–87, First Sec. (Political/Econ.), Embassy in Jakarta, Indonesia 1987–94, First Sec., FCO (Head of BBC World Service Section) 1994–97, Deputy High Commr in Kingston, Jamaica and British Trade Commr to Cayman Islands 1997–2001, Amb. to Panama 2002–06 (retd). *Leisure interests:* reading and researching British history in Indonesia, Jamaica and Panama, playing golf, riding motorcycles, photography. *Address:* c/o Foreign and Commonwealth Office, King Charles Street, London, SW1A 2AH, England (office). *Telephone:* (20) 7008-1500 (office). *Website:* www.fco.gov.uk (office).

MALCOLM, Steven J., BCE; American energy industry executive; *Chairman, President and CEO, The Williams Companies Inc.;* b. Sept. 1948, St Louis, MO; m. Gwen Malcolm; one d.; ed Univ. of Missouri–Rolla, Northwestern Univ.; began career in refining, marketing and transportation depts, Cities Gas Co.; joined Williams Cos Inc. 1984, Dir of Business Devt, Williams Natural Gas Co. 1984–86, Dir of Gas Man. 1986–89, Vice-Pres. of Gas Man. and Supply 1989–93, Sr Vice-Pres. and Gen. Man. Mid-Continent Region, Williams Field Services 1993–94, Sr Vice-Pres. and Gen. Man. Gathering and Processing 1994–96, Sr Vice-Pres. and Gen. Man. Midstream Gas and Liquids, Williams Energy Services 1996–98, Pres. and CEO Williams Energy Services 1998–2001, apptd Dir The Williams Cos Inc. 2001, Pres. and COO 2001–02,

Pres. and CEO 2002–03, Chair., Pres. and CEO 2002–; mem. Bd Tusla Area United Way, Tusla Community Foundation, YMCA, St John Medical Center, Boy Scouts of America Indian Nations Council; mem. Univ. of Tusla Advancement and Athletics Cttees, YMCA Exec. Cttee; mem. Business Roundtable, Cttee to Encourage Corp. Philanthropy, Nat. Petroleum Council; fmr mem. Nat. Energy Services Asscn. *Address:* The Williams Companies, Inc., 1 Williams Center, Tusla, OK 74172, USA (office). *Telephone:* (918) 573-2000 (office). *Fax:* (918) 573-6714 (office). *Website:* www.williams.com (office).

MALCOMSON, James Martin, MA, PhD, FBA; British economist and academic; *Professor of Economics, University of Oxford;* b. 23 June 1946, Staunton-on-Wye; s. of E. Watlock Malcomson and Madeline (Stuart) Malcomson; m. Sally Claire Richards 1979; one d. (deceased); ed Gonville and Caius Coll., Univ. of Cambridge, Harvard Univ., USA; Research Fellow, Lecturer, Sr Lecturer, Univ. of York 1971–85; Prof. of Econs, Univ. of Southampton 1985–98; Prof. of Econs, Univ. of Oxford 1999–; Fellow, All Souls Coll. Oxford 1999–; Fellow, Econometric Soc. 2005. *Publications:* numerous articles in scientific journals. *Leisure interests:* walking, music, film, theatre. *Address:* All Souls College, Oxford, OX1 4AL (office); Department of Economics, Manor Road Building, Manor Road, Oxford, OX1 3UQ, England (office). *Telephone:* (1865) 279379 (office). *Fax:* (1865) 279299 (office). *E-mail:* james.malcomson@economics.ox.ac.uk (office). *Website:* www.economics.ox.ac.uk (office).

MALCORRA, Susana; Argentine engineer and international organization official; *Under-Secretary-General and Head of Department of Field Support, United Nations;* b. 1954; m.; one s.; ed Univ. of Rosario; grad. trainee with IBM, eventually becoming Dir of Public Sector, later assigned to IBM's corp. HQ in USA where she oversaw relations between HQ and Mexico and the Andean region of Latin America –1993; various admin. positions with Telecom Argentina 1993–2003, COO and Exec. Dir 1995–2001, CEO 2001–02; co-f. Vectis Management 2002; Deputy Exec. Dir (Admin) WFP 2004–07 (led initial phase of operational response to tsunami emergency Dec. 2004), Deputy Exec. Dir and COO Jan.–March 2008, UN Under-Sec.-Gen. and Head of Dept of Field Support 2008–; Founding mem. Argentine chapter, Int. Women's Forum; mem. Advisory Bd of Business School of Univ. of San Andres, Buenos Aires, Advisory Bd of Equidad. *Address:* Department of Field Support, United Nations, First Avenue at 46th Street, New York, NY 10017, USA (office). *Website:* www.un.org/Depts/dpko/dpko/dfs.shtml (office).

MALECELA, Cigwiyemisi John Samwel; Tanzanian politician and diplomatist; b. 1934, Dodoma; m. Ezerina Mwaipopo; one s. three d.; ed Bombay Univ., India and Univ. of Cambridge, UK; Admin. Officer, Civil Service 1960–61; Consul in USA and Third Sec. to the UN 1962; Regional Commr, Mwanza Region 1963; Perm. Rep. to the UN 1964–68; Amb. to Ethiopia 1968; E African Minister for Communications, Research and Social Services, E African Community 1969–72; Minister of Foreign Affairs 1972–75, of Agric. 1975–80, of Mines 1980–81, of Transport and Communications 1982–85; Regional Commr, Iringa 1987–89; High Commr in UK 1989–90; Prime Minister and First Vice-Pres. of Tanzania 1990–95; Minister without Portfolio 1995; Vice-Chair. Chama Cha Mapinduzi Party 1992–95; Vice-Chair. Desert Locust Control Org. for East Africa; mem. Commonwealth Group on S Africa 1985; Order of Merit of First Degree (Egypt), First Order of Independence (Equatorial Guinea). *Leisure interests:* reading, sports. *Address:* PO Box 2324, Dodoma, Tanzania.

MALEK, Redha; Algerian politician and diplomatist; b. 1931, Batna; s. of Malek Ahmed and Ladjouze Zoulikha; m. Rafida Cheriet 1963; two s. one d.; ed in Algiers and Paris; Ed.-in-Chief El-Moudjahid (weekly newspaper of FLN); mem. Algerian del. to negotiations of Evian 1961–62, Drafting Cttee of Program of Tripoli setting out FLN political programme 1962, mem. Cen. Cttee FLN 1979–; Drafting Cttee of Nat. Charter 1976; Amb. to Yugoslavia 1963–65, to France 1965–70, to USSR 1970–77, to USA 1979–82, to UK 1982–84; Minister of Information and Culture 1978–79; Pres. Conseil Nat. Consultatif 1992; Minister of Foreign Affairs 1992–93; mem. High Council of State 1992–94; Prime Minister of Algeria 1993–94 (removed by armed forces leaders); Pres. Alliance Nat. Républicaine 1995; involved in negotiations for release of 52 American hostages in Iran 1980–81; Harold Weill Medal, New York Univ. *Publications:* Tradition et Révolution 1993, L'Algérie à Evian 1995. *Address:* 2 Rue Ahmed Bey, Algiers, Algeria.

MALENCHENKO, Col Yuri Ivanovich; Russian/Ukrainian cosmonaut; b. 22 Dec. 1961, Svetlovodsk, Ukraine; m.; one s.; ed Kharkov Higher Mil. Aviation School, Zukovsky Mil. Aviation Eng Acad.; army service 1979–; mil. pilot of 3rd class, flew more than 800 hours in fighters; mem. staff Y. Gagarin Cosmonauts' Training Centre 1987–, cosmonaut-explorer 1995–; participant in flight to space station Mir Aug.–Sept. 1994; achieved manual docking with the cargo spaceship Progress after two failed automatic attempts. *Address:* Yuri Gagarin Cosmonauts' Training Centre, Zvezdny gorodok, Moscow Region, Russia.

MÄLER, Karl-Göran, PhD; Swedish economist and academic; *Professor and Director, Beijer International Institute of Ecological Economics;* b. 3 March 1939, Sollefteå; s. of Karl Markus Mäler and Henny Kristina Mäler; m. Sara Aniyar; two d.; ed Stockholm Univ.; Prof. of Econs, Stockholm School of Econs; Dir Beijer Int. Inst. of Ecological Econs, Royal Swedish Acad. of Sciences; Founding mem. European Asscn of Environmental and Resource Economists (EAERE); Co-organizer Ecological and Environmental Econs Research and Training Activity at Int. Centre for Theoretical Physics, Trieste, Italy; Dr hc (Haifa); Volvo Environment Prize 2002, EAERE European Lifetime Achievement Award in Environmental Econs (co-recipient) 2005, Older Linné Medal in Gold, Royal Swedish Acad. of Science. *Publications:* Environmental Economics: A Theoretical Inquiry 1974, Priskompensation Och Planeringsosakerhet I Forsvaret: Utredning Utford Pa Uppdrag Av 1978 ars Forsvarskommitte (co-author) 1981, Environmental Decision Making (co-author) 1984, Environment and Development: An Economic Approach (co-author) 1992, Economic Science, 1981–1990: The Sveriges Riksband (ed.) 1992, Poverty, Institutions, and the Environmental-Resource Base (co-author) 1994, Current Issues in Environmental Economics (co-ed.) 1995, Rights to Nature: Ecological, Economic, Cultural, and Political Principles of Institutions for the Environment (co-ed.) 1996, Biodiversity Loss: Economic and Ecological Issues (co-ed.) 1997, The Economics of Transnational Commons (co-ed.) 1997, The Environment and Emerging Development Issues (co-ed.) 2001, The Economics of Non-Convex Ecosystems (co-ed.) 2004. *Leisure interest:* bird watching. *Address:* Beijer Institute, Royal Swedish Academy of Sciences, Box 50005, 104 05 Stockholm, Sweden (office). *Telephone:* (8) 673-95-30 (office). *Fax:* (8) 15-24-64 (office). *E-mail:* karl@beijer.kva.se (office). *Website:* www.beijer.kva.se (office).

MALER, Leopoldo Mario, LLB; Argentine artist and art foundation executive; b. 2 April 1937, Buenos Aires; s. of Abraham Maler and Esther Kraiselburd; m. 1st Silvia Oclander 1967; m. 2nd Joyce Pieck 1973; m. 3rd María Rosa Baquero 1988; one s.; ed Univ. of Buenos Aires; journalist, BBC World Service (Latin American Service) 1961–64, 1967–74, UN Radio, New York 1980–82; Dean, Parsons School of Design, Dominican Repub. 1983–85; Dir Napa Contemporary Arts Foundation 1988–91; Examiner Prof., Leeds Polytechnic and Middlesex Polytechnic Depts of Art, UK 1976–78; one-man show Otros Diluvios, Centro Cultural, Buenos Aires 1987; monuments at Olympic Park, Korea, Parque de las Naciones, Madrid, Lamentin, Guadaloupe (Madonna and Child); Ed. NACA Journal 1992–; Guggenheim Fellow 1977; First Grand Prix, 14th Int. Biennale, São Paulo 1977, Gen. Motors Prize, Biennale of Sports in the Arts, Montevideo 1982, Gandhi Prize for Social Communication, Buenos Aires 1984, City of Madrid Medal for Artistic Merit 1991. *Film:* Man in Silence 1964 (Best Short Film, London Film Festival 1964). *Ballet:* X IT, The Place, London 1969. *Leisure interests:* scuba-diving, psychology, sailing, music. *Address:* Apdo Postal 25320, Santo Domingo, Dominican Republic. *Telephone:* (809) 696-0072.

MALESKI, Denko, PhD; Macedonian diplomatist; *Professor of Law, University of Cyril & Methodius;* b. 14 Nov. 1946, Skopje; s. of Vlado Maleski and Maria Alivantova; m. Miriana Ivanskova 1970; three d.; ed Univs of London, Skopje and Ljubljana; Prof. of Int. Politics, Univ. Cyril & Methodius, Skopje 1981–91, currently Prof. of Law; Visiting Prof. (Fulbright Scholar), Bowling Green State Univ., Ohio, USA 1990; Minister of Foreign Affairs 1991–93; Amb. and Perm. Rep. of Macedonia to UN, New York 1993–96; Borjan Tanevski Foundation Award 2005. *Publications:* Contemporary Political Systems 1985; numerous articles on democracy, political systems and int. relations. *Leisure interests:* reading, jogging. *Address:* University of Cyril & Methodius, PO Box 576, Bulevar Krste Misirkov b.b., 1000 Skopje, Macedonia.

MALEWEZI, Rt Hon. Justin Chimera, BA; Malawi teacher, educational administrator and politician; b. 23 Dec. 1944, Ntchisi; s. of the late Canon John Julius Malewezi and of Bartlet Rachel Malewezi; m. Felicity Rozina Chizalema 1970; two s. two d.; ed Columbia Univ., New York; secondary school teacher 1967–69, headmaster 1969–74, educ. admin. 1974–78; Deputy Sec., Ministry of Finance and Prin. Sec. in various ministries 1978–89; Head of Civil Service 1989–91; Vice-Pres. of Malawi 1994–99, 1999–2003; unsuccessful cand. presidential elections 2004. *Leisure interests:* tennis, football. *Address:* c/o Office of the Vice-President, PO Box 30399, Capital City, Lilongwe 3; PO Box 30086, Lilongwe 3, Malawi (home).

MALFITANO, Catherine; American singer (soprano) and stage director; b. 18 April 1948, New York City; d. of Maria Maslova and Joseph Malfitano; one d.; ed Manhattan School of Music; debut at Central City Opera 1972; has appeared at the world's leading opera houses, including the Metropolitan Opera, Lyric Opera of Chicago, Vienna State Opera, La Scala, Bavarian State Opera, Paris Opera, Royal Opera Covent Garden, Berlin's Deutsche Opera and State Opera, Teatro Comunale Florence, San Francisco Opera, Netherlands Opera, Los Angeles Opera, Houston Grand Opera, Théâtre du Chatelet Paris, Grand Théâtre du Genève, Liceu Barcelona, Hamburg State Opera and Théâtre Royal de la Monnaie Brussels; numerous recitals worldwide, orchestral concerts and cabaret performances; private voice teacher and gives masterclasses worldwide; debut as Stage Dir with Madama Butterfly at Central City Opera 2005, followed by Poulenc's La Voix humaine at Theatre Royal de la Monnaie, Brussels 2006; mem. Faculty, Depts of Voice and Chamber Music and Ensembles, Vocal, Manhattan School of Music 2008–; Hon. PhD (De Paul Univ.); Emmy Award (for Tosca). *Opera roles include:* Ottavia in L'incoronazione di Poppea, La Femme in La Voix humaine, Kostelnicka in Jenůfa, Lulu, Marie in Wozzeck, Madama Butterfly, Herodias in Salome, Eugene Onegin, Jenny in Mahagonny, Erisbe in L'Ormindo, Annina in Saint of Bleecker Street, Euridice, Polly Peachum in Three Penny Opera, Lucia di Lammermoor, Gretel, Marzelline and Leonore in Fidelio, Thérèse in Les Mamelles de Tirésias, Konstanze in Die Entführung aus dem Serail, Susanna in Le nozze di Figaro, Zerlina and Donna Elvira in Don Giovanni, Cleopatra in Antony and Cleopatra, Fiorilla in Il Turco in Italia, Emilia Marty in The Makropulos Case, the three heroines in Les Contes d'Hoffmann, the three heroines in Il Trittico, Violetta in La Traviata, Lady Macbeth of Mtsensk, Rose and Anna Maurrant in Street Scene, Manon, Tosca, Carmen, Regina, La Fanciulla del West, Kundry in Parsifal, Senta in Der Fliegende Holländer, Kat'a Kabanova, Stiffelio; sang in the world premieres of Carlisle Floyd's Bilby's Doll, Thomas Pasatieri's Washington Square and The Seagull, Conrad Susa's Transformations, William Bolcom's Beatrice in A View from the Bridge, McTeague, Medusa and Victoria in A Wedding. *Operas directed include:* Madama Butterfly, Central City Opera 2005, La Voix Humaine, La Monnaie 2006, The Saint of Bleecker Street, Central City Opera

2007, Tosca, Florida Grand Opera 2008, Rigoletto, Washington National Opera 2008, Don Giovanni, San Francisco Opera/Merola 2008. *Address:* Manhattan School of Music, 120 Claremont Avenue, New York, NY 10027, USA (office). *Telephone:* (917) 304-8079 (home). *E-mail:* Divamomcat@aol.com (office). *Website:* www.msmnyc.edu/voice (office).

MALHOUTRA, Manmohan (Moni), MA; Indian international official and consultant; *Trustee, Indira Gandhi Memorial Trust and Jawaharlal Nehru Memorial Fund;* b. 15 Sept. 1937, Izatnagar; s. of Col Gopal Das Malhoutra and Shukla Malhoutra; m. Leela Nath 1963; two d.; ed Delhi Univ., Balliol Coll., Oxford, UK; entered Indian Admin. Service 1961; mem. Prime Minister's Secr. 1966–73; joined Commonwealth Secr. 1974; Dir Sec.-Gen.'s Office and Int. Affairs Div. 1977–82, Asst Commonwealth Sec.-Gen. 1982–93; Conf. Sec. to Commonwealth Heads of Govt Meetings, London 1977, Lusaka 1979, Melbourne 1981, also at Asia-Pacific Regional Heads of Govt Meetings; led Commonwealth Secr. team in Observer Group at pre-independence elections in Zimbabwe 1980; elections in Uganda 1980; Sec. Commonwealth Southern Africa Cttee; Head of Secr. of Commonwealth Group of Eminent Persons on South Africa 1986; Chef de Cabinet, Commonwealth Sec.-Gen.'s Office 1982–90, Head Commonwealth Secr. Human Resource Devt Group 1983–93; mem. Bd Dirs Int. Inst. for Democracy and Electoral Assistance, Stockholm 1996–2003; Sec.-Gen. Rajiv Gandhi Foundation, New Delhi 2001–07; Trustee, Indira Gandhi Memorial Trust, Jawaharlal Nehru Memorial Fund; Rhodes Scholar 1958. *Publications:* First Proof (contrib.) 2004, New Century: Whose Century (ed. and publr) 2000, India: The Next Decade (ed. and publr) 2006. *Leisure interests:* reading, music, tennis, travel. *Address:* 118 Golf Links, New Delhi 110 003, India (home). *Telephone:* (11) 24643630 (home). *Fax:* (11) 24643630 (home). *E-mail:* moni.malhoutra@airtelmail.in (home).

MALICK, Terrence; American film director; b. 30 Nov. 1943, Waco, Texas; ed Center for Advanced Film Studies, American Film Inst.; Golden Berlin Bear Award 1999, Chicago Film Critics Asscn Award 1999, Golden Satellite Award 1999 (all for The Thin Red Line). *Films directed and written include:* Badlands (also producer) 1973, Days of Heaven 1978 (New York Film Critics Award, Nat. Soc. of Film Critics Award, Cannes Film Festival Award), The Thin Red Line 1998, The New World (also producer) 2005, The Unforeseen (exec. producer) 2006. *Address:* c/o DGA, 7920 Sunset Boulevard, Los Angeles, CA 90046 (office); c/o Harley Williams, 1900 Avenue of the Stars, Floor 17, Los Angeles, CA 90067, USA.

MALIELEGAOI, Tuila'epa Sailele; Samoan politician; *Prime Minister and Minister of Foreign Affairs;* fmr Deputy Prime Minister and Minister of Finance, Trade, Industry and Commerce and Tourism; Prime Minister of Samoa 1998–; concurrently Minister of Foreign Affairs; mem. Human Rights Protection Party. *Address:* Prime Minister's Department, PO Box L 1861, Apia, Samoa. *Telephone:* 63122. *Fax:* 21339. *E-mail:* pmdept@ipasifika.net (office).

MALIK, Art; British actor; m.; two d. *Television:* The Jewel in the Crown, Chessgame, The Far Pavilions, The Black Tower, Death is Part of the Process, After the War, Shadow of the Cobra, Stolen, Cleopatra 1999, In the Beginning 2000, The Seventh Scroll 2001. *Films:* Richard's Things, A Passage to India, Underworld, Living Daylights, Side Streets, City of Joy 1992, Wimbledon Poisoner 1994, True Lies 1994, A Kid in King Arthur's Court 1995, Path to Paradise 1997, Booty Call 1997, Side Streets 1998, Tabloid 2001, Out Done 2002, Tempo 2003, Fakers 2004, Dean Spanley 2008. *Theatre:* Othello (RSC), Cymbeline and Great Expectations (Royal Exchange, Manchester).

MALIK, Gunwantsingh Jaswantsingh, BSc, MA; Indian diplomatist; b. 29 May 1921, Karachi; s. of the late Jaswant Singh Malik and Balwant Kaur Malik (née Bhagat); m. Gurkirat Kaur 1948 (divorced 1982); two s.; ed Downing Coll., Cambridge, UK, Gujrat Coll., Ahmedabad; RAF 1943–46; Indian Foreign Service 1947–79, Second Sec., Indian Embassy, Brussels 1948–50, Addis Ababa 1950; Under-Sec. Ministry of External Affairs 1950–52; First Sec. and Chargé d'affaires Argentina 1952–56; in Japan 1956–59; Counsellor (Commercial) and Asst Commr Singapore 1959–63; Dir Ministry of Commerce 1963–64; Jt-Sec. Ministry of External Affairs 1964–65; Amb. to Philippines 1965–68, to Senegal, concurrently to Côte d'Ivoire, Mauritania, The Gambia and Upper Volta 1968–70, to Chile (also Accred to Peru, Ecuador and Colombia) 1970–74, to Thailand 1974–77, to Spain 1977–79; Leader trade del. to S. America 1964; mem. del. to ECAFE 1965, to Group of 77 in Lima 1971, to Gov. Body of UNDP 1971, to UNCTAD III 1972, to ESCAP 1975; Chair. Tech. and Drafting Cttee, ESCAP 1976; Deputy Chair. Cttee of the Whole 1977; Dir Indian Shaving Products 1986–88; Sec. Asscn Indian Diplomats 1983–84, 1989–91, Vice-Pres. 1985–86, Pres. 1986–87; Vice-Chair. Delhi Chapter Soc. for Int. Devt 1985–89; Chair. Ahluwalia Baradi Trusts 1988–93; Vice-Pres. Alliance Française de Delhi 1990–98, Pres. 2000–02; Chair. Maharani Voyages Pvt. Ltd 1995–2004. *Publications:* numerous literary, political and economic articles. *Leisure interests:* photography, writing, touring. *Address:* C224 Defence Colony, New Delhi 110 024, India (home). *Telephone:* (11) 41550925 (home). *Fax:* (11) 41550379 (home).

MALIK, Iftikhar Ali, BA; Pakistani business executive; *CEO, Guard Group of Industries;* b. 30 Dec. 1944, Lahore; ed FC Coll., Lahore; currently CEO Guard Group (autofilter, brake lining and brake oil mfrs); Chair. Pakistan Automobile Spare Parts Importers and Dealers Asscn 1985–86; mem. Exec. Cttee Lahore Chamber of Commerce and Industry 1980, Pres. 1990; Vice-Pres. and Zonal Chair. Fed. of Pakistan Chambers of Commerce and Industry 1994–97, Pres. and Life Mem. 2001–02; Life Mem. SAARC Chamber of Commerce and Industry (currently Vice-Chair.), Indo–Pak Chamber of Commerce and Industry; Mem. Man. Cttee, ECO Chamber of Commerce and Industry; Chair. Punjab Olympic Asscn; Vice-Chair. Mumtaz Bakhtawar

Trust Hosps; Special Lifetime Mem. Confed. of Asia Pacific Chambers of Commerce and Industry; Vice-Chair. Pakistan Olympic Asscn. *Address:* Guard Group of Industries, 80 Badami Bagh, POB 465, Lahore (office); 57-FCC, Gulberg III, Lahore, Pakistan (home). *Telephone:* (42) 7725616 (office); (42) 5757996 (home). *Fax:* (42) 7722627 (office). *E-mail:* guard@brain.net.pk (office). *Website:* www.mbmt.org.

MALIK, Shahid, MA; Pakistani diplomatist; *High Commissioner to India;* m. Ghazala Malik; joined Foreign Service Acad. 1972, worked as section officer, Ministry of Foreign Affairs; fmr directing staff mem. Lahore Civil Services Acad.; Deputy High Commr, New Delhi 1992–95, High Commr to India 2006–; served as Political Affairs Counsellor, Washington, DC, also postings to embassies in Tokyo and Rome; Dir-Gen. and Additional Foreign Sec., Ministry of Foreign Affairs 2001–02; High Commr to Canada 2002–06 (also accred to Guyana 2003–06). *Address:* High Commission of Pakistan, 2/50g Shanti Path, Chanakyapuri, New Delhi 110 021, India (office). *Telephone:* (11) 26110601 (office). *Fax:* (11) 26872339 (office). *E-mail:* pakhc@nda.vsnl.net.in (office).

MALIKI, Nuri Kamal (Jawad) al-; Iraqi politician; *Prime Minister;* b. (Nouri Kamel al-Maliki), 1 July 1950, Hindiya; m.; four c.; ed Baghdad Univ.; official of Dawa party, fled Iraq to Syria 1980; returned to Iraq as one of Dawa leaders serving as spokesman and adviser to Dawa leader and Iraq interim Prime Minister Ibrahim al-Jaafari 2003; helped draft new constitution; mem. cttee tasked to purge Iraq Baathist legacy; Prime Minister of Iraq 2006–. *Address:* Office of the Prime Minister, Baghdad, Iraq.

MALIKI, Riyad Najib al-, PhD; Palestinian politician; *Minister of Foreign Affairs and of Information;* b. 31 May 1955, Bethlehem; Prof., Coll. of Eng., Bir Zeit Univ. 1981–96; Founder and Dir-Gen. Panorama (community devt centre) 1991–; Minister of Foreign Affairs and of Information 2007–; mem. Exec. Bd Pugwash (Conf. on Int. Affairs, Science and Nobel Peace Prize) 1995–, World Movt for Democracy 1997–; columnist, Al-Ayyam (weekly newspaper); European Peace Prize 2000, Italian Peace Prize 2005. *Address:* Ministry of Foreign Affairs, POB 1336, Ramallah; Ministry of Foreign Affairs, POB 4017, Gaza, Palestinian Autonomous Areas (office). *Telephone:* (2) 2405040 (office); (8) 2829260 (office). *Fax:* (2) 2403772 (office); (8) 2868971 (office). *E-mail:* info@mofa.gov.ps (office). *Website:* www.mofa.gov.ps (office).

MALINVAUD, Edmond, LenD; French economist; b. 25 April 1923, Limoges; s. of Auguste Malinvaud and Andrée Ballet; m. Elisabeth Compagnon 1952; two d.; ed Lycée Gay-Lussac, Limoges, Lycée du Parc, Lyon, Univ. of Paris, Ecole polytechnique; with Inst nat. de statistique et des études économiques 1948–66, Insp.-Gen. 1966–74, Man. Dir 1974–87; Prof. Collège de France 1987–93, Hon. Prof. 1993–; Researcher, Cowles Foundation for Research in Econs, Chicago 1951; Prof., Ecole pratique des hautes études 1957–93; Prof., Univ. of Calif. at Berkeley 1961, 1967; Dir Ecole nat. de la statistique et de l'admin. économique 1962–66; Chair. Int. Econometric Soc. 1963: Assoc. Prof., Law Faculty, Univ. of Paris 1969–71; Vice-Chair. Soc. de Statistique de Paris 1971–73, Chair. 1974; Dir of Econ. Projections, Ministry of Econ. and Finance 1972–74; mem. Bd Banque de France 1972–88; Dir Banque nat. de Paris 1973–81; Vice-Pres. Asscn française des sciences économiques 1985–87; Chair. Int. Econ. Asscn 1974–77; Chair. Int. Statistical Inst. 1979–81; Admin. Groupe des assurances nationales 1981–89; Pres. l'Acad. pontificale des sciences sociales 1994–2003; Hon. Prof., Coll. de France 1993; Dr hc (Univs of Basle, Louvain, Helsinki, Geneva, Lausanne, Montréal, Rome, Frankfurt, Milan, Lisbon, Athens, Santiago de Compostela, Bonn, Bielefeld); Commdr, Légion d'honneur, Commdr, Palmes académiques, Grand Croix, Ordre nat. du mérite; Médaille d'argent, CNRS, Paolo Baffi Prize for Economics, Recktenwald Prize for Econs. *Publications:* Initiation à la compatibilité nationale 1957, Méthodes statistiques de l'économétrie 1964, Leçons de théorie micro-économique 1968, La croissance française 1972, Réexamen de la théorie du chômage 1980, Théorie macroéconomique 1981, Essais sur la théorie du chômage 1983, Voies de la recherche macroéconomique 1991, Equilibre général dans les économies de marché 1993, Diagnosing Unemployment 1994, Macroeconomic Theory, Vols A and B 1998, Vol. C 2000. *Address:* 42 avenue de Saxe, 75007 Paris, France (home).

MALJERS, Floris; Dutch business executive; b. 12 Aug. 1933, Middelburg; m. J. H. de Jongh 1958; two s. one d. (deceased); ed Univ. of Amsterdam; joined Unilever 1959; Man. Dir Unilever, Colombia 1964, Unilever, Turkey 1966; Man. Dir Vdberg & Jurgens, Netherlands 1970; mem. Parent Bd of Unilever and Head of Man. Edible Fats Group 1974; Chair. Unilever NV 1984–94, Vice-Chair. Unilever PLC 1984; Chair. Supervisory Bd Philips, Electronics NV, 1994; Dir Amoco 1994–98, ABN/Amro Bank, KLM, Royal Dutch Airlines 1991–, Philips Electronics, Guinness 1994–98; Gov. European Policy Forum 1993–; Chair. Bd Trustees Utrecht Univ. Hosp. 1994–, Rotterdam School of Man., Erasmus Univ. 1999–, now Prof. Emer.; Hon. KBE 1992. *Address:* PO Box 11550, 2502 AN The Hague; Room F2-30, Department of Strategy and Business Environment, Rotterdam School of Management, Erasmus University, Burg. Oudlaan 50, PO Box 1738, 3000 DR Rotterdam, Netherlands. *Telephone:* (10) 408-2210. *Fax:* (10) 408-9013.

MÄLK, Raul; Estonian diplomatist, economist and fmr journalist; *Permanent Representative, European Union;* b. 14 May 1952, Parnu, Estonia; ed Tartu Univ., Leningrad Inst. of Political Studies; economist and researcher, Inst. of Econs, Estonian Acad. of Sciences 1975–77; Sr Ed., Deputy Ed.-in-Chief, Ed.-in-Chief Estonian Radio 1977–90; Deputy Head Office of Chair. Supreme Soviet of Estonia 1990–92; adviser to Minister of Foreign Affairs 1992–93; Head Office of Minister of Foreign Affairs 1993–94; Deputy Perm. Under-Sec. Ministry of Foreign Affairs 1994–96; Amb. to UK 1996–2001, also accred to Ireland 1996–2003, Amb. to Portugal 2000–03; Minister of Foreign Affairs 1998–99; Head Estonian dels for negotiations with Russia, Finland, Latvia 1994–96; Dir-Gen. Policy Planning Dept, Ministry of Foreign Affairs 2001–07;

Perm. Rep. of Estonia to EU 2007–; Order of the White Star, Third Class (Estonia), also decorations from Portugal, Latvia, Malta and Poland; Estonian Journalists' Union Award 1990. *Leisure interests:* theatre, music, attending sports events. *Address:* Ministry of Foreign Affairs, Islandi square 1, 15049 Tallinn, Estonia (office). *Telephone:* 3222273925 (office). *Fax:* 3222274333 (office). *E-mail:* vminfo@vm.ee (office). *Website:* www.vm.ee (office).

MALKOVICH, John; American actor and producer; b. 9 Dec. 1953, Christopher, Ill.; s. of Dan Malkovich and Joe Anne Malkovich; m. Glenne Headley 1982 (divorced 1988); m. 2nd Nicoletta Peyran; one s. one d.; ed Eastern Illinois and Illinois State Univs; co-f. Steppenwolf Theatre, Chicago 1976; mem. Creative Bd of Dirs Artists Ind. Network; Co-founder Mr. Mudd (production co.) 1998; has directed three fashion shorts (Strap Hangings, Lady Behave, Hideous Man) for London-based designer Bella Freud. *Theatre appearances include:* True West 1982, Death of a Salesman 1984, Burn This 1987; Dir Balm in Gilead 1984–85, Arms and the Man 1985, Coyote Ugly 1985, The Caretaker 1986, Burn This 1990, A Slip of the Tongue 1992, Libra 1994, Steppenwolf 1994. *Films include:* Places in the Heart 1984, The Killing Fields 1984, Eleni 1985, Making Mr. Right 1987, The Glass Menagerie 1987, Empire of the Sun 1987, Miles from Home 1988, The Accidental Tourist (exec. producer) 1988, Dangerous Liaisons 1989, Jane, La Putaine du roi 1989, Queen's Logic 1989, The Sheltering Sky 1989, The Object of Beauty 1991, Shadows and Fog 1992, Of Mice and Men 1992, Jennifer Eight, Alive, In the Line of Fire, Mary Reilly 1994, The Ogre 1995, Mulholland Falls 1996, Portrait of a Lady 1996, Con Air 1997, The Man in the Iron Mask 1997, Rounders 1998, Time Regained 1998, Being John Malkovich 1999, The Libertine 1999 (also dir), Ladies Room 1999, Joan of Arc 1999, Shadow of the Vampire 2000, Les Âmes fortes 2001, Je Rentre à la Maison 2001, Hotel 2001, Knockaround Guys 2001, The Dancer Upstairs (dir and producer) 2002, Ripley's Game 2003, Johnny English 2003, Um Filme Falado 2003, The Libertine (also producer) 2004, The Hitchhiker's Guide to the Galaxy 2005, Colour Me Kubrick: A True...ish Story 2005, Art School Confidential (also producer) 2006, Klimt 2006, The Call 2006, Eragon 2006, Drunkboat 2007, In Tranzit 2008, Beowulf 2007, Gardens of the Night 2007, The Great Buck Howard 2008, Changeling 2008, The Mutant Chronicles 2008, Burn After Reading 2008, Disgrace 2008, Afterwards 2008. *Television includes:* Death of a Salesman 1985, RKO 281 1999, Les Misérables 2000, Napoleon (miniseries) 2002. *Address:* Mr. Mudd, 5225 Wilshire Boulevard, Suite 604, Los Angeles, CA 90036, USA; c/o Artists Independent Network, 32 Tavistock Street, London, WC2E 7PB, England (office). *Telephone:* (323) 932-5656 (Mr Mudd). *Fax:* (323) 932-5666 (Mr Mudd). *Website:* www.mrmudd.com.

MALLABY, Sir Christopher Leslie George, Kt, GCMG, GCVO, BA; British diplomatist and business executive; b. 7 July 1936, Camberley, Surrey; s. of Brig. A. W. S. Mallaby and M. C. Mallaby (née Jones); m. Pascale Thierry-Mieg 1961; one s. three d.; ed Eton Coll., King's Coll., Cambridge; diplomatic postings in Moscow 1961–63, Berlin 1966–69, New York 1970–74, Moscow 1974–77, Bonn 1982–85; Head of Arms Control, Soviet and E European and Planning Depts, FCO 1977–82; Deputy Sec. to Cabinet 1985–88; Amb. to FRG (now Germany) 1988–92, to France 1993–96; Man. Dir UBS Warburg (later UBS Investment Bank) 1996–2006; Chair. Primary Immunodeficiency Asscn 1996–2002, Advisory Bd Great Britain Centre, Humboldt Univ. Berlin 1998–2005, Advisory Bd German Studies Inst., Birmingham Univ. 1999–2006, European Org. for Research and Treatment of Cancer 2000–; Dir Charter European Investment Trust 1996–2007, Sun Life and Provincial Holdings PLC 1996–2000, EDF Trading 1999–2003, Vodafone Germany 2000–; Adviser to RMC 1996–2000, Herbert Smith 1997–2001; Trustee, Tate Gallery 1996–2002, Reuters (now Thomson-Reuters) 1998–; Founder Trustee Entente Cordiale Scholarships 1996–2008 (Chair. 2001–08); Chair. Somerset House Trustees 2002–06; Hon. Fellow, GB Centre, Humboldt Univ. 2005; Dr hc (Univ. of Birmingham) 2004; Grand Cross, Order of Merit (Germany); Grand Officier, Légion d'honneur, Commdr, Ordre des Palmes académiques. *Leisure interests:* grandchildren. *E-mail:* christopher.mallaby@tiscali.co.uk (home).

MALLET, W. George, GCSL, GCMG, CBE; Saint Lucia politician (retd); b. 24 July 1923, Colón, Panama; m. Beryl Bernadine Leonce; ed RC Boys' School, Castries Intermediate Secondary School; marketing man. of a Castries commercial firm; mem. Castries City Council 1952–64; elected to Legis. Council 1958; Minister for Trade, Industry, Agric. and Tourism 1964–79; mem. Opposition 1979–82; Deputy Prime Minister and Minister for Trade, Industry and Tourism 1982–92; Deputy Prime Minister and Minister for Foreign Affairs, Trade and Industry 1992–96; Gov.-Gen. of Saint Lucia 1996–97. *Address:* PO Box 216, Castries (office); The Morne, Castries, Saint Lucia (home). *Telephone:* 452-2318 (office); 453-7252 (home). *Fax:* 452-4677 (office).

MALLINCKRODT, Georg Wilhelm von; German banker; *President, Schroders PLC;* b. 19 Aug. 1930, Eichholz; s. of Arnold von Mallinckrodt and Valentine von Mallinckrodt (née von Joest); m. Charmaine Brenda Schroder 1958; two s. two d.; ed Schule Schloss Salem; with AGFA, Munich 1948–51; with Munchmeyer & Co., 1951–53; with Kleinwort & Co., London 1953–54; with J. Henry Schroder Bank Corp., NY 1954–55, 1957–, with J. Henry Schroder & Co. Ltd 1960, Dir Schroders PLC 1977, Chair. 1985–95, Pres. 1995–; Chair. J. Henry Schroder Bank AG, Zurich 1984–2003, Schroder Inc., NY 1984–; Dir Schroders Australia Holdings Ltd, Sydney 1984–2001, Schroder & Co. Inc., NY 1986–2000, Schroder Int. Merchant Bankers Ltd, Singapore 1988–2000, Siemens PLC 1989–2001; with Union Bank of Switzerland, Geneva 1956–57; Adviser, McGraw Hill 1986–89, Bain & Co.; Chair., Council of World Econ. Forum; Vice-Pres., German-British Chamber of Commerce, Trustee, Christian Responsibility in Public Affairs, Inst. of Business Ethics; Hon. DCL (Bishop's Univ., Québec) 1994, Hon. KBE 1997, Freeman of the City 2004; Annual Sternberg Interfaith Award 2005; Cross of the Order of Merit (Fed. Repub. of Germany) 1990;; Commdr.'s Cross of Order of Merit 2001. *Leisure interests:* opera, shooting. *Address:* Schroders PLC, 31 Gresham Street, London, EC2V 7QA, England (office). *Telephone:* (20) 7658-6370 (office). *Fax:* (20) 7658-2211 (office). *E-mail:* george.mallinckrodt@schroders.com (office). *Website:* www.schroders.com (office).

MALLOCH-BROWN, Baron (Life Peer), cr. 2007, of St Leonard's Forest in the County of West Sussex; **(George) Mark Malloch-Brown,** , KCMG, MA, PC; British government minister, fmr business executive and international organization official; *Minister for Africa, Asia and the United Nations;* b. 16 Sept. 1953, London; m.; four c.; ed Magdalene Coll., Cambridge, Univ. of Michigan, USA; Political Corresp., Economist 1977–79; worked for UNHCR first in Thailand in charge of field operations for Cambodian refugees 1979–81, then in Geneva as Deputy Chief of Emergency Unit 1981–83; Founder Economist Devt Report 1983–86; lead int. partner, Sawyer Miller Group (communications management firm), advising govts political leaders and corpns 1986–94; mem. Soros Advisory Cttee on Bosnia and Herzegovina 1993–94; Dir of External Affairs, IBRD 1994–96, Vice-Pres. for External Affairs 1996–99, for UN Affairs 1996–99, Admin. UNDP 1999–2005, Chief of Staff in Exec. Office of UN Sec.-Gen. 2005–06, Deputy Sec.-Gen. April–Dec. 2006; Distinguished Visiting Fellow, Yale Center for the Study of Globalization 2007; Vice-Chair. Quantum Group of Funds (hedge fund group) 2007; Vice-Chair. Open Soc. Inst. 2007; Minister for Africa, Asia and UN 2007–, also attending Cabinet; Chair. UN Devt Group; fmr Vice-Chair. Bd of Refugees Int., Washington, DC, USA; Dr hc (Michigan State) 2003, (Catholic Univ., Lima) 2004, (Pace Law School) 2005, (Walden Univ.) 2008; numerous awards including one of Time Magazine's 100 Most Influential People in the World 2005. *Address:* Foreign and Commonwealth Office, King Charles Street, London, SW1A 2AH, England (office). *Telephone:* (20) 7008-1500 (office). *E-mail:* psmallochbrowninfo@fco.gov.uk (office). *Website:* www.fco.gov.uk (office).

MALLON, Séamus; Northern Irish politician, teacher and playwright; b. 17 Aug. 1936, Markethill, Co. Armagh, Northern Ireland; m.; one d.; ed Christian Bros; Grammar School, Newry, St Joseph's Coll. of Educ., Belfast; Chair. Social Democratic and Labour Party (SDLP) 1973–74, Deputy Leader 1979–2001; mem. Nat. Ass. 1973–74, Armagh Dist Councillor 1973–86; mem. Nat. Convention 1974–75; elected to Nat. Ass. 1982 but disqualified; mem. Irish Senate 1982, New Ireland Forum 1983–84, Forum for Peace and Reconciliation 1994–95, Nat. Forum and Talks 1996–98, British-Irish Inter-Parl. Body; MP, House of Commons for Newry and Armagh 1986–2005; mem. NI Ass. for Newry and Armagh 1998–2000; (Ass. suspended 11 Feb. 2000); Deputy First Minister (desig.) 1998–99, Deputy First Minister 1999–2000; Hon. LLD (Queen's Belfast) 1999, (NCEA) 2000, (Nat. Univ. Ireland) 2002. *Leisure interests:* golf, fishing, literature. *Address:* 2 Bridge Street, Newry, Co. Down, BT35 8AE (office); 5 Castleview, Markethill, Armagh, BT60 1QP, Northern Ireland (home). *Telephone:* (28) 3026-7933 (office); (28) 3755-1411 (home). *Fax:* (28) 3026-7828 (office).

MALLOUM, Brig.-Gen. Félix; Chadian army officer; b. 1932, Fort-Archambault (now Sarh); ed Mil. Schools, Brazzaville, Fréjus, Saint-Maixent; served in French Army, Indo-China 1953–55, Algeria; joined Chad Nat. Army; Lt 1961, Capt. 1962, Col 1968; fmr Head of Mil. Corps at the Presidency; Chief of Staff of the Army Dec. 1972–Sept. 1973; C-in-C of the Armed Forces 1972–73; under house arrest June 1973, released April 1975 after coup deposed Pres. Tombalbaye; Head of State, Chair. Supreme Mil. Council 1975–79, Pres. Council of Ministers, Minister of Defence and Ex-Servicemen 1975–79; resgnd March 1979 after signing Kano Peace Agreement with Front Nat. du Tchad.

MALLY, Komlan; Togolese politician; *Minister for Health;* b. 12 Dec. 1960, Adiva; ed Ecole Nationale d'Administration, Univ. of Benin, Lomé; Prefect, Wawa Pref. 1996–99, Golfe Pref. 2002–06; mem. Parl. 2007–; Minister of Towns and Town Planning 2006–07; Prime Minister 2007–08 (resgnd); Minister of State and Minister of Health 2008–; mem. Rassemblement du peuple togolais (RPT). *Address:* Ministry of Health, rue Branly, BP 386, Lomé (office); Rassemblement du peuple togolais, place de l'Indépendance, BP 1208, Lomé, Togo (office). *Telephone:* 221-35-24 (office); 226-93-83 (office). *Fax:* 222-20-73 (office). *E-mail:* rpttogo@yahoo.fr (office).

MALLYA, Vijay; Indian business executive and politician; *Chairman, United Breweries Group;* fmrly with American Hoechst Corpn (now Aventis) USA, UK; Man. Brewing and Spirits Divs, United Breweries (UB) Group (manufacturers of Kingfisher Beer) 1980, Chair. 1983–; est. Kingfisher Airlines; Chair. Hoechst Marion Roussel India (Aventis), Aventis CropScience; f. software co., USA 1993; mem. Rajya Sabha (Parl.) for Karnataka 2002–; Nat. Working Pres. Janata Party; Dr hc (Univ. of Southern Calif., Irvine). *Leisure interests:* sports, yachting. *Address:* UB Group, UB Anchorage, 5th Floor, 100/1, Richmond Road, Bangalore 560 025, India (office). *E-mail:* cmo@ubmail.com (office). *Website:* www.theubgroup.com (office).

MALOFEEV, Anatoly Aleksandrovich; Belarusian politician; b. 14 May 1933, Gomel; one d.; ed Gomel Railway Coll., Belarus State Inst. of Nat. Econ., Higher Party School; worked as locksmith, Minsk, then Gomel and Minsk carriage repair plants 1949–62; mil. service; mem. CPSU 1954–91; various posts on CP cttees Gomel, at Dept of Chemical and Light Industries of Cen. Cttee of CP of Belarus, Chair. Gomel Regional Exec. Cttee of CP of Belarus, mem. Cen. CPSU Cttee 1986–91, Politburo 1990–91; USSR People's Deputy 1989–91; Deputy Supreme Soviet of Belorussia 1982–92; First Sec. Cen. Cttee of CP of Belorussia 1990–93; mem. Chamber of Reps 1996–2000, 2000–, Chair. 1997–2000; Chair. Parl. Comm. for Econ. Policies and Reforms 1996, Cttee on Int. Affairs and Ties with the CIS 2000–; Order Red Banner of Labour (twice),

Award of the Fatherland (3rd degree) 1999, Hon. Charter of Council of Ministers, Hon. Charter of Nat. Ass. *Address:* Sovetskaya Str. 11, 220010 Minsk, Belarus (office). *Telephone:* (17) 222-63-98 (office); (17) 222-62-37 (office). *Fax:* (17) 222-6461 (office). *E-mail:* mizhn@house.gov.by (office).

MALONE, John C., BS, MS, PhD; American telecommunications industry executive; *Chairman, Liberty Media Corporation;* b. 7 March 1941, Milford, Conn.; m. Leslie Malone; ed Yale and Johns Hopkins Univs; fmr Pres. Jerrold Electronics Corpn; Pres. Tele-Communications Inc. (TCI), Denver 1973–96, Chair. and CEO (until merger with AT&T) 1996–99; mem. Bd Dirs and Chair. Liberty Media Corpn Denver 1999–, CEO Liberty Media International (formed by spinoff of Liberty Media's non-North American operations) 2004–, Chair. Liberty Global, Inc.; Chair. and CEO Discovery Holding Co.; Chair. The DIRECTV Group, Inc. 2008–; mem. Bd of Dirs Bank of New York, IAC/InterActiveCorp, Expedia, Inc.; mem. Bd of Dirs Nat. Cable TV Asscn (NCTA) 1974–77, 1980–93; Dr hc (Denver Univ.) 1992; NCTA Vanguard Award, TVC Magazine Man of the Year Award 1981, Wall Street Transcript's Gold Award for cable industry's best CEO 1982, 1985, 1986, 1987, Wall Street's Transcript Silver Award 1984, 1989, Women In Cable's Betsy Magness Fellowship Honoree, Univ. of Pennsylvania Wharton School Sol C. Snider Entrepreneurial Center Award of Merit for Distinguished Entrepreneurship, American Jewish Cttee Sherrill C. Corwin Human Relations Award, Communications Tech. Magazine Service and Tech. Award, Bronze Award 1993 Financial World CEO of the Year Competition, Hopkins Distinguished Alumnus Award 1994. *Address:* Liberty Media Corpn, 12300 Liberty Blvd ., Englewood, CO 80112, USA (office). *Telephone:* (720) 875-5400 (office). *Fax:* (720) 875-7469 (office). *E-mail:* info@libertymedia.com (office); info@directv.com (office). *Website:* www.libertymedia.com (office); www.directv.com (office).

MALONE, Thomas Francis, ScD; American geophysicist; b. 3 May 1917, Sioux City, Iowa; s. of John and Mary (Hourigan) Malone; m. Rosalie A. Doran 1942; five s. one d.; ed S Dakota State School of Mines and Tech. and MIT; mem. of Staff MIT 1941–43, Asst Prof. 1943–51, Assoc. Prof. 1951–54; Dir Travelers Weather Service and Travelers Weather Research Center for Travelers Insurance Co., Hartford, Conn. 1954–56, Dir of Research 1956–69, Second Vice-Pres. 1964–66, Vice-Pres. 1966–68, Sr Vice-Pres. 1968–70; Dean of Graduate School, Univ. of Connecticut 1970–73; Dir Holcomb Research Inst., Butler Univ. 1973–83, Dir Emer. 1983–; Sec.-Gen. Scientific Cttee on Problems of Environment 1970–72; Pres. American Meteorological Soc. 1960–62, American Geophysical Union 1961–64, Inst. of Ecology 1978–81, Vice-Pres. Int. Council of Scientific Unions 1970–72, Treas. 1978–84; Foreign Sec. Nat. Acad. of Sciences 1978–82, Chair. Bd on Atmospheric Sciences and Climate 1981–84; Scholar in Residence St Joseph Coll., Conn. 1983; Distinguished Scholar, NC State Univ. 1990–98; mem. Scientific Advisory Cttee on Climate Impact Assessment and Response, UNEP 1992– Advisory Cttee on Accreditation, Conn. Dept of Higher Educ. 2000–02; Fellow Royal Irish Acad. 1982–, Nat. Sciences Resources for the Future 1983–84, American Acad. of Arts and Sciences 1999–; Exec. Scientist, Connecticut Acad. of Science and Eng 1987–91; mem. NAS, AAAS, American Geophysical Union; Univ.'s Distinguished Scholar Emer., NC State Univ. 1999–; Hon. DEng; Hon. LHD; Hon. ScD (Bates Coll.) 1988; Losey Award, Inst. of Aerospace Sciences 1960; Charles Franklin Brooks Award 1964 and Cleveland Abbe Award 1968 (American Meteorological Soc.), Int. Meteorological Soc. Prize 1984, World Meteorological Org. Gold Medal 1984, St Francis of Assisi Prize for Environment 1991, AAAS Award for Int. Scientific Co-operation, Irving Award American Distance Learning Consortium 1997. *Publications:* numerous articles in scientific journals. *Address:* 5 Bishop Road, Apt 203, West Hartford, CT 06119, USA. *Telephone:* (860) 236-2426 (home). *Fax:* (860) 527-2161 (office); (860) 233-6250 (home). *E-mail:* tfmalone@aol.com (office); tfmalone@aol.com (home).

MALOUF, David George Joseph, AO, BA; Australian writer and poet; b. 20 March 1934, Brisbane, Qld; s. of G. Malouf; ed Brisbane Grammar School and Univ. of Queensland; Hon. Fellow, Australian Acad. of the Humanities; Gold Medal, Australian Literature Soc. 1974, 1982, Age Book of the Year, NSW Premier's Award for Fiction, Vance Palmer Award, Pascal Prize, Commonwealth Writers' Prize and Prix Femina Etranger, for The Great World 1991, inaugural IMPAC Dublin Literary Award 1993, Neustadt Int. Prize for Literature 2000, many other awards. *Publications include:* poetry: Bicycle and other poems 1970, Neighbours in a Thicket 1974, First Things Last 1981, Selected Poems 1991, Poems 1959–89 1992; novels: Johnno 1975, An Imaginary Life 1978, Child's Play 1982, Fly Away Peter 1982, Harland's Half Acre 1984, 12 Edmonstone Street 1985, The Great World 1990, Remembering Babylon 1993, The Conversations at Curlow Creek 1996, Dream Stuff 2000; short stories: Antipodes 1983, Dream Stuff 2000, Every Move You Make 2006, The Complete Stories 2007; play: Blood Relations 1987; opera librettos: Voss 1986, Mer de Glace 1991, Baa Baa Black Sheep 1993, Jane Eyre 2000. *Address:* c/o Rogers, Coleridge & White, 20 Powis Mews, London, W11 1JN, England (office); c/o Barbara Mobbs, 35A Sutherland Crescent, Darling Point, Sydney, NSW 2027 (office); 53 Myrtle Street, Chippendale, NSW 2008, Australia (home). *Telephone:* (20) 7221-3717 (office). *Fax:* (20) 7229-9084 (office).

MALPAS, Sir Robert, Kt, CBE, BSc, FEng, FIMechE, FIChemE, FRSA; British business executive; b. 9 Aug. 1927, Birkenhead; s. of the late Cheshyre Malpas and of Louise Marie Marcelle Boni; m. Josephine Dickenson 1956; ed Taunton School, St George's Coll., Buenos Aires, Argentina, Univ. of Durham; joined ICI Ltd 1948, with ICI Europa, Brussels 1966–75, CEO ICI Europa Ltd 1973–75, Dir ICI 1975–78; Pres. Halcon Int. Inc., New York 1978–82; Man. Dir BP PLC 1983–89; Chair. Power Gen PLC 1989–90, Cookson Group PLC 1991–98; Dir (non-exec.) Bd BOC Group 1981–96, Eurotunnel 1987–2000 (Chair. 1996–98), Barings PLC 1989–95, Repsol SA (Spain) 1989–2002; mem. Advisory Bd SpecialChem Paris 1996–2000; Chair. Ferghana Pnrs 1998–2003, Evolution PLC 2000–05; Exec. Dir ENAGAS Spain 2002–06; currently Chair. RL Capital; Pres. SCI 1988–89; Sr Vice-Pres. Royal Acad. of Eng 1989–92; Chair. LINK 1986–93, Natural Environment Research Council 1993–96,; Hon. FRSC; Order of Civil Merit, Spain 1968; hon. degrees from Loughborough, Newcastle, Surrey, Bath, Durham, Sheffield Hallam, Westminster Univs. *Leisure interests:* theatre, opera, reading, music, sports. *Address:* 2 Spencer Park, London, SW18 2SX, England (home). *Telephone:* (20) 8877-4250 (home). *Fax:* (20) 8877-1197 (office). *E-mail:* bobmalpas@aol.com (home).

MALTBY, Per Eugen, DPhil; Norwegian astrophysicist and academic; *Professor, University of Oslo;* b. 3 Nov. 1933, Oslo; s. of Olaf K. Maltby and Else M. (née Raastad) Maltby; m. Elisabet Ruud 1956; two c.; ed Univ. of Oslo; Research Asst, Univ. of Oslo 1955–60, lecturer 1963–66, Assoc. Prof. 1967–82, Prof. 1983–, Chair., Astronomy Dept 1975–77; Research Fellow, Calif. Inst. of Tech. 1960–61, Sr Research Fellow 1964–65; amanuensis Univ. of Bergen 1961–63; Visiting Scientist CSIRO, Sydney 1974–75; Chair. Norwegian Council for Natural Science Research 1978–80; mem. Norwegian Acad. of Sciences and Letters, Int. Astronomical Union, American Astronomical Soc., European Physics Soc., Norwegian Physics Soc. *Address:* Postboks 1029, Blindern, 0315 Oslo 3 (office); Vaekerøvn 126A, 0383 Oslo, Norway (home).

MALTSEV, Col Gen. Leonid Semenovich, MA; Belarusian army general and government official; *Minister of Defence;* b. 29 Aug. 1949, Slonim Dist, Grodno Region; ed Minsk Suvorov Mil. High School, Kiev Higher Combined Arms Command School, Frunze Mil. Acad.; commdr of platoon, co. and battalions in Grouping of Soviet Forces, Germany 1970s; Motorised Rifle Regiment Deputy Commdr, Commdr, Chief of Staff then Commdr of Motorised Rifle Div. in Far E Dist 1979–92; First Deputy Commdr of Combined Arms and Services of Belarus Mil. Dist, 28th Arms Corps Commdr, Chief of Gen. Staff, First Deputy Minister of Defence then Minister of Defence of Repub. of Belarus 1992–97; First Deputy Chief, CIS Mil. Cooperation Coordination Staff 1997–2000; Deputy State Sec., Security Council of Belarus 2000–01; Minister of Defence 2001–. *Address:* Ministry of Defence, vul. Kamunistychnaya 1, 220034 Minsk, Belarus (office). *Telephone:* (17) 239-23-79 (office). *Fax:* (17) 289-19-74 (office). *Website:* www.mod.mil.by (office).

MALYSHEV, Andrey Borisovich; Russian nuclear engineer; *Chairman, Federal Nuclear Regulatory Authority;* b. 26 Sept. 1959, Moscow; m.; one d.; ed Moscow Power Eng Inst.; began career as engineer, Atomenergoproekt State Research and Devt Design Inst. 1982, apptd Dir-Gen. 1997; Deputy Minister, Ministry of Atomic Energy 2002–03; Chair. Fed. Nuclear Regulatory Authority 2003–; Hon. Builder of Russia Award. *Publications:* reports, articles and conf. papers. *Leisure interest:* tennis. *Address:* Federal Nuclear Regulatory Authority, Taganskaya st. 34, 109147 Moscow, Russia (office). *Telephone:* (495) 912-15-68 (office). *Fax:* (495) 912-40-41 (office). *E-mail:* tshishkova@gan.ru (office). *Website:* www.ran.ru (office).

MAŁYSZ, Adam; Polish professional ski jumper; b. 3 Dec. 1977; m. Izabela Malysz; one d.; ed coached by Heinz Kuttin (nat. coach) and by his uncle, Jan Szturc, Austria; debut for Poland in Czech Repub. 1994; World Champion, Normal Hill, Lahti, Finland 2001, runner-up, Large Hill 2001; Winner, World Cup in ski jumping 2001, 2002, 2003 (first ski jumper to win three consecutive overall World Cup titles); Four Ski-Jumps competition 2001; Winner, Polish Championships 2002; Silver and Bronze Medals, Olympic Games 2002; World Champion, Val di Fiemme, Italy 2003; Winner, Large Hill, World Cup: Lahti, 2003, Oslo, Norway 2003, Zakopane, Poland 2005, Harrachov, Czech Repub. 2005; Winner, Ski Flying, World Cup, Tauplitz, Austria 2005; Second Place, Large Hill, World Cup: Zakopane 2004, Titisee-Neustadt, Germany 2005, Innsbruck, Austria 2005; Third Place, Large Hill, Kuopio, Finland 2005; mem. KS Wisla Ustronianka Ski Club, Wisla; nicknamed "The Flying Pole", "The Polish Batman". *Leisure interests:* football, cars. *Address:* ul. Kopydło 59, 43-374 Wisła (office); c/o Polski Zwiazek Narciarski, ul. Mieszczanska 18/3, 30-313 Kraków, Poland. *Telephone:* (12) 260-99-70. *Fax:* (12) 269-71-12. *E-mail:* office@pzn.pl. *Website:* www.pzn.pl.

MAMATGELDIYEV, Maj.-Gen. Agageldy, MD; Turkmenistani army officer and politician; trained as physician; career in Turkmenistan Armed Forces, rank of Maj.-Gen.; fmr Head of Turkmen Border Guard Service; Minister of Defence 2003–09. *Address:* c/o Ministry of Defence, 744000 Aşgabat, ul. 1995 4, Turkmenistan.

MAMATSASHVILI, Teimuraz; Georgian diplomatist, engineer and economist; b. 10 Nov. 1942, Tbilisi; s. of David Mamatsashvili and Maria Robakidze; m. Irina Arkhangelskaya 1967; two d.; ed Georgian Ploytech. Inst., Tbilisi, Acad. of Foreign Trade, Moscow; Sr Engineer, Inst. of Metrology, Tbilisi 1965–70; Sr Engineer, Trade Representation of USSR in Australia 1973–77; Sr Engineer, Deputy Dir, Dir Licensmash co. (part of Licensintorg Corpn), Moscow 1977–89; Trade Rep. to Tokyo, Japan 1989–92; Minister of Foreign Econ. Relations 1992–93; Amb. to UK 1995–2004, to Ireland 1998–2004; Perm. Rep. to Int. Maritime Org. 1995–; Gov. EBRD 1996–; two state Orders of USSR 1979, 1989. *Leisure interests:* hunting, video filming, gardening. *Address:* c/o Ministry of Foreign Affairs, 9 April 4, 380018 Tbilisi (office); 4 Uznadze St., Appt. 31, Tbilisi, Georgia (home).

MAMBA, Clifford Sibusio, BSc; Swazi diplomatist; *Permanent Secretary for Foreign Affairs and Trade;* b. 5 May 1963, Manzini; m.; ed Univ. of Middlesex, UK and Seoul Inst. of Int. Affairs and Strategic Studies, Repub. of Korea; Amb. to Repub. of Korea then the EU 1991–96; Amb. to Malaysia 1996–2000; Perm. Rep. to UN 2000; currently Perm. Sec. for Foreign Affairs and Trade; fmr Chair. African, Caribbean and Pacific Group of States Cttee of Ambs, ACP Ambassadorial Sub-cttee for Sugar; Dean, Southern African Devt Community ambs 1996. *Leisure interests:* sports, reading, travel. *Address:* c/o Ministry of Foreign Affairs and Trade, POB 518, Mbabane, Swaziland. *Telephone:* 4042661. *Fax:* 4042669.

MAMBERTI, Archbishop Dominique François Joseph; French ecclesiastic and diplomatist; *Secretary for Relations with States, Roman Curia;* b. 7 March 1952, Marrakesh, Morocco; ordained priest 1981; traveled to Rome to study diplomacy at Pontifical Ecclesial Acad. 1984, joined Vatican diplomatic service 1986, has held posts in Algeria, Chile, UN, New York, Lebanon, has also worked in Secr. of State Section for Foreign Affairs, Apostolic Del. to Somalia 2002–04, Apostolic Nuncio (Amb.) to Sudan 2002–06, to Eritrea 2004–06, Sec. for Relations with States, Roman Curia 2006–; Titular Archbishop of Sagona 2002–. *Address:* Secretariat of State, Roman Curia, Palazzo Apostolico Vaticano, Citta del Vaticano 00120 Rome, Italy (office). *Telephone:* (06) 69883014 (office). *Fax:* (06) 69885364 (office). *E-mail:* vati032@relstat-segstat.va (office). *Website:* www.vatican.va/roman_curia/secretariat_state (office).

MAMEDOV, Etibar; Azerbaijani politician; *Chairman, National Independence Party (Istiklal);* led opposition movt against Popular Front of Azerbaijan (PFA); Founding Chair. Nat. Independence Party (Istiklal) 1992–; elected to Parl. 1995; cand. in Presidential elections 1998, 2003; formed new political alliance between Istiklal and Democratic Party of Azerbaijan to oppose Govt 2000. *Address:* National Independence Party (NIP–Milli Istiklal), Baku, Azadliq Avenue 179, Azerbaijan (office). *Website:* www.amip.info (office).

MAMEDOV, Georgy Enverovich, PhD, CHisSc; Russian diplomatist; *Ambassador to Canada;* b. 9 Sept. 1947, Moscow; m.; one s. one d.; ed Moscow Inst. of Int. Relations; researcher Inst. of USA and Canada 1970–77, mem. staff USSR Embassy in USA 1972–73, 1977–81, Sec., Counsellor, Deputy Chief, then Chief Dept of USA and Canada, USSR Ministry of Foreign Affairs 1981–91, Deputy Minister of Foreign Affairs of Russia 1991–2003; Amb. to Canada 2003–; mem. State Cttee on Defence Industry 1996–98. *Address:* Embassy of the Russian Federation, 285 Charlotte Street, Ottawa, K1N 8L5, Canada (office). *Telephone:* (613) 235-4341 (home). *Fax:* (613) 236-6342 (office). *E-mail:* rusemb@magma.ca (office).

MAMERT, Jean Albert; French public servant; b. 26 March 1928; s. of Paul Mamert and Marthe Maynadier; m. Monique Petit 1966; one s. one d.; ed Lycée et Faculté de Droit, Montpellier, Inst. d'Études Politiques, Paris, Ecole Nat. d'Admin, Paris; Auditor 1955, later Master of Requests, Council of State 1962–; Tech. Counsellor of Govt for Constitutional Problems, 1958–59, Sec.-Gen. Constitutional Consultative Cttee 1958; Chief of Prime Minister's Office Jan.–July 1959; Sec.-Gen. Econ. and Social Council 1959–72; Dir-Gen. Cino del Duca 1978; mem. EEC Econ. and Social Cttee 1970–74; with Michelin Group 1972–78, Pres. Pneumatiques Michelin SA, Spain 1974–78; Dir-Gen. Editions Mondiales 1978–80; Pres. Société Lorraine de matériel minier et métallurgique (SLMM) 1980; Dir France-Soir 1983–84; Dir Avenir-Publicité 1984–89; Gen. Del. Asscn Nat. des Socs par Action 1986–89, Pres. 1989–97; Vice Prin. SICOVAM 1986–; Dir 1996–; mem. Operations Comm. of the Bourse (Paris Stock Exchange) 1996–; Hon. Pres. and Dir Nat. Asscn of Jt Stock Cos (ANSA) 1997–; Chevalier Légion d'honneur. *Address:* 15 place du Général Catroux, 75017 Paris (office); 89 rue de l'Assomption, 75016 Paris, France.

MAMET, David Alan, BA; American playwright, screenwriter and director; b. 30 Nov. 1947, Chicago; s. of Bernard Morris Mamet and Lenore June Mamet (née Silver); m. 1st Lindsay Crouse 1977 (divorced); m. 2nd Rebecca Pidgeon 1991; ed Goddard Coll., Plainfield, Vt; Artist-in-Residence, Goddard Coll. 1971–73; Artistic Dir St Nicholas Theatre Co., Chicago 1973–75; Guest Lecturer, Univ. of Chicago 1975, 1979, NY Univ. 1981; Assoc. Artistic Dir Goodman Theatre, Chicago 1978; Assoc. Prof. of Film, Columbia Univ. 1988; Hon. DLitt (Dartmouth Coll.) 1996; Outer Critics Circle Award for contrib. to American theatre 1978. *Films directed:* House of Games 1986, Things Change 1987, Homicide 1991, Oleanna 1994, The Spanish Prisoner 1997, The Winslow Boy 1999, Catastrophe 2000, State and Main 2000, Heist 2001, Spartan 2004, Redbelt 2008. *Films written include:* The Postman Always Rings Twice 1981, The Verdict 1982, About Last Night 1986, The Untouchables 1987, House of Games 1987, Things Change 1988, We're No Angels 1989, Homicide 1991, Glengarry Glen Ross 1992, Hoffa 1992, Oleanna 1994, American Buffalo 1996, The Edge 1997, The Spanish Prisoner 1997, Wag the Dog 1997, Ronin 1998, State and Main 2000, Hannibal 2001, Heist 2001, Spartan 2004, Edmond 2005, Redbelt 2008. *Works include:* The Duck Variations 1971, Sexual Perversity in Chicago 1973 (Village Voice Obie Award 1976), The Reunion 1973, Squirrels 1974, American Buffalo (Village Voice Obie Award 1976) 1976, (New York Drama Critics Circle Award 1977), A Life in the Theatre 1976, The Water Engine 1976, The Woods 1977, Lone Canoe 1978, Prairie du Chien 1978, Lakeboat 1980, Donny March 1981, Edmond 1982 (Village Voice Obie Award 1983), The Disappearance of the Jews 1983, The Shawl 1985, Glengarry Glen Ross (Pulitzer Prize for Drama, New York Drama Critics Circle award) 1984, Speed-the-Plow 1987, Bobby, Gould in Hell 1989, The Old Neighborhood 1991, Oleanna 1992, Ricky Jay and his 52 Assistants 1994, The Village (novel) 1994, Death Defying Acts 1996, Boston Marriage 1999, The Wicked Son 2006; screenplays: The Postman Always Rings Twice 1979, The Verdict 1980, The Untouchables 1986, House of Games 1986, Things Change (with Shel Silverstein) 1987, We're No Angels 1987, A Life in the Theatre (also dir) 1989, Oh Hell! 1991, Homicide 1991, Hoffa 1991, Glengarry Glen Ross 1992, The Rising Sun 1992, Oleanna 1994, The Edge 1996, The Spanish Prisoner 1996, Wag the Dog 1997, State and Main 2000, The Winslow Bo 1999, Boston Marriage 2001, Heist 2001, Hannibal 2001, Spartan 2004; children's books: Mr Warm and Cold 1985, The Owl (with Lindsay Crouse) 1987, The Winslow Bay 1999; essays: Writing in Restaurants 1986, Some Freaks 1989, On Directing Film 1990, The Hero Pony 1990, The Cabin 1992, A Whore's Profession (also screenplay adaptation) 1993, The Cryptogram 1994, Passover 1995, Make-Believe Town: Essays and Remembrances 1996, Plays 1996, Plays 2 1996, The Duck and the Goat 1996, The Old Religion 1996, True and False 1996, The Old Neighborhood 1998, Jafsie and John Henry 2000, Bambi vs Godzilla (non-fiction) 2007. *Address:* c/o Howard Rosenstone, Rosenstone/Wender Agency, 38 East 29th Street, 10th Floor, New York, NY 10016, USA.

MAMI, Cheb; Algerian rai singer and songwriter; b. (Mohamed Khélifati), 11 July 1966, Graba-el-Oved, Saïda; signed to Disco Maghreb, after winning second prize in Ihan wa chabab contest on the radio 1982; numerous live performances at rai festivals, tours worldwide; military service, Algeria 1987–89; collaborations with Sting, K-Mel, Gordon Cyrus, Simon Law; World Music Award for Best Selling Arabic Artist 2001. *Recordings include:* albums: Douni El Bladi 1986, Prince Of Rai 1989, Let Me Rai 1990, Fatma Fatma, Saida 1994, Let Me Cry 1995, Douni El Bladi 1996, 100% ARABICA (with Cheb Khaled), Meli Meli 1999, Dellali 2001, Lazrag Saani 2001, Du Sud au Nord 2004, Layali 2006. *Address:* c/o EMI Music France, 118 rue du Mont Cenis, 75891 Paris, Cedex 18, France. *Website:* www.chebmami.net.

MAMMEDYAROV, Elmar Maharram oğlu, PhD; Azerbaijani diplomatist; *Minister of Foreign Affairs;* b. 2 July 1960, Baku; m.; two s.; ed Kyiv State Univ. School of Int. Relations and Int. Law, Ukrainian SSR, USSR Diplomatic Acad.; Second Sec. then First Sec., Ministery of Foreign Affairs 1982–88, Dir Div. of State Protocol 1991–92, First Sec. Perm. Mission to UN, New York 1992–95, Deputy Dir Dept of Int. Orgs 1995–98, Counsellor, Embassy in Washington, DC 1998–2003; Amb. to Italy 2003–04; Minister of Foreign Affairs 2004–. *Address:* Ministry of Foreign Affairs, 1009 Baku, S. Qurbanov küç. 4, Azerbaijan (office). *Telephone:* (12) 596-90-00 (office). *Fax:* (12) 498-84-80 (office). *E-mail:* press-service@mfa.gov.az (office). *Website:* www.mfa.gov.az (office).

MAMUT, Alexander Leonidovich; Russian business executive and lawyer; b. 29 Jan. 1960, Russia; s. of Leonid Mamut; ed Moscow State Univ.; lawyer 1985–; Founder and Head ALM Consulting Co. 1990–; business activities 1989–; Founder and mem. Bd Dirs Bank Imperial 1990–; Founder and Chair. Exec. Bd Co. on Project Financing 1993–, later Jt Stock Interbanking Credit Org. Co. for Project Financing (COPF) 1996–2000; Chair. Troika-Dialog; mem. Council on Industrial Policy and Business of Russian Govt 1994–; adviser to Head of Admin. Russian Presidency 1998–; mem. Bd Dirs Sobinbank 1999–; mem. Observation Council Bank Moskovsky Delovoy Mir MDM-Bank 1999–, Chair. 1999–2001. *Address:* MDM Bank, Sadovnicheskaya str. 3, 113035 Moscow, Russia (office). *Telephone:* (495) 797-95-00 (office).

MAN, Gen. Chu Huy; Vietnamese politician and soldier; b. 1913, Nghe An Province; one s. three d.; Col in Viet Nam People's Army 1950; Commdr of Dien Bien Phu 1954; mem. Cen. Cttee of Lao Dong Party; promoted to Maj.-Gen., Chief Commdr in Western Highlands 1960–75; mem. Politburo of CP of Viet Nam 1976–; promoted to Gen., Dir of Political Dept of Viet Nam People's Army 1976–; Vice-Pres. Council of State 1981–86; promoted to four-star Gen. 1982; Adviser to Ministry of Defence 1986–. *Address:* 36 A Ly Nam De, Hanoi, Viet Nam.

MANABE, Syukuro (Suki), DSc; American (b. Japanese) meteorologist and academic; *Senior Meteorologist, Atmospheric and Oceanic Science Program, Princeton University;* b. 21 Sept. 1931, Ehime Pref.; s. of Seiichi Manabe and Sueko Manabe (née Akashi); m. Nobuko Nakamura 1962; two d.; ed Tokyo Univ., Japan; Research Meteorologist, Gen. Circulation Research Section, US Weather Bureau, Washington, DC 1958–63; Sr Research Meteorologist, Geophysical Fluid Dynamics Lab., Environmental Science Services Admin., Washington, DC 1963–68, Nat. Oceanic and Atmospheric Admin., Princeton, NJ 1968–97, mem. Sr Exec. Service, USA 1979–96, Sr Scientist 1996–97; Dir Global Warming Research Program, Frontier Research System for Global Change 1997–2001; Lecturer with rank of Prof., Atmospheric and Oceanic Sciences Program, Princeton Univ. 1968–1997; Visiting Research Collaborator, Atmospheric and Oceanic Science Program, Princeton Univ. 2002–03, Sr Meteorologist 2005–; mem. NAS; Foreign mem. Academia Europaea, Royal Soc. of Canada; Fellow, American Geophysical Union, AAAS; Hon. DS (McGill Univ.) 2004; Hon. mem. American Meteorological Soc., Japan Meteorological Soc., Royal Meteorological Soc.; Fujiwara Award, Japan Meteorological Soc. 1966, Rossby Research Medal, American Meteorological Soc. 1992, Blue Planet Prize, Asahi Glass Foundation 1992, Revelle Medal, AGU 1993, Asahi Prize (Asahi Shimbun Foundation) 1995, Volvo Environmental Prize, Volvo Foundation 1997, Milankovitch Medal, European Geophysical Soc. 1998, and many other awards. *Publications:* more than 140 papers in scientific journals. *Leisure interests:* swimming, running. *Address:* Program in Atmospheric and Oceanic Sciences, Princeton University, Sayre Hall, 300 Forrestal Road, Princeton, NJ 08540 (office); 6 Governors Lane, Princeton, NJ 08540-3666, USA (home). *Telephone:* (609) 258-2790 (office); (609) 924-0734 (home). *Fax:* (609) 258-2850 (office); (609) 924-6360 (home). *E-mail:* manabe@princeton.edu (office); nmana6@aol.com (home). *Website:* www.aos.princeton.edu (office).

MANAGADZE, Irakli; Georgian economist and central banker; *President and Chairman of the Board, National Bank of Georgia;* b. 27 Oct. 1967, Tbilisi; s. of Nodar Managadze and Manana Janelidze; m. Nino Simonia; one d.; ed State Univ., Tbilisi; Attaché, Ministry of Foreign Affairs 1991–92, Sr. Specialist, State Cttee. of External Econ. Relations 1992–93; Chief State Adviser, Econ. and Political Reform Comms., Georgian Cabinet of Ministers 1993–94; Asst. Exec. Dir. World Bank 1994–96, Institutional Specialist, Municipal and Social Infrastructure Div., European Dept. IV 1996–98; Pres. and Chair. Bd., Nat. Bank of Georgia 1998–. *Address:* National Bank of Georgia, Leonidze 3-5, 380005 Tbilisi, Georgia (office). *Telephone:* (32) 996505 (office). *Fax:* (32) 999346 (office). *E-mail:* alexandrac@nbg.gov.ge (office). *Website:* www.nbg.gov.ge (office).

MANAGADZE, Nodar Shotayevich; Georgian film director and scriptwriter; b. 19 March 1943, Tbilisi; s. of Shota Managadze and Gabilaia Ketevan; m. Janelidze Manana 1966; one s.; ed Rustaveli Theatre Inst., Tbilisi; Dir Georgian Films 1988–; mem. Supervisory Council Kartuli Pilmi JSC 1994–; Lecturer Faculty of Cinema Tbilisi Ivane Javakhishvili State Univ. 1996–. *Films include:* Molodini (Waiting) 1970, Tsutisopeli (Life) 1971, The Warmth of Your Hands 1972 (1st Prize Tbilisi Film Festival 1972, A Common Wall 1973, The Silver Siren 1973 (1st Prize Naples Film Festival 1973), Ivane Kotorashvilis ambavi (The Story of Ivane Kotorashvili) 1974, How the Fine Fellow was Married 1974, Gatsotskhlebuli legendebi (Living Legends) 1979 (participant of Cannes Film Festival, Best Film, Sitges Film Festival 1988), Kashkhali mtashi 1979, The Dam in the Mountains 1980, Gazapkhuli gadis 1983, Spring is on the Wane 1984, Ei, Maestro (Special Prize, San Remo Film Festival 1988, First Prize, Baku Film Festival 1988) 1987, Noah 1990, Epiphany (Grand Prix, Tbilisi Film Festival 1994, Special Prize, Sochi Int. Film Festival 1994) 1994, The Migration of the Angel 2001 (Best Dir, Tambov Orthodox Christian Countries Film Festival 2001). *Leisure interests:* mountains, music, sports. *Address:* Bakradze str. 11, 380009, Tbilisi, Georgia. *Telephone:* (32) 93-27-17; (32) 99-99-71. *Fax:* (32) 51-09-10. *E-mail:* nmanagadze@yahoo.com (home).

MANANDHAR, Krishna Bahadur, MA; Nepalese central banker; *Chairman and Acting Governor, Nepal Rastra Bank (Central Bank);* ed Tribhuvan Univ., Univ. of Manchester, UK; Research Officer, Centre for Econ. Devt and Admin, Kathmandu 1973; Section Officer, Planning Comm. 1973–74; served as Asst Research Officer, Asst Controller, later Deputy Chief Controller at Nepal Rastra Bank (Cen. Bank), Exec. Dir Foreign Exchange Dept *c.* 2003, Deputy Gov. Nepal Rastra Bank –2007, Chair., Acting Gov. and Chair. Man. Cttee 2007–; mem. Bd of Dirs Rastriya Banijya Bank 1998–99, Nepal Arab Bank 1999–; Trustee and mem. Senate, Kathmandu Univ. *Address:* Nepal Rastra Bank, Central Office, Baluwatar, PO Box 73, Kathmandu, Nepal (office). *Telephone:* (1) 4412963 (office). *Fax:* (1) 4410159 (office). *E-mail:* gsd@nrb.org.np (office). *Website:* www.nrb.org.np (office).

MANASIEVSKI, Jovan; Macedonian politician; *Chairman, Liberal-Democratic Party (Liberalno-Demokratska Partija);* b. 21 May 1968, Gostivar; ed Skopje Univ., St Cyril and Methodius; Counsellor to Mayor of Skopje, responsible for Communications and Co-ordination of Int. Co-operation 1997–2002; mem. Parl. 2002–, Minister of Labour and Social Policy 2004, Deputy Prime Minister and Minister of Defence –2006; mem. Liberal-Democratic Party (Liberalno-Demokratska Partija), Chair. 2006–. *Address:* Liberal-Democratic Party (Liberalno-Demokratska Partija), 1000 Skopje, Partizanski odredi 89, Macedonia (office). *Telephone:* (2) 3063675 (office). *E-mail:* contact@ldp.org.mk (office). *Website:* www.ldp.org.mk (office).

MANASSEH, Leonard Sulla, OBE, RA, AADipl, FRIBA, FCSD; British architect; b. 21 May 1916, Singapore; s. of the late Alan Manasseh and Esther Manasseh (née Elias); m. 1st 1947 (divorced 1956); two s.; m. 2nd Sarah Delaforce 1957; two s. one d. (deceased); ed Cheltenham Coll., The Architectural Asscn School of Architecture; Asst Architect, CREN London and Guy Morgan & Partners; teaching staff, Architectural Asscn and Kingston School of Art 1941–43; served Fleet Air Arm 1943–46; Asst Architect, Herts. County Council 1946–48; Sr Architect, Stevenage New Town Devt Corpn 1948–50; partner, Leonard Manasseh Partnership 1950–; teaching staff, Architectural Asscn 1951–59; opened office in Singapore and Malaysia with James Cubitt & Partners 1953–54; mem. Council, Architectural Asscn 1959–66, Pres. 1964–65, Council of Industrial Design 1965–68, Council RIBA 1968–70, 1976–82 (Hon. Sec. 1979–81), Council, Nat. Trust 1977–91, Ancient Monuments Bd 1978–84, Bd, Chatham Historic Dockyard Trust 1984–97; Pres. Franco-British Union of Architects 1978–79; RA Rep. Bd of Govs Dulwich Schools Foundation 1987–95; Surveyor to Dulwich Picture Gallery 1987–94, Chair. 1988–93; Pres. Royal West of England Acad. 1989–94; Past Pres. Royal Watercolour Asscn. *Work includes:* houses, housing and schools, industrial work, power stations, research centres, municipal offices, conservation plan for Beaulieu Estate, Nat. Motor Museum, Beaulieu, Wellington Country Park, Stratfield Saye, Pumping Station, Weymouth, British Museum refurbishment, additions to Old Royal Observatory, Greenwich, Service Yard, Hampstead Heath, for City of London 1992. *Radio:* The Reunion (BBC Radio 4 Festival of Britain) 2003. *Publications:* Office Buildings (with 3rd Baron Cunliffe) 1962, Snowdon Summit Report (Countryside Comm.) 1974, Eastbourne Harbour Study (Trustees, Chatsworth Settlement) 1976; planning reports and studies. *Leisure interests:* photography, travel, painting, watching aeroplanes, being optimistic. *Address:* 6 Bacon's Lane, Highgate, London, N6 6BL, England. *Telephone:* (20) 8340-5528. *Fax:* (20) 8347-6313.

MANCEL, Jean-François; French politician; b. 1948; s. of Michel Mancel and Renée Baque; six c.; ed Faculté de droit et Inst d'études politiques, École nationale d'administration, Paris; Pres. Conseil Général, Oise; Pres. Oise Departmental Ass. 1985–2004; Deputy to Nat. Ass. 1978– (RPR 1978–2002, UMP 2002–); mem. Conseil Municipal of Beauvais 1977–89, of Novillers 1995–2001; Conseiller Général de L'Oise 1979–2004; Sec.-Gen. RPR 1995–97; mem. European Parl. 1984–86. *Leisure interests:* skiing, tennis. *Address:* Conseil Général de l'Oise, 1 rue Cambry, BP 941, 60024 Beauvais; Rassemblement pour la République, 123 rue de Lille, 75007 Paris, France. *Telephone:* 3-44-06-60-67 (office). *Fax:* 3-44-06-63-01 (office). *E-mail:* jfmancel@assemblee-nationale.fr (office).

MANCHAM, Sir James Richard Marie, Kt, FRSA; British politician, lawyer and international consultant; b. 11 Aug. 1939, Victoria, Mahé, Seychelles; s. of the late Richard and Evelyne (née Tirant) Mancham; m. 1st Heather Jean Evans 1963 (divorced 1974); one s. one d.; m. 2nd Catherine Olsen 1985; one s.; ed Univ. of Paris and Middle Temple, London; called to the Bar, Middle Temple 1961; mem. Legis. Council of the Seychelles 1961; mem. Govt Council 1967; Founder and Leader, SDP 1964, revived 1992–; mem. Legis. Ass. 1970–76, of Nat. Ass. 1976–77; Chief Minister 1970–75, Prime Minister 1975–76; Pres. of the Republic of Seychelles 1976–77 (deposed by coup); int. trade consultant 1981–; Chair. Mahé Publications Ltd 1984–, Airominor Ltd 1987–; Pres. Berlin-European Airways 1988–90; Founder and Chair. Crusade for the Restoration of Democracy in Seychelles 1990–; Leader of the Opposition, Pres. Democratic Party 1992–; Lecturer in Geopolitics of the Indian Ocean, Int. Univ. of Japan 1996; Hon. KBE 1976; Officier, Légion d'honneur, Grand Chevalier La Chaire de Rôtisseur and numerous medals and decorations. *Publications:* Reflections and Echoes from the Seychelles, Paradise Raped 1983, Galloo: The Undiscovered Paradise 1984, New York's Robin Island 1985, Peace of Mind 1989, Adages of An Exile 1991, Oh, Mighty America 1998. *Leisure interests:* travel, water sports, tennis, writing. *Address:* PO Box 29, Mahé, Seychelles.

MANCHIN, Joseph, III, BA; American politician and business executive; *Governor of West Virginia;* b. 24 Aug. 1947, Farmington, WV; m.; three c.; ed Farmington High School, Univ. of West Virginia; operated a chain of family-owned retail stores; Dir Enersystems –2004; elected to State House of Dels 1982, 1984, to State Senate 1986, 1988, 1992; Sec. of State for West Virginia 2000–04; Gov. of West Virginia 2005–. *Address:* Office of the Governor, 1900 Kanawha Boulevard, E, Charleston, WV 25305, USA (office). *E-mail:* Governor@WVGov.org (office). *Website:* www.wvgov.org (office).

MANCINI, Ange; French government official; Prefect of French Guiana 2002–06, of Martinique 2007–. *Address:* Préfecture, 82 rue Victor Sévère, BP 647–648, 97262 Fort-de-France Cédex, Martinique (office). *Telephone:* 5-96-39-36-00 (office). *Fax:* 5-96-71-40-29 (office). *E-mail:* contact.prefecture@martinique.pref.gouv.fr (office). *Website:* www.martinique.pref.gouv.fr (office).

MANCINO, Nicola; Italian politician and lawyer; b. 15 Oct. 1931, Montefalcione, Avellino; fmr communal, prov. and regional councillor, Chair. Campania Regional Exec. Council (twice), Christian Democrat (DC) Prov. Sec., Avellino, Regional Sec. Campania; elected Senator from Avellino 1976, 1979, 1983, 1987; Chair. DC Parl. Group 1984; Minister of Interior 1992–94, Pres. of Senate 1996–2001; Vice-Pres. Consiglio Superiore della Magistratura (Magistrates' Governing Body) 2006–. *Address:* Consiglio Superiore della Magistratura, Piazza Indipendenza 6, 00185 Rome, Italy (office). *Telephone:* (6) 444911 (office). *Fax:* (6) 4457175 (office). *E-mail:* seg-seggen@cosmag.it (office). *Website:* www.csm.it (office).

MANCUSO, Frank G.; American film industry executive; b. 25 July 1933, Buffalo; m. Fay Mancuso; one s. one d.; ed State Univ., NY; joined Paramount Pictures Corpn, Buffalo, NY 1962; Vice-Pres. and Gen. Sales Man. Paramount Pictures Corpn of Canada Ltd, Toronto 1970–72, Pres. and subsequently head of Paramount's Western Div., LA, USA 1972-76, Vice-Pres., Gen. Sales Man. Paramount's Motion Picture Div., New York 1976–78, Sr Vice-Pres. 1978–79, Exec. Vice-Pres. in charge of Distribution and Marketing 1979–80, Pres. Paramount Distribution 1980–83, Pres. Motion Picture Group of Paramount Pictures Corpn 1983–84; Chair. and CEO Paramount Pictures Corpn 1984–91; Chair., CEO MGM 1993–99; Consultant Santa Monica, Calif. 1999–; Vice-Pres. Variety Clubs Int. and of Motion Picture Pioneers; Chair. of Bd of Will Rogers Memorial Fund; Dir Will Rogers Memorial Fund, NY-Cornell Medical Center, Burke Rehabilitation Center, UCLA Medical Center, Museum of Broadcasting, Acad. of Motion Picture Arts and Sciences, Motion Picture Asscn and other orgs; Sherrill G. Corwin Human Relations Award, American Jewish Cttee 1985. *Address:* c/o Metro-Goldwyn-Mayer Inc., 10250 Constellation Blvd., Los Angeles, CA 90067-6421, USA.

MANCUSO, Salvatore; Colombian paramilitary leader; *Leader, Autodefensas Unidas de Colombia (AUC);* b. Montería; s. of Salvatore Mancuso and Gladys Gómez; m. Martha Elena Dereix; ed Universidad Javeriana de Bogotá; son of Italian immigrant whose family are ranchers in Monteria area; joined army 1990, deserted from army 1990 to found paramilitary group Los Tangeueros 1990; Chief Lt Autodefensas Unidas de Colombia (AUC) (paramilitary umbrella group) 1992–2004, Leader 2004–; wanted for extradition to USA Nov. 2004 for trafficking cocaine and money laundering; initiated disarmament of some AUC forces as part of peace negotiations with Govt Dec. 2004. *E-mail:* auc_inspeccion@yahoo.es. *Website:* www.colombialibre.org.

MANDABA, Jean-Luc; Central African Republic politician and medical practitioner; Minister of Health 1981; imprisoned for political opinions 1982, case against him subsequently dismissed; Vice-Chair. Mouvement de Libération du Peuple Centrafricain; Prime Minister of Cen. African Repub. 1993–95. *Address:* c/o Office of the Prime Minister, Bangui, Central African Republic.

MANDAL, Badri Prasad; Nepalese politician; Deputy Prime Minister, Minister of Home Affairs, of Agric. and of Co-operatives and Local Devt 2002–03; Ministry of Forests and Soil Conservation Feb.–July 2005, of Agric. and Co-operatives July 2005–06; mem. Nepali Sadbhavana Party (NSP), Acting Pres. 2002, now leader of Mandal faction. *Address:* Nepali Sadbhavana Party (NSP) (Nepal Goodwill Party), Shantinagar, New Baneshwor, Kathmandu, Nepal (office). *Telephone:* (1) 4488068 (office). *Fax:* (1) 4470797 (office).

MANDELA, Nelson Rolihlahla; South African politician, lawyer, international affairs consultant and fmr head of state; b. 1918, Umtata, Transkei; s. of Chief of Tembu tribe; m. 1st Evelyn Mandela 1944 (divorced 1957, died 2004); four c. (three deceased); m. 2nd Winnie Mandela (q.v.) 1958 (divorced 1996); two d.; m. 3rd Graca Machel (widow of the late Pres. Machel of Mozambique) 1998; ed Univ. Coll. of Fort Hare, Univ. of the Witwatersrand; legal practice, Johannesburg 1952; Nat. organizer African Nat. Congress (ANC); on trial for treason 1956–61 (acquitted 1961); arrested 1962, sentenced to five years' imprisonment Nov. 1962; on trial for further charges 1963–64, sentenced to life imprisonment June 1964; released Feb. 1990; Deputy Pres. ANC 1990–91, Pres. 1991–97, mem. Nat. Exec. Cttee 1991–; Pres. of South Africa 1994–99; Chancellor Univ. of the North 1992–; Jt Pres. United World Colls 1995–; Hon. Fellow Magdalene Coll., Cambridge 2001; Hon. Freeman of London; Freedom of City of Glasgow 1981; Hon. Citizen of Rome 1983; Freeman of Dublin 1988; Hon. Bencher Lincoln's Inn 1994; Hon. QC 2000; Order of the Niger 1990; Hon. LLD (Nat. Univ. of Lesotho) 1979, (City Coll. of City Univ. of New York) 1983, (Lancaster) 1984, (Strathclyde) 1985, (Calcutta) 1986, (Harare) 1987, (Kent) 1992, Hon. DLitt (Texas Southern Univ.) 1991; Dr hc (Complutense) 1991; Hon. DCL (Oxford) 1996, Cambridge (1996); Hon. LLD (London) 1996, Bristol (1996), (Nottingham) 1996, (Warwick) 1996, (De Montfort) 1996, (Glasgow Caledonian) 1996; Jawaharlal Nehru Award (India) 1979, Bruno Kreisky Prize for Human Rights 1981, Simon Bolivar Int. Prize (UNESCO) 1983, Third World Prize 1985, Sakharov Prize 1988, Gaddafi Human Rights Prize 1989, Bharat Ratna (India) 1990, Jt winner Houphouët Prize (UNESCO) 1991, Nishan-e-Pakistan 1992, Asturias Prize 1992, Liberty Medal (USA) 1993; shared Nobel Prize for Peace 1993; Mandela-Fulbright Prize 1993, Tun Abdul Razak Award 1994, Anne Frank Medal 1994, Int. Freedom Award 2000, Johannesburg Freedom of the City Award 2004, Amnesty Int. Amb. of Conscience Award 2006. *Publications:* No Easy Walk to Freedom 1965, How Far We Slaves Have Come: South Africa and Cuba in Today's World (with Fidel Castro) 1991, Nelson Mandela Speaks: Forging a Non-Racial Democratic South Africa 1993, Long Walk to Freedom 1994. *Address:* c/o ANC, 51 Plein Street, Johannesburg 2001, South Africa (office). *Telephone:* (11) 3307000 (office). *Fax:* (11) 3360302 (office). *E-mail:* info@anc.org.za (office).

MANDELBAUM, Michael, MA, PhD; American academic and writer; *Senior Fellow, Council on Foreign Relations;* ed Yale Univ., King's Coll. Cambridge, UK, Harvard Univ.; mem. Faculty, Harvard Univ., MA, Columbia Univ., NY, US Naval Acad., Annapolis 1975–90; Christian A. Herter Prof. of American Foreign Policy, Nitze School of Advanced Int. Studies, Johns Hopkins Univ. 1990–, Dir of American Foreign Policy Program; currently Sr Fellow, Council on Foreign Relations; Assoc. Dir Aspen Inst. Congressional Project on American Relations with the Fmr Communist World; foreign affairs columnist Newsday. *Publications:* The Nuclear Question: The United States and Nuclear Weapons, 1946–1976 1979, The Nuclear Revolution: International Politics Before and After Hiroshima 1981, The Nuclear Future 1983, Reagan and Gorbachev (co-author) 1987, The Fate of Nations: The Search for National Security in the 19th and 20th Centuries 1988, Making Markets: Economic Transformation in Eastern Europe and the Post-Soviet States (co-ed.) 1993, The Global Rivals (co-author) 1988, Western Approaches to the Soviet Union (ed.) 1988, The Rise of Nations in the Soviet Union (ed.) 1991, Central Asia and the World (ed.) 1994, The Strategic Quadrangle: Russia, China, Japan and the United States in East Asia (ed.) 1995, The Dawn of Peace in Europe 1996, Postcommunism: Four Perspectives (co-ed.) 1996, The Social Safety Net in Postcommunist Europe (co-ed.) 1997, The New Russian Foreign Policy (ed.) 1998, The New European Diasporas (ed.) 2000, The Ideas that Conquered the World: Peace, Democracy and Free Markets in the Twenty-First Century 2002, The Meaning of Sports: Why Americans Watch Baseball, Football and Basketball and What They See When They Do 2004, The Case for Goliath: How America Acts as the World's Government in the Twenty-First Century 2007; numerous articles in professional journals. *Address:* Council on Foreign Relations, 1779 Massachusetts Avenue, NW, Washington, DC 20036, USA (office). *Telephone:* (202) 663-5669 (office). *Fax:* (202) 986-2984 (office). *E-mail:* dcmeetings@cfr.org (office). *Website:* www.cfr.org (office).

MANDELBROT, Benoit B., PhD; French/American mathematician, physicist, economist and academic; *Sterling Professor Emeritus, Yale University;* b. 20 Nov. 1924, Warsaw, Poland; s. of Charles Mandelbrot and Belle Lurie Mandelbrot; m. Aliette Kagan 1955; two s.; ed Ecole Polytechnique, Paris, California Inst. of Technology, Pasadena, Faculté des Sciences, Paris; Jr mem. and Rockefeller Scholar, Inst. for Advanced Study, Princeton, NJ 1953–54; Jr Prof. of Math., Univ. of Geneva 1955–57, Univ. of Lille and Ecole Polytechnique, Paris 1957–58; Research Staff mem. IBM Thomas J. Watson Research Center, New York 1958–74, IBM Fellow 1974–93, now Fellow Emer.; Abraham Robinson Adjunct Prof. of Math. Sciences, Yale Univ. 1987–99, Sterling Prof. 1999–, Sterling Prof. Emer. 2005–; Prof., Acad. of Sciences of Paris 1995; Battelle Fellow, Pacific Northwest Nat. Lab. 2006–; Visiting Prof., Harvard Univ. 1962–64, 1979–80, 1984–87; Einstein Coll. of Medicine 1970; Visitor, MIT 1953, Univ. Paris 1966, Coll. de France 1973, etc.; Fellow, American Acad. of Arts and Sciences, American Philosophical Soc., American Physical Soc., American Geophysical Union, Soc. Française de Physique; mem. NAS, European Acad. of Arts, Sciences and Humanities (Paris), Int. Statistical Inst., Soc. Mathématique de France, American Math. Soc.; Foreign Assoc. Norwegian Acad. of Sciences; Officier, Légion d'honneur; Hon. DSc (Syracuse) 1986, (Laurentian) 1986, (Boston) 1987, (State Univ. of NY) 1988, (Bremen) 1988, (Guelph) 1989, (Dallas) 1992, (Union) 1993, (Buenos Aires) 1993, (Tel-Aviv) 1995, (Open Univ.) 1998, (Athens) 1998, (St Andrews) 1999, (Emory) 2002; MD hc (Bari) 2006; Hon. DHL (Pace) 1989, (Torino) 2005; Barnard Medal for Meritorious Service to Science 1985, Franklin Medal for Signal and Eminent Service in Science 1986, Alumni Distinguished Service Award for Outstanding Achievement, California Inst. of Tech. 1988, Humboldt Prize 1988, 'Science for Art' Prize 1988, Harvey Prize for Science and Tech. 1989, Wolf Prize for Physics 1993, John Scott Award 1999, L.F. Richardson Medal for Geophysics 2000, Procter Prize of Sigma Xi 2002, Japan Prize for Science and Tech. 2003, Sierpinski Prize for Math. 2005, Władysław Orlicz Prize 2005 and numerous other awards. *Publications include:* Logique, langage et théorie de l'information (with L. Apostel and A. Morf) 1957, Les objets fractals: forme, hasard et dimension 1975, 1984, 1989, 1995, Fractals: Form, Chance and Dimension 1977, The Fractal Geometry of Nature 1982, La geometria fractal de la naturaleza 1987, Fractals and Scaling in Finance: Discontinuity, Concentration, Risk 1997, Fractales, hasard et finance 1997, Multifractals and l/f Noise: Wild Self-Affinity in Physics 1999, Nel mondo dei frattali 2001, Gaussian Self-Affinity and Fractals, Globality, The Earth, l/f Noise and R/S 2002, Fractals, Graphics and Mathematical Education (with M.L. Frame) 2002, Fractals and Chaos: The Mandelbrot Set and Beyond 2004, The (Mis)Behavior of Markets: A Fractal View of Risk, Ruin and Reward (with R. L. Hudson) 2004. *Leisure interest:* music. *Address:* 75 Cambridge Parkway, E509, Cambridge, MA 02142, USA (home). *Telephone:* (617) 693-1791 (office); (617) 620-6598 (office). *E-mail:* benoit.mandelbrot@yale.edu (office). *Website:* www.math.yale.edu/mandelbrot (office).

MANDELSON, Baron (Life Peer), cr. 2008, of Foy in the County of Herefordshire and Hartlepool in the County of Durham; **Rt Hon. Peter Benjamin Mandelson,** PC; British politician; *Secretary of State for Business, Enterprise and Regulatory Reform;* b. 21 Oct. 1953; s. of the late George Mandelson and of Mary Mandelson (née Morrison); ed St Catherine's Coll., Oxford; joined TUC Econ. Dept 1977–78; Chair. British Youth Council 1978–80; Producer, London Weekend TV 1982–85; Dir of Campaigns and Communications, Labour Party 1985–90; MP for Hartlepool 1992–2004; an Opposition Whip 1994–97, Shadow Frontbench Spokesman on Civil Service 1995–96, Dir Tony Blair's election campaign 1997; Minister without Portfolio 1997–98; Sec. of State for Trade and Industry July–Dec. 1998, for NI 1999–2001, for Business, Enterprise and Regulatory Reform 2008–; EU Commr for Trade 2004–08; Chair. UK-Japan 21st Century Group 2001–04; mem. Council London Borough of Lambeth 1979–82; industrial consultant SRU Group 1990–92; mem. Int. Advisory Cttee Centre for European Policy Studies 1993–. *Publications:* Youth Unemployment: Causes and Cures 1977, Broadcasting and Youth 1980, The Blair Revolution: Can New Labour Deliver? 1996, Pro-Europe, Pro-Reform: A Progressive Vision of the EU 2001, The European Union in the Global Age 2007. *Leisure interests:* country walking, swimming, reading. *Address:* Department of Business, Enterprise and Regulatory Reform, 1 Victoria Street, London SW1H 0ET (office); House of Lords, London, SW1A 0PW, England. *Telephone:* (20) 7215-5000 (office); (20) 7219-5353 (House of Lords). *Fax:* (20) 7215-0105 (office). *E-mail:* enquiries@berr.gsi.gov.uk (office). *Website:* www.berr.gov.uk (office).

MANDELSTAM, Stanley, PhD, FRS; British physicist and academic; *Professor Emeritus of Physics, University of California, Berkeley;* b. 12 Dec. 1928, Johannesburg, S Africa; s. of Boris Mandelstam and Beatrice Mandelstam (née Liknaitzky); ed Univ. of Witwatersrand, S Africa, Univs of Cambridge and Birmingham; Boese Postdoctoral Fellow, Columbia Univ., USA 1957–58; Asst Research Physicist, Univ. of California, Berkeley 1958–60, Prof. of Physics 1963–94, Prof. Emer. 1994–; Prof. of Math. Physics, Univ. of Birmingham 1960–63; Prof. Associé, Univ. de Paris Sud 1979–80, 1984–85; Fellow, American Acad. of Arts and Sciences; Dirac Medal and Prize, Int. Centre for Theoretical Physics 1991, Dannie Heinemann Prize in Math. Physics 1992. *Publications:* papers on theoretical particle physics. *Leisure interests:* reading, music. *Address:* Department of Physics, 447 Birge Hall, University of California, Berkeley, CA 94720 (office); 1800 Spruce Street, Berkeley, CA 94720, USA (home). *Telephone:* (510) 642-5237 (office); (510) 540-5318 (home). *Fax:* (510) 643-8497 (office). *E-mail:* smandelstam@lbl.gov (office). *Website:* www.physics.berkeley.edu/research/faculty/mandelstam.html (office).

MANDIĆ, Andrija; Montenegrin metallurgical engineer, business executive and politician; *President, Serb People's Party of Montenegro (SPP) (Srpska Narodna Stranka Crne Gore);* b. 19 Jan. 1965, Šavnik; m.; two c.; ed Faculty of Tech. and Metallurgy, Univ. of Montenegro; Co-owner of smelting plant that produced aluminium alloys in Montenegro; mem. Parl. of Montenegro; Co-Founder Serb People's Party of Montenegro (SPP) (Srpska Narodna Stranka Crne Gore) 1997, Pres. 2002–; fmr Deputy Minister of the Economy. *Address:* Serb People's Party of Montenegro (SPP) (Srpska Narodna Stranka Crne Gore), 81000 Podgorica, Vojislava Grujića 4, Montenegro (office). *Telephone:* (81) 652149 (office). *E-mail:* sns@cg.yu (office); pobjeda@andrijamandic.com. *Website:* www.sns.cg.yu (office); www.andrijamandic.com.

MANDIL, Claude; French administrative official, engineer and business executive; b. 9 Jan. 1942, Lyon; s. of Léon Mandil and Renée Mandil (née Mizraki); m. Annick Goubelle 1966; four s. one d.; ed Lycée Pasteur de Neuilly and Ecole Polytechnique; mining engineer, Metz 1967–71, Rennes 1971–74; Délégation à l'Aménagement du Territoire et à l'Action régionale (DATAR) 1974–77; Inter-Dept Dir and Regional Del. Agence nat. de Valorisation de la Recherche, Anvar 1978–81; Tech. Adviser to Prime Minister 1981–82; Dir-Gen. Inst. of Industrial Devt (IDI) 1983, Pres. 1984–88; Dir-Gen. Bureau des recherches géologiques et minières 1988; Dir-Gen. Energies et Matières Premières, Ministry of Industry and Land Devt 1990–98; Deputy Man. Dir Gaz de France 1998–2000; Pres. Institut français du pétrole 2000–03; Exec. Dir IEA 2003–07 (retd); Officier, Ordre nat. du Mérite, Officier, Légion d'honneur, decorations from Germany and Norway. *Leisure interest:* music. *Address:* 6 rue du Plateau Saint Antoine, 78150 Le Chesnay, France (home).

MANDINGA, Vítor; Guinea-Bissau politician; Minister of Finance 2005–07. *Address:* c/o Ministry of Finance, Rua Justino lopes 74a, CP 67, Bissau, Guinea Bissau (office).

MANDOKI, Luis; Mexican film director, writer and producer; b. 1954, Mexico City; m. Olivia Mandoki; one s. two d.; ed studied fine arts in Mexico and at San Francisco Art Inst., London Coll. of Printing, London Int. Film School; directed first short film Silent Music which won an award at Int. Amateur Film Festival of Cannes Film Festival 1976; directed short films and documentaries for Instituto Nacional Indigenista (Nat. Inst. for the Indigenous), Conacine (Nat. Comm. of Film) and Centro de Produccion de Cortometraje (Center for the Production of Short Films); film Motel selected to represent Mexico in film festivals world-wide 1984; film Voces inocentes selected to represent Mexico at Academy Awards for Best Foreign Film 2005. *Films directed:* Mundo mágico 1980, Campeche, un estado de animo (also producer) 1980, El secreto (Ariel Award, Mexican Acad. of Film 1980) 1980, Papaloapan 1982, Mundo mágico (segment La venganza de Carlos Mango) 1983, Motel (aka Murderer in the Hotel) 1984, Gaby: A True Story (also developer and co-producer) 1987, Noche de Califas (producer) 1987, White Palace 1990, Born Yesterday 1993, When a Man Loves a Woman (aka To Have and to Hold) 1994, Message in a Bottle 1999, Meeting Genevieve 2000, Amazing Grace 2000, Angel Eyes (Ojos de ángel) 2001, Trapped (aka 24 Stunden Angst) (also producer) 2002, Voces inocentes (Innocent Voices) (also screenplay and producer) (Glass Bear, 14plus: Best Feature Film, Berlin Int. Film Festival 2005, Jury Prize for Best Feature Film, RiverRun Int. Film Festival 2006) 2004, Fraude: México 2006 (aka Stolen) (documentary) (also producer) 2007. *Television:* The Edge 1989, Utopia (series) (exec. producer) 2003, ¿Quien es el Señor Lopez? (series) (also producer) 2006. *Address:* c/o William Morris Agency, One William Morris Place, Beverly Hills, CA 90212, USA (office). *Telephone:* (310) 859-4000 (office). *Fax:* (310) 859-4462 (office). *Website:* www.wma.com (office).

MANDUR, László, BSc; Hungarian politician; *Deputy Speaker, Hungarian National Assembly;* b. 12 Feb. 1958, Csömör; m.; three c.; ed Coll. of Transport and Communication, Győr, Univ. of Econs, Budapest; clerk of works at Ferihegy II Airport; worked at Betonútépítő Construction Co. 1979–81; mem. of Hungarian Socialist Workers' Party 1979–89; mem. of staff, Young Communist League of Budapest Cttee, then Dist Sec. and later Budapest Sec. 1981–89; founding mem., Hungarian Socialist Party (MSZP) 1989, mem. of party exec. and faction leader, Budapest Dist III Ass. 1994–97, Co-Chair. MSZP Nat. Econs Section 1998–2000, mem. Budapest Party Council 1999–2000, MSZP Budapest Pres. 2000–04, mem. Nat. Exec. 2004–; Man. Dir Budapest Radio Kft. 1989–97; mem. Bd, then Chair., Hortobágy Fishery Rt. 1995–97; Chair. Antenna Hungaria Rt. 1996–98; mem. Supervisory Bd, Hajógyári Sziget Asset Man. Rt. 1996–99; Man. Dir Antel Invest Kft. 1997–98; Man. Dir Honline Kft. 1999; mem. Bd Budapest Waterworks Rt. 1999–2000; Man. Dir Trangon Bt. 2000–02; mem. Hungarian Nat. Ass. 2002–, Deputy Speaker 2002–; Commdr, Ordre Nat. du Mérite 2004. *Publications:* Mr. Producer (co-author) 1993. *Address:* Hungarian National Assembly, 1357 Budapest, Kossuth tér 1–3, Hungary (office). *Telephone:* (1) 441-4000 (office); (1) 441-4175 (office). *Fax:* (1) 441-4041 (office). *Website:* www.parlament.hu (office).

MANESSIS, Aristovoulos; Greek professor of law; *Professor Emeritus, University of Athens;* b. 23 March 1922, Argostoli; s. of Ioannis Manessis and Eustathia Vlysma; m. Mary Manoledaki 1961; ed Univs of Thessaloniki, Paris and Heidelberg; Lecturer in Constitutional Law, Univ. of Thessaloniki 1957, Prof. 1961–68 (dismissed by mil. regime); Prof. of Public Law, Univ. of Amiens 1970–74; Prof. and Dean, Faculty of Law, Univ. of Thessaloniki 1974–80; mem. Special Supreme Court 1976–77, 1987–88; Prof. of Constitutional Law, Univ. of Athens 1980, Dean, Faculty of Law 1982–83, 1987–88, Prof. Emer. 1988–; Pres. Union of Greek Constitutionalists 1984–89; Pres. Council of Studies of Greek Parl. 1987–; mem. Acad. of Athens 1992–; Dr hc (Amiens) 1980, (Thrace) 1990. *Publications:* The Law of Necessity 1953, The Guarantees of the Observance of the Constitution (Vol. 1) 1956, (Vol. 2) 1965, The Legal and Political Status of the President of the Republic 1975, Constitutional Law 1980, Constitutional Theory and Practice 1980, Civil Liberties 1982, Law, Politics, Constitution 1984, The Constitutional Revision of 1986 1989, The Constitution in the 21st Century 1993, Problems Regarding the Protection of Human Rights 1995; in French: Deux Etats nés en 1830, Ressemblances et dissemblances constitutionnelles entre la Belgique et la Grèce 1959, L'évolution des institutions politiques de la Grèce 1986, La protection constitutionnelle des droits de l'homme en Grèce et dans les autres Etats membres de l'Union Européenne 1993. *Leisure interest:* listening to classical music. *Address:* 14A, J. Gennadiou Street, 11521 Athens, Greece. *Telephone:* (1) 7210644. *Fax:* (1) 3234064.

MANFREDI, Valerio Massimo; Italian archaeologist, academic and writer; *Professor of Archaeology, Bocconi University;* b. 1943; specialist in topography of the ancient world; has taken part in many archaeological excavations in Italy and abroad; has taught at Università Cattolica, Milan, Venice Univ., Loyola Univ., Chicago and Ecole Pratique des Hautes Etudes, Paris, currently Prof. of Archaeology Bocconi Univ., Milan; corresp. on antiquities for publs Panorama and Il Messaggero; Commendatore della Repubblica; Premio Rhegium Julii, Premio Hemingway 2004. *Television:* Stargate (LA7-TV). *Publications include:* Xenophon's Anabasis (translator), Lo Scudo di Talos, Palladion, Il Faraone delle Sabbie, L'Oracolo, Le Paludi di Hesperia, La Torre della Solitudine, Alexandros: Child of a Dream, Alexander: The Sands of Amon, Alexander: The Ends of the Earth, Chimaira Akropolis 2001, L'ultima Legione (The Last Legion: Spartan) 2002, Il Tiranno (trans. as Tyrant) 2003, L'impero del draghi 2005, Zeus e altro racconti 2006, L'armata Perduta 2007, Idi di Marzo 2008. *Leisure interests:* motorcycling. *Address:* Laura Grandi (Agent), Via Caradosso 12, 20123, Milan (office); Via delle Grazie 31, 41010, Piumazzo, Modema, Italy (home). *Telephone:* 059-931519 (home). *Fax:* 059-931519 (home). *E-mail:* toilos@tim.it (home).

MANGAL, Mohammad Gulab; Afghan politician; *Governor, Helmand Province;* b. Paktika Prov.; fmr UN worker; fmr Loya Jirga (grand council) Del. from Paktia Prov.; Gov. of Paktika Prov. 2004–06, of Laghman Prov. 2006–08, of Helmand Prov. 2008–. *Address:* Office of the Governor, Lashkhar Gah, Helmand Province, Afghanistan (office).

MANGANELLI, Antonio; Italian police officer; *Chief of Police;* b. 8 Dec. 1950, Avellino, Campania; ed graduated in law at Univ. of Naples, post-graduate degree in Clinical Criminology at Univ. of Modena; has lectured on criminal police techniques at Italian Police Acad.; apptd Dirigente superiore 1996, directed Cen. Witness Protection Service; fmr Questore of both Palermo and Naples; apptd Prefetto di prima classe by Council of Ministers 2000, assigned to post of Criminal Police Dir and Deputy Dir of Public Security, First Deputy Dir of Public Security 2001–07, Chief of Police 2007–. *Publications:* several scientific publs on kidnapping investigations and criminal police techniques, including handbook on investigation techniques (co-authored with Franco Gabrielli). *Address:* Office of the Chief of Police, c/o Ministry of Internal Affairs, Piazzale del Viminale, Via Agostino Depretis 7, 00184 Rome, Italy (office). *Telephone:* (06) 4651 (office). *E-mail:* info@poliziastato.it (office). *Website:* www.poliziastato.it (office).

MANGANYI, Noel Chabani, DLitt, DPhil; South African civil servant and psychologist; b. 13 March 1940; s. of Frans Manganyi and Sophie Manganyi; m. 1st Esmé Kakana (divorced); m. 2nd Dr Peggy Sekele 1990; two d.; Post Doctoral Fellow School of Medicine, Yale Univ. 1973–75; Prof. of Psychology Univ. of Transkei 1976–80; Prof., Sr Research Fellow Witwatersrand Univ. 1981–90; in active forensic practice of psychology as expert witness for defence of anti-apartheid activists at Supreme Court, SA –1991; Vice-Chancellor Univ. of the North, Pietersburg 1991–92; Exec. Dir PSI Jt Educ. Trust 1993–94; Dir-Gen. of Nat. Educ. 1994–99; currently Advisor to Vice-Chancellor and Principal of Univ. of Pretoria; Founder, Violence and Health Resources Project, Witwatersrand Univ. 1986; mem. several psychology orgs. *Publications:* Treachery and Innocence: Psychology and Racial Difference in South Africa 1991, A Black Man Called Sekoto; 7 other books and 12 articles in scientific and professional journals. *Address:* Private Bag X212, Pretoria 0001, South Africa.

MANGESHKAR, Lata; Indian singer, actress and songwriter; b. 18 Sept. 1929, Indore; d. of actor and singer Dinanath Mangeshkar; sister of Asha Bhosle; Indian film playback singer; first sang in Kiti Hasaal 1942; has recorded thousands of songs in 20 Indian languages; Hon. Citizenship of Republic of Suriname 1980, Hon. Citizenship of Houston, Texas, USA 1987; Hon. DLitt (Pune Univ.) 1990; Filmfare Awards 1958, 1962, 1965, 1969 (refused to be considered for this award after 1969 to encourage new talent), Filmfare Lifetime Achievement Award 1993, Filmfare Special Award 1994, National Awards, Best Female Playback Singer 1972, 1975, 1990, Maharashtra State Award, Best Playback Singer 1966, 1967, Bengal Film Journalist's Award, Best Female Playback Singer 1964, 1967, 1968, 1969, 1970, 1971, 1973, 1975, 1981, 1985, Key of the City of Georgetown, Guyana 1980, Dada Saheb Phalke Award 1989, Videocon Screen Lifetime Achievement Award 1996, Rajiv Gandhi Award 1997, Lux Zee Cine Lifetime Achievement Award 1998, IIFA London, Lifetime Achievement Award 2000, Noorjehan Award 2001, Maharashtra Ratna 2001, Bharat Ratna 2001; Lata Mangeshkar Award instituted by Government of Madya Pradesh 1984. *Films include:* Pahill Mangala Gaur 1942, Chimukla Sansaar 1943, Maakhe Baal 1943, Gajabhau 1944, Badi Maa 1945, Jeevan Yaatra 1946, Subhadra 1946, Mandir 1948, Chattapati Shivaji 1953, Pukar 2000. *Recordings include:* albums: soundtracks: Sargam 1979, Darr 1993, Hum Aapke Hain Koun...! 1994, Dilwale Dulhania Le Jayeng 1995, Dil To Pagal Hai 1997, Lagaan 2001; solo: Lata In Concert – An Era In An Evening 1997, Saadgi 2007. *Address:* c/o Lata Mangeshkar Foundation, 45121 Cougar Circle, Fremont, CA 94539, USA; 'Prabhu Kunj', 101 Peddar Road, 400026 Mumbai, India.

MANGLA, P. B., MA, MLibSc, MSLS, MInfSc, DLSc; Indian professor of library and information science; *Professor Emeritus, Delhi University;* b. 5 July 1936, India; s. of Radha Krishan; m. Raj Mangla 1961; one s. one d.; ed Univ. of Punjab, Univ. of Delhi, Columbia Univ., New York and in London; Prof. and Head of Dept of Library Sciences, Univ. of Tabriz, Iran 1970–72, Visiting Prof. 1974–75; UNESCO expert, Guyana 1978–79; Prof. and Head of Dept of Library and Information Sciences, Univ. of Delhi 1972–, Dean Faculty of Arts 1976–78, 1984–88, Chair. Bd of Research Studies 1979–85; Library Consultant, Reserve Bank of India, Bombay 1992–93; Library Adviser, YMCA New Delhi 1992–; various other admin. posts in Delhi and numerous other univs 1972–; Chair. Manpower Devt Cttee of Nat. Information System in Science and Tech. 1977–; Sr Vice-Pres. and Founder-mem. Indian Asscn of Academic Librarians 1981–83; mem. Bd Int. Fed. of Library Asscns and Insts 1983– (Vice-Pres. 1987–89, 1989–91), Inst. of Information Scientists; Nat. Prof., UGC 1984–86; Chair. Bd of Eds Univ. of Delhi Annual Reports 1989–96; mem. Editorial Bd Third World Libraries (USA) 1989–, Journal of Library and Information Science, Education for Information, Amsterdam 1982–, Review in Library and Information Science, USA, LIBRI (Copenhagen), Third World Libraries (Chicago), Int. Journal of Information and Library Research (UK) 1989–; Special Adviser, IFLA Regional Section for Asia and Oceania 1991–; Chair. Programme Implementation Cttee, Nat. Service Scheme, Delhi Univ. 1989–, Governing Body Deshbandhu Coll., Delhi Univ. 1990–95, Dyal Singh Coll., Delhi Univ. 2001–04, Univ. Grants Cttee (UGC) Panel of Library and Information Science 1992–; Prof., Mangla Research Foundation 2001, Dyal Singh Coll., Delhi Univ. 2001–04 (Prof. Emer. 2004–); mem. Steering Cttee Inflibnet (UGC) 1990–99; mem. Planning Comm. (Govt of India) Working Group on Modernization of Libraries and Informatics for 7th, 8th and 9th Five-Year Plans; mem. Research Cttee INSDOC New Delhi 2000–02, Nat. Inst. of Science Communication and Information Resources 2002–; mem. Nat. Advisory Cttee Nat. Library 2002–, Expert Cttee Asiatic Soc. 2002–, Working Group on Libraries, Nat. Knowledge Comm. 2006, Search Cttee for Chair., Inflibnet (UGC) 2006; mem. Bd of Man., Nat. Library of India (Kolkata) 2004–; Fellow, Indian Library Asscn; Rockefeller Foundation (New York) Merit Scholarship 1961–62, British Council sponsorship 1979, 1980, 1987, 1989, IDRC (Canada) sponsorship 1983, 1991, Int. Library Movt Award (India)

1984, Shiromani Award for Human Excellence 1991, IFLA Gold Medal 1991, Distinguished Services Award and Citation, Punjab Library Asscn 1997, Library and Information Science: Parameters and Perspectives, two-vol. Festchrift 1997, Certificate of Honour, IASLIC 2006; several memorial lectures; Hon. Fellow Indian Library Asscn. *Publications:* author/ed. of numerous books and specialist reviews in India and overseas. *Leisure interests:* travel, reading. *Address:* EB-210 Maya Enclave, New Delhi 110064, India. *Telephone:* (11) 2512-0458; (11) 2512-0331 (home). *E-mail:* manglapb@yahoo.co.in (home).

MANGOAELA, Percy Metsing, BSc, BEd, LLB; Lesotho diplomatist and international civil servant; *Chairman, Lesotho Telecommunications Authority;* b. 26 Aug. 1942, Berea; m.; two d.; ed Memorial Univ. of Newfoundland, Dalhousie Univ., Canada, Makerere Univ., Kampala and Harvard Univ., USA; radio news reporter Dept of Information and Broadcasting 1966–68; joined Lesotho civil service 1968, Asst Sec., Ministry of Foreign Affairs, then Desk Officer, Int. Orgs and N America –1970; Dir of Civil Aviation 1973–76, Prin. Sec., Ministry of Transport and Communications 1976–79, 1990; Deputy Co-ordinator UN Transport and Communications Decade for Africa, UN Econ. Comm. for Africa 1979–89; Prin. Sec., Depts of Trade and Industry and Consumer Affairs 1991–92; 92;.

MANGOLD, Klaus; German business executive; b. 6 June 1943, Pforzheim; m.; two c.; ed Univ. of Munich, Univ. of Heidelberg, Univ. of Geneva; Asst Man. German-Mexican Chamber of Commerce, Mexico City 1972–73; Section Jr Barrister Thyssen 1973–75; Man. Union of German Textile Industry, Stuttgart 1976; mem. Bd Dirs Rhodia AG (Rhone Poulenc Group) 1983–90; Chair. Bd Quelle-Schickedanz AG, Fürth 1991–94; mem. Bd Dirs Daimler-Benz AG and Chair. Bd Daimler-Benz InterServices AG 1995–2003; mem. Bd Dirs DaimlerChrysler Services AG, Berlin 1998–2003, Chair. 1998–2003; Chair. Cttee on Eastern European Econ. Relations 2000–05; Exec. Adviser to Chair. DaimlerChrysler AG for Cen. and Eastern Europe and Cen. Asia 2003–; mem. of numerous supervisory and advisory bds including Rothschild & Cie, France and Germany, Chubb Corpn, USA, Rhodia, SA, France, Metro AG, Germany, Jenoptik AG, Germany, Magna International Inc., Canada; Chevalier, Légion d'honneur. *Publications:* Die Zukunft der Dienstleistung (ed.) 1997, Die Welt der Dienstleistung (ed.) 1998. *Address:* DaimlerChrysler AG, Siemenstr. 7, 70469 Stuttgart, Germany (office). *Telephone:* (711) 2574-3300 (office). *Fax:* (711) 2574-8008 (office).

MANGOLD, Robert Peter, MFA; American artist; b. 12 Oct. 1937, N Tonawanda, NY; ed Cleveland Inst. of Art and Yale Univ.; Instructor School of Visual Arts, New York 1963–, Hunter Coll. 1964–65, Cornell Univ. Skowhegan Summer Art School 1968; one-man exhbns Daniel Weinberg Gallery, LA 1984, Akron Art Museum 1984, Pace Gallery 1992, Le Consortium Dijon, France 1992; retrospective Exhbn Stedelijk Museum, Amsterdam 1982; has participated in numerous exhbns notably at Whitney Museum, New York 1968, 1973, 1979, 1983, Solomon R. Guggenheim Museum, New York 1971, Documenta, Kassel, W Germany 1972, 1977, 1982, Museum of Contemporary Art, Chicago 1974, Ritter Klagenfurt, Austria 1992–93; work represented in numerous public collections in USA, UK and Europe including Whitney Museum, Solomon R. Guggenheim Museum, Museum of Fine Arts, Houston, Tate Gallery, London, Kunsthaus, Zürich and Stedelijk Museum, Amsterdam; Guggenheim Grant 1969; Nat. Council on Arts Award 1966.

MANGOPE, Chief Lucas Manyane; South African politician and tribal chief; b. 27 Dec. 1923, Motswedi, Zeerust; s. of Manyane Mangope and Semakaleng Mangope; m. Leah Tscholofelo Dolo 1951; four s. three d.; ed St Peter's Coll. and Bethel Coll.; worked in the Dept of Bantu Admin and Devt, later taught at Motswedi; succeeded his father as Chief of the Bahurutshe-Boo-Manyane 1959; Vice-Chair. Tswana Territorial Authority 1961–68, Chief Councillor, Exec. Council 1968–72; Chief Minister of Bophuthatswana Homeland 1972–77; fmr Prime Minister, Minister of Finance, Minister of Law and Order; Pres. 1977–94; leader South African United Christian Democratic Party; mem. North-West Prov. legislature. *Leisure interests:* soccer, tennis, choral music. *Address:* PO Box 245, Buhrmannsdrif 2867, South Africa (office). *Telephone:* (18) 3814044 (office). *Fax:* (18) 3185979 (office).

MANGUEL, Alberto; Canadian (b. Argentine) writer, editor and translator; b. 1948, Buenos Aires, Argentina; Fellow, Simon Guggenheim Foundation, S. Fischer Stiftung; Officier, Ordre des Arts et des Lettres; Premio Lanacion 1971, Harbourfront Festival Prize 1992, Canadian Authors' Asscn Prize 1992, Prix France-Culture 2000, Premio German Sánchez Ruiperez 2002, Prix Poitou-Charentes 2004, Prix Roger Caillois 2004. *Publications:* (in English) novels: News from a Foreign Country Came (McKitterick Prize 1992) 1991, Stevenson Under the Palm Trees 2004, The Library at Night 2006; collections: In Another Part of the Forest: The Flamingo Anthology of Gay Literature (with Craig Stephenson) 1968, The Gates of Paradise: The Flamingo Anthology of Erotic Literature 1969, Black Water: The Flamingo Anthology of Fantastic Literature 1990; non-fiction: The Dictionary of Imaginary Places 1980, Into the Looking-Glass Wood: Essays on Books, Reading and the World 1985, A History of Reading (TLS Int. Book of the Year, Prix Médicis 1998) 1996, Reading Pictures 2001, A Reading Diary 2005, With Borges 2006, Homer's The Iliad and The Odyssey: A Biography 2007, The City of Words 2008; ed. of numerous anthologies, many trans. *Address:* Guillermo Schavelzon Agency, Calle Muntaner 339 5, 08021 Barcelona, Spain (office). *Telephone:* (93) 2011310 (office). *Fax:* (93) 2006886 (office). *E-mail:* info@schavelzon.com (office). *Website:* www.schavelzon.com (office).

MANGWANA, Sam; Democratic Republic of the Congo singer, musician (guitar) and songwriter; b. 1945, Kinshasa, Zaire (now Democratic Repub. of the Congo); ed studied singing in the Salvation Army choir; mem. Tabu Ley

Rochereau's Africa Fiesta, c. 1962, Franco's TPOK Jazz 1972; formed Festival des Maquisards with Dizzy Mandjeku 1968; established La Belle Sonora label; founder, African All Stars 1976, based in Abidjan, toured Africa, Europe and the USA; now lives in Paris. *Recordings include:* albums: Sam and Les Maquisards 1968, Sam and African All Stars Vols 1 and 2 1982, Maria Tebbo, Rumba Music 1991, Gallo Negro (featuring Papa Noël) 1998, Sam Mangwana Plays Dino Vangu 2000. *Address:* c/o Alison Loerke, 12501 11th Avenue NW, Seattle, WA 98177, USA (office).

MANHIRE, William (Bill), BA, MLitt, MPhil; New Zealand poet, writer and academic; *Professor of Creative Writing and English Literature, Victoria University of Wellington;* b. 27 Dec. 1946, Invercargill; s. of Jack Manhire and Madeline Mary Manhire; m. Barbara Marion McLeod 1970; one s. one d.; ed S Otago Dist High School, Otago Boys' High School, Univ. of Otago at Dunedin, Univ. Coll., London, UK; Lecturer in English, Vic. Univ., Wellington 1973, f. creative writing programme 1976, Prof. of Creative Writing and English Literature 1997–; Dir Int. Inst. of Modern Letters 2001–; Fiction Ed. Victoria Univ. Press 1976–96; Fulbright Visiting Prof. in NZ Studies, Georgetown Univ., USA Jan.–June 1999; inaugural Te Mata Estate New Zealand Poet Laureate 1997–99; Nuffield Fellowship 1981; Companion NZ Order of Merit; Hon. DLitt (Otago); NZ Book Award 1977, 1984, 1992, 1996, Montana Book Award 1994, Katherine Mansfield Fellowship 2004, NZAF Arts Laureate 2005, Montana NZ Book Award 2006, Prime Minister's Award for Poetry. *Publications:* Malady 1970, The Elaboration 1972, Song Cycle 1975, How to Take Your Clothes Off at the Picnic 1977, Dawn/Water 1980, Good Looks 1982, Locating the Beloved and Other Stories 1983, Zoetropes: Poems 1972–82 1984, Maurice Gee 1986, The Brain of Katherine Mansfield 1988, The New Land: A Picture Book 1990, The Old Man's Example 1990, Milky Way Bar 1991, An Amazing Week in New Zealand 1993, Fault 1994, South Pacific 1994, Hoosh 1995, My Sunshine 1996, Songs of My Life 1996, Sheet Music: Poems 1967–1982 1996, Mutes and Earthquakes 1997, What to Call Your Child 1999, Doubtful Sounds: Essays and Interviews 2000, Collected Poems 2001, Collected Poems 2001, Under the Influence (memoir) 2003, Lifted (poems) 2005, Pine 2005; editor: New Zealand Listener Short Stories Vol. 1 1977, Vol. 2 1978, Some Other Country: New Zealand's Best Short Stories (with Marion McLeod) 1984, Six by Six 1989, Soho Square 1991, 100 New Zealand Poems 1994, Denis Glover: Selected Poems 1995, Spectacular Babies (with Karen Anderson) 2001, The Wide White Page: Writers Imagine Antarctica 2004, 121 New Zealand Poems 2006, The Goose Bath 2006, Still Shines When You Think of It (with Peter Whiteford). *Leisure interest:* swimming. *Address:* Creative Writing Programme, International Institute of Modern Letters, Victoria University of Wellington, PO Box 600, Wellington, New Zealand (office). *Telephone:* (4) 463-6808 (office). *Fax:* (4) 463-6865 (office). *E-mail:* bill .manhire@vuw.ac.nz (office). *Website:* www.vuw.ac.nz/modernletters (office).

MANIATOPOULOS, Constantinos S.; Greek EU official and business executive; b. 1941; m. Theodora Hiou; one s.; ed Athens and Paris; fmrly employed in energy and industry sectors; Chair. and Man. Dir EKO Petroleum Co., Greece; Special Adviser to Minister of Energy; mem. Bd various nat. advisory bodies; Gen. Sec. Tech. Chamber of Greece; Dir-Gen. for Energy, EC (now EU) Comm. 1986–95. *Address:* 13 Makedonias Street, Kifissia, Athens, Greece; 10 Akti Miaouli, 18538 Piraeus (office).

MANIGAT, Leslie Francois; Haitian politician and academic; *Secretary-General, Rassemblement des Démocrates Nationalistes et Progressistes (RDNP);* b. 16 Aug. 1930, Port-au-Prince; m. 2nd Mirlande Manigat 1970; f. School of Int. Studies at Univ. of Haiti, first Dir; fmr Research Assoc. Johns Hopkins Univ., Washington, DC; fmr Prof. Inst. of Political Studies, Paris; then with Univ. of West Indies, Trinidad and Tobago; with Simón Bolívar Univ., Caracas 1978; returned from 23 years in exile 1986; Pres. of Haiti Jan. 1988 (first democratically elected Pres. of Haiti), overthrown by Lt-Gen. Henri Namphy June 1988; Sec.-Gen. Rassemblement des Démocrates Nationalistes et Progressistes (RDNP), unsuccessful presidential cand. 2006. *Address:* Rassemblement des Démocrates Nationalistes et Progressistes (RDNP), 234 route de Delmas, Delmas, Port-au-Prince, Haiti. *Telephone:* 246-3313.

MANIGLIA FERREIRA, Adm. Ramón Orlando; Venezuelan government official and naval officer; mem. Navy, fmr Navy Commdr, C-in-C 2003, rank of Vice-Adm., then Three-Sun Adm. 2005; Inspector Gen. Nat. Armed Forces 2004–05; Minister of Nat. Defence 2005–06. *Address:* c/o Ministry of National Defence, Edif. 17 de Diciembre, planta baja, Base Aérea Francisco de Miranda, La Carlota, Caracas, Venezuela (office).

MANIK, K. D. Ahmed; Maldivian government official; *Commissioner of Elections;* Deputy Minister of Environment and Construction –2005; Commr of Elections and Registrar of Political Parties 2005–. *Address:* Office of the Commissioner of Elections, PA Complex, 3rd Floor, Hilaalee Magu, Malé, Maldives (office). *Telephone:* 3324426 (office). *Fax:* 3323997 (office). *E-mail:* info@elections.gov.mv (office). *Website:* www.elections.gov.mv (office).

MANIKU, M. U.; Maldivian business executive; Founder-Chair. Universal Enterprises Pvt. Ltd; fmr Special Econ. Adviser to the Pres.; Chair. Maldives Asscn of Tourism Industry. *Address:* Maldives Association of Tourism Industry, Gadhamoo Building, 3rd Floor, Henveyru, Malé, Maldives (office). *Telephone:* 3326640 (office). *Fax:* 3326641 (office). *E-mail:* mati@dhivehinet .net.mv (office).

MANILOV, Col-Gen. Valery Leonidovich, PhD; Russian civil servant and army officer; *Representative of Primorsky Federal District, Federation Council;* b. 10 Jan. 1939, Tulchin, Ukraine; m.; one d.; ed Odessa Higher Infantry School, Mil.-Political Acad., Gen. Staff Mil. Acad.; service in Odessa, Baikal mil. commands, S Group of armed forces, service in Afghanistan; on staff Ministry of Defence 1988–; Head Information Service of Jt Armed Forces of CIS 1992–93; Asst to Sec. Russian Security Council July–Oct. 1993, Deputy

Sec. 1993–96; First Deputy Head of Gen. Staff. 1998–2000; mem. Acad. of Mil. Sciences, Russian Acad. of Natural Sciences, Int. Acad. of Informatization; mem. Council of Fed., Rep. Primorsky Territory 2001–. *Address:* Council of Federation, B. Dmitrovka 26, 103426 Moscow, Russia. *Telephone:* (495) 252-89-77.

MANILOW, Barry; American singer, musician (piano) and songwriter; b. (Barry Alan Pincus), 17 June 1946, New York, NY; s. of Harold Manilow and Edna Manilow; ed New York Coll. Music, Juilliard School of Music; worked in mailroom, CBS; film ed. WCBS-TV; Dir Music Ed Sullivan's Pilots; Dir Music, conductor and producer for Bette Midler; Amb. for Prince's Trust 1996; solo artist 1974–; Producer of the Year 1975, After Dark magazine Ruby Award 1976, Photoplay Gold Medal 1976, Grammy Award for Song of the Year (for I Write The Songs) 1977, Emmy Award (for The Barry Manilow Special) 1977, American Music Awards for Favorite Male Artist 1978–80, Grammy Award for Best Male Pop Vocal Performance (for At The Copa from Copacabana) 1979, Songwriters Hall of Fame Hitmaker Award 1991, Starlight Foundation Humanitarian of the Year 1991, Soc. of Singers Ella Award 2003. *Theatre:* Barry Manilow on Broadway (jt recipient Tony Award 1977) 1976, Barry Manilow at the Gershwin (Broadway) 1989, Copacabana (West End, London) 1994. *Television appearance:* Copacabana (film) 1985. *Recordings include:* albums: Barry Manilow I 1973, Barry Manilow II 1974, Tryin' To Get The Feelin' 1975, This One's For You 1976, Live 1977, Even Now 1978, One Voice 1979, Barry 1980, A Nice Boy Like Me 1980, If I Should Love Again 1981, Live In Britain 1982, I Wanna Do It With You 1982, Here Comes The Night 1982, Oh, Julie! 1982, 2.00 AM Paradise Café 1984, Manilow 1985, Live On Broadway 1987, Swing Street 1987, Barry Manilow 1989, Songs To Make The Whole World Sing 1989, Because It's Christmas 1990, Showstoppers 1991, Hidden Treasures 1993, Singin' With The Big Bands 1994, Another Life 1995, Summer of '78 1996, Manilow Sings Sinatra 1998, Here At The Mayflower 2001, A Christmas Gift Of Love 2002, Two Nights Live 2004, Scores: Songs From Copacabana and Harmony 2004, The Greatest Songs of the Fifties 2006, The Greatest Songs of the Sixties 2006, The Greatest Songs of the Seventies 2007, In the Swing of Christmas 2007, Beautiful Ballads and Love Songs 2008, The Greatest Songs of the Eighties 2008, Happy Holiday! 2008. *Publication:* Sweet Life: Adventures on the Way to Paradise 1987. *Address:* William Morris Agency, 1325 Avenue of the Americas, New York, NY 10019, USA (office). *Telephone:* (212) 586-5100 (office). *Fax:* (212) 246-3583 (office). *Website:* www.wma.com (office); www.manilow.com.

MANIN, Yuri Ivanovich, BSc, PhD, DPhysMathSci (habil.); Russian/German mathematician and academic; *Professor Emeritus, Max Planck Institute for Mathematics;* b. 16 Feb. 1937, Simferopol; s. of Ivan Manin and Rebecca Miller; m. Xenia Semenova; one s.; ed Moscow State Univ.; Researcher Steklov Math. Inst. Moscow 1960–, now Prin. Researcher; Prof. of Math. Moscow State Univ. 1965–91; Visiting Prof. several univs including Harvard Univ., Columbia Univ. 1991–93; Prof. MIT 1992–93; Scientific mem. Max Planck Inst. for Math., Bonn 1993–, Dir, Man. Dir 1995, now Prof. Emer.; Bd of Trustees Prof., Northwestern Univ. 2002–; Corresp. mem. Russian Acad. of Sciences, Göttingen Acad. of Sciences; Foreign mem. Royal Netherlands Acad. of Arts and Sciences; mem. Academia Europaea; mem. Pontifical Acad. of Science, Vatican; mem. Acad. Leopoldina Germany; mem. American Acad. of Arts and Sciences; foreign mem. French Acad. des Sciences; Order 'pour le Mérite' for Arts and Sciences (Germany) 2007, Grosses Verdienstkreuz mit Stern (Germany) 2008; Dr hc (Sorbonne, Univ. Pierre et Marie Curie, Paris VI) 1999, (Warwick) 2006; Abel Bicentennial DPhil hc (Oslo) 2002; Lenin Prize 1967, Brouwer Gold Medal 1987, Frederic Esser Nemmers Prize 1994, Rolf Schock Math. Prize (Royal Swedish Acad. of Sciences) 1999, King Faisal Prize for Science 2002, Georg Cantor Medal of German Math. Soc. 2002. *Publications:* Frobenius Manifolds, Quantum Cohomology and Moduli Spaces 1999; author, co-author of 11 monographs and about 220 scientific papers. *Leisure interests:* literary criticism, linguistics, cultural studies. *Address:* Max Planck Institute for Mathematics, Vivatsgasse 7, 53111 Bonn, Germany (office). *Telephone:* (228) 402271 (office). *Fax:* (228) 402277 (office). *E-mail:* manin@mpim-bonn.mpg.de (office). *Website:* www.mpim-bonn.mpg.de/index.html (office).

MANKELL, Henning; Swedish playwright and writer; b. 3 Feb. 1948, Stockholm; m. 3rd Eva Bergman 1998; four s.; merchant seaman 1964–66; Dir Teatro Avenida, Maputo, Mozambique 1987–; co-f. Leopard publishing house 2001–; German Crime Prize 1999, Macallan CWA Golden Dagger Award 2001, Author of the Year, Germany 2002, Premio Pepe Carvalho, Spain 2007. *Plays include:* The Amusement Park 1068, Tale on the Beach of Time 1997, Labyrinten (trans. as The Labyrinth) 2000. *Publications include:* fiction: Bergsprängaren (trans. as The Rock Blaster) 1973, Vettvillingen (trans. as The Mad Man) 1978, Fångvårdskolonin som försvann (trans. as The Prison Colony that Disappeared) 1979, Dödsbrickan (trans. as The Death Badge) 1980, En seglares död (trans. as The Death of a Sailor) 1981, Daisy Sisters 1982, Sagan om Isidor (trans. as The Tale of Isidor) 1984, Leopardens Öga (trans. as The Eye of the Leopard) 1990, Comédia infantil 1995, Vindens Son 2000, Tea-bag 2001, Djup (trans. as Depth) 2004, Italienska Skor (trans. as Italian Shoes) 2006; crime fiction: Mördare utan ansikte (trans. as Faceless Killers; Acad. of Swedish Crime Writers' Prize 1991, Scandinavian Crime Soc. Prize 1991) 1991, Hundarna i Rīga (trans. as The Dogs of Rīga) 1992, Den vita lejoninnan (trans. as The White Lioness) 1993, Mannen som log (trans. as The Man Who Smiled) 1994, Villospår (trans. as Sidetracked) 1995, Den femte kvinnan (trans. as The Fifth Woman) 1996, Steget efter (trans. as One Step Behind) 1997, Brandvägg (trans. as Firewall) 1998, Pyramiden (trans. as The Pyramid) 1999, Danslärarens återkomst (trans. as The Return of the Dancing Master) 1999, Innan Frosten (trans. as Before the Frost) 2002, Kennedys Hjärna (trans. as Kennedy's Brain) 2005; juvenile fiction: Sandmålaren (trans. as The Sand Painter) 1974, Hunden som sprang mot en stjärna (trans. as The Dog that ran towards a star) 1990, Skuggorna Växer i Skymningen (trans. as The Shadows grow in the Dark) 1991, Katten som Àlskade Regn 1992, Eldens Hemlighet (trans. as Secrets in the Fire) 1995, Pojken som sov med snö i sin säng (trans. as The Boy who slept with snow in his bed) 1996, A Bridge to the Stars 1998; short stories: Anton och det Gripenstedtska sommarnöjet (trans. as Anton and the Summerhouse of Gripenstedtessays) 1974; essays: Jag dör, men minnet lever, I sand och i lera 1999. *Address:* c/o Leopard förlag AB, S:t Paulsgatan 11, 118 46 Stockholm, Sweden (office). *Telephone:* (8) 203-14-0 (office). *Fax:* (8) 462-99-44 (office). *E-mail:* info@leopardforlag.se (office). *Website:* www.henningmankell.com.

MANKIEWICZ, Frank, MS, AB, LLB; American public affairs executive; b. 16 May 1924, New York; s. of Herman J. and Sara Mankiewicz; m. Holly Jolley 1952 (divorced); two s.; m. 2nd Patricia O'Brien 1988; ed Columbia Univ., Univ. of Calif., Berkeley and Los Angeles; mem. Calif. and DC Bars; practised as lawyer, Los Angeles 1955–61; served with Peace Corps as Country Dir, Lima, Peru and later as Regional Dir for Latin America; Press Sec. to Senator Robert F. Kennedy 1966–68; syndicated columnist (with Tom Braden), Washington and co-presenter, nightly newscast on CBS television affiliate 1968–71; Campaign Dir presidential campaign of George McGovern 1972; Pres. Nat. Public Radio 1977–83; Vice-Chair. Gray and Co. (now Hill and Knowlton) Washington, 1983–2006; Hon. DHL (Lincoln Univ.) 1983; UCLA Public Service Award 1988;. *Publications:* Perfectly Clear: Nixon from Whittier to Watergate 1974, U.S. *v.* Richard Nixon: The Final Crisis 1976, With Fidel: A Portrait of Castro and Cuba 1977, Remote Control: Television and the Manipulation of American Life 1977. *Leisure interests:* baseball, literature, US political history. *Address:* Hill and Knowlton, 600 New Hampshire Avenue, Suite 601, NW, Washington, DC 20037 (office); 2022 Columbia Road, NW, Washington, DC, USA (home). *Telephone:* (202) 944-5104 (office). *Fax:* (202) 944-1961 (office). *E-mail:* frank.mankiewicz@hillandknowlton.com. *Website:* www.hillandknowlton.com.

MAŃKO, Dariusz, PhD; Polish business executive; *President of the Management Board, Grupa Kęty SA;* b. 1968; ed Agricultural Univ., Poznań, Acad. of Econs, Katowice; sales rep. and later Head of Marketing and Devt, SAPA POLAND 1993–96; joined Grupa Kęty SA 1996, Man., ZML Kęty SA 1996–99, CEO and Gen. Dir, Metalplast-Bielsko SA 1999–2000, mem. Man. Bd Grupa Kęty SA 2000–, Pres. 2005–. *Address:* Grupa Kęty SA, Kościuszki 111 str., 32–650 Kęty, Poland (office). *Telephone:* (33) 8446000 (office). *Fax:* (33) 8446100 (office). *E-mail:* kety@gk-kety.com.pl (office). *Website:* www.gk-kety.com.pl (office).

MANLEY, Albert Leslie; South African diplomatist; b. 1945, Cape Town; s. of Albert George Rowan Manley and Mary Leslie Manley; m. Charlene Manley 1988; three s. one d.; ed Univ. of Free State; entered Dept of Foreign Affairs 1969, Desk Officer for Middle East 1974–76, Planning Section of Ministry, Pretoria and Cape Town 1981–82, other posts 1982–86; Vice-Consul in Lourenço Marques (now Maputo) 1970–74; Counsellor for Political Affairs at Embassy, London 1977–81; Perm. Rep. to UN, New York 1987–88, Geneva 1988–92; Head Int. Econs, Foreign Ministry 1992–94, Head Int. Devt and Econ. Affairs 1995–98; Minister at South African Embassy and Mission to the EU, Brussels 1998; currently Chief Dir (acting) of Econ. and Social Affairs, Dept of Foreign Affairs; Fellow, Center for Int. Affairs, Harvard Univ., USA 1994–95. *Leisure interests:* golf, music, books. *Address:* Department of Foreign Affairs, 1234 Church Street, Arcadia, Pretoria 0002, South Africa (office). *Telephone:* (12) 3511360 (office). *Fax:* (12) 3511331 (office). *E-mail:* manleya@foreign.gov.za (office). *Website:* www.dfa.gov.za (office).

MANLEY, John, PC, BA, LLB; Canadian business executive, lawyer and fmr politician; *Senior Counsel, McCarthy Tétrault LLP;* b. 5 Jan. 1950, Ottawa; s. of John Joseph Manley and Mildred Charlotte Scharf; m. Judith Manley; one s. two d.; ed Carleton Univ., Univ. of Ottawa; fmrly practitioner in business and income tax law, Ottawa; law clerk to Chief Justice of Canada 1976–77; Chair. Ottawa-Carleton Bd of Trade 1985–86; mem. Parl. 1988–; Minister of Industry 1993–2000, also Minister responsible for Atlantic Canada Opportunities Agency, Canada Econ. Devt and Western Econ. Diversification 1996–97; Minister of Foreign Affairs 2000–02; Chair. Ad Hoc Cabinet Cttee on Public Security and Anti-terrorism; Deputy Prime Minister of Canada and Minister of Infastructure and Crown Corpn 2002–03; Minister of Finance 2002–03; Political Minister for Ont. 2002–03; Chair. Cabinet Cttees on Econ. Union and on Social Union 2002–03; retd from politics 2003; Sr Counsel, McCarthy Tétrault LLP, Ottawa 2003–; mem. Bd of Dirs Nortel Networks 2004–, CIBC 2005–; Chair. Ind. Task Force on the Future of North America, Council on Foreign Relations 2005; named Chair. of govt panel on future of Canada's presence in Afghanistan 2007; Dr hc (Ottawa) 1998; Internet Person of the Year 2000, Newsmaker of the Year, Time Canada 2001. *Leisure interest:* marathon runner. *Address:* McCarthy Tétrault LLP, Suite 1400, The Chambers, 40 Elgin Street, Ottawa, ON K1P 5K6, Canada (office). *Telephone:* (613) 238-2109 (office). *Fax:* (613) 563-9386 (office). *Website:* www.mccarthy.ca (office).

MANN, Emily Betsy, BA, MFA; American writer, theatre director and playwright; *Artistic Director, McCarter Theatre;* b. 12 April 1952, Boston, Mass; d. of Arthur Mann and Sylvia Mann (née Blut); m. Gary Mailman; one s. from previous m.; ed Harvard Univ., Univ. of Minnesota; Resident Dir Guthrie Theater, Minneapolis 1976–79; Dir Brooklyn Acad. of Music Theater Co., Brooklyn, NY 1980–81; freelance writer and dir, New York 1981–90; Artistic Dir McCarter Theatre, Princeton, NJ 1990–; mem. Soc. of Stage Dirs and Choreographers, Theater Communications Group, New Dramatists, PEN, Writer's Guild; mem. Exec. Bd Dramatists' Guild; BUSH Fellowship 1975–76, Obie Awards for Directing 1981, 2002, Obie Award for Playwriting 1981, New Drama Forum Assсn Rosamond Gilder Award 1983, NEA Asscns Grant 1984, Tony Award for Outstanding Regional Theater 1984, Guggenheim Fellowship

1985, McKnight Fellowship 1985, CAPS Award 1985, NEA Playwrights Fellowship 1986, Brandeis Univ. Women of Achievement Award 1995, Douglass Coll. of NJ Woman of Achievement Award 1996, Rosamond Gilder Award for Outstanding Achievement in the Theater 1999, Harvard Univ. Alumnae Recognition Award 1999, Nat. Conf. for Community and Justice Award 2004, Leader of the Year Award, Princeton Regional Chamber of Commerce 2005. *Plays directed include:* Suddenly Last Summer, Loeb Drama Center 1971, The Bull Gets the Matador Once in a Lifetime, Agassiz Theater 1972, Macbeth, Loeb Drama Center 1973, Matrix, Guthrie Theater 1975, The Birthday Party, Guthrie Theater 1975, Cold, Guthrie Theater 1976, Ashes, Guthrie 2 Theater 1977, Cincinnati Playhouse 1980, Annulla, Guthrie Theater 1977, New Theater of Brooklyn 1989, Dark Pony and Reunion, Guthrie Theater 1978, The Farm, Actors Theater of St Paul 1978, On Mount Chimborazo, Guthrie 2 Theater, 1978, Surprise Surprise, Guthrie 2 Theater 1978, The Roads in Germany, Theater in the Round 1978, The Glass Menagerie, Guthrie Theater 1979, McCarter Theatre 1990, He and She, Brooklyn Acad. of Music 1980, Still Life (Obie Award), Goodman Theater 1980, American Place Theater 1981, Dwarfman Master of a Million Shapes, Goodman Theater 1981, A Doll's House, Oregon Contemporary Theater 1982, Hartford Stage Co. 1986, Through the Leaves, Empty Space Theater 1983, A Weekend Near Madison, Astor Place Theater 1983, The Value of Names, Hartford Stage Co. 1984, Execution of Justice, Guthrie Theater 1985, Virginia Theater (Broadway) 1986, Hedda Gabbler, La Jolla Playhouse 1987, Betsey Brown, American Music Theater Festival 1989, McCarter Theatre 1991, Miss Julie, McCarter Theatre 1992, Three Sisters, McCarter Theatre 1992, Cat on a Hot Tin Roof, McCarter Theatre 1992, Twilight: Los Angeles 1992 (LA Nat. Asscn for the Advancement of Colored People (NAACP) Award for Best Dir), Mark Taper Forum/McCarter Theatre 1993, The Perfectionist, McCarter Theatre 1993, The Matchmaker, McCarter Theatre 1994, Having our Say, McCarter Theatre 1995, Booth Theater (Broadway) 1995, The Mai, McCarter Theatre 1996, Betrayal, McCarter Theatre 1997, The House of Bernarda Alba, McCarter Theatre 1997, Safe as Houses, McCarter Theatre 1998, Meshugah, McCarter Theatre 1998, Fool for Love, McCarter Theatre 1999, The Cherry Orchard, McCarter Theatre 2000, Romeo and Juliet, McCarter Theatre 2001, Because He Can, McCarter Theatre 2001, All Over, McCarter Theatre and Roundabout Theater Co. 2002, The Tempest, McCarter Theatre 2003, Anna in the Tropics, McCarter Theatre/Broadway 2003, Last of the Boys, McCarter Theatre 2004, The Bells, McCarter Theatre 2005, Miss Witherspoon, McCarter Theatre/Playwright's Horizons 2005. *Plays translated and adapted include:* Nights and Days (Les nuits et les jours, Pierre Laville) 1985, Miss Julie 1992, The House of Bernarda Alba 1997, Meshugah 1998, Uncle Vanya 2003. *Plays included in publications:* New Plays USA 1, New Plays 3, Coming to Terms: American Plays and the Vietnam War 1985, The Ten Best Plays of 1986, Out Front 1988, Testimonies: Four Plays by Emily Mann (Theater Communications Group Inc.) 1997. *Publications include:* plays: Annulla Allen: The Autobiography of a Survivor 1977, Still Life (six Obie Awards 1981, Fringe First Award 1985) 1982, Execution of Justice (Helen Hayes Award, Bay Area Theater Critics Circle Award, HBO/USA Award, Playwriting Award Women's Cttee Dramatists Guild for Dramatizing Issues of Conscience) 1986, Having Our Say: The Delaney Sisters' First 100 Years (LA NAACP Award for Best Play) 1994, Greensboro: A Requiem 1996; musicals: Betsey Brown: A Rhythm and Blues Musical (co-author with Ntozake Shange); screenplays: Fanny Kelly (unproduced) 1981, You Strike a Woman, You Strike a Rock: The Story of Winnie Mandela (unproduced mini-series) 1988, The Greensboro Massacre (unproduced) 1992, Having Our Say (Christopher Award, Peabody Award) 1999, Political Stages (co-ed.) 2002. *Address:* McCarter Theatre, 91 University Place, Princeton, NJ 08540-5121, USA (office). *Telephone:* (609) 258-6502 (office). *Fax:* (609) 497-0369 (office). *E-mail:* emann@mccarter.org (office). *Website:* www.mccarter.org.

MANN, Hugo; German business executive; m.; three c.; worked as carpenter, opened first furniture store in 1938, later f. Wertkauf retail chain, sold to Wal-Mart for $500 million in 1997; fmr Head of Mann Mobilia GmbH, Germany. *Address:* c/o Mann Mobilia, Spreewaldallee 38–40, Autobahnkreuz Mannheim/Viernheim, 68309, Mannheim, Germany (office). *Telephone:* (621) 7161-402 (office). *Fax:* (621) 7161-432 (office).

MANN, Michael K.; American producer, director and writer; b. 5 Feb. 1943, Chicago; ed Univ. of Wisconsin, London Film School; Exec. Producer (TV) Miami Vice, Crime Story, Drug Wars: Camarena Story, Drug Wars: Cocaine Cartel, Police Story, Starsky and Hutch; mem. Writers Guild, Directors Guild; two Emmy Awards. *Films include:* The Jericho Mile (TV film, dir, scriptwriter) (Best Dir Award, Directors Guild) 1979, Thief (dir, exec. producer, scriptwriter) 1981, The Keep (dir, scriptwriter) 1981, Manhunter (dir, scriptwriter) 1986, Last of the Mohicans (dir, co-producer, scriptwriter) 1992, Heat (dir, co-producer, scriptwriter) 1995, The Insider (dir, producer) 1999, Ali 2001, Collateral (dir, producer) (Best Dir, Nat. Bd of Review) 2004, The Aviator (producer) (Best Film, BAFTA Awards 2005), Miami Vice 2006. *Address:* c/o Creative Artists Agency, 9830 Wilshire Boulevard, Beverly Hills, CA 90212, USA.

MANN, Yuri Vladimirovich, DPhilSc; Russian literary scholar and historian; *Professor, Russian State Humanitarian University;* b. 9 June 1929, Moscow; s. of Vladimir Mann and Sonja Mann; m. Galina Mann 1956; two s.; ed Moscow Univ.; school teacher, Moscow 1952–56; Prof. of Russian Literature, Gorky Inst. of World Literature –1992; Prof., Russian State Humanitarian Univ. 1992–; Visiting Prof., Chicago Univ., USA 1991; Chief Ed. Complete Academic Works of N. V. Gogol (23 vols); mem. CPSU 1952–90, Russian PEN Centre 1995, Acad. of Natural Sciences 1996. *Publications include:* The Grotesque in Literature 1966, Russian Philosophical Aesthetics 1820s–1830s 1969, The Poetics of Russian Romanticism 1976, The Poetics of Gogol 1978, In Search of a Live Soul–Gogol's Dead Souls 1984, The Dialectics

of Image 1987, The Aksakov Family 1992, Beyond the Mask of Laughter: The Life of Nikolai Gogol 1994, The Dynamics of Russian Romanticism 1995, The Poetics of Gogol: Variations on the Theme 1996, Russian Literature XIX Century. Romanticism 2001, Gogol: The Life and the Creation 1809–1845 2004, Exploring Gogol 2005, 19th Century Russian Literature (Romanticism) 2007, Creations of Gogol: Meaning and Form 2007, Turgenev and the Others 2008. *Address:* Russian State Humanitarian University, Ul. Chayanov 15, Moscow 125267 (office); 3 Tverskaya-Yamskaya 44, Apt 5, Moscow 125047, Russia (home). *Telephone:* (495) 250-66-92 (office); (495) 250-52-97 (home). *E-mail:* ymann@si.ru (home).

MANNAI, Jassim Abdullah al-, PhD; Bahraini business executive and international organization official; *Director-General and Chairman, Arab Monetary Fund;* b. 1948; ed Univ. of the Sorbonne, Paris, France and Harvard Business School; Exec. Vice-Pres. Gulf Investment Corpn, Kuwait 1987–94; CEO and Chair. Arab Trade Financing Program, Abu Dhabi 1994–; Dir-Gen. and Chair. Arab Monetary Fund, Abu Dhabi 1994–; Chair. Inter Arab Rating Co. EC (mem. Fitch IBCA Group) 1995–2001. *Publications:* numerous articles on economic and financial issues in various publs. *Address:* Office of the Director-General, Arab Monetary Fund Building, Corniche Road, PO Box 2818, Abu Dhabi, United Arab Emirates (office). *Telephone:* (2) 6171400 (office). *Fax:* (2) 6326454 (office). *E-mail:* centralmail@amfad.org.ae (office). *Website:* www.amf.org.ae (office).

MANNING, Sir David Geoffrey, Kt, GCMG, BA; British diplomatist; b. 5 Dec. 1949, Portsmouth, Hants.; s. of John Robert Manning and Joan Barbara Manning; m. Catherine Marjory Parkinson 1973; ed Ardingly Coll., Oriel Coll. Oxford, Johns Hopkins Univ., USA; Third Sec., FCO (Mexico, Cen. America Dept) 1972; Third, later Second Sec., Warsaw 1974–76; Second, later First Sec., New Delhi 1977–80; E European and Soviet Dept FCO 1980–82; Policy Planning Staff, FCO 1982–84; First Sec. (Political Internal), Paris 1984–88; Counsellor on loan to Cabinet Office 1988–90; Counsellor, Head of Political Section, Moscow 1990–93; Head, Eastern Dept (fmrly Soviet Dept), FCO 1993–94; British mem. of ICFY Contact Group on Bosnia April–Nov. 1994; Head of Planning Staff 1994–95; Amb. to Israel 1995–98; Deputy Under-Sec. of State, FCO 1998–2000; Perm. Rep. to NATO Jan.–Aug. 2001; Foreign Policy Adviser to Prime Minister 2001–03; Head of Cabinet Office Defence and Overseas Secr. 2001–03; Amb. to USA 2003–07. *Address:* c/o Foreign and Commonwealth Office, King Charles Street, London, SW1A 2AH, UK (office).

MANNING, Jane, OBE, FRAM, FRCM, GRSM; British singer (soprano), lecturer and writer; *Visiting Professor, Royal College of Music;* b. 20 Sept. 1938, Norwich; d. of the late Gerald Manning and Lily Thompson; m. Anthony Payne 1966; ed Norwich High School for Girls, RAM, London and Scuola di Canto, Cureglia, Switzerland; London debut concert 1964; since then active world-wide as freelance soprano soloist with special expertise in contemporary music; more than 350 BBC broadcasts; regular tours of USA since 1981 and of Australia since 1978; appearances at all leading European festivals and concert halls; New York début 1983; more than 300 world premières including several operas; Founder/Artistic Dir Jane's Minstrels (ensemble) 1988; many recordings including complete vocal works of Messiaen and Satie; Vice-Pres. Soc. for Promotion of New Music 1996–; Visiting Prof., Mills Coll., Oakland, Calif. 1981, 1982, 1983, 1986, Royal Coll. of Music 1995–; visiting lecturer, univs in UK, USA, Canada, Australia, NZ and Scandinavia; Arts and Humanities Research Council (AHRC) Creative Arts Research Fellow, Kingston Univ. 2003–07; mem. Exec. Cttee Musicians' Benevolent Fund; Hon. Prof., Keele Univ. 1996–2002; Hon. DUniv (York) 1988, Hon. DMus (Keele) 2004, (Dunelm) 2007; Special Award for Services to British Music, Composers' Guild of GB 1973. *Publications:* New Vocal Repertory (Vol. I) 1986, (Vol. II) 1998, A Messiaen Companion 1995, A Practical Guide to the Performance of the sprech-stimme in Pierrot Lunaire; contrib. to History of Musical Performance. *Leisure interests:* cooking, ornithology, cinema, philosophy, theatre, reading. *Address:* 2 Wilton Square, London, N1 3DL, England (home). *Telephone:* (20) 7359-1593 (home). *E-mail:* janetone@gmail.com (home). *Website:* www.classical-artists/janemanning.com.

MANNING, Patrick Augustus Mervyn, BSc; Trinidad and Tobago politician; *Prime Minister and Minister of Tobago Affairs;* b. 17 Aug. 1946, San Fernando, Trinidad; s. of Arnold Manning and Elaine Manning; m. Hazel Anne-Marie Kinsale 1972; two s.; ed Presentation Coll., San Fernando and Univ. of the West Indies; refinery operator Texaco, Trinidad 1965–66; Parl. Sec. 1971–78, Minister 1978–86; Minister of Information and of Industry and Commerce 1981, of Energy 1981–86; Leader of the Opposition 1986–90; Prime Minister 1991–95, 2001–, also Minister of Tobago Affairs; Minister of Finance 2001–07; fmr Minister of Nat. Security; Leader People's Nat. Movt (PNM) 1987–. *Leisure interests:* table tennis, chess, reading. *Address:* Office of the Prime Minister, Whitehall, Maraval Road, Port of Spain; People's National Movement, 1 Tranquillity Street, Port of Spain, Trinidad. *Telephone:* 622-1625 (office); 625-1533. *Fax:* 622-0055 (office). *E-mail:* opm@trinidad.net; opm@ttgov.gov.tt (office). *Website:* www.opm.gov.tt.

MANNING, Peyton, BA; American football player; b. 24 March 1976, New Orleans; s. of Archie Manning and Olivia Manning; m. Ashley Thompson 2001; ed Isidore Newman High School, New Orleans, Univ. of Tenn.; quarterback; holds 42 Nat. Collegiate Athletic Asscn (NCAA), South Eastern Conference (SEC) and Univ. of Tenn. records, including 33 Univ. of Tenn. single game, season and career records; first pick in 1998 Nat. Football League (NFL) draft by Indianapolis Colts 1998, holds several NFL passing records including throwing 49 touchdown passes 2004, led Colts to Super Bowl XLI championship 2007; f. Peyback Foundation 1999; Gatorade Circle of Champions National Player of the Year in high school; voted third-best quarterback in SEC history; named in SEC All-Decade Team; Maxwell Trophy (for coll. football's best player) 1997; Associated Press (AP) Most Valuable Player of the

NFL 2003 (jtly with Steve McNair) 2004, Bert Bell Award 2003, 2004, AP NFL Offensive Player of the Year 2004, Walter Payton NFL Man of the Year Walter Payton NFL Man of the Year 2005, Pro Bowl Most Valuable Player 2005, Super Bowl XLI Most Valuable Player 2007; named to Pro Bowl team 2000–01, 2003–07. *Publications:* Manning: A Father, His Sons and a Football Legacy (with Archie Manning) 2000. *Address:* IMG, 1 Erieview Plaza, Suite 1300, Cleveland, OH 44114; Indianapolis Colts, 7001 West 56th Street, Indianapolis, IN 46254, USA. *Telephone:* (216) 522-1200. *Fax:* (216) 522-1145. *E-mail:* karnold@imgworld.com. *Website:* www.imgfootball.com; www.peytonmanning.com; www.colts.com.

MANNING, Robert Joseph; American journalist; *President and Editor-in-Chief, Bobcat Books Inc.;* b. 25 Dec. 1919, Binghamton, NY; s. of Joseph James Manning and Agnes Pauline Brown; m. 1st Margaret Marinda Raymond 1944 (died 1984); three s.; m. 2nd Theresa Slomkowski 1987; US Army service 1942–43; Nieman Fellow, Harvard Univ. 1945–46; State Dept and White House Corresp. United Press. 1944–46, Chief UN Corresp. United Press. 1946–49; Writer, Time magazine 1949–55, Senior Ed. 1955–58, Chief, London Bureau, Time, Life, Fortune, Sports Illustrated magazines 1958–61; Sunday Ed., New York Herald Tribune 1961–62; Asst Sec. of State for Public Affairs, US Dept of State 1962–64; Exec. Ed. Atlantic Monthly 1964–66, Ed.-in-Chief 1966–80; Vice-Pres. Atlantic Monthly Co. 1966–80; Ed.-in-Chief Boston Publishing Co. 1981–87; Pres., Ed.-in-Chief Bobcat Books Inc., Boston 1987–; Fellow, Kennedy Inst. of Politics, Harvard Univ. 1980; mem. AAAS; Dr hc (Tufts Univ.), (St Lawrence Univ.). *Publications include:* Who We Are 1976, The Swamp Root Chronicle 1992, The Vietnam Experience (25 vols). *Address:* 1200 Washington Street, Apt 507, Boston, MA 02118, USA. *E-mail:* bobcat1225@rcn.com (office).

MANNINGHAM-BULLER, Dame Eliza(beth) Lydia, DCB; British fmr government official; b. 14 July 1948; d. of Sir Reginald Manningham-Buller (later Viscount Dilhorne) and Lady Mary Lilian Lindsay; m. 1991; ed Northampton High School, Benenden School, Kent and Lady Margaret Hall, Oxford Univ.; fmr English teacher; joined MI5 Security Service 1974, worked on case of KGB defector Oleg Gordievsky and on Lockerbie disaster, served as MI5 liaison officer at British Embassy in Washington, DC, Dir for Surveillance and Tech. Operations 1993, Dir of Irish Counter-terrorism, Dir of Finance and Information Tech., Deputy Dir-Gen. 1997–2002, Dir-Gen. 2002–07 (retd); Hon. Fellow, Lady Margaret Hall, Oxford 2003, Northampton Univ. 2008; Dr hc (Cranfield) 2003, (Open) 2005. *Address:* c/o MI5 Security Service, POB 3255, London, SW1P 1AE, England (office).

MANOLIČ, Josip, (Joža); Croatian politician and lawyer; b. 22 March 1920, Kalinovac; m. Marija Manolić (née Eker); three d.; ed Zagreb Univ.; mem. youth orgs and trade union activist 1938–; mem. anti-fascist movt; Sec. Dist Cttee League of Communist Youth of Croatia; Chief Dept of Nat. Security in Bjelovar 1945–46 (dismissed); worked in Ministry of Internal Affairs of Croatia 1948–60; Interior Affairs Secr. in Zagreb 1960–65; mem. of Parl. Repub. of Croatia, Pres. Legis. Body of Constitutional Comm. 1965–71; mandate suspended because of nationalist activities; Co-founder Croatian Democratic Union (HDZ) first Chair. Exec. Cttee 1989, elected Vice-Pres. 1990; mem. of Croatian Parl. 1990–; Pres. Croatian Govt 1990–91, Vice-Pres. Presidency of Repub. of Croatia –1999; Pres. House of Counties of Croatian Parl. 1992–94; Pres. Emergency Bd of Croatia; Dir Bureau for the Protection of Constitutional Order 1991–93; Founder Croatian Ind. Democrats (HND), Pres. of HND; an organizer of Croatian army; certificate for participation in anti-Fascist struggle 1941–45, certificate for participation in the defence of the homeland 1991–92. *Publication:* Manolić 1989–95 (collection of interviews). *Leisure interest:* chess. *Address:* Nazorova Str. 57, 41000 Zagreb, Croatia (office). *Telephone:* (1) 4848476 (office).

MANOOGIAN, Richard A., BA; American business executive; *Chairman and CEO, Masco Corporation;* b. 1937; s. of Alex Manoogian and Marie Manoogian; ed Yale Univ.; joined Masco Corpn 1958, apptd Dir 1964, Vice-Pres. 1964–68, Pres. 1968–85, Chair. and CEO 1985–; mem. Bd of Dirs JPMorgan Chase 1978–, Bank One Corpn, Ford Motor Co. 2001–, Metaldyne Corpn, Detroit Renaissance, The American Business Conf., MSX Int.; Life Pres. Armenian Gen. Benevolent Union; Chair. Detroit Inst. of Arts, Alex and Marie Manoogian Foundation; Dir Yale Univ. Art Gallery; mem. Henry Ford Museum, Michigan Business Roundtable, Mackinac Island State Park Comm., American Fed. of Arts, American Asscn of Museums, Museum Trustees Asscn, Chief Execs Org. (YPO); Trustee Greenfield Village, Community Foundation of Southeastern Michigan, Archives of American Art (Smithsonian Inst.), Center for Creative Studies, Fine Arts Cttee of the State Dept, Nat. Gallery of Art. *Address:* Masco Corporation, 21001 Van Born Road, Taylor, MI 48180, USA (office). *Telephone:* (313) 274-7400 (office). *Fax:* (313) 792-6135 (office). *Website:* www.masco.com (office).

MANOROHANTA, Cécile; Malagasy politician and academic; fmr Dir of Research and Dean of Universite Nord, Antsiranana Prov.; Nat. Vice-Pres. ruling Tiako i Madagasikara (I Love Madagascar—TIM) party; Minister of Defence (first woman) 2007–09 (resgnd). *Publications:* A Quantitative Study of Voice in Malagasy (UCLA Working Papers in Linguistics 6: Papers in African Linguistics 1) 2001; numerous papers on linguistics in professional journals. *Address:* c/o Ministry of National Defence, BP 08, Ampahibe, 101 Antananarivo, Madagascar (office).

MANSBRIDGE, Peter; Canadian broadcaster and journalist; *Anchor, Prime Time News, Canadian Broadcasting Corporation;* b. 1948, London; m. Wendy Mesley (divorced); served in Royal Canadian Navy; fmr airline freight man.; disc jockey and newscaster CBC Radio, Churchill 1968, Reporter CBC Radio, Winnipeg 1971, Reporter CBC TV News 1972–85, Reporter The National, Saskatchewan 1975, with Parl. Bureau, Ottawa 1976–80, Co-Anchor Quarterly Report, Anchor Sunday Report 1985, Anchor The National 1988–92, Anchor of news segment on The National 1992–, Anchor Prime Time News 1992–; Gemini Award 1988, 1989, 1990, 1993. *Address:* Prime Time News, Canadian Broadcasting Corporation, 181 Queen Street, Ottawa, ON K1P 1K9, Canada (office). *Telephone:* (613) 288-6000 (office). *Fax:* (613) 724-5074 (office). *Website:* www.cbc.ca (office).

MANSELL, Kevin B.; American retail executive; *President, Kohl's Department Stores;* b. St Louis; ed Univ. of Missouri; various buying and merchandising roles, Venture Stores Div., May Dept Stores 1975; Divisional Merchandise Man. Kohl's Dept Stores 1982–87, Gen. Merchandise Man. 1987–96, Sr Exec. Vice-Pres. of Merchandising and Marketing 1998–99, Dir 1999–, Pres. 1999–. *Address:* Kohl's Department Stores, N56 W17000 Ridgewood Drive, Menomonee Falls, WI 53051-5660, USA (office). *Telephone:* (262) 703-7000 (office). *Fax:* (262) 703-6143 (office). *Website:* www.kohls.com (office).

MANSELL, Nigel, OBE; British racing driver; b. 8 Aug. 1953, Upton-on-Severn; s. of Eric Marshall and Joyce Marshall; m. Rosanne Perry; two s. one d.; ed Matthew Boulton Polytechnic, Solihull Tech. Coll.; began racing in karts; won 11 regional Championships 1969–76; Formula Ford and Formula Three 1976–79; Formula Two, later Formula One 1980; Lotus team 1981–84; Williams-Honda team 1985–87; Williams-Judd team 1988; Ferrari team 1989–90; Williams-Renault team 1991–92 and 1994 (part-time); McLaren team 1995; first competed in a Grand Prix, Austria 1980; won 31 Grand Prix races 1980–94, record since beaten by Michael Schumacher; Formula One World Drivers Champion 1992; American Newman-Haas Indy Car Team 1993; Indy Car Champion 1993; special constable; owner of Woodbury Park Golf and Country Club 1993–; Hon. DEng (Birmingham) 1993; BBC Sports Personality of the Year 1986, 1992. *Publications:* Mansell and Williams (with Derick Allsop) 1992, Nigel Mansell's IndyCar Racing (with Jeremy Shaw) 1993, My Autobiography (with James Allen) 1995, Driven to Win (with Derick Allsop). *Leisure interests:* golf, fishing, flying. *Address:* c/o Nicki Dance, Woodbury Park Golf and Country Club, Woodbury Castle, Woodbury, Exeter, Devon, EX5 1JJ, England. *Telephone:* (1395) 233382 (office). *Fax:* (1395) 232978 (office). *E-mail:* nickidance@woodburypark.co.uk.

MANSER, Michael John, CBE, RA, DIPL. ARCH., PRIBA, RWA; British architect; b. 23 March 1929, London; s. of the late Edmund G. and Augusta M. Manser; m. Dolores Josephine Bernini 1953; one s. one d.; ed School of Architecture, The Polytechnic of Cen. London; Chair. The Manser Practice (architects) 1961–; architectural corresp. The Observer 1964–66; wide variety of architectural projects including pvt. housing, industrial buildings, research labs, schools, swimming pools, commercial and domestic renovation and refurbishment, hotels, offices, air ferry terminals, London Underground stations, health bldgs; Pres. RIBA 1983–85; Academician Royal Acad. 1994; RIBA Rep. RSA 1987–93 (Chair. Art for Architecture Award Scheme 1990–); mem. Council Nat. Trust 1991–93; Assessor Art in the Workplace Awards 1988–; Chair. Art and Work Awards 1996–; mem. Royal Acad. Council 1998–Architectural Cttee 1998–, City of Westminster Public Art Panel 1999–, Works Cttee 1999–, Remuneration Cttee 2000–, Audit Cttee 2000–; Royal W of England Academician 1993–; City of Westminster Public Art Panel 2001; Chair. Nat. Homebuilder Design Awards 1998, RIBA Awards Cttee 1998–2002; Chair. British Architectural Library Trust 2008–; Hon. FRAIC; Civic Trust Award 1967, Civic Trust Commendation 1973, European Architectural Heritage Award 1975, Dept of Environment Good Design in Housing Award 1975, Structural Steel Design Award 1976, 1995, RIBA Award Commendation 1977; RIBA Award, RIBA Regional Award 1991, Royal Fine Art Comm. and Sunday Times Bldg of the Year Finalist 1991, Quarternario Int. Award for Innovative Tech. in Architecture Finalist 1993, Civic Trust Award 1993, RIBA Award and Regional Award 1995, Manser Medal RIBA Housing Award 2001, RIBA Award 2002 Buildings listed for Preservation in 2002. *Publications:* Planning Your Kitchen (co-author), Psychiatry in the Elderly (co-author), Companion to Contemporary Architectural Thought (co-author) 1993; contributions to nat. and tech. press. *Leisure interests:* architecture, music, books, gardening, boats. *Address:* The Manser Practice, Bridge Studios, Hammersmith Bridge, London, W6 9DA; 76 Whitehall Court, London, SW1A 2EL, England. *Telephone:* (20) 8741-4381 (office). *E-mail:* manser@manser.co.uk (office).

MANSFIELD, Eric Harold, MA, ScD, F.I.M.A., F.R.Eng., FRAeS, FRS; British scientist and academic; b. 24 May 1923, Croydon, Surrey; s. of Harold G. Mansfield and Grace Pfundt Mansfield; m. 1st 1947 (divorced 1973); m. 2nd Eunice Shuttleworth-Parker 1974; two s. one d.; ed St Lawrence Coll., Ramsgate, Trinity Hall, Cambridge; various grades, Structures Dept, Royal Aircraft Est., Farnborough 1943–83, Chief Scientific Officer 1980–83; Visiting Prof. Univ. of Surrey 1984–90; mem. British Nat. Cttee for Theoretical and Applied Mechanics 1973–79, Gen. Ass. Int. Union of Theoretical and Applied Mechanics 1976–80; originator of Neutral Hole Theory, The Inextensional Theory for thin plates, Wrinkled Membrane Theory (modern version), Theory of Gravity-induced Wrinkles in Vertical Membranes, Theory for Objects Supported by Surface Tension, Theory for the Collapse of Rigid-Plastic Plates; Bronze Medal, Royal Aeronautical Soc. 1967, James Alfred Ewing Gold Medal for Eng Research 1991, Royal Medal, Royal Soc. 1994. *Publications:* Bending and Stretching of Plates 1964, Bridge: the Ultimate Limits 1986; articles in professional journals. *Leisure interests:* bridge, palaeontology, snorkelling, walking Poppy the dog. *Address:* Primrose Cottage, Alresford Road, Cheriton, Hants., SO24 0QJ, England (home). *Telephone:* (1962) 771280 (home).

MANSFIELD, Michael, QC, BA, FRSA; British barrister; *Professor of Law, Westminster University;* b. 12 Oct. 1941, London; s. of Frank Mansfield and Marjorie Sayers; m. 1st Melian Mansfield 1967 (divorced 1992); three s. two d.; m. 2nd Yvette Mansfield 1992; one s.; ed Highgate School and Keele Univ.;

began practising 1967; est. Tooks Court chambers 1984; specialist in civil liberties work; Prof. of Law, Westminster Univ. 1997–; films for BBC TV: Inside Story 1991, Presumed Guilty; Pres. Amicus, Haldane Soc., NCRM; Patron Acre Lane Neighbourhood Chambers, Brixton 1997–; Hon. Fellow, Kent Univ.; Hon. LLD (South Bank Univ.) 1994, (Univ. of Herts.) 1995, (Keele Univ.) 1995, (Westminster Univ.) 2005. *Radio:* Moral Maze, BBC Radio 4 1995–98. *Publications:* Presumed Guilty 1994, Home Lawyer 2004. *Leisure interests:* my children, drumming. *Address:* Tooks Chambers, 8 Warner Yard, London, EC1R 5EY, England (office). *Telephone:* (20) 7841-6100 (office). *Fax:* (20) 7841-6199 (office). *Website:* www.tooks.co.uk (office).

MANSFIELD, Sir Peter, Kt, BSc, PhD, FRS; British physicist and academic; *Professor Emeritus in Residence, University of Nottingham;* b. 9 Oct. 1933, London; s. of the late S. G. Mansfield and R. L. Mansfield; m. Jean M. Kibble 1962; two d.; ed William Penn School, Peckham and Queen Mary Coll., London, Univ. of London; Research Assoc. Dept of Physics, Univ. of Ill. 1962; lecturer, Univ. of Nottingham 1964, Sr Lecturer 1967, Reader 1970, Prof. of Physics 1979–94, Prof. Emer. in Residence 1995–; MRC Professorial Fellow 1983–88; Sr Visitor, Max Planck Inst. for Medical Research, Heidelberg 1972–73; Fellow, Queen Mary Coll. 1985; Pres. Soc. of Magnetic Resonance in Medicine 1987–88; Hon. FRCR 1992; Hon. FInstP 1996; Hon. mem. British Inst. of Radiology (BIR) 1993; Hon. DrMed (Strasbourg) 1995; Hon. DSc (Univ. of Kent at Canterbury) 1996; Royal Soc. Wellcome Foundation Gold Medal and Prize 1985, Duddell Medal, Inst. of Physics 1988, Royal Soc. Mullard Medal 1990, ISMAR Prize 1992, Barclay Medal, BJR 1993, Gold Medal, European Asscn of Radiology 1995, Garmisch-Partenkirchen Prize for MRI 1995, Rank Prize 1997, Nobel Prize for Medicine (jtly) 2003; several other awards. *Publications:* NMR Imaging in Biomedicine 1982, NMR Imaging (co-ed.) 1990, MRI in Medicine 1995; some 200 scientific publs in learned journals. *Leisure interests:* reading, languages, flying. *Address:* Magnetic Resonance Centre, Department of Physics and Astronomy, University of Nottingham, NG7 2RD, England (office). *Telephone:* (115) 9514740 (office). *Fax:* (115) 9515166 (office). *E-mail:* pamela.davies@nottingham.ac.uk (office). *Website:* (office).

MANSFIELD, Terence Arthur, PhD, FRS; British biologist and academic; *Professor Emeritus, University of Lancaster;* b. 18 Jan. 1937, Ashby-de-la-Zouch, Leics.; s. of Sydney W. Mansfield and Rose Mansfield (née Sinfield); m. Margaret M. James 1963; two s.; ed Univs of Nottingham and Reading; Research Fellow, Univ. of Reading 1961–65; Lecturer and Prof., Univ. of Lancaster 1965–87, Dir Inst. of Environmental and Biological Sciences 1987–94, Provost of Science and Eng 1994–97, Research Prof. 1996–2001, Prof. Emer. 2001–; mem. Agric. and Food Research Council 1989–93. *Publications:* Physiology of Stomata (co-author) 1968, Stomatal Physiology (co-ed.) 1981, Plant Adaptation to Environmental Stress (co-ed.) 1993, Disturbance of the Nitrogen Cycle (co-ed.) 1998, Glimpses of the Victorians at Church 2004; numerous chapters and journal articles on aspects of botanical science. *Leisure interests:* cricket, hill-walking, church history. *Address:* 25 Wallace Lane, Forton, Preston, PR3 0BA, England (home). *Telephone:* (1524) 791338 (home).

MANSHA, Mian Mohammad; Pakistani industrialist; *Chairman, Nishat Group;* s. of Mian Mohammad Yahya; Chair. Nishat Group, conglomerate with interests in banking, insurance, textiles and cement, including Muslim Commercial Bank, Nishat Mills, D.G. Khan Cement. *Address:* Nishat Chunian, 31-Q, Gulberg II, Lahore 54660, Pakistan (office). *Telephone:* (42) 5761730 (office). *Fax:* (42) 5878696 (office). *E-mail:* info@nctex.com (office). *Website:* www.nctex.com (office).

MANSHARD, Walther, Dr rer. nat; German geographer, academic and international civil servant; *Professor, Geographisches Institut, University of Freiburg;* b. 17 Nov. 1923, Hamburg; s. of Otto and Ida Manshard; m. Helga Koch 1951; one d.; ed Univ. of Hamburg; Asst lecturer, Univ. of Southampton, UK 1950–52; lecturer, Univ. of Ghana 1952–60; Dozent, Univ. of Cologne 1960–63; Prof. Univ. of Giessen 1963–70; Prin. Dir UNESCO Dept of Environmental Sciences 1970–73; Prof., Head of Dept Univ. of Freiburg 1973–77, 1980–; Vice-Rector, UN Univ., Tokyo 1977–80; Sec.-Gen. and Treas. Int. Geographical Union 1976–84; Sr Adviser UN Univ. 1990–93; Hon. DLitt 1991. *Publications:* Die geographischen Grundlagen der Wirtschaft Ghanas 1961, Tropisches Afrika 1963, Agrargeographie der Tropen 1968, Afrika–Südlich der Sahara 1970, Tropical Agriculture 1974, Die Städte des tropischen Afrika 1977, Renewable Natural Resources and the Environment 1981, Entwicklungsprobleme in Agrarräumen Tropen-Afrikas 1988, Umwelt v. Entwicklung in den Tropen 1995. *Address:* Geographisches Institut, University of Freiburg, Werderring 4, 79085 Freiburg i. Br.; Schwarzwaldstrasse 24, 79189 Bad Krozingen, Germany. *Telephone:* (761) 2033571 (office); (7633) 3488 (home). *Fax:* (761) 2033575 (office); (7633) 101253 (home). *E-mail:* walthermanshard@geographie.uni-freiburg.de (office). *Website:* www.geographie.uni-freiburg.de (office).

MANSINGH, Lalit, MA; Indian diplomatist; *Professor Emeritus, Foreign Service Institute;* b. 29 April 1941, Cuttack; s. of the late Mayadhar Mansingh and of Hemalata (née Behura) Mansingh; m. Indira Singh 1976; one s. one d.; ed Utkal Univ., Orissa, Indian School of Int. Studies, New Delhi; lecturer in political science 1961–63; joined diplomatic service 1963, Deputy Chief of Mission to Kabul 1971–74, to Brussels 1976–80, to Washington, DC 1989–92, Amb. to UAE 1980–83; High Commr to Nigeria 1993–95, to London 1998–99; Jt Sec. Dept of Econ. Affairs, Ministry of Finance 1984–85; Dir Gen. Indian Council for Cultural Relations 1985–89; Dean Foreign Service Inst., New Delhi 1995–96, currently Prof. Emer.; Perm. Sec. Ministry of External Affairs 1997–98; Amb. to USA 2001–04; mem. Exec. Cttee, Peace and Conflict Studies; mem. Indian Council for Sustainable Devt (TERI); mem. Int. Advisory Council, APCO Worldwide, Washington DC; mem. Governing Council, Development Alternatives; mem. Governing Body, Gram Vikas, Orissa; Univ. Gold Medals for top ranking graduate in History and Political Science. *Publication:* Indian Foreign Policy: Agenda for the 21st Century (Ed.-in-Chief) 1998. *Leisure interests:* classical music, dance, fine arts, theatre. *Address:* N-38 Panchsheel Park, New Delhi 110 017, India (home). *Telephone:* (11) 4175-1178 (office). *E-mail:* lalitmansingh@yahoo.com (office).

MANSON, Marilyn; American singer and songwriter; b. (Brian Warner), 5 Jan. 1969, Canton, OH; m. Dita Von Teese 2005 (divorced 2007); fmr music journalist; founder mem., Marilyn Manson & the Spooky Kids 1989–, later just Marilyn Manson; numerous TV appearances, tours; Kerrang! Icon Award 2005. *Recordings include:* albums: Portrait of an American Family 1994, Smells Like Children 1995, Antichrist Superstar 1996, Mechanical Animals 1998, The Last Tour on Earth 1999, Holy Wood (In the Shadow of the Valley of Death) 2000, Genesis of the Devil 2001, Live 2002, The Word According to Manson 2002, The Golden Age of Grotesque 2003, White Trash 2003, From Obscurity 2 Purgatory 2004, Eat Me, Drink Me 2007, The High End of Low 2009. *Publication:* The Long Hard Road Out of Hell (autobiog.) 1997. *Address:* CAA, 162 Fifth Avenue, 6th Floor, New York, NY 10010, USA (office). *Telephone:* (212) 277-9000 (office). *Fax:* (212) 277-9099 (office). *Website:* www.caa.com (office); www.marilynmanson.com.

MANSUROV, Tair Aimukhametovich, PhD; Kazakhstani diplomatist and regional governor; *Governor, North Kazakhstan Region;* b. 1 Jan. 1948, Sarkand, Taldykorgan Region, Kazakhstan; s. of Aimukhamet Mansurov and Maken Tursynbekova; m. Saule Bakirova 1973; one s. two d.; ed Kazakh Politechnical Inst., Almaty, Higher Party School at Cen. Cttee of CP, Moscow; worked in construction orgs Alma-Ata, Chief Engineer Almaatacentrestroy 1965–79; Chief, Dept of Construction, Alma-Ata Regional CP Cttee 1979–87; First Sec. Leninskiy Dist CP Cttee, Alma-Ata 1979–87; Instructor, Dept of Construction, Cen. CP Cttee, Moscow 1988–91; Second Sec. Karaganda Region CP Cttee 1989–91; Chief of Section, Dept of Econs, Cen. CP Cttee, Moscow 1988–91; Deputy to Supreme Soviet of USSR 1988–91; Pres. Kazakhstan Devt Fund, Moscow 1991–93; Amb. to Russian Fed. 1994–2002, concurrently Amb. to Finland 1996–2002; Amb. at Large and Advisor to Pres. of Kazakhstan 2002–03; Gov. N Kazakhstan Region 2003–; mem. Acad. of Creativity, Int. Acad. of High School, Acad. of Social Sciences; Kurmet Order 1996, Order of St Daniel the Prince of Muscovy, Order of Dostyk, Order of Friendship; several medals. *Publications:* Faces of Sovereignty: Sovereignty in the Prism of Social History, Kazakhstan and Russia: Sovereignization, Integration, Experience of Strategic Partnership, Kazakh–Russian Relations in the Epoch of Changes, scientific and feature books about diplomatist N. Turiakulov. *Leisure interest:* literature. *Address:* Kazakhstan Constitution str. 58, 150011 Petropavlovsk, Kazakhstan. *Telephone:* (7152) 464125; (7152) 462048. *Fax:* (7152) 365588.

MANTASHE, Gwede, MA; South African trade union official and politician; *Secretary-General, African National Congress (ANC);* b. Transkei; ed Univ. of South Africa; Br. Chair. Matla Coal, Nat. Union of Mineworkers 1982–84, Regional Sec. Witbank 1985–88, Nat. Organizer 1988–93, Regional Coordinator 1993–94, Asst Gen. Sec. 1994–98, Gen. Sec. 1998–2006; mem. Cen. Cttee and Politburo SA Communist Party, Chair. 2007–; fmr mem. Exec. Cttee Congress of South African Trade Unions (COSATU); Sec.-Gen. African Nat. Congress 2007–; Dir Samancor 1995–; Exec. Dir Devt Bank of Southern Africa 2006–; Chair. Tech. Task Team, Jt Initiative for Priority Skills Acquisition. *Address:* African National Congress, 54 Sauer Street, Johannesburg 201, South Africa (office). *Telephone:* (11) 3761000 (office). *Fax:* (11) 3761134 (office). *E-mail:* nmtyelwa@anc.org.za (office). *Website:* www.anc.org.za (office).

MANTEGA, Guido, MA, PhD; Brazilian economist, academic and government official; *Minister of Finance;* b. 7 April 1949, Genoa, Italy; s. of Giuseppe Mantega and Anna Costa Mantega; m. Eliana Berger Mantega; ed School of Econs and Admin, Universidade de Sao Paulo, Inst. of Devt Countries, Univ. of Sussex, UK; Prof. of Econs, School of Business Admin, Fundação Getúlio Vargas 1981–; Budget Dir and Head, Office of Municipal Dept of Planning, São Paulo, 1982–92; Prof. of Econs, Pontifícia Universidade Católica de São Paulo-PUC-SP 1984–87; mem. Coordination of Econ. Program for Brazilian Labor Party (PT) in presidential elections 1984, 1989, 1998; Econ. Advisor to President Luiz Inácio Lula da Silva 1993–2002; coordinator PT's Econ. Program 2002; Minister of Planning, Budget, and Admin 2003–04; Pres. Banco Nacional de Desenvolvimento Econômico e Social (BNDES) 2004–06; Minister of Finance 2006–. *Publications:* numerous articles and books including Acumulação Monopolista e Crises no Brasil 1981, A Economia Política Brasileira 1984, Custo Brasil: Mito ou Realidade 1997. *Address:* Ministry of Finance, Esplanada dos Ministérios, Bloco P, 5° andar, 70048-900 Brasília, DF, Brazil (office). *Telephone:* (61) 3412-2515 (office). *Fax:* (61) 3412-1721 (office). *E-mail:* gabinete.df.gmf@fazenda.gov.br (office). *Website:* www.fazenda.gov.br (office).

MANTEGAZZA, Sergio, Dipl. Bus. Admin; Swiss travel industry executive; *President, Globus Group of Cosmos, Lugano;* b. 31 Oct. 1927, Mendrisio; s. of Antonio Mantegazza; m.; two s. one d.; ed Instituto Elvetico, Lugano, Gademann Handelsschule, Zurich; Man. Globus Gateway Tours, Lugano, Switzerland 1945–48, Gen. Man. 1948–52, Dir 1952–56, Man. Dir 1956–60, Pres. 1960–; Hon. Consul of Mexico in Lugano; Order of San Gregorio Magno 1992. *Address:* Globus Travel Services SA, Via alla Roggia, 6916 Grancia, Switzerland (office). *Telephone:* (91) 985-71-11 (office). *Fax:* (91) 985-73-78 (office). *E-mail:* smante@globuscosmos.ch (office). *Website:* www.globusandcosmos.com (office).

MANTEL, Hilary Mary, CBE, BJur, FRSL; British writer; b. 6 July 1952, Hadfield, Derbyshire; d. of Henry Thompson and Margaret Mary Thompson; m. Gerald McEwen 1973; ed Harrytown Convent, Cheshire, London School of

Econs, Sheffield Univ. *Radio:* The Giant, O'Brien (drama) 2002, Learning to Talk (5 plays) 2003. *Publications:* Every Day is Mother's Day 1985, Vacant Possession 1986, Eight Months on Ghazzah Street 1988, Fludd (Winifred Holtby Memorial Award, Southern Arts Literature Prize, Cheltenham Festival Prize) 1989, A Place of Greater Safety (Sunday Express Book of the Year Award 1993) 1992, A Change of Climate 1994, An Experiment in Love (Hawthornden Prize 1996) 1995, The Giant, O'Brien 1998, Giving up the Ghost 2003, Learning to Talk 2003, Beyond Black 2005, Wolf Hall 2009. *Address:* A. M. Heath & Co., 6 Warwick Court, London, WC1R 5DJ, England (office). *Telephone:* (20) 7242-2811 (office). *Fax:* (20) 7242-2711 (office). *Website:* www.amheath.com (office).

MANUEL, Trevor Andrew; South African politician; *Minister of Finance;* b. 31 Jan. 1956, Cape Town; s. of Abraham J. Manuel and Philma van Söhnen; m. Lynn Matthews; three s.; ed Harold Cressy High School; mem. Labour Party Youth 1969–71, Policy Man. on Devt 1989–; construction technician 1974–81; Sec. Kensington Civic Asscn 1977–82; Founding mem. Western Cape United Democratic Front (UDF) 1980s, Sec. Regional Exec. UDF 1983–90, mem. UDF Nat. Exec. Cttee 1983–86, 1989–90; Organizer CAHAC 1981–82; field worker Educational Resource and Information Centre 1982–84; in detention 1985, 1987–88, 1989, restricted 1985–86, 1986–90 (when not in detention); Publicity Sec. ANC Western Cape; mem. ANC Nat. Exec. Cttee 1991–; Minister of Trade and Industry, Govt of Nat. Unity 1994–96; Minister of Finance 1996–. *Address:* Private Bag X115, Pretoria 0001, South Africa. *Telephone:* (012) 315-5372. *Fax:* (012) 323-3262.

MANUELLA, Sir Tulaga, GCMG, MBE; Tuvaluan accountant and fmr Governor-General; b. 26 Aug. 1936; s. of Teuhu Manuella and Malesa Moevasa; m. Milikini Uinifaleti; two s. three d.; sub-accountant and ledger keeper 1953–55; clerical officer 1955–57; Sr Asst, then Asst Accountant, Treasury 1957–75; Asst Accountant, Tuvalu Govt; Accountant, then Acting Financial Sec., Ministry of Finance 1976–84; Financial Sec. Financial Div. Church of Tuvalu 1984–86; Pacific Conf. of Churches, Suva, Fiji 1987–91; Co-ordinator of Finance and Admin. Ekalesia Kelisiano 1992–94; Gov.-Gen. of Tuvalu 1994–1998; Chancellor Univ. of the S Pacific 1997–2000; Patron Pacific Islands Soc. in Britain and Ireland 1995. *Address:* c/o Office of the Governor-General, PO Box 50, Vaiaku, Funafuti, Tuvalu (office).

MANUKYAN, Vazgen Mikayelovich, PhD; Armenian politician and mathematician; *Leader, National Democratic Union;* b. 13 Feb. 1946, Leninakan (now Gyumri); s. of Mikael Manukyan and Astkhik Manukyan; m. Vardui Rafaelovna Ishkhanyan; three d.; ed Yerevan State Univ., Siberian Dept of USSR Acad. of Sciences; Prof., Yerevan State Univ. 1972–95; political activities since 1960s, one of founders and leaders Club of Armenian Culture 1967, mem. and co-ordinator Cttee Karabakh 1988–; mem. of Bd, co-ordinator Armenian Pan-Nat. Movt 1989–90, Leader Nat. Democratic Union 1991–; Deputy, Armenian Supreme Soviet 1990–91; Prime Minister of Armenia 1990–91; State Minister of Armenia Sept.–Oct. 1992; mem. Council of Nat. Security at Pres. 1992–93; Minister of Defence 1992–93; Chair. Cttee on Econ. Reform, State Comm. on Land Reform and Privatization; mem. Parl. 1991–; one of leaders of opposition; cand. for the presidency 1996. *Publications:* It is Time to Jump off the Train 1990, Armenian Dream of a Deadlock of Survival 2002. *Address:* National Assembly, Marshal Bagramian Prosp. 26, 375016 Yerevan, Armenia (office); Bachramyan str, I Tupik, H.9, Apt 4, 375019, Yerevan, Armenia (home). *Telephone:* (10) 523412 (office); (10) 526006 (home). *Fax:* (10) 523766 (home). *E-mail:* vmanukyan@netsys.am (home); astgh@netsys.am (home).

MANWANI, Harish, BA, MA; Indian business executive; *Chairman, Hindustan Unilever Limited;* m.; two d.; ed Mumbai Univ., Advanced Man. Program, Harvard Business School, USA; joined Hindustan Lever Ltd (HLL) in 1976, Div. Vice-Pres. Marketing, Detergents 1995, mem. Bd as Dir for Personal Products 1995, also held regional responsibility for Cen. Asia and Middle East Business Group, moved to UK as Sr Vice-Pres. (Global Hair Care and Oral Care) and Exec. Vice-Pres. Latin America Business Group 2000–01, Pres. (Home and Personal Care), Latin America Business Group 2001–04, also served as Chair. Unilever's Latin America Advisory Council, Pres. and CEO (Home and Personal Care), N America Business Group 2004–05, joined Unilever Exec. as Pres. Asia and Africa 2005–, also Chair. (non-exec.) HLL 2005–; mem. Exec. Bd Indian School of Business. *Leisure interests:* spending time with family, playing golf and bridge. *Address:* Hindustan Lever Ltd, Hindustan Lever House, 165/166 Backbay Reclamation, Mumbai 400 020, India (office). *Telephone:* (22) 3983-0000 (office). *Fax:* (22) 2287-1970 (office). *E-mail:* webmaster@unilever.com (office). *Website:* www.hll.com (office).

MANZ, Wolfgang; German pianist; b. 6 Aug. 1960, Düsseldorf; m. Julia Goldstein 1985; two s. one d.; studied with Drahomir Toman, Prague and Karlheinz Kämmerling, Hanover; teacher, High School of Music, Karlsruhe 1994–98; concert tours UK, Germany, Belgium and Japan; performed Promenade Concerts, London 1984, Gilels Memorial Concert, Düsseldorf 1986, Karajan Foundation, Paris 1987; First Prize Mendelssohn Competition, Berlin 1981, Second Prize, Leeds Piano Competition 1981, Second Prize Brussels Queen Elizabeth Competition 1983, Van Cliburn Int. Piano Competition Award, Texas 1989. *Recordings include:* Chopin Studies, Beethoven Triple Concerto, with English Chamber Orchestra, solo recital Liszt, Schumann and Debussy, Dohnanyi Piano Quintet. *Leisure interests:* composing, swimming, gardening. *Address:* Pro Classics, Dr Eckhardt van den Hoogen, Wöhlerstrasse 2, 41515 Grevenbroich, Germany (office). *Telephone:* (181) 211670 (office). *Fax:* (181) 211660 (office). *E-mail:* mail@classics.de (office). *Website:* www.proclassics.de (office).

MANZONI, Giacomo, MusM; Italian composer; b. 26 Sept. 1932, Milan; m. Eugenia Tretti 1960; one s.; ed Bocconi Univ., Milan, Univ. of Tübingen and Conservatorio Verdi, Milan; Ed. Il Diapason (music review) 1956; music critic, l'Unità 1958–66; music ed. Prisma 1968; mem. editorial staff, Musica/Realtà 1980–; Prof., Conservatorio Verdi 1962–64, 1974–91, Conservatorio Martini, Bologna 1965–68, 1969–74, Scuola di Musica Fiesole 1988–2004, Accad. Musicale Pescarese 1993–96; mem. Accad. Nazionale di Santa Cecilia, Rome 1994–; has given master courses in composition in Buenos Aires, Granada, Tokyo, Santiago, Beijing, etc.; Dr hc (Udine); Premio Abbiati 1989. *Compositions include:* La Sentenza 1960, Atomtod 1965, Musica notturna 1966, 'Insiemi' 1967, Ombre (alla memoria di Che Guevara) for chorus and orchestra 1968, Per M. Robespierre 1975, Parole da Beckett 1971, Masse: omaggio a E. Varèse 1977, Ode 1982, Scene Sinfoniche per il Dr. Faustus 1984, Dedica (su testi di Maderna) 1985, Dr. Faustus: Scene dal romanzo di T. Mann 1989, 10 versi di E. Dickinson 1989, Malinamusik 1991, Finale e aria (I. Bachmann) 1991, Il deserto cresce (F. Nietzsche) 1992, Moi, Antonin A. (Artaud) 1997, Trame d'Ombre (da Zeami) 1998, O Europa! (A. József) 1999; Sul passaggio del tempo (R. Sanesi) 2001, Sembianti 2003, Studio da concerto for violin, winds and percussion 2005, Mercurio transita davanti al sole 2006, and other chamber music; Una voce chiama, for voice, viola and live electronics (F. Fortini) 1994, Quanto oscura selva trovai (Dante), for trombone, chorus and live electronics 1995, Oltre la soglia, for voice and string quartet 2000, Pensiero XX di G. Leopardi for narrator and string quartet 2001, Vergers for choir 2006; film and incidental music. *Publications:* A. Schoenberg 1975, Scritti 1991, Tradizione e Utopia 1994; translations of Adorno and Schönberg. *Address:* Viale Papiniano 31, 20123 Milan, Italy. *Telephone:* (02) 4817955. *E-mail:* gmanz@libero.it (home).

MAO, Rubai; Chinese politician; *Chairman, Environment Protection and Resources Conservation Committee, National People's Congress;* b. 1938, Yangzhou City, Jiangsu Prov.; ed Nanjing Univ.; joined CCP 1959; Deputy Dir then Dir Meteorological Office of Tibet (Deputy Sec. CCP Party Cttee); Deputy Sec. CCP Tibet Autonomous Regional Cttee 1984, Vice-Chair. Tibet Autonomous Region 1986–93; Vice-Minister of State Construction Ministry 1993–97; Sec. CCP Ningxia Hui Autonomous Regional Cttee 1997–2002; Chair. People's Congress of Ningxia Hui Autonomous Region 1998–2002; mem. 15th CCP Cen. Cttee 1997–2002; Vice-Chair. Environment Protection and Resources Conservation Cttee of 10th Nat. People's Congress 2002, Chair. 2003–; mem. Standing Cttee 10th Nat. People's Congress; Pres. Meteorology Soc. *Address:* Standing Committee, National People's Congress, Beijing, People's Republic of China (office). *Fax:* (10) 63098439 (office).

MAO, Zhiyong; Chinese party official; b. 1929, Yueyang Co., Hunan Prov.; joined CCP 1952; Sec. CCP Yueyang Co. Cttee 1964–66; Deputy CCP Sec. of Yueyang Pref. and Deputy CCP Sec. of Changde Pref., Hunan 1966–71; Deputy Sec.-Gen. CCP Hunan Prov. Cttee 1972–73, First Sec., Sec. 1977–88; mem. 5th NPC 1978–80; Sec. CCP Jiangxi Prov. Cttee 1988–95; Chair. Standing Cttee Jiangxi Prov. People's Congress 1993–98; mem. 11th CCP Cen. Cttee 1977–82, 12th CCP Cen. Cttee 1982–87, 13th CCP Cen. Cttee 1987–92, 14th CCP Cen. Cttee 1992–97; mem. 8th NPC 1993–98; Vice-Chair. 9th CPPCC Nat. Cttee 1998–2003. *Address:* National Committee of Chinese People's Political Consultative Conference, 23 Taipingqiao Street, Beijing, People's Republic of China (office).

MAOATE, Terepai, PhD; Cook Islands politician; *Deputy Prime Minister and Minister of Finance and Economic Development;* Prime Minister and Minister of Finance 2000–02, Deputy Prime Minister and Minister of Finance 2005, currently Deputy Prime Minister and Minister of Finance and Econ. Devt, Financial Intelligence Unit, Public Expenditure and Review Cttee, Health, Ombudsman, Devt Investment Bd, Small Business Enterprise Centre, Attorney-Gen., Commerce Comm., Nat. Superannuation, Parl. Services and Broadcasting; fmr Gov. Asian Devt Bank; Leader, Democratic Party. *Address:* Ministry of Finance and Economic Management, POB 120, Rarotonga, Cook Islands (office). *Telephone:* 22878 (office). *Fax:* 23877 (office). *E-mail:* cifinsec@mfem.gov.ck (office). *Website:* www.mfem.gov.ck (office).

MAOR, Galia, BA, MBA; Israeli economist and banker; *President and CEO, Bank Leumi le-Israel BM;* b. 1943; m.; three c.; ed Hebrew Univ. of Jerusalem; joined Bank of Israel 1963, held numerous supervisory positions including Head of Open Market Operations, Supervisor of Banks 1982–89, Sr Dir Banking Systems, currently mem. Advisory Cttee; pvt. consultancy 1989–91; joined Bank Leumi as Deputy Gen. Man. 1991, Pres. and CEO 1995–; mem. Bd of Govs Hebrew Univ. of Jerusalem; Chair. Friends of Yeladim (Council for the Child in Placement), Friends of Acad. of the Hebrew Language, Israeli Cttee of INSEAD; Dr hc (Open Univ.), (Netanya Coll.); Recannati Award for Women's Excellence in Man. 2001, Women's Excellence Award, Hadassah 2001, Woman of the Year, Globes magazine 2008; ranked by Fortune magazine amongst 50 Most Powerful Women in Business outside the US (34th) 2002, (42nd) 2003, (36th) 2004, (32nd) 2005, (32nd) 2006, (35th) 2007, ranked by Forbes magazine amongst 100 Most Powerful Women (88th) 2006, (83rd) 2007. *Address:* Bank Leumi le-Israel BM, PO Box 2, 24–32 Yehuda Halevi Street, Tel-Aviv 65546, Israel (office). *Telephone:* 3-5148111 (office). *Fax:* 3-5661872 (office). *Website:* www.bankleumi.co.il (office).

MAPFUMO, Thomas Tafirenyika Mukanya; Zimbabwean musician (mbira, guitar), singer and songwriter; b. 2 July 1945, Marondera; important figure in local Shona music 1970s–; singer in local bands, including The Cosmic Dots, the Springfields; f. Hallelujah Chicken Run Band 1973, Black Spirits 1976; performed with The Pied Pipers 1977; f. Acid Band 1977–, later banned from the radio, renamed Blacks Unlimited 1978; Mapfumo imprisoned for subversion 1977; researcher in traditional Zimbabwean folk music. *Recordings include:* albums: Hokoya! 1977, Mbira Music of Zimba 1980, Gwindingwe 1980, Mabesa 1983, Congress 1983, The Chimurenga Singles 1983, Ndangariro 1984, Corruption 1984, Mr Music 1985, Chimurenga For Justice 1986, Zimbabwe-Mozambique 1987, Nyamaropa Nhimutimu 1989,

Shumba 1990, The Spirit of the Eagle 1991, Chimurenga Masterpis 1991, Hondo 1993, Chimurenga Int'l 1993, Vanhu Vatema 1994, Chimurenga: African Spirit Music 1997, Rise Up 2006. *Address:* Adastra, 2 Star Row, North Dalton, Driffield, East Yorkshire YO25 9UR, England (office). *Telephone:* (1377) 217662 (office). *Fax:* (1377) 217754 (office).

MAPLE, M. Brian, AB, MS, PhD; American physicist and academic; *Director, Institute for Pure and Applied Physical Sciences, University of California, San Diego;* ed San Diego State Univ., Univ. of Calif., San Diego; Asst Research Physicist, Univ. of Calif., San Diego 1969–75, Asst Prof. of Physics 1973–75, Assoc. Prof. 1975–81, Prof. 1981–90, Bernd T. Matthias Endowed Chair. in Physics 1990–, Dir Center for Interface and Materials Science 1990–, Dir Inst. for Pure and Applied Physical Sciences 1995–; Visiting Scientist, Univ. of Chile, Santiago 1971–73; Visiting Prof., Instituto de Fisica José Balseiro, Argentina 1974; Assoc. Research Physicist, Univ. of Calif., Santa Barbara Inst. for Theoretical Physics 1980; Chair. Gordon Conf. on Superconductivity 1990, 2000; mem. American Physical Soc. 1977– (Fellow 1985–), Calif. Catalysis Soc. 1977–, American Vacuum Soc. 1977–, Materials Research Soc. 1977–; Fellow AAAS 1997–; mem. Advisory Bd Superconductivity Review 1989–, CONNECT 1990–, Journal of Physics: Condensed Matter 1997–; mem. numerous int. advisory cttees; Humboldt Research Award 1998, Frank H. Spedding Award 1999, American Physical Soc. James C. McGroddy Prize for New Materials 2000, Berndt T. Matthias Prize 2000. *Publications:* numerous papers on solid state physics and surface physics; Valence Fluctuations in Solids (Co-Ed.) 1982, Superconductivity in Ternary Compounds (Co-Ed.) 1982, Handbook on the Physics and Chemistry of Rare Earths (Co-Ed.) 2000. *Address:* Department of Physics, University of California, San Diego, 9500 Gilman Drive, MC 0319, La Jolla, CA 92093-3968, USA (office). *Telephone:* (858) 534–3968 (office). *Fax:* (858) 534–1241 (office). *E-mail:* mbmaple@ucsd.edu (office). *Website:* mbmlab.ucsd.edu (office).

MAPONYA, Richard John; South African business executive; b. 24 Dec. 1926, Pietersburg; s. of late Godfrey Kgabane Maponya and Mary Machichane Maponya (née Mogashoa); m. Marina Nompinti Sondlo (died 1992); two s. four d.; ed Kagiso Teacher's Training Coll., Pietersburg; Proprietor Maponya's Supply Stores 1952–; Dir Maponya's Bus Services 1965, Maponya's Funeral Parlour (Pty) Ltd 1976, Afro Shopping Construction Enterprises (Pty) Ltd, Maponya's Discount Supermarket 1983–, Maponya's Bottle Store, Maponya's Motors (Pty) Ltd, Maponya Motors Property Holdings (Pty) Ltd, Maponya's Orlando Restaurant (Pty) Ltd, Maponya's Stud Farm, Lebowa Devt Corpn, numerous other cos; Man. Dir MA Africa (Pty) Ltd, Mountain Motors, Soweto 1978–; Propr BMW Agency, Soweto; Chair. Kilimanjaro Investments (East London-based bottler); race horse owner; Founder and Pres. NAFCOC 1965; Chair. Trade and Transport Cttee, Soweto Council; mem. Urban Bantu Council 1965–76; Pres. Black Proprietors Garage Owners' Asscn. *Leisure interests:* racing, music. *Address:* PO Box 783045, Sandton 2146, South Africa.

MAPP, Wayne, LLB, LLM, PhD; New Zealand lawyer and politician; *Minister of Defence, of Research, Science and Technology, Associate Minister for Economic Development and for Tertiary Education;* b. 12 March 1952, Te Kopuru; ed Auckland Univ., Univ. of Cambridge, UK; lawyer in pvt. practice 1978–82; Lecturer in Commercial Law, Auckland Univ. 1984–94, Assoc. Prof. 1994–96; mem. New Zealand Nat. Party 1982–, Divisional Policy Chair., Auckland 1993–96; MP for North Shore 1996–, mem. Select Cttees on Foreign Affairs, Defence and Trade 1997–99, on Justice and Law Reform 1997–2002, on Māori Affairs 1999–2001, 2003–04, on Social Services 2002, on Educ. and Science 2003–04, Transport and Industrial Relations 2005–06, on Privileges 2005–08; Spokesman for Defence 1999–2002, for Justice 1999–2002, for Disarmament and Arms Control 2002–03, for Foreign Affairs 2002–03, for Housing 2002–03, for Constitutional and Treaty of Waitangi Issues 2003–04, for Immigration 2003–04, for Labour and Industrial Relations 2004–06; Assoc. Spokesman for Treaty of Waitangi 1999–2002, for Constitutional and Treaty of Waitangi Issues 2004–05; Minister of Defence, of Research, Science and Tech., Assoc. Minister for Econ. Devt and for Tertiary Educ. 2008–. *Address:* Ministry of Defence, POB 12703, Molesworth Street, Wellington, New Zealand (office). *Telephone:* (4) 496-0999 (office). *Fax:* (4) 496-0859 (office). *E-mail:* info@defence.govt.nz (office). *Website:* www.defence.govt.nz (office).

MAPURANGA, Machivenyika Tobias, BA, MA, PhD; Zimbabwean diplomatist; *Ambassador to USA;* b. 22 March 1947; m. Shupikayi V. D. Mapuranga; five c.; ed Univs of London, Oxford and Edinburgh, UK; Lecturer, Univ. of Ibadan, Jos Campus, Nigeria 1975–76, Univ. of Jos 1975–79, Univ. of Zimbabwe 1979–80; Counsellor and Chargé d'affaires a.i. to Zambia 1980–81, Amb. to Tanzania 1982–86, Deputy Sec., Political and Econ. Affairs, Ministry of Foreign Affairs 1986–87, Special Rep. of OAU Sec.-Gen. to Rwanda 1993–94, Head of OAU Del. to Arusha Peace Talks, Asst Sec.-Gen. in several depts of OAU, Deputy Perm. Sec., Political and Econ. Affairs, Ministry of Foreign Affairs 1995–96, Perm. Rep. to UN 1996–99, Chair. Fourth Cttee (Special Political and Decolonization), UN Gen. Ass. 1997, Chair. Non-Aligned Movement Political Cttee 1997, Head of Zimbabwean Del. to Commonwealth Summit in Australia 1999, Perm. Sec., Ministry of Foreign Affairs 1999–2001, Amb. to Ghana 2001–05, to USA 2005–. *Address:* Embassy of Zimbabwe, 1608 New Hampshire Avenue, NW, Washington, DC 20009, USA (office). *Telephone:* (202) 332-7100 (office). *Fax:* (202) 483-9326 (office). *E-mail:* info@zimbabwe-embassy.us (office). *Website:* www.zimbabwe-embassy.us (office).

MAQBOOL, Lt-Gen. Khalid, MSc; Pakistani army officer (retd) and government administrator; b. 1948; ed Staff Coll., Quetta, Nat. Defence Coll., Rawalpindi, Naval Postgraduate Inst., Monterey, USA; commissioned in Pakistan Army 1966, saw action with infantry regt in Kashmir Sector 1971, Commdr of Corps, Infantry Div./Brigade, Chief Instructor, Nat. Defence Coll. and Command and Staff Coll., Quetta, Defence and Mil. Attaché to USA for two and half years; Chair. Nat. Accountability Bureau 2000–01; Gov. of Punjab Prov. 2001–08 (resgnd); Chancellor Univ. of Sargodha; Hilal-e-Imtiaz (Mil.), Hilal-e-Imtiaz. *Address:* c/o Office of the Governor, Lahore, Punjab, Pakistan.

MAQUEDA, Juan Carlos; Argentine politician, lawyer and university teacher; b. 29 Dec. 1949, Río Tercero; ed La Salle Coll. and Catholic Univ. of Córdoba; Prof. of Law, Catholic Univ. of Córdoba 1977–80, Adjunct Prof. of Natural Law 1980, Prof. of History of Political Insts of Argentina 1981, Asst Prof. of Natural Law 1981–82, 1983–84, Prof. 1984–85, Adjunct Prof. of Constitutional Law 1985, Prof. of Political Theory 1986; Tech. Sec., Faculty of Law and Social Sciences, Univ. of Córdoba 1980–86; mem. Justicialista party; Prov. Deputy, Córdoba 1986–91; Deputy to Nat. Ass. 1991–99; Minister of Educ., Prov. of Córdoba 1999–2001; Pres. Constitutional Convention of Prov. of Córdoba Aug. 2001; Senator from Córdoba 2001–03, Vice-Pres. Nat. Senate 2001, Pres. 2002; mem. Fed Council of Nat. Culture and Educ. 1999–2001; Vice-Pres. Argentine Group, Parliamentarians for Global Action. *Publications include:* El Pensamiento Político Español del Siglo XVI 1980, Los Partidos Políticos: Ordenamiento Legal 1985, Sistemas Electorales y los Sistemas de Partidos 1985, La Nueva Constitución de Córdoba: Labor Constituyente y Debates 1987, Labor Parlamentaria en la Cámera de Diputados de la Provincia de Córdoba y Debates 1988, 1989. *Address:* c/o Senado, Hipólito Yrigoyen 1849, 3° Piso, 1310 Buenos Aires, Argentina (office). *E-mail:* juan.maqueda@senado.gov.ar (office). *Website:* www.senado.gov.ar (office).

MARADONA, Diego Armando; Argentine fmr professional football player and football manager; *Head Coach, Argentina national football team;* b. 30 Oct. 1960, Lanús, Buenos Aires; s. of Diego Maradona and Dalma Salvadora Franco; m. Claudia Villafane; two d.; with Boca Juniors, Argentina 1981–82, Barcelona Football Club 1982–84; with Naples Football Club 1984–91, Seville (Spain) 1992–93, Boca Juniors 1997, Badajoz 1998; won Youth World Cup with Argentina nat. team 1979, won World Cup with Argentina nat. team 1986; founded Maradona Producciones; fmr Amb. for UNICEF; banned from football for 15 months after drugs test; convicted by Naples Court on charges of possession of cocaine, 14-month suspended sentence and fine of 4 million lire, Sept. 1991; Fed. Court in Buenos Aires ruled he had complied with the treatment; suspended for 15 months for taking performance-enhancing drugs in World Cup Finals June 1994; indicted for shooting an air rifle at journalists Aug. 1994; resgnd as coach of Deporto Mandiyu 1994; Capt. of Argentina 1993; host La Noche del Diez (talk show) 2005; Dir of Football Boca Juniors football club 2005–06; Head Coach, Argentina nat. football team 2008–; South American Player of the Year 1979, World Footballer of the Year 1986, Footballer of the Century Award, Féd. Int. de Football Asscn (France) 2000. *Publication:* El Diego (autobiog.) 2005. *Address:* Asociación del Fútbol Argentino, Viamonte 1366, C1053ACB Buenos Aires, Argentina (office). *Telephone:* (11) 4370-7900 (office). *E-mail:* fmolina@afa.org.ar (office). *Website:* www.afa.org.ar (office); www.diegomaradona.com.

MARAFINO, Vincent Norman, MBA; American business executive; b. 8 June 1930, Boston; m. Doris M. Vernall 1958; three d.; ed San Jose State Coll. and Santa Clara Univ.; served with USAF 1953–55; Chief Accountant, American Standard Advance Tech. Lab., Mountain View, Calif. 1956–59; with Lockheed Missiles & Space Co., Sunnyvale, Calif. 1959–70; Asst Controller, Lockheed Corpn Burbank, Calif. 1970–71, Vice Pres., Controller 1971–77, Sr Vice-Pres. Finance 1977–83, Exec. Vice-Pres., Chief Financial and Admin. Officer 1983–88, Vice-Chair. of Bd and Chief Financial and Admin. Officer 1988–95; mem. Bd of Dirs Lockheed Missiles and Space Co., Inc.; Chair. Bd of Dirs Lockheed Finance Corpn; mem. Bd of Trustees Holy Cross Medical Center, Mission Hills; mem. Financial Execs Inst., American Inst. of CPAS. *Address:* c/o Lockheed Corporation, 6801 Rockledge Drive, Bethesda, MD 20817, USA.

MARAGALL, Pasqual, PhD; Spanish civil servant and academic; b. 13 Jan. 1941, Barcelona; m.; three c.; ed Barcelona Univ., New School for Social Research, New York; lecturer in Econs Barcelona Univ.; Mayor of Barcelona 1982–97, organizer of 1992 Olympic Games in Barcelona; mem. Partit dels Socialistes de Catalunya, Pres. 2000–07; Pres. Council of Municipalities and Regions of Europe 1991–97, Cttee of the Regions of EU 1996–98; Pres. Govt of Catalonia 2003–06; Insignia Order of the Légion d'honneur 1993, Hon. OBE; Hon. DLitt (Winchester Art School, UK), Dr hc (Johns Hopkins USA) 1997, Laurea hc (Reggio Calabria Italy) 1998; Medal of the Council of Europe 1984, Olympic Golden Award 1992, Golden Medal Award Spanish Inst. New York 1993. *Address:* Catalan Socialist Party, Nicaragua 75, E-08029 Barcelona, Spain. *Telephone:* (934) 955400 (office). *Fax:* (934) 955430 (office). *E-mail:* pmaragall@psc.es (office). *Website:* www.psc.es (office).

MARAINI, Dacia; Italian writer and poet; b. 13 Nov. 1936, Fiesole; d. of Fosco Maraini and Alliata Topazia; ed Collegio S.S. Annunziata, Florence and Rome; Prix Formentor for L'Età del Malessere (The Age of Discontent) 1962. *Plays include:* La famiglia normale 1967, Centocelle gli anni del fascismo 1971, Dialogo di una prostituta con un solo cliente 1973, Da Roma a Milano 1975, Don Juan 1976, Due Donne di Provincia 1978, Erzbeth Bartory 1980, Donna Lionora giacubina 1981, I Sogni di Clitennestra 1981, Dramma d/amore al circo Bagno Balò 1981, Lezioni d'Amore 1982, Bianca Garofani 1982, Delitto 1987, Charlotte Corday 1989, Celia Carli 1990, Commedia Femminile 1994, Camille 1995. *Publications:* La Vacanza 1962, L'Età del Malessere 1962, Crudeltà All' Aria Aperta 1966, A Memoria 1967, Mio Marito 1968, Memoirs of a Female Thief 1973, Donne mie 1974, Donna in Guerra 1975, Mangiami Pure 1978, Lettere a Marina 1981, Dimenticato di Dimenticare 1983, Il treno per Helsinki 1984, Isolina 1985, Devour me too 1987, La Bionda, la bruna e l'asino 1987, La Lunga Vita di Marianna Ucria 1990, L'Uomo tatuato 1990, Viaggiando con passo de volpe 1991, Bagheria 1993, Voci 1994, La ragazza con la treccia 1994, Mutino, Orlov e il gatto che si crede pantera 1995, Dolce per sé 1997, Se amando troppo 1998, Buio 1999, La nave per Kobe 2001,

Colomba 2004, Il gioco dell'universo 2007, Il treno dell'ultima notte 2008. *Address:* c/o Rizzoli, RCS Libri, Via Mecenate 91, 20138 Milan (office); Via Beccaria 18, 00196 Rome, Italy (home). *Telephone:* 3611795 (home). *Website:* www.rcslibri.it (office); www.daciamaraini.it.

MARAJ, Rashid Muhammad al-, BS; Bahraini banking official and fmr government official; *Governor, Central Bank of Bahrain;* ed Univ. of Houston, USA, Strathclyde Univ., UK; Engineer, Ministry of Industry and Devt 1979–80; Asst Under-Sec. for Econ. Affairs, Ministry of Finance and Nat. Economy 1981–95; Under-Sec., Ministry of Transport 1995–99; Gen. Man. and CEO, Arab Petroleum Investments Corpn, Saudi Arabia 1999–2005; Gov. Cen. Bank of Bahrain 2005–. *Address:* Central Bank of Bahrain, POB 27, Building 96, Block 317, Road 1702, Manama, Bahrain (office). *Telephone:* 17547777 (office); 17547500 (office). *Fax:* 17530399 (office); 17537799 (office). *E-mail:* governor@cbb.gov.bh (office); info@cbb.gov.bh. *Website:* www.cbb.gov.bh (office).

MARANDA, Pierre Jean, MA, LPh, PhD, FRSC; Canadian anthropologist and academic; *Professor Emeritus, Laval University;* b. 27 March 1930, Québec; s. of Lucien Maranda and Marie-Alma Rochette; m. Elli-Kaija Köngäs 1962 (deceased); two s.; ed Laval Univ., Québec, Univ. of Montreal and Harvard Univ.; Asst Prof. of Classics, Univ. Laval 1955–58; Research Fellow, Harvard Univ. 1966–70; Dir of Research Ecole Pratique des Hautes Etudes, Paris 1968–69; Assoc. Prof. of Anthropology Univ. of BC 1969–71, Prof. 1971–75; Prof. Collège de France, Paris 1975; Research Prof. Laval Univ. 1976–96, Prof. Emer. 1996–; Pres. Steering Cttee of Cultural Hypermedia Encyclopedia of Oceania 1996–; Visiting Prof., Fed. Univ. of Rio de Janeiro 1983, Univ. of Toronto, ISISSS 1985, 1987, Univ. of British Columbia 1986, Université Omar Bongo, Libreville, Gabon 1991, 1992, Ecole des hautes études en sciences sociales, Paris 1994; Dr hc (Memorial Univ., Newfoundland) 1985; Médaille du Collège de France 1975, Canada Council Molson Prize in the Social Sciences and Humanities 1997. *Films:* Behind the Masks (with Claude Lévi-Strauss), Nat. Film Bd of Canada 1974, The Lau of Malaita, Solomon Islands (with Leslie Woodhead), Granada TV 1987. *Publications:* Structural Models in Folklore and Transformational Essays (with E. K. Köngäs) 1963, Echanges et communications (co-ed. with J. Pouillon) 1970, Structural Analysis of Oral Tradition (co-ed. with E. K. Köngäs) 1971, Introduction to Anthropology: A Self-Guide 1972, Mythology (ed.) 1972, French Kinship: Structure and History 1974, Mythology 1974, Soviet Structural Folkloristics 1974, Symbolic Production symbolique (ed.) 1977, L'Appropriation sociale de la logique (ed.) 1978, Imposer la bâtardise francophone (co-ed. with Eric Waddell) 1982, Automatic Text Reading: An Attempt at Artificially Intelligent Interpretation 1984, Dialogue conjugal 1985, DISCAN: A Computer Programme for Discourse Analysis 1989, L'unité dans la diversité culturelle: Une geste bantu, Vol. 1: Le sens des symboles fang, mbede, eshira 1993, Masques démasqués (co-ed. with Andrée Gendreau) 1993, Lo spazio semiotico dell'Andromaque di Racine 1994, Sémiotique de l'igname à Malaita, Iles Salomon 1995, A Semiotic Encyclopedia of the Lau People (Malaita, Solomon Islands) (computer diskette) 1997, Cultural Hypermedia Encyclopedia of Oceania (with Pierre Jordan and Christine Jourdan) (3rd edn) 1998, The Double Twist: From Ethnography to Morphodynamics (ed.) 2001, Peuples des eaux, gens des îles: l'Océanie (co-author) 2001; more than 90 articles in scientific journals. *Leisure interests:* skiing, swimming, tennis, bridge, music, art. *Address:* Département d'Anthropologie, Université Laval, Québec, PQ G1K 7P4, Canada (office). *Telephone:* (418) 656-5867 (office); (418) 999-8570 (home); (418) 656-2131. *Fax:* (418) 656-2831 (office). *E-mail:* pierre.maranda@ant.ulaval.ca (office); pmaranda@videotron.ca (home). *Website:* www.oceanie.org (office).

MARAPANE, Tilak Janaka; Sri Lankan politician; fmr Attorney-Gen.; Minister of Defence and of Transport, Highways and Aviation 2001–04. *Address:* c/o Ministry of Defence, 15/5 Baladaksha Mawatha, POB 572, Colombo 3, Sri Lanka.

MARAT, Allan, DJur; Papua New Guinea politician; *Attorney-General and Minister of Justice;* ed Univ. of Oxford; Leader People's Progress Party; Deputy Prime Minister, Minister for Trade and Industry, Papua New Guinea 2002–06; Attorney-Gen. and Minister of Justice 2007–. *Address:* Department of the Attorney-General, POB 591, Waigani, NCD, Papua New Guinea (office). *Telephone:* 3230138 (office). *Fax:* 3230241 (office). *Website:* www.justice.gov.pg (office).

MARBER, Patrick; British writer and director; b. 19 Sept. 1964, London; s. of Brian Marber and Angela Benjamin; m. Debra Gillett; one s.; ed Wadham Coll., Oxford; Evening Standard Award for Best Comedy 1995, Writers' Guild Award for Best West End Play 1995 (both for Dealer's Choice), Evening Standard Best Comedy Award 1997, Critics' Circle Award for Best Play 1997, Olivier Award 1998, New York Drama Critics' Award 1999 (all four for Closer). *Plays directed and/or written include:* Dealer's Choice 1995, Blue Remembered Hills 1996, '1953' 1996, Closer 1997, The Old Neighbourhood 1998, The Caretaker 2000, Howard Katz 2001. *Television work includes:* The Day Today, Paul Calf Video Diary, Knowing Me Knowing You, 3 Fights 2 Weddings and a Funeral, The Curator, After Miss Julie. *Publications include:* Dealer's Choice 1995, After Miss Julie 1996, Closer 1997, Howard Katz 2001. *Address:* c/o Judy Daish Associates Ltd, 2 St Charles Place, London, W10 6EG, England (office). *Telephone:* (20) 8964-8811 (office). *Fax:* (20) 8964-8966 (office).

MARÇAL, Rev. Arlindo; Timor-Leste diplomatist and clergyman; *General Secretary, Christian Democrat Party;* fmr Head of East Timor Protestant Church; Vice-Pres. Constituent Ass. 2001–02; Pres. Adviser Council of Int. Habitat for Humanity 2001–; Gen.-Sec. Christian Democrat Party 2002–; Founding mem. Yayasan Hak (human rights org.); Amb. to Indonesia 2003–07. *Address:* Partido Democrata Cristão (Christian Democrat Party), Former Escola Cartilha, Rua Quintal Kiik, Bairro Economico, Dili, Timor-Leste (office). *Telephone:* 3324683 (office). *E-mail:* arlindom@octa4.net.au (office).

MARCANO, Luis Herrera, DIur; Venezuelan diplomatist and academic; *Professor of Law, Universidad Central de Venezuela;* b. 13 Dec. 1931, Caracas; m. Maria Sardi de Herrera; ed Universidad Cen. de Venezuela; staff mem. Ministry of Foreign Affairs 1950–55, adviser 1956–57, Dir Int. Orgs 1958, Dir Office of the Commrs for Guyana 1965–67, Dir Int. Policy 1968, Adviser to the Minister 1969–72, 1978, mem. Foreign Relations Advisory Comm. 1979–84, Amb. and mem. Comm. for Maritime Delimitation with Colombia 1980, mem. Council of Legal Advisers 1984–, legal adviser 1990–91, Co-ordinator of Pro Tempore Secr. of Rio Group 1990, external adviser 1992–99, adviser to Ministers of Interior and Justice 1999; Amb. and Deputy Perm. Rep. to UN, New York 2000; Amb. and Deputy Chief of Mission in Washington, DC 2001, Chargé d'affaires (acting) 2002–03; Prof. of Public Int. Law, Universidad Cen. de Venezuela 1963–, Dir School of Law 1978–81, Dean Faculty of Legal and Political Sciences 1981–84; also currently external adviser in legal matters to Latin American and Caribben Econ. System (SELA); Exec. Sec. Organizing Comm., Universidad Simón Rodríguez 1972–76; mem. Interamerican Juridical Cttee, OAS 1982–, Pres. 1990–92; legal adviser Latin American Econ. System 1986–90; adviser to UN Truth Comm. for El Salvador 1992–93, mem. UN Comm. of Inquiry for Burundi 1995–96; adviser to Petróleos de Venezuela 1985–86. *Address:* c/o Faculty of Law and Political Science, Universidad Central de Venezuela, Apdo Postal 1050, Ciudad Universitaria, Los Chaguaramos, Caracas, 1051, Venezuela (office). *Website:* www.ucv.ve (office).

MARCEAU, Félicien, (pseudonym of Louis Carette); French writer; b. 16 Sept. 1913, Cortenberg, Belgium; s. of Louis Carette and Marie Lefèvre; m. 2nd Bianca Licenziati 1953; ed Coll. de la Sainte Trinité à Louvain and Univ. de Louvain; mem. Acad. Française 1975; Officier, Légion d'honneur, Ordre nat. du Mérite, Commdr des Arts et des Lettres; Prix Prince Pierre de Monaco 1974; Grand Prix du Théâtre 1975. *Publications:* Novels: Chasseneuil 1948, Capri petite île 1951, Chair et Cuir 1951, L'Homme du Roi 1952, En de secrètes noces 1953, Bergère Légère 1953, Les Élans du cœur 1955 (Prix Interallié), Les Belles Natures 1957, Creezy 1969 (Prix Goncourt), Le corps de mon ennemi 1975, Appelez-moi Mademoiselle 1984, La Carriole du Père Juniet 1985, Les passions partagées 1987, Un Oiseau dans le Ciel 1989, Les ingénus 1992, La Terrasse de Lucrezia 1993, Le Voyage de noces de Figaro 1994, La grande fille 1997, La Fille du Pharaon 1998, L'affiche 2000; plays: L'oeuf 1956, La bonne soupe 1958, La preuve par quatre 1965, Un jour j'ai rencontré la vérité 1967, Le babour 1969, L'ouvre-boîte 1972, L'homme en question 1973, A nous de jouer 1979; essays: Casanova ou l'anti-Don Juan 1951, Balzac et son monde 1955, Le roman en liberté 1977, Une insolente liberté: Les aventures de Casanova 1983, L'Imagination est une science exacte 1998; memoirs: Les années courtes 1968. *Leisure interest:* painting. *Address:* c/o Les Editions Gallimard, 5 rue Sébastien-Bottin, 75007 Paris; Academie Française, 23 quai de Conti, 75006 Paris, France. *Telephone:* 1-49-54-42-00; 1-44-41-43-06.

MARCEAU, Sophie; French actress; b. (Sophie Danièle Sylvie Maupu), 17 Nov. 1966, Paris; d. of Benoît Maupu and Simone Morisset; one s.; Meilleur Espoir Féminin (for César) 1982, (for Molière) 1991 and several foreign prizes. *Films include:* La Boum 1980, La Boum 2 1982 (César Award), Fort Saganne 1984, Joyeuses Pâques 1985, L'Amour Braque 1985, Police 1985, 'Round Midnight (uncredited) 1986, Descente aux Enfers 1986, Chouans! 1987, L'etudiante 1988, Mes nuits sont plus belles que vos jours 1989, Pacific Palisades 1989, Pour Sacha 1991, La note bleue 1991, Fanfan 1993, La fille de D'Artagnan 1994, Braveheart 1995, L'Aube à l'envers (Dir) 1995, Al di là delle nuvole (Beyond the Clouds) 1995, Firelight 1995, Anna Karenina 1997, Marquise 1997, The World is Not Enough 1998, Lost & Found 1999, A Midsummer Night's Dream 1999, La fidelité 2000 (Cabourg Romantic Film Festival Award), Belphégor – Le fantôme du Louvre (Belphecor: Curse of the Mummy) 2001, Parlez-moi d'amour (Dir) 2002 (Best Director, Montréal World Film Festival), Alex and Emma 2003, Je reste! 2003, Les clefs de bagnole (The Car Keys) 2003, À ce soir (aka Nelly) 2004, Anthony Zimmer 2005, Lezioni di volo 2006, La Disparue de Deauville 2007, Female Agents 2007. *Stage appearances include:* Eurydice 1991, Pygmalion 1993. *Publication:* Menteuse 1996. *Leisure interests:* countryside, music, reading, travel. *Address:* c/o Artmédia, 20 avenue Rapp, 75007 Paris, France (office). *Telephone:* 1-44-31-22-00. *E-mail:* infos@marceau.as (office). *Website:* www.sophie-marceau.ifrance.com.

MARCHAND, Philippe, LenD; French politician and lawyer; b. 1 Sept. 1939, Angoulême, Charente; s. of Guy Marchand and Madeleine Bonat; m. Marie-Odile Filliau 1965; three s.; ed Collège de Parthenay, Univ. of Poitiers; lawyer at Saintes bar 1965–92; local councillor, Charente-Maritime 1976–2001, Saintes 1982–2001; Socialist Deputy for Charente-Maritime 1978–90, Vice-Pres. Assemblée Nationale 1985–86; Vice-Pres. Socialist Group in Parl. 1990–91; Titular Judge, High Court 1987; mem. Nat Comm. on Information Tech. and Freedom 1982–86, 1988–; Minister-del. in Ministry of the Interior 1990–91, Minister of the Interior 1991–92; regional councillor, Poitou-Charentes 1992–; mem. Comm. Nat. de Déontology de la Sécurité; Officier Légion d'honneur, Grand Cross of the Orden Isabel la Católica (Spain). *Address:* c/o Parti Socialiste, 10 rue de Solférino, 75333 Paris, France (office).

MARCHANT, Ian; British energy industry executive; *CEO, Scottish and Southern Energy;* worked for Coopers & Lybrand including a two-year secondment to Dept of Energy working on electricity privatization; joined Southern Electric 1992, Finance Dir and mem. Bd of Dirs 1996–98, Finance Dir Scottish and Southern Energy (after merger of Southern Electric and Scottish Hydro Electric) 1998–2002, mem. Bd Dirs 1998–, CEO 2002–, lead Dir for Corp. Responsibility, mem. Nomination Cttee; Chair. UK Business

Council for Sustainable Energy; Dir (non-exec.) Maggie's Cancer Centres, John Wood Group PLC 2006–; mem. Forum for Renewable Energy Devt in Scotland, Ofgem's Environmental Advisory Group, Energy Research Partnership.

MARCHENKO, Grigori Alexandrovich; Kazakhstani politician and banker; b. 26 Dec. 1959, Almaty; m.; ed Moscow State Inst. of Int. Relations, Georgetown Univ., USA; engineer-designer and acting Deputy Head, Dept of Sr Mans Ministry of Non-Ferrous Metals, Kazakh SSR 1984–85; Trans., Ed. and Leader Marketing Information Group, Kazakh Scientific Research Inst. 1986–88; acting head Design Bureau of Semiconductor Machine Building, Chair. Scientific Production Co-operative Centre 1988–90; Asst to Vice-Pres. of Kazakhstan 1992–93; Deputy Gov. Nat. Bank of Kazakhstan 1994–96, Gov. 1999–2004; First Deputy Prime Minister of Kazakhstan 2004–06; Chair. Nat. Securities Comm. of Kazakhstan 1996–98; Pres. DB Securities of Kazakhstan 1998–99; Pew Fellow, Georgetown Univ. 1994. *Address:* c/o Office of the Prime Minister, Beibitshilik 11, 473000 Astana, Kazakhstan (office).

MARCHIONNE, Sergio; Italian/Canadian business executive; *CEO, Fiat SpA;* b. 1952; Chartered Accountant, Tax Specialist Deloitte & Touche 1983–85; Group Controller Lawson Mardon Group, Toronto 1985, later Dir of Corp. Devt; Exec. Vice-Pres. Glenex Industries 1989–90; Vice-Pres. of Finance and Chief Financial Officer Acklands Ltd 1990–92; Vice-Pres. for Legal and Corp. Devt, Chief Financial Officer and Sec. Lawson Group 1992–94, Exec. Vice-Pres. for Corp. Devt and Chief Financial Officer Algroup (following Algroup's acquisition of Lawson Group) 1994–96, CEO 1996–99, CEO Lonza Group Ltd (following demerger) 2000–01, Chair. 2002; CEO SGS Group Geneva 2002, Chair. SGS 2006–; mem. Bd Fiat SpA 2003–, CEO 2004–, CEO Fiat Auto 2005– (renamed Fiat Group Automobiles 2007), also Chair. CNH Case New Holland (Group co. operating in the agricultural and construction equipment business) 2006–; mem. Bd Dirs UBS AG 2007–, Vice-Chair. 2008–; mem. Bd Serono SA, Chair. Audit Cttee; Chair. European Automobile Mfrs Asscn; Perm. mem. Fondazione Giovanni Agnelli; mem. Gen. Council Assonime; mem. Canadian Inst. of Chartered Accountants; Cavaliere del Lavoro; Hon. LLD (Univ. of Windsor), hon. degree in Econs (Univ. of Cassino), Hon. MA (CUOA Foundation), degree ad honorem in Industrial Eng and Man. (Polytechnic Univ., Turin). *Address:* Fiat SpA, 250 Via Nizza, 10126 Turin, Italy (office). *Telephone:* (011) 0061111 (office). *Fax:* (011) 0063798 (office). *E-mail:* info@fiatgroup.com (office). *Website:* www.fiatgroup.com (office).

MARCHUK, Guriy Ivanovich; Russian mathematician; b. 8 June 1925, Petro-Khersonets Village, Orenburg Region; m.; three c.; ed Leningrad State Univ.; Sr Research Assoc., Head of Dept, Inst. of Physics and Energetics, Obninsk 1953–62; Inst. of Math. of Siberian Br. of USSR Acad. of Sciences 1962–64; Prof., Novosibirsk Univ. 1962–80; Deputy Chair., Chair. of Presidium, Siberian Br. of USSR Acad. of Sciences 1964–79; Dir Computing Centre of Siberian Br. of USSR Acad. of Sciences 1964–79; Deputy Chair. USSR Council of Ministers and Chair. State Cttee for Science and Tech. 1980–86; Dir Dept of Computing Math. (now Inst.), Acad. of Sciences 1980–, Adviser to Dir 1999–; Corresp. mem. USSR (now Russian) Acad. of Sciences 1962–68, mem. 1968–, Vice-Pres. 1975–78, Pres. 1986–91, Chair. Scientific Council on Medicine 1987–91; Deputy to USSR Supreme Soviet 1979–89; Lenin Prize 1961, A. Karpinski Prize, Hamburg 1988; Order of Lenin (four times), Keldysh Gold Medal 1981, Chebyshev Gold Medal 1996 and other decorations. *Publications:* works on problems of computational math. and physics of atmosphere. *Address:* Institute of Numerical Mathematics, Gubkin Str. 8, 117333, Moscow, Russia. *Telephone:* (495) 938-17-69. *Fax:* (495) 938-18-21.

MARCHUK, Gen. Yevgen Kirilovich, CJur; Ukrainian politician; b. 28 Jan. 1941, Dolinivka, Kirovograd Region; m.; two s.; ed Kirovograd Pedagogical Inst.; worked as school teacher of Ukrainian and German Languages; with Ukrainian KGB (State Security Cttee) 1963–91, Deputy Chair. 1990–91; Chair. Nat. Security Service of Ukraine 1991; State Minister of Defence, Nat. Security and Emergencies 1991–94; Deputy Prime Minister July 1994, First Deputy Prime Minister 1994–95; Prime Minister of Ukraine 1995–96; mem. Verkhovna Rada (United Social Democratic Party faction) 1996–; Head Cttee of Social Policy and Labour 1998–; Sec. Ukrainian Nat. Security and Defence Council 2000–03; Minister of Defence 2003–04; Pres. Ukrainian Transport Union 1998; presidential cand. 1999. *Address:* c/o National Security and Defence Council of Ukraine, Domandarma Kameneva Str. 8, 01133 Kiev, Ukraine. *Telephone:* (44) 291-60-27.

MARCINKEVIČIUS, Justinas; Lithuanian poet, playwright and translator; b. 10 March 1930, Važatkiemis, Lithuania; s. of Motiejus Marcinkevičius and Ieva Marcinkevičius; m. Genovaitė Kalvaitytė 1955; two d.; ed Univ. of Vilnius; began literary career 1953; fmr Vice-Chair. Bd Union of Lithuanian Writers; mem. CPSU 1957–90; USSR People's Deputy 1989–91; mem. Lithuanian Acad. of Science 1990, Lithuanian Council of Culture and Art 1991; Order of the Grand Duke Gediminas; awards include State Prizes (twice), People's Poet of Lithuania, J.G. Horder Award 1997, Polish PEN Centre Award 1997, J.G. Herder Award 1998, Santarvé Award 1999, Nat. Award of Lithuania 2001, Award of the Baltic Assembly 2001. *Publications include:* in trans.: I Ask to Speak 1955, The Twentieth Spring 1955, The Pine that Laughed 1961, Blood and Ashes 1961, Hands that Share out the Bread 1963, The Wall 1965, Mindaugas 1968, The Cathedral 1971, Mazhvidas 1977, The Tender Touch of Life 1978, The Only Land 1984, For the Living and the Dead 1988, Lullaby to the Homeland and the Mother 1992, By the Rye and by the Hearth 1993, Poems from the Diary 1993, The Harmony of the Flowing River 1995, A Step 1998, The Tree of Knowledge 2001, The Spider's Wedding 2002, Carmina minora 2000, Dienos drobulé 2002. *Address:* c/o Lietuviškos knygos, J. Basanavičiaus g. 5, 01118 Vilnius, Lithuania (office). *E-mail:* info@booksfromlithuania.lt (office). *Website:* www.booksfromlithuania.lt (office).

MARCINKIEWICZ, Kazimierz; Polish politician; b. 20 Dec. 1959, Gorzów Wielkopolski; ed Wrocław Univ., Adam Mickiewicz Univ., Poznan; worked as teacher; mem. Solidarity Ind. Self-Governing Trade Union 1983–90; Founding mem. Christian-Nat. Union party (ZChN) 1989; Supt Bd of Educ. in Gorzów Wielkopolski 1990–92; Deputy Minister of Nat. Educ. 1992–93; consultant and Deputy Dir Voivodship Methodological Centre in Gorzów 1993–95; mem. main Bd of ZChN and head of bd in Gorzów Wielkopolski 1994; Deputy third Sejm representing Electoral Action Solidarity-ZChN, later Deputy Chair. and Chair., Sejm Educ., Science and Youth Comm., also Deputy Chief, Special Comm. on Admin. Reform; Head of Cabinet 1999–2000; left ZChN and f. Right Wing Alliance 2001, then head Parliamentary Club of Law and Justice party; Deputy fourth Sejm and Chair. of State Treasury Comm.; Prime Minister of Poland 2005–06; ed and publr ind. educational periodical Pokolenie; Co-founder, Ed. and Publr of Aspekty (Catholic weekly); Cyberpolitician 2003. *Publications:* numerous articles on economics. *Address:* c/o Law and Justice (Prawo i Sprawiedliwość—PiS), 02-018 Warsaw, ul. Nowogrodzka 84/86, Poland. *Telephone:* (22) 6215035. *Fax:* (22) 6216767. *E-mail:* biuro@pis.org.pl. *Website:* www.pis.org.pl.

MARCKER, Kjeld Adrian, PhD; Danish molecular biologist and academic; *Professor of Molecular Biology, Århus University;* b. 27 Dec. 1932, Nyborg; s. of Kjeld A. C. Marcker and Minna C. Callesen; m. Anne Birgit Hansen 1964; three d.; ed Nyborg Gymnasium and Univ. of Copenhagen; Dept of Physical Chem., Univ. of Copenhagen 1958; Carlsberg-Wellcome Fellow, MRC Lab. of Molecular Biol., Cambridge 1962, mem. staff 1964; Fellow, King's Coll. Cambridge 1968; Prof. in Molecular Biology, Århus Univ. 1970–; mem. Royal Danish Acad., Danish Acad. of Tech. Science, Academiae Europaeae; Novo Medical Prize 1971; Anders Jahre Medical Prize 1973. *Publications:* articles in scientific journals. *Leisure interests:* soccer, bird-watching, history. *Address:* Laboratory of Gene Expression, Department of Molecular Biology, University of Århus, Gustav Wieds Vej 10, 8000 Århus C (office); Tjoernehegnet 32, 8541 Skoedstrup, Denmark (home). *Telephone:* 86-22-01-18 (home). *E-mail:* KM@mb.au.dk (home).

MARCOS, Imelda Romualdez; Philippine politician and social leader; b. 2 July 1929, Tacloban City; d. of Vicente Orestes Romualdez and Remedios Trinidad; m. Ferdinand E. Marcos 1954 (died 1989); one s. two d.; Gov. of Metro Manila 1975–86; Roving Amb.; visited Beijing 1976; took part in negotiations in Libya over self-govt for southern provs 1977; leader Kilusan Bagong Lipunan (New Society Movt) 1978–81; mem. Batasang Pambansa (Interim Legis. Ass.) 1978–83; Minister of Human Settlements 1978–79, 1984–86, of Human Settlements and Ecology 1979–83; mem. Cabinet Exec. Cttee 1982–84; Chair. Southern Philippines Devt Authority 1980–86; indicted for embezzlement 1988, acquitted 1990; returned to Philippines Nov. 1991; sentenced to 18–24 years' imprisonment for criminal graft Sept. 1993; convicted of two charges of corruption, sentenced to 9–12 years on each Sept. 1993; sentenced on appeal to Supreme Court; faced four charges of graft Sept. 1995; presidential cand. 1992, 1998; mem. Philippine House of Reps for first dist of Leyte 1995–2001; opened Marikina City Footwear Museum in Manila in which most of the exhibits are her own footwear 2001; arrested on charges of corruption and extortion committed during her husband's presidency 2001; acquitted of 32 counts of graft 2008; voted 'Muse of Manila' 1950. *Records include:* Imelda Papin featuring songs with Mrs Imelda Romualdez Marcos 1989.

MARCUS, Claude, DEcon; French advertising executive (retd); b. 28 Aug. 1924, Paris; s. of Jack Marcus and Louise Bleustein; m. Claudine Pohl 1948; one s. three d.; ed Faculté des Lettres, Aix and Faculté de Droit, Paris; fmr Vice-Chair. Supervisory Bd, Man. Dir Publicis, Chair. Publicis Int.; fmr Chair. Perm. Comm. Advertising Profession/Consumer Unions; Chevalier, Légion d'honneur, Officier, Ordre nat. du Mérite, Médaille des Evadés, Chevalier, Ordre des Palmes académiques et de l'Economie nationale. *Leisure interests:* antiques, tennis. *Address:* 12 rue Félicien David, 75016 Paris, France. *Telephone:* 1-44-43-70-02. *Fax:* 1-45-20-18-01 (home). *E-mail:* claudius6@wanadoo.fr (home).

MARCUS, Rudolph Arthur; American chemist and academic; *Arthur Amos Noyes Professor of Chemistry, California Institute of Technology;* b. 21 July 1923, Montreal, Canada; s. of Myer Marcus and Esther Marcus; m. Laura Hearne 1949 (deceased 2003); three s.; ed McGill Univ., Montreal; worked for Nat. Research Council of Canada 1946–49; Univ. of N Carolina 1949–51; Asst Prof., Polytech. Inst. of Brooklyn 1951–54, Assoc. Prof. 1954–58, Prof. 1958–64; Prof., Univ. of Ill. 1964–68; Arthur Amos Noyes Prof. of Chem., Calif. Inst. of Tech. 1978–; Visiting Prof. of Theoretical Chem., Univ. of Oxford, UK 1975–76; Visiting Linnett Prof. of Chem., Univ. of Cambridge, UK 1996; mem. Courant Inst. of Math. Sciences, New York Univ. 1960–61, Council, Gordon Research Confs 1965–68, Chair. Bd of Trustees and mem. Bd 1966–69; Chair. Div. of Physical Chem., ACS 1964–65; mem. Exec. Cttee American Physical Soc. Div. of Chemical Physics 1970–72, Advisory Bd ACS Petroleum Research Fund 1970–72, Review Cttee Argonne Nat. Lab. Chem. Dept 1966–72 (Chair. 1968–69), Brookhaven Nat. Lab. 1971–73, Radiation Lab., Univ. of Notre Dame 1976–78, External Advisory Bd, NSF Center for Photoinduced Charge Transfer 1990–, Nat. Research Council/NAS, Cttee on Climatic Impact; Chair. Cttee on Kinetics of Chemical Reactions 1975–77, Panel on Atmospheric Chem. 1975–78, Cttee on Chemical Sciences 1977–79, Cttee Survey Opportunities in Chem. 1982–86, Math. Panel, Int. Benchmarking of US Research Fields 1996–98, Advisory Cttee for Chem., NSF 1977–80, Review Cttee, Chem. Depts, Princeton Univ. 1972–78, Polytech. Inst. of New York 1977–80, Calif. Inst. of Tech. 1977–78, Cttee for Accountability of Federally Funded Research, COSEPUP 2000–01; Adviser, State Key Lab. for Structural Chem. of Unstable and Stable Species, Beijing 1995, Center for Molecular Sciences, Chinese Acad. of Sciences, Beijing 1995–; mem.

Editorial Bds Laser Chem. 1982–, Advances in Chemical Physics 1984–, World Scientific Publishing 1987–, International Reviews in Physical Chemistry 1988–, Progress in Physics, Chemistry and Mechanics (China) 1989–, Journal of the Chemical Society Perkin Transactions 2 1992–, Chemical Physics Research (India) 1992–, Trends in Chemical Physical Research (India) 1992–; Hon. Ed. International Journal of Quantum Chemistry 1996–; mem. NAS, American Philosophical Soc. (mem. Council 1999–), Int. Acad. of Quantum Molecular Science; Foreign mem. Royal Society, London, Chinese Acad. of Sciences; Assoc. mem. Center for Advanced Studies, Univ. of Ill. 1968–69; Fellow, American Acad. of Arts and Sciences, Co-Chair. Exec. Cttee Western Section; Foreign FRSC 1991–; NSF Sr Post-Doctoral Fellowship 1960–61; Alfred P. Sloan Fellowship 1960–63; Fulbright-Hays Sr Scholar 1971–72; numerous lectureships; Hon. FRSC, Hon. Fellow, Univ. Coll., Oxford 1995–, Hon. Prof., Fudan Univ., Shanghai 1994–, Inst. of Chem., Chinese Acad. of Sciences, Beijing 1995–, Hon. Visitor, Nat. Science Council, Taiwan 1999, Hon. mem. American Philosophical Soc. 1990 (Council mem. 1999), Int. Soc. of Electrochemistry, Korean Chemical Soc. 1996, Int. Soc. for Theoretical Chemical Physics, Literary and Historical Soc., Univ. Coll., Dublin 2004, European Acad. of Science 2004, Hon. Citizen of Winnipeg 1995, Key to City of Taipei, Taiwan 1999; Hon. DSc (Chicago) 1983, (Polytechnic Univ.) 1986, (Gothenburg) 1987, (McGill) 1988, (New Brunswick) 1993, (Queen's) 1993, (Oxford) 1995, (Yokohama Nat. Univ.) 1996, (Univ. of NC) 1996, (Univ. of Ill.) 1997, (Technion–Israel Inst. of Tech.) 1998, (Univ. Politécnica de Valencia, Spain) 1999, (Northwestern Univ.) 2000, (Univ. of Waterloo, Canada) 2002; Anne Molson Prize for Chem. 1943, Alexander von Humboldt Foundation Sr US Scientist Award 1976, ACS Irving Langmuir Award in Chem. Physics 1978, R. A. Robinson Medal, Faraday Div., Royal Soc. of Chem. (RSC) 1982, C. F. Chandler Medal (Univ. of Columbia) 1983, Wolf Prize 1985, ACS Peter Debye Award in Physical Chem. 1988, ACS Willard Gibbs Medal 1988, Centenary Medal, Faraday Div., RSC 1988, Nat. Medal of Science 1989, ACS Theodore William Richards Medal 1990, Evans Award (Ohio State Univ.) 1990, ACS Edgar Fahs Smith Award, ACS Remsen Award, ACS Pauling Medal 1991, Nobel Prize for Chem. 1992, Hirschfelder Prize in Theoretical Chem. (Univ. of Wisconsin) 1993, American Acad. of Achievement Golden Plate Award 1993, Lavoisier Medal (Soc. Française de Chimie) 1994, ACS Auburn-Kosolapoff Award 1996, ACS Award in Theoretical Chem., ACS Oesper Award 1997, Top 75 Award, Chemical and Eng News, ACS 1998. *Achievements include:* devt of the Marcus Theory of electron transfer reactions in chemical systems and RRKM Theory of unimolecular reactions. *Publications:* numerous articles in scientific journals, especially Journal of Chemical Physics and Journal of Physical Chem. *Leisure interests:* music, history, tennis and skiing. *Address:* Noyes Laboratory, Caltech Chemistry 127-72, California Institute of Technology, Pasadena, CA 91125 (office); 331 South Hill Avenue, Pasadena, CA 91106, USA (home). *Telephone:* (626) 395-6566 (office). *Fax:* (626) 792-8485 (office). *E-mail:* ram@caltech.edu (office). *Website:* www.cce.caltech.edu/faculty/marcus/index (office).

MARCUS, Ruth Barcan, BA, MA, PhD; American academic and author; *Senior Research Scholar, Reuben Post Halleck, Emerita, Yale University;* b. 2 Aug. 1921, New York; d. of Samuel Barcan and Rose Post; m. Jules A. Marcus 1942 (divorced 1976); two s. two d.; ed New York and Yale Univs; Research Assoc. Inst. for Human Relations, Yale Univ. 1945–47; Assoc. Prof. Roosevelt Univ. 1959–64; Prof. and Chair. Dept of Philosophy, Univ. of Ill. 1964–70; Prof. Northwestern Univ. 1970–73; Reuben Post Halleck Prof. of Philosophy, Yale Univ. 1973–93, Sr Research Scholar 1994–, now Senior Research Scholar, Reuben Post Halleck, Emer.; Visiting Distinguished Prof., Univ. of Calif., Irvine 1994–99; Adviser, Oxford Univ. Press New York 1980–90; Guggenheim Fellow 1953–54; NSF Fellow 1963–64; Fellow, Center for Advanced Studies, Stanford Univ. 1979, Inst. for Advanced Study in the Humanities, Univ. of Edin. 1983, Wolfson Coll. Oxford 1985, 1986, Clare Hall, Cambridge 1988 (Perm. mem. Common Room); Fellow, American Acad. of Arts and Sciences; mem. and Pres. Inst. Int. de Philosophie, Paris 1990–93, Hon. Pres. 1993–; Chair. Nat. Bd of Officers, American Philosophical Asscn 1977–83; Pres. Asscn for Symbolic Logic 1983–86; Pres. Elizabethan Club 1988–90; mem. Council on Philosophical Studies (Pres. 1988–), Steering Cttee, Fed. Int. Soc. de Philosophie 1985–99; mem. numerous editorial bds; Hon. DHumLitt (Illinois) 1995; Medal, Coll. de France 1986, Wilbur Cross Medal, Yale Univ. 2000. *Publications:* The Logical Enterprise (ed. with A. Anderson and R. Martin) 1975, Logic Methodology and Philosophy of Science (ed.) 1986, Modalities 1993, 1995; articles in professional journals. *Address:* Department of Philosophy, Box 208306, Yale University, New Haven, CT 06520, USA (office). *Telephone:* (203) 432-1672. *Fax:* (203) 432-7950 (office). *E-mail:* ruth.marcus@yale.edu (office). *Website:* www.yale.edu/philos (office).

MARCY, Geoffrey W., BA, PhD; American astronomer and academic; *Professor of Astronomy and Director, Center for Integrative Planetary Science, University of California, Berkeley;* b. 29 Sept. 1954, Los Angeles, Calif.; s. of Robert Misrahi and Gloria Isaacs; m. Dr Susan Kegley 1994; ed Granada Hills High School, Los Angeles, Univ. of California, Los Angeles, Univ. of California, Santa Cruz; Carnegie Fellow, Carnegie Inst. of Washington 1982–84; Prof. of Physics and Astronomy, San Francisco State Univ. 1984–96, Distinguished Univ. Prof. 1997–99, Adjunct Prof. of Physics and Astronomy 1999–; Prof. of Astronomy, Univ. of California, Berkeley 1999–, Dir Center for Integrative Planetary Science 2000–; a Prin. Invesigator for NASA's Space Interferometry Mission 2001; mem. Cttee on the Status of Women in Astronomy (American Astronomical Soc. —AAS) 1994–97, Publs Bd, Publs of the Astronomical Soc. of the Pacific 1997–2002, Bd of Dirs, Astronomical Soc. of the Pacific 1997–99, Bd of Councillors, American Astronomical Soc. 1998–2000, NASA Working Group: Origins of Solar Systems 1998–2000, NASA Working Group: Terrestrial Planet Finder 1998–2001; mem. NAS 2002; Fellow, Calif. Acad. of Sciences 1996; ABC News Hour Person of the Week 26

Jan. 1996, Manne Siegbahn Award, Physics Cttee of Swedish Acad. 1996, Bunyan Lecturer, Stanford Univ. 1997, Alumnus of the Year, Univ. of California, Santa Cruz 1997, first Int. Astronomical Union Comm. 51 Bioastronomy Medal of Honor 1997, first Certificate of Recognition, Extrasolar Planetary Foundation 1999, UCLA Alumni Professional Achievement Award 1999, Invited Lecture and Exhibit, Centennial Meeting of American Physical Soc. 1999, G. Darwin Lecturer, Royal Astronomical Soc. 2000, California Scientist of the Year 2000, NSF Distinguished Lecturer 2000, NAS Henry Draper Medal 2001, Sackler Lecturer, Univ. of Leiden 2001, AAS Beatrice Tinsley Prize 2002, Carl Sagan Award, American Astronautical Soc. and Planetary Soc. 2002, NASA Medal for Exceptional Scientific Achievement 2003 Discover Magazine: Space Scientist of the Year 2003, Shaw Prize in Astronomy (Lecture) 2005, Niels Bohr Lecturer, Niels Bohr Inst. 2005, George Gamow Lecturer, Univ. of Colorado 2006, NASA Astrobiology Inst. 'Getting to the Core of Exoplanets: From Gas Giants to Ice Giants' 2007, Lecture: Nat. Air and Space Museum: New Worlds, Yellowstone, and Life in the Universe 2007. *Achievements include:* discovered 70 of first 100 known extrasolar planets; discovered first system of planets around a Sun-like star (Upsilon And), discovered first transiting planet around another star (HD209458), discovered first cand. Saturn-mass planets (HD46375, HD16141), discovered first extrasolar planet orbiting beyond 5 AU (55 Cancri d, co-discovered first Neptune-sized planets: Gliese 436b and 55 Cancri e. *Publications:* numerous scientific papers in professional journals. *Address:* 417 Campbell Hall, University of California, Berkeley, CA 94720, USA (office). *Telephone:* (510) 642-1952 (office). *Fax:* (510) 642-3411 (office). *E-mail:* gmarcy@astro.berkeley.edu (office). *Website:* astro.berkeley.edu/~gmarcy (office).

MÅRDH, Per-Anders, MD, PhD; Swedish university professor and physician; *Professor of Clinical Bacteriology, University of Uppsala;* b. 9 April 1941, Stockholm; s. of Gustav-Adolf Mårdh and Inga-Greta Mårdh (née Bodin); ed Univ. of Lund; Assoc. Prof., Univ. of Lund 1973; Dir WHO Collaboration Centre for Sexually Transmitted Diseases, Univ. of Lund 1980–85, then Uppsala Univ. 1985–; Prof. of Clinical Bacteriology, Univ. of Uppsala 1984–; Founder Scandinavian Asscn for Travel Medicine and Health 1990; Chair. Healthy Travel and Tourism Centre, Simrishamn; mem. Bd Int. Tourist Health Org., Osterlen Acad.; Fernström's Award for young prominent research workers 1982. *Publications:* as ed.: Genital Infections and Their Complications 1975, Chlamydia trachomatis in Genital and Related Infections 1982, Chlamydial Infections 1982, International Perspectives on Neglected Sexually Transmitted Diseases 1983, Gas Chromatography/Mass Spectrometry in Applications in Microbiology 1984, Sexually Transmitted Diseases 1984, Bacterial Vaginosis 1984, Coagulase–negative Staphylococci 1986, Infections in Primary Health Care 1986, Genital Candida-infection 1990, Vaginitis/Vaginosis 1991, Travel and Migration Medicine 1997; Author: Chlamydia 1988, Swedish Red Houses 1991, Travel Well Travel Healthy 1992, Travel Medicine 1994. *Leisure interests:* art, skiing. *Address:* Department of Obstetrics and Gynaecology, Lund University Hospital, 221 85 Lund, Sweden (office). *Telephone:* (46) 17-13-20 (office); (46) 12-98-08 (home). *Fax:* (46) 15-78-68 (office). *E-mail:* per-anders.mardh@med.lu.se (office); per-anders.mardh@telia.com (home). *Website:* www.med.lu.se (office).

MAREE, John B., BComm, AMP; South African business executive; b. 13 Aug. 1924, Middelburg, Cape; s. of Dr John Maree; m. Joy du Plessis 1950; one s.; ed Univ. of the Witwatersrand and Harvard Business School, USA; Chair. Eskom Electricity Council 1985–97, Nedcor Group of Cos 1990–97, Denel Ltd 1992–95, Powertech Ltd 1997; Dir Devt Bank of SA, Old Mutual; Fellow, Inst. of Marketing Man.; Hon. DCom; Star of SA 1985, Order for Meritorious Service (Gold) 1989, Chevalier, Légion d'honneur, Order of Cloud and Banner, People's Repub. of China; one of top 5 Businessmen of the Year 1981. *Leisure interests:* golf, gardening. *Address:* 52 4th Road, Hyde Park, Sandton 2196, South Africa (home). *Telephone:* (11) 881-4363 (office); (11) 788-8812 (home). *Fax:* (11) 881-4799 (office). *E-mail:* drmaree@nedbank.co.za (office).

MARES, Petr, PhD; Czech politician and academic; b. 15 Jan. 1953; m.; two d.; ed Charles Univ., Prague, Warsaw Univ., Poland; engineer, Strojinvestav Eng Co. 1989–81; researcher, Inst. of Czechoslovak History 1981–84; record keeper, Dept of Archives, Gen. Trade Union 1987–88; researcher, Dept of History and Theory of Film-Making, Czechoslovak Films Inst. 1988–90; Sec. Chair. of Political Sciences, Faculty of Social Sciences, Charles Univ. 1990, Vice-Dean for Study Affairs, Head Dept of American Studies Inst. of Int. Studies –1996; Fellow, Univ. of Calgary, Canada 1996; Chair. Cttee for Science, Educ., Culture and Youth, Chamber of Deputies 1998–2002; Deputy Prime Minister for Minorities of Czech Repub. 2002–04; Chair. Freedom Union –2004. *Publications include:* History of the Lands of the Czech Crown: Part II (co-author) 1992, United States Presidents 1994, History and NATO (co-author) 1997; many articles in professional journals. *Address:* c/o Office of the Government, nábř. Edvarda Beneše 4, 118 01 Prague 1, Czech Republic (office).

MARGELOV, Mikhail Vitalyevich; Russian politician; *Member of the Russian Federal Assembly;* b. 22 Dec. 1964, Moscow; m.; one s.; trans., Int. Dept, CPSU Cen. Cttee 1984–86; Arabic teacher, Higher KGB School 1986–89; Chief Ed. Arab Dept, ITAR-TASS 1989–90; with consulting cos World Resources, Boston Consulting Group, Ban & Co. 1990–95; with Video Int. 1995–; co-ordinator Boris Yeltsin Presidential election campaign; First Deputy Head Dept of Man., Russian Presidium 1996–97, Head of Dept of Public Relations 1997–98; Head of Advisory Group to the Chair., State Customs Cttee 1998; Head of Political Advisory Group, Novosti Information Agency 1999; Head of Russian Information Centre 1999–2000; Rep. for Pskov region, Russian Fed. Ass. 2000–, mem. Council of the Fed., Chair. Int. Affairs Cttee 2001–. *Address:* Nekrasov str. 23, Office 241, 180001 Pskov (office);

Council of the Federation, Bolshaya Dmitrovka str. 26, Moscow, Russia (office). *Telephone:* (88112) 16-08-31 (office); (495) 292-13-58 (office).

MARGÉOT, HE Cardinal Jean, PhL, STL; Mauritian ecclesiastic; *Bishop Emeritus of Port-Louis;* b. 3 Feb. 1916, Quatre-Bornes; s. of Joseph Margéot and Marie Harel; ed Séminaire Français, Rome, Pontifical Gregorian Univ., Rome, Italy; ordained priest 1938, Bishop of Port-Louis 1969–93, Bishop Emer. 1993–; cr. Cardinal-Priest of S. Gabriele Arcangelo all'Acqua Traversa 1988; Grand Officer Order of the Star and Key 1997. *Address:* c/o Eveche, rue 13 Msgr Gonin, Port-Louis; Bonne Terre, Vacoas, Mauritius. *Telephone:* (208) 3068 (Port-Louis); (424) 5716 (Vacaos). *Fax:* (208) 6607 (Port-Louis); (426) 5190 (Vacaos). *E-mail:* jmargeot@bow.intnet.mu (office).

MARGETTS, Sir Robert John, Kt, CBE, FREng, FIChemE; British insurance industry executive; *Chairman, Legal & General Group Plc;* b. 1946; ed Univ. of Cambridge; trained as chemical engineer; joined ICI PLC 1970, various positions including Dir 1992–2000, Vice-Chair. 1998–2000; Chair. Legal & General Group Plc 2000–; Chair. UK Natural Environment Research Council (NERC) 2000–06, BOC Group 2001–06, Huntsman Corpn (Europe), Ensus PLC 2006–; Dir (non-exec.) Anglo-American PLC; mem. UK Council for Science and Tech.; Hon. Fellow, Imperial Coll. 1999, City & Guilds 2001, Hon. Freeman City of London 2004, Salters Company 2004; Hon. DEng (Univ. of Sheffield) 1997, Hon. DSc (Cranfield Univ.) 2003. *Address:* Legal & General Group Plc, One Coleman Street, London, EC2R 5AA, England (office). *Telephone:* (20) 3124-2000 (office). *Fax:* (20) 7528-6222 (office). *E-mail:* info@ legalandgeneralgroup.com (office). *Website:* www.legalandgeneralgroup.com (office).

MARGOLIASH, Emanuel, MD; American biochemist and academic; *Professor, Laboratory of Molecular Biology, University of Illinois, Chicago;* b. 10 Feb. 1920, Cairo, Egypt; s. of Wolf Margoliash and Bertha Margoliash (née Kotler); m. Sima Beshkin 1944; two s.; ed Mission Laïque Française, Cairo, American Univ. of Beirut, Lebanon; Research Fellow, Dept of Experimental Pathology, Hebrew Univ., Jerusalem 1945–48; served as Medical Officer in the Israel Army 1948–49; Sr Asst in Experimental Pathology, Cancer Research Labs, Hadassah Medical School, Hebrew Univ., Jerusalem 1951; worked under Prof. D. Keilin, Molteno Inst., Univ. of Cambridge, England 1951–53; Acting Head, Cancer Research Labs, Hadassah Medical School, Hebrew Univ., Jerusalem 1954–58, Lecturer in Experimental Pathology, 1955; worked at Nobel Inst., Dept of Biochem. under a fellowship of the Dazian Foundation for Medical Research 1958; Research Assoc., Dept of Biochem., Univ. of Utah Coll. of Medicine, Salt Lake City, Utah, USA 1958–60; Research Assoc., McGill-Montreal Gen. Hospital Research Inst., Montreal, Canada 1960–62; Research Fellow and Head, Protein Section, Dept of Molecular Biology, Abbott Laboratories, North Chicago, Ill. 1962–71; Professorial Lecturer, Dept of Biochem., Univ. of Chicago, Ill. 1964–71; Prof. of Biochem. and Molecular Biology, Northwestern Univ., Evanston, Ill. 1971–90, Chair. Dept of Biochem., Molecular Biology and Cell Biology 1979–82, Owen L. Coon Prof. of Molecular Biology 1988–90, Prof. Emer. 1990–; Prof., Lab. of Molecular Biology, Dept of Biological Sciences, Univ. of Ill., at Chicago 1989–, Co-ordinator 1989–93; mem. Nat. Acad. of Sciences and numerous scientific socs; Fellow, American Acad. of Arts and Sciences, American Acad. of Microbiology; mem. Editorial Bd of Journal of Biological Chem. 1966–72, Biochemical Genetics 1966–80, Journal of Molecular Evolution 1971–82, Biochem. and Molecular Biology Int. 1981–99; mem. Int. Union of Biochem. Cttee on Nomenclature 1962–, Advisory Cttee, Mich. State Univ. Atomic Energy Comm. Plant Research Lab. 1967–72; Co-Chair. Gordon Research Conf. on Proteins 1967; Keilin Memorial Lectureship of the Biochemical Soc. 1970; Harvey Soc. Lectureship 1970–71; mem. Publs Cttee, American Soc. of Biological Chemists Inc. 1973–76; mem. of Exec. Cttee of US Bioenergetics Group of the Biophysical Soc. 1980–; Rudi Lemberg Fellow, Australian Acad. of Science 1981; Guggenheim Fellow 1983. *Publications:* more than 275 scientific papers and volumes. *Address:* Department of Biological Sciences, (M/C 066), The University of Illinois at Chicago, 845 W Taylor Street, Chicago, IL 60607-7060, USA. *Telephone:* (312) 996-8268. *Fax:* (312) 996-2805.

MARGRETHE II, HM, Queen of Denmark; b. 16 April 1940; d. of the late King Frederik IX and Queen Ingrid; m. Count Henri de Laborde de Monpezat (now Prince Consort Henrik of Denmark) 1967; two s., HRH Crown Prince Frederik and HRH Prince Joachim; ed Univs of Copenhagen, Århus and Cambridge, Sorbonne, Paris and London School of Econs; succeeded to the throne 14 Jan. 1972; has undertaken many official visits abroad with her husband, travelling extensively in Europe, the Far East, N and S America; Hon. KG 1979; Hon. Freedom of City of London 2000; Hon. Bencher of the Middle Temple 1992; Hon. Fellow Lucy Cavendish Coll. Cambridge 1989, Girton Coll. Cambridge 1992; Hon. LLD (Cambridge) 1975; Dr hc (London) 1980, (Univ. of Iceland) 1986, (Oxford) 1992, (Edin.) 2000; Medal of the Headmastership, Univ. of Paris 1987. *Achievements (miscellaneous):* illustrated J.R.R. Tolkien's Lord of the Rings (1977), Historierne om Regnar Lodbrog, Norse Legends as told by Jorgen Stegelmann (1979), Bjarkemaal (1982), Poul Oerum's Comedy in Florens (1990) and Cantabile poems by HRH the Prince Consort (2000), designed costumes for TV Theatre's The Shepherdess and the Chimney-sweep (1987), scenography and costumes for the ballet A Folk Tale, Royal Theatre (1991), découpages for TV film about the Hans Christian Andersen fairy tale Snedronningen (1999–2000), scenography and costumes for Tivoli pantomime ballet Kaerlighed i Skarnkassen (2001), illustrations for Karen Blixen's Seven Gothic Tales (2002). *Publications:* (trans.) All Men are Mortal (with HRH the Prince Consort) 1981, The Valley 1988, The Fields 1989, The Forest (trans.) 1989. *Address:* Amalienborg, 1257 Copenhagen K; PO Box 2143, 1015 Copenhagen K, Denmark. *E-mail:* hofmarskallatet@kongehuset.dk (office). *Website:* www.kongehuset.dk (office).

MARGULIS, Gregoriy, DSc; American (b. Russian) researcher, academic and educator; *Professor of Mathematics, Yale University;* b. 24 Feb. 1946, Moscow, Russia; ed Moscow High School and Moscow Univ.; Jt Scientific Fellow, Inst. for Problems in Information Transmission, Moscow 1970–74, Sr Research Fellow 1974–86, Leading Research Fellow 1986–91; Prof. of Math., Yale Univ., New Haven, Conn. 1991–; mem. NAS 2001; Foreign Hon. Mem. American Acad. of Arts and Science 1991; Hon. Fellow, Tata Inst. of Fundamental Research 1996; Dr hc (Bielefeld) 2000; Young Mathematicians' Prize, Moscow Math. Soc. 1968, Fields Medal, Int. Congress of Mathematicians, Helsinki 1978 (prevented by Soviet Govt from travelling to Helsinki to receive medal), Medal of Collège de France 1991, Humboldt Prize 1995, Wolf Foundation Prize in Mathematics 2005. *Publications:* numerous articles in math. journals on ergodic theory, dynamical systems, discrete subgroups of Lie groups, geometry, number theory, combinatorics. *Address:* Yale University, Department of Mathematics, 438 DL, PO Box 208283, New Haven, CT 06520-208283, USA (office). *Telephone:* (203) 432-7318 (office). *E-mail:* margulis@math.yale.edu (office). *Website:* www.math.yale.edu (office).

MARGULIS, Lynn, AB, MS, PhD, FAAS; American evolutionist, university professor and author; *Distinguished University Professor, Department of Geosciences, University of Massachusetts;* b. 5 March 1938, Chicago; d. of Morris and Leone Wise Alexander; m. 1st Carl Sagan 1957; m. 2nd T.N. Margulis 1967; three s. one d.; ed Univs of Chicago, Wisconsin and Calif. at Berkeley; Research Assoc. Dept of Biology, Brandeis Univ. 1963–64, Lecturer 1963–65, Biology Co-ordinator, Peace Corps, Colombia Project 1965–66; Consultant and Staff mem. The Elementary Science Study, Educational Services 1963–67; Adjunct Asst Prof. Dept of Biology, Boston Univ. 1966–67, Asst Prof. 1967–71, Assoc. Prof. 1971–77, Prof. 1977–88, Univ. Prof. 1986–88; Distinguished Univ. Prof., Dept of Geosciences, Univ. of Massachusetts, Amherst 1988–; Visiting Prof., Dept of Marine Biology, Scripps Inst. of Oceanography Jan.–March 1980, Dept of Geology and Planetary Science Calif. Inst. of Tech. 1980, Dept of Microbiology, Universidad Autónoma de Barcelona, Spain 1985, 1986; NASA-Ames Planetary Biology and Microbial Ecology Summer Research Programme 1980, 1982, 1984; Guggenheim Foundation Fellow 1979; Sherman Fairchild Distinguished Scholar, Calif. Inst. of Tech. 1977; mem. NAS 1983, Russian Acad. of Natural Science 1998, American Acad. of Arts and Sciences 1999; Faculty Merit Publication Award, Boston Univ. 1967, Sherman Fairchild Fellowship, Calif. Inst. of Tech. 1980, NASA Public Service Award 1981, Nat. Medal of Service 1999, Presidential Medal of Science 1999, Collegium Helveticum 2001, Alexander von Humboldt Prize 2002; 13–16 hon. doctorate degrees. *Films:* Eukaryosis: Origin of Nucleated Cells (documentary video) and approx. 20 others on microscopic life. *Publications:* Origin of Eukaryotic Cells 1970, Origins of Life I (ed.) 1970, Origins of Life II (ed.) 1971, Origins of Life: Planetary Astronomy (ed.) 1973, Origins of Life: Chemistry and Radioastronomy (ed.) 1973, Limits of Life (ed. with C. Ponnamperuma) 1980, Symbiosis in Cell Evolution 1981, Early Life 1982, Five Kingdoms: An Illustrated Guide to the Phyla of Life on Earth (with K.V. Schwartz) 1982, Origins of Sex (with D. Sagan) 1986, Microcosmos: Four billion years of evolution from our bacterial ancestors (with D. Sagan) 1986, 1991, Garden of Microbial Delights 1988, Biospheres From Earth to Space (with D. Sagan) 1988, Global Ecology (with René Fester) 1989, Handbook Protoctista (ed.) 1990, Mystery Dance (with D. Sagan) 1991, Symbiosis as a Source of Evolutionary Innovation: Speciation and Morphogenesis (ed. with R. Fester) 1991, Environmental Evolution: the Effect of the Origin and Evolution of Life on Planet Earth (ed. with L. Olendzenski) 1992, Concepts of Symbiogenesis (ed.) 1992, Diversity of Life: The Five Kingdoms 1992, Symbiosis in Cell Evolution: Microbial Communities in the Archaean and Proterozoic Eons 1993, Illustrated Glossary of the Protoctista (with H. McKhann and L. Olendzenski) 1993, The Illustrated Five Kingdoms. A Guide to the Diversity of Life on Earth (with K.V. Schwartz and M. Dolan) 1993, What is Life? (with D. Sagan) 1995, Slanted Truths (with D. Sagan) 1997, What Is Sex? (with D. Sagan) 1998, Early Life (with M.F. Dolan) 2002, Acquiring Genomes: A Theory of the Origins of Species (with D. Sagan) 2003, Peces Luminosos: Historias de Ciencia y Amor 2003, Mind, Life and Universe: Conversations with great scientists of our time (ed. with Eduardo Punset) 2008; interactive CD: Five Kingdoms. *Leisure interests:* fiction, poetry, Spain, pre-Columbian Mexican culture, hiking, cycling, swimming. *Address:* Department of Geosciences, Morrill Science Center, University of Massachusetts, Amherst, MA 01003, USA (office). *Telephone:* (413) 545-3244 (office). *Fax:* (413) 545-1200 (office). *E-mail:* celeste@geo.umass.edu (office). *Website:* www .geo.umass.edu (office); www.sciencewriters.org (home).

MARIAM, Lt-Col Mengistu Haile; Ethiopian fmr head of state and army officer; b. 26 May 1937, Addis Ababa; m. Wubanchi Bishaw 1968; one s. two d.; ed Holeta Mil. Acad.; served in Army's Third Div., attaining rank of Maj.; mem. Armed Forces Co-ordinating Cttee (Derg) June 1974–; took leading part in overthrow of Emperor Haile Selassie Sept. 1974, Head of Derg Exec. Cttee Nov. 1974; First Vice-Chair. Provisional Mil. Admin. Council (PMAC) 1974–77, Chair. (Head of State) 1977–91; Pres. of Democratic Repub. of Ethiopia 1987–91 (overthrown in coup); Chair. PMAC Standing Cttee; Chair. Council of Ministers 1976–91, OAU 1983–84; Sec.-Gen. Workers' Party of Ethiopia 1984–91; accused of genocide in absentia; now living in Zimbabwe as political refugee; convicted of genocide 2006. *Leisure interests:* swimming, tennis, chess, reading, watching films. *Address:* PO Box 1536, Gunhill Enclave, Harare, Zimbabwe. *Telephone:* 745254.

MARIANI, Carlo Maria; Italian artist; b. 25 July 1935, Rome; s. of Anastasio Mariani and Anita de Angelis; m. 1st B. Brantsen 1959 (divorced 1983); m. 2nd Carol Lane 1990; one s. one d.; ed Acad. of Fine Arts, Rome; lives and works in Rome and New York; participated in Documenta 7, Kassel 1982, Venice Biennale 1982, 1984, 1990, Sydney Biennial 1986 and numerous other group exhbns in USA, Canada, UK, USSR, Europe and S America; Fetrinelli Prize, Accademia dei Lincei 1998.

MARIANI-DUCRAY, Francine, LenD; French museum director; *Director, Musées de France;* b. 7 Oct. 1954, Paris; m. Pierre Mariani; three c.; ed Ecole nationale d'administration (ENA) Paris, Inst. d'études politiques de Paris; joined Ministry of Culture 1979; Tech. Adviser to François Léotard, Minister of Culture and Communication 1986–88; a Dir Musée du Louvre 1988–91; Dir of Gen. Admin, Ministry of Culture 1993–98; Head of Gen. Inspections of Admin of Cultural Affairs, Ministry of Culture and Communication 1998–2001; Dir Musées de France 2001–; Pres. Réunion des musées nationaux (RMN) 2001–03; Commdr, Ordre des Arts et des Lettres, Chevalier du mérite; Chevalier, Légion d'honneur 2005. *Address:* Siège de la Direction des musées de France, 6 rue des Pyramides, 75001 Paris (office); 19 rue des Hauts Closeaux, 92310 Paris, France (home). *Telephone:* 1-40-15-34-03 (office); 1-45-34-04-32 (home). *Fax:* 1-40-15-34-10 (office). *E-mail:* francine.mariani-ducray@culture.gouv.fr (office). *Website:* www.dmf.culture.gouv.fr (office).

MARÍAS FRANCO, Javier; Spanish writer and translator; b. 20 Sept. 1951, Madrid; s. of Julián Marías Aguilera and the late Dolores Franco Manera; ed Institución Libre de Enseñanza, Colegio Estudio, Universidad Complutense de Madrid; trans. and writer of film screenplays 1969–; Ed. Alfaguara 1974; lecturer at various univs worldwide; mem. Int. Parliament of Writers (exec. council 2001–); Chevalier, Ordre des Arts et des Lettres, Premio Comunidad de Madrid 1998; Premio Nacional de Traducción (for translation of Tristram Shandy) 1979, Alberto Moravia Int. Prize, Rome 2000, Grinzane Cavour prize, Turin 2000. *Publications:* novels: Los dominios del lobo 1971, Travesía del horizonte 1972, El Monarca del tiempo 1978, El hombre sentimental (Premio Herralde de Novela, Premio Ennio Flaiano 2000) 1986, El Siglo 1982, Todas las almas (Premio Ciudad de Barcelona) 1989, Corazón tan blanco (Premio de la Crítica 1993, Prix L'Oeil et la Lettre 1993, Int. IMPAC Prize 1997) 1992, Mañana en la batalla piensa en mí (Premio Fastenrath de la Real Academia Española de la Lengua 1995, Premio Internacional de Novela Rómulo Gallegos 1995, Prix Fémina Étranger, France 1996, Premio Arzobispo Juan de San Clemente 1995, Premio Letterario Internazionale Mondello-Cittá di Palermo 1998) 1994, Negra espalda del tiempo 1998, Tu rostro mañana, 1. Fiebre y lanza (Premio Salambó 2003) 2002, Your Face Tomorrow 2: Dance and Dream 2006; other fiction: Gospel (screenplay) 1969, Mientras ellas duermen (short stories) 1990, Cuando fui mortal (short stories) 1996, Mala índole (short story) 1998; non-fiction: Pasiones pasadas (articles and essays) 1991, Vidas escritas (articles) 1992, Literatura y fantasma (articles and essays) 1993, Vida del fantasma (articles) 1995, Si yo amaneciera otra vez (articles and poems) 1997, Miramientos (articles) 1997, Mano de sombra (articles) 1997, Desde que te vi morir (articles and poems) 1999, Seré amado cuando falte (articles) 1999, Salvajes y sentimentales (articles) 2000, A veces un caballero (articles) 2001; numerous translations; contrib. to anthologies, including Cuentos únicos 1989, El hombre que parecia no querer nada 1996; contrib. to journals and newspapers, including El País, El Diario de Barcelona, Hiperión, Revista de Occidente. *Address:* Mercedes Casanovas Agencia Literaria, Iradier 24, 08017 Barcelona, Spain (office). *Website:* www.javiermarias.es.

MARIÁTEGUI CHIAPPE, Sandro; Peruvian politician; b. 5 Dec. 1922; s. of José Carlos Mariátegui; m. Matilde de Zela; one d.; Deputy for Lima 1963–68; Minister of Finance and Trade 1965–67; Founder Acción Popular Party, Sec.-Gen. 1985–87; Senator 1980–; Pres. of Senate 1982–83; Prime Minister and Minister of Foreign Affairs April–Oct. 1984. *Address:* Av. Ramírez Gastón 375, Miraflores, Lima, Peru.

MARIĆ, Ljerka, BSc; Bosnia and Herzegovina economist and government official; *Director, Directorate for Economic Planning;* Minister of Finance, Canton of Fojnica 1998; Asst Minister of Finance and the Economy, Bosnian Fed. 2000; fmr Adviser to the Prime Minister; Minister of Finance and the Treasury of the Insts of Bosnia and Herzegovina 2003–07; currently Dir Directorate for Econ. Planning, Council of Ministers. *Address:* Directorate for Economic Planning, Ministry of Finance and the Treasury, 71000 Sarajevo, trg Bosne i Hercegovine 1, Bosnia and Herzegovina (office). *Telephone:* (33) 205345 (office). *Fax:* (33) 471822 (office). *E-mail:* trezorbih@trezorbih.gov.ba (office). *Website:* www.trezorbih.gov.ba (office).

MARICAN, Tan Sri Dato' Mohamed (Mohd) Hassan, FCA; Malaysian petroleum industry executive; *Acting Chairman, President and CEO, Petroliam Nasional Berhad (PETRONAS);* b. 18 Oct. 1952, Sungai Petani; m. Puan Sri Datin Sri Noraini Mohd Yusoff; ed Malay Coll., Kuala Kangsar; with Touche Ross & Co. 1972–80; Partner, Hanafiah Raslan and Mohamed 1980–89; Sr Vice-Pres. of Finance, Petroliam Nasional Berhad (PETRONAS) 1989–95, Pres. and CEO 1995–, Acting Chair. 2004–, also mem. Bd of Dirs and Chair. PETRONAS subsidiaries PETRONAS Dagangan Berhad, PETRONAS Gas Berhad, Malaysia Int. Shipping Corpn Berhad, Engen Ltd SA; Chair. Perusahaan Otomobil Nasional Berhad (Proton) 2000–03; mem. Malaysian Inst. of Accountants, Malaysian Asscn of CPAs, Commonwealth Business Council; Dato' Setia Sultan Mahmud Terengganu, with title of Dato' 1992, Seri Paduka Mahkota Terengganu, with title of Dato' 1996, Panglima Setia Mahkota, with title Tan Sri 1997, Commdr, Légion d'honneur 2000, Friendship Medal (Viet Nam) 2001, Panglima Negara Bintang Sarawak, with title of Datuk Seri 2003. *Address:* Petroliam Nasional Berhad (PETRONAS), Tower 1, PETRONAS Twin Towers, Kuala Lumpur City Centre, Kuala Lumpur 50088, Malaysia (office). *Telephone:* (3) 20515000 (office). *Fax:* (3) 20265050 (office). *E-mail:* webmaster@petronas.com.my (office). *Website:* www.petronas.com.my (office).

MARIE, Aurelius John Baptiste Lamothe, MBE; Dominican fmr head of state and lawyer; b. 23 Dec. 1904, Portsmouth, Dominica; s. of Bright Percival Marie and Lily Marie; m. Bernadette Dubois 1964; fmr magistrate; Pres. of Dominica 1980–83. *Leisure interests:* gardening, reading, hiking. *Address:* Zicack, Portsmouth, Dominica.

MARIN, Angel; Bulgarian army officer (retd) and politician; *Vice-President;* b. 8 Jan. 1942, Batak; m.; two c.; ed secondary school in Devin, Higher Mil. Artillery School, Shoumen, civilian degree in Radio Electronics Eng, Mil. Artillery Acad., Leningrad (now St Petersburg), USSR, univ. degree in mil. educ.; began mil. career as Lt-Engineer, held various positions in Missile Force, including Commdr Missile Launcher Unit, Commdr Start Platoon and Commdr Start Battery 1965–74, Commdr Separate Missile Div., Stara Zagora 1978–80, Commdr Artillery Regt, Stara Zagora 1980–82, Chief of Missile Force and Artillery, Second Div., Stara Zagora 1982–87, Chief of Missile Force and Artillery, Third Army, Sliven 1987–90, Commdr Missile Force and Artillery of the Ground Force of Bulgarian Armed Forces 1990–98, promoted to Maj.-Gen. 1991, dismissed from Army due to disagreement with the manner of army reform, retd 1998; Vice-Pres. of Bulgaria 2002–; graduated with distinction and a gold medal in 'Command of Chief of Staff HQ and Operative-Tactical', Mil. Artillery Acad., Leningrad. *Publication:* The Last War. *Address:* Office of the Vice-President, bul. Dondukov 2, 1123 Sofia, Bulgaria (office). *Telephone:* (2) 923-93-33 (office). *E-mail:* press@president.bg (office). *Website:* www.president.bg (office).

MARIN, Vice-Adm. Gheorghe, PhD; Romanian naval officer; *Chief of the General Staff;* b. 1 Jan. 1952, Negru-Vodă, Constanţa dist; m. Elena Marin; one d.; ed Mircea cel Bătrân Naval Acad., Constanţa, Faculty of Econ. Planning and Cybernetics, Econ. Studies Acad., Bucharest; Navigation and Communication Officer FPB (M) Squadron 1974–78; CO, Fast Patrol Boat 1980–81; Staff Officer, N3 1981–85; Chief Software Programming Section, Naval Informatics Centre 1985–89; Chief Naval Informatics Center 1989–95; CO Electronic Warfare Brigade within Naval Forces 1995–99; Supt, Mircea cel Bătrân Naval Acad. 1999–2003; Dir of Gen. Staff 2003–04, Chief of Naval Forces Staff 2004–06, Chief of Gen. Staff 2006–; Dr hc (Dunarea de Jos Univ.); Knight, Ordinul Naţional Steaua României, Grande Ufficiale, Ordine al Merito della Repubblica Italiana. *Publications:* more than 20 books and 70 articles. *Address:* Office of the Chief of the General Staff, Ministry of National Defence, 050561 Bucharest 5, Str. Izvor 13–15, Sector 5, Romania (office). *Telephone:* (21) 4023400 (office). *Fax:* (21) 3195698 (office). *E-mail:* sefsmg@mapn.ro (office). *Website:* www.defense.ro (office).

MARIN, Jean-Claude; French lawyer and judge; *Chief Public Prosecutor of Paris;* First Advocate Gen., Court of Cassation, Dir of Criminal Affairs and Pardons 2002–04, Solicitor and Chief Public Prosecutor of the Repub. of Paris 2004–. *Address:* Tribunal de Grande Instance de Paris, 4 blvd du Palais, 75055 Paris RP, France (office). *Telephone:* 1-44-32-51-51 (office). *Fax:* 1-43-29-12-55 (office). *E-mail:* info@tgi-paris.justice.fr (office). *Website:* www.tgi-paris.justice.fr (office).

MARIN, Maguy; French choreographer and artistic director; b. 2 June 1951, Toulouse; s. of Antonio Marin and Luisa Calle; ed Conservatoire de Toulouse; joined Maurice Béjart's Ballet du XXème siècle; joined Ballet Théâtre de l'Arche (subsequently Compagnie Maguy Marin) 1979; Chevalier, Ordre des Arts et Lettres; Grand Prix Nat. de la choréographie 1983. *Choreographic works include:* May B 1981, Babel Babel 1982, Jaleo 1983, Hymen 1984, Calambre 1985, Cinderella 1985, Eden 1986, Leçons de Ténèbres 1987, Coups d'états 1988, Groosland 1989, Cortex 1991, Made in France 1992, Ay Dios 1993, Waterzooï 1993, Ramdam 1995, Aujourd'hui peut-être 1996, Pour ainsi dire 1999, Quoi qu'il en soit 1999, Points de fuite 2001, Les applaudissements ne se mangent pas (One Can't Eat Applause) 2002, Ça, quand même 2004, Umwelt 2005, Ha! Ha! 2006. *Address:* Compagnie Maguy Marin, Centre Chorégraphique National de Rillieux-la-Pape, 30 Ter, avenue Général Leclerc, BP 106, 69143 Rillieux-la-Pape Cedex, France (office). *Telephone:* (4) 72-01-12-30 (office). *Fax:* (4) 72-01-12-31 (office). *E-mail:* info@compagnie-maguy-marin.fr (home). *Website:* www.compagnie-maguy-marin.fr (home).

MARIN GONZALEZ, Manuel, MA; Spanish international official; *President, Congress of Deputies;* b. 21 Oct. 1949, Ciudad Real; m. Carmen Ortiz; two c.; ed Madrid Univ., Coll. of Europe, Bruges and Univ. of Nancy; joined Spanish Socialist Party 1974; mem. Parl. for Ciudad Real, La Mancha 1977–86, 2000–; Sec. of State for Relations with the EEC 1982–85; EEC (now EU) Commr for Social Affairs, Employment, Educ. and Training 1986–89, for Co-operation and Devt 1989–94, for External Relations with the Mediterranean (South), Near and Middle East, Latin America and Asia (except Japan, People's Repub. of China, Repub. of Korea, Hong Kong, Macao, Taiwan) 1995–99, Vice-Pres. of Comm. 1993–99, Pres. (Acting) 1999; Spokesman, Foreign Affairs Cttee, Congress of Deputies 2001–04, Pres. Congress of Deputies 2004–; Grand Cross, Order of Isabel la Católica. *Address:* Congress of Deputies, Carrera de San Jerónimo s/n, 28071 Madrid, Spain (office). *Telephone:* (91) 3906000 (office). *Fax:* (91) 4298707 (office). *Website:* www.congreso.es (office).

MARINAC, Darko, BEng, PhD; Croatian business executive; *President of the Management Board, Podravka d.d.;* b. 1950, Zagreb; ed Zagreb Univ., Croatian Chamber of the Economy, Cologne Business School, Germany; joined Pliva (pharmaceutical group) 1975, Project Man. 1978, later Dir-Gen., penicillin plant, Dir, Veterinary and Agro-Chemical Div. 1984, Dir, Research and Devt Div. 1990–92, also Vice-Pres., Man. Bd 1996–99; Integration Dir, Polfa Krakow and Lachema Brno 1999–2000; Pres., Man. Bd, Podravka d.d. 2000–; Pres., Man. Bd, Croatian Employers' Asscn 2004–. *Address:* Podravka d.d., A. Starčevića 32, 48000 Koprivnica, Croatia (office). *Telephone:* (48) 6510 (office). *Fax:* (48) 622008 (office). *E-mail:* podravka@podravka.com (office). *Website:* www.podravka.com (office).

MARINHO, Roberto Irineu; Brazilian media executive; *President, Organizações Globo;* b. 13 Oct. 1947, Rio de Janeiro; s. of Roberto Marinho; m. 1st

Aparecida Marinho; one s.; m. 2nd Karen Marinho; ed Getúlio Vargas Foundation; joined O Globo newspaper 1963; reporter ABC TV, New York 1969–70; Dir Rio Gráfica 1971–77; Vice-Pres. TV Globo 1978–98, Vice-Pres. Organizações Globo (media conglomerate) 1998–2003, CEO 2002–03, Pres. 2003–; Amigo do Livro Prize, Câmara Brasileira do Livro 2004. *Leisure interests:* coffee production. *Address:* Organizações Globo, Rua Irineu Marinho 70, Cidade Nova, 20230-901 Rio de Janeiro, Brazil. *Website:* www.globo.com.br.

MARINI, Franco; Italian politician; b. 9 April 1933, S. Pio; fmr trade union leader; mem. European Parl. (Italian Popular Party) 1999–2004; Pres. Senato della Repubblica 2006–08; mem. Partito Democratico. *Address:* Partito Democratico, Piazza Saint'Anastasia 7, 00186 Rome, Italy (office). *Telephone:* (06) 675471 (office). *Fax:* (06) 67547319 (office). *E-mail:* info@partitodemocratico.it (office). *Website:* www.partitodemocratico.it (office).

MARININA, Col. Aleksandra Borisovna, PhD; Russian writer and fmr criminologist; b. (Marina Anatolyevna Alekseyeva), 16 June 1957, Lviv, Ukraine; m. Col Sergey Zatochny; ed Moscow State Univ.; fmr mem. of staff, Acad. of Internal Affairs; began writing detective stories 1991–; mem. of staff, Moscow Inst. of Justice, Ministry of Internal Affairs 1994–97. *Films for television:* Kamenskaya (48 episodes). *Publications:* Death and Some Love, Ghost of Music, Stolen Dream, I Died Yesterday, Men's Game, Forced Murderer, Black List, Requiem, When Gods Laugh, He Who Knows (vols 1–2), and numerous others. *Leisure interests:* collecting hand bells, reading, Verdi operas, computer solitaire. *Address:* COP Literary Agency, Zhukovskogo str. 4, Apt 29, 103062 Moscow (office); Verhnaya Krasnoselskaya str. 9, Apt 44, 107140 Moscow, Russia (home). *Telephone:* (495) 928-84-56 (office); (495) 975-45-35 (home). *Fax:* (495) 928-84-56 (office). *E-mail:* alexandra@marinina.ru (office). *Website:* www.marinina.ru (home).

MARINO, Dan; American fmr professional football player; b. 15 Sept. 1961, Pittsburgh; s. of Daniel Marino and Veronica Marino; m. Claire Marino; three s. two d. (one adopted); ed Cen. Catholic High School, Univ. of Pittsburgh; quarterback for Miami Dolphins (Nat. Football League–NFL) 1983–1999, retd 2000, returned to org. in Jan. 2004 as Sr Vice-Pres. of Football Operations but resgnd three weeks later; holds 25 NFL records and tied for five others; records include most passing yards (61,361), most completions (4,967), most passing touchdowns (420), most passing yards in a season (5,084 in 1984); f. Dan Marino Foundation; Dir Business Devt, Dreams Inc. 2000–; host on HBO's weekly football programme 'Inside the NFL' and CBS's NFL Today; 16-time winner of AFC Offensive Player of the Week; NFL Man of the Year award 1998; College Football Hall of Fame 2002, Pro Football Hall of Fame 2005. *Publication:* Marino–On the Record, Dan Marino: My Life in Football 2005. *Address:* 1304 SW 160th Avenue, Suite 113, Sunrise, FL 33326, USA. *Website:* www.danmarino.com (office); www.danmarinofoundation.org.

MARINOS, Ioannis, (Kritovoulos, Popolaros, W.), BA; Greek journalist and politician; *Chairman, Structural Reforms Committee, Ministry of Economy and Finance;* b. 20 July 1930, Hermoupolis; ed School of Law, Univ. of Athens; journalist, To Vima (daily political journal) 1953–65, columnist 1992–; journalist, Economicos Tachydromos, Ed.-in-Chief 1956, Ed. and Dir 1964–96, consultant/columnist 1996–; political commentator in Ta Nea (daily) 1972–75; commentator for many radio and TV stations in Greece; mem. European Parl., European Popular Party 1999–2004; currently Chair., Structural Reforms Cttee, Ministry of Economy and Finance; mem. Bd Music Hall of Athens, Red Cross, Amnesty Int; Hon. PhD (Aristotelian Univ. Salonika) 1999; more than 30 awards including Best European Journalist of 1989 (EC Comm. and Asscn of European Journalists) and awards from UN and Athens Acad. *Publications:* The Palestinian Problem and Cyprus 1975, For a Change Towards Better 1983, Greece in Crisis 1987, Common Sense 1993, Constitutional Reform: Ideas & Proposals (co-author) 2007. *Leisure interests:* literature, history, classical music, fishing. *Address:* 26 Nikis Street, Athens 105 57 (office); 2 Kontziadon Street, Piraeus 185 37, Greece (home). *Telephone:* (210) 3210280 (office); (210) 4526823 (home). *Fax:* (210) 3210281 (office). *E-mail:* jmarinos@dolnet.gr (office).

MARIO, Ernest, BS, MS, PhD; American business executive and pharmacist; *Chairman and CEO, Reliant Pharmaceuticals Inc.;* b. 12 June 1938, Clifton, NJ; s. of Jerry Mario and Edith Mario; m. Mildred Martha Daume 1961; three s.; ed Rutgers Coll. of Pharmacy, New Brunswick, NJ, Univ. of Rhode Island; Vice-Pres. Mfg Operations, Smith Kline 1974–77; joined E. R. Squibb & Sons 1977, Vice Pres. Mfg for U.S. Pharmaceuticals Div. 1977–79, Vice-Pres. Gen. Man., Chemical Div. 1979–81, Pres. Chemical Eng Div. and Sr Vice-Pres. 1981–83, Pres. and CEO Squibb Medical Products 1983–86, mem. Bd 1984–85; Pres. Glaxo Inc. 1986–89, Chair. 1989–91, apptd to Bd of Glaxo Holdings PLC 1988, Chief Exec. 1989–93, Deputy Chair. 1992–93; Co-Chair. CEO ALZA Corpn 1993–97, Chair., CEO 1997–2001; Chair. and CEO Apothogen, Inc. 2002; Chair. IntraBiotics Pharmaceuticals, Inc. 2002–03; Chair. and CEO Reliant Pharmaceuticals Inc. 2003–; mem. Bd of Dirs Boston Scientific Corpn, Maxygen, Inc., Pharmaceutical Product Devt Inc.; Chair. American Foundation for Pharmaceutical Educ.; Trustee Duke Univ., Rockefeller Univ., Univ. of RI Foundation. *Leisure interests:* golf, swimming. *Address:* Reliant Pharmaceuticals, Inc., 110 Allen Road, Liberty Corner, NJ 07938, USA (office). *Telephone:* (908) 580-1200 (office). *Fax:* (908) 542-9405 (office). *Website:* www.reliantrx.com (office).

MARION, Jean-Luc, LèsL, PhD; French professor of philosophy; *Professor, University of Paris, Sorbonne;* b. 3 July 1946, Meudon; s. of the late Jean E. Marion and of Suzanne Roussey; m. Corinne Nicolas 1970; two s.; ed Lycée Int. de Sèvres, Ecole Normale Supérieure (Ulm), and Univ. of Paris, Sorbonne; Asst Prof., Univ. of Paris, Sorbonne 1973–81, Prof. 1995–, Dir Centre d'Etudes Cartésiennes 1995–; Dir Ecole Doctorale V 1998–95; Prof., Univ. of Poitiers 1981–88; Prof., Univ. of Paris X (Nanterre) 1988–95; John Nuveen Prof., Univ. of Chicago 1992–; Visiting Prof., Washington Univ. 1990, Villanova Univ. 2000, Boston Coll. 2001–03; Assoc. Prof., Laval Univ., Canada 1993–96; Dir serie Epiméthée, Presses Universitaires de France, Paris 1981–; Co-Dir Les Études Philosophiques (journal); mem. Faculty Steering Cttee, Chicago Centre in Paris 2001–04; mem. Acad. Française 2008–; Chevalier des Palmes académiques; Dr hc (Utrecht Univ.); Prix Charles Lambert, Acad. des Sciences Morales et Politiques 1978, Grand Prix de Philosophie, Acad. Française 1992. *Publications:* Sur l'ontologie grise de Descartes 1975, L'idole et la distance 1977, Sur la théologie blanche de Descartes 1981, Dieu sans l'être 1982, Sur le prisme métaphysique de Descartes 1986, Prolégomènes à la charité 1986, Réduction et Donation 1989, La croisée du visible 1991, Questions cartésiennes 1991, Questions cartésiennes II 1996, Hergé. Tintin le terrible 1996, Etant donné 1997, De surcroît 2001, Le phénomène érotique 2003, Le visible et le révélé 2005, Le Visilbe et le révélé 2005. *Leisure interest:* running. *Address:* Université de Paris Sorbonne, 1 rue Victor Cousin, 75005 Paris, France (office); University of Chicago, Swift Hall, 1025 East 58th Street, Chicago, IL 60637, USA (office); 28 rue Serpente, #311, 75006 Paris, France. *Telephone:* 1-53-10-58-58 (Paris) (office). *E-mail:* Jean-Luc.Marion@ens.fr (office); jmarion@uchicago.edu (office).

MARJORIBANKS, Kevin, BSc, MA, PhD, F.A.S.S.A., FACE, FRSS; Australian academic; *Head, Graduate School of Education, University of Adelaide;* b. 25 July 1940, Sydney; s. of Hugh Marjoribanks and Irene Marjoribanks; m. Janice Lily 1962; one s. one d.; ed Univ. of NSW, Univ. of New England, Harvard Univ., USA, Univ. of Toronto, Canada; Teaching Fellow Harvard Univ. 1967–69; Asst Prof. Univ. of Toronto 1969–70; lecturer in Sociology, Univ. of Oxford 1970–75; Prof. of Educ. Univ. of Adelaide 1974–, Pro-Vice-Chancellor 1986–87, Vice-Chancellor 1987–93, Head Grad. School of Educ. 1996–; Visiting Prof., Oxford Univ. 1994–95. *Publications:* Environments for Learning 1974, Families and Their Learning Environments 1979, Ethnic Families and Children's Achievements 1980, The Foundations of Students' Learning 1991, Families, Schools and Children's Learning 1994, Australian Education 1999, Family and School Capital 2002. *Leisure interests:* writing, music, reading. *Address:* School of Education, University of Adelaide, Education Building, 245 North Terrace, Adelaide SA 5005 (office); 81 Molesworth Street, North Adelaide, SA 5006, Australia (home). *Telephone:* (8) 8303-3784 (office); (8) 8267-5613 (home). *Fax:* (8) 8303-3604 (office). *E-mail:* kevin.marjoribanks@adelaide.edu.au (office).

MARK, Alan F., DCNZM, CBE, PhD, FRSNZ; New Zealand botanist and academic; *Professor Emeritus of Botany, University of Otago;* b. 19 June 1932, Dunedin; s. of Cyril L. Mark and Frances E. Marshall; m. Patricia K. Davie 1957; two s. two d.; ed Mosgiel District High School, Univ. of Otago and Duke Univ., N Carolina; Otago Catchment Bd, Dunedin 1959–61; Sr Research Fellow, Hellaby Indigenous Grasslands Research Trust 1961–65, Adviser in Research 1965–2000, Chair. Bd Govs 2000–; Lecturer, Univ. of Otago 1960, Sr Lecturer 1966, Assoc. Prof. 1969, Prof. of Botany 1975–98, Prof. Emer. 1998–; Visiting Asst Prof., Duke Univ. 1966; Hon. mem. NZ Alpine Club 2002; Fulbright Travel Award 1955, James B. Duke Fellowship 1957, Loder Cup 1975, NZ 1990 Commemoration Medal, The Inaugural Awards of NZ (Conservation/Environment) 1994, Hutton Medal (Botanical/Conservation Research), Royal Soc. of NZ 1997. *Publications:* New Zealand Alpine Plants (with N. M. Adams) 1973; more than 150 scientific papers. *Leisure interests:* nature conservation, enjoying the outdoors. *Address:* Department of Botany, University of Otago, Box 56, Dunedin (office); 205 Wakari Road, Helensburgh, Dunedin, New Zealand (home). *Telephone:* (3) 479-75-73 (office); (3) 476-32-29 (home). *Fax:* (3) 479-75-83. *E-mail:* amark@otago.ac.nz (office). *Website:* www.botany.otago.ac.nz/staff/mark (office).

MARK, Mary Ellen; American photographer; b. 1940, Philadelphia; m. Martin Bell; has photographed prostitution in India, street children in USA, heroin addiction in London, African famines; photographer Magnum agency, Life magazine, The New Yorker; contribs to New York Times Magazine, Rolling Stone, Vanity Fair; Hon. DFA (Univ. of the Arts) 1992, (Pennsylvania) 1994, (Center for Creative Studies, Detroit) 2001, (Columbia Coll., Chicago) 2004, (Kenyon Coll. 2004); first prize, Robert F. Kennedy Journalism 1985, Philippe Halsman Award, American Soc. of Magazine Photographers, Infinity Award for Journalism, Erna and Victor Hasselblad Foundation Grant, Walter Annenberg Grant, Guggenheim Fellowship, Matrix Award, Dr Erich Salomon Award, Cornell Capa Award 2001. *Publications:* Passport 1974, Ward 81 1979, Falkland Road 1981, Mother Teresa's Mission of Charity in Calcutta 1985, The Photo Essay: Photographers at Work, Mary Ellen Mark: 25 Years 1991, Streetwise 1992, Indian Circus 1993, Portraits 1995, Cry for Help 1996, Mary Ellen Mark: American Odyssey 1999, Mary Ellen Mark 55 2001, Photo Poche 2002, Twins 2003, Exposure 2005, Extraordinary Child 2007, Seen Behind the Scene: Forty Years of Photographing on Set 2008. *Address:* Mary Ellen Mark Library, 37 Greene Street, 4th Floor, New York, NY 10013, USA (office). *E-mail:* library@falkland.com (office). *Website:* www.maryellenmark.com.

MARK, Reuben, AB, MBA; American business executive; b. 21 Jan. 1939, Jersey City, NJ; s. of Edward Mark and Libbie Mark (née Berman); m. Arlene Slobzian 1964; two s. one d.; ed Middlebury Coll. and Harvard Univ.; with Colgate-Palmolive Co., New York 1963–, Pres., Gen. Man. Venezuela 1972–73, Canada 1973–74, Vice-Pres., Gen. Man. Far East Div. 1974–75, Household Products Div. 1975–79, Group Vice-Pres. Domestic Operations 1979–81, Exec. Vice-Pres. 1981–83, COO 1983–84, Pres. 1983–86, CEO 1984–, Chair. 1986–; Lecturer in Business Admin., Univ. of Connecticut 1977; mem. Bd Dirs Soap and Detergent Asscn. *Address:* Colgate-Palmolive Co., 300 Park Avenue, New York, NY 10022, USA.

MARK, Sir Robert, Kt, GBE, QPM; British fmr police official; b. 13 March 1917, Manchester; s. of the late John and Louisa Hobson Mark; m. Kathleen

Mary Leahy 1941 (died 1997); one s. one d.; ed William Hulme's Grammar School, Manchester; Constable to Chief Supt, Manchester Police 1937–42, 1947–56; Chief Constable of Leicester 1957–67; Asst Commr, Metropolitan Police (London) 1967–68, Deputy Commr 1968–72, Commr 1972–77; Royal Armoured Corps 1942–47, Lt Phantom (GHQ Liaison Regt) NW Europe 1944–45, Maj. Control Comm. for Germany 1945–47; mem. Standing Advisory Council on Penal System 1966; Assessor to Lord Mountbatten's Inquiry into Prison Security 1966; mem. Advisory Cttee on Police in NI 1969; Dir Automobile Asscn 1977–87, Control Risks Ltd 1981–87; Visiting Fellow, Nuffield Coll., Oxford 1970–78; Lecture tour of N America for World Affairs Council and FCO Oct. 1971; Dimbleby Memorial Lecturer, BBC TV 1973; Hon. Freeman, City of Westminster 1977; KStJ; Hon. LLM (Leicester) 1966; Hon. DLitt (Loughborough) 1976; Hon. LLD (Liverpool) 1978, (Manchester) 1978; Queen's Police Medal 1965. *Publications:* numerous articles in the national press and in legal and police journals; Edwin Stevens Lecture to the Laity at the Royal Society of Medicine 1972, Policing a Perplexed Society 1977, In the Office of Constable (autobiog.) 1978. *Address:* Esher, Surrey, KT10 8LU, England (home).

MARKELL, Jack, BA, MBA; American business executive and state official; *Governor of Delaware;* b. 26 Nov. 1960, Newark, Del.; m.; two c.; ed Brown Univ., Univ. of Chicago; fmr Sr Vice-Pres. for Corp. Devt, Nextel; fmr Consultant for McKinsey and Co. Inc.; Founder Del. Money School; State Treasurer of Delaware 1999–2009; Gov. of Delaware 2009–; Chair. Information Services Task Force 2001, Del. Coll. Investment Plan Bd; Co-Chair. Gov.'s Task Force for Financial Independence 2002, Deferred Compensation Council; mem. Bd of Pardons, Cash Man. Policy Bd, Del. Econ. Financial Advisory Cttee, Employee Benefits Cttee, Strategic Econ. Devt Council; Democrat. *Address:* Office of the Governor, Legislative Hall, Dover, DE 19901, USA (office). *Website:* www.state.de.us/governor (office).

MARKHAM, Kenneth Ronald, PhD, FRSNZ, FNZIC; New Zealand research chemist (retd); *Research Associate, Industrial Research Ltd;* b. 19 June 1937, Christchurch; s. of Harold W. Markham and Alicia B. Markham; m. E. P. Eddy 1966; two d.; ed Victoria Univ. of Wellington, Melbourne Univ.; Tech. Trainee, Dominion Lab., Wellington 1955–62; Scientist, Chem. Div., Distinguished Scientist Industrial Research (DSIR) Ltd, Lower Hutt 1962–65, Scientist, Organic Chem. Section, Chem. Div., DSIR 1968–75, Section Leader, Natural Products Section 1976–92, Group Leader Chem. Div. 1980–87, Sr Research Fellow 1987, Plant Chem., Team Man. 1992–2004, Research Assoc. 2004–; Post-Doctoral Fellow, Botany Dept, Univ. of Texas 1965–66, Asst Prof. 1967; Monsanto Chemicals Research Fellow 1960; Hon. Research Assoc., Biological Sciences, Vic. Univ. of Wellington 1998–; mem. Ed. Advisory Bd int. journal Phytochemical Analysis 1990–, Int. Journal of Flavonoid Research 1998–; Int. Corresp., Groupe Polyphenols 1992–; Easterfield Award, Royal Inst. of Chem. 1971, NZ Govt Ministerial Award for Excellence in Science 1990, Science and Tech. Medal, Royal Soc. of NZ 1997, Pergamon Phytochemistry Prize 1999. *Publications:* The Systematic Identification of Flavonoids (with Mabry and Thomas) 1970, Techniques of Flavonoid Chemistry 1982, Flavonoids: Chemistry, Biochemistry and Applications (co-ed. with O. M. Andersen) 2006; 18 invited chapters on flavonoids, spectroscopy and Hebe, 255 scientific papers on phytochemistry and its interpretation in int. journals 1960–; one patent on UV screens. *Leisure interests:* philately, swimming, stock market, photography, world news, petanque, palms, genealogy. *Address:* Industrial Research Ltd (IRL), PO Box 31310, Lower Hutt (office); 160 Raumati Road, Paraparaumu, New Zealand (home). *Telephone:* (4) 931-3577 (office); (4) 905-5285 (home). *Fax:* (4) 569-0055 (office). *E-mail:* k.markham@irl.cri.nz (office); kpmarkham@paradise.net.nz (home). *Website:* www.irl.cri.nz (office).

MARKHAM, Richard J.; American business executive; *Partner, Care Capital LLC;* b. 26 Sept. 1950, Hornell, New York; ed Purdue Univ. School of Pharmacy; Dist Man. Merck Sharp & Dohme Div., Merck & Co. Inc., served successively as Product Man., Sr Product Man., Dir of Market Planning 1973–86, Exec. Dir of Marketing Planning 1986–87, Vice-Pres. of Marketing 1987–89, Vice-Pres. Merck Sharp & Dohme Int. 1989–91, Sr Vice-Pres. Merck & Co. 1993; mem. Bd of Dirs Marion Merrell Dow Inc. 1993, Pres. and COO 1993–95; COO Hoechst Marion Roussel 1995–97, CEO 1997–99; CEO Aventis Pharma 1999–2002, Chair. Man. Bd Aventis Pharma AG 1999–2002, Vice-Chair. 2002–, COO 2002–05; Pnr Care Capital LLC 2004–; mem. Bd of Dirs Pharmaceutical Research and Mfrs Asscn; mem. Bd of Trustees Health Care Inst., NJ. *Address:* Care Capital, LLC, 47 Hulfish Street, Suite 310, Princeton, NJ 08542, USA (office). *Telephone:* (609) 683-8300 (office). *Fax:* (609) 683-5787 (office). *E-mail:* info@carecapital.com (office). *Website:* www.carecapital.com (office).

MARKL, Hubert, Dr rer. nat (Habil.); German biologist and academic; *Professor of Biology, University of Konstanz;* b. 17 Aug. 1938, Regensburg; ed Univ. of Munich, Ludwig Maximilian Univ., Munich, Univ. of Frankfurt am Main; research internships, Harvard and Rockefeller Univs, USA 1965–66; Dozent, Univ. of Frankfurt am Main 1967–68; Full Prof. and Dir Zoological Inst., Tech. Univ. of Darmstadt 1968–74; Prof. of Biology, Univ. of Konstanz 1974–, Prof., Univ. of Konstanz, Ruhestand 2003–; Heinrich Hertz Visiting Prof., Univ. of Karlsruhe 1994–95; Vice-Pres. Deutsche Forschungsgemeinschaft (German Research Foundation) 1977–83, Pres. 1986–91; Pres. newly founded Berlin-Brandenburgische Akad. der Wissenschaften 1993; Chair. Gesellschaft Deutscher Naturforscher und Ärzte 1993–94; Pres. Max Planck Soc. 1996–2002; mem. German Acad. of Natural Scientists Leopoldina, Berlin-Brandenburg Acad. of Sciences, Bavarian Acad. of Sciences, Göttingen Acad. of Sciences, Heidelberg Acad. of Sciences, Rhine-Westphalian Acad. of Sciences, Academia Europaea, American Acad. of Arts and Sciences, AAAS, Indian Acad. of Sciences; Hon. Mem. Soc. of German Chemists 1997–; Bundesverdienstkreuz 1992, Order of Merit Star (Poland), Verdienstorden des Landes Baden-Württemberg 1997, Großes Verdienstkreuz mit Stern 1999, Bayerischer Verdienstorden 2001, Bayerische Verfassungsmedaille in Silber 2002; Hon. Dr rer. nat (Saarland) 1992, (Potsdam) 1999; Hon. PhD (Dublin) 1997; Hon. DHumLitt (Jewish Theological Seminary, New York) 2000; Hon. DrPhil (Tel-Aviv) 2001, (Hebrew Univ., Jerusalem) 2001, (Weizmann Inst. of Science, Rehovot) 2002; Lorenz Oken Medal, Gesellschaft Deutscher Naturforscher und Ärzte 1984, Karl Vossler Prize 1985, Arthur Burkhardt Prize 1989, Karl Winnacker Prize 1991, Ernst Robert Curtius Prize 1995, Prognos Prize 1997, Pro meritis scientiae et litterarum, Bayerischen Staatsministeriums für Wissenschaft, Forschung und Kunst 2002, Harnack Medal, Max-Planck-Gesellschaft 2004, Ehrenring der Eduard-Rhein-Stiftung 2004, Hanns Martin Schleyer Prize 2005. *Publications:* Biophysik (co-ed.) 1977, 1982 (English: Biophysics 1983), Evolution of Social Behavior (ed.) 1980, Natur und Geschichte (co-ed.) 1983, Neuroethology and Behavioral Physiology (co-ed.) 1983, Evolution, Genetik und menschliches Verhalten 1986, Natur als Kulturaufgabe 1986, Wissenschaft: Zur Rede gestellt 1989, Wissenschaft im Widerstreit 1990, Die Fortschrittsdroge 1992, Wissenschaft gegen Zukunftsangst 1998, Schöner neuer Mensch? 2002; numerous scientific papers in professional journals on sensory physiology and social behaviour of animals, nature conservation and environmental protection, promotion and support of science and research. *Address:* Fachbereich Biologie, Universität Konstanz, Postfach M 612, 78457 Konstanz, Germany (office). *Telephone:* (7531) 88-2725 (office); (7531) 43716 (home). *Fax:* (7531) 88-4345 (office). *E-mail:* hubert.markl@uni-konstanz.de (office). *Website:* www.uni-konstanz.de/FuF/Bio/forsch/zoology/markl (office).

MARKÓ, Béla; Romanian politician; *Leader, Democratic Alliance of Hungarians in Romania;* b. 8 Sept. 1951, Târgul Secuiesc; m.; three c.; ed Faculty of Philology, Univ. of Babeş-Bolyai, Cluj-Napoca; poetry teacher, Santana de Mures Elementary School 1974–76; Ed. Igaz Szo Literary Magazine 1976–89; Ed.-in-Chief Lato Literary Magazine 1989; sr mem. Democratic Alliance of Hungarians in Romania (DAHR) 1989, Vice-Pres. 1989–93, mem. Standing Cttee 1990–91, Pres. in Senate 1991–92, elected Leader 1993, re-elected 1995, 1999, 2003; Senator for Mures 1990–, mem. Culture and Education Comms 1992, Foreign Policy and Culture Comms 1992–96; State Minister in charge of coordinating activities in fields of culture, educ. and European integration 2004–07; advocated autonomy for parts of Transylvania where ethnic Hungarians (Magyar) in a majority; signed cooperation agreement with Pres. Ion Iliescu's Social Democratic Party, leading to schism in DAHR 2000; mem. Writers' Union in Romania 1978–, Writers' Union in Hungary 1990–; Sec.-Gen. PEN Group of Hungarian Writers in Romania 1990–; Sec. Writers' Union Subsidiary in Târgu Mureş 1990–96. *Publications:* poetry: 18 vols –1974, Notes on a Happy Pear Tree 1999, Comme un échiquier ferme 2001, Despre natura metaforelor, Timp canibal 1997; one vol. of Hungarian literature for 11th grade 1980–83, 1990–2002, two vols of essays and literary analysis, three vols of studies and political discourses, trans. into Hungarian of some plays by Lucian Blaga and Radu Stanca. *Address:* Democratic Alliance of Hungarians in Romania, 024015 Bucharest, Str. Avram Iancu 8, Romania (office). *Telephone:* (21) 3144356 (office). *E-mail:* elhivbuk@rmdsz.ro (office). *Website:* www.rmdsz.ro (office).

MARKOPOULOS, Christos, DSc; Greek politician and nuclear chemist; *President, Federation of Balkan Non-Governmental Organizations for Peace and Co-operation;* b. 25 Dec. 1925, Athens; s. of Antony Markopoulos and Paraskevi Vergopoulou; m. 1st Sapfo Mazaraki 1954 (divorced 1960); one s.; m. 2nd Kleopatra Papadopoulou 1974; two s.; ed Varvakios High School, Teachers' Acad., Athens, Univ. of Athens, Leicester Coll. of Tech., UK; Nat. State Chem. Lab. 1956–59; Group Leader, Greek Atomic Energy Comm. 1962–69, Dir Radio-immunochem. 1977–81; Asst Prof., Nat. Tech. Univ. of Athens 1965; Sr Researcher, Imperial Coll., London 1968; Visiting Scientist, Tech. Hochschule, Darmstadt, FRG; Visiting Prof., Univ. of Bologna 1973; Pres. Hellenic Nuclear Soc. 1975–81; mem. Steering Cttee, European Nuclear Soc. 1979–81; mem. Cen. Cttee, Panhellenic Socialistic Movement (PASOK) 1975–93; mem. European Parl. 1981–84 (mem. Energy, Research and Tech. Comm.); Amb.-at-Large for West European Countries 1984–85; mem. Nat. Parl. of Greece 1985–89 (Pres. Foreign Affairs Cttee 1986–87); Head of Greek Parl. Del. in Council of Europe 1986–88 (Vice-Pres. Parl. Ass. 1987–88); Minister in charge of Int. Orgs 1988–89; Pres. Panhellenic Movt for Nat. Independence, World Peace and Disarmament 1981–90; Founder Int. Peace Olympiad Bureau, Co-ordinator First Peace Olympiad 1989; Founder and Pres. Movt for Peace, Human Rights and Nat. Independence 1991–2001 (Hon. Pres. 2001–), Fed. of Balkan Non-Governmental Orgs for Peace and Co-operation 1993–; Pres. Int. Organizing Cttee, 2nd European Conf. on Peace, Democracy and Co-operation in Balkans 1996; Pro Merito Medal, Parl. Ass. Council of Europe 1986, Model of Council of Europe 1988, Medal of Civilization, UNESCO 1989, Diploma and Medal for Contrib. to Peace and Welfare of Humanity, Int. Peace Bureau 1992, Honour Award for Contrib. to Progress of Science of Chem., Asscn of Greek Chemists 1997, Honour Prize for Participation in Nat. Resistance against German occupation 1999. *Publications:* Organic Chemistry (2 vols) 1963 and 1971, Inorganic Chemistry (2 vols) 1968 and 1971, Introduction to Modern Chemistry 1973, The Dominance of Prota and the Theory of Enforced Randomness 1991, Order and Anarchy 1996, Chance and Order 1997, Alexander and Diogenes 1999, Conjectures and Arpisms 1999; and numerous articles on nuclear disarmament, peace, int. affairs, European relations and human rights. *Leisure interests:* swimming, classical music. *Address:* 23 Kzitonos, 16121 Athens (office); 34 Eratous Street, 15561 Holargos, Athens, Greece (home). *Telephone:* (1) 7211929 (office); (1) 6524687 (home). *Fax:* (1) 7211035 (office); (1) 6526847. *E-mail:* febang@otenet.gr (office); ch_marko@otenet.gr (home).

MARKOV, Sergey Aleksandrovich; Russian politician and academic; *Director, Institute of Political Studies;* b. 18 April 1958, Dubna, Moscow Region; s. of Aleksander Nikolayevich Markov and Anna Dmitriyevna Markova; m. Nina Leonidovna Markova; one d.; ed Moscow State Univ.; teacher, Moscow Inst. of Radio Electronics and Automatics, Moscow Inst. of Political Sciences; consultant, Security Council, Russian Fed.; Visiting Scholar, Univ. of Wisconsin-Madison; Sr Consultant, Nat. Democratic Inst. of Int. Relations 1997–; Dir Inst. of Political Studies 1997–; consulting expert, numerous nat. and int. orgs including Security Council at Russian Presidium, State Duma, Nat. Democratic Inst. of Int. Relations, Chase Manhattan Bank, ING Baring, Renaissance Capital 1990–; Exec. Dir Asscn of Consulting Centres, Russian Asscn of Political Sciences 1991–; Ed.-in-Chief, internet publr for strana.ru; Prof., Moscow State Univ.; Prof., Higher School of Econs 2000–; Co-Chair. Moscow Carnegie Centre 1994–97; Chair. Organizing Cttee Civil Forum 2001; Co-ordinator Nat. Civil Council on Foreign Policy 2002–. *Leisure interests:* tennis, swimming, cycling. *Address:* Institute of Political Studies, Zubovsky Boulevard 4, Entrance 8, 119021 Moscow Russia (office). *Telephone:* (495) 201-80-50 (office). *Fax:* (495) 201-81-70 (office). *E-mail:* markov@fep.ru (office). *Website:* www.fep.ru (office).

MARKOVÍC, Ante; Croatian politician; b. 25 Nov. 1924, Konjic; ed Zagreb Univ.; Sec. League of Communist Youth; Engineer, Designer and Head Test Dept, Rade Koncar factory, Dir-Gen. 1961–86; Pres. Exec. Council of Croatia 1982–86; Pres. Presidency of Croatia 1986–88; Pres. Fed. Exec. Council 1989–91.

MARKOVIĆ, Predrag; Serbian politician and publisher; b. 7 Dec. 1955, Cepure; ed Univ. of Belgrade; Ed. Student, Vreme (newspapers), Vidici (magazine); Owner Stubovi kulture publishing house 1993–; Pres. G17 PLUS Man. Bd 2000–01, Pres. Political Council, mem. Exec. Bd 2001–02, Vice-Pres. G17 PLUS party 2003–; Pres. Nat. Ass. of Serbia 2004–; Acting Pres. of Serbia March–July 2004; fmr Pres. Asscn of Publrs of Serbia and Montenegro; mem. PEN, Serbian Literary Soc. *Publications:* Morali su doći nasmejani lavovi 1983, Otemenost duše 1989. *Address:* G17 PLUS, Trg Republike 5, 11000 Belgrade, Serbia (office). *Telephone:* (11) 3344930 (office). *Fax:* (11) 3344459 (office). *Website:* www.g17plus.org.yu (office).

MARKOWITZ, Harry M., PhD; American economist and professor of finance; *President, Harry Markowitz Company;* b. 24 Aug. 1927, Chicago; s. of Morris Markowitz and Mildred Gruber; m. Barbara Gay; research staff, Rand Corpn Santa Monica, Calif. 1952–60, 1961–63; Tech. Dir Consolidated Analysis Centers, Ltd, Santa Monica 1963–68; Prof. UCLA 1968–69; Pres. Arbitrage Man. Co., New York 1969–72; in pvt. practice as consultant, New York 1972–74; research staff, T. J. Watson Research Center, IBM, Yorktown Hills, NY 1974–83; Speiser Prof. of Finance, Baruch Coll., City Univ. of New York 1982–90, Vice-Pres. Inst. of Man. Science 1960–62; Pres. Harry Markowitz Co. 1984–; Dir Research Daiwa Securities Trust Co. 1990–2000; Fellow, Econometric Soc., American Acad. of Arts and Sciences; Pres. American Finance Asscn 1982; Nobel Prize in Econs (with W. F. Sharpe and M. H. Miller), 1990. *Publications:* Portfolio Selection: Efficient Diversification of Investments 1959, Mean-Variance Analysis in Portfolio Choice 1987; co-author, SIMSCRIPT Simulation Programming Language 1963; co-ed. Process Analysis of Economic Capabilities 1963. *Address:* 1010 Turquoise Street, Suite 245, San Diego, CA 92109, USA.

MARKS, David Joseph, MBE, RIBA; British architect; b. 15 Dec. 1952, Stockholm, Sweden; s. of Melville Marks and Gunilla Marta Loven; m. Julia Barfield; one s. two d.; ed Int. School of Geneva, Switzerland, Kingston Polytech. School of Architecture, Architectural Asscn School of Architecture, London; fmrly with Tetra Ltd, Richard Rogers Partnership; co-f. Marks Barfield Architects with Julia Barfield 1989, London Eye Co. 1994, as Man. Dir raised the finance for Devt of the London Eye; lectures include The Prince's Foundation Urban Villages Forum 2000, Royal Inst. 2001, RIBA 2000, Royal Acad. of Arts 2000, 2001, British European Group Conf., Rome 2001, Berlin 2001; Royal Inst. of Chartered Surveyors Award, RIBA Award for Architecture 2000, London Tourism Awards 2000, London First Millennium Award, American Inst. of Architects Design Award 2000, European Award for Steel Structures 2001, Blueprint Award 2001, Prince Philip Designers Prize, Special Commendation 2001, Faculty of Bldg, Barbara Miller Trophy 2001, Pride of Britain Award for Innovation 2001, Design Week Special Award 2001, D&AD Awards, Silver and Gold 2001, Queen's Award for Enterprise (Innovation) 2003, and several other awards. *Leisure interests:* family pursuits. *Address:* Marks Barfield Architects, 50 Bromells Road, London, SW4 0BG, England (office). *Telephone:* (20) 7501-0180 (office). *Fax:* (20) 7498-7103 (office). *E-mail:* dmarks@marksbarfield.com (office). *Website:* www.marksbarfield.com (office).

MARKS, Dennis Michael, BA; British music and arts executive, broadcaster, writer and film producer and director; b. 2 July 1948, London; s. of Samuel Marks and Kitty Ostrovsky; m. 1st Deborah Cranston 1972; one s. one d.; m. 2nd Sally Groves 1992; ed Haberdashers' Aske's School, Elstree, Trinity Coll., Cambridge; Dir and Producer BBC TV Music and Arts 1972–78; co-f. Bristol Arts Unit 1978–81; f. Third Eye Productions 1981–85; Ed. Music Features BBC TV 1985–88, Asst Head of Music and Arts 1988–91, Head of Music BBC TV 1991–93; Gen. Dir English Nat. Opera (ENO) 1993–97; Pres. Int. Music Centre, Vienna 1989–92; Italia Prize 1989, Royal Philharmonic Soc. Award 1990, Int. Emmy 2008. *Radio:* Faultline, Appian Way, Composers' Days (BBC Radio 3) 2004. *Television:* producer and dir of several hundred documentaries and operas 1972–2004. *Publications:* Great Railway Journeys 1981, Repercussions (Afro-American Music) 1985. *Leisure interests:* cookery, travel. *Address:* 12 Camden Square, London, NW1 9UY, England (office). *E-mail:* dennismarks@blueyonder.co.uk (office).

MARKS, Matthew Stuart, BA; American art dealer and gallery owner; *Owner, Matthew Marks Gallery;* b. 14 Nov. 1962, New York City; s. of Dr. Paul Marks; ed Bennington Coll.; consultant Pace Editions Inc., New York 1982–86, Assoc. Pace Gallery 1985–87; Dir Anthony D'Offay Gallery, London 1987–89; opened first gallery 1989; moved to garage-door warehouse on 22nd Street in 1994; now shows prominent modern artists such as painters Jasper Johns, Brice Marden and Ellsworth Kelly, sculptor Robert Gober, as well as photographers Andreas Gursky, Inez van Lamsweerde and Nan Goldin; has held exhibits of work by Willem de Kooning, Lucian Freud and Cy Twombly. *Address:* Matthew Marks Gallery, 523 West 24th Street, New York, NY 10011, USA (office). *Telephone:* (212) 243-0200 (office). *E-mail:* info@matthewmarks.com (office). *Website:* www.matthewmarks.com (office).

MARKS, Michael, CBE; British business executive; *Founding Partner, NewSmith Capital Partners LLP;* b. 28 Dec. 1941, London; one s. two d.; ed St Paul's School, London; joined Smith Bros 1958, Dir 1975, Chief Exec. 1987, Chief Exec. and Exec. Chair. Smith New Court 1995; Co-Head Global Equities Group, Merrill Lynch 1995–98, Exec. Chair. Merrill Lynch Europe, Middle East & Africa 1997–2003, Exec. Vice-Pres. Merrill Lynch & Co. 2001–03, Chair. Merrill Lynch Investment Mans (MLIM) 2001–03, mem. Exec. Man. Cttee Merrill Lynch; mem. Int. Markets Advisory Bd, Nat. Asscn of Securities Dealers 1991–, Bd London Stock Exchange 1994–2004; Chair. London Investment Banking Asscn 1998–2002; Vice-Pres. British Bankers Asscn 1998–; Founding Pnr NewSmith Capital Partners LLP 2003–; Dir (non-exec. Old Mutual plc 2004–, RIT Capital Partners plc 2004–. *Address:* NewSmith Capital Partners LLP, Lansdowne House, 57 Berkeley Square, London, W1J 6ER, England (office). *Telephone:* (20) 7518-3700 (office). *Fax:* (20) 7518-3701 (office). *E-mail:* enquiries@newsmithcapital.com (office). *Website:* www.newsmithcapital.com (office).

MARKS, Michael E., MA, MBA; American business executive; *Managing Partner, Bigwood Capital, LLC;* ed Oberlin Coll., Harvard Business School; fmr Pres. and CEO Metcal, Inc. (precision heating instrument co.); mem. Bd of Dirs Flextronics Corpn (electronics mfg services provider) 1991–, Chair. 1993–2003, 2006–08, CEO 1994–2006, Pres. 2003; Founder and Man. Partner, Bigwood Capital, LLC (pvt. equity firm), Palo Alto, Calif. 2007–; mem. Kohlberg Kravis Roberts & Co. (pvt. equity firm), Menlo Park, Calif. 2006–07, Sr Advisor 2007–08; mem. Bd of Dirs SanDisk Corpn, Milpitas, Calif. 2003–, Schlumberger Ltd, Houston, Tex., Sun Microsystems, Inc., Santa Clara, Calif. *Address:* Bigwood Capital LLC, 245 Lytton Avenue, Suite 250, Palo Alto, CA 94301-1465 USA (office). *Telephone:* (650) 473-5465 (office).

MARKS, Paul Alan, MD; American oncologist and cell biologist; b. 16 Aug. 1926, New York; s. of Robert R. Marks and Sarah (Bohorad) Marks; m. Joan Harriet Rosen 1953; two s. one d.; ed Columbia Coll. and Columbia Univ.; Fellow, Columbia Coll. of Physicians and Surgeons 1952–53, Assoc. 1955–56, mem. of Faculty 1956–82, Dir Haematology Training 1961–74, Prof. of Medicine 1967–82, Dean Faculty of Medicine and Vice-Pres. Medical Affairs 1970–73, Dir Comprehensive Cancer Center 1972–80, Vice-Pres. Health Sciences 1973–80, Prof. of Human Genetics and Devt 1969–82, Frode Jensen Prof. of Medicine 1974–80; Prof. of Medicine and Genetics, Cornell Univ. Coll. of Medicine, New York 1982–; Prof. Cornell Univ. Grad. School in Medical Sciences 1983–; Attending Physician Presbyterian Hosp., New York 1967–83; Pres. and CEO Memorial Sloan-Kettering Cancer Center 1980–99, Pres. Emer. 2000; Attending Physician Memorial Hosp. for Cancer and Allied Diseases 1980–; mem. Sloan-Kettering Inst. for Cancer Research 1980–; Adjunct Prof. Rockefeller Univ. 1980–; Visiting Physician, Rockefeller Univ. Hosp. 1980–; Trustee Hadassah Medical Centre, Jerusalem 1996–2000; mem. Advisory Cttee to Dir, NIH 1993–96, NIH External Advisory Cttee-Intramural Research Program Review 1993–94; mem. editorial bds of several scientific journals; Gov. Weizmann Inst. 1976–96; Dir Revson Foundation 1976–91; Master American Coll. of Physicians; mem. Inst. of Medicine, NAS; Fellow Royal Soc. of Medicine, London; research focus is on histone deacetylase inhibitors, mechanism of action and potential as anti-cancer agents; Dr hc (Urbino) 1982, (Tel Aviv) 1992, (Columbia Univ., NY) 2000; Hon. PhD (Hebrew Univ., Jerusalem) 1987; Recognition for Acad. Accomplishments, Chinese Acad. of Medical Sciences 1982, Centenary Medal, Institut Pasteur 1987, Pres.'s Nat. Medal of Science 1991, Gold Medal for Distinguished Academic Accomplishments, Coll. of Physicians and Surgeons of Columbia Univ., New York, Japan Foundation for Cancer Research Award 1995, John Jay Award for Distinguished Professional Achievement, Columbia Coll. 1996, Lifetime Achievement Award Greater NY Hosp. Asscn 1997, Humanitarian Award, Breast Cancer Foundation 2000, The John Stearns Award for Lifetime Achievement in Medicine, NY Acad. of Medicine 2002; and other awards. *Publications:* over 400 articles in scientific journals. *Leisure interest:* tennis. *Address:* Memorial Sloan-Kettering Cancer Center, 1275 York Avenue, New York, NY 10021 (office); P.O. Box 1485, Washington, CT 06793, USA (home). *Telephone:* (212) 639-6568 (office). *Fax:* (212) 639-2861 (office). *E-mail:* paula_marks@mskcc.org (office).

MARKS, Tobin J., BS, PhD; American chemist and academic; *Vladimir N. Ipatieff Professor of Catalytic Chemistry, Northwestern University;* b. 25 Nov. 1944, Washington, DC; ed Univ. of Md, MIT; Asst Prof. of Chemistry, Northwestern Univ., Evanston, IL 1970–74, Assoc. Prof. 1974–78, Prof. 1978, Charles E. & Emma H. Morrison Prof. of Chemistry 1986–, Prof. of Materials Science and Eng 1987–, Vladimir N. Ipatieff Prof. of Catalytic Chemistry 1999–; presenter of numerous hon. lectures at univs in USA and abroad; mem. Editorial Bd several journals including Topics in Catalysis, Journal of Molecular Catalysis, Chemistry of Materials, Nouveau Journal de Chimie, Organometallics; mem. Corp. Tech. Advisory Bd, Dow Corning Corpn 1994–, Dow Chemical Co. 1995–; mem. AAAS, American Acad. of Arts and Sciences, NAS, ACS (Councillor, Inorganic Chemistry Div. 1980–85), Materials

Research Soc.; ACS Award in Organometallic Chemistry 1989, ACS Award in Organic Chemistry 1994, Royal Soc. of Chemistry Centenary Medal 1997, Univ. of Pittsburgh Francis Clifford Phillips Award 1998, Italian Chemical Soc. Paolo Chini Award 1999, ACS Cotton Medal 2000, ACS Linus Pauling Medal 2001, ACS Willard Gibbs Medal 2001, Royal Soc. of Chemistry Frankland Medal 2003, German Chemical Soc. Karl Ziegler Medal 2003. *Address:* WCAS Chemistry, Northwestern University, 2145 Sheridan Road, Evanston, IL 60208, USA (office). *Telephone:* (847) 491-5658 (office). *Fax:* (847) 491-7713 (office). *E-mail:* t-marks@northwestern.edu (office). *Website:* www.chem.northwestern.edu/brochure/marks.html (office).

MARKWORT, Helmut; German journalist, publisher, editor and presenter; *Publisher, Editor-in-Chief and CEO, Focus Magazine;* b. 8 Dec. 1936, Darmstadt; s. of August Markwort and Else Markwort (née Volz); started in journalism 1956, various posts in local media –1966; founder Ed.-in-Chief of several magazines and radio stations; Publr, Ed.-in-Chief and CEO Focus Magazine 1993–; Man. Focus TV 1996–; Publr Focus Money 2000–; Head of Bd Tomorrow Focus AG 2001–, Playboy Publishing Deutschland AG 2002–; presenter Bookmark 2004–, Der Sonntags Stammtisch 2007–Dir Hubert Burda Media Holding GmbH 1991–; Nat. Merit Cross (1st Class) 1999; 'Horizont Mann der Medien' Award 1983, 1993, Advertising Age 'Marketing Superstar' 1994, Hildegard von Bingen Award for Journalism, BDS Mittelstandspreis Award, Bavarian's Merit Medal 1996, Premio Capo Circeo 2004, Reinhold Maier Medal 2007, Karl Carstens Award 2007. *Leisure interests:* football, theatre. *Address:* Focus Magazine, Arabella str. 23, 81925 Munich, Germany (office). *Fax:* (89) 92502026 (office). *Website:* www.focus.de (office).

MARLEY, Rita; Jamaican singer, songwriter and philanthropist; b. (Alpharita Constantia Anderson), 25 July 1946, Santiago de Cuba, Cuba; d. of Leroy Anderson and Cynthia 'Beda' Jarrett; m. Bob Marley 1966 (died 1981); two s. one d. and three d. from various relationships; grew up in upper level of Beachwood, Kingston, Jamaica; was singing with female ska trio named The Soulettes (later became the I-Threes), recording for Studio One, when she met her future husband mid-1960s; became involved in Rastafari Movt 1966, remains active mem. Ethiopian Orthodox Church; following her husband's death, recorded albums under her own name and looked after his estate; currently lives in Konkonuru, nr Aburi, Ghana; honoured by Clutch magazine as one of 21 International Women of Power 2008. *Films:* The Mighty Quinn (actress and reggae music consultant) 1989, The Reggae Movie (special thanks) 1995, How High (writer and performer, One Draw) 2001, Africa Unite (exec. producer) 2008. *Albums:* Pied Piper (single, on Club Ska '67) 1967, Rita Marley 1980, Who Feels It Knows It 1981, Harambe (Working Together for Freedom) 1988, We Must Carry on 1988, Beauty of God's 1990, Good Girls Cult 1990, One Draw 1990, Sings Bob Marley . . . and Friends 2003, Play Play 2004, Sunshine After Rain 2005, Gifted Fourteen Carnation 2006. *Publication:* No Woman No Cry (book).

MARLOWE, Hugh (see Patterson, Harry).

MARMOLEJO, Francisco José Ruiz; Colombian international organization official; *Acting Secretary-General and Executive Director, Amazon Cooperation Treaty Organization;* b. Cali; ed Nat. Univ. of Colombia, Fed. Univ. of Pará, Brazil, Univ. of Las Palmas, Gran Canaria; previous posts include Environmental Del. Comptroller, Colombia, Chair. Technological Transfer Nat. Program (Pronatta), mem. Panel of Experts on the Amazon, Co-Dir Ecofondo (org. of environmental NGOs); Exec. Dir Amazon Cooperation Treaty Org. (Organización del Tratado de Cooperación Amazónica) 2003–, Acting Sec.-Gen. 2007–. *Address:* Amazon Cooperation Treaty Organization, SHIS–QI 05, Conjunto 16, casa 21, Lago Sul, Brasília, DF 71615-160, Brazil (office). *Telephone:* (61) 3248-4119 (office). *Fax:* (61) 3248-4238 (office). *E-mail:* fjruiz@otca.org.br (office). *Website:* www.otca.org.br (office).

MARMOT, Sir Michael Gideon, Kt, MBBS, PhD, FFPHM, FRCP, FAcMedSci; British academic and director of health research; *Director, International Institute for Society and Health and Professor of Epidemiology and Public Health, University College London;* b. 26 Jan. 1945; s. of Nathan Marmot and Alice Marmot (née Weiner); m. Alexandra Naomi Ferster 1971; two s. one d.; ed Univ. of Sydney and Univ. of California, Berkeley; Resident Medical Officer, Royal Prince Alfred Hosp. 1969–70; Fellowship in Thoracic Medicine 1970–71; Resident Fellow and Lecturer Univ. of Calif., Berkeley 1971–76 (fellowships from Berkeley and American Heart Asscn); Lecturer then Sr Lecturer in Epidemiology, London School of Hygiene and Tropical Medicine, Univ. Coll. London 1976–85, Prof. of Epidemiology and Public Health Medicine 1985–; Dir Int. Centre for Health and Society, Univ. Coll. London 1994–; Hon. Consultant in Public Health Medicine, Bloomsbury and Islington Dist Health Authority 1985–; Visiting Prof. Royal Soc. of Medicine 1987; MRC Research Professorship 1995; Chair. Comm. on Social Determinants of Health, WHO 2004–; mem. Faculty of Community Medicine; Foreign Assoc. mem. Inst. of Medicine (Nat. Acads of Sciences); Hon. MD (Univ. of Sydney) 2006; Balzan Prize for Epidemiology 2004, Harveian Oration 2006. *Publications:* Status Syndrome (Bloomsbury and Times Holt) 2004; numerous articles in learned journals. *Leisure interests:* viola, tennis. *Address:* Department of Epidemiology and Public Health, University College London, 1–19 Torrington Place, London, WC1E 6BT (office); Wildwood Cottage, 17 North End, London, NW3 7HK, England (home). *Telephone:* (20) 7679-1717 (office). *Fax:* (20) 7813-0242 (office). *E-mail:* m.marmot@ucl.ac.uk (office). *Website:* www.ucl.ac.uk/epidemiology/staff/marmot (office); www.ucl.ac.uk/iish (office).

MARONI, Roberto; Italian politician; *Minister of Internal Affairs;* b. 15 March 1955, Varese; m.; two s.; graduated in law; worked in banks for ten years, then head of legal office of a US multinational for eight years; entered politics 1979; co-f. Lega Lombarda party (subsequently Lega Nord); elected Councillor, Varese; apptd mem. Lega Lombarda Nat. Council; Deputy 1992–; became Leader of party in Chamber of Deputies; elected Lega Nord Deputy in Gen. Elections March 1994; Minister of Internal Affairs 1994–95, 2008–, of Labour and Social Affairs 2001–06. *Leisure interests:* football, playing saxophone. *Address:* Ministry of Internal Affairs, Piazzale del Viminale, Via Agostino Depretis 7, 00184 Rome (office); Lega Nord, Via C. Bellerio 41, 20161 Milan, Italy (office). *Telephone:* (06) 4651 (office); (02) 66234236 (office). *Fax:* (02) 66234402 (office). *E-mail:* webmaster@leganord.org (office). *Website:* www.interno.it (office); www.leganord.org (office).

MAROONE, Michael E.; American automobile retail executive; *President and Chief Operating Officer, AutoNation Inc.;* b. 1953; fmr CEO and Pres. Maroone Group –1997, Pres. New Vehicle Dealer Div., AutoNation Inc. (after acquisition of Maroone Group by AutoNation) 1997–98, Group Pres. 1998–, COO 1999–, mem. Bd of Dirs 2005–; Pnr Fla Panthers ice hockey team; Ford Motor Co. Chairman's Award, Time magazine Quality Dealer. *Address:* AutoNation Inc., 110 SE 6th Street, Fort Lauderdale, FL 33301, USA (office). *Telephone:* (954) 769-6000 (office). *Fax:* (954) 769-6537 (office). *Website:* corp.autonation.com (office).

MAROSI, Ernő, PhD; Hungarian art historian; *Vice-President for the Social Sciences, Hungarian Academy of Sciences;* b. 18 April 1940, Miskolc; s. of Ferenc Marosi and Magdolna Kecskés; m. Julia Szabó; ed Budapest University of Arts and Sciences; Lecturer, Dept of Art History (Budapest Acad. of Arts and Sciences) 1963, Prof. 1991; mem. Research Group Hungarian Acad. of Sciences, then Deputy Dir of Research Inst. 1974–91, Head of Dept 1974–91, Dir 1991–; mem. Int. Cttee of UNESCO on the History of Art 1991–; Sec. of TMB (Nat. Postgrad. Degree Granting Board), Special Cttee on the History of Art, Architecture and Archaeology; Corresp. mem. of Hungarian Acad. of Sciences 1993–2001, mem. 2001–, currently Vice-Pres. (for the social sciences). *Publications:* A középkori müvészet világa (The World of Arts of the Middle Ages) 1969, A román kor müvészete (The Arts of the Romanesque Age) 1972, Bevezetés a müvészettörténetbe (Introduction to the History of Arts) 1973, Magyar falusi templomok (Village Churches in Hungary) 1975, Emlék márványból vagy homokköböl (Relics from Marble or Sandstone) 1976, Die Anfänge der Gotik in Ungarn 1984, Magyarországi müvészet 1300–1470 körül (Arts in Hungary 1300–1470) 1984, A budavári szoborlelet (jtly) 1989. *Address:* Office of the Vice-President for the Social Sciences, Hungarian Academy of Sciences, Roosevelt tér 9, 1051 Budapest, Hungary (office). *Telephone:* (1) 302-4808 (office). *Fax:* (1) 331-4379 (office).

MAROVIĆ, Svetozar; Montenegrin politician and fmr head of state; b. 21 March 1955, Kotor, Montenegro; s. of Jovo Marović and Ivana Marović; m. Djina Marović; two c.; ed Univ. of Montenegro; Dir Municipal Public Accounting Dept in Budva; mem. Presidency of Cen. Cttee of League of Communists of Montenegro; Sec.-Gen. of Democratic Socialist Party of Montenegro, currently Deputy Chair.; mem. Parl. of Montenegro, Speaker 1998–2002; mem. Chamber of Citizens Parl. of Yugoslavia 1997; Pres. of Serbia and Montenegro 2003–06; November's Award, Budva. *Leisure interest:* volleyball. *Address:* c/o Office of the President, Belgrade, Serbia (office).

MARQUAND, David Ian, FBA, FRHistS, FRSA; British academic, author and fmr politician; *Visiting Fellow, Department of Politics, University of Oxford;* b. 20 Sept. 1934, Cardiff, Wales; s. of Rt Hon. Hilary Marquand and Rachel Marquand; m. Judith M. Reed 1959; one s. one d.; ed Emanuel School, Magdalen Coll., Oxford, St Antony's Coll., Oxford, Univ. of California, Berkeley, USA; Sr Scholar, St Antony's Coll. Oxford 1957–58; Teaching Asst, Univ. of California 1958–59; editorial writer, The Guardian 1959–61; Research Fellow, St Antony's Coll. Oxford 1962–64, Hon. Fellow 2003–; Lecturer in Politics, Univ. of Sussex 1964–66; MP (Labour) for Ashfield, Notts. 1966–77; del. to Council of Europe and WEU assemblies 1970–73; Opposition Spokesman on Treasury Affairs 1971–72; Chief Adviser, Sec.-Gen. EC 1977–78; Prof. of Contemporary History and Politics, Univ. of Salford 1978–91; Prof. of Politics, Univ. of Sheffield 1991–96, Dir Political Economy Research Centre 1993–96, Hon. Prof. 1997–; Prin. Mansfield Coll. Oxford 1996–2002, Hon. Fellow; Visiting Fellow, Dept of Politics, Univ. of Oxford 2002–; Jt Ed. The Political Quarterly 1987–96; Hon. DLitt (Salford, Sheffield), Hon. Dr of Political Science (Bologna); George Orwell Memorial Prize 1979, Isaiah Berlin Prize for Lifetime Achievement in Political Studies. *Publications:* Ramsay Macdonald 1973, Parliament for Europe 1979, The Unprincipled Society 1988, The Progressive Dilemma 1991, The New Reckoning 1997, Religion and Democracy 2000, Decline of the Public 2004, Britain Since 1918 2008. *Leisure interest:* walking. *Address:* Department of Politics and International Relations, Manor Road, University of Oxford, Oxford, OX1 3UQ (office); Mansfield College, Oxford, OX1 3TF, England (office). *Telephone:* (1865) 751026 (office). *Fax:* (1865) 278725 (office). *E-mail:* david.marquand@politics.ox.ac.uk (office); david.marquand@mansfield.ox.ac.uk (office). *Website:* www.politics.ox.ac.uk (office).

MARQUARDT, Klaus Max, Dr rer. pol; German business executive; b. 18 Dec. 1926, Berlin; s. of Dr Arno Marquardt and Ruth Marquardt; m. Brigitte Weber; three d.; ed Realgymnasium Berlin, Univ. Berlin and Tech. Univ. Berlin; mem. Bd ARAL AG –1971, Chair. 1971–86; Pres. Petroleum Econ. Asscn 1979–86; Chair. Supervisory Bd, Westfalenbank AG, Bochum; mem. Supervisory Bd Energieversorgung Sachsen Ost AG, Dresden; Grosses Bundesverdienstkreuz. *Address:* Roggenkamp 14, 44797 Bochum, Germany (office). *Telephone:* (234) 791091 (office). *Fax:* (234) 791091 (office).

MARQUES AMADO, Luis Filipe; Portuguese economist and politician; *Minister of Foreign Affairs;* b. 17 Sept. 1953; m.; two c.; ed Universidade Técnica de Lisboa, Inst. of Nat. Defense, Simon Fraser Univ., Canada; fmr Auditor, Court of Auditors; fmr mem. Regional Legis. Ass. of Madeira; mem. Assembléia da República (Ass. of the Repub.); Sec. of State for Internal Admin

1995–97, for Foreign Affairs and Co-operation 1997–99, 1999–2002; Minister of Nat. Defence and Maritime Affairs 2005–06, of Foreign Affairs 2006–; fmr Visiting Prof., Georgetown Univ., USA. *Address:* Ministry of Foreign Affairs, Palácio das Necessidades, Largo do Rilvas, 1399-030 Lisbon, Portugal (office). *Telephone:* (21) 3946000 (office). *Fax:* (21) 3946053 (office). *E-mail:* gii@mne.gov.pt (office). *Website:* www.min-nestrangeiros.pt (office).

MÁRQUEZ, Gabriel García (see GARCÍA MÁRQUEZ, Gabriel).

MÁRQUEZ DE LA PLATA IRARRAZAVAL, Alfonso; Chilean politician; b. 19 July 1933, Santiago; s. of Fernando Márquez de la Plata Echenique and Rosa Yrarrazaval Fernández; m. María de la Luz Cortes Heyermann 1957; one s. one d.; ed Universidad Católica de Chile; Vice-Chair. Sociedad Nacional de Agricultura 1969–73, Chair. 1973–77; Chair. Banco de Santiago 1977–78; Minister of Agric. 1978–80; mem. Govt Legislative Comm. 1981–83; Dir A.F.P. Provida 1981–83, Compañía de Cervecerías Unidas 1981–83, Banco de Crédito e Inversiones 1981–83; Co-Proprietor and Admin. Sociedad Agrícola Caren Ltda; Govt Minister-Sec.-Gen. 1983–84, Minister of Labour and Social Security 1984–88; Chair. Nat. TV Council 1989–92; Espiga de Oro, Colegio Ingenieros Agrónomos 1998. *Publications:* El Salto al Futuro 1992, El Gobierno Ideal 1993, Mirando al Futuro 1998, Una Persecución Vergonzosa 2001, El Peligro Totalitario 2002. *Address:* Av. Presidente Kennedy 4150, Dp. 901, Santiago, Chile. *Telephone:* (2) 2084229. *Fax:* (2) 2061731. *E-mail:* almarruez@mi.cl (home).

MARR, Andrew William Stevenson, BA; British journalist; b. 31 July 1959, Glasgow, Scotland; s. of Donald Marr and Valerie Marr; m. Jackie Ashley 1987; one s. two d.; ed Dundee High School, Craigflower School, Loretto School, Trinity Hall, Cambridge; gen. reporter, business reporter The Scotsman 1982–84, Parl. Corresp. 1984–86, Political Ed. 1988; Political Ed. The Economist 1988–92; Political Corresp. The Independent 1986–88, Chief Commentator 1992–96, Ed. 1996–98, Ed.-in-Chief 1998; columnist The Express and The Observer 1998; Political Ed. BBC 2000–05; presenter Start the Week, BBC Radio 4 2002–; presenter morning interview programme, Sunday AM (BBC) 2005–; Chair. Jury Bd Samuel Johnson Prize for Non-Fiction 2001; What The Papers Say Award for Columnist of the Year 1995, British Press Award for Columnist of the Year 1995, Creative Freedom Award for Journalist of the Year 2000, Channel 4 Political Awards Journalist Award 2001, Royal Television Soc. Television Journalism Award for specialist journalism 2001, Voice of the Listener and Viewer Award for Best Individual Contributor on TV 2002, BAFTA Richard Dimbleby Award 2004. *Publications:* The Battle for Scotland 1992, Ruling Britannia 1996, The Day Britain Died 2000, My Trade: A Short History of British Journalism 2004, A History of Modern Britain (also TV series; winner, British Documentary Award for Best Series 2008) 2007. *Leisure interests:* reading, wining and dining, painting. *Address:* Room 3200, BBC Television Centre, Wood Lane, London, W12 7RJ, England (office). *Website:* www.bbc.co.uk (office).

MARRA, Thomas M.; American business executive; *President and COO, Hartford Financial Services Group Inc.;* ed St Bonaventure Univ.; joined Hartford Life Inc. as Assoc. Actuary 1980, Vice-Pres. and Dir, Individual Annuity Div. 1990–94, Sr Vice-Pres. and Dir 1994–96, Exec. Vice-Pres. 1996–2000, COO 2000–07, Pres. Hartford Life, Inc. 2002–07, Exec. Vice-Pres. Hartford Financial Services Group Inc. (The Hartford) 1990–2007, Dir Investment Products Div. 1998–2000, mem. Bd of Dirs 2002–, Pres. and COO 2007–; Chair. American Council of Life Insurers; mem. Bd of Trustees St Bonaventure Univ., Bushnell Performing Arts Center, Hartford, Conn.; Fellow, Soc. of Actuaries; mem. American Acad. of Actuaries. *Address:* Hartford Financial Services Group Inc., One Hartford Plaza, 690 Asylum Avenue, Hartford CT 06115-1900, USA (office). *Telephone:* (860) 547-5000 (office). *Fax:* (860) 547-2680 (office). *E-mail:* info@thehartford.com (office). *Website:* www.thehartford.com (office).

MARRACK, Philippa C., PhD, FRS; British/American immunologist and academic; *Senior Faculty Member, National Jewish Medical and Research Center, Howard Hughes Medical Institute;* b. 28 June 1945, Ewell, Surrey; ed Univ. of Cambridge and Univ. of California, San Diego; Postdoctoral Fellow, MRC Lab. for Molecular Biology, Cambridge 1970–71; Research Bye Fellow, Girton Coll., Cambridge 1970–71; Postdoctoral Fellow, Damon Runyon Soc. for Cancer Research, Dept of Biology, Univ. of California, San Diego, La Jolla 1971–73; Postdoctoral Fellow, Dept of Microbiology, Univ. of Rochester, NY 1973–74, Assoc. 1974–75, Asst Prof. 1975–76, Asst Prof. of Oncology, Dept of Microbiology and James P. Wilmot Cancer Center, Univ. of Rochester School of Medicine and Dentistry 1976–79, Assoc. Prof. of Oncology 1979–82; Established Investigator, American Heart Assсn, Dallas, Tex. 1976–81; mem. Dept of Medicine, Nat. Jewish Hosp. and Research Center, Denver, Colo 1979–; Assoc. Prof., Depts of Biophysics, Biochemistry and Genetics and Dept of Medicine, Univ. of Colorado Health Sciences Center 1980–85, Prof., Dept of Biochemistry and Molecular Genetics and Dept of Medicine 1985–, Prof., Dept of Microbiology and Immunology 1988–94, Prof., Dept of Immunology 1994–; Investigator, Howard Hughes Medical Inst., Denver 1986–; Head, Nat. Jewish Center for Immunology and Respiratory Medicine Denver 1988–90, Head, Div. of Basic Immunology, Nat. Jewish Medical and Research Center 1998–99, currently Sr Faculty mem., Integrated Dept of Immunology; Distinguished Prof., Univ. of Colorado 1993; mem. Laskar Award Selection Cttee 1993–; mem. Advisory Bd Cancer Research Inst. 1986–; mem. Council American Assсn of Immunologists 1995–, Vice-Pres. 1999–2000, Pres. 2000–01; Charter Bd mem. Molecular Medicine Soc. 1995–; Sec.-Gen. Tri-Annual Meeting, Int. Union of Immunologists 1995–; Vice-Pres. Int. Union of Immunological Socs 1998–; mem. Trudeau Inst. 1997–, Scientific Advisory Bd Sandler Foundation 1999–; Advisory Ed. Journal of Experimental Medicine 1985–, Therapetic Immunology 1992–; Assoc. Ed. Cell 1987–; Contributing Ed. Molecular Medicine 1995–; mem. Editorial Bd Cellular Immunology 1983–, Proceedings of the National Academy of Science 1997–, Journal of Autoimmunity 1997–; mem. NAS 1989–, British Soc. for Immunology, American Assсn of Immunologists, American Heart Assсn (Basic Science Council); Fellow, American Acad. of Arts and Sciences 1991–; Hon. mem. Scandinavian Soc. for Immunology 1990–; Hon. DSc (Univ. of Rochester) 1991, (Macalester Coll.) 1996; Arthur B. Lorber Award for Distinguished Service, Nat. Jewish Center for Immunology and Respiratory Medicine 1990, Prize Winner and Lecturer, Royal Soc. Wellcome Foundation 1990, Feodor Lynen Medal for Special Achievement and Distinguished Service Award 1990, Ernst W. Bertner Memorial Award, M. D. Anderson Cancer Center 1992, Christopher Columbus Discovery Award for Biomedical Research 1992, Paul Ehrlich and Ludwig Darmstädter Prize (Germany) 1993, William B. Coley Award for Distinguished Research in Fundamental Immunology, Cancer Research Inst. 1993, Dickson Prize in Medicine, Univ. of Pittsburgh 1995, Behring-Heidelberger Lecture Award 1995, FASEB Excellence in Science Award 1995, Louisa Gross Horwitz Prize, Columbia Univ. 1995, Rabbi Shai Schacknai Memorial Prize, Hadassah Univ. 1998, Howard Taylor Ricketts Prize, Univ. of Chicago 1999, Interscience Conf. on Antimicrobial Agents and Chemotherapy Award 1999, Irvington Inst. Scientific Leadership Award in Immunology 2001, L'Oréal-UNESCO For Women in Science Award 2004. *Publications:* more than 250 articles in scientific journals on devt, specificity, activation and life history of T cells. *Address:* Kappler/Marrack Laboratory, Howard Hughes Medical Institute, National Jewish Medical and Research Center, 1400 Jackson Street, 5th Floor, Goodman Building, Denver, CO 80206, USA (office). *Telephone:* (303) 398-1322 (office). *Fax:* (303) 398-1396 (office). *E-mail:* marrackp@njc.org (office). *Website:* nationaljewish.org/faculty/marrack.html (office); www.kmlab.njc.org (office); www.hhmi.org (office).

MARRAKCHI, Ahmad, PhD; Tunisian university administrator; b. 9 Feb. 1935, Sfax; m.; four c.; ed Toulouse Univ., France; Assoc. Prof., then Prof., Univ. of Tunis; Dir Tunis Nat. School of Eng (ENIT) 1975–85; est. Faculty of Tech. at Univ. of Qatar, Dean of Faculty and adviser to Pres. of Univ. 1990–99; mem. French Soc. of Electricians, European Soc. for Engineers Training; Founding mem. and Pres. Tunisian Soc. of Electronics Specialists; Fellow, Islamic Acad. of Sciences. *Address:* c/o Islamic Academy of Sciences, PO Box 830036, Amman, Jordan (office). *Telephone:* 5522104 (office). *Fax:* 5511803 (office).

MARRINER, Sir Neville, Kt, CBE, FRCM, FRAM; British music director and conductor; *Life President, Academy of St Martin in the Fields;* b. 15 April 1924, Lincoln, England; s. of Herbert H. Marriner and Ethel M. Marriner; m. Elizabeth M. Sims 1955; one s. (Andrew Stephen Marriner) one d.; ed Lincoln School, Royal Coll. of Music; Founder and Dir Acad. of St Martin-in-the-Fields, London 1956–, now Life Pres.; Musical Dir LA Chamber Orchestra 1969–78; Dir South Bank Festival of Music 1975–78, Dir Meadowbrook Festival, Detroit 1979–84; Music Dir Minn. Orchestra 1979–86, Stuttgart Radio Symphony Orchestra 1984–89, Barbican Summer Festival 1985–87; Fellow, Trinity Coll. of Music, Hong Kong Acad. for Performing Arts; Kt of the Polar Star 1984, Officier, Ordre des Arts et Lettres 1995; Hon. DMus (Hull) 1998, (Royal Scottish Acad.) 1999; Tagore Gold Medal, six Edison Awards (Netherlands), two Mozart Gemeinde Awards (Austria), three Grand Prix du Disque (France), two Grammy Awards (USA), Shakespeare Prize. *Recordings include:* Dvořák Serenades, Haydn Violin Concerto in C, Mozart Serenade K361, Il Barbiere di Siviglia, all Schubert's Symphonies, The English Connection (Vaughan Williams' The Lark Ascending, Elgar Serenade and Tippett Corelli Fantasia), Trumpet Concertos (with Hakan Hardenberger), Mendelssohn Piano Works (with Murray Perahia), Mozart Haffner Serenade, Bach Concertos, Suites and Die Kunst der Fuge, Vivaldi's The Four Seasons, Concerti Grossi by Corelli, Geminiani, Torelli, Locatelli and Manfredini, Mozart Symphonies, Concertos, Serenades and Divertimenti, Handel Messiah, Opera overtures and Water and Fireworks music, Die Zauberflöte 1980, Handel Arias (with Kathleen Battle), Il Turco in Italia and Don Giovanni, Verdi's Oberto 1997, Sylvia McNair: Love's Sweet Surrender 1998, Brahms Symphonies 1–4 1998, Schumann Symphonies 1–4 1998, complete Symphonies of Beethoven, Tchaikovsky, Weber, Gounod, Cantatas of Bach (with Fischer-Dieskau, Janet Baker), Haydn Symphonies. *Address:* Academy of St Martin in the Fields, Raine House, Raine Street, London, E1 9RG, England (office). *Telephone:* (20) 7702-1377 (office). *Fax:* (20) 7481-0228 (office). *E-mail:* info@asmf.org (office). *Website:* www.asmf.org (office).

MARRIOTT, J. W. (Bill), Jr, BA; American business executive; *Chairman and CEO, Marriott International Inc.;* b. 25 March 1932, Washington., DC; s. of J. Willard Marriott and Alice Sheets Marriott; m. Donna Marriott; three s. one d.; ed Univ. of Utah; ship's service supply officer, USS Randolph 1954–56; joined The Hot Shoppes (family-owned restaurant chain, later renamed Marriott) 1956, various positions including Head of Hotels Div., Pres. Marriott Corpn 1964–97, Chair. and CEO Marriott Int. Inc. 1997–; mem. Bd of Trustees Nat. Geographic Soc., Naval Acad. Endowment Trust, Nat. Urban League; CEO of the Year Award, Chief Executive Magazine 1988. *Publications include:* The Spirit to Serve: Marriott's Way (co-author) 1997. *Address:* Marriott International Inc., Corporate Headquarters, One Marriott Drive, Washington, DC 20058, USA (office). *Telephone:* (301) 380-3000 (office). *Fax:* (301) 380-3969 (office). *Website:* www.marriottnewsroom.com (office).

MARRON, Donald Baird; American banker; b. 21 July 1934, Goshen, NY; m. Catherine D. Calligar; ed Bronx High School of Science, NY and Baruch School of Business; investment analyst, New York Trust Co. 1951–56, Lionel D. Edie Co. 1956–58; Man. Research Dept George O'Neill & Co. 1958–59; Pres. D. B. Marron & Co. Inc. 1959–65, Mitchell Hutchins & Co. Inc. (merger with D. B. Marron & Co. Inc.) 1965–69, Pres., CEO 1969–77; Pres. PaineWebber Inc. (merger with Mitchell Hutchins & Co. Inc.) 1977–88, CEO 1980, Chair. Bd

1981–2001; co-founder, fmr Chair. Data Resources Inc.; fmr Dir New York Stock Exchange; mem. Bd Fannie Mae; mem. Advisory Bd Carlyle Group 2005–; Vice-Pres. Bd of Trustees Museum of Modern Art, now Pres.; mem. Council on Foreign Relations Inc., Pres.'s Cttee on The Arts and the Humanities Inc.; Trustee Center for Strategic and Int. Studies, George Bush Presidential Library. *Address:* c/o Museum of Modern Art, 11 West 53rd Street, New York, NY 10019, USA (office).

MARS, Forrest Edward, Jr; American business executive; b. 1931; s. of the late Forrest Mars, Sr; brother of John Franklin Mars (q.v.); m. Virginia Cretella 1955 (divorced 1990); four d.; ed Yale Univ.; CEO Mars, Inc. –2000, also Chair., Co-Pres. *Address:* c/o Mars Inc., 6885 Elm Street, McLean, VA 22101-3810, USA (office).

MARS, John Franklin; American business executive; *Chairman, Mars Inc.;* b. 1935; s. of the late Forrest Mars, Sr; brother of Forrest Edward Mars, Jr (q.v.); m.; two c.; ed Yale Univ.; Chair. Kal Kan Foods, Inc.; Co-Pres. Mars, Inc. 1973–, CEO 2000, now Chair. *Address:* Mars, Inc., 6885 Elm Street, McLean, VA 22101-3810, USA (office). *Telephone:* (703) 821-4900 (office). *Fax:* (703) 448-9678 (office). *Website:* www.mars.com (office).

MARS-JONES, Adam; British writer; b. 26 Oct. 1954, London; s. of the late Sir William Mars-Jones; partner Keith King; ed Westminster School, Trinity Hall, Cambridge and Univ. of Virginia, USA; film critic, The Independent 1989–97, The Times 1999–2001; Somerset Maugham Award 1982. *Publications:* Lantern Lecture (short stories) 1981, Mae West is Dead 1983, The Darker Proof (with Edmund White) 1987, Monopolies of Loss 1992, The Waters of Thirst (novel) 1993, Blind Bitter Happiness (essays) 1997, Pilcrow 2008. *Address:* 38 Oakbank Grove, Herne Hill, London, SE24 0AJ, England (home).

MARSALIS, Wynton; American musician (trumpet), music administrator and composer; b. 18 Oct. 1961, New Orleans; s. of Ellis Marsalis and Dolores Marsalis; three c.; ed Berks. Music Center, Tanglewood, Juilliard School, New York; played with New Orleans Philharmonic age 14; joined Art Blakey and the Jazz Messengers 1980; toured with Herbie Hancock 1981; formed own group with brother Branford Marsalis 1982; leader Wynton Marsalis Septet; in addition to regular appearances in many countries with his own jazz quintet, he follows a classical career and has performed with the world's top orchestras; regularly conducts masterclasses in schools and holds private tuition; Artistic Dir Lincoln Center Jazz Dept, New York 1990–; numerous hon. doctorates; Edison Award, Netherlands, Grand Prix du Disque, eight Grammy Awards in both jazz and classical categories, Pulitzer Prize for Music 1997, Algur H. Meadows Award, Southern Methodist Univ. 1997, Ronnie Scott Award for Int. Trumpeter 2007. *Compositions:* Soul Gestures in Southern Blues 1988, Blood on the Fields (oratorio) 1994, Jazz/Syncopated Movements 1997. *Recordings include:* All American Hero 1980, Wynton 1980, Wynton Marsalis 1981, Think of One 1983, English Chamber Orchestra 1984, Hot House Flowers 1984, Baroque Music: Wynton Marsalis, Edita Gruberova, Raymond Leppard and the English Chamber 1985, Black Codes (From the Underground) 1985, J Mood 1985, Live at Blues Alley 1986, Tomasi/Jolivet: Trumpet Concertos 1986, Carnaval 1987, Baroque Music for Trumpets 1988, The Majesty of the Blues 1989, Crescent City Christmas Card 1989, Tune in Tomorrow (soundtrack) 1991, Quiet City 1989, 24 1990, Trumpet Concertos 1990, Blue Interlude 1992, Citi Movement 1992, In This House, On This Morning 1992, Hot Licks: Gypsy 1993, On the Twentieth Century 1993, Joe Cool's Blues 1994, Live in Swing Town 1994, In Gabriel's Garden 1996, Jump Start and Jazz 1996, Live at Bubba's 1996, One By One 1998, The Marcial Suite 1998, At the Octoroon Ball: String Quartet No. 1 1999, Big Train 1999, Fiddler's Tale 1999, Reeltime 1999, Sweet Release and Ghost Story 1999, Goin' Down Home 2000, Immortal Concerts: Jody 2000, The London Concert 2000, All Rise 2002, Angel Eyes 2002, The Magic Hour 2004, Two Men with the Blues (with Willie Nelson) 2008, He and She 2009. *Publications:* Sweet Swing Blues on the Road 1994, Marsalis on Music 1995, Requiem 1999. *Address:* c/o Laurel J. Wicks, Ted Kurland Associates, 173 Brighton Avenue, Boston, MA 02134, USA (office). *Telephone:* (617) 254-0007 (office). *Fax:* (617) 782-3577 (office). *E-mail:* laurel@tedkurland.com (office); info@wyntonmarsalis.org (office). *Website:* www.wyntonmarsalis.org.

MARSH, Baron (Life Peer), cr. 1981, of Mannington in the County of Wiltshire; **Richard William Marsh,** Kt, PC; British public servant and politician; b. 14 March 1928; s. of William Marsh; m. 1st Evelyn Mary Andrews 1950 (divorced 1973); two s.; m. 2nd Caroline Dutton 1973 (died 1975); m. 3rd Felicity McFadzean 1979; ed Jennings School, Swindon, Woolwich Polytechnic and Ruskin Coll., Oxford; Health Services Officer, Nat. Union of Public Employees 1951–59; mem. Clerical and Admin. Whitley Council for Health Service 1953–59; MP for Greenwich 1959–71; Parl. Sec. Ministry of Labour 1964–65; Jt Parl. Sec. Ministry of Tech. 1965–66; Minister of Power 1966–68, of Transport 1968–69; Dir Michael Saunders Man. Services 1970–71, Nat. Carbonizing Ltd 1970–71, Concord Rotaflex 1970–71; Chair. British Railways Bd 1971–76, Newspaper Publishers Assen Ltd 1976–89, Allied Investments Ltd 1977–82, British Iron & Steel Consumers' Council 1977–82, Lee Cooper Licensing Services 1980–83, Dual Fuel Systems 1981, Lee Cooper Group 1983, TV-am 1983–84 (Deputy Chair. 1981–83), Lopex PLC 1986–97, Laurentian Financial Group PLC 1986–; Dir Imperial Life of Canada UK 1983–90; Chair. British Industry Cttee on SA Ltd 1989–, Mannington Man. Services 1989–; Chair. and Chief Exec. Laurentian Holdings Co. 1989; Chair. China and Eastern Investments Trust, Hong Kong 1990–98 (Dir 1987–98); Adviser Nissan Motor Co. 1981–, Fujitec 1982–92, Taisei 1992–, Income & Growth Trust 1995–. *Publication:* Off the Rails (memoirs) 1978. *Address:* House of Lords, London, SW1A 0PW, England.

MARSH, Rodney William, MBE; Australian professional cricket coach and fmr professional cricketer; b. 4 Nov. 1947, Armadale, Western Australia; m.; three s.; ed Univ. of Western Australia; Australian Test cricketer (wicket-keeper) 1970–84; Test career 96 matches, 355 dismissals (343 caught, 12 stumped), batting average 26.51 (three centuries); One-day international career 92 matches, 124 dismissals (120 caught, four stumped), batting average 20.08; Head Coach Commonwealth Bank Cricket Acad. 1991–2001; Dir England and Wales Cricket Board Nat. Acad. 2001–; Wisden Cricketer of the Year 1982. *Publication:* (with Jack Pollard) The Glovemen 1994. *Leisure interests:* golf, watching Aussie rules football. *Address:* ECB National Academy, c/o Andrew Walpole, Media Relations Manager, Lord's Cricket Ground, London, NW8 8QZ, England (office); 4 Briar Avenue, Medindie, South Australia 5081, Australia (home). *E-mail:* rodney.marsh@ecb.co.uk (office); rmarsh@bettanet.net.au (home).

MARSHALL, Barry J., FRS, FAA, AC; Australian gastroenterologist and academic; b. 30 Sept. 1951, Kalgoorlie; ed Univ. of Western Australia; physician, Royal Perth Hosp. 1974–83; Research Fellow, gastroenterologist, Prof. of Medicine, Univ. of Va, USA 1986–96; currently Hon. Research Fellow, Helicobacter pylori Research Lab., Univ. of Western Australia School of Biomedical and Chemical Sciences, Sir Charles Gairdner Hosp., Perth; Albert Lasker Award 1995, Dr. A. H. Heineken Prize for Medicine 1998, Australian Achiever Award 1998, Florey Medal 1998, Buchanan Medal, Royal Soc. of Medicine, London 1998, Benjamin Franklin Award for Life Sciences 1999, Poppy Award, Australian Inst. of Political Sciences 2000, Nobel Prize for Medicine 2005. *Research:* collaborated with Robin Warren on research leading to culture of Helicobacter pylori 1982 and recognition of assen between H.pylori, gastritis, peptic ulcer and gastric cancer. *Leisure interests:* computers, electronics, photography. *Address:* H.pylori Research Laboratory, Sir Charles Gairdner Hospital, Verdun Street, Nedlands, WA 6009, Australia (office). *E-mail:* bmarshall@hpylori.com.au (office). *Website:* www.hpylori.com.au (office); www.eftelcorporate.com.au/~bjmrshll.

MARSHALL, Hon. (Cedric) Russell, CNZM, BA; New Zealand politician and diplomatist; *President, New Zealand Institute of International Affairs;* b. 15 Feb. 1936, Nelson; s. of Cedric Thomas Marshall and Gladys Margaret (née Hopley) Marshall; m. Barbara May Watson 1961; two s. one d.; ed Nelson Coll., Christchurch Teachers' Coll., Trinity Theological Coll., Auckland, Victoria Univ.; teacher at various schools 1955–56; Methodist Minister in Christchurch 1960–66, Masterton 1967–71; MP for Wanganui (Labour) 1972–90; Minister of Educ. 1984–87, of Foreign Affairs 1987–90, of Disarmament and Arms Control 1987–89, of Pacific Island Affairs 1989–90; Sr Opposition Whip 1978–79; Chair. NZ Comm. for UNESCO 1990–99, NZ Rep., UNESCO Exec. Bd 1995–99; Chancellor, Victoria Univ. of Wellington 2000–01; High Commr to UK and Nigeria and Amb. to Ireland 2002–05; Chair. Africa Information Centre Trustees 1991–95, Commonwealth Observer Group, Seychelles 1993, Commonwealth Observer Mission to S Africa 1994, Cambodia Trust (Aotearoa-NZ) 1994–2001, Polytechnics Int. NZ 1994–2001, Educ. NZ 1998–2001, Tertiary Educ. Advisory Comm. 2000–01, Cambodia Trust (UK) 2002–05, Tertiary Educ. Comm. 2005–07; Pres. NZ Inst. of Int. Affairs 2007–; mem. Commonwealth Observer Group, Lesotho 1993, Victoria Univ. (Wellington) Council 1994–2002, Nelson Mandela Trustees 1995–2008; Labour. *Leisure interests:* classical music, genealogy. *Address:* New Zealand Institute of International Affairs, Victoria University of Wellington, PO Box 600, Wellington, New Zealand (office). *Telephone:* (4) 463-5356 (office). *Fax:* (4) 463-6568 (office). *E-mail:* russell.marshall@paradise.net.nz (office); nziia@vuw.ac.nz (office). *Website:* www.victoria.ac.nz/nziia (office).

MARSHALL, Garry Kent, BS; American actor, director and writer; b. 13 Nov. 1934, New York City; s. of Anthony Wallace Marsciarelli and Marjorie Irene Ward; brother of Penny Marshall; m. Barbara Marshall; one s. two d.; ed Northwestern Univ., Evanston, Ill.; served in US Armed Forces during Korean War; writer for Stars and Stripes newspaper and Production Chief, Armed Forces Radio Network; copy boy then reporter, Daily News, NY 1956–59; joke writer for Joey Bishop and Phil Foster; career as stand-up comedian; began tv career as writer for The Tonight Show with Jack Parr 1959; Exec. Producer, American Broadcasting Co. (TV network), Paramount Studios 1970s; star on Hollywood Walk of Fame. *Film appearances include:* Toller Hecht auf krummer Tour 1961, Psych-Out 1968, Maryjane 1968, Goldfinger, Grand Theft Auto 1977, The Way They Were (TV) 1981, Lost in America 1985, Jumpin' Jack Flash 1986, But Seriously Folks (TV) 1986, Beaches 1988, Murphy Brown (TV) 1988, Pretty Woman 1990, Secret Agent 00 Soul 1990, Soapdish 1991, A League of Their Own 1992, Hocus Pocus 1993, The Last Shot (TV) 1993, Exit to Eden 1994, Statistically Speaking 1995, With Friends Like These 1998, Never Been Kissed 1999, Runaway Bride 1999, Can't Be Heaven 2000, This Space Between Us 2000, It's a Shame About Ray 2000, Tomcats 2001, The Hollywood Sign 2001, The Majestic 2001, Orange County 2002, Mother Ghost 2002, The Long Ride Home 2003, They Call Him Sasquatch 2003, Devil's Night 2003, Lucky 13 2005, Chicken Little (voice) 2005, Mute 2005, Keeping Up with the Steins 2006. *Films written, directed or produced:* Young Doctors in Love 1982, The Flamingo Kid 1984, Nothing in Common 1986, Overboard 1987, The Lottery 1987, Beaches 1988, Pretty Woman 1990, Frankie and Johnny 1991, Exit to Eden 1994, Dear God 1996, The Twilight of the Golds 1997, The Other Sister 1999, Runaway Bride 1999, The Princess Diaries 2001, Raising Helen 2004, Princess Diaries 2: The Royal Engagement 2004, Rogue Farm 2004, Georgia Rule 2007. *Television shows written, directed or produced:* Make Room for Daddy 1953, The Jack Paar Show 1959–61, The Joey Bishop Show 1961–65, The Danny Thomas Show 1961–64, The Dick Van Dyke Show 1961–66, The Lucy Show 1962–68, Gomer Pyle, U.S.M.C. 1964, I Spy 1965–68, Hey Landlord 1966–67, Love American Style 1969, The Odd Couple 1970–75, The Little People 1972–74, Me and the Chimp 1972, Happy Days 1974–84, Laverne and Shirley 1976–83, Blansky's

Beauties 1977, Mork & Mindy 1978–82, Angie 1979–80, Who's Watching the Kids 1978, Joanie Loves Chachi 1982–83, Herndon 1983, Nothing in Common 1987, Murphy Brown 1994. *Address:* c/o Creative Artists Agency Inc., 9830 Wilshire Boulevard, Beverly Hills, CA 90212-1825, USA (office). *Telephone:* (310) 288-4800 (office). *Fax:* (310) 288-4800 (office). *Website:* www.caa.com (office).

MARSHALL, Margaret Anne, OBE; British singer (soprano); b. 4 Jan. 1949, Stirling; d. of Robert Marshall and Margaret Marshall; m. Dr Graeme G. K. Davidson 1970; two d.; ed High School of Stirling and Royal Scottish Acad. of Music and Drama; first opera appearance in Orfeo ed Euridice, Florence 1977; has since sung at La Scala, Covent Garden, Glyndebourne, Scottish Opera, Barcelona, Hamburg, Cologne and Salzburg; concert performances in maj. European and US cities and festivals with maj. orchestras; numerous recordings; first prize Munich Int. Competition 1974, James Gulliver Award for Performing Arts in Scotland. *Leisure interests:* squash, golf, cooking. *Address:* Woodside, Main Street, Gargunnock, Stirling, FK8 3BP, Scotland.

MARSHALL, (Carole) Penny; American actress and director; b. 15 Oct. 1943, New York; d. of Anthony Marshall and Marjorie Ward; sister of Garry Marshall; m. 1st Michael Henry (divorced), one d.; m. 2nd Robert Reiner 1971 (divorced 1979); ed Univ. of New Mexico; Co-founder Parkway Productions. *Films include:* appeared in: How Sweet It Is 1967, The Savage Seven 1968, The Grasshopper 1979, '1941' 1979, Movers and Shakers 1985, She's Having a Baby 1988, The Hard Way 1991, Special Delivery 1999, Looking for Comedy in the Muslim World 2005, Everybody Wants to Be Italian 2007, Alice Upside Down 2007, Blonde Ambition 2007; directed: Jumpin' Jack Flash 1986, Big 1988, Awakenings (also producer) 1990, A League of their Own (also producer) 1992, Renaissance Man (also producer) 1994, The Preacher's Wife 1996, The Time Tunnel: The Movie 1999, Jackie's Back 1999, Riding in Cars with Boys 2001; other produced: Calendar Girl 1993, Getting Away With Murder 1996, With Friends Like These 1998, Risk 2003, Cinderella Man 2005, Bewitched 2005. *Television includes:* The Odd Couple 1971–75, Laverne and Shirley 1976–83. *Address:* Parkway Productions, 7095 Hollywood Blvd, Suite 1009, Hollywood, CA 90028, USA. *Telephone:* (323) 874-6207. *Fax:* (323) 874-3124.

MARSHALL, Sir Peter, Kt, KCMG, CVO; British diplomatist; b. 30 July 1924, Reading; s. of the late R. H. Marshall and Winifred Marshall; m. 1st Patricia R. Stoddart 1957 (died 1981); one s. one d.; m. 2nd Judith Tomlin (née Miller) 1989; ed Tonbridge School and Corpus Christi Coll., Cambridge; RAFVR 1943–46; served HM Foreign (later Diplomatic) Service 1949–83; Aide to British Amb., Washington, DC 1952–56; Head of Chancery, Baghdad 1961, Bangkok 1962–64, Paris 1969–71; Deputy Dir Treasury Centre for Admin. Studies 1965–66; Counsellor, UK Mission, Geneva 1966–69; Head, Financial Relations Dept, FCO 1971–73, Asst Under-Sec. of State 1973–75; Minister, UK Mission to UN, New York 1975–79; Perm. Rep. UK Mission, Geneva 1979–83; Commonwealth Deputy Sec.-Gen. (Econ.) 1983–88; Chair. Royal Commonwealth Soc. 1988–92, Commonwealth Trust 1989–92; Chair. Jt Commonwealth Socs Council 1993–2003; Pres. Queen Elizabeth House, Oxford 1990–94; Visiting Lecturer, Diplomatic Acad. of London 1989–2001; Hon. Fellow, Corpus Christi Coll., Cambridge 1989, Univ. of Westminster 1992. *Publications:* The Dynamics of Diplomacy 1989, The United Kingdom – The United Nations (contrib.) 1990, Diplomacy Beyond 2000 (ed.) 1996, Positive Diplomacy 1997, Are Diplomats Really Necessary? (ed.) 1999, The Information Explosion (ed.) 1999. *Leisure interests:* music, golf. *Address:* 26 Queensdale Road, London, W11 4QB, England (home). *Telephone:* (20) 7229-1921 (home). *E-mail:* jupetermarshall@aol.com (home).

MARSHALL, Ray, PhD; American economist, academic and fmr government official; *Professor Emeritus, Lyndon B. Johnson School of Public Affairs, University of Texas;* b. 22 Aug. 1928, Oak Grove, La.; m. Patricia Williams 1946; one s. three d.; ed Millsaps Coll., Miss., Louisiana State Univ., Univ. of Calif. at Berkeley; Fulbright Research Scholar, Finland; post-doctoral research, Harvard Univ.; Instructor San Francisco State Coll.; Assoc. Prof. and Prof. Univs of Miss., Ky, La.; Prof. of Econs, Univ. of Texas 1962–67, Prof. of Econs 1969, Chair. Dept 1970–72, Prof. of Econs and Public Affairs, Lyndon B. Johnson School of Public Affairs 1981, Rapoport Prof. Econs and Public Affairs, Prof. Emer. 1998–, fmrly Dir Center for Study of Human Resources; US Sec. of Labor 1977–81; Co-Chair. Comm. on the Skills of the American Workforce; Trustee German Marshall Fund and Carnegie Corpn of NY 1982–90; mem. Comm. on Future of Labor/Man. Relations; Hon. degrees (Maryland, Cleveland State, Millaaps Coll., Bates Coll., Rutgers, Ind., Tulane, Utah State, St Edward's); Lifetime Achievement Award, Industrial Relations Research Asscn 2001. *Publications:* The Negro Worker 1967, The Negro and Apprenticeship 1967, Cooperatives and Rural Poverty in the South 1971, Human Resources and Labor Markets 1972, Anthology of Labor Economics 1972, Human Resources and Labor Markets 1975, Labor Economics: Wages, Employment and Trade Unionism 1976, The Role of Unions in the American Economy 1976, An Economic Strategy for the 1980s 1981, Work and Women in the Eighties 1983, Unheard Voices: Labor and Economic Policy in a Competitive World 1987, Economics of Education 1988, Losing Direction: Families, Human Resource Development and Economic Performance 1991, Thinking for a Living (with Marc Tucker) 1992, Back to Shared Prosperity (ed.) 2000. *Address:* c/o University of Texas, L.B.J. School of Public Affairs, Drawer Y, University Station, Austin, TX 78713, USA. *Telephone:* (512) 471-6242 (office); (512) 345-1828 (home). *Fax:* (512) 345-8491 (home). *E-mail:* ray.marshall@mail.utexas.edu (office). *Website:* www.utexas.edu/lbj (office).

MARSHALL, Robin, BSc, PhD, FRS, FRAS, FInstP; British physicist and academic; *Research Professor of Particle Physics and Life Sciences, University of Manchester;* b. 5 Jan. 1940, Skipton, Yorks.; s. of the late Robert Marshall and Grace Eileen Marshall; m. 1963 (divorced 2002); two s. one d.; ed Ermysted's Grammar School, Skipton, Univ. of Manchester; Research Scientist, DESY, MIT, Daresbury Lab., Rutherford Appleton Lab. 1965–92; Sr Prin. Scientific Officer (Individual Merit) Rutherford Appleton Lab. 1985–92; Prof. of Experimental Physics and Head, Particle Physics Group, Univ. of Manchester 1992–2005, Research Prof. of Particle Physics and Life Sciences 2005–; Dir and Co. Sec. Frontiers Science and TV Ltd; mem. Council Royal Soc., Royal Soc. Rep. on Univ. of Manchester Ass., Chair. Royal Soc. Univ. Fellowship Cttee; Trustee, Museum of Science and Industry, Manchester; Max Born Medal and Prize, German Physical Soc. 1997. *Publications:* more than 200 scientific papers. *Leisure interests:* painting and drawing, movies. *Address:* Department of Physics and Astronomy, University of Manchester, Manchester, M13 9PL, England (office). *Telephone:* (161) 275-4170 (office); (161) 275-4175 (office). *Fax:* (161) 275-4246 (office). *E-mail:* R.Marshall@man.ac.uk (office); Robin.Marshall@manchester.ac.uk (office). *Website:* macnode1.hep.man.ac.uk/~robin (office).

MARSHALL, Ruth Ann, BBA, MBA; American business executive; ed Southern Methodist Univ., Dallas, Tex.; began her career at IBM, numerous managerial and exec. positions over 18-year period; served as Group Exec. Vice-Pres. two Electronic Payment Service cos, MAC Regional Network and Buypass Corpn, Sr Exec. Vice-Pres. combined cos following acquisition by Concord EFS; Pres. MasterCard N America 1999, Pres., Americas, MasterCard Int. –2006 (retd); mem. Bd of Dirs Global Payments Inc. 2006–, American Standard Corpn, Pella Corpn, ConAgra Foods, Inc. 2007–; mem. Bd several civic and academic orgs, including Citymeals-on-Wheels, The PGA First Tee, Cox School of Business at Southern Methodist Univ.; Credit Card Management's Leader of the New Millennium Award 1999, ranked by Fortune magazine amongst 50 Most Powerful Women in Business in the US 2003, ranked by Forbes magazine amongst 100 Most Powerful Women (88th) 2004, (41st) 2005. *Leisure interest:* competitive sports (especially golf), piano, travel. *Address:* 4923 Fisher Island Drive, Fisher Island, FL 33109, USA.

MARSHALL OF KNIGHTSBRIDGE, Baron (Life Peer), cr. 1998, of Knightsbridge in the City of Westminster; **Colin (Marsh) Marshall,** Kt; British business executive; b. 16 Nov. 1933, Edgware, Middlesex; s. of Marsh Marshall and Florence M. Marshall; m. Janet Cracknell 1958; one d.; ed Univ. Coll. School, Hampstead; cadet purser, later Deputy Purser, Orient Steam Navigation Co. 1958–64; with Hertz Corpn 1958–64; with Avis Inc. 1964–79, Exec. Vice-Pres. and COO New York 1971–75, Pres. and COO, New York 1975–76, Pres. and CEO, New York 1976–79; Exec. Vice-Pres. and Sector Exec. Norton Simon Inc., 1979–81; Dir and Deputy Chief. Exec. Dir Sears Holdings PLC 1981–83; Chief Exec. British Airways 1983–95, Deputy Chair. 1989–93, Exec. Chair. 1993–95, Chair. (non-exec.) 1996–2004; Chair. Inchcape 1996–2000, Siebe PLC (now Invensys PLC) 1996–2003; fmr Deputy Chair. Royal Bank of Scotland; Deputy Chair. British Telecommunications 1996–2001, Dir 1995–2001; Dir Grand Metropolitan PLC 1988–95, Midland Group 1989–, HSBC Holdings 1992–2004, US Air 1993–96, Qantas 1993–96, 2000–01; Chair. Int. Advisory Bd British American Business Council 1994–; Pres. Commonwealth Youth Exchange Council 1998–; Deputy Pres. CBI 1995–96, 1998 (Pres. 1996–98); Chair. Britain in Europe 1998–, Chatham House 1999–, CBI Int. Advisory Bd 2002–, Royal Inst. of Int. Affairs –2003; mem. Bd IBM UK Ltd 1990–1995, Panel 2000 1998–99; Hon. DLitt (Suffolk, USA) 1984, (Westminster) 1999, Hon. LLD (Bath) 1989, (American Univ. London) 1993, (Lancaster) 1997, Hon. DSc (Buckingham) 1990, (Cranfield) 1997, Dr of Business (London Guildhall) 2000. *Leisure interests:* tennis, skiing. *Address:* Britain in Europe, 85 Frampton Street, London, NW8 8NQ, England. *Telephone:* (20) 7725-4200 (office). *Fax:* (20) 7725-4201 (office). *Website:* info@britainineurope.org.uk (office).

MARŠIĆANIN, Dragan; Serbian politician and diplomatist; *Ambassador to Switzerland;* worked in private sector for several cos including Elektron, Novi Kolektiv, Belgrade Water Utility; Chair. Vracar municipality –1996; fmr Sec. Democratic Party of Serbia, currently Vice-Pres.; fmr Minister of Economy; Speaker, Nat. Assembly –2004; cand. in presidential election 2004 (finished fourth); currently Amb. to Switzerland. *Address:* Embassy of Serbia, Seminarstr. 5, 3006 Bern, Switzerland (office). *Telephone:* 313526353 (office). *Fax:* 313514474 (office). *E-mail:* info@ynamb.ch (office). *Website:* www.ynamb.ch.

MARTEL, Yann; Canadian writer; b. 1963, Salamanca, Spain; ed Trent Univ.; grew up in Alaska, BC, Costa Rica, France, Ont. and Mexico; fmr tree planter, dishwasher, security guard; became professional writer 1990. *Publications:* Facts Behind the Helsinki Roccamatios (short stories) (Journey Prize) 1993, Self (novel) 1996, Life of Pi (novel) (Hugh MacLennan Prize for Fiction 2001, Man Booker Prize 2002, Boeke Prize 2003) 2001, We Ate the Children Last (short stories) 2004. *Leisure interests:* yoga, writing, volunteer in a palliative care unit. *Address:* c/o Knopf Canada, Random House of Canada Ltd, One Toronto Street, Unit 300, Toronto, ON M5C 2VC, Canada (office). *Telephone:* (416) 364-4449 (office). *Fax:* (416) 364-6863 (office). *Website:* www.randomhouse.ca (office).

MARTELLI, Claudio; Italian politician; b. 24 Sept. 1943, Milan; m.; four c.; mem. Italian Socialist Party (PSI) 1967–93, mem. Secr. 1973–75, Leader PSI Group, Milan Municipal Council 1975–79; elected Deputy 1979, 1983, 1987, 1992; Deputy Prime Minister 1989–92, Minister of Justice 1991–93; MEP for Italian Democratic Socialists (SDI) 1999–2004, mem. Cttee on Foreign Affairs, Human Rights, Common Security and Defence Policy, mem. Interparliamentary Del. for Relations with South-East Europe; Spokesman League of Socialists 2000–; Ed.-in-Chief La Sinistra Sociale socialist review. *Address:* c/o Socialisti Democratici Italiani (SDI) (Italian Democratic Socialists), Piazza S. Lorenzo in Lucina 26, 00186 Rome, Italy.

MARTENS, Wilfried A. E., DLaws, Lic. Notary, Bac. Thomistic Phil.; Belgian politician and lawyer; *President, European People's Party;* b. 19 April 1936,

Sleidinge; ed Katholieke Universiteit Leuven (Louvain); lawyer, Court of Appeal, Ghent 1960; fmr Leader Vlaamse Volksbeweging; Adviser to Harmel Cabinet 1965, to Vanden Boeynants Cabinet 1966; Head of Mission to Tindemans Cabinet (Community Affairs) 1968; Pres. Christelijke Volkspartij-Jongeren (CVP Youth Org. 1967–71), Pres. CVP 1972–79; mem. Parl. for Ghent-Eeklo 1974–91, mem. Senate for Brussels-Halle-Vilvoorde 1991–94; Co-founder European People's Party (EPP) 1976, Pres. Working Cttee on Policy 1976–77, Pres. 1990–, Pres. EPP Group, European Parl. 1994–99; Prime Minister 1979–81, 1981–92; Minister of State 1992–; Pres. European Union of Christian Democrats 1993–96; Pres. Christian Democratic Int. 2000–01; Charles V Prize (for contrib. to EU) 1998; numerous Belgian and int. awards. *Address:* European People's Party, 10 rue du Commerce, 1000 Brussels, Belgium (office). *Telephone:* (2) 285-41-59 (office). *Fax:* (2) 285-41-55 (office). *E-mail:* presid@epp.eu (office). *Website:* www.epp.eu (office).

MÅRTENSON, Jan; Swedish diplomatist; b. 14 Feb. 1933, Uppsala; m.; two s. two d.; ed Univ. of Uppsala; held various Foreign Ministry and diplomatic posts until 1966; Head Section UN Dept Ministry for Foreign Affairs, Stockholm 1966–67, Head Information Dept 1973–75; Deputy Dir Stockholm Int. Peace Research Inst. 1968–69; Sec.-Gen. Swedish Prep. Cttee for UN Conf. on Human Environment 1970–72; Chef de Cabinet for King of Sweden 1975–79; Asst Sec.-Gen. Centre for Disarmament, UN Dept of Political and Security Council Affairs 1979–82, Under-Sec.-Gen. for Disarmament Affairs 1983–87; Chair. UN Appointments and Promotions Bd 1984–86; Sec.-Gen. Int. Conf. on Relationship between Disarmament and Devt 1987; Dir-Gen. UN Office, Geneva 1987–92, Under-Sec.-Gen. and Head UN Centre for Human Rights, Geneva 1987–92, Co-ordinator UN Second Decade Against Racism 1987; Amb. to Switzerland and Liechtenstein 1993–95; Amb.-at-Large, Ministry of Foreign Affairs 1996–98; Marshal of the Diplomatic Corps 1999–2004; Chair. Int. Club, Stockholm, Travellers' Club, Stockholm. *Publications:* some 50 books; articles on disarmament and human rights. *Leisure interests:* gardening, fishing. *Address:* Karlaplan 14, 115 20 Stockholm, Sweden (home). *Telephone:* (8) 660-98-39 (home). *E-mail:* jm@swedishvision.se (office).

MÅRTENSSON, Arne, MBA; Swedish banker; *Chairman, Svenska Handelsbanken;* b. 10 Oct. 1951, Vänersborg; s. of Aldo Mårtensson and Ingrid Mårtensson; m. 2nd Heléne Melin-Mårtensson 1996; ed Stockholm School of Econs, Harvard Business School, USA; Industrial Devt Dept, Svenska Handelsbanken 1972–75, Vice-Pres. and Head Credit Dept, Regional Unit, Western Sweden 1975–77, Sr Vice-Pres. Admin., Cen. Sweden 1977–80, Sr Vice-Pres. and Area Man. Stockholm City 1980–84, Exec. Vice-Pres. and Gen. Man., Western Sweden, 1984–89, Pres. Stockholm 1989–91, Group Chief Exec. 1991–2001, Chair. 2001–; Deputy Chair. Telefonaktiebolaget LM Ericsson; mem. (non-exec.) Bd Holmen AB, Industrivärden AB, Swedish Industry and Stock Exchange Cttee, Sandvik AB, Skanska AB, ICC Sweden, V & S Vin & Spirit AB, Stockholm School of Econs Advisory Bd (Chair.), mem. Int. Business Council of World Econ. Forum, Industrial Council, Royal Swedish Acad. of Eng Sciences; Econ. Dr. hc. *Leisure interests:* sailing, jogging, skiing. *Address:* Svenska Handelsbanken, 106 70 Stockholm, Sweden (office). *Telephone:* (8) 22-92-20 (office). *Fax:* (8) 701-11-95 (office). *Website:* www.handelsbanken.se/ireng (office).

MARTIN, Carolyn (Biddy), PhD; American academic and university administrator; *Chancellor, University of Wisconsin;* b. Lynchburg, Va; ed Coll. of William and Mary, Middlebury Coll., Univ. of Wisconsin; Asst Prof., Dept of German Studies, Cornell Univ. 1985–91, Assoc. Prof. 1991–97, Prof. 1997–2008, Chair Dept of German Studies 1994–97, Sr Assoc. Dean, Coll. of Arts and Sciences 1996; Provost Cornell Univ. 2000–08; Chancellor Univ. of Wisconsin, Madison 2008–. *Address:* Office of the Chancellor, University of Wisconsin, Madison, WI 53706, USA (office). *Telephone:* (608) 263-2400 (office). *Website:* chancellor.wisc.edu (office).

MARTIN, Chris; British singer, musician (guitar, piano) and songwriter; b. 2 March 1977, Devon, England; m. Gwyneth Paltrow 2003; one d. one s.; ed Univ. Coll. London; mem., Coldplay 1998–; BRIT Award for Best British Group 2001, MTV Award for Best UK and Ireland Act 2002, Billboard Group of the Year 2002, Ivor Novello Songwriters of the Year 2003, Grammy Awards for Record of the Year (for Clocks) 2004, for Song of the Year, for Best Pop Performance by a Duo or Group (both for Viva la Vida) 2009, Q Award for Best Act in the World 2005, Digital Music People's Choice Award for best official site, for Best Digital Music Community (for Coldplay.com) 2005, MTV Europe Music Awards for Best UK & Ireland Act, for Best Song (for Speed of Sound) 2005, American Music Award for Favorite Alternative Music Artist 2005, BRIT Award for Best British Single (for Speed of Sound) 2006, Echo Award for Best Int. Group, Germany 2006, ASCAP Award for Song of the Year (for Speed of Sound) 2006, World Music Award for Best Rock Act 2008. *Recordings include:* albums: Parachutes (BRIT Award for Best Album, Grammy Award for Best Alternative Album 2001) 2000, A Rush Of Blood To The Head (BRIT Award for Best British Album, NME Award for Best Album 2003) 2002, X&Y (BRIT Award for Best British Album 2006, Juno Award for Int. Album of the Year 2006) 2005, Viva la Vida (Grammy Award for Best Rock Album 2009) 2008. *Address:* c/o Dave Holmes, 3–D Management, Los Angeles, CA , USA (office); c/o Parlophone, Fifth Floor, EMI House, 43 Brook Green, London, W6 7EF, England (office). *Website:* www.coldplay.com.

MARTIN, Hon. Clare, BA; Australian organization official and fmr politician; *CEO, Australian Council of Social Service;* b. 15 June 1952, Sydney; d. of Prof. Noel Desmond Martin and Bernice Martin (née Downey); m. David Alderman; one s. one d.; ed Loreto Convent, Normanhurst, Sydney Univ.; Sr Political Journalist and Broadcaster ABC (TV and Radio) 1978–95; MLA (Australian Labour Party—ALP) for Fannie Bay NT 1995–; Shadow Minister for Statehood, then Shadow Minister for the Arts 1995–96, Ethnic Affairs

1995–96, Correctional Services 1995–97, Lands, Planning and Environment 1995–97, Arts and Museums 1995–2001, Urban Devt 1996–97, Housing 1996–99, Asian Relations, Trade and Industry 1997–99, Racing and Gaming 1997–99, Young Territorians 1997–99; Leader ALP 1999–2007; Minister for Communications Science and Advanced Tech. 2001–02; Northern Territory Chief Minister 2001–07; Minister for Arts and Museums 2001–07, Young Territorians 2001–07, Women's Policy 2001–07, Sr Territorians 2001–07, Territory Devt 2002–07, Indigenous Affairs 2002–07; Treasurer 2001–07; CEO Australian Council of Social Service 2008–; fmr Bd mem. YWCA NT; mem. Jt Ethics Cttee Menzies School Health Research, Royal Darwin Hosp. *Leisure interests:* being fit, reading, music, sport, family. *Address:* Australian Council of Social Service, Level 2, 619 Elizabeth Street, Redfern, NSW 2016 (office); Tenancy 1, 10 Parap Place, Parap Shopping Village, Parap, NT 0820, Australia (home). *Telephone:* (2) 9310-6200 (office). *Fax:* (2) 9310-4822 (office). *E-mail:* info@acoss.org.au (office). *Website:* www.acoss.org.au (office).

MARTIN, Sir Clive Haydn, Kt, OBE, TD, DL, FCMA, FCIS; British business executive; *Chairman, MPG Ltd;* b. 20 March 1935; s. of Thomas Stanley Martin and Dorothy Gladys Martin; m. Linda Constance Basil Penn 1959; one s. three d.; ed St Alban's School, Haileybury and Imperial Service Coll., London School of Printing and Graphic Arts; nat. service in Germany 1956–58; Man. Dir Staples Printers Ltd (now MPG Ltd) 1972–85, Chair. 1972–; ADC to The Queen 1982–86; Alderman, City of London 1985–2005, Sheriff 1996–97, Lord Mayor of London 1999–2000; Master, Stationers' and Newspaper Makers' Co. 1997–98; CO, Hon. Artillery Co. 1978–80, Regimental Col 1981–83, Master Gunner, Tower of London 1981–83; Master, Chartered Secretaries and Admin.s' Co. 2004–05; Fellow Inst. of Paper, Printing and Publishing; Hon. DCL (City Univ.); Dr hc (London Inst.) 2001 Hon. Col, 135 Ind. Geographic Squadron, Royal Engineers 1999–2004; Hon. Col, The London Regiment 2001–. *Leisure interests:* ocean racing (owner and skipper, British Sardinia Cup Team 1984), walking, cycling. *Address:* MPG Ltd., The Gresham Press, Old Woking, Surrey, GU22 9LH, England (office). *Telephone:* (1483) 757501 (office). *Fax:* (1483) 724629 (office).

MARTIN, G. Steven, PhD, FRS; American/British biochemist, biologist and academic; *Judy C Webb Professor of Cell and Developmental Biology, University of California, Berkeley;* b. 19 Sept. 1943, Oxford, England; s. of Kurt Martin and Hanna Martin; m. Gail Zuckman 1969; one s.; ed Manchester Grammar School, Univ. of Cambridge; Postdoctoral Fellow, Virus Lab., Univ. of California, Berkeley 1968–71; mem. of staff, Imperial Cancer Research Fund, London 1971–75; Asst Prof. Dept of Zoology, Univ. of Calif., Berkeley 1975–79, Assoc. Prof. 1979–83, Prof. 1983–89, also Asst Research Virologist Cancer Research Lab. 1975–79, Assoc. Research Virologist 1979–83, Research Virologist 1983–, Prof. Dept of Molecular and Cell Biology 1989–, Richard and Rhoda Goldman Prof. of Cell and Developmental Biology 2002, now Judy C. Webb Prof. of Cell and Developmental Biology, also Head, Div. of Cell and Developmental Biology 1999–2004; John Simon Guggenheim Memorial Foundation Fellowship 1991–92, American Cancer Soc. Scholar Award in Cancer Research 1991–92. *Publications:* articles in various learned journals including Nature, Science, Cell. *Leisure interests:* hiking, bicycling, reading. *Address:* Department of Molecular and Cell Biology, University of California, Berkeley, 16 Barker Hall #3204, Berkeley, CA 94720-3204, USA (office). *Telephone:* (510) 642-1508 (office). *Fax:* (510) 643-1729 (office). *E-mail:* gsm@berkeley.edu (office). *Website:* mcb.berkeley.edu/faculty/CDB/martins.html (office).

MARTIN, Sir George Henry, Kt, CBE; British music industry executive, producer and composer (retd); b. 3 Jan. 1926; s. of Henry Martin and Bertha Beatrice Martin; m. 1st Sheena Rose Chisholm 1948; one s. one d.; m. 2nd Judy Lockhart Smith 1966; one s. one d.; ed Bromley Co. School, Kent, Guildhall School of Music and Drama; Sub-Lt RNVR 1944–47; worked at BBC 1950; with EMI Records Ltd 1950–65, produced all records featuring The Beatles and numerous other artists; formed AIR Group of cos 1965, Chair. 1965–; built AIR Studios 1969; built AIR Studios, Montserrat 1979; completed new AIR Studios, Lyndhurst Hall, Hampstead 1992; co. merged with Chrysalis Group 1974, Dir 1978–; Chair. Heart of London Radio 1994–; scored the music for 15 films; Hon. Fellow Guildhall School of Music; Hon. mem. Royal Acad. of Music; Hon. DMus (Berklee Coll. of Music, Boston) 1989, MA (Salford) 1992; Grammy Awards 1964, 1967 (two), 1973, 1993, 1996; Ivor Novello Awards 1963, 1979. *Publications:* All You Need Is Ears 1979, Making Music 1983, Summer of Love 1994. *Leisure interests:* boats, sculpture, tennis, snooker. *Address:* George Martin Music, AIR Studios, Lyndhurst Hall, Lyndhurst Road, Hampstead, London, NW3 5NG, England (office). *Telephone:* (20) 7794-0660 (office). *Fax:* (20) 7916-2784 (office). *E-mail:* info@georgemartinmusic.com (office). *Website:* www.georgemartinmusic.com.

MARTIN, Harold; New Caledonian politician and head of state; *President;* b. 6 April 1954, Nouméa; Pres. Council on the Regulation and Establishment of Agricultural Prices 1991, 1993, 1994–95; Pres. Territorial Congress 1997–98, 2004–07; Pres. 2007–, also responsible for mining and taxes; Pres. L'Avenir Ensemble (Future Together Party) 2007–; Mayor of Païta. *Address:* Office of the President, 8 route des Artifices, BP M2, 98849 Nouméa Cédex (office); L'Avenir Ensemble, 19 blvd Extérieur, Faubourg Blanchot, Nouméa, New Caledonia. *Telephone:* 246565 (office); 870371 (AE) (office). *Fax:* 246580 (office); 870379 (AE) (office). *E-mail:* cellule.communication@gouv.nc (office). *Website:* www.gouv.nc (office); www.avenirensemble.nc (office).

MARTIN, James Grubbs, PhD; American healthcare industry executive and fmr politician; *Corporate Vice-President, Carolinas HealthCare System;* b. 11 Dec. 1935, Savannah, Ga; s. of Arthur M. and Mary J. (Grubbs) Martin; m. Dorothy A. McAulay 1957; two s. one d.; ed Davidson (NC) Coll. and Princeton Univ.; Assoc. Prof. of Chem., Davidson Coll. 1960–72; mem. 93rd–98th Congresses from NC; Gov. of North Carolina 1985–93; Corp. Vice-Pres.

Carolinas HealthCare System 1995–; mem. Bd of Dirs Duke Energy Co. 1994, Palomar Medical Technologies, Inc., aaiPharma Inc., Family Dollar Stores, Inc. 1997–; fmr mem. Bd of Dirs James G. Cannon Medical Research Center, J. A. Jones Construction 1993; mem. Bd of Visitors, McColl Graduate School of Business, Queens Univ. of Charlotte; Trustee Davidson Coll. 1998–; Dr hc Queens Univ. of Charlotte 1997; ACS Charles Lathrop Parsons Award 1983. *Leisure interests:* golf, sailing, music. *Address:* c/o Carolinas Healthcare System, PO Box 32861, Charlotte, NC 28232-2861, USA (office). *Telephone:* (704) 355-5314 (office). *Fax:* (704) 355-0300 (office). *E-mail:* jgmartin@carolinas.org (office). *Website:* www.carolinashealthcare.org (office).

MARTIN, Kevin J., BA, MA, JD; American government official; *Chairman, Federal Communications Commission;* b. Charlotte, NC; m. Catherine Jurgensmeyer Martin; two s.; ed Univ. of NC, Duke Univ., Harvard Law School; fmr law clerk for US Court Dist Judge William M. Hoeveler; fmrly with Wiley, Rein & Fielding; later with US Office of the Ind. Counsel; Legal Advisor to Fed. Communications Comm. (FCC) Commr 1997–99; Deputy Gen. Counsel to Bush campaign, Austin, Tex. 1999–2000; fmr Prin. Tech. and Telecommunications Advisor, Bush-Cheney Transition team, later Special Asst to the Pres. for Econ. Policy; fmr mem. staff Nat. Econ. Council; Commr FCC 2001–, Chair. 2005–; Chair. Fed.-State Jt Bd on Separations, Fed.-State Jt Conf. on Advanced Telecommunications Services, mem. Fed.-State Jt Bd on Universal Service. *Address:* Federal Communications Commission, 445 12th Street, SW, Washington, DC 20554, USA (office). *Telephone:* (202) 418-1000 (office). *Fax:* (202) 418-2801 (office). *E-mail:* Kevin.Martin@fcc.gov (office). *Website:* www.fcc.gov/commissioners/martin (office).

MARTIN, Sir Laurence Woodward, Kt, MA, PhD, DL; British academic; *Professor Emeritus, University of Newcastle upon Tyne;* b. 30 July 1928, St Austell, Cornwall; s. of Leonard Martin and Florence Mary Woodward; m. Betty Parnall 1951; one s. one d.; ed St Austell Grammar School, Christ's Coll., Cambridge, Yale Univ.; RAF Flying Officer 1948–51; Asst Prof. MIT 1956–61; Assoc. Prof. Johns Hopkins Univ. 1961–64; Prof. Univ. of Wales 1964–68, King's Coll. London 1968–78; Vice-Chancellor Univ. of Newcastle 1978–90, Emer. Prof. 1991–; Arleigh Burke Chair in Strategy, Center for Strategic and Int. Studies, Washington, DC 1998–2000; Visiting Prof. Univ. of Wales 1985–90; Dir Royal Inst. of Int. Affairs 1991–96; Fellow, King's Coll., London; Lees Knowles Lecturer, Cambridge; Reith Lecturer BBC; Hon. DCL (Newcastle) 1991. *Radio:* Reith Lectures 1981. *Publications:* Peace Without Victory 1958, The Sea in Modern Strategy 1967, Arms and Strategy 1973, The Two Edged Sword 1982, The Changing Face of Nuclear War 1987, British Foreign Policy (jtly) 1997. *Leisure interests:* travel, walking, fishing. *Address:* 35 Witley Court, Coram Street, London, WC1N 1HP, England (home). *E-mail:* lmartin@csis.org (office).

MARTIN, Lynn; American academic, consultant and fmr politician; *Chair, Deloitte & Touche Council on the Advancement of Women;* b. 26 Dec. 1939, Chicago, Ill.; m. Harry Leinenweber; two d.; ed Univ. of Illinois; mem. Winnebago Co. Bd 1972–76; mem. Ill. House of Reps 1977–79, Senate 1979–81; mem. House of Reps 1981–91; Sec. of Labor 1991–93; Vice-Chair. House Repub. Conf. 1982–86; Co-Chair. Bi-partisan Ethics Task Force; mem. House Rules Cttee, House Budget Cttee, Cttee on Public Works and Transportation, Cttee on DC; fmr Prof., Harvard Univ. and J.L. Kellogg Graduate School of Man., Northwestern Univ.; currently Chair. Deloitte & Touche Council on Advancement of Women; Chair. The Future of the Health Care Labor Force in a Graying Society (Univ. of Illinois task force); mem. Bd of Dirs Proctor & Gamble Co., Constellation Energy Group Inc., Dreyfus Funds, Ryder System Inc., SBC Communications Inc.; mem. Int. Advisory Council, Coco-Cola Co.; International ATHENA Award 2002. *Address:* c/o Deloitte Touche Tohmatsu, 111 South Wacker Drive, Chicago, IL 60606-4301, USA. *Website:* www.deloitte.com (office).

MARTIN, Rt Hon. Michael John; British politician; *Speaker, House of Commons;* b. 3 July 1945, Glasgow, Scotland; s. of Michael Martin and Mary Martin; m. Mary McLay 1966; one s. one d.; ed St Patrick's Boys' School, Glasgow; fmr sheet metal worker; AUEW Shop Steward, Rolls Royce, Hillington 1970–74, TU Organizer 1976–79; Councillor for Fairfield Ward, Glasgow Corpn 1973–74, for Balornock Ward, Glasgow Dist Council 1974–79; MP for Glasgow, Springburn 1979–2005, Glasgow North East 2005–; Parl. Pvt. Sec. to Rt Hon Denis Healey 1981–83; mem. Select Cttee for Trade and Industry 1983–86; Chair. Scottish Grand Cttee 1987–97; mem. Speaker's Panel of Chair. 1987–2000; Dep. Speaker of House of Commons 1997–2000, Speaker 2000–; mem. Coll. of Piping 1989–; Dr hc (Glasgow Univ.) 2003, Hon. Fellow of the Chartered Inst. of Bankers in Scotland 2003. *Leisure interests:* hill walking, local history, piping. *Address:* House of Commons, London, SW1A 0AA, England (office). *Telephone:* (20) 7219-3000 (office).

MARTIN, Micheál, MA; Irish politician; *Minister of Foreign Affairs;* b. 16 Aug. 1960, Cork; s. of Paddy Martin; m. Mary O'Shea; one s.; ed Colaiste Chríost Rí, Univ. Coll., Cork; fmr secondary school teacher; elected to Cork Corpn 1985, Alderman 1991; fmr Chair. Arts Cttee; Lord Mayor of Cork 1992–93; mem. Dáil Éireann 1989–; fmr Chair. Oireachtas All Party Cttee on the Irish Language; fmr mem. Dail Cttee on Crime, Dail Cttee on Finance and Gen. Affairs; Minister for Educ. 1997–2000, for Health and Children 2000, for Enterprise, Trade and Employment –2008, of Foreign Affairs 2008–; Nat. Chair. Fianna Fail Nat. Exec. 1988–; Nat. Chair. Ogra Fianna Fail; mem. Bd Cork Opera House, Graffiti Theatre Co., Nat. Sculpture Factory, Everyman Palace Theatre, Crawford Gallery, College of Commerce and several school bds; fmr mem. Governing Body Univ. Coll., Cork; won Cork Examiner Political Speaker of the Year Award 1987. *Address:* Department of Foreign Affairs, 80 St Stephen's Green, Dublin 2, Ireland (office). *Telephone:* (1) 4780822 (office). *Fax:* (1) 4781484 (office). *E-mail:* minister@dfa.ie (office). *Website:* www.dfa.ie (office).

MARTIN, Rt Hon Paul, PC, BA, LLB; Canadian politician; b. 1938, Windsor, Ont.; s. of the late Paul Martin and Eleanor Martin; m. Sheila Ann Cowan 1965; three s.; ed Univs of Ottawa and Toronto; worked in legal branch of ECSC; called to Bar, Ont. 1966; with Power Corpn of Canada, Montreal; Chair. and CEO Canada Steamship Lines; Dir of seven major Canadian cos; MP for LaSalle-Émard, Montreal 1988–; cand. for leadership of Liberal Party 1990, Leader 2003–06; Co-Chair. Nat. Platform Cttee, Liberal Party of Canada 1993; Minister of Finance 1993–2002, also Minister Responsible for Fed. Office of Regional Devt 1993–95; Prime Minister of Canada 2003–06; Chair. G-20 (int. group) 1999–2002. *Publications:* Creating Opportunity: The Liberal Plan for Canada (jtly), Making History: The Politics of Achievement, Hell or High Water: My Life In and Out of Politics (auto-biog.) 2008. *Address:* Room 418-N Centre Block, House of Commons, Ottawa, ON K1H 7R3, Canada (office). *Telephone:* (613) 992-4284 (office). *Fax:* (613) 992-4291 (office). *E-mail:* martip@parl.gc.ca (office). *Website:* www.paulmartin.ca.

MARTIN, Ricky; Puerto Rican singer and actor; b. (Enrique Martin Morales), 24 Dec. 1971, San José, PR; two s.; mem. Latin pop band, Menudo 1984–89; solo artist 1989–; worked as actor and singer in Mexico; f. Ricky Martin Foundation 2000; American Music Award for Favorite Latin Artist 2000, Int. Humanitarian Award 2005. *Television:* Alcanzar una Estrella II (Mexican soap opera), played Miguel in General Hospital (US series). *Theatre:* Marius in Les Misérables (Broadway). *Film:* Hercules (voice in Spanish-language version). *Recordings include:* albums: Ricky Martin 1991, Me Amarás 1993, A Medio Vivir 1995, Vuelve (Grammy Award for Best Latin Pop Album) 1998, Ricky Martin 1999, Sound Loaded 2000, La Historia 2001, Almas de Silencio 2003, Life 2005, MTV Unplugged (Latin Grammy Awards for Best Male Pop Vocal Album and Best Long Form Music Video 2007) 2006. *Address:* Columbia Records, Sony BMG Music Entertainment, 550 Madison Avenue, New York, NY 10022-3211, USA (office). *Telephone:* (212) 833-7100 (office). *Fax:* (212) 833-7416 (office). *Website:* www.sonybmg.com (office); www.rickymartin.com; www.rickymartinfoundation.org.

MARTIN, Steve; American actor, comedian and writer; b. 14 Aug. 1945, Waco, Tex.; s. of Glenn Martin and Mary Lee Martin; m. 1st Victoria Tennant 1986 (divorced 1994); m. 2nd Anne Stringfield 2007; ed Long Beach State Coll., UCLA; TV writer for several shows; nightclub comedian; TV special Steve Martin: A Wild and Crazy Guy 1978; Georgie Award, American Guild of Variety Artists 1977, 1978, American Cinematheque Career Achievement Honour 2004, John F. Kennedy Center for Performing Arts Mark Twain Prize for American Humor 2005, Kennedy Center Honor 2007. *Recordings:* Let's Get Small 1977 (Grammy Award), A Wild and Crazy Guy 1978 (Grammy Award), Comedy is Not Pretty 1979, The Steve Martin Bros. *Films include:* The Absent Minded Waiter 1977, Sgt Pepper's Lonely Hearts Club Band 1978, The Muppet Movie 1979, The Jerk 1979 (also screenwriter), Pennies from Heaven 1981, Dead Men Don't Wear Plaid (also writer) 1982, The Man With Two Brains (also writer) 1983, The Lonely Guy 1984, All of Me 1984 (Nat. Soc. of Film Critics Actor's Award), Three Amigos (also writer and exec. producer) 1986, Little Shop of Horrors 1986, Roxanne (also screenwriter and exec. producer) 1987, Planes, Trains and Automobiles 1987, Dirty Rotten Scoundrels 1988, Parenthood 1989, My Blue Heaven 1990, LA Story (also writer and exec. producer) 1991, Grand Canyon 1991, Father of the Bride 1991, Housesitter 1992, Leap of Faith 1992, A Simple Twist of Fate (also writer and exec. producer) 1994, Mixed Nuts 1994, Father of the Bride 2 1995, Sgt Bilko 1996, The Spanish Prisoner 1997, The Out of Towners 1999, Bowfinger (also writer) 1999, Joe Gould's Secret 2000, Novocaine 2001, Bringing Down the House 2003, Looney Tunes: Back in Action 2003, Cheaper by the Dozen 2003, Jiminy Glick in La La Wood 2004, Shopgirl (also screenplay and producer) 2005, Cheaper by the Dozen 2 2005, Pink Panther (also screenplay) 2006. *Recording:* The Crow: New Songs for the Five-String Banjo 2009. *Publication:* The Pleasure of My Company 2003, Born Standing Up (autobiog.) 2007. *Address:* c/o Michelle Bega, Rogers & Cowan, 1888 Century Park East, Suite 500, Los Angeles, CA 90067 (office); ICM, 8942 Wilshire Boulevard, Beverly Hills, CA 90211, USA.

MARTIN, Todd Christopher; American fmr professional tennis player; b. 8 July 1970, Hinsdale, Ill.; s. of Dale Martin and Lynn Martin; m. Amy Martin; one s.; ed Northwestern Univ.; winner, New Haven Challenger 1989; turned professional 1990; semi-finalist Stella Artois Grass Court Championships, London 1993, Champion 1994, Champion (doubles with Pete Sampras q.v.) 1995; finalist, Australian Open 1994, Grand Slam Cup, Munich 1995; semi-finalist, US Open 1994, Wimbledon 1994, 1996, Paris Open 1998; Champion, Scania Stockholm Open 1998; winner of 13 pro titles; mem. US Davis Cup Team 1994–99; Pres. ATP Players' Council 1995–97, 1998–99; est. Todd Martin Devt Fund, Lansing, Mich. 1994; Special Adviser, USA Tennis High Performance Program 2003–; announced retirement 2004; contrib. ESPN; mem. Bd of Dirs Tim and Tom Gullickson Foundation; currently coaching Mardy Fish; Adidas/ATP Tour Sportsmanship Award 1993, 1994, ATP Tour Most Improved Player 1993. *Address:* POB 4165, Vero Beach, FL 32963; c/o Todd Martin Development Fund, Court One North, 1609 Lake Lansing Road, Lansing, MI 48912, USA.

MARTIN, Valerie; American writer; b. 1948, Missouri. *Publications:* Love: Short Stories 1976, Set in Motion (novel) 1978, Alexandra (novel) 1980, A Recent Martyr (novel) 1987, The Consolation of Nature and Other Stories 1988, Mary Reilly (novel) 1990, The Great Divorce (novel) 1994, Italian Fever (novel) 1999, Salvation: Scenes from the Life of St Francis (biog.) 2001, Property (novel) (Orange Prize for Fiction) 2003, The Unfinished Novel and Other Stories 2006, Trespass 2007. *Address:* c/o Alfred A. Knopf, 299 Park Avenue, Fourth Floor, New York, NY 10171, USA (office).

MARTÍN DELGADO, José María, DenD; Spanish university rector; b. 26 June 1947, Málaga; s. of Rafael Martín Delgado and María Jesús Martín

Delgado; m. Irene Martín Delgado 1973; one s. two d.; ed Univs of Granada and Bologna; Prof. of Fiscal and Tax Law, Univ. of Granada, Univ. Autónoma de Madrid, Univ. Autónoma de Barcelona, Univ. La Laguna and Univ. of Málaga (fmr Dean Faculty of Law) 1969–; Rector Univ. of Málaga 1984–94; Minister of Culture, Junta de Andalucía 1994–96; Rector Universidad Internacional de Andalucía 1996–; mem. Spanish Asscn of Fiscal Law, Int. Fiscal Asscn; Dr hc (Dickinson Coll., Pa). *Publications:* Análisis Jurídico del Fondo de Previsiones para Inversiones, Ordenamiento Tributario Español 1977, Sistema Democrático y Derecho Tributario. *Leisure interests:* reading, music, fishing, tennis. *Address:* Universidad Internacional de Andalucía, Monasterio de Santa María de las Cuevas, Américo Vespucio nº2, Isla de la Cartuja, 41092 Seville (office). *Telephone:* (95) 446-2299 (office). *Fax:* (95) 446-2288 (office). *E-mail:* unia@uia.es (office). *Website:* www.unia.es (office).

MARTÍN FERNÁNDEZ, Miguel; Spanish banker; *Head of Internal Audit Office, Banco de España;* b. 9 Nov. 1943, Jerez de la Frontera; m. Anne Catherine Cleary 1972; one s. two d.; ed Univ. Complutense, Madrid; Head Budget and Finance Sections, Ministry of Finance 1969–72, Deputy Dir 1972–76; Economist, World Bank, Latin American Region 1976–77, Alt. Exec. Dir for Spain, Italy and Portugal, World Bank 1977–78; Dir-Gen. Treasury, Ministry of Finance 1978–79; Under-Sec. for Budget and Public Expenditure 1979–81; Pres. Inst. for Official Credit 1982; Head Annual Accounts Centre, Banco de España 1983–84; Under-Sec. Economy and Finance 1984–86; Dir-Gen. Banco de España 1986–92, Deputy Gov. 1992–2000, Head Internal Audit Office 2000–; Gran Placa de la Orden del Mérito Postal, Encomienda del Mérito Agrícola. *Address:* Banco de España, Calle Alcalá 50, 28014 Madrid, Spain (office).

MARTIN-LÖF, Per Erik Rutger, PhD; Swedish mathematician, philosopher and academic; *Professor of Logic, Department of Mathematics, Stockholm University;* b. 8 May 1942, Stockholm; s. of Sverker Emil Bernhard Martin-Löf and Gertrud Cecilia Benedicks; m. Kerstin Maria Birgitta Forsell; one s. two d.; ed Stockholm Univ.; Asst, Math. Statistics, Stockholm Univ. 1961–64, Doctoral Scholar, Faculty of Science 1965–66, 1967–68, Docent, Math. Statistics 1969–70, Prof. of Logic 1994–; State Scholar of Swedish Inst., Moscow Univ. 1964–65; Amanuensis, Math. Inst., Århus Univ., Denmark 1966–67; Asst Prof., Dept of Math., Univ. of Ill., Chicago, USA 1968–69; Researcher in Math. Logic, Swedish Natural Science Research Council 1970–81, in Logic 1981–83, Prof. of Logic 1983–94; mem. Academia Europaea, Royal Swedish Acad. of Sciences; Dr hc (Leiden) 2004, (Marseilles) 2004. *Publications:* Notes on Constructive Mathematics 1970, Intuitionistic Type Theory 1984. *Leisure interest:* ornithology. *Address:* Department of Mathematics, Stockholm University, 106 91 Stockholm (office); Barnhusgatan 4, 111 23 Stockholm, Sweden (home). *Telephone:* (8) 16-45-32 (office); (8) 20-05-83 (home). *Fax:* (8) 612-67-17 (office). *E-mail:* pml@math.su.se (office). *Website:* www.matematik.su.se (office).

MARTIN-LÖF, Sverker, MSc (Eng), DTech; Swedish construction industry executive; *Chairman, Skanska AB;* b. 1943, Stockholm; ed Royal Inst. of Tech., Stockholm; worked at Swedish Pulp and Paper Research Inst.; fmr Pres. MoDo Chemetics; fmr Tech. Dir Mo och Domsjö AB; fmr Pres. Sunds Defibrator AB; Pres. Svenska Cellulosa Aktiebolaget SCA 1988–2002, Chair. 2002–; Chair. Skanska AB 2001–; Vice-Chair. AB Industrivärden, Telefonaktiebolaget LM Ericsson, Svenskt Näringsliv; Chair. SSAB Svenskt Stål AB; mem. Bd of Dirs LM Ericsson, Confed. of Swedish Enterprise, Boliden 2002–, Svenska Handelsbanken AB; Hon. PhD (Mid-Sweden Univ., Sundsvall). *Address:* Skanska AB, Klarabergsviadukten 90, 111 91 Stockholm, Sweden (office). *Telephone:* (8) 753-88-00 (office). *Fax:* (8) 755-12-56 (office). *E-mail:* info@skanska.com (office). *Website:* www.skanska.com (office).

MARTIN MATEO, Ramón; Spanish professor of administrative law; b. 31 Aug. 1928, Valladolid; s. of Andrés Martín Mateo and Julia Martín Mateo; m. Clara Abad Lobejón 1966; four c.; Prof. of Admin. Law, Univs of País Vasco, Madrid, Valladolid and Alicante; Rector Univ. of Alicante 1986; Order Mérito Civil; Order of Andrés Bello (Venezuela). *Publications:* D°- Administrativo Económico 1974, Manual de Derecho Administrativo, Bioética y Derecho 1987, Liberalización de la Economía: Más Estado, menos Administración, La eficacia social de la jurisdicción contencioso-administrativa 1989, Tratado de Derecho Ambiental (3 vols) 1991–97. *Leisure interests:* mountaineering, music. *Address:* c/o Universidad de Alicante, Carretera de S. Vicente del Raspeig, 03690 Alicante, Spain. *E-mail:* Ramon.Martin@ua.es (office).

MARTÍN VILLA, Rodolfo; Spanish politician and business executive; b. 3 Oct. 1934, Santa María del Páramo, León; m. María Pilar Pena Medina; two c.; ed Escuela Superior de Ingenieros Industriales, Madrid; Leader of Madrid Section, Sindicato Español Universitario, Nat. Leader 1962–64; Sec.-Gen. Syndical Org. 1969–74; mem. Council of the Realm; Nat. Econ. Adviser, Nat. Inst. of Industry; Nat. Econ. Adviser, Banco de Crédito Industrial, later Pres.; Civil Gov. of Barcelona and Prov. Head of Falangist Movement 1974–75; Minister for Relations with Trade Unions 1975–76, of the Interior 1976–79, of Territorial Admin. 1980–82; mem. Parl. (for Unión de Centro Democrático) 1977–83; First Deputy Prime Minister 1981–82; mem. Parl. (for Partido Popular) 1989–; mem. Exec. Cttee, Partido Popular 1989–; Chair. Endesa (Co.) 2000–02; mem. Sr Corps of Inspectors of State Finance; fmr mem. special group of industrial engineers assisting Treasury. *Address:* Partido Popular (PP), Génova 13, 28004 Madrid, Spain. *Telephone:* (91) 5577300. *Fax:* (91) 3085587.

MARTINA, Dominico (Don) F.; Netherlands Antilles politician; *Leader, Movimentu Antiyas Nobo;* fmr finance officer, Govt of Curaçao; head, Govt social affairs Dept; f. Movimentu Antiyas Nobo 1979, Leader 1979–; MP 1979–; Prime Minister of Netherlands Antilles 1979–84, 1985–88. *Address:* Movimentu Antiyas Nobo, Landhuis Morgenster, Willemstad, Curaçao, Netherlands Antilles. *Telephone:* (9) 468-4781.

MARTINEAU, Rt Hon. Paul, PC, QC; Canadian lawyer, judge and politician; b. 10 April 1921, Bryson, Québec; s. of Alphonse Martineau and Lucienne Lemieux; m. 1st Hélène Neclaw 1946 (died 2000); two d.; m. 2nd Jolanta Bak; legal practice at Campbells Bay, Québec 1950–, at Hull, Québec 1966–; fmr Crown Attorney for District of Pontiac, Québec; MP 1958–65; Parl. Asst to Prime Minister 1959–61; Deputy Speaker of House of Commons 1961–62; Minister of Mines and Tech. Surveys 1962–63; mem. Royal Comm. on Admin. of Justice 1967–70; Puisne Judge Superior Court Prov. of Québec 1980–96; Progressive Conservative. *Leisure interests:* painting, travelling. *Address:* 1204 Mountain Road, Aylmer, PQ J9H 5E1, Canada (home). *Telephone:* (819) 827-2065 (home). *Fax:* (819) 827-9169.

MARTINELLI BERROCAL, Ricardo, MA, MBA; Panamanian business executive, politician and head of state; *President;* b. 11 March 1952, Panama City; s. of Ricardo Martinelli Pardini and Gloria Berrocal de Martinelli; m. Marta Linares de Martinelli; three c.; ed Staunton Mil. Acad., USA, Univ. of Arkansas, INCAE Business School, Costa Rica; Dir Social Security Fund 1994–96; Chair. Bd of Dirs Panama Canal Authority and Minister for Canal Affairs 1999–2003; Pres. Cambio Democrático Party 1998–; Pres. of Panama 2009; Chair. Importadora Ricamar SA, Supermercados 99; Chair. Bd of Dirs Central Azucarera La Victoria, Plastigol SA; Dir Gold Mills de Panamá, Global Bank, Panasal SA, Televisora Nacional de Panamá, Direct TV, Desarrollo Norte SA, Molino de Oro, AVIPAC, Calox Panameña. *Address:* Office of the President, Palacio Presidencial, Valija 50, Panamá 1; Cambio Democrático, Parque Lefevre, Plaza Carolina, arriba de la Juguetería del Super 99, Panamá, Panama (office). *Telephone:* 227-4062 (office); 217-2643 (office). *Fax:* 227-0076 (office); 217-2645 (office). *E-mail:* cambio.democratico@hotmail.com (office). *Website:* www.presidencia.gob.pa (office).

MARTINEZ, Arthur C., MBA; American business executive; *Chairman and CEO Emeritus, Sears, Roebuck & Co.;* b. 25 Sept. 1939, NY; s. of Arthur F. Martinez and Agnes (Caulfield) Martinez; m. Elizabeth Rusch 1966; two c.; ed Polytechnic Univ., Harvard Univ., joined Exxon Chemical Co. 1960; Int. Paper Co. 1967–69; Talley Industries 1969–70; exec. positions in int. finance, RCA Corpn New York 1970–80; Sr Vice-Pres. and Chief Financial Officer, Saks 1980–84, Exec. Vice-Pres. for Admin. 1984-87; Sr Vice-Pres. and Group Chief Exec. Retail Div. BATUS Inc. 1987–90; Chair. and CEO Sears Merchandise Group, Sears, Roebuck & Co. 1992–95; fmr Vice-Chair. and mem Bd of Dirs Saks Fifth Avenue, New York; Chair., CEO Sears, Roebuck & Co. 1995–2000, now Chair. and CEO Emer.; Chair. Supervisory Bd ABN AMRO Holding NV 2006–; mem. Bd of Dirs PepsiCo, Inc. 1999–, Int. Flavors & Fragrances Inc. 2000–, Liz Claiborne, Inc.; fmr Chair. Bd of Dirs Nat. Retail Fed.; fmr mem. Bd of Dirs Amoco Corpn, Ameritech Corpn, Fed. Reserve Bank of Chicago, Martha Stewart Omni Media Inc.; Trustee Chicago Symphony Orchestra. *Leisure interests:* gardening, golf, tennis. *Address:* c/o Sears, Roebuck & Company, 3333 Beverly Road, Hoffman Estates, IL 60179, USA.

MARTINEZ, Conchita; Spanish fmr professional tennis player; b. 16 April 1972, Monzón; d. of Cecilio Martínez and Conchita Martínez; turned professional 1988; reached last 16 French Open 1988, quarter-finals French Open 1989, 1990, 1991, 1992, 1993, semi-finals Italian Open 1991, French Open 1994, Australian, French and US Opens and Wimbledon 1995, French and US Opens 1996, quarter-finals Olympic Games 1992; with Arantxa Sanchez-Vicario (q.v.) won Olympic Doubles silver medal 1992 and bronze medal 1996; Wimbledon Singles Champion 1994 (first Spanish woman to win title); has won 43 WTA tour titles; Spanish Fed. Cup Team 1988–96, 1998, 2000–01; retd April 2006; currently commentator for Eurosport Spain, Canal+ and DirecTV in USA; Tournament Dir Andalucía Tennis Experience 2009–; WTA Tour Most Impressive Newcomer 1989, Most Improved Player, Tennis Magazine 1994, ITF Award of Excellence 2001, Int. Tennis Hall of Fame 2001. *Leisure interests:* golf, horse riding, music, soccer, cinema, beach volleyball, skiing. *Address:* Office of the Tournament Director, Andalucía Tennis Experience, Club de Tenis Puente Romano, Marbella, Málaga, Spain. *E-mail:* comunicacion@andaluciatennis.com. *Website:* www.andaluciatennis.com.

MARTINEZ, Mel; American politician and lawyer; *Senator from Florida;* b. 1947; m. Kitty Martinez; three c.; ed Florida State Univ. Coll. of Law; lawyer, Orlando 1973–98; Chair. Orange Co., Fla 1998–2001, providing urban services to residents; US Sec. of Housing and Urban Devt 2001–03; Senator from Florida 2005–; Chair. of Gov. Jeb Bush's Growth Man. Study Comm., of Bd Greater Orlando Aviation Authority, of Bd Orlando/Orange Co. Expressway Authority. *Address:* 317 Hart Senate Office Building, Washington, DC 20510, USA (office). *Telephone:* (202) 224-3041 (office). *Fax:* (202) 228-5171 (office). *Website:* martinez.senate.gov (office).

MARTÍNEZ, Tomás Eloy, MA; Argentine novelist, essayist, journalist and academic; *Professor and Director, Latin American Studies Program, Rutgers University;* b. 1934, Tucumán; ed Univ. of Tucumán, Univ. of Paris VII; film critic La Nación, Buenos Aires 1957–61; production chief Primera Plana, Buenos Aires 1962–69; European correspondent based in Paris, Abril 1969–70; Ed. Panorama 1970–72, cultural supplement of La Opinión 1972–75; Literary Ed. El Nacional, Caracas 1975–77, Consultant Ed. 1977–78; f. and production chief El Diario de Caracas 1979; co-f. Siglo 21, Guadalajara 1991; founder and Ed. literary supplement, Primer Plano for Página/12, Buenos Aires 1991–95; columnist La Nación, Buenos Aires 1996–, New York Times Syndicate 1996–; numerous conferences, courses in univs throughout Europe and America; Prof. Univ. of Maryland 1984–87; currently Distinguished Prof. and Dir of Latin American Studies programme Rutgers Univ., NJ; Fellow Woodrow Wilson Center for Int. Scholars, Washington, DC,

Guggenheim Foundation, Kellogg Inst., Univ. of Notre-Dame, IN; Dr hc (John F. Kennedy Univ., Buenos Aires), (Univ. of Tucumán); Premio Alfaguara de Novela 2002. *Screenplays include:* (with Augusto Roa Bastos) El último piso 1962, El terrorista 1962, El demonio en la sangre 1964, La Madre María 1974. *Publications:* Estructuras del cine argentino (essay) 1961, Sagrado (novel) 1969, La pasión según Trelew (non-fiction) 1974, Los testigos de afuera (essay) 1978, Lugar común la muerte (short stories) 1979, El retrato del artista enmascarado (essay) 1982, La novela de Perón 1985, La mano del amo 1991, Santa Evita 1995, Las memorias del General (novel) 1996, El suelo argentino (non-fiction) 1999, Ficciones verdaderas (short stories) 2000, El vuelo de la reina 2002, El cantor de Tango 2004; numerous essays. *Address:* Spanish and Portuguese Department, Rutgers University, 105 George Street, New Brunswick, NJ 08901, USA (office). *Telephone:* (732) 932-9412, ext. 27 (office). *E-mail:* eloy@rci.rutgers.edu. *Website:* span-port.rutgers.edu (office).

MARTINEZ, Victor Hipólito; Argentine politician, lawyer and law professor; b. 24 Nov. 1924, Córdoba; m. Fanny Munte; three s.; ed Univ. of Córdoba; Rep. to the Prov. Ass. of Córdoba 1967; Mayor of Córdoba 1963–66; Dir of newspaper Los Principios 1970–72; Vice-Pres. of Argentina 1983–89. *Address:* Senado de la Nación Argentina, Hipólito Yrigoyen 1849, C.P. 1089, Buenos Aires, Argentina.

MARTÍNEZ DE PERÓN, María Estela (Isabelita); Argentine politician and fmr dancer; b. 6 Feb. 1931, La Rioja Prov.; m. Gen. Juan Domingo Perón (Pres. of Argentina 1946–55, 1973–74) 1961 (died 1974); joined troupe of travelling folk dancers; danced in cabaret in several S American countries; met her future husband during his exile in Panama, lived in Spain 1960–73, returned to Argentina with Juan Perón, became Vice-Pres. of Argentina 1973–74, Pres. 1974–76 (deposed by mil. coup); Chair. Peronist Party 1974–85; detained under house arrest 1976–81; settled in Madrid, Spain 1985; arrested 2007 on Argentine warrent to testify about forced disappearances during her presidency, extradition denied by Spanish courts 2008.

MARTÍNEZ MARTÍNEZ, José Manuel; Spanish business executive; *Chairman and CEO, MAPFRE SA;* ed Madrid Univ.; graduated as public works engineer, economist and actuary; began career at MAPFRE in 1972, first assigned to newly created dept of eng and construction risk insurance, acquired his first man. experience as Chief Exec. of re-insurance subsidiary, co. merged into holding co. Corporación MAPFRE 1985, Chief Exec. MAPFRE's listed holding co., Chair. MAPFRE VIDA 1996–2001, Chair. and CEO MAPFRE SA 2001–, Chair. Fundación MAPFRE; mem. Bd of Dirs Consorcio Espafrol de Seguros, Consorcio de Compensacion de Seguros Fundación Carolina (Govt-sponsored foundation for Latin American scholarships); Hon. mem. Fundación Carlos III 2002, Alumni Asscn of ENAE Business School, Madrid 2006; Distingued Service Award, Int. Insurance Soc. 1995, Los Mejores de 1997, La Verdad newspaper, Murcia 1997, Award International Character 2001, Academia Nacional de Seguros e Previdencia (Brazil) 2001, Dirigentes Award, Dirigentes Magazine 2002, Management Award, Confederación Española de Directivos y Ejecutivos 2006, Insurance Hall of Fame Award, Int. Insurance Soc. 2007, Gold Medal, Latin American Commerce Chambers (AICO) 2007, Tiepolo Award, Italian Chamber in Spain and Chamber of Commerce of Madrid 2007. *Address:* MAPFRE SA, Carretera de Pozuelo-Majadahonda 52, 28220 Majadahonda, Madrid, Spain (office). *Telephone:* (91) 581-11-00 (office). *Fax:* (91) 581-11-34 (office). *E-mail:* info@mapfre.com (office). *Website:* www.mapfre.com (office).

MARTÍNEZ SISTACH, HE Cardinal Lluís, DCL; Spanish ecclesiastic; *Archbishop of Barcelona;* b. 29 April 1937, Barcelona; ed Pontifical Lateran Univ., Rome; ordained priest in Barcelona 1961; worked with Catholic Action and was notary on Barcelona's archdiocesan tribunal; elected pres. of Spain's asscn of canonists in 1983, and taught canon law for several years; Auxiliary Bishop of Barcelona and Titular Bishop of Aliezira 1987–91; Bishop of Tortosa 1991–97; Archbishop of Tarragona 1997–2004, of Barcelona 2004–; cr. Cardinal 2007; mem. Apostolic Signature (a Vatican court) and Pontifical Council for Legis. Texts. *Address:* Arzobispado, Carrer del Bisbe 5, 08002 Barcelona, Spain (office). *Telephone:* (93) 270-1012 (office). *Fax:* (93) 270-1303 (office). *E-mail:* web@palau.arqbcn.org (office). *Website:* www.arqbcn.org (office).

MARTÍNEZ SOMALO, HE Cardinal Eduardo; Spanish ecclesiastic; b. 31 March 1927, Baños de Río Tobía; ordained 1950; elected Bishop of Tagora 1975, consecrated 1975, then Archbishop; cr. Cardinal 1988; mem., fmr Prefect of the Congregation for Divine Worship and the Discipline of the Sacraments; Prefect of Congregation for Insts of Consecrated Life and for Socs of Apostolic Life 1992–; Chamberlain of the Holy Roman Soc.; mem. Pontifical Comm. for Latin America, Congregations for Evangelization of Peoples, for the Clergy, for Catholic Educ. *Address:* Palazzo delle Congregazioni, Piazza Pio XII 3, 00193 Rome, Italy.

MARTINI, HE Cardinal Carlo Maria, SJ; Italian ecclesiastic; *Archbishop Emeritus of Milan;* b. 15 Feb. 1927, Turin; ed Pontifical Gregorian Univ., Rome; ordained priest 1952; Chair of Textual Criticism, Pontifical Biblical Inst., Rector 1969; elected Pontifical Gregorian Univ. "rector magnificus"; Archbishop of Milan 1980–2002, Archbishop Emer. 2002–; Consultant to Sacred Congregations for the Bishops, Doctrine of Faith, Religions and Catholic Educ.; mem. Pontifical Council for Culture; cr. Cardinal-Priest of S. Cecilia 1983; Pres. CCEE (Consilium Conferentiarum Episcopalium Europae) 1987–93; participated in Papal Conclave 2005. *Publications include:* Belief or Non-Belief?: A Confrontation (with Umberto Eco) 2001. *Address:* c/o Palazzo Arcivescovile, Piazza Fontana 2, 20122 Milan, Italy. *Telephone:* (02) 85-561.

MARTINI-URDANETA, Alberto, Dr rer. pol, DScS; Venezuelan politician, lawyer and diplomatist; *Judge, Supreme Court;* b. 2 April 1930, Trujillo; m.; five c.; ed Cen. Univ. of Venezuela; clerk at Third Court of First Instance, Fed. Dist 1949–51, Sec. Labour Third Court of First Instance 1954–62; Substitute Judge, Labour Court of First Instance 1956, Judge 1957; Legal Counsellor to Ministry for Foreign Relations 1958; f. mem. (1956) and Sec.-Gen. Venezuelan Inst. of Social Legislation 1960–69; Pres. Venezuelan Industrial Bank 1971; Minister of Labour 1972–74; Dir-Gen. Venezuelan Inst. for Social Legis. 1978–79; Perm. Rep. to UN and other int. orgs, Geneva 1979–81, Perm. Rep. to UN, New York 1981–84; Supreme Court Judge 1999–; Chair. numerous int. cttees and orgs, including several ILO cttees and confs. *Publications:* Suspensión del Contrato de Trabajo, Regimenes Especiales de Trabajo, La Relación de Trabajo y El Hecho Social; numerous articles on labour and social matters. *Address:* c/o La Sede del Tribunal Supremo de Justicia, Avenida Brarlt, Caracas, Venezuela.

MARTINO, Antonio; Italian politician and university lecturer; b. 22 Dec. 1944, Messina, Sicily; s. of Gaetano Martino; Lecturer in Monetary History and Politics, Chair. Faculty of Political Science, mem. Bd of Dirs Libera Università Internazionale degli Studi Sociali (LUISS), Rome; fmr mem. Liberal Party (PLI); joined Forza Italia party 1994, Parl. Deputy 1994–; Minister for Foreign Affairs 1994–95, of Defence 2001–06. *Address:* Forza Italia, Via dell'Umiltà 36, 00187 Rome, Italy (office). *Telephone:* (06) 67311 (office). *Fax:* (06) 6788255 (office). *E-mail:* lettere@forza-italia.it (office). *Website:* www.forza-italia.it (office).

MARTINO, HE Cardinal Renato Raffaele, JCD; Italian ecclesiastic; *President, Pontifical Council for Justice and Peace and Pontifical Council for Migrants and Itinerant People;* b. 23 Nov. 1932, Salerno; ordained priest 1957; entered Diplomatic Service of the Holy See, serving in Nicaragua, the Philippines, Lebanon and Brazil 1962–80; Titular Archbishop of Segermes 1980; Apostolic Pro-Nuncio to Thailand and Singapore and Apostolic Del. to Laos and Malaysia 1980, Apostolic Del. to Brunei Darussalam 1983; Perm. Observer of the Holy See to the UN 1986–2002, participated in Conf. of Sustainable Devt, Rio de Janeiro, Brazil 1992, Conf. on Population Devt, Cairo, Egypt 1994, Summit on Women, Beijing, China 1995, Conf. on Sustainable Devt, Johannesburg, SA 2002; Pres. Pontifical Council for Justice and Peace 2002–; Pres. Pontifical Council for Migrants and Itinerant People 2006–; cr. Cardinal (Cardinal-Deacon of S. Francesco di Paola ai Monti) 2003; participated in papal conclave April 2005; decorations from govts of Italy, Portugal, Thailand, Argentina, Venezuela, Lebanon; eight hon. doctorates. *Address:* Pontifical Council for Justice and Peace, Piazza S. Calisto 16, 00153 Rome, Italy (office). *Telephone:* (06) 69879911 (office). *Fax:* (06) 69887205 (office). *E-mail:* pcjustpax@justpeace.va (office).

MARTINON, David, DEA; French civil servant; *Spokesman for the President;* b. 13 May 1971, Leiden, Netherlands; ed Institut d'études politiques, École nationale d'administration; began career as communications officer, États généraux de l'opposition 1990; communications adviser, Acte Public Communication 1991–94, Ministry of Defence 1995–98; Deputy Spokesman, Ministry of Foreign Affairs 1998–2001; Diplomatic Adviser to Minister of the Interior, Nicolas Sarkozy 2002–04, 2005–07; served as Dir of Int. Relations, Union pour un Mouvement Populaire (UMP); Chief of Staff, presidential campaign of Nicolas Sarkozy 2006–07; Spokesman for the Pres. 2007–. *Address:* Palais de l'Elysée, 55 rue du faubourg Saint-Honoré, 75008 Paris, France (office). *Telephone:* 1-42-92-81-00 (office). *E-mail:* dmartinon@u-m-p.org (office). *Website:* www.elysee.fr (office).

MARTINS, Peter; American ballet director, choreographer and former dancer; *Ballet Master-in-Chief, New York City Ballet;* b. 27 Oct. 1946, Copenhagen, Denmark; m. 1st Lise la Cour (divorced 1973); one c.; m. 2nd Darci Kistler (q.v.) 1991; one d.; pupil of Vera Volkova and Stanley Williams with Royal Danish Ballet; Dir NY City Ballet; Teacher, School of American Ballet 1975, NY Ballet 1975, Ballet Master 1981–83, Co-Ballet Master-in-Chief 1983–89, Ballet Master-in-Chief 1989–; Artistic Adviser, Pa Ballet 1982–; mem. Royal Danish Ballet 1965–67, Prin. Dancer (including Bournonville repertory) 1967; Guest Artist, NY Ballet 1967–70, Prin. Dancer 1970–83; Guest Artist Regional Ballet Cos, USA, also Nat. Ballet, Canada, Royal Ballet, London, Grand Theatre, Geneva, Paris Opera, Vienna State Opera, Munich State Opera, London Festival Ballet, Ballet Int., Royal Danish Ballet; Dance magazine Award 1977; Cue's Golden Apple Award 1977, Award of Merit, Phila Art Alliance 1985. *Choreographed Broadway musicals include:* Dream of the Twins (co-choreographer) 1982, On your Toes 1982, Song and Dance 1985. *Choreographed works include:* Calcium Light Night 1977, Tricolore (Pas de Basque Section) 1978, Rossini Pas de Deux 1978, Tango-Tango (ice ballet) 1978, Dido and Aeneas 1979, Sonate di Scarlatti 1979, Eight Easy Pieces 1980, Lille Suite 1980, Suite from L'Histoire du Soldat 1981, Capriccio Italien 1981, The Magic Flute 1981, Symphony No. 1 1981, Délibes Divertissement 1982, Piano-Rag-Music 1982, Concerto for Two Solo Pianos 1982, Waltzes 1983, Rossini Quartets 1983, Tango 1983, A Schubertiad 1984, Mozart Violin Concerto 1984, Poulenc Sonata 1985, La Sylphide 1985, Valse Triste 1985, Eight More 1985, We Are the World 1985, Eight Miniatures 1985, Ecstatic Orange, Tanzspiel 1988, Jazz 1993, Symphonic Dances 1994, Barber Violin Concerto 1994, Mozart Piano Concerto (No. 17) 1994, X-Ray 1995. *Publication:* Far From Denmark (autobiog.) 1982. *Address:* New York City Ballet, New York State Theater, 20 Lincoln Center Plaza, New York, NY 10023, USA. *Telephone:* (212) 870-5567. *Website:* www.nycballet.com.

MARTINSON, Ida Marie, PhD; American nurse; *Professor Emerita, School of Nursing, University of California, San Francisco;* b. 8 Nov. 1936, Mentor, Minn.; m. Paul Martinson 1962; one s. one d.; ed St Luke's Hosp. School of Nursing, Duluth, Minn. and Univs of Minnesota and Illinois; Instructor in Tuberculosis Nursing, St Luke's Hosp., Duluth 1957–58; Instructor in Nursing, Thornton Jr Coll., Harvey, Ill. 1967–69; Asst Prof. and Chair. of Research, Univ. of Minn. School of Nursing 1972–74, Assoc. Prof. and Dir of Research 1974–77, Prof. and Dir of Research 1977–82; Prof. Dept of Family

Health Care Nursing, Univ. of Calif., San Francisco 1982–2003, now Prof. Emer., Chair. 1982–89; Carl Walter and Margaret Davis Walter Visiting Prof. at Payne Bolton School of Nursing, Case Western Reserve Univ., Cleveland, Ohio 1994–96; Chair. and Prof., Dept of Health Sciences, Hong Kong Polytechnic Univ. 1996–2000, now Advisor, Hong Kong Polytechnic Univ. Honor Soc. of Nursing; Fellow, American Acad. of Nursing; mem. Inst. of Medicine, NAS 1981–, mem. Governing Council 1984–86; Pres. Children's Hospice Int. 1986–88; Co-founder of Children's Cancer Foundation, Taiwan; f. East Asia Forum of Nursing Schools (EAFONS); Sigma Theta Tau Int. Soc. of Nursing 1999. *Publications:* Home Care: A manual for implementation of home care for children dying of cancer 1978, Home Care: A manual for parents (with D. Moldow) 1979, Family Nursing 1989, Home Care Health Nursing 1989; more than 100 articles in journals, 56 book chapters (1994) and one film; ed. of several books on home and family nursing. *Leisure interests:* skiing, walking, reading. *Address:* Department of Family Health Care Nursing, Box 0606, 521 Parnassus Ave, Nursing 431Y, University of California, San Francisco, San Francisco CA 94143-0606, USA (office). *Telephone:* (415) 476-4668 (office). *Fax:* (415) 753-2161 (office). *E-mail:* ida.martinson@nursing.ucsf.edu (office). *Website:* nurseweb.ucsf.edu/www/ix-fd.shtml (office).

MARTIROSSIAN, Radick Martirosovich, PhD; Armenian scientist; b. 1 May 1936, Madagis, Nagorno Karabakh; s. of Martiros A. Martirossian and Astkhik G. Harutunian; m. Rena A. Kasparova 1965, two s.; ed Yerevan State Univ. and Lebedev Physics Inst. of Acad. of Sciences, Moscow; Dir Inst. of Radiophysics and Electronics, Nat. Acad. of Sciences of Armenia 1980–; Rector, Yerevan State Univ. Oct. 1993–; mem. Armenian Acad. of Sciences, 'Intercosmos' and 'Radioastronomy' scientific councils; research areas: microwave quantum amplifiers, remote sensing, microwave telecommunications, radioastronomy; Armenian State Prize in Science and Eng 1988, Ukrainian State Prize 1989; Gagarin Medal for Space Research. *Leisure interest:* chess. *Address:* Yerevan State University, 1 Alex Manoogian Street, 375049 Yerevan, Armenia. *Telephone:* (10) 55-46-29. *Fax:* (10) 15-10-87.

MARTO, Michel, MA, PhD; Jordanian economist and politician; b. 21 Aug. 1940, Jerusalem; s. of Issa Marto; m. Lucy Peridakis 1970; one s. two d.; ed Middle East Tech. Univ., Ankara, Univ. of Southern Calif., LA; Dir Econ. Research, Central Bank of Jordan 1969–70, Deputy Gov. 1989–97; Dir Econ. Research, Royal Scientific Soc. 1970–75; economist, World Bank, Washington DC 1975–77; Deputy Gen. Man. Jordan Fertilizer Industry 1977–79; Deputy Gen. Man. Bank of Jordan 1979–86, Man. Dir 1986–89; Chair. Jordanian Securities Comm. 1997–98; Minister of Finance 1998–2003; Chevalier, Ordre du mérite national, France; Commdr Légion d'honneur; Al-Hussein Distinguished Service Medal, Jordanian Star Medal (1st Class), Jordanian Independence Medal (1st Class), Omicron Delta Epsilon (Honor Soc. in Econs), USA, Phi Kappa Phi (Top Univ. Grad.), USA. *Publications:* various articles on economic topics in specialist journals. *Leisure interests:* reading, music, theatre. *Address:* c/o Ministry of Finance, PO Box 85, Amman 11118 (office); PO Box 2927, Amman 11181, Jordan. *Telephone:* (6) 5926745 (home). *Fax:* (6) 5930718 (home). *E-mail:* michelmarto@hotmail.com.

MARTONYI, János, PhD; Hungarian politician and lawyer; b. 5 April 1944, Kolozsvár (now Cluj-Napoca, Romania); m.; one s. one d.; ed József Attila Univ., Szeged, City of London Coll., Hague Acad. of Int. Law, Hungarian Acad. of Sciences; Trade Sec., Brussels 1979–84; Head of Dept, Ministry of Foreign Trade 1984–89; Commr for Privatization 1989–90; State Sec. Ministry of Int. Econ. Relations 1990–91, Ministry of Foreign Affairs 1991–94, Minister of Foreign Affairs 1998–2004; Prof., Loránd Eötvös Univ., Budapest 1990; Head Inst. of Private Int. Law, József Attila Univ., Szeged 1997; Visiting Prof., Colls of Europe, Bruges, Belgium and Natolin, Poland; Man. Partner, Martonyi és Kajtár, Baker and McKenzie (law firm), Budapest office 1994–98; mem. Budapest Chamber of Attorneys, Hungarian Lawyers' Soc.; Commdr Légion d'honneur, Grosses Goldenes Ehrenzeichen (Austria) 2000. *Publications:* numerous papers in various languages. *Address:* Martonyi es Kajtar Baker & McKenzie Attorneys at Law, Andrássy út 102, 1062 Budapest, Hungary (office). *Telephone:* (1) 302-3330 (office). *Fax:* (1) 302-3331 (office). *E-mail:* janos.martonyi@bakernet.com (office). *Website:* www.bakernet.com/BakerNet/Locations/Europe+Middle+East/Offices/Budapest/default.htm (office).

MARTRE, Henri Jean François; French telecommunications and space engineer; b. 6 Feb. 1928, Bélesta; s. of Marius Martre and Paule Maugard; m. Odette Coppier 1953; three d.; ed Ecole Polytechnique; telecommunications engineer 1952–59; Deputy Head of telecommunications service in the production of armaments 1961–64, Head of Bureau Département Electronique, then Head Industrial Bureau of the Cen. Service of Telecommunications to the Ministerial Del. for Armaments 1964–66, Deputy Dir Industrial Affairs 1966, Dir of Programmes and Industrial Aspects of Armaments 1971–74, Gen. Engineer First Class for Armaments 1974, Gen. Del. for Armaments 1977–83, State Admin. Société Nat. Industrielle Aérospatiale 1974–77, also SNECMA, Société Française d'Equipements pour la Navigation Aérienne; mem. Atomic Energy Cttee 1977–83; Pres. and Dir-Gen. Société Aérospatiale 1983–92; Vice-Pres. Surveillance Council for the Airbus Industry 1986–92; Pres. Club d'information et de reflexion sur l'économie mondiale (Cirem) 1987–98, Asscn européenne des constructeurs de matériel aérospatial 1988 (Hon. Pres. 1988), Groupement des industries françaises aéronautiques et spatiales (Gifas) 1990–93, France-Japan Cttee 1991–, Edifrance 1992–94, Asscn Française de Normalisation (AFNOR) 1993–2002, Supervisory Bd ESL Network 1996–; Vice-Pres., Supervisory Bd KLM; mem. Bd of Dirs Siemens-France 1994–99, Renault 1996–, France Telecom 2003–; Vice-Pres. Conseil de Surveillance de Bertin & Cie 1996, Pres. 1997–99; mem. Conseil supérieur de l'aviation marchande 1998–; Trustee Sogepa-Advisory Council Banque de France; Grand-Croix Légion d'honneur, Commdr, Ordre nat. du Mérite, Médaille de l'Aéronautique, Grand Officer Order of Merit (Germany), Order of the Crown (Belgium), Order of the Pole Star (Sweden), Commdr Legion of Merit (USA), Commdr White Rose (Finland), Order of Mil. Merit (Brazil), Order of the Sacred Treasure (Japan). *Leisure interests:* skiing, sailing. *Address:* 13 rue du Clos Fenquières, 75015 Paris, France (home). *Telephone:* 1-45-33-77-06 (office); 1-45-33-08-82 (home). *Fax:* 1-45-33-77-06 (office). *E-mail:* henri.martre@noos.fr (office).

MARTY, Martin E., MDiv, PhD, STM; American academic and ecclesiastic; *Fairfax M. Cone Distinguished Service Professor Emeritus of the History of Modern Christianity, Divinity School, University of Chicago;* b. 5 Feb. 1928, West Point, Neb.; s. of Emil A. Marty and Anne Louise Wuerdemann Marty; m. 1st Elsa Schumacher 1952 (died 1981); seven c.; m. 2nd Harriet Lindemann 1982; ed Concordia Seminary, St Louis, Lutheran School of Theology, Chicago and Univ. of Chicago; Lutheran Minister 1952–63; Prof. of History of Modern Christianity Univ. of Chicago 1963–, Fairfax M. Cone Distinguished Service Prof. 1978–98, now Emer.; Assoc. Ed. The Christian Century 1956–85, Sr Ed. 1985–98; Sr Scholar in Residence, Park Ridge Center 1985, Pres. 1985–89; Pres. American Soc. of Church History 1971, American Catholic History Asscn 1981, American Acad. of Religion 1988; Dir Fundamentalism project American Acad. of Arts and Sciences 1988–, The Public Religion Project 1996–99; Fellow, AAAS, Soc. of American Historians; more than 70 hon. degrees; Nat. Book Award for Righteous Empire 1972, Nat. Medal Humanities 1997. *Publications:* many books and numerous articles on religious history, theology and cultural criticism. *Leisure interests:* good eating, baroque music, calligraphy. *Address:* 175 East Delaware #85081, Chicago, IL 60611, USA (home). *Telephone:* (312) 640-1558 (office). *E-mail:* memarty@aol.com (home). *Website:* www.illuminos.com (office).

MARTYNOV, Vladlen Arkadyevich, DEconSci; Russian economist; b. 14 Dec. 1929, Saratov; s. of Arkady Martynov and Evdokiya Martynova; m. Liya Romanova 1955; m.; one s.; ed Leningrad Univ.; mem. CPSU 1952–91; lecturer, Leningrad Eng Inst. 1955–57; Sr researcher, Head of Sector, Deputy Dir Inst. of World Economy and Int. Relations (IMEMO) 1957–89, Dir 1989–; Corresp. mem. USSR (now Russian) Acad. of Sciences 1987–94, mem. 1994–; mem. CPSU Cen. Cttee 1990–91; USSR State Prize 1977. *Publications:* articles on agriculture of industrially developed countries and capitalist economies. *Leisure interests:* classical music, swimming. *Address:* Institute of World Economy and International Relations (IMEMO), Profsoyuznaya Str. 23, GSP-7, 117859 Moscow, Russia. *Telephone:* (495) 120-43-32 (office); (495) 429-66-41 (home). *Fax:* (495) 310-7027 (office). *E-mail:* imemoran@glas.apc.org (office).

MARTYNOW, Syarhey M.; Belarusian politician and diplomatist; *Minister of Foreign Affairs;* b. 22 Feb. 1953; m.; two s.; ed Moscow State Inst. of Int. Econ. Relations, USSR; with Dept of Int. Econ. Orgs, Ministry of Foreign Affairs, USSR 1975–80, Asst to Minister of Foreign Affairs 1980–88, Deputy Head Dept of Int. Orgs 1988–91; Deputy Perm. Rep. of Repub. of Belarus to UN, New York, 1991–92; Chargé d'Affaires, Washington, DC, 1992–93; Amb. to USA 1993–97; First Deputy Minister of Foreign Affairs 1997–2001; Amb. to Belgium, Head of Mission to European Communities and Head of Mission to NATO 2001–03; Minister of Foreign Affairs 2003–; Vice-Chair. First Cttee (Int. Security and Disarmament) of UN Gen. Ass. 1988–97; fmr Vice-Pres. Amendment Conf. of the State Parties to the (1963) Treaty Banning Nuclear Tests in the Atmosphere in Outer Space and Under Water; three-times Chair. Nuclear Disarmament Group of UN Disarmament Comm., several-times Vice-Chair. and Rapporteur UN Disarmament Comm., Chair. 1998; Pres. Conf. on Disarmament, Geneva 2000; mem. UN Cttee on Econ., Cultural and Social Rights, Geneva 2001–; mem. Minsk Int. Educational Centre. *Address:* Ministry of Foreign Affairs, 220030 Minsk, vul. Lenina 19, Belarus (office). *Telephone:* (17) 227-29-22 (office). *Fax:* (17) 227-45-21 (office). *E-mail:* mail@mfabelar.gov.by (office). *Website:* www.mfa.gov.by (office).

MARUF, Taha Mohi ed-Din, LLB; Iraqi fmr politician; b. 1924, Sulaimaniyah; s. of Muhyiddin and Fatima Marouf; ed Coll. of Law, Univ. of Baghdad; worked as lawyer; joined Diplomatic Service 1949; Minister of State 1968–70; Minister of Works and Housing 1968; Amb. to Italy, concurrently non-resident Amb. to Malta and Albania 1970–74; Vice-Pres. of Iraq 1974–2003; mem. Higher Cttee of Nat. Progressive Front 1975–2003; Chair. African Affairs Bureau of Revolutionary Command Council 1976–2003; taken into custody by coalition forces May 2003.

MARURAI, Jim; Cook Islands politician; *Prime Minister, Minister of Education, Human Resources and Police, Head of State Telecommunications and Information Broadcasting;* m. Tuainekore Au Tamariki Marurai (died 2005); ed Tereora Coll., Rarotonga, Otago Univ., NZ; Minister of Educ. 1999–; Prime Minister, Minister of Educ., Human Resources and Police, Head of State Telecommunications and Information Broadcasting 2004–; mem. Democratic Party. *Address:* Office of the Prime Minister, Private Bag, Rarotonga, Cook Islands (office). *Telephone:* 29301 (office). *Fax:* 20856 (office). *E-mail:* jmarurai@oyster.net.ck (office); rosita@oyster.net.ck (office). *Website:* www.cook-islands.gov.ck (office).

MARUSIN, Yury Mikhailovich; Russian singer (tenor); b. 8 Dec. 1945, Kizel, Perm Region; ed Leningrad State Conservatory; soloist, Maly Opera and Ballet Theatre, Leningrad 1972–80; soloist, Mariinsky Theatre 1980–90; guest soloist, Wiener Staatsoper 1986–91; USSR State Prize 1985, Best Foreign Singer Diploma (Italy) 1982, People's Artist of USSR 1983. *Repertoire includes:* over 50 parts in operas. *Address:* IMC Artists Management Inc., 51 MacDougal Street, Suite 300, New York, NY 10012, USA. *Telephone:* (212) 560-2221 (office). *E-mail:* imcartist@onebox.com (office).

MARUSTE, Rait, PhD; Estonian judge; *Judge, European Court of Human Rights;* b. 27 Sept. 1953, Pärnu; s. of Albert Maruste and Mare Maruste; m.

Mare Maruste (née Nurk) 1976; one s. one d.; ed Pärnu Jaagupi Secondary School, Tartu Univ., University of Leningrad; Lecturer, Faculty of Law, Tartu Univ. 1977–85, Docent 1985–92, Head of Dept of Criminal Law and Procedure 1991; cand. for doctorate 1991–93; studies abroad at HEUNI, Finland, 1991, Åbo Akademi Univ., Finland 1991, Max Planck-Inst., Freiburg, Germany 1991, Univ. of Cambridge, UK 1992, Max Planck Inst., Heidelberg, Germany 1995, Centre For Advanced Studies, Oslo, Norway 2001; Chief Justice of Supreme Court 1992–98, Chair. (ex-officio) Constitutional Review Chamber 1998–; Judge (Section IV), European Court of Human Rights (ECHR) 1998–; Chair. and Founding mem. Estonian Academic Law Soc., Bd of Estonian Law Centre Foundation, 1995–1998; mem. Int. Soc. for the Reform of Criminal Law, Estonian Working Group for Accession to ECHR, Editorial Bd of law journal Juridica 1993–1998, Comm. of Europe Drafting Cttee on Status of Judges in Europe 1998, Int. Justice in the World Prize Jury 2001–; Order of the White Star (Second Class). *Publications include:* Human Rights and Principles of Fair Trial 1993, Constitution and Its Review (in Estonian) 1997; more than 100 articles in journals. *Leisure interests:* sailing, skiing. *Address:* European Court of Human Rights, Council of Europe, 67075 Strasbourg - Cedex, France (office); Pikk Str. 94, Apt. 27, 2400 Tartu, Estonia (home). *Telephone:* (3) 88-41-20-18 (office); (7) 436696 (home). *Fax:* (3) 88-41-27-30 (office). *Website:* www.echr.coe.int (office).

MARX, Anthony W., BA, MA, PhD; American political scientist, academic and university administrator; *President, Amherst College;* m. Karen Barkey; one s., one d.; ed Wesleyan, Yale, Princeton Univs; lived in Brazil and SA 1984–89, co-founder Khanya Coll.; fmr consultant to UNDP; Asst to Pres. of Univ. of Pa; Assoc. Prof. of Political Science, Columbia Univ., Co-Dir Center for Historical Social Studies, Faculty Dir Masters of Int. Affairs, Dir Undergraduate Studies and of Dept's Honors Program, co-founder Columbia Urban Educators Program 2001; Dir Mellon Foundation's Sawyer Seminar on Democracy and Inequality 2001–02; Pres. Amherst Coll. 2003–; fmr Fellow US Inst. of Peace, Nat. Humanities Center, Howard Foundation, Harry Frank Guggenheim Foundation; John Simon Guggenheim Fellow; American Political Science Asscn Ralph Bunche Award 1999, American Sociological Asscn Barrington Moore Award 2000. *Publications include:* Lessons of Struggle: South African Internal Opposition 1960–1990 1992, Making Race and Nation: A Comparison of the United States, South Africa and Brazil 1998, Faith in Nations: Exclusionary Origins in Nationalism 2002; numerous articles. *Address:* Amherst College, Amherst, MA 01002-5000, USA (office). *Telephone:* (413) 542-2000 (office). *E-mail:* marx@amherst.edu (office). *Website:* www.amherst.edu (office).

MARY, Sister Avelin, PhD, FIBR; Indian marine biologist; *Director, Sacred Heart Marine Research Centre;* b. 5 May 1942; d. of M. P. Raj and Annapooranam; ed Marathwada Univ., Aurangabad; Asst Prof. in Zoology 1977; postdoctoral position, New York Aquarium 1985; involved in bioactive marine natural products research 1986–; Reader in Zoology, St Mary's Coll, Tuticorin 1993–, Prin. 1997–; postdoctoral research at Osborne Labs of Marine Science, NY, USA; involved in research projects into biofouling (biological coating acquired on ships during years at sea) at Duke Univ. Marine Lab., USA, Univ. of Delaware, Fu Jen Univ., Taiwan, Tulane Univ., Univ. of Hawaii; has isolated 12 active compounds from Indian Ocean soft coral as non-toxic antifoulants; Dir of Research, Sacred Heart Marine Research Centre, Tuticorin, India 2000–; RC nun belonging to Congregation of Mother of Sorrows, Servants of Mary; Scientist of the Year, Nat. Environmental Science Acad. (NESA) 2002, Netaji Subhash Chandra Bose Nat. Award for Excellence, Jagruthi Kiran Foundation 2003. *Publications:* numerous scientific papers on marine biology. *Leisure interests:* reading, computer art design. *Address:* c/o Sacred Heart Marine Research Centre, St Mary's College Campus, Tuticorin, 628001, Tamil Nadu, India (office); c/o SHRC Poseidon Ocean Sciences, Inc., The Chanin Building, Suite 2805, 122 East 42nd Street, New York, NY 10168, USA (office). *Telephone:* (461) 2325400 (office). *E-mail:* info@poseidonsciences.com (office); avelinmary@yahoo.com (home). *Website:* www.poseidonsciences.com/shmrc.html (office).

MAS, Artur; Spanish politician; *Leader, Convergència i Unió;* ed Liceu Francès de Barcelona, L'Escola Aula, Faculties of Law and Econs, Univ. of Barcelona; joined Dept of Trade and Tourism, Generalitat, Barcelona 1982; est. Partnership for Commercial Promotion of Catalonia (COPCA); mem. list Convergència i Unió, Barcelona 1987, selected for municipal elections 1991, elected Deputy to Parl. of Catalonia 1995, Spokesperson for Generalitat 2000, Regional Minister 2001; Leader Convergència I Unió (CiU) Coalition 2000–; Pres. Convergència Democràtica de Catalunya (CDC) 1997–, Sec.-Gen. 2000–; Dir Investment Co., Catalan Industrial Group 1988–; mem. Admin. Bd Caixa d'Estalvis de Catalunya. *Leisure interest:* French literature. *Address:* Convergència Democràtica de Catalunya, Córcega 331-333, 08037 Barcelona, Spain (office).

MAS-COLELL, Andreu, PH.D.; Spanish economist; *Head of Department of Economics and Business, Pompeu Fabra University;* b. 29 June 1944, Barcelona; m.; three c.; ed Univs. of Barcelona and Valladolid, Univ. of Minnesota, U.S.A.; teacher Econ. Sciences, Univ. of Madrid 1966–68; Asst. Research Economist, Univ. of Calif. at Berkeley, U.S.A. 1972–75, Asst. Prof. of Econs. and Math. 1975–77, Assoc. Prof. 1975–78, Prof. 1979–81, Research Fellow at MSRI and Ford Visiting Prof. 1985–86; Visiting Scholar Univ. of Bonn, Germany 1976–77; Visiting Prof. Autonomous Univ. of Barcelona 1981–82; Visiting Prof. Pompeu Fabra Univ. 1993, Prof. 1995–99, Head of Dept. of Econs. and Business 1997–; Prof. of Econs. Harvard Univ. 1981–95 (first Louis Berkman Prof. of Econs. 1988); mem. Council Econometric Soc. 1982–89, Exec. Cttee. 1986–94, Second Vice-Pres. 1991, First Vice-Pres. 1992, Pres. 1993; Ed. Journal of Mathematical Economics 1985–89, Econometria 1988–92; Assoc. Ed. Economic Theory 1990–94, Mathematics of Social Sciences 1990–97; mem. or chair. of numerous advisory panels and cttees.; Sloan Fellow 1978–80, Guggenheim Fellow 1985–86, Fellow American Acad. of Arts and Sciences 1985–, Econometric Soc. 1978–, Foreign Assoc. NAS 1997–; Dr. h.c. (Alicante) 1992 recipient of N.S.F. grants 1978–79, 1981–84, 1985–87, 1992–95 and grants from Spanish Educ. Sec. 1996–99; King Juan Carlos Prize in Econs. 1989, Generalitat de Catlayuna Narcís Monturiol Medal for Scientific Merit 1990, Co-recipient of Fundació Catalana per a la Recerca Science Prize 1994. *Publications include:* Non-cooperative Approaches to the Theory of Perfect Competition (ed.) 1982, The Theory of General Economic Equilibrium: A Differentiable Approach 1985, Contributions to Mathematical Economics, in Honor of Gérard Depardieu (with W. Hildebrand) 1986, Equilibrium Theory and Applications (co-ed.) 1991, Microeconomic Theory (with M. Whinston and J. Green) 1995, Cooperation: Game Theoretic Approaches (co-ed.) 1997; numerous articles in learned journals. *Address:* Department of Economics and Business, Pompeu Fabra University, Ramon Trias Fargas, 25, 08005 Barcelona, Spain (office). *Telephone:* (935) 42-24-98 (office). *Fax:* (935) 42-18-60 (office). *E-mail:* andreu.mas@econ.upf.es (office). *Website:* www.econ.upf.es (office).

MASÁR, Vladimír, Ing.; Slovak banker; *Chairman, Deloitte Slovakia;* b. 2 May 1958, Partizánske; s. of Vladimír Masár and Jolana Masárová; m. Dagmar Glasová 1983; one s. two d.; ed Univ. of Econs Bratislava; State Bank of Czechoslovakia 1981–90; Deputy Dir City Br., Gen. Credit Bank 1990–91; Dir Credit Dept Tatra Bank-Slovakia 1992; State Sec. Ministry of Finance of Slovakia 1992; Gov. Nat. Bank of Slovakia 1993–99; Chair. Deloitte Slovakia 2000–. *Leisure interests:* swimming, tennis. *Address:* Deloitte Slovakia, Apolla BC, Prievozská 2/B, 821 09 Bratislava, Slovakia (office). *Telephone:* (2) 5824-9130 (office). *Fax:* (2) 5824-9222 (office). *E-mail:* vmasar@deloittece.com (office). *Website:* www.deloitte.sk (office).

MASARSKY, Mark Veniaminovich, CandPhilSc; Russian business executive and journalist; b. 19 June 1940, Muryinskoye, Novgorod Region; m. Olga Yevgen'yevna Fedosova; one s. one d.; ed Rostov Univ.; teacher, Taganrog Radio-Tech. Inst. 1965–67, Rostov Univ. 1967–70, Khabarovsk Polytechnical Inst. 1970–75; Corresp. Young Communist 1977–82; f. and mem. Gold-diggers of Petchora co-operative 1982–87; f. and Chair. Volkhov Jt-stock co. 1987–, Russian Gold co.; one of founders of Moscow Commodity Exchange; Pres. Int. Asscn of Factory Leaders 1992–2001; Chair. Entrepreneurs Council, Moscow Govt 1996–; mem. Bd Dirs Russian Bank of Reconstruction and Devt, Novobank Volkhov-Presnaya Investment Co., ITAR-TASS Co.; mem. Expert-Analytical Council to Pres. Yeltsin; mem. Conciliatory Comm. on Public Accord Agreement; mem. Bd Public Chamber, Pres.'s Admin. *Publications:* The Convincing, Time of Orders and Times of Troubles. *Address:* Entrepreneurs Council, Moscow Government, Novy Arbat 36, Moscow, Russia. *Telephone:* (495) 290-87-04.

MASCARENHAS GOMEZ MONTEIRO, António Manuel; Cape Verde politician and lawyer; m. Maria Monteiro 1967; one s. two d.; ed Univ. of Lisbon, Univ. of Coimbra, Catholic Univ. Louvain, Belgium; Asst and researcher, Inter-university Centre Public Law, Belgium 1974–77; Sec.-Gen. Nat. Ass. 1977–80; Judge of Supreme Court 1980–90; Pres. of Cape Verde 1991–2001; f. Asscns of Magistrates of Cape Verde 1977; Pres. Third Conference on Regional System of Human Rights Protection in Africa, America and Europe, Strasbourg 1992; mem. OAU Mission to Angola 1992; Pres. Colloquium on Constitutional Transition in Africa at Catholic Univ. Louvain 1993; Presidential Medal of Freedom 1991. *Publications:* Reflexions sur la compétence d'un gouvernement démissionnaire 1977, La notion de l'expédition des affaires courantes 1977, La Charte Africaine des Droits de l'Homme et des Peuples 1991. *Address:* c/o Presidência da República, C.P. 100, Praia, Santiago, Cape Verde.

MASCHLER, Thomas Michael; British publisher; *Managing Director and Publisher, Jonathan Cape Ltd;* b. 16 Aug. 1933, Berlin; s. of Kurt Leo Maschler and Rita Masseron; m. 1st Fay Coventry 1970 (divorced 1987); one s. two d.; m. 2nd Regina Kulinicz 1988; ed Leighton Park School, Reading; Production Asst, André Deutsch 1955–56; Ed., MacGibbon and Kee 1956–58; Fiction Ed., Penguin Books 1958–60; Editorial Dir, Jonathan Cape Ltd 1960–70, Man. Dir 1960–, Chair. 1970–91, Publr 1991–; Dir Random House 1987. *Film:* The French Lieutenant's Woman (assoc. producer) 1981. *Publications:* Declarations (ed.) 1957, New English Dramatists series (ed.) 1959–63, Publisher (memoir) 2005. *Address:* Jonathan Cape Ltd, Random House, 20 Vauxhall Bridge Road, London, SW1V 2SA, England (office). *Telephone:* (20) 7840-8400 (office). *Fax:* (20) 7233-6117 (office). *Website:* www.randomhouse.co.uk (office).

MASEFIELD, (John) Thorold, KStJ, CMG, MA; British diplomatist; b. 1 Oct. 1939, Kampala, Uganda; s. of Dr Geoffrey Bussell Masefield and Mildred Joy Thorold Rogers; m. Jennifer Mary Trowell MBE 1962; two s. one d. (and one d. deceased); ed Repton School, Derbyshire, St John's Coll. Cambridge; joined Commonwealth Relations Office 1962, Pvt. Sec. to Perm. Under-Sec. 1963–64, Second Sec. Kuala Lumpur 1964–65, Warsaw 1966–67, FCO 1967–69, First Sec. UK Del. to Disarmament Conf., Geneva 1970–74, Deputy Head Planning Staff. FCO 1974–77, Far Eastern Dept 1977–79, Counsellor, Head of Chancery, Consul-Gen. Islamabad 1979–82, Head Personnel Services Dept FCO 1982–85, Head Far Eastern Dept 1985–87, Fellow Center for Int. Affairs, Harvard Univ. 1987–88, Resident Chair. Civil Service Selection Bd 1988–89; High Commr in Tanzania 1989–92; Asst Under-Sec. of State for S and SE Asia and the Pacific, FCO 1992–94; High Commr in Nigeria 1994–97 (also Accred to Benin and Chad); Gov. and C-in-C of Bermuda 1997–2001; Chair. Brockenhurst Parish Council 2007–, School Gov. *Leisure interests:* fruit and vegetables. *Address:* c/o Foreign and Commonwealth Office, Whitehall, London, SW1A 2AH, England.

MASEKELA, Hugh; South African musician (trumpet); b. 1939, nr Johannesburg; ed Guildhall School of Music, London, Manhattan School of Music, New York; co-f. The Jazz Epistles 1959; fmrly in voluntary exile from early 1960s, in UK, USA, Ghana, Nigeria, Guinea and Botswana; f. Botswana Int. School of Music 1986; Musical Dir Graceland; Kora All African Music Award for Best Male Artist in Southern Africa 2005. *Compositions include:* wrote Sarafina (Broadway musical). *Recordings include:* Grrr 1966, The Promise of a Future 1968, Masekela 1968, Home is Where the Music Is (with Dudu Pukwana) 1972, The African Connection 1973, Techno Bush 1984, I Am Not Afraid (with Hedzoleh Soundz), Tomorrow 1987, Beatin' Aroun De Bush 1992, Stimela 1994, Reconstruction 1994, Black to the Future 1998, Boys Doin' It 1998, Sixty 2000, Time 2002, Still Grazing 2004, Revival 2005. *Publication:* Still Grazing: The Musical Journey of Hugh Masekela 2003. *Address:* Ritmo Artists, PO Box 684705, Austin, TX 78768-4705, USA (office). *Telephone:* (512) 447-5661 (office). *Fax:* (512) 447-5886 (office). *E-mail:* info@ritmoartists.com (office). *Website:* www.ritmoartists.com (office).

MASEKO, Zola; South African film director; b. 1967; ed Nat. Film and TV School, Beaconsfield, England; born and raised in exile, Tanzania and Swaziland; joined Umkhonto We Sizwe (armed wing of African Nat. Congress) 1987; made first documentary Dear Sunshine 1992; returned to S Africa 1994; developed three-part tv series Homecoming 2005; joined Pistoleros Films 2005. *Films directed include:* The Foreigner (also writer) 1997, The Life and Times of Sarah Baartman 1998, The Return of Sarah Baartman 2002, Children of the Revolution 2002, A Drink in the Passage (Special Jury Award, Fespaco) 2002, Drum (also writer, Etalon d'Or de Yennenga Award Fespaco 2005) 2004. *Address:* Pistoleros Films, 5 Wandel Street Gardens, Cape Town 8001, South Africa (office). *Telephone:* (21) 4614336 (office). *Website:* www.pisoleros.co.za (office).

MASERA, Rainer Stefano, DPhil; Italian banker; *Chairman, SanPaulo IMI SpA;* b. 6 May 1944, Como; s. of Francesco Masera; m. Giovanna Aveta; two c.; ed La Sapienza Univ., Rome, Univ. of Oxford, UK; economist, Bank for Int. Settlements, Basle 1971–75; mem. staff, then Head Int. Dept, Research Dept, Bank of Italy 1975–77, Head Research Dept 1982–84, Cen. Dir for Econs Research 1985–88; Alt. mem. EEC Monetary Cttee 1977–81; Dir-Gen. Istituto Mobiliare Italiano (IMI) 1988–; Chair. SanPaolo IMI SpA 1998–; fmr Minister of the Budget. *Publications:* L'Unificazione Monetaria e lo SME 1980, A European Central Bank 1989, International Monetary and Financial Integration 1988, Prospects for the European Monetary System 1990, Intermediari, Mercati e Finanza d'Impresa 1991. *Leisure interests:* tennis, skiing. *Address:* Istituto Mobiliare Italiano, Viale dell'Arte 25, 00144 Rome; SanPaolo IMI SpA, Piazza San Carlo 156, 10121 Turin, Italy (office). *Telephone:* (011) 5551 (office). *Fax:* (011) 555-2989 (office). *Website:* www.sanpaolo.it (office).

MASERI, Attilio, MD, FRCP; Italian cardiologist; b. 12 Nov. 1935; s. of Adriano Maseri and Antonietta Albini; m. Countess Francesca Maseri Florio di Santo Stefano 1960 (died 2000); one s.; ed Classical Lycée Cividale, Padua Univ. Medical School; Research Fellow Univ. of Pisa 1960–65, Columbia Univ., New York, USA 1965–66, Johns Hopkins Univ., Baltimore, USA 1966–67; Asst Prof., Univ. of Pisa 1967–70, Prof. of Internal Medicine 1970, Prof. of Cardiovascular Pathophysiology, Prof. of Medicine (Locum) 1972–79, Sir John McMichael Prof. of Cardiovascular Medicine, Royal Postgraduate Medical School, Hammersmith Hosp., Univ. of London 1979–91; Prof. of Cardiology and Dir Inst. of Cardiology, Catholic Univ. of Rome 1991–; Fellow American Coll. of Cardiology; Life mem. Johns Hopkins Soc. of Scholars; Kt of Malta; King Faisal Int. Prize 1992; Distinguished Scientist Award, American Coll. of Cardiology 1996. *Publications:* Myocardial Blood Flow in Man 1972, Primary and Secondary Angina 1977, Perspectives on Coronary Care 1979, Ischaemic Heart Disease 1995; articles in major int. cardiological and medical journals. *Leisure interests:* skiing, tennis, sailing. *Address:* Via Zandonai 9-11, 00194 Rome, Italy.

MASHEKE, Gen. Malimba; Zambian politician and army officer; b. 1941; fmr Army Commdr; Minister of Defence 1985–88, of Home Affairs 1988–89; Prime Minister of Zambia 1989–91; fmr Chair. United Nat. Independence Party (UNIP); currently Chair. Interreligious and Int. Fed. for World Peace (IIFWP), Zambia chapter; mem. Forum for Democracy and Devt. *Address:* c/o United National Independence Party (UNIP), POB 30302, Lusaka, Zambia.

MASHELKAR, Raghunath Anant, BChemEng, PhD; Indian research scientist; *Director General, Council of Scientific and Industrial Research (CSIR);* b. 1 Jan. 1943, Mashel, Goa; m. Mrs. Vaishali R. Mashelkar; two d. one s.; ed Univ. of Bombay; Dir-Gen. Council of Scientific and Industrial Research and Sec., Govt of India Dept of Scientific and Industrial Research July 1995–; Pres. Physical Science, Nat. Acad. of Sciences 1991; Gen. Pres. Indian Science Congress 1999–2000; Chancellor, Assam Univ. 2000–; Fellow, Indian Acad. of Sciences 1983, Indian Nat. Science Acad. 1984, Nat. Acad. of Eng 1987, Third World Acad. of Sciences 1991; numerous honorary degrees including DSc (hc) from Univs of Salford, UK 1993, Kanpur 1995, Indian School of Mines 1997, Bundelkhand Univ. 2000, Guwahati Univ. 2000, Anna Univ. 2000, Univ. of London 2001, (Univ. of Wis.) 2002, (Banaras Hindu Univ.) 2002, (Allahabad Univ.) 2002, (MS Univ. of Baroda) 2003, (Kalyani Univ.) 2004; numerous awards and prizes including Shanti Swarup Bhatnagar Prize 1982, 2001, UDCT Outstanding Alumni Medal 1985, Fed. of Indian Chambers of Commerce and Industry Award 1987, Padmashri 1991, GD Birla Award for Scientific Research 1993, Goyal Prize 1996, JRD Tata Corporate Leadership Award 1998, Padma Bhushan 2000. *Publications:* author or co-author of 236 research papers on macromolecules in books and learned journals since1968; books: Intellectual Property and Competitive Strategies in the 21st Century (with S.A. Khan) 2003, Advances in Transport Processes Vol. 1 1980, Vol. 2 1982, Vol. 3 1983, Vol. 4 1986, Transport Phenomena in Polymeric Systems Vol. 1 (ATP Vol. 5) 1987, Vol. 2 (ATP Vol. 6) 1989, Advances in Transport Phenomena in Fluidizing Systems (ATP Vol. 7) 1987, Vol. 8 1992, Vol. 9 1993, Frontiers in Chemical Reaction Engineering Vol. 1 1984, Vol. 2 1984, Recent Trends in Chemical Reaction Engineering Vol. 1 1987, Vol. 2 1987, Reactions and Reaction Engineering 1987, Heat Transfer Equipment Design 1988, Reading in Solid State Chemistry 1994, Dynamics of Complex Fluids 1998, Structure and Dynamics in the Mesophasic Domain 1999, co-authored 28 patents 1988–2003. *Address:* Council of Scientific and Industrial Research, Anusandhan Bhavan, 2 Rafi Marg, New Delhi 110 001 (office); CSIR/Science Centre, Lodi Garden's Gate No. 2, Lodi Estate, New Delhi 110 003, India (home). *Telephone:* (11) 23710472, 23717053 (office); (11) 24618851, 24649359 (home). *Fax:* (11) 23710618 (office). *E-mail:* dgcsir@csir.res.in (office). *Website:* www.csir.res.in (office).

MASHKOV, Vladimir Lvovich; Russian actor; b. 27 Nov. 1963, Tula; s. of Lev Petrovich Mashkov and Natalya Ivanovna Nikiforova; m. 1st Tatyana Lvovna Mashkova; one d.; 2nd Ksenia Borisovna Mashkova; ed Moscow Art Theatre School; actor and Stage Dir Oleg Tabakov Theatre-Studio 1988–; main roles in most productions; staged five productions; various film roles; numerous awards including K. Stanislavsky Prize for Best Direction 1994, Crystal Turandot Prize for Best Play 1995, Baltic Pearl for fast career growth 1997; various awards for best actor in film and theatre. *Plays (as stage director):* Star House by Local Time, Passions for Bumbarash, The Death-Defying Act, The Threepenny Opera, Number 13 2001. *Film roles include:* Zelyonyy ogon kozy (The Goat's Green Fire) 1989, Ha-bi-assy 1990, Delay - raz! (aka Do It - One!) 1990, Lyubov na ostrove smerti (Love at the Death Island) 1991, Alyaska, ser! (Alaska, Sir!) 1992, Moi Ivan, toi Abraham (Me Ivan, You Abraham) 1993, Moscow Nights, Limita 1994, Katya Ismailova 1994, American Daughter 1995, Koroli i kapusta (Cabbages and Kings; voice) 1996, Noch pered Rozhdestvom (voice) 1997, Vor (The Thief) 1997, Sirota kazanskaya (Sympathy Seeker) (also dir) 1997, Sochineniye ko dnyu pobedy (Composition for Victory Day) 1998, Dve luny, tri solntsa (Two Moons, Three Suns) 1998, Mama (Mummy) 1999, Russkiy bunt (The Captain's Daughter) 2000, Dancing at the Blue Iguana 2000, 15 Minutes 2001, An American Rhapsody 2001, The Quickie 2001, Behind Enemy Lines 2001, Oligarkh 2002, Papa (also writer, dir and producer) 2004, Statski sovetnik 2005, The Good Shepherd 2006. *Television includes:* Casus Improvisus 1991, Dvadtsat minut s angelom 1996, Idiot (mini-series) 2003. *Address:* Oleg Tabakov Theatre-Studio, Chaplygina str. 12A, Moscow, Russia. *Telephone:* (495) 916-21-21 (Theatre); (495) 925-73-44 (Yelena Chukhrai Art Agency). *E-mail:* grtagent@mtu-net.ru (office); v_mashkoff@mtu-net.ru (home).

MASIMOV, Karim K., DEcon; Kazakhstani economist and politician; *Prime Minister;* b. 15 June 1965, Tselinograd (now Astana); ed Beijing Linguistic Inst., Wuhan Univ., China and Kazakh State Acad. of Man.; began career as sr economist at Ministry of Labour; fmr sr specialist, Kazakh Ministry of Foreign Econ. Affairs, Urumqi, China; fmr CEO Kazakh Trading House, Hong Kong; Chair. Almaty Merchant Bank 1995–97, Jt Stock Co. Halyk Bank of Kazakhstan 1997–2000; Minister of Transport and Communications 2001–04; Chief Policy Adviser to Pres. Nazarbayev 2004–06; Deputy Prime Minister 2006–07; Minister of Economy and Budget Planning April–Oct. 2006; Prime Minister 2007–; Dr hc (Peoples' Friendship Univ., Russia) 2007. *Address:* Office of the Prime Minister, 010000 Astana, Beibitshilik 11, Kazakhstan (office). *Telephone:* (7172) 32-31-04 (office). *Fax:* (7172) 32-40-89 (office). *Website:* www.government.kz (office).

MASIRE, Quett Ketumile Joni, LLD, JP; Botswana fmr head of state; *Congo Facilitator, Southern African Development Community;* b. 23 July 1925, Kanye; s. of Joni Masire and Gabaipone Masire; m. Gladys Olebile Molefi 1957; three s. three d.; ed Kanye and Tiger Kloof; f. Seepapitso Secondary School 1950; reporter, later Dir, African Echo 1958; mem. Bangwaketse Tribal Council, Legis. Council; fmr mem. Exec. Council; Founder-mem. Botswana Democratic Party; mem. Legis. (now Nat.) Ass. March 1965; Deputy Prime Minister 1965–66; attended Independence Conf., London Feb. 1966; Vice-Pres. and Minister of Finance 1966–80 and of Devt Planning 1967–80, Pres. of Botswana 1980–98; Chair. Southern African Devt Community 1999, Congo Facilitator 1999–; Hon. GCMG; Hon. LLD (Williams Coll.) 1980, (Sussex) 1986, (St John); Naledi Ya Botswana (Star of the Nation) 1986. *Leisure interest:* watching football. *Address:* PO Box 70, Gaborone, Botswana (home). *Telephone:* 353391 (home).

MASIRE-MWAMBA, Gabaipone Mmasekgoa, BSc, MBA; Botswana business executive and international organization official; *Deputy Secretary-General, Commonwealth Secretariat;* ed Univ. of London, UK, Univ. of Pittsburgh, USA; fmr Chief Exec. Investment Promotion Agency (BEDIA); fmr Group Man. of Corp. Business and Regulatory Affairs, Botswana Telecommunications Corpn; fmr UK Business Devt Man., Commonwealth Telecommunications Org.; Deputy Sec.-Gen. Commonwealth Secr. 2008–. *Address:* Commonwealth Secretariat, Marlborough House, Pall Mall, London, SW1Y 5HX, England (office). *Telephone:* (20) 7747-6385 (office). *Fax:* (20) 7839-9081 (office). *E-mail:* info@commonwealth.int (office). *Website:* www.commonwealth.int (office).

MASKAWA, Toshihide, PhD; Japanese physicist and academic; *Professor of Physics, Kyoto Sangyo University;* b. 7 Feb. 1940; ed Nagoya Univ.; Research Assoc., Nagoya Univ. 1967; Research Assoc., Kyoto Univ. 1970–76, Prof. 1980–2003, Prof. Emer. 2003–, Dir Yukawa Inst. for Theoretical Physics 1997–99; Assoc. Prof., Univ. of Tokyo 1976–80; Prof. of Physics, Kyoto Sangyo Univ. 2007–; mem. Japanese Science Council 1997–2000; Nishina Memorial Award 1979, JJ Sakurai Prize (American Inst. of Physics) 1985, Japan Acad. Award 1985, Asahi Award 1994, Sino-Japanese Cultural Award 1995, Nagoya Univ. Grad. School of Science Lecture Award 2002, European Physical Soc. High-energy Elementary Particle Physics Prize 2007, Nobel Prize for Physics (jtly) 2008. *Address:* Kyoto Sangyo University, Faculty of Science, Motoyama,

Kamigamo, Kita-Ku, Kyoto 603-8555, Japan (office). *Website:* www.kyoto-su.ac.jp/department/sc/index.html (home).

MASKIN, Eric Stark, AB, AM, PhD; American economist and academic; *Albert O. Hirschman Professor of Social Science, Institute for Advanced Study;* b. 12 Dec. 1950, New York City; s. of Meyer Maskin and Bernice Rabkin Maskin; m. Gayle Sawtelle; one s. one d.; ed Harvard Univ.; Research Fellow, Jesus Coll., Univ. of Cambridge, UK 1976–77; Asst Prof. of Econs, MIT 1977–80, Assoc. Prof. 1980–81, Prof. 1981–84, Visiting Prof. 1999–2000; Overseas Fellowship, Churchill Coll., Univ. of Cambridge 1980–82; Prof. of Econs, Harvard Univ. 1985–2000, Louis Berkman Prof. of Econs 1997–2000; Visiting Overseas Fellowship, St John's Coll., Univ. of Cambridge 1987–88; Albert O. Hirschman Prof. of Social Science, Inst. for Advanced Study, Princeton 2000–; Visiting Prof. of Econs Princeton Univ. 2000–; research areas have included game theory and mechanism design theory; has delivered lectures at int. insts including Hebrew Univ., Jerusalem, Wuhan Univ., Seoul Nat. Univ., Univ. of Tokyo, Stockholm School of Econs; Dir, Summer School in Econ. Theory, Hebrew Univ. of Jerusalem 2008–; mem. American Econ. Asscn, NAS, Econometric Soc. (Pres. 2003), Game Theory Soc. (Pres.-elect 2008–(10)), European Econ. Asscn; mem. Educ. Advisory Bd, J. S. Guggenheim Foundation 2007–; mem. Scientific Council, J. J. Laffont Foundation, Toulouse Sciences Economiques; Ed., Economics Letters 1992–; Assoc. Ed., Social Choice and Welfare 1983–, Games and Economic Behavior 1988–, Review of Economic Design 1993–, QR Journal of Theoretical Economics 2000–, International Journal of Game Theory 2003–; Advisory Ed., Division of Labor and Transaction Costs 2005–, Economics 2006–; Editorial Adviser, Journal of Developing Areas 2001–; Fellow, American Acad. of Arts and Sciences 1994–; Corresponding Fellow, British Acad. 2003–; Monash Distinguished Visiting Scholar, Monash Univ. 2003; Hon. Prof., Wuhan Univ. 2004, Tsinghua Univ. 2007, Hon. Fellow, St John's Coll., Cambridge 2004; Hon. MA, Univ. of Cambridge 1977, Hon. DHumLitt (Bard Coll.) 2008, Dr hc (Corvinus Univ., Budapest) 2008; Galbraith Teaching Prize, Harvard Univ. 1990, 1992, Erik Kempe Award in Environmental Econs 2007, Jt Winner, Nobel Prize in Econs (with Leo Hurwicz and Roger B. Myerson) 2007, EFR – Business Week Award, Rotterdam 2008. *Publications:* co-ed.: Economic Analysis of Markets and Games 1992, Recent Developments in Game Theory 1999, Planning, Shortage and Transformation 2000; more than 100 articles in academic journals. *Leisure interests:* clarinet, opera. *Address:* School of Social Science, Institute for Advanced Study, Einstein Drive, Princeton, NJ 08540, USA (office). *Telephone:* (609) 734-8309 (office). *Fax:* (609) 951-4458 (office). *E-mail:* maskin@ias.edu (office). *Website:* www.sss.ias.edu (office).

MASLYUKOV, Yuri Dmitriyevich; Russian politician; b. 30 Sept. 1937, Leninabad, Tajik SSR; m. Svetlanana Ivanov Maslyukova; one s.; ed Leningrad Inst. of Mechanics, Higher Mil. Artillery School; Sr engineer, Deputy Head of Dept, Izhevsk Research Inst. of Tech. of Ministry of Defence Industry 1962–70; chief engineer, Deputy Dir Izhevsk Machine Construction Factory 1970–74; Head, Main Dept of Tech., Ministry of Defence Industry 1974–79; Deputy Minister of Defence Industry 1974–82; First Deputy Chair. USSR State Planning Cttee 1982–85; Deputy Chair., First Deputy Chair., USSR Council of Ministers 1985; Chair. State Comm. on Mil. and Industrial Problems 1985; Chair. USSR State Planning Cttee 1985–91; Deputy Chair. USSR Council of Ministers, Chair. State Mil. Industrial Comm. 1991; leading expert, Voronezh Co. SOKOL 1993–94; Dir.-Gen. Yugtrustinvest 1994–95; mem. CPSU Cen. Cttee 1986–91, Cand. mem. of Politburo 1988, mem. 1989; Deputy USSR Supreme Soviet 1990–91; mem. USSR Presidential Council 1991; mem. State Duma 1993–98, 1999–; Chair. Cttee on Econ. Policy 1995–98; Minister of Industry and Trade of Russian Fed. July–Sept. 1998; First Deputy Chair. of Govt 1998–99; mem. Cen. Cttee CP of Russian Fed. 1997; Chair. Cttee on Industry, Construction and Scientific Tech. 1998–99, 2000–; Adviser to V. Semenikhin Inst. of Automation 1999–2000; mem. Co-ordination Council, Movt of People's Patriotic Union of Russia. *Address:* State Duma, Okhotny Ryad 1, 103265 Moscow, Russia (office). *Telephone:* (495) 292-04-98, (office); (495) 292-03-15. *Fax:* (495) 292-37-63 (office).

MASMANIDIS, Costas, BSc, PhD; Greek chemist, business executive and international organization executive; *Secretary-General, Black Sea Economic Cooperation (BSEC) Business Council;* b. 1946, Thessaloniki; ed Aristotelian Univ., Thessaloniki, Univ. of Cincinnati, USA; Post-doctoral Research Fellow, Rensselaer Polytechnic Inst., Troy, NY; 18-year career as Gen. Man. with Dow Chemical Co. in int. positions in USA, Switzerland, SA and Balkan countries and as Man. Dir of Greek subsidiary, and with int. positions as Country Man., Corp., sales and market Man.; currently Sec.-Gen. Black Sea Econ. Cooperation (BSEC) Business Council, Istanbul; Founding mem. and twice-elected Pres. Hellenic Asscn of Chemical Industries; mem. CEFIC; fmr Sec.-Gen. Athens-Piraeus Industry Asscn, Hellenic-Chinese Chamber of Commerce and Industry; fmr mem. Bd of Dirs Hellenic-American Chamber of Commerce and Industry; fmr mem. Gen. Council Fed. of Greek Industries. *Publications include:* Globalisation, Dematerialisation and the New Economy: The Transformation of Business and the Workplace at the Dawn of the 21st Century 2000, SME Innovation and Competitiveness (training manual), The Prospects of Business Cooperation in the Countries of the Mediterranean (study). *Address:* BSEC Business Council, Müsir Fuad Pasa Yalisi, Eski Tersane, 80860 Istinye, İstanbul, Turkey (office). *Telephone:* (212) 229-1144 (office). *Fax:* (212) 229-0332 (office). *E-mail:* info@bsec-business.org (office). *Website:* www.bsec-business.org (office).

MASOL, Vitaliy Andreyevich, PhD; Ukrainian politician (retd); b. 14 Nov. 1928, Olshivka, Chernigov Region; s. of Andrei Dmitrievich Masol and Lidiya Grigorievna Masol; m. Nina Vasilievna Masol 1978; one s.; ed Kiev Polytechnic Inst., Inst. of Econ. Man.; foreman, shop foreman, deputy chief engineer, Novokramatorsk machine-construction plant 1951–63, Dir 1963–71; mem. CPSU 1956–91; Gen. Dir of production unit of heavy machine-construction factories in Kramatorsk, Ukraine 1971–72; First Deputy Chair. of Gosplan for Ukrainian SSR 1972–79; Deputy Chair. Ukrainian Council of Ministers 1979–87, Chair. (Prime Minister) 1987–90 (resgnd following mass student demonstrations), re apptd 1994–95; mem. of CPSU Cen. Auditing Cttee 1981–86; Chair. Planning and Budget Comm., USSR Supreme Soviet 1982–87; mem. Cen. Cttee CPSU 1989–91; Deputy to USSR Supreme Soviet 1979–89, USSR People's Deputy 1989–91; mem. Parl. of Ukraine 1990–98, Higher Council of Pres. of Ukraine 1997–; adviser to Rostok bank; several orders, including Order of Lenin (twice), Order of Count Yaroslav Mudry 1998; numerous awards. *Leisure interest:* tourism. *Address:* Desyatinnaya str. 8, Apt 8, Kiev 252025, Ukraine.

MASON, Sir (Basil) John, Kt, C.B., DSc, FRS; British meteorologist; b. 18 Aug. 1923, Docking, Norfolk; s. of the late John Robert and Olive Mason; m. Doreen Sheila Jones 1948; two s.; ed Fakenham Grammar School and Univ. Coll., Nottingham; commissioned, Radar Branch, RAF 1944–46; Shirley Research Fellow, Univ. of Nottingham 1947; Asst lecturer in Meteorology, Imperial Coll., London 1948–49, lecturer 1949; Warren Research Fellow, Royal Soc. 1957; Visiting Prof. of Meteorology, Univ. of Calif. 1959–60; Prof. of Cloud Physics, Imperial Coll. of Science and Tech., Univ. of London 1961–65; Dir-Gen. Meteorological Office 1965–83, Pres. Royal Meteorological Soc. 1968–70; mem. Exec. Cttee World Meteorological Org. 1965–75, 1977–83; Chair. Council, Univ. of Surrey 1971–75; Pro-Chancellor Univ. of Surrey 1979–85; Pres. Inst. of Physics 1976–78; Treas. and Sr Vice-Pres. Royal Soc. 1976–86; Dir Fulmer Research Inst. 1976–78; Pres. BAAS 1982–83; Dir Royal Soc. Project on Acidification of Surface Waters 1983–90; mem. Advisory Bd Research Councils 1983–86; Pres. UMIST 1986–94, Chancellor 1994–96; Chair. Grad. School for Environment, Imperial Coll., London 1995–98; Chair. ICSU/WMO Scientific Cttee for World Climate Research Prog., Co-ordinating Cttee for Marine Science and Tech. 1987–89; Pres. Nat. Soc. for Clean Air 1989–91, Asscn for Science Educ. 1992–93, Nat. Soc. of Environmental Eng 1999–2003; Foreign mem. Norwegian Acad. of Science 1993; Bakerian Lecture, Royal Soc. 1971; Halley Lecture, Oxford Univ. 1977; Lecturer, Linacre Coll., Oxford 1990; Rutherford Lecture, Royal Soc. 1990; Hon. Fellow Imperial Coll. of Science and Tech. 1974, UMIST 1979; Hon. DSc (Nottingham) 1966, (Durham) 1970, (Strathclyde) 1975, (City Univ.) 1980, (Sussex) 1983, (E Anglia) 1988, (Plymouth Polytechnic) 1990, (Heriot-Watt) 1991, (UMIST) 1994, (Reading) 1998; Hugh Robert Mill Medal, Royal Meteorological Soc. 1959, Charles Chree Medal and Prize, Physical Soc. 1965, Rumford Medal, Royal Soc. 1972, Glazebrook Medal and Prize, Inst. of Physics 1974, Symons Memorial Gold Medal, Royal Meteorological Soc. 1975, Naylor Prize and Lectureship, London Math. Soc. 1979, Royal Medal, Royal Soc. 1991. *Publications:* The Physics of Clouds 1957, Clouds, Rain and Rain-making 1962, Acid Rain 1992. *Leisure interests:* music, foreign travel, biography. *Address:* Department of Environmental Science, Imperial College, London, SW7 (office); 64 Christchurch Road, East Sheen, London, SW14, England (home). *Telephone:* (20) 7594-9287 (office); (20) 8876-2557 (home). *Fax:* (20) 7581-0245 (office).

MASON, Sir John (see Mason, Sir (Basil) John).

MASON, Dame Monica, DBE; British (b. South African) ballet company artistic director; *Director, Royal Ballet;* b. 6 Sept. 1941, Johannesburg, SA; d. of Richard Mason and E. Fabian; m. Austin Bennett 1968; ed Johannesburg, Nesta Brooking School of Ballet, UK and Royal Ballet School, London; joined Royal Ballet in Corps de Ballet 1958, Soloist 1963, Prin. 1968, Sr Prin. –1989; selected by Kenneth MacMillan to create role of Chosen Maiden in Rite of Spring 1962; other roles created for her include: Diversions, Calliope Rag in Elite Syncopations, Electra, Mistress in Manon, Romeo and Juliet, Midwife in Rituals, Adieu 1980, Nursey in Isadora, Summer in The Four Seasons, The Ropes of Time; appeared in mime roles including Carabosse in The Sleeping Beauty and Lady Capulet in MacMillan's Romeo and Juliet; recently created role of Mrs Grose in William Tuckett's The Turn of the Screw; Répétiteur and Asst to Prin. Choreographer, Royal Ballet 1980–84, Prin. Répétiteur 1984–91, Asst Dir Royal Ballet 1991–2002, Dir 2002–; Hon. DUniv (Surrey) 1996. *Repertory includes:* Odette/Odile in Swan Lake, Princess Aurora in The Sleeping Beauty, title role in Giselle, Prelude and Mazurka in Les Sylphides, leading role in Raymonda Act III, dramatic parts including Hostess in Les Biches and the Black Queen in Checkmate; other major roles include: leading role in MacMillan's Song of the Earth, Nijinska's Les Noces and Nureyev's Kingdom of the Shades scene from La Bayadère; appeared in first performances by Royal Ballet of Hans van Manen's Adagio Hammerklavier, Jerome Robbins' Dances at a Gathering and In the Night, Balanchine's Liebeslieder Walzer and Tudor's Dark Elegies; other roles include: the Lilac Fairy in The Sleeping Beauty, Empress Elisabeth and Mitzi Caspar in MacMillan's Mayerling, title role in The Firebird, Variations in Frederick Ashton's Birthday Offering, the Fairy Godmother and Winter Fairy in Cinderella, Lady Elgar in Enigma Variations, Queen of Denmark in Helpmann's Hamlet. *Address:* Royal Opera House, Covent Garden, London, WC2E 9DD, England (office). *Telephone:* (20) 7212-9712 (office). *Fax:* (20) 7212-9121 (office). *E-mail:* monica.mason@roh.org.uk (office). *Website:* www.royalopera.org/ballet (office).

MASON, Paul James, CB, PhD, FRS; British meteorologist (retd); *Professor Emeritus, University of Reading;* b. 16 March 1946, Southampton; s. of Charles Ernest Edward Mason and Phyllis Mary Mason (née Swan); m. Elizabeth Mary Slaney 1968; one s. one d.; ed Univs of Nottingham and Reading; Scientific Officer, then Prin. Scientific Officer, Meteorological Office 1967–79, Head Meteorological Research Unit, Cardington 1979–85, Asst Dir Boundary Layer Br., Meteorological Office 1985–89, Deputy Dir Physical Research, Meteorological Office 1989–91, Chief Scientist 1991–2003; Dir

Univs Weather Research Network (UWERN), Univ. of Reading 2003–06, Prof. Emer. 2006–; mem. Council Royal Meteorological Soc. 1989–90, Pres. 1992–94; Chair. Steering Cttee Global Climate Observing System 2002–06; mem. Editorial Bd Boundary Layer Meteorology 1988–98; L.G. Groves Prize for Meteorology 1980, Buchan Prize, Royal Meteorological Soc. 1986, Mason Medal, Royal Meteorological Soc. 2006. *Publications:* scientific papers in meteorology and fluid dynamics journals. *Leisure interests:* walking, travel. *Address:* Department of Meteorology, University of Reading, PO Box 243, Earley Gate, Reading, Berks., RG66 6BB, England (office). *Telephone:* (118) 378-8957 (office). *E-mail:* p.j.mason@reading.ac.uk (office).

MASON, Peter, BA, MBA; Australian investment banker; *Chairman, AMP Ltd;* Dir Mayne Group Ltd 1992–2005; fmr Deputy Chair. Children's Hosp. Sydney; fmr Chair. and CEO Schroders Australia Ltd, Group Man. Dir Schroders Asia Pacific; Chair. JP Morgan Chase Bank Australia 2000–05, Ord Minnett Holdings Pty 2004–05; mem. Bd AMP Ltd 2003–, Chair. 2005–, mem. Remuneration Cttee, Audit Cttee; fmr Chair. Children's Hosp. Fund; fmr Dir Lloyds Bank Australia, UK; Dir Australian Research Alliance for Children and Youth; Sr Adviser UBS Investment Bank Australasia; Govt Appointee, Univ. of NSW Council; Order of Australia. *Address:* AMP Ltd, Level 24, 33 Alfred Street, Sydney 2000, Australia (office). *Telephone:* (2) 9257-5000 (office). *Fax:* (2) 8275-0199 (office). *Website:* www.ampgroup.com (office).

MASON, Sir Ronald, Kt, KCB, DSc, FRS, CChem, FRSC, CEng, FIM; British professor of chemical physics (retd) and civil servant; *Chairman, University College London Hospitals Charities;* b. 22 July 1930, Wales; s. of David John Mason and Olwen Mason (née James); m. 1st E. Pauline Pattinson 1953; m. 2nd E. Rosemary Grey-Edwards 1979; three d.; ed Quaker's Yard Grammar School and Univs of Wales and London; Research Assoc., Univ. Coll. London (UCL) 1953–60, Fellow 1995–; Lecturer, Imperial Coll. London 1960–63; Prof., Univ. of Sheffield 1963–70; Prof., Univ. of Sussex 1970–88; Chief Scientific Adviser, Ministry of Defence 1977–83; Pro-Vice-Chancellor, Univ. of Sussex 1977–78; many visiting professorships in Australia, Canada, France, Israel, NZ and USA 1965–83, Int. Relations, Univ. Coll. of Wales; Chair. Hunting Ltd 1986–87, British Ceramics Research Ltd 1990–98, UCL Hosps Nat. Health Service Trust 1993–2001, Science Applications Int. Corpn (UK) Ltd 1993–96; Pres. British Hydromechanics Research Asscn 1986–95, Inst. of Materials 1995–96; Chair. Council for Arms Control, London 1986–91; mem. UN Disarmament Studies Comm. 1983–91; Chair. UCL Hosps Charities 2004–; Hon. Fellow, Univ. of Glamorgan 1987; Hon. FIMechE 1993; Hon. DSc (Wales) 1986, (Keele) 1993; medals of various learned socs. *Publications:* many scientific research publs on structural chem. and chemical physics of surfaces, author/ed. of 10 monographs, papers on defence policies and tech. *Leisure interests:* gardening, travelling, music, opera. *Address:* 2nd Floor, Trustees Department, University College London Hospitals Charities, 140 Hampstead Road, London, NW1 2BX, England (office). *Telephone:* (20) 7380-9664 (office). *E-mail:* masons@chestnuts100.freeserve.co.uk. *Website:* www.uclh.org (office).

MASON OF BARNSLEY, Baron (Life Peer), cr. 1987, of Barnsley in South Yorkshire; **Roy Mason,** PC, DL; British politician; b. 18 April 1924, Barnsley, Yorks; s. of Joseph and Mary Mason; m. Marjorie Sowden 1945; two d.; ed Carlton Junior School, Royston Sr School and London School of Econs (T.U.C. Course); mine worker 1938–53; branch official, Nat. Union of Mineworkers 1947–53; mem. Yorkshire Miners' Council 1949–53; MP for Barnsley (now Barnsley Cen.) 1953–87; Minister of State (Shipping), Bd of Trade 1964–67; Minister of Defence (Equipment) 1967–68; Postmaster-Gen. April–June 1968; Minister of Power 1968–69; Pres. Bd of Trade 1969–70; Sec. of State for Defence 1974–76, for Northern Ireland 1976–79; Opposition Spokesman for Agric., Fisheries and Food 1979–81; Hon. DUniv (Sheffield Hallam Univ.) 1993, Hon. DCL (Univ. of Northumbria) 2005. *Publication:* Paying the Price. *Leisure interests:* fly-fishing, philately, cravatology. *Address:* House of Lords, Westminster, London, SW1A 0PW (office); 12 Victoria Avenue, Barnsley, S. Yorks., S70 2BH, England (home).

MASORIN, Adm. Vladimir; Russian naval officer; *Navy Commander-in-Chief;* b. 24 Aug. 1947, Beloye, Tver region; ed Black Sea Nakhimov Naval School, Naval Acad., Gen. Staff Acad.; Chief of Staff 1993–96, First Deputy Commdr Kola Flotilla 1993–96, Commdr Caspian Flotilla 1996–2002, Black Sea Fleet 2002–05, Chief of Navy Staff 2005, Navy C-in-C 2005–. *Address:* c/o Ministry of Defence, ul. Myasnitskaya 37, 105175 Moscow, Russia (office). *Telephone:* (495) 293-38-54 (office). *Fax:* (495) 296-84-36 (office). *Website:* www .mil.ru (office).

MASOUD, Ahmad Wali, MA; Afghan diplomatist and politician; *Leader, Nizat-i Melli-i Afghanistan (National Movement of Afghanistan);* b. 1 Nov. 1964, Kabul; brother of the late Ahmed Shah Masoud, leader of Northern Alliance mil. forces in Afghanistan, and of Ahmad Zia Masoud; m. Beheshta Masoud; three d.; ed Muslim Public School, Peshawar, Pakistan, Mid-Cornwall Coll. of Further Educ., Polytechnic of Cen. London and Westminster Univ., UK; Foreign News Reporter, Times Newspaper 1989; Ed. Ariana News Bulletin 1989–1992; Rep. Jamiat-i Islami (Islamic Soc.), main political faction in Afghanistan, fighting Russian occupation 1989–92; Second Sec., Embassy of Afghanistan, London 1992, First Sec. and Chargé d'affaires a.i. 1993, Minister Counsellor and Chargé d'affaires a.i. 1993–2003, Amb. to UK 2003–07; currently Leader, Nizat-i Melli-i Afghanistan (Nat. Movt of Afghanistan), Kabul. *Address:* Nizat-i Melli-i Afghanistan, Kabul, Afghanistan (office).

MASOUD, Ahmad Zia; Afghan diplomatist and politician; *First Vice-President;* b. 1 May 1956, brother of the late Ahmad Shah Masoud and Ahmad Wali Masoud; ed Lycée Esteqlal and Kabul Polytechnic Inst.; mem. Shora-e-Nizar Movt; Amb. to Russian Fed. (non-resident Envoy to Moldova, Armenia, Azerbaijan, Georgia and Belarus), Moscow 2002–04; First Vice-Pres. 2004–. *Address:* c/o Office of the President, Gul Khana Palace, Presidential Palace, Kabul, Afghanistan (office). *E-mail:* president@afghanistangov.org (office). *Website:* www.president.gov.af (office).

MASRI, Munib al-; Palestinian business executive; *Chairman, Palestinian Development and Investment Company;* b. Nablus; m.; six c.; ed Univ. of Texas, USA; fmr Jordanian cabinet minister; f. Edgo (eng services co.), London, UK; served as emissary of King Hussein of Jordan to Palestinian leader Yasser Arafat's HQ during fighting between Jordanian troops and Palestinian fighters 1970; acted as mediator between Israeli Prime Minister Benjamin Netanyahu and Yasser Arafat mid-1990s; first Palestinian businessman to return to Palestinian territories following Oslo agreements in 1994; Founder and Chair. Palestine Devt and Investment Co. (Padico) 1994; f. Paltel phone co.; mem. Palestinian Cen. Council. *Address:* Palestine Development and Investment Company, POB 316, Nablus, Palestinian Autonomous Areas (office). *Telephone:* (9) 2384354 (office). *Fax:* (9) 2384355 (office). *E-mail:* padico@padico.com (office). *Website:* www.padico.com (office).

MASRI, Taher Nashat, BBA; Jordanian politician and diplomatist; *Senator, Jordanian Parliament (Upper House);* b. 5 March 1942, Nablus; s. of Nashat Masri and Hadiyah Solh; m. Samar Bitar 1968; one s. one d.; ed Al-Najah Nat. Coll., Nablus and North Texas State Univ., USA; with Cen. Bank of Jordan 1965–73; mem. Parl. (Lower House) 1973–74, 1984–88, 1989–97; Minister of State for Occupied Territories Affairs 1973–74; Amb. to Spain 1975–78, to France 1978–83, also accred to Belgium 1979–80, Rep. to EEC 1978–80; Perm. Del. to UNESCO 1978–83; Amb. to UK 1983–84; Minister of Foreign Affairs 1984–88, Jan.–June 1991; Deputy Prime Minister and Minister of State for Econ. Affairs April–Sept. 1989; Chair. Foreign Relations Cttee 1989–91, 1992–93; Prime Minister and Minister of Defence June–Nov. 1991; Speaker Nat. Ass. 1993–94; Senator 1998–2001, 2005–; fmr Rep. to Arab League; mem. and Rapporteur, Royal Comm. for Drafting the Nat. Charter 1990; Chair. Bd Princess Haya Cultural Center for Children 1992–; Pres. Nat. Soc. for the Enhancement of Freedom and Democracy (JUND) 1993–97, Jordanian-Spanish Friendship Asscn 1998–, Bd of Trustees Jordan Univ. for Science and Tech., Irbid 1998–; Commr for Civic Socs with Arab League, Cairo (stationed in Amman) 2002–; mem. and Head, Political Cttee of the Royal Comm. for Drafting the Nat. Agenda 2005–; mem. Alkuods Al-Sharif Defending Asscns 1996–2001, 2003–, Advisory Cttee Anna Lindh Euro-Mediterranean Foundation for the Dialogue between Cultures 2004–; Grand Cordon, Jewelled Al-Nahda (Order of the Renaissance) (Jordan), Order of Al-Nahda (1st Degree) (Jordan), Order of Al-Kawkab (Jordan) 1974, Gran Cruz de Mérito Civil (Spain) 1977, Order of Isabel la Católica (Spain) 1978, Commdr, Légion d'honneur 1981, Grand Officier, Ordre Nat. du Mérite, Order of Merit (Grand Cross, First Class, FRG), Kt Grand Cross (Italy); Hon. GBE; Grand Cordon, Ordre Nat. de Cedre (Lebanon), Grand Decoration of Honour in Gold with Sash for Services (Austria), Order of Diplomatic Service Merit and Gwanghawa Medal (Repub. of Korea); numerous awards. *Address:* PO Box 5550, Amman 11183, Jordan. *Telephone:* (6) 4642227 (office); (6) 5920600 (home). *Fax:* (6) 4642226 (office). *E-mail:* t.n.masri@index.com.jo (office).

MASSA, Sergio; Argentine politician and government official; *Cabinet Chief;* b. 28 April 1972, Buenos Aires; m.; two c.; ed Belgrano Univ.; joined Unión del Centro Democrático 1989, then joined Partido Justicialista; Social Devt Adviser in Vice-Presidential campaign of Ramon Ortega 1999; Exec. Dir Nat. Agency for Social Security Admin (ANSES) 2002–07; elected mem. Chamber of Deputies 2005 but relinquished seat to stay at ANSES; Mayor of Tigre 2007– (currently on leave); Cabinet Chief 2008–; Lifetime Mem. Club Atlético Tigre 2007–. *Address:* Office of the Cabinet Chief, Julio A. Roca 782, C1067APB, Buenos Aires, Argentina (office). *Telephone:* (11) 4331-1951 (office). *E-mail:* infosig@jgm.gov.ar (office). *Website:* www.jgm.gov.ar (office).

MASSAD, Carlos, MA, PhD; Chilean banker and economist; b. 29 Aug. 1932, Santiago; m.; five c.; ed Univ. of Chile, Chicago Univ.; Dir of Dept of Econs, Univ. of Chile 1959–64; Vice-Pres. Cen. Bank of Chile 1964–67, Pres. 1967–70, Gov. 1996–2003 (resgnd); Exec. Dir of IMF 1970–74; mem. of Advisory Cttee, World Bank 1978–81; various posts, Econ. Comm. for Latin America (CEPAL) 1970–92; Exec. Pres., Eduardo Frei Montalva Foundation 1993–94; Minister of Health 1994–96; Euromoney Best Cen. Banker of Latin America 1997, The Banker Cen. Bank Gov. For the Americas Region of the Year 2001. *Publications:* Macroeconomics 1979, Rudiments of Economics 1980, Adjustment With Growth 1984; Economic Analysis: An Introduction to Microeconomics 1986, Internal Debt and Financial Stability (Vol. 1) 1987, (Vol. 2) 1988, The Financial System and Resource Distribution: Study based on Latin America and the Caribbean 1990, Elements of Economics: An Introduction to Economic Analysis 1993, On Public Health and Other Topics 1995, Macroeconomía en un mundo interdependiente (with Guillermo Patillo) 2000; and numerous articles. *Address:* c/o Central Bank of Chile, Agustinas 1180, Castilla 967, Santiago, Chile (office).

MASSÉ, Hon. Marcel, PC, MP, OC, QC, BA, LLB, BPhilEcon; Canadian banker and civil servant; *Executive Director for Canada, World Bank Group;* b. 23 June 1940, Montreal; m. Josée M'Baye 1965; three s. one d.; ed Univ. of Montreal, McGill Univ., Montreal, Univ. of Warsaw, Poland, Oxford Univ., UK; called to Bar, Québec 1963; Admin. and Econs Div., World Bank, Washington, DC 1967–71; Econ. Adviser, Privy Council Office, Ottawa 1971–73; Deputy Minister of Finance, Prov. of NB 1973–74, Chair. Cabinet Secr. 1974–77; Deputy Sec. Cabinet for Fed. Prov. Relations, Ottawa 1977–79, Deputy Sec. Cabinet (Operations), Privy Council Office 1979, Sec. to the Cabinet and Clerk of the Privy Council Office 1979–80; Pres. Canadian Int. Devt Agency, Ottawa 1980–82; Under-Sec. of State for External Affairs, Ottawa 1982–85; Canadian Exec. Dir IMF, Washington 1985–89; Pres. Canadian Int. Devt Agency (CIDA) 1989–93; Sec. to Cabinet for Intergovernmental Affairs March–June 1993; MP for Hull-Aylmer 1993–99; Pres. of the Privy Council and Minister of Intergovernmental Affairs and responsible for Public Service Renewal 1993–96; Pres. of Treasury Bd 1996–99, Exec. Dir Inter-American Devt Bank 1999–2002; Exec. Dir for Canada, World Bank Group 2002–; Hon. DCL (Acadia Univ.) 1983; Hon. LLD (New Brunswick) 1984; Dr hc (Univ. du Québec) 1992, (Ottawa Univ.) 1996. *Address:* 1818 H Street, NW, Washington, DC 20433, USA (office). *Telephone:* (202) 458-0077 (office). *Fax:* (202) 477-4155 (office). *E-mail:* mmasse@worldbank.org (office). *Website:* www.worldbank.org (office).

MASSE, Hon. Marcel; Canadian politician; *President, Société Héritage de Champlain;* b. 1936, Saint-Jean-de-Matha, Québec; s. of Rosaire Masse and Clermont; m. Cécile Martin 1960; one s. one d.; ed Ecole normale Jacques-Cartier, Univ. of Montreal, Sorbonne, City of London Coll., European Inst. of Business Admin.; fmr teacher of ancient history, Lanaudière Regional School Bd; Dir Lavalin (eng co.) 1974–84 (also Project Dir for UNDP, Vice-Pres., Vice-Pres. of Marketing and Commercial Devt); mem. Québec Nat. Ass. 1966–73 (held portfolios of Minister of State for Educ., Minister responsible for Public Service, for Inter-Governmental Affairs, Minister of Planning and Devt); Minister of Communications 1984–85, 1985–86, of Energy, Mines and Resources 1986–89, of Communications 1989–90, responsible for La Francophonie 1990, of Defence 1991–93; Chief Consultant CFC (consultancy) 1994–95; Del.-Gen. of Québec to France 1996–97; Pres. Comm. franco-québécoise sur les lieux de mémoire communs 1997–2006, Comm. des biens culturels du Québec 1997–2000; f. Société Héritage de Champlain 2005, now Pres.; fmr Pres. Wilfrid Pelletier Foundation; Dir numerous orgs including Montreal Symphony Orchestra, Canadian Writers' Foundation, Canadian Refugee Foundation, Lanaudière Summer Festival, Club de Dakar, Jeunesses Musicales du Canada; Progressive Conservative; Officier, Légion d'honneur, Ordre du Québec. *Leisure interests:* reading, music, fishing, skiing. *Address:* CP 1030, Saint-Donat, PQ J0T 2C0, Canada (office).

MASSENGALE, Martin Andrew, BS, MS, PhD; American university administrator, agronomist and academic; *Director, Center for Grassland Studies, Foundation Distinguished Professor and President Emeritus, University of Nebraska;* b. 25 Oct. 1933, Monticello, Ky; s. of the late Elbert G. Massengale and Orpha Conn Massengale; m. Ruth A. Klingelhofer 1959; one s. one d.; ed W Kentucky Univ. and Univ. of Wis.; Asst Agronomist and Asst Prof., Univ. of Ariz., Tucson 1958–62, Assoc. Agronomist and Assoc. Prof. 1962–65, Agronomist and Prof. 1965–66, Agronomist, Prof. and Head of Dept 1966–74, Assoc. Dean, Coll. of Agric. and Assoc. Dir Agricultural Experiment Station 1974–76; Vice-Chancellor for Agric. and Natural Resources, Univ. of Nebraska, Lincoln 1976–81, Chancellor Univ. of Nebraska 1981–91, Interim Pres. 1989–91, Pres. 1991–94, Pres. Emer. 1994–, Dir Center for Grassland Studies and Foundation Distinguished Prof. 1994–; Pres. Crop Science Soc. of America 1973–74, Grazing Lands Forum 1997–98; Chair. Agronomic Science Foundation; mem. numerous cttees, nat. panels, advisory bds etc. including Chair., Exec. Comm. and Advisory Bd to US Sec. of Agric., US Senate and House of Reps Agric. and Appropriations Cttees; Fellow, AAAS, American Soc. of Agronomy, Crop Science Soc. of America and other professional socs; Hon. Lifetime Trustee, Neb. Council on Econ. Educ. 1999; Dr hc (Neb. Wesleyan Univ., Senshu Univ., Tokyo), Distinguished Alumni (Western Kentucky) 2002; numerous honours and awards including Triumph of Agri Award 1999, Nebraska Agriculture Relations Co. Honoree 2000, Nebraska LEAD Alumni Asscn 'Friend of LEAD' Award 2001, Outstanding Pres.'s Award, All-American Football Foundation 2001, Alpha Gamma Rho Brothers of the Century Award 2004; mem. US Dept of Agric. Charter Hall of Fame 2004, Nebraskaland Foundation Wagonmaster Award 2006, Gamma Sigma Delta Distinguished Achievement in Agric. Award 2008. *Publication:* Renewable Resource Management for Forestry and Agriculture (co-ed.) 1978; numerous peer-reviewed articles in scientific journals. *Leisure interests:* reading, travel, golf, photography. *Address:* 220 Keim Hall, University of Nebraska, Lincoln, NE 68583-0953 (office); 3436 West Cape Charles Road, Lincoln, NE 68516, USA (home). *Telephone:* (402) 472-4101 (office); (402) 420-5350 (home). *Fax:* (402) 472-4104 (office). *E-mail:* mmassengale1@unl.edu (office). *Website:* www.grassland.unl.edu (office).

MASSERET, Jean-Pierre; French politician; b. 23 Aug. 1944, Cusset (Alliers); s. of Lucien Masseret and Claudia Rollet; m. Marie-Hélène Roddier 1967; three c.; ed Institut des Hautes Etudes de Défense Nationale; fmr Chief Insp., Inland Revenue; mem. staff of Minister for War Veterans 1981–86; Senator for Moselle 1983–, Vice-Chair. Senate Finance Cttee; Minister of State attached to Minister of Defence, with responsibility for War Veterans 1997–2001; Mayor of Havange (Moselle) 1995–97; Pres., Lorraine Regional Council 2004–, mem. Parti Socialiste Political Cttee; mem. Parl. Ass. of WEU, of Council of Europe, Socialist Party Nat. Office; fmr Chair. Lorraine Athletics League 1986–92; fmr regional champion runner. *Address:* Senat, Palais du Luxembourg, 75291 Paris Cedex 06, France (office). *Telephone:* 1-42-34-20-64 (office). *Fax:* 1-42-34-42-62 (office). *E-mail:* jp.masseret@senat.fr (office). *Website:* www.senat.fr (office).

MASSEY, Anna, CBE; British actress; b. Sussex; d. of Raymond Massey and Adrienne Allen; m. 1st Jeremy Huggins 1958 (divorced 1963); one s.; m. 2nd Prof. Uri Andres 1988; ed in London, New York, France, Switzerland and Italy. *Films include:* Gideon's Day 1958, Peeping Tom 1960, The Trip to Biarritz 1962, Bunny Lake Is Missing 1965, De Sade 1969, The Looking Glass War 1969, Frenzy 1972, The Vault of Horror 1973, A Doll's House 1973, A Little Romance 1979, Sweet William 1980, Five Days One Summer 1982, Another Country 1984, The Little Drummer Girl 1984, The Chain 1984, The McGuffin 1985, Killing Dad 1989, Journey into the Shadows (Best Actress, Locarno Film Festival 1984), Sacred Hearts (Royal TV Soc. Award 1986) 1985, Foreign Body 1986, La couleur du vent 1988, The Tall Guy 1989, Mountains of the Moon 1990, Impromptu 1991, Emily's Ghost 1992, Angels & Insects 1995,

Haunted 1995, The Grotesque 1995, Sweet Angel Mine 1996, Driftwood 1997, The Slab Boys 1997, Déjà Vu 1997, Captain Jack 1999, Mad Cows 1999, Room to Rent 2000, Dark Blue World 2001, Possession 2002, The Importance of Being Earnest 2002, The Machinist 2004, Mrs. Palfrey at the Claremont 2005, The Gigolos 2006, The Oxford Murders 2008, Affinity 2008. *Theatre roles:* debut in The Reluctant Debutante aged 17; subsequent appearances in School for Scandal, The Doctor's Dilemma, The Right Honourable Gentleman, The Miracle Worker, The Glass Menagerie, The Prime of Miss Jean Brodie; appeared with Nat. Theatre in 1970s and 1980s in Heartbreak House, Close of Play, Summer, The Importance of Being Earnest (Best Supporting Actress Award, Soc. of West End Theatre 1983, Best Supporting Actress, British Theatre Asscn 1986), A Kind of Alaska (Best Supporting Actress, British Theatre Asscn 1986), Family Voices, King Lear, Mary Stuart (1996); also appeared at The Royal Court in Spoiled, The Seagull. *Radio:* many radio plays and narration of This Sceptred Isle BBC Radio 1999. *Television includes:* A Midsummer Night's Dream 1964, Hay Fever 1968, Before the Party 1969, David Copperfield 1969, A Woman Sobbing 1972, The Pallisers (series) 1974, Churchill's People (series) 1974, The Love of a Good Woman 1976, The Mayor of Casterbridge (mini-series) 1978, Mrs Danvers in Rebecca 1979, The Corn is Green 1979, Afternoon Off 1979, You're Not Watching Me, Mummy 1980, Lady Nelson in I Remember Nelson (mini-series) 1982, The Cherry Orchard, The Critic 1982, Mansfield Park (mini-series) 1983, Journey into the Shadows: Portrait of Gwen John 1983, Sakharov 1984, Anna Karenina 1985, Season's Greetings 1986, The Christmas Tree 1986, Hotel du Lac (Royal TV Soc. Award 1986, BAFTA Award for Best Actress 1987) 1986, The Day After the Fair 1987, A Hazard of Hearts 1987, Tears in the Rain 1988, Sun Child 1988, Under a Dark Angel's Eye (mini-series) 1989, Shalom Joan Collins 1989, Around the World in 80 Days (mini-series) 1989, A Tale of Two Cities (mini-series) 1989, Sea Dragon 1990, Mistress of Suspense (series) 1990, The Man from the Pru 1990, The Return of the Psammead (series) 1993, Murder In Mind 1994, Nice Day at the Office (series) 1994, A Respectable Trade (mini-series) 1998, Come and Go 2000, The Sleeper 2000, He Knew He was Right (mini-series) 2004, Belonging 2004, Agatha Christie: A Life in Pictures 2004, The Robinsons (series) 2005, A Good Murder 2006, Pinochet in Suburbia 2006, Oliver Twist 2007. *Publication:* Telling Some Tales (autobiog.) 2006. *Address:* c/o Markham and Froggatt Ltd, 4 Windmill Street, London, W1P 1HF, England (office).

MASSON, Jacques, LenD; French banker; b. 17 April 1924, Paris; s. of Georges Masson and Yvonne Masson (née Poutot); m. Annie Bedhet 1946; one s. two d. (one deceased); ed Faculté de Droit, Paris, Ecole Nat. d'Organisation Economique et Sociale and Centre de Perfectionnement dans l'Admin des Affaires; joined Banque Nat. de Paris (BNP) 1950, Asst Dir 1963, Dir in charge of Paris branches 1964, Dir 1972, Asst Dir-Gen. 1978, Dir-Gen. 1982–87, Hon. Dir-Gen. 1987; Prof., Inst. Technique de banque du Conservatoire nat. des arts et métiers 1971–; Dir Basaltes 1988–; mem. Banking Comm.; Pres. BNP Bail; Chair. Bd Dirs Groupement des Cartes Bancaires CB 1988–93; Dir SILEC, Nouvelles Galeries, Devanlay, Soc. Nouvelle des Basaltes, Econoler France, Soc. Cheddito France SA; mem. Supervisory Bd, SOVAC; Chevalier, Légion d'honneur, Officier, Ordre Nat. du Mérite. *Address:* 34 rue du Docteur Blanche, 75016 Paris, France (home).

MASTELLA, Clemente; Italian journalist and politician; *Mayor of San Giovanni di Ceppaloni;* b. 5 Feb. 1947, Ceppaloni, Benevento; m. Sandra Lonardo; early career as journalist, RAI Naples; mem. Parl. 1976–; Mayor of San Giovanni di Ceppaloni 1987–1992, 2003–; Co-founder Centro Cristiano Democratico party (after dissolution of Christian Democracy party) 1994; Minister of Labour 1994–95; Co-founder Cristiano Democratici per la Repubblica, then Unione Democratici per la Repubblica 1998; Sec. Popolari—UDEUR (Alleanza Popolare—Unione Democratici per l'Europa) (Union of Democrats for Europe) 1999–; Deputy Speaker of the House 2001–06; Minister of Justice 2006–08 (resgnd). *Address:* Popolari—UDEUR (Alleanza Popolare—Unione Democratici per l'Europa) (Union of Democrats for Europe), Largo Arenula 34, 00186 Rome, Italy. *Telephone:* (06) 684241. *Fax:* (06) 68210615. *E-mail:* info@popolariudeur.it. *Website:* www.popolariudeur.it; www.clementemastella.it.

MASTER, Simon Harcourt; British publisher; b. 10 April 1944, Caterham; s. of Humphrey R. Master and Rachel B. Plumbly; m. Georgina M. C. Batsford 1969; two s.; ed Ardingly Coll. Sussex; Publishing Dir Pan Books Ltd 1973–80, Man. Dir 1980–87; Chief Exec. Random House UK and Exec. Vice-Pres. Random House Int. Group 1987–89, Group Man. Dir Random Century Group 1989–90, Group Deputy Chair. 1989–2006, Chair., CEO Gen. Books Div., Random House UK 1992–2006; Chair., Arrow Books 1990–92; Dir (non-exec.) HMSO 1990–95; mem. Council Publrs Asscn 1989–95 (Vice-Pres. 1995–96, 2000–2001, Pres. 1996–97, 2001–02); mem. Advisory Panel, London Book Fair 2008. *Leisure interests:* gardening, golf, classic cars, scuba diving.

MASTERSON, Patrick, PhD, MRIA; Irish university professor; *President, European University Institute;* b. 19 Oct. 1936, Dublin; s. of Laurence Masterson and Violet Masterson; m. Frances Lenehan; one s. three d.; ed Belvedere Coll., Castleknock Coll., Univ. Coll., Dublin, Univ. of Louvain; mem. staff Dept of Metaphysics, Univ. Coll., Dublin 1963–72, Prof. Faculties of Arts, Philosophy and Sociology 1972–80, Dean of the Faculty of Philosophy and Sociology 1980–83, Registrar 1983–86, Pres. 1986–93; Pres. European Univ. Inst., Florence 1994–; Vice-Chancellor Nat. Univ. of Ireland 1987, 1988, 1993; Grande Oficial, Ordem do Mérito da República Portuguesa, Grande Ufficiale della Repubblica Italiana; Dr hc (Caen, Trinity Coll. Dublin, New York). *Publications:* Atheism and Alienation: A Study of the Philosophical Sources of Contemporary Atheism 1971, Images of Man in Ancient and Medieval Thought: (Studia Gerardo Verbeke ab amicis et collegis dictata) 1976. *Leisure interests:* modern art, reading, theatre, fishing. *Address:* Office of the President, European University Institute, Badia Fiesolana, Via dei Roccettini

9, 50016 San Domenico di Fiesole (FI), Italy. *Telephone:* (055) 4685310. *Fax:* (055) 4685312.

MASTERSON, Valerie, CBE; British singer; b. Birkenhead; d. of Edward Masterson and Rita McGrath; m. Andrew March; one s. one d.; Prof. of Singing, RAM, London 1992–; Pres. British Youth Opera 1994–99, Vice-Pres. 2000–; has sung with D'Oyly Carte Opera, Glyndebourne, Royal Opera House, Covent Garden and English Nat. Opera and on TV and radio; also in major opera houses abroad including Paris, Aix-en-Provence, Toulouse, Munich, Geneva, San Francisco and Chicago; Hon. FRCM 1992; Hon. FRAM 1993; Hon. DLitt (South Bank Univ.) 1999; Award for Outstanding Individual Performance of the Year in a New Opera, Soc. of West End Theatre 1983. *Opera roles include:* La Traviata, Manon, Semele, Merry Widow, Louise, Lucia di Lammermoor, Mireille; other leading roles in Faust, Alcina, Die Entführung aus dem Serail, Le Nozze di Figaro, Così fan Tutte, La Bohème, Magic Flute, Julius Caesar, Rigoletto, Orlando, Der Rosenkavalier, Xerxes, The Pearl Fishers, Die Fledermaus etc. *Recordings include:* Julius Caesar, La Traviata, Elisabetta Regina d'Inghilterra, Bitter Sweet, Ring Cycle, recitals and various Gilbert and Sullivan discs. *Leisure interests:* tennis, swimming. *Address:* c/o Music International, 13 Ardilaun Road, London, N5 2QR, England (office). *Telephone:* (20) 7359-5183 (office). *Fax:* (20) 7226-9792 (office). *E-mail:* music@musicint.co.uk (office). *Website:* www.musicint.co.uk (office).

MASUDA, Hiroya; Japanese politician; b. 20 Dec. 1951; ed Univ. of Tokyo; began career at Ministry of Construction 1977; Dir Traffic Enforcement Div., Traffic Dept, Chiba Pref. Police HQ 1982–86; Dir Railway Traffic Div., Dept of Planning, Ibaraki Pref. 1986–93; Dir River Admin Policy Planning, Gen. Affairs Div., River Bureau, Ministry of Construction 1993–94, Dir Construction Disputes Settlement, Construction Industry Div., Econ. Affairs Bureau 1994–95; Gov. of Iwate Pref. 1995–2007; Minister for Internal Affairs and Communications, Minister of State for Decentralization Reform, Correcting Regional Disparities, Regional Govt (doshu-sei) and Privatization of the Postal Services 2007–08 (resgnd). *Address:* c/o Ministry of Internal Affairs and Communications, 2-1-2, Kasumigaseki, Chiyoda-ku, Tokyo 100-8926, Japan (office).

MASUI, Yoshio, PhD, FRS, OC, FRSC; Canadian (b. Japanese) biologist and academic; *Professor Emeritus, Department of Zoology, University of Toronto;* b. 1931, Kyoto; s. of Fusa-Jiro Masui and Toyoko Masui; m. Yuriko Masui 1959; one s. one d.; ed Kyoto Univ.; teacher of biology, Konan High School, Kobe; Research Asst, Biology Dept, Konan Univ. 1955–61, Lecturer 1961–65, Asst Prof. 1965–68, Prof. Emer. 1997–; Lecturer, Biology Dept, Yale Univ. 1969; Assoc. Prof., Zoology Dept, Univ. of Toronto 1969–78, Prof. 1978–97, Prof. Emer. 1997–; Visiting Prof. Tokyo Univ. 1999, Hiroshima Univ. 2000, Konan Univ. 2002–04; discovered Maturation Promoting Factor (MPF), cytostatic factor (CSF) proteins in the cytoplasm of cells that controls cell div.; Manning Award 1991, Gairdner Int. Award 1992, Albert Lasker Medical Research Award 1998. *Publications:* numerous scientific papers. *Address:* Department of Zoology, University of Toronto, 25 Harbord Street, Toronto, Ont. M5S 3G5 (office); 32 Overton Crescent, Don Mills, North York, Toronto, Ont. M3B 2V2, Canada (home). *Telephone:* (416) 978-3493 (office); (416) 444-6972 (home). *Fax:* (416) 978-8532 (office). *E-mail:* masui@zoo.utoronto.ca (office). *Website:* www.zoo.utoronto.ca (office).

MASUKO, Osamu; Japanese automotive industry executive; *Representative Director, President and Chief Business Ethics Officer, Mitsubishi Motors Corporation;* ed Waseda Univ.; joined Mitsubishi Corpn 1972, Man. Korea Team, Motor Vehicle Dept 1990–91, Man. Indonesia Team 1991–95, Asst Gen. Man. Motor Vehicle Dept 1995–97, Chief Adviser, P.T. Krama Yudhi Tiga Berlian Motors, Jakarta 1997–2002, Gen. Man. Motor Vehicle Unit 2002–03, Sr Vice Pres. and Div. COO Motor Vehicle Business Div. 2003–04, Man. Dir and Head Overseas Operations 2004–05, Pres., COO, Chief Business Ethics Officer Mitsubishi Motors Corpn Jan.–April 2005, Rep. Dir, Pres. and Chief Business Ethics Officer April 2005–. *Address:* Mitsubishi Motors Corpn, 2-16-4 Konan, Minato-ku, Tokyo 108-8410, Japan (office). *Telephone:* (3) 6719-2111 (office). *Fax:* (3) 6719-0059 (office). *E-mail:* info@mitsubishi-motors.co.jp (office). *Website:* www.mitsubishi-motors.co.jp (office).

MASUR, Kurt; German conductor; b. 18 July 1927, Brieg, Silesia, Poland; ed Nat. Music School, Breslau, Hochschule für Musik, Leipzig; theatre conductor in Erfurt and Leipzig 1948–55, conductor, Dresden Philharmonic 1955–58, Chief Conductor 1967–72; Gen. Musical Dir, Mecklenburg State Theatre 1958–60; Prin. Musical Dir, Komische Oper in East Berlin 1960–64; Musical Dir Dresden Philharmonic 1967–72; Conductor, Leipzig Gewandhaus Orchestra 1970–96, Music Dir 1996–; UK début with New Philharmonia Orchestra 1973; début in USA with Cleveland Orchestra 1974; Music Dir Conductor New York Philharmonic 1991–2002; Prin. Conductor London Philharmonic Orchestra 1991–2007; Music Dir Orchestre Nat. de France 2002–08, Conductor Laureate 2008–; has toured extensively in Europe and the USA; Freeman of City of Leipzig; Hon. Pres. Kulturstiftung, Leipzig; Officier, Légion d'honneur, Bundesverdienstkreuz; Hon. Citizen of Brieg (Poland), Commdr Cross of Merit (Poland) 1999; hon. degrees from seven American univs and Univ. of Leipzig. *Address:* Masur Music International Inc., Ansonia PO Box 231478, New York, NY 10023, USA (office). *Telephone:* (646) 623-5803 (office). *Fax:* (212) 414-8276 (office). *E-mail:* info@kurtmasur.com (office). *Website:* www.kurtmasur.com (office).

MASUREL, Jean-Louis Antoine Nicolas, MBA; French industrialist and vintner; b. 18 Sept. 1940, Cannes; s. of Antoine and Anne-Marie Masurel (née Gallant); m. 1st 1964; two d.; m. 2nd Martine Fabrega 1987; ed Hautes Etudes Commerciales, Graduate School of Business Admin., Harvard Univ.; with Morgan Guaranty Trust Co., New York, last position Sr Vice-Pres. New York 1964–80; Sr Exec. Vice-Pres. Banque de Paris & des Pays Bas 1980–82; Deputy Pres. Banque Paribas 1982–83; Man. Dir Moët-Hennessy 1983–89, Vice-Chair. 1987; Man. Dir LVMH Moët-Hennessy Louis Vuitton 1987–89; Pres. Arcos Investissement SA 1989–, Hediard SA 1991–95; Hon. Pres. Harvard Business School Club de France 1993–96; mem. Supervisory Bd Peugeot SA 1987–, 21 Centrale Pnrs SA; Dir Soc. des Bains de Mer (SBM), Monaco 1994–; Sr Int. Adviser, BBL Investment Banking 1997–99, ING Barings 1999–2001; Dir Banque du Gothard SAM, Monaco 1998–, Oudart SA 1999–; Gov. American Hosp. in Paris; wine producer in Néoules (Domaine de Trians-Var); Chevalier des Arts et des Lettres 1996; Chevalier Légion d'honneur 2001. *Leisure interests:* hunting, skiing. *Address:* Arcos Investissement, 10a rue de la Paix, 75002 Paris; Domaine de Trians, 83136 Néoules, France (home). *Telephone:* 1-42-96-01-96. *Fax:* 1-42-96-01-70. *E-mail:* jlmasurel@wanadoo.fr (office). *Website:* www.trians.com (home).

MASUZOE, Yoichi, LLB; Japanese academic, politician and research institute director; b. 29 Nov. 1948, Fukuoka Pref.; ed Univ. of Tokyo; Research Fellow, Univ. of Tokyo 1971–73, L'Institut d'Histoire des Relations Internationales Contemporaines, Univ. of Paris, France 1973–75, L'Institut d'Hautes Etudes Internationales, Univ. of Geneva, Switzerland 1976–78; Assoc. Prof. of Political Science and History, Univ. of Tokyo 1979–89; Dir Masuzoe Inst. of Political Economy 1989–; mem. House of Councillors (Senator) 2001–, fmr Dir Budget Cttee, Research Comm. on Constitution, Pres. Cttee on Foreign Affairs and Defence 2005–07; Minister of Health, Labour and Welfare 2007–08 (resgnd); mem. Liberal Democratic Party (LDP), Chair. Senate Policy Bd 2006–; Ed.-in-Chief Cahiers Du Japon 1998–2001. *Publications:* Akai bara wa saitaka (Politics in France) 1983, Sengyo to siteno seijika (Political Leadership) 1989, Sengo Nihon no Gen'ei (Dangerous Cult) 1995, 20 Seiki Enerugi Kakumei no Jidai (The Meaning of the 20th Century) 1998, Years of Trial: Japan in the 1990s 2000. *Address:* Masuzoe Institute of Political Economy, 3-48-1 Daita, Setagaya-ku, Tokyo 155-0033 (office); Liberal-Democratic Party (LDP), 1-11-23, Nagata-cho, Chiyoda-ku, Tokyo 100-8910, Japan (office). *Telephone:* (3) 3581-6211 (office). *E-mail:* koho@ldp.jimin.or.jp (office). *Website:* www.masuzoe.gr.jp (office); www.jimin.jp (office).

MATACZYNSKI, Maciej; Polish lawyer and business executive; *Chairman, PKN Orlen;* ed Faculty of Law of Adam Mickiewicz Univ. (Fulbright Scholar), T.M.C. Assera Inst., The Hague, Netherlands; Tutor, European Law Professorship, Faculty of Law, Adam Mickiewicz Univ., Poznań 2003–; legal adviser on civil law contracts 2004–; Sec. and Ind. mem. Supervisory Bd PKN Orlen Feb.–Nov. 2006, currently Chair. Supervisory Bd, Chair. Nomination and Remuneration Cttee, mem. Corp. Governance Cttee; mem. Supervisory Bd TC Debica SA. *Publications:* numerous law publs in Poland and abroad. *Address:* PKN Orlen, 09-411 Plock, ul. Chemikow 7, Poland (office). *Telephone:* (24) 3650000 (office). *Fax:* (24) 3654040 (office). *E-mail:* info@orlen.pl (office). *Website:* www.orlen.pl (office).

MATAKI, Tateo; Japanese advertising industry executive; *Chairman, Dentsu Inc.;* Exec. Vice-Pres. Dentsu Inc. 1999–2002, Pres. and COO 2002–03, Pres. and CEO 2004–07, Chair. 2007–; Dir Japan Productivity Center for Socio-Econ. Devt (JPC-SED) 2003. *Address:* Dentsu Inc., 1-8-1 Higashi-shimbashi, Minato-ku, Tokyo 105-7001, Japan (office). *Telephone:* (3) 6216-5111 (office). *Fax:* (3) 5551-2013 (office). *Website:* www.dentsu.com (office).

MATANE, Sir Paulias Nguna, Kt, CMG, OBE, GCMG, KsfJ; Papua New Guinea diplomatist; *Governor-General;* b. 21 Sept. 1931, Viviran, Rabaul; s. of Ilias and Elta (Toto) Matane; m. Kaludia Peril 1957; two s. two d.; senior positions in Dept of Educ. 1957–69; mem. Public Service Bd 1969; Head, Dept of Lands, Surveys and Mines 1969, of Business Devt 1970–75; Amb. to USA and Mexico 1975–80, Perm. Rep. to UN 1975–81, High Commr in Canada 1977–81; Sec., Dept of Foreign Affairs and Trade 1980–85; Chair. Cttee on the Philosophy of Educ. for Papua New Guinea 1986–88, Cocoa Industry Investigating Cttee of Cocoa Quality in Papua New Guinea 1986–88, Ocean Trading Co. Pty Ltd 1989–91, Newton Pacific (PNG) Pty Ltd 1989–; Censorship Bd of PNG 1990–93; Dir Triad Pacific (PNG) Pty Ltd 1987–96 (Chair. 1987–91); Presenter weekly radio programme Insait Long Komuniti 1998–, weekly programme on EMTV 1990–; Columnist The Time Traveller, in The National Newspaper 1999–; Dir Nat. Museum and Art Gallery (Bd of Trustees) 1995–99, Pres. 1999–; Dir Nat. Library and Archives 1996–; Chair. Community Consultative Cttee on East New Britain Provincial Govt of Autonomy –2004; Gov.-Gen. of Papua New Guinea 2004–; mem. Nat. Investment and Devt Authority, Nat. Tourism Authority, Nat. Citizenship Advisory Cttee, Univ. of Papua New Guinea Council; Hon. DTech (Papua New Guinea) 1985; Hon. DPhil (Papua New Guinea) 1985; 10th Independence Anniversary Medal 1985, UN 40th Anniversary Medal, Silver Jubilee Medal 2001. *Publications:* My Childhood in New Guinea, A New Guinean Travels through Africa, Two New Guineans Travel through South East Asia, What Good is Business?, Aimbe the Magician, Aimbe the Challenger, Aimbe the School Dropout, Aimbe the Pastor, Kum Tumun of Minj, Two Papua New Guineans Discover the Bible Lands (later retitled Travels Through the Bible Lands) 1987, To Serve with Love 1989, Chit-Chats 1991, East to West–The Longest Train Trip in the World 1991, Let's Do It PNG, Trekking through the New Worlds, Voyage to Antarctica 1996, Laughter Made in PNG 1996, Amazing Discoveries in 40 Years of Marriage 1996, The Word Power 1998, The Other Side of Port Moresby . . . In Pictures 1998, A Trip of a Lifetime 1998, Waliling Community United Church Then and Now 1998, Coach Adventures Down Under 1999, Some Answers to our Management Problems in the Public and Private Sectors 1999, More Answers to Our Management Problems 1999, Chit-Chats (vol. 3) 2000, Management for Excellence 2001, Exploring the Holy Lands 2001, Travels Through South-East Asia (Vols 1 and 2) 2001, Humour: The Papua New Guinean Way, Ripples in the South Pacific Ocean, India: a

Splendour in Cultural Diversity, Papua New Guinea: The Land of Natural Beauty, Diversity: The Time Traveller. *Leisure interests:* reading, squash, writing, travel, gardening, swimming. *Address:* Paulias Matane Foundation Inc., Government House, P.O. Box 79, Port Moresby, NCD, Papua New Guinea (office). *Telephone:* 3202020 (office). *Fax:* 3202020 (office). *E-mail:* ggeneral@global.net.pg (office).

MATANZIMA, Chief Kaiser; South African politician and lawyer; b. 1915, St Mark's Dist; s. of the late Mhlobo Matanzima; m. Nozuko Jayinja 1954; four s. five d.; ed Lovedale Missionary Institution and Fort Hare Univ. Coll.; Chief, Amahale Clan of Tembus, St Mark's District 1940; mem. United Transkeian Gen. Council 1942–56; Perm. Head Emigrant Tembuland Regional Authority and mem. Exec. Cttee Transkeian Territorial Authority 1956–58; Regional Chief of Emigrant Tembuland 1958–61; Presiding Chief Transkeian Territorial Authority 1961–63; Chief Minister of Transkei 1963–76, Prime Minister 1976–79; Pres. Repub. of Transkei 1979–85; Leader, Transkei Nat. Party 1987–88; Chancellor, Univ. of Transkei 1977–88; Freeman of Umtata 1982; Hon. LLD (Fort Hare). *Publication:* Independence My Way 1977. *Address:* Qamata, Bizana District, Transkei, South Africa.

MATASKELEKELE, Kalkot; Ni-Vanuatu lawyer, judge and head of state; *President;* fmr Judge on Supreme Court; Pres. of Vanuatu 2004–. *Address:* Office of the President, Port Vila, Vanuatu (office).

MATENDA KYELU, Athanase; Democratic Republic of the Congo politician; *Minister of Finance;* Admin., Fed. of Businesses of the Democratic Repub. of Congo (FEC) –2003; mem. Parl. 2003–; Minister of Public Works and Infrastructure 2004–06, of Finance 2007–; mem. People's Party for Reconstruction and Democracy (PPRD). *Address:* Ministry of Finance, Boulevard du 30 juin, BP 12998, KIN I, Kinshasa–Gombe, Democratic Republic of the Congo (office). *Telephone:* (12) 31197 (office). *Website:* www.minfinrdc.cd (office).

MATEPARAE, Lt-Gen. Jerry, MA; New Zealand army officer and government official; *Chief, New Zealand Defence Force;* b. Nov. 1954; m. Janine Mateparae; five c.; ed Officer Cadet School, Portsea, Australia, Univ. of Waikato; enlisted Regular Force of NZ Army 1972; mem. Royal NZ Infantry Regiment (RNZIR) 1976; appointments included command at platoon, co. and battalion level in NZ Infantry Battalions, also served with NZ Special Air Service, commanded First Battalion RNZIR; other appointments included Chief Instructor NZ Army's Tactical School, Staff Officer Operations, NZ Army Training Group, Army Gen. Staff and Dir of Force Devt, HQ NZ Defence Force; apptd NZ Army's Land Commdr 1999; joint command of NZ forces in East Timor 1999–2001; re-apptd Land Component Commdr in HQ of Joint Forces New Zealand 2001; Chief of Army 2002–06; Chief NZ Defence Force (first Maori) 2006–; Assoc. Fellow, NZ Inst. of Man.; Additional Officer NZ Order of Merit 1999. *Address:* Chief of Defence Force, Defence House, Wellington, New Zealand (office). *Telephone:* (4) 496-0999 (office). *Fax:* (4) 496-0859 (office). *Website:* www.nzdf.mil.nz (office).

MATEŠA, Zlatko, MA; Croatian politician, judge, academic and organization executive; *Assistant Dean, Zagreb School of Economics and Management;* b. 17 June 1949, Zagreb; m.; two c.; ed Zagreb Univ., Henley Man. College, UK, J. F. Kennedy School of Govt, Harvard, USA; Asst Judge, Judge Zagreb Municipal Court 1978–; Asst Man., Man. Legal Dept INA-Trade (Industrija Nafte Asscn) 1978–82, Dir Legal and Personnel Dept 1982–85, Dir Joint Admin. Services 1985–89, mem. Man. Bd, Vice-Pres. 1989–90; Asst to Gen.-Man. INA-HQ 1990–92; mem. Croatian Democratic Union (HDZ); Dir Agency for Reconstruction and Devt of Govt of Croatia 1992–93; Minister without Portfolio 1993–95; Minister of Economy Sept.–Nov. 1995; Prime Minister of Croatia 1995–2000; currently Asst Dean Zagreb School of Econs and Man.; Pres. Croatian Olympic Cttee. *Leisure interests* flying, water polo. *Address:* Zagreb School of Economics and Management, Jordanovac 110, 10000 Zagreb, Croatia (office). *Telephone:* (1) 2354242 (office). *Fax:* (1) 2354243 (office). *E-mail:* zlatko.matesa@zsem.hr (office). *Website:* www.zsem.hr (office).

MATEU PI, Meritxell; Andorran diplomatist and politician; *Minister of Foreign Affairs, Culture and Co-operation;* b. 19 Jan. 1966; ed Paul Valéry Univ., Montpellier and Inst. of Int. Relations, Paris, France; Amb. to France 1995–99, also Perm. Rep. to Council of Europe and UNESCO; Amb. to EU, Belgium and Luxembourg 1997–98, to Netherlands 1998–99, to Denmark 1999, to Germany 1999–2004, to Slovenia 2001; Minister of Housing, Higher Educ. and Research 2001–07, of Foreign Affairs, Culture and Co-operation 2007–. *Address:* Ministry of Foreign Affairs, Carrer Prat de la Creu, 62-64, AD500 Andorra la Vella, Andorra (office). *Telephone:* 875700 (office). *Fax:* 869559 (office). *E-mail:* exteriors.gov@andorra.ad (office). *Website:* www .maecc.ad (office).

MATEV, Lachezar Nikolov, MA, MSc, PhD; Bulgarian diplomatist; *Ambassador to UK;* b. 5 Aug. 1951, Sofia; m. Bisserka Mateva; two c.; ed Tech. Univ., Sofia, Sofia Univ., Moscow Diplomatic Acad.; mem. Bd, Higher Educ. Council, Ministry of Education 1977–82; Eastern European Countries Dept, Ministry of Foreign Affairs 1982; First Sec., Embassy in Prague 1982–89; Foreign Econ. Policy and Econ. Organisations Directorate 1992–93; Co-founder and Man. Dir Int. Business Devt magazine, 1992–93; Man. Dir VECCO Ltd; Head UN Agencies Section, Foreign Econ. Policy Dept 1993–95; mem., then Head, Bulgarian Del. to UNDP Exec. Bd 1994–95; Counsellor, Embassy in Madrid 1995–98; Head of Unit, European Integration Directorate, Ministry of Foreign Affairs, mem. Accession Negotiations Team, mem. Inter-Ministerial Cen. Coordination Unit for Nat. Plan for Econ. Devt, mem. Inter-Ministerial Cttee for Intellectual Rights' Protection, mem. Cttee on Use of Atomic Energy for Peaceful Purposes 1998–2002; Minister Plenipotentiary, Embassy in London 2002–05, Amb. to UK 2005–, also Perm. Rep. to IMO 2007–; Kt Commdr, Royal Order of St Francis 2006. *Leisure interests:* art, classical and opera music, theatre, tennis, swimming, karate, basketball, rowing, skiing, gardening, business and finance. *Address:* Bulgarian Embassy, 186–188 Queen's Gate, London, SW7 5HL, England (office). *Telephone:* (20) 7581-0781 (office). *Fax:* (20) 7584-4948 (office). *E-mail:* ambass.office@bulgarianembassy.org.uk (office). *Website:* www.bulgarianembassy-london.org (office).

MATHAS, Theodore (Ted) A., AB, JD; American insurance executive; *President and CEO, New York Life Insurance Company;* b. 1967, Norfolk, Va; m. Keryn Mathas; three c.; ed Stanford Univ., Univ. of Virginia; attorney, Debevoise & Plimpton –1995; joined Asset Man. Div., New York Life Insurance Co. 1995, Pres. Eagle Strategies Corpn (subsidiary co.) 1996–99, also Pres. NYLIFE Securities Inc. 1997–99, COO for career agency distribution system 1999–2001, COO Life & Annuity 2001–04, mem. Exec. Man. Cttee 2002–, mem. Bd Dirs and Vice-Chair. 2006–07, COO 2006–08, Pres. 2007–, CEO 2008–; Dir Haier New York Life Insurance Ltd, Shanghai, Max New York Life Insurance Co. Ltd, New Delhi. *Address:* New York Life Insurance Co., 51 Madison Avenue, Suite 3200, New York, NY 10010, USA (office). *Telephone:* (212) 576-7000 (office). *Fax:* (212) 576-8145 (office). *E-mail:* info@newyorklife.com (office). *Website:* www.newyorklife.com (office).

MATHÉ, Georges, MD; French professor of medicine; b. 9 July 1922, Sermages; s. of Adrien and Francine (née Doridot) Mathé; m. Marie-Louise Servier 1954; one d.; ed Lycée Banville, Moulins and Univ. de Paris; Head of Clinic, Medical Faculty, Paris Univ. 1952–53, Assoc. Prof. of Cancer Research Fac. Medicine, Paris 1956–67; Head, Dept of Haematology, Inst. Gustave-Roussy 1961; Tech. Counsellor, Ministry of Health 1964–66; Dir Inst. de Cancérologie et d'Immunogénétique 1964–84; Prof. of Experimental Cancerology, Faculté de Médecine, Univ. de Paris-Sud, Villejuif 1966; Ed.-in-Chief Biomedicine and Pharmacotherapy; Co-ed. Medical Oncology & Tumor Pharmacotherapy; consultant Swiss Hospital of Paris –1991, Hosp. of Oncology, Sofia; mem. Cen. Cttee Rassemblement pour la Répub.; Vice-Pres. Bd of Dirs INSERM 1972–73; Prés. Comité Consultatif de la Recherche Scientifique et Tech. 1972–75, Medical Oncology Soc., Comité cancer, European Hospital of Rome; mem. Royal Soc. of Medicine, New York Acad. of Sciences; Commdr, Légion d'honneur, Grand Officier; Ordre nat. du Mérite, Commendatore dell'Ordine al Merito della Repub. Italiana; Médaille d'or des hôpitaux de Paris, Grand Prix Humanitaire de France, Medawar Laureate Transplantation Soc. 2002; numerous foreign and international scientific awards. *Publications:* Le métabolisme de l'eau (with J. Hamburger) 1952, La greffe (with J.L. Amiel) 1962, Aspects histologiques et cytologiques des leucémies et hématosarcomes (with G. Séman) 1963, L'aplasie myélolymphoide de l'irradiation totale (with J.L. Amiel) 1965, Sémiologie médicale (with G. Richet) 1965 (3rd edn 1977), La chimiothérapie des cancers 1966 (3rd edn 1974), Le cancer 1967, Bone Marrow Transplantation and White Cells Transfusions (with J. L. Amiel and L. Schwarzenberg) 1971, La santé: est-elle au dessus de nos moyens? (with Catherine Mathé) 1970, Natural History and Modern Treatment of Hodgkin's Disease (with M. Tubianan) 1973, Histocytological typing of the neoplastic diseases of the haematopoietic and lymphoid tissues (with H. Rappaport) 1973, Cancérologie générale et clinique (with A. Cattan) 1974, Le temps d'y penser 1974, Immunothérapie active des cancers: immunoprévention et immunorestauration 1976, Cancer Active Immunotherapy; Immunoporphylaxis and Immunorestoration: An Introduction 1976, Cancer Chemotherapy: Its Role in the Treatment Strategy of Hematologic Malignancies and Solid Tumors (with A. Clarysse and Y. Kenis) 1976, Dossier Cancer 1977, L'homme qui voulait être guéri 1985 (novel), Nagasaki (play), Le Sexe des Dieux et des Diables 1992 (play), Le Sida sidère la science, le sexe et les sceaux 1995. *Leisure interests:* novel writing, theatre. *Address:* c/o Institut national de la santé et de la recherche médicale, 101 rue de Tolbiac, 75654 Paris Cedex 13, France (office); Le Fonbois, 10 Rue du Bon Puits, Arpajon, 91290 La Norville, France (home). *Telephone:* 64-90-03-58 (home).

MATHER, Graham Christopher Spencer, MA; British politician, solicitor and administrator; *President, European Policy Forum;* b. 23 Oct. 1954, Preston, Lancs.; s. of Thomas Mather and Doreen Mather; m. 1st Fiona Marion McMillan Bell 1981 (divorced 1995); two s.; m. 2nd Geneviève Elizabeth Fairhurst 1997; ed Hutton Grammar School, New Coll., Oxford (Burnet Law Scholar); Asst to Dir-Gen. Inst. of Dirs 1980, est. Policy Unit 1983, Head of Policy Unit 1983–86; Deputy Dir Inst. of Econ. Affairs 1987, Gen. Dir 1987–92; Pres. European Policy Forum 1992–, European Media Forum 1997–, European Financial Forum 1999–; MEP for Hampshire North and Oxford 1994–99; Visiting Fellow, Nuffield Coll. Oxford 1992–99; mem. Competition Appeals Tribunal 2000; mem. Monopolies and Mergers Comm. 1989–94, Westminster City Council 1982–86; Conservative parl. cand. for Blackburn 1983; Vice-Pres. Strategic Planning Soc. 1993–, Asscn of Dist Councils 1994–97; mem. Public Policy Advisory Bd, Queen Mary and Westfield Coll. London 1993–; Consultant Tudor Investment Corpn 1992–. *Publications:* Striking out Strikes (with C.G. Hanson) 1988; Europe's Constitutional Future (contrib.) 1990, Making Decisions in Britain 2000; papers and contribs to journals. *Address:* European Policy Forum, 49 Whitehall, London, SW1A 2BX, England (office). *Telephone:* (20) 7839-7565 (office). *Fax:* (20) 7839-7339 (office). *E-mail:* graham.mather@epfltd.org (office). *Website:* www.epfltd.org (office).

MATHER, John C., BA, PhD; American astrophysicist; *Senior Project Scientist, James Webb Space Telescope, Goddard Space Flight Center, National Aeronautics and Space Administration (NASA);* b. 7 Aug. 1946, Roanoke, Va; s. of Robert Eugene Mather and Martha Belle Cromwell Mather; m. Jane Anne Hauser; ed Swarthmore Coll., Pa, Univ. of California, Berkeley; began career as NAS Research Assoc., Goddard Inst. for Space Studies, NASA, becoming Project Scientist for Cosmic Background Explorer satellite (COBE) 1974–76, Study Scientist, Goddard Space Flight Center 1976–88, Head of Infrared Astrophysics Br. 1988–89, 1990–93, Study Scientist, James Webb Space Telescope (JWST) 1995–99, Sr Project Scientist 1999–; mem. NAS

1997–, American Acad. of Arts and Sciences 1998–; Fellow, American Physical Soc. 1996–, Int. Soc. for Optical Eng 2007–; Hon. DSc (Swarthmore Coll.) 1994, (Maryland) 2008; Goddard Sr Fellow, holder of numerous awards including John C. Lindsay Memorial Award 1990, NASA Exceptional Scientific Achievement Award 1991, Nat. Air and Space Museum Trophy 1991, American Inst. of Aeronautics and Astronautics Space Science Award 1993, American Acad. of Arts and Sciences Rumford Prize 1996, Univ. of Ariz. Marc Aaronson Memorial Prize 1998, Franklin Inst. Benjamin Franklin Medal 1999, Gruber Cosmology Prize 2006, Nobel Prize for Physics (with George F. Smoot) 2006. *Publications:* The Very First Light (co-author with John Boslough) 1996, 2008. *Address:* Mail Code 443, National Aeronautics and Space Administration, Goddard Space Flight Center, Greenbelt, MD 20771, USA (office). *Telephone:* (301) 286-6885 (office). *Fax:* (301) 286-5558 (office). *E-mail:* john.c.mather@nasa.gov (office). *Website:* astrophysics.gsfc.nasa.gov/staff/CVs/John.Mather (office).

MATHER, Richard Martin, BArch; British architect; *Director, Rick Mather Architects;* b. 30 May 1937; s. of the late Richard John Mather and Opal Martin; ed School of Architecture and Allied Arts, Univ. of Oregon; Assoc. Teacher, Univ. Coll. London, Univ. of Westminster, Harvard Grad. School of Design 1967–88; Prin. Rick Mather Architects 1973–; RIBA External Examiner to Univs and Colls in England and Scotland 1986–; Consultant Architect, Architectural Asscn 1978–92 (mem. Council 1992–96), Univ. of East Anglia 1988–92, Univ. of Southampton 1996; Trustee, Victoria & Albert Museum 2000–; Ellis F. Lawrence Medal, Univ. of Oregon School of Architecture 2005. *Major works include:* Times Headquarters Bldg, London (RIBA Award 1992), All Glass Structure, London (RIBA Award 1994), Arco Bldg, Keble Coll., Oxford (RIBA Award 1996, Civic Trust Award 1997), Sloane Robinson Bldg, Keble Coll., Oxford (Civic Trust Award 2005) 2002–, ISMA Centre, Univ. of Reading 1998 (RIBA Award 1999), Neptune Court, Nat. Maritime Museum (Civic Trust Award 2000), Wallace Collection 2000, Dulwich Picture Gallery (RIBA Crown Estates Conservation Award 2001, AIA Business Week/Architectural Record Award 2001, Civic Trust Award 2002), London Southbank Centre Masterplan 2000–, Virginia Museum of Fine Arts (Architectural Review/MIPIM Future Projects Award 2004), USA 2001–, Greenwich World Heritage Site Masterplan 2002–, Ashmolean Museum Masterplan 2002–, Natural History Museum Masterplan 2003–, Barking London Road, New Art & Design Acad., John Moores Univ., Liverpool 2005–, New Library and Archive Bldg, The Queen's Coll. 2006–, New Music Room, Corpus Christi Coll. 2006–, Acland Site Redevelopment, Keble Coll. Oxford 2006–, Barking River Roding Masterplan 2006–, West End One, Milton Keynes 2006–. *Publications:* Zen Restaurants: Rick Mather 1992, Rick Mather: Urban Approches 1992, Rick Mather Architects Monograph 2006. *Leisure interests:* gardens, skiing, food. *Address:* Rick Mather Architects, 123 Camden High Street, London, NW1 7JR, England (office). *Telephone:* (20) 7284-1727 (office). *Fax:* (20) 7267-7826 (office). *E-mail:* info@rickmather.com (office). *Website:* www.rickmather.com (office).

MATHEWS, (Forrest) David, PhD; American educationalist and foundation executive; *President, CEO and Trustee, Charles F. Kettering Foundation;* b. 6 Dec. 1935, Grove Hill, Ala; s. of Forrest Lee and Doris Mathews; m. Mary Chapman 1960; two d.; ed Univ. of Alabama and Columbia Univ.; Infantry Officer US Army Reserves 1959–67; Pres. Univ. of Alabama 1969–80, Lecturer and Prof. of History 1969–80; Sec. of Health, Educ. and Welfare 1975–77; Chair. Nat. Council for Public Policy Educ. 1980–; Dir Acad. Educ. Devt 1975–2003; Pres., CEO and Trustee Charles F. Kettering Foundation 1981–; mem. Bd Dirs Nat. Civic League 1996–2005; mem. numerous advisory and other bds including Acad. for Educ. Devt, Nat. Civic League, Exec. Cttee of Public Agenda; Trustee Nat. March of Dimes 1977–85, John F. Kennedy Center for Performing Arts 1975–77, Woodrow Wilson Int. Center for Scholars 1975–77, Miles Coll. 1978–, Teachers Coll., Columbia Univ. 1977–95, Gerald R. Ford Foundation 1988–; 16 hon. degrees; numerous awards. *Publications:* works on history of Southern USA, higher educ. in public policy, including The Changing Agenda for American Higher Education, The Promise of Democracy, Is There a Public for Public Schools? 1996, Politics for People: Finding a Responsible Voice 1999, Why Public Schools? Whose Public Schools? 2003, Reclaiming Public Education by Reclaiming Our Democracy 2006. *Leisure interest:* gardening. *Address:* The Charles F. Kettering Foundation, 200 Commons Road, Dayton, OH 45459 (office); 6050 Mad River Road, Dayton, OH 45459, USA. *Telephone:* (937) 434-7300 (office). *Fax:* (937) 428-5353 (office).

MATHEWSON, Sir George (Ross), Kt, CBE, MBA, PhD, FRSE, CEng, MIEE, CIMgt; British banking executive; b. 14 May 1940; s. of George Mathewson and Charlotte Gordon (née Ross); m. Sheila Alexandra Graham (née Bennett) 1966; two s.; ed Perth Acad., St Andrews Univ., Canisius Coll., Buffalo, NY, USA; Asst Lecturer, St Andrews Univ. 1964–67; various posts in Research and Devt, Avionics Engineer, Bell Aerospace, Buffalo, NY 1967–72; joined Industrial & Commercial Finance Corpn, Edinburgh 1972, Area Man., Aberdeen 1974, Asst Gen. Man. and Dir 1979; Chief Exec. and mem. Scottish Devt Agency 1981–87; Dir of Strategic Planning and Devt, Royal Bank of Scotland Group 1987–90, Deputy Group Chief Exec. 1990–92, Group Chief Exec. 1992–2000, Exec. Deputy Chair. 2000–01, Chair. 2001–06 (retd); Dir Scottish Investment Trust PLC (Chair. Nominations Cttee and Chair.'s Advisory Group) 1981–, IIF Inc. 2001–, Santander Central Hispano, SA 2001–; Pres. British Bankers' Asscn 2002–05; Fellow, Chartered Inst. of Bankers in Scotland 1994–; Hon. LLD (Dundee) 1983, (St Andrews) 2000; Hon. DUniv (Glasgow) 2001. *Publications include:* several articles on eng and finance. *Leisure interests:* rugby, tennis, business. *Address:* c/o The Royal Bank of Scotland PLC, 36 St Andrew Square, Edinburgh, EH2 2YB, Scotland (office).

MATHIAS, Charles McCurdy; American politician and lawyer; b. 24 July 1922, Frederick, Md; s. of Charles McCurdy Mathias, Sr and Theresa Trail Mathias; m. Ann Hickling Bradford 1958; two s.; ed Haverford Coll., Yale Univ. and Univ. of Md; apprentice seaman 1942, commissioned Ensign 1944, sea duty, Pacific 1944–46; Capt. US Naval Reserve (retd); admitted to Md Bar 1949, to US Supreme Court Bar 1954; Asst Attorney-Gen. of Md 1953, 1954; City Attorney, Frederick, Md 1954–59; mem. Md House of Dels 1958; mem. US House of Reps 1960–68; Senator from Md 1969–87, Chair. Senate Rules and Admin. Cttee 1981–87; Chair. of Bd First American Bankshares 1993–99; Milton S. Eisenhower Distinguished Professor in Public Policy, Johns Hopkins School for Advanced Int. Studies 1987; Hon. Chair. Nat. Comm. on the Voting Rights Act; Republican; Légion d'honneur (France); Order of Orange-Nassau (Netherlands); Order of Merit (FRG); Hon. KBE (UK). *Address:* c/o National Commission on the Voting Rights Act, Lawyers' Committee for Civil Rights Under Law, 1401 New York Avenue, NW, Suite 400, Washington, DC 20005; 51 Louisiana Avenue, NW, Washington, DC 20001 (office); 3808 Leland Street, Chevy Chase, MD 20815, USA (home).

MATHIAS, Peter, CBE, MA, DLitt, FBA, FRHistS; British professor of economic history (retd); b. 10 Jan. 1928, Somerset; s. of John Samuel Mathias and Marian Helen Love; m. Elizabeth Ann Blackmore 1958; two s. one d.; ed Colstons Hosp., Bristol, Jesus Coll. Cambridge and Harvard Univ., USA; Research Fellow, Jesus Coll. 1952–55; Lecturer, History Faculty, Cambridge Univ. 1955–68, Tutor and Dir of Studies, Queens' Coll., Sr Proctor, Cambridge Univ. 1965–66; Chichele Prof. of Econ. History, Oxford Univ. and Fellow of All Souls Coll. 1969–87; Master of Downing Coll., Cambridge 1987–95; Pres. Int. Econ. History Asscn 1974–78, Hon. Pres. 1978–; Pres. Business Archive Council 1984–95, Vice-Pres. 1995–; Chair. British Library Advisory Council 1994–99; Vice-Pres. Royal Historical Soc. 1975–80 (Hon. Vice-Pres. 2001–), Int. Inst. of Econ. History Francesco Datini Prato 1987–99; Hon. Treas. British Acad. 1979–88, Econ. History Soc. 1967–88 (Pres. 1989–92, Vice-Pres. 1992–); Chair. Central European Univ. Press Advisory Bd 2002–; mem. Advisory Bd of the Research Councils 1983–88; Chair. History of Medicine Panel, Wellcome Trust 1980–88; Syndic Fitzwilliam Museum 1987–98; Chair. Fitzwilliam Museum Enterprises Ltd 1990–99, Friends of Kettle's Yard 1989–95, Bd of Continuing Educ., Cambridge Univ. 1991–95; Curator Bodleian Library, Oxford 1972–87; mem. Academia Europaea 1989, Beirat WissenschaftsKolleg, Berlin 1992–98, foreign mem. Royal Danish Acad., Royal Belgian Acad.; Trustee GB-Sasakawa Foundation 1994–, Chair. 1997–2005, Pres. 2005–; Hon. Fellow Jesus Coll., Queens' Coll., Downing Coll. Cambridge; Order of the Rising Sun (Japan) 2003; Hon. LittD (Buckingham, Birmingham, Hull, Warwick, de Montfort, East Anglia); Dr hc (Russian Acad. of Sciences) 2002, (Kansai Univ., Japan) 2006; Maria Theresa Medal, Univ. of Pavia 2002. *Publications:* Brewing Industry in England 1700–1830 1959, Retailing Revolution 1967, Tradesmen's Tokens 1962, The First Industrial Nation 1969, 1983, The Transformation of England 1979, L'economia britannica dal 1815 al 1914 1994; Cinque lezioni di teoria e storia 2003, Gen. Ed. Cambridge Economic History of Europe 1968–90, History of Mankind vol. 6 (UNESCO) 2007. *Leisure interests:* travel, New Hall porcelain. *Address:* 33 Church Street, Chesterton, Cambs., CB4 1DT, England (office). *Telephone:* (1223) 329824 (home). *Fax:* (1223) 329824 (office). *E-mail:* pm314@cam.ac.uk (office).

MATHIES, Richard A., BS, MS, PhD, FRSC; American chemist and academic; *Dean, College of Chemistry, University of California, Berkeley;* b. 1946, Seattle; m. JoAnne Mathies; two c.; ed Univ. of Washington, Cornell Univ.; Helen Hay Whitney Fellow, Yale Univ. 1974–76; Asst Prof., Coll. of Chem., Univ. of California, Berkeley 1976, Alfred P. Sloan Fellow 1979–81, Gilbert Newton Lewis Prof. 2008–, also Dean, Coll. of Chem. 2008–, Co-Founder and Dir Center for Analytical Biotechnology; Dir Microchip Biotechnologies; mem. Advisory Bd Alameda Capital, Affymetrix; mem. American Optical Soc., American Soc. for Photobiology, AAAS; Fellow, Optical Soc. of America 2004; NY Acad. of Sciences Harold Lamport Award 1983, American Soc. for Photobiology Research Award 1989, Frederick Conf. on Capillary Electrophoresis Award 1998, Asscn for Lab. Automation Research Award 2001, Optical Soc. of America Ellis R. Lippincott Award 2004. *Achievements include:* work in developing energy transfer fluorescent labels that was critical to the early completion of the Human Genome Sequence. *Publications:* author of over 380 publs and 35 patents on photochemistry, photobiology, bioanalytical chemistry and genome analysis tech. *Address:* Office of the Dean, College of Chemistry, University of California, Berkeley, CA 94720-1776, USA (office). *Telephone:* (510) 642-4192 (office). *Fax:* (510) 642-3599 (office). *E-mail:* rich@zinc.cchem.berkeley.edu (office). *Website:* chem.berkeley.edu (office).

MATHIESEN, Arni M., MSc; Icelandic politician; b. 2 Oct. 1958, Reykjavík; s. of Matthías Á. Mathiesen and Sigrún Þorgilsdóttir Mathiesen; m. Steinnun Kristín Fridjónsdóttir 1991; three d.; ed Flensborgarskóli, Hafnarfjödur, Univs of Edin. and Stirling, Scotland, UK; qualified as veterinarian 1983; worked as veterinary officer for fish diseases 1985–95; Man.-Dir of Acquaculture, Faxalax hf. 1988–89; Chair. Flensborgarskóli Student Asscn 1977–78; Vice-Pres. Icelandic Asscn of Young Conservatives (SUS) 1985–87; Pres. Asscn of Young Conservatives (Stefnir), Hafnarfjödur 1986–88; elected mem. of Parl.; mem. Independence Party; Rep. of Iceland to Nordic Council 1991–95; mem. Parl. Cttee on EFTA and EEC 1995–99; Minister of Fisheries 1999–2005, of Finance 2005–09 (resgnd); fmr Chair. Prevention of Cruelty to Animals; mem. Bd Guarantee Div., Acquaculture Loans 1990–94, Bd Icelandic Veterinary Asscn 1986–87, Bd of Búnadarbanki Islands; mem. Salary Council, Confed. of Univ. Grads 1985–87; mem. Flensborgarskóli School Bd 1990–99; fmr mem. Bd of Búnadarbanki Islands, Agricultural Loan Fund. *Address:* Independence Party, Háaleitisbraut 1, 105 Reykjavík, Iceland (office). *Telephone:* 5151700 (office). *Fax:* 5151717 (office). *E-mail:* xd@xd.is (office). *Website:* www.xd.is (office).

MATHIESEN, Matthias (Árnason), CandJuris; Icelandic politician and lawyer; b. 6 Aug. 1931, Hafnarfjörður; s. of Árni M. Mathiesen and Svava E. Mathiesen; m. Sigrún Thorgilsdóttir 1956; two s. one d.; ed Univ. of Iceland; Chief Exec. Hafnarfjörður Savings Bank 1958–67, Chair. 1967–2005; Advocate, Supreme Court 1967–74, 1991–; mem. Althing (Parl.) 1959–91, Speaker Lower Chamber 1970–71; Rep. of Althing to Nordic Council 1965–74, mem. Presidium 1970–71, 1973–74, Pres. 1970–71, 1980–81; Del. North Atlantic Ass., NATO 1963–69, 1972, Chair. Icelandic Del. 1964–67, Pres. of Ass. 1967–68; mem. Bd E Thorgilsson & Co. Ltd, Hafnarfjörður 1973–2001, Chair. 1982–2001; Dir Nat. Bank of Iceland 1961–74, 1980–83; Icelandic mem. of Bd of Govs World Bank Group (IBRD, IDA, IFC) 1983–85; Minister of Finance 1974–78, Minister of Commerce (including Banking) and of Nordic Co-operation 1983–85, for Foreign Affairs 1985–87, of Communications 1987–88; mem. Cen. Cttee, Independence Party 1965–91. *Address:* Hringbraut 59, Hafnarfjörður, Iceland (home). *Telephone:* (91) 5-02-76 (home).

MATHIEU, Georges Victor Adolphe, LèsL; French artist; b. 27 Jan. 1921, Boulogne; s. of Adolphe Mathieu d'Escaudoeuvres and Madeleine Dupré d'Ausque; ed Facultés de droit et des lettres, Lille; Teacher of English; Public Relations Man., US Lines; ed. US Lines, Paris Review 1953–63; exhibited at Paris 1950, New York 1952, Japan 1957, Scandinavia 1958, England, Spain, Italy, Switzerland, Germany, Austria and S America 1959, Middle East 1961–62, Canada 1963; special exhbn of work held at Musée Municipal d'Art Moderne, Paris 1963; exhbn of 100 paintings, Galerie Charpentier, Paris 1965; designed gardens and bldgs for BC transformer factory, Fontenay-le-comte 1966; 16 posters for Air France exhibited at Musée Nat. d'Art Moderne, Paris 1967; exhbn of 10 tapestries at Musée de la Manufacture Nat. des Gobelins 1969; designed 18 medals for Paris Mint 1971, new 10F coin 1974; works exhibited in numerous countries including shows in Antibes 1976, Ostend 1977, Grand Palais, Paris 1978, Wildenstein Gallery, New York, Dominion Gallery, Montreal 1979, Musée de la Poste, Paris 1980, Galerie Kasper, Morges, Switzerland 1983, Théâtre municipal de Brives 1984; retrospective show, Palais des Papes, Avignon 1985; Galerie Calvin, Geneva 1985, Wally Findlay Galleries 1986, Galerie Schindler, Berne 1986, Galerie du Luxembourg 1986, Galerie Protée, Paris, Stockholm 1990, Boulogne sur Mer 1992, Museum of Modern Art, Toulouse 1995; creator of Tachisme; mem. Acad. of Fine Arts; Officier, Légion d'honneur, des Arts et des Lettres; Ordre de la Couronne de Belgique. *Principal works:* Hommage à la Mort 1950, Hommage au Maréchal de Turenne 1952, Les Capétiens Partout 1954, La Victoire de Denain 1963, Hommage à Jean Cocteau 1963, Paris, Capitale des Arts 1965, Hommages aux Frères Boisserée 1967, Hommage à Condillac 1968, La prise de Bergen op Zoom 1969, Election de Charles Quint 1971, Matta-Salums 1978, La Libération de Paris 1980, La Libération d'Orléans par Jeanne d'Arc 1982, Monumental sculpture in Neuilly 1982, in Charenton 1982, Ceiling-painting in Boulogne-Billancourt town hall 1983, Massacre des 269 1985, Le Paradis des orages 1988, L'Immortalité ruinée 1989, La Complainte silencieuse des enfants de Bogotá 1989, Rumeur de paradis 1991. *Publications:* Au-delà du Tachisme, Le privilège d'Etre, De la Révolte à la Renaissance, La Réponse de l'Abstraction lyrique, L'abstraction prophétique, Le massacre de la sensibilité 1996, Désormais seul en face de Dieu 1998. *Address:* c/o Institut de France, 23 quai Conti, 75006 Paris, France (office).

MATHIS, Edith; Swiss singer (soprano); b. 11 Feb. 1938, Lucerne; m. Bernhard Klee; ed Lucerne Conservatoire; début Lucerne (in The Magic Flute) 1956; sang with Cologne Opera 1959–62; appeared Salzburg Festival 1960, Deutsche Oper, W Berlin 1963; début Glyndebourne (Cherubino in Le Nozze di Figaro) 1962, Covent Garden (Susanna in Le Nozze di Figaro) 1970, Metropolitan Opera House, New York (Pamina in The Magic Flute) 1970, Berne City Opera 1990; sang to Mendelssohn, Brahms and Schubert, Wigmore Hall, London 1997; mem. Hamburg State Opera 1960–75. *Address:* Bureau de Concerts de Valmalete, 7 rue Hoche, 92300 Paris, France (office). *Telephone:* 1-47-59-78-59 (office). *Fax:* 1-47-59-87-50 (office). *Website:* www.valmalete.com (office).

MATHIS-EDDY, Darlene, PhD; American poet and academic; *Professor Emerita, Ball State University;* b. 19 March 1937, Elkhart, Ind.; d. of the late William Eugene Mathis and Fern Roose Paulmer Mathis; m. Spencer Livingston Eddy, Jr 1964 (died 1971); ed Goshen Coll. and Rutgers Univ.; Instructor in English, Douglass Coll. 1962–64; Instructor in English, Rutgers Univ. 1964, 1965, Rutgers Univ. Coll. (Adult Educ.) 1967; Asst Prof. in English, Ball State Univ. 1967–71, Assoc. Prof. 1971–75, Prof. 1975–99, Poet-in-Residence 1989–93, Prof. Emer., English and Humanities 1999–, Ralph S. Whitinger Lecturer, Ball State Univ. Honors Coll. 1998–99; Adjunct Prof., Core Program and Coll. Seminar Program, Univ. of Notre Dame, Ind. 2001–06; Consulting Ed. Blue Unicorn 1995–; Founding Ed. The Hedge Row Press 1995–; mem. Comm. on Women for the Nat. Council of Teachers of English 1976–79; Poetry Ed. BSU Forum; Vice-Pres. Programs, American Asscn of Univ. Women, Elkhart Br.; Pres. American Asscn of Univ. Women 2008–; Woodrow Wilson Nat. Fellow 1959–62, Rutgers Univ. Grad. Honors and Honors Dissertation Fellow 1964–65, 1966–67, Notable Woodrow Wilson Nat. Fellow 1991; numerous creative arts, creative teaching, research grants and awards. *Publications:* Leaf Threads, Wind Rhymes 1986, The Worlds of King Lear 1971, Weathering 1992, Reflections: Studies in Light 1993; Contributing Ed. Snowy Egret 1988–90; numerous poems in literary reviews; book reviews and essays in numerous journals; articles in American Literature, English Language Notes, etc. *Leisure interests:* gardening, music, antiques, reading, sketching, photography, bird watching, cooking. *Address:* 1840 West Cobblestone Boulevard, Elkhart, IN 46514-4961, USA (home). *Telephone:* (574) 266-4394 (home). *Website:* www.nd.edu/~collegeseminar (office).

MATHUR, Arun; Indian civil servant; Admin., Union Territories of Dadra and Nagar Haveli, Daman and Diu –2006. *Address:* c/o Office of the Administration of Dadra and Nagar Haveli, Administrator's Bungalow, Moti Daman, Daman 396 210, India.

MATHUR, Murari Lal, PhD; Indian mechanical engineer and academic; *Professor Emeritus, Faculty of Engineering, University of Jodhpur;* b. 10 July 1931, Masuda; s. of late Dr S. D. Mathur and Lalti Devi; m. Vimla Mathur 1961; one s. three d.; ed Govt Coll., Ajmer, Birla Engineering Coll., Pilani, Glasgow Univ., UK; Asst Prof., MBM Eng Coll., Govt of Rajasthan 1952–57; Deputy Dir of Tech. Educ. and Sec. Bd of Tech. Educ., Govt of Rajasthan 1957–58; Prof. and Head Mechanical Eng Dept, Univ. of Jodhpur 1963–85, Prof., Dean Faculty of Eng 1966–68, 1974, 1977–80, Vice-Chancellor 1985–90, Prof. Emer. 1991–; Chair. Automotive Prime-Movers Sectional Cttee, Indian Bureau of Standards; Co-ordinator Solar Passive House Project; design consultant heat exchanger and heat recovery equipment; consultant Cen. Silk Bd and other industries; Fellow, Inst. of Engineers (India); Sri Chandra Prakash Memorial Gold Medal, Pres. of India's Prize, Inst. of Engineers Award. *Films:* has produced two educational films. *Publications:* books on thermal eng, internal combustion engines, gas turbines and jet propulsion, thermodynamics, fluid mechanics and machines, machine drawing and heat transfer; over 80 research papers. *Leisure interests:* reading, writing, lecturing on educational topics and topics concerning energy and environment, social service. *Address:* Alok Villa, 17-A, Shastri Nagar, Jodhpur 342 003, Rajasthan, India (home). *Telephone:* 2433207 (home); (98) 29253207 (mobile) (home).

MATHUR, Shiv Charan; Indian politician; *Governor of Assam;* b. 14 Feb. 1926, Madhi-Qanungo; s. of the late Durga Prasad Ji; m.; one s. two d.; Gen. Sec. Rajasthan Students' Congress 1945–47; Chair. Municipal Bd, Bhilwara 1956–57; mem. Rajasthan Pradesh Congress Cttee 1967–, All India Congress Cttee 1972–; mem. Third Lok Sabha 1964–97; mem. Rajasthan State Legis. Ass. 1967–77, 1980–91, 1998–, Chair. Public Undertakings Cttee 1980–81, Convenor Rules Cttee 1985–87, Chair. Subordinate Legislation Cttee 1987–88, Estimates Cttee 1998–2003, Admin. Reforms Comm. 1999–2003, mem. Rules Cttee 2004; Minister for Educ., Power, PWD and Public Relations, Rajasthan Cabinet 1967–72, for Food and Civil Supplies, Agric., Animal Husbandry, Dairy and Planning 1973–77; Chief Minister of Rajasthan 1981–85, 1988–89; mem. Tenth Lok Sabha 1991–96, Chair. Cttee on Privileges 1991–96, Convenor Sub-Cttee on Energy 1994–96; Gov. of Assam 2008–; mem. Exec. Cttee, Commonwealth Parl. Asscn 1994–96; Life Chair. Social Policy Research Inst., Janput 1985–. *Address:* Office of the Governor of Assam, Assam Sachivalaya Complex Dispur, Guwahati, 781006 Assam, India (office). *Telephone:* (361) 2540500 (office). *Fax:* (361) 2731832 (office). *E-mail:* info@assamgovt.nic.in (office). *Website:* assamassembly.gov.in/biodata-governor.html (office).

MATIBA, Kenneth; Kenyan politician; Chair. Kenya Breweries 1968–79; founder, Kenya Football League; fmr Chair. Kenya Football Fed.; entered Parl. 1979; resgnd from Govt over election-rigging 1988; imprisoned for 10 months for leading multi-party democracy movt July 1990; Chair. FORD-Asili Party; contested presidential election Dec. 1992; Founder and Chair. Alliance Hotels and Resorts; owner The People Daily newspaper. *Leisure interest:* mountain climbing. *Address:* Alliance Hotels and Resorts, POB 49839, 00100 Nairobi; c/o Forum for the Restoration of Democracy—Asili (FORD—Asili), Anyany Estate, POB 72595, Nairobi, Kenya. *E-mail:* alliance@africaonline.co.ke.

MATIN, Abdul, MA, PhD; Pakistani economist; *Member, Higher Education Commission;* b. 1 March 1932, Sawabi; s. of Dur Jamil Khan; m. Azra Matin 1959; three s.; ed Univ. of Peshawar and Univ. of Bonn, FRG; Chair. Dept of Econs, Univ. of Peshawar and Dir Bd of Econs, North-West Frontier Prov. (NWFP) 1959–70; Chief Economist, Govt of NWFP 1970–72; Minister and Deputy Perm. Rep., Pakistan Mission at UN, New York 1973–76; Exec. Dir ADBP, Islamabad 1977–85; Vice-Chancellor Univ. of Peshawar 1987–89; Vice-Pres. and mem. of Cen. Cttee, Pakistan Tehrik-i-Insaaf (Movt for Justice) 1996–; Chair. of Task Forces to Regulate Pvt. Educational Insts in NWFP 1999–, to Reform Higher Secondary Govt Schools in NWFP 2000–; mem. Nat. Comm. on Manpower, Govt of Pakistan, Educ. Inquiry Cttee, NWFP, Prov. Finance Comm., NWFP 2002–, Health Regulatory Authority, NWFP 2003–, Higher Educ. Comm. of Pakistan 2003–, Econ. Reform Comm., NWFP 2004, Search Cttee for Vice-Chancellors, NWFP; Chair. Govt Working Group on Transport Policy 1991–92, Universities Services Reforms and Man. Cttee, Govt of NWFP 1998; mem. Bd of Man. Quaid-e-Azam Mazar 2000–, Pakistan Bait-ul-Mal; engaged in research project 'Revival and Reconstruction of Muslim World'; prepared policy draft for Nat. Centre for Rehabilitation of Child Labour 2001; Hamdard Foundation Award for Outstanding Services 1992, Khawaja Farid Sang, Lahore 2004. *Publications:* Industrialization of NWFP 1970; 85 articles on the problems, policies and pattern of econ. devt in professional journals. *Leisure interests:* extension lectures, public speeches, involvement in discourses on rectification of West-Ummah relations. *Address:* House No. 27, Street No. 9, Sector D-3, Phase I, Hayatabad, Peshawar, NWFP, Pakistan (home). *Telephone:* 5817144 (home). *Fax:* 5817144 (home).

MATIN, M. A., FRCS; Bangladeshi ophthalmologist and politician; b. 1 Dec. 1937, Pabna; ed Dhaka Medical Coll.; worked in Royal Eye Hosp. and King's Coll. Hosp., London 1964–67; Assoc. Prof. of Ophthalmology, Inst. of Postgraduate Medicine and Research, Dhaka 1967–72, Prof., then Head of Dept 1972–; Hon. Col and Consultant Ophthalmologist, Combined Mil. Hosp., Dhaka 1976; MP 1979–, re-elected MP (BNP) 2001–; Minister of Civil Aviation and Tourism 1979, Minister of Youth Devt and of Health and Population Control 1981, Minister of Home Affairs 1981–82, Minister of Commerce 1984, Minister of Works 1985, Deputy Prime Minister in charge of Ministry of Home

Affairs 1986–88; Deputy Prime Minister 1988–89; Minister of Health and Family Planning 1988, 1989, of Home Affairs 1988–89; Adviser in charge of Home Affairs, of Shipping, and of Liberation War Affairs 2007–09; fmr Sec.-Gen. and Pres. Bangladesh Ophthalmological Soc. and Pres. Bangladesh Medical Services Asscn; Vice-Chair. Bangladesh Medical Research Council and Vice-Pres. Bangladesh Coll. of Physicians and Surgeons; Alim Memorial Gold Medal; Int. Award, Asian Pacific Acad. of Ophthalmology 1981. *Address:* c/o Ministry of Home Affairs, Bangladesh Secretariat, School Building, 2nd and 3rd Floors, Dhaka 1000; Shantinagar, Dhaka, Bangladesh (home).

MATLOCK, Jack Foust, Jr, MA; American diplomatist; b. 1 Oct. 1929, Greensboro; s. of Jack Foust Matlock and Nellie McSwain; m. Rebecca Burrum 1949; four s. one d.; ed Duke and Columbia Univs and Russian Inst.; Instructor, Dartmouth 1953–56; joined foreign service, State Dept 1956, Official in Washington 1956–58, Embassy Official, Vienna 1958–60, Consul Gen., Munich 1960–61, Embassy Official, Moscow 1961–63, Accra 1963–66, Zanzibar 1967–69, Dar es Salaam 1969–70, Country Dir for USSR, State Dept 1971–74, Deputy Chief of Mission, Embassy in Moscow 1974–78, Diplomat-in-Residence, Vanderbilt Univ. 1978–79, Deputy Dir, Foreign Service Inst., Washington 1979–80, Amb. to Czechoslovakia 1981–83, to USSR, 1987–91; Special Asst to Pres. and Sr Dir European and Soviet Affairs, Nat. Security Council 1983–87; Sr Research Fellow Columbia Univ. 1991–93, Kathryn and Shelby Collum Davis Prof. 1993–96; George F. Kennan Prof., Inst. for Advanced Study, Princeton, NJ 1996–2001; John L. Weinberg/Goldman Sachs and Co. Visiting Prof. of Public and Int. Affairs, Woodrow Wilson School of Public and Int. Affairs, Princeton Univ. 2001–04; mem. American Acad. of Diplomacy, Council on Foreign Relations, American Philosophical Soc.; Dickey Fellow Dartmouth Coll. 1992; Hon. mem. Latvian Acad. of Sciences 2002 Hon. LLD (Greensboro Coll.) 1989, Albright Coll. (1992), Connecticut Coll. (1993); Superior Honor Award, US State Dept, Presidential Meritorious Service Award, McIver Award for Distinguished Public Service 1994 and many others. *Publications:* Ed. Index to J. V. Stalin's Works 1971, Autopsy on an Empire: The American Ambassador's Account of the Collapse of the Soviet Union 1995, Reagan and Gorbachev: How the Cold War Ended 2004. *Address:* 940 Princeton-Kingston Road, Princeton, NJ 08540, USA. *Telephone:* (609) 252-1953 (home). *Fax:* (609) 252-9373 (home). *E-mail:* jfmatlo@attglobal.net (home).

MATLYUBOV, Lt-Gen. Bahodir Ahmedovich; Uzbekistani government official; *Minister of Internal Affairs;* b. 10 March 1952, Samarqand, Uzbek SSR, USSR; ed Samarqand State Univ.; held various positions at Samarqand Regional Internal Affairs Directorate 1978–94; Head, Buxoro Regional Internal Affairs Directorate 1994–97; held several sr positions in Ministry of Internal Affairs including Chair. State Cttee on Demonopolization and Competition and Business Support, Chair. State Customs Cttee 2004, First Deputy Minister of Internal Affairs 1997–2006, Minister of Internal Affairs 2006–; Shon-Saraf (Glory) Order (First and Second degree). *Address:* Ministry of Internal Affairs, 100029 Tashkent, Yu. Rajaby ko'ch. 1, Uzbekistan (office). *Telephone:* (71) 139-73-36 (office). *Fax:* (71) 133-89-34 (office). *Website:* www.mvd.uz (office).

MATOKA, Peter Wilfred, PhD; Zambian politician, international civil servant and diplomatist; b. 8 April 1930, Mwinilunga, NW Prov.; m. Grace J. Mukahlera 1957; two s. one d.; ed Rhodes Univ., S Africa, American Univ., Washington, DC, Univ. of Zambia, Univ. of Warwick, UK; civil servant, Northern Rhodesia Govt 1954–64; mem. of Parl. of Zambia 1964–78; Minister of Information and Postal Services 1964–65, of Health 1965–66, of Works and Housing 1967, of Power, Transport and Works 1968; mem. Cen. Cttee, United Nat. Independence Party (UNIP) 1967, 1971–78; Minister for Luapula Prov. 1969; High Commr of Zambia in UK 1969–70, concurrently accred to the Holy See (Vatican); Minister for the S Prov. 1970, of Health 1971–72, of Local Govt and Housing 1972–77, of Devt Planning 1977, of Econ. and Tech. Co-operation 1977–78; Chief Whip, Nat. Ass. 1973–78; Sr Regional Adviser, UN Econ. Comm. for Africa, Addis Ababa 1979–83; High Commr in Zimbabwe 1984–88; Chair. Social and Cultural Sub-Cttee of Cen. Cttee of UNIP 1988–90, of Science and Tech. Sub-Cttee 1990–91; Sr Lecturer, Social Devt Studies Dept, Univ. of Zambia 1995–; Chair. WHO Africa Region 1966; Pres. Africa, Caribbean and Pacific Group of States 1977; Chair. Nat. Inst. of Scientific Research 1977; Chair. Zambia-Kenya and Zambia-Yugoslavia Perm. Comms 1977; Chair. Lusaka MULPOC 1977; Chair. and Man. Dir FilZam Projects and Investments Services Centre Ltd 1992–; Vice-Chair. Nat. Tender Bd 1977; Life mem. CPA; mem. Perm. Human Rights Comm. of Zambia 1997–; Nat. Consultant on Child Labour Issues 1997–; Kt of St Gregory (Vatican) 1964; Kt, Egypt and Ethiopia, Grand Commdr of the Companion Order of Freedom 2006. *Leisure interests:* gardening, television, walking. *Address:* University of Zambia, PO Box 32379, Lusaka (office); Ibex Hill, P.O. Box 50101, Lusaka, Zambia (home). *Telephone:* (1) 291777 (office); (1) 260221 (home). *Fax:* (1) 253952 (office). *E-mail:* registra@unza.zm (office).

MATOLCSY, György; Hungarian politician and economist; b. 1955, Budapest; m.; two c.; ed Budapest Univ. of Economic Sciences; jr official, Industrial Org. Inst. 1977–78; mem. staff Ministry of Finance 1978–81, mem. Secr. 1981–85; Fellow, Finance Research Inst. 1985–90; Political State Sec. Prime Minister's Office 1990–91; Dir Privatization Research Inst. 1991; Dir EBRD, London 1991–94; Dir Property Foundation, Inst. for Privatization Studies 1995–99; Minister of Econ. Affairs 1999–2002; econ. strategist, Hungarian Civic Union (Magyar Polgári Szövetség—Fidesz). *Address:* Magyar Polgári Szövetség, Budapest, Hungary (office). *E-mail:* info@hirlap.com (office). *Website:* www.fidesz.hu (office).

MATOMÄKI, Tauno, MSc (Eng); Finnish business executive; *Chairman and CEO, Rosenlew RKW Finland Ltd;* b. 14 April 1937, Nakkila; s. of Niilo Matomäki and Martta Matomäki; m. Leena Matomäki (née Nilsson) 1963; one s. three d.; ed Tech. Univ., Helsinki; joined Rauma-Repola 1967, various positions, Pres. and CEO 1987–, Pres. and CEO Repola Ltd 1991–; Chair. and CEO Rosenlew RKW Finland Ltd; Chair. Bd Dirs Rauma Ltd, United Paper Mills Ltd, Pohjolan Voima Ltd, Finnyards Ltd, UPM-Kymmene, Confed. of Finnish Industries, Finnish Employers' Confed.; mem. Bd Dirs Effjohn AB; mem. Supervisory Bd Teollisuuden Voima Oy (Chair.), Kansallis-Osake-Pankki, Pohjola Insurance Co., Ilmarinen Pension Insurance Co., Polar Rakennusosakeyhtiö, Uusi Suomi Oy; Kt, Order of the White Rose of Finland (First Class). *Address:* Rosenlew RKW Finland Ltd, 28101 Pori, Finland (office). *Telephone:* (39) 11141 (office).

MATORI, Abdul Djalil; Indonesian politician; mem. PKB Party, Nahdlatul Ulama; Minister of Defence 2001–04; expelled from Muslim Clerics party; attended impeachment proceedings of Pres. Wahid May 2002. *Address:* c/o Ministry of Defence, Jalan Medan Merdeka Barat, 13–14, Jakarta Pusat, Indonesia (office).

MATORIN, Vladimir Anatolievich; Russian singer (bass); b. 2 May 1948, Moscow; s. of Anatoly Ivanovich Matorin and Maria Tarasovna Matorina; m. Svetlana Sergeyevna Matorina; one s.; ed Gnessin Pedagogical Inst. (now Acad.) of Music; soloist, Moscow Stanislavsky and Nemirovich-Danchenko Music Theatre 1974–91, Bolshoi Theatre 1991–; numerous int. tours; winner, All-Union Glinka Competition of vocalists and Int. Competition of Singers in Geneva, Merited Artist of Russia, People's Artist of Russia. *Opera roles include:* Boris Godunov, Ivan Susanin, King René (Iolanthe), Gremin (Eugene Onegin), Dosifei (Khovanshchina), Count Galitsky (Prince Igor), Don Basilio (Barber of Seville), Count (Invisible City of Kitezh) and more then 65 others. *Leisure interests:* poetry, sacred music, travelling by car. *Address:* Bolshoi Theatre of Russia, Teatralnaya pl. 1, 103009 Moscow (office); Ulansky per. 21, korp. 1 Apt. 53, 103045 Moscow, Russia (home). *Telephone:* (495) 692-38-86 (Bolshoi Opera); (495) 680-44-17 (home). *Fax:* (495) 680-44-17.

MATOTO, 'Otenifi Afu'alo, BA, MA; Tongan civil servant and politician; *Minister for Finance and Information;* m. Lavinia Matoto; two d.; ed Univ. of Auckland, New Zealand, Univ. of Durham, UK; Asst Teacher, Tonga High School 1968; joined Ministry of Finance as an Asst Sec. in 1971, twice acted as Devt Officer 1971–77, Sec. of Finance 1977–83; Man., Devt and Planning, Bank of Tonga 1983, held various managerial positions 1983–99; Man. Dir Tonga Devt Bank 1999–2006; Minister for Public Enterprises 2006–07, for Public Enterprises and Information 2007–, for Finance and Information 2008–; mem. bds or chair. numerous govt agencies, statutory bodies and cttees; mem. exec. cttees numerous professional and business asscns; Treas. Tonga Rugby Football Union (TRFU) 1975–82; Chair. TRFU Referees' Asscn early 1980s–early 1990s; mem. Nuku'alofa Rotary Club 1974–, served as Pres. for several years; ordained Minister of the Constitutional Free Church of Tonga. *Leisure interest:* sports, especially rugby. *Address:* Ministry of Finance, Treasury Building, PO Box 87, Vuna Road, Kolofo'ou, Nuku'alofa, Tonga (office). *Telephone:* 23066 (office). *Fax:* 21010 (office). *E-mail:* minfin@candw.to (office).

MATSUDA, Iwao; Japanese politician; b. 19 May 1937; ed Univ. of Tokyo; elected mem. House of Reps 1986, 1990 1993; Parl. Vice Minister, Ministry of Educ., Science, Culture and Sports 1991–92; elected mem. House of Councillors 1998, 2004; Sr State Sec. for Int. Trade and Industry 2000–01; Sr Vice Minister of Economy, Trade and Industry 2001; Chief Dir Cttee on Economy and Industry 2002–04; Chair. Research Cttee on Int. Affairs 2004–05; Minister of State for Science and Tech. Policy, for Food Safety and for Information Tech. 2005–06. *Address:* Liberal-Democratic Party—LDP (Jiyu-Minshuto), 1-11-23, Nagata-cho, Chiyoda-ku, Tokyo 100-8910, Japan. *Telephone:* (3) 3581-6211. *E-mail:* koho@ldp.jimin.or.jp. *Website:* www.jimin.jp.

MATSUDA, Masatake; Japanese transport industry executive; *Director and Adviser, East Japan Railway Company;* b. 1936, Hokkaido; ed Hokkaido Univ.; began career with Japan Nat. Railway (JNR) 1961, held positions successively as Planning Man. Office of Planning Man., Planning Man. Hokkaido HQ, Dir-Gen. Reconstruction Promotion HQ, Man.-Dir and Gen. Man. Corp. Planning HQ E Japan Railway Co. (JR East–co. created following privatisation of JNR 1987), Vice-Pres., Pres. 1993, Chair. JR East –2006, Dir and Adviser 2006–; Dir Mizuho Holdings Inc.; Pres. World Exec. Council, Int. Union of Railways (UIC), Vice-Pres. UIC 2003–04; apptd mem. Prime Ministerial Advisory Panel tasked with overseeing Privatisation of Semigovernmental Expressway Corpns 2003, resgnd from panel in protest of privatisation scheme. *Address:* East Japan Railway Company, 2-2 Yoyogi 2-chome, Shibuya-ku, Tokyo 151-8578, Japan (office). *Telephone:* (3) 5334-1310 (office). *Fax:* (3) 5334-1297 (office). *Website:* www.jreast.co.jp (office).

MATSUDA, Seiko; Japanese singer and actress; b. (Noriko Kamachi), 10 March 1962, Fukuoka; m. 1st Masaki Kanda 1985 (divorced 1998); one c.; m. 2nd Hiroyuki Hatano 1998 (divorced 2000). *Films:* Nogiku no haka 1981, Yume De Aetera 1982, Natsufuku no Ibu 1984, Karibu: Ai no shinfoni 1985, Final Vendetta 1996, Armageddon 1998, Drop Dead Gorgeous 1999, Partners 2000, Gedo 2000, Sennen no koi – Hikaru Genji monogatari 2002, Shanghai Baby 2007, Hotaru no Haka 2008. *Television:* The Big Easy (series) 1996, Tattahitotsuno takaramono (film) 2004, Yo nimo kimyo na monogatari: Aki no tokubetsu hen 2005. *Recordings include:* albums: Squall 1980, North Wind 1980, Silhouette 1981, Kaze Tachi Nu 1981, Pineapple 1982, Candy 1982, Utopia 1983, Canary 1983, Tinkerbell 1984, Windy Shadow 1984, The Ninth Wave 1985, Sound of My Heart 1985, Supreme 1986, Strawberry Time 1987, Citron 1988, Precious Moment 1989, Seiko 1990, We Are Love 1990, Eternal 1991, Nouvelle Vague 1992, Sweet Memories 1992, A Time For Love 1993, Diamond Expression 1993, Glorious Revolution 1994, It's Style 1995, Was It The Future 1996, Guardian Angel 1996, Vanity Fair 1996, Sweetest Time

1997, My Story 1997, Forever 1998, Seiko Matsuda Remixes 1999, 20th Party 2000, Love & Emotion Vol. 1 2001, Love & Emotion Vol. 2 2001, Area 62 2002, Sunshine 2004, Fairy 2006, Baby's Breath 2007, My Pure Melody 2008. *Publication:* Yume de Aetara 1982. *Address:* c/o Sony Music Entertainment (Japan) Inc., 1-4 Ichigaya-Tamachi, Shinjuku-ku, Tokyo 162-8715, Japan. *E-mail:* office@seikomatsuda.jp (office). *Website:* www.seikomatsuda.net.

MATSUHISA, Nobuyuki (Nobu); Japanese chef; b. Tokyo; m.; two d.; served apprenticeship in sushi bars in Tokyo; opened sushi bar in Peru, later moving to Argentina, Japan and Alaska; opened Matsuhisa restaurant in Beverly Hills, Calif. 1987, Aspen, Colo 1999; opened Nobu restaurant in New York 1994, London 1997, Tokyo 199, now manages 14 restaurants. *Address:* c/o Matsuhisa, 120 North La Cienega Blvd., Beverly Hills, CA 90211, USA (office). *Telephone:* (310) 659-9639 (office).

MATSUI, Hideki; Japanese baseball player; b. 12 June 1974, Kanazawa; ed Seiryo High School, Kanazawa; left fielder; drafted out of high school by Yomiuri Giants of Japanese Cen. League 1993 (number one selection), played 1993–2003, won three Japanese Series titles, hit Japan career 332 home runs with overall batting average of .308; left Japan to sign with NY Yankees 2003–, major league debut 31 March 2003; operates Hideki Matsui House of Baseball, Neagari; nine times Japanese League All-Star; three Japanese League Most Valuable Player awards; American League All-Star Team 2003; runner-up American League Rookie of the Year 2003. *Address:* c/o New York Yankees, Yankee Stadium, East 161st Street and River Avenue, New York, NY 10452, USA. *Telephone:* (718) 293-4300. *Fax:* (718) 293-8431. *Website:* newyork.yankees.mlb.com.

MATSUMOTO, Hiroshi, BEng, MEng, PhD; Japanese engineer, academic and university administrator; *President, Kyoto University;* b. 17 Nov. 1942; ed Kyoto Univ.; Research Assoc., Dept of Electronics, Kyoto Univ. 1967–69, Research Assoc., Dept of Electrical Eng 1969–74, Assoc. Prof., Ionosphere Research Lab., Kyoto Univ. 1974–81, Assoc. Prof., Radio Atmospheric Science Center 1981–87, Prof. 1987–2000, also Head of Research Inst. for Sustainable Humanosphere 2004–05, Exec. Vice-Pres. Kyoto Univ. 2005–08, Pres. 2008–; numerous awards including Shida-Rinzaburo Award 1999, Russian Fed. of Cosmonautics Gagarin Medal 2006, Hasegawa Nagata Award 2008. *Address:* Office of the President, Kyoto University, Yoshida-Honmachi, Sakyo-ku, Kyoto 606-8501, Japan (office). *Telephone:* (75) 753-7531 (office). *Fax:* (774) 334598 (office). *Website:* www.kyoto-u.ac.jp/en (office).

MATSUMOTO, Ken, MA; Japanese business executive; b. 2 Feb. 1935, Shanghai, China; s. of Shigeharu and Hanako Matsumoto; m. Junko Masuda 1969; one s.; ed Gakushuin High School, Swarthmore Coll., USA, Univ. of Tokyo; mem. Bd Dirs Auburn Steel Co. Inc., Auburn, NY 1973–77; Sr Man. Export Dept-I, Nippon Steel Corpn 1977–84; Dir Research Div., The Fair Trade Center 1984–90, Man. Dir 1990–; Bancroft Scholarship. *Leisure interests:* tennis, skiing. *Address:* 5-11-38, Miyazaki, Miyamae-ku, Kawasaki-shi, Kanagawa-ken, 216 Japan. *Telephone:* (44) 854-0693.

MATSUMOTO, Masayoshi; Japanese business executive; *President and CEO, Sumitomo Electric Industries;* mem. Bd of Dirs Sumitomo Electric Industries 1999–, fmr Sr Man. Dir, fmr Pres. and COO, now Pres. and CEO; Vice-Chair. Optoelectronic Industry and Tech. Devt Asscn. *Address:* Sumitomo Electric Industries, 5-33 Kitahama 4-chome, Chuo-ku, Osaka 541-0041, Japan (office). *Telephone:* (6) 6220-4141 (office). *E-mail:* info@sei.co.jp (office). *Website:* www.sei.co.jp (office).

MATSUMOTO, Masayuki; Japanese engineer and transport industry executive; *President, Central Japan Railway Company;* joined Japanese Nat. Railways (now Japan Railways–JR) 1972, Tech. Dir E Japan Railway Co. 2000, sr positions with Transport & Rolling Stock Dept 2001–02, Vice-Pres. Cen. Japan Railway Co. (JR Tokai) –2004, Pres. 2004–; Dir Ricoh Leasing Co. Ltd 2003; Exec. Man.-Dir Ricoh Co. Ltd 2004–; mem. Inst. of Electrical Engineers of Japan, Inst. of Electronics, Information and Communication Engineers, Information Processing Soc. of Japan. *Address:* Central Japan Railway Company, 1-1-4 Meieki, Nakamura-ku, Nagoya 450-6101, Japan (office). *Telephone:* (3) 3274-9727 (office). *Fax:* (3) 5255-6780 (office). *Website:* www.jr-central.co.jp (office).

MATSUO, Kenji; Japanese insurance industry executive; *President, Meiji Yasuda Life Insurance Company;* Dir Meiji Life Insurance Co. –2003, mem. Bd of Dirs Meiji Yasuda Life Insurance Co. 2004– (after merger of Meiji Life Insurance Co. and Tasuda Mutual Life Insurance Co.), Man. Dir and Gen. Man. Real Estate Dept –2005, Pres. 2005–, mem. Nominating Cttee, Compensation Cttee; mem. Bd of Dirs Life Insurance Asscn of Japan, Nikon Corpn; Dir (non-voting) Société Generale Group 2006–. *Address:* Meiji Yasuda Life Insurance Co., 1-1, Marunouchi 2-chome, Chiyoda-ku, Tokyo 100-0005, Japan (office). *Telephone:* (3) 3283-8293 (office). *Fax:* (3) 3215-8123 (office). *E-mail:* info@meijiyasuda.co.jp (office). *Website:* www.meijiyasuda.co.jp (office).

MATSUO, Minoru, DEng; Japanese university administrator and professor of engineering; b. 4 July 1936, Kyoto; ed Kyoto Univ.; Asst Prof. School of Eng, Kyoto Univ. 1964–65, Assoc. Prof. 1965–72; Assoc. Prof. School of Eng, Nagoya Univ. 1972–78, Prof. 1978–98, Univ. Senator 1987–89, Dean 1989–92, Dir Center for Integrated Research in Science and Eng 1995–97, Pres. of Nagoya Univ. 1998–2004. *Publications include:* Reliability in Geotechnical Design 1984. *Address:* c/o Nagoya University, Furo-cho, Chikusa-ku, Nagoya, 464–8601, Japan (office). *Website:* www.nagoya-u.ac.jp/en (office).

MATSUSHITA, Masaharu, BIur; Japanese business executive; *Honorary Chairman and Executive Adviser, Matsushita Electric Industrial Co. Ltd;* b. 17 Sept. 1912, Tokyo; s. of Eiji Matsushita and Shizuko Hirata; m. Sachiko Matsushita; two s. one d.; ed Tokyo Imperial Univ.; Mitsui Bank 1935–40; with Matsushita Electric Industrial Co. Ltd 1940–, Auditor 1944–47, Dir and mem. Bd 1947–49, Exec. Vice-Pres. 1949–61, Pres. 1961–77, Chair. Bd 1977–2000, Hon. Chair. and Exec. Adviser 2000–; Dir Matsushita Electronics Corpn 1952–72, 1985–, Chair. 1972–85; Auditor, Matsushita Real Estate Co. Ltd 1952–68, Dir 1968–; Dir Matsushita Communication Industrial Co. Ltd 1958–70, Chair. 1970–86; Dir Matsushita Seiko Co. Ltd 1956–87, Kyushu Matsushita Electric Co. Ltd 1955–87, Matsushita Reiki Co. Ltd (fmrly Nakagawa Electric Inc.) 1961–87, Matsushita Electric Corpn of America 1959–74 (Chair. 1974–); Pres. Electronics Industries Asscn of Japan 1968–70; Rep. Dir Kansai Cttee for Econ. Devt 1962–, Dir 1975–; mem. Standing Cttee, Osaka Chamber of Commerce 1966–; Standing Dir Kansai Econ. Fed. 1970–, Vice-Pres. 1977–; Blue Ribbon Medal 1972, Commdr of Order of Orange-Nassau (Netherlands) 1975. *Address:* Matsushita Electric Industrial Co. Ltd, 1006 Ouza Kadoma, Kadoma-shi, Osaka 571-8501, Japan (office). *Telephone:* (6) 6908-1121 (office). *Fax:* (6) 6908-2351 (office). *Website:* www.panasonic.co.jp/global (office).

MATSUSHITA, Yasuo, LLB; Japanese banker; b. 1 Jan. 1926; ed Univ. of Tokyo; joined Ministry of Finance 1950, Dir Commercial Banks Div., Banking Bureau 1971–72, Dir Secretarial Div., Minister's Secr. 1972–74, Dir-Gen. Kinki Finance Bureau 1974–75, Deputy Dir-Gen. Budget Bureau 1975–78, Deputy Vice-Minister 1978–80, Dir-Gen. Budget Bureau 1980–82, Admin. Vice-Minister of Finance 1982–86; Dir Taiyo Kobe Bank 1986–87, Pres. 1987–90; Chair. Mitsui Taiyo Kobe Bank 1990–92, renamed Sakura Bank 1992–94, Rep. Dir and Advisor, Sakura Bank June–Dec. 1994; Gov. Bank of Japan 1994–98, resgnd following arrest of sr bank official on bribery charges 12 March 1998. *Leisure interests:* reading, tennis. *Address:* c/o Bank of Japan, 2-1-1, Chuo-ku, Tokyo 108-8660, Japan.

MATSUURA, Koichiro; Japanese international organization official and diplomatist; *Director-General, United Nations Educational, Scientific and Cultural Organization (UNESCO);* b. 1937, Tokyo; ed Univ. of Tokyo, Haverford Coll., Pa; began diplomatic career 1959; Dir-Gen. Econ. Co-operation Bureau, Ministry of Foreign Affairs 1988, Dir-Gen. N American Affairs Bureau 1990; Deputy Minister for Foreign Affairs; Amb. to France 1994–98; Chair. UNESCO's World Heritage Cttee 1998–99; Dir-Gen. UNESCO 1999–. *Address:* Office of the Director-General, UNESCO, 7 place de Fontenoy, 75352 Paris 07 SP, France (office). *Telephone:* 1-45-68-10-00 (office). *Fax:* 1-45-67-16-90 (office). *E-mail:* scg@unesco.org (office). *Website:* www.unesco.org (office).

MATSUYAMA, Yoshinori, LLD; Japanese psychologist and academic; b. 5 Dec. 1923, Kyoto; m. Michiko Kinugasa 1949; one s. two d.; ed Doshisha and Osaka Univs; Prof. of Psychology, Doshisha Univ. 1959–93, Pres. 1973–79, 1980–83, Chancellor 1985 (Chair. Bd of Trustees 1985–93); Hon. LLD (Wesleyan Univ., Conn. and Amherst Coll., Mass.). *Publications:* A Study on Behaviour Disorders 1957, A Study on Anxiety 1961, Psychology of Motivation 1967, Human Motivation 1981. *Address:* 90 Matsubaracho Ichijoji Saky-ku, Kyoto 606-8156; c/o Doshisha University, Karasuma Imadegawa, Kamigyo-ku, Kyoto 602-80, Japan (office). *E-mail:* ji-shomu@mail.doshisha.ac.jp (office).

MATSUYEV, Denis Leonidovich; Russian pianist; *Artistic Director, Crescendo;* b. 11 June 1975, Irkutsk; s. of Leonid Matsuyev and Irina Gomelskaya; ed Moscow State Conservatory (pupil of Prof. Sergei Dorensky); concerts 1993–; Soloist, Moscow State Academic Philharmonic Soc. 1995–; recitals in Paris, New York, Munich, Hamburg, Athens, Salzburg, Tokyo, Moscow and St Petersburg; played with State Symphony Orchestra of Russian Fed., Hon. Ensemble of Russia (St Petersburg), Tokyo Symphony, Budapest Philharmonic, Seoul Philharmonic; debut in London at Andrew Lloyd Webber Festival 1996; numerous tours in USA; Founder and Artistic Dir Crescendo (classical music and jazz festival) 2005–; Grand Prix Int. Piano Contest in SA 1993, 1st Prize, 11th Int. Tchaikovsky Competition, Moscow 1998. *Address:* Marshal Zhukov prosp. 13, Apt 4, 123308 Moscow, Russia (home). *Telephone:* (495) 290-17-04 (home).

MATTARELLA, Sergio; Italian politician and lecturer in law; b. 23 July 1941, Palermo; m.; three c.; ed Palermo Univ.; fmr mem. Nat. Council and Cen. Leadership Christian Democrat Party, Deputy Political Sec. 1990–92; now mem. Italian Popular Party; Deputy for Palermo-Trapani-Agrigento-Caltanissetta 1983–, for Sicilia 1 1994–; fmr Minister for Relations with Parl., Minister for Educ. –1990, Deputy Prime Minister 1998–2001, Minister for Defence 1999–2001; fmr Deputy Chair. Bicamerale; fmr Vice-Pres. Parl. Cttee on Terrorism; fmr mem. Parl. Inquiry Cttee on Mafia; mem. Third Standing Comm. on Foreign and EC Affairs; Political Ed. Il Popolo 1992–94; Prof. of Parl. Law Palermo Univ. *Address:* c/o Camera dei Deputati, Piazza di Monte Citorio 1, 00186 Rome, Italy (office).

MATTHÄUS, Lothar (Loddar); German professional football manager and fmr professional football player; b. 21 March 1961, Erlangen; professional debut with Borussia Mönchengladbach 1979; with Bayern Munich 1984–88, 1992–2000 (won UEFA Cup 1996); with Inter Milan 1988–92 (won Italian Championship 1989, won UEFA Cup 1991); with New York Metro Stars Mar.–Nov. 2000; Sports Dir Rapid Vienna 2001–02; Man. Partizan Belgrade, Serbia and Montenegro 2002–03; Coach Hungarian Nat. Team Dec. 2003–; with German nat. team 1980–96, 1998–2000 (captain 1990, won World Cup 1990), played in 25 World Cup matches, played for nat. team 150 times; World Sportsman of the Year 1990, World Footballer of the Year 1990, 1991, European Footballer of the Year 1990. *Address:* c/o Hungarian Football Federation, Budapest, Hungary (office). *Website:* www.mlsz.hu.

MATTHÄUS-MAIER, Ingrid; German banking executive and fmr politician; *Spokeswoman of the Board of Managing Directors, KfW Bankengruppe;* b. 9 Sept. 1945, Werlte, Aschendorf Co.; d. of Heinz-Günther Matthäus and

Helmtraud Matthäus (née von Hagen); m. Robert Maier 1974; one s. one d.; ed studied law in Giessen and Münster; Research Asst, Münster Higher Admin. Court, then Admin. Court Judge in Münster; joined Free Democratic Party (Freie Demokratische Partei—FDP) 1969, mem. North Rhine-Westphalian Exec. Cttee and of Fed. Exec. Cttee FDP; Fed. Chair. Young Democrats 1972; mem. Bundestag 1976, Chair. Finance Cttee 1979–82, resgnd all posts, left FDP and resgnd seat in Bundestag in protest at coalition change of FDP 1982; joined SPD 1982; re-elected to Bundestag 1983, Deputy Chair. SPD Parl. Group (in charge of fiscal, budgetary/borrowing, banking, stock exchange and monetary affairs) 1988, mem. Exec. Cttee SPD 1995–99, Titular mem. Mediation Cttee 1995, resgnd seat in Bundestag 1999; mem. Bd of Man. Dirs KfW Bankengruppe 1999–2006, Spokeswoman of Bd of Man. Dirs 2006–, responsible for Secr. of Man. Affairs/Legal Affairs, Secr. of Domestic Credit Affairs, Communications and Internal Auditing, also responsible for Berlin Br.; mem. Supervisory Bd Deutsche Telekom AG, Deutsche Post AG, Bonn Deutsche Steinkohle AG, Herne 2007–, EVONIK Industries AG (fmrly, Essen –2009, RAG Aktiengesellschaft, Essen, Salzgitter Mannesmann Handel GmbH, Dusseldorf; ranked by Fortune magazine amongst 50 Most Powerful Women in Business outside the US (31st) 2007, ranked by the Financial Times amongst Top 25 Businesswomen in Europe (17th) 2006, (15th) 2007. *Address:* c/o Christine Volk, KfW, Palmengartenstraße 5–9, 60325 Frankfurt, Germany (office). *Telephone:* (69) 7431-4466 (office). *Fax:* (69) 7431-4141 (office). *E-mail:* christine.volk@kfw.de (office); ingrid.matthaus-maier@kfw.de (office). *Website:* www.kfw.de (office).

MATTHES, Ulrich; German actor; b. 9 May 1959, Berlin; s. of Günter Matthes and Else Matthes; with Düsseldorfer Schauspielhaus 1986–87, Bayerisches Staatstheater, Munich 1987–89, Kammerspiele, Munich 1989–92, Schaubühne, Berlin 1992–98, Deutsches Theater, Berlin; Förderpreis, Kunstpreis Berlin 1991, O.E. Hasse-Preis 1992, Bayerischer Filmpreis 1999.

MATTHEW, Norman; Marshall Islands politician; *Minister of Internal Affairs;* Senator for Aur Atoll; Minister of Internal Affairs 2008–; fmr mem. United People's Party (UPP), now mem. Aelon Kein Ad (Our Islands) party; del. to Asia Pacific Parl. Forum. *Address:* Ministry of Internal Affairs, POB 18, Majuro MH 96960, Marshall Islands (office). *Telephone:* (625) 8240 (office). *Fax:* (625) 5353 (office). *E-mail:* rmihpo@ntamar.net (office).

MATTHEWS, Peter Hugoe, LittD, FBA; British professor of linguistics; *Professor Emeritus, University of Cambridge;* b. 10 March 1934, Oswestry; s. of John Hugo Matthews and Cecily Eileen Elmsley Hagarty; m. Lucienne Marie Jeanne Schleich 1984; one step-s. one step-d.; ed Montpellier School, Paignton, Clifton Coll., St John's Coll., Cambridge; lecturer, Univ. Coll. of N Wales, Bangor 1960–65, at Ind. Univ., Bloomington 1963–64; Lecturer, Reader and Prof., Univ. of Reading 1965–80; Visiting Prof. Deccan Coll., Pune 1969–70; Sr Research Fellow King's Coll., Cambridge 1970–71; Fellow, Nias Wassenaar, Holland 1977–78; Prof. and Head of Dept of Linguistics, Univ. of Cambridge 1980–2001, Fellow of St John's Coll. 1980–, Praelector 1987–2001, Prof. Emer. 2001–; Pres. Philological Soc. 1992–96, Vice-Pres. 1996–; Hon. mem. Linguistics Soc. of America 1994–. *Publications:* Inflectional Morphology 1972, Morphology 1974, Generative Grammar and Linguistic Competence 1979, Syntax 1981, Grammatical Theory in the United States from Bloomfield to Chomsky 1993, The Concise Oxford Dictionary of Linguistics 1997, A Short History of Structural Linguistics 2001, Linguistics: A Very Short Introduction 2003. *Leisure interests:* cycling, gardening. *Address:* St John's College, Cambridge, CB2 1TP (office); 10 Fendon Close, Cambridge, CB1 7RU, England (home); 22 Rue Nina et Julien Lefevre, 1952 Luxembourg. *Telephone:* (1223) 338768 (office); (1223) 247553 (home). *Website:* www.mml .cam.ac.uk/ling (office).

MATTHEWS, Robert Charles Oliver, CBE, MA, FBA; British economist and academic; *Professor Emeritus of Political Economy, University of Cambridge;* b. 16 June 1927, Edin.; s. of Oliver Harwood Matthews and Ida Finlay; m. Joyce Lloyds 1948 (died 2006); one d.; ed Edin. Acad. and Corpus Christi and Nuffield Colls, Oxford; Asst Univ. Lecturer, then Lecturer, Cambridge 1949–65; Drummond Prof. of Political Economy 1965–75, All Souls Coll., Oxford; Master of Clare Coll., Cambridge 1975–93, Fellow 1993–; Prof. of Political Economy, Cambridge 1980–91, now Prof. Emer.; Chair. Social Science Research Council 1972–75; Fellow, St John's Coll., Cambridge 1950–65, All Souls Coll., Oxford 1965–75; Hon. Fellow Corpus Christi Coll., Oxford; Hon. DLitt (Warwick Univ.) 1981, (Abertay) 1996. *Publications:* A Study in Trade Cycle History 1954, The Trade Cycle 1958, Economic Growth: A Survey (with F. H. Hahn) 1964, Economic Growth: Trends and Factors (ed.) 1981, British Economic Growth 1856–1973 (with C. H. Feinstein and J. Odling-Smee) 1982, Slower Growth in the Western World (ed.) 1982, Contemporary Problems of Economic Policy (ed., with J. R. Sargent) 1983, Economy and Democracy (ed.) 1985, Mostly Three-Movers; collected chess problems 1995 and articles in learned journals. *Leisure interest:* chess problems. *Address:* Clare College, Cambridge, CB2 1TL, England. *Telephone:* (1223) 333200.

MATTHEWS, Sir Terence H. (Terry), Kt, OBE, BSc; British/Canadian telecommunications industry executive; *Chairman, Mitel Networks Corporation;* b. 1943, Newport, Wales; m.; four c.; ed Univ. of Wales, Swansea; emigrated to Ottawa, Canada 1969; co-f. Mitel Corpn (with Michael Cowpland) 1972, Chair. 1972–85, Chair. Mitel Networks Corpn (communications system div.) 2001–; f. Newbridge Networks Corpn 1986, Chair. and CEO 1986–2000; f. March Networks Corpn 2000, Chair. and CEO 2000–; f. Celtic House Int.; Founding Chair. Celtic Manor Resort (host of Ryder Cup 2010); Chair. Convedia Corpn, DragonWave, Tundra Semiconductor Corpn; Fellow Inst. of Electrical Engineers; mem. Royal Acad. of Eng; Hon. PhD (Univs of Wales, Glamorgan and Swansea, Carleton Univ., Ottawa). *Address:* Mitel Networks Corporation, 350 Legget Drive, POB 13089, Kanata, Ont. K2K 2W7, Canada (office). *Telephone:* (613) 592-2122 (office). *Fax:* (613) 592-4784 (office). *Website:* www.mitel.com (office).

MATTHIAS, Stefanos; Greek judge (retd); b. 27 May 1935, Athens; m.; one d.; ed Univ. of Athens, Univ. of Poitiers, France; judge 1961–2002; Pres. Supreme Civil and Penal Court 1996–2002; Dir Nat. School for Judges 1994–96; First Class Honour Cross. *Publications:* more than 40 studies and articles on pvt. law and on European Convention on Human Rights. *Leisure interest:* painting. *Address:* 26 Niriidon Str., 17561 Paleon Faliron, Greece (home). *Telephone:* (210) 9882632 (home); (210) 9827466 (home). *E-mail:* stefmatt@otenet.gr (home).

MATTHIESSEN, Peter, BA; American writer and editor; *Founding Editor, The Paris Review;* b. 22 May 1927, New York; s. of Erard A. Matthiessen and Elizabeth (née Carey) Matthiessen; m. 1st Patricia Southgate 1951 (divorced); m. 2nd Deborah Love 1963 (died 1972); three s. one d.; m. 3rd Maria Eckhart 1980; ed Sorbonne, Paris, Yale Univ.; co-founder and now Founding Ed. The Paris Review 1953–; ordained a Zen Monk 1981; fmr corresp., New Yorker; Trustee New York Zoological Soc. 1965–78; mem. American Acad. of Arts and Letters 1974–, Nat. Inst. of Arts and Science 1986–; Atlantic Prize 1950, American Acad. of Arts and Letters Award 1963, National Book Award 1978, John Burroughs Medal 1981, African Wildlife Leadership Foundation Award 1982, Gold Medal for Distinction in Natural History 1985, Orion-John Hay Award 1999, Soc. of Conservation Biologists Award 1999, Heinz Award for Arts and Humanities 2000, Lannan Lifetime Achievement Award 2002, Harvard Nat. History Museum Roger Tory Peterson Medal 2003. *Publications:* Race Rock 1954, Partisans 1955, Raditzer 1960, Wildlife in America 1959, The Cloud Forest 1961, Under the Mountain Wall 1963, At Play in the Fields of the Lord 1965, The Shore Birds of North America 1967, Oomingmak: The Expedition to the Musk Ox Island in the Bering Sea 1967, Sal si puedes 1969, Blue Meridian 1971, The Tree Where Man Was Born 1972, The Wind Birds 1973, Far Tortuga 1975, The Snow Leopard 1978, Sand Rivers 1981, In the Spirit of the Crazy Horse 1983, Indian Country 1984, Midnight Turning Grey 1984, Nine-Headed Dragon River 1986, Men's Lives 1986, Partisans 1987, On the River Styx 1989, Killing Mr Watson 1990, African Silences 1991, Baikal 1992, Shadows of Africa 1992, East of Lo Monthang: In the Land of Mustang 1995, Lost Man's River 1997, Bone by Bone (novel) 1999, Tigers in the Snow 2000, Peter Matthiessen Reader: Non Fiction 1959-1991 2000, An African Trilogy 2000, Sal si Puedes – Cesar Chávez and the New American Revolution 2000, Birds of Heaven: Travels with Cranes 2001, Ends of the Earth: Voyages to Antarctica 2003, Shadow Country: A New Rendering of the Watson Legend (Nat. Book Award for Fiction) 2008. *Address:* The Paris Review, 62 White Street, New York, NY 10013, USA (office). *Website:* www .parisreview.com (office).

MATTHIESSEN, Poul Christian, MA, DSc (Econs); Danish demographer and academic; b. 1 Feb. 1933, Odense; s. of Jens P. E. Matthiessen and Laura C. Nielsen; m. Ulla Bay 1986; two d.; Research Asst, Copenhagen Telephone Co. 1958–63; Lecturer in Statistics and Demography, Univ. of Copenhagen 1963–70, Prof. of Demography 1971–95; Pres. Carlsberg Foundation 1993–2002; Chair. Carlsberg's Bequest in Memory of Brewer J. C. Jacobsen 1993–2003; mem. Bd of Dirs Museum of Nat. History at Frederiksborg Castle 1993–2002; mem. European Population Cttee 1972–2000, Royal Danish Acad. of Science and Letters 1982, Academia Europaea 1988; mem. Supervisory Bd Carlsberg A/S 1989–2003, Chair. Supervisory Bd Carlsberg A/S 1993–2003; mem. Supervisory Bd Royal Scandinavia 1993–2001, Fredericia Bryggeri 1993–97, Falcon Bryggerier AB 1998–2001; mem. Bd of Dirs Den Berlingske Fond 1999–2008. *Publications:* Infant Mortality in Denmark 1931–60 1964, Growth of Population: Causes and Implications 1965, Demographic Methods (Vol. I–III) 1970, Some Aspects of the Demographic Transition in Denmark 1970, The Limitation of Family Size in Denmark (Vol. I–II) 1985, Population and Society 2007. *Leisure interests:* literature, history, architecture. *Address:* The Royal Society of Sciences and Letters, H.C. Andersens Boulevard 37, 1553 Copenhagen V (office). *Telephone:* 33-43-53-36 (office). *E-mail:* pcm@post.tele .dk (office).

MATTHÖFER, Hans; German politician; b. 25 Sept. 1925, Bochum; m. Traute Mecklenburg 1951; ed Univs of Frankfurt am Main and Madison, Wis., USA; Mem. of Social Democratic Party (SPD) 1950–; mem. Econ. Dept IG Metall 1953, Head of Educ. and Training Dept 1961; mem. OECD Washington and Paris 1957–61; mem. Bundestag (Parl.) 1961–87; mem. Bundestag Cttees for Econ., Econ. Co-operation, Law, Foreign Affairs; Parl. Sec. of State, Ministry of Econ. Co-operation 1972–74; mem. Exec. Cttee SPD 1973–85, mem. Presidency and Treas. 1985–87; Minister for Research and Tech. 1974–78, of Finance 1978–82, of Posts and Telecommunications April–Oct. 1982; Chair. BG-AG Holding Co. 1987–97; Adviser to Bulgarian Govt 1997–2000; Vice-Pres. Latin America Parliamentarians' Group 1961, 1983; mem. hon. Presidium of German Section, Amnesty Int. 1961; Pres. Deutsche Stiftung für Entwicklungsländer (Foundation for Overseas Devt) 1971–73; Vice-Chair. Enquiry Comm. on Tech. Assessment of Bundestag 1984–86; Publisher of Vorwärts 1985–88; Pres. German Supporting Cttee for ORT 1989–; Großkreuz den Bundesverdienstorden 1983, Gran Cruz del Mérito Civil (Spain) 1989, Gran Maestre de la Orden del Mayo al Mérito (Argentina) 1985, Gran Cruz de la Orden de Bernardo O'Higgins (Chile) 1992. *Publications:* Der Unterschied zwischen den Tariflöhnen und den Effektivverdiensten in der Metallindustrie der Bundesrepublik 1956, Technological Change in the Metal Industries 1961/62, Der Beitrag politischer Bildung zur Emanzipation der Arbeitnehmer–Materialien zur Frage des Bildungsurlaubs 1970, Streiks und streikähnliche Formen des Kampfes der Arbeitnehmer im Kapitalismus 1971, Für eine menschliche Zukunft—Sozialdemokratische Forschungs- und Technologiepolitik 1976, Humanisierung der Arbeit und

Produktivität in der Industriegesellschaft 1977, 1978, 1980, Agenda 2000-Vorschläge zur Wirtschafts- und Gesellschaftspolitik 1993; numerous articles on trades unions, research, technology, development, politics, economics and finance. *Leisure interests:* chess, reading. *Address:* Georg-Rückert Strasse 2, Apt. 306, 65812 Bad Soden, Germany (home). *Telephone:* (6196) 201306.

MATTHUS, Siegfried; German composer; b. 13 April 1934, Mallenuppen, E Prussia; s. of the late Franz Matthus and of Luise Perrey; m. Helga Spitzer 1958; one s.; ed Hochschule für Musik, Berlin, Acad. of Arts and Music, Berlin (masterclass with Hanns Eisler); composer and consultant, Komische Oper, Berlin 1964–2002; Prof. 1985–; Artistic Dir Chamber Opera Festival, Rheinsberg 1991; mem. Acad. of Arts of GDR, Acad. of Arts of W Berlin, Acad. of Arts, Munich; Nat. Prize 1972, 1984, Bundesverdienstkreuz (First Class) 2000. *Compositions include:* Te Deum, 10 operas, one oratorio, concertos, orchestral and chamber music, etc. *Leisure interests:* swimming, jogging, carpentry. *Address:* Elisabethweg 10, 13187 Berlin (home); Seepromenade 15, 16348 Stolzenhagen, Germany (home). *Telephone:* (30) 4857362 (Berlin) (home); (33397) 21736 (Stolzenhagen) (home). *Fax:* (30) 48096604 (Berlin) (home); (33397) 71400 (Stolzenhagen) (home). *E-mail:* smatthus@aol.com (home).

MATTILA, Karita Marjatta; Finnish singer (soprano); b. 5 Sept. 1960, Somero; d. of Arja Mattila and Erkki Mattila (née Somerikko); m. Tapio Kuneinen 1992; ed Sibelius Acad., Finland and studied with Liisa Linko-Malmio, and Vera Rozsa in London; operatic debut at Finnish Nat. Opera as the Countess (Marriage of Figaro) 1983; appeared with Brussels Opera as Countess, Eva, Rosalinde 1984–85; debut at Royal Opera House, Covent Garden as Fiordiligi 1986, subsequent appearances as Pamina, Countess and Agathe 1986–89, Donna Elvira 1992, Musetta 1994, Elisabeth de Valois 1996, Elsa 1997, Chrysothemis 1997; appeared at Barenboim-Ponnelle Festival, Paris 1986, Tel-Aviv 1987, 1990; debut at Metropolitan Opera as Donna Elvira 1990, Eva in Meistersinger 1993, Lisa 1995, Musetta 1996, Elsa in Lohengrin 1998, Amelia in Simon Boccanegra 1999, Fidelio 2000, Chrysothemis 2002, Jenůfa 2003; debut at Opéra Nat. de Paris as Elsa 1996, Hanna Glawari 1997, Lisa 2001; Théâtre du Châtelet: Elisabeth de Valois 1996, Desdemona 2001, Arabella 2002; appearances at Salzburg Festival: Donna Anna 1999, Fiordiligi 2000, Jenůfa 2001; has also appeared in Washington, Houston, Chicago and San Francisco; recitals throughout Europe; has worked under maj. conductors, including Sir Colin Davis, Claudio Abbado, von Dohnanyi, Giulini, Sinopoli, Solti, Haitink, Maazel, Levine; first prize Finnish Nat. Singing Competition 1981, first prize BBC Singer of the World, Cardiff 1983, Evening Standard Award 1997, Acad. du Disque Lyrique Award 1997, Grammy Award for Best Opera 1998, Pro Finlandia 2001, Musical America Musician of the Year 2005. *Recordings:* over 50 solo and opera recordings. *Leisure interests:* sport, yoga, golf, sailing. *Address:* IMG Artists, The Light Box, 111 Power Road, London, W4 5PY, England (office). *Telephone:* (20) 8233-5800 (office). *Fax:* (20) 8233-5801 (office). *E-mail:* jvanderveen@imgartists.com (office); tapio.kuneinen@pp.inet.fi (home). *Website:* www.imgartists.com (office).

MATTINGLY, Mack Francis, BS; American business executive, diplomatist and fmr politician; b. 7 Jan. 1931, Anderson, Ind.; s. of Joseph Hilbert and Beatrice Wayts Mattingly; m. 1st Carolyn Longcamp 1957 (deceased); two d.; m. 2nd Leslie Ann Davisson 1998; ed Indiana Univ.; served USAF 1951–55; Account Supervisor, Arvin Industries, Ind. 1957–59; Marketing Man. IBM Corpn 1959–79; owner M's Inc. 1975–80; US Senator from Georgia 1981–87; Asst Sec.-Gen. for Defence Support, NATO, Brussels 1987–90; Amb. to Seychelles 1992–93; speaker and author on defence and foreign policy matters; fmr Chair. Southeastern Legal Foundation, Georgia Ports Authority; mem. Cumberland Island Asscn; mem. Bd of Dirs, Novecon Tech., Compu-Credit Corpn; US Trustee to Puerto Rico Conservation Trust; fmr trustee and dir of several corpns, foundations, etc; Republican; Sec. of Defense Distinguished Service Medal for Outstanding Public Service 1988 and other awards from public service and USAF. *Publications:* numerous articles, speeches and book chapters. *Address:* 4315 10th Street, East Beach, St Simons Island, GA 31522, USA (home). *Telephone:* (912) 638-5430 (home). *E-mail:* mlmattingly@comcast.net (home).

MATTIS, Gen. James N.; American army officer; *Supreme Allied Commander Transformation, NATO; Commander, United States Joint Forces Command;* ed Cen. Washington State Univ., Amphibious Warfare School, Marine Corps Command and Staff Coll., Nat. War Coll.; entered US Marine Corps and commissioned as Second Lt 1972; as a Lt, served as rifle and weapons platoon commdr in 3rd Marine Div., as a Capt., commanded rifle co. and weapons co. in 1st Marine Brigade; as Maj., commanded Recruiting Station Portland; as Lt-Col, commanded 1st Bn, 7th Marines, one of Task Force Ripper's assault bns in Operation Desert Shield and Desert Storm; as Col, commanded 7th Marines (Reinforced); as Brig.-Gen., commanded 1st Marine Expeditionary Brigade and then Task Force 58, during Operation Enduring Freedom in southern Afghanistan; as Maj.-Gen., commanded 1st Marine Div. during initial attack (2003) and subsequent stability operations in Iraq during Operation Iraqi Freedom; in first tour as Lt-Gen., commanded Marine Corps Combat Devt Command and served as Deputy Commdt for combat Devt; commanded I Marine Expeditionary Force, Camp Pendleton, Calif. 2006–07; served as Commdr of US Marine Forces Cen. Command; rank of Gen. 2007; Supreme Allied Commdr Transformation, NATO 2007–; Commdr US Jt Forces Command (USJFCOM), Norfolk, Va 2007–; Kuwait Liberation Medal (Kuwait), Kuwait Liberation Medal (Saudi Arabia), Marine Corps Recruiting Service Ribbon (with Bronze Service Star), Sea Service Deployment Ribbon (with one Silver and two Bronze Service Stars), Humanitarian Service Medal, Global War on Terrorism Service Medal, Global War on Terrorism Expeditionary Medal, Iraq Campaign Medal, Afghanistan Campaign Medal, Southwest Asia Service Medal (with two Bronze Service Stars), Nat. Defense Service Medal (with two Bronze Service Stars), Marine Corps Expeditionary Medal, Navy and Marine Corps Meritorous Unit Commendation, Navy Unit Commendation, Jt Meritorious Unit Award, Presidential Unit Citation, Combat Action Ribbon, Navy and Marine Corps Achievement Medal, Meritorious Service Medal (with two Gold Award Stars), Bronze Star (with Combat Valor Device), Legion of Merit, Defense Superior Service Medal, Navy Distinguished Service Medal, Defense Distinguished Service Medal (with Oak Leaf Cluster). *Address:* US Joint Forces Command, 1562 Mitscher Avenue, Suite 200, Norfolk, VA 23551-2488, USA (office). *Telephone:* (757) 836-6555 (office). *E-mail:* info@jfcom.mil (office). *Website:* www.jfcom.mil (office).

MATTSON, Mark Paul, BS, MS, PhD; American neuroscientist; *Chief, Laboratory of Neurosciences and Chief, Cellular and Molecular Neurosciences Section, National Institute on Aging;* b. 1 April 1957, Rochester, Minn.; m. Joanne Mattson (née Youngblood) 1983; one s. one d.; ed Iowa State Univ., North Texas State Univ., Univ. of Iowa; Postdoctoral Researcher in Developmental Neuroscience, Colorado State Univ. 1986–87; Asst Prof. of Anatomy and Neurobiology, Univ. of Kentucky 1989–93, joined faculty Sanders-Brown Research Center on Aging, Univ. of Kentucky Medical Center 1989, Assoc. Prof. 1993–97, Prof. 1997–2000, Dir Confocal Laser Scanning Microscope Facility 1992–2000; Chief, Lab. of Neurosciences, Nat. Inst. on Aging, also Chief, Cellular and Molecular Neurosciences Section 2000–; Prof. of Neuroscience, Johns Hopkins Univ. 2000–; Ed.-in-Chief, Journal of Molecular Neuroscience; Assoc. Ed. Journal of Neuroscience, Journal of Neurochemistry, Journal of Neuroscience Research; mem. AAAS, Soc. for Neuroscience, Int. Brain Research Org., American Soc. for Cell Biology, NY Acad. of Sciences; numerous awards including Metropolitan Life Foundation Medical Research Award, Alzheimer's Asscn Zenith Award, Jordi Folch Pi Award, Santiago Grisolia Chair Prize and several Grass Lectureship Awards. *Publications include:* Telomerase, Aging and Disease 2001, Diet-Brain Connection: Impact on Memory, Mood, Aging and Disease 2002, Stem Cells: A Cellular Fountain of Youth (Jt Ed.) 2002, Sleep And Aging (Ed.) 2005; more than 300 original research articles and more than 80 review articles. *Address:* Laboratory of Neurosciences, Biomedical Research Center, 05C214, 251 Bayview Boulevard, Suite 100, Baltimore, MD 21224-6825, USA (office). *Telephone:* (410) 558-8463 (office). *Fax:* (410) 558-8465 (office). *E-mail:* mattsonm@grc.nia.nih.gov (office). *Website:* www.grc.nia.nih.gov/branches/irp/mmattson.htm (office).

MATUBRAIMOV, Almambet Matubraimovich; Kyrgyzstani politician; b. 1952, Osh Region, Kyrgyzstan; ed Tashkent Inst. of Light and Textile Industry; worker in sovkhoz Kursheb Osh Region; master, sr master, textile factory KKSK 1977–80; army service 1980–82; head of workshop, head of production textile factory KKSK (later Bishkek) 1982–84, Dir 1984–90; Chair. Exec. Cttee Sverdlov Region, Frunze (later Bishkek) 1990–91; First Deputy Minister of Industry Repub. of Kyrgyzstan 1991–93; First Deputy Prime Minister 1991–93; Chair. People's Council of Repub. of Kyrgyzstan (Uluk Kenesh) 1995–99; in opposition to Pres. Akayev 1999; worked in Mining Br. 1999–2005; Plenipotentiary of the Pres. for Southern Region 2005–06, Plenipotentiary on Econ. Cooperation with Eurasian Countries 2006; Deputy in Jogorku Jenesh (Parl.) 2006–. *Address:* Uluk Kenesh, 720003 Bishkek, Kyrgyzstan.

MATUSCHKA, Mario, Graf von, DJur; German diplomatist; b. 27 Feb. 1931, Oppeln, Silesia; s. of Michael, Graf von Matuschka and Pia, Gräfin Stillfried-Rattonitz; m. Eleonore, Gräfin von Waldburg-Wolfegg 1962; two s. two d.; ed St Matthias Gymnasium, Breslau, Domgymnasium, Fulda and Univs of Fribourg, Paris and Munich; entered foreign service 1961; Attaché, German Observer's Mission at UN, New York 1961–62; Vice-Consul, Consul, Salzburg 1963–66; Second Sec. Islamabad 1966–68; First Sec. Tokyo 1968–71; Foreign Office, Bonn 1971–75, 1978–80, 1982–88, 1990–93; Economic Counsellor, London 1975–78; Deputy Chief of Protocol, UN, New York 1980–82; State Sec., Chief of Protocol, Land Berlin 1988–90; Amb. and Perm. Rep. of Germany to OECD 1993–96; Diplomatic Adviser to Commr Gen., Expo 2000, Hanover 1996–97, Dir Holy See's Pavilion June–Oct. 2000; Sec. Gen. Internationaler Club La Redoute e.V. 1997–2000, mem. Bd 2000–02; Head of Del. Blessed Clemens August 2002–; Sovereign Mil. Order of Malta 1961, Order of Merit (Germany) 1990, decorations from Japan 1972, Portugal 1989, Holy See 2002. *Publication:* Manuale Prayer Book for German Asscn SMRO (co-ed.) 2005. *Address:* Drachenfelsstraße 45, 53757 St Augustin, Germany (home). *Telephone:* (2241) 337707 (home). *Fax:* (2241) 337707 (home). *E-mail:* grafmatuschka@aol.com (home).

MATUTE AUSEJO, Ana María; Spanish writer; b. 26 July 1926, Barcelona; d. of Facundo Matute and Mary Ausejo; m. 1952 (divorced 1963); one s.; ed Damas Negras French Nuns Coll.; collaborated on literary magazine Destino; Visiting Lecturer, Indiana Univ. 1965–66, Oklahoma Univ. 1969–; Writer-in-Residence, Univ. of Virginia 1978–79; mem. Real Academia Española de la Lengua 1996–; Hon. mem. Hispanic Soc. of America, American Asscn of Teachers of Spanish and Portuguese; Dr hc (Univ. of Leon); Highly Commended Author, Hans Christian Andersen Jury, Lisbon 1972, Gold Medal, Circulo de Bellas Artes de Madrid, 2006, Premio Nacional de las Letras Españolas 2007. *Children's books:* El País de la Pizarra 1956, Paulina 1961, El Sal Tamontes Verde 1961, Caballito Loco 1961, El Aprendiz 1961, Carnavalito 1961, El Polizón del Ulises (Lazarillo Prize) 1965. *Publications include:* Los Abel 1948, Fiesta Al Noroeste (Café Gijón Prize) 1952, Pequeño Teatro (Planeta Prize) 1954, Los Niños Tontos 1956, Los Hijos Muertos (Nat. Literary Prize and Critics Prize) 1959, Primera Memoria (Nadal Prize) 1959, Tres y un sueño 1961, Historias de la Artamila 1961, El Río 1963, El Tiempo 1963, Los Soldados lloran de noche 1964 (Fastenrath Prize 1969), El Arrepentido y otras Narraciones 1967, Algunos Muchachos 1968, La Trampa 1969, La Torre Vigia 1971, Olvidado Rey Gudu 1974, Sólo un pie descalzo 1983, La virgen de

Antioquía y otros relatos 1990, De ninguna parte 1993, La oveja negra 1994, El árbol de oro y otros relatos 1995, El verdadero final de la bella durmiente 1995, Todos mis cuentos 2000. *Leisure interests:* painting, drawing, the cinema. *Website:* www.anamaria-matute.com.

MATUTES JUAN, Abel; Spanish international organization official and politician; b. 31 Oct. 1941, Ibiza; s. of Antonio and Carmen Matutes; m. Nieves Prats; one s. three d.; ed Univ. of Barcelona; studies in law and econs; fmr entrepreneur in tourism and property in island of Ibiza; fmr Lecturer in Econs and Public Finance, Univ. of Barcelona; Deputy Chair. Ibiza & Formentera Tourist Bd 1964–69; Mayor of Ibiza 1970–71; Senator for Ibiza and Formentera 1977–82; Deputy Alianza Popular 1982–85; Deputy Nat. Chair. Alianza Popular; mem. Community Comm. 1986–94; EC Commr for Credits and Investments, Small and Medium-Sized Enterprises and Financial Eng 1986–89, for American Policy, Latin American Relations 1989–93, for Energy and Euratom Supply Agency, Transport 1993–95; Nat. Vice-Pres., then mem. Exec. Cttee. political party Partido Popular (fmrly Alianza Popular) 1979–; mem. European Parl. 1994–96, Pres. Comm. for External Relations and Security of European Parl. 1994–96; Minister of Foreign Affairs 1996–2000; Pres. and Founder, Matutes Group of Companies; Pres. Foundation Empresa y Crecimiento; Exec. Vice-Pres. EXCELTUR (Hoteliers Asscn); mem. Eurogroup, Spanish Group of the Trilateral Comm.; mem. Bd of Dirs, BSCH, FCC, Insecc, Balearia, Assecurationi Internationali di Previdenza; mem. Royal Spanish Acad. of Econs and Financial Sciences; Dr hc (Complutense Univ., Madrid), (Univ. of Santiago, Chile) more than 40 nat. and foreign decorations and hons including Grand Cross of the Order of Merit (FRG), Grand Official Legion of Honor Order (France), Grand Gold Cross of Austrian Repub., Grand Cross Order of Merit (Italy), Grand Cross Order of Carlos III (Spain) Hon. Cttee Mem., Royal Inst. for European Studies. *Leisure interests:* tennis, sailing. *Address:* P.O. Box 416, Ibiza, Spain (office). *Telephone:* (971) 313811 (office). *Fax:* (971) 311864 (office). *E-mail:* matutes@fiesta-hotels.com (office).

MATVEYENKO, Valery P., DrTech; Russian physicist; *Director, Institute of Continuous Media Mechanics, Russian Academy of Sciences;* b. 9 Feb. 1948, Kizel, Perm region; m.; one d.; ed Perm State Polytech. Inst.; eng., jr, then sr researcher Urals Scientific Centre at the Russian Acad. of Sciences 1972–79; scientific sec., head of laboratory, Deputy Dir Inst. of Continuous Media Mechanics at the Urals branch of the Russian Acad. of Sciences 1979–93, Dir 1993–; mem. Russian Acad. of Sciences (corresp. mem. 1997–2001); State Prize of Russian Federation 1998; order of Friendship of Peoples, various medals. *Publications include:* over 140 scientific works, two monographs. *Leisure interests:* fishing. *Address:* Institute of Continuous Media Mechanics, Urals branch of the Russian Academy of Sciences, Koroleva str. 1, Perm 614013, Russia (office). *Telephone:* 3422-13 68 61 (office). *Fax:* 3422-13 60 87 (office). *E-mail:* mvp@icma.ru (office).

MATVEYEV, Victor A., Dr Phys., Math., Sciences; Russian physicist; *Director, Institute of Nuclear Research, Russian Academy of Sciences;* b. 11 Dec. 1941, Taiga, Novosibirsk region; m.; two c.; ed Leningrad State Univ.; Jr then Sr Researcher, Head of Sector, United Inst. of Nuclear Research 1965–78, Deputy Dir 1978–87, Dir 1987–; mem. Editorial Bd Yadernaya Fyzika (journal); mem. Russian Acad. of Sciences (corresp. mem. 1991–94); Lenin Prize. *Publications include:* Gravitation and Elementary Particle Physics 1980, Nonconservation of Barrion Numbers in Extreme Conditions 1988; numerous scientific papers on relativistic quark models of elementary particles, quantum field theory. *Address:* Institute of Nuclear Research, Russian Academy of Sciences, 60 let Okryabra prosp. 7a, Moscow 107312, Russia (office). *Telephone:* (495) 135-77-60 (office); (495) 334-00-71 (office). *Website:* www.inr.ac.ru (office).

MATVIYENKO, Valentina Ivanovna; Russian politician; *Governor of St Petersburg City;* b. 7 April 1949, Shepetovka, Ukrainian SSR; m. Vladimir Vasilyevich Matviyenko; one s.; ed Leningrad Inst. of Chem. and Pharmaceuticals, Acad. of Social Sciences at CPSU Cen. Cttee, Acad. of Diplomacy USSR Ministry of Foreign Affairs; Komsomol work 1972–84; First Sec. Krasnogvardeisk Dist CP Cttee, Leningrad 1984–86; Deputy Chair. Exec. Cttee Leningrad City Council 1986–89; USSR Peoples' Deputy, mem. Supreme Soviet 1989–92; mem. of Presidium, Chair. Cttee on Family, Motherhood and Childhood Protection Affairs 1989–91; Russian Amb. to Malta 1991–94, to Greece 1997–98; rank of Amb. Extraordinary and Plenipotentiary; Dir Dept on Relations with Federal Subjects, Parl. and Public Orgs Ministry of Foreign Affairs 1995–97, Deputy Prime Minister responsible for social issues 1998–2003, Chair. Comm. on Int. Humanitarian Aid and Religious Orgs; Presidential Rep. in the North-Western Fed. Okrug 2003; mem. Security Council of the Russian Fed. 2003; Gov. of St Petersburg 2003–; Badge of Honour 1976, Order of the Red Banner of Labour 1982, Order for Service to the Homeland (3rd Class) 1999; ranked by Forbes magazine amongst 100 Most Powerful Women (31st) 2008. *Address:* Office of the Mayor (Governor and Premier of the City Government of St Petersburg), 191060 St Petersburg, Smolnyi, Russia (office). *Telephone:* (812) 276-45-01 (office); (812) 276-18-27 (office). *E-mail:* gov@gov.spb.ru (office). *Website:* www.gov.spb.ru (office).

MATYJASZEWSKI, Krzysztof, PhD; Polish chemist and academic; *University Professor, Carnegie Mellon University;* b. 8 April 1950; s. of Henryk and Antonina Matyjaszewski; m. Malgorzata Matyjaszewska; one s. one d.; ed Technical Univ. of Moscow, USSR, Polish Acad. of Sciences, Polytechnical Univ. of Łódź; Post-doctoral Fellow, Univ. of Florida 1977–78; Research Assoc., Polish Acad. of Sciences 1978–84; Research Assoc., CNRS, France 1984–85; Invited Prof., Univ. of Paris, France 1985; Asst Prof., later Assoc. Prof., later Prof., Carnegie Mellon Univ., Pittsburg, Pa 1985–98, Head, Chem. Dept 1994–98, J.C. Warner Prof. of Natural Sciences 1998–, Univ. Prof. 2004–; Elf Chair, Acad. des sciences, Paris 1998; Adjunct Prof., Dept of Chemical and Petroleum Eng, Univ. of Pittsburgh 2000–, Polish Acad. of Sciences, Łódź 2000–; Visiting Prof., Univ. of Paris 1985, 1990, 1997, 1998, Univ. of Freiburg, Germany 1988, Univ. of Bayreuth, Germany 1991, Univ. of Strasbourg, France 1992, Univ. of Bordeaux, France 1996, Univ. of Ulm, Germany 1999, Univ. of Pisa, Italy 2000, Mich. Molecular Inst. 2004; Ed. Progress in Polymer Science, Central European Journal of Chemistry; present or past mem. Editorial Bd numerous journals including Macromolecules, Macromolecular Chemistry and Physics, Journal of Polymer Science, Journal of Inorganic and Organometallic Polymers, Journal of Macromolecular Science, Pure and Applied Chemistry, Int. Journal of Polymeric Materials, Chinese Journal of Polymer Science, Int. Journal of Applied Chemistry, Chemistry Central Journal; ACS Polymeric Materials Science and Eng Fellow 2001; IUPAC Fellow 2002–, Corresp. mem. IUPAC Comm. on Polymer Nomenclature; Chair. ACS Polymer Curriculum Devt Award Cttee ACS, mem. Program Cttee, Polymer Chem. Div., Chair. Int. Cttee, Polymer Chem. Div.; mem. US Nat. Acad. of Eng, Polish Acad. of Sciences; Dr hc (Ghent) 2002, (Russian Acad. of Sciences) 2006, (Tech. Univ. of Łódź) 2007, (Athens) 2009; Award of Scientific Sec. of Polish Acad. of Sciences 1974, Award of Polish Chemical Soc. 1980, Award of Polish Acad. of Sciences 1981, Award of Presidential Young Investigator, NSF 1989, ACS Carl S. Marvel-Creative Polymer Chem. Award 1995, Reed Lecturer, Rensellaer Polytechnic Inst. 1998, Milkovitch Lecturer, Univ. of Akron 1998, Humboldt Award for Sr US Scientists 1999, ACS Pittsburgh Award 2001, ACS Polymer Chem. Award 2002, ACS Cooperative Research Award in Polymer Science and Eng 2004, Award of Foundation for Polish Science 2004, Macro Group Medal (UK) 2005, ACS Hermann F. Mark Sr Scholar Award 2007. *Publications:* co-author/ed. ten books, 65 book chapters, more than 1,000 scientific papers, 33 US and 108 int. patents. *Address:* Department of Chemistry, Carnegie Mellon University, 4400 Fifth Avenue, Pittsburgh, PA 15213, USA (office). *Telephone:* (412) 268-3209 (office). *Fax:* (412) 268-6897 (office). *E-mail:* km3b@andrew.cmu.edu (office). *Website:* polymer.chem.cmu.edu (office).

MATYUKHIN, Gen. Vladimir Georgyevich, DTechSci; Russian business executive and government official; *Head, Federal Information Technology Agency;* b. 4 Feb. 1945, Moscow; ed Moscow Inst. of Energy, Moscow State Univ.; mem. staff Moscow Pedagogical Inst. 1962–64; engineer Construction Bureau, Moscow Inst. of Energy 1964–73; service in state security organs 1969–; Deputy Dir-Gen. Fed. Agency of Govt Telecommunications and Information 1993–99, Dir-Gen. 1999–2003; First Deputy Minister of Defence –2004, Head of State Defence Procurements Cttee –2004; rank of Gen. (Army) 2004; Head, Fed. Information Tech. Agency 2004–; mem. Acad. of Cryptography, Acad. of Int. Communication; several medals including For Labour Valour 1986, For Services to the Motherland 1999, For Military Merit 2000, St Daniil of Moscow Second degree 2000, First degree 2007. *Publications:* numerous journal articles. *Leisure interests:* photography, floriculture. *Address:* c/o Ministry of Communications and Information Technology, ul. Tverskaya 7, 103375 Moscow, Russia (office). *Telephone:* (495) 771-80-71 (office). *Fax:* (499) 503-98-70 (office). *E-mail:* mvgpr@minsyaz.ru (office). *Website:* www.minsvyaz.ru (office).

MAU, Vladimir Alexandrovich, DrEcon, PhD; Russian politician and economist; *Rector, Academy of National Economy;* b. 29 Dec. 1959, Moscow; m. Dr Irina Starodoubrovskaia; one s.; ed Moscow Plekhanov Inst. of Nat. Econs, Inst. of Econs USSR Acad. of Sciences, Acad. de Grenoble, Université Pierre Mendès, France; with Inst. of Econs, USSR (now Russian) Acad. of Sciences 1981–91, Inst. for the Economy in Transition; Sr Lecturer, Econ. Dept, Moscow State Univ. 1988–92; Head of Dept, Inst. of Econ. Policy 1991; Adviser to Chair., Govt of Russian Fed. 1992; mem. Bd Dirs and Head of Dept, Inst. for the Economy in Transition 1993; Adviser to Deputy Mayor of Moscow 1993, to First Deputy Chair., Govt of Russian Fed. 1993–94; Prof., High School of Econs 1993–2002; Adviser to Leader of the Faction in the State Duma of Russia 1994–95; Deputy Dir, Inst. for the Economy in Transition and Head of Dept for Political Studies of Econ. Reforms 1994–97; Dir Working Centre for Econ. Reform, Govt of Russian Fed. 1997–2002; Lecturer, Stanford Univ. Overseas Dept 1997–; Rector Acad. of Nat. Economy (under Govt of Russian Fed.) 2002–; Fowler Hamilton Fellow, Christ Church, Univ. of Oxford 1997; mem. Editorial Bd Mir Rossii (Universe of Russia) Journal 1993–97, Otkrytaya Politika (Open Policy) Journal 1994–, Voprosy Ekonomiki (Problems of Economics) Journal, Vestnik Yevropy (Herald of Europe) Journal, Rossikyskoe Predprinimatelstvo (Russian Entrepreneurship) Journal Scientific Sec., Economic Heritage; mem. Editorial Council, Journal of Economic Transition, RAND Corpn; Ed.-in-Chief Ekonomicheskaya Politika (Economic Policy) journal 2006–; Hon. Economist of Russian Fed. 2000. *Publications:* 600 articles in books, scientific journals, magazines and newspapers in Russian, English, French, German, Italian on history of econ. thought, political economy, social and political issues of market reforms, econ. policy; 29 books including In The Quest of Planification 1990, History of Economic Studies in the USSR: Outlines for Conception 1992, Reforms and Dogma: 1914–1929 1993, Economy and Power 1995, Political History of Economic Reform in Russia 1985–1994 1996, Economy and Law (Constitutional Problems of Economic Reforms in Russia) 1998, Economic Reform: Through the Prism of Constitution and Politics 1999, The Laws of Revolution: Experience of Perestroika and Our Future (with Irina Starodubrovskaia) 1991, Russian Economic Reforms as Seen by an Insider: Success or Failure? 2000, Challenge of Revolution (with Irina Starodubrovskaia) 2001, Great Revolutions from Cromwell to Putin 2001, Constitutional Economics (with Peter Barenboimand and Vladimir Lafitsky) 2002, From Crisis to Growth 2005. *Leisure interest:* history, reading. *Address:* Academy of National Economy, Vernadskogo Prospekt 82, 119571, Moscow, Russia (office). *Telephone:* (495) 434-83-89 (office). *Fax:* (495) 433-24-85 (office). *E-mail:* rector@ane.ru (office). *Website:* www.ane.ru (office).

MAUCHER, Helmut Oswald, Diplom-Kaufmann; German business executive; *Honorary Chairman, Nestlé AG;* b. 9 Dec. 1927, Eisenharz (Allgäu); ed Frankfurt Univ.; completed commercial apprenticeship at Nestlé factory in Eisenharz, Germany, then transferred to Nestlé, Frankfurt; various man. positions within the Nestlé Co. in Germany 1964–80, Pres. and CEO Nestlé-Gruppe Deutschland, Frankfurt 1975–80, Exec. Vice-Pres. and mem. Exec. Cttee Nestlé SA, Vevey, Switzerland 1980–81, CEO 1981–90, Chair. Bd 1990–2000 and CEO 1990–97, Hon. Chair. 2000–; Chair. Bd Trustees Stiftung Demoskopie Allensbach Germany, Frankfurt Inst. for Advanced Studies; mem. Bd Koç Holding AS, Istanbul, Union Bancaire Privée, Geneva, Int. Course of Studies Bachelor and Master Philosophy and Econs, Bayreuth Univ.; mem. Bd of Trustees, Fondation Simón I. Patiño Geneva; mem. Advisory Council, Deutsche Vermögensberatung AG, Frankfurt; mem. Int. Advisory Cttee, Fitch Rating Agency, London and New York; Order El Aguila Azteca (Mexico) 1993, Grosses Goldenes Ehrenzeichen mit dem Stern für Verdienste um die Republik Oesterreich 1993, Das Grosse Verdienstkreuz des Verdienstordens mit Stern der Bundesrepublik Deutschland 1997, Das Osterreichische Ehrenkreuz für Wissenschaft und Kunst 1. Klasse 1999; Dr hc (Autonomous Univ. of Guadalajara, Mexico) 1989, (European Business School, Ostrich-Winkel, Germany) 1997, (Tech. Univ., Munich) 1998; Fortune Magazine Gold Medal 1984, Leadership Award for Corporate Statesmanship, International Institute for Management Development (IMD) 1993, IMD-Maucher Nestlé Chair 1993, Appeal of Conscience Foundation Award, New York 1995, INTERNORGA Prize, Hamburg 1996, Manager Magazine Business Hall of Fame 1997, Scopus Award, Hebrew Univ., Jerusalem 1999, Preis Soziale Marktwirtschaft, Konrad-Adenauer Stiftung e.V. 2004. *Publication:* Leadership in Action (translated from German 'Marketing ist Chefsache' into several languages). *Address:* c/o Nestlé AG, Avenue Nestlé 55, 1800 Vevey, Switzerland.

MAUD, Hon. Sir Humphrey John Hamilton, KCMG, MA, FRCM; British diplomatist (retd); *Chairman, Commonwealth Disaster Management Agency Ltd;* b. 17 April 1934, Oxford; s. of Lord and Lady Redcliffe-Maud; m. Maria Eugenia Gazitua 1963; three s.; ed Eton Coll., King's Coll., Cambridge, Nuffield Coll., Oxford; Instructor in Classics, Univ. of Minn., USA 1958–59; joined Diplomatic Service 1959, Third Sec. Madrid 1961–63, Third, later Second Sec. Havana 1963–65, at FCO 1966–68, Cabinet Office 1968–69, First Sec. Paris 1970–74, Sabbatical at Nuffield Coll., Oxford (Econs) 1974–75, Head Financial Relations Dept, FCO 1975–79, Minister, Madrid 1979–82, Amb. to Luxembourg 1982–84; Asst Under-Sec. of State (Econ. and Commercial) 1985–88; High Commr in Cyprus 1988–89; Amb. to Argentina 1990–93 (reopened diplomatic relations between Britain and Argentina 1990 after the Falklands War); Commonwealth Deputy Sec.-Gen. 1993–99; currently Chair. Commonwealth Disaster Man. Agency Ltd; mem. Nat. Youth Orchestra 1949–52; Chair. Pall Mall Initiatives 2000–; Chair. Trustees Musequality 2007–. *Publications:* Round Table (various articles). *Leisure interests:* music, golf, bird-watching. *Address:* 88 St James's Street, London, SW1A 1PL (office); 31 Queen Anne's Grove, London, W4 1HW, England (home). *Telephone:* (20) 7930-3570 (office); (20) 8994-2808 (home). *Fax:* (20) 7839-4700 (office); (20) 8995-1165 (home). *E-mail:* hmaud@cdma.org.uk (office). *Website:* www.cdma.org.uk (office).

MAUDE, Rt Hon Francis (Anthony Aylmer), PC, MA; British politician and business executive; b. 4 July 1953; s. of Baron Maude of Stratford-upon-Avon; m. Christina Jane Hadfield 1984; two s. three d.; ed Abingdon School, Corpus Christi Coll., Cambridge; called to Bar 1977 (Forster Boulton Prize); Councillor Westminster City Council 1978–84; MP for Warwicks. N 1983–92, for Horsham 1997–; Parl. Pvt. Sec. to Minister of State for Employment 1984–85; an Asst Govt Whip 1985–87; Parl. Under-Sec. of State Dept of Trade and Industry 1987–89; Minister of State, FCO 1989–90; Financial Sec. to HM Treasury 1990–92; Chair. Govt's Deregulation Task Force 1994–97; Shadow Chancellor 1998–2000, Shadow Foreign Sec. 2000–01; Chair. Prestbury Holdings, Jubilee Investment Trust, Incepta Group plc 2004–05; Chair., Conservative Party 2005–07; Dir Salomon Brothers 1992–93, Asda Group 1992–99, Utek 2006–; Man. Dir Morgan Stanley and Co. 1993–97; Deputy Chair. Benfield Group Ltd 2003–; Deputy Chair., Huntsworth plc. *Leisure interests:* skiing, cricket, reading, music. *Address:* House of Commons, London, SW1A 0AA (office). *Telephone:* (20) 7219-2494 (office). *Fax:* (20) 7219-2990 (office). *E-mail:* francismaudemp@parliament.uk (office). *Website:* www.parliament.uk (office); www.francismaude.com (office).

MAULDE, Bruno Guy André Jean de, LenD; French banker; b. 27 March 1934, Toulouse; s. of Guy de Maulde and Suzanne Mazars; m. Dominique Le Henaff 1958; three d.; ed Inst. of Political Studies, Toulouse, Nat. Coll. of Admin.; Insp. des Finances 1962; Adviser, External Econ. Relations Dept, Finance Ministry 1967–68; Alt. Exec. Dir IMF for France 1968–70; Financial attaché, Embassy, USA 1968–70, in New York 1970–71; French Treasury Adviser 1971–74, Asst Dir 1974–77, Deputy Dir 1977–78; Deputy Man. Dir Caisse Nat. de Crédit Agricole 1979–81; Financial Minister, Embassy of France and Exec. Dir IMF and IBRD, Washington 1981–85; Chair. and CEO Crédit du Nord 1986–93; Chair. Conseil des Bourses de Valeurs (CBV) 1990–94; Dir Compagnie Financière de Paribas 1993–94; Dir of various other corpns and public insts; mem. Council of Monetary Policy, Banque de France 1994–97; Chevalier, Légion d'honneur, Ordre nat. du Mérite, Croix de la Valeur militaire, Officier du Mérite agricole. *Leisure interest:* yachting. *Address:* Rozaven, 29930 Pont-Aven, France.

MAUNG, Deputy Sr Gen. Aye, BSc; Myanma military officer; *Vice-Chairman, State Peace and Development Council;* b. 25 Dec. 1937, Kon Balu; m.; ed Defence Services Acad.; joined Myanma Army 1959, C-in-C 1993–; Deputy C-in-C Defence Services; Vice-Chair. State Law and Order Restoration Council (SLORC) 1994–97, State Peace and Devt Council 1997–.

Address: c/o Office of the Chairman of the State Peace and Development Council, 15–16 Windermere Park, Yangon, Myanmar (office). *Telephone:* (1) 282445 (office).

MAUNG, Cynthia, MD; Myanma physician; *Director, Mae Tao Clinic;* b. 6 Dec. 1959, Rangoon; m. Kyaw Hein; two d.; ed Univ. of Rangoon; trained at North Okkalapa Gen. Hosp.; worked in rural clinic in Karen State; participated in nationwide anti-govt protests in 1988, fled to Thailand several months later; f. Mae Tao Clinic in Thailand to treat refugees fleeing from Myanmar; John Humphries Freedom Award 1999, American Women's Medical Asscn Pres.'s Award 1999, Jonathan Mann Award 1999, Van Hueven Goedhart Award, Foundation for Human Rights in Asia Special Award 2001, Ramon Magsaysay Award 2002, Global Concern for Human Life Award, Chou-Ta Kuan Foundation 2005, Unsung Heroes of Compassion Award 2005, World's Children's Hon. Award 2007, Asia Democracy and Human Rights Award 2007, Catalonia Int. Prize (jtly) 2008. *Address:* Mae Tao Clinic, PO Box 67, Mae Sot, Tak 63110, Thailand (office). *Telephone:* (55) 563-644 (office). *Fax:* (55) 544-655 (office). *E-mail:* win7@loxinfo.co.th (office). *Website:* www.maetaoclinic.org (office).

MAUNG MAUNG KHA, U; Myanma politician; mem. Cen. Exec. Cttee Burma Socialist Programme Party (BSPP); Minister for Industry and Labour 1973–74, for Industry 1974–75, for Mines 1975–77, Prime Minister of Burma (now Myanmar) 1977–88; mem. State Council 1977–88. *Address:* c/o Office of the Prime Minister, Yangon, Myanmar.

MAUPIN, Armistead Jones, Jr; American writer; b. 13 May 1944; s. of Armistead Jones Maupin and the late Diana Jane (née Barton) Maupin; ed Univ. of North Carolina; reporter, News and Courier, Charleston, SC 1970–71; Associated Press, San Francisco 1971–72; Account Exec. Lowry Russom and Leeper Public Relations 1973; columnist, Pacific Sun Magazine 1974; publicist, San Francisco Opera 1975; serialist, San Francisco Chronicle 1976–77, 1981, 1983; Commentator K.R.O.N.-TV San Francisco 1979; serialist, San Francisco Examiner 1986; Exec. Producer Armistead Maupin's Tales of the City 1993; contrib. to New York Times, Los Angeles Times and others; numerous awards, including: Freedom Leadership Award, Freedoms Foundation 1972, Communications Award, Metropolitan Elections Comm., LA 1989, Exceptional Achievement Award, American Libraries Asscn 1990, Outstanding Miniseries Award, Gay and Lesbian Alliance Against Defamation 1994. *Film:* The Night Listener (adapted from his book, exec. prod.) 2006. *Publications:* Tales of the City (Big Gay Read Award 2006) 1978, More Tales of the City 1980, Further Tales of the City 1982, Babycakes 1984, Significant Others 1987, Sure of You 1989, 28 Barbary Lane 1990, Back to Barbary Lane 1991, Maybe the Moon 1992, The Essential Clive Baker (co-author) 1999, The Night Listener 2000, Michael Tolliver Lives 2007; librettist: Heart's Desire 1990. *Address:* c/o Literary Bent, PO Box 4109990, Suite 528, San Francisco, CA 94141 (office); c/o Amanda Urban, 40 West 57th Street, Floor 16, New York, NY 10019, USA. *E-mail:* inquiries@literarybent.cor (office).

MAURA, Carmen, BA; Spanish actress; b. 15 Sept. 1945, Madrid; d. of Antonio Maura; worked as a cabaret singer and translator; has appeared in numerous films including many of Pedro Almodóvar's works. *Other films include:* El espíritu 1969, Mantis 1971, El hombre oculto (The Man In Hiding) 1971, El asesino está entre los trece 1973, Un casto varón español 1973, Tanata 1974, Don Juan 1974, Vida íntima de un seductor cínico 1975, La encadenada (A Diary of a Murderess) 1975, El love feroz 1975, Leonor 1975, Pomporrutas imperiales 1976, La petición (The Request) 1976, Una pareja como las demás 1976, Ir por lana 1976, La mujer es cosa de hombres 1976, El libro del buen amor II (The Book of Good Love 2) 1976, Tigres de papel (Paper Tigers) 1977, ¿Qué hace una chica como tú en un sitio como éste? (What's a Girl Like You Doing in a Place Like This?) 1978, Mi blanca Varsovia 1978, Menos mi madre y mi hermana 1978, Folle... folle... fólleme Tim! 1978, De fresa, limón y menta (Strawberry, Lemon and Mint) 1978, Los ojos vendados (Blindfolded Eyes) 1978, Tal vez mañana... 1979, Café, amor y estereofonía 1979, La mano negra (The Black Hand) 1980, Aquella casa en las afueras (That House in the Outskirts) 1980, Pepi, Luci, Bom y otras chicas del montón (Pepi, Luci, Bom and Other Girls Like Mom) 1980, El hombre de moda (Man of Fashion) 1980, Gary Cooper, que estás en los cielos (Gary Cooper, Who Art in Heaven) 1980, Femenino singular 1982, Entre tinieblas (Dark Habits) 1983, El Cid cabreador 1983, ¿Qué he hecho yo para merecer esto!! (What Have I Done to Deserve This?) 1984, Extramuros (Beyond the Walls) 1985, Sé infiel y no mires con quién (Be Wanton and Tread No Shame) 1985, Matador 1986, Delirios de amor 1986, Tata mía (Dear Nanny) 1986, La ley del deseo (Law of Desire) 1987, 2.30 A.M. 1988, Mujeres al borde de un ataque de nervios (Women on the Verge of a Nervous Breakdown) (Best Actress, European Film Awards 1989) 1988, Bâton rouge 1988, ¡Ay, Carmela! (Best Actress, European Film Awards 1991) 1990, Cómo ser mujer y no morir en el intento (How to Be a Woman and Not Die Trying) 1991, Chatarra 1991, Sur la terre comme au ciel (In Heaven as on Earth) 1992, La reina anónima (The Anonymous Queen) 1992, Louis, enfant roi (Louis, the Child King) 1993, Sombras en una batalla (Shadows in a Conflict) 1993, Cómo ser infeliz y disfrutarlo (How to Be Miserable and Enjoy It) 1994, El rey del río 1995, Parella de tres 1995, El palomo cojo (The Lame Pigeon) 1995, Le bonheur est dans le pré (Happiness is in the Field) 1995, Amores que matan 1996, Vivir después 1997, Tortilla y cinema 1997, Alliance cherche doigt 1997, Elles 1997, Alice et Martin 1998, El entusiasmo (Enthusiasm) 1998, El cometa (The Comet) 1999, Lisboa 1999, Superlove 1999, Carretera y manta (To the End of the Road) 2000, Le harem de Mme Osmane 2000, La comunidad 2000, El apagón 2001, El palo (The Hold-Up) 2001, Arregui, la noticia del día 2001, Clara y Elena 2001, Assassini dei giorni di festa (Killers on Holiday) 2002, Valentín 2002, 800 balas (800 Bullets) 2002, Le ventre de Juliette 2003, Le pacte du silence 2003, 25 degrés en hiver (25 Degrees in Winter) 2004, La promesa 2004, Al otro lado 2004, Entre vivir y soñar 2004, Reinas 2005, Free Zone 2005, Volver (Goya Award for Best Supporting Actress 2007) 2006, El Menor de los males 2007, La Virgen negra 2008, The Garden of Eden 2008, Que parezca un accidente 2008. *Television includes:* Juan y Manuela (series) 1974, Suspiros de España (series) 1974, El coleccionismo y los coleccionistas (series) 1979, Cervantes (mini-series) 1980, La huella del crimen: El crimen de la calle Fuencarral 1984, Sal gorda (Coarse Salt) 1984, La mujer de tu vida: La mujer feliz 1988, Mieux vaut courir 1989, A las once en casa (series) 1998, Famosos y familia (series) 1999, Une mère en colère 2000, Arroz y tartana 2003, Mentir un peu 2004, Mentir un peu 2006, Círculo rojo (series) 2007.

MAURER, Ueli; Swiss communications consultant and politician; *Member, Federal Council;* b. 1 Dec. 1950, Wetzikon; m.; six c.; Dir Zürich Farmers Asscn 1994–2008; mem. Zürich Cantonal Parl. 1978–86 (Pres. 1991); mem. House of Reps 1991; mem. Schweizerischen Volkspartei (Swiss People's Party), Pres. 1996–2008, Pres. Zürich Div. 2008; mem. Swiss Federal Council 2009–, also Head of Fed. Dept of Defence, Civil Protection and Sports 2009–; fmr Pres. Swiss Vegetable Farmers Asscn, Farmers Machinery Asscn (Maschinenring). *Address:* Swiss Federal Council, Bundeshaus Ost, 3003 Berne, Switzerland (office). *Telephone:* (324) 50 58 (office). *Fax:* (323) 57 82 (office). *E-mail:* postmaster.vbs@gs-vbs.admin.ch (office). *Website:* www.admin.ch (office).

MAURESMO, Amélie; French professional tennis player; b. 5 July 1979, Saint-Germain-en-Laye; began to play tennis aged four; turned professional 1994; won both Jr French Open and Wimbledon titles 1996; finalist, Australian Open 1999; semi-finalist, US Open singles 2002, 2006; quarter-finalist, French Open singles 2003, 2004; silver medal, Olympic Games, Athens 2004; winner of two Grand Slam singles titles, Australian Open 2006, Wimbledon 2006; ranked World No. 1 Sept.–Oct. 2004; doubles finalist with Svetlana Kuznetsova, Wimbledon 2005; lives in Geneva, Switzerland; Int. Tennis Fed. Jr World Champion 1996. *E-mail:* agence@interactive-one.fr. *Website:* www.ameliemauresmo.fr (office).

MAURÍCIO, Armindo Cipriano; Cape Verde politician; currently Minister of Defence and Parl. Affairs. *Address:* Ministry of Defence and Parliamentary Affairs, Palácio do Governo, Várzea, Praia, Santiago, Cape Verde (office). *Telephone:* 61-03-44 (office). *Fax:* 61-20-81 (office). *E-mail:* armindo.mauricio@palgov.cv (office).

MAUROY, Pierre; French politician; b. 5 July 1928, Cartignies; s. of Henri Mauroy and Adrienne Bronne; m. Gilberte Deboudt 1951; one s.; ed Lycée de Cambrai, Ecole normale nationale d'apprentissage, Cachan; Nat. Sec. Jeunesses socialistes 1950–58; Tech. Teacher, Colombes 1952; Sec.-Gen. Syndicat des collèges d'enseignement tech. section, Féd. de l'Educ. Nat. 1955–59; Fed. Sec. for the North, Section Française de l'Internationale Ouvrière 1961, mem. Political Bureau 1963, Deputy Sec.-Gen. 1966; mem. Exec. Cttee, Féd. de la gauche démocratique et socialiste 1965–68; Gen. Councillor, Cateau 1967–73; Vice-Pres. Gen. Council, Nord Département 1967–73; Municipal Councillor, Lille 1971, First Deputy Mayor 1971, Mayor 1973–2001; First Sec. and Nat. Co-ordinating Sec., Northern Fed., Parti Socialiste 1971–79; Deputy (Nord) to Nat. Ass. 1973–81, 1986, Senator 1992–; First Sec. Parti Socialiste 1989–92; Pres. Socialist Int. 1992–99, Regional Council, Nord-Pas-de-Calais 1974; Pres. Nat. Fed. Léo Lagrange youth centres 1972–81, Hon. Pres. 1981–84; mem. European Parl. 1979–81, Vice-Pres. Political Cttee; Political Dir Action socialiste Hebdo newspaper 1979–81; Prime Minister of France 1981–84; Pres. World Fed. of Twinned Towns 1983–92; Pres. Communauté urbaine de Lille 1989–, Comm. pour la décentralisation 1999–; founder, Pres. Jean Jaurès Foundation 1992–; Grand cordon de l'ordre de la Répub. de Tunisie, Grand Croix, Ordre nat. du Mérite, Chevalier de la Légion d'Honneur. *Publications:* Héritiers de l'avenir 1977, C'est ici le chemin 1982, A gauche 1985, Parole de Lillois 1994, Léo Lagrange (biog.) 1997, Mémoires: vous mettrez du bleu au ciel 2003. *Address:* Sénat, 75291 Paris Cedex 06 (office); 17–19 rue Voltaire, 59000 Lille, France (home). *E-mail:* p.mauroy@senat.fr (office). *Website:* www.senat.fr (office).

MAURSTAD, Toralv; Norwegian actor and theatre director; b. 24 Nov. 1926, Oslo; s. of Alfred and Tordis Maurstad; m. Beate Eriksen; one s.; ed Universitet i Uppsala and Royal Acad. of Dramatic Art, London; trained as concert pianist; debut in Trondheim 1947; Oslo Nye Teater 1951; Oslo Nat. Theatre 1954; Man. Dir Oslo Nye Teater (Oslo Municipal Theatre) 1967–78; Man. Dir Nat. Theatre 1978–86, actor/Dir Nat. Theatre 1987–; Norwegian Sr Golf Champion 1992; Kt First Class, Order of St Olav (Norway), Order of Oranian (Netherlands); Oslo Critics' Award, Ibsen Prize, Amanda, Aamot Statuette. *Plays acted in or directed include:* Young Woodley 1949, Pal Joey 1952, Peer Gynt 1954, Long Day's Journey 1962, Teenage Love 1963, Hamlet 1964, Arturo Ui (in Bremen, Germany) 1965, Brand (Ibsen) 1966, Of Love Remembered (New York) 1967, Cabaret 1968, Scapino 1975, Two Gentlemen of Verona 1976, The Moon of the Misbegotten 1976, Same Time Next Year 1977, Twigs 1977 (also TV production), Sly Fox 1978, Whose Life is it Anyway? 1979, Masquerade 1980, Amadeus 1980, Much Ado about Nothing 1981, Kennen Sie die Milchstrasse? 1982, Duet for One 1982, Hamlet 1983, Private Lives (with Liv Ullman) 1993, Dear Liar 1996, The Pretenders 1998, Copenhagen 2000, Enigma Variation 2001, Waiting for Godot 2005, Rigoletto (opera) 2005, Twelfth Night 2005. *Films:* Fant 1937, Trysil-Knut 1942, Kranes konditori 1951, Andrine og Kjell 1952, Cirkus Fandango 1954, Hjem går vi ikke 1955, Line 1961, Kalde Spor 1962, Om Tilla (About Tilla) 1963, Svarta palmkronor (Black Palm Trees) 1968, Hennes meget kongelige høyhet 1968, Song of Norway 1970, Flåklypa Grand Prix (voice) 1975, Glade vrinsk (writer) 1975, Etter Rubicon (After Rubicon) 1987, Det var en gang (voice) 1994, Jakten på nyresteinen (Chasing the Kidney Stone; voice) 1996, Solan, Ludvig og Gurin med reverompa (Gurin with the Foxtail; voice) 1998, Olsenbanden Junior på rocker'n 2004. *Radio plays:* Doll's House, Peer Gynt, Masquerade. *Television:* Gengangere 1962, Frydenberg 1965, Ett köpmanshus i skärgården (mini-series) 1972, Spyship (mini-series) 1983, The Last Place on Earth (mini-series) 1985, # Konsultasjon eller helbredelsens kunst (dir) 1988, Olsenbandens første kupp (mini-series) 2001, Enigmavariasjoner 2002, Hotel Cesar (episode) 2004. *Publication:* Du Store Min (autobiog.). *Leisure interests:* skiing, hunting, fishing, golf, tennis. *Address:* Nationaltheatret, Stortingsgt. 15, Oslo 1 (office); Box 58, Holmenkollen, 0712, Norway (home); Thorleif, Hangsvei 20, Voksenkollen 0712, Oslo, Norway. *Telephone:* 22-14-18-84 (home). *Fax:* 22-14-10-80 (home). *E-mail:* toralv@maurstad.no (home).

MAVRIKOS, George; Greek trade union official and international organization executive; *General Secretary, World Federation of Trade Unions;* Deputy Pres. Gen. Confed. of Workers in Greece; Sec. All Workers Militant Front (PAME) (a CP of Greece-affiliated trade union); Vice-Pres. WFTU and Coordinator of its European Office –2005, Gen. Sec. WFTU 2005–. *Address:* World Federation of Trade Unions, 40 Zan Moreas Str., 117 45 Athens, Greece (office). *Telephone:* (21) 09236700 (office). *Fax:* (21) 09214517 (office). *E-mail:* info@wftucentral.org (office). *Website:* www.wftucentral.org (office).

MAVROMMATIS, Andreas V.; Cypriot diplomatist, barrister and human rights expert; *Chairman, Mass Media Complaints Committee;* b. 9 June 1932, Larnaca; s. of Vladimiros Mavrommatis and Marthe Mavrommatis (née Andreou); m. Mary Cahalane 1955; one s. three d.; ed Greek Gymnasium, Limassol, Lincoln's Inn, London; practising advocate 1954–58; magistrate 1958–60; Dist Judge 1960–70; Minister of Labour and Social Insurance 1970–72; Special Adviser on Foreign and Legal Affairs to Pres. of Cyprus 1972–75; Perm. Rep. to UN Office at Geneva 1975–78, to UN, New York 1979–82; Greek Cypriot Interlocutor in Intercommunal Talks 1982–89; Perm. Rep. to UN, New York 1989–92; Adviser to the Pres. of the Repub., mem. of Working Group on the Cyprus Question July–Dec. 1992; Govt Spokesman Dec. 1992–; Pres. Fédération Internationale des Corps et Asscns Consulaires 1995–; Chair. Mass Media Complaints Cttee 1997–, UN Cttee Against Torture (CAT) 1997–; Special Rapporteur of the Comm. on Human Rights on the situation of human rights in Iraq 1999–2004; fmr Pres. ECOSOC; Chair. UN Cttee on Relations with the Host Country; Hon. Consul Gen. of Indonesia 1994–. *Publication:* Treaties in Force in Cyprus. *Leisure interests:* reading, walking. *Address:* 10 Platon Street, Engomi, Nicosia, Cyprus (office). *Telephone:* 351878 (office). *Fax:* 357111 (office). *E-mail:* avmavro@cytanet.com.cy (office).

MAVRONICOLAS, Kyriakos, FRCS; Cypriot ophthalmologist and politician; b. 1955, Paphos; m. Irene (Roula) Kokkinidou; two c.; ed First Gymnasium, Paphos, Nat. and Kapodistrian Univ. of Athens Medical School, Athens Law School; began career as ophthalmologist, Nicosia 1960, practised in UK 1981–87; fmr Gen. Sec. Democratic Students' Movement (AGONAS); Sec. Athens Br., Socialist Party (EDEK), becoming EDEK Dist Sec., Nicosia 1989–93, later Party First Vice-Pres.; Deputy Pres. Social Democrat Movement (KISOS); Minister of Defence 2003–06. *Address:* c/o Ministry of Defence, 4 Emmanuel Roides Avenue, 1432 Nicosia, Cyprus (office).

MAVROYIANNIS, Andreas D., DipLaw; Cypriot diplomatist; *Permanent Representative, United Nations;* b. 20 July 1956, Agros; m. Calliopi Efthyvoulou; one s. one d.; ed Univ. of Thessalonica, Greece, Université de Droit et de Sciences Economique, Paris, Université de Paris X, Nanterre; joined Ministry of Foreign Affairs 1987; served at Embassy in Paris 1989–93, also in Political Div., Cyprus Question Div., EU Div., and as Assoc. European Correspondent; Dir, Office of Minister of Foreign Affairs 1995–97, 2002–03; Amb. to Ireland 1997–99, to France 1999–2002 (non-resident to Andorra, Tunisia, Morocco); Acting Perm. Sec., Ministry of Foreign Affairs 2003; Perm. Rep. to UN, New York 2003–, also High Commr to St Lucia 2003–; Chair. UN Cttee on Relations with Host Country 2003–; Rep. at Cttee of Legal Advisers on Public Int. Law (CAHDI), Council of Europe 1988–92; Rep. Prep. Comm. for High Authority, Law of the Sea 1989; mem. Greek Cypriot negotiating team in bi-communal talks for solution of Cyprus issue 2002–03; Lecturer, Cyprus Mediterranean Inst. of Man., Cyprus Acad. for Public Admin, Law School of Univ. of Athens; Diploma of The Hague Acad. of Int. Law 1984. *Publications:* articles and reviews in scholarly journals and newspapers. *Address:* Office of the Permanent Representative of Cyprus to the United Nations, 13 East 40th Street, New York, NY 10016, USA (office). *Telephone:* (212) 481-6023 (office). *Fax:* (212) 685-7316 (office). *E-mail:* cyprus@un.int (office). *Website:* www.un.int/cyprus (office).

MAWER, Sir Philip John Courtney, Kt, MA, DPA, FRSA; British parliamentary official and church official; *Parliamentary Commissioner for Standards;* b. 30 July 1947; s. of Eric Douglas Mawer and Thora Constance Mawer; m. Mary Ann Moxon 1972; one s. two d.; ed Hull Grammar School, Univ. of Edinburgh, Univ. of London; Sr Pres. EU Student Rep. Council 1969–70; joined Home Office 1971; Pvt. Sec. to Minister of State 1974–76; Nuffield and Leverhulme Travelling Fellowship 1978–79; Sec. Lord Scarman Inquiry into Brixton Riots 1981; Asst Sec. Head of Industrial Relations, Prison Dept 1984–87; Prin. Pvt. Sec. to Home Sec. Douglas Hurd 1987–89; Under-Sec. Cabinet Office 1989–90; Sec.-Gen. Church of England Synod 1990–2002; Sec.-Gen. Archbishops' Council 1999–2002; Parl. Commr for Standards 2002–; Dir (non-exec.) Ecclesiastical Insurance Group 1996–2002; Trustee All Churches Trust 1992–; mem. Governing Body SPCK 1994–2002; Patron Church Housing Trust 1996–; Hon. Lay Canon of St Alban's Cathedral 2003; Hon. DLitt (Hull) 2006. *Leisure interests:* family, friends. *Address:* Office of the Parliamentary Commissioner for Standards, House of Commons, London, SW1A 0AA, England (office). *Telephone:* (20) 7219-0311 (office). *Fax:* (20) 7219-0490 (office). *E-mail:* standardscommissioner@parliament.uk (office). *Website:* www.parliament.uk (office).

MAWHINNEY, Baron (Life Peer), cr. 2005; **Brian Stanley,** Kt, PC, PhD; British parliamentarian and company director; b. 26 July 1940; s. of Frederick Stanley Arnot Mawhinney and Coralie Jean Mawhinney; m. Betty Louise Oja 1965; two s. one d.; ed Royal Belfast Academical Inst., Queen's Univ. Belfast, Univ. of Michigan, USA, Univ. of London; Asst Prof. of Radiation Research, Univ. of Iowa, USA 1968–70; lecturer, subsequently Sr Lecturer, Royal Free Hosp. School of Medicine 1970–84; mem. MRC 1980–83; MP for Peterborough 1979–97, for Cambridgeshire NW 1997–2005; Parl. Under-Sec. of State for Northern Ireland 1986–90; Minister of State, Northern Ireland Office 1990–92, Dept of Health 1992–94; Sec. of State for Transport 1994–95; Chair. Conservative Party 1995–97; Opposition Front Bench Spokesman on Home Affairs 1997–98; Pres. Conservative Trade Unionists 1987–90; mem. Gen. Synod of Church of England 1985–90; Chair. Football League 2003–. *Publication:* Conflict and Christianity in Northern Ireland (co-author) 1976, In the Firing Line–Faith, Power, Politics, Forgiveness 1999. *Leisure interests:* sport, reading. *Address:* House of Lords, London, SW1A 0PW, England (office). *Telephone:* (1733) 261868 (office). *Fax:* (1733) 266887 (office). *Website:* www.parliament.uk (office).

MAXIM, His Holiness Patriarch; Bulgarian ecclesiastic; *Head, Bulgarian Orthodox Church;* b. (Marin Naydenov Minkov), 29 Oct. 1914, Oreshak, Lovech region; ed Sofia Acad. of Theology; served the Church in Ruse and Lovech 1935; became monk and took name Maxim 1941; apptd Archimandrite and Coadjutor in the Ruse diocese 1947; Rep. of Bulgarian Church in Moscow, Russia 1950–55; apptd Sec.-Gen. of the Holy Synod 1955; ordained Bishop 1956; Metropolitan of Lovech 1960–71; elected Metropolitan of Sofia and Patriarch of Bulgaria 1971–; his position was challenged when several bishops questioned the authority of the Patriarchy 1992, schism was resolved by Int. Orthodox Synod that recognised Patriarch Maxim as sole head of Church in Bulgaria 1998; active in public and political affairs; strong supporter of legislation prohibiting governmental interference in religious affairs 2002; Foundation Prize Laureate, Foundation for the Unity of Orthodox Christian Nations 2005. *Address:* Office of the Bulgarian Patriarchy, 1090 Sofia, Oborishte Str. 4, Synod Palace, Bulgaria (office). *Telephone:* (2) 87-56-11 (office). *Fax:* (2) 89-76-00 (office).

MAXWELL, Ian, MA; British/French publisher; b. 15 June 1956, Maisons-Laffitte, France; s. of the late (Ian) Robert Maxwell and of Elisabeth Meynard; brother of Kevin Maxwell; m. 1st Laura Plumb 1991 (divorced 1998); m. 2nd Tara Dudley Smith 1999; ed Marlborough Coll. and Balliol Coll., Oxford; Man. Dir Pergamon Press France 1980–81; Jt Man. Dir Pergamon Pres. GmbH 1980; Marketing Dir Pergamon Press Inc. 1982–83; Dir Sales Devt BPCC PLC 1985–86; Dir Group Marketing BPCC PLC (now Maxwell Communication Corpn PLC) 1986; Chair. Agence Centrale de Presse, Paris 1986–89; Dir TFI TV station, Paris 1987–89; CEO Maxwell Pergamon Publrs 1988–89; Jt Man. Dir Maxwell Communication Corpn 1988–91; Acting Chair. Mirror Group Newspapers 1991; Dir New York Daily News –1991, Telemonde Holdings 1997–; publishing consultant Westbourne Communications Ltd 1993; Publr Maximov Publs Ltd. 1995–; Chair. Derby Co. Football Club 1984–87, Vice-Chair. 1987–91; mem. Nat. Theatre Devt Council 1986; Pres. Club d'Investissement Media 1988. *Leisure interests:* skiing, water skiing, watching football.

MAXWELL DAVIES, Sir Peter, Kt, CBE, MusB, FRCM, FRSAMD, FRNCM; British composer and conductor; *Master of the Queen's Music;* b. 8 Sept. 1934, Manchester, England; s. of Thomas Davies and Hilda (née Howard) Davies; ed Leigh Grammar School, Royal Manchester Coll. of Music, Manchester Univ.; studied with Goffredo Petrassi, Rome 1957 and with Roger Sessions, Milton Babbitt, Earl Kim, Princeton Univ., NJ, USA (Harkness Fellow) 1962–64; Dir of Music, Cirencester Grammar School 1959–62; Harkness Fellowship, Grad. School, Princeton Univ. 1962–64; lecture tours in Europe, Australia, USA, Canada, Brazil; Visiting Composer, Univ. of Adelaide 1966; Prof. of Composition, Royal Northern Coll. of Music, Manchester 1965–80 (Fellow 1978); Pres. Schools Music Assen 1983–, Composers' Guild of GB 1986–, Nat. Fed. of Music Socs 1989–, Cheltenham Arts Festival 1994–96, Soc. for Promotion of New Music 1995–; Visiting Fromm Prof. of Composition, Harvard Univ. 1985; f. and Co-Dir (with Harrison Birtwistle q.v.) Pierrot Players 1967–71; f. and Artistic Dir The Fires of London 1971–87; f. and Artistic Dir St Magnus Festival, Orkney Islands 1977–86, Pres. 1986–; Artistic Dir Dartington Summer School of Music 1979–84; Assoc. Conductor and Composer Scottish Chamber Orchestra 1985–94, Composer Laureate 1994–; Conductor and Composer, BBC Philharmonic Orchestra (Manchester) 1992–2001; Assoc. Conductor and Composer Royal Philharmonic Orchestra 1992–2001; Master of the Queen's Music 2004–; Fellowship British Acad. of Composers and Songwriters 2005; mem. Accademia Filarmonica Romana 1979, Royal Swedish Acad. of Music 1993, Bayerische Akad. der Schönen Künste 1998; hon. mem. Royal Acad. of Music 1979, Guildhall School of Music and Drama 1981, Royal Philharmonic Soc. 1987, Royal Scottish Acad. 2001; Hon. Fellow Royal Incorporation of Architects in Scotland 1994, Hon. Fellow Univ. of Highlands and Islands 2004, Freeman of the City of Salford; Officier, Ordre des Arts et des Lettres 1988; several hon. degrees including Hon. DMus (Edin.) 1979, (Manchester) 1981, (Bristol) 1984, (Open Univ.) 1986, (Glasgow) 1993, (Durham) 1994, (Hull) 2001, (Kingston) 2005; Hon. DLitt (Warwick) 1986, (Salford) 1999; Hon. DUniv (Heriot-Watt) 2002; Olivetti Prize 1959, Koussevitsky Award 1964, Koussevitsky Recording Award 1966, Cobbett Medal for services to chamber music 1989, First Award of Assen of British Orchestras, for contribs to orchestras and orchestral life in UK 1991, Gulliver Award for Performing Arts in Scotland 1991, Nat. Fed. of Music Socs Charles Groves Award for outstanding contrib. to British Music 1995, Royal Philharmonic Soc. Award for Large-scale Composition (for Symphony No. 5) 1995, Inc. Soc. of Musicians Distinguished Musicians Award 2001. *Compositions include:* Sonata for trumpet and piano 1955, Alma redemptoris mater for ensemble 1957, St Michael sonata for 17 wind instruments 1957, Prolation for orchestra 1958, Five Klee Pictures for percussion, piano and strings 1959, Five Motets for soli, chorus and ensemble 1959, O Magnum Mysterium for chorus, instruments and organ 1960, Te Lucis ante Terminum 1961, String Quartet 1961, Frammenti di Leopardi for soprano, contralto and chamber ensemble 1962, First Fantasia on John Taverner's In Nomine for orchestra 1962, Veni Sancte Spiritus for soli, chorus and orchestra 1963, Second Fantasia on John Taverner's In Nomine 1964, Ecce Manus Tradentis for mixed chorus and instruments 1964, Shepherd's Calendar for young singers and instrumentalists 1965, Notre Dame des Fleurs 1966, Revelation and Fall for soprano and instrumental ensemble 1966, Antechrist for chamber ensemble 1967, Missa super L'Homme Armé for speaker and ensemble 1968, Stedman Caters for instruments 1968, Nocturnal Dances (ballet) 1969, St Thomas Wake-Foxtrot for orchestra 1969, Worldes Blis 1969, Eram quasi Agnus (instrumental motet) 1969, Eight Songs for a Mad King for male singer and ensemble 1969, Vesalii Icones for dancer and ensemble 1969, Taverner (opera) 1970, From Stone to Thorn for mezzo-soprano and instrumental ensemble 1971, Blind Man's Buff (masque) 1972, Hymn to Saint Magnus for chamber ensemble and mezzo-soprano 1972, Renaissance Scottish Dances 1973, Stone Litany for mezzo-soprano and orchestra 1973, Fiddlers at the Wedding 1974, Miss Donnithorne's Maggot for mezzo-soprano and chamber ensemble 1974, The Kestrel Paced Round the Sun 1975, Ave Maris Stella for chamber ensemble 1975, Three Studies for Percussion 1975, The Blind Fiddler for soprano and chamber ensemble 1975, Stevie's Ferry to Hoy (beginner's piano solo) 1975, Three Organ Voluntaries 1976, Kinloche His Fantassie (with Kinloch) 1976, Anakreontika (Greek songs for mezzo-soprano) 1976, Orchestral Symphony No. 1 1976, The Martyrdom of St Magnus (chamber opera) 1976, Runes from a Holy Island 1977, Westerlings (unaccompanied part songs) 1977, A Mirror of Whitening Light for chamber ensemble 1977, Le Jongleur de Notre Dame (Masque) 1978, The Two Fiddlers 1978, Salome (ballet) 1978, Black Pentecost (for voices and orchestra) 1979, Solstice of Light (for Tenor, Chorus and Organ) 1979, The Lighthouse (chamber opera) 1979, Cinderella (pantomime opera for young performers) 1979, A Welcome to Orkney (chamber ensemble) 1980, Orchestral Symphony No. 2 1980, Little Quartet (string quartet) 1980, The Yellow Cake Revue (for voice and piano) 1980, The Medium 1981, The Bairns of Brugh 1981, Piano Sonata 1981, Little Quartet No. 2 (for string quartet) 1981, Lullabye for Lucy 1981, Brass Quintet 1981, Songs of Hoy (Masque for children's voices and instruments) 1981, The Pole Star 1982, Sea Eagle (for horn solo) 1982, Image, Reflection, Shadow (for chamber ensemble) 1982, Sinfonia Concertante (for chamber orchestra) 1982, Into the Labyrinth (tenor and chamber orchestra) 1983, Sinfonietta Accademica (chamber orchestra) 1983, Unbroken Circle 1984, Guitar Sonata 1984, The No. 11 Bus 1984, One Star, At Last (carol) 1984, Orchestral Symphony No. 3 1984, The Peat Cutters 1985, Violin Concerto 1985, First Ferry to Hoy 1985, An Orkney Wedding, with Sunrise 1985, Sea Runes (vocal sextet) 1986, Jimmack the Postie (overture) 1986, Excuse Me 1986, House of Winter 1986, Trumpet Concerto 1987, Resurrection (opera in one act with prologue) 1987, Oboe Concerto 1988, Cello Concerto 1988, Mishkenot (chamber ensemble) 1988, The Great Bank Robbery 1989, Orchestral Symphony No. 4 1989, Hymn to the Word of God (for tenor and chorus) 1990, Concerto No. 4 for clarinet 1990, Caroline Mathilde (ballet) 1990, Tractus 1990, Dangerous Errand (for tenor soli and chorus) 1990, The Spiders' Revenge 1991, First Grace of Light 1991, Strathclyde Concerto No. 5 for violin and viola, No. 6 for flute 1991, Ojai Festival Overture 1991, A Selkie Tale (music-theatre work for performance by children) 1992, The Turn of the Tide (for orchestra and children's chorus and instrumental groups) 1992, Strathclyde Concerto No. 7 for double bass 1992, Sir Charles his Pavan 1992, Strathclyde Concerto No. 8 for bassoon 1993, A Spell for Green Corn: The MacDonald Dances 1993, Orchestral Symphony No. 5 (Royal Philharmonic Soc. Award for Large-Scale Composition 1995) 1994, Cross Lane Fair (for orchestra) 1994, Strathclyde Concerto No. 9 for six woodwind instruments 1994, The Three Kings (for chorus, orchestra and soloists) 1995, The Beltane Fire (choreographic poem) 1995, The Doctor of Myddfai (opera) 1995, Orchestral Symphony No. 6 1996, Strathclyde Concerto No. 10 for orchestra 1996, Piccolo Concerto 1996, Job (oratorio for chorus, orchestra and soloists) 1997, Mavis in Las Vegas–Theme and Variations 1997, Orkney Saga I: Fifteen keels laid in Norway for Jerusalem-farers 1997, The Jacobite Rising (for chorus, orchestra and soloists) 1997, Piano Concerto 1997, Orkney Saga II: In Kirkwall, the first red Saint Magnus stones 1997, Sails in St Magnus I–III 1998, A Reel of Seven Fishermen 1998, Sea Elegy (for chorus, orchestra and soloists) 1998, Roma Amor Labyrinthus 1998, Reel with Northern Lights 1998, Swinton Jig 1998, Temenos with Mermaids and Angels (for flute and orchestra) 1998, Spinning Jenny 1999, Sails in Orkney Saga III: An Orkney Wintering (for alto saxophone and orchestra) 1999, Trumpet quintet (for string quartet and trumpet) 1999, Mr Emmet Takes a Walk 1999, Horn Concerto 1999, Orkney Saga IV: Westerly Gale in Biscay, Salt in the Bread Broken 2000, Orchestral Symphony No. 7 2000, Orchestral Symphony No. 8 (Antarctic Symphony) 2000, Canticum Canticorum 2001, De Assumtione Beatae Mariae Virginis 2001, Crossing Kings Reach 2001, Mass 2002, Missa Parvula 2002, Naxos Quartet No. 1 2002, Piano Trio 2002, Naxos Quartet No. 2 2003, No. 3 2003, No. 4 2004, No. 5 2004, Children's Games 2004, Judas Mercator for trombone solo 2004, Fanfare for Carinthia for four trumpets 2004, Tecum Principium for flute and marimba 2004, The Fall of the Leafe for string orchestra 2004, Lullay, my child and weep no more for SATB chorus 2004, Naxos Quartet No. 6 and No. 7 2005, O Verbum Patris for SATB chorus & organ 2005, The Golden Rule (anthem with lyrics by Andrew Motion, for the 80th birthday of HM Queen Elizabeth II) 2006, A Little Birthday Music (for the 80th birthday of HM Queen Elizabeth II) 2006, Liber Pulsationis Fabulatoris for chorus (dedicated to Sir Paul McCartney) 2008; has written music for films: The Devils, The Boyfriend and many piano pieces, works for choir, instrumental works and realizations of fifteenth and sixteenth-century composers. *Address:* c/o Intermusica, 16 Duncan Terrace, London, N1 8BZ, England (office). *Telephone:* (20) 7278-5455 (office). *Fax:* (20) 7278-8434 (office). *E-mail:* mail@intermusica.co.uk (office). *Website:* www.maxopus.com (office).

MAY, Elaine; American actress, film director and screenwriter; b. 21 April 1932, Philadelphia; d. of Jack Berlin; m. 1st Marvin May (divorced); one d.; m. 2nd Sheldon Harnick 1962 (divorced 1963); appeared on radio and stage as child; performed Playwright's Theater, Chicago; appeared in student production Miss Julie, Univ. of Chicago; with Mike Nichols (q.v.) and others in improvisatory theatre group, The Compass (nightclub), Chicago 1954–57; improvised nightclub double-act with Mike Nichols, appeared New York Town Hall 1959; An Evening with Mike Nichols and Elaine May, Golden Theater, New York 1960–61; numerous TV and radio appearances; weekly appearance NBC radio show Nightline. *Films:* Luv 1967, A New Leaf (also Dir) 1972, The Heartbreak Kid (Dir) 1973, Mikey and Nicky (Dir) 1976 (writer, Dir remake 1985), California Suite 1978, Heaven Can Wait (co-author screenplay) 1978, Ishtar (writer and Dir) 1987, In The Spirit 1990, The Birdcage 1996 (co-author screenplay), Primary Colors (co-author screenplay) 1998, The John Cassavetes Collection (director) 1999, Small Time Crooks 2000. *Publications:* Better Part of Valour (play) 1983, Hotline 1983, Mr. Gogol and Mr. Preen 1991, Death Defying Acts 1995.

MAY, Baron (Life Peer), cr. 2001, of Oxford in the County of Oxfordshire; **Robert McCredie May,** Kt, OM, AC, PhD, FRS, FAAS; Australian biologist and academic; *President-Elect, British Association for the Advancement of Science;* b. 1 Aug. 1936, Sydney; s. of Henry W. May and Kathleen M. McCredie; m. Judith Feiner 1962; one d.; ed Sydney Boys' High School, Univ. of Sydney; Gordon MacKay Lecturer in Applied Math., Harvard Univ., USA 1959–61; at Univ. of Sydney 1962–73, Sr Lecturer in Theoretical Physics 1962–64, Reader 1964–69, Personal Chair 1969–73; Class of 1877 Prof. of Biology, Princeton Univ., USA 1973–88, Chair. Univ. Research Bd 1977–88; Royal Soc. Research Prof., Dept of Zoology, Univ. of Oxford and Imperial Coll., London, UK 1988–95; Chief Scientific Adviser to UK Govt and Head, Office of Science and Tech. 1995–2000; Pres. Royal Soc., British Ecological Soc. 2000–05; Crossbench Peer in House of Lords 2001–, mem. Science and Tech. Select Cttee 2006–, Science and Cttee Sub-cttees: I (Scientific Aspects of Ageing) 2005, I (Allergy/Waste Reduction) 2007–08, Systematics and Taxonomy Enquiry 2008, Draft Climate Change Bill Jt Cttee 2007; fmr Ind. mem. Jt Nature Conservancy Councils; Overseas mem. Australian Acad. of Sciences 1991–; Foreign mem. NAS 1992–; mem. Academia Europaea 1994–; Fellow, Merton Coll., Oxford 1988–; Foreign mem. NAS 1992–; fmr Chair. Bd of Trustees, Natural History Museum, London; Trustee, British Museum 1989–, Royal Botanic Gardens, Kew 1991–95, WWF (UK) 1990–94, Nuffield Foundation (Exec. Trustee) 1993–, BAAS 2006– (also Hon. Fellow, Pres.-Elect 2009); hon. degrees from univs including Uppsala (1990), Yale (1993), Sydney (1995), Princeton (1996), (ETH) 2003; Croonian Lecturer, Hitchcock Lecturer, John M. Prather Lecturer, Weldon Memorial Prize, Univ. of Oxford 1980, Award of MacArthur Foundation 1984, Medal of Linnean Soc. of London 1991, Marsh Christian Prize 1992, Frink Medal, Zoological Soc. of London 1995, Crafoord Prize 1996, Copley Medal, Royal Soc. 2007. *Publications:* Stability and Complexity in Model Ecosystems 1973, Exploitation of Marine Communities (ed.) 1974, Theoretical Ecology: Principles and Applications (ed.) 1976, Population Biology of Infectious Diseases (ed.) 1982, Exploitation of Marine Ecosystems (ed.) 1984, Perspectives in Ecological Theory (ed.) 1989, Population Regulation and Dynamics (ed.) 1990, Infectious Diseases of Humans: Transmission and Control (with R. M. Anderson) 1991, Large Scale Ecology and Conservation Biology 1994, Extinction Rates 1995, Evolution of Biological Diversity 1999, Virus Dynamics: the Mathematical Foundations of Immunology and Virology (with Martin Nowak) 2000. *Leisure interests:* tennis, running, hiking. *Address:* House of Lords, Westminster, London, SW1A 0PW (office); The BA, Wellcome Wolfson Building, 165 Queen's Gate, London, SW7 5HD, England. *Telephone:* (20) 7219-6958 (office); (870) 770-7101. *Fax:* (870) 770-7102. *Website:* www.parliament.uk (office); www.the-ba.net.

MAY, Rt Hon Theresa Mary, MA; British politician; b. 1 Oct. 1956; d. of Rev. Hubert Brasier and Zaidee Brasier (née Barnes); m. Philip John May 1980; ed St Hugh's Coll., Oxford; worked for Bank of England 1977–83; with Inter-Bank Research Org. 1983–85; with Asscn for Payment Clearing Services 1985–97 (Head of European Affairs Unit 1989–96); mem. (Conservative Party) Merton London Borough Council 1986–94; contested (Conservative Party) Durham NW 1992, Barking June 1994; MP (Conservative) for Maidenhead 1997–; Opposition Frontbench Spokeswoman on Educ. and Employment 1998–99; Shadow Sec. of State for Educ. and Employment 1999–2001; Shadow Sec. for Transport, Local Govt and the Regions 2001–02; Chair. Conservative Party 2002–03; Shadow Sec. of State for Environment and Transport 2003–04, for the Family 2004–05, for the Family and Culture, Media and Sport 2005; Shadow Leader, House of Commons 2005–, Shadow Minister for Women 2007–. *Publications:* articles: Women in the House: The Continuing Challenge, in Parliamentary Affairs Vol. 57 number 4 2004. *Leisure interests:* walking, cooking. *Address:* House of Commons, London, SW1A 0AA, England (office). *Telephone:* (20) 7219-5206 (office). *Fax:* (20) 7219-1145 (office). *E-mail:* mayt@parliament.uk (office). *Website:* www.tmay.co.uk (office).

MAY, Thomas; German university administrator; *Chancellor, Ludwig-Maximilians-Universität München;* b. 1958, Hildesheim; ed Univ. of Hamburg, Univ. Munich; Adviser, Deutsche Forschungsgemeinschaft (DFG, German Research Foundation) 1987–95; Deputy Sec.-Gen. German Council of Science and Humanities (Wissenschaftsrat) 1995–2003; Chancellor Ludwig-Maximilians-Universität München 2003–. *Address:* Office of the Chancellor, Ludwig-Maximilians-Universität München, Geschwister-Scholl-Platz 1, 80539 Munich, Germany (office). *Telephone:* (89) 2180-3269 (office). *Fax:* (89) 2180-6324 (office). *E-mail:* Kanzler@lmu.de (office). *Website:* www.uni-muenchen.de (office).

MAYAKI, Ibrahim Assane, PhD; Niger politician; *Chief Executive Officer, NEPAD;* b. 24 Sept. 1951, Niamey; s. of Assane Adamou Mayaki and Marie Mosconi; m. Marly Perez Marin 1976; one s. one d.; ed Ecole nationale d'admin de Québec, Canada, Univ. of Paris II, France; fmr Prof. of Public Admin in Niger and Venezuela; worked in uranium sector in Niger at Soc. des mines de l'air (SOMAIR), subsidiary of COGEMA Group; Minister of Foreign Affairs and Co-operation 1996–97; Prime Minister of Niger 1997–2000; Guest Prof. of Int. Relations, Univ. of Paris XI 2000–04, researcher at Research Centre on Europe and the Contemporary World (CREMOC) 2000–04; Exec. Dir The Hub (initiative to coordinate agricultural devt in Western and Cen. Africa) 2004–09; CEO New Partnership for Africa's Devt (NEPAD) 2009–; Grand Officier, Ordre Nat. Niger. *Publications:* several books on public affairs, planning and local devt; Quand la caravane passe... (autobiog.). *Leisure interest:* taekwondo (5th dan). *Address:* NEPAD Secretariat, Block B, Gateway Park Corner Challenger & Columbia Avenues Midridge Office Park, Midrand 1685, South Africa (office). *Telephone:* (11) 256-3600 (office). *E-mail:* ibrahimassanem@gmail.com (office). *Website:* www.nepad.org (office).

MAYALEH, Adib, PhD; Syrian central banker; *Governor, Central Bank of Syria;* ed Univ. of Aix-en-Provence, France; fmr Editing Advisor, Arab Group for Press, Advertising and Publication, Iqtisadyia Magazine; fmr mem. and Pres. Monetary and Credit Bd; fmr Advisor, French Commercial Del. to Syria; fmr Prof. of Econs, Damascus Univ.; Gov. Cen. Bank of Syria 2005–; Second Vice-Chair. Intergovernmental Group of Twenty-Four on Int. Monetary Affairs and Devt 2007. *Address:* Central Bank of Syria, place du 17 avril, Damascus, Syria (office). *Telephone:* (11) 2212642 (office). *Fax:* (11) 2248329 (office). *E-mail:* info@bcs.gov.sy (office). *Website:* www.banquecentrale.gov.sy (office).

MAYALL, Richard (Rik) Michael; British comedian, actor and writer; b. 7 March 1958, Harlow, Essex; s. of John Mayall and Gillian Mayall; m. Barbara Robbin; one s. two d.; ed Univ. of Manchester; f. 20th Century Coyote theatre co.; Hon. MA (Worcester) 2007. *Theatre includes:* The Common Pursuit 1988, Waiting for Godot 1991–92, The Government Inspector, Cell Mates 1995, A Family Affair 2000, The New Statesman 2006, 2007, Alan B'Stards Extremely Secret Weapon 2006, The New Statesman Episode 2006: The Blair B'Stard Project 2006. *Live Stand Up includes:* The Comic Strip 1981, Kevin Turvey and Bastard Squad 1983, Rik Mayall, Ben Elton, Andy De La Tour (UK tour & Edin. Fringe) 1983, Rik Mayall and Ben Elton 1984–85, (Australian tour) 1986, 1992, Rik Mayall and Andy De La Tour 1989–90, Rik Mayall and Adrian Edmondson (UK tours) 1993, 1995, 1997, 2001. *Films include:* Kevin Turvey Investigates (video) 1981, Eye of the Needle 1981, An American Werewolf in London 1981, Shock Treatment 1981, Couples and Robbers 1982, Whoops Apocalypse 1986, Dangerous Brothers Present: World of Danger (video) 1986, Eat the Rich 1987, Little Noises 1991, Drop Dead Fred 1991, Carry On Columbus 1992, Horse Opera 1993, Bottom Live (video) 1993, Bottom Live: The Big Number 2 Tour (video) 1995, Remember Me? 1997, Bring Me the Head of Mavis Davis (Best Actor, San Remo Film Festival 1997) 1997, Bottom Live 3: Hooligan's Island (video) 1997, Merlin – The Return 1999, Guest House Paradiso 1999, Blackadder Back and Forth 1999, Bottom 2001: An Arse Oddity 2001, Kevin of the North 2001, Day of the Sirens 2002, Oh Marbella! 2003, Cold Dark 2003, Chaos and Cadavers 2003, Sindy: The Fairy Princess (video) 2003, Bottom Live 2003: Weapons Grade Y-Fronts Tour (video) 2003, Churchill: The Hollywood Years 2004; provided voices for animations including Tom Thumb in The World of Peter Rabbit and Friends – The Tale of Two Bad Mice 1994, Toad in Willows in Winter (Emmy Award 1997) 1996, The Robber King in The Snow Queen 1995, Prince Froglip in The Princess and the Goblin 1993, Hero Baby in How to be a Little Sod 1995, Bud Tucker in Double Trouble (video game) 1996, Young William Tell in Oscar's Orchestra 1996, Le château des singes (A Monkey's Tale) 1999, Hogs of War (video game; voice) 2000, Valiant 2005. *Radio includes:* The Sound of Trumpets (BBC Radio 4) 1999, A Higher Education (BBC Radio 4) 2000. *Television includes:* A Kick Up the Eighties (series) 1981, Kevin Turvey: The Man Behind the Green Door 1982, The Young Ones (also creator and co-writer, two series, BBC) 1982, 1984, The Comic Strip Presents (Channel Four) 1983–84, 1992, George's Marvellous Medicine (five episodes, Jackanory, BBC) 1985, Saturday Live (series) 1986, Comic Relief 1986, Filthy Rich and Catflap (series) 1987, The New Statesman (four series, YTV) 1987–88, 1990, 1994 (Int. Emmy Award 1989, BAFTA Best New Comedy 1990, Special Craft Gold Medal Best Performer/Narrator), Jake's Journey 1988, Grim Tales (two series 1989, 1990), Bottom (three series, BBC) 1990, 1992, 1994 (British Comedy Awards Best New Comedy 1992), Rik Mayall Presents Briefest Encounter (Granada TV) (British Comedy Awards Best Comedy Actor 1993) 1993, Rik Mayall Presents Dancing Queen 1993, A. B'Stard Exposed 1994, Rik Mayall Presents The Big One 1995, Rik Mayall Presents Dirty Old Town 1995, Rik Mayall Presents Clair de lune 1995, Look at the State We're In! (mini-series) 1995, How to Be a Little Sod (series) 1995, The Wind in the Willows (voice) 1995, Wham Bam Strawberry Jam! (BBC) 1995, The Alan B'Stard Interview with Brian Walden 1995, The Canterville Ghost 1997, In the Red 1998, Watership Down (series; voice) 1999, Jellikins (series; voice) 1999, Tom and Vicky (series; voice) 1999, The Bill 1999, Jonathan Creek 1999, Jesus Christ Superstar 2000, The Knock (series) 2000, Murder Rooms 2000, Tales of Uplift and Moral Improvement (series) 2001, Believe Nothing (series) 2002, ABBA: Our Last Video Ever 2004, Shoebox Zoo (series; voice) 2004, King Arthur's Disasters (series; voice) 2005, All About George (series) 2005, King Arthur's Disasters (second series), Comic Strip presents Pampas Grass 2005,. *Address:* c/o Aude Powell, The Brunskill Management Ltd, Suite 8A, 169 Queen's Gate, London, SW7 5HE, England (office). *Telephone:* (20) 7581-3388 (London) (office); (1768) 881430. *Fax:* (20) 7589-9460 (London) (office); (1768) 881850.

MAYANJA, Rachel N., BL, LLM; Ugandan UN official; *Special Adviser to the Secretary-General on Gender Issues and Advancement of Women, United Nations;* three c.; ed Makarere Univ., Harvard Univ. Law School, USA; early career in UN Div. for Equal Rights for Women, Centre for Social Devt and Humanitarian Affairs; served in UN peacekeeping missions in Namibia (UNTAG) 1989–90 and Iraq/Kuwait (UNIKOM) 1992–94; sr positions in UN Office of Human Resources Man. including Chief of Common System, Specialist Services, Sec. to Sec.-Gen.'s Task Force on reform of Human Resources Man. 1999, Dir of Human Resources Man. Div., UN FAO 2000–04; Special Adviser to Sec.-Gen. on Gender Issues and Advancement of Women 2004–. *Address:* Office of the Special Adviser on Gender Issues and Advancement of Women (OSAGI), Department of Economic and Social Affairs, Two United Nations Plaza, 12th Floor, New York, NY 10017, USA (office). *Telephone:* (212) 963-5086 (office). *Fax:* (212) 963-1802 (office). *E-mail:* osagi@un.org (office). *Website:* www.un.org/womenwatch/osagi (office).

MAYAWATI, Kumari, BA, BEd, LLB; Indian lawyer and politician; *Chief Minister of Uttar Pradesh and President, Bahujan Samaj Party;* b. 15 Jan. 1956, Badalpur, Gautam Budh Nagar Dist, UP; d. of Sri Prabhu Das and Smt. Ram Rati Ji; ed Delhi Univ., Meerut Univ.; Chief Minister of UP (first Dalit Chief Minister of an Indian state) 1995, 1997, 2002–03, 2007–; Pres. Bahujan Samaj Party 2003–; fmr mem. Legis. Ass. UP 1996–; mem. UP Legis. Council 2007–; fmr mem. Parl. (Lok Sabha); currently mem. Parl. (Rajya Sabha); several honours and awards, ranked by Forbes magazine amongst 100 Most Powerful Women (59th) 2008. *Publications:* Bahujan Samaj Aur Uski Rajniti (Hindi version) 2000, (English version) 2001, Bahujan Movement Ka Safarnama (two vols) 2006. *Leisure interests:* Indian cuisine, clean environment and welfare of Bahujan Samaj. *Address:* Office of the Chief Minister, Government of Uttar Pradesh, Suchna Bhawan, Park Road, Lucknow, 226001 (office); C-57, Indrapuri, New Delhi, 110012 (home); 13A Mall Avenue, Lucknow, 226001, India (home). *Telephone:* (11) 2621122 (home). *Fax:* (11) 2239401. *E-mail:* upinformation@gmail.com (office). *Website:* www.upgov.nic.in (office).

MAYER, Colin, MA, DPhil; British academic; *Peter Moores Dean and Professor of Management Studies, Saïd Business School, University of Oxford;* b. 12 May 1953, London; s. of the late Harold Charles Mayer and of Anne Louise Mayer; m. Annette Patricia Haynes 1979; two d.; ed St Paul's School, London, Oriel Coll., Oxford, Wolfson Coll., Oxford, Harvard Univ., USA; HM Treasury, London 1976–78; Harkness Fellow, Harvard Univ. 1979–80; Fellow in Econs, St. Anne's Coll., Oxford 1980–86, Price Waterhouse Prof. of Corp. Finance, City Univ. Business School 1987–92; Prof. of Econs and Finance, Univ. of Warwick 1992–94; Peter Moores Prof. of Man. Studies, Saïd Business School, Oxford 1994–2006, Dean 2008–, Dir Oxford Financial Research Centre 1994–2006, del. Oxford Univ. Press 1996–; Chair. OXERA Ltd 1987–2006; Assoc. Ed. Annals of Finance, Journal of Int. Financial Man., European Financial Man. Journal, Fiscal Studies, Scottish Journal of Political Economy, Oxford Review of Econ. Review of Finance; mem. Exec. Cttee Royal Econ. Soc. 2002–; Fellow, Wadham Coll. Oxford 1994–2006, St Edmund Hall 2006–; Gov. St Paul's School London 2002–06; Hon. Fellow St Anne's Coll., Oxford Univ. 1993, Oriel Coll. *Publications:* Economic Analysis of Accounting Profitability (co-author) 1986, Risk, Regulation and Investor Protection (co-author) 1989, European Financial Integration (co-author) 1991, Capital Markets and Financial Intermediation (co-author) 1993, Hostile Takeovers (co-author) 1994, Asset Management and Investor Protection (co-author) 2002; contribs to academic journals and books. *Leisure interests:* piano, jogging, reading philosophy and science. *Address:* Saïd Business School, University of Oxford, Park End Street, Oxford, OX1 1HP (office); Wadham College, Oxford, OX1 3PN, England. *Telephone:* (1865) 288919 (office). *Fax:* (1865) 288805 (office). *E-mail:* colin.mayer@sbs.ox.ac.uk (office). *Website:* www.finance.ox.ac.uk (office); www.sbs.ox.ac.uk (office).

MAYER, HE Cardinal Paul Augustin, OSB; German ecclesiastic; b. 23 May 1911, Altötting; professed Brother of Order of Saint Benedict 1931, ordained priest 1935, consecrated Bishop (Titular See of Satrianum) 1972, then Archbishop; Sec. of Religious and Secular Insts 1971; Pro-Prefect of Sacraments (later Divine Worship and the Discipline of the Sacraments) 1984, Prefect 1985–88; cr. Cardinal-Priest of S. Anselmo all'Aventino 1985; Pres. 'Ecclesia Dei' 1988–91 (retd), now Pres. Emer. *Address:* c/o Palazzo della Congr. per la Dottrina della Fede, Piazza del S. Uffizio 11, 00193 Rome; via Rusticucci 13, 00193 Rome, Italy (home). *Telephone:* (06) 69885213.

MAYER, Peter, BA, MA; American/British book publisher; *President, Overlook Press, New York; Gerald Duckworth Publishers, London;* b. 28 March 1936, Hampstead, London, England; s. of Alfred Mayer and Lee Mayer; one d.; ed Columbia Univ., New York, Christ Church, Oxford; Grad. Fellow, Indiana Univ.; Fulbright Fellow, Freie Universität Berlin 1959; worked with Orion Press before joining Avon books for 14 years; Publr and Pres. Pocketbooks 1976–78; Chief. Exec. Penguin Books Ltd, London 1978–96, later Chair. Penguin USA; exec. positions with The Overlook Press (co-f. with his father 1970) 1996–, acquired Ardis Publrs 2001, Duckworth Publrs 2003, Nonesuch Press 2005; mem. Bd Asscn of American Publrs –2003, Bd Frankfurt Bookfair Fellowship, Bd Nat. Book Foundation –2003), New York Univ. Publrs Advisory Bd, Scholastic Bd of Dirs, German Book Office; Chevalier and Officier, Ordre des Arts et des Lettres 1996; Most Distinguished Publr of the Year 1995, Foundation of Publrs' and Booksellers' Asscn's in India Award for Oustanding Contrib. to Int. Publishing 1996, London Book Fair/Trilogy Lifetime Achievement Award 2008. *Publications:* An Idea is Like a Bird 1963, The Pacifist Conscience (ed.) 1966. *Address:* Duckworth Publishers, 90–93 Cowcross Street, London, EC1M 6BF, England (office); The Overlook Press, 141 Wooster Street, New York, NY 10012, USA. *Telephone:* (20) 7490-7300 (London) (office); (212) 673-2223 (New York) (office). *Fax:* (20) 7490-0080 (London) (office); (212) 673-2296 (New York) (office). *E-mail:* info@duckworth-publishers.co.uk (office); sales@overlookpress.com (office). *Website:* www.ducknet.co.uk (office); www.overlookpress.com (office).

MAYER, Thomas; German conductor; ed State Acad. of Music, Berlin; worked in opera houses of Beuthen, Leipzig, Teplitz and Aussig, subsequently Asst to Erich Kleiber, Fritz Busch and Arturo Toscanini, Teatro Colón, Buenos Aires; directed German opera season, Santiago, Chile and State Symphony Orchestra of Montevideo, Uruguay; conducted at Metropolitan Opera, New York 1974, subsequently Dir Venezuelan Symphony Orchestra, Halifax and Ottawa orchestras, Canada; guest conductor with many orchestras in Europe, N America and Australia; a regular conductor of Sinfonie Orchestra Berlin (West) and Berlin Symphony Orchestra (East) 1974–.

MAYER-KUCKUK, Theo, Dr rer. nat; German nuclear physicist; *Scientific Director, Magnus-Haus;* b. 10 May 1927, Rastatt; m. Irmgard Meyer 1965; two s.; ed Univ. of Heidelberg; Research Fellow, Max Planck Institut für Kernphysik, Heidelberg 1953–59, Scientific mem. 1964; Research Fellow, Calif. Inst. of Tech., Pasadena 1960–61; Dozent, Univ. of Heidelberg 1962, Tech. Univ. Munich 1963; Prof. of Physics, Univ. of Bonn 1965–92, Dir Inst. of Nuclear and Radiation Physics 1965–92; Vice-Pres. Int. Union of Pure and Applied Physics (IUPAP) 1984–90; Pres. German Physical Soc. 1990–92, Vice-Pres. 1992–96; Scientific Dir Magnus-Haus Berlin 1994–; mem. Acad. of Sciences of Nordrhein-Westfalen 1982; Röntgenpreis, Univ. of Giessen 1964. *Publications:* Kernphysik, Atomphysik, Der gebrochene Spiegel 1989; research papers and review articles in physics journals. *Leisure interest:* sailing. *Address:* Institut für Strahlen- und Kernphysik der Universität Bonn, Nussallee 14, 53113 Bonn (office); Magnus-Haus, am Kupfergraben 7, 10117 Berlin (office); Dreiserstr.26, 12587 Berlin, Germany (home). *Telephone:* (228) 732201 (office); (30) 6409-5993 (home). *Fax:* (30) 6495-8134 (home). *E-mail:* temka@web.de (home).

MAYFIELD, Rt Rev. Christopher John, MA, MSc; British ecclesiastic; *Lord Bishop of Manchester;* b. 18 Dec. 1935; s. of Dr Roger Mayfield and Muriel Mayfield; m. Caroline Roberts 1962; two s. one d.; ed Sedbergh School, Gonville & Caius Coll. Cambridge and Linacre House, Oxford, Cranfield Univ.; ordained deacon 1963, priest 1964; curate, St Martin-in-the-Bull Ring, Birmingham 1963–67; Lecturer, St Martin's, Birmingham 1967–71; Vicar of Luton 1971–80; Archdeacon of Bedford 1979–85; Bishop Suffragan of Wolverhampton 1985–93; Bishop of Manchester 1993–2002; Lord Bishop of Manchester, House of Lords 1998; Hon. Asst Bishop, Worcester; Dr hc (Manchester Univ.) 2002. *Leisure interests:* marriage, evangelism, walking, watching cricket and rugby. *Address:* Harewood House, 54 Primrose Crescent, St Peter's, Worcester, WR5 3HT, England (home). *Telephone:* (1905) 764822 (home). *E-mail:* caroline@mayfieldc.freeserve.co.uk (home).

MAYHEW JONAS, Dame Judith, DBE, LLM; New Zealand politician, lawyer and academic; b. 18 Oct. 1948, Dunedin; m. 1976 (divorced 1986); m. 2nd Christopher Jonas 2003; ed Otago Girls' High School, Univ. of Otago, NZ; barrister and solicitor, NZ 1973, solicitor, England and Wales 1993; Lecturer in Law, Univ. of Otago 1970–73; Lecturer in Law and Sub-Dean, Univ. of Southampton, UK 1973–76, King's Coll., London 1976–89; Dir Anglo-French law degree, Sorbonne, Paris 1976–79; Dir of Training and Employment Law, Titmuss Sainer Dechert 1989–94; mem. Bd London Guildhall Univ. 1992–2002; mem. Court and Council Imperial Coll., London 2001–03; Dir of Educ. and Training, Wilde Sapte 1994–99; City and Business Adviser to Mayor of London 2000–; mem. Court of Common Council Corpn of London 1986–2004, Chair. Policy and Resources Cttee 1997–2003; Special Adviser to Chair. of Clifford Chance 2000–03; Chair. Bd Govs 1999–2003; Chair. Royal Opera House, London 2003–08, Ind. Schools' Council 2008–, New West End Co. 2008–; Dir Gresham Coll. 1990–, London First Centre 1996–, Int. Financial Services London (fmrly British Invisibles) 1996–, London First 1997–, 4Ps 1997–, London Devt Agency 2000 (Chair. Business and Skills Cttee –2004, Vice-Chair. 2003–), Cross River Partnership; Trustee Natural History Museum 1998–; Dir (non-exec.) Merrill Lynch 2006–; Gov. Birkbeck Coll. London 1993–; Provost King's Coll., Cambridge 2003–05; Trustee Natural History Museum; Hon. LLD (Otago) 1998, (City Univ. London) 1999; named New Zealander of the Year in the UK 2004. *Leisure interests:* opera, theatre, old English roses, tennis. *Address:* New West End Company, 3rd Floor, Morley House, 320 Upper Regent Street, London W1B 3BE, England (office). *Telephone:* (20) 7462-0680 (office). *E-mail:* info@newwestend.com (office). *Website:* www.newwestend.com (office).

MAYHEW OF TWYSDEN, Baron (Life Peer), cr. 1997, of Kilndown in the County of Kent; **Patrick Barnabas Burke Mayhew,** Kt, PC, QC; British politician and barrister; b. 11 Sept. 1929, Cookham, Berks.; s. of the late A. G. H. Mayhew and Sheila M. B. Roche; m. Jean Elizabeth Gurney 1963; four s.; ed Tonbridge School and Balliol Coll., Oxford; Pres. Oxford Union Soc. 1952; called to Bar (Middle Temple) 1955; QC 1972; MP (Conservative) for Tunbridge Wells (now Royal Tunbridge Wells) 1974–97; Parl. Sec., Dept of Employment 1979–81; Minister of State, Home Office 1981–83; Solicitor-Gen. 1983–87; Attorney-Gen. 1987–92; Sec. of State for Northern Ireland 1992–97; Dir (non-exec.) Western Provident Asscn 1998–, Vice-Chair. 2000–; Chair. Prime Minister's Advisory Cttee on Business Appointments 1999–. *Leisure interests:* country pursuits, sailing. *Address:* House of Lords, Westminster, London, SW1A 0PW, England (office). *Telephone:* (20) 7219-3000 (office).

MAYNE, David Quinn, PhD, DSc, FRS, FREng, FIEE, FIEEE, FIC; British engineer and academic; *Professor Emeritus and Senior Research Fellow, Imperial College London;* b. 23 April 1930, Germiston, S Africa; s. of Leslie Harper Mayne and Jane Quin; m. Josephine Mary Hess 1954; three d.; ed Christian Brothers' Coll., Boksburg, Univ. of The Witwatersrand, S Africa; Lecturer, Univ. of the Witwatersrand 1951–54, 1957–59; Research Engineer,

British Thomson Houston Co. 1955–56; Lecturer, Imperial Coll. of Science, Tech. and Medicine 1959–66, Reader 1967–70, Prof. 1970–89; Prof. of Electrical and Computer Eng, Univ. of California, Davis 1989–96, Prof. Emer. 1997–, Head Dept of Electrical Eng 1984–88, Sr Research Fellow Science Research Council 1979; Sr Research Fellow Dept of Electrical and Electronic Eng, Imperial Coll., Univ. of London 1996–; Visiting Research Fellow, Harvard Univ., USA 1970; Visiting Prof. Univ. of Calif., Berkeley, Univ. of Newcastle, Australia, IIT, Delhi, Academia Sinica, Beijing, Univ. of California, Santa Barbara, Univ. of Wisconsin, Madison; Fellow, Int. Fed. of Automatic Control 2008; Hon. Prof., Beihang Univ., Beijing 2008; Hon. DTech (Lund) 1995; Heaviside Premium 1979, 1984, Harold Hartley Medal 1984, IEEE Control Systems Award 2009. *Publications:* Differential Dynamic Programming 1970; 250 papers in professional journals on optimization, optimal control, adaptive control and optimization-based design. *Leisure interests:* walking, cross-country skiing, music. *Address:* Department of Electrical and Electronic Engineering, Imperial College, London, SW7 2BT (office); 123 Elgin Crescent, London, W11 2JH, England (home). *Telephone:* (20) 7594-6287 (office); (20) 7792-0972 (home). *Fax:* (20) 7594-6282 (office). *E-mail:* d.mayne@imperial.ac.uk (office). *Website:* (office).

MAYNE, (David) Roger, BA; British photographer and artist; b. 5 May 1929, Cambridge; s. of A. B. Mayne and D. Mayne (née Watson); m. Ann Jellicoe 1962; one d. one s.; ed Balliol Coll., Oxford; self-taught in photography; photographs of London and other city street scenes 1955–61; taught at Bath Acad. of Art, Corsham 1966–69; works in Museum of Modern Art, New York, Metropolitan Museum of Art, New York, Art Inst. of Chicago, Bibliothèque Nationale, Paris, Nat. Gallery of Australia, Canberra, V & A Museum, London, Arts Council of GB. *Publications:* Things Being Various (with others) 1967, The Shell Guide to Devon (with Ann Jellicoe) 1975, The Street Photographs of Roger Mayne 1986, 1993, Roger Mayne Photographs 2001. *Leisure interests:* listening to music, looking at art exhbns, watching sport, mountains. *Address:* c/o Lindsay Stewart, Quartet, 8 Lower John Steet, London, W1F 9AU, England. *Telephone:* www.rogermayne.com.

MAYNE, Thom, BArch, MArch; American architect and artist; *Principal, Morphosis;* b. 19 Jan. 1944, Waterbury, Conn.; ed Univ. of Southern California, Harvard Univ. Grad. School of Design; Prof., UCLA 1992–; Co-founder and Bd mem. Southern Calif. Inst. of Architecture (SCI-ARC) 1972–99; Co-founder and Prin. of Morphosis (architectural office), Santa Monica, Calif. 1972–; Elliot Noyes Chair, Harvard Univ. Grad. School of Design 1988; Eliel Saarinen Chair, Yale School of Architecture, Yale Univ. 1991; visiting position at Calif. State Coll. at Pomona 1971; Visiting Prof., Miami Univ. School of Fine Arts 1982, Washington Univ. in St Louis School of Architecture 1984, Univ. of Tex. School of Architecture 1984, Univ. of Pa Grad. School of Fine Arts 1985, Columbia Univ. Grad. School of Architecture, Planning and Preservation 1986, Univ. of Cincinnati Coll. of Design, Architecture, Art and Planning 1990, Hochschule für Angewandte Kunst, Vienna, Austria 1991, Tech. Univ. of Vienna 1993, Univ. of Sarajevo, Bosnia and Herzegovina 1994, Tech. Univ. of Kraków, Poland 1994, Summer Studio, Univ. of Ore. School of Architecture and Allied Arts 1995–96, The Berlage Inst., Amsterdam, Netherlands 1993, 1996, Tech. Univ. of Graz, Austria 1996–97; Visiting Master Teacher, Clemson Univ. Coll. of Architecture, Arts and Humanities 1991; Plym Distinguished Professorship in Architecture, Univ. of Ill. at Urbana-Champaign 1992–93; Bannister Fletcher Visiting Prof., The Bartlett School of Architecture 1995; Baumer Distinguished Prof., Ohio State Univ. Knowlton School of Architecture 1997; Workshop Leader, Research Inst. for Experimental Architecture 1997; Baird Visiting Prof., Cornell Univ. School of Architecture 1999; mem.-Elect American Acad. of Design 1992; Fellow, American Inst. of Architecture 2006; works in collections: Avery Library, Columbia Univ., New York, Aedes Gallery und Architekturforum, Berlin, Denver Art Museum, Colo, Diane Farris Gallery, Vancouver, Fonds Regional d'Art Contemporaire du Center (FRAC), Orléans, France, Gwenda Jay Gallery, Chicago, The Israel Museum, Jerusalem, Österreichisches Museum für Angewandte Kunst (MAK), Vienna, Merry Norris Contemporary Art, Los Angeles, Museo Nacional de Bellas Artes, Buenos Aires, New York Museum of Modern Art, San Francisco Museum of Modern Art; Rome Prize Fellowship, American Acad. in Rome 1987, Brunner Prize in Architecture, American Acad. of Arts and Letters 1992, Alumni of the Year, Univ. of Southern California 1995, AIA Los Angeles Gold Medal 2000, Chrysler Design Award of Excellence 2001, Pritzker Architecture Prize 2005. *Works include:* Freidland Jacobs Communications, Los Angeles 1996, Salick Healthcare Office Bldg (8150), Los Angeles 1997, Landa Residence, Manhattan Beach, Calif. 1997, Sun Tower, Seoul, S Korea 1997, ASE Design Center, Taipei, Taiwan 1997, SHR Perceptual Management, Scottsdale, Ariz. 1998, Lutece, Las Vegas, Nev. 1999, Int. Elementary School, Long Beach, Calif. 1999, Tsunami Asian Grill, Las Vegas 1999, Diamond Ranch High School, Pomona 1999, Univ. of Toronto Grad. Student Housing 2000, Hypo Alpe-Adria Centre, Klagenfurt, Austria 2002, Silent Collisions, Charleroi, Belgium 2003, Caltrans Dist 7 HQ, Los Angeles 2004, Science Educ. Resource Center, Science Center School, Los Angeles 2004, Univ. of Cincinnati Student Recreation Center 2005, Nat. Oceanic and Atmospheric Admin (NOAA) Satellite Operation Facility, Suitland, Md 2005, San Francisco Fed. Bldg 2006, Wayne L. Morse US Courthouse, Eugene, Ore. 2006, Matano House, Paso Robles, Calif. 2006. *Address:* Morphosis, 2041 Colorado Avenue, Santa Monica, CA 90404, USA (office). *Telephone:* (310) 453-2247 (office). *Fax:* (310) 829-3270 (office). *E-mail:* studio@morphosis.net (office); Thom.Mayne@aud .ucla.edu. *Website:* www.morphosis.net (office); www.aud.ucla.edu.

MAYOR, Michel G. E., MPhys, PhD, DrAstron; Swiss astronomer and academic; *Professor, University of Geneva;* b. 12 Jan. 1942, Lausanne; m. Francoise Mayor-Pirolet; one s. two d.; ed Univs of Lausanne and Geneva; Researcher, Cambridge Observatory 1971; Pres. Int. Astronomical Union (IAU) Comm. on Galactic Structure 1988–91, Swiss Soc. for Astrophysics and Astronomy 1990–93; Researcher, Univ. of Hawaii 1994–95; currently Prof. of Astronomy, Univ. of Geneva; Dir Geneva Observatory 1998–2002; Foreign Assoc., Acad. Française des Sciences; Chevalier de la Légion d'honneur 2004; Dr hc (Catholic Univ. of Louvain, Belgium, Swiss Inst. of Tech., Lausanne, Fed. Univ. of Rio Grande del Norte, Brazil, Uppsala Univ.); Charles Louis de Saulces de Freycinet Prize, Acad. Française des Sciences 1983, IAU Comm. of Bioastronomy Medal 1997, Prix Marcel Benoist 1998, Astronomical Soc. of France Janssen Prize 1998, Observatory of the Côte d'Azur Adion Medal 1998, Balzan Prize for Physics, Natural Sciences and Medicine 2000 (jt recipient), Einstein Medal 2004, Shaw Prize for Astronomy 2005. *Achievements include:* discovered first extrasolar planet, "51 Peg b" 1995. *Publications:* New Worlds in the Cosmos: The Discovery of Exoplanets (with Pierre-Yves Frei) 2003; more than 300 scientific papers. *Address:* Observatoire de Genève, 51 chemin des Maillettes, 1290 Sauverny, Switzerland (office). *Telephone:* (22) 379-2460 (office). *Fax:* (22) 379-2205 (office). *E-mail:* Michel.Mayor@obs.unige.ch (office). *Website:* www.unige.ch/sciences/astro (office).

MAYOR ZARAGOZA, Federico, DrPhar; Spanish politician, biologist and university official; *President, Fundación Cultura de Paz;* b. 27 Jan. 1934, Barcelona; s. of Federico Mayor and Juana Zaragoza; m. María Angeles Menéndez 1956; two s. one d.; ed Univ. Complutense of Madrid; Prof. of Biochemistry, Faculty of Pharmacy, Granada Univ. 1963–73; Rector, Granada Univ. 1968–72; Prof. of Biochemistry, Autonomous Univ., Madrid 1973, Chair. Severo Ochoa Molecular Biology Centre (Higher Council of Scientific Research) 1974–78; Under-Sec. Ministry of Educ. and Science 1974–75; mem. Cortes (Parl.) for Granada 1977–78; Chair. Advisory Cttee for Scientific and Tech. Research 1974–78; Deputy Dir-Gen. UNESCO 1978–81, Dir-Gen. 1987–99; Minister for Educ. and Science 1981–82; Dir Inst. of the Sciences of Man, Madrid 1983–87; mem. European Parl. 1987; Pres. Scientific Council, Ramón Areces Foundation, Madrid 1989–, First Mark Communications 2000–, European Research Council Expert Group 2002–; Founder and Pres. Fundación Cultura de Paz 1999–; Co-Chair. Alliance of Civilizations, UN 2005–06; Pres. Initiative for Science in Europe (ISE) 2007–; mem. Club of Rome 1981–; Academician, Royal Acad. of Pharmacy; mem. European Acad. of Arts, Sciences and Humanities, Int. Cell Research Org. (ICRO), AAAS, The Biochemical Soc. (UK), French Soc. of Biological Chem., ACS, Academia de Bellas Artes, and numerous other orgs; Grand Cross, Alfonso X El Sabio, Orden Civil de la Sanidad Carlos III, Caro y Cuervo (Colombia), Commdr Placa del Libertador (Venezuela), Grand Officier, Ordre Nat. du Mérite (France); Dr hc (Westminster) 1995. *Publications:* A contraviento (poems) 1987, Mañana siempre es tarde 1987 (English version: Tomorrow Is Always Too Late 1992), Aguafuertes (poems) 1991 (English version: Patterns 1994), La nueva página 1994, Memoria del futuro 1994, La paix demain? 1995, Science and Power 1995, UNESCO: Un idéal en action 1996, El fuego y la esperanza (poems) 1996, Terral (poems) 1998 (English version: Land Wind 1998), Un mundo nuevo (English version: The World Ahead: Our Future in the Making) 1999, Los nudos gordianos 1999, La fuerza de la palabra 2005, Un diálogo ibérico enel marco europeo y mundial 2006, Alzaré mi voz (poems) 2007, Voz de vida, voz debida 2007, Tiempo de acción 2008, En pie de paz (poems) 2008; numerous specialized works, trans., articles. *Leisure interests:* reading, writing, music. *Address:* Fundación Cultura de Paz, Velázquez 14, 3° D, 28001 Madrid (office); Mar Caribe 15, Interland, Majadahonda, 28220 Madrid, Spain (home). *Telephone:* (91) 4261555 (office). *Fax:* (91) 4316387 (office). *E-mail:* f.mayor@fmayor.e.telefonica.net (office). *Website:* www.fund -culturadepaz.org (office).

MAYORSKY, Boris Grigoryevich; Russian diplomatist; *Adviser, Ministry of Foreign Affairs;* b. 19 May 1937, Odessa, Ukraine; m.; two d.; ed Moscow Inst. of Int. Relations, UNO Translation Courses; with Africa Div. USSR Ministry of Foreign Affairs 1961; on staff USSR Embassy, Ghana 1961–64; attaché 1964–65; with UN European Secr., Geneva 1966–69, WHO, Geneva 1969–70; First Sec., Head of Sector Law Div. USSR Ministry of Foreign Affairs 1970–73, adviser, Comm. on Law Problems of Space 1973–89; First Deputy Head, Head Dept on Int. Scientific and Tech. Co-operation 1989–92; Amb. to Kenya 1992–2000, to Spain 2000–02; currently Adviser to Ministry of Foreign Affairs. *Address:* Ministry of Foreign Affairs, Smolenskaya-Sennaya 32/34, 119200 Moscow, Russia (office). *Telephone:* (495) 244-16-06 (office). *Fax:* (495) 230-21-30 (office). *E-mail:* ministry@mid.ru (office). *Website:* www.mid.ru (office).

MAYOUX, Jacques Georges Maurice Sylvain; French banker and business executive; b. 18 July 1924, Paris; s. of Georges Mayoux and Madeleine de Busscher; one s. one d.; ed Ecole des Hautes Etudes Commerciales, Ecole Libre des Sciences Politiques, Faculté de Droit et des Lettres de Paris; studied at Ecole Nat. d'Admin 1949–51; personal adviser to Minister of Finance 1958, Asst Gen. Sec. Comité Interministeriel pour les Questions de Coopération Economique Européenne 1958–63; mem. Gen. Council, Banque de France 1963–73; Gen. Man. Caisse Nat. de Crédit Agricole 1963–75; Prof., Inst. d'Etudes Politiques 1964–72; Chair., Gen. Man. Agritel 1972–75, SACILOR (Aciéries et laminoirs de Lorraine) 1978–82, SOLLAC (Soc. Lorraine de laminage continu) 1980–82; Pres. SOLMER 1980–81, Société Générale SA 1982–86 (Hon. Pres. 1986, Hon. Chair.), Cen. Cttee for Rural Renovation 1971, Fondation H.E.C. 1978–90; Pres. French-Canadian Chamber of Commerce 1986–90; Vice-Chair. Goldman Sachs Europe 1989–; Insp. Général des Finances 1976–87; Vice-Pres. Admin. Council Euris 1990–; mem. Supervisory Bd Harpener Gesellschaft 1980–86, Conseil Ordre de la Légion d'honneur 1993–; Gov. American Hosp. in Paris; Commdr, Légion d'honneur, Commdr, Ordre nat. du Mérite, Officier des Arts et Lettres; Commdr, Order of the Phoenix (Greece). *Address:* Société Générale, 38 rue de Bassano, 75008 Paris (office); Goldman Sachs (Europe), 2 rue de Thann, 75017 Paris, France (office); 65 avenue Foch, 75115 Paris, France (home). *Telephone:*

1-42-12-11-30 (office). *Fax:* 1-42-12-11-99 (office). *E-mail:* jacques.mayoux@gs.com (office).

MAYRHUBER, Wolfgang; Austrian airline industry executive; *Chairman and CEO, Deutsche Lufthansa AG;* b. 22 March 1947, Waizenkirchen; ed Tech. Coll. of Steyr, Bloor Inst., Canada, Massachusetts Inst. of Tech., USA; joined Deutsche Lufthansa AG 1970, various positions including engineer, Engine Overhaul Facility, Hamburg, man. posts in Maintenance, Repair and Overhaul (MRO) Operation, Exec. Vice-Pres. and COO of Tech. Operations 1992–94, Chair. of Exec. Bd Lufthansa Technik AG 1994–2000, apptd to Exec. Bd Deutsche Lufthansa AG 2001–02, Deputy Chair. 2002–03, Chair. and CEO 2003–; Chair. Supervisory Bd Lufthansa CityLine; Vice-Chair. Bd of Dirs AMECO Corpn, Beijing, People's Repub. of China; mem. Supervisory Bd Fraport AG, Eurowings Luftverkehrs AG, Munich Re Group (Münchener Rückversicherungs-Gesellschaft AG), BMW Group; mem. Bd of Dirs Swiss International Air Lines Ltd, HEICO Corpn, Fla, USA; mem. Steering Cttee Asscn of European Airlines, Chair. 2006; Chair. Strategy and Policy Cttee IATA, mem. Bd Govs IATA. *Address:* Deutsche Lufthansa AG, Von-Gablenz-Strasse 2–6, 50679 Cologne, Germany (office). *Telephone:* 696960 (office). *Fax:* 696966818 (office). *E-mail:* konzernkommunikation@dlh.de (office). *Website:* www.lufthansa.com (office).

MAYS, Willie; American fmr baseball player; b. 6 May 1931, Westfield; s. of William Howard Mays and Ann Mays; Nat. League Rookie of the Year 1951; played for the New York Giants 1951–57, San Francisco Giants (after team relocation) 1958–72, New York Mets 1972–73; career statistics include 3,283 hits and 660 home runs; two-time Most Valuable Player; 12 Gold Gloves; played in a record-tying 24 All-Star games; participated in four World Series; retd, signed ten-year contract as goodwill amb. and part-time coach for the New York Mets; Special Asst to Team Pres., San Francisco Giants 1986–; Associated Press Athlete of the Year Award 1954, elected to the Baseball Hall of Fame 1979, All-Century Major League Baseball Team, 100 Greatest World Athletes. *Address:* San Francisco Giants, Pacific Bell Park, 24 Willie Mays Plaza, San Francisco, CA 94107, USA (office). *Telephone:* (415) 972-2000 (office). *Website:* www.sfgiants.com (office).

MAYSTADT, Philippe, MA, PhD; Belgian politician and international finance executive; *President, European Investment Bank;* b. 14 March 1948, Verviers; three c.; ed Claremont Grad. School, Los Angeles and Catholic Univ. of Louvain; Asst Prof., Catholic Univ. of Louvain 1970–77, Prof. 1989–2007; Adviser, Office of Minister for Regional Affairs 1974; Deputy for Charleroi 1977–91; Sec. of State for Regional Economy and Planning 1979–80; Minister of Civil Service and Scientific Policy 1980–81, for the Budget, Scientific Policy and Planning 1981–85, of Econ. Affairs 1985–88; Deputy Prime Minister 1986–88; Minister of Finance 1988–98, of Foreign Trade 1995–98; Deputy Prime Minister 1995–98; Pres. Parti Social Chrétien 1998–99; mem. Senate June–Dec. 1999; Pres. European Investment Bank 2000–; Chair. IMF Interim Cttee 1993–98; Finance Minister of the Year, Euromoney magazine 1990. *Publications:* Listen and then Decide 1988, Market and State in a Globalized Economy 1998, Comprendre l'économie: l'Etat et le marché à l'heure de la mondialisation 1998. *Address:* European Investment Bank, 100 Boulevard Konrad Adenauer, 2950 Luxembourg (office). *Telephone:* 4379-94464 (office). *Fax:* 4379-64474 (office). *E-mail:* p.maystadt@eib.org (office). *Website:* www.eib.org (office).

MAZAHERI, Tahmasb, MS; Iranian civil engineer, government official and banking official; b. 1953; ed Univ. of Tehran; fmr univ. lecturer; Head Bonyad Mostazafan and Janbazan Foundation 1985–91; Sec.-Gen Bank Markazi Jomhouri Islami Iran (Cen. Bank) 1991–94, Gov. 2007–; Minister of Econ. Affairs and Finance 2001–04, Deputy Minister of Econ. Affairs and Finance 2005–06; Man. Dir Export Devt Bank of Iran (EDBI) 2007–08. *Address:* c/o Bank Markazi Jomhouri Islami Iran, POB 15875-7177, 144 Mirdamad Blvd, Tehran, Iran (office).

MAZANKOWSKI, Rt Hon. Donald Frank, PC, OC; Canadian politician and business consultant; b. 27 July 1935, Viking, Alberta; s. of the late Frank Mazankowski and Dora Lonowski; m. Lorraine E. Poleschuk 1958; three s.; ed High School; MP 1968–93; Minister of Transport and Minister responsible for Canadian Wheat Board 1979; Minister of Transport 1984–86; Pres. Treasury Bd 1987–88; Minister responsible for Privatization, Regulatory Affairs and Operations 1988, of Agric. 1989–91, of Finance 1991–93; Deputy Prime Minister 1986–93, Pres. of the Queen's Privy Council for Canada 1989–91; business consultant 1993–; fmr Chair. Inst. of Health Econs, Canadian Genetics Diseases Network, Alberta Premier's Advisory Council on Health; Gov. Univ. of Alberta; dir numerous cos; Progressive Conservative Party; Albert Order of Excellence 2003; Hon. DEng (Tech. Univ. of Nova Scotia) 1987; Hon. LLD (Univ. of Alberta) 1993; Paul Harris Fellow, Rotary International, Alberta Centennial Medal 2005. *Leisure interests:* fishing, golf. *Address:* PO Box 1350, Vegreville, Alberta, T9C 1S5, Canada (Office and Home). *Telephone:* (780) 410-0728. *Fax:* (780) 410-0748. *E-mail:* donmaz@shaw.ca.

MAZEAUD, Pierre, Docteur en droit; French politician; *President, Fondation Charles de Gaulle;* b. 24 Aug. 1929, Lyon; s. of Jean Mazeaud and Paulette Duirat; m. 1st Marie Prohom 1953 (divorced 1960); two d.; m. 2nd Sophie Hamel 1967; one s. one d.; ed Lycée Louis-le-Grand et Faculté de droit de Paris; Judge of Tribunal of Instance, Lamentin, Martinique 1961; in charge of conf., Faculty of Law, Paris 1955; Tech. Adviser to Prime Minister 1961; Judge of Tribunal of Great Instance, Versailles 1962; Tech. Adviser to Minister of Justice 1962; Tech. Adviser to Jean Foyer's Cabinet 1962–67; Tech. Adviser to Minister of Youth and Sports 1967–68; Deputy for Hauts-de-Seine 1968–73, for Haute-Savoie 1988–98, Vice.-Pres. Assemblée Nationale 1992–93, 1997–98, Vice-Pres. Groupe des députés sportifs 1968; Minister responsible for Youth and Sport 1973–76; Councillor of State 1976; Pres. Law Comm. of Assemblée Nationale 1987–88, 1993–98; Vice-Pres. l'Assemblée Nationale 1992–93, 1997–98; Titular Judge, High Court 1987–97; Mayor, Saint-Julien-en-Genevois 1979–89; regional councillor, Rhône-Alpes 1992–98, Pres. Commission des finances de Rhône-Alpes; mem. Constitutional Council 1998–, Pres. 2004–07; Pres. Fondation Charles de Gaulle 2007–; Vice-Pres. Cttee de réflexion sur la modernisation et le rééquilibrage des institutions 2007–; in charge of courses IEP (l'Institut d'études politiques) d'Aix-en-Provence; Professeur, IEP Paris 1999–; mem. Acad. des Sciences Morales et Politiques 2005–, Acad. des Sports; Officier, Légion d'honneur, Commdr de la Légion d'honneur, Officier du Mérite sportif. *Achievements include:* climbed Mount Everest 1978 (oldest man to do so). *Publications:* Montagne pour un homme nu 1971, Everest 78 1978, Sport et Liberté 1980, Nanga Parbat – montagne cruelle 1982, Des cailloux et des mouches ou l'échec à l'Himalaya 1985, Rappel au Règlement 1995. *Leisure interests:* mountaineering, skiing, swimming. *Address:* Fondation et Institut Charles de Gaulle, 5 rue de Solférino, 75007 Paris, France (office). *Telephone:* 1-44-18-66-77 (office). *Fax:* 1-44-18-66-99 (office). *E-mail:* contact@charles-de-gaulle.org (office). *Website:* www.charles-de-gaulle.org (office); r (office).

MAZOWIECKI, Tadeusz; Polish politician, journalist and writer; *Chairman, Polska Fundacja im. Roberta Schumana;* b. 18 April 1927, Płock; s. of Bronisław Mazowiecki and Jadwiga Mazowiecka; widower; three s.; ed Warsaw Univ.; Chair. Acad. Publishing Co-operative, Warsaw 1947–48; mem. Catholic Asscn PAX; contrib. to daily and weekly PAX Publs, dismissed 1955; Co-Founder, mem. of Bd, Vice-Pres. Warsaw Catholic Intelligentsia Club (KIK) 1956; Co-Founder and Chief Ed. Catholic monthly Więź (Bond) 1958–81; Deputy to Sejm (Parl.) (Catholic Group ZNAK) PRL (Polish People's Repub.) 1961–72; mem. of various opposition groups and protest movts 1968–89; Co-Founder and mem. Council Soc. for Acad. Courses (Flying Univ.) 1977–89; co-founder and Chair. Polska Fundacja im. Roberta Schumana 1991–; Head, Team of Experts, Lenin Shipyard, Gdańsk 1980; Co-Ed. Solidarity Trades Union Statutes; adviser to Solidarity Nat. Consultative Comm.; organizer and First Chief Ed. of Solidarity weekly 1981–89; interned 1981–82; participant, Round Table plenary debates, Co-Chair. group for union pluralism, mem. group for political reforms, team for mass-media, co-ordinator negotiation teams from opposition 1989; Prime Minister of Poland (first non-communist prime minister in Cen. and Eastern Europe after World War II) 1989–90; Deputy to Sejm (Parl.) 1991–2001; Chair. Democratic Union (Unia Demokratyczna) 1990–94, merged with Liberal Democratic Congress to form Freedom Union—Unia Wolności) 1994–95, left party in protest against coalitions with SLD and Samoobrona 2002; tabled compromise text of preamble to new Polish constitution which resolved issue of reference to God 1997; Chair. Parl. Comm. for European Integration 1997–2001; UN Special Rapporteur of Comm. on Human Rights investigating human rights situation in Fmr Yugoslavia 1992–95; mem. PEN Club; Order of White Eagle 1995, Officier Légion d'honneur 1998; Dr hc (Louvain) 1990, (Genoa) 1991, (Giessen) 1993, (Poitiers) 1994, (Exeter) 1998, (Acad. of Econs, Katowice) 1999, (Warsaw) 2003; Hon. LLD (Exeter) 1997; Peace Prize (Anglican Church, New York) 1990, Premio Napoli 1992; Andrzej Strug Award 1990, Freedom Award (American Jewish Congress) 1990, Giorgio La Pira Award of Peace and Culture 1991, Polish-German Award 1994, St Adalbert Award 1995, European Human Rights Award 1996, Robert Schuman Medal 2005. *Publications include:* Cross-Roads and Values 1971, The Second Face of Europe 1979, Internment 1984. *Address:* Biuro Tadeusza Mazowieckiego, Polska Fundacja im. Roberta Schumana, Al. Ujazdowskie 37, 00-540 Warsaw, Poland (office). *Telephone:* (22) 6212161 (office); (22) 6217555 (office). *Fax:* (22) 6297214 (office). *E-mail:* t.mazowiecki@schuman.org.pl (office). *Website:* schuman.org.pl (office).

MAZRUI, Ali A., MA, DPhil; Kenyan political scientist and academic; *Albert Schweitzer Professor in the Humanities and Director, Institute of Global Cultural Studies, State University of New York, Binghamton;* b. 24 Feb. 1933, Mombasa; s. of Al'Amin Ali Mazrui and Safia Suleiman Mazrui; m. 1st Molly Vickerman 1962 (divorced 1982); three s.; m. 2nd Pauline Ejima Uti-Mazrui 1991; two s.; ed Columbia Univ., USA, Univs of Manchester and Oxford, UK; Lecturer in Political Science, Makerere Univ., Uganda 1963–65, Prof. of Political Science 1965–72, Dean of Social Sciences 1967–69; Assoc. Ed. Transition Magazine 1964–73, Co-Ed. Mawazo Journal 1967–73; Visiting Prof. Univ. of Chicago 1965; Research Assoc. Harvard Univ. 1965–66; Dir African Section, World Order Models Project 1968–73; Visiting Prof. Northwestern Univ., USA 1969, McGill and Denver Univs 1969, London and Manchester Univs 1971, Dyason Lecture Tour of Australia 1972; Vice-Pres. Int. Political Science Asscn 1970–73, Int. Congress of Africanists 1967–73, Int. Congress of African Studies 1978–85, Int. African Inst. 1987–, World Congress of Black Intellectuals 1988–; Fellow, Center for Advanced Study in the Behavioral Sciences, Stanford 1972–73; Prof. of Political Science, Univ. of Michigan 1973–91; Sr Visiting Fellow, Hoover Inst. on War, Revolution and Peace, Stanford 1973–74; Dir Centre for Afro-American and African Studies 1979–81; Research Prof. Univ. of Jos, Nigeria 1981–86; Andrew D. White Prof.-at-Large, Cornell Univ. 1986–92, currently Sr Scholar in Africana Studies; Albert Schweitzer Prof. in the Humanities, State Univ. of New York, Binghamton 1989–, also Dir Inst. of Global Cultural Studies; Ibn Khaldun Prof.-at-Large School of Islamic and Social Sciences, Leesbury, Va 1997–; Walter Rodney Distinguished Prof. Univ. of Guyana, Georgetown 1997–98; Albert Luthuli Prof.-at-Large in the Humanities and Devt Studies, Univ. of Jos, Nigeria; Reith Lecturer 1979; Presenter BBC TV series The Africans 1986; mem. World Bank's Council of African Advisers; Int. Org. Essay Prize 1964, Northwestern Univ. Book Prize 1969. *Publications:* Towards a Pax Africana 1967, On Heroes and Uhuru-Worship 1967, The Anglo-African Commonwealth 1967, Violence and Thought 1969, Protest and Power in Black Africa (co-ed.) 1970, The Trial of Christopher Okigbo 1971, Cultural Engineering and Nation Building in East Africa 1972, Africa in World Affairs: The Next Thirty Years (co-ed.) 1973, A World Federation of Cultures: An African Perspective 1976, Political Values and the Educated Class in Africa 1978, Africa's International Relations 1978, The African Condition (Reith Lectures) 1980, Nationalism and New States in Africa (co-author) 1984, The Africans: A Triple Heritage 1986, Cultural Forces in World Politics 1989, Africa Since 1935 (Vol. VIII of UNESCO General History of Africa; ed.) 1993, The Power of Babel: Language and Governance in Africa's Experience 1998. *Leisure interests:* travel, dining out, swimming, reading thrillers and mystery novels. *Address:* State University of New York, Institute of Global Culture Studies, Office of Schweitzer Chair, P.O. Box 6000, Binghamton, NY 13902 (office); 313 Murray Hill Road, Vestal, NY 13850, USA (home). *Telephone:* (607) 777-4494 (office). *Website:* www.binghamton.edu/igcs (office).

MAZUKA, Michiyoshi; Japanese business executive; *Chairman, Fujitsu Limited;* ed Gakushuin Univ.; joined Fujitsu Ltd 1971, has held several sr exec. positions including Chief Dir of Higashi Nihon Sales, Man. Exec. Officer, Sr Man. Dir and Vice-Pres., with fujitsureseller.com 2005, with Fujitsu America Inc. 2006–08, later Corp. Sr Vice-Pres. Fujitsu Ltd –2008, Chair. 2008–. *Address:* Fujitsu Headquarters, Shiodome City Center, 1-5-2 Higashi-Shimbashi, Minato-ku, Tokyo 105-7123, Japan (office). *Telephone:* (3) 6252-2220 (office). *Fax:* (3) 6252-2783 (office). *E-mail:* info@fujitsu.com (office). *Website:* www.fujitsu.com (office).

MAZUMDAR-SHAW, Kiran, BSc; Indian business executive; *Chairman and Managing Director, Biocon India Ltd;* b. 23 March 1953, Bangalore; m. John Shaw 1997; ed Bishop Cotton Girls School, Mount Carmel Coll., Bangalore, Bangalore Univ., Ballarat Coll., Melbourne Univ., Australia; trainee Brewer, Carlton & United Breweries, Melbourne and trainee Maltster, Barrett Bros & Burston, Australia 1975–77; Brewery Consultant, Jupiter Breweries Ltd, Calcutta (now Kolkata) 1975–76; Tech. Man. Standard Malting Corpn, Baroda 1976; Trainee Man. Biocon Ltd, Cork, Repub. of Ireland 1978; Chair. and Man. Dir Biocon India Ltd 1978–; Dir Pharmacia United Ltd, Bangalore 1987–94; Chair. Syngene Int., Bangalore 1994–; Chair. Clinigene Int., Bangalore 2000–; mem. Bd Bio-Ventures for Global Health; Chair. and Mission Leader Confed. of Indian Industries Nat. Task Force on Biotechnology; Council mem. Basic Chemicals, Pharmaceuticals and Cosmetics Export Promotion Council 1983–; Vice-Pres. Asscn of Women Entrepreneurs of Karnataka (AWAKE) 1983–89, Indo-American Chamber of Commerce, Bangalore 1986–87; mem. Prime Minister's Council on Trade and Industry in India, Confed. of Indian Industries, Greater Mysore Chamber of Industries, Advisory Cttee, Dept of Biotechnology, Young Presidents' Org., Research Council, CFTRI, Bangalore Agenda Task Force, Bd of Science Foundation, Ireland; mem. Bd Govs ndian Inst. of Man. Bangalore; Trustee Karnataka Chitrakala Parishat; Chair. All India Art Exhbn; participated in various int. seminars; Padma Shri 1989, Padma Bhushan 2005; Hon. DSc (Ballarat) 2004; Dr hc (Manipal Acad. of Higher Educ.) 2005; Gold Award for Best Woman Entrepreneur, Inst. of Marketing Man. 1982, AWAKE Outstanding Contrib. Award 1983, Rotary Award for Best Model Employer 1983, Jaycees Outstanding Young Person Award 1987, Int. Women's Asscn (Chennai) Woman of the Year 1998–99, Nat. Award for Best Small Industry, Sir M. Visveswaraya Memorial Award, Fed. of Karnataka Chambers of Commerce and Industry 2002, Rajyotsava Award 2002, Ernst & Young Entrepreneur of the Year Award in Healthcare and Life Sciences Category 2002, Australian Alumni High Achiever Award, IDP Australian Alumni Asscn 2003, Whirlpool GR8 Women Award for Science and Tech. 2004, The Economic Times Business Woman of the Year Award 2004, Indian Chamber of Commerce Lifetime Achievement Award 2005, ranked by Fortune magazine amongst 50 Most Powerful Women in Business outside the US (44th) 2005, (48th) 2006, (50th) 2007, ranked by Forbes magazine amongst 100 Most Powerful Women (99th) 2008. *Publication:* Ale and Arty. *Leisure interest:* trekking. *Address:* Biocon India Ltd, 20th K M, Hosur Road, Electronic City, Bangalore, 560100 India (office). *Telephone:* (80) 28082808 (office). *Fax:* (80) 28523423 (office). *E-mail:* contact.us@biocon.com (office). *Website:* www.biocon.com (office).

MAZUROK, Yuri Antonovich; Ukrainian singer (baritone); b. 18 July 1931, Krasnik, Poland (now Ukraine); one s.; ed Lvov Inst. and Moscow Conservatoire; debut with Bolshoi Opera 1963, Prin. of the co. 1964–2001; has performed worldwide; retd from the stage 2001; awards include Prague Spring Vocal Competition 1960, Int. Enesco Singing Competition, Bucharest 1961, First Prize at World Fair, Montreal 1967, USSR People's Artist 1976. *Operatic roles include:* Eugene (Eugene Onegin), Prince Yeletsky (The Queen of Spades), Andrei (War and Peace), Figaro (The Barber of Seville), Scarpia (Tosca) and Escamillo (Carmen) and especially Verdi repertoire, including René (Un Ballo in Maschera), Rodrigo (Don Carlos), Germont (La Traviata). *Address:* c/o Bolshoi Theatre, Teatralnaya Pl. 1, 103009 Moscow, Russia (office).

MAZURSKY, Paul, BA; American film writer, director and actor; b. (Irwin Mazursky), 25 April 1930, Brooklyn, NY; s. of David Mazursky and Jean Gerson; m. Betsy Purdy 1953; two d.; ed Brooklyn Coll.; stage, TV and film actor 1951–; night club comedian 1954–60; writer, Danny Kaye Show 1963–67; co-writer, I Love You, Alice B. Toklas (film) 1968; mem. Bd of Govs Acad. of Motion Picture Arts and Sciences; Dr hc (Brooklyn Coll.). *Films include:* as writer and Dir, Bob & Carol & Ted & Alice 1969, Alex in Wonderland 1970, Blume in Love 1972, Harry & Tonto 1973, Next Stop, Greenwich Village 1976, An Unmarried Woman 1977–78, Willie & Phil 1979–80, Tempest 1982, Moscow on the Hudson 1984; as writer, producer and Dir, Down and Out in Beverly Hills 1986, Moon Over Parador 1988, Enemies A Love Story 1989, Scenes From a Mall 1991, The Pickle 1993, Faithful 1996, Yippee (documentary) 2006; as actor films include: Fear and Desire 1953, Blackboard Jungle 1955, Deathwatch 1966, Alex in Wonderland 1970, The Other Side of the Wind 1972, Blume in Love 1973, A Star Is Born 1976, An Unmarried Woman 1978, A Man, a Woman and a Bank 1979, History of the World: Part I 1981, Tempest 1982, Moscow on the Hudson 1984, Into the Night 1985, Down and Out in Beverly Hills 1986, Punchline 1988, Scenes from the Class Struggle in Beverly Hills 1989, Enemies: A Love Story 1989, Scenes from a Mall 1991, Man Trouble 1992, The Pickle 1993, Carlito's Way 1993, Love Affair 1994, Miami Rhapsody 1995, Faithful 1996, 2 Days in the Valley 1996, Touch 1997, Why Do Fools Fall in Love 1998, Antz (voice) 1998, Crazy in Alabama 1999, The Majestic (voice) 2001, Da wan 2001, Do It for Uncle Manny 2002, I Want Someone to Eat Cheese With 2006, Cattle Call 2006. *Television:* Winchell 1998, A Slight Case of Murder 1999, Once and Again (series) 1999–2002, The Sopranos (series) 2000–01, Coast to Coast 2004, Curb Your Enthusiasm (series) 2004. *Publications:* Show Me the Magic (autobiog.). *Address:* c/o Ken Kamins, 8942 Wilshire Boulevard, Beverly Hills, CA 92011, USA.

MAZZARELLA, David; American newspaper editor; *Editorial Director, Stars and Stripes;* b. 1938; with Assoc. Press, Lisbon, New York, Rome 1962–70; with Daily American, Rome 1971–75, Gannett News, Washington, DC 1976–77, The Bridgewater, Bridgewater, NJ 1977–83; Ed., Sr Vice-Pres. USA Today –1999; Ombudsman Stars and Stripes (newspaper for American military services) 2000–01, Ed. Dir 2001–. *Address:* Stars and Stripes, 529 14th Street NW, Suite 350, Washington, DC 20450, USA. *Telephone:* (202) 761-0900. *Fax:* (202) 761-089. *E-mail:* mazzarellad@stripes.osd.mil. *Website:* www.stripes.com.

MAZZONI DELLA STELLA, Vittorio; Italian banker; b. 21 May 1941, Siena; ed Univ. of Florence; joined Monte dei Paschi di Siena bank, Naples 1966, worked in Rome, then Siena brs, then in Market and Econ. Research Dept, apptd Man. 1976, mem. Bd of Dirs 1990, Deputy Chair. 1991–, Deputy Chair. Monte dei Paschi Banque, Paris 1991; mem. Bd of Dirs Sindibank, Barcelona 1991; Chair. ICLE (MPS banking group), Rome 1991; mem. Bd Dirs Centro Finanziaria SpA, Rome 1987–; mem. Bd Dirs and Exec. Cttee Deposit Protection Fund, Rome 1991–; mem. Bd Asscn of Italian Bankers (ABI) 1991–; elected Prov. Councillor, Siena 1980, Deputy Chair. Prov. Council 1980–82, Mayor 1983–90; Chair. Chigiana Foundation (music acad.), Siena 1991–. *Address:* Monte dei Paschi di Siena, Siena, Italy.

MBA-ABESSOLE, Paul, PhD, DTheol; Gabonese ecclesiastic and government official; *Deputy Prime Minister, Minister of Culture, the Arts, Educating the Population, Reconstruction Projects and Human Rights;* b. 9 Oct. 1939, Ngnung-Ako, Kango; ed Univ. de Paris, Inst. Catholique de Paris, France; teacher of French 1964–65; religious instructor 1965–73; curate 1973–76; political refugee in France 1983–89; typesetter 1984, 1986–87; returned to Gabon 1989; Founder and Leader Morena-bûcheron 1990, renamed Rassemblement nat. des bûcherons 1991, then Rassemblement pour le Gabon 2000; presidential cand. 1993, 1998; Mayor of Libreville 1996–; Pres. of World Conf. of Mayors 1999; apptd Minister of State for Human Rights and Missions 2002–03, currently Deputy Prime Minister, also Minister of Agric., Livestock and Rural Devt, in charge of Human Rights 2003–07, of State in the Office of Pres. 2007, of Reform, Human Rights, the Fight against Poverty and Illicit Enrichment 2007, currently of Culture, the Arts, Educating the Population, Reconstruction Projects and Human Rights. *Leisure interest:* reading. *Address:* c/o Office of the Prime Minister, PO Box 546, Libreville, Gabon (office). *Telephone:* 77-89-81 (office).

MBA NGUEMA, Gen. Antonio; Equatorial Guinean military officer; Minister of Nat. Defence 2004–. *Address:* Ministry of National Defence, Malabo, Equatorial Guinea. *Telephone:* (09) 27-94.

MBABAZI, Amama, LLB; Ugandan lawyer and politician; *Minister for Security;* b. 16 Jan. 1949, Mpiro, Kigezi; m. Jacquleine Susan Mbabazi; three s. three d.; ed Makerere Univ., Kampala and Law Devt. Centre; Advocate of Courts of Judicature, Uganda; worked as State Attorney in Attorney Gen.'s Chambers; Sec. Ugandan Law Council; Dir. Legal Services, Ugandan Nat. Liberation Army 1979; Pnr Kategaya Mbabazi & Tumwesigye Advocates, Kampala 1981; MP for Kinkizi West; fmr Minister of State for Regional Affairs, Ministry of Foreign Affairs; fmr Minister of State in charge of Political Affairs, Office of Pres.; Minister of State for Defence 1986–92, then Minister of Defence, currently Minister for Security 2007–; mem. Ugandan Law Soc. 1977–; elected. Del. to Constitute Ass. on Ugandan Constitution 1995; fmr head of bds of dirs of several state and pvt. cos; Nalubaale Medal of Honour. *Address:* Ministry of Security, Kampala, Uganda (office). *E-mail:* ambabazi@uganda.co.ug (office).

MBANEFO, Arthur Christopher Izuegbunam, FCA; Nigerian financial consultant and fmr diplomatist; b. 11 June 1930; m.; one s.; Minister for Commerce and Industries, Eastern Region of Nigeria (Repub. of Biafra) 1968–70; staff mem. Price Waterhouse & Co., London 1970–71; fmr Pnr, Akintola Williams & Co., Chartered Accountants; f. Arthur Mbanefo and Assocs (corp. and financial consulting co.) 1986; Pro-Chancellor and Chair. of Council, Univ. of Lagos 1984–86, Obafemi Awolowo Univ. 1986–90, Ahmadu Bello Univ. 1990–93; Perm. Rep. to UN, New York 1999–2003, Chair. G77 2000, Chair. Bd of Trustees UNITAR 2000–04; Dir Orient Petroleum Resources Ltd; Fellow, Inst of Chartered Accountants in England and Wales, Inst. of Chartered Accountants of Nigeria, Nigerian Inst. of Man. (mem. Council 1979–87); Pro-Chancellor and Chair. of Council Ahmadu Bello Univ. 1990–93, Obafemi Awolowo Univ. 1986–90, Univ. of Lagos 1984–86; f. Asscn of Accountancy Bodies of W Africa 1982, Pres. 1987; Hon. Yoruba Chieftaincy, Distinguished Order of Fed. Repub. of Nigeria 1981, Odu of Onitsha 1994, Commdr Order of the Niger 2002; several nat. and int. awards and medals, including from Govts of Italy and Brazil. *Address:* c/o Orient Petroleum

Resources Ltd, Lion House, Abuja Estate, Enugu-Onitsha Express Way, Awka, Nigeria.

M'BAREK, Sghair Ould; Mauritanian politician; b. 1954, Néma; m.; four c.; ed Univ. of Nouakchott; Minister of Nat. Educ. 1992–93, 1997–98, 2000, of Rural Devt and the Environment 1994–95, of Health and Social Affairs 1995, of Commerce and Tourism 1998–99, of Equipment and Transport 1999, of Justice 2001–03; Prime Minister of Mauritania 2003–07. *Address:* c/o Office of the Prime Minister, Nouakchott, Mauritania (office).

MBASOGO, Lt-Col Teodoro Obiang Nguema; Equatorial Guinean politician and army officer; *President and Supreme Commander of the Armed Forces;* ed in Spain; fmr Deputy Minister of Defence; overthrew fmr Pres. Macias Nguema in coup; Pres. of Equatorial Guinea 1979–; Supreme Commdr of the Armed Forces 1979–; Minister of Defence 1986. *Address:* Oficina del Presidente, Malabo, Equatorial Guinea.

M'BAYE, Kéba; Senegalese judge; b. 5 Aug. 1924, Kaolack; s. of Abdoul M'baye and Coura M'bengue; m. Mariette Diarra 1951; three s. five d.; ed Ecole Nat. de la France d'Outre-mer; Judge of Appeal, Supreme Court of Senegal, First Pres. 1964; fmr Chair. Int. Comm. of Jurists, Chair. Comm. on Codification of Law of Civil and Commercial Liabilities; Vice-Chair. Exec. Cttee, Int. Inst. of Human Rights (René Cassin Foundation); mem. Supreme Council of Magistrature, Int. Penal Law Asscn (and Admin. Council), Int. Criminology Asscn, Société de Législation comparée, Int. Olympic Cttee (mem. Exec. Bd); Judge, Int. Court of Justice, The Hague 1982–91 (Vice-Pres. 1987–91); fmr mem. various UN bodies, fmr mem. or Chair. Comm. on Human Rights and other such cttees and various symposia organized by Int. Asscn of Legal Sciences, Red Cross, Unidroit and UNESCO; fmr Pres. and mem. Int. Cttee on Comparative Law, Int. African Law Asscn, Int. Cttee for Social Science Documentation; Hon. Pres. World Fed. of UN Asscns. *Publications:* numerous publs on Senegalese law, the law of Black Africa and human rights. *Leisure interest:* golf. *Address:* Rue G, angle rue Léon Gontran Damas, BP 5865, Dakar, Senegal. *Telephone:* (221) 25-55-01.

MBEKI, Thabo Mvuyelwa, MA; South African politician and fmr head of state; b. 18 June 1942, Idutywa; s. of the late Govan Mbeki and of Epainette Mbeki; m. Zanele Dlamini 1974; ed Lovedale, Alice, St John's Umtata, Univs of London and Sussex; Leader African Students Org. 1961; Youth Organizer for African Nat. Congress (ANC), Johannesburg 1961–62; six weeks' detention, Byo 1962; left SA 1962; official, ANC offices, London, England 1967–70; mil. training, USSR 1970; Asst Sec. ANC Revolutionary Council 1971–72; Acting ANC Rep., Swaziland 1975–76; ANC Rep., Nigeria 1976–78, mem. ANC, Nat. Exec. Cttee 1975, re-elected 1985; Dir Information and Publicity, ANC 1984–89, Head of Dept of Int. Affairs 1989–93, Del. on Talks about Talks with SA Govt 1990, Chair. ANC 1993; First Deputy Pres. of South Africa 1994–99; Pres. ANC 1997–2007; Pres. of South Africa 1999–2008 (resgnd); mem. Bd IOC 1993; Pres. African Union 2002–03; Hon. KCMG, KStJ. *Address:* ANC, 54 Sauer Street 2001, Johannesburg 2001, South Africa (office). *Telephone:* (11) 3761000 (office). *Fax:* (11) 3761134 (office). *E-mail:* nmtyelwa@anc.org.za (office). *Website:* www.anc.org.za (office).

MBETE, Baleka; South African politician; b. 24 Sept. 1949, Durban; ed Inanda Seminary, Durban, Lovedale Teachers' Coll., King William's Town, E Cape; teacher Isibonelo High School, KwaMashu, Durban 1975; went into exile, teacher Matter Dolorosa High School, Mbabane, Swaziland 1976–77; joined African Nat. Congress (ANC) 1976, worked in ANC Dept of Information and Publicity (Radio Freedom) and Women's Section, Dar es Salaam, Tanzania 1977–81, Public Relations work for ANC, Nairobi, Kenya 1981–83, worked in ANC underground political structures, Gaborone, Botswana 1983–86, mem. ANC Regional Women's Cttee and Regional Political Cttee, Harare, Zimbabwe 1986–87, Admin. Sec., Exec. Cttee, Lusaka, Zambia 1987–90, Sec.-Gen. ANC Women's League 1991–93, mem. ANC Nat. Exec. Cttee 1991–, Chair. ANC Parl. Caucus 1995–, Nat. Chair. ANC 2007–; Deputy Speaker, Nat. Ass. 1996–2004, Speaker 2004–; Acting Deputy Pres. Sept. 2008–; mem. Presidential Panel, Truth and Reconciliation Comm. 1995–. *Address:* c/o African National Congress, 54 Sauer Street, Johannesburg 201, South Africa (office). *Telephone:* (11) 3761000 (office). *Fax:* (11) 3761134 (office). *E-mail:* nmtyelwa@anc.org.za (office). *Website:* www.anc.org.za (office).

M'BOW, Amadou-Mahtar, LèsL; Senegalese academic; b. 20 March 1921, Dakar; m. Raymonde Sylvain 1951; one s. two d.; ed Faculté des Lettres, Univ. de Paris; Prof., Coll. de Rosso, Mauritania 1951–53; Dir Service of Fundamental Educ. 1953–57; Minister of Educ. and Culture 1957–58; Prof. Lycée Faidherbe, St Louis 1958–64; Ecole Normale Supérieure, Dakar 1964–66; Minister of Educ. 1966–68; Minister of Culture, Youth and Sports 1968–70; Asst Dir-Gen. for Educ., UNESCO 1970–74; Dir-Gen. UNESCO 1974–87; Hon. Prof., Faculty of Humanities, Ind. Univ. of Santo Domingo (Dominican Repub.), Ecole Normale Supérieure, Dakar 1979, Nat. Independent Univ. of Mexico 1979, Escuela Superior de Administración y Dirección de Empresas, Barcelona 1984; mem. Acad. du Royaume du Maroc; Assoc. mem. Acad. of Athens; Grand Cross of the Order of the Liberator (Venezuela), Grand Cross of the Order of the Sun (Peru), Commdr and Grand Officier, Ordre National (Ivory Coast), Commdr des Palmes académiques (France), Officier, Ordre du Mérite (Senegal), Commdr de l'Ordre national de Haute Volta, Bintang Jasa Utama (Order of Merit, Indonesia), Kawkab Star (Jordan), Order of Merit (Syria) and numerous other decorations; 46 hon. doctorates, 35 decorations, freedom of 11 cities (1987) including Dr hc (Univ. of the Andes, State Univ. of Mongolia, State Univ. of Haiti, Khartoum, Sri Lanka, Tribhuvan Univ. Nepal, Pontifical Catholic Univ. of Peru, Buenos Aires, Granada, Sherbrooke, W Indies, Open Univ. UK, Belfast, Sofia, Nairobi, Philippines, Malaya, Venice, Uppsala, Moscow, Paris); Prix Terre des Hommes, Canada. *Publications:*

numerous monographs, articles in educational journals, textbooks, etc. *Address:* B.P. 5276, Dakar-Fann, Senegal; B.P. 434, Rabat, Morocco.

MBOWENI, Tito, MA; South African politician and banker; *Governor, South African Reserve Bank;* b. 16 March 1959, Tzaneem, Nothern Prov.; ed Nat. Univ. of Lesotho and Univ. of E Anglia; mem. ANC 1980 (ANC, Zambia 1988), fmr Deputy Head Dept of Econ. Planning, Co-ordinator for Trade and Industry; Minister of Labour, Govt of Nat. Unity 1994–99; Gov. SA Reserve Bank 1999–; Hon. Prof. of Econs (Univ. of S Africa) 2002–03; Hon. DComm (Univ. of Natal) 2001. *Leisure interests:* fly-fishing, soccer. *Address:* South African Reserve Bank, 370 Church Street, PO Box 427, Pretoria 0001, South Africa (office). *Telephone:* (12) 3133911 (office); (12) 3133526 (office). *Fax:* (12) 3134181 (office). *E-mail:* mpho.mtimkulu@resbank.co.za (office). *Website:* www.resbank.co.za (office).

MBUSA NYAMWISI, Antipas; Democratic Republic of the Congo politician; *Minister of Foreign Affairs and International Co-operation;* fought with Rally for Congolese Democracy (RCD) against Govt 1998–99; Founder and Chair. RCD-Kisangani Party (later Forces for Renewal Party) 1999–; Minister of Regional Co-ordination 2003–07, of Foreign Affairs and Int. Co-operation 2007–; unsuccessful cand. in 2006 presidential election. *Address:* Ministry of Foreign Affairs and International Co-operation, place de l'Indépendence, BP 7100, Kinshasa-Gombe, Democratic Republic of the Congo (office). *Telephone:* (12) 32450 (office).

MBYWANGI, Margarita; Paraguayan politician; *Minister for Indigenous Affairs;* b. 1962, Canindeyú; three c.; captured by settlers and sold into forced labour at age of four; Chief (cacique) of Aché Tribe 1992–; mem. Movimiento Popular Tekojojá (MPT); Minister for Indigenous Affairs 2008–. *Address:* c/o Movimiento Popular Tekojoja, Asunción, Paraguay (office). *E-mail:* joaquinbonett@gmail.com (office).

MDLALOSE, Frank Themba, BSc, UED, MB, CH.B.; South African politician and fmr diplomatist; b. 29 Nov. 1931, Nqutu Dist KwaZulu; s. of Jaconiah Zwelabo Mdlalose and Thabitha Mthembu; m. Eunice Nokuthula 1956; three s. two d.; ed Univ. of Fort Hare, Rhodes Univ. and Univ. of Natal; Intern, King Edward VII Hosp., Durban 1959; pvt. medical practice, Pretoria 1960–62, Steadville, Ladysmith, Natal, Atteridgeville 1962–70; medical practitioner, Madadeni 1970–78; Nat. Chair. Inkatha 1977; Minister of Health, KwaZulu 1983–90, Acting Minister of Educ. 1990, Minister without Portfolio 1991–94; Premier, KwaZulu-Natal 1994; Amb. to Egypt –2002 (retd); Hon. DrIur (Zululand) 1998. *Publication:* My Life (autobiog.) 2006. *Address:* PO Box 14110, Madadeni 2951, South Africa. *Telephone:* (34) 3291201.

MEACHER, Rt Hon. Michael Hugh, PC, MP; British politician; b. 4 Nov. 1939, Hemel Hempstead, Herts.; s. of late George H. and Doris M. (née Foxell) Meacher; m. 1st Molly C. (née Reid) 1962 (divorced 1985); two s. two d.; m. 2nd Lucianne Craven 1988; ed Berkhamsted School, New Coll., Oxford and London School of Econs; Lecturer in Social Admin., Univ. of York and LSE 1966–70; MP for Oldham West 1970–97, for Oldham West and Royton 1997–; Jr Minister, Dept of Industry 1974–75, Dept of Health and Social Security 1975–76, Dept of Trade 1976–79; mem. Nat. Exec. Cttee of Labour Party 1983–88, Shadow Cabinet 1983–97, Shadow Spokesman for Health and Social Security 1983–87, for Employment 1987–89, for Social Security 1989–92, for Overseas Devt 1992–93, for Citizens' Rights 1993–94, for Transport 1994–95, for Employment 1995–96, for Environmental Protection 1996–97; Minister of State for the Environment 1997–2003; mem. Treasury Select Cttee 1980–83; cand. for deputy leadership of Labour Party 1983; mem., parl. rep. for UNISON; mem. Child Poverty Action Group and other voluntary orgs. *Publications:* Taken for a Ride: Special Residential Homes for the Elderly Mentally Infirm: A Study of Separatism in Social Policy 1972, Socialism with a Human Face 1982, Diffusing Power 1992; over 1,000 articles on econ., industrial and social policy, regional devt, defence issues, the welfare state, media reform, civil service reform, the police, etc. *Leisure interests:* sport, music, reading. *Address:* House of Commons, Westminster, London, SW1A 0AA (office); 34 Kingscliffe Gardens, London, SW19 6NR, England (home). *Telephone:* (20) 7219-6461 (office). *Fax:* (20) 7219-5945 (office). *E-mail:* massonm@parliament.uk (office). *Website:* www.epolitix.com/webminster/michael-meacher (office).

MEAD, Carver Andress, MS, PhD; American computer scientist and academic; *Gordon and Betty Moore Professor of Engineering and Applied Science, Emeritus, California Institute of Technology;* b. 1 May 1934, Bakersfield, Calif.; ed Calif. Inst. of Tech.; began teaching at Calif. Inst. of Tech. 1957, est. Dept of Computer Science, currently Gordon and Betty Moore Emer. Prof. of Eng and Applied Science; pioneer of very-large-scale integrated (VSLI) circuit technology; developed first techniques for designing complex microchips, cr. gallium-arsenide (GaAs) transistor and first software compilation of a silicon chip; f. Actel Corpn, Silicon Compilers, Synaptics, Sonic Innovations, Foveon Inc., Silerity, Cascade Semiconductor Design; owns over 50 patents; Fellow American Physical Soc.; mem. Nat. Acad. of Eng; Hon. DSc (Univ. of Lund), D. Hon. (Univ. of Southern Calif.); Achievement Award, Electronics Magazine 1981, Harry Goode Memorial Award 1985, Phil Kaufman Award 1996, Lemelson-MIT Prize 1999, Computer Hisotyr Museum Fellow Award 2002, Nat. Medal of Tech. 2002. *Publications:* Introduction to VLSI Systems (co-author with Lynn Conway) 1980, Analog VLSI and Neural Systems 1989; over 100 articles in scientific journals. *Address:* California Institute of Technology, Computer Science Department, 1200 East California Boulevard, MC 256-80, Pasadena, CA 91125, USA (office). *Telephone:* (626) 395-2814 (office). *Website:* www.cs.caltech.edu (office).

MEAKINS, Ian; British business executive; *CEO, Alliance UniChem plc;* fmrly with Bain & Co., Procter and Gamble; founding pnr Kalchas Group; joined United Distillers 1991, several sr positions with Diageo including Pres.

European Major Markets and Global Supply; currently CEO Alliance UniChem plc, mem. Bd of Dirs. *Address:* Alliance UniChem plc, 2 The Heights, Brooklands, Weybridge, Surrey KT13 0NY, England (office). *Telephone:* (1932) 870-550 (office). *Fax:* (1932) 870-555 (office). *Website:* www .alliance-unichem.com (office).

MEARSHEIMER, John J., BS, MA, PhD; American academic; *R. Wendell Harrison Distinguished Service Professor of Political Science, University of Chicago;* ed Univ. of Southern Calif., Cornell Univ., West Point Mil. Acad.; served as officer in USAF 1970–75; Research Fellow, Brookings Institution 1979–80; Research Assoc., Center for Int. Affairs, Harvard Univ. 1980–82; Asst Prof., Political Science Dept, Univ. of Chicago 1982–84, Assoc. Prof. 1984–87, Prof. 1987–96, R. Wendell Harrison Distinguished Service Prof. 1996–, also Co-Dir Program on Int. Security Policy; Visiting Scholar, Olin Inst. for Strategic Studies, Harvard Univ. 1992–93; mem. American Acad. of Arts and Sciences, IISS, Chicago Council on Global Affairs, Council on Foreign Relations; mem. or fmr mem. editorial bds International Security, Security Studies, International History Review, JFQ: Joint Forces Quarterly, Journal of Transatlantic Studies, Asian Security, China Security; Clark Award for Distinguished Teaching, Cornell Univ., Quantrell Award for Distinguished Teaching, Univ. of Chicago 1985, George Kistiakowsky Scholar, American Acad. of Arts and Sciences 1986–87, Distinguished Scholar Award, Int. Studies Asscn 2004. *Publications:* Conventional Deterrence (Edgar S. Furniss, Jr Book Award) 1983, Nuclear Deterrence: Ethics and Strategy (jt ed.) 1985, Liddell Hart and the Weight of History 1988, The Tragedy of Great Power Politics (Joseph Lepgold Book Prize) 2001, The Israel Lobby and US Foreign Policy (with Stephen M. Walt) 2007; contribs to Perspectives on International Relations, London Review of Books, Middle East Policy, Foreign Policy, International Relations, New Republic, International Security, New York Times, Chicago Tribune and numerous chapters in books. *Address:* Political Science Department, University of Chicago, 5828 South University Avenue, Chicago, IL 60637, USA (office). *Telephone:* (773) 702-8667 (office). *Fax:* (773) 702-1689 (office). *E-mail:* j-mearsheimer@uchicago.edu (office). *Website:* www .uchicago.edu (office).

MÉBIAME, Léon; Gabonese politician; b. 1 Sept. 1934, Libreville; ed Coll. Moderne, Libreville, Centre de Préparation aux Carrières Administratives, Brazzaville, Ecole Fédérale de Police, Ecole Nat. de Police, Lyon, France; posted to Chad 1957–59; Police Supt 1960; further studies at Sûreté Nat. Française, Paris; Deputy Dir Sûreté Nat., Gabon 1962–63, Dir 1963–67; successively Under-Sec. of State for the Interior, Minister Del. for the Interior and Minister of State in charge of Labour, Social Affairs and the Nat. Org. of Gabonese Women 1967; Vice-Pres. of the Govt, Keeper of the Seals and Minister of Justice Jan.–July 1968; Vice-Pres. of the Govt in charge of Co-ordination 1968–75, Pres. Nat. Consultative Council 1972; Prime Minister 1975–90; Minister of Co-ordination, Housing and Town Planning 1975–76, of Land Registry 1976–78, of Co-ordination, Agric., Rural Devt, Waters and Forests 1978–79, in Charge of State Corpns 1980–82, for Merchant Marine and Civil Service 1982–83, of Transport and Civil and Commercial Aviation 1989–90; Presidential Cand. Dec. 1993; Commdr Etoile Equatoriale; Grand Officier, Order nat. de Côte d'Ivoire, du Mérite Centrafricain; Chevalier, Etoile Noire du Bénin. *Address:* c/o Office du Premier Ministre, B.P. 546, Libreville, Gabon.

MEBOUTOU, Michel Meva'a; Cameroonian politician; b. Prov. du Sud. Francophone; Minister of Finance and the Budget –2004; mem. Bd of Govs IMF; mem. Bulu tribe. *Address:* c/o Ministry of Finance and the Budget, Quartier Administratif, Yaoundé, Cameroon (office).

MECHANIC, David, MA, PhD; American sociologist and academic; *University Professor and Rene Dubos Professor of Behavioral Sciences and Director, Institute for Health, Health Care Policy and Aging Research, Rutgers University;* b. 21 Feb. 1936, New York; s. of Louis Mechanic and Tillie Mechanic (née Penn); m. Kate Mechanic; two s.; ed City Coll. of New York and Stanford Univ.; mem. Faculty, Univ. of Wisconsin 1960–79, Prof. of Sociology 1965–73, John Bascom Prof. 1973–79, Dir Center for Medical Sociology and Health Services Research 1971–79, Chair. Dept of Sociology 1968–70; Prof. of Social Work and Sociology, Rutgers Univ. 1979–, Univ. Prof. and Dean Faculty of Arts and Sciences 1981–84, Univ. Prof. and Rene Dubos Prof. of Behavioral Sciences 1984–, Dir Inst. for Health, Health Care Policy and Aging Research 1985–; mem. various advisory panels etc.; mem. NAS; mem. Inst. of Medicine of NAS, American Acad. of Arts and Sciences; Guggenheim Fellowship 1977–78; numerous awards. *Publications:* author of 12 books and about 400 papers and chapters and ed. of 11 books on sociological and health care subjects. *Address:* Institute for Health, Health Care Policy and Aging Research, Rutgers University, 30 College Avenue, New Brunswick, NJ 08901, USA (office). *Telephone:* (732) 932-8415 (office). *Fax:* (732) 932-1253 (office). *E-mail:* mechanic@rci.rutgers.edu (office). *Website:* www.ihhcpar .rutgers.edu (office).

MECHANIC, William M. (Bill), PhD; American film industry executive; b. Detroit, Mich.; ed Michigan State Univ., Univ. of Southern California; Dir of Programming SelecTV 1978–80, Vice-Pres. Programming 1980–82; Vice-Pres. Pay TV, Paramount Pictures Corpn 1982–84; Vice-Pres. Pay TV Sales, Walt Disney Pictures and TV 1984–85, Sr Vice-Pres. Video 1985–87, Pres. Int. Theatrical Distribution and Worldwide Video 1987–93; Pres. and COO 20th Century Fox Film Entertainment 1993–96, Chair. and CEO 1996–2000; f. Pandemonium LLC (ind. production co.) 2000; mem. Bd of Councilors, School of Cinema Arts, Univ. of Southern Calif.; mem. Bd of Govs Acad. of Motion Picture Arts and Sciences (Execs Br) 2002–05. *Films include:* Dark Water (producer) 2005, The New World (exec. producer) 2005. *Address:* Pandemon-ium LLC, 100 North Crescent Drive, Suite 125, Beverly Hills, CA 90210-5449, USA.

MEČIAR, Vladimír, DrIur; Slovak politician; *Chairman, People's Party— Movement for a Democratic Slovakia;* b. 26 July 1942, Zvolen; s. of Jozef Mečiar and Anna (née Tomková) Mečiarová; m. Margita Mečiarová (née Bencková); two s. two d.; ed Komenský Univ., Bratislava; clerk 1959–69; various posts in Czechoslovak Union of Youth 1967–68; expelled from all posts and CP; employed as manual worker because of his attitude to Soviet occupation of Czechoslovakia, Heavy Eng Works, Dubnica nad Váhom 1970–73; clerk, later commercial lawyer for Skloobal Nemšová 1973–90; politically active again after collapse of communist system 1989; Minister of Interior and Environment, Govt of Slovak (Fed.) Repub. 1990, Deputy to House of Nations, Fed. Ass. 1990–92; Chair. People's Party— Movt for a Democratic Slovakia (LS-HZDS) 1991–; Prime Minister of Slovakia 1990–91, 1992, 1994–98; Opposition mem. Parl. 2002–; presidential cand. 2004 elections; Order of Maltese Cross 1995; Dr hc (Lomonosov Univ., Moscow) 1995, (Braća Karić Univ., Yugoslavia) 1996; Peutinger Award (Germany) 1995. *Publications:* Slovakia, Be Self-Confident!, Slovak Taboo. *Leisure interests:* sport, music, literature, hiking. *Address:* People's Party—Movement for a Democratic Slovakia (Ludová strana—Hnutie za Demokratické Slovensko), 830 00 Bratislava, Tomášikova 32A, POB 49, Slovakia (office). *Telephone:* (2) 4822-0203 (office). *Fax:* (2) 4822-0223 (office). *E-mail:* predseda@hzds.sk (office). *Website:* www.hzds.sk (office).

MECKSEPER, Friedrich; German painter and printmaker; b. 8 June 1936, Bremen; s. of Gustav Meckseper and Lily Ringel-Debatin; m. Barbara Müller 1962; one s. two d.; ed State Art Acad., Stuttgart, State Univ. for the Visual Arts, Berlin; apprentice mechanic, Robert Bosch GmbH, Stuttgart 1952–55; more than 100 solo and group exhbns of his prints, collages and paintings in Europe, USA, Australia and Japan; represented in many major museums of contemporary art and at print biennials world-wide; Prof. of Art, Int. Summer Acad., Salzburg 1977–79; Guest Lecturer, London 1968; German-Rome Prize 1963, Prize of the 7th Biennale, Tokyo 1970, of the 6th Biennale, Fredrikstad 1982, of the 1st Kochi Int. Print Triennial, Japan 1990. *Publications:* Friedrich Meckseper, Etchings 1956–1994; catalogue raisonné of the graphic work 1994. *Leisure interests:* locomotives, steamboats, ballooning, paintings, etchings, books. *Address:* Landhausstrasse 13, 10717 Berlin, Germany.

MEDAK, Peter; British film director; b. 23 Dec. 1940, Budapest, Hungary; m. Julia Migenes 1989; two s. four d.; worked with AB-Pathe, London 1956–63; Dir Universal Pictures 1963–, Paramount Pictures 1967–; has directed several operas, plays and series for US TV; Evening Standard Award for Best Dir: The Krays 1990. *Films directed include:* Negatives 1968, A Day in the Death of Joe Egg 1970, The Ruling Class 1973, Third Girl From the Left 1973, Ghost in the Noonday Sun 1975, The Odd Job 1978, The Changeling 1979, Zorro, Zorro, The Gay Blade 1981, Breaking Through 1984, The Men's Club, The Krays 1990, La Voix Humaine 1991, Let Him Have It 1991, Romeo is Bleeding 1994, Pontiac Moon 1994, Hunchback of Notre Dame 1996, Species 2 1997, David Copperfield 1998, Feast of All Saints 2000. *Address:* c/o William Morris Agency, Beverly Hills, California (office); Armstrong and Hirsch (Attorneys), 1885 Century Park East, Suite 1888, Century City, CA 90067 (office); c/o Duncan Health (agent), ICM UK, London W1, England; Scott J. Feinstein, 16255 Ventura Boulevard, Suite 625, Encino, CA 91436, USA. *Telephone:* (323) 650-9770 (office); (213) 448-6769. *Fax:* (323) 650-5867 (office). *E-mail:* petermedak@mac.com (office).

MEDELCI, Mourad, LèsSc, DèsSc; Algerian government official; *Minister of Foreign Affairs;* b. 30 April 1943, Tlemcen; m.; five c.; ed Univ. of Algiers; began career working in Algerian energy industry 1970–80; Sec.-Gen., Ministry of Commerce 1980–88; Minister of Trade 1988–89, 1999–2001, of Finance 2001–02, 2005–07, of Foreign Affairs 2007–; Minister Delegate of the Budget 1990–91; Adviser to Pres. of Algeria 2002–05; Gov. for Algeria, Islamic Devt Bank; Vice-Pres. Emir Abdelkader Foundation 1996; founding mem. Asscn for Int. Relations 1997; Founder and Pres. Asscn for Promotion of Eco-effectiveness and Quality in Enterprises (APEQUE) 1998; mem. African Peer Review (APR) Panel of Eminent Persons 2004. *Address:* Ministry of Foreign Affairs, place Mohamed Seddik Benyahia, el-Mouradia, Algiers, Algeria (office). *Telephone:* (21) 69-23-33 (office). *Fax:* (21) 69-21-61 (office). *Website:* www.mae.dz (office).

MEDGYESSY, Péter, PhD; Hungarian politician, economist and diplomatist; b. 19 Oct. 1942, Budapest; m. 2nd Katalin Csaplár; one s. one d. (from previous marriage); ed Budapest Univ. of Econs (then Karl Marx Univ.); held several positions in Ministry of Finance, Dept of Finance, Dept of Prices, Dept of Int. Finances; fmr Dir-Gen. Dept of State Budget; Deputy Minister of Finance 1982–87; Minister of Finance 1987–88; Deputy Prime Minister in interim Govt of Miklós Németh (q.v.) 1988–89; Pres., Chief Exec. Magyar Paribas 1990–94; Pres. and CEO Hungarian Bank for Investment and Devt Ltd 1994–96; Minister of Finance 1996–98; Chair. Bd Dirs Inter-Europa Bank 1998–2001; Vice-Pres. Atlasz Insurance Co. 1998–2001; Prime Minister of Hungary 2002–04 (resgnd), Man. Prime Minister Aug.–Sept. 2004; Amb. at Large 2004–; Prof., Coll. of Finance and Accounting, Budapest; Pres. Hungarian Econ. Soc.; Dir Int. Inst. of Public Finance, Saarbrücken; mem. Presidium Hungarian Bank Asscn 1996–, Council of World Econ. Forum; Commdr's Cross with Star, Order of Merit of Hungarian Repub. 1998, Chevalier de la Légion d'honneur 2000, Officer's Cross 2004, Order of Crown of Belgium 2002, Order of the Rising Sun – Gold and Silver Star (Japan) 2002, Grand Cross, Order of Merit (Chile) 2003, Grand Cross, Order of Merit (Norway) 2003, Grand Cross, Order of Merit (Germany) 2004; Medal of Irish Hungarian Econ. Asscn 2005. *Publications:* several articles on budgetary and exchange rate policies and monetary system in financial and econ. publs. *Leisure interests:* nature, music. *Address:* c/o Office of the Prime Minister, Kossuth Lajos tér 1–3, 1055 Budapest. *Telephone:* (1) 441-4000. *Fax:* (1) 441-

4543. *E-mail:* medgyessyp@meh.hu (office). *Website:* www.medgyessy.hu (office).

MEDINA, Danilo; Dominican Republic politician; *Secretary of State to the Presidency;* b. Arroyo Cano, San Juan de la Maguana; s. of Juan Pablo Medina and Amelia Sánchez; m. Cándida Montilla; three d.; ed Universidad Autónoma de Santo Domingo (UASD), INTEC; f. San Juan de la Maguana br., Frente Revolucionario Estudiantil Nacionalista, UASD; joined Partido de la Liberación Dominicana 1973, mem. Cen. Cttee 1983–; elected Deputy, Nat. Congress 1986, Pres. Chamber of Deputies 1990–94; Sec. of State to the Presidency 1996–; Presidential Cand. 2000. *Address:* Administrative Secretariat of the Presidency, Palacio Nacional, Avda México, esq. Dr Delgado, Santo Domingo, Dominican Republic (office). *Telephone:* 686-4771 (office). *Fax:* 688-2100 (office). *E-mail:* prensa@presidencia.gov.do (office). *Website:* www.presidencia.gov.do (office).

MEDINA ESTÉVEZ, HE Cardinal Jorge Arturo, DTheol, DCL; Chilean ecclesiastic; *Prefect Emeritus of Divine Worship and the Discipline of the Sacraments;* b. 23 Dec. 1926, Santiago de Chile; ed Major Seminary of Santiago; ordained priest 1954; mem. Major Seminary of Santiago, Theological Faculty of Santiago; attended Second Vatican Council early 1960s; Auxiliary Bishop of Rancagua and Titular Bishop of Tibili 1984–87, consecrated 1985, Bishop of Rancagua 1987–93, of Valparaíso 1993–96; Pro-Prefect Congregation for Divine Worship and the Discipline of the Sacraments 1996–98, Prefect 1998–2002, Prefect Emer. 2002–; cr. Cardinal-Deacon of S. Saba 1998, currently Sr Cardinal Deacon; participated in Papal Conclave 2005, as Cardinal Proto-Deacon, announced to the world the election of Pope Benedict XVI. *Address:* c/o Congregation for Divine Worship and the Discipline of the Sacraments, Piazza Pio XII 10, 00193 Rome, Italy. *Telephone:* (06) 69884316.

MEDINA-MORA ICAZA, Eduardo, LLB; Mexican politician; *Procurator-General;* b. 30 Jan. 1957, México; ed Nat. Univ. of Mexico; fmr Asst Dir Desc, Corp. Strategic Planning Dir; fmr Coordinator of Advisers to Under-Secr. of Fisheries; fmr Head of Dept of Promotion and Market Research, Conasupo; fmr adviser to NAFTA Negotiating Team for Agric., Norms, Unfair Trading Practices, Investment and Rules of Origin; fmr legal adviser to Nat. Agric. and Fisheries Bd; fmr nat. adviser to Business Co-ordination Bd; fmr Dir Tech. Secr. Alliance for the Mexico-US Border; Gen. Dir Center for Research and Nat. Security (CISEN) 2000–05; Sec. of Public Security 2005–06; Procurator Gen. 2006–; mem. and Tech. Sec., Nat. Security Cabinet; mem. Nat. Security Council; mem. Mexican Coll. of Lawyers, ABA. *Address:* Office of the Procurator-General, Avda Paseo de la Reforma 211–213, Col. Cuauhtémoc, Del. Cuauhtémoc, 06500 México DF, Mexico (office). *Telephone:* (55) 5346-0114 (office). *Fax:* (55) 5346-0908 (office). *E-mail:* ofproc@pgr.gob.mx (office). *Website:* www.pgr.gob.mx (office).

MEDINA-QUIROGA, Cecilia, Licenciada en Ciencias Jurídicas y Sociale, DIur; Chilean jurist and academic; *President, Inter-American Court of Human Rights (Corte Interamericana de Derechos Humanos);* b. 1935, Concepción; ed Univ. of Chile, Santiago, Univ. of Utrecht, Netherlands; Prof. of Int. Law of Human Rights, Faculty of Law, Univ. of Chile, Founder and Co-Dir Human Rights Centre; Visiting Prof., Harvard Law School, USA; has also taught at Lund Univ., Int. Inst. of Human Rights, Univ. of Toronto, UN Univ. for Peace, Univ. of Utrecht and in Sweden; mem. UN Human Rights Cttee 1995–2002, Chair. 1999–2000, author of General Comment 28 on the rights of men and women as set out in Article 3 of the Int. Covenant on Civil and Political Rights; Judge, Inter-American Court of Human Rights (Corte Interamericana de Derechos Humanos) 2004–, Vice-Pres. 2007–08, Pres. 2008–; mem. Int. Comm. of Jurists 2004–; selected by UN Human Rights Council for group of ind. experts assigned to investigate Nov. 2006 Beit Hanoun incident Dec. 2006; Gruber Prize for Women's Rights, Peter Gruber Foundation Int. Awards 2006. *Publications:* Nomenclature and Hierarchy: Basic Latin American Sources (co-author) 1979, Chile: La Nueva Constitución, Democracia y Derechos Humanos, Cuadernos ESIN, No. 18 1981, The Battle of Human Rights: Gross, Systematic Violations and the Inter-American System 1988, Derecho Internacional de los Derechos Humanos. Manual de Enseñanza (ed.) 1990, SIM Special No. 13, Training Course on International Human Rights Law: Selected Lectures, Peace Palace, The Hague, 16 Sept.–4 Oct. 1991 (ed.) 1992, Special Issue on The Americas, NQHR, Vol. 10, No. 2 (ed.) 1992, Constitución, Tratados y Derechos Esenciales Introducción y Selección de textos, Corporación Nacional de Reparación y Reconciliación 1994, Sistema Jurídico y Derechos Humanos. El derecho nacional y las obligaciones internacionales de Chile en materia de Derechos Humanos (co-ed.) 1996; numerous book chapters and articles in professional journals. *Address:* Corte Interamericana de Derechos Humanos, Apdo Postal 6906-1000, San José, Costa Rica (office). *Telephone:* (506) 234-0581 (office). *Fax:* (506) 234-0584 (office). *E-mail:* corteidh@corteidh.or.cr (office). *Website:* www.corteidh.or.cr (office).

MEDIU, Fatmir; Albanian politician; b. 21 Jan. 1967, Durrës; m. Xhuljeta Mediu; two c.; ed Faculty of Geology and Mines, Tirana Univ.; engineer Albpetrol Enterprise, Fier 1990–91; joined Republican Party 1990, Chair. Fier Dist Br. 1991–92, Deputy Chair. Albanian Republican Party 1992–97, Chair. 1997–; elected mem. Parl. 2001, Chair. Republican Parl. Group 2001–05, Chair. Parl. Comm. on Stability Pact and European Integration 2001–05, mem. Comm. for Legislation and Foreign Affairs 2001–05, mem. Del. to European Parl. 2001–05; Minister of Defence 2005–08 (resgnd); Pres. Building Democracy Foundation, Tirana 1998; mem. Int. Foundation, Washington DC, USA 1999, Exec. Cttee East–West Parliamentarian Practice, Amsterdam, Netherlands 2001, Parliamentarians for Global Action, New York 2002. *Address:* c/o Ministry of Defence, Bulevardi Dëshmoret e Kombit, PO Box 203/1, Tirana, Albania (office).

MEDOJEVIĆ, Nebojša; Montenegrin politician; *President, Movement for Changes (Pokret za Promjene—PZP);* b. 13 June 1966, Pljevlja; m.; one s. one d.; ed Faculty of Electrical Eng., Univ. of Montenegro; Founder and Pres. Students Forum-Movt for Peace 1989; Founder Montenegrin Movt against Facism 1992; Co-founder Social-Democratic Party 1989, mem. of Presidency 1992–99; worked as Privatisation Man, Agency for Econ. Restructuring and Foreign Investments 1991–99; Leader Centre for Transition, Podgorica 1999–2002; Exec. Dir Group for Change 2002–06; Pres. and Leader, Movt for Changes (Pokret za Promjene—PZP); mem. Parl. 2006–; cand. for Pres. of Montenegro 2008. *Publications include:* Montenegrin Economy in Transition, Mass Voucher Privatisation, Public Procurements, Privatisation and Corruption, Conflict of Interests; has published more than 100 articles on problems of post-Communism transition. *Address:* Movement for Changes (Pokret za Promjene—PZP), 81000 Podgorica, bul. Ivana Crnojevica 107/1, Montenegro (office). *Telephone:* (81) 667010 (office). *E-mail:* gzpkotor@cg.yu (office); nm@nebojsamedojevic.org. *Website:* www.promjene.org (office); www.nebojsamedojevic.com.

MEDVEDCHUK, Viktor, DIur; Ukrainian politician and lawyer; *Chairman, Social Democratic Party of Ukraine (United);* b. 7 Aug. 1954, Pochet Village, Aban Rayon, Krasnoyarsk Territory (Russia); m.; two d.; ed Nat. Taras Shevchenko Univ. of Kiev; lawyer, Kiev City Bar Asscn 1978–89; Head, Legal Advice Office, Shevchenko Dist, Kiev 1989–91; Pres. Union of Lawyers of Ukraine; fmr Head of the Supreme Board of Experts of the Ukrainian Bar; Pres. Int. Law Co. B.I.M. 1991–; mem. Social Democratic Party of Ukraine (SDPU) (later Social Democratic Party of Ukraine (United)—SDPU(U)) 1994–, SDPU(U) Cen. Council 1995–98, Head, SDPU Comm. on Legal Reform 1995–96, mem. SDPU(U) Politburo 1995–, Deputy Chair. SDPU(U) 1996–98, Chair. 1998–, mem. SDPU(U) Parl. faction 2001–; Adviser to Pres. of Ukraine on Tax Policy Issues 1996–2000; Nat. Deputy of Ukraine to 2nd Verkhovna Rada 1997, mem. Cttee on Law and Order 1997–98, Coordinating Council on Legal Reforms affiliated to Pres. of Ukraine 1997–2000, Supreme Econ. Council affiliated to Pres. of Ukraine, State Comm. on Admin. Reforms in Ukraine, Nat. Deputy to 3rd Verkhovna Rada 1998, Deputy Chair. Verkhovna Rada 1998–2000, mem. Supreme Legal Council, Coordinating Council on Local Self-Govt, Deputy Chair. Coordinating Council on Internal Affairs, First Deputy Chair. Verkhovna Rada of Ukraine 2000–01, Nat. Deputy to 4th Verkhovna Rada, Head, SDPU(U) Parl. faction May–June 2002; Head, Admin of Pres. of Ukraine 2002–04; Head, Nat. Council on Youth Policies affiliated to Pres. of Ukraine 1999–; Head, Comm. on State Awards and Heraldry 2002–, Organizing Cttee on Conduct of the Year of Ukraine in the Russian Fed. 2002–03, Working Group for putting forward suggestions on ensuring publicity and openness in work of public authorities 2002–; Chair. Comm. for guaranteeing smooth work of int. experts checking export of Kolchuga reconnaissance radio-electronic stations 2002–, Ukraina Nat. Palace Supervisory Bd 2002–, Organizing Cttee for carrying out the Year of the Russian Fed. in Ukraine 2002–, Public Service Coordinating Cttee under Pres. of Ukraine 2003–, Organizing Cttee for commemorating the Eastern (Crimean) War of 1853–1856 2003–, Coordinating Comm. for the reconstruction of the Zhashkiv-Chervonoznamyanka section of the Kiev-Odesa motorway 2003–, Organizing Cttee for celebrating the 150th anniversary of Ivan Franko's birthday 2003–, Supervisory Bd of Nat. Acad. of Public Admin under Pres. of Ukraine 2004–; Deputy Chair. Information Policy Council under Pres. of Ukraine 2002–; Co-Chair. Coordinating Cttee for charting and publishing the Nat. Atlas of Ukraine 2002–; mem. Bd USSR Union of Lawyers from Ukraine 1990–91, Coordinating Cttee on Struggle against Corruption and Organised Crime affiliated to Pres. of Ukraine 1994–99, Council of Employers and Producers affiliated to Pres. of Ukraine 1995–2000, Nat. Council for Security and Defence of Ukraine 2002–; mem. Ukrainian Acad. of Law, Int. Slavic Acad., Acad. of Econs; Honoured Lawyer of Ukraine 1992; Hon. Award of Ukrainian Pres. – Order 'For Merit' (3rd Class) 1996, (2nd Class) 1998, Order 'For Merit' 2000, Hon. Award of Ukrainian Pres. – Order of Prince Yaroslav the Wise (5th Class) 2004, Slovak Order of the White Cross (2nd Class) 2004. *Address:* Social Democratic Party of Ukraine (United), vul. Ivan-Franko 18, 01030 Kiev, Ukraine (office). *Telephone:* (44) 536-15-71 (office). *Fax:* (44) 536-15-78 (office). *E-mail:* sdpuo@sdpuo.com (office); international@sdpuo.com (office). *Website:* www.sdpuo.com (office); www.medvedchuk.org.ua (home).

MEDVEDEV, Armen Nikolayevich, Cand. of Arts; Russian film critic, film producer, journalist and civil servant; b. 28 May 1938, Moscow; m.; one d.; ed All-Union Inst. of Cinematography; mem. staff, Bureau of Propaganda of Soviet Cinema, USSR (now Russian) State Cttee on Cinematography 1959–, mem. Bd Dirs 1984–87, First Deputy Chair. 1987–89, Chair. 1992–99; Prof., All-Union Inst. of Cinematography; Ed.-in-Chief Soviet Film (magazine) 1966–72; Deputy Ed.-in-Chief Iskusstvo Kino (magazine) 1972–75, 1976–82, Ed.-in-Chief 1982–84; Ed.-in-Chief All-Union Co. Soyuzinformkino 1975–76; Head Dept of Culture and Public Educ., USSR Council of Ministers 1989–91; fmr consultant Govt of USSR 1991; Pres. Rolan Bykov Int. Fund of Devt of Cinema and TV for Children and Youth 1999–; Pres. 18th Int. Film Festival for Children and Young People 2001; Chair. Jury, Open Russian Film Festival, Sochi 2004; mem. Jury, XXVIth Moscow Int. Film Festival 2004; Hon. Worker of Arts; several decorations, including Order for Service to Motherland; numerous awards. *Films produced:* Velikiy polkovodets Georgiy Zhukov 1995, Khrustalyov, mashinu! Khrustalyov, My Car!) 1998. *Television role:* Krasnaya ploschad (Red Square) (mini-series) 2004. *Publications:* several books on cinema; articles and essays. *Address:* Koshtoyanz str. 6, Apt 225, 117454 Moscow, Russia. *Telephone:* (495) 133-12-19.

MEDVEDEV, Dmitrii Anatolyevich, PhD; Russian business executive, government official and head of state; *President;* b. 14 Sept. 1965, Leningrad (now St Petersburg); s. of Prof. Anatoly Afanasevich Medvedev and Yulia Veniaminovna Medvedeva (née Shaposhnikova); m. Svetlana Vladimirovna

Linnik 1982; one s.; ed Leningrad State Univ.; Asst Prof., Leningrad State Univ. 1990–99; Adviser to Chair. Leningrad City Council and Expert Consultant, Cttee for External Relations, St Petersburg Mayor's Office 1990–95, mem. Exec. Cttee on Int. Relations 1991–95; Deputy Chief of Staff, Govt of Russian Fed. 1999–2000; Deputy Head, then First Deputy Head of the Presidential Admin 2000–03, Head 2003–05; First Deputy Prime Minister 2005–08; Pres. of Russia 2008–; mem. Bd of Dirs OAO Gazprom 2000–08, Chair. 2000–01, 2002–08, Deputy Chair. 2001–02; Order in the Name of Russia 2004. *Leisure interests:* British hard rock, including Deep Purple, Black Sabbath, Pink Floyd and Led Zeppelin, swimming, jogging, chess, yoga, reading the works of Mikhail Bulgakov and the Harry Potter books of J. K. Rowling, football (follows FC Zenit St Petersburg). *Address:* Office of the President, 103132 Moscow, Staraya pl. 4 (office). *Telephone:* (495) 925-35-81 (office). *Fax:* (495) 206-07-66 (office). *E-mail:* president@gov.ru (office). *Website:* www.kremlin.ru (office).

MEDVEDEV, Nikolai Pavlovich; Russian politician; b. 26 Nov. 1952, Anayevo, Mordovia; m.; one s. one d.; ed Mordovian State Pedagogical Inst., Higher Comsomol School, Cen. Comsomol Cttee; with Saransk Professional Tech. School; worked in Comsomol orgs 1975–83; instructor, Saransk City CP Cttee, Sec. CP Cttee Saransk Machine-construction Factory 1983–90; Deputy Chair. Saransk City Soviet 1990–; RSFSR Peoples' Deputy; mem. Presidium, Supreme Soviet; mem. Comm. on Int. Relations at Soviet of Nationalities 1990–93; Head of Dept, Admin. of Russian Presidency 1993–94; Dir Inst. of Regional Policy 1995–97; Deputy Minister on Co-operation with CIS countries 1994–95; mem. State Duma (Yabloko group) 1996–99; Dir Moscow Inst. of Regional Policy 2000–. *Publications:* several books including Establishment of Federalism in Russia, National Policy in Russia: From Unitarism to Federalism, International Conflicts and Political Stability. *Address:* Moscow Institute of Regional Policy, Moscow, Russia.

MEDVEDEV, Nikolai Yakovlevich, DrSc; Russian energy industry executive; *Chief Geologist and Deputy Director-General, OJSC Surgutneftegas;* b. 1943; Chief Geologist Neftyanaya Kompaniya Surgutneftegas 2000–03, Chief Geologist and Deputy Dir-Gen. OJSC Surgutneftegas 2000–, Chair. March–May 2006. *Address:* OJSC Surgutneftegas, 1 Kukuevitskogo Street, Surgut 628400, Tyumen, Russia (office). *Telephone:* (3462) 42-61-33 (office). *Fax:* (3462) 33-32-35 (office). *Website:* www.surgutneftegas.ru (office).

MEDVEDEV, Roy Aleksandrovich, PhD; Russian historian and sociologist; b. 14 Nov. 1925, Tbilisi; s. of Aleksandr Romanovich Medvedev and Yulia Medvedeva; twin brother of Zhores Medvedev (q.v.); m. Galina A. Gaidina 1956; one s.; ed Leningrad State Univ., Acad. of Pedagogical Sciences of USSR; mem. CPSU –1969, 1989–91; worker at mil. factory 1943–46; teacher of history, Ural Secondary School 1951–53; Dir of Secondary School in Leningrad region 1954–56; Deputy to Ed.-in-Chief of Publishing House of Pedagogical Literature, Moscow 1957–59; Head of Dept, Research Inst. of Vocational Educ., Acad. of Pedagogical Sciences of USSR 1960–70, Senior Scientist 1970–71; freelance author 1972–; People's Deputy of USSR, mem. Supreme Soviet of USSR 1989–91; mem. Cen. Cttee CPSU 1990–91; Co-Chair. Socialist Party of Labour 1991–2003. *Publications:* Vocational Education in Secondary School 1960, Faut-il réhabiliter Staline? 1969, A Question of Madness (with Zhores Medvedev) 1971, Let History Judge 1972, On Socialist Democracy 1975, Qui a écrit le 'Don Paisible'? 1975, La Révolution d'octobre était-elle inéluctable? 1975, Solschenizyn und die Sowjetische Linke 1976, Khrushchev–The Years in Power (with Zhores Medvedev) 1976, Political Essays 1976, Problems in the Literary Biography of Mikhail Sholokhov 1977, Samizdat Register 1978, Philip Mironov and the Russian Civil War (with S. Starikov) 1978, The October Revolution 1979, On Stalin and Stalinism 1979, On Soviet Dissent 1980, Nikolai Bukharin–The Last Years 1980, Leninism and Western Socialism 1981, An End to Silence 1982, Khrushchev 1983, All Stalin's Men 1984, China and Superpowers 1986, L'URSS che cambia (with G. Chiesa) 1987, Time of Change (with G. Chiesa) 1990, Brezhnev: A Political Biography 1991, Gensek s Lybianki: A Political Portrait of Andropov 1993, 1917. The Russian Revolution 1997, Capitalism in Russia? 1998, The Unknown Andropov 1998, Post-Soviet Russia 2000, The Unknown Stalin (with Zhores Medvedev) 2001, Putin 2004, Solzhenitsyn and Sakharov (with Zhores Medvedev) 2004, Moscow Model of Yuri Luzhkov 2005, Putin 2007, Divided Ukraine 2007; and over 400 professional and general articles. *Leisure interest:* allotment gardening. *Address:* c/o Z. A. Medvedev, 4 Osborn Gardens, London, NW7 1DY, England; Abonnement Post Box 258, 125475 Moscow A-475; Dybenko str 2 apt 20, 125475 Moscow A-475, Russia (home). *Telephone:* (495) 597-61-20 (home).

MEDVEDEV, Zhores Aleksandrovich, PhD; British/Russian biologist; b. 14 Nov. 1925, Tbilisi; s. of Aleksandr Romanovich Medvedev and Yulia Medvedeva; twin brother of Roy Medvedev (q.v.); m. Margarita Nikolayevna Buzina 1951; two s.; ed Timiriazev Acad. of Agricultural Sciences, Moscow, Inst. of Plant Physiology, USSR Acad. of Sciences; joined Soviet Army 1943, served at front as a pvt.; Scientist, later Sr Scientist, Dept of Agrochemistry and Biochemistry, Timiriazev Acad. 1951–62; Head of Lab., Molecular Radiobiology, Inst. of Medical Radiology, Obninsk 1963–69; Sr Scientist All-Union Scientific Research Inst. of Physiology and Biochemistry of Farm Animals, Borovsk 1970–72; Sr Scientist, Nat. Inst. for Medical Research, London 1973–92; mem. New York Acad. of Sciences, American Gerontological Soc., Biochemical Soc., Genetic Soc.; Soviet citizenship restored 1990; Book Award, Moscow Naturalist Soc. 1965, Aging Research Award of US Aging Asscn 1984, René Schubert Preis in Gerontology 1985. *Publications:* Protein Biosynthesis and Problems of Heredity, Development and Ageing 1963, Molecular-Genetic Mechanisms of Development 1968, The Rise and Fall of T. D. Lysenko 1969, The Medvedev Papers 1970, A Question of Madness (with Roy Medvedev) 1971, Ten Years After 1973, Khrushchev – The Years in Power

(with Roy Medvedev) 1976, Soviet Science 1978, The Nuclear Disaster in the Urals 1979, Andropov 1983, Gorbachev 1986, Soviet Agriculture 1987, The Legacy of Chernobyl 1990, The Unknown Stalin (with Roy Medvedev) 2001, Stalin and the Jewish Problem 2003, Solzhenitsyn and Sakharov (with Roy Medvedev) 2004, Nutrition and Longevity 2007; more than 400 papers and articles on gerontology, genetics, biochemistry, environment, history and other topics. *Leisure interests:* social research and writing, gardening. *Address:* 4 Osborn Gardens, London, NW7 1DY, England (home). *Telephone:* (20) 8346-4158 (home). *E-mail:* zhmedvedev@yahoo.co.uk (home).

MEEK, Paul Derald, BS; American business executive; b. 15 Aug. 1930, McAllen, Tex.; s. of William Van Meek and Martha Mary Meek (née Sharp); m. Betty Catherine Robertson 1954; four d.; ed Univ. of Tex.; with Tech. Dept Humble Oil & Refining Co., Baytown, Tex. 1953–55; Cosden Oil & Chem. Co. 1955–76, Pres. 1968–76; Dir American Petrofina Inc. (now FINA), Dallas 1968–, Vice-Pres., COO 1976–83, Pres., CEO 1983–86, Chair. Bd, Pres., CEO 1984–86, Chair. Bd 1986–98; mem. Advisory Council Coll. Eng Foundation, Univ. of Tex. 1979–; Co-Chair. Industrial Div. United Way of Metropolitan Dallas 1981–82; Chair. Public Utilities Comm. of Tex. 1989–92; Trustee Southwest Research Inst.; mem. American Petroleum Inst., Dallas Wildcat Comm. (Chair. 1987–88). *Publication:* (contrib.) Advances in Petroleum Chemistry and Refining 1957. *Address:* c/o FINA Inc., PO Box 2159, 8350 North Central Expressway, Dallas, TX 75221, USA.

MEESE, Edwin, III, BA, JD; American academic, lawyer and fmr government official; *Ronald Reagan Distinguished Fellow and Chairman, Center for Legal and Judicial Studies, The Heritage Foundation;* b. 1931; s. of Edwin Meese, Jr and Leone Meese; m. Ursula Meese; one s. one d.; ed Yale Univ. and Univ. of Calif., Berkeley; taught law at Univ. of San Diego Law School, Dir Center for Criminal Justice Policy and Man.; sr position under Gov. Reagan, State Capitol, Sacramento, Calif.; Reagan's Campaign Chief of Staff, presidential elections 1980, Dir Transition Org. 1980–81; Counsellor to Pres. Reagan and mem. Nat. Security Council, Domestic Policy Council and Cabinet 1981–85; US Attorney Gen. 1985–88; Ronald Reagan Distinguished Fellow and Chair. Center for Legal and Judicial Studies, The Heritage Foundation, Washington 1988–; Distinguished Visiting Fellow, Hoover Inst., Stanford Univ., Calif. 1988–; mem. Iraq Study Group, US Inst. of Peace 2006; Distinguished Sr Fellow, Inst. for United States Studies, Univ. of London 1996–2003; mem. Bd of Dirs Capital Research Center, Landmark Legal Foundation, Center for the Study of the Presidency, American Prosecutors Research Inst.; retd Col US Army Reserve; Harvard Univ. John F. Kennedy School of Govt Medal 1986. *Publications:* With Reagan: The Inside Story 1992, Making America Safer (co-ed.) 1997, Leadership, Ethics and Policing (co-author) 2004. *Leisure interest:* collecting models of police patrol cars. *Address:* The Heritage Foundation, 214 Massachusetts Avenue, NE, Washington, DC 20002, USA. *Telephone:* (202) 608-6180. *Fax:* (202) 547-0641. *E-mail:* staff@heritage.org. *Website:* www .heritage.org/about/staff/EdwinMeese.cfm.

MEGAWATI, Sukarnoputri; Indonesian politician and fmr head of state; *Chairman, Partai Demokrasi Indonesia Perjuangan (Indonesian Democratic Struggle Party);* b. 23 Jan. 1947, Jogjakarta; d. of the late Achmed Sukarno (fmr Pres. of Indonesia) and Fatmawati; m. 1st Surendro (deceased); m. 2nd Hassan Gamal Ahmad Hassan; m. 3rd Taufik Kiemas; three c.; mem. House of Reps (Partai Demokrasi Indonesia–PDI) 1987; Leader PDI 1993–96 (deposed); Chair. Partai Demokrasi Indonesia Perjuangan (PDI-P) 1996–; Vice-Pres. of Indonesia 1999–2001, Pres. 2001–04; ranked by Forbes magazine amongst 100 Most Powerful Women (eighth) 2004. *Address:* c/o Partai Demokrasi Indonesia Perjuangan, Jalan Raya Pasar Minggu, Lenteng Agung, Jakarta, Indonesia.

MEGHJI, Hon. Zakia Hamdan; Tanzanian politician and teacher; b. 31 Dec. 1946; secondary school teacher 1971–72; tutor at women's training cooperative and at Moshi Cooperative Coll. 1972–78; tutor, World Cooperative Coll. 1978–86; Dist Commr 1988–90; Regional Commr 1990; Exec. Sec., Dept of Econs and Social Welfare 1991; Minister of Natural Resources and Tourism 1994–2006, of Finance 2006–08; mem. Chama Cha Mapinduzi party. *Address:* c/o Chama Cha Mapinduzi, Kuu Street, POB 50, Dodoma, Tanzania (office). *Telephone:* 2180575 (office). *E-mail:* katibumkuu@ccmtz.org (office). *Website:* www.ccmtz.org (office).

MEGRET, Bruno André Alexandre, MSc; French politician and engineer; *Leader, Mouvement national républicain;* b. 4 April 1949, Paris; s. of Jacques Megret and Colette Constantinides; m. Catherine Rascovsky 1992; two s.; ed Lycée Louis-le-Grand, Paris, Univ. of California at Berkeley, École Polytechnique; Head of Dept Nat. Devt Programme 1975–76; Dist Engineer, Eng Dept, Essonne Département 1977–79; tech. adviser, Office of Minister for Overseas Service 1979–81; Deputy Dir Infrastructure and Transport Ile-de-France Region 1981–86; Deputy Front nat. d'Isère 1986–88, Vice-Pres. Front nat. Parl. Group 1987–98, expelled from Front nat. Dec. 1998; Founder and Leader Mouvement nat. républicain (MNR) 1999–; mem. European Parl. 1989–99; Regional Councillor Provence-Côte d'Azur 1992–, Special Adviser to Mayor of Vitrolles 1997; mem. and Hon. Pres. Comités d'action républicaine. *Publications:* Demain le chêne 1982, L'Impératif du renouveau 1986, La Flamme 1990, L'Alternative nationale 1996, La Troisième voie 1997, La Nouvelle Europe 1998, Le Chagrin et l'espérance 1999, Pour que vive la France 2000, La France à l'endroit 2001. *Address:* Mouvement national républicain, 15 rue Cronstadt, 75015 Paris, France (office). *Telephone:* (1) 56-56-64-34 (office). *Fax:* (1) 56-56-52-47 (office). *Website:* www.m-n-r.com (office); www.bruno-megret.com (home).

MEGUID, Nagwa Abdel, PhD; Egyptian geneticist and academic; *Professor of Human Genetics, National Research Centre;* Clinical Researcher and Geneticist, Nat. Research Centre, Cairo, now Prof. of Human Genetics;

L'Oreal-UNESCO For Women in Science Award 2002. *Publications:* numerous articles in scientific journals. *Address:* National Research Centre, El Buhoth Street, Dokki, Giza, 12311 Cairo, Egypt (office). *Telephone:* (2) 7617590 (office). *Fax:* (2) 3370597 (office). *E-mail:* meguid@nrc.org.eg (office). *Website:* www.nrc.sci.eg (office).

MÉHAIGNERIE, Pierre; French politician and engineer; b. 4 May 1939, Balazé, Ille et Vilaine; s. of Alexis Méhaignerie and Pauline Méhaignerie (née Boursier); m. Julie Harding 1965; one s. one d.; ed Lycée Saint-Louis, Paris, Ecole nationale supérieure agronomique, Rennes, Ecole nationale supérieure de sciences agronomiques appliquées, Paris; engineer, Génie Rural des Eaux et Forêts, Dept of Agric. 1965–67; technical counsellor, Ministry of Agric. 1969–71, Ministry of Cultural Affairs 1971–73; mem. Nat. Ass. for Ille-et-Vilaine 1973–76, 1981–86, 1988–93, 1995–; County Councillor for Vitré-Est 1976–2001, elected Mayor of Vitré April 1977–; Sec. of State to Minister of Agric. 1976–77; Minister of Agric. 1977–81, of Housing, Transport and Urban Affairs 1986–88, of Justice 1993–95; Pres. Finance Comm., Nat. Ass. 1995–97, 2002–07; mem. European Parl. 1979; Vice-Pres. Union pour la démocratie française 1988–2002; Pres. Conseil Gen. d'Ille et Vilaine 1982–2001, Pres. Centre des démocrates sociaux 1982–94; Secrétaire général Union pour une Majorité Populaire 2004–; Commdr du Mérite agricole. *Publications:* Aux Français qui ne veulent plus être gouvernés de haut 1995, Bretagne: désir d'avenir 1998. *Address:* Mairie, BP 70627, 35506 Vitré Cedex (office); Assemblée Nationale, 75355 Paris; 76 rue du Rachapt, 35500 Vitré, France (home). *Telephone:* 2-99-75-07-28 (office); 1-40-63-66-17 (office). *E-mail:* pmehaign@club-internet.fr (office). *Website:* www.pierre-mehaignerie.org (office).

MEHDORN, Hartmut; German transport industry executive; b. 31 July 1942, Berlin; m. Hélène Mehdorn (née Vuillequez); three c.; began career as operating asst, Focke Wulf Bremen (renamed Fokker GmbH) 1966, led design and production of Airbus A 300 1974, Head of Production 1978–80; mem. Exec. Cttee and Head of Production, Planning and Purchase, Airbus Industrie AG 1980–84; Man. Dir Mfg, MBB (Messerschmidt Bölkow Blohm) 1984–86, mem. Man. Bd 1986–89; Pres. German Airbus GmbH 1989–94; mem. Bd and Exec. Cttee German Aerospace AG (Daimler Benz Aerospace AG) 1993; Chair. Heidelberger Printing Machines (Heideldruck) AG 1995–98; Chair. Deutsche Bahn (DB) AG 1999–2003, Chair. and CEO 2003–09 (resgnd); Chair. Supervisory Bd Vattenfalls Europe AG, DB Cargo AG, DB Wetz AG, DB Regio AG, DB Reise & Touristik AG; mem. Exec. Cttee SAP AG 2002–; mem. Advisory Bd Baden-Württemberg Commerzbank AG 2000–; mem. Supervisory Bd DEVK (Deutsche Eisenbahn Versicherung Lebensversicherung) AG, Lufthansa Technik AG, West LB AG; hon. mem. Senate Univ. of Heidelburg 1999–. *Address:* c/o Deutsche Bahn AG, Potsdamer Platz 2, 10785 Berlin, Germany (office).

MEHRA, K. S.; Indian civil servant; various positions in Admin of Andaman and Nicobar Islands, Govt of Arunachal Pradesh, Govt of Delhi; Jt Sec. Ministry of Textiles –1999; mem. of staff, Municipal Corpn of Delhi 1999–2001; Admin. Union Territory of Lakshadweep 2001–04; Chair. Lakshadweep Devt Corpn; ex-officio Insp.-Gen. of Police. *Address:* c/o Administrator's Office, Kavaratti, Lakshadweep, India.

MEHTA, Aman, BEcons; Indian banker (retd) ; b. 1946, India; m.; two c.; ed Delhi Univ.; with Mercantile Bank Ltd 1967–69; joined Hongkong and Shanghai Banking Corpn Ltd (HSBC) 1969, roles in various depts including Operations, Credit, Br. and Area Man., Merchant Banking, Man. Corp. Planning 1985, Chair. and Chief Exec. HSBC USA Inc. 1993–95, Deputy Chair. HSBC Bank Middle East 1995–98, Gen. Man. Int. and later Exec. Dir Int. HSBC 1998, CEO 1999–2004; Chair. HSBC Bank Malaysia Berhad 1999–2004, Dir HSBC Bank Australia, HSBC Investment Bank Asia Holdings Ltd, HSBC Holdings BV Netherlands; Man. Dir The Saudi British Bank 1988–91, Group Gen. Man. 1991–92. *Address:* c/o Hongkong and Shanghai Banking Corporation Limited, Level 34, HSBC Main Building, 1 Queen's Road Central, Hong Kong Special Administrative Region, People's Republic of China (office).

MEHTA, Goverdhan, BSc, MSc, PhD; Indian organic chemist, academic and international organization official; *President, International Council for Science;* b. 1943, Jodhpur; ed Univ. of Poona; Hon. Prof. Jawaharlal Nehru Centre for Advanced Scientific Research, Bangalore 1990–; Vice-Chancellor Univ. of Hyderabad 1994–98; Prof. of Organic Chemistry and fmr Dir Indian Inst. of Science, Bangalore; mem. Exec. Bd Int. Council for Science (ICSU) 1999–2002, Pres. 2005–, fmr Chair. ICSU Nat. Cttee; Co-Chair. Inter-Acad. Council; Fellow, Int. Union of Pure and Applied Chem., fmr Chair. Int. Cttee; Officier dans l'Ordre Palmes Academiques, France, Padma Shri, India; DSc hc (Univ. of Marseilles); Humboldt Research Prize, Germany, Third World Acad. of Sciences Medal. *Publications:* more than 370 papers in int. journals. *Address:* International Council for Science, 5 rue Auguste Vacquerie, 75016 Paris, France (office). *Telephone:* 1-45-25-03-29 (office). *Fax:* 1-42-88-94-31 (office). *E-mail:* secretariat@icsu.org (office). *Website:* www.icsu.org (office).

MEHTA, Ajai Singh (Sonny); American (b. Indian) publishing company executive; *Chairman and Editor-in-Chief, Knopf Publishing Group;* b. 1942, India; m. Gita Mehta; one s.; ed Lawrence School, Sanawar, and Univ. of Cambridge; fmrly with Pan and Picador Publs, UK; Pres. Alfred A. Knopf Div. of Random House (now Knopf Publishing Group, New York) 1987–, now Chair. and Ed.-in-Chief. *Address:* Alfred A. Knopf Inc., 1745 Broadway, New York, NY 10019, USA. *Website:* www.randomhouse.com/knopf.

MEHTA, Adm. Sureesh; Indian naval officer; *Chief of Naval Staff and Chairman, Joint Chiefs of Staff Committee;* b. 18 Aug. 1947; m. Maria Teresa Mehta; two c.; ed Nat. Defence Acad., Defence Services Staff Coll., Wellington, Nat. Defence Coll., New Delhi; commissioned in Indian Navy 1967, joined Fleet Air Arm and flew Sea Hawk jet fighters from carrier INS Vikrant 1967, carried out instructional duties as Directing Staff in Defence Services Staff Coll., earlier appointments included command of frigate INS Beas and guided missile frigate INS Godavari, also commanded Naval Air Stations, INS Garuda, C-in-C Eastern Naval Command 2005–06, other operational Flag appointments have included Flag Officer Naval Aviation, Fleet Commdr Western Fleet during Kargil Crisis 1999, has held various staff appointments in Flag rank at New Delhi, including Asst Controller Carrier Projects, Asst Chief of Personnel (Human Resources Devt), Controller of Personnel Services, Chief of Personnel, Dir-Gen. Coast Guard, Deputy Chief of Naval Staff, Chief of Naval Staff 2006–, currently Chair. Jt Chiefs of Staff Cttee; Ati Vishist Seva Medal 1995, Param Vishist Seva Medal 2005. *Address:* Office of the Chief of Naval Staff, Integrated Headquarters of Ministry of Defence (Navy), Sena Bhawan, New Delhi, 110 0111, India (office). *E-mail:* webmasterindiannavy@nic.in (office). *Website:* indiannavy.nic.in (office).

MEHTA, Ved (Parkash), MA; American (naturalized) writer and academic; b. 21 March 1934, Lahore, Pakistan (fmrly British India); s. of Amolak Ram and Shanti Mehta (née Mehra); m. Linn Cary 1983; two d.; ed Arkansas School for the Blind, Pomona Coll., Calif., Balliol Coll., Oxford, UK, Harvard Univ.; staff writer, New Yorker magazine 1961–94; Visiting Scholar, Case Western Reserve 1974; Visiting Prof. of Literature, Bard Coll. 1985, 1986; Noble Foundation Visiting Coll. of Art and Cultural History, Sarah Lawrence Coll. 1988; Fellow, New York Inst. for the Humanities 1988–92; Visiting Fellow (Literature), Balliol Coll., Oxford 1988–89; Visiting Prof. of English, New York Univ. 1989–90; Rosenkrantz Chair in Writing, Yale Univ. 1990–93, Lecturer in History 1990, 1991, 1992, Lecturer in English 1991–93; Assoc. Fellow, Berkeley Coll. (a constituent of Yale Coll.) 1988–, Residential Fellow 1990–93; Arnold Bernhard Visiting Prof. of English and History, Williams Coll. 1994; Randolph Visiting Distinguished Prof. of English and History, Vassar Coll., NY 1994–96; Sr Fellow, Freedom Forum, Media Studies Center and Visiting Scholar, Columbia Univ., New York 1996–97; Fellow, Center for Advanced Study in Behavioral Sciences 1997–98; mem. Council on Foreign Relations 1979–, Usage Panel, American Heritage Dictionary 1982; Hon. Fellow, Balliol Coll. Oxford 1999; Hon. DLtrs (Pomona Coll.) 1972, (Williams Coll.) 1986; Hon. DLitt (Bard Coll.) 1982; Hon. DUniv (Stirling, Scotland) 1988; Hon. LHD (Bowdoin) 1995; Hazen Fellow 1956–59, Harvard Prize Fellow 1959–60, Residential Fellow, Eliot House 1959–61, Guggenheim Fellow 1971–72, 1977–78, Ford Foundation Travel and Study Grantee 1971–76, Public Policy Grantee 1979–82, MacArthur Prize Fellow 1982–87, Asscn of Indians in America Award 1978, Signet Medal, Harvard Univ. 1983, Distinguished Service Award, Asian/Pacific American Library Asscn 1986, New York City Mayor's Liberty Medal 1986, Centenary Barrows Award, Pomona Coll. 1987, New York Public Library Literary Lion Medal 1990, and Literary Lion Centennial Medal 1996, New York State Asian-American Heritage Month Award 1991, South Asian Literary Asscn Lifetime Achievement Award 2004. *Television:* writer and narrator of documentary film, Chachaji: My Poor Relation (DuPont Columbia Award for Excellence in Broadcast Journalism 1977–78) (PBS) 1978, (BBC) 1980. *Publications:* Face to Face (Secondary Educ. Annual Book Award 1958, serial reading on BBC Light Programme 1958, dramatization on BBC Home Programme 1959) 1957, Walking the Indian Streets 1960, Fly and the Fly Bottle 1963, Delinquent Chacha (novel) 1967, Portrait of India 1970, John Is Easy to Please 1971, Mahatma Gandhi and His Apostles 1977, The New India 1978, Photographs of Chachaji 1980, A Family Affair: India Under Three Prime Ministers 1982, Three Stories of the Raj (fiction) 1986, Rajiv Gandhi and Rama's Kingdom 1995, A Ved Mehta Reader: The Craft of the Essay 1998; Continents of Exile (autobiography): Daddyji 1972, Mamaji, 1979, Vedi 1982 (serial reading on BBC Book at Bedtime 1990), The Ledge Between the Streams 1984, Sound-Shadows of the New World 1986, The Stolen Light 1989, Up at Oxford 1993, Remembering Mr. Shawn's New Yorker 1998, All For Love 2001, Dark Harbor 2003, The Red Letters (concluding volume) 2004. *Leisure interest:* daydreaming. *Fax:* (212) 472-7220 (home). *E-mail:* vedmehta@aol.com (home). *Website:* www.vedmehta .com.

MEHTA, Zarin, FCA; Indian music administrator; b. 28 Oct. 1938, Bombay; s. of the late Mehli Mehta and of Tehmina Daruvala Mehta; brother of Zubin Mehta (q.v.); m. Carmen Lasky 1966; two c.; CA, London 1957, accountant Frederic B. Smart & Co., London 1957–62, Coopers & Lybrand, Montreal 1962–81; Dir Orchestre Symphonique de Montréal 1973–81, Man. Dir 1981–90; Exec. Dir and COO Ravinia Festival, Ill. 1990–99, CEO 1999–2000; Exec. Dir New York Philharmonic 2000–; mem. Ordre de Comptables Agréés du Québec. *Address:* New York Philharmonic, Administrative Offices, Avery Fisher Hall, 10 Lincoln Center Plaza, New York, NY 10023, USA (office). *Telephone:* (212) 875-5900 (office). *Website:* www .newyorkphilharmonic.org (office).

MEHTA, Zubin; Indian conductor; *General Music Director, Bavarian State Opera;* b. 29 April 1936, Bombay; s. of the late Mehli Mehta and of Tehmina Daruvala Mehta; m. 1st Carmen Lasky 1958 (divorced); one s. one d.; m. 2nd Nancy Diane Kovack 1969; ed Vienna Acad. of Music, studied under Hans Swarowsky; first professional conducting in Belgium, Yugoslavia and UK (Liverpool); Music Dir Montreal Symphony 1961–67, Los Angeles Philharmonic Orchestra 1962–78; Music Dir New York Philharmonic Orchestra 1978–91; Music Dir Israel Philharmonic 1969–, appointed Dir for Life 1981; Gen. Music Dir Bavarian State Opera 1998–; conductor at festivals of Holland, Prague, Vienna, Salzburg and Spoleto; debut at La Scala, Milan 1969; conducts regularly with the Vienna and Berlin Orchestras; winner of Liverpool Int. Conductors' Competition 1958; Music Dir Maggio Musicale, Florence 1969, 1986–; Dr hc (Tel-Aviv Univ.), Weizmann Inst. of Science, The Hebrew Univ. of Jerusalem, Jewish Theological Seminary, Westminster Choir Coll., Princeton, Brooklyn Coll., Colgate Univ.); co-winner Wolf Prize 1996,

Kennedy Center Honor 2006, Praemium Imperiale Award for Music, Tokyo 2008; Commendatore (Italy), Médaille d'Or Vermeil (City of Paris), Commdr, Ordre des Arts et des Lettres (France), Great Silver Medal of Service (Austria) 1997, Padma Vibhushan (India) 2001. *Leisure interest:* cricket. *Address:* c/o Askonas Holt Ltd, Lincoln House, 300 High Holborn, London, WC1V 7JH, England (office); Bayerische Staatsoper, Max-Joseph-Platz 2, 80539 München, Germany; Israel Philharmonic Orchestra, 1 Huberman Street, Box 11292, 61112 Tel-Aviv, Israel. *Telephone:* (20) 7400-1700 (office). *Fax:* (20) 7400-1799 (office). *E-mail:* info@askonasholt.co.uk (office). *Website:* www.askonasholt.co.uk (office).

MEI, Baojiu; Chinese opera singer; b. Feb. 1934, Beijing; s. of Mei Lanfang; actor, Mei Lanfang Peking Opera Co. 1951–62, actor (First Class) Beijing Peking Opera Troupe 1962–; head, Mei Lanfang Peking Opera Troupe. *Plays:* Phoenix Returning to Its Nest, The Imperial Concubine Getting Drunk, Xiang Yu Bidding Farewell to Yu Ji, Yuzhoufeng. *Recordings include:* Masterpieces of Beijing Opera, Famous Arias from Beijing Opera. *Films:* A Great Master Recaptured 2006. *Address:* Peking Opera Troupe, Haihu West lane No. 30, Fengtai District, Beijing 100077, People's Republic of China (office).

MEIDANI, Rexhep Qemal, DèsSc; Albanian academic and fmr head of state; *Professor, University of New York, Tirana (UNYT);* b. 17 Aug. 1944, Tirana; m.; two c.; ed Univs of Caen and Paris XI, France, Univ. of Tirana; scientific collaborator, C.E.N., Saclay, France 1974–96; Asst, then Lecturer, then Docent, Univ. of Tirana and Univ. of Pristina, Kosova 1966–96, Prof. of Theoretical Physics 1987–, Dean of Faculty of Natural Sciences 1988–92; Visiting Scientist and Visiting Prof., Italy, France, Germany, UK, USA, Greece etc.; mem. Socialist Party of Albania 1996–97, 2002–, Gen. Sec. 1996–97; mem. Parl. 1997; Pres. of Albania 1997–2002; currently Prof., New York Univ. of Tirana; Chair. Bd Albanian Centre for Human Rights 1994–96, Ed.-in-Chief Human Rights quarterly 1994–96; Co-Founder Citizens of Helsinki, Democratic Albania; mem. Albanian Cttee for Understanding and Cooperation in the Balkans 1986–90; Co-Ed. Bulletin of Natural Sciences 1978–89, Ed.-in-Chief 1989–94; Co-Ed. Balkan Physics Letters 1992–96; mem. Acad. of Sciences 2003, Club of Madrid, Int. Cttee for Democracy in Cuba, Int. Raoul Wallenberg Foundation, Editorial Advisory Bd World Leaders Magazine, European Asscn of Law Students (Elsa), Albania, War Invalids' Asscn against Nazism; Hon. Amb. of Millennium Goals, Amb. for Peace, Int. Hon. Citizen, New Orleans, USA 2002; Order 'Naim Frasheri', Third Class 1981, Nat. Order Golden Star of Romania 1999, Order of King Tomislav (Croatia) 2001, Nat. Order of Merit (Grade of Companion of Honour) (Malta) 2002; Hon. PhD (Istanbul Tech. Univ.) 1998, Dr hc (Aristotle Univ. of Thessaloniki) 1998, (Sofia Univ.) 1998, Hon. DHumLitt (American Univ., Rome) 1999, (Univ. of Bridgeport, Conn.) 2001, Preside d'Onore (Università Mediterranea René Cassin, Bari) 1999, Hon. DSc (Portsmouth, UK) 2002; Prize of the Repub., Second Class 1988, Gold Medal of Merit of the City of Athens 1998, Great Cross of Salvation (Greece) 1998, Médaille du Mérite (U.P. Universelle) 1998, Honorary Medal of the Centre Democritos (Greece) 1998, F. Lux Award, Clark Univ., Worcester, Mass, USA 2000, Golden Key of the City of Worcester 2000, Golden Key of the City of Prague, Czech Repub. 2001, Jan Masaryk Medal, Univ. of Economics, Prague 2001, Medal of the Robert Schumann Foundation, Paris 2001, Chancellor's Int. Medallion of Distinction, New Orleans Univ. 2002, Golden Key of the City of New Orleans 2002. *Publications:* President Meidani and Kosovo 2000, The Balkans – A General Outlook. Montenegro, Bosnia, Kosovo, FYR of Macedonia, Serbia: Near-Term Challenges 2001, Dall'Indipendenza verso L'Interdipendenza dell'Integrazione 2002, Globalization, Integration and the Albanian Nation 2002, Jus Gentium 2003, Politics, Moral and State 2003, Agreement with Myself 2004, The Traps of Nation-State 2005, Politics in Vivo-in Vitro 2006, Las trampas del Estado-nacion 2007, Is it deterministic the quantum theory? 2007, On space-time 2008; numerous scientific monographs and books and hundreds of scientific and political articles published in Albania; many articles in int. scientific publs and numerous others on political and social problems. *Address:* University of New York Tirana, Rr. Komuna e Parisit prane Kopshtit Botanik, PO Box 2301, Tirana (office); Bulevardi Zogu I, Pallati 57, Shkalla 1, Ap. 12, Tirana, Albania (home). *Telephone:* (42) 273056 (office); (4) 271887 (home). *Fax:* (42) 273059 (office). *E-mail:* rmeidani@hotmail.com (home); rmeidani@gmail.com (home); rmeidani@rmeidani.info (home).

MEIER, Beat H., PhD; Swiss chemist and academic; *Head, Department of Chemistry and Applied Sciences, Eidgenössische Technische Hochschule Zürich (ETH Zürich);* b. 1954, Solothurn; ed Eidgenössische Technische Hochschule Zürich; Post-Doctoral Researcher, Los Alamos Nat. Labs, USA 1985–87; Staff Scientist, Eidgenössische Technische Hochschule Zürich (ETH Zürich) 1987, Prof. 1998–, also Head, Dept of Chem. and Applied Sciences; Prof. of Physical Chem., Nijmegen Univ., Netherlands 1994–98. *Address:* Laboratorium fur Physikalische Chemie, HCI D 225, Wolfgang-Pauli-Str. 10, 8093 Zürich, Switzerland (office). *Telephone:* (44) 632-44-01 (office). *Fax:* (1) 632-1621 (office). *E-mail:* beat.meier@nmr.phys.chem.ethz.ch (office). *Website:* www.ethz.ch (office); www.nmr.ethz.ch/~beme (office).

MEIER, Richard Alan, BArch, FAIA; American architect; b. 12 Oct. 1934, Newark, NJ; s. of Jerome Meier and Carolyn Meier (née Kaltenbacher); m. Katherine Gormley 1978 (divorced); one s. one d.; ed Cornell Univ.; with Frank Grad & Sons, NJ 1957, Davis, Brody & Wisniewski, New York 1958–59, Skidmore, Owings & Merrill 1959–60, Marcel Breuer & Assocs 1961–63; Prof. Architectural Design Cooper Union 1962–73; Prin. Architect, Richard Meier & Assocs, New York 1963–80, Richard Meier & Partners 1980–; Visiting Critic, Pratt Inst. 1960–62, 1965, Princeton 1963, Syracuse Univ. 1964; Architect American Acad. in Rome 1973–74; Visiting Prof. of Architecture, Yale Univ. 1975, 1977, Harvard 1977; Eliot Noyes Visiting Critic in Architecture 1980–81; Visiting Prof., UCLA 1987, 1988, 1990, 2000; Univ. Professorship, Cornell Univ. 2000–04, mem. Advisory Council; mem. Jerusalem Comm.; Fellow, American Acad. of Arts and Sciences; mem. Bd Trustees Cooper-Hewitt Museum, Bd Dirs American Acad. and Inst. of Arts and Sciences; Hon. FRIBA; Dr hc (NJ Inst. of Tech.) 1987, (Universita di Napoli) 1991, (Parsons School of Deisgn) 1996, 1998, (Pratt School of Fine Arts) 1999, (Univ. of Bucharest) 2001, (NC State Univ.) 2004, (Mercy Coll.) 2004; Nat. AIA Awards: 1969, 1971, 1974, 1976, 1977, 1983–85, 1987, 1990, 1993, 2000, 2002, 2003, 2005, 2006, Regional AIA Awards: 1968, 1971, 1972, 1974, 1976, 1982, 1984–87, 1989, 1990–93, 1996–2001, 2003–05, Progressive Architecture Award 1979, 1989–91, 1996, Architectural Record Award of Excellence for House Design 1964, 1968, 1969, 1977, Nat. Inst. of Arts and Letters Award in Architecture 1972, Pritzker Architecture Prize 1984, RIBA Gold Medal 1987, Progressive Architecture Gold Medal 1997, AIA Gold Medal 1998, Praemium Imperiale 1997; Commdr des Arts et Lettres (France) 1992, Deutscher Architektur Preis 1993, 1995, AIA Twenty-Five Year Award 2000, World Architecture Award 2001, Pratt Legend Award 2004, American Acad. of Arts and Letters Gold Medal 2008, Acad. Royale des Sciences, des lettres et des Beaux-Arts 1991. *Major works:* Smith House, Darien, Conn. 1965–67, Westbeth Artists' Housing, New York 1967–70, Saltzman House, East Hampton, New York 1967–69, House in Old Westbury, Old Westbury, New York 1969–71, Bronx Devt Center 1970–77, Douglas House, Harbor Springs, Mich. 1971–76, Shamberg House, Chappaqua, New York 1972–77, The Atheneum, New Harmony, Ind. 1975–79, Hartford Seminary, Conn. 1978–81, Museum for Decorative Art, Frankfurt am Main, Germany 1979–85, High Museum of Art, Atlanta, Ga 1980–83, Renault HQ, France 1981, Museum für Kunsthandwerk, Germany 1984, Grotta House NJ 1984–89, The Getty Center, Los Angeles, Calif. 1985–97, Museum of Contemporary Art, Barcelona, Spain 1987–95, Canal+ Headquarters, Paris, France 1988–92, Rachofsky House, Dallas, Tex. 1991–96, US Courthouse, Islip, New York 1993–2000, Sandra Day O'Connor US Courthouse, Phoenix, Ariz. 1994–2000, City Hall and Cen. Library, The Hague 1995, Neugebauer House, Naples, Fla 1995–98, Int. Center for Possibility Thinking, Garden Grove, Calif. 1996–2003, Jubilee Church, Rome, Italy 1996–2003, J. Paul Getty Center 1997, San Jose Civic Center, San Jose, Calif. 1998–2005, 173/176 Perry Street Condominiums, New York 1999–2002, 66 Restaurant, New York 2002–03, Burda Collection Museum, Baden-Baden, Germany 2001–04, Charles Street Apartments, New York 2003–06, and others. *Publications:* Richard Meier Museums, Building the Getty, Richard Meier, Richard Meier Architect 1–4, American Dream: The Houses at Sagaponac, Architecture in Detail: The Getty Center, Between Nature and Culture, Building the Getty/Richard Meier, Dives in Misericordia Church Rome: Project by Richard Meier Vols 1–3, Five Architects, Getty Center Design Process, Meier/Stella – Art and Architecture, Richard Meier, Richard Meier Architect (Monacelli Press), Richard Meier in Europe, Richard Meier Sculpture: 1992–1994, Richard Meier: The Architect as Designer and Artist, Richard Meier: Barcelona Museum of Contemporary Art, Richard Meier: Building for Art, Richard Meier: Collages, Richard Meier Details, Weishaupt Forum. *Address:* Richard Meier & Partners, 475 10th Avenue, Floor 6, New York, NY 10018, USA (office). *Telephone:* (212) 967-6060 (office). *Fax:* (212) 967-3207 (office). *E-mail:* mail@richardmeier.com (office). *Website:* www.richardmeier.com (office).

MEIMARAKIS, Evangelos; Greek lawyer and politician; *Minister of National Defence;* b. 14 Dec. 1953, Athens; m. Ioanna Kolokota; two d.; ed Athens Univ. Law School, Panteion Univ.; founding mem. New Democracy youth group ONNED, fmr Pres.; mem. Parl. (New Democracy party) 1989–, New Democracy Political Planning and Programme Sec. 2000–01, Cen. Cttee Sec. 2001–06; Deputy Minister for Culture, responsible for sports 1992–1993; Minister of Nat. Defence 2006–. *Address:* Ministry of National Defence, Odos Mesogeion 227–231, 154 51 Athens, Greece (office). *Telephone:* (210) 6598607 (office). *Fax:* (210) 6443832 (office). *E-mail:* minister@mod.mil.gr (office). *Website:* www.mod.gr (office); www.meimarakis.gr.

MEINER, Richard; German publisher; b. 8 April 1918, Dresden; s. of Felix Meiner and Elisabeth Meiner (née Gensel); m. Ursula Ehlert 1947; one s. one d.; mil. service 1937–45; f. Richard Meiner Verlag, Hamburg 1948–64; Dir Verlage Felix Meiner 1964–81, Felix Meiner Verlag GmbH, Hamburg 1981–98; Mil. Medal; Gold Medal of Union of German Booksellers 1983; Medal of Honour of German Bücherei Leipzig 1987; Hon. Fellow German Soc. for Philosophy in Germany 1988; Bundesverdienstkreuz I. Klasse 1989. *Publications:* Verlegerische Betreuung der Philosophischen Bibliothek, Corpus Philosophorum Teutonicorum Medii Aevi, G.W.F. Hegel, Gesammelte Werke. Krit. Ausgabe, G.W.F. Hegel, Vorlesungen, Kant-Forschungen, Nicolai de Cusa Opera omnia. Krit. Ausgabe, Handbuch PRAGMATIK, Studien zum achtzehnten Jahrhundert und weitere philosophische Reihen und Einzelmonographien. *Leisure interests:* tennis, skiing. *Address:* c/o Felix Meiner Verlag GmbH, Richardstrasse 47, 22081 Hamburg, Germany.

MEINWALD, Jerrold, MA, PhD, FAAS; American chemist and academic; *Goldwin Smith Professor Emeritus of Chemistry, Cornell University;* b. 16 Jan. 1927, New York, NY; s. of Dr Herman Meinwald and Sophie Baskind; m. 1st Dr Yvonne Chu 1955 (divorced 1979); two d.; m. 2nd Dr Charlotte Greenspan 1980; one d.; ed Brooklyn and Queen's Colls, Univ. of Chicago and Harvard Univ.; Instructor in Chem., Cornell Univ. 1952–54, Asst Prof. 1954–58, Assoc. Prof. 1958–61, Prof. 1961–72, Acting Chair. of Chem. 1968, Prof. of Chem. 1973–80, Goldwin Smith Prof. of Chem. 1980–2005, Andrew Mellon Foundation Prof. 1993–95, Goldwin Smith Prof. Emer. 2006–, Grad. School Prof. 2006–; Prof. of Chem., Univ. of California, San Diego 1972–73; Visiting Prof., Harvard Medical School 1997; Chemical Consultant, Schering-Plough Corpn 1957–2000, Procter & Gamble Pharmaceuticals 1958–96, Cambridge Neuroscience Research Inc. 1987–93; mem. Scientific Advisory Bd Entomed 2002–04; Consultant on Chemical Ecology, Max-Planck Soc. 1995–97; mem. of Visiting Cttee for Chem., Brookhaven Nat. Lab. 1969–73;

numerous lectureships in USA, Canada, UK, Australia, NZ, France, Czechoslovakia, Switzerland, Belgium, China, Taiwan, Brazil, Japan; mem. Editorial Bd Organic Reactions 1967–78, Journal of Chemical Ecology 1974–, Insect Science and its Application 1979–91, Chemistry and Biochemistry 2004–, Proceedings of the National Academy of Science 2007–; Alfred P. Sloan Foundation Fellow 1958–62, Guggenheim Fellow 1960–61, 1976–77, NIH Special Postdoctoral Fellow 1967–68, Fogarty Int. Scholar 1983–84; Distinguished Scholar-in-Residence, Hope Coll., Holland, Mich. 1984; NAS Exchange Scholar to Czechoslovakia 1987; Fellow, Center for Advanced Study in the Behavioral Sciences (Stanford) 1990–91; Research Dir Int. Centre of Insect Physiology and Ecology, Nairobi 1970–77; mem. Advisory Bd Petroleum Research Fund 1970–73, Advisory Bd Research Corpn 1978–83, Advisory Council Dept of Chem., Princeton Univ. 1978–82, Advisory Bd (Chem. Section) NSF 1979–82, Scientific Advisory Bd Native Plants Inc. 1987–93; Organizing Chair. Sino-American Symposium on the Chem. of Natural Products, Shanghai 1980, UNESCO's Working Group on Co-operation in the Field of Natural Products Chem. 1982–87, Chem. Program Cttee Alfred P. Sloan Foundation 1985–91; mem. Bd Dirs Xerces Soc. 1994–, Scientific Cttee PROBEM/Amazonia 1996–2003; Pres. Int. Soc. of Chemical Ecology 1988–89; mem. NAS, American Philosophical Soc.; Fellow, American Acad. of Arts and Sciences (Sec. 2006–), Japan Soc. for the Promotion of Science; Hon. PhD (Göteborg) 1989; ACS Edgar Fah Smith Award 1977, ACS E. Guenther Award 1984, Distinguished Scientist-Lecturer Award, Kalamazoo Section of ACS 1985, ACS A.C. Cope Scholar Award 1989, Tyler Prize in Environmental Science 1990, ACS Gustavus John Esselen Award for Chem. in the Public Interest 1991, Silver Medal, Int. Soc. of Chemical Ecology 1991, J. Heyrovsky Medal, Czech Acad. of Sciences 1996, ACS Roger Adams Award in Organic Chem. 2005. *Publications:* Advances in Alicyclic Chemistry Vol. I (co-author) 1966, Explorations in Chemical Ecology (co-ed.) 1987, Pheromone Biochemistry (co-author) 1987, Chemical Ecology: The Chemistry of Biotic Interaction (co-ed.) 1995; more than 400 research articles in major chemical journals. *Leisure interests:* playing flute, baroque flute and recorder. *Address:* Department of Chemistry and Chemical Biology, Cornell University, Ithaca, NY 14853 (office); 429 Warren Road, Ithaca, NY 14850, USA (home). *Telephone:* (607) 255-3301 (office); (607) 257-0035 (home). *Fax:* (607) 255-3407 (office). *E-mail:* circe@cornell.edu (office). *Website:* www.chem.cornell.edu/faculty/index.asp?fac=40 (office).

MEIRELLES, Fernando; Brazilian film director; b. 11 Sept. 1955, São Paulo; ed Universidade de São Paulo; trained as architect; created experimental video productions at univ.; producer of TV programmes including Crig Rá, O Mundo no Ar, Ernesto Varella, TV Mix, Comédia da Vida Privada, Cidade dos Homens; Dir Rá-Tim-Bum (children's series, TV Cultura) 1989–90; Co-Founder 02 Filmes Co. (largest commercial production co. in Brazil); debut as feature film director 1997; several awards for Rá-Tim-Bum including New York Film and TV Festival Gold Medal, Cannes Film Festival Lion and Clio Awards; over 20 other prizes. *Films include:* O Menino Maloquinho (Crazy Kid) 1997, E no Meio Passa um Trem (short film) 1998, Domesticas (Maids) 2000, Cidade de Deus (City of God) 2001, Palace II (short film) 2001, The Constant Gardener 2005, Blindness 2008. *Address:* Rua Heliopolis, 410, Vila Hamburguesa, São Paulo, SP 05318-010, Brazil (office). *Telephone:* (11) 36448040 (office). *Fax:* (11) 36410415 (office). *Website:* www.ozfilmes.com (office).

MEIRELLES, Henrique de Campos, BCE, MBA; Brazilian central banker; *Governor, Central Bank of Brazil;* b. 31 Aug. 1945; m. Eva Missini; ed Univ. of São Paulo, Fed. Univ. of Rio de Janeiro and Harvard Business School, USA; Man. Dir BankBoston Leasing 1974, Vice-Pres., São Paulo 1978, Head Commercial Bank in Brazil 1980, Deputy Country Man. 1981, Pres. and Regional Man. in Brazil 1984, Pres. and COO BankBoston Corpn 1996, Pres. FleetBoston's Global and Wholesale Bank and mem. Bd of Dirs, also Office of the Chair. FleetBoston Financial 1999–2002; Fed. Dep. for Goías state 2002; Gov. Cen. Bank of Brazil 2003–; mem. Bd of Dirs Raytheon Corpn, New York, New England Conservatory, Inst. of Contemporary Art, Acción Int.; mem. Advisory Council Sloan School of Man., MIT, Harvard Business School Initiative on Global Corp. Governance, Boston Coll. Carroll School of Man., Center for Latin American Issues of the George Washington Univ., Brazilian-American Chamber of Commerce, New York, Adolfo Ibañez Univ., Santiago, Chile; Founding Pres. Latin American Leasing Fed.; Chair. Emer. Brazilian Asscn of Int. Banks; Chair. Soc. for the Revitalization of the City of São Paulo, Travessia Foundation; mem. Exec. Cttee US-Brazilian Business Council, American Chamber of Commerce, São Paulo. *Address:* Banco Central do Brasil, SBS, Q.03, Bloco B, CP 08670, 70074-900 Brasília, DF, Brazil (office). *Telephone:* (61) 3414-1000 (office). *Fax:* (61) 3223-1033 (office). *E-mail:* presidencia@bcb.gov.br (office). *Website:* www.bcb.gov.br (office).

MEIRING, Gen. Georg Lodewyk, MSc; South African army officer; b. 18 Oct. 1939, Ladybrand; m. Anna Maria G. Brink; three s. two d.; ed Univ. of Orange Free State; joined S African Army as a signals officer 1963, later Dir of Signals; Officer Commdg Witswatersrand Command, Johannesburg 1981–82; Chief of Army Staff, Logistics, S African Defence Force (SADF), Pretoria 1982–83; Gen. Officer Commdg SW Africa Territory Defence Forces, Windhoek 1987–89; Gen. Officer Commdg Far North, Pietersburg 1989–90; Deputy Chief, S African Army, SADF, Pretoria 1983–87, 1990–93, Chief 1993–94; Chief S African Nat. Defence Force (SANDF) 1994–98; several mil. decorations. *Leisure interests:* hunting, gardening, reading, walking. *Address:* Private Bag X414, Pretoria 0001, South Africa.

MEISEL, Steven; American photographer; *Principal Photographer, Vogue;* b. New York City; ed Parsons School of Design; began career as lecturer Parsons School of Design; worked as illustrator Women's Wear Daily; professional photographer 1980–; currently prin. photographer for American and Italian versions of Vogue magazine; photographer for advertising campaigns of designers Versace, Yves Saint Laurent, Prada, Dolce & Gabbana, Valentino; exhbn of photography at White Cube2 Gallery, London 2001. *Publications include:* Sex. Erotic Fantasies. Madonna (with Madonna) 1992, Stern Portfolio No. 32: Steven Meisel 2003. *Address:* c/o Vogue, Condé Nast Publications, 4 Times Square, New York, NY 10036, USA (office). *Telephone:* (212) 286-2860 (office).

MEISER, Richard Johannes, MD; German professor of internal medicine; b. 10 Aug. 1931, Cottbus; s. of Richard W. Meiser and Hasmig Bunyadian; ed gymnasium and studies in philosophy and medicine; Univ. Prof. in Internal Medicine (Haematology), Univ. of Saarland 1971–; Pres. Univ. of Saarland 1983–92; Vice-Pres. for Int. Affairs, West German Rectors' Conf. (WRK) 1987; Officier, Ordre Nat. du Mérite (France); Officier, Ordre de Mérite (Luxembourg). *Publications:* studies on macroglobulinemia in tropical splenomegaly (1966/67), on the metabolism of mycloma cells (1970), on tropical parasites, on combination chemotherapy (1981); Aktuelle Probleme und Perspektiven des Arztrechts (co-ed.) 1989. *Leisure interests:* literature, souvenirs. *Address:* Domagkstrasse 2, 6650 Homburg-Saar, Germany (home). *Telephone:* (6841) 5868 (home).

MEISNER, HE Cardinal Joachim; German ecclesiastic; *Archbishop of Cologne and Primate of Germany;* b. 25 Dec. 1933, Breslau; s. of Walter Meisner and Hedwig Meisner; ed Univ. of Erfurt, Pastoral Seminary at Neuzelle; ordained priest 1962; Chaplain of St Ägidien, Heiligenstadt 1963–66, St Crucis, Erfurt 1966; Caritas-Rector Diocese of Erfurt 1966–75; Auxiliary Bishop of Erfurt-Meiningen and Titular Bishop of Vina 1975–80; Bishop of Berlin 1980–89; cr. Cardinal-Priest of S. Pudenziana 1983; Archbishop of Cologne and Primate of Germany 1988–; Hon. Citizen of Miguel Pereira, Brazil 1992; Hon. PhD (Jesuit Univ., Manila) 1990. *Publications:* Das Auditorium Coelicum am Dom zu Erfurt 1960, Nachreformatorische katholische Frömmigkeitsformen in Erfurt 1971, various articles in magazines. *Leisure interest:* Christian art. *Address:* Kardinal-Frings-Str. 10, 50668 Cologne, Germany (office). *Telephone:* (221) 16420 (office). *Fax:* (221) 16421700 (office). *E-mail:* erzbischof@erzbistum-koeln.de (office). *Website:* www.erzbistum-koeln.de (office).

MEJÍA, HE Cardinal Jorge María; Argentine ecclesiastic; *Archivist Emeritus of Vatican Secret Archives;* b. 31 Jan. 1923, Buenos Aires; ordained priest 1945; Titular Archbishop of Apollonia 1986; Official of Justice and Peace 1986–94; Sec. of Bishops 1994–98; Archivist of Vatican Secret Archives and Librarian of Vatican Library 1998–2003, Archivist Emer. 2003–; cr. Cardinal-Deacon of S. Girolamo della Carità 2001. *Address:* c/o Palazzo Apostolico Vaticano, 00120 Città del Vaticano, Italy. *Telephone:* (06) 69883314. *Website:* www.vatican.va/library_archives/vat_secret_archives/index.htm.

MEJIA CARRANZA, Aristides; Honduran government official; *Vice-President;* Pres. Supreme Electoral Tribunal 2005; Minister of Nat. Defence 2006–08; Vice-Pres. 2008–; mem. Liberal Party. *Address:* Office of the President, Palacio José Cecilio del Valle, Blvd Juan Pablo II, Tegucigalpa, Honduras (office). *Telephone:* 232-6282 (office). *Fax:* 231-0097 (office). *Website:* www.presidencia.gob.hn (office).

MEJÍA DOMÍNGUEZ, Rafael Hipólito; Dominican Republic politician; Pres. of the Dominican Repub. 2000–04. *Address:* c/o Administrative Secretariat of the Presidency, Palacio Nacional, Avda México, esq. Dr Delgado, Santo Domingo, D.N., Dominican Republic (office).

MEKSI, Aleksandr; Albanian politician and engineer; fmr construction engineer and restorer of medieval architecture; mem. Democratic Party; Prime Minister of Albania 1992–97. *Address:* c/o Council of Ministers, Tirana, Albania.

MEKSI, Ermelinda, DEcon; Albanian politician and statistician; b. 1957, Tirana; ed European Univ. of Tirana, other pvt univs in Albania; economist 1978–80; Asst Prof. of Econs, Tirana Univ. 1981–87; co-f. Socialist Party 1991, mem. Presidency 1991–; mem. Parl. (Socialist Party) 1992–; Minister of State for Devt and Econ. Cooperation 1997–98; Minister of Econ. Cooperation and Trade 1998–2000; Head of Albanian Parl. Del. to European Parl. 2002–03; Deputy Prime Minister and State Minister of European Integration 2003; Minister of European Integration 2003–05; chief negotiator for Albanian WTO Accession 2000, Stability Pact and Stabilization and Asscn Agreement negotiations with EC 2004–06; mem. Parl. Cttee on Economy, Finances and Privatization; Visiting Prof. La Sapienza Univ., Rome 1992–93, Univ. of Bari, Univ. of Dublin, Kosovo Univ., Univ. La Signora del Buon Consiglio, Tirana, Marin Barleti Univ., Tirana, European Univ., Tirana; del. to several int. orgs including EC, World Bank, IMF, EBRD, UNDP, WTO, European Investment Bank. *Publications:* author of several publications and co-author of several reference books and school texts. *Address:* Albanian Parliament, Tirana, Albania (office). *E-mail:* e_meksi@yahoo.com (office).

MELAMID, Aleksandr; Russian artist; b. 14 July 1945, Moscow; ed Stroganov School and Acad. of Art, Vilnius; initial artistic training at Moscow Art School; originator (with Vitaliy Komar) of 'Sots-art'; mem. of USSR Union of Artists, expelled for "distortion of Soviet reality and non-conformity with the principles of Socialist realism" 1972; moved to Israel 1977, to USA 1978. *Principal works include:* Young Marx 1976, Colour Writing 1972, Quotation 1972, Post Art 1973, Factory for Producing Blue Smoke 1975, Poster Series 1980. *Publications include:* Turkey (Around the world program) 1957, Painting by Numbers: Komar and Melamid's Scientific Guide to Art (co-ed.) 1999, When Elephants Paint: The Quest of Two Russian Artists to Save the Elephants of Thailand 2000.

MELANDRI, Giovanna, BEcons; Italian politician; b. 28 Jan. 1962, New York, USA; m.; one d.; ed Univ. of Rome; mem. Exec. Cttee Legambiente

1988–94; mem. Nat. Direction of Partito Democratico della Sinistra 1991–2007 (mem. Exec. Cttee, in charge of Communication Policy 1996–98), mem. Partito Democratico 2007–; mem. Camera dei Deputati (Chamber of Deputies) 1994–; mem. Young Progressive Networks of Policy Network 2005–; Minister of Culture 1998–2001, for Youth and Sports 2006–08; Shadow Minister for Communication 2008–; promoter, Emily in Italia (initiative of 50 women active in politics and soc. promoting women in politics) 1998–; Officier, Légion d'honneur 2003. *Publications:* (ed.): Ambiente Italia (annual environmental report of Legambiente) 1989–94, Italian World Watch Magazine 1986–91, Digitalia, l'ultima rivoluzione 1998, Cultura, paesaggio e turismo 2006), Come un chiodo: la moda, le ragazze, l'alimentazione 2007. *Address:* Partito Democratico, Piazza Saint'Anastasia 7, 00186 Rome, Italy (office). *Telephone:* (06) 675471 (office). *Fax:* (06) 67547319 (office). *E-mail:* info@partitodemocratico.it (office); melandri_g@camera.it (office). *Website:* www.partitodemocratico.it (office); www.giovannamelandri.it (office).

MELCHETT, 4th Baron, cr. 1928; **Peter Robert Henry Mond Melchett,** LLB, MA; British organic farmer, environmentalist and fmr politician; *Policy Director, Soil Association;* b. 24 Dec. 1948, Norfolk; s. of Lord Julian Melchett (died 1973) and Sonia Melchett; one s. one d.; ed Eton Coll., Univ. of Cambridge, Keele Univ., Staffs.; mem. Labour Party; House of Lords Peer 1973–99; Govt Minister, Depts of Environment and Industry 1975–77; Minister of State, NI Office 1977–79; Pres. Ramblers Asscn 1981–84; Chair. Community Industry 1979–86; Special Lecturer School of Biological Sciences, Nottingham Univ. 1984–2002; joined Greenpeace UK 1985, Chair. and Exec. Dir (arrested and remanded in prison for two days after destroying six acres of genetically modified (GM) maize at farm in Lyng, cleared of causing criminal damage, Norfolk Crown Court 2000) 1989–2000; Chair. Greenpeace Japan 1995–2001; Consultant, Corp. Responsibility Dept, Burson-Marsteller UK (public relations co.) 2002–04; Policy Dir Soil Asscn (organic foods certification body) 2002–; mem. BBC Rural Affairs Committee 2004–, Dept of Educ. School Meals Review Panel 2005; Patron Prisoners Abroad. *Address:* The Soil Association, South Plaza, Marlborough Street, Bristol, BS1 3NX, England (office). *Telephone:* (117) 987 4561 (office); (20) 7831-6262 (office). *E-mail:* pmelchett@soilassociation.org (office). *Website:* www.soilassociation.org (office).

MELCHIOR, Torben, LLM; Danish judge; *President, Supreme Court;* b. 19 Aug. 1940; ed Univ. of Copenhagen, Harvard Law School, USA; civil servant, Ministry of Justice 1966–81, Head, Directorate of Family Law 1982–86; High Court Judge 1986–90; Justice of Supreme Court 1991, Pres. Supreme Court 2004–. *Address:* Supreme Court, Prins Jørgens Gård 13, 1218 Copenhagen, Denmark (office). *Telephone:* 33-63-27-50 (office). *Fax:* 33-15-00-10 (office). *Website:* www.hoejesteret.dk (office).

MELÉNDEZ, Florentín, MA, PhD; Salvadorean academic and international organization official; *President, Inter-American Commission on Human Rights (IACHR—Comisión Interamericana de Derechos Humanos);* ed Nat. Univ. of El Salvador, Complutense Univ. of Madrid, Spain; worked at UN and in public and pvt. insts in El Salvador on issues related to human rights; joined Inter-American Comm. on Human Rights (IACHR—Comisión Interamericana de Derechos Humanos), OAS 2004, Pres. 2004–; Special Rapporteur for rights of persons deprived of liberty in Americas; prepared Draft Declaration of Principles on Protection of Persons Deprived of Freedom; has also been Rapporteur for Argentina, Bolivia, Mexico and Dominican Repub.; del. on several occasions to Inter-American Court of Human Rights; visiting lecturer on human rights at several univs; Freedom Award, Marcelino Pan Y Vino/MAPAVI Foundation 2007. *Publications:* numerous books and compilations on human rights. *Address:* Inter-American Commission on Human Rights, 1889 F Street, NW, Washington, DC 20006, USA (office). *Telephone:* (202) 458-6002 (office). *Fax:* (202) 458-3992 (office). *E-mail:* cidhoea@oas.org (office). *Website:* www.cidh.oas.org (office).

MELEŞCANU, Teodor Viorel, PhD; Romanian jurist and politician; b. 10 March 1941, Brad, Hunedoara Co.; m. Felicia Meleşcanu; one d.; ed Moise Nicoara High School, Arad, Bucharest Univ., Univ. Inst. for Higher Int. Studies, Geneva; with Ministry of Foreign Affairs 1966; mem. numerous dels to UN confs; First Sec. UN, Geneva; Secretary, Ministry of Foreign Affairs, Minister of Foreign Affairs 1992–96, also Deputy Prime Minister; Senator (for Prahova constituency) 1996–2000, Minister of Defence 2007–08; Assoc. Prof. of Int. Law, Univ. of Bucharest 1996–; researcher, Romanian Inst. for Int. Studies 1996–; Founder and Pres. Alliance for Romania (social democratic party) 1997–2001, merged into Nat. Liberal Party (Partidul Naţional Liberal—PNL) 2001, First Vice-Pres. 2001–; presidential cand. 2000; mem. Asscn of Int. Law and Int. Relations (ADIRI), Int. Law Comm. (UN) (First Vice-Chair. 55th Session, Chair. 56th Session). *Publications:* Responsibility of States for the Peaceful Use of Nuclear Energy 1973, International Labour Organization Functioning and Activity, numerous studies and articles. *Leisure interests:* sports (tennis and ski), hunting and fishing. *Address:* National Liberal Party (NLP), 011866 Bucharest, Bd. Aviatorilor 86, Romania (office). *Telephone:* (21) 2310795 (office). *Fax:* (21) 2310796 (office). *E-mail:* dre@pnl.ro (office). *Website:* www.pnl.ro (office).

MELETINSKY, Eleazar Moiseyevich, DLit; Russian philologist; b. 22 Oct. 1918, Kharkov, Ukraine; s. of Moise Meletinsky and Raisa Margolis; m. Elena Andreyevna Kumpan; ed Moscow Inst. of History, Philosophy and Literature; army service World War II 1941–43; Prof. Tashkent Univ. 1944–46; Head of Chair. Petrozavodsk Univ. 1946–49; arrested, imprisoned in Gulag 1949–54; Sr Researcher Inst. of World Literature USSR Acad. of Sciences 1956–92; Dir Inst. of Higher Humanitarian Studies 1992–2005; Prize Pitré 1971, USSR State Prize 1990; Order of the Patriotic War (Second Class). *Publications:* The Hero of Fairy Tales 1958, The Origin of the Heroic Epos 1963, Edda and the First Epic Form 1968, Poetics of Myth 1976, Paleosifirian Epic Mythology 1979, The Medieval Novel 1983, Introduction to Historic Poetics or Epics and the Novel 1986, Historical Poetics of the Novella 1990, On Literary Archetypes 1994, From Myth to Literature 2001, Notes of Work of Dostojevsky 2001, The Beginning of the Psychological Novel 2002; and works on problems of semiotics, history of folklore, mythology. *Address:* c/o Institute of Higher Humanitarian Studies, Miusskaya str. 6, 125267 Moscow (office); Ndakova 12, Apt. 36, 119415, Moscow, Russia (home). *Telephone:* (495) 133-15-98 (home).

MELINESCU, Gabriela; Romanian poet, editor, essayist and translator; b. 16 Aug. 1942, Bucharest; ed Univ. of Philology, Bucharest; began career as Ed. Femeia and Luceafarul magazines; based in Sweden 1975–; trans. of works by Swedenborg, Strindberg, Brigitta Trotzig, Goran Sonevi; Albert Bonniers Prize 2002, Nichita Stanescu Prize 2002, Inst. of Romanian Culture Prize 2004. *Publications:* poetry: Ceremonie de iarna 1965, Fiintele abstracte 1967, Interiorul legii 1968, Boala de origine divina 1970, Juramantul de saracie, castitate si supunere (Writers' Union Prize) 1972, Inginarea lumiir 1972, Impotriva celui drag 1975, Zeul fecunditatii 1977, Oglinda femeii 1986, Lumina spre lumina 1993; prose: Jurnal suedez Vols I–III, Bobinocarii 1969, Catargul cu doua corabii (juvenile) 1969, Viata cere viata (jtly) (non-fiction) 1975, Copiii rabdarii 1979, Lupii urca in cer 1981, Vrajitorul din Gallipoli 1986, Regina strazii 1988, Omul pasare (Swedish Acad. De Nio Prize) 1991; contrib. to Crossing Boundaries: An International Anthology of Women's Experiences in Sport 1999. *Address:* c/o Editura Polirom, Bd. Copou nr. 4, 700506 Iaşi, Romania. *E-mail:* office@polirom.ro.

MELKERT, Ad, MA; Dutch politician, banker and UN official; *Under-Secretary-General and Associate Administrator, United Nations Development Programme (UNDP);* b. 1956, Gouda; m. Mónica León Borquez; two d.; ed Univ. of Amsterdam; Pres., Council of European Nat. Youth Cttees 1979–81; Sec.-Gen. Youth Forum of the EC 1981–84; Pres. Nat. Cttee, UN Int. Youth Year 1984–85; Asst to Gen. Sec., Dir Internal Affairs, Netherlands Org. for Int. Devt Co-operation 1984–86; mem. Parl. 1986–; Minister of Social Affairs and Employment 1994–98; Parliamentary Leader Partij van de Arbeid (PvdA – Labour Party) 1998–2002, Party Leader 2001–02 (resgnd after 2002 election defeat); Exec. Dir for Moldova, World Bank (IBRD) 2002–06; Under-Sec.-Gen. and Assoc. Admin. UNDP 2006–. *Address:* United Nations Development Programme, One United Nations Plaza, New York, NY 10017, USA (office). *Telephone:* (212) 906-5000 (office). *Fax:* (212) 906-5364 (office). *Website:* www.undp.org (office).

MELLO, Craig C., BS, PhD; American geneticist and academic; *Howard Hughes Medical Investigator and Professor, Program in Molecular Medicine, University of Massachusetts Medical School;* b. 18 Oct. 1960, New Haven, Conn.; ed Fairfax High School, Va, Brown Univ., Harvard Univ.; Postdoctoral Fellow, Fred Hutchinson Cancer Research Center; joined faculty, Univ. of Massachusetts Medical School 1994, currently Prof. in Program in Molecular Medicine, Howard Hughes Medical Investigator 2000–; affiliated with Center for AIDS Research, Interdisciplinary Grad. Program, Cell Biology, Cancer Center, Program in Cell Dynamics; mem. NAS 2005; Warren Triennial Prize, Massachusetts Gen. Hosp., Wiley Prize in Biomedical Sciences (co-recipient), Rockefeller Univ. 2003, NAS Award in Molecular Biology (co-recipient) 2003, Lewis S. Rosenstiel Award for Distinguished Work in Medical Research (co-recipient), Brandeis Univ. 2005, Gairdner Foundation Int. Award 2005, Massry Prize (co-recipient) 2005, Paul Ehrlich and Ludwig Darmstaedter Prize (co-recipient) 2006, inaugural recipient Dr Paul Janssen Award for Biomedical Research, Johnson & Johnson 2006, Nobel Prize in Physiology or Medicine (co-recipient with Andrew Fire) for the discovery of RNA interference 2006. *Publications:* numerous scientific papers in professional journals. *Address:* Biotech Two, Suite 219, Program in Molecular Medicine, University of Massachusetts, 373 Plantation Street, Worcester, MA 01605, USA (office). *Telephone:* (508) 856-2254 (office). *E-mail:* Craig.Mello@umassmed.edu (office). *Website:* umassmed.edu (office); www.hhmi.org/research/investigators/mello.html (office).

MELLOR, Rt Hon. David, PC, QC, FZS; British lawyer, journalist, fmr politician and broadcaster; b. 12 March 1949; s. of Douglas H. Mellor; m. Judith Hall 1974 (divorced 1996); two s.; ed Swanage Grammar School, Christ's Coll. Cambridge; called to Bar (Inner Temple) 1972; apptd QC 1987; Chair. Cambridge Univ. Conservative Asscn 1970; fmr Vice-Chair. Chelsea Conservative Asscn; MP for Putney 1979–97; Parl. Under-Sec. of State, Dept of Energy 1981–83, Home Office 1983–86, Minister of State, Home Office 1986–87, FCO 1987–88; Minister for Health 1988–89; Minister of State, Home Office 1989–90; Minister for the Arts July–Nov. 1990; Chief Sec. to Treasury 1990–92; Sec. of State for Nat. Heritage April–Sept. 1992; Consultant Middle East Broadcasting Centre, Middle East Economic Digest, Abela Holdings, RACAL Tacticom, British Aerospace, Ernst & Young, G.K.N.; mem. Bd Amor Holdings, English Nat. Opera 1993–95; Chair. Sports Aid Foundation 1993–97, Football Task Force 1997–99; Deputy Chair. Trustees London Philharmonic Orchestra 1989–90; presenter Six-O-Six BBC Radio 5 1993–99, The Midnight Hour, BBC 2 1997–99, Across the Threshold (series) 1998–, Classic FM 1998–; sports columnist, Evening Standard 1997–2008; Exec. Dir Three Delta LLP 2006–; music critic, Mail on Sunday 2000–; fmr mem. Council Nat. Youth Orchestra; Special Trustee Westminster Hosp. 1979–86; Hon. Assoc. British Veterinary Asscn (for work for animal welfare) 1986; Variety Club Award for BBC Radio Personality of the Year 1994. *Leisure interests:* classical music, football, reading. *Address:* 1st Floor, 14 Hay's Mews, London, W1J 5PT, England (office). *Telephone:* (20) 7514-5522 (office). *Fax:* (20) 7499-1811 (office). *E-mail:* jacki@davidmellorconsultancy.co.uk.

MELLOR, David Hugh, MA, MEng, MS, PhD, ScD, FBA, FAHA; British philosopher and academic; *Professor Emeritus of Philosophy, University of Cambridge;* b. 10 July 1938, London; s. of S. D. Mellor and E. N. Mellor (née Hughes); ed Newcastle Royal Grammar School, Manchester Grammar School and Pembroke Coll., Cambridge; Harkness Fellowship in Chem. Eng, Univ. of Minnesota, USA 1960–62, MIT School of Chem. Eng Practice 1962; Tech. Officer, ICI 1962–63; research student in philosophy 1963–68; Fellow, Pembroke Coll., Cambridge 1964–70; Fellow, Darwin Coll., Cambridge 1971–2005, Vice-Master 1983–87; Asst Lecturer in Philosophy, Univ. of Cambridge 1965–70, Lecturer 1970–83, Reader in Metaphysics 1983–86, Prof. of Philosophy 1986–99, Prof. Emer. 1999–, Pro-Vice-Chancellor 2000–01; Hon. Prof. of Philosophy, Univ. of Keele 1989–92; Visiting Fellow in Philosophy, ANU 1975; Radcliffe Fellow in Philosophy 1978–80; Visiting Prof., Auckland Univ., NZ 1985; Pres. British Soc. for the Philosophy of Science 1985–87, Aristotelian Soc. 1992–93; Hon. PhD (Lund) 1997. *Publications:* The Matter of Chance 1971, Real Time 1981, Matters of Metaphysics 1991, The Facts of Causation 1995, Real Time II 1998, Probability: A Philosophical Introduction 2005; numerous articles on philosophy of science, metaphysics and philosophy of mind. *Leisure interest:* theatre. *Address:* 25 Orchard Street, Cambridge, CB1 1JS, England (home). *Telephone:* (1223) 740017 (home). *E-mail:* dhm11@cam.ac.uk (home). *Website:* people.pwf.cam.ac.uk/dhm11 (office).

MELLOR, James R., BEE, MS; American business executive and electrical engineer; b. 1931; m. Suzanne Mellor; three c.; ed Univ. of Michigan; Research Engineer, then Section Man. in charge of Electronics Systems Design, Hughes Aircraft Co. 1955–58; various eng and man. positions Litton Industries, including Corpn Vice-Pres., Pres. Data Systems Div., Vice-Pres. of Business Devt, Vice-Pres. of Eng, Dir of Advanced Devt, Sr Vice-Pres. Communications and Electronics Data Systems Group 1970–73, Exec. Vice-Pres. Defense Systems Group 1973–77; Dir AM Int. Inc. 1977–81, also Pres. and COO; joined Gen. Dynamics 1981, Exec. Vice-Pres. Marine, Land Systems and Int. 1986–91, Pres. and COO 1991–93, Pres. and CEO 1993–94, Chair. and CEO 1994–97, Consultant and mem. Bd Dirs 1997–; Chair. USEC Inc. 1998–; Chair. AmerisourceBergen Corpn 2004–06 (retd); received three patents relating to large screen display and digital computing tech.; Consultant to Dept of Defense 1972–75; fmr Chair. Shipbuilders Council of America, Computer and Business Equipment Mfrs Asscn; currently mem. Bd Dirs, Pinkerton Inc., Computer Sciences Corpn, Net2Phone Inc., USEC Inc.; fmr mem. Bd Dirs Bergen Brunswig Corpn, Armed Forces Communications and Electronics Asscn, Nat. Security Industrial Asscn, US Navy League, Bd of Councillors Univ. of Southern Calif. Business School; currently mem. Nat. Advisory Cttee, Univ. of Michigan, United States—Egypt Pres.'s Council; Officer Order of the Crown (Belgium) 1987; Business Leader Recipient, Ellis Island Medals of Honour 1998. *Address:* c/o AmerisourceBergen Corporation, 1300 Morris Drive, Suite 100, Chesterbrook, PA 19087-5594, USA (office).

MELNIKOV, Vitaly Vyacheslavovich; Russian film director and screenwriter; b. 1 May 1928, Mazanovo, Amur Prov.; m. Tamara Aleksandrovna Melnikova; ed All-Union State Inst. of Cinema (VGIK) under S. I. Yutkevich and M. I. Romm; series of documentary films 1953–64; Artistic Dir Golos studio 1989–; Sec. St Petersburg Union of Cinematographers; People's Artist of Russia 1986, Venice Film Festival Prize 1981. *Films include:* Barbos Visits Bobik 1965, Nachalnik Chukotki (Chief Chukotky) 1966, Mama vyshla zamuzh (Mum's Got Married) 1969, Sem nevest efreytora Zbrueva (The Seven Brides of Lance-Corporal Zbruyev) 1970, Zdravstvuy i proshchay (Hello and Goodbye!) 1972, Xenia, Fyodor's Favourite Wife 1974, Starshiy syn (The Elder Son) (also writer) 1975, Zhenitba (Marriage) (also writer) 1977, September Holiday 1979, Dve strochki melkim shriftom (Two Lines in Small Print) (also writer) 1981, Unikum (One of a Kind) (also writer) 1983, Vyyti zamuzh za kapitana (To Marry a Captain) 1985, Pervaya vstrecha – poslednyaya vstrecha (First Meeting – Last Meeting) 1987, Tsarskaya okhota (The Royal Hunt) 1990, Chicha 1992, The Vareny's Last Case 1994, Tsarevich Alexei (also writer) 1996, Night Lights 2000, Lunoi byl polon sad (The Garden Was Full of Moon) 2000, Bednyy, bednyy Pavel (Poor, Poor Pavel) (also writer) 2003. *Television includes:* Chuzhaya zhena i muzh pod krovatyu (Another Man's Wife and Husband Under Bed) 1984, Otpusk v sentyabre (also writer) 1987. *Address:* Svetlanovsky proyezd 105, Apt 20, 195269 St Petersburg, Russia. *Telephone:* (812) 532-51-88.

MELNIZKY, Walter, DJur; Austrian judge; b. 1 Nov. 1928, Vienna; s. of Ernst Melnizky and Maria Melnizky; m. Gertrude Melnizky 1953; one s.; ed Univ. of Vienna; judge 1954–57, 1962–69; Public Prosecutor 1957–62; Gen. Prosecutor 1969–86; Pres. Supreme Court 1987–93; Chair. Court of Arbitration Gen. Medical Council of Vienna 1995–; Pres. Austrian Automobile and Motorcycle Touring Club (ÖAMTC) 1981–2001; consultant, Syndicus Asscn of Public Experts 1988–; Komturkreuz des Landes Niederösterreich und Burgenlandes, Grosses Goldenes Ehrenzeichen am Bande (Austria), Grosses Verdienstkreuz mit Stern und Schulterband (Germany). *Publications:* numerous juridical essays, especially on traffic law and criminal law. *Leisure interests:* classical music, opera. *Address:* c/o ÖAMTC, Schubertring 1–3, 1010 Vienna; Hannplatz 4/14, 1190 Vienna, Austria (home). *Telephone:* (1) 711-99-702; (1) 368-73-74 (home). *Fax:* (1) 368-73-74 (home).

MELROSE, Donald Blair, DPhil, FAA; Australian physicist and academic; *Professor, University of Sydney;* b. 13 Sept. 1940, Hobart, Tasmania; s. of the late Andrew B. Melrose and of Isla L. Luff; m. Sara C. Knabe 1969; one s. one d.; ed N Sydney Boys' High School, John Curtin High School, Fremantle, Univs of Western Australia and Tasmania, Univ. of Oxford, UK; Research Fellow, Univ. of Sussex, UK 1965–66; Research Assoc., Belfer Grad. School of Science, Yeshiva Univ., New York, USA 1966–68; Research Fellow, Center for Theoretical Physics, Univ. of Maryland, USA 1968–69; Sr Lecturer in Theoretical Physics, ANU 1969–72, Reader 1972–79; Prof. of Theoretical Physics, Univ. of Sydney 1979–, Dir Research Centre for Theoretical Astrophysics 1991–99, Head of School 2001–02, Prof. of the Univ. 2000–; Australian Research Council Professorial Research Fellow 2003–07; Rhodes Scholar for Tasmania 1962, Pawsey Medal, Australian Acad. of Science 1974,

Walter Boas Medal, Australian Inst. of Physics 1986, Thomas Ranken Lyle Medal, Australian Acad. of Science 1987, Harrie Massey Medal and Prize, Inst. of Physics 1998. *Publications:* Plasma Physics (two vols) 1980, Instabilities in Space and Laboratory Plasmas 1986, Electromagnetic Processes in Dispersive Media (with R. C. McPhedran) 1991, Plasma Astrophysics (with J. G. Kirk and E. R. Priest) 1994; more than 200 papers in scientific journals. *Leisure interests:* rugby union, surfing, jogging, squash. *Address:* School of Physics, Room 454, University of Sydney, Sydney, NSW 2006 (office); 8/84 Milray Avenue, Wollstonecraft, NSW 2065, Australia (home). *Telephone:* (2) 9351-4234 (office); (2) 9438-3635 (home). *Fax:* (2) 9351-7726 (office); (2) 9351-7726 (office). *E-mail:* d.melrose@physics.usyd.edu.au (office). *Website:* www.physics.usyd.edu.au/~melrose (office).

MELROY, Col (retd) Pamela Ann, MSc; American astronaut and air force officer (retd); b. 17 Sept. 1961, Palo Alto, Calif.; d. of David Melroy and Helen Melroy; m. Douglas W. Hollett; ed Wellesley Coll., Massachusetts Inst. of Tech.; participated in US Air Force ROTC program 1983; Undergraduate Pilot Training, Reese Air Force Base, Tex. 1985; flew KC-10 as Copilot, Aircraft Commdr and Instructor Pilot, Barksdale Air Force Base, La 1985–91; attended Air Force Test Pilot School, Edwards Air Force Base, Calif. 1991; Test Pilot, C-17 Combined Test Force 1991–94; logged over 5,000 hours in flight time in over 45 different aircraft; Astronaut Cand., NASA 1994; Shuttle Pilot training, Johnson Space Center 1995–96, has since served on Columbia Reconstruction Team, CAPCOM duties at mission control, as Pilot on STS-92 Discovery 2000, STS-112 Atlantis 2002, as Commdr STS-120 2007; logged over 38 days in space; mem. Soc. of Experimental Test Pilots, Order of Daedalians, 99s (Int. Org. of Women Pilots); Air Force Meritorious Service Medal, First Oak Leaf Cluster; Air Medal, First Oak Leaf Cluster; Aerial Achievement Medal, First Oak Leaf Cluster; Expeditionary Medal, First Oak Leaf Cluster. *Address:* NASA Johnson Space Center, 2101 NASA Parkway, Houston, TX 77058, USA. *Telephone:* (281) 483-0123. *Website:* www.nasa.gov.

MELVILLE-ROSS, Timothy David, CBE, FCIS, FIOB, FRSA, CIMgt; British business executive; *Chairman, DTZ Holdings PLC;* b. 3 Oct. 1944, Westward Ho, Devon; s. of the late Antony Melville-Ross and Anne Fane; m. Camilla Probert 1967; two s. one d.; ed Uppingham School and Portsmouth Coll. of Tech.; BP 1963–73; Rowe Swann & Co. (stockbrokers) 1973–74; Nationwide Bldg Soc. 1974–94, Dir and Chief Exec. 1985–94; Dir Monument Oil & Gas PLC 1992–99; Dir-Gen. Inst. of Dirs 1994–99; Deputy Chair. Monument Oil and Gas PLC 1997–99; Dir Bovis Homes Ltd 1997–2008 (Chair. 2005–08), DTZ Holdings PLC (Chair. 2000–), Equity Trust SARL 2003–05; Chair. Investors in People UK 1999–2006; Chair. Supervisory Bd Bank Insinger de Beaufort NV 2000–05; Deputy Chair. Royal London Mutual Insurance 2003–05, Chair. 2006–; Chair. Manganese Bronze PLC 2003–; Chair. Higher Educ. Funding Council 2008–. *Leisure interests:* reading, music, bridge, sport, the countryside. *Address:* DTZ Holdings PLC, 1 Curzon Street, London, W1A 5PZ (office); Little Bevills, Bures, Suffolk, CO8 5JN, England (home). *Telephone:* (20) 7643-6039 (office); (1787) 227424 (home). *Fax:* (20) 7643-6062 (home). *E-mail:* tim.melville-ross@dtz.com (office). *Website:* www.dtz.com (office).

MEMBE, Bernard Kamillius, MA; Tanzanian politician; *Minister of Foreign Affairs and International Relations;* b. 9 Nov. 1953; ed Univ. of Dar es Salaam and John Hopkins Univ., USA; Nat. Security Analyst, Office of the Pres. 1977–90; Ambassadorial Adviser, Ministry of Foreign Affairs 1992–2000; mem. Parl. (Chama Cha Mapinduzi Party—CCM) for Mtama 2000–; Deputy Minister of Home Affairs Jan.–Oct. 2006, of Energy and Minerals 2006–07; Minister of Foreign Affairs and Int. Relations 2007–. *Address:* Ministry of Foreign Affairs and International Relations, POB 9000, Dar es Salaam, Tanzania (office). *Telephone:* (22) 2111906 (office). *Fax:* (22) 2116600 (office). *E-mail:* bmembe@parliament.go.tz (office).

MEMMI, Albert; French writer; b. 15 Dec. 1920, Tunis; s. of François Memmi and Marguerite née Sarfati; m. Germaine Dubach 1946; three c.; ed Lycée Carnot, Tunis, Univ. of Algiers and Univ. de Paris à la Sorbonne; Teacher, Lycée Carnot, Tunis 1953, Teacher of Philosophy, Tunis 1955; Dir Psychological Centre, Tunis 1953–57; moved to France 1956; attached to Centre Nat. de la recherche Scientifique 1957, Researcher, CNRS, Paris 1959–; Chargé de conférences, Ecole pratique des hautes études 1958, Asst Prof. 1959–66, Prof. 1966–70; Prof., Inst. de Psychanalyse, Paris 1968–; Prof., Univ. of Paris 1970–, Dir, Social Sciences Dept 1973–76, Dir, Anthropological Lab.; mem. Acad. des Sciences d'Outre-mer; Vice-Pres., Pen-Club 1976–79; Managing Agent, Syndicat des Écrivains de Langue Française (SELF) 1981; Vice-Pres., Comité Nat. Laïcité-République 1991; mem. Comité de patronage du MRAP; mem. Ligue Internationale Contre le Racisme et l'Anti-sémitisme (LICRA); Hon. Cttee Mem. l'Union Rationaliste, Comité Culturel Tunisien en France 1995; Scientific Cttee Mem. Cahiers Francophones d'Europe Centre-Orientale 1996; Cttee Mem. sponsoring Association des Anciens Elèves du Lycée Carnot de Tunis 1996; Hon. Mem. Association des Etudes Françaises en Afrique Australe 1996; Advisory mem., Institut des Études Transrégionales du Centre d'Études, Int. Study Centre, Princeton Univ. 1995; mem. l'Acad. des Sciences d'Outremer, l'Accademia Internazionale, l'Acad. de la Méditerranée; Officier Légion d'honneur; Commdr Ordre de Nichan Iftikhar; Officier des Palmes académiques, Officier des Arts et Lettres, Officier Ordre de la République Tunisienne; Chevalier des affaires culturelles du Burkina Faso; Dr hc (Ben Gurion) 1999, (Beer Schéba); Hon. Prof. Walker Aims Univ., Washington Univ., l'école des H.E.C.; Prix de Carthage 1953, Prix Fénéon 1953, Prix Simba 1978, Prix de l'Union Rationaliste 1994, Grand Prix Littéraire de l'Afrique du Nord, Grand Prix Littéraire du Maghreb 1995, Prix littéraire Tunisie-France 1999, Chalom du Crif 2000, Grand Prix de la ville de Bari 2000, Prix de l'Afrique méditeranéenne 2002, Prix de la Fondation Ignacio Silone 2003, Grand Prix de la Francophonie décerné par l'Académie Française

2004. *Publications include:* novels: Le Statue de Sel (trans. as The Pillar of Salt) 1953, Strangers 1955, Agar 1955, Le Scorpion 1969, Le Désert 1977, Le Pharaon 1988; poems: Le Mirliton du ciel 1990, short stories: Le nomade immobile 2000, Térésa et autre femmes 2004; non-fiction: Portrait du colonisé 1957, Portrait d'un Juif 1962, Anthologie des écrivains Maghrebins 1964, 1969, Anthologie des écrivains nord-africains 1965, Les français et le racisme 1965, The Liberation of the Jew 1966, Dominated Man 1968, Decolonisation 1970, Juifs et Arabes 1974, Entretien 1975, La terre intérieure 1976, La dependance 1979, Le racisme 1982, Ce que je crois 1984, Les écrivains francophones du Maghreb 1985, L'Écriture colorée 1986, Bonheurs 1992, A contre-courants 1993, Ah, quel bonheur 1995, Le Juif et l'autre 1995, L'Exercice du bonheur 1996, Le Buveur et l'amoureux 1996, Feu sur 40 idées recues 1999, Dictionnaire à l'usage des incrédules 2002, Portrait du décolonisé, arabo-musulman et de quelques autres 2004, contrib. to Le onde 1989–94, Le Figaro 1995, New York Times, L'Action. *Leisure interest:* writing. *Address:* 5 rue Saint Merri, 75004 Paris, France. *Telephone:* 1-40-29-08-31. *Fax:* 1-42-74-25-22.

MEN, Mikhail Aleksandrovich, CandSci; Russian politician; *Governor of Ivanovo Oblast;* b. 12 Nov. 1960, Semkhoz, Moscow Region; s. of Aleksander Men; m.; three c.; ed Moscow Gubkin Inst. of Gas and Oil, Moscow State Inst. of Culture; Russian Acad. of State Service; fmr stage director, amateur theatre and clubs of Moscow 1983–91; bass guitarist and singer for rock band Most 1986; mem. Moscow Region Duma 1993–95; mem. State Duma (Parl.) 1995–99; Deputy Chair. Cttee on Culture 1995–2005; Chair. All-Union Christian Union 1996–; Chair. Aleksander Men Foundation; elected Vice-Gov. Moscow Region 2000–02 (resgnd); Deputy Mayor of Moscow 2002–05; Gov. of Ivanovo Oblast 2005–. *Publication:* Culture and Religion 2001. *Leisure interests:* music, sport. *Address:* 153002 Ivanovo, ul. Pushkina 9, Russia (office). *Telephone:* (4932) 47-17-19 (office). *Fax:* (4932) 47-17-19 (office). *E-mail:* git@adminet.ivanovo.ru (office). *Website:* www.ivreg.ru/biography/gubernator.html (office); www.menn.ru (home).

MENA KEYMER, Carlos Eduardo; Chilean lawyer, academic and fmr diplomatist; m.; two c.; fmr Under-Sec. of Navy; Amb. to Brazil 2000–03; Vice-Pres. Ejecutivo del Comité de Inversiones Extranjeras (Exec. Cttee on Foreign Investments) 2006–; Pres. Empresa Portuaria Arica (cargo handling co.). *Address:* Empresa Portuaria Arica, Máximo Lira 389, Arica, Chile (office). *Telephone:* 58) 25-5078 (office). *Fax:* (58) 23-2284 (office). *E-mail:* puertoarica@puertoarica.cl (office). *Website:* www.puertoarica.cl (office).

MÉNAGE, Gilles Marie Marcel; French government official and organization official; *Secretary-General, l'Institut François Mitterrand;* b. 5 July 1943, Bourg-la-Reine (Hauts-de-Seine); s. of Georges Ménage and Jeanne Paillottet; m. 1st Marie-France Beaussier (divorced); two d.; m. 2nd Doris Lenz; one s. one d.; ed Lycée Lakanal, Sceaux, Lycée Berthollet, Annecy, Inst. d'Études Politiques, Paris and Ecole Nat. d'Admin; civil admin., Ministry of Interior 1969; Deputy Prefect, Head of Staff for Prefect of Tarn-et-Garonne 1969–70, then for Prefect of Haute-Vienne and Limousin 1970–74; Tech. Adviser to Sec. of State for Posts and Telecommunications (PTT) 1974; Head of Staff for Pierre Lelong, Sec. for PTT 1974–76; Deputy Prefect and Special Adviser to Prefect of Paris 1976–77; Head of Staff for Prefect/Sec.-Gen. of Préfecture de Paris 1977–81; Sr Lecturer, Inst. d'Etudes Politiques, Paris 1976–77, Inst. Int. d'Admin. Publique 1980–81; Tech. Adviser, then Deputy Head of Staff for Pres. of France 1982–88, Chief of Staff 1988–92; Chair. Electricité de France 1992–95; working on energy project for Ministry of Industry 1996–97; Prefect 1997–; Chair. Int. Consortiums Consultants 1998–; Pres. 'Les florilèges du Château féodal de Madaillan' 2002; Sec. Gen. l'Institut François Mitterrand 2003–; Pres. 'Les Florilèges de Quercy, Gascogne, Guyenne' 2004; Chevalier, Ordre nat. du Mérite, Chevalier, Légion d'honneur. *Publications:* La France face aux dangers de guerre 1981, L'oeil du pouvoir: les Affaires de l'État (1981–1986) 1999, L'oeil du pouvoir: Face aux terrorismes (1981–1986) 2000, L'oeil du pouvoir: Face au terrorisme moyen oriental (1981–86) 2001. *Leisure interests:* skiing, music, organizing concerts for talented young musicians. *Address:* l'Institut François Mitterrand, 10 rue Charlot, 75003 Paris (office); EDF, 38 rue Jacques Ibert, 75177, Paris Cedex 17 (office); Château de Noilhac, 47140 Penne d'Agenais, France (home); International Consortiums, Château de Noilhac, 47140 Penne d'Agenais (office). *Telephone:* 1-40-42-82-85 (office); (5) 53-41-36-01 (home). *E-mail:* gilles.menage@libertysurf.fr (office). *Website:* www.mitterrand.org (office).

MENAGHARISHVILI, Irakli Afinogenovich; Georgian politician; b. 18 May 1951, Tbilisi; s. of Afinogen Menagarishvili and Ekaterine Jorbenadze; m. Manana Mikaberidze 1975; two s.; ed Tbilisi State Inst. of Medicine; leader Comsomol Orgs 1976–80; head of City Public Health Dept 1980–82; First Deputy Minister of Public Health 1982–86, Minister 1986–91, 1992–93; Dir Georgian Cen. of Strategic Studies; Co-ordinator of Humanitarian Aid of State Council of Georgia 1991–92; Deputy Prime Minister 1993–95; Minister of Foreign Affairs 1995–2004. *Address:* c/o Ministry of Foreign Affairs, 4 Chitadze Street, 380008 Tbilisi, Georgia.

MENARD, John R., Jr, BA; American retail executive; *President and CEO, Menards Inc.;* m. (divorced); six c.; ed Univ. of Wis. at Eau Claire; opened his first home-improvement store in 1972; founder, Pres. and CEO Menards Inc. 1972–; mem. Bd of Dirs Polaris Industries Pnrs L.P. 2001–; sponsors Menards Racing team. *Address:* Menards Inc., 4777 Menard Drive, Eau Claire, WI 54703-9604, USA (office). *Telephone:* (715) 876-5911 (office). *Fax:* (715) 876-2868 (office). *Website:* www.menards.com (office); www.teammenard.net.

MENCHÚ TUM, Rigoberta; Guatemalan human rights activist; b. 9 Jan. 1959, San Miguel Uspantán; d. of the late Vicente Menchu and Juana Menchu; m. Angél Canil 1995; one c.; began campaigning for rights of Indians as teenager; fled to Mexico after parents and brother were killed by security forces 1980; co-ordinated protests in San Marcos against 500th anniversary of arrival of Columbus in Americas 1992; f. Rigoberta Menchú Tum Foundation, Guatemala City; Int. Goodwill Amb. UNESCO 1996–; cand. for Pres. 2007; Pres. UN Indigenous Initiative for Peace 1999; Commdr, Légion d'honneur 1996; numerous hon. degrees; Nobel Peace Prize 1992. *Publications:* I, Rigoberta (trans. into 12 languages) 1983, Rigoberta: Grandchild of the Mayas (co-author) 1998. *Address:* Fundacion Rigoberta Menchú Tum, Avenida Simeón Cañas 4-04 Zona 2, Ciudad de Guatemala, Guatemala (office). *Telephone:* 2230-2431 (office). *Fax:* 2221-3999 (office). *E-mail:* guatemala@frmt.org (office). *Website:* www.frmt.org (office).

MENDELSOHN, John, BA, MD; American physician, medical researcher and administrator; *President, University of Texas M. D. Anderson Cancer Center;* b. 31 Aug. 1936, Cincinnati; m. Anne Mendelsohn; three s.; ed Harvard Coll., Harvard Medical School; residency training in internal medicine at Brigham and Womans' Hosp., Boston; Research Fellow, NIH, Washington Univ. Medical School, St Louis; mem. faculty, later Asst Prof., then Prof., Univ. of Calif., San Diego 1970–85, est. National Cancer Inst.-designated cancer centre, Dir 1976–85; with Memorial Sloan-Kettering Cancer Center 1985–96, Chair. Dept of Medicine, held Winthrop Rockefeller Chair in Medical Oncology, also served for five years as Co-head of Program in Molecular Pharmacology and Therapeutics; Prof. and Vice-Chair. of Medicine, Cornell Univ. Medical Coll.; fmr Attending Physician at both Memorial and New York Hosps; Pres. Univ. of Tex. M.D. Anderson Cancer Center, Houston, Tex. 1996–; Founding Ed. Clinical Cancer Research; fmr mem. editorial bds numerous leading scientific journals; Vice-Chair. BioHouston; mem. Bd Greater Houston Partnership, Bd Houston Tech. Center, Bd Center for Houston's Future, Houston Forum; mem. NAS Inst. of Medicine 1997; Fulbright Scholar, Raymond Bourgine Award 1997, Gold Medal of Paris 1997, honoured by Bristol-Myers Squibb Co. with unrestricted grant for promising research at M.D. Anderson Cancer Center 1997, Joseph H. Burchenal Clinical Research Award, American Asscn for Cancer Research 1999, Jill Rose Award, Breast Cancer Research Foundation 1999, Simon Shubitz Prize, Univ. of Chicago 2002, David A. Karnofsky Memorial Award, American Soc. of Clinical Oncology 2002, Bristol-Myers Squibb Freedom to Discover Award for Distinguished Achievement in Cancer Research 2004, jointly honoured with his wife for public service by Woodrow Wilson Int. Center for Scholars 2005, Fulbright Lifetime Achievement Medal 2005, Dan David Prize 2006. *Publications:* The Molecular Basis of Cancer (Sr Ed.); more than 300 scientific papers and articles for journals and books. *Address:* President's Office, University of Texas M.D. Anderson Cancer Center, 1515 Holcombe Blvd, Box 0091, Houston, TX 77030, USA (office). *Telephone:* (713) 792-6000 (office). *Website:* www.mdanderson.org (office).

MENDES, Sam, CBE; British theatre director and film director; b. 1 Aug. 1965; s. of Valerie Mendes and Peter Mendes; m. Kate Winslet (q.v.) 2003; one s.; ed Magdalen Coll. School, Oxford and Peterhouse, Cambridge; fmr artistic Dir Minerva Studio Theatre, Chichester; Artistic Dir Donmar Warehouse 1992–2002; Co-Dir The Bridge Project (theatre Co. est. with Kevin Spacey at Old Vic Theatre, London and Brooklyn Acad. of Music, NY) 2007–; Critics' Circle Award 1989, 1993, 1996, Olivier Award for Best Dir 1996, Tony Award 1998, LA Critics' Award, Broadcast Critcs' Award, Toronto People's Choice Award, Golden Globe Award (all 1999), Shakespeare Prize, Directors' Guild of Great Britain lifetime achievement award 2005. *Films:* American Beauty (Acad. Award for Best Dir, Best Film 2000) 1999, Road to Perdition 2002, Jarhead 2005, Revolutionary Road 2008, Away We Go 2009. *Plays directed include:* London Assurance (Chichester), The Cherry Orchard (London), Kean (Old Vic, London), The Plough and the Stars (Young Vic, London) 1991, Troilus and Cressida (RSC) 1991, The Alchemist (RSC) 1991, Richard III (RSC) 1992, The Tempest (RSC) 1993; Nat. Theatre debut with The Sea 1991, The Rise and Fall of Little Voice (Nat. and Aldwych) 1992, The Birthday Party 1994, Othello (also world tour); Assassins, Translations, Cabaret, Glengarry Glen Ross, The Glass Menagerie, Company, Habeas Corpus, The Front Page, The Blue Room, To the Green Fields Beyond (all at Donmar Warehouse) 1992–2000; Uncle Vanya and Twelfth Night (Donmar Warehouse, Olivier Award for Best Dir 2003, Olivier Special Award 2003) 2002, Oliver! (London Palladium), Cabaret, The Blue Room (Broadway, NY). *Leisure interest:* cricket. *Address:* Creative Artists Agency, 2000 Avenue of the Stars, Los Angeles, CA 90067, USA (office). *Telephone:* (424) 288-2000 (office). *Fax:* (424) 288-2900 (office). *Website:* www.caa.com (office).

MENDES, Sérgio; Brazilian singer and songwriter; b. 11 Feb. 1941, Niterói; s. of Benedicto Mendes; m. Gracinha Leporace; ed Music Conservatory of Niterói; pioneered Bossa Nova movt in Brazil with Antonio Carlos Jobim, João Gilberto and Moacyr Santos; f. Bossa Rio Sextet in 1958, toured Brazil, Europe, Middle East and Japan; Bossa Nova Festival, New York 1962; moved to Calif., USA 1964; f. Brasil 64 band, toured USA, tour with Frank Sinatra 1967, tour of Japan 1968, Europe 1980; recorded albums with Black Eyed Peas 2006, 2008; continues to tour around the world. *Recordings include:* Brasileiro (Grammy Award for Best World Music Album 1992) 1992, Timeless (Latin Grammy Award for Best Brazilian Pop Album 2006) 2006, Encanto 2008, over 40 albums. *Address:* c/o Concord Music Group, Inc., 23307 Commerce Park Road, Cleveland, OH 44122 USA (office). *Website:* www.concordmusicgroup.com (office); www.sergiomendesmusic.com.

MENDES CABEÇADAS, Adm. José Manuel; Portuguese naval officer; b. 1943, Lisbon; m. Sibylle Ninette; two s. one d.; ed Naval Acad., Portuguese Naval War Coll.; began career in Portuguese Navy 1961; several sea duty tours with various ships, Commdr NRP Quanza and NRP Oliveira e Carmo; held positions successively as Dir Communication Centre, Lake Niassa and Ministry of Defence, Dir Naval Radio Station, Metangula, Mozambique, Staff Officer Personnel and Org. Div., Staff Officer Intelligence Div., Naval

Command, Head of 1st Section Directorate of Personnel, Teacher of Man. Portuguese Naval War Coll.; assigned to Mil. Rep. to NATO, Brussels 1984, later Exec. Asst Iberian Atlantic Area, NATO HQ; Exec. Asst to Chief of Naval Command 1996–2000; Dir of Portuguese Naval War Coll. 2000–02; Chief of Naval Staff May–Nov. 2000; Chief of Defence 2002–06; apptd Vice Adm. 2000, Adm. 2002; Grand Officier Ordem Militar de Avis Distinguished Service Gold Medal, 2 Distinguished Service Silver Medals, Mil. Merit Medals 1st, 2nd and 3rd Class, 2 Navy Cross Medals 2nd Class. *Address:* c/o Ministry of National Defence, Av. Ilha de Madeira, 1400-204 Lisbon, Portugal (office).

MENDES DA ROCHA, Paulo; Brazilian architect; b. 25 Oct. 1928, Vitória; ed Faculty of Architecture and Urban Planning, Mackenzie Univ., São Paulo; started pvt. practice 1955; Prof. Faculty of Architecture and Urban Planning, Univ. of São Paulo 1959–98; won nat. competition to design part of Paulistano Athletic Club in Sao Paulo; fmr Pres. Brazilian Inst. of Architects; Mies van der Rohe Award for Latin American Architecture, Barcelona, 2000, Pritzker Prize 2006. *Major works include:* Club Atletico Paulistano, Pinacoteca of São Paulo restoration project, Museu Brasileiro de Escultura (MuBE) project, Cultural Center FIESP, Pinacoteca de São Paulo, Poupatempo Itaquera, Urban Bus Terminal Parque D. Pedro II. *Publications include:* Paulo Mendes da Rocha: Projects 1967/2006 (with Rosa Artigas) 2007. *Address:* c/o The Hyatt Foundation, Media Information Office, 8002 Ashcroft Avenue, Los Angeles, CA, USA.

MÉNDEZ GUTIÉRREZ, Gonzalo; Bolivian government official and academic; b. Cochabamba; ed Universidad Mayor de San Simón, Univ. of Amberes, Catholic Univ. of Louvain, Belgium; fmr Nat. Dir of Academic Planning, Universidad Católica Boliviana; fmr Prof. Universidad Andina Simón Bolívar; fmr Dir of Finance and Planning, Municipality of Cochabamba; Minister of Nat. Defence 2005–06 (resgnd). *Address:* c/o Ministry of National Defence, Plaza Avaroa, esq. Pedro Salazar y 20 de Octubre 2502, La Paz, Bolivia (office).

MÉNDEZ PINELO, Gen. César Augusto; Guatemalan politician and army officer; 28 years of service in Guatemalan Armed Forces, rank of Gen.; fmr Mil. Attaché, Embassy in Honduras; served with Mil. Intelligence Dept; Minister of Nat. Defence –2004.

MENDILLO, Jane, BA, MBA; American investment manager and business executive; *President and CEO, Harvard Management Company, Inc.;* ed Yale Univ.; man. consultant with Bain & Co., Boston, Mass –1987; joined Harvard Management Co. (Harvard Univ.'s endowment arm) 1987, mem. Internal Equities Man. Team 1987–89, Vice-Pres. for Pvt. Equity 1989–91, Vice-Pres. for Trusts 1992–96, Vice-Pres. of External Investments 1997–2002, Pres. and CEO 2008–; Chief Investment Officer, Wellesley Coll. 2002–08; mem. Yale Univ. Investment Cttee 2002–08, Partners HealthCare System Investment Cttee (includes Massachusetts Gen. Hosp. and Brigham and Women's Hosp.), Harvard-Yenching Inst. Investment Cttee, Dimock Community Health Center Bd of Visitors, Roxbury; mem. Boston Security Analysts Soc., Inc., Boston Cttee on Foreign Relations, Boston Econ. Club; 100 Women in Hedge Funds Industry Leadership Award 2007, ranked by Forbes magazine amongst 100 Most Powerful Women (42nd) 2008. *Address:* Harvard Management Company, Inc., 600 Atlantic Avenue, Suite 15, Boston, MA 02210-2211, USA (office). *Telephone:* (617) 523-4400 (office). *E-mail:* general@hmc.harvard.edu (office). *Website:* www.hmc.harvard.edu (office).

MENDIS, Sunil; Sri Lankan business executive and banker; joined Hayleys Ltd 1962, mem. Bd of Dirs 1977–2004, Chair. and CEO 1993–2004; Gov. Central Bank of Sri Lanka 2004–06, Chair. Monetary Bd 2004–06; mem. Nat. Council for Econ. Devt 2004–06; mem. Bd of Govs South East Asian Central Banks (SEACEN) Research and Training Centre 2004–; fmr mem. Bd of Dirs Bank of Ceylon, US Educational Foundation in Sri Lanka, Private Sector Infrastructure Devt Co. Ltd, Export Devt Bd, Bd Investment, Presidential Salaries Comm. *Address:* c/o Central Bank of Sri Lanka, 30 Janadhipathi Mawatha, Colombo 1, Sri Lanka (office).

MENDONCA E MOURA, Alvaro; Portuguese politician and diplomatist; *Permanent Representative, European Union;* b. 17 March 1951, Oporto; m.; four c.; ed Univ. of Colmbra; Embassy Attaché 1975–78; Third Sec. 1978; Second Sec. 1978–82; First Sec. 1982–90; Counsellor 1990–93; Minister 1993–2002; Amb. 2002–; posted to Perm. Del. to EFTA, GATT, Geneva 1979, posted to Embassy, Pretoria, S Africa 1985, Chargé d'affaires a.i. 1988–89; Dir forAfrican Affairs, Ministry of Foreign Affairs 1990–91; Chef de Cabinet, Sec. of State for Foreign Affairs and Co-operation 1991–92; Chef de Cabinet, Minister for Foreign Affairs 1992–95; Amb. in Vienna, Perm. Rep. to UN Office in Vienna 1995; non-resident Amb. in Ljubljana 1996; non-resident Amb. in Bratislava 1996; Amb., Perm. Rep. to UN Office and other Int. Orgs, Geneva 1999; Amb., Perm. Rep. to EU 2002–; Head of Portuguese Del. to UN Comm. on Crime Prevention and Criminal Justice 1996, 1997, 1998, 1999; Chair. Preparatory Cttee, Cttee of Whole of UN Gen. Ass.'s Special Session on Narcotic Drugs 1997–98; Vice-Chair. UN Human Rights Comm. 2001–02; Chair. Gen. Ass., World Intellectual Property Org. 2001–02; Prof., Dept of Int. Relations, Lusiada Univ., Lisbon; mem. High-Level Group of Experts appointed by UN Sec. Gen. to review Int. Drug Control Programme, to strengthen UN machinery for Int. Drug Control, Vienna, New York 1998. *Address:* Permanent Mission of Portugal, 12/22 Avenue de Cortenbergh, 1040 Brussels, Belgium (office). *Telephone:* (2) 286-42-11 (office). *Fax:* (2) 231-00-26 (office). *E-mail:* reper@reper-portugal.be (office). *Website:* www.reper-portugal.be (office).

MENDONÇA PREVIATO, Lucia, PhD; Brazilian biophysicist, parasitologist and academic; b. 17 Feb. 1949, Maceió, Alagoas; currently Prof. of Biophysics and Parasitology, Biophysics Inst., Fed. Univ. of Rio de Janeiro; Nat. Order for Scientific Merit 2002, L'Oréal-UNESCO for Women in Science Award 2004. *Publications:* numerous articles in scientific journals on the study of *Trypanosoma cruzi*, the protozoan parasite responsible for Chagas disease. *Address:* Biophysics Institute, Federal University of Rio de Janeiro, Rio de Janeiro 21944–170, Brazil (office). *E-mail:* luciamp@biof.ufrj.br (office). *Website:* www.biof.ufrj.br (office).

MENDOZA, June, AO, OBE, RP, ROI; British portrait painter; b. Melbourne; d. of John Morton and Dot Mendoza; m. Keith Mackrell; one s. three d.; ed Lauriston School for Girls, Melbourne, St Martin's School of Art, London; portraits include HM Queen Elizabeth II, HM Queen Elizabeth, the Queen Mother, HRH The Prince of Wales, Diana, Princess of Wales, Baroness Thatcher, Prime Ministers of Fiji, Australia, Philippines, Singapore, Pres. of Iceland, Philippines and many other govt, academic, industrial, regimental, theatrical and sporting personalities, series of internationally known musicians, large boardroom and family groups; large canvas for the House of Commons (440 portraits) of the House in session, for Australian House of Reps (170 portraits) for Parl., Canberra; has made numerous TV appearances and lectures regularly in UK and overseas; mem. Royal Soc. of Portrait Painters, Royal Inst. of Oil Painters; Freeman of City of London 1997; Hon. Mem. Soc. of Women Artists; Hon. DLitt (Bath, Loughborough); Dr hc (Open Univ.). *Leisure interests:* classical and jazz music, theatre. *Address:* 34 Inner Park Road, London, SW19 6DD, England (home). *Telephone:* (20) 8788-7826 (home). *Fax:* (20) 8780-0728 (home). *E-mail:* keithmackrell@btinternet.com (home). *Website:* www.junemendoza.co.uk (home).

MENEM, Carlos Saul, DJur; Argentine politician; *President, Partido Justicialista, La Rioja Province;* b. 2 July 1935, Anillaco, La Rioja; s. of Saul Menem and Muhibe Akil; m. 1st Zulema Fátima Yoma 1966 (divorced); one s. (deceased) one d.; m. 2nd Cecilia Bolocco 2001; one s.; ed Córdoba Univ.; f. Juventud Peronista (Peron Youth Group), La Rioja Prov. 1955; defended political prisoners following Sept. 1955 coup; Legal Adviser, Confederación General del Trabajo, La Rioja Prov. 1955–70; cand. Prov. Deputy 1958; Pres. Partido Justicialista, La Rioja Prov. 1963–; elected Gov. La Rioja 1973, re-elected 1983, 1987; imprisoned following mil. coup 1976–81; cand. for Pres. Argentine Repub. for Partido Justicialista 1989; Pres. of Argentina 1989–99; Vice-Pres. Conf. of Latin American Popular Parties (COPPAL) 1990–; arrested for alleged involvement in illegal arms sales during his presidency June 2001, charged July 2001, placed under house arrest for five months; Presidential Cand. 2003. *Publications:* Argentine, Now or Never, Argentina Year 2000, The Productive Revolution (with Eduardo Duhalde). *Leisure interests:* flying, tennis. *Address:* Partido Justicialista, Buenos Aires, Argentina.

MENENDEZ, Robert (Bob), BA; American politician; *Senator from New Jersey;* b. 1 Jan. 1954, New York City; m. Jane Jacobsen (divorced); one s. one d.; ed St Peter's Coll., Jersey City, Rutgers Univ., Newark; entered public service when he launched a successful petition drive to reform his local school bd 1973, elected to Union City Bd of Educ. 1974; admitted to NJ Bar 1980; Mayor of Union City 1986–92, simultaneously served in New Jersey Gen. Ass. 1987–91 and New Jersey Senate 1991–93; mem. US House of Reps for NJ 13th Congressional Dist 1993–2006, fmr Vice-Chair. House Democratic Caucus, Chair. 2002, Chair. Democratic Task Force on Educ. 2001–03, Democratic Task Force on Homeland Security 2001–03; Chair. Credentials Cttee, Democratic Nat. Convention 2004; highest-ranking Hispanic in Congressional history; apptd to Senate by Gov. Jon Corzine of NJ to fill the seat made vacant by Corzine's resignation from the Senate to serve as Gov. of New Jersey 2006–, re-elected in midterm elections Nov. 2006, mem. Banking, Housing and Urban Affairs Cttee, Energy and Natural Resources Cttee, Budget Cttee; Democrat. *Address:* 502 Senate Hart Office Building, Washington, DC 20510, USA (office). *Telephone:* (202) 224-4744 (office). *Fax:* (202) 228-2197 (office). *Website:* menendez.senate.gov (office); www.menendez2006.com (office).

MENEZES, Fradique Bandeira Melo de; São Tomé and Príncipe head of state and business executive; *President and Commander-in-Chief of the Armed Forces;* b. 1942; m. (deceased); ed Instituto Superior de Psicologia Aplicada, Lisbon, Portugal and Univ. of Brussels, Belgium; fmr Minister for Foreign Trade; fmr Amb. to Belgium and Netherlands; mem. Acção Democrática Independente (ADI) Party; Pres. of São Tomé e Príncipe 2001–, also C-in-C of Armed Forces. *Address:* Office of the President, São Tomé, São Tomé e Príncipe (office).

MENG, Fengchao; Chinese engineer and business executive; *Deputy Chairman and President, China Communications Construction Company Ltd;* served in various positions at Ministry of Railways and its eng affiliates; Chair. China Zhongtie Major Bridge Eng Group Co. Ltd 1982–98; Vice-Pres. China Railway Eng Co. 2000–04; Pres. China Harbour Eng Co. (Group) 2005, mem. Bd of Dirs and Pres. China Communications Construction Group 2005–06, Deputy Chair. and Pres. China Communications Construction Co. Ltd 2006–. *Address:* China Communications Construction Co. Ltd, B88 Andingmenwai Dajie, Beijing 100011 (office); China Communications Construction Co. Ltd, 85 Deshengmenwai Street, Xicheng District, Beijing 100088, People's Republic of China (office). *Telephone:* (10) 82016655 (office). *Fax:* (10) 82016500 (office). *E-mail:* zhangbz@ccccltd.cn (office); info@ccgrp.com.cn (office). *Website:* www.ccgrp.com.cn (office).

MENG, Jianzhu; Chinese politician; *Minister of Public Security;* b. July 1947, Wuxian Co., Jiangsu Prov.; joined CCP 1968; Deputy Political Instructor and Deputy Leader of Boat Fleet, Supply Marketing and Transport Station, Qianwei Farm (also Sec. CCP Shanghai Communist Youth League) 1968–73, Sec. CCP Party Br. 1973–76, mem. CCP Qianwei Farm Party Cttee 1976–77 (also Leader, Publicity Dept), Sec. Cork Gen. Plant, Qianwei Farm, CCP Party Br. 1977–81, Dir Political Dept, Qianwei Farm 1977–81, Deputy Sec., later Dir CCP Party Cttee 1981–86; Sec. CCP Chuansha Co. Cttee,

Shanghai 1986–90, Jiading Co. Cttee, Shanghai 1990–91; Sec. Rural Work Cttee, CCP Shanghai Municipal Cttee 1991–92; Deputy Sec.-Gen. Shanghai Municipal Govt 1992–93; Vice-Mayor and Chair. Shanghai Econ. Restructuring Comm. 1993–96; Deputy Sec. Shanghai Municipal Cttee 1996; Sec. Jiangxi Prov. Cttee 2001–07, Chair. Standing Cttee Jiangxi People's Congress 2001; Alt. mem. 15th CCP Cen. Cttee 1997–2002, mem. 16th CCP Cen. Cttee 2002–07, mem. 17th CCP Cen. Cttee 2007–; Minister of Public Security 2007–; State Councillor 2008–. *Address:* Ministry of Public Security, 14 Dongchangan Jie, Dongcheng Qu, Beijing 100741, People's Republic of China (office). *Telephone:* (10) 65122831 (office). *Fax:* (10) 65136577 (office). *Website:* www .mps.gov.cn (office).

MENG, Xuenong, MSc; Chinese politician; b. 1949, Penglai, Shandong Prov.; ed Chinese Univ. of Science and Tech., Anhui Prov.; joined CCP 1972; worked in No. 2 Motor Vehicle Plant, Beijing 1969–71, (also Sec. CCP Communist Youth League 1971–74); Office Sec., Beijing Automobile Industry Co. 1971–74 (also Deputy Sec., later Sec. CCP Communist Youth League); Office Sec. Org. Dept CCP Zhejiang Prov. Cttee 1977–80, later Sec. of Gen. Office of Prov. Cttee; fmr Deputy Sec. CCP Communist Youth League Beijing Municipal Cttee; Gen. Man. Beijing Hotel Allied Co. 1986–87 (also Deputy Sec., later Sec. CCP Communist Youth League); Dir Admin for Industry and Commerce, Beijing 1987–93 (also Sec. CCP Leading Party Group); worked under Hu Jintao, Pres. of People's Repub. of China; Vice-Mayor of Beijing 1993–98, Exec. Vice-Mayor 1998–2002, Mayor 2003–04, mem. CCP Standing Cttee, Beijing Municipal Cttee; Deputy Dir Construction Comm. for Project for Diverting Water from the South to the North 2003–07 (mem. CCP Leading Party Group 2004–07); mem. 16th CCP Cen. Cttee 2002–07, 17th CCP Cen. Cttee 2007–; Acting Gov. Shanxi Prov. 2007–08, Gov. 2008 (resgnd). *Address:* c/o Office of the Governor, People's Government, Taiyuan, Shanxi Province, People's Republic of China (office).

MENGES, Chris; British cinematographer and film director; b. 15 Sept. 1940, Kingston, Herefordshire; m. 2nd Judy Freeman 1978; five c. from 1st marriage; TV cameraman on documentaries filmed in Africa, Asia and S America. *Films include:* camera operator: Poor Cow 1967, If.... 1968; cinematographer: Abel Gance: The Charm of Dynamite 1968, Loving Memory 1969, Kes 1969, Black Beauty (dir of photography) 1971, Gumshoe 1971, A Sense of Freedom 1979, Black Jack 1979, Bloody Kids 1979, Star Wars: Episode V – The Empire Strikes Back (dir of photography: studio second unit) 1980, The Gamekeeper 1980, Babylon 1980, East 103rd Street 1981, Looks and Smiles 1981, Warlords of the 21st Century 1982, Couples and Robbers 1982, Angel 1982, Local Hero 1983, Winter Flight 1984, Which Side Are You On? 1984, Comfort and Joy 1984, The Killing Fields (Acad. Award) 1984, Marie 1985, Fatherland 1986, The Mission (Acad. Award) 1986, Singing the Blues in Red, Shy People 1987, High Season 1987, Michael Collins (LA Film Critics Award 1997) 1996, The Boxer (dir of photography) 1997, The Pledge 2001, Dirty Pretty things 2002, The Good Thief 2002, Criminal (dir of photography) 2004, Tickets 2005, The Three Burials of Melquiades Estrada 2005, North Country 2005; Dir: East 103rd Street (also producer) 1981, A World Apart 1988, Criss-Cross 1992, The Life and Death of Chico Mendes, Second Best 1994, The Lost Son 1999, North Country 2005. *Television includes:* Auditions 1980, A Question of Leadership 1981, Tales Out of School: Made in Britain 1982, Walter 1982, Walter and June 1983, The Red and the Blue: Impressions of Two Political Conferences – Autumn 1982 1983, Concert for George 2003.

MENGISTU HAILE MARIAM (see MARIAM, Mengistu Haile).

MENKEN, Alan; American composer; b. 22 July 1949, New York; ed New York Univ.; began composing and performing Lehman Engel Musical Theater Workshop, BMI. *Theatre music includes:* God Bless You Mr Rosewater 1979 (Off-Broadway debut), Little Shop of Horrors (with Howard Ashman), Kicks, The Apprenticeship of Duddy Kravitz, Diamonds, Personals, Let Freedom Sing, Weird Romance, Beauty and the Beast, A Christmas Carol. *Film music includes:* Little Shop of Horrors 1986, The Little Mermaid 1988 (two Acad. Awards 1989), Beauty and the Beast 1990 (two Acad. Awards 1991), Lincoln 1992, Newsies 1992, Aladdin 1992 (two Acad. Awards 1993), Life with Mikey 1993, Pocahontas (with Stephen Schwartz) 1995 (Golden Globe Award 1996, two Acad. Awards 1996), The Shaggy Dog 2006. *Address:* The Shukat Company, 340 West 55th Street, Apt 1A, New York, NY 10019, USA. *Telephone:* (212) 582-7614 (office).

MENKERIOS, Haile, MA; South African (b. Eritrean) diplomat and economist; *Assistant Secretary General for Political Affairs, United Nations;* b. 1 Oct. 1946, Adi Felesti; s. of Drar Menkerios and Negusse Giorgis; m. Hebret Berhe 1979 (divorced); one s. one d.; ed Addis Ababa, Brandeis and Harvard Univs, USA; teaching asst, Harvard Univ. 1971–73; combatant in Eritrean People's Liberation Army (EPLA) 1973–74; Head of Tigrigna Section, Dept of Information and Propaganda, Eritrean People's Liberation Front (EPLF) 1974–75, mem. Foreign Relations Cttee 1976–77, mem. Cen. Council 1977–2001, Asst to Head of Dept of Foreign Relations 1977–79, Head of African Relations 1977–79, Research Div., Dept of Conscientization, Educ. and Culture 1979–86; Dir Research and Information Centre of Eritrea 1986–87; Head, Research and Policy Div., Dept of Foreign Relations 1987–90; Gov. of East and South Zone of Eritrea 1990–91; mem. Eritrean Nat. Council 1991–2001; Rep. of Provisional Govt of Eritrea to Ethiopia 1991–93; Special Envoy of Pres. to Somalia 1991–96, to the Greater Lakes Region 1996–97; mem. High Level Horn of Africa Cttee on Somalia 1993–95; Amb. of State of Eritrea to Ethiopia and OAU 1993–96; Amb., Perm. Rep. of State of Eritrea to UN 1997–2001; Sr Adviser to Special Envoy of Sec.-Gen. to the Inter-Congolese Dialogue, Moustapha Niasse 2002–03; Dir Africa Div., UN Dept of Political Affairs 2003–05; Sec.-Gen.'s Deputy Special Rep. for UN Mission in the Democratic Repub. of the Congo (MONUC) 2005–07; UN Asst Sec.-Gen. for Political Affairs 2007–. *Publications include:* various articles on African politics. *Leisure interests:* reading, sports. *Address:* UN Secretariat, DPA, S-3570A, New York, NY 10017 (office); 222 East 34th Street, Apt 1502, New York, NY 10016, USA (home). *Telephone:* (212) 963-4049 (office). *Fax:* (212 963-1323 (office). *E-mail:* menkerios@un.org (office). *Website:* www.un.org (office).

MENON, Mambillikalathil Govind Kumar (Goku), MSc, PhD, FRS; Indian physicist; *Adviser, Department of Space, Indian Space Research Organization;* b. 28 Aug. 1928, Mangalore; s. of Kizhekepat Sankara Menon and Mambillikalathil Narayaniamma; m. Indumati Patel 1955; one s. one d.; ed Jaswant Coll., Jodhpur, Royal Inst. of Science, Bombay, Univ. of Bristol, UK; Research Assoc., Univ. of Bristol 1952–53; Sr Award of Royal Comm. for Exhbn of 1851, Univ. of Bristol 1953–55; Reader, Tata Inst. of Fundamental Research, Bombay 1955–58; Assoc. Prof. 1958–60, Prof. and Dean of Physics Faculty 1960–64, Sr Prof. and Deputy Dir (Physics) 1964–66, Dir Tata Inst. of Fundamental Research 1966–75; Sir C.V. Raman Prof., Indian Nat. Science Acad. 1986–91; M.N. Saha Distinguished Fellow 1994–99; Dr Vikram Sarabhai Distinguished Prof., Indian Space Research Org. 1999–2004, Adviser, Dept of Space 2004–; Chair. Electronics Comm. and Sec. to Govt of India Dept of Electronics 1971–78; Chair. Indian Space Research Org. 1972; Scientific Adviser to Minister of Defence, Dir-Gen. Defence Research and Devt Org. and Sec. for Defence Research 1974–78; Dir-Gen. Council of Scientific and Industrial Research 1978–81; Sec. to Govt of India, Dept of Science and Tech. 1978–82, Dept of Environment 1981–82; Chair. Comm. for Additional Sources of Energy; Chair. Science Advisory Cttee to Cabinet 1982–85; Scientific Adviser to Prime Minister 1986–89 and mem. Govt Planning Comm. (with rank of Minister of State) 1982–89; Minister of State for Science and Tech. and for Educ. 1989–90; MP 1990–96; Chair. Cosmic Ray Comm. ICSU/IUPAP 1973–75, Bharat Electronics Ltd, Bharat Dynamics Ltd (Missiles); Pres. Asia Electronics Union 1973–75, Indian Science Congress Asscn 1981–82, India Int. Centre, New Delhi 1983–88, 2007–, Int. Council of Scientific Unions 1988–93, Indian Statistical Inst. 1990–; mem. Bd Dirs Escorts Ltd; Vice-Pres. IUPAP, Third World Acad. of Sciences 1983–88; mem. Pontifical Acad. of Sciences, Rome, Bd Inst. for Advanced Studies (UNU), Tokyo; Fellow, Indian Acad. of Sciences (Pres. 1974–76), Indian Nat. Science Acad. (Pres. 1981–82); Chair. Indian Inst. of Tech., Bombay 1997–2003, Indian Inst. of Information Tech. 1999–2004, Indian Inst. of Tech. Delhi 2003–06; Hon. Pres. Asia Electronics Union; Hon. Fellow, Nat. Acad. of Sciences, India (Pres. 1987–88), Tata Inst. of Fundamental Research, Inst. of Electronics and Telecommunications Eng of India, Indian Inst. of Science, Bangalore, Nat. Inst. of Educ., Inst. of Physics (UK) 1997; Hon. mem. IEEE; Foreign Hon. mem. American Acad. of Arts and Sciences, Russian Acad. of Sciences; Padma Shri 1961, Padma Bhushan 1968, Padma Vibhushan 1985; Hon. DEng (Stevens Inst. of Tech., USA); Hon. DSc (Jodhpur, Delhi, Sardar Patel, Roorkee, Banaras Hindu, Jadavpur, Sri Venkateswara, Allahabad, Andhra, Utkal, North Bengal, Aligarh Muslim, Guru Nanak Dev and Bristol Univs and Indian Inst. of Tech., Madras and Kharagpur); Shanti Swarup Bhatnagar Award for Physical Sciences, Council of Scientific and Industrial Research 1960; Repub. Day (Nat.) Awards, Khaitan Medal, Royal Asiatic Soc. 1973; Cecil Powell Medal, European Physical Soc. 1978, G.P. Chatterjee Award of Indian Science Congress Asscn 1984, Award for Professional Excellence 1984, Pandit Jawaharlal Nehru Award for Sciences, Madhya Pradesh State Govt 1983, Om Prakash Bhasin Award for Science and Tech. 1985, C.V. Raman Medal of Indian Nat. Science Acad. 1985, Fourth J.C. Bose Triennial Gold Medal of Bose Inst. 1984, Sri Ashutosh Mukherjee Award of Indian Science Congress Asscn 1988; Abdus Salam Medal, Third World Acad. of Sciences 1997. *Publications:* 160 papers on cosmic ray and elementary particle physics. *Leisure interests:* bird-watching, photography. *Address:* K-5 (rear), Hauz Khas Enclave, New Delhi 110016 (office); C-178 (first floor), Sarvodaya Enclave, New Delhi 110017, India (home). *Telephone:* (11) 26511454 (office); (11) 26966096 (home). *Fax:* (11) 26510825 (home). *E-mail:* mgkmenon@nic.in.

MENON, Raghu; Indian civil servant, government official and airline executive; *Chairman and Managing Director, Air-India Ltd;* officer of Indian Admin. Service of Assam-Nagaland cadre 1974, served in Ministry of Information and Broadcasting, apptd Jt Sec., Ministry of Civil Aviation 2002, Special Sec. and Financial Advisor –2008, Chair. and Man. Dir Air-India Ltd (state-owned airline merged with Indian airline under Nat. Aviation Co. of India Ltd) 2008–. *Address:* Air-India Ltd, 3rd Floor, Tower-II, Jeevan Bharati 124, Connaught Circus, New Delhi, 110 001, India (office). *Telephone:* (11) 23731225 (office). *E-mail:* info@home.airindia.in (office). *Website:* home .airindia.in (office).

MENON, Shiv Shankar, MA; Indian diplomatist; *Foreign Secretary;* b. 5 July 1949; m. Mohini Sathe; ed Delhi Univ.; joined Foreign Service 1972, Second Sec., Embassy in Beijing 1974–77; UnderSec. in charge of Africa and then China 1977–79; First Sec., Embassy in Vienna 1979–83, also Alt. Gov. IAEA Bd and Deputy Perm. Rep. to UN Orgs; Dir Dept of Atomic Energy, Mumbai 1983–86; Counsellor and DCM, Embassy in Beijing 1986–89; Deputy Chief of Mission, Embassy in Tokyo 1989–92; Jt Sec. in charge of N E Div. 1992–95; Amb. to Israel 1995–97; High Commr to Sri Lanka 1997–2000; Amb. to China 2000–03; High Commr to Pakistan 2003–06; Foreign Sec. 2006–; Madhav Award 2000. *Address:* Ministry of External Affairs, South Block, New Delhi 110 011, India (office). *Telephone:* (11) 23011127 (office). *Fax:* (11) 23011463 (office). *Website:* meaindia.nic.in (office).

MENSAH, Joseph Henry, MSc; Ghanaian politician; *Senior Minister, responsible for Public Sector Reform and the National Institutional Renewal Programme;* b. 31 Oct. 1928; ed Achimota Coll., Univ. Coll. of Gold Coast (now Univ. of Ghana), London School of Econs, UK and Stanford Univ., USA; Asst

Insp. of Taxes 1953; Research Fellow, Univ. Coll. of Gold Coast 1953–57; Lecturer in Econs, Univ. of Ghana 1957–58; Economist, UN HQ, New York 1958–61; Chief Economist, Prin. Sec. and Exec. Sec. of Nat. Planning Comm. Ghana 1961–65; Economist, UN Dir, Div. of Trade and Econ. Co-operation and Econ. Comm. for Africa (ECA) 1965–69; Commr of Finance April–July 1969; mem. Parl. for Sunyani (Progress Party) 1969–72; Minister of Finance 1969–72, of Econ. Planning 1969–71; arrested Jan. 1972, released July 1973; re-arrested 1975; sentenced to eight years' imprisonment with hard labour Oct. 1975, released June 1978, in exile in London 1982; returned to Ghana Feb. 1995; mem. Parl. for Sunyani East (New Patriotic Party) 1996–2000, Minority Leader in Parl. 1997–2000; re-elected mem. Parl. for Sunyani East 2000, Majority Leader in Parl.; fmrly Minister in Charge of Govt Business, Minister for Parl. Affairs; currently Sr Minister, responsible for Public Sector Reform and the Nat. Institutional Renewal Programme; Chair. Nat. Plan. Comm. *Address:* c/o Office of Majority Leader, Parliament, Accra, Ghana (office).

MENSHIKOV, Oleg Yevgenyevich; Russian actor; b. 8 Nov. 1960, Serpukhov, Moscow Region; ed Shchepkin Higher School of Theatre Art, Maly Theatre; Laurence Olivier Prize for Yesenin 1991, Film Critics' Prize for Best Actor of 1994, prizes for best men's role at Festivals Kinotaurus 1996, Baltic Pearl 1996, other awards. *Theatre roles include:* Ganya Ivolgin (Idiot after Dostoyevsky) 1981, Sergey (Sports Scenes of 1981) 1986, Caligula (Caligula) 1989, Yesenin (When She Danced) London 1991, Ikharev (Gamblers) London 1992, Nizhinsky (N. Nizhinsky) 1993. *Film roles include:* Rodnya (Kinfolk) 1981, Polyoty vo sne i nayavu (Flights in Dreams and in Reality) 1982, Kiss, Polosa prepyatstviy (Stripe of Obstacles) 1984, Mikhailo Lomonosov 1984, Po glavnoy ulitse s orkestrom (Through Main Street with an Orchestra) 1986, Moy lyubimyy kloun (My Favourite Clown) 1986, Moonzund (also singer) 1987, Bryzgi shampanskogo (Splashes of Champagne) 1988, Zhizn po limitu (Limited Life) 1989, Lestnitsa (The Stairway) 1989, Yama (The Pit) 1990, Dyuba-Dyuba 1993, Utomlyonnye solntsem (Burnt by the Sun) 1994, Kavkazskiy plennik (Prisoner of the Caucasus) 1996, Sibirskiy tsiryulnik (The Barber of Siberia) 1998, Mama (Mummy) 1999, Est-Ouest (East-West) 1999, Statski sovetnik 2005; appeared in films of dirs N. Mikhalkov, A. Proshkin, A. Muratov, D. Khvan, S. Bodrov, R. Balayan, V. Kozakov, A. Sakharov. *Television includes:* Pokrovskiye vorota (Pokrov Gates) 1982, Potseluy (The Kiss) 1983, Volodya bolshoy, Volodya malenkiy (Big and Small Volodya) 1985, Prime Suspect 6 2003, Doctor Zhivago (mini-series) 2005, Zolotoy telenok (mini-series) 2006. *Address:* Maly Kozykhinsky per. 8/18, Apt 3, Moscow, Russia. *Telephone:* (495) 299-02-17 (home).

MENSHOV, Vladimir Valentinovich; Russian film director and actor; b. 17 Sept. 1939, Baku; m. Vera Alentova (q.v.) 1963; one d.; ed Moscow Arts Theatre Studio School, All-Union State Inst. of Cinema (VGIK) 1970; RSFSR State Prize 1978, Acad. Award for Moscow Does Not Believe in Tears 1980, USSR State Prize 1981, RSFSR Artist of Merit 1984, Prize of American Guild of Cinema Owners. *Leading roles in:* A Man in His Place 1973, Last Meeting 1974, Personal Opinions 1977, Time for Reflection 1983, The Intercept 1986, Where is Nofelet? 1987, The Town Zero 1988, Red Mob 1993, Russian Ragtime 1993. *Films include:* Loss (Rozygrysh) 1977, Moscow Does Not Believe in Tears 1980, Love and Doves 1984, Shirly-Myrly 1995, Envy of Gods 2000, Spartak i Kalashnikov 2002, Nochnoy dozor 2004, Vremya sobirat' kamni 2005, Dnevnoy dozor (Day Watch) 2006. *Address:* 3-d Tverskaya-Yamskaya 52, Apt. 29, 125047 Moscow, Russia. *Telephone:* (495) 250-85-43.

MENTRÉ, Paul; French civil servant and diplomatist; *Inspector-General of Finances;* b. 28 June 1935, Nancy; s. of Paul Mentré and Cécile de Loye; m. 1st Sabine Brundsaux 1958 (divorced 1975); two d.; m. 2nd Gaëlle Bretillot 1975; two s.; m. 3rd Jehanne Collard 1992; ed Ecole Polytechnique, Ecole Nat. d'Admin; Insp. of Finance 1960; Special Asst, French Treas. 1965–70; Deputy Dir of the Cabinet of the Minister of Finance (V. Giscard d'Estaing) 1971–73; Under-Sec. Ministry of Economy and Finance 1971–72; Dir Crédit National 1973–75, Crédit Lyonnais 1973–75; Gen. Del. for Energy 1975–78; Financial Minister, French Embassy in Washington, DC 1978–82; Exec. Dir IMF and World Bank 1978–81; Insp.-Gen. of Finances 1981–; Man. Dir Banque Nationale de Paris 1986–87, Dir-Gen. 1987–90; Pres. Dir-Gen. Crédit Nat. 1987–90; Pres. Crédit sucrier 1990, technopole de Caen Synergia 1991–94, Valréal 1992–, Trouville-Deauville Dist 1995– (Communauté de communes Cœur Côte Fleurie from 2002); Exec. Sec. Cttee for the Monetary Union of Europe; Dir European Investment Bank 1987–91; Prof., Ecole des Hautes Etudes Commerciales; mem. Supervisory Council Crédit local de France 1987–90, French-German Council of Econ. Advisers; Dir Affine; Founder Victimes et Citoyens (support group for victims of road traffic accidents) 2001, Pres. 2004–; Chevalier, Ordre nat. du Mérite, des Arts et Lettres, Saudi Royal Order. *Publications:* Imaginer l'avenir, Gulliver enchaîné 1982, L'Amerique et nous, L'insoutenable légèreté du fort 1989, articles on economic issues in Le Figaro, Le Monde and Les Echos. *Leisure interests:* tennis, skiing. *Address:* Communauté de Communes Coeur Côte Fleurie, 12 Rue Robert Fossorier BP 30086, 14803 Deauville Cedex (office); c/o Ministry of the Economy, Finance and Industry, 139 rue de Bercy, 75572 Paris Cedex 12 (office); 18 rue de Bourgogne, 75007 Paris, France (home). *Telephone:* 2-31-88-54-49 (office); 1-40-04-04-04 (office). *Fax:* 2-31-88-19-76 (office); 1-43-43-75-97 (office). *E-mail:* info@coeurcotefleurie.org (office). *Website:* www.coeurcotefleurie.org (office); www.minefi.gouv.fr (office).

MENZEL, Jiří; Czech film and theatre director and actor; b. 23 Feb. 1938; s. of Josef Menzel and Božena Jindřichová; ed Film Acad. of Performing Arts, specialized in film directing, 1957–61; film Dir and actor 1962–89; Head of Dept of Film Directing, Film Acad. of Performing Arts, Prague 1990–92; Producer of Studio 89 1991–; Dir Vinohradské divadlo (theatre) 1997, 1998–, Artistic Dir 2000; mem. Supervisory Bd O.P.S., Prague, European City of Culture 2000 1999; Officier, Ordre des Arts et des Lettres (France) 1990, Medal of Merit 1996; Oscar Prize, Santa Monica 1968 for Closely Observed Trains, Akira Kurosawa Prize for Lifelong Merits in Cinematography, San Francisco 1990, Ennio Flaiano, Prize for Lifetime Achievement in Cinematography, Pescara, Italy 1996; Czech Lion Prize, Czech Film and TV Acad. (for lifetime career) 1997, Golden Seal Prize (Yugoslavia) 1997. *Recent film roles:* Jak si zaslouzit princeznu (How to Deserve a Princess) 1995, Ma je pomsta (Revenge is Mine) 1995, Truck Stop 1996, Drákuluv svagr (mini TV series) 1996, Une trop bruyante solitude (Too Loud a Solitude) 1996, Franciska vasárnapjai (Every Sunday) 1997, Vsichni moji blízcí (All My Loved Ones, USA) 1999, Ab ins Paradies (When Grandpa Loved Rita Hayworth) 2001, Potonulo groblje (The Sunken Cemetery) 2002, Útek do Budína 2002, Világszám! 2004. *Films directed include:* Ostre sledované vlaky (Closely Observed Trains) 1966, Vesnicko má strediskovà (My Sweet Little Village) 1985, Konec starych casu (The End of the Good Old Days) (Grand Prize of the Int. Film Producers' Meeting, Cannes 1990) 1989, Skrivánci na niti (Skylarks on the String) 1990, The Beggar's Opera 1991, The Life and Extraordinary Adventures of Private Ivan Chonkin 1994, Ten Minutes Older: The Cello 2002, Obsluhoval jsem anglického krále (I Served the King of England) 2006. *Opera directed:* Dalibor by Smetana Cagliari 1999. *Plays directed:* Pré by J. Suchý, Prague 1999, A Midsummer Night's Dream, Český Krumlov 2000. *Publication:* Tak nevím (novel) 1998. *Leisure interest:* literature. *Address:* Studio 89, Krátký film Praha a.s., Jindřišská 34, 112 07 Prague 1 (office); Divadlo na Vinchradech, Náměstí míru 7, 120 00 Prague 2, Czech Republic (home). *Telephone:* (2) 22520452 (office). *Fax:* (2) 22520452. *E-mail:* dnv@anet.cz.

MER, Francis Paul, LèsL (Econs); French business executive; *Chairman, Supervisory Board, Group Safran;* b. 25 May 1939, Pau, Basses Pyrénées; s. of René Mer and Yvonne Casalta; m. Catherine Bonfils 1964; three d.; ed Lycée Montesquieu, Bordeaux, Ecole Nationale Supérieure des Mines, Paris and Ecole Polytechnique; mining engineer, Ministry of Industry 1966; tech. adviser, Abidjan 1967–68; Chair. Inter-ministerial Cttee on European Econ. Co-operation 1969–70; Head of Planning, Saint-Gobain Industries 1971; Dir of Planning, Compagnie Saint-Gobain-Pont-à-Mousson 1973; Dir of Planning, later Dir-Gen. Saint-Gobain Industries 1973; Dir Société des Maisons Phénix 1976–78; Asst Dir-Gen. Saint-Gobain-Pont-à-Mousson 1978–82, Pres.-Dir-Gen. de Pont-à-Mousson SA 1982–86; Pres.-Dir-Gen. Usinor-Sacilor 1986–2002, Chair. Usinor Group 2001–02; Pres. Chambre syndicale de la sidérurgie française 1988–, Conservatoire Nat. des Arts et Métiers 1989–, Eurofer 1990–97, Asscn nat. de Recherche Technique 1991–, Centre d'études prospectives et d'informations internationales 1995–2000; Pres. Int. Iron and Steel Inst. (INSI) 1997–98; Dir Crédit Lyonnais 1997–, Electricité de France 1997–, Air France 1997–; Minister of the Economy, Finance and Industry 2002–2004; Chair. Fondation pour L'Innovation Politique 2004; mem. Bd of Dirs Inco 2005–; Chair. Supervisory Bd Group Safran 2006–; Commdr, Légion d'honneur, Ordre nat. du Mérite. *Address:* Groupe Safran, 2 Boulevard du Général Martial Valin, 75724 Paris Cedex 15 (office); 9 rue Bobierre-de-Vallière, 92340 Bourg-la-Reine, France (home). *Telephone:* 1-40-60-80-80 (office). *Fax:* 1-40-60-81-02 (office). *E-mail:* webmaster@safran-group.com (office); f.mer@laposte.net (office). *Website:* www.safran-group.com (office).

MERAFHE, Lt-Gen. Mompati, LLB; Botswana politician; *Vice-President;* b. 6 June 1936, Serowe; two s. three d.; ed Univ. of S Africa; police officer, later Deputy Commr of Police 1960–77; Commdr Botswana Defence Force, ranked Maj.-Gen. 1977, Lt-Gen. 1988; MP for Mahalapye; fmr Cabinet Minister for Public Admin; Minister of Foreign Affairs 1994, 1996–2008; Vice-Pres. 2008–. *Address:* c/o Office of the President, Private Bag 001, Gaborone, Botswana (office). *Telephone:* 3950825 (office). *Fax:* 3950858 (office). *E-mail:* op.registry@gov.bw (office). *Website:* www.gov.bw/government/ministry_of_state_president.html#office_of_the_president (office).

MERCADO CASTRO, Patricia; Mexican politician; b. 1957, Ciudad Obregon, Sonora; m.; two c.; ed Universidad Nacional Autónoma de México; began career as legal adviser to seamstresses' union; held several positions in agencies designed to promote more equality between the sexes; influenced by Liberation Theology of S American bishops in 1970s; only woman on 90-person strike cttee at bus and truck manufacturer, Dina 1983, Pres. Mujeres Trabajadoras Unidas 1985–91; mem. Advisory Bd Instituto Mexicano de Investigación de Familia y Población 1992; Man. Dir Grupo de Información y Reproducción Elegida 1992–96; Exec. Dir Equidad de Género, Ciudadanía, Trabajo y Familia 1997–2001; lost primary for presidential candidacy for Democracia Social to Gilberto Rincón 2000; Pres. México Posible (political party) 2002–03, led party in mid-term elections that failed to achieve sufficient votes for nat. registration 2003; Pres. Partido Alternativa Socialdemócrata y Campesina (now Partido Socialdemócrata) Jan.–Aug. 2005, party presidential cand. 2006. *Address:* c/o Partido Socialdemócrata, Avda Insurgentes Sur 1942, Col. Florida, Del. Alvaro Obregón, 01030 México, DF, Mexico. *Telephone:* (55) 9150-5191. *Fax:* (55) 9150-5190. *E-mail:* info@alternativa.org.mx. *Website:* www.alternativa.org.mx.

MERCADO JARRÍN, Gen. Luis Edgardo; Peruvian politician and army officer; b. 19 Sept. 1919, Barranco, Lima; s. of Dr Alejandro Mercado Ballón and Florinda Jarrín de Mercado; m. Gladys Neumann Terán de Mercado 1951; one s. four d.; ed Colegio la Libertad de Moquegua, Escuela Militar de Chorrillos; commissioned 1940, Gen. of Div. 1970–; Prof. Escuela Militar, Escuela de Artillería, Escuela Superior de Guerra, Centro de Altos Estudios Militares, etc.; Dir of Army Intelligence; del. of Peruvian Army to several inter-American army confs; guest lecturer to US Army, Fort Holabird and Fort Bragg; Commdt-Gen. Centro de Instrucción Militar del Perú 1968; Minister of Foreign Affairs 1968–71; Army Chief of Staff Jan.–Dec. 1972; Prime Minister and Minister of War 1973–75; decorations include Grand Cross of Orden Militar de Ayacucho and Orden al Mérito Militar, Orden del Sol and orders from Colombia, Portugal, Argentina, Bolivia, Brazil and Venezuela. *Publications:* La Política y la Estrategia Militar en la Guerra Contrasubversiva en América Latina, El Ejército de Hoy en Nuestra Sociedad en Período de Transición y en el Campo Internacional, El Ejército y la Empresa; contributor to magazine of Interamerican Defense Coll., USA, Revista Militar del Perú, Brazilian Military Journal. *Leisure interests:* tennis, riding, classical music, reading (contemporary mil. philosophy, sociology and econ.). *Address:* Avenida Velasco Astete 1140, Chacarrilla del Estanque, Lima, Peru. *Telephone:* 256823.

MERCADO RAMOS, Fernando, BA, JD; Puerto Rican politician and lawyer; *Secretary of State;* b. 18 June 1957, Lares; s. of Tomas Mercado-Estremere and Luz M. Ramos-Valez; m. Michelle Waters; two s.; ed Univ. of Puerto Rico, Univ. of Madrid, Spain; teacher of psychology and sociology Colegio Nuestra Señora del Carmen Rió Piedras 1979–1981; legal counsel Culture Comm., House of Reps 1982–84; Exec. Dir Comm. of the Govt 1985–88, Sec.-Gen. 1989–92; judge Court of the First Instance 1992, Sec.-Gen. 1999; Sec.-Gen. Partido Popular Democrático 1999–2000; Sec. of State 2001–; mem. American Acad. of Judicial Educ. 1996–, American Judicature Soc., American Bar Asscn Judicial Admin. Div., American Judges' Asscn, Colegio de Abogados de Puerto Rico 1981–. *Publications include:* Grito a la Intimidad 1976, Un Pensamiento en Viaje 1990, Un Nuevo Lider: Esperanza de una Nueva Generación 1991. *Leisure interests:* reading, swimming, writing. *Address:* Office of the Secretary of the State, Department of State, P.O.B. 3271, San Juan, PR 00902-3271, Puerto Rico (office). *Telephone:* (787) 723-4343 (office). *Fax:* (787) 725-7303 (office). *E-mail:* fmercado@estado.gobierno.pr (office). *Website:* www.estado .gobierno.pr (office).

MERCIECA, Mgr Joseph, BA, SThD, JUD; Maltese ecclesiastic; *Archbishop of Malta;* b. 11 Nov. 1928, Victoria, Gozo; s. of Saverio Mercieca and Giovanna Vassallo; ed Gozo Seminary, Gregorian Univ. and Lateran Univ., Rome; ordained priest 1952; Rector Gozo Seminary 1952–69; Judge of Roman Rota 1969–74; ordained Titular Bishop of Gemelle in Numidia, apptd Auxiliary Bishop of Malta 1974; Vicar-Gen. 1975–76; Consultor, Congregation of the Sacraments and Congregation for the Doctrine of Faith, Vatican City 1976; Archbishop of Malta, Pres. Maltese Episcopal Conf. 1976–; mem. Apostolic Segnatura, Rome 1991. *Address:* Archbishop's Curia, Floriana (office); Archbishop's Palace, Mdina, Malta (home). *Telephone:* 21234317 (office). *Fax:* 21223307 (office).

MERCKX, Eddy; Belgian fmr cyclist; b. 17 June 1945, Meen, Brussels sel-Kiezegem; m. Claudine Merckx; one s. one d.; world amateur champion 1963, first professional race 1964, winner World Road Championships 1967, 1971, 1974, Tours of Italy 1968, 1970, 1972, 1973, 1974, Tours de France 1969, 1970, 1971, 1972, 1974 (shares record for most wins, holds record (34) for most stage wins), Tours of Belgium 1970, 1971, Tour of Spain 1973, Tour of Switzerland 1974, 32 major classics; broke the then world hour record, Mexico City 1972; retd 1978 with 525 wins in 1,800 races; involved with manufacture of bicycles which bear his name 1980–; Belgian Sportsman of the Year 1969–74 (record), Belgian Athlete of the Century. *Address:* S'Herenweg 11, 1869 Meise, Belgium (home). *Telephone:* (2) 269-62-72 (home). *Fax:* (2) 269-93-67 (home). *E-mail:* info@eddymerckx.be (home). *Website:* www.eddymerckx.be (home).

MEREDOV, Rashid Ovezgeldyyevich; Turkmenistani politician; *Deputy Prime Minister, responsible for the police and army, and Minister of Foreign Affairs;* b. 1960, Ashgabat; ed Faculty of Law, Moscow State Univ.; Deputy Dir Nat. Inst. for Democracy and Human Rights –1999, Dir 2001–05; apptd Speaker in Majlis (Nat. Ass.) 1999, Chair. –2001; Minister of Foreign Affairs 2001–, Deputy Chair. of the Govt 2003–05; Deputy Prime Minister, responsible for the police and army 2007–; For the Love of Fatherland Medal, Gayrat Medal, Galkynysh Order. *Address:* Ministry of Foreign Affairs, 744000 Aşgabat, pr. Magtymguly 83, Turkmenistan (office). *Telephone:* (12) 26-62-11 (office). *Fax:* (12) 35-42-41 (office). *E-mail:* mfatm@online.tm (office).

MEREZHKO, Viktor Ivanovich; Russian scriptwriter; b. 28 July 1937, Olginfeld, Rostov-on-Don Region; m. (wife deceased); one s. one d.; ed Ukrainian Inst. of Polygraphy, Lvov, All-Union Inst. of Cinematography; engineer Molot Publrs, Rostov-on-Don 1961–64; freelance 1968–; TV broadcaster and Head of History Programming; Vice-Pres. TV-6 Ind. TV; Chair. Kinoshock Festival, Nika Prize Cttee; State Prize 1986. *Plays include:* I'm a Woman, Cry, Caucasian Roulette. *Films include:* over 45 film scripts, including Zdravstvuy i proshchay (Hello and Goodbye) 1972, Odinozhdy odin (One Once) 1974, Tryn-trava 1976, Zhuravl v nebe (Crane In the Sky) 1977, Vas ozhidayet grazhdanka Nikanorova (Citizen Nikanorova Waits for You) 1978, Ukhodya – ukhodi 1978, Tryasina (Quagmire) 1978, Kholostyaki 1980, Rodnya (Kinfolk) 1981, Otstavnoy kozy barabanshchik 1981, Polyoty vo sne i nayavu (Flights in Dreams and in Reality) 1983, Polosa vezeniya (Goldfishes) 1983, Osobyy sluchay 1983, Yesli mozhesh, prosti… (If You Can, Forgive…) 1984, Aplodismenty, aplodismenty… (Applause, Applause…) 1984, Prosti (Forgive Me) (also actor) 1986, Odinokaya zhenshchina zhelayet poznakomitsya (Lonely Woman Seeks Lifetime Companion) 1986, Zabavy molodykh (Joys of Youth) 1987, 9 maya 1987, Under the Blue Sky (Fipressi Prize, Venice Festival 1987), Shag (aka Message from the Future) 1988, Avtoportret neizvestnogo (Selfportrait of an Unknown Man) 1988, Martokhela monadire (Lonely Hunter) 1989, Sobachiy pir (Dogs' Feast) 1990, Nochnye zabavy (Night Fun) 1991, Yesli by znat… (If We'd Only Known) 1993, Kurochka Ryaba (Ryaba My Chicken) 1994, Greshnye apostoly lyubvi 1995, Ligne de vie (Line of Life) 1996, The Two from Big Road 1996, Kavkazskaya ruletka (Caucasus Roulette) 2002, Lisa Alisa (video) 2003; actor: Yesli yest parusa 1969, Pod nebom golubym 1989, Dikiy plyazh 1990, Russkiy roman (Russian Romance) 1993. *Television includes:* scriptwriter: Saga o kriminale (series) 2001, Provintsialy (series) (also actor) 2002. *Leisure interest:* collecting

side-arms. *Address:* Usiyevicha str. 8, Apt 133, 125319 Moscow, Russia (home). *Telephone:* (495) 217-57-58; (495) 155-74-59 (home).

MERIDOR, Dan; Israeli politician and lawyer; b. 1947, Jerusalem; m.; four c.; ed Hebrew Univ.; served in Israel Defence Forces (IDF) as tank commander in 1967 Six Day War, continued to serve as captain in IDF reserves; practised law Jerusalem 1973–82; fmr mem. Likud Party; Cabinet Sec. of Govt 1982–84; mem. Knesset 1984–2003; Minister of Justice 1988–92, of Finance 1996–97; Chair. Foreign Affairs and Defense Cttee 1997–2001; Minister without Portfolio responsible for Nat. Defence and Diplomatic Strategy 2001–03; Leader Centre Party 2001; has been Knesset observer to the Council of Europe. *Address:* c/o Office of the Prime Minister, POB 187, 3 Rehov Kaplan, Kiryat Ben-Gurion, Jerusalem 91919, Israel.

MERIKAS, George, MD; Greek politician and professor of medicine; b. 5 May 1911, Agios Andreas; s. of Emmanuel Merikas and Helen (née Kritikou) Merikas; m. Irene (née Koutsogianni) Merikas 1945 (died 1971); two s. one d.; ed Medical School, Univ. of Athens; Assoc. Prof. of Medicine, Univ. of Athens 1953, Prof. 1970–78; Dir Dept of Medicine, Evangelismos Hosp., Athens 1960–70; Fulbright Grant, Univ. of Cincinnati Medical School 1964–65; mem. Acad. of Athens 1978–, Pres. 1988–89; Minister of Health, Welfare and Social Services 1989–90; Pres. Nat. AIDS Cttee in Greece 1988–; mem. Accad. Tiberina, New York Acad. of Sciences, Asscn for the Advancement of Sciences. *Publications:* Hepatitis Associated Antigen in Chronic Liver Disease 1970, Australia Antigen in the Liver 1972, Hepatitis B Core Antigen and Antibody in Primary Liver Cancer 1975, Internal Medicine (two vols) 1976, Cholesterol Gall-Stone Dissolution by CDC 1976. *Leisure interests:* literature, history. *Address:* 6 Vasileos Irakliou Str., 10682 Athens, Greece. *Telephone:* (1) 8210719.

MERIMÉE, Jean-Bernard, LenD; French diplomatist; *Special Adviser to Secretary-General on European Affairs, United Nations;* b. 4 Dec. 1936, Toulouse (Haute-Garonne); s. of Jacques Merimée and Germaine Merimée (née Larrieu); m. Anna Mirams 1965; one s. two d.; ed Lycées Pasteur, Neuilly-sur-Seine and Louis-le-Grand, Paris, Institut d'Etudes Politiques de Paris, Ecole Nat. d'Admin, Paris; with Cen. Admin, Ministry of Foreign Affairs 1965, with Sec.-Gen. 1972–75; Second then First Sec. to UK 1966–72; Chief of Mission of Co-operation, Côte d'Ivoire 1975–78, Chief of Protocol 1978–81; Amb. to Australia 1982–85, to India 1985–87, to Morocco, Rabat 1987–91; Amb. and Perm. Rep. to Security Council and Chief of Perm. Mission to UN, New York 1991–95; Amb. to Italy, Rome 1995–98, to Repub. of San Marino (resident in Rome) 1997–98, to Cen. Admin 1998–99; Perm. Rep. to UN 1999, Special Adviser to Sec.-Gen. on European Affairs with rank of Under-Sec.-Gen. 1999–; Dir Groupe Benjelloun (mobile telephone, banking and insurance cos), Morocco; mem. Advisory Bd BMCE Bank, France; Officier, Légion d'honneur, Officier, Ordre nat. du Mérite, Commdr of the Order of Christ (Portugal), Grand Officer of the Order of the Phoenix (Greece), Kt of the Dannebrog (Denmark), Officer of the Oak Crown (Luxembourg), Merit Commdr of the Supreme Order of Malta. *Address:* Office of the Secretary-General, United Nations, New York, NY 10017, USA. *Telephone:* (212) 963-1234. *Fax:* (212) 963-4879. *E-mail:* inquiries@un.org. *Website:* www.un.org.

MÉRINDOL, Nicolas, BA, MBA; French certified public accountant and banking executive; *CEO, Caisse Nationale des Caisses d'Epargne;* ed Institut Supérieur de Gestion, Institut Nat. des Techniques Economiques et Comptables; began career with Renault in Argentina and France; later worked at Caisse des Dépôts; joined Exec. Cttee of Groupe Caisse d'Epargne 1988, moved to Caisse d'Epargne de Picardie 1991, served as Finance and Risk Man. Dir before joining Man. Bd of regional savings bank, apptd Dir for Org. 1996, later Dir of Financial Planning at Caisse Nationale des Caisses d'Epargne, mem. Man. Bd Caisse Nationale des Caisses d'Epargne with responsibility for banking operations and finance 2002–03, responsible for Commercial Banking Div. and Corp. Strategy 2003–06, CEO Caisse Nationale des Caisses d'Epargne 2006–; Chair. Crédit Foncier; Chair. Supervisory Bd Banque Palatine, Compagnie 1818; Chair. European Banking Industry Cttee 2006, Vice-Chair. 2007–; mem. Nat. Council for Sustainable Devt; mem. Bd Dirs Nat. Agency for Personal Care Services 2006–; mem. Bd Fund for Social Cohesion, Steering Cttee France Investissement. *Address:* Caisse Nationale des Caisses d'Epargne, 50 avenue Pierre Mendès, 75201 Paris Cedex 13, France (office). *Telephone:* 1-58-40-40-02 (office). *Fax:* 1-58-40-50-30 (office). *E-mail:* info@groupe.caisse-epargne.com (office). *Website:* www.groupe.caisse -epargne.com (office).

MERINI, Alda; Italian poet and author; b. 21 March 1931, Milan; m. 1st (died 1981); four c.; m. 2nd Michael Pierri 1983; ed Laura Solera Mantegazza; also studied piano; discovered and guided by Giacinto Spagnoletti from age 15; collaborated with friend Salvatore Quasimodo 1950–53; period of silence and isolation 1961–72, alternating periods of health and illness until 1979 and again in 2004; Prix Librex-Guggenheim 'Eugenio Montale' for poetry 1993. *Publications:* La presenza di Orfeo 1953, Nozze romane 1955, Paura di Dio 1955, Tu sei Pietro 1961, Destinati a morire 1980, Le rime petrose 1983, Le satire della Ripa 1983, Le più belle poesie 1983, La Terra Santa 1984, La Terra Santa e altre poesie 1984, L'altra verità. Diario di una diversa 1986, Fogli bianchi 1987, Testamento 1988, Delirio amoroso 1989, Il tormento delle figure 1990, Vuoto d'amore 1991, Valzer 1991, Balocchi e poesie 1991, Le parole di Alda Merini 1991, La vita felice: aforismi 1992, Ipotenusa d'amore 1992, Aforismi 1992, La palude di Manganelli o Il monarca re 1992, Rime dantesche 1993, Le zolle d'acqua 1993, Se gli angeli sono inquieti 1993, La presenza di Orfeo: 1953–1962 1993, Titano amori intorno 1994, 25 poesie autografe 1994, Doppio bacio mortale 1994, Reato di vita. Autobiografia e poesia 1994, Il fantasma e l'amore 1994, La pazza della porta accanto 1995, Ballate non pagate 1995, Sogno e poesia 1995, Lettera ai figli 1995, La Terra Santa: Destinati a morire – La Terra Santa – Le satire della ripa – Le rime petrose –

Fogli bianchi 1996, Aforismi 1996, Un'anima indocile 1996, Refusi 1996, Immagini a voce 1996, La vita felice: sillabario 1996, La vita facile (Premio Viareggio 1996, Premio Procida-Elsa Morante 1997) 1997, La volpe e il sipario 1997, Orazioni piccole 1997, Curva in fuga 1997, Ringrazio sempre chi mi dà ragione 1997, Lettere a un racconto prose lunghe e brevi 1998, Fiore di poesia 1951–1997 1998, Eternamente vivo 1998, 57 poesie 1998, Favole, orazioni, salmi 1998, L'uovo di Saffo. Alda Merini e Enrico Baj 1999, Le ceneri di Dante: con una bugia di ceneri 1999, Aforismi e magie 1999, La poesia luogo del nulla. Poesie e parole con Chicca Gagliardo e Guido Spaini 1999, Il ladro Giuseppe. Racconti degli anni Sessanta 1999, Lettera a Maurizio Costanzo 1999, Vanni aveva mani lievi 2000, Le poesie di Alda Merini 1997–1999 2000, Superba è la notte 1996–1999 2000, Una poesia 2002, Tre aforismi 2000, Amore 2000, Due epitaffi e un testamento 2000, L'anima innamorata 2000, Corpo d'amore: un incontro con Gesù 2001, Maledizioni d'amore 2002, Il paradiso 2002, Anima 2002, Ora che vedi Dio 2002, Un aforisma 2002, Folle, folle, folle d'amore per te 2002, Magnificat. Un incontro con Maria 2002, Il maglio del poeta 2002, Silenzio 2002, La vita 2002, La carne degli angeli 2003, Più bella della poesia è stata la mia vita 2003, Alla tua salute, amore mio: poesie, aforismi 2003, Poema di Pasqua 2003, Clinica dell'abbandono 2004, Cartes (Des) 2004, Dopo tutto anche tu 2004. *E-mail:* info@aldamerini.com (office). *Website:* www.aldamerini.com (office).

MERINO LUCERO, Beatriz, MA; Peruvian lawyer, politician and government official; *Defensora del Pueblo (Ombudsman);* b. 1949, Lima; ed Universidad Nacional Mayor de San Marcos, London School of Econs, UK, Harvard Univ. Law School, USA; lawyer fmrly specializing in tax and int. trade; elected Senator (Movimiento Libertad) 1990–92; mem. Congreso (Frente Independiente Moralizador) 1995–2000; Dir Master Tax and Fiscal Policy, Univ. of Lima 2000–01; elected Head of Sunat (tax agency) 2001–03; Pres. Council of Ministers (Prime Minister) June–Dec. 2003; member of the Inter-American Dialogue, Washington, DC –2005; Defensora del Pueblo (Ombudsman) 2005–; Orden 'El Sol del Perú' en el Grado de Gran Cruz 2006; María Elena Moyano Prize, Ministry of Women and Social Devt, Vaso de Leche Award of the Women of Peru, Woman of the Year, OWIT Peru, Robert G. Storey International Award for Leadership, Center for American and International Law 2004. *Address:* Defensora del Pueblo, Jr. Ucayali N° 388, Lima, Peru (office). *Telephone:* (1) 3110300 (office). *E-mail:* centrodeatencionvirtual@defensoria.gob.pe (office). *Website:* www.defensoria.gob.pe (office).

MERKEL, Angela Dorothea, Dr rer. nat; German politician; *Chancellor;* b. 17 July 1954, Hamburg; d. of Horst Kasner and Herlind Kasner; m. 1st Ulrich Merkel (divorced 1982); m. 2nd Joachim Sauer 1998; ed Univ. of Leipzig; Research Assoc. in quantum chem., Zentralinstitut für physikalische Chemie, East Berlin 1978–90; joined Demokratischer Aufbruch (DA) 1989, Press Spokesperson 1990; Deputy Spokesman for Govt of Lothar de la Maizière, March–Oct. 1990; joined CDU (Christian Democratic Union) 1990, mem. Bundestag 1990–, Deputy Fed. Chair. 1991–98, CDU Chair. Fed. State of Mecklenburg-Vorpommern 1993–2000, Gen. Sec. CDU 1998–2000, Chair. 2000–, also Parl. Leader 2002–05; Fed. Minister for Women and Young People 1991–94, for Environment, Nature Conservation and Nuclear Safety 1994–98; Chancellor 2005–; Pres. European Council and Chair. G8 2007; mem. Council of Women World Leaders; Bundesverdienstkreuz 2008; Dr hc (Hebrew Univ. of Jerusalem) 2007, (Univ. of Leipzig) 2008, (Univ. of Tech., Wrocław) 2008; ranked by Forbes magazine amongst 100 Most Powerful Women (first) 2006, (first) 2007, (first) 2008, named a Hero of the Environment 2007, Charlemagne Prize for distinguished services to European unity 2008. *Publication:* Der Preis des Überlebens: Gedanken und Gespräche über zukünftige Aufgaben der Umweltpolitik (The Price of Survival: Ideas and Conversations about Future Tasks for Environmental Policy) 1997. *Leisure interests:* reading, hiking, gardening. *Address:* Office of the Federal Chancellery, Willy-Brandt str. 1, 10557 Berlin, Germany (office). *Telephone:* (30) 40000 (office). *Fax:* (30) 40002357 (office). *E-mail:* internetpost@bundeskanzler.de (office). *Website:* www.bundeskanzler.de (office); www.angela-merkel.de.

MERKELBACH, Reinhold, DPhil; German professor of classics; *Professor Emeritus, University of Cologne;* b. 7 June 1918, Grenzhausen; s. of Paul Merkelbach and Gertrud Stade; m. Lotte Dorn 1941; one s. two d.; ed Schondorf Gymnasium, Univs of Munich and Hamburg; Asst at Classics Inst. Univ. of Cologne 1950–57, Prof. 1961–83, Prof. Emer. 1983–; Prof. Erlangen Univ. 1957–61; mem. Rheinisch-Westfälisch Akad. der Wissenschaften 1979–; Corresp. mem. British Acad. 1986–; Dr. hc Besançon 1978. *Publications:* Untersuchungen zur Odyssee 1951, Die Quellen des griechischen Alexanderromans 1954, Roman und Mysterium im Altertum 1961, Isisfeste 1962, (with M. West) Fragmenta Hesiodea 1968, (with F. Solmsen and M. West) Hesiodi Opera 1970, 1989, Mithras 1984, Die Hirten des Dionysos 1988, Platons Menon 1988, (with M. Totti) Abrasax I–IV 1990–96, Die Bedeutung des Geldes für die Geschichte der griechisch-römischen Welt 1992, Isis regina—Zeus Sarapis 1995, Hestia und Erigone 1996, Philologica 1997, (with J. Stauber) Steinepigramme aus dem griechischen Osten 1998–2001, Griechische Inschriften jenseits des Euphrat (with J. Stauber) 2005; many edns of Greek inscriptions, Ed. of Zeitschrift für Papyrologie und Epigraphik, Epigraphica anatolica, Beiträge zur klassischen Philologie. *Address:* Im Haferkamp 17, 51427 Bergisch-Gladbach, Germany. *Telephone:* (2204) 60727. *Fax:* (2204) 60727.

MERKIN, J. Ezra; American business executive; *Chairman, GMAC Financial Services;* ed Columbia Coll., New York, Harvard Univ. Law School, Cambridge, Mass; Man. Pnr, Gabriel Capital Group (and its predecessor) 1985–2008; Chair. GMAC Financial Services 2008–; Trustee and Chair. Investment Cttees Yeshiva Univ. and of UJA/Fed. of New York; Trustee, Carnegie Hall, New York, Beyeler Foundation and Museum, Basel, Switzerland, Gruss Foundation; mem. Bd of Visitors Columbia Coll.; Gov. Levy Econs Inst. of Bard Coll., Annandale-on-Hudson, NY; Pres. Fifth Avenue Synagogue, New York; Vice-Chair. Ramaz School, New York. *Address:* GMAC Financial Services, 200 Renaissance Center, Detroit, MI 48265-2000, USA (office). *Telephone:* (313) 556-5000 (office). *Fax:* (815) 282-6156 (office). *E-mail:* info@gmacfs.com (office). *Website:* www.gmacfs.com (office).

MERKLEY, Jeffery (Jeff) A., BA, MA; American politician; *Senator from Oregon;* b. 24 Oct. 1956, Myrtle Creek, Ore.; m. Mary Merkley; two c.; ed Stanford Univ., Princeton Univ.; Presidential Man. Fellow, Office of the US Sec. of Defense, Washington, DC 1982–91; Man. Pnr, Computer Medics 1989–91; Exec. Dir Portland Habitat for Humanity 1991–94; Dir of Housing Devt at Human Solutions 1995–96; Pres. World Affairs Council of Oregon 1996–2003, mem. Bd of Trustees 1991–; mem. Oregon State House of Reps 1998–2009, Speaker 2007–09; Senator from Oregon 2009–; Founder People's Investment Opportunity Program, Walk for Humanity; Democrat. *Address:* Office of Senator Jeff Merkley, US Senate, Washington, DC 20510, USA (office). *Website:* www.senate.gov (office).

MERLINI, Cesare; Italian international affairs scholar and fmr professor of nuclear technologies; b. 29 April 1933, Rome; m.; two s. two d.; lecturer in Nuclear Technologies 1967–76; Prof. of Nuclear Technologies, Turin Polytechnic 1976–85; Dir Istituto Affari Internazionali, Rome 1970–79, Pres. 1979–2000, fmr Chair., currently Pres. Bd of Trustees; Pres. Exec. Cttee Consiglio per le Relazioni fra Italia e Stati Uniti (Council for USA and Italy) 1983–92; mem. Bd of Dirs and Exec. Cttee Unione Tipografico-Editrice Torinese publrs SpA, Turin, Chair. 1999–; mem. Trilateral Comm. 1973–2001, Council, Int. Inst. for Strategic Studies, London 1993–99, Gen. Council, Aspen Inst. Italia, Rome; mem. Bd of Dirs, Asscn Jean Monnet, Paris, ISPI, Milan. *Publications:* Fine dell'atomo? Passato e futuro delle applicazioni civili e militari dell'energia nucleare 1987, L'Europa degli Anni Novanta: Scenari per un futuro imprevisto (co-author and ed.) 1991; co-author and ed. of numerous books on nuclear energy and int. strategy, author of numerous articles on European and int. affairs and of scientific publs on nuclear reactors and related technological and eng problems. *Address:* Consiglio per le Relazioni fra Italia e Stati Uniti, Piazzale Flaminio 19, 00186 Rome, Italy (office). *Telephone:* (6) 3222546 (office). *Fax:* (6) 3201867 (office). *E-mail:* consiusa@tin.it (office).

MERLONI, Vittorio, CBE; Italian industrialist; *Chairman, Indesit Company;* b. 30 April 1933, Fabriano, Ancona; m. Franca Carloni; four c.; ed Univ. of Perugia; Chair. Merloni Elettrodomestici SpA 1970– (renamed Indesit Co. 2005–), Fineldo (family holding co. that controls Indesit Co. and other Group interests); mem. Confederazione Generale dell'Industria Italiana (Confindustria) 1976–, Pres. 1980–84; mem. Bd Dirs Assocs of Harvard Business School 1981–94; Pres. Assonime (Asscn for Italy's limited liability cos) 2001–05; mem. Consiglio Nazionale dell'Economia e del Lavoro (Nat. Council of Economy and Labour); mem. two dels to China; honorary doctorate of Management Engineering (Politecnico University of Milan) 2001; Cavaliere di Gran Croce al merito della Repubblica, Cavaliere del Lavoro 1984; Leonardo Award 2004, GEI Award 2005. *Leisure interests:* racing cars, boats. *Address:* Indesit Company SpA, Viale Aristide Merloni 47, 60044 Fabriano (AN), Italy (office). *Telephone:* (0732) 6611 (office). *Fax:* (0732) 662380 (office). *Website:* www.indesitcompany.com (office).

MERMAZ, Louis; French politician and professor of history; b. 20 Aug. 1931, Paris; m. Annie d'Arbigny; 3 c.; teacher Lycée le Mans, Lycée Lakanal, Sceaux; Jr Lecturer in Contemporary History, Univ. of Clermont-Ferrand; Sec.-Gen. Convention des institutions républicaines 1965–69; mem. Socialist Party Nat. Secr. 1974–79, 1987–; mem. Nat. Ass. for Isère 1967–68, 1973–90, 1997–2001; Mayor of Vienne 1971–2001; Conseiller Gén. Canton of Vienne-Nord 1973–79, Vienne-Sud 1979–88; Pres. Conseil gén. of Isère 1976–85; Chair. Socialist Party Exec. Cttee 1979; Minister of Transport May–June 1981, of Equipment and Transport May–June 1988, of Agric. and Forests 1990–92, for Relations with Parl. and Govt Spokesman 1992–93; Pres. Nat. Ass. 1981–86, Socialist Group in Nat. Ass. 1988–90, Asscn Mer du Nord-Méditerranée 1989–94; mem. Senate for Isère 2001–; Chevalier Légion d'honneur. *Publications:* Madame Sabatier, Les Hohenzollern, L'autre volonté 1984, Madame de Maintenon 1985, Les Geôles de la République 2001. *Address:* Sénat, Palais du Luxembourg, 15 rue du Vaugirard, 75005 Paris (office); Permanence Parlementaire, 2 rue des Célestes, 38200 Vienne, France. *Telephone:* 1-42-34-28-58 (office); 4-74-85-47-58. *E-mail:* l.mermaz@senat.fr (office). *Website:* www.senat.fr/senfic/mermaz_louis01020h.html (office).

MERNISSI, Fatema, PhD; Moroccan sociologist and writer; b. 1941, Fez; ed Univ. of Paris (Sorbonne) and in the USA; sociologist, feminist and expert in the Koran; Prof. Univ. Mohammed V, Rabat. *Publications include:* The Veil and the Male Elite: A Feminist Interpretation of Women's Rights in Islam 1992, Islam and Democracy: Fear of the Modern World 1994, The Forgotten Queens of Islam 1994, Dreams of Trespass: Tales of a Harem Girlhood 1994, Fear of Modernity or The Political Harem, Women's Rebellion and Islamic Memory 1996, Dreams on the Threshold, Les Ait Débrouille 1997, Scheherazade Goes West 2001, Beyond the Veil: Male-Female Dynamics in Muslim Society 2003, Les Sindbads Marocains: Voyage dans le Maroc civique 2004. *E-mail:* fatema@mernissi.net (office). *Website:* www.mernissi.net.

MERO, Muhammad Mustafa, PhD; Syrian politician; b. 1940, Tal-Mineen, Damascus; m.; two s. three d.; ed Damascus Univ.; Mayor of Daraa 1980–86, of Al-Hasaka 1986–93; Gov. of Aleppo 1993–2000; Prime Minister of Syria 2000–03. *Address:* c/o Office of the Prime Minister, rue Chahbandar, Damascus, Syria (office).

MERON, Theodor, LLM, MJ, JSD; American judge and academic; *Appeals Judge, United Nations International Criminal Tribunal for the Former*

Yugoslavia; b. 28 April 1930, Kalisz, Poland; ed Univ. of Jerusalem, Harvard Univ. Law School, Univ. of Cambridge, UK; fmr Legal Adviser, Israeli Foreign Ministry, fmr Amb. of Israel to Canada, later to UN in Geneva, resgnd 1977; US citizen 1984–; Visiting Prof. of Law, New York Univ. School of Law 1975, Prof. of Law 1977, Charles L. Denison Prof. of Int. Law 1994–2003, Charles L. Denison Prof. of Law Emer. and Judicial Fellow 2006–; Prof. of Int. Law, Grad. Inst. of Int. Studies, Geneva, Switzerland 1991–95; Ed.-in-Chief American Journal of Int. Law 1993–98; elected Judge UN Criminal Tribunal for the Fmr Yugoslavia (ICTY) 2001, Pres. 2003–05, also mem. Appeals Chamber (ICTY) and UN Criminal Tribunal for Rwanda (ICTR) 2001–; fmr Counsellor on Int. Law US Dept of State; mem. Council on Foreign Relations; Public mem. US Del. to CSCE Conf. on Human Dimension, Copenhagen; numerous visiting lectureships in univs in Europe and USA; mem. Inst. of Int. Law; Officier, Légion d'Honneur (France) 2007; Int. Bar Asscn Rule of Law Award, American Soc. of Int. Law Hudson Medal 2006, American Council of Learned Soc. Haskins Prize 2008. *Publications include:* Investment Insurance in International Law, Henry's Wars and Shakespeare's Laws 1994, Bloody Constraint: War and Chivalry in Shakespeare 1998, War Crimes Law Comes of Age: Essays 1999, International Law in the Age of Human Rights 2003; numerous articles and publs on int. law and human rights. *Address:* UN Criminal Tribunal for the Former Yugoslavia, Public Information Unit, PO Box 13888, 2501 The Hague, Netherlands (office); New York University School of Law, Vanderbilt Hall, 40 Washington Square South, Room 304, New York, NY 10012-1099, USA. *Telephone:* (70) 512-8840 (office); (212) 998-6191. *Fax:* (70) 512-5252 (office). *E-mail:* meront@juris.law.nyu.edu. *Website:* www.un .org/icty (office); http://its.law.nyu.edu/facultyprofiles/profile .cfm?personID=20122 (office).

MÉRORÈS, Léo, LLB, MA, PhD; Haitian diplomatist and UN official; *President, Economic and Social Council (ECOSOC);* b. 21 April 1943; m.; ed State Univ. of Haiti, Ecole de Commerce Maurice Laroche, Port-au-Prince, New York Univ., USA; early career as salesman, Enterprises Gerard Theard, Port-au-Prince 1961; worked part-time as accountant and Asst to Head of Credit Dept, Shapiro & Sons Textile Corpn, New York, USA 1969–73; UNDP Deputy Resident Rep. in Togo and Madagascar 1978–84, worked in UNDP office in Rwanda 1974–78, UNDP Deputy Resident Rep. for Liberia, Mali and Cameroon 1984–92, responsible for UNDP offices in Gabon and Burundi 1989–92, a Prin. Counsellor for UNDP working with Econ. Community of West African States (ECOWAS) countries 1992–2001, consultant on man. and econ. co-operation issues for several UN entities, including Dept of Econ. and Social Affairs, UN Office for Project Services (UNOPS) and UNDP 2001–04; Chargé d'affaires, Perm. Mission to UN, New York 2004–05, Perm. Rep. to UN 2005–; Vice-Pres. ECOSOC, representing Group of Latin America and Caribbean 2006–08, Pres. ECOSOC 2008–. *Address:* Permanent Mission of Haiti to the United Nations, 801 Second Avenue, Room 600, New York, NY 10017, USA (office). *Telephone:* (212) 370-4840 (Perm. Mission) (office); (212) 963-4640 (ECOSOC) (office). *Fax:* (212) 661-8698 (Perm. Mission) (office); (212) 963-5935 (ECOSOC) (office). *E-mail:* haiti@un.int (office); ecosocinfo@un .org (office). *Website:* www.un.org/ecosoc (office).

MERRILL, Susan L., JD; American lawyer and securities industry executive; *Executive Vice President, Enforcement, Financial Industry Regulatory Authority, Inc.;* b. 1957; m.; two c.; ed Univ. of Maryland, Brooklyn Law School; moved to New York to pursue acting career; judicial clerk for Hon. Francis Van Dusen, US Court of Appeals of the Third Circuit 1986–87; Assoc. Davis Polk & Wardell (law firm), New York 1987, Pnr 1994–2004; Chief Enforcement Officer, NYSE Group Inc. (fmrly New York Stock Exchange) 2004–07, Exec. Vice Pres., Enforcement, Financial Industry Regulatory Authority, Inc. (formed after consolidation of NYSE Mem. Regulation with Nat. Asscn of Securities Dealers) 2007–. *Address:* Financial Industry Regulatory Authority, Inc., 1735 K Street, NW, Washington, DC 20006, USA (office). *Telephone:* (301) 590-6500 (office). *Website:* www.finra.org (office).

MERSCH, Yves; Luxembourg central banker; *Governor, Luxembourg Central Bank;* b. 1 Oct. 1949; ed Univ. of Paris; called to the Bar, Luxembourg 1974; Public Law Asst, Univ. Paris-XI 1974; Budget Asst, Ministry of Finance 1975; mem. staff IMF, Washington, DC, USA 1976–77; Ministry of Finance, Fiscal Affairs and Structural Policies 1977–80; Adviser, Ministry of Finance, Monetary Affairs and Int. Financial Relations 1981; Govt Commr Luxembourg Stock Exchange 1985; Dir Treasury 1989; Gov. Luxembourg Cen. Bank 1998–; mem. Governing Council, European Cen. Bank. *Address:* Banque Centrale du Luxembourg, 2 boulevard Royal, 2983, Luxembourg (office). *Telephone:* 4774-1 (office). *Fax:* 4774-4901 (office). *E-mail:* info@bcl.lu (office). *Website:* www.bcl.lu (office).

MERSON, Michael H., MD; American physician and academic; *Director, Center for Interdisciplinary Research on AIDS, Yale University;* b. 7 June 1945, New York; ed Amherst Coll., State Univ. of New York Downstate Medical Center, Johns Hopkins Univ.; joined Center for Disease Control, Atlanta 1972; worked in several countries including Brazil and Bangladesh; joined WHO 1978, Medical Officer Dir WHO Diarrhoeal Diseases Control Programme 1978–87, Dir Acute Respiratory Infections Control Programme 1987–90; Exec. Dir Global Programme on AIDS 1990–95; Dean and Chair Dept of Epidemiology and Public Health, Yale Univ. School of Medicine 1995–2005, Lauder Prof. of Public Health 2001–, Dir and Prin. Investigator Center for Interdisciplinary Research on AIDS (CIRA), also Dir of Admin. and Int. Research Cores 2005–; Prin. Investigator Yale's AIDS Int. Training and Research Program (AITRP), St. Petersburg, Russia and extension activities in China and South Africa, Prin. Investigator Int. Clinical, Operational and Health Services Research and Training Award (ICOHRTA) Program, Pretoria, South Africa; Co-investigator Bill and Melinda Gates Foundation, Global Health Program; Surgeon Gen. Exemplary Service Medal, S. Flem-

ming Award, Frank Bobbott Alumni Award, Award for Outstanding Contribution to the Campaign Against HIV/AIDS (Russia). *Publications:* International Health: Diseases, Programs, Systems and Policies (co-ed.); over 150 articles on subjects from food-borne diseases to effectiveness of HIV interventions and numerous book chapters (jtly). *Address:* Yale Center for Interdisciplinary Research on AIDS, 40 Temple Street, Suite 1B, New Haven, CT 06510, USA (office). *Telephone:* (203) 764-8474 (office). *Fax:* (203) 764-4353 (office). *E-mail:* michael.merson@yale.edu (office). *Website:* cira.med.yale.edu (office).

MERTIN, Klaus, Dr rer. pol; German banker; b. 9 March 1922; Chair. of Supervisory Bd Deutsche Bank Berlin AG, Berlin, Dierig Holding AG, Augsburg; Deputy Chair. of Supervisory Bd Deutsche Centralbodenkredit AG, Berlin, Cologne; mem. of Supervisory Bd AG für Industrie und Verkehrswesen, Frankfurt, Badenwerk AG, Karlsruhe, Daimler-Benz AG, Stuttgart, Gerling-Konzern-Versicherungs-Beteiligungs AG, Cologne, Heidelberger Druckmaschinen AG, Heidelberg, Karstadt AG, Essen, Rheinmetall Berlin AG, Düsseldorf, Salamander AG, Kornwestheim, Schindler Aufzügefabrik GmbH, Berlin; mem. of Advisory Bd Barmenia Versicherungen, Wuppertal; mem. of Admin. Council Deutsche Bank Compagnie Financière Luxembourg, Luxembourg; mem. of Exec. Council Schott Glaswerke, Mainz. *Address:* Deutsche Bank AG, Taunusanlage 12, 60325 Frankfurt am Main, Germany (office).

MERTLÍK, Pavel, PhD, Hab. Dozent; Czech economist and politician; *Chief Economist, Raiffeisenbank, Prague;* b. 7 May 1961, Havlíčkův Brod; m. Dana Mertlík; two s.; ed School of Econs, Prague, Charles Univ., Prague; Prof. of Econs, Prague School of Econs 1983–88; Research Fellow, Inst. of Forecasting of the Czech Repub. 1989–91; Prof. of Econs, Charles Univ. 1991–95; Research Fellow, Czech Nat. Bank 1995–98; mem. Czech Social Democratic Party 1995–; Minister of Finance and Deputy Prime Minister 1998–2001; Chief Economist, Raiffeisen Bank, Prague 2001–. *Publications:* numerous articles on price theory, monopolies, econ. transformation and privatization. *Leisure interests:* cycling, fishing, skiing. *Address:* Raiffeisenbank, Olbrachtova 9, 14021, Prague 4, Czech Republic (office). *Telephone:* (2) 2114-1800 (office). *Fax:* (2) 2114-2800 (office). *E-mail:* pavel.mertlik@rb.cz (office). *Website:* www .rb.cz (office).

MERTON, John Ralph, MBE (Mil.); British artist; b. 7 May 1913, London; s. of Sir Thomas Ralph Merton, KBE and Violet Margery Harcourt Sawyer; m. Viola Penelope von Bernd 1938; three d. (one deceased); ed Eton. Coll., Balliol Coll., Oxford; 20 pictures exhibited at Colnaghi, Bond Street, London 1938; served World War II, Lt Col Air Photo Reconnaissance Research Unit 1944; exhbn Christopher Wood Gallery, London 1995; 63 pictures exhibited at Fine Art Soc. Gallery, Bond Street, London 2003; Legion of Merit, USA 1944. *Portraits include:* Daphne Wall 1946, Jane Dalkeith (now Duchess of Buccleuch) (Royal Acad. 'A' Award) 1958, Triple Portrait of HRH The Princess of Wales 1988, drawing of HM The Queen as Head of the Order of Merit 1989, James Meade (winner Nobel Prize for Econs) 1987, Paul Nitze 1991, Lord and Lady Romsey with a Mirror Reflecting Broadlands 1997. *Publication:* A Journey Through an Artist's Life (limited edn) Book 1 1994, Book 2 2003. *Leisure interests:* music, making things, underwater photography. *Address:* Pound House, Pound Lane, Oare, Nr Marlborough, Wiltshire, SN8 4JA, England. *Telephone:* (1672) 563539.

MERTON, Robert C., PhD; American economist and academic; *John and Natty McArthur University Professor, Harvard Business School;* b. 31 July 1944, New York; s. of Robert K. Merton (q.v.) and Suzanne Merton; m. June Rose 1966 (separated 1996); two s. one d.; ed Columbia Univ., Calif. Inst. of Tech., Mass. Inst. of Tech.; Instructor in Econs, MIT 1969–70; Asst Prof. of Finance, Alfred P. Sloan School of Man. 1970–73, Assoc. Prof. 1973–74, Prof. 1974–80, J.C. Penney Prof. of Man. 1980–88; Visiting Prof. of Finance, Harvard Univ. Business School 1987–88, George Fisher Baker Prof. of Business Admin. 1988–98, John and Natty McArthur Univ. Prof. 1998–; Research Assoc. Nat. Bureau of Econ. Research 1979–; Sr Adviser, Office of Chair., Salomon Inc. 1988–93; Prin., Co-Founder Long-Term Capital Man. Greenwich, Conn. 1993–99; Sr Adviser, JP Morgan & Co. 1999–2001; Co-Founder and Dir, Integrated Finance Ltd (IFL) 2002–07, Chief Science Officer and Dir, Trinsum Group (after merger of IFL and Marakon) 2007–08; Sr Fellow, Int. Asscn of Financial Engineers; Fellow, Econometric Soc., American Acad. of Arts and Sciences, Financial Man. Asscn 2000; mem. NAS, American Finance Asscn (Dir 1982–84, Pres. 1986, Fellow 2000); mem. numerous editorial bds; Hon. Prof., HEC School of Man. (École des Hautes Études Commerciales), Paris 1995–; Hon. MA (Harvard) 1989; Hon. LLD (Chicago) 1991; Hon. DEconSc (Lausanne) 1996; Dr hc (Paris-Dauphiné) 1997, Dr hc (Universidad Nacional Mayor de San Marcos, Lima, Peru) 2004; Hon. DrManSc (Nat. Sun Yat-sen Univ., Taiwan) 1998; DSc hc (Athens Univ. of Econs and Business) 2003, (Claremont Graduate Univ.) 2008; Leo Melamed Prize, Univ. of Chicago Business School 1983, Financial Engineer of the Year Award, Int. Asscn of Financial Engineers 1993, shared Nobel Prize for Econs 1997 for devising Black-Scholes Model for determining value of derivatives, Michael Pupin Medal for Service to the Nation, Columbia Univ. 1998, Distinguished Alumni Award, Calif. Inst. of Tech. 1999, numerous other awards. *Publications:* The Collected Scientific Papers of Paul A. Samuelson, Vol. III (Ed.) 1972, Continuous-Time Finance 1990, Casebook in Financial Engineering: Applied Studies in Financial Innovation (co-author) 1995, The Global Financial System: A Functional Perspective (co-author) 1995, Finance (co-author) 2000, numerous articles in professional journals. *Address:* Graduate School of Business, Harvard University, 353 Baker Library, Soldiers Field, Boston, MA 02163, USA (office). *Telephone:* (617) 495-6678 (office). *Fax:* (617) 495-8863 (office). *E-mail:* rmerton@hbs.edu (office). *Website:* www.people.hbs.edu/rmerton (home).

MERWIN, William Stanley, AB; American poet, dramatist, writer and translator; b. 30 Sept. 1927, New York, NY; m. Diane Whalley 1954; ed Princeton Univ.; playwright-in-residence Poet's Theatre, Cambridge, MA 1956–57; Poetry Ed. The Nation 1962; Assoc., Theatre de la Citié, Lyons 1964–65; Special Consultant in Poetry, Library of Congress, Washington, DC 1999; Acad. of American Poets Fellowship 1973; mem. Acad. of American Poets, American Acad. of Arts and Letters; Yale Series of Younger Poets Award 1952, Bess Hokin Prize 1962, Ford Foundation grant 1964, Harriet Monroe Memorial Prize 1967, PEN Translation Prize 1969, Rockefeller Foundation grant 1969, Pulitzer Prize in Poetry 1971, Shelley Memorial Award 1974, NEA grant 1978, Bollingen Prize 1979, Aiken Taylor Award 1990, Maurice English Award 1990, Dorothea Tanning Prize 1994, Lenore Marshall Award 1994, Ruth Lilly Poetry Prize 1998. *Publications:* poetry: A Mask for Janus 1952, The Dancing Bears 1954, Green with Beasts 1956, The Drunk in the Furnace 1960, The Moving Target 1963, The Lice 1967, Three Poems 1968, Animae 1969, The Carrier of Ladders 1970, Signs 1971, Writings to an Unfinished Accompaniment 1973, The First Four Books of Poems 1975, Three Poems 1975, The Compass Flower 1977, Feathers from the Hill 1978, Finding the Islands 1982, Opening the Hand 1983, The Rain in the Trees 1988, Selected Poems 1988, Travels 1993, The Vixen 1996, The Folding Cliffs 1998, Migration: New and Selected Poems (Nat. Book Award for Poetry) 2005, Present Company 2007, The Shadow of Sirius (Pulitzer Prize for Poetry 2009) 2008; plays: Darkling Child (with Dido Milroy) 1956, Favor Island 1957, The Gilded West 1961, adaptations of five other plays; other: A New Right Arm, West Wind: Supplement of American Poetry (ed.) 1961, The Miner's Pale Children 1970, Houses and Travellers 1977, Unframed Originals: Recollections 1982, Regions of Memory: Uncollected Prose 1949–1982 1987, The Essential Wyatt (ed.) 1989, The Lost Upland 1993, The Ends of the Earth (essays) 2005, Summer Doorways (memoir) 2005; translator: Selected Translations 1948–1968 1968, Selected Translations 1968–1978 1979, Sir Gawain and the Green Knight: A New Verse Translation 2004. *Address:* Steven Barclay Agency, 12 Western Avenue, Petaluma, CA 94952, USA (office). *Telephone:* (707) 773-0654 (office). *Fax:* (707) 778-1868 (office). *Website:* www.barclayagency.com (office).

MERZ, Friedrich; German politician and lawyer; b. 11 Nov. 1955, Brilon; m. Charlotte Gass; one s. two d.; judge, Saarbrücken Dist Court 1985–86; lawyer 1986–, Asscn of Chemical Industry 1986–89, Regional Court of Appeal, Cologne 1992–; mem. European Parl. 1989–94; mem. Bundestag 1994–, Parl. Leader CDU 2000–02. *Address:* Bundeshaus, Platz der Republik, 11011 Berlin, Germany (office). *Telephone:* (30) 22772888 (office). *Fax:* (30) 22776436. *E-mail:* friedrich.merz@bundestag.de (office). *Website:* www.friedrich-merz.de (home).

MERZ, Hans-Rudolf, Dr rer. pol; Swiss management consultant and politician; *President of Federal Council and Head of Federal Department of Finance;* b. 10 Nov. 1942, Herisau; m.; three s.; ed Univ. of St Gallen; Asst Lecturer, Univ. of St Gallen 1967–69; Sec., FDP St Gallen; Man. Appenzell Ausserhoden Industrial Asscn 1969–74; Deputy Dir UBS Wolfsberg training centre 1974–77; worked in pvt. practice as ind. consultant 1977–2003; Chair. Helvetia Patria Insurance Co., AG Cilander Textile Finishing, Anova Holding 1977–2003; elected Rep. Council of States 1997, served as Chair. Finance Cttee, mem. Foreign Affairs and Security Cttee; Vice-Pres. OCSE del.; elected to Fed. Council 2003, Head of Fed. Dept of Finance 2004–, Vice-Pres. Fed. Council 2008, Pres. 2009–. *Address:* Federal Department of Finance, Bernerhof, Bundesgasse 3, 3003 Bern, Switzerland (office). *Telephone:* 313226033 (office). *Fax:* 313233852 (office). *E-mail:* info@gs-efd.admin.ch (office). *Website:* www.efd.admin.ch (office).

MESA GISBERT, Carlos Diego; Bolivian politician; b. 12 Aug. 1953; fmr historian and journalist; Vice-Pres. of Bolivia 2002–03, Pres. 2003–05 (resgnd); mem. Bolivian History Acad. *Address:* c/o Ministry of the Presidency, Palacio de Gobierno, Plaza Murillo, La Paz, Bolivia (office).

MESELSON, Matthew Stanley, PhB, PhD; American biologist and academic; *Thomas Dudley Cabot Professor of the Natural Sciences and Principle Investigator, Meselson Laboratory, Harvard University;* b. 24 May 1930, Denver, Colo; s. of Hymen Avram and Ann Swedlow Meselson; m. 1st Katherine Kaynis 1960; m. 2nd Sarah Leah Page 1969; two d.; m. 3rd Jeanne Guillemin 1986; ed Univ. of Chicago, Univ. of Calif. (Berkeley) and Calif. Inst. of Tech.; Research Fellow, Calif. Inst. of Tech. 1957–58, Asst Prof. of Physical Chem. 1958–59, Sr Research Fellow in Chemical Biology 1959–60; Assoc. Prof. of Biology, Harvard Univ. 1960–64, Prof. of Biology 1964–76, Thomas Dudley Cabot Prof. of Nat. Sciences 1976–; Chair. Fed. of American Scientists 1986–88; mem. NAS, Inst. of Medicine, American Acad. of Arts and Sciences, Acad. Santa Chiara, American Philosophical Soc., Council on Foreign Relations; Life Mem. New York Acad. of Sciences; Foreign mem. Royal Soc., Acad. des Sciences, Russian Acad. of Sciences; Fellow, AAAS; Hon. DSc (Oakland Coll.) 1966, (Columbia) 1971, (Chicago) 1975; Hon. ScD (Yale) 1987, (Northwestern) 2003; Dr hc (Princeton) 1988; Prize for Molecular Biology, NAS 1963, Eli Lilly Award in Microbiology and Immunology 1964, Public Service Award, Fed. of American Scientists 1972 Alumni Medal, Univ. of Chicago Alumni Asscn 1971, Alumni Distinguished Service Award, Calif. Inst. of Tech. 1975, Lehman Award of New York Acad. of Sciences 1975, Leo Szilard Award, American Physical Soc. 1978, Presidential Award of New York Acad. of Sciences 1983, MacArthur Fellow 1984–89, Scientific Freedom and Responsibility Award, AAAS 1990, Thomas Hunt Morgan Medal, Genetics Soc. of America 1995, Public Service Award, American Soc. for Cell Biology 2002, Linus Pauling Award 2004, Lasker Award for Special Achievement in Medical Science 2004, Mendel Medal, British Genetics Soc. 2008. *Publications:* numerous papers on the biochemistry and molecular biology of nucleic acids and on arms control of biological and chemical weapons, in various numbers of Proceedings of NAS and of Scientific American, etc. *Address:* Sherman Fairchild Building, 7 Divinity Avenue, Harvard University, Cambridge, MA 02138, USA (office). *Telephone:* (617) 495-7899 (office); (617) 495-2264 (office). *Fax:* (617) 496-2444 (office). *Website:* mcb.harvard.edu/meselson (office).

MESFIN, Seyoum; Ethiopian politician; *Minister of Foreign Affairs;* b. Jan. 1949, Tigray; m.; four c.; ed Bahir Dar Polytechnic Inst., Addis Ababa Univ.; exec. mem. Tigray People's Liberation Front (TPLF); Chair. Foreign Affairs Cttee, Ethiopian People's Revolutionary Democratic Front (EPRDF); Minister of Foreign Affairs 1991–. *Address:* Ministry of Foreign Affairs, PO Box 393, Addis Ababa, Ethiopia (office). *Telephone:* (11) 5517345 (office). *Fax:* (11) 5514300 (office). *E-mail:* mfa.addis@telecom.net.et. *Website:* www.mfa.gov.et.

MESGUICH, Daniel Elie Emile; French actor and theatre and opera director; b. 15 July 1952, Algiers; s. of William Mesguich and Jacqueline Boukabza; m. Danielle Barthélémy 1971; one s. three d.; ed Lycée Thiers, Marseille, Sorbonne, Paris and Conservatoire Nat. Supérieur d'Art Dramatique; actor 1969–; stage dir 1972–; f. Théâtre du Miroir 1974; Prof. Conservatoire Nat. Supérieur d'Art Dramatique 1983–; Dir Théâtre Gérard Philippe, Saint-Denis 1986–88, Théâtre de la Métaphore, Lille 1991–98; numerous appearances on stage, film and TV and dir of numerous stage plays and operas; Chevalier, Ordre Nat. du Mérite; Officier des Arts et des Lettres. *Films:* Molière 1977, La Fille de Prague avec un sac très lourd 1978, Dossier 51 1978, L'Amour en fuite 1978, Clair de femme 1979, La Banquière 1980, Allonz'enfants 1981, La Chanson du mal-aimé 1981, Les Iles 1982, La Belle captive 1982, L'Araignée de satin 1982, Contes clandestins 1983, Les Mots pour le dire 1983, Paris vu par 20 ans après 1984, Le Radeau de la Méduse 1988, 1998, L'Autrichienne 1989, Toussaint Louverture 1989, La Femme fardée 1990, Jefferson in Paris 1994, Tiré à part 1997, Le divorce 2000, Le Tango des Rasherski 2003. *Plays directed:* Shakespeare: Hamlet, Le Roi Lear, Romeo et Juliet, Titus Andronicus, La Tempête, Antoine et Cleopâtre; Racine: Andromaque, Britannicus, Esther, Mithridate; Molière: Don Juan; Chekhov: Platonov. *Operas directed:* Le Grand Macabre (Ligeti), Le Ring (Wagner), Bal Masqué (Verdi), La Vie Parisienne (Offenbach), Wozzeck (Berg), Le fou (Landowski), Elephant Man (Laurent Petit Guard), Damnation de Faust (Berlioz). *TV roles include:* Kafka: la lettre au père 1975, Le Cardinal de Retz 1975, Lazare Carnot ou Le glaive de la révolution 1978, Joséphine ou la comédie des ambitions 1979, Aéroport: Charter 2020 1980, Médecins de nuit 1980, Dans quelques instants 1981, La Sorcière 1982, Napoleón, La Vie de Berlioz 1983, Le Château 1984, Grand hôtel 1986, La Garçonne 1988, Döende dandyn, Den 1989, Les Nuits révolutionnaires 1989, Mon dernier rêve sera pour vous 1989, L'Affaire Dreyfus 1995, L'"Allée du roi 1996, Un pique-nique chez Osiris 2001. *Publications:* L'Eternel éphémère 1991, Le Passant composé 2004. *Address:* Agence A, Monita Derrieux, 34 rue Vivienne, 75002 Paris, France. *E-mail:* daniel.mesguich@wanadoo.fr (home).

MESHAAL, Khalid, BSc; Palestinian politician; *Head of Political Bureau, Hamas—Harakat al-Muqawama al-Islamiyya;* b. 1956, Silwad, West Bank; m.; four s. three d.; ed Kuwait Univ.; joined Muslim Brotherhood 1971; f. List of the Islamic Right (student org.), Kuwait Univ.; Physics Teacher, Kuwait 1978–84; Founding mem. Islamic Resistance Movt (Hamas—Harakat al-Muqawama al-Islamiyya) 1987, mem. Political Bureau, Chair. 1996–, Political Leader (in exile), Hamas 2004–. *Address:* Hamas Political Bureau, Damascus, Syria.

MESHKOV, Aleksey Yuryevich; Russian diplomatist and politician; *Ambassador to Italy;* b. 22 Aug. 1959, Moscow; m. Galina Ivanovna Meshkova; two s. two d.; ed Moscow State Inst. of Int. Relations; with diplomatic service 1981–; referent, attaché then Third Sec., USSR Embassy, Spain 1981–86, First Sec., Counsellor then Sr Counsellor (Russian Embassy) 1992–97; Third, Second, First Sec. then Head of Div., Dept of Co-operation in Science and Tech., Ministry of Foreign Affairs 1986–92, Deputy Head, Dept of European Co-operation 1997–98, Head, Dept of Foreign Policy Planning 1999–2001, mem. Collegiate Ministry of Foreign Affairs 2000–, Deputy Minister of Foreign Affairs 2001–04; Amb. to Italy 2004–; Order of Friendship. *Address:* Embassy of the Russian Federation, Via Gaeta 5, 00144 Rome, Italy (office). *Telephone:* (06) 4941680 (office). *Fax:* (06) 491031 (office). *E-mail:* ambrus@ambrussia.it (office). *Website:* www.ambrussia.it (office).

MESIĆ, Stjepan (Stipe); Croatian lawyer and head of state; *President;* b. 24 Dec. 1934, Orahovica; m. Milka Mesić (née Dudunić); two d.; ed gymnasium in Požega and Univ. of Zagreb; active in student politics; lawyer in Orahovica and Našice; compulsory mil. service; became a municipal judge after passing judicial exams; ind. cand. in municipal council elections 1966; Mayor of Orahovica 1967; mem. Parl. of Socialist Repub. of Croatia 1967; indicted for 'acts of enemy propaganda', served one-year prison sentence in Stara Gradiška prison for participation in Croatian Spring Movt 1975; Sec. Croatian Democratic Union (Hrvatska demokratska zajednica—HDZ), later Chair. Exec. Council; Prime Minister first govt of Repub. of Croatia 1990; mem. Presidency of Socialist Fed. Repub. of Yugoslavia, subsequently Pres. until resgnd 1991; Speaker Croatian Parl. 1992–94; left HDZ and f. Croatian Ind. Democrats (Hrvatski Nezavisni Demokrati—HND) 1994, merged with Croatian People's Party (Hrvatska narodna stranka—HNS) 1997, later Exec. Vice-Pres.; Pres. Repub. of Croatia 2000– (re-elected 2005); Hon. mem. Int. Foundation of Raoul Wallenberg 2002; Hon. Citizen of Podgorica, Montenegro 2007; State Order of the Star of Romania 2000, Grand Star of the Decoration of Honour for Merit (Austria) 2001, Golden Order Gjergj Kastrioti Skënderbeu (Albania) 2001, Grand Cross of the Order of Saviour (Greece) 2001, Order of St Michael and St George (UK), Kt of the Grand Cross with Grand Sash (Italy) 2001, Grand Order of the Crown of Malaysia 2002, Order of the Grand Cross with Chain (Hungary) 2002, DOSTYK Medal of the First Degree (Kazakhstan) 2002, Medal for Merit (Chile) 2004, Grand Order of King

Tomislav with Sash and Grand Star (Croatia) 2005; Charles Univ. Medal (Czech Repub.) 2001, Crans Montana Forum Award 2002, ABA Award 2002, Gold Medal of the Presidency of the Italian Repub. 2004, Raoul Wallenberg Award 2006, Int. League of Humanists Award 2007. *Publications:* The Break-up of Yugoslavia: Political Memoirs 1992, 1994. *Leisure interests:* nanbudo (martial art), swimming, golf. *Address:* Office of the President, 10000 Zagreb, Pantovčak 241, Croatia (office). *Telephone:* (1) 4565191 (office). *Fax:* (1) 4565299 (office). *E-mail:* office@president.hr (office). *Website:* www .predsjednik.hr (office).

MESKÓ, Attila, MA, PhD, DSc; Hungarian geophysicist and academic; *Secretary-General, Hungarian Academy of Sciences;* b. 23 April 1940, Budapest; s. of Illés Meskó and Ida Tóth; m. Andrea Bodoky; two d.; ed Lóránd Eötvös Univ.; asst and research worker, Lóránd Eötvös Geophysical Inst., Hungarian Acad. of Sciences, Seismological Observatory and Dept of Sciences, Observatory and Dept of Geophysics 1958–59, 1964–73; consultant with seismic prospecting co. 1966–83; Assoc. Prof. in Geophysics 1973–80; Head of Research Group for Environmental Physics and Geophysics 1985–93; Deputy Sec.-Gen. Hungarian Acad. of Sciences 1999–2005, Sec.-Gen. 2005–; Pres. Geophysical Cttee Hungarian Acad. of Sciences 1979–92, Earth Sciences Dept, Lóránd Eötvös Univ. 1994–, Asscn of Hungarian Geophysicists 1998–; Corresp. mem. Hungarian Acad. of Sciences 1990, Full mem. 1995; State Prize 1978, Publication Award, Academic Publishers 1986, Eötvös Memorial Medal 1993, OTKA Arnold Ipolyi Award 2000. *Publications:* numerous books, including Digital Filtering, Applications in Geophysical Exploration for Oil 1984, Gravity and Magnetics in Oil Prospecting, Seismic Safety of the Paks Nuclear Power Plant 1997; numerous papers in scientific journals. *Leisure interest:* music. *Address:* Hungarian Academy of Sciences, Roosevelt tér 9., 1051 Budapest, Hungary (office). *Telephone:* (1) 269-0114 (office); (1) 311-9812 (office); (1) 355-9546 (home). *Fax:* (1) 312-9812 (office); (1) 355-9546 (home). *Website:* www.mta.hu/?id=852 (office).

MESSAGER, Annette; French artist; b. 30 Nov. 1943, Berck-sur-Mer; d. of André Messager and Marie L. Messager (née Chalessin); ed Ecole Nationale Supérieure des Arts Décoratifs; Chevalier, Ordre des Arts et des Lettres, Chevalier de la legion d'honneur 2004, Officier, Ordre National du Mérite 2008; Prix National de Sculpture 1996, Lion d'Or de la Biennale de Venice 2005. *Address:* c/o Marian Goodman, 79 rue du Temple, 75003 Paris (office); 146 boulevard Camelinat, 92240 Malakoff, France. *Telephone:* 1-42-53-45-77.

MESSAS, David, LPh; rabbi; b. 15 July 1934, Meknès, Morocco; s. of Shalom Messas; Dir Edmond-Fleg Univ. Centre, Ecole Maimonde de Boulogne-Billancourt 1968, Tout Familial (student's forum) 1973; Rabbi for Algerons community, Synagogue du Brith Shalom 1984; Chief Rabbi of Geneva 1989–94, of Paris 1995; Chevalier Légion d'honneur, Chevalier Ordre des Palmes Académiques, Prix de Jérusalem. *Address:* c/o Consistoire Israélite de Paris, 17 rue Saint Georges, 75009 Paris, France.

MESSER, Thomas Maria, BA, MA; American museum director; *Director Emeritus, Solomon R. Guggenheim Museum;* b. 9 Feb. 1920, Bratislava, Czechoslovakia; s. of Richard Messer and Agatha (Albrecht) Messer; m. Remedios García Villa 1948 (died 2002); ed Thiel Coll., Greenville, Pa, Boston and Harvard Univs, Univ. of the Sorbonne, Paris; Dir Roswell Museum, New Mexico 1949–52; Dir American Fed. of Arts, New York 1952–56, Trustee and First Vice-Pres. 1972–75; Dir Inst. of Contemporary Art, Boston 1956–61; Dir Solomon R. Guggenheim Museum, New York 1961–88, Dir Emer. 1988–; Pres. Asscn of Art Museum Dirs 1974–75 (Hon. mem. 1988–); Chair. Int. Cttee for Museums and Collections of Modern Art, Int. Council of Museums 1974–77, Hon. Chair. 1977–; Chair. Int. Exhbns Cttee 1976–78, US/ICOM (Nat. Cttee of Int. Council of Museums) 1979–81; Adjunct Prof. of Art History, Harvard Univ. 1960; Barnard Coll. 1965, 1971; Sr Fellow, Center for Advanced Studies, Wesleyan Univ. 1966; Trustee Center for Inter-American Relations (now Americas Soc.) 1974–, Exec. Council Int. Council of Museums 1983–85; Vice-Chair. US Int. Council of Museums Cttee of American Asscn of Museums, Washington, DC 1979–81; Pres. MacDowell Colony Inc. 1977–80; Dir Solomon R. Guggenheim Foundation 1980–90, Trustee 1985–90, Dir Emer. 1988–; mem. Advisory Bd, Palazzo Grassi Venice 1986–97; Trustee Fontana Foundation, Milan 1988–; Chair. Arts Int., Inst. of Int. Educ. 1988–90; Trustee, Inst. of Int. Educ. 1991–99, Hon. Trustee 1999–, Fontana Foundation 1996–; Curatorships Schirn Kunsthalle, Frankfurt 1988–99, Sr Adviser La Caixa Foundation, Barcelona 1990–94; Visiting Prof. Frankfurt Goethe Univ. 1991–; fmr mem. Museum Advisory Panel of Nat. Endowment for the Arts, Art Advisory Panel to Commr of Internal Revenue Service 1974–77; mem. Council Nat. Gallery of the Czech Repub. 1994–99; Trustee Isamo Noguchi Foundation, New York and Tokyo 1998–; Hon. mem. Inst. of Int. Educ. 1999–; Kt, Royal Order of St Olav (Norway), Cross of Merit (FRG) 1975, Officer, Order of Leopold II (Belgium) 1978, Austrian Cross of Merit 1980, Royal Danish Kt Order 1983, Orden de Isabel la Católica 1984, Great Cross of Merit (FRG) 1986, Officier, Légion d'honneur 1989; Hon. DFA (Univ. of Massachusetts); Goethe Medal 1990. *Major retrospective exhibitions at the Guggenheim Museum include:* Edvard Munch, Vasily Kandinsky, Egon Schiele, Paul Klee and Alberto Giacometti. *Publications:* The Emergent Decade: Latin American Painters and Paintings in the 1960s 1966, Edvard Munch 1973, Vasily Kandinsky 1997; museum catalogues on Vasily Kandinsky, Paul Klee, Edvard Munch, Egon Schiele, etc.; articles and contribs to numerous art journals. *Leisure interests:* music and literature, cultural pursuits. *Address:* 303 E 57th Street, New York, NY 10022 (office); 35 Sutton Place, New York, NY 10022, USA (home). *Telephone:* (212) 486-1393 (office); (212) 355-8611 (home). *E-mail:* tmmesser@aol.com (office).

MESSIER, Jean-Marie Raymond Pierre; French business executive; b. 13 Dec. 1956, Grenoble; s. of Pierre Messier and Janine Delapierre; m. Antoinette Fleisch 1983; three s. two d.; ed Lycée Champollion, Grenoble, Ecole polytechnique, Ecole Nat. d'Admin.; Inspecteur des Finances 1982; Dir Office of Minister in charge of privatization at Ministry of Econ., Finance and Privatization, then Tech. Adviser to Minister 1986–88; Man. Pnr, Lazard Frères et Cie 1989–94; Chair. Fonds Partenaires 1989–94; Dir, Gen. Man. and Chair. Exec. Comité Général des Eaux group (now Vivendi) 1994, Chair. and Man. Dir 1996–2002; Chair. and Man. Dir Cégétel 1996–2000, Cie Immobi-lière Phénix 1994–95, Cie Générale d'Immobilier et de Services (CGIS) 1995–96, SGE 1996–97; Dir Canal Plus 1995 (merged with Universal and Vivendi 2000 to form Vivendi Universal), Chair. and CEO 2000–02; fmr Dir LVMH, Strafor-Facom, Saint-Gobain, UGC, Daimler-Benz, New York Stock Exchange 2001–02; Founder and CEO Messier Pnrs LLC, NY 2003–; mem. Bd of Dirs Rentabiliweb 2007–. *Publication:* j6m.com: faut-il avoir peur de la nouvelle économie? 2000, My True Diary 2002. *Leisure interests:* flying, skiing, tennis. *Address:* Messier Partners LLC, One Rockerfeller Plaza, 15th Floor, New York, NY 10001, USA (office).

MESSNER, Hon. Anthony, AM, FCA; Australian government official and chartered accountant; b. 24 Sept. 1939, East Melbourne, Vic.; s. of Colin Thomas Messner and Thelma Luxford Messner; ed South Australia Inst. of Tech., Adelaide; practised as chartered accountant 1965–75, 1990–97; mem. Fed. Senate for S Australia 1975–90; Minister for Veterans' Affairs, Asst Treas. 1980–83; Shadow Minister for Social Security 1983–85, for Finance and Taxation 1985–87, for Communications 1987–88, for Public Admin 1988–89; Admin. Norfolk Island 1997–2003; consultant 2003–; Centennial Medal 2001. *Leisure interests:* rugby, reading biographies and history, music, cricket. *Address:* 59 Bride Road, Nowra, NSW 2541 (office); 100 Kanearoo Road, Berry, NSW 2535, Australia (home). *Telephone:* (2) 4422-1611 (office); (2) 4464-2768 (home). *Fax:* (2) 4464-2768 (home). *E-mail:* messnert@optusnet.com.au (office).

MESSNER, Reinhold; Italian mountaineer, lecturer and author; b. 17 Sept. 1944, Brixen; one s. three d.; ed Univ. of Padua; began climbing aged four with his father; joined expedition to Nanga Parbat (8,000m), N Pakistan 1970; with pnr Peter Habeler became first person to climb Mount Everest without supplementary oxygen; later climbed Everest alone by North Col route without oxygen; the first person to climb all the world's 8,000m peaks in Himalayas and adjoining ranges; made first crossing of Antarctica on foot (2,800 km) since Shackleton 1989–90; collaborated with Dir Werner Herzog in filming his story Schrei aus Stein 1991; f. int. org. Mountain Wilderness; f. Ortles Museum, Sulden and Juval Museum (collections of Asiatica), 'Dolo-mites'/Monte Rite Museum 2002, Firmian Museum, Bozen 2006; mem. European Parl. (for the Green Party) 1999–2004; ITAS 1975, Primi Monti 1968, DAV 1976, 1979, Sachbuchpreis for Donauland 1995, Coni 1998, Bambi Lifetime Award 2000, Royal Geographical Soc.'s Gold Medal 2001. *Publica-tions:* Free Spirit: A Climber's Life 1991, Antarctica 1992, To the Top of the World 1999, Moving Mountains 2001, The Second Death of George Mallory 2001, The Naked Mountain 2003. *Address:* c/o MMM Firmian, Sigmundskro-nerstr. 53, 39100 Bozen (office); Castle Juval, 39020 Kastelbell, Italy (home). *Telephone:* (0471) 631265 (office). *Fax:* (0471) 633890 (office). *E-mail:* info@ reinholdmessner.it (office). *Website:* www.reinhold-messner.de (office).

MESTEL, Leon, BA, PhD, FRS; British astronomer and academic; *Professor Emeritus of Astronomy, University of Sussex;* b. 5 Aug. 1927, Melbourne, Australia; s. of Rabbi Solomon Mestel and Rachel née Brodetsky; m. Sylvia L. Cole 1951; two s. two d.; ed West Ham Secondary School, London and Trinity Coll., Cambridge; ICI Research Fellow, Univ. of Leeds, 1951–54; Common-wealth Fund Fellow, Princeton Univ. Observatory 1954–55; Univ. Asst Lecturer in Math., Cambridge 1955–58, Univ. Lecturer 1958–66; Fellow, St John's Coll., Cambridge 1957–66; Visiting mem. Inst. for Advanced Study, Princeton 1961–62; J. F. Kennedy Fellow, Weizmann Inst. for Science, Israel 1966–67; Prof. of Applied Math., Univ. of Manchester 1967–73; Prof. of Astronomy, Univ. of Sussex 1973–93, Prof. Emer. 1993–; Eddington Medal 1993, Gold Medal 2002 Royal Astronomical Soc. *Publications:* Stellar Magnetism 1999 (paperback 2003); papers, lecture notes, reviews, conf. reports on different branches of theoretical astrophysics. *Leisure interests:* reading, music. *Address:* Department of Applied Mathematics and Theoretical Physics, Centre for Mathematical Sciences, Wilberforce Road, Cambridge CB3 0WA; 1 Highsett, Hills Road, Cambridge CB2 1NX, England. *Telephone:* (1223) 337910 (office); (1223) 355233 (home). *Fax:* (1223) 765900 (office). *E-mail:* L.Mestel@damtp.cam.ac.uk (office); mestel@mestel.fsnet.co.uk (home).

MESTIRI, Mohamed Said; Tunisian professor of medicine; b. 22 June 1919, Tunis; s. of Tahar Mestiri and Khedija Kassar; m. Zohra Chenik (d. of fmr Prime Minister Mohamed Chenik) 1950; four s. one d.; ed Lycée Carnot, Tunis, Faculty of Medicine, Algiers; Intern and Resident, Algiers Hosp. and Sadiki Hosp., Tunis 1947–51; Asst Surgeon, Sadiki Hosp. 1951–57; Chief Surgeon, H. Thameur Hosp. Tunis 1957–64; Chief, Dept of Gen. Surgery, La Rabta Hosp. 1965–85; Prof. of Surgery, Faculty of Medicine, Tunis 1970–85, Hon. Prof. 1985–; Founder and Pres. Tunisian Soc. of Surgery 1973–85; Foreign mem. French Acad. of Surgery; Foreign Corresp. mem. Nat. Acad. of Medicine (France), Royal Belgian Acad. of Medicine; mem. Int. Soc. of Surgery; Hon. mem. Soc. Belge de Chirurgie; Commdr of Beylical Order Nichan Iftikhar 1957, Medal of Bizerta 1962, Chevalier of Tunisian Ind., Commdr Order of Tunisian Repub. *Publications include:* Moncef Bey: Le Règne 1988, Moncef Bey: L'Exil 1990, Le Ministère Chenik 1991, Le Métier et la Passion (memoirs) 1995, Abulcasis, grand Maître de la Chirurgie arabe 1997, La Chirurgie arabe ancienne et son Impact en occident 1998. *Leisure interests:* swimming, bridge. *Address:* 5 avenue Ferhat Hached-Gammarth, 2070 La Marsa, Tunisia. *Telephone:* (1) 746-965. *Fax:* (1) 775-663 (office); (1) 746-905 (home). *E-mail:* said.mestiri@med.mail.com (home).

MESTRALLET, Gérard; French business executive; *Chairman and CEO, Suez SA;* b. 1 April 1949, Paris; ed Ecole Polytechnique, Ecole nationale d'Admin; joined Cie de Suez (provider of electricity, natural gas, water and waste man. services) 1984, Special Asst 1984–86, Deputy Chief Exec. for Industrial Affairs 1986–91, Chair. and CEO Suez 1995–97, Chair. Exec. Bd Suez Lyonnaise des Eaux (water treatment subsidiary co.) 1997–2001, Chair. and CEO Cie de Suez 2001–, Chair. Suez Énergie Services, Suez Environment, Electrabel, Houlival, Suez-Tractebel (Belgium); Exec. Dir and Chair. Man. Cttee Société Générale de Belgique 1991–95; Chair. Hisusa (Spain); Vice-Chair. Aguas de Barcelona (Spain); mem. Bd Dirs Saint-Gobain (France), Pargesa Holding SA (Switzerland); mem. Bd Trustees AXA; Chair. Paris EUROPLACE Asscn; mem. Council of French Inst. of Dirs; Rep. of Govt of France in negotiations with Walt Disney Co. to est. Euro Disney Theme Park 1995; mem. Advisory Bd CECIA (Council of Int. Advisers) 2000–08; Person of the Year Award, French-American Chamber of Commerce, NY Chapter 2001. *Leisure interest:* cycling. *Address:* Suez SA, 16 rue de la Ville l'Evêque, 75008 Paris, France (office). *Telephone:* 1-40-06-46-00 (office). *Fax:* 1-40-06-66-10 (office). *E-mail:* info@suez.com (office). *Website:* www.suez.com (office).

MESTRE, Philippe, LLB; French politician and civil servant; b. 23 Aug. 1927, Talmont, Vendee; s. of Raoul Mestre and Anne Lapie; m. Janine Joseph 1951; one s. two d.; ed Paris Univ.; Admin. Overseas France 1951; Pvt. Sec. to High Commr, Congo 1957–60, to Indre-et-Loir Prefect 1967, to Prime Minister Raymond Barre 1978–81; Tech. Adviser to Pierre Messmer (Minister of Defence) 1964–69, to Prime Minister Jacques Chaban-Delmas 1969–70, 1971–72; Pres. Inter-ministerial Mission of Repatriation from Overseas Territories 1969–70; Prefect of Gers 1970–71, of Calvados 1973–76, of Loire-Atlantique 1976–78, of Mayotte 2001–02; Pres. Serpo 1981–93; Deputy of Vendée 1981–86, 1986–93; Vice-Pres. Nat. Ass. 1986–88; Minister of War Veterans 1993–95; fmr Vice-Pres. Union pour la Démocratie Française (UDF); Commdr Légion d'honneur, Officier Ordre nat. du Mérite, du Mérite agricole, Croix de la Valeur militaire. *Publications:* Quand flambait le bocage 1969, Demain, rue Saint-Nicaise 1990 (Prix Claude Farrère), Devant douze fusils 2000 (Prix des Ecrivains de Vendée). *Address:* c/o Union pour la démocratie française, 133 bis, rue de l'Université, 75007 Paris (office); 95 rue de Rennes, 75006 Paris, France (home). *Telephone:* 1-53-59-20-00 (office). *Fax:* 1-53-59-20-59 (office). *Website:* www.udf.org (office).

MESYATS, Gennady Andreyevich, DSc; Russian physicist and academic; *Vice-President, Russian Academy of Sciences;* b. 28 Feb. 1936, Kemerovo; s. of Andrei Mesyats and Anna Mesyats; m. Nina Alexandrovna (née Mashukova) Mesyats 1959; one s.; ed Tomsk Polytechnical Inst.; Sr Research Physicist, Research Inst. for Nuclear Physics, Tomsk Polytechnical Inst. 1961–64, Head of Lab. 1966–71; Deputy Dir Inst. of Atmospheric Optics, Tomsk 1971–76; Dir and Prof., Inst. of High Current Electronics, Tomsk 1976–86; Dir and Prof., Inst. of Electrophysics 1987–; Corresp. mem. USSR (now Russian) Acad. of Sciences 1979, mem. 1984–, Pres. Ural Div. 1986–99, Vice-Pres. of Acad. 1987–; Int. Chair. Supreme Attestation Comm. 1999–; Pres. Demidov Foundation; Vice-Pres. Int. Unit of Science and Eng Fellowships; mem. Russian Electrical Eng Acad.; Hon. Prof. Tomsk Polytechnic Univ. 1996, Russian Technological Univ. 2000; Dr hc (Urals State Technical Univ.) 1996; Order of Red Banner of Labour 1971, Badge of Honour 1981, Order of Lenin 1986, Order for Services to the Motherland 1996, 1999; Walter Dine Int. Prize 1990, Ervin Marx Award in Pulsed Power 1991, State Prize of USSR 1978, USSR Council of Ministers Prize 1990, A. G. Stoletov Prize 1996, State Prize of Russia 1999, Global Energy Prize 2003. *Publications:* Techniques for the Production of High-Voltage Nanosecond Pulses 1963, Generation of High-Power Nanosecond Pulses 1974, Field Emission and Explosive Processes in Gas Discharges 1982, High-Power Nanosecond X-Ray Pulses 1983, Pulsed Electrical Discharge in Vacuum 1989, Ectons 1994, About Our Science 1995, Pulsed Gas Lasers 1995, Explosive Electron Emission 1998, Physics of Pulsed Breakdown in Gases 1998, Ectons in a Vacuum Discharge: Breakdown, the Spark and the Arc 2000. *Leisure interests:* reading fiction, studying Russian history, writing articles. *Address:* Russian Academy of Sciences, 14 Leninsky Prospekt, Moscow GSP-1 117901 (office); Apt 29, 3 Akademika Petrovskogo, Moscow 117900, Russia (home). *Telephone:* (495) 237-53-12 (office); (495) 952-50-81. *E-mail:* mesyats@pran.ru (office).

MÉSZÁROS, Márta; Hungarian film director and screenwriter; b. 19 Sept. 1931, Budapest; d. of László Mészáros; m. 2nd Jan Nowicki; ed Moscow Film School; emigrated with family to USSR 1936; now lives in Hungary; Golden Bear Award OCIC 1975, Béla Balázs Prize 1977, Artist of Merit 1989. *Films include:* End of September 1973, Free Breath 1973, Adopted Child 1975, Nine Months 1976, The Two of Them 1977, En Route 1979, Heritage 1980, Diary for my Children 1982, Fata Morgana Land 1983, Diary for my Loves 1986, Diary III 1989, Bye bye chaperon rouge 1989, Napló apámnak, anyámnak (Diary for My Father and Mother) 1990, A Magzat 1993, Siódmy pokój 1995, A Szerencse lányai 1999, Kisvilma - Az utolsó napló (Little Vilna: The Last Diary) 2000, Csodálatos mandarin (The Miraculous Mandarin) 2001, A Temetetlen halott 2004. *Address:* c/o MAFILM Studio, Lumumba utca 174, 1149 Budapest, Hungary. *Telephone:* (1) 183-1750.

META, Ilir; Albanian politician and economist; *Chairman, Socialist Movement for Integration;* b. 24 March 1969, Skrapar; m. Monika Kryemadhi; one s. two d.; ed Tirana Univ.; elected Deputy 1992–; Co-founder Euro-Socialist Youth Forum of Albania (FRESSH) (Deputy Chair. 1992–95, Chair. 1995–2001); Deputy Chair. Parl. Comm. for Foreign Relations 1996–97; fmr Deputy Prime Minister 1998–99, Sec. of State for European Integration (Ministry of Foreign Affairs) and Minister of Government Co-ordination March–Oct. 1998; Prime Minister of Albania 1999–2002; Deputy Prime Minister and Minister of Foreign Affairs 2002–03; presidential cand. 2003; mem. Socialist Party of Albania (Steering Council 1992–2004, Deputy Chair. and Int. Sec. 1993–96), left party 2004; Co-founder and Chair. Socialist Movt for Integration (Lëvizja Socialiste për Integrim—LSI) 2004–; mem. Socialist Youth Int. (Vice-Chair. 1993–96), Int. Comm. on the Balkans; Visiting Lecturer, Faculty of Econs, Tirana Univ. *Leisure interest:* sports. *Address:* Socialist Movement for Integration (Lëvizja Socialiste për Integrim), Rruga Smai Frasheri 20/10, Tirana, Albania (office). *Telephone:* (4) 270412 (office). *Fax:* (4) 270413 (office). *E-mail:* imeta@ilirmeta.com; secretariat@lsi.al (office). *Website:* www.lsi.al (office); www.ilirmeta.com.

METCALF, Donald, AC, BSc (Med), MD, FRCPA, FRACP, FAA, FRS; Australian immunologist, hematologist and academic; *Professor Emeritus, University of Melbourne;* b. 26 Feb. 1929, Mittagong, NSW; m. Josephine Metcalf; four d.; ed Sydney Univ.; Demonstrator of Bacteriology, Univ. of Sydney 1950–51, Resident Medical Officer, Royal Prince Alfred Hosp., Sydney 1953–54; Carden Fellow in Cancer Research, The Walter and Eliza Hall Inst. of Medical Research, Melbourne 1954–56, Head, Cancer Research Lab., 1958–64, Head, Cancer Research Unit and Asst Dir 1965–96, Research Prof. of Cancer Biology, Univ. of Melbourne 1986–96, Prof. Emer. 1996–; Visiting Scientist, Harvard Medical School, Boston, USA, Roswell Park Memorial Inst., Buffalo, NY, USA, Swiss Inst. for Experimental Cancer Research, Lausanne, Radiobiological Inst., Rijswijk, Netherlands, Univ. of Cambridge, UK; Foreign Assoc. NAS; Hon. mem. Alpha Omega Alpha Medical Society (USA) 1998; Hon. DSc (Sydney); Hon. MD (Oslo); Syme Prize for Research, Univ. of Melbourne 1964, Britannica Australia Award for Medicine 1966, AMA-BMA Prize for Medical Research 1968, Mollison Prize for Research on Pathology, AMA 1968, Royal Soc. of Victoria Research Medal 1974, Gold Medal, Australian Cancer Soc. 1980, Wellcome Prize, Royal Soc. (shared) 1986, Bristol-Myers Award for Distinguished Achievement in Cancer Research, Hammer Prize for Cancer, Koch Prize (FRG), Gairdner Foundation Int. Award (Canada), Alfred P. Sloan Prize, General Motors Cancer Research Foundation (shared), Bertner Foundation Award, M. D. Anderson Cancer Center, Rabbi Shai Shacknai Prize, Hadassah Univ., Jerusalem, Albert Lasker Clinical Medical Research Award 1993, Louisa Gross Horwitz Prize, Columbia Univ., Jessie Stevenson Kovalenko Medal, NAS, Kantor Family Prize for Cancer Research Excellence, Hipple Cancer Research Center (inaugural recipient), Ernst Neumann Award, Int. Soc. for Experimental Hematology 1995, Royal Medal, Royal Soc., London 1995, Amgen Australia Prize (shared) 1996, The Warren Alpert Foundation Prize, Harvard Medical School 1996, Chiron Int. Award, Nat. Acad. of Medicine, Italy 2000, Prime Minister's Prize for Science 2001, honoured by Australia Post with issue of commemorative stamp 2002. *Publications:* Haemopoietic Cells 1971, Hemopoietic colonies: In Vitro Cloning of Normal and Leukemic Cells 1977, Clonal Culture of Hemopoietic Cells: Techniques and Applications 1984, The Hemopoietic Colony Stimulating Factors 1984, Molecular Control of Blood Cells 1988, Normal and Malignant Hematopoiesis: New Advances (Pezcoller Foundation Symposia, Vol. 6) 1995, Hemopoietic Colony-Stimulating Factors: From Biology to Clinical Applications (co-author) 1995, Summon up the Blood: In Dogged Pursuit of the Blood Cell Regulators 2000; more than 400 peer-reviewed scientific papers and 200 other scientific papers. *Address:* The Walter and Eliza Hall Institute of Medical Research, 1G Royal Parade, Parkville, Vic. 3050, Australia (office). *Telephone:* (3) 9345-2555 (office). *Website:* www.wehi.edu.au (office).

METCALF, John Wesley, BA, CM; Canadian author and editor; *Editor, Canadian Notes and Queries;* b. 12 Nov. 1938, Carlisle, UK; s. of Thomas Metcalf and Gladys Moore; m. Myrna Teitelbaum 1975; three s. three d.; ed Beckenham and Penge Grammar School and Univ. of Bristol; emigrated to Canada 1962; Writer-in-Residence, Univs of NB 1972–73, Loyola of Montreal 1976, Ottawa 1977, Concordia Univ. Montreal 1980–81, Univ. of Bologna 1985; Sr Ed. Porcupine's Quill Press 1989–, Ed. Canadian Notes and Queries (literary magazine) 1997–; Sr Ed. Biblioasis Press 2005–. *Publications:* The Lady Who Sold Furniture 1970, The Teeth of My Father 1975, Girl in Gingham 1978, Selected Stories 1982, Kicking Against the Pricks 1982, Adult Entertainment 1986, What is a Canadian Literature? 1988, Volleys 1990, How Stories Mean 1992, Shooting the Stars 1992, Freedom from Culture: Selected Essays 1982–1992 1994, Acts of Kindness and of Love (jtly) 1995, Forde Abroad 2003, An Aesthetic Underground 2003, Standing Stones: The Best Stories of John Metcalf 2004, Shut Up He Explained 2007. *Leisure interest:* collecting modern first editions. *Address:* 128 Lewis Street, Ottawa, ON K2P 0S7, Canada. *Telephone:* (613) 233-3200. *Website:* www.biblioasis.com.

METHENY, Patrick (Pat) Bruce; American jazz musician (guitar); b. 12 Aug. 1954, Lee's Summit, MO; ed Univ. of Miami; taught guitar at Univ. of Miami and Berklee Coll. of Music; fmrly guitarist with Gary Burton Quintet; has performed and recorded with musicians and composers, including Ornette Coleman, Herbie Hancock and Steve Reich; formed Pat Metheny Group 1978–; Boston Music Awards for Outstanding Jazz Album, Outstanding Guitarist, Outstanding Jazz Fusion Group 1986, Grammy Award for Best Instrumental Composition 1990, 1993, Best Contemporary Jazz Performance 1995, Best Rock Instrumental Performance 1996, Orville H. Gibson Award for Best Jazz Guitarist 1996, Best Guitarist (Jazz Times Magazine) 2000. *Recordings include:* albums: Bright Size Life 1976, Watercolours 1977, Pat Metheny Group 1978, New Chautauqua 1979, An Hour With Pat Metheny 1979, American Garage 1980, As Falls Wichita, So Falls Wichita Falls 1981, Offramp 1981, 80/81 1981, Travels 1983, Rejoicing 1983, Works 1984, First Circle 1984, Song X (with Ornette Coleman) 1985, Still Life (Talking) 1987, Works II 1988, Letter From Home 1989, Question And Answer (with Roy Haynes and Dave Holland) 1990, Secret Story 1992, Under Fire (film-score) 1992, Zero Tolerance For Silence 1992, I Can See Your House From Here 1993, The Road To You: Recorded Live In Europe 1993, Dream Teams 1994, Zero Tolerance for Silence 1994, We Live Here 1995, This World 1996, Quartet 1996, The Sign Of Four 1996, Imaginary Day 1997, Beyond the Missouri Sky

1997, Passaggio Per Il Paradiso (film-score) 1998, Like Minds 1998, All The Things You Are 1999, A Map Of The World (film-score) 1999, Last Train Home 1999, Jim Hall and Pat Metheny 1999, Trio 99>00 2000, Trio Live 2000, Move To The Groove 2001, Parallel Universe 2001, Sassy Samba 2001, Speaking Of Now 2002, One Quiet Night 2003, The Way Up (Grammy Award for Best Contemporary Jazz Album 2006) 2005, Metheny Mehldau 2006, Day Trip 2008. *Address:* Ted Kurland Associates, 173 Brighton Avenue, Boston, MA 02134-2003, USA (office). *Telephone:* (617) 254-0007 (office). *Fax:* (617) 782-3524 (office). *E-mail:* agents@tedkurland.com (office). *Website:* www.tedkurland.com (office); www.patmetheny.com.

METIA, Lotoala; Tuvaluan politician; *Minister of Finance, Economic Planning and Industries;* Auditor Gen. 1990–97, 2002; fmr Sec. for Commerce, Tourism and Trade; mem. Parl. 2006–, Minister of Finance, Econ. Planning and Industries 2006–; fmr Chair. Tuvalu Telecommunications Corpn. *Address:* Ministry of Finance, Economic Planning and Industries, PMB, Vaiaku, Funafuti, Tuvalu (office). *Telephone:* 20408 (office). *Fax:* 20210 (office).

METZ, Johann Baptist, DPhil, DTheol; German professor of theology; b. 5 Aug. 1928, Auerbach; s. of Karl M. Metz and Sibylle Müller; ed Univs of Bamberg, Innsbrück and Munich; Prof. of Fundamental Theology, Univ. of Münster 1963–; Prof. of Philosophy of Religion, Univ. of Vienna, Austria 1993–; mem. Founding Comm. of Univ. of Bielefeld 1966; consultant to Papal Secr. Pro Non Credendibus 1968–73; Adviser to German Diocesan Synod 1971–75; mem. Advisory Council, Inst. für die Wissenschaften vom Menschen (Vienna) 1982–; mem. Advisory Council Wissenschaftszentrum Nordrhein-Westfalen/Kulturwissenschaftliches Inst. 1989–2000; numerous guest professorships; Dr hc (Univ. of Vienna); awards from Univ. of Innsbrück and Boston Coll., Mass. *Publications:* books on theological and political themes in several languages. *Address:* Katholisch-Theologische Fakultät, Seminar für Fundamentaltheologie, Johannisstrasse 8–10, 4400 Münster (office); Kapitelstrasse 14, 48145 Münster, Germany. *Telephone:* (251) 83-2631 (office); (251) 36662 (home). *Fax:* (251) 36662 (home). *E-mail:* j.metz@uni-muenster.de.

METZGER, Henry, AB, MD, FAAS; American (b. German) scientific researcher; b. 23 March 1932, Mainz, Germany; s. of Paul Alfred Metzger and Anne (Daniel) Metzger; m. Deborah Stashower 1957; two s. one d.; ed Univ. of Rochester, Columbia Univ.; emigrated to USA 1938; Intern, then Asst Resident, Col-Presbyterian Medical Center 1957–59; Research Assoc., NIAMD, NIH 1959–61, Medical Officer, Arthritis and Rheumatism Branch, Bethesda, MD 1963–73, Chief, Section on Chemical Immunology 1973–, Chief, Arthritis and Rheumatism Branch, Nat. Inst. of Arthritis and Musculoskeletal and Skin Diseases 1983–94, Dir Intramural Research Program 1987–98; Fellow Helen Hay Whitney Foundation, Dept of Biology, Univ. of Calif., San Diego 1961–63; Pres. American Asscn of Immunologists 1991–92; Pres. Int. Union of Immunological Socs 1992–95; mem. Health Research Council BMFT, German Govt 1994–97; mem. NAS; Hon. mem. Chilean and French Socs of Immunology; several awards. *Publications:* over 200 scientific papers and contribs to scientific journals. *Address:* 3410 Taylor Street, Chevy Chase, MD 20815, USA (home).

METZLER-ARNOLD, Ruth; Swiss accountant and politician; *Global Head of Investor Relations, Novartis Pharmaceuticals Corporation;* b. 23 May 1964; m.; ed Univ. of Freiburg; chartered accountant, UBS Berne 1989–90, PricewaterhouseCoopers AG, St Gallen 1990–99; Dist Judge, Appenzell 1992–95; Canton Judge, Appenzell Inner Rhodes 1995–96; Minister of Finance, Govt of Appenzell Inner Rhodes 1996–99; mem. Swiss Fed. Council, Head of Fed. Dept of Justice and Police 1999–2003; Vice-Pres. of Switzerland 2003; currently Global Head of Investor Relations, Norvartis Pharmeuticals Corpn; Pres. Schweizer Sporthilfe (Swiss Sport Aid Foundation); mem. Christian Democratic People's Party. *Publication:* Grissini & Alpenbitter 2004. *Address:* Novartis Pharma S.A.S., 2/4, rue Lionel Terray, 92500 Rueil-Malmaison, France (office); Brenden, 9050 Appenzell, Switzerland (home). *Telephone:* 1-55-47-60-00 (office). *Fax:* 1-55-47-60-50 (office). *Website:* www.novartis.fr (office).

MEYER, Sir Christopher John Rome, Kt, KCMG, MA; British diplomatist; b. 22 Feb. 1944, Beaconsfield; s. of the late Flight Lt R. H. R. Meyer and Mrs E. P. L. Landells; m. 1st Françoise Hedges 1976; two s. one step-s.; m. 2nd Catherine Laylle 1997; two step-s.; ed Lancing Coll., Lycée Henri IV, Paris, Peterhouse Coll., Cambridge and Johns Hopkins School of Advanced Int. Studies, Bologna, Italy; Foreign Office 1966–67; Army School of Educ. 1967–68; Third Sec., later Second Sec. Moscow 1968–70; Second Sec. Madrid 1970–73; FCO 1973–78; First Sec. Perm. Representation of UK at EC 1978–82; Counsellor and Head of Chancery, Moscow 1982–84; Head of News Dept, FCO 1984–88; Visiting Fellow, Center for Int. Affairs, Harvard 1988–89; Minister (Commercial), Washington, DC 1989–92, Minister and Deputy Head of Mission 1992–93; Press Sec. to Prime Minister 1994–96; Amb. to Germany 1997, to USA 1997–2003; Chair. Press Complaints Comm. 2003–09; Dir (non-exec.) GKN plc, Arbuthnot Banking Group; mem. Int. Advisory Bd Fleishman-Hillard; Gov. English Speaking Union; mem. Exec. Cttee Pilgrims Soc.; Hon. Fellow, Peterhouse, Cambridge 2001; mem. Worshipful Co. of Stationers and Newspaper Makers 2009; Freeman of the City of London 2009. *Radio:* BBC Radio 4: presenter and scriptwriter of How to Succeed at Summits, Corridors of Power 2006, Lying Abroad 2007. *Television:* presenter of Mortgaged to the Yanks (BBC 4) 2006. *Publication:* DC Confidential 2005. *Leisure interests:* jazz, history, football. *Address:* c/o Press Complaints Commission, Halton House, 20–23 Holborn, London, EC1N 2JD, England (office).

MEYER, (Donatus) Laurenz (Karl); German politician; b. 2 Feb. 1948, Salzkotten; m.; four d.; ed Univ. of Münster; fmr mem. staff VEW AG, Dortmund; mem. Hamm City Council 1975–95; Parl. Group Chair. Christian Democratic Union (CDU), Hamm 1989–95; mem. Land Parl. of N Rhine-Westphalia (NRW) 1990–2002, Econ. Policy Spokesman of Land Parl. of NRW 1990–99, Vice-Chair. CDU Parl. Group of Land Parl. of NRW 1997–99, Chair. 1999–2000, Vice-Pres. Land Parl. of NRW 2000, Treas. CDU of NRW 1997–2001; mem. Fed. Party Exec., Sec.-Gen. CDU Germany 2000–04, currently Chair. Economy and Tech. Group; mem. Bundestag 2002–; Order of Merit (FRG). *Leisure interests:* tennis, golf. *Address:* Christlich-Demokratische Union, Konrad-Adenauer-Haus, Klingelhöferstrasse 8, 10785 Berlin, Germany (office). *Telephone:* (30) 220700 (office). *Fax:* (30) 22070111 (office). *E-mail:* laurenz.meyer@cdu.de (office). *Website:* www.laurenz-meyer.de; www.cdu.de (office).

MEYER, Edgar, BMus; American composer and double bassist; b. 24 Nov. 1960, Tulsa, Okla; s. of Edgar A. Meyer and Anna Mary Metzel; m. Cornelia (Connie) Heard 1988; one s.; ed Georgia Inst. of Tech., Atlanta, Indiana School of Music, Bloomington; began playing bass aged five under tutelage of father; began composing pop songs and classical pieces as a child; studied with Stuart Stanley at univ.; formed 'bluegrass' band Strength in Numbers, Nashville, Tenn. 1984; signed to MCA label; regular bass player, Santa Fe Chamber Music Festival 1985–93; appeared with concert artists Emanuel Ax (piano) and Yo-yo Ma (cello); collaborated with Katty Mattea on album Where Have You Been (Grammy Award, Country Music Award, Acad. of Country Music Asscn Award) 1990; premiere of Concerto for Bass 1993; joined Chamber Music Soc., Lincoln Center, New York 1994; formed band Quintet for Bass and String Quartet, soloist debut performance 1995; premiere of Double Concerto for Bass and Cello 1995; premiere of Violin Concerto 2000; recitals with Amy Dorfman, Bela Flack and Mike Marshall; performed at Aspen, Caramoor and Marlboro Festivals; debuted with Boston Symphony Orchestra, Tanglewood, Mass 2000; Visiting Prof., RAM, London, UK; Winner, Zimmerman-Mingus Competition, Int. Soc. of Bassists 1981, Avery Fisher Prize 2000, Grammy Award for the Best Crossover Album 2001. *Music includes:* albums: Unfolding 1986, The Telluride Sessions (Strength in Numbers) 1989, Dreams of Flight 1987, Love of a Lifetime 1988, Appalachia Waltz 1996, Uncommon Ritual 1997, Short Trip Record 1999, Bach Unaccompanied Cello Suites Performed on a Double Bass 1999, Appalachian Journey (Grammy Award 2001) 2000, Perpetual Motion 2000. *Address:* c/o IMG Artists, Lovell House, 616 Chiswick High Road, London, W4 5RX, England (office). *Telephone:* (20) 7957-5800 (office). *Fax:* (20) 7957-5801 (office). *E-mail:* artistseurope@imgartists.com (office). *Website:* www.imgartists.com (office).

MEYER, Robert; Norwegian photohistorian; b. 2 Oct. 1945, Oslo; m. Ingebjørg Ydstie 1985; one s. one d.; ed Fotoskolan, Univ. of Stockholm; photographer, Norwegian State Police 1963–64; advertising photographer 1964–; freelance photographer 1964–71; debut exhbn LYS, Oslo 1970; photojournalist, Norwegian Broadcasting, Oslo 1971–77; Ed. and Publr Ikaros 1976–80; full-time photohistorian engaged in research work 1977–; Prof. Inst. of Photography (SHDK) Bergen 1990–; Munch stipend 1981; art stipend 1988–90; two book prizes. *Publications:* Norsk fotohistorisk Journal 1976–78, Jim Bengston i Photographs 1981, Slow Motion 1985, Simulo 1987, Norsk Landskapsfotografi 1988, Den glemte tradisjonen 1989, Splint 1991. *Address:* Institute of Photography Strømgt. 1, 5015 Bergen (office); Professor Hansteens gate 68, 5006 Bergen, Norway (home). *Telephone:* 55-31-22-14 (office); 55-31-07-93 (home). *Fax:* 55-32-67-56.

MEYER, Robert B., BA PhD; American physicist and academic; *Professor, Department of Physics, Brandeis University;* ed Harvard Univ.; Sloan Foundation Research Fellow 1971–75; Researcher, Dept of Physics, Harvard Univ.; fmr Visiting Prof. Chalmers Inst. of Tech., Göteborg, Sweden, Ecole Supérieure de Physique et de Chimie Industrielles de la Ville de Paris, France; joined Dept of Physics, Brandeis Univ. 1978, becoming Prof. of Physics; Fellow, American Physical Soc. 1992–; Joliot Curie Medal of City of Paris, Special Recognition Award, Soc. for Information Display, LVMH Science for Art Prize Vinci of Excellence, Benjamin Franklin Medal in Physics 2004, Oliver Buckley Prize, American Physical Soc., George Gray Medal, British Liquid Crystal Soc. *Address:* Brandeis University, Department of Physics, MS 057, PO Box 549110, Waltham, MA 02454-9110, USA (office). *Telephone:* (781) 736-2870 (office). *Fax:* (781) 736-2915 (office). *E-mail:* meyer@brandeis.edu (office). *Website:* www.physics.brandeis.edu/faculty/meye.htm (office).

MEYER, Roelof (Roelf) Petrus, BComm, LLB; South African fmr politician; b. 16 July 1947, Port Elizabeth; m. 1st Carené Lubbe 1971; two s. two d.; m. 2nd Michèle de la Rey 2002; ed Fickburg High School, Univ. of the Free State; practised as attorney, Pretoria and Johannesburg –1980; MP for Johannesburg West 1979–97; Deputy Minister of Law and Order 1986–88, of Constitutional Devt 1988–91 and of Information Services 1990–91; Minister of Defence and of Communication 1991–92, of Constitutional Devt and of Communication 1992–94, of Provincial Affairs and Constitutional Devt 1994–96; Sec.-Gen. Nat. Party 1996–97; Co-Founder United Democratic Movt 1997, Deputy Pres. 1998–2000; MP 1998–2000; Tip O'Neill Chair. in Peace Studies, Univ. of Ulster 2000–01; Chair. Civil Soc. Initiative 2000–; Chief Govt Negotiator at Multi-Party Negotiating Forum for new SA Constitution; Nat. Party, fmr Chair. Standing Cttee on Nat. Educ., fmr Chair. Standing Cttee on Constitutional Devt, fmr Parl. Whip. *Leisure interests:* reading, outdoor life, jogging. *Address:* PO Box 2271, Brooklyn Square, Pretoria 0075 (office); 732 Skukuza Street, Faerie Glen, 0043 Pretoria, South Africa (home). *Telephone:* (12) 3341826 (office); (82) 9900004. *Fax:* (12) 3341867 (office). *E-mail:* roelf.meyer@tilca.com (office); rmeyer@lantic.net (home). *Website:* www.tilca.com (office).

MEYER, Ron; American business executive; *President and Chief Operating Officer, Universal Studios;* b. 1944; m. Kelly Chapman; one s. three d.; served in US Marine Corps; with Paul Kohner Agency 1965–70; agent William Morris Agency 1970–75; co-founder and Pres. Creative Artists Agency 1975–95;

Pres., COO, Universal Studios 1995–. *Address:* Universal Studios Inc., 100 Universal City Plaza, Universal City, CA 91608, USA (office). *E-mail:* cindy.gardner@nbcuni.com (office). *Website:* www.nbcuni.com (office).

MEYER, Thomas J, BS, PhD; American chemist and academic; *Kenan Professor of Chemistry, University of North Carolina and; Associate Laboratory Director, Los Alamos National Laboratory;* ed OH Univ., Stanford Univ.; Woodrow Wilson Graduate Fellow, Stanford Univ. 1963–64, NSF Graduate Fellow 1965–66; NATO Postdoctoral Research Fellow, Univ. Coll., London, England 1967; Asst Prof. of Chemistry, Univ. of NC 1968–72, Assoc. Prof. 1972–75, Prof. 1975–82, M. A. Smith Prof. of Chemistry 1982–87, Kenan Prof. of Chemistry 1987–, Chair. Dept of Chemistry 1985–90, Vice-Provost for Graduate Studies and Research 1994–99; Visiting Prof., Sydney Univ., Australia 1976; Visiting Scientist, Xerox Webster Research Center, Webster, NY 1978; Visiting Scientist, Sandia Nat. Lab. 1981; Visiting Prof., Univ. Louis Pasteur, Strasbourg, France 1983; Visiting Scientist, Centre d'Etudes Nucleaires, Grenoble, France 1983; Visiting Prof., Univ. de Rennes, France 1986, Univ. di Ferrara, Italy 1992, Univ. of Buenos Aires, Argentina 1993; Assoc. Lab. Dir, Los Alamos Nat. Lab., NM 2000–; Dir Triangle Univs Licensing Consortium 1989–95, Triangle Univs Center for Advanced Studies Inc. 1994–, NC Biotechnology Center 1994–, Associated Univs Inc. 1995–97, NC Bd of Science and Tech. 1995–99, Research Triangle Inst. 1995–; mem. numerous socs including ACS, American Asscn of Univ. Profs, AAAS (Fellow 1981–), American Acad. of Arts and Sciences 1994–; mem. Editorial Bd Inorganic Chemistry 1983–87, Journal of the American Chemical Soc. 1983–87, Accounts of Chemical Research 1991–, Structure and Bonding 1997–, Journal of Photochemistry and Photobiology A 1998–; ACS Charles H. Stone Award 1982, ACS Award in Inorganic Chemistry 1990, ACS Southern Chemist of the Year Award 1992, Royal Australian Chemical Inst. Nyholm Award 1996, Inter-American Photochemical Soc. Award 1997, ACS Remsen Award 1999; numerous hon. lectures in USA and abroad. *Address:* Strategic and Supporting Research Directorate, Los Alamos National Laboratory, MS A127 ALDSSR, Los Alamos, NM 87545, USA (office). *Telephone:* (505) 667-8597 (office). *Fax:* (505) 667-5450 (office). *E-mail:* tjmeyer@lanl.gov (office). *Website:* www.lanl.gov/orgs/ssr/meyer.htm (office).

MEYER, Wilhelm Olaf, MArch, ARIBA, MIA, MBA; South African architect; b. 14 May 1935, Pretoria; s. of Dr F. Meyer; m. Angela Winsome 1961; one s. one d.; ed Univs of Witwatersrand and Pennsylvania; Partner, Moerdyk & Watson, Pretoria 1961; f. own practice, Wilhelm O Meyer & Partners, Johannesburg 1966, Consultant 1993–; Founder mem. Urban Action Group, Johannesburg 1971; mem. Council SA Council of Architects 1973–, Pres. 1983, 1985; Co-Founder, COPLAN Jt architectural practice with P.S.I. Hong Hong 1983; Pres.-in-Chief, Interbou 84 1984; opened architectural practice jtly in London 1986; mem. Bd Faculty, School of Architecture, Univ. of Witwatersrand 1988–93; Gen. Consultant for Standard Bank Bldgs nationwide 1993; Dir Pancom Devt Co. 1993–; many other appointments; work includes urban design, apt. bldgs, univ. bldgs, churches, Marine Parade Hotel, Durban, Johannesburg Civic Centre and Johannesburg Art Gallery; Medal of Honour for Architecture, SA Akad. vir Wetenskap en Kuns 1980; numerous other awards and competition prizes. *Publications:* contribs to architectural journals. *Leisure interests:* music, windsurfing. *Address:* 64 Galway Road, Parkview 2193, Johannesburg, South Africa.

MEYER-LANDRUT, Andreas, PhD; German diplomatist; b. 31 May 1929, Tallinn, Estonia; s. of Bruno and Käthe Meyer-Landrut (née Winter); m. Hanna Karatsony von Hodos 1960; one s. one d.; m. 2nd Natali Somers (née Seferov); ed Univs of Göttingen and Zagreb; entered foreign service 1955, in Moscow, Brussels and Tokyo 1956–68, Amb. to Congo (Brazzaville) 1969; in Foreign Office, Bonn 1971–80, Head of Sub-Dept for Policy towards Eastern Europe and GDR 1974–78, Dir Dept of Relations to Asia, Near and Middle East, Africa and Latin America 1978–80, Amb. to USSR 1980–83, 1987–89; State Sec. to Foreign Office 1983–87; Head of Fed. Pres.'s Office and State Sec. 1989–94; Man. Daimler Chrysler AG in Moscow 1994–2002; Adviser to German cos in Russia and CIS countries; Hon. Pres. German-Russian Forum Berlin; Hon. mem. German Equestrian Fed.; Grand Commdr Order of Merit. *Publications:* Mit Gott und langen Unterhosen: Erlebnisse eines Diplomaten in der Zeit des Kalten Krieges 2003. *Address:* Malaja Bronnaja ul. 20A, 103104 Moscow, Russia (office); Auswärtiges Amt für BO, MOS 11013 Berlin PF 117. *Telephone:* (495) 290-4930 (office); (495) 200-6231 (office); (495) 200-62-31 (home). *Fax:* (495) 291-8605 (office); (495) 209-1672 (home). *E-mail:* Andreas.Meyer-Landrut@gmx.net (office).

MEYEROWITZ, Elliot Martin, AB, MPhil, PhD, FAAS; American biologist and academic; *George W. Beadle Professor of Biology and Chairman, Division of Biology, California Institute of Technology;* b. 22 May 1951, Washington, DC; m. Joan Agnes Kobori; two c.; ed Columbia Univ., New York, Yale Univ., New Haven, Conn.; Jane Coffin Childs Memorial Fund Postdoctoral Fellow, Dept of Biochemistry, Stanford Univ. School of Medicine, Calif. 1977–79; Asst Prof. of Biology, California Inst. of Tech., Pasadena 1980–85, Assoc. Prof. 1985–89, Prof. of Biology 1989–2002, Exec. Officer for Biology 1995–2000, Chair. Div. of Biology 2000–, George W. Beadle Prof. of Biology 2002–; Visiting A. F. Wood Prof., Univ. of Florida, Gainesville 2000; European Flying Fellowship in Plant Molecular Biology, Grad. School of Experimental Plant Sciences, Univ. of Ghent, Belgium, Institut des Sciences Vegetales, France, Max-Planck-Institut für Zuchtungsforschung, Germany 2001; mem. Editorial Bd Mechanisms of Development 1990–, Molecular Biology of the Cell 1991–, Cell 1991–, Trends in Genetics 1993–, Current Biology 1993–, Development 1994–, BioEssays 1996–, Current Opinion in Plant Biology 1997–, Genome Biology 1999–, Journal of Biology 2001–, Philosophical Transactions of the Royal Society B 2006–; mem. Scientific Advisory Bd Kumho Life and Environmental Science Lab. 1997–, Yale-Peking Univ. Jt Center for Plant Molecular Genetics 2001–, Temasek Life Sciences Lab. 2002–05; mem. Scientific Advisory Cttee, Inst. of Molecular Biology and Biotechnology, Heraklion, Crete 2001–07; mem. American Acad. of Arts and Sciences 1991–, NAS 1995–, American Philosophical Soc. 1998; Foreign Assoc. Acad. des sciences, France 2002–; Foreign mem. Royal Soc. (UK) 2004–; Assoc. mem. European Molecular Biology Org. 2008; Dr hc (École Normale Supérieure, Lyon) 2007; Huebschman Prize in Biology, Columbia Univ. 1972, John S. Nicholas Award for Outstanding Biology Dissertation, Yale Univ. 1977, Sloan Foundation Research Fellowship, Calif. Inst. of Tech. 1981, Pelton Award, Botanical Soc. of America and Conservation and Research Foundation 1994, Gibbs Medal, American Soc. of Plant Physiologists 1995, Genetics Soc. of America Medal 1996, Science pour l'Art Science Prize, LVMH Moët-Hennessy-Louis Vuitton 1996, Mendel Medal and Mendel Lecturer, Genetical Soc. of GB 1997, Int. Prize for Biology, Japan Soc. for the Promotion of Science 1997, Jean Weigle Memorial Lecturer, Univ. of Geneva 1998, Richard Lounsbery Award, NAS 1999, Annual Biology Lecturer, ETH, Zürich 2001, Wilbur Cross Medal, Yale Univ. 2001, Ross Harrison Prize, Int. Soc. of Developmental Biologists 2005, Balzan Prize 2006. *Publications:* more than 200 articles in scientific journals. *Address:* Division of Biology, California Institute of Technology, Mail Code 156-29, 1200 East California Boulevard, Pasadena, CA 91125, USA (office). *Telephone:* (626) 395-6889 (office). *Fax:* (626) 449-0756 (office). *E-mail:* meyerow@caltech.edu (office). *Website:* www.caltech.edu/~meyerowitz (office).

MEYEROWITZ, Joel; American photographer; b. 1938, Bronx, New York; s. of Hy Meyerowitz; one s.; fmr art dir in an advertising firm; began photography career in 1962; early advocate of colour photography mid-1960s; gave lessons in colour photography at Cooper Union, New York 1971; commissioned by St Louis Art Museum, Missouri to photograph Eero Saarinen's Gateway Arch 1977; photographed Empire State Bldg 1978; produced and directed his first film, POP, an intimate diary of a three-week road trip made with his son and father 1998; cr. The World Trade Center Archive of more than 8,000 images, documenting destruction and recovery at Ground Zero and immediate neighbourhood following attacks on World Trade Center 2001; works in collection of ATT Collection, Boston Museum of Fine Art, Carnegie Inst. Museum of Art, Chicago Art Inst., George Eastman House, IBM Collection, Int. Center of Photography, New York, Merrill Lynch Collection, Metropolitan Museum of Art, Museum of Modern Art, New York, Miami Art Museum, Museum of Photographic Art, Philadelphia Museum of Art, San Francisco Museum of Modern Art, San Jose Museum of Art, Seagram Collection, St Louis Museum, Stedelijk Museum, Toledo Museum of Art, Virginia Museum, Whitney Museum of American Art, US Trust Company, Gund Collection, Hallmark Cards Collection; Guggenheim Fellow, NEA Award, NEH Award. *Publications:* Cape Light 1979, St Louis & the Arch 1981, A Summer's Day 1985, Wild Flowers 1986, The Arch 1988, Creating a Sense of Place 1990, Redheads 1991, Bay/Sky 1993, At the Water's Edge 1993, The Nutcracker 1993, Città e Destino (City and Destiny), La natura delle città (The Nature of Cities) 1995, Bystander: A History of Street Photography 1994, Joel Meyerowitz (Phaidon 55 series) 2001, Tuscany: Inside the Light 2003, Aftermath: The World Trade Center Archives 2006. *Website:* www.joelmeyerowitz.com.

MEYROWITZ, Carol; American business executive; *President and CEO, The TJX Companies, Inc.;* joined Hit or Miss div., The TJX Companies, Inc. 1983, later held sr man. positions with Hit or Miss and Chadwick's of Boston, Sr Exec. Vice-Pres. and Pres. The Marmaxx Group (co.'s largest div.) 2001–05, Pres. The TJX Companies, Inc. 2005–, mem. Bd of Dirs and CEO 2007–, mem. Cttee of Exec. Man. 2007–; advisory consultant, Berkshire Partners LLC, Boston 2005–; ranked by Fortune magazine amongst 50 Most Powerful Women in Business in US (26th) 2006, (31st) 2007, (27th) 2008. *Address:* The TJX Companies, Inc., 770 Cochituate Road, Framingham, MA 01701, USA (office). *Telephone:* (508) 390-1000 (office). *Fax:* (508) 390-2828 (office). *E-mail:* info@tjx.com (office). *Website:* www.tjx.com (office).

MEZHIROV, Aleksandr Petrovich; Russian poet; b. 26 Sept. 1923, Moscow; s. of Pyotr Izraelevich Mezhirov and Yelizaveta Semyonovna Mezhirova; m. Yelena Yaschenko; one d.; ed Moscow Univ.; served in Soviet Army 1941–45; Prof. in Literary Inst., Moscow 1966–91; State Prize for Poetry 1986, Georgian State Prize 1989. *Publications:* more than 50 vols of poetry, including Long is the Road 1947, Returns 1955, Poems and Translations 1962, Ladoga Ice 1965, Selected Works (2 Vols) 1981, The Blind Turning 1983, The Outline of Things 1984, Prose in Poetry 1985, Bormotucha 1990, The What That Has No Name 1995, Ground Wind 1997, Apologia of a Circus 1997; trans. Georgian and Lithuanian poetry, articles, critical reviews, essays on history of Russian econs. *Leisure interest:* billiards.

MEZOUAR, Salaheddine, MSc(Econ); Moroccan politician and administrator; *Minister of the Economy and Finance;* b. 11 Dec. 1953, Meknès; m.; two c.; ed Institut européen d'admin des affaires (INSEAD), Fontainebleau, France, Institut supérieur de commerce et d'admin des entreprises (ISCAE), Casablanca, Université des sciences sociales, Grenoble, France; held admin. and financial posts with Régies d'Eau et d'Électricité de Rabat et de Tanger early 1980s; Chief Financial Officer Franco-Tunisian electrical, plumbing, refrigeration and maintenance co. based in Tunis –1986; Chief of Div. and in charge of mission, Office d'exploitation des Ports (ODEP) 1986–91; joined Spanish co. specializing in manufacture of tissue where he served as Gen. Man. of subsidiary Settat and Commercial Dir of group for Morocco, Africa and Middle East 1991; Pres. Moroccan Asscn of Textile Industries and Clothing (AMITH) 2002; also served as Pres. Textile and Leather Fed. in Gen. Confed. of Moroccan Enterprises (CGEM); Minister of Industry, Trade and Upgrading of the Economy 2004–07, of the Economy and Finance 2007–; mem. Cen. Cttee Rassemblement nat. des Indépendants; fmr Vice-Pres. Raja athletic club; fmr capt. nat. basketball team. *Address:* Ministry of the

Economy and Finance, Blvd Muhammad V, Quartier Administratif, Chellah, Rabat, Morocco (office). *Telephone:* (3) 7677501 (office); (3) 7677200 (office). *Fax:* (3) 7677527 (office). *E-mail:* daag@daag.finances.gov.ma (office). *Website:* www.finances.gov.ma (office).

MGALOBLISHVILI, Grigol, BA, MA; Georgian diplomatist and politician; b. 7 Oct. 1973; m.; two c.; ed Tbilisi State Univ., Istanbul Univ., Oxford Univ., UK; interpreter, Georgian Trade Mission in Turkey 1995–96; attaché, Dept of Western European Countries, Ministry of Foreign Affairs 1996–98; First Sec. Embassy in Ankara 1998–2000, Political Counsellor 1998–2002; Deputy Dir Dept of US, Canada and Latin American Countries, Ministry of Foreign Affairs 2003–04, Dir Dept of European and Euro-integration 2004; Amb. to Turkey 2004–08; Prime Minister of Georgia Nov. 2008–Feb. 2009. *Address:* c/o Chancellery of the Government, 0105 Tbilisi, P. Ingorovka 7, Georgia (office).

M'HENNI, Hedi; Tunisian politician; fmr Minister of Public Health; Minister of Interior and Local Devt 2003–04, of Nat. Defence 2004–05; Sec.-Gen. of the governing Rassemblement constitutionnel démocratique 2005–. *Address:* c/o Ministry of National Defence, blvd Bab Menara, 1030 Tunis, Tunisia (office).

MICELI, Felisa; Argentine economist and fmr government official; ed Univ. of Buenos Aires; Dir-Sec. Bank of the Province of Buenos Aires 1983–87; worked at Ecolatina consultancy firm in early 1990s; Rep. of Ministry of Economy at Cen. Bank 2002–03; Chair. Banco de la Nación Argentina 2003–05; Minister of the Economy 2005–07 (resgnd). *Address:* c/o Ministry of the Economy, Hipólito Yrigoyen 250, 1310 Buenos Aires, Argentina (office).

MICHAEL, Rt Hon. Alun Edward, BA; British politician; b. 22 Aug. 1943, Brynewran, Wales; s. of the late Leslie Charles Michael and Elizabeth (Betty) Michael; m.; two s. three d.; ed Keele Univ.; journalist South Wales Echo 1966–71; Youth and Community Worker, Cardiff 1972–84; Area Community Education Officer, Grangetown and Butetown 1984–87; mem. Cardiff City Council 1973–89 (fmr Chair. Finance, Planning, Performance Review and Econ. Devt, Chief Whip, Labour Group); mem. House of Commons (Labour and Co-op) for Cardiff S and Penarth 1987–; Opposition Whip 1987–88; Opposition Frontbench Spokesman on Welsh Affairs 1988–92, on Home Affairs and the Voluntary Sector 1992–97; Minister of State, Home Office 1997–98; Sec. of State for Wales 1998–99; First Sec. of Nat. Ass. for Wales 1999–2000; Minister of State for Rural Affairs and Local Environmental Quality, Dept for the Environment, Food and Rural Affairs 2001–05, Minister of State for Industry and Regions 2005–06; mem. Nat. Ass. for Wales for Mid and W Wales 1999–2001; mem. numerous parl. groups and cttees.; Vice-Pres. YHA. *Leisure interests:* opera, reading, long-distance running, mountain-walking, National Parks, classical music. *Address:* House of Commons, London, SW1A 0AA, England (office). *Telephone:* (20) 7219-5980 (office). *Fax:* (20) 7219-5930 (office). *E-mail:* alunmichaelmp@parliament.uk (office).

MICHAEL, George; British singer, songwriter and producer; b. (Georgios Kyriacos Panayiotou), 25 June 1963, Finchley, London; s. of Jack Kyriacus Panayiotou and the late Lesley Panayiotou; ed Bushey Meads School; debut in group The Executive 1979; formed (with Andrew Ridgeley) Wham! 1981–86, numerous consecutive hits; toured UK, France, USA, China, etc.; launched solo career 1986–; chose to release all further music free online 2004–; BRIT Awards for Best British Group 1985, Outstanding Contribution to British Music 1986, Best British Male Artist 1988, Best British Male Solo Artist 1997, Ivor Novello Awards for Songwriter 1985, 1989, Grammy Award (for I Knew You Were Waiting For Me, duet with Aretha Franklin) 1988, British Rock Industry Award for Best Male Artist 1988, Nordoff-Robbins Silver Clef Award 1989, American Music Awards for Favorite Pop/Rock Male Artist, Soul R&B Male Artist 1989, ASCAP Golden Note Award 1992. *Recordings include:* albums: with Wham!: Fantastic 1983, Make It Big 1984, Music From The Edge of Heaven 1986, The Final 1986; solo: Faith (Grammy Award for Best Album 1989, American Music Awards for Favorite Album 1989) 1987, Listen Without Prejudice: Vol. 1 (BRIT Award for Best British Album 1991) 1989, Older 1996, Older and Upper 1998, Ladies and Gentlemen: The Best of George Michael 1998, Songs from the Last Century 1999, Patience 2004, Twenty Five 2006. *Publication:* George Michael: Bare (autobiog. with Tony Parsons) 1990. *Address:* Connie Filippello Publicity, 49 Portland Road, London, W11 4LJ, England (office). *Telephone:* (20) 7229-5400 (office). *Fax:* (20) 7229-4804 (office). *E-mail:* Cfpublicity@aol.com (office). *Website:* www.georgemichael.com.

MICHAEL, HM King; Romanian fmr ruler; b. 25 Oct. 1921, Foishor Castle, Sinaïa; s. of the late King Carol II and Princess Helen of Greece; m. Princess Anne of Bourbon-Parma 1948; five d.; declared heir apparent, ratified by Parl. 4 Jan. 1926; proclaimed King 1927, deposed by his father 1930; succeeded to the throne of Romania following his father's abdication 1940; led coup d'état against pro-Nazi dictator, Ion Antonescu 1944; forced to abdicate following communist takeover of Romania 30 Dec. 1947; subsequently ran chicken farm in Herts., UK; went to Switzerland as test pilot 1956; has also worked for Lear Inc.; started electronics co. and worked as stockbroker; deported from Romania on first visit since exile Dec. 1990; returned to Romania 1992; Romanian citizenship and passport restored 1997; undertook official mission for Romania's integration into NATO and EU 1997; Collar and Grand Master, Order of Carol I of Romania, Order of Faithful Service, Order of Crown of Romania and Star of Romania, Grand Cross, Royal Victorian Order, Grand Cross, Légion d'honneur, Grand Cross, Order of Leopold (Belgium), Collar, Order of Annunciata, Grand Cross, Order of St Saviour (Greece), Marshal, Romanian Armed Forces. *Leisure interest:* restoring Second World War jeeps. *Address:* Villa Serena, CP 627, 1290 Versoix, Switzerland (office). *Telephone:* (22) 755-29-68 (office). *Fax:* (22) 755-29-69 (office). *E-mail:* msregele@swissonline.ch (office).

MICHAELS, Lorne; Canadian television and film producer; *Executive Producer, Saturday Night Live;* b. 17 Nov. 1944, Toronto; m. 1st Rosie Schuster (divorced); m. 2nd Susan Forristal (divorced); m. 3rd Alice Barry; three c.; ed Univ. of Toronto; fmr writer and producer CBC; fmr writer Rowan Martin's Laugh-In (TV show) NBC 1968, creator and Exec. Producer Saturday Night Live 1975–, Exec. Producer Late Night with Conan O'Brien; f. Broadway Video Inc. (production co.) 1975; ten Emmy Awards including Emmy Award for Best Writing in a Variety/Comedy Series 2002, Mark Twain Prize for American Humor 2004. *Films produced include:* Gilda Live (also writer) 1980, Three Amigos (also co-writer) 1986, Wayne's World 1992, Wayne's World II 1993, Lassie 1994, Tommy Boy 1995, Kids in the Hall: Brain Candy 1996, A Night at the Roxbury 1998, Superstar 1999, The Ladies Man 2000, Enigma 2001, Mean Girls 2004. *Television includes:* Things We Did Last Summer 1977, The Paul Simon Special (also writer) 1977, Steve Martin's Best Show Ever (also writer) 1981, The Coneheads 1983, The New Show 1984, The Kids in the Hall 1988, Sunday Night 1988, Frosty Returns 1992. *Address:* c/o Saturday Night Live, NBC Television Network, 30 Rockefeller Plaza, New York, NY 10112, USA (office). *Telephone:* (212) 664-4444 (office). *Fax:* (212) 664-4085 (office). *Website:* www.lornemichaels.com; www.nbc.com/Saturday_Night_Live (office).

MICHAELS-MOORE, Anthony, BA; British singer (baritone); b. 8 April 1957, Grays, Essex; s. of John Frederick Moore and Isabel Shephard; m. Ewa Bozena Migocki 1980; one d.; ed Gravesend School for Boys, Univ. of Newcastle, Royal Scottish Acad. of Music and Drama, Fenham Teacher Training Coll.; prin. baritone, Royal Opera House, Covent Garden 1987–97; roles in all British opera cos; debut La Scala, Milan (Licinius in La Vestale) 1993, New York Metropolitan Opera (Marcello in La Bohème) 1996, Vienna Staatsoper (Lescaut in Manon) 1997, San Francisco Opera (Eugene Onegin) 1997, Paris Bastille (Sharpless in Madama Butterfly) 1995; specializes in 19th-century baritone repertoire; winner Luciano Pavarotti/Opera Co. of Phila Prize 1985, Royal Philharmonic Soc. Award Winner 1997. *Television appearances include:* BBC Proms (Beethoven's Missa Solemnis, Mahler's Symphony No. 8), Carmina Burana recorded at La Scala, Milan 1996. *Music:* major recordings include: Carmina Burana, Lucia di Lammermoor, La Vestale, La Favorite, Falstaff and Il Tabarro, Aroldo. *Radio:* regular BBC Radio 3 broadcasts, Verdi operas from Royal Opera House, Met Opera relays from New York. *Leisure interests:* clay pigeon shooting, computer games, oriental food. *Address:* IMG Artists, The Light Box, 111 Power Road, London W4 5PY, England (office). *Telephone:* (20) 7957-5800 (office). *Fax:* (20) 7957-5801 (office). *E-mail:* sthomson@imgartists.com (office); amichaelsmoore@aol.com (office). *Website:* www.imgartists.com (office); www.anthony-michaels-moore.com.

MICHAL, Jiři, BSc; Czech business executive; *Chairman and CEO, Zentiva a.s.;* ed Univ. of Chem. and Tech., Prague; joined Zentiva a.s. 1974, various man. roles including Operational Dir, Chief Financial Officer, becoming CEO and Chair. 1993–; Vice-Pres. Czech Chemical Industry Asscn. *Address:* Zentiva a.s., U Kabelovny 130, 10237 Prague 10, Czech Republic (office). *Telephone:* (267) 241111 (office). *Fax:* (272) 702402 (office). *E-mail:* zentiva@zentiva.cz (office). *Website:* www.zentiva.eu (office).

MICHALCZEWSKI, Dariusz, (The Tiger); Polish/German boxer; b. 5 May 1968, Gdańsk; m.; two s.; amateur boxer 1982–91; 133 wins in 150 amateur fights; professional boxer 1991–; 48 wins in 49 professional fights; European champion, Göteborg 1991; became World Boxing Org. (WBO) light-heavyweight champion 1994 and defended the title 23 times; defeated by Julio César González Oct. 2003; won WBO cruiserweight title in 1994 (abandoned 1995); won World Boxing Asscn (WBA), Int. Boxing Fed. (IBF) light-heavyweight titles in 1997. *Address:* Waldeweg 134B, 22393 Hamburg, Germany (office). *Telephone:* (40) 68912656 (office). *Website:* www.dariusz-tiger.de.

MICHALIK, Archbishop Józef, DTheol; Polish ecclesiastic; *Archbishop of Przemyśl and Chairman, Conference of Polish Episcopate;* b. 20 April 1941, Zambrów; ed Acad. of Catholic Theology, Warsaw, Angelicum, St Thomas Pontifical Univ., Rome; ordained priest, Łomża 1964; Vice-Chancellor Bishops' Curia, Łomża 1973–78; fmr lecturer Higher Theological Seminary, Łomża, Rector Pontifical Polish Coll., Rome 1978–86; staff mem. Pontifical Laity Council 1978–86; Bishop of Gorzów 1986–92; Chair. Episcopate Cttee for Academic Ministry 1986–95; Bishop Zielona Góra and Gorzów 1992–93; Archbishop of Przemyśl 1993–; Chair. Episcopate's Council for Poles Abroad, Councils of Episcopates of Europe Cttee for Laity; mem. Main Council of Conf. of Polish Episcopate, (Chair. 2004–), Vatican Congregation for Bishops. *Publications:* My Talks with God 1976, La Chiesa e il suo rinnovamento secondo Andrea Frycz Modrzewski 1973, Brothers Look at Your Vocation 1991, Bóg i Ojczyzna, Wiara i Naród 1998, Mocą Twoją Panie 1998, Pan was potrzebuje 2000. *Address:* Pl. Katedralny 4/A, 37-700 Przemyśl, Poland (office). *Telephone:* (16) 6786694 (office). *Fax:* (16) 6782674 (office). *E-mail:* michalik@episkopat.pl (office). *Website:* www.przemysl.opoka.org.pl (office).

MICHAUD, Jean-Claude Georges; French broadcasting executive; b. 28 Oct. 1933; s. of Maurice Michaud and Suzanne Michaud; one s. one d. (from fmr marriage); ed Lycée Louis-le-Grand, Paris and Ecole Normale Supérieure, Paris; Counsellor, Ministry of Educ. 1961–62, Ministry of Information 1962–64; Asst Dir Television ORTF 1964–68, Counsellor to Dir-Gen. 1968–70; man. position, Librairie Hachette 1970–73; Deputy Dir for External Affairs and Co-operation, ORTF 1973–74; Dir of Int. Affairs and Co-operation, Télédiffusion France 1975–80, Dir of Commercial Affairs 1982–83, Overseas Dir 1983–85; Pres.-Dir-Gen. Soc. Française Radio-Télévision d'Outre-Mer (RFO) 1986–89; Pres. Dir-Gen. Sofratev 1989–98. *Publication:* Teoria e Storia nel Capitale di Marx 1960, Alain Peyrefitte 2002. *Leisure interests:* walking, skiing, reading. *Address:* 55 boulevard du Montparnasse, 75006 Paris, France (home). *Telephone:* 1-45-49-06-90 (home). *Fax:* 1-42-22-58-43 (home). *E-mail:* michaud.jeanclaude@wanadoo.fr (home).

MICHAUX-CHEVRY, Lucette; French politician and lawyer; b. 5 March 1929, Sainte-Claude, Guadeloupe; d. of Edouard Chevry and Florentine Labry; m. Émile Michaux (deceased); two c.; lawyer Basse-Terre 1955–; Municipal Councillor, Sainte-Claude 1959–65; mem. Departmental Council of Guadeloupe 1976, Chair. 1982–85; f. Political Party for Guadeloupe (LPG) 1984; mem. Regional Council 1984; Deputy to Nat. Ass. 4th Constituency of Guadeloupe 1986; Mayor of Gourbeyre 1987; State Sec. for French-speaking World, Govt of France 1986–88; Chair. Regional Council of Guadeloupe 1992–2004; Deputy to Nat. Ass. 1993; Nat. Minister with special responsibility for Humanitarian Measures and Human Rights 1993–95; Senator from Guadeloupe (RPR) 1995–; Mayor of Basse-Terre 1995–2001; Pres. Objectif Guadeloupe 2000–; mem. Comm. of Foreign Affairs and Nat. Defence. *Address:* Sénat, 15, rue de Vaugirard, 75291 Paris Cédex 06, France. *Telephone:* 1-42-34-20-00 (office). *Fax:* 1-42-34-26-77 (office). *E-mail:* l.michaux-chevry@senat.fr (office). *Website:* www.senat.fr (office).

MICHEL, James Alix; Seychelles politician and head of state; *President;* b. 16 Aug. 1944; ed Teacher Training Coll., Seychelles; teacher 1960–61; with Cable & Wireless Telecommunications 1962–71; treas. and sec. staff union 1970–71; Accountant, Asst Man., then Man. Hotel des Seychelles 1971–74; mem. Exec. Cttee Seychelles People's United Party and Co-ordinator of Party Brs, also Ed. of The People 1974–77; Minister of State, Admin and Information 1977–79; mem. Cen. Exec. Cttee Seychelles People's Progressive Front 1978–, also Sec.; Chief of Staff Seychelles People's Defence Forces 1979–93; Minister of Educ., Information, Culture and Telecommunications 1979–86, of Educ., Information, Culture and Sports 1986–89, of Finance 1989–91, of Finance and Information 1991–93, of Finance, Information, Communications and Defence, also First Desig. Minister to discharge the functions of Pres. 1993–96; Vice-Pres. (retaining portfolios for Finance, Information and Communications) 1996; Vice-Pres. (with portfolios of Econ. Planning and Environment and Transport) 1998–2000; Vice-Pres. and Minister of Finance, Econ. Planning, Information Tech. and Communications 2001–04; Pres. of the Seychelles, with additional responsibility for Defence, Police, Information and Public Relations, Legal Affairs and Risk and Disaster Man. 2004–, and Minister of Finance 2005–06; Patron Seychelles Football Fed.; Foreign mem. Russian Acad. of Natural Sciences; Gran Croce dell'Ordine al Merito Melitense, Kt of Malta, Outstanding Civilian Service Medal, US Army Dept 1995. *Address:* Office of the President, State House, POB 55, Victoria, Mahé, Seychelles (office). *Telephone:* 224155 (office). *Fax:* 224985 (office). *Website:* www.virtualseychelles.sc.

MICHEL, Louis; Belgian politician; *Commissioner for Development and Humanitarian Aid, European Commission;* b. 2 Sept. 1947, Tirlemont; fmr lecturer at Inst. Supérieur de Commerce Saint-Louis; Prof. of Dutch, English and German Literature, Ecole Normale provinciale de Jodoigne 1968–78; Alderman of Jodoigne 1977–83, Mayor 1983–; Sec.-Gen. Parti Réformateur Libéral (PRL) 1980–82, Pres. 1982–90; Pres. Fed. of Local and Provincial PRL Office Holders 1990–92; Pres., parl. group in Council of Walloon Region 1991–92, in House of Reps 1992–95; MP 1978–99; Pres. PRL 1995–2001; Deputy Pres. of Liberal Int.; Deputy Prime Minister and Minister of Foreign Affairs July 1999–2004; Rep. of Belgium to EU Special Convention on a European Constitution 2001–; EU Commr for Devt and Humanitarian Aid 2004–; mem. Parl. Comms on Finance, Budget, Institutional Reforms and Comm. charged with supervising electoral expenditures; mem. Benelux Inter parl. Consultative Council; Commdr Order of Leopold. *Address:* European Commission, 200 rue de la Loi, 1049 Brussels, Belgium (office). *Telephone:* (2) 299-11-11 (office). *Fax:* (2) 295-01-38 (office). *Website:* europa.eu (office).

MICHEL, Mohamedou Ould; Mauritanian government official and fmr diplomatist; fmr Minister of Planning; fmr Amb. to Australia, fmr Amb. to USA; currently Sr Adviser to the Pres. of Mauritania. *Address:* c/o Office of the President, BP 184, Nouakchott, Mauritania. *Telephone:* 525-26-36.

MICHEL, Pauline, LèsL; Canadian poet, writer, scenarist and songwriter; b. 1944, Asbestos, PQ; ed École normale Marguerite Bourgeois, Univ. of Sherbrooke, Laval Univ.; fmr Professor, Cegep de Sherbrooke, Université du Québec à Montréal; numerous poetry and song tours and recitals in Canada, Africa, France; scenarist for TV and films; Parl. Poet Laureate 2004–06; mem. Union des écrivaines et des écrivains Québécois, Writers' Union of Canada, League of Canadian Poets; Ministry of Cultural Affairs grant, Canadian Embassy in Paris bursary 1980; Winner Québec en chansons, Prix Adate. *Plays:* Farfelu ou Les sens ensorceleurs, Au fil de l'autre, On perd la boule. *Films:* as co-scenarist, actress, singer in La Caresse d'une ride (documentary), Les héritières d'Esther Blondin; consultant for Les Cheveux en quatre (documentary). *Recordings:* albums: Animagerie, Au coeur d'la vie 1979, Contrastes 1980, Hello moineau 1985, Le tour du monde 2000. *Music:* Sors de ta cage (comedy musical). *Radio:* À deux voix, Le jardin des ombres. *Writing for television:* scenarist for L'animagerie, You-hou (Radio-Canada), Le Château des enfants, Télé-Métropole, Télé-Ressources, Passe-Partout (consultant) (Télé-Québec), À la Claire Fontaine (TV Ontario), Hello Moineau (coproduction for Francophonie countries), La Maison de Ouimzie/Wimzie's House (broadcast in 100 countries), Dossi, Rémi et compagnie (France). *Publications include:* novels: Les yeux d'eau 1975, 2002, Mirage 1978, 2004, Le papillon de Vénus 1999, Eyes of Water 2006; short stories: Frissons d'enfants/Haunted Childhoods 2006; play: Au fil de l'autre 2004; poetry: L'oeil sauvage 1988, Funambule/Tightrope 2006; children's book: Cannelle et pruneau dans les feuilles de thé 1992; songbooks: Le tour du monde 2000, Hello Moineau 1985, Demeurez dans mon amour 1987, Voyez comme ils s'aiment 1988; contrib. of novellas and poems to anthologies. *Leisure interests:* music, dance, cinema. *Address:* 3315 Ridgewood Avenue, Apt 6, Montréal, PQ H3V 1BY (home). *Telephone:* (514) 344-0588 (home). *E-mail:* pmichel@aei.ca (home).

MICHELBERGER, Pál, DSc; Hungarian engineer; b. 4 Feb. 1930, Vecsés; s. of Pál Michelberger and Mária Komáromy; m. Ilona Torma; one s. one d.; ed Technical Univ., Budapest; Assoc. Prof., Tech. Univ., Budapest 1963–68, Prof. 1968–, Rector 1990–94; mem. Bd of Mans, IKARUS Motor Coach Factory 1991–95, Hungarocamion Transport Co. 1992–94; Chair. Cttee for Machine Design, Scientific Soc. for Mechanical Eng, Co-Pres. 1976–90, Vice-Pres. 1990–93; Councillor, Fed. Int. des Techniques de l'Automobile 1974, Vice-Pres. 1978, Pres. 1992–94; Pres. (elect) Hungarian Rectors' Conf. 1994–95; mem. Perm. Cttee European Rectors' Conf. 1991–94; mem. Russian Acad. of Transportation 1992, Acad. Europaea 1993–, European Acad. of Science and Arts 1998–; Corresp. mem. Hungarian Acad. of Sciences 1982, mem. 1990 (Vice-Pres. 1993), Verein Deutscher Ingenieure 1983–; Hon. Pres. Hungarian Accreditation Cttee; A. G. Pattantyus Prize 1973, L. Eötvös Prize 1994, Széchenyi Prize 1995, O. Benedikt Prize 1998, Pázmány Prize 1999. *Publications:* seven books and numerous articles on vehicle dynamics. *Leisure interest:* music. *Address:* Szabadság út 141, 2040, Budaörs (office); c/o Technical University, Műegyetem rakpart 3-9, 1521 Budapest, Hungary. *Telephone:* (1) 463-1111 (office); (22) 422-668 (home). *Fax:* (1) 463-1783.

MICHELIN, François; French business executive; b. 15 June 1926, Clermont-Ferrand; s. of Etienne Michelin and Madeleine (née Calliès) Michelin; m. Bernadette Montagne 1951; Man. Dir Compagnie Générale des Etablissements Michelin, Michelin & Cie 1959–66, Jt Man. Dir 1966–99; Man. Dir Cie Financière Michelin, Manufacture française des pneumatiques Michelin; Dir Peugeot SA; Conseiller d'Etat en service extraordinaire 1989. *Publication:* Et pourquoi pas? (jtly) (Prix de l'excellence, Maxim's Business Club 1999) 1998. *Leisure interest:* tennis. *Address:* c/o Compagnie Générale des Établissements Michelin, 12 cours Sablon, 63000 Clermont-Ferrand, Cedex 9, France (office).

MICHELL, Keith; Australian actor; b. 1 Dec. 1926, Adelaide, Australia; s. of Joseph Michell and Maud (née Aslat) Michell; m. Jeanette Sterk 1957; one s. one d.; ed Port Pirie High School, Adelaide Univ. Teacher's Coll. and School of Arts, Old Vic. Theatre School; started career as art teacher; first stage appearance Playbox, Adelaide 1947; with Young Vic. Theatre Co. 1950–51, first London appearance in And So To Bed 1951; Artistic Dir, Chichester Festival Theatre 1974–77; Top Actor Emmy Award 1971, British Film Award 1973, Logie Award 1974 and numerous others. *Stage appearances include:* Troilus and Cressida 1954, Romeo and Juliet 1954, Macbeth 1955, Don Juan 1956, Irma La Douce 1958, The Art of Seduction 1962, The Rehearsal 1963, Robert and Elizabeth 1964, The King's Mare 1966, Man of La Mancha 1968–69, Abelard and Heloise 1970, Hamlet 1972, Dear Love 1973, The Crucifer of Blood 1979, Captain Beaky Christmas Show 1981–82, The Tempest 1982, On the Rocks 1982, Amadeus 1983, La Cage aux Folles 1984–85, Jane Eyre 1986, Portraits 1987, The Royal Baccarat Scandal 1988, Henry VIII 1991, Aspects of Love 1992, Scrooge 1993–94, Monsieur Amilcar 1995, Brazilian Blue 1995, Family Matters 1998, All the World 2001, 2003, The Artisan's Angel (Ramazzini) (actor and dir) 2004. *Television includes:* The Six Wives of Henry VIII 1972, Keith Michell in Concert at Chichester 1974, Captain Beaky and His Band, Captain Beaky, Vol. 2, The Story of the Marlboroughs, Jacob and Joseph, The Story of David, The Tenth Month, The Day Christ Died, My Brother Tom 1987, Capt. James Cook 1988, Murder She Wrote (series) 1988, The Prince and the Pauper 1996. *Television/video:* The Gondoliers, The Pirates of Penzance, Ruddigore, The Six Wives of Henry VIII. *Films include:* Dangerous Exile, The Hell Fire Club, Seven Seas to Calais, The Executioner, House of Cards, Prudence and the Pill, Henry VIII and His Six Wives, Moments, The Deceivers. *Publications:* Shakespeare Sonnet series of lithographs 1974, Captain Beaky (illustrations for poems) 1975, Captain Beaky Vol. 2 1982, Alice in Wonderland 1982, Keith Michell's Practically Macrobiotic Cookbook 1987. *Leisure interests:* cooking, painting, writing. *Address:* c/o Curtis Brown, Haymarket House, 28-29 Haymarket, London, SW1Y 4SP, England. *Telephone:* (20) 7393-4400 (office).

MICHELL, Robert H., PhD, FRS, FMedSci; British biochemist and academic (retd); *Royal Society Research Professor, University of Birmingham;* b. 16 April 1941, Yeovil; s. of Rowland C. Michell and Elsie L. (Hall) Michell; m. 1st June Evans 1967 (divorced 1971); m. 2nd Esther Margaret Oppenheim 1992; two s. one d.; ed Crewkerne School, Univ. of Birmingham; Research Fellow, Univ. of Birmingham 1965–66, 1969–70, Harvard Medical School 1966–68; Lecturer, Univ. of Birmingham 1970–81, Sr Lecturer 1981–84, Reader 1984–86, Prof. of Biochemistry 1986–87, Royal Soc. Research Prof. 1987–; mem. European Molecular Biology Org. 1991, Council, Royal Soc. 1996–97; CIBA Medal, Biochemical Soc. 1988, Royal Soc. UK-Canada Rutherford Lecturer 1994, Biochemical Soc. Morton Lecturer 2002. *Publications include:* Membranes and their Cellular Functions (with J. B. Finean and R. Coleman) 1974, 1978, 1984, Membrane Structure (ed. with J. B. Finean) 1981, Inositol Lipids and Transmembrane Signalling (co-ed. with M. J. Berridge) 1988, Inositol Lipids in Cell Signalling (co-ed. with A. H. Drummond and C. P. Downes) 1989. *Leisure interests:* birdwatching, photography, modern literature, wildernesses. *Address:* School of Biosciences, University of Birmingham, Edgbaston, Birmingham, B12 2TT (office); 59 Weoley Park Road, Selly Oak, Birmingham, B29 6QZ, England (home). *Telephone:* (121) 414-5413 (office). *Fax:* (121) 414-5925 (office); (870) 137-7947. *E-mail:* r.h.michell@bham.ac.uk (office). *Website:* www.biosciences.bham.ac.uk (office).

MICHELS, Sir David Michael Charles, Kt; British leisure industry executive; *President, British Hospitality Association;* b. 1943; ed London Hotel School; various sales and marketing positions including Man.-Dir, Grand Metropolitan 1966–81; joined Ladbroke Group PLC 1981, Sales and Marketing Dir Ladbroke Hotels 1981–83, Man.-Dir Leisure Div. 1983–95,

Man.-Dir Ladbroke Hotels 1985–97; Sr Vice-Pres. of Sales and Marketing, Hilton Int. (following acquisition of Ladbroke Group by Hilton Group PLC 1987) 1987–89, Deputy Chair. Hilton UK and Exec. Vice-Pres. Hilton Int. 1989–91, CEO Stakis PLC 1991–99, apptd mem. Bd Hilton Group PLC 1999 (after acquisition of Stakis by Hilton Group), CEO 1999–2000, Group CEO 2000–06 (after reunification of Hilton International with Hilton Hotel Corpn); mem. Bd of Dirs British Land Co. PLC 2003–, easyJet plc 2006–, Strategic Hotels & Resorts 2006–, Sr Ind. Dir Marks and Spencer Group plc 2006–08, Deputy Chair. 2008–; Pres. British Hospitality Asscn 2006–; fmr Dir Arcadia Group PLC, Hilton Hotel Corpn –2006; fmr Pres. Hilton in the Community Foundation; Trustee Anne Frank Trust; Hon. Fellow, Acad. of Food & Wine Service 2003. *Address:* British Hospitality Association, Queens House, 55-56 Lincoln's Inn Fields, London, WC2A 3BH, England (office). *Telephone:* (0845) 880-7744 (office). *Fax:* (20) 7404-7799 (office). *E-mail:* info@bha.org.uk (office). *Website:* www.bha.org.uk (office).

MICHELSEN, Axel, DPhil; Danish biologist and academic; b. 1 March 1940, Haderslev; s. of Erik Michelsen and Vibeke Michelsen; m. Ulla West-Nielsen 1980 (died 2008); two s. one d.; ed Univ. of Copenhagen; Asst Prof. of Zoophysiology and Zoology, Univ. of Copenhagen 1963–72; Prof. of Biology, Odense Univ. 1973–2005; Chair. Danish Science Research Council 1975–78, Danish Nat. Cttee for Biophysics 1980–90, Danish Nat. Cttee for ICSU 1986–2000, 2004–06, Max-Planck Gesellschaft Fachbeirat 1977–81, Carlsberg Lab. 2003–; Dir Carlsberg Foundation 1986–, Centre for Sound Communication 1994–2003; mem. Royal Danish Acad. of Sciences and Letters, Akad. der Naturforscher Leopoldina, Academia Europaea; Corresp. mem. Akad. der Wissenschaften und der Literatur (Mainz), Bayerische Akad. der Wissenschaften, Akad. der Wissenschaften zu Göttingen; Kt, Order of Dannebrog (First Class) 1990; Alexander von Humboldt Prize 1990. *Publications:* The Physiology of the Locust Ear 1971, Sound and Life 1975, Time Resolution in Auditory Systems 1985, The Dance Language of Honeybees 1992. *Leisure interests:* wines, beekeeping, gardening. *Address:* Institute of Biology, University of Southern Denmark, Campusvej 55, 5230 Odense M (office); The Carlsberg Foundation, 35 H.C. Andersens Boulevard, 1553 Copenhagen V (office); Rosenvænget 74, 5250 Odense SV, Denmark (home). *Telephone:* 65-50-24-66 (Odense) (office); 33-43-53-63 (Copenhagen) (office); 61-26-35-82 (home); 66-11-75-68 (home). *Fax:* 65-93-04-57 (Odense) (office). *E-mail:* a.michelsen@biology.sdu.dk (office). *Website:* www.amichelsen-biology.sdu.dk (office); www.sdu.dk/ansat/a.michelsen.aspx (office); www.carlsbergfondet.dk (office).

MICHENER, Charles Duncan, BS, PhD, FAAS; American entomologist and academic; *Professor Emeritus of Entomology, University of Kansas;* b. 22 Sept. 1918, Pasadena, Calif.; s. of Harold and Josephine Rigden Michener; m. Mary Hastings 1940; three s. one d.; ed Univ. of California, Berkeley; Tech. Asst in Entomology, Univ. of Calif. 1939–42; Asst Curator, Lepidoptera and Hymenoptera, American Museum of Natural History, New York 1942–46, Assoc. Curator 1946–48, Research Assoc. 1949–; Curator, Snow Entomological Museum, Univ. of Kansas 1949–89, Dir 1974–83; Assoc. Prof. of Entomology, Univ. of Kansas 1948–49, Prof. 1949–89, Prof. Emer. 1989–, Chair. Dept of Entomology 1949–61, 1972–75, Watkins Dist Prof. of Entomology 1959–89, of Systematics and Ecology 1969–89; State Entomologist, S. Div. of Kansas 1949–61; Ed. Evolution 1962–64; American Ed. Insectes Sociaux (Paris), 1954–55, 1962–90; Assoc. Ed. Annual Review of Ecology and Systematics 1970–90; Pres. Soc. for the Study of Evolution 1967, Soc. of Systematic Zoology 1969, American Soc. of Naturalists 1978, Int. Union for the Study of Social Insects 1977–82 (Vice-Pres. Western Hemisphere Section 1979–80); mem. NAS, American Acad. of Arts and Sciences; Corresp. mem. Acad. Brasileira de Ciências; Guggenheim Fellow to Brazil 1955–56, Africa 1966–67; Fellow, Royal Entomological Soc. of London; Foreign Hon. mem. Russian Entomological Soc., Soc. of Systematic Biology, Netherlands Entomological Soc.; Morrison Prize, New York Acad. of Sciences 1943, Fulbright Scholar, Australia 1957–58, Founder's Award, American Entomological Soc. 1981, Thomas Say Award, Entomological Soc. of America 1997, C. V. Riley Award, Entomological Soc. of America 1999, Distinguished Research Medal, Int. Soc. of Hymenopterists 2002. *Publications:* Comparative External Morphology, Phylogeny and a Classification of the Bees (Hymenoptera) 1944, American Social Insects (with M. H. Michener) 1951, The Nest Architecture of the Sweat Bees (with S. F. Sakagami) 1962, A Classification of the Bees of the Australian and S. Pacific Regions 1965, The Social Behaviour of the Bees 1974, Kin Recognition in Animals (with D. Fletcher) 1987, The Bee Genera of North and Central America (with R. J. McGinley and B. N. Danforth) 1994, The Bees of the World 2000. *Leisure interests:* travel, field work. *Address:* Entomology Division, Natural History Museum, University of Kansas, PSB, 1501 Crestline Drive, Lawrence, KS 66045 (office); 1706 West 2nd Street, Lawrence, KS 66044, USA (home). *Telephone:* (785) 864-4610 (office); (785) 843-4598 (home). *Fax:* (785) 864-5260 (office). *E-mail:* michener@ku.edu (office).

MICHIE, David Alan Redpath, OBE, FRSA; British painter and academic; *Professor Emeritus of Painting, Heriot Watt University;* b. 30 Nov. 1928, St Raphael, France; s. of James Beattie Michie and Anne Redpath; m. Eileen Michie 1951 (died 2003); two d.; ed Hawick High School, Edinburgh Coll. of Art; Lecturer in Drawing and Painting, Gray's School of Art, Aberdeen 1957–61; Vice-Prin., Edinburgh Coll. of Art 1974–77, Head of School of Drawing and Painting 1982–90, Prof. of Painting 1988–90; Prof. Emer., Heriot Watt Univ. 1991–; Visiting Artist to Acad. of Fine Art, Belgrade 1979, to Art Studio Dept, Univ. of Calif. at Santa Barbara 1992; mem. Edinburgh Festival Soc. 1976–, Royal Scottish Acad. 1972, Royal Glasgow Inst. of Fine Art (RGI) 1983, Royal West of England Acad. (RWA) 1991–2000, Museums and Galleries Comm. 1991–96, Scottish Int. Trust 2004–; Founding Fellow, Inst. of Contemporary Scotland 2000; Guthrie Award, RSA 1964, David Cargill Award, R.G.I. 1977, Lothian Region Award 1977, Sir William Gillies Award,

RSA 1980, Glasgow City of Culture Award, RGI 1990, Cornelissen Prize, RWA 1992. *Leisure interest:* music. *Address:* 17 Gilmour Road, Edinburgh, EH16 5NS, Scotland (home). *Telephone:* (131) 667-2684 (home).

MICHNIK, Adam; Polish journalist and historian; *Editor-in-Chief, Gazeta Wyborcza;* b. 17 Oct. 1946, Warsaw; m.; one s.; ed Adam Mickiewicz Univ., Poznań; active in anti-communist movt 1965–80, spent six years in prison; Co-Founder and mem. Cttee for the Defence of Workers (KOR) 1976–80; Biuletyn Informacyjny, Krytyka, Zapis (ind. periodicals); activist Solidarity Self-governing Ind. Trade Union in the 1980s; imprisoned 1985–86; participant Round Table plenary debates 1989; Deputy to Sejm (Parl.) 1989–91; Ed.-in-Chief Gazeta Wyborcza (daily) 1989–; mem. Int. Advisory Bd, Council on Foreign Relations; Officer's Cross of Merit (Hungary) 1998, Bernardo O'Higgins Commdr's Order (Chile) 1999, Order for Contrib. to Polish-German Reconciliation, European Univ. Viadriana, Frankfurt 2000, Grand Prince Gedymin Order (Lithuania) 2001, Grand Cross of Merit (Germany) 2001; Dr hc (New School for Social Research, New York, Univ. of Minnesota, Univ. of Michigan, Connecticut Coll.); French Pen Club Freedom Award 1982, Robert F. Kennedy Human Rights Award 1986, Alfred Jurzykowski Foundation Award, La Vie Man of the Year 1989, Shofar Award 1991, Brucke-Preis (Germany) 1995, Award of the European Journalists Asscn 1995, Medal of Imre Nagy 1995, OSCE Prize in Journalism and Democracy 1996, The Golden Pen (Bauer Verlag) 1998, The Francisco Cerecedo Journalist Prize 1999, Int. Press Inst. Freedom Hero 2000, Carl Bertelsmann Prize 2001, Erasmus Prize 2001, Dan David Prize 2006. *Publications:* Cienie zapomnianych przodków (The Shadows of the Forgotten Ancestors) 1975, Kościół, Lewica, Dialog (Church, The Left, Dialogue) 1977, Penser la Pologne 1983, Szanse polskiej Demokracji (Chances for Polish Democracy) 1984, Z dziejów honoru w Polsce. Wypisy więzienne (From the History of Honour in Poland. Prison Notes) 1985, Takie czasy: Rzecz o kompromisie (Such Other Times: Concerning Compromise) 1985, Listy z Białołęki (Letters from Białołęka), Polskie pytania (Polish Questions) 1987, Druga faza rewolucji 1990, Między Panem a Plebanem 1995, Diabeł naszego czasu 1995, Letters From Freedom 1998, Confessions of a Converted Dissident – Essay for the Erasmus Prize 2001; many articles in Gazeta Wyborcza, Der Spiegel, Le Monde, Libération, El País, Lettre Internationale, New York Review of Books, The Washington Post and others. *Address:* Gazeta Wyborcza, ul. Czerska 8/10, 00-732 Warsaw, Poland (office). *Telephone:* (22) 5504000 (office); (22) 5554002 (office). *Fax:* (22) 8416920 (office). *E-mail:* contact@agora.pl (office).

MICHON, John Albertus, MSc, PhD; Dutch psychologist and academic; *Professor Emeritus of Psychonomics, Leiden University;* b. 29 Oct. 1935, Utrecht; s. of the late J. J. Michon and of S. Ch. A. de Ruyter; m. Hetty Sommer 1960; one s. one d. (deceased); ed Utrecht Mun. Gymnasium and Univs of Utrecht and Leiden; Research Assoc. Inst. for Perception, Soesterberg 1960–73, Head, Dept of Road User Studies 1969–73; Co-Founder, Netherlands Psychonomics Foundation 1968, Sec. 1968–72, Pres. 1975–80; Prof. of Experimental Psychology and Traffic Science, Univ. of Groningen 1971–92, Dir Inst. for Experimental Psychology 1971–92, Chair. Traffic Research Center 1977–92, Chair. Dept of Psychology 1978, 1983–92, Assoc. Dean, Faculty of Social Sciences 1983–86; mem. Bd Center for Behavioral, Cognitive and Neurosciences 1990–92, co-f. Dept of Cognitive Science 1990; Dir Netherlands Inst. for the Study of Criminality and Law Enforcement 1992–98; Prof. of Criminal Research, Leiden Univ. 1992–98, Sr Research Prof. of Psychonomics 1998–, now Emer. Prof.; Pres. Int. Soc. for the Study of Time 1983–86, now Hon. mem.; Co-Founder, mem. Bd European Soc. for Cognitive Psychology 1984–90; Vice-Chair. Nat. Council for Road Safety 1977–86; Ed.-in-Chief, Acta Psychologica 1971–74; Visiting Prof. Carnegie Mellon Univ., Pittsburgh, Pa 1986–87; Co-ordinator EEC DRIVE Project Generic Intelligent Driver Support 1988–92; Chair. Steering Cttee for the Cognitive Sciences, Netherlands Org. for Scientific Research NWO 2002–; mem. Royal Netherlands Acad. of Arts and Sciences 1981 (Chair. Behavioral and Social Sciences Section 1988–98, Chair. Accreditation Cttee Research Schools 2000–07); mem. Academia Europaea (London), European Acad. of Sciences and Arts (Salzburg), Social Sciences Council (SWR) 1994–2003; Kt, Order of the Dutch Lion 2002; Dr hc (Liège) 1995; NATO Science Fellowship 1965, NIAS Fellowship 1976, Honda Foundation Lecturing Award 1977, Medal of Honour, Netherlands Psychonomics Soc. 2005. *Publications:* Timing in Temporal Tracking 1967, Sociale Verkeerskunde 1976, Handboek der Psychonomie 1976, 1979, Beïnvloeding van Mobiliteit 1981, Time, Mind and Behaviour 1985, Guyau and the Idea of Time 1988, Handboek der Sociale Verkeerskunde 1989, Soar: A Cognitive Architecture in Perspective 1992, Generic Intelligent Driver Behaviour 1993, Nederlanders over Criminaliteit en Rechtshandhaving 1997; approx. 250 articles and chapters in scientific journals and books. *Leisure interests:* visual arts (painting, graphics), music (bassoon playing). *Address:* Department of Psychology, Leiden University, Wassenaarseweg 52, PO Box 9555, 2300 RB Leiden, Netherlands (office). *Telephone:* (71) 5274036 (office); (71) 5273630 (office). *E-mail:* michonja@xs4all.nl (home). *Website:* www.fsw.leidenuniv.nl (office); www.xs4all.nl/~michonja (home).

MICHOT, Yves Raoul; French aviation executive; b. 4 Nov. 1941, Nantes; s. of Raoul Michot and Lucienne Ruffel; m. Michèle Gouth 1964; two s. one d.; ed Ecole Polytechnique and Ecole Nationale Supérieure d'Aeronautique; Brétigny Flight Test Centre 1965–73; Govt Concorde Project Man. 1973–75; Tech. Adviser to Nat. Armament Dir 1975–78, to Minister of Defence 1978–80; Mirage 2000 Program Man., Ministry of Defence 1980–84; Mil. Programs Gen. Man. Aérospatiale 1984, Programs Gen. Man. 1985; Exec. Vice-Pres. Aérospatiale 1987, Exec. Vice-Pres. and COO 1989, Sr Exec. Vice-Pres. and COO and Pres. Aérospatiale 1995–99, Pres., Dir-Gen. 1996–99, Pres. Bd Dirs 1999; fmr Pres. European Asscn of Aerospace Industries (AECMA),; Pres. Club d'affaires franco-singapourien 1998–; Chair. Défense Conseil Int. –2007;

Pres. Descartes Prize Grand Jury 2001, 2002; Officier, Légion d'Honneur, Commdr, Ordre Nat. du Mérite, Médaille de l'Aéronautique. *Address:* 3 rue Chabrier, 78370 Plaisir, France (home).

MICKELSON, Philip (Phil), BS; American professional golfer; b. 16 June 1970, San Diego, Calif.; s. of Philip Mickelson and Mary Mickelson; m. Amy McBride 1996; one s. two d.; ed Arizona State Univ.; jr career won 34 San Diego County titles, three Nat. Collegiate Athletics Asscn (NCAA) Championships, three Jack Nicklaus Awards as Nat. Coll. Player of the Year, mem. Walker Cup team 1989, 1991, US Amateur Championships 1990, played in World Amateur Team Championship 1990, Tucson Chrysler Classic 1991; turned professional 1992; Professional Golf Asscn (PGA) titles Northern Telecom Open 1991 (last amateur player to win PGA event and first since 1985), 1995, 1996, Buick Invitational Calif. 1993, 2000, 2001, The International 1993, Mercedes Championships 1994, 1998, Phoenix Open 1996, GTE Byron Nelson Golf Classic 1996, NEC World Series of Golf 1996, Bay Hill Invitational 1997, Sprint International 1997, Pebble Beach Nat. Pro-Am, 1998, BellSouth Classic 2000, MasterCard Colonial 2000, The Tour Championship 2000, Canon Greater Hartford Open 2001, 2002, Bob Hope Chrysler Classic 2002, 2004, US Masters 2004, 2006, US PGA Championship 2005, Players Championship 2007, World Golf Championship–Calif. 2009; mem. Presidents Cup team 1994, 1996, 1998, 2000, 2003, Dunhill Cup team 1996, Ryder Cup team 1995, 1997, 1999, 2002 (postponed from 2001), 2004, 2008; scored 59, lowest score in professional strokeplay history, at Grand Slam of Golf in Hawaii 2004 (only achieved on three other occasions on PGA tour); sponsored the Special Operations Warrior Project 2004 to support US troops; Co-Chair. American Jr Golf Asscn; involved in golf course design; Golf World Amateur of the Year 1991, ESPY Award Best Championship Performance 2004, ESPY Award Best Male Golfer 2004,. *Leisure interests:* football, flying. *Address:* c/o Steve Loy, Gaylord Sports Management, 13845 North Northsight Blvd, Suite 200, Scottsdale, AZ 85260, USA (office). *E-mail:* sloy@gaylordsports.com (office). *Website:* www.gaylordsports.com (office); www.phil-mickelson.com (office).

MICKLETHWAIT, John; British journalist and writer; *Editor-in-Chief, The Economist;* ed Magdalen Coll., Oxford; fmrly with Chase Manhattan Bank; joined The Economist 1987, as Media Correspondent, then established Los Angeles office 1990–93, Ed. business section 1993–97, New York Bureau Chief 1997–99, US Ed. 1999–2006, Ed.-in-Chief 2006–; Harold Wincott Press Award for Young Financial Journalist 1989. *Publications:* The Witch Doctors (with Adrian Wooldridge) (Financial Times/Booz Allen Global Business Book Award 1997) 1996, A Future Perfect: The Challenge and Hidden Promise of Globalisation (with Adrian Wooldridge) 2000, The Company: A Short History of a Revolutionary Idea (with Adrian Wooldridge) 2003, The Right Nation (with Adrian Wooldridge) 2004, God is Black (with Adrian Wooldridge) 2009; contrib. articles to the New York Times, Los Angeles Times, Wall Street Journal, Guardian, Spectator and the New Statesman, Boston Globe. *Address:* The Economist, 25 St James's Street, London, SW1A 1HG, England (office). *Website:* www.economist.com (office).

MICOSSI, Stefano; Italian economist and international official; *Professor of European Integration, College of Europe, Bruges;* b. 27 Oct. 1946, Bologna; m. Daniela Zanotto; one s. one d.; ed Università Statale di Milano, Yale Univ., USA; economist, Bank of Italy Research Dept 1974–78, Head 1980–84, Asst Dir 1984–86, Dir Int. Div. 1986–88; seconded to IMF as Asst to Italy's Exec. Dir 1978–80; Dir of Econ. Research Confindustria (Confed. of Italian Industries) 1988–94; Prof. of Macroeconomic Policy Int. Free Univ. of Social Sciences 1989–94, Prof. of Monetary Theory and Policy 1993–94; Prof. of Int. Monetary Econs, Coll. of Europe, Bruges 1990–94, Prof. of European Integration 1999–; Dir-Gen. for Industry, EC 1994–99; Dir-Gen. Asscn of Italian Ltd Cos (ASSONIME) 1999–. *Publications:* Jt Ed. Adjustment and Integration in the World Economy 1992, The Italian Economy 1993, Inflation in Europe 1997 and books on the European Monetary System 1988, numerous articles in professional journals. *Address:* ASSONIME, Piazza Venezia 11, 00187 Rome, Italy.

MIĆUNOVIĆ, Branislav; Montenegrin theatre director and politician; *Minister of Culture, Sports and Media;* Prof. of Acting, Faculty of Dramatic Arts, Belgrade and Faculty of Dramatic Arts, Cetinje; fmr Theatre Dir at Yugoslav Drama Theatre, Belgrade, Serbian Nat. Theatre, Croatian Nat. Theatre, Nat. Theatre, Tuzla, Nat. Theatre, Nis, Zvezdara Theatre, Belgrade; directed works by Aleksandra Popovic, Velimir Lukic, Ljubomir Simovic, Veljko Radovic, Jordan Plevneša, Goran Stefanovskog, Iva Bresan, Gordan Mihic; Dir Montenegrin Nat. Theatre 2003–07; Minister of Culture, Sports and Media 2008–; mem. Cttee for the Arts Theatre, Montenegrin Acad. of Sciences and Arts. *Address:* Ministry of Culture, Sports and Media, 81000 Podgorica, Vuka Karadžića 3, Montenegro (office). *Telephone:* (81) 231561 (office). *Fax:* (81) 231540 (office). *E-mail:* min.kulture.rcg@cg.yu (office). *Website:* www.ministarstvokulture.vlada.cg.yu (office).

MIDDELHOEK, André, PhD; Dutch civil servant; b. 13 Dec. 1931, Voorburg; s. of J. Middelhoek; m. Trudy van den Broek 1982; two d.; ed Univ. of Amsterdam; Cen. Planning Office, Govt of Netherlands 1958–69, Deputy Dir 1966–69; lecturer, Int. Inst. for Social Studies, The Hague 1960–69; Dir-Gen. of the Budget, Ministry of Finance 1969–77; mem. Court of Auditors of European Communities 1977–93; Pres. European Court of Auditors 1993–96; Pres. Cttee of Wise Men 1999–; Commdr, Order of Netherlands Lion; Grand Croix, Couronne de Chêne (Luxembourg). *Publications:* publs on econs, econ. planning, public finance, policy analysis, EU finance and audit. *Leisure interests:* swimming, tennis, genealogy, hiking. *Address:* Marnixlaan 108, 3090 Overijse, Belgium (home). *Telephone:* (2) 687-55-53 (home). *Fax:* (2) 688-39-41 (home). *E-mail:* andremiddelhoek@heynet.be (home).

MIDDELHOFF, Thomas, MBA, PhD; German business executive; *Chairman, Polestar Group Ltd;* b. 11 May 1953, Düsseldorf; m.; five c.; ed Münster Univ., Univ. des Saarlandes; fmr Lecturer in Marketing, Univ. of Münster; Head of Sales and Marketing, Middelhoff GmbH (family-owned textile co.) 1983; Man. Asst to CEO, Mohndruck Graphische Betriebe GmbH 1986–87, Man. Dir 1989–90, Chair. of Man. Bd 1990; Man. Dir Elsnerdruck GmbH, Berlin 1987–88; mem. Bd responsible for multimedia, Bertelsmann publishing 1990–94, Head of Corp. Devt and Coordinator for Multimedia 1994–97, Chair. and CEO Bertelsmann AG 1998–2004; Partner, Investcorp International Ltd, currently Advisory Dir; Chair. Supervisory Bd, KarstadtQuelle AG 2004–05, of Bd of Man. 2005–, also Chair. Supervisory Bd Arcandor AG (new name for holding group 2007) 2004–, CEO 2005–; Chair. Thomas Cook Group PLC 2005–, Polestar Group Ltd 2004–06, 2007–, Moneybookers.com, London 2007–, Senator Entertainment AG 2006–; mem. Bd of Dirs New York Times Co., Apcoa Parking; Vernon A. Walters Award 1998. *Address:* Polestar Group Ltd, 1 Apex Business Park, Boscombe Road, Dunstable, Beds., LU5 4SB (office); Investcorp International Ltd, 48 Grosvenor Street, London, W1K 3HW, England (office). *Telephone:* (1582) 678900 (Polestar) (office); (20) 7629-6600 (Investcorp) (office). *Fax:* (1582) 678901 (Polestar) (office); (20) 7499-0371 (Investcorp) (office). *E-mail:* info@polestar-group.com (office); info@investcorp.com (office). *Website:* www.polestar-group.com (office); www.investcorp.com (office).

MIDDENDORF, J. William, II, BS, MBA; American fmr government official, diplomatist and business executive; b. 22 Sept. 1924, Baltimore, Md; s. of the late Henry Stump and Sarah Boone Middendorf; m. Isabelle J. Paine 1953; two s. two d.; ed Holy Cross Coll., Harvard Univ. and New York Grad. School of Business Admin; USN service during World War II; in Credit Dept of Bank of Manhattan Co. (now Chase Manhattan Bank) 1947–52; Analyst, Wood Struthers and Co. Inc. (brokerage firm), New York 1952–58, Pnr 1958–62; Sr Pnr Middendorf, Colgate and Co. (investment firm), New York 1962–69; US Amb. to Netherlands 1969–73; Under-Sec. of the Navy 1973–74, Sec. 1974–76; Pres. and CEO First American Bankshares, Washington, DC 1977–81; Pres. and CEO Middendorf & Co., Inc., Washington, DC 1989–, Chair. Middendorf SA 1989–; US Amb. to OAS 1981–85, to EC 1985–87; Chair. Presidential Task Force on Project Econ. Justice 1985–86; mem. Bd of Dirs and Sec.-Treasurer, Int. Republican Inst.; Trustee Heritage Foundation 1989–; numerous hon. degrees; State Dept Superior Honor Award 1974, Dept of Defense Distinguished Public Service Award 1975, 1976, USN Public Service Award 1976, Ludwig Von Mises Inst. Free Market Award 1985, Arleigh Burke Award 1998; numerous other awards; Grand Master of Order of Naval Merit (Brazil) 1974, Distinguished Service Medal (Brazil) 1976, Order of Arab Repub. of Egypt (Class A) 1979, Grand Officer of the Order of Orange Nassau, Netherlands 1985,. *Athletic achievements:* US Nat. Sculling Champion in Masters Div. 1979, won a world masters championship in rowing at the 1985 Toronto Masters Games. *Compositions:* has composed seven symphonies, an opera and numerous marches and concertos. *Publications:* Investment Policies of Fire and Casualty Insurance Companies. *Address:* 565 West Main Road, Little Compton, RI 02837, USA.

MIDDLEMAS, Robert Keith, DPhil, DLitt, FRSA; British historian and academic; *Professor Emeritus, University of Sussex;* b. 26 May 1935, Alnwick; s. of Robert James Middlemas and Eleanor Mary Middlemas (née Crane); m. Susan Mary Tremlett 1958; one s. three d.; ed Stowe School, Pembroke Coll., Cambridge; nat. service 2nd Lt Northumberland Fusiliers 1953–55; Clerk, House of Commons 1958–67; Lecturer in History, Univ. of Sussex 1967–76, Reader 1976–86, Prof. 1986–95, Prof. Emer. 1995–; Visiting Prof., Stanford Univ. and Hoover Inst. 1984, Univ. of Beijing 1989; Dir, ESL and Network Ltd 1998–, Chair. 2003–07; mem. UK Nat. Cttee UNESCO 1980–86, Co-Founder and Ed., Catalyst, A Journal of Public Debate 1985–87; Council mem., Research Cttee mem., Foundation for Mfg and Industry 1993–99; Consultant and mem. Advisory Bd, ESL and Network, SA 2000–09. *Publications:* The Master Builders 1963, The Clydesiders 1965, Baldwin (jtly) 1969, Diplomacy of Illusion 1972, Thomas Jones: Whitehall Diary (ed.) 1969–72, Cabora Bassa: Engineering and Politics 1975, Politics in Industrial Society 1979, Power and the Party: Communism in Western Europe 1980, Industry, Unions and Government 1984, Power, Competition and the State (three vols) 1986–91, Orchestrating Europe: Informal Politics of the Community Since 1973 1995, Kinship and Survival 2009. *Leisure interests:* rifle shooting (UK nat. team, Canada 1958), sailing, fishing, landscape gardening, building follies. *Address:* West Burton House, West Burton, Pulborough, West Sussex, RH20 1HD, England (home). *Telephone:* (1798) 831516 (home). *Fax:* (1798) 831040 (home).

MIDDLETON, (John) Christopher, MA, DPhil; British academic; *David J. Bruton Centennial Professor Emeritus of Modern Languages, University of Texas;* b. 10 June 1926, Truro; s. of Hubert S. Middleton and Dorothy M. Miller; m. 1953 (divorced); one s. two d.; ed Felsted School and Merton Coll. Oxford; Lektor in English, Univ. of Zürich 1952–55; Asst Lecturer in German, King's Coll. Univ. of London 1955–57, Lecturer 1957–66; Prof. of Germanic Languages and Literature Univ. of Texas 1966–98, David J. Bruton Centennial Emer. Prof. 1998–; Sir Geoffrey Faber Memorial Prize 1964, Guggenheim Poetry Fellowship 1974–75, Nat. Endowment for Humanities Poetry Fellowship 1980, Tieck-Schlegel Trans Prize 1985, Max Geilinger Stiftung Prize 1987, Soeurette Diehl Fraser Award for Trans, Texas Inst. of Letters 1993, Camargo Foundation Fellow 1999. *Publications:* Torse 3, poems 1948–61 1962, Nonsequences/Selfpoems 1965, Our Flowers and Nice Bones 1969, The Lonely Suppers of W.V. Balloon 1975, Carminalenia 1980, 111 Poems 1983, Two-Horse Wagon Going By 1986, Selected Writings 1989, The Balcony Tree 1992, Some Dogs 1993, Andalusian Poems 1993, Intimate Chronicles 1996, The Swallow Diver 1997, Twenty Tropes for Doctor Dark 2000, The Word Pavilion and Selected Poems 2001, Of the Mortal Fire 2003, The Anti-Basilisk 2005, The Tenor on Horseback 2007, Collected Poems 2008; prose: Pataxanadu and Other Prose 1977, Serpentine 1985, In the Mirror of the Eighth King 1999, Crypto-Topographia 2002; trans: Ohne Hass und Fahne (with W. Deppe and H. Schönherr) 1958, Modern German Poetry 1910–60 (with M. Hamburger) 1962, Germany Writing Today 1967, Selected Poems, by Georg Trakl 1968, Selected Letters, by Friedrich Nietzsche 1969, Selected Poems, by Friedrich Hölderlin and Eduard Mörike 1972, Selected Poems of Goethe 1983, Slected Stories, by Robert Walser 1983, Andalusian Poems (with Leticia Garza-Falcón) 1993, Faint Harps and Silver Voices: Selected Translations 2000; essays and other writings. *Address:* 1112 W 11th Street, Apt 201, Austin, TX 78703 (home); Department of Germanic Studies, University of Texas, Austin, TX 78712, USA (office). *Telephone:* (512) 471-4123 (office). *Website:* www.utexas.edu/depts/german/faculty/middleton.html (office).

MIDDLETON, Peter, BA; British business executive and diplomatist; b. 10 Feb. 1940; s. of Roy Middleton and Freda Middleton; m. 1st Yvonne Summerson 1968 (divorced 1996); two s. one d.; m. 2nd Anita Mehra 1996; ed Univ. of the Sorbonne, Paris and Univ. of Hull; joined a monastery, Paignton, Devon; joined the Foreign Service, two-year posts in both Indonesia and Tanzania 1969–77; Sr Embassy Counsellor Paris 1977–82; joined Midland Bank 1985, Midland Int. 1985–87; with Thomas Cook 1987–92; CEO Lloyd's of London (Insurance) 1992–95; Chief Exec. Salomon Bros Int. 1995–98; Chair. London Luton Airport 1999–2000; Transaction Dir Nomura Int. PLC 2000–; Chair. Football League 1998–2000; Chief Exec. World Professional Billiards and Snooker Asscn 1999–2000; Chair. Dome Europe 2000–; Hon. LLD (Teesside) 1997. *Leisure interests:* music, horse-racing, soccer. *Address:* Nomura International PLC, Nomura House, 1 St Martin's-le-Grand, London, EC1A 4NP, England (office).

MIDDLETON, Sir Peter Edward, GCB, MA; British business executive and fmr civil servant; *Chairman, Camelot Group;* b. 2 April 1934; m. 1st Valerie Ann Lindup 1964 (died 1987); one s. (deceased) one d.; m. 2nd Connie Owen 1990; ed Sheffield City Grammar School, Univs of Sheffield and Bristol; Sr Information Officer, HM Treasury 1962, Prin. 1964, Asst Dir, Centre for Admin. Studies 1967–69, Pvt. Sec. to Chancellor of Exchequer 1969–72, Treasury Press Sec. 1972–75, Head, Monetary Policy Div. 1975, Under-Sec. 1976, Deputy Sec. 1980–83, Perm. Sec. 1983–91; Deputy Chair., Barclays Group 1991–98, Chair. 1999–2004, Chair., BZW Div. 1991–98; Chair., Sheffield Urban Regeneration Co. Ltd 2001–06; mem. Council Univ. of Sheffield 1991–, Pro-Chancellor 1997–99, Chancellor 1999–; mem. Bd United Utilities Group PLC 1994–2007, Vice-Chair. 1998–99, Chair. 1999–2000, Deputy Chair. 2000–07; non-exec. mem. Bd Bass PLC/Six Continents 1992–2001, Dir 1992–2001, General Accident Fire and Life Assurance Corpn PLC (now CGU PLC) 1992–98; Chair., Camelot Group 2004–; Chair., Marsh & McLennan UK 2005–; Chair., Reyniers & Co.; Sr Adviser, Fenchurch Advisory Pnrs 2005–; mem. Council Manchester Business School 1985–92; Gov. London Business School 1984–90, Ditchley Foundation 1985–; mem. Nat. Econ. Research Asscn 1991–2008; Chair. Inst. of Contemporary History 1993–2001, Dir 2001–; Chair. Centre for Effective Dispute Resolution 2004–; Pres. British Bankers' Asscn 2004–06; mem. Financial Reporting Council 1997–98; Dir Int. Monetary Conf. 2001–02; Vice-Chair. Bankers Benevolent Fund 2005–; Chair. Creative Sheffield 2006–; Chair. Bridge Int. Trust 2008–; Chair. Burford Advisors LLP 2008–; Chair. European Asscn for Banking & Financial History 2008; Visiting Fellow, Nuffield Coll., Oxford 1981–89; Hon. DLitt (Sheffield) 1984. *Leisure interests:* music, walking, outdoor sports. *Address:* Camelot Group plc, Tolpits Lane, Watford, Herts., WD18 9RN, England (office). *Telephone:* (1923) 425000 (office). *Website:* www.camelotgroup.co.uk (office).

MIDDLETON, Stanley, BA, MEd, FRSL; British writer and schoolteacher (retd); b. 1 Aug. 1919, Bulwell, Nottingham; s. of Thomas Middleton and Elizabeth Ann Middleton (née Burdett); m. Margaret Shirley Charnley (née Welch) 1951; two d.; ed Bulwell St Mary's School, Bulwell Highbury School, High Pavement School, Nottingham, Nottingham Univ. Coll., Univ. of Nottingham; fmr English teacher; fmr Head of English High Pavement Coll., Nottingham, retd 1981; Judith Wilson Fellow Emmanuel Coll., Cambridge 1982–83; Hon. MA (Nottingham) 1975, Hon. MUniv (Open) 1995, Hon. DLitt (De Montfort) 1998, (Nottingham Trent) 2000. *Radio Plays include:* The Captain from Nottingham (BBC), A Little Music at Night (BBC). *Publications:* A Short Answer 1958, Harris's Requiem 1960, A Serious Woman 1961, The Just Exchange 1962, Two's Company 1963, Him They Compelled 1964, The Golden Evening 1968, Wages of Virtue 1969, Brazen Prison 1971, Holiday (Booker Prize) 1974, Still Waters 1976, Two Brothers 1978, In a Strange Land 1979, The Other Side 1980, Blind Understanding 1982, Entry into Jerusalem 1983, The Daysman 1984, Valley of Decision 1985, An After Dinner's Sleep 1986, After a Fashion 1987, Recovery 1988, Vacant Places 1989, Changes & Chances 1990, Beginning to End 1991, A Place to Stand 1992, Married Past Redemption 1993, Catalysts 1994, Toward the Sea 1995, Live and Learn 1996, Brief Hours 1997, Against the Dark 1997, Necessary Ends 1999, Small Change 2000, Love in the Provinces 2002, Brief Garlands 2004, Sterner Stuff 2005, Mother's Boy 2006, Her Three Wise Men 2008. *Leisure interests:* music, painting. *Address:* 42 Caledon Road, Sherwood, Nottingham, NG5 2NG, England. *Telephone:* (115) 962-3085.

MIDLER, Bette; American singer, entertainer and actress; b. 1 Dec. 1945, Honolulu; m. Martin von Haselberg 1984; one d.; ed Univ. of Hawaii; début as actress in film Hawaii 1965; mem. of cast in Fiddler on the Roof, New York 1966–69, Salvation, New York 1970, Tommy, Seattle Opera Co. 1971; nightclub concert performer 1972–; After Dark Ruby Award 1973, Grammy Award 1973, Special Tony Award 1973, Emmy Award 1978. *Film appearances include:* The Rose (two Golden Globe Awards) 1979, Jinxed 1982, Down and Out in Beverly Hills 1986, Ruthless People 1986, Outrageous Fortune 1987, Big Business 1988, Beaches 1989, Stella 1990, For The Boys (Golden Globe Award) 1991, Hocus Pocus 1993, Gypsy (TV), The First Wives Club 1996, That Old Feeling 1997, Get Bruce 1999, Isn't She Great? 1999, Drowning Mona 2000, What Women Want 2001, Stepford Wives 2004, Then She Found Me 2007, The Women 2008. *Recordings include:* The Divine Miss M. 1973, Bette Midler 1973, Broken Blossom 1977, Live at Last 1977, Thighs and Whispers 1979, New Depression 1979, Divine Madness 1980, No Frills 1984, Some People's Lives 1991, Best Of 1993, Bette of Roses 1995, Experience the Divine 1997, Bathhouse Betty 1998, From a Distance 1998, Bette 2000. *Television includes:* The Tonight Show (Emmy Award) 1992, Gypsy 1993, Seinfeld 1996, Diva Las Vegas 1997, Murphy Brown 1998. *Publications:* A View From A Broad 1980, The Saga of Baby Divine 1983. *Address:* c/o All Girl Productions, 100 Universal City Plaza, Universal City, CA 91608 (office); c/o Warner Bros. Records, 3300 Warner Boulevard, Burbank, CA 91505, USA. *Fax:* (818) 866-5871.

MIDORI; Japanese violinist; b. 25 Oct. 1971, Osaka; d. of Setsu Goto; ed Professional Children's School, Juilliard School of Music, NY Univ.; began violin studies with mother aged four; moved to USA 1982; début with New York Philharmonic 1982; recording début 1986 aged 14; now makes worldwide concert appearances; founder and Pres. Midori and Friends (foundation) 1992; Dorothy B. Chandler Performing Arts Award, New York State Asian-American Heritage Month Award, Crystal Award (Japan), Suntory Award 1994. *Leisure interests:* cooking, reading, listening to music, art. *Address:* c/o Intermusica Artists Management Ltd, 16 Duncan Terrace, London, N1 8BZ, England (office); Opus 3 Artists, 470 Park Avenue South, 9th Floor North, New York, NY 10016, USA (office); c/o Midori and Friends, 850 Seventh Avenue, Suite 1103, New York, NY 10019 (office). *Telephone:* (20) 7278-5455 (office); (212) 584-7500 (office). *Fax:* (20) 7278-8434 (office); (646) 300-8200 (office). *E-mail:* mail@intermusica.co.uk (office); info@opus3artists.com (office); violin@gotomidori.com. *Website:* www.intermusica.co.uk (office); www.opus3artists.com (office); www.gotomidori.com; www.midoriandfriends.org.

MIDWINTER, John Edwin, OBE, PhD, DSc, FRS, FREng, FIEE, FIEEE, FInstP; British professor of optoelectronics (retd); b. 8 March 1938, Newbury, Berks.; s. of the late H.C. Midwinter and of V.J. (née Rawlinson) Midwinter; m. Maureen A. Holt 1961; two s. two d.; ed King's Coll., London; Sr Scientific Officer, Royal Radar Establishment 1967–68; Sr Research Physicist, Perkin-Elmer Corpn, USA 1968–70; Head, Fibre Optic Devt, British Telecom Research Labs 1971–77, Head Optical Communications Technology 1977–84; British Telecom Prof. of Optoelectronics, Univ. Coll., London 1984–91, Head, Dept of Electronic and Electrical Eng 1988–98, Pender Prof. of Electronic Eng 1991–2004, Vice-Provost 1994–99, Dir Univ. Coll., London Adastral Park Campus 2000–03; Vice-Pres. IEE 1994, Deputy Pres. 1998–2000, Pres. 2000–01; Dir Young Engineers 2004–05; Hon. DSc (Nottingham) 2000, (Loughborough) 2001, (Queen Univ. Belfast) 2004; IEE-J.J. Thompson Medal 1987, Faraday Medal 1997, IEEE Eric Sumner Award and Medal 2002. *Publications:* Applied Non-Linear Optics 1972, Optical Fibers for Transmission 1977; over 200 papers on lasers, non-linear optics and optical communications. *Leisure interests:* walking, skiing, writing.

MIELI, Paolo; Italian journalist; *Director, Corriere della Sera;* b. 25 Feb. 1949, Milan; two s.; ed classical lycée, La Sapienza Univ., Rome; Asst to Chair of History of Political Parties, Univ. of Rome; Corresp., Political Commentator at Home, Head of Cultural Desk and then Cen. Man. Ed., Espresso (weekly) 1967–85; worked for La Repubblica 1985–86; Leader Writer, La Stampa 1986–90, Ed.-in-Chief 1990–92; Ed. Corriere della Sera 1992–97, Dir 2004–; apptd Pres. RAI (Radiotelevisione Italiana) March 2003 (resgnd after five days); Prof. of Contemporary History, Univ. of Milan; mem. Bd Govs Storia Illustrata, Pagina and has collaborated with Tempi Moderni, Questi Istituzioni, Mondo operaio; Premio Spoleto 1990; Premio Mediterraneo 1991, Premio Alfio Russo 1995. *Publications:* Litigo a Sinistra, Il Socialismo Diviso, Storia del Partito Socialista Negli Anni della Repubblica, Le Storie – La Storia 1999, Storia e Politica: Risorgimento, fascismo e comunismo 2001, La goccia cinese 2002. *Leisure interests:* ancient history, skiing. *Address:* Corriere della Sera, Via Solferino 28, 20121 Milan (office); Via Medaglie d'Oro 391, 00136 Rome, Italy (home). *Telephone:* (02) 2827979 (office). *Fax:* (02) 29009705 (office). *E-mail:* pmieli@corriere.it (office).

MIERS, Sir David, KBE, CMG, MA; British diplomatist (retd); b. 10 Jan. 1937, Liverpool; s. of the late Col R. Miers, DSO and Honor Bucknill; m. Imelda Wouters 1966; two s. one d.; ed Winchester Coll. and Univ. Coll., Oxford; joined diplomatic service 1961; served Tokyo 1963, Vientiane 1966, Paris 1972, Tehran 1977, Beirut 1983; Asst Under-Sec. FCO 1986; Amb. to Greece 1989–93; to Netherlands 1993–96; Chair. Soc. of Pension Consultants 1998–, British-Lebanese Asscn 1998–, Anglo-Hellenic League 1999–. *Leisure interest:* open air.

MIERZEJEWSKI, Jerzy; Polish painter and academic; b. 13 July 1917, Kraków; s. of Jacek Mierzejewski and Stanisława Brzezińska; m. Krystyna Szner (died 1994), one s. one d.; ed Acad. of Fine Arts, Warsaw; Lecturer and Prof. State Film School, Łódź; fmr Dean Film Photography Dept and Film Directory Dept, fmr Rector; fmr Pres. Union of Polish Artists and Designers, State Film School, Łódź; works in perm. collections Nat. Museum, Warsaw, Muzeum Sztuki, Łódź, Stedelijk Museum, Amsterdam and in numerous pvt. collections; Kt's Cross of Polonia Restituta Order 1975; Minister of Culture and Art Prize (II Class) 1963, Grant-Pollok-Krasner Foundation Award 1992, 1996, Jan Cybis Award 1997, Golden Frog, Int. Film Festival of the Art of Cinematography Camerimage 1997. *Films include:* Jan Matejko 1954, Jacek Mierzejewski 1968. *Paintings include:* My Brother 1985, Garden 1986, Lake 1992, Hospital 1992, Double Landscape 1995, Brunch 1998, Studio X 1998, Sielanka 1999, Pilgrim 2000, The Moment 2001, Friend 2002. *Exhibitions include:* 30 one-man exhbns; group exhbns include Selective Eye, Crown Town Gallery, Los Angeles 1970. *Publications include:* Composition of Film Picture

1955, Some Aspects of Continuity of Film 1963. *Address:* ul. Śmiała 63, 01-526 Warsaw, Poland (home). *Telephone:* (22) 8392243 (home).

MIFSUD BONNICI, Carmelo (Carm), LLD; Maltese lawyer, politician and academic; *Minister for Justice and Home Affairs;* b. 17 Feb. 1960, Floriana; s. of fmr Pres. Ugo Mifsud Bonnici; m. Sandra Gatt; three s.; ed St Aloysius' Coll., Birkirkara, De La Salle Coll., Cottonera, Univ. of Malta; practised in criminal, civil and commercial fields; Sr Lecturer in Roman Law, Univ. of Malta; Pres. MKSU as a univ. student; active in Partit Nazzjonalista (Nationalist Party) Youth Movt (MZPN) 1982–, held several posts in Exec.; mem. Parl. 1998–, perm. mem. several cttees, including Privileges and Laws; mem. Malta Environment and Planning Authority 2001–03; Parl. Sec., Ministry for Justice and Home Affairs 2003–08; Minister for Justice and Home Affairs 2008–. *Publications:* Zewg Minuti Flimkien 1998 Il-Principji Hemm Jibqghu 2003. *Address:* Ministry for Justice and Home Affairs, Auberge D'Aragon, Independence Square, Valletta VLT 2000, Malta (office). *Telephone:* 22957000 (office). *Fax:* 22957348 (office). *E-mail:* mjha@gov.mt (office). *Website:* www.mjha.gov.mt (office).

MIFSUD BONNICI, Ugo, BA, LLD; Maltese politician, lawyer and fmr head of state; *Member, Council of Europe Commission for Democracy Through Law (Venice Commission);* b. 8 Nov. 1932, Cospicua; s. of Carmelo Mifsud Bonnici and Maria Mifsud Bonnici (née Ross); m. Gemma Bianco; two s. one d.; ed Royal Univ. of Malta; practising lawyer 1955–87; mem. Parl. 1966–94; Opposition Spokesman for Educ. 1972–87; Pres. Gen. Council and Admin. Council of Nationalist Party 1977–87; Minister of Educ. 1987, of Educ. and Interior 1990–92, of Educ. and Human Resources 1992–94, Pres. of Malta 1994–99; currently Lecturer on History of Law and Human Rights, Univ. of Malta, also Lecturer on Comparative Law, Int. Maritime Law Inst.; Chair. Cttee of Guarantee under the Law for the Protection of the Cultural Heritage; mem. Council of Europe Comm. for Democracy Through Law (Venice Comm.) 2002–; Hon. DLitt (Univ. of Malta) 1995, (Univ. of Paris IV) 1999. *Publications:* Biex il-futur jerga' jibda 1976, Il-linja t-tajba 1981, Biex il-futur rega' beda 1992, Il-Manwal tal-President 1997, Kif Sirna Republika 1999, Introduction to Comparative Law 2004; newspaper articles. *Address:* c/o Venice Commission, Council of Europe, 67075 Strasbourg Cedex, France; 18 Erin Serracino Inglott Road, Cospicua, Malta (home). *Telephone:* 826975 (home). *E-mail:* ugomb@maltanet.net (home). *Website:* www.venice.coe.int.

MIGAŠ, Jozef, DPhil, CSc; Slovak politician; b. 7 Jan. 1954, Pušovce; m. Alena Migašová; one s. one d.; ed Univ. of Kiev; fmrly with Acad. of Sciences, Košice, Political Univ., Bratislava; f. Party of the Democratic Left, Chair. 1996–2001; diplomatist 1993–96; Chair. Nat. Council of the Slovak Repub. 1998–2002. *Address:* c/o National Council of the Slovak Republic, na'meste A. Dubčeka 1, 812 80 Bratislava (office); c/o Office of the Government of the Slovak Republic, nám. Slobody 1, 813 70 Bratislava 1, Slovakia. *Telephone:* (7) 593-41-201 (office); (7) 593-41-111. *Fax:* (7) 544-15-460 (office). *E-mail:* migajoze@nrsr.sk (office). *Website:* www.nrsr.sk (office).

MIGIRO, Asha-Rose Mtengeti, LLB, LLM, PhD; Tanzanian lawyer, politician, academic and UN official; *Deputy Secretary-General, United Nations;* b. 9 July 1956, Songea; m. Prof. Cleophas Migiro; two d.; ed Univ. of Dar-es-Salaam, Univ. of Konstanz, Germany; Head, Dept of Constitutional and Admin. Law, Univ. of Dar-es-Salaam 1992–94, fmr Sr Lecturer, Faculty of Law; mem. Parl. (Chama Cha Mapinduzi party); Minister of Community Devt, Gender and Children's Affairs 2000–06, of Foreign Affairs and Int. Co-operation 2006–07; Deputy Sec.-Gen. UN 2007–. *Address:* Office of the Deputy Secretary-General, United Nations, United Nations Plaza, New York, NY 10017 USA (office). *Telephone:* (212) 963-1234 (office). *Fax:* (212) 963-4879 (office). *Website:* www.un.org (home).

MIGNON, Emmanuelle; French civil servant; b. 1968; ed École supérieure des sciences économiques et commerciales, Institut d'études politiques de Paris, École nationale d'administration; OSCE electoral observer, Bosnia and Herzegovina 1997; adviser to Minister of the Interior, Nicolas Sarkozy 2002–04; Educ. Dir, Union pour un Mouvement Populaire (UMP) 2004–06; Chief of Staff, Office of the Pres. 2007–08; adviser to the Pres. 2008–; Pres., Chambord Admin. Council 2007–; Nat. Commr, Scouts Unitaires de France 1990–. *Address:* Palais de l'Elysée, 55 rue du faubourg Saint-Honoré, 75008 Paris, France (office). *Telephone:* 1-42-92-81-00 (office). *E-mail:* emignon@u-m-p.org (office). *Website:* www.elysee.fr (office).

MIGRANYAN, Andranik Movsesovich, CandHisSc; Russian/Armenian civil servant; *Professor, Moscow Institute of International Relations;* b. 10 Feb. 1949, Yerevan; m.; one d.; ed Moscow State Inst. of Int. Relations, Inst. of Int. Workers' Movt USSR Acad. of Sciences; teacher, Prof. Moscow Inst. of Automobile Construction 1976–85; leading researcher Inst. of Econ. and Political Studies Acad. of Sciences 1985–88; Head Cen. for Studies of Social-Political Problems and Interstate Relations of CIS 1992–93; mem. Pres.'s Council 1993–; Chief Expert Cttee on CIS countries of State Duma 1993–96; Chair. Bd Scientific Council on CIS Countries; Prof. Moscow State Inst. of Int. Relations (MGIMO) 1994–; co-f. Politika Fund; Vice-Pres. Reforma Fund. *Address:* Reforma Fund, Staromonetny per.10, 109180 Moscow (office); MGIMO, Vernadskogo prosp. 76, 117454, Moscow, Russia (office). *Telephone:* (095) 433-34-95.

MÍGUEZ BONINO, Rev. José, PhD; Argentine professor of theology, clergyman and international church official; *Professor Emeritus, Protestant Institute for Higher Theological Studies;* b. 5 March 1924, Santa Fé; s. of José Míguez Gándara and Augustina Bonino; m. Noemi Nieuwenhuize 1947; three s.; ed Facultad Evangélica de Teología, Emory Univ., Union Theological Seminary, New York; Methodist minister in Bolivia, later in Argentina 1945–; Prof. of Theology, Facultad Evangélica de Teología, Buenos Aires 1954–70, Rector 1960–70; Prof. of Systematic Theology and Ethics, Protestant Inst. for Higher Theological Studies, Buenos Aires 1970–86, Prof. Emer. 1986–, Dean of Post-Graduate Studies 1973–86; mem. Cen. Cttee of World Council of Churches (WCC) 1968–75, a Pres. Presidium of WCC 1976–82; Visiting Prof., Facoltà Valdese di Teologia, Rome 1963, Union Theological Seminary, New York 1967–68, Selly Oak Coll., Birmingham, UK 1974, Faculté de Théologie Protestante, Strasbourg Univ. 1981, Harvard Univ. 2001–02; Observer at II Vatican Council 1962–64; Pres. Perm. Ass. for Human Rights (APDH), Argentina; mem. Nat. Constitutional Ass. 1994–, Nuremberg Human Rights Award Jury 1995–99; Hon. PhD (Candler School of Theol., Free Univ. of Amsterdam 1980); Hon. DD (Aberdeen) 1987. *Publications:* Concilio abierto 1968, Integración humana y unidad cristiana 1968, Ama y haz lo que quieras 1972, Theology in a Revolutionary Situation (trans. in Dutch, German, Italian) 1975, Espacio para ser hombres 1975, Christians and Marxists 1976, Toward a Christian Political Ethic 1983, Rostros del Protestantismo en América Latina 1996; articles in Concilium, Expository Times, Evangelische Kommentare, Evangelio y Poder: poder del evangelio y poder político, Teología y Economía 2003. *Leisure interests:* swimming, playing tennis. *Address:* Camacuá 252, 1406 Buenos Aires (office); F. Madero 591, 1706 V. Sarmiento (Haedo) Rov., Buenos Aires, Argentina (home). *Telephone:* (1) 4654-2184 (home). *Fax:* (11) 4656-4239 (office). *E-mail:* jmiguez@arnet.com.ar (home).

MIHAJLOV, Mihajlo; Serbian author, scholar and human rights administrator; b. 26 Sept. 1934, Pančevo; s. of Nicholas Mihajlov and Vera Daniloff; ed High School, Sarajevo and Zagreb Univ.; served in armed forces 1961–62; freelance writer and trans., magazines, newspapers and radio 1962–63; Asst Prof. of Modern Russian Literature, Zagreb Univ. 1963–65; freelance writer, western press 1965–66, 1970–74; imprisoned 1966–70, 1974–77; lectures, USA, Europe and Asia 1978–79; Visiting Lecturer, Yale Univ. 1981; Visiting Prof. of Russian Literature and Philosophy, Univ. of Virginia 1982–83; Visiting Prof. Ohio State Univ. 1983–84, Univ. of Siegen 1984, Univ. of Glasgow 1985; Commentator on Ideological Matters, Radio Free Europe/Radio Liberty Inc. 1986; Sr Fellow, Program on Transitions to Democracy, Elliott School of Int. Affairs, George Washington Univ. 1994–99, Adjunct Fellow, Hudson Inst. 1999; Vice-Pres. Democracy Int.; Chair. Democracy Int. Comm. to Aid Democratic Dissidents in Yugoslavia 1990; mem. Editorial Bd int. magazine Kontinent 1975–84, Tribuna Magazine, Paris and Forum Magazine, Munich, Contributing Ed. Religion in Communist Dominated Areas, New York; mem. Int. PEN (French br. 1977, American 1982); mem. Int. Helsinki Group, Cttee for the Free World; mem. Bd Int. Gesellschaft für Menschenrechte 1982–, Bd of Consultants, Centre for Appeals for Freedom 1980, Nat. Cttee of Social Democrats USA 1989, Advisory Bd CAUSA Int. 1986; Special Analyst for Intellectual and Ideological Events in the Soviet Union and Eastern Europe, Research Div. of Radio Free Europe 1985–86; Fellow, Nat. Humanities Cen.; Trustee, World Constitution and Parl. Asscn 1982–; Int. League for Human Rights Award 1978, Council against Communist Aggression Award 1975, 1978, Ford Foundation Award for the Humanities 1980. *Publications:* Moscow Summer 1965, Russian Themes 1968, Underground Notes 1976, 1982, Unscientific Thoughts 1979, 2004, Planetary Consciousness 1982, Djilas versus Marx 1990, Homeland is Freedom 1994; hundreds of articles in newspapers, magazines and scholarly books (weekly column in Belgrade daily Borba (renamed Nasa Borba 1995) 1990–). *Leisure interests:* classical music, motoring. *Address:* Obilićev Venac 6, Stan 5, 11000 Belgrade, Serbia (home). *Telephone:* (11) 303-3218 (home). *E-mail:* mishamih@yahoo.com (home).

MIHAJLOVIĆ, Svetozar; Bosnia and Herzegovina politician; fmr Vice-Pres. of Serb Repub. of Bosnia and Herzegovina; co-Prime Minister of Bosnia and Herzegovina 1999–2000; Minister for Civil Affairs and Communications 2001–03. *Address:* c/o Ministry for Civil Affairs and Communications, Vojvode Putnika 3, 71000 Sarajevo, Bosnia and Herzegovina (office).

MIHÓK, Peter, PhD; Slovak business administrator and fmr diplomatist; *President, Slovak Chamber of Commerce and Industry;* b. 18 Jan. 1948, Topoľčianky; s. of Augustin Mihók and Johanna Mihoková; m. Elena Škulová 1971; two d.; ed Econ. Univ., Bratislava; with Czechoslovak Chamber of Commerce 1971–78; Commercial Counsellor, Embassy, Morocco 1978–82; Dir Foreign Relations Dept; Incheba (Foreign Trade Co.) 1982–90; Dir Foreign Dept, Office of Govt of Slovakia 1990–91; Vice-Pres. Czechoslovak Chamber of Commerce and Industry (CCI) 1991–92; Dir Int. Politics Dept, Ministry of Foreign Affairs of Slovakia 1991; Plenipotentiary of Govt of Slovakia in EU, Head Negotiator in Brussels 1991–94; Pres. Slovak CCI 1992–; Vice-Chair. Supervisory Bd Heineken Slovakia 1998–, Globtel Orange Bratislava 2001–; Vice-Chair. World Chamber Fed. Paris 2001–; Pres. Ecosoc Slovakia 2000–; Deputy Pres. Eurochambers 2001–; mem. Supervisory Bd Incheba a.s. Bratislava 1999–, Chair. 2004–; mem. Presidency, European Econ. and Social Cttee, Brussels 2004–; mem. Advisory Body to Pres. of Slovakia; mem. Econ. Council of Govt of Slovakia, Chair. Govt Pricing Cttee; mem. Council Slovak Electricity Works; Vice-Chair. Omnia Group, Kooperativa; mem. Scientific Council, Econ. Univ. Bratislava; Gold Medal of Hungarian CCI 1999, Officer, Order of Léopold II, Belgium 1995, Officier Ordre du Mérite, France 1996, Prominent of Economy, Slovakia 1997, Great Silver Order, Austria 1998, Commendatore Ordine, Stella della Solidarita Italiana 2003, Gold Medal, House of Europe 2003. *Publication:* Advertising in the Market Economy. *Leisure interests:* literature, philately, swimming. *Address:* Slovak Chamber of Commerce and Industry, Gorkého 9, 816 03 Bratislava, Slovakia (office). *Telephone:* (2) 5443-3291 (office). *Fax:* (2) 5413-1159 (office). *E-mail:* predseda@scci.sk (office). *Website:* www.scci.sk (office).

MIHOV, Gen. Miho, MA; Bulgarian air force officer; *Adviser to the President;* b. 1 Feb. 1949, Sennik; s. of Dimitar Mihov and Stanka Mihov; m. 1973; one s. one d.; ed Benkovski Air Force Acad., Dolna Mitropolia, Rakovski Nat. War Coll., Sofia, Gen. Staff Coll., Moscow, USAF Special Operations School;

Training Flight Air Unit Deputy Commdr/Instructor; Air Squadron Deputy Commdr, Commdr, Air Regt, Deputy Commdr, Commdr; Air Corps Deputy Commdr; Air Defence Div. Commdr, Air Force Commdr; Chief of Gen. Staff of the Bulgarian Armed Forces 1997–2002; Adviser to Pres. of Bulgaria 2002–; Order of Merit and Valour; Medal for Service to the Bulgarian Armed Forces; Medal for the 40th Anniversary of the Victory over Hitler and Fascism; Medals and Orders of Distinguished Service; Order of Merit of Aviation (presented by King of Spain); Order presented by King of Sweden; Order presented by Pres. of Repub. of Bulgaria; Legion of Merit (USA). *Leisure interests:* hunting, skiing. *Address:* 2 Dondoukov blvd, 1123 Sofia, Bulgaria. *Telephone:* (2) 923-91-08 (office). *Fax:* (2) 981-75-79 (office). *E-mail:* mihov@president.bg (office). *Website:* www.president.bg (office).

MIIKE, Takashi; Japanese film director; b. 24 Aug. 1960, Yao, Osaka; ed Yokohama Film School; worked in television for a decade before becoming Asst Dir to Shohei Imamura; directed first theatrically distributed film Shinjuku Triad Society 1995; int. debut with Audition 2000. *Films include:* The New Generation 1996, Full Metal Yakuza 1997, Rainy Dog 1997, The Bird People in China 1998, Andromedia 1998, Blues Harp 1998, Man, A Natural Girl (TV mini-series) 1999, Ley Lines 1999, Silver 1999, Salaryman Kintaro 1999, Dead or Alive 2000, MPD Psycho (TV mini-series) 2000, City of Lost Souls 2000, Guys from Paradise 2000, Dead or Alive 2: Birds 2000, Making of 'Gemini' 2000, Family 2 2001, Love Cinema Vol. 6 2001 (also known as Visitor Q 2002), Ichi the Killer 2001, Agitator 2001, The Happiness of the Katakuris 2001, Dead or Alive: Final 2002, Graveyard of Honor 2002, Shangri-La 2002, Pandora 2002, Deadly Outlaw: Rekka 2002, The Man in White 2003, Zeburaaman 2004, Gozu 2004.

MIKEREVIĆ, Dragan, PhD, DSc; Bosnia and Herzegovina politician; *Vice-President, Party of Democratic Progress;* b. 12 Feb. 1955, Doboj; m.; two c.; ed Univ. of Novi Sad; fmr Chief of Finance Dept, Municipality of Doboj, later Pres. Municipality Ass.; fmr Financial Dir Health Assurance Bureau, Republika Srpska; fmr Prof. of Econs, Univ. of Banja Luka, later Man. and mem. of research teams, Inst. for Economy, Univ. of Banja Luka; mem. Party of Democratic Progress 1999–, currently Vice-Pres.; Chair. Council of Ministers (Prime Minister) of Bosnia and Herzegovina 2002, Minister for European Integration 2001–02; Prime Minister of Serb Repub. (Republika Srpska) of Bosnia and Herzegovina 2003–05. *Address:* c/o Office of the Prime Minister, 78000 Banja Luka, Republika Srpska, Bosnia and Herzegovina. *Telephone:* (51) 331333.

MIKHAILOV, Felix Trofimovich; Russian philosopher; b. 12 April 1930, Chimkent, Kazakhstan; ed Moscow State Univ.; researcher, Head of Chair 2nd Pirogov Moscow Inst. of Med. (now Russian State Med. Univ.) 1957–72; Head of Lab. Research Inst. of Methods of Teaching, USSR (now Russian) Acad. of Pedagogical Sciences 1972–74, Head of Lab. Research Inst. of Gen. and Pedagogical Psychology 1974–84; Chief Researcher, Head of Sector Inst. of Philosophy, USSR (now Russian) Acad. of Sciences 1994–; visiting reader univs in USA, UK, Canada; mem. Russian Acad. of Educ. *Publications:* numerous books, papers and articles on problems of human self-consciousness, including The Mystery of Humans. *Address:* Institute of Philosophy, Russian Academy of Sciences (IF RAN), Volkhonka str. 14m building 5, 119842 Moscow, Russia (office). *Telephone:* (495) 203-91-09 (office).

MIKHAILOV, Nikolai Vasilyevich, DPhil; Russian politician; *Co-Chairman, Russian-American Commission on Economic and Technical Co-operation;* b. 14 May 1937, Sevsk, Bryansk Region; m.; one s.; ed Moscow Bauman Higher School of Tech.; with defence industry enterprises 1961–96; Dir-Gen., Vympel Co. 1986–96; Deputy Sec. Security Council of Russian Fed. 1996–97; State Sec., First Deputy Minister of Defence of Russian Fed. 1997–2000; Co-Chair. Russian-American Comm. on Econ. and Tech. Co-operation 1998–, mem. Bd of Dirs AFC Systema Co. 2001–; USSR State Prize, State Prize of Russian Fed. 1997. *Publications:* (titles in trans.) Global World and Global Problems: Science and Labour in a Modern World; Military Defence Complex: Analyses and Challenges; Science and Knowledge: From Modern Times to the Future. *Leisure interests:* sports, music, classic literature. *Address:* Systema Financial Corporation, Leont'yevsky per. 10, 103009 Moscow (office); Raspletina str. 39, bied 14, 123060, Moscow, Russia (home). *Telephone:* (495) 730-15-14 (office); (495) 598-04-34 (home); (495) 105-44-21 (home). *Fax:* (495) 730-03-07 (office). *E-mail:* nmikhailov@sistema.ru (office); nmikhailov@mtu-net.ru (home). *Website:* www.sistema.ru (office).

MIKHAILOV, Viktor Nikitovich, DTechSc; Russian physicist and politician; *Director, Institute of Strategic Stability;* b. 12 Feb. 1934, Sopronovo, Moscow Region; m.; one s.; ed Moscow Inst. of Physics and Eng; on staff All-Union Research Inst., Arsamas; worked with group of nuclear bomb constructors; f. Scientific School of Explosive Nuclear Fission; Prof., Deputy, First Deputy Minister of Machine Construction of USSR (later USSR Ministry of Atomic Energy) 1988–1992; Minister of Atomic Energy Russian Fed. 1992–98; Scientific Leader Russian Fed. Nuclear Centre, VNII of Experimental Physics 1992–; Dir Inst. of Strategic Stability 1999–; Chair. Scientific Council 1998–; fmr mem. Security Council of Russia; mem. Russian Acad. of Sciences 1997–; Order of Honor 2005; Lenin Prize 1967, USSR State Prize 1992, Russian Fed. State Prize 1997. *Publication:* more than 200 works on nuclear energy problems. *Address:* ISS Minatom Russia, Luganskaya 9, 115304 Moscow, Russia (office). *Telephone:* (495) 321-35-47 (office); (495) 321-46-33 (office). *Fax:* (495) 321-40-56 (office). *E-mail:* mikhailov@niiit.ru (office). *Website:* www.iss.niiit.ru (office).

MIKHAILOV, Vyacheslav Aleksandrovich, DrHist; Russian politician; b. 13 April 1938, Dubovka, Volgograd Region; m.; two d.; ed Lvov State Univ.; teacher, secondary school, Lecturer, Lvov State Univ.; Head of Sector, Inst. of Marxism-Leninism at CPSU Cen. Cttee 1987–90; Head, Div. of Nat. Policy,

CPSU Cen. Cttee 1990–91; scientific consultant, I and World (magazine), Head, Centre on Int. Problems and Protection of Human Rights 1991–93; Prof., Moscow Inst. of Int. Relations (MGIMO) 1992–93, 1999–; Deputy Chair. State Cttee on Problems of Fed. and Nationality 1993–95; First Deputy Minister on Problems of Nationality and Regional Policy Jan.–July 1995, Minister 1995–98, 1999–2000; First Deputy Sec. Security Council 1998–99; Chair. Expert Council on Nat., Migration Policy and Interaction with Religious Asscns under the Plenipotentiary Rep. of the Russian Pres. in the Cen. Fed. Dist 2003. *Publications:* three monographs on nat. problems and numerous articles. *Address:* MGIMO, Vernadskogo Prosp. 76, 117454 Moscow, Russia (office). *Telephone:* (495) 206-43-26 (office).

MIKHALKOV, Nikita Sergeyevich; Russian film director; b. 21 Oct. 1945, Moscow; s. of Mikhalkov Sergey Vladimirovich and Konchalovskaya Natalia Petrovna; m. 1st Anastasya Vertinskaya 1966; m. 2nd Tatyana Mikhalkova 1973; two s. two d.; ed Shchukin Theatre School, State Film Inst. under Mikhail Romm; mem. State Duma 1995 (resgnd); First Sec. Russian Union of Cinematographers 1997–98, Chair. 1998–; Artistic Dir TRITE Studio; first worked as actor in films: Strolling Around Moscow, A Nest of Gentlefolk, The Red Tent; mem. Bd of Dirs Pervyi Kanal; Chevalier, Légion d'honneur; RSFSR People's Artist 1984, Felix Prize for Best European Film 1993, State Prize of Russian Fed., Honoured Artist of Russia, Special Lion for Overall Work, Venice Film Festival 2007 and several other awards. *Films directed:* A Quiet Day at the End of the War, At Home Among Strangers, A Stranger at Home 1975, The Slave of Love 1976, An Unfinished Piece for Mechanical Piano 1977, Five Evenings 1978, Several Days in the Life of I. I. Oblomov 1979, Kinsfolk 1982, Without Witnesses 1983, Dark Eyes 1987, Urga 1990 (Prize at Venice Biennale 1991), Anna from 6 to 18 1994, Burned by the Sun (Acad. Award for Best Foreign Film) 1994. *Film appearance:* Persona non grata 2005. *Play:* An Unfinished Piece for Mechanical Piano, Rome 1987. *Leisure interests:* sport, hunting. *Address:* Maly Kozikhinsky per. 4, Apt. 16–17, 103001 Moscow, Russia.

MIKHALKOV, Sergey Vladimirovich; Russian playwright, poet and children's writer; b. 13 March 1913, Moscow; m. 1st Natalia Konchalovskaya (deceased); two s.; m. 2nd; ed Literary Inst., Moscow; began writing 1928, verses for children 1935; co-author (with El-Registan) Soviet Anthem 1943; mem. CPSU 1950–91; Chief Ed. Fitil 1962–; First Sec. Moscow Br., RSFSR Union of Writers 1965–70, Chair. of Union 1970–91; Deputy to Supreme Soviet of RSFSR 1967–70, to USSR Supreme Soviet 1970–89; author Anthem of Russian Fed. (new version) 2000; mem. Comm. for Youth Affairs, Soviet of Nationalities; fmr Corresp. mem. Acad. of Pedagogical Sciences 1970; Order For Service to Fatherland (Second Class) 2003; numerous awards. *Film script:* Frontovye podrugi (Frontline Friends) 1941. *Plays:* Tom Kenti (after Mark Twain) 1938, Krasnyi galstuk (Red Neckerchief), Selected Works 1947, Ilya Golovin, Ya khochu domoi (I Want to Go Home) 1949, Raki (Lobsters) 1952, Zaika-Zaznaika 1955, Sombrero 1958, Pamyatnik Sebe (A Monument to Oneself) 1958, Dikari (Campers) 1959, Collected Works (4 vols) 1964, Green Grasshopper 1964, We Are Together, My Friend and I 1967, In the Museum of Lenin 1968, Fables 1970, Disobedience Day 1971, The Funny Bone (articles) 1971, Collected Works (3 vols) 1970–71, Selected Works 1973, Slap in the Face 1974, Bibliographical Index 1975, The Scum 1975, The Lodger 1977, Echo 1980, Almighty Kings 1983, Fables 1987, A Choice for Children (English trans.) 1988. *Publications:* Dyadya Styopa (Uncle Steve) 1936 and Collected Works (poems, stories, plays) in two vols. *Address:* Tchaikovskogo str. 28/35, Apt 67, 121069 Moscow, Russia. *Telephone:* (495) 291-78-15.

MIKHALKOV-KONCHALOVSKY, Andrey Sergeyevich; Russian film director and scriptwriter; b. 20 Aug. 1937, Moscow; s. of Sergey Mikhalkov and Natalia Konchalovskaya; m. 1st Natalia Arinbasarova 1946; m. 2nd Irina Ivanova 1960; one s. two d.; ed USSR State Inst. of Cinema, Moscow 1961–65; worked in Hollywood 1979–93; RSFSR People's Artist 1980. *Films include:* Roller and Violin (with A. Tarkovsky) 1959, Malchik i golub (The Boy and the Pigeon) 1961, Ivanovo detstvo (Ivan's Childhood) (actor) 1962, Mne dvadtsat let (I am Twenty) (actor) 1964, Pervyy uchitel (The First Teacher) 1965, Istoriya Asi Klyachinoy, kotoraya lyubila, da ne vyshla zamuzh (The Story of Asya Klyachina, Who Loved but Did Not Marry) 1966, Dvoryanskoe gnezdo (A Nest of Gentlefolk) 1969, Dyadya Vanya (Uncle Vanya) 1971, Romans o vlyublyonnykh (Romance of Lovers) 1974, Siberiada 1979, Split Cherry Tree 1982, Maria's Lovers (also composer of song Maria's Eyes) 1984, Runaway Train 1985, Duet for One 1986, Shy People 1987, Homer and Eddie 1988, Tango and Cash 1989, The Inner Circle 1991, Kurochka Ryaba (Ryaba My Chicken) (also producer) 1994, Lumière et compagnie (Lumière and Company) 1996, Dom durakov (House of Fools) (also producer) 2002, Moscow Chill (producer) 2005; scriptwriter (with Tarkovsky) Andrei Rublev 1969; also opera dir and theatre dir (productions at La Scala, Bastille, Mariinski Theatre). *Television includes:* The Odyssey (Odissea) 1997, The Lion in Winter 2003. *Address:* Mosfilmovskaya str. 1, Russkaya Ruletka, 119858 Moscow (Studio); Malaya Gruzinskaya 28, Apt 130, 123557 Moscow, Russia (home). *Telephone:* (495) 143-93-09 (Studio); (495) 253-50-21 (home). *Fax:* (495) 143-91-89.

MIKHEEV, Vladimir Andreyevich, DrPhysSc, FInstP, FIMechE; Ukrainian physicist and engineer; *Consultant Engineer, Oxford Instruments NanoScience Ltd;* b. 5 Aug. 1942; m. Tatiana Mikheeva 1969; one s. one d.; ed Kharkov Polytechnic; researcher 1964–86; discovery of quantum diffusion 1972–77; Head of Lab. of Ultralow Temperatures, Inst. for Low Temperature Physics and Eng, Ukrainian Acad. of Science 1986–; Visiting Prof., Royal Holloway and Bedford New Coll. 1992; Consultant Engineer, Tech. Devt, Oxford Instruments NasnoScience Ltd 1994–; Ed. Research Matters –2004; Lenin Prize for Science and Tech. *Publications:* more than 120 articles published worldwide. *Address:* Oxford Instruments NanoScience Ltd, Tubney Woods, Abingdon, Oxon., OX13 5QX (office); 35 Browning Drive, Bicester,

Oxon., OX26 2XN, England (home). *Telephone:* (1865) 393200 (office). *Fax:* (1865) 393333 (office). *E-mail:* vladimir.mikheev@oxinst.co.uk (office). *Website:* www.oxford-instruments.com (office).

MIKI, Shigemitsu; Japanese financial executive; *President and Co-CEO, Mitsubishi Tokyo Financial Group Incorporated;* b. 1935; Pres. and Co-CEO Mitsubishi Tokyo Financial Group Inc. (MTFG) 2001–; Pres. Bank of Tokyo Mitsubishi Ltd (BTM) 2001–; Chair. Japanese Bankers Asscn –2003; Counsellor Policy Bd, Bank of Japan; Vice-Chair. Exec. Bd Nippon-Keidanren 2003–; mem. Bd of Dirs Mitsubishi Motors Corpn 2002–; Dir Japan Int. Medical Tech. Foundation (JIMTEF); Trustee Financial Accounting Standards Foundation, Accounting Standards Bd of Japan (ASBJ). *Address:* Mitsubishi Tokyo Financial Group Incorporated, 10-1 Yurakucho 1-chome, Chiyoda-ku, Tokyo 100-0006, Japan (office). *Telephone:* (3) 3240-8111 (office). *Fax:* (3) 3240-8203 (office). *Website:* www.mtfg.co.jp (office).

MIKITA, Kunio; Japanese business executive; *Chairman, Mediceo Paltac Holdings Company Ltd;* b. 23 Oct. 1943; ed Kinki Univ.; joined Daisho Co. Ltd (named changed to Paltac 1976) 1966, mem. Bd of Dirs 1990–, Man. Dir 1995–96, Exec. Vice-Pres. 1996–98, Pres. 1998–2004, Rep. Dir and CEO 2004–, apptd Exec. Vice-Pres. Mediceo Paltac Holdings Co. Ltd (following acquisition of Paltac) 2005, later Vice-Pres. and Rep. Dir, Chair. 2008–. *Address:* Mediceo Paltac Holdings Co. Ltd, 7-15, Yaesu 2-chome, Chuo-ku, Tokyo 104-8464, Japan (office). *Telephone:* (3) 3517-5800 (office). *Fax:* (3) 3517-5011 (office). *E-mail:* info@mediceo-paltac.co.jp (office). *Website:* www.mediceo-paltac.co.jp (office).

MIKKELSEN, Brian, MA; Danish politician; *Minister of Justice;* b. 31 Jan. 1966, Copenhagen; m. Eliane Wexøe Mikkelsen; four c.; ed Univ. of Copenhagen; Business Man. Conservative Secondary School Students 1985–86, Nat. and Scandinavian Chair. 1986–87; mem. Nat. Exec. Cttee, Conservative Youth 1987–89, Nat. Chair. 1989–90; mem. Exec. Cttee Christian Democratic Youth Org. 1989–90; mem. Nat. Exec. Conservative People's Party 1989–91, 1998–, Deputy Chair., Conservative People's Party Parl. Group 1999–; mem. Parl. 1994–; Minister for Culture 2001–08, of Justice 2008–; Ed. The Conservative Season 2004; Exec. mem. Ledøje-Smørum FC 1983–84, FOF 1987–89, Tech. Council 1997–2001; mem. Danish Youth Council 1989–91, Holbæk Coll. of Educ. Council 1994–2001, Railway Council 1996–2001, Council for the Danish Centre for Human Rights 1998–2001, Danish Cultural Inst. Council 1998–2001, Danish Road Safety Council 2000–01, VL Group 7 2000–01, ARTE Council 2000–01; mem. World Anti-Doping Agency Foundation Bd 2002–03, Vice-Pres. 2004–06, mem. Exec. Cttee 2007–08. *Publications:* Nicaragua 1986, Namibia on the Road to Democracy 1988, The Conservative Breakthrough 1991, Land and Small Businesses 1994. *Address:* Ministry of Justice, Slotsholmsgade 10, 1216 Copenhagen, Denmark (office). *Telephone:* 72-26-84-00 (office). *Fax:* 33-93-35-10 (office). *E-mail:* jm@jm.dk (office). *Website:* www.jm.dk (office).

MIKKELSEN, Richard, MSc(Econ); Danish central banker (retd); b. 27 April 1920, Copenhagen; m. Ester Overgaard 1944 (died 1993); at Banken for Slagelse og Omegn 1937–45; apptd Asst Danmarks Nationalbank 1945, Head of Section 1954, Asst Head Dept 1961, Head Dept 1961, Dir 1966, Asst Gov. 1971, Gov. 1982–90; Attaché, Danish-OEEC Del., Paris 1955–57; mem. Bd European Monetary Agreement 1970–72; Industrial Mortgage Fund 1971–81; mem. Bd Mortgage Credit Council, Supervisor 1972–81; mem. Bd Export Finance Corpn 1975–90; mem. Steering Cttee and Bd Employees Capital Pension Fund 1980–91, Industrial Mortgage Credit Fund 1981–91, Monetary Cttee of EEC 1982–90; Nordic Financial Cttee 1982–90, Econ. Policy Cttee of OECD 1982–90; Chair. Financing Fund of 1992 1992–96; Commdr Order of Dannebrog. *Publication:* Monetary History of Denmark, 1960–90. *Address:* c/o Danmarks Nationalbank, Havnegade 5, 1093 Copenhagen K, Denmark. *Telephone:* 33-63-63-63.

MIKLOŠ, Ivan, DipEngEcon; Slovak politician and economist; *Vice-Chairman, Slovak Democratic and Christian Union–Democratic Party (SDKÚ-DS);* b. 2 June 1960, Svídník; m.; two c.; ed Univ. of Econs, Bratislava, LSE, UK; Asst, Univ. of Econs, Bratislava 1983–87, Chief Asst 1987–90; Adviser to Deputy Prime Minister responsible for Econ. Reform 1990; Dir Govt Dept of Econ. and Social Policy 1990–91; Minister of Privatization 1991–92; Exec. Dir and Pres. MESA 10 Org. 1992–98; Deputy Prime Minister 1998–06; Minister of Finance 2002–06; First Deputy Chair. Civil Democratic Union 1992–93; Chair. Democratic Party 1993–2000; mem. Slovak Democratic and Christian Union-Democratic Party (SDKÚ-DS) 2001–, Vice-Chair. 2002–; Mem. of Parl. 2006–; First Vice-Pres. East-West Inst., New York 1998; mem. Windsor Group 1993–, Int. Advisory Bd, New Atlantic Initiative 1995–, World Econ. Forum – Global Leaders of Tomorrow 1999–; Hon. PhD (Alma Coll., Mich., USA) 2000; named by Euromoney magazine Minister of Finance of the Year 2004. *Publications include:* numerous articles in specialized and popular press. *Leisure interests:* tennis, windsurfing, skiing. *Address:* Slovenská demokratická a kresťanská únia-Demokratická strana—SDKÚ-DS, Ružinovská 28, 827 35 Bratislava, Slovakia (office). *Telephone:* (2) 4341-4102 (office). *Fax:* (2) 4341-4106 (office). *E-mail:* sdku@sdkuonline.sk (office). *Website:* www.sdkuonline.sk (office).

MIKLOŠKO, Jozef, Doz, RnDr, DrSc; Slovak politician, mathematician, diplomatist, journalist and writer; *Chairman, Union of Christian Seniors of Slovakia;* b. 31 March 1939, Nitra; s. of Ondrej Mikloško and Marta (née Kutlíková) Mikloško; m. Mária Bitterová 1964; two s. two d.; ed Pedagogical Univ., Bratislava, Komenský Univ., Bratislava; teacher, Nové Zámky 1961–62; scientific worker, Inst. of Tech. Cybernetics, Slovak Acad. of Sciences, Bratislava 1963–90; Lecturer, Faculty of Mathematics and Physics, Komenský Univ., Bratislava 1969–89; Head. Int. Base Lab. for Artificial Intelligence 1985–90; Vice-Chair. Christian-Democratic Movt 1990; Deputy to Slovak Nat. Council 1990–91; Fed. Deputy Premier for Human Rights in Czechoslovak Fed. Repub. 1990–92; Deputy to House of the People, Fed. Ass. June–Dec. 1992; Adviser to Pres. of Slovakia 1993–95; Head DACO publishing house 1995–2000, 2005–; Sec. Justice and Peace Comm. 1995–2000; Lecturer and Vice-Rector Trnava Univ. 1996–2000; Amb. to Italy, Malta and San Marino 2000–05; Chair. Solidarity Foundation 1993–97, Schiller Foundation for Protection of Life and Human Rights 1995–2000; Chair. Asscn of Slovak Catholic Publishers 2006–08, Asscn of Christian Seniors of Slovakia 2007–; mem. World Ecological Acad., Moscow 1994–, Int. Informatization Acad., Moscow 1995–, Slovak Asscn of Writers 1995–, Slovak Asscn of Journalists 1997–2000; Deputy to Town Council, Bratislava V 1994–2000; Grande Ufficiale d'Italia 2006; Laudis et Honoris Signum (Italy) 2001, Gold Star for European Culture 2005. *Publications:* Strong Secret: When We Were Young 1995, Farewell 1996, Very Top Secret: When We Were Free 1999, Top Secret: When We Were Italian 2006, Whom Maria Took To Heaven 2006, When We Were Young: After 60 Years 2007; five scientific books, 65 scientific publications, 200 newspaper articles, 30 blogs. *Leisure interests:* literature, blogging, music, sport, history, church. *Address:* Malokarpatská 22, 90021 Svätý Jur, Slovakia (home). *Telephone:* (2) 4497-0689 (home). *E-mail:* mikloskojozef@zoznam.sk (home); ambasciatore.sk@virgilio.it (home). *Website:* www.jozefmiklosko.sk (home); www.jozefmiklosko.blog.sme.sk (home).

MIKOLAJ, Ján, CSc; Slovak engineer, academic and politician; *Deputy Prime Minister and Minister of Education;* b. 19 Oct. 1953; ed Žilina Transport Univ.; Asst Prof., later Assoc. Prof., Road Construction Dept, Žilina Transport Univ. 1983–, mem. Scientific Council, Civil Eng Faculty 1992, Prof. and Head of Construction Implementation Dept, now the Dept of Construction Techs and Man. 1999–; Gen. Dir Slovak Road Admin 1995–98; elected to Nat. Council of Slovak Repub. (Slovak Nat. Party—Slovenská národná strana) 2002, 2006; Deputy Prime Minister and Minister of Educ. 2008–. *Address:* Ministry of Education, Stromová 1, 813 30 Bratislava, Slovakia (office). *Telephone:* (2) 5937-4111 (office). *Fax:* (2) 5937-4335 (office). *E-mail:* kancmin@minedu.sk (office). *Website:* www.minedu.sk (office).

MIKOSZ, Andrzej; Polish lawyer and politician; b. 17 Oct. 1965, Poznań; ed Adam Mickiewicz Univ., Poznań; Pnr Ziemski i Partnerzy (law firm), Poznań 1993–1996; co-f. Głowacki, Grynhoff, Hałaziński, Mikosz (law firm) 1996–1997; mem. Polish Securities and Exchanges Comm. and advisor to Minister of Agric. and Rural Devt 1998–2000; lawyer Weil, Gotshal and Manges, Warsaw 2000–02; Dir of Capital Markets practice, Lovells (law firm), Warsaw 2002–05; Minister of the Treasury 2005–2006. *Publications:* numerous papers on company law, capital markets and corporate governance. *Address:* c/o Ministry of the Treasury, ul. Krucza 36, 00–522 Warsaw, Poland (office).

MIKOV, Mihail Raikov; Bulgarian politician and academic; *Minister of the Interior;* b. 16 June 1960, Kula; m.; two c.; ed St Clement of Ohrid Univ.of Sofia; Assoc. Prof. of Criminal Law, St Clement of Ohrid Univ. of Sofia; mem. Parl. (Socialist Party) for dist of Vidin 1997–, Chair. Parl. Group of leftist Coalition for Bulgaria 2005–, mem. Legal Matters Cttee, European Integration Cttee; Minister of the Interior 2008–. *Address:* Ministry of the Interior, 1000 Sofia, ul. 6-ti Septemvri 29, Bulgaria (office). *Telephone:* (2) 982-20-14 (office). *Fax:* (2) 982-20-47 (office). *E-mail:* info@mvr.bg (office). *Website:* www.mvr.bg (office).

MIKULSKI, Barbara Ann, BA, MSW; American politician; *Senator from Maryland;* b. 20 July 1936, Baltimore; d. of William Mikulski and Christina Eleanor Kutz; ed Mount St Agnes Coll. and Univ. of Maryland; Baltimore Dept Social Services 1961–63, 1966–70; York Family Agency 1964; VISTA Teaching Center 1965–70; Teacher, Mount St Agnes Coll. 1969; Teacher, Community Coll., Baltimore 1970–71; Democratic Nominee to US Senate 1974, to 1976; mem. US House of Reps (96th–99th Congresses) from 3rd Md Dist 1977–87; Senator from Maryland 1987–, first woman Democrat elected to US Senate in her own right; mem. Democratic Nat. Strategy Council; Adjunct Prof., Loyola Coll. 1972–76; mem. Nat. Bd of Dirs Urban Coalition; mem. Nat. Asscn of Social Workers; Democrat; Hon. Fellow, American Acad. of Nursing 2007; Polish Order of Merit 2001, Commdr's Cross and Star (Poland) 2001; Hon. LLD (Goucher Coll.) 1973, (Hood Coll.) 1978, (Bowie State Univ.) 1989, (Morgan State Univ.) 1990, (Massachusetts) 1991; Hon. DHL (Pratt Inst.) 1974. *Address:* 503 Hart Office Building, Washington, DC 20510, USA (office). *Telephone:* (202) 224-4654 (office). *Fax:* (202) 224-8858 (office). *Website:* mikulski.senate.gov (office).

MÍL, Jaroslav, MBA; Czech business executive; *General Director, Czech Confederation of Industry;* b. 10 Aug. 1958, Prague; ed Electrotechnology Faculty, Czech Tech. Univ., Prague, Sheffield Business School, UK; various tech. positions, then Dir responsible for Procurement and Fuel Cycles, Czech Power Co. (ČEZ) 1985–2000, Chair. Bd and CEO 2000–03, Chair. Bd and CEO Elektrárny Opatovice (EOP) 2000; mem. Bd of Govs World Nuclear Fuel Market, Atlanta, USA 1993–99, Bd of Dirs Škoda-ÚJP Praha 1994–2000, Supervisory Bd Severočeské doly 1998–99, Bd Czech Asscn of Employers in Energy Sector 2000–; Gen. Dir Czech Confed. of Industry 2003–; Chair. Bd Radioactive Waste Repository Authority 1997–2000; fmr mem. ICC, Bd Dirs EURELECTRIC, European Nuclear Council, Int. Advisory Cttee of Soc. for Strategic Man.; mem. Bd Dirs Czech Tech. Univ. *Leisure interests:* family, skiing, golf, squash, cycling, hiking. *Address:* Czech Confederation of Industry, Mikulandska 7, 113 61 Prague 1, Czech Republic (office). *Telephone:* (2) 24915250 (office). *Fax:* (2) 24915252 (office). *E-mail:* spcr@spcr.cz (office). *Website:* www.spcr.cz (office).

MILAKNIS, Valentinas Pranas; Lithuanian business executive and politician; *Chairman, Alna AB Company;* b. 4 Oct. 1947, Rokiskis; m. Sofija Milakniene; one s. one d.; ed Kaunas Polytech. Inst.; fmr engineer, then Head of Group, Head of Sector, Deputy Chief Engineer Control System Planning and Design Construction Bureau, Municipal Econ. Planning Inst. 1970–89; apptd Man. Dir, then Dir-Gen. Alna AB Co. 1989, currently Chair.; Minister of Nat. Economy 1999–2000; Dir-Gen. LRT (Lithuanian public TV and radio broadcaster) 2001–03. *Leisure interest:* shooting. *Address:* Alna AB, A. Domaševiciaus 9, 2001 Vilnius, Lithuania (office). *Telephone:* (2) 31-22-44 (office). *E-mail:* info@alna.lt (office). *Website:* www.alna.com (office).

MILANI, Cesare (Chez), BA, LLB; South African trade union official and lawyer; *General Secretary, Federation of Unions of South Africa;* b. 27 Nov. 1966, Cape Town; m.; one d.; ed Stellenbosch Univ., Univ. of South Africa School of Business Leadership; Nat. Legal Adviser (HOS PERSA) 1994–97; Gen. Sec. Fed. of Unions of SA (FEDUSA) 1997–; mem. Pres. Mbeki's Working Group, NEDLAC Exec. Cttee and Man. Cttee, CCMA Governing Body. *Leisure interests:* antiques, sailing. *Address:* FEDUSA, PO Box 2096, Northcliff 2115, Pretoria (office); PO Box 412, Featherbrook Estate, 1746, South Africa (office). *Telephone:* (11) 4765188 (office); (11) 4765189 (office). *Fax:* (11) 4765131 (office). *E-mail:* chez@fedusa.org.za (office). *Website:* www.fedusa.org.za (office).

MILBERG, Joachim, Dr-Ing; German automotive industry executive and engineer; *Chairman of the Supervisory Board, BMW AG;* b. 10 April 1943, Westphalia; ed Technische Universität Berlin; Research Asst, Inst. of Machine Tools and Production Tech., Berlin Tech. Univ. 1970–72; exec. employee, Werkzeugmaschinenfabrik Gildemeister AG (machine tools factory) 1972–78, Head of Automatic Tuning Machines division 1978–81; Prof. of Machine Tools and Man. Science, Munich Tech. Univ. 1981–93; mem. Bd of Man. BMW (Production) 1993–98, (Eng and Production) 1998–99, Chair. Bd of Man. 1999–2002, mem. Supervisory Bd 2002–04, Chair. 2004–; Hon. Dr-Ing. *Address:* Bayerische Motoren Werke AG, Petuelring 130, 80788, Munich, Germany (office). *Telephone:* (89) 382-0 (office). *Fax:* (89) 382-244-18 (office). *E-mail:* info@bmwgroup.com (office). *Website:* www.bmw.com (office); www .bmwgroup.com (office).

MILBRADT, Georg, Dr rer pol; German politician and academic; b. 23 Feb. 1945, Eslohe, Sauerland; m. Angelika Meeth; two s.; ed Univ. of Münster; Asst, Inst. of Finance, Univ. of Münster 1970–80, Guest Prof. 1985–; Deputy Prof. of Finance and Econs, Univ. of Mainz 1980–83; Head, Dept of Finance, Münster 1983–90, later responsible for econ. devt and property man.; mem. CDU 1991–, Fed. Admin 2000–; Minister of Finance, Saxony State 1990–2001; mem. Bundesrates (Upper House of Parl.) Cttee on Mediation; mem. Saxony State Parl. 1994–; Minister-Pres. of Saxony April 2002–08 (resgnd); Regional Deputy Chair. Sächsischen Union 1999; Chair. Bd Sächsischen Aufbaubank, Dresden Airport, Sächsischen Landesbank; Deputy Chair. Bd Leipzig-Halle Airport; Chair. Tariff Community of German Länder (TdL); Bundesvierdienstkreuz 2005. *Leisure interests:* literature, computers. *Address:* CDU, Konrad-Adenauer-Haus, Klingelhöferstrasse 8, 10785 Berlin, Germany (office). *Telephone:* (30) 220700 (office). *Fax:* (30) 22070111 (office). *E-mail:* info@cdu.de (office). *Website:* www.cdu.de (office); www.georg-milbradt.de (office).

MILBURN, Rt Hon. Alan, PC, BA; British politician; b. 27 Jan. 1958; m. Mo O'Toole 1982 (divorced 1992); m. Ruth Briel; two s.; ed Stokesley Comprehensive School, Lancaster Univ.; co-ordinator Trade Union Studies Information Unit, Newcastle 1984–90; Sr Business Devt Officer N Tyneside Municipal Borough Council 1990–92; MP for Darlington 1992–; Opposition Front Bench Spokesman on Health 1995–96, on Treasury and Econ. Affairs 1996–97; Minister of State, Dept of Health 1997–98; Chief Sec. to Treasury 1998–99, Sec. of State for Health 1999–2003; Chancellor of the Duchy of Lancaster 2004–05; Chair. Parl. Labour Party Treasury Cttee 1992–95; mem. Public Accounts Cttee 1994–95; Chair. Charities Scrutiny Cttee 2004–; mem. Nutritional Advisory Bd, PepsiCo UK 2007–. *Address:* House of Commons, London, SW1A 0AA, England (office). *Website:* www.parliament.uk (office); www.alanmilburn.co.uk (home).

MILCHAN, Arnon; American film producer; b. 6 Dec. 1944, Palestine (now Israel). *Plays produced:* Tomb, It's So Nice To Be Civilized, Amadeus (Paris production). *Films include:* Black Joy 1977, The Medusa Touch (exec. producer) 1978, Dizengoff 99 1979, The King of Comedy 1983, Can She Bake a Cherry Pie? (actor) 1983, Once Upon a Time in America (also actor) 1984, Brazil 1985, Legend 1985, Stripper (exec. producer) 1986, Man on Fire 1987, Big Man on Campus 1989, The Adventures of Baron Munchausen 1989, Who's Harry Crumb 1989, The War of the Roses 1989, Pretty Woman 1990, Q&A 1990, Guilty by Suspicion 1991, Switch (exec. producer) 1991, JFK (exec. producer) 1991, Memoirs of an Invisible Man (exec. producer) 1992, The Mambo Kings 1992, The Power of One 1992, Under Siege 1992, That Night 1992, Heaven and Earth 1993, Sommersby 1993, Falling Down (exec. producer) 1993, Made in America 1993, Free Willy (exec. producer) 1993, Striking Distance 1993, The Nutcracker (exec. producer) 1993, Six Degrees of Separation 1993, The Client 1994, Natural Born Killers (exec. producer) 1994, Second Best 1994, The New Age 1994, Cobb (exec. producer) 1994, Boys on the Side 1995, Under Siege 2 1995, Free Willy 2: The Adventure Home 1995, Empire Records 1995, Copycat 1995, Heat (exec. producer) 1995, The Sunchaser 1996, A Time to Kill 1996, Tin Cup (exec. producer) 1996, Bogus 1996, The Mirror Has Two Faces 1996, Murder at 1600 1997, L.A. Confidential 1997, Free Willy 3: The Rescue (exec. producer) 1997, The Devil's Advocate 1997, Breaking Up (exec. producer) 1997, The Man Who Knew Too Little 1997, Dangerous Beauty 1998, City of Angels (exec. producer) 1998, Goodbye Lover (exec. producer) 1998, The Negotiator 1998, Simply Irresistible (exec. producer) 1999, A Midsummer Night's Dream (exec. producer) 1999, Entrapment (exec. producer) 1999, Fight Club (exec. producer) 1999, Up at the Villa (exec. producer) 2000, Big Momma's House (exec. producer) 2000, Tigerland 2000, Freddy Got Fingered (exec. producer) 2001, Joy Ride (exec. producer)

2001, Don't Say a Word 2001, Black Knight 2001, Joe Somebody (exec. producer) 2001, High Crimes 2002, Life or Something Like It 2002, Unfaithful (exec. producer) 2002, Daredevil 2003, Down with Love (exec. producer) 2003, Runaway Jury 2003, The Girl Next Door (exec. producer) 2004, Man on Fire 2004, First Daughter (exec. producer) 2004, Elektra 2005, Mr. & Mrs. Smith 2005, Bee Season (exec. producer) 2005, Stay (exec. producer) 2005, Just My Luck 2006, The Sentinel 2006. *Television includes:* Masada (mini-series) (supervising producer) 1981, Free Willy (series; exec. producer), The Client (series; exec. producer) 1995, Michael Hayes (series; exec. producer) 1997, The Hunt for the Unicorn Killer 1999, Noriega: God's Favorite (exec. producer) 2000. *Address:* New Regency Enterprises, 10201 West Pico Boulevard, Building 12, Los Angeles, CA 90035, USA.

MILEDI, Ricardo, MD, FRS, FAAS, MRI; Mexican/American neurobiologist and academic; *Distinguished Professor, Neurobiology and Behavior, University of California, Irvine;* b. 15 Sept. 1927, Mexico DF; m. Ana Mela Garces 1955; one s.; ed Universidad Nacional Autónoma de Mexico; Research Fellow, Instituto Nacional de Cardiología, Mexico 1954–56; Visiting Fellow, John Curtin School of Medical Research, Canberra, Australia 1956–58; Hon. Research Assoc., Dept of Biophysics, Univ. Coll. London 1958–59, Lecturer 1959–62, Reader 1962–65, Prof. of Biophysics 1965–75, Foulerton Research Prof. of the Royal Soc. 1975–85, Foulerton Research Prof. and Head of Dept of Biophysics 1978–85; Distinguished Prof., Neurobiology and Behavior, Dept of Psychobiology, School of Biological Sciences, Univ. of California, Irvine 1984–; Fellow, Third World Acad. of Sciences, American Acad. of Arts and Sciences; mem. NAS 1989, European Acad. of Arts, Sciences and Humanities 1995, Mexican Acad. of Medicine 1995, Mexican Acad. of Sciences 1995; Hon. mem. Hungarian Acad. of Sciences; Dr hc (Univ. del País Vasco, Leioa, Spain) 1992, (Trieste Univ., Italy) 2000, (Univ. of Chihuahua, Mexico) 2000; King Faisal Foundation Int. Prize for Science, Principe de Asturias Prize (Spain) 1999, Royal Soc. Medal 1999, Univ. of California (Irvine) Medal. *Publications:* more than 500 published papers. *Leisure interest:* hiking. *Address:* Department of Neurobiology and Behavior, University of California, 1215 Bio Sci II, Mail Code 4550, Irvine, CA 92697-4550 (office); 9 Gibbs Court, Irvine, CA 92616, USA (home). *Telephone:* (949) 824-4730 (office); (949) 856-2677 (home). *Fax:* (949) 824-6090 (office). *E-mail:* rmiledi@uci.edu (office). *Website:* neurobiology .uci.edu (office).

MILES, (Henry) Michael (Pearson), OBE; British business executive; *Chairman, Schroders;* b. 19 April 1936; s. of the late Brig. H. G. P. Miles and Margaret Miles; m. Carol Jane Berg 1967; two s. one d.; ed Wellington Coll., Nat. Service, Duke of Wellington's Regt; joined John Swire & Sons 1958, Dir John Swire & Sons (HK) Ltd 1970–99, Chair. 1984–88; Man. Dir John Swire & Sons (Japan) Ltd 1973–76; Man. Dir Cathay Pacific Airways Ltd 1978–84, Chair. 1984–88; Chair. Swire Pacific 1984–88; Exec. Dir John Swire & Sons Ltd 1988–99, Adviser to Bd 1999–; Dir Johnson Matthey PLC 1990–2003, Chair. (non-exec.) 1998–2002; Chair. (non-exec.) Schroders 2003–; Dir (non-exec.) Baring PLC 1989–95 (Jt Deputy Chair. 1994–95), Portals Holdings 1990–95, BICC 1996–2002, HSBC Holdings 1984–88, ING Baring Holdings Ltd 1989–2002, BP PLC 1994–, Pacific Assets Trust PLC 1997–2003, Balfour Beatty 1996–2002; Chair. Hong Kong Tourist Asscn 1984–88, Korea-Europe Fund Ltd; Vice-Pres. China-Britain Business Group 1992–2000; Gov. Wellington Coll. 1988–. *Leisure interests:* golf, tennis. *Address:* Schroders, 31 Gresham Street, London, EC2V 7QA (office); Shalbourne House, Shalbourne, nr Marlborough, Wilts., SN8 3QH, England (home). *Telephone:* (20) 7658-6000 (office). *Website:* www.schroders.com (office).

MILES, Michael A., Jr., BA, MBA; American retail executive; *President and Chief Operating Officer, Staples Inc.;* ed Yale and Harvard Univs; began career at Bain & Company; joined PepsiCo Inc. as Dir of Strategic Planning, Restaurants 1993, Div. Vice Pres. Pizza Hut 1994, then Sr Vice-Pres. Concept Devt and Franchise, Pizza Hut (after Yum Brands Inc. spinoff from PepsiCo that included Pizza Hut) 1996–99, COO Pizza Hut Inc. 2000–03; COO Staples Inc. 2003–, Pres. 2006–. *Address:* Staples Inc., 500 Staples Drive, Framingham, MD 01702, USA (office). *Telephone:* (508) 253-5000 (office). *Fax:* (508) 253-8989 (office). *Website:* www.staples.com (office).

MILES, Roy Edward; British art dealer and writer; b. 9 Feb. 1935, Liverpool; s. of Edward Marsh and Elsa McKinley; m. Christine Rhodes 1970 (died 1997); ed Bembridge School, Isle of Wight, Sorbonne, Paris; dealer in British art and fine paintings; organizer of major exhbns of Victorian and Russian art; Gold Medal for Art 1943. *Television:* contribs to numerous art programmes. *Publications:* Priceless: Memoirs and Mysteries of Britain's No. 1 Art Dealer (autobiog.) 2003; articles in magazines, newspapers and journals. *Leisure interests:* classical music, history. *Address:* 10 Ennismore Gardens, London, SW7 1NP, England. *Telephone:* (20) 7581-7969 (home).

MILES, Sarah; British actress; b. 31 Dec. 1941, Ingatestone, Essex; m. Robert Bolt 1967 (divorced 1976), remarried 1988 (died 1995); ed Royal Acad. of Dramatic Art (RADA), London; first film appearance in Term of Trial 1962; with Nat. Theatre Co. 1964–65; Shakespeare stage season 1982–83; Assoc. mem. RADA. *Theatre appearances include:* Vivat! Vivat Regina!, Asylum 1988. *Films include:* Term of Trial 1962, The Servant 1963, The Ceremony 1963, Those Magnificent Men in Their Flying Machines 1965, I Was Happy Here 1965, Blowup 1966, Ryan's Daughter 1970, Lady Caroline Lamb 1972, The Hireling 1973, The Man Who Loved Cat Dancing 1973, Pepita Jiménez 1975, The Sailor Who Fell From Grace With the Sea 1976, The Big Sleep 1978, Priest of Love 1981, Venom 1982, Ordeal by Innocence 1984, Steaming 1985, Hope and Glory 1987, White Mischief 1987, Hope and glory 1987, Dotkniecie reki (The Silent Touch) 1992, Jurij 2001, I giorni dell'amore e dell'odio (Days of Grace) 2001, The Accidental Detective 2003. *Television includes:* Great Expectations 1974, James A. Michener's Dynasty 1976, Walter and June 1983, Harem 1986, Queenie 1987, A Ghost in Monte Carlo 1990, Dandelion

Dead (mini-series) 1994, Ring Around the Moon, The Rehearsal, Poirot: The Hollow 2004. *Publications:* Charlemagne (play) 1992, A Right Royal Bastard (memoirs) 1993, Serves Me Right (memoirs) 1994, Bolt from the Blue (memoirs) 1996.

MILHAUD, Charles; French banking executive; b. 1943; science grad.; has spent entire career with Groupe Caisse d'Epargne, joined Caisse d'Epargne de Sète 1964, CEO 1967–80, CEO, then Chair. Man. Bd Caisse d'Epargne des Bouches du Rhône et de la Corse 1980–99, Chair. Man. Bd Centre Nat. des Caisses d'Epargne (thereafter Caisse Nationale des Caisses d'Epargne when it was cr. in Sept. 1999) 1999–2008 (resgnd), Chair. Caisses d'Epargne Foundation for Social Solidarity; Chair. Supervisory Bd Natixis, Financière OCEOR; Chair. French Banking Fed. 2006–07; Vice-Pres. Nexity; mem. Municipal Council of Marseille 2008–; Officier, Ordre nat. du Mérite 2001, Légion d'honneur 2005. *Address:* c/o Caisse Nationale des Caisses d'Epargne, 50 avenue Pierre Mendès, 75201 Paris Cedex 13, France (office).

MILIBAND, Rt Hon David Wright, BA, MSc; British politician; *Secretary of State for Foreign and Commonwealth Affairs;* b. 15 July 1965; s. of the late Ralph Miliband and Marion Miliband (née Kozak); m. Louise Shackelton 1998; one s.; ed Corpus Christi Coll., Oxford, Massachusetts Inst. of Tech., USA; Research Fellow Inst. of Public Policy Research 1989–94; Sec. Comm. on Social Justice 1992–94; Head of Policy, Office of Leader of Opposition 1994–97; Head, Prime Minister's Policy Unit 1997–2001; Minister of State, Dept for Educ. and Skills 2002–04; Minister for the Cabinet Office 2004–05; Minister of Communities and Local Govt 2005–06; Secretary of State for the Environment, Food and Rural Affairs 2006–07, for Foreign and Commonwealth Affairs 2007–; MP (South Shields) 2001–. *Publications:* Reinventing the Left (ed.) 1994, Paying for Inequality: The Economic Cost of Social Injustice (jt ed.) 1994. *Leisure interests:* supporting Arsenal Football Club, Hoping for South Shields Football Club. *Address:* Foreign and Commonwealth Office, King Charles Street, London, SW1A 2AH (office); House of Commons, London, SW1A 0AA (office); Ede House, 143 Westoe Road, South Shields, NE33 3PD, England (office). *Telephone:* (20) 7008-1500 (FCO) (office); (191) 456-8910 (office). *Fax:* (191) 456-5842 (office). *E-mail:* milibandd@parliament.uk (office). *Website:* www.fco.gov.uk (office); www.davidmiliband.info (office).

MILIBAND, Rt Hon. Edward (Ed) Samuel, PC, BA, MSc; British politician; *Secretary of State for Energy and Climate Change;* b. 24 Dec. 1969, London; s. of the late Ralph Miliband and Marion Kozak; brother of David Miliband; ed London School of Econs, Corpus Christi Coll., Oxford; Special Adviser to Chancellor of Exchequer 1997, becoming Chair., Treasury Council of Econ. Advisers; MP (Labour) for Doncaster N 2005–; Parl. Sec. to Cabinet Office 2006, Chair. All-Party Group on Young People, Minister for Third Sector 2006–07, Minister for Cabinet Office and Chancellor, Duchy of Lancaster 2007–08; Sec. of State for Energy and Climate Change 2008–; Visiting Lecturer, Dept of Govt, Harvard Univ., USA 2003, also Visiting Scholar, Center for European Studies. *Address:* House of Commons, London SW1A 0AA, England (office). *Telephone:* (20) 7276-1234 (office). *E-mail:* milibande@parliament.uk (office). *Website:* www.edmilibandmp.com (office).

MILINGO, Most Rev. Archbishop Emmanuel, DipEd; Zambian ecclesiastic; *Archbishop Emeritus of Lusaka;* b. 13 June 1930; s. of Yakobe Milingo and Tomaida Lumbiwe; m. Maria Sung 2001 (divorced); ed St Mary's Presbyterial School, Fort Jameson and Kasina Junior Seminary and Kachebere Major Seminary, Nyasaland (now Malawi); studied Pastoral Sociology (Diploma), Rome, Univ. Coll. Dublin, Ireland; curate, Minga Mission 1958–61; Parish Priest, St Ann's Mission, Chipata 1963–66; Sec. for Mass Media, Zambia Episcopal Conf. 1966–69; Archbishop of Lusaka 1969–83, Archbishop Emer. 1983–; Special Del. to Pontifical Comm. for Pastoral Care of Migrants, Refugees and Pilgrims 1983–; drew worldwide headlines in 2001 when he married a Korean woman in a large ceremony in New York organised by the Unification Church ('Moonies'), later expressed regret and contrition to Pope John Paul II, subsequently spent a year in seclusion, returning to Rome in 2002. *Publications:* Amake Joni, Demarcations, The World in Between, The Flower Garden of Jesus the Redeemer, My Prayers are Not Heard, Precautions in the Ministry of Deliverance, Against Satan, The World in Between: Christian Healing and the Struggle for Spiritual Survival, Confessions of an Excommunicated Catholic (auto-biog.); has produced his own CD . *Leisure interests:* writing and preaching to make Jesus Christ known and loved. *E-mail:* emmanuelmilingo@hotmail.com (home). *Website:* www.archbishopmilingo.org.

MILINKEVICH, Alyaksandr, PhD; Belarusian politician; *Leader, Movement for Freedom;* b. 25 July 1947, Grodno; m. (twice); two c. from first m.; ed Grodno Teacher Inst., USSR Acad. of Sciences, European Centre for Security Research, Garmisch-Partenkirchen, FRG; early career as teacher, Hrodna 1969–72; Jr Researcher, USSR Acad. of Sciences (Belarus) 1972–78; Assoc. Prof., Grodno State Univ. 1978–80, 1984–90; Head, Dept of Physics, Univ. of Setif, Algeria 1980–84; Deputy Chair. Hrodna Admin Exec. Cttee 1990–96; Leader, Ratusha (Town Hall) Org. 1996–2003; Pres. Grodna-93 football team; Founder and Head, Ratusha Resource Centre 1997 (closed by authorities 2003); headed presidential campaign of Syamyon Domash 2001; contested presidential election as cand. for coalition of United Democratic Forces 2006; Founder and Leader, Movt for Freedom (human rights group); European Parl. Sakharov Prize 2006. *Address:* c/o United Civic Party (Abyadnanya Hramadzyanskaya Partya Belarusi), 220123 Minsk, vul. Khoruzhey 22, Belarus (office). *Telephone:* (17) 289-50-09 (office). *Fax:* (17) 283-50-09 (office). *E-mail:* ucpb@ucpb.org (office); info@milinkevich.org. *Website:* www.ucpb.org (office); en.milinkevich.org.

MILINTACHINDA, Piamsak; Thai international organization official; *Director-General, Department of Technical and Economic Cooperation, Ministry of Foreign Affairs;* b. 1950, Bangkok; ed Chulalongkorn Univ. and Wayne State Univ., USA; Attaché, Dept of Econ. Affairs, Ministry of Foreign Affairs 1977–80; Second Sec., Royal Thai Embassy, Singapore 1981–84; First Sec. Dept of ASEAN Affairs, Ministry of Foreign Affairs 1985–87, Deputy Dir-Gen. 1999; Counsellor, Perm. Mission to UN, New York 1988–91; Dir North American Div., Dept of American and South Pacific Affairs, Ministry of Foreign Affairs 1992–94; Minister, Deputy Perm. Rep. to WTO, Geneva 1995–99; Deputy Dir-Gen. Dept of European Affairs, Ministry of Foreign Affairs 2000–01; Amb., Deputy Exec. Dir APEC Secr. 2002, Exec. Dir 2003–05; Dir-Gen. Dept of Tech. and Econ. Cooperation (DTEC) 2004–. *Address:* Department of Technical and Economic Cooperation, Ministry of Foreign Affairs, 443 Sri Ayudhya Road, Bangkok, Thailand 10400 (office). *Telephone:* (2) 643-5000 (office). *Fax:* (2) 225-6155 (office). *Website:* www.dtec.thaigov.net (office).

MILIUS, John Frederick; American film writer, director and actor; b. 11 April 1944, St Louis; s. of William Styx Milius and Elizabeth (née Roe) Milius; m. 1st Renée Fabri 1967; two s.; m. 2nd Celia K. Burkholder 1978; ed Univ. of Southern Calif.; wrote screenplays: The Devil's 8 1969, Evel Knievel 1971, Jeremiah Johnson 1972, The Life and Times of Judge Roy Bean 1973, Magnum Force 1973, Purvis FBI (for TV) 1974, Apocalypse Now 1979 (Acad. Award for Best Screenplay 1980), 1941 (with Francis Ford Coppola q.v.) 1979, Geronimo: An American Legend (co-writer), Clear and Present Danger (co-writer), Apocalypse Now Redux; wrote and directed: Dillinger 1973, The Wind and the Lion 1975, Big Wednesday 1978, Conan the Barbarian 1981, Red Dawn 1984, Farewell to the King 1989, Navy Seals 1990, Flight of the Intruder 1991, The Texas Rangers 1994, The Northmen 1999; acted in Go West, Young Man! 2003, Easy Riders, Raging Bulls 2003, Riding Giants 2004. *Address:* c/o Jeff Berg International Creative Management, 8942 Wilshire Boulevard, Beverly Hills, CA 90211, USA (office).

MILLAN, Rt Hon. Bruce, PC, CA; British politician (retd); b. 5 Oct. 1927, Dundee, Scotland; s. of David Millan; m. Gwendoline Fairey 1953; one s. one d.; ed Harris Acad., Dundee; worked as chartered accountant (Inst. of Chartered Accountants of Scotland) 1950–59; MP for Craigton Div. of Glasgow 1959–83, for Govan Div. of Glasgow 1983–88; EEC (now EU) Commr for Regional Policy 1989–95; Parl. Under-Sec. of State for Defence (RAF) 1964–66, for Scotland 1966–70; Minister of State, Scottish Office 1974–76, Sec. of State for Scotland 1976–79; Opposition Spokesman for Scotland 1979–83; Labour; Hon. Fellow (Paisley) 1991, Hon. FRSE 1995; Hon. LLD (Dundee) 1989, (Abertay Dundee) 1994, (Glasgow) 1995; Hon. DLitt (Heriot-Watt) 1991; Dr hc (Panteios, Athens) 1995, (Sheffield Hallam) 1996. *Address:* 1 Torridon Avenue, Glasgow, G41 5LA, Scotland (home). *Telephone:* (141) 427-6483 (home).

MILLAR, Fergus Graham Burtholme, MA, DPhil, DLitt, FBA, FSA; British historian and academic (retd); *Professor Emeritus of Ancient History, University of Oxford;* b. 5 July 1935, Edinburgh, Scotland; s. of J. S. L. Millar and J. B. Taylor; m. Susanna Friedmann 1959; two s. one d.; ed Edinburgh Acad., Loretto School, Trinity Coll., Oxford; Fellow, All Souls Coll., Oxford 1958–64; Fellow and Tutor in Ancient History, The Queen's Coll., Oxford 1964–76; Prof. of Ancient History, Univ. Coll., London 1976–84; Camden Prof. of Ancient History, Univ. of Oxford 1984–2002, currently Emer. Prof. of Ancient History; Fellow, Brasenose Coll. Oxford 1984–2002; Pres. Soc. for the Promotion of Roman Studies 1989–92 (Vice-Pres. 1977–89, 1992–2001, Hon. Vice-Pres. 2001–; Pres. Classical Asscn 1992–93; Publications Sec. British Acad. 1997–2002; Corresp. mem. German Archaeological Inst. 1977, Bavarian Acad. 1987, Finnish Acad. 1989, Russian Acad. 1999, American Acad. 2003; Hon. DPhil (Helsinki) 1994, Hon. DLitt (St Andrews Univ.) 2004; Premio Cultori di Roma 2005, Kenyon Medal for Classical Studies, British Acad. 2005. *Publications:* several historical studies, The Roman Near East 1993, The Crowd in Rome in the Late Republic 1998, The Roman Republic in Political Thought 2002. *Address:* Oriental Institute, Pusey Lane, Oxford, OX1 2LE (office); 80 Harpes Road, Oxford, OX2 7QL, England (home). *Telephone:* (1865) 288093 (office); (1865) 515782 (home). *Fax:* (1865) 278190 (office). *E-mail:* fergus.millar@bnc.ox.ac.uk (office).

MILLER, Aleksei Borisovich, PhD; Russian business executive; *Deputy Chairman of the Board of Directors and Chairman of the Management Committee (CEO), OAO Gazprom;* b. 31 Jan. 1962, Leningrad (now St Petersburg); m.; one s.; ed N.A. Voznesenskii Leningrad Inst. of Finance and Econs; engineer-economist, Gen. Planning Div., LenNIIProekt – Leningrad Civil Construction Research and Design Inst.; researcher, Leningrad Inst. of Finance and Econs 1990–91; mem. Cttee on Foreign Econ. Relations, Office of the Mayor of St Petersburg 1991–96; Dir of Devt and Investments, Morskoy Port of St Petersburg Open Jt Stock Co. 1996–99; Dir-Gen. Balttiiskaya Truboprovodnaya Sistema (Baltic Pipeline System) 1999–2000; Deputy Minister of Energy 2000–01; Deputy Chair. Bd of Dirs and Chair. Man. Cttee (CEO) OAO Gazprom 2001–; Medal for Outstanding Services to the Fatherland (2nd degree), Order for Services to Energy Co-operation (2nd degree), Hungary, St Mesrop Mashtots Order, Armenia, Dostyk Order (2nd degree) Kazakhstan, Sergei Radonezhskii Order of the Russian Orthodox Church, Patriarchal Merit Certificate; named by Expert magazine (Russian business weekly) Person of the Year (jtly) 2005. *Address:* OAO Gazprom, 117997 Moscow, ul. Nametkina 16, V-420, GSP-7, Russia (office). *Telephone:* (495) 719-30-01 (office). *Fax:* (495) 719-83-33 (office). *E-mail:* gazprom@gazprom.ru (office). *Website:* www.gazprom.ru (office).

MILLER, Andrew, CBE, MA, PhD, FRSE; British academic; *Secretary and Treasurer, Carnegie Trust for the Universities of Scotland;* b. 15 Feb. 1936, Kelty, Fife; s. of William Hamilton Miller and Susan Anderson (née Auld) Miller; m. Rosemary Singleton Hannah Fyvie 1962; one s. one d.; ed Beath High School, Univ. of Edinburgh; Asst Lecturer in Chem., Univ. of Edin.

1960–62; Post-Doctoral Fellow, CSIRO Div. of Protein Chem., Melbourne 1962–65; Staff Scientist MRC Lab. of Molecular Biology, Cambridge 1965–66; Lecturer in Molecular Biophysics, Oxford Univ. 1966–83; First Head European Molecular Biology Lab., Grenoble Antenne, France 1975–80; Prof. of Biochem., Univ. of Edinburgh 1984–94, Vice-Dean of Medicine 1991–93, Vice-Provost, Medicine and Veterinary Medicine 1992–93, Vice-Prin. 1993–94; Prin. and Vice-Chancellor, Univ. of Stirling 1994–2001, Prof. Emer. 2001–; Interim Chief Exec. Cancer Research, UK 2001–02; mem. Science and Eng Research Council Biological Sciences Cttee 1982–85; mem. Council Inst. Laue-Langevin, France 1981–85; mem. Univ. Grants Cttee, Biological Sciences Cttee 1985–88; Dir of Research, European Synchrotron Radiation Facility, Grenoble 1986–91; Fellow, Wolfson Coll., Oxford 1967–83, Hon. Fellow 1995–; mem. Univ. Funding Council-Biological Science Advisory Panel, Medical Advisory Panel 1989; mem. Council, Grenoble Univ. 1990–91, Royal Soc. of Edin. 1986 (Gen. Sec. 2001–05), Council Open Univ. 2001–05; mem. Minister of Educ.'s Action Group on Standards in Scottish Schools 1997–99, Scottish Exec. Science Strategy Group 1999–2000, UNESCO UK Science Cttee 2000–02; Adviser to Wellcome Trust on UK-French Synchrotron 1999–2000; Chair. Int. Centre for Mathematical Sciences, Edin. 2001–05; Visiting Prof., Univ. of Edin. 2001–03; Leverhulme Emer. Fellow 2001–03; Bd mem. Food Standards Agency; Deputy Chair. Scottish Food Advisory Cttee 2003–05; Sec. and Treas., Carnegie Trust for the Univs of Scotland 2004–; Hon. DUniv (Stirling) 2002, (Open) 2006. *Publications:* Minerals in Biology (co-ed.) 1984; 170 research papers. *Leisure interests:* reading, walking, music. *Address:* Carnegie Trust for the Universities of Scotland, Andrew Carnegie House, Pittencrieff Street, Dunfermline, Fife, KY12 8AW, Scotland (office). *Telephone:* (1383) 724990 (office). *Fax:* (1383) 749799 (office). *E-mail:* amiller@carnegie-trust.org (office). *Website:* www.royalsoced.org.uk (office).

MILLER, Axel, LenD; Belgian banking executive; b. 20 Feb. 1965, Uccle; one s. three d.; ed Université Libre de Bruxelles; fmr Partner, Clifford Chance (law firm) for 14 years specializing in finance, mergers and acquisitions, int. commercial law; Gen. Counsel, Dexia Group 2001–02, mem. Man. Bd 2002–, Man. Dir and Chair. Man. Bd 2003–08, CEO Dexia SA 2006–08, Group Head, Personal Financial Services 2003–, mem. Strategy and Appointments Cttees, mem. Man. Bd Dexia Bank 2002–, Dexia BIL, mem. Bd of Dirs Dexia Crédit Local; Vice-Pres. Financial Security Assurance Holdings; mem. Man. Bd Fédération des entreprises de Belgique; mem. Bd of Dirs Ethias, Crédit du Nord, LVI Holding (Carmeuse group). *Address:* c/o Dexia Group, Place Logier 11, Brussels 1210, Belgium (office).

MILLER, Hon. Dame Billie Antoinette; Barbadian politician and lawyer; b. 8 Jan. 1944; d. of the late Frederick Edward Miller; ed Queen's Coll., Barbados, King's Coll., Univ. of Durham, UK; elected mem. Parl. for City of Bridgetown 1976, Mininster of Health and Nat. Insurance 1976–81, of Educ. 1981–85, of Educ. and Culture 1985–86; apptd to Senate 1986, Leader of Opposition Business; re-elected mem. Parl. 1991, Deputy Leader of Opposition 1993–94; Sr Minister and Minister of Foreign Affairs and Foreign Trade 1994–2008; Chair. Exec. Cttee Commonwealth Parl. Asscn 1991–99, NGO Planning Cttee for Int. Conf. on Population and Devt, Cairo, Egypt 1994, IDB's Advisory Council on Women in Devt, Washington, DC 1996–2002, Caribbean Tourism Org. 1997–98, Asscn of Caribbean States' Ministerial Council 2000–01; Pres. Int. Planned Parenthood Fed., Western Hemisphere Region 1991–97, African, Caribbean and Pacific States Council of Ministers 1998, 32nd Regular Session of the Gen. Ass. of OAS 2002; Pres. Bd Dirs Interamerican Parl. Group on Population and Devt for the Caribbean and Latin America, New York; Co-ordinator of CARICOM Ministerial Spokespersons with Responsibility for External Negotiations in Bilateral, ACP-EU, WTO and FTAA Matters 2002–; Vice-Chair. Commonwealth Ministerial Action Group 2000–02, 6th WTO Ministerial Conf. 2005; mem. Int. Planned Parenthood Fed. Cen. Council, Planned Parenthood Fed. of America Inc., UN Population Fund's Advisory Panel for Activities Concerning Women, Inter-American Dialogue; Hon. Fellow, Honors Coll., Florida International Univ. 2001; Grand Officer, Nat. Order of Benin 2000, Nat. Order of Juan Mora Fernandez, Costa Rica 2001; Dame of St Andrew 2003; Queen's Silver Jubilee Medal 1977, Barbados Centennial Award 2000, Grantley Adams Award, Barbados Labour Party 2001, Woman of Great Esteem Award, Kingdom Ministries, USA 2002, Dame Elsie Payne Award of Excellence, Queen's Coll. Asscn 2002, The Dame Billie Miller Lecture Series on Women in Govt in association with Medgar Evers Coll., CUNY 2004. *Publications:* numerous papers and articles on population and women's issues. *Leisure interests:* reading, interior design, Ikebana. *Address:* c/o Ministry of Foreign Affairs and Foreign Trade, 1 Culloden Road, St Michael, Barbados (office).

MILLER, Bode; American professional skier; b. 12 Oct. 1977, Franconia, NH; s. of Jo Miller; ed Carrabassett Valley Acad., Me; World Cup debut: Park City, UT, USA 1996; mem. US Nat. Team 1996–; Gold Medals, Combined and Giant Slalom events, World Championships, St Moritz, Switzerland 2003, Silver Medal, Super-G; Silver Medals, Combined and Giant Slalom events, Winter Olympic Games, Salt Lake City, USA 2002; 12 World Cup wins (six Giant Slalom, four Slalom, two Combined); won Alpine Skiing World Cup 2005, 2008; won Super G World Cup 2007; left US Ski Team 2007; f. Team America (ind. race team) 2007; f. SkiSpace.com (social networking and information site for skiers and snowboarders). *Leisure interest:* reggae and rap music. *Address:* c/o US Ski and Snowboard Association, Box 100, 1500 Kearns Blvd, Park City, UT 84060, USA. *Website:* www.skispace.com.

MILLER, David, LLB, MA; Canadian/American politician; *Mayor of Toronto;* b. USA; m. Jill Arthur; two c.; ed Faculty of Law, Univ. of Toronto, Harvard Univ., USA; trained in employment and immigration law; fmr Partner Aird & Berlis law firm, Toronto; cand. for New Democratic Party (NDP) in fed. elections, Parkdale-High Park constituency 1993, by-election in York S-Weston 1996; elected to Municipality of Metropolitan Toronto Council 1994–97, City of Toronto Council 1997–2003; Mayor of Toronto 2003–; mem. Bd Man. Bloor West Village Business Improvement Area, Colborne Lodge, Mackenzie House, Spadina House Community, Junction Gardens Business Improvement Area, Swansea Town Hall Community Centre; mem. Bd of Dirs Runnymede Hosp.; mem. Admin Cttee, Humber York Community Council, ABC Ad Hoc Cttee, Humber Watershed Alliance, Labour Relations Advisory Panel, Oak Ridges Moraine Steering Cttee, Toronto Transit Comm.; mem. Law Soc. of Upper Canada. *Address:* Toronto City Hall, 2nd Floor, 100 Queen Street West, Toronto, ON M5H 2N2, Canada (office). *Telephone:* (416) 397-2489 (office). *Fax:* (416) 696-3687 (office). *E-mail:* mayor_miller@toronto.ca (office). *Website:* www.toronto.ca (office).

MILLER, David A. B., BSc, PhD, FRS, FRSE; British physicist and academic; *Director, E.L. Ginzton Laboratory, Stanford University;* b. 19 Feb. 1954, Hamilton; ed Heriot-Watt Univ., St Andrews Univ.; Research Assoc., Heriot-Watt Univ. Dept of Physics 1979–80, Lecturer 1980–81; mem. Tech. Staff, AT&T Bell Laboratories, Holmdel, NJ, USA 1981–87, Head Photonics Switching Device Research Dept 1987–92, Head Photonics Research Dept 1996; Prof. of Electrical Eng, Stanford Univ. 1996, W. M. Keck Foundation Prof. of Electrical Eng 1997–, Prof. by Courtesy of Applied Physics 1997–, Dir Stanford Univ. Solid State and Photonics Lab. 1997–, Dir E.L. Ginzton Lab. 1997–, Co-Dir Stanford Photonics Research Center; Fellow Optical Soc. of America 1988–, American Physical Soc. 1988–, IEEE 1995–; Vice-Pres. Int. Comm. for Optics 1999–2002; Dir Optical Soc. of America 2000–03; mem. Editorial Bd Semiconductor Science and Technology 1987–90, Optical and Quantum Electronics 1988–, Applied Physics Reviews 1991–97; Dr hc (Vrije Universiteit) 1997, Hon. DEng (Heriot-Watt) 2003 Adolph Lomb Medal, Optical Soc. of America 1986, R. W. Wood Prize, Optical Soc. of America 1986, Int. Comm. for Optics Prize 1991, Third Millennium Medal, IEEE 2000. *Achievements:* holder of 58 patents. *Publications:* over 200 papers on optics and optoelectronics. *Address:* E.L. Ginzton Laboratory, Stanford University, Room AP213, 450 Via Palou, Stanford, CA 94305–4088, USA (office). *Telephone:* (650) 723-0111 (office). *Fax:* (650) 725-9355 (office). *E-mail:* dabm@ee.stanford.edu (office). *Website:* www.ee.stanford.edu/~dabm/ (office).

MILLER, Edward A., PhD; American engineer; worked on USAF experimental RVX-1 and RVX-2 re-entry vehicles and MK III intercontinental ballistic missile (ICBM) Atlas launch vehicle; fmr Project Engineer and Program Man., General Electric, responsible for design, construction, deployment, operation and recovery of Corona's satellite recovery vehicle (first man-made object recovered from Earth orbit); fmr Leader, Itek Corpn's Viking Lander Program, helped obtain first imagery transmitted from surface of Mars in 1974; Asst Sec. of the Army 1975–77, led R&D programme that resulted in advanced weapons systems, including Apache and Blackhawk helicopters, Abrams M1 Tank, Patriot High Altitude Air Defense System; Army Distinguished Civilian Service Decoration; recognized as an Eminent Engineer by Nat. Eng Honor Soc. (Tau Beta Pi) 1976, named a Pioneer of Space Tech. 1985, honoured by Dir of CIA for his role as Corona Pioneer 1995, Charles Stark Draper Prize, Nat. Acad. of Eng (co-recipient) 2005. *Address:* c/o National Academy of Engineering, 500 Fifth Street, NW, Washington, DC 20001, USA. *E-mail:* NAEMembershipOffice@nae.edu.

MILLER, Edward D., MD, FRCP, FRCA; American anesthesiologist, academic and university administrator; *Dean, Medical Faculty, School of Medicine, Johns Hopkins University;* b. 1 Feb. 1943, Rochester, NY; ed Ohio Wesleyan Univ., Univ. of Rochester School of Medicine and Dentistry; intern, Univ. Hosp., Boston 1968–69; Chief Resident in Anesthesiology, Peter Bent Brigham Hosp., Boston 1969–71; Research Fellow in Physiology, Harvard Medical School 1971–73; Dir of Anesthesia Research, Brooke Army Medical Center, Fort Sam Houston, Tex. 1973–75; Asst Prof. of Anesthesiology, Univ. of Virginia 1975–79, Assoc. Prof. 1979–82, Prof. of Anesthesiology 1982–83, Prof. of Anesthesiology and Surgery 1983–86; E.M. Papper Prof. of Anesthesiology and Chair., Dept of Anesthesiology, Coll. of Physicians and Surgeons, Columbia Univ. 1986–94; Mark C. Rogers Prof. and Dir Dept of Anesthesiology and Critical Care Medicine, Johns Hopkins Univ. 1994–, Interim Dean 1996–97, CEO 1997–, Vice-Pres. School of Medicine 1997–, Dean of Medical Faculty, Johns Hopkins Univ. School of Medicine 1997–, est. Center for Innovation in Quality Patient Care; mem. Asscn of Univ. Anesthesiologists (Pres. 1990–92); Ed. Anesthesia and Analgesia 1982–92; fmr Ed. Critical Care Medicine; fmr Chair. Food and Drug Asscn Advisory Cttee on Anesthesia and Life Support Drugs; mem., Inst. of Medicine, NAS, Maryland's Health Care Access and Cost Comm.; Bd mem. Greater Baltimore Cttee, Mercantile Safe Deposit and Trust Fund. *Address:* 100 SOM Administration, The Johns Hopkins University School of Medicine, 733 North Broadway, Baltimore, MD 21205, USA (office). *Telephone:* (410) 955-3180 (office). *Fax:* (410) 955-0889 (office). *E-mail:* emiller@jhmi.edu (office). *Website:* webapps.jhu.edu (office).

MILLER, George H., BS, MS, PhD; American physicist and academic; *Laboratory Director and President, Lawrence Livermore National Security LLC;* ed Coll. of William and Mary; Physicist, Lawrence Livermore Nat. Lab., Univ. of California 1972–80, A-Div. Leader and Program Leader, Thermonuclear Design and Computational Physics Devt 1980–85, Assoc. Dir for Nuclear Design 1985–89, Assoc. Dir for Defense and Nuclear Techs 1990–, Assoc. Dir for Nat. Security 1996–2000, Assoc. Dir for Nat. Ignition Facility programs 2000–05, Interim Dir 2005–06, Lab. Dir and Pres. Lawrence Livermore Nat. Security LLC 2006–; Special Scientific Adviser on Weapon Activities, US Dept of Energy, Washington, DC 1989–90; mem. Sr Man. Group, Univ. of California; mem. American Physical Soc.; Fellowship Awards from NSF, Gulf Gen. Atomics. *Address:* Lawrence Livermore National Security LLC, 2300 First Street, Suite 204, Livermore, CA 94550, USA (office). *Telephone:* (925) 453-3580 (office). *Fax:* (925) 454-1447 (office). *Website:* www.llnsllc.com (office).

MILLER, George 'Kennedy', AO, MB, BS; Australian film director, producer, writer and physician; b. 3 March 1945, Chinchilla, Queensland; s. of James Miller and Angela Miller (née Balson); m. Sandy Gore 1985; one d.; ed Sydney Boys' High School, Univ. of New South Wales Medical School; Resident Medical Officer, St Vincent's Hosp., Sydney 1971–72; f. Kennedy Miller film co. with the late Byron Kennedy 1977, Chair. 1977–; Pres. Jury Avoriaz Film Festival 1984; mem. Jury Cannes Film Festival 1988; Chair. Byron Kennedy Memorial Trust 1984–; mem. Bd Dirs Museum of Contemporary Art, Sydney 1987–; Best Dir, Australian Film Inst. 1982, Best Dir TV Drama, Penguin Awards 1983, Grand Prix Avoriaz 1983, Best Foreign Film, LA Film Critics 1983 and numerous other prizes and awards. *Films include:* dir: Violence In the Cinema, Part 1 (also writer) 1971, Mad Max (also writer) 1979, Mad Max 2 (also writer) 1981, Twilight Zone: The Movie (segment 4) 1983, Mad Max Beyond Thunderdome (also producer and writer) 1985, The Witches of Eastwick 1987, Lorenzo's Oil (also producer and writer) 1992, 40,000 Years of Dreaming (also producer and writer) 1997, Babe: Pig in the City (also producer and writer) 1998, Happy Feet (also producer and writer) (BAFTA Award for Best Animated Film 2007) 2006; producer: The Chain Reaction (assoc. producer) 1980, The Year My Voice Broke 1987, Dead Calm 1989, Flirting 1991, Video Fool for Love 1995, Babe (also writer) (Golden Globe Award for Best Picture 1996) 1995, 40,000 Years of Dreaming 1997, Babe: Pig in the City 1998, Happy Feet (Acad. Award for Best Animated Feature Film 2007) 2006. *Television includes:* dir: Ryan (series) 1973, Bellamy (series; episode 1.02 The Carver Gang) 1981, The Dismissal (mini-series) (also exec. producer and writer) 1983, The Last Bastion (mini-series; co-dir) 1984; producer: Cowra Breakout (mini-series) 1984, Bodyline: It's Not Just Cricket (mini-series) 1984, The Riddle of the Stinson 1987, Vietnam (mini-series) 1987, The Dirtwater Dynasty (mini-series) 1988, The Clean Machine 1988, Fragments of War: The Story of Damien Parer 1988, Bangkok Hilton (mini-series) 1989. *Leisure interests:* art, music, sport. *Address:* 30 Orwell Street, King's Cross, NSW 2011, Australia. *Telephone:* (2) 357-2322.

MILLER, Heidi G., PhD; American investment banker; *CEO, Treasury and Security Services, JPMorgan Chase & Co.;* b. 1953; m. Brian Miller; two c.; ed Princeton Univ., Yale Univ.; began career at Chemical Bank in 1979, Man. Dir and Group Head, Emerging Markets 1987–92; Vice-Pres. and Asst to Pres. Travelers Group Inc. 1992–98, later Chief Risk Officer of its Salomon Smith Barney unit, Chief Financial Officer Travelers Group Inc. 1995–98; Chief Financial Officer Citigroup Inc. 1998–2000; Sr Exec. Vice-Pres. Strategic Planning and Admin and mem. Bd of Dirs Priceline.com 2000–01; Vice-Chair. Marsh & McLennan Co. Inc. 2001–; Exec. Vice-Pres., Chief Financial Officer and mem. Bd Dirs Bank One, Chicago 2002–04, Exec. Vice-Pres. and CEO Treasury and Security Services, JPMorgan Chase & Co. (following merger with Bank One) 2004–; mem. Bd of Dirs General Mills Inc., Mead Corpn and Merck & Co. Inc., Local Initiatives Support Corpn 2004–; Trustee Princeton Univ.; ranked by Fortune magazine amongst 50 Most Powerful Women in Business in the US (50th) 2002, (29th) 2004, (28th) 2005, (25th) 2006, (27th) 2007, named by US Banker magazine amongst 25 Women to Watch 2004, also named amongst the 25 Most Powerful Women in Banking (fourth) 2005, (first) 2007, (first) 2008; named by Global Finance magazine amongst Ones to Watch 2005. *Address:* JPMorgan Chase & Co., 270 Park Avenue, New York, NY 10017, USA (office). *Telephone:* (212) 270-6000 (office). *Fax:* (212) 270-1613 (office). *Website:* www.jpmorganchase.com (office).

MILLER, Jacques Francis, AO, BA, MD, PhD, DSc, FAA, FRS; Australian medical research scientist and academic; *Professor Emeritus, University of Melbourne;* b. (Jacques Francis Meunier), 2 April 1931, Nice, France; s. of the late Maurice Miller and Fernande Debarnot; m. Margaret D. Houen 1956; ed Univs of Sydney and London; Jr Resident Medical Officer, Royal Prince Alfred Hosp., Sydney 1956; pathological research, Univ. of Sydney 1957, fmr Prof. of Experimental Immunology, now Prof. Emer.; cancer research, Chester Beatty Research Inst., London 1958–65; Head, Experimental Pathology and Thymus Biology Unit, Walter and Eliza Hall Inst., Melbourne 1966–; various other professional appointments; Foreign Assoc., NAS; numerous awards and honours including Esther Langer-Bertha Teplitz Memorial Prize 1965, Paul Ehrlich-Ludwig Darmstaedter Prize 1974, Inaugural Sandoz Prize for Immunology 1990, Florey-Faulding Medal and Prize 2000, Copley Medal, Royal Soc. 2001, Prime Minister's Prize for Science 2003. *Publications:* more than 400 papers in scientific journals, mostly on immunology and cancer research. *Leisure interests:* art, photography, music, literature. *Address:* Walter and Eliza Hall Institute of Medical Research, 1G Royal Parade, Parkville, Vic. 3050 (office); 5 Charteris Drive, East Ivanhoe, Vic. 3079, Australia (home). *Telephone:* (3) 9345-2555 (office); (3) 9499-3481 (home). *Fax:* (3) 9347-0852 (office). *Website:* www.wehi.edu.au.

MILLER, James Clifford, III, PhD; American business executive, academic and government official; *Chairman, Board of Governors, United States Postal Service;* b. 25 June 1942, Atlanta, Ga; s. of James Clifford Miller, Jr and Annie Moseley; m. Demaris Humphries 1961; one s. two d.; ed Univs of Georgia and Virginia; Asst Prof. Ga State Univ. Atlanta 1968–69; Economist, US Dept of Transport 1969–72; Assoc. Prof. of Econs Texas A & M Univ. 1972–74; Economist, US Council of Econ. Advisers, Washington, DC 1974–75; Asst Dir US Council of Wage and Price Stability 1975–77; Resident Scholar, American Enterprise Inst. 1977–81; Admin., Office of Information and Regulatory Affairs, Office of Man. and Budget and Exec. Dir Presidential Task Force on Regulatory Relief 1981; Chair. Fed. Trade Comm., Washington, DC 1981–85; Dir Office of Man. and Budget 1985–89; Distinguished Fellow, Center for Study of Public Choice, George Mason Univ. 1988–, Chair. Citizens for a Sound Econ. 1988–2002; Chair. The CapAnalysis Group 2002–04; Chair. Bd of Govs, US Postal Service 2004–, Chair. Audit and Finance Cttee; Thomas Jefferson Fellow 1965–66; DuPont Fellow 1966–67, Ford Foundation Fellow 1967–68. *Publications:* Why the Draft? The Case for a Volunteer Army 1968, Economic Regulation of Domestic Air Transport; Theory and Policy 1974, Perspectives on Federal Transportation Policy 1975, Benefit – Cost Analyses of Social Regulation 1979, Reforming Regulation 1980, The Federal Trade Commission: The Political Economy of Regulation 1987, The Economist as Reformer 1989, Fix the U.S. Budget! 1994, Monopoly Politics 1999. *Leisure interests:* politics, econs. *Address:* Board of Governors, United States Postal Service, 475 L'Enfant Plaza, SW, Washington, DC 20260-0010, USA. *Telephone:* (202) 268-2500 (office). *Fax:* (202) 268-4860 (office). *Website:* www.usps.com (office).

MILLER, Jonathan; American media executive; b. 1957; early career Vice-Pres. of Programming and NBA Entertainment with Nat. Basketball Asscn; CEO and Man. Dir Nickelodeon UK, then Man. Dir Int.; Pres. and CEO USA Broadcasting 1997–1999; Pres. and CEO USA Electronic Commerce Solutions 1999–2000; Pres. and CEO USA Information and Services (USAIS) 2000–2002; Chair. and CEO America Online Inc. (later AOL LLC) 2002–06. *Address:* c/o AOL LLC, 22000 AOL Way, Dulles, VA, 20166-9323, USA (office).

MILLER, Sir Jonathan Wolfe, Kt, CBE, MB, BCh, FRA, FRCP; British stage director, film director, physician and writer; b. 21 July 1934, London; s. of the late Emanuel Miller; m. Helen Rachel Collet 1956; two s. one d.; ed St Paul's School, St John's Coll., Cambridge and Univ. Coll. Hosp. Medical School, London; co-author of and appeared in Beyond the Fringe 1961–64; Dir John Osborne's Under Plain Cover, Royal Court Theatre 1962, Robert Lowell's The Old Glory, New York 1964 and Prometheus Bound, Yale Drama School 1967; Dir at Nottingham Playhouse 1968–69; Dir Oxford and Cambridge Shakespeare Co. production of Twelfth Night on tour in USA 1969; Research Fellow in the History of Medicine, Univ. Coll., London 1970–73; Assoc. Dir Nat. Theatre 1973–75; mem. Arts Council 1975–76; Visiting Prof. in Drama, Westfield Coll., Univ. of London 1977–; Exec. Producer Shakespeare TV series 1979–81; Artistic Dir Old Vic 1988–90; Research Fellow in Neuropsychology, Univ. of Sussex; Fellow, Univ. Coll. London 1981–, Royal Coll. of Physicians; mem. American Acad. of Arts and Sciences; Hon. Fellow, St John's Coll. Cambridge, Royal Coll. of Physicians (Edin.) 1998; Dr hc (Open Univ.) 1983, Hon. DLitt (Leicester) 1981, (Kent) 1985, (Leeds) 1996, (Cambridge) 1996; Royal Television Soc. Silver Medal 1981, Royal Soc. of Arts Albert Medal 1992. *Productions:* for Nat. Theatre, London: The Merchant of Venice 1970, Danton's Death 1971, The School for Scandal 1972, The Marriage of Figaro 1974; other productions The Tempest, London 1970, Prometheus Bound, London 1971, The Taming of the Shrew, Chichester 1972, The Seagull, Chichester 1973, The Malcontent, Nottingham 1973, Arden Must Die (opera) 1973, The Family in Love, Greenwich Season 1974, The Importance of Being Earnest 1975, The Cunning Little Vixen (opera) 1975, All's Well That Ends Well, Measure For Measure, Greenwich Season 1975, Three Sisters 1977, The Marriage of Figaro (ENO) 1978, Arabella (opera) 1980, Falstaff (opera) 1980, 1981, Otello (opera) 1982, Rigoletto (opera) 1982, 1984, Fidelio (opera) 1982, 1983, Don Giovanni (opera) 1985, The Mikado (opera) 1986, Tosca (opera) 1986, Long Day's Journey into Night 1986, Taming of the Shrew 1987, The Tempest 1988, Turn of the Screw 1989, King Lear 1989, The Liar 1989, La Fanciulla del West (opera) 1991, Marriage of Figaro (opera), Manon Lescaut (opera), Die Gezeichneten (opera) 1992, Maria Stuarda (opera), Capriccio (opera), Fedora (opera), Bach's St Matthew Passion 1993, Der Rosenkavalier (opera), Anna Bolena (opera), Falstaff (opera), L'Incoronazione di Poppea (opera), La Bohème (opera) 1994, Così fan Tutte (opera) 1995, Carmen (opera) 1995, Pelléas et Mélisande (opera) 1995, She Stoops to Conquer, London 1995, A Midsummer Night's Dream, London 1996, The Rake's Progress, New York 1997, Ariadne auf Naxos, Maggio Musicale, Florence 1997, Falstaff, Berlin State Opera 1998, The Beggar's Opera 1999, Tamerlano, Sadler's Wells, Paris and Halle 2001, Jenufa, Glimmerglass Opera 2006, The Cherry Orchard, Sheffield Crucible 2007, La Bohème, ENO, London 2009. *Films:* Take a Girl Like You 1969 and several films for television including Whistle and I'll Come to You 1967, Alice in Wonderland 1966, The Body in Question (series) 1978, States of Mind (series) 1983, The Emperor 1987, Jonathan Miller's Opera Works (series) 1997, Brief History of Disbelief (series) 2005. *Publications:* McLuhan 1971, Freud: The Man, his World, his Influence (ed.) 1972, The Body in Question 1978, Subsequent Performances 1986, The Don Giovanni Book: Myths of Seduction and Betrayal (ed.) 1990, On Reflection 1998, Nowhere in Particular 2001. *Leisure interest:* deep sleep.

MILLER, Karl Fergus Connor, FRSL; British academic, writer and editor; b. 2 Aug. 1931; s. of William Miller and Marion Miller; m. Jane Elisabeth Collet 1956; two s. one d.; ed Royal High School, Edinburgh and Downing Coll., Cambridge; Asst Prin., HM Treasury 1956–57; BBC TV producer 1957–58; Literary Ed., The Spectator 1958–61, New Statesman 1961–67; Ed., The Listener 1967–73; Lord Northcliffe Prof. of Modern English Literature, Univ. Coll., London 1974–92; Ed., London Review of Books 1979–89, Co-Ed. 1989–92; James Tait Black Prize 1975, Scottish Arts Council Book Award 1993. *Publications:* Poetry from Cambridge 1952–54 (ed.) 1955, Writing in England Today: The Last Fifteen Years (ed.) 1968, Memoirs of a Modern Scotland (ed.) 1970, A Listener Anthology, August 1967–June 1970 (ed.) 1970, A Second Listener Anthology (ed.) 1973, Cockburn's Millennium 1975, Robert Burns (ed.) 1981, Doubles: Studies in Literary History 1985, Authors 1989, Rebecca's Vest (autobiog.) 1993, Boswell and Hyde 1995, Dark Horses (autobiog.) 1998, Electric Shepherd: A Likeness of James Hogg 2003. *Leisure interest:* football. *Address:* 26 Limerston Street, London, SW10 0HH, England. *Telephone:* (20) 7351-1994.

MILLER, Lajos; Hungarian singer (baritone); b. 23 Jan. 1940, Szombathely; s. of Lajos Miller and Teréz Sebestyén; m. Zsuzsa Dobránszky; one s.; ed studied at Music Acad. of Budapest under Jenö Sipos; mem. Hungarian State Opera 1968–; roles include Verdi's Renato, Rodrigo, Simon Boccanegra, Don Carlos, Rolando in Battaglia di Legnano, Iago, Nabucco, Conte di Luna, Miller, Germont, Gluck's Orpheus, Orestes, Mozart's Don Giovanni, Guglielmo, Giordano's Carlo Gérard, Leoncavallo's Silvio, Rossini's Figaro, Guglielmo Tell, Tchaikovsky's Eugene Onegin, Yeletsky, Puccini's Scarpia, Bizet's Escamillo, Berio's Commandante Ivo, Donizetti's Enrico, Rimsky-Korsakov's Grasnoi, Puccini's Sharplesshas; sung with major cos in France, Germany, Italy, Monaco, Switzerland, Austria, UK, USA, Belgium, Venezuela, Canada, Chile, Japan, Argentina, Russia; Grand Prix, Fauré singing contest, Paris 1974, First Prize, Toti dal Monte singing contest, Treviso, Italy 1975, Liszt Prize 1975, Kossuth Prize 1980. *TV films:* Orfeusz Es Eurydike (Rainieri de Calzabigi and Christoph Willibald Gluck) 1985, Enrico (Lucia di Lammermoor), Marcello (Tabarro), Silvio (Pagliacci), Loth (Madarasz Loth), two portrait films 1995, Angelica (Ibert), L'elisir d'amore (Donizetti), Rigoletto (Verdi), Bank Ban 2002. *Leisure interests:* tennis, surfing, skiing, photography, making films. *E-mail:* info@lajosmiller.com (office). *Website:* www.lajosmiller.com.

MILLER, Leslie O.; Bahamian politician; fmr Minister of Trade and Industry. *Address:* c/o Ministry of Trade and Industry, Manx Building, West Bay Street, POB N-4849, Nassau, The Bahamas (office).

MILLER, Leszek, MPolSci; Polish politician; b. 3 July 1946, Żyrardów; m. Aleksandra Borowiec; one s.; ed Higher School of Social Sciences; electrician Enterprise of Linen Industry, Żyrardów 1963–70; mem. Polish United Workers' Party (PZPR) 1966–90, Staff mem. Cen. Cttee 1977–86; First Sec. Voivodeship's Cttee of Skierniewice 1986–89, mem. Cen. Cttee 1989–90, mem. Politburo Cen. Cttee 1989–90; Participant Round Table Talks 1989; Deputy to Sejm (Parl.) 1991– (Chair. Left Alliance Caucus 1997–2001); Minister of Labour and Social Policy 1993–96, of Interior and Admin. 1997; Minister, Head Council of Ministers Office 1996; Chair. Democratic Left Alliance (SLD) 1999–; mem. and Co-founder Social Democracy of Repub. of Poland 1990–2001 (Gen. Sec. 1990–93, Vice-Chair. 1993–97, Chair. 1997–2001); Prime Minister of Poland 2001–04 (resgnd); Kt's Cross of Polonia Restituta Order 1984, Golden Cross of Merit 1979, Chevalier of the Order of the Smile; Goodwill Amb., Polish Cttee of UNICEF 2000. *Leisure interests:* angling, literature. *Address:* c/o Chancellery of the Prime Minister, Al. Ujazdowskie 1/3, 00-583 Warsaw, Poland (office).

MILLER, Sir Peter North, Kt, MA, DSc; British insurance broker; b. 28 Sept. 1930, London; s. of Cyril T. Miller and Dorothy N. Miller; m. Jane Miller 1991; one s.; two s. one d. by previous marriage; ed Rugby School and Lincoln Coll. Oxford; joined Thos. R. Miller & Son (Insurance) 1953, Partner 1959, Sr Partner 1971–, Chair. of Miller Insurance Group 1971–83, 1988–96; mem. Cttee Lloyds Insurance Brokers' Asscn 1973–77, Deputy Chair. 1974-75, Chair. 1976–77; mem. Cttee of Lloyds 1977–80, 1982–89; Chair. of Lloyds 1984–87; mem. Cttee on Invisible Exports 1975–77; mem. Insurance Brokers' Registration Council 1977–81; Chair. British Cttee of Bureau Veritas 1980–2001; one of Her Majesty's Lts for City of London 1987–; Hon. Fellow Lincoln Coll., Oxford 1992–; Commendatore, Ordine al Merito della Repubblica Italiana 1989. *Leisure interests:* all forms of sport (except cricket), particularly running, riding, tennis and sailing, wine, music. *Address:* c/o Miller Insurance Group, Dawson House, 5 Jewry Street, London, EC3N 2PY (office); Quinneys, Camilla Drive, Westhumble, Dorking, Surrey, RH5 6BU, England. *Telephone:* (20) 7488-2345.

MILLER, Robert; Canadian electronics industry executive; f. Future Electronics 1968, now third-largest wholesale electronics distributor in world; supporter of Alcor Life Extension Foundation. *Address:* Future Electronics, 237 Hymus Boulevard, Pointe-Claire, PQ H9R 5C7, Canada (office). *Telephone:* (514) 694-7710 (office). *Fax:* (514) 695-3707 (office). *Website:* www.futureelectronics.com (office).

MILLER, Robert (Bob) G., BA, MBA; American business executive; ed Univ. of Missouri, Kansas City, Iowa State Univ.; joined Albertson's Inc. 1961, Exec. Vice Pres. Retail Operations 1989–91; CEO Fred Meyer Inc. 1991–99; Vice-Chair. and COO The Kroger Co. (following acquisition of Fred Meyer Inc. by Kroger) 1999; Chair. Rite Aid Corpn 1999–2007, CEO 1999–2003, remains mem. Bd of Dirs; mem. Bd of Dirs Harrah's Entertainment Inc. 1999–, Nordstrom, Inc. 2005–; Chair. Wild Oats Markets, Inc. *Address:* Rite Aid Corporation, 30 Hunter Lane, Camp Hill, PA 17011, USA (office). *Telephone:* (717) 761-2633 (office). *Fax:* (717) 975-5871 (office). *E-mail:* contacttheboard@riteaid.com (office). *Website:* www.riteaid.com (office).

MILLER, Robert Joseph (Bob), BA, JD; American lawyer and politician; *Principal, Dutko Worldwide;* b. 30 March 1945, Evanston, Ill.; s. of Ross Wendell Miller and Coletta Jane Doyle; m. Sandra Ann Searles; one s. two d.; ed Santa Clara and Loyola Univs; First Legal Advisor, Las Vegas Metropolitan Police Dept 1973–75; JP 1975–78; Deputy Dist Attorney, Clark Co., Las Vegas 1971–73, Dist Attorney 1979–86; Lt Gov. of Nevada 1987–89, 1989–90, Gov. 1989–99; Chair. Nev. Comm. on Econ. Devt, Nev. Comm. on Tourism 1987–91; mem. Nat. Govs Asscn (Vice-Chair. Exec. Cttee 1995–96, Chair. 1996–97, fmr Chair. Cttee on Justice and Public Safety, Chair. Legal Affairs Cttee 1992–94, Lead Gov. on Transport 1992–); Sr Partner, Jones Vargas, Las Vegas 1999–2005; Prin., Dutko Worldwide, Las Vegas 2005–; Co-Chair. Russian Heritage Highway Foundation; Democrat; Hon. Consul Officer of Repub. of Bulgaria. *Address:* Dutko Worldwide, 900 South Pavilion Center, Las Vegas, NV 89133, USA (office). *Telephone:* (702) 240-0831 (office). *Fax:* (702) 240-0331 (office). *Website:* www.dutkoworldwide.com (office).

MILLER, Robert Stevens (Steve), Jr, AB, MBA, JD; American business executive; *Executive Chairman, Delphi Corporation;* b. 4 Nov. 1941, Portland, Ore.; s. of Robert Stevens Miller and Barbara Weston Miller; m. Margaret Rose Kyger 1966; three s.; ed Stanford Univ. and Harvard Law School; mem. financial staff, Ford Motor Co., Dearborn, Mich. 1968–71; Investment Man., Ford Motor de Mexico, Mexico City 1971–73; Dir of Finance, Ford Asia Pacific, Melbourne, Australia 1974–77; Vice-Pres. (Finance), Ford Motor de Venezuela, Caracas 1977–79; Vice-Pres.-Treas., Chrysler Corpn, Detroit, Mich. 1980–81, Exec. Vice-Pres. (Finance) 1981–85, 1985–88, Exec. Vice-Pres. 1988–92; Sr Partner James D. Wolfensohn Inc. 1992–93; Chair. Morrison Knudson Corpn 1995–96; Chair. Waste Man. Inc. 1998–99, Pres. and CEO 1999, now Dir; Chair. and CEO Federal-Mogul Corpn 2000–05; Chair. and CEO Delphi Corpn 2005–07, Exec. Chair. 2007–; mem. Bd of Dirs United Airlines, Reynolds American, Symantec Corpn, Waste Management, Inc.; mem. Int. Advisory Bd, Creditanstalt Bankverein, Vienna, Austria. *Leisure interest:* model railroading. *Address:* Delphi Corpn, 5725 Delphi Drive, Troy, MI 48098-2815, USA (office). *Telephone:* (248) 813-2000 (office). *Fax:* (248) 813-2670 (office). *E-mail:* info@delphi.com (office). *Website:* www.delphi.com (office).

MILLER, Stuart A., BS, JD; American real estate executive; *CEO and President, Lennar Corporation;* b. 1957; s. of the late Leonard Miller and Susan Miller; m. Vicki Miller, four c.; ed Harvard Univ., Univ. of Miami; joined Lennar Corpn 1981, Vice-Pres. 1992–97, CEO and Pres. 1997–, Chair. LNR Property Corpn 1997–; mem. Jt Center for Housing Studies Policy Advisory Bd, Harvard Univ.; America's Most Powerful People, Forbes 2000. *Address:* Lennar Corporation, 700 NW 107th Avenue, Suite 400, Miami, FL 33172, USA (office). *Telephone:* (305) 559-4000 (office). *Fax:* (305) 229-6453 (office). *Website:* www.lennar.com (office).

MILLER, Thomas J., MA, PhD; American diplomatist; b. 1948, Chicago; ed Univ. of Michigan; mem. Sr Foreign Service at rank of Minister-Counselor; joined State Dept 1976; analyst for Vietnam, Laos and Cambodia 1976–77; Special Asst to Under-Sec. for Political Affairs 1977–79; Deputy Prin. Officer, US Consulate, Chiang Mai, Thailand 1979–81; served twice on Israeli Desk (once as Dir); Head Office of Maghreb Affairs; Acting Dir of an office on counter-terrorism; political section, Athens Embassy 1985–87, Deputy Chief of Mission, Athens 1994–97; Special Coordinator for Cyprus (with rank of Amb.) 1997–99; Amb. to Bosnia and Herzegovina 1999–2001, to Greece 2001–04; retd from US State Dept 2005; mem. Int. Advisory Bd Hellenic-American Heritage Council; Equal Opportunity Award (Dept. of State), Superior Honor Award (five times) (Dept of State), Meritorious Award (Dept of State) and many others. *Address:* c/o Hellenic American Heritage Council, 1100 New Hampshire Avenue, NW, Washington, DC 20037, USA.

MILLER, Walter Geoffrey Thomas, AO; Australian diplomatist; *Vice-President, Australian Institute of International Affairs;* b. 25 Oct. 1934, Tasmania; s. of Walter T. Miller and Gertrude S. Galloway; m. Rachel C. Webb 1960; three s. one d.; ed Launceston High School, Univs of Tasmania and Oxford; served in Australian missions in Kuala Lumpur, Djakarta and at UN, New York; Deputy High Commr, India 1973–75; Amb. to Repub. of Korea 1978–80; Head, Int. Div. Dept of the Prime Minister and Cabinet, Canberra 1982; Deputy Sec. Dept of Foreign Affairs 1985–86; Amb. to Japan 1986–89; Dir-Gen. Office of Nat. Assessments Canberra 1989–95; High Commr to NZ 1996–2000; Vice-Pres. Australian Inst. of Int. Affairs 2005–; Rhodes Scholar 1956. *Leisure interests:* international relations, literature, ballet, tennis, reading, golf. *Address:* 124 Kent Street, Sydney, NSW 2000 (office); 85 Union Street, McMahons Point, NSW 2060, Australia (home). *Telephone:* (2) 9247-2709 (office).

MILLER, William Hughes, BS, AM, PhD; American chemist and academic; *Kenneth S. Pitzer Distinguished Professor of Chemistry, University of California, Berkeley;* b. 16 March 1941, Kosciusko, MS; ed Georgia Inst. of Tech., Harvard Univ.; NATO Postdoctoral Fellow, Univ. of Freiburg, Germany 1967–68; Jr Fellow, Harvard Univ. 1967–69; Asst Prof., Dept of Chem., Univ. of Calif., Berkeley 1969–72, Assoc. Prof. 1972–74, Prof. 1974–, Miller Research Prof. 1978–79, 1998–99, Vice-Chair. Dept of Chem. 1984–88, Chair. 1989–93, Chancellor's Research Prof. 1998–2001, Kenneth S. Pitzer Distinguished Prof. 1999–; Sr Staff Scientist, Chemical Sciences Div., Lawrence Berkeley Nat. Lab. 1969–; mem. Editorial Bd Chemical Physics 1973–96, Nouveau Journal de Chimie 1977–87, International Journal of Quantum Chemistry 1979–89, Journal of Physical Chemistry 1983–89, Advances in Quantum Chemistry 1987–, Theoretical Chemistry Accounts 1997–; mem. ACS 1980–, Int. Acad. of Quantum Molecular Science 1985–, NAS 1987–; Fellow AAAS 1983–, American Physical Soc. 1984– (Vice-Chair. and later Chair., Div. of Chemical Physics 1997–2000), American Acad. of Arts and Sciences 1993–; Hon. Prof., Univ. of Shandong 1994; Int. Acad. of Quantum Molecular Science Annual Prize 1974, Humboldt Foundation Sr Scientist Award 1981, E. O. Lawrence Award 1985, ACS Irving Langmuir Award in Chemical Physics 1990, ACS Award in Theoretical Chem. 1994, J. O. Hirschfelder Prize in Theoretical Chem. 1996, ACS Ira Remsen Award 1997, Royal Soc. of Chem. Faraday Div. Spiers Medal 1998, ACS Peter Debye Award Award in Physical Chem. 2003, Welch Award in Chem. 2007. *Publications:* more than 300 articles in scientific journals. *Leisure interest:* playing 'old time' banjo. *Address:* Department of Chemistry, University of California, Berkeley, CA 94720, USA (office). *Telephone:* (510) 642-0653 (office). *Fax:* (510) 642-6262 (office). *E-mail:* millerwh@berkeley.edu (office). *Website:* neon.cchem.berkeley.edu (office).

MILLER, Zell Bryan, MA; American fmr politician; b. 24 Feb. 1932, Young Harris, Ga; s. of Stephen G. Miller and Birdie Bryan; m. Shirley Carver 1954; two s.; ed Young Harris Coll., Univ. of Ga; Prof. of Political Science and History, Univ. of Ga, Young Harris Coll. 1959–64, 1999–; mem. Ga Senate 1960–64; Dir Ga Bd of Probation 1965–67; Deputy Dir Ga Dept of Corrections 1967–68; Exec. Sec. to Gov. of Ga 1968–71; Exec. Dir Democratic Cttee of Ga 1971–72; mem. State Bd of Pardons and Paroles, Atlanta 1973–75; Lt-Gov. of Ga 1975–90; Gov. of Ga 1990–98, Senator from Ga 2000–05; Pres. Council of

State Govts 1991; Vice-Chair. Southern Gov.'s Asscn 1991; mem. American Battle Monuments Comm. 2005–; contrib. Fox News Channel 2005–. *Publications:* The Mountains Within Me, Great Georgians, They Heard Georgia Singing. *Address:* 1175 Peachtree Street, NE, #100–300, Atlanta, GA 30361, USA (office).

MILLER SMITH, Charles, MA; British business executive; *Chairman, Scottish Power PLC;* b. 7 Nov. 1939, Glasgow; s. of William Smith and Margaret Wardrope; m. Dorothy Adams 1964 (died 1999); one s. two d.; ed Glasgow Acad. and St Andrews Univ.; Financial Dir Vinyl Products, Unilever 1970–73, Head of Planning 1974; Finance Dir Walls Meat Co. 1976; Vice-Chair. Industan Lever 1979–81; Speciality Chemicals Group 1981; Chief Exec. PPF Int. 1983; Chief Exec. Quest Int. 1986; Financial Dir Unilever Bd 1989; Exec. Unilever Foods 1993–94; Exec. Dir ICI PLC 1994–95, Chief Exec. 1995–99, Chair. 1999–2001; Chair. (non-exec.) Scottish Power PLC 2000–; Dir HSBC Holdings PLC 1996–; Int. Adviser, Goldman Sachs 2001–05; currently European Adviser, Warburg Pincus LLC; mem. Defence Man. Bd, Ministry of Defence; Hon. LLD (St Andrews) 1995. *Leisure interests:* reading, walking. *Address:* Scottish Power PLC, Corporate Office, 1 Atlantic Quay, Glasgow, G2 8SP, Scotland (office). *Telephone:* (141) 248-8200 (office). *Fax:* (141) 248-8300 (office). *Website:* www.scottishpower.plc.uk (office).

MILLERON, Jean-Claude; French economist and international finance official; b. 8 Jan. 1937, Paris; s. of Pierre A. Milleron and Geneviève Hédouin; m. Marie-France Dannaud 1966; two s. one d.; ed Ecole Polytechnique, Paris, Ecole Supérieure des Sciences Econ., Paris; with Nat. Inst. of Statistics and Econ. Studies (INSEE), Paris 1963–70, Dir-Gen. 1987–92; Visiting Research Dept of Econs, Univ. of Calif., Berkeley 1970–71; Deputy Dir Nat. School of Statistics and Econ. Admin. (ENSAE), Paris 1971–78; Head of Dept of Econs, Planning Commissariat-Gen., Paris 1978–81; Dir of Forecasting, Ministry of Econ. and Finance 1982–87; Dir-Gen. INSEE 1986–92; Under-Sec.-Gen. Dept of Econ. and Social Information and Policy Analysis, UN, New York 1992–97; Special Adviser to French Minister of Econ., Finance and Industry 1997–98; apptd Exec. Dir of IMF and IBRD 1998; apptd Financial Minister, Embassy in Washington, DC 1998; Fellow, Econometric Soc. *Publications:* various books and articles on econ. theory and public econs. *Leisure interests:* jogging, hiking, opera. *Address:* c/o Ministry of the Economy, Finance and Industry, 139 rue de Bercy, 75572 Paris, France.

MILLETT, Baron (Life Peer), cr. 1998, of St Marylebone in the City of Westminster; **Peter Julian Millett,** PC; British judge (retd); b. 23 June 1932; s. of the late Dennis Millett and Adele Millett; m. Ann Harris 1958; three s. (one deceased); ed Harrow School and Univ. of Cambridge; called to Bar, Middle Temple 1955, Lincoln's Inn 1959, Singapore 1976, Hong Kong 1979; at Chancery Bar 1958–86; Lecturer in Practical Conveyancing and Examiner Council of Legal Educ. 1962–76; mem. Gen. Council of the Bar 1971–75; Judge, High Court of Justice, Chancery Div. 1986–94, Lord Justice of Appeal 1994–98, Lord of Appeal in Ordinary 1998–2004; mem. House of Lords 1998–; Non-Perm. Judge of the Court of Final Appeal, Hong Kong 2000–; Hon. Fellow, Trinity Hall Cambridge; Hon. LLD (Queen Mary and Westfield Coll., London). *Address:* House of Lords, Westminster, London, SW1A 0PQ (office); Essex Court Chambers, 24 Lincoln's Inn Fields, London, WC2A 3EG, England (office). *Telephone:* (20) 7219-3202 (office); (20) 7813-8000 (office). *Fax:* (20) 7219-5979 (office); (20) 7813-8080 (office).

MILLIKEN, Hon. Peter Andrew Stewart, LLB, MA; Canadian politician and lawyer; *Speaker, House of Commons;* b. 12 Nov. 1946, Kingston, Ont.; s. of John Andrew Milliken and Catherine Margaret Milliken; ed Queen's Univ., Kingston, Wadham Coll., Oxford, UK, Dalhousie Univ., Halifax; called to Bar of Ont., Solicitor of Supreme Court of Ont. 1973; solicitor, Cunningham, Little, Kingston (law firm) 1973–78, PNR, Cunningham, Little, Bonham and Milliken 1978–89; MP for Kingston and the Islands 1988–; served as Asst House Leader, Vice-Chair. Standing Cttee on Privileges and Elections; Parl. Sec. to Leader of Govt in House of Commons 1993–96; Deputy Chair. Cttees of Whole House 1996, Deputy Speaker and Chair. Cttees of Whole House 1997, elected Speaker of House of Commons 2001–; Chair. Bd of Internal Economy; Lecturer in Business Law, School of Business, Kingston 1973–81; Hon. Pres. United Empire Loyalists' Asscn of Canada; Hon. LLD (State Univ. of New York) 2001. *Publication:* Question Period: Developments from 1960 to 1967 1968. *Address:* Speaker's Office, Parliament Buildings, Centre Block, Room 222-N, Ottawa, ON K1A 0A6 (office); Quaker Valley, R.R. No. 1, Elginburg, ON K0H 1M0, Canada (home). *Telephone:* (613) 992-5042 (office); (613) 548-7889 (home). *Fax:* (613) 947-2816 (office). *E-mail:* SpkrOff@parl.gc.ca (home); millip9@parl.gc.ca (office). *Website:* www.parl.gc.ca/information/about/people/House/Speaker/index_e.html (office); www.petermilliken.org (home).

MILLON, Charles, LèsScEcon; French politician and international organization official; *President, Unir Pour Lyon;* b. 12 Nov. 1945, Belley, Ain; s. of Gabriel Millon and Suzanne Gunet; m. Chantal Delsol 1970; three s. two d.; ed Ecole Sainte-Marie, Lyon, Faculté de Droit et de Sciences Economiques de Lyon; univ. tutor 1969; legal and taxation adviser 1970–; Mayor of Belley 1977–2001; Deputy 1981–86, 1988–93, First Vice-Pres. Ass. Nat. 1986–88, Leader Union pour la Démocratie Française in Nat. Ass. 1989; Minister of Defence 1995–97; Local Councillor, Ain 1985–88; Vice-Pres. Regional Council, Rhône-Alpes 1981–88, Pres. 1988–99, Pres. 1988–98; Founder and Pres. la Droite Movt 1998–99; Leader Droite Libérale Chrétienne 1999–2003; Municipal Councillor and Urban Community Councillor, Lyon 2001–; Pres. Unir Pour Lyon 2001–; Amb. to FAO 2003–07. *Publications:* L'Extravagante histoire des nationalisations 1984, L'Alternance-vérité 1986, La Tentation du Conservatisme 1995, La Paix civile 1998, Lettre d'un ami impertinent 2002. *Leisure interests:* reading, walking, mountaineering. *Address:* Groupe Unir Pour Lyon, 4 rue de la République, BP 1099, 69202 Lyon Cedex 01 (office); 11 bis rue des Barons, 01300 Belley, France (home). *Telephone:* 4-72-07-77-56 (office). *Fax:* 4-72-07-91-47 (office). *Website:* www.millon.org (office).

MILLS, Dame Barbara Jean Lyon, DBE, QC, MA; British lawyer; *Adjudicator, HM Revenue and Customs;* b. 10 Aug. 1940; m.; four c.; ed St Helen's School, Northwood and Lady Margaret Hall, Oxford; called to bar, Middle Temple, London 1963, Bencher 1990; Jr Prosecuting Counsel to Inland Revenue 1977, Sr Prosecuting Counsel 1979; Jr Treasury Counsel, Cen. Criminal Court 1981; Recorder, Crown Court 1982–92; QC 1986; Dept of Trade and Industry Insp. under Section 177 of Financial Services Act 1986 (re Jenkins-British Commonwealth) 1986; mem. Criminal Injuries Compensation Bd 1988–90; Legal Assessor to Gen. Medical Council and Gen. Dental Council 1988–90; mem. Parole Bd 1990; Dir Serious Fraud Office 1990–92; mem. Gen. Advisory Council of BBC 1991–92; QC (NI) 1991; Dir of Public Prosecutions and Head, Crown Prosecution Service 1992–98; Adjudicator for HM Revenue and Customs (fmrly Adjudicator for HM Revenue and Customs and Excise), Valuation Office Agency, Public Guardianship Office and Insolvency Service 1999–; Chair. Forum UK 1999–2001, Council of Man., Women's Library 2000–; Dir (non-exec.) Royal Free Hampstead Nat. Health Service Trust 2000–; Gov. London Guildhall Univ. 1999–; Trustee Victim Support 1999–; mem. The Competition Comm. 2001–; Hon. Vice-Pres., Inst. for Study and Treatment of Delinquency 1996; Hon. Fellow, Lady Margaret Hall, Oxford 1991, Soc. for Advanced Legal Studies 1997; Companion of Honour, Inst. of Man. 1993; Hon. LLD (Hull, Nottingham Trent) 1993, (London Guildhall) 1994. *Address:* The Adjudicator's Office, 6th Floor, Haymarket House, 28 Haymarket, London, SW1Y 4SP (office); 72 Albert Street, London, NW1 7NR, England. *Telephone:* (20) 7930-2292 (office); (20) 7388-9206. *Fax:* (20) 7930-2298 (office); (20) 7388-3454. *E-mail:* adjudicators@gtnet.gov.uk (office). *Website:* www.adjudicatorsoffice.gov.uk (office).

MILLS, Hayley Cathrine Rose Vivien; British actress; b. 18 April 1946, London; d. of the late Sir John Mills and Lady Mills (Mary Hayley Bell); m. Roy Boulting 1971 (divorced 1977); two s.; Elmhurst Ballet School, Inst. Alpine Vidamanette; first film appearance in Tiger Bay 1959; on contract to Walt Disney; first stage appearance as Peter Pan 1969; Silver Bear Award, Berlin Film Festival 1958, British Acad. Award; Special Oscar (USA), TV Best Actress Award 1982. *Films include:* Pollyanna 1960, The Parent Trap 1961, Whistle Down the Wind 1961, Summer Magic 1962, In Search of the Castaways 1963, The Chalk Garden 1964, The Moonspinners 1965, The Truth about Spring 1965, Sky West and Crooked 1966, The Trouble with Angels 1966, The Family Way 1966, Pretty Polly 1967, Twisted Nerve 1968, Take a Girl Like You 1970, Forbush and the Penguins 1971, Endless Night 1972, Deadly Strangers 1975, The Diamond Hunters 1975, What Changed Charley Farthing? 1975, The Kingfisher Caper 1975, Appointment with Death 1987, After Midnight 1990, 2BPerfectlyHonest 2004, Stricken 2005. *Stage appearances include:* The Wild Duck 1970, Trelawny 1972, The Three Sisters 1973, A Touch of Spring 1975, Rebecca 1977, My Fat Friend 1978, Hush and Hide 1979, The Importance of Being Earnest (Royal Festival Theatre, Chichester), The Summer Party 1980, Tally's Folly 1982, The Secretary Bird 1983, Dial M for Murder 1984, Toys in the Attic 1986, The Kidnap Game 1991, The King and I (Australian and New Zealand tour) 1991–92, The Card 1994, Fallen Angels 1994, Dead Guilty 1995–96, Brief Encounter 1997–98, The King and I (US tour) 1997–98, Suite in Two Keys (New York) 2001, A Little Night Music (USA) 2001, The Vagina Monologues (New York) 2001, Humble Boy (UK) 2004. *Television appearances include:* The Flame Trees of Thika 1981, Parent Trap II 1986, Good Morning Miss Bliss, Murder She Wrote, Back Home, Tales of the Unexpected, Walk of Life 1990, Parent Trap III, IV, Wild at Heart (series) 2007–09. *Publication:* My God (with Marcus Maclaine) 1988. *Leisure interests:* riding, reading, children, cooking, travel. *Address:* c/o Chatto and Linnit, 123A Kings Road, London, SW3, England. *Telephone:* (20) 7352-7722 (office). *Website:* www.hayleymills.com.

MILLS, Ian Mark, BSc, DPhil, FRS; British chemist and academic; *Professor Emeritus of Chemical Spectroscopy, University of Reading;* b. 9 June 1930; s. of John Mills and Marghuerita Alice Gertrude Mills (née Gooding); m. Margaret Maynard 1957; one s. one d.; ed Leighton Park School, Univ. of Reading, St John's Coll. Oxford; Research Fellow, Univ. of Minn. 1954–56; Research Fellow in Theoretical Chem., Corpus Christi Coll., Cambridge 1956–57; Lecturer in Chem. Univ. of Reading 1957–64, Reader 1964–66, Prof. of Chemical Spectroscopy 1966–95, Prof. Emer. 1995–, Leverhulme Emer. Research Fellow 1996–98; Ed. Molecular Physics 1972–77, 1995–2004; mem. and Chair. of various cttees of IUPAC; Vice-Pres. Faraday Div. of RSC 1984–86; mem. British Nat. Cttee for IUPAC of RSC 1992–2000, Chair. 1998–2000; Pres., Consultative Cttee on Units of the Bureau Int. des Poids et Mesures 1995–; Chair. British Standards Inst. Cttee on Symbols and Units 1996–2004; mem. Council, Royal Inst. 2000–03; Lomb Medal 1960, Fellow 1974, Lippincott Medal of Optical Soc. of America 1982, RSC Spectroscopy Award 1990. *Publications:* Quantities, Units and Symbols in Physical Chemistry (co-author) 1988; various papers in learned journals on quantum mechanics and molecular spectroscopy. *Leisure interests:* sailing, walking. *Address:* Department of Chemistry, University of Reading, Reading, RG6 6AD (office); 57 Christchurch Road, Reading, RG2 7BD, England (home). *Telephone:* (118) 931-8456 (office); (118) 987-2335 (home). *Fax:* (118) 931-6331 (office). *E-mail:* i.m.mills@reading.ac.uk (office).

MILLS, John Evans Atta, PhD; Ghanaian politician, academic and head of state; *President;* b. 21 July 1944, Cape Coast, Cen. Region; m. Ernestina Naadu; ed Univ. of Ghana, London School of Econs, School of Oriental and African Studies, London Univ., Stanford Law School, Calif.; Lecturer, Faculty of Law, Univ. of Ghana 1971–80, Assoc. Prof. of Law 1992; Visiting Prof., Temple Law School, Phila, USA 1978–79, 1986–87, Leiden Univ., Netherlands 1985–86; Acting Commr Internal Revenue Service 1986–93, Commr 1993–96;

Nat. Democratic Congress cand. in presidential election 2000, 2004, 2008; Vice-Pres. of Ghana 2000, Pres. 2009–. *Address:* Office of the President, POB 1627, Osu, Accra -North, Ghana (office). *Telephone:* (21) 665415. *Website:* www.ghanacastle.gov.gh.

MILNE, Alasdair David Gordon, BA; British broadcasting official; b. 8 Oct. 1930, Cawnpore (Kanpur), India; s. of Charles Gordon Shaw Milne and Edith Reid Clark; m. Sheila Kirsten Graucob 1954 (died 1992); two s. one d.; ed Winchester Coll., New Coll., Oxford; served with 1st Bn, Gordon Highlanders 1949; joined BBC 1954, Deputy Ed. 1957–61, Ed. of Tonight Programme 1961–62, Head of Tonight Productions 1963–65; Partner Jay, Baverstock, Milne & Co. 1965–67; rejoined BBC 1967, Controller BBC Scotland 1968–72, Dir of Programmes, BBC TV 1973–77, Man. Dir TV 1977–82, Deputy Dir-Gen. BBC 1980–82, Dir-Gen. 1982–87; Chair., Darrell Waters Ltd 1988–90; Dir ABU TV Ltd 1988–93; Pres. Commonwealth Broadcasting Asscn 1984–87; BBC Visiting Prof., Univ. of Miami 1989; Hon. Fellow New College, Oxford; Dr hc (Stirling) 1983; Cyril Bennett Award 1987. *Publication:* DG: The Memoirs of a British Broadcaster 1988. *Leisure interests:* piping, salmon fishing, golf. *Address:* 30 Holland Park Avenue, London, W11 3QU, England.

MILNES, Sherrill, MMusEd; American singer; b. 10 Jan. 1935, Hinsdale, IL; s. of James Knowlton and Thelma Roe Milnes; m. 2nd Nancy Stokes 1969; one s.; one s. one d. by first marriage; m. 3rd Maria Zouves 1996; ed Drake Univ., Northwestern Univ.; studied with Boris Goldovsky, Rosa Ponselle, Andrew White, Hermanes Baer; with Goldovsky Opera Co. 1960–65, New York City Opera Co. 1964–67, debut with Metropolitan Opera Co., New York 1965, leading baritone 1965–; has performed with all American city opera cos and major American orchestras 1962–73; performed in Don Giovanni, Vespri Siciliani and all standard Italian repertory baritone roles, Metropolitan Opera and at San Francisco Opera, Hamburg Opera, Frankfurt Opera, La Scala, Milan, Covent Garden, London, Teatro Colón, Buenos Aires, Vienna State Opera, Paris Opera and Chicago Lyric Opera; founder and Artistic Dir VOICE (Vocal and Operatic Intensive Creative Experience) 2001–; Chair. of Bd Affiliate Artists Inc.; Order of Merit (Italy) 1984; three hon. degrees; three Grammy Awards, Sanford Medal, Yale Univ., Opera News Award 2008. *Recordings:* over 60 albums 1967–; most recorded American opera singer 1978. *Leisure interests:* table tennis, swimming, horse riding. *Address:* The VOICExperience Foundation, PO Box 1576, Plain Harbor, FL 34682-1576, USA (office). *E-mail:* voicexp@aol.com (office). *Website:* www.voiceexperiencefoundation.com (office).

MILNOR, John W., PhD; American mathematician and academic; *Distinguished Professor of Mathematics and Director, Institute for Mathematical Sciences, State University of New York, Stony Brook;* b. 20 Feb. 1931, Orange, NJ; ed Princeton Univ.; faculty, Princeton Univ. 1953–55, Alfred P. Sloan Fellow 1955–59, Prof. of Math. 1960–62, Henry Putman Prof. of Math. 1962; on staff, State Univ. of New York, Stony Brook 1988–, currently Distinguished Prof. of Math. and Dir Inst. for Math. Sciences; Ed. Annals of Mathematics 1962–; mem. NAS 1963, American Acad. of Arts and Sciences, American Philosophy Soc., American Math. Soc.; Hon. DSc (Syracuse Univ.) 1965, (Univ. of Chicago) 1967; Putnam Fellow, Princeton Univ. 1949–50, Fields Medal, Int. Congress of Mathematicians, Stockholm 1962, Nat. Medal of Science 1967, Leroy P. Steele Prize, American Math. Soc. 1982, Wolf Prize (Israel) 1989, Leroy P. Steele Prize for Math. Exposition 2004. *Publications:* Morse Theory, Characteristic Classes (with Stasheff), The h-Cobordism Theorem, Dynamics in One Complex Variable, Singular Points of Complex Hypersurfaces, Topology from the Differentiable Viewpoint; numerous articles in math. journals on differential topology, differential geometry and algebraic topology. *Address:* Institute for Mathematical Sciences, State University of New York, 5D-148 Math Tower, Stony Brook, NY 11794-3660, USA (office). *Telephone:* (516) 642-7318 (office). *Fax:* (516) 632-7631 (office). *E-mail:* jack@math.sunysb.edu (office). *Website:* www.math.sunysb.edu (office).

MILO, Paskal, PhD; Albanian politician; *Chairman, Social Democracy Party;* b. 22 Feb. 1949, Vlorë; s. of Koço Petromilo and Parashqevi Petromilo; m. Liliana Balla-Milo 1976; one s. two d.; ed Univ. of Tirana; journalist 1971–74; high school teacher 1975–80; Lecturer in History, Univ. of Tirana 1981–91, Dean Faculty of History and Philology 1991–92, Prof. 1996; Sec. of State for Educ. 1991; mem. Parl. (Social Democratic Party—SDP) 1992–96, 1997–, Chair. Parl. Comm. for Educ. and Science 1992–96, Minister of Foreign Affairs 1997–2001, for European Integration 2001–02; left SDP to form Social Democracy Party (Partia Demokracia Sociale—PDS) 2003, Chair. 2003–; Chair. SE European Co-operation Process (SEECP); mem. Parl., Council of Europe 2006–. *Publications:* The End of an Injustice 1984, Albania and Yugoslavia 1918–27 1992, A Good Understanding and Cooperation in the Balkans, From Utopia to Necessity 1997, Albania and the Balkan Entente 1997, Constitutional Rights and Minorities in the Balkans: A Comparative Analysis 1997, The Soviet Union and Albania's Foreign Policy 1944–46 1997, Albania in East-West Relations 1944–45 1998, European Union: Identity, Integration, Future 2002, Diary of a Foreign Minister: Kosova Conflict 1997-2001 2009, Kosova from Rambouillet to Independence 2009. *Leisure interests:* football, music. *Address:* Partia Demokracia Sociale, Bulevardi 'Zogu i I', ish klinika dentare, Tirana, Albania (office). *Telephone:* (4) 274487 (office); (4) 250973 (home). *Fax:* (4) 274487 (office). *E-mail:* paskalmilo@yahoo.it (home).

MILOŠOSKI, Antonio, MA; Macedonian lawyer, politician, diplomatist and researcher; *Minister of Foreign Affairs;* b. 29 Jan. 1976, Tetovo; m.; ed SS. Cyril and Methodius Univ., Skopje, Friedrich Wilhelm Univ. Bonn, Germany, Gerhard Merkator Univ. of Duisburg, Germany; mem. Exec. Cttee Youth Force Union of Internal Macedonian Revolutionary Org—Democratic Party for Macedonian Nat. Unity 1995–97, Vice-Pres. 1997–98; Chair. Office of the Deputy Prime Minister of FYR Macedonia 1999–2000; Govt Spokesman 2000–01; Counsellor to the Prime Minister Jan.–May 2001; Research Fellow, Inst. for Political Science, Gerhard Merkator Univ., Duisburg 2005–06; Minister of Foreign Affairs 2006–; Founder Youth Euro-Atlantic Forum (MEAF); columnist, Dnevnik (newspaper) 2000. *Address:* Ministry of Foreign Affairs, 1000 Skopje, Dame Gruev 6, Former Yugoslav Republic of Macedonia (office). *Telephone:* (2) 3110333 (office). *Fax:* (2) 3115790 (office). *E-mail:* mailmnr@mfa.gov.mk (office). *Website:* www.mfa.gov.mk (office).

MILOW, Keith; British artist; b. 29 Dec. 1945, London; s. of Geoffrey Keith Milow and the late Joan Ada; ed Camberwell School of Art and Royal Coll. of Art; experimental work at Royal Court Theatre, London 1968; teacher, Ealing School of Art 1968–70; Artist in Residence, Univ. of Leeds (Gregory Fellowship) 1970; worked in New York (Harkness Fellowship) 1972–74; teacher, Chelsea School of Art 1975, School of Visual Arts, New York City 1981–85; works in public collections in six countries, including Tate Modern and Victoria and Albert Museum, London, Guggenheim Museum and Museum of Modern Art, New York; lives and works in Amsterdam; Calouste Gulbenkian Foundation Visual Arts Award 1976; equal First Prize Tolly Cobbold/Eastern Arts 2nd Nation Exhbn 1979; Arts Council of GB Major Award. *Address:* Warmoesstraat 10, 1012 JD Amsterdam, Netherlands (home). *Telephone:* (20) 420-05-74 (home). *E-mail:* keithmilow@dds.nl (office). *Website:* www.keithmilow.com (office).

MILSOM, Stroud Francis Charles, QC, FBA; British academic; b. 2 May 1923, Merton, Surrey; s. of Harry Lincoln Milsom and Isobel Vida Collins; m. Irène Szereszewski 1955 (died 1998); ed Charterhouse School, Trinity Coll. Cambridge and Univ. of Pennsylvania Law School (as Commonwealth Fund Fellow); Fellow, Trinity Coll. 1948–55; Fellow, Tutor and Dean, New Coll. Oxford 1956–64; Prof. of Legal History, LSE 1964–76; Prof. of Law, Cambridge Univ. 1976–90, Fellow of St John's Coll. 1976–; called to Bar 1947, Hon. Bencher, Lincoln's Inn 1970, QC 1985; Literary Dir, Selden Soc. 1964–80, Pres. 1985–88; mem. Royal Comm. on Historical Manuscripts 1975–98; Foreign mem. American Philosophical Soc.; Hon. LLD (Glasgow) 1981, (Chicago) 1985, (Cambridge) 2003; Ames Prize, Harvard 1972, Swiney Prize, RSA 1974. *Publications:* Novae Narrationes 1963, Introduction to reissue of History of English Law (Pollock and Maitland) 1968, Historical Foundations of the Common Law 1969, 1981, Legal Framework of English Feudalism 1976, Studies in the History of the Common Law 1985, A Natural History of the Common Law 2003. *Address:* St John's College, Cambridge, CB2 1TP; 113 Grantchester Meadows, Cambridge, CB3 9JN, England (home). *Telephone:* (1223) 354100 (home).

MILTON-THOMPSON, Sir Godfrey James, KBE, MA, MB (Cantab.), FRCP, DCH; British naval surgeon; *Chairman, St John Council for Cornwall;* b. 25 April 1930, Birkenhead, Cheshire; s. of the late Rev. James Milton-Thompson and May L. Hoare; m. Noreen H. F. Fitzmaurice 1952; three d.; ed Eastbourne Coll., Queens' Coll. Cambridge and St Thomas's Hosp., London; joined RN 1955, Sr Specialist in Medicine, RN Hosp., Malta 1962–66; Consultant Physician, RN Hospital, Plymouth 1966–69, 1971–75; Hon. Research Fellow, St Mark's Hosp. 1969–70; Prof. of Naval Medicine 1975–80; promoted Surgeon Capt. 1976; Royal Coll. of Defence Studies 1981, Deputy Medical Dir-Gen. (Naval) 1982–84, Medical Dir-Gen. (Naval) 1985–90, Deputy Surgeon-Gen. (Research and Training) 1985–87; promoted Surgeon Rear Adm. 1984, Surgeon Rear-Adm. (Operational Medical Services) 1984; Surgeon Gen., Defence Medical Services in the rank of Surgeon Vice-Adm. 1988–90; Hon. Physician to HM the Queen 1982–90; Chair. Cornwall Community Healthcare Trust 1991–93; Chair. Bd of Govs, St Mary's School, Wantage 1996–2006; Vice-Pres. British Digestive Foundation 1997–; Warden, St Katharine's House, Wantage 1993–98; Hon. Col, 211 (Wessex) Field Hosp., RAMC (V) 1990–95; Chair. St John Council for Cornwall 2000–; Kt of Justice, Order of St John 1989; Errol-Eldridge Prize 1974, Gilbert Blane Medal 1976. *Publications:* contrib. to medical and scientific literature on gastroenterology. *Leisure interests:* fishing, literature, collecting East Anglian paintings, archery. *Address:* Pool Hall, Menheniot, Cornwall, PL14 3QT, England.

MILUTINOVIĆ, Milan, LLM; Serbian politician, diplomatist and lawyer; b. 19 Dec. 1942, Belgrade; s. of Aleksandar Milan Milutinović and Ljubica Vladimir Jokić; m. Olga Branko Spasojević; one s.; ed Belgrade Univ.; mem. Presidency of Socialist Youth Union of Yugoslavia 1969–71; MP 1969–74; Sec. Communal Cttee of League of Communists 1972–74; Sec. for Ideology, City Cttee of League of Communists 1974–77; Minister of Science and Educ. of Serbian Repub. 1977–82; Dir Serbian Nat. Library 1983–87; Head of Sector for Press, Information and Culture, Sec. for Foreign Affairs 1987–89; Amb. to Greece 1989–95; Minister of Foreign Affairs, Fed. Repub. of Yugoslavia 1995–98; Pres. of Serbia 1997–2002; accused of crimes against humanity and violations of the customs of war by UN War Crimes Tribunal 2001, charged with crimes against humanity and war crimes by Int. Court of Justice 2003, provisionally released 2005 pending trial; Order of Merit with Silver Star 1974, Medal for work with Gold Coronet 1980. *Publications include:* University – Eppur si muove! 1985. *Leisure interest:* philately. *Address:* c/o Office of the President, Andrićev venac 1, 11000 Belgrade; Koste Glavinica 9, 11000 Belgrade, Serbia (home).

MILYUKOV, Yuri Aleksandrovich, CandPhysMathSc; Russian banker; *President, Moscow Commodity Exchange;* b. 29 April 1957; m.; two s.; ed Moscow Inst. of Physics Eng; researcher, Lebedev Inst. of Physics USSR (now Russian) Acad. of Sciences 1984–87; Chair. Council of Altair 1989–91; f. Moscow Commodity Exchange (MTB) 1990–, Pres. 1993–; mem. Council on Business, Govt of Russian Fed. 1992–; mem. Bd Dirs, Russian Industrialists and Entrepreneurs Union 1992–; mem. Presidium, All-Russian Movt Businessmen for New Russia 1993–94; mem. Co-ordination Council, Round Table of Russian Business 1994–; mem. Beer Lovers Party; mem. Cen. Cttee 1995–; mem. Political Consultative Council of Russian Presidency 1996; Chair. Rosmed; Chair. Russian Union of Stock Exchanges 1991–; Chair. Stock Cttee,

Moscow Stock Exchange 1996–; First Deputy Chair. Bd MDM Bank 1997–. *Leisure interest:* theatre. *Address:* Stock Exchange, Mira Prospekt 69, 129223 Moscow (office); MDM Bank, Zhitnaya Str. 14, 117049 Moscow, Russia (office). *Telephone:* (495) 187-98-26 (office); (495) 797-95-00.

MIMURA, Akio, BS; Japanese business executive; *Representative Director and Chairman, Nippon Steel Corporation;* b. 2 Nov. 1940; ed Tokyo Univ.; with Fuji Iron & Steel 1963–70 (remained with co. following merger with Yawata Steel to form Nippon Steel Corpn 1970), Man. Dir 1998–2000, Vice-Pres. 2000–03, Rep. Dir and Pres. 2003–08, Rep. Dir and Chair. 2008–; Vice-Chair. (fmly Chair.) Japan Iron and Steel Fed. Industry Asscn (JISF); Vice-Chair. Int. Iron and Steel Inst. (ISII) 2006–07. *Address:* Nippon Steel Corpn, 6-3 Otemachi 2-chome, Chiyoda-ku, Tokyo 100-8071, Japan (office). *Telephone:* (3) 3242-4111 (office). *Fax:* (3) 3275-5607 (office). *E-mail:* info@www .nsc.co.jp (office). *Website:* www.nsc.co.jp (office); www.worldsteel.org (office).

MIN, Huifen; Chinese musician and university professor; b. Nov. 1945, Yixing Co., Jiangsu Prov.; ed Shanghai Conservatory of Music; Prof., Shanghai Conservatory of Music 1993–; mem. 5th Nat. Cttee CPPCC 1978–83, 6th Nat. Cttee 1983–88, 7th Nat. Cttee 1988–93, 8th Nat. Cttee 1993–98; leading player of erhu (traditional instrument); First Prize, Nat. Erhu Playing Competition 1963, Shanghai Literature and Art Award 1988, Nat. Gold Record Award 1989. *Recordings include:* 15 albums including Erhu Solos, River of Sorrow, Wishes of the Honghu Lake People. *Address:* Shanghai Conservatory of Music, Room 1101 Building 151, Weihai Road, Shanghai 200003, People's Republic of China.

MIN, Keh-sik, MS; South Korean business executive; b. 1941; ed Univ. of California, Berkeley, USA; fmr Man. Dir Daewoo Shipbuilding; fmr Pres. and COO, Research and Devt Centre, Hyundai Heavy Industries Co. Ltd, becoming Pres. 2001, Dir, Vice-Chair., Co-CEO and Chief Tech. Officer 2007–; Pres., S Korea Br., Int. Conf. on Control, Automation and Systems (ICCAS), also mem. Advisory Council. *Address:* Hyundai Heavy Industries Co. Ltd, 1, 1, Jeonha-dong, Dong-gu, Gyeonsang nam-do, Ulsan 682-792, Republic of Korea (office). *Telephone:* (52) 202-2114 (office); (52) 230-3899 (office). *Fax:* (52) 230-3450 (office). *E-mail:* ir@hhi.co.kr (office). *Website:* www.hhi.co.kr (office).

MINAH, Francis Misheck, LLM; Sierra Leonean politician and lawyer; b. 19 Aug. 1929, Pujehun; m. Gladys Emuchay; four c.; ed Methodist Boys' High School, Freetown, King's Coll. (London Univ.), Grays Inn, London; Pres. Sierra Leone Students' Union of GB and Ireland 1960–62; mem. House of Reps. 1967–87; Minister of Trade and Industry 1973–75, of Foreign Affairs 1975–77, of Justice 1977–78; Attorney-Gen. 1978; Minister of Finance 1978–80, of Health 1980–82; Attorney-Gen. and Minister of Justice 1982–84; First Vice-Pres. 1985–87; UNESCO Fellowship to study community devt in India and Liberia; barrister-at-law.

MINANI, Thomas; Burundian politician; fmr Dir-Gen. Coffee Office; Minister of Commerce and Industry 2003–05; mem. FRODEBU.

MINAYEV, Valery V., Dr Econ., Cand.His.; Russian economist and historian; *Pro-rector, Russian State University of Humanities;* b. 1949, Moscow region; ed Moscow State Inst. of Archives and History; teacher, Prof., Chair. Russian State Univ. of Humanities 1973–2002, Pro-rector 2002–; Deputy Chair. Scientific Council; mem. editorial bd of journals Novy Istorichesky Vestnik, Yurisprudentsya, Popular Economic Encyclopaedia; mem. Russian Academy of National Sciences; medal of 850th anniversary of Moscow. *Publications include:* more than 70 scientific papers and monographs, including On Periodization of Demographic History 1995, The Formation of the Labour Market in Modern Russia: Population and Crises 2001, Problems of the Labour Market in Classical Theoretical Schools 2001, Tolerance and Polycultural Society 2002. *Address:* Russian State University of Humanities, Miusskaya pl. 6, Moscow 125267, Russia. *Telephone:* (4095) 250-61-31. *Fax:* (495) 250-62-11.

MINC BAUMFELD, Carlos, MSc, PhD; Brazilian geographer, academic and politician; *Minister of the Environment;* b. 12 July 1951, Rio de Janeiro; m.; two c.; ed Fed. Univ. of Rio de Janeiro, Tech. Univ. of Lisbon, Univ. of Paris I (Sorbonne); Co-founder Partido Verde 1986; now mem. Partido dos Trabalhadores; State Deputy for Rio de Janeiro 1986–; Asst Prof., Dept of Geography, Fed. Univ. of Rio de Janeiro; Sec. for the Environment, State Govt of Rio de Janeiro 2006–08; Minister of the Environment 2008–; UNEP Global Award 500 1989. *Publications:* Como Fazer Movimento Ecológico 1985, A Reconquista da Terra 1986, Ecologia e Política no Brasil 1987, Despoluindo a Política 1994, Ecologia e Cidadania 1997. *Address:* Ministry of the Environment, Esplanada dos Ministérios, Bloco B, 5° andar, 70068-900 Brasília, Brazil (office). *Telephone:* (61) 3317-1058 (office). *Fax:* (61) 3317-1755 (office). *E-mail:* carlos.minc@mma.gov.br (office). *Website:* www.mma.gov.br (office); www.minc.com.br.

MINCATO, Vittorio; Italian business executive; *Chairman, Fondazione CUOA;* b. 14 May 1936, Torrebelvicino, Vicenza; joined Ente Nazionale Idrocarburi (Eni) Group SpA (oil and gas co.) 1957, various positions including Admin. and Finance Man. Lanerossi (textile co.) 1957–77, Admin. Man. Eni SpA 1977–84, Asst to Chair. 1984–88, Man. Human Resources and Org. 1988–92, Chair. Savio (textile machinery) and Head of Fertilizers Section, EniChem 1990–92, Deputy Chair. and Man. Dir EniChem 1993–95, Chair. EniChem 1996–98, Man. Dir Eni SpA 1998–2005, CEO 2002–05, fmr Dir numerous other Eni cos including Agip, Lanerossi, Immobiliare Metanopoli, Sofid and Polimeri Europa; Chair. Poste Italiane SpA 2005–08, Fondazione CUOA 2007–; mem. Bd of Dirs Il Sole 24 Ore SpA 2000–, Fondazione Eni Enrico Mattei, Exec. Bd Assonime (Asscn of Italian Ltd Liability Cos) 2001–, Bd Dirs Fondazione Teatro alla Scala, Man. Bd Assolombarda (industrialists'

asscn); Cavaliere del Lavoro 2002. *Leisure interests:* classical music (especially Wagner), reading. *Address:* Fondazione CUOA, Villa Valmarana Morosini, Altavilla Vicentina, Italy (office). *Telephone:* (04) 44333711 (office). *Fax:* (04) 44333999 (office). *E-mail:* direzione@cuoa.it (office). *Website:* www.cuoa.it (office).

MINCHIN, Nicholas (Nick), BEcons, LLB; Australian politician; b. NSW; m. Kerry Minchin; two s. one d.; ed Australian Nat. Univ.; various positions with Liberal Party Fed. Secr. including Deputy Fed. Dir 1977–83; State Dir S Australian Liberal Party 1985–93; elected to Commonwealth Parl. as Liberal Senator for S Australia 1993; Parl. Sec. to Leader of the Opposition 1994–96, to the Prime Minister (upon election win) 1996–97; Special Minister of State and Minister Assisting the Prime Minister 1997–98; Minister for Industry, Science and Resources 1998–2001; Minister for Finance and Admin and Deputy Leader of the Govt in the Senate 2001–07. *Address:* 36 Grenfell Street, Kent Town, SA 5067, Australia (office). *Telephone:* (2) 6277-7400 (Parl.) (office). *Fax:* (2) 6273-4110 (Parl.) (office). *E-mail:* senator.minchin@aph.gov .au (office). *Website:* www.aph.gov.au/senator_minchin (office).

MINCKWITZ, Bernhard von; German business executive; b. 11 Aug. 1944, Göttingen; m. Cornelia Böhning; fmr mem. Man. Bd Bertelsmann AG; mem. Bd Süddeutscher Verlag, Man. Dir Süddeutscher Verlag Hüthig Fachinformationen –2002; mem. Sponsorship Foundation for Chinese Excellent Students from Poor Families 2005–. *Address:* c/o Süddeutscher Verlag GmbH, Emmy-Noether-Str. 2, 80992 Munich, Germany (office).

MINDADZE, Aleksandr Anatol'yevich; Russian scriptwriter; b. 28 April 1949, Moscow; m. Galina Petrovna Orlova; two d.; ed All-Union State Inst. of Cinematography; screenplays since 1972; has worked with dir Vadim Abdrashitov since 1976; Merited Worker of Art of Russia, State Prize of Russia 1984, Silver Pegas Prize of Cultural Asscn Ennio Flaiano 1985, USSR State Prize 1991, co-recipient of Golden Ram Award with Vadim Abdrashitov for their contribution to Russian cinema 1994. *Film scripts include:* Vesenniy prizyv (Spring Selection) 1976, Slovo dlia zashchity (Speech for the Defence) (Prize of All-Union Film Festival, Prize of Lenin's Komsomol) 1976, Spring Mobilization (A. Dovzhenko Silver Medal) 1977, Povorot (The Turning Point) 1978, Okhota na lis (A Fox Hunt) 1980, Predel zhelaniy 1982, Ostanovilsya poyezd (The Train Has Stopped) 1982, Parad planet (Parade of the Planets) 1984, Plyumbum, ili opasnaya igra (Plumbum, or The Dangerous Game) 1986, Sluga (The Servant) 1988, Armavir 1991, Pyesa dlya passazhira (Play for a Passenger) (Silver Bear, Berlin Int. Film Festival) 1995, Vremya tantsora (Time of the Dancer) (Grand Prix, Kinotavr Film Festival, Sochi 1997 and several int. awards) 1998, Magnitnye buri (Magnetic Storms) 2003, Trio 2003, Kosmos kak predchuvstvie (Golden Eagle Award) 2005, Otryv (The Soar) (White Elephant Award, Munich Film Festival) 2007, Minnesota 2009. *Address:* Usiyevicha str. 8, Apt 89, 125319 Moscow, Russia (office). *Telephone:* (499) 155-75-34 (home). *E-mail:* mindadze@mail.ru (home).

MINDAOUDOU, Aichatou, PhD; Niger politician, lawyer and academic; *Minister of Foreign Affairs, Co-operation and African Integration;* ed Univ. of the Sorbonne, Paris, France; Minister of Social Devt, Population and Women 1996–99, of Foreign Affairs 1999–2000, of Foreign Affairs, Co-operation and African Integration 2001–; Sr Lecturer in Int. Law. *Address:* Ministry of Foreign Affairs and Co-operation and African Integration, BP 396, Niamey (office); PO Box 11529, Niamey, Niger (home). *Telephone:* 72-29-07 (office); 72-35-15 (home). *Fax:* 73-52-31 (office). *E-mail:* indo-ai@ifrance.com (home).

MINETA, Norman Yoshio, BS; American politician, transport industry executive, communications consultant and fmr government official; *Vice-Chairman, Hill & Knowlton, Inc.;* b. 12 Nov. 1931, San Jose, Calif.; s. of Kay Kunisaku Mineta and Kane Mineta (née Watanabe); m. Danealia Mineta; two s. two step-s.; ed Univ. of Calif., Berkeley; agent/broker Mineta Insurance Agency 1956–89; mem. Advisory Bd, Bank of Tokyo in Calif. 1961–75; mem. San Jose City Council 1967–71; Vice-Mayor, City of San Jose 1969–71, Mayor 1971–75; mem. House of Reps from 13th (now 15th) Calif. Dist 1975–95, Sub cttee on Surface Transportation 1989–92; Sr Vice-Pres. and Man. Dir Transportation Systems and Services, Lockheed Martin 1995–2001; US Sec. of Transportation, Washington, DC 2001–06 (resgnd); Vice-Chair. Hill & Knowlton, Inc., Washington, DC 2006–; Chair. Nat. Civil Aviation Revenue Comm. 1997; Commr San Jose Human Relations Comm. 1962–64, San Jose Housing Authority 1966–; mem. Bd of Regents, Santa Clara Univ., Smithsonian Nat. Bd 1996–; Hon. DH (Rust Coll.) 1993; Presidential Medal of Freedom 2006. *Address:* Hill & Knowlton, Inc., 607 14th Street, NW, Suite 300, Washington, DC 20005, USA (office). *Telephone:* (202) 333-7400 (office). *Fax:* (202) 333-1638 (office). *Website:* www.hillandknowlton.com (office).

MINFORD, (Anthony) Patrick (Leslie), CBE, PhD; British economist and academic; *Professor of Applied Economics, Cardiff Business School;* b. 17 May 1943; s. of Leslie Mackay Minford and Patricia Mary Sale; m. Rosemary Irene Allcorn 1970; two s. one d.; ed Horris Hill, Winchester Coll., Univ. of Oxford, London School of Econs; Econ. Asst, Ministry of Overseas Devt 1966; Economist, Ministry of Finance, Malawi 1967–69; Econ. Adviser Courtaulds Ltd 1970–71; HM Treasury 1971–73; HM Treasury Del. Washington, DC 1973–74; Visiting Hallsworth Fellow, Univ. of Manchester 1974–75; Edward Gonner Prof. of Applied Econs, Univ. of Liverpool 1976–97; Visiting Prof., Cardiff Business School 1993–97, Prof. of Applied Econs 1997–; Dir Merseyside Devt Corpn 1988–89; mem. Monopolies and Mergers Comm. 1990–96, Treasury Panel of Independent Econ. Forecasters 1993–96; Ed. Nat. Inst. for Econ. and Social Research Review 1975–76, Liverpool Quarterly Econ. Bulletin 1980–. *Publications:* Substitution Effects, Speculation and Exchange Rate Stability 1978, Unemployment – Cause and Cure 1983, Rational Expectations and the New Macroeconomics 1983, The Housing Morass 1987, The Supply-Side Revolution in Britain 1991, The Cost of Europe (ed.)

1992, Rational Expectations Macroeconomics 1992, Markets not Stakes 1998, Britain and Europe: Choices for Change (with Bill Jamieson) 1999, Advanced Macroeconomics: A Primer (with David Peel) 2002, Money Matters: Essays in honour of Alan Walters 2004, Should Britain Leave the EU? – An Economic Analysis of a Troubled Relationship (co-author) 2005, An Agenda for Tax Reform 2006; articles in journals. *Address:* Cardiff Business School, University of Wales Cardiff, Cardiff, CF10 3EU, Wales (office). *Telephone:* (29) 2087-5728 (office). *Fax:* (29) 2087-4419 (office). *E-mail:* MinfordP@cardiff.ac.uk (office). *Website:* www.cf.ac.uk/carbs/faculty/minfordp/index.html (office).

MINGOS, David Michael Patrick, BSc, DPhil, FRSC, FRS; British scientist and academic; *Principal, St Edmund Hall, Oxford;* b. 6 Aug. 1944, Basra, Iraq; s. of Vasso Mingos and Rose Enid Billie Griffiths; m. Stacey Mary Hosken 1967; one s. one d.; ed Harvey Grammar School, Folkestone, King Edward VII School, Lytham, Univ. of Manchester, Univ. of Sussex; Fulbright Fellow Northwestern Univ. Ill., USA 1968–70; ICI Fellow, Univ. of Sussex 1970–71; Lecturer, Queen Mary Coll., London 1971–76; Lecturer in Inorganic Chem., Univ. of Oxford 1976–90, Reader 1990–92; Fellow, Keble Coll., Oxford 1976–92; Univ. Assessor 1991–92; Sir Edward Frankland BP Prof. of Inorganic Chem., Imperial Coll., London 1992–99, Visiting Prof. 1999–2002; Dean, Royal Coll. of Science 1996–99; Prin. St Edmund Hall, Oxford 1999–; visiting professorships in USA, Canada, France, Germany, Switzerland and consultant for various UK and US chemical cos; Gov. Harrow School; mem. numerous editorial bds; Hon. DSc (UMIST) 2000, (Sussex) 2001; Corday Morgan Medal, Noble Metal Prize, Tilden Medal of RSC, Manchott Prize 1995, Michael Collins Award for Innovation in Microwave Chemistry 1996, Alexander von Humboldt Forschungs Prize 1999. *Publications:* An Introduction to Cluster Chemistry 1989, Essentials of Inorganic Chemistry 1 1996, Essential Trends in Inorganic Chemistry 1998, Essentials of Inorganic Chemistry 2 1998, Regional Ed. Journal of Organometallic Chemistry, Series Ed. Structure and Bonding. *Leisure interests:* cricket, tennis, walking, gardening, travel. *Address:* St Edmund Hall, Oxford OX1 4AR, England (office). *Telephone:* (1865) 279003 (office). *Fax:* (1865) 279030 (office). *E-mail:* michael.mingos@seh.ox.ac.uk (office). *Website:* www.seh.ox.ac.uk (office).

MINKIN, Vladimir Isaakovich; Russian chemist; b. 4 March 1935; m.; one d.; ed Rostov State Univ.; Asst, Docent, Prof. Rostov State Univ.; Corresp. mem. USSR (now Russian) Acad. of Sciences 1990, mem. 1994; works on physical and organic chem., quantum chem. of organic compounds, organic photochemistry; mem. Comm. of IUPAC; USSR State Prize. *Publications include:* Dipole Moments in Organic Chemistry 1968, Quantum Chemistry of Organic Compounds 1986. *Leisure interests:* chess, literature. *Address:* Institute of Physical and Organic Chemistry, Stachki pr. 194/3, 344104 Rostov on Don, Russia. *Telephone:* (8632) 28-54-88 (office).

MINKS, Wilfried; German stage director and designer; b. 21 Feb. 1930, Binai, Czechoslovakia; twin s.; ed Akad. der Künste, Berlin; theatre engagements in Ulm through Intendant Kurt Hübner (worked with Peter Zadek, Peter Palitzsch); Hübner (Intendant), Zadek, Minks, Bremen 1962–73; worked as stage designer with Fassbinder, Gruber, Stein, Zadek, Palitzsch; Prof. of Stage Design, Hochschule für Bildende Kunst, Hamburg 1970–; cr. German Pavilion, Expo 1970, Osaka, Japan; began working as theatre dir 1971; screenplay and direction for film Die Geburt der Hexe 1980. *Television production design:* Ein ungebetener Gast 1963, Der Spaßvogel 1964, Der Nebbich 1965, Die Unberatenen 1966, Der Kirschgarten 1966, Maß für Maß 1968, Rotmord (also writer) 1969, Das Kaffeehaus 1970, Die Jungfrau von Orleans (also dir and writer) 1974, Die Geisel 1977. *Address:* Wellingsbüttler Landstraße 166, 22337 Hamburg, Germany. *Telephone:* (40) 503600.

MINNELLI, Liza; American singer and actress; b. 12 March 1946, Los Angeles; d. of the late Vincente Minnelli and Judy Garland; m. 1st Peter Allen 1967 (divorced 1972); m. 2nd Jack Haley, Jr 1974 (divorced 1979); m. 3rd Mark Gero 1979 (divorced 1992); m. 4th David Gest 2002 (divorced 2007). *Films:* Charlie Bubbles 1968, The Sterile Cuckoo 1969, Tell Me That You Love Me, Junie Moon 1971, Cabaret (played Sally Bowles) 1972 (Acad. Award for Best Actress, The Hollywood Foreign Press Golden Globe Award, the British Acad. Award and David di Donatello Award, Italy), Lucky Lady 1976, A Matter of Time 1976, New York, New York 1977, Arthur 1981, Rent-a-Cop 1988, Arthur 2: On the Rocks 1988, Sam Found Out 1988, Stepping Out 1991, Parallel Lives 1994. *Television includes:* Liza, Liza with a Z (Emmy Award) 1972, Goldie and Liza Together 1980, Baryshnikov on Broadway 1980 (Golden Globe Award), A Time to Live 1985 (Golden Globe Award), My Favourite Broadway: The Leading Ladies 1999. *Theatre:* Best Foot Forward 1963, Flora, the Red Menace 1965 (Tony Award), Chicago 1975, The Act 1977–78 (Tony Award), Liza at the Winter Garden 1973 (Special Tony Award), The Rink 1984, Victor-Victoria 1997, Liza's at the Palace 2008. *Recordings:* Liza with a Z, Liza Minnelli: The Singer, Liza Minnelli: Live at the Winter Garden, Tropical Nights, The Act, Liza Minnelli: Live at Carnegie Hall, The Rink, Liza Minnelli at Carnegie Hall, Results 1989, Maybe This Time 1996, Minnelli on Minnelli 2000, Liza's Back 2002, The Very Best of Liza Minnelli: Life is a Cabaret! 2002. *E-mail:* askliza@officiallizaminnelli.com (office). *Website:* www.officiallizaminnelli.com.

MINNER, Ruth Ann; American fmr politician; b. 17 Jan. 1935, Milford, Del.; m. 1st Frank Ingram (deceased); three s.; m. 2nd Roger Minner (died 1991); ed Delaware Tech. and Community Coll.; receptionist to Gov. of Del. 1972–74; mem. Del. House of Reps 1974–82, House Majority Whip; mem. Del. Senate, Del. to Gen. Ass. 1982–92; Lt-Gov. 1993–2001, Gov. of Del. 2001–09; Democrat. *Leisure interest:* family. *Address:* c/o Office of the Governor, Legislative Hall, Wilmington, DE 19801, USA (office).

MINNICK, Mary E., BS, MBA; American business executive and fmr beverage industry executive; *Partner, Lion Capital LLP;* b. 27 Nov. 1959, Evanston, Ill.;

ed Bowling Green State Univ., Duke Univ.; joined The Coca-Cola Co. in 1983, later Pres. S Pacific Div., The Coca-Cola Co., later Pres. Coca-Cola Japan, Exec. Vice-Pres. The Coca-Cola Co. and Pres. and COO Coca-Cola Asia 2001–05, Exec. Vice-Pres. and Pres. Marketing, Strategy, and Innovation, Coca-Cola Co. 2005–07 (resgnd); Pnr, Lion Capital LLP, London 2007–; mem. Bd of Dirs Target Corpn, Heineken; mem. Dean's Council, John F. Kennedy School of Govt, Harvard Univ.; mem. Bd Visitors, Fuqua School of Business, Duke Univ.; Alumni Wf360 (Womenfuture); ranked by Fortune magazine amongst 50 Most Powerful Women in Business in the US (30th) 2005, (31st) 2006, ranked by Forbes magazine amongst 100 Most Powerful Women (85th) 2005. *Address:* Lion Capital LLP, 21 Grosvenor Place, London, SW1X 7HF, England (office). *Telephone:* (20) 7201-2200 (office). *Fax:* (20) 7201-2222 (office). *Website:* www.lioncapital.com (office).

MINOGUE, Kylie Ann, OBE; Australian singer and actress; b. 28 May 1968, Melbourne, Vic.; started acting in Skyways 1980, The Sullivans 1981, The Henderson Kids 1984–85, then Neighbours 1986–88 (all TV series); solo artist 1988–, first female vocalist to have her first (released) five singles obtain silver discs in UK; numerous tours, concerts, television and radio performances world-wide; launched own range of lingerie 2003; Ordre des Arts et des Lettres 2008; Woman of the Decade award 1989, nine Logies (Australian TV Industry awards), six Music Week Awards (UK), three Australian Record Industry Asscn Awards, three Japanese Music Awards, Irish Record Industry Award, Canadian Record Industry Award, World Music Award, Australian Variety Club Award, MO Award (Australia), Amplex Golden Reel Award, Diamond Award (Belgium), MTV Video of the Year (for Did it Again) 1998, MTV Awards for Best Pop Act, Best Dance Act 2002, BRIT Award for Best Int. Female Solo Artist 2002, 2008, Grammy Award for Best Dance Recording (for Come into my World) 2004, Music Industry Trusts' Award 2007, Q Idol Award 2007. *Recordings include:* albums: Kylie 1988, Enjoy Yourself 1989, Rhythm of Love 1990, Let's Get To It 1991, Kylie – Greatest Hits 1992, Kylie Minogue 1994, Kylie Minogue (Impossible Princess) 1997, Intimate And Live 1998, Light Years 2000, Hits + 2000, Fever (BRIT Award for Best Int. Album 2002) 2001, Confide In Me (compilation) 2002, Body Language 2003, X 2007. *Films:* The Delinquents 1989, Streetfighter 1994, Biodome 1996, Sample People 1999, Cut 1999, Sample People 2000, Moulin Rouge 2001. *Play:* The Tempest 1999. *Publications:* Kylie 1999, Kylie La La La (with William Baker) 2003, The Showgirl Princess (juvenile) 2006. *Address:* Terry Blamey Management Pty Ltd, 329 Montague Street, Albert Park, Vic. 3206, Australia (office); Terry Blamey Management, PO Box 13196, London, SW6 4WF, England (office). *Telephone:* (20) 7371-7627 (office). *Fax:* (20) 7731-7578 (office). *E-mail:* info@terryblamey.com (office). *Website:* www.kylie.com (office).

MINOR, Halsey; American computer industry executive; *Chairman and CEO, Grand Central Communications Inc.;* ed Univ. of Virginia; investment banker Merrill Lynch Capital Markets, San Francisco 1991; f. Global Publishing Corpn, San Francisco; f. CNET: The Computer Network (later CNET Networks), San Francisco 1992, Chair., CEO 1992–2000; Chair. Emer. 2000–; f. Grand Central Communications Inc., Chair., CEO 2003–. *Address:* Grand Central Communications Inc., Inc., 50 Fremont Street, San Francisco, CA 94105, USA (office). *Telephone:* (415) 344-3200 (office). *Fax:* (415) 344-3250 (office). *Website:* www.grandcentral.com (office).

MINOVES TRIQUELL, Juli F., MA, MPhil; Andorran economist, politician, diplomatist and international organization official; b. 15 Aug. 1969, Andorra la Vella; ed Lycée Comte de Foix, Andorra, Music School of the Lyceum of Barcelona, Spain, Fribourg Univ., Switzerland, Yale Univ., USA; teacher of Catalan, Migrosklubschule, Bern, Switzerland 1989–91; Special Corresp. of Radio Andorra, Gulf War 1991; Asst Prof. of Constitutional Law and Political Economy, Dept of Political Science, Yale Univ. 1993; Counsellor, first Perm. Mission of Andorra to the UN, New York 1993–94; Deputy Perm. Rep. and Chargé d'affaires 1994–95, Perm. Rep. 1995–2004; Alt. Head of Andorran Del. to World Summit on Social Devt, Copenhagen; Special Plenipotentiary Rep. of Andorran Govt in negotiations to establish diplomatic relations with various govts 1994–95; Amb. to USA and Canada 1996; Vice-Pres. UN Gen. Ass. 1997; Head of Andorran del. to UN Special Ass. Rio+5 1997; Chief of Cabinet a.i. of the Minister of Foreign Affairs 1997–99; mem. special group of UN diplomats for inspections in Iraq 1998; Head of Andorran del. for the establishment of an Int. Criminal Court, Rome, 1998; Amb. to Spain 1998, to Finland and Switzerland 1999, to UK 2000; Minister of Foreign Affairs, Culture and Co-operation 2001–07; Vice-Pres. and mem. of the Bureau, Liberal International, London; Great Cross, Order of Merit of Portugal 1997; Tristaina de periodisme journalism award 1986, Crédit Suisse Award for stock exchange research 1988, El futur de les Valls Research Award 1989, Grad. Fellowship, Foundation Crèdit Andorrà 1991. *Publications:* articles in Andorra 7 weekly magazine 1986–88, Segles de Memòria (novel) (Fiter i Rossell Award) 1989, Les Pedres del Diable (short stories) (Sant Carles Borromeu Award 1992). *Address:* Liberal International, 1 Whitehall Place, London, SW1A 2HD, England (office). *Telephone:* (20) 7839-5905 (office). *Fax:* (20) 7925-2685 (office). *E-mail:* all@liberal-international.org (office). *Website:* www.liberal-international.org (office).

MINOW, Newton N., JD; American lawyer; *Counsel, Sidley Austin LLP;* b. 17 Jan. 1926, Milwaukee, Wis.; s. of Jay A. Minow and Doris Minow (née Stein); m. Josephine Baskin 1949; three d.; ed Northwestern Univ.; Law Clerk to Supreme Court Chief Justice Vinson 1951; Admin. Asst to Gov. of Illinois 1952–53; served Stevenson's law firm 1955–57, Partner 1957–61; Chair. Fed. Communications Comm. 1961–63; Exec. Vice-Pres. Gen. Counsel Encyclopaedia Britannica, Chicago 1963–65; mem. Bd of Trustees, Rand Corpn 1965–75, 1976–86, 1987, Chair. 1970–72; Partner, Sidley Austin LLP (fmrly Leibman, Williams, Bennett, Baird & Minow and fmrly Sidley & Austin) 1965–91, Counsel 1991–; mem. Bd Trustees, Carnegie Corpn of New York

1987–97, Chair. 1993–97; Annenberg Univ. Prof., Northwestern Univ. 1987–; Dir The Annenberg Washington Program 1987–96; Trustee Northwestern Univ. 1975–87, Life Trustee 1987–; Life Trustee, Univ. of Notre Dame; Chair. Arthur Andersen & Co. Public Review Bd 1974–83, Public Broadcasting Service 1978–80; Democrat; Hon. Chair. and Dir Chicago Educational TV Asscn; Hon. LLD (Wisconsin) 1963, (Brandeis) 1963, (Northwestern Univ.) 1965, (Columbia Coll.) 1972, (Notre Dame) 1994, (Santa Clara) 1998. *Publications:* Equal Time: The Private Broadcaster and the Public Interest 1964, Presidential Television (co-author) 1973, Electronics and the Future (co-author) 1977, For Great Debates (co-author) 1987, Abandoned in the Wasteland: Children, Television and the First Amendment 1995. *Leisure interest:* reading. *Address:* Sidley Austin LLP, 1 S Dearborn Street, Chicago, IL 60603 (office); 179 E Lake Shore Drive, Chicago, IL 60611, USA (home). *Telephone:* (312) 853-7555 (office). *Fax:* (312) 853-7036 (office). *E-mail:* nminow@sidley.com (office). *Website:* www.sidley.com (office).

MINTER, Alan; British fmr boxer; b. 17 Aug. 1951, Penge, London; s. of Sidney Minter and Anne Minter; m. Lorraine Bidwell 1974; one s. one d.; ed Sarah Robinson School, Ifield; amateur boxer 1965–72; Amateur Boxing Asscn (ABA) champion 1971; Olympic bronze medallist 1972; 145 amateur fights, 125 wins; professional boxer 1972–82; won British middleweight championship 1975; won Lonsdale Belt outright 1976; won European championship from Germano Valsecchi Feb. 1977, lost it to Gratien Tonna Sept. 1977; forfeited British title Feb. 1977, regained it Nov. 1977; won vacant European title v. Angelo Jacopucci July 1978, retained it v. Tonna Nov. 1978; relinquished British title Nov. 1978; won world middleweight title from Vito Antuofermo, Las Vegas March 1980 (first British boxer to win a world championship in USA for 63 years); retained title v. Antuofermo June 1980, lost it to Marvin Hagler Sept. 1980; lost European title to Tony Sibson Sept. 1981; retd from boxing Feb. 1982. *Publication:* Minter: An Autobiography 1980. *Leisure interest:* golf.

MINTOFF, The Hon. Dominic, BSc, BE&A, MA, A&CE; Maltese politician and architect (retd); b. 6 Aug. 1916, Cospicua; s. of Lawrence Mintoff and Concetta née Farrugia (deceased); m. Moyra de Vere Bentinck 1947 (died 1997); two d.; ed Univs of Malta and Oxford; civil engineer in Great Britain 1941–43; practised in Malta as architect 1943–; rejoined and helped reorganize Maltese Labour Party 1944; elected to Council of Govt and Exec. Council 1945; mem. Legis. Ass. 1947; Deputy Leader of Labour Party, Deputy Prime Minister and Minister for Works and Reconstruction 1947–49; resgnd Ministry, Leader of Labour Party 1949–85; Prime Minister and Minister of Finance 1955–58; Leader of the Opposition 1962–71; Prime Minister 1971–84, also Minister of Foreign and Commonwealth Affairs 1971–81 (redesigned Ministry of Foreign Affairs 1978), of the Interior 1976–81, 1983–84; Special Adviser to Prime Minister 1985–87; mem. House of Reps 1987–98; Chair. Malta Counter Trade Co. Ltd. *Publications:* several scientific, literary and artistic works. *Leisure interests:* swimming, water skiing, bocci, horse riding. *Address:* The Olives, Tarxien, Malta. *Telephone:* (21) 692404 (home). *Fax:* (21) 697966 (home).

MINTON, Mark C., BA, MA; American diplomatist; *Ambassador to Mongolia;* ed Columbia Univ., Yale Univ.; served for three years in US Army; career mem. Foreign Service, began his career as a Political Officer in Tokyo 1977, served on Policy Planning Staff, Washington, DC, followed by assignment with Office of Soviet Union Affairs, Consul Gen. in Sapporo, Japan 1984, served in subsequent assignments with Dept of State's Exec. Secr., as Pearson Fellow with US Senate and as Deputy Dir (Japanese Affairs) at Dept of State, Minister-Counselor for Political Affairs, Embassy in Seoul 1992, returned to Washington, DC as Dir of Korean Affairs, Minister-Counselor for Political Affairs, US Mission to the UN, New York 1998, Deputy Chief of Mission, Embassy in Seoul –2006, served for over six months as Chargé d'affaires a.i., then Amb. to Mongolia 2006–; fmr Diplomat-in-Residence, CUNY. *Address:* Embassy of the USA, PO Box 1021, Ikh Toiruu 59/1, Ulan Bator 13, Mongolia (office). *Telephone:* (11) 329095 (office). *Fax:* (11) 320776 (office). *E-mail:* pao@usembassy.mn (office); webmaster@us-mongolia.com (office). *Website:* mongolia.usembassy.gov (office).

MINTON, Yvonne Fay, CBE; Australian singer (mezzo-soprano); b. 4 Dec. 1938, Sydney; d. of R. T. Minton; m. William Barclay 1965; one s. one d.; ed Sydney Conservatorium of Music, studied in London with H. Cummings and Joan Cross; sang with several opera groups in London; debut at Covent Garden 1965, prin. mezzo-soprano 1965–71; US debut at Lyric Opera, Chicago (Octavian in Der Rosenkavalier) 1972; guest artist, Cologne Opera 1969–, Australian Opera 1972–73, also with Hamburg State Opera and at Bayreuth, Paris, Salzburg, Metropolitan Opera, New York, Munich and San Francisco; many concert appearances; created role of Thea in Tippett's The Knot Garden 1970; Hon. ARAM. *Recordings include:* Der Rosenkavalier, Figaro, La Clemenza di Tito, Mozart's Requiem, Elgar's The Kingdom. *Leisure interests:* reading, gardening.

MINTZ, Shlomo; Israeli violinist; b. 30 Oct. 1957, Moscow, USSR; s. of Abraham Mintz and Eve (née Labko) Mintz; m. Corina Ciacci; two s.; ed Juilliard School of Music, New York, USA; went to Israel when very young; many concert tours; Premio Accad. Musicale Chigiana, Siena, Italy 1984; Music Dir, conductor, soloist Israel Chamber Orchestra 1989–93; Artistic Adviser Limburg Symphony Orchestra, Netherlands 1994; Principal Guest Conductor, Zagreb Philharmonic Orchestra 2008–; guest conductor and soloist for numerous orchestras world-wide; Premio Accademia Musicale Chigiana, Diapason D'Or, Grand Prix du Disque, Gramophone Award, Edison Award. *Recordings include:* Violin Concertos by Mendelssohn and Bruch (Grand Prix du Disque, Diapason d'Or) 1981, J. S. Bach Complete Sonatas and Partitas for Solo Violin, The Miraculous Mandarin by Bartok (with Chicago Symphony Orchestra, conducted by Abbado), Compositions and Arrangements by Kreisler (with Clifford Benson, piano), Twenty-four Caprices by Paganini, Two Violin Concertos by Prokofiev (with London Symphony Orchestra, conducted by Abbado), The Four Seasons by Vivaldi (with Stern, Perlman, Mehta). *Address:* Christa Morneweg Concert Management (office). *E-mail:* concert@morneweg.ch (office). *Website:* www.morneweg.ch (office); www.shlomo-mintz.com.

MINUTO-RIZZO, Alessandro, LLD; Italian diplomatist and international organization official; *Deputy Secretary-General, NATO;* b. 10 Sept. 1940, Rome; m.; two s.; mem. staff Directorate of Cultural Affairs, Ministry of Foreign Affairs, Rome 1969–72; First Sec. Washington, DC 1972–75; Counsellor, Prague 1975–80; Head Eastern Europe Desk, Directorate for Econ. Affairs 1980–81, Head EEC External Relations Desk 1981–86; Minister Counsellor OECD, Paris 1986–92; Minister Plenipotentiary Jan. 1992; Diplomatic Counsellor of Minister for Budget and Econ. Planning 1992–96, of Minister for Co-ordination of European Policies (a.i.) 1995–96; Deputy Chief of Cabinet, Ministry of Foreign Affairs Jan.–Oct. 1996, Co-ordinator for EU Affairs 1996–97; Diplomatic Counsellor of Minister of Defence 1997–2000; Amb. to Cttee for Policy and Security of EU 2000–01; Deputy Sec.-Gen. NATO 2001–; Del. to Council, ESA 1986–92; Chair. Admin. and Financial Cttee 1993–96; Chair. Ass. of Parties of Eutelsat 1989; mem. Man. Bd Italian Space Agency 1994–95; Chair. EU Cttee for Territorial Devt 1996. *Address:* NATO, blvd Léopold III, 1110 Brussels, Belgium (office). *Telephone:* (2) 707-49-06 (office). *Fax:* (2) 707-46-66 (office). *E-mail:* sgoffice@hq.nato.int (office). *Website:* www.nato.int (office).

MIOT, Jean Louis Yves Marie; French journalist; b. 30 July 1939, Châteauroux (Indre); s. of René Miot and Madeleine Moreau; two s. three d.; ed Lycée Jean Giraudoux de Châteauroux and Univ. de Poitiers; Ed. Centre Presse, Poitiers 1964–68; journalist, French Antilles 1968–70; Ed.-in-Chief, later Political Dir Havre-Presse 1970–74; Man. Dir France Antilles Martinique Guadeloupe, launched France-Guyane (weekly) 1974–76; Head, Legis. Elections Service, Le Figaro 1977–78; Man. Dir Berry Républicain, Bourges 1978; Dir Groupe de Presse Robert Hersant 1978–79; Political corresp. L'Aurore 1979–80; mem. Man. Bd Société de Gestion and Assoc. Dir Le Figaro 1980–93; Pres. Advisory Bd Le Figaro 1993–96; Pres. Syndicat de la Presse Parisienne 1986–96; Pres. Féd. Nat. de la Presse Française 1993–96; Pres. Agence-France-Presse (AFP) 1996–99, Syndicat des agences de presse de nouvelles (SANOV) 1996–99; Pres.-Dir Gen. Codalie, Financière-CDP and CD-Presse 1999–; mem. Conseil Econ. et Social 1993–96, Comm. de réflexion sur la justice 1997; Dir Société Financière de Radio-Diffusion (SOFIRAD) 1995; Chevalier, Légion d'honneur, Officier de l'Etoile Civique, Officer, Order of Lion (Senegal). *Address:* SARL Codalie, 59 avenue Victor Hugo, 75116 Paris (office); CD-Presse, 3 chemin du Clos, 95650 Puiseux-Pontoise (office); 10 rue Maître Albert, 75005 Paris, France (home). *Telephone:* 1-46-34-70-21 (office). *Fax:* 1-46-34-70-21 (office). *E-mail:* janmio@wanadoo.fr (home).

MIOU-MIOU; French actress; b. (Sylvette Héry), 22 Feb. 1950, Paris; one d. by the late Patrick Dewaere; one d. by Julien Clerc; worked as child in Les Halles wholesale market; apprenticed in upholstery workshop; with comedian Coluche helped create Montparnasse café-theatre 1968; stage appearance in Marguerite Duras' La Musica 1985. *Films:* La cavale 1971, Themroc 1972, Quelques missions trop tranquilles 1972, Elle court la banlieue 1972, Les granges brûlées 1972, Les aventures de Rabbi Jacob 1972, Les valseuses 1973, La grande Vadrouille 1974, Lily aime-moi 1974, Pas de Problème 1974, Un génie, deux associés, une cloche 1975, La marche triomphale 1975, F. comme Fairbanks 1976, On aura tout vu 1976, Jonas qui aura vingt ans en l'an 2000 1976, Portrait de province en rouge 1977, Dites-lui que je l'aime 1977, Les routes du Sud 1978, Au revoir à lundi 1978, Le grand embouteillage 1978, La Dérobade 1978, La femme flic 1980, Est-ce bien raisonnable? 1980, La gueule du loup 1981, Joséphа 1981, Guy de Maupassant 1982, Coup de foudre 1983, Attention, une femme peut en cacher une autre! 1983, Canicule 1983, Blanche et Marie 1984, Tenue de soirée 1986, Ménage, Les portes tournantes 1988, La lectrice 1988, Milou en mai 1990, Netchaiev est de retour 1991 La Totale! 1991, Le Bal des Casse-Pieds 1992, Tango 1993, Germinal 1993, Montparnasse–Pondichéry 1994, Un indien dans la ville 1994, Ma femme me quitte 1996, Le Huitiéme jour 1996, Nettoyage à sec 1997, Elles 1997, Hors jeu 1998, Tout va bien, on s'en va 2000, Mariages! 2004, L'Après-midi de monsieur Andesmas 2004, L'Un reste, l'autre part 2005, Riviera 2005, Les Murs porteurs 2005, The Science of Sleep 2006, Avril 2006, Family Hero 2006, Les Murs porteurs 2007, Affaire de famille 2008, Le Grand alibi 2008, Mia et le Migou (voice) 2008, Pour un fils 2009.

MIQDAD, Faisal al-; Syrian diplomatist; *Deputy Foreign Minister;* fmr Deputy, then Acting Amb. to UN New York, Perm. Rep. 2002–05; Deputy Foreign Minister 2006–. *Address:* Ministry of Foreign Affairs, ave Shora, Muhajireen, Damascus, Syria (office). *Telephone:* (11) 3331200 (office). *Fax:* (11) 3320686 (office).

MIRABAUD, Pierre G.; Swiss banker and national organization official; *Chairman, Swiss Bankers Association;* b. 1948; ed Univ. of Geneva; past positions with Banque Rivaud SA, Morgan Guaranty Trust, Blunt Ellis & Loewi, Swiss Bank Corpn; joined Mirabaud & Cie 1976, Pnr 1979, Sr Pnr 1995–; Chair. Swiss Pvt. Bankers Asscn 1990–93, Swiss Bankers Asscn 2003–; Vice-Chair. Bd Avenir Suisse –2003; founder and Chair. Pro Democratia Foundation; Chair. Bd Quantum Endowment Fund NV; mem. Bd Geneva Int. Airport. *Address:* Swiss Bankers Association, PO Box 4182, 4002 Basel, Switzerland (office). *Telephone:* (61) 295-93-93 (office). *Fax:* (61) 272-53-82 (office). *E-mail:* office@sba.ch (office). *Website:* www.swissbanking.org (office).

MIRAKHOR, Abbas, PhD; Iranian international banking executive and economist; *Executive Director, International Monetary Fund;* b. 1 July 1941, Tehran; m. Loretta Thomas 1965; two s.; ed Kansas State Univ., USA; Asst and Assoc. Prof. and Chair. Dept of Econs, Univ. of Alabama 1968–77, Prof.

and Chair. Dept 1977–79, Vice-Chancellor 1979–80; Az-Zahra Univ., Tehran; Prof. and Chair. Grad. Study Dept, Alabama A&M Univ. 1980–83; Prof. of Econs Fla Inst. of Tech. 1983–84; Economist, IMF 1984–87, Sr Economist 1987–90, Exec. Dir 1990–; Quaid-e-Azam Star for Service to Pakistan 1999, Order of Companion of Volta for Service to Ghana 2005; IEEE Eng Man. Soc. First Paper Prize 1972, Islamic Development Bank Annual Prize for Research in Islamic Econs (jtly) 2003. *Publications:* numerous articles on econs. *Address:* International Monetary Fund, 700 19th Street, NW, Washington, DC 20431, USA (office). *Telephone:* (202) 623-7370 (office). *Fax:* (202) 623-4966 (office). *E-mail:* amirakhor@imf.org (office). *Website:* www.imf.org (office).

MIRANI, Aftab Shahban; Pakistani politician; b. Shikarpur; s. of Ghulam Kadir Shahban Mirani and Begum Sharfunisa Shahban Mirani; m.; one s. three d.; ed studies in farm man. and agric. in USA; fmr Pres. Shikarpur Municipality; mem. Sindh Prov. Ass. (Pakistan People's Party) 1977–90; Chief Minister of Sindh –1990; mem. Nat. Ass. 1990–; Minister of Defence 1993–96; Vice Chair. and Treasurer, Shaheed Zulfikar Ali Bhutto Institute of Science and Technology. *Leisure interests:* walking, swimming. *Address:* c/o Pakistan People's Party (PPP), 8, St 63, F-8/4, Islamabad, Pakistan.

MIRAPEIX LUCAS, Ferran, LenD, MBA; Andorran politician; *Minister of Finance;* b. 7 Sept. 1957; ed Univ. of Barcelona, Spain, LSE, UK, Northwestern Univ., USA; Finance Counselor of Comú de Sant Julià 2000–03, Chief Finance Counselor 2004–05; Minister of Finance 2006–; Vice-Pres. Liberal Party of Andorra. *Address:* Ministry of Finance, Carrer Prat de la Creu 62–64, Andorra la Vella Ad 500, Andorra (office). *Telephone:* 875700 (office). *E-mail:* finances.gov.ad (office). *Website:* www.finances.ad (office).

MIRICIOIU, Nelly, Diploma of Bacalaureat (Piano) and Degree (Voice); Romanian/British singer (soprano); b. 31 March 1952, Adjud; d. of Voicu Miricioiu and Maria Miricioiu; ed Octav Bancila Music School, Iasi, George Eunescu Conservatoire; professional debut as Queen of the Night in The Magic Flute in Romania 1970; western European debut as Violetta in Scottish Opera production of La Traviata 1981; debut at Covent Garden as Nedda in I Pagliacci 1982, at La Scala as Lucia in Lucia di Lammermoor 1983; has since appeared at many of the other opera houses of the world including Verona, San Francisco, Vienna, Berlin, Hamburg, Madrid, Florence, Moscow, Monte Carlo, New York Met and in recitals and concerts (e.g. Salzburg, Concertgebouw, Royal Festival Hall); repertoire includes Mimi (La Bohème), Julietta (I Capuleti e I Montecchi), Gilda (Rigoletto), Elvira (Ernani), Marguerite and Elena (Mefistofele), Michaela (Carmen), Marguerite (Faust), Violetta (La Traviata), Manon Lescaut, Anna Bolena, Roberto Devereux, Lucrezia Borgia and Maria Stuarda (by Donizetti), Tancredi (Rossini), Elisabeth (Don Carlos) 1996, Il Pirata and Norma (Bellini), Emma d'Antiochia (Mercadante), Tosca (Puccini), I Vespri Siciliani (Verdi), Jerusalem (Verdi), Giovanna d'Arco (Verdi), Semiramide (Rossini); has worked with many leading conductors and dirs, singing leading roles such as Tosca with Jose Carreras, Jose Cura, Neil Schicoff, Mimi in La Bohème with Placido Domingo, Violetta in La Traviata with Franco Bonisolli, with Roberto Alagna, Renato Bruson, Alfredo Kraus, and many other leading artists; began 20-year series of Vara Matinee Concerts at Amsterdam Concertgebouw in 1986; made first recording, recital at Wigmore Hall, London 1986; debut in roles of Elizabeth in Don Carlos (Verdi), title roles in Luisa Miller (Verdi) and Silvana in La Fiamma (Respighi), Rome Opera 1997; debuts as Cio Cio San in Madam Butterfly (Puccini) for Hamburg State Opera, Fedora (Giordano) for Teatro Colon Buenos Aires, title role in Semiramide (Rossini) for Opera de Genève (also in a concert version at Queen Elizabeth Hall, London); debut Norma (Bellini) at Teatro dell'Opera Di Roma and in Athens 1999; debut as Francesca in Francesca da Rimini (Zandonai) at Vara Matinee Concert, Amsterdam 2000 and as Adriana Lecouvreur (Cilea) at La Scala, Milan 2000; debut as Imogen in II Pirata (Bellini), Washington, DC 2001; debut in title role in Iris (Mascagni) at Vara Matinee series 2003 and role of Helene in Jerusalem (Verdi) in concert version for Frankfurt Opera 2003; performed in premier of Emma D'Antiochia (Mercadante) at Royal Festival Hall 2003, title role in world premier of Maria Vittoria (Respighi) 2004; master-classes at Alderburgh 2000, Vilar Young Person, Royal Opera House, Covent Garden 2000, London 2002, RAM, London 2003, 2005, Opera Studio, Israeli Opera 2004, Dutch IVC 2004, S' Hertogenbosh 2004, Grachten Festival Amsterdam 2007; jury mem. Maria Callas Grand Prix 2003, London Int. Music Festival 2003, Athens 2003, S' Hertogenbosh 2004; winner of 10 int. competitions, including Second Prize, Francisco Vinas 1974 (First Prize not awarded) First Prize, Maria Callas Competition, Athens 1974, Second Prize, Paris 1975, Second Prize, Geneva 1976, Gold Medal, Katia Popova Competition 1977, First Prize, S' Hertogenbosh Competition 1978, First Prize, Ostende 1980, American Biographical Insts Award 1994, Romanian Medal of Cultural Merit 2004. *Recordings include:* Puccini's Tosca, Mercadante's Orazi e Curiazi, Donizetti's Rosamunda d'Inghilterra (with Renee Fleming and Bruce Ford) and Maria De Rudenz (Maria), Rossini's Ricdardo e Zoraide, Pacini's Maria d' Inghilterra (Maria) 1998, Mascagni's Cavalleria Rusticana (Santuzza) and a live recording in Rome of Respighi's La Fiamma (Silvana) and Nelly Miricioiu Live at the Concertgebouw, Nelly Miricioiu – A Rossini Gala 2000, Nelly Miricioiu – Bel Canto Portrait 2001 Roberto Devereux (Elizabetta) recorded at Covent Garden 2002 (released in 2003), Mercadante's Emma D'Antiochia 2005. *Leisure interests:* literature, television, cooking, socializing. *Address:* c/o Zemsky/Green Artists Management, 104 West 73rd Street, New York, NY 10023, USA (office); c/o Royal Opera House (Contracts), Covent Garden, London, WC2E 9DD, England. *Telephone:* (212) 579-6700 (office); (20) 7240-1200; (1923) 829679 (home). *Fax:* (212) 579-4723 (office); (1923) 827487 (home). *E-mail:* agreen@zemskygreen.com (office); bzemsky@zemskygreen.com (office); info@roh.org.uk; ram36@dial.pipex.com (home); kirk@dial.pipex.com (home). *Website:* www.zemskygreen.com (office); www.royaloperahouse.org (office); www.opera-singer.com (home).

MIRONOV, Oleg Orestovich, LLD; Russian lawyer; b. 5 June 1939, Pyatigorsk; m.; one s.; ed Saratov Inst. of Law; local investigator Pyatigorsk 1964; teacher, Prof. Constitutional Law Dept Saratov Inst. of Law; State Duma Deputy with CP of Russian Fed. 1993–95; mem., State Duma for Saratov Region 1995–98; mem. Cttee on Law and Legal Reform; mem. Central Cttee of CP of Russian Fed. –1998; Commr on Human Rights (Ombudsman) in Russian Fed. 1998–2003; mem. Interparl. Ass. of CIS, Acad. of Social Sciences, Russian Acad. of Lawyers; Honoured Jurist of Russian Fed. *Publications:* about 200 articles including monographs on problems of constitutional law, theory of state and law, politology. *Leisure interests:* mountain tourism, sports. *Address:* c/o Office of the Commissioner on Human Rights in the Russian Federation, Myasnitskaya str. 47, Moscow, Russia. *Telephone:* (495) 207-76-30 (office).

MIRONOV, Sergei Mikhailovich, CandJur; Russian engineer and politician; *Chairman, Sovet Federatsii (Federation Council);* b. 14 Feb. 1953, Pushkin, Leningrad Oblast; m.; one s. one d.; ed Leningrad (now St Petersburg) Plekhanov Mining Inst., St Petersburg State Tech. Univ., North-Western Acad. of Civil Service, St Petersburg State Univ.; army service 1971–73; engineer, Rusgeophysica (production co.) 1978–86; Sr Geophysicist, USSR Ministry of Geology, Mongolia 1987–91; Exec. Dir Russian Trade Chamber 1991–93, Construction Corpn – Restoration of St Petersburg 1994–95; mem., First Deputy Chair., then Chair. Legis. Ass. of St Petersburg 1995–2000; Head, Political Council The Will of Petersburg (Volya Peterburga) regional political movt 2000–01; Rep. of St Petersburg Ass. to Fed. Council, June 2001, Chair. Fed. Council Dec. 2001–; Founder and Chair. Russian Leader Party of Life 2003, Chair. A Just Russia (Spravedlivaya Rossiya) (merger of Motherland, Russian Party of Life and Russian Pensioners' Party) 2006–; unsuccessful presidential cand. 2004; Order of Merit for the Fatherland (Third degree) 2008. *Address:* Sovet Federatsii (Federation Council), 103426 Moscow, ul. B. Dmitrovka 26 (office); A Just Russia (Spravedlivaya Rossiya), 107031 Moscow, ul. B. Dmitrovka 32/1, Russia (office). *Telephone:* (495) 203-90-74 (Federation Council) (office); (495) 650-38-80 (A Just Russia) (office). *Fax:* (495) 203-46-17 (office). *E-mail:* VPParfenov@mironov.ru (home); info@spravedlivo.ru (office). *Website:* www.council.gov.ru (office); www.spravedlivo.ru (office); www.mironov.ru; mironov.info.

MIRONOV, Yevgeniy Vitalyevich; Russian actor; b. 29 Nov. 1966, Saratov; s. of Vitaly Sergeyevich Mironov and Tamara Petrovna Mironova; ed Saratov School of Theatre Art, Studio School of Moscow Art Theatre; actor, Oleg Tabakov Theatre-Studio 1990–; Merited Artist of Russia 1996. *Theatre roles include:* David Schwartz (Matrosskaya Tishina, A. Galich), Aleksander Aduyev (Common Story, Goncharov), Bumbarash (Passions over Bumbarash, Kim), Orestes (Oresteia, Aeschylus), Ivan Karamazov (The Brothers Karamazov and Hell, Dostoyevsky), Maratov (The Last Night of the Last Tsar, Radzinsky). *Films include:* roles in films by A. Kaidanovsky, A. Mitta, V. Todorovsky, Khotinenko, D. Yevstigneyev, N. Mikhalkov, S. Gazarov, including Zhena kerosinshchika (Kerosene Salesman's Wife) 1988, Pered rassvetom (Before Sunrise) 1989, Delay – raz! (Do It – One!) 1990, Lyubov (Love) (Prize for Best Kinotaurus Festival 1992, Constellation-92, Young Stars of Europe, Geneva 1992, Cinema Critics Prize-Best Actor of the Year 1992) 1991, Zateryannyy v Sibiri (Lost In Siberia) 1991, Kak zhivyote, karasi? (How's Life, Crucians?) 1992, Ankor, eshchyo ankor! (Encore, Once More Encore!) (Prize of Cinema Critics, Best Actor of the Year 1993) 1992, Poslednyaya subbota (The Last Saturday) 1993, Limita (Nika Prize 1995) 1994, Utomlyonnye solntsem (Burnt by the Sun) (Prize for Supporting Actor, Constellation-95) 1994, Musulmanin (The Mussulman) (Cinema Critics Prize, Best Actor of the Year 1995) 1995, Revizor (Inspector) (Prize for Best Actor Role, Ural Festival 1996) 1996, Zmeinyy istochnik 1997, Mama (Mummy) 1999, Dnevnik ego zheny (His Wife's Diary) 2000, V avguste 44-go (In August of 1944) 2001, Dom durakov (House of Fools) 2002, Prevrashcheniye (Metamorphosis) 2002, Igra v modern 2003, Vecherniy zvon (video) 2004, Na Verkhney Maslovke 2005, Pobeg 2005, Kosmos kak predchuvstvie 2005. *Television includes:* Dvadtsat minut s angelom 1996, Idiot (mini-series) 2003. *Address:* Oleg Tabakov Theatre-Studio, Chaplygina str. 12A, Moscow, Russia. *Telephone:* (495) 916-21-21 (office); (495) 264-15-58 (home).

MIROW, Thomas; German economist and banking executive; *President, European Bank for Reconstruction and Development (EBRD);* b. 6 Jan. 1953, Paris, France; m. Barbara Mirow; two d.; ed Univ. of Bonn; Asst and later Chef de Cabinet to fmr Chancellor Willy Brandt 1975–83; Dir Hamburg Press Office 1983–87; Political and Man. Consultant 1988–91; State Minister and Head of Chancellery, Hamburg State Admin 1991–93, State Minister for Urban Devt and Head of Chancellery 1993–97, State Minister for Econs 1997–2001; mem. EC High-Level Group on Lisbon Strategy 2004, Personal Rep. of Fed. Chancellor for Lisbon Strategy and Dir-Gen. for Econ. Policy, Fed. Chancellery 2005, State Sec. Fed. Finance Ministry 2005–08; Pres. EBRD 2008–; Chair. Supervisory Bd Hamburger Hafen- und Lagerhaus AG (Hamburg Port) 1997–2001, Flughafen Hamburg GmbH 1997–2001; mem. Supervisory Bd Daimler Chrysler Luft- und Raumfahrtholding (Daimler Chrysler Aerospace Holding) 1997–2001; Man. Dir Alstertor Schienenlogistik Beteiligung GmbH 2002–05; mem. Admin. Council Hamburgische Landesbank 1997–2001; mem. Bd of Supervisory Dirs Kreditanstalt für Wiederaufbau 1997–2001; Sr Adviser Ernst & Young AG 2002–05; Adviser MM Warburg Bank 2002–05. *Address:* European Bank for Reconstruction and Development, One Exchange Square, London, EC2A 2JN, England (office). *Telephone:* (20) 7338-6000 (office). *Fax:* (20) 7338-6100 (office). *Website:* www.ebrd.com (office).

MIRRA, Dave; American professional BMX rider; b. 4 April 1974, Chittenango, NY; s. of Michael Mirra and Linda Mirra; brother of Tim Mirra; nicknamed 'Miracle Boy'; has won more medals (18) than any other BMX rider at X Games; subject of several video games about BMX riding. *E-mail:* mirrafan@davemirra.com. *Website:* www.davemirra.com.

MIRREN, Dame Helen, DBE; British actress; b. 26 July 1945, London; m. Taylor Hackford 1997; first experience with Nat. Youth Theatre culminating in appearance as Cleopatra in Antony and Cleopatra, Old Vic 1965; joined RSC 1967 to play Castiza in The Revenger's Tragedy and Diana in All's Well that Ends Well; Dr hc (St Andrews) 1999. *Other roles include:* Cressida in Troilus and Cressida, Hero in Much Ado About Nothing, RSC, Stratford 1968; Win-the-Fight Littlewit in Bartholomew Fair, Aldwych 1969, Lady Anne in Richard III, Stratford, Ophelia in Hamlet, Julia in The Two Gentlemen of Verona, Stratford 1970 (the last part also at Aldwych), Tatyana in Enemies, Aldwych 1971; title role in Miss Julie, Elyane in The Balcony, The Place 1971; with Peter Brook's Centre Int. de Recherches Théâtrales, Africa and USA 1972–73; Lady Macbeth, RSC, Stratford 1974 and Aldwych 1975; Maggie in Teeth 'n' Smiles, Royal Court 1975; Nina in The Seagull and Ella in The Bed Before Yesterday, Lyric for Lyric Theatre Co. 1975; Margaret in Henry VI (Parts 1, 2 and 3), RSC 1977–78; Isabella in Measure for Measure, Riverside 1979; The Duchess of Malfi, Manchester Royal Exchange 1980 and Round-house 1981; The Faith Healer, Royal Court 1981; Antony and Cleopatra 1983, 1998, The Roaring Girl, RSC, Barbican 1983, Extremities (Evening Standard Award) 1984, Madame Bovary 1987, Two Way Mirror 1989; Sex Please, We're Italian, Young Vic 1991; The Writing Game, New Haven, Conn. 1993, The Gift of the Gorgon (New York) 1994; A Month in the Country 1994, Orpheus Descending 2001, Dance of Death (New York) 2001, Phaedra (London) 2009. *Films include:* Age of Consent 1969, Savage Messiah, O Lucky Man! 1973, Caligula 1977, The Long Good Friday, Excalibur 1981, Cal (Best Actress, Cannes) 1984, 2010 1985, White Nights 1986, Heavenly Pursuits 1986, The Mosquito Coast 1987, Pascali's Island 1988, When the Whales Came 1988, Bethune: The Making of a Hero 1989, The Cook, the Thief, His Wife and Her Lover 1989, The Comfort of Strangers 1989, Where Angels Fear to Tread 1990, The Hawk, The Prince of Jutland 1991, The Madness of King George 1995, Some Mother's Son 1996, Teaching Mrs Tingle 1998, The Pledge 2000, No Such Thing 2001, Greenfingery 2001, Gosford Park (Screen Actors' Guild Award for Best Supporting Actress) 2002, Calendar Girls 2003, The Clearing 2004, Raising Helen 2004, The Hitchhiker's Guide to the Galaxy (voice) 2005, Shadowboxer 2005, The Queen (Best Actress, Venice Film Festival, Nat. Bd of Review, Los Angeles Film Critics Asscn, Toronto Film Critics Asscn, Nat. Soc. of Film Critics 2006, Golden Globe for Best Actress (drama) 2006, Screen Actors' Guild Award for Outstanding Performance by a Female Actor in a Leading Role 2007, Best British Actress, London Film Critics' Circle Awards 2007, Best Int. Actress, Irish Film and Television Awards 2007, BAFTA Award for Best Actress 2007, Acad. Award for Best Actress 2007) 2006, National Treasure Book of Secrets 2007. *Television includes:* Miss Julie, The Apple Cart, The Little Minister, As You Like It, Mrs. Reinhardt, Soft Targets 1982, Blue Remembered Hills, Coming Through, Cause Celebre, Red King White Knight, Prime Suspect (BAFTA Award) 1991, Prime Suspect II 1992, Prime Suspect III 1993, Prime Suspect IV: Scent of Darkness 1995 (Emmy Award 1996), Prime Suspect V: Errors of Judgement 1996, Painted Lady 1997, The Passion of Ayn Rand 1998, Prime Suspect VI 2004, Elizabeth I (Golden Globe Award for Best Actress in a mini-series or film made for TV 2007, Screen Actors' Guild Award for Outstanding Performance by a Female Actor in a Television Movie or Mini-series 2007) 2005, Prime Suspect VII (Emmy Award for Best Actress in a Mini–series 2007) 2006. *Publication:* In the Frame (autobiog.) 2007. *Address:* c/o Ken McReddie Ltd, 36–40 Glasshouse Street, London, W1B 5DL, England (office).

MIRRLEES, Sir James Alexander, Kt, MA, PhD, FBA; British professor of economics; *Distinguished Professor at Large, Chinese University of Hong Kong;* b. 5 July 1936, Scotland; s. of the late George B. M. Mirrlees; m. 1st Gillian M. Hughes 1961 (died 1993); two d.; m. 2nd Patricia Wilson 2001; ed Univ. of Edinburgh and Trinity Coll., Cambridge; Adviser, MIT Center for Int. Studies, New Delhi 1962–63; Asst Lecturer in Econs and Fellow, Trinity Coll., Univ. of Cambridge 1963, Univ. Lecturer 1965; Research Assoc. Pakistan Inst. of Devt Econs 1966–67; Fellow, Nuffield Coll. and Edgeworth Prof. of Econs, Univ. of Oxford 1968–95; Prof. of Political Economy, Univ. of Cambridge 1995–2003; Distinguished Prof. at Large, Chinese Univ. of Hong Kong 2003–; Adviser to Govt of Swaziland 1963; Visiting Prof., MIT 1968, 1970, 1976, 1987; Ford Visiting Prof., Univ. of California, Berkeley 1986; Visiting Prof., Yale Univ. 1989; Laureate Prof., Univ. of Melbourne, Australia; mem. Treasury Cttee on Policy Optimization 1976–78; Pres. Econometric Soc. 1982, Royal Econ. Soc. 1989–92, European Econ. Asscn 2000; Hon. FRSE, Foreign Hon. mem. American Acad. of Arts and Sciences, NAS, Hon. mem. American Econ. Asscn; Hon. DLitt (Warwick) 1982, (Portsmouth) 1997, (Oxford) 1998, Hon. DScS (Brunel) 1997, Hon. DSc (Social Sciences) (Edin.) 1997, Dr hc (Peking, Chinese Univ. of Hong Kong, Macao, Liège, Helsinki School of Econs); Nobel Prize for Econ. 1996. *Publications:* jt author of three books and articles in academic journals. *Leisure interests:* music, travel, computing. *Address:* Chinese University of Hong Kong, Shatin, Hong Kong Special Administrative Region, People's Republic of China (office). *Telephone:* 2609-7831 (office); 2603-6670 (home). *Fax:* 2603-6586 (office). *E-mail:* jam28@cam.ac.uk (office).

MIRSAIDOV, Shukurulla Rakhmatovich, DEcon; Uzbekistan politician; b. 14 Feb. 1938, Leninabad; m.; four c.; ed Tashkent Finance and Econ. Inst.; mem. CPSU 1962–91; on staff State Planning Org. 1964–84; Head Cen. Statistical Dept, Uzbek SSR 1984–85; Chair. Tashkent City Council 1985–86; Head of Dept, CP of Uzbekistan 1988–89; Deputy Premier of Uzbekistan SSR 1989–90; Chair. Council of Ministers 1990–92; Vice-Pres. of Uzbekistan 1991–92; State Sec. for Pres. Karimov 1992; rep. Int. Fund for Privatization and Investments in Uzbekistan 1992–95; now in pvt. business. *Address:* International Fund for Privatization, Tashkent, Uzbekistan.

MIRVISH, David, CM; Canadian theatrical producer; b. 29 Aug. 1944; s. of the late Edwin Mirvish, CBE and Anne Macklin; producer and owner of the Old Vic Theatre, London and The Royal Alexandra and The Princess of Wales Theatres, Toronto; productions and co-productions include: Candide and Too Clever by Half (London), Into the Woods (London), Les Misérables (Canada), The Good Times Are Killing Me (New York), Miss Saigon, Crazy for You, Tommy (Toronto); Dir Williamstown Theatre Festival, USA –1992, Nat. Gallery of Canada, Nat. Theatre School of Canada 1989–91, Toronto French School; mem. Canadian Cultural Property Export Review Bd 1983–86; Rayne Award (Royal Nat. Theatre); Toronto Theatre Alliance (Dora) Humanitarian Award, Toronto Arts Award 1994. *Address:* Mirvish Productions, 284 King Street West, Suite 400, Toronto, Ont. M5V 1J2, Canada (office); The Old Vic, Waterloo Road, London, SE1 8NB, England (office). *Telephone:* (20) 7928-2651 (London) (office); (416) 593-0351 (Toronto) (office). *Fax:* (416) 593-9221 (office). *E-mail:* webmaster@mirvishproductions.com (office). *Website:* www .mirvishproductions.com (office).

MIRZA, Fehmida, MB BS; Pakistani politician, physician and business executive; *Speaker, National Assembly;* b. 20 Dec. 1956, Karachi; d. of Qazi Abdul Majeed Abid; m. Zulfikar Ali Mirza; two s. two d.; ed Liaquat Medical Coll., Jamshoro; physician at MCH Centre, then School Health Centre 1983–89; Dir Mirza Sugar Mills 1989–99, CEO 1999–; mem. Nat. Ass. representing Badin 1997–, Speaker 2008–; mem. Pakistan People's Party. *Address:* Office of the Speaker, National Assembly of Pakistan, Parliament House, Islamabad, Pakistan (office). *Telephone:* (51) 9221082 (office). *Fax:* (51) 9221106 (office). *Website:* www.na.gov.pk (office).

MIRZA, Jamil Ahmed; Pakistani artist and industrialist; b. 21 Feb. 1921, Delhi, India; c. of Mirza Noor Ahmed and of Sughra Begum; m.; three s. two d.; ed St. Joseph High School, Bombay (now Mumbai), India, Sir J.J. School of Art, Bombay; Film Art Dir, Calcutta (now Kolkata), India 1945–49; f. Elite Publishers Ltd, Karachi 1951, developed photo-offset printing, electronic colour scanning and invented computerised Urdu calligraphy 1981; Fellow, Sir J.J. School of Arts 1944; mem. Rotary Club 1965, Dist Gov. 1974; DLitt hc (Karachi) 1999; numerous art, civil and professional awards, including First Prize, Dolly Gursetji Mural Decoration 1942, three Best Entry Awards, All India Art in Industry 1943, Tamgha-I-Imtiaz (Medal of Distinction), Govt of Pakistan 1982, Rotary Int. Meritorious Services Award 1993, Lifetime Achievement Award, Pakistan Asscn of Printing and Graphics Art Industry 2001. *Exhibitions include:* Bombay Art Soc. 1928–43, The Children's Royal Acad., London, UK 1936, Royal Drawing Soc., London, UK 1936–37, All India Art Industry 1943–45. *Publications include:* Urdu Lexicon of Ligatures 1995. *Leisure interests:* painting, travelling, sports. *Address:* Elite Publishers Ltd, D-118, SITE, Karachi 75700 (office); Al-Noor, 23-B/6, PECHS, Karachi 75400, Pakistan (home). *Telephone:* (21) 2573435–39 (office); (21) 4547880 (home). *Fax:* (21) 2564720 (office); (21) 4559011 (home). *E-mail:* elite@elite.com.pk (office); amj@elite.com.pk (home). *Website:* www.elite.com.pk (office).

MIRZAEV, Ruslan Erkinovích; Uzbekistan politician; *Minister of Defence;* Sec. Nat. Security Council –2005; Minister of Defence 2005–. *Address:* Ministry of Defence, 100000 Tashkent, Ak. Abdullayev k'och. 100, Uzbekistan (office). *Telephone:* (71) 169-82-43 (office). *Fax:* (71) 169-82-28 (office).

MIRZIYOYEV, Shavkat Miromonovich; Uzbekistani politician; *Prime Minister;* b. 1957, Samarqand, Uzbek SSR, USSR; ed Tashkent Inst. of Irrigation, Eng and Agric. Mechanization; Pro-Rector Tashkent Inst. of Irrigation and Mechanization of Agric. –1996; Hokim (Gov.) Jizzax Viloyat 1996–2001, Samarqand Viloyat 2001–03; mem. Oly Majlis (Parl.) 1999–; Prime Minister 2003–. *Address:* Office of the Cabinet of Ministers, 100078 Tashkent, Mustaqillik maydoni 5, Uzbekistan (office). *Telephone:* (71) 139-82-95 (office). *Fax:* (71) 139-84-63 (office). *Website:* www.gov.uz (office).

MIRZOEFF, Edward, CVO, CBE, MA; British television producer, director and executive producer; b. 11 April 1936, London; s. of the late Eliachar Mirzoeff and of Penina Asherov; m. Judith Topper 1961; three s.; ed Hasmonean Grammar School, London, The Queen's Coll. Oxford; market researcher, Social Surveys (Gallup Poll) Ltd 1958–59, Public Relations Exec., Duncan McLeish & Assocs 1960–61; Asst Ed., Shoppers' Guide 1961–63; with BBC TV 1963–2000, Exec. Producer, Documentaries 1983–2000; Dir and producer of many film documentaries including: (with Sir John Betjeman) Metro-land 1973, A Passion for Churches 1973, The Queen's Realm 1977; Police – Harrow Road 1975, The Regiment 1977, The Front Garden 1979, The Ritz 1981, The Englishwoman and The Horse 1981, Elizabeth R (marking the Queen's 40th anniversary) 1992, Torvill and Dean – Facing the Music 1994, Treasures in Trust 1995, John Betjeman – The Last Laugh 2001; Ed., 40 Minutes (BBC) 1985–89; Exec. Producer, many documentary series including Real Lives 1985, Pandora's Box 1992, The Ark 1993, True Brits 1994, Situation Vacant 1995, The House 1995, Full Circle with Michael Palin 1997, The Fifty Years War: Israel and the Arabs 1998; Producer, Richard Dimbleby Lectures 1972–82, A. J. P. Taylor Lectures (three series); Exec. Producer, The Lord's Tale (Channel 4) 2002, A Very English Village 2005, The Lie of the Land (Channel 4) 2007; Chair. BAFTA 1995–97 (Vice-Chair., TV 1991–95); Trustee BAFTA 1999–; Trustee Grierson Trust 1999–, Vice-Chair. 2000–02, Chair. 2002–06; Vice-Pres. The Betjeman Soc. 2006–; mem. Bd Dirs' and Producers' Rights Soc. 1999–2007, Salisbury Cathedral Council 2002–, Ability Media Board 2009–; BAFTA Awards: Best Documentary 1981, Best Factual Series 1985, 1989, Alan Clarke Award for outstanding creative contribution to TV 1995; Samuelson Award, Birmingham Festival 1988, BFI TV Award 1988, British Video Award 1992, Broadcasting Press Guild Award 1996, Royal Philharmonic Soc. Music Award 1996, Int. Emmy 1996. *Leisure interests:* lunching with friends, opera. *Address:* 9 Westmoreland Road, London, SW13 9RZ, England (home).

MIRZOYAN, Edvard Mikhailovich; Armenian composer; b. 12 May 1921, Gori, Georgian SSR; s. of Mikhail Mirzoyan and Luciné Mirzoyan; m. Elena M. Stepanyan 1951; two c.; ed Yerevan Conservatory, Moscow Conservatory; teacher Komitas Conservatory, Yerevan, Armenia 1948–, Prof. 1965–; mem. CPSU 1952–90; Pres. Union of Composers of Armenian SSR 1957–91; Sec. USSR Union of Composers 1962–90; mem. Cen. Cttee of Armenian CP 1964–90; Deputy of Supreme Soviet of Armenian SSRCP 1959–90; People's Deputy of USSR 1989–91; mem. USSR Supreme Soviet 1990–91; Pres. Armenian Peace Fund 1978–; Armenian Meritorious Artist 1958; Armenian People's Artist 1963; USSR People's Artist 1981; Order of Cyril and Methodius, Bulgaria 1981. *Compositions include:* Symphonic Dances 1946, Soviet Armenia (cantata), To the Heroes of the War (Symphonic poem), Symphony of Light (ballet), Symphony for strings and timpani 1962, Sonata for cello and piano 1967, Poem for Piano, Lyrical Picture Shushanik 1973, In Memory of Aram Khachaturyan 1988, Album for my Granddaughter 1988, Poem for Cello and Piano 1995, Circle Seasons based on the words of Chinese poets 1997, Requiem for Chorus a capella 2008; string quartet, romances, instrumental pieces, songs, film-music. *Address:* c/o Armenian Composers' Union, Demirchyan Street 25, Apt 9, 375002 Yerevan, Armenia. *Telephone:* (10) 52-92-59. *Fax:* (10) 72-36-39.

MIRZOYEV, Gasan Borisovich; Russian lawyer; *President, Guild of Russian Lawyers;* b. 11 Dec. 1947, Baku, Azerbaijan; ed Azerbaijan State Univ., Moscow Inst. of Man.; State Arbiter of Moscow 1987–; Founder and Chair. Moscow State Centre on Legal Assistance, later Moscow Legal Centre 1993–, leading to creation of Russian Lawyers Guild; Rector and mem. Russian Bar Acad.; Vice-Pres. Russian Acad. of Natural Sciences; Pres. Human Rights Bd Int. Informatization Acad.; mem. Political Council, Union of Right Forces; Pres. Guild of Russian Lawyers 1994–; Deputy State Duma of Russian Fed. 1999–; Chair. Ed. Bd Rossiyskiy Advokat; Merited Lawyer of Russia. *Publications:* over 100 including monographs on problems of legal protection of business in Russia and protection of human rights; essays and articles. *Leisure interest:* chess. *Address:* Guild of Russian Lawyers, Maly Poluyaroslavsky per. 3/5, 107120 Moscow, Russia (office). *Telephone:* (495) 916-12-48 (office). *Fax:* (495) 975-24-16 (office). *E-mail:* grusadvocat@mtu-net .ru (office).

MIRZOYEV, Ramason Zarifovich; Tajikistani diplomatist; b. 15 Feb. 1945, Kulyab Region; m.; six c.; ed Tadjik Inst. of Agric.; worked with construction teams Kulyab Region; in Afghanistan 1975–78; worked in CP bodies and orgs 1983–; USSR People's Deputy 1989–92; Deputy Chair. USSR Supreme Soviet 1989–91; Man. Council of Ministers Repub. of Tajikistan 1992–95; Amb. to Russian Fed. 1995–2001, to Iran 2001. *Address:* Ministry of Foreign Affairs, Rudaki Prosp. 42, 73405 Dushanbe, Tajikistan. *Telephone:* (2) 211808.

MIRZOYEV, Vladimir V.; Russian stage director; b. 21 Oct. 1957; m.; one s. two d.; ed Moscow State Inst. of Theatre Arts; Artistic Dir Studio Domino of the Union of Theatre Workers 1987–89; lived and worked in Canada, f. theatre co. Horizontal Eight, Toronto 1989–93; Stage Dir Moscow Stanislavsky Drama Theatre 1994–; stage dir for productions at Moscow Vakhtangov Theatre, Lenkom Theatre, Vilnius Theatre of Russian Drama, Maryinsky Theatre and for television. *Plays include:* Possibilities, Feast Day (Studio Domino), Proposal, Bear, Caligula (studio Horizontal Eight, Toronto), Cyrano de Bergerac, Amphitrion (Moscow Vakhtangov Theatre), Two Women (Lenkom Theatre), Twelfth Night, Marriage, Khlestakov (Moscow Stanislavsky Drama Theatre), Tartuffe (Vilnius Theatre of Russian Drama). *Publications include:* contrib. to journal Sovietski Teatr 1981-87.

MISSNED, HH Sheikha Mozah bint Nasser al-, BA; Qatari d. of Nasser bin Abdullah al-Missned; m. HH Sheikh Hamad bin Khalifa ath-Thani, Amir of Qatar; five s. (including Sheikh Tamim bin Hamad bin Khalifa ath-Thani) two d.; ed Univ. of Qatar; Chair. Qatar Foundation for Educ., Science and Community Devt 1995–; Pres. Supreme Council for Family Affairs 1998–; Vice-Chair. Supreme Educ. Council 2002–; UNESCO Special Envoy for Basic and Higher Educ. 2003; founder Int. Fund for Higher Educ. in Iraq 2003; mem. UN High-Level Group of the Alliance of Civilizations 2005; Dr hc (Virginia Commonwealth Univ., USA) 2003, (Texas A & M Univ., USA); ranked by Forbes magazine amongst 100 Most Powerful women (79th) 2007. *Address:* The Royal Palace, POB 923, Doha, Qatar (office). *Website:* www .mozahbintnasser.qa.

MISTRETTA, Charles A., PhD; American biomedical engineer, physicist and academic; *John R. Cameron Professor, Department of Biomedical Engineering, University of Wisconsin;* ed Univ. of Illinois and Harvard Univ.; James Picker Advanced Fellow in Academic Radiology 1972–74; apptd Prof., Depts of Medical Physics and Radiology, Univ. of Wisconsin, Madison, currently John R. Cameron Prof., Dept of Biomedical Eng, Coll. of Eng; Fellow, American Asscn of Physicists in Medicine; Laufman-Greatbatch Prize, Asscn for the Advancement of Medical Instrumentation 1983, J. Allyn Taylor Int. Prize in Medicine, Robarts Research Inst. and Univ. of Western Ontario (co-recipient) 1998. *Publications:* more than 120 articles in medical journals on investigations of non-invasive techniques for magnetic resonance imaging of cardiovascular system. *Address:* Clinical Science Center, University of Wisconsin, Box 3252, Module E3 E1/398, 600 Highland Avenue, Madison, WI 53792, USA (office). *Telephone:* (608) 263-8313 (office); (608) 265-9685 (office). *Fax:* (608) 263-0876 (office). *E-mail:* camistre@facstaff.wisc.edu (office); camistre@wisc .edu (office). *Website:* www.engr.wisc.edu/bme (office).

MISTRY, Dhruva, MA, RA, FRBS; Indian sculptor; b. 1 Jan. 1957, Kanjari, Gujarat; s. of Pramodray Mistry and Kantaben Mistry; ed M.S. Univ. of Baroda and Royal Coll. of Art, London; British Council Scholar, RCA 1981–83; Artist in Residence in association with Arts Council of Britain at Kettle's Yard Gallery with Fellowship at Churchill Coll., Cambridge 1984–85; freelance

Sculptor-Agent, Nigel Greenwood Gallery, London 1983–97; Sculptor in Residence, Victoria and Albert Museum, London 1988; Rep. GB for the Grand Rodin Prize Exhbn, Japan 1990; Prof., Head of Sculpture and Dean, Faculty of Fine Arts, M.S. Univ. of Baroda 1999–2002; youngest Royal Academician since J.M.W. Turner when elected 1991; first Indian to be elected Fellow, Royal Soc. of British Sculptors 1993; lives and works in Vadodara; Hon. CBE 2001; Hon. DUniv (Univ. of Central England) 2007; The Madame Taussaud's Award for Art at the RCA 1983, Jack Goldhill Award, Royal Acad. of Arts 1991, Award for the Design of Humanities Prize Medal, London 1994, Design and Pres.'s Award for Victoria Square Sculptures 1995, The Landscape Inst. and Marsh Fountain of the Year Award 1995, Award of Excellence, Gujarat Gaurav Samiti 2006. *Major commissions include:* Mitchell Beazley 1982, Peter Moores Foundation, Liverpool 1983, Merseyside Devt Corpn, Liverpool 1984, Churchill Coll., Cambridge 1985, Nitchiman Corpn, Japan 1987, Glasgow Garden Festival 1988, British Art Medal Soc., London 1988, Nat. Museum of Wales, Cardiff 1989, Hunterian Art Gallery, Glasgow 1990, Victoria Square, The City Council, Birmingham 1992, Quaglino's, London 1993, Int. Classical Music Awards, London 1993, Tamano City Project, Uno, Japan 2002, Petronet LNG Ltd, Dahej 2004. *Public collections include:* Arts Council, London, Birmingham Museum and Art Gallery, Birmingham Contemporary Art Soc., London, Churchill Coll., Cambridge, Cartwright Hall, Bradford, City Art Gallery, Manchester, City of Stoke-on-Trent, Dept of Fine Arts, Punjab Univ., Chandigarh, Fukuoka Art Museum and Asian Art Gallery, Fukuoka, Glynn Vivian Art Gallery, Swansea, Govt Museum and Art Gallery, Chandigarh, Hunterian Art Gallery, Glasgow, Harris Museum and Art Gallery, Preston, Jigyo-Chuo-Koen Park, Fukuoka, Lalit Kala Akademi, New Delhi, Leicestershire Educ. Authority, Laing Art Gallery, Newcastle-upon-Tyne, LNG Petronet Ltd, Dahej, Milton Keynes Devt Corpn, Merseyside Devt Corpn, Liverpool, Nat. Museum of Wales, Cardiff, Oriana, P&O Cruises, Osians Archive, New Delhi, Peter Moores Foundation, Liverpool, Roopankar Museum of Fine Art, Bhopal, RCA, London, Southampton Art Gallery, Sculpture at Goodwood, Tate Gallery, London, British Council, London, British Museum, London, British Library, London, Hakone Open Air Museum, Japan, Ulster Museum, Belfast, Victoria & Albert Museum, London, Walker Art Gallery, Liverpool, West Zone Culture Centre, Udaipur, Yorkshire Sculpture Park, West Bretton, Tamano City Council, Uno, Japan. *Publications:* (exhbn catalogues) Sculptures and Drawings 1985, Cross-sections 1988, Dhruva Mistry, Bronzes 1985–1990. *Leisure interests:* photography, reading, walking. *Address:* 76 Anu Shakti Nagar, Sama, Vadodara 390 008, Gujarat, India (office). *Telephone:* (265) 2712949 (office); (93) 76214788 (mobile). *E-mail:* dhruva@dhruvamistry.com (home). *Website:* www.dhruvamistry.com (home).

MISTRY, Pallonji; Indian construction industry executive; *Chairman, Shapoorji Pallonji Group;* b. 1 June 1929; m.; four c.; fmr Chair. Forbes Gokak –2003, Associated Cement Cos Ltd –2004; currently Chair. Shapoorji Pallonji Group; largest individual shareholder in Tata Sons (holding co.); Hon. Mem. World Zarathushti Chamber of Commerce 2004. *Address:* Shapoorji Pallonji & Co. Ltd, Shapoorji Pallonji Centre, 41/44 Minoo Desai Marg, Colaba, Mumbai 400005, India (office). *Telephone:* (22) 67490263 (office). *Fax:* (22) 66338176 (office). *Website:* www.shapoorji.com (office).

MISTRY, Rohinton, BA, BSc; Canadian author; b. 3 July 1952, Bombay (now Mumbai), India; m. Freny Elavia 1975; ed St Xavier's High School, Bombay, Univ. of Bombay, Univ. of Toronto and York Univ., Canada; moved to Canada 1975; bank clerk, Toronto 1975–85; began writing short stories 1982; writings have been translated into more than 25 languages; Hon. PhD (Ottawa) 1996, (Toronto) 1999, (York) 2003; Gov.-Gen.'s Award for Fiction 1991, Commonwealth Writers' Prize for Best Book 1992, 1996, First Novel Award, W.H. Smith/Books in Canada 1992, Giller Prize 1995, Winifred Holtby Prize, RSL 1996, Los Angeles Times Fiction Prize 1997, ALOA Prize for Asscn Fiction (Denmark) 1997, Kiriyama Pacific Rim Book Prize for Fiction 2002, Canadian Authors' Asscn Award for Fiction 2003, Guggenheim Fellowship 2005. *Publications include:* Tales from Firozsha Baag (short stories) 1987, Such a Long Journey (novel) 1991, A Fine Balance (novel) 1995, Family Matters (novel) 2002, The Scream 2008; essays and articles in various languages and periodicals. *Address:* c/o Bruce Westwood, Westwood Creative Artists Ltd, 94 Harbord Street, Toronto, ON M5S 1G6, Canada (office). *Telephone:* (416) 964-3302 (office). *Fax:* (406) 975-9209 (office). *E-mail:* wca_office@wcaltd.com (office). *Website:* www.wcaltd.com (office).

MITA, Katsushige, BEE; Japanese business executive; *Chairman Emeritus, Hitachi Ltd;* b. 6 April 1924, Tokyo; s. of Yoshitaro and Fuji Mita; m. Toriko Miyata 1957 (died 1989); two d.; ed Univ. of Tokyo; joined Hitachi Ltd 1949; Gen. Man. Omika Works Aug.–Nov. 1971, Kanagawa Works 1971–75, Dir 1975; Man. Computer Group 1976–78, Exec. Man. Dir 1977–79, Sr Exec. Man. Dir 1979–80, Exec. Vice-Pres. 1980–81; Pres. and Rep. Dir Hitachi Ltd 1981–91, Chair. and Rep. Dir 1991–2000, Chair. Emer. 2000–, Hon. Chair. Advisory Bd The Hitachi Center for Tech. and Int. Affairs; Vice-Chair. Keidanren (Japan Fed. of Econ. Orgs) 1992–; mem. Int. Business Program Advisory Council, The Fletcher School, Tufts Univ., Medford, Mass, USA; Dr hc (Tufts Univ., USA) 1991; Blue Ribbon Medal (Japan) 1985, Officier, Légion d'honneur 1993, DSPN Dato (Malaysia) 1993; Will Rogers Award (USA) 1994. *Leisure interests:* golf, gardening. *Address:* 2423-277, Nara-machi, Aoba-ku, Yokohama-shi, Kanagawa-ken, 227, Japan (home).

MITA, Toshia; Japanese energy industry executive; *President, Chubu Electric Power Company, Inc.;* b. 12 Nov. 1946, Aichi Pref.; ed Seikei Univ.; joined Chubu Electric Power Co., Inc. 1969, served in various man. positions including Dir Hekinan Thermal Power Station 1995–97, Atsumi Thermal Power Station 1997–99, Kawagoe Thermal Power Station 1999–2001, Thermal Power Centre 2001–03, Tokyo Br. 2003–05, Man. Dir and Gen. Man. Sales

Dept 2005–06, Pres. 2006–. *Address:* Chubu Electric Power Co., Inc., 1 Higashi-shincho, Higashi-ku, Nagoya 461-8680, Japan (office). *Telephone:* (52) 951-8211 (office). *Fax:* (52) 962-4624 (office). *E-mail:* info@chuden.co.jp (office). *Website:* www.chuden.co.jp (office).

MITARAI, Fujio, BA; Japanese business executive; *Chairman and CEO, Canon Inc.;* b. 23 Sept. 1935, Kamae, Oita (Kyushu); m. Chizuko Mitarai (died 2002); several c.; ed Chuo Univ.; joined Canon Camera Co. Inc. 1961, transferred to newly est. Canon USA 1966, Pres. and CEO Canon USA Inc. 1979–89, Vice-Pres. Canon Inc. –1995, Pres. and CEO 1995–2006, Chair. and CEO 2006–; Corp. Auditor Dai-ichi Mutual Life Insurance Co.; Vice-Chair. Nippon Keidanren (Japan Business Fed.) 2002–06, Chair. 2006–, Chair. Cttee on Corp. Governance 2000–; Person of the Year Award, Photographic Mfrs and Distributors Asscn 1999, named by BusinessWeek one of the world's top 25 managers 2001, recipient Business Reformer Commendation from govt of Japan 2002. *Leisure interest:* golf. *Address:* Canon Corporate Headquarters, 30-2 Shimomaruko 3-chome, Ohta-ku, Tokyo 146-8501, Japan (office). *Telephone:* (3) 3758-2111 (office). *Fax:* (3) 5482-5135 (office). *E-mail:* info@canon.com (office). *Website:* www.canon.com (office).

MITCHELL, Arthur; American dancer, choreographer and artistic director; b. 27 March 1934, New York; s. of Arthur Mitchell and Willie Mae Mitchell; ed School of American Ballet; with Ballet Theater Workshop 1954; with John Butler Co., 1955; Prin. Dancer, New York City Ballet 1955–72; dancer, choreographer and actor, Spoleto Festival of Two Worlds 1960; Founder and Artistic Dir American Negro Dance Co. 1966–; Founder, Choreographer and Artistic Dir Nat. Ballet Co., Brazil 1967; Founder, Dir and Choreographer Dance Theater of Harlem, New York City 1969–; Teacher of Dance, Karel Shook Studio, Melissa Hayden School, Cedarhurst, Long Island, Jones-Haywood School of Ballet, Washington; Choreographer (with Rod Alexander) Shinbone Alley; has appeared in numerous productions; hon. degrees include: Hon. DArts (Columbia Coll., Chicago) 1975; Hon. DFA (NC School of the Arts) 1981, (Fordham Univ.) 1983, (Princeton Univ., Williams Coll.) 1986, (Juilliard School) 1990; Hon. DA (Harvard) 1987; awards include: Ebony Magazine American Black Achievement Award 1983; Paul Robeson Award, Actors Equity Asscn, NAACP Image Awards Hall of Fame 1986; Arnold Gringrich Memorial Award 1987; Banquet of the Golden Plate 1989; Kennedy Center Honor for Lifetime Achievement 1993; Handel Medallion, City of New York, American Acad. of Arts and Letters Award for Distinguished Service to the Arts, Barnard Coll. Medal of Distinction, Zenith Award for Fine Arts 1994, Nat. Medal of Arts 1995. *Address:* Dance Theater of Harlem, 466 West 152nd Street, New York, NY 10031, USA (office).

MITCHELL, Basil George, MA, DD, FBA; British philosopher and academic; *Fellow Emeritus, Oriel College, Oxford;* b. 9 April 1917, Bath; s. of George William Mitchell and Mary Mitchell; m. Margaret Eleanor Collin 1950; one s. three d.; ed King Edward VI School, Southampton and The Queen's Coll., Oxford; served in RN 1940–46, Lt 1942, Instructor Lt 1945; Lecturer, Christ Church, Oxford 1946–47; Fellow and Tutor in Philosophy, Keble Coll., Oxford 1947–67, Fellow Emer. 1981; Nolloth Prof. of the Philosophy of the Christian Religion, Univ. of Oxford and Fellow of Oriel Coll. 1968–84, Fellow Emer. 1984–; Stanton Lecturer, Univ. of Cambridge 1959–62; Edward Cadbury Lecturer, Univ. of Birmingham 1966–67; Gifford Lecturer, Univ. of Glasgow 1974–76; Norton Lecturer, Southern Baptist Theological Seminary, Louisville 1989; Visiting Prof., Princeton Univ., USA 1963, Colgate Univ., USA 1976; mem. Church of England Doctrine Comm. 1978–85; Chair. Ian Ramsey Centre, Oxford 1985–89; Hon. DD (Glasgow) 1977; Hon. DLitHum (Union Coll., Schenectady) 1979; Nathaniel Taylor Lecturer, Yale Univ., USA 1986, Sarum Lecturer, Univ. of Oxford 1992. *Publications:* Faith and Logic (ed.) 1957, Law, Morality and Religion in a Secular Society 1967, The Philosophy of Religion (ed.) 1971, The Justification of Religious Belief 1973, Morality: Religious and Secular 1980, How to Play Theological Ping Pong and Other Essays on Faith and Reason 1990, Faith and Criticism 1994, An Engagement with Plato's Republic (with J. R. Lucas) 2003. *Leisure interests:* gardening, flower arranging. *Address:* Bartholomew House, 9 Market Street, Woodstock, Oxon., OX20 1SU, England. *Telephone:* (1993) 811265 (home).

MITCHELL, David, MA; British writer; b. Jan. 1969, Southport; m. Keiko Mitchell; one d.; ed Univ. of Kent; worked in Waterstone's, Canterbury 1990–91; taught English in Japan 1994–2002; one of Granta's Best of Young British Novelists 2003. *Publications:* Ghostwritten (Mail on Sunday/John Llewellyn Rhys Prize, James Tait Black Memorial Prize) 1999, Number9-Dream 2001, Cloud Atlas (British Book Awards for Richard & Judy Best Read of the Year 2005, South Bank Show Literary Fiction Award, Geoffrey Faber Memorial Prize 2005) 2004, Black Swan Green 2006. *Address:* c/o Sceptre, Hodder Headline Ltd, 338 Euston Road, London, NW1 3BH, England.

MITCHELL, Sir Derek, Kt, KCB, CVO; British fmr civil servant and company director; b. 5 March 1922, Wimbledon; s. of the late Sidney Mitchell and Gladys Mitchell; m. Miriam Jackson 1944 (died 1993); one s. two d.; ed St Paul's School, London and Christ Church, Oxford; served Royal Armoured Corps and HQ London District 1942–45; served in HM Treasury 1947–63, Prin. Pvt. Sec. to Chancellor of the Exchequer 1962–63; Prin. Pvt. Sec. to Prime Minister 1964–66; Deputy Under-Sec. of State, Dept of Econ. Affairs 1966–67, Ministry of Agric., Fisheries and Food 1967–69; Econ. Minister, British Embassy, Washington and Exec. Dir IBRD, IMF, etc. 1969–72; Second Perm. Sec. (Overseas Finance) HM Treasury 1973–77; Dir Guinness Mahon 1977–78; Sr Adviser, Shearson Lehman Brothers International 1979–88; Dir Bowater Corpn 1979–84, Bowater Industries PLC 1984–89, Bowater Inc. 1984–93, Standard Chartered PLC 1979–89; mem. Nat. Theatre (now Royal Nat. Theatre) Bd 1977–96; mem. Bd French Theatre Season 1997 1996–98; Trustee Nat. Theatre (now Royal Nat. Theatre) Foundation 1982–2002, Chair. 1989–2002; mem. Council of Univ. Coll., London 1978–82, Port of London Authority 1979–82; Independent Dir The Observer Ltd 1981–93; Dir The Peter Hall Production Co. Ltd 1989–90; Trustee Nuffield Trust (fmrly Nuffield Prov. Hosps Trust) 1978–99. *Address:* 9 Holmbush Road, Putney, London, SW15 3LE, England (home). *Telephone:* (20) 8788-6581 (home). *Fax:* (20) 8788-6948 (home).

MITCHELL, Duncan, MSc, PhD, FRSSAf; South African professor of physiology; *Professor Emeritus, Brain Function Research Group, School of Physiology, University of Witwatersrand;* b. 10 May 1941, Germiston; s. of Thomas Mitchell and Maud K. (née Abercrombie) Mitchell; m. Lily May Austin 1966; one s. one d.; ed St John's Coll., Johannesburg, Univ. of Witwatersrand; mem. scientific staff, Research Org. of Chamber of Mines of SA 1964–72, Nat. Inst. for Medical Research, London 1973–75; Prof. of Physiology, Medical School, Univ. of Witwatersrand 1976–2006, Prof. Emer. 2007–; Gold Medal, Zoological Soc. of SA 2000. *Publications:* more than 200 papers in thermal, pain and sleep physiology. *Leisure interests:* nature conservation, ballet. *Address:* School of Physiology, University of the Witwatersrand, Medical School, 7 York Road, Parktown, 2193 Johannesburg, South Africa (office); 73A Fourth Street, Linden, Johannesburg 2195 (home). *Telephone:* (11) 717-2359 (office); (11) 888-2671 (home); (83) 260-7205 (home). *Fax:* (11) 643-2765 (office). *E-mail:* Duncan.Mitchell@wits.ac.za (office); duncanmitch@gmail.com (home). *Website:* hermes.wits.ac.za/www/health/physiology/staff/duncan.htm (office).

MITCHELL, Hon. Fred, JR, MPA, BA, LLB; Bahamian politician; b. 5 Oct. 1953, Nassau; ed St. Augustine's Coll., Antioch Univ., OH and John F. Kennedy School of Govt, Harvard Univ., USA, Univ. of Buckingham, UK; elected to Senate; fmr Chair. Senate Select Cttee on Culture; Public Relations Consultant, Al Dillette & Assocs; fmr Opposition Spokesman on Foreign Affairs, Labour and Immigration; Minister of Foreign Affairs and Public Service 2002-7; Founding-mem. Bahamas Cttee on S Africa; mem. Progressive Liberal Party; mem. New Providence Human Rights Asscn. *Address:* c/o Ministry of Foreign Affairs, East Hill Street, PO Box N-3746, Nassau, Bahamas (office).

MITCHELL, George John, BA, LLB; American business executive, lawyer, diplomatist and fmr politician; *Special US Envoy to the Middle East;* b. 20 Aug. 1933, Waterville, Me; s. of George J. Mitchell and Mary Mitchell; m. Heather M. Mitchell; ed Bowdoin Coll., Brunswick, Me, Georgetown Univ., Washington, DC; served in US Army 1954–56; called to Bar 1960; trial attorney, US Dept of Justice, Washington, DC 1960–62; Exec. Asst to Senator Edmund Muskie 1962–65; Pnr, Jensen & Baird, Portland 1965–77; US Attorney for Maine 1977–79; US Dist Judge 1979–80; US Senator from Maine (Democrat) 1980–95, Majority Leader, US Senate 1988–95; Chair. Maine Democratic Cttee 1966–68; mem. Nat. Cttee Maine 1968–77; Special Adviser to Pres. Clinton for Econ. Initiatives in Ireland 1995–2000; Chair. Cttee on NI 1995; Chancellor Queen's Univ., Belfast 1999–; Adviser Thames Water 1999–; mem. Bd of Dirs The Walt Disney Co. 1994–2006, Chair. 2004–06; joined Verner, Liipfert, Bernhard McPherson & Hand (law firm) 1995–2002; Pnr, DLA Piper LLP, Washington, DC 2002–04, Chair. Global Bd, Co-Chair. Govt Controversies Practice Group 2005–; Special US Envoy to the Middle East 2009–; mem. Bd of Dirs Staples Inc., Boston Red Sox (professional baseball team); headed investigation into alleged steroid use by major league baseball players 2007; Hon. KBE 1999; Hon. LLD (Queen's, Belfast) 1997; Philadelphia Liberty Medal 1998, Presidential Medal of Freedom 1999, Houphouët-Boigny Peace Prize (jtly 1999, Tipperary Int. Peace Award 2000, Truman Inst. Peace Prize, German Peace Prize, UN Educational Peace Prize, Harry Hopkins Medal, Harry S. Truman Good Neighbor Award 2007. *Publications:* Men of Zeal (with William S. Cohen), World on Fire, Not for America Alone: The Triumph of Democracy and the Fall of Communism, Making Peace. *Address:* Department of State, 2201 C St, NW, Washington, DC 20520 (office); DLA Piper, 1200 19th Street, NW, Washington, DC 20036, USA (office). *Telephone:* (202) 647-4000 (office); (202) 861-3833 (DLA Piper) (office). *Fax:* (202) 647-6738 (office); (202) 689-8562 (DLA Piper) (office). *E-mail:* george.mitchell@dlapiper.com (office). *Website:* www.state.gov (office); www.dlapiper.com (office).

MITCHELL, Rt Hon. Sir James Fitzallen, BSc, C.Biol, KCMG, PC; Saint Vincent and the Grenadines politician, agronomist, biologist and hotelier; b. 15 May 1931, Bequia, Grenadines; s. of Reginald Mitchell and Lois (née Baynes) Mitchell; m. Patricia Parker 1965 (divorced); four d.; ed St Vincent Grammar School, Imperial Coll. of Tropical Agric., Trinidad and Univ. of British Columbia; Agricultural Officer, Saint Vincent 1958–61; Ed. Pest Control Articles and News Summaries, Ministry of Overseas Devt, London 1964–65; MP for the Grenadines 1966–2001; Minister of Trade, Agric., Labour and Tourism 1967–72; MP (as an ind.) for the Grenadines 1972–79, re-elected in by-election 1979–2001; Premier of St Vincent 1972–74; Prime Minister of Saint Vincent and the Grenadines 1984–2000, also Minister of Finance and Planning and fmr Minister of Foreign Affairs; Founder New Democratic Party 1975, then Pres.; Chair. Caribbean Democrat Union 1991; Vice-Chair. Int. Democrat Union 1992–; Chair. Hotel Frangipani, Gingerbread, and several other cos; mem. Inst. of Biologists, London 1965–; Order of the Liberator (Venezuela) 1972, Grand Cross Knights of Malta 1998, Order of Propitious Clouds, Grand Cross Don Infanta (Portugal), Chevalier d'Honneur, Chaine de Rotisseur 1995, and other awards. *Publications include:* World Fungicide Usage 1965, Caribbean Crusade 1989, Guiding Change in the Islands 1996, A Season of Light 2001, Beyond the Island (autobiography) 2005. *Leisure interests:* sailing, farming. *Address:* Hotel Frangipani, Box One, Bequia, Saint Vincent (office). *Telephone:* (458) 3255 (office). *Fax:* (458) 3824 (office). *E-mail:* frangi@vincysurf.com (office).

MITCHELL, John; New Zealand professional rugby coach and fmr professional rugby union player; b. 23 March 1964, Hawera; made 134 appearances for Waikato Chiefs rugby team (86 as Capt.) and set record for most tries scored in a NZ season (21); made six mid-week appearances for NZ; Asst Coach England rugby team 1997–2000; returned to coach Waikato Chiefs 2001 season; All Blacks Coach 2001–03, team finished 3rd in World Cup 2003; Coach Waikato Nat. Provincial Championship Team 2003–4; Head Coach, Emirates Western Force, WA 2005–. *Address:* Emirates Western Force, PO Box 146, Floreat, WA 6014, Australia. *Telephone:* (8) 9383-7714. *Website:* www.rugbywa.com.au.

MITCHELL, Joni, CC; Canadian singer, songwriter, visual artist and poet; b. (Roberta Joan Anderson), 7 Nov. 1943, Fort Macleod, Alberta; d. of William A. Anderson and Myrtle Anderson (née McKee); m. 1st Chuck Mitchell 1965 (divorced); m. 2nd Larry Klein 1982; one d. by Brad McGrath; ed Alberta Coll.; Jazz Album of Year and Rock-Blues Album of Year for Mingus, Downbeat Magazine 1979, Juno Award 1981, Century Award, Billboard Magazine 1996, Polar Music Prize (Sweden) 1996, Gov. Gen.'s Performing Arts Award 1996, Nat. Acad. of Songwriters Lifetime Achievement Award 1996; inducted into Rock & Roll Hall of Fame 1997, into Nat. Acad. of Popular Music–Songwriters Hall of Fame 1997, into Canadian Songwriters Hall of Fame 2007, Grammy Award for Best Pop Instrumental Performance (for One Week Last Summer) 2008, Jack Richardson Producer of the Year 2008. *Recordings include:* albums: Song to a Seagull, Clouds, Ladies of the Canyon 1970, Blue 1971, For the Roses, Court and Spark 1974, Miles of Aisles, The Hissing of Summer Lawns 1975, Hejira 1976, Don Juan's Reckless Daughter, Mingus 1979, Shadows and Light 1980, Wild Things Run Fast 1982, Dog Eat Dog 1985, Chalk Mark in a Rain Storm 1988, Night Ride Home 1991, Turbulent Indigo (Grammy Awards for Best Pop Album, Best Art Direction 1996) 1994, Hits 1996, Misses 1996, Taming the Tiger 1998, Both Sides Now (Grammy Award for Best Traditional Pop Vocal Album 2001) 2000, Travelog 2002, Songs of a Prairie Girl 2005, Shine 2007. *Dance:* The Fiddle and the Drum (score for ballet with the Alberta Ballet) 2007. *Songs include:* Both Sides Now, Michael from Mountains, Urge for Going, Circle Game. *Television includes:* Joni Mitchell: Intimate and Interactive (Gemini Award 1996). *Publication:* Joni Mitchell: The Complete Poems and Lyrics. *Address:* Macklam Feldman Management, 1505 W 2nd Avenue, Suite 200, Vancouver, BC V6H 3Y4, Canada (office). *Telephone:* (604) 734-5945 (office). *Fax:* (604) 732-0922 (office). *E-mail:* feldman@slfa.com (office). *Website:* jonimitchell.com.

MITCHELL, Julian, BA; British author; b. 1 May 1935, Epping, Essex, England; s. of the late William Moncur Mitchell and Christine Mitchell (née Browne); ed Winchester and Wadham Coll., Oxford; mem. Literature Panel, Arts Council 1966–69, Welsh Arts Council 1988–92; John Llewellyn Rhys Prize 1965; Somerset Maugham Award 1966. *Publications:* novels: Imaginary Toys 1961, A Disturbing Influence 1962, As Far As You Can Go 1963, The White Father 1964, A Circle of Friends 1966, The Undiscovered Country 1968; biography: Jennie: Lady Randolph Churchill (with Peregrine Churchill), A Disgraceful Anomaly 2003; plays: Half Life 1977, The Enemy Within 1980, Another Country 1981 (SWET Award 1982, filmed 1984), Francis 1983, After Aida (or Verdi's Messiah) 1986, Falling over England 1994, August 1994 (adapted from Uncle Vanya, filmed 1995). *Films:* Arabesque 1965, Vincent and Theo 1990, Wilde 1997; television plays and adaptations; translation of Pirandello's Henry IV. *Television:* more than 50 TV plays. *Leisure interests:* fishing, local history. *Address:* 6/47 Draycott Place, London, SW3 3DB, England (home). *Telephone:* (20) 7589-1933 (home).

MITCHELL, Katie; British theatre director; *Associate Director, Royal National Theatre;* b. 23 Sept. 1964; d. of Michael Mitchell and Sally Mitchell; Pres. Oxford Univ. Dramatic Soc. 1984; awarded a Winston Churchill Memorial Trust Award to research Eastern European theatre in Russia, Lithuania, Georgia, Poland and Germany 1989; f. Classics on a Shoestring Theatre Co. 1990; Assoc. Dir RSC 1997–98; Assoc. Dir Royal Court Theatre, London 2001–03; Assoc. Dir Abbey Theatre, Dublin 2000-02; Assoc. Dir Royal Nat. Theatre 2003–; Evening Standard Award for Best. Dir 1996. *Plays directed:* Arden of Faversham, Vassa Zheleznova and Women of Troy (with Classics on a Shoestring) 1990–91; A Woman Killed with Kindness 1991, The Dybbuk 1992, Ghosts 1993, Henry VI 1994, Easter 1995, The Phoenician Women 1996, The Mysteries 1997, The Beckett Shorts 1997, Uncle Vanya 1998 (RSC); Rutherford and Son 1994, The Machine Wreckers 1995, The Oresteia 1999, Ivanov 2002, Three Sisters 2003, Iphigenia at Aulis 2004, The Idiot 2008 (Royal Nat. Theatre); Endgame 1996 (Donmar Warehouse); Don Giovanni 1996, Jenůfa 1998, Katya Kabanova 2001, Jephtha 2003, The Sacrifice 2007 (Welsh Nat. Opera); Attempts on Her Life 1999 (Piccolo Theatre, Milan); The Maids 1999 (Young Vic, London); The Country 2000, Mountain Language Ashes to Ashes 2001, Nightsongs 2002, Forty Winks 2004 (Royal Court); The Last Ones 1996, Iphigenia in Aulis 2001 (Abbey Theatre, Dublin); The Seagull 2006, The Waves 2006, Attempts on her Life (Nat. Theatre) 2006; The Jewish Wife/A Respectable Wedding (Young Vic) 2007; St Matthew Passion (Glyndebourne) 2007. *TV work includes:* The Widowing of Mrs Holroyd 1995, The Stepdaughter 2000 (BBC), Turn of the Screw 2004. *Address:* c/o Leah Schmidt, The Agency, 24 Pottery Lane, London, W11 4LZ, England.

MITCHELL, Keith Claudius, MS, PhD; Grenadian politician; *Leader, New National Party;* b. 12 Nov. 1946, St George's; m. Marietta Mitchell; one s.; ed Presentation Coll., Grenada, Univ. of West Indies, Barbados, Howard Univ. and American Univ., Washington, DC; cand. for Grenada Nat. Party in 1972 elections; Gen. Sec. New Nat. Party 1984–89, Leader 1989–; Minister of Communication, Works, Public Utilities, Transportation, of Civil Aviation and Energy 1984–87, of Communications, Works, Public Utilities, Co-operatives, Community Devt, Women's Affairs and Civil Aviation 1988–89; Prime Minister of Grenada and Minister of Finance, External Affairs, Mobilization, Trade and Industry, Information and Nat. Security 1995–99; Prime Minister and Minister of Nat. Security and Information 1999–2008, re-elected 2003, also Minister of Finance 2007–08; Capt. Grenada Nat. Cricket Team 1971–74; Order of the Brilliant Star (Taiwan) 1995. *Leisure interest:* playing cricket. *Address:* New National Party (NNP), Upper Lucas Street, St. George's, Grenada (office). *Telephone:* 440-1875 (office). *Fax:* 440-1876 (office). *E-mail:* nnpadmin@spiceisle.com (office). *Website:* nnpnews.com (office).

MITCHELL, Pat, MA; American broadcasting executive and television producer; *President and CEO, Paley Center for Media;* m. Scott Seydel; six c.; ed Univ. of Georgia; fmr news anchor and producer WBZ-TV Boston; first woman to host and produce her own nat. talk show, Woman to Woman 1980s; Co-Founder, developer of series, specials, documentaries, VU Productions –1992; has worked for NBC, CBS and ABC; Head CNN Productions, Time Inc. TV –2000; Pres. and CEO Public Broadcasting Service (PBS) 2000–06; Pres. and CEO Paley Center for Media (fmly Museum of TV and Radio), New York 2006–; mem. Council on Foreign Relations, Women's Advisory Council of the Kennedy School of Govt, US–Afghan Women's Council; mem. Bd of Dirs Bank of America, Participant Productions, Sun Microsystems, Human Rights Watch; mem. Bd of Trustees Sundance Inst. (currently Vice Chair.), Mayo Clinic; Founding mem. American chapter, Global Green USA; Dr hc (Emerson Coll.), (Hollins Univ.), (Bloomsburg Univ.), (Converse Coll.); Business Hall of Fame, Georgia State Univ. *Television includes:* Woman to Woman (Emmy Award for Best Daytime Talk Program 1984), CNN Perspectives, Cold War (Peabody Award), Millennium: A Thousand Years of History. *Address:* Paley Center for Media, 25 West 52nd Street, New York, NY 10019, USA (office). *Telephone:* (212) 621-6800 (office). *Website:* www.paleycenter.org (office).

MITCHELL, Thomas Noel, PhD, LittD; Irish academic; b. 7 Dec. 1939; s. of Patrick Mitchell and Margaret Mitchell; m. Lynn S. Hunter 1965; three s. one d.; ed Nat. Univ. of Ireland, Trinity Coll. Dublin and Cornell Univ. NY; Instructor Cornell Univ. 1965–66; Asst Prof. Swarthmore Coll. 1966–73, Assoc. Prof. 1973–78, Prof. of Classics 1978–79; Prof. of Latin, Trinity Coll. Dublin 1979–91, Fellow 1980–, Sr Dean 1985–87, Sr Lecturer 1987–90, Provost 1991–2001; Cornell Visiting Prof. Swarthmore Coll. 1986; mem. Royal Irish Acad. (Vice-Pres. 1989); mem. American Philosophical Soc. 1996–; Distinguished Visiting Prof. Victoria Univ. Melbourne 2001–; Visiting Fellow, The Hoover Inst. Stanford Univ. Calif. 2002; Chair. Bd St James Hosp., Dublin, Press Council of Ireland 2007–; Hon. Fellow, RCPI 1992, R.C.S.I. 1993; Hon. LLD (Queen's Univ. Belfast) 1992, (Nat. Univ. of Ireland) 1992; Hon. D.Hum.Litt. (Swarthmore) 1992, (Lynn Univ., USA) 1998, (State Univ. of New York) 1998; Hon. PhD, (Charles Univ., Prague) 1998, (Dublin Inst. of Tech.) 1999; Hon. DLitt (Victoria Univ. of Tech.) 2000. *Publications:* Cicero, The Ascending Years 1979, Cicero, Verrines II.1. 1986, Cicero the Senior Statesman 1990; numerous articles and reviews on Cicero and Roman History. *Leisure interest:* gardening. *Address:* The Rubrics, Trinity College, Dublin 2 (office); Dodona, Blackwood Lane, Malahide, Co. Dublin, Ireland (home). *Telephone:* (1) 6081843 (office).

MITCHISON, John Murdoch, FRS, FRSE, FIBiol; British cell biologist; b. 11 June 1922, Oxford; s. of the late Lord Mitchison and of Naomi M. Mitchison (née Haldane); m. Rosalind Mary Wrong 1947 (died 2002); one s. three d.; ed Winchester Coll., Trinity Coll., Univ. of Cambridge; Army Operational Research 1941–46; Sr and Research Scholar, Trinity Coll., Univ. of Cambridge 1946–50, Fellow 1950–54; Lecturer in Zoology, Univ. of Edinburgh 1953–59, Reader in Zoology 1959–62, Prof. of Zoology 1963–88, Dean of Faculty of Science 1984–85, Univ. Fellow 1988–92, Prof. Emer. 1988– and Hon. Fellow; J.W. Jenkinson Memorial Lecturer, Univ. of Oxford 1971–72; mem. Edinburgh Univ. Court 1971–74, 1985–88; mem. Council Scottish Marine Biological Asscn 1961–67; mem. Exec. Cttee Int. Soc. for Cell Biology 1964–72; mem. Biology Cttee SRC 1976–79, Science Bd 1976–79; mem. Royal Comm. on Environmental Pollution 1974–79, Academia Europaea 1989; mem. Working Group of Biological Manpower, Dept of Educ. and Science 1968–71; Pres. British Soc. for Cell Biology 1974–77; mem. Advisory Cttee on Safety of Nuclear Installations, Health and Safety Exec. 1981–84. *Publications:* The Biology of the Cell Cycle 1971, numerous papers in scientific journals. *Address:* Institute of Cell, Animal and Population Biology, West Mains Road, Edinburgh, EH9 3JT (office); Great Yew, Ormiston, East Lothian, EH35 5NJ, Scotland (home). *Telephone:* (1875) 340530. *Fax:* (131) 667-3210 (office). *E-mail:* jmmitchison@ed.ac.uk (office).

MITCHISON, (Nicholas) Avrion, DPhil, FRS; British professor of zoology and comparative anatomy; b. 5 May 1928, London; s. of the late Baron Mitchison and Naomi Mitchison; m. Lorna Margaret Martin 1957; two s. three d.; ed Leighton Park School and Univ. of Oxford; Lecturer, later Reader in Zoology, Univ. of Edin. 1956–62; Head, Div. of Experimental Biology, Nat. Inst. for Medical Research, Mill Hill 1962–71; Jodrell Prof. of Zoology and Comparative Anatomy, Univ. Coll. London 1970–89; Scientific Dir Deutsches Rheuma-Forschungszentrum, Berlin 1990–96; Sr Fellow, Dept of Immunology, Univ. Coll. London 1996–; Hon. Dir Imperial Cancer Research Fund, Tumour Immunology Unit, Univ. Coll. London; Hon. MD (Edin.); Paul Ehrlich Prize, Mitchison Prize for Rheumatology est. in his honour. *Address:* Department of Immunology, University College London, Windeyer Building, 46 Cleveland Street, London, W1P 6DB (office); 14 Belitha Villas, London, N1 1PD, England (home). *Telephone:* (20) 7380-9349. *Fax:* (20) 7380-9357. *E-mail:* n.mitchison@ucl.ac.uk (office).

MITHI, Mukut; Indian government official; b. 1954; m. Smt. Pomaya Mithi; mem. Indian Nat. Congress (INC), later of Arunachal Congress, broke from latter to form Arunachal Congress (Mithi)—AC(M) 1998, AC(M) later merged with INC 1999; Chief Minister of Arunachal Pradesh 1999–2003; Lt-Gov. Puducherry (fmrly Pondicherry) 2006–08 (resgnd). *Leisure interests:* basketball, jogging, singing, dancing. *Address:* c/o Office of the Lieutenant-Governor, Puducherry, India.

MITREVA, Ilinka, MA, PhD; Macedonian politician and academic; b. 11 Feb. 1950, Skopje; ed Univ. of Skopje, Univ. of Belgrade; taught French Literature at Faculty of Philology, then Head of Group of Romance Languages and Literature, Philological Faculty, Univ. of Skopje 1974–94; mem. Sobranie (Ass.) 1994–, Head of Ass. Group for Co-operation with European Parl.; Minister of Foreign Affairs 2001, 2002–06; Head of Macedonian Parl. Del. in Cen. European Initiative; mem. Initiative Bd for NATO Club; Chevalier, Ordre nat. du Mérite. *Address:* c/o Ministry of Foreign Affairs, Dame Gruev 6, 1000 Skopje, Republic of Macedonia (office).

MITRI, Tariq; Lebanese politician and academic; *Minister of Culture;* b. 1950, Tripoli; fmr Prof., Balamand Univ.; Dir Faith and Unity Bureau, WCC, Geneva mid-1980s, later Co-ordinator Islamic-Christian Dialogue; Minister of Environment and Admin. Devt 2005–06; Minister of Culture 2006–, Acting Minister of Foreign Affairs and Emigrants 2006–08; Co-founder Centre of Christian-Muslim Studies; active mem. in several groups and orgs concerning Muslim-Christian dialogue in Middle East and world-wide. *Address:* Ministry of Culture, Immeuble Hatab, rue Madame Curie, Verdun, Beirut (office); Ministry of Foreign Affairs and Emigrants, rue Sursock, Achrafieh, Beirut, Lebanon. *Telephone:* (1) 744250 (Ministry of Culture) (office); (1) 333100 (Ministry of Foreign Affairs) (office). *Fax:* (1) 756303 (Ministry of Culture) (office). *E-mail:* omarhala_48@hotmail.com (office); info@emigrants.gov.lb (office). *Website:* www.culture.gov.lb (office); www.emigrants.gov.lb (office).

MITROFANOV, Aleksey Valentinovich; Russian politician and writer; b. 16 March 1962, Moscow; s. of Zoya Mitrofanova; m. Marina Lillevyali; ed Moscow Inst. of Int. Relations; with Ministry of Foreign Affairs 1985–88; researcher, Inst. of USA and Canada 1988–91; producer TV programmes, Leisure Centre Sokol; mem. Higher Council, Liberal Democratic Party of Russia 1991–93; Minister of Foreign Affairs, Shadow Cabinet of Liberal Democratic Party 1992–96; mem. State Duma 1993–; Deputy Chair. Cttee on Int. Relations 1993–96, Chair. Cttee on Geopolitics 1996–99; joined A Just Russia 2007. *Films:* scriptwriter: Pchiojka (A Little Bee), Yuliya 2006; numerous documentaries including Yury Andropov 1993, Andrey Gromyko 1993. *Publications include:* Steps of New Geopolitics, Secret Visit of Professor Voland, t.A.T.u Come Back 2006. *Leisure interest:* chess. *Address:* State Duma, 103265 Moscow, Okhotny ryad 1, Russia. *Telephone:* (495) 292-83-10 (office). *Fax:* (495) 292-94-64 (office). *Website:* www.duma.ru (office); alexeymitrofanov.ru (home).

MITROFANOV, Alexandr; Czech political journalist; b. 27 June 1957, Rostov, Russia; m.; one s. one d.; ed Rostov State Univ., Russia; Ed. Škodovák, Škoda Plzeň 1980–88, Právo Lidu 1991–92; contrib. to Právo 1992–, Political Commentator; undertook sabbatical study in UK 1994, 1997; Křepelky Prize, Czech Literary Fund 1994, Ferdinand Peroutka Prize for Journalism 2001. *Publications:* Behind the Façade of Lidový dům, Czech Social Democracy, People and Events 1992–1998 1998, Politics Under Lid (with Markéta Maláčova) 2002, three chapters in Erratic Paths of Social Democracy 2005. *Leisure interests:* reading, writing books. *Address:* Právo, Slezská 13, 121 50 Prague 2, Czech Republic (office). *Telephone:* (2) 21001315 (office). *Fax:* (2) 21001276 (office). *E-mail:* alexandr.mitrofanov@pravo.cz (office). *Website:* www.pravo.cz (office).

MITROFANOVA, Eleonora Valentinovna, DrEcon; Russian economist, politician and government official; *Head, Russian Center for International Scientific and Cultural Cooperation, Ministry of Foreign Affairs;* b. 11 June 1953, Moscow; three s. one d.; ed Moscow State Inst. of Int. Relations; worked at Research Inst. of Marine Transport 1976–91; Dir-Gen. Explex law co., Moscow 1991–93; mem. State Duma, Russian Fed. 1993–97, mem. Cttee on Budget, Taxation, Banking and Finance; Auditor, Chamber of Russian Fed. 1997–2001; First Deputy Minister of Foreign Affairs 2001–04, Head, Foreign Ministry Agency for Relations with Russians Abroad 2004–; Deputy Dir-Gen. on Admin. Problems, UNESCO 2001–03; Head, Russian Center for Int. Scientific and Cultural Cooperation (Roszarubezhcenter), Ministry of Foreign Affairs 2004–; mem. Int. Man. Acad. (Order 'Friendshipnations') 2003; Order of People's Friendship 2003. *Address:* Russian Centre for International Scientific and Cultural Cooperation, 125009 Moscow, 14 Vozdivzhenka Street, Russia (office). *Telephone:* (495) 290-12-45 (office). *Fax:* (495) 200-32-48 (office). *E-mail:* mitrofanova@rusintercenter.ru (office). *Website:* www .rusintercenter.ru (office).

MITROPOLSKY, Yuriy Alekseyevich, DMathSc; Ukrainian mathematician; *Scientific Consultant, Department of Mathematics and Cybernetics, Ukrainian Academy of Sciences;* b. 3 Jan. 1917, Shishaki, Poltava Region; s. of Alexy Savvich Mitropolsky and Vera Vasilevna (née Charnish) Mitropolskaya; m. Olexandra (née Lihacheva) Mitropolskaya 1941; one s. one d.; ed Kiev State Univ., Kazakh State Univ.; army service 1943–45; scientific researcher, Inst. of Bldg Mechanics 1946–51; Inst. of Math. Ukrainian Acad. of Sciences 1951–58, Dir 1958–88, Hon. Dir 1988–; mem. Ukranian Acad. of Sciences 1961, Acad.-Sec. Dept of Math. and Cybernetics 1963–93, Scientific Consultant 1993–; lecturer, Prof. Ukranian State Univ. 1949–89; mem. USSR (now Russian) Acad. of Sciences 1984; Foreign Corresp. mem. Accademia di Bologna 1971–; Lenin Prize 1965; Hero of Socialist Labour 1986. *Publications:* over 500 scientific articles and papers and 25 monographs including Group-theoretical Approach in Asymptotic Methods of Nonlinear Mechanics 1988, Nonlinear Mechanics, Groups and Symmetry 1995, Nonlinear Mechanics, One-Frequency Oscillations 1997. *Leisure interest:* travel. *Address:* Ukrainian Academy of Sciences, Vladimirskaya 54, 01034, Kiev 34 (office); B. Khemelnitskogo Street 42, Apt. 10, 01030 Kiev 30, Ukraine (home). *Telephone:* (44) 235-23-84, (44) 235-31-93 (office); (44) 235-20-10 (home). *Fax:* (44) 235-20-10 (office).

MITROPOULOS, Efthimios; Greek international organization official; *Secretary-General, International Maritime Organization;* b. 30 May 1939, Piraeus; m.; one s. one d.; ed Aspropyrgos Merchant Marine Acad., Hellenic Coast Guard Acad.; with Greek Merchant Navy 1959–62; Coast Guard Officer, Corfu and Piraeus 1964–65; mem. Greek Del. to IMO 1966–77, becoming Head; Harbour Master, Corfu 1977–79; joined IMO Secr. 1979, Head of Navigation Section 1985–89, Sr Deputy Dir for Navigation and Related Matters 1989–92, Dir Maritime Safety Div. 1992–2003, Asst Sec.-Gen. 2000–03, Sec.-Gen. 2004–; Chancellor, World Maritime Univ., Malmo, Sweden 2004–; Chair. Int. Maritime Law Inst., Malta 2004–; Gov. Royal Nat. Lifeboat Inst.; mem. Hellenic Inst. of Marine Tech., Shipmasters' Union of Greece, Int. Fed. of Shipmaster's Asscns, Propeller Club, Royal Automobile Club; Fellow, Royal Inst. of Navigation; Hon. Citizen of Galaxidi, Greece; Hon. Mem., Int. Asscn of Marine Aids to Navigation and Lighthouse Authorities; Hon. Fellow, Nautical Inst., Inst. of Marine Eng, Science and Tech.; Officier de l'Orde du Mérite Maritime de la France, Mil. Valour Medal and Phoenix Order (Hellenic Repub.), Commendatore, Order of Merit (Italy), St Marcus Cross, Patriarchate of Alexandria and All Africa, Grand Commdr, Order of the Phoenix (Hellenic Repub.), Medal for Valour & Honour (Hellenic Coast Guard), Grand'Ufficiale, Order of Merit (Italy); hon. degrees from Nicola Vaptsarov Naval Acad., Bulgaria, Maritime Univ., Constanza, Romania, Schiller Int. Univ., Dalian Maritime Univ., China, Chung-Ang Univ., Seoul, Repub. of Korea, Univ. of Messina, Italy, City Univ., London, Univ. of the Aegean, Greece, Odessa Nat. Maritime Acad.; numerous awards, including Coastguard Award (Grand Cross), Argentina, 15 November Medal, Uruguay, Medal of Naval Merit, Brazil, US Coast Guard Distinguished Public Service Award, Colombian Navy Medal for 'Servicios Distinguidos a la Dirección General Marítima', Silver Bell Award, The Seamen's Church Institute, New York, Danish Shipowners' Asscn Maritime Award, Union of Greek Shipowners Environment Award 2006, Interferry Person of Distinction 2006, Int. Hall of Fame Award, New York 2007, Seatrade Personality of the Year 2008, Turkish Shipping Golden Anchor Lifetime Achievement Award 2008. *Publications:* Tankers: Evolution and Technical Issues 1969, Studies in Shipping Economics 1970, Safety of Navigation 1971, Categories and Types of Merchant Ships 1973, Collision Avoidance at Sea 1975, Separation of Traffic at Sea 1976, Shipping Economics and Policy 1981. *Leisure interests:* swimming, diving, fishing, football, classical music, naval history. *Address:* 7 Cornwall House, Cornwall Gardens, London, SW7 4AE (home); International Maritime Organization, 4 Albert Embankment, London, SE1 7SR, England (office). *Telephone:* (20) 7735-7611 (office). *Fax:* (20) 7587-3210 (office). *E-mail:* secretary-general@imo.org (office). *Website:* www.imo.org (office).

MITSOTAKIS, Constantine; Greek politician; b. 18 Oct. 1918, Chania, Crete; m. Marika Yianoukou; one s. three d.; ed Univ. of Athens; served in army 1940–41; active in Cretan resistance against Nazi occupation, twice arrested and sentenced to death; after War, republished newspaper KIRYX; MP for Chania 1946–74, 1977–; Under-Sec. of State for Finance, then Acting Minister for Communications and Public Works 1951; Minister for Finance 1963–64, for Econ. Co-ordination 1965; arrested by mil. junta 1967, released, under house arrest, escaped and lived in exile; returned to Greece 1974; f. Neoliberal Party; joined New Democracy Party 1978, Leader 1984–93; Minister for Econ. Co-ordination 1978-80, for Foreign Affairs 1980–81; Prime Minister of Greece, also with responsibility for the Aegean 1990–93. *Address:* 1 Aravantinou Street, 106 74 Athens, Greece.

MITTA, Aleksander Naumovich; Russian film director; b. 29 March 1933, Moscow; ed Moscow Inst. of Construction Eng, All-Union Inst. of Cinematography; with Mosfilm studio 1961; Prof., Hamburg Univ. 1995–; Merited Worker of Arts of Russia 1974. *Films include:* The Fearless Ataman 1961, Drug moy Kolka (My Friend Kolka) 1961, Bez strakha i upryoka (No Fear, No Blame) 1962, Bolshoy fitil 1963, Zvonyat, otkroyte dver (Someone is Ringing, Open the Door) (Grand Prix Int. Festival in Venice) 1965, Gori, gori, moya zvezda (Twinkle, Twinkle, My Star) 1969, Tochka, tochka, zapyataya... (Period, Period, Comma...) 1972, Moskva, lyubov moya (Moscow, My Love) 1974, Skaz pro to, kak tsar Pyotr arapa zhenil (How Czar Peter the Great Married Off His Moor) 1976, Klouny i deti 1976, Ekipazh (The Crew) (Prize of All-Union Film Festival) 1980, Skazka stranstviy (The Story of the Voyages) 1982, Safety Margin 1988, Shag (A Step) 1988, Zateryannyy v Sibiri (Lost in Siberia) 1991, Raskalyonnaya subbota 2002. *Television includes:* Alfred Schnittke and His Friends 1994, Border of the State (series) 1999–2000, Granitsa. Tayozhnyy roman (mini-series) 2000, Red-Hot Weekend 2003, Swan Paradise 2005. *Publication:* Cinema Between Hell and Paradise. *Leisure interest:* watching films on DVD. *Address:* Malaya Gruzinskaya str. 28, Apt 105, 123557 Moscow, Russia (home). *Telephone:* (495) 253-51-57 (Moscow) (home). *Fax:* (495) 253-73-20 (home).

MITTAL, Lakshmi Niwas; Indian steel industry executive; *Chairman and CEO, ArcelorMittal Steel Company NV;* b. 15 June 1950, Sadulpur, Rajasthan; m. Usha Mittal; one s. one d.; ed St Xavier's Coll., Calcutta; began career in family's steel-making business; Founder, Chair., CEO The LNM Group; f. Caribbean Ispat 1989; acquired Ispat Mexicana 1992, Ispat Sidbec, Canada 1994, Ispat Hamburger Stahlwerke, Germany 1995, Karmet, Kazakhstan 1995, Irish Ispat 1996, Thyssen's Long Product Div., Germany 1997, Ispat Unimetal Group 1999, Chair., CEO of all mem. cos of LNM Group Inc., Ispat Int. NV, Ispat Karmet, Ispat Indo, Ispat Coal, Chair. and CEO Mittal Steel Co. NV (after merger with Int. Steel Group) 2004–06, Chair. and CEO ArcelorMittal (after merger with Arcelor) 2006–, Dir (non-exec.) ArcelorMittal South Africa; mem. Bd Dirs ICICI Bank Ltd, Goldman Sachs; mem. Exec. Cttee Int. Iron and Steel Inst., Foreign Investment Council in Kazakhstan, Int. Investment Council in South Africa, World Econ. Forum's Int. Business Council, Advisory Bd Kellogg School of Man., USA; Padma Vibhushan 2008; Steelmaker of the Year Award 1996, Eighth Hon. Willy Korf Steel Vision

Award 1998, Fortune European Businessman of the Year 2004, Wall Street Journal Entrepreneur of the Year 2004, Sunday Times Business Person of 2006, Financial Times Man of the Year 2006, Die Welt Gewinner 2006, Time magazine Newsmaker of the Year 2006, Dwight D. Eisenhower Global Leadership Award 2007. *Leisure interests:* swimming, yoga, golf. *Address:* ArcelorMittal, Hofplein 20, 3032 Rotterdam, Netherlands (office); Ispat International (UK) Ltd, 7th Floor, Berkeley Square House, Berkeley Square, London, W1J 6DA, England (office). *Telephone:* (10) 217880050 (Rotterdam) (office); (20) 7629-7988 (London) (office). *Fax:* (10) 2178850 (Rotterdam) (office). *E-mail:* contact@arcelormittal.com (office). *Website:* www.arcelormittal.com (office).

MITTAL, Som, BEng; Indian engineer and computer industry executive; *President, National Association of Software and Services Companies;* b. 7 Feb. 1952; ed Indian Inst. of Tech., Kanpur, Indian Inst. of Man., Ahmedabad; has worked for Larsen & Toubro, Escorts and Compaq; set up SRF Ltd jt venture; worked for Wipro Infotech, CEO Business Solutions Div. 1993–94; fmr Pres. and CEO Digital Equipment (India) Ltd, Bangalore; Head of Services Business for Asia-Pacific and Japan region, Hewlett-Packard –2007; Vice-Chair. Nat. Asscn of Software and Services Cos (NASSCOM), Chair. 2003–04, Pres. 2008–; mem. Nat. Council and fmr Chair. Confed. of Indian Industry; mem. Exec. Council and past Pres. (South) Mfrs Asscn of Information Tech.; mem. Chief Minister's Task Force (Govt of Karnataka), Governing Council Indian Inst. of Information Tech.; Founder-mem. Bd of Educ. Standards. *Address:* NASSCOM, 607, 5th Floor, Oxford Towers, Airport Road, Kodihalli, Bangalore, 560 008, India (office). *Telephone:* (80) 41151705 (ext. 706) (office). *Fax:* (80) 41151707 (office). *E-mail:* president@nasscom.in (office). *Website:* www.nasscom.in (office).

MITTAL, Sunil Bharti; Indian telecommunications executive; *Chairman and Group Managing Director, Bharti Enterprises;* s. of Sat Paul Mittal; m.; two s. one d.; ed Punjab Univ., Harvard Univ., USA; Founder Bharti Enterprises 1976–, Dir 1995–, Chair. and Group Man. Dir 2001–; Chair. Indo-US Jt Business Council; mem. Nat. Council of Confed. of Indian Industry, Fed. of Indian Chambers of Commerce and Industry; Hon. Consul of Seychelles, Hon. Fellow Inst. of Electronics and Telecommunication Engineers of India; Padma Bhushan 2007; Hon. DSc (Govind Ballabh Pant Univ. of Agric. and Tech.); Communication World Telecom Man of the Year 1997, Business India Businessman of the Year 2002, GSM Asscn Chairman's Award 2008. *Address:* Bharti Tele-Ventures Ltd, Qutab Ambience (at Qutab Minar), Mehrauli Road, New Delhi 110 030, India (office). *Telephone:* (11) 41666000 (office). *Fax:* (11) 41666011 (office). *E-mail:* corpcomm@bharti.com (office). *Website:* www.airtel.in (office).

MITTERRAND, Gen. Jacques; French aerospace executive; b. 21 May 1918, Angoulême, Charentes; s. of Joseph Mitterrand and Yvonne Mitterrand (née Lorrain); brother of the late François Mitterrand; m. Gisèle Baume 1948; two d.; ed St Paul Coll., Angoulême, St Louis Lycée, Paris, St Cyr Mil. Acad.; served in Air Force 1937–75; participated in devt and institution of French Nuclear Force; mem. Del. to NATO Perm. Group, Washington, DC 1961–64; Gen., Asst Commdr French Strategic Air Forces 1965–67, Commdr 1970–72; Deputy Chief of Staff of Air Force 1968, of Armed Forces 1968–70; Insp. Gen. of Air Force 1972–75; mem. Supreme Air Council 1970–75; Chair. Bd and Chief Exec., Soc. Nat. Industrielle Aérospatiale (SNIAS) 1975–81; Counsellor to Chair. French Atomic Energy Agency 1975; First Vice-Chair. French Aerospace Industries Asscn (GIFAS), Chair. 1981–84; Chair. Asscn Européenne des Constructeurs de Matériel Aérospatial (AECMA) 1978–83; Pres. Office Gén. de l'Air (Oga) 1984–93, Hon. Pres. 1993–; Vice-Chair. Supervisory Bd of Airbus Industry; Vice-Pres. Turbomeca 1983; mem. Bd Inst. of Air Transport; Dir Intertechnique, Turbomeca, Hurel Dubois; Grand Croix, Légion d'honneur, Croix de guerre, Croix de la Valeur militaire, Croix du Combattant; Médaille de l'Aéronautique. *Address:* Oga, 33 Avenue des Champs-Elysées, Paris 75008 (office); 87 boulevard Murat, 75016 Paris, France (home).

MITYUKOV, Mikhail Alekseyevich, CandJurSc; Russian politician, lawyer and academic; b. 7 Jan. 1942, Ust-Uda, Irkutsk Region; m. Ludmila Aleksandrovna Mityukova; two s. one d.; ed Irkutsk State Univ.; worked in Khakassia Autonomous Region (now Repub.), Deputy Chair. regional court 1968–87; Sr Teacher, Head of Chair of History and Law Abakan State Pedagogical Inst. 1987–90; Russian Fed. People's Deputy and mem. Supreme Soviet, Deputy Chair. then Chair. Cttee on Law 1990–93; First Deputy Minister of Justice 1993–94; mem. State Duma (Parl.) 1993–95, First Deputy Chair. 1994–95; participated in drafting new Russian Constitution; First Deputy Sec., Security Council of Russia 1996–98; Plenipotentiary Rep. of Russian Pres. in Constitutional Court 1998–2005; Prof., State Univ. (RGU) 1995–; Merited Jurist of the Russian Fed. award, several medals. *Publications:* over 200 scientific works and monographs including Constitutional Courts on Post-Soviet Territory 1999, A History of Constitutional Justice in Russia 2002. *Address:* c/o Ipat'yevski per. 9–14, 103132 Moscow, Russia (office).

MITZNA, Amram, MA; Israeli politician and army general (retd); *Chairman, Israel Labour Party; Mayor, Haifa;* b. 20 Feb. 1945, Kibbutz Dovrat; m.; three c.; ed Haifa Univ., Harvard Univ.; joined Israeli Armed Forces 1963; served as Brig. in Six-Day War 1967, Yom Kippur War 1973; resgnd in protest at Israeli treatment of Palestinians in Sabra and Shatila, Lebanon 1982; re-apptd Defence Force Commdr in West Bank during Palestinian uprising 1987–93, later Gen. of the Cen. Region Command, retd from army 1993, rank of Maj. Gen.; Mayor of Haifa 1993–; Chair. Israel Labour Party 2002–, advocates removal of West Bank and Gaza settlements and direct negotiations with Palestinian leadership. *Address:* Knesset Residence, Kiryat Ben-Guryon, Jerusalem 91950, Israel (office). *Telephone:* (2) 6753810 (office). *Fax:* (2) 6753715 (office). *E-mail:* amitzna@knesset.gov.il (office).

MIURA, Satoshi; Japanese telecommunications executive; *President and CEO, Nippon Telegraph and Telephone Corporation (NTT);* b. 3 April 1944; joined Nippon Telegraph and Telephone Corpn 1967, held several exec. positions including Sr Vice-Pres. and Exec. Man., Personnel Dept 1996–97, Sr Vice-Pres. and Exec. Man. Personnel and Industrial Relations Dept 1997–98, Exec. Vice-Pres. and Exec. Man. Personnel and Industrial Relations 1998–99, Exec. Vice-Pres. and Deputy Sr Exec. Man. NTT East Provisional HQ 1999–2002, Sr Exec. Vice-Pres. NTT East 1999–2002, Pres. 2002–07, Sr Exec. Vice-Pres. NTT 2005–07, Pres. 2007–. *Address:* Nippon Telegraph and Telephone Corporation, 3-1, Otemachi 2-chome, Chiyoda-ku, Tokyo 100-8116 Japan (office). *Telephone:* (3) 5205-5581 (office). *Fax:* (3) 5205-5589 (office). *E-mail:* info@ntt.co.jp (office). *Website:* www.ntt.co.jp/index_e.html (office).

MIYAHARA, Hideo, ME, DE; Japanese computer scientist, university administrator and academic; *President, Osaka University;* ed Osaka Univ.; Asst Prof., Dept of Applied Math. and Physics, Faculty of Eng, Kyoto Univ. 1973–80; Assoc. Prof., Dept of Information and Computer Sciences, Faculty of Eng Science, Osaka Univ. 1980–86, Prof., Computation Centre 1986–89, Prof., Dept of Information and Computer Sciences, Faculty of Eng Science 1989–, Dir Computation Centre 1995–98, Dean Faculty of Eng Science 1998–2000, Dean Grad. School of Information Science and Tech. 2000–03, Pres. Osaka Univ. 2003–; Visiting Scientist, IBM Thomas J. Watson Research Center, USA 1983–84; Chair. Japan Cttee of Univs for Int. Exchange (JACUIE); Fellow, Information Processing Soc. of Japan, IEEE. *Publications:* numerous scientific papers in professional journals on performance evaluation of computer communication networks, broadband ISDN and multimedia systems. *Address:* Office of the President, Osaka University, 1-1 Yamadaoka, Suita, Osaka 565-0871, Japan (office). *Telephone:* (6) 6850-6585 (office). *Fax:* (6) 6850-6589 (office). *E-mail:* miyahara@ist.osaka-u.ac.jp (office). *Website:* www.osaka-u.ac.jp (office).

MIYAHARA, Kenji, BA; Japanese business executive; *Chairman, Sumitomo Corporation;* ed Kyoto Univ.; joined Sumitomo Shoji Kaisha 1958, Pres. and CEO Sumitomo Corpn of America 1990–96, Pres. and CEO Sumitomo Corpn 1996–2001, Chair. 2001–; Chair. Japan Foreign Trade Council Inc. 2000–04, Japan–Viet Nam Econ. Cttee 2003–, Japan Fed. of Trading Cos (JFTC) 2004–; Vice-Chair. Japan Fed. of Econ. Orgs (KEIDANREN) 2004; Counsellor, Bank of Japan 2004–; mem. Panel of Conciliators and Arbitrators, Int. Centre for the Settlement of Investment Disputes (ICSID); mem. US–Japan Pvt. Sector/Govt Comm. 2002–03; Hon. Chair. Japan Foreign Trade Council Inc. 2004–. *Address:* Sumitomo Corporation, 1-8-11 Harumi, Chuo-ku, Tokyo 104-8610, Japan (office). *Telephone:* (3) 5166-5000 (office). *Fax:* (3) 5166-6292 (office). *Website:* www.sumitomocorp.co.jp (office).

MIYAHARA, Koji; Japanese shipping industry executive; *President,* Sr Man. Dir Nippon Yusen Kabushiki Kaisha (NYK Line) –2004, Pres. 2004–, Chief Exec. CSR Man. HQ, Chair. Bulk/Energy Resources Transportation Strategy Cttee, Dir-Gen. NYK Cool Earth Project. *Address:* Nippon Yusen Kabushiki Kaisha, 3-2, Marunouchi 2-chome, Chiyoda-ku, Tokyo 100-0005, Japan (office). *Telephone:* (3) 3284-5151 (office). *Fax:* (3) 3284-6359 (office). *E-mail:* info@nyk.com (office). *Website:* www.nyk.com (office).

MIYAKE, Issey; Japanese fashion designer; b. (Kazunaru Miyake), 22 April 1939, Hiroshima; ed Tama Art Univ. Tokyo and La Chambre Syndicale de la Couture Parisienne, Paris; Asst Designer to Guy Laroche, Paris 1966–68, to Hubert de Givenchy, Paris 1968–69; Designer, Geoffrey Beene (ready-to-wear firm), New York 1969–70; est. Miyake Design Studio, Tokyo 1970; Dir Issey Miyake Int., Issey Miyake & Assocs, Issey Miyake Europe, Issey Miyake USA and Issey Miyake On Limits (Tokyo); Exec. Adviser and Planner, First Japan Culture Conf., Yokohama 1980; developed Pleats Please universal form of contemporary clothing combining technology, functionality and beauty 1993, exhibited at Pompidou Centre, Paris; embarked upon A-POC (A Piece of Cloth) project with Dai Fujiwara and team of young designers 1998; est. Miyake Issey Foundation 2004; work has been exhibited in Paris, Tokyo and at MIT and appears in collections of Metropolitan Museum of Art, New York and Victoria & Albert Museum, London; Dr hc (RCA) 1993; Japan Fashion Editors' Club Awards, 1974, 1976, Mainichi Design Prize 1977, Pratt Inst. New York Award for Creative Design 1980, International Award, Council of America Fashion Designers 1984, Neiman-Marcus Award 1984, Award of Les Oscars 1985 de la Mode, Paris for Best Collection Presented by a Foreign Designer 1985, Award of the Japanese magazine for the textile industry Senken Shimbun 1986, Mainichi Newspaper Fashion Awards 1977, 1984, 1996, Kyoto Prize for Arts and Philosophy 2007. *Address:* Tokyo Headquarters, Miyake Design Studio, 1-23, Ohyama-cho, Shibuya-ku, Tokyo 151, Japan (office). *Telephone:* (3) 3481-6411 (office).

MIYAKO, Harumi; Japanese singer; b. 22 Feb. 1948, Kyoto City; d. of the late Shoji Matsuda (Yi Jong Tack) and of Matsuyo Kitamura; m. Hiroomi Asatsuki 1978 (divorced 1982); Pnr Ikko Nakamura; ed pvt. music schools; began traditional Japanese dancing lessons aged 6, ballet lessons aged 9, joined a theatrical co. aged 11; winner Colombia Nationwide Popular Song Contest aged 15 1963; recording debut with release of Komaru kotoyo (You Upset Me) 1964; began career singing traditional enka (ethnic) music; appeared on every annual New Years Eve Contest Kohaku uta gassen, NHK 1965–85; retd as singer 1984; worked as music producer and news commentator; special performance on music programme Kohaku uta gassen, NHK 1989; re-launched music career singing modern pop music 1990; annual concerts in Budo-Kan; regular appearances on TV music programmes; has released more than 115 records; Rookie of the Year Award 1964, Nihon Kayo Taisho (Japan

Annual Pop Grand Prize) 1976, Nihon Record Taisho (Japan Record Annual Grand Prize) 1976. *Singles include:* Komaru kotoyo 1964, Anko tsubaki wa koi no hana (New Artist Award, Japanese Recording Industry) 1964, Namida no renraku fune 1965, Bakattcho debune 1965, Sukini natta hito 1968, Kita no shuka kara (Record of the Year, Japan Popular Music Award) 1976, I Want to Become an Everyday Woman 1984, Sennen No Koto 1990, Sakure Shigure 1993, Nana no ran 1994, Ajia Densetsu 1996, Jashu mon 1998, Ohara zessho 2000. *Address:* c/o Nippon Columbia Co. Ltd, 4-14-14 Akasaka, Minato-ku, Tokyo 107-8011, Japan (office). *Website:* miyakoharumi.net (office).

MIYAMOTO, Mikihiko; Japanese insurance executive; Pres. Yasuda Mutual Life Insurance Co. Ltd –2004; Chair. Meiji Yasuda Life Insurance Co. (cr. through merger of Yasuda Mutual and Meiji Life Insurance Cos 2004) Jan. 2004–06 (resgnd). *Address:* c/o Meiji Yasuda Life Insurance Company, 19-1 Nishi-Shinjuku, Shinjuku-ku, Tokyo 169-8701, Japan (office).

MIYAMOTO, Yuji, MA; Japanese diplomatist; *Ambassador to People's Republic of China;* b. 3 July 1946, Fukuoka; m.; one s. one d.; ed Kyoto Univ., Harvard Univ. Grad. School of Arts and Sciences; joined Ministry of Foreign Affairs 1969, worked in China and Mongolia Div. 1973–75, Devt Cooperation Div. 1975-78; First Sec., Perm. Mission to UN, New York 1978–81; First Sec., Embassy of Japan, Beijing 1981–83; Deputy Dir Soviet Union Div., Ministry of Foreign Affairs 1983–85, Dir of Arms Control and Disarmament 1985–87, Pvt. Sec. to Minister for Foreign Affairs 1987–89, Dir of Policy Planning Div. 1989–90, Dir of China and Mongolia Div. 1990–91; Research Assoc., IISS, London 1991–92; Sr Supervisor, Foreign Service Training Inst., Ministry of Foreign Affairs 1992, Vice-Pres. –1994; Consul Gen., Consulate Gen. of Japan, Atlanta, Ga, USA 1994–97; Minister to People's Repub. of China 1997, Minister Extraordinary and Plenipotentiary –2001; Dir-Gen. for Arms Control and Scientific Affairs 2001–02; Amb. to Myanmar 2002–04; Amb. in charge of Okinawan Affairs, Rep. of Govt of Japan 2004–06; Amb. to People's Repub. of China 2006–. *Address:* Embassy of Japan, 7 Ri Tan Lu, Jian Guo Men Wai, Beijing 100600, People's Republic of China (office). *Telephone:* (10) 65322361 (office). *Fax:* (10) 65324625 (office).

MIYASHITA, Sohei; Japanese politician; mem. LDP; fmr civil servant in Finance Ministry; mem. for Nagano House of Reps 1979–2004; Dir-Gen. Defence Agency 1991–92, Environment Agency 1994–95; Minister of Health and Welfare 1998–99; Chair. Social Security Reform Study Group 2001–. *Address:* c/o Liberal Democratic Party, 1-11-23 Nagata-cho, Chiyoda-ku, Tokyo 100-8910, Japan (office).

MIYATO, Naoteru, BA; Japanese insurance industry executive; *President and Representative Director, T&D Holdings, Inc.;* b. 20 May 1943; ed Keio Univ.; joined Daido Life 1967, positions included Pres. Daido Int., New York and Gen. Man. Research Dept, Gen. Man. Gen. Marketing Dept 1994–99, mem. Bd of Dirs Taiyo Life, Daido Life 1994–, Man. Dir 1996–99, Sr Man. Dir March–July 1999, Pres. and Rep. Dir 1999–2004, Pres. and Rep. Dir T&D Holdings, Inc. (holding co.) 2004–. *Address:* T&D Holdings Inc., 2-7-9 Nihonbashi, Chuo-Ku, Tokyo 103-0027, Japan (office). *Telephone:* (3) 3231-8685 (office). *Fax:* (3) 3231-8893 (office). *E-mail:* info@td-holdings.co.jp (office). *Website:* www.td-holdings.co.jp (office).

MIYAZAKI, Hayao; Japanese film producer, film director and animator; b. 5 Jan. 1941, Tokyo; ed Gakushuin Univ.; started career as animator Toei Douga Studios 1963; joined A Pro 1971, moved to Nippon Animation 1973; directed first TV series Mirai Shonen Conan 1978; moved to Tokyo Movie Shinsha 1979, directed first film Rupan Sansei: Kariosutoro no shiro 1979; f. Ghibli Studios with Isao Takahata 1981–; Mononoke Hime and Sen to Chihiro no Kamikakushi both set Japanese box office records; Venice Film Festival lifetime achievement award 2005. *Films:* as writer/dir: Rupan Sansei: Kariosutoro no Shiro (Lupin III: The Castle of Cagliostro) 1979, Kaze no tani no Nausicaa (Nausicaa of the Valley of the Wind) 1984, Tenku no Shiro no Laputa (Floating Island of Laputa) 1986, Tonari no Totoro (My Neighbour's Totoro) 1988, Majo no Takkyubin (Kiki's Delivery Service) 1989, Kurenai no Buta (The Red Pig) 1992, On Your Mark 1995, Mononoke Hime (Princess Mononoke) 1997, Tonari no Yamada-kun (My Neighbour Yamada) 1999, Sen to Chihiro no Kamikakushi (Spirited Away) (Japanese Acad. Award for Best Film 2002, Hong Kong Film Award for Best Asian Film 2002, Berlin Int. Film Festival Golden Bear Award 2002, Best Animation Acad. Award 2003) 2001, Kujira Tori 2001, Hauru no ugoku Shiro (Howl's Moving Castle) (Venice Film Festival Golden Osella, Nebula Award 2007) 2004, Yadosagashi 2006, Mizugumo monmon 2006, Hoshi wo katta hi 2006; as producer: Yanagawa horiwari monogatarai (The Story of Yanagawa's Canals) 1987, Omohide poro poro (Memories of Yesterday) 1991, Heisei tanuki gassen pompoko (The Raccoon War) 1994, Mimi wo Sumaseba (Whisper of the Heart) 1995, Neko no ongaeshi (The Cat Returns) 2002. *Website:* www.studioghiblidvd.co.uk.

MIYET, Bernard; French diplomatist; *Chairman, Société des auteurs, compositeurs et éditeurs de musique (Sacem);* b. 16 Dec. 1946, Bourg de Péage; m. Dominique Bourguignon 1974; one d.; ed Inst. of Political Studies, Grenoble, Nat. School of Admin. (ENA); Chief of Staff, Ministry of Communications 1981–82; Chair. and CEO Soc. Française de radiodiffusion 1983–84; Special Adviser to Chair. Schlumberger Ltd 1985; Consul Gen. of France, LA 1986–89; Deputy Dir-Gen. Office of Cultural, Scientific and Tech. Relations, Ministry of Foreign Affairs, Paris 1989–91; Amb. and Perm. Rep. of France to UN, Geneva 1991–93; Amb. responsible for audio-visual services to GATT Uruguay Round, Ministry of Foreign Affairs, Paris 1993–94; Amb. and Perm. Rep. of France to OSCE, Vienna 1994–97; UnderSec.-Gen. for Peacekeeping Operations, UN, New York 1997–2000; Chair. Soc. des auteurs, compositeurs et éditeurs de musique (Sacem) 2001–; Pres. Gesac (European grouping of socs of authors and composers) 2005–; Chevalier, Ordre nat. du Mérite; Commdr des Arts et Lettres. *Leisure interests:* opera, cinema, theatre. *Address:* Sacem, 225 avenue Charles de Gaulle, 92528 Neuilly-sur-Seine Cedex, France (office). *Telephone:* (1) 47-15-41-07 (office). *Fax:*)1) 47-15-41-32 (office). *E-mail:* dominique.ramond@sacem.fr (office). *Website:* www.sacem.fr (office).

MIYOSHI, Shunkichi; Japanese business executive; b. 16 March 1929; ed Univ. of Tokyo; joined NKK Corpn 1951, mem. Bd Dirs 1982–, Man. Dir 1985–88, Sr Man. Dir 1988–90, Exec. Vice-Hon. Adviser 2002–; Pres. 1990–92, Pres. 1992–97, Chair. of Bd 1997–2002; Pres. Iron and Steel Inst. of Japan 1992–94; Chair. Japan Inst. of Construction Eng 1997–, Japan Vocational Ability Devt Asscn 1998–, Weights and Measures Admin. Council 1998–; Vice-Chair. Japan Fed. of Employers' Asscns 1997–; Dir Japan Iron and Steel Fed. 1992–97, Vice-Chair 1993–94, 1996–97; Exec. mem. Bd of Dirs Japan Fed. of Econ. Orgs 1992–97; mem. Coal Mining Council 1992–97, Electric Power Devt Co-ordination Council 1996–2001 (disbanded), Trade Council 1997–, Cen. Environment Council 1997–99, Electric Power Devt Cttee 2001–; Trustee Japan Asscn of Corp. Executives 1995–. *Address:* NKK Corporation, 1-1-2 Marunouchi, Chiyoda-ku, Tokyo 100-8202, Japan (office). *Telephone:* (3) 3212-7111. *Fax:* (3) 3214-8401.

MIYOSHI, Toru, LLB; Japanese judge (retd); b. 31 Oct. 1927; ed Univ. of Tokyo; Asst Judge, Tokyo Dist Court and Tokyo Family Court 1955; Judge, Hakodate Dist Court and Hakodate Family Court 1965; Judge, Tokyo Dist Court (Presiding Judge of Div.) 1975; Pres. Research and Training Inst. for Court Clerks 1982; Pres. Oita Dist Court and Oita Family Court 1985; Pres. Nagano Dist Court and Nagano Family Court 1986; Chief Judicial Research Official of Supreme Court 1987; Pres. Sapporo High Court 1991, Tokyo High Court 1992; Justice of Supreme Court 1992; Chief Justice of Supreme Court 1995–97; mem. Advisory Council to Consider the Direct Election of the Prime Minister 2001.

MIZOTE, Kensei; Japanese politician; b. 13 Sept. 1942; ed Faculty of Law, Univ. of Tokyo; with Fuji Steel Co. (now Nippon Steel Corpn) 1966–71; Vice-Pres. Koyo Dockyard Co. Ltd 1971–79, Pres. 1979–87; Mayor of Mihara City, Hiroshima Pref. 1987–93; mem. House of Councillors for Hiroshima Pref. 1993–, Chair. Cttee on Gen. Affairs 2001, Cttee on Rules and Admin 2004, mem. Cttee on Budget and Finance 2001; Parl. Vice-Minister of Int. Trade and Industry 1997; Chair. Finance Sub-cttee, New Constitution Drafting Cttee, LDP 2005, Coastal Shipping Activation Sub-cttee, Special Cttee on Marine Transportation and Shipbuilding 2006; Minister of State, Chair. Nat. Public Safety Comm. and Minister of State for Disaster Man. 2006–07. *Address:* c/o National Public Safety Commission, 2-1-2, Kasumigaseki, Chiyoda-ku, Tokyo 100-8974, Japanese (office).

MIZRAHI, Isaac; American fashion designer; b. 14 Oct. 1961, Brooklyn, New York; s. of Zeke Mizrahi and Sarah Mizrahi; ed Yeshiva, Flatbush, High School of Performing Arts, Manhattan, Parsons School of Design; apprenticed to Perry Ellis 1982, full-time post 1982–84; worked with Jeffrey Banks 1984–85, Calvin Klein 1985–87, Mark Morris, Twyla Tharp, Bill T. Jones and Mikhail Baryshnikov; started own design firm in partnership with Sarah Hadad Cheney 1987, first formal show 1988, first spring collection Nov. 1988, first menswear line launched April 1990, announced closure of firm Oct. 1998; partnered with Target Stores to launch a collection of women's sportswear and accessories 2002, cr. home collection for Target 2005; appeared off-Broadway in one-man show Les Mizrahi 1999; hosted The Isaac Mizrahi Show on Oxygen Network 1999; wrote and directed Supermodelhero, which first appeared online in 2005 and is currently being developed into a major motion picture; three CFDA Designer of the Year Awards 1980s, Drama Desk Award for costume design in The Women 2002. *Address:* c/o Target Corporation, 1000 Nicollet Mall, Minneapolis, MN 55403, USA. *Telephone:* (612) 304-6073. *Fax:* (612) 696-3731. *Website:* target.com/isaac_group/index.jhtml.

MIZRAHI, Valerie, PhD; Zimbabwean biologist and academic; *Principal Investigator and Director, Molecular Mycobacteriology Research Unit, University of the Witwatersrand;* ed Univ. of Cape Town, S Africa; postdoctoral work at Pennsylvania State Univ., USA 1983–86; held positions with South African Council for Scientific and Industrial Research, Smith Kline & French Research & Devt; fmr Head of Molecular Biology Unit, South African Inst. for Medical Research –2000; Prin. Investigator and Dir Molecular Mycobacteriology Research Unit, Univ. of the Witwatersrand (jtly funded by South African MRC, Nat. Health Lab. Services (fmrly South African Inst. for Medical Research) and the Univ.) 2000–; Int. Research Scholar, Howard Hughes Medical Inst., Chevy Chase, Md 2000, 2005; Fellow, Royal Soc. of South Africa; mem. Third World Acad. of Sciences, Acad. of Science of South Africa; Order of the Mapungubwe in Silver 2007; L'Oréal-UNESCO For Women in Science Award 2000, DST Distinguished Woman Scientist Award 2006, Gold Medal of the South African Soc. for Biochemistry and Molecular Biology 2006. *Publications:* numerous articles in medical journals. *Address:* Molecular Mycobacteriology Research Unit, Department of Molecular Medicine and Haematology, University of the Witwatersrand, Witwatersrand 2050, South Africa (office). *E-mail:* mizrahiv@pathology.wits.ac.za (office). *Website:* www.wits.ac.za/myco (office).

MIZUKOSHI, Koshi; Japanese metal industry executive; *Chairman and Representative Director, Kobe Steel Ltd (KOBELCO);* b. 1 Sept. 1938, Seoul, S Korea; m.; two s.; ed Univ. of Tokyo; joined Planning and Business Admin Dept, Kobe Steel Ltd (KOBELCO) 1961, Inspection Section, Devt Dept 1965–73, Man. Corp. Planning Dept 1973–78, Asst to Pres. 1978–81, Gen. Man. Planning and Admin Dept, Iron and Steel Div.'s Production Group 1983–91, Man. Dir 1991–93, Sr Man. Dir 1993–96, mem. Bd of Dirs 1989–, Rep. Dir 1996–, Exec. Vice-Pres. 1996–99, CEO and Pres. 1999–2004, Chair. 2004–; Vice-Chair. Kansai Econ. Fed.; mem. Bd of Dirs Foundation for Biomedical Research and Innovation, Kansai Int. Public Relations Promotion Office. *Address:* Kobe Steel Ltd, Shinko Building, 10-26 Wakinohamacho 2-

chome, Kobe 651-8585, Japan (office). *Telephone:* (78) 261-5111 (office). *Fax:* (78) 261-4123 (office). *E-mail:* info@kobelco.co.jp (office). *Website:* www .kobelco.co.jp (office).

MKAPA, Benjamin William, BA; Tanzanian politician, journalist and diplomatist; b. 12 Nov. 1938, Masasi; s. of William Matwani and Stephania Nambanga; m. Anna Joseph Maro 1966; two s.; ed Makerere Univ. Coll.; Admin. Officer, Dist Officer 1962; Foreign Service Officer 1962; Man. Ed. Tanzania Nationalist and Uhuru 1966, The Daily News and The Sunday News 1972; Press Sec. to Pres. 1974; Founding Dir Tanzania News Agency 1976; High Commr in Nigeria 1976; Minister for Foreign Affairs 1977–80, for Information and Culture 1980–82; High Commr in Canada 1982–83; Amb. to USA 1983–84; Minister for Foreign Affairs 1984–90; MP for Nanyumbu 1985–95; Minister for Information and Broadcasting 1990–92, for Science, Tech. and Higher Educ. 1992–95; Pres. of Tanzania and C-in-C of Armed Forces 1995–2005; Chair. Chama Cha Mapinduzi (CCM) party 1996–2005; Dr hc (Soka Univ., Tokyo) 1998; Hon. DHumLitt (Morehouse Coll., Atlanta, USA) 1999. *Leisure interest:* reading. *Address:* c/o Office of the President, PO Box 9120, Dar es Salaam, Tanzania.

MKHATSHWA, Smangaliso, ThM, PhD; South African ecclesiastic and local government official; *Executive Mayor of Tshwane;* b. 26 June 1939, Barberton, Mpumalanga; s. of Elias Mkhatshwa and Maria Mkhatshwa (née Nkosi); ed Pax Coll., Pietersburg, St Peter's Seminary, KwaZulu Natal, Univ. of Leuven, Belgium; ordained Roman Catholic priest 1965, worked as a pastor in Witbank until 1970, seconded to Church's Gen. Secr., Pretoria; detained for four months under the Internal Security Act following Soweto uprising 1976, restricted by five-year banning order to Pretoria magisterial dist 1977–83, apptd Parish Priest of St Charles Lwanga, Soshanguve; Sec.-Gen. Southern African Catholic Bishops' Conf. 1981–88; Patron of the United Democratic Front 1983; detained in the Ciskei in Oct. 1983 and charged with subversion, incitement to public violence and addressing an unlawful meeting, found not guilty and released in March 1984; detained under emergency regulations in 1986, released and successfully sued the state for torture and assault; Sec.-Gen. Inst. for Contextual Theology 1988–94; mem. Parl. (African Nat. Congress—ANC) 1994–, mem. Reconstruction and Devt Standing Cttee and Educ. Standing Cttee; Deputy Minister of Educ. 1996–99; mem. ANC Nat. Exec. Cttee 1997–; Trustee Kagiso Trust, Matla Trust; Pres. Cen. Transvaal Civics Assen (later renamed SANCO Pretoria); Exec. Mayor of Tshwane 2000–; Dr hc (Tübingen, Germany, and Georgetown and Univ. Coll. of New Rochelle, USA); Steve Biko Human Rights Award, Indicator Newspaper Award. *Publications:* articles on theology and politics. *Leisure interests:* tennis, music, reading, theatre. *Address:* Office of the Executive Mayor of Tschwane, PO Box 440, Pretoria 0001, South Africa (office). *Telephone:* (12) 358-4905 (office). *Fax:* (12) 323-5117 (office). *Website:* www.tshwane.gov.za (office).

MKRTUMYAN, Yuri Israelovich, CandHisSc; Armenian ethnographer; b. 1 Jan. 1939, Tbilisi; ed Moscow State Univ.; lab. asst, jr researcher Inst. of Archaeology and Ethnography, Armenian Acad. of Sciences 1962–71, Prof. 1996–; Sr Lecturer Yerevan State Univ. 1971–89; Head Chair of Ethnography, Yerevan State Univ. 1989–94; Sec. CP Cttee Yerevan State Univ.; mem. Cen. CPSU Cttee, mem. Bureau Cen. Cttee Armenian CP 1990–91; counsellor to Minister of Foreign Affairs, Repub. of Armenia April–June 1994; Amb. to Russia 1994–96; Dir Inst. of Ethnography and Archaeology 1997–. *Publications:* over 40 scientific works on theoretical and regional ethnography in Russian, Armenian and English. *Address:* Institute of Ethnography and Archaeology, Armenian Academy of Sciences, Charentsa Street 15, 375025 Yerevan, Armenia. *Telephone:* (10) 55-68-96 (office).

MKULO, Mustapha; Tanzanian politician; *Minister of Finance, Planning, Economy and Empowerment;* fmr Dir-Gen. Nat. Social Security Fund; Deputy Minister of Finance –2008, Minister of Finance, Planning, Economy and Empowerment 2008–. *Address:* Ministry of Finance, Planning, Economy and Empowerment, PO Box 1154, Zanzibar, Tanzania (office). *Telephone:* (24) 231169 (office).

MLADIĆ, Gen. Ratko; Bosnia and Herzegovina fmr military leader; b. 12 March 1943, Kalinovik; m.; one s.; Serb nationalist; began mil. career as tank officer, Yugoslav People's Army (YPA), Bosnia and Herzegovina; gained popularity among Serb population for supporting their claim to enclave of Krajina during civil war in Croatia 1991; apptd CO YPA 1992; commanded siege of Sarajevo 1992–94; supported creation of a 'Greater Serbia' and opposed any peace settlement of Bosnian civil war, including Gen. Framework Agreement for Peace in Bosnia and Herzegovina 1995; indicted as war criminal 1995; given protection by Slobodan Milošević until his arrest by Yugoslav authorities and extradition to Int. Criminal Tribunal for the Fmr Yusoslavia (ICTY), The Hague 2001; went into hiding 2001; US Govt increased reward offered for information leading to his arrest to US $5m 2002; report issued by Netherlands Inst. for War Documentation held Mladić to be principally responsible for massacre of up to 8,000 people in Srebrenica in 1995.

MLAMBO-NGCUKA, Phumzile, BA, MPhil; South African politician; b. 3 Nov. 1955, KwaZulu Natal, Clermont Township; m. Bulelani Ngcuka; one c.; ed Nat. Univ. of Lesotho; teacher in KwaZulu Natal 1981–83; founder and Dir Young Women's Int. Programme, YWCA World Office, Geneva, Switzerland 1984–87; Dir TEAM (NGO), Cape Town 1987–89; Dir World Univ. Services 1990–92; est. Phumelela Services 1993–94; MP 1994–, Chair., Public Service Portfolio Cttee 1994; Deputy Minister, Dept of Trade and Industry (DTI) 1996–99; Minister of Minerals and Energy 1999–2005; Deputy Pres. 2005–08 (resgnd); founding mem., Guguletu Community Devt Corpn (GCDC); mem. Nat. Exec. Cttee, African Nat. Congress 1997–. *Address:* African National Congress, 54 Sauer Street, Johannesburg 2001, South Africa (office). *Telephone:* (11) 3761000 (office). *Fax:* (11) 3761134 (office). *E-mail:* nmtyelwa@anc.org.za (office). *Website:* www.anc.org.za (office).

MLECHIN, Leonid M.; Russian journalist and writer; b. 12 June 1957; m.; one s.; ed Moscow State Univ.; staff, head of division, Deputy Ed.-in-Chief weekly Novoye Vremya 1979–93; Deputy Ed.-in-Chief newspaper Izvestia 1993–96; political reviewer All-Russian State Cttee on Radio and Television 1996–97; writer and narrator Particular Dossier (TV-Tsentr) 1997–. *Publications include:* more than 20 books, including detective stories, novels, historical non-fiction, and biographies of Yevgeny Primakov and the chairmen of the KGB. *Address:* TV-Tsentr, ul. B. Tatarskaya 33/1, Moscow 113184, Russia (office). *Telephone:* (495) 215-18-12 (office); (495) 217-75-50 (office).

MLECZKO, Andrzej; Polish graphic designer and illustrator; b. 5 Jan. 1949, Tarnobrzeg; one d.; ed Kraków Technical Univ.; illustrator of books, paintings, drawings; contrib. to magazines in Poland and abroad 1971–; worked as theatre consultant for Kochanowski 1975–80, for Slowacki 1980–92; Andrzej Mleczko Author's Gallery, Kraków 1983–, Warsaw 2002–; has designed over 10,000 graphics, drawings and posters; member of the Polish Artists Society 1974–. *Publications:* numerous albums and books. *Address:* Andrzej Mleczko Author's Gallery, ul. św. Jana 14, 31-018 Kraków (office); ul. Marszatkowska 140, 00-061 Warsaw, Poland (office). *Telephone:* (12) 4217104 (office); (22) 8295760 (office). *Fax:* (12) 4217104 (office). *E-mail:* galeria@pro.onet.pl (office). *Website:* www.mleczko.onet.pl (office).

MLYNÁRIK, Ján, CSc, PhD; Slovak historian and academic; *Professor, Charles University;* b. 11 Feb. 1933, Filakova; m.; five c.; ed Charles Univ., Prague; Prof., Acad. of Music and Dramatic Arts, Bratislava 1957–59, Acad. of Performing Arts (AMU), Prague 1959–60; manual worker (for political reasons) 1970–81; political prisoner in Ruzyne 1981–82; expelled from Czechoslovakia 1982; Prof., Univ. of Munich 1982–89; worked on Radio Free Europe 1982–89; mem. Parl. 1990–92; Prof., Charles Univ., Prague 1990–. *Publications include:* Way to the Stars 1989, M. R. Štefánik 1999. *Leisure interests:* literature, music. *Address:* Charles University, nám. J. Palacha 2, Prague 1, 11000 Czech Republic (office). *Telephone:* (2) 22319762 (office). *Fax:* (2) 222328405 (office).

MMARI, Geoffrey Raphael Vehaeli, DipEd, PhD; Tanzanian university teacher and administrator; *Provost, Tumaini University, Dar es Salaam College;* b. 24 June 1934, Moshi; s. of the late Vehaeli Mmari and Luisia Mmari; m. Salome Mmari 1959; one s. three d.; ed Univ. of E Africa, Univ. of N Iowa, USA, Univ. of Dar es Salaam; teacher and admin. 1966–69; univ. teacher 1969–; Vice-Chancellor Sokoine Univ. of Agric. 1984–88, Univ. of Dar es Salaam 1988–91; Co-ordinator Open Univ. Planning Office 1991–, Vice-Chancellor Open Univ. of Tanzania 1993–2005; Provost, Tumaini Univ., Dar es Salaam Coll. 2005–; Chair. Higher Educ. Accreditation Council, Nat. Examinations Council, Media Council of Tanzania, Tanzania Family Planning Assen, Media Council of Tanzania; mem. Council Mzumbe Univ., Sokoine Univ. of Agric., State Univ. of Zanzibar, Math. Assen of Tanzania; Drum Major for Justice Award 2003. *Publications:* Mwalimu: The Influence of Julius Nyerere (ed. with Colin Legum) 1995; ed. secondary math. books series; articles in journals and chapters in books 1960–. *Leisure interests:* reading, travelling, walking. *Address:* Tumaini University, Dar es Salaam College, PO Box 77588, Dar es Salaam, Tanzania (office). *Telephone:* (22) 276-0426 (office); (22) 276-0335 (office); (22) 260-2359 (home). *E-mail:* tudarco@yahoo.com (office).

MNANGAGWA, Emmerson; Zimbabwean politician; *Minister of Defence;* b. 15 Sept. 1946; fmr Admin. Sec. Zimbabwe African Nat. Union-Patriotic Front (ZANU-PF); Head Cen. Intelligence Org. 1980s; Minister of State Security; fmr Minister of Justice, Legal and Parl. Affairs 1989–2000; Speaker of Parl. 2000–05; Minister of Rural Housing 2005–09, of Defence 2009–. *Address:* Ministry of Defence, Defence House, cnr Kwame Nkuruma and 3rd Streets, Harare, Zimbabwe (office). *Telephone:* (4) 700155 (office). *Fax:* (4) 727501 (office). *Website:* www.mod.gov.zw (office).

MO, Shaoping; Chinese lawyer; *Senior Partner, Beijing Mo Shaoping Law Firm;* b. 1958; m.; one d.; ed Chinese Acad. of Social Sciences; China's leading advocate for political dissidents; in pvt. practice since 1992; f. Beijing Mo Shaoping Law Firm, Sr Partner 1995–. *Address:* Beijing Mo Shaoping Law Firm, Waterside Pavilion, Inside Zhongshan Park, Dongcheng District, Beijing, People's Republic of China (office). *Telephone:* (10) 66055431 ext. 328-302 (office). *Fax:* (10) 66058311 (office). *E-mail:* shaoping@public.bta.net .cn (office).

MO, Timothy; British author; b. 30 Dec. 1950, Hong Kong; s. of Peter Mo Wan Lung and Barbara Helena Falkingham; ed Mill Hill School and St John's Coll., Univ. of Oxford; fmrly worked for Times Educational Supplement and New Statesman; fmr reporter for Boxing News and PAYE clerk; Hawthornden Prize. *Publications include:* The Monkey King 1979 (Geoffrey Faber Memorial Prize 1979), Sour Sweet 1982, An Insular Possession 1986, The Redundancy of Courage 1991 (E. M. Forster Award 1992), Brownout on Breadfruit Boulevard 1995, Renegade or Halo 2 1999 (James Tait Black Memorial Prize 1999). *Leisure interests:* weight training, scuba diving. *Address:* c/o Paddleless Press, BCM Paddleless, London, WC1N 3XX, England. *Telephone:* timothymo@eudoramail.com.

MO, Yan; Chinese novelist; b. (Guan Moye), 1955, Gaomi, Shandong Prov.; ed PLA Acad. of Arts, Beijing Normal Univ.; joined PLA 1976. *Publications:* Red Sorghum, Thirteen Steps, The Herbivora Family, Jiuguo, The Republic of Wine 1992, Garlic Ballads 1995, Big Breasts and Wide Hips 1996, Shifu You'll Do Anything for a Laugh 2001, Life and Death Are Wearing Me Out 2008.

Address: c/o Arcade Publishing, 116 John Street, #2810, New York, NY 10038, USA (office). *Website:* www.arcadepub.com (office).

MOBERG, Anders C.; Swedish food retail executive; b. Almhult; with IKEA 1970–98, Chief Exec. 1986–98; Chief of Int. Affairs, Home Depot (US home improvements co.) 1998–2003; Pres. and CEO Royal Ahold NV, Netherlands 2003–07. *Address:* c/o Royal Ahold NV, Piet Heinkode 167–173, 1019 GM Amsterdam, Netherlands (office).

MOBY; American musician (guitar, drums, keyboards) and producer; b. (Richard Melville Hall), 11 Sept. 1965, Harlem, New York; s. of James Hall and Elizabeth Hall; ed Royle Grammar School, Darien, CT, Univ. of Connecticut; cr. first band 1979, new wave/punk rock band Vatican Commandos 1980, new wave band AWOL 1982; DJ The Beat, Port Chester, New York 1984, Mars, Palladium, Palace de Beauté, MK, New York 1989; production and remixes for Metallica, Smashing Pumpkins, Michael Jackson, Depeche Mode, Soundgarden, Blur, David Bowie, Orbital, Prodigy, Freddie Mercury, Brian Eno, B-52s, Ozzy Osbourne, John Lydon, Butthole Surfers, Erasure, Aerosmith, OMD, Pet Shop Boys, Jon Spencer Blues Explosion; numerous tours, festival appearances, TV and radio broadcasts; owner tea shop Teany, New York; mem. BMI, PMRS, AF of M, SAG, AFTRA; MTV Web Award 2002, Q Magazine Best Producer Award 2002, MTV Video Music Award for Best Cinematography in a Video (for We Are All Made Of Stars) 2002. *Compositions for film:* Double Tap (score) 1997, contrib. to numerous other film soundtracks. *Recordings include:* albums: Moby 1992, The Story So Far 1993, Ambient 1993, Early Underground 1993, Move (EP) 1994, Underwater 1995, Everything is Wrong (Spin Magazine Album of the Year) 1995, Voodoo Child: The End of Everything 1996, Animal Rights 1996, Rare: Collected B-Sides 1989–1993 1996, Everything is Wrong: Non-stop DJ Mix By Evil Ninja Moby 1996, I Like To Score 1997, Play 1999, Mobysongs 2000, 18 2002, Play: The B Sides 2004, Hotel 2005, Last Night 2008. *Address:* DEF, 51 Lonsdale Road, London, NW6 6RA, England (office); c/o Mute, 429 Harrow Road, London, W10 4RE, England. *Telephone:* (20) 7328-2922 (office). *Fax:* (20) 7328-2322 (office). *E-mail:* info@d-e-f.com (office). *Website:* www.moby.com.

MOCK, Alois, LLD; Austrian politician; *Honorary Chairman, Austrian People's Party;* b. 10 June 1934, Euratsfeld; s. of August Mock and Mathilde Mock; m. Dr Edith Mock (née Partik) 1963; ed Univ. of Vienna, Johns Hopkins Univ., Bologna and Free Univ., Brussels; mem. Austrian mission to OECD 1962–66; Pvt. Sec. to Fed. Chancellor 1966, Head of Private Office 1968; Minister of Educ. 1969–70; mem. Parl. 1970–99 (retd due to illness); Leader, Austrian People's Party (Österreichische Volkspartei— ÖVP) 1979–89, Hon. Chair. 1995–; Leader of Opposition 1979–87; Vice-Chancellor 1987–89; Minister of Foreign Affairs 1987–95; Pres. European Democratic Union, Vienna 1979–88; Pres. European Democratic Union 1979–98, Int. Democratic Union, London 1983–87; Co-founder Cen. European Cooperative (Pentagonale) 1989, later grew to 16 countries of Cen. European Initiative. *Publication:* Standpunkte 1983. *Address:* c/o Österreichische Volkspartei, Lichtenfelsgasse 7, 1010 Vienna, Austria.

MOCUMBI, Pascoal Manuel, MD; Mozambican medical doctor and fmr politician; *High Commissioner, European-Developing Countries Clinical Trials Programme (EDCTP);* b. 10 April 1941, Maputo; s. of Manuel Mocumbi Malume and Leta Alson Cuhle; m. Adelina Isabel Bernardino Paindane 1970; two s. two d.; ed Lausanne Univ. of Lausanne; founding mem. Frente de Libertação de Moçambique 1962, Rep. FRELIMO Algeria –1967, 1967–1974, Head, Information Dept; Dir José Macamo Hosp., Maputo 1976; Provincial Health Dir, Chief Medical Officer, Clinical Doctor Beira Central Hosp., Sofala 1976–80; Clinical Doctor Maputo Hosp. 1980–87; Asst Lecturer, Faculty of Health, Eduardo Mondlane Univ., Maputo 1984–85; mem. National Assembly, FRELIMO Political Cttee 1980–87, Minister of Health 1980–87, Minister of Foreign Affairs 1987–94; Prime Minister of Mozambique 1994–2004; High Commissioner, European-Developing Countries Clinical Trials Programme (EDCTP) 2004–. *Leisure interests:* jogging, squash, reading. *Address:* 1874 Av. Armando Tivane, Maputo, Mozambique (home). *Telephone:* (1) 495517 (home). *E-mail:* pascoal.mocumbi@tvcabo.co.mz (home).

MOCZULSKI, Leszek Robert, LLM; Polish politician, lawyer, journalist and historian; b. 7 June 1930, Warsaw; s. of Stanisław Moczulski and Janina Moczulska (née Reimer); m. 1st Małgorzata Moczulska (née Smogorzewska) 1951 (deceased); m. 2nd Maria-Ludwika (née Różycka) Moczulska 1968; two d.; ed Acad. of Political Science, Warsaw, Warsaw Univ.; reporter on Życie Warszawy (daily) 1950–53, on dailies and weeklies, including Dookoła Świata, Warsaw 1955–57; imprisoned on charges of slandering Poland in foreign press 1957–58, acquitted; assoc. (pseud. Leszek Karpatowicz) Więź (monthly) 1959–62; Head History Section Stolica (weekly) 1961–77; ed. of underground journals Opinia 1977–78, Droga 1978–80, Gazeta Polska 1979–80; arrested Aug. 1980 and sentenced to seven years on charge of attempting to overthrow regime, amnestied Aug. 1984; sentenced to four years on charge of heading illegal org. March 1985, amnestied Sept. 1986; victim of reprisals 1946–89, including repeated 48-hour custody (250 times 1976–80), forbidden to publish, refused passport, prevented from finishing PhD; mem. Polish Journalists' Assen 1951–, Theatre Authors and Composers' Union 1960– (mem. Bd 1972–77), Polish Historical Soc.; active in Movt for Rights of Man and Citizen (ROPCiO) 1977–80; Deputy to Sejm (Parl.) 1991–97; Hon. Chair. Parl. Club of Confed. of Independence of Poland (KPN) 1993–97; Chair. Parl. Cttee for Polish Connection Abroad 1993–97; mem. Confed. for an Independent Poland (KPN) 1979– (one of founders, temporary chair. 1979–80, Chair. 1980–); mem. Polish del. to Parl. Ass., Council of Europe 1992–93, 1994–96; Gold Badge of Honour, Officer's Cross of Polonia Restituta Order (London) 1987. *Publications:* numerous contribs on history, politics and int. affairs, over 20 books including Wojna polska (War) 1939 1972, Rewolucja bez rewolucji (Revolution Without Revolution) 1979, Trzecia Rzeczpospolita – zarys ustroju politycznego (A Constitutional System for Independent Poland) 1984, U progu niepodległości (Gateway to Independence) 1990, Bez wahania (Without Hesitation) 1992, Trzy drogi (Three Ways) 1993, Demokracja bez demokracji (Democracy Without Democracy) 1995, Geopolityka (Geopolitics) 1999, Investigation 2001. *Leisure interests:* horse riding, old automobiles, sailing, old maps. *Address:* ul. Jaracza 3 m. 4, 00-378 Warsaw, Poland. *Telephone:* (22) 625 26 39 (home). *E-mail:* lmski@poczta.onet.pl (home). *Website:* www.moczulski.pl.

MODI, Narendra Damodardas, MA; Indian politician; *Chief Minister of Gujarat;* b. Sept. 1950, Vadnagar, Mehsana Dist; ed Gujarat Univ.; mem. Nava Nirman Andolan movt 1972–77; joined Bharatiya Janata Party 1986, Gen. Sec. for Gujarat 1988, elected to Ass. 1995, Nat. Sec., Delhi 1995, re-elected in Gujarat 1998, Gen. Sec. for Himachal Pradesh, the Punjab and Haryana 1998–2001, Nat. Gen. Sec. 1999–; Chief Minister of Gujarat 2001–03, 2003–. *Publications include:* Sangharsha ma Gujarat (Gujarat under Struggle), Setu Bandh, Patra Roop Guruji. *Address:* Office of the Chief Minister, Block No. 1, 5th Floor, New Sachivalaya, Ganghinagar, 382 010, Gujarat, India (office). *Telephone:* (79) 23232611 (office); (79) 23232601 (home). *Fax:* (79) 23222101 (office); (79) 23222020 (home). *E-mail:* cm@gujaratindia.com (office). *Website:* www.gujaratindia.com (office).

MODI, Vinay Kumar, BTechChemEng; Indian industrialist; b. 31 May 1943, Modinagar; s. of the late Rai Bahadur Gujar Mal Modi and Dayawati Modi; m. Chander Bala 1965; one s. one d.; ed Scindia School, Gwalior, Indian Inst. of Tech., Kanpur; Dir Modi Industries Ltd 1965–; Vice-Chair. and Man. Dir Modi Rubber Ltd 1976–; Chair. Gujarat Guardian Ltd, Modi Mirrlees Blackstone Ltd, Shree Acids and Chemicals Ltd; various awards from govt for export performance; prizes from several asscns. *Publications:* various articles on steel, tyres and cement production. *Leisure interests:* golf, tennis, billiards. *Address:* DDA Shopping Centre, New Friends Colony, New Delhi 110065 (office); Modi Bhavan, Civil Lines, Modinagar 201204, India (office); 55A, Friends Colony (East), New Delhi 110065 (home). *Telephone:* (11) 6835766 (office); (11) 6830703 (office); (11) 6833088 (home); (11) 6833633 (home). *Fax:* (11) 6830868 (office); (11) 6846175 (home). *E-mail:* modivinay@hotmail.com (office).

MODIANO, Patrick Jean; French novelist; b. 30 July 1945, Boulogne-Billancourt; s. of Albert Modiano and Luisa Colpyn; m. Dominique Zehrfuss 1970; two d.; ed schools in Biarritz, Chamonix, Deauville, Thônes, Barbizon, coll. in Paris; Chevalier des Arts et des Lettres; Prix Roger Nimier 1968, Prix Felix Fénéon 1969, Grand Prix de l'Académie française 1972, Prix Goncourt 1978, Prix Pierre de Monaco 1984, Grand Prix du Roman de la Ville de Paris 1994, Grand Prix de Littérature Paul Morand de l'Académie française 2000. *Publications:* La place de l'étoile 1968, La ronde de nuit 1969, Les boulevards de ceinture 1972, Lacombe Lucien (screenplay) 1973, La polka (play) 1974, Villa triste (novel) 1975, Interrogatoire d'Emmanuel Berl 1976, Livret de famille (novel) 1977, Rue des boutiques obscures 1978, Une jeunesse 1981, Memory Lane 1981, De si braves garçons (novel) 1982, Poupée blonde 1983, Quartier perdu 1985, Dimanches d'août 1986, Une aventure de Choura 1986, La fiancée de Choura 1987, Remise de peine (novel) 1988, Catherine Certitude 1988, Vestiaire de l'enfance (novel) 1989, Voyage de noces 1990, Fleurs de ruine (novel) 1991, Un cirque passe (novel) 1992, Chien de printemps 1993, Du plus loin de l'oubli 1995, Dora Bruder 1997, Des inconnues 1999, La petite bijou 2001, Accident nocturne 2003, Un pedigree 2005. *Address:* c/o Editions Gallimard, 5 rue Sébastien Bottin, 75007 Paris, France.

MODROW, Hans, DR.; German politician; b. 27 Jan. 1928, Jasenitz, Ueckermuende Dist; s. of Franz Modrow and Agnes (née Krause) Modrow; m. Annemarie Straubing 1950; two d.; apprentice locksmith 1942–45; served in German army in Second World War; prisoner of war –1949; mem. SED 1949; First Sec. of East Berlin City Cttee 1953–61; mem. East Berlin City Council 1953–71; SED Party School 1954–58; cand. mem. SED Cen. Cttee 1958–67, mem. Cen. Cttee 1967–90; Deputy to People's Chamber (Volkskammer) 1958–90; First Sec. SED Dist Cttee, Berlin-Köpernick 1961–67; Head Dept for Agitation and Propaganda, SED Cen. Cttee 1967–71; First Sec., SED Dresden Dist Cttee 1973–89; Prime Minister of GDR 1989–90; mem. Bundestag 1990–94, Hon. Chair. Party of Democratic Socialism 1990–; MEP 1999–; on trial for alleged vote-rigging April 1993; found guilty and fined May 1993; to stand trial again for the same offence after appeal court decision that fine was too small; retrial ordered Nov. 1994; given nine-month suspended sentence for electoral fraud 1995; Order of Merit of Fatherland 1959, Silver 1969, Gold 1975, Karl Marx Order 1978. *Publications:* Aufbruch und Ende 1991, Ich wollte ein neues Deutschland, Die Perestroika–wie ich sie sehe. *Leisure interests:* politics, culture, sport (active skier). *Address:* Karl-Marx-Allee 62, 10243 Berlin, Germany. *Telephone:* (30) 2912789.

MOE, George Cecil Rawle, CHB, QC, MA, LLM; Barbadian fmr politician and barrister-at-law; b. 12 March 1932, Barbados; s. of Cecil S. Moe and Odessa M. (née Marshall) Moe; m. Olga Louise Atkinson 1957; two s. one d.; ed Harrison Coll., Univ. of Oxford, UK and Columbia Univ., New York, USA; called to the Bar, Middle Temple, London; Magistrate 1960–62; Acting Asst Legal Draftsman 1962–63; Acting Crown Counsel 1963–66; Sr Crown Counsel 1967–71; Acting Perm. Rep. to UN 1970–71; Attorney-Gen. and Minister of Legal Affairs 1971–76, also Minister of External Affairs 1972–76; Leader of Senate 1972–76; pvt. practice 1976–79; Puisne Judge (Belize) 1979–81, Chief Justice (Belize) 1982–85; Justice of Appeal, Eastern Caribbean Supreme Court 1985–91, apptd Justice of Appeal, Supreme Court of Barbados 1991. *Leisure interests:* music, cricket, gardening, swimming. *Address:* c/o Supreme Court, Judiciary Office, Coleridge Street, Bridgetown (office); PO Box 1004, Bridgetown, Barbados. *Telephone:* 432-2357.

MOE, Thorvald, PhD; Norwegian economist; *Deputy Secretary General, Ministry of Finance;* b. 4 Oct. 1939, Oslo; s. of Thorvald Moe and Marie Cappelen Moe; m. Nina Kjeldsberg 1968; one s. one d.; ed Stanford Univ.; held various sr posts in Ministry of Finance; Dir-Gen. Econ. Policy Dept Ministry of Finance 1978–86, Chief Econ. Adviser and Deputy Perm. Sec. 1989–97; Amb. to OECD 1986–89; Deputy Sec.-Gen. OECD 1998–2002; Deputy Sec. Gen. Ministry of Finance 2002–; Head Norwegian Del. to Econ. Policy Cttee at OECD 2002–. *Leisure interests:* history, tennis. *Address:* Ministry of Finance, Akersgt. 40, POB 8008, Dep., 0030 Oslo, Norway (office). *Telephone:* 22-24-90-90 (office). *Fax:* 22-24-95-10 (office). *E-mail:* arkiv.postmottak@finans.dep.no (office). *Website:* odin.dep.no/fin (office).

MOELLER, Bernd, DTheol; German academic; *Professor Emeritus of Church History, University of Göttingen;* b. 19 May 1931, Berlin; s. of the late Max Moeller and Carola Bielitz; m. Irene Müller 1957; three d.; ed Univs of Erlangen, Mainz, Basle, Munich and Heidelberg; Research Asst Univ. of Heidelberg 1956–58, Privatdozent 1958–64; Prof. of Church History, Univ. of Göttingen 1964–now Emer., Rector 1971–72; Chair. Verein für Reformationsgeschichte, Heidelberg 1976–2001; mem. Akad. der Wissenschaften zu Göttingen, Academia Europaea; Dr hc (Zürich) 1998. *Publications:* Reichsstadt und Reformation 1962, Geschichte des Christentums in Grundzügen 1965, Spätmittelalter 1966, Oekumenische Kirchengeschichte (with R. Kottje) I-III 1970–74, Deutschland im Zeitalter der Reformation 1977, Die Reformation und das Mittelalter 1991, Kirchengeschichte. Deutsche Texte (1699–1927) 1994, Städtische Predigt in der Frühzeit der Reformation (with K. Stackmann) 1996, Luther – Rezeption 2001, Albrecht Dürer's Vier Apostel (with K. Arndt) 2003, Deutsche Biogrphische Enzyklopädie der Theologie und der Kirchen I–II 2005. *Address:* Herzberger Landstrasse 26, 37085 Göttingen, Germany. *Telephone:* (551) 42850.

MOERSCH, Karl; German politician and journalist; b. 11 March 1926, Calw/Württemberg; s. of Karl F. Moersch; m. Waltraut Schweikle 1947; one s.; ed Univ. of Tübingen; journalist in Ludwigshafen, Bad Godesberg (Deutscher Forschungsdienst) and Frankfurt (Ed. of Die Gegenwart) 1956–58; Head of Press Dept, Freie Demokratische Partei (FDP) 1961–64; freelance journalist 1964–; fmr mem. Bundestag; Parl. Sec. of State, Minister of State, Ministry of Foreign Affairs 1970–76; mem. Exec. Bd of UNESCO 1980–85; Ludwig-Uhland Prize 1997. *Publications:* Kursrevision–Deutsche Politik nach Adenauer 1978, Europa für Anfänger 1979, Sind wir denn eine Nation? 1982, Bei uns im Staate Beutelsbach 1984, Geschichte der Pfalz 1987, Sueben, Württemberger und Franzosen 1991, Sperrige Landsleute 1996, Es geht seltsam zu – in Württemberg 1998, Immer wieder war's ein Abenteuer–Erinnerungen 2001, Kontrapunkt Baden-Württemberg 2002; contrib. numerous articles to newspapers, etc. *Address:* Gebhard-Müller-Allee 14, 71638 Ludwigsburg, Germany (home). *Telephone:* (7141) 905745. *Fax:* (7141) 905643.

MOESER, James, BMus, MMus, DMus; American concert organist, university administrator and academic; *Professor of Music, University of North Carolina;* b. Colorado City, Tex.; m. Dr Susan Dickerson Moeser; one s. one d.; ed Univ. of Texas, Univ. of Michigan; Asst Prof. and Chair. Organ Dept, Univ. of Kansas 1966–75, Dean School of Fine Arts 1975–86, later Althaus Distinguished Prof. of Organ; Dean Coll. of Arts and Architecture and Exec. Dir Univ. Arts Services, Pennsylvania State Univ. 1986–92; Vice-Pres. for Academic Affairs and Provost Univ. of S Carolina 1992–96; Chancellor Univ. of Nebraska at Lincoln 1996–2000; Chancellor Univ. of N Carolina at Chapel Hill 2000–08, Prof. of Music 2009–; apptd by FBI to Nat. Security Higher Educ. Advisory Bd 2005; serves on Coll. Bd's Nat. Comm. on Writing and two Asscn of American Univs cttees; selected by Nat. Collegiate Athletic Asscn for its Presidential Task Force on the Future of Div. I Intercollegiate Athletics and its fiscal responsibility sub-cttee; mem. CEO Group of Six (group of pres and chancellors from major athletic confs); fmr mem. Bd of Dirs Nat. Asscn of State Univs and Land Grant Colls, Chair. Tech.-Transfer Coll. Comm.; fmr mem. Kellogg Comm. on the Future of State and Land-Grant Univs; Fulbright Scholar in Berlin and Paris, honoured by Grad. School at Texas with Outstanding Alumnus Award 2001. *Address:* Department of Music, University of North Carolina, 3320 Hill Hall, Chapel Hill, NC 27599-9100, USA (office). *Telephone:* (919) 962-1039 (office). *Website:* http://music.unc.edu (office).

MOFAZ, Lt-Gen. Shaul, BA, MBA; Israeli politician and army officer; *Deputy Prime Minister and Minister of Transport;* b. 1948, Teheran, Iran; m. Orit Mofaz; four c.; ed Bar-Ilan Univ., US Marine Corps Command and Staff Coll., Va, USA; immigrated to Israel 1957; paratrooper, Israel Defense Forces (IDF) 1966, served in Six-Day War 1967; command positions in Paratroop Brigade; Commdr Paratroop Reconnaissance Unit 1973; Deputy Commdr Paratroop Brigade; infantry brigade commdr 1982; Commdr IDF Officers' School 1984; Commdr Paratroop Brigade 1986–88; promoted Brig.-Gen. 1988; Commdr Reserve Armour Div. 1988–90; Commdr Galilee Div. 1990–92; Commdr IDF forces in Judea and Samaria 1993–94; promoted Maj.-Gen. 1994; GOC Southern Command 1994–96; Chief of Planning Directorate Gen. Staff 1996–97; Deputy Chief IDF Gen. Staff 1997; 16th Chief of Gen. Staff 1998–2002; Minister of Defence 2002–06; Deputy Prime Minister and Minister of Transport 2006–; left Likud party to join newly formed Kadima party Dec. 2005. *Address:* Ministry of Transport, Government Complex, 5 Bank of Israel Street, Jerusalem, Israel (office). *Telephone:* 2-6663190 (office). *Fax:* 2-6663195 (office). *E-mail:* dover@mot.gov.il (office). *Website:* www.mot.gov.il (office).

MOFFAT, Sir Brian Scott, Kt, OBE, FCA; British business executive; *Deputy Chairman and Senior Independent Director, HSBC Holdings PLC;* b. 6 Jan. 1939; s. of Festus Moffat and Agnes Moffat; m. Jacqueline Cunliffe 1964; one s. (and one s. deceased) one d.; ed Hulme Grammar School; with Peat Marwick Mitchell & Co. 1961–68; joined British Steel Corpn (later British Steel PLC, now Corus Group PLC) 1968, Man. Dir Finance 1986–91, Chief Exec. 1991–99, Chair. 1993–2003; Dir (non-exec.) HSBC Holdings PLC 1998–, Deputy Chair. and Sr Ind. Dir (non-exec.) 2001–; Dir (non-exec.) Enterprise Oil PLC 1995–2002, Bank of England 2000–, Nosmas Holdings BV 2003–; Hon. DSc (Warwick) 1998, (Sheffield) 2001. *Leisure interests:* farming, fishing, shooting. *Address:* Springfield Farm, Earlswood, Chepstow, Monmouthshire, NP6 6AT, England (home). *Telephone:* (1291) 650959. *Fax:* (1291) 650747.

MOFFAT, Leslie Ernest Fraser, BSc, MB, CH.B., MBA, FRCSE, FRCS (GLASG.), FRCPE; British urologist; b. 3 Nov. 1949; m.; three d.; ed Univs of Edinburgh and Stirling; Professorial House Officer posts City Hosp., Royal Infirmary, Edin. 1974–75; Sr House Officer Dept of Surgery, Royal Infirmary, Edin. 1976, Surgical Registrar 1977–79; Munro Prosector, Royal Coll. of Surgeons Edin. 1977–78; Research Registrar, Clinical Shock Study Group, Western Infirmary, Glasgow 1980–81; Urological Sr Registrar, Glasgow Teaching Hosps 1982–86; Clinical Sr Lecturer, Univ. of Aberdeen 1986–; Pres. Grampian Div. BMA 1994; Trustee Prostate Cancer charity, Hammersmith Hosp., London; Chair. Urological Cancer Working Party in Scotland; Founding Ed. UroOncology 1999–; Chair. Urological Cancer Working Party in Scotland 1999–; Medical and Specialist Adviser to Cancer BACUP; Urological Consultant to British Antarctic Survey; Hon. Consultant Royal Marsden Hosp. London; Burgess of Aberdeen 1999. *Publications:* Prostate Cancer – The Facts (co-author), Urological Cancer: A Practical Guide to Management; over 105 publs including 6 book chapters. *Leisure interests:* country life, opera. *Address:* UroOncology, Polwarth Building, Medical School, Foresterhill, Aberdeen, AB25 2ZD (office); Tillery House, Udny, Ellon, Aberdeenshire, Scotland (home). *Telephone:* (1224) 849136 (office); (1651) 842898 (home). *Fax:* (1224) 403618 (office). *E-mail:* uro-oncology@abdn.ac.uk (office).

MOFFATT, Henry Keith, ScD, FRS; British mathematician and academic; *Professor Emeritus of Mathematical Physics, University of Cambridge;* b. 12 April 1935, Edinburgh, Scotland; s. of the late Frederick Henry Moffatt and Emmeline Marchant Fleming; m. Katharine (Linty) Stiven 1960; two s. (one deceased) two d.; ed Univs of Edinburgh and Cambridge; Asst Lecturer, then Lecturer, Univ. of Cambridge 1961–76, Prof. of Math. Physics 1980–2005, Prof. Emer. 2005–; Fellow, Trinity Coll., Cambridge 1961–76, 1980–, Tutor 1971–74, Sr Tutor 1975; Prof. of Applied Math., Bristol Univ. 1977–80; Dir Isaac Newton Inst. for Mathematical Sciences 1996–2001; Pres. Int. Union of Theoretical and Applied Mechanics 2000–04, Vice-Pres. 2004–08; part-time Prof. Ecole Polytechnique, Paris 1992–99; Chair. Int. de Recherche Blaise Pascal 2002–03; Leverhulme Emer. Fellow 2003–05; Ed. Journal of Fluid Mechanics 1966–83; mem. Academia Europaea 1994; Foreign mem. Royal Netherlands Acad. of Arts and Sciences 1991, Acad. des Sciences, Paris 1998, Acad. Scienzia Lincei 2001, NAS (USA) 2008; Officier des Palmes académiques 1998; Dr hc (INPG Grenoble) 1987, (State Univ. of New York) 1990, (Edin.) 2001, (Eindhoven Tech. Univ.) 2006, (Glasgow) 2007; Smiths Prize 1960, Panetti-Ferrari Prize and Gold Medal 2001, Euromech Fluid Mechanics Prize 2003, Sr Whitehead Prize, London Math. Soc. 2005, Hughes Medal, Royal Soc. 2005. *Publications:* Magnetic Field Generation in Electrically Conducting Fluids 1978, Topological Fluid Mechanics (ed. with A. Tsinober) 1990, Topological Aspects of the Dynamics of Fluids and Plasmas (jt ed.) 1992. *Leisure interests:* French country cooking, hill walking. *Address:* DAMTP, Centre for Mathematical Sciences, Wilberforce Road, Cambridge, CB3 0WA (office); Trinity College, Cambridge, CB2 1TQ (office); 6 Banhams Close, Cambridge, CB4 1HX, England (home). *Telephone:* (1223) 363338 (office). *Fax:* (1223) 765900 (office). *E-mail:* hkm2@damtp.cam.ac.uk (office). *Website:* www.damtp.cam.ac.uk (office); .

MOFFETT, David McKenzie, BA, MBA; American mortgage executive; b. 22 Feb. 1952, Daytona Beach, Fla; s. of James Denny Jr and Dorothy McCall; m. 1st Cynthia Ann Daugherty 1973 (divorced 1977); m. 2nd Katherine Anne Martin 1979; three c.; ed Univ. of Oklahoma, Southern Methodist Univ.; planning analyst, First Nat. Bank & Trust Co. 1975–76, financial analyst 1978, Vice-Pres. 1978–80, Sr Vice-Pres. 1981–86, Exec. Vice-Pres. 1987–93; Chief Financial Officer Star Banc Corpn (merged with Firstar Corpn) 1993–98, Chief Financial Officer and Vice-Chair. Firstar Corpn 1998–2001, Chief Financial Officer, Vice-Chair. and Dir US Bancorp 2001–07 (after Firstar merger with US Bancorp 2001); CEO Fed. Home Loan Mortgage Corpn (Freddie Mac) Sept. 2008–March 2009; Sr Adviser The Carlyle Group 2007–08; fmr Chair. Chief Financial Officers' Council, Financial Services Roundtable; Chair. Bd of Dirs Ebay Inc. 2007–, MBIA Insurance Corpn 2007–, E.W. Scripps Inc. 2007–, Building Materials Holding Corpn 2007–; mem. Chief Financial Officers' Roundtable, Bank Admin Inst.; mem. Advisory Bd Price Coll. of Business, Univ. of Oklahoma; mem. Nat. Asset/Liability Man. Asscn, Bank Admin Inst.; Chair.'s Award, First Nat. Bank 1980. *Leisure interests:* running, golf, skiing, scuba diving, cycling. *Address:* c/o Freddie Mac, 8200 Jones Branch Drive, McLean, VA 22102, USA (office).

MOFFETT, James R., BS, MS; American geologist and mining executive; *Chairman, Freeport-McMoRan Copper & Gold;* ed Univ. of Texas at Austin, Tulane Univ.; consulting geologist 1964–69; Co-f. McMoRan Oil & Gas Co. 1969, merged with Freeport Minerals Co. to form Freeport-McMoRan Inc., Chair. and CEO 1984–97, mem. Bd of Dirs 1992–, currently Chair. Freeport-McMoRan Copper & Gold Inc. and Pres. Commr of PT Freeport Indonesia (mining unit), also Co-Chair. McMoRan Exploration Co.; serves on numerous boards; mem. Mining Foundation of the Southwest; Hon. DSc (Louisiana State Univ.); Hon. Dr of Financial Econs (Univ. of New Orleans); Horatio Alger Asscn of Distinguished Americans Award 1990, Norman Vincent Peale Award, Horatio Alger Asscn of Distinguished Americans 2000, mem. American Mining Hall of Fame. *Address:* Freeport-McMoRan Copper & Gold, One North Central Avenue, Phoenix, AZ 85004-4414, USA (office). *Telephone:*

(602) 366-8100 (office). *E-mail:* info@fcx.com (office). *Website:* www.fcx.com (office).

MOGAE, Festus Gontebanye, MA; Botswana politician and fmr head of state; *Secretary-General's Special Envoy for Climate Change, United Nations;* b. 21 Aug. 1939, Serowe; s. of Ditlhabano and Dithunya Mogae; m. Barbara Gemma Modise 1968; three d.; ed Moeng Secondary School, North West London Polytechnic, Univs of Oxford and Sussex; Planning Officer, Ministry of Devt Planning 1968–69, Ministry of Finance and Devt Planning 1970, Sr Planning Officer 1971, Dir Econ Affairs 1972–74, Perm. Sec. 1975–76; Alt. Exec. Dir of IMF 1976–78, Exec. Dir 1978–80; Alt. Gov. for Botswana, IMF 1971–72, African Devt Bank 1971–76, IBRD 1973–76; Dir Botswana Devt Corpn 1971–74 (Chair. 1975–76), De Beers Botswana Mining Co. Ltd 1975–76, Bangwato Concessions Ltd 1975–76, BCL Sales Ltd 1975–76, Bank of Botswana 1975–76 (Gov. 1980–81); Gov. IMF 1981–82; Perm. Sec. to Pres. of Botswana 1982–89, Minister of Finance and Devt Planning 1989–98, Vice-Pres. 1992–98; Pres. of Botswana 1998–2008; UN Sec.-Gen.'s Special Envoy for Climate Change 2008–; Pres. Botswana Soc., Botswana Soc. of the Deaf; mem. Jt Devt Cttee of World Bank and IMF on the transfer of real resources to developing countries 1992–, Kalahari Conservation Soc., Commonwealth Parl. Assoc., Parliamentarians for Global Action, Global Coalition for Africa; Rep., Commonwealth Fund for Tech. Co-operation 1971–; est. Champions for an HIV-Free Generation; Hon. Fellowship, Botswana Inst. of Bankers 1999; Officier, Ordre Nat. Côte d'Ivoire 1979, Mali 1997, Presidential Order of Honour of Botswana 1989, Grand Cross, Légion d'honneur 2008; Hon. LLD (Botswana) 1998; Achievement Awards for AIDS Leadership (USA 2000, Gaborone 2001), Nat. Leadership Award, Africa-America Inst. 2002, Mo Ibrahim Prize 2008. *Leisure interests:* reading, tennis, music. *Address:* United Nations, New York, NY 10017, USA (office). *Telephone:* (212) 963-1234 (office). *Fax:* (212) 963-4879 (office). *Website:* www.un.org (office).

MOGG, John Frederick; British civil servant and fmr EU official; *Chairman, Ofgem;* b. 5 Oct. 1943, Brighton; s. of Thomas W. Mogg and Cora M. Mogg; m. Anne Smith 1967; one d. one s.; ed Univ. of Birmingham; fmrly with Rediffusion group; First Sec. UK Perm. Representation at EC, Brussels 1979–82; various appointments in UK civil service 1982–89; Deputy Head, European Secr. Cabinet Office 1989–90; Deputy Dir-Gen. Internal Market and Industrial Affairs, European Comm. 1990–93, Dir-Gen. Internal Market (fmrly DG XV) Directorate-Gen. 1993–2002; mem. Gas and Electricity Markets Authority 2003; Chair. (non-exec.) Ofgem 2003–. *Address:* Ofgem, 9, Millbank, London, SW1P 3GE, England (office). *Telephone:* (20) 7901-7000 (office). *Fax:* (20) 7901-7066 (office). *E-mail:* enquiries@energywatch.org.uk (office). *Website:* www.ofgem.gov.uk (office).

MOGGACH, Deborah, BA, DipEd, FRSL; British writer; b. 28 June 1948, London; d. of Richard Hough and Helen Charlotte Hough; m. Anthony Moggach 1971 (divorced); one s. one d.; ed Camden School for Girls, Univ. of Bristol, Univ. of London; Chair. Soc. of Authors 1999–2001; mem. PEN. *Television:* (dramas) To Have and To Hold 1986, Stolen 1990, Goggle-Eyes (adaptation) 1993 (Writers' Guild Award for Best Adapted TV Serial), Seesaw 1998, Close Relations 1998, Love in a Cold Climate (adaptation) 2001, Final Demand 2003, The Diary of Anne Frank 2009. *Film:* Pride and Prejudice (adaptation) 2005. *Play:* Double Take. *Publications:* novels: You Must Be Sisters 1978, Close to Home 1979, A Quiet Drink 1980, Hot Water Man 1982, Porky 1983, To Have and To Hold 1986, Driving in the Dark 1988, Stolen 1990, The Stand-in 1991, The Ex-Wives 1993, Seesaw 1996, Close Relations 1997, Tulip Fever 1999, Final Demand 2001, These Foolish Things 2004, In the Dark 2007; short stories: Smile 1987, Changing Babies 1995. *Leisure interests:* swimming in rivers, walking round cities. *Address:* Curtis Brown, 28–29 Haymarket, London, SW1Y 4SP, England (office). *Telephone:* (20) 7396-6600 (office). *Fax:* (20) 7396-0110 (office).

MOGGIE, Datuk Leo, MA, MBA; Malaysian politician; b. 1 Oct. 1941, Kanowit, Sarawak; ed Univs of Otago and Pennsylvania State Univ.; Dist Officer, Kapit, Sarawak 1966–68; Dir Borneo Literature Bureau, Kuching, Sarawak 1968–69; attached to Office of Chief Minister, Kuching 1969–72; Deputy Gen. Man. Borneo Devt Corpn Kuching 1973–74; elected to Sarawak State Legis. Ass. and Parl.; Sec.-Gen. Sarawak Nat. Party (SNAP) 1976; Minister of Welfare Services, State Govt of Sarawak 1976–77, of Local Govt 1977–78; Minister of Energy, Telecommunications and Posts 1978–89, of Works and Public Utilities 1989–90, of Public Works 1990–95. *Address:* c/o Ministry of Public Works, Jalan Sultan Salahuddin, 50580 Kuala Lumpur, Malaysia.

MOGWE, Archibald Mooketsa, MBE, BA, PMS, PH; Botswana politician, diplomatist and teacher; b. 29 Aug. 1921, Kanye; s. of Rev. Morutwana T. Mogwe and Mary (née Leepo) Mogwe; m. Lena Mosele Senakhomo 1953; one s. two d.; ed schools in Bechuanaland Protectorate, teacher training in S Africa, Univs of Reading and Oxford; teacher 1944–57; Educ. Officer 1957–64; transferred to Secr. 1964, Perm. Sec. 1966; worked in Foreign Office 1966–, Sr Perm. Sec., Sec. to Cabinet and Head of Public Service 1968–74; Minister of Foreign Affairs 1974–84, of Mineral Resources and Water Affairs 1984–89, 1990–94; Amb. to USA 1996–2002. *Leisure interests:* soccer, classical music, shooting. *Address:* c/o Ministry of Foreign Affairs, Private Bag 00368, Gaborone, Botswana. *Telephone:* 3600700. *E-mail:* empofu@gov.bw.

MOHAMAD, Goenawan; Indonesian poet, writer and journalist; b. 29 July 1941, Batang, Cen. Java; leader of Tempo magazine in Indonesia, forcibly closed twice by Suharto New Order admin; est. Inst. for Studies in the Free Flow of Information; mem. Int. Advisory Bd ARTICLE 19 human rights group; several awards for journalism, including Int. Ed. of the Year, World Press Review 1999, Dan David Prize 2006. *Publications include:* Potret Seorang Penyair Muda Sebagai Si Malin Kundang (The Portrait of A Young Poet as

Malin Kundang) 1972, Seks, Sastra, Kita (Sex, Literature, Us) 1980, Pariksit dan Interlude 2001, Setelah Revolusi Tak Ada Lagi (Once the Revolution No Longer Exists) 2001, Kata, Waktu (Word, Time) 2001. *Address:* Tempo Interaktif, Kebayoran Center Blok A11–A15, Jl. Kebayoran Baru – Mayestik, Jakarta 12440, Indonesia (office). *Telephone:* (21) 725-5625 (office). *Fax:* (21) 720-6995 (office). *E-mail:* iklannews@tempo.co.id (office). *Website:* www.tempointeractive.com (office).

MOHAMED, Caabi el Yachroutou; Comoran politician; Minister of Finance 1993–94; Prime Minister of Comoros April–Oct. 1995; Interim Pres. 1995–96; Vice-President with responsibility for Finance, the Budget, the Economy, Foreign Trade, Investments and Privatizations –2006; mem. Rally for Democracy and Renewal. *Address:* c/o Ministry of Finance, the Budget and Privatization, BP 324, Moroni, The Comoros.

MOHAMEDOU, Mohamed Mahmoud Ould, PhD; Mauritanian academic and politician; *Minister of Foreign Affairs and Co-operation;* ed Univ. Panthéon-Sorbonne, Paris, City Univ. of New York; fmr Research Dir Int. Council on Human Rights, Geneva; fmr Prof. of Political Science, Harvard Univ., Assoc. Dir Program on Humanitarian Policy and Conflict Research, Harvard School of Public Health; Minister of Foreign Affairs and Co-operation 2008–. *Publications:* Societal Transition to Democracy in Mauritania 1995, Iraq and the Second Gulf War, State-Building and Regime Security 1998, Contre-Croisade: Origines et Conséquences du 11 Septembre 2004. *Address:* Ministry of Foreign Affairs and Co-operation, BP 230, Nouakchott, Mauritania (office). *Telephone:* 525-26-82 (office). *Fax:* 525-28-60 (office).

MOHAMMAD, Haji Din; Afghan provincial governor and fmr rebel leader; *Governor of Kabul Province;* fmr mem. Yunus Khalis faction, Hizb-i Islami; fmr Mujahidin commdr; Gov. Nangarhar Prov. 2002–05, Kabul Prov. 2005–. *Address:* Office of the Governor, Kabul, Afghanistan (office).

MOHAMMAD HUSSEINI, Khial; Afghan politician; Deputy Gov. of Ghazni Prov. –2004, Gov. 2004–05; lawmaker representing Ghazni Prov. in Afghan Parl. 2005–. *Address:* Wolasi Jirga (House of Representatives), Kabul, Afghanistan (office).

MOHAMMAD-NAJJAR, Mostafa; Iranian politician; *Minister of Defence and Armed Forces Logistics;* b. 1956; ed Org. of Industrial Man.; trained as mechanical engineer; participated in suppression of Kurdish insurgency 1978–79; joined Islamic Revolution Guards Corps 1979, various logistical and admin. positions, Head of Expeditionary Force in Lebanon 1980s, Commdr of Guard Operations in Middle E region 1990s; Minister of Defence and Armed Forces Logistics 2005–; mem. Bd of Dirs Defence Industries Org. *Address:* Ministry of Defence and Armed Forces Logistics, Shahid Yousuf Kaboli Street, Sayed Khandan Area, Tehran, Iran (office). *Telephone:* (21) 21401 (office). *Fax:* (21) 864008 (office). *E-mail:* info@mod.ir (office). *Website:* www.mod.ir (office).

MOHAMMED, Gen. Atta; Afghan military commander; *Governor of Balkh Province;* b. 1965, Qalander Shah Colony, Mazar e Sharif; m. 1992; six c.; ed Bakhter High School and at univ. in Tajikistan; fought Soviet occupation in Mazar-i-Sharif as Mujahed mil. officer under the command of Ustad Zabiullah 1980s, following assassination of Ustad Zabiullah was selected as Deputy Commdr of Mujahed forces that belonged to Zabiullah 1987; his forces captured Balkh from forces of communist govt 1993; rank of Lt-Gen. 1993; apptd Chief of Politics and Mil. of Jamiat e Mili Islami (Islamic Soc.) and mem. High Comm. of Islamic Govt of Afghanistan 1993; apptd Commdr 7th Army Corps 1994; led troops to recapture northern provs 2001; promoted to Gen. 2002; Gov. of Balkh Prov. 2004–; Medal of Educ., Ministry of Educ., Shining Star of Educ., Educ. Presidency, title of Man of Peace, Univ. of Mazar e Sharif, honoured by Ministry of Information, Culture and Tourism and by Ministry of Women's Affairs, numerous other honours and awards. *Address:* Office of the Governor, Mazar-i-Sharif, Balkh Province, Afghanistan (office). *Telephone:* (70) 500500 (mobile) (office). *Fax:* +873763036469 (office). *E-mail:* The_Balkh_Government@yahoo.com (office).

MOHAN, Ramesh, PhD; Indian university vice-chancellor and fmr professor of English; b. 20 March 1920, Meerut (UP); s. of Madan Mohan and Kamal Kumari; m. Vimala Mangalik 1943; three s.; ed Lucknow Univ., Leeds Univ., UK; Lecturer in English, Lucknow Univ. 1942–55, Reader 1955–61, Prof. and Head Dept of English and Modern European Languages 1961–67; Dir Cen. Inst. of English and Foreign Languages, Hyderabad 1967–85; Vice-Chancellor, Meerut Univ. 1985–88; Visiting Prof. Univ. of Ill., Urbana, USA 1971, 1975; Consultant, Indira Gandhi Nat. Open Univ., New Delhi 1988–90; Pres. Indian Asscn of English Studies 1975–80, Asscn of Indian Univs 1982–83; mem. Bd of Dirs, American Studies Research Centre 1969–89, Exec. Council, Univ. of Hyderabad 1974–77, Exec. Bd Sahitya Akademi, New Delhi 1978–88, Bd of Dirs, US Educational Foundation of India 1980–81, Governing Council, Indian Inst. of Science, Bangalore 1980–81, Univ. Grants Comm. 1982–85, Council, Asscn of Commonwealth Univs 1982–83, Governing Body, Indian Inst. of Advanced Studies, Simla 1984–87; Wilhelm and Jacob Grimm Prize (GDR) 1986. *Publications:* The Political Novels of Anthony Trollope 1961, George Meredith and the Political Novel 1968, Teaching of English at the University Level in India 1968, Syllabus Reform in English 1977, Some Aspects of Style and Language in Indian English Fiction 1978, Indian Writing in English (Ed.) 1978, English by Air 1979, Stylistics and Literary Interpretation 1980, Symphony (collection of poems) 1984, Nehru as a Man of Letters 1989, Radhakrishnan and Higher Education in India 1989, Religion and National Secularism 1993, English in India: Status and Creativity 1993, Crisis in Higher Education 1994, Let Me Say (essays and addresses) 1996, Benjamin Disraeli: Political Novelist 1999; numerous papers on teaching of English and higher educ. in India. *Leisure interests:* music, theatre, reading, writing, jigsaw puzzles. *Address:* Shanti Sadan 36, Nehru Road, Meerut, Uttar Pradesh, India. *Telephone:* 642339.

MOHAQQEQ, Haji Mohammad; Afghan politician and fmr rebel leader; *Founder and Leader, Hizb-i Wahdat-i Islami Mardum-i Afghanistan (People's Islamic Unity Party of Afghanistan);* b. Charkent Dist, Balkh Prov.; ed Mazar-e-Sharif; Chair. Political Cttee and Admin. of Northern Areas, Hizb-i-Wahdat-i Islami (Islamic Unity Party); fmr Minister of the Interior; led several attacks against Taliban Govt; Minister of Planning, Interim Govt 2001–04; presidential cand. 2004; Founder and Leader Hizb-i Wahdat-i Islami Mardum-i Afghanistan (People's Islamic Unity Party of Afghanistan); Deputy Chair. Jabahai Tafahim Millie (Nat. Understanding Front); mem. Hazara community. *Address:* Hizb-i Wahdat-i Islami Mardum-i Afghanistan, Kabul, Afghanistan (office).

MOHIEDDIN, Zakaria; Egyptian politician and army officer; b. 7 May 1918; s. of the late Abdul Magid Mohieddin and Zeinab Abdul Magid; m. Naila Moustafa 1950; one s. two d.; ed Mil. Coll. and Staff Officers' Coll., Cairo; fmr Lecturer, Mil. Coll. and Staff Officers' Coll. and Dir-Gen. Intelligence; mem. Revolutionary Council 1952; Minister of the Interior 1953–58; Minister of the Interior UAR 1958–62, Vice-Pres. UAR and Chair. Aswan Dam Cttee 1961–62; mem. Nat. Defence Cttee 1962–69, Presidency Council 1962–64; mem. Exec. Cttee Arab Socialist Union 1964–69; Deputy Prime Minister 1964–65, 1967–68; Prime Minister and Minister of the Interior 1965–66. *Leisure interests:* fishing, shooting, rowing, poultry farming. *Address:* 52 El-Thawra Street, Dokki, Cairo, Egypt (office). *Telephone:* 7499421 (office). *Fax:* 7614680 (office). *E-mail:* mem@mzdh.com (office).

MOHL, Andrew, BSc; Australian financial services executive; *CEO, AMP Group Ltd;* b. 1955; with Fed. Reserve Bank of New York 1983–84; fmr Deputy Head of Research, Reserve Bank of Australia; Man. Dir ANZ Funds Man. –1996; Gen. Man. of Retail Distribution, AMP Financial Services 1996, Man. Dir AMP Asset Man., Man. Dir AMP Australian Financial Services 1999–2002, CEO AMP Group Ltd 2002–. *Address:* AMP Group Ltd, AMP Sydney Cove Building, 33 Alfred Street, Sydney, NSW 2000, Australia (office). *Telephone:* (2) 9257-7001 (office). *Fax:* (2) 8275-0199 (office). *E-mail:* vicky-toppinen@amp.com.au (office). *Website:* www.ampgroup.com (office).

MÖHLER, Hanns, BSc, MSc, PhD; German pharmacologist and academic; *Professor of Pharmacology, Eidgenössische Technische Hochschule Zürich and University of Zurich;* b. 8 March 1940, Ehingen; m.; two c.; ed Univs of Bonn, Tübingen and Freiburg; research work at Michigan State Univ., USA and MRC Labs, London, UK; apptd Vice-Dir (Science) Research Dept, Hoffmann-La Roche, Basel; qualified as Univ. Lecturer at Univ. of Freiburg, later promoted to Assoc. Prof.; Prof. of Pharmacology, Dept of Chem. and Applied Biosciences, ETH Zürich 1989–, Faculty of Medicine, Univ. of Zurich 1989–, Head of Inst. of Pharmacology; Co-ed. of numerous journals; mem. European Acad. of Sciences 1991–; Fellow, Collegium Helveticum 2004–; Golden Kraepelin Medal, German Inst. for Psychiatric Research 2003. *Publications:* a textbook on biochemistry, Pharmacology of GABA and Glycine Neurotransmission (Handbook of Experimental Pharmacology) 2000, The GABA Receptors (with by S. J. Enna) 2007; numerous scientific papers in professional journals on the neurobiology of the brain and molecular pharmacology of the action of drugs. *Address:* Institute of Pharmacology and Toxicology, Irchel Campus Y17, University of Zurich, Winterthurerstrasse 190, 8057 Zurich, Switzerland (office). *Telephone:* (44) 635-59-11 (office). *E-mail:* mohler@pharma.uzh.ch (office). *Website:* www.pharma.uzh.ch (office).

MOHN, Christoph; German electronics and telecommunications executive; *Chief Executive Officer, Lycos Europe NV;* b. 1965; s. of Reinhard Mohn; great-great-grand s. of Carl Bertelsmann (f. co. 1835); ed Westfälische Wilhelms-Universität, Münster; fmr intern, Bantam Doubleday Dell; with Bertelsmann Music Group (BMG), Hong Kong and New York, USA 1991–94; specialist in electronics and telecommunications, McKinsey & Co. (Germany) 1994–96; Vice-Pres. Telemedia (subsidiary of Bertelsmann) 1996–97; CEO Lycos Europe NV 1997–, responsible for expansion of co. into 13 European countries. *Address:* Lycos Europe NV, Carl-Bertelsmann-Strasse 29, 33332 Gütersloh, Germany (office). *Telephone:* (52) 418071000 (office). *Fax:* (52) 418071450 (office). *Website:* www.lycos-europe.com (office).

MOHN, Elisabeth (Liz); German media industry executive; *Chairwoman of the Executive Board, Bertelsmann Verwaltungsgesellschaft mbH;* b. 21 June 1941, Wiedenbrück; m. Reinhard Mohn 1982; three c.; joined Bertelsmann group's book club unit 1958, Chief Exec. Bertelsmann Admin Co. 2002–; Man. Dir and mem. Supervisory Bd Bertelsmann Trust 2002–, currently Chair. Exec. Bd Bertelsmann Verwaltungsgesellschaft, Vice-Chair. Exec. Bd Bertelsmann Stiftung, Deputy Chair. Bertelsmann Foundation; Founder and Pres. Assistance for Stroke Victims Foundation 1993–; Pres. Neue Stimmen (singing competition) 1987–; mem. European Acad. of Sciences, Salzburg 1997–, Club of Rome 1999–; Dr hc (Univ. of Tel-Aviv) 2005; Vernon A. Walters Award, Atlantik-Brucke 2008. *Address:* Bertelsmann AG, Carl-Bertelsmann-Strasse 270, 33311, Gütersloh, Germany. *Telephone:* (5241) 80-22 01 (office). *Fax:* (5241) 73611 (office). *E-mail:* liz.mohn@bertelsmann.de (office). *Website:* www.bertelsmann.com (office).

MOHN, Reinhard; German publisher; *Chairman Emeritus, Bertelsmann AG;* b. 29 June 1921; m. Elisabeth Mohn 1982; army service 1939–43; POW in N Africa and USA 1943–46; Pres. and CEO Bertelsmann AG 1947–81, Chair. Supervisory Bd 1981–91, now Chair. Emer.; Founder, mem. Cttee Bertelsmann Foundation, Chair. 1991–98. *Publications:* Success Through Partnership 1988, Humanity Wins 2000. *Address:* Bertelsmann AG, Carl-Bertelsmann-Strasse 270, 33311 Gütersloh, Germany. *Telephone:* (5241) 800 (office). *Fax:* (5241) 809662 (office). *Website:* www.bertelsmann.de (office).

MOHOHLO, Linah Kelebogile, BEcons, MA; Botswana economist and central banker; *Governor, Bank of Botswana;* ed George Washington Univ., USA and Univ. of Exeter, UK; joined Bank of Botswana 1976, served in various positions including Deputy Dir of Research 1988, Dir Financial Markets Dept 1989, Deputy Gov. 1997–99, Gov. 1999–; worked with African Dept and Monetary and Exchange Affairs Dept, IMF, Washington, DC 1989–97; fmr Commr, Comm. of Africa; mem. Africa Emerging Markets Forum, Africa Progress Panel; mem. Advisory Bd Diamond Empowerment Fund; Cen. Bank Gov. of the Year for Africa and Middle East, Financial Times magazine 2001, Cen. Bank Gov. of the Year for Sub-Saharan Africa, Euromoney 2001, Presidential Order of Honour 2004, Africa's Banking Regulator of the Year 2007; apptd Eminent Person by UN Sec.-Gen. 2001. *Address:* Bank of Botswana, PO Box 712, Private Bag 154, 17938 Khama Crescent, Gaborone, Botswana (office). *Telephone:* 3606000 (office). *Fax:* 3913890 (office). *E-mail:* selwej@bob.bw (office). *Website:* www.bankofbotswana.bw (office).

MOHORITA, Vasil; Czech politician and business executive; *Head of External Relations, Zbrojovka;* b. 19 Sept. 1952, Prague; s. of Vasil Mohorita and Ludmila Mohoritová; m. Vlasta Mohoritová 1976; one s. one d.; ed Komsomol Coll., Moscow and CP of Czechoslovakia (CPCZ) Political Coll., Prague; joined CP of Czechoslovakia (Komunistická strana Československa—KSC) 1970, mem. Cen. Cttee 1988–90, First Sec. Cen. Cttee 1989–90; Chair. Youth Union's Czechoslovak Cen. Cttee 1987–89; mem. Czechoslovak Nat. Front Presidium 1987; Deputy, Czechoslovak Nat. Council 1986–90; mem. Presidium Fed. Ass. Jan.–Oct. 1990, Deputy to Fed. Ass. House of People 1990–92; Chair. Communist Deputies Club Jan.–Nov. 1990; agent for Valemo, Parfia, Jamiko, CIS Group; Chair. Bd of Supervisors E.R. Tradings; Head of Sales, Frut Ovo (pvt. co.); mem. Party of Democratic Left 1993–97; Chair. Party of Democratic Socialism 1997–98; Head of External Relations, Zbrojovka, Brno 2000–. *Publications:* numerous articles. *Leisure interests:* reading historical and political literature, playing the guitar, basketball, tennis. *Address:* Zbrojovka, Lazaretni 7, 615 00, Brno, Czech Republic. *Website:* www.zbrojovkabrno.com.

MOHRT, Michel, LenD; French writer and editor; b. 28 April 1914, Morlaix; s. of Fernand Mohrt and Amélie Mohrt (née Gélébart); m. Françoise Jarrier 1955; one s.; ed Law School, Rennes; lawyer, Marseilles Bar –1942; Prof., Yale Univ., Smith Coll., UCLA, USA 1947–52; Ed. and Head English Trans Section Les Editions Gallimard 1952–; mem. Acad. française 1985; Officier, Légion d'honneur, Croix de guerre; Grand Prix de la Critique littéraire 1970, Grand Prix de Littérature de l'Acad. française 1983. *Publications:* novels: Le répit, Mon royaume pour un cheval 1949, Les nomades, le serviteur fidèle, La prison maritime (Grand Prix du roman de l'Acad. française 1962) 1961, La campagne d'Italie 1965, L'ours des Adirondacks 1969, Deux Indiennes à Paris 1974, Les moyens du bord 1975, La guerre civile 1986, Le Télésiège 1989, Un soir à Londres 1991, On liquide et on s'en va 1992, L'Ile des fous 1999; essays: Les intellectuels devant la défaite de 1870, Montherlant, homme libre 1943, Le nouveau roman américain 1956, L'air du large 1969, L'air du large II 1988; plays: Un jeu d'enfer 1970, La maison du père 1979, Vers l'Ouest 1988, L'Air du temps 1991. *Leisure interests:* sailing, painting. *Address:* c/o Editions Gallimard, 5 rue Sébastien-Bottin, 75007 Paris; 4 bis rue du Cherche-Midi, 75006 Paris, France (home). *Telephone:* 1-42-22-42-12 (home).

MOHTASHAMI, Ali Akbar, DTheol; Iranian politician; *Secretary-General, International Conference on Palestinian Intifada;* b. 30 Aug. 1946, Tehran; s. of Seyed Hossein and Fatemeh Mohtashami; m. Fatemeh Mohtashami 1968; two s. five d.; studied theology in Iran and Iraq; mil. training in Palestinian camps, Lebanon; went to Paris with Ayatollah Khomeini 1978; returned to Iran and took part in overthrow of monarchy 1979; mem. political advisory office of Ayatollah Khomeini; Dir of Ayatollah's representative delegation in Foundation of the Oppressed 1980; mem. IRIB Supervisory Council 1980–81; Amb. to Syria 1981–85; a founder of Hezbollah in Lebanon; Minister of the Interior 1985; mem. Parl. 1989–91; Chair. Parl. Cttee on Defence; Sec.-Gen. IPU Group of Iran (Chair. 1989–91); mem. Cttee to Protect the Islamic Revolution of Palestine, Cen. Council of Combatant Clergy; Sec.-Gen. of Int. Conf. on Intifada; Deputy Chair. Bd of Trustees Qods Inst.; Social Adviser to Pres. of Iran; Man. Bayan newspaper (banned June 2000). *Publications include:* Plurality, From Iran to Iran (Memoirs) 1965–79. *Leisure interests:* study, sport (especially mountaineering and swimming). *Address:* General Secretariat of International Conference on Palestinian Intifada, 11 Khorshid Street, Pastor Avenue, Tehran (office); Islamic Consultative Assembly, Tehran (office); 11, Adib-ol-Mamalek Street, Ray Street, Tehran, Iran (home). *Telephone:* (21) 6135672 (office); (21) 361892 (home). *Fax:* (21) 6460046 (office). *E-mail:* info@gods-path.org (office). *Website:* www.gods-path.org (office).

MOI, Daniel Arap; Kenyan politician; b. 1924, Sacho, Baringo district; m. Lena Moi (died 2004); seven c.; ed African Mission School, Kabartonjo A.I.M. School and Govt African School, Kapsabet; teacher 1945–57; Head Teacher, Govt African School, Kabarnet 1946–48, 1955–57, teacher Tambach Teacher Training School, Kabarnet 1948–54; African Rep. mem., Legis. Council 1957–63; Chair. Kenya African Democratic Union (KADU) 1960–61; mem. House of Reps 1961–; Parl. Sec., Ministry of Educ. April–Dec. 1961; Minister of Educ. 1961–62, Local Govt 1962–64, Home Affairs 1964–67; Pres. Kenya African Nat. Union (KANU) for Rift Valley Province 1966–67; Vice-Pres. of Kenya 1967–78, concurrently Minister of Home Affairs; Pres. of Kenya and C-in-C of the Armed Forces 1978–2002; Minister of Defence 1979–2002; Chair. KANU –2003; Chair. OAU 1981–82; mem. Rift Valley Educ. Bd, Kalenjin Language Cttee; Chair. Rift Valley Provincial Court; Kt of Grace, Order of St John 1980. *Address:* c/o Office of the President, Harambee House, Harambee Avenue, PO Box 30510, Nairobi, Kenya.

MOISEEV, Andrey Sergeyevich; Russian athlete; b. 3 June 1979, Rostov-na-Donu; competes in Modern Pentathlon, including shooting, fencing, swimming, showjumping and 3,000m run; coached by Audrey Tropin; winner Gold Medal (team), World Championships, Moscow 2004; winner Gold Medal (relay), World Championships, Moscow 2004; winner Gold Medal (individual), World Cup, Budapest 2004, Olympic Games, Athens 2004; winner Silver Medal (individual), World Cup Final, Moscow 2001, World Cup, Most 2003; winner Bronze Medal (individual), World Cup, Wahrendorf 2001; winner Bronze Medal (team), World Championships, Street 2001; winner Gold Medal (individual), Olympic Games, Beijing 2008; mem. Dynamo Rostov Club. *Address:* c/o All-Russia Athletic Federation, 8, Luzhnetskaya nab., Moscow 119871, Russia. *Website:* eng.rusathletics.com.

MOISEIWITSCH, Benjamin Lawrence, PhD, MRIA; British mathematician and academic; *Professor Emeritus of Applied Mathematics, University of Belfast;* b. 6 Dec. 1927, London; s. of Jacob Moiseiwitsch and Chana Kotlerman; m. Sheelagh Mary Penrose McKeon 1953; two s. two d.; ed Royal Liberty School, Romford and Univ. Coll., London; Lecturer in Applied Math., Univ. of Belfast 1952–62, Reader in Applied Math. 1962–68, Prof. of Applied Math. 1968–93, Prof. Emer. 1993–, Head, Dept of Applied Math. and Theoretical Physics 1977–89, Dean Faculty of Science 1972–75. *Publications include:* Variational Principles 1966, Integral Equations 1977. *Leisure interest:* music. *Address:* Department of Applied Mathematics and Theoretical Physics, The Queen's University of Belfast, Belfast, BT7 1NN (office); 21 Knocktern Gardens, Belfast, BT4 3LZ, Northern Ireland (home). *Telephone:* (28) 9027-3158 (office); (28) 9097-6040 (home). *Fax:* (28) 9023-9182 (office). *E-mail:* b.moiseiwitsch@qub.ac.uk (office); b.moiseiwitsch@btinternet.com (home). *Website:* www.qub.ac.uk/mp/amtpt (office); www.b.moiseiwitsch .btinternet.co.uk (home).

MOÏSI, Dominique; French professor of international relations; *Deputy Director, Institut français des relations internationales;* b. 21 Oct. 1946, Neuilly-sur-Seine; s. of Jules Moïsi and Charlotte Tabakman; m. Diana Pinto-Moïsi 1977; two s.; ed Lycée Buffon, Paris, Institut d'études politiques, Paris, Faculté de droit de Paris, Harvard Univ., USA; Visiting Lecturer, Hebrew Univ. of Jerusalem 1973–75; Asst Lecturer, Univ. of Paris X 1975–89; Deputy Dir Inst français des relations internationales 1979–; Lecturer, Ecole Nationale d'Admin 1980–85, Ecole des hautes études en sciences sociales 1988–; Sec.-Gen. Groupe d'étude et de recherche des problèmes internationaux 1975–78; Assoc. Prof., Johns Hopkins Univ. European Centre, Bologna 1983–84; Visiting Prof., Collège d'Europe, Warsaw, Poland; Ed. Politique étrangère 1983–; Prof., Inst. d'études politiques, Paris; mem. Bd of Dirs Salzburg Seminar, Aspen Inst., Berlin; editorial writer for Financial Times and Die Zeit. *Publications include:* Crises et guerres au XXe siècle: analogies et différences 1981, Le nouveau continent: plaidoyer pour une Europe renaissante (with Jacques Rupnik) 1991, Les cartes de la France à l'heure de la mondialisation (jtly) 2000, Politique étrangère (jtly) 2003. *Leisure interests:* music, cinema, tennis, skiing. *Address:* Institut français des relations internationales (IFRI), 27 rue de la Procession, 75015 Paris (office); 4 rue Saint-Florentin, 75001 Paris, France (home). *Telephone:* 1-40-61-60-00 (office). *Fax:* 1-40-61-60-60 (office). *E-mail:* moisi@ifri.org (office). *Website:* www.ifri.org (home).

MOISIU, Alfred, DMilSc; Albanian fmr head of state; b. 1 Dec. 1929, Shkodër; s. of Spiro Moisiu; m. (wife deceased); one s. three d.; ed High School of Tirana, mil. eng school in Leningrad (now St Petersburg) and Acad. of Mil. Eng, Moscow, USSR, Defence Acad., Tirana, NATO Mil. Coll. Rome, Italy; participant in Nat. Liberation War 1943–45; platoon commdr, Jt Officers' School, Tirana 1948–49; Instructor, Skanderbeg Mil. Acad., Tirana 1949–51; assigned to Eng Directory, Ministry of Defence 1958–66; Commdr, Pontoon Brigade, Kavaja 1966–71; Head of Eng and Fortification Directory, Ministry of Defence 1971–81; Deputy Minister of Defence 1981–82, Minister 1991–92, Adviser on Defence 1992–94, Vice-Minister of Defence for Defence Policy 1994–97; Commdr of Eng Co., Burrel 1982–84; Pres. of Albania 2002–07; Pres. Albanian Atlantic Asscn (pro-NATO NGO) 1994; Freeman of Bajram Curri, of Bari, Italy; Order of the Red Star, Order for Mil. Services, Skanderbeg Order (2nd Class), Order of St Michael (UK), Order of St George (UK), Order of King Tomisllov with Great Band (Denmark), Gold Medal of the Peizen Leoson (Kosova), Great Cross of Merit (Poland), Great Order of King Vyztautos the Great (Lithuania); Dr of Mil. Sciences 1979; Medal for Mil. Services, Medal of Liberation, Medal of the 10th Army Anniversary. *Publications:* Kosova Between War and Peace (memoirs); has published many articles and studies in Albania and abroad on mil. affairs, defence and regional security policy, and about events in Kosovo. *Address:* c/o Office of the President, Bulevardi Dëshmorët e Kombit, Tirana (office); Rr. Elbasanit, Pall. Amerikan 2, N214, Tirana; Rr. Myztezim Kolliçi, Pall.3/1, Tirana, Albania (home). *Telephone:* (4) 2375201; (4) 2274834. *Fax:* (4) 2375201; (4) 2274834. *E-mail:* alfredmoisiu@ yahoo.com.

MOITINHO DE ALMEIDA, José Carlos de Carvalho, LenD; Portuguese judge; *Judge, Supreme Court of Portugal;* b. 17 March 1936, Lisbon; m. Maria de Lourdes Saraiva De Menezes 1959; one s. one d.; Asst to Public Prosecutor 1963–68; Public Prosecutor, Court of Appeal, Lisbon 1962–72; Chef du Cabinet to Minister of Justice 1972–73; Deputy Attorney-Gen. 1974–79; Dir Office of European Law 1980–86; fmr Judge, Court of Justice of European Union and Pres. Third and Sixth Chambers; Judge, Supreme Court of Portugal 2000–; Croix de Guerre, Ordre du Mérite (Luxembourg), Ordem de Merito (Portugal). *Publications:* Le contrat d'assurance dans le droit portugais et comparé, La publicité mensongère, Droit communautaire, ordre juridique communautaire, Les libertés fondamentales dans la CEE. *Leisure interests:* swimming, gardening. *Address:* Vivenda Panorama, Av. do Monaco, 2675 Estoril, Portugal (home). *Telephone:* (21) 3218900 (office); (21) 4682997 (home). *Fax:* (21) 4647999 (home). *E-mail:* jcmoitinho@mail.telepac.pt (home).

MOJADDEDI, Sibghatullah; Afghan religious leader and politician; *Speaker, Meshrano Jirga; Leader, Jebha-i-Nejat-i-Melli;* b. 1929; ed Al-Azhar Univ., Cairo, Egypt; imprisoned for involvement in plot to assassinate Soviet Prime Minister Nikita Krushchev 1959–64; f. Jami'at Ulamai Mohammadi (Org. of Muslim Clergy) 1972; f. Jebha-i-Nejat-i-Melli Afghanistan (Nat. Liberation Front of Afghanistan) 1979, Leader 1979–; acting Pres. Unity Govt 1992; Head Govt of Mujaheddin Council, Kabul 1992–94; currently Speaker, Meshrano Jirga (House of Elders). *Address:* Jebha-i-Nejat-i-Melli (National Liberation Front), Pashtun, Afghanistan (office).

MOJSOV, Lazar, DIur; Macedonian journalist, politician and diplomatist (retd); b. 19 Dec. 1920, Negotino, Macedonia; s. of Dono Mojsov and Efka Mojsov; m. Liljana Jankov 1945; two d.; ed Belgrade Univ.; fmr mem. Anti-Fascist Ass. for the Nat. Liberation of Macedonia; fmr Public Prosecutor, Macedonia; Minister of Justice, Macedonia 1948–51; Dir New Macedonia 1953–58; Pres. Supreme Court of Macedonia 1953; fmr Head of Press Dept, Fed. Govt of Macedonia; mem. Yugoslav Fed. Parl. and Parl. of Macedonia; mem. Exec. Bd, Socialist League of Working People of Yugoslavia; mem. Exec. Cttee of Cen. Cttee, Macedonian League of Communists; mem. Cen. Cttee League of Communists of Yugoslavia –1989 (Pres. of Presidium 1980–81); Amb. to USSR 1958–61; Dir Inst. for Study of Workers' Movements 1961–62; Dir and Chief Ed. Borba 1962–64; Pres. Int. Cttee of Fed. Conf. of Socialist Alliance of Working People of Yugoslavia 1965; Amb. to Austria 1967–69; Perm. Rep. to UN 1969–74; Chair. Security Council 1973; Deputy Fed. Sec. for Foreign Affairs 1974–78, Fed. Sec. 1982–84; mem. Collective State Presidency of Yugoslavia 1984–89, Vice-Pres. 1986–87, Pres. 1987–88; Pres. 32nd UN Gen. Ass. 1977; Partisan Memorial Medal 1941; Order of Merit for Exceptional Achievements First Class, Order of Merit for Services to the Nation, First and Third Class, Order of Brotherhood and Unity. *Publications:* The Bulgarian Workers' Party (Communist) and the Macedonian National Question 1948, Vasil Glavinov: First Propagator of Socialism in Macedonia 1949, Concerning the Question of the Macedonian National Minority in Greece 1954, The World Around Us 1977, Historical Themes 1978, Dimensions of Non-alignment 1980, Past and Present 1981, Nonalignment Yesterday, Today and Tomorrow 1990. *Leisure interest:* philately.

MOKOSE, Lincoln Ralechate; Lesotho diplomatist and politician; *Minister of Forestry and Land Reclamation;* b. 24 Feb. 1949, Kolonyama; m.; two s. one d.; ed Nat. Univ. of Lesotho and Birmingham Univ.; began career as Asst Teacher in various high schools in Lesotho and Swaziland 1971–91; Pres. Nat. Univ. of Lesotho Student Union 1978–80; Chief Insp., Ministry of Educ. 1992–98; fmr High Commr to S Africa 1998; Amb. to Denmark, also attributed to Poland and The Russian Federation 1998–2002; elected mem. Parl. 2002; Deputy Speaker, Nat. Ass. 2002–03; Minister of Forestry and Land Reclamation 2003–. *Address:* Minister of Forestry and Land Reclamation, P. O. Box 92, Maseru 100, Lesotho (office). *Telephone:* 22313057 (office). *Fax:* 22310515 (office). *Website:* www.lesotho.gov.ls/forestry (office).

MOLCHANOV, Vladimir Kyrillovich; Russian journalist; b. 7 Oct. 1950, Moscow; s. of Kyrill Molchanov; m. Consuella Segura; one d.; ed Moscow State Univ.; with Press Agency Novosti 1973–86; observer USSR State Cttee for TV and Radio 1987–91; artistic Dir studio of independent co. REN-TV 1991–, Observer Reuter-TV 1994–; regular appearances in his own TV programmes Before and After Midnight 1987–93, Before and After 1994–, Panorama 2000–, Longer than Age 2000–; mem. Acad. of Russian TV, Acad. of Natural Sciences; Prize of Journalists' Union as the Best TV Journalist 1990 and other awards. *Publications:* TV films: Remembrance, I, You, He and She, People and Years, Zone, I Still Have More Addresses, Tied with One Chain, August of 1991 (screenplays), Retribution Must Come (M. Gorky Prize 1982). *Leisure interest:* life in the country. *Address:* REN-TV, Zubovsky blvd 17, Moscow, Russia. *Telephone:* (495) 255-90-77 (office).

MOLDAZHANOVA, Gulzhan, MBA; Russian business executive; *CEO, Basic Element;* ed Kazakh State Univ., Lomonosov Moscow State Univ., Finance Acad. of Govt of Russian Fed., Antwerp Univ., Belgium; sr man. at Sibirsky Aluminium (Sibal, later renamed Basic Element—Basel) 1995–2000, Dir Sales and Marketing, Russian Aluminium Co. (RUSAL) 2000–02, Dir for Strategy and Corp. Devt 2002–04, mem. Bd of Dirs and Man. Dir Aluminium Business, Basic Element Co. (RUSAL's major shareholder) 2004–06, CEO Basic Element 2006–; named by The Wall Street Journal amongst Ten Managers to Watch In Top Firms in Europe 2004, ranked by Fortune magazine amongst 50 Most Powerful Women in Business outside the US (22nd) 2006, (20th) 2007, ranked by Forbes magazine amongst 100 Most Powerful Women (37th) 2008. *Address:* Basic Element, 30 ul. Rochdelskaya, Moscow 123022, Russian Federation (office). *Telephone:* (495) 720-50-25 (office). *Fax:* (495) 720-53-95 (office). *E-mail:* info@basicelement.ru (office). *Website:* www.basicelement.ru (office).

MOLEFE, Popo Simon; South African politician; b. 26 April 1952, Sophiatown; m. 1st Olympia Molefe (divorced); three c.; m. 2nd Boitumelo Plaatje 1991; ed Naledi High School; microfilm machine operator, photographic printing machine operator 1976–78; mem. SASM 1973–76; mem. Black Peoples' Convention 1974, 1977; First Chair. Azanian People's Org. (AZAPO), Soweto Br. 1979–81; mem. Gen. and Allied Workers Union 1980–83; Sec. Transvaal Region, United Democratic Front 1983, Nat. Gen. Sec. 1983–91; mem. Nat. Exec. Cttee African Nat. Congress (ANC) 1991–; charged with treason and murder after detention in 1985, convicted at Delmas Treason Trial, sentenced to ten years' imprisonment after being held in custody for four years 1988, released 1989; Chair. ANC Nat. Elections Comm. 1992–94, ANC Alexandra Br. 1990; Vice-Chair. ANC PWV Region 1990–94; Premier NW

Prov. Govt 1994–2004; Sec. Nat. Organizing Comm. of ANC. *Address:* Private Bag X2018, Mmabatho 8681; African National Congress, PO Box 61884, Marshalltown 2107, South Africa.

MOLELEKI, Monyane, MA; Lesotho politician; *Minister of Natural Resources;* b. 5 Jan. 1951, Mohlaka-oa-Tuka, Maseru Dist; m.; one s. two d.; ed Nazareth Primary School, Christ the King High School, Moscow State Univ.; Head Teacher, St Thomas Secondary School 1972–73; reporter and sub-ed., The Echo newspaper 1973–74; news reader, reporter and sub-ed., Radio Lesotho 1974–75; Extension Educator, Media Section, Inst. of Extra Mural Studies (IEMS), Nat. Univ. of Lesotho 1983–87, Admin. 1985–86; Public Relations Man. Lesotho Highlands Devt Authority (LHDA) 1988–91; mem. Parl. for Senqunyane Constituency 1993, later for Machache No. 38 Constituency; Minister of Natural Resources 1993–94, 1998, of Information and Broadcasting 1996–98, of Foreign Affairs 2004–07, of Natural Resources 2007–; Co-founder and Pres. Matela Multi-Purpose Co-Operative 1973–75; mem. Maseru Beautification Cttee 1984–91, Matlama Football Club Cttee 1984–91 (fmr Sec.-Gen.). *Address:* Ministry of Natural Resources, POB 772, Maseru 100, Lesotho (office). *Telephone:* 22322334 (office). *Fax:* 22313602 (office). *Website:* www.lesotho.gov.ls/natural (office).

MOLIN, Yuri Nikolaevich; Russian chemist and physicist; *Advisor, Russian Academy of Sciences;* b. 3 Feb. 1934; s. of N. N. Molin and A. F. Kuramova; m. 1st N. G. Molina 1965; two d.; m. 2nd M. Iakovleva 2005; ed Moscow Inst. of Physics and Tech.; worked in USSR Acad. of Sciences Inst. of Chemical Physics 1957–59; various posts in USSR (now Russian) Acad. of Sciences Inst. of Chem. Kinetics and Combustion 1959–, Dir 1971–93, Head of Lab. 1993–, Advisor 2004–; teacher in Univ. of Novosibirsk 1966–, Prof. 1974–; mem. USSR (now Russian) Acad. of Sciences 1981; Fellow, Int. Electron Paramagnetic Resonance Soc. 1998; Mendeleev Lecture 1992; Lenin Prize 1986. *Publications:* Spin Exchange 1980, Spin Polarization and Magnetic Effects in Radical Reactions 1984, Infrared Photochemistry 1985. *Leisure interest:* mountain walking. *Address:* Institute of Chemical Kinetics and Combustion, Novosibirsk 630090, Russia (office). *Telephone:* (383) 333-16-07 (office); (383) 330-25-21 (home). *Fax:* (383) 330-73-50 (office). *E-mail:* molin@ns.kinetics.nsc.ru (office).

MOLINA, Alfred; British actor; b. 24 May 1953, London; m. Jill Gascoigne; ed Guildhall School of Music and Drama; on stage has appeared with RSC and at Nat. Theatre, Royal Court Theatre, Donmar Warehouse, Minskoff Theater, Broadway. *Films include:* Indiana Jones and the Raiders of the Lost Ark 1981, Anyone for Denis 1982, Number One 1984, Eleni 1985, Ladyhawke 1985, A Letter to Brezhnev 1985, Prick Up Your Ears 1987, Manifesto 1988, Not Without My Daughter 1991, American Friends 1991, Enchanted April 1991, When Pigs Fly 1993, The Trial 1993, American Friends 1993, White Fang 2: Myth of the White Wolf 1994, Maverick 1994, Hideaway 1995, The Perez Family 1995, A Night of Love 1995, The Steal, Species 1995, Before and After 1996, Dead Man 1996, Scorpion Spring 1996, Mojave Moon 1996, Anna Karenina 1997, The Odd Couple II 1997, Boogie Nights 1997, The Man Who Knew Too Little 1997, The Imposters 1998, Magnolia 1999, Dudley Do-Right 1999, The Trial 2000, Chocolat 2000, Texas Rangers 2001, Agatha Christie's Murder on the Orient Express 2001, Pete's Meteor 2002, Road to Perdition 2002, Frida 2003, My Life Without Me 2003, Coffee and Cigarettes 2003, Spider-Man II 2004, Steamboy 2004, Sian Ka'an (voice) 2005, The Da Vinci Code 2006, The Moon and the Stars 2006, As You Like It 2006, The Hoax 2006, Orchids 2006, The Moon and the Stars 2007, Silk 2007, The Ten Commandments 2007. *Television includes:* role of Blake in series El Cid, Year in Provence, Nervous Energy, Ladies Man (series). *Website:* www.alfred-molina.com (office).

MOLINA, Mario J., PhD; American/Mexican scientist and academic; *Professor of Chemistry, University of California, San Diego;* b. 19 March 1943, Mexico City; s. of Roberto Molina-Pasquel and Leonor Henriquez; m. Guadalupe Alvarez; one c.; ed Acad. Hispano Mexicana, Univ. Nacional Autónoma de Mexico (UNAM), Univ. of Freiburg and Univ. of Calif. at Berkeley; Asst Prof., UNAM 1967–68; Research Assoc., Univ. of California, Berkeley 1972–73; Research Assoc., Univ. of California, Irvine 1973–75, Asst Prof. 1975–79, Assoc. Prof. 1979–82; Sr Research Scientist, Jet Propulsion Lab., Calif. 1983–89; Prof., Dept of Earth, Atmospheric and Planetary Sciences and Dept of Chem., MIT 1989–97, Inst. Prof. 1997–2003; Prof., Dept of Chem. and Biochemistry, Univ. of California, San Diego 2003–; Pres. Centro Mario Molina; mem. NAS, Inst. of Medicine; 20 hon. degrees; Max Planck Research Award 1994–96, UNEP Ozone Award 1995, Nobel Prize for Chem. 1995, Volvo Environment Prize 2004; many other awards and distinctions. *Publications:* numerous book chapters and articles in scientific journals. *Leisure interests:* music, reading, tennis. *Address:* University of California, San Diego, UHA 3050E, 9500 Gilman Drive #0356, La Jolla, CA 92093-0356 (office); 3535 Lebon Drive, Apt 2210, San Diego, CA 92122, USA (home). *Telephone:* (858) 534-1696 (office). *Fax:* (858) 534-1697 (office). *E-mail:* mjmolina@ucsd.edu (office). *Website:* www-chem.ucsd.edu/research/profile.cfm?cid=C04871 (office); www.centromariomolina.org (office).

MOLINA BARRAZA, Col Arturo Armando; Salvadorean fmr head of state and army officer; b. 6 Aug. 1927, San Salvador; s. of Mariano Molina and Matilde Barraza de Molina; m. María Elena Contreras de Molina; four s. one d.; ed Escuela Militar, El Salvador, Escuela Superior de Guerra, Mexico, Escuela de Infanteria, Spain; Section and Co. Commdr, Escuela Militar; Artillery Garrison, Asst Dir Escuela de Armas, Section and Dept Chief, Staff HQ; Del. 6th Conf. of American Armed Forces, Peru 1965, 7th Conf. Buenos Aires; Gen. Co-ordinator, 2nd and 3rd Confs of Defence Council of Cen. American States; Dir Exec. Comm. for Shipping; Dir Nat. Cttee of Caritas, El Salvador; Pres. of El Salvador 1972–77.

MOLINA CONTRERAS, Gen. Jorge Alberto; Salvadorean army officer and politician; *Minister of National Defence;* Del. to UN Conf. to Review Progress made in Implementation of Programme of Action to Prevent, Combat and Eradicate the Illicit Trade in Small Arms and Light Weapons in All Its Aspects, New York 2006; fmr Jt Chief of Staff of the Armed Forces; Minister of Nat. Defence 2008–; rank of Brig.-Gen. 2005, Maj.-Gen. 2006, Gen. 2007. *Address:* Ministry of National Defence, Alameda Dr Manuel E. Araújo, Km 5, Carretera a Santa Tecla, San Salvador, El Salvador (office). *Telephone:* 2250-0100 (office); 2250-0325 (office). *E-mail:* fuerzaarmada@faes.gob.sv (office). *Website:* www.fuerzaarmada.gob.sv (office).

MOLINA SÁNCHEZ, César Antonio, LicenDer; Spanish writer and politician; *Minister of Culture;* b. 1952, La Coruña; fmr Prof. of Literary Theory and Criticism, Complutense Univ., Prof. of Humanities and Journalism, Univ. Carlos III; worked for Cambio 16 (magazine) and Diario 16 (newspaper) 1985–96, becoming Deputy Dir; Man. Dir Círculo de Bellas Artes 1996–2004; Dir Cervantes Inst. 2004–07; Minister of Culture 2007–; Deputy (Spanish Socialist Workers' Party–PSOE) for A Coruña 2008–. *Publications:* Épica 1974, Proyecto preliminar para una arqueología de campo (poetry) 1978, Últimas horas en Lisca Blanca 1979, La estancia saqueada (poetry) 1983, La revista Alfar y la prensa literaria de su época (1920-1930) 1984, Antología de la poesía Gallega contemporánea 1984, Gobierno de un jardín 1986, Derivas 1987, El fin de Finisterre 1988, Prensa literaria en Galicia (1809-1920) 1989, Prensa literaria en Galicia (1920-1960) 1989, Medio siglo de Prensa literaria española (1900-1950) 1990, Sobre el iberismo y otros escritos de literatura portuguesa 1990, Las ruinas del mundo 1991, El fin de Finisterre 1992, Para no ir a parte alguna 1994, Sobre la inutilidad de la poesía 1995, Nostalgia de la nada perdida; ensayo sobre narrativa contemporánea 1996, Vivir sin ser visto 2000, A fin de Fisterra (poetry) 2001, A Coruña, agua y luz 2001, Olas en la noche 2001, Regresar a donde no estuvimos 2003, Viaje a la Costa da morte 2003, En el mar de Ánforas 2005, En honor de Hermes 2005, Fuga del amor 2005, El rumor del tiempo 2006, Custode delle antiche forme (poetry) 2007, Eume 2007, Esperando a los años que no vuelven 2007. *Address:* Ministry of Culture, Plaza del Rey 1, 28071 Madrid, Spain (office). *Telephone:* (91) 7017000 (office). *Fax:* (91) 7017352 (office). *E-mail:* contacte@mcu.es (office). *Website:* www.mcu.es (office).

MOLISA, Sela; Ni-Vanuatu politician; *Minister of Finance;* b. 15 Dec. 1950, Santo; s. of Mandei Rongtuhun and Ruth Rongtuhun; two s. one d.; ed Onesua High School, Malaba Coll., Efate, Univ. of the S Pacific, Fiji, Fifi School of Medicine; banker 1974–77; Gen. Man. Co-operative Fed. 1977–81; mem. Parl. 1982–; Minister of Internal Affairs 1983, of Foreign Affairs 1983–87, of Finance 1987–91, 2002–04 (resgnd), 2008–, of Trade, Commerce and Industry 1996, of Finance and Econ. Man. 1998–99, of Lands and Natural Resources 2001–02; apptd Govt Special Rep. to negotiate with rebels during attempted secession of Santo from Vanuatu 1980; involved in design and implementation of Vanuatu Comprehensive Reform Programme 1997–; mem. Vanua'aku Pati. *Leisure interests:* reading, swimming, listening to music, watching sports. *Address:* Ministry of Finance, PMB 058, Port Vila (office); POB 252, Port Vila, Vanuatu (home). *Telephone:* 23032 (office); 23081 (home). *Fax:* 27937 (office); 23081 (home).

MÖLK, Ulrich, DPhil; German academic; *Professor of Romance Literature, Akademie der Wissenschaften, University of Göttingen;* b. 29 March 1937, Hamburg; s. of Heinrich Mölk and Berta Mölk; m. Renate Mölk 1962; ed Univs of Hamburg and Heidelberg; Prof. of Romance Literature, Univ. of Giessen 1967; Prof. of Romance Literature, Akad. der Wissenschaften, Univ. of Göttingen 1974–, Dir Inst. für Lateinische und Romanische Philologie des Mittelalters 1974–2005; mem. Acad. of Göttingen, Vice-Pres. 1990–92, Pres. 1992–94. *Publications:* Guiraut Riquier, Las cansos 1962, Trobar clus 1968, Répertoire métrique de la poésie lyrique française 1972, Trotzki, Literaturkritik 1973, Trobadorlyrik 1982, Flaubert, Une Nuit de Don Juan, Edition 1984, Vita und Kult des hl. Metro von Verona 1987, Lohier et Malart 1988, Romanische Frauenlieder 1989, Die europäische Bedeutungsgeschichte von 'Motiv' 1992, Julien Sorel vor dem Schwurgericht 1994, Impressionistischer Stil 1995, Literatur und Recht 1996, Europäische Jahrhundertwende 1999, Albéric: le poème d'Alexandre 2000, Das älteste französische Kreuzlied 2001, Prousts Venedig 2002, Estetismo e decadentismo 2004. *Address:* Akademie der Wissenschaften, Theaterstrasse 7, 37073 Göttingen (office); Höltystr. 7, 37085 Göttingen, Germany (home). *Telephone:* (551) 395331 (office). *Fax:* (551) 395365 (office). *E-mail:* jhwroma@gwdg.de (office). *Website:* www.uni-goettingen.de/de/sh/1397 (office).

MOLL, Kurt; German singer (bass); b. 11 April 1938, Buir; m. Ursula Pade 1968; one s. two d.; ed Staatliche Hochschule für Musik, Cologne; operatic debut in Cologne; subsequently sang operatic roles at Aachen, Mainz, Wuppertal, Hamburg; appeared Bayreuth 1968, Salzburg 1970, La Scala, Milan 1972, Covent Garden, London 1975, Metropolitan Opera, New York 1978; Prof. Staatliche Hochschule für Musik, Cologne 1991–; mem. Hamburg, Bavarian and Vienna State Operas. *Address:* Voigtelstr. 22, 50933 Cologne, Germany.

MÖLLER, Erwin; German business executive; b. 23 Jan. 1939; m.; ed Tech. Univ. of Darmstadt; Chair. Supervisory Bd Metaleurop SA, Foutenay-sous-Bois, VTG Vereinigte Tanklager und Transportmittel GmbH, Hamburg; Chair. Exec. Bd Preussag AG; mem. Supervisory Bd Hannoversche Lebensversicherung AG, Hannover, Kabelmetal Electro GmbH, Hannover, Salzgitter Stahl GmbH, Düsseldorf; mem. Governing Council DSL Bank, Bonn; Chair. Bd and Dir Amalgamated Metal Corp. PLC, London; Hon. Consul Grand-Duchy of Luxembourg.

MOLLER, Gordon Desmond, ONZM, DipArch, FNZIA, FRSA; New Zealand architect; *Chairman, Moller Architects;* b. 26 July 1940, Hastings; s. of Oscar

Carl Moller and Winifred Daisy Moller; m. Sylvia Anne Liebezeit 1962; one s. two d.; ed Wellington Coll., Hutt Valley High School, Univ. of Auckland; Dir Craig Craig Moller architectural practice 1969–2002, Chair. Moller Architects 2003–; Chair. Arts Marketing Bd, Aotearoa 1994, 1995, Site Safe NZ 2002, 2003, Construction Information Ltd 2006, Greenbuild 2007; Pres. Wellington Architectural Centre 1972, 1973; Professorial Teaching Fellow, Victoria Univ. School of Architecture 1990, 1991; Pres. NZ Inst. of Architects 2003–06; Co-Convenor Auckland City Urban Design Panel 2003–; mem. Design Consortium Wellington Civic Centre 1992, 1998; Ed. New Zealand Architects 1976–83; Trustee, Wellington City Gallery Foundation 1998–2006; mem. NZ Registered Architects Bd 2006–08; Dir Auckland Theatre Co. 2006–; Trustee NZ Architectural Publications Trust 2003–; Chair. Judging Panel NZ Govt Starter Home Design Competition 2008/09; Hon. Mem. Royal Australian Inst. of Architects; Hon. DLitt (Victoria Univ. of Wellington) 2006; NZ Inst. of Architects Gold Medal 2006, 50 design awards 1970–2007. *Designs include:* School of Architecture, Wellington 1994, Sky Tower, Auckland 1994–97, numerous houses, Macau Tower and Entertainment Centre, Macau 1999–2001, Point Apartments, Auckland 2000, New Galleries, Te Papa Wellington 2001, Viaduct Point Apartments, Auckland 2002, Sky City Conf. Centre 2002, Sky City Grand Hotel 2003, 67-storey Elliott Tower Auckland 2006, new Houses of Parliament, Muscat, Oman 2008–12, 30-storey commercial office building, Auckland 2008–11. *Leisure interests:* photography, music, motoring, landscape gardening, design, travel, visual and performing arts. *Address:* 121 Customs Street West, Auckland (home); Level 13, West Plaza, 3 Albert Street, Auckland, New Zealand (office). *Telephone:* (9) 357-0686 (office); (9) 357-1140 (office). *Fax:* (9) 357-0689 (office). *E-mail:* gordon@mollerarchitects.com (office). *Website:* www.mollerarchitects.com (office).

MØLLER, Mærsk Mc-Kinney; Danish shipping industry executive; *Senior Partner, A.P. Møller-Mærsk A/S;* b. 13 July 1913, Copenhagen; s. of Arnold Peter Møller and Chastine Estelle Møller (née Mc-Kinney); m. Emma Mc-Kinney Møller (née Neergaard Rasmussen) 1940 (died 2005); three d.; Pnr, A. P. Møller, Copenhagen 1940–65, Sr Pnr 1965–; Chair. A/S Dampskibsselskabet Svendborg 1965–2003, Dampskibsselskabet af 1912 A/S 1965–2003, A.P. Møller-Mærsk A/S 2003, Odense Steel Shipyard Ltd; mem. Int. Council Morgan Guaranty Trust Co., New York 1967–84; mem. Bd of Dirs IBM Corpn, USA 1970–84 (Advisory Bd 1984–93), Mærsk Olie og Gas A/S; Chair. The A. P. Møller and Chastine Mc-Kinney Møller Foundation; Hon. mem. Baltic Exchange, London 1991; Danish Order of the Elephant 2000; Grand Cross, Order of Dannebrog; Hon. KBE 1990; Peace and Commerce Medal, US Dept of Commerce 1991. *Address:* A.P. Møller-Mærsk A/S, Esplanaden 50, 1098 Copenhagen K, Denmark (office). *Telephone:* 33-63-33-63 (office). *Fax:* 33-63-41-08 (office). *Website:* www.apmoller.com (office).

MØLLER, Per Stig, MA, PhD; Danish politician; *Minister for Foreign Affairs;* b. 1942; s. of Poul Møller and Lis Møller; ed Univ. of Copenhagen; Lecturer, Sorbonne Univ., Paris 1974–76; Cultural Ed. Radio Denmark 1973–74, Deputy Head, Culture and Soc. Dept 1976–79, Chief of Programmes 1979–84; Vice-Chair. Radio Council 1985–86, Chair. 1986–87; Commentator, Berlingske Tidende 1984–2001; Chair. Popular Educ. Asscn (FOF) 1983–89; mem. Parl. (Danish Conservative Party) 1984–, mem. Exec. Cttee 1985–89, 1993–98, Chair. 1997–98, Parl. Leader 1997–98, Foreign Policy Spokesman 1998–2001; mem. Council of Europe 1987–90, 1994–97, 1998–2001; Minister for the Environment 1990–93; Chair. Security Policy Cttee 1994–96, mem. Foreign Policy Cttee 1994–2001; Minister for Foreign Affairs 2001–; Nat. Chair. Union of Conservative Gymnasium Students 1960–61, Vice-Chair. Conservative Students' Asscn 1961–62, Pres. Students' Union; Chevalier, Ordre Nat. du Lion 1975, Chevalier des Arts et des Lettres 1986, Grosskreuz des Verdienstordens der Bundesrepublik Deutschland 2002, Commdr of the first class of the Order of the Dannebrog 2002, Commdr, Ordre Nat. du Benin 2003, Grand-Croix de l'Ordre de la Couronne de Chêne 2003, Order of Stara Planina (1st Class) 2006, Commdr Grand Cross, Royal Order of the Polar Star, Sweden 2007, Grand Cross of the Order of the South Cross, Brazil 2007, Grand Cross, Commdr of the Order for Merits to Lithuania 2007; Sound and Environment Award 1993, Georg Brandes Award 1996, Einer Hansen Research Fund Award 1997, G-1930s Politician of the Year 1997, Cultural Award of the Popular Educ. Asscn 1998, Raoul Wallenberg Medal 1998, Kaj Munk Award 2001, Rosenkjaer Award 2001, Robert Schumann Medal 2003, Nersornaat Medal of Merit in Gold 2005. *Publications include:* La Critique dramatique et littéraire de Malte-Brun 1971, Erotismen 1973, København-Paris (trans.) 1973, På Sporet af det forsvundne Menneske 1976, Livet I Gøgereden 1978, Fra Tid til Anden 1979, Tro, Håb og Faellesskab 1980, Midt I Redeligheden 1981, Orwells Håb og Frygt 1983, Nat uden Daggry 1985, Mulighedernes Samfund 1985, Stemmer fra Øst 1987, Historien om Estland, Letland og Litauen 1990, Kurs mod Katastrofer? 1993, Miljøproblemer 1995, Den naturlige Orden: Tolv år der flyttede Verden 1996, Spor: Udvalgte Skrifter om det åbne Samfund og dets Vaerdier 1997, Magt og Afmagt 1999, Munk 2000, Mere Munk 2003. *Address:* Ministry of Foreign Affairs, Asiatisk Plads 2, 1448 Copenhagen K, Denmark (office). *Telephone:* 33-92-00-00 (office). *Fax:* 32-54-05-33 (office). *E-mail:* um@um.dk (office). *Website:* www.um.dk (office).

MØLLER, Stig, LLM; Danish university administrator; *Director of Administration, University of Aarhus;* b. 29 Aug. 1939; ed Univ. of Copenhagen; Capt. of the Reserve 1963; Sec. Ministry of the Interior 1966–71, Ministry of Pollution Reduction 1971–73; Tutor in Admin. Law, Univ. of Copenhagen 1968–71; Teacher of Public Law, School of Admin 1968–79; Acting Head of Office, Dept of the Environment 1974–76, Head of Office 1976–79; Dir of Admin, Univ. of Aarhus 1979–; mem. Man. Group for Co-operation of Nordic Univ. Dirs of Admin (Chair. 1982–88) 1979–2000; mem. Bd of Dirs Ejendomsselskab AS, Aarhus Univ. Research Foundation. *Address:* University of Aarhus, Nordre Ringgade 1, 8000 Århus C, Denmark (office). *Telephone:* (89) 42-11-11 (office). *Fax:* (86) 19-70-29 (office). *E-mail:* au@au.dk (office). *Website:* www.au.dk/en/direktor (office).

MOLLISON, Patrick Loudon, CBE, MD, FRCP, FRCOG, FRCPath, FRS; British haematologist, medical writer and academic; *Professor Emeritus of Haematology, University of London;* b. 17 March 1914, London; s. of William M. Mollison and Beatrice M. Walker; m. 1st Margaret D. Peirce 1940 (divorced 1964); three s.; m. 2nd Jennifer A. Jones 1973; ed Univ. of Cambridge and St Thomas's Hosp. Medical School, London; worked in London Blood Transfusion Service for MRC 1939–43, then in RAMC; Dir, MRC Blood Transfusion Research Unit (later Experimental Haematology Unit) at Post grad. Medical School; in charge of Haematology Dept, St Mary's Hosp., London 1960–79; Prof. of Haematology, Univ. of London 1962–79, Prof. Emer.; Hon. Consultant Immunohaematologist, N London Blood Transfusion Centre 1983–2000; several awards and honours including Landsteiner Award, American Asscn of Blood Banks 1960, Presidential Award, Int. Soc. of Blood Transfusion 2000. *Publications:* Blood Transfusion in Clinical Medicine 1951; some 200 papers in scientific journals. *Leisure interests:* opera, gardening. *Address:* 60 King Henry's Road, London, NW3 3RR, England (home). *Telephone:* (20) 7722-1947 (home).

MOLLOY, Patrick; Irish business executive; *Chairman, CRH plc;* b. 4 Jan. 1938; m. Ann Lynch; three s. two d.; ed Trinity Coll. Dublin, Harvard Business School, USA; Asst Gen. Man. Bank of Ireland 1975–78, Gen. Man. Area East 1978–83, Man. Dir 1983–91, Group CEO 1991–98; apptd Dir (non-exec.) CRH plc 1997, Chair. 2000–; Chair. Blackrock Clinic, Enterprise Ireland; Dir Waterford Wedgwood plc. *Leisure interests:* fishing, shooting. *Address:* CRH plc, Belgard Castle, Clondalkin, Dublin 22, Ireland. *Telephone:* (1) 4041000 (office). *Fax:* (1) 4041007 (office). *Website:* www.crh.com (office).

MOLLOY, Robert M., BComm; Irish politician (retd); b. 6 July 1936, Salthill, Galway; s. of Michael Edward Molloy and Rita (Stanley) Molloy; m. Phyllis Barry 1972; two s. two d.; ed St Ignatius Coll., Univ. Coll., Galway; became mem. Dáil Éireann (House of Reps) 1965, retd 2002, House Cttee of Public Accounts 1965–69, House Cttee on Constitution 1967; Parl. Sec. to Minister for Educ. 1969–70; Minister for Local Govt 1970–73, for Defence 1977–79, of Energy 1989–92, of State to the Govt 1997–2002, and fmrly at the Dept of the Environment and Local Govt with special responsibility for Housing and Urban Renewal; mem. Galway Co. Council 1967–70, 1974–77, 1985–91, Galway Borough Council 1967–70, 1985–91; Mayor of Galway 1968–69; Chair., Galway Harbour Bd 1974–77, 1985–91, Lough Corril Navigation Trustees 1985–91; Chair., House Cttee on Bldg Land; mem., House Cttee on State-Sponsored Bodies 1982–87, 1994–, on the Irish Language 1992–, on Enterprise and Econ. Strategy 1994–; mem. Council of Europe 1996–, Governing Body, Univ. Coll. Galway 1977, Exec. Inter-Parl. Asscn; Dir, Salthill Failte Ltd 1985–91, Galway Harbour Co. 2003–, Bord Iascaigh Mhara (Irish Sea Fisheries Board) 2007–. *Leisure interests:* swimming, sailing, golf. *Address:* St Mary's, Rockbarton, Salthill, Galway, Ireland (home). *Telephone:* (91) 521765 (home).

MOLNÁR, Károly, PhD, DSc; Hungarian academic and politician; *Minister without Portfolio responsible for Science, Research and Innovation;* ed Tech. Univ. of Budapest; Asst, Dept of Chemical and Food Eng, Tech. Univ. of Budapest 1967–71, Sr Asst 1971–78, Assoc. Prof. 1978–91, Prof. 1991–, Head of Dept of Process Eng 1988–2008, Vice-Dean Faculty of Mechanical Eng 1992–94, Dean 1994–2001, Vice-Rector for Educ. 2000–04, Rector 2004–08; Minister without Portfolio responsible for Science, Research and Innovation 2008–; Chair. Bd of Dirs Tisza Chemical Group PLC 1994–96, Deputy Chair. 1996–98; Chair. Hungarian Rectors Conf. 2006–08; Chair. Bd of Dirs Paks Nuclear Power Plant Ltd 2002–08; Chair. Complex Cttee on Chemical and Processing Eng, Hungarian Acad. of Sciences, Technological Scientific Council and Heat and Mass Transfer Cttee, Hungarian Scientific Soc. of Energy Econs; mem. European Fed. of Chemical Eng, Int. Solar Energy Soc.; Commdr, Order of Merit 2005; János András Segner Award 1986, Gold Medal of Excellent Inventor 1986, 1991, Géza Szikla Award 1992, Lóránd Eötvös Award 1996, Pro Facultate Award 2002, Pro Universitate et Scientia Award 2002, Int. Socrates Award 2006, Széchenyi Award 2007, Arnold Ipolyi Award, Imre Szabó Award. *Address:* c/o Office of the Prime Minister, 1055 Budapest, Kossuth Lajos tér 1–3, Hungary (office). *Telephone:* (1) 441-4000 (office). *Fax:* (1) 268-3050 (office). *E-mail:* webmaster@meh.hu (office). *Website:* www.meh.hu (office).

MOLNÁR, Lúdovít, Dr rer. nat, DSc; Slovak computer scientist and university administrator; *Rector, Slovak University of Technology;* b. 11 Oct. 1940, Komjatice Dist; m.; three c.; ed Slovak Univ. of Tech., Bratislava; various teaching positions, Slovak Univ. of Tech., Bratislava 1962–, currently Rector; research periods in UK 1969–70, 1991, USSR 1974, Italy 1978, Cyprus 1983. *Publications include:* numerous computer tech. manuals and textbooks. *Leisure interest:* literature. *Address:* Office of the Rector, Slovak University of Technology, Vazovova 5, 812 43 Bratislava 16, Slovakia (office). *Telephone:* (2) 52497196 (office). *Fax:* (2) 57294333 (office). *E-mail:* molnar@rstu.vm.stuba.sk (office). *Website:* www.stuba.sk (office).

MOLONEY, Thomas Walter, MA, MBA, MPH; American academic, organization official and consultant; b. 8 Feb. 1946, New York; s. of Thomas Walter Moloney and Anne Heney; ed Colgate Univ., Columbia Univ.; Program Dir Nat. Center for the Deaf-Blind, New York 1971–72; Special Asst to Dir and Dean, Cornell Univ. Medical Center 1973–74; Asst Vice-Pres. Robert Wood John Foundation 1975–80; Visiting Lecturer, Princeton Univ. 1975–80; Sr Vice-Pres., The Commonwealth Fund, New York 1980–92; Dir of Public Policy and Health Programmes, Inst. for the Future 1992–99; Man. Pnr Futures Inc. (consulting firm) 1997–; mem. Bd Dirs New England Medical Center, Boston 1982–89; mem. Bd Grantmakers in Health, New York 1984–, Chair. 1984–88;

Policy Scholar Eisenhower Center, Columbia Univ., New York 1992–, Inst. of Health Policy Studies, Univ. of California, San Francisco 1992–; mem. Nat. Bd of Medical Examiners 1986–90, Health Advisory Cttee, Gen. Accounting Office, Washington, DC 1987–; Bd, Foundation Health Services Research, Washington, DC 1989 and other bds; Fellow, American Acad. of Arts and Sciences; mem. Inst. of Medicine, NAS. *Publications:* Ed. New Approaches to the Medicaid Crisis 1983; numerous articles. *Address:* Futures Inc., Floor 8, 1170 North Ocean Boulevard, Palm Beach, FL 33480 (office); 72 Norwood Avenue, Upper Montclair, NJ 07043, USA.

MOLONEY, Tom; British publishing executive; b. 1959; joined Emap PLC (radio and magazines outfit) 1981, apptd Group Man. Dir Emap Metro and Elan 1989, Chief Exec. Consumer Magazines UK 1995–99, has overseen launch of magazines Heat, More, Q and Empire, mem. Exec. Bd 1995–2007, COO then Pres. and CEO Emap USA 1999–2001, Group COO 2001–03, CEO 2003–07.

MOLSON, Eric H., AB; Canadian brewing industry executive; *Chairman, Molson Coors Brewing Company;* b. 16 Sept. 1937, Montreal, PQ; s. of Thomas H. P. Molson and Celia F. Cantlie; m. Jane Mitchell 1966; three c.; ed Selwyn House School, Montreal, Bishop's Coll. School, Lennoxville, Le Rosey, Switzerland, Princeton and McGill Univs and US Brewers' Acad. New York; served as apprentice brewer with Molson Breweries of Canada Ltd, rising through various appointments to Pres., Chair. Molson Inc. (now Molson Coors Brewing Co.) 1988–. *Address:* Molson Coors Brewing Co., 1555 Notre Dame Street East, Montreal, PQ H2L 2R5, Canada (office). *Telephone:* (514) 597-1786 (office). *Fax:* (514) 598-6866 (office). *Website:* www.molson.com (office).

MOLTERER, Wilhelm, MSc; Austrian politician; b. 14 May 1955, Steyr; s. of Johann Kletzmayr and Anna Kletzmayr, Josef Molterer and Cäcilia Molterer (adoptive parents); m. Brigitte Molterer; two c.; ed Fed. Agricultural Coll., St Florian and Johannes Kepler Univ., Linz; Research Asst Dept of Agric. Policy, Univ. of Linz 1979–81; Head Econ. Policy Div., Austrian Farmers Fed. 1981–84, Dir 1989–93; Municipal Councillor, Sierning 1985–87; Sec. Office of Fed. Minister Dr. Josef Riegler 1987–89; mem. Nat. Council 1990–94; Sec. –Gen. Austria People's Party (ÕAP) 1993–94, Parl. Group Leader 2003–07, Chair. 2007–08; Fed. Minister of Agric. and Forestry 1994–2003 (and Environment and Water Man. 2000–03), of Finance 2007–08, Vice-Chancellor of Austria 2007–08. *Address:* Austrian People's Party, Lichtenfelsgasse 7, 1010 Vienna, Austria (office). *Telephone:* (1) 401-26-0 (office). *Fax:* (1) 401-26-10-9 (office). *E-mail:* email@oevp.at (office). *Website:* www.oevp.at (office).

MOLTMANN, Jürgen, DTheol; German theologian and academic; *Professor and Rector, Wuppertal Church University;* b. 8 April 1926, Hamburg; m. Dr. Elisabeth Moltmann-Wendel; four d.; POW during Second World War; with Dept of Theology, Univ. of Göttingen 1948–52, Prof. of Theology 1957–; fmr Minister, Bremen; Prof. and Rector Wuppertal Church Univ. 1958–; co-ed. Deutsch-Polnsiche Hefte 1959–68; Visiting Prof. in USA 1967–68; Dir CONCILIUM 1979–94; Italian Prize of Literature, Isle of Elba 1971, Amos Comenius Medal, Bethlehem, Pa 1992, Ernst Bloch Prize of the City of Ludwigshafen 1995, Grawemeyer Award on Religion, Louisville, Ky 2000 Dr hc (Duke Univ.), (Bethlehem Theological Seminary), (Kalamazoo Coll.), (Raday Kolleg, Budapest), (St Andrews Univ.), (Emory Univ.), (Univ. of Leuven), (Univ. of Iasi), (Nottingham Univ.), (Managua, Nicaragua). *Publications:* Christliche Petzel und das Calvinismus in Bremen 1958, Prädestination und Perseveranz 1961, Anfänge Dialektische Theologie 1963, Theologie der Hoffnung (Theology of Hope) (Isle of Elba Literary Prize) 1964, Mensch 1971, Der gekreuzigte Gott (The Crucified God) 1972, Der Sprache der Befreiung 1972, Das Experiment Hoffnung 1974, Kirche in der Kraft des Geistes 1975, Zukunft der Schöpfung 1977, Trinität und Reich Gottes 1980, Gott in der Schöpfung (God in Creation) 1985, Das Weg Jesu Christi (The Way of Jesus Christ) 1989, Der Geist des Lebens (The Spirit of Life) 1991, Das Kommen Gottes (The Coming of God) (Grawemeyer Religion Award) 1995, Experiences in Theology 1999, Science and Wisdom 2002, In the End – the Beginning: The Life of Hope 2004. *Address:* Liebermeister Strasse 12, 72076 Tübingen, Germany.

MOLYNEAUX OF KILLEAD, Baron (Life Peer), cr. 1997, of Killead in the County of Antrim; **James Henry Molyneaux,** KBE, PC; British politician; b. 27 Aug. 1920, Killead, Co. Antrim; s. of William Molyneaux and Sarah Gilmore; ed Aldergrove School, Co. Antrim; served in RAF 1941–46; mem. Antrim Co. Council 1964–73; Vice-Chair. Eastern Special Care Hosp. Man. Cttee 1966–73; Chair. Antrim Branch NI Asscn for Mental Health 1967–70; Hon. Sec. S Antrim Unionist Asscn 1964–70; MP for Antrim South 1970–83, for Lagan Valley 1983–97; Vice-Pres. Ulster Unionist Council 1974; Leader Ulster Unionist Party, House of Commons 1974–97; Leader Ulster Unionist Party 1979–95; mem. NI Ass. 1982–86; fmr JP (resgnd 1987); Deputy Grand Master of Orange Order and Hon. Past Grand Master of Canada; Sovereign Grand Master, Commonwealth Royal Black Inst. 1971–98. *Leisure interests:* music, gardening. *Address:* House of Lords, Westminster, London, SW1A 0PW (office); Aldergrove, Crumlin, BT29 4AR, Co. Antrim, Northern Ireland. *Telephone:* (28) 9442-2545 (Crumlin).

MOLYVIATIS, Petros; Greek diplomatist and politician; b. 12 June 1928, Chios; m. Niovi Christaki; one d. one s.; ed Univ. of Athens; Gen. Sec. Presidency of the Repub. 1980–85, 1990–95, fmr Diplomatic Adviser to the Pres.; mem. Parl. 1996–, fmr mem. Standing Cttees on Defence, Foreign Affairs, European Affairs; fmr mem. Greek dels to UN, NATO; fmr Amb.; Minister of Foreign Affairs 2004–06. *Address:* c/o Ministry of Foreign Affairs, Odos Akadimias 1, 106 71 Athens, Greece (office).

MOMPER, Walter; German politician; *President of Lower House, Berlin Chamber of Deputies;* b. 21 Feb. 1945, Sulingen; mem. Berlin Chamber of Deputies 1975–95, 1999–; party whip, SPD, Berlin 1985–89, Chair. –1992; Gov. Mayor of Berlin 1989–91; Vice-Pres. Lower House, Berlin 1999–2001, Pres. 2001–. *Address:* Abgeordnetenhauses, Seydelstrasse 28, 10117 Berlin, Germany. *Telephone:* 20623698.

MONAGENG, Sanji Mmasenono, LLB; Botswana judge; *Judge, Pre-Trial Division, International Criminal Court;* b. 9 Aug. 1950, Serowe; ed Univ. of Botswana, Court Adm. Course, RIPA International, London, UK, Int. Criminal Law Course, Grotius Centre for Int. Law Studies, Leiden Univ., The Hague, Netherlands; magistrate 1987–97; CEO and Exec. Sec. Law Soc. of Botswana 1997–2006; Judge of High Court of Repub. of the Gambia, under Commonwealth Fund for Tech. Cooperation Programme 2006–08; Judge of High Court of Kingdom of Swaziland 2008–; mem. and Commr African Comm. on Human and Peoples' Rights 2003–, Chair. 2007–; Judge, Pre-Trial Div., ICC, The Hague, Netherlands 2009–; secondment as Deputy Chief Adjudication Officer to UN Observer Mission to S Africa, Johannesburg March–May 1994, to Law Soc. of Zimbabwe Feb.–March 199, to Law Soc. of England and Wales, London, UK Jan.–March 2005; Residency at Brandies Univ., Boston, USA Sept. 2005; Chair. Ethics, Law and Human Rights sector of Nat. AIDS Council in Botswana; sits on numerous bds, including Nat. Broadcasting Bd of Botswana, Open Soc. Initiative of Southern Africa, Human Rights Trust of Southern Africa; Co-founder Transparency International (Botswana Chapter), Dirs Inst. of Botswana; mem. Int. Bar Asscn, Int. Soc. for the Reform of Criminal Law, Int. Asscn of Women Judges, Emang Basadi Women's Org., Women in Law and Devt in Africa (WILDAF), Media Inst. of Southern Africa (Botswana Chapter); Trustee, Southern Africa Litigation Centre. *Address:* International Criminal Court, PO Box 19519, 2500 CM The Hague, The Netherlands (office). *Telephone:* (70) 515-85-15 (office). *Fax:* (70) 515-85-55 (office). *E-mail:* otp.informationdesk@icc-cpi.int (office). *Website:* www.icc-cpi.int (office).

MONBERG, Torben Axel, DPhil; Danish anthropologist; b. 25 July 1929, Copenhagen; s. of Axel S. S. Monberg and Elna Elsa Johansson; m. 1st Bodil B. Melbye (died 1976); m. 2nd Hanne Birthe (née Schou) 1985; one s. two d.; ed Univ. of Copenhagen; Asst Prof. of Cultural Sociology, Univ. of Copenhagen 1965–69, Prof. 1969–75; Chief Curator Nat. Museum of Denmark 1975–80; Prof., Univ. of Hawaii 1972; field work on Rennell and Bellona Islands 1958–84, on Tikopia (with Raymond Firth) 1966; mem. Danish Acad. of Sciences; Hon. Chief, Bellona Island, Solomon Islands 1984; Hon. Fellow Asscn for Social Anthropology in Oceania. *Publications:* From the Two Canoes, Oral Traditions of Rennell and Bellona Islands (with Samuel H. Elbert) 1965, The Religion of Bellona Island 1966, Mobile in the Trade Wind 1976, Mungiki, Kulturen og dens religion på øen Bellona i Stillehavet 1979, Bellona Island: Beliefs and Ritual Practices 1991; scientific and popular papers. *Address:* Veksebovej 10, 3480 Fredensborg, Denmark. *Telephone:* 42-28-10-31. *Fax:* 42-28-45-31.

MONCADA, Salvador Enrique, MD, PhD, DSc, FRS, FRCP; British academic, physician and scientist; *Director, Wolfson Institute for Biomedical Research, University College London;* b. 3 Dec. 1944, Tegucigalpa, Honduras; s. of Salvador Moncada and Jenny Seidner; m. 1st 1966; one s. (deceased) one d.; m. 2nd HRH Princess Esmeralda of Belgium 1998; one s. one d.; ed Univ. of El Salvador; Assoc. Prof. of Pharmacology and Physiology, Univ. of Honduras 1974–75; Section Leader, Wellcome Research Laboratories, Beckenham, Kent 1975–77, Head of Prostaglandin Research 1977–84, Dir of Therapeutic Research 1984–86, Dir of Research 1986–95; Dir Wolfson Inst. for Biomedical Research, Univ. Coll. London 1996–; Foreign mem. NAS 1994; Hon. mem. Asscn of Physicians of GB and Ireland 1997, American Soc. of Hematology 1999; Hon. DMed (Universidad Complutense de Madrid) 1986, (Antwerp) 1997, Academico de Honor de la Real Academia Nacional de Medicina 1993; Hon. DSc (Sussex) 1994, (Mount Sinai School of Medicine New York), (Nottingham) 1995, (Univ. Pierre and Marie Curie, Paris) 1997, (Edin.) 2000; Prince of Asturias Prize for Science and Tech. 1990, Amsterdam Prize for Medicine 1992, First Roussel Uclaf Prize, Royal Medal 1994, Louis and Artur Lucian Award 1997, Galen Medal in Therapeutics, Dale Medal, Gold Medal of the Spanish Soc. of Cardiology 1999, Gold Medal of the Royal Soc. of Medicine 2000. *Publications:* Nitric Oxide from L-Arginine: A Bioregulatory System (co-ed.) 1990, The Biology of Nitric Oxide (Vols 1–7) 1992–2000. *Leisure interests:* theatre, literature, music, walking, diving. *Address:* The Wolfson Institute for Biomedical Research, University College London, Gower Street, London, WC1E 6BT, England (office). *Telephone:* (20) 7679-6666 (office). *Fax:* (20) 7209-0470 (office). *E-mail:* s.moncada@ucl.ac.uk (office). *Website:* www.ucl.ac.uk/wibr (office).

MONCAYO GALLEGOS, Gen. Paco, MSc, PhD; Ecuadorean army officer (retd) and politician; *Mayor of Quito;* b. 1941; m. Marta de Moncayo; four c.; fmr Pres. of Rumiñahui Bank; fmr C-in-C of Armed Forces; fmr Head of the Ministry of Agric.; fmr Nat. Deputy; Mayor of Quito 2000–; currently Co-Pres. United Cities and Local Govts; mem. Acad. of Ecuadorian History; lectures in Geopolitics and Int. Law at Ecuador Cen. Univ. University; Simón Bolívar Medal, UNESCO 2004. *Address:* Alcaldía de Quito, Quito, Ecuador (office); c/o United Cities and Local Governments, Carrer Avinyó, 15, 08002 Barcelona, Spain. *E-mail:* info@cities-localgovernments.org. *Website:* www.cities-localgovernments.org.

MONDALE, Walter Frederick, LLB; American fmr politician and lawyer; *Senior Counsel, Dorsey and Whitney LLP;* b. 5 Jan. 1928, Ceylon, Minn.; s. of Rev. and Mrs Theodore Sigvaard Mondale; m. Joan Adams 1955; two s. one d.; ed Minnesota public schools, Macalester Coll., Univ. of Minnesota and Univ. of Minnesota Law School; admitted to Minn. Bar 1956, pvt. practice 1956–60; Attorney-Gen., Minn. 1960–64; US Senator from Minnesota 1964–77; Vice-Pres. of the US 1977–81; mem. Nat. Security Council 1977–81; fmr Regent Smithsonian Inst.; Counsel with firm Winston and Strawn 1981–87; Pnr,

Dorsey and Whitney LLP (law firm) 1987–93, now Sr Counsel and Pnr International/Corporate practice group; Amb. to Japan 1993–96; fmr mem. Bd Control Data, Columbia Pictures; Democrat-Farm Labor Party; Democratic Cand. for Presidency 1984. *Publication:* The Accountability of Power: Towards a Responsible Presidency 1975. *Leisure interest:* fishing. *Address:* Dorsey and Whitney LLP, Suite 1500, 50 South Sixth Street, Minneapolis, MN 55402-1498, USA (office). *Telephone:* (612) 340-6307 (office). *Fax:* (952) 516-5673 (office). *E-mail:* mondale.walter@dorsey.com (office). *Website:* www.dorsey.com (office).

MONEO, José Rafael, DArch; Spanish architect and academic; *Josep Lluis Sert Professor of Architecture, Harvard University;* b. 9 May 1937, Tudela, Navarra; s. of Rafael Moneo and Teresa Vallés; m. Belén Feduchi 1963; three d.; ed Madrid Univ. School of Architecture; Fellow, Acad. in Rome 1963–65; Asst Prof. Madrid School of Architecture 1966–70; Prof. Barcelona School of Architecture 1970–80; Visiting Fellow, Inst. for Architecture and Urban Studies, Cooper Union School of Architecture New York 1976–77; Chair. Dept of Architecture Harvard Univ. Grad. School of Design 1985–90, Josep Lluís Sert Prof. 1992–; mem. American Acad. of Arts and Sciences, Accad. di San Luca di Roma, Real Academia de Bellas Artes de San Fernando de España; Hon. Fellow, American Inst. of Architects; Dr hc (Leuven) 1993; Premio di Roma 1962; Gold Medal for Achievement in Fine Arts, Govt of Spain 1992; Brunner Memorial Prize, American Acad. of Arts and Letters; Schock Prize in the Visual Arts 1993, Pritzker Award 1996, Int. Union of Architects Gold Medal 1996, Antonio Feltrinelli Prize 1998, RIBA Gold Medal 2003 and other distinctions. *Work includes:* Bankinter Bank, Madrid, Nat. Museum of Roman Art, Mérida, Thyssen Bornemisza Museum, San Pablo Airport, Seville, Manzana Diagonal, Barcelona, Davis Museum, Wellesley Coll. USA, City Hall Extension, Murcia 1998, Barcelona Concert Hall 1999, Kursaal Concert Hall, San Sebastian 1999, Audrey Jones Beck Building, Houston Museum of Fine Arts 2000, Cathedral of Our Lady of the Angels, Los Angeles 2002, Chivite Winery, Arínzano, Navarra 2002, Arenberg Campus Library, CU Leuven 2002, Gen. and Royal Archive of Navarra, Pamplona 2003, Gregorio Marañón Mother's and Children's Hosp., Madrid 2003, Bank of Spain Extension, Madrid 2006, Contemporary Art Center of Aragon Beulas Foundation, Huesca 2004, Prado Museum Extension, Madrid 2007, Lab. for Integrated Science and Engineering (LISE) Building, Harvard Univ. 2007, Chace Center, Rhode Island School of Design 2008, Museum of the Roman Theater, Cartagena 2008, Library Univ. of Deusto, Bilbao 2009, Lab. Novartis Campus, Basel 2009. *Address:* Calle Cinca 5, Madrid 28002, Spain. *Telephone:* (1) 5642257. *Fax:* (1) 5635217. *E-mail:* r.moneo@rafaelmoneo.com (office). *Website:* www.gsd.harvard.edu/people/faculty/moneo (office).

MONGE, Luis Alberto; Costa Rican politician; b. 29 Dec. 1925, Palmares, Alajuela; s. of Gerardo Monge Quesada and Elisa Álvarez Vargas; ed Univs of Costa Rica and Geneva; mem. Cen. de Trabajadores Rerum Novarum 1947, subsequently Pres.; fmr Vice-Pres. Inter-American Labor Confed. (CIT); militant mem. Nat. Liberation Army 1948; mem. Nat. Constituent Ass. (Social Democrat) 1949; Co-Founder Nat. Liberation Party 1951, Sec.-Gen. for 12 years; worked for ILO, Geneva for 3 years; Sec.-Gen. Interamerican Labor Org. (ORIT) for 6 years; served at Ministry of the Presidency, Govt of José Figueras 1955; mem. Legis. Ass. 1958, 1970, Pres. of Congress 1970–74; Prof. Inter-American School of Democratic Educ. and Dir Center of Democratic Studies for Latin America (CEDAL); Pres. of Costa Rica 1982–86.

MONGELLA, Gertrude; Tanzanian international organization official; *President, Pan African Parliament (PAP);* b. 1945; four c.; ed Univ. of Dar Es Salaam; fmr teacher; mem. Parl. 1980–93; Minister of State, Prime Minister's Office 1982–88, Minster of Lands, Tourism and Natural Resources 1985–87, Minister without Portfolio 1987–90; High Commr to India 1991–92; UN Asst Sec.-Gen. and Sec.-Gen., Fourth World Conf. on Women, Beijing 1993–95, UN Under-Sec. and Special Envoy to UN Sec.-Gen. on Women's Issues and Devt 1996–97; Sr Advisor to Exec. Sec. of Econ. Comm. for Africa (ECA) on Gender Issues 1997–; mem. Parl. for Ukerewe Constituency 2000–04; Pres. Pan African Parl. (consultative ass. of the African Union) 2004–; Head of African Union's election monitoring team during Zimbabwe presidential election 2002; WHO Goodwill Amb. for Africa Region 2003–04; Chair. Int. Advisory Bd African Press Org. 2008–; Delta Prize for Global Understanding 2005. *Address:* Pan-African Parliament, Gallagher Estate, Private Bag X16, Midrand 1685, Johannesburg, South Africa (office). *Telephone:* (11) 5455000 (office). *Fax:* (11) 5455136 (office). *E-mail:* secretariat@panafricanparliament.org (office). *Website:* www.pan-africanparliament.org (office).

MONGUNO, Shettima Ali; Nigerian politician and educationist (retd); b. 1926, Monguno District, Borno Province; s. of Rahma and Fanna Monguno; m. 1st Ashe Monguno (divorced); m. 2nd Meta Monguno 1948 (died 1994); two s. five d.; m. 3rd Fatima Monguno 2001; ed Borno Middle School, Bauchi Teacher Training Coll., Katsina Higher Teachers' Coll., Univ. of Edin., Coll. of Arts, Science and Tech., Zaria, Moray House Coll. of Educ., Edin.; teacher, Yerwa Central Elementary School 1947–49, Borno Middle School 1952–56; MP (Kaga Marghi) 1959–66; Educ. Sec., Borno Native Admin 1952–58; Councillor for Educ., Borno Native Authority 1961–65; Fed. Minister of the Air Force 1965, of Internal Affairs 1965–66; Fed. Commr for Trade and Industry 1967–71, for Mines and Power, Petroleum and Energy 1971–75; Chair. Scholarship Bd, N Nigeria 1966–67; Chair. Borno Local Educ. Cttee 1966–67; Pres., OPEC 1972–73; Chair. Maiduguri Metropolitan Council 1976–79; Founding Pro-Chancellor, Calabar Univ. 1976–80, Univ. of Nigeria 1980–84; mem. Constituent Ass. 1978–79; Deputy Nat. Chair., Nat. Party of Nigeria (NPN) 1980–84; political detainee 1984–85 (cleared by mil. tribunal); del. to UN Gen. Ass., UNCTAD 1968, 1974 and many other int. confs; mem. Bd of Trustees West African Examinations Council –1976; Chair. Bd of Dirs, FRUCO Co.

Nigeria Ltd 1987–2000; Chair. Bd of Trustees, Borno Educ. Endowment Fund 1986–87; Co-Pres. Provisional World Constitution and Parl. Asscn 1992–; mem. Bd of Trustees, World Environmental Movt for Africa (WEMFA) –1986; mem. Commonwealth Countries League Educ. Fund 1996–, Transparency Int. Nigeria 1997–; Life mem. Britain-Nigeria Asscn; Patron and Life mem. Nigeria-USA Council 1998; Hon. Citizen cities of Oklahoma, Lima, Quito, Louisville; Hon. Mayor Oklahoma City; Key to City of New York 1967; Distinguished Friend of Council, W African Exams Council 2002; numerous decorations including First Class Hons, Repub. of Egypt 1970, Order of the Two Niles (Sudan) 1970, First Class Nat. Honour (Cameroon) 1970, Honour of the Empire of Ethiopia 1970, Commdr, Order of Fed. Repub. (Nigeria) 1982; Hon. DLitt (Sokoto) 1984, (Maiduguri) 1996, (Univ. of Nigeria Nsuka) 2001; numerous awards including UNESCO Medal for Campaign against Illiteracy 1991, Borno State Merit Award. *Publications:* Corruption – Why it Thrives in Nigeria 1983. *Leisure interests:* gardening, reading, cycling, farming. *Address:* 5 Muhammed Monguno Road, Old Gra, Maiduguri, Borno State (office); PO Box 541, Maiduguri, Borno State, Nigeria (home). *Telephone:* (76) 231170, 342140. *Fax:* (76) 231170, 342140.

MONICELLI, Mario; Italian film director and screenwriter; b. 15 May 1915; ed Università degli Studi, Pisa; fmr asst to Pietro Germi; writer of film Riso Amaro; film dir 1949–; Golden Lion, Venice Film Festival, Silver Medal, Berlin Film Festival, Silver Laurel Medal, San Francisco Film Festival. *Films include:* I ragazzi della via Paal (The Boys of Via Paal) 1935, Pioggia d'estate (as Michele Badiek) 1937, Totò cerca casa (Totò Looks for an Apartment) 1949, Al diavolo la celebrità (Fame and the Devil) 1949, È arrivato il cavaliere! 1950, Vita da cani 1950, Guardie e ladri (Cops and Robbers) 1951, Totò e i re di Roma 1951, Totò e le donne (Toto and the Women) 1952, Le infedeli (The Unfaithfuls) 1953, Proibito (Forbidden) 1954, Totò e Carolina (Toto and Carolina) 1955, Un eroe dei nostri tempi (A Hero of Our Times) 1955, Donatella 1956, Il medico e lo stregone (Doctor and the Healer) 1957, Padri e figli (Like Father, Like Son) 1957, I soliti ignoti (Persons Unknown; aka Big Deal of Madonna Street) 1958, Lettere dei condannati a morte 1959, La grande guerra (The Great War) 1959, Risate di gioia (Joyful Laughter) 1960, Boccaccio '70 (segment 'Renzo e Luciana') 1962, I compagni (The Organizer) 1963, Alta infedeltà (High Infidelity; segment 'Gente Moderna') 1964, Casanova '70 1965, Le fate (The Queens; segment 'Fata Armenia') 1966, L'Armata Brancaleone 1966, La ragazza con la pistola (Girl with a Pistol) 1968, Capriccio all'italiana (Caprice Italian Style; segment 'La bambinaia') 1968, Toh, è morta la nonna! (Oh, Grandmother's) 1969, Brancaleone alle crociate (Brancaleone at the Crusades) 1970, Le coppie (The Couples; segment 'Il frigorifero') 1970, La Mortadella (Lady Liberty) 1971, Vogliamo i colonnelli (We Want the Colonels) 1973, Romanzo popolare (aka Come Home and Meet My Wife) 1974, Amici miei (My Friends) 1975, Signore e signori, buonanotte (Goodnight, Ladies and Gentlemen) 1976, Caro Michele (Dear Michael) 1976, Un borghese piccolo piccolo (An Average Little Man) 1977, I nuovi mostri (The New Monsters; segments 'Autostop' and 'First Aid') 1977, Viaggio con Anita (A Trip with Anita) 1979, Temporale Rosy 1980, Camera d'Albergo 1981, Il Marchese del Grillo 1981, Amici miei atto II (All My Friends Part 2) 1982, Lovers and Liars, Bertoldo, Bertoldino e... Cacasenno 1984, Le due vite di Mattia Pascal (The Two Lives of Mattia Pascal) 1985, Speriamo che sia femmina (Let's Hope It's a Girl) (also wrote screenplay) 1986, I Picari (The Rogues) 1988, 12 registi per 12 città (segment 'Verona') 1989, Il male oscuro (Dark Illness) 1990, Rossini! Rossini! 1991, Parenti serpenti (Dearest Relatives, Poisonous Relations) 1992, Cari fottutissimi amici (Dear God-damned Friends) 1994, Facciamo paradiso (Looking for Paradise) 1995, Esercizi di stile (segment 'Idillio edile') 1996, Topi di appartamento 1997, I Corti italiani (segment 'Topi di appartamento') 1997, Panni sporchi (Dirty Linen) 1999, Un amico magico: il maestro Nino Rota 1999, Un altro mondo è possibile (Another World Is Possible) 2001, Lettere dalla Palestina (Letters from Palestine) 2003, Firenze, il nostro domani 2003. *Television includes:* La moglie ingenua e il marito malato 1989, Come quando fuori piove (mini-series) 2000. *Address:* Via del Babuino 135, Rome, Italy. *Telephone:* (06) 6780448.

MONK, Meredith Jane; American composer, director and choreographer; b. 20 Nov. 1942, New York; d. of Theodore G. Monk and Audrey Lois Monk (née Zellman); ed Sarah Lawrence Coll.; Founder and Artistic Dir House Foundation for the Arts 1968–; formed Meredith Monk & Vocal Ensemble 1978–; mem. American Acad. of Arts and Sciences 2006; Dr hc (Bard Coll.) 1988, (Univ. of the Arts) 1989, (Juilliard School of Music) 1998, (San Francisco Art Inst.) 1999, (Boston Conservatory) 2001; Golden Eagle Award 1981, Nat. Music Theatre Award 1986, German Critics' Award for Best Recording of the Year 1981, 1986, MacArthur Genius Award 1995, Samuel Scripps Award 1996, United States Artists Fellow 2006 and many other awards. *Works include:* Break 1964, 16 Millimeter Earrings 1966, Juice: A Theatre Cantata 1969, Key 1971, Vessel: An Opera Epic 1971, Paris 1972, Education of the Girlchild 1973, Quarry 1976, Songs from the Hill 1976, Dolmen Music 1979, Specimen Days: A Civil War Opera 1981, Ellis Island 1981, Turtle Dreams Cabaret 1983, The Games 1983, Acts from Under and Above 1986, Book of Days 1988, Facing North 1990, Three Heavens and Hells 1992, ATLAS: An Opera in Three Parts 1991, New York Requiem 1993, Volcano Songs 1994, American Archaeology 1994, The Politics of Quiet 1996, Steppe Music 1997, Magic Frequencies 1998, Micki Suite 2000, Eclipse Variations 2000, mercy 2001, Possible Sky 2003, Impermanence 2004, Stringsongs 2005, Songs of Ascension 2008. *Leisure interests:* gardening, horseback riding. *Address:* The House Foundation, 260 West Broadway, Suite 2, New York, NY 10013, USA (office). *Telephone:* (212) 904-1330 (office). *Fax:* (212) 904-1305 (office). *E-mail:* monk@meredithmonk.org (office). *Website:* www.meredithmonk.org (office).

MÖNKH-ORGIL, Tsendiin; Mongolian politician; *Minister of Justice and Home Affairs;* b. 1964, Sühbaatar prov.; ed Moscow Higher School of Int. Relations, Harvard Univ., USA; Attaché, Int. Orgs Dept, Ministry of Foreign

Affairs 1998–91; Third, then Second Sec. for Political and Legal Affairs, Perm. Mission to UN, New York 1991–95; with int. law firm, Washington DC 1996; Dir-Gen. Mönh-Orgil, Idesh, Lynch 1997; apptd Deputy Minister of Law and Internal Affairs 2000; Minister of Foreign Affairs 2004–06 (resgnd); Minister of Justice and Home Affairs 2007–. *Address:* Ministry of Justice and Home Affairs, Government Building 5, Khudaldaany Gudamj 61A, Chingletei District, Ulan Bator, Mongolia (office). *Telephone:* (11) 325225 (office). *Fax:* (11) 325225 (office). *E-mail:* forel@moj.pmis.gov.mn. *Website:* www.pmis.gov .mn (office).

MONKS, John Stephen, BA; British trade union official; *Secretary-General, European Trade Union Confederation;* b. 5 Oct. 1945, Manchester; s. of Charles Edward Monks and Bessie Evelyn Monks; m. Francine Jacqueline Schenk 1970; two s. one d.; ed Univ. of Nottingham; joined TUC Org. Dept 1969, Asst Sec. Employment and Manpower Section 1974, Head Org., Employment Law and Industrial Relations Dept 1977–87, Deputy Gen.-Sec. 1987–93, Gen.-Sec. 1993–2003; Sec.-Gen. European Trade Union Confed. (ETUC) 2003–; mem. Council Advisory, Conciliation and Arbitration Service (ACAS) 1979–95; mem. British Govt and EU Competitiveness Councils 1997; Visiting Prof., School of Man., Manchester Business School 1996–; Trustee People's History Museum 1988–, Chair. 2005–; Dr hc (Nottingham, UMIST, Salford, Cranfield, Cardiff, Kingston, Southampton and Open Univs). *Leisure interests:* hiking, music, squash. *Address:* European Trade Union Confeder-ation, 5 Boulevard Roi Albert II, 1210 Brussels, Belgium (office). *Telephone:* (2) 224-04-11 (office). *Fax:* (2) 224-04-54 (office). *E-mail:* etuc@etuc.org (office). *Website:* www.etuc.org (office).

MONNIER, Claude Michel, PhD; Swiss journalist; *Adviser to General Management, Edipresse Suisse SA;* b. 23 March 1938, Rwankéri, Rwanda; s. of Henri Monnier and Olga Pavlov; m. Estela Troncoso Balandrán 1958; two s.; ed Univs of Geneva and Mexico, Grad. Inst. of Int. Studies, Geneva; educational tour in Asia and America 1956–58; Research Fellow, Swiss Nat. Fund for Scientific Research, Tokyo 1963–66; Tokyo Corresp. Journal de Genève 1963–66, Foreign Ed. 1966–70, Ed.-in-Chief 1970–80; Ed. Le Temps Stratégique, Genève 1982–2001; mem. Bd French-speaking Swiss TV and radio 1989–2000; mem. Academic Council, Univ. of Lausanne 1998–2005, Bd Médias et Société Foundation, Geneva; Adviser to Gen. Man. Edipresse Suisse SA 2001–. *Publications:* Les Américains et sa Majesté l'Empereur: Etude du conflit culturel d'où naquit la constitution japonaise de 1946 1967, Alerte, citoyens! 1989, L'année du Big-Bang 1990, La terre en a marre 1991, La déprime, ça suffit! 1992, Dieu, que la crise est jolie! 1993, Les Rouges nous manquent 1994, La bonté qui tue 1995, Envie de bouffer du lion 1996, Programme d'un agitateur 1997, Le temps des règlements de compte 1998, Le Culte suspect de l'action 1999, La trahison de l'an 2000 2000, Morts de trouille 2001, Il faut nous faire soigner! 2002, Où est ta victoire, George W. 2003, La Suisse devient folle 2004, Et maintenant, on fait quoi? 2005. *Leisure interests:* walking, light aircraft flying. *Address:* Chemin de Saussac 2, 1256 Troinex, Geneva, Switzerland (home). *Telephone:* (22) 322-34-92 (office); (22) 343-95-55 (home). *Fax:* (22) 343-95-55 (home).

MONOD, Jérôme; French business executive; b. 7 Sept. 1930, Paris; s. of Olivier Monod and Yvonne (née Bruce) Monod; m. Françoise Gallot 1963; three s.; ed Wesleyan Univ., USA, Institut d'Etudes Politiques, Ecole Nat. d'Admin; Auditeur, Cour des Comptes 1957; Rapporteur, Study mission of Sec.-Gen. for Algerian Affairs 1958; Chargé de mission, Prime Minister's Office 1959–62; Conseiller Référendaire à la Cour des Comptes 1963; Chief Exec. Dél. à l'Aménagement du Territoire 1967–75; Special Asst to Prime Minister Jacques Chirac 1975–1976; Sec.-Gen. Rassemblement pour la République (RPR) 1976–78; Chair. Bd, Centre Français du Commerce Extérieur 1980–83; Pres. French Canadian Chamber of Commerce in Paris 1984–86; Vice-Pres. Société Lyonnaise des Eaux 1979–80, Chair. and CEO 1980–97; Vice-Chair. General Waterworks Corpn (USA) 1983–93; Vice-Chair., Compagnie de Suez 1995–97, Chair. Supervisory Bd, Suez Lyonnaise des Eaux 1997–2000, Chair. Lyonnaise des Eaux de Casablanca 1997–2000; Chair. Sino French Holding (China) 1996–; Adviser to Pres. of France 2000–02; mem. Bd of Dirs Total (Cie Française des Pétroles), Aguas de Barcelona (Spain), Dic-Degrémont (Japan), Lyonnaise American Holding (USA), Groupe GTM, GTM-Entrepose, Métropole Télévision; mem. Consulta-tive Council Banque de France, Business Advisory Council, IFC (USA); mem. Int. Advisory Bd, NatWest Bank; mem. Steering Cttee, European Round Table 1995–2000; Commdr, Légion d'honneur, Officier des Arts et des Lettres, Chevalier des Palmes académiques. *Publications:* L'aménagement du terri-toire 1971, Transformation d'un pays: pour une géographie de la liberté 1975, Propositions pour la France 1977, Manifeste pour une Europe souveraine 1999, L'Aménagement du territoire 2002, Essai sur la Gouvernance publique 2004, L'aménagement du territoire 2006. *Leisure interests:* swimming, climbing. *Address:* Presses Universitaires de France, 6 avenue Reille, 75685 Paris Cedex 14 (office); 15, rue de Verneuil, 75007 Paris, France (home).

MONORY, Jacques; French painter; b. 25 June 1934, Paris; s. of Luis José Monory and Angèle Foucher; m. 2nd Sabine Monirys 1959 (divorced 1968); one s.; m. 3rd Paule Moninot 1993; ed Ecole des Beaux Arts de Paris, Ecole des Arts Appliqués, Paris; Diplomé de l'Ecole des Arts Appliqués; work repre-sented in numerous public collections in Europe, USA and Japan. *Films:* Ex 1968, Brighton Belle 1973, La Voleuse (video) 1986, Le Moindre Geste peut faire signe 1986. *Publications:* Document bleu 1970, Diamondback 1979, Rien ne bouge assez vite au bord de la mort 1984, Quick 1985, Eldorado 1991, 3' 30" 1993, Angèle 2005. *Leisure interests:* shooting, swimming. *Address:* 9 Villa Carnot, 94230 Cachan, France (home). *Telephone:* 1-46-65-08-67 (home). *Fax:* 1-46-65-08-67 (home). *E-mail:* jacques.monory@wanadoo.fr (office). *Website:* www.jacquesmonory.com (office).

MONREAL LUQUE, Alberto, DEconSc; Spanish politician and economist; *President, Eurotabac;* b. 18 Nov. 1928, Madrid; s. of Federico Monreal and Irene Luque; m. María Elena Alfageme 1961; two s. one d.; ed Univ. de Madrid; mem. Cuerpo de Economistas del Estado 1957–; Prof., Faculty of Econ. Sciences, Univ. de Madrid 1957–68; Tech. Sec. Ministry of Public Works 1965–68; Sec. of State, Ministry of Educ. and Science 1968–69; Minister of Finance 1969–73; Pres. Tabacalera (Tobacco Monopoly Co.) 1974–82; Pres. Eurotabac 1994–; Econ. Consultant, Superior Council of Commerce, Ministry of the Economy; Deputy Chair. Grupo Anaya (publrs). *Address:* Eurotabac, Monte Esquinza 34, 28010, Madrid, Spain (office). *Telephone:* (91) 3104218 (office). *Fax:* (91) 3104286 (office). *E-mail:* eurotabac@retemail.es (office).

MONTAGNA, Gilberto Luis Humberto; Argentine civil engineer; b. 1936; m.; four c.; Sec. Chamber of Food Industrialists (CIPA) 1964–84, Vice-Pres. 1984; Sec. Fed. of Food and Derivatives Industries (FIPAA) 1975–84, Pres. 1984–87; Sec. to Coordinator of Food and Derivates Industry (COPAL) 1975–79, now Pres.; Sec. Industrial Transitory Comm. (COTEI) of Unión Industrial Argentina (UIA) 1978–79, mem. Advising Exec. Comm. of UIA Comptrolling 1979–81, First Vice-Pres. UIA 1981–89, Pres. 1989; Tech. Adviser, ILO, Geneva 1978; Alt. Del. to ILO 1979, 1980, 1981; Founder, currently Vice-Pres. Action for Pvt. Initiative; Vice-Pres. Establecimientos Modelo Terrabusi SAIC; Dir Terra Garba Sacai y F, Atilena SCA. *Address:* c/o Unión Industrial Argentina, Avda Leandro N Arem 1067, 11°, 1001 Buenos Aires, Argentina.

MONTAGNIER, Luc, LèsL, DMed; French research scientist, academic and international organization official; *President World Foundation for AIDS Research and Prevention;* b. 18 Aug. 1932, Chabris; s. of Antoine Montagnier and Marianne Rousselet; m. Dorothea Ackermann 1961; one s. two d.; ed Univs of Poitiers and Paris; Asst in Faculty of Science, Paris 1955–60, Attaché 1960, Head 1963, Head of Research 1967; Dir of Research CNRS 1974–; Head of Lab. Inst. of Radium 1965–71; Head of Viral Oncology Unit, Pasteur Inst. 1972–, Prof., Pasteur Inst. 1985–; Vice-Pres. Scientific Council AIDS Research Agency 1989–; Pres. World Foundation for AIDS Research and Prevention (WFARP) 1993–; Prof., Queens Coll., New York 1997–2001; mem. Acad. nat. de Médecine 1989, Acad. des Sciences 1996; Commdr Légion d'honneur 1994, Grand Officier 2009, Commdr Ordre nat. du Mérite; Lauréat du CNRS 1964, 1973, Prix Rosen de Cancérologie 1971, Prix Galien 1985, Prix de la Fondation Louis-Jeantet 1986, Prix Lasker 1986, Prix Gairdner 1987, Japan Prize 1988, King Faisal Prize 1993, Warren Alpert Foundation Prize 1998, Prince of Asturias Prize for Science 2000, Nobel Prize for Medicine (jtly) 2008 and many other prizes. *Publications:* Vaincre le SIDA 1986, SIDA: les faits, l'espoir 1987, SIDA et infection par VIH (jtly) 1989, Des virus et des hommes 1994, Oxidative Stress in Cancer, AIDS and Neurodegenerative Diseases (jtly) 1997, New Concepts in Aids Pathogenesis (jtly), Virus (jtly) 2000, numerous scientific papers. *Leisure interests:* piano playing, swimming. *Address:* World Foundation for AIDS Research and Prevention, UNESCO, 1 rue Miollis, 75732 Paris, France (office). *Telephone:* 1-45-68-45-45 (office). *Fax:* 1-42-73-37-45 (office). *E-mail:* lucmontagnier@hotmail.com (office).

MONTAGUE, Sir Adrian Alastair, Kt, CBE, KB, MA; British energy industry executive; *Chairman, British Energy PLC;* b. 28 Feb. 1948; s. of the late Charles Edward Montague and Olive Montague (née Jones); m. 1st Pamela Evans 1970 (divorced 1982, died 2000); one s. two d.; m. 2nd Penelope Webb 1986; one s.; ed Trinity Hall, Cambridge; admitted solicitor 1973; with Linklater & Paines Solicitors, London 1971–94, Partner 1979; Dir Kleinwort Benson (subequently Dresdner Kleinwort Benson) where he was Co-Head merged Global Project Finance businesses of Kleinwort Benson and Dresdner Bank 1994–97; Chief Exec. Pvt. Finance Initiative Taskforce, HM Treasury 1997–2000; Deputy Chair. Partnerships UK PLC 2000–01; Deputy Chair. Network Rail 2001–04; Chair. British Energy PLC 2002–, Friends Provident PLC 2005–; Dir Michael Page International PLC 2001–, Chair. (non-exec.) 2002–; Chair. (non-exec.) Partnerships for Health PLC; Chair. Infrastructure Investors Ltd 2005–; Dir CellMark AB, Gothenburg; Sr Int. Adviser to Société Générale, Paris 2001–04; mem. Strategic Rail Authority 2000–01; fmr Pvt. Finance Adviser to Deputy Prime Minister. *Address:* British Energy PLC, 1 Sheldon Square, Paddington, London, W2 6TT, England (office). *Telephone:* (20) 7266-8350 (office). *E-mail:* adrian.montague@british-energy.com (office). *Website:* www.british-energy.com (office).

MONTAGUE, Diana, ARCM; British singer (mezzo-soprano); b. 8 April 1953, Winchester; d. of Mr and Mrs N. H. Montague; m. 1st Philip Doghan 1978; one s.; m. 2nd David Rendall 1990; one s. two d.; ed Testwood School, Totton, Hants., Winchester School of Art and Royal Northern Coll. of Music; professional debut at Glyndebourne 1977; Prin. Mezzo-Soprano, Royal Opera House, Covent Garden 1978; freelance artist 1984–; has toured throughout Europe and USA appearing at Metropolitan Opera and Bayreuth, Aix-en-Provence, Salzburg and Glyndebourne festivals; sang at Promenade Concerts, London 1991; Ariadne auf Naxos for Opera North 1998. *Leisure interests:* horse-riding, country life in general. *Address:* Intermusica, 16 Duncan Terrace, London, N1 8BZ, England (office). *Telephone:* (20) 7239-0191 (office). *Fax:* (20) 7278-844 (office). *E-mail:* mail@intermusica.co.uk (office). *Website:* www.intermusica.co.uk (office).

MONTANA, Claude; French fashion designer; b. 1949, Paris; m. Wallis Franken 1993; began career designing jewellery in London, then worked for leather and knitwear firms; first ready-to-wear show 1976; f. Claude Montana Co. 1979; opened boutiques in Paris 1983, 1986; f. Montana Fragrances Co. 1984; designer in charge of Haute Couture, House of Lanvin 1990-92; designed men's wear for Complice, Italy; mem. Chambre Syndicale du Pret-a-Porter.

MONTANA, Joseph C., Jr (Joe), B.B.A.; American fmr professional football player; b. 11 June 1956, New Eagle, Pa; s. of Joseph C. Montana, Sr and

Theresa Montana; m. 1st Kim Monses 1975 (divorced); m. 2nd Cass Castillo (divorced 1983); m. 3rd Jennifer Wallace 1984; two d.; ed Univ. of Notre Dame; quarterback, San Francisco 49ers 1979–93, Kansas City Chiefs 1993–94, Nat. Football League (NFL); commentator NBC TV 1995–; career statistics include 3,409 completions, 40,551 passing yards, 273 touchdowns, 92.3 passer rating; mem. NFL Super Bowl championship teams 1982, 1985, 1989; played in Pro Bowl 1982–85; voted Most Valuable Player in the Super Bowl 1982, 1985, 1990 (record), NFL Player of the Year 1989, 1990; pnr Target-Chip Ganassi Racing Team 1995–; New Business Devt Dept, Viking Components Inc. 1999; elected to Pro Football Hall of Fame 2000. *Publication:* Cool Under Fire (with Alan Steinberg) 1989. *Address:* c/o IMG, 1 Erieview Plaza, Suite 1300, Cleveland, OH 44114, USA.

MONTAÑO, Jorge, PhD; Mexican diplomatist; b. 16 Aug. 1945, Mexico City; s. of Jorge Montaño and Lucia Montaño; m. Luz María Valdes; one s. one d.; ed Nat. Autonomous Univ. of Mexico, London School of Econs, UK; posts with Nat. Inst. of Fine Arts, Ministry of Public Educ., Nat. Autonomous Univ. of Mexico; Dir-Gen., Office for UN Specialized Agencies, then Dir-in-Chief for Multilateral Affairs, Ministry of Foreign Affairs 1979–82; fmr Int. Affairs Adviser to Pres. Salinas de Gortari; fmr univ. lecturer, Mexico and UK; Perm. Rep. to UN 1989–93; Amb. to USA 1993–95. *Publication:* The United Nations and the World Order 1945–1992 1992. *Address:* Chimalistac No. 6, Colonia San Angel, 01070 México, DF, Mexico. *Telephone:* (5) 661-9765.

MONTAZERI, Ayatollah Hussein Ali; Iranian religious leader; b. 1922, Najafabad, Isfahan; s. of Montazeri Ali and Sobhani Shah Baigom; m. Rabbani, Khadijeh 1942; three s. four d.; ed Isfahan Theological School; teacher of science and philosophy, Theological School, Qom; arrested after riots over Shah's land reform 1963; visited Ayatollah Khomeini in Iraq 1964; arrested several times and exiled to rural parts of Iran 1964–74; imprisoned 1974–78; Leading Ayatollah of Tehran 1979–80; returned to Qom Feb. 1980; named Grand Ayatollah 1984; resgnd as successor to Ayatollah Khomeini March 1989; placed under house arrest in Qom 1997, released 2003. *Address:* Madresseh Faizieh, Qom, Iran.

MONTEALEGRE, Eduardo, ScB, MBA; Nicaraguan politician; b. 9 May 1955; ed Brown Univ., Harvard Univ., USA; early career as business exec. and dir of several financial insts, positions included Man. BANIC Corpn and Asst Dir Cen. Bank of Nicaragua; lived in exile in USA during Sandanista rule 1979–90 serving as Vice Pres. Banking Investment Group, Shearson Lehman Hutton before forming Montealegre & Co (pvt. financial advisory co.); Chief of Staff in the Presidency 1998, 2003, Minister of Foreign Affairs 1999–2000, of Treasury and Public Credit 2002–03; mem. Constitutionalist Liberal Party (PLC) –2005; co-f. Alianza Liberal Nicaragüense (ALN) 2005, presidential cand. 2006. *Address:* c/o Alianza Liberal Nicaragüense (ALN), Managua, Nicaragua.

MONTEGRIFFO, Peter Cecil Patrick, LLB; British barrister; *Partner, Hassans;* b. 28 Feb. 1960, Gibraltar; s. of Dr Cecil Montegriffo and Lily Zammitt; m. Josephine Perera 1985; two s.; ed Bayside Comprehensive School, Univ. of Leeds and Lincoln's Inn/Council of Legal Educ.; called to the Bar 1982; practitioner in law firm J. A. Hassan & Partners (now Hassans), Pnr 1988–; mem. Exec. Gibraltar Labour Party/Asscn for Advancement of Civil Rights (GLP/AACR) 1982–88, Deputy Leader 1988–89; Leader Gibraltar Social Democrats (GSD) 1989–91; Deputy Chief Minister and Minister for Trade and Industry 1996–2000. *Publications:* contributions to International Trust Laws, Practical Guide to Offshore Trusts, Offshore Materials, Asset Protection, Jordans (Changes and Development of Corporate Tax System). *Leisure interests:* literature, economics, music, travel. *Address:* Hassans, 57 Line Wall Road, Gibraltar (office); 14 Admiral's Place, Old Naval Hospital, Gibraltar (home). *Telephone:* 79000 (office); 79912 (home). *Fax:* 71966 (office); 42772 (home). *E-mail:* peter.montegriffo@hassans.gi (office); pcm@gibnet.gi (home). *Website:* www.gibraltarlaw.com/pcmontegriffo.htm (office).

MONTEIRO, António Isaac; Guinea-Bissau politician; fmr Minister of Rural Devt and Agric.; fmr Del. to FAO; Minister of Foreign Affairs, Int. Co-operation and Communities 2005–07. *Address:* c/o Ministry of Foreign Affairs, International Co-operation and Communities, Rua Gen. Omar Torrijo, Bissau, Guinea-Bissau (office).

MONTEIRO, António Victor Martins; Portuguese diplomatist; *Ambassador to France;* b. 22 Jan. 1944, Angola; m.; two d.; ed Univ. of Lisbon; Perm. Rep. to FAO 1978; Deputy Chief of Protocol, Ministry of Foreign Affairs 1979; joined Perm. Mission to UN 1981, apptd Deputy Perm. Rep. 1984; Chief of Cabinet, Sec. of State for Foreign Affairs and Co-operation 1987; Head of Temporary Mission for Peace Process Structures in Angola 1991, Rep. to Jt Political and Mil. Comm.; Dir-Gen. for Political and Econ. Affairs 1993, Dir-Gen. for External Policy 1994; apptd Perm. Rep. to UN 1996; Co-ordinator Cttee for Perm. Co-ordination of the Community of Portuguese-Speaking Countries 1996; Amb. to France –2004; Minister of Foreign Affairs and Portuguese Communities Abroad 2004–05; High Rep. of the UN for Elections in Côte d'Ivoire 2005; Amb. to France 2006–. *Address:* Embassy of Portugal, 3 rue de Noisiel, 75116 Paris, France (office); Rua Joao de Deus, No. 15–2E, 1200-694 Lisbon, Portugal (home). *Telephone:* 1-47-27-35-29 (office); (21) 3870313 (home). *Fax:* 1-44-05-94-02 (office). *E-mail:* avmmonteiro@hotmail.com (home); mailto@embaixada-portugal-fr.org (office). *Website:* www.embaixada-portugal-fr.org (office).

MONTENEGRO RIZZARDINI, Gloria, PhD; Chilean ecologist, botanist and academic; *Professor and Director of Botany, Faculty of Agronomy and Forestry Sciences, Pontificia Universidad Catolica de Chile;* b. 16 July 1941, Santiago; m.; two c.; ed Pontifical Catholic Univ. of Chile and Univ. of Texas, Austin, USA; currently Dir of Botany and of Research and Graduate Studies, Prof. of Botany and Phytochemistry, Faculty of Agronomy and Forestry Sciences, Pontificia Universidad Catolica de Chile; Visiting Prof., Univ. of Texas at Austin, Univ. of Arizona, Tucson, USA; Pres. Advisory Bd COPEC-PUC Foundation for Science and Natural Resources, Fundación para la Investigación en Ciencia y Tecnología en Recursos Naturales; fmr Pres. Botanical Soc. of Chile, Latin-American Botany Asscn, Int. Soc. for Mediterranean Ecosystems; mem. Scientific Advisory Bd TWAS-TWNSO-Global Environmental Facility projects; mem. Exec. Cttee and Regional Coordinator of the Latin America Plant Science Network; mem. Int. Cooperative Biodiversity Group; Exec. mem. UNESCO Group 'Women, Science & Technology in Latin America'; mem. Bd 'Comunidad-Mujer in Chile Group' (for improvement of women's rights); Fellow, Latin American Acad. of Sciences, Third World Acad. of Sciences; Gold Medal of Providencia Co. (Chile), L'Oréal-UNESCO Women in Science Award 1998, Pontificia Univ. Catolica de Chile Monseñor Carlos Casanueva Prize for Distinguished Prof. 2008, named one of the 100 Leading Women in Chile 2008. *Publications:* Landscape Disturbance and Biodiversity in Mediterranean-Type Ecosystems (co-ed.) 1998, Fire and Climatic Change in Temperate Ecosystems of the Western Americas (co-ed.) 2003; several patents and scientific publs. *Address:* Facultad de Agronomia e Ingenieria Forestal, Pontificia Universidad Católica de Chile, Av. Vicuña Mackenna 4860, Santiago, Chile (office). *Telephone:* 354-5726 (office). *Fax:* 354-5702 (office). *E-mail:* gmonten@puc.cl (office). *Website:* www.investigacionbotanica.puc.cl (office).

MONTGOMERIE, Colin Stuart, OBE; British professional golfer; b. 23 June 1963, Glasgow, Scotland; s. of James Montgomerie; m. Eimear Wilson 1990 (divorced 2004); one s. two d.; ed Strathallan School, Leeds Grammar School, Houston Baptist Univ., Texas, USA; won Scottish Stroke Play Championship 1985, Scottish Amateur Championship 1987; turned professional 1987; won Portuguese Open 1989, Scandinavian Masters 1991, 1999, 2001, Heineken Dutch Open, Volvo Masters 1993, Peugeot Open de España, Murphy's English Open, Volvo German Open 1994, Volvo German Open, Trophée Lancôme, Alfred Dunhill Cup 1995, Dubai Desert Classic, Murphy's Irish Open 1996, 1997, 2001, Canon European Masters, Million Dollar Challenge 1996, World Cup (Individual), Andersen Consulting World Champion 1997, PGA Championship 1998, 1999, 2000, German Masters 1998, Compaq European Grand Prix 1997, King Hassan II Trophy 1997, British Masters 1998, Benson and Hedges Int. Open 1999, BMW Int. Open 1999, Cisco World Matchplay 1999, Loch Lomond Invitational 1999, Skins Game (US) 2000, Novotel Perrier Open de France 2000, Ericsson Australian Masters 2001, Volvo Masters Andalucia, TCL Classic 2002, Macao Open 2003; mem. European Ryder Cup team from 1991–2004 (undefeated in Ryder Cup singles), apptd Capt. European Ryder Cup team 2009; Hon. LLD (St Andrews); seven times winner of Volvo Order of Merit Trophy 1993–99. *Publications:* Real Monty: The Autobiography of Colin Montgomerie, The Thinking Man's Guide to Golf. *Leisure interests:* music, cars, DIY, films. *Address:* c/o IMG, Pier House, Strand-on-the-Green, London, W4 3NN, England. *Website:* www.colinmontgomerie.com.

MONTGOMERY, David; American photographer; *Visiting Research Professor, University of East London;* b. 8 Feb. 1937, Brooklyn, New York; m. 1st (divorced); two d.; m. 2nd Martine King 1983; one s. one d.; ed Midwood High School, Brooklyn Coll., Juilliard School of Music; toured USA as musician; freelance photographer/dir 1960–; regular contrib. to Sunday Times Colour Magazine, Vogue, Tatler, Rolling Stone, Esquire, Fortune, New York Sunday Times, House and Garden magazines; has contributed to many books on home style: four in association with Tricia Guild of Designers Guild, a definitive English flower book for Pulbrook & Gould and four books on New Age aromatherapy entitled 'Romance', 'Relaxation', 'Vitality' and 'Well Being'; did photography for Nicky Haslam's book 'Sheer Opulence'; commissioned by Royal Mail to do a special edition stamp for the Millennium issue; has also photographed for major retailers, including Harrods, John Lewis, The Body Shop; has also shot major advertising campaigns for Designers Guild, Colefax and Fowler, Jane Churchill, Sandersons; has worked on campaigns for brands including Rolex, Saab, Fiat; Visiting Research Prof., Univ. of E London 2007–; has photographed HM Queen Elizabeth II, HM Queen Elizabeth the Queen Mother, TRH Duke and Duchess of York, Rt Hon. Margaret Thatcher, Rt Hon Pierre Trudeau, Mick Jagger, Clint Eastwood, Lord Mountbatten, Lord Hume, HM King Hussein, HRH Queen Noor, Rt Hon Edward Heath, Rt Hon James Callaghan, Baron Thyssen-Bornemisza, Prince and Princess Thurn und Taxis, HE Cardinal Basil Hume, Jimi Hendrix, The Rolling Stones, Sir Paul McCartney, Chrissie Hynde, Pierce Brosnan, Barbra Streisand, S Club 7, Atomic Kitten; teaches at Univ. of East London 2007–; numerous awards for photography and advertising. *Publications:* contribs to New York Times/Sunday Times, Vogue, Homes and Gardens, Rolling Stone. *Leisure interests:* flowers and fish keeping, photography, day-dreaming, jazz music. *Address:* Studio B, 11 Edith Grove, London, SW10 0JZ; 23 Langton Street, Chelsea, London SW10 0JL, England (home). *Telephone:* (20) 7823-3723 (office); (20) 7351-5665 (home).

MONTGOMERY, David John, BA; British newspaper executive; *Executive Chairman, Mecom Group plc;* b. 6 Nov. 1948, Bangor, Northern Ireland; s. of William John Montgomery and Margaret Jean Montgomery; m. 1st Susan Frances Buchanan Russell 1971 (divorced 1987); m. 2nd Heidi Kingstone 1989 (divorced 1997); m. 3rd Sophie, Countess of Woolton 1997; ed Queen's Univ., Belfast; Sub-Ed., Daily Mirror London, Manchester 1973–76, Asst Chief Sub-Ed. 1976–80; Chief Sub-Ed. The Sun 1980; Asst Ed. Sunday People 1982; Asst Ed. News of the World 1984, Ed. 1985–87; Ed. Today 1987–91 (Newspaper of the Year 1988); Man. Dir News UK 1987–91; Chief Exec. London Live TV 1991–92, Dir 1991–92; Chief Exec. Mirror Group 1992–99; Dir Satellite Television PLC 1986–91, News Group Newspapers 1986–91, Donohue Inc. 1992–95, Newspaper Publishing 1994–98, Scottish Media Group 1995–99, Press Asscn 1996–99; Founder and Exec. Chair. Mecom Group plc 2000–; Chair. Tri-Mex Group PLC 1999–, Yava 2000–, Africa Lakes PLC 2000–,

Integrated Educ. Fund Devt Bd, NI 2000–, Espresso 2001–; with other investors acquired Berliner Verlag (Berliner Zeitung and Berliner Kurier newspapers), Germany, Chair. Supervisory Bd 2005–. *Leisure interests:* music, family. *Address:* Mecom Group plc, Empire House, 175 Piccadilly, London, W1J 9EN (office); ALC, 7–10 Chandos Street, London, W1G 9DQ; 15 Collingham Gardens, London, SW5 0HS, England. *Telephone:* (20) 7491-6660 (Mecom) (office); (20) 7323-5440 (office); (20) 7373-1982 (home). *Fax:* (20) 7491-6666 (Mecom) (office). *E-mail:* info@mecom.co.uk (office); dmontgomery@tri-mex.com (office). *Website:* www.mecom.co.uk (office); www.berlinonline.de/berliner-zeitung (office).

MONTGOMERY, R. Lawrence (Larry), BS; American retail executive; *Chairman, Kohl's Department Stores;* b. 1949; ed Ferris State Univ.; Pres., Block's Div., Allied Stores Corpn 1985–87; Sr Vice-Pres., L. S. Ayres Div., May Dept Stores 1987–88; Sr Vice-Pres. and Dir of Stores, Kohl's Dept Stores 1988–93, Exec. Vice-Pres. 1993–96, Vice-Chair. 1994–2000, mem. Bd of Dirs 1994–, CEO 1999–2002, Chair. 2002–. *Address:* Kohl's Department Stores, N56 W17000 Ridgewood Drive, Menomonee Falls, WI 53051-5660, USA (office). *Telephone:* (262) 703-7000 (office). *Website:* www.kohls.com (office).

MONTGOMERY, Tim; American fmr athlete; b. 28 Jan. 1975, Gaffney, SC; pnr Marion Jones (q.v.); one d.; ed Gaffney High School, Blinn Coll. JC, Norfolk State Coll.; fmrly American football and baseball player; ran 100m in 9.96 seconds age 19; world record holder (9.78 seconds 100m), Grand Prix Final, 2002; ran fastest 60m (6.48 seconds), Dortmund 2002; coached by Trevor Graham; runner-up: JUCO Indoor 1994, USA Championships 100m 1997, USA Indoors 60m 1997, USATF Outdoor Championship 100m 2002, Golden Gala 100m 2002, Norwich Union Grand Prix 100m 2002; winner: Bislett Golden Gala 100m 2001, Zurich 100m 2001, Sparkassen 100m 2002, Engen Grand Prix 100m 2002, Prefontaine 100m 2002, DN Galan 100m 2002, Weltklasse 100m 2002, Memorial Van Damme 100m 2002, Grand Prix Final 100m 2002; Bronze Medal: World Championships 100m 1997; Silver Medal: Olympics 4x100m relay 1996, 1999, Goodwill Games 100m 2001,World Indoors 60m 2001, World Championships 100m 2001; Gold Medal: World Championships 4x100m relay 1999, Olympics 4x100m relay 2000; arrested on fed. heroin distribution charges 2008. *Address:* c/o Vector Sports Management, 417 Keller Parkway, Keller, TX 76248, USA (office). *E-mail:* info@vectorsportsmgmt.com (office). *Website:* www.vectorsportsmgmt.com (office).

MONTGOMERY, William D., BA, MBA; American diplomatist; b. 8 Nov. 1945, Carthage, Mo.; m. Lynne Germain; one s. two d.; ed Buckness and George Washington Univs, Nat. War Coll.; served US Army 1967–70; joined Foreign Service 1974, Econ.-Commercial Officer, Belgrade, Commercial Officer, Moscow, Political Officer, Moscow, Deputy Chief of Mission, Dar es Salaam; several posts in Dept of State; Deputy Chief of Mission, Sofia 1989–91; Amb. to Bulgaria 1993–96; Special Adviser to Pres. and Sec. of State for Bosnian Peace Implementation 1996–97; Amb. to Croatia 1998–2000, to Yugoslavia 2000–01, to Serbia and Montenegro 2001–04 (retd); several Army decorations including Bronze Star; Distinguished Honor Award and other awards from Dept of State; Order of Prince Trpimir, Croatia, Order of Star Planina, First Class, Bulgaria, Order of Madara Horseman, First Class, Bulgaria. *Leisure interests:* skiing, tennis. *Address:* c/o Department of State, 2201 C Street, NW, Washington, DC 20520, USA.

MONTI, Mario; Italian international organization official and economist; *President, Bocconi University;* b. 19 March 1943, Varese; m.; two c.; ed Bocconi Univ., Milan and Yale Univ., USA; Assoc. Prof., Univ. of Trento 1969–70; Prof., Univ. of Turin 1970–79; Prof. of Monetary Theory and Policy, Bocconi Univ. 1971–85, Prof. of Econs, Dir Inst. of Econs 1985–94, f. Paolo Baffi Centre for Monetary and Financial Econs 1985, f. Innocenzo Gasparini Inst. of Econ. Research 1989, Rector, Bocconi Univ. 1989–94, Pres. 1994; Econ. Commentator, Corriere della Sera 1978–94; Rapporteur, Treasury Cttee on Savings Protection 1981, Chair. Treasury Cttee on Banking and Financial System 1981–82, mem. Competition Act Drafting Cttee 1987–88, mem. Treasury Cttee on Debt Man. 1988–89, on Banking Law Reform 1989–91; mem. working party preparing Italy for single market 1988–90; mem. Macroeconomic Policy Group, European Comm. and Center for Econ. Policy Studies (CEPS) 1985–86; mem. EC responsible for Internal Market, Financial Services and Financial Integration, Customs, Taxation 1995–99, for Competition 1999–2004; Int. Adviser, Goldman Sachs Int. 2005–; Pres. Bocconi Univ., Milan 2005–. *Address:* Bocconi University, Via Sarfatti 25, 20136 Milan, Italy (office). *Telephone:* (02) 58361 (office). *Website:* www.uni-bocconi.it (office).

MONTIEL, Eduardo Luis, DBA MS; Nicaraguan politician; b. San Sebastián, Managua; Eduardo Montiel Argüello; m. 1st; two c.; m. 2nd Eugenia Argeñal; ed Harvard Business School, MIT, USA; early career as industrial engineer; Dean, Instituto Centroamericano de Administración de Empresas (INCAE); Pres. Del. Comisión de Promoción de Inversiones; Adviser, govt enterprises in Latin America, USA, Europe; Minister of Finance and Public Credit 2004–05; mem. Editorial Council. *Publications include:* more than 70 publications. *Address:* Frente a la Asamblea Nacional, Apdo 2170, Managua, Nicaragua (office).

MONTILLA AGUILERA, José, LLB; Spanish politician; *President, Government of Catalonia;* b. 15 Jan. 1955, Iznájar, Cordoba; m.; five c.; ed Univ. of Barcelona; mem. Partit dels Socialistes de Catalunya (PSC) 1978–, mem. Exec. Comm. 1987–, Sec. 1994, First Sec. 2000; mem. City Council, Sant Joan Despí 1979–83; mem. Council and Mayor, Cornellá de Llobregat 1983–2004; Second Vice-Pres., Barcelona Del. 1987–95, First Vice-Pres. 1999; Deputy, Barcelona Congress 2004–; Minister of Industry, Tourism and Trade 2004–06; Pres. Govt of Catalonia 2006–. *Address:* Government of Catalonia, Plaça de Sant Jaume 4, 08002 Barcelona, Spain (office). *Telephone:* (93) 4024600 (office). *Fax:* (93) 3183488 (office). *E-mail:* gbpresident.presidencia@gencat.cat (office). *Website:* www.gencat.cat/president (office).

MONTKIEWICZ, Zdzislaw; Polish business executive; b. 28 June 1944, Sokolów Podlaski; ed Mil. Tech. Acad.; mem. staff Polish Acad. of Sciences 1972–74, Ministry of Foreign Affairs 1974–78, UN Security Council 1978–82; Dir-Gen. Dernan & Sental Manufacturing and Financial Group 1983–88; Dir-Gen. Poland office, IBM World Trade/Europe/Middle East/Africa Corpn 1988–91; Pres. Ciech SA 1994–97; Pres. Prudential/Prumerica Financial Poland 1997–2001; Pres. Man. Bd Powszechny Zaklad Ubezpieczen (PZU) SA (state-controlled insurer) 2002–03; Founder-mem. Polish Trade and Finance Union; mem. Zacheta Art Soc. *Leisure interest:* reading historical books. *Address:* c/o Powszechny Zaklad Ubezpieczen SA, al. Jana Pawla II 24, 00-133 Warsaw, Poland (office).

MONTWILL, Alexander, PhD, DSc, MRIA, FInstP; Irish physicist and academic; *Professor Emeritus, Department of Physics, University College Dublin;* b. 28 Oct. 1935, Riga, Latvia; s. of Stanislaw Montwill and Jadwiga Huszcza; m. Ann O'Doherty 1966; one s. four d.; ed Belvedere Coll., Westland Row Christian Brothers' School, Dublin and Univ. Coll. Dublin; lecturer, Univ. Coll. Dublin 1959–81, Assoc. Prof. 1981–85, Prof. of Experimental Physics 1985, Prof. Emer. 2002–, Head Dept of Physics 1986–95; Visiting Assoc. Prof. City Coll. of New York 1966–68; Visiting Scientist, CERN, Geneva 1965–. *Television includes:* Understanding the Universe (six-part series), RTE. *Radio includes:* 150 segments on physics, RTE . *Publications:* 50 publs on high-energy physics; Let There Be Light: The Story of Light from Atoms to Galaxies (with Ann Breslin) 2008. *Leisure interest:* bridge. *Address:* Department of Physics, University College, Belfield, Dublin 4, Republic of Ireland. *Telephone:* (1) 7162230 (office); (1) 2894763 (home). *Fax:* (1) 2837275 (office). *E-mail:* alex_montwill@hotmail.com (home).

MONTY, Jean C., MA, MBA; Canadian business executive; *Chairman, BCE Emergis Inc.;* b. 26 June 1947, Montreal; m. Jocelyne Monty; two s.; ed Coll. Sainte-Marie, Montreal and Univs of W. Ontario and Chicago; Merrill Lynch, New York, Toronto and Montreal 1970–74; Bell Canada, Montreal 1974; Pres. Télébec Ltée. 1976; Nat. Defence Coll. Kingston, Ont. 1979–80; Bell Canada 1980–92, Pres. 1989, Pres. and CEO 1991–92; Pres. and COO Northern Telecom Ltd 1992, Pres. and CEO 1993–98; Chair. and CEO Bell Canada Enterprises (BCE) Inc. 1998–2002 (resgnd), Chair. BCE Emergis Inc. 2004–; Dir Bombardier Inc., Centria Inc., Fiera Capital Inc., Contramax Inc.; mem. Supervisory Bd Lagardère Group, Paris. *Leisure interest:* golf. *Address:* BCE Emergis Inc., 1000, rue de Sérigny, bureau 600, Longueuil, PQ J4K 5B1, Canada. *Telephone:* (450) 928-6000. *Website:* www.emergis.com (office).

MONYAKE, Lengolo Bureng, MSc, UED; Lesotho government official; b. 1 April 1930, Lesotho; s. of Bureng L. Monyake and Leomile Monyake; m. Molulela Mapetla 1957; two s. one d.; ed Fort Hare Univ. Coll., Univ. of Toronto, Carleton Univ., London School of Econs; Headmaster, Jordan High School 1958–61; Dir of Statistics, Govt of Lesotho 1968–74, Perm. Sec. 1974–76, Deputy Sr Perm. Sec. 1976–78; Amb. 1979–83; Man. Dir Lesotho Nat. Devt Corpn 1984–86; Minister for Foreign Affairs 1986–88, for Works 1988; Alt. Exec. Dir IMF 1988–90, Exec. Dir 1990–92; Deputy Exec. Sec. Southern African Devt Community 1993–98; currently with African Peer Review Mechanism (APRM), Lesotho; also currently Pres. Eighteenth Episcopal Dist, Connectional Lay Org., African Methodist Episcopal Church, Lesotho. *Leisure interests:* tennis, table tennis, music, photography. *Address:* PO Box 526, Maseruloo, Lesotho, South Africa. *E-mail:* lmonyake@amec-connectionallay.org.

MOODY, Robert Vaughn, OC, BA, MA, PhD, FRSC; Canadian (b. British) mathematician and academic; *Professor Emeritus of Mathematics, Department of Mathematical and Statistical Sciences, University of Alberta; Adjunct Professor of Mathematics, University of Victoria;* b. 28 Nov. 1941; ed Univ. of Sask., Univ. of Toronto; Asst Prof., Dept of Math., Univ. of Sask. 1966–70, Assoc. Prof. 1970–76, Prof. 1976–89; Asst Prof., New Mexico State Univ., Las Cruces 1967–68; with Mathematisches Institüt, Universität Bonn 1973–74, Centre de Recherche de Mathematiques Appliquées, Montreal 1983–84; Prof., Concordia Univ., Montreal 1984–86; apptd Prof., Dept of Math., Univ. of Alberta 1989, Chair. Review Cttee, Dept of Math. and Statistics 1990, now Prof. Emer. of Math., Dept of Math. and Statistical Sciences; Scientific Dir Banff Int. Research Station for Math. Innovation and Discovery 2001–03; Guest Prof., Gesamthochschule Wuppertal Jan.–June 1979, Université de Paris VI Jan.–June 1979, Tata Inst. for Math., Bombay, India 1987; mem. Bd Fields Inst. for Research in Math. Sciences 1988–91, Council, Acad. of Science, RSC 1990–93; mem. Scientific Advisory Bd, Centre de Recherches de Mathematique, Université de Montréal 1993–96, Scientific Advisory Panel, Fields Inst. for Research in Math. Sciences 1993–98; mem. Editorial Bd Nova Journal of Algebra and Geometry1992–98, Canadian Journal of Mathematics, Canadian Mathematics Bulletin; mem. Publs Cttee, Canadian Math. Soc. 1982–85, 1988–90; mem. PIMS Scientific Review Panel 1997–; mem. Aspen Inst. for Physics 1982, 1983, 1984, 1986, 1987, 1990, 1997; co-discoverer of Kac-Moody algebra; Dr hc (Université de Montréal) 2000; Coxeter-James Lectureship, Canadian Math. Soc. 1978, Japan Soc. for the Promotion of Science Fellowship 1981, Eugene Wigner Medal (jtly with Victor Kac) for "work on affine Lie algebras that has influenced many areas of theoretical physics", Int. Cttee for Group Theoretical Methods in Math. and Physics 1994, Jeffrey-William Lectureship, Canadian Math. Soc. 1994, Ireland Lectureship, Univ. of New Brunswick 1995, Kaplan Award for Science, Univ. of Alberta 1995, Britten Lectureship, McMaster Univ. 1996, Alberta Science and Tech. Award for Outstanding Research 1996, Frontiers of Mathematics Lectureship, Texas A&M Univ. 1996, CRM/Fields Inst. Prize 1998, Killam Prize 2002, Lansdowne Professorship, Univ. of Victoria 2004, Golden Jubilee Professorship, Benares Hindu Univ., Varanasi 2004. *Publications:* six books and more than 70 articles. *Address:* Department of Mathematical and Statistical Sciences, 632 Central Academic Building, University of Alberta, Edmonton, Alberta T6G 2G1, Canada (office). *Telephone:* (780) 492-3396 (office). *Fax:* (780) 492-6826 (office). *E-mail:* mathsci@math.ualberta.ca (office). *Website:* www.math.ualberta.ca/~rvmoody/rvm (office).

MOODY-STUART, Sir Mark, KCMG, MA, PhD, FGS; British company director and geologist; *Non-Executive Chairman, Anglo American PLC;* b. 15 Sept. 1940, Antigua, West Indies; s. of Sir Alexander Moody-Stuart and Judith Moody-Stuart (née Henzell); m. Judith McLeavy 1964; three s. one d.; ed Shrewsbury School and St John's Coll., Cambridge; with Shell Internationale Petroleum Mij. 1966–67, Koninklijke Shell E & P Lab. 1967–68, worked with Shell cos in Spain, Oman, Brunei 1968–72, Chief Geologist, Australia 1972–76, Shell UK 1977–78, Brunei Shell Services Man. 1978–79, Gen. Man. Shell 1978–79, Man. Western Div. Shell Nigeria 1979–82, Gen. Man. Shell Turkey 1982–86, Chair. and CEO Shell Malaysia 1986–89, Exploration and Production Co-ordinator, Royal Dutch/Shell 1990, Dir Shell Transport & Trading Co. PLC 1990–2005, Chair. 1997–2001, Man. Dir Royal Dutch/Shell Group 1991–2001, Chair. Cttee of Man. Dirs 1998–2001; Chair. (non-exec.) Anglo American PLC 2002–, mem. Remuneration, Safety and Sustainable Devt and Nomination Cttees; Jt Chair. G8 Task Force on Devt of Renewable Sources of Energy 2000; mem. Bd Dirs Accenture 2001–, HSBC Holdings PLC 2001–, Saudi Aramco 2007–; Chair. Business Action for Sustainable Devt 2001–02, Global Compact Foundation 2006–; Pres. Liverpool School of Tropical Medicine 2001–08; Fellow, Geological Soc. of London (Pres. 2002–04); mem. UN Sec.-Gen.'s Advisory Council for the Global Compact 2001–04, Bd UN Global Compact 2006–; mem. Bd Global Reporting Initiative 2001–07, Bd Int. Inst. for Sustainable Devt 2002–; Gov. Nuffield Hosps 2001–08; Hon. FIChemE 1997; Hon. Fellow, St John's Coll., Cambridge 2001; Hon. DBA (Robert Gordon) 2000; Hon. LLD (Aberdeen) 2001; Hon. DSc (Royal Holloway, London); Cadman Medal Inst. of Petroleum 2002. *Publications:* papers in scientific and other journals. *Leisure interests:* sailing, travel, reading. *Address:* Anglo American PLC, 20 Carlton House Terrace, London, SW1Y 5AN, England (office). *Telephone:* (20) 7968-8709 (office). *Fax:* (20) 7698-8687 (office). *E-mail:* mmoodystuart@angloamerican.co.uk (office). *Website:* www.angloamerican.co.uk (office).

MOONEY, Harold Alfred (Hal), MA, PhD; American biologist and academic; *Paul S. Achilles Professor of Environmental Biology and Senior Fellow, by courtesy, Woods Institute for the Environment, Stanford University;* b. 1 June 1932, Santa Rosa, Calif.; s. of Harold Walter Stefany and Sylvia A. Hart; m. Sherry L. Gulmon 1974; three d.; ed Univ. of California, Santa Barbara and Duke Univ.; Instructor to Assoc. Prof., UCLA 1960–68; Assoc. Prof., Stanford Univ. 1968–73, Prof. 1975–, Paul S. Achilles Prof. of Environmental Biology 1976–; fmr Chair. US Nat. Research Council Cttee on Ecosystem Man. for Sustainable Marine Fisheries; served as Coordinator of UN Global Biodiversity Assessment 1995; fmr Pres. Ecological Soc. of America; Guggenheim Fellow 1974; mem. NAS, American Philosophical Soc.; Foreign mem. Russian Acad. of Sciences; Fellow, American Academy of Arts and Sciences; Hon. mem. British Ecological Soc.; Mercer Award, Ecology Soc. of America 1961, Humboldt Award 1988, ECI Prize in Terrestrial Ecology, Inst. of Ecology Prize (Germany) 1990, Max Planck Research Award in Biosciences 1992, Eminent Ecologist Award (co-recipient), Ecological Soc. of America 1996, Ramon Margalef Prize in Ecology and Environmental Sciences 2007. *Publications:* 12 books. *Address:* Department of Biological Sciences, Room 477, Herrin Labs, Stanford University, Stanford, CA 94305-5020 (office); 2625 Ramona Street, Palo Alto, CA 94306, USA (home). *Telephone:* (650) 723-1179 (office). *Fax:* (650) 723-9253 (office). *E-mail:* hmooney@stanford.edu (office). *Website:* www.stanford.edu/dept/biology (office).

MOONVES, Leslie (Les); American television industry executive; *President and CEO, CBS Corporation;* b. 6 Oct. 1949, Valley Stream, Long Island, NY; m. Nancy Moonves 1979; two s. one d.; ed Bucknell Univ.; trained as actor at Neighbourhood Playhouse, NY; performed in numerous stage and tv productions; began to produce plays for Broadway and LA 1977; TV Exec., Twentieth Century Fox TV, Saul Ilson Productions and Catalina Productions 1978–85; Vice-Pres. Lorimar TV 1985–89, Pres. 1989–93; Pres. Warner Bros. TV 1993–95; Pres. CBS Entertainment and Group Exec. Vice-Pres., CBS TV 1995–98, Pres. and CEO CBS TV 1998–2003, elected to Corp. Bd of Dirs 1999, Chair. and CEO 2003–, oversees productions of UPN, CBS Enterprises, CBS News, CBS Sports, CBS Entertainment, King World Productions; Co-Pres. and Co-COO Viacom Inc. (after Viacom acquired CBS) 2000-05, Pres. and CEO CBS Corpn (after CBS split from Viacom) 2005–; Co-Chair. LA Bd of Govs, Museum of TV & Radio; mem. Nat. Collegiate Athletic Asscn (NCAA) Advisory Bd; mem. Bd of Dirs LA Free Clinic; mem. Bd of Trustees, Entertainment Industries Council; Trustee, American Film Inst., Nat. Council of Families and TV. *Address:* CBS Corporation, 51 West 52nd Street, New York, NY 10019, USA (office). *Telephone:* (212) 975-4321 (office); (212) 258-6000 (office). *Fax:* (212) 975-4516 (office); (212) 258-6464 (office). *Website:* www.cbscorporation.com (office).

MOORBATH, Stephen Erwin, DPhil, DSc, FRS; British scientist and academic; *Professor Emeritus, Department of Earth Sciences, University of Oxford;* b. 9 May 1929, Magdeburg, Germany; s. of Heinz Moorbath and Else Moorbath; m. Pauline Tessier-Varlêt 1962; one s. one d.; ed Lincoln Coll., Oxford; Asst Experimental Officer, Atomic Energy Research Est., Harwell 1948–51; Scientific Officer, AERE 1954–56; Research Fellow, Univ. of Oxford 1956–61, Sr Research Officer, 1962–78, Reader in Geology 1978–92, Prof. of Isotope Geology 1992–96, Prof. Emer. 1996–, Professorial Fellow, Linacre Coll. 1990–96, Fellow Emer. 1996; Research Fellow, MIT, USA 1961–62; several awards. *Publications:* numerous contribs to books and scientific journals. *Leisure interests:* music, philately, travel, linguistics. *Address:* Department of Earth Sciences, Oxford University, Parks Road, Oxford, OX1 3PR (office); 53 Bagley Wood Road, Kennington, Oxford, OX1 5LY, England (home). *Telephone:* (1865) 282147 (office); (1865) 739507 (home). *Fax:* (1865) 272072 (office). *E-mail:* stephen.moorbath@earth.ox.ac.uk (office). *Website:* www.earth.ox.ac.uk (office).

MOORCOCK, Michael John, (Edward P. Bradbury, Desmond Read); British novelist; b. 18 Dec. 1939, London; s. of Arthur Moorcock and June Moorcock; m. 1st Hilary Bailey 1963 (divorced 1978); one s. two d.; m. 2nd Jill Riches 1978 (divorced 1983 m. 3rd Linda M. Steele 1983; ed Michael Hall School, Sussex; worked as musician and journalist; Ed. Outlaws Own 1951–53, Tarzan Adventures 1957–59, Sexton Blake Library 1959–61, Current Topics 1961–62; Ed. New Worlds 1963–96, Consulting Ed. 1996–; August Derleith Prize, World Fantasy Lifetime Achievement Award 2000, Science Fiction Hall of Fame 2002, Priz Utopiales 2004, named Damon Knight Grand Master, Science Fiction and Fantasy Writers of America 2008. *Films:* The Final Programme 1973, The Land that Time Forgot 1975. *Records:* Warrior on the Edge of Time (Hawkwind) 1975, The New World's Fair 1975, The Brothel in Rosenstrasse 1982, Roller Coaster Holiday 2004. *Publications include:* The Eternal Champion sequence 1963–98, Behold the Man (Nebula Award 1967) 1968, Condition of Muzak (Guardian Fiction Prize 1977) 1976, Gloriana (World Fantasy Award 1979) 1977, Byzantium Endures 1981, The Laughter of Carthage 1984, Mother London 1988, Jerusalem Commands 1992, Blood 1994, The War Amongst Angels 1996, Tales from the Texas Woods 1997, King of the City 2000, Silverheart (co-author) 2000, London Bone 2001, The Dreamthief's Daughter 2001, The Skrayling Tree 2003, The Lives and Times of Jerry Cornelius 2004, Wizardry and Wild Romance 2004, The White Wolf's Son 2005, The Vengeance of Rome 2006. *Leisure interests:* climbing, travelling, walking, cats, birds. *Address:* c/o Morhaim Literary Agency, 30 Pierrepont Street, Brooklyn, NY 11201, USA (office); c/o Agence Hoffman, 77 Boulevard St Michel, 75005 Paris, France (office); PO Box 1230, Bastrop, TX 78602, USA (home). *Telephone:* (718) 222-8400 (Brooklyn) (office). *Fax:* (512) 321-5000 (Brooklyn) (office). *E-mail:* mjm@multiverse.org (office). *Website:* www.multiverse.org.

MOORE, Ann S., BSc, MBA; American publisher and media executive; *Chairman and CEO, Time Inc.;* b. 1950, McLean, Va; m. Donovan Moore; one s.; ed Vanderbilt Univ., Nashville, Harvard Univ. Business School; financial analyst, Time Inc. 1978, served in various exec. positions including Publr and Pres. People magazine (est. spin-offs Teen People, Instyle, Real Simple, People en Español 2001), cr. Sports Illustrated for Kids 1989, Exec. Vice-Pres. Time Inc. 2001–02, Chair. and CEO 2002–, responsible for Time magazine, People, Fortune, Money, Entertainment Weekly and 135 other titles (first woman in position); mem. Bd of Dirs Avon Products Inc., Wallace Foundation; Adweek's Publishing Exec. of the Year 1998, MIN Magazine's Consumer Magazine Player of the Year 1999, named one of Advertising Age's Women to Watch 2001, ranked by Fortune magazine amongst 50 Most Powerful Women in Business in the US 1998–2001, (11th) 2002, (13th) 2003, (13th) 2004, (13th) 2005, (15th) 2006, (19th) 2007, first Annual AOL Time Warner Civic Leadership Award 2003, ranked by Forbes magazine amongst 100 Most Powerful Women (20th) 2004, (38th) 2005, (53rd) 2006, (57th) 2007, (93rd) 2008. *Leisure interests:* Washington Redskins, cooking, reading. *Address:* Time Inc., Rockefeller Plaza, New York, NY 10019, USA (office). *Telephone:* (212) 484-8000 (office). *Website:* www.timewarner.com (office).

MOORE, Carole Irene, MS; Canadian librarian; *Chief Librarian, University of Toronto;* b. 15 Aug. 1944, Berkeley, Calif., USA; ed Stanford and Columbia Univs; Reference Librarian, Columbia Univ. Libraries 1967–68; Reference Librarian, Univ. of Toronto Library 1968–73, Asst Head, Reference Dept 1973–74, Head 1974–80, Head, Bibliographic Processing Dept 1980–86, Assoc. Librarian, Tech. Services 1986–87, Chief Librarian, Univ. of Toronto Library 1986–, Research Libraries Group Dir 1994–96; mem. Preservation of Research Library Materials Cttee, Asscn of Research Libraries 2004–06; mem. Bd of Dirs Univ. of Toronto Press 1994–; Columbia Univ. School of Library Service Centenary Distinguished Alumni Award 1987. *Publications:* Labour Relations and the Librarian (ed.) 1974, Canadian Essays and Collections Index 1972–73 1976. *Leisure interest:* gardening. *Address:* University of Toronto Libraries, Chief Librarian's Office, 130 St George Street, Room 2015, Toronto, ON M5S 1A5, Canada (office). *Telephone:* (416) 978-2292 (office). *Fax:* (416) 971-2099 (office). *E-mail:* carole.moore@utoronto.ca (office). *Website:* www.library.utoronto.ca (office).

MOORE, Charles Hilary, MA; British journalist; *Group Consulting Editor, The Daily Telegraph (UK);* b. 31 Oct. 1956, Hastings; s. of Richard Moore and Ann Moore; m. Caroline Baxter 1981; twin s. and d.; ed Eton Coll. and Trinity Coll. Cambridge; editorial staff, Daily Telegraph 1979–81, leader writer 1981–83; Asst Ed. and Political Columnist, The Spectator 1983–84, Ed. 1984–90, fortnightly columnist ('Another Voice') 1990–95; weekly columnist, Daily Express 1987–90; Deputy Ed. Daily Telegraph 1990–92; Ed. Sunday Telegraph 1992–95, Daily Telegraph 1995–2003, Group Consulting Ed. Daily Telegraph (UK) 2003–; Chair. Policy Exchange; Trustee T. E. Utley Memorial Fund, Benenden Council, ShareGift. *Publications:* 1936 (co-ed. with C. Hawtree) 1986, The Church in Crisis (with A. N. Wilson and G. Stamp) 1986, A Tory Seer: The Selected Journalism of T. E. Utley (co-ed. with S. Heffer) 1986. *Address:* c/o Daily Telegraph, 11 Buckinghham Palace Road, London, SW1 0DT, England (office).

MOORE, Demi; American actress; b. (Demi Guynes), 11 Nov. 1962, Roswell, New Mexico; d. of Danny Guynes and Virginia Guynes; m. 1st Bruce Willis (q.v.) (divorced 2000); three d.; m. 2nd Ashton Kutcher 2005; began acting with small part in TV series; worked as a model, Los Angeles; f. Moving Pictures (production co.). *Films include:* Choices 1981, Parasite 1982, Blame It on Rio 1984, No Small Affair 1984, St Elmo's Fire 1985, One Crazy Summer

1986, About Last Night 1986, Wisdom 1986, The Seventh Sign 1988, We're No Angels 1989, Ghost 1990, Nothing But Trouble 1991, Mortal Thoughts (also co-producer) 1991, The Butcher's Wife 1991, A Few Good Men 1992, Indecent Proposal 1993, Disclosure 1994, The Scarlet Letter 1995, Now and Then 1995, Striptease 1996, The Juror 1996, The Hunchback of Notre Dame (voice) 1996, Deconstructing Harry 1997, G.I. Jane (also producer) 1997, Passion of Mind 2000, The Hunchback of Notre Dame II (voice) 2002, Charlie's Angels: Full Throttle 2003, Half Light 2006, Bobby 2006, Flawless 2007, Mr. Brooks 2007; producer: Austin Powers: International Man of Mystery 1997, Austin Powers: The Spy Who Shagged Me 1999, Austin Powers in Goldmember 2002. *Television:* General Hospital (series), Bedroom, The Magic 7, numerous episodes of series. *Theatre:* The Early Girl (Theater World award). *Address:* Moving Pictures, 1453 Third Street, Suite 420, Santa Monica, CA 90401, USA. *Telephone:* (310) 576-0577.

MOORE, Gillian, MBE, BMus, MA, FRCM; British music administrator; *Head of Contemporary Culture, Southbank Centre;* b. 20 Feb. 1959, Glasgow; d. of Charles Moore and Sara Queen; pnr Bruce Nockles; one s.; ed Univ. of Glasgow, Royal Scottish Acad. of Music and Drama, Univ. of York, Harvard Univ.; Educ. Dir London Sinfonietta 1983–93, Artistic Dir 1998–2006; Head of Educ., Southbank Centre, London 1993–98, also Music Audience Devt Man. 1996, Head of Contemporary Culture 2006–; Artistic Dir ISCM World Music Days, Manchester 1997–98; Visiting Prof., Royal Coll. of Music 1996–; Gov. Nat. Youth Orchestra of GB; mem. British Govt Nat. Curriculum Working Group on Music; Hon. Mem. Guildhall School of Music 1993; Dr hc (Brunel) 2006; Sir Charles Groves Award for Outstanding Contrib. to British Music 1992, Asscn of British Orchestras Award for Contrib. of Most Benefit to Orchestral Life in the UK 1999, Leslie Boosey Award 2008. *Address:* Southbank Centre, Belvedere Road, London, SE1 8XX (office); 108 Waller Road, London, SE14 5LU, England (home). *Telephone:* (871) 663-2501 (office); (20) 7639-6680 (home). *Fax:* (20) 7639-6675 (home). *Website:* www.southbankcentre.co.uk (office).

MOORE, Gordon Earle, PhD, FIEEE, FRSEng; American fmr semiconductor executive; *Chairman Emeritus, Intel Corporation;* b. 3 Jan. 1929, San Francisco; m.; two c.; ed Univ. of Calif., Berkeley, Calif. Inst. of Tech.; with Fairchild Semiconductor –1968; Co-founder and Exec. Vice-Pres. Integrated Electronics (Intel, world's largest manufacturer of microprocessors) 1968–75, Pres. and CEO 1975–79, Chair. and CEO 1979–87, Chair. 1987–97, Chair. Emer. 1997–; Dir Gilead Sciences Inc.; mem. Nat. Acad. of Eng; mem. Bd Trustees Calif. Inst. of Tech.; Nat. Medal of Tech. 1990. *Address:* Intel Corpn, 2200 Mission College Boulevard, Santa Clara, CA 95052-8119, USA (office). *Telephone:* (408) 765-8080 (office). *Fax:* (408) 765-9904 (office). *Website:* www.intel.com (office).

MOORE, James; Canadian politician; *Minister of Canadian Heritage and Official Languages;* b. 10 June 1976, New Westminster; MP 2000–; Parl. Sec. to Minister Public Works and Govt Services 2006–07; Sec. of State for Official Languages, Pacific Gateway and the Vancouver-Whistler Olympics 2007–08; Minister of Canadian Heritage and Official Languages 2008–; mem. Canadian Alliance Party 2000–03, Conservative Party of Canada 2003–. *Address:* Canadian Heritage, 15 rue Eddy, Gatineau, PQ K1A 0M5, Canada (office). *Telephone:* (819) 997-0055 (office). *Fax:* (819) 953-5382 (office). *Website:* www.pch.gc.ca (office).

MOORE, Hon. John Colinton, AO, BCom, AASA; Australian fmr politician and company director; b. 16 Nov. 1936, Rockhampton; s. of T. R. Moore and D. S. Moore; m. 2nd Jacquelyn Moore; two s. one d. from previous m.; ed Armidale School, Queensland Univ.; stockbroker 1960; mem. Brisbane Stock Exchange 1962–74; Vice-Pres. and Treas. Queensland Liberal Party 1967–73, Pres. 1973–76, 1984–90; MP for Ryan 1975–2001; Minister for Business and Consumer Affairs 1980–82; Opposition Spokesman for Finance 1983–84, for Communications 1984–85, for Northern Devt and Local Govt 1985–87, for Transport and Aviation 1987, for Business and Consumer Affairs 1987–89, for Business Privatization and Consumer Affairs 1989–90; Shadow Minister for Privatization and Public Admin. 1994, for Privatization 1994–95, for Industry, Commerce and Public Admin. 1995–96; Minister for Industry, Science and Tourism 1996–97, of Industry, Science and Tech. 1997–98, for Defence 1998–2001; Vice-Pres. Exec. Council 1996–98; Dir William Brandt & Sons (Australia), Phillips, First City, Brandt Ltd, Merrill Lynch, Pierce, Fennell and Smith (Australia) Ltd, Citinat, Agricultural Investments Australia Ltd; mem. various int. dels, Council Order of Australia, Advisory Council General Motors, Australia. *Leisure interests:* tennis, cricket, reading, golf. *Address:* PO Box 2191, Toowong, Brisbane 4066; 47 Dennis Street, Indooroopilly, Brisbane, Australia (home). *Telephone:* 419 704764 (office); (7) 3217-7427 (home). *Fax:* (7) 3876-8088 (office). *E-mail:* john_moore1@bigpond.com.au (home).

MOORE, Capt. John Evelyn, RN, FRGS; British editor, author and naval officer (retd); b. 1 Nov. 1921, Sant' Ilario, Italy; s. of William John Moore and Evelyn Elizabeth (née Hooper); m. 1st Joan Pardoe 1945; one s. two d.; m. 2nd Barbara Kerry; ed Sherborne School, Dorset; entered RN 1939, specialized in hydrographic surveying, then submarines: commanded HM Submarines Totem, Alaric, Tradewind, Tactician, Telemachus; RN staff course 1950–51; Commdr 1957; attached to Turkish Naval Staff 1958–60; subsequently Plans Div., Admiralty, 1st Submarine Squadron, then 7th Submarine Squadron in command; Capt. 1967; served as Chief of Staff, C-in-C Naval Home Command; Defence Intelligence Staff; retd list at own request 1972; Ed., Jane's Fighting Ships 1972–87; Ed., Jane's Naval Review 1982–87; Hon. Prof. of Int. Relations, Aberdeen Univ. 1987–90, St Andrews Univ. 1990–92. *Publications:* Jane's Major Warships 1973, The Soviet Navy Today 1975, Submarine Development 1976, Soviet War Machine (jtly) 1976, Encyclopaedia of World's Warships 1978, World War 3 1978, Seapower and Politics 1979, Warships of the Royal Navy 1979, Warships of the Soviet Navy 1981, Submarine Warfare: Today and Tomorrow (jtly) 1986; ed. The Impact of Polaris 1999. *Leisure interests:* gardening, archaeology. *Address:* 1 Ridgelands Close, Eastbourne, East Sussex, BN20 8EP, England. *Telephone:* (1323) 638836.

MOORE, Julianne, BA; American actress; b. 3 Dec. 1961, Fayetteville, NC; m. 1st John Gould Rubin (divorced 1995); m. 2nd Bart Freundlich; one s. one d.; ed Boston Univ. School for Arts; with the Guthrie Theater 1988–89. *Stage appearances include:* Serious Money 1987, Ice Cream with Hot Fudge 1990, Uncle Vanya, The Road to Nirvana, Hamlet, The Father, The Vertical Hour 2006. *Film appearances include:* Tales from the Darkside 1990, The Hand That Rocks the Cradle 1992, The Gun in Betty Lou's Handbag 1992, Body of Evidence 1993, Benny and Joon 1993, The Fugitive 1993, Short Cuts 1993, Vanya on 42nd Street 1994, Roommates 1995, Safe 1995, Nine Months 1995, Assassins 1995, Surviving Picasso 1996, Jurassic Park: The Lost World 1997, The Myth of Fingerprints 1997, Hellcab 1997, Boogie Nights 1997, The Big Lebowski 1998, Eyes Wide Shut, The End of the Affair 1999, Map of the World 1999, Magnolia 1999, Cookie's Fortune 1999, An Ideal Husband 1999, Hannibal 2000, The Shipping News 2002, Far From Heaven (Best Actress, Venice Film Festival) 2002, The Hours 2002, Marie and Bruce 2004, Laws of Attraction 2004, The Forgotten 2004, Trust the Man 2005, Freedomland 2005, Children of Men 2006, Next 2007, I'm Not There 2007, Savage Grace 2007, Blindness 2008. *Television appearances include:* As the World Turns (series), The Edge of Night (series), Money, Power Murder 1989, Lovecraft 1991, I'll Take Manhattan, The Last to Go, Cast a Deadly Spell. *Publication:* Freckleface Strawberry (juvenile) 2007. *Address:* c/o Kevin Huvane, Creative Artists Agency, 9830 Wilshire Boulevard, Beverly Hills, CA 90212, USA.

MOORE, Michael, CBE, MA, MBA; British business executive; b. 15 March 1936; s. of Gen. Sir Rodney Moore and Olive Marion Robinson; m. Jan Moore; one s.; ed Eton Coll., Magdalen Coll., Oxford and Harvard Business School, USA; called to the Bar 1961; Chair. Tomkins PLC 1984–95, Quicks Group PLC 1993–, Linx Printing Technologies PLC 1993–, London Int. Group PLC 1994–, Status Holdings PLC 2000–; Jt Deputy Chair., Clerical Medical & Gen. Life Assurance Soc. 1996–; Chair. Nat. Soc. for Prevention of Cruelty to Children (NSPCC) 1988–95; Chair. Which? 1997–; Trustee Public Concern at Work 1996–. *Leisure interests:* reading, music (especially opera), visiting ruins, tennis. *Address:* 35 New Bridge Street, London, EC4V 6BJ, England.

MOORE, Michael Francis; American writer and filmmaker; b. 23 April 1954, Davison, Mich.; m. Kathleen Glynn 1991; ed Davison High School; elected to Davison, Mich. school bd aged 18; active in student politics; began career as journalist with The Flint Voice, later Ed., expanded into The Mich. Voice; Ed. Mother Jones magazine, San Francisco 1986–88; Founder and mem. Bd of Dirs Traverse City (Mich.) Film Festival. *Television includes:* Pets or Meat: The Return to Flint 1992, TV Nation (NBC series) 1994–95, 1997, And Justice for All (dir) 1998, The Awful Truth (series) 1999. *Films:* Roger and Me (writer, dir, producer) 1989, Canadian Bacon (writer, producer, dir) 1994, The Big One (dir) 1997, Bowling for Columbine (screenwriter, dir, producer; Jury Award, Cannes Film Festival 2003, Acad. Award for Best Documentary 2003) 2002, Fahrenheit 9/11 (dir; Palme d'Or, Cannes Film Festival, US People's Choice Award for Best Film 2005) 2004, Sicko 2007. *Film appearances:* Pony Express 1953, Lucky Number 1999, EdTV 1999. *Publications:* Downsize This!: Random Threats from an Unarmed America 1996, Stupid White Men (Book of the Year, British Book Awards 2003) 2001, Adventures in a TV Nation (with Kathleen Glynn) 2002, Dude, Where's My Country? 2003, Will They Ever Trust Us Again?: Letters from the War Zone 2004. *Address:* c/o Random House Inc., 1745 Broadway, Suite B1, New York, NY 10019-4305, USA (office). *E-mail:* mike@michaelmoore.com. *Website:* www.michaelmoore.com.

MOORE, Rt Hon. Michael Kenneth, PC, MP; New Zealand politician and international organization official; b. 28 Jan. 1949, Whakatane; s. of the late Alan Moore and Audrey Moore; m. Yvonne Dereaney 1975; fmr social worker, printer etc.; MP for Eden 1972–75, Papanui, Christchurch 1978–84, Christchurch N 1984–96, Waimakariri 1996–99; Minister of Overseas Trade and Marketing, also Minister of Tourism and Publicity and of Recreation and Sport 1984–87; Minister of Overseas Trade and Marketing and of Publicity 1987–88, 1989–90, of External Relations and Int. Trade 1988–90; Minister of Foreign Affairs Jan.–Oct. 1990; Prime Minister Sept.–Oct. 1990; Leader of the Opposition 1990–93; fmr Assoc. Minister of Finance; Dir-Gen. WTO 1999–2002. *Publications include:* A Pacific Parliament, Hard Labour, Fighting for New Zealand 1993, Children of the Poor 1996, A Brief History of the Future 1998. *Address:* c/o Privy Council, Government of New Zealand, Parliament Buildings, Wellington, New Zealand.

MOORE, Nicholas G., JD, BS; American business executive; *Senior Counselor, Bechtel Group Inc.;* m. Jo Anne Moore; four c.; ed St Mary's Coll., Calif., Hastings Coll. of Law, Univ. of Calif., Berkeley; joined Coopers & Lybrand 1968, Pnr 1974, Head of Tax Practice, San José office 1974–81, Man. Partner San José Office 1981, mem. firm council 1984, Exec. Cttee 1988, Vice-Chair. W Region 1991–92, Client Service Vice-Chair. 1992, Chair., CEO Coopers & Lybrand USA 1994, Chair. Coopers & Lybrand Int. 1997, Global Chair. and CEO PricewaterhouseCoopers LLP (formed from merger of Coopers & Lybrand Int. and Price Waterhouse) 1999–2001; currently Sr Counselor Bechtel Group Inc.; mem. Bd of Dirs, Network Appliance Inc. 2002–, Bechtel Group, Inc., Network Appliance Inc., Brocade Communications Systems, Inc., Hudson Highland Group, Inc., Gilead Sciences, Inc.; mem. Calif. Bar Asscn; Trustee Financial Accounting Foundation 1997–, St. Mary's Coll. of Calif.; Chair. Co-operation Ireland; mem. Bd of Trustees Cttee for Econ. Devt; Vice-Chair. Business Cttee, Metropolitan Museum of Art. *Address:* Bechtel Group, Inc., 50 Beale Street, San Francisco, CA 94105-1895, USA (office). *Telephone:* (415) 768-1234 (office). *Fax:* (415) 768-9038 (office). *Website:* www.bechtel.com (office).

MOORE, Sir Patrick Alfred Caldwell-, Kt (see Caldwell-Moore, Sir Patrick Alfred, Kt).

MOORE, Sir Roger, Kt; British actor; b. 14 Oct. 1927, London; m. 1st Doorn van Steyn (divorced 1953); m. 2nd Dorothy Squires 1953 (divorced 1969, died 1998); m. 3rd Luisa Mattioli; two s. one d.; ed Royal Acad. of Dramatic Art; Special Amb. for UNICEF 1991–; Dag Hammarskjold Inspiration Award, UNICEF 2007. *Films include:* Crossplot 1969, The Man With the Golden Gun 1974, That Lucky Touch 1975, Save Us From Our Friends 1975, Shout At The Devil 1975, Sherlock Holmes in New York 1976, The Spy Who Loved Me 1976, The Wild Geese 1977, Escape To Athena 1978, Moonraker 1978, Esther, Ruth and Jennifer 1979, The Sea Wolves, 1980, Sunday Lovers 1980, For Your Eyes Only 1980, Octopussy 1983, The Naked Face 1983, A View to a Kill 1985, Bullseye! 1990, Fire, Ice and Dynamite 1990, Bed and Breakfast 1992, The Quest 1996, Spice World 1997, The Enemy 2001, Boat Trip 2002, The Fly Who Loved Me (voice) 2004, Here Comes Peter Cottontail: The Movie (voice) 2005. *Television appearances include:* The Alaskans (series) 1959, The Saint (series) 1962–69, The Persuaders (series) 1972–73, The Man Who Wouldn't Die 1992, Dream Team (series) 1999, Foley and McColl: This Way Up 2005. *Publications:* James Bond Diary 1973, My Word is My Bond (auto-biog.) 2008.

MOORE OF LOWER MARSH, Baron (Life Peer), cr. 1992, of Lower Marsh in the London Borough of Lambeth; **John Edward Michael Moore;** British politician; b. 26 Nov. 1937; s. of Edward O. Moore; m. Sheila S. Tillotson 1962; two s. one d.; ed London School of Econs; with Royal Sussex Regt Korea 1955–57; Pres. Students' Union LSE 1959–60; banking and stockbroking, Chicago 1962–65; Dir Dean Witter Int. Ltd 1968–79, Chair. 1975–79; underwriting mem. Lloyds 1978–92; Exec. Chair. Crédit Suisse Asset Man. 1991–, Energy Saving Trust Ltd 1992–95 (Pres. 1995–); mem. Parl. for Croydon Cen. 1974–92; Parl. Under-Sec. of State, Dept of Energy 1979–83; Econ. Sec. to HM Treasury June–Oct. 1983, Financial Sec. to HM Treasury Oct. 1983–86; Sec. of State for Transport 1986–87, for Dept of Health and Social Security 1987–88, for Social Security 1988–89; Dir Monitor Inc. 1990– (Chair. Monitor Europe 1990–), Blue Circle Industries 1993–, Camelot PLC 1994–96, Rolls-Royce PLC (Deputy Chair. 1996–2003, Acting Chair. 2003–05), Crédit Suisse Investment Man. Australia 1995–, Cen. European Growth Fund PLC 1995–, BEA Assocs USA 1996–98, TIG Inc. 1997–, Pvt. Client Partners, Zurich 1999–; mem. Court of Govs LSE 1977–. *Address:* Crédit Suisse Asset Management Ltd, Beaufort House, 15 St. Botolph Street, London, EC3A 7JJ (office); House of Lords, Westminster, London, SW1A 0PW, England. *Telephone:* (20) 7426-2626 (office). *Fax:* (20) 7426-2618 (office).

MOORES, Sir Peter, Kt, CBE, DL, KB; British business executive; b. 9 April 1932; s. of Sir John Moores; m. Luciana Pinto 1960 (divorced 1984); one s. one d.; ed Eton Coll., Christ Church, Oxford, Wiener Akademie der Musik und darstellender Kunste; worked opera, Glyndebourne and Vienna State Opera; Dir The Littlewoods Org. 1965–93 (Chair. 1977–80); f. Peter Moores Foundation 1964; pioneered opera recordings in English trans. by EMI and Chandos; supported recordings by Opera Rara of rare 19th-Century Italian opera; annual Peter Moores Foundation Scholarships awarded to promising young opera singers, Royal Northern Coll. of Music; endowed Faculty Directorship and Chair of Man. Studies, Oxford Univ. 1992; est. Scotland Beef Project, Barbados (land conservation and self-supporting farming practice) 1993, Transatlantic Slave Trade Gallery, Merseyside Maritime Museum 1994; Benefactor, Chair of Tropical Horticulture, Univ. of W. Indies, Barbados 1995; f. Compton Verney House Trust 1993, Peter Moores Foundation 1998; Dir Singer & Friedlander 1978–92, Scottish Opera 1988–92; Trustee Tate Gallery 1978–85; Gov. BBC 1981–83; Hon. RNCM 1985, DL of Lancashire 1992; Hon. MA (Christ Church, Oxford) 1975,); Gold Medal of Italian Repub. 1974, Gramophone Award for Special Achievement 2008. *Leisure interests:* opera, shooting, visual arts. *Address:* Parbold Hall, Parbold, nr Wigan, Lancs., WN8 7TG, England (home).

MOORMAN van KAPPEN, Olav, LLD; Dutch legal historian and academic; *Professor Emeritus of Legal History, Nijmegen University;* b. 11 March 1937, The Hague; s. of Karel S. O. van Kappen and Johanna J. Moorman; m. Froukje A. Bosma 1963; one s. one d.; ed Huygens Lyceum and Utrecht Univ.; Research Asst Faculty of Law, Utrecht Univ. 1961–64, Jr Lecturer 1965–68; Sr Lecturer Faculty of Law, Amsterdam Univ. 1968–71; Asst Prof. Faculty of Law, Leyden Univ. 1971–72; Prof. of Legal History, Nijmegen Univ. 1971–2000, Co. Dir Gerard Noodt Inst. for Legal History 1972–2000, Emer. Prof. 2000–; Visiting Prof. Munster Univ. 1982–83, Poitiers Univ. 1986, 1991 Düsseldorf Univ. 1989–90, Univ. René Descartes (Paris V) 1992, 1995, 1999; mem. Bd of Govs Netherlands School for Archivists 1979–81, Chair. 1981–95; mem. Netherlands Council of Archives 1979–89, Vice-Pres. 1986–89, Pres. 1990–95; mem. Nat. Council of Cultural Heritage 1990–95; mem. editorial Bd, Legal History Review 1983–; mem. Dutch Soc. of Sciences at Haarlem 1982, Royal Netherlands Acad. of Sciences 1986; Corresp. mem. Acad. of Sciences, Göttingen 1996; Dr hc (Univ. René Descartes (Paris V)); Cross of Merit 1st Class (FRG), Officier, Ordre des Palmes Académiques (France), Officier, Ordre van Oranje-Nassau (Netherlands). *Publications:* over 360 books and numerous articles on various aspects of legal history. *Address:* Institute of Legal Science of Nijmegen University, PO Box 9049, 6500 KK Nijmegen, Netherlands. *Telephone:* (24) 3612186. *Fax:* (24) 3616145.

MOOSA, Mohammed Valli, BSc; South African politician and international organization executive; *Chairman, Congress Steering Committee, International Union for the Conservation of Nature;* b. 9 Feb. 1957, Johannesburg; m. Elsabé Wessels; ed Lenasia State Indian High School, Univ. of Durban-Westville; active in South African Students' Org., Nat. Indian Congress and other political and trade-union activities; teacher 1979–82; involved in est. of Anti-South African Indian Council Cttee 1982, revival of Transvaal Indian Congress 1983; Founder mem. and fmr mem. Nat. Exec. Cttee United Democratic Front; fmr Leader Mass Democratic Movt; detained 1987, escaped 1988; planned Defiance Campaign; detained 1989; involved in Conf. for a Democratic Future 1989; mem. Nat. Reception Cttee for released African Nat. Congress (ANC) leaders 1989–90; with ANC 1990–, mem. Nat. Exec. Cttee 1991, fmr mem. Nat. Working Cttee, rep. of negotiating team Convention for a Democratic South Africa 1991–94; Deputy Minister of Prov. Affairs and Constitutional Devt 1994, Minister 1996–99, Minister of Environmental Affairs and Tourism 1999–2004; Pres. Int. Union for the Conservation of Nature 2004–08, Chair. Congress Steering Cttee. *Address:* IUCN Headquarters, Rue Mauverney 28, Gland 1196, Switzerland (office). *Telephone:* (22) 999-00-00 (office). *Fax:* (22) 999-00-02 (office). *E-mail:* webmaster@iucn.org (office). *Website:* www.iucn.org (office).

MOQBEL, Zarar Ahmad; Afghan politician; *Minister of Refugees and Repatriation;* Deputy Minister of Interior Affairs –Sept. 2005, Acting Minister of Interior Affairs Sept. 2005–March 2006, Minister of Interior Affairs 2006–08, of Refugees and Repatriation 2008–. *Address:* Ministry of Refugees and Repatriation, Jungaluk, off Darlaman Road, Kabul, Afghanistan (office). *E-mail:* afgmorr@afgmorr.com (office).

MORA GRAMUNT, Gabriel; Spanish architect; b. 13 April 1941, Barcelona; s. of Evaristo Mora Gramunt and Josefa Mora Gramunt; m. Carmina Sanvisens Montón 1985; one s.; ed Tech. Univ. of Architecture, Barcelona (ETSAB); Assoc. Piñón-Viaplana 1967; tutor, ETSAB 1973; in partnership with Jaume Bach Nuñez, Bach/Mora Architects 1976–; Prof. of History of Modern Architecture, EINA School of Design 1978; Design Tutor, ETSAB 1978–; Visiting Prof. Univ. of Dublin 1993; various professional awards. *Work includes:* Grass Hockey Olympic Stadium, Terrassa 1992, cen. telephone exchange, Olympic Village, Barcelona 1992, apt bldgs, agric. complex, health clinic etc. *Publications include:* Junge Architekten in Europa (jtly) 1983, Young Spanish Architects (jtly) 1985. *Address:* Passatge Sant Felip, 12 bis, 08006 Barcelona, Spain.

MORA RODAS, Nelson Alcides, Dr en Derecho; Paraguayan lawyer, politician and academic; ed Nat. Coll. of the Capital, Faculty of Social Sciences, Nat. Univ. of Asunción, Catholic Univ. of Colombia, Bogotá, Univ. of Salamanca, Spain, Colegio Mayor de Nuestra Sra. del Rosario, Bogotá, Nat. War Coll., Asunción; Titular Prof. of Criminal Procedural Law, Catholic Univ., Villarrica; taught classes, courses and held confs at Nat. Univ. of Asunción, Visiting Prof., Faculty of Law and Social Sciences; fmr civil employee, Ministry of Justice and Labour; fmr Sec. of Court; fmr solicitor for Prosecutor Gen.; fmr Judge of First Instance in Penal and Civil Law; mem. Court of Criminal Appeal; Amb. to Colombia 1995–2003; Solicitor Gen. 2003–04; Minister of the Interior 2004–05, of Nat. Defence 2007–08; mem. Asoc. Nacional Republicana–Partido Colorado (Nat. Republican Asscn–Colorado Party); Degree of Grand Cross 'Academic Excellence', the Hispano-American Acad. of Sciences and Letters and Univ. Piloto of Colombia, Bogotá 1997, Grand Cross of Boyacá (Colombia) 2003. *Publications:* Amarras fraternas, Colombia Paraguay 1999, Delincuencias Internacional Organizada. Drogas. Narcotráfico. Espacio Judicial Común 2000, Código Penal Paraguayo, Doctrina, Comentarios, Concordancias, Leyes Especiales 2000, Cerca del amanecer 2001. *Address:* Asociación Nacional Republicana–Partido Colorado, Casa de los Colorados, 25 de Mayo 842, Asunción, Paraguay (office). *Telephone:* (21) 44-4137 (office). *Fax:* (21) 49-7857 (office). *Website:* www.anr.org.py (office).

MORA WITT, Galo, PhD; Ecuadorean writer, musician and politician; *Minister of Culture;* b. 1957, Loja; ed Salesiana Univ.; guitarist and singer with Pueblo Nuevo 1978–; adviser to Casa de la Cultura Ecuatoriana 1996–2004; Minister of Culture 2008–. *Publications include:* Un pájaro redondo para jugar (Memoria y Fútbol) 2002, Memorial de una Lumbrera (biografía de Pío Jaramillo Alvarado); numerous essays and articles. *Address:* Ministry of Culture, Avda Portugal E9-138 y República del Salvador, Quito, Ecuador (office). *Website:* www.ministeriodecultura.gov.ec (office).

MORAES DE ABREU, José Carlos; Brazilian business executive; *President of the Administrative Council, Itaúsa-Investimentos Itaú SA;* b. 15 July 1922; ed Universidade de São Paulo; Man. Dir Itaúsa-Investimentos Itaú SA 1966, Exec. Vice-Pres. 1966–76, 1979–83, Pres. 1976–79, 1983–, Dir Gen. and mem. Admin. Council 2001–, Pres. Admin. Council 2008–, Vice-Pres. Itautec Philco, mem. Itaubanco Share Options Cttee; mem. Nat. Monetary Council 1975– 84; Hon. LLB (São Paulo) 1944. *Address:* Itaúsa-Investimentos Itaú SA, Praça Alfredo Edydio de Souza Aranha 100, Torre Itaúsa, São Paulo 04344-902, SP, Brazil (office). *Telephone:* (11) 5019-1677 (office). *Fax:* (11) 5019-1114 (office). *E-mail:* info@itausa.com.br (office). *Website:* www.itausa.com.br (office).

MORAHAN, Christopher Thomas; British theatre, television and film director; b. 9 July 1929, London; s. of the late Thomas Morahan and Nancy Barker; m. 1st Joan Murray 1954 (died 1973); m. 2nd Anna Carteret 1974; two s. three d. (one deceased); ed Highgate School and Old Vic Theatre School; Dir Greenpoint Films and Head, plays, BBC TV 1972–76; Assoc. Dir Royal Nat. Theatre 1977–88; BAFTA Best TV Series 1984, Int. Emmy 1984, 1993, 1994, Evening Standard Best Dir 1984, Prix Italia 1987, and many other awards. *Stage productions include:* Little Murders, This Story of Yours, The Caretaker, Flint, Melon, Major Barbara, The Handyman, Letter of Resignation, Racing Demon, Equally Divided, The Importance of Being Earnest, Semi Detached, Quartet, The Retreat from Moscow, Beyond a Joke, Heartbreak House, Naked Justice, the Winslow Boy, Hock and Soda Water; for Nat. Theatre: State of Revolution, The Philanderer, Brand, Richard III, Strife, The Wild Duck, Man and Superman, Wild Honey, The Devil's Disciple. *Films include:* All Neat in Black Stockings 1968, Diamonds for Breakfast 1968, Clockwise 1986, Paper Mask (also producer) 1990, Unnatural Pursuits 1991. *Radio includes:* Art, BBC Radio 3. *Television includes:* The Hooded Terror (producer) 1963, Pygmalion (producer) 1973, Emergency-Ward 10 (series) 1975, Ghost Squad (series) 1961, The Road 1963, Malatesta 1964, Fable 1965, Coming Up for Air 1965, Nineteen Eighty Four 1965, A Game, Like, Only a Game 1966, Talking to a Stranger (mini-series) 1966, The Ragged Trousered Philanthropists 1967, The Gorge 1968, The Letter 1969, Lay Down Your Arms 1970, Uncle Vanya 1970, Hearts and Flowers 1970, Lulie IV 1971, The Bankrupt 1972, The Common 1973, Fathers and Families (mini-series) 1977, The Jewel in the Crown (mini-series) (also producer) 1984, In the Secret State 1985, After Pilkington 1987, Troubles 1988, The Heat of the Day 1989, Can You Hear Me Thinking? 1990, Old Flames 1990, Ashenden (mini-series) 1991, Common Pursuit 1992, The Bullion Boys (also producer) 1993, Summer Days Dream 1994, It Could Be You 1995, The Peacock Spring 1996, Element of Doubt, A Dance to the Music of Time (two episodes) 1997. *Leisure interests:* photography, birdwatching. *Address:* c/o Whitehall Artists, 10 Lower Common South, London, SW15 1BP; Highcombe Farmhouse, The Devil's Punchbowl, Thursley, Godalming, Surrey, GU8 6NS, England. *Telephone:* (20) 8785-3737; (1428) 607031. *Fax:* (20) 8788-2340 (office). (1428) 607989. *E-mail:* chrismorahan@solutions-inc.co.uk (home).

MORAIS, José Pedro de; Angolan politician and economist; *Minister of Finance;* b. 20 Dec. 1955; ed in France; fmr Sec. of State for Construction Materials; Minister of Planning and Econ. Co-ordination 1992; Angola's nominee to Bd of IMF 1990s; Minister of Finance 2002–. *Address:* Ministry of Finance, Avda 4 de Fevereiro 127, CP 592, Luanda, Angola (office). *Telephone:* 222338548 (office). *Fax:* 222338548 (office). *E-mail:* cdi@minfin.gv.ao (office). *Website:* www.angola-portal.ao/MINFIN (office).

MORALES, Armando; Nicaraguan artist; b. 15 Jan. 1927, Granada; ed Inst. Pedagógico de Varones, Managua, Escuela de Bellas Artes, Managua and Pratt Graphic Art Center, New York; first solo exhbn Lima 1959, subsequently at Toronto, New York, Washington, DC, Panama, Bogotá, Detroit, Caracas, Mexico City; Group exhbns all over N and S America and in Europe; named Alt. Del. to UNESCO 1982; juror, Exposicion Pinturerias, Cultural Foundation Artencion, Mexico City 1994; Order of Ruben Dario 1982; numerous awards for painting in the Americas including Carnegie Int. 1964 and award at Arte de América y España Exhbn, Madrid.

MORALES, Erik; Mexican boxer; b. Tijuana; s. of Jose Morales; brother of Diego Morales; m. America Morales; three c.; began boxing at age of five, had 114 amateur fights (108-6); trained by father in family boxing gym, Tijuana and by Fernando Fernandez; winner of 11 major amateur titles in Mexico; professional debut 1993; has had over 50 professional fights 2005; known as Erik "El Terrible" Morales; winner Mexican Super Bantamweight (SB) Title against Enrique Jupiter, Tijuana 1995, N American Boxing Fed. (NABF) SB Title against Juan Torres, Las Vegas, Nev. 1995, 1st NABF SB Defence against Alberto Martinez, Las Vegas 1995, 2nd NABF SB Defence against Kenny Mitchell, Tijuana 1995, 3rd NABF SB Defence against Rudy Bradley, Las Vegas 1996, 4th NABF SB Defence against Hector Acero-Sanchez, Las Vegas 1996, World Boxing Council (WBC) SB Title against Daniel Zaragoza, El Paso 1997, 1st WBC SB Defence against John Lowey, Tijuana 1997, 2nd WBC SB Defence against Remigio Molina, Tijuana 1998, 3rd WBC SB Defence against Jose Luis Bueno, Indio, Calif. 1998, 4th WBC SB Defence against Junior Jones, Tijuana 1998, 6th WBC SB Defence against Juan Carlos Ramirez, Las Vegas 1999, 7th WBC SB Defence against Reynante Jamiloi, Tijuana 1999, 8th WBC SB Defence against Wayne McCullough, Detroit, Mich. 1999, 9th WBC SB Defence against Marco Antonio Barerra, Las Vegas 2000, WBC Interim Featherweight Title against Kevin Kellery, El Paso, Tex. 2000, WBC Featherweight Title against Guty Espadas, Las Vegas 2001, 1st WBC Featherweight Defense against Injin Chi, LA 2001, Defence of Title fights against Croft 2003, Velardez 2003, WBC Super Featherweight Title against Jesus Chavez 2004, Int. Boxing Asscn (IBA) Jr Lightweight Title against Carlos Hernandez 2004, IBA Super Featherweight Title and WBC Int. Super Featherweight Title against Manny Pacquiao, Las Vegas 2005; boxing promoter and man.; owner web boxing magazine box-latino.com; NABF Boxer of the Year 1996. *Leisure interests:* computer enthusiast. *Address:* c/o World Boxing Organization - Latino, Maza 557, Oficina 17, 1220 Buenos Aires, Argentina (office). *Telephone:* (11) 4931-7608 (office). *E-mail:* anaboxlatino@hotmail.com (office). *Website:* www.box-latino.com (office).

MORALES, Geraldo Rubén; Argentine politician; *President, Unión Cívica Radical;* b. 18 July 1959, Jujuy; m.; three s.; ed Universidad Nacional de Jujuy; began career at Instituto de Seguros, Dir Liquidation Dept 1980–89; Asst in Political Econs, Universidad Nacional de Jujuy 1985–92, Head of Macro econs 1992–93; Fed. Deputy for Jujuy state 1989–2000, Chair. Fed. Finance Cttee 1991–92, Leader Unión Cívica Radical (UCR) in Chamber of Deputies 1993; Minister for Social Devt 2000–01; Senator for Jujuy 2001–; Pres. Unión Cívica Radical (UCR) 2006–; unsuccessful cand. in governorship elections for Jujuy 1995, 1999. *Address:* Unión Cívica Radical, Alsina 1786, 1088 Buenos Aires (office); Hipólito Yrigoyen 1708, Piso 5, Of. 503, Buenos Aires, Argentina. *Telephone:* (11) 4375-2000 (UCR) (office); (11) 43795936. *E-mail:* morales@senado.gov.ar; presidencia@ucr.org.ar (office). *Website:* www.ucr.org.ar; morales.radicales.org.ar.

MORALES AIMA, Juan Evo; Bolivian politician and head of state; *President;* b. 29 Oct. 1959, Orinoca, Oruru; s. of Dionisio Morales Choque and Maria Mamani; fmr llama herder and trumpet player; farmed piece of land in Chapare for coca production 1980s; Founder and Leader, Movimiento al Socialismo (MAS) 1987; became leader of the 'cocaleros' (coca producers) following US attempts to eradicate cocaine production (Plan Dignity) 1998; expelled from govt after three policemen were killed in farmers' riots; mem. Congress; ran second in presidential elections 2002, succeeded in gaining resignation and exile of Pres. Gonzalo Sanchez de Lozada on issue of Bolivian gas exports 2003; Pres. of Bolivia 2006–. *Address:* Office of the President, Palacio de Gobierno, Plaza Murillo, La Paz; Movimiento al Socialismo, La Paz, Bolivia (office). *Telephone:* (2) 237-1082 (office). *Fax:* (2) 237-1388 (office). *E-mail:* despacho@presidencia.gov.bo (office). *Website:* www.presidencia.gov.bo (office); www.masbolivia.org (office).

MORALES ANAYA, Juan Antonio, PhD; Bolivian economist and social scientist; *President, Banco Central de Bolivia;* ed Catholic Univ. of Leuven, Belgium; Dir of Socio-Econs Research Inst. 1974–95; Catholic Univ. of Bolivia 1974–95; Dir Cen. Bank of Bolivia 1993–95, now Pres. *Address:* Banco Central de Bolivia, Avda Ayacucho esq. Mercado, Casilla Postal 3118, La Paz, Bolivia (office). *Telephone:* 37-4151 (office). *Fax:* 39-2398 (office). *E-mail:* jam@mail.bcb.gov.bo (office); vmarquez@mail.bcb.gov.bo. *Website:* www.bcb.gov.bo (office).

MORALES BERMÚDEZ, Gen. Francisco; Peruvian politician and army officer; b. 4 Oct. 1921, Lima; grandson of the late Col Remiro Morales (President of Peru, 1890–94); m. Rosa Pedraglio de Morales Bermúdez; four s. one d.; ed Chorillos Mil. School; Founder mem. Dept of Research and Devt, Army Gen. Staff; taught at School of Eng and at Army Acad. of War; Chief of Staff of First Light Div., Tumbes; Asst Dir of Logistics, Dir of Econ., War Ministry; advanced courses at Superior Acad. of War, Argentina and Centre for Higher Mil. Studies, Peru; apptd to reorganize electoral registration system 1962; Minister of Econ. and Finance 1968–74; Chief of Army Gen. Staff 1974–75: Prime Minister, Minister of War and Commdr-Gen. of Army Feb.–Aug. 1975; Pres. of Peru 1975–80.

MORALES CARAZO, Jaime René; Nicaraguan business executive and politician; *Vice-President;* b. 10 Sept. 1936, Granada; s. of the late Carlos A. Morales and Anita Carazo Arellano; m. Amparo Vázquez Rovelo; two c.; f. Nicaraguan Devt Investments SA (INDES) in 1960s; mem. Nicaraguan Democratic Force 1983–93, Constitutional Liberal Party 1993–2002, Chair. Honour, Ethics and Justice Cttee 1993–2002, mem. Nat. Cttee 1993–2002; personal adviser (with rank of Minister) to the Pres. of Nicaragua 1997–2001, Chair. Nat. Council on Sustainable Devt 1997–2001; Deputy in Nat. Ass. 2001–06; Vice-Pres. of Nicaragua 2007–. *Address:* Office of the President, Casa Presidencial, Managua, Nicaragua (office). *Website:* www.presidencia.gob.ni (office).

MORALES TRONCOSO, Carlos; Dominican Republic politician; *Secretary of State for Foreign Affairs;* b. 29 Sept. 1940; m. Luisa Alba de Morales; four d.; ed Louisiana State Univ.; several positions at Gulf & Western Americas Corpn 1976–84; Vice-Pres. of Dominican Repub. 1990–94; Sec. of State for Foreign Affairs 1994–96, 2004–; mem. Instituto Americano de Ingenieros Químicos (AICHE); Dr hc (Dominican Chamber of Commerce of New York) 1984; Gulf & Western Americas Industrialist of the Year 1982. *Publications:* De Lo Privado a Lo Público 2002. *Address:* Secretariat of State for Foreign Affairs, Avenida Independencia 752, Santo Domingo, DN, Dominican Republic (office). *Telephone:* 535-6280 (office). *Fax:* 535-5772 (office). *E-mail:* postmaster@serex.gov.do (office). *Website:* www.serex.gov.do (office).

MORAN, 2nd Baron, (cr. 1943), of Manton; (Richard) John McMoran Wilson, KCMG; British diplomatist (retd); b. 22 Sept. 1924, London; s. of the late Sir Charles McMoran Wilson, 1st Baron Moran and Dorothy Dufton; m. Shirley Rowntree Harris 1948; two s. one d.; ed Eton Coll., King's Coll., Cambridge; served in World War II; HMS Belfast 1943, Sub-Lt RNVR in motor torpedo boats and HM Destroyer Oribi 1944–45; Foreign Office 1945; Third Sec., Ankara 1948, Tel Aviv 1950; Second Sec., Rio de Janeiro 1953; First Sec., Foreign Office 1956; Washington, DC 1959; Foreign Office 1961; Counsellor, S Africa 1965; Head of W African Dept of FCO 1968–73, concurrently Amb. to Chad 1970–73; Amb. to Hungary 1973–76, to Portugal 1976–81; High Commr in Canada 1981–84; sits as ind. Cross Bench peer, House of Lords; Chair. All Party Conservation Group of both Houses of Parl. 1992–2000, Wildlife and Countryside Link 1992–95, Regional Fisheries Advisory Cttee, Welsh Region, NRA 1989–94, Jt Fisheries Policy and Legislation Working Group (The Moran Cttee) 1997, Salmon and Trout Asscn 1997–2000 (Exec. Vice-Pres. 2000–); Pres. Welsh Salmon and Trout Angling Asscn 1988–95, 2001–, Radnorshire Wildlife Trust 1994–; Vice-Chair. Atlantic Salmon Trust 1983–95, Vice-Pres. 1995–; mem. Council Royal Soc. for the Protection of Birds 1989–94 (Vice-Pres. 1997–98), Agricultural Sub-Cttee 1991–95, 1997–2000; Grand Cross of the Order of the Infante (Portugal) 1978. *Publications:* (as John Wilson) C.B., a Life of Sir Henry Campbell-Bannerman 1973 (Whitbread Award for Biography), Fairfax 1985, William Robert Grove: the Lawyer who Invented the Fuel Cell (jt author) 2007. *Leisure interests:* fishing, fly-tying, bird watching. *Address:* House of Lords, Westminster, London, SW1A 0PW, England (office). *Telephone:* (20) 7219-3000 (office); (1985) 560-257 (home).

MORÁN LÓPEZ, Fernando; Spanish politician, diplomatist and author; b. 1926, Avilés; m. María Luz Calvo-Sotelo; one s. two d.; ed Institut des Hautes Etudes Internationales, Paris, London School of Econs, Madrid Univ.; began diplomatic career 1954; Asst Consul, Spanish Consulate-Gen., Buenos Aires 1956; Sec. Spanish Embassy, Pretoria; transferred to Ministry of Foreign Affairs 1963, specialized in African affairs, Asst Dir-Gen. for Africa, Near and Middle East, Political Dir Dept of Foreign Policy, later in charge of Africa, Near and Middle East 1971, Dir-Gen. of African Affairs 1975–77; First Sec. Spanish Embassy, Lisbon; Consul-Gen. Spanish Embassy, London 1974; Partido Socialista Popular cand. for elections to Congress of Deputies 1977; elected Partido Socialista Obrero Español Senator for Asturias, Socialist Spokesman for Foreign Affairs in Senate; Minister of Foreign Affairs 1982–85; Perm. Rep. to the UN 1985–87; MEP 1989–99; Légion d'honneur, Grand Cross of Carlos III, Grand Cross Order of Isabel la Católica 1985, Grand Cross of Christ (Portugal). *Publications:* También se muere el Mar 1958, Una política exterior para España, El día en que 1997, Palimpsesto 2002. *Leisure interests:*

literature, theatre. *Address:* Alvárez de Baena 5, 28006 Madrid, Spain (home). *Telephone:* (91) 5643719 (home).

MORANO, Nadine; French politician; *Spokesperson, Union pour un Mouvement Populaire (UMP);* b. 6 Nov. 1963, Nancy; elected mem. of Nat. Ass. for Meurthe-et-Moselle constituency 2002–07, re-elected 2007, Vice-Pres. working groups on Nat. Security and Youth, Integration and Citizenship, friendship groups between France and Brunei, Chad and Luxembourg, mem. Comm. on Family, Social and Cultural Affairs, friendship groups between France and China, Italy, Madagascar, Qatar; Regional Councillor for Lorraine; mem. Union pour un Mouvement Populaire (UMP), Spokesperson 2007–, also serves as Gen. Del. for Employment; mem. Génération Entreprise. *Address:* 1 rue St Waast, BP 158, 54206 Toul (office); Palais Bourbon, 75355 Paris 07, France (office). *Telephone:* 3-83-64-24-43 (office). *Fax:* 3-83-63-13-95 (office). *E-mail:* deputee@nadine-morano.com (office). *Website:* www.nadine-morano.com (office).

MORATINOS CUYAUBÉ, Miguel Ángel; Spanish diplomatist and politician; *Minister of Foreign Affairs and Co-operation;* b. 8 June 1951, Madrid; m. Dominique Maunac; three c.; Dir Eastern Europe Co-ordination Desk 1974–79; First Sec., Spanish Embassy, Yugoslavia 1979–80, Chargé d'Affaires 1980–84; political adviser, Spanish Embassy, Rabat 1984–87; Deputy Dir-Gen. for N Africa 1987–91; Dir-Gen. Inst. for Co-operation with the Arab World 1991–93; apptd Dir-Gen. of Foreign Policy for Africa and the Middle East 1993; Amb. to Israel June–Dec. 1996; EU Special Rep. for the Middle East Peace Process Dec. 1996–2003; Minister of Foreign Affairs and Co-operation 2004–; Commdr of Civil Merit, Knight of the Order of Civil Merit, Officer of the Order of Isabel la Católica, Commdr of the Order of the Repub. of Tunisia, Commdr of the Orange-Nassau Order of the Netherlands; Arab Journalists Assn Co-operation Prize 1994. *Address:* Ministry of Foreign Affairs and Co-operation, Plaza Marqués de Salamanca 8, 28071 Madrid, 2806 Spain (office). *Telephone:* (91) 3798300 (office). *Fax:* (91) 3667098 (office). *E-mail:* buzonweb@mae.es (office). *Website:* www.mae.es (office).

MORATTI, Letizia Brichetto Arnaboldi; Italian media industry executive and politician; *Mayor of Milan;* m. Gianmarco Moratti; two c.; Pres. RAI 1994–96; Dir (non-exec.) BSkyB May–Sept. 1999, Chair. News Corpn Europe 1998–99; Minister of Educ., Univ. and Scientific Research 2001–06; Mayor of Milan 2006–. *Address:* Comune di Milano, Piazza della Scala 2, 20100 Milan, Italy (office). *Telephone:* (02) 88451 (office). *Fax:* (02) 88450418 (office). *Website:* www.comune.milano.it (office).

MORAUTA, Sir Mekere, Kt, BEcons; Papua New Guinea politician and banker; b. 12 June 1946; s. of Morauta Hasu and Morikoai Elavo; m. Roslyn Morauta; two s.; ed Univ. of Papua New Guinea, Flinders Univ. of S. Australia; research officer, Dept of Labour 1971; economist, Office of the Econ. Adviser 1972; fmr dir of numerous cos; Sec. for Finance, Govt of Papua New Guinea 1973–82; Man. Dir Papua New Guinea Banking Corpn 1983–92; Chair. Nat. Airline Comm. 1992–94; Gov. Bank of Papua New Guinea 1993–94; Exec. Chair. Morauta Investments Ltd 1994–97; MP for Moresby NW 1997–; Minister for Planning and Implementation 1997, for Fisheries 1998–99; Prime Minister and Treas. of Papua New Guinea 1999–2002; mem. Bd of Dirs Angco; Hon. DTech (Univ. of Tech., Lae) 1987. *Publications:* numerous econs-related papers. *Address:* c/o Prime Minister's Office, PO Box 639, Naigani, NCD, Papua New Guinea (office).

MORAVČÍK, Jozef, LLD, CSc; Slovak politician; b. 19 March 1945, Očová Zvolen Dist; m.; two d.; ed Charles Univ., Komenský Univ.; clerk with Chemapol (trade co.) Bratislava; lecturer Law Faculty, Komenský Univ., Bratislava 1972–85, Head of Dept of Business Law 1985–90; Dean, Law Faculty 1990–91; Deputy to Slovak Nat. Council 1991–92; mem. Movt for Democratic Slovakia (MDS) 1991–94; Minister of Foreign Affairs of ČSFR July–Dec. 1992; Chair. Council of Ministers of CSCE July–Dec. 1992; Minister of Foreign Affairs, Slovak Repub. 1993–94; Prime Minister of Slovakia March–Dec. 1994; Chair. Democratic Union of Slovakia 1994–97; Chair. Policy Planning Council 1997–; Mayor of Bratislava 1998–2002. *Address:* Magistrát hlavného mesta SR Bratislavy, Primaciálne hám. 1, PO Box 192, 814 22 Bratislava, Slovakia (office). *Telephone:* (7) 5443-5324 (office). *Fax:* (7) 5443-5405 (office). *E-mail:* primator@bratislava.sk (office). *Website:* www.bratislava.sk (office).

MORAVEC, Ivan; Czech pianist and academic; b. 9 Nov. 1930, Prague; m. 1st (deceased); m. 2nd; one s., one d.; ed Conservatoire, Prague 1946–51; teacher, Acad. of Musical Arts, Prague 1969–, Prof. 2000–; soloist with Czech Philharmonic Orchestra; concert tours Europe, USA, Japan; festivals Salzburg, Edin., Aldeburgh, Prague Spring, Schleswig-Holstein, Tanglewood, etc.; Charles IV Prize 2000, Cannes Classical Award 1999, Platinum Disc Award, Supraphon 2000, Medal for Merit 2000, Int. Prize Charles Univ. 2000, Harmonie Prize 2001, Classical Award for Lifetime Achievement, Cannes 2002. *Music:* Recordings for Nonesuch, Supraphon, Dorian, Vox, Moss, Connoisseur Soc., Hänssler (numerous record of the year listings in High Fidelity, Stereo Review, New York Times, Time Magazine, Newsweek). *Leisure interest:* culture. *Address:* c/o Linda Marder, 127 West 96th Street, #13B, New York, NY 10025, USA (office); Pod Vyhlídkou 520, 160 00 Prague 6, Czech Republic (home). *Telephone:* (212) 864-1005 (office); (2) 23123696 (home). *Fax:* (212) 864-1066 (office); (2) 33343696 (home). *E-mail:* lymarder@aol.com (office). *Website:* www.cramermarderartists.com (office); www.ivanmoravec.net.

MORCELI, Noureddine; Algerian athlete; b. 28 Feb. 1970, Tenes; coached by his brother Abderrahmane Morceli; world champion, 1,500m Tokyo 1991, Stuttgart 1993, Gothenburg 1995; fmr world record-holder at 1,500m, one mile, 2,000m, 3,000m; gold medal Atlanta 1996; announced intention to compete in 2003 over 5,000m and 10,000m, but did not race 2003–04; IAAF Athlete of the Year 1994. *Address:* c/o Ministry of Youth and Sports, 3 rue Mohamed Belouizdad, Algiers, Algeria.

MORCHIO, Giuseppe; Italian automobile industry executive; b. 20 Nov. 1947, Rapallo, Genoa; m.; 2 c.; ed Genoa Polytechnic Univ.; began career in cable sector of Manuli Group; Dir of Logistics Pirelli Group 1980, then Vice-Pres. Mfg, Quality and Logistics, Pirelli Group Worldwide, then Corp. Exec. Vice-Pres., Pirelli SpA; Chair. and CEO Pirelli Neumáticos, Barcelona; Pres. and CEO Pirelli Tyre North America; CEO Pirelli Cavi SpA Holding 1993–95; Chair. and CEO Pirelli Cavi e Sistemi SpA 1995–2003; Dir 1999–2003; CEO Fiat SpA 2003–2004 (resgnd); Chair. Fiat Auto, Iveco, Magneti Marelli, Coamu, Teksid (all with Fiat Group) 2003–04; mem. Bd CNH, Ferrari, Banco di Desio e della Brianza; mem. Exec. Cttee Bd Dirs Confindustria (business asscn). *Leisure interest:* sailing. *Address:* c/o Fiat SpA, Corporate Headquarters, Via Nizzi 250, 10126 Turin, Italy (office).

MORDACQ, Patrick; French government official (retd) and international consultant; b. 20 May 1934, Bordeaux; m. Marie Thérèse de Yturbe 1967; one s. one d.; ed Ecole Nat. d'Admin; Commissariat Gen. du Plan d'Equipement et de la Productivité 1963–67; Office of Minister of Equipment and Housing 1968; Head, Office of Foreign Investment, Treasury 1969; Deputy Chair. Comm. of Industry for VIth Plan 1970; Head, Office of Loans, Aid and Guarantees to Business, Treasury 1971–74; Finance Dir Groupe Jacques Borel Int. 1974–77; Head, Finance Service, Commissariat Gen. du Plan d'Equipement et de la Productivité 1977; Financial Counsellor, French Embassy, Bonn 1979; Head, Regulation of Finance, Treasury 1984–86; Govt Commr Centre Nat. des Caisses d'Epargne et de Prévoyance 1984–86; CEO Comm. des Opérations de Bourse 1986–91; Dir for France, EBRD (London) and Financial Counsellor, French Embassies, Poland, Romania and Bulgaria 1991–96; Conseiller-Maître, Cour des Comptes 1996–2002; Chair. Bd of Auditors, OECD 2002–07; consultant, institutional building projects (public finance man.) 2002–; Chevalier, Légion d'honneur, Officier, Ordre nat. du Mérite, Commdr, Bundesverdienstkreuz (Germany). *Address:* 5 rue Pierre le Grand, 75008 Paris, France (home). *E-mail:* p.mordacq@free.fr (home).

MORDECHAI, Yitzhak, MA; Israeli politician and fmr army officer; b. 1944, Iraq; m. (divorced); two c.; ed Staff and Command Colls, Tel-Aviv and Haifa Univs; emigrated to Israel aged five; served in Israeli Defence Forces (IDF) 1962–95, Commdr of a paratroop unit in the Sinai, 1967 Six Day War, paratroop bn on Suez Canal front, 1973 Yom Kippur War, Chief Infantry and Paratroopers Officer 1983–86, apptd Head of IDF HQ Training Dept, rank of Maj.-Gen. 1986, Officer in Command of IDF Southern Command 1986, of Cen. Command 1989, of Northern Command 1991; joined Likud party 1995; mem. Knesset (Parl.) 1996–2001, Minister of Defence 1996–99, of Transport and Energy 1999–2001, also fmr Deputy Prime Minister; convicted on three counts of indecent acts towards subordinates, received suspended sentence 2001; mem. Likud-Tzomet-Gesher group. *Address:* c/o Likud, 38 Rehov King George, Tel-Aviv 61231, Israel (office).

MORDKOVITCH, Lydia, MA, PhD, FRNCM, ARAM; British (b. Russian) violinist; *Professor of Violin, Royal Academy of Music;* b. 30 April 1944, Saratov, Russia; ed School for Talented Children, Kishinev, Stoliarski School, Odessa, Nejdanova Conservatoire, Odessa, Tchaikovsky Conservatoire, Moscow and studied with David Oistrakh; went to Israel 1974; has lived in UK since 1980; Sr Lecturer, Kishinev Inst. of Art 1970–73; Sr Lecturer, Rubin Acad. of Music, Jerusalem 1974–80; Prof. of Violin, Royal Northern Coll. of Music, Manchester, England 1980–, RAM, London 1995–; soloist in recitals, concerts, on radio and TV, USSR, then Europe, USA, S and Cen. America 1974–; Hon. mem. RAM; winner, Young Musicians Competition, Kiev 1967, Long-Thibaud Competition, Paris 1969, Gramophone Award (for Shostakovich concertos) 1990, three Diapason d'Or Awards, Woman of the Year Award, American Biog. Inst. 1996, 1997, 1998, 1999, 2000, Outstanding Woman of the 20th Century, Outstanding Woman of the 21st Century, American Biog. Inst. *Recordings:* over fifty records and CDs for RCA, Chandos, Collins and Carlton. *Leisure interests:* theatre, literature, art. *Address:* c/o Alex Durston Management, 68 High Street, Malmesbury, Wiltshire SN16 9AT, England (office); Royal Academy of Music, Marylebone Road, London, NW1 5HT, England (office). *Telephone:* (1666) 824748 (office); (20) 7873-7373 (office). *Fax:* (1666) 8247374 (office). *E-mail:* ad@admus.demon.co.uk (office). *Website:* www.ram.ac.uk (office).

MOREAU, Jeanne, FBA; French actress; b. 23 Jan. 1928, Paris; d. of Anatole-Désiré Moreau and Katherine Buckley; m. 1st Jean-Louis Richard 1949 (divorced); one s.; m. 2nd William Friedkin 1977 (divorced); ed Collège Edgar-Quinet, Conservatoire national d'art dramatique; stage actress with Comédie Française 1948–52; Théâtre Nat. Populaire 1953; Pres. Cannes Film Festival July 1975; Paris Int. Film Festival 1975; Pres. Acad. des Arts et Techniques du Cinéma 1986–88; Pres. Comm. des avances sur recettes 1993–94; mem. Acad. des Beaux-Arts, Inst. de France (Acad. of Modern Art) 2000–, jury of December Prize 2001–; Fellow, BAFTA; Hon. Acad. 1998; Officier, Légion d'honneur, Officier Ordre nat. du Mérite, Commdr des Arts et Lettres; Molière Award 1988, European Cinema Prize, Berlin 1997, Golden Bear, Int. Film Festival, Berlin 2000. *Plays include:* L'heure éblouissante, La machine infernale, Pygmalion, La chatte sur un toit brûlant, La bonne soupe, La chevauchée sur le lac de Constance, Lulu, L'intoxe, Night of the Iguana, Le récit de la Servante Zerline 1986, La Célestine 1989, Un trait de l'espirit 2000. *Films include:* Dernier amour (Last Love) 1949, Pigalle-Saint-Germain-des-Prés 1950, L'homme de ma vie (The Man in My Life) 1952, Il est minuit, docteur Schweitzer (aka Dr. Schweitzer) 1952, Dortoir des grandes (Girls' Dormitory) 1953, Julietta 1953, Touchez pas au grisbi (Hands Off the Loot) 1954, Les intrigantes (The Plotters) 1954, Secrets d'alcove 1954, La Reine Margot (Queen Margot) 1955, M'sieur la Caille 1955, Les hommes en blanc (Men in White) 1955, Gas-Oil 1955, Le salaire du péché (The Wages of Sin) 1956,

Jusqu'au dernier (Until the Last One) 1957, Les louves (The She-Wolves) 1957, L'étrange Monsieur Steve 1957, Trois jours à vivre (Three Days to Live) 1957, Échec au porteur (Not Delivered) 1958, Ascenseur pour l'échafaud (Lift to the Scaffold) 1958, Le dos au mur (Back to the Wall) 1958, Les amants (The Lovers) 1958, Les quatre cents coups (The Four Hundred Blows) 1959, Les liaisons dangereuses (Dangerous Liaisons) 1959, Matisse ou Le talent de bonheur (voice) 1960, 5 Branded Women (1960), Moderato cantabile 1960, Le dialogue des Carmélites 1960, La notte 1961, Une femme et une femme (A Woman Is a Woman) (uncredited) 1961, Jules et Jim 1962, Eve 1962, Le procès (The Trial) 1962, La baie des anges (Bay of Angels) 1963, Peau de banane (Banana Peel) 1963, Le feu follet (Will o' the Wisp) 1963, The Victors 1963, Le journal d'une femme de chambre (The Diary of a Chambermaid) 1964, The Train 1964, The Yellow Rolls-Royce 1964, Mata-Hari 1964, Viva Maria! 1965, Campanadas a medianoche (Chimes at Midnight) 1965, Mademoiselle 1966, L'amour à travers les âges 1967, Le plus vieux métier du monde (The Oldest Profession in the World) 1967, The Sailor from Gibraltar 1967, La mariée était en noir (The Bride Wore Black) 1968, The Immortal Story (Une histoire immortelle) 1968, Great Catherine 1968, Le corps de Diane (Diana's Body) 1969, The Deep 1970, Monte Walsh 1970, L'humeur vagabonde (Vagabond Humour) 1972, Comptes rebours (aka Reckonings Against the Grain) 1971, Chère Louise (Dear Louise) 1972, Nathalie Granger 1972, Joanna Francesa 1972, Le jardin qui bascule (The Garden That Tilts) 1974, Je t'aime 1974, Les valseuses (Going Places, USA) 1973, La race des 'seigneurs' (aka Elite Group) 1974, Pleurs 1974, Hu-Man 1975, Souvenirs d'en France 1975, Lumière (also writer and dir) 1976, Monsieur Klein 1976, The Last Tycoon 1976, Le petit théâtre de Jean Renoir 1976, L'adolescente (also writer) 1978, Madame Rosa 1978, Your Ticket Is No Longer Valid 1981, Plein Sud 1981, Mille milliards de dollars (A Thousand Billion Dollars) 1982, Querelle 1982, Au-delà de cette limite votre billet n'est plus valable 1982, La truite (The Trout) 1982, Lillian Gish (producer and dir), Le paltoquet 1986, Sauve-toi Lola 1986, Le miraculé (1987, Jour après jour (Day After Day) 1989, Nikita 1990, Alberto Express 1990, La femme fardée 1990, Anna Karamazova 1991, La Vieille qui marchait dans la Mer (The Old Lady Who Walked in the Sea) 1991, To Meteoro vima tou pelargou (The Suspended Step of the Stork) 1991, Bis ans Ende der Welt (Till the End of the World) 1991, L'amant (The Lover) (voice) 1992, La nuit de l'océan 1992, À demain 1992, L'absence (The Absence) 1993, Map of the Human Heart 1993, Je m'appelle Victor (My Name Is Victor) 1993, A Foreign Field 1993, The Summer House 1994, Les cent et une nuits de Simon Cinéma (A Hundred and One Nights of Simon Cinema) 1995, Al di là delle nuvole (Beyond the Clouds) 1995, I Love You, I Love You Not 1996, The Proprietor 1996, Amour et confusions (Love and Confusions) 1997, Un amour de sorcière (Witch Way Love) 1997, Ever After 1998, Il manoscritto del principe (The Prince's Manuscript) 2000, Genesys (video game) 2001, Lisa 2001, Cet amour-là 2001, The Will to Resist 2002, La petite prairie aux bouleaux (The Birch-Tree Meadow) (writer) 2003, Akoibon 2005, Le temps qui reste 2005, Go West (also assoc. producer) 2005, Time to Leave 2005. *Television includes:* Le petit théâtre de Jean Renoir (The Little Theatre of Jean Renoir) 1970, Saint, martyr et poète 1975, L'arbre 1982, L'intoxe 1983, Vicious Circle 1985, The Last Seance 1986, Le tiroir secret (mini-series) 1986, L'ami Giono: Ennemonde 1990, Clothes in the Wardrobe 1992, Catherine the Great 1995, Belle Époque (mini-series; voice) 1995, Balzac 1999, Les Misérables (mini-series) 2000, Zaïde, un petit air de vengeance 2001, Les parents terribles 2003, La Contessa di Castiglione 2005, Les rois maudits (mini-series) 2005. *Leisure interest:* reading. *Address:* c/o Spica Productions, 4 Square du Roule, 75008 Paris, France.

MOREL, Claude Sylvestre Anthony; Seychelles diplomatist; *Ambassador to France;* b. 25 Sept. 1956, Victoria, Mahé; m. Margaret Morel; one s. one d.; ed Seychelles Coll., Univ. of Lille, France, Cairo Inst. of Diplomatic Studies, Inst. Int. d'Admin Publique, Paris; Chief of Protocol, Ministry of Foreign Affairs 1983–87, Dir Bilateral/Multilateral Affairs 1987–88; Chargé d'affaires, Embassy, Paris 1988–90; Dir-Gen. Ministry of Foreign Affairs 1990–96; Amb. to EU (also accred to Benelux and Germany) 1997–98; Perm. Rep. to UN and Amb. to USA and Canada 1998–2005; Prin. Sec., Ministry of Foreign Affairs 2005–07; Amb. to France (also accred to UK 2007–, to Monaco 2008–) and Perm. Rep. to UNESCO and FAO 2007–. *Leisure interests:* sports in general, travelling. *Address:* Seychelles Embassy, 51 avenue Mozart, 75016 Paris, France (office). *Telephone:* 1-42-30-57-47 (office). *Fax:* 1-42-30-57-40 (office). *E-mail:* ambsey@aol.com (office).

MOREL, Pierre Jean Louis Achille; French diplomatist; *Special Representative for Central Asia, European Union;* b. 27 June 1944, Romans (Drôme); s. of André Morel and Janine Vallernaud; m. Olga Bazanoff 1978; three c.; ed Lycée du Parc, Lyon, Paris, Ecole nat. d'admin; Europe Dept, Ministry of Foreign Affairs 1971–73, Analysis and Forecasting Centre 1973–76, First Sec. then Second Counsellor, Embassy, Moscow 1976–79, Ministerial Rep., Gen. Secr. Interministerial Cttee on European Econ. Co-operation 1979–81, Office of Pres. of Repub., Technical Adviser to Gen. Secr. 1981–85, Dir Political Affairs, Ministry of Foreign Affairs 1985–86, Amb. and France's Rep. Disarmament Conf. Geneva 1989, Head French Del. Preparatory Cttee Conf. on Security and Co-operation in Europe 1990, Diplomatic Adviser, Office of Pres. of Repub. 1991–92, Amb. to Georgia 1992–93, to Russia (also Accred to Moldova, Turkmenistan, Mongolia, Tajikistan and Kyrgyzstan) 1992–96, to China 1996–2002; Amb. to Holy See 2002–05; Advisor to the Policy Planning Centre, Ministry of Foreign Affairs 2005–06; EU Special Rep. for Central Asia 2006–; Officier, Légion d'honneur, Officier Ordre nat. du Mérite. *Publications:* trans. Mantrana 1984, Sauts de Temps 1989, Serpentara 1998 by Ernst Jünger. *Address:* c/o Council of the European Union, Rue de la Loi, 175, B-1048 Brussels, Belgium (office). *Telephone:* (2) 281 64 51 (office). *Fax:* (2) 281 51 46 (office). *E-mail:* pierre.morel@consilium.europa.eu (office). *Website:* www.consilium.europa.eu (office).

MORELLET, François Charles Alexis Albert; French painter and sculptor; b. 30 April 1926, Cholet, Maine-et-Loire; s. of Charles Morellet and Madeleine Guérineau; m. Danielle Marchand 1946; three s.; ed Lycée Charlemagne, Institut Nat. des Langues et Civilisations Orientales, Paris; Commercial Dir then Man. Dir Morellet-Guérineau 1948–76; artist 1942–; Grand prix nat. de sculpture 1987. *Works include:* mural at 22 Reade Street, Lower Manhattan, New York 1988, neon piece, Grande halle de la Villette, Paris 1988, steel sculpture, La Défense, Paris 1991, neon piece, Debis Potsdamerplatz, Berlin 1998, transparent films on glass, Obayashi Corpn, Tokyo 1998, neon pieces, Bundestag, Berlin 2000, marble piece, Jardin des Tuileries, Paris 2000, Gold Leaves, French Embassy, Berlin 2003, Musée des Beaux-Arts, Angers 2006, Musée d'Orsay, Paris 2006, Bundestag Elisabeth Lüders-Haus, Berlin 2003, Cité Internationale de Lyon, Palais des Congrès, Lyon 2006. *Publication:* Mais comment taire mes commentaires 1999. *Leisure interests:* travel, underwater fishing. *Address:* 83 rue Porte Baron, 49300 Cholet (home). *Telephone:* (2) 41-62-23-81 (office). *Fax:* (2) 41-71-04-74 (office). *E-mail:* f.morellet@wanadoo.fr (office).

MORENILLA, José María, DR.IUR; Spanish judge; b. 29 Aug. 1926, Granada; s. of Carlos Morenilla and Clotilde Morenilla; m. Joanne Allard 1962; one s. one d.; ed School of Law, Granada, Columbia Univ., Univ. of Granada; Judge of First Instance 1952; Legal Adviser (in int. law) Ministry of Justice 1978–87; Supreme Court Judge Criminal Section 1987–90, Admin. Section 1990–; Agent/Rep. of Spanish Govt before European Comm. of Human Rights 1988–90; apptd Judge European Court of Human Rights 1990; Cross of Honour of San Raimundo de Peñafort. *Publications:* Organization of the Courts and Judicial Reform in the United States 1968, Poder Judicial en los Estados Unidos 1979, La Igualdad (Jurídica) de la Mujer en España 1980, Medidas Alternativas de la Prisión 1983, Protección Internacional de los Derechos Humanos 1984, Convenio Europeo de Derechos Humanos – Ámbito, Organos, Procedimientos 1985. *Leisure interests:* music (opera), reading. *Address:* Juan Ramón Jiménez 2, 9°C, 28036 Madrid, Spain. *Telephone:* (91) 4574591.

MORENO, Glen, BA, JD; American business executive; *Chairman, Pearson plc;* b. 1943, Calif.; ed Stanford Univ., Delhi Univ., Harvard Law School; sr positions at Citigroup in Europe and Asia 1969–87; CEO Fidelity Int. 1987–91; Sr Ind. Dir Man Group plc, non-exec. Dir 1994–; Chair. Pearson plc 2005–; mem. Bd of Dirs Fidelity Int.; Trustee Prince of Liechtenstein and Liechtenstein Global Trusts; Gov. Ditchley Foundation. *Address:* Pearson plc, 80 Strand, London, WC2R ORL, England (office). *Telephone:* (20) 7010-2306 (office). *Fax:* (20) 7010-6601 (office). *Website:* www.pearson.com (office).

MORENO BARBER, Javier, Licenciado en Ciencias Químicas, Master of Journalism; Spanish journalist and editor; *Director, El País;* b. 1963, Paris, France; ed Univ. of Valencia, Autonomous Univ. of Madrid; worked in Germany –1992; worked for econs section of El País 1992–94, Man. Ed. Mexican edn of newspaper 1994, returned to to Spain and co-ordinated Latin American edn, served as special envoy to several int. events, Head of Econs section 1999–2002, corresp. in Berlin 2002–03, Dir econ. daily Cinco Dias 2003–06, Dir El País 2006–, apptd cttee to undertake extensive redesign of newspaper Feb. 2007, completed Oct. 2007. *Address:* El País, Miguel Yuste 40, 28037 Madrid, Spain (office). *Telephone:* (91) 337-8200 (office). *Fax:* (91) 337-7758 (office). *E-mail:* redaccion@elpais.com (office). *Website:* www.elpais.com (office).

MORENO BARBERA, Admiral Antonio; Spanish naval officer; *Chief of Defence Staff;* b. 17 April 1940, Madrid; m. Pepa Deckler Andreu; four c.; ed Naval War Coll.; began career in Spanish Navy 1956; apptd Lt JG 1961; served on board destroyer Alava, submarines Almirante García de los Reyes S-31, Delfín S-61, Marsopa S-63, Submarine Flotilla Staff; Commdr submarines Tonina S-62 and Galerna S-71 1975–83; Commdg Officer frigate Asturias F-74 1983–89; Commdr Submarine Flotilla 1988–92; shore assignments include Leading Lecturer on Logistics, Naval Warfare Coll., Lecturer on Tactics, Submarine School, Chief of Tactical Studies, Dept at Naval Staff, Exec. Asst to Chief of Naval Staff; Commdr of Fleet of Amphibious Force (Delta Group) 1992–94; Chief of Rota Naval Base 1994–95; Chief of the Jt Defence Staff 1995–97; Chief of Naval Staff 1997–99; Chief of Defence Staff 1999–; apptd Vice-Admiral 1994, Admiral 1997; Grand Cross of St Hermenegildo, Commdr US Legion of Merit four Naval Merit Crosses, Sahara Medal (Combat Zone), Brazilian Naval Merit Medal, Naval Merit Grand Cross, Mil. Merit Grand Cross, Chilean Great Star Mil. Merit Cross, Brazilian Naval Merit Grand Cross. *Address:* Ministry of Defence, Paseo de la Castellana 109, 28071 Madrid, Spain (office). *Telephone:* (91) 3955000 (office). *Fax:* (91) 5563958 (office). *E-mail:* infodefensa@mde.es (office). *Website:* www.mde.es.

MORENO FERNANDEZ, Abelardo; Cuban diplomatist; *Permanent Representative, United Nations;* m.; one d.; joined Ministry of Foreign Affairs 1961; Perm. Sec. to UN, Geneva 1964–68, Deputy Rep. to UN Security Council, New York 1990–91, Minister Counsellor to UN 1992–95; Deputy Dir for Political Affairs, Ministry of Foreign Affairs 1995, Dir for Multilateral Affairs 1995–2000, Deputy Minister for Foreign Affairs 2000–09; Perm. Rep. to UN, New York 2009–; Prof., Higher Inst. for Int. Relations, Cuba; Visiting Lecturer, Columbia Univ., Higher Inst. for Int. Relations, Geneva, Indian Inst. for Non-Aligned Studies. *Address:* Permanent Mission of Cuba to the United Nations, 315 Lexington Avenue and 38th Street, New York, NY 10016, USA. *Telephone:* (212) 689-7215 (office). *Fax:* (212) 779-1697 (office). *E-mail:* cuba@un.int (office). *Website:* www.un.int/cuba (office).

MORENO GARCÉS, Lenín, Licenció en Administración Pública; Ecuadorean politician and organization executive; *Vice-President;* b. 19 March 1953, Nuevo Rocafuerte; s. of Senator Prof. Servio Moreno; m. Rocio Gonzalez; three d.; ed Instituto Nacional Mejía, Colegio Nacional Sebastián Benalcázar,

Universidad Cen. del Ecuador; Dir Centro de Formación Profesional Continental 1976–78; Sales Man., Satho 1982–84; Marketing Man., Zitro 1985–86; Dir OMC Publigerencia Andina 1986–92; Admin. Dir Ministry of Govt 1996–97; Exec. Dir Cámara de Turismo de Pichincha 1997–99, Exec. Dir Federación Nacional de Cámaras de Turismo 1997–99; Exec. Dir Cámara de Turismo de Pichincha 1997–99; Dir Nat. Council on Disabilities (CONADIS) 2001–04; Academic Dir Eventa Foundation 2004–06; Vice-Pres. of Ecuador 2007–. *Publications:* several books, including Filosofía para la vida y el trabajo, Teoría y Práctica del Humor, Ser Feliz es Fácil y Divertido, Los Mejores Chistes del Mundo, Humor de los Famosos, Trompabulario, Ríase no sea enfermo, Cuentos no Ecológicos. *Address:* Palacio de Carondelet, Quito, Ecuador (office). *Telephone:* (2) 258-4000 (office). *E-mail:* info@presidencia.gov.ec (office). *Website:* www.presidencia.gov.ec/modulos.asp?id=26 (office); www.leninmoreno.com.

MORENO-MEJÍA, Luis Alberto, BA, MBA; Colombian diplomatist and international organization official; *President, Inter-American Development Bank;* b. 3 May 1953, Philadelphia, USA; m. Gabriela Febres-Cordero 1970; one s. one d.; ed Florida Int. Univ., Thunderbird Univ., Phoenix, Ariz. and Harvard Univ.; Div. Man. Praco 1977–82; exec. producer of nationwide nightly news programme and other entertainment and children's programmes 1982–90; Neiman Fellow, Harvard Univ. 1990–91; Pres. Inst. de Foment Industrial 1991–92; Minister of Econ. Devt 1992–94; telecommunications adviser and pvt. consultant, Luis Carlos Sarmiento Org., Bogotá 1994–97; Pnr Westsphere Andean Advisers 1997–98; Campaign Man. of Andrés Pastrana 1994; Amb. to USA 1998–2005; Pres. IDB, Washington, DC 2005–; Orden al Mérito Civil Ciudad de Bogotá, en el Grado de Gran Cruz, awarded by Mayor of Bogotá 1990, Orden al Mérito Industrial – José Gutiérrez Gómez, Colombian Nat. Business Asscn 2002, Orden de Boyacá en el Grado de Gran Cruz awarded by the Pres. of Colombia 2002; King of Spain Prize for journalistic excellence. *Publications include:* articles on Colombian and int. politics and econs for publs in Colombia and USA; writings have appeared in New York Times, Boston Globe, Miami Herald, El Tiempo, Foreign Affairs en Español and Semana. *Address:* Inter-American Development Bank (IDB), 1300 New York Avenue, NW, Washington, DC 20577, USA (office). *Telephone:* (202) 623-1000 (office). *Fax:* (202) 623-3096 (office). *E-mail:* pic@iadb.org (office). *Website:* www.iadb.org.

MORENO OCAMPO, Luis; Argentine lawyer; *Chief Prosecutor, International Criminal Court;* b. 1953, Buenos Aires; ed Univ. of Buenos Aires; Deputy Public Prosecutor in trials against mil. junta 1985–87; Dist Attorney, Fed. Circuit, City of Buenos Aires 1987–92; in pvt. practice (specializing in corruption control programmes and ethical advice for large cos) 1992–; Chief Prosecutor (first in position), Int. Criminal Court 2003–; Sub-Dir Research Centre, Univ. of Buenos Aires Law School 1984, currently Adjunct Prof. of Penal Law; Visiting Prof. of Law, Harvard Univ., USA; co-f. Poder Ciudadano; mem. Advisory Cttee Transparency Int., Pres. for Latin America and the Caribbean. *Film appearance:* (as himself) The Devil Came on Horseback 2006. *Publications include:* In Self Defense: How to Avoid Corruption 1993, When Power Lost the Trial: How to Explain the Dictatorship to Our Children 1996. *Address:* International Criminal Court, Maanweg 174, 2516 AB, The Hague, The Netherlands (office). *Telephone:* (70) 5158515 (office). *Fax:* (70) 5158555 (office). *Website:* www.icc-cpi.int.

MORENO-RAZO, Alma Rosa, BA, MA, PhD; Mexican economist, financial officer and fmr diplomatist; *Chief Administrative Officer, Grupo Financiero Banorte SAB de CV;* ed Instituto Tecnológico Autónomo de México, El Colegio de México, New York Univ., USA; fmr Deputy Dir for Planning, Promotion and Tech. Assistance, Nat. Bank of Public Works and Services (Banobras); fmr Exec. Dir Reconstruction and Syndicated Loans Multibanco Comermex; held various positions at Ministry of Finance and Public Credit, Gen. Co-ordinator for Income and Tax Policies 1998–99, Pres. Nat. Service for Tax Admin (SAT) 1999–2000, Head of Liaison Unit with Mexican Congress, Special Adviser to Sec. of Finance on Income Policies and Federalism, Dir-Gen. for Income Policies; Visiting Researcher, Centre for Econ. Investigation and Educ. in Mexico 2000–01; Amb. to UK 2001–2004; currently Chief Admin. Officer, Grupo Financiero Banorte SAB de CV. *Address:* Grupo Financiero Banorte SAB de CV, Ave. Revolucion No 3000, Sur Primavera, 64830 Monterrey NL, Mexico (office). *Telephone:* (81) 8319-7200 (office). *Fax:* (81) 8318-5042 (office). *Website:* www.banorte.com (office).

MORETTI, Nanni; Italian actor and filmmaker; b. (Giovanni Moretti), 19 Aug. 1953, Brunico, Bolzano; m.; one c.; co-f. Sacher Film S.r.l. (film production co.) 1986; est. Cinema Nuovo Sacher 1991; founder and artistic Dir Sacher Film Festival 1996; co-f. Tandem (film distribution co.) 1997; jury mem., Cannes Int. Film Festival 1997; jury Pres., Venice Int. Film Festival 2001. *Films include:* as actor, dir and writer: Io sono un autarchico (I am Self Sufficient, also producer) 1976, Ecce Bombo 1978, Sogni d'oro (Sweet Dreams, Special Prize Venice Int. Film Festival) 1981, Bianca 1983, La Messa è finita (The Mass is Ended, Silver Bear Berlin Int. Film Festival 1986) 1985, Palombella rossa (Red Wood-Pigeon, also producer) 1989, Aprile (also producer) 1998, La Stanza del figlio (The Son's Room, also producer, Palme d'Or Cannes Film Festival) 2001, as dir: La Cosa (the Thing, also producer, writer) 1990, Caro diario (Dear Diary, also producer, writer, 3 David di Donatello Awards, Best Dir Cannes Int. Film Festival) 1994, L'unico paese al mondo 1994, Il Giorno della prima di Close Up (Opening Day of Close Up) 1996, The Last Customer (also producer) 2003, Il caimano 2006; also actor in: Domani accadrà (It's Happening Tomorrow) 1988, Il Portaborse 1991, La Seconda Volta (The Second Time) 1996, Trois vies & une seule mort (Three Lives and Only One Death) 1996, Quiet Chaos 2008. *Address:* Sacher Film S.r.l., Via Piramide Cestia 1, 00153 Rome (office); Via Pindemonte 22, 00152 Rome, Italy (home). *Telephone:* (06) 5745353 (office). *Fax:* (06) 5740483 (office).

MORGAN, Most Rev. Dr Barry, PhD; British ecclesiastic; *Archbishop of Wales;* b. 1947, Neath, Wales; m. Hilary Morgan 1969; one s. one d.; ed Ystalyfera Grammar School, Swansea Valley, Univ. Coll., London, Selwyn Coll., Cambridge, Westcott House, Cambridge, Univ. of Wales; ordained deacon 1972, priest 1973; subsequently curate in parish of St Andrews Major, Michaelston-le-Pit, Glam.; Chaplain and Lecturer, St Michael's Coll. and Univ. of Wales, Cardiff; Warden of Church Hostel, Bangor; Chaplain and Lecturer in Theology, Univ. of Wales, Bangor; Dir of Ordinands and In-service Training Adviser, Diocese of Bangor; Rector of Wrexham; Archdeacon of Meironnydd and Rector of Criccieth with Treflys 1986; elected and consecrated Bishop of Bangor 1993–99; Bishop of Llandaff 1999–2003; Archbishop of Wales 2003–; led Clergy School, Diocese of Kerala, India 2002; rep. Church in Wales on WCC; has served on several comms and working parties; Fellow, Bangor Univ. 1994, Univ. of Wales Inst. 2003, Cardiff 2004, Lampeter 2004. *Publications include:* O Ddydd i Ddydd 1980, The History of the Church Hostel and Anglican Chaplaincy at the University College of North Wales, Bangor 1986, Concepts of Mission and Ministry in Anglican Chaplaincy Work 1988, Ministry in the Church in Wales – The Shape of Things to Come? 2002, Strangely Orthodox – R.S. Thomas and his Poetry of Faith 2006. *Leisure interest:* golf. *Address:* Llys Esgob, The Cathedral Green, Llandaff, Cardiff, CF5 2YE, Wales (office). *Telephone:* (29) 2056-2400 (office). *Fax:* (29) 2056-8410 (office). *E-mail:* archbishop@churchinwales.org.uk (office). *Website:* www.churchinwales.org.uk (office).

MORGAN, David, BEcons, MSc, PhD; Australian banking executive; *Managing Director and CEO, Westpac Banking Corporation;* b. 14 March 1947, Melbourne; s. of Raymond K. Morgan and Verna Morgan; m. Roslyn Joan Kelly; two c.; ed La Trobe Univ., Univ. of London, UK, Harvard Univ., USA; Sr Economist Dept of Fiscal Affairs, IMF, Washington DC 1976–79; Asst Sec. Foreign Investment Br., Fed. Treasury 1980–81, Fiscal and Monetary Policy Br. 1982–83, mem. Taxation Policy Div., Treasury Dept Canberra 1983–85; First Asst Sec.-Gen. Financial and Econ. Policy, Commonwealth Treasury 1986–87; Deputy Sec. of Finance 1987, of Econs 1989; Deputy Man. Dir Westpac Financial Services Group 1990, Chief Gen. Man. Asia Pacific Div., Westpac, Sydney 1990, Man. Dir Westpac Financial Services Group 1990–91, Group Exec. Retail Banking, Westpac Banking Corpn 1992–94, Group Exec. Institutional and Int. Banking 1994–97, Exec. Dir Westpac Banking Corpn 1997–, Man. Dir and CEO 1999–, mem. Social Responsibility Cttee; mem. Union Club. *Leisure interests:* wine, tennis, classical music. *Address:* Westpac Banking Corporation, Level 25, 60 Martin Place, Sydney 2000, Australia (office). *Telephone:* (2) 9226-3143 (office). *Fax:* (2) 9226-1539 (office). *Website:* www.westpac.com.au (office).

MORGAN, Edwin George, OBE, MA; Scottish poet, writer, translator and academic; *The Scots Makar (National Poet of Scotland);* b. 27 April 1920, Glasgow; ed Rutherglen Acad., High School of Glasgow, Univ. of Glasgow; RAMC 1940–46; Asst Lecturer, Univ. of Glasgow 1947–50, Lecturer 1950–65, Senior Lecturer 1965–71, Reader 1971–75, Titular Prof. of English 1975–80, Prof. Emeritus 1980–; Visiting Prof., Univ. of Strathclyde 1987–90; Hon. Prof., Univ. Coll., Wales 1991–95; Poet Laureate of Glasgow 1997–2006; The Scots Makar (Nat. Poet of Scotland) 2004–; has trans poetry from Hungarian, Italian, French, German, Russian, Spanish and Anglo-Saxon; Cholmondeley Award for Poetry 1968, Scottish Arts Council Book Awards 1968, 1973, 1975, 1977, 1978, 1983, 1984, 1991, 1992, Hungarian PEN Memorial Medal 1972, Soros Translation Award 1985, Queen's Gold Medal for Poetry 2000, Saltire Soc. and Scottish Arts Council Lifetime Achievement Award 2003. *Plays:* various plays and opera librettos. *Publications:* poetry: The Vision of Cathkin Braes 1952, The Cape of Good Hope 1955, Starryveldt 1965, Scotch Mist 1965, Sealwear 1966, Emergent Poems 1967, The Second Life 1968, Gnomes 1968, Proverbfolder 1969, Penguin Modern Poets 15 (with Alan Bold and Edward Brathwaite) 1969, The Horseman's Word: A Sequence of Concrete Poems 1970, Twelve Songs 1970, The Dolphin's Song 1971, Glasgow Sonnets 1972, Instamatic Poems 1972, The Whittrick: A Poem in Eight Dialogues 1973, From Glasgow to Saturn 1973, The New Divan 1977, Colour Poems 1978, Star Gate: Science Fiction Poems 1979, Poems of Thirty Years 1982, Grafts/Takes 1983, Sonnets from Scotland 1984, Selected Poems 1985, From the Video Box 1986, Newspoems 1987, Themes on a Variation 1988, Tales from Limerick Zoo 1988, Collected Poems 1990, Hold Hands Among the Atoms 1991, Sweeping Out the Dark 1994, Virtual and Other Realities 1997, Demon 1999, New Selected Poems 2000, Cathures 2002, Love and a Life 2003, Tales from Baron Munchausen 2005, The Play of Gilgamesh 2006, A Book of Lives (Sundial Scottish Arts Council Book of the Year 2008) 2007, Beyond the Sun 2007; prose/editor: Collins Albatross Book of Longer Poems: English and American Poetry from the Fourteenth Century to the Present Day (ed.) 1963, Scottish Poetry 1–6 (co-ed.) 1966–72, New English Dramatists 14 (ed.) 1970, Essays 1974, East European Poets 1976, Hugh MacDiarmid 1976, Scottish Satirical Verse (ed.) 1980, Twentieth Century Scottish Classics 1987, Nothing Not Giving Messages (interviews) 1990, Crossing the Border: Essays in Scottish Literature 1990, Language, Poetry and Language Poetry 1990, Collected Translations 1996, Evening Will Come They Will Sew the Blue Sail 1991, James Thomson: The City of Dreadful Night (ed.) 1993. *Address:* Clarence Court, 234 Crow Road, Glasgow, G11 7PD, Scotland (home). *Website:* www.edwinmorgan.com (home).

MORGAN, Gwyn, BSc (MechEng), PEng; Canadian business executive; *Executive Vice-Chairman, EnCana Corporation;* b. 4 Nov. 1945, Carstairs, Alberta; s. of Ian Morgan and Margaret Morgan; ed Univ. of Alberta and Cornell Univ, NY; Petroleum Engineer, Alberta Energy Resources Conservation Bd –1970; Man. Operations and Eng, Consolidated Natural Gas Ltd, Consolidated Pipelines Ltd, Norlands Petroleums Ltd 1970–75; joined Alberta Energy Co. Ltd 1975, positions including Pres. and CEO, Founding Pres. and CEO EnCana Corpn (following merger of Alberta Energy Co. Ltd and Pan

Canadian Energy Corpn) 2002–05, Exec. Vice-Chair. 2005–; Dir HSBC Bank North America, SNC-Lavalin Inc., Alcan Inc., American Petroleum Inst., Inst. of the Americas; Founding mem. Canadian Asscn of Petroleum Producers Bd of Govs; mem. Advisory Bd Accenture Energy; Past Pres. Ind. Petroleum Asscn of Canada; fmr Vice-Chair. Canadian Council of Chief Execs (fmrly Business Council on Nat. Issues); fmr Dir Public Policy Forum; fmr mem. Bd of Man. Calgary Foothills Gen. Hosp.; Trustee Fraser Inst.; Hon. Col (retd) 410 Tactical Fighter Squadron, Canadian Air Force; Univ. of Western Ont. Ivey Business Leader Award 2002, Alberta Business Hall of Fame, Univ. of Alberta Canadian Business Leader Award 2002, Canadian CEO of the Year 2005. *Leisure interests:* hiking, skiing, cycling, ocean sailing, physical fitness. *Address:* EnCana Corporation, Suite 1800, 855 2nd Street SW, PO Box 2850, Calgary, Alberta T2P 2S5, Canada (office). *Telephone:* (403) 645-2000 (office). *Fax:* (403) 645-4644 (office). *Website:* www.encana.com (office).

MORGAN, Howard James, MA; British artist; b. 21 April 1949, N Wales; s. of Thomas James Morgan and Olive Victoria Morgan (née Oldnall); m. Susan Ann Sandilands 1977 (divorced 1998); two s. one d.; one s. one d. (with Sarah Milligan); ed Fairfax High School, Sutton Coldfield, Univ. of Newcastle-upon-Tyne; career artist; comms by HM The Queen, HM The Queen of The Netherlands, HRH Prince Michael of Kent, TRH The Prince & Princess of Hanover, Tom Stoppard, Philip Larkin, Francis Crick, Paul Maurice Dirac, Dame Antoinette Sibley (Nat. Portrait Gallery, London), Mr & Mrs Neil McConnell; perm. display of work at Nat. Portrait Gallery, London; mem. Royal Soc. of Portrait Painters 1986–. *Leisure interests:* riding, 1938 Citröen, books. *Address:* Studio 401½, Wandsworth Road, Battersea, London, SW8 6JP; 12 Rectory Grove, Clapham Old Town, London, SW4 0EA, England (home). *Telephone:* (20) 7720-1181 (Studio). *E-mail:* howard@howard-morgan .co.uk (office). *Website:* www.howard-morgan.co.uk (office).

MORGAN, Rt Hon. (Hywel) Rhodri, PC, MA; British politician; *First Minister, National Assembly for Wales;* b. 29 Sept. 1939; s. of the late Thomas John Morgan and of Huana Morgan; m. Julie Edwards 1967; one s. two d.; ed St John's Coll. Oxford, Harvard Univ., USA; Research Officer, Cardiff City Council, Welsh Office and Dept of Environment 1965–71; Econ. Adviser, Dept of Trade and Industry 1972–74; Industrial Devt Officer, S Glamorgan Co. Council 1974–80; Head of Bureau for Press and Information, European Comm. Office for Wales 1980–87; Labour MP for Cardiff W, House of Commons 1987–2001; Opposition Spokesman on Energy 1988–92, Welsh Affairs 1992–97; Sec. for Econ. Devt, Nat. Ass. for Wales 1999–2000; First Minister, Nat. Ass. for Wales 2000–. *Publication:* Cardiff: Half and Half a Capital 1994. *Leisure interests:* long-distance running, wood carving, marine wildlife. *Address:* Welsh Assembly Government, Cardiff Bay, Cardiff, CF99 1NA (office); Lower House, Michaelston-le-Pit, Dinas Powys, South Glamorgan, CF64 4HE, Wales (home). *Telephone:* (29) 2089-8765 (office); (29) 2051-4262 (home). *Fax:* (29) 2089-8198 (office). *E-mail:* rhodri.morgan@wales.gsi .gov.uk (office).

MORGAN, James N., PhD; American economist and academic; *Senior Research Scientist Emeritus, Institute for Social Research, University of Michigan;* b. 1 March 1918, Corydon, Ind.; s. of John Jacob Brooke and Rose Ann Davis Morgan; m. Gladys Lucille Hassler 1945; three s. one d.; ed Northwestern Univ. and Harvard; Asst Prof. of Econs, Brown Univ. 1947–49; Carnegie Research Fellow, Inst. for Social Research, Univ. of Mich. 1949–51, Fellow, Center for Advanced Study in the Behavioral Sciences 1955–56, Program Dir Survey Research Center, Inst. for Social Research 1956–88, Prof. of Econs 1957–88, Prof. Emer. 1988–, Sr Research Scientist Emer., Inst. for Social Research 2005–; Fellow, Wissenschaftskolleg zu Berlin 1983–84, American Statistical Asscn, American Gerontological Asscn; mem. NAS, American Acad. of Arts and Sciences; Distinguished Faculty Award 1997, Woytinsky Lecture 1999. *Publications:* Income and Welfare in the United States 1962, Economic Behavior of the Affluent 1965, Economic Survey Methods 1971, Five Thousand American Families (ed.) (10 vols) 1972–84, Economics of Personal Choice 1980, Household Survey of Grenada 1985; numerous articles in scientific journals. *Leisure interests:* travel, photography. *Address:* Institute for Social Research, University of Michigan, 426 Thompson Street, Ann Arbor, MI 48104 (office); 1217 Bydding Road, Ann Arbor, MI 48103, USA (home). *Telephone:* (734) 764-8388 (office); (734) 668-8304 (home). *Fax:* (734) 647-4575 (office). *E-mail:* jnmorgan@umich.edu (office). *Website:* www.isr.umich.edu (office).

MORGAN, Keith John, BSc, MA, DPhil, FRSC, FRACI, FAIM; British/Australian university vice-chancellor and academic; *Visiting Professor, Hiroshima University;* b. 14 Dec. 1929; s. of C. F. J. Morgan and W. Morgan; m. Hilary A. Chapman 1957 (divorced 1999); one d.; ed Manchester Grammar School and Brasenose Coll. Oxford; Sr Research Fellow, Ministry of Supply 1955–57; ICI Research Fellow 1957–58; Lecturer, Univ. of Birmingham 1958–64; AEC Research Fellow, Purdue Univ. 1960–61; Lecturer, Univ. of Lancaster 1964–65, Sr Lecturer 1965–68, Prof. 1968–86, Pro-Vice-Chancellor 1973–78, Sr Pro-Vice-Chancellor 1978–86, Prof. Emer. 2003–; Vice-Chancellor, Univ. of Newcastle, NSW 1987–93, Prof. Emer. 1993–; Prof., Univ. of Electro-Communications, Tokyo 1993–95; Visiting Prof., Hiroshima Univ. 1995–99, Sr Research Fellow 2003, currently Visiting Prof.; Visiting Prof. Nagoya Univ. 2002; Chair. Hunter Foundation for Cancer Research –1993; Deputy Chair. Hunter Tech. Devt Centre 1987–93, Hunter Econ. Devt Council 1989–93, Hunter Fed. Task Force 1991–93; Ed. Higher Education Forum 2003–, Higher Education Research in Japan 2003–; Hon. DSc (Newcastle) 1993. *Publications:* various scientific, managerial, economic and educational papers. *Leisure interests:* Mozart, mountains, cricket. *Address:* 9B Castle Hill, Lancaster, LA1 1YS, England (home). *E-mail:* keith.j.morgan@lineone.net (home).

MORGAN, Baron (Life Peer), cr. 2000, of Aberdyfi in the County of Gwynedd; **Kenneth Owen Morgan,** DPhil, DLitt (Oxon.), FBA, FRHistS; British historian and academic; *Emeritus Professor, University of Wales;* b. 16 May 1934, Wood Green; s. of David James Morgan and Margaret Morgan (née Owen); m. Jane Keeler 1973 (died 1992); one s. one d.; ed University Coll. School, London, Oriel Coll., Univ. of Oxford; Lecturer, History Dept, Univ. Coll., Swansea 1958–66, Sr Lecturer 1965–66; Fellow and Praelector, Modern History and Politics, The Queen's Coll., Univ. of Oxford 1966–89; Prin., Univ. Coll. of Wales, Aberystwyth 1989–95; Pro-Vice-Chancellor, Univ. of Wales 1989–93, Vice-Chancellor 1993–95, Prof. 1989–99, Emer. Prof. 1999–; Ed. Welsh History Review 1961–2003; Jt Ed. 20th Century British History 1994–99; mem. House of Lords Constitutional Cttee 2001–04; Election Commentator BBC Wales 1964–79; Fellow American Council of Learned Socs Columbia Univ. 1962–63, Visiting Prof. 1965; Visiting Prof. Univ. of Witwatersrand 1997–2000, Univ. of Bristol 2000, Univ. of Rouen 2003; Hon. Fellow Univ. Coll., Swansea 1985, Hon. Prof. 1995–; Hon. Fellow The Queen's Coll., Oxford 1992, Univ. of Wales, Cardiff 1997, Trinity Coll., Carmarthen 1998, Oriel Coll. Oxford 2003; Supernumerary Fellow, Jesus Coll., Oxford 1991–92; Hon. DLitt.; Hon. DLitt (Wales), (Glamorgan) 1997, (Greenwich) 2004. *Radio:* regular commentator (also on TV) on politics and modern history 1964–. *Publications:* Wales in British Politics 1963, David Lloyd George 1963, Freedom or Sacrilege? 1966, Keir Hardie 1967, The Age of Lloyd George 1971, Lloyd George: Family Letters (ed.) 1973, Lloyd George 1974, Keir Hardie: Radical and Socialist 1975, Consensus and Disunity 1979, Portrait of a Progressive (with Jane Morgan) 1980, Rebirth of a Nation: Wales 1880–1980 1981, David Lloyd George 1981, Labour in Power 1945–51 1984, The Oxford Illustrated History of Britain (ed.) 1984, Labour People 1987, The Oxford History of Britain (ed.) 1988, The Red Dragon and The Red Flag 1989, Academic Leadership 1991, The People's Peace: British History 1945–90 1992, Modern Wales: Politics, Places and People 1995, Young Oxford History of Britain and Ireland (Gen. Ed.) 1996, Callaghan: A Life 1997, Crime, Protest and Police in Modern British Society (ed.) 1999, The Twentieth Century 2000, The Great Reform Act 2001, Michael Foot: A Life 2007. *Leisure interests:* music, sport, travel, architecture. *Address:* House of Lords, London, SW1A 0PW (office); The Croft, 63 Millwood End, Long Hanborough, Witney, Oxon., OX29 8BP, England. *Telephone:* (20) 7219-8616 (office); (1993) 881341 (home). *Fax:* (1993) 881341 (home). *E-mail:* k.morgan@online.rednet.co.uk (home).

MORGAN, Michèle, (pseudonym of Simone Roussel); French actress; b. 29 Feb. 1920; d. of Louis Roussel; m. 1st Bill Marshall; one s.; m. 2nd Henri Vidal (deceased); studied with R. Simon, Paris; actress 1936–; mem. Jury, Cannes Festival 1972, Pres. 1971; Grand Officier, Légion d'honneur, Officier, Ordre nat. du Mérite, Commdr des Arts et des Lettres; Hon. César 1992, Career Golden Lion, Venice Film Festival, 1996, Victoire (France) for Best Actress 1946, 1948, 1950, 1952, 1955, Médaille de vermeil, Paris 1967. *Films include:* Le Mioche 1936, Mes tantes et moi 1936, Gigolette 1936, Gribouille 1937, Le Récif de corail 1938, Orage 1938, Quai des brumes 1938, La Loi du nord 1939, L'Entraîneuse 1940, Les Musiciens du ciel 1940, My Life with Caroline 1941, Remorques 1941, Joan of Paris 1942, Untel père et fils 1943, Two Tickets to London 1943, Higher and Higher 1943, Passage to Marseille 1944, Symphonie pastorale 1946 (Cannes Festival Prize for Best Actress), The Chase 1946, The Fallen Idol 1948, Aux yeux du souvenir 1948, Fabiola 1949, La Belle que voilà 1950, Maria Chapdelaine 1950, Le Château de verre 1950, L'Étrange Madame X 1951, Les sept péchés capitaux 1952, Minute de vérité 1952, Les orgueilleux 1953, Obsession 1954, Oasis 1955, Napoléon 1955, Les grandes manoeuvres 1955, Marguerite de la nuit 1955, Marie Antoinette 1956, Si Paris nous était conté 1956, The Vintage 1957, Retour de manivelle 1957, Le miroir à deux faces 1958, Femmes d'un été 1959, Pourquoi viens-tu si tard? 1959, Les scélérats 1959, Fortunat 1960, Le puits aux trois vérités 1961, Les lions sont lâches 1961, Rencontres 1962, Le crime ne paie pas 1962, Landru 1963, Constance aux Enfers 1963, Il Fornaretto di Venezia 1963, Méfiez-vous, mesdames 1963, Les yeux cernés 1964, Dis-moi qui tuer 1965, Les centurions 1966, Benjamin 1968, Le chat et la souris 1975, Ils vont tous bien 1989. *Plays include:* Le Tout pour le tout 1979, Chéri 1981, Les Monstres sacrés 1993. *Television includes:* Silent the Song 1952, Camille 1953, La Bien-aimée 1967, Le Tout pour le tout 1981, Le Tiroir secret 1968, La Veuve de l'architecte 1995, Des gens si bien élevés 1997, La Rivale 1999. *Publications:* Mes yeux ont vu 1965, Avec ces yeux-là 1977, Le fil bleu 1993. *Address:* Agents Associés, 201 rue du Faubourg Saint-Honoré, 75008 Paris, France.

MORGAN, Peter William Lloyd, MBE, MA; British business executive; b. 9 May 1936, Neath; s. of the late Matthew Morgan and of Margaret Gwynneth (née Lloyd) Morgan; m. Elisabeth Susanne Davis 1964; three d.; ed Llandovery Coll., Trinity Hall, Cambridge; served Royal Signals 1954–56; joined IBM UK Ltd 1959, Data Processing Sales Dir 1971–74, Group Dir of Data Processing Marketing, IBM Europe, Paris 1975–90, Dir IBM UK Ltd 1980–87, IBM UK Holdings Ltd 1987–89; Dir Gen. Inst. of Dirs 1989–94; Dir South Wales Electricity PLC 1989–95, Chair. 1996; Dir Nat. Provident Inst. 1990–95, Chair. 1996–99; Dir Firth Holdings PLC (now Hyder Consulting PLC) 1994–, Zergo Holdings PLC (now Baltimore Technologies PLC) 1994–, (Chair. 2000–), Oxford Instruments PLC 1999–; Chair. Pace Micro Tech. PLC 1996–99, KSCL Ltd 1999–2000, Technetix PLC 2002–; Dir IDP SA (Paris) 2000–02; Dir Asscn of Lloyds' Mems 1997–, Council mem. Lloyds of London 2000–, Dir Lloyds.com 2001–; mem. Econ. and Social Cttee, EU 1994–2002, Advisory Cttee Business and the Environment 2001–; Master, Co. of Information Technologists; Radical of the Year, Radical Soc. 1990. *Leisure interests:* music, history, gardening, skiing, wine, dog walking. *Address:* Baltimore Technologies PLC, Innovation House, Mark Road, Hemel Hempstead, Herts., HP2 7DN, England (office). *Telephone:* (118) 903-8905 (office); (1428) 642757 (home). *Fax:* (1653) 600066 (office); (1428) 643684 (home).

E-mail: petermorgan@baltimore.com (home). *Website:* www.baltimore.com (office).

MORGAN, Piers Stefan; British journalist; b. 30 March 1965, Guildford; s. of Anthony Pughe-Morgan and Gabrielle Oliver; m. Marion E. Shalloe 1991; three s.; ed Cumnor House Preparatory School, Chailey School, Sussex, Lewes Priory Sixth Form Coll. and Harlow Journalism Coll.; reporter, Surrey and S London newspapers 1987–89; Showbusiness Ed. The Sun 1989–94; Ed. The News of the World 1994–95, Daily Mirror (later The Mirror) 1995–2004; co-founder Press Gazette Ltd, owner of Press Gazette 2005–07; Editorial Dir newspaper for children, First News 2006–; Atex Award for Nat. Newspaper Ed. of Year 1994, What the Papers Say Newspaper of the Year Award 2001, GQ Ed. of the Year 2002, British Press Awards Newspaper of the Year 2002, Magazine Design and Journalism Awards Columnist of the Year Award (Live Magazine) 2007. *Television:* presenter: The Importance of Being Famous (Channel 4) 2004, Morgan & Platell (Channel 4) 2005–06, You Can't Fire Me, I'm Famous (BBC1) 2006–07, Piers Morgan on Sandbanks (ITV 1) 2008; judge: America's Got Talent (NBC) 2006–, Britain's Got Talent (ITV 1) 2007–. *Publications:* Private Lives of the Stars 1990, Secret Lives of the Stars 1991, Phillip Schofield, To Dream a Dream 1992, Take That, Our Story 1993, Take That: On the Road 1994, The Insider (memoir) 2005, Don't You Know Who I Am? 2007, God Bless America 2009. *Leisure interests:* cricket, Arsenal Football Club. *Address:* William Morris Agency Inc., Centre Point, 103 New Oxford Street, London, WC1A 1DD, England (office). *Telephone:* (20) 7534-6800 (office). *Fax:* (20) 7534-6900 (office). *Website:* www.firstnews.co.uk.

MORGAN, William Newton, MArch, FAIA; American architect; *President, William Morgan Architects;* b. 14 Dec. 1930, Jacksonville, Fla; s. of Thomas Morgan and Kathleen Fisk Morgan; m. Bernice Leimback 1954; two s.; ed Duncan U. Fletcher High School, Harvard Coll., Harvard Grad. School of Design, Università degli Studi per Stranieri, Perugia and Univ. of Rome, Italy; USN 1952–55; Lehman Fellow, Harvard Univ. 1956–57; Fulbright Grantee, Italy 1958–59; Pres. William Morgan Architects, P.A. 1961–; Wheelwright Fellow, Harvard Grad. School of Design 1964–65, Visiting Critic 1981–82; AIA Fellowship 1978; Nat. Endowment of the Arts Fellow 1980; Adjunct Prof. of Art History, Jacksonville Univ. 1995–, Univ. of N Florida 1997, Univ. of Florida 1998; Beineke-Reeves Distinguished Prof. of Architecture, Univ. of Florida 1998–2000; mem. Savannah Coll. of Art and Design Advisory Bd 2003–06; mem. Soc. of American Archaeology Presentation, Vancouver, BC 2008; numerous awards and distinctions, including AIA Honor for Design Excellence 1974, AIA Honor for Research and Recording Ancient American Architecture 1998, Gibbons Eminent Scholar of Architecture and Urban Design, Univ. of S Florida 1990. *Architectural designs include:* Florida State Museum, Gainsville 1969–70, Jacksonville Police Admin. Bldg 1971–75, Pyramid Condominium, Ocean City, Md 1972–74, First Dist Court of Appeal, Tallahassee 1983–85, Westinghouse HQ, Orlando 1984–86, US Embassy, Khartoum 1987–91, US Courthouses, Fort Lauderdale 1976–78, Tallahassee 1992–98, Neiman-Marcus, Fort Lauderdale 1980–82. *Publications:* Prehistoric Architecture in the Eastern United States 1980, Prehistoric Architecture in Micronesia 1988, Ancient Architecture of the Southwest 1994, Pre-Columbian Architecture in Eastern North America 1999, Earth Architecture: From Ancient to Modern 2008; numerous articles. *Leisure interest:* furniture design and building. *Address:* 1945 Beach Avenue, Atlantic Beach, FL 32233, USA (home). *E-mail:* wnmorgan@aol.com (office). *Website:* www.williammorganarchitects.com (office).

MORGAN OF HUYTON, Baroness (Life Peer), cr. 2001, of Huyton in the County of Lancashire; **Sally Morgan,** MA; British politician; b. 28 June 1959, Liverpool; d. of Albert Edward Morgan and Margaret Morgan; m. John Lyons 1984; two s.; ed Belvedere Girls' School, Univs of Liverpool, Durham and London; secondary school teacher 1981–85; Labour Party Student Organizer 1985–87; Sr Targeting Officer 1987–93; Dir of Campaigns and Elections 1993–95; Head of Party Liaison for Leader of Opposition 1995–97; Political Sec. to Prime Minister 1997–2001; Minister of State for Women June–Nov. 2001; Dir of Govt Relations 2001–05; mem. House of Lords 2001–; mem. Bd Dirs Olympic Delivery Authority; Dir (non-exec.) Carphone Warehouse PLC, Southern Cross Healthcare PLC; adviser to Bd, ARK, Lloydspharmacy. *Leisure interests:* relaxing with friends, cooking, gardening, walking. *Address:* House of Lords, London, SW1A 0PW, England (office). *Telephone:* (20) 7219-5500 (office). *E-mail:* morgan@parliament.uk (office).

MORGENTHAU, Robert Morris, LLB; American lawyer; *Manhattan District Attorney;* b. 31 July 1919, New York; s. of Henry Morgenthau, Jr and Elinor (née Fatman) Morgenthau; m. 1st Martha Pattridge (deceased); one s. four d.; m. 2nd Lucinda Franks 1977; one s. one d.; ed Deerfield Acad., Amherst Coll., Yale Univ.; barrister, New York 1949; Assoc. of Patterson, Belknap & Webb, New York 1948–53, Partner 1954–61; US Attorney S. Dist New York 1961–62, 1962–70; Dist Attorney New York County (Manhattan) 1975–; mem. New York Exec. Cttee State of Israel Bonds; Democratic Candidate for Gov., New York 1962; mem. Bd of Dirs P.R. Legal Defense and Educ. Fund; Trustee Baron de Hirsch Fund, Fed. of Jewish Philanthropies; Co. Chair. New York Holocaust Memorial Comm.; Pres. Police Athletic League 1962; mem. Bar Asscn City of New York; Democrat; Dr hc (New York Law School) 1968, (Syracuse Law School) 1976, (Union Univ., Albany Law School) 1982, (Colgate Univ.) 1988, Frank Hogan Award, NY State Dist Attorney's Asscn 2000, Lone Sailor Award, USN Memorial Foundation 2000, Award for Excellence in Public Service, NY State Bar Asscn 2001. *Address:* Office of District Attorney, One Hogan Place, New York, NY 10013, USA (office). *Telephone:* (212) 335-9000 (office). *Website:* www.manhattanda.org (office).

MORGRIDGE, John P., MBA; American computer industry executive; *Chairman, Cisco Systems Inc.;* ed Univ. of Wis., Stanford Univ.; Capt.

USAF 1957–60; Vice-Pres. Honeywell Inc. 1960–80; Vice-Pres. Stratus Computer 1980–86; Pres. and COO Grid Systems 1987–88; Pres. and CEO Cisco Systems Inc. 1988–95, Chair. 1995–; Lecturer (part-time), Grad. School of Business, Stanford Univ. 1997–; mem. Bd of Dirs American Leadership Forum for Silicon Valley, The Nature Conservancy, Business Execs for Nat. Security, Wis. Alumni Research Foundation, Cisco Foundation, Cisco Learning Inst., CARE, Interplast; mem. Tech. Advisory Bd Milwaukee Public Schools, Advisory Council Stanford Business School; Hon. DSc (Univ. of Wis.) 1994, Hon. LHD (Lesley Coll.), Hon. PhD (Northern Ill. Univ., The American Int. Univ. in London, Carleton Univ.) Ernest C. Arbuckle Award, Stanford Univ. 1996. *Address:* Cisco Systems Inc., 170 West Tasman Drive, San Jose, CA 95134-1706, USA (office). *Telephone:* (408) 526-4000 (office). *Fax:* (408) 526-4100 (office). *Website:* www.cisco.com (office).

MORI, Hanae; Japanese fashion designer; b. 1926, Shimane; m.; two s.; graduate in Japanese literature; began career as costume designer for films in 1950s and has designed for over 500 films; opened first shop in Shinjuku, Tokyo 1951; now has 67 Hanae Mori shops in Japan, a store in New York, three shops in Paris and one in Monaco; first overseas show New York 1965; couture business and ready-to-wear; mem. Chambre Syndicale de la Haute Couture, Paris (first Asian mem.) 1977–; retrospective exhbn at The Space, Hanae Mori Bldg Tokyo 1989; Co-Founder Asscn for 100 Japanese books; launched Hanae Mori perfume brand 1995; Order of Cultural Merit 'Bunka Koro Sha' (Japan), Chevalier Légion d'honneur, Ordre des Arts et Lettres; numerous awards and prizes, including Neiman Marcus Award 1973. *Address:* Hanae Mori Haute Couture, 5 place de l'Alma, 75008 Paris, France (office). *Telephone:* 1-47-23-52-03 (office). *Fax:* 1-47-23-62-82 (office). *Website:* www.hanaemori.com (office); www.hanaemoriusa.com (office).

MORI, Hideo, BA; Japanese business executive; b. 1 April 1925, Osaka City; s. of Shigekazu Mori and Ikue Mori; m. Masako (née Okano) Mori; two s.; ed Kyoto Univ. 1947; joined Sumitomo Chemical Co. Ltd 1947, Dir 1977, Man. Dir 1980, Sr Man. Dir 1982, Pres. 1985–93, Chair. 1993–2000, now Co. Counselor; Chair. Sumitomo Pharmaceuticals Co. Ltd, ICI-Pharma Ltd, Japan Upjohn Ltd, Nippon Wellcome KK; Dir and Counsellor Japan Petrochemical Ind. Asscn; Exec. Dir Japan Fed. of Employers' Asscns; Dir Japan Tariff Asscn, Nihon Singapore Polyolefin Co. Ltd; Pres. Japan Chemical Industry Asscn 1990; mem. Bd of Exec. Dirs, Fed. of Econ. Orgs (Keidanren); Blue Ribbon Medal 1987. *Leisure interest:* golf. *Address:* c/o Sumitomo Chemical Co. Ltd, 2-27-1, Shinkawa 2-chome, Chuo-ku, Tokyo 104-8260, Japan. *Telephone:* (3) 5543-5102. *Fax:* (3) 5543-5901. *Website:* www.sumitomo-chem.co.jp (office).

MORI, Immanuel (Manny), BA; Micronesian politician and head of state; *President;* b. 25 Dec. 1948, Fefan Island, Chuuk State; m. Elina Ekiek (deceased); four d.; ed Xavier High School, Chuuk and Univ. of Guam; began career at Citicorp Credit-Guam Bank 1973, Asst Man., Saipan Branch 1974–76; Asst Admin. Trust Territory Social Security Admin 1976–79; Nat. Revenue Officer, State of Chuuk 1979–81; Controller, Federated States of Micronesia Devt Bank 1981–84, Pres. and CEO 1984–97; Exec. Vice-Pres. Bank of Federated States of Micronesia 1997–99; mem. Micornesian Congress 1999–2003, 2004–, Vice-Chair. Judiciary and Govt Operations Cttee 1999–2003, Health Educ. and Social Affairs Cttee 1999–2003, Chair. Ways and Means Cttee 2001–03, Vice-Chair. External Affairs Cttee 2004–05, Chair. Resources and Devt Cttee 2005–07; Gen.-Man. and CEO Chuuk Public Utility Corpn 2004–07; President of Federated States of Micronesia 2007–. *Address:* Office of the President, PO Box PS-53 Palikir, Pohnpei FM 96941, Federated States of Micronesia (office). *Telephone:* 320-2228 (office). *Fax:* 320-2785 (office). *E-mail:* ppetrus@mail.fm (office). *Website:* www.fsmpio.fm (office).

MORI, Kazuhisa, BSc; Japanese nuclear non-profit organization representative; *Executive Advisor, Japan Atomic Industrial Forum, Inc.;* b. 17 Jan. 1926, Hiroshima; s. of Tsunezo Mori and Kayo Mori; m. Reiko Iizuka 1953; two s.; ed Kyoto Univ.; mem. editorial staff, Chuokoron-sha Inc. 1948–55; Chief of Nuclear Energy Devt Electric Power Devt Co., Ltd 1956–65; Man. Programming Div. Tokyo Channel 12 TV, Ltd 1963–65; with Japan Atomic Industrial Forum, Inc. (JAIF) 1956–, Exec. Man. Dir 1978, Vice-Chair. 1996, Exec. Vice-Chair. 1998, currently Exec. Advisor; Dir Nuclear Safety Research Asscn 1965–; Vice-Pres. Japan Atomic Energy Relations Org. 1976–; Councillor, Univ. Alumni Asscn 1994–; Chevalier, Ordre nat. du Mérite (France), Order of Civil Merit Seogryu Medal (Korea). *Publications:* Economics of Atomic Power 1956, Atomic Power 1960. *Leisure interests:* fishing, Go (traditional Japanese game). *Address:* Japan Atomic Industrial Forum, Inc., 2-13 Shiba-Daimon 1-chome, Minato-ku, Tokyo 105-8605 (office); 5-20, Sakuragaoka 1-chome, Kugenuma, Fujisawa City, Kanagawa, Japan. *Telephone:* (3) 5777-0761 (office); (466) 26-6228 (home). *Website:* www.jaif.or.jp (office).

MORI, Shigefumi, MA, DrSci; Japanese mathematician and academic; *Professor, Research Institute of Mathematical Sciences, Kyoto University;* b. 23 Feb. 1951, Nagoya; ed Kyoto Univ.; Asst, Kyoto Univ. 1975, Prof., Research Inst. of Mathematical Sciences 1990–; Lecturer in Math., Univ. of Nagoya 1980, Asst Prof. 1982–88, Prof. 1988–90; Visiting Prof., Harvard Univ. 1977–80, Inst. for Advanced Study, Princeton, NJ 1981–82, Columbia Univ., New York 1985–87, Univ. of Utah, USA 1987–89, 1991–92; mem. Japan Acad. 1999–; Iyanaga Prize, Japan Math. Soc. 1983, Chunichi Culture Prize 1984, Japan Math. Soc. Autumn Prize (co-recipient) 1988, Inoue Science Prize 1989, Cole Prize in Algebra, American Math. Soc. 1990, Japan Acad. Prize (co-recipient) 1990, Fields Medal, Int. Congress of Mathematicians, Kyoto 1990, Japanese Govt Prize (Person of Cultural Merits) 1990, Fujiwara Award, Fujiwara Foundation of Science 2004. *Publications:* numerous articles in math. journals on algebraic geometry. *Address:* Research Institute of Mathematical Sciences, Kyoto University, Kyoto 606-8502, Japan (office). *Tele-*

phone: (75) 753-7227 (office). *Fax:* (75) 753-7276 (office). *E-mail:* mori@kurims.kyoto-u.ac.jp (office). *Website:* www.kurims.kyoto-u.ac.jp (office).

MORI, Shosuke; Japanese energy industry executive; *President, Kansai Electric Power Company Inc.;* ed Kyoto Univ.; joined Kansai Electric Power Co. Inc. 1963, Gen. Man., Systems Eng Div. 1989–94, Exec. Officer and Gen. Man., Corporate Planning Office 1994–97, mem. Bd of Dirs and Man., Power Systems Div. 1997–99, Man. Dir 1999–2001, Exec. Vice-Pres. 2001–05, Pres. 2005–. *Address:* Kansai Electric Power Co. Inc., 6-16 Nakanoshima 3-chome, Kita-ku, Osaka 530-8270, Japan (office). *Telephone:* (6) 6441-8821 (office). *Fax:* (6) 6447-7174 (office). *E-mail:* info@kepco.co.jp (office). *Website:* www.kepco.co.jp (office).

MORI, Yoshiro; Japanese politician; b. 14 July 1937; m. Chieko Mori; one s. one d.; ed Waseda Univ.; with Sankei Newspapers, Tokyo 1960–62; mem. House of Reps, for Ishikawa Pref. Dist 1 1969–96, Dist 2 1996–; Deputy Dir-Gen. Prime Minister's Office 1975–76; Deputy Chief Cabinet Sec. 1977–78; Dir Educ. Div., Policy Research Council, Liberal Democratic Party (LDP) 1978–81, Deputy Sec.-Gen. LDP 1978–79, 1984–85, Chair. Special Cttee on Educational Reform, Policy Research Council 1984–87, Acting Chair. Policy Research Council 1986, Acting Chair. Gen. Council 1986–87, Chair. Nat. Org. Cttee 1987–88, Chair. Research Comm. on Educational System, Policy Research Council 1989–91, Chair. Policy Research Council 1991–92, Sec.-Gen. LDP 1993–95, Chair. Gen. Council 1996–98, Sec.-Gen. LDP 1998–2001; Chair. Standing Cttee on Finance, House of Reps 1981–82, on Rules and Admin. 1991; Minister of Educ. 1983–84, of Int. Trade and Ind. 1992–93, of Construction 1995–96; Prime Minister of Japan 2000–01. *Address:* c/o Liberal Democratic Party, 1-11-23 Nagata-cho, Chiyoda-ku, Tokyo, 100-8910, Japan.

MORIKAWA, Kosuke, PhD; Japanese scientist and academic; *Research Director, Biomolecular Engineering Research Institute (BERI);* b. 28 Sept. 1942, Tokyo; m. Keiko Tanaka 1966; ed Koyamadai High School, Tokyo Univ.; instructor Tokyo Univ. 1971–75, research assoc. Århus Univ., Denmark 1975–77, MRC Lab. of Molecular Biology, Cambridge, UK 1978–80; instructor Kyoto Univ. 1980–86, Dir First Dept Protein Eng Research Inst. 1986–, Research Dir Biomolecular Eng Research Inst. (BERI) 1996–. *Leisure interest:* listening to classical music, particularly by Bach and Mozart. *Address:* Department of Structural Biology, Biomolecular Engineering Research Institute, 6-2-3 Furuedai, Suita, Osaka 565-0874 (office); 1-22-16 Hiyoshidai, Takatsuki, Osaka 569-1022, Japan. *Telephone:* (726) 89- 0519 (home); (6) 6872-8211 (office). *Fax:* (6) 6872-8219. *E-mail:* morikawa@beri.or.jp (office). *Website:* www.beri.or.jp (office).

MORIKAWA, Toshio, LLB; Japanese banker; b. 3 March 1933, Tokyo; m. Sawako Morikawa; two d.; ed Univ. of Tokyo; joined Sumitomo Banking Corpn (now Sumitomo Mitsui Banking Corpn) 1955, Dir 1980–84, Man. Dir 1984–85, Sr Man. Dir 1985–90, Deputy Pres. 1990–93, Pres. 1993–97, Chair. 1997–2001, Advisor 2001–; mem. Bd Dirs NEC Corpn 2000–; Chair. Fed. of Bankers' Asscns 1994–95. *Leisure interests:* golf, driving. *Address:* c/o Sumitomo Mitsui Financial Group Inc., 1-2, Yurakucho 1-Chome, Chiyoda-ku, Tokyo 100-0006, Japan. *Telephone:* (3) 5512-3411 (office). *Fax:* (3) 5512-4429 (office). *Website:* www.smbc.co.jp (office); www.smfg.co.jp (office).

MORILLON, Gen. Philippe; French army officer and politician; b. 24 Oct. 1935, Casablanca, Morocco; m. 1st Anne Appert 1958 (deceased); three d.; m. 2nd Christine Gaudry 1998; ed Ecole Militaire de Saint-Cyr, Ecole Supérieure, Army Staff Coll.; platoon leader, French Foreign Legion during Algerian war of independence; fmr Div. Commdr of French units stationed in Germany; mil. expert, Assemblée Nationale 1984–86; Deputy Under-Sec. for Int. Relations, Ministry of Defence 1988–90; Deputy Commdr, then Commdr UN Protection Force (UNPROFOR) in Bosnia-Herzegovina 1992–93; Adviser on Defence to Govt of France 1993; Commdr Force d'Action Rapide 1994–96; mem. European Parl. (Union pour la démocratie française, mem. Group of the Alliance of Liberals and Democrats for Europe) 1999–, Chair. Cttee on Fisheries, mem. Conf. of Cttee Chairmen, Cttee on Foreign Affairs, Sub-cttee on Security and Defence, Del. to ACP-EU Jt Parl. Ass., Del. to Euro-Mediterranean Parl. Ass.; Pres. Asscn L'envol pour les enfants européens; fmr Pres. French Inter-ministerial Coordinating Cttee for the 12th World Youth Day, Paris 1997; Commdr Ordre nat. du Mérit 1988, Grand Officier de la Légion d'honneur 1993; Servitor Pacis Award, Path to Peace Foundation 1999. *Publications:* Croire et Oser 1993, Paroles de Soldat 1996, Mon Credo 1999, Le Testament de Massoud 2005. *Leisure interest:* reading. *Address:* European Parliament, Bâtiment Altiero Spinelli, 09G205, 60 rue Wiertz, 1047 Brussels, Belgium (office); Ministère de la Défense, 14 rue Saint-Dominique, 75700 Paris, France. *Telephone:* (2) 284-5506 (office). *Fax:* (2) 284-9506 (office). *E-mail:* philippe.morillon@europarl.europa.eu (office). *Website:* www.europarl.eu.int/members/expert/alphaOrder/view.do?language=EN&id=4332.

MORIN, Edgar, Lic. en Hist. et Géog., Lic. en Droit et Sciences écon.; French scientific researcher and philosopher; *Director Emeritus, Centre national de la recherche scientifique (CNRS);* b. 8 July 1921, Paris; s. of Vidal Nahoum and Luna Beressi; m. Edwige Lannegrace; two d.; resistance fighter 1942–44; Head, Propaganda Dept, French mil. govt, Germany 1945; Ed.-in-Chief Paris newspaper 1947–50; researcher, CNRS 1950–, Dir of Research 1970–93, Dir Emer. 1993–; Dir Review Arguments 1957–62, Communications 1972–; Dir Centre d'études transdisciplinaires (sociologie, anthropologie, politique) (Cetsap), of Ecole des hautes études en sciences sociales 1977–93; Commdr, Légion d'honneur, Commdr des Arts et des Lettres; Dr hc (Brussels, Perugia, Palermo, Geneva, Natal, João Pessoa, Odense, Porto-Alegre, Milan, Guadalajara); Prix européen de l'Essai Charles Veillon 1987, Prix média de l'Asscn des Journalistes Européens 1992, Prix Internacional Catalunya 1994, Prix int. Nonino 2004. *Publications include:* L'Homme et la mort 1951, Le Cinéma ou l'homme imaginaire 1956, Autocritique 1959, Le Vif du sujet 1969, Le Paradigme perdu: la nature humaine 1973, La méthode (six vols) 1977–2004, De la nature de l'URSS 1983, Penser l'Europe 1987, Vidal et les siens 1989, Terre-Patrie 1993, Mes démons 1994, Amour, poésie, sagesse 1998; numerous other publs. *Leisure interests:* music, theatre, movies, literature. *Address:* 7 rue Saint-Claude, 75003 Paris, France (home). *Telephone:* 1-42-78-90-99 (home). *Fax:* 1-48-04-86-35 (home). *E-mail:* loridant@ehess.fr (office).

MORIN, Hervé; French politician; *Minister of Defence;* b. 17 Aug. 1961, Pont-Audemer; m. Catherine Broussot; one s. one d.; ed Deauville Lycée, Ecole Jeanne d'Arc, Caen, Univ. of Caen, Univ. of Paris II, Inst. of Political Studies, Paris; Dir of Services, Nat. Ass. 1987–93, 1998; Lecturer, Univ. of Paris V 1989–95; Municipal Councillor 1989–95; mem. Gen. Council of Eure 1992–2004; Tech. Adviser on Nat. Affairs and the Environment, Office of the Minister of Defence 1993–95; Mayor of Epaignes 1995–; Pres. Cormeilles Town Community 1995–; mem. Union pour la Démocratie Française (UDF) 1998–2007, Leader Parl. Group 2002–07; mem. Nouveau Centre 2007–, Leader 2008–; Deputy for Eure 1998–; Spokesperson for François Bayrou during presidential campaign 2002; Regional Councillor for Haute-Normandie 2004–; Minister of Defence 2007–; Pres. France-Niger Group, Nat. Ass.; Pres. Asscn for the Reunification of Normandy 1999–. *Address:* Ministry of Defence, 14 rue Saint Dominique, 75007 Paris, France (office). *Telephone:* 1-42-19-30-11 (office). *Fax:* 1-47-05-40-91 (office). *E-mail:* courrier-ministre@sdbc.defense.gouv.fr (office). *Website:* www.defense.gouv.fr (office); www.herve-morin.net.

MORIN, Jean, LenD; French civil servant; b. 23 June 1916, Melun; s. of Alexis Morin and Berthe France; m. Janine Lamouroux 1942; one s. two d.; ed Ecole Libre des Sciences Politiques, Inst de Statistique, Paris; Sec.-Gen. Inst Scientifique des Recherches Economiques et Sociales 1939; Auditeur, Cour des Comptes 1941; Dir of Personnel, Ministry of the Interior 1944; Prefect, Manche 1946; Deputy Dir du Cabinet to Pres. of Provisional Govt 1946, to Minister of Foreign Affairs 1947–48; Tech. Adviser, Minister of the Interior 1948–49; Prefect, Maine-et-Loire 1949; Conseiller Référendaire, Cour des Comptes 1949; Prefect, Haute-Garonne and Extraordinary Insp.-Gen. of Admin. (5th Region) 1958–60; Del.-Gen. in Algeria 1960–62; Sec.-Gen. of Merchant Navy 1962–68; Pres. Ass., Inter-Governmental Maritime Consultative Org. 1962–68; Pres. Société auxiliaire minière du Pacifique (Saumipac) 1968–72, Cie française industrielle et minière du Pacifique 1969–72; Dir Publicis SA 1970, Vice-Pres. 1972, Dir Publicis Conseil, Pres. 1972–73, mem. Conseil de Surveillance de Publicis SA 1987–90; Pres. Communication et Publicité 1972, Intermarco 1974–84, Comité de surveillance Intermarco (Amsterdam); Chair. and Man. Dir Régie-Presse 1974–83; Vice-Pres. Comité de surveillance Holding Farner (Zürich); Pres. Inst. de la Mer 1974–97, now Hon. Pres., Acad. de Marine 1990–92; Hon. Préfet, Conseiller Maître Cour des Comptes; Grand Croix, Légion d'honneur, Croix de guerre, Médaille de la Résistance avec rosette, Grand Croix, and other French and foreign decorations. *Publication:* De Gaulle et l'Algérie 1999. *Leisure interests:* history, bridge. *Address:* c/o Cour des Comptes, 13 rue Cambon, 75001 Paris (office); 19 avenue du Maréchal-Franchet-d'Esperey, 75016 Paris, France. *Telephone:* 1-46-47-59-10.

MORIN, Roland Louis, LenD; French public servant; *Vice-President, Commission Nationale des Comptes de Campagne et des Financements Politiques;* b. 6 Sept. 1932, Taza, Morocco; s. Fernand Morin and Emilienne Morin (née Carisio); m. Catherine Roussy 1961; one s. one d.; ed Lycée Gouraud, Rabat, Faculty of Law and Humanities, Bordeaux and Ecole Nat. d'Admin; auditor, Audit Office 1960; Asst to Prime Minister and Chargé de Mission, Algeria 1960–61; Pvt. Recorder Comm. for Verification of Public Accounts, Asst to Recorder-Gen. 1964; Tech. Counsellor Louis Joxe Cabinet (Minister of State for Admin. Reform) 1966–67, Edmond Michelet Cabinet (Minister of State for Public Office) 1967-68; Referendary Counsellor Audit Office 1967; Asst to Prime Minister, Departmental Head for Econ. and Financial Programmes and Affairs 1968; Dir of Financial Affairs, Gen. Del. for Scientific and Tech. Research 1969, Asst to Del.-Gen. 1970, Asst Del.-Gen. 1974, Dir 1978; rejoined Audit Office 1980; Prof. Inst. d'Etudes Politiques de Paris 1965–90; Chargé de Mission with Jean-Pierre Chevènement (Minister of State, Minister for Research and Tech.) 1981–82, Dir Gen. Research and Tech., Ministry of Research and Industry 1982–86; Conseiller maître, Cour des comptes 1986, Pres. 1993–2000, Hon. Pres. 2000–; mem. Comité nat. d'évaluation de la recherche (CNER) 1989–94, Commission nationale des comptes de campagne et des financements politiques (CNCCFP) 1997–2000 (Vice-Pres. 2000–); Officier, Légion d'honneur, Ordre nat. de Mérite, Chevalier des Palmes académiques, Mérite agricole. *Publications:* Les sociétés locales d'économie mixte et leur contrôle 1964, Théorie des grands problèmes économiques contemporains. *Leisure interest:* tennis. *Address:* 24 Résidence des Gros-Chênes, 91370 Verrières-le-Buisson (home); Villa Ej-Jemaïa, 903 rocade des Playes, 83140 Six-Fours-les-Plages, France. *E-mail:* Service-juridique@cnccfp.fr. *Website:* www.cnccfp.fr.

MORISHITA, Yoichi; Japanese electronics executive; *Executive Advisor, Matsushita Electric Industrial Company Ltd;* ed Kwansei Gakuin Univ.; joined Matsushita Electric Industrial Co. Ltd 1957, Man. Electric Motor Osaka Sales Office, Electric Motor Dept 1971–87, apptd mem. Bd of Dirs 1987, Man.-Dir and Dir Living Sales Div. 1989–90, Sr Man.-Dir 1990–91, Head Consumer Products Business Group 1991–92, Exec. Vice-Pres. 1992–93, Pres. 1993–2000, Chair. 2000–06, Exec. Advisor 2006–; Chair. Kansai Electric Industry Devt Centre 1993, Telecommunications Council 1998, Japan Security Systems Asscn 1998; Acting Chair. Japan Electonics and Information Tech. Industries Asscn (JEITA) 2001; Vice-Chair. Electric Industries Asscn of Japan 1993, Japan Fed. of Econ. Orgs (Keidanren) 1999; Commr Tax Comm. 1997, Industrial Structure Council 1999; mem. Keidanren Cttee on China. *Address:* Matsushita Electric Industrial Company Ltd, 1006 Oaza Kadoma,

Kadoma, Osaka 571-8501, Japan (office). *Telephone:* (6) 6908-1121 (office). *Fax:* (6) 6908-2351 (office). *Website:* matsushita.co.jp (office).

MORISSETTE, Alanis Nadine; Canadian rock singer and songwriter; b. 1 June 1974, Ottawa; signed contract as songwriter with MCA Publishing aged 14, recorded two albums for MCA's recording div.; moved to Toronto, later to LA, USA; BRIT Award for Best Int. Newcomer 1996, four Grammy Awards, including Album of the Year and Best Rock Album, MTV European Music Award for Best Female Artist 1996. *Recordings include:* albums: Alanis 1991, Now Is The Time 1992, Jagged Little Pill 1995, Space Cakes (live) 1998, Supposed Former Infatuation Junkie 1998, Alanis Unplugged (live) 1999, Under Rug Swept 2002, Feast On Scraps: Inside Under Rug Swept 2002, So-called Chaos 2004, Jagged Little Pill Acoustic 2005, Flavors of Entanglement 2008. *Film appearances:* Anything for Love 1993, Dogma 1999, Jay and Silent Bob Strike Back 2001, De-Lovely 2004. *Television appearances:* acted in serial You Can't Do That on Television aged 10, host of Music Works series 1994. *Address:* Red Light Management, 9200 Sunset Boulevard, Los Angeles, CA 90069, USA (office). *E-mail:* info@redlightmanagement.com (office). *Website:* www.redlightmanagement.com (office); www.alanismorissette.com.

MORITA, Tomijiro; Japanese insurance executive; *Chairman, Dai-ichi Mutual Life Insurance Company;* b. 1941; m.; ed Univ. of Tokyo; joined Dai-ichi Mutual Life Insurance Co. 1964, Vice Pres. 1996–97, Pres. 1997–2004, Chair. 2004–; mem. Bd of Dirs Japan Productivity Centre for Socio-Econ. Devt (JPC-SED), Odakyu Group; mem. Exec. Cttee Japan-US Business Council 2003–. *Address:* Dai-ichi Mutual Life Insurance Co., 13-1 Yurakucho 1-chome, Chiyoda-ku, Tokyo 100-8411, Japan (office). *Telephone:* (3) 3216-1211 (office). *Fax:* (3) 5221-4360 (office). *E-mail:* info@dai-ichi-life.co.jp (office). *Website:* www.dai-ichi-life.co.jp (office).

MORITS, Yunna Petrovna; Russian poet; b. 2 June 1937, Kiev, Ukraine; m. Yuri Grigor'yevich Vasil'yev; one s.; ed Gorky Literary Inst.; began publishing poetry 1954; has participated in int. poetry festivals London, Cambridge, Toronto, Rotterdam, other locations; has made recordings of recitations of her poetry; mem. Russian PEN, Exec. Cttee, Russian Acad. of Natural Sciences; Golden Rose, Italy 1996, Triumph Prize, Russia 2000, A. D. Sakharov Prize for Civil Courage of Writer 2004. *Publications:* eleven collections of poetry (trans. in many languages), including The Vine 1970, With Unbleached Thread 1974, By Light of Life 1977, The Third Eye 1980, Selected Poems 1982, The Blue Flame 1985, On This High Shore 1987, In the Den of Vice 1990, The Face 2000, In This Way 2000, By the Law to the Postman Hello 2005, and six books for children including The Great Secret for a Small Company 1987, A Bunch of Cats 1997, Move Your Ears 2003; poems appeared in journal Oktyabr 1993–97; also short stories, essays, scripts for animated cartoons. *Leisure interests:* painting and drawing (more than 300 works published). *Address:* 129010 Moscow, Astrakhansky per. 5, Apt 76, Russia (home). *Telephone:* (495) 680-08-16 (home). *E-mail:* morits@owl.ru (home). *Website:* morits.ru.

MORITZ, Michael J., MA, MBA; British/American investment industry executive; *Managing Partner, Sequoia Capital;* b. 1954, Cardiff, Wales; m.; two c.; ed Howardian High School, Cardiff, Christ Church, Oxford, Wharton School, Univ. of Pennsylvania; worked as a reporter for Time 1984–86; Co-founder Technologic Pnrs (tech. newsletter and conf. co.) 1984–86; joined Sequoia Capital, Menlo Park, California 1986, currently Man. Pnr; mem. Bd of Dirs Flextronics 1993–2005, Yahoo! 1995–2003, Google Inc. 1999–2007; internet co. investments include Google, Yahoo!, PayPal, eBay, Apple Computer, Cisco, Webvan, YouTube, eToys; Hon. Student, Christ Church, Oxford 2005; listed first in Forbes' Midas List of the top dealmakers in the technology industry 2006, 2007, ranked amongst TIME 100 2007. *Publications:* Going For Broke: The Chrysler Story (with Barry Seaman) 1981, The Little Kingdom: The Private Story of Apple Computer 1984. *Address:* Sequoia Capital, 3000 Sand Hill Road, Building 4, Suite 180, Menlo Park, CA 94025, USA (office). *Telephone:* (650) 854-3927 (office). *Fax:* (650) 854-2977 (office). *E-mail:* moritz@sequoiacap.com (office). *Website:* www.sequoiacap.com (office).

MORIYAMA, Raymond, OC, MArch, FRAIC, RCA, FRSA, FAIA; Canadian architect and planner; *Principal, Moriyama and Teshima Architects;* b. 11 Oct. 1929, Vancouver; s. of John Michi and Nobuko Moriyama; m. Sachiko Miyauchi 1954; three s. two d.; ed Univ. of Toronto, McGill Univ.; Raymond Moriyama Architects and Planners 1958–70; Partner, Moriyama and Teshima Architects 1970–, Prin. 1980–; Design Tutor, Univ. of Toronto 1961–63; Chair. Ecological Research Ltd 1970; Chair. Mid-Canada Conf., Task Force on Environmental and Ecological Factors 1969–70; mem. Bd and Life mem. Royal Canadian Inst.; Dir Canadian Guild of Crafts 1973–75; mem. of Council, Ont. Coll. of Arts 1972–73; mem. Advisory Cttee, MBA Programme in Arts Admin, York Univ. 1982; Founding mem. Asia Pacific Foundation of Canada 1982; mem. Bd, Multilingual TV; mem. Bd of Trustees, Royal Ont. Museum; mem. Council's Advisory Cttee, N York Gen. Hosp.; Chancellor Brock Univ. 2001–07; Fellow, Toronto Soc. of Architects 1998; Int. FRIBA; several exhbns of architectural work of office; numerous TV documentaries; Regeneration Suite dedicated to work of Raymond Moriyama; Order of Ontario 1992, Order of Rising Sun Gold Rays with Rosette 2004; 10 hon. doctorates, including Univ. of Toronto, McGill Univ., York Univ.; Civic Awards of Merit (Toronto and Scarborough), Gov.-Gen.'s Medal for Architecture (four times), P.A. Award 1989, Toronto Arts Award 1990, Winner, int. competition for Nat. Saudi Arabian Museum, Riyadh 1996–99, Gold Medal, Royal Architectural Inst. of Canada 1997, Best Architect in Toronto Award 1997, 1998 and many other awards. *Works include:* Japanese Canadian Cultural Centre/Noor Cultural Centre, Toronto 1954–2005, Ontario Science Centre, Toronto 1964–69, Scarborough Civic Centre 1968–74, Niagara Falls and River 100 Year Plan, and Work with 16 univs 1968–, Toronto Reference Library 1973–77, Meewasin Valley 100 Year Plan, Saskatoon 1974–76, Science North, Sudbury 1980–84, Ottawa City Hall 1987–91, Canadian Embassy, Tokyo, Japan 1988–92, Canadian War Museum, Ottawa 2001–05, 124 km Wadi Hanifa Reclamation/Bioremediation, Riyadh, Saudi Arabia 2003. *Publications:* Great American Goose Egg Co. (Canada) Ltd, The Global Living System and Mid-Canada Task Force Committee on Ecological and Environmental Factors 1970, Can Your Life Become a Work of Art 1975, The Satisfactory City: The Survival of Urbanity 1975, Into God's Temple of Eternity, Drive a Nail of Gold, TANT – Time, Appropriateness, Nature and Transition 1982, Architect as Nature's Collaborator (lecture at McGill Univ.) 1996, In Search of a Soul (documentary on the concept and realization of the new Canadian War Museum in Ottawa). *Leisure interests:* fishing, sailing. *Address:* 32 Davenport Road, Toronto, ON M5R 1H3, Canada (home). *Telephone:* (416) 925-4484 (home). *Fax:* (416) 925-4736 (home). *E-mail:* rm@mtarch.com (office). *Website:* www.mtarch.com (office).

MORJANE, Kamel; Tunisian international organization official, diplomatist and government official; *Minister of National Defence;* b. 9 May 1948, Hammam-Sousse; m. Dorra Ben Ali,; two c.; ed Faculty of Law and Nat. School of Admin, Univ. of Tunis, Graduate Inst. of Int. and Devt Studies, Univ. of Geneva, Switzerland; worked as journalist; fmr Asst Prof. Univ. of Geneva; joined staff UNHCR 1977, Dir, Human Resources 1988–89, SW Asia, Middle East and N Africa Div. 1990–94, Africa Div. 1994–96, Asst High Commr 2001–05; apptd Perm. Rep. to UN, Geneva 1996, later UN Sec.-Gen.'s Special Rep. for Democratic Repub. of Congo 1999–2001; Minister of Defence 2005–; Grand Officier, Ordre Sept Novembre, Grand Officier, Ordre de la République, Médaille de la Jeunesse (Tunisia), Commandeur, Ordre Mano (Togo). *Address:* Ministry of National Defence, blvd Bab Menara, 1030 Tunis, Tunisia (office). *Telephone:* (71) 560-240 (office). *Fax:* (71) 561-804 (office). *E-mail:* defnat@defense.tn (office). *Website:* www.defense.tn (office).

MØRK, Truls; Norwegian cellist; b. 25 April 1961, Bergen; s. of John Mørk and Turid Otterbech; two s. one d.; ed studied under his father, with Frans Helmerson at Swedish Radio Music School, in Austria with Heinrich Schiff and in Moscow with Natalia Shakovskaya; debut, BBC Promenade Concerts 1989; has since appeared with leading European, American and Australian orchestras, including the Berlin Philharmonic, New York Philharmonic, Philadelphia Symphony, Cincinnati Philharmonic, Rotterdam Philharmonic, London Philharmonic, Pittsburgh Symphony, City of Birmingham Symphony, Orchestre de Paris, NHK Symphony, Royal Concertgebouw and Cleveland, Los Angeles and Gewandhaus Symphony Orchestras; regular appearances at int. chamber music festivals; founder Int. Chamber Music Festival in Stavanger, Artistic Dir –2003; prizewinner Moscow Tchaikovsky Competition 1982, first prize Cassado Cello Competition, Florence 1983, W Naumburg Competition, New York 1986, UNESCO Prize European Radio-Union Competition, Bratislava 1983. *Recordings include:* Schumann, Elgar and Saint-Saëns concertos, Tchaikovsky Rococo Variations, recitals of cello works by Grieg, Sibelius, Brahms, Rachmaninov and Myaskovksy, Dvořák and Shostakovich cello concertos, Haydn cello concertos with Norwegian Chamber Orchestra, Britten Cello Symphony and Elgar Cello Concerto with Sir Simon Rattle and the City of Birmingham Symphony Orchestra, Britten Cello Suites (Grammy Award 2002), Schumann Cello Concerto with Paavo Jarvi and Orchestre Philharmonique de Radio France 2005. *Address:* Harrison Parrott, 5–6 Albion Court, London, W6 0QT, England (office). *Telephone:* (20) 7229-9166 (office). *Fax:* (20) 7221-5042 (office). *E-mail:* info@harrisonparrott.co.uk (office). *Website:* www.harrisonparrott.com (office).

MORLEY, Rt Hon. Elliot, BEd; British politician; *Prime Minister's Special Representative to the Gleneagles Dialogue on Climate Change;* b. 6 July 1952, Liverpool; m.; two c.; ed Hull Coll. of Educ.; served as Dept Head, Greatfield High School; Councillor, Hull City Council 1979–86; MP for Scunthorpe 1987–, mem. Select Cttee on Agric. 1987–89, Environmental Audit Cttee 2003–06; Shadow Minister for Fisheries, Countryside and Animal Welfare 1989–97; Minister for Fisheries, Animal Health and Welfare, and the Countryside, Ministry of Agric., Fisheries and Food 1997–2001, for Fisheries, Water and Nature Protection, Dept for Environment, Food and Rural Affairs (DEFRA) 1997–2003; Minister for Environment and Agri-Environment 2003–05, for Environment and Climate Change 2005–06; Prime Minister's Special Rep. to the Gleneagles Dialogue on Climate Change 2006–; Pres. and Chair. GLOBE International 2006–; fmr Pres. Hull Teachers' Asscn; Vice-Pres. Wildlife and Countryside Link, Asscn of Drainage Authorities. *Address:* House of Commons, Westminster, London, SW1 0AA, England (office). *Telephone:* (1724) 842000 (office). *E-mail:* morleye@parliament.uk (office). *Website:* www.elliotmorley.co.uk.

MORLEY, Malcolm, ARCA; British artist; b. 7 June 1931, London; ed Royal Coll. of Art and Camberwell School of Arts and Crafts, London; discover art serving a three-year term in Wormwood Scrubs prison; began to produce paintings in an abstract expressionist style from 1956; moved to New York 1958; influenced by Barnett Newman, Andy Warhol and Roy Lichtenstein; began to be more expressionist and to incorporate collage into his work 1970s; returned to a more precise photo-realist style 1990s; 1st Annual Turner Prize, The Tate Gallery, London 1984, 1991, Skowhegan School of Painting and Sculpture Award 1992. *Address:* c/o Sperone Westwater, 415 West 13 Street, New York, NY 10014, USA. *Telephone:* (212) 999-7337. *Fax:* (212) 999-7338. *E-mail:* info@speronewestwater.com. *Website:* www.speronewestwater.com.

MOROSS, Manfred David, BSc, MBA; British business executive; b. 30 Aug. 1931; s. of Dr H. Moross and A. Moross; m. Edna Fay Jacobson 1956; three s. one d.; ed Witwatersrand and Harvard Univs; Dir Whitehall Financial Group, New York, Whitehall Investment Corpn, New York, Siem Industries Inc., Bermuda; Hon. PhD Weizmann Inst. of Science. *Leisure interests:* tennis, reading. *Address:* 7 Princes Gate, London, SW7, England (home). *Telephone:* (20) 7589-9020 (home). *Fax:* (20) 7581-8497.

MOROZ, Oleksandr Oleksandrovych; Ukrainian politician; *Leader, Socialist Party of Ukraine;* b. 29 Feb. 1944, Buda, Kyiv Oblast; m. Valentina Andriyivna Moroz (née Lavrinenko); two d.; ed Ukrainian Agric. Acad., Higher CP School; trained as engineer in Kyiv; engineer and mechanic in state farm professional school, dist and regional enterprises of Selkhoztechnika 1965–76; sec. regional trade union, First Sec. Dist CP Cttee; Head of Agric. Div. Regional CP Cttee; Co-founder and Leader, Socialist Party of Ukraine 1991–; People's Deputy of Ukrainian SSR, then mem. Verkhovna Rada (Parl.) 1994–, Chair. 1994–98, 2006–07; presidential cand. 1994, 1999, 2004. *Publications:* author or co-author of a number of legal projects including Code on Land: Where Are We Going?, Choice, Subjects for Meditation; several articles. *Address:* Socialist Party of Ukraine, 02100 Kyiv, vul. Bazhova 12, Ukraine (office). *Telephone:* (44) 573-58-97 (office). *E-mail:* pr@spu.in.ua (office). *Website:* www.spu.in.ua (office).

MOROZOV, Oleg Viktorovich, CPhilSc; Russian politician; *Deputy Speaker, State Duma;* b. 5 Nov. 1953, Kazan; m.; one d.; ed Kazan State Univ.; docent, Kazan State Univ.; Head of Div. Tatar Regional CP Cttee 1987–89; instructor, Asst to Sec., CPSU Cen. Cttee 1989–91; consultant, Office of USSR Pres. 1991–92; Deputy Dir-Gen. Biotekhnologiya; mem. State Duma 1993– (re-elected as mem. Otechestvo—Vsya Russia Movt 1999), Head, Regions of Russia Deputy Group, currently Deputy Speaker State Duma; mem. Deputies' group New Regional Politics 1994–96; Chair. Deputies' Group Russian Regions 1997–; joined Yedinstvo Party 2001. *Leisure interests:* collecting toy hippopotamuses, serious classical music. *Address:* State Duma, Okhotny ryad 1, 103265 Moscow, Russia. *Telephone:* (495) 292-83-52 (office). *Fax:* (495) 292-91-69 (office). *Website:* www.duma.gov.ru.

MOROZOV, Vladimir Mikhailovich; Russian singer (bass); *Head of Vocal Training Department, Herzen State Pedagogical University;* b. 12 Feb. 1933, Leningrad; m.; one s.; ed Leningrad State Conservatory; soloist with Kirov (now Mariinsky) Opera 1959–; Prof. and Head of Vocal Training Dept, Herzen State Pedagogical Univ. of Russia; mem. CPSU 1965–91; Glinka Prize 1974, USSR State Prize 1976, RSFSR People's Artist 1976, USSR People's Artist 1981. *Roles include:* Varlaam (Boris Godunov), Ivan the Terrible (The Women from Pskov), Grigory (Quiet Flows the Don), Peter the Great (Peter I), Dosifey (Khovanshchina). *Address:* Herzen State Pedagogical University of Russia, St Petersburg, 48 Moika Emb., St Petersburg 191186, Russia.

MORPARIA, Kalpana; Indian banker; *Chief Strategy and Communications Officer, ICICI Group;* ed Mumbai Univ.; Sr Legal Officer, ICICI Bank Ltd 1975–96, Gen. Man. in charge of Legal, Planning, Treasury and Corp. Communications Depts 1996–98, Sr Gen. Man. in charge also of Human Resources Devt, Planning and Strategic Support Group and Special Projects Dept 1998–2001, apptd Exec. Dir 2001, currently Head, Corp. Center and Official Spokesperson, ICICI Bank Ltd, Jt Man. Dir 2006–07, Chief Strategy and Communications Officer, ICICI Group 2007–, mem. Fraud Monitoring Cttee, Share Transfer and Shareholders'/Investors' Grievance Cttee, Asset-Liability Man. Cttee, Cttee of Dirs; mem. Bd of Dirs Dr Reddy's Laboratories Ltd ADS; Women Achievers Award in the Field of Finance and Banking, Indian Merchants' Chamber (Ladies Wing) 1999, ranked jt 93rd by Forbes magazine amongst 100 Most Powerful Women 2006. *Address:* ICICI Bank Ltd, ICICI Bank Towers, Bandra Kurla Complex, Mumbai, 400 051, India (office). *Telephone:* (22) 26531414 (office). *Fax:* (22) 26531167 (office). *Website:* www.icicibank.com (office).

MORPURGO, Michael, OBE; British writer; b. 5 Oct. 1943, St Albans, Hertfordshire; m. Clare Morpurgo; co-f., Farms for City Children project; Children's Laureate 2003–05; Writer-in-Residence, The Savoy Hotel, London 2007; Whitbread Children's Book Award 1995, Smarties Book Prize 1996, Bronze Prize in 6–8 years group 2003, Children's Book Awards 1996, 2000, 2002. *Publications include:* Beyond the Rainbow Warrior, Billy the Kid, Black Queen, Colly's Barn, Conker, Dear Olly, Escape from Shangri-La, Farm Boy, Friend or Foe, From Hearabout Hill, Grania O'Malley, Joan of Arc, Kensuke's Kingdom, King of the Cloud Forests, Long Way Home, Marble Crusher, Mr Nobody's Eyes, My Friend Walter, Out of the Ashes, Red Eyes at Night, Sam's Duck, Snakes and Ladders, The Butterfly Lion, The Nine Lives of Montezuma, The Rainbow Bear, The Sleeping Sword, The War of Jenkins' Ear, The White Horse of Zennor, The Wreck of the Zanzibar, Toro! Toro!, Twist of Gold, Waiting for Anya, War Horse, Wartman, Who's a Big Bully Then?, Why the Whales Came, Wombat Goes Walkabout, The Last Wolf 2002, Private Peaceful (Prix Sorcières for children's novel, France, Blue Peter Book Award 2005) 2003, The Amazing Story of Adolphus Tips 2005, Alone on a Wide Wide Sea 2006, On Angel Wings 2006, Born to Run 2007, Kaspar Prince of Cats 2008. *Address:* c/o HarperCollins Publishers, 77–85 Fulham Palace Road, Hammersmith, London W6 8JB, England (office). *Website:* www.harpercollins.co.uk (office).

MORRICONE, Ennio; Italian film score composer; b. 10 Nov. 1928, Rome; s. of Mario Morricone and Libera Morricone; m. Maria Travia; two s. two d.; ed Acad. of Santa Cecilia, Rome; Hon. Acad. Award 2007. *Film scores:* Il Federale 1961, La Voglia matta 1962, Diciottenni al sole 1962, La Cuccagna 1962, Il Successo 1963, Le Monachine 1963, I Basilischi 1963, Duello nel Texas (as Dan Savio) 1963, La Scoperta dell'America 1964, I Motorizzati 1964, ...e la donna creò l'uomo 1964, I Maniaci 1964, Prima della rivoluzione 1964, I Due evasi di Sing Sing 1964, Per un pugno di dollari (as Leo Nichols) 1964, Le Pistole non discutono 1964, I Malamondo 1964, Thrilling 1965, Slalom 1965, Non son degno di te 1965, Menage all'italiana 1965, Idoli controluce 1965, La Battaglia di Algeri 1965, Una Pistola per Ringo 1965, Gli Amanti d'oltretomba 1965, Altissima pressione 1965, I Pugni in tasca 1965, Centomila dollari per Ringo 1965, Il Ritorno di Ringo 1965, Per qualche dollaro in più 1965, La Ragazza del bersagliere 1966, Per Firenze 1966, Navajo Joe (as Leo Nichols) 1966, Mi vedrai tornare 1966, Matchless 1966, I Lunghi giorni della vendetta 1966, Un Fiume di dollari 1966, Sette pistole per i MacGregor 1966, Agent 505 - Todesfalle Beirut 1966, Uccellacci e uccellini 1966, El Greco 1966, Un Uomo a metà 1966, Das Gewisse Etwas der Frauen 1966, La Resa dei conti 1966, Il Buono, il brutto, il cattivo 1966, Sette donne per i MacGregor 1966, Scusi, facciamo l'amore? 1967, Pedro Páramo 1967, Il Giardino delle delizie 1967, Dalle Ardenne all'inferno 1967, L'Avventuriero 1967, Le Streghe 1967, OK Connery 1967, I Crudeli (as Leo Nichols) 1967, Per pochi dollari ancora (theme) 1967, La Cina è vicina 1967, L'Harem 1967, La Ragazza e il generale 1967, Faccia a faccia 1967, Arabella 1967, Tepepa 1968, Il Mercenario 1968, Mangiala 1968, Italia vista dal cielo 1968, Grazie, zia 1968, Il Grande silenzio 1968, ...e per tetto un cielo di stelle 1968, Ecce Homo 1968, Diabolik 1968, Escalation 1968, Da uomo a uomo 1968, La Bataille de San Sebastian 1968, Comandamenti per un gangster 1968, Teorema 1968, Partner 1968, Roma come Chicago 1968, Gli Intoccabili 1968, C'era una volta il West 1968, Vergogna schifosi 1969, Senza sapere niente di lei 1969, Queimada 1969, Giotto 1969, La Donna invisibile 1969, Dio è con noi 1969, L'Assoluto naturale 1969, Fräulein Doktor 1969, Cuore di mamma 1969, L'Alibi 1969, Galileo 1969, Gentleman Jo... uccidi 1969, La Monaca di Monza 1969, Metti una sera a cena 1969, Un Bellissimo novembre 1969, Ruba al prossimo tuo 1969, Un Tranquillo posto di campagna 1969, I Marziani hanno dodici mani 1969, H2S 1969, Sai cosa faceva Stalin alle donne? 1969, Un Esercito di cinque uomini 1969, La Stagione dei sensi 1969, Una Breve stagione 1969, Le Clan des Siciliens 1969, Zenabel 1969, Uccidete il vitello grasso e arrostitelo 1970, Metello 1970, Giochi particolari 1970, La Califfa 1970, Two Mules for Sister Sara 1970, L'Uccello dalle piume di cristallo 1970, La Moglie più bella 1970, Indagine su un cittadino al di sopra di ogni sospetto 1970, Hornets' Nest 1970, Città violenta 1970, I Cannibali 1970, Quando le donne avevano la coda 1970, Le Foto proibite di una signora per bene 1970, Vamos a matar, compañeros 1970, Oceano 1971, Gli Occhi freddi della paura 1971, Incontro 1971, Forza 'G' 1971, La Classe operaia va in paradiso 1971, Tre nel mille 1971, Il Gatto a nove code 1971, Una Lucertola con la pelle di donna 1971, Veruschka 1971, Krasnaya palatka 1971, Il Decameron 1971, La Tarantola dal ventre nero 1971, Giornata nera per l'ariete 1971, Il Giorno del giudizio 1971, Sans mobile apparent 1971, Addio, fratello crudele 1971, Sacco e Vanzetti 1971, L'Istruttoria è chiusa: dimentichi 1971, Malastrana 1971, Giù la testa 1971, Maddalena 1971, Le Casse 1971, 4 mosche di velluto grigio 1971, ¡Viva la muerte... tua! 1971, La Violenza: Quinto potere 1972, Questa specie d'amore 1972, Quando la preda è l'uomo 1972, Perché? 1972, Il Maestro e Margherita 1972, Lui per lei 1972, Guttoso e il 'Marat morto' di David 1972, Fiorina la vacca 1972, Il Diavolo nel cervello 1972, Les Deux saisons de la vie 1972, D'amore si muore 1972, Crescete e moltiplicatevi 1972, La Cosa buffa 1972, Chi l'ha vista morire? 1972, Bianchi bandinelli e la Colonna Traiana 1972, Anche se volessi lavorare, che faccio? 1972, Mio caro assassino 1972, Le Tueur 1972, Cosa avete fatto a Solange? 1972, Bluebeard 1972, J. and S. - storia criminale del far west 1972, L'Attentat 1972, Sbatti il mostro in prima pagina 1972, Un Uomo da rispettare 1972, Il Ritorno di Clint il solitario 1972, Quando le donne persero la coda 1972, La Vita, a volte, è molto dura, vero Provvidenza? 1972, Vaarwel 1973, Sepolta viva 1973, Quando l'amore è sensualità 1973, Libera, amore mio... 1973, Che c'entriamo noi con la rivoluzione? 1973, Allonsanfan 1973, Le Serpent 1973, Le Moine 1973, La Proprietà non è più un furto 1973, Revolver 1973, Rappresaglia 1973, Ci risiamo, vero Provvidenza? 1973, Giordano Bruno 1973, Il Mio nome è Nessuno 1973, Il Giro del mondo degli innamorati di Peynet 1974, Fatti di gente per bene 1974, La Cugina 1974, L'Anticristo 1974, Spasmo 1974, Mussolini: Ultimo atto 1974, Sesso in confessionale 1974, Il Fiore delle mille e una notte 1974, Le Trio infernal 1974, Milano odia: la polizia non può sparare 1974, Le Secret 1974, Storie di vita e malavita 1975, Il Sorriso del grande tentatore 1975, Labbra di lurido blu 1975, Gente di rispetto 1975, Macchie solari 1975, L'Ultimo treno della notte 1975, Peur sur la ville 1975, Leonor 1975, Der Richter und sein Henker 1975, Per le antiche scale 1975, The Human Factor 1975, Una Vita venduta 1976, Todo modo 1976, San Babila ore 20 un delitto inutile 1976, René la canne 1976, Per amore 1976, Film 1976, La Donna della domenica 1976, Il Deserto dei Tartari 1976, Attenti al buffone 1976, L'Arriviste 1976, Ariel Limon 1976, L'Agnese va a morire 1976, Salò o le 120 giornate di Sodoma 1976, Der Dritte Grad 1976, Divina creatura 1976, 1900 1976, L'Eredità Ferramonti 1976, Stato interessante 1977, Il Prefetto di ferro 1977, Il Mostro 1977, The Dragon, the Odds 1977, Corleone 1977, Le Ricain 1977, Exorcist II: The Heretic 1977, Orca 1977, Holocaust 2000 1977, Autostop rosso sangue 1977, L'Immoralità 1978, Forza Italia! 1978, Il Gatto 1978, One, Two, Two: 122, rue de Provence 1978, Pedro Páramo 1978, Così come sei 1978, La Cage aux folles 1978, Ten to Survive 1979, Il Prato 1979, Il Ladrone 1979, Dedicato al mare Egeo 1979, Le Buone notizie 1979, Il Giocattolo 1979, Viaggio con Anita 1979, L'Umanoide 1979, Bloodline 1979, La Luna 1979, I... comme Icare 1979, Uomini e no 1980, Si salvi chi vuole 1980, The Fantastic World of M.C. Escher 1980, Bugie bianche 1980, Windows 1980, Un Sacco bello 1980, Stark System 1980, Ogro 1980, Nouvelles rencontres 1980, The Island 1980, L'Oeil 1980, La Banquière 1980, La Cage aux folles II 1980, La Dame aux camélias 1980, Il Pianeta azzurro 1981, Bianco, rosso e Verdone 1981, Occhio alla penna 1981, La Disubbidienza 1981, So Fine 1981, Le Professionnel 1981, La Tragedia di un uomo ridicolo 1981, Porca vacca 1982, Nana 1982, Il Bandito dagli occhi azzurri 1982, Espion, lève-toi 1982, A Time to Die 1982, The Thing 1982, White Dog 1982, Blood Link 1982, Maja Plisetskaja 1982, Hundra 1983, Le Ruffian 1983, El Tesoro de las cuatro coronas 1983, Copkiller 1983, La Chiave 1983, Le Marginal 1983, Sahara 1983, Pelota 1984, Once Upon a Time in America 1984, Les Voleurs de la nuit 1984, Code Name: Wild Geese 1984, Red Sonja 1985, Kommando Leopard 1985, Il Pentito 1985, La Cage aux folles 3 – 'Elles' se marient 1985, La Venexiana 1986, La Gabbia 1986, The Mission 1986, Quartiere 1987, Mosca addio 1987, Il Giorno prima 1987, The Untouchables 1987, Gli Occhiali d'oro 1987, Il Cuore di mamma 1988, Frantic 1988, A Time of Destiny 1988, Rampage 1988, Nuovo cinema Paradiso 1989,

Casualties of War 1989, Fat Man and Little Boy 1989, Tre colonne in cronaca 1990, Tempo di uccidere 1990, ¡Átame! 1990, Dimenticare Palermo 1990, Stanno tutti bene 1990, The Big Man 1990, Tracce di vita amorosa 1990, State of Grace 1990, Hamlet 1990, Mio caro dottor Gräsler 1991, Ilona und Kurti 1991, Money 1991, La Domenica specialmente 1991, Bugsy 1991, A Csalás gyönyöre 1992, Beyond Justice 1992, City of Joy 1992, La Villa del venerdì 1992, Love Potion No. 9 1992, Roma imago urbis 1993, In the Line of Fire 1993, Il Lungo silenzio 1993, La Scorta 1993, Jona che visse nella balena 1994, Una Pura formalità 1994, Wolf 1994, Love Affair 1994, Disclosure 1994, L'Uomo proiettile 1995, The Night and the Moment 1995, Pasolini, un delitto italiano 1995, L'Uomo delle stelle 1995, Ninfa plebea 1996, I Magi randagi 1996, Tashunga 1996, La Sindrome di Stendhal 1996, Vite strozzate 1996, Sostiene Pereira 1996, La Lupa 1996, Naissance des stéréoscopages 1997, Con rabbia e con amore 1997, Cartoni animati 1997, Marianna Ucrìa 1997, U Turn 1997, Lolita 1997, The Thing: Terror Takes Shape 1998, Bulworth 1998, La Leggenda del pianista sull'oceano 1998, Il Fantasma dell'opera 1998, Lucignolo 1999, In the Line of Fire: The Ultimate Sacrifice 2000, Canone inverso - making love 2000, Mission to Mars 2000, Vatel 2000, Sensitive New-Age Killer 2000, Malèna 2000, La Ragion pura 2001, Cowboys Don't Kiss in Public 2001, Un Altro mondo è possibile 2001, Aida degli alberi 2001, Threnody 2002, Senso '45 2002, Ripley's Game 2002, Il Diario di Matilde Manzoni 2002, L'Ultimo pistolero 2002, Arena Concerto 2003, Al cuore si comanda 2003, La Luz prodigiosa 2003, The Wages of Sin 2003, 72 metra 2004, Kill Bill: Vol. 2 2004, Guardiani delle nuvole 2004, Sorstalanság 2005, Karol, un uomo diventato papa 2005, Eridendo l'uccise 2005, Libertas 2005, Fateless 2005. *Television scores:* The Virginian (series theme) 1962, Lo Squarciagola 1966, 1943: un incontro 1969, La Sciantosa 1970, Nessuno deve sapere (series) 1971, Correva l'anno di grazia 1870 1971, L'Uomo e la magia 1972, L'Automobile 1972, Moses the Lawgiver 1975, Drammi gotichi 1976, Noi lazzaroni (series) 1978, Le Mani sporche 1978, Invito allo sport (series) 1978, Orient-Express (series) 1979, The Life and Times of David Lloyd George (series) 1981, Marco Polo (series) 1982, The Scarlet and the Black 1983, Wer war Edgar Allan? 1984, Die Försterbuben 1984, Via Mala (series) 1985, C.A.T. Squad 1986, I Promessi sposi (series) 1988, Gli Indifferenti (series) 1988, Camillo Castiglioni oder die Moral der Haifische 1988, Gli Angeli del potere 1988, C.A.T. Squad: Python Wolf 1988, Il Principe del deserto (series) 1989, The Endless Game 1990, Voyage of Terror: The Achille Lauro Affair 1990, Cacciatori di navi 1990, Una Storia italiana 1992, Piazza di Spagna (series) 1993, Missus 1993, La Piovra series 1–10 1984–99, Genesi: La creazione e il diluvio 1994, Abraham 1994, Jacob 1994, Joseph 1995, Moses (title music) 1996, Il Barone (series) 1996, Samson and Delilah 1996, In fondo al cuore 1997, Nostromo (series) 1997, David (theme) 1997, Solomon 1997, Ultimo 1998, I Guardiani del cielo 1998, Il Quarto re 1998, La Casa bruciata 1998, Ultimo 2 - La sfida 1999, Nanà 1999, Esther 1999, Padre Pio - Tra cielo e terra 2000, Perlasca, un eroe italiano 2002, Un Difetto di famiglia 2002, Il Papa buono 2003, Musashi (series) 2003, Maria Goretti 2003, Charlie Chaplin - Les années suisses 2003, Il Cuore nel pozzo 2005. *Address:* c/o Gorfaine/Schwartz Agency Inc., 4111 West Alameda Avenue, Suite 509, Burbank, CA 91505, USA (office). *Telephone:* (818) 260-8500 (office).

MORRILL, Rev. John Stephen, DPhil, FBA; British historian and academic; *Professor of British and Irish History, University of Cambridge;* b. 12 June 1946, Manchester; s. of William Henry Morrill and Marjorie Morrill (née Ashton); m. Frances Mead 1968 (died 2007); four d.; ed Altrincham Grammar School, Trinity Coll., Oxford; Research Fellow, Trinity Coll. Oxford 1970–74, Hon. Fellow 2006–; Lecturer in History, Univ. of Stirling 1974–75; Fellow, Selwyn Coll. Cambridge 1975–, Sr Tutor 1989–92, Vice-Master 1994–2005; Lecturer in History, Cambridge Univ. 1975–92, Reader in Early Modern History 1992–98, Prof. of British and Irish History 1998–; mem. Council, Royal Historical Soc. 1988–92, Vice-Pres. 1992–96; Chair. Communications and Activities Cttee, British Acad. 1998–, mem. Council 1998–, Vice-Pres. 2000–02; mem. and Trustee Arts and Humanities Research Council 2000–04, Chair. Rescue Cttee 2001–04; ordained Perm. Deacon, RC Diocese of East Anglia 1996; mem. Acad. of Finland 2001; Hon. DLitt (Univ. of East Anglia) 2001; Hon. DUniv (Surrey) 2001. *Publications:* Cheshire 1630–1660 1974, The Revolt of the Provinces 1976, Reactions to the English Civil War 1981, Oliver Cromwell and the English Revolution 1989, The Impact of the English Civil War 1991, Revolution and Restoration 1992, The Nature of the English Revolution 1992, The British Problem 1534–1707 1996, The Oxford Illustrated History of Tudor and Stuart Britain 1996, Revolt in the Provinces 1998, Soldiers and Statesmen of the English Revolution (co-author) 1998; 40 articles in learned journals. *Leisure interests:* music, theology, whisky, cricket. *Address:* Selwyn College, Cambridge, CB3 9DQ (office); 1 Bradford's Close, Bottisham, Cambridge, CB25 9DW, England (home). *Telephone:* (1223) 335895 (office); (1223) 811822 (home). *Fax:* (1223) 335837 (office). *E-mail:* jsm1000@cam.ac.uk (office).

MORRIS, Christopher, FCA; British chartered accountant; *Partner, Begbies Traynor;* b. 28 April 1942; s. of Richard Archibald Sutton Morris, MC and Josephine Fanny Mary (née Galliano) Morris; m. Isabel Ramsden (divorced); two s.; qualified 1967; Pnr, Head of UK insolvency arm Touche Ross & Co. (later Deloitte) 1972–2000; Sr Partner Corp. Recovery; Pnr Begbies Traynor 2004–; cases have included liquidation of Laker Airways 1982, British Island Airways, British Air Ferries, Rush & Tompkins, London & County Securities, Polly Peck Int., Banco Ambrosiano, Bank of Credit and Commerce International (BCCI); Fellow Soc. of Practitioners of Insolvency. *Leisure interests:* racing, wine, the countryside. *Address:* Begbies Traynor, 32 Cornhill, London, EC3V 3BT, England (office). *Telephone:* (20) 7398-3800 (office). *Fax:* (20) 7398-3799 (office). *Website:* www.begbies-traynor.com (office).

MORRIS, Sir Derek James, Kt, MA, DPhil; British economist and academic; *Provost, Oriel College, University of Oxford;* b. 23 Dec. 1945, Harrow; s. of Denis William Morris and Olive Margaret Morris; m. Susan Mary Whittles 1975; two s.; ed Harrow Co. Grammar School, St Edmund Hall and Nuffield Coll., Oxford; Research Fellow, Univ. of Warwick 1969–70; Fellow and Tutor of Econs Oriel Coll., Oxford 1970–98, now Provost; Econ. Dir Nat. Econ. Devt Office 1981–84; Chair. Oxford Econ. Forecasting Ltd 1984–98; mem. Monopolies and Mergers Comm. 1991–95, Deputy Chair. 1995–98, Chair. Competition (fmrly Monopolies and Mergers) Comm. 1998–2004; Chair. Morris Review of Actuarial Profession 2004; Hon. Fellow, St Edmund Hall, Oxford 2002, Trinity Coll., Dublin 2004; Dr hc (Univ. Coll., Dublin) 2004, (Univ. of East Anglia) 2006. *Publications include:* The Economic System in the UK (ed.) 1971, Industrial Economics and Organisation (with D. Hay) 1985, Chinese State-Owned Enterprises and Economic Reform 1994; numerous journal articles on econs. *Leisure interests:* skiing, rugby, history. *Address:* Oriel College, Oxford, OX1 4EW, England (office). *Telephone:* (1865) 276543 (office). *E-mail:* lodge@oriel.ox.ac.uk (office). *Website:* www.oriel.ox.ac.uk (office).

MORRIS, Desmond John, DPhil; British zoologist; b. 24 Jan. 1928, Purton, Wilts.; s. of Capt. Harry Howe Morris and Marjorie Morris (née Hunt); m. Ramona Joy Baulch 1952; one s.; ed Dauntsey's School, Wilts., Birmingham Univ. and Oxford Univ.; zoological research worker Univ. of Oxford 1954–56; Head of Granada TV; Head of Film Unit Zoological Soc. of London 1956–59, Curator of Mammals 1959–67; Dir Inst. of Contemporary Arts, London 1967–68; Research Fellow at Wolfson Coll., Oxford 1973–81; privately engaged in writing books on animal and human behaviour 1968–73, 1981–2006 and making television programmes; artist; mem. Scientific Fellow Zoological Soc. of London; Hon. DSc (Reading) 1998. *Television:* Zootime (Granada) 1956–67, Life in the Animal World (BBC) 1965–67, The Human Race (Thames TV) 1982, The Animals Roadshow (BBC) 1987–89, The Animal Contract 1989, Animal Country 1991–95, The Human Animal 1994, The Human Sexes 1997. *Publications:* The Reproductive Behaviour of the Ten-spined Stickleback 1958, The Story of Congo 1958, Curious Creatures 1961, The Biology of Art 1962, Apes and Monkeys 1964, The Mammals: A Guide to the Living Species 1965, The Big Cats 1965, Men and Snakes (with Ramona Morris) 1965, Zootime 1966, Men and Apes (with Ramona Morris) 1966, Men and Pandas (with Ramona Morris) 1966, Primate Ethology (Editor) 1967, The Naked Ape 1967, The Human Zoo 1969, Patterns of Reproductive Behaviour 1970, Intimate Behaviour 1971, Manwatching: A Field-Guide to Human Behaviour 1977, Gestures, Their Origins and Distribution 1979, Animal Days (autobiog.) 1979, The Giant Panda 1981, The Soccer Tribe 1981, Inrock (fiction) 1983, The Book of Ages 1983, The Art of Ancient Cyprus 1985, Bodywatching 1985, The Illustrated Naked Ape 1986, Dogwatching 1986, Catwatching 1986, The Secret Surrealist 1987, Catlore 1987, The Human Nestbuilders 1988, The Animals Roadshow 1988, Horsewatching 1988, The Animal Contract 1990, Animal-Watching 1990, Babywatching 1991, Christmas Watching 1992, The World of Animals 1993, The Naked Ape Trilogy 1994, The Human Animal 1994, Body Talk: A World Guide to Gestures 1994, The Illustrated Catwatching 1994, Illustrated Babywatching 1995, Catworld: A Feline Encyclopedia 1996, Illustrated Dogwatching 1996, The Human Sexes 1997, Illustrated Horse-Watching 1998, Cool Cats: The 100 Cat Breeds of the World 1999, Body Guards: Protective Amulets and Charms 1999, Cosmetic Behaviour and the Naked Ape 1999, The Naked Eye 2000, Dogs, a Dictionary of Dog Breeds 2001, People-Watching 2002, The Silent Language 2004, The Nature of Happiness 2004, The Naked Woman: A Study of the Female Body 2004, Watching: Encounters with Humans and Other Animals (autobiog.) 2006, The Naked Man 2008, Baby, The Story of a Baby's First Two Years 2008. *Leisure interest:* archaeology. *Address:* c/o Jonathan Cape, 20 Vauxhall Bridge Road, London, SW1V 2SA, England. *Fax:* (1865) 512103. *E-mail:* dmorris@ ukstudio.org. *Website:* www.desmond-morris.com.

MORRIS, Doug; American record company executive, producer and songwriter; *Chairman and Chief Executive Officer, Universal Music Group;* b. Nov. 1938; ed Columbia Univ.; fmr songwriter music publisher Robert Mellin Inc.; writer and prod. Laurie Records from 1965, later Vice-Pres. and Gen. Man.; f. Big Tree label (sold to Atlantic Records 1978); Pres. ATCO Records (part of Warner Music) 1978–80, Pres. Atlantic Records 1980–90, Co-Chair. and Co-CEO Atlantic Recording Group 1990–94, Pres. and COO, then Chair. Warner Music USA 1994; co-cr. Interscope Records; Chair. and CEO MCA Music Entertainment Group (now Universal Music Group) 1995–, f. Universal Records, apptd to Vivendi Universal Management Bd 2005; co-f. (with Jimmy Iovine q.v.) Jimmy and Doug's Farm Club project, comprising a record label, website and cable TV show 1999–; jt owner Pressplay subscription-based music download website; bd mem. The Robin Hood Foundation, The Cold Spring Harbor Laboratory; Dir Rock and Roll Hall of Fame; NARAS President's Merit Award 2003. *Compositions include:* Sweet Talkin' Guy, The Chiffons 1996. *Address:* Universal Music Group, 2200 Colorado Avenue, Santa Monica, CA 90404, USA (office). *Website:* www.umusic.com (office); www.farmclub.com (office).

MORRIS, Errol, BA; American film director; b. 5 Feb. 1948, Hewlett, New York; m. Julia Sheehan 1984; one s.; ed Univ. of Wisconsin; f. Fourth Floor Productions Inc., Cambridge, Mass; has directed numerous tv commercials. *Films include:* Gates of Heaven 1980, Vernon, Florida 1982, The Thin Blue Line 1988, The Dark Wind 1991, A Brief History of Time 1991, Fast, Cheap and Out of Control 1997, Mr. Death: The Rise and Fall of Fred A. Leuchter, Jr. 1999, The Fog of War: Eleven Lessons from the Life of Robert S. McNamara (Acad. Award for Best Documentary 2004) 2003, Standard Operating Procedure (Grand Jury Silver Bear, Berlin Film Festival) 2008. *Publication:* Standard Operating Procedure (with Philip Gourevitch) 2008. *Address:* Fourth Floor Productions Inc., 650 Cambridge Street, Cambridge, MA 02141, USA (office). *Telephone:* (617) 876-4499 (office).

MORRIS, Baroness (Life Peer), cr. 2005, of Yardley in the County of West Midlands; **Estelle Morris,** BEd; British politician; b. 17 June 1952; d. of Charles Richard Morris and Pauline Morris; ed Whalley Range High School, Manchester, Coventry Coll. of Educ., Warwick Univ.; teacher 1974–92; Councillor, Warwick Dist Council 1979–91, Labour Group Leader 1981–89; MP for Birmingham, Yardley 1992–; Opposition Whip 1994–95, Opposition Front-bench Spokeswoman on Educ. 1995–97; Parl. Under-Sec. of State, Dept for Educ. and Employment (DfEE) 1997–98, Minister of State 1998–2001, Sec. of State for Educ. and Skills 2001–02; Minister of State for the Arts, Dept for Culture, Media and Sport 2003–05; Privy Councillor; Pro Vice-Chancellor Sunderland Univ. 2005–07; Chair. Strategy Bd Inst. of Effective Educ., Univ. of York; Hon. Degrees (Warwick) 2003, (Wolverhampton) 2004, (Leeds Metropolitan) 2004, (Bradford) 2005, (Birmingham) 2006, (Manchester Metropolitan, Cumbria) 2007, (Sunderland) 2008. *Address:* House of Lords, London, SW1A 0PW, England (office). *Telephone:* (20) 7219-3000 (office). *Website:* www.parliament.uk (office).

MORRIS, James Humphry (see Morris, Jan).

MORRIS, James Peppler; American singer (bass-baritone); b. 10 Jan. 1947; s. of James Morris and Geraldine Peppler; m. 1st Joanne F. Vitali 1971; one d.; m. 2nd Susan Quittmeyer 1987; one s. one d. (twins); ed Univ. of Maryland, Peabody Conservatory and Acad. of Vocal Arts; debut at Metropolitan Opera, New York 1970; opera and concert appearances throughout USA, Canada, S. America, Europe, Japan and Australia. *Recordings include:* Wotan in the New Ring Cycles, The Flying Dutchman, operas by Wagner, Offenbach, Mozart, Verdi, Donizetti, Bellini. *Title roles include:* The Flying Dutchman, Don Giovanni, Le Nozze di Figaro, Macbeth, Boris Godunov, Faust, Billy Budd, Otello. *Address:* Columbia Artists' Management Inc., 1790 Broadway, New York, NY 10019-1412, USA (office). *Telephone:* (212) 841 9500 (office). *Fax:* (212) 841 9744 (office). *E-mail:* info@cami.com (office). *Website:* www.cami.com (office).

MORRIS, James T., BA, MBA; American international organization official and business executive; b. 18 April 1943, Terre Haute, Ind.; m. Jacqueline Harrell Morris; three c.; ed Indiana Univ., Butler Univ.; Chief of Staff to Mayor of Indianapolis 1967–73; Dir of Community Devt, Lilly Endowment 1973, Vice-Pres., Pres. 1984–89; Chair. and CEO IWC Resources Corpn, Ind. Water Co. 1989–; Exec. Dir UN WFP 2002–07; Chair. NCAA Foundation; Chair. Bd of Trustees Ind. Univ.; Treas. US Olympic Cttee; mem. Bd Govs American Red Cross; Inductee, Ind. Acad.; Dr hc (Butler Univ.), (Ind. Univ.), (Vincennes Univ.), (Rose Hufman Inst. of Tech.), (Univ. of Southern Ind.), (Martin Univ.), (Franklin Coll.), (Marian Coll.), (Wabash Coll.), (Univ. of Notre Dame); Medal of Freedom, Ellis Island, New York, Whitney Young Award, Indianapolis Urban League, Charles L. Whistler Award, Int. Citizen of the Year, Int. Center of Indianapolis and numerous other awards. *Address:* c/o World Food Programme, Via Cesare Giulio Viola 68, Parco dei Medici, 00148 Rome, Italy. *Telephone:* (06) 6513-3030.

MORRIS, Jan, (James Humphry Morris), CBE, MA, FRSL; British writer; b. 2 Oct. 1926, Somerset, England; ed Christ Church Coll., Oxford; editorial staff, The Times 1951–56, The Guardian 1957–62; Commonwealth Fellowship, USA 1954; mem. Yr Academi Gymreig, Gorsedd of Bards, Welsh Nat. Eisteddfod; Hon. Fellow, Univ. Coll. Wales, Univ. of Wales, Bangor; Hon. FRIBA; Hon. Student, Christ Church Oxon.; Dr hc (Univ. of Wales) 1993, (Univ. of Glamorgan) 1996. *Publications:* as James Morris: Coast to Coast (aka I Saw the USA) 1956, Sultan in Oman 1957, The Market of Seleukia (aka Islam Inflamed: A Middle East Picture) 1957, Coronation Everest 1958, South African Winter 1958, The Hashemite Kings 1959, Venice 1960, South America 1961, The Upstairs Donkey (juvenile) 1962, The World Bank: A Prospect (aka The Road to Huddersfield: A Journey to Five Continents) 1963, Cities 1963, The Outriders: A Liberal View of Britain 1963, The Presence of Spain 1964, Oxford 1965, Pax Britannica: The Climax of an Empire 1968, The Great Port: A Passage through New York 1969, Places 1972, Heaven's Command: An Imperial Progress 1973, Farewell the Trumpets: An Imperial Retreat 1978; as Jan Morris: Conundrum 1974, Travels 1976, The Oxford Book of Oxford 1978, Destinations: Essays from 'Rolling Stone' 1980, The Venetian Empire: A Sea Voyage 1980, My Favourite Stories of Wales 1980, The Small Oxford Book of Wales, Wales The First Place, A Venetian Bestiary 1982, The Spectacle of Empire 1982, Stones of Empire: The Buildings of the Raj 1983, Journeys 1984, The Matter of Wales: Epic Views of a Small Country 1984, Among the Cities 1985, Last Letters from Hav: Notes from a Lost City 1985, Stones of Empire: The Buildings of the Raj 1986, Scotland, The Place of Visions 1986, Manhattan, '45 1987, Hong Kong: Xianggang 1988, Pleasures of a Tangled Life 1989, Ireland Your Only Place 1990, City to City 1990, O Canada 1992, Sydney 1992, Locations 1992, Travels with Virginia Woolf (ed.) 1993, A Machynlleth Triad 1994, Fisher's Face 1995, The Princeship of Wales 1995, The World of Venice 1995, 50 Years of Europe 1997, Hong Kong: Epilogue to an Empire 1997, Lincoln: A Foreigner's Quest 1999, Our First Leader 2000, A Writer's House in Wales 2001, Trieste and the Meaning of Nowhere 2001, A Writer's World: Travels 1950–2000 2003, Hav (fiction) 2006, Portmeirion (with others) 2006. *Address:* c/o AP Watt Ltd, 20 John Street, London, WC1N 2DR, England (office); Trefan Morys, Llanystumdwy, Gwynedd LL52 0LP, Wales (home). *Telephone:* (20) 7405-6774 (office); (1766) 522222 (home). *Fax:* (20) 7831-2154 (office). *E-mail:* apw@apwatt.co.uk (office); janmorris1@msn.com (home). *Website:* www.apwatt.co.uk (office).

MORRIS, Mark William; American choreographer and dancer; *Artistic Director, Mark Morris Dance Group;* b. 29 Aug. 1956, Seattle, Wash.; s. of William Morris and Maxine Crittenden Morris; Artistic Dir Mark Morris Dance Group 1980–; Dir of Dance, Théâtre Royal de la Monnaie, Brussels 1988–91; Co-Founder White Oak Dance Project (with Mikhail Baryshnikov q.v.) 1990; performed with various dance cos including Lar Lubovitch Dance Co., Hannah Kahn Dance Co., Laura Dean Dancers and Musicians, Eliot Feld Ballet, Koleda Balkan Dance Ensemble; cr. over 100 works for Mark Morris Dance Group including Mythologies 1986, L'Allegro, il Penseroso ed il Moderato 1988, Dido and Aeneas 1989, The Hard Nut 1991, Grand Duo 1993, Lucky Charms 1994, Rondo 1994, The Office 1994, I Don't Want to Love 1996, Peccadillos 2000, V 2001; has cr. dances for many other ballet cos including San Francisco Ballet, Paris Opera Ballet and American Theatre Ballet, Boston Ballet; cr. King Arthur (for ENO) 2006; Guggenheim Fellowship 1986; Fellow MacArthur Foundation 1991; New York Dance and Performance Award 1984, 1990. *Address:* Mark Morris Dance Group, 3 Lafayette Avenue, Brooklyn, NY 11217, USA. *Telephone:* (718) 624-8400 (office). *Fax:* (718) 624-8900 (office). *Website:* www.mmdg.org (office).

MORRIS, Michael G., MSc, LLB; American energy industry executive; *President, CEO and Chairman, American Electric Power Company Inc.;* b. 1946, Fremont, Ohio; m. Linda Morris; two s.; ed Detroit Coll. of Law, E Michigan Univ.; f. and fmr Pres. ANR Gathering Co.; fmr Pres. Colorado Interstate Gas (CIG); fmr Exec. Vice-Pres. ANR Pipeline Co.; fmr Pres. CMS Marketing, Services and Trading; Pres. and CEO Consumers Energy –1997; Pres., CEO and Chair. Northeast Utilities System 1997–2003; Pres., CEO and Chair. American Electric Power 2004–; Dir St Francis Care Inc., Nuclear Electric Insurance Ltd, American Gas Asscn, Spinnaker Exploration, Flink Ink Corpn, Webster Financial Corpn, Cincinnati Bell; 2nd Vice-Chair. Edison Electrical Inst.; mem. US Dept of Energy Electricity Advisory Bd, Nat. Govs Asscn Task Force on Electricity Infrastructure, CT Gov.'s Council on Econ. Competitiveness and Tech.; mem. Michigan Bar Asscn; Trustee, Bushnell Overseers; fmr Chair. CT Business and Industry Asscn; fmr mem. Bd, Detroit Coll. of Law, Inst. of Gas Tech., E Michigan Univ. Foundation, Olivet Coll. Leadership Advisory Council, Library of Michigan Foundation. *Address:* American Electric Power Company Inc., Corporate Headquarters, 1 Riverside Plaza, Columbus, OH 43215–2372, USA (office). *Telephone:* (614) 716-1000 (office). *Fax:* (614) 223-1823 (office). *Website:* www.aep.com (office).

MORRIS, Michael Jeremy, MA; British performing arts producer; *Co-Director, Artangel;* b. 30 March 1958, London; s. of Lawrence Morris and Monica Morris; m. Sarah Culshaw 1991; one s. one d.; ed Oundle School, Keble Coll. Oxford and City Univ., London; Assoc. Dir of Theatre, Inst. of Contemporary Arts 1981–84, Dir of Performing Arts 1984–87; mem. Drama and Dance Panel, British Council 1984–90; Founding Dir Cultural Industry Ltd (presenting and producing contemporary theatre, music and dance) 1987–; Co.-Dir Artangel (commissioning outstanding artists to create new work) 1991–, Artangel Media 2000–; Dir first production and co-author of libretto of Michael Nyman's opera The Man Who Mistook His Wife for a Hat 1986; Dir first production and author of libretto of Mike Westbrook's opera Coming Through Slaughter 1994; has commissioned and produced projects by Robert Wilson, Michael Clark, William Forsythe, Brian Eno and Laurie Anderson, John Berger and Simon McBurney, amongst many others; Dir Cultural Industry Ltd. *Leisure interests:* world music, fine wine, foreign food, popular art. *Address:* Artangel, 31 Eyre Street Hill, London, EC1R 5EW, England (office). *Telephone:* (20) 7713-1400 (office). *Fax:* (20) 7713-1401 (office). *E-mail:* info@artangel.org.uk (office). *Website:* www.artangel.org.uk (office).

MORRIS, Sir Peter John, Kt, AC, MB, BS, PhD, FRCS, FMedSci, FRS; Australian surgeon and academic; *Chairman, British Heart Foundation;* b. 17 April 1934, Horsham, Vic.; s. of Stanley Henry Morris and Mary Lois (née Hennessy) Morris; m. Jocelyn Mary Gorman 1960; three s. two d.; ed Univ. of Melbourne; Resident Surgical Officer, St Vincent's Hosp. 1958–61; Surgical Registrar, Southampton Gen. Hosp., UK 1963–64; Clinical Assoc. and Fellow, Mass. Gen. Hosp., Boston, USA 1964–66; Asst Prof. of Surgery, Medical Coll., Richmond, Va, USA 1967; Dir Tissue Transplantation Labs, Univ. of Melbourne, Australia 1968–74; Reader in Surgery 1971–74; Consultant Surgeon, Lymphona Clinic, Cancer Inst., Melbourne 1969–74; Nuffield Prof. of Surgery, Univ. of Oxford, UK 1974–2002 (now Prof. Emer.), Dir Oxford Transplant Centre; Pres. The Transplantation Soc. 1984–86, European Surgical Asscn 1996–98, Int. Surgical Soc. 2001–; Vice-Chair. Clinical Medicine Bd, Univ. of Oxford 1982–84; Vice-Pres. Royal Coll. of Surgeons of England 2000–01, then Pres.; Chair. Council, Inst. of Health Sciences, Univ. of Oxford 2000–; Council mem. MRC, London 1983–87; Ed. Transplantation 1979–; Fellow, Balliol Coll., Univ. of Oxford 1974–; mem. UFC 1989–92; Gov. Health Foundation 1998–2003; Pres. Royal Coll. of Surgeons of England 2001–04, Medical Protection Soc.; currently Chair. British Heart Foundation, Dir Centre for Evidence in Transplantation; Hon. FRCSE, FACS 1986, FRACS 1996, FRCP, FRCPE; Hon. Fellow, American Coll. of Surgeons, American Surgical Asscn, Royal Australasian Coll. of Surgeons, Japan Surgical Soc., German Surgical Soc., Coll. of Physicians and Surgeons of Glasgow; Hon. Prof., Univ. of London; Hon. DSc (Hong Kong) 2000, (Imperial Coll.) 2003; Selwyn Smith Prize (Australia), Lister Medal (UK) 1998, Hamilton Fairley Medal, Royal Coll. of Physicians 2005; Medawar Prize, TTS 2006. *Publications:* Kidney Transplantation 1978 (revised sixth edn) 2008, Tissue Transplantation 1982, Transient Ischaemic Attacks 1982, Progress in Transplantation 1984, Oxford Textbook of Surgery (with R. Malt) 1993, (second edn with W. Wood) 2001. *Leisure interests:* golf, tennis, cricket. *Address:* Royal College of Surgeons, 35–43 Lincoln's Inn Fields, London, WC2A 3PE (office); 19 Lucerne Road, Oxford, OX2 7QB, England (home). *Telephone:* (20) 7869-6604 (office). *Fax:* (20) 7869-6644 (office). *E-mail:* ntalawila@rceng.ac.uk (office); pmorris@rcseng.ac.uk (office); peterj.morris@virgin.net (home). *Website:* www.transplantevidence.com (office).

MORRIS, Richard Graham Michael, CBE, MA, DPhil, FRS, FRSE, FMedSci; British neuroscientist and academic; *Royal Society/Wolfson Professor of Neuroscience, University of Edinburgh;* b. 27 June 1948, Worthing; s. of

Robert Morris and Edith Morris; m. Hilary Ann Lewis 1985; two d.; ed Univs of Cambridge and Sussex; Lecturer in Psychology, Univ. of St Andrews 1977–86, MRC Research Fellow 1983–86; Reader, then Prof. of Neuroscience, Univ. of Edin. 1986–, Dir Centre for Neuroscience 1993–97, Chair. Dept of Neuroscience 1998, currently Dir Centre for Cognitive and Neural Systems, Royal Soc./Wolfson Prof. of Neuroscience 2006–; Sec. Experimental Psychology Soc. 1983–87; Chair. UK Brain Research Asscn 1990–94; mem. MRC Neuroscience Research Grants Cttee 1983–87, Neuroscience and Mental Health Bd 1993–97, Innovation Bd 1998–2000, MRC Strategy Group 2000–02; Forum Fellow at World Econ. Forum 2000; Life Sciences Co-ordinate OST Foresight Project on Cognitive Systems 2002–04; Pres. Fed. of European Neuroscience Socs 2006–08; Fellow, American Acad. of Arts and Sciences 2004, AAAS 2006; Decade of the Brain Lecturer 1998, Zotterman Lecturer 1999, Yngve Zotterman Prize, Karolinska Inst. 1999, Henry Dryerre Prize, Royal Soc. of Edin. 2000, BNA Outstanding Contrib. to Neuroscience 2002, EJN European Neuroscience Award 2004, Feldberg Prize 2006, Santiago Grisola Award 2007. *Publications:* Parallel Distributed Processing (ed.) 1988, Neuroscience: Science of the Brain, 1994, 2003, Long-Term Potentiation (co-ed. with T. V. P. Bliss and G. L. Collingridge) 2004, scientific papers on neural mechanisms of memory. *Leisure interest:* sailing. *Address:* Centre for Cognitive and Neural Systems, University of Edinburgh, 1 George Square, Edinburgh, EH8 9JZ, Scotland (office). *Telephone:* (131) 650-3518 (office); (7795) 225620 (mobile) (office); (131) 441-5501 (home). *Fax:* (131) 650-4579 (office). *E-mail:* Richard.G.M.Morris@ed.ac.uk (office). *Website:* www.ccns .sbms.mvm.ed.ac.uk/staff/people/morris_richard.htm (office).

MORRIS, Richard Keith, OBE, BPhil, MA, FSA; British writer, archaeologist and composer; *Director, Institute for Medieval Studies, University of Leeds;* b. 8 Oct. 1947, Birmingham; s. of John Richard Morris and Elsie Myra Wearne; m. Jane Whiteley 1972; two s. one d.; ed Denstone Coll., Staffs., Pembroke Coll., Oxford and Univ. of York; musician, writer 1971–; Research Asst, York Minster Archaeological Office 1972–75; Churches Officer, Council for British Archaeology 1975–77, Research Officer, 1978–88, Dir 1991–99; Hon. Lecturer, School of History, Univ. of Leeds 1986–88, Dir Inst. for Medieval Studies 2003–; Lecturer, Dept of Archaeology, Univ. of York 1988–91; Commr, English Heritage 1996–, Chair. Advisory Cttee 2003–; Chair. Ancient Monuments Advisory Cttee for England 1996–2001, Historic Settlements and Landscapes Cttee 2001–03, Bede's World 2001–; mem. Heritage Lottery Fund Expert Panel 2005–; Trustee, Nat. Coal Mining Museum for England 2003–08; Hon. Visiting Prof., Univ. of York 1995; Hon. Vice-Pres. Council for British Archaeology; Frend Medal, Soc. of Antiquaries 1992. *Opera:* Lord Flame (jtly). *Music:* Five Auden Songs. *Film:* Nothing but Names (screenplay). *Publications:* Cathedrals and Abbeys of England and Wales 1979, The Church in British Archaeology 1983, Churches in the Landscape 1989, Guy Gibson (jtly) 1994, Cheshire: The Biography of Leonard Cheshire, VC, OM 2000, The Triumph of Time 2008. *Leisure interests:* aviation history, natural history, 20th-century music and opera. *Address:* Institute for Medieval Studies, Parkinson Building, University of Leeds, Leeds, LS2 9JT (office); 13 Hollins Road, Harrogate, N Yorks., HG1 2JF, England (home). *Telephone:* (113) 343-3617 (office); (1423) 50429 (home). *Fax:* (113) 343-3616 (office). *E-mail:* r.k .morris@leeds.ac.uk (office); r.k.morris@dsl.pipex.com (home). *Website:* www .leeds.ac.uk/ims/about/staffdetails.html#morris (office).

MORRIS OF ABERAVON, Baron (life Peer), cr. 2001, of Aberavon in the County of West Glamorgan and of Ceredigion in the County of Dyfed; **John Morris,** Kt, KG, PC, QC, LLD; British politician and barrister; b. 5 Nov. 1931, Aberystwyth; s. of the late D. W. Morris and of Mary Olwen Ann Morris; m. Margaret M. Lewis JP 1959; three d.; ed Ardwyn, Aberystwyth, Univ. Coll. of Wales, Aberystwyth, Gonville and Caius Coll., Cambridge and Acad. of Int. Law, The Hague; commissioned Royal Welch Fusiliers and Welch Regt; called to Bar, Gray's Inn 1954, Bencher 1985; Labour MP for Aberavon 1959–2001; Parl. Sec. Ministry of Power 1964–66; Jt Parl. Sec. Ministry of Transport 1966–68; Minister of Defence Equipment 1968–70; Sec. of State for Wales 1974–79; a Recorder, Crown Court 1982–97; Legal Affairs and Shadow Attorney-Gen. 1983–97; Attorney-Gen. 1997–99; Chancellor Univ. of Glamorgan; fmr Deputy Gen. Sec. and Legal Adviser, Farmers' Union of Wales; mem. UK Del., Consultative Ass., Council of Europe and WEU 1963–64; mem. Cttee of Privileges 1994–97, Select Cttee on Implementation of the Nolan Report 1995–97; Chair. Nat. Pneumoconiosis Jt Cttee 1964–66, Nat. Road Safety Advisory Council 1967–68, Jt Review of Finances and Man. British Railways 1966–67; mem. N Atlantic Ass. 1970–74; HM Lord Lt for Dyfed; Pres. London Welsh Asscn; Hon. Fellow Univ. Coll. of Wales, Aberystwyth and Swansea, Trinity Coll., Carmarthen, Gonville and Caius Coll. Cambridge; Hon. LLD (Wales). *Address:* c/o House of Lords, London, SW1A 0PW, England (office). *Telephone:* (20) 7219-3470 (office).

MORRIS OF HANDSWORTH, Baron (Life Peer), cr. 2006, of Handsworth in the County of West Midlands; **William (Bill) Morris,** FRSA, OJ; British trade union official (retd); b. 19 Oct. 1938, Jamaica; s. of William Morris and Una Morris; m. Minetta Morris 1957 (died 1990); two s.; ed Mizpah School, Manchester, Jamaica; Dist Officer, Transport & Gen. Workers' Union (TGWU), Nottingham 1973, Dist Sec. Northampton 1977, Nat. Sec. Passenger Services 1979–85, Deputy Gen. Sec. TGWU 1986–92, Gen. Sec. 1992–2003; mem. TUC Gen. Council 1988–2003; mem. Comm. for Racial Equality 1977–87, IBA Gen. Advisory Council 1981–86, ITF Exec. Bd 1986–, Prince of Wales Youth Business Trust 1987–90, BBC Gen. Advisory Council 1987–88, Employment Appeals Tribunal 1988–, Royal Comm. on Lords Reform 1999, Bd of Govs South Bank Univ. 1997, Comm. for Integrated Transport 1999–; Dir (non-exec.) Court of the Bank of England 1998–; Dir Unity Trust Bank 1994–2003; Chancellor Univ. of Tech., Jamaica 2000–, Staffordshire Univ. 2004–; Chair. Morris Enquiry 2003–04; mem. Cricket Bd for England and Wales; Hon. Fellow City & Guilds 1992, Royal Soc. of Arts; Dr hc (S Bank

Univ.) 1994, (Open Univ.) 1995; Hon. DLitt (Westminster) 1998 and several other hon. degrees; Public Figure of the Year, Ethnic Multicultural Media Awards (EMMA) 2002. *Leisure interests:* walking, gardening, watching sports, jazz concerts. *Address:* House of Lords, London, SW1A 0PW, England. *Telephone:* (20) 7219-3485. *E-mail:* morrisw@parliament.uk.

MORRISON, Graham, MA, DipArch, RIBA; British architect; b. 2 Feb. 1951, Kilmarnock, Scotland; s. of Robert Morrison and Robina S. Morrison; m. Michelle Lovric; one s. one d.; ed Brighton Coll., Jesus Coll., Cambridge; Partner, Allies and Morrison 1983–; mem. RIBA council 1991–94, Dir RIBA Journal 1993–97; External Examiner, Univ. of Cambridge 1994–97, Univ. of Portsmouth 2003–05; Royal Fine Arts Commr 1998–99; Special Prof. of Architecture, Univ. of Nottingham 2004–05; mem. Arts Council Architecture Advisory Cttee 1996–97, CABE Design Review Cttee 2000–04, London Advisory Cttee, English Heritage 2001–; RIBA Awards to Allies and Morrison for The Clove Bldg 1991, Pierhead, Liverpool 1995, Sarum Hall School 1996, Nunney Square, Sheffield 1996, Newnham Coll. Cambridge 1996, British Embassy, Dublin 1997, Abbey Mills Pumping Station, Stratford 1997, Goldsmiths Coll., London 1998, Blackburn House, London 2000, Blackwell 2003, Extension to Horniman Museum London 2004, One Piccadilly Gardens, Manchester 2004, 85 Southwark Street (RIBA London Bldg of the Year Award) 2004, BBC Media Village, White City 2005, Fitzwilliam Coll. Gatehouse and Auditorium 2005; Nat. Winner for Corp. Workplace Bldg, British Council for Offices Awards 2004, Architectural Practice of the Year Award, The Building Awards 2004. *Exhibitions include:* New British Architecture, Japan 1994, Allies and Morrison Retrospective, USA Schools of Architecture 1996–98; also exhbns in Helsinki, Delft, Strasbourg 1999. *Publication:* Allies and Morrison 1996. *Leisure interest:* Venice. *Address:* Allies and Morrison, 85 Southwark Street, London, SE1 0HX (office); 5 Winchester Wharf, 4 Clink Street, Southwark, London, SE1 9DL, England (home). *Telephone:* (20) 7921-0100 (office); (20) 7357-8757 (home). *Fax:* (20) 7921-0101 (office). *E-mail:* gmorrison@alliesandmorrison.co.uk (office); gm@ gmorrison.plus.com (home). *Website:* www.alliesandmorrison.com (office).

MORRISON, James Douglas, AO, PhD, DSc, FAA, FRSE; Australian mass spectrometrist; *Foundation Professor Emeritus of Chemistry, La Trobe University;* b. 9 Nov. 1924, Glasgow, Scotland; s. of James K. Morrison and Rose Ann Wheeler; m. Christine B. Mayer 1947; three s.; ed Lenzie Acad., Scotland and Univ. of Glasgow; Instructor, Dept of Chem., Univ. of Glasgow 1946–48; Research Officer, CSIRO 1949, Chief Research Officer 1965–67; Foundation Prof. of Chem., La Trobe Univ. 1967–90, Prof. Emer. 1990–; Resident Head, Chisholm Coll. 1972–77; Adjunct Prof., Univ. of Utah 1975–, Univ. of Delaware 1987–; Commonwealth Fund Fellow, Chicago Univ. 1956–57; Visiting Prof., Princeton Univ. 1964, Univ. of Utah 1971; mem. Council, Royal Soc. of Victoria, Pres. 1975–76; mem. Council, Australian Acad. of Science, Vice-Pres. 1986–87; Fellow, Royal Australian Chemical Inst.; Rennie and Smith Medals, Royal Australian Chemical Inst. *Publications:* articles in scientific journals. *Leisure interests:* fossil hunting, Byzantine studies, travel. *Address:* 40 Central Avenue, Mooroolbark, Vic. 3138, Australia.

MORRISON, Sir Kenneth Duncan, Kt, CBE; British retail industry executive (retd); *Executive Chairman, Wm Morrison Supermarkets PLC;* joined Wm Morrison Supermarkets PLC 1952, Chair. and Man. Dir 1956–97, Exec. Chair. 1997–2008 (retd). *Address:* c/o Wm Morrison Supermarkets PLC, Hilmore House, Thornton Road, Bradford, West Yorkshire BD8 9AX, England (office).

MORRISON, Robert S., BA, MBA; American business executive; *Chairman and CEO, 3M Company;* b. 4 April 1942, Chicago; s. of Forrest John Morrison and Grayce Morrison Scheck Hopkins; m. Susan E. Brennan 1988; five c.; ed Coll. of the Holy Cross, Univ. of Pennsylvania; Asst Brand Man. Procter & Gamble 1969–72, Brand Man. 1972–75, Assoc. Advertising Man. 1975–81, Div. Man. 1981–83; Vice-Pres. Marketing Kraft Inc. 1983–85, Group Vice-Pres., Pres. Refrigerated Products Group 1985–89, Pres. Kraft Gen. Foods Canada 1989–91, Gen. Foods USA 1991–95, Chair. and CEO Kraft Foods Inc. 1994–97; Chair., CEO and Pres. Quaker Oats Co. 1997–2001; Vice-Chair. Pepsi Co. Inc. 2001–03; Chair. and CEO 3M Co. 2005–; mem. Bd of Dirs Aon Corpn, Illinois Tool Works Inc., Econ. Club of Chicago, Grocery Manufacturers of America; mem. Bd of Trustees Lyric Opera of Chicago, Ravinia Festival, Highland Park, Chicago Urban League; Decorated Silver Star, Purple Heart. *Leisure interests:* golf, tennis, skiing. *Address:* 3M Company, 3M Center, St Paul, MN 55144, USA (office). *Telephone:* (651) 733-1110 (office). *Fax:* (651) 733-9973 (office). *Website:* www.mmm.com (office).

MORRISON, Toni, MA; American novelist and academic; *Goheen Professor in the Humanities Emerita, Princeton University;* b. (Chloe Anthony Wofford), 18 Feb. 1931, Lorain, Ohio; d. of George Wofford and Ella Ramah (Willis) Wofford; m. Harold Morrison 1958 (divorced 1964); two c.; ed Lorain High School, Howard Univ., Cornell Univ.; taught English and Humanities, Tex. Southern Univ. 1955–57, Howard Univ. 1957–64; Ed., then Sr Ed. Random House, New York 1965–85; Assoc. Prof. of English, State Univ. of New York 1971–72, Schweitzer Prof. of the Humanities 1984–89; Robert F. Goheen Prof. of the Humanities, Princeton Univ. 1989–, now Emer.; Visiting Lecturer Yale Univ. 1976–77, Bard Coll. 1986–88; Clark Lecturer Trinity Cambridge 1990; Massey Lecturer Harvard Univ. 1990; mem. Council, Authors Guild, American Acad. of Arts and Sciences, American Acad. of Arts and Letters, Authors League of America, Nat. Council on the Arts; Commdr Ordre des Arts et des Lettres; Ohioana Book Award 1975, American Acad. and Inst. of Arts and Letters Award 1977, Nat. Book Critics Circle Awards 1977, 1997, NY State Gov.'s Arts Award 1987, Nobel Prize for Literature 1993, Nat. Book Foundation Medal 1995, Nat. Humanities Medal 2000. *Publications:* The Bluest Eye 1970, Sula 1974, The Black Book (ed) 1974, Song of Solomon 1977,

Tar Baby 1983, Dreaming Emmett (play) 1986, Beloved 1987 (Pulitzer Prize and Robert F. Kennedy Book Award 1988), Jazz 1992, Playing in the Dark: Whiteness and the Literary Imagination (lectures) 1992, Race-ing Justice, Engendering Power (ed, essays) 1992, Honey and Rue (song cycle) 1993, Nobel Prize Speech 1994, Birth of a Nation'hood: Gaze, Script and Spectacle in the O. J. Simpson Trial 1997, Paradise 1998, Collected Essays of James Baldwin (ed) 1998, Love 2003, A Mercy 2008; co-author, for children: The Big Box (poems) 1999, The Book of Mean People 2002, The Ant or the Grasshopper, The Lion or the Mouse 2003. *Address:* Program in Creative Writing, Princeton University, Room 305, 185 Nassau Street, Princeton, NJ 08544, USA (office). *Telephone:* (609) 258-1071 (office). *Fax:* (609) 258-1454 (office). *Website:* www.princeton.edu (office).

MORRISON, Van, OBE; British singer, songwriter and musician; b. (George Ivan Morrison), 31 Aug. 1945, Belfast, Northern Ireland; one d.; left school aged 15; joined The Monarchs, playing in Germany; founder and lead singer, Them 1964–67; solo artist 1967–; BRIT Award for Outstanding Contribution to British Music 1994, Q Award for Best Songwriter 1995, Grammy Award for Best Pop Collaboration with Vocals 1995, BMI Icon Award 2004, Ronnie Scott Award for Int. Male Singer 2007. *Recordings include:* albums: Blowin' Your Mind 1967, Astral Weeks 1968, Moondance 1970, His Band and Street Choir 1970, Tupelo Honey 1971, Saint Dominic's Preview 1972, Hardnose the Highway 1973, It's Too Late To Stop Now 1974, Veedon Fleece 1974, This Is Where I Came In 1977, A Period of Transition 1977, Wavelength 1978, Into the Music 1979, Common One 1980, Beautiful Vision 1982, Inarticulate Speech of the Heart 1983, Live At The Royal Opera House, Belfast 1984, A Sense of Wonder 1984, No Guru, No Method, No Teacher 1986, Poetics Champion Compose 1987, Irish Heartbeat 1988, Avalon Sunset 1989, Enlightenment 1990, Hymns to the Silence 1991, Bang Masters 1990, The Best of Van Morrison 1993, Too Long in Exile 1993, A Night in San Francisco 1994, Days Like This 1995, Songs of the Mose Allison: Tell Me Something 1996, The Healing Game 1997, Tell Me Something 1997, Brown Eyed Girl 1998, The Masters 1999, Super Hits 1999, Back On Top 1999, The Skiffle Sessions: Live in Belfast 1998 2000, You Win Again 2000, Down The Road 2002, What's Wrong With This Picture? 2003, Magic Time 2005, Pay the Devil 2006, Keep it Simple 2008. *Address:* c/o Polydor Ltd, Black Lion House, 72–80 Black Lion Lane, Hammersmith, London, W6 9BE, England. *Website:* www.vanmorrison.co.uk.

MORRITT, Rt Hon. Sir (Robert) Andrew, Kt, PC, CVO, QC; British judge; *The Chancellor of The High Court;* b. 5 Feb. 1938, London; s. of Robert Augustus Morritt and Margaret Mary Morritt (née Tyldesley Jones); m. Sarah Simonetta Merton 1962; two s.; ed Eton Coll., Magdalene Coll., Cambridge; 2nd Lt Scots Guards 1956–58; called to Bar, Lincoln's Inn 1962, QC 1977, Bencher 1984, Treas. 2005; Jr Counsel to Sec. of State for Trade in Chancery Matters 1970–77, to Attorney-Gen. in Charity Matters 1972–77; Attorney-Gen. to HRH The Prince of Wales 1978–88; a Judge of High Court of Justice, Chancery Div. 1988–94; a Lord Justice of Appeal 1994–2000; Vice-Chancellor, Co. Palatine of Lancaster 1991–94; The Chancellor of The High Court 2000–; Pres. Council of the Inns of Court 1997–2000; mem. Gen. Council of Bar 1969–73, Advisory Cttee on Legal Educ. 1972–76, Top Salaries Review Body 1982–87. *Leisure interests:* fishing, shooting. *Address:* Royal Courts of Justice, Strand, London, WC2A 2LL, England (office). *Telephone:* (20) 7947-7477 (office). *Fax:* (20) 7947-6572 (office). *E-mail:* elaine.harbert@judiciary.gsi.gov.uk (office). *Website:* www.hmcourts-service.gov.uk (office).

MORSCHAKOVA, Tamara Georgyevna, DJurSc; Russian judge; b. 28 March 1938, Moscow; m.; one d.; ed Moscow State Univ.; jr researcher, Inst. of State and Law, USSR Acad. of Sciences 1958–71; Sr researcher, chief, then leading researcher All-Union Research Inst. of Soviet Construction and Law 1971–91; mem. Scientific-Consultative Council, Supreme Court of Russian Fed. 1985–; Prof., Moscow State Juridical Acad. 1987–; Justice, Constitutional Court of Russian Fed. 1991–95, Deputy Chair. 1995–2002, Councillor 2002–; Head of Chair, State Univ. Higher School of Economics 2001–; Honoured Jurist of Russian Fed.; Honoured Scientist of Russian Fed. *Publications:* books include Efficiency of Justice 1975, Reform of Justice 1990, Commentary to Legislation on Judiciary 2003, Criminal Procedure Law 2003. *Address:* c/o Constitutional Court of Russian Federation, 103132 Moscow, Ilyinka str. 21, Russia (office). *Telephone:* (495) 206-16-29 (office). *Website:* www.ksrf.ru (office).

MORSE, Sir (Christopher) Jeremy, Kt, KCMG; British banker; b. 10 Dec. 1928, London; s. of the late Francis J. Morse and Kinbarra (née Armfield-Marrow) Morse; m. Belinda M. Mills 1955; three s. one d.; ed Winchester Coll., and New Coll., Oxford; fmrly with Glyn, Mills & Co., Dir 1964; Dir, Legal and Gen. Assurance Society Ltd 1963–64, 1975–87; Exec. Dir, Bank of England 1965–72, Dir (non-exec.) 1993–97; Alt. Gov., IMF 1966–72; Chair. of Deputies of 'Cttee of Twenty', IMF 1972–74; Deputy Chair., Lloyds Bank Ltd 1975–77, Chair. 1977–93; Chair., Lloyds Merchant Bank Holdings 1985–88; Dir (non-exec.) ICI 1981–93, Zeneca 1993–99; Chair. Cttee of London Clearing Bankers 1980–82, City Communications Centre 1985–87; mem. Council, Lloyd's 1987–98; mem. NEDC 1977–81; Pres., Inst. Int. d'Études Bancaires 1982–83, Int. Monetary Conf. 1985–86, Banking Fed. of EC 1988–90, Chartered Inst. of Bankers 1992–93; Vice-Pres., Business in the Community 1986–98; Chair., City Arts Trust 1977–79, Per Jacobsson Foundation 1987–99, Governing Bodies Asscn 1994–99; Chancellor, Bristol Univ. 1988–2003; Pres., Classical Asscn 1989–90; Fellow, All Souls Coll., Oxford 1953–68, 1983–, Sub-Warden 2004–06; Chair. Trustees, Beit Memorial Fellowships for Medical Research 1976–2003; Fellow, Winchester Coll. 1966–83, Warden 1987–97; Hon. Life mem. British Chess Fed. 1988–, Hon. Master of Chess Composition, FIDE 2006–; Hon. DLitt (City) 1977, Hon. DSc (Aston) 1984, Hon. LLD (Bristol) 1989. *Publication:* Chess Problems: Tasks and Records 1995. *Leisure interests:* poetry, golf, problems and puzzles, coarse gardening. *Address:* 102A Drayton Gardens, London, SW10 9RJ, England (home). *Telephone:* (20) 7370-2265 (home).

MORTADA, Hani; Syrian government official, academic and paediatrician; *Minister of Higher Education;* b. 1939, Damascus; m.; three c.; ed Damascus Univ.; Head Paediatrics Dept, Faculty of Medicine, Damascus Univ. 1987–92, Dean Faculty of Medicine 1991–2000, Pres. Damascus Univ. 2000–03; Minister of Higher Educ. 2003–. *Address:* Ministry of Higher Education, ave Kasem Amin, ar-Rawda, Damascus, Syria (office). *Telephone:* (11) 2129870 (office). *Fax:* (11) 3327719 (office). *E-mail:* mhe@scs-net.org (office). *Website:* www.moufadaleh.org (office).

MORTELL, Michael Philip, MSc, MS, PhD; Irish mathematician and university administrator; *Professor of Applied Mathematics, University College, Cork;* b. 9 Feb. 1941, Cork; m. Patricia Yule 1967; two d.; ed Charleville Christian Bros School, Univ. Coll., Cork and California Inst. of Tech., USA; Asst Prof. and Assoc. Prof., Center for Application of Math., Lehigh Univ., USA 1967–72; Lecturer in Math., Univ. Coll. Cork 1972–89, Registrar 1979–89, Pres. 1989–99, Prof. Applied Math. 1999–; Visiting Prof., Univ. of British Columbia, Canada 1976–77, Univ. of Queensland, Australia 1979; Visiting Assoc., California Inst. of Tech. and New York Univ. 1999–2000; Foundation Fellow, Univ. of Auckland, NZ 2003; Vice-Chancellor Nat. Univ. of Ireland; Chair. Conf. of Heads of Irish Univs; Hon. LLD (Univ. of Dublin, Queen's Univ. Belfast, Limerick Univ.). *Publications:* some 40 papers on nonlinear acoustics. *Leisure interests:* reading, art, gardening, sport. *Address:* Department of Applied Mathematics, University College, Cork, Ireland (office). *Telephone:* (21) 4903402 (office). *Fax:* (21) 4270813 (office). *E-mail:* m.mortell@ucc.ie (office). *Website:* euclid.ucc.ie (office).

MORTENSEN, Viggo Peter, Jr, BA; American/Danish actor, poet, photographer, painter and jazz musician; b. 20 Oct. 1958, New York City; s. of Viggo P. Mortensen (Danish) and Grace Mortensen (American); m. Exene Cervenka 1987 (separated 1990, divorced 1998); one s.; ed St Lawrence Univ., Canton, NY; spent early childhood in Manhattan, family travelled widely and spent several years living in Venezuela, Argentina and Denmark (where he worked as a truck driver); worked as trans. for Swedish ice hockey team during Winter Olympics, Lake Placid 1980; began acting in New York, studying with Warren Robertson; appeared in several plays and movies, eventually moved to Los Angeles; Owner Perceval Press (publishing co.). *Stage appearances:* Tybalt in Romeo and Juliet, Indiana Repertory Theatre, Indianapolis 1985–86, Nazi capt. in Bent, Coast Playhouse, West Hollywood, Calif. 1987, Live at Beyond Baroque, Beyond Baroque, Venice, Calif. 1999, Beyond Baroque Live 2, Beyond Baroque 2004. *Films:* Witness 1985, Salvation! 1987, Prison 1988, Fresh Horses 1988, The Reflecting Skin 1990, Tripwire 1990, Leatherface: Texas Chainsaw Massacre III 1990, Young Guns II 1990, The Indian Runner 1991, Boiling Point 1993, Deception 1993, Carlito's Way 1993, The Young Americans 1993, American Yakuza 1993, The Crew 1994, Floundering 1994, Ewangelia wedlug Harry'ego 1994, Gimlet 1995, Crimson Tide 1995, The Passion of Darkly Noon 1995, Black Velvet Pantsuit 1995, The Prophecy 1995, The Portrait of a Lady 1996, Albino Alligator 1996, Daylight 1996, G.I. Jane 1997, La Pistola de mi hermano 1997, A Perfect Murder 1998, Psycho 1998, A Walk on the Moon 1999, 28 Days 2000, The Lord of the Rings: The Fellowship of the Ring 2001, The Lord of the Rings: The Two Towers 2002, The Lord of the Rings: The Return of the King 2003, Hidalgo 2004, A History of Violence 2005, Alatriste 2006, Eastern Promises 2007, Appaloosa 2008, Good 2008. *Television:* George Washington (miniseries) 1984, Search for Tomorrow (series) 1985, Once in a Blue Moon 1990, Vanishing Point 1997. *Achievements:* painted the large murals in his artist's studio in film A Perfect Murder 1998. *Albums:* 1991 (poetry) 1991, Don't Tell Me What to Do (music and poetry) 1994, One Less Thing to Worry About (music and poetry; with others) 1997, Live at Beyond Baroque (with others) 1999, One Man's Meat 1999, The Other Parade (music and poetry; with others) 1999, Pandemoniumfromamerica (with Buckethead) 2003, Beyond Baroque Live 2 (with others) 2004, Please Tomorrow (with Buckethead) 2004, This That and the Other (with Buckethead) 2004, Intelligence Failure (with Buckethead) 2005. *Publications:* Ten Last Night (poetry) 1993, Recent Forgeries (also illustrator, with accompanying CD) 1998, Coincidence of Memory (also illustrator) 2002, Sign Language (also photographer) 2002, Un hueco en el sol 2003; audiobooks: Myth: Dreams of the World 1996, The New Yorker Out Loud (contrib.) 1998; non-fiction: The Horse Is Good (also photographer) 2004, Twilight of Empire: Responses to Occupation (co-author) 2004, Strange Familiar: The Work of Georg Gudni (co-author) 2005; photography: Hole in the Sun 2002, 45301 2003, Miyelo (with Mike Davis, James Mooney, and Sonny Richards) 2004, Mo Te Upoko-o-te-ika/For Wellington 2004, Linger 2005. *Leisure interests:* horse riding, San Lorenzo football club (Buenos Aires), New York Mets professional baseball team, Montréal Canadiens professional ice hockey team. *Address:* c/o Jenny Rawlings, Creative Artists Agency, 9830 Wilshire Blvd, Beverly Hills, CA 90212-1825, USA (office). *Telephone:* (310) 288-4545 (office). *Fax:* (310) 288-4800 (office). *Website:* www.caa.com (office).

MORTIER, Gerard; Belgian music director; *Director-General, Paris Opéra;* b. 25 Nov. 1943, Ghent; ed Univ. of Ghent; engaged in journalism and communications 1966–67; Admin. Asst Flanders Festival 1968–72; Artistic Planner, Deutsche Oper am Rhein, Düsseldorf 1972–73; Asst Admin. Frankfurt Opera 1973–77; Dir of Artistic Production, Hamburg Staatsoper 1977–79; Tech. Programme Consultant, Théâtre Nat. de l'Opéra, Paris 1979–81; Dir-Gen. Belgian Nat. Opera, Brussels 1981–91; Dir Salzburg Music Festival 1992–2001; Fellow, Wissenschaftskolleg (Inst. for Advanced Study), Berlin 2001–02; Dir, Kultur Ruhr triennial arts festival 2002; Dir-Gen. Paris Opéra 2004–09; announced as Gen. Man. and Artistic Dir New York City

Opera 2007, resgnd 2008; Artistic Dir designate, Teatro Real, Madrid (2010–); mem. Acad. of Arts, Berlin; Dr hc (Antwerp), (Salzburg); Commdr, Ordre des Arts et des Lettres 2000, Chevalier, Légion d'honneur 2005, Grand Officier Ordre de Leopold 2005. *Address:* c/o Opéra National de Paris, 120 rue de Lyon, 75012 Paris, France (office). *Telephone:* 1-40-01-16-06 (office). *Fax:* 1-40-01-20-59 (office). *E-mail:* gmortier@operadeparis.fr (office). *Website:* www.opera-de-paris.fr (office).

MORTIER, Roland F. J., DPhil; Belgian academic; *Professor Emeritus, Université Libre de Bruxelles;* b. 21 Dec. 1920, Ghent; s. of the late Arthur Mortier and Berthe Baudson; m. Loyse Triffaux 1948; one s.; ed Antwerp Atheneum, Univ. Libre de Bruxelles and Univ. of Ghent; Prof., Univ. Libre de Bruxelles 1955–85, Prof. Emer. 1990–; Visiting Prof., Univs of Toronto, Stanford, Yale, Paris, Cologne, Jerusalem, London, Cleveland, Maryland, Duisburg, Pisa; Vice-Pres. Inst. des Hautes Etudes de Belgique; Past Pres. Soc. Diderot, FCLA, ISECS; mem. Acad. Royale de Langue et de Littérature Françaises, Belgium, Inst de France 1993; Foreign mem. Hungarian Acad. of Sciences; Corresp. Fellow, British Acad., Academia Europaea; other professional appointments and affiliations; Hon. mem. of the Acad. of Japan 2003; Chevalier, Légion d'honneur 2001; Dr hc (Montpellier, Göttingen, Jerusalem); Prix Francqui 1965, Prix Montaigne 1983, Prix Counson 1985, Prix de l'Union rationaliste de France 1993, Giltsilver Medal of the Acad. Française 2001, Grand Prix de la Francophonie of the Acad. Française 2006. *Publications:* Diderot en Allemagne 1954, Clartés et Ombres du Siècle des Lumières 1969, Le Tableau littéraire de la France au XVIIIe Siècle 1972, La Poétique des Ruines en France 1974, L'Originalité, une nouvelle catégorie esthétique 1982, Le coeur et la raison 1990, Anacharsis Cloots, ou l'Utopie Foudroyée 1995, Les combats des lumières 2000, Le prince d'Albanie 2000; critical edns of Voltaire and Diderot, of Prince de Ligne 2001, Le 18[e]siècle français au quotidien 2002, Selected Works of the Prince de Ligne (3 vols) 2006. *Leisure interests:* reading, walking, swimming, travel. *Address:* 10 avenue Général de Longueville, BP 12, 1150 Brussels, Belgium (home). *Telephone:* (2) 772-01-94 (home). *Fax:* (2) 772-01-94 (home).

MORTIMER, Hugh Roger, LVO, BSc, MA; British diplomatist; *Deputy Head of Mission, British Embassy, Berlin;* b. 19 Sept. 1949, Salisbury; ed Cheltenham Coll., Univ. of Surrey, King's Coll. London; joined FCO 1973, served Rome, Singapore, UN, New York; on secondment to German Ministry of Foreign Affairs 1990; Deputy Head of Mission, Berlin 1991–94, 2005–; FCO 1994–95, Ankara 1997–2000; Amb. to Slovenia 2001–05. *Leisure interests:* jogging, guitar playing, cinema. *Address:* British Embassy, Wilhelmstr. 70–71, 10117 Berlin, Germany (office). *Telephone:* (30) 204570 (office). *Fax:* (30) 20457594 (office). *E-mail:* info@britischebotschaft.de (office). *Website:* www.britischebotschaft.de (office).

MORTON, Donald Charles, PhD, FAA; Canadian astronomer; *Researcher Emeritus, Herzberg Institute of Astrophysics, National Research Council of Canada;* b. 12 June 1933; s. of Charles O. Morton and Irene M. Wightman; m. Winifred Austin 1970; one s. one d.; ed Univ. of Toronto and Princeton Univ., NJ; astronomer, US Naval Research Lab. 1959–61; from Research Assoc. to Sr Research Astronomer (with rank of Prof.), Princeton Univ. 1961–76; Dir Anglo-Australian Observatory (Epping and Coonabarabran, NSW) 1976–86; Dir-Gen. Herzberg Inst. of Astrophysics, Nat. Research Council of Canada 1986–2000, Researcher Emer. 2001–; mem. Int. Astronomical Union, Royal Astronomical Soc. (Assoc. 1980), Astronomical Soc. of Australia (Pres. 1981–83, Hon. mem. 1986), Canadian Astronomical Soc., Canadian Asscn of Physicists; Fellow Australian Acad. of Science 1984–. *Publications:* research papers in professional journals. *Leisure interests:* mountaineering, running. *Address:* Herzberg Institute of Astrophysics, National Research Council of Canada, 5071 W Saanich Road, Victoria, BC V9E 2E7, Canada (office). *Telephone:* (250) 363-8313 (office). *Fax:* (250) 363-0045 (office). *E-mail:* don.morton@nrc-cnrc.gc.ca (office). *Website:* www.hia-iha.nrc-cnrc.gc.ca (office).

MOSA, Markus; German business executive; *CEO, Edeka Zentrale AG;* b. 1967, Brühl bei Köln; m.; two c.; joined Spar Handels AG 1994, Schenefeld 1994, held several positions –1999, joined Netto Marken-Discount 1999, fmr Spokesman of Exec. Bd, Edeka AG (acquired Netto), Hamburg, Chief Financial Officer Edeka Zentrale AG –2008, CEO 2008–. *Address:* Edeka Zentrale AG & Co. KG, New-York-Ring 6, 22297 Hamburg, Germany (office). *Telephone:* (40) 63-77-0 (office). *Fax:* (40) 63-77-22-31 (office). *E-mail:* info@edeka.de (office). *Website:* www.edeka.de (office).

MOSBACHER, Robert Adam, BSc; American energy industry executive and fmr government official; *Chairman, Mosbacher Energy Company;* b. 11 March 1927, New York; s. of Emil Mosbacher and Gertrude (née Schwartz) Mosbacher; m. Georgette Paulsin 1986; one s. three d.; ed Washington and Lee Univs; ind. oil and gas producer 1948–89, serving as Chair. and CEO Mosbacher Energy Co., Houston 1986–; Sec. of Commerce, Washington 1989–92; returned to Mosbacher Energy Co., also Vice-Chair. Mosbacher Power Group, Houston 1992–; Dir Texas Bankshares, Houston, New York Life Insurance Co.; Chair. Bd of Dirs, Choate School, Wallingford, Conn.; Dir Aspen Inst. Center for Strategic and Int. Studies; Chair. Nat. Finance, George Bush for Pres.; Pres. Ford Finance Cttee; Gen. Campaign Chair., then Chief Fundraiser 1992 Republican Presidential Campaign; Gen. Chair. Finance, Republican Nat. Cttee, Washington, DC 1992–; currently Chair. Int. Econ. Alliance, Greater Houston Partnership; Dir Texas Heart Inst.; mem. Mid-Continent Oil and Gas Asscn (fmr Chair.), American Petroleum Inst. (Dir, Exec. Cttee), US Oil and Gas Asscn (mem. Exec. Cttee), Nat. Petroleum Council (Chair. 1984–85), All American Wildcatters Asscn (fmr Chair.), American Asscn Petroleum Landmen; Hon. LLD (Lee Univ.) 1984. *Address:* Mosbacher Energy Corp., 712 Main Street, Suite 2200, Houston, TX 77002, USA.

MOSBAKK, Kurt; Norwegian politician; *Chairman, Norwegian Tourist Board;* b. 21 Nov. 1934, Orkdal; s. of Henrik Mosbakk and Jenny Mosbakk; m. Grete Tidemandsen 1975; two s. one d.; ed Norwegian Coll. Econs and Business Admin; Pvt. Sec. to Minister of Defence 1964–65; Minister of Trade and Shipping 1986–88; County Exec. of Østford 1988–; Deputy Chair. Norwegian Defence Comm. 1990–92; fmr Deputy Mayor Lørenskog; Chair. Akershus Co. Labour Party 1969–74; Chief Co. Exec. Finnmark Co. 1976; Chair. Bd Norwegian State Housing Bank 1988–; Chair. Norwegian Tourist Bd 1990–. *Leisure interest:* literature. *Address:* NORTRA, Drammensvn 40, PO Box 2893 Solli, 0230 Oslo, Norway.

MOSCOSO DE GRUBER, Mireya Elisa; Panamanian politician and fmr head of state; b. 1 July 1946, Panama; d. of Plinio Antonio Moscoso and Elisa Rodríguez de Moscoso; m. Arnulfo Arias (died 1988); one s.; ed Colegio Comercial María Inmaculada, Miami Dade Community Coll., USA; fmr Exec. Sec. Social Security Agency; fmr Sales Man., Deputy Man. and Gen. Man. Arkapal SA (coffee co.); Govt rep. on numerous int. missions; spent ten years in exile in USA; Pres. Partido Arnulfista; Pres. of Panama 1999–2004; fmr Pres. Arias Foundation, Madrid; fmr mem. Asscn of Boquete Coffee Growers, Asscn of Milk Producers, Nat. Asscn of Ranchers. *Address:* c/o Partido Panameñista, Avda Perú y Calle 38e, No 37–41, al lado de Casa la Esperanza, Apdo 9610, Panamá 4, Panama (office).

MOSCOVICI, Pierre; French politician; b. 16 Sept. 1957; s. of Serge Moscovici and Marie Bromberg; ed Univ. of Paris X, I, IV, Ecole nat. d'administration; official, Cour des Comptes 1984–88; Adviser, pvt. office of Minister of Nat. Educ., Youth and Sport 1988–89, Special Adviser to Minister 1989–90; Head. Gen. Planning Comm.'s Public Sector Modernization and Finance Dept 1990; mem. Parti Socialiste (PS) Nat. Council and Nat. Bureau 1990, Nat. Sec. responsible for policy research and devt 1990–92, 1995–97, Nat. Treas. 1992–94; mem. Doubs Gen. Council, Sochaux-Grand-Charmont canton 1994–2001; Montbéliard municipal councillor 1995–2001; Regional Councillor Franche Comté 1998–2004 mem. European Parl. 1994–97; Nat. Ass. Deputy for 4th Doubs constituency 1997, 2007–; Minister Del. attached to Minister for Foreign Affairs, with responsibility for European Affairs 1997–2002; Rep. Convention on the Future of Europe 2002; Regional Councillor Franche-Comté. *Publications include:* A la recherche de la gauche perdue 1994, L'urgence, plaidoyer pour une autre politique 1997, Au coeur de l'Europe 1999, L'Europe, une puissance dans la mondialisation 2001, Les 10 questions qui fâchent les Européens 2004, L'Europe est morte, vive l'Europe 2006. *Leisure interests:* tennis, skiing. *Address:* 51 avenue des Allies, 25200 Montbéliard (office); Assemblée Nationale, 126 rue de la Université, 75355 Paris 07 SP, France. *Telephone:* 3-81-32-31-69 (office). *Fax:* 3-81-32-31-67 (office). *E-mail:* pmoscovici@assemblee-national.fr (office). *Website:* www.assemblee-nationale.fr.

MØSE, Erik; judge; *Judge, International Criminal Tribunal for Rwanda;* b. 1950; ed Univ. of Oslo, postgraduate studies in Geneva, Switzerland; Lecturer, Univ. of Oslo 1981–; Head of Div., Ministry of Justice –1986; fmr Deputy Judge; Supreme Court Advocate at Solicitor Gen.'s Office 1986–93; Judge, Court of Appeals, Oslo 1993–99; Vice-Pres. Int. Criminal Tribunal for Rwanda 1999–2003, Pres. 2003–07, Judge 2007–; fmr Chair. Council of Europe's Steering Cttee for Human Rights, Cttee for drafting European Convention for the Prevention of Torture, and several other cttees; Fellow Univ. of Essex, UK; Commdr, Royal Norwegian Order of Merit; Dr hc (Essex). *Publications:* numerous books and publs on human rights. *Address:* International Criminal Tribunal for Rwanda, Arusha International Conference Centre, PO Box 6016, Arusha, Tanzania (office). *Telephone:* (212) 963-2850 (UN, New York) (office); (27) 250-4369 (Arusha) (office); (27) 250-4372 (Arusha) (office). *Fax:* (212) 963-2848 (UN, New York) (office); (27) 250-4000 (Arusha) (office); (27) 250-4373 (Arusha) (office). *E-mail:* ictr-press@un.org (office). *Website:* www.ictr.org (office).

MOSELEY BRAUN, Carol, BA, JD; American business executive, lawyer and fmr politician; *President, Ambassador Organics, Good Food Organics;* b. 16 Aug. 1947; d. of Joseph J. Moseley and Edna A. Moseley (née Davie); m. Michael Braun 1973 (divorced 1986); one s.; ed Univ. of Illinois-Chicago, Univ. of Chicago, Kennedy School of Govt, Harvard Univ.; fmr Asst Attorney, Davis, Miner & Barnhill; fmr Attorney, Jones, Ware & Grenard; fmr Asst US Attorney for Northern Dist of Ill.; mem. Ill. House of Reps 1978–88; Cook Co. Recorder of Deeds 1988; Senator from Ill. (first African-American woman to be elected to Senate) 1993–99; Amb. to NZ and Samoa 1999–2001; Stewart Mott Visiting Prof., Morris Brown Coll. 2001; Prof. of Business Law, DePaul Univ. Grad. School of Business 2001–02; business consultant, CMBraun LLC 1998–; f. Moseley Braun LLC (law firm), Chicago; Founder and Pres. Ambassador Organics, Good Food Organics (organic food products) 2005–; sought Democratic party presidential candidacy 2004; mem. two corp. bds; Hon. PhD; 11 Hon. doctorates in law, letters and political science; numerous awards. *Address:* Ambassador Organics, 1634 East 53rd Street, 2nd Floor, Chicago, IL 60615, USA (office). *Telephone:* (773) 288-3700 (office). *Fax:* (773) 288-3708 (office). *E-mail:* cmbraun@@ambassadororganics.com (office). *Website:* www.ambassadororganics.com (office).

MOSER, Baron (Life Peer), cr. 2001, of Regents Park in the London Borough of Camden; **Claus Adolf Moser,** KCB, CBE, FBA; British statistician and academic; b. 24 Nov. 1922, Berlin; s. of the late Dr. Ernest Moser and Lotte Moser; m. Mary Oxlin 1949; one s. two d.; ed Frensham Heights School, London School of Econs; RAF 1943–46; Asst Lecturer in Statistics, LSE 1946–49, Lecturer 1949–55, Reader in Social Statistics 1955–61, Prof. of Social Statistics 1961–70; Statistical Adviser Cttee on Higher Educ. 1961–64; Dir LSE Higher Educ. Research Unit 1964–; Dir Royal Opera House Covent Garden 1965–87, Chair. 1974–87; Dir Cen. Statistical Office, Head of Govt Statistical Service 1967–78; Visiting Fellow, Nuffield Coll. 1972–80; Vice-

Chair. N. M. Rothschild and Sons 1978–84, Dir 1978–90; Dir The Economist 1979–93, Chair. Economist Intelligence Unit 1978–84; Warden of Wadham Coll., Oxford 1984–93, Pres. 1989–90; Chair. Askonas Holt Ltd 1990–2002, British Museum Devt Trust 1993–2004, Basic Skills Agency 1997–2002; Dir Equity & Law Life Assurance Soc. 1980–87, Int. Medical Statistics Inc. 1982–88, Octopus Publishing Group 1982–87, Property and Reversionary Investments 1986–87; Chancellor Univ. of Keele 1986–2002, Open Univ. of Israel 1994–2004; Pres. British Asscn 1989–95; Pro-Vice-Chancellor Oxford Univ. 1991–93; Trustee Soros Foundation 1993–1997; Gov. Royal Shakespeare Theatre 1982–93, British American Arts Asscn 1982–, Pilgrim Trust 1982–99, Nat. Comm. on Educ. 1991–95; mem. Gov. Body, Royal Ballet School 1974–87; Hon. Fellow RAM 1970, LSE 1976, Inst. of Educ., Univ. of London 1997, RIBA 2005; Commdr Ordre nat. du Mérite 1976, Commdr's Cross, Order of Merit (FRG) 1986; Hon. DScS (Southampton) 1975, (Leeds, Surrey, Keele, York, Sussex, City Univs) 1977, Hon. DTech (Brunel) 1981, Hon. DSc (Wales) 1990, (Liverpool) 1991, Hon. DScEcon (London) 1991, Dr hc (Brighton) 1994. *Publications:* Measurement of Levels of Living 1957, Survey Methods in Social Investigation 1958, Social Conditions in England and Wales (co-author) 1958, British Towns (co-author) 1961 and papers in statistical journals. *Leisure interest:* music. *Address:* 3 Regents Park Terrace, London, NW1 7EE, England (home). *Telephone:* (20) 7485-1619 (home).

MOSES, Edwin (Ed), BSc, MBA; American athlete, sports administrator, diplomatist and business executive; b. 31 Aug. 1955, Dayton, Ohio; m. Myrella Bordt Moses 1982; ed Fairview High School and Morehouse Coll., Atlanta, Ga; won gold medal for 400m hurdles, Olympic Games, Montreal 1976 (in world record time), LA 1984; one of only three men to break 48 secs for 400m hurdles; holds record for greatest number of wins consecutively in any event; winner 122 straight races 1977–87, lost to Danny Harris June 1987; at one time held 13 fastest times ever recorded; retd 1988, comeback 1991, 2nd comeback 2003; competed int. for USA in bobsleigh and 2- and 4-man sleds; mem. Jt Olympic Cttee Athletes Comm., Exec. Bd of US Olympic Cttee, Bd of Dirs Jesse Owens Foundation; US Rep. to Int. Amateur Athletic Fed. 1984–; Pres. Int. Amateur Athletics Asscn; dynamics engineer, Pomona, Calif.; fmr Chair. US Olympic Cttee Substance Abuse Cttee; Founding Partner Platinum Group (representing athletes' business interests); Financial Consultant with Solomon Smith Barney; Vice-Chair US Olympic Foundation; Jesse Owens Int. Award 1981, US Track and Field Hall of Fame 1994, Speaker of the Athletes' Oath at 1984 Olympic Games. *Leisure interests:* aviation, scientific breakthroughs in athletics, scuba diving. *Address:* Robinson-Humphrey Co., 3333 Peachtree Road NE, Atlanta, GA 30326, USA.

MOSES, Lincoln Ellsworth, PhD; American professor of statistics; *Professor Emeritus, Stanford University;* b. 21 Dec. 1921, Kansas City; s. of Edward Walter Moses and Virginia (née Holmes) Moses; m. 1st Jean Runnels 1942; m. 2nd Mary Louise Coale 1968; two s. three d.; ed Stanford Univ.; Asst Prof. of Educ., Columbia Univ. 1950–52; Asst Prof. of Statistics, Stanford Univ. and Stanford Medical School 1952–55, Assoc. Prof. 1955–59, Prof. 1959–, now Emer., Assoc. Dean of Humanities and Sciences 1965–68, 1985–86, Dean of Graduate Studies 1969–75; (First) Admin. Energy Information Admin, US Dept of Energy 1978–80; Guggenheim Fellow, Fellow at Center for Advanced Study in Behavioral Sciences. *Publications:* (with Herman Chernoff) Elementary Decision Theory 1959, Biostatistics Casebook (jt ed.) 1980, Think and Explain with Statistics 1986. *Leisure interests:* birds, chess. *Address:* Department of Health Research and Policy, Division of Biostatistics, HRP Building, Stanford University School of Medicine, Stanford, CA 94305-5405, USA (office). *Telephone:* (650) 851-8182 (home); (650) 723-6910 (office). *Fax:* (650) 725-6951 (office). *Website:* www.stanford.edu/dept/HRP (office).

MOSHAHED, Ahmad; Afghan diplomatist and government official; *Chairman, Independent Administrative Reform and Civil Service Commission;* Amb. to Iran in Transitional Govt 2004; Minister of Educ. 2004; currently Chair. Ind. Admin. Reform and Civil Service Comm., Kabul. *Address:* Independent Administrative Reform and Civil Service Commission, Shah Mahmood Khan Ghazi Watt, Prime Minister's Compound Opposite the Vice President's Office, Kabul, Afghanistan (office). *Website:* www.iarcsc.gov.af.

MOSHER, Gregory Dean, BFA; American theatre producer, director and academic; *Director of University Arts Initiatives and Adjunct Assistant Professor of Theatre Arts, Columbia University;* b. 15 Jan. 1949, New York; s. of Thomas Edward Mosher and Florence Christine Mosher; ed Oberlin Coll., Ithaca Coll., Juilliard School; Dir Stage 2 Goodman Theatre, Chicago 1974–77, Artistic Dir 1978–85; Artistic Dir Lincoln Center Theater 1985–92, Resident Dir 1992–2004; Dir Univ. Arts Initiatives and Adjunct Asst Prof. of Theatre Arts, Columbia Univ., New York 2004–; Chevalier, Ordre des Arts et des Lettres; two Tony Awards (as producer of revivals: Anything Goes, Our Town), Obie Award, Margo Jefferson, Outer Critics. *Productions include:* new works by Tennessee Williams, Studs Terkel, David Mamet, John Guare, Michael Weller, Wole Soyinka, Elaine May, David Rabe, Mbongeni Ngema, Edward Albee, Spalding Gray, Arthur Miller, Leonard Bernstein, Stephen Sondheim, Richard Nelson, Jerome Robbins; producer: Samuel Beckett's first directing work in US, Krapp's Last Tape 1979, Bosoms and Neglect 1979, Endgame 1980, The Man Who Had Three Arms 1983, Hurlyburly 1984, The Flying Karamazov Brothers "Juggling and Cheap Theatrics" 1986, The House of Blue Leaves 1986, The Front Page 1987, Death and the King's Horseman 1987, The Regard of Flight 1987, The Comedy of Errors 1987, Anything Goes 1987, Sarafina! 1988, Speed-the-Plow (Broadway and RNT) 1988, Our Town 1988, The Tenth Man 1989, Some Americans Abroad 1990, Six Degrees of Separation 1990, Monster in a Box 1991, Mule Bone 1991, Two Shakespearean Actors 1992, A Streetcar Named Desire 1992, Freak 1998, James Joyce's The Dead 2000. *Plays directed:* Glengarry Glen Ross (David Mamet), Broadway 1984–85, American Buffalo 1975, A Life in the Theater 1977,

Edmond 1982, Glengarry Glen Ross 1984, Speed-the-Plow (David Mamet), Danger: Memory (Miller premiere) 1987, Broadway 1988, London 1989, Our Town (50th anniversary production, Thornton Wilder), Broadway 1988, Oh Hell, Lincoln Center Theater 1989, Uncle Vanya 1990, Mr Gogol and Mr Preen 1991, A Streetcar Named Desire 1992, Stanley (producing dir) 1997. *Films:* American Buffalo 1996 (producer), The Prime Gig 2000 (dir). *Television includes:* King Lear (actor) 1974, The Comedy of Errors (dir) 1987, Uncle Vanya (dir) 1991, A Life in the Theatre (dir) 1993, The House of Blue Leaves (exec. producer) 1987. *Address:* Arts Initiative at Columbia University, 206 Prentis Hall, 632 West 125th Street, Mail Code 5011, New York, NY 10027, USA (office). *Telephone:* (212) 851-1872 (office). *E-mail:* gm2127@columbia.edu (office). *Website:* www.cuarts.com (office).

MOSHINSKY, Elijah, BA; British opera director; b. 8 Jan. 1946; s. of Abraham Moshinsky and Eva Moshinsky; m. Ruth Dyttman 1970; two s.; ed Melbourne Univ. and St Antony's Coll. Oxford; apptd to Royal Opera House 1973, Assoc. Producer 1979–; work for Royal Opera includes original productions of Peter Grimes 1975, Lohengrin 1978, The Rake's Progress 1979, Un Ballo in Maschera 1980; Macbeth 1981, Samson et Dalila 1981, Tannhäuser 1984, Otello 1987, Die Entführung aus dem Serail 1987, Attila 1990, Simon Boccanegra 1991, Stiffelio 1993, Aida 1994, Otello 1994, The Makropoulos Case 1996, The Queen of Spades 1998; has also produced work for ENO, Australian Opera, Metropolitan Opera, New York, Holland Festival, Maggio Musicale, Florence etc. *Theatre productions include:* Troilus and Cressida (Nat. Theatre) 1976, The Force of Habit (Nat. Theatre) 1976, Three Sisters (Albery) 1987, Light Up the Sky (Globe) 1987, Ivanov (Strand) 1989, Much Ado About Nothing (Strand) 1989, Another Time (Wyndham's) 1989, Shadowlands (Queen's) 1989, Cyrano de Bergerac 1992, Genghis Cohn 1993, Danton 1994; Dir Matador (Queen's) 1991, Becket (Haymarket) 1991, Reflected Glory (Vaudeville) 1992, Richard III 1998, The Female Odd Couple (Apollo) 2001; productions for BBC TV of works by Shakespeare, Ibsen and Sheridan. *Leisure interests:* painting, telephone conversation.

MOSIER, Frank Eugene; American business executive; b. 15 July 1930, Kersey, Pa; s. of Clarence Mosier and Helen Mosier; m. Julia M. Fife 1961; one s. one d.; ed Univ. of Pittsburgh; joined Standard Oil Co. Cleveland 1953, Vice-Pres. (supply and distribution) 1972–76, (supply and transport) 1976–77, Sr Vice-Pres. (marketing and refining) 1977–78, (supply and transport) 1978–82, (downstream petroleum dept) 1982–85, Exec. Vice-Pres. 1985–86, Pres. and COO 1986–88, BP America Inc. (following 1987 merger of BP and Standard Oil), Cleveland, Pres. 1987–88, Vice-Chair. 1988–91 (retd), Vice-Chair. Advisory Bd 1991–93; mem. Bd of Dirs Associated Estates Realty Corpn 1993–; fmr mem. Bd of Dirs Boykin Lodging Co. *Address:* c/o Board of Directors, Associated Estates Realty Corporation, 5025 Swetland Court, Richmond Heights, OH 44143-1467, USA.

MOSIMANN, Anton, OBE; Swiss chef and restaurateur; *Chairman, Mosimann's Ltd;* b. 23 Feb. 1947; s. of Otto Mosimann and Olga Mosimann; m. Kathrin Roth 1973; two s.; ed pvt. school in Switzerland; apprentice, Hotel Baeren, Twann; worked in Canada, France, Italy, Sweden, Japan, Belgium, Switzerland 1962–; cuisinier at Villa Lorraine, Brussels, Les Prés d'Eugénie, Eugénie-les-Bains, Les Frères Troisgros, Roanne, Paul Bocuse, Collonges au Mont d'Or, Moulin de Mougins; joined Dorchester Hotel, London 1975, Maître Chef des Cuisines 1975–88; owner, Mosimann's (fmr Belfry Club) 1988–, Mosimann's Party Service 1990–, The Mosimann Acad. 1995–, Creative Chefs 1996–; World Pres. Les Toques Blanches Internationales 1989–93; Visiting Prof., Univ. of Strathclyde 2003; Pres. Royal Warrant Holders' Asscn 2006–07; Hon. mem. Chefs' Asscns of Canada, Japan, Switzerland, SA, Freedom of City of London 1999; Croix de Chevalier du Mérite Agricole, Ordre Nat. du Mérite Agricole (France) 2006; Dr of Culinary Arts hc (Johnson and Wales Univ., USA), Hon. DSc (Bournemouth Univ.) 1998, Hon. Prof., Thames Valley Univ. 2004; Personalité de l'Année Award 1986,; Royal Warrant of Appointment to HRH the Prince of Wales 2000, Restauranteur of the Year, Int. Food and Beverage Forum, Rhode Island 2000, Lifetime Achievement Award (Hotel & Caterer) 2004, numerous awards in int. cookery competitions. *Television programmes include:* Anton Goes to Sheffield 1986 (Glenfiddich Award), Cooking with Mosimann (series) 1990, Anton Mosimann Naturally 1991–92, Natürlich, Leichtes Kochen (Swiss TV) 1997, Mosimann's Culinary Switzerland (Swiss TV) 1998. *Publications:* Cuisine à la Carte 1981, A New Style of Cooking: The Art of Anton Mosimann 1983, Cuisine Naturelle 1985, Anton Mosimann's Fish Cuisine 1988, The Art of Mosimann 1989, Cooking with Mosimann 1989, Anton Mosimann—Naturally 1991, The Essential Mosimann 1993, Mosimann's World 1996, Mosimann's Fresh 2006. *Leisure interests:* classic cars, collecting antiquarian cookery books, enjoying fine wine; passionate about food and travelling especially to food markets of the Far East. *Address:* c/o Mosimann's, 11B West Halkin Street, London, SW1X 8JL, England (office). *Telephone:* (20) 7235-9625 (office). *Fax:* (20) 7245-7847 (office). *E-mail:* amosimann@mosimann.com (office). *Website:* www.mosimann.com (office).

MOSISILI, Bethuel Pakalitha, BA, MEd; Lesotho politician; *Prime Minister and Minister of Defence and Public Service;* b. 14 March 1945, Waterfall; m.; two s. two d.; ed Univ. of Botswana, Lesotho and Swaziland, Univ. of Wis., USA, Univ. of SA, Simon Fraser Univ., Canada; joined Basutoland Congress Party 1967; Deputy Headmaster Bereng High School 1972–73; Asst Lecturer in African Languages, Univ. of Botswana, Lesotho and Swaziland 1973–76; Lecturer in African Languages, Nat. Univ. of Lesotho 1976–83; Sr Lecturer, Univ. of Fort Hare, SA 1983–84, Univ. of Transkei 1985–88, Univ. of Zululand 1989–92; mem. Parl. 1993–; Minister of Educ. and Training, Sports, Culture and Youth Affairs 1993–95; apptd Deputy Prime Minister 1995; Minister of Home Affairs and Local Govt 1995–98; Prime Minister of Lesotho and Minister of Defence and Public Service 1998–; fmr Deputy Leader Lesotho

Congress for Democracy, Leader 1998–; mem. Lesotho Educational Research Asscn, African Languages Asscn of SA, S African Pedagogical Soc. *Address:* Office of the Prime Minister, Government Office Complex, Phase 1 Qhobosheaneng, 50, PO Box 527, Maseru 100, Lesotho (office). *Telephone:* 22325043 (office). *Fax:* 22320662 (office). *E-mail:* mmajobo@cabinet.gov.ls (office). *Website:* www.lesotho.gov.ls (office).

MOSKOVSKY, Col-Gen. Aleksey Mikhailovich; Russian army officer; *Deputy Minister of Defence and Head of Armaments;* b. 1947, Smolensk; ed Kiev Higher Military Engineering Radio Technical School, Novosibirsk State Univ.; worked in devt and testing of armaments and mil. tech.; Deputy State Mil. Insp. of Russia, Sec. Council of Defence 1997–98; Deputy Sec. Russian Council of Security 1998–2001, supervised security in defence, tech. and scientific areas; Deputy Minister of Defence, Head of Armaments 2001–; State Prize of Russian Fed., Prize of Council of Ministers for devt of new weapons. *Address:* Ministry of Defence, 105175 Moscow, ul. Myasnitskaya 37, Russia (office). *Telephone:* (495) 293-38-54 (office). *Fax:* (495) 296-84-36 (office). *Website:* www.mil.ru (office).

MOSLEY, Max Rufus; British fmr racing driver and lawyer; *President, Fédération Internationale de l'Automobile;* b. 13 April 1940, London; s. of the late Sir Oswald Mosley and of the Hon. Lady Diana Mosley (née Freeman-Mitford); m. Jean Marjorie Taylor 1960; two s.; ed Christ Church Oxford; called to Bar (Gray's Inn) 1964; fmr Dir March Cars Ltd, Legal Adviser to Formula One Constructors Asscn, fmr Formula Two racing driver, Co-Founder March Grand Prix Team; Pres. Fed. Int. du Sport Automobile (FISA) 1991–93, Fed. Int. de l'Automobile 1993–; Chair. Mfrs Comm. 1986–91; Hon. Pres. European Parl. Automobile Users Group 1994–99; Chair. European New Car Assessment Programme 1997–2004; Vice-Chair. Supervisory Bd ERTICO Intelligence Transport Systems Europe 1999–2001, Chair. 2001–04, Pres. and Spokesperson 2004–06; Founder-mem. Institut du Cerveau et de la Moelle Epiniere 2005, EC CARS 21 High Level Group 2005; Patron EU eSafety Aware Communications Platform; Hon. Pres. Nat. Road Safety Council of Armenia 2006; Order of Merit (Italy) 1994, Order of Madarksi Kannik, First Degree (Bulgaria) 2000, Castrol/Inst. of the Motor Industry Gold Medal 2000, Quattroruote Premio Speciale per la Sicurezza Stradale (Italy) Gold Medal 2001, Goldene VdM-Dieselring (Germany) 2001, Order of Merit (Romania) 2004, Visitante Ilustre de la Ciudad de Asuncion (Ecuador) 2004, Chevalier, Ordre de la Légion d'honneur 2006, Commdr, Ordre de Saint Charles (Monaco) 2006; Hon. DCL (Northumbria) 2005. *Leisure interests:* walking, snowboarding. *Address:* Fédération Internationale de l'Automobile, 8 place de la Concorde, 75008 Paris, France (office). *Telephone:* 1-43-12-44-55 (office). *Fax:* 1-43-12-44-66 (office). *Website:* www.fia.com (office).

MOSLEY, Nicholas (see Ravensdale, 3rd Baron).

MOSLEY, Walter; American writer; b. 1952, Los Angeles; m. Joy Kellman 1987 (divorced); ed Goddard Coll., Johnson State Coll., City Coll. CUNY; Artist-in-Residence Africana Studies Inst., NY Univ. 1996; mem. Bd of Dirs Nat. Book Awards, Poetry Soc. of America –2007; past Pres. MWA; American Library Asscn Literary Award 1996, O. Henry Award 1996, Anisfield Wolf Award 1996, TransAfrica Int. Literary Prize 1998. *Publications include:* Devil in a Blue Dress (Shamus Award) 1990, A Red Death 1991, White Butterfly 1992, Black Betty 1994, RL's Dream 1995, A Little Yellow Dog 1996, Gone Fishin' 1997, Always Outnumbered, Always Outgunned 1997, Blue Light 1998, Walkin' the Dog 1999, Fearless Jones 2001, Futureland: Nine Stories of an Imminent Future 2001, Bad Boy Brawly Brown 2002, Fear Itself 2003, Six Easy Pieces (short stories) 2003, What Next: An African American Initiative Toward World Peace 2003, The Man in My Basement 2004, Little Scarlet 2004, Cinnamon Kiss 2005, 47 (for young adults) 2006, Fortunate Son 2006, Killing Johnny Fry 2007, This Year You Write Your Novel 2007, Blonde Faith 2007, Diablerie 2008, The Long Fall 2009; contribs to New York Times, Library of Contemporary Thought, New Yorker, GQ, Esquire, USA Weekend, Los Angeles Times Magazine, Savoy. *Address:* W. W. Norton, 500 Fifth Avenue, Floor 6, New York, NY 10110, USA (office). *Website:* www.waltermosley.com.

MOSONYI, György, DipEng; Hungarian business executive; *Group CEO, MOL Group;* b. 1949; ed Veszprém Univ.; joined Shell Int. Petroleum Co. (SIPC) 1974 as Lubricant Sales Rep., Commercial Dir 1986–92, Man. Dir, Shell-Interag Kft. 1992–93, Chair. and CEO, Shell Hungary Rt. 1994–99, also Chair., Cen. European Region and Gen. Man., Shell Bohemian; Group CEO and mem. Bd of Dirs MOL Group 1999–; Chair., Tiszai Vegyi Kombinát (TVK) Rt. 2002–; Chair. AEGON Hungary Általános Biztosíto Rt.; Chair. Jt Ventures Asscn of Hungary; Dir Panrusgas; mem. Bd of Dirs American Chamber of Commerce. *Address:* MOL Group, Október huszonharmadika u.18, 1502 Budapest, Hungary (office). *Telephone:* (1) 209-0000 (office). *Fax:* (1) 464-1335 (office). *Website:* www.mol.hu (office).

MOSS, Andrew, LLB, CA; British insurance executive; *Group CEO, Aviva PLC;* b. March 1958; m. Susan Moss; four c.; ed Christ Church Coll., Oxford; accountancy training, Coopers & Lybrand; Vice-Pres. and Head of Fiduciary Compliance, Citibank NA 1988–89; Asst Dir Group Treasury, Midland Montagu/HSBC Markets 1989–95, Head of Group Asset and Liability Man. HSBC Group 1995–97, Chief Financial Officer, Investment Banking and Markets, HSBC Group 1997–2000; Dir Finance, Risk Man. and Operations, Lloyd's of London 2000–04; Group Finance Dir Aviva PLC 2004–07, Group CEO 2007–; mem. Asscn of Corp. Treasurers, CFO Forum. *Leisure interests:* golf, rugby, gardening. *Address:* Aviva PLC, St Helen's, 1 Undershaft, London, EC3P 3DQ, England (office). *Telephone:* (20) 7283-2000 (office). *Fax:* (20) 7662-2753 (office). *E-mail:* aviva_info@aviva.com (office). *Website:* www.aviva.com (office).

MOSS, Bernard K., MD, PhD, FAAS; American virologist and academic; *Section Head and Laboratory Chief, Laboratory of Viral Diseases, National Institute of Allergy and Infectious Diseases;* b. 26 July 1937, New York; ed New York Univ., New York Univ. School of Medicine and Massachusetts Inst. of Tech.; Intern, Children's Hosp. Medical Center, Boston, Mass 1961–62; Investigator, Lab. of Biology of Viruses, Nat. Inst. of Allergy and Infectious Diseases, NIH, Bethesda, Md 1966–70, Head, Macromolecular Biology Section 1971–84, Chief, Lab. of Viral Diseases 1984–; Foundation for Microbiology Lectureship 1980–81; Wellcome Visiting Prof. in Microbiology, American Soc. of Microbiology 1987; Adjunct Prof., George Washington Univ. Grad. Genetics Program, Washington, DC 1994–, Adjunct mem. Inst. for Biomedical Science 1996–; Adjunct Prof., Univ. of Maryland; Head, WHO Collaborating Center for Research on Viral Vectors for Vaccines 1988–2001; mem. Vaccinia Sub-cttee of Nat. Vaccine Program Interagency Group 1988–, Poxvirus Subgroup of Int. Cttee on Taxonomy of Viruses 1992–95, 1997–, WHO Advisory Cttee on Variola Virus 1999–, Fellowship Recruitment Cttee of AAAS 2000–; Ed. Virology 1992–; mem. Editorial Bd Journal of Virology 1972–, AIDS Research and Human Retroviruses 1989–, Current Opinion in Biotechnology 1990–; mem. Editorial Advisory Bd Advances in Virus Research Member 1984–, NIH Catalyst 1993–; mem. American Soc. for Microbiology, American Soc. of Biological Chemists, NAS 1987–, American Soc. for Virology 1994– (currently Pres.), American Acad. of Microbiology 1996–; NSF Research Fellowship 1958, US Public Health Service (PHS) Postdoctoral Fellowship 1963–66, PHS Commendation Medal 1979, PHS Meritorious Service Medal 1984, Science Digest magazine 100 Most Innovative Scientists of 1985, PHS Distinguished Service Medal 1986, Solomon A. Berson Medical Alumni Achievement Award, New York Univ. 1987, Dickson Prize for Medical Research, Univ. of Pittsburgh 1988, Invitrogen Eukaryotic Expression Award 1991, ICN Int. Prize in Virology, ICN Pharmaceuticals Research 1994, Sackler Scholarship, Univ. of Tel-Aviv 1996, J. Allyn Taylor Int. Prize in Medicine, Robarts Research Inst. 1997, Cancer Research Campaign Lecturer, Univ. of Glasgow, UK 1999, Bristol-Myers Squibb Award for Distinguished Achievement in Infectious Disease Research 2000. *Publications:* more than 560 articles in scientific journals. *Address:* Laboratory of Viral Diseases, National Institute of Allergy and Infectious Diseases, NIH, Building 4, Room 229, 4 Center Drive, MSC 0445, Bethesda, MD, 20892-0445, USA (office). *Telephone:* (301) 496-9869 (office). *Fax:* (301) 480-1147 (office). *E-mail:* bmoss@niaid.nih.gov (office); bmoss@nih.gov (office). *Website:* www.niaid.nih.gov/dir/labs/lvd/moss.htm (office).

MOSS, Kate; British model; b. 16 Jan. 1974, Addiscombe; d. of Peter Edward Moss and Linda Rosina; one d. with fmr pnr Jefferson Hack; ed Croydon High School; has modelled for Face, Harpers and Queen, Vogue, Dolce & Gabbana, Katherine Hamnett, Versace (q.v.), Yves Saint Laurent; exclusive contract world-wide with Calvin Klein (q.v.) 1992–; designed Kate Moss collection for Topshop 2007; named Female Model of the Year VH-1 Awards 1996. *Film:* Unzipped 1996. *Publication:* Kate 1994. *Address:* Storm Model Management, 1st Floor, 5 Jubilee Place, London, SW3 3TD, England. *Telephone:* (20) 7376-7764.

MOSS, Sir Stirling, Kt, OBE; British racing driver; b. 17 Sept. 1929, London; s. of Alfred Moss and Nora Aileen Moss; m. 1st Katherine Stuart Moson 1957 (divorced 1960); m. 2nd Elaine Barbarino 1964 (divorced 1968); one d.; m. 3rd Susie Paine 1980; one s.; ed Haileybury and Imperial Service Coll.; bought his first racing car, a Cooper 500, with prize money from show-jumping 1947; British Champion 1951; built his own car, the Cooper-Alta 1953; drove in H.W.M. Formula II Grand Prix team 1950, 1951, Jaguar team 1950, 1951; Leader of Maserati Grand Prix team 1954; mem. Mercedes team 1955; leader of Maserati Sports and Grand Prix teams 1956, Aston Martin team 1956; mem. Vanwall, Aston Martin, Maserati teams 1958; winner of Tourist Trophy (TT) race, UK 1950, 1951, 1953, 1955, 1958, 1959, 1960, 1961, Gold Coupe des Alpes (three rallies without loss of marks) 1954, Italian Mille Miglia 1955, Sicilian Targa Florio 1955, eight int. events including New Zealand, Monaco Grand Prix, Nurburgring 1,000 km. (FRG) 1956, Argentine 1,000 km. UK, Pescara (Italy), Moroccan Grand Prix 1957, 11 events incl. Argentine, Netherlands, Italian Grand Prix and Nurburgring 1,000 km. 1958, 19 events including New Zealand, Portuguese, US Grand Prix 1959, 19 events including Cuban, Monaco, Austrian, S African Grand Prix 1960, 27 events including Monaco, German, Pacific Grand Prix, Nassau Tourist Trophy 1961; competed in 529 events, finishing in 387, winning 211, during motor racing career 1947–62; retd from racing after accident at Goodwood, UK April 1962, made comeback 1980, subsequently taking part in numerous vintage car races; many business ventures, consultancy work on vehicle evaluation, property conversion, design; Man. Dir Stirling Moss Ltd; Dir 28 cos; also journalism and lecturing; Pres. or Patron of 28 car clubs; Hon. FIE 1959; Gold Star, British Racing Drivers' Club 10 times 1950–61, Driver of the Year (Guild of Motoring Writers) (twice), Sir Malcolm Campbell Memorial Award 1957. *Publications include:* Stirling Moss 1953, In the Track of Speed 1957, Le Mans '59 1959, Design and Behaviour of the Racing Car 1963, All But My Life 1963, How to Watch Motor Racing 1975, Motor Racing and All That 1980, My Cars, My Career 1987, Stirling Moss: Great Drives in the Lakes and Dales 1993, Motor Racing Masterpieces 1995, Stirling Moss (a biog.) 2001, Stirling Moss Scrapbook 1955 2005. *Leisure interests:* theatre and cinema, designing houses, model making, motor trials, historic racing, interior decorating, woodwork. *Address:* c/o Stirling Moss Ltd, 46 Shepherd Street, Mayfair, London, W1J 7JN (office); 44 Shepherd Street, London, W1J 7JN, England (home). *Telephone:* (20) 7499-3272/7967. *Fax:* (20) 7499-4104. *E-mail:* stirlingmossltd@aol.com (office).

MÖSSBAUER, Rudolf L., PhD; German physicist and academic; *Professor Emeritus, Technical University of Munich;* b. 31 Jan. 1929, Munich; s. of Ludwig Mössbauer and Erna Mössbauer; m.; one s. two d.; ed Tech.

Hochschule, Munich; Research Asst Max-Planck Inst., Heidelberg 1955–57; Research Fellow, Tech. Hochschule, Munich 1958–60; Research Fellow, Calif. Inst. of Tech. 1960, Sr Research Fellow 1961, Prof. of Physics Dec. 1961; Prof. of Experimental Physics, Tech. Univ. of Munich 1964–72, 1977–97, Prof. Emer. 1997–; Dir Inst. Max von Laue and of German-French-British High Flux Reactor, Grenoble, France 1972–77; Foreign mem. American Acad. of Arts and Sciences, Accad. Nazionale di Roma; mem. Deutsche Physische Gesellschaft, Deutsche Gesellschaft der Naturforscher, Leopoldina, American Physical Soc., European Physical Soc., Indian Acad. of Sciences, American Acad. of Sciences, NAS, Russian Acad. of Sciences, Pontifical Acad. of Sciences, Hungarian Acad. of Sciences; Grosses Bundesverdienstkreuz; Hon. DSc (Oxford) 1973, (Lille) 1973, (Leicester) 1975, (Birmingham) 1999; Dr hc (Grenoble) 1974; Research Corpn Award 1960, Röntgen Prize, Univ. of Giessen 1961, Elliot Cresson Medal of Franklin Inst., Philadelphia 1961, Nobel Prize for Physics 1961. *Publications:* papers on recoilless nuclear resonance absorption and on neutrino physics. *Leisure interests:* piano, hiking, photography, languages. *Address:* Fachbereich Physik, Physik Department E 15, Technische Universität Munich, 85747 Garching, Germany (office). *Telephone:* (89) 28912522 (office). *Fax:* (89) 28912680 (office). *E-mail:* beatrice.vbellen@ph.tum.de (office). *Website:* www.e15.physik.tu-muenchen.de (office).

MOSTAFAVI, Mohsen, Diploma in Architecture; Iranian architect and academic; *Dean, Graduate School of Design, Harvard University;* m. Homa Farjadi; ed Architectural Asscn School of Architecture, London, Univ. of Essex, Univ. of Cambridge, UK; fmr Design Critic, Univ. of Cambridge; fmr Visiting Prof., Frankfurt Acad. of Arts (Stadelschule); fmrly taught at Univ. of Pennsylvania School of Design; Assoc. Prof. of Architecture, Grad. School of Design, Harvard Univ. 1990–95, Dir MArch I Program 1992–95, Dean 2008–; Chair. Architectural Asscn, School of Architecture, London 1995–2004; fmr Arthur L. and Isabel B. Wiesenberger Prof. in Architecture, Cornell Univ. –2007, Gale and Ira Drukier Dean, Coll. of Architecture, Art and Planning, Cornell Univ. 2004–07; mem. Steering Cttee Aga Khan Award for Architecture; jury mem. Holcim Foundation for Sustainable Construction; fmr mem. Design Cttee, London Devt Agency; winner of Pritzker Prize 2000. *Publications:* Architecture and Continuity (co-author) 1983, On Weathering: the Life of Buildings in Time (co-author, American Inst. of Architects Prize) 1993, Delayed Space (co-author) 1994 Approximations 2002, Surface Architecture 2002 (CICA Bruno Zevi Book Award), Logique Visuelle 2003, Landscape Urbanism: a Manual for the Machinic Landscape 2004, Structure as Space 2006; contribs to The Architectural Review, AAFiles, Arquitectura, Bauwelt, Casabella, Centre, Daidalos. *Address:* Office of the Dean, Graduate School of Design, Harvard University, 48 Quincy Street, Gund Hall, Cambridge, MA 02138, USA (office). *Telephone:* (617) 495-4364 (office). *Website:* www.gsd.harvard.edu (office).

MOTE, Clayton Daniel (Dan), Jr, MS, DSc; American university administrator and professor of mechanical engineering; *President, University of Maryland;* m. Patricia Mote; one d. one s.; ed Univ. of Calif., Berkeley; mem. Faculty, Dept of Mechanical Eng, Univ. of Calif., Berkeley 1967–98, Vice-Chancellor, Chair in Mechanical Systems and Pres. UC Berkeley Foundation 1991–98; Glenn L. Martin Inst. Prof. of Mechanical Eng and Pres. Univ. of Maryland, College Park 1998–; consultant to US Congress on educational issues; Pres. Atlantic Coast Conf. 2004–05; fmr Vice-Chair., Basic Research Cttee, US Dept of Defense; mem. Nat. Acads Cttee, Senate Energy Sub-Cttee, US Senate Energy and Natural Resources Cttee; mem. Leadership Council, Nat. Innovation Initiative, Council on Competitiveness; mem. Council, Nat. Acad. of Eng; Fellow AAAS, Int. Acad. of Wood Science, Acoustical Soc. of America; holds patents in USA, Norway, Finland and Sweden; Hon. mem. ASME Int.; two hon. doctorates; Humboldt Prize, FRG, Berkeley Citation, UC Berkeley Distinguished Eng Alumnus, J.P. Den Hartog Award, ASME Int. Tech. Cttee on Vibration and Sound 2005. *Publications:* over 300 articles, books and chapters in books on dynamics of gyroscopic systems and biomechanics. *Address:* Office of the President, University of Maryland, Main Administration Building, College Park, MD 20742-5025, USA (office). *Telephone:* (301) 405-5803 (office). *E-mail:* president@umd.edu (office). *Website:* www.umd.edu (office).

MOTEGI, Toshimitsu; Japanese politician; *Minister of State for Financial Services and Administrative Reform;* b. 7 Oct. 1955; ed Faculty of Econs, Univ. of Tokyo, John F. Kennedy School of Govt, Harvard Univ., USA; joined Marubeni Corpn 1978; political journalist, Yomiuri Shimbun 1983–84; Man. Consultant, Mckinsey & Co. 1984–93; mem. House of Reps (Tochigi Pref. 5th Dist) 1993–, Dir Cttee on Foreign Affairs 1997, Cttee on the Budget 2004–07, Chair. Cttee on Health, Labour and Welfare 2007–; Vice-Minister for Int. Trade and Industry 1999–2002; Sr Vice-Minister for Foreign Affairs 2002–03; Minister of State for Okinawa and Northern Territories Affairs, Science and Tech. Policy, and Information Tech. 2003–08; Minister of State for Financial Services and Admin. Reform 2008–; Deputy Sec. Gen., LDP 1998–2006, Chief Deputy Sec. Gen. 2006–. *Address:* Financial Services Agency, 3-1-1, Kasumigaseki, Chiyoda-ku, Tokyo 100-8967, Japan (office). *Telephone:* (3) 3506-6000 (office). *Website:* www.fsa.go.jp (office); www.kantei.go.jp (office).

MOTEJL, Otakar, DIur; Czech judge and politician; *Ombudsman;* b. 10 Sept. 1932, Prague; s. of Jirí Motejl and Eliška Motejl; m. Anna Motejl (died 1995); one d.; ed Charles Univ., Prague; solicitor in Banska Bystrica, Slovakia 1955–1966, later in Kladno and Prague; researcher Law Inst., Ministry of Justice 1966–1968; Judge, Supreme Court of Prague 1968–1970; resumed law practice 1970–89; mem. Cttee for Investigation of Events of 17 Nov. 1989 (Velvet Revolution); Pres. Supreme Court of Czech and Slovak Fed. Repub. 1990–92, Supreme Court of Czech Repub. 1993–98; Minister of Justice 1998–2000; Ombudsman 2000–; Commdr, Légion d'honneur 2000. *Publications include:* articles in law journals. *Leisure interests:* literature, music. *Address:* Office of the Ombudsman, Údolní 39, 60200 Brno, Czech Republic (office). *Telephone:* (5) 42542777 (office). *Fax:* (5) 42542112 (office). *E-mail:* podatelna@ochrance.cz (office). *Website:* www.ochrance.cz (office).

MOTION, Andrew Peter, MLitt, FRSA; British biographer and poet; b. 26 Oct. 1952, London; s. of Andrew R. Motion and Catherine G. Motion; m. 1st Joanna J. Powell 1973 (divorced 1983); m. 2nd Janet Elisabeth Dalley 1985; two s. one d.; ed Radley Coll. and Univ. Coll., Oxford; Lecturer in English, Univ. of Hull 1977–81; Ed. Poetry Review 1981–83; Poetry Ed. Chatto & Windus 1983–89, Editorial Dir 1985–87; Prof. of Creative Writing Univ. of E Anglia, Norwich 1995–2003; Chair. Literature Advisory Panel Arts Council of England 1986–98; Poet Laureate 1999–2009; Chair of Creative Writing, Royal Holloway Coll., University Coll. London 2003–; Chair., Museums, Libraries and Archives Council 2008–; mem. Poetry Soc. (vice-pres.); Hon. DLitt (Hull) 1996, (Exeter) 1999, (Brunel) 2000, (A.P.U.) 2001, (Open Univ.) 2002; Arvon/Observer Prize 1982, Dylan Thomas Award 1987, Whitbread Biography Award 1993. *Publications:* poetry collections: The Pleasure Steamers 1978, Independence 1981, The Penguin Book of Contemporary British Poetry (ed., anthology) 1982, Secret Narratives 1983, Dangerous Play (Rhys Memorial Prize) 1984, Natural Causes 1987, Love in a Life 1991, The Price of Everything 1994, Salt Water 1997, Selected Poems 1996–97 1998, Public Property 2001, Here to Eternity: An Anthology of Poetry (ed.) 2001, The Cinder Path 2009; poems as Poet Laureate: Remember This: An Elegy on the Death of HM Queen Elizabeth The Queen Mother 2002, A Hymn for the Golden Jubilee 2002, On the Record (for Prince William's 21st birthday) 2003, Spring Wedding (for the wedding of Prince Charles and Camilla Parker Bowles) 2005, The Golden Rule (anthem for 80th birthday of HM Queen Elizabeth II, with music by Sir Peter Maxwell-Davies) 2006, Diamond Wedding (for the Diamond Wedding Anniversary of HM Queen Elizabeth II and HR Duke of Edinburgh) 2007; non-fiction: The Poetry of Edward Thomas 1981, Philip Larkin 1982, The Lamberts (Somerset Maugham Award 1987) 1986, Philip Larkin: A Writer's Life 1993, William Barnes Selected Poems (ed.) 1994, Keats 1997, Wainewright the Poisoner 2000, In the Blood: A Memoir of my Childhood 2006, Ways of Life: Selected Essays and Reviews, 1994–2006 2008; fiction: The Pale Companion 1989, Famous for the Creatures 1991, The Invention of Dr Cake 2003; other: additional texts for a performance of Haydn's Seven Last Words of Our Saviour on the Cross 2003. *Leisure interest:* fishing. *Address:* c/o Faber & Faber, Bloomsbury House, 74–77 Great Russell Street, London, WC1B 3DA, England (office). *Website:* www.faber.co.uk (office).

MOTLANTHE, Kgalema; South African trade union official, politician and fmr head of state; *Deputy President;* b. 19 July 1949, Johannesburg; three c.; mem. UmKhonto we Sizwe (ANC mil wing), detained during student protests 1976, arrested again 1977, spent 10 years in detention at Robben Island 1977–87; Educ. Officer Nat. Union of Mineworkers 1987–92, Sec.-Gen. 1992–97; Sec.-Gen. ANC 1997–2007, Deputy Pres. Dec. 2007–; mem. Parl. July 2008–; Minister without Portfolio July–Sept. 2008; Acting Pres. of South Africa Sept. 2008–May 2009, Deputy Pres. 2009–. *Address:* c/o The Presidency, Union Bldgs, West Wing, Government Avenue, Pretoria 0001 (office); African National Congress, 54 Sauer Street, Johannesburg 2001, South Africa (office). *Telephone:* (12) 3005200 (office); (11) 3761000 (office). *Fax:* (12) 3238246 (office); (11) 3761134 (office). *E-mail:* president@po.gov.za (office); nmtyelwa@anc.org.za (office). *Website:* www.gov.za/president/index.html (office); www.anc.org.za (office).

MOTSPAN, Dumitru; Moldovan politician; b. 3 May 1940, Selishte vill.; engineer, worked as head agric. enterprises, head local admin.; Chair. Agrarian-Democratic Party; Deputy Chair. of Parl. 1994–97, Chair. 1997–2000. *Address:* Parliament House, Stefan Celmari prosp. 105, 277033 Chişinău, Moldova (office). *Telephone:* (2) 23-25-28 (office).

MOTSUENYANE, Samuel Mokgethi, BSc (Agric.); South African business executive and diplomatist; b. 11 Feb. 1927, Potchefstroom; s. of the late Solomon P. Motsuenyane and Christina D. Motsuenyane; m. Jocelyn Mashinini 1954; six s.; ed N Carolina State Univ., USA, Jan Hofmeyr School of Social Work; Nat. Organizing Sec. African Nat. Soil Conservation Asscn 1952–59; NC State Univ., USA 1960–62; Pres. NAFCOC 1968–92; Chair. African Business Publications, African Business Holdings, NAFCOC Permanent, Venda Nat. Devt Corpn, New-Real African Investments; Dir African Devt and Construction Holdings, NAFCOC Nat. Trust, Barlow Rand, Blackchain Ltd, numerous other cos; Chancellor, Univ. of the North (SA) 1985–90; Pres. Motsuenyane Comm. to investigate torture and disappearances in ANC detention camps 1992–93; Amb. to Saudi Arabia (also accred to Yemen, Kuwait and Oman) 1996–2000; Leader South African Observer Mission to the Presidential Elections in Zimbabwe 2002; Pres. Boy Scouts of SA 1976–81; Leader of Senate 1994–96; serves on bds of numerous cos and orgs; Dr hc (Univ. of Witwatersrand) 1983; Hon. DEconSc (Cape Town) 1986; Harvard Business Award 1977. *Publications:* numerous articles. *Leisure interests:* gardening, reading. *Address:* c/o Ministry of Foreign Affairs, Private Bag X152, Pretoria 0001, South Africa. *Telephone:* (12) 3511000.

MOTTAKI, Manouchehr, MA; Iranian diplomatist and politician; *Minister of Foreign Affairs;* b. 1953, Bandar Gaz, Golestan; ed Bangalore Univ., India, Tehran Univ.; joined Islamic Revolutionary Guards Corps (IRGC) 1979, IRGC Liaison Officer to Ministry of Foreign Affairs (MOF) 1979–80; Deputy of Islamic Consultative Ass. (Majlis) 1980–84, 2004–; Head of Political Bureau, MOF 1984–85; Amb. to Turkey 1985–89, to Japan 1994–99; Dir-Gen. of W European Affairs, MOF 1989; Deputy Foreign Minister for Int. Affairs 1989–92, for Consular and Parl. Affairs 1992–4; Adviser to Minister of Foreign Affairs 1999–2001; Vice-Pres. Islamic Culture and Communications Org. 2001–04; Campaign Man. for Presidential Cand. Ali Larijani 2005; Minister of Foreign Affairs 2005–. *Address:* Ministry of Foreign Affairs, Shahid Abd al-

Hamid Mesri Street, Ferdowsi Avenue, Tehran, Iran (office). *Telephone:* (21) 61151 (office). *Fax:* (21) 33212763 (office). *E-mail:* matbuat@mfa.gov.ir (office). *Website:* www.mfa.gov.ir (office).

MOTTISTONE, 4th Baron, cr. 1933, of Mottistone; **David Peter Seely,** CBE, FIET, FCIPD; British naval officer (retd); b. 16 Dec. 1920, London; s. of Maj.-Gen. J. E. B. Seely, 1st Lord Mottistone, and Lady Mottistone (née Murray of Elibank); m. Anthea Christine McMullan 1944; two s. three d. (one deceased); ed Royal Naval Colls, Dartmouth and Greenwich; promoted to Commdr, RN 1955, Special Asst NATO Chief of Allied Staff, Malta 1956–58, in command HMS Cossack 1958–59, rank of Capt. RN 1960, Deputy Dir, Signals Div., Admiralty 1961–63, in command HMS Ajax and 24th Escort Squadron 1964–65, Naval Adviser to UK High Commr, Ottawa 1965–66, retd from RN in protest at govt's defence policy 1967; Peer of Parl. 1966–99, Peer of the Realm 1966–; Dir of Personnel and Training, Radio Rentals Group of Cos 1967–69; Dir, Distributive Industries Training Bd 1969–75, Cake & Biscuit Alliance 1975–82; Lord Lt of Isle of Wight 1986–95, Gov., Capt. and Steward of Isle of Wight 1992–95; KStJ 1990; Hon. DLitt (Bournemouth) 1994. *Leisure interest:* yachting. *Address:* The Old Parsonage, Mottistone, Isle of Wight, PO30 4EE, England (home).

MOTTLEY, Mia Amor, QC; Barbadian lawyer and politician; *Leader, Barbados Labour Party;* b. 1 Oct. 1965; ed Merryvale Private School, The UN Int. School, Queen's Coll., London School of Econs, UK; called to the Bar of England and Wales, Inner Bar of Barbados 2002; Opposition Senator, Senate of Barbados and Shadow Minister of Culture and Community Devt 1991–94, served on several Jt Select Cttees including Praedial Larceny and Domestic Violence; MP 1994–; Minister of Educ., Youth Affairs and Culture 1994–2001; Gen. Sec. Barbados Labour Party 1996–2008, Leader 2008–; Chair. Caribbean Community (CARICOM) Standing Cttee of Ministers of Educ. 1996, 1997; Deputy Prime Minister, Attorney-Gen., Leader of Govt Business in House of Ass. and Minister of Home Affairs 2001–06; Deputy Prime Minister, Leader of Govt Business in House of Ass. and Minister of Econ. Affairs and Devt 2006–08; Leader of the Opposition 2008–; mem. Nat. Security Council of Barbados, Barbados Defence Bd, Privy Council of Barbados 2002. *Address:* Barbados Labour Party, Grantley Adams House, 111 Roebuck Street, Bridgetown, Barbados. *Telephone:* 429-1990 (office). *Fax:* 427-8792 (office). *E-mail:* will99@caribsurf.com (office). *Website:* labourparty.wordpress.com (office).

MOTTRAM, Sir Richard Clive, KCB, GCB, BA; British civil servant; b. 23 April 1946; s. of John Mottram and Florence Yates; m. Fiona Margaret Erskine 1971; three s. one d.; ed King Edward VI Camp Hill School, Birmingham, Univ. of Keele; joined Civil Service 1968, assigned to Ministry of Defence, Asst Pvt. Sec. to Sec. of State for Defence 1971–72, Prin. Naval Programme and Budget 1973, Cabinet Office 1975–77, Pvt. Sec. to Perm. Under-Sec., Ministry of Defence 1979–81, Pvt. Sec. to Sec. of State for Defence 1982–86, Asst Under-Sec. of State (programmes) 1986–89, Deputy Under-Sec. of State (Policy) 1989–92, Perm. Sec. Office of Public Service and Science, Cabinet Office 1992–95, Ministry of Defence 1995–98, Dept of the Environment, Transport and the Regions 1998–2001, Dept for Transport, Local Govt and the Regions 2001, for Work and Pensions 2002–05, Intelligence, Security and Resilience, Cabinet Office 2005–07 (retd); Hon. DLitt (Keele) 1996. *Leisure interests:* cinema, theatre, tennis. *Address:* c/o Cabinet Office, 70 Whitehall, London, SW1A 2AS, England (office).

MOTULSKY, Arno Gunther, BS, MD; American medical geneticist and academic; *Professor Emeritus of Medicine and Genome Sciences, University of Washington;* b. 5 July 1923, Germany; s. of Herman Motulsky and Rena Motulsky (née Sass); m. Gretel Stern 1945; one s. two d.; ed YMCA Coll., Chicago, Yale Univ., Univ. of Illinois Medical School; Intern, Fellow, Asst and Sr Resident (Internal Medicine) Michael Reese Hosp., Chicago 1947–51; Staff mem. in charge of Clinical Investigation, Dept of Hematology, Army Medical Service Graduate School, Walter Reed Army Medical Center; Research Assoc. in Internal Medicine, George Washington Univ. School of Medicine, Washington 1952–53, Instructor 1953–55, Asst Prof. 1955–58, Assoc. Prof. 1958–61, Prof. Dept of Medicine 1961–, Prof. Dept of Genetics 1961–, Dir Medical Genetics Training Program 1961–89, Dir Center for Inherited Diseases 1972–89; Prof. Emer. of Medicine and Genome Sciences 1994–; Pres. Int. Congress of Human Genetics 1986; Ed. American Journal of Human Genetics 1969–75, Human Genetics 1969–98; mem. American Soc. of Human Genetics, NAS 1976, American Acad. of Arts and Sciences 1978, American Philosophical Soc.; Hon. DSc (Illinois) 1982; Hon. MD (Würzburg) 1991; William Allan Memorial Award 1970, Alexander von Humboldt Award 1984, San Remo Int. Prize for Genetic Research 1988, Excellence in Educ. Award 1999. *Publications:* Human Genetics – Problems and Approaches (with F. Vogel) 1996; more than 300 medical and scientific articles. *Leisure interests:* reading, collecting African art, antique maps. *Address:* University of Washington, Medicine and Genome Sciences, Health Sciences Bldg K336-B, PO Box 357730, Seattle, WA 98195-7730 (office); 4347 53rd NE, Seattle, WA 98105, USA (home). *Telephone:* (206) 543-3593 (office). *Fax:* (206) 685-7301 (office). *E-mail:* agmot@u.washington.edu (office). *Website:* depts.washington .edu/medgen/faculty/motulsky.html (office).

MOTYL, Vladimir Yakovlevich; Russian film director; b. 26 June 1927, Lepel, Belarus; s. of Yakov Motyl and Vera Levina; m. Ludmila Podaruyeva; one d.; ed Sverdlovsk Inst. of Theatre, Ural State Univ.; Chief Stage Dir Sverdlovsk Theatre of Young Spectators 1955–57; work in cinema 1957–; mem. Exec. Bd Union of Cinematographers; Sec. Union of Cinematographers of Moscow; Founder film studio Serial; Artistic Dir Higher Courses for Scriptwriters and Film Dirs 1995–; Merited Worker of Arts 1992; State Prize of Russian Fed. 1997, Prize of the Union of Cinematographers 1963, Prize of All-Union Film Festival 1964, Hon. Diploma Best Films of the World, Int. Film Festival, Belgrade 1977, Prize of Golden Ostap Film Festival, St Petersburg 1995. *Films include:* Deti Pamira (Children of Pamir) 1963, Zhenya, Zhenechka and Katyusha (jtly, also writer) 1967, Beloe solntse pustyni (White Sun of the Desert) 1970, Zvezda plenitelnogo schastya (The Star of Fascinating Happiness) (also writer) 1975, Forest 1980, Les (also writer) 1987, Chest imeyu (I Have Honour) (writer) 1987, Rasstanemsya, poka khoroshiye (also writer) 1991, Okhlamon (Blockhead) (writer) 1993, Nesut menya koni (Gone with the Horses) (also writer) 1996. *Television includes:* Neveroyatnoye pari, ili istinnoye proisshestviye, blagopoluchno zavershivsheyesya sto let nazad (Incredible Bet, or True Event That Ended Happily Hundred Years Ago) 1984, Once There Lived Shishlov... 1987, Veliky Vanya 1987. *Leisure interests:* travelling, history, sciences. *Address:* Higher Courses for Scriptwriters and Film Directors, Bolshoi Tishinsky per. 12, 123557 Moscow (office); Dovzhenko str. 12, korp. 1, Apt 45, 119590 Moscow, Russia (home). *Telephone:* (495) 253-64-88 (office); (495) 143-68-00 (home).

MOTZFELDT, Jonathan; Greenlandic politician; b. 25 Sept. 1938, Qassimut, Greenland; m. Kristjana Gudrum Gudmundsdóttir 1992; ed Greenland Teacher's College, Univ. of Copenhagen; teacher; Lutheran pastor; mem. and Vice-Chair. Greenland Ass. 1971–79; mem. Greenland Parl. (Landsting) 1979–, Chair. 1979–88, 1997, 2002; Prime Minister of Greenland 1979–91, 1997–2002; Co-Founder Siumut Party, Chair. 1977–79, 1980–87, 1998–2001; Hon. Dr rer. pol (Fairbanks USA); Nersornaat in gold, K; Ordre de la Couronne (Belgium) and other foreign decorations and medals. *Address:* Greenland Home Rule Government, PO Box 1015, 3900 Nuuk, Greenland. *Telephone:* 395000. *Fax:* 325002. *Website:* www.homerule.gl (office).

MOTZFELDT, Josef; Greenlandic politician; b. 1941; trained as teacher; Minister for Trade, Traffic and Vocational Training 1984–88; mem. Parl. 1987–; Chair. Inuit Ataqatigiit Party 1994–2007; Minister of Economy 1999–2001, Minister of Economy (Greenland Home Rule Govt) 2002–03 Jan. 2003; Minister of Finance and Foreign Affairs, Vice-Premier, Minister for Nordic Cooperation 2003–07; Greenland Homerule Silver Award. *Films:* Tukuma (co-dir) 1984. *Address:* c/o Inuit Ataqatigiit, POB 321, 3900 Nuuk, Greenland (office). *Telephone:* 346229 (office); 311394 (home). *Fax:* 323232 (office). *E-mail:* tuusi@gh.gl (office). *Website:* www.ia.gl (office).

MOUALLEM, Walid; Syrian diplomatist; *Minister of Foreign Affairs;* b. 1941; ed Cairo Univ.; joined diplomatic corps 1964; held positions at missions in Saudi Arabia, Spain; fmr charge d'affaires London, UK; Amb. to Romania 1975–80; Head, Foreign Ministry Bureau, Damascus 1984–90; Amb. to USA 1990–2000; Deputy Minister of Foreign Affairs 2005–06, Minister of Foreign Affairs 2006–. *Address:* Ministry of Foreign Affairs, rue ar-Rashid, Damascus, Syria (office). *Telephone:* (11) 3331200 (office). *Fax:* (11) 3327620 (office).

MOUBARAK, Samir, PhD; Lebanese diplomatist; *Ambassador to Spain;* b. 3 March 1943, Beirut; s. of Moussa Moubarak and Nada Aboussouan; ed Ecole des Hautes Etudes Commerciales, Paris, Sorbonne, Paris; Political Section, Ministry of Foreign Affairs, Beirut 1967–69; mem. Lebanese Del., Perm. Mission of Lebanon to UN, New York 1969–73; First Sec., Embassy, Paris 1973–77, Chargé d'affaires a.i., Embassy, Madrid; Special Adviser to Minister of Foreign Affairs, Beirut 1977–82; Amb. to Sweden 1982–88; Amb., Ministry of Foreign Affairs 1988–94; Perm. Rep. of Lebanon to UN, New York 1994–99, Vice-Pres. 50th Session UN Gen. Ass. 1995, Vice-Pres. ECOSOC, New York 1996; Amb. to Spain 1999–. *Address:* Lebanese Embassy, Paseo de la Castellana 178, 3° Izqda, 28046 Madrid, Spain (office). *Telephone:* (91) 3451368 (office). *Fax:* (91) 3455631 (office). *E-mail:* leem_e@teleline.es (office).

MOUGEOTTE, Etienne Pierre Albert; French journalist; *Editor in Chief, Le Figaro Magazine;* b. 1 March 1940, La Rochefoucauld; s. of Jean Mougeotte and Marcelle Thonon; m. Françoise Duprilot 1972; one s. two d.; ed Lycée Buffon, Lycée Henri-IV, Paris, Inst. d'études politiques de Paris, Inst. Français de presse; reporter, France-Inter 1965-66, Beirut Corresp. 1966–67; Ed. Europe Numéro 1 1968–69; Chief Reporter, Asst Ed.-in-Chief Information Première (TV) 1969–72; Producer l'Actualité en question 1972; journalist Radio-Télé Luxembourg 1972–73; Ed.-in-Chief Europe 1 1973, News Dir 1974–81; monthly contrib. Paradoxes 1974–; Editorial Dir Journal du Dimanche 1981–83, Télé 7 Jours 1983–87; Dir Gen. Broadcasting TF1 1987–89, Dir Gen. 1987–89, Vice-Pres. Broadcasting 1989–; Vice-Pres. French Fed. of Press Agencies 1975–81; mem. Interprofessional communication group (Gic) 1985–87; Pres. Nat. Videocommunication Syndicate 1982–87, TF1 Films, Tricom; Dir TF1 1991–2007; Pres. TF1 Films Productions; Dir TFI Films 1991–2007, Pres. TFI Films and TFI Digital 2000–07; Assoc. Prof. École de Journalisme, Univ. of Paris Sciences Po 2004–; Ed.-in-Chief Le Figaro Magazine 2007–; Officier Légion d'honneur, Ordre nat. du Mérite. *Leisure interests:* tennis, golf. *Address:* Société du Figaro SA, 14 boulevard Haussman, 75009 Paris, France (office). *Website:* www.lefigaro.fr/lefigaromagazine (office).

MOUKHTAR, Gamal ed-Din; Egyptian institute director and academic; *President, Arab Academy for Science, Technology and Maritime Transport;* fmr Chair. Egyptian Antiquities Org.; currently Pres. Arab Acad. for Science, Tech. and Maritime Transport, Alexandria. *Publications include:* Cairo: The Site and the History (co-author) 1988, Alexandria: The Site and the History (co-author) 1993, Sinai: The Site and the History (co-author) 1998. *Address:* Arab Academy for Science, Technology and Maritime Transport, PO Box 1029, Alexandria, Egypt (office). *Telephone:* (3) 5565429 (office). *Fax:* (3) 5622525 (office). *E-mail:* info@aast.edu (office). *Website:* www.aast.edu (office).

MOULAERT, Jacques, LLD, MPA; Belgian banker; *Honorary Chair, ING Bank Belgium SA;* b. 23 Oct. 1930, Ostend; s. of the late Albert Moulaert and of Marie de Neckere; m. Christiane Laloux 1957; four d.; ed St Barbara Coll. Ghent, Univ. of Ghent and Harvard Univ., USA; Gen. Sec. Aleurope SA 1961; Asst Man. Compagnie Lambert 1967; Man. Compagnie Bruxelles Lambert

(CBL) 1972; Man. Dir Groupe Bruxelles Lambert 1979; Chair. Bd Bank Brussels Lambert (BBL) 1993–2001; Hon. Chair., ING Bank Belgium SA; Officier, Ordre de la Couronne; Commdr, Ordre de St-Sylvestre; Commdr, Ordre de Léopold. *Address:* 2, Tailleur de Pierre, 1380 Lasne (home); ING Bank Belgium, 24 avenue Marnix, 1000 Brussels, Belgium (office). *Telephone:* (2) 547-29-29 (office); (2) 633-10-52 (home). *Fax:* (2) 547-31-00 (office); (2) 633-64-15 (home). *E-mail:* info@bbl.be (office).

MOULAYE, Mohamed, DSc; Mauritanian politician and public official; b. 1 Oct. 1936, Ouagadougou, Burkina Faso; s. of El Hassan Moulaye and Maimouna Dem; m. Ginette Marcin 1962; three s. five d.; Founder-mem. Asscn de la Jeunesse de Mauritanie 1956; Sec.-Gen. Section PRM Boutilimit 1960; mem. Nat. Ass. 1965–75; Directeur des finances 1966; Contrôleur financier 1967–75; Minister of Finance 1975–77, 1979; Parl. rapporteur to Comm. des Finances; fmr mem. IPU; Dir Office of Pres. of Mauritania 1979–80; Conseiller Econ. et Financier du Chef de l'Etat, Président de la Comm. Centrale des Marchés Publics; Pres. Parti du Centre démocratique mauritanien 1992, now Democratic Centre Party; First Vice-Pres. Action pour le Changement; mem. Conseil général, Banque Centrale de Mauritanie 1980–; Dir Personnel Air Afrique, Financial Dir 1985–; Chair. and Man. Dir Arrachad, Nouackchott 1990; Chevalier, Ordre nat. du Mérite. *Leisure interests:* reading, cinema. *Address:* BP 289, Nouackchott, Mauritania.

MOULINE, Larbi; Moroccan business executive, diplomatist and consultant; b. 10 Nov. 1934, Rabat; s. of Mohamed Mouline and Habiba Balafrej; m. Naima Mouline 1959; three s. one d.; ed Ecole Nat. Supérieure des Mines, St Etienne, France; Man. Dir O.C.P. (phosphate co.) 1959–74, Pres. Amicale des Hors-Cadres; Gen. Man. Sonasid (steel co.) 1975–83; Amb. to India 1984–86, to Greece 1987–88; Adviser to Minister of Privatization and Econ. Affairs, Minister of Agric. 1989–94; now pvt. consultant; Sec.-Gen. Asscn des Intervenants Scientifiques (ASSIST), Rabat; Kt of the Throne (Morocco), Order of Phoenix (Greece). *Publications:* A Study on Economic Development Linked to a Steel Complex in Morocco 1977, A Study on Mechanization in Phosphate Mines. *Leisure interests:* reading, music, golf, travel. *Address:* 27 rue Cadi Sanhaji, Souissi, Rabat, Morocco. *Telephone:* (37) 750282. *Fax:* (37) 639501. *E-mail:* imouline@iam.net.ma (home).

MOULTON, Alexander Eric, CBE, MA, FREng, FIMechE, FRSA; British engineer; b. 9 April 1920, Stratford-on-Avon; s. of John Coney Moulton and Beryl Latimer Moulton; ed Marlborough Coll., King's Coll., Cambridge; worked in Engine Research Dept, Bristol Aeroplane Co. 1939–44, Personal Asst to Sir Roy Fedden 1940–42; est. Research Dept of George Spencer, Moulton & Co. Ltd, originating work on rubber suspensions for vehicles and designing Flexitor, Works Man. then Tech. Dir 1945–56; f. Moulton Developments Ltd, Man. Dir 1956–, devt work on own designs of rubber suspensions including Hydrolastic and Hydragas 1956, Chair. 1956–67, Man. Dir 1956–; designed Moulton Coach; f. Moulton Bicycles Ltd to produce own design Moulton Bicycle 1962, Chair. and Man. Dir 1962–67, Dir 1967–; Dir Alex Moulton Ltd; Dir SW Regional Bd, Nat. Westminster Bank 1982–87; Fellow Plastics and Rubber Inst.; Royal Designer for Industry; Dr hc (RCA); Hon. DSc (Bath); Design Centre Award 1964, Amb. Award 1964, Bidlake Memorial Plaque 1964, Gold Medal Milan Triennale 1964, Queens Award to Industry for Tech. Innovation (Moulton Developments Ltd) 1967, Soc. of Industrial Artists and Designers Design Medal 1976, Council of the Inst. of Mechanical Engineers James Clayton Prize, Crompton Lanchester Medal (from Automobile Div.), Thomas Hawksley Gold Medal, 1979. *Publications:* various papers on vehicle suspension. *Leisure interests:* steamboating, canoeing, cycling. *Address:* The Hall, Bradford-on-Avon, Wiltshire, BA15 1AJ, England. *Telephone:* (1225) 862991.

MOUNGAR, Fidèle; Chadian politician and physician; *Leader, Action tchadienne pour l'unité et le socialisme;* b. Logone Region; fmr head of surgery, Peronne Hosp., Somme, France; Prime Minister of Chad 1993; currently Leader Action tchadienne pour l'unité et le socialisme (ACTUS), Collectif des partis pour le changement (COPAC). *Address:* Action tchadienne pour l'unité et le socialisme, N'Djamena, Chad (office). *E-mail:* actus@club-internet.fr (office).

MOUNT, (William Robert) Ferdinand, MA, FRSL, FSA; British writer and journalist; b. 2 July 1939, London; s. of the late Robert Mount and Julia Mount; m. Julia Margaret Lucas 1968; two s. (one deceased), one d.; ed Eton Coll., Christ Church, Oxford; Political Ed., The Spectator 1977–82, 1985, Literary Ed. 1984–85; Head, Prime Minister's Policy Unit 1982–84; Dir, Centre for Policy Studies 1984–91; Political Columnist, The Standard 1980–82, The Times 1984–85, Daily Telegraph 1985–90; Ed., Times Literary Supplement 1991–2002; Sr Columnist, The Sunday Times 2002–04; Vice-Chair., Power Comm. 2004–05; mem. RSL (mem. of Council 2002–05); Hon. Fellow (Univ. of Wales, Lampeter) 2002. *Publications:* Very Like a Whale 1967, The Theatre of Politics 1972, The Man Who Rode Ampersand 1975, The Clique 1978, The Subversive Family 1982, The Selkirk Strip 1987, Of Love and Asthma 1991 (Hawthornden Prize 1992), The British Constitution Now 1992, Communism 1992, Umbrella 1994, The Liquidator 1995, Jem (and Sam) 1998, Fairness 2001, Mind the Gap: The New Class Divide in Britain 2004, Heads You Win 2004, The Condor's Head 2007, Cold Cream: My Early Life and Other Mistakes 2008. *Address:* 17 Ripplevale Grove, London, N1 1HS, England (home). *Telephone:* (20) 7607-5398 (home).

MOUNTAIN, Ross; New Zealand UN official; *Acting Special Representative for Iraq, United Nations;* Inter-Agency Liaison Officer, Div. of Social Affairs, UN, Geneva 1973–75, Coordinator UN Non-Governmental Liaison Service 1975–83; Chief of Information Section, UNDP European Office 1976–85; Deputy Resident Rep. in S Pacific, Fiji 1985–88; UNDP Resident Rep. ad interim and Dir UN Information Centre, Kabul, Afghanistan 1988–91; UN Special Coordinator for Emergency Relief Operations, UNDP Resident Rep. to World Food Programme and UN Population Fund (UNFPA) Rep. in Liberia 1991–93; UNDP Rep. and UN Humanitarian Affairs Coordinator, Haiti, on secondment from UN Resident Coordinator and UNDP Resident Coordinator for Eastern Caribbean, Barbados 1993–95; UN Resident Coordinator in Lebanon and Resident Rep. of UNDP and UNFPA 1995–98; Asst Emergency Relief Coordinator and Dir Geneva Office, Office for the Coordination of Humanitarian Relief (OCHA) 1998–2003; UN Acting Special Rep. for Iraq Dec. 2003–; fmr Humanitarian Coordinator ad interim for E Timor Crisis, Special Humanitarian Envoy for floods in Mozambique, Special Humanitarian Coordinator for Liberia, Head OCHA Crisis Task Team for Iraq. *Address:* Office of the Special Representative for Iraq, United Nations, New York, NY 10017, USA. *Telephone:* (212) 963-1234. *Fax:* (212) 963-4879. *E-mail:* inquiries@un.org. *Website:* www.un.org/Depts/oip.

MOUNTCASTLE, Vernon Benjamin, Jr, MD; American neurophysiologist (retd) and academic; *Professor Emeritus, Krieger Mind-Brain Institute, Johns Hopkins University;* b. 15 July 1918, Shelbyville, Ky; s. of Vernon B. Mountcastle and Anna-Francis Marguerite Waugh; m. Nancy Clayton Pierpont 1945; two s. one d.; ed Roanoke Coll., Salem, Va and Johns Hopkins Univ. School of Medicine; House Officer, Surgery, The Johns Hopkins Hosp. Baltimore, Md 1943; with USN Amphibious Forces 1943–46; through jr ranks, The Johns Hopkins Univ. School of Medicine 1948–59, Prof. of Physiology 1959, Dir of Dept of Physiology 1964–80, Univ. Prof. of Neuroscience 1980–92, Prof. Emer. 1992–; Dir Bard Labs of Neurophysiology, Johns Hopkins Univ. 1981–91; Pres. Neurosciences Research Foundation 1981–85; Dir Neuroscience Research Program 1981–84; Penfield Lecturer, American Univ., Beirut 1971; Sherrington Lecturer, Liverpool Univ. 1974; Sherrington Lecturer, Royal Soc. of Medicine, London, Mellon Lecturer, Univ. of Pittsburgh 1976, Visiting Prof. Collège de France, Paris 1980 and numerous other hon. lectureships; Nat. Pres. Soc. for Neuroscience 1971–72; mem. NAS, American Acad. of Arts and Sciences, American Phil. Soc.; Foreign Fellow, Royal Soc. (UK); Hon. DSc (Pennsylvania) 1976, (Roanoke) 1968, (Northwestern) 1985; Hon. MD (Zurich) 1983, (Siena) 1984; Lashley Prize, American Philosophical Soc. 1974, F.O. Schmitt Prize and Medal, MIT 1975, Gold Medal, Royal Soc. of Medicine 1976, Horwitz Prize, Columbia 1978, Gerard Prize, Soc. for Neuroscience 1980, Int. Prize, Fyssen Foundation Paris 1983, Lasker Award 1983, Nat. Medal of Sciences 1986, McGovern Prize and Medal, AAAS 1990, Neuroscience Award Fidia Fed. 1990, Australia Prize 1993, Neuroscience Prize, NAS 1998. *Publications:* The Mindful Brain (with G. M. Edelman) 1978, Medical Physiology (two vols) (ed. and major contrib.) 14th edn 1980, Perceptual Neuroscience: The Cerebral Cortex 1998, The Sensory Hand 2005; more than 50 articles in scientific journals on the physiology of the central nervous system, especially on the neuronal mechanisms in sensation and perception. *Leisure interests:* gardening. *Address:* The Krieger Mind-Brain Institute, Johns Hopkins University, 3400 N Charles Street, Baltimore, MD 21218 (office); 15601 Carroll Road, Monkton, MD 21111, USA (home). *Telephone:* (410) 516-4271 (office); (410) 472-2514 (home). *Fax:* (410) 516-8648 (office). *E-mail:* mountcastle@mbi.mb.jhu.edu (office). *Website:* www.mb.jhu.edu (office).

MOUNTER, Julian D'Arcy, MA; British journalist, television director, producer and broadcasting executive; b. 2 Nov. 1944, Cornwall; s. of Francis Mounter and Elizabeth Moore; m. Patricia A. Kelsall-Spurr 1983; two s.; ed Skinners Grammar School, Tunbridge Wells, Grenville Coll., Univ. of Leicester; reporter with various local newspapers 1961–65; journalist, The Times 1966–71; Weekend World, London Weekend TV 1971–73; Head of Current Affairs and Documentaries, Westward TV 1973–74; Reporter/Dir Panorama and Midweek, BBC TV 1974–78; Ed., Inside Business, Thames TV 1978–79, Exec. Producer, Current Affairs 1979–81, Controller, Children's and Young Adults' Dept 1981–84; Dir Programmes and Production, Thorn-EMI Satellite and Cable 1984–86; Dir Cosgrove Hall Ltd 1981–84, JRA Ltd 1980–85, Cameralink Ltd 1980–85, Blackwell Videotec Ltd 1980–85; Dir-Gen. and CEO Television New Zealand 1986–91; Chair. South Pacific Pictures Ltd, Broadcast Communications Ltd 1988–91; Dir The Listener, Visnews (UK) Ltd 1987–89, Reuters TV Ltd 1989–91; Chief Exec. and Pres. Star TV Ltd Hutchvision Ltd, Media Assets Ltd, Asia News Ltd 1992–93; Chair. New Media Investments 1994–98, Majestic Films and TV Ltd 1993–95, Swoffers Ltd 1995–96, Renown Leisure Group Ltd 1995–; CEO and Man. Dir Seven Network Ltd 1998–2000; Chair. and CEO Media Consultants and Investments 2001–; mem. Bd Dirs CTV Ltd 1994–99; Dir Int. Council of Nat. Acad. of Television Arts and Sciences, New York 1993–2005, Assoc. Dir 2005–; Trustee, Int. Inst. of Communications 1988–95; Hon. Visiting Fellow, Univ. of Leicester 2005; Queen's Medal for Services to NZ 1990; various press and TV awards. *Leisure interests:* ocean sailing, naval history, music. *Address:* Centre for Mass Communication Research, University of Leicester, University Road, Leicester, LE1 7RH, England (office); Media Consultants and Investments, 1 Rozell Terrace, Mount Durand, St Peter Port, GY1 1EB, Guernsey (office). *Fax:* (1481) 713390 (Leicester) (office). *E-mail:* executive@mediahelp.tv (office); cmcr@le.ac.uk (office). *Website:* www.le.ac.uk/cmcr (office).

MOUREAUX, Philippe; Belgian politician; b. 12 April 1939, Etterbeek; m.; four c.; secondary school teacher 1961–62; Asst, subsequently Prof., Université Libre de Bruxelles 1967–; Adviser, Deputy Prime Minister's Office 1972–73, on staff Prime Minister's Office 1973–74, Chef de cabinet to Deputy Prime Minister 1977–80, Minister of the Interior and Institutional Reforms 1980, of Justice and Institutional Reforms 1980–81, Minister and Chair. Exec. of French Community, responsible for cultural affairs, budget and foreign affairs 1981–85, Feb.–May 1988, Deputy Prime Minister and Minister for the Brussels Region and Institutional Reforms 1988–89, 1990–92, of Social Affairs 1992–93; Minister of State 1995–; Co-Pres. Conférence intergouvernementale et interparlementaire pour le renouveau institutionnel 1999-2000; mem. Parti

Socialiste. *Address:* Administration communale, Rue du Comte de Flandre, 20, 1080 Brussels, Belgium. *Telephone:* (2) 412-37-00. *Fax:* (2) 412-37-02. *E-mail:* pmoureaux@molenbeek.irisnet.be.

MOURINHO FELIX, José Mario Santos; Portuguese football manager; *Manager, FC Internazionale Milano;* b. 26 Jan. 1963, Setubal; s. of Felix Mourinho and Maria Júlia Mourinho; m. Tami Mourinho; two c.; completed UEFA coaching course after studying in Britain 1987; worked as fitness trainer at various clubs and coached jr team Vitoria Setubal then asst Estrela Amadora 1990–92; interpreter, Sporting Lisbon 1992–1993, interpreter and Asst Coach Porto 1993–1996, Asst Coach Barcelona, Spain, 1996–2000, Coach Benfica 2000, Uniao de Leiria 2000–01, Porto 2002–04, Man. and First Team Coach Chelsea FC, England 2004–07; Manager, FC Internazionale Milano 2008–; won UEFA Cup 2003 with Porto, Portuguese Championship 2003, 2004, Portuguese Cup 2003, Champions League 2004; with Chelsea English Championship 2005, 2006, League Cup 2007; univ. degree in Physical Educ. specializing in Football Methodology; BBC Sports Personality of the Year Coach of the Year Award 2005. *Address:* FC Internazionale Milano, Via Durini 24, 20122 Milan, Italy (office). *Telephone:* (02) 77151 (office). *Fax:* (02) 781514 (office). *Website:* www.inter.it (office).

MOUSAWI, Faisal Radhi al-, MB, BCh, FRCSE; Bahraini government official and orthopaedic surgeon; b. 6 April 1944, Bahrain; one s. three d.; ed Univ. of Cairo, Egypt; fmr Rotary Intern, Cairo Univ. Hosp.; House Officer, Sr House Officer, Dept of Surgery, Govt Hosp., Bahrain; Sr House Officer, Accident and Orthopaedic Surgery, Cen. Middx Hosp., London; Orthopaedic Surgery, St Helier Hosp., Carshalton, Surrey; Gen. Surgery, Nelson Hosp., London, St Bartholomew's Hosp., London; Registrar, Orthopaedic Surgery, Whittington Hosp., London, Gen. and Traumatic Surgery, Wexford Co. Hosp., Ireland; locum consultant, Whittington Hosp. 1983–84; Consultant Orthopaedic Surgeon, Salmaniya Medical Centre, Bahrain 1976–, Chair. Dept of Surgery 1982–84, Chief of Medical Staff June–Aug. 1982, Chair. Dept of Orthopaedic Surgery; Asst Prof. Coll. of Medicine and Medical Sciences, Arabian Gulf Univ.; Asst Under-Sec., Ministry of Health 1982–85, Minister of Health 1995–2002; Chair. Shura Council 2002–06; mem. Scientific Council, Arab Bd for Surgery 1979–; Chair. Arab Bd Cttee for Sub-specialities in Surgery, Arab Bd for Orthopaedic Surgery 1990–, Chair. Training Cttee 1988–; Chair. Nat. Arab Bd Cttee and Co-ordinator, Arab Bd Programme in Surgery, Bahrain; Examiner, Ministry of Health Qualification Examination 1982–, Royal Coll. of Surgeons, Ireland, Part B Fellowship Examination; mem. Editorial Bd Bahrain Medical Bulletin; Founding mem. and Pres. Gulf Orthopaedic Asscn; mem. European Soc. for Sport Medicine, Knee Surgery and Arthroscopy; Fellow, British Orthopaedic Asscn, Royal Coll. of Surgeons, Ireland. *Publications:* numerous papers and articles. *Leisure interest:* tennis. *Address:* c/o Shura Council, PO Box: 2991, Shaikh Duaij Road, Ghudaibiya, Bahrain (office). *Website:* www.shura.gov.bh (office).

MOUSKOURI, Joanna (Nana); Greek singer and politician; b. 13 Oct. 1934, Athens; d. of Constantin and Alice Mouskouri; m. 1st George Petsilas; one s. one d.; m. 2nd Andre Chapelle; ed Athens Nat. Conservatory; singer 1956–; living in Paris 1962–; has given concerts world-wide; numerous TV appearances including Numéro 1 1979 and Nana Mouskouri à Athènes 1984; UNICEF Amb. 1993–94, Special Rep. for the Performing Arts and Hon. Spokesperson; mem. European Parl. 1994–; has received 300 Gold and Platinum Discs world-wide; Gran Cruz Placa de Plata (Dominican Repub.) 2006, Officier Légion d'honneur 2007, Grand Commdr Order of Benefaction (Greece) 2007; Greek Broadcasting Festival Award 1959, Barcelona Festival Award, No. 1 French Female Singer 1979; No. 1 Female Singer World-wide, Canada 1980 and numerous other awards and prizes. *Songs include:* L'enfant au tambour, Les parapluies de Cherbourg, C'est bon la vie, Plaisir d'amour, Ave Maria, L'amour en héritage, Only love, White Rose of Athens, Je chante avec toi, Liberté. *Publications:* Chanter ma vie 1989, Memoirs 2007. *Leisure interests:* collecting antique jewellery, antiques and paintings, swimming. *Address:* c/o Polygram, 20 rue des Fossés Saint-Jacques, 75005 Paris, France (office); Aharnon 289, GR112 53, Athens, Greece (home). *Telephone:* (22) 7521068 (home). *Fax:* (22) 7522293 (home). *E-mail:* nemaprod@bluewin.ch (home). *Website:* www.nanamouskouri.net.

MOUSSA, Amre Mahmoud, LLB; Egyptian politician and diplomatist; *Secretary-General, League of Arab States;* b. 3 Oct. 1936, Cairo; ed Cairo Univ.; joined Ministry of Foreign Affairs 1957; served in several diplomatic posts abroad, including Amb. to India 1983–86; Perm. Rep. to the UN 1990–91; Minister of Foreign Affairs 1991–2001; Sec.-Gen., League of Arab States (Arab League) 2001–. *Address:* League of Arab States, POB 11642, Tahrir Square, Cairo, Egypt (office). *Telephone:* (2) 3934499 (office). *Fax:* (2) 5740331 (office). *E-mail:* secretary-general@las.int (office). *Website:* www.arableagueoline.org (office).

MOUSSA, Pierre L.; French banker; b. 5 March 1922, Lyon; m. Anne-Marie Trousseau 1957; ed Ecole Normale Supérieure; Insp. of Finances 1946–50; Tech. Adviser to Sec. of State for Finance 1949–51, Dept of External Econ. Relations 1951–54, Dir Econ. Affairs and Planning, Ministry for Overseas Territories 1954–59; Dir of Civil Aviation, Ministry of Public Works and Transport 1959–62; Dir Dept of Operations for Africa, World Bank 1962–64; Pres. French Fed. of Assurance Cos 1965–69; Pres. Banque de Paris et des Pays-Bas 1969–81, Chair. 1978–81; Chair. Finance and Devt Inc. 1982–86, Pallas Holdings 1983–92, Dillon, Read Ltd 1984–87, France Développement (Frandev) 1986–90, Cresvale Partners 1987–94, Pallas Invest 1988–90, Pallas Monaco 1988–96, The Managed Convertible Fund 1990–95, Pallas Ltd 1992–93, Strand Assocs Ltd 1993–, Strand Partners Ltd 1993–94, The Prometheus Fund 1993–95, Forum pour l'Afrique 1995–, West Africa Growth Fund 1997–, Fondation pour l'Entreprise Africaine 1999–; dir numerous cos; Officier, Légion d'honneur 1976, Officier, Ordre nat. du Mérite. *Publications:* L'économie de la zone franc, Les chances économiques de la communauté Franco-Africaine, Les nations prolétaires, Les Etats-Unis et les nations prolétaires, La roue de la fortune: souvenirs d'un financier 1989, Caliban naufragé: les relations Nord-Sud à la fin du XXe siècle 1994. *Address:* 49 Devonshire Close, London, W1G 7BG (office); 14 Pelham Place, South Kensington, London, SW7 2NH, England (home). *Telephone:* (20) 7436-4500 (office). *Fax:* (20) 7323-0885 (office). *E-mail:* pierremoussa@btinternet.com (office).

MOUSSAVI, Farshid, BSc, DipArch; British (b. Iranian) architect; *Professor of Architecture, Harvard University;* b. 1965, Tehran; m. Alejandro Zaera-Polo; ed Univ. Coll. London, Bartlett School of Architecture, Harvard Univ., USA, Dundee Univ., RIBA; moved to London with family 1979; worked with Renzo Piano workshop, Genoa; with Office for Metropolitan Architecture, Rotterdam 1991–93; Co-Founder and Owner (with husband Alejandro Zaera-Polo) Foreign Office Architects Ltd, London 1995–; Unit Master, Architectural Asscn School of Architecture 1993–2000; Visiting Prof., Princeton Univ., UCLA, Columbia Univ., Berlage Inst., Amsterdam, Hoger Architecture Inst., Belgium; Prof. and Head of Architecture Inst., Acad. of Fine Arts, Vienna 2002–05; Kenzo Tange Visiting Design Critic, Harvard Design School 2005; currently Prof. of Architecture, Harvard Univ.; represented UK at Architecture Biennale, Venice, Italy 2002; mem. Int. Design Cttee (IDC), London; mem. Design and Architecture Advisory Group to British Council; mem. Aga Khan Award for Architecture Steering Cttee 2005– (Chair. Jury 2004); mem. jury RIBA Gold Medal; numerous awards including Architect of the Year Award, Spain, Charles Jencks Award 2005, Architectural Digest Award 2007. *Architectural works include:* Yokohama Int. Ferry Terminal, Japan 1996–2002 (Eric Miralles Prize for Architecture 2003, Kanagawa Architecture Prize); Belgo Restaurant Notting Hill Br., London 1998, Bristol 1999, New York 1999; Bluemoon Hotel, Groningen, Netherlands; Municipal Police HQ, Joiosa, Spain 2000–; Public Square and Theatre, nr Alicante 2001–; Coastal Park, nr Barcelona 2002–; T'Raboes Harbour Facilities, Amersfoort, Netherlands 2002–; Meydan Retail Complex and Multiplex, Istanbul, Turkey 2007 (European Business Award for the Environment, Urban Land Inst. Award for Excellence, Prime Property Award, ArkiPARC Award); Carabanchel Social Housing (RIBA European Award 2008); John Lewis Dept Store and Cineplex, Leicester, UK 2008. *Publications include:* The Yokohama Project 2002, Foreign Office Architects Ltd's ARC 2002; numerous monographs. *Address:* Foreign Office Architects, 55 Curtain Road, London, EC2A 3PT, England (office). *Fax:* (20) 7033-9801 (office). *E-mail:* london@f-o-a.net (office). *Website:* www.f-o-a.net (office).

MOUSSAVI, Mir Hussein; Iranian politician; b. 1942, Iran; m. Zahra Rahnavard; ed Nat. Univ., Tehran; trained as an architect; joined Islamic Soc. at univ. in Tehran and active in Islamic socs since; imprisoned briefly for opposition to the Shah 1973; a Founder-mem. Islamic Republican Party (IRP) 1979; apptd Chief Ed. IRP newspaper Islamic Republic 1979; Foreign Minister Aug.–Oct. 1981; elected Prime Minister by Majlis (consultative ass.) 1981–89, Adviser to the Pres. 1989; currently mem. Shura-ye Tashkhis-e Maslahat-e Nezam—Council to Determine the Expediency of the Islamic Order. *Address:* c/o Office of the President, Palestine Avenue, Azerbaijan Intersection, Tehran, Iran.

MOUSTIERS, Pierre Jean (Rossi), LenD; French author and producer; b. 13 Aug. 1924, La Seyne (Var); ed Univs of Aix-Marseilles and Neuchâtel; Attaché, Office des Changes, French zone in Germany 1947–49; Chief of Information Services, Nat. Information and Protection Centre for Construction (CNIP) 1950–60; medical del., pharmaceutical lab. Merck, Darmstadt 1961, later regional insp.; Literary Critic, Nice-Matin 1970, Radio-Marseille; Officier des Arts et Lettres, Médaille des Combattants de la Résistance; Hommes et Lectures Prize 1962, Grand Prix de littérature sportive, Prix Jean Giono, Italy 1986. *Play:* Les Trois Chaînes (Théâtre de Boulogne-Billancourt) 1976. *Television:* L'hiver d'un gentilhomme 1973, La mort du Pantin 1975, Une place forte 1976, Un crime de notre temps 1977, La ronde de nuit (Grand Prix du Scénario) 1978, Le Coq de Bruyére 1980, Le Curé de Tours (Prix Acad. Balzac for TV adaptation 1980) 1980, Antoine et Julie 1981, Bel Ami 1983, L'Affaire Caillaux (Sceptre d'Or) 1985, Le Coeur du Voyage 1986, L'Eté de la Révolution 1989, Les Grandes Familles 1989, L'Interdiction 1992, Pris au piège 1993, Eugénie Grandet 1993, Un si bel orage 1995. *Publications:* Le journal d'un geôlier 1957, La mort du Pantin 1961, Le pharisien 1962, La paroi (Grand Prix du Roman, Acad. française1969) 1969, L'hiver d'un gentilhomme (Prix des Maisons de la Presse 1972) 1971, Une place forte (Grand Prix littéraire de Provence 1975, Prix Louis Philippe Kammans) 1974, Un crime de notre temps (Prix des libraires 1977) 1976, Prima Donna 1978, Le Coeur du voyage 1981, La grenade 1984, Un Aristocrate à la lanterne 1986, L'Eclat 1990, Un si bel orage 1991, La Flambée 1993, L'Or du torrent 1995, A l'Abri du Monde (Prix Chateaubriant) 1997, Saskia 1999, Ce fils unique 2000; Hervé Bazin ou le romancier en mouvement (essay) 1973, Ce Fils Unique 2000, De Rêve et de Glace 2001, Le Dernier Mot d'un Roi (Prix du roman historique) 2003, Demain, dès l'Aube 2005, L'avenir ne s'oublie pas 2006. *Leisure interests:* mountaineering, reading, painting and drawing, taxidermy. *Address:* Campagne Sainte Anne, boulevard des Acacias, 83100 Toulon, France. *E-mail:* pierremoustiers@wanadoo.fr. *Website:* www.pierremoustier.com.

MOUT, Marianne Elisabeth Henriette Nicolette, DLitt; Dutch historian and academic; *Professor of Central European Studies and of Modern History, Leiden University;* b. 31 May 1945, Wassenaar; d. of Arie Mout and Maria Helena van Tooren; m. 1st Robbert Salomon van Santen (divorced 1979); m. 2nd Peter Felix Ganz 1987; ed Rijnlands Lyceum, Wassenaar, Univ. of Amsterdam; research student, Czechoslovakia 1966, 1967; Asst Keeper, Jewish Historical Museum, Amsterdam 1969; Ed., Martinus Nijhoff publrs

1970; Lecturer in Modern History, Utrecht Univ. 1975–76; Sr Lecturer in Dutch History, Leiden Univ. 1976–94, Prof. of Cen. European Studies 1990–, Prof. of Modern History 1994–; Man. Ed. Tijdschrift voor Geschiedenis 1981–86; Fellow, Netherlands Inst. for Advanced Studies, Wassenaar 1987–88, 1993–94; Pres. Conseil Int. pour l'édition des oeuvres complètes d'Erasme; mem. Bd Inst. of Netherlands History (Instituut voor Nederlandse Geschiedenis) 1989–; mem. Royal Netherlands Acad. of Arts and Sciences; Corresp. mem. Austrian Acad. of Sciences. *Publications:* Komenský v Amsterodamu (with J. Polišenský) 1970, Bohemen en de Nederlanden in de zestiende eeuw 1975, Plakkaat van Verlatinge 1581 1979, Die Kultur des Humanismus 1998; numerous articles, mainly on 16th–17th century Dutch and Cen. European history of ideas and cultural history; ed. and co-ed. of several books, including Gerhard Oestreich, Antiker Geist und moderner Staat bei Justus Lipsius 1989, Erasmianism Idea and Reality 1997. *Address:* Department of History, PB 9515, 2300 RA Leiden (office); Oranje Nassaulaan 27, 2361 LB Warmond, Netherlands (home). *Telephone:* (71) 5272759 (office); (71) 5272651 (office). *Fax:* (71) 5272652 (office). *E-mail:* m.e.h.n.mout@hum.leidenuniv.nl (office). *Website:* www.geschiedenis.leidenuniv.nl (office).

MOUTAWAKIL, Nawal el-; Moroccan sports administrator, politician and fmr athlete; *Minister of Youth and Sports;* b. 15 April 1962, Casablanca; m.; two c.; ed Iowa State Univ., USA; gold medallist, 400m hurdles, Olympic Games, Los Angeles 1988 (first Moroccan, African and Muslim woman to win Olympic Gold); Asst Coach, Iowa State Univ.; Dir Nat. School of Track and Field, Casablanca br. 1991; currently Minister of Youth and Sports; Vice-Pres. Moroccan Track and Field Fed. 1992; mem. Moroccan Nat. Olympic Cttee; Sec. of State for Sport and Youth 1997; Sr Exec., Fondation Banque Marocaine du Commerce Exterieur; mem. Athletes' Comm., Int. Asscn Athletics Feds 1989–, mem. Council 1995–, mem. Devt Sub-Comm. for Women; mem. Int. Olympic Cttee (first Muslim woman) 1998–, (mem. Working Group on Women and Sport 1996–), mem. Electoral Coll.; mem. Comité Int. des Jeux Mediterranéens, Comité Int. des Jeux de la Francophonie, Laureus World Sports Acad.; mem. Rassemblement national des indépendants; Chevalier, Ordre nat. du Mérite Exceptionnel (Morocco) 1983, Chevalier, Ordre nat. du Lion (Senegal) 1988; one of Outstanding Arab Women 2008. *Address:* Ministry of Youth and Sports, blvd ibn Sina, Rabat, Morocco. *Telephone:* (3) 7680028. *Fax:* (3) 7680145.

MOUTINOT, Laurent; Swiss lawyer and politician; *President, Council of State of Geneva;* b. 2 March 1953, Geneva; m.; three c.; advocate, Geneva Bar 1978–97; Pres. Asloca romande 1990–93, Vice-Pres. Asloca suisse 1990–97; Deputy Grand Council of Geneva 1993–97; Leader of Parl. Group 1994–96; elected (Parti socialiste) to Council of State of Geneva (Département de l'aménagement, de l'équipement et du logement) 1997–, Vice-Pres. 2001–02, Pres. 2002–03, 2007–. *Address:* Conseil d'Etat, Rue David-Dufour 5, case postale, 1211 Geneva 8, Switzerland (office). *Telephone:* (22) 3274940 (office). *Website:* www.geneve.ch/chancellerie/conseil (office).

MOUTON, Jacques; French banker; *Honorary Chairman, Caisse Nationale des Caisses d'Epargne;* b. 1937; Chair. Supervisory Bd and Chair. Remuneration and Selection Cttee, Caisse Nationale des Caisses d'Epargne 2003–07, Hon. Chair. 2007–. *Address:* Caisse Nationale des Caisses d'Epargne, 50 avenue Pierre-Mendès, 75201 Paris Cedex 13, France (office). *Telephone:* 1-58-40-41-42 (office). *Fax:* 1-58-40-48-00 (office). *E-mail:* info@caisse-epargne.fr (office). *Website:* www.caisse-epargne.fr (office).

MOVAHEDIAN ATTAR, Rasoul; Iranian diplomatist; *Ambassador to UK;* m. Azam Kolahdouzan; fmr Advisor to Minister of Foreign Affairs, fmr Head of Dept for Soviet Union, Eastern Europe, N America in Ministry of Foreign Affairs, fmr Amb. to Czech Repub. and Slovakia, to Portugal, Amb. to UK 2006–. *Address:* Embassy of Iran, 16 Prince's Gate, London, SW7 1PT, England (office). *Telephone:* (20) 7225-3000 (office). *Fax:* (20) 7589-4440 (office). *E-mail:* info@iran-embassy.org.uk (office). *Website:* www.iran-embassy.org.uk (office).

MOWAT, Farley McGill, OC, BA; Canadian writer; b. 12 May 1921, Belleville, Ont.; s. of Angus Mowat and Helen Mowat (née Thomson); m. 1st Frances Mowat 1947; two s.; m. 2nd Claire Mowat 1963; ed Toronto Univ.; served in the Canadian Army 1939–45; Arctic exploration 1947–49; full-time writer 1950–; Hon. DLitt (Laurentian Univ.) 1970, (Univ. of Victoria) 1982, (Lakehead Univ.) 1986, (Univ. Coll. of Cape Breton) 1996; Hon. DLaws (Lethbridge, Toronto, Prince Edward Island, Queen's Univ.); Hon. DH (McMaster Univ., Hamilton) 1994; Hon. LLD (Queen's Univ.) 1995; Gov.-Gen.'s Award, Canadian Centennial Medal, Leacock Medal for Humour, Hans Christian Andersen Award, Anisfield Wolf Award, Mark Twain Award, Gemini Award (Best Documentary Script), Award of Excellence (Atlantic Film Festival) 1990, Canadian Achievers Award, Take Back the Nation Award, Council of Canadians 1991, Author's Award, Author of the Year, Foundation for Advancement of Canadian Letters 1993, Fourth Nat. Prize for Foreign Literature Books, Beiyue Literature and Art Publishing House, People's Repub. of China 1999, Jubilee Commemorative Medal 2002, Nat. Outdoor Book Award for Lifetime Achievement 2005. *Publications:* People of The Deer 1952, The Regiment 1955, Lost in The Barrens 1956, The Dog Who Wouldn't Be 1957, Coppermine Journey 1958, The Grey Seas Under 1958, The Desperate People 1959, Ordeal by Ice 1960, Owls in the Family 1961, The Serpent's Coil 1961, The Black Joke 1962, Never Cry Wolf 1963, Westviking 1965, The Curse of the Viking Grave 1966, Canada North 1967, The Polar Passion 1967, This Rock Within the Sea 1968, The Boat Who Wouldn't Float 1969, Sibir 1970, A Whale for the Killing 1972, Tundra 1973, Wake of the Great Sealers (with David Blackwood) 1973, The Snow Walker 1975, Canada North Now 1976, And No Birds Sang 1979, The World of Farley Mowat 1980, Sea of Slaughter 1984, My Discovery of America 1985, Virunga (Woman in the Mist, USA) 1987, The New Founde Land 1989, Rescue the Earth 1990, My Father's Son 1992, Born Naked 1993, Aftermath 1995, A Farley Mowat Reader 1997; TV documentary: Sea of Slaughter 1990, The Farfarers 1998, Walking on the Land 2000, High Latitudes 2002, No Man's River 2004, Bay of Spirits 2006, Otherwise 2008. *Leisure interests:* travel, all facets of nature. *Address:* c/o Writers Union of Canada, 24 Ryerson Avenue, Toronto, Ont., M4T 2P3 (office); 18 King Street, Port Hope, Ont., L1A 2R4, Canada.

MOXLEY, John Howard, III, MD, FACP; American physician and business executive; *Managing Director, North American Health Care Division, Korn/Ferry International;* b. 10 Jan. 1935, Elizabeth, NJ; s. of John Howard Moxley, Jr and Cleopatra Mundy Moxley; m. Doris Banchik; three s.; ed Williams Coll. and Univ. of Colorado School of Medicine; hosp. posts 1961–63; Clinical Assoc., Nat. Cancer Inst., Solid Tumor Branch 1963–65; Sr Resident Physician, Peter Bent Brigham Hosp. 1965–66; mem. Lymphoma Task Force Nat. Cancer Inst. 1965–77; Instructor in Medicine and Asst to the Dean, Harvard Medical School 1966–69; Dean Univ. of Md School of Medicine and Assoc. Prof. of Medicine 1969–73; Vice-Chancellor for Health Sciences and Dean of School of Medicine, Univ. of Calif., San Diego and Assoc. Prof. of Medicine 1973–80; Asst Sec. of Defense for Health Affairs, Dept of Defense, Washington, DC 1979–81; Sr Vice-Pres., Corp. Planning and Alternative Services, American Medical Int. Inc. 1981–87; Pres. and CEO MetaMedical Inc., Beverly Hills, Calif. 1987–89; Man. Dir, N American Health Care Div., Korn/Ferry Int. 1989–; Dir Nat. Fund for Medical Educ. 1986–, Chair. 1993–; Fellow American Fed. for Clinical Research; mem. Inst. of Medicine (NAS), American Soc. of Clinical Oncology, American Medical Asscn; Dir Henry M. Jackson Foundation for the Advancement of Mil. Medicine 1983, Naval Studies Bd; Sec. of Defense Medal for Distinguished Public Service and other awards. *Publications:* numerous papers in scientific journals. *Address:* Korn/Ferry International, 1900 Avenue of the Stars, Suite 2600, Los Angeles, CA 90067 (office); 8180 Manitoba Street 210, Playa del Rey, CA 90293, USA (home). *Telephone:* (310) 843-4123 (office). *E-mail:* moxleyj@kornferry.com (office). *Website:* www.kornferry.com (office).

MOXON, (Edward) Richard, MB, BChir, FRCP; British medical doctor; b. 16 July 1941, Leeds; s. of the late Gerald Richard Moxon and Margaret Forster Mohun; m. Marianne Graham 1973; two s. one d.; ed Shrewsbury School, St John's Coll., Cambridge and St Thomas' Hosp. Medical School, London; with Hosp. for Sick Children, Great Ormond St, London 1969; Research Fellow in Infectious Diseases, Children's Hosp. Medical Center, Boston, Mass, USA 1971–74; Asst Prof. of Pediatrics, Johns Hopkins Hosp., Baltimore, Md, USA 1974–80, Dir Eudowood Pediatric Infectious Diseases Unit 1982–84; Action Research Prof. of Paediatrics, Univ. of Oxford 1984–; Group Leader, Molecular Infectious Diseases Group (Pathogenic Bacteria), The Weatherall Inst. of Molecular Medicine, John Radcliffe Hosp. 1988–; Visiting Scientist, Dept of Molecular Biology, Washington Univ., St Louis, Mo. 1990–91; Fellow, Jesus Coll. Oxford 1984–; Founder and Chair. Oxford Vaccine Group 1994–; mem. Steering Group, Encapsulated Bacteria, WHO 1987–93; Chair. MRC Sub-Cttee Polysaccharide Vaccines 1986–90; Convenor, BPA Immunology and Infectious Diseases Group 1984–89; mem. American Soc. Clinical Investigation; Founding Fellow, Acad. of Medical Sciences 1998; Fellow Infectious Diseases Soc. of America, American Soc. Pediatric Research; Mitchell Lecturer, Royal Coll. of Physicians 1992, Bob Deich Memorial Lecturer, Univ. of Rochester, NY 1995, Teale Lecturer, Royal Coll. of Physicians 1998, Burroughs-Wellcome Lecturer, Univ. of Pennsylvania 1998, Dolman Lecturer, Univ. of British Columbia 1999, J. H. P. Jonxis Lecturer, Beatrix Children's Hosp., Groningen, Netherlands 2001. *Publications:* Neonatal Infections (with D. Isaacs) 1991, A Practical Approach to Paediatric Infectious Diseases (with D. Isaacs) 1996, Longman Handbook of Neonatal Infections (with D. Isaacs) 1999; Modern Vaccines (editorial adviser) 1990, Progress in Vaccinology (ed.) 2000; more than 300 scientific articles on infections, molecular basis of bacterial virulence and vaccines published in major journals. *Leisure interests:* music, literature, sports. *Address:* Department of Paediatrics, The Weatherall Institute of Molecular Medicine, University of Oxford, John Radcliffe Hospital, Headington, Oxford, OX3 9DS (office); 17 Moreton Road, Oxford, OX2 7AX, England (home). *Telephone:* (1865) 221074 (office); (1865) 222349 (office). *Fax:* (1865) 220479. *E-mail:* richard.moxon@paediatrics.ox.ac.uk (office). *Website:* www.imm.ox.ac.uk (office).

MOYANA, Kombo James, MA, MPhil, PhD; Zimbabwean banker; b. 4 July 1942, Chipinge; m.; one s. three d.; ed Columbia Univ., New York, USA; Research Fellow, Inst. de Développement Economique et de Planification, Dakar 1972; Fellow, UNITAR, New York 1973; int. finance economist, Div. of Money, Finance and Devt UNCTAD, New York and Geneva 1974–80; seconded to Ministry of Econ. Planning and Devt of Govt of Zimbabwe 1980; Deputy Gov. Reserve Bank of Zimbabwe 1980, Gov. 1983; Alt. Gov. IMF 1983; Pres. Inst. of Bankers (Zimbabwe) 1985–86; Exec. Sec. Preferential Trading Area of Eastern, Cen. and Southern African States –1991; CEO Trade & Investment Bank Ltd; Chair. Asscn of African Cen. Banks 1991–93. *Leisure interest:* farming. *Address:* PO Box 1283, Harare, Zimbabwe. *Telephone:* 790731; 7910721.

MOYANO, Hugo; Argentine trade union official; *Secretary-General, Confederación General del Trabajo (CGT);* b. 9 Jan. 1944, La Plata; Rep., Mar del Plata Div., Sindicato de Choferes de Camiones (trade union) 1962, Sec.-Gen. 1962–72, Sec.-Gen. Sindicato de Choferes de Camiones, Buenos Aires 1987–91, 1991–2003; Sec.-Gen. Mar del Plata Br., Partido Justicialista (PJ) 1983, becoming Sec. and Vice-Pres. Parl. Transport Comm.; Global Vice-Pres. Road Transport Div., Int. Fed. of Transport Workers 1998–; Sec.-Gen. Confederación Argentina de Trabajadores del Transporte 2003–05; Sec.-Gen. Confederación General del Trabajo (CGT) 2005–. *Address:* Confederación General del Trabajo, Azopardo 802, C1107ADN Buenos Aires, Argentina (office). *Telephone:* (11) 4343-1883 (office). *Website:* www.cgtra.org.ar (office).

MOYERS, William (Bill) D., FAAS; American journalist and broadcaster; *Executive Editor, Public Affairs Television, Inc.;* b. 5 June 1934, Hugo, Okla; s. of Henry Moyers and Ruby Johnson; m. Judith Davidson 1954; two s. one d.; ed Univ. of Texas, Edinburgh Univ. and Southwestern Baptist Theological Seminary; Exec. Asst to Senator Lyndon Johnson 1959–60; Assoc. Dir US Peace Corps 1961–63, Deputy Dir 1963; Special Asst to Pres. Johnson 1963–66, Press Sec. to Pres. 1965–66; Publr of Newsday, Long Island, NY 1966–70; host of This Week, weekly current affairs TV programme 1970; Ed.-in-Chief Bill Moyers Journal, Public Broadcasting Service 1971–76, 1978–81; Contrib. Newsweek 1974–76; Chief Corresp. CBS Reports 1976–78, Sr News Analyst, CBS News 1981–86; Exec. Ed. Public Affairs TV Inc. 1987–; news analyst, NBC News 1995–; Pres. Florence and John Schumann Foundation 1991–; mem. American Philosophical Soc.; Emmy Awards 1983–90, Gold Baton Award 1991, 1999, American Jewish Cttee Religious Liberty Award 1995, Walter Cronkite Award 1995, Fred Friendly First Amendment Award 1995, Charles Frankel Prize 1997, George Peabody Award 2000. *Publications:* Listening to America 1971, The Secret Government 1988, Joseph Campbell and the Power of Myth 1988, A World of Ideas 1989, Healing and the Mind 1993, Genesis: A Living Conversion 1996, Fooling with Words 1999. *Address:* Public Affairs Television Inc., 450 West 33rd Street, New York, NY 10001, USA.

MOYNIHAN, 4th Baron, cr. 1929; **Colin Berkeley Moynihan,** MA; British organization official and business executive; *Chairman, British Olympic Association;* b. 13 Sept. 1955; m. Gaynor-Louise Metcalf 1992; two s. one d.; ed Monmouth School, Univ. Coll., Oxford; World Gold Medal for Lightweight Rowing, Int. Rowing Fed. 1978, World Silver Medal for Rowing 1981, Silver Medal for Rowing, Olympics 1980; Personal Asst to Chair. Tate and Lyle Ltd 1978–80, Man. Tate and Lyle Agribusiness 1980–82; CEO Ridgways Tea and Coffee Merchants 1982–83, Chair. 1983–87; Minister for Sport 1987–90; Chair. CMA Consultants 1993–; Man. Dir Ind. Power Corpn plc 1996–2001; Chair. and CEO Consort Resources Group 2000–03; Exec. Chair. Clipper Windpower Europe Ltd 2004–, Dir Clipper Windpower PLC 2005–; Dir Rowan Group 1996–; Chair. British Olympic Asscn 2005–; Gov. Sports Aid Foundation (London and SE) 1980–82; Freeman City of London 1978. *Leisure interests:* reading, sport, music. *Address:* House of Lords, London, SW1A 0PW, England (office). *Telephone:* (20) 7219-3000 (office); (20) 7820-1978 (home). *Fax:* (20) 7820-7808 (home). *E-mail:* c.moynihan@cmagroup.org.uk (office). *Website:* www.parliament.uk/about_lords/about_lords.cfm (office); www.olympics.org.uk.

MOYO, Jonathan, MPA, PhD; Zimbabwean politician; b. 12 Jan. 1957; m.; fmr mem. Zimbabwe African Nat. Union-Patriotic Front (ZANU-PF); Minister of State for Information and Publicity 2000–05; fmr mem. Pres. Robert Mugabe's 'Gang of Four' politicians; architect of Zimbabwe's highly controlled press regime; currently mem. Parl. (ind.). *Leisure interests:* philosophy, classics, music, composition, tennis, scriptwriting. *Address:* Parliament Buildings, Harare, Zimbabwe (office). *Website:* www.parlzim.gov.zw (office).

MOZILO, Angelo R., BSc; American financial services industry executive; b. 1938, New York, NY; ed Fordham Univ., NY; Co-founder Countrywide Financial Corpn 1969, Chair. and CEO –2008 (following takeover by Bank of America); Co-founder IndyMac Bank (f. as Countrywide Mortgage Investment, spun off as ind. bank 1997, collapsed and seized by fed. regulators July 2008); Chair. Countryside Home Loans Inc.; Pres. Mortgage Bankers Asscn of America (MBA) 1991–92, mem. Bd of Dirs 1992–; mem. Bd of Dirs Jt Center for Housing Studies, Harvard Univ., The Home Depot 2006–; mem. Bd of Trustees Nat. Housing Endowment, Fordham Univ., Gonzaga Univ., St Francis High School, Calif.; Hon. LLD (Pepperdine Univ.); Ellis Island Medal of Honor, Albert Schweitzer Award, Boy Scouts of America James E. West Fellowship Award, Jane Wyman Humanitarian Service Award, Arthritis Foundation, Special Achievement Award for Humanitarian Service, Nat. Italian American Foundation, Housing Person of the Year Award 2004; inducted into Hall of Fame, Nat. Asscn of Home Builders. *Address:* c/o Countrywide Financial Corpn, 4500 Park Granada, Calabasas, CA 91302-1613, USA. *Telephone:* (818) 225-3000.

MPAHLWA, Mandisi B. M.; South African politician; *Minister of Trade and Industry;* fmr Deputy Minister of Finance; Minister of Trade and Industry 2004–. *Address:* Ministry of Trade and Industry, House of Trade and Industry, 11th Floor, cnr Prinsloo and Pretorius Streets, Pretoria 0002 (office); Private Bag X84, Pretoria 0001, South Africa (office). *Telephone:* (12) 3109791 (office). *Fax:* (12) 3222701 (office). *E-mail:* alec@dti.pwv.gov.za (office). *Website:* www.dti.gov.za (home).

MPALANYI-NKOYOYO, Most Rev. Livingstone, DD; Ugandan ecclesiastic; *Archbishop of Uganda and Bishop of Kampala;* b. 4 Oct. 1939, Namukozi Village, Ssingo Co., Mityana Dist; s. of the late Erisa Wamala Nkoyoyo; m. Ruth Nkoyoyo; three s. two d.; ed Bishop Lutaaya Theological Coll., Buwalasi Theological Coll., Legoni Trinity Coll. Ghana, Cranmer Theological House; worked as a mechanic 1959–62; lay reader, Church of Uganda 1962; curate, Kasubi Parish 1970, priest 1971–74; Parish Priest, Nsangi Parish 1975–76; Archdeacon, Namirembe Archdeaconry 1977; Asst Bishop, Namirembe Diocese 1980; Suffragan Bishop, Mukono Area 1982; Bishop, Mukono Diocese 1984; Archbishop of Uganda and Bishop of Kampala 1995–. *Address:* Church of Uganda, PO Box 14123, Mengo, Kampala, Uganda (office). *Telephone:* (41) 270218 (office); (41) 271138 (home). *Fax:* (41) 251925 (office). *E-mail:* couab@uol.co.ug (office).

MPINGA KASENDA, PhD; Democratic Republic of the Congo politician and university professor; b. 30 Aug. 1937, Tshilomba; ed Elisabethville (now Lubumbashi) High School of Social Sciences, Catholic Univ. of Lovanium and Univ. of Bordeaux, France; teacher, Tshilomba Secondary School 1957–59; studied at Lubumbashi and Lovanium Univ. 1959–65; Asst Lecturer, Lovanium Univ. 1965–66, Prof. 1966–70; Adviser to the Chancellor, Nat. Univ. of Zaïre and to the Minister of Public Admin. 1971–72; mem. Political Bureau Mouvement Populaire de la Révolution (MPR) 1972, mem. Perm. Cttee 1974–80; Deputy People's Commr 1975, First State Commr 1977–80; Dir Makanda Kabobi Inst. (MPR school) 1974–; Commdr, Nat. Order of Zaïre and Democratic People's Repub. of Korea, Grand Officier Ordre du Mérite nat. (Mauritania). *Publications:* Ville de Kinshasa, Organisation politique et administrative 1968, L'administration publique du Zaïre 1973, Les reformes administratives au Zaïre 1975. *Address:* Institut Makanda Kabobi, avenue de la Gombe, Kinshasa (office); 384 Quartier Gombele, Kinshasa/Lemba, POB 850, Democratic Republic of the Congo (home).

MPOMBO, George W.; Zambian politician; *Minister of Defence;* mem. Nat. Ass. (Movt for Multi-party Democracy—MMD) 2001–, Minister of Energy and Water Devt 2003-05, Minister for Copperbelt Prov. 2005-06, Minister of Defence 2006–. *Address:* Ministry of Defence, PO Box 31931, Lusaka, Zambia (office). *Telephone:* (1) 252366 (office).

MRAD, Abd ar-Rahim; Lebanese politician; fmr Minister of Educ.; Minister of National Defence 2004–05. *Address:* c/o Ministry of National Defence, Yarze, Beirut, Lebanon (office).

MRAMBA, Basil; Tanzanian politician; ed Makerere Univ., City Univ. Grad. School, London, UK, Harvard Grad. School of Business, USA; Man. Asst, Williamson Diamond Mwadui 1964–69; Manpower Devt Dir Nat. Development Corpn 1969–72; Dir Gen. Small Scale Industries Org-SIDO 1973–80; mem. Parl. 1980–95; Minister of Trade and Industry 1995–2000, 2006–08; Minister of Finance 2000–06; Minister of Infrastructure Devt 2006. *Address:* c/o Ministry of Industry, Trade and Marketing, POB 9503, Dar es Salaam, Tanzania (office).

MRAMOR, Dušan, DEcon; Slovenian economist and academic; *Professor of Finance, University of Ljubljana;* b. 1 Nov. 1953, Ljubljana; ed Univ. of Ljubljana; fmr Visiting Prof., Indiana Univ., USA, Cen. European Univ., Budapest, Wirtschaftuniversität, Vienna, Assoc. Dean, Faculty of Econs, Univ. of Ljubljana, Chair. Man. Board, Univ. of Ljubljana; fmr mem. Prime Minister's Strategic Econ. Council; Minister of Finance 2002–04; Prof. of Finance, Univ. of Ljubljana 2004–; fmr Pres. Expert Council Agency for the Securities Market; fmr Pres. Bd of Dirs Univ. of Ljubljana; mem. Expert Council Slovenian Inst. of Auditing, Coordinating Cttee Slovenian Asscn of Economists, Slovenian Asscn of Accountants. *Address:* Faculty of Economics, University of Ljubljana, Kardeljeva ploscad 17, Ljubljana, 1000, Slovenia (office). *Telephone:* (1) 5892400 (office). *Fax:* (1) 5892698 (office). *E-mail:* dusan.mramor@ef.uni-lj.si (office). *Website:* www.ef.uni-lj.si/pedagogi/pe_pedagog.asp?id=51 (office).

MROCZKOWSKI, Marek, MEconSc; Polish business executive; *CEO, Unipetrol a.s.;* ed Warsaw School of Econs; with Polski Koncern Naftowy ORLEN SA 1994–2001; Pres. and CEO, POLKOMTEL SA 2001–02; Pres. and CEO, ELANA SA, Torun 2003–04; currently CEO, Unipetrol a.s., also Vice-Chair., Bd of Dirs. *Address:* Unipetrol a.s. 110 05 Prague, Czech Republic (office). *Website:* www.unipetrol.cz (office).

MROUDJAE, Ali; Comoran politician; *Leader, Parti Comorien pour la Démocratie et le Progrès;* b. 2 Aug. 1939, Moroni; s. of Chohezi Mroudjae and Charif Zahara; m. Nourdine Batouli 1967; three s. five d.; Minister of Foreign Affairs and Co-operation 1979–82; Prime Minister of the Comoros 1982–85; Minister of State for Internal and Social Affairs Jan.–Sept. 1985; numerous other portfolios; currently Leader Parti Comorien pour la Démocratie et le Progrès (PCDP). *Leisure interests:* reading, swimming, travelling. *Address:* PCDP, Route Djivani, BP 179, Moroni; BP 58, Rond Point Gobadjou, Moroni, Comoros. *Telephone:* (73) 1733 (PCDP); (73) 1266. *Fax:* (73) 0650 (PCDP).

MROŻEK, Sławomir; Polish writer; b. 26 June 1930, Borzęcin nr Brzesk; m.; fmr cartoonist, satirist and journalist; mem. Polish Writers' Asscn 1951–71, 1978–; numerous prizes include Silver Cross of Merit 1953, Julian Brano Prize 1954, Kościelscy Foundation Award (Switzerland) 1962, Prix de l'Humour Noir 1964, Alfed Jurzykowski Award 1964, 1985, State Prize (Austria) 1972, Prix Crédit Industriel et Commercial Paris Théâtre (France) 1993. *Publications include:* prose includes: Maleńkie lato (novel) 1956, The Elephant (short stories) 1957, Wesele w Atomicach (Wedding in Atomice) 1959, The Rain (short stories) 1962, Moniza Clavier (short story) 1967, The Ugupu Bird (short stories) 1968, Dwa listy 1974, Małe listy 1981, Dziennik powrotu 2000; plays include: The Police 1958, What a Lovely Dream, Indyk (Turkey) 1961, Karol 1961, Striptease 1964, Tango 1964, On the High Seas, Vatzlav 1970, Druga zmiana (Second Service) 1970, Testarium 1970, Blessed Event 1973, Rzeźnia (Butchery) 1973, Emigrants 1974, Garbus (Humpback) 1975, Utwory sceniczne nowe 1976, Krawiec (Tailor) 1977, Drugie danie (Second Dish), Pieszo 1983, Miłość na Krymie (Love in Crimea) 1993, Wielebni 2001; series of satirical drawings: Polska w obrazach (Poland in Pictures) 1957, Postępowiec (Progressive man) 1960, Rysunki 1982, Polska w obrazach i polskie cykle (Poland in Pictures and the Other Polish Series) 1998. *Address:* Związek Literatów Polskich, ul. Królewska 84 m. 18, 30-079 Kraków, Poland (office). *Telephone:* (12) 636-29-66 (office).

MROZIEWICZ, Robert; Polish politician and historian; *Professor, Collegium Civitas, Polish Academy of Sciences;* b. 20 Sept. 1942, Warsaw; m. Elżbieta Nowik; two s.; ed Univ. of Warsaw; Asst, Warsaw Univ. 1965–68, Polish Inst. of Int. Affairs 1968–70; Inst. of History, Polish Acad. of Sciences 1971–89, Asst Prof., Inst. of History 1985, currently Prof., Collegium Civitas; Minister-Adviser, Ministry of Foreign Affairs; Deputy Perm. Rep. to UN, New York, then Perm. Rep. of UN, New York 1990–92; Under-Sec. of State in Ministry of Foreign Affairs; Pres. of UN Social and Economic Council 1992–97,

Pres. of Gen. Ass. 1992; Under-Sec. of State for Co-operation with Abroad and Integration with NATO in Ministry of Nat. Defence 1997; mem. Solidarity Trade Union 1980–99; Commdr's Cross of Order Polonia Restituta 1995. *Publications:* author and co-author of six monographs and various scientific articles. *Address:* Collegium Civitas, Palace of Culture and Science, Plac Defilad 1, 12 piętro, 00-901 Warsaw, Poland (office). *Telephone:* (22) 625-7187 (office). *Fax:* (22) 656-7175 (office). *Website:* www.collegium.edu.pl (office).

MSIKA, Joseph; Zimbabwean politician; *Vice-President;* m. Maria Msika; Co-Vice-Pres. Zimbabwe African Nat. Union (ZANU) Dec. 2000–; Co-Vice-Pres. of Zimbabwe 2001–. *Address:* Office of the Vice-Presidents, Munhumutapa Building, Samora Machel Avenue, Private Bag 7700, Harare, Zimbabwe (office). *Telephone:* (4) 707091 (office).

MSIMANG, Mendi, BA; South African diplomatist and civil servant; *Treasurer, African National Congress;* b. 1928, Johannesburg; m. Mantombazana Tshabalala; four c. from previous marriage; ed Univ. Coll. of Rome, Lesotho; with Rand Steam Laundries, organizer Laundry Workers' Union; asbestos assayer Costa Rican consulate; joined ANC, Personal Sec. to then Sec.-Gen. Walter Sisulu; with Nelson Mandela (q.v.) and Oliver Tambo's law practice –1960; left for UK; Rep. ANC Mission to UK and Ireland; Co-Founder South Africa in Fact (ANC newsletter); Ed. Spotlight on South Africa (ANC journal); Admin. Sec. ANC Nat. Exec. Cttee in Exile, E Africa br.; collaborated with Oliver Tambo to est. Solomon Mahlangu Freedom Coll., Tanzania; ANC Educ. Officer; Admin. Sec. Treas.-Gen. of ANC's office, Zambia; ANC Chief Rep. to India 1969, to UK 1988; returned to SA 1990; elected mem. ANC Nat. Exec. Cttee 1991, Nat. Ass. 1994 (fmr Chair.); fmr Chair. ANC Parl. Caucus; High Commr to UK 1995–98; Treasurer ANC 1998–; Chair. Nelson Mandela Children's Fund; Vice-Pres. Royal Over-Seas League, London; Fellow Rotarian, Rotary Club of London. *Leisure interests:* watching football, golf, jazz/blues, reading, theatre. *Address:* P.O. Box 25929, Monument Park, Pretoria 0105, South Africa.

MSUYA, Cleopa David, BA; Tanzanian politician and civil servant (retd); b. 4 Jan. 1931, Chomvu Usangi, Mwanga Dist; s. of David Kilenga and Maria Ngido; m. Rhoda Christopher 1959; four s. two d.; ed Old Moshi and Tabora Secondary Schools, Makerere Univ. Coll., Uganda; Civil Service, Community Devt Officer 1956–61, Commr for Community Devt 1961–64, Prin. Sec. to Ministry of Community Devt and Nat. Culture 1964, to Ministries of Land Settlement and Water Devt 1965–67, to Ministry of Econ. Affairs and Devt Planning 1967–70 and to Treas. 1970–72; Minister of Finance 1972–75, 1983–85, for Finance, Econ. Affairs and Planning 1985–89, for Industries 1975–80, for Industries and Trade 1990–95; Prime Minister 1980–83, 1994–95; First Vice-Pres. 1994–95; mem. Nat. Ass. 1995–2000; Gov. ADB, IMF; mem. Bd Dirs of several public corpns. *Address:* c/o Office of the Prime Minister and First Vice-President, PO Box 980, Dodoma, Tanzania.

MSWATI III, HM The King of Swaziland; Makhosetive; b. 19 April 1968; s. of the late King Sobhuza II and Queen Ntombi Laftwala; m. to 13 wives (Emakhosikati); 24 c.; ed Sherborne School, UK; crowned King of Swaziland 25 April 1986. *Leisure interests:* swimming, rugby. *Address:* Lozitha Palace, Mbabane, Swaziland.

MTETWA, Beatrice; Zimbabwean lawyer; *President, Law Society of Zimbabwe;* lawyer, Kantor and Immerman law firm, Harare; Speaker, The Bar Conf., UK 2004; Dir The Zimbabwe Independent newspaper; lawyer for Foreign Corresps Asscn of Zimbabwe; Council mem. Law Soc. of Zimbabwe, currently Pres.; mem. Zimbabwe Lawyers for Human Rights; Human Rights Lawyer of the Year 2003, Cttee to Protect Journalists Int. Press Freedom Award 2005, Bindmans Law and Campaigning Award 2006, Burton Benjamin Award 2008. *Address:* c/o Zimbabwe Lawyers for Human Rights, 6th Floor Beverly Court, 100 Nelson Mandela Avenue, Harare; Kantor and Immerman, MacDonald House, 10 Selous Avenue, Harare (office); c/o The Zimbabwean Independent, Zimind Publishers (Private) Limited, Suites 23 and 24, One Union Avenue, Harare, Zimbabwe. *Telephone:* (4) 7043512 (office). *Fax:* (4) 704436 (office). *E-mail:* kanim@ecoweb.co.zw (office).

MU, Guoguang; Chinese university professor; b. 22 Jan. 1931, Jinxi City, Liaoning Prov.; m. Chi Yuanxiang; one s. one d.; ed Nankai Univ.; Prof., Nankai Univ., Pres. 1986–95, Chair. Academic Cttee, Dir Inst. of Modern Optics; Pres. Chinese Optical Soc.; mem. Chinese Acad. of Sciences 1991; mem. 4th Presidium of Depts, Chinese Acad. of Sciences 2000–; Fellow, Optical Soc. of America, Third World Acad. of Sciences, Int. Soc. of Optical Eng; Hon. PhD (Kyoto Limengkom); several scientific awards. *Publications:* Optics (univ. textbook). *Leisure interest:* swimming. *Address:* Nankai University, Institute of Modern Optics, 94 Weijin Road, Tianjin 300071, People's Republic of China (office). *Telephone:* (22) 2350-2275 (office); (22) 2350-1688 (home). *Fax:* (22) 23240-3118 (office); (22) 2350-2896 (home). *E-mail:* mugg@nankai.edu.cn (home).

MUASHER, Marwan Jamil, MS, PhD; Jordanian politician and diplomatist; *Senior Vice-President for External Affairs, Communications and United Nations Affairs, World Bank Group;* b. 14 June 1956, Amman; two c.; ed American Univ. of Beirut, Lebanon, Purdue Univ., USA; Asst Research Engineer, Univ. of Petroleum and Minerals, Saudi Arabia 1983–84; Dir Computer Centre, Jordan Electric Power Co. 1984; Sr Consultant Special System Co. 1984–85; Head, Computer Unit and Monitory System, Ministry of Planning 1985–87, Dir Socio-Econ. Information Centre, Nat. Information System 1987–90; Press Adviser to Prime Minister 1990–91; Head, Jordan Information Bureau, USA 1991–94; Amb. to Israel 1995–96, to USA and Mexico 1997–2002; Minister of Information 1996, of Foreign Affairs 2002–04; Deputy Prime Minister and Minister of State for Prime Ministry Affairs and Govt Performance 2004–05; Senator 2006–07; Sr Vice-Pres. for External Affairs, Communications and UN Affairs, World Bank, Washington, DC

2007–; political columnist, Jordan Times 1983–90; Al-Kawkab Medal, First Order (Jordan) 2000, Dr hc (Purdue Univ.) 1999, Independence Medal 2000, Diplomat of the Year Award, LA Int. Affairs Council 2000. *Publications:* The Arab Center 2008. *Address:* The World Bank, 1818 H Street, NW, Washington, DC 20433, USA (office). *Telephone:* (202) 473-1000 (office). *Fax:* (202) 477-6391 (office). *Website:* www.worldbank.org (office).

MUBARAK, Gamal; Egyptian politician and business executive; *Secretary of the Policies Committee, National Democratic Party (NDP);* s. of Pres. Hosni Mubarak and Suzanne Mubarak; ed American Univ., Cairo; started career with Bank of America, served for six years in London; Sec. Policies Cttee NDP 2002–, also mem. Gen. Secr.; spokesman for US-Egyptian Business Advisory Body. *Address:* National Democratic Party (NDP), Cairo, Egypt (office). *Website:* www.ndp.org.eg (office).

MUBARAK, (Muhammad) Hosni, BMilSci, BA; Egyptian air force officer and head of state; *President;* b. 4 May 1928, Kafr El-Moseilha, Minuffya Governorate; m. Suzanne Sabet; two s.; ed Mil. Acad., Air Acad.; joined Air Force 1950, Lecturer Air Force Acad. 1952–59; Commdr Cairo West Air Base 1964; Dir-Gen. Air Acad. 1967–69; Air Force Chief of Staff 1969–72; C-in-C 1972–75; promoted to Lt-Gen. 1974; Vice-Pres. of Egypt 1975–81; Pres. 1981– (cand. of NDP); Vice-Pres. Nat. Democratic Party (NDP) 1979, Pres. 1982; mem. Higher Council for Nuclear Energy 1975–; Sec.-Gen. NDP and Political Bureau 1981–82, Chair. 1982–; Chair. OAU 1989–90, 1993–94, Arab Summit 1996–, GI5 1998, 2000; Pres. Emergency Arab Summit 2000, D-8 Summit 2001, COMESA Summit 2001; Order of Star of Honour 1964, 1974, Medal of the Star of Sinai of the First Order 1983 and numerous other foreign decorations; Dr hc (Bulgaria) 1998, (Beijing) 1999, (St Johns) 1999, (George Washington) 1999; Louise Michel Prize 1990, Prize of Democratic Human Rights, Social and Political Studies Centre, Paris 1990, UN Prize of Population 1994 and numerous other awards and honours. *Leisure interest:* squash. *Address:* Presidential Palace, Abdeen, Cairo, Egypt.

MUBARAK, HE Suzanne, BA, MA; Egyptian sociologist and national organization official; *President, National Council for Women;* b. 28 Feb. 1941, Menya; m. Pres. Hosni Said Mubarak; two s.; ed St Claire School, Heliopolis, Cairo, American Univ. in Cairo (AUC); Founder and Chair., Integrated Care Soc. 1977–; First Lady of Egypt 1981–; Pres. First and Second Nat. Conf. on Women 1994–96; f. Suzanne Mubarak Museum for Children 1996; initiated Unified Law on Children 1996; Pres., Nat. Council for Women 2000–; founder and Chair., Egyptian Soc. for Childhood and Devt; f. Egyptian Children's Literature Centre for Documentation, Research and Information; Pres. of Advisory Bd to Nat. Council for Childhood and Motherhood; Pres., Egyptian Nat. Women Cttee; Pres. of Egyptian Section, Int. Bd of Books for Young People (IBBY); Pres., Egyptian Red Crescent Soc.; initiated Nat. Campaign for Safe Blood Transfusion; Vice-Pres. Comm. on Ethics of Scientific Knowledge and Tech. (COMEST); Head of Egyptian Del. to UN World Conf. to Review and Appraise the Achievements of UN Decade for Women, Equality, Devt and Peace, Nairobi, Kenya 1985; Hon. Chair., Int. Symposium on Children's Books, UNICEF, Cairo 1986; Paul Harris Fellow, Rotary Foundation, Rotary Int. 1992; Dr hc (Iwa Univ., Seoul, South Korea) 1999, (American Univ. in Cairo) 2000, (American Univ. in Spain) 2000; DIur, Westminster Coll., New Wilmington, Pa, USA, Degree of Prof. Counsellor, Shanghai Univ., China 1999; Maurice Pate Award, UNICEF Exec. Bd 1989, Highest Award, Rehabilitation Int. Centre 1989, Enrique de la Mata Int. Prize for Peace, Together for Peace Foundation 1992, Health for All Gold Medal, WHO 1994, Int. Book Award, Int. Book Cttee 1995, Award of Highest Honour, Soka Univ. 1995, American World Book Asscn Award for Publ., Award of Arab Publrs Fed. 1996, Avicenne Medal, UNESCO 1997, Prize of Tolerance, European Acad. of Sciences and Arts 1998, Rotary Award 1999. *Publications:* Social Action Research in Urban Egypt: A Case Study of Primary School Upgrading in Bulaq (thesis) 1982. *Address:* The National Council for Women, 1113 Corniche El-Nil, 1st Floor, PO Box 11625, Cairo, Egypt (office). *Telephone:* (202) 5747758 (office); (202) 5748708 (office). *Fax:* (202) 5749472 (office); (202) 5749364 (office). *E-mail:* ncw@ncwegypt.com (office). *Website:* www.ncwegypt.com (office).

MUDASSIR HUSAIN, Justice Syed J. R., BA, LLB; Bangladeshi judge (retd); b. 1 March 1940, Hobigonj; s. of the late Advocate Syed Md. Mumidul Husain and Syeda Honse-Ara-Akther Khatun; m. Syeda Mazida Khatun; three d. one s.; ed Dhaka Univ.; enrolled as Advocate of High Court of E Pakistan 1965; part-time Lecturer, Central Law Coll. Dhaka 1966–78; Examiner and Question Setter, Dept of Law, Univ. of Dhaka; reporter, Bangladesh Law Reports 1973–77; apptd Asst Attorney Gen. 1977; enrolled as Advocate of Appellate Div. 1980; apptd Deputy Attorney Gen. 1984; apptd Judge, High Court Div. 1992, Judge of the Appellate Div. 2002; Chief Justice, Supreme Court 2004–07 (retd); rep. World Intellectual Property Org. 2003. *Leisure interest:* reading books, watching world television, watching cricket and football. *Address:* c/o Supreme Court, Dhaka 1000; Flat 1 – BA-RC Tower, 74 Elephant Road, Dhaka 1205, Bangladesh (home). *Telephone:* (2) 8652523 (home).

MUDAVADI, Wycliffe Musalia; Kenyan economist and politician; *Deputy Prime Minister and Minister of Local Government;* b. 21 Sept. 1960, Vihiga Dist; m.; three c.; fmr employee Tysons Ltd (property consultants firm) –1989; land economist, Nat. Housing Corpn 1984–89; mem. Parl. for Sabatia 1989–; Minister of Supplies and Marketing 1989–92, of Finance 1992–97, of Agric. 1997–99, of Transport and Communications 1999–2002, Deputy Prime Minister and Minister of Local Govt 2008–; Vice-Pres. of Kenya Nov.–Dec. 2002; Nat. Vice-Chair. Kenya African Nat. Union 2002–; Founder Rainbow Alliance; mem. Inst. of Surveyors. *Address:* Office of the Deputy Prime Minister and Ministry of Local Government, Jogoo House 'A', Taifa Rd, POB 30004, Nairobi (home); Kenya African National Union, KICC POB 72394,

Nairobi, Kenya (office). *Telephone:* (20) 217475 (office). *Website:* www.localgovernment.go.ke (office).

MUDD, Daniel H., BA, MPA; American business executive; b. 1959; s. of Roger Mudd; m.; four c.; ed Univ. of Virginia, John F. Kennedy School of Govt at Harvard Univ.; served as officer in US Marine Corps, including combat service in Beirut, Lebanon; Robert Bosch Foundation Fellowship, Germany 1989; Vice-Pres. of Business Devt, GE Capital 1991–93, Man. Dir Int. Financing 1993–95, Pres. and CEO European Fleet Services, Brussels 1995–96, Pres. Asia Pacific 1996–99, Pres. and CEO Japan 1999–2000; Vice-Chair. and COO Fannie Mae, Washington, DC 2000–04, interim CEO 2004–05, Pres. and CEO 2005–08, mem. Bd of Dirs 2000–08; mem. Bd of Dirs Fortress Investment Group LLC, Center for the Study of the Presidency, Homes for Working Families, Hampton Univ.; mem. Bd of Mans Univ. of Virginia. *Address:* c/o Fannie Mae, 3900 Wisconsin Avenue, NW, Washington, DC 20016-2892, USA. *Telephone:* (202) 752-7000. *E-mail:* headquarters@fanniemae.com. *Website:* www.fanniemae.com.

MUDD, Roger Harrison, MA; American news broadcaster (retd); b. 9 Feb. 1928, Washington; s. of Kostka Mudd and Irma Iris (née Harrison) Mudd; m. Emma Jeanne Spears 1957; three s. one d.; ed Washington and Lee Univ. and Univ. of N Carolina; served with US Army 1945–47; teacher Darlington School, Rome, Ga 1951–52; reporter Richmond (Va) News Leader 1953; News Dir Station WRNL, Richmond 1953–56; reporter, radio and TV Station WTOP, Washington 1956–61; Corresp. CBS 1961–80; Chief Washington Corresp. NBC 1980–87, Congressional Corresp. MacNeil/Lehrer News Hour 1987–92; Host The History Channel 1995–2004 (retd); Prof. of Journalism, Princeton Univ. 1992–94, Washington & Lee Univ. 1995–96; Dir Berlin Comm. 1996–99, Va Foundation for Ind. Colls. 1997–, Nat. Portrait Gallery Comm. 1997–; mem. Bd of Dirs Media Gen. 1998–2001, Civil War Trust 1999–2001; five Emmy Awards; George Foster Peabody Award, Joan Shorenstein Award for Distinguished Washington Reporting. *Publication:* Great Minds of History 1999. *Address:* 7167 Old Dominion Drive, McLean, VA 22101, USA (home).

MUDENGE, Isack Stanislaus Gorerazvo, BA, PhD; Zimbabwean politician; *Minister of Minister of Higher and Tertiary Education;* b. 17 Dec. 1941, Bawa, Zimuto, Masvingo; ed Univ. of Rhodesia and Nyasaland, Gonakudzingwa, Univ. of York, UK and Univ. of London, UK; Lecturer, then Sr Lecturer Fourah Bay Coll., Sierra Leone and Nat. Univ. of Lesotho 1971–80; joined Zimbabwe African Nat. Union (ZANU) party 1963, mem. Cen. Cttee 1993–; Sec. for External Affairs, ZANU Br., Lesotho 1977–80; Permanent Sec. of Foreign Affairs 1980–85; Permanent Rep. to the UN, New York 1985–90, Chair. Co-ordinating Cttee of the Non-aligned Nations at the UN 1986–89, Vice-Pres. UN Gen. Ass. 1989; Sec. for Educ. ZANU, Munyambe S. Dist 1990–91; Sr Permanent Sec. of Political Affairs 1990–92; Deputy Sec. for Commissariat and Culture, Masvingo Prov. 1991–93; Minister of Higher Educ. 1992–95; Deputy Sec. for Educ., Politburo ZANU; Minister of Foreign Affairs 1995–2005, of Higher Educ. and Tech. (now of Higher and Tertiary Educ.) 2005–; mem. Int. Cttee for the Release of the ZANU Leadership Arrested in Zambia 1975–76; Int. Treas. World Univ. Service, Geneva 1974–76, Pres. 1976–78; Treas. Int. Congress of African Studies 1976–78, 1986–92, Pres. 1992–; Exec. mem. Bd of the Donors on African Educ., World Bank 1993. *Publications:* A Political History of Munhumutapa: 1400–1902; contribs to Journal of Southern African Studies 1979–80; several other books and articles in learned journals. *Address:* Ministry of Higher Education and Technology, cnr Fourth St and Samora Machel Ave, Union Avenue, POB UA275, Harare, Zimbabwe (office). *Telephone:* (4) 796440 (office). *Fax:* (4) 790923 (office). *E-mail:* thesecretary@mhet.ac.zw (office). *Website:* www.mhet.ac.zw (office).

MUDGE, Dirk; Namibian politician; b. 16 Jan. 1928, Otjiwarongo; m. Stienie Jacobs; two s. three d.; Chair. of Turnhalle Constitutional Conf. 1977; Vice-Chair. of Nat. Party and mem. SW Africa Exec. Council Sept. 1977; formed Republican Party of SW Africa 1977; Chair. Democratic Turnhalle Alliance (now DTA of Namibia) 1977; mem. Constituent Ass. 1978–79, Nat. Ass. 1979–83; Pres. Ministers' Council 1980–83, Minister for Finance and Governmental Affairs 1985–89; mem. Nat. Ass. 1991–93. *Address:* DTA of Namibia, P.O. Box 173, Windhoek 9000, Namibia.

MUDIMBE, Valentin-Yves, (Hermano Matro); American academic and writer; *Newman Ivey White Professor of Literature, Duke University;* b. 12 Aug. 1941, Likasi Jadolville, Democratic Republic of the Congo; ed Univ. of Lovanium, Catholic Univ. of Louvain, Univ. of Besançon; specialist in phenomenology and structuralism; fmr Lecturer, Univs of Louvain, Paris-Nanterre, Zaïre and Haverford Coll.; Dir of Studies, Ecole des Hautes-Etudes, Paris 1988–89; Louis H. Jordon Lecturer, School of West African Studies, Univ. of London; Samuel Fischer Prof., Free Univ. of Berlin; Prof., Literature Program, Stanford Univ. 1994–2000; currently Newman Ivey White Prof. of Literature, Duke Univ., NC, USA; Visiting Prof., El Colegio de Mexico, Univ. of Antioquia, Colombia, Cologne Univ.; Gen.-Sec., Soc. for African Philosophy in N America (SAPINA) 1988–99; Chair. Bd African Philosophy, Univ. of London, Int. Africa Inst., SOAS; Hon. Corresponding mem., Belgian Acad. of Overseas Sciences; Chevalier de la Pleiade, Ordre de la Francophone et du Dialogue des Cultures 1997; Dr hc (Université de Paris Denis Diderot, Paris VII (La Chancellerie des Universités de Paris, Sorbonne) 1997, (Catholic Univ. of Leuven) 2006. *Publications include:* L'odeur du père 1982, The Invention of Africa 1988, Parables and Fables 1991, The Idea of Africa 1994, Tales of Faith 1997; Ed.: The Surreptitious Speech 1992, Nations, Identities, Cultures 1997, Diaspora and Immigration 1999; Co-Ed.: Africa and the Disciplines 1993, Le corps glorieux des mots et des êtres 1994; seventy articles; three collections of poetry, four novels. *Address:* Duke University, Literature Program, 101 Science Bldg, Box 90670, Durham, NC 27708, USA (office). *Telephone:* (919) 684-4240 (office). *Fax:* (919) 684-4127 (office). *E-mail:* vmudimbe@duke.edu (office). *Website:* fds.duke.edu/db/aas/Literature/faculty/vmudimbe (office).

MUDRINIĆ, Ivica, BASc; Croatian business executive; *President and CEO, T-Hrvatski Telekom dd;* b. 1955; ed Univ. of Toronto, Canada; began career in Product Devt Dept, Motorola Communications –1985; f. MX Engineering Inc. 1985; returned to Croatia 1990, becoming Adviser for Communications to Croatian Pres., Asst Minister for Maritime Affairs, Transport and Communications 1991–92, Minister 1992–94; Pres., Telecommunications Council 1994–96; Pres. Man. Bd, Hrvatska Radiotelevizija 1996–98; CEO, Hrvatska pošta i telekomunikacije 1998–99, Pres., T-Hrvatski Telekom (following liberalisation) 1999–, then Pres. and CEO. *Address:* T-Hrvatski Telekom dd, Savska cesta 32, 10000 Zagreb, Croatia (office). *Telephone:* (1) 4911000 (office). *Fax:* (1) 4911011 (office). *E-mail:* info@t.ht.hr (office). *Website:* www.t.ht.hr (office).

MUELLER, Edward A., BS, MBA; American telecommunications industry executive; *CEO, Qwest Communications International, Inc.;* b. St Louis; ed Univ. of Missouri, Washington Univ.; joined Southwestern Bell 1968, held several sr positions including Pres. and CEO Southwestern Bell, Pres. and CEO Pacific Bell 1997–99, Pres. SBC Int. Operations 1999–2000; Pres. and CEO Ameritech 2000–02; CEO Williams-Sonoma, Inc. 2003–07, mem. Bd of Dirs 2005–; CEO Qwest Communications Int., Inc., Denver 2007–. *Address:* Qwest Communications International, Inc., 1801 California Street, Denver, CO 80202, USA (office). *Telephone:* (303) 992-1400 (office). *Fax:* (303) 992-1724 (office). *Website:* www.qwest.com (office).

MUELLER, Robert Swan, III, MA, JD; American lawyer and federal official; *Director, Federal Bureau of Investigation (FBI);* b. 7 Aug. 1944, New York City; s. of Robert Swan Mueller, Jr and Alice Mueller (née Truesdale); m. Ann Standish 1966; two d.; ed Princeton Univ., New York Univ. and Univ. of Virginia; Capt. US Marine Corps 1967–70; Assoc. Pillsbury, Madison & Sutro, San Francisco 1973–76; Asst US Attorney, US Attorney's Office, Northern Dist Calif., San Francisco 1976–80, Chief, Special Prosecutions Unit 1980–81, Criminal Div. 1981–82; Chief, Criminal Div. Mass. Dist, US Attorney's Office, Boston 1982–85, First Asst US Attorney in Boston 1985, US Attorney for Mass. Dist 1986–87, Deputy US Attorney for Mass. Dist 1987–88; Pnr Hill and Barlow, Boston 1988–89; Asst to Attorney Gen. for criminal matters, US Dept of Justice, Washington, DC 1989–90, Asst Attorney Gen. for criminal div. 1990–93, Interim US Attorney, Northern Dist Calif. 1998–2001; Dir FBI 2001–; lawyer, Hale & Dorr, Washington 1993; Bronze Star, Purple Heart, Vietnamese Cross of Gallantry. *Address:* Department of Justice, Federal Bureau of Investigation, J. Edgar Hoover Building, 950 Pennsylvania Avenue, NW, Washington, DC 20530, USA (office). *Telephone:* (202) 324-3000 (office). *Website:* www.fbi.gov (office).

MUELLER-STAHL, Armin; German actor; b. 17 Dec. 1930, Tilsit, East Prussia (now Sovetsk, Russia); ed Berlin Conservatory; began career with music studies (violin), subsequently became actor; moved to FRG 1980; Hon. DHumLitt (Chicago); Bundesfilmpreis 1981, Silver Bar Award 1992. *Films include:* Heimliche Ehen 1956, Königskinder (Royal Children) 1962, ...und Deine Liebe auch 1962, Christine 1963, Nackt unter Wölfen (Naked Among Wolves) 1963, Preludio 11 1964, Alaskafüchse 1964, Tödlicher Irrtum 1970, Der Dritte (The Third) 1972, Januskopf 1972, Die Hosen des Ritters Bredow 1973, Kit & Co. 1974, Jakob, der Lügner (Jacob the Liar) 1975, Nelken in Aspik 1976, Die Flucht (The Flight) 1977, Lola 1981, Die Flügel der Nacht 1982, Die Sehnsucht der Veronika Voss 1982, Der Westen leuchtet 1982, Trauma 1983, Viadukt (aka The Train Killer) 1983, Un dimanche de flic (A Cop's Sunday) 1983, L'homme blessé (The Wounded Man) 1983, Eine Liebe in Deutschland (A Love in Germany) 1983, Tausend Augen (Thousand Eyes) 1984, Rita Ritter 1984, Glut (Embers) 1984, Oberst Redl (Colonel Redl) 1985, Die Mitläufer 1985, Vergeßt Mozart (Forget Mozart) 1986, Bittere Ernte (Angry Harvest) 1986, Momo 1986, Der Joker (Lethal Obsession) 1987, Killing Blue (Midnight Cop) 1988, Das Spinnennetz (Spider's Web) 1989, Schweinegeld (aka C*A*S*H: A Political Fairy Tale, UK) 1989, A Hecc 1989, Music Box 1989, Avalon 1990, Kafka 1991, Bronsteins Kinder (Bronstein's Children) 1991, Night on Earth 1991, Utz 1992, The Power of One 1992, Far from Berlin 1992, Red Hot 1993, Der Kinoerzähler (The Film Narrator) 1993, The House of the Spirits 1993, Taxandria 1994, The Last Good Time 1994, Holy Matrimony 1994, A Pyromaniac's Love Story 1995, Theodore Rex (video) 1995, Shine (Australian Film Prize 1996), Conversation with the Beast 1996, Der Unhold (The Ogre) 1996, The Assistant 1997, The Game 1997, The Peacemaker 1997, The Commissioner 1998, The X-Files 1998, The Thirteenth Floor 1999, The Third Miracle 1999, Jakob the Liar 1999, The Long Run 2000, Mission to Mars (uncredited) 2000, Pilgrim 2000, The Story of an African Farm 2004, The Dust Factory 2004, Local Color 2006, Ich bin die Andere 2006, Eastern Promises 2007, Leningrad 2007. *Television includes:* Fünf Patronenhülsen (Five Cartridges) 1960, Flucht aus der Hölle (mini-series) 1960, Die Letzte Chance 1962, Der Andere neben dir 1963, Wolf unter Wölfen (mini-series) 1964, Ein Lord am Alexanderplatz 1967, Columbus 64 1966, Wege übers Land (mini-series) 1968, Die Dame aus Genua 1969, Kein Mann für Camp Detrick 1970, Die Verschworenen (mini-series) 1971, Die Sieben Affären der Dona Juanita (mini-series) 1973, Das Unsichtbare Visier (series) 1973, Stülpner-Legende (series; uncredited) 1973, Die Eigene Haut 1974, Geschlossene Gesellschaft 1978, Die Längste Sekunde 1980, Collin (mini-series) 1981, Ferry oder Wie es war 1981, Ja und Nein 1981, Die Gartenlaube 1982, Ich werde warten 1982, An uns glaubt Gott nicht mehr (God Does Not Believe in Us Anymore) 1982, Ausgestoßen 1982, Der Fall Sylvester Matuska 1982, Flucht aus Pommern 1982, Ruhe sanft, Bruno 1983, Tatort - Freiwild 1984, Hautnah 1985, Gauner im Paradies 1986, Auf den Tag genau 1986, Unser Mann im Dschungel (aka Amazonas Mission) 1987, Amerika (mini-series) 1987, Franza 1987, Jokehnen oder Wie lange fährt man von Ostpreußen nach Deutschland? (mini-series)

1987, Tagebuch für einen Mörder 1988, In the Presence of Mine Enemies 1997, 12 Angry Men 1997, Jesus 1999, Crociati (Crusaders) (mini-series) 2001, Die Manns - Ein Jahrhundertroman (mini-series) 2001, The Power of Knowledge (series) 2005. *Publications:* Verordneter Sonntag (Lost Sunday), Drehtage, Unterwegs Nach Hause (On the Way Home).

MUFAMADI, Fholisani Sydney, MSc; South African politician; b. 28 Feb. 1959, Alexandra, Johannesburg; m. Nomusa Kumalo; one s. two d.; ed Univ. of London, UK; pvt. teacher, Lamula Secondary School 1980; Gen. Sec. Gen. and Allied Workers' Union 1982; Publicity Sec. United Democratic Front (UDF); Asst Gen. Sec. Congress of South African Trade Unions 1985; mem. Nat. Peace Cttee, helped draft Nat. Peace Accord 1991; mem. African Nat. Congress (ANC) Nat. Exec. Cttee, ANC Working Cttee, Cen. Cttee of South African Communist Party, Political Bureau; ANC Rep. at Transitional Exec. Council on Law and Order, Safety and Stability 1993–94; Minister of Safety and Security, Govt of Nat. Unity 1994–99, of Prov. Affairs and Local Govt 1999–2008 (resgnd); Hon. DSc (Igbinedion Univ., Okada). *Leisure interest:* reading. *Address:* African National Congress, 54 Sauer Street, Johannesburg 2001, South Africa (office). *Telephone:* (11) 3761000 (office). *Fax:* (11) 3761134 (office). *E-mail:* nmtyelwa@anc.org.za (office). *Website:* www.anc.org.za (office).

MUFTI, Hania, MSc; Jordanian lawyer and international organization executive; *Director, Middle East and North Africa Division, Human Rights Watch;* b. Amman; ed in Jordan and Lebanon and Univ. of Bath, UK; more than 20 years' professional experience in human rights research and advocacy; Researcher, Middle East Research Dept, Amnesty Int.'s Secr., London, UK 1981–97; Dir Middle East and North Africa Div., Human Rights Watch, London 2000–. *Publications:* author of numerous reports for Amnesty International, including Iraq: The World Would Not Listen 1994, Kuwait: Three Years of Unfair Trials 1994, Iraq: Human Rights Abuses in Iraqi Kurdistan Since 1991 1995, Bahrain: A Human Rights Crisis 1995. *Address:* Human Rights Watch, 2nd Floor, 2-12 Pentonville Road, London, N1 9HF, England (office). *Telephone:* (20) 7713-1995 (office). *Fax:* (20) 7713-1800 (office). *E-mail:* hrwuk@hrw.org (office). *Website:* www.hrw.org (office).

MUGABE, Robert Gabriel, BA, BAdmin, BEd, MSc (Econ), LLM; Zimbabwean politician, head of state and fmr teacher; *President;* b. 21 Feb. 1924, Kutama; m. 1st Sarah Mugabe (died 1992); one s. (deceased); m. 2nd Grace Marufu 1996; ed Kutama and Empandeni Mission School, Fort Hare Univ. Coll., S Africa, Univs of S Africa and London; teacher, at Drifontein Roman Catholic School, Umvuma 1952, Salisbury S Primary School 1953, in Gwelo 1954, Chalimbana Teacher Training Coll. 1955, in Accra, Ghana 1958–60; entered politics 1960; Publicity Sec. of Nat. Dem. Party 1960–61; Publicity Sec. Zimbabwe African People's Union 1961; detained Sept.–Dec. 1962, March–April 1963; escaped to Tanzania April 1963; Co-Founder of Zimbabwe African Nat. Union (ZANU) Aug. 1963; Sec.-Gen. Aug. 1963; in detention in Rhodesia 1964–74; Pres. ZANU; mem. Politburo ZANU 1984–; Jt Leader of Patriotic Front (with Joshua Nkomo) 1976–79; contested Feb. 1980 elections as Leader of ZANU (PF) (name changed to ZANU 1984) Party, Pres. 1988–; Minister of Defence 1980–87, also fmrly of Public Works, Industry and Tech.; Prime Minister of Zimbabwe 1980–87; Pres. of Zimbabwe 1988–; Chancellor Univ. of Zimbabwe; apptd Amb. for southern Africa, African Union 2003; Newsmaker of the Year Award (S African Soc. of Journalists) 1980, Africa Prize 1988; Dr hc (Ahmadu Bello Univ., Nigeria) 1980; Int. Human Rights Award (Howard Univ., Washington) 1981, Jawarhalal Nehru Award 1992. *Address:* Office of the President, Munhumutapa Building, Samora Machel Avenue, Private Bag 7700, Causeway, Harare, Zimbabwe. *Telephone:* (4) 707091 (office).

MUGLER, Thierry; French fashion designer; b. 1946, Strasbourg; ed in Strasbourg; fmr ballet dancer, Opéra du Rhin, Strasbourg; later window-dresser and clothing designer, Gudule boutique, Paris; designer of fashion collection for André Peters, London; subsequently began career as freelance clothing designer in Amsterdam, later in Paris where he launched Café de Paris collection; designer of menswear and fashion accessories; launched own Thierry Mugler fashion label, Paris 1973; launched Thierry Mugler Diffusion fashion co.; opened own boutique, Place des Victoires, Paris; clothing also sold in dept stores in USA and Japan; launched range of perfumes. *Address:* Thierry Mugler Parfums, 10 Cavendish Place, London, W1G 9DN, England (office). *Telephone:* (20) 7307-6700 (office). *Fax:* (20) 7307-6705 (office). *Website:* www.thierrymugler.com (office).

MUHAMMAD VI, HM The King of Morocco; b. 21 Aug. 1963, Rabat; s. of the late King Hassan II; m. Lalla Salma Bennani 2002; one s. (Crown Prince Moulay Hassan, b. 2003) one d. (b. 2007); ed Collège Royal, Université Mohammed V, Faculté des Sciences Juridiques, Economiques et Sociales de Rabat; Head Moroccan del., 7th Summit of Non-Aligned Nations, New Delhi 1983, 10th Franco–African Conf., Vittel 1983; apptd Co-ordinator Admin. and Services, Armed Forces 1985; rank of Gén. de Div. 1994; Hon. Pres. Asscn Socio–Culturelle du Bassin Méditerranéen 1979–; Chair. Org. Cttee 9th Mediterranean Games, Casablanca 1982; succeeded to the throne on the death of his father 23 July 1999. *Address:* Royal Palace, Rabat, Morocco.

MUHAMMAD, Ali Nasser; Yemeni politician; b. 1939, Dathina Rural District; active mem. of Nat. Liberation Front (NLF) 1963–67; Gov. of the Islands 1967, of Second Prov. 1968; mem. Nat. Front Gen. Command March 1968; Minister of Local Govt 1969, of Defence 1969–77, of Educ. 1974–75; mem. Front Exec. Cttee 1970; mem. Presidential Council of People's Democratic Repub. of Yemen 1971–78, Chair. June–Dec. 1978; Chair. Council of Ministers (Prime Minister) 1971–85; mem. Supreme People's Council (SPC) 1971, Chair. Presidium of SPC (Head of State) 1980–86 (overthrown in coup Jan. 1986); mem. Political Bureau of Nat. Front 1972–75, of United Political Org. Nat. Front 1975–78, of Yemen Socialist Party (YSP) 1978–86, Sec.-Gen. of YSP 1980–86.

MUHAMMED, Magaji, BA; Nigerian government official and diplomatist; b. 31 Dec. 1940, Dutsinma, Katsina State; ed Ahmadu Bello Univ.; Dist Officer Idoma, Wukari and Tiv Div., Prin. Asst Sec. Mil. Gov.'s Office, Kaduna 1965–75; fmr Admin., Kaduna Capital Territory, Perm. Sec. 1975; joined Civil Service 1980, Dir Project Implementation, Ministry of Industries, Dir Commercial and Industrial Incentives, Ministry of Trade and Industries; Amb. to Saudi Arabia 2000–03; Minister of Industry –2005, of Internal Affairs 2005–06 (resgnd). *Address:* c/o Ministry of Internal Affairs, Area 1, Secretariat Complex, Garki, Abuja, Nigeria (office).

MUHAMMEDOV, Hojamuhammet; Turkmenistani politician; b. 1966, Aşgabat; ed Turkmen Inst. of Nat. Economy; started career as forwarding agent, Turkmenengilazyksenagat Asscn, Ministry of Trade and Consumer Co-operation 1983, then worked as construction engineer, engineer of Supplies Dept of Turkmenhimsnabbyt, stock keeper, Dept of State Cttee for Logistics of Turkmenistan; Deputy Dir, then Dir Harytimpeks Co., Ministry of Trade and Foreign Econ. Relations, then Dir Gulistan state trade centre 1998–2005; Deputy Chair. State Commodity and Raw Materials Exchange 2005, Chair. 2006; Chair. Supreme Supervisory Chamber of Turkmenistan July–Nov. 2007; Deputy Chair. of the Govt, responsible for the Textile Industry, Trade and the Chamber of Commerce and Industry 2007–09. *Address:* c/o Office of the President and the Council of Ministers, 744000 Aşgabat, Turkmenistan. *Telephone:* (12) 35-45-34.

MUHEIM, Franz Emmanuel, LèsL; Swiss diplomatist (retd) and academic; b. 27 Sept. 1931, Berne; s. of Hans Muheim and Hélène Ody; m. Radmila Jovanovic 1962; ed Univs of Fribourg, Geneva and Paris; joined Fed. Dept of Foreign Affairs 1960, served successively in Belgrade, Rabat and London 1961–70, Council of Europe, UN and Int. Orgs Section, Dept of Foreign Affairs, Berne 1971–77, Deputy Head of Mission, Minister Plenipotentiary, Washington, DC 1978–81, Deputy Dir Political Affairs and Head, Political Div. Europe and N America, with rank of Amb., Berne 1982–83, Dir Int. Orgs, Dept of Foreign Affairs 1984–89, Head of Swiss dels to int. confs including UNESCO, Int. Red Cross, Non-Aligned Movement; Amb. to UK 1989–94; Pres. Swiss Red Cross 1996–2001; Vice-Pres. Int. Fed. of Red Cross and Red Crescent Socs 1996–2001; Fellow, Center for Int. Affairs, Harvard Univ., USA 1981–82; Prof., Bologna Center of Johns Hopkins Univ. 1995–96; Pres. Fribourg Festival of Sacred Music. *Publications:* Einblick in die Schweizerische Aussenpolitik: Festschrift für Staatssekretär Raymond Probst (co-ed.) 1984, Les organisations internationales entre l'innovation et la stagnation (contrib.) 1984, Multilateralism Today, Geburtstag von a. Ständerat Franz Muheim 1993. *Leisure interests:* walking, mountaineering, skiing, photography, classical music. *Address:* Es Chesaux, 1646 Echarlens, Switzerland (home). *Telephone:* (26) 9152474 (home). *Fax:* (26) 9152450 (home). *E-mail:* franz.e.muheim@mcnet.ch (home).

MUHITH, Abul Maal Abdul, BA, MA, MPA; Bangladeshi diplomatist and politician; *Minister of Finance;* b. 1934; s. of Abu Ahmad Abdul Hafiz and Sayed Shahar Banu Chowdhury; m. Sayed Sabia Muhith; two s. one d.; ed Dhaka Univ., Univ. of Oxford, UK, Harvard Univ., USA; Gen.-Sec. Cen. Cttee, Pakistan Civil Service Asscn 1960–69; Econ. Councillor, Embassy in Washington, DC 1969–71, Chief of Mission 1971–72, chargé d'affairs 1972–77; Sec. of Planning, Pakistan Civil Service 1972, Sec., External Resource Dept, Ministry of Finance and Planning 1977–8, Minister of Finance and Planning 1982–83, of Finance 2009–; Visiting Fellow, Princeton Univ. 1984, 1985; Tamgha e Khidmat Award (Govt of Pakistan) 1966. *Address:* Ministry of Finance, Bangladesh Secretariat, Bhaban 7, 1st 9-Storey Building, 3rd Floor, Dhaka 1000 (office). *Telephone:* (2) 8690202 (office). *Fax:* (2) 865581 (office). *Website:* www.mof.gov.bd (office).

MÜHLEMANN, Lukas, MBA; Swiss business executive; b. 1950; ed Univ. of St Gallen and Harvard Univ.; fmr systems engineer IBM; man. consultant McKinsey & Co. 1977–94, Prin. 1982, Dir 1986, Man. Dir McKinsey's Swiss offices 1989, mem. Bd Dirs McKinsey & Co., Inc., New York 1990; CEO Swiss Re 1994, Man. Dir 1994, Deputy Chair. 1996; CEO Credit Suisse Group 1997–2002, Chair. Bd Dirs 2000–02, mem. Bd Dirs Credit Suisse, Credit Suisse First Boston; mem. Bd Tonhalle Foundation, Zurich, Zurich Opera House, Banco Gen. de Negocios; Pres. Harvard Club of Switzerland. *Address:* c/o Credit Suisse Group, Paradeplatz 8, P.O. Box 1, CH- 8070 Zurich, Switzerland.

MUHTADEE BILLAH, HRH Crown Prince, Haji al-; Brunei; b. 17 Feb. 1974, Istana Darul Hana, Bandar Seri Begawan; s. of HM Sultan Haji Hassanal Bolkiah Mu'izuddin Waddaulah and HM Raja Isteri Pengiran Anak Hajah Saleha; m. HRH Pengiran Anak Isteri Pengiran Anak Sarah binti Pengiran Salleh Ab Rahaman 2004; ed Univ. of Brunei Darussalam, Oxford Centre for Islamic Studies, England; proclaimed Crown Prince 10 Aug. 1998; attachments to various govt ministries and depts, and to private cos. *Address:* c/o Istana Nurul Iman, Bandar Seri Begawan, BA 1000, Brunei (office). *Website:* www.crownprince.bn.

MUHYIDDIN, Tan Sri Dato' Haji Mohd Yassin bin; Malaysian politician; *Minister of International Trade and Industry;* b. 1947; Chief Minister of Johor 1982–95; Minister of Youth and Sports 1995–99, of Domestic Trade and Consumer Affairs 1999–2004, of Agric. and Agro-Based Industry 2004–08, of Int. Trade and Industry 2008–; currently Vice-Pres. United Malays Nat. Org. *Address:* Ministry of International Trade and Industry, Blok 10, Kompleks Pejabat Kerajaan, Jalan Duta, 50622 Kuala Lumpur, Malaysia (office). *Telephone:* (3) 62033022 (office). *Fax:* (3) 62012337 (office). *E-mail:* webmiti@miti.gov.my (office). *Website:* www.miti.gov.my (office).

MUIR, Richard John Sutherland, CMG, BA; British diplomatist; *Ambassador to Kuwait;* b. 25 Aug. 1942, London; s. of John Muir and Edna Hodges; m. Caroline Simpson 1965; one s. one d; ed Stationers' Co. School and Univs of Reading and Strasbourg; entered HM Diplomatic Service 1966; Second Sec. Jeddah 1967–70, Tunis 1970–72; FCO 1972–75; First Sec. Washington, DC 1975–79; Prin. Dept of Energy 1979–81; Counsellor, Jeddah 1981–85; FCO 1985–91; Under-Sec. and Chief Insp. Diplomatic Service 1991–94; Amb. to Oman 1994–98, to Kuwait 1999–. *Leisure interests:* walking, sailing, fishing, opera. *Address:* United Kingdom Embassy, PO Box 2, 13001 Safat, Arabian Gulf Street, Kuwait City, Kuwait (office); c/o Foreign and Commonwealth Office, London, SW1A 2AH, England. *Telephone:* 2403336 (office). *Fax:* 2426799 (office). *E-mail:* general@britishembassy-kuwait.org (office). *Website:* www.britishembassy-kuwait.org (office).

MUIR, William (Bill) F., BEng, MBA; American business executive; *President, GMAC Financial Services;* b. 28 Dec. 1954, Freeport, NY; ed Cornell Univ., Harvard Univ.; joined General Motors (GM) at Treas.'s Office, New York 1983, Dir of Foreign Exchange and Int. Cash Man. 1986–87, Dir of Overseas Borrowings 1987–89, Dir of Corp. Finance and Investor Relations 1989–90, Gen. Dir of Business Devt 1990–92, Vice-Pres. of Nat. Accounts, GMAC Financial Services 1992–95, Vice-Pres. of Eastern US Operations 1995–96, Exec.-in-Charge of Operations, later Exec. Dir of Planning, GM's Delphi Automotive Systems 1996, Exec. Vice-Pres. and Chief Financial Officer GMAC Financial Services Feb. 1998–2004, Chair. GMAC's Insurance Group 1999–, Pres. GMAC Financial Services 2004–, mem. Bd of Dirs GMAC Commercial Finance, GMAC Bank. *Address:* GMAC Financial Services, 200 Renaissance Center, Detroit, MI 48265-2000, USA (office). *Telephone:* (313) 556-5000 (office). *Fax:* (815) 282-6156 (office). *E-mail:* info@gmacfs.com (office). *Website:* www.gmacfs.com (office).

MUJAHID, Jamila; Afghan journalist and broadcaster; *President, Afghanistan Women in Media Network;* b. Kabul; m. Sayed Amin; five c.; ed in Afghanistan; broadcaster with Radio-Television Afghanistan from 1980, evening news broadcaster on TV and radio 1985–96; worked for NGOs during Taleban regime; first female broadcaster to appear on Radio-Television Afghanistan announcing the departure of the Taleban 2001; Pres., Afghanistan Women in Media Network, Kabul 2002–, publishing monthly magazine, Hefat and running 'The Voice of Afghan Women' radio station (Dir of radio station 2003, relaunched 2005–); Ed., Malalai women's magazine 2003–. *Address:* Afghanistan Women in Media Network, Afghan Media and Culture Centre, Behind Ministry of Planning, Malik Ashgar Crossroads, Kabul, Kabul Province, Afghanistan (office). *E-mail:* ainakabul@ainaworld.org (office).

MUJAWAR, Ali Muhammad, BA, MA, PhD; Yemeni academic and politician; *Prime Minister;* b. 1953, Shabwa; ed Algiers Univ., Algeria and Grenoble Univ., France; mem. Higher Studies Cttee, Business Dept, Univ. of Aden 1990–2000, Head, Business Man. Dept, Faculty of Econs 1994–96, Dean of Faculty of Oil and Minerals 1996–99, Dean, Faculty of Man. Studies 2001–03; Gen. Man. Al-Barah Cement Factory 1999–2000; fmr Deputy Minister of Civil Service and Insurance, Minister of Fisheries 2003–06, of Electricity and Water 2006–07, Prime Minister 2007–. *Address:* Office of the Prime Minister, San'a, Yemen (office). *Telephone:* (1) 274662 (office).

MUJOTA, Fehmi; Kosovo politician; *Minister of Defence;* fmr mem. Kosovo Liberation Army; fmr Mayor Shtime Municipality; mem. Democratic Party of Kosovo; mem. Kosovo Ass., First Vice Chair. Cttee for Public Services, Local Admin and Media; Minister of Defence 2008–. *Address:* Office of the Minister of Defence, c/o Office of the Government, Rruga Nënë Terezë, 10000 Prishtina (office); Democratic Party of Kosovo, Rruga Nënë Terezë 20, 10000 Prishtina, Kosovo (office). *Telephone:* (44) 156774 (office). *E-mail:* pdk@pdk-ks.org (office). *Website:* www.ks-gov.net (office); www.pdk-ks.org (office).

MUJURU, Joyce Teurai-Ropa; Zimbabwean politician; *Vice-President;* b. 15 April 1955, Mount Darwin; m. Tapfumanei Ruzambu Solomon Mujuru (Nhongo) 1977; four d.; ed Women's Univ. in Africa, Zimbabwe; Minister of Youth, Sport and Recreation 1980–81, of Community Devt and Women's Affairs 1981–88, of Community and Co-operative Devt 1989–92, of Rural Resources and Water Devt 1996–2004; Vice-Pres. of Zimbabwe 2004–; Gov. and Resident Minister of Mashonaland Cen. Prov. 1993–96; Liberation Medal, War Veteran Order of Merit. *Leisure interests:* church and women's meetings, knitting, sewing, cooking, outdoor life. *Address:* Office of the Vice-President, Munhumutapa Building, Samora Machel Avenue, Private Bag 7700, Causeway, Harare (office); No. 9 Tara Township, Ruwa (home); Box 57, Ruwa, Zimbabwe (home). *Telephone:* (4) 707091 (office).

MUKAI, Chiaki, MD, PhD; Japanese astronaut, surgeon and academic; *Visiting Professor, International Space University;* b. 6 May 1952, Tatebayashi, Gunma Pref.; m. Makio Mukai; ed Keio Girls' High School, Tokyo, Keio Univ. School of Medicine; science astronaut, NASDA (renamed JAXA–Japan Aerospace Exploration Agency 2003) 1983–, first Japanese woman in space having logged 566 hours; NASA experience includes Japanese Payload Specialist, First Material Processing Test (Spacelab-J), STS-47 1985, back-up Payload Specialist, Neurolab (STS-90) Mission, flew aboard STS-65 1994, STS-95 Discovery 1998, Deputy Mission Scientist for STS-107; bd certified for medicine 1977, as cardiovascular surgeon 1989; Resident in Gen. Surgery, Keio Univ. Hosp. 1977–78; mem. Medical Staff, Shimizu Gen. Hosp., Shizuoka Pref. 1978–79, Emergency Surgery Staff, Saiseikai Kanagawa Hosp., Kanagawa Pref. 1979–80; Resident in Cardiovascular Surgery, Keio Univ. Hosp. 1980–82, Chief Resident 1982–83; mem. Medical Staff in Cardiovascular Surgery, Saiseikai Utsunomiya Hosp., Tochigi Pref. 1982–83; Asst Prof., Dept of Cardiovascular Surgery, Keio Univ. 1983–87, Visiting Assoc. Prof., Dept of Surgery 1992–98, Visiting Prof. 1999–; Visiting Scientist, Div. of Cardiovascular Physiology, Space Biomedical Research Inst., NASA Johnson Space Center 1987–88; Research Instructor, Dept of Surgery, Baylor Coll. of Medicine, Houston, Tex. 1992–; Visiting Prof., Int. Space Univ. Strasbourg, France 2004–; mem. American Aerospace Medical Asscn, Japan Soc. of Microgravity Applications, Japan Soc. of Aerospace and Environmental Medicine, Japanese Soc. for Cardiovascular and Thoracic Surgery, Japan Surgical Soc. *Leisure interests:* snow skiing, Alpine competitive skiing, bass fishing, scuba diving, tennis, golf, photography, American literature, travel. *Address:* International Space University, Strasbourg Central Campus, Parc d'Innovation, 1 rue Jean-Dominique Cassini, 67400 Illkirch-Graffenstaden, France (office); Japan Aerospace Exploration Agency, 7-44-1 Jindaiji, Higashi-Machi, Chofu-shi, Tokyo 182-8522, Japan (office). *Telephone:* 3-88-65-54-30 (France) (office); (281) 483-0123 (Japan) (office). *Fax:* 3-88-65-54-47 (France) (office). *Website:* www.isunet.edu (office); www.jaxa.jp/index_e.html (office).

MUKAMBAYEV, Usup Mukambayevich; Kyrgyzstani politician and lawyer; *President's Representative in Parliament;* b. 28 Jan. 1941, Dzholgolot, Kyrgyzia; m. Prof. Galina Mukumbayeva; two d.; ed Kyrgyz State Univ., higher courses at State Security Cttee of USSR; shepherd, Kolkhoz Ak-Suy Region; army service; Sec. CP Cttee of State Security Cttee 1974–78; Deputy Head of Admin, State Security Cttee, Osh Region 1978–80, Head of Admin, State Security Cttee, Talass and Osh Regions 1980–86; First Deputy Chair. State Security Cttee, Kyrgyz Repub. 1986–91; Minister of Justice 1991–93; mem. Parl. (Zhogorku Kenesh) of Kyrgyzstan 1987–2000, Chair. Legis. Ass. 1996–2000, Pres.'s Rep. in Parl. 2001–; Academician, Int. Acad. of Turk Nations, Moscow 1997; Honoured Lawyer of the Kyrgyz Repub. 1993; Order of the Red Star 1985; Dank Medal 2000. *Publications:* Constitutional Development of Kyrgyzstan 1999, About the Activity of the Legislative Assembly of Zhogorku Kenesh of the Kyrgyz Republic 2000. *Leisure interest:* walking on mountain routes. *Address:* Office of the President, 720003 Bishkek (office); 176 Kurenkeeva str. Bishkek, Kyrgyzstan (home). *Telephone:* (312) 62-63-95 (office); (312) 66-13-28 (office); (312) 67-00-37 (home). *Fax:* (312) 21-86-27 (office).

MUKASA, Shinji; Japanese construction industry executive; *President and CEO, Obayashi Corporation;* Exec. Vice-Pres. Obayashi Corpn –1997, apptd Pres. 1997, currently Pres. and CEO; Pres. and Dir Overseas Construction Asscn of Japan Inc. (OCAJI); Dir Global Infrastructure Fund Research Foundation. *Address:* Obayashi Corporation, Shinagawa Intercity Tower B, 2-15-2 Konan, Minato-ku, Tokyo 108-8502, Japan (office). *Telephone:* (3) 5769-1910 (office). *Fax:* (3) 5769-1910 (office). *Website:* www.obayashi.co.jp (office).

MUKASEY, Michael Bernard, BA, LLB; American lawyer, government official and fmr judge; b. 1941, Bronx, New York; m. Susan Mukasey 1974; one s. one d.; ed Columbia Univ., Yale Law School; Assoc., Webster Sheffield Fleishchmann Hithcock & Brookfield (law firm), New York City 1967–72; Asst US Attorney, US Dist Court for the Southern Dist of New York 1972–76, Chief Judge, Chief Official Corruption Unit 1975–76; Assoc. then Pnr, Patterson Belknap Webb & Tyler 1976–87, 2006–07; Judge, US Dist Court for the Southern Dist of New York 1988–2006, Chief Judge 2000–06 (retd); US Attorney Gen., Dept of Justice, Washington, DC 2007–09; advisor to Rudy Giuliani Republican presidential nomination campaign 2007; Dr hc (Brooklyn Law School) 2002; numerous awards including Learned Hand Medal, Fed. Bar Council. *Address:* c/o Department of Justice, 950 Pennsylvania Avenue, NW, Washington, DC 20530-0001, USA.

MUKERJEA, Pratim (Peter), MBA; British/Indian broadcasting executive; *Chairman, INX Media Pvt. Ltd;* b. London; s. of Khrishna Mukerjea and Baloram Mukerjea; m. Indrani Mukerjea; two s. one d.; ed business studies, Hatfield, Herts.; began career with Heinz (UK), later with British Store House and advertising agency O&M (UK office); fmr Regional Group Account Dir, DDB Needham Advertising, Hong Kong; fmr Account Dir, Ogilvy & Mather, New Delhi and London; Sales Dir (Hong Kong, later India and Middle East) Star TV 1993–97, Exec. Vice-Pres. 1997–99, CEO Star India 1999–2007; Co-founder, with his wife, and Chief Strategy Officer INX Media Pvt. Ltd 2007–, currently Chair.; mem. Bd Dirs ESPN STAR Sports, Hathway, Media Content and Communications Services (India) for Star News. *Address:* INX Media Pvt. Ltd, INX House, Dr Dadasaheb Bhadkamkar Marg, Grant Road (E), Mumbai 400 007, India (office). *Telephone:* (22) 66019999 (office). *Fax:* (22) 66019898 (office). *E-mail:* pavan.chawla@inxtv.in (office). *Website:* www.inxnetwork.in (office).

MUKHAMEDOV, Irek Javdatovich, OBE; Russian/Tatar ballet dancer; *Guest Artist, Royal Ballet;* b. 8 Feb. 1960; m. Maria Zubkova; one s. one d.; ed Moscow Choreographic Inst.; joined Moscow Classical Co.; debut with Bolshoi Ballet in title role of Grigorovich's Spartacus 1981; other roles include Ivan IV in Ivan the Terrible, Jean de Brienne in Raymonda, Basil in Don Quixote, Romeo in Grigorovich's Romeo and Juliet, Boris in Grigorovich's The Golden Age; toured extensively with Bolshoi Ballet and made worldwide guest appearances; joined The Royal Ballet 1990; Covent Garden debut in MacMillan's pas de deux Farewell (with Darcey Bussell) 1990; f. Irek Mukhamedov & Co. 1991–; appeared in musical The King and I, London 1995. *Address:* c/o Knight Ayton Management, 114 St Martin's Lane, London, WC2N 4BE, England (office). *Telephone:* (20) 7836-5333 (office). *Fax:* (20) 7836-8333 (office). *E-mail:* info@knightayton.co.uk (office). *Website:* www.knightayton.co.uk (office).

MUKHAMEJANOV, Baurzhan A., PhD; Kazakhstani politician; *Minister of Internal Affairs;* b. 1960; ed Kirov Kazakh State Univ.; fmr Deputy Head of Presidential Admin; Minister of Justice 1997–2000, of Internal Affairs 2005–. *Address:* Ministry of Internal Affairs, 010000 Astana, Manasa 4, Kazakhstan (office). *Telephone:* (7172) 34-36-01 (office). *Fax:* (7172) 34-17-38 (office). *E-mail:* press@mvd.kz (office). *Website:* www.mvd.kz (office).

MUKHAMEJANOV, Ural; Kazakhstani politician; b. Nov. 1948, Kustanai; ed Novosibirsk Inst. of Cooperative Trade; fmr Inspector, Personnel Policy Dept of Presidential Admin; mem. Majlis (Ass.) from Kustanai district, Chair. (Speaker) of Majlis 2004–07; mem. Fatherland Republican Political Party (Otan); Order of Kurmet. *Address:* 010000 Astana, Parliament House, Kazakhstan (office). *Telephone:* (7172) 15-30-19 (office). *Fax:* (7172) 33-30-99 (office). *E-mail:* Smimazh@parlam.kz (office). *Website:* www.parlam.kz (office).

MUKHAMETSHIN, Farid Khairullovich, DScS; Russian/Tatar politician; *Chairman, State Council of Tatarstan;* b. 22 May 1947, Almetyevsk, Tatarstan; m.; two c.; ed Almetyevak Higher Professional Tech. School, Ufa Inst. of Oil; metal turner in factories; CP functionary; Sec. Almetyevsk City CP Cttee; Chair. Exec. Cttee, Almetyevsk City Soviet; Deputy Chair. Council of Ministers, Minister of Trade of Tatar ASSR 1970–91; Chair. Supreme Soviet of Tatarstan Repub. 1991–94; mem. Council of Fed. 1991–94, 1998–; Prime Minister of Tatarstan Repub. 1995–98; Chair. State Council of Tatarstan 1998–; del. to Council of Europe, Chair. Regional Comm.; Leader Tatarstan New Age political movt 1999–. *Address:* Parliament Buildings, Svobody pl. 1, 420060 Kazan, Tatarstan, Russia. *Telephone:* (8432) 67-63-00 (office). *Fax:* (8432) 92-73-59 (office). *E-mail:* first@gossov.tatarstan.ru (office). *Website:* www.gossov.tatarstan.ru (office).

MUKHERJEE, Bharati, BA, MA, PhD; American (b. Indian) academic and writer; *Professor, English Department, University of California, Berkeley;* b. 27 July 1940, Kolkata; s. of Sudhir Lal Mukherjee and Bina Banerjee; m. Clark Blaise 1963; two s.; ed Univs of Calcutta, Baroda and Iowa; Prof. of English, McGill Univ.; lecturer, Skidmore Coll.; Lecturer in Literature and Creative Writing, Queen's Coll., New York; Prof. Univ. of Calif. at Berkeley 1990–. *Publications:* The Tiger's Daughter 1971, The Tiger's Daughter and Wife 1975, Days and Nights in Calcutta (with Clark Blaise) 1977, Darkness 1985, The Sorrow and the Terror (with Clark Blaise) 1987, The Middleman and Other Stories (Nat. Book Critics Circle Award for Fiction) 1988, Jasmine 1989, The Holder of the World 1993, Leave it to Me 1996, Desirable Daughters 2002, The Tree Bride 2004. *Address:* English Department, University of California, 334 Wheeler Hall, Berkeley, CA 94720 (office); 130 Rivoli Street, San Francisco, CA 94117, USA. *Telephone:* (510) 642-2765 (office); (415) 681-0345. *Fax:* (415) 759-9810. *E-mail:* mukhster@aol.com. *Website:* english.berkeley.edu (office).

MUKHERJEE, Pranab Kumar, LLB, MA; Indian politician; *Minister of External Affairs;* b. 11 Dec. 1935, Kirnahar, Birbhum Dist, W Bengal; s. of Kamada Kinkar Mukherjee and Rajlakshmki Mukherjee; m.; two s. one d.; ed Univ. of Calcutta; started career as lecturer; Ed. Palli-O-Panchayat Sambad (Bengali monthly); Founder-Ed. Desher Dak (Bengali weekly) 1967–71; mem. Rajya Sabha 1969–, Leader 1980–88; Deputy Minister of Industrial Devt, Govt of India 1973; Deputy Minister for Shipping and Transport Jan.–Oct. 1974; Minister of State, Ministry of Finance 1974–75; Minister for Revenue and Banking 1975–77; Minister of Commerce 1980–82, of Finance Jan.–Sept. 1982, 1982–85, of Commerce 1993–95, of External Affairs 1995–96, of Defence 2004–06, of External Affairs 2006–; Deputy Chair. Planning Comm. with Cabinet rank; f. Rashtriya Samajwadi Congress 1987–; mem. Exec. Cttee Congress (I) Party 1972–73, All India Congress Cttee 1986; Treas. Congress (I) Party, mem. Working Cttee, Deputy Leader in Rajya Sabha; Pres. W Bengal Pradesh Congress Cttee; Hon. DLitt. *Publications:* Bangla Congress: An Aspect of Constitutional Problems in Bengal 1967, Mid-term Election 1969, Off the Track 1987, Challenges Before the Nation 1992. *Leisure interests:* reading, gardening, music. *Address:* Ministry of External Affairs, South Block, New Delhi 110 011 (office); S-22, Greater Kailash-II, New Delhi 110 048 (office); 13 Talkatora Road, New Delhi 110 001, India (home); 2-A, 1st Floor, 602/7 Kabi Bharti Sarni (Lake Road), Kolkata 700 029. *Telephone:* (11) 23011127 (ministry) (office); (11) 3737623 (office); (11) 6474025; (11) 6435656 (home). *Fax:* (11) 23011463 (ministry) (office). *E-mail:* pkm@sansad.nic.in (office). *Website:* meaindia.nic.in (office).

MUKHTAR, Chaudhry Ahmed; Pakistani politician and business executive; *Minister of Defence, with additional charge of Commerce and Textile Industry;* Owner Service Shoe business and several other cos in Pakistan; sr leader of Pakistan People's Party, Gujrat Dist; fmr Minister of Commerce in Govt of Benazir Bhutto 1993–96; mem. Parl. for Gujrat-II 2008–; Minister of Defence, with additional charge of Commerce and Textile Industry 2008–; Chair. Pakistan International Airlines. *Address:* Ministry of Defence, Pakistan Secretariat, No. II, Rawalpindi 46000, Pakistan (office). *Telephone:* (51) 9271107 (office). *Fax:* (51) 9271113 (office). *E-mail:* tahir@mod.gov.pk (office). *Website:* www.mod.gov.pk (office).

MUKHTAR, Mansur, BSc, MPhil, PhD; Nigerian economist, academic and politician; *Minister of Finance;* b. 21 Sept. 1959; ed Ahmadu Bello Univ., Univs of Cambridge and Sussex, UK; economist, Central Bank of Nigeria 1980–81; Asst Lecturer, Bayero Univ. 1981–82, Lecturer and Head Dept of Econs 1988–90; special adviser to Minister of Agric. and Natural Resources 1990–92; economist, World Bank, Washington, DC 1992–97, Admin. Young Professionals Program 1997–2000; Deputy Gen. Man. of Strategic Man. and Econs Div., United Bank for Africa PLC 2000–01; Dir Portfolio Man. and Strategy, Debt Man. Office, Ministry of Finance 2001–03, Dir Gen. 2003–07; Exec. Dir African Devt Bank, Tunis 2007–09; Minister of Finance 2009–; mem. Program Implementation Monitoring Cttee 1998–99, Sub-Cttee on Economy and Finance, Presidential Policy Advisory 1999; Officer of the Fed. Repub. of Nigeria; several prizes, grants and awards. *Address:* Ministry of Finance, Ahmadu Bello Way, Central Area, PMB 14, Garki, Abuja, Nigeria (office). *Telephone:* (9) 2346290 (office). *Fax:* susman@nigeria.gov.ng (office). *Website:* www.fmf.gov.ng (office).

MULALLY, Alan R., BS, MS, MA; American automotive industry executive; *President and CEO, Ford Motor Company;* b. 4 Aug. 1945, Oakland, Calif.; m. Jane Connell; three s. two d.; ed Univ. of Kan., Sloan School of Man., Massachusetts Inst. of Tech.; joined The Boeing Co. 1969, numerous eng and program man. positions including contributions on 727, 737, 747, 757, 767 airplanes, Vice-Pres. of Eng, Vice-Pres. and Gen. Man. 777 program, Sr Vice-Pres. of Airplane Devt, Boeing Commercial Airplanes Group 1994–97, Sr Vice-Pres. The Boeing Co. and Pres. Boeing Information, Space and Defense Systems 1997–98, Exec. Vice-Pres. The Boeing Co. and Pres. Boeing Commercial Airplanes 1998–2006, CEO 2001–06; Pres. and CEO Ford Motor Co. 2006–; fmr Chair. Bd of Govs Aerospace Industries Asscn; fmr Co-Chair. Washington Competitive Council; fmr mem. Advisory Bds NASA, Univ. of Washington, Univ. of Kansas, MIT; fmr mem. Scientific Advisory Bd USAF; mem. Nat. Acad. of Eng; Fellow, AIAA 1995 (Pres. –2006), Royal Acad. of Eng; Hon. Fellow, Royal Aeronautical Soc. 1999; Industry Engineer of the Year, Nat. Soc. of Professional Engineers 1978, Tech. Man. Award, American Inst. of Aeronautics and Astronautics 1986, Univ. of Kan. Eng School Distinguished Eng Service Award 1994, Reed Aeronautics Award, American Inst. of Aeronautics and Astronautics 1996, Engineer of the Year, Design News magazine 1996. *Leisure interests:* tennis and golf. *Address:* Ford Motor Company, 1 American Road, Dearborn, MI 48126-2798, USA (office). *Telephone:* (313) 322-3000 (office). *Fax:* (313) 845-6073 (office). *E-mail:* info@ford.com (office). *Website:* www.ford.com (office).

MULAMBA NYUNYI WA KADIMA, Gen. (Léonard); Democratic Republic of the Congo politician, army officer and diplomatist; b. 1928, Luluabourg (now Kananga); s. of Kadima Mulamba and Ngalula Mulamba; m. Adolphine N'galula 1956; six s. two d.; ed Mil. School, Luluabourg; commissioned 1954; Maj. and Deputy Dir of Cabinet, Ministry of Defence 1961–64; Lt-Col 1962; Col, Chief of Staff and Commr of Eastern Prov. (now Haut Zaïre) after re-occupation of Kivu Province 1964–65; Prime Minister 1965–66; Pres. Soc. nationale d'Assurances (SONAS) 1966; Amb. to India 1967–69; Amb. to Japan 1969–76, also accred to Repub. of Korea 1971–76; Amb. to Brazil 1976–79; Général de Division, Général de Corps d'Armée 1979; Mil. Medal, Cross of Bravery, Commdr Ordre de la Couronne (Belgium), Grand Officier Ordre nat. du Léopard (Zaïre), Ordre du Mérite (Cen. African Republic), Compagnon de la Révolution. *Leisure interests:* hunting, reading. *Address:* c/o Chancellerie des Ordres Nationaux, BP 2014, Kinshasa, Democratic Republic of Congo.

MULARONI, Antonella; San Marino lawyer, judge and politician; *Secretary of State for Foreign and Political Affairs, Telecommunications and Transport;* b. 27 Sept. 1961; ed Univ. of Bologna, Italy; qualified as lawyer and notary public 1987; Political Sec. to Sec. of State for Finance, Budget and Econ. Planning 1986–87, Dir Office for Relations with San Marino Communities Abroad, Dept of Foreign Affairs 1987–90; Deputy Perm. Rep. of Repub. of San Marino to Council of Europe 1989–90; served as lawyer and notary public 1991–2001; mem. (People's Alliance) Great and Gen. Council (Parl.) 1993–2001, 2008–; Judge European Court of Human Rights 2001–08; Sec. of State for Foreign and Political Affairs, Telecommunications and Transport 2008–; fmr mem. San Marino Christian Democratic Party Cen. Cttee; Founding mem. People's Alliance of San Marino Democrats 1993, Co-ordinator Jan.–June 1993, Pres. of Ass. 1998–99. *Address:* Secretariat of State for Foreign and Political Affairs and Economic Planning, Palazzo Begni, Contrada Omerelli, 47890 San Marino (office). *Telephone:* 0549 882312 (office). *Fax:* 0549 882814 (office). *E-mail:* info.affariesteri@gov.sm (office). *Website:* www.esteri.sm (office).

MULARONI, Pier Marino; San Marino politician; *Secretary of State for Labour, Co-operation and Youth Policies;* mem. Christian Democratic Party; apptd Capt.-Regent 1997; Sec. of State for Finance, Transport, the Budget and Relations with Azienda Autonoma di Stato Filatelica e Numismatica (AASFN) and Azienda Autonoma di Stato per i Servizi Pubblici (AASS) 2002, currently Sec. of State for Labour, Co-operation and Youth Policies. *Address:* Secretariat of State for Labour, Co-operation and Youth Policies, Palazzo Mercuri, Contrada del Collegio 38, 47890 San Marino (office). *Telephone:* 0549 882532 (office). *Fax:* 0549 882535 (office). *E-mail:* segr.lavoro@omniway.sm (office). *Website:* www.lavoro.segreteria.sm (office).

MULCAHY, Anne M., BA; American business executive; *Chairman and CEO, Xerox Corporation;* b. 21 Oct. 1952, Rockville Centre, NY; ed Marymount Coll., Tarrytown, NY; joined Xerox Corpn, Stamford, CT 1976, various sales and sr man. positions 1976–92, Vice-Pres. Human Resources 1992–95, Vice-Pres. and Staff Officer Customer Relations 1995–97, Chief Staff Officer 1997–99, Corp. Sr Vice-Pres. 1998–99, Pres. Gen. Markets Operations 1999–2000, Pres. and COO 2000–01, CEO 2001–02, Chair. and CEO 2002–; mem. Bd Dirs Catalyst, Citigroup Inc., Fuji Xerox Co. Ltd, Target Corpn, The Washington Post Co.; Chair. Corp. Governance Task Force of the Business Roundtable; mem. Business Council; ranked by Fortune magazine amongst 50 Most Powerful Women in Business (fourth) 2003, (fourth) 2004, (second) 2005, (second) 2006, (second) 2007, ranked by Forbes magazine amongst 100 Most Powerful Women (42nd) 2004, (sixth) 2005, (fifth) 2006, (13th) 2007, (tenth) 2008, named by The Wall Street Journal one of 50 Women to Watch 2005. *Address:* Office of the CEO, Xerox Corporation, 45 Glover Avenue, PO Box 4505, Norwalk, CT 06856-4505, USA (office). *Telephone:* (203) 968-3000 (office). *E-mail:* officeoftheceo@xerox.com (office). *Website:* www.xerox.com (office).

MULCAHY, Sir Geoffrey John, Kt, BSc, MBA; British business executive; *Chairman, Javelin Group;* b. 7 Feb. 1942, Sunderland; s. of Maurice Mulcahy and Kathleen Mulcahy (née Blenkinsop); m. Valerie Elizabeth Mulcahy 1965; one s. one d.; ed King's School, Worcester, Univ. of Manchester, Harvard Univ.; started career in labour relations, marketing and planning with Esso Corpn; Finance Dir Norton Abrasives' European Div., then with British

Sugar; joined Woolworth Holdings (now Kingfisher PLC) 1983, first as Group Financial Dir, then Group Man. Dir 1984–86, CEO 1986–93, Chair. 1990–95, Group CEO Kingfisher Group 1995–2002; Chair. Javelin Group; Dir (non-exec.) Brown & Jackson 2005–. *Leisure interest:* sailing, squash. *Address:* Javelin Group Ltd, 71 Victoria Street, London SW1H 0HW, England (office). *Telephone:* (20) 7961-3200 (office). *Fax:* (20) 7961-3299 (office). *E-mail:* info@javelingroup.com (office). *Website:* www.javelingroup.com (office).

MULDOON, Paul Benedict, BA, FRSL; Irish poet and academic; *Howard G. B. Clark '21 University Professor in the Humanities and Professor of the Council of the Humanities and Creative Writing, Princeton University;* b. 20 June 1951, Portadown, NI; s. of Patrick Muldoon and Brigid Regan; m. Jean Hanff Korelitz 1987; one s. one d.; ed St Patrick's Coll., Armagh, Queen's Univ., Belfast; radio and TV producer, BBC NI 1973–86; has taught at Univs of Cambridge, East Anglia, Columbia Univ., New York, Univ. of California, Berkeley, Univ. of Massachusetts 1986–; Lecturer, Princeton Univ., NJ 1987–88, 1990–95, Dir Creative Writing Program 1993, Prof. 1995–, Howard G. B. Clark '21 Prof. in the Humanities and Prof. of Council of Humanities and Creative Writing 1998–, Founder, Princeton Poetry Festival 2009–; Visiting Prof., Univ. of Massachusetts 1989–90, Bread Loaf School of English 1997–; Poetry Ed., The New Yorker 2007–; mem. Aosdána, Poetry Soc. of GB (Pres. 1996–), American Acad. of Arts and Sciences 2000–, American Acad. of Arts and Letters 2008–; Hon. Prof. of Poetry, Univ. of Oxford 1999–2004; Eric Gregory Award 1972, Sir Geoffrey Faber Memorial Awards 1980, 1991, Guggenheim Fellowship 1990, American Acad. of Arts and Letters Award for Literature 1996, Irish Times Poetry Prize 1997, Pulitzer Prize for Poetry 2003, Griffin Prize 2003, Shakespeare Prize 2004. *Publications:* poetry: Knowing My Place 1971, New Weather 1973, Spirit of Dawn 1975, Mules 1977, Names and Addresses 1978, Immram 1980, Why Brownlee Left 1980, Out of Siberia 1982, Quoof 1983, The Wishbone 1984, Selected Poems 1968–83 1986, Meeting the British 1987, Madoc: A Mystery 1990, Incantata 1994, The Prince of the Quotidian 1994, The Annals of Chile (T.S. Eliot Prize) 1995; Kerry Slides 1996, New Selected Poems 1968–1994 1996, Hopewell Haiku 1997, The Bangle (Slight Return) 1998, Hay (poems) 1999, Poems 1968–1998 2001, Horse Latitudes 2006; for children: The O-O's Party 1981, The Last Thesaurus 1995, The Noctuary of Narcissus Batt 1997; other: Monkeys (TV play) 1989, Shining Brow (opera libretto) 1993, Six Honest Serving Men (play) 1995, Bandanna (opera libretto) 1999, To Ireland, I (essays) 2000; ed.: The Scrake of Dawn 1979, The Faber Book of Contemporary Irish Poetry 1986, The Essential Byron 1989, Moy Sand and Gravel (Pulitzer Prize for Poetry) 2002; trans.: The Astrakhan Cloak, by Nuala Ni Dhomhnaill 1993, The Birds, by Aristophanes (with Richard Martin) 1999. *Leisure interest:* electric guitar. *Address:* Creative Writing Program, Room 122, Lewis Center for the Arts, 185 Nassau Street, Princeton University, Princeton, NJ 08544, USA (office). *Telephone:* (609) 258-4708 (office). *E-mail:* muldoon@princeton.edu (office). *Website:* www.paulmuldoon.net.

MULDOWNEY, Dominic John, BPhil; British composer; b. 19 July 1952, Southampton; s. of William Muldowney and Barbara Muldowney (née Lavender); m. Diane Ellen Trevis 1986; one d.; ed Taunton's Grammar School, Southampton and Univ. of York; Composer-in-Residence, Southern Arts Asscn 1974–76; Music Dir Royal Nat. Theatre 1976–97; Prof. of Composition, RAM 1999–; has composed music for British and int. festivals, for many films and TV and over 50 scores for the theatre; Prix Italia 1993, 1997, Sony Awrd 1997. *Compositions include:* Piano Concerto 1983, Saxophone Concerto 1984, Sinfonietta 1986, Ars Subtilior 1987, Lonely Hearts 1988, Violin Concerto 1989, Three Pieces for Orchestra 1990, Percussion Concerto 1991, Oboe Concerto 1992, Trumpet Concerto 1993, Concerto for 4 Violins 1994 The Brontës (ballet) 1995, Trombone Concerto 1996, Clarinet Concerto 1997, The Fall of Jerusalem (oratorio) 1998, God's Plenty (ballet) 1999, Red Razzmatazz (opera) 2005, War Oratorio 2007, The Last Confession 2007, Tsunami 2008. *Leisure interest:* driving through France and across America. *Address:* c/o Carlin Music, 3 Bridge Approach, Chalk Farm, London, NW1 8BD, England (office). *E-mail:* info@carlinmusic.com (office). *Website:* www.carlinmusic.com (office).

MULIOKELA, Wamundila; Zambian politician and business executive; *Chairman, ZESCO Ltd;* mem. Parl. 2001–06; fmr Deputy Minister of Mines and Minerals; Deputy Minister of Defence –2005, Minister of Defence 2005–06; Chair. ZESCO Ltd (power utility) 2006–. *Address:* ZESCO Ltd, Great East Road, Stand No 6949, 10101 Lusaka, Zambia. *Website:* www.zesco.co.zm.

MULISCH, Harry; Dutch novelist, poet and dramatist; b. 29 July 1927, Haarlem; ed Haarlem Lyceum; Knight, Order of Orange Nassau 1977. *Publications:* Archibald Strohalm (novel) 1952, Tussen hamer en aambeeld (novella) 1952, Chantage op het leven (short story) 1953, De Diamant (novel) 1954, De Sprong der Paarden en de Zoete Zee (novel) 1955, Het mirakel (short stories) 1955, Het Zwarte licht (novel) 1957, Manifesten (essays) 1958, Het Stenen Bruidsbed (novel) 1959, Tanchelijn (play) 1960, Voer voor Psychologen (autobiog.) 1961, Wenken voor de bescherming van uw gezin en uzelf, tijdens de Jongste Dag (essays) 1961, De Knop (play) 1961, De Zaak 40/61 (non-fiction) 1963, Bericht aan de Rattenkoning (essay) 1966, Wenken voor de Jongste Dag (essays) 1967, Het woord bij de daad (essays) 1968, Reconstructie (essays) 1969, De Verteller (novel) 1970, Paralipomena Orphica (essays) 1970, De Verteller verteld: Kommentaar, Katalogus, Kuriosa en een Katastrofestuk (essay) 1971, De Toekomst van gisteren (essay) 1972, Oidipous Oidipous (play) 1972, Woorden, woorden, woorden (poems) 1973, De Vogels (poems) 1974, Tegenlicht (poems) 1975, Twee Vrouwen (novel) 1975, Kind en Kraai (poems) 1975, Mijn Getijdenboek (autobiog.) 1975, Oude Lucht (short stories) 1977, De Aanslag (novel) 1982, Opus Gran (poems) 1982, De Kamer (short stories) 1984, Hoogste Tijd (novel) 1985, De Pupil (novel) 1987, De Elementen (novel) 1988, De Ontdekking van de Hemel (novel) 1992, De Procedure (novel) 1999, Het Theater, de brief en de waarheid (novel) 2000, Siegfried (novel) 2001. *Address:* Van Miereveldstraat 1, 1071 DW Amsterdam, Netherlands. *E-mail:* info@mulisch.nl. *Website:* www.mulisch.nl.

MULKI, Hani, MSc, PhD; Jordanian diplomatist and politician; b. 15 Oct. 1951; s. of Fawzi Mulki and Bashira Mulki; m. Sheila Mulki; two s.; ed Rensselaer Polytechnic Inst., New York, USA; fmr Sec.-Gen. Higher Council for Science and Tech.; fmr Minister of Industry and Trade, Sully, Water and Irrigation; Amb. to Egypt and the Arab League –2004; Minister of Foreign Affairs 2004–05; mem. Senate 2005–07; Special Adviser to King of Jordan 2005–; Amb. to Egypt 2008–; Perm. Rep. to the Arab League 2008–; fmr Pres. Royal Scientific Soc.; Commdr, Royal Order of the Nordic Star (Sweden) 1989, Grand Cordon, Order of Istiklal 1993, Je Maintiendrai Medal (Netherlands) 1996, Grand Cordon, Order of Al Kawkab 1998, Return of the Insignia of Danish Orders 1998, Grand Officier, Ordre Nat. du Mérite (France) 1998. *Address:* c/o Ministry of Foreign Affairs, PO Box 35217, Amman 11180 (office); 37 Damascus Street, Abdoun, Amman, Jordan (home). *Telephone:* (6) 592-4444 (home). *E-mail:* hani-mulki@gmail.com (home).

MULLAJONOV, Faizulla Maksudjonovich; Uzbekistan banking official; *Chairman, Central Bank of the Republic of Uzbekistan;* b. Tajiki kishlak, Namangan region; currently Chair. Cen. Bank of the Repub. of Uzbekistan. *Address:* Central Bank of the Republic of Uzbekistan, 100001 Tashkent, O'zbekiston shox ko'ch. 6, Uzbekistan (office). *Telephone:* (71) 112-61-94 (office). *Fax:* (71) 133-00-44 (office). *E-mail:* webmaster@cbu.st.uz (office). *Website:* www.cbu.uz (office).

MULLAN, Peter, BSc; British actor and film director; b. 1954, Glasgow; ed Univ. of Glasgow; debut with Wildcat Theatre Co. 1988; Hon. MA (Caledonian Univ., Glasgow) 2000. *Film appearances include:* Riff-Raff 1990, The Bid Man 1991, Shallow Grave 1994, Braveheart 1995, Ruffian Hearts 1995, Good Day for the Bad Guys 1995, Trainspotting 1996, Fairytale: A True Story, My Name is Joe (Best Actor Award, Cannes Film Festival 1998) 1998, Duck 1998, Miss Julie 1999, Mauvaise passe 1999, Ordinary Decent Criminal 2000, The Claim 2000, Session 9 2001, The Magdalene Sisters 2002, Entering Blue Zone 2002, Young Adam 2002, Kiss of Life 2003, Kono yo no sotoe–Club Shinchugun 2004, Criminal 2004, Blinded 2004, Waves 2004, On a Clear Day 2005, Cargo 2006, Children of Men 2006, True North 2006, The Last Legion 2007, Dog Altogether 2007, Boy A 2007. *Films written and directed include:* Good Day for the Bay Guys 1995, Fridge 1996, Orphans (Golden Lion Award, Venice Film Festival 1998) 1997, The Magdalene Sisters (Golden Lion Award, Venice Film Festival 2002) 2002. *Films produced include:* Caesar 2000. *Television includes:* Rab C. Nesbitt (series) 1990, Jute City (film) 1991, Nightlife (film) 1996, Cardiac Arrest (series) 1996–97, Bogwoman (film) 1997.

MULLEN, Larry, Jr; Irish musician (drums); b. 31 Oct. 1961, Dublin; founder mem., the Feedback 1976, renamed the Hype, finally renamed U2 1978–; major concerts include Live Aid Wembley 1985, Self Aid Dublin, A Conspiracy of Hope (Amnesty Int. Tour) 1986, Smile Jamaica (hurricane relief fundraiser) 1988, Very Special Arts Festival, White House, Washington, DC 1988; numerous tours worldwide; Grammy Award for Best Rock Performance by a Duo or Group with Vocal (for Desire) 1988, BRIT Awards for Best Int. Act 1988–90, 1992, 1998, 2001, Best Live Act 1993, Outstanding Contribution to the British Music Industry 2001, JUNO Award 1993, World Music Award 1993, Grammy Award for Song of the Year, Record of the Year, Best Rock Performance by a Duo or Group with Vocal (all for Beautiful Day) 2000, Grammy Awards for Best Pop Performance by a Duo or Group with Vocal (for Stuck In A Moment You Can't Get Out Of), for Record of the Year (for Walk On), for Best Rock Performance by a Duo or Group with Vocal (for Elevation) 2001, American Music Award for Favorite Internet Artist of the Year 2002, Ivor Novello Award for Best Song Musically and Lyrically (for Walk On) 2002, Golden Globe for Best Original Song (for The Hands That Built America, from film Gangs of New York) 2003, Grammy Awards for Best Rock Performance by a Duo or Group with Vocal, Best Rock Song, Best Short Form Music Video (all for Vertigo) 2004, Nordoff-Robbins Silver Clef Award for lifetime achievement 2005, Q Award for Best Live Act 2005, Digital Music Award for Favourite Download Single (for Vertigo) 2005, Meteor Ireland Music Award for Best Irish Band, Best Live Performance 2006, Grammy Awards for Song of the Year, for Best Rock Performance by a Duo or Group with Vocal (both for Sometimes You Can't Make it on Your Own), for Best Rock Song (for City of Blinding Lights) 2006; Portuguese Order of Liberty 2005. *Films:* Rattle and Hum 1988. *Recordings include:* albums: Boy 1980, October 1981, War 1983, Under a Blood Red Sky 1983, The Unforgettable Fire 1984, Wide Awake In America 1985, The Joshua Tree (Grammy Award for Album of the Year, Best Rock Performance by a Duo or Group with Vocal) 1987, Rattle and Hum 1988, Achtung Baby (Grammy Award for Best Rock Performance by a Duo or Group with Vocal 1992) 1991, Zooropa (Grammy Award for Best Alternative Music Album) 1993, Passengers (film soundtrack with Brian Eno) 1995, Pop 1997, The Best Of 1980–90 1998, All That You Can't Leave Behind (Grammy Award for Best Rock Album 2001) 2000, The Best Of 1990–2000 2002, How To Dismantle An Atomic Bomb (Meteor Ireland Music Award for Best Irish Album 2006, Grammy Awards for Album of the Year, for Best Rock Album 2006) 2004, No Line on the Horizon 2009. *Address:* Principle Management, 30–32 Sir John Rogersons Quay, Dublin 2, Ireland (office). *E-mail:* candida@numb.ie (office). *Website:* www.u2.com.

MULLEN, Adm. Michael (Mike) Glenn, MSc; American naval officer; *Chairman, Joint Chiefs of Staff;* b. 4 Oct. 1946, Los Angeles, Calif.; m.; two s.; ed Naval Postgraduate School, Monterey, Calif., Harvard Business School; served as jr officer aboard USS Collett, USS Blandy, USS Fox, USS Sterrett, held command posts aboard USS Noxubee, USS Goldsborough, USS Yorktown, as Flag Officer commanded Cruiser-Destroyer Group Two and George

Washington Battle Group, fmr Commdr US Second Fleet/NATO Striking Fleet Atlantic; non-operational posts have included Co. Officer and Exec. Asst to Commdt of Midshipmen, US Naval Acad., Annapolis, Dir Surface Officer Distribution, Bureau of Naval Personnel; posts with Chief of Naval Operations include Deputy Dir and Dir of Surface Warfare, Deputy Chief of Naval Operations for Resources, Requirements and Assessments, 32nd Vice-Chief of Naval Operations 2003–04; served as Commdr Allied Jt Force Command Naples, Chief of Naval Operations 2004–07; Chair. Jt Chiefs of Staff 2007–; Jt Chiefs of Staff Identification Badge, Navy Surface Warfare Badge (Officer), Defense Distinguished Service Medal, Navy Distinguished Service Medal (2), Defense Superior Service Medal, Legion of Merit Decoration (6), Meritorious Service Medal, Navy and Marine Corps Commendation Medal, Navy and Marine Corps Achievement Medal, Navy Unit Commendation Ribbon, Navy Meritorious Unit Commendation Ribbon, Navy 'E' Ribbon, Navy Expeditionary Medal, Nat. Defense Service Medal (3), Armed Forces Expeditionary Medal, Viet Nam Service Medal, Global War on Terrorism Service Medal, Humanitarian Service Medal (2), Navy Overseas Service Ribbon (4), Navy Sea Service Deployment Ribbon (2), Repub. of Viet Nam Gallantry Cross Unit Citation Medal, Repub. of Viet Nam Civil Actions Unit Citation Ribbon. *Address:* Office of the Chairman of the Joint Chiefs of Staff, 9999 Joint Staff Pentagon, Washington, DC 20318-9999, USA (office). *Website:* www.jcs.mil (office).

MÜLLER, Claus, Dr rer. nat; German mathematician, consultant and academic; *Professor Emeritus, University of Aachen;* b. 20 Feb. 1920, Solingen; s. of Michael Müller and Grete (née Porten) Müller; m. Irmgard Döring 1947; two s. one d.; ed Univs of Bonn and Munich; service in German army and navy 1941–45; Asst Prof., Göttingen Univ. 1945–46; Lecturer, Bonn Univ. 1947–55; Lecturer, Univ. Coll., Hull 1949; Prof. and Dir Inst. of Math. Sciences, Tech. Univ. of Aachen 1955–85, Prof. Emer. 1985–; Fellow Peterhouse, Cambridge 1948; Visiting Prof., Princeton Inst. 1952, Courant Inst., New York, Math. Research Center Madison, Boeing Scientific Research Lab. 1955–65; Saragossa Acad. 1968, North-Rhine Acad. 1970. *Publications:* Foundations of the Mathematical Theory of Electromagnetic Waves, Spherical Harmonics, Analysis of Spherical Symmetries 1997; specialist articles in math. *Leisure interest:* music. *Address:* Horbacher Strasse 33, 52072 Aachen, Germany. *Telephone:* (241) 12661.

MÜLLER, Gerhard, Dr rer. nat; German chemist and academic; *Professor of Chemistry, University of Konstanz;* b. 7 March 1953, Rehren, Lower Saxony; ed Tech. Univ. of Munich; Postdoctoral Assoc., Univ. of Calif., Berkeley 1980–81; Postdoctoral Assoc. Max-Planck-Inst. für Kohlenforschung, Mulheim 1982–83; Research Assoc., Tech. Univ. of Munich 1983–89, Lecturer 1989; Prof. of Chemistry, Univ. of Konstanz 1990–, Vice-Dean, Dept of Chemistry 1992–93, 1995–96, Dean 1993–95, Vice-Pres. of Research 1998–2000; mem. German Nat. Cttee, Int. Union of Crystallography 1994–2000, Chair. Div. of Molecular Compounds 1992–2000; Asst Ed. Zeitschrift für Naturforschung B 1986–; mem. German Chemical Soc., German Crystallographic Soc., Nat. Geographic Soc. *Address:* Fachbereich Chemie, Universität Konstanz, Postfach 5560-M723, Universitaetsstrasse 10, 78464 Konstanz, Germany (office). *Telephone:* (7531) 88-3735 (office). *Fax:* (7531) 88-3140 (office). *E-mail:* gerhard.mueller@chemie.uni-konstanz.de (office). *Website:* www.chemie.uni-konstanz.de/~haffke/german/arb/ag/agmuel.htm (office).

MÜLLER, Gerhard, DTheol; German ecclesiastic; b. 10 May 1929, Marburg/Lahn; s. of Karl Müller and Elisabeth Landau; m. Ursula Herboth 1957; two s.; ed Marburg, Göttingen and Tübingen; priest in Hanau/Main 1956–57; Deutsche Forschungsgemeinschaft scholarship, Italy 1957–59; Asst, Ecumenical Seminar, Univ. of Marburg 1959–61, Docent, Faculty of Theology 1961–66; Guest Lecturer, German Historical Inst., Rome 1966–67; Prof. of Historical Theology (Modern Church History), Univ. of Erlangen 1967–82; Evangelical-Lutheran Bishop of Brunswick 1982–94; mem. Mainz, Netherlands Acads and Braunschweiger Wissenschaftliche Gesellschaft; Hon. Prof., Univ. of Göttingen 1983–; Hon. DTheol (St Andrews). *Publications:* Franz Lambert von Avignon und die Reformation in Hessen 1958, Nuntiaturberichte aus Deutschland 1530–1532 (two vols) 1963, 1969, Die römische Kurie und die Reformation 1523–1534 1969, Die Rechtfertigungslehre 1977, Reformation und Stadt 1981, Zwischen Reformation und Gegenwart 1983, Zwischen Reformation und Gegenwart II 1988, Causa Reformationis 1989, Die Mystik oder das Wort? 2000; ed. works of Andreas Osiander and a 36-vol. theological encyclopaedia. *Address:* Sperlingstrasse 59, 91056 Erlangen, Germany (home). *Telephone:* (9131) 490939 (home). *Fax:* (9131) 490939 (home). *E-mail:* gmuellerdd@arcor.de (home).

MÜLLER, K. Alex, PhD; Swiss physicist; b. 20 April 1927, Basel; ed Swiss Fed. Inst. of Tech.; Project Man., Battelle Institute, Geneva 1958–62; Lecturer, Univ. of Zurich 1962, Titular Prof. 1970, Prof. 1987–; joined IBM Zurich Research Lab., Rüschlikon 1963, Man. Dept of Physics and Fellow 1973–92, Researcher 1985–, Fellow Emer. 1992–98; Fellow, American Physical Soc.; mem. European Physics Soc.; Foreign Assoc. mem. NAS, Russian, Slovenian, Polish and Sachsen Acads of Sciences; Hon. mem. Swiss Physical Soc., Zurich Physical Soc., Acad. of Ceramics; Hon. DSc (Geneva) 1987, (Tech. Univ. of Munich) 1987, (Università degli Studi di Pavia) 1987, (Leuven) 1988, (Boston) 1988, (Tel-Aviv) 1988, (Tech. Univ. of Darmstadt) 1988, (Nice) 1989, (Universidad Politecnica, Madrid) 1989, (Bochum) 1990, (Università degli Studi di Roma) 1990, (Trondheim) 1992, (Metz) 1995, (Salzburg) 1995, (Regensburg) 1996, (Cottbus, Germany) 1997, (Leipzig) 2000, (Bar Ilan) 2006, (Tbilisi) 2007; with G. Bednorz: Marcel-Benoist Prize 1986, Nobel Prize for Physics (with G. Bednorz) for discovery of new superconducting materials 1987, 13th Fritz London Memorial Award, UCLA 1987, Dannie Heineman Prize, Minna James Heineman Stiftung, Acad. of Sciences, Gottingen, Germany 1987, Robert Wichard Pohl Prize, German Physical Soc. 1987, Hewlett-Packard Europhysics Prize 1988, Int. Prize for New Materials Research, American Physical Soc. 1988, Minnie Rosen Award, Ross Univ., New York 1989, Special Tsukuba Award (Japan) 1989, Int. 'Aldo Villa' Prize, Italian Ceramic Soc. 1991. *Publications:* more than 400 publs on structural phase transitions, critical and multicritical phenomena, the behaviour of ferroelectrica at low temperatures and superconductivity in cuprates. *Address:* University of Zürich, Physik-Institut, Winterthurerstr. 190, 8057 Zürich (office); Haldenstr. 54, 8909 Hedingen, Switzerland (home). *Telephone:* (44) 6355749 (office). *Fax:* (44) 6355704 (office). *Website:* www.physik.uzh.ch (office).

MÜLLER, Klaus-Peter; German banker; *Chairman of the Supervisory Board, Commerzbank AG;* b. 16 Sept. 1944, Duppach; m.; one d.; apprenticeship in banking, Bankhaus Friedrich Simon KGaA, Düsseldorf 1962–64; with Düsseldorf Br., Commerzbank AG 1966–68, New York Rep. Office and Br. 1968–73, Jt Man. Düsseldorf and Duisburg Br. 1973–82, Jt Man. New York Br. 1982–86, Exec. Vice-Pres. 1986–90, Head of Corp. Banking Dept 1990–2001, Head, East German Operations 1990–, mem. Bd of Man. Dirs 1990–, Chair. 2001–08, Chair. Supervisory Bd 2008–; Pres. Asscn of German Banks, Berlin 2005–; Hon. Prof., Frankfurt School of Finance and Man. 2007; Dr hc (Finance Acad. of Russian Fed.) 2004. *Address:* Commerzbank AG, 60261 Frankfurt/Main, Germany (office). *Telephone:* (69) 13620 (office). *Fax:* (69) 285389 (office). *E-mail:* info@commerzbank.com (office). *Website:* www.commerzbank.com (office).

MÜLLER, Lothar; German financier; b. 27 Jan. 1927, Munich; m. Irmgard Mueller; one s. three d.; with tax authority of Bavaria 1954; Head, Bavarian Finance Ministry 1977–79; Pres. Landeszentralbank, Bavaria 1979–94; mem. Cen. Bank Council of the Deutsche Bundesbank; Bayerischer Verdienstorden, Grosses Bundesverdienstkreuz. *Publications:* publs on public finance, company and tax law, monetary and economic policy. *Address:* Waldparkstrasse 35C, 85521 Riemerling, Germany. *Telephone:* (89) 28893200. *Fax:* (89) 28893890.

MÜLLER, Peter; German lawyer and politician; *Minister-President of Saarland;* b. 25 Sept. 1955, Illingen; m. Astrid Gercke-Müller; three s.; ed Lebach Grammar School, Univs of Bonn and Saarbrücken; trainee lawyer 1983–86; Asst Lecturer, Univ. of Saarland 1983–86, later Chair. Constitutional and Admin. Law; Judge, Saarbrücken Regional Court –1990; mem. CDU Parl. Party, Saarland Parl. 1990–; Minister Pres. of Saarland 1999–; Dr hc (Tokyo) 2001. *Publication:* Nach dem Pisa-Shock. Plädoyers für eine Bildungreform (co-ed.) 2002, Bevölkeningsentoicklung und Grundgesetz, ins Festschrift für Georg Ress 2005. *Leisure interests:* active footballer, plays chess and skat, clarinet and saxophone. *Address:* Landtag des Saarlandes, Postfach 101833, 66081 Saarbrücken (office); Saarländische Staatskanzlei, Am Ludwigsplatz 14, Postfach 102431, 66024 Saarbrücken, Germany (office). *Telephone:* (681) 5011122 (office). *Fax:* (681) 5011262 (office). *E-mail:* p.mueller@staatskanzlei.saarland.de (office). *Website:* www.saarland.de (office); www.staatskanzlei.saarland.de (office).

MULLER, Steven, PhD; American academic and university administrator; *Distinguished Professorial Lecturer and FPI Fellow, Paul H. Nitze School of Advanced International Studies (SAIS) and President Emeritus, Johns Hopkins University;* b. 22 Nov. 1927, Hamburg, Germany; s. of Werner A. Muller and Marianne Muller (née Hartstein); m. 1st Margie Hellman 1951; two d.; m. 2nd Jill E. McGovern 2000; ed Hollywood High School, Los Angeles, Univ. of Calif., Los Angeles, Univ. of Oxford, UK, Cornell Univ.; Instructor in Political Science, Wells Coll. 1953; US Army 1954–55; Research Fellow in Social Science, Cornell Univ. 1955–56; Asst Prof. of Political Science, Haverford Coll. 1956–58; Asst Prof. of Govt, Cornell Univ. 1958–61, Assoc. Prof. and Dir Center for Int. Studies 1961–66, Vice-Pres. for Public Affairs 1966–71; Provost, Johns Hopkins Univ. 1971–72, Pres. 1972–90, Pres. Emer. 1990–, Distinguised Professorial Lecturer and FPI Fellow, Paul H. Nitze School of Advanced Int. Studies 1993–; Pres. Johns Hopkins Hosp. 1972–83; Chair. 21st Century Foundation 1990–96; Chair. of Bd St Mary's Coll. of Maryland; Co-Chair. American Inst. for Contemporary German Studies; Dir Law/Gibb Corpn, Org. Resources Counselors, Inc., Atlantic Council of the US, German Marshall Fund of the US; fmr mem. Bd of Dirs, CSX Corpn, Millipore Corpn, Beneficial Corpn, Alex. Brown & Sons Inc., Van Kampen Closed End Funds; Commdr's Cross of the Order of Merit (FRG). *Publications:* Documents on European Government 1963, From Occupation to Cooperation 1992 (co-ed.), In Search of Germany 1996 (co-ed.), Universities in the Twenty-First Century 1996; articles in learned journals. *Leisure interest:* philately. *Address:* Johns Hopkins University, Paul H. Nitze School of Advanced International Studies, 1619 Massachusetts Avenue, NW, Suite 406, Washington, DC 20036 (office); 2315 Bancroft Place, NW, Washington, DC 20008-4005, USA (home). *Telephone:* (202) 663-5821 (office); (202) 387-2777 (home). *Fax:* (202) 663-5822 (office); (202) 387-6777 (home). *E-mail:* kareese@jhu.edu (office); catalina53@juno.com (home). *Website:* www.sais-jhu.edu (office).

MÜLLER, Werner, PhD; German politician and business executive; *Chairman of the Executive Board, Evonik Industries AG;* b. 1 June 1946, Essen; m.; two c.; ed Univs of Mannheim, Duisberg and Bremen; Lecturer, Univ. of Applied Sciences, Ludwigshafen 1970–72; part-time Lectureships, Univs of Mannheim and Regensburg 1970–73; Head of Market Research, Rheinisch-Westfälische electricity co. (RWE) 1973–80; Gen. Rep. and Chief Exec. VEBA AG (power co.) 1980–92, mem. Exec. Bd VEBA Kraftwerke Ruhr AG, Gelsenkirchen 1992–97; ind. industrial consultant 1997–98; apptd Adviser to Gerhard Schroder, Minister-Pres. of Lower Saxony 1991; Fed. Minister of Econ. and Tech. 1998–2002; Chair. Exec. Bd RAG AG, Essen 2003–07, also Chair. Exec. Bd RAG Beteiligungs-AG (renamed Evonik Industries AG 2007), Essen 2006–; Chair. Supervisory Bd, Deutsche Bahn AG 2005–. *Address:*

Evonik Industries AG, Rellinghauser Straße 1–11, 45128 Essen (office); Deutsche Bahn AG, Potsdamer Platz 2, 10785 Berlin, Germany (office). *Telephone:* (201) 177-01 (Essen) (office); (30) 297-0 (Berlin) (office). *Fax:* (201) 177-3475 (Essen) (office); (30) 29761919 (Berlin) (office). *E-mail:* info@evonik.com (office); info@db.de (office). *Website:* www.evonik.com (office); www.db.de (office).

MÜLLER-SEIDEL, Walter, DPhil; German professor of modern literature; b. 1 July 1918, Schöna; s. of Martin Müller-Seidel and Rosa (née Seidel) Müller; m. Ilse Peters 1950; one s.; ed Univs of Leipzig and Heidelberg; lecturer Univ. of Cologne 1958, Privat-dozent 1958–59; Prof. Univ. of Munich 1960–65; Ordinary Prof. 1965, now Emer.; mem. Bayerische Akad. der Wissenschaften 1974. *Publications:* Versehen und Erkennen: Eine Studie über Heinrich von Kleist 1961, Probleme der literarischen Wertung 1965, Theodor Fontane: Soziale Romankunst in Deutschland 1975, Die Geschichtlichkeit der deutscher Klassik 1983, Die Deportation des Menschen, Kafkas Erzählung 'In der Strafkolonie' im europäischen Kontext 1986, Arztbilder im Wandel. Zum literarischen Werk Arthur Schnitzlers 1997, Alfred Erich Hoche: Lebensgeschichte im Spannungsfeld von Psychiatrie 1999, Strafrecht und Literatur 1999. *Address:* Pienzenauerstrasse 164, 81925 Munich, Germany. *Telephone:* (89) 988250.

MULLIEZ, Vianney; French retail executive; *Chairman of the Supervisory Board, Groupe Auchan;* b. 5 March 1963, Roubaix; m.; three c.; ed Ecole des Hautes Etudes Commerciales, Paris; worked eight years with PricewaterhouseCoopers; f. MBV & Associés (accountancy firm); Dir of Finance, Auchan France 1998–2000, Dir for Int. Devt 2000–04, Pres. Immochan International (subsidiary co.) 2004, Chair. Supervisory Bd Groupe Auchan 2006–; Pres. Supervisory Bd Asscn Familiale Mulliez 2006–. *Leisure interest:* golf. *Address:* Groupe Auchan, 40 avenue de Flandre, PO Box 139, 59964 Croix Cedex, France (office). *Telephone:* (3) 20-81-68-00 (office). *Fax:* (3) 20-81-69-09 (office). *E-mail:* info@groupe-auchan.com (office). *Website:* www.groupe-auchan.com (office).

MULLIN, Leo F., BS, MBA; American business executive; m. Leah Mullin; one s. one d.; ed Harvard Univ., Harvard School of Arts and Sciences, Harvard Business School; began career as man. consultant McKinsey & Co. 1967, Pnr 1973–76; Sr Vice-Pres. Strategic Planning, Consolidated Rail Corpn (Conrail), Phila 1976–81; sr man. positions First Chicago 1981–93, Pres. and COO 1993–95; Vice-Chair. Unicorn Corpn and Commonwealth Edison 1995–97; Chair. and CEO Delta Air Lines Inc. 1997–2004 (resgnd); mem. Bd of Dirs Bellsouth Corpn, Johnson & Johnson, Juvenile Diabetes Research Foundation; fmr mem. Bd of Dirs Air Transport Asscn (ATA), Int. Air Transport Asscn (IATA); mem. Business Council, Atlanta Chamber of Commerce, Robert W. Woodruff Arts Center; mem. Bd of Trustees GA Research Alliance. *Address:* c/o Board of Directors, Johnson & Johnson, One Johnson & Johnson Plaza, New Brunswick, NJ 08933, USA (office).

MULLIS, Kary Banks, PhD; American biochemist; b. 28 Dec. 1944, Lenoir, NC; s. of Cecil Banks Mullis and Bernice Alberta Barker Fredericks Mullis; two s. one d.; ed Georgia Inst. of Tech., Univ. of California, Berkeley; Lecturer in Biochem. Univ. of Calif., Berkeley 1972; Postdoctoral Fellow, Univ. of Kan. Medical School 1973–76, Univ. of Calif., San Francisco 1977–79; researcher Cetus Corp. 1979–86; Dir Molecular Biology Xytronyx, Inc., San Diego 1986–88; consultant 1988–96; Chair. StarGene, Inc.; Vice-Pres. Histotec, Inc., Vyrex Inc.; Visiting Prof. Univ. of SC; Partner in Questar Int. 1998; devised polymerase chain reaction; Preis Biochemische Analytik Award 1990, Allan Award 1990, Gairdner Foundation Award 1991, Nat. Biotech. Award 1991, R&D Magazine Scientist of the Year 1991, Koch Award 1992, Chiron Corpn Award 1992, Japan Prize 1992, Calif. Scientist of the Year 1992, shared Nobel Prize for Chem. 1993, Japanese Science and Tech. Foundation Award 1993. *Publications:* numerous articles.

MULLOVA, Viktoria; Russian violinist; b. 27 Nov. 1959, Moscow; d. of Yuri Mullov and Raissa Mullova; one s. two d.; ed studied in Moscow at Cen. Music School and Moscow Conservatory under Leonid Kogan; left USSR 1983; has appeared with most major orchestras and conductors and at int. festivals; lives in London; First Prize, Sibelius Competition, Helsinki 1980, Gold Medal, Tchaikovsky Competition, Moscow 1982. *Recordings include:* more than 20 discs including Beethoven Violin Concerto, Mendelssohn Violin Concerto with the Orchestre Revolutionnaire et Romantique, John Eliot Gardiner, Mozart Violin Concertos Nos 1, 3 & 4, Orchestra of the Age of Enlightenment; on Onyx Classics: Vivaldi Violin Concertos, Bach's Six Solo Sonatas and Partitas. *Address:* Askonas Holt Ltd, Lincoln House, 300 High Holborn, London, WC1V 7JH, England (office). *Telephone:* (20) 7400-1700 (office). *Fax:* (20) 7400-1799 (office). *E-mail:* info@askonasholt.co.uk (office); info@viktoriamullova.com (office). *Website:* www.askonasholt.co.uk (office); www.viktoriamullova.com.

MULRONEY, Rt Hon. (Martin) Brian, PC, CC, LLD; Canadian fmr politician, business executive and lawyer; *Senior Partner, Ogilvy Renault;* b. 20 March 1939, Baie Comeau, Québec.; s. of Benedict Mulroney and Irene Mulroney (née O'Shea); m. Mila Pivnicki 1973; three s. one d.; ed St Thomas Coll. High School, Chatham, St Francis Xavier Univ., Antigonish, NS, Université Laval, Québec; called to Bar of Québec 1965; Partner, Ogilvy, Cope, Porteous, Montgomery, Renault, Clarke & Kirkpatrick, Montreal 1965–76, Sr Partner, Ogilvy Renault 1993–; Exec. Vice-Pres. (Corp. Affairs), Iron Ore Co. of Canada 1976–77, Pres. and Dir 1977–83; Leader, Progressive Party of Canada 1983–93; mem. Parl. 1983–93; Leader of Opposition 1983–84; Prime Minister of Canada 1984–93 (resgnd); Co-Chairman of the United Nations Summit on Children; Chair. Forbes Global (New York), Int. Advisory Bd Barrick Gold Corpn, Toronto, Bd Quebecor World Inc.; Chair. and Dir Persona Communications, Inc., St John's; Dir Barrick Gold Corpn, Archer Daniels Midland Co., Cendant Corpn, Trizec Properties Inc., AOL Latin America, Quebecor Inc., Quebecor World Inc., Quebecor Media, Montreal, Lion Capital LLP, London, Said Holdings Ltd, Bermuda; mem. Int. Advisory Council, JP Morgan Chase & Co., New York, China Int. Trust and Investment Corpn, Beijing, Independent News and Media PLC, Dublin, Magna International, Toronto; Sr Counsellor to Hicks, Muse, Tate & Furst, Dallas; Trustee Montreal Heart Inst. Foundation, Freedom Forum, Int. Advisory Council Les Hautes Etudes Commerciales Univ. of Montreal, World Trade Center Memorial Foundation, Council on Foreign Relations; Grand Officier Ordre nat. du Québec; several hon. degrees; numerous awards. *Publication:* Where I Stand 1983. *Leisure interests:* tennis, swimming. *Address:* Ogilvy Renault, 1981 McGill College Avenue, Suite 1100, Montreal, PQ H3A 3C1 (office); 47 Forden Crescent, Westmount, PQ H3Y 2Y5, Canada (home). *Telephone:* (514) 847-4779 (office). *Fax:* (514) 286-1238 (office). *E-mail:* bmulroney@ogilvyrenault.com (office). *Website:* www.ogilvyrenault.com (office).

MULUZI, Bakili; Malawi politician, business executive and fmr head of state; b. 17 March 1943, Machinga; m. Patricia Shanil; seven c.; ed Huddersfield Tech. Coll., Thirsted Tech. Coll. and coll. in Denmark; clerk, colonial civil service of Nyasaland; fmr Sec.-Gen. Malawi Congress Party (resgnd 1982); mem. Parl. 1975; held various Cabinet portfolios including Educ. and Minister without Portfolio; business interests in transport, merchandise distribution and real estate; Leader, United Democratic Front 1992–; Pres. of Malawi 1994–2004; arrested on fraud and corruption charges 2006; Hon. DJur (Lincoln, MO, Glasgow); Hon. Dr rer. pol (Nat. Chengchi, Taipei). *Publications:* Democracy with a Price 2000, Mau Anga: The Voice of a Democrat 2002. *Leisure interests:* reading, watching football, assisting the needy. *Address:* c/o United Democratic Front (UDF), POB 5446, Limbe, Malawi.

MULVA, James J. (Jim), MBA; American oil industry executive; *Chairman and CEO, ConocoPhillips Company;* b. 1946, Green Bay, Wis.; ed Univ. of Texas; served as US Navy Officer 1969–73; joined Phillips Petroleum Co. 1973, Chief Financial Officer 1990–93, Sr Vice-Pres. 1993–94, Exec. Vice-Pres. 1994, Pres. and COO 1994–99, Chair., Pres. and CEO 1999–2002, Pres. and CEO ConocoPhillips Co. (cr. following merger of Phillips Petroleum Co. and Conoco Co.) 2002–04, Chair. and CEO 2004–; Chair. American Petroleum Inst. 2006; mem. Bd Dirs General Electric, M.D. Anderson Cancer Center; mem. The Business Council, The Business Roundtable; Trustee, Boys and Girls Clubs of America; Petroleum Exec. of the Year 2002. *Address:* ConocoPhillips Company, Conoco Center, 600 North Dairy Ashford, Houston, TX 77079-1175 (office); PO Box 2197, Houston, TX 77252, USA (office). *Telephone:* (281) 293-1000 (office). *Fax:* (281) 293-1440 (office). *Website:* www.conocophillips.com (office).

MUMBA, Nevers; Zambian politician and evangelist; b. 18 May 1960, Chinsali; s. of Sunday Mumba; nephew of Kenneth Kaunda, first Pres. of Zambia; m. Florence Mumba; five c.; ed Nations Inst., Dallas, Tex., USA; Founder and Pres. Victory Ministries International, Chair. Bd Victory Coll.; made his name as TV evangelist; Co-founder and Nat. Chair. Nat. Citizen's Coalition (NCC); presidential cand. 2001; disbanded NCC and joined ruling Movt for Multiparty Democracy 2003; Vice-Pres. of Zambia 2003–04; Dr hc (Univ. of Mich. –Flint, USA). *Leisure interest:* boxing. *Address:* c/o Office of the Vice-President, POB 30208, Lusaka, Zambia (office).

MUMBENGEGWI, Samuel, PhD; Zimbabwean politician; began career as primary school teacher; Lecturer, Morgenster Teachers Coll.; Civil Servant, Ministry of Educ. 1980–87, Ministry of Higher Educ. and Tech. 1988–94; Deputy Sec. of Planning, Ministry of Higher Educ. and Tech. 1994; Head of Appointments, Promotions and Conditions, Public Service Comm. 1994–2000; mem. Parl. 2000–; Minister of Educ., Sports and Culture 2000–01, of Higher Educ. and Tech. 2001–03, of Industry and Int. Trade 2003–05, of Indigenisation and Empowerment 2005–07, of Finance 2007–08. *Address:* c/o Ministry of Finance, Blocks B, E and G, Composite Building, Corner Samora Machel Avenuee and Fourth Street, Private Bag 7705, Causeway, Harare, Zimbabwe (office).

MUMBENGEGWI, Simbarashe Simbanenduku, BA, DipEd; Zimbabwean diplomatist, politician and public servant; *Minister of Foreign Affairs;* b. 20 July 1945, Chivi Dist; s. of the late Chivandire Davis Mumbengegwi and Dzivaidzo Shuvai Chimbambo; m. Emily Charasika 1983; one s. four d.; ed Monash Univ., Melbourne, Australia, Univ. of Zimbabwe; active in Zimbabwe African Nat. Union (ZANU) Party 1963–, in exile, Australia 1966–72, Deputy Chief Rep. in Australia and Far East 1973–76, Chief Rep. 1976–78, Chief Rep. in Zambia 1978–80, mem. Cen. Cttee 1984–94; elected MP 1980, 1985; Deputy Minister of Foreign Affairs 1981–82, Minister of Water Resources and Devt 1982, of Housing 1982–84, of Public Construction and Nat. Housing 1984–88, of Transport 1988–90; Perm. Rep. to UN 1990–95; Amb. to Belgium, the Netherlands and Luxembourg, Perm. Rep. to EU 1995–99; Perm. Rep. to Org. for the Prohibition of Chemical Weapons (OPCW) 1997–99, Chair. Conf. of the State Parties 1997–98, mem. Exec. Council 1997–99; Amb. to the UK and Ireland 1999–2005; Minister of Foreign Affairs 2005–. *Leisure interests:* reading, photography, jogging, tennis, golf. *Address:* Ministry of Foreign Affairs, Munhumutapa Building, Samora Machel Avenue, POB 4240, Causeway, Harare, Zimbabwe (office). *Telephone:* (4) 727005 (office); (4) 705420 (office). *Fax:* (4) 705161 (office); (4) 727175 (office).

MUMFORD, David Bryant, PhD; American mathematician and academic; *University Professor, Division of Applied Mathematics, Brown University;* b. 11 June 1937, Three Bridges, Sussex, England; s. of William Bryant Mumford and Grace Schiott; m. 1st Erika Jentsch 1959 (died 1988); three s. one d.; m. 2nd Jenifer Moore 1989; ed Harvard Univ.; Prof. of Math., Harvard Univ. 1967–77, Higgins Prof. 1977–97, Chair. Math. Dept 1981–84, MacArthur Fellow 1987–92; Prof. of Math., Brown Univ. 1996–; Pres. Int. Math. Union

1995–98; mem. NAS, American Acad. of Arts and Sciences, American Philosophical Soc., Norwegian Acad. of Sciences and Letters; Hon. DSc (Warwick) 1983, (Norwegian Univ. Science and Tech.) 2000, (Rockefeller); Fields Medal 1974. *Publications:* Geometric Invariant Theory 1965, Abelian Varieties 1970, Algebraic Geometry I 1976, Two and Three Dimensional Patterns of the Face 1999, Indra's Pearls 2002. *Leisure interest:* sailing. *Address:* Brown University, Division of Applied Mathematics, Room 210, 182 George Street, Providence, RI 02912 (office); 15 Sleeper Street, #505, Boston, MA 02210, USA (home). *Telephone:* (401) 863-3441 (office); (617) 670-2989 (home). *Fax:* (401) 863-1355 (office). *E-mail:* david_mumford@brown.edu (office). *Website:* www.dam.brown.edu/people/mumford (office).

MUMUNI, Alhaji Muhammad, LLB, LLM, BL; Ghanaian politician; *Minister of Foreign Affairs, Regional Integration and NEPAD;* b. 28 July 1949; ed Univ. of Ghana, Ghana Law School; fmr Nat. Service Coordinator for the North; fmr Legal Officer, Bank for Housing and Construction; fmr Dist Magistrate; mem. Parl. for Kumbungu 1997–2004, mem. Judiciary Cttee, Standing Orders Cttee; Minister of Employment and Social Welfare 1997–2000, of Foreign Affairs, Regional Integration and NEPAD 2009–; Vice-Pres. 86th Session, Institutional Labour Congress, Geneva 1998. *Address:* Ministry of Foreign Affairs, Treasury Road, POB M53, Accra, Ghana (office). *Telephone:* (21) 664951 (office). *Fax:* (21) 680017 (office). *E-mail:* ghmaf00@ghana.com (office).

MUN, Il-bong; North Korean politician; mem. Supreme People's Ass.; Minister of Finance 2000–. *Address:* Ministry of Finance, Pyongyang, Democratic People's Republic of Korea (office).

MUNAVVAR, Mohamed; Maldivian lawyer; *President, Maldivian Democratic Party;* fmr Attorney-Gen., Repub. of the Maldives; arrested Aug. 2004, transferred to house arrest Oct.–Dec. 2004 (charges withdrawn); legal advisor to Maldivian Democratic Party –2007, Pres. 2007–. *Address:* Maldivian Democratic Party (MDP), 1st Floor, M. Gloryge, Fareedhee Magu, Malé, Maldives (office). *Telephone:* 3340044 (office). *Fax:* 3322960 (office). *E-mail:* secretariat@maldiviandemocraticparty.org (office). *Website:* www.maldiviandemocraticparty.org (office).

MUNDA, Arjun; Indian politician; Chief Minister of Jharkhand 2003–05 (resgnd), reappointed March, 2005–Sept. 2006 (resgnd); mem. Bharatiya Janata Party. *Address:* c/o Chief Minister's Secretariat, Ranchi 834 001, India.

MUNDELL, Robert Alexander, PhD; Canadian professor of economics; *Professor of Economics, Columbia University;* b. 24 Oct. 1932, Kingston, Ont.; s. of William Campbell Mundell and Lila Teresa Mundell; m. Barbara Sheff 1957 (divorced 1972); two s. one d.; ed Univ. of British Columbia, Univ. of Washington, Massachusetts Inst. of Tech., London School of Econs, Univ. of Chicago; Instructor, Univ. of BC 1957–58; economist, Royal Comm. on Price Spreads of Food Products, Ottawa 1958; Asst Prof. of Econs, Stanford Univ., USA 1958–59; Prof. of Econs, Johns Hopkins Univ., School of Advanced Int. Studies, Bologna, Italy 1959–61; Sr Economist, IMF 1961–63; Visiting Prof. of Econs, McGill Univ. 1963–64, 1989–90; Prof. of Int. Econs, Grad. Inst. of Int. Studies, Geneva, Switzerland 1965–75; Prof. of Econs Univ. of Chicago 1966–71; Prof. of Econs and Chair. Dept of Econs, Univ. of Waterloo, Ont. 1972–74; Prof. of Econs Columbia Univ., USA 1974–; Ed. Journal of Political Economy 1966–71; Annenburg Distinguished Scholar in Residence, Univ. of Southern Calif. 1980; Richard Fox Visiting Prof. of Econs, Univ. of Pa 1990–91; First Rockefeller Visiting Research Prof. of Int. Econs, Brookings Inst. 1964–65; Guggenheim Fellow 1971; Marshall Lectures, Cambridge Univ. 1974; Distinguished Lecturer, Ching-Hua Inst., Taipei, Taiwan 1985; Pres. N American Econ. and Financial Asscn 1974–78; Dr hc (Univ. of Paris) 1992, (People's Univ. of China) 1995; Jacques Rueff Prize and Medal 1983, Nobel Prize for Econs 1999. *Publications:* The International Monetary System: Conflict and Reform 1965, Man and Economics 1968, International Economics 1968, Monetary Theory: Interest, Inflation and Growth in the World Economy 1971, Global Disequilibrium in the Lloyd Economy (co-author) 1989, Building the New Europe (co-author) 1991, Inflation and Growth in China (co-author) 1996; numerous papers and articles in journals. *Leisure interests:* painting, tennis, hockey, skiing, art history. *Address:* Department of Economics, Columbia University, 420 West 118th Street, New York, NY 10027; 35 Claremont Avenue, New York, NY 10027, USA (home); Palazzo Mundell, Santa Colomba, Siena, Italy (June–Aug.). *Telephone:* (212) 854-3669 (office); (212) 749-0630 (Home, USA); (0577) 57068 (Italy). *Fax:* (212) 854-8059.

MUNDIE, Craig James, BS, MS; American computer software industry executive; *Chief Research and Strategy Officer, Microsoft Corporation;* b. 1949, Cleveland; m.; one d.; ed Georgia Inst. of Tech.; Software Developer, Systems Equipment Corpn (SEC), then at Data Gen. Corpn (which acquired SEC) 1972; Co-founder and CEO Alliant Computer Systems Corpn 1982–92; Gen. Man. Advanced Consumer Tech., Microsoft Corpn, Redmond, WA 1992–93, Vice Pres. Advanced Consumer Tech. Group 1993–96, Sr Vice Pres. Consumer Platforms Div. 1996–2001, Sr Vice Pres. Advanced Strategies and Policies 2001–06, Chief Research and Strategy Officer 2006–; mem. Nat. Security Telecommunications Advisory Cttee 2000–, Markle Foundation Task Force on Nat. Security in the Information Age 2002–, Council on Foreign Relations 2002–; Trustee Fred Hutchinson Cancer Research Center, Seattle; mem. Advisory Bd Coll. of Computing, Ga Inst. of Tech. *Address:* Microsoft Corporation, 1 Microsoft Way, Redmond, WA 98052-6399, USA (office). *Telephone:* (425) 882-8080 (office). *Fax:* (425) 936-7329 (office). *Website:* www.microsoft.com (office).

MUNEKUNI, Yoshihide, BA; Japanese automobile executive; b. Hiroshima; ed Hosei Univ.; joined Honda Motor Co. Ltd 1966, career assignments include Dir then Exec. Vice-Pres. America Honda Motor Co. Inc., Pres. and Dir Honda N America Inc. 1989–90, Chair. Honda N America Inc. 1990–95, COO Automobile Sales Operations Honda Motor Co. Ltd 1995–97, Chair. and Rep. Dir 1997; Chair. Japan Automobile Mfrs Asscn (JAMA) 2002–04; mem. Japan–USA Govt-Business Forum 2002.

MUNEOKA, Shoji; Japanese steel industry executive; *President and Representative Director, Nippon Steel Corporation;* joined Nippon Steel Corpn in 1970, served as Dir of Sec., later Man. Dir and Vice-Pres. –2008, Pres. and Rep. Dir Nippon Steel Corpn 2008–, also Chair. associated co. based in Shanghai; Chair. Japanese Iron and Steel Fed. *Address:* Nippon Steel Corpn, 6-3 Otemachi 2-chome, Chiyoda-ku, Tokyo 100-8071, Japan (office). *Telephone:* (3) 3242-4111 (office). *Fax:* (3) 3275-5607 (office). *E-mail:* info@www.nsc.co.jp (office). *Website:* www.nsc.co.jp (office); www.worldsteel.org (office).

MUNGIU, Cristian; Romanian film director and producer; b. 27 April 1968, Iaşi; ed Univ. of Iaşi, Univ. of Film, Bucharest; fmr teacher and jurnalist; directed eight short films at film school, including The Hand of Paulista that was Romania's entry in the 1999 Student Acad. Awards, graduated from film school 1998; made several short films, then his first feature film, Occident 2002, which won prizes in several film festivals and was featured in Director's Fortnight at Cannes Film Festival 2002; formed Mobrafilms production co. 2006. *Films:* writer and dir: Zapping 2000, Nici o întâmplare 2000, Corul pompierilor 2000, Occident (aka West) 2002, Lost and Found (segment 'Turkey Girl') 2005, 4 luni, 3 săptămâni şi 2 zile (4 Months, 3 Weeks & 2 Days; also producer) (Palme d'Or, Cannes Film Festival (first Romanian dir) 2007) 2007; producer: Bucuresti-Berlin 2005, Offset (exec. producer) 2006; other: Teen Knight (first asst dir) 1998, Train de vie (Train of Life; second asst dir) 1998.

MUNGOSHI, Charles Muzuva; Zimbabwean writer, poet and playwright; b. 2 Dec. 1947, Chivhu; m. Jesesi Jaboon 1976; four s. one d.; ed secondary school; clerk in bookshop, Harare 1969–74; Ed. with the Literature Bureau 1974–81; Dir and Ed. publisher in Zimbabwe 1981–88; Writer-in-Residence, Univ. of Zimbabwe 1985–87; Visiting Arts Fellow, Univ. of Durham 1990; Writer-in-Residence Univ. of Florida, Gainesville (USA) 2000; Hon. DLitt (Zimbabwe) 2004; Noma Award for Publishing in Africa, Book Centre/PEN Award, Commonwealth Writers Award (Africa Region). *Film:* The Axe (writer and Dir) 1999. *Publications:* (novels) Makunun'unu Maodzamwoyo (in Shona) 1970, Waiting for the Rain 1975, Ndiko Kupindana Kwamazuva (in Shona) 1975, Kunyarara Hakusi Kutaura? (in Shona) 1983; (short stories) Coming of the Dry Season 1972, Some Kinds of Wounds 1980, Setting Sun and Rolling World 1987, One Day Long Ago: Tales from a Shona Childhood (folk tales) 1991, Walking Still 1997; (poetry) The Milkman Doesn't Only Deliver Milk 1981. *Leisure interests:* travelling reading, acting. *Address:* P.O. Box 1688, Harare (office); 47/6156 Uta Crescent, Zengeza 1, Chitungwiza, Zimbabwe. *E-mail:* muzuva47@yahoo.com.

MUNITZ, Barry, PhD; American foundation administrator, academic and university administrator; b. 26 July 1941, Brooklyn, New York; s. of Raymond J. Munitz and Vivian LeVoff Munitz; m. Anne Tomfohrde 1987; ed Brooklyn Coll., Princeton Univ., Univ. of Leiden, Netherlands; Asst Prof. of Literature and Drama, Univ. of Calif., Berkeley 1966–68; Staff Assoc., Carnegie Comm. on Higher Educ. 1968–70; mem. Presidential staff, then Assoc. Provost Univ. of Ill. 1970–72, Academic Vice-Pres. 1972–76; Vice-Pres., Dean of Faculties, Cen. Campus Univ. of Houston 1976–77, Chancellor 1977–82; Pres., COO Federated Devt Co. 1982–91; Vice-Chair. Maxxam Inc., LA 1982–91; Chancellor Calif. State Univ., Long Beach 1991–98, Prof. of English Literature, UCLA 1991–; Pres., CEO J. Paul Getty Trust, LA 1998–2006 (resgnd); Woodrow Wilson Fellow 1963; mem. Bd of Advisors Leeds Weld and Co. *Publications:* The Assessment of Institutional Leadership 1977; articles and monographs. *Address:* c/o J. Paul Getty Trust, Suite 400, 1200 Getty Center Drive, Los Angeles, CA 90049, USA (office).

MUNJAL, Brijmohan Lall; Indian business executive; *Chairman and Managing Director, Hero Group;* b. 1923, Kamalia, Pakistan; started career making bicycle parts; Chair., Man. Dir Hero Group (bicycle manufacturer), Hero Honda Motors Ltd (Honda partner for making motorcycles); Padma Bhushan; Ernst & Young Entrepreneur of the Year Award, Madras Man. Asscn Business Leadership Award 2002. *Address:* Hero Honda Motors Ltd, 34 Community Centre, Basant Lok, Vasant Vihar, New Delhi 110057, India (office). *Telephone:* (11) 26142451 (office). *Fax:* (11) 26143321 (office). *Website:* www.herohonda.com (office).

MUNK OLSEN, Birger, DLitt; Danish professor of medieval culture and philology; *Professor, Saxo Institute, University of Copenhagen;* b. 26 June 1935, Copenhagen; m. 1st Annalise Bliddal 1964 (divorced 1988); m. 2nd Gudrun Haastrup 1994; two d.; ed Ecole Normale Supérieure, Sorbonne, Paris and Pontificia Univ. Gregoriana, Rome; Assoc. Prof. of Romance Philology, Univ. of Copenhagen 1961–68; Lecturer Univ. Paris-Sorbonne 1968–74; Prof. of Romance Philology, Univ. of Copenhagen 1974–83, Prof. of Medieval Culture and Philology 1983–; Chair. Danish Nat. Research Council for the Humanities 1987–90; Danish Rep. Standing Cttee for the Humanities, European Science Foundation 1988–92; mem. Royal Danish Acad. 1985– (Vice-Pres., Chair. Humanities Section 1989–95, Pres. 1996–2004), Danish Council for Research Planning and Policy 1987–89, Acad. Europaea 1988– (Exec. Council 1989–92); Corresp. mem. Acad. des Inscriptions et Belles Lettres (Inst. de France) 1996, mem. 1998–; Vice-Pres. Soc. Int. de Bibliographie Classique 1994–99, Pres. 1999–2004; Hon. mem. Academia Româna 2000; mem. European Science and Tech. Ass. (ESTA) 1997–2000, Corresp. Fellow Royal Soc. of Edin. 2001; Prix Brunet 1984; Kt Order of Dannebrog, Officier Légion d'Honneur, Ordre Nat. du Mérite, Commander Ordinul Naţional Pentru Merit (Romania) Dr hc (Paris) 2003. *Publications:* Les 'Dits' de Jehan de Saint-Quentin 1978, L'étude des auteurs classiques latins aux XI^{e}et XIIe siècles, Vols I–IV 1982–89, I classici nel canone scolastico altomedievale 1991, L'atteggiamento medievale di fronte alla cultura classica

1994, La réception de la littérature classique au Moyen Age 1995. *Address:* Ny Kongensgade 20, 1557 Copenhagen V, Denmark; 51 rue de Tolbiac, 75013 Paris, France; Torshoj 1, Veddinge, 4540 Faarevejle, Denmark. *Telephone:* 33-91-91-81 (Copenhagen); 1-45-84-27-18 (Paris); 20-21-72-17 (Faarevejle). *Fax:* 35-32-81-55 (office). *E-mail:* bmo@hum.ku.dk (office).

MUNRO, Alice, BA; Canadian writer; b. 10 July 1931, Wingham, Ont.; d. of Robert E. Laidlaw and Anne Chamney; m. 1st James A. Munro 1951 (divorced 1976); three d.; m. 2nd Gerald Fremlin 1976; ed Univ. of Western Ontario; Gov.-Gen.'s Award for Literature 1978, 1986, Canadian Booksellers' Award 1972, Marian Engel Award 1986, Canada-Australia Literary Prize 1994, Lannan Literary Award 1995, WH Smith Literary Award 1996, Fiction Prize, Nat. Book Critics Circle 1999, Giller Prize 1999, O. Henry Award 2001. *Publications:* Dance of the Happy Shades 1968 (Gov.-Gen.'s Award for Literature 1968), A Place for Everything 1970, Lives of Girls and Women 1971, Something I've Been Meaning to Tell You 1974, Who Do You Think You Are? (aka The Beggar Maid) 1978, The Moons of Jupiter 1982, The Progress of Love 1986, Friend of My Youth 1990, Open Secrets 1994, Selected Stories 1996, The Love of A Good Woman 1998, Hateship, Friendship, Courtship, Loveship, Marriage 2001, Runaway (short stories) 2005, The View from Castle Rock 2006, Too Much Happiness 2009. *Address:* William Morris Agency, 1325 Avenue of the Americas, Floor 16, New York, NY 10019, USA (office); PO Box 1133, Clinton, ON, N0M 1L0, Canada (home).

MUNRO, J. Richard, BA; American publishing executive; b. 26 Jan. 1931, Syracuse, NY; m. Carol Munro; three s.; ed Colgate, Columbia and New York Univs; joined Time Inc. 1957; Pres. Pioneer Press Inc. (Time subsidiary) 1969; Publr Sports Illustrated 1969–71; Vice-Pres. Time Inc. 1971–75, Group Vice-Pres. for Video 1975–79, Exec. Vice-Pres. 1979–80, Pres. 1980–86, CEO 1980–90, Chair. 1986–90, Chair. Exec. Comm. 1990–96, also Dir; Chair. Genentech Inc. 1997; mem. Bd of Chancellors Juvenile Diabetes Research Foundation Int. (JDRF); fmr Dir IBM Corpn; Trustee RAND Corpn 1984-1994; Hon. LittD (Richmond Univ.) 1983; Purple Heart with two Clusters.

MUNROE-BLUM, Heather, OC, BA, MSW, PhD; Canadian university administrator, epidemiologist and academic; *Principal and Vice-Chancellor, McGill University;* b. Montreal; m. Len Blum; one d.; ed McMaster Univ., Wilfrid Laurier Univ., Univ. of NC, USA; fmr Prof. York Univ., McMaster Univ.; fmr Prof. Univ. of Toronto, Dean of Social Work, Gov., Vice-Pres. Research and Int. Relations 1994–2002; Prof. Dept of Epidemiology and Biostatistics, McGill Univ., Prin. and Vice-Chancellor 2003–; fmr mem. Bd of Dirs and Int. Review Panel, Medical Research Council of Canada (now Canadian Insts of Health Research); fmr founding mem. Medical and Related Sciences Discovery Dist Bd (MARS); mem. Bd of Dirs NeuroScience Canada Partnership, NeuroScience Canada Foundation, McGill Univ. Health Centre, McCord Museum, Canadian Council of Christians and Jews, Max Bell Foundation, McGill–Queen's Univ. Press, Montreal Int., La Chambre de commerce du Montréal métropolitan, Trafalgar School for Girls, La Conf. du Montréal, Four Seasons Hotels Inc.; fmr mem. Int. Review German Academic Exchange Service, Swiss Nat. Science Foundation, Nat. Inst. of Mental Health; fmr mem. Prime Minister's Advisory Council on Science and Tech. Expert Panel on Canada's Role in Int. Science and Tech.; mem. Asscn of Univs and Colls of Canada, American Asscn of Univs, Conf. des recteurs et des principaux des Universités du Québec, Universitas 21; Assoc. Sr Fellow, Massey Coll.; Specially Elected Fellow, Acad. of Science, RSC; McMaster Univ. Distinguished Alumni Award, Univ. of NC at Chapel Hill School of Public Health Outstanding Alumni Award. *Publications:* more than 60 works, including four books. *Address:* Office of the Principal and Vice-Chancellor, James Administration Building, Room 506, McGill University, 845 Sherbrooke Street West, Montréal, PQ H3A 2T5, Canada (office). *Telephone:* (514) 398-4180 (office). *Fax:* (514) 398-4768 (office). *Website:* www.mcgill.ca/principal (office).

MUNS ALBUIXECH, Joaquín, PhD; Spanish economist, academic and international civil servant; *Professor Emeritus, University of Barcelona;* b. 25 June 1935, Barcelona; m. M. Tardà; one s.; ed Univ. of Barcelona and London School of Econs; Economist, Nat. Studies Div. of OECD 1962–63; Asst Prof. of Econs Univ. of Barcelona 1963–65, Prof. of Econs, Univ. of Barcelona 1968–73, Sr Prof. of Int. Econ. Org. 1973–2005, Jean Monnet Prof. of European Integration 1991–2005, Prof. Emer. 2005–; Economist, Western Hemisphere Dept of IMF 1965–68, Exec. Dir IMF 1978–80; Exec. Dir IBRD 1980–82; Econ. Adviser to Barcelona City Council 1968–73; Econ. Adviser to Govt of Spain and to various public and pvt. insts 1973–78; Adjunct Prof. SIS American Univ. 1982; mem. European Parl. (Liberal Group) 1987–89; mem. Vatican Council of Econ. Advisers 1988–94; mem. Governing Council Bank of Spain 1994–2004; economic journalist; Cross of St George (Catalonia) 1984; Outstanding Researcher Catalan Foundation for Research and Innovation (FCRI) 1995, King Juan Carlos Prize for Econs 2008. *Publications:* (in English): Adjustment, Conditionality and International Financing (ed.) 1984; (in Spanish): Industrialization and Growth in the Developing Countries 1972, The European Option for the Spanish Economy 1973, The International Economic Crisis: Thoughts and Proposals 1975, Crisis and Reform of the International Monetary System 1978, History of the Relations between Spain and the IMF 1958–82, Twenty-five Years of the Spanish Economy 1986, The EMU and its Future 1992, Radiography of the Crisis 1993, Spain and the World Bank 1994, Spain and the Euro: Risks and Opportunities (Ed.) 1997, The Culture of Stability and the Consensus of Washington (with M. Guitián) 1999, Readings on Economic Integration: The European Union (ed.) 2005, Compilation of the Principal Documents of the Relations Spain-IMF 1958-2007 (comp, 16 vols) 2008. *Leisure interests:* travel, music. *Address:* Diagonal 690, 08034 Barcelona (office); C. Muntaner, 268, 08021 Barcelona, Spain (home). *Telephone:* (93) 4021939 (office); (93) 2094534 (home). *Fax:* (93) 4021934 (office); (93) 4140697 (home). *E-mail:* jmuns@ub.edu (office). *Website:* www.ub.edu/muns/personal.html (office).

MUNTEANU, Mihai; Moldovan singer (tenor); b. 15 Aug. 1943, Kriva, Briceni; s. of Ion Muntean and Elizaveta Muntean; m. Rosentul Galina Andrian 1969; one s. one d.; ed Kishinev Inst. of Arts, La Scala, Milan; Prin. Tenor with Moldovan State Acad. Theatre of Opera and Ballet 1971–, Gen. Dir 1996–97; Prof. Chair of Vocal Arts, Music Acad. of Moldova 1993–; Provost Art Inst., Mil. Acad. Stefan Cel Mare 1996–; Pres. Centre for Devt and Support of Culture Mihai Munteanu 1998–; Hon. Prof., Modern Humanitarian Inst. Moscow 1997–; Verdi Award 1978, USSR People's Artist, 1986, Moldovan State Award 1984, Award of the Republic 1993. *Opera roles include:* Lensky (Eugene Onegin), Riccardo (Un Ballo in Maschera), Don Carlo (Don Carlo), Cavaradossi (Tosca), Calaf (Turandot), Hermann (The Queen of Spades), Radames (Aida), Turriddu (Cavalleria Rusticana), Otello (Otello), Canio (Pagliacci), Manrico (Il Trovatore), Samson (Samson et Dalila), Ismael (Nabucco), Don José (Carmen), Don Alvaro (La Forza del Destino), Pinkerton (Madame Butterfly); performances and concerts throughout the world. *Leisure interests:* collecting books, family, children, music. *Address:* 16 N. Iorga str., Apt 13, 2012 Chişinău, Moldova. *Telephone:* 911-7577 (office); (2) 23-75-19. *Fax:* (2) 23-75-19. *E-mail:* mihai.muntean@excite.com (home).

MÜNTEFERING, Franz; German politician; b. 16 Jan. 1940, Neheim; s. of Franz Müntefering and Anna Schlinkmann; m. Ankepetra Rettich 1995; two d.; apprenticeship in industrial admin. 1954–57; industrial admin. in eng firm 1957–61; mil. training 1961–62; mem. Social Democratic Party of Germany (SPD) 1966–, sub-Dist Chair. Hochsauerland 1984–88, mem. Dist Exec. W Westphalia 1984–, Dist Chair. 1992–98, mem. Exec. Cttee 1991–, Fed. Business Man. 1995–99, Chair. state org. North Rhine Westphalia 1998–2001, Gen. Sec. 1999, Chair. SPD 2002–05; mem. Sudern City Council 1969–79; mem. Bundestag 1975–92, Parl. Business Man. SPD Bundestag Parl. Group 1991–92; mem. North Rhine Westphalia Landtag 1996–98; Fed. Minister of Transport, Construction and Housing 1998–99, Vice-Chancellor and Minister of Labour and Social Affairs 2005–07 (resgnd); mem. IG Metall (Eng TU) 1967–. *Address:* c/o Sozialdemokratische Partei Deutschlands (SPD) (Social Democratic Party of Germany), Willy-Brandt-Haus, Wilhelmstr. 141, 10963 Berlin, Germany.

MUNTIANAS, Viktoras; Lithuanian engineer and politician; b. 11 Nov. 1951, Marijampolė; ed Marijampolė Secondary School No 3, Vilnius Civil Eng Inst. (now Vilnius Gediminas Tech. Univ.), Vilnius Higher School for Party Studies; Jr Research Fellow, Lithuanian Construction and Architecture Research Inst. 1978–79; construction site man., later Chief Engineer, Kaunas Construction Plant 1979–85; Deputy Chair., Exec. Cttee of Kėdainiai Dist 1986–90; Gov., Kėdainiai Dist 1990–93; Gov. AB Ūkio Bankas, Kėdainiai Br. 1994–96; Vice-Pres., Trust Vikonda 1996–97; mem., Municipal Bd, later Mayor, Kėdainiai Dist 1997–2004; mem. Seimas 2004–; Deputy Chair. Bd of Seimas 2004–06, Speaker 2006–08, mem. Cttee on Budget and Finance 2004–06, Comm. on Anti-corruption 2004–06; mem. Labour Party Group 2004–06, Ass. of Elders, Parl. Group for Relations with France, Seimo Delegacija Lietuvos ir Ukrainos Aukščiausiosios Rados Asamblėjoje; mem. CPSU –1989; mem. and Deputy Chair., Labour Party 2003–06; mem. and Chair. Civil Democracy Party 2006–. *Leisure interests:* hunting, sports, angling. *Address:* c/o Seimas, Gedimino pr. 53, Vilnius 01109, Lithuania. *Telephone:* (5) 239-6559. *E-mail:* viktoras.muntianas@lrs.lt (office). *Website:* www.lrs.lt (office).

MUOI, Do; Vietnamese politician; b. 1917, Hanoi; joined movt against French colonial rule 1936; imprisoned by French; escaped in 1945 and took part in anti-Japanese uprising in Ha Dong Prov.; political and mil. leader in provs of Red River delta during struggle against French 1951–54; Alt. mem. Cen. Cttee Communist Party of Viet Nam (CPV) 1955–60, mem. 1960–; Alt. mem. Political Bureau CPV 1976–82, now mem. Gen. Sec. of Cen. Cttee CPV 1987–; Deputy to Nat. Ass. 2nd, 4th, 5th, 6th, 7th and 8th Legislatures; Minister of Commerce 1969; Deputy Prime Minister and Minister of Building 1976–87; Vice-Chair. Council of Ministers in charge of Economy 1987–; Prime Minister 1988–91; Sec. Gen. CPV 1991–98; Vice-Chair. Nat. Defence Council 1989; Order of the October Revolution (USSR) 1987 and several Vietnamese decorations. *Address:* Communist Party of Viet Nam, 1 Hoang Van Thu, Hanoi; Council of Ministers, Hanoi, Viet Nam.

MURAD, Ferid, BA, MD, PhD; American pharmacologist and academic; *John S. Dunn Distinguished Chair Physiology and Medicine Director, Institute of Molecular Medicine, University of Texas;* b. 14 Sept. 1936, Whiting, Indiana; s. of John and Henrietta Josephine Murad; m. Carol A. Leopold 1958; one s. four d.; ed DePauw Univ., Ind. and Western Reserve Univ., Cleveland, Ohio; Dir Clinical Research Center, School of Medicine, Univ. of Va 1971–81, Div. of Clinical Pharmacology 1973–81, Prof. Depts of Internal Medicine and Pharmacology 1975–81; Prof. Depts. of Internal Medicine and Pharmacology, Stanford Univ. 1981–89, Acting Chair. Dept of Medicine 1986–88; Chief of Medicine Palo Alto Veterans Admin. Medical Center, Calif. 1981–86; Adjunct Prof. Dept of Pharmacology, Northwestern Univ., Chicago 1988–96; Chair. Dept of Integrative Biology and Pharmacology, Univ. of Texas Medical School, Houston 1997– also Prof., now John S. Dunn Distinguished Chair in Physiology, Dir Depts of Pharmacology and Physiology, Medicine Dir Inst. of Molecular Medicine 1999–; Vice-Pres. Pharmaceutical Research and Devt, Abbott Laboratories 1988–92; CEO and Pres. Molecular Geriatrics Corpn, Lake Bluff, Ill. 1993–95; Ciba Award 1988, Albert and Mary Lasker Award for Basic Research 1996, Nobel Prize in Medicine or Physiology 1998, AAMC Research Award 2002, Grisalin Award 2005. *Publications:* more than 405 publs and books, including Discovery of Some of the Biological Effects of Nitric Oxide and its Role in Cellular Signaling (Nobel Lecture 1998) 1999. *Leisure interests:* golf, carpentry. *Address:* Imm, University of Texas, 1825 Pressler,

Suite 530, Houston, TX 77030, USA (office). *Telephone:* (713) 500-2433 (office). *Fax:* (713) 500-2498 (office). *E-mail:* ferid.murad@uth.tmc.edu (office). *Website:* www.uth.tmc.edu/uth_orgs/imm/centers/cellsignal.html (office).

MURADOV, Sakhat, DTechSc; Turkmenistani politician (retd); b. 7 May 1932, Ivanovo, Russia; s. of Nepes Muradov and Nursoltan Muradova; m. Sona Muradova 1954; two s. one d.; ed Turkmenistan Agric. Inst.; fmr mem. CP; Head Dept of Science and Educ. Central Cttee Turkmenistan CP 1965–70; Rector Turkmenistan State Univ. 1970–79; Minister for Higher Educ. 1979–85; Rector Turkmenistan Polytechnic Inst. 1985–90; Deputy to Supreme Soviet of Turkmenistan, 8th and 12th Convocations, fmr First Deputy Chair. Supreme Soviet of Turkmenistan, Chair. 1990–92; Chair. Turkmenistan Majlis (legislature) 1992–2001; Order of Red Banner of Labour (twice), Star of Pres. of Turkmenistan, Certificate of Honour (Presidium of Turkmenistan Supreme Soviet). *Publications:* three books, more than 50 articles. *Leisure interests:* sport, tourism, literature. *Address:* c/o Turkmenistan Majlis, 17 Bitarap Turkmenistan, 744000 Ashkhabad, Turkmenistan. *Telephone:* (3632) 35-31-25. *Fax:* (3632) 35-31-47.

MURAKAMI, Haruki, BA; Japanese writer; b. 12 Jan. 1949, Kyoto; m. Yoko Takahashi 1971; ed Kobe High School, Waseda Univ.; owner Peter Cat jazz club, Tokyo 1974–81; began writing in 1978, lived in Europe 1986–89, USA 1991–95; Visiting Scholar, Princeton Univ. 1991–93; Una's Lecturer in the Humanities, Univ. of Calif., Berkeley 1992; Writer-in-Residence, Tufts Univ. 1993–95, Harvard Univ. 2005–06; Franz Kafka Prize 2006, Jerusalem Prize 2009. *Publications:* fiction: Hear the Wind Sing (Gunzo Literature Award for Budding Writers) 1979, Pinball 1980, A Wild Sheep Chase (Noma Literary Award for New Writers) 1982, Hard-Boiled Wonderland and The End of the World (Junichi Tanizaki Award) 1985, Norwegian Wood 1987, Dance Dance Dance 1988, South of the Border, West of the Sun 1992, Wind-Up Bird Chronicle (Yomiuri Literary Award 1996) 1994–95, Sputnik Sweetheart 1999, Kafka on the Shore 2002, After Dark 2004; short stories: Slow Boat to China 1983, A Perfect day for Kangaloos 1983, Dead Heat 1985, The Elephant Vanishes 1986, TV People 1990, Phantoms of Lexington 1998, After the Quake 2000, Blind Willow, Sleeping Woman (Frank O'Connor Int. Short Story Award, Kiriyama Prize 2007) 2006; non-fiction: Underground 1997, The Place That was Promised (Kuwahara Takeo Award) 1998, What I Talk About When I Talk About Running 2008; essays: A Young Reader's Guide to Short Fiction 1997; has translated works by F. Scott Fitzgerald, Raymond Carver, Truman Capote, Paul Theroux, John Irving, J. D. Salinger. *Leisure interests:* running marathons, music, jazz, classical etc. *Address:* ICM, 40 West 57th Street, New York, NY 10019, USA (office). *Telephone:* (212) 556-5600 (office). *Website:* www.icmtalent.com (office).

MURAKAMI, Ryunosuke (Ryū); Japanese writer and film director; b. 19 Feb. 1952, Sasebo City, Nagasaki; m. Tazuko Takahashi 1976; fmr rock band drummer, TV talk show host; writer and film-maker 1976–. *Films:* adaptations of many of his novels, including Almost Transparent Blue (writer and dir) 1978, Daijôbu, mai furendo (writer and dir) 1983, Raffles Hotel (writer and dir) 1989, Topâzu (writer and dir) 1992, Ôdishon (writer) 1999, Kyoko (writer and dir) 2000, Hashire! Ichiro (from novel Hashire! Takahashi) 2001. *Publications:* novels: Kagirinaku tōmei ni chikai burrū (trans. as Almost Transparent Blue) (Akutagawa Prize, Gunzou Prize) 1976, Hashire! Takahashi, Ôdishon, Topâzu (trans. as Tokyo Decadence), Raffles Hotel, Daijôbu, mai furendo (trans. as All Right, My Friend), Kyoko (trans. as Because of You), 69 1987, Coin Locker Babies 1995, In the Miso Soup (Yomiuri Literary Award 1998) 1997, Exodus (serialised) 1998–99, Piercing 2007, Audition 2009; non-fiction: Ano kane de nani ga kaeta ka 2003. *Address:* c/o Kodansha International Ltd, Otowa YK Building, 1-17-14 Otowa, Bunkyo-ku, Tokyo 112-8652, Japan.

MURAKAMI, Seiichiro, LLB; Japanese politician; b. 11 May 1952; ed Tokyo Univ.; elected to House of Reps for Ehime Pref. 1986–; Sec. of State for Finance 1992–93; Chair. Parl. Cttee on Coal Problems 1994–95, on Finance 1997–98; apptd Deputy Sec.-Gen. Liberal Democratic Party (LDP) 1995, Commr Policy Research Council 1999; Sr Vice-Minister on Finance 2000–02; Minister of State for Regulatory Reform, for Industrial Revitalization Corpn of Japan, for Admin. Reform, for Special Zones of Structural Reform and for Regional Revitalization 2004–05. *Address:* c/o Liberal-Democratic Party–LDP (Jiyu-Minshuto), 1-11-23, Nagata-cho, Chiyoda-ku, Tokyo 100-8910, Japan (office).

MURAKAMI, Takashi, MA, PhD; Japanese artist and designer; b. 1963, Tokyo; ed Univ. of Fine Arts, Tokyo; trained in classical Nihon-gah style of Japanese traditional painting; pop artist whose style fuses historic Japanese painting with contemporary cartoons; made debut as modern artist with solo exhbn Takashi, Tamiya 1991; invited to participate in PS1 Int. Studio Program on Rockefeller Foundation Asian Cultural Council fellowship grant, NY 1994; f. Hirpon Factory (Kaikai Kiki—production studio) Asaka City, Saitama 1994; Guest Prof., Dept of Art, UCLA, Calif. 1998; worked for French fashion house Louis Vuitton (LV) and cr. LV 'Murakami bag' 2003; his recurring character, Mr DOB, appears on t-shirts, posters, key-chains and mugs worldwide; work has been exhibited in Asia, America and Europe; curator Super Flat exhbn (showcase of contemporary Japanese artists), Little Boy exhbn; directed artwork for Kanye West's album, Graduation, 2007; has participated in numerous group exhbns in Japan, Korea, USA, Italy, Denmark, Norway, Sweden, Finland, Austria, Australia, France, New Caledonia, Philippines 1991–. *Solo Exhibitions include:* Gallery Ginza Surugadai, Tokyo 1989, Art Gallery at Tokyo Nat. Univ. of Fine Arts and Music 1991, Aoi Gallery, Osaka 1991, Rontgen Kunst Inst. 1992, Nasubi Gallery, Tokyo 1993, Gallery Koto, Okayama 1994, Emmanuel Perrotin, Paris (France) 1995, Yngtingagatan, Stockholm (Sweden) 1995, Feature Inc., NY 1996, Gavin Brown Enterprize, NY 1996, Ginza Komatsu, Tokyo 1996, Univ. of Buffalo Art Gallery, NY 1997, Blum & Poe, Santa Monica, CA 1998, Tomio

Koyama Gallery, Tokyo 1998, Marianne Boesky Gallery, NY 1999, Bard Coll. Museum of Art 1999, Issey Miyake Men, Aoyama, Tokyo 2000, Grand Cen. Terminal, NY 2001, Museum of Fine Arts, Boston, 2001, Galerie Emmanuel Perrotin, Paris 2001, Museum of Contemporary Art, Tokyo 2001, Cartier Foundation, Paris 2002, Pacifico Yokohama Exhibition Hall 2003, 2004, Museum of Contemporary Art, Los Angeles 2007, Brooklyn Museum, NY 2008. *Address:* c/o Kornelia Tamm Fine Arts, 28 Willa Cather Road, Santa Fe, NM 87540, USA (office). *E-mail:* ktamm@valstar.net (office).

MURALITHARAN, Muttiah; Sri Lankan professional cricketer; b. 17 April 1972, Kandy; s. of Muttiah Sinnasamy; ed St Anthony's Coll.; right-arm off-break bowler, lower-order right-hand batsman; teams: Tamil Union Cricket and Athletic Club, Lancashire, Kent, Sri Lanka; quickest and youngest player to reach 400 Test wickets (in 72 matches) and 500 Test wickets (in 87 matches); world's highest wicket-taker 2000, 2001; took 532 wickets (average 22.86) in 91 Tests; 369 wickets (average 22.11) in 238 one-day ints; 1,015 first-class wickets (average 19.10) in 175 matches; Wisden Cricketer of the Year 1999, CEAT Int. Cricketer of the Year 2000, rated Best Ever Test Bowler by Wisden Dec. 2002. *Address:* c/o Board of Control for Cricket in Sri Lanka, A. P. B. Tennekoon, 35 Maitland Place, Colombo 7, Sri Lanka. *Telephone:* (1) 691439. *E-mail:* cricket@sri.lanka.net.

MURALITHARAN, Vinayagamoorthy, (ColKaruna); Sri Lankan politician and fmr rebel leader; *Minister of National Integration;* b. 1966; m. Nira Muralitharan; three c.; joined Liberation Tigers of Tamil Eelam 1983, commdr in charge of Batticaloa and Amparai dists Eastern Prov. 1987–2004; Founder and Leader, Tamil Makkal Viduthalai Pulikal breakaway group after defection to govt 2004 (recognized as political party 2007); apptd mem. Parl. for United People's Freedom Alliance (UPFA) 2008–; Minister of Nat. Integration 2009–. *Address:* c/o Tamileela Makkal Viduthalai Pulikal, Colombo, Sri Lanka.

MURALIYEV, Amangeldy Mursadykovich; Kyrgyzstani politician; b. 7 Aug. 1947, Kum-Aryk; ed Bishkek Polytechnical Inst., Acad. of Nat. Econ. USSR Govt; Eng Frunze (Bishkek) factories 1970–80; Dir heavy machine construction factory 1980–82, Kyrgizavtomash factory 1982–88; Chair, Frunze City Council 1988–91; Chair State Cttee on Economy, State Sec. 1991–92; Min. Chair Fund of State Property 1994–96; Deputy Prime Minister 1996; Gov. Osh region 1996–99; Prime Minister of Kyrgyzstan 1999–2000; Minister of Econ. Devt, Industry and Trade (acting) 2004–2006; Co-ordinator Political Bd Union Party of Kyrgyzstan 2001–; Pres. Kyrgyzstan Stock Exch. 2001–; Pres. Kyrgyzstan Football Union; mem. Kyrgyzstan Eng Acad. *Address:* Kyrgyz Stock Exchange, Moskovskaya 172, 720010 Bishkek, Kyrgyzstan (office).

MURANO, Elsa A., BSc, MSc, DrSc; American food scientist, academic, university administrator and fmr government official; *President, Texas A&M University;* b. (Elsa Casales), 14 Aug. 1959, Havana, Cuba; m. Peter S. Murano; ed Miami Dade Coll., Florida Int. Univ., Virginia Tech Univ.; Asst Prof., Dept of Microbiology, Immunology and Preventative Medicine, Iowa State Univ. 1990–95; Assoc. Prof., Dept of Animal Science, Texas A&M Univ. 1995–97, becoming Sadie Hatfield Prof. in Agric., also Assoc. Dir Center for Food Safety, Inst. for Food Science and Eng 1995–97, Dir 1997–2001, Vice Chancellor and Dean Coll. of Agric. and Life Sciences 2005–07, also Dir Tex. Agricultural Experiment Station (now Tex. AgriLife Research) 2005–07, Pres. Texas A&M Univ. 2008–; US Under-Sec. of Agric. for Food Safety, Washington, DC 2001–04. *Publications:* author or co-author of seven books, book chapters and monographs, numerous scholarly papers, abstracts and related materials. *Address:* Office of the President, 1246 TAMU, Texas A&M University, College Station, TX 77843-1246, USA (office). *Telephone:* (979) 845-2217 (office). *Fax:* (979) 845-5027 (office). *E-mail:* president@tamu.edu (office). *Website:* www.tamu.edu/president (office).

MURAOKA, Takamitsu, PhD, FAHA; Japanese academic; b. 9 Feb. 1938, Hiroshima; m. Keiko Kageyama 1965; two s. one d.; ed Tokyo Kyoiku, The Hebrew Univ., Jerusalem; Lecturer in Semitic Languages, Dept of Near Eastern Studies, Univ. of Manchester, UK 1970–80; Prof. of Middle Eastern Studies, Chair. Dept, Melbourne Univ. 1980–91; Prof. of Hebrew, Univ. of Leiden 1991–2003; Ed. Abr-Nahrain (Leiden) 1980–92; Visiting Prof., Univ. of Göttingen, Germany 2001–02; Research Fellow, Netherlands Inst. of Near Eastern Studies 2004–06; Hon. Prof. in Semitic Languages, Presbyterian Coll. and Theological Seminary, Seoul 2006–07; Hon. Fellow, Acad. of the Hebrew Language 2006–; Alexander von Humboldt Research Award 2001–02. *Publications:* A Greek-Hebrew/Aramaic Index to I Esdras 1982, Emphatic Words and Structures in Biblical Hebrew 1985, Classical Syriac for Hebraists 1987, A Grammar of Biblical Hebrew (with P. Joüon) 1991, 2006, Studies in Qumran Aramaic (ed.) 1992, A Greek-English Lexicon of the Septuagint (Twelve Prophets) 1993, Studies on the Hebrew of the Dead Sea Scrolls and Ben Sira (co-ed. with J. F. Elwolde) 1997, A Grammar of Egyptian Aramaic (with B. Porten) 1998, 2003, Classical Syriac – A Basic Grammar with a Chrestomathy 1997,2005, Hebrew/Aramaic Index to the Septuagint Keyed to the Hatch-Redpath Concordance 1998, A Greek-English Lexicon of the Septuagint – chiefly of the Pentateuch and the Twelve Prophets 2002. *Leisure interest:* angling. *Address:* Wijttenbachweg 57, 2343 XW Oegstgeest, Netherlands (home).

MURATA, Makoto, BEng; Japanese business executive; b. 26 Dec. 1926, Nagano Pref.; s. of Ichiro Murata and Misue Murata; m. Yukio Kurashina 1953; one s.; ed Univ. of Tokyo; joined Showa Denko KK (SDK) 1948, Dir 1973, Man. Dir 1978–83, Senior Man. Dir 1983–87, Rep. Dir and Exec. Vice-Pres. 1983–87, Rep. Dir, Pres. and CEO 1987–97, Rep. Dir, Chair. 1997–2001, Adviser 2001–; Chair. Japan Ammonium Sulphate & Urea Industry Asscn 1988–90, Japan Carbon Asscn 1991–93, Acetic Acid Mfrs Asscn 1991–93,

Japan Hygienic Olefine and Styrene Plastics Asscn 1993–94, Japan Petrochemical Industry Asscn 1993–94, Japan Chemical Industry Asscn 1996–98, Asscn for the Progress of New Chem. 1998–2000, Japan Chemical Innovation Inst. 1999–2000, Chemical Products Council of MITI 1999–2000; Exec. mem. Bd Dirs, Japan Fed. of Econ. Orgs (Keidanren) 1994–2001. *Leisure interest:* golf. *Address:* Showa Denko KK, 1-313-9, Shiba Daimon, Minato-ku, Tokyo 105-8518 (office); 2–12, Miyazaki 6-chome, Miyamae-ku, Kawasaki, Japan (home). *Telephone:* (3) 5470-3111 (office); 44-854-2551 (home). *Fax:* (3) 3436-2625 (office). *E-mail:* pr-office@hq.sdk.co.jp (office). *Website:* www.sdk.co.jp (office).

MURATA, Ryohei, LLB; Japanese diplomatist; b. 2 Nov. 1929, Kyoto; s. of Tahei Murata and Yoshiko Murata; m. Reiko Akama 1958; one d.; ed Kyoto Univ.; joined Ministry of Foreign Affairs 1952; Deputy Dir-Gen. Middle Eastern and African Affairs Bureau 1974–76, Treaties Bureau 1976–78; Amb. to UAE 1978–80; Dir-Gen. Middle Eastern and African Affairs Bureau 1980–82, Econ. Affairs Bureau 1982–84; Amb. to Austria 1985–87; Deputy Minister for Foreign Affairs 1987, Vice-Minister 1987–89; Amb. to USA 1989–91, to Germany 1992–94; Adviser to the Foreign Minister 1994–2002, to the Sanwa Bank and to Hotel Okura 1995–2001, to The Nippon Foundation 2000–. *Publications:* Between Friends 1985, OECD 2000, Ocean, World and Japan 2001, Why Has the Quality of the Foreign Ministry Deteriorated? 2002, Japanese Foreign Policy in Perspective 1952–2002 2003. *Leisure interest:* contract bridge. *Address:* The Nippon Foundation, 1-2-2, Akasaka, Minato-ku, Tokyo (office); No. 1003 DearStage Sakaimachi-Nishiki, 514 Kikuyacho, Nakagyo-ku, Kyoto 604-8127, Japan (home). *Telephone:* (3) 6229-5209 (office); (75) 212-4807 (home). *Fax:* (3) 6229-5120 (office); (75) 212-4807 (home). *E-mail:* r_murata@ps.nippon-foundation.or.jp (office).

MURATA, Yoshitaka; Japanese politician and government official; b. 30 July 1944, Shizuoka City; ed Univ. of Tokyo for Foreign Studies, Kyoto Univ., Univ. of Grenoble and Ecole Nat. d'Admin, France; joined Ministry of Finance 1968, seconded as Sec., Embassy in Beijing, People's Repub. of China 1974–76, Sec. to Minister of Labour 1978; Dir Office of Public Relations 1985–88, Dir Local Taxation Agency in Capital Area 1986–87, Dir Research Div., Int. Finance Bureau 1987–89; elected to House of Reps for Okayama Constituency 1990–; various positions in House include Dir Cttee on Rules and Admin, Cttee on Transport, Cttee on Finance and Monetary Affairs, Cttee on Audit and Oversight of Admin, Chair. Standing Cttee on Economy, Trade and Industry 1990–2004; various positions in Cabinet include Parl. Sec. of Econ. Planning, of Finance and of Monetary Affairs Agency 1990–2004; Chair. of Nat. Public Safety Comm. and Minister of State for Disaster Man. and for Nat. Emergency Legislation 2004–05; fmr Deputy Sec.-Gen. and Dir of Transportation Div., Policy Research Council, Liberal Democratic Party (LDP). *Address:* c/o Liberal-Democratic Party–LDP (Jiyu-Minshuto), 1-11-23, Nagata-cho, Chiyoda-ku, Tokyo 100-8910, Japan (office).

MURATOVA, Kira Georgievna; Russian/Ukrainian film director; b. 5 Nov. 1934, Soroki, Moldavia; m. 1st Alexandre Muratov (divorced); m. 2nd Yevgeni Golubenko; ed All-Union Inst. of Cinematography with Sergey Gerasimov; debut feature film with A. Muratov On Steep Bank; acted in several films; USSR State Prize 1989, Int. Andrzey Wajda Prize 2000. *Films include:* Our Harvest Bread 1965, Short Meetings 1968, Long Partings 1972 (Fipressi Prize, Locarno 1987), Cognizing the White World 1980, Among Grey Stones 1983, Change of Fate 1988, Asthenic Syndrome 1990 (Nika Prize 1990), The Sentimental Militiaman 1991, Animations 1994, Three Stories 1997, The Tuner (Best Film Int. Eurasia Film Festival) 2004, Spravka 2005, Dva v odnom 2007. *Address:* Proletarsky blvd 14B, apt 15, 270015 Odessa, Ukraine. *Telephone:* 28-65-51 (home).

MURAYAMA, Tomiichi; Japanese politician (retd); b. 3 March 1924, Oita Prefecture; m. Yoshie Murayama; two d.; ed School of Political Science and Econs, Meiji Univ.; fmr sec. of a trade union of Oita Pref. Govt employees; entered local govt 1955; mem. Japanese Socialist Party (JSP), now Social Democratic Party of Japan (SDPJ), renamed Democratic League 1995, renamed Shakai Minshuto (Social Democratic Party); Chair. Oita Pref. of JSP, Chair. Diet Affairs Cttee 1991–93, Chair. SDPJ 1993–96; mem. House of Reps 1972–; Prime Minister 1994–96; mem. Lower House's Cttee on Social and Labour Affairs; retd from politics 2000. *Publications:* several books on social and labour affairs. *Leisure interest:* drama appreciation. *Address:* Social Democratic Party, 1-8-1, Nagata-cho, Chiyoda-ku, Tokyo 100-0014 (office); 3-2-2 Chiyomachi, Oita, Oita 870, Japan (home). *Telephone:* (3) 3580-1171 (office); (975) 32-0033 (home). *Fax:* (3) 3580-0691. *E-mail:* sdpjmail@omnics.co .jp (office). *Website:* www.omnics.co.jp (office).

MURCH, Walter; American film editor and sound designer; b. 1943, New York City; m. Muriel Murch; two c.; ed Johns Hopkins Univ., Univ. of Southern California; worked with George Lucas, Francis Ford Coppola and Anthony Minghella as film ed. and sound designer; Acad. Award for Best Sound (Apocalypse Now), BAFTA Award and two Acad. Awards (The English Patient). *Films include:* The Godfather (sound-effects ed.) 1972, American Graffiti (sound designer) 1973, The Godfather, Part II (sound designer) 1974, The Conversation (ed. and sound designer) 1974, Julia (ed.) 1977, Apocalypse Now (and sound designer) 1979, Return to Oz (Dir) 1985, The Unbearable Lightness of Being (ed.) 1988, The English Patient (ed. and sound mixer) 1996, The Talented Mr Ripley (ed.) 1999, K-19: Widowmaker (sound and ed.) 2002, Cold Mountain (sound and ed.) 2003. *Publication:* In the Blink of an Eye: A Perspective on Film Editing (with Francis Ford Coppola q.v.) 1995. *Address:* c/o Mirisch Agency, 1801 Century Park E, Suite 1801, Los Angeles, CA 90067, USA (office).

MURDOCH, Elisabeth, BA; British media executive; *Chair and CEO, Shine Ltd;* b. 22 Aug. 1968; d. of Rupert Murdoch (q.v.) and Anna Maria Murdoch (née Torv); m. 1st Elkin Kwesi Pianim (divorced); two d.; m. 2nd Matthew Freud 2001; one d.; ed Vassar Coll., Poughkeepsie, New York; presentation and promotions asst, Nine Network Australia 1990–91, researcher and producer 1991–93, Man. of Programming and Promotion Fox TV LA 1993, Programme Dir KSTU Fox 13 Salt Lake City 1993–94, Dir of Programme Acquisitions FX Cable Network LA 1994–95, Pres., CEO, EP Communications 1995–96 (Peabody Award for Broadcast Excellence 1995); Gen. Man. Broadcasting Dept, BSkyB Ltd 1996, Dir of Programming 1996–98, Man. Dir Sky Networks 1998–2000; Dir Future Publishing 2000–; Co-Founder Shine Ltd 2001, Chair. and CEO 2001–. *Address:* Shine Ltd, Primrose Studios, 109 Regent's Park Road, London, NW1 8UR, England (office). *Telephone:* (20) 7985-7013 (office). *Fax:* (20) 7985-7191 (office). *E-mail:* nichola.kemp@ shinelimited.com (office). *Website:* www.shinelimited.com (office).

MURDOCH, James; American media executive; *Chairman and CEO of Europe and Asia, News Corporation;* b. 1972; s. of Rupert Murdoch (q.v.); m. Kathryn Hufschmid; one c.; ed Horace Mann High School, New York, Harvard Univ.; f. record label Rawkus Entertainment 1995; joined News Corpn 1996, Pres. News Digital Media 1997–99, Exec. Vice-Pres. News Corpn 1999–, mem. Exec. Cttee News Digital systems; CEO and Chair. Star TV 2000–03; Dir (non-exec.) BSkyB 2003, CEO 2003–07, Chair. (non-exec.) 2007–; Chair. and CEO Europe and Asia, News Corpn 2007–; mem. Bd YankeeNets, Inner City Scholarship Fund, Jump Start, Harvard Lampoon Trustees. *Leisure interests:* reading, painting. *Address:* News Corp, News International Ltd, 1 Virginia Street, London, E98 1XY, England (office). *Telephone:* (20) 7782-6000 (office). *Fax:* (20) 7895-902 (office). *Website:* www.newsint.co.uk (office).

MURDOCH, Lachlan Keith, BA; business executive; *Executive Chairman, Illyria Pty Ltd;* b. 8 Sept. 1971, London; s. of Keith Rupert Murdoch (q.v.) and Anna Maria Murdoch (q.v.); m. Sarah Murdoch 1999; two s.; ed Trinity School, Manhattan, Aspen Country Day School, Andover, Mass, Princeton Univ.; Dir Queensland Press Ltd 1994–2005, Chair. 1996–2005; Dir News Corporation 1996–, Deputy COO 2000–05, Adviser 2005–; Deputy Chair. Star Group Ltd 1995–2005; Dir News Ltd 1995–2005, Chair. 1997–2005; Dir Foxtel Management 1998–2005; Dir Gemstar TV International Inc. 2001–04; Dir NDS Group 2002–05; currently Exec. Chair. Illyria Pty Ltd; Dir Asia Pacific Business Coalition on HIV/AIDS (Aus) Ltd 2006–; Dir Surf Life Saving Australia Foundation 2007–08; Cannes Lions Media Person of the Year 2005. *Leisure interests:* rock climbing, sailing, reading. *Address:* 33 Nickson Street, Surry Hills, Sydney, NSW 2010, Australia (office).

MURDOCH, (Keith) Rupert, AC; American (b. Australian) publisher, broadcaster and media business developer; *Chairman and CEO, News Corporation;* b. 11 March 1931, Melbourne, Victoria; s. of the late Sir Keith Murdoch and of Dame Elisabeth Murdoch; m. 1st Patricia Booker (divorced); one d.; m. 2nd Anna Maria Torv 1967 (divorced); two s. one d.; m. 3rd Wendi Deng 1999; two d.; ed Geelong Grammar School, Victoria and Worcester Coll., Oxford; inherited Adelaide News 1954; has since built up News Corporation (Group CEO 1979–, Chair. 1991–); has acquired newspapers, broadcasting and other interests in Australia, UK, USA, Latin America, Europe and Asia, including: Australia – newspapers: The Australian (nat.), Daily Telegraph, Sunday Telegraph, Daily Mirror (Sydney), Sunday Sun (Brisbane), The News and Sunday Mail (Adelaide), The Sunday Times (Perth); USA – New York Post; UK – newspapers: Sun, News of the world (nat., acquired 1969); acquired Times Newspapers Ltd 1981, group includes The Times, The Sunday Times, The Times Literary Supplement, The Times Educational Supplement, The Times Higher Education Supplement; Dir Times Newspapers Holdings 1981–, Chair. 1982–90, 1994–; magazines: Weekly Standard (US politics); film: Fox Film Entertainment; TV: British Sky Broadcasting (UK), STAR (Asia), Fox Broadcasting Co., Fox Cable Networks; other interests include lifestyle portal MySpace.com, book publr HarperCollins and ownership of 35 US TV stations; Chair. and CEO Fox Entertainment Group USA 1992–; mem. Bd of Dirs Associated Press 2008–; Commdr of the White Rose (First Class) 1985; Kt, Order of St Gregory the Great 1998. *Leisure interests:* sailing, skiing. *Address:* News International, 1 Virginia Street, London, E98 1EX, England (office); News Corporation Ltd, 2 Holt Street, Surry Hills, Sydney, NSW 2010, Australia (office); News Corporation, 1211 Avenue of the Americas, New York, NY 10036, USA (office). *Telephone:* (2) 9288-3000 (Sydney) (office); (212) 852-7017 (New York) (office). *Fax:* (2) 9288-3292 (Sydney) (office); (212) 852-7145 (New York) (office). *Website:* www.newscorp.com (office).

MURDOCH MANN, Anna Maria, MA; Australian media executive; b. 30 June 1944, Scotland; d. of J. Torv; m. 1st Rupert Murdoch (q.v.) 1967 (divorced 1999); two s. one d.; m. 2nd William Mann 1999; ed New York Univ., USA; journalist, Daily Telegraph, Daily Mirror, Sunday Mirror, Australia; Dir, Vice-Pres. News America Publishing Inc., News America Holdings; Dir News Corpn Ltd 1990–98; Chair. Bd Regents, Children's Hosp., LA; Pres. Bd Children's Inst. Int. (fmr Sec.); fmr Chair. Friends of NIDA (Nat. Inst. of Dramatic Art) in America Foundation, New York; mem. Bd of Dirs Lincoln Center for the Performing Arts. *Publications:* In Her Own Image 1985, Family Business 1988, Coming to Terms 1991. *Address:* 25 Sutton Place, New York, NY 10022-2453, USA (office).

MURERWA, Herbert; Zimbabwean politician; m.; mem. Zimbabwe African Nat. Union-Patriotic Front (ZANU-PF); High Commr to UK 1984–1990; Minister of Environment and Tourism 1990–95, of Industry and Commerce 1995–96, of Finance and Econ. Devt 1996–2000, 2002, of Higher Educ. and Tech. 2000–01, of Int. Trade and Tech. 2001–02; Minister of Higher Educ. and Tech. and Acting Minister of Finance and Econ. Devt –2005, Minister of Finance and Econ. Devt 2005–07. *Address:* c/o Ministry of Finance and Economic Development, Blocks B, E and G, Composite Bldg, cnr Samora Machel Ave and Fourth St, Private Bag 7705, Causeway, Harare, Zimbabwe (office).

MURIGANDE, Charles; Rwandan politician; *Minister for Cabinet Affairs;* b. 15 Aug. 1958, Butare; Gen. Sec. Rwandese Patriotic Front (RPF) 1998–; Minister of Foreign Affairs and Regional Co-operation 2002–08, for Cabinet Affairs 2008–. *Address:* c/o Office of the President, BP 15, Kigali, Rwanda (office). *Telephone:* 59062000 (office). *Fax:* 572431 (office). *E-mail:* info@presidency.gov.rw. *Website:* www.presidency.gov.rw.

MURILLO JORGE, Marino Alberto, BEcons; Cuban politician; *Minister of Economy and Planning;* ed Coll. of Nat. Defence; fmr Dir of Audits and Econs, Ministry of Food; fmr Vice-Minister of Econs and Planning –2009; Minister for Internal Trade; Minister of Economy and Planning 2009–, also Vice-Pres. Council of Ministers, Partido Comunista de Cuba. *Address:* Ministry of Economy and Planning, 20 de Mayo, entre Territorial y Ayestarán, Plaza de la Revolución, Havana, Cuba (office). *Telephone:* (7) 881-8789 (office). *Fax:* (7) 33-3387 (office). *E-mail:* mep@ceniai.inf.cu (office).

MURKOWSKI, Frank Hughes, BA; American banker and fmr state official; b. 28 March 1933, Seattle, Wash.; s. of Frank Michael and Helen (Hughes) Murkowski; m. Nancy R. Gore 1954; two s. four d. including Lisa Murkowski; ed Ketchikan High School, Santa Clara Univ., Seattle Univ.; service with US Coast Guard 1955–57; with Pacific Nat. Bank of Seattle 1957–59, Nat. Bank of Alaska, Anchorage 1959–67, Vice-Pres. in Charge of Business Devt, Anchorage 1965–67; Commr, Dept of Econ. Devt, Alaska State, Juneau 1967–70; Pres. Alaska Nat. Bank of the North, Fairbanks 1971–80; Pres. Alaska State Chamber of Commerce 1977; Senator from Alaska 1981–2002, Chair. Cttee on Energy and Natural Resources 1995–2001; Gov. of Alaska 2002–07; Vice-Pres. Bd of Trade, BC (Canada) and Alaska; mem. American Bankers Asscn, Alaska Bankers Asscn (fmr Pres.); Republican. *Leisure interests:* hunting, fishing, skiing, tennis, golf. *Address:* c/o Office of the Governor, State Capitol, PO Box 110001, Juneau, Alaska 99811-0001, USA.

MURKOWSKI, Lisa, BEcons, LLB; American politician and lawyer; *Senator from Alaska;* d. of Frank Hughes Murkowski; m. Verne Martell; two s.; ed Georgetown Univ., Williamette Coll. of Law; worked in pvt. law practice for eight years; served as Anchorage Dist Court Attorney for two years; elected to Alaska State House of Reps 1998, 2000, 2002, served as House Majority Leader 2003; apptd Senator from Alaska 2002–04, elected 2004–, apptd Deputy Whip and Chair. Class of New Senators, mem. Energy and Natural Resources Cttee, Chair. Sub cttee on Water and Power, mem. Sub cttees on Energy, and Public Lands and Forests, Environment and Public Works Cttee, Sub cttees on Transportation and Infrastructure, Fisheries, Wildlife and Water, Veteran Affairs and Indian Affairs; mem. Alaska Fed. of Republican Women, Midnight Sun Republican Women, Anchorage Republican Women's Club. *Leisure interests:* skiing, fishing, camping. *Address:* 709 Hart Senate Building, Washington, DC 20510 (office); 510 L Street, Suite 550, Anchorage, Alaska 99501, USA. *Telephone:* (202) 224-6665 (DC) (office); (907) 271-3735 (Alaska) (office). *Fax:* (202) 224-5301 (DC) (office); (907) 276-4081 (Alaska) (office). *Website:* murkowski.senate.gov (office).

MŪRNIECE, Linda; Latvian politician; *Minister of the Interior;* b. 28 Jan. 1970, Dobele; ed Jūrmala Secondary School no. 1, Univ. of Latvia; Insp., State Police 1992–93; Chief Insp. and Asst to Head, State Econ. Sovereignty Protection Dept, Security Police 1993–95; Chief Insp., Press Centre, Ministry of the Interior 1995–97; Head of Advertising, VEF Bank 1997–2001; New Era Party Project Man. May–July 2002; mem. Saeima 2002–; Sec. Nat. Security Cttee 2002–04; Parl. Sec., Ministry of the Interior 2002–2004; Deputy Chair., Defence and Internal Affairs Cttee 2002–; Deputy Chair., New Era Party Parl.Group March–Oct. 2004; Chair., Cttee on Supervising Prevention and Combating of Corruption, Contraband and Organised Crime 2004–; Parl. Sec., Ministry of Defence Jan.–Dec. 2005, Minister of Defence 2006, of the Interior 2009–. *Address:* Ministry of the Interior, Čiekurkalna 1, līnija 1, korp. 2, Rīga, 1026, Latvia (office). *Telephone:* 6721-9263 (office). *Fax:* 6722-9686 (office). *E-mail:* kanceleja@iem.gov.lv (office). *Website:* www.iem.gov.lv (office).

MUROFUSHI, Minoru, BA; Japanese business executive; *Counselor, ITOCHU Corporation;* ed Tokyo Univ.; joined C Itoh 1956, Gen. Man. Coal Dept, New York 1963–71, Vice-Pres. C Itoh (America) (now ITOCHU) 1971, mem. Bd 1985, Chief Exec. 1990–98, also Chair. Bd 1999, now Counselor; currently Vice-Chair. Tokyo Chamber of Commerce and Industry; mem. Bd HSBC Holdings 1992–2002, Exec. Cttee, Trilateral Comm. Pacific Asia Group 1999-2000, Competitiveness Comm. organized by Prime Minister Obuchi 2000-2001. *Address:* ITOCHU Corporation, 5-1 Kita-Aoyama 2-chome, Minato-ku, Tokyo 107-8077, Japan. *Telephone:* (3) 3497-2022 (office). *Fax:* (3) 3497-2002 (office).

MUROMACHI, Kaneo; Japanese banking executive; *Chairman, UFJ Holdings Inc.;* Sr Man.-Dir Sanwa Bank 1997–99, Pres. 1999–2001, Pres. and CEO 2001–02; Sr Adviser to UFJ Bank (created by merger of Sanwa Bank and Tokai Bank) 2004; Chair. UFJ Holdings Inc. 2004–; Special mem. The Tax Comm. 2002; Dir Inamori Foundation, Foundation for Advanced Studies on Int. Devt (FASTID) 2003–; Councillor, Grad. School of Int. Man., IUJ Business School, Japan. *Address:* UFJ Holdings Inc., 5–6 Fushimimachi 3-chome, Chuo-ku, Osaka-shi, Osaka, Japan (office). *Telephone:* (6) 6228-7111 (office). *Fax:* (3) 3212-5870 (office). *Website:* www.ufj.co.jp/index.html (office).

MURPHY, Dervla Mary; Irish author and critic; b. 28 Nov. 1931, Cappoquin; d. of Fergus Murphy and Kathleen Rochfort-Dowling; one d.; ed Ursuline Convent, Waterford; American Irish Foundation Literary Award 1975, Ewart-Biggs Memorial Prize 1978, Irish American Cultural Inst. Literary Award 1985. *Publications:* Full Tilt 1965, Tibetan Foothold 1966, The Waiting Land 1967, In Ethiopia with a Mule 1968, On a Shoestring to Coorg 1976, Where the Indus is Young 1977, A Place Apart 1978, Wheels Within Wheels 1979, Race to the Finish? 1981, Eight Feet in the Andes 1983, Muddling Through in Madagascar 1985, Ireland 1985, Tales from Two Cities 1987, Cameroon with Egbert 1989, Transylvania and Beyond 1992, The Ukimwi Road 1993, South from the Limpopo 1997, Visiting Rwanda 1998, One Foot in Laos 1999, Through the Embers of Chaos: Balkan Journeys 2002, Through Siberia by Accident 2005, Silverland: A Winter Journey Beyond the Urals 2006, In Corners of Cuba 2008. *Leisure interests:* reading, music, cycling, swimming, walking. *Address:* Lismore, Co. Waterford, Ireland.

MURPHY, Edward (Eddie) Regan; American film actor; b. 3 April 1951, Brooklyn, New York; s. of Vernon Lynch (stepfather) and Lillian Lynch; m. 2nd Nicole Mitchell 1993 (divorced 2006); five c.; feature player in Saturday Night Live TV show 1980–84; film debut in 48 Hours 1982; tours with own comedy show; comedy albums: Eddie Murphy 1982, Eddie Murphy: Comedian 1983, How Could It Be 1984, So Happy 1989; has also released seven record albums of comedy and songs; f. Eddie Murphy Productions (production co.) 1996; recipient of numerous awards and nominations. *Films include:* 48 Hours 1982, Trading Places 1983, Delirious 1983, Best Defence 1984, Beverly Hills Cop 1984, The Golden Child 1986, Beverly Hills Cop II 1987, Eddie Murphy Raw 1987, Coming to America 1988, Harlem Nights 1989, 48 Hours 2 1990, Boomerang 1992, Distinguished Gentleman 1992, Beverly Hills Cop III 1994, The Nutty Professor 1996, Dr. Dolittle 1998, Holy Man 1998, Life 1998, Bowfinger 1999, Toddlers 1999, Pluto Nash 1999, Nutty Professor II: The Klumps 2000, Shrek 2001 (voice), Dr Doolittle 2 2001, Showtime 2002, I Spy 2002, Daddy Day Care 2003, Shrek 4–D 2003 (voice), Haunted Mansion 2003, Shrek 2 (voice) 2004, Dreamgirls (Golden Globe for Best Supporting Actor 2007, Screen Actors' Guild Award for Outstanding Performance by a Male Actor in a Supporting Role 2007) 2006, Norbit 2007, Shrek the Third (voice) 2007, Meet Dave 2008. *Address:* c/o William Morris Agency, 1 William Morris Place, Beverly Hills, CA 90212; Eddie Murphy Productions, 152 West 57th Street, 47th Floor, New York, NY 10019, USA. *Telephone:* (212) 399-9900 (Eddie Murphy Productions).

MURPHY, Gerry, MBS, PhD, FInstD, CCMI; Irish business executive; b. 1955; m.; two s.; ed Univ. Coll. Cork, Univ. Coll. Dublin; fmrly with Grand Metropolitan PLC (now Diageo), Ireland, UK and USA 1978–91; CEO Greencore Group PLC, Dublin 1991–95, Exel PLC (fmrly NFC) 1995–2000, Carlton Communications PLC 2000–03, Kingfisher PLC 2003–08; Dir (non-exec.) Abbey Nat. 2004, Reckitt Benckiser 2005–. *Address:* c/o Kingfisher PLC, 3 Sheldon Square, London, W2 6PX, England (office).

MURPHY, Glenn K., BA; Canadian retail executive; *Chairman and CEO, Gap Inc.;* b. Montreal; ed Univ. of Western Ont.; began career with A.C. Nielsen; 14 years in category man., marketing, procurement and operations, Loblaw Cos Ltd, becoming Exec. Vice-Pres. Loblaws Supermarkets 1997–2000; Pres. and CEO Chapters Inc. 2000; Chair. and CEO Shoppers Drug Mart 2001–07; mem. Bd of Dirs Gap Inc. 2007–, Chair. and CEO 2007–. *Address:* Gap Inc., Two Folsom Street, San Francisco, CA 94105, USA (office). *Telephone:* (650) 952-4400 (office). *Fax:* (415) 427-2553 (office). *Website:* www.gap.com (office).

MURPHY, James (Jim); British politician; *Secretary of State for Scotland;* b. 1967, Glasgow; m. Claire Murphy; two s. one d.; ed Strathclyde Univ.; Pres. Nat. Union of Students, Scotland 1992–94, Nat. Union of Students, UK 1994–96; Dir Endsleigh Insurance 1994–96; Project Man. Scottish Labour Party 1996–97; MP for Eastwood constituency (now East Renfrewshire) 1997–, mem. Public Accounts Cttee 2000–01, Parl. Pvt. Sec. to Sec. of State for Scotland 2001–02, Govt whip 2002–05, Parl. Sec. at Cabinet Office 2005–06, Minister of State for Employment and Welfare Reform 2006–07, for Europe 2007–08; Sec. of State for Scotland 2008–. *Address:* Scotland Office, Dover House, Whitehall, London SW1A 2AU, England (office). *Telephone:* (20) 7270-6754 (office). *Fax:* (20) 7270-6812 (office). *E-mail:* scotlandoffice.ministers@scotland.gsi.gov.uk (office). *Website:* www.scotlandoffice.gov.uk (office).

MURPHY, John Michael; British artist; b. 7 Sept. 1945, St Albans; s. of James Murphy and Maureen (née Tarrant) Murphy; ed St Michael's Coll., Hitchin, Luton and Chelsea Schools of Art; has participated in several group exhbns in Britain, Europe and USA; Arts Council of GB Award 1980. *Address:* c/o Lisson Gallery, 67 Lisson Street, London, NW1 5DA, England.

MURPHY, Paul Peter, PC, MA; British politician; *Secretary of State for Wales;* b. 25 Nov. 1948; s. of the late Ronald Murphy and Marjorie Murphy; ed Oriel Coll., Oxford; man. trainee Co-operative Wholesale Soc. 1970–71; Lecturer in History and Govt, Ebbw Vale Coll. of Further Educ. 1971–87; mem. Torfaen Borough Council 1973–87 (Chair. Finance Cttee 1976–86); Sec. Torfaen Constituency Labour Party 1974–87; MP for Torfaen 1987–; Opposition Front Bench Spokesman for Wales 1988–94, on NI 1994, on Foreign Affairs 1994–95, on Defence 1995–97; Minister of State, NI Office 1997–99; Sec. of State for Wales 1999–02, 2008–, for NI 2002–05; Chair. Intelligence and Security Cttee, Cabinet Office 2005–, Local Govt and the Regions Cttee 2008–; Hon. Fellow, Oriel Coll. Oxford; Kt of St Gregory 1997, Kt Commdr of the Constantinian Order of St George. *Leisure interest:* music. *Address:* The Wales Office, Office of the Secretary of State for Wales, Gwedyr House, Whitehall, London SW1A 2ER, England (office). *Telephone:* (20) 7270-0534 (office); (1495) 750078 (constituency office) (office). *E-mail:* wales.office@walesoffice.gsi.gov.uk (home). *Website:* www.walesoffice.gov.uk (office).

MURPHY, Thomas (Tom); Irish playwright and theatre director; b. 23 Feb. 1935, Tuam, Co. Galway; s. of John (Jack) Murphy and Winifred Shaughnessy; ed Tuam Vocational School, Vocational Teachers' Training Coll., Dublin; metalwork teacher 1957–62; playwright and theatre Dir 1962–; Writer-in-Asscn Druid Theatre Co., Galway 1983–86, Abbey Theatre 1986–89; Tom Murphy at the Abbey (Irish Nat. Theatre), six-play season 2001; Mem. Irish Acad. of Letters, Aosdána; Hon. DLitt (Trinity Coll., Dublin) 1998, (Galway NUI) 2000; Irish Acad. of Letters Award 1972, Harveys Award 1983, 1985, Sunday Tribune Arts Award 1985, Independent Newspapers Award

1983, 1989, Drama-Logue Critics' Award 1995, Irish Times ESB Theatre Awards Special Tribute 1997, 2000, Irish Times Theatre Award for Best Play 2005. *Stage plays:* On the Outside 1959, A Whistle in the Dark 1961, A Crucial Week in the Life of a Grocer's Assistant 1966, The Orphans 1968, Famine 1968, The Morning After Optimism 1971, The White House 1972, The Vicar of Wakefield (adaptation) 1974, On the Inside 1974, The Sanctuary Lamp 1975, The J. Arthur Maginnis Story 1976, The Blue Macushla 1980, The Informer (adaptation) 1981, The Gigli Concert 1983, Conversations on a Homecoming 1985, Bailegangaire 1985, A Thief of a Christmas 1986, Too Late for Logic 1989, The Patriot Game 1991, She Stoops to Folly 1995, The Wake 1998, Too Late for Logic 1998, The House 2000, The Cherry Orchard 2003, The Drunkard 2003, Alice Trilogy 2005, The Last Days of a Reluctant Tyrant 2009. *Publications:* The Seduction of Morality (novel) 1994. *Leisure interests:* music, gardening. *Address:* Alexandra Cann Representation, 2 St Thomas Square, Newport, Isle of Wight PO30 1SN, England (office); 4 Garville Road, Dublin 6, Ireland (home). *Telephone:* (1983) 556866 (office). *E-mail:* alex@alexandracann.co.uk (office).

MURPHY, William P., Jr, MD; American physician, biomedical engineer and business executive; *CEO, Small Parts Inc.;* b. 1923, Boston, Mass; s. of William Parry Murphy; m.; ed Harvard Univ., Univ. of Ill. School of Medicine, MIT; cr. first invention, a residential snow blower, at high school; practised medicine at St Francis Hosp., Honolulu, Hawaii and Peter Bent Brigham Hosp., Boston; medical consultant to US Army during Korean War, cr. first dialysis machines for use during war and flexible sealed blood bags for transfusions with colleague Dr. Carl Walter; f. Medical Devt Corpn (renamed Cordis Corpn 1959) 1957, purchased by Johnson & Johnson 1996; cr. first motor-driven angiographic injectors, disposable vascular diagnostic catheters, hollow-fiber artificial kidneys, medical procedural trays, physiologic cardiac pacemakers, externally programmable and dual chamber demand pacemakers; f. Small Parts Inc. 1963, currently CEO; mem. Bd of Dirs Bioheart Inc.; co-founder and CEO Hyperion Inc., Miami 1986–2003; est. FIRST (Fore Inspiration and Recognition of Science and Tech.) 1989; Founding Fellow, American Soc. for Artificial Internal Organs and American Inst. for Medical and Biological Eng 1993; holds 17 US patents; numerous awards including Distinguished Service Award, Int. Soc. for Artificial Organs 1981, Distinguished Service Award, N American Soc. of Pacing and Electrophysiology 1985, Jay Malina Award, Beacon Council 2003, Lemelson-MIT Lifetime Achievement Award 2003. *Publications:* over 30 medical papers. *Leisure interests:* sailing his antique steam-powered tugboat. *Address:* Small Parts, Inc, 13980 N.W. 58th Court, POB 4650, Miami Lakes, FL 33014-0650, USA (office). *Telephone:* (800) 220-4242. *E-mail:* parts@smallparts.com (office). *Website:* www.smallparts.com (office).

MURPHY-O'CONNOR, HE Cardinal Cormac, STL, PhL; British ecclesiastic; *Archbishop Emeritus of Westminster;* b. 24 Aug. 1932, Reading, Berks.; s. of the late Dr Patrick George Murphy-O'Connor and Ellen Theresa Cuddigan; ed Prior Park Coll., Bath, The Venerable English Coll., Rome and Gregorian Univ., Rome; ordained Priest 1956; Asst Priest, Corpus Christi Parish, Portsmouth 1956–63, Sacred Heart Parish, Fareham 1963–66; Pvt. Sec. Chaplain to Bishop of Portsmouth 1966–70; Parish Priest, Portswood, Southampton 1970–71; Rector Venerable English Coll., Rome 1971–77; Bishop of Arundel and Brighton 1977–2000; Archbishop of Westminster 2000–09, Emer. 2009–; cr Cardinal 2001; First Chair. Bishops' Cttee for Europe 1980–83; Jt Chair. Anglo-RC Int. Comm. 1983–2000; Chair. TVS Religious Advisers Panel 1985–90; Pres. Catholic Bishops' Conf. of England and Wales 2000– (Dept for Mission and Unity 1993–); Vice-Pres. Council of the Episcopal Confs of Europe 2001–; mem. Presidential Cttee of Pontifical Council for the Family 2001–, Congregation for Divine Worship and the Discipline of the Sacraments 2001–, Admin of Patrimony of the Holy See 2001–, Council for the Study of Org. and Econ. Problems of the Holy See 2001–, Pontifical Council for Culture 2002–, Pontifical Comm. for Cultural Heritage of the Church 2002–, Pontifical Council for Promoting Christian Unity 2002–; Hon. Bencher of the Inner Temple 2001, Freeman of the City of London 2001, Prior of British and Irish Del. of Constantinian Order 2002, Bailiff Grand Cross of Sovereign Mil. Order of Malta 2002; Hon. DD (Lambeth) 1999. *Publications:* The Family of the Church 1984, At the Heart of the World 2004. *Leisure interests:* music, walking, reading, sport. *Address:* Diocese of Westminster, Vaughan House, 46 Francis Street, London, SW1P 1QN, England (office). *Telephone:* (20) 7798-9009 (office). *E-mail:* vhreception@rcdow.org.u (office). *Website:* www.rcdow.org.uk (office).

MURR, Elias; Lebanese government official, lawyer and business executive; *Deputy Prime Minister and Minister of National Defence;* b. 1962, Bteghrin; s. of Michel Murr; m. Karine Lahoud 1992; three c.; fmr Ed.-in-Chief Al-Jumhouriyah newspaper; business interests in finance and real estate; Minister of the Interior 2000–04; Deputy Prime Minister and Minister of Defence 2005–. *Address:* Ministry of National Defence, Yarze, Beirut, Lebanon (office). *Telephone:* (5) 920400 (office). *Fax:* (5) 951014 (office). *E-mail:* ministry@lebarmy.gov.lb (office). *Website:* www.lebarmy.gov.lb (office).

MURRAY, Bill; American actor and writer; b. 21 Sept. 1950, Evanston, Ill.; m. 1st Margaret Kelly 1980 (divorced 1996); four s.; m. 2nd Jennifer Butler; ed Loyola Acad., Regis Coll., Denver, Second City Workshop, Chicago; performer off-Broadway Nat. Lampoon Radio Hour; regular appearances TV series Saturday Night Live; appeared in radio series Marvel Comics' Fantastic Four; Emmy Award for best writing for comedy series 1977. *Films include:* Meatballs 1977, Mr Mike's Mondo Video 1979, Where the Buffalo Roam 1980, Caddyshack 1980, Stripes 1981, Tootsie 1982, Ghostbusters 1984, The Razor's Edge 1984, Nothing Lasts Forever 1984, Little Shop of Horrors 1986, Scrooged 1988, Ghostbusters II 1989, What About Bob? 1991, Mad Dog and Glory 1993, Groundhog Day 1993, Ed Wood 1994, Kingpin 1996, Larger Than Life 1996, Space Jam 1996, The Man Who Knew Too Little 1997, With Friends Like These 1998, Veeck as in Wreck 1998, Rushmore 1998, Wild Things 1998, The Cradle Will Rock 1999, Hamlet 1999, Company Man 1999, Charlie's Angels 2000, The Royal Tenenbaums 2001, Osmosis Jones 2001, Lost in Translation (Golden Globe, Best Actor Musical or Comedy 2004, BAFTA Award, Best Actor in a Leading Role) 2003, Coffee and Cigarettes 2003, Garfield: The Movie (voice) 2004, The Life Aquatic with Steve Zissou 2004, Broken Flowers 2005, The Lost City 2005, Garfield 2 (voice) 2006, The Darjeeling Limited 2007, Get Smart 2008, City of Ember 2008; co-producer, dir, actor film Quick Change 1990; Writer, NBC-TV series Saturday Night Live 1977–80. *Publications:* Cinderella Story: My Life in Golf 1999. *Leisure interest:* golf. *Address:* c/o Jessica Tuchinsky, Creative Artists Agency, 9830 Wilshire Boulevard, Beverly Hills, CA 90212, USA.

MURRAY, Denis James, OBE; British journalist; *Ireland Correspondent, BBC Television;* b. 7 May 1951; s. of the late James Murray and Helen Murray; m. Joyce Linehan 1978; two s. two d.; ed St Malachy's Coll. Belfast, Trinity Coll. Dublin, Queen's Univ. Belfast; grad. trainee, Belfast Telegraph 1975–77, also reporter; Belfast Reporter, Radio Telefís Éireann 1977–82; Dublin Corresp. BBC 1982–84, NI Political Corresp. 1984–88, Ireland Corresp. 1988–. *Leisure interests:* music, reading, sports, family. *Address:* BBC, Broadcasting House, Ormeau Avenue, Belfast, BT2 8HQ, Northern Ireland (office). *Telephone:* (28) 9033-8000 (office). *Website:* www.bbc.co.uk (office).

MURRAY, John Loyola, BL, SC; Irish judge; *Chief Justice, Supreme Court;* b. 27 June 1943, Limerick; s. of John C. Murray and Catherine Casey; m. Gabrielle Walsh 1969; one s. one d.; ed Crescent Coll., Rockwell Coll., Univ. Coll. Dublin and King's Inns, Dublin; Pres. Union of Students of Ireland 1964–66; barrister-at-law 1967; Bencher, King's Inns 1986; SC, Bar of Ireland 1981; Attorney-Gen. Aug.–Dec. 1982, 1987–91; mem. Council of State 1987–91; Judge, Court of Justice of European Communities 1991–99; Judge, Supreme Court 1999–, Chief Justice 2004–; Hon. LLD (Limerick). *Leisure interests:* yachting, travel, art. *Address:* Supreme Court, Four Courts, Inns Quay, Dublin 7, Ireland (office). *Website:* www.courts.ie (office).

MURRAY, Joseph Edward, MD, DSc; American plastic surgeon (retd); b. 1 April 1919, Milford, Mass; s. of William A. Murray and Mary DePasquale; m. Virginia Link 1945; three s. three d.; ed Holy Cross Coll. and Harvard Univ.; Chief Plastic Surgeon, Peter Bent Brigham Hosp. Boston 1964–86, Emer. 1986–; Chief Plastic Surgeon, Children's Hosp. Medical Center, Boston 1972–85, now Emer.; Prof. of Surgery, Harvard Medical School 1970–86; mem. American Surgical Asscn, American Soc. of Plastic and Reconstructive Surgery, American Asscn of Plastic Surgeons etc.; Hon. Fellow, Royal Australasian Coll. of Surgeons, Royal Coll. of Surgeons of England; Hon. DSc (Holy Cross Coll.) 1965, (Rockford (Ill.) Coll.) 1966, (Roger Williams Coll.) 1986; Hon. award, American Acad. of Arts and Sciences 1962, Gold Medal, Int. Soc. of Surgeons 1963, Nobel Prize for Medicine (jtly) 1990, Bigelow Medal, Boston Surgical Soc. 1992, Pontifical Medal 1997, Massachusetts Medical Lifetime Achievement Award 1998. *Achievements:* performed first human kidney transplant 1954. *Leisure interests:* tennis, biking, swimming. *Address:* 108 Abbott Road, Wellesley, MA 02481, USA. *Telephone:* (781) 235-4356 (home). *Fax:* (781)-235-2612 (office). *E-mail:* josmurray@aol.com (office).

MURRAY, Leslie (Les) Allan, BA, AO; Australian poet; b. 17 Oct. 1938, Nabiac, NSW; s. of the late Cecil Allan Murray and Miriam Pauline Murray (née Arnall); m. Valerie Gina Morelli 1962; three s. two d.; ed Univ. of Sydney; translator, Australian Nat. Univ. 1963–67; in Prime Minister's Dept 1970–71; Acting Ed., Poetry Australia 1973–80; Ed., New Oxford Book of Australian Verse 1985–97; Literary Ed., Quadrant 1989–; Petrarca Prize (Germany) 1995, T. S. Eliot Prize 1997, Queen's Gold Medal for Poetry 1999, Mondello Prize (Italy) 2004. *Publications:* The Ilex Tree (with Geoffrey Lehmann) 1965, The Weatherboard Cathedral 1969, Poems Against Economics 1972, Collected Poems 1976, Selected Poems: The Vernacular Republic 1979, The Boys Who Stole the Funeral (verse novel) 1980, Selected Poems 1986, Dog Fox Field 1990, The Paperbark Tree (selected prose) 1991, Translations from the Natural World 1992, Fivefathers (ed.) 1995, Subhuman Redneck Poems 1996, A Working Forest (prose) 1997, Fredy Neptune (verse novel) 1998, Conscious & Verbal 1999, Learning Human – New Selected Poems 2001, Poems the Size of Photographs 2002, New Collected Poems 2003, The Best Australian Poems (ed.) 2004, The Biplane Houses 2006. *Leisure interests:* cinema, gossip, ruminative driving. *Address:* Margaret Connolly & Associates, 16 Winton Street, Warrawee, NSW 2074, Australia (office).

MURRAY, Hon. Lowell, PC, BA, MA, LLD; Canadian politician; b. 26 Sept. 1936, New Waterford, Nova Scotia; s. of the late Daniel Murray and Evelyn Young; m. Colleen Elaine MacDonald 1981; two s.; ed St Francis Xavier Univ., NS, Queen's Univ., Ont.; fmr Chief of Staff to Minister of Justice and Minister of Public Works; Progressive Conservative Nat. Campaign Chair. in Gen. Election 1977–79, 1981–83; Senator 1979–, Co-Chair. Jt Senate-House of Commons Cttee on Official Languages 1980–84; Chair. Standing Cttee on Banking, Trade and Commerce 1984–86; Chair. Standing Senate Cttee on Nat. Finance 1995–96, 1999–2004, Chair. Standing Senate Cttee on Social Affairs, Science and Tech. 1997–99; Leader of Govt in the Senate 1986–93 and Minister of State for Fed.-Provincial Relations 1986–91; Minister responsible for Atlantic Canada Opportunities Agency 1987–88; Acting Minister for Communications 1988–89; mem. Bd Dirs Sony of Canada 1995–; mem. Bd Trustees Inst. for Research on Public Policy 1984–86, Trilateral Cttee 1985–86, Council of the Fed. Advisory Panel on Fiscal Imbalance 2005–06; Progressive Conservative. *Address:* The Senate, Room 502, Victoria Building, Ottawa, ON K1A 0A4, Canada (home). *Telephone:* (613) 995-2407 (office). *Fax:* (613) 947-4730 (office). *E-mail:* murral@sen.parl.gc.ca (office).

MURRAY, Noreen Elizabeth, CBE, PhD, FRS, FRSE; British geneticist and academic; *Professor Emerita, Institute of Cell Biology, University of Edinburgh;* b. 26 Feb. 1935, Burnley, Lancs.; d. of John Parker and Lilian G. Parker; m. Prof. Sir Kenneth Murray 1958; ed Lancaster Girls' Grammar School, King's Coll., Univ. of London, Univ. of Birmingham; Research Assoc. Dept of Biological Sciences, Stanford Univ., Calif. 1960–64; Research Fellow Botany School, Univ. of Cambridge 1964–67; at Dept of Molecular Biology, Univ. of Edinburgh, Lecturer, then Sr Lecturer 1974–80, Reader 1982–88, Prof. of Molecular Genetics 1988–, now Emer.; mem. MRC Molecular Genetics Unit 1968–74; Group Leader, European Molecular Biology Lab., Heidelberg 1980–82; mem. European Molecular Biology Org. 1981–, Biotech. and Biosciences Research Council 1994–97; Pres. Genetical Soc. of GB 1987–90; founder and mem. Darwin Trust, Edinburgh; jtly invented first phage vectors for cloning DNA 1974; Dr hc (Birmingham) 1995, (UMIST) 1995, (Warwick) 2001, Hon. DSc (Lancaster) 2008;Fellow King's Coll. London 2006; Gabor Medal, Royal Soc. 1989, AstraZeneca Award, Biochemical Soc. (UK) 2005. *Publications:* numerous articles in specialist publs and journals. *Leisure interest:* gardening. *Address:* Institute of Cell Biology, University of Edinburgh, King's Buildings, Mayfield Road, Edinburgh EH9 3JR, Scotland (office). *Telephone:* (131) 650-5374 (office). *Fax:* (131) 668-3870 (office). *E-mail:* Noreen.Murray@ed.ac.uk (office). *Website:* www.icmb.ed.ac.uk/staff/murray (office).

MURRAY, Patty, BA; American politician; *Senator from Washington;* b. 11 Oct. 1950, Bothell, Wash.; d. of David L. Johns and Beverly A. Johns (née McLaughlin); m. Robert R. Murray 1972; one s. one d.; ed Washington State Univ.; teacher, Shoreline Community Coll. 1984–87; campaigned against proposed closure of Wash. State Parent Educ. Programme 1980; fmr mem. Wash. State Senate; instructor Shoreline Community Coll. Seattle 1984–88; Senator from Wash. 1993–, Vice-Chair. Senate Democratic Policy Cttee, mem. Budget Cttee, Appropriations Cttee; Democrat. *Address:* 173 Russell Senate Office Bldg, Washington, DC 20510 (office); 528 NW 203rd Place, Seattle, WA 98177, USA. *Telephone:* (202) 224-2621 (office). *Fax:* (202) 224-0238 (office). *Website:* murray.senate.gov (office).

MURRAY, Robin MacGregor, MD, DSc, FRCP; British psychiatrist and academic; *Professor of Psychiatry, Institute of Psychiatry at the Maudsley, King's College London;* b. 31 Jan. 1944, Glasgow, Scotland; s. of James. A. C. Murray and Helen MacGregor; m. Shelagh Harris 1970; one s. one d.; ed Glasgow and London Univs; jr posts with Glasgow Univ., Dept of Medicine 1970–72, with Maudsley Hosp. 1972–75; Sr Lecturer Inst. of Psychiatry, London 1978–82, Dean 1982–89, Prof. of Psychological Medicine 1989–99, Prof. of Psychiatry 1999–; Lilly Int. Fellow Nat. Inst. for Mental Health, Bethesda, Md 1976–77; Pres. Asscn of European Psychiatrists 1995–96; Gaskell Gold Medal and Research Prize (Royal Coll. of Psychiatrists) 1976, Sr Leverhulme Research Fellow (Royal Soc.) 1993; Hon. mem. Asscn of European Psychiatry 2002; Kurt Schneider Award 1994, Adolf Meyer Award 1997, Paul Hoch Award 1998, Stanley Dean Award 1999, Hilton Distinguished Investigator Award of the Nat. Alliance for Research into Schizophrenia and Depression (NARSAD) 1999, Fifth Castilla del Pino Award for Achievement in Psychiatry 2002, Psykiatriyhdistys Suomen Medal, Finnish Psychiatric Soc. 2003. *Publications:* Schizophrenia 1996, Psychosis in the Inner City 1998, First Episode Psychosis (co-author) 1999; publs on schizophrenia, depression, psychiatric genetics and epidemiology, alcoholism and analgesic abuse. *Leisure interests:* Scottish and Jamaican music, swimming. *Address:* Department of Psychiatry, Institute of Psychiatry, de Crespigny Park, London, SE5 8AF, England (office). *Telephone:* (20) 7703-6091. *Fax:* (20) 7701-9044. *Website:* www.iop.kcl.ac.uk (office).

MURRAY, Simon, CBE; British banker and author; b. 25 March 1940, Leicester; s. of Patrick G. Murray and Maxine M. K. Murray; m. Jennifer A. Leila Mather 1966; one s. two d.; ed Bedford School (Sr Exec. Programme) and Stanford Business School; joined French Foreign Legion 1960, served for five years in 2nd Foreign Parachute Regt (2ème REP), fought in Algerian War of Independence against guerillas of Front de Libération Nationale; Jardine Matheson & Co., Ltd 1966–73; Dir Matheson & Co., London 1973–75; Man. Dir Jardine Eng Corpn 1975–80; Founder and Man. Dir Davenham Investments Ltd 1980–84; Group Man. Dir Hutchison Whampoa Ltd 1984–93, now mem. Bd Dirs; pioneered mobile phones in Hong Kong and developed in the UK the mobile phone system now know as Orange; Exec. Chair. (Asia/Pacific) Deutsche Bank 1993–98; Founder and Chair. Simon Murray & Assocs; Chair. Gleacher Partners Asia, Hong Kong; advisor, Bain & Company (Asia), Inc., N. M. Rothschild & Sons Ltd, UK, China Nat. Offshore Oil Corpn; mem. Bd Dirs Cheung Kong (Holdings) Ltd, Hong Kong, Hermes International, France; Officier, Ordre nat. du Mérite; Hon. LLD (Bath) 2005. *Achievement:* oldest man, aged 63, to walk unsupported to the South Pole 2004. *Publication:* Legionnaire: An Englishman in the French Foreign Legion 1978 (made into a film called Simon: An English Legionnaire 2002). *Leisure interests:* flying helicopters with his wife Jennifer (first woman to fly solo round the world in a helicopter), squash, jogging, reading. *Address:* Gleacher Partners (Asia) Ltd, 2108 Gloucester Tower, The Landmark, 11 Pedder Street, Central, Hong Kong (office). *Telephone:* 2501-1399 (office).

MURRAY, Stuart, FRAIA, RIBA, DipArch, ASTC; Australian architect and planner; b. 27 Oct. 1926, Sydney; s. of Cyril Hargreaves Murray and Daphne Williams; m. 1st Elizabeth Grime 1952 (divorced 1965); two s. two d.; m. 2nd Adrienne Solti 1982; ed Fort Street High School, Sydney, Sydney Tech. Coll. School of Architecture and Univ. of Sydney; Office of Burley Griffin 1944–46; Office of Sydney Ancher 1947–49; Office of Denis Clarke Hall, London 1950–52; partner, Ancher Mortlock & Murray 1953–64; Dir Ancher Mortlock Murray & Woolley, Architects 1965–75; Stuart Murray & Assocs, Architects & Planners 1976–; Dir N Sydney Planning Consultants 1968–72; work includes: Canberra Housing, Nat. Heritage List 1960, Elizabeth Bay Apartments, RAIA Heritage List 1967, Great Hall, Univ. of Newcastle (winner, Limited Competition 1968) 1971, Aeronautics School, Univ. of Sydney 1974, North Sydney Devt Control Plan 1974, Polo Club, Forbes, NSW 1987, school and univ. bldgs, homes and apts etc.; Town Hall, Waverley, Sydney: Winner, Nat. Competition 1957 (unbuilt). *Publications:* papers on civic design and urban environment. *Leisure interests:* architecture, art, music, literature, philosophy, cooking, travel, walking. *Address:* Stuart Murray & Associates, Suite 1, 144 High Street, North Sydney, NSW 2060, Australia (office). *Telephone:* (2) 9955-4779 (office). *Fax:* (2) 9955-3653 (office).

MURTAGH, Peter, BA; Irish journalist; *Managing Editor, The Irish Times;* b. 9 April 1953, Dublin; s. of Thomas Murtagh and Olive de Lacy; m. Moira Gutteridge 1988; one s. one d.; ed The High School, Dublin and Trinity Coll. Dublin; reporter, The Irish Times 1981–84, Foreign Ed., Opinion Ed., Managing Ed. 1997–; Ed. Insight, The Sunday Times, London 1985; reporter, Deputy Foreign Ed. and News Ed. The Guardian, London 1986–94; Ed. The Sunday Tribune, Dublin 1994–97; Journalist of the Year, Ireland 1983; Reporter of the Year, UK 1986. *Publications:* The Boss: Charles J. Haughey in Government (with J. Joyce) 1983, Blind Justice: The Sallins Mail Train Robbery (with J. Joyce) 1984, The Rape of Greece 1994, Irish Times Book of the Year 1999–2008. *Leisure interests:* family, newspapers, Ireland. *Address:* The Irish Times, Tara Street, Dublin 2 (office); Somerby Road, Greystones, Co. Wicklow, Ireland (home). *Telephone:* (1) 6758000 (office). *Fax:* (1) 6615302 (office). *E-mail:* pmurtagh@irish-times.ie (office). *Website:* www.irishtimes.com (office).

MURTEIRA NABO, Francisco Luís, MBA; Portuguese economist and business executive; *Chairman, Galp Energia SGPS SA;* b. 1939, Evora; ed Instituto Superior de Economia e Gestao, Escola de Direccao e Negocios-AESE; Chief Alderman, City Hall, Lisbon 1976–81; Chair. Portuguese Radio Marconi Co. 1978–82; Vice-Pres. Sorefame 1982–83; Sec. of State for Transport 1983–85; Admin. Companhia Industrial de Portugal e Colónias 1986–87; Deputy Sec. for Educ., Health and Social Affairs, Office of Macao 1987–89, Deputy Sec. for Econ. Affairs, Admin of Macao 1989–90, Head of Govt of Territory of Macao 1990–91; Minister of Social Equipment (Public Works) 1995–96; Chair. Portugal Telecom, SGPS, SA 1996–2003 (also Chair. Exec. Cttee); Chair. Galp Energia SGPS SA 2005–; Pres. Câmara do Comércio e Indústria Luso-Chinesa (Portuguese-Chinese Chamber of Commerce and Industry); mem. Direcção da Associação Comercial de Lisboa (Directorate of Commercial Asscn of Lisbon), Institut Européen d'Admin des Affaires (INSEAD); Chair. Proforum (Asscn for the Devt of Eng); fmr Dir (non-exec.) BPG (Banco Portugues de Gestao, SA), Companhia de Seguros Sagres, SA, Holdomnis – Gestao e Investimentos, SA, Templo – Gestao e Investimentos, SA, Seng Heng Bank, BES – Banco Espirito Santo, SA; Pres. Portuguese Economists Asscn; fmr Pres. COTEC Portugal (Asscn for Business Innovation); mem. Conselho Superior de Ciência, Tecnologia e Inovação (Supreme Council for Science, Tech. and Innovation); Trustee, Fundação Oriente. *Address:* GALP – Petróleos e Gás de Portugal SGPS SA, Rua Tomás da Fonseca, Torre C, Edifício Galp Energia, 1600-209 Lisbon, Portugal (office). *Telephone:* (21) 724-25-00 (office); (21) 724-08-66 (office). *Fax:* (21) 724-29-65 (office); (21) 724-05-73 (office). *E-mail:* investor.relations@galpenergia.com (office). *Website:* www.galpenergia.com (office).

MURTHY, N.R. Narayana, MSc; Indian business executive; *Chief Mentor, Infosys Technologies Ltd;* m; two c.; co-f. Infosys Technologies Ltd 1981, Chair. 1981–2006, CEO 1981–2002, Chief Mentor 2002–; mem. Prime Minister's Council on Trade and Industry; mem. Bd Dirs Reserve Bank of India; mem. Asian Exec. Bd, Wharton Business School; Nikkei Asia Award, Wharton School Dean's Medal, Max Schmidheiny Foundation Freedom Prize 2001, Ernst & Young Global World Entrepreneur of the Year 2003. *Address:* Infosys Technologies, Plot 44, 3rd Cross, Electronic City, Hosur Road, Bangalore 561 229, India (office). *Telephone:* (80) 28520261 (office). *Fax:* (80) 28520352 (office). *E-mail:* infosys@inf.com (office). *Website:* www.inf.com (office).

MUSA, Said, LLB; Belizean politician and attorney-at-law; b. 19 March 1944, San Ignacio; s. of Hamid Musa and Aurora Musa (née Gibbs); ed St John's Coll., Belize City, Manchester Univ., England; called to the Bar London 1966; worked as barrister, Gray's Inn, London 1966–67; circuit magistrate Belize 1967–68, Crown Counsel 1968–70; lawyer pvt. practice 1970–79, 1984–89, 1993–98 (Sr Counsel 1983–); Pres. Public Service Union 1969; f. People's Action Cttee, Soc. for Promotion of Educ. and Research (SPEAR) 1969; obliged to leave public service because of political activities; joined People's United Party (PUP); Chair. Fort George Div. PUP 1974–; Chair. PUP 1986–94, Deputy Leader 1994–96, Leader 1996–; Co-Founder Journal of Belizean Affairs 1972; apptd Senator to Nat. Ass. by George Price 1974; negotiator in talks to safeguard territorial integrity of Belize on independence 1975–81; mem. House of Reps for Fort George constituency 1979–84, 1993–98; Attorney-Gen. and Minister for Educ., Sports and Culture 1979–84; Minister of Foreign Affairs, Econ. Devt and Educ. 1989–93 (negotiated recognition of Belizean sovereignty by Guatemala 1991); Leader of the Opposition 1996–98; Prime Minister of Belize 1998–2008, concurrently Minister of Finance and Foreign Affairs, then Minister of Finance and Econ. Devt 1998–2003, of Nat. Devt and the Public Service 2004–08, of Finance 2005–08. *Publications:* People's Assemblies, People's Government and articles in nat. press. *Leisure interests:* reading, int. affairs, human rights, music, tennis. *Address:* People's United Party, 3 Queen Street, Belize City, Belize (office). *Telephone:* 223-2428 (office). *Fax:* 223-3476 (office).

MUSEMINARI, Rosemary; Rwandan diplomatist and politician; *Minister of Foreign Affairs and Co-operation;* b. 1962; m.; five d.; ed Makerere Univ., Kampala; Lecturer, Nsamizi Inst. of Social Policy, Entebbe, Uganda 1986–94; returned to Rwanda 1994, Head of Dept for Social Services 1994–99; Sec.-Gen.

Nat. Red Cross Soc. of Rwanda 1999–2000; Amb. to UK (also accred Scandinavian countries and Ireland) to 2000–05; Minister of State for Regional Cooperation 2005–08, Minister of Foreign Affairs and Co-operation 2008–; Chair. Foreign Affairs Ministers COMESA 2007–. *Address:* Ministry of Foreign Affairs and Co-operation, blvd de la Révolution, BP 179, Kigali, Rwanda (office). *Telephone:* 574522 (office). *Fax:* 572904 (office). *Website:* www .minaffet.gov.rw (office).

MUSEVENI, Gen. Yoweri Kaguta; Ugandan head of state; *President and Commander-in-Chief of Armed Forces;* b. 1944, Ntungamo, Mbarara; s. of Amos Kaguta and Esteri Kokundeka; m. Janet Kataaha; four c.; ed Mbarara High School, Ntare School, Univ. Coll. of Dar es Salaam; Research Asst Office of fmr Pres. Milton Obote 1971; in Tanzania planning overthrow of regime of Idi Amin 1971–79; f. Front for Nat. Salvation (FRONASA) 1972; taught at Moshi Co-operative Coll., Tanzania 1972; participated in Tanzanian invasion of Uganda 1979; Defence Minister in interim Govt of Uganda Nat. Liberation Front (UNLF) following overthrow of Amin 1979–80; following election of Dr Obote, amid allegations of ballot-rigging, in 1980, spent five years as leader of Nat. Resistance Army (NRA) waging a guerrilla war 1981–86; Pres. of Uganda (following overthrow of Govt by NRA forces) and Minister of Defence, then Pres. and C-in-C of Armed Forces 1986–; Chair. Preferential Trade Area (PTA) 1987–88, 1992–93, OAU 1990–91. *Publications:* Selected Essays 1985, Selection of Speeches and Writings, Vol. I: What is Africa's Problem? 1992, Vol. II 1997, Sowing the Mustard Seed – The Struggle for Freedom and Democracy 1997. *Leisure interest:* football. *Address:* Office of the President, Parliament Building, P.O. Box 7168, Kampala, Uganda. *Telephone:* (41) 258441. *Fax:* (41) 256143. *E-mail:* info@gouexecutive.net (office). *Website:* www.gouexecutive .net (office).

MUSGRAVE, Thea, CBE, MusDoc; British composer; b. 27 May 1928, Edinburgh; d. of James Musgrave and Joan Musgrave (née Hacking); m. Peter Mark 1971; ed Edinburgh Univ. and Paris Conservatoire (under Nadia Boulanger); Lecturer, Extra-Mural Dept, Univ. of London 1958–65; Visiting Prof., Univ. of California, Santa Barbara 1970; Guggenheim Fellow 1974–75, 1982–83; Distinguished Prof., Queen's Coll., City Univ. of New York 1987–2002; Hon. DMus (CNAA, Smith Coll., Old Dominion Univ.); Koussevitzky Award 1972, 2000. *Works include:* Chamber Concertos 1, 2 & 3 1966, Concerto for Orchestra 1967, Clarinet Concerto 1968, Beauty and the Beast (ballet) 1969, Night Music 1969, Horn Concerto 1971, The Voice of Ariadne (chamber opera) 1972–73, Viola Concerto 1973, Space Play 1974, Mary, Queen of Scots (opera) 1976–77, A Christmas Carol (opera) 1978–79, An Occurrence at Owl Creek Bridge (radio opera) 1981, Harriet, A Woman Called Moses 1980–84, Black Tambourine for women's chorus and piano 1985, Pierrot 1985, For the Time Being for chorus 1986, The Golden Echo 1987, Narcissus 1988, The Seasons (orchestral) 1988, Rainbow (orchestral) 1990, Simón Bolívar (opera) 1993, Autumn Sonata 1993, Journey through a Japanese Landscape (marimba concerto) 1993, On the Underground (vocal) 1994, Helios (oboe concerto) 1995, Phoenix Rising (orchestral) 1997, Canta, Canta (clarinet and ensemble) 1997, Lamenting with Ariadne 1999, The Mocking Bird (baritone and ensemble) 2000, Pontalba (opera) 2003, Turbulent Landscapes (orchestral) 2004, Wood, Metal, Skin (concerto for percussion and orchestra) 2004, Journey into Light (soprano and orchestra) 2005, Two's Company (duet for oboe and percussion) 2005; chamber music, songs, choral music, orchestral music. *Leisure interests:* cooking, cinema, reading. *Address:* Chester Novello, 14–15 Berners Street, London, W1T 3LJ, England (office). *Telephone:* (20) 7612-7400 (office). *Website:* www.chesternovello.com (office); www .theamusgrave.com (home).

MUSGROVE, Ronnie, JD; American state official and lawyer; *Governor of Mississippi;* b. 29 July 1956; m. Melanie Ballard; three c.; ed Northwest Miss. Jr Coll., Univ. of Miss.; partner Smith, Musgrove & McCord, Miss.; Lt Gov. State of Miss. 1996–99, Gov. of Miss. 2000–; Fellow Miss. Bar Foundation; mem. Miss. State Bar, Miss. Bar Asscn, Miss. Young Lawyers' Asscn, Panola Co. Bar Asscn, Tri Co. Bar Asscn. *Address:* Office of the Governor, P.O.B. 139, Jackson, MS 39205, USA (office).

MUSHARRAF, Gen. (retd) Pervez; Pakistani fmr army officer and fmr head of state; b. 11 Aug. 1943, Delhi, India; s. of Syed Musharraf Uddin; m. Sehba Farid 1968; one s. one d.; ed St Patrick's High School, Karachi, Forman Christian Coll., Lahore, Command and Staff Coll., Quetta, Nat. Defence Coll., Rawalpindi, Royal Coll. of Defence Studies, UK; spent early childhood in Turkey 1949–56; joined Pakistan Mil. Acad. 1961; commd in Artillery Regt 1964; fought in 1965 war with India (Imtiazi Sanad Gallantry Award); spent much of mil. career in Special Services Group; Company Commdr Commando Battalion Indo-Pakistan War 1971; Dir-Gen. Mil. Operations, Gen. HQ 1993–95; apptd C-in-C of Pakistani Army Oct. 1998, Chair. Jt Chiefs of Staff Cttee 1999, led mil. coup 1999, Chief of Staff 1999–2007; Chief Exec. Nat. Security Council of Pakistan 1999–2002; Pres. of Pakistan 2001–08 (resgnd). *Publication:* In the Line of Fire: A Memoir 2006. *Leisure interests:* squash, tennis, golf, reading, mil. history. *Address:* c/o Office of the President, Aiwan-e-Sadr, Islamabad, Pakistan (office).

MUSHKETIK, Yuri Mikhailovich; Ukrainian writer; b. 21 March 1929, Verkiivka, Chernigiv Region; s. of Mikhail Petrovich Mushketik and Uliana Onufriivna Mushketik; m. Lina Sergiivna Mushketik (née Lushnikova); two d.; ed Kiev State Univ.; mem. CPSU 1951–91; Chair. Bd Union of Writers of Ukraine 1987–; Ed.-in- Chief Dripro journal; Chair. Nat. Cttee of UNESCO; first works published 1952; T. Shevchenko Ukrainian State Prize 1980. *Publications include:* Fires in the Middle of the Night 1959, Black Bread 1960, The Heart and the Stone 1961, Drop of Blood 1964, A Bridge Across the Night 1975, White Shadow 1975, Position 1979, Pain 1981, The Boundary 1987, Selected Works (2 vols) 1989, Hetman's Treasure (novel) 1993, Brother Against Brother (novel) 1995. *Leisure interests:* reading American literature,

history of Ukrainian Cossacks. *Address:* Suvorova Str. 3, Apt. 10, 252010 Kiev, Ukraine. *Telephone:* (44) 290-80-04.

MUSIN, Aslan Yespulayevich; Kazakhstani government official; *Chairman, Majlis (Parliament);* b. 2 Jan. 1954; ed Almaty Inst. of Econs; fmr Akim (Gov.) Aktobe and Atyrau Oblasts; Minister of Econ. Affairs and Budget Planning 2006–07; Deputy Prime Minister Jan.–Sept. 2007; Chair. Majlis (Parl.) 2007–. *Address:* Office of the Chairman, 010000 Astana, Parliament House, Kazakhstan (office). *Telephone:* (7172) 15-30-19 (office). *Fax:* (7172) 33-30-99 (office). *E-mail:* Smimazh@parlam.kz (office). *Website:* www.parlam.kz (office).

MUSOKE, Rt Hon Kintu; Ugandan politician, journalist and publisher; *Senior Adviser to President;* b. Masaka; Minister of Information 1989–91; Minister for Presidency 1991–94; Minister of State for Security; Prime Minister of Uganda 1994–2000; currently Sr Adviser to Pres. of Uganda; Chair. Advisory Cttee, USA Presidential Emergency Fund for Aids Relief (PEPFAR). *Address:* c/o Office of the Prime Minister, PO Box 341, Kampala (office); PO Box 15025, Kampala, Uganda (home). *Telephone:* (41) 4257370 (home). *Fax:* (41) 4235459 (office). *E-mail:* kintumusoke@hotmail.com (home).

MUSOKOTWANE, Situmbeko; Zambian economist and government official; *Minister of Finance and National Planning;* economist with Bank of Zambia, fmr Deputy Gov.; held several cabinet positions including Sec. to the Treasury and Deputy Sec. to the Cabinet; econ. advisor to Pres. of Zambia –2008; Minister of Finance and Nat. Planning 2008–; fmr Prof., Univ. of Zambia; fmr Dir ZCCM Investments Holdings plc. *Address:* Ministry of Finance and National Planning, Finance Bldg, POB 50062, Lusaka, Zambia (office). *Telephone:* (21) 1252121 (office). *Fax:* (21) 1251078 (office). *E-mail:* info@mofnp.gov.zm (office). *Website:* www.mofnp.gov.zm (office).

MUSONDA, Moses, PhD; Zambian diplomatist, academic and government official; *Permanent Secretary for Education;* ed Bryn Mawr Univ.; fmr Pro Vice-Chancellor, Univ. of Zambi; fmr Amb. to People's Repub. of China and to Malta; Amb. to UK –2002, High Commr to India 2002–04; Perm. Sec. for Educ. 2004–. *Address:* Ministry of Education, 15102 Ridgeway, POB RW50093, Lusaka, Zambia. *Telephone:* (1) 227636. *Fax:* (1) 222396.

MUSONGE, Peter Mafany; Cameroonian politician; b. 3 Dec. 1942; ed Stanford Univ.; fmr Gen. Man. Cameroon Devt Corpn (CDC); mem. Rassemblement démocratique du peuple camerounais (RDPC); Prime Minister of Cameroon 1996–2004. *Address:* c/o Office of the Prime Minister, Yaoundé, Cameroon.

MUSONI, James; Rwandan politician; *Minister of Finance and Economic Planning;* Commr Gen., Rwanda Revenue Authority –2005; Minister for Commerce, Industry, Investment Promotion, Tourism and Cooperatives 2005–06, of Finance and Economic Planning 2006–; mem. Front Patriotique Rwandais. *Address:* Ministry of Finance and Economic Planning, BP 158, Kigali, Rwanda. *Telephone:* 575756 (office). *Fax:* 577581 (office). *E-mail:* mfin@rwanda1.com (office). *Website:* www.minecofin.gov.rw (office).

MUSSA, Michael; American economist and academic; *Senior Fellow, Institute for International Economics;* b. 1944; ed Univs of Calif. and Chicago; Asst Prof. of Econs Univ. of Rochester; Research Fellow, LSE and Grad. Inst. of Int. Studies; William H. Abbott Prof. of Int. Business, Univ. of Chicago Grad. School of Business 1980–; Research Assoc. Nat. Bureau of Econ. Research 1981–; fmr mem. US Council of Econ. Advisers; fmr Visiting Prof. Asian and Research Depts of IMF; Econ. Counsellor and Dir Research Dept IMF 1991–2001, Special Adviser to Man. Dir 2001–; currently Sr Fellow, Inst. for Int. Econs. *Address:* Institute for International Economics, 1750 Massachusetts Avenue, NW, Washington, DC 20036, USA (office). *Telephone:* (202) 328-9000 (office). *Fax:* (202) 695-3225 (office). *Website:* www.iie.com (office).

MUSSELWHITE, Charlie, (Memphis Charlie); American blues-harp player; b. 31 Jan. 1944, Kosciusko, Miss.; s. of the late Ruth Maxine Musselwhite; m. Henrietta; ed Memphis Tech. High School; concerts tours in USA; performed on albums with Bonnie Raitt, The Blind Boys of Alabama, Tom Waits, Mickey Hart and INXS; Presenter, weekly radio show Charlie's Back Room (KRSH); 22 W.C.Handy awards, Lifetime Achievement Awards (Monterey Blues Festival, San Javier Jazz Festival, Spain), Mississippi Gov.'s Award for Excellence in the Arts, Pete Pedersen Lifetime Achievement Award, Howlin' Wolf Award, Trophées France Blues 2000, 2002. *Recordings include:* Stand Back! 1967, Louisiana Fog 1968, Stone Blues 1968, Tennessee Woman 1968, Memphis, Tennessee 1970, The Harmonica According to Charlie Musselwhite 1979, Curtain Call Cocktails 1982, Mellow-Dee 1986, Ace of Harps 1990, Signature 1991, Where Have All the Good Times Gone? 1992, In My Time 1993, Memphis Charlie 1993, The Blues Never Die 1994, Takin' Care of Business 1995, Rough News 1997, Continental Drifter 1999, Best of the Vanguard Years 2000, One Night in America 2002, Sanctuary 2004, Delta Hardware 2006, Rough Dried 2007. *E-mail:* henri@sonic.net (office). *Address:* c/o The Rosebud Music Booking Agency (office). *Telephone:* (415) 386-3456 (office). *Fax:* (1225) 743787 (office). *Website:* www.charliemusselwhite.com (home); www.realworldrecords.com (office); www.rosebudus.com (office).

MUSTAFAJ, Besnik; Albanian academic and politician; b. 23 Sept. 1958, Bajram Curri City; m.; two c.; ed Tirana Univ.; Prof. of Foreign Literature, Faculty of History and Philology, Tirana Univ. 1983–91; founding mem. Democratic Party of Albania (DPA) 1990–, Sec. for Int. Relations 1999–2005; elected MP 1991, Deputy Chair. Foreign Relations Comm. 2001–05, Deputy Chair. of Perm. Del. to European Parl. 2001–05; Amb. to France and Perm. Rep. to UNESCO, Paris 1992–97; Minister of Foreign Affairs 2005–07 (resgnd); co-founder Albanian Helsinki Cttee 1990; Founding Chair. Albanian Writers' Pen Club. *Publications:* Vera pa kthim (The Summer of no Return)

1989, Gjinkallat e vapës (The Cicadas of the Heat) 1994, Një sagë e vogël (A Little Saga) 1995, Daullja prej letre (The Paper Drum) 1996, Boshti (The Void) 1998; several books and papers on poetry and aesthetics. *Address:* c/o Ministry of Foreign Affairs, Bulevardi Gjergj Fishta 6, Tirana, Albania (office).

MUSTAPHA, Faisz, PC, LLB, HE; Sri Lankan lawyer and diplomatist; m. Ameena Mustapha; fmr lawyer; mem. Perm. Court of Arbitration 1993–; Chair. Sri Lanka Comm. on Elimination Discrimination and Monitoring Fundamental Rights; fmr Chair. and mem. Finance Comm.; mem. Sri Lanka Law Comm.; Deputy-Pres. Bar Asscn; fmr Chair. Sri Lanka Human Rights Comm.; Trustee Lt-Gen. Denzil Kobbekaduwa Trust; High Commr to UK 2002–05 (also accred as Amb. to Ireland 2003–05); currently Pres.'s Counsel, mem. Presidential Panel of Legal/Constitutional Experts 2006–, Presidential Comm. of Inquiry into failed finance cos 2007–. *Address:* c/o President's Secretariat, Republic Sq., Colombo 1, Sri Lanka. *Telephone:* (911) 2324801. *Fax:* (11) 2331246. *E-mail:* gosl@presidentsl.org. *Website:* www.presidentsl .org.

MUSTAPHA, Shettima, BSc, PhD; Nigerian politician; *Minister of Defence;* b. 26 Nov. 1939, Nguru; ed Ahmadu Bello Univ., Zaria, Univ. of Cambridge, UK, Purdue Univ., USA; Commr, Borno State 1979–83; cand. for Vice-Pres. in 1983 election; held as political prisoner 1983–85; Regional Head of Jos Office, Fed. Agric. Coordinating Unit, Fed. Ministry of Agric. 1985–89, Head of Agric. Projects Monitoring and Evaluation Unit 1989–90, Minister of Agric. and Natural Resources 1990–92; Nat. Treas. People's Democratic Party 1998–2001; fmr Chair. Savannah Bank of Nigeria plc; Minister of Defence 2008–; fmr consultant to World Bank, IFAD, FAO, UNDP; Fellow, Genetics Soc. of Nigeria; mem. American Soc. of Agronomy, Agricultural Soc. of Nigeria; Hon. Fellow, Entomological Soc. of Nigeria; Officer, Order of the Fed. Repub. *Address:* Ministry of Defence, Ship House, Central Area, Abuja, Nigeria (office). *Telephone:* (9) 2340534 (office). *Fax:* (9) 2340714 (office). *E-mail:* mamed@nigeria.gov.ng (office).

MUSTILL, Baron (Life Peer), cr. 1992, of Pateley Bridge in the County of North Yorkshire; **Michael John Mustill,** Kt, PC, FBA; British judge, author and arbitrator (retd); b. 10 May 1931; s. of Clement Mustill and the late Marion Mustill; m. 1st Beryl R. Davies (divorced); m. 2nd Caroline Phillips; two s. one step d.; ed Oundle School and St John's Coll., Cambridge; called to Bar, Gray's Inn 1955, Bencher 1976, QC 1968; Deputy Chair. Hants. Quarter Sessions 1971; Recorder, Crown Court 1972–78; Judge, High Court, Queen's Bench Div. 1978–85; Presiding Judge, NE Circuit 1981–84; a Lord Justice of Appeal 1985–92; Lord of Appeal in Ordinary 1992–97; Pres. British Maritime Law Asscn 1995–, Chartered Inst. of Arbitrators 1995–98, Asscn of Average Adjusters 1996–97, Seldon Soc. 1997–2000; Yorke Distinguished Visiting Fellow, Univ. of Cambridge 1996–; mem. Comité Maritime Arbitration 1996–, Indian Council of Arbitration; Hon. Prof. of Law, Univ. of Birmingham 1995–. *Publications:* The Law and Practice of Commercial Arbitration in England (with S. C. Boyd) 1982, Anticipatory Breach of Contract 1990; articles in legal journals. *Address:* Essex Court Chambers, 24 Lincoln's Inn Fields, London, WC2A 3ED (office); House of Lords, Westminster, London, SW1A 0PW; 42 Laurier Road, London, NW5 1SJ, England (home). *Telephone:* (20) 7813-8000 (office); (20) 7485-3726 (home). *Fax:* (20) 7813-8080 (office).

MUSTONEN, Olli; Finnish pianist, composer and conductor; b. 7 June 1967, Helsinki; s. of Seppo Mustonen and Marja-Liisa Mustonen; m. Sole Mustonen; began studies with harpsichord, studied piano with Ralf Gothóni and Eero Heinonen, composition with Einojuhani Rautavaara; has played with many of the world's leading orchestras; has appeared at festivals including Berlin, Hollywood Bowl, BBC Proms and Salzburg; Artistic Dir Turku Music Festival 1990–92, Ludus Mustonalis concert series; co-founder and Dir, Helsinki Festival Orchestra; Conductor, Tapiola Sinfonietta 2003–; Edison Award 1992, Gramophone Award for Best Instrumental Recording 1992. *Major compositions:* Fantasia (for piano and strings) 1985, Toccata (for piano, string quartet and double bass) 1989, two Nonets (for two string quartets and double bass) 1995, 2000, Triple Concerto (for three violins and orchestra) 1998, Jehkin Iivana Sonata for piano 2006, Sinuhe Sonata for solo oboe 2005–06. *Leisure interests:* mathematics, nature, politics, sports. *Address:* c/o Van Walsum Management Ltd, 11 York Road, London, SE1 7NX, England (office). *Telephone:* (20) 7902-0520 (office). *Fax:* (20) 7902-0520 (office). *E-mail:* vwm@ vanwalsum.com (office). *Website:* www.vanwalsum.co.uk (office).

MUSYOKA, (Stephen) Kalonzo, LLB; Kenyan lawyer and politician; *Vice President and Minister of Home Affairs;* b. 24 Dec. 1953, Tseikuru village, Mwingi Dist; m. Pauline Musyoka; four c.; ed Univ. of Nairobi; lawyer with Kaplan & Stratton Advocates; Sr Pnr, Musyoka & Wambua Advocates; mem. Parl. 1985, Deputy Speaker, Nat. Ass. 1988–93; Sec. Kitui branch, Kenya African Nat. Union (KANU) Party 1985–88, fmr Nat. Organizing Sec. 1988, Vice-Chair. 2002; Asst Minister for Work, Housing and Planning 1986–88; Minister of Foreign Affairs 1992–98, 2002–04; fmr Minister of Educ., Tourism and Information; Minister of the Environment and Natural Resources 2004–05; defected from KANU to launch Liberal Democratic Party just before Dec. 2002 presidential elections, Leader, Orange Democratic Movement—Kenya 2007–; unsuccessful cand. in presidential elections 2007; Vice Pres. of Kenya and Minister of Home Affairs 2008–. *Address:* Kenya National Assembly, Parliament Buildings, PO Box 41842, Nairobi (office); Rehani House, 9th Floor, Koinange Street, PO Box 67121, Nairobi, Kenya (office). *Telephone:* (20) 221291 (Parliament) (office); (20) 213460 (office). *Fax:* (20) 336589 (Parliament) (office); (20) 214787 (office). *E-mail:* odmk2007@yahoo .com (home). *Website:* www.bunge.go.ke (office); odmk.org (office).

MUTA, Taizo, BSc, MSc, DSc; Japanese theoretical physicist, university administrator and academic; *President, Hiroshima University;* b. 1 June 1937; ed Kyushu Univ., Tokyo Univ.; Research Assoc., Faculty of Science, Kyoto

Univ. 1965–71, Asst Prof., Research Inst. for Fundamental Physics 1971–82; Prof., Faculty of Science, Hiroshima Univ. 1982–, mem. Senate 1991, Presidential Aide 1993–95, Dean Faculty of Science 1995–99, Vice-Pres. 1999–2001, Prof., Grad. School of Science 2000–, Pres. 2001–. *Publications:* Foundations of Quantum Chromodynamics: An Introduction to Perturbative Methods in Gauge Theories (World Scientific Lecture Notes in Physics, Vol. 5) 1984, 1990 International Workshop of Strong Coupling Gauge Theories and Beyond, July 28–31, 1990, Nagoya, Japan 1991, International Workshop on Electroweak Symmetry Breaking: November 12–15, 1991 Hiroshima (co-author) 1992; numerous scientific papers in professional journals on the theory of elementary particles, quantum chromodynamics and dynamical symmetry breaking in quantum field theory. *Leisure interests:* astronomy, fishing, skiing. *Address:* Office of the President, Hiroshima University, 3-2 Kagamiyama 1-chome, Higashi-Hiroshima 739-8511, Japan (office). *Telephone:* (82) 422-7111 (office). *Fax:* (82) 424-6179 (office). *E-mail:* muta@ hiroshima-u.ac.jp (office). *Website:* www.hiroshima-u.ac.jp (office).

MUTALIBOV, Ayaz Niyazi Oğlu; Azerbaijani politician; b. 12 May 1938, Baku; m. Adilia Khanum; two s.; ed M. Azizbekov Azerbaijani Inst. of Oil and Chem.; mem. CPSU 1963–91; engineer, later Dir Baku Refrigerator Manu-facturing Plant; Dir Baku Asscn for Production of Refrigerators and House-hold Equipment 1974–77; Second Sec. of Narimanov Dist Party Cttee 1977–79; Minister of Local Industry for Azerbaijan SSR 1979–82; Vice-Chair. Council of Ministers Azerbaijan SSR 1982–89, Chair. 1989–91; Pres. Gosplan for Repub. 1982–89; First Sec., Cen. Cttee Azerbaijan CP 1990–91; USSR People's Deputy 1989–91; mem. CPSU Politburo 1990–91; Pres. of Azerbaijan 1991–92 (resgnd); charged with organizing a coup and impeached 1992, arrested in Moscow in 1996, released due to ill health; elected Chair. Civic Unity Party 2000; candidature for 2003 presidential elections blocked by electoral comm.; arrest warrant issued by Prosecutor-Gen. of Azerbaijan 2005; currently lives in Moscow. *Address:* c/o Cultural-Educational Fund of Ayaz Mutalibov 'For the Progress of Azerbaijan', Pokrovskii bulv. 4/17/23, 101000, Moscow, Russia. *Telephone:* (095) 145-65-06. *Fax:* (095) 724-20-22.

MUTALOV, Abdulkhashim Mutalovich, PhD; Uzbekistan politician and business executive; b. 27 April 1947, Telyau, Tashkent Region; s. of Abdurahmonov Mutal and Abdurahmonova Turihon; m. Mutalova Hurinisa; one s.; ed All-Union Inst. of Food Industry; worker, Tashkent Factory of Bread Products; army service 1965–79; Dir Akhangaran Enterprise of Bread Products 1979–86; Deputy Minister of Bread Products Uzbek SSR 1986–87, Minister 1987–91; Deputy Chair. Cabinet of Ministers 1991–92; Prime Minister of Uzbekistan 1992–96; Chair. State grain co. Uzdon Makhsulot 1996–; Orden Znak Pochota 1986. *Publications:* Main Directions in Formation of Free-Market Relations in Grain-Processing Enterprises of the Republic of Uzbekistan 1993. *Leisure interests:* tennis. *Address:* Tegirmon Novvovhona Jihozlari LLC (Bakery Equipment Co.), Tashkent (office); Turob Tula Street 28–57, Chilanzar District, Tashkent, Uzbekistan (home). *Telephone:* (712) 984652 (office); (712) 1394184 (home). *Fax:* (712) 984656 (office). *E-mail:* gulnaz@corp.uzreport.com (home).

MUTAMBARA, Arthur, BSc, MSc, PhD; Zimbabwean politician; *Leader, Movement for Democratic Change;* b. 25 May 1966; ed Univ. of Zimbabwe, Univ. of Oxford, UK, MIT, USA; active in student politics in 1980s; worked as man. consultant, McKinsey and Co.; fmr Prof. of Business Strategy, Kellogg Business School, Northwestern Univ., USA; Man. Dir Africa Tech. and Business Inst. 2003–; leader of pro-Senate faction Movt for Democratic Change (MDC) party 2006–; arrested for political activities, released without charge, March and May 2006. *Address:* Movement for Democratic Change, Harvest House, 6th Floor, cnr Angwa Street and Nelson Mandela Avenue, Harare, Zimbabwe (office). *Website:* www.mdczimbabwe.org (office).

MUTASA, Didymus Noel Edwin; Zimbabwean politician; *Minister of State for National Security;* b. 27 July 1935, Rusape; ed Goromonzi Govt School, Univ. of Birmingham, UK; began career as clerk and admin. officer in civil service; Co-founder Southern Region Fed. Services Asscn 1960; Co-founder Cold Comfort Soc.(multi-racial farming cooperative) 1964–70; arrested 1970, held in solitary confinement, Sinoia Prison 1970–72; in exile 1972–79; Founder mem. Zimbabwe African Nat. Union (ZANU) Br., Birmingham, UK and Dist Chair. ZANU UK 1975; joined ZANU HQ, Maputo, Mozambique 1977, Deputy Sec. for Finance, ZANU Cen. Cttee 1978; mem. Parl. for Manicaland 1980–, Speaker of Parl. 1980–90, Sec. for Transport and Welfare 1984–, Minister for Political Affairs 1990, Anti-Corruption and Anti-Monopolies Programme Minister 2003–05, Minister of State for Nat. Security 2005–. *Address:* Ministry of National Security, Chaminuka Building, POB 2278, Harare (office); Zimbabwe African National Union—Patriotic Front, corner of Rotten Row and Samora Machel Avenue, POB 4530, Harare, Zimbabwe. *Telephone:* (4) 700501 (office); (4) 753329 (ZANU—PF) (office). *Fax:* (4) 732660 (office); (4) 774146 (ZANU—PF) (office). *Website:* www.zanupfpub .co.zw (office).

MUTAWAKIL, Wakil Ahmad; Afghan politician; served as spokesman and personal sec. to Taliban leader Mullah Mohammad Omar –1999; Foreign Minister in Taliban Govt of Islamic Emirate of Afghanistan 1999–2002; surrendered in Kandahar to govt troops following ousting of regime Feb. 2002, held for three years under house arrest in Kabul 2002–05; now part of present govt under admin of Hamid Karzai; cand. in parl. elections Sept. 2005.

MUTEBI II, HM Kabaka of Buganda; (Ronald Muwenda Mutebi); b. 13 April 1955, Mmengo; s. of the late Kabaka Sir Edward Fredrick Walugembe Mutesa II (King Freddy) and Lady Sarah Nalule Kisosonkole; m. Lady Sylvia Nagginda 1999; ed Kingsmead Preparatory School, Sussex, Bradford Public School, Reading, Magdalene Coll., Cambridge, UK; lived in exile in England following overthrow of his father Mutesa II by fmr Pres. of Uganda Milton

Obote 1966–86; Assoc. Ed. African Concord; returned to Uganda 1986; crowned 37th Kabaka (King) of Buganda, marking restoration of ancient kingdom of Buganda, 31 July 1993. *Leisure interest:* squash. *Address:* Mmengo Palace, PO Box 58, Kampala, Uganda.

MUTHARIKA, Bingu Wa, BCom, MA, PhD; Malawi politician, economist and head of state; *President;* b. Feb. 1934, Thyolo; m. Ethel Zvauya Nyoni; three d. one s.; ed Univ. of Delhi, India, George Washington Univ., USA, Univ. of Nairobi, Kenya, Pacific Western Univ., USA; accounts clerk, Soche Authority 1957–58; admin. officer, Civil Service 1963–64; Sr Prin., Civil Service, Zambia 1965–66; Chief, Africa Trade Centre, UN Econ. Comm. for Africa 1966–75; loan officer, World Bank 1975–78; several UN posts 1978–90 including Dir African Trade and Devt Finance; Sec.-Gen. COMESA 1991–97; fmr Minister for Econ. Planning and Devt; Pres. of Malawi 2004–, also C-in-C of Malawi Defence Force and Police Service, Minister of Agric. and Food Security and Minister of Educ., Science and Tech.; fmr mem. United Democratic Front; est. Democratic Progressive Party 2005; Founder and Pres. Reach Int.; mem. COMESA, Asscn of African Cen. Banks, Conf. of African Ministers of Finance, African Fed. of Chambers of Commerce and Industry, Fed. of Nat. Asscns of Women in Business in E and S Africa; Agricola Prize (FAO) 2008. *Publications:* Towards Multinational Economic Cooperation in Africa 1972, One Africa, One Destiny 1995, Out of Poverty: The Resumption of Economic Growth in Malawi 2003, Mabizinesi Aphindu 2003; numerous articles in int. journals. *Address:* Office of the President and Cabinet, Private Bag 301, Capital City, Lilongwe 3, Malawi (office). *Telephone:* 1789311 (office). *Fax:* 1788456 (office). *Website:* www.malawi.gov.mw/opc/opc.htm (office).

MUTHURAMAN, B., BTech; Indian steel industry executive; *Managing Director, Tata Steel;* b. 26 Sept. 1944; ed Indian Inst. of Tech. (IIT), Madras, Xavier's Labour Research Inst., Jamshedpur, Advanced Man. Programme, Centre Européen d'Éducation Permanente (CEDEP)/Institut Européen d'Admin des Affaires (INSEAD), France; joined Tata Steel as grad. trainee 1966, worked in areas of Iron-making and Eng Devt for 10 years, spent 19 years in Marketing and Sales Div. rising to Vice-Pres., selected to head Cold Rolling Mill Project 1995, Exec. Dir (Special Projects) 2000–01, Man. Dir Tata Steel 2001–; Chair. Tata Sponge Iron Ltd, Tata Steel KZN (Pty) Ltd, SA, TM International Logistics Ltd, The Tinplate Co. of India Ltd, Natsteel Asia Pte Ltd, Natsteel Asia (S) Pte Ltd, Singapore, Millennium Steel Public Co. Ltd, Bangkok; mem. Bd Dirs Tata Inc., New York, Tata Int. Ltd, Tata Industries Ltd, Mumbai, The Dhamra Port Co. Ltd; Chair. Bd of Govs Xavier Labour Relations Inst., Jamshedpur, Nat. Inst. of Tech., Jamshedpur, Research Council of Nat. Metallurgical Lab., Jamshedpur; Pres. Indian Inst. of Metals; mem. Bd of Dirs Int. Iron and Steel Inst., Brussels (mem. Exec. Cttee), West Bengal Industrial Devt Corpn Ltd, CEDEP; mem. UN Global Compact Bd, Nat. Council of Confed. of Indian Industries; mem. Bd Govs IIT, Kharagpur; Hon. Rotarian, Jamshedpur Rotary Club (East and West); Distinguished Alumnus Award, IIT, Madras 1997, Tata Gold Medal, Indian Inst. of Metals 2002, CEO of the Year Award, Indian Inst. of Materials Man. 2002, Nat. HRD Network Pathfinders Award in the CEO Category 2004, CEO of the Year, Business Standard 2005, CEO with Human Resources Orientation Award, World HRD Congress at Mumbai 2005, Management Man of the Year 2006–2007 Award, Bombay Man. Asscn 2007. *Leisure interests:* playing cricket and golf, reading literature on general management, finance, marketing and business. *Address:* The Tata Iron and Steel Co. Ltd, Bombay House, 24 Homi Mody Street, Mumbai 400 001, India (office). *Telephone:* (22) 6665-8282 (office). *Fax:* (22) 6665-8113 (office); (22) 6665-7725 (office). *E-mail:* muthuraman@tatasteel.com (office). *Website:* www.tatasteel.com (office).

MUTI, Riccardo; Italian conductor; *Music Director, Chicago Symphony Orchestra;* b. 28 July 1941, Naples; s. of Domenico Muti and Gilda Sellitto; m. Cristina Mazzavillani 1969; two s. one d.; ed San Pietro Conservatory, Majella, Naples and Milan Conservatory of Music; Prin. Conductor, Maggio Musicale, Florence 1969–81; Prin. Conductor, Philharmonia Orchestra, London 1973–82, Music Dir 1979–82, Conductor Laureate 1982–; Prin. Guest Conductor Philadelphia Orchestra 1977–80, Prin. Conductor and Music Dir 1980–92, Conductor Laureate 1992–; Music Dir La Scala, Milan 1986–2005; Prin. Conductor Filarmonica della Scala 1988–2005; Prin. Guest Conductor Designate Teatro dell'Opera, Rome, New York Philarmonic; Music Dir, Chicago Symphony Orchestra 2009–; concert tours in USA with Boston, Chicago and Philadilphia Orchestras; concerts at Salzburg, Edinburgh, Lucerne, Flanders and Vienna festivals; also conducted Berlin Philharmonic, Bayerische Rundfunk Sinfonie Orchester, Vienna Philharmonic, New York Philharmonic and Concertgebouw Amsterdam; opera: Florence, Munich, Covent Garden, La Scala, Ravenna, Vienna, Accad. di Santa Cecilia (Rome), Accademico Dell'Accademia Cherubini (Florence); Grand Golden Medal of the City of Monaco, Grand Silver Ehrenkreuz Medal (Austria), Officer Order of Merit (Germany), Verdienstkreuz (First Class, Germany) 1976, Cavaliere Gran Croce (Italy) 1991, Légion d'honneur (France), Hon. KBE 2000, Russian Order of Friendship 2001, Silver Medal of the Salzburg Mozarteum 2001; Hon. mem. American Acad. of Arts & Sciences; Hon. PhD (Weizmann Inst. of Science), Dr hc (Pennsylvania, Philadelphia, Bologna, Urbino, Milan, Cremona, Lecce); Guido Cantelli Award 1967, Diapason d'Oro, Premio Critica Discografia Italiana, Prix Académie nat. du disque 1977, Deutscher Schallplatten Preis, 'Bellini d'Oro', Abbiati Prize, Grand Prix du disque for La Traviata (Verdi), Requiem in C minor (Cherubini) 1982, Disco d' Oro for Music for Films, Wolf Prize 2000. *E-mail:* info@riccardomuti.com. *Website:* www.riccardomuti.com.

MUTKO, Vitalii Leontyevich, CandEconSci; Russian mechanical engineer and politician; *Minister of Sport, Tourism and Youth Policy;* b. 8 Dec. 1958, Kurinskaya, nr Tuapse, Krasnodar Territory; m.; two d.; ed Leningrad (now St Petersburg) Construction Vocational School No. 226, Petrokrepost (now

Shlisselburg) Nautical School, Leningrad Region, Leningrad River Vocational Coll., Leningrad Inst. of Water Transport, Faculty of Law, St Petersburg State Univ., St Petersburg State Univ. of Econs and Finance; served as seaman on ships from NW River Steam Navigation and Leningrad sea port 1977–78, originally worked on Vladimir Ilich river steamship, later transferred to work on river-sea dry cargo ship, also worked in port of Hamburg; Komsomol activist during his studies 1978, headed coll. Komsomol org., headed local trade union coll. cttee; joined CPSU 1979; following graduation, worked at Exec. Cttee of Kirov Dist Soviet of People's Deputies in Leningrad 1983, worked as an instructor and Head of Dept for Social Issues, Sec., later Chair. Exec. Cttee 1990, set up Council of Chairmen 1990; Deputy, Kirov Regional Council 1990, Head of Admin of Kirov Dist 1991; organized meetings of workers from Kirov factory against Aug. putsch conspirators 1991; Deputy Mayor of St Petersburg and Chair. of Mayor's Cttee on Social Issues 1992–95; Curator of Zenit St Petersburg Football Club 1992–95, Pres. 1995–2003; authorized rep. of Vladimir Putin in presidential elections 2000; headed electoral staff of St Petersburg Gov. cand. Valentina Matviyenko 2000; Pres. Russian Football Premier League 2001–03; Fed. Council rep. from St Petersburg Govt 2003–08, Chair. Comm. on Youth and Sport Affairs, mem. Cttee on Fed. and Regional Policy Issues, Comm. on Control of Maintenance of Activity of Fed. Council; Pres. Russian Football Union 2005; mem. Tech. and Devt Cttee of FIFA 2006–; Senator for St Petersburg (for second time) 2007–; mem. presidential cttee on devt of physical culture and sport, highest standard sport, and on preparation and direction of 2014 XXII Winter Olympic Games and XI Winter Paralympics in Sochi 2007–; Minister of Sport, Tourism and Youth Policy 2008–; Pres. Special Olympics Cttee for St Petersburg, Golden Pelican (charity); Order of Honour 1994, Order of Friendship 2002; medals dedicated 'In Commemoration of the 300th Anniversary of St Petersburg', 'In Commemoration of the 1000th Anniversary of Kazan'. *Address:* Federal Agency for Physical Culture and Sport, 105064 Moscow, 18 ulitsa Kazakova (office); Federal Agency for Tourism, 103084 Moscow, 47 ulitsa Myasnitskaya, Russia (office). *Telephone:* (495) 263-08-40 (Sport) (office); (495) 105-72-56 (Sport) (office); (495) 208-29-37 (Tourism) (office); (495) 207-79-07 (Tourism) (office). *Fax:* (495) 263-07-61 (Sport) (office). *E-mail:* info@rossport.ru (office); rustourism@ropnet.ru (office). *Website:* www .rossport.ru (office); www.russiatourism.ru (office).

MUTO, Kabun; Japanese politician; b. 18 Nov. 1926; s. of Kaichi Muto; m. Hisako Koketsu 1951; two s.; ed Kyoto Univ.; worked in family brewing business; mem. House of Reps 1967–; Parl. Vice-Minister of Home Affairs 1972–73, Minister of Agric., Forestry and Fisheries 1979–80, of Int. Trade and Industry Feb.–Dec. 1990, of Foreign Affairs April–Aug. 1993, Dir-Gen. Man. and Coordination Agency (State Minister) and Minister for Women's Affairs 1996–97; Chair. Liberal-Democratic Party (LDP) Commerce and Industry Div. 1974–76; Deputy Sec.-Gen. LDP 1978–79; mem. Standing Cttee on Budget, House of Reps, LDP Finance Cttee; Vice-Pres. LDP Cttee on Small and Medium Enterprises, LDP Tax Policy Cttee etc. *Publications:* Kusa-no-Ne Minshushugi (Grassroots Democracy), Jiminto Saisei no Teigen, Nihon no Sentaku (Japan's Choice) etc. *Address:* c/o Liberal-Democratic Party—LDP (Jiyu-Minshuto), 1-11-23, Nagata-cho, Chiyoda-ku, Tokyo 100-8910, Japan.

MUTOLA, Maria Lurdes; Mozambican athlete; b. 27 Oct. 1972, Maputo; d. of João Mutola and Catarina Mutola; ed Eugene High School, Ore., USA; gold medallist, 800m, World Indoor Championships 1993, 1995, 1997, 2001, 2003, 2004; winner 800m World Cup 1992, 1994, 1998, 2002; winner 800m Grand Prix Final 1993, 1995, 1999, 2001; gold medallist, 800m, World Championships 1995, 2001, 2003; bronze medallist, 800m, Olympic Games, Atlanta 1996, gold medallist 800m, Sydney 2000; winner 800m World Athletics Final 2003; world record holder at 1,000m indoor; African record holder at 800m and 1,000m (outdoor); between 1992 and 1995 she won 42 consecutive races; won all six Golden League races 2003 winning US$1 million prize; f. Lurdes Mutola Foundation 2001; Hon. UN Amb. 2003–. *Address:* c/o Lurdes Mutola Foundation, 25th of September Ave, Times Square Building, Block II, 1st Floor, Door 12, Maputo, Mozambique. *Website:* www.mariamutola.com; www .flmutola.org.mz.

MUTTER, Anne-Sophie; German violinist; b. 29 June 1963, Rheinfelden/ Baden; m. 1st Dithelf Wunderlich 1989 (deceased); m. 2nd André Previn 2002 (divorced 2006); studied with Prof. Aida Stucki, Winterthur, Switzerland; began musical career playing piano and violin 1969; played in the Int. Music Festival, Lucerne 1976; début with Herbert von Karajan at Pfingstfestspiele, Salzburg 1977; soloist with major orchestras of the world; also plays with string trio and quartet; Guest Teacher RAM, London 1985; est. foundation promoting gifted young string players throughout the world; Hon. Pres. Mozart Soc., Univ. of Oxford 1983; Youth Music Prize (FRG) for violin 1970, for piano 1970, for violin 1974; Artist of the Year, 'Deutscher Schallplattenpreis', Grand Prix Int. du Disque, Record Acad. Prize, Tokyo 1982, Internationaler Schallplattenpreis 1993; Order of Merit (of Germany, of Bavaria), Herbert von Karajan Award 2003. *Recordings include:* Mozart: Five Violin Concertos 2005, Bach, Gubaidulina: Violin Concertos (with the Trondheim Soloists) 2008, Mendelssohn's Violin Concerto 2009. *Leisure interests:* graphic arts, sport. *Address:* Kaye Artists Management, Barratt House, 7 Chertsey Road, Woking, GU21 5AB, England (office); Effnerstrasse 48, 81925 Munich, Germany; c/o London Symphony Orchestra, Barbican Hall, London, EC1, England. *Telephone:* (89) 984418 (Germany). *Fax:* (89) 9827186 (Germany).

MUZAFFAR, Chandra, PhD; Malaysian political scientist, academic and international organization executive; *President, International Movement for a Just World;* b. 10 March 1947, Bedong, Kedah; m.; two d.; ed Univ. of Singapore; Lecturer, Science Univ. of Malaysia 1970–83, Sr Research Fellow 1992–97; Prof. and first Dir Centre for Civilizational Dialogue, Univ. of

Malaya 1997–99; Founder-Pres. multi-ethnic social reform group Aliran Kesedaran Negara (Nat. Consciousness Movt) 1977–91; mem. Exec. Cttee Asian Comm. on Human Rights 1985; arrested by Malaysian Govt under Internal Security Act Oct. 1987, released without conditions Dec. 1987; nominated as monitor by Human Rights Watch 1988; Pres. Int. Movt for a Just World (JUST), Kuala Lumpur 1997–; Deputy Pres. Kealidan (Nat. Justice Party) 1999–2001; mem. Bd Dirs Integrity Inst., Malaysia 2004–, and several int. NGOs; Weigand Distinguished Visitor Fellowship, Duke Univ., USA 2000; Harry J. Benda Prize for distinguished scholarship on SE Asia, Asscn of Asian Studies, North America 1989. *Publications:* author or ed. of 20 books on religion, human rights, Malaysian politics, and int. relations, including Rights, Religion, and Reform 2002, Muslims, Dialogue, Terror 2003, Global Ethic or Global Hegemony? 2005; more than 500 articles in local and int. journals. *Leisure interest:* reading. *Address:* International Movement for a Just World, PO Box 288, 46730 Petaling Jaya, Selangor, Malaysia (office). *Telephone:* (3) 7960-3207 (office); (3) 6201-5170 (home). *Fax:* (3) 7960-3245 (office). *E-mail:* cmuzaffar@just-international.org (office). *Website:* www.just-international.org (office).

MUZI-FALCONI, Livio; Italian diplomatist; *President, Commission for Historic Archives;* b. 1 Sept. 1936, Oslo, Norway; s. of Baron Filippo Muzi Falconi and Marion Barton; m. Marina Chantre 1961; two s. two d.; ed Tamalpais School for Boys, San Rafael, Calif., Lowell High School, Univ. of San Francisco, Univ. of Genoa; joined Italian diplomatic corps 1960; Lt, Italian Air Force 1962; Vice-Consul Buenos Aires 1963–67; First Sec. Madrid Embassy 1967–70; Dept of Migratory Affairs Ministry of Foreign Affairs 1970–72; Counsellor London Embassy 1972–77; Consul Gen. Addis Ababa 1977–79; Coordinator European Affairs Ministry of Foreign Affairs 1979–83; Amb. to Nigeria (also Accred to Benin) 1983–87; Minister Embassy, London 1987–92; Deputy Head Italian State Protocol 1992–95; Chief of Protocol Exec. Office of Sec.-Gen. of UN 1995–98; elected rep. Italian diplomatic and other Trade Unions 1969–73, 1977–79, 1992–95; Head of Task Force, Ministry of Foreign Affairs; Hon. KCMG 1991; Grand Official Order of Repub. 1990. *Address:* Via A. Gramsci 9, 00197 Rome, Italy (home). *Telephone:* (6) 36914276 (office). *Fax:* (6) 36918630 (office). *E-mail:* livio.muzi@esteri.it (office).

MUZITO, Adolphe; Democratic Republic of the Congo economist and politician; *Prime Minister;* b. 1957; ed Univ. of Kinshasa; Regional Finance Insp., Finance Inspectorate Gen. 2007; Minister of the Budget 2007–08; Prime Minister 2008–; Sec.-Gen. Parti Lumumbiste Unifie 2007–. *Address:* Office of the Prime Minister, Kinshasa, Democratic Republic of the Congo (office).

MUZOREWA, Abel Tendekayi, MA, DD, DHL; Zimbabwean ecclesiastic; b. 14 April 1925, Old Umtali; s. of Philemon Haadi Muzorewa and Hilda Takaruda Muzorewa (née Munangatire); m. Margaret Muzorewa (née Chigodora); four s. one d.; ed Old Umtali Secondary School, Nyadiri United Methodist Mission, Cen. Methodist Coll., Fayette, Mo., Scarritt Coll., Nashville, Tenn., USA; Pastor, Chiduku N Circuit 1955–57; studied in USA 1958–63; pastor, Old Umtali Mission 1963; Dir of Youth Work, Rhodesia Annual Conf. 1965; Jt Dir of Youth Work, Rhodesia Christian Council 1965; Travelling Sec. Student Christian Movt 1965; Resident Bishop, United Methodist Church 1968–92; Pres. African Nat. Council (ANC) 1971–85, All-Africa Conf. of Churches; Rep. of UANC at Geneva Conf. on Rhodesia 1976; mem. Transitional Exec. Council to prepare transfer to majority rule in Rhodesia 1978–79, Prime Minister of Zimbabwe Rhodesia, Minister of Defence and Combined Operations June—Dec. 1979; attended Lancaster House Conf. 1979; contested March 1980 election as Leader of UANC; detained Nov. 1983–Sept. 1984; fled to USA 1985, returned to Zimbabwe Nov. 1986; Pres. of United Parties 1994–98; presidential cand. 1995; Pres. Coll. of Bishops United Methodist Church of Cen. Africa 1988–92; Bishop of Zimbabwe and Head of United Methodist Church; Hon. DD (Cen. Methodist Coll., Mo.) 1960; UN Prize for Outstanding Achievement in Human Rights 1973. *Publications:* Manifesto for African National Council 1972, Rise Up and Walk (autobiog.) 1978. *Leisure interests:* vegetable and flower growing, poultry raising. *Address:* PO Box 3408, Harare; PO Box 353, Borrowdale, Harare, Zimbabwe. *Telephone:* (4) 704127. *Fax:* (4) 745303.

MVOUBA, Isidore; Republic of the Congo politician; *Prime Minister, responsible for the Co-ordination of Government Action and Privatization;* b. 1954, Kindamba; with Chemin de fer Congo Océan 1977; mem. Parti Congolais du Travail; Countryside Dir for Sassou Nguesso 1992, 2002; Prin. Pvt. Sec. for Head of State 1997–99; fmr Minister for Transport, Civil Aviation and the Merchant Navy; Prime Minister, responsible for the Co-ordination of Govt Action and Privatization 2005–. *Address:* Office of the Prime Minister, Brazzaville, Republic of the Congo (office). *Telephone:* 81-10-67 (office). *Website:* www.congo-site.net (office).

MWAANGA, Vernon Johnson; Zambian diplomatist, politician and business executive; b. 1939; ed Hodgson Tech. Coll., Lusaka, Stanford Univ., USA and Oxford Univ., UK; joined Zambian independence movt 1960; mem. United Nat. Independence Party (UNIP) 1961, later Regional Party Sec., Monze and Choma Areas; Deputy High Commr for Zambia in UK 1964–65; Amb. to USSR 1965–68; Perm. Rep. to UN 1968–72; Ed.-in-Chief Times of Zambia 1972–73; Minister of Foreign Affairs 1973–75, 1991–92; apptd Minister of Information and Broadcasting Services 2002; Nat. Sec. Movt for Multi-party Democracy (MMD) –2005; mem. UNIP Cen. Cttee 1975; Chair. Curray Ltd, Bank of Credit and Commerce (Zambia) Ltd, Zambia Safaris Ltd; mem. Int. Public Relations Asscn; Fellow, London Inst. of Dirs. *Address:* c/o Movement for Multi-party Democracy (MMD), POB 30708, Lusaka, Zambia.

MWAKAWAGO, Daudi Ngelautwa; Tanzanian politician; b. Sept. 1939; ed Makerere Univ., Uganda, Victoria Univ. of Manchester, England; Tutor at Kivukoni Coll., Dar es Salaam 1965–72, Vice-Prin. 1970, Prin. 1971, 1977; Nat. MP 1970–75; Minister for Information and Broadcasting 1972–77; Constituent MP 1975; mem. Party of Constitution Comm. 1976; mem. Constituent Ass. 1977, Cen. Cttee Chama cha Mapinduzi 1977–; Minister of Information and Culture 1982–84, of Labour and Manpower Devt 1984–86, of Industries and Trade 1986–88; Perm. Rep. to UN, New York 1994–2003; Special Rep. of the UN Sec.-Gen. to Sierra Leone 2003–06; fmr mem. Historical Asscn of Tanzania, Nat. Adult Educ. Asscn of Tanzania, African Adult Educ. Asscn, Income Tax Local Cttee, Bd of Inst. of Adult Educ., Nat. Advisory Council on Educ.; fmr Dir Nat. Devt Corpn, Nat. Museum; Chair. Wildlife Corpn 1979–; Vice-Chair. Co-operative Coll., Moshi; mem. TIRDO.

MWAKWERE, Chirau Ali; Kenyan politician and diplomatist; b. 1945; Amb. to Zimbabwe –2004; Minister of Foreign Affairs June 2004–05. *Address:* c/o Ministry of Foreign Affairs, Treasury Building, Harambee Avenue, POB 30551, Nairobi, Kenya (office).

MWANSA, Kalombo T., LLB, LLM, MPhil, PhD; Zambian politician and professor of law; *Minister of Home Affairs;* b. 9 Sept. 1955, Nchelenge; m. 1983; two s. two d.; ed Univ. of Zambia, Harvard Univ., USA, Univs of Cambridge and London, UK; Tutor in Law, Univ. of Zambia 1979–80, Lecturer in Law and Criminology 1983–88, Acting Dean of Law School 1992–93; Perm. Sec. Ministry of Home Affairs 1993–98; Acting Chair. Police and Prisons Service Comm. 1994–96; Perm. Sec. of Admin, Cabinet Office 1998–99; Deputy Sec. to Cabinet 1999–2002, Acting Sec. 2001, 2002; Minister of Foreign Affairs 2002–04, of Home Affairs 2004–05, 2008–, of Mines and Mineral Devt 2005–08; nominated mem. Parl. 2002–; Livingstone Scholar, Jesus Coll. Cambridge 1982–83; Commonwealth Scholar, SOAS 1988–92; awards from Lusaka Hindu Asscn, Law Asscn of Zambia. *Publications include:* Property Crime in Zambia, Death Penalty in Zambia, Zambia Police and Crime Prevention, Juvenile Delinquency in Zambia. *Leisure interests:* reading, vegetable gardening, soccer. *Address:* Ministry of Home Affairs, POB 32862, Lusaka, Zambia (office). *Telephone:* (21) 1213505 (office).

MWAPE, Augustine Festus Lupando; Zambian politician; *Ambassador to China;* fmr engineer, teacher; mem. Parl. for Lukashya constituency; Minister of Communications and Transport –2003; Deputy Minister of Northern Prov. –2004; Vice-Pres. of Zambia 2004–06; Ambassador to China 2007–; Spontaneous Award, Ngoma Awards. *Address:* Zambian Embassy, Dong Si Jie, San Li Tun, Beijing, 100600, People's Republic of China (office). *Telephone:* (10) 65321554 (office). *Fax:* (10) 65321891 (office).

MWEMWENIKARAWA, Nabuti; I-Kiribati politician; Minister for Finance and Econ. Devt –2007. *Address:* c/o Ministry of Finance and Economic Development, POB 67, Bairiki, Tarawa, Kiribati (office).

MWENCHA, J.E.O. (Erastus), MA, MBS; Kenyan economist and international finance official; m.; three c.; ed Univ. of Nairobi, York Univ., Canada; entered civil service 1974, becoming Prin. Industrial Devt Officer; Dir Kenya Medical Research Inst.; Dir Kenya Industrial Research and Devt Inst.; Sec. Industrial Sciences Advisory Council; Sr Industrial Expert, Econ. Comm. for Africa 1983; Dir of Industry, Energy and Environment, Preferential Trade Area for Eastern and Southern Africa 1987–97; Acting Sec.-Gen. Common Market for Eastern and Southern Africa (COMESA) 1997–98, Sec.-Gen. 1998–2008; Order of the Moran of the Burning Spear 1998. *Publications:* contrib. to The Free Trade Area of the Common Market for Eastern and Southern Africa (COMESA). *Leisure interests:* playing golf, ardent Christian. *Address:* c/o COMESA Centre, Ben Bella Road, P.O. Box 30051, 10101 Lusaka, Zambia (office).

MWINYI, Ali Hassan; Tanzanian fmr head of state, teacher and diplomatist; b. 8 May 1925, Kivure, Mkuranga Dist, Tanganyika; m. Siti A. Mwinyi 1960; five s. four d.; ed secondary school, Dole, Zanzibar, Zanzibar Teachers' Training Coll., Durban Univ. Inst. of Educ. and Hall Univ., UK; moved to Zanzibar as a child; primary schoolteacher at Mangapwani, Zanzibar 1945–50; Headteacher, Bumbwini Primary School 1950–54; Tutor, Zanzibar Teachers' Training Coll. 1956–61, later Prin.; joined Shiraz Party (ASP) 1964; Prin. Perm. Sec. of Educ. Zanzibar 1964–65; Asst Gen. Man. Zanzibar State Trading Corpn 1965–70; Asst Treasurer Makadara ASP Br., Zanzibar 1966–70; Chair. E African Currency Bd 1964–70, Nat. Kiswahili Council (BAKITA) 1964–77, Zanzibar Censorship Board 1964–65, Tanzania Food and Nutrition Council (LISHE); Minister of State, Office of Pres., Tanzania 1970; Minister for Health 1972–75, for Home Affairs 1975–77; Amb. to Egypt 1977–82; Minister of Natural Resources and Tourism 1982–83, of State in Vice-Pres.'s Office 1983–84; interim Pres. of Zanzibar Feb.–April 1984, Pres. April 1984; Vice-Pres. of Tanzania 1984–85, Pres. 1985–95, also fmr Minister of Defence and Nat. Service; fmr C-in-C of Armed Forces; mem. Chama Cha Mapinduzi (CCM or Revolutionary Party), Vice-Chair. 1984–90, Chair. 1990–96; Chair. Commonwealth Observer Mission to Regional and Gen. Elections in Guyana 6–19th Dec. 1997, OAU Mission to Regional and Gen. Elections in Nigeria Feb.–March 1998, Nat. Advisory Bd on the Control of HIV/AIDS; mem. Tanzania-Britain Soc.; fmr mem. Council Univ. of Dar es Salaam; Patron Tanzania Union Govt and Health Employees, Dar es Salaam Islamic Club, Tanzania Railway Workers Union, Muslims' Asscn for the Revertees, Shinyanga Orphanage Centre, Union of Tanzania Press Club, Tanzania Heralds for Youth Services, Publishers' Asscn of Tanzania, Tanga Muslim Org., Tanzania Muslim Hajj Trust; Hon. Life mem. Tanzania Law Soc. *Address:* c/o State House, Dar es Salaam, Tanzania.

MWINYI, Hussein Ali, MD; Tanzanian physician and politician; *Minister of Defence and National Service;* b. 23 Dec. 1966; ed Azania Secondary School, Tambaza High School, Marmara Univ., Turkey, Hammersmith Hosp., UK; doctor, Ministry of Health 1993–97, specialist doctor 1997–98; Lecturer in Medicine, Hubert Kairuki Memorial Univ. 1998–2000; Deputy Minister of Health 2000–05; MP for Kwahani 2005–; Minister of State for Union Affairs 2006–08; Minister of Defence and Nat. Service 2008–; mem. Chama Cha

Mapinduzi (CCM—Revolutionary Party of Tanzania). *Address:* Ministry of Defence and National Service, PO Box 9544, Dar es Salaam, Tanzania (office). *Telephone:* (22) 2117153 (office). *Fax:* (22) 2116719 (office).

MWIRARIA, Daudi; Kenyan politician; b. 3 Sept. 1938, Meru; ed Univ. of London, UK and Univ. of E Africa; statistician for E African Common services org. 1962, then Dir E African Statistical Dept; Sec., Common Market, E African Community; Perm. Sec. in various ministries 1977–88; retd from Civil Service to enter politics 1992, MP (Democratic Party–DP) for N Imenti 1992–; Minister of Finance 2003–06 (resgnd); founder mem. and Leader Cen. Kenya Parl. Group; Deputy Chair. DP. *Leisure interests:* reading, farming, photography, golfing. *Address:* c/o Democratic Party of Kenya (DP), Continental House, POB 56396, Nairobi 30007 Kenya (office).

MYAGKOV, Andrei Vasilyevich; Russian actor; b. 8 July 1938, Leningrad; ed Leningrad Inst. of Chemical Tech., Studio-School, Moscow Art Theatre; began acting in Sovremennik Theatre 1965–77, with Moscow Art Theatre 1977–; USSR State Prize, RSFSR State Prize, RSFSR People's Artist. *Theatre includes:* Aduyev in Ordinary Story, Trubetskoy in Decembrists, Repetilov in Trouble from Intelligence, Misail in Boris Godunov. *Films include:* Pokhozhdeniya zubnogo vracha (Adventures of a Dentist) 1965, Staryy dom (The Old House) 1969, Bratya Karamazovy (The Brothers Karamazov) 1969, Moya sudba 1970, Nezhdannyy gost (The Uninvited Guest) 1972, Grossmeyster 1972, Nadezhda (Hope) 1973, Utrenniy obkhod (Morning Round) 1974, Strakh vysoty (Fear of the Height) 1975, Vy mne pisali… 1976, Sluzhebnyy roman (Office Romance) 1977, Primite telegrammu v dolg 1979, Garazh 1979, Rassledovaniye 1980, 4:0 v polzu Tanechki (4:0 for Tanechka) 1982, Poslesloviye (Epilogue) 1983, Oglyanis!… (Turn Back!…) 1983, Letargiya 1983, Polosa prepyatstviy (Stripe of Obstacles) 1984, Zhestokiy romans (A Cruel Romance) 1984, Poslednyaya doroga (The Last Road) 1986, Ot zarplaty do zarplaty (From Pay to Pay) 1986, Chelovek, kotoryy bral intervyu 1986, Svobodnoye padeniye 1987, Silnee vsekh inykh veleniy (Above All Else) 1987, Kuvyrok cherez golovu 1987, Mat (Mother) 1989, Vinovata li ya… (Am I Guilty…) 1992, Na Deribasovskoy khoroshaya pogoda, ili na Brayton Bich opyat idut dozhdi (There's Good Weather in Deribasovskaya, It's Raining Again in Brighton Beach) 1992, Osenniye soblazny (Autumn Temptations) 1993, Iskusstvo umirat (The Art of Dying) 1995, Privet, duralei! (Hello, Fools!) (voice) 1996, Kontrakt so smertyu 1998, Skaz pro Fedota-streltsa (The Tale of Fedot, the Shooter) 2002. *Television includes:* Ironiya sudby, ili S lyogkim parom! (Irony of Fate) 1975, Dni Turbinykh 1976, Iz zapisok Lopakhina (From Lopakhin's Notes) 1977, Aktivnaya zona (Active Zone) 1979, Gonki po vertikali (Vertical Races) 1983, 32oe dekabrya 2004. *Address:* General Yermolov str. 6, Apt 42, 121293 Moscow, Russia. *Telephone:* (495) 148-93-64.

MYAING, U Linn, BSc; Myanma diplomatist; b. 15 Oct. 1947, Yangon; m. Daw Thi Thi Ta; two d.; ed Defence Studies Acad.; commissioned as officer in Myanmar Navy 1967–93; Deputy Dir Americas Div., Political Dept, Ministry of Foreign Affairs 1993–94, served first as Counsellor, then as Minister Counsellor, Perm. Mission to UN and other Int. Orgs, Geneva 1994–97, Deputy Dir Gen. Ministry of Foreign Affairs, also attached as Minister, Deputy Perm. Rep. to Perm. Mission of Myanmar, Geneva 1998–99, Amb. to France (also accred to UNESCO) 1999–2001 (also accred to Belgium, the Netherlands, Switzerland and EU) 2000–01, Amb. to USA 2001–07. *Address:* Ministry of Foreign Affairs, Nay Pyi Taw, Myanmar (office). *Website:* www.mofa.gov.mm (office).

MYASNIKOV, Vladimir Stepanovich, DrHist; Russian historian and sinologist; *Head, Centre for Chinese and Russian Relations and Deputy Director, Institute of Far East, Russian Academy of Sciences;* b. 15 May 1931, Moscow; ed Moscow State Inst. of Int. Relations; researcher Inst. of Sinology 1956–60, Inst. of Peoples of Asia 1963–64, Inst. of Econs of World Socialist System 1964–66; researcher, Scientific Sec., Head of Div. Inst. of Far East, Russian Acad. of Sciences 1966–85, Deputy Dir 1985–, Head Centre for Chinese and Russian Relations 1992–; Corresp. mem. Russian Acad. of Sciences 1990, mem. 1997. *Publications:* over 150 published works, books, monographs. *Address:* Institute of Far East, Russian Academy of Sciences, Nakhimovsky prosp. 32, 117218 Moscow (office); Novocheremoushkinskaya str. 49, 160 Moscow, Russia (home). *Telephone:* (495) 124-07-22 (office). *Fax:* (495) 718-96-56 (office). *E-mail:* ifes@cemi.rssi.ru (office).

MYASOYEDOV, Boris Fedorovich; Russian chemist; b. 2 Oct. 1930; m.; one s.; ed Moscow I. Mendeleyev Inst. of Chem. and Tech.; Jr, Sr Researcher, Head of Lab, Deputy Dir V. Vernadsky Inst. of Geochem. and Analytical Chem.; Corresp. mem. USSR (now Russian) Acad. of Sciences 1990, mem. 1994; research in chem. of radioactive elements, radionucleides, creation and application of chem. sensors and analysers; USSR State Prize, V. Khlopin Prize Acad. of Sciences. *Publications:* Chemical Sensors: Possibilities and Perspectives 1990. *Leisure interests:* music, stamp collecting. *Address:* Institute of Geochemistry and Analytical Chemistry, Kosygin str. 19, 117975 Moscow, Russia. *Telephone:* (495) 137-41-47 (office); (495) 420-90-81 (home). *Fax:* (495) 938-20-54.

MYERS, A. Maurice (Maury), BA, MBA; American business executive; b. 1941, Long Beach, Calif.; m. Jean Myers; three d.; ed Calif. State Univ. at Fullerton, Long Beach State Univ.; began career in financial man. training programme, Ford Motor Co.; fmr Sr Dir Passenger Market Devt, Continental Airlines; joined Aloha Air Group, Honolulu 1983, Pres. and CEO –1994; Pres. and COO America W Airlines, Phoenix 1994–96; Chair., Pres. and CEO Yellow Corpn 1996–99; Chair., Pres. and CEO Waste Man. Inc. 1999–2004; Ellis Island Medal of Honor 2002. *Address:* c/o Waste Management Incorporated, 1001 Fannin Street, Suite 4000, Houston, TX 77002, USA (office).

MYERS, Barton, MArch, FAIA; American/Canadian architect, planner and academic; *President, Barton Myers Associates Inc.;* b. 6 Nov. 1934, Norfolk, Va; s. of Barton Myers and Meeta Myers (née Burrage); m. Victoria George 1959; one d.; ed Norfolk Acad., U.S. Naval Acad. and Univ. of Pennsylvania; Partner, A. J. Diamond & Barton Myers, Toronto 1968–75; Founder and Prin. Barton Myers Assocs Inc., Toronto 1975–86, Barton Myers Assocs Inc., LA 1981–; Asst Prof. of Architecture Univ. of Toronto 1968–70; mem. Advisory Cttee Nat. Capital Comm., Ottawa 1968–74; Founder and Pres. Bd of Dirs, Trace Magazine 1980–82; Visiting Prof., Harvard Grad. School of Design 1981; Sr Prof., School of Architecture and Urban Design, UCLA 1981–; mem. AIA, Soc. of Architectural Historians, GSA Nat. Register of Peer Professionals; numerous design awards, including Royal Architectural Inst. of Canada Gold Medal 1994, several AIA awards including Los Angeles Gold Medal 2002. *Major works by Diamond & Myers Assocs include:* York Square, Toronto; Ont. Medical Asscn, Toronto; Myers & Wolf Residences, Toronto; Housing Union Bldg, Univ. of Alberta Citadel Theatre, Edmonton; Dundas-Sherborne Housing, Toronto. *Major works by Barton Myers Assocs Inc. include:* Seagram Museum, Waterloo, Ont.; Howard Hughes Center, LA; Wang Tower, LA; Performing Arts Center, Portland, Ore.; Pasadena City Center; Music Center Expansion, LA; CBC Network HQ, Toronto; Cerritos Center for the Performing Arts, Calif.; Woodsworth Coll., Univ. of Toronto; NW Campus Housing, UCLA; Art Gallery of Ont. expansion (competition winner); York Univ. Fine Arts Bldg expansion, Toronto; New Jersey Performing Arts Center, Newark (New Jersey Golden Trowel Award, Int. Masonry Inst., Chicago Athenaeum Award 1998); The Ice House Renovation, Beverly Hills, Calif.; UCSD/Scripps Ocean Atmosphere Research Facility, La Jolla, Calif.; Univ. of New Mexico, Albuquerque (Master Devt Plan); Hall of Justice, Sacramento, Calif. (Historical Preservation Award Calif. Preservation Foundation 2002); House and studio at Toro Canyon, Montecito, Calif. (CCAIA Honor Award in Design 2000, AIA PIA Housing Award for Innovation in Housing Design 2002); 421 South Beverly Drive, Beverly Hills, Calif. (Beverly Hills Architectural Design Award 2002); Tempe Center for the Arts, Tempe, Ariz. 2006. *Publications:* Barton Myers Selected and Current Works (in The Master Architect series) 1994, New Stage for a City (monograph) 1998, Barton Myers: 3 Steel Houses (House Design series) 2004. *Leisure interests:* travel, reading. *Address:* Barton Myers Associates Inc., 1025 Westwood Boulevard, Los Angeles, CA 90024, USA (office). *Telephone:* (310) 208-2227 (office). *Fax:* (310) 208-2207 (office). *E-mail:* b_myers@bartonmyers.com (office). *Website:* bartonmyers.com (office).

MYERS, Dale Dehaven, BSAE; American engineer, business executive and consultant; b. 8 Jan. 1922, Kansas City, Mo.; s. of Wilson A. Myers and Ruth Myers; m. Marjorie Williams 1943; two d.; ed Univ. of Washington, Seattle; Aerophysics Dept, N American 1946, Chief Engineer, Missile Div. 1954, Vice-Pres. and Program Man. Hound Dog Air-Launched Missile Program 1957; Vice-Pres. and Program Man., Apollo Command and Service Modules, N American 1964; Assoc. Admin. for Manned Space Flight, NASA Headquarters 1970–74, Deputy Admin., NASA 1986–89; US Govt Rep. to AGARD 1988–89; Pres. N American Aircraft Operations, Rockwell Int. Corpn 1974–77, Corporate Vice-Pres. 1974–77; Under-Sec., Dept of Energy, Washington 1977–79; Pres. and COO Jacobs Eng Group Inc., Pasadena 1979–84; Pres. Dale Myers and Assocs, Leucadia, 1984–86, 1989–; mem. Bd of Dirs Ducommun Inc., 1982–86, Jacob's Eng Group 1979–86, MacNeal Schwendler Corpn 1990–98, SYS 1984–86, SAIC's GSC 1993–97, San Diego Aerospace Museum 1992–2004; mem. NASA Advisory Comm. 1984–86, NASA Aero Comm. 1994–97; Fellow, American Astronautical Soc.; mem. Nat. Acad. of Engineers 1974, Int. Acad. of Astronautics 1991; Hon. Fellow, AIAA; Hon. PhD (Whitworth Coll.); NASA Public Service Award 1969, NASA Distinguished Service Medal 1971, 1974, DSM (Dept of Energy) 1979. *Leisure interests:* golf, old cars. *Address:* PO Box 232518, Encinitas, CA 92023, USA. *Telephone:* (760) 753-4043 (office); (760) 753-5770 (home).

MYERS, Margaret Jane (Dee Dee), BS; American broadcaster, magazine editor and fmr government official; *President, Dee Dee Myers & Associates;* b. 1 Sept. 1961, Quonset Point, RI; d. of Stephen George Myers and Judith Ann Burleigh; one d.; ed Univ. of Santa Clara; Press Asst Mondale for Pres. Campaign, LA 1984, to deputy Senator Art Torres, LA 1985; Deputy Press Sec. to Mayor Tom Bradley, LA 1985–87, Tom Bradley for Gov. Campaign 1986; Calif. Press Sec. Dukakis for Pres. Campaign, LA 1988; Press Sec. Feinstein for Gov. Campaign, LA and San Francisco 1989–90; Campaign Dir Jordan for Mayor Campaign, San Francisco 1991; Press Sec. Clinton for Pres. Campaign, Little Rock 1991–92, White House, Washington 1993–94; Co-Host Equal Time, CNBC, Washington 1995–97; Contributing Ed. Vanity Fair magazine, Washington 1995–; founder and Pres. Dee Dee Myers & Associates; mem. Bd Trustees, Calif. State Univ. 1999–2004 (Vice-Chair. 2000–01); lecturer on politics, current affairs and women's issues; consultant to NBC TV drama The West Wing; Robert F. Kennedy Award, Emerson Coll., Boston 1993. *Publication:* Why Women Should Rule the World 2008. *Leisure interests:* running, cycling, music, major league baseball. *Address:* 5146 Klingle Street, NW, Washington, DC 20016-2655; c/o Vanity Fair, Condé Nast Publications, 4 Times Square, 17th Floor, New York, NY 10036, USA (office). *Website:* www.vanityfair.com (office).

MYERS, Mike; Canadian actor and writer; b. 25 May 1963, Toronto, Ont.; s. of Eric Myers and Bunny (née Hind) Myers; m. Robin Ruzan 1993 (divorced 2005); Canadian Comedy Award 2000. *Stage appearances:* The Second City, Toronto 1986–88, Chicago 1988–89; actor and writer: Mullarkey & Myers 1984–86. *Television includes:* John and Yoko (TV film) 1985, Saturday Night Live 1989–94 (Emmy Award for Outstanding Writing in a Comedy or Variety Series 1989), Russell Gilbert Show 1998, Dir The Bacchae (TV Film) 1999. *Films:* Wayne's World 1992, So I Married an Axe Murderer 1992, Wayne's World II 1993, Austin Powers: International Man of Mystery 1997, Meteor 1998, McClintock's Peach 1998, Just Like Me 1998, It's A Dog's Life 1998, 54 1998, Austin Powers: The Spy Who Shagged Me 1998, Pete's Meteor 1999, Shrek (voice) 2001, Austin Powers in Goldmember 2002, View from the Top

2003, Shrek 4–D (voice) 2003, Nobody Knows Anything 2003, Cat in the Hat 2003, Shrek 2 (voice) 2004, Shrek the Third (voice) 2007, The Love Guru 2008. *Address:* c/o David O'Connor, Creative Artists Agency, 9830 Wilshire Boulevard, Beverly Hills, CA 90212, USA.

MYERS, Norman, CMG, BA, MA, PhD, FLS, FRSA; British scientist; *Fellow, Green College, Oxford;* b. 24 Aug. 1934, Whitewell, Yorks.; s. of John Myers and Gladys Myers (née Haworth); m. Dorothy Mary Halliman 1965 (separated 1992); two d.; ed Clitheroe Royal Grammar School, Lancs., Keble Coll., Oxford, Univ. of California, Berkeley, USA; Dist Officer, Kenya Admin 1958–61; taught French and English at Delamere School for Boys, Nairobi 1961–65; freelance author and journalist, professional photographer, lecturer and broadcaster on African wildlife 1966–69; ind. scientist and consultant in Environment and Devt with focus on the tropics 1972–; has worked for many int. orgs and govt agencies; Man. Dir Norman Myers Scientific Consultancy Ltd 1982–; mem. Editorial Bd Global Environmental Change, Biodiversity and Conservation, Ecological Economics, The Environmentalist, Environmental Conservation; Environment, Development and Sustainability; Ecoscience, World Forest Resource Management, Forest Ecology and Management, Futures; Fellow, Green Coll. Oxford 2000–; Adjunct Prof. of Environmental Science, Nicholas School of the Environment, Duke Univ., USA; Visiting Prof., Harvard Univ., Cornell Univ., Stanford Univ., Univ. of Califonia, Berkeley, USA; Amb. to World Wide Fund (WWF) for Nature UK; Foreign Assoc., NAS; mem. American Asscn of Environmental and Resource Economists, American Inst. of Biological Sciences; Fellow, AAAS, World Acad. of Art and Science; Hon. Visiting Fellow, Green Coll., Oxford; Order of the Golden Ark (Netherlands) 1983, Kt of the Golden Ark (Netherlands) 1992; hon. science degree (Univ. of Kent) 2003; Gold Medal, WWF Int. 1983, Gold Medal, New York Zoological Soc. (now the Wildlife Conservation Soc.) 1986, Volvo Environment Prize 1992, UNEP Sasakawa Environment Prize 1995, Blue Planet Prize 2001 (one of only two people world-wide to receive all three leading environmental prizes), Pew Fellow in Environment, Liveable City Award, City of London, Haas Int. Alumnus Award, Univ. of California, Berkeley. *Publications:* The Long African Day 1972, The Sinking Ark (five scientific/literary awards) 1979, Conversion of Tropical Moist Forests (report to NAS) 1980, A Wealth of Wild Species (four book clubs and two science awards) 1983, The Primary Source: Tropical Forests and Our Future 1984, Economics of Ecosystem Management (co-ed.) 1985, The Gaia Atlas of Planet Management 1985, The Gaia Atlas of Future Worlds: Challenge and Opportunity in an Age of Change 1990, Population, Resources and the Environment: The Critical Challenges (for UN Population Fund) 1991, Tropical Forests and Climate (ed.) 1992, Ultimate Security: The Environmental Basis of Political Stability 1993, Scarcity or Abundance: A Debate on the Environment (co-author) 1994, Environmental Exodus: An Emergent Crisis in the Global Arena (co-author) 1995, Perverse Subsidies (co-author) 1998, Hotspots: Earth's Biologically Richest and Most Endangered Terrestrial Ecoregions (co-author) 1999, Towards a New Green Print for Business and Society (in Japanese) 1999, Perverse Subsidies: How Tax Dollars Undercut the Environment and the Economy (co-author) 2001, New Consumers: The Influence of Affluence on the Environment (co-author) 2004, The New Gaia Atlas of Planet Management (co-author) 2005, Institutional Roadblocks: Why Policy Processes Often Fail to Deliver (co-author) 2008; more than 300 scientific papers in professional journals on ecology, conservation biology, energy, population growth, environmental policy, environmental sociology and anthropology. *Leisure interests:* marathon running, mountaineering, professional photography. *Address:* Upper Meadow, Douglas Downes Close, Quarry Road, Headington, Oxford, OX3 8FS, England. *Telephone:* (1865) 750387. *Fax:* (1865) 741538. *E-mail:* myers1n@aol.com (office).

MYERS, Richard B., BS, MBA; American air force officer; b. 1942, Kansas City, Mo.; m.; two d. one s.; ed Kansas State Univ., Auburn Univ., Air Command/Staff Coll., Ala, US Army War Coll., Pa and Harvard Univ.; commissioned 2nd Lt, USAF 1965; fighter pilot, Vietnam 1969; various assignments to Commdr US Forces, Japan and 5th Air Force, Yakota Air Base, Japan 1993–96; Asst to Chair. Jt Chiefs of Staff, The Pentagon, 1996–97; rank of Gen. 1997; Commdr Pacific Air Forces, Hickam Air Force Base, Hawaii 1997–98; C-in-C N American Aerospace Defense Command/US Space Command, Peterson Air Force Base, Colo 1998–2000; Vice-Chair. Jt Chiefs of Staff 2000–01, Chair. 2001–05 (retd); mem. NATO Mil. Cttee; Defense Distinguished Service Medal with Oak Leaf Cluster, Distinguished Service Medal, Legion of Merit, Distinguished Flying Cross with Oak Leaf Cluster, Meritorious Service Medal with Three Oak Leaf Clusters, Air Medal with 18 Oak Leaf Clusters, Air Force Commendation Medal, Presidential Medal of Freedom 2005. *Address:* c/o Office of the Chairman of the Joint Chiefs of Staff, Washington, DC 20318-9999, USA (office).

MYERSON, Jacob M., MA; American economist and diplomatist; b. 11 June 1926, Rock Hill, SC; s. of Solomon Myerson and Lena Myerson (née Clein); m. 1st Nicole Neuray 1965 (died 1968); one d.; m. 2nd Helen Hayashi 1974 (died 1995); ed Washington, DC, Pennsylvania State Coll., George Washington Univ.; entered US Foreign Service 1950; Economic Analyst for the Office of the US High Commr, Berlin 1950–52, mem. US Regional Mission for the OEEC and Marshall Plan, Paris 1953–56; State Dept Desk Officer for EC and European Free Trade Area Affairs 1956–60; Chief of Political Section of US Mission to the European Communities, Brussels 1960; Special Asst to the Under-Sec. of State, Officer in Charge of NATO Political Affairs, State Dept, then Deputy Political Adviser and Counsellor to the US Mission to NATO, Brussels 1965–68, Adviser to the US del. at several ministerial sessions of the N Atlantic Council 1966–70; Econ. Counsellor US Mission to the European Communities, Brussels, then Deputy Chief and Minister Counsellor 1970–75; Amb. to UN Econ. and Social Council, New York 1975–77; Minister Counsellor for Econ. and Commercial Affairs, US Embassy, Paris 1977–80; Deputy Sec.-

Gen. of the OECD 1980–88; Order of the Sacred Treasure (Japan) 1990; Rivkin Award American Foreign Service Assoc. 1969. *Leisure interest:* modern and contemporary art. *Address:* 2 rue Lucien-Gaulard, 75018 Paris, France.

MYERSON, Roger B., AB, SM, PhD; American economist and academic; *Glen A. Lloyd Distinguished Service Professor of Economics, University of Chicago;* b. 29 March 1951, Boston, Mass; m. Regina Weber Myerson; two c.; ed Harvard Univ.; Asst Prof. of Managerial Econs and Decision Sciences, Northwestern Univ. 1976–79, Assoc. Prof. 1979–82, Prof. 1982–2001; Visiting Researcher, Universität Bielefeld, Germany 1978–79; Visiting Prof. of Econs, Univ. of Chicago 1985–86, 2000–01, Prof. of Econs 2001–07, Glen A. Lloyd Distinguished Service Prof. of Econs 2007–; Fellow, Econometric Soc. 1983–, American Acad. of Arts and Sciences 1993–; Assoc. Ed. Journal of Economic Theory 1983–93; mem. Editorial Bd International Journal of Game Theory 1982–92, Games and Economic Behavior 1989–97; Dr hc (Universität Basel, Switzerland) 2002; Nobel Prize in Econs (with Leo Hurwicz and Eric S. Maskin) 2007. *Publications:* Game Theory: Analysis of Conflict 1991, Probability Models for Economic Decisions 2005; more than 80 articles in academic journals. *Address:* Department of Economics, University of Chicago, 1126 East 59th Street, Chicago, IL 60637, USA (office). *Telephone:* (773) 834-9071 (office). *Fax:* (773) 702-8490 (office). *E-mail:* myerson@uchicago.edu (office). *Website:* home.uchicago.edu/~rmyerson (office).

MYINT, U Myo; Myanma diplomatist; fmr Amb. to Singapore and to Thailand; currently Man. Dir Myanma Sugarcane Enterprise (state owned co.). *Address:* Myanma Sugarcane Enterprise, Thiri Mingala Lane, off Kaba Aye Pagoda Road, Yangon, Myanmar. *Telephone:* (1) 666041. *Fax:* (1) 666107.

MYINT MAUNG, U; Myanma diplomatist and administrator; b. 10 March 1921, Magwe; m.; three c.; ed Univ. of Rangoon; joined Army 1942; has held the following positions: Head of Co-operative Dept; Chief of Admin. Div. of Burma Socialist Programme Party, also mem. Party Inspection Cttee; mem. Pyithu Hluttaw (People's Congress) for Magwe Constituency; mem. Bd of Dirs of People's Bank of the Union of Burma, Exec. Cttee of Burma Sports and Physical Fitness Cttee, Cen. Cttee of Burma Red Cross Soc.; Chair. Resettlement Cttee of Cen. Security and Admin. Cttee, Independence Award Cttee; Perm. Rep. to UN 1975–77; Minister of Foreign Affairs 1977–79; Amb. to China –1989; mem. State Council and Attorney-Gen. 1988. *Address:* c/o Ministry of Foreign Affairs, Yangon, Myanmar.

MYNBAYEV, Sauat M., CandEcon; Kazakhstani politician; *Minister of Energy and Mineral Resources;* b. 19 Nov. 1962, Taldy-Kurgan; s. of Mukhametbai Mynbayev and Oralbaeva Rakhima; m. Kaliyeva Zhanar Mynbayev; one s. one d.; ed Moscow State Univ.; teacher, Almaty Inst. of Nat. Economy, later Assoc. Prof. 1989–; Pres. Kazakhstan Exchange 1991–92; First Deputy Chair. and Dir Kazkommerts Bank 1992–95; Deputy Minister of Finance and Dir of Treasury 1995–98, Minister of Finance 1998–99; Deputy Head of Pres.'s Admin. 1999; Minister of Agric. 1999–2001; apptd Pres. Devt Bank of Kazakhstan 2001; Dir European Bank of Devt from Kazakhstan 2001; Deputy Prime Minister of Kazakhstan 2003–06; Minister of Industry and Trade 2004–06, of Energy and Mineral Resources 2007–. *Address:* Ministry of Energy and Mineral Resources, 010000 Astana, Beibitshilik 37, Kazakhstan (office). *Telephone:* (7172) 31-71-33 (office). *Fax:* (7172) 31-71-64 (office). *E-mail:* ministr@minenergo.kegoc.kz (office). *Website:* www.minenergo.kz (office).

MYNERS, Baron (Life Peer), cr. 2008, of Truro in the County of Cornwall; **Paul Myners,** CBE, FRSA; British publishing executive and government official; *Financial Services Secretary and Minister for the City;* b. 1 April 1948; m. Alison Myners; one s. four d.; ed Univ. of London; teacher with Inner London Educ. Authority 1971–72; finance writer, Daily Telegraph 1972–75; with N. M. Rothschild (merchant bank) 1974–85; CEO Gartmore Investment Man. 1985–87, Chair. 1987–2001; Deputy Chair. Powergen 1999–2001; Exec. Dir Nat. Westminster Bank 1999–2000; Chair. Guardian Media Group 2001–08, also Publisher The Guardian and The Observer newspapers; Financial Services Sec. and Minister for the City, HM Treasury 2008–, also Govt Spokesperson for HM Treasury in House of Lords; mem. Financial Reporting Council 1995–2004, Company Law Review Consultative Cttee 1998–2000; Court of Dirs of Bank of England 2005–; Chair. Low Pay Comm. 2006–; fmr mem. Bd of Dirs (non-exec.) mmO₂2001–, Bank of NY, Marks & Spencer 2002 (interim Chair. 2004); Chair. Tate Galleries –2009; Visiting Fellow, Nuffield Coll., Oxford; mem. Royal Acad. Trust, United Response; Dr hc (Univ. of Exeter). *Leisure interest:* London Symphony Orchestra. *Address:* House of Lords, London, SW1A 0PW, England. *Telephone:* (20) 7219-5353 (House of Lords); (20) 7270-5696. *E-mail:* fsst.action@hm-treasury.gsi.gov.uk. *Website:* www.hm-treasury.gov.uk.

MYRATGULYEV, Amandurdy; Turkmenistani government official; Head of Main State Tax Service 2004–05; Deputy Prime Minister and Minister of the Economy and Finance 2005–07. *Address:* c/o Ministry of the Economy and Finance, ul. 2008 4, 744000 Aşgabat, Turkmenistan (office).

MYRDAL, Jan; Swedish writer; b. 19 July 1927, Stockholm; s. of the late Gunnar Myrdal and Alva Reimer; m. 1st Nadja Wiking 1948; m. 2nd Maj Liedberg 1953; m. 3rd Gun Kessle (died 2007) 1956; one s. one d.; Sunday columnist (politics, culture) Stockholms-Tidningen 1963–66, Aftonbladet 1966–72; Chair. and Publr Folket i Bild/Kulturfront 1971–72, columnist 1972–; Hon. DLit (Upsala Coll., NJ) 1980; Hon. PhD (Nankai Univ., China) 1993; Chevalier, Ordre des Arts et Lettres 1990. *Works include:* films: Myglaren 1966, Hjalparen 1968, Balzac or The Triumphs of Realism 1975, Mexico: Art and Revolution 1991; TV documentaries: Democratic Kampuchea 1978–79, Guerilla Base Area of Democratic Kampuchea 1979, China 1979, 20 films on history of political caricature and posters 1975–87. *Publications:* (in Swedish) novels: Hemkomst 1954, Jubelvår 1955, Att bli och vara 1956,

Badrumskranen 1957, Karriär 1975, Barndom 1982, En annan värld 1984; drama: Folkets Hus 1953, Moraliteter 1967, Garderingar 1969, B. Olsen 1972; travel: Resa i Afghanistan 1960, Bortom berg och öknar 1962, Turkmenistan 1966, En världsbild (co-author) 1977, Sidenvägen 1977, Indien väntar 1980; politics: Kina: Revolutionen går vidare 1970, Albansk utmaning 1970, Ett 50-tal 1972, lag utan ordning, Kinesiska frågor, Tyska frågor 1976, Kina efter Mao Tse-tung 1977, Kampuchea och kriget 1978, Kampuchea hösten 1979, Den albanska utmaningen 1968–86, 1987, Mexico, Dröm och längtan 1996; art: Bartom Bergen 1983; essays: Söndagsmorgon 1965, Skriftställning 1968, Skriftställning II 1969, Skriftställning III 1970, Skriftställning IV 1973, V 1975, Klartexter 1978, Skriftställning X 1978, Balzac und der Realismus (in German) 1978, Strindberg och Balzac 1981, Ord och Avsikt 1986, Det nya Stor, Tyskland 1992, När Västerlandet trädde fram 1992, Inför nedräkningen 1993, När morgondagarna sjöng 1994, En fest i Liu Lin 1994, När morgondagarna sjöng 1994, Mexico - Dröm och längtan 1995, Rölvag as an example 1995, Maj, en kärlek 1998, Om vin 1999, Det odelbara ordet 2002, Gubbsjuka 2002, Meccano 2005, Sälja krig som margarin 2005; autobiography: Rescontra 1962, Samtida bekännelser 1964, Inför nedräkningen 1993, När morgondagarna sjöng 1994, En kärlek 1998, Maj: En kärlek 1998; art: Ansikte av sten, Angkor 1968, Ondskan tar form 1976; Dussinet fullt 1981, Den trettonde 1983, Franska revolutionens bilder 1989, 5 ar av frihet 1830–35 1991, När Västerlandet tradde fram 1992, André Gill 1995, Drömmen om det goda samhallet; Kinesiska affischer 1966–1976 1996; wine: Jan Myrdal on vin 1999; biography: August Strindberg and Ole Edvart Roelvag 1997, Johan August Strindberg 2000; (in English) Report from a Chinese Village 1965, Chinese Journey 1965, Confessions of a Disloyal European 1968, Angkor: an essay on art and imperialism 1970, China: The Revolution Continued 1971, Gates to Asia 1971, Albania Defiant 1976, The Silk Road 1979, China Notebook 1975–78 1979, Return to a Chinese Village 1984, India Waits 1984, Childhood 1991, Another World 1993, 12 Going on 13 1995. *Leisure interests:* collecting Meccano, computing for fun. *Address:* Kalvängen 70 D, 739 91 Skinnskatteberg, Sweden (home). *Telephone:* (223) 51-012 (home). *Fax:* (223) 51-007 (home). *E-mail:* myrdal@myrdal.pp.se (home). *Website:* www.myrdal -kessle.se.

MYSEN, Bjorn O., MA, PhD; American research scientist; *Senior Scientist, Geophysical Laboratory, Carnegie Institution of Washington;* b. 20 Dec. 1947, Oslo, Norway; s. of Martin Mysen and Randi Mysen; m. Susanna Laya 1975; two c.; ed Univ. of Oslo and Pennsylvania State Univ.; Carnegie Foundation Fellow 1974–77; Sr Scientist, Experimental Geochemist, Carnegie Inst., Washington, DC 1977–; Visiting Scientist, Bayerisches Geoinstitut, Germany 1988; Research Assoc., CNRS-Orléans, France 1994; Visiting Prof., Institut de Physique du Globe, Paris, France 2001, 2004, Inst. for Study of the Earth's Interior, Univ. of Okayama at Misasa, Japan 2006, 2007; mem. Royal Norwegian Acad. of Science and Letters 1985; Fellow, Mineralogy Soc. of America 1991; F. W. Clarke Medal 1977, Reusch Medal 1978, ISI Highly Cited 2001, George W. Morey Award, American Ceramical Soc. 2006. *Publications:* Structure and Properties of Silicate Melts 1988, Silicate Glasses and Melts – Properties and Structure 2005; seven edited books and more than 250 other scientific publs. *Address:* Geophysical Laboratory, Carnegie Institution of Washington, 5251 Broad Branch Road, NW, Washington, DC 20015, USA (office). *Telephone:* (202) 478-8975 (office). *Fax:* (202) 478-8901 (office). *E-mail:* mysen@gl.ciw.edu (office); bmysen@ciw.edu (office). *Website:* www.gl.ciw.edu/ ~mysen (office).

MYŚLIWSKI, Wiesław; Polish writer; b. 25 March 1932, Dwikozy, nr Sandomierz; m. Wacława Stec; one s.; ed Catholic Univ. of Lublin; worked at People's Publishing Cooperative until 1976, Ed., quarterly magazine Regiony 1975–99; Ed., fortnightly Sycyna 1994–99; numerous awards include Stanis-ław Piętak Prize 1968, 1973, Prize of Ministry of Culture and Art 1971, State Prize 1986, Reymont Prize 1997, Alfred Jurzykowski Foundation Award, New York 1998. *Publications include:* novels: Nagi sad (Naked Orchard) 1967, Pałac (Palace, also screenplay 1980) 1970, Kamień na kamieniu (Stone on Stone) 1984, Widnokrąg (Horizon) (Nike Literary Prize 1997) 1996, Traktat o Tuskaniu fasoli (Treatise on Shelling Beans) (Nike Literary Prize 2007) 2006; screenplays: Przez dziewięć mostów (Across Nine Bridges) 1972, Klucznik (Housemaster) (TV) 1979, Droga (The Road) (TV) 1981, Kamień na kamieniu (Stone on Stone) 1995; plays: Złodziej (Thief) 1973, Klucznik (Steward) 1978, Drzewo (Tree) 1989, Requiem dla gospodyni (Requiem for the Housewife) 2000. *Address:* ul. Nowoursynowska 119C, 02-797 Warsaw, Poland (home).

MYTARAS, Dimitris; Greek artist; b. 1934, Chalkis; s. of Basilis Mytaras and Efrosini Mytaras; m. Chariklia Mytaras 1961; one s.; ed Athens School of Fine Arts and Ecole des Arts Décoratifs, Paris; Prof., Athens School of Fine Arts; has exhibited in many of the world's capitals and has participated in most important Biennales; assoc. with Kreonidis Gallery, Athens, Metropolis Art Galleries, New York, the Inter Art Group, Tokyo and Galerie Flak, Paris; main periods of his painting are: Mirrors 1960–64, Dictatorship 1966–70, Epitaphs 1971–76, Portraits 1977–87, Theatre Scenes 1988–91. *Publications:* D. Mytaras: Peinture 1982, D. Mytaras: Peinture 1990, D. Mytaras: Drawings 1994, D. Mytaras: Parepiptonda. *Address:* Kamariotou 15, 115–24 N Filothei, Athens, Greece. *Telephone:* 6913658. *Fax:* 6928327.

MYTTON, Graham Lambert, PhD, FRSA; British marketing consultant; b. 21 Oct. 1942, Sanderstead; s. of Peter Mytton and Joan Jackson; m. Janet Codd 1966; two d.; ed Trinity School, Croydon, Purley Grammar School and Univs of Liverpool, Manchester and Dar es Salaam; Man. BBC Radio studio 1964–66; Research Fellow, Zambia Broadcasting 1970–73; radio producer, BBC African Service 1973–75; current affairs producer, BBC Radio Four 1976; Head, Hausa Language Section, BBC African Service 1976–82; Head, Int. Broadcasting Audience Research, BBC World Service 1982–91, Head, Audience Research and Correspondence 1991–96, Controller, Marketing 1996–98; ind. consultant and trainer in audience, opinion and market research 1998–; Dir Intermedia, Washington, DC 2001–; AT&T Guest Lecturer, George Washington Univ. 1995; Silver Medal, Market Research Soc. 1997. *Publications:* Mass Communications in Africa 1983, Global Audiences (ed.) 1993, Handbook on Radio and TV Audience Research 1993. *Leisure interests:* stamp collecting, singing. *Address:* Roffeys, The Green, Coldharbour, Dorking, Surrey, RH5 6HE, England (office). *Telephone:* (1306) 712122 (office). *Fax:* (1306) 712958 (office). *E-mail:* gmytton@gn.apc.org (office).

MZALI, Mohamed, Lic en Phil; Tunisian politician; b. 23 Dec. 1925, Monastir; m.; six c.; ed Sadiky School, Tunis, Univ. of Paris; teacher, Sadiky School, Lycée Alaoui and Univ. of Zitouna 1950–56; Chef de Cabinet, Ministry of Educ. 1956–58; mem. Nat. Ass. 1959–; Dir of Youth and Sports, President's Secr. 1959–64; Dir-Gen. Radiodiffusion Télévision Tunisienne 1964–67; Sec. of State for Nat. Defence 1968–69; Minister of Youth and Sports 1969–70, of Educ. 1969–70, 1971–73, 1976–80, of Health 1973–76; Co-ordinator of Govt Activities, Dept of the Pres. March–April 1980; Prime Minister 1980–84, Prime Minister and Minister of the Interior 1984–86; mem. Neo-Destour Party (now Parti Socialiste Destourien) 1947–, mem. Cen. Cttee 1971–, Sec.-Gen. 1980–86; mem. IOC (First Vice-Pres. 1976–80) 1976–; Municipal Councillor, Tunis 1960, 1963; First Vice-Pres. Tunis Town Council 1960–63, Pres. Culture, Youth and Sports Comm. 1960–66; Pres. Ariana Town Council 1959–72; Founder El Fikr (monthly cultural review) 1955; Pres., Tunisian Olympic Cttee 1962–, Union des Ecrivains Tunisiens 1970–; Pres. Int. Cttee Jeux Méditerranéens 1979–; mem. Arab Language Acad., Cairo 1976–, Baghdad 1978–, Damascus 1980–, Jordan 1980–; mem. French Sports Acad. 1978–; Living in France in self-imposed exile; fined and sentenced to 15 years forced labour after *in absentia* conviction for corruption 1987; Grand Cordon, Ordre de l'Indépendance, Ordre de la République, Grand Officier, Légion d'honneur and numerous foreign decorations. *Publications:* La Démocratie 1955, Recueil d'Editoriaux d'El Fikr 1969, Prises de positions 1973, Etudes 1975, Points de vue 1975, Les Chemins de la pensée 1979, The Word of the Action 1984, Olympism Today 1984.

MZIMELA, Rev. Sipo E., MA, PhD; South African ecclesiastic, civil servant and politician; b. 1937, Durban; m.; three d.; ed General Theological Seminary and New York Univ., USA; in exile 1961, W Germany 1964–74, USA 1974, African Nat. Congress (ANC) Rep. to USA and UN 1974–80; ordained Episopal Priest New York 1976; worked with SA refugees; Rector Episcopal Church of the Epiphany, Ventnor, NJ and Adjunct Prof., New York Univ. 1981–83; Head, Dept of Religion and Lecturer, St Paul's United Theological Coll., Limuru, Kenya 1984–87; Founder SA Educ. Fund 1987; Assoc. Priest, St Bartholomew's Episcopal Church, Atlanta 1988–94, Assisting Priest 2005–; Inkatha Freedom Party Rep. to USA 1990; fmr Minister of Works, KwaZulu Govt 1994; Minister of Correctional Services, Govt of Nat. Unity 1994–99; mem. Parl. for Inkatha Freedom Party, later mem. Parl. and Chief Whip United Democratic Movt; returned to USA 2002; Asst Prof. of Religious Studies, Agnes Scott Coll. 2004. *Publications include:* Apartheid – South African Nazism, Whither South Africa Now?, Marching to Slavery – South Africa's Descent to Communism. *Address:* St Bartholomew's Episcopal Church, 1790 LaVista Road NE, Atlanta GA 30329, USA. *Telephone:* (404) 634-3336. *E-mail:* babs@stbartsatlanta.org.

N

NÄÄTÄNEN, Risto Kalervo, PhD; Finnish psychologist and academic; *Director, Cognitive Brain Research Unit, University of Helsinki;* b. 14 June 1939, Helsinki; s. of Prof. Esko K. Näätänen and Rauni Näätänen (née Raudanjoki); m. Marjatta Kerola 1960; three s.; ed Univ. of Helsinki; Asst Dept of Psychology, Univ. of Helsinki 1965–69, Prof. of Psychology 1975–, Dir Cognitive Brain Research Unit 1991–; Researcher Acad. of Finland 1969–75, Research Prof. 1983–, Acad. Prof. 1995–; Scientific Organizer (with Prof. G. Rizzolatti) of European Science Foundation Winter School 1990; Fellowships, Dept of Psychology, UCLA 1965–66, Univ. Dundee, Scotland 1979–80, Univ. Marburg, Germany 1980–81, The Neurosciences Inst., New York 1985–86, Inst. for Advanced Study, Berlin 1988–89; Vice-Pres. Fed. of European Psychophysiology 1994–96, Pres. 1996–; mem. Brain Research Soc. of Finland (Pres. 1983–91), Int. Brain Research Org. (Governing Council 1985–91), Nordic Psychophysiology Soc. (Pres. 1992–95), Advisory Council, Int. Assen for the Study of Attention and Performance, Governing Council, Fed. of European Psychophysiology Socs.; mem. Finnish Acad. of Science and Letters 1980–, Academia Europaea 1991– (Council 2000–); Foreign mem. Russian Acad. of Sciences 1994–; Kt (First Class), Order of the White Rose of Finland; Dr hc (Jyväskylä), (Tartu) 2000; Purkinje Medal (Prague) 1988, Finnish Cultural Foundation Prize 1990, First Science Prize (Finland) 1997, State Traffic Safety Medal 1992. *Publications:* Selective Attention and Evoked Potentials 1967, Road-User Behaviour and Traffic Accidents (with H. Summala) 1976, Attention and Brain Function 1992, The Orienting Response in Information Processing (with E.N. Sokolov, J.A. Spinks & H. Lyytinen; numerous articles. *Leisure interests:* sports, the Green Movement, traffic safety. *Address:* Cognitive Brain Research Unit, The Department of Psychology, PO Box 9, Siltavuorenpenger 20 C, University of Helsinki, 00014 Helsinki (office); Mäkipellontie 12 D, 00320 Helsinki, Finland (home). *Telephone:* (9) 19129445 (office). *E-mail:* risto.naatanen@helsinki.fi (office). *Website:* www.cbru.helsinki.fi (office).

NABIULLINA, Elvira Sakhipzadovna, PhD; Russian economist and government official; *Minister of Economic Development;* b. 29 Oct. 1963, Ufa, Bashkortostan; ed M.V. Lomonosov Moscow State Univ.; Chief Specialist, Russian Union of Industrialists and Businessmen on econ. policy 1992–94; Deputy Head, Dept of Econ. Reform 1994–96, Head of Dept 1996–97; Deputy Minister of the Economy 1997–98; Vice-Pres. Bd of Dirs Promtorgbank 1998–99; Exec. Dir Euroasian (rating service) 1999; First Deputy Minister of Econ. Devt and Trade 2000–07, Minister of Econ. Devt 2007–; Vice-Pres. Fund Centre of Strategic Devt 1999–2000, Pres. 2003–05, Head of Research Group 2005–07; Head of Advisory Council of Organizing Cttee on Preparation and Maintenance of Presidency of the Russian Fed. in G8 2005–06; fmr mem. Pres.'s Expert Council on Priority Nat. Projects and Demography; World Fellow, Yale Univ., USA 2007. *Address:* Ministry of Economic Development, 125993 Moscow, ul. 1-ya Tverskaya-Yamskaya 1/3, Russia (office). *Telephone:* (495) 200-03-47 (office). *E-mail:* presscenter@economy.gov.ru (office). *Website:* www.economy.gov.ru (office).

NACHTIGALL, Dieter, Dr rer. nat; German physicist; b. 4 Feb. 1927, Berge; s. of Walter Nachtigall and Emma (née Eisermann) Nachtigall; two s. one d.; ed Humboldt Univ., Berlin; schoolteacher, GDR 1946–49, Lecturer, Teacher's Coll. 1949–50; Scientific Asst and Lecturer, Tech. Univ. of Dresden 1956–59; Research Group Leader Nuclear Research Establishment, Juelich, FRG 1959–65; Research Assoc. CERN, Geneva 1965–66; Group Leader EURATOM BCNM, Geel 1966–71; Prof. of Physics Educ., Paed. Hochschule, Dortmund 1971–81, Univ. of Dortmund 1981–92, Prof. Emer. 1992–, Dean Dept of Physics 1990–92; Advisory Prof., East China Normal Univ., Shanghai 1989–, Guangxi Normal Univ. 1995; mem. Int. Comm. on Physics Educ. 1987–93; Hon. Prof. Xian Highway Inst. 1988, Normal Univ. of Chengdu/Sichuan 1993, South West China Normal Univ. at Chongqing 1994; Medal of Int. Comm. on Physics Educ. 1998. *Publications:* Table of Specific Gamma Ray Contents 1969, Physikalische Grundlagen für Dosimetrie und Strahlenschutz Thiemig 1971, Skizzen zur Physik-Didaktik Lang 1986, Neues Physiklernen-Das Teilchen-Konzept Lang 1989, Das Feldkonzept 1990, Das Wellenkonzept 1990, Internalizing Physics – Making Physics Part of One's Life (UNESCO) 1995. *Address:* Otto Hahn Strasse 4, 44224 Dortmund (office); Auf'm Hilmkamp 15, 58739 Wickede Wiehagen, Germany (home). *Telephone:* (231) 7552989 (office); (2377) 3548 (home). *Fax:* (231) 7555175 (office); (2377) 6134 (home). *E-mail:* nachtigall@didaktik.physik.uni-dortmund.de (office); dieternachtigall@t-online.de (home).

NACHTWEY, James, FRPS; American photojournalist and war photographer; b. 1948, Syracuse, NY; ed Leominster High School and Dartmouth Coll.; influenced by imagery from Vietnam War and American Civil Rights Movt became self-taught photographer; held a series of odd jobs, including as a truck driver; also worked on merchant ships; started work as newspaper photographer, New Mexico 1976; moved to New York and began working as freelance photographer 1980; worked for Black Star 1980–85; contract photographer Time magazine 1984–; covered first overseas assignment in Northern Ireland 1981; worked in SA, Latin America, Middle East, Russia, Eastern Europe, fmr Soviet Union shooting pictures of war, conflict and famine, and images of sociopolitical issues (pollution, crime and punishment) in Western Europe and USA; covered elections in SA 1994, invasion of Iraq 2003, tsunami in SE Asia 26 Dec. 2004; made series of photographs about attacks on World Trade Center 11 Sept. 2001; compiled a photo essay on effects of Sudan conflict on civilians; has worked on extensive photographic essays in El Salvador, Nicaragua, Guatemala, Lebanon, the West Bank and Gaza, Israel, Indonesia, Thailand, India, Sri Lanka, Afghanistan, the Philippines, South Korea, Somalia, Sudan, Rwanda, SA, Russia, Bosnia, Chechnya, Kosovo, Romania, Brazil and USA; mem. Magnum Photos 1986–2001; Co-founding mem. VII Photo Agency 2001; Hon. DFA (Massachusetts Coll. of Art); numerous honours and awards, including Common Wealth Award, Martin Luther King Award, Dr Jean Mayer Global Citizenship Award, Henry Luce Award, Robert Capa Gold Medal (five times), World Press Photo Award (twice), Magazine Photographer of the Year (seven times), Int. Center of Photography Infinity Award (three times), Leica Award (twice), Bayeaux Award for War Corresps (twice), Alfred Eisenstaedt Award, Canon Photo Essayist Award, W. Eugene Smith Memorial Grant in Humanistic Photography, Dan David Prize, Dan David Foundation and Tel-Aviv Univ. 2003, Heinz Foundation Achievement Award 2006, TED (Technology Entertainment Design) Prize (co-recipient) 2007. *Address:* c/o Time magazine, 1271 Avenue of the Americas, New York, NY 10020-1393, USA (office). *Telephone:* 212-522-1212 (office). *Fax:* 212-522-0602 (office). *Website:* www.time.com (office); www.jamesnachtwey.com.

NADAL PARERA, Rafael (Rafa); Spanish professional tennis player; b. 3 June 1986, Manacor, Majorca; s. of Sebastian Nadal and Ana Maria Parera; ed coached by Toni Nadal; began playing tennis age four; turned professional 2001; played his only jr Grand Slam event at Wimbledon in 2002 and reached semi-finals; won first ATP match defeating Ramon Delgado in Majorca to become the ninth player in open era to win an ATP match before 16th birthday; became second-youngest player to be ranked among world's top 100 singles players 2003; reached fourth round at Australian Open 2005, semi-final 2008, winner 2009; winner, French Open 2005, 2006, 2007, 2008; runner-up, Wimbledon 2006, 2007, winner 2008; quarter-finalist, US Open 2006, semi-finalist 2008; semi-finalist, Masters Cup 2006, 2007; gold medal, men's singles, Olympic Games, Beijing 2008; clay-court winning streak of 81 matches (longest among male players in open era) April 2005–May 2007; youngest player in history to win Davis Cup at first attempt; 34 career singles titles; five career doubles titles; ranked World No. 1 since 18 Aug. 2008; asteroid 128036 Rafaelnadal named in his honour; ATP Newcomer of the Year 2003, ATP Most Improved Player 2005, Laureus World Newcomer of the Year 2006, Prince of Asturias Award 2008. *Leisure interests:* playing PSP, soccer and golf, fishing, going out with friends in Majorca. *Address:* c/o Carlos Costa, IMG, Via Augusta, 200 4th Floor, 08021 Barcelona, Spain (office). *Telephone:* (93) 2003455 (office). *Fax:* (93) 2005924 (office). *E-mail:* kc@rafaelnadal.com. *Website:* www.rafaelnadal.com.

NADAR, Shiv; Indian business executive, engineer and philanthropist; *Chairman and CEO, HCL Technologies;* b. 18 July 1945, Tamil Nadu; m.; one c.; Systems Analyst, Cooper Eng; Sr Man. Trainee, DCM Ltd 1968; f. Hindustan Computers Ltd (later HCL) 1976, CEO HCL Technologies Ltd 1991, currently Chair. and Chief Strategy Officer; Dr hc (Madras); Padma Bhushan 2008. *Address:* HCL Technologies Ltd, A10/11, Sector 3, Noida 201 301, Uttar Pradesh, India (office). *Telephone:* (120) 2520-917 (office). *Fax:* (120) 2526-907 (office). *E-mail:* webhost@hcl.in (office). *Website:* www.hcl.in (office).

NADER, Ralph, AB, LLB; American lawyer, author and consumer advocate; b. 27 Feb. 1934, Winsted, Conn.; s. of Nadra Nader and Rose Bouziane; ed Princeton and Harvard Univs; admitted to Conn. Bar 1958, Mass Bar 1959, also US Supreme Court; US Army 1959; law practice in Hartford, Conn. 1959–; Lecturer in History and Govt, Univ. of Hartford 1961–63; Founder and fmr Head of Public Citizen Inc. 1980; Lecturer, Princeton Univ. 1967–68; Co-founder Princeton Project 55 1989; launched political movt Democracy Rising 2001; Green Party cand. for presidential election 1996, 2000, ind. cand. 2004, 2008; mem. ABA; f. Clean Water Action Project, Disability Rights Center, Public Interest Research Groups (PIRGs), Center for Study of Responsive Law, Center for Auto Safety, Pension Rights Center, Project for Corp. Responsibility; Contributing Ed. Ladies Home Journal 1973–81, syndicated columnist, In the Public Interest 1972–; f. The Multinational Monitor (monthly magazine); Nieman Fellows Award 1965–66, named one of ten Outstanding Young Men of Year by the US Jr Chamber of Commerce 1967, Woodrow Wilson Award, Princeton Univ. 1972. *Film appearance:* (as himself) Fun with Dick and Jane 2005. *Publications:* Unsafe at Any Speed 1965, Who Runs Congress? 1972, The Consumer and Corporate Accountability 1974, Taming the Giant Corporation (co-author) 1976, The Menace of Atomic Energy (with John Abbotts) 1979, The Lemon Book 1980, Who's Poisoning America? 1981, The Big Boys 1986, Winning the Insurance Game (co-author) 1990, Good Works 1993, No Contest: Corporate Lawyers and the Perversion of Justice in America 1996, The Ralph Nader Reader 2000, Crashing the Party 2002, Civic Arousal 2004, It Happened in the Kitchen: Recipes for Food and Thought, Why Women Pay More (with Frances Cerra Whittelsley), Children First! A Parent's Guide to Fighting Corporate Predators, The Seventeen Traditions 2007. *Address:* Democracy Rising, PO Box 18485, Washington, DC 20036; PO Box 19312, Washington, DC 20036, USA. *E-mail:* info@nader.org. *Website:* www.democracyrising.us; www.nader.org.

NADINGAR, Emmanuel; Chadian politician; *Minister of Petroleum;* Deputy Chief of Staff, Govt of Chad –2004; Minister of Nat. Defence, Veterans and Victims of War 2004–07, of Petroleum 2007–. *Address:* Ministry of Petroleum, BP 816, N'Djamena, Chad (office). *Telephone:* 52-56-03 (office). *Fax:* 52-36-66 (office). *E-mail:* mme@intnet.td (office). *Website:* www.ministere-petrole.td (office).

NADIR, Asil; Turkish-Cypriot business executive; b. 1 May 1941, Paphos; s. of Irfan Nadir; m. Ayesha Nadir twice (divorced twice); two s.; ed Univ. of

Istanbul; settled in East End of London, England 1963; formed Wearwell cash-and-carry clothing co., Tower Hamlets 1967; est. cardboard-box factory for fruit-packing in Northern Cyprus following partition of island in 1974; Chair. Polly Peck Int. PLC 1980–90; business expanded to include citrus fruit, colour television factory in Turkey, hotels, leisure complexes, Pizza Hut franchise in Turkey, etc.; acquired control of Sansui electronics co.; bought tropical fruit arm of Del Monte Co., making Polly Peck world's third largest fruit trader; cos became largest employers in Northern Cyprus; owner of several leading Turkish newspapers; set up charitable trust Nadir Health and Educ. Foundation 1989; Polly Peck empire valued at nearly £2 billion when it collapsed and was placed in hands of administrators Oct. 1990; arrested 15 Dec. 1990 following inquiries into his business affairs by Inland Revenue and Serious Fraud Office; indicted on counts of theft and false accounting, faced further charges, rearrested Sept. 1991; declared bankrupt Nov. 1991; jumped bail and fled to "Turkish Federated State of Northern Cyprus" May 1993; pledged to return to UK to clear his name Sept. 2003. *Address:* c/o Dome Hotel, Kyrenia, "Turkish Federated State of Northern Cyprus".

NAFEH, Ibrahim; Egyptian journalist; *President, Arab Journalists' Union;* b. 1934, Suez; m.; two c.; diplomatic corresp., Cairo Radio 1956–60; Econ. Ed. Al-Gumhuriya newspaper 1960–62; Econ. Ed. Al-Ahram newspaper 1962–67, Head Econ. Dept 1974–75, Chief Ed. 1975, Chair. and Ed.-in-Chief 1975–82, Chair. and Exec. Ed. 1982–2005; Middle East specialist in IBRD, Information Dept 1971–73; currently Pres. Arab Journalists' Union. *Publication:* Translation into Arabic of Lester Pearson's Report: Partners in Development 1971. *E-mail:* info-faj@faj.org.eg (office). *Website:* www.faj.org.eg (office).

NAFISI, Azar, PhD; Iranian writer and academic; *Director, Dialogue Project, School of Advanced International Studies, Johns Hopkins University;* b. 1962; m.; one d.; ed Oklahoma Univ., USA; fmrly teacher, Tehran Univ., Allemeh Tabatabai Univ.; fmrly visiting fellow, Oxford Univ.; currently Dir of the Dialogue Project, School of Advanced Int. Studies, Johns Hopkins Univ., Washington, DC, USA. *Publications:* Anti-Terra: A Study of Vladimir Nabokov's Novels 1994, Reading 'Lolita' in Tehran: A Memoir in Books 2003, La Voce Verde 2006, Things I've Been Silent About 2009; contrib. numerous chapters and articles on promotion of democracy, human rights in Muslim societies, women's rights, literature, culture. *Address:* Steven Barclay Agency, 12 Western Avenue, Petaluma, CA 94952, USA (office); The Paul H. Nitze School of Advanced International Studies, Johns Hopkins University, The Rome Building, Room 731, 1619 Massachusetts Avenue, Washington, DC 20036, USA (office). *Telephone:* (707) 773-0654 (office); (202) 663-5785 (office). *Fax:* (707) 778-1868 (office). *E-mail:* steven@barclayagency.com (office); anafisi@jhu.edu (office); info@azarnafisi.com (office). *Website:* www.barclayagency.com/nafisi.html (office); www.sais-jhu.edu (office); www.azarnafisi.com.

NAG, Rajat M.; Canadian engineer, economist and banker; *Managing Director-General, Asian Development Bank;* ed Indian Inst. of Tech., Delhi, Univ. of Saskatchewan, London School of Econs, UK; worked as energy and water resources planning specialist with int. consulting firm, becoming chief economist; worked as economist/financial analyst for five years at Bank of Canada; joined Asian Devt Bank (ADB) as Project Economist in Agric. Dept 1986, assigned to ADB's Nepal Resident Mission 1991–94, held various sr positions in ADB's Programs Dept (West) and in Financial Sector and Industry Div., Infrastructure Dept (West), mem. man. cttee that formulated proposals for re-organization of ADB operations 2001, Deputy Dir Programs Dept (West) 2000–02, Dir Gen. Mekong Dept 2002–06, Special Advisor to ADB Pres. on Regional Econ. Cooperation and Integration 2005–06, Dir Gen. newly amalgamated Southeast Asia Dept 2006, Man. Dir-Gen. ADB 2006–. *Address:* Asian Development Bank, 6 ADB Avenue, 1500 Mandaluyong City, Philippines (office). *Telephone:* (2) 632-4444 (office). *Fax:* (2) 636-2444 (office). *E-mail:* mediacenter@adb.org (office). *Website:* www.adb.org (office).

NAGA, Fayza Abu an-, MPolSci; Egyptian diplomatist and politician; *Minister of International Co-operation;* b. 12 Nov. 1951, Port Said; d. of Mohamed Abu an-Naga and Amina an-Nagari; m. Hisham El Zimaity; one s.; ed Cairo Univ., Geneva Univ.; joined foreign service 1975, served at Perm. Mission of Egypt to UN 1979–84, 1992–96, Aide to Minister of State for Foreign Affairs Boutros Boutros Ghali 1984–91, Political and Special Asst to UN Sec.-Gen. Boutros Boutros Ghali 1992–96; Asst Foreign Minister for African Affairs 1997–99; Perm. Rep. to UN, Geneva 1999–2001; Minister of State for Foreign Affairs (first woman) 2001–04; Minister of Int. Co-operation 2004–; mem. Council, Bd of Trustees, Bibliotheca Alexandrina; Dr hc (Qafqaz Univ., Azerbaijan) 2007. *Address:* Ministry of International Co-operation, 8 Sharia Adly, Cairo, Egypt (office). *Telephone:* (2) 23910008 (office). *Fax:* (2) 23908159 (office). *E-mail:* ministeroffice@mic.gov.eg (office). *Website:* www.mic.gov.eg (office).

NAGAI, Kiyoshi, PhD, FRS; Japanese biologist; *Professor, Structural Studies Division, MRC Laboratory of Molecular Biology;* s. of Otoyi Nagai and Naoko Nagai (née Matsumoto); m. Yoshito Mayima 1974; one s. one d.; ed Osaka Univ. Morimoto Lab.; Prof. MRC Lab. of Molecular Biology 1981–; Leader, Nagai Group (research projects); Fellow Darwin Coll. Cambridge 1993–; organizer RNA Club (Darwin Coll.), Novartis Medal and Prize, Biochem. Soc. 2000. *Leisure interests:* reading, playing cello in chamber groups. *Address:* Structural Studies Division, Medical Research Council Laboratory of Molecular Biology, Hills Road, Cambridge, CB2 2QH, (office); 100 Mowbray Road, Cambridge, CB1 7TG, England. *Telephone:* (1223) 402292 (office). *Fax:* (1223) 213556 (office). *E-mail:* kn@mrc-lmb.cam.ac.uk (office). *Website:* www2.mrc-lmb.cam.ac.uk (office).

NAGAKURA, Saburo, DrSc; Japanese scientist; b. 3 Oct. 1920, Shizuoka Pref.; m. Midori Murayama 1953; one s.; ed Shizuoka High School and Tokyo Imperial Univ.; Assoc. Prof., Univ. of Tokyo 1949–59, Prof. 1959–81; Head of Physical Organic Chem. Lab., Inst. of Physical and Chemical Research 1961–81; mem. Science Council of Japan 1972–75; mem. Science Council, Ministry of Educ., Science and Culture 1974–86, 1988–96, Univ. Council 1987–93; Dir-Gen. Inst. for Molecular Science 1981–87; Pres. Int. Union of Pure and Applied Chem. 1981–83, Chem. Soc. of Japan 1984–85, Okazaki Nat. Research Insts 1985–88, Grad. Univ. for Advanced Studies 1988–95, Japanese Centre for Int. Studies in Ecology 1993–, Kanagawa Acad. of Science and Tech. 1995–; mem. Japan Acad., Int. Acad. of Quantum Molecular Science, Deutsche Akad. der Naturforscher Leopoldina; Foreign mem. Royal Swedish Acad. of Sciences; Foreign Fellow Indian Nat. Science Acad.; Hon. mem. Royal Institution, London, Chem. Soc. of Japan, Korean Acad. of Science and Tech.; Hon. Fellow Chinese Chem. Soc., Indian Acad. of Sciences; Hon. DSc (Nebraska); Chem. Soc. of Japan Prize 1966, Asahi Prize 1971, Japan Acad. Prize 1978, Jawaharlal Nehru Birth Centenary Medal 1996; Person of Cultural Merit 1985, Order of Cultural Merit 1990. *Publications:* Electronic Theory for Organic Chemistry 1966 and many publs on electronic structure and dynamic behaviour of excited molecules. *Leisure interest:* appreciation of Japanese paintings. *Address:* 2-7-13 Higashi-cho, Kichijoji, Musashino, Tokyo 1800002, Japan. *Telephone:* (422) 22-5777.

NAGANO, Kent; American conductor; *Music Director, Montréal Symphony Orchestra and Bayerische Staatsoper;* b. 22 Nov. 1951, Berkeley, Calif.; ed studied under Ozawa, Boulez and Bernstein; first achieved int. recognition when he conducted Boston Symphony Orchestra in performance of Mahler's Symphony No. 9 1984; conducted US premiere of Messiaen's The Transfiguration; debut at Paris Opera conducting world premiere of Messiaen's St François d'Assise; debut, Metropolitan Opera, New York conducting Poulenc's Dialogues de Carmelites 1994; Music Dir Berkeley Symphony Orchestra, Calif. 1978–2009; Music Dir Opera de Lyon 1988–99; Music Dir Hallé Orchestra 1991–2000; Artistic Dir Deutsches Symphonie-Orchester Berlin 2000–07; Prin. Conductor and Music Dir Los Angeles Opera 2001–06; Music Dir Montréal Symphony Orchestra 2006–, Bayerische Staatsoper 2006–; Officier, l'Ordre des Arts et Lettres 1992, Order of the Rising Sun, Gold Rays 2009; Grammy Awards for Busoni's Dr Faust with Opéra National de Lyon, Prokofiev's Peter and the Wolf, with the Russian Nat. Orchestra. *Address:* c/o Van Walsum Management Ltd, The Tower Building, 11 York Road, London, SE1 7NX, England (office). *Telephone:* (20) 7902 0520 (office). *Fax:* (20) 7902 0521 (office). *E-mail:* vwm@vanwalsum.com (office). *Website:* www.vanwalsum.co.uk (office); www.osm.ca; www.bayerische.staatsoper.de.

NAGAO, Makoto, MEng, PhD; Japanese academic and engineer; *President, National Institute of Information and Communications Technology (NICT);* b. 4 Oct. 1936; ed Kyoto Univ.; pioneer of natural language processing and intelligent image processing tech.; led research developing first machine translation systems and digital library systems; Asst Prof., Faculty of Eng, Kyoto Univ. 1961–67, Lecturer 1967–68, Assoc. Prof. 1968–73, Prof. 1973–, Dir Data Processing Centre 1986–90, Dean Faculty of Eng 1997, Pres. Kyoto Univ. 1997–2003; Visiting Assoc. Prof., Dept of Informatics, Grenoble Univ. 1969–70; Pres. Japan Asscn of Nat. Univs 2001–03; Pres. Nat. Inst. of Information and Communications Tech. (NICT) 2004–; Pres. Japanese Cognitive Science Soc. 1988–90, Int. Asscn for Machine Tech. (IAMT) 1991–93, Asia–Pacific Asscn for Machine Tech. (AAMT) 1992–96, Asscn for Nat. Language Training (NLP) 1994–96, Inst. of Electronics, Information and Communication Engineers (IEICE) 1998–99, Information Processing Soc. of Japan (IPSJ) 1999–2000, Japan Library Asscn 2002–; Fellow IEEE 1999; mem. Science Council of Japan 2000–03; Hon. DSc (Univ. of Nottingham, UK) 1999 IEEE Emmanuel R. Piore Award 1993, Bunka-shou Culture Prize 1994, IEICE Distinguished Achievement and Contribs Award 1997, IPSJ Contribs Award 1997, IAMT Medal of Honour 1997, Japanese Govt Purple Ribbon Medal 1997, JSAI Achivement Award 1998, NHK Broadcast Cultural Award 1998, C&C Prize 1999, Takayanagi Kinen-shou Memorial Award 2000, Asscn for Computational Linguistics Lifetime Achievement Award 2003, Japan Prize for Information and Media Tech. 2005. *Publications:* in English: A Structural Analysis of Complex Aerial Photographs 1980, Machine Translation: How Far Can it Go? 1989, Knowledge and Inference 1990; in Japanese: Engineering for Pattern Recognition and Language Understanding 1989, Artificial and Human Intelligence 1992, Digital Library 1994, Natural Language Processing (co-author) 1996, What is Understanding? 2001. *Address:* National Institute of Information and Communications Technology (NICT), Incorporated Administrative Agency, 4-2-1 Nukui-Kitamachi, Koganei, Tokyo 184-8795 (office); 39-1 Kitaikeda, Iwakura, Sakyo, Kyoto, Japan (home). *Telephone:* (42) 327-7523 (office). *Fax:* (42) 327-7586 (office). *E-mail:* nagao-sec@nict.go.jp (office). *Website:* www.nict.go.jp (office).

NAGARE, Masayuki; Japanese sculptor; b. 1923, Nagasaki; m. (divorced); one d.; ed Ritsumeikan Univ.; enrolled in Zen Temple; apprentice to a sword maker; fighter pilot volunteer, World War II; several solo exhbns. *Works include:* Cloud Fortress, New York, Nagare Park, Okushiri, as well as over 2,000 other pieces. *Address:* c/o Jason McCoy Gallery, 41 East 57th Street, New York, NY 10022, USA.

NAGASE, Jinen; Japanese politician; b. 3 Oct. 1943; joined Ministry of Labour 1966, Sec. to Minister of Labour 1982–84, Dir Employment Security Bureau, Measures for the Aged Dept, Employment Measures Div. 1984–86, Dir Labour Relations Bureau, Labour Legislation Div. 1986–88 (resgnd from Ministry); mem. House of Reps for Toyama Prefecture 1st Dist (LDP) 1990–, Deputy Chair. LDP Diet Affairs Cttee 1994, State Sec. for Health and Welfare 1995–96, Dir LDP Environment Div. 1996, Chair. LDP Social Affairs Div. 1996, Dir LDP Labour Admin Div. 1997, Deputy Sec.-Gen. LDP and Chief Dir House Cttee on Health and Wefare 1998, Sr State Sec. for Labour 1999–2000, Chair. House Standing Cttee on Judicial Affairs 2000, Sr State Sec. for Justice

2000–01, Sr Vice-Minister of Justice 2001–02, Chief Dir of House Cttee on Health, Labour and Welfare 2002–03, Chief Deputy Chair. Policy Research Council 2004, Dir Jt Meeting of Both Houses on the Reform of Pension and Other Social Security Systems 2005, Deputy Chief Cabinet Sec. 2005–06, Minister of Justice 2006–07. *Address:* c/o Ministry of Justice, 1-1-1, Kasumigaseki, Chiyoda-ku, Tokyo 100-8977, Japan (office).

NAGASHIMA, Shigeo, BA; Japanese baseball player; b. 20 Feb. 1936, Chiba Pref.; s. of Toshi Nagashima and Chiyo Nagashima; m. Akiko Nishimura 1965; two s. two d.; ed St Paul's Univ., Tokyo; professional baseball player, Tokyo Yomiuri Giants 1958–74, Man. 1975–81, 1993–2001; Rookie of the Year 1958, Most Valuable Player of the Year (five times), Best Average Hitter of the Year (six times), Most Home-run Hitter of the Year (twice), Most Runs batted in Hitter of the Year (five times), Man. of Champion Team of the Year three times. *Leisure interest:* golf. *Address:* 3-29-19, Denenchofu, Ohta-ku, Tokyo 145, Japan. *Fax:* (3) 3722-3766.

NAGEL, Andrés; Spanish artist; b. 15 Aug. 1947, San Sebastián; qualified as an architect; subject of books 'Nagel' by Edward Lucie-Smith 1992 and 'Una Decada' by Lluisa Borràs 2003. *Address:* Caserío Parada 36, 20015 San Sebastián, Guipúzcoa, Spain (office).

NAGEL, Günter; German landscape architect; b. 2 Feb. 1936, Dresden; s. of Heinrich Nagel and Erna (née Hempel) Nagel; m. Helga Jähnig 1962; one c.; ed Dresden, Humboldt Univ., Berlin and Berlin Tech. Univ.; Scientific Asst Garden and Landscape Design, Berlin Tech. Univ. 1962–70, lectureship in Design, Garden and Landscape; freelance landscape architect; lectureships at Fine Arts Univ., Berlin (Prof. 1974) and Tech. Univ. Brunswick 1970–74; Prof. and Dir Inst. for Park Planning and Garden Architecture, Univ. of Hannover 1977–2000, Vice-Pres. Univ. of Hannover 1986–88; mem. German Soc. for Garden Design and Preservation of Natural Resources; mem. Deutscher Werkbund; mem. Bd of Trustees, Fritz Schumacher Foundation and Karl Foerster Foundation; Dir Acad. of Arts, Berlin, German Acad. of Town and Country Planning. *Publications:* Gärten in Cornwall 1975, Freiräume in der Stadtentwicklung 1978, Erholungsraum Stadtlandschaft 1980, Stadtumbau Grunfunktionen im Hamburger Hafen 1983, Gestaltung und Nutzung des Freiraums Strasse 1985, Verbesserung des Wohnumfeldes 1985, Qualität öffentlicher Freiräume 1986. *Address:* c/o Institut für Grünplanung und Gartenarchitektur, Universität Hannover, Herrenhäuser Strasse 2, 30419 Hannover, Germany.

NAGEL, Ivan; German professor of aesthetics and history of performing arts; b. 28 June 1931, Budapest, Hungary; ed Univ. of Heidelberg, Univ. of Paris, France, Univ. of Frankfurt and Univ. of Durham, UK; Theatre and Music Critic, Deutsche Zeitung 1959–61, Süddeutsche Zeitung 1969–71; Artistic Adviser, Münchner Kammerspiele 1962–69; Gen. Man. Deutsches Schauspielhaus, Hamburg 1972–79; Pres. Int. Theatre Inst. 1972–79; Cultural Corresp. Frankfurter Allgemeine, New York 1980–83; Fellow, Wissenschaftkolleg, Berlin 1983–84, 1988–89; Dir State Theatre, Stuttgart 1985–88; Prof. of Aesthetics and History of the Performing Arts, Hochschule der Künste, Berlin 1988–96; Dir Drama Section Salzburg Festival 1997–98; Founder and Pres. Theater der Welt (int. theatre festival), Hamburg 1979, 1989, Cologne 1981, Stuttgart 1987; mem. Akad. der Künste, Berlin, Akad. für Sprache und Dichtung, Darmstadt and Akad. der Darstellenden Künste, Frankfurt; mem. PEN Club; Hon. PhD 2008; Berlin Merit Order 2002, Fed. Merit Order 2003; Merck Award 1988, Kortner Award 1998, Moses Mendelssohn Award 2000, Ernst Bloch Award 2003, Heinrich Mann Award 2005. *Publications:* Autonomie und Gnade: Über Mozarts Opern 1985 (English trans. Autonomy and Mercy 1991), Gedankengänge als Lebensläufe: Versuche über das 18. Jahrhundert 1987, Kortner Zadek Stein 1989, Johann Heinrich Dannecker: Ariadne auf dem Panther 1993, Vier Regisseure: Bondy, Castorf, Sellars, Wilson 1996, Der Künstler als Kuppler: Goyas Nackte und Bekleidete Maja 1997, Streitschriften 2001, Falschwörterbuch 2004, Drama und Theater 2006. *Leisure interest:* music. *Address:* Keithstr. 10, 10787 Berlin, Germany (home). *Telephone:* (30) 2114710 (home). *Fax:* (30) 2114710 (home). *E-mail:* ivannagel@gmx.de (office).

NAGEL, Thomas, BA, BPhil, PhD; American academic; *Professor of Philosophy and Law, School of Law, New York University;* b. 4 July 1937, Belgrade, Serbia; s. of Walter Nagel and Carolyn Baer Nagel; m. 1st Doris Blum 1968 (divorced 1972); m. 2nd Anne Hollander 1979; ed Cornell and Harvard Univs and Univ. of Oxford, UK; Asst Prof. of Philosophy, Univ. of Calif., Berkeley 1963–66; Asst Prof. of Philosophy, Princeton Univ. 1966–69, Assoc. Prof. 1969–72, Prof. 1972–80; Prof. of Philosophy, New York Univ. 1980–, Prof. of Philosophy and Law 1986–, Fiorello LaGuardia Prof. of Law 2001–03, Univ. Prof. 2002–; Fellow, American Acad. of Arts and Sciences, British Acad.; Rolf Schock Prize in Logic and Philosophy, Royal Swedish Acad. of Sciences 2008. *Publications:* The Possibility of Altruism 1970, Mortal Questions 1979, The View from Nowhere 1986, What Does It All Mean? 1987, Equality and Partiality 1991, Other Minds 1995, The Last Word 1997, The Myth of Ownership (with Liam Murphy) 2002, Concealment and Exposure and other essays 2002. *Address:* School of Law, New York University, 40 Washington Square South, 418, New York, NY 10012, USA (office). *Telephone:* (212) 998-6225 (office). *Fax:* (212) 995-4179 (office). *E-mail:* nagelt@juris.law.nyu.edu (office). *Website:* philosophy.fas.nyu.edu (office).

NAGGAR, Zaghloul Raghib an-, PhD; geologist and academic; b. 17 Nov. 1933; ed Univ. of Wales, UK; taught at Ain Shams Univ., Cairo, King Saud Univ., Riyadh, Univ. Coll. of Wales, Aberystwyth, Kuwait Univ., Univ. of Qatar, Doha; fmr Prof. of Geology, King Fahd Univ. of Petroleum and Minerals, Dhahran; now at Arab Devt Inst.; mem. Geological Soc., London, Geological Soc. of Egypt, American Soc. of Petroleum Geologists, Tulsa; Fellow, Inst. of Petroleum, London, Islamic Acad. of Sciences, mem. Council 1994; Secondary Educ. Award (Egypt), Best Papers Award (Arab Petroleum Congress) 1970. *Address:* c/o Islamic Academy of Sciences, PO Box 830036, Amman, Jordan (office). *Telephone:* 5522104 (office). *Fax:* 5511803 (office). *Website:* www.elnaggarzr.com.

NAHODHA, Shamsi Vuai; Tanzanian politician; currently Chief Minister, Supreme Revolutionary Council of Zanzibar; Branch Vice-Pres., Commonwealth Parl. Assсn. *Address:* Office of the Chief Minister, POB 239, Zanzibar, Tanzania (office). *Telephone:* (24) 2311126 (office). *Fax:* (24) 233788 (office).

NAHORNY, Włodzimierz; Polish pianist and composer; b. 5 Nov. 1941, Radzyń Podlaski; m. Anna Woźniakowska; has performed in numerous concerts in Europe 1964–, including Int. Jazz Workshop, Hamburg 1965–69, Jazz Festival, Edin. 2000, Shanghai Music Festival 2001, Algiers 2002, Novosibirsk 2003, Sarajevo 2004, Kowno 2004, Rome 2004, Paris 2004, Expo 2005, Nagoya, Japan 2005; First Prize, Jazz nad Odrą, Int. Jazz Festival, Vienna 1967, Musician of the Year, Jazz Forum magazine 1967, First Prize, Polish Song Festival, Opole 1972, 1973, Meritorious Activist of Culture 1974, 1986, Grand Prix Jazz Melomani, Łódź 1997, Fryderyk Polish Music Award 2000, Bronze Medal, Meritorius of Culture Gloria Artist 2005. *Compositions:* soundtracks: Rondo, Pełnia; for theatre: Medea, Księżniczka Turandot; songs: Her Portrait, Chianti, Śpiewnik Nahornego (Nahorny's Songbook) 2003. *Recordings:* Nahorny-Chopin Polish Fantasy, Nahorny-Szymanowski Myths, Nahorny-Karłowicz Concerto Dolce Far Niente, Ballet 'Polish Fantasy', Baltics Opera, Gdansk; for theatre: Lanie Robertson, I Love O'Keeffe, Dir Cristoff Kolberger. *Leisure interests:* books, garden, theatre. *Address:* ul. Nałęczowska 62/14, 02-922 Warsaw, Poland (office). *Telephone:* (22) 642-76-81 (home). *Fax:* (22) 642-76-81 (home). *E-mail:* nahorny@konto.pl (home).

NAHYAN, Sheikh Abdullah bin Zayed an-; United Arab Emirates government official and diplomatist; *Minister of Foreign Affairs;* Minister of Information and Culture –2006, Minister of Foreign Affairs 2006–; mem. Council of Ministers; Chair. Emirates Media Inc. *Address:* Ministry of Foreign Affairs, POB 1, Abu Dhabi, United Arab Emirates (office). *Telephone:* (2) 4444488 (office). *Fax:* (2) 4449100 (office). *E-mail:* mofa@mofa.gov.ae (office). *Website:* www.mofa.gov.ae (office).

NAHYAN, Sheikh Hamdan bin Zayed an-; United Arab Emirates politician; fmr Minister of State for Foreign Affairs, currently Deputy Prime Minister and Minister of Public Works:. *Address:* Ministry of Public Works, POB 878, Abu Dhabi, United Arab Emirates (office). *Telephone:* (2) 6260606 (office). *Fax:* (2) 6260026 (office). *E-mail:* falshamsi@mpw.ae (office). *Website:* www.mopw.gov.ae (office).

NAHYAN, HH Sheikh Khalifa bin Zayed an-, (Ruler of Abu Dhabi); United Arab Emirates; *President;* b. 1948, al-Ain; s. of the late HH Sheikh Zayed bin Sultan al-Nahyan; apptd Ruler of Abu Dhabi's Rep. in Eastern Region of Abu Dhabi and Head of Courts Dept in Al-Ain on his father's accession as Ruler of Abu Dhabi 1966, Crown Prince of Abu Dhabi and Head of Abu Dhabi Defence Force 1969; Prime Minister of Abu Dhabi and Minister of Defence and Finance 1971–74, first Chair. Abu Dhabi Exec. Council 1974; Deputy Prime Minister of UAE 1973; Supreme Commdr UAE Armed Forces 1976; Chair. Supreme Petroleum Council late 1980s–, Abu Dhabi Fund for Devt, Abu Dhabi Investment Authority, Research and Wildlife Devt Agency; Pres. of UAE and Ruler of Emirate of Abu Dhabi 2004–. *Leisure interests:* falconry, fishing, reading history and poetry. *Address:* Office of the President of the United Arab Emirates and Ruler of Abu Dhabi, Manhal Palace, PO Box 280, Abu Dhabi, United Arab Emirates (office). *Telephone:* 6652000 (office). *Fax:* 6651962 (office).

NAHYAN, HH Sheikh Mohammed bin Zayed al-, (Crown Prince of Abu Dhabi); United Arab Emirates government official; *Deputy Supreme Commander of the UAE Armed Forces;* b. 1961; m.; nine c.; ed Royal Mil. Acad., Sandhurst, UK; Deputy Crown Prince of Abu Dhabi 2003–04, Crown Prince of Abu Dhabi 2004–; Chief of Staff of the Armed Forces of the UAE 1993–2005, Deputy Supreme Commdr of the UAE Armed Forces 2005–; Chair. Exec. Bd 2004–; mem. Abu Dhabi Exec. Council, Deputy Chair. 2004–; mem. Supreme Petroleum Council; Chair. Abu Dhabi Council for Econ. Devt, Abu Dhabi Educ. Council 2005–; Head of Mubadala Devt Co. 2002–; Head of UAE Offsets Group; Pres. Emirates Center for Strategic Studies and Research; Special Adviser to his brother Sheikh Khalifa Bin Zayed Al-Nahyan; numerous decorations. *Address:* Abu Dhabi Council for Economic Development, PO Box 44484, Abu Dhabi, United Arab Emirates (office). *Telephone:* (2) 6913300 (office). *Fax:* (2) 6913400 (office). *E-mail:* info@adced.ae (office). *Website:* www.adced.ae (office).

NAHYAN, HE Sheikh Nahyan bin Mubarak an-; United Arab Emirates university chancellor and politician; *Minister of Education;* b. 1948; Chancellor, United Arab Emirates Univ. 1976–, Higher Colls of Tech. 1988, Abu Dhabi Petroleum Univ. (ADPU), Zayed Univ.; Minister of Higher Educ. and Scientific Research 1990–2004, Minister of Educ. 2004–; Chair. Union Nat. Bank, Abu Dhabi Group (construction co.), Bank Alfalah Ltd; Hilal-i-Pakistan Award, Pres. of Pakistan. *Address:* Ministry of Education, POB 295, Abu Dhabi (office); United Arab Emirates University, POB 15551 Al-Ain, United Arab Emirates (office). *Telephone:* (2) 6213800 (office); (3) 7544375 (office). *Fax:* (2) 6313778 (office); (3) 7540555 (office). *E-mail:* moe@uae.gov.ae (office); chancellor@uaeu.ac.ae (office). *Website:* www.moe.gov.ae (office); www.uaeu.ac.ae (office).

NAHYAN, Sheikh Sultan bin Zayed an-; United Arab Emirates government official and soldier; *Deputy Prime Minister;* b. 1955; ed in Abu Dhabi, Lebanon, Sandhurst Mil. Acad., UK; Commdr Western Mil. Dist 1976; Gen. Commdr UAE Armed Forces 1978; now Deputy Commdr Abu Dhabi Defence

Forces; Deputy Prime Minister 1991–. *Address:* PO Box 831, Abu Dhabi, United Arab Emirates. *Telephone:* (2) 651881.

NAIDOO, Beverley, PhD; South African/British writer and educationalist; b. 21 May 1943, Johannesburg, South Africa; d. of Ralph Henry Trewhela and Evelyn Levison; m. Nandhagopaul Naidoo 1969; one s. one d.; ed Univs of Witwatersrand, York and Southampton; NGO worker, SA 1964; detained without trial, SA 1964; teacher, London then Dorset, UK 1969–89; educ. adviser on English and cultural diversity, Dorset 1990–97; writer 1985–; int. writers' workshops and readings 1991–; Hon. Visiting Fellow, School of Educ., Univ. of Southampton 1992–2006; Hon. DLitt (Southampton) 2002, (Exeter) 2007; Hon. DUniv (Open Univ.) 2003; The Other Award, UK 1985, Child Study Children's Book Cttee Award, USA 1986, 1998, Vlag en Wimpel Award, Netherlands 1991, African Studies Asscn Africana Children's Book Award, USA 1998, 2004, Arts Council Writer's Award, UK 1999, Smarties Silver Medal for Children's Books, UK 2000, Carnegie Medal for Children's Literature, UK 2000, Jane Addams Book Award, USA 2002, 2004. *Plays:* The Playground, Polka Theatre, London 2004. *Radio:* The Other Side of Truth (BBC) 2003. *Publications:* Censoring Reality: An Examination of Non-fiction Books on South Africa 1985, Journey to Jo'burg 1985, Chain of Fire 1989, Through Whose Eyes? Exploring Racism: Reader, Text and Context 1992, Letang and Julie (series – illustrator Petra Rohr-Rouendaal) 1994, No Turning Back 1995, Where is Zami? (illustrator Petra Rohr-Rouendaal) 1998, The Other Side of Truth 2000, Out of Bounds 2001, Baba's Gift (with Maya Naidoo, illustrator Karin Littlewood) 2003, The Great Tug of War and Other Stories 2003, Web of Lies 2004, Burn My Heart 2007. *Leisure interests:* reading, theatre, walking. *Address:* c/o Hilary Delamere, The Agency, 24 Pottery Lane, London, W11 4LZ, England (office). *Telephone:* (20) 7727-1346 (office). *Fax:* (20) 7727-9037 (office). *E-mail:* info@theagency.co.uk (office). *Website:* www.theagency.co.uk (office); www.beverleynaidoo.com.

NAIDOO, Jayaseelan (Jay); South African trade union official, banker and business executive; *Chairman, Development Bank of Southern Africa;* b. 20 Dec. 1954, Durban; m. Mrs Lucie Pagé 1992; two s. one d.; ed Sastri Coll., Durban and Univ. of Durban-Westville; mem. SASO 1977; involved in community orgs, Natal 1976–79; studies interrupted by political events 1978; Organizer Fed. of South African Trade Unions (FOSATU) 1980; Gen. Sec. Sweet Food & Allied Workers Union 1982, Congress of South African Trade Unions (COSATU) 1985–93; Minister, Office of the Pres., Govt of Nat. Unity 1994–96; Minister of Posts and Telecommunications and Broadcasting 1996–99; Chair. Devt Bank of Southern Africa 2000–, Global Alliance for Improved Nutrition 2003–; mem. Bd Dirs J&J Group 2000–, ITU Telecom 2007–; mem. Health Advisory Comm. Clinton Global Initiative 2007–; Chevalier, Légion d'honneur 2006. *Leisure interests:* jazz, skiing cross-country, family, cuisine. *Address:* Development Bank of Southern Africa, PO Box 1234, Halfway House, Midrand 1685, South Africa (office). *Telephone:* (11) 783-0770 (office). *Fax:* (11) 388-3063 (office). *E-mail:* jay@jandjgroup.com (office). *Website:* www.dbsa.org (office); www.jandjgroup.com (office); www.gainhealth.org (office).

NAIDU, Chandrababu, MA; Indian politician; b. 20 April 1951; ed S.V. Univ. Tirupathi; Minister of Finance and Revenue 1994–95; Chief Minister of Andhra Pradesh 1995–2004; Pres. Telugu Desam (Telugu Nation). *Address:* c/o Block C, Room No. 404, AP Secretariat, Hyderabad, Andhra Pradesh, India.

NAIDU, K. Muppavarapu Venkaiah, BA, BL; Indian politician; *President, Bharatiya Janata Party (BJP);* b. 1 July 1949, Chavatapalem, Nellore Dist, Andhra Pradesh; s. of the late Rangaiah Naidu and Ramanamma Naidu; m. M. Usha; one s. one d.; fmr agriculturalist; political activist, imprisoned during Nat. Emergency 1975–77; Pres. Youth Wing of Janata Party, Andhra Pradesh (AP) 1977–80, State Univ. of Bharatiya Janata Party (BJP—Indian People's Party) 1988–93, Student Union, Andhra Univ. 1973–74; Vice-Pres. Youth Wing of All-India BJP 1980–83, Leader of BJP Legis. Party, AP 1980–85, Gen. Sec. All-India BJP 1993–2002, Pres. BJP 2002–; mem. Legis. Ass., AP 1978–83, 1983–85; elected to Rakya Sabha 1998; Minister of Rural Devt 2000–02. *Address:* Bharatiya Janata Party (BJP), 11 Ashok Road, New Delhi 110 001, India (office). *Telephone:* (11) 3382234 (office). *Fax:* (11) 3782163 (office). *E-mail:* bjpco@del3.vsnl.net.in (office). *Website:* www.bjp.org (office).

NAILATIKAU, Ratu Epeli, OBE; Fijian government official, diplomatist and army officer; *Vice President;* b. 5 July 1941, Levuka, Ovalau; s. of Ratu Edward Cakobau and Vasemaca Tuiburelevu; m. Adi Koila Mara; one s. one d.; ed Levuka Public School and Queen Victoria School; completed mil. training in New Zealand, seconded to 1st Battalion, Royal New Zealand Infantry Regt in Sarawak, Malaysia 1966, Brig.-Gen., Fiji Infantry Regt 1987–88, Commdr of Armed Forces 1982–88; fmr High Commr to UK; fmr Amb. to Denmark, Egypt, Germany, Israel and Holy See, to the Pacific 1998–99; Perm. Sec. for Foreign Affairs and External Trade 1999–2000; Deputy Prime Minister 2000–01; Minister for Fijian Affairs 2000–01; Speaker of House of Reps 2001–06, Chair. Parl. Appropriations and House Cttees 2001–06; Minister of Foreign Affairs and Trade 2007 (in Cdre Josaia Bainimarama's interim govt), Minister of Foreign Affairs, Int. Co-operation and Civil Aviation 2007–08, of Prov. Devt and Multi-Ethnic Affairs 2008–09; Vice-Pres. of Fiji 2009–; LVO, Meritorious Service Decoration, Venerable Order of the Hospital of Saint John of Jerusalem. *Address:* c/o Office of the President, Government House, Berkley Crescent, Government Buildings, POB 2513 Suva, Fiji (office). *Telephone:* 3314244 (office). *Fax:* 3301645 (office). *Website:* www.fiji.gov.fj/publish/president.shtml (office).

NA'IM, Abdullahi Ahmed An-, LLB, Dip.Crim., PhD; Sudanese/American academic; *Charles Howard Candler Chaired Professor of Law, Emory University;* b. 19 Nov. 1946, Shendi, Sudan; ed Univ. of Khartoum, Univs of Cambridge and Edin., UK; Lecturer and Assoc. Prof. of Law, Univ. of Khartoum 1976–85; Rockefeller Fellow, Columbia Univ. Center for Study of Human Rights 1981–82; Visiting Prof., UCLA 1985–87; Fellow, Woodrow Wilson Int. Center for Scholars 1987–88; Ariel F. Sallows Prof. of Human Rights, Univ. of Sask., Canada 1988–91; Olof Palme Visiting Prof., Uppsala Univ., Sweden 1991–92; Visiting Fellow, Harvard Law School Human Rights Program 1991; Scholar-in-Residence, Ford Foundation Office for Middle East and N Africa, Cairo, Egypt 1992–93; Prof. of Law and Sr Fellow of Law and Religion Program, Emory Univ. 1995–, Charles Howard Candler Chaired Prof. of Law 1999–; Visiting Prof., Utrecht Univ. 1999, Harvard Law School 2003; Wiarda Chair, Faculty of Law, Utrecht Univ. 2005–06; Global Legal Scholar, Warwick Univ. School of Law, UK 2007–09; Scholar-in-Residence, Ford Foundation, New York, NY May–Dec. 2007; Extraordinary Prof., Human Rights Center, Univ. of Pretoria, South Africa 2009–(10); Exec. Dir Human Rights Watch/Africa, Washington DC 1993–95; Commr, Int. Comm. of Jurists; mem. Bd Urban Morgan Inst. for Human Rights, Cairo Inst. for Human Rights Studies, Int. Council on Human Rights Policy, Geneva; mem. ed. bds Human Rights Quarterly, Int. Politics; Dr J.P. van Praag Award of Dutch Humanist Ethical Soc. 1999, Marion Creekmore Award for Internationalization, Emory Univ. *Publications:* Sudanese Criminal Law: The General Principles of Criminal Responsibility 1985, The Second Message of Islam by Ustadh Mahmoud Mohamed Taha (English trans.) 1987, Toward an Islamic Reformation: Civil Liberties, Human Rights and International Law 1990, Human Rights in Africa: Cross-Cultural Perspectives (co-ed.) 1990, Cry of the Owl by Francis Deng (Arabic trans.) 1991, Human Rights in Cross Cultural Perspectives: Quest for Consensus (ed.) 1992, Human Rights and Religious Values (co-ed.) 1995, Proselytization and Communal Self-Determination in Africa (ed.) 1999, The Politics of Memory: Truth, Healing and Social Justice (ed.) 2002, Cultural Transformation and Human Rights in Africa (ed.) 2002, Human Rights Under African Constitutions (ed.) 2003, African Constitutionalism and the Role of Islam 2006, Islam and the Secular State 2008; numerous writings, including 60 articles and 28 short articles and book reviews. *Address:* School of Law, Emory University, 1301 Clifton Road, Atlanta, GA 30322, USA (office). *Telephone:* (404) 727-1198 (office). *E-mail:* Abduh46@law.emory.edu (office). *Website:* www.law.emory.edu/aannaim (office).

NAIPAUL, Sir V(idiadhar) S(urajprasad), Kt, CLit, BA, FRSL; Trinidadian-born writer; b. 17 Aug. 1932, Chaguanas; m. 1st Patricia Ann Hale 1955 (died 1996); m. 2nd Nadira Khannum Alvi 1996; one d. (adopted); ed Queen's Royal Coll., Port-of-Spain and Univ. Coll. Oxford; for two years freelance broadcaster with the BBC, producing programmes for the Caribbean area; fiction reviewer on New Statesman 1958–61; grant from Trinidad Govt to travel in Caribbean and S America 1961; in India 1962–63, 1975, 1988–89, in Uganda 1965–66, in USA 1969, 1978–79, 1987–88, in Argentina 1972, 1973–74, 1977, 1991, in Venezuela 1977, 1985, in Iran, Pakistan, Malaysia and Indonesia 1979–80, 1995; mem. Soc. of Authors; Hon. DLitt (Univ. of the W Indies, St Augustine) 1975, (St Andrews) 1979, (Columbia) 1981, (Cambridge) 1983, (London) 1988, (Oxford) 1992; John Llewelyn Rhys Memorial Prize 1958, Somerset Maugham Award 1961, Phoenix Trust Award 1962, Hawthornden Prize 1964, W. H. Smith Award 1968, Booker Prize 1971, Jerusalem Prize 1983, Ingersoll Prize 1986, David Cohen British Literature Prize 1993, Nobel Prize for Literature 2001. *Publications:* The Mystic Masseur 1957, The Suffrage of Elvira 1958, Miguel Street 1959, A House for Mr Biswas 1961, The Middle Passage 1962, Mr Stone and the Knights Companion 1963, An Area of Darkness 1964, The Mimic Men 1967, A Flag on the Island 1967 (collection of short stories), The Loss of El Dorado 1969, In a Free State 1971, The Overcrowded Barracoon (essays) 1972, Guerrillas 1975, India: A Wounded Civilization 1977, A Bend in the River 1979, A Congo Diary 1980, The Return of Eva Perón 1980, Among the Believers 1981, Finding the Centre 1984, The Enigma of Arrival 1987, A Turn In The South 1989, India: A Million Mutinies Now 1990, A Way in the World 1994, Beyond Belief 1998, Letters Between a Father and Son 1999, Reading and Writing: a Personal Account 2000, Half a Life 2001, Literary Occasions 2004, Magic Seeds 2004, A Writer's People 2007. *Address:* Aitken Alexander Associates Ltd, 18–21 Cavaye Place, London, SW10 9PT, England. *Telephone:* (20) 7373-8672. *Fax:* (20) 7373-6002. *E-mail:* reception@aitkenalexander.co.uk. *Website:* www.aitkenalexander.co.uk.

NAIR, Dileep, BMechEng, MPA; Singaporean international organization official; ed McGill Univ., Montreal, Canada, Kennedy School of Govt, Harvard Univ., USA; with Housing and Devt Bd 1974–79; joined Admin. Service 1979, various posts including Dir in charge of expenditure control, Deputy Sec. Ministry of Trade and Industry 1986–89, Ministry of Defence 1989–97; CEO Post Office Savings Bank of Singapore 1997–98, Man. Dir Devt Bank of Singapore (DBS) 1998–2000; Under-Sec.-Gen. for Internal Oversight Services, UN 2000–05; fmr Vice-Pres. Singapore Indian Devt Asscn; mem. Hindu Advisory Bd; mem. Bd of Govs Raffles Inst.; Colombo Plan Scholar 1969–73. *Address:* c/o UN Office of Internal Oversight Services, United Nations Plaza, New York, NY 10017, USA (office).

NAIR, Mira; Indian film director and producer; b. 1957, Bhubaneswar, Orissa; m. 1st Mitch Epstein; m. 2nd Mahmood Mamdan; one s.; ed Irish Catholic boarding school, Simla, Univ. of Delhi and Harvard Univ., USA; performed with experimental theatre co., Calcutta (now Kolkata); began career as documentary and feature film-maker at Harvard Univ.; Asst Prof., School of the Arts, Columbia Univ., New York. *Films:* India Cabaret (American Film Festival Award for Best Documentary of 1985) 1985, Children of Desired Sex (documentary), Salaam Bombay! (Cannes Film Festival Camera d'Or Award for Best First Feature by a New Dir, Prix du Publique) 1988, Mississippi Masala (three awards at Venice Film Festival) 1991, Buddha, The Perez Family 1996, Kama Sutra 1996, My Own Country 1998, The Laughing Club of India 1999, Monsoon Wedding (Golden Lion Award,

Venice Film Festival) 2002, Hysterical Blindness 2002, Vanity Fair 2005, The Namesake 2006, Migration 2007, New York, I Love You 2008, 8 2008. *Address:* Film Department, School of the Arts, Columbia University, 513 Dodge Hall, 2960 Broadway, New York, NY 10027, USA (office). *Telephone:* (212) 854-2815 (office). *E-mail:* film@columbia.edu (office). *Website:* wwwapp.cc.columbia.edu/art/app/arts/index.jsp (office).

NAIRNE, Rt Hon. Sir Patrick Dalmahoy, PC, GCB, MC, MA; British civil servant and university administrator; b. 15 Aug. 1921, London; s. of the late C.S. Nairne and E.D. Nairne; m. Penelope Chauncy Bridges 1948; three s. three d.; ed Radley Coll., Univ. Coll., Oxford; entered civil service 1947; Pvt. Sec. to First Lord of Admiralty 1958–60; Defence Sec. 1965–67; Deputy Sec., Ministry of Defence 1970–73; Second Perm. Sec., Cabinet Office 1973–75; Perm. Sec., Dept of Health and Social Security 1975–81; Master, St Catherine's Coll. Oxford 1981–88; Chancellor, Essex Univ. 1983–97; Dir, Cen. ITV 1982–92; Chair., W Midlands Bd 1990–92, Nuffield Council on Bioethics 1991–96; mem. Civil Service Security Appeals Panel 1982, Cttee of Inquiry into the events leading to the Argentine invasion of the Falklands 1982; UK Monitor, Anglo-Chinese Agreement on Hong Kong 1984; Gov. and mem. Council of Man., Ditchley Foundation 1988–2004; Chair., Comm. on the Conduct of Referendums 1996; Church Commr 1993–98; Chair. Advisory Bd, Museum of Modern Art, Oxford 1988–98, Pres. 1998; Chair., Irene Wellington Educational Trust 1986–2002; Pres. Radleian Soc. 1980–83; Pres., Seamen's Hosp. Soc. 1982–2002, Oxfordshire Craft Guild 1993–97; mem. Radley Coll. Council 1975–99; Trustee, Nat. Maritime Museum 1981–91, Joseph Rowntree Foundation 1982–96, Nat. AIDS Trust 1987–96, Oxford School of Drama 1998; Hon. LLD (Leicester) 1980, (St Andrews) 1984; Hon. DUniv (Essex) 1983. *Painting exhibitions:* Clarges Gallery, London 1971, 1977, 1983, 1997, 1999; Oliver Swann Gallery, London 1989, 1992. *Leisure interests:* watercolour painting, calligraphy. *Address:* Yew Tree, Chilson, Chipping Norton, Oxon., OX7 3HU, England (home). *Telephone:* (1608) 676456 (home). *E-mail:* pat.nairne@btinternet.com (home).

NAISH, Bronwen, ARMCM; British musician (double bass and musical saw); *Examiner, Associated Board of the Royal Schools of Music;* b. 19 Nov. 1939, Burley, Hants.; d. of E.F.E. Naish and G.J. Grant; m. Roger Best 1959 (divorced 1981); two s. three d.; ed Holyhead Grammar School and Royal Manchester Coll. of Music; began playing double bass 1966; performance and teaching in northern England and sub-prin. bass, Northern Sinfonia 1967–73; debut recital, King's Hall, Newcastle-upon-Tyne 1971; London debut, Purcell Room 1974; returned to N Wales to concentrate on solo career 1976; Channel Island tours 1980, 1988; Australian tour 1988; est. Slap & Tickle with pianist Maurice Horhut 1988; Edin. Fringe Festival 1989, 1990; commissioning new works for musical saw (recent acquisition) 1990; examiner, Assoc. Bd of Royal Schools of Music. *Publication:* Another String to my Bow 1982. *Leisure interests:* beekeeping, do-it-yourself. *Address:* Moelfre, Cwm Pennant, Garndolbenmaen, Gwynedd, LL5 9AX, North Wales (home). *Telephone:* (20) 8299-2931 (home). *Fax:* (1766) 530356 (home). *E-mail:* bnaish@onetel.com (home).

NAJDER, Zdzisław Marian, PhD; Polish civic leader and author; b. 31 Oct. 1930, Warsaw; s. of Franciszek Najder and Józefa Najder (née Kowalska); m. Halina Paschalska 1965; one s.; ed Warsaw Univ., Univ. of Oxford, UK; Asst Inst. for Literary Research of Polish Acad. of Sciences 1952–57; Sr Asst Aesthetics, Warsaw Univ. 1958–59; on staff, Twórczość (monthly) 1957–81; taught Polish literature at Columbia and Yale Univs, USA 1966 and Univ. of Calif., Berkeley, USA 1966–67; Prof. of Philosophy, Univ. of Calif., Davis 1967–68, Regents' Prof. 1968–69; Prof. of English Literature, Northern Ill. Univ., USA 1971–72; Visiting Scholar, Stanford Univ., Calif. 1974–75; adviser to Solidarity Trade Union 1980–90; Visiting Fellow, St Antony's Coll., Oxford 1981, 1988; Head, Polish section of Radio Free Europe, Munich 1982–87; charged with spying, sentenced to death in absentia by Warsaw Mil. Tribunal 1983, stripped of Polish citizenship 1985, sentence revoked 1989, case dismissed 1990; mem. editorial staff Kontakt, Paris 1988–91; Chair. Nat. Civic Cttee 1990–92; Chief Adviser to the Prime Minister 1992; Pres. Civic Inst. 1991–97, Atlantic Club 1991–93; Chair. Joseph Conrad Soc. (Poland) 1994–; Prof. of English Literature, Univ. of Opole 1997–2003; Adviser to Chair. Cttee for European Integration 1998–2001; Prof., European Acad., Cracow 2005–; mem. Polish Writers' Union 1956–83, PEN Club 1957–, Nat. Council for European Integration 1999–2004; f. Polish Agreement for Independence 1976; founder and Pres., Club of Weimar 2005–; Commdr's Cross, Order of Polonia Restituta 1983; Commdr, Ordre Nat. du Mérite (France) 1991; Chevalier Légion d'Honneur (France) 2004; Juliusz Mieroszewski Award 1982, Prize of Modern Language Asscn 1984, Polish PEN Club Prize 1988. *Publications:* studies and essays including Conrad's Polish Background 1964, Nad Conradem 1965, Values and Evaluations 1975, Życie Conrada-Korzeniowskiego 1981, Ile jest dróg? 1982, Wymiary polskich spraw 1990, Jaka Polska 1993, Z Polski do Polski poprzez PRL 1995, Conrad in Perspective: Essays on Art and Fidelity 1997, W sercu Europy 1998, Sztuka i wierność 2000. *Leisure interests:* travel, walks in forest, 12th-century Romanesque art. *Telephone:* (22) 8448536 (home). *Fax:* (22) 8448536 (home). *E-mail:* zdzislaw.najder@list.pl (home).

NAJMIDDINOV, Safarali Mahsudinovich; Tajikistani politician; *Minister of Finance;* ed Tajik State Univ.; fmr Chief Accountant and Head of Dept of Finance, State Cttee of Statistics; Head of Trade Dept, Municipality of Dushanbe 1982–92; Deputy Minister of Trade 1991–2000; Minister of Finance 2000–. *Address:* Ministry of Finance, 734067 Dushanbe, Nazarov 64/14, Tajikistan (office). *Telephone:* (37) 881-25-79 (office). *E-mail:* nii_finance@mail.tj (office).

NAKADAI, Tatsuya; Japanese actor; b. 13 Dec. 1932, Tokyo; m. Tomoye Ryu 1957 (died 1996); ed Haiyuza Actors' Training School; worked with Masaki Kobayashi and Akira Kurosawa; stage work comprises both shingeki (modern theatre) featuring a highly acclaimed Hamlet and roles in other Shakespeare, Gorky, Ibsen and Chekhov adaptations, and avant-garde, including work with Kobo Abe's theatre group. *Films:* Kabe atsuki heya (The Thick-Walled Room) 1953, Shichinin no samurai (The Seven Samurai) 1954, Hi no tori 1956, Fukuaki no seishun 1956, Sazae-san 1956, Oshidori no mon (Lovebirds' Gate) 1956, Ôban 1957, Arakure (Untamed) 1957, Hikage no musume 1957, Zoku Ôban: Fû unhen 1957, Kiken na eiyu (A Dangerous Hero) 1957, Zokuzoku Ôban: Dôto uhen 1957, Sazae-san no seishun (Sazae's Youth) 1957, Kuroi kawa (Black River) 1957, Haha sannin (A Boy and Three Mothers, USA) 1958, Kekkon no subete (All About Marriage) 1958, Buttuke honban (Go and Get It) 1958, Enjo (Conflagration) 1958, Hadaka no taiyo (Naked Sun) 1958, Yajû shisubeshi 1959, Kagi (The Key) 1959, Ginza no onéchan (Three Dolls in Ginza, USA) 1959, Anyakôro 1959, Ningen no joken I (No Greater Love) 1959, Ningen no joken II (The Road to Eternity) 1959, Musume tsuma haha (Daughters, Wives and a Mother) 1960, Aoi yaju (The Blue Beast, USA 1965) 1960, 'Minagoroshi no uta' yori kenjû-yo saraba! (Get 'em All, USA 1961) 1960, Qnna ga kaidan o agaru toki (When a Woman Ascends the Stairs) 1960, Qginsama (Love Under the Crucifix, USA 1965) 1960, Yojimbo (The Bodyguard) 1961, Tsuma to shita onna to shite (As a Wife, As a Woman) 1961, Ningen no joken III (A Soldier's Prayer) 1961, Eien no hito (Immortal Love) 1961, Tsubaki Sanjûrô 1962, Karami-ai (The Inheritance, USA 1964) 1962, Yushu heiya (Madame Aki) 1963, Tengoku to jigoku (Heaven and Hell) 1963, Shiro to kuro (Pressure of Guilt) 1963, Gojuman-nin no isan (Legacy of the 500,000) 1963, Miren 1963, Onna no rekishi (A Woman's Life) 1963, Seppuku (Harakiri, USA) 1964, Jigoku sakusen 1964, Kaidan (Ghost Story) 1964, Chi to suna (Fort Graveyard) 1965, Saigô no shinpan 1965, Dai-bosatsu tôge (The Sword of Doom, USA) 1966, Tanin no kao (The Face of Another) 1966), Jinchoge (Daphne), Yotsuya kaidan 1966 (Illusion of Blood) 1966, Gohiki no shinshi (Cash Calls Hell) 1966, Satsujin kyo jidai (The Age of Assassins) 1967, Kojiro 1967, Jôi-uchi: Hairyô tsuma shimatsu (Samurai Rebellion) 1967, Tabiji 1967, Oggi a me... domani a te! (Today We Kill, Tomorrow We Die!) 1968, Kiru (Kill!, USA) 1969, Rengo kantai shirei chôkan: Yamamoto Isoroku (Admiral Yamamoto) (narrator) 1968, Nikudan (The Human Bullet) 1968, Goyokin (Official Gold) 1969, Eiko e no 5,000 kiro (5,000 Kilometres to Glory) 1969, Nihonkai daikasen (Battle of the Japan Sea) 1969, Hitokiri (Tenchu!, USA 1970) 1969, Tengu-to (Blood End) 1969, Jigokuhen (Portrait of Hell) 1969, Ezo yakata no ketto (Duel at Ezo) 1970, Bakumatsu (The Ambitious) 1970, Buraikan (Outlaws) 1970, Zatôichi abare-himatsuri (Blind Swordsman's Fire Festival) 1970, Tenkan no abarembo (Will to Conquer, USA 1971) 1970, Inochi bonifuro (At the Risk of My Life) 1971, Gekido no showashi: Okinawa kessen (The Battle of Okinawa) 1971, Shussho Iwai (Prison Release Celebration) 1972, Ôshô 1973, Kanashimi no Belladonna (Belladonna) (voice) 1973, Ningen kakumei (The Human Revolution, USA) 1973, Asayake no uta (Rise, Fair Sun, USA 1975) 1973, Karei-naru ichizoku 1974, Seishun no mon (The Gate of Youth, USA 1976) 1975, Tokkan (Battle Cry) 1975, Wagahai wa neko de aru (I Am a Cat) 1975, Kinkanshoku 1975, Banka 1976, Fumô chitai 1976, Sugata Sanshiro 1977, Jo-oh-bachi (Queen Bee) 1978, Kumokiri nizaemon (Bandit vs. Samurai Squad) 1978, Hi no tori (The Firebird) 1978, Buru kurisumasu (Blue Christmas) 1978, Yami no karyudo (Hunter in Darkness) 1979, Kagemusha (Kagemusha the Shadow Warrior), 203 kochi (The Battle of Port Arthur) 1980, Nihon no atsui hibi bôsatsu: Shimoyama shigen (Willful Murder) 1981, Kirûin Hanako no shôgai (Onimasa) 1982, Uchû senkan Yamato: Kanketsuhen (Final Yamato) (narrator) 1983, Ran (Chaos) 1985, Shokutaku no nai ie (The Empty Table) 1985, Atami satsujin jiken 1986, Hachiko monogatari 1987, Yushun (Oracion, USA) 1988, Return From the River Kwai 1988, Ni-ni-roku (Four Days of Snow and Blood, USA 1989, Kagerô 1991, Goh-hime (Basara – The Princess Goh) 1992, Toki rakujitsu (The Distant Setting Sun) 1992, Yao shou du shi (The Wicked City) 1992, Kozure Ôkami: Sono chîsaki te ni 1993, Gekko no natsu (Summer of the Moonlight Sonata 1993, East Meets West 1995, Miyazawa Kenji son ai 1996, "Hideyoshi" (TV series) 1996, Ame agaru (After the Rain) 1999, Kin'yû fushoku rettô: Jubaku (Jubaku: Spellbound) 1999, Sukedachiya sukeroku (Vengeance for Sale) 2001, Shiroi inu to Waltz wo (To Dance with the White Dog) 2002, Hi wa mata noboru 2002, Ashura no gotoku (Like Asura) 2003.

NAKAE, Toshitada; Japanese journalist; b. 4 Oct. 1929, Chiba City; m. Yohko Nakae 1959; three s.; ed Tokyo Univ.; local reporter Asahi Shimbun 1953–58, econ. reporter 1958–72, Econ. Ed. 1972–76, Asst Man. Ed. 1976–78, Man. Ed. 1978–83, Dir 1982–97, Pres. 1989–96, Special Adviser 1996–; Pres. Japan Newspaper Publrs' and Eds' Asscn 1991–95; Commdr des Arts et des Lettres 1994; Newspaper Culture Award 2007. *Publications:* (in English trans.) Cities 1966, The Pulitzer Prize Story 1970, The News Media 1971, The Economy of Cities 1971. *Leisure interests:* driving, listening to music, karaoke. *Address:* 1-11-1-401 Hamadayama, Suginami-ku, Tokyo, Japan. *Telephone:* (3) 3302-7087. *Fax:* (3) 3302-7087 (home).

NAKAE, Yosuke; Japanese diplomatist; *Honorary President, Institute for Japan–China Relations;* b. 30 Dec. 1922, Osaka; s. of Yasuzo Nakae and Itsu Kawase; m. Yasuko Takakura 1959; one s. one d.; ed Kyoto Univ.; Dir-Gen. of Asian Affairs Bureau, Ministry of Foreign Affairs 1975; Amb. to Yugoslavia 1978, to Egypt 1982, to People's Repub. of China 1984–87; Commr, Japan Atomic Energy Comm. 1987–91; Pres.'s Adviser, Mitsubishi Heavy Industries Co. Ltd 1991–99; Pres., Inst. for Japan-China Relations 1992–2004, Hon. Pres. 2004–; Grand Cordon of the Order of the Sacred Treasure 1995. *Ballet scenarios performed include:* Creature 1975, Mobile et Immobile 1983, Friendship Across the Strait 1987, Magpies' Bridge 1998. *Publications:* ballet scenarios: Creature 1975, Mobile et Immobile – Mirage à l'Abu-Simbel 1983, Friendship Across the Strait 1987, Magpies' Bridge 1998; books: Future of China 1991, An Unbefitting Ambassador Talks 1993, Memoirs of Sino-Japanese Diplomacy 2008. *Leisure interest:* writing scenarios for ballet.

Address: 3-21-5, Eifuku, Suginami, Tokyo 168-0064, Japan (home). *Telephone:* (3) 3325-7359 (home). *Fax:* (3) 3325-7359 (home).

NAKAGAWA, Shoichi; Japanese politician; b. 19 July 1953, Hokkaido; s. of Ichiro Nakagawa; ed Tokyo Univ.; with Industrial Bank of Japan 1978–83; mem. for Hokkaido, House of Reps 1983–, Chief Dir Finance Cttee 1991, Dir Budget Cttee 1993, Chief Dir Agric., Forestry and Fisheries Cttee 1993, Chair. Communications Cttee 1995, Dir Research Comm. on the Constitution 2000; Deputy Chair. LDP Policy Research Council 1995, Deputy Chief Sec., LDP 1996, Acting Chair. LDP Exec. Council 1997, Chair. Special Cttee on Agric., Forestry and Fisheries Trade Policy 1999, Chair. Special Cttee on Int. Fisheries 2000, Chair. Research Comm. on Trade in Agricultural, Forestry and Fishing Products 2001, Chair. LDP Public Relations HQ 2001, Chair. Party Org. HQ 2002, Chair. Policy Research Council 2006–; Minister of Agric., Forestry and Fisheries 1998–99, 2005–06, of Economy, Trade and Industry 2003–05, of Finance 2008–09 (resgnd). *Address:* c/o LDP, 1-11-23, Nagata-cho, Chiyoda-ku, Tokyo 100-8910, Japan (office).

NAKAJIMA, Fumio, DLitt; Japanese philologist and academic; *Professor Emeritus of English Philology, University of Tokyo;* b. 11 Nov. 1904, Tokyo; m. Chizu Takaba 1935; ed First Prefectural School, First Nat. Coll. and Univ. of Tokyo; Asst Prof., Univ. of Keijo, Seoul 1928, Assoc. Prof. 1933, Prof. of English Philology 1939; Prof. of English Philology, Univ. of Tokyo 1947–65, Prof. Emer. 1965–; Prof. Tsuda-juku Coll. 1965–73, Pres. 1973–80; Pres. English Literary Soc. of Japan 1952–64, Shakespeare Soc. of Japan 1964–75; mem. Japan Acad. 1974–; Order of the Sacred Treasure (Second Class) 1975. *Publications:* Imiron 1939, Eigo-no-Joshiki 1944, Bunpo-no-Genri 1949, Eibunpo-no-taikei 1961, Eigo-no-Kozo 1980, Nihongo-no-Kozo 1985. *Address:* 2-24-10, Nishi-koigakubo, Kokubunji, Tokyo 185, Japan. *Telephone:* (423) 24-5580.

NAKAMURA, Hisao; Japanese business executive; b. 11 Nov. 1923, Kyoto Pref.; s. of Kinjiro Nakamura and Masao Nakamura; m. Fusako Nagai 1955; one s. one d.; ed Kyoto Univ.; joined Kuraray Co. Ltd 1950, Dir 1972, Man. Dir 1976, Exec. Vice-Pres. 1981, Pres. 1985–93, Chair. 1993–; Chair. Kurray Trading Co. Ltd 1984–; Pres. Kyowa Gas Chemical Industries Co. Ltd 1985–. *Leisure interests:* golf, car-driving, reading. *Address:* 1-12-39 Umeda, Kita-ku, Osaka 530; 52 Nigawa-dai, Takarazuka, Hyogo 665, Japan.

NAKAMURA, Kenzo, PhD; Japanese physicist and academic; *Head, Physics Division 3, Institute of Particle and Nuclear Studies, High Energy Accelerator Research Organization (KEK);* ed Univ. of Tokyo; Research Assoc., Physics Dept, Univ. of Tokyo 1973–84, Inst. for Cosmic Ray Research 1988–95; Assoc. Prof., Nat. Lab. for High Energy Physics (KEK) 1984–88, Head, Experimental Planning and Program Coordination Div. 1995, currently Head, Physics Div. 3, Inst. of Particle and Nuclear Studies, High Energy Accelerator Research Org. (KEK); mem. Kamiokande Collaboration and Super-Kamiokande Collaboration 1987–; Asahi Prize (Super-Kamiokande Group) for discovery of neutrino mass 1998. *Publications:* numerous articles in scientific journals. *Address:* KEK-IPNS, Room No. 4-307 (Building No. 4), 1-1 Oho, Tsukuba, Ibaraki 305-0801, Japan (office). *Telephone:* (298) 645435 (office). *Fax:* (298) 647831 (office). *E-mail:* kenzo.nakamura@kek.jp (office). *Website:* psux1.kek.jp/~kekps (office).

NAKAMURA, Kunio; Japanese electronics industry executive; *Chairman, Panasonic Corporation;* b. 5 July 1939, Shiga; ed Osaka Univ.; joined Matsushita Electric Industrial Co. Ltd (MEICL) 1962, Dir Tokyo Special Sales Office, Corp. Consumer Sales Div. 1985–89, Dir Corp. Man. Div. for the Americas and Chair. Matsushita Electric Corpn of America 1993–96, Man. Dir 1996–97, Sr Man. Dir 1997–2000, Pres. MEICL 2000–06, Chair. 2006– (named changed to Panasonic Corpn Oct. 2008), Pres. Panasonic Co. 1989–92, Pres. Panasonic UK Ltd 1992–93; Pres. AVC Co. 1997–2000. *Address:* Panasonic Corpn, Corporate Headquarters, 1006 Oaza Kadoma, Kadoma City, Osaka 571-8501, Japan (office). *Telephone:* (6) 6908-1121 (office). *Fax:* (6) 6908-2351 (office). *E-mail:* info@panasonic.net (office). *Website:* panasonic.net (office).

NAKAMURA, Kuniwo; Palauan former head of state; *Leader, Ta Belau Party;* Vice-Pres. of Palau 1989–92; Pres. of Palau 1993–2001; Leader Ta Belau Party. *Address:* Ta Belau, c/o Olbiil era Kelulau, Koror, PW 96940, Palau (office).

NAKAMURA, Mutsuo, LLB, LLM, LLD; Japanese university administrator and academic; *President, Hokkaido University;* b. 7 Feb. 1939; ed Hokkaido Univ.; Instructor of Law, Hokkaido Univ. 1963–70, Assoc. Prof. 1970–74, Prof. 1974–2001, mem. Senate 1984–88, Dean Faculty of Law 1988–90, Vice-Pres. Hokkaido Univ. 1997–99, Pres. 2001–. *Address:* Office of the President, Hokkaido University, Kita 8, Nishi 5, Kita-ku, Sapporo 060-0808, Japan (office). *Telephone:* (11) 706-2111 (2000) (office). *Fax:* (11) 706-4885 (office). *E-mail:* nakamura@general.hokudai.ac.jp (office). *Website:* www.hokudai.ac.jp (office).

NAKAMURA, Shozaburo; Japanese politician; fmr businessman; mem. LDP; mem. for Minami Kanto bloc, House of Reps; fmr Dir-Gen. Environment Agency, Parl. Vice-Minister of Finance (three times); Minister of Justice 1998–99 (resgnd). *Leisure interests:* skiing, scuba diving. *Address:* c/o Ministry of Justice, 1-1-1, Kasumigaseki, Chiyoda-ku, Tokyo 100, Japan.

NAKAMURA, Shuji, DEng; Japanese physicist and academic; *Professor of Materials Science,, University of California, Santa Barbara;* b. 22 May 1954, Shikoku; ed Univ. of Tokushima; Research and Devt (R&D) Dept, Nichia Chemical Industries Ltd 1979–84, Group Head, R&D 1st Section 1985–88, Group Head, R&D 2nd Section 1989–93, Sr Researcher, Dept of Devt 1993–99; Visiting Research Assoc., Dept of Electronic Eng, Univ. of Fla 1988–89; Prof., Materials Science Dept, Univ. of Calif., Santa Barbara 1999–, also Dir Center for Solid State Lighting and Displays; numerous awards including Sakurai Award 1995, Nishina Memorial Award 1996, Okochi Memorial Award 1997, Julius-Springer Prize for Applied Physics 1999, Takayanagi Award 2000, Carl Zeiss Research Award 2000, Honda Award 2000, Crystal Growth and Crystal Technology Award 2000, Asahi Award 2001, Optical Soc. of America Nick Holonyak Award 2001, Franklin Institute Medal in Eng 2002, Millennium Tech. Prize 2006. *Achievements:* inventor of solid-state white lights made from LEDs; holder of 80 Japanese and 10 US patents. *Publications:* 220 specialist articles. *Address:* Materials Science Department, University of California, Santa Barbara, CA 93106, USA (office). *Telephone:* (805) 893-5552 (office). *Fax:* (805) 893-8983 (office). *E-mail:* shuji@engineering.ucsb.edu (office). *Website:* www.cnsi.ucla.edu/Bios/UCSB/Nakamura_CV.htm (office).

NAKAMURA, Toshikazu, PhD; Japanese clinical professor of medicine; *Professor and Chairman, Division of Molecular Regenerative Medicine, Osaka University Graduate School of Medicine;* ed Osaka Univ. Grad. School of Science; Assoc. Prof., School of Medicine, Univ. of Tokushima 1980–88; Prof., Faculty of Science, Kyushu Univ. 1988–93; Prof., Biomedical Research Center, Osaka Univ. Medical School 1993–2001, Prof., Div. of Molecular Regenerative Medicine, Osaka Univ. Grad. School of Medicine 2001–; Princess Takamatsu Cancer Research Award, Academic Award, Mochida Memorial Foundation, Osaka Science Award, Inoue Prize for Science, and other awards. *Publications:* numerous articles in scientific and medical journals. *Address:* Division of Molecular Regenerative Medicine, Course of Advanced Medicine, B7, Osaka University Graduate School of Medicine, Suita, Osaka 565-0871, Japan (office). *Telephone:* (6) 6879-3783 (office). *Fax:* (6) 6879-3789 (office). *E-mail:* nakamura@onbich.med.osaka-u.ac.jp (office). *Website:* www.med.osaka-u.ac.jp (office).

NAKANE, Chie; Japanese social anthropologist and academic; *Professor Emerita, University of Tokyo;* b. 30 Nov. 1926, Tokyo; d. of Minoru Nakane and Chiyo Nakane; ed Univ. of Tokyo; lived in China in 1940s; embarked on career investigating Asian societies including Japan, India, China and Tibet; Prof. of Social Anthropology, Inst. of Oriental Culture, Univ. of Tokyo (first woman prof.) 1979–87, Dir Inst. 1980–82, now Prof. Emer.; Visiting Prof., Univ. of Chicago, USA, SOAS, London, UK; Prof.-at-Large, Cornell Univ., USA; mem. Japan Acad. (first and only woman mem.) 1995; Fellow, Center for Advanced Studies in Behavioral Sciences USA 1973–74; Foreign mem., American Philosophical Soc. 1977; mem. UNESCO World Comm. on Culture and Devt 1993–95; mem. Jury, Rolex Awards for Enterprise 1980, 2002; Hon. mem., Royal Anthropological Inst. of GB and Ireland 1975, Int. Union for Anthropological and Ethnological Sciences 2005; Imperial Order of Culture 2001; Japan Foundation Award 1987. *Publications:* Garo and Khasi – A Comparative Study in Matrilineal Systems 1967, Kinship and Economic Organization in Rural Japan 1967, Japanese Society 1970, Social Anthropology – A Comparative Study of Asian Societies 1987, Recent Trends in Mongolian, Tibetan and Vietnamese Studies (ed.), Acta Asiatica 76 1999, Caste, Its Diversity and Fluidity (article) 2002, Development Processes of Tibet Politico-Religious Systems (article) 2007. *Leisure interest:* oil painting. *Address:* The Japan Academy, 7–32 Ueno Park, Tokyo 110-0007, (office); 1404 Takanawa, 4-24-55, Minato-ku, Tokyo 108–0074, Japan (home). *Telephone:* (3) 3822-2101 (office); (3) 3473-4321 (home). *Fax:* (3) 3822-2105 (office). *Website:* www.japan-acad.go.jp (office).

NAKANISHI, Koji, BSc, PhD; Japanese chemist and academic; *Centennial Professor of Chemistry, Columbia University;* b. 11 May 1925, Hong Kong; ed Nagoya Univ., Harvard Univ., USA; Asst Prof., Dept of Chem., Nagoya Univ. 1955–58, Prof. 1958–63; Prof., Dept of Chem., Tohoku Univ. 1963–69; Dir of Research, Int. Center for Insect Physiology and Ecology, Nairobi, Kenya 1969–77; Prof., Dept of Chem., Columbia Univ., New York, USA 1969–80, Centennial Prof. 1981–, Chair., Dept of Chem. 1987–90, Dir of Research, Chem. Unit, Biosphere 2 Center 2001–; Dir Suntory Inst. for Bioorganic Research, Osaka 1979–81; mem. American Acad. of Arts and Sciences 1973–; Hon. mem. Pharmaceutical Soc. of Japan 1991–, mem. 2002–; Hon. mem. Chemical Soc. of Japan 1997–; Fellow NY Acad. of Sciences 1980–, Academia Nazionale delle Scienze, Italy 1993–, AAAS 1996–; numerous awards including Chemical Soc. of Japan Award in Pure Chem. 1954, Asahi Cultural Prize 1968, ACS Guenther Award 1978, Royal Soc. of Chem. Centenary Medal 1979, Japan Acad. Prize 1990, Swedish Acad. of Pharmaceutical Sciences Scheele Award 1992, Czech Acad. of Sciences Heyrovsky Gold Medal 1995, Nakanishi Prize est. jtly by ACS and Chemical Soc. of Japan 1996, King Faisal Int. Prize (Saudi Arabia) 2003, Tetrahedron Prize 2004. *Publications:* author, co-author or ed. of nine books; co-ed nine-vol. series on natural products; more than 780 articles in scientific journals. *Leisure interest:* magic. *Address:* Department of Chemistry, Columbia University, 3000 Broadway, Mail Code 3114, New York, NY 10027 (office); 560 Riverside Drive, NY 10027, USA (home). *Telephone:* (212) 663-7605 (office). *Fax:* (212) 932-1289 (office). *E-mail:* kn5@columbia.edu (office). *Website:* www.columbia.edu/cu/chemistry/faculty/kj.html (office).

NAKANISHI, Shigetada, PhD; Japanese biochemist and academic; *Director, Osaka Bioscience Institute;* b. Ogaki; ed Kyoto Univ.; earned degree in medicine; Post-doctoral Fellow, Nat. Cancer Inst., NIH, Bethesda, Md, USA 1971; returned to Kyoto Univ. 1974; currently Dir Osaka Bioscience Inst.; mem. NAS 2000–; Person of Cultural Merit 2006; Bristol-Myers Squibb Award for Distinguished Achievement in Neuroscience Research 1995, Keio Medical Science Prize (co-recipient) 1996, Gruber Neuroscience Prize, The Peter and Patricia Gruber Foundation 2007. *Achievements include:* pioneered research into communication between nerve cells in the brain; with research team unravelled molecular detail of information transfer and processing, and provided pharmacologists with many new possibilities for drug design. *Publications:* Systems Biology: The Challenge of Complexity (co-ed.) 2009; numerous scientific papers in professional journals. *Address:* Osaka

Bioscience Institute, 6-2-4 Furuedai, Suita, Osaka 565-0874, Japan (office). *Telephone:* (6) 6872-4850 (office). *Fax:* (6) 6871-6686 (office). *E-mail:* nakanishi@obi.or.jp (office). *Website:* www.obi.or.jp (office).

NAKASONE, Hirofumi; Japanese politician; *Minister of Foreign Affairs;* b. 28 Nov. 1945; s. of Yasuhiro Nakasone (fmr Prime Minister of Japan); ed Keio Univ.; with Asahi Chemical Industry Co. Ltd 1968; Sec. to Prime Minister Yasuhiro Nakasone 1983; mem. House of Councillors (Liberal Democratic Party— LDP) 1986–; Parl. Vice-Minister, Ministry of Int. Trade and Industry 1990; Chair. Standing Cttee on Commerce and Industry, House of Councillors 1993, Cttee on Orgs Involved with Women's Issues, Social Educ. and Religion, LDP 1995; Head Deputy Chair. LDP Diet Affairs Cttee, House of Councillors 1996; Chair. Standing Cttee on Rules and Administration, House of Councillors 1997; Chair. LDP Policy Bd, House of Councillors 1998, Special Cttee on Managing Debts of Japan Nat. Railway Settlement Corpn and Reform of Nat. Forestry Services 1998; Minister of Educ., Science, Sports and Culture and Minister of State for Science and Tech. 1999–2000; Minister of Foreign Affairs 2008–. *Address:* Ministry of Foreign Affairs, 2-11-1, Shiba-Koen, Minato-ku, Tokyo 105-8519, Japan. *Telephone:* (3) 3580-3311. *Fax:* (3) 3581-2667 (office). *E-mail:* webmaster@mofa.go.jp (office). *Website:* www.mofa.go.jp (office).

NAKASONE, Yasuhiro; Japanese politician; b. 27 May 1918, Takasaki, Gunma Prov.; s. of Matsugoroh and Yuku Nakasone; m. Tsutako Kobayashi 1945; one s. (Hirofumi Nakasone) two d.; ed Tokyo Imperial Univ.; mem. House of Reps; fmr Minister of State, Dir-Gen. of Science and Tech. Agency; Chair. Nat. Org. LDP, Jt Cttee on Atomic Energy, Special Cttee on Scientific Tech., Chair. LDP Exec. Council 1971–72, Sec.-Gen. LDP 1974–76, Chair. 1977–80; Minister of Transport 1967–68; Minister of State and Dir-Gen. Defence Agency 1970–71; Minister of Int. Trade and Industry 1972–74; Minister of State and Dir-Gen. of Admin. Man. Agency 1980–82; Prime Minister of Japan 1982–87; Chair. and Pres. Int. Inst. for Global Peace 1988–89, Inst. for Int. Policy Studies 1988–; after involvement in Recruit affair resigned from LDP, rejoined April 1991. *Publications:* Ideal of Youth, Frontier in Japan, The New Conservatism, Human Cities – A Proposal for the 21st Century 1980, Tenchiyujou (autobiog.) 1996. *Leisure interests:* golf, swimming, painting. *Address:* 3-22-7, Kamikitazawa, Setagaya-ku, Tokyo, Japan (home). *Telephone:* (3) 3304-7000 (home).

NAKATA, Hideo; Japanese film director; b. 19 July 1961, Okayama; ed Univ. of Tokyo; began career as Asst Dir, Nikkatsu Studios; worked under supervision of Masaru Konuma; directorial debut with God's Hand (TV film) 1992; adapted horror novel Ringu by Suzuki Koji into feature film 1998. *Films directed include:* God's Hand (TV) 1992, Don't Look Up/Ghost Actress (also writer) 1996, Ringu 1998, Chaos 1999, Ringu 2 (also writer) 1999, Sadistic and Masochistic 2000, Sleeping Bride 2000, Dark Water (also writer) 2002, Last Scene 2002, Samara: The Ring 2 2005, The Eye 2006, Out 2006, The Entity 2006. *Address:* c/o United Talent Agency Inc., 9560 Wilshire Boulevard, Suite 500, Beverly Hills, CA 90212, USA (office). *Telephone:* (310) 273-6700 (office). *Fax:* (310) 247-1111 (office).

NAKAYAMA, Kyoko, BA; Japanese politician and diplomatist; *Minister of State for Social Affairs and Gender Equality, Minister of Public Records Management and National Archives, and Minister of State for the Abduction Issue;* b. 26 Jan. 1940; ed Univ. of Tokyo; with Ministry of Foreign Affairs 1964–66; Ministry of Finance 1966–75, 1978–93, Deputy Dir-Gen. Minister's Secr.) 1993; with IMF, Washington, DC 1975–78; Exec. Vice-Pres. The Japan Foundation 1993–99; Amb. to Uzbekistan 1999–2002; Councillor of Cabinet Secr. (for the Abduction Issue) 2002–04; Special Advisor to Prime Minister (for Abduction Issue) 2006–08; mem. House of Councillors 2007–; Minister of State for Social Affairs and Gender Equality, Minister of Public Records Man. and Nat. Archives, and Minister of State for the Abduction Issue 2008–. *Address:* Cabinet Office, 1-6-1, Nagata-cho, Chiyoda-ku, Tokyo 100-8914, Japan (office). *Telephone:* (3) 5253-2111 (office). *E-mail:* info@cao.go.jp (office). *Website:* www.cao.go.jp (office).

NAKAYAMA, Masaaki; Japanese politician; mem. House of Reps; fmr Dir-Gen. Man. and Co-ordination Agency; fmr Posts and Telecommunications Minister; Chair. House of Reps Budget Cttee, Liberal Democratic Party's cttee on election system; Minister for Construction and Dir-Gen. Nat. Land Agency 1999–2000. *Address:* c/o Ministry of Construction, 2-1-3, Kasumigaseki, Chiyoda-ku, Tokyo 100-0013, Japan (office).

NAKAYAMA, Nariaki; Japanese politician; b. 7 June 1943; ed Univ. of Tokyo; entered Ministry of Finance 1966, Chief of Ebara Tax Office 1971, Head of Budget Bureau 1978, Dir Tokai Local Finance Bureau 1980, Dir for Minister's Secr. 1982; with World Bank, Washington, DC, USA 1975; mem. House of Reps for Miyazaki Pref. 1986–, Chair. Cttee on Commerce and Industry 1999, Special Cttee on Disasters 2000, Cttee on Health, Labour and Welfare 2003; Parl. Vice-Minister for Educ. 1990; Dir Environment Div., LDP 1992, Commerce and Industry Div. 1996, Deputy Chair. Research Comms 2002, Deputy Sec.-Gen. 2003; Vice-Minister of Int. Trade and Industry 2000–01, of Economy, Trade and Industry 2001–04; Minister of Educ., Culture, Sports, Science and Tech. 2004–05; Minister of Land, Infrastructure and Transport Sept. 2008 (resgnd). *Address:* c/o Liberal-Democratic Party–LDP (Jiyu-Minshuto), 1-11-23, Nagata-cho, Chiyoda-ku, Tokyo 100-8910, Japan (office).

NAKAYAMA, Taro, MD, PhD; Japanese politician; b. 27 Aug. 1924, Osaka; ed Osaka Medical Coll.; mem. Osaka Pref. Ass. 1955–68; mem. House of Councillors 1968-86, Parl. Vice-Pres. Labor Party 1971; Chair. Cttee on Cabinet 1976, Chair. Cttee on Rules and Admin 1979; Dir-Gen. Prime Minister's Office 1980; Chief Okinawa Devt Agency 1980; Chair. Parl. Affairs Cttee of LDP 1982, LDP Financial Cttee 1988, LDP Political Reform HQ 1998, LDP Research Comm. on Foreign Affairs 1999; mem. Gen. Council of LDP 1998–; mem. House of Reps 1986–; Minister of Foreign Affairs 1989–91; Chair. Research Comm. on Constitution of House of Reps 2000–; Chair. Asian Population and Devt Asscn and Chair. or Pres. numerous int. parliamentarians' friendship leagues including Japan–India Parliamentarians' Friendship League; Grand Cordon, First Order of Rising Sun, 1997. *Publications:* five books including Scientific Strategy for the Post-Oil Age 1979. *Address:* 1-7-1 Nagata-Cho, Chiyoda-ku, Tokyo, Japan.

NAKIB, Falah an-; Iraqi civil engineer and politician; b. Samarra; s. of Gen. Hassan al-Naqib; fmr mem. Iraqi Nat. Congress, Iraq Nat. Movt; apptd Gov. Salahaddin Prov. by US-led admin; Interim Minister of the Interior 2004–05. *Address:* c/o Office of the Minister of the Interior, Green Zone, Baghdad, Iraq.

NALBANDIAN, Edvard, PhD; Armenian diplomatist; *Minister of Foreign Affairs;* b. 1956; m.; one d.; ed Moscow State Inst. of Int. Relations, Inst. of Oriental Studies, USSR Nat. Acad. of Sciences; worked at USSR Embassy in Lebanon 1978–83; at USSR Ministry of Foreign Affairs, Moscow 1983–86; Counsellor of USSR Embassy (then Russian Fed. Embassy) in Egypt 1986–92; Chargé d'Affaires in Egypt 1992–93, Amb. to Egypt 1994–98 (also accred Marocco and Oman), to France 1999–2008 (also accred to Israel, the Vatican and Andorra) 2004–08; Minister of Foreign Affairs 2008–; Special Rep. of the Pres. of Armenia to Int. Org. of Francophony 2006; Commdr, Légion d'honneur 2001, Grand Cross of St Gregory (Holy See) 2003; Award of Friendship of Nations (USSR) 1982, Mkhitar Gosh Medal 2001. *Address:* Ministry of Foreign Affairs, 0010 Yerevan, Republic Square, Government House 2, Armenia (office). *Telephone:* (10) 54-40-41 (office). *Fax:* (10) 54-39-25 (office). *E-mail:* info@armeniaforeignministry.com (office). *Website:* www.armeniaforeignministry.com (office).

NAŁĘCZ, Maciej; Polish scientist; b. 27 April 1922, Warsaw; s. of Aleksander Nałęcz and Stefania Nałęcz; m. Zofia Bozowska 1952; one s.; ed Warsaw Tech. Univ.; scholarship to Case Inst. of Tech., Cleveland, USA 1961–62; Assoc. Prof. 1962–72, Prof. 1972–; Corresp. mem. Polish Acad. of Sciences (PAN) 1967–73, Ordinary mem. 1974–, Presidium mem. and Sec. Tech. Sciences Section 1972–80, Deputy Gen. Sec. PAN 1981–83, Deputy to Sejm (Parl.) 1985–89; Dir Inst. of Automatic Control 1962–72; Chair. Biomedical Eng Cttee of Section IV 1972–; Dir Inst. of Biocybernetics and Biomedical Eng 1975–93; Dir Int. Centre of Biocybernetics 1988–; Chair. Nat. Cttee for Pugwash Confs. 1972–, elected Chair. Pugwash Council 1974, 1977, 1982, 1987, 1992–97; Visiting Prof. Polytechnic Inst. of Brooklyn 1967–68, Univ. of Hanover, W Germany 1990; Distinguished Visiting Prof. Ohio State Univ. 1979–80, Campinas Univ., Brazil 1985, Cleveland Clinic Foundation 1985, Waseda Univ., Japan 1988; Scholar in Residence, Int. Fogarty Foundation, NIH, USA 1991–92; mem. Int. Measurement Confed. (IMEKO), Cttee on Data for Science and Tech. (CODATA) of ICSU, Exec. Cttee Int. Fed. of Automatic Control 1972–, Int. Soc. of Artificial Organs, Admin. Bd Int. Fed. for Medical and Biological Eng 1988–94, Gen. Bd European Soc. of Engineers and Physicians (Co-founder) 1991–, Int. Acad. for Medical and Biological Eng 1997–; Co-founder and Vice-Pres. European Soc. for Eng and Medicine (ESEM) 1995–98; Foreign mem. USSR (now Russian) Acad. of Sciences 1976–, Georgian Acad. of Sciences 1996–; Hon. mem. World Org. of Gen. Systems and Cybernetics 1979, Soc. for Theoretical and Applied Electrotechnics 1980, Polish Soc. for Medical Eng 1995; Kt's, Officer's, Commdr's with Star Cross (and Great Cross 2002), Order Polonia Restituta, Order Banner of Labour, 2nd Class 1972, 1st Class 1978; State Prize, 2nd Class 1972, Nobel Peace Prize (for Pugwash) 1995; Award med tack för värdefull insats (Sweden) 1957, Copernicus Medal, Polish Acad. of Science, Križik Medal, Czechoslovakian Acad. of Science 1988, Int. Fogarty Center Medal, USA 1991. *Publications:* The Technology of Hall Generators and Their Use in Measurement and Conversion 1972, Trends in Control Components 1974, Control Aspects of Biomedical Engineering (ed. and contrib.) 1987, Computers in Medicine (ed. and contrib.) 1987, Problems of Biocybernetics and Biomedical Engineering (ed. and contrib.) Vols I–VI 1990–91, State of Art and Development of BME in Poland (monograph, ed. and co-author) 1994, Biocybernetics and Biomedical Engineering 2000 (nine vols, monograph, ed. and co-author) 2003. *Leisure interest:* summer house. *Address:* International Centre of Biocybernetics, Polish Academy of Sciences, ul. Trojdena 4, 02-109 Warsaw, Poland (office). *Telephone:* (22) 658-28-77 (office). *Fax:* (22) 658-28-72 (office). *E-mail:* maciej.nalecz@ibib.waw.pl (office).

NALLET, Henri Pierre; French politician; *Vice-President, Fondation Jean Jaurès;* b. 6 Jan. 1939, Bergerac (Dordogne); s. of Jean Nallet and France Lafon; m. Thérèse Leconte 1963; one s.; ed Inst. d'Etudes Politiques, Bordeaux; Sec.-Gen. Jeunesse Étudiante Catholique 1963–64; Inst. de Formation des Cadres Paysans 1965–66; Féd. Nat. des Syndicats d'Exploitants Agricoles (FNSEA) 1966–70; Dir of Research, Dept of Econ. and Rural Sociology, Inst. Nat. de Recherche Agronomique (INRA) 1970–81; agricultural adviser, Secr. Gen. of Presidency of Republic 1981–85; Minister of Agric. 1985–86; Socialist Deputy to Nat. Ass. 1986–88; Minister of Agric. and Forestry 1988–90, Garde des Sceaux, Minister of Justice 1990–92; Conseiller-Gen. of Yonne 1988–2001; Mayor of Tonnerre 1989–2000; Conseiller d'état 1992–; Deputy for Yonne 1997–99; Pres. Del. of Nat. Ass. to EU; mem. Parl. Ass. of Council of Europe and of WEU; Consultant IBRD 1992–, EU 1992–; Vice-Chair. European Socialist Party 1997–2003; Nat. Sec. for Int. Affairs of Socialist Party 1999–2003; Directeur Général Relations Extérieures Groupe de Recherche Servier; Pres. World Council of Nutrition 1985–87; Vice-Pres. Fondation Jean Jaurès 1997–; Officier Légion d'honneur 2001. *Publications:* Tempête sur la justice 1992, Les Réseaux multidisciplinaires. La Documentation française 1999, Le multilateralisme: une réforme possible 2004. *Address:* 22 rue Garnier, 92578 Neuilly-sur-Seine Cedex, France. *E-mail:* fondation@jean-jaures.org (office). *Website:* www.jean-jaures.org (office).

NAM, Duck-woo, PhD; South Korean politician, economist and government official; b. 10 Oct. 1924; s. of Nam Sang-Bom and Cha Soon Yoo; m. Hye Sook Choi 1953; two s. one d.; ed Kook Min. Coll., Seoul, Seoul Nat. Univ. Oklahoma State and Stanford Univs.; with Bank of Korea 1952–54; Asst Prof., Assoc. Prof., Prof., Dean of Econ. Dept, Kook Min Coll. 1954–64; Prof. Sogang Univ. and Dir Research Inst. for Econ. and Business 1964–69; Minister of Finance 1969; Gov. for Korea, IMF, IBRD, ADB 1969–72, Chair. Bd of Govs. Asian Devt Bank 1970; Deputy Prime Minister and Minister of Econ. Planning Bd 1974–78; Special Asst for Econ. Affairs to the Pres. Jan.–Dec. 1979; Prime Minister of Repub. of Korea 1980–82; mem. Advisory Cttee on Evaluation of Econ. Devt Plan, Nat. Mobilization Bd 1964–69; Adviser to Korea Devt Bank 1964–69; Assoc. mem. Econ. and Scientific Council 1967–69. *Publications:* History of Economic Theory 1958, History of Economic Theory (co-author) 1962, Price Theory 1965, The Determinants of Money Supply and Monetary Policy: in the case of Korea 1954–64 1966, Social Science Research and Population Policy (jt author) 1980, Changes in the Pattern of Trade and Trade Policy in a Pacific Basin Community 1980. *Leisure interests:* reading, music appreciation.

NAM, Joong-soo, BBA, MBA, PhD; South Korean telecommunications executive; *President and CEO, KT Corporation;* ed Seoul Nat. Univ., Univ. of Massachusetts and Duke Univ. Fuqua School of Business, USA; joined KT Corpn 1981, Vice-Pres. IMT-2000 Business Group –2001, Chief Financial Officer 2001–03, Pres. and CEO KT Freetel Co. (mobile affiliate) 2003–05, Pres. and CEO KT Corpn 2005–. *Address:* KT Corporation, 206 Jungja-dong, Bundang-gu Songnam, Kyonggi 463-711, Republic of Korea (office). *Telephone:* (31) 727-0114 (office). *Fax:* (31) 727-0949 (office). *E-mail:* info@kt.co.kr (office). *Website:* www.kt.co.kr (office).

NAM, Young-sun; South Korean business executive; *Co-CEO of Powder and Financial Division and President, Hanwha Chemical Corporation;* b. 2 April 1953; ed Yonsei Univ.; Gen. Man. Hanwha Chemical Corpn 1994–2003, Co-CEO Powder and Financial Div. 2003–, Pres. Hanwha Chemical Corpn 2005–. *Address:* Hanwha Chemical Corpn, Hanwha Building, 1 Changgyo-dong, Chung-ku, Seoul 100-797, Republic of Korea (office). *Telephone:* (2) 729-2700 (office); (2) 729-1114 (office). *Fax:* (2) 729-1762 (office). *E-mail:* hanwhacorp@hanwha.co.kr (office). *Website:* english.hanwhacorp.co.kr (office).

NAM HONG, Hor, LLB, ML; Cambodian diplomatist and politician; *Deputy Prime Minister and Minister of Foreign Affairs and International Co-operation;* b. 15 Nov. 1935, Phnom-Penh; m.; five c.; ed Univ. of Phnom-Penh, Univ. of Paris, L'Ecole Royale d'Admin, France; Amb. to Cuba 1973–75; Khmer Rouge prisoner 1975–79; Vice-Minister of Foreign Affairs 1980–82; Amb. to fmr USSR 1982–89; Minister of Foreign Affairs 1990–93, 1998–, currently Deputy Prime Minister and Minister of Foreign Affairs and Int. Co-operation; mem. Nat. Ass. 1998–; mem. Supreme Nat. Council of Cambodia 1991–93, Amb. to France 1993–98; mem. Cambodian People's Party (CPP); Grand Officer of Monisaraphon, Ordre Nat. du Mérite, Grand Cross, Royal Order of Cambodia, Order of the White Elephant (Thailand), Grand Collier, Royal Order of Cambodia. *Leisure interests:* reading, swimming, gymnastics. *Address:* Ministry of Foreign Affairs and International Co-operation, 3 rue Samdech Hun Sen, Khan Chamkarmon, Phnom-Penh, Cambodia (office). *Telephone:* (23) 214441 (office). *Fax:* (23) 216144 (office). *E-mail:* mfaicinfo@mfaic.gov.kh (office). *Website:* www.mfaic.gov.kh (office).

NAMALIU, Rt Hon. Sir Rabbie Langanai, KCMG, PC, BA, MA; Papua New Guinea politician; b. 3 April 1947, Raluana, E New Britain Prov.; s. of Darius Namaliu and Utul Ioan Namaliu; m. 1st Margaret Nakikus 1978 (died 1993); two s. one step-d.; m. 2nd Kelina Tavul 1999; one s.; ed Keravat High School, Univ. of Papua New Guinea, Univ. of Victoria, BC, Canada; fmrly scholar and Fellow, Univ. of Papua New Guinea; tutor and Lecturer in History, Univ. of Papua New Guinea; Prin. Pvt. Sec. to Chief Minister 1974; fmr Prov. Commr, E New Britain and Chair. Public Services Comm.; held sr positions in the Office of the Prime Minister and Leader of the Opposition under Mr Somare; MP for Kokopo Open 1982–; Minister for Foreign Affairs and Trade 1982–84, for Primary Industry 1984–85; Deputy Leader, Pangu Pati 1985–88, Leader 1988–92; Prime Minister 1988–92; Speaker Nat. Parl. 1994–97; Sr Minister for State 1997–98, for Petroleum and Energy 1998–99; Minister of Foreign Affairs and Immigration 2002–06, of Finance 2006–07, of the Treasury 2007; Pres. African Caribbean Pacific Council of Ministers 1984; Co-Pres. ACP/EEC Jt Council of Ministers 1984; Vacation Scholar, ANU 1968; Visiting Fellow, Univ. of Calif., Center for Pacific Studies, Santa Cruz, Calif., USA 1976; Hon. MA, LLD, (Victoria, BC) 1983; Independence Medal 1975, Queen's Silver Jubilee Medal 1977, Pacific Man of the Year 1988. *Leisure interests:* reading, fishing, walking, golf. *Address:* c/o Department of Finance and Treasury, POB 710, Waigani, Vulupindi Haus, NCD, Papua New Guinea; POB 6655, Boroko, National Capital District, Papua New Guinea.

NAMBIAR, Vijay K.; Indian diplomatist; *Chef de Cabinet to the Secretary-General, United Nations;* b. Aug. 1943, Poona; m. Malini Nambiar; two d.; ed Bombay Univ.; joined Foreign Service 1967, early years specializing in Chinese language and serving in Hong Kong and Beijing; subsequent posts included Belgrade, Yugoslavia in mid-1970s; numerous bilateral and multilateral postings in Beijing, Belgrade and New York in 1970s and 1980s, also Jt Sec. (Dir Gen.) for E Asia 1988 and multilateral affairs at New Delhi HQ 1980s; Amb. to Algeria 1985–88, to Afghanistan 1990–92, to Malaysia 1993–96, to China 1996–2000, to Pakistan 2000–01; Perm. Rep. to UN, New York 2002–04; Deputy Nat. Security Adviser (DNSA) and Head, Nat. Security Council Secr. 2005–06; Under-Sec.-Gen. and Special Adviser to UN Sec.-Gen., New York 2006–07, Chef de Cabinet (Chief of Staff), UN Sec.-Gen. 2007–. *Address:* Office of the Secretary-General, United Nations, New York, NY 10017, USA (office). *Telephone:* (212) 963-1234 (office). *Fax:* (212) 963-4879 (office). *Website:* www.un.org (home).

NAMBU, Yoichiro, ScD; American (b. Japanese) physicist and academic; *Harry Pratt Judson Distinguished Service Professor Emeritus, Department of Physics and Enrico Fermi Institute, University of Chicago;* b. 18 Jan. 1921, Tokyo; s. of Kichiro Nambu; ed Univ. of Tokyo; Prof., Osaka City Univ. 1950–56; Researcher, Inst. for Advanced Study, Princeton, NJ, USA 1952–54; Research Assoc., Dept of Physics and Enrico Fermi Inst., Univ. of Chicago 1954–56, Assoc. Prof. 1956–58, Prof. 1958–77, Harry Pratt Judson Distinguished Service Prof. 1977–91, Emer. 1991–, Chair. Dept of Physics 1974–77; mem. NAS 1971–, American Acad. of Arts and Sciences 1971–; Hon. Mem. Japan Acad. 1984–; Govt of Japan Order of Culture 1978; Hon. DSc (Northwestern Univ.) 1987, (Osaka Univ.) 1996; Nat. Medal of Science, American Physical Soc., Dannie Heineman Prize for Math Physics 1970, J. Robert Oppenheimer Prize 1976, Max Planck Medal 1985, Dirac Medal, Int. Center for Theoretical Physics 1986, Sakurai Prize, American Physical Soc. 1994, Wolf Prize in Physics 1994, Gian Carlo Wick Medal, World Fed. of Scientists 1996, Bogoliubov Prize, Jt Inst. for Nuclear Research 2003, Benjamin Franklin Medal in Physics, Franklin Inst. 2005, Pomeranchuk Prize, Inst. of Theoretical and Experimental Physics, Russia 2007, Nobel Prize for Physics (jtly) 2008. *Address:* Enrico Fermi Institute, University of Chicago, 5640 South Ellis Avenue, Chicago, IL 60637, USA (office). *Telephone:* (773) 702-7286 (office). *Fax:* (773) 834-2222 (office). *E-mail:* nambu@theory.uchicago.edu (office). *Website:* www.physics.uchicago.edu (office).

NAMIR, Ora; Israeli politician and diplomatist; b. 1 Sept. 1930; m. Mordechai Namir; ed Levinsky and Givat Hashlosha teacher seminaries, Hunter Coll., New York; officer in Israel Defence Forces during War of Independence; Sec., Mapai Knesset faction 1951–55; Sec.-Gen. Na'amat (Working Women and Volunteers Org.), Tel-Aviv 1967–74; mem. Knesset 1973–96, Chair. Prime Minister's Cttee on the Status of Women 1975–78, Educ. and Culture Cttee 1977–84, Labour and Social Welfare Cttee 1984–92; Minister of the Environment 1992, of Labour and Social Affairs 1992–96; Amb. to China (also accred to Mongolia) 1996–2000. *Publications:* Report of the Committee for the Status of Women; articles in Israeli press. *Address:* c/o Ministry of Foreign Affairs, 9 Yitzhak Rabin Blvd, Kiryat Ben-Gurion, Jerusalem 91035, Israel.

NAMOLOH, Maj.-Gen. (retd) Charles Dickson Ndaxu Phillip; Namibian military officer, government official and politician; *Minister of Defence;* b. 28 Feb. 1950, Odibo; s. of Phillip Hidishange Namoloh and Fransiska Kaimba Nghihangakenwa; ed St Mary's Mission Anglican School, Indira Gandhi Univ., Delhi; graduated from northern centre as guerrilla detachment commdr 1975, from Vystrel Field Acad. as motorised Infantry Brigade Commdr 1982; fmr High Commr to India; currently Minister of Defence; Head of Politics, Security and Defence Cttee, South African Devt Community; Swapo Highest Medal of Ongulumbashe 1989, Order of the Eagle 2004. *Address:* Ministry of Defence, Private Bag 13307, Windhoek, Namibia (office). *Telephone:* (61) 2042005 (office). *Fax:* (61) 232518 (office). *E-mail:* cnamoloh@mod.gov.na (office). *Website:* www.mod.gov.na (office).

NAMPHY, Lt-Gen. Henri; Haitian politician and soldier; fmr Chief of Haitian Gen. Staff; Head of State and Pres. Nat. Governing Council (formed after overthrow of Jean-Claude Duvalier q.v., in coup) 1986–88; Vice-Chair. Legis. 1987–88; now living in exile in Dominica.

NAMYSŁOWSKI, Zbigniew; Polish jazz musician (trombone) and composer; b. 9 Sept. 1939, Warsaw; m. Maria Małgorzata Ostaszewska; two d. one s.; ed in Warsaw; trombone player, leader of Modern Dixielanders 1957–60, sideman with Zygmunt Wichary Group 1960, New Orleans Stompers 1960–61, alto sax player and leader of Jazz Rockers 1961–62, Air Condition 1980–82, Zbigniew Namysłowski Quartet and Quintet 1973–; Air Condition 1980–83; Kalatówki Big Band 2001–03, sideman in the Wreckers 1962–63, Krzysztof Komeda Quintet 1965; mem. Polish Composer Asscn 1972–; participant in festivals include Students' Group Festival, Wrocław (Award for the Best Soloist – trombone) 1957, Int. Jazz Festival, Prague (Award for the Best Soloist) 1964, Lugano 1961, Tauranga (New Zealand) 1969, 1978, Bombay (now Mumbai) 1969, 1978, Paris 1974, Ivrea (Italy) 1979, Montréal 1984, Copenhagen 1989, Århus 1989, several times Jazz Jamboree, Warsaw and Molde, Kongsberg, Bergen (Norway), Zürich, Christianstadt, Stockholm, North Sea-Haag, Pori Jazz Festival (Finland), Red Sea (Israel) 1991, Int. Festival Wien, Kuwait 2002 and others; has toured in countries including Denmark, USA, Italy, New Zealand, Australia, India, Netherlands, Greece, Canada, Mexico, Sweden, Norway, Switzerland; State Prize (First Class) 1984, Fryderyk (Polish music award for Best Polish Jazz Record of the Year– Zbigniew Namysłowski Quartet and Zakopane Highlanders Band) 1995, Jazz Forum Award 1997, 1998, Gold Cross of Merit 1974, Meritorious Activist of Culture Award 1982. *Compositions include:* Der Schmalz Tango 1976, Convenient Circumstances 1980, Speed Limit 1981, Kuyawiak Goes Funky 1984, After Perturbation 1985, Quiet Afternoon 1985, Double-Trouble Blues 1985, Cuban Tango Mojito 1986, Seven-Eleven 1987, Western Ballade 1992, Oriental Food 1994, Mazurka Uborka 1996. *Recordings include:* Polish Jazz– Zbigniew Namysłowski Quartet, Kuyawiak Goes Funky, Zbigniew Namysłowski with Symphony Orchestra, Song of the Pterodactil, Jasmine Lady, Song of Innocence, Double Trouble, Open, Without Talk; adaptations of compositions by Mozart, Gershwin and Chopin for string quartet, clarinet and jazz band. *Leisure interests:* travelling, tennis, skiing, bicycling. *E-mail:* quartet@poczta.onet.pl (office).

NAN, Zhenzhong; Chinese journalist and politician; b. May 1942, Lingbao, He'nan Prov.; ed Zhengzhou Univ.; joined Xinhua News Agency 1964, fmrly Vice-Chief, then Chief Shandong Br., Xinhua News Agency, Assoc. Ed. then Ed.-in-Chief, Office of Gen. Editing 1986, Vice-Pres. Xinhua News Agency 1993–2000, Ed.-in-Chief 2000–07 (retd); Vice-Chair. All-China Journalists' Asscn; joined CCP 1978; Del., 13th CCP Nat. Congress 1987–92, 14th CCP Nat. Congress 1992–97, 15th CCP Nat. Congress 1997–2002, 16th CCP Nat.

Congress 2002–07; Deputy, 9th NPC 1998–2003, 10th NPC 2003–08, mem. NPC Standing Cttee, Vice-Chair. NPC Foreign Affairs Cttee 2003; awarded title China's Prominent Journalist of the Year 1984, winner, first Fan Chanjiang News Awards 1991. *Publications:* The Responsibility System of Agricultural Production in China 1981, I Learn to Be a Journalist 1985, The Eyes of a Correspondent 1988, The Reflections of a Correspondent 1993, Selected Works by Nan Zhenzhong 1996, The Ability to Discover 1999, The Strategic View of a Correspondent 1999, On Success – A Discussion with Young Journalists 2003. *Address:* c/o Xinhua (New China) News Agency, 57 Xuanwumen Xidajie, Beijing 100803, People's Republic of China (office).

NANDAN, Satya Nand, CF, CBE, LLB; Fijian diplomatist and lawyer; *Secretary-General, International Seabed Authority;* b. 10 July 1936, Suva; s. of Shiu Nandan and Rajkuar Nandan; m. 1st Sreekumari Nandan 1966 (died 1971); m. 2nd Zarine Merchant 1976; one s.; ed DAV Coll. Suva, John McGlashan Coll. Dunedin, NZ, Univs of Wellington, NZ and London, UK, and Lincoln's Inn, London; called to Bar, Lincoln's Inn 1965; barrister and solicitor, Supreme Court of Fiji 1966–; pvt. law practice, Suva 1965–70; Counsellor then Amb. Perm. Mission of Fiji to UN 1970–76; Leader, Fiji Del. to Third UN Conf. on Law of Sea 1973–82; Amb. to EEC (also accred to Belgium, France, Italy, Luxembourg, Netherlands) 1976–80; Perm. Sec. for Foreign Affairs, Fiji 1981–83; UN Under-Sec.-Gen. for Ocean Affairs and the Law of the Sea and Special Rep. of UN Sec.-Gen. for Law of the Sea 1983–92; mem. Perm. Mission of Fiji to UN 1993–96; Chair. UN Conf. on Straddling Fish Stocks and Highly Migratory Fish Stocks 1993–95; Rep. of Fiji to Int. Seabed Authority 1994–95, Sec.-Gen. 1996–2008; Pres. Meeting of States Parties, 1982 UN Convention on the Law of the Sea 1994–96; Int. Law Adviser to Govt of Fiji 1994–95; Chair. Conf. on Conservation and Man. of Highly Migratory Fish Stocks in Cen. and Western Pacific 1997–2000, UN Int. School 1996–2000, 2005–08; mem. Int. Advisory Group, Maritime and Port Authority of Singapore 1997–2000; del. to numerous int. confs etc.; Visiting Lecturer, Columbia Univ. New York and Univ. of Virginia, Charlottesville; Sr Visiting Fellow, US Inst. of Peace 1992; many other professional appointments; Grand Cross, Order of Merit (FRG) 1996, Companion Order of Fiji 1999; Hon. LLD (Newfoundland) 1995; Dr hc (Univ. of the South Pacific) 1996. *Publications include:* Commentary on 1982 UN Convention on Law of Sea (seven vols) (ed.); numerous articles on UN and aspects of Law of the Sea. *Leisure interests:* history, int. law, reading, swimming. *Address:* International Seabed Authority, 14–20 Port Royal Street, Kingston, Jamaica (office); 301 East 48th Street, New York, NY 10017, USA (home). *Telephone:* (876) 922-9105 (office). *Fax:* (876) 967-3011 (office). *E-mail:* snandan@isa.org.jm (office). *Website:* www.isa.org.jm (office).

NANO, Fatos Thanas, PhD; Albanian politician; b. 16 Sept. 1952, Tirana; m. Xhoana Nano; ed Tirana Univ.; taught political economy in Faculty of Econs, Tirana Univ.; fmr Sec.-Gen. of Council of Ministers, Deputy Chair. Jan.–Feb. 1991, Chair. (Prime Minister) Feb.–June 1991; Chair. Socialist Party of Albania (Partia Socialiste e Shqipërisë) 1991–; stripped of immunity from prosecution to face charges of embezzlement July 1993; convicted of misappropriation of state funds, of dereliction of duty and of falsifying state documents April 1994; sentenced to 12 years' imprisonment; released and pardoned March 1997; Prime Minister of Albania 1997–98, 2002–05; Founder Movt for Solidarity 2007.

NAOURI, Jean-Charles; French financier and business executive; *Chairman, President and CEO, Groupe Rallye;* b. 8 March 1949, Algeria; served as Sr Adviser to Finance Minister Pierre Beregovoy 1982–86; Founder and Chair. Fonciere Euris (pvt. equity fund), has roles in several cos by Euris including Censor, Fimalac 2002–, Chair. Casino Group 2003–, CEO 2005–, Man. SCI Penthiévre 2003–, Chair., Pres. and CEO Groupe Rallye, Chair. Finatis; Caisse Nationale des Caisses d'Epargne 2004–mem. Bd of Dirs HSBC France; mem. Supervisory Bd Groupe Marc de Lacharriére; Man. Pnr, Rothschild et Compagnie Banque;. *Address:* Groupe Rallye, 83 rue du Faubourg Saint Honoré, Paris 75008 (office); Groupe Casino, 24, rue de la Montat, Saint Etienne 42100, France (office). *Telephone:* 1-44-71-13-62 (Paris) (office); 4-77-45-31-31 (Saint Etienne) (office). *Fax:* 1-44-71-13-60 (Paris) (office). *E-mail:* info@rallye.fr (office). *Website:* www.rallye.fr (office); www.groupe-casino.fr (office).

NAPIER, John; British stage designer; b. 1 March 1944; s. of James Edward Thomas Napier and Lorrie Napier (née Godbold); m. 1st Andreanne Neofitou; one s. one d.; m. 2nd Donna King; one s. one d.; ed Hornsey Coll. of Art, Cen. School of Arts and Crafts; production designs include: A Penny for a Song, Fortune and Men's Eyes, The Ruling Class, The Fun War, Muzeeka, George Frederick (ballet), La Turista, Cancer, Isabel's a Jezebel, Mister, The Foursome, The Lovers of Viorne, Lear, Jump, Sam Sam, Big Wolf, The Devils (ENO), The Party, Knuckle, Kings and Clowns, Lohengrin (Covent Garden), Macbeth, Richard III, Hedda Gabler, Twelfth Night, The Greeks, Nicholas Nickleby, Cats, Starlight Express, Time, Les Misérables, Miss Saigon, Sunset Boulevard, Burning Blue, Jesus Christ Superstar, Idomeneo (Glyndebourne), Who's Afraid of Virginia Woolf?, An Enemy of the People, Peter Pan, Martin Guerre, Candide, Jane Eyre, Nabucco (Metropolitan Opera), South Pacific, Skellig 2003, Aladdin (Old Vic), Equus 2007; Designer, co-Dir, Siegfried & Roy Show, Las Vegas 1990; film designs include Hook 1991; numerous stage and TV set designs world-wide; Hon. Fellow London Inst. 2001; Royal Designer for Industry, Royal Soc. of Arts 1996, five Tony Awards. *Leisure interest:* photography. *Address:* c/o Macnaughton Lord Representation, Unit 10, The Bromhouse Studios, 50 Sullivan Road, London, SW6 3DX, England. *Telephone:* (20) 7384-9517. *Fax:* (20) 7371-7563. *E-mail:* info@mlrep.com.

NAPIER, John Alan, MA (Econs); British business executive; *Chairman, Royal & Sun Alliance Insurance Group plc;* b. 22 Aug. 1942; s. of the late William Napier and Barbara Napier (née Chatten); m. 1st Gillian Reed 1961; two s. one d.; m. 2nd Caroline Denning 1992; one d. two step-s. one step-d.; ed Colchester Royal Grammar School and Emmanuel Coll., Cambridge; jr and middle man. positions, Int. Publishing Corpn and Reed Int. 1960–69; Man. Dir Index Printers 1969–72; Man. Dir QB Newspapers 1972–76; Exec. Dir (Australia) James Hardie Industries 1976–86; Group Man. Dir AGB PLC 1986–90; Group Man. Dir Hays PLC 1991–98; Chair. Booker PLC 1998–2000; Exec. Chair. Kelda Group PLC 2000–02, Chair. (non-exec.) Sept. 2002–; Chair. Yorkshire and Humber Rural Affairs Forum 2002–; Chair. Royal & Sun Alliance Insurance Group plc 2003–. *Leisure interests:* rural matters, outdoor activities, people, philosophy. *Address:* Royal & Sun Alliance Insurance Group plc, 9th Floor, One Plantation Place, 30 Fenchurch Street, London, EC3M 3BD, England (office). *Telephone:* (20) 7111-7000 (office). *Website:* www.royalsunalliance.com (office).

NAPIER, HE Cardinal Wilfrid Fox, B.PH., B.TH., MA; South African ecclesiastic; *Archbishop of Durban;* b. 8 March 1941, Matatiele; s. of Thomas D. Napier and Mary Davey; ed Little Flower School, Ixopo, Natal, Nat. Univ. of Ireland, Galway and Catholic Univ., Louvain, Belgium; ordained priest 1970; Asst Pastor, St Anthony's Parish, Lusikisiki 1971; Parish Priest, St Francis Parish, Tabankulu 1973; Apostolic Admin., Diocese of Kokstad 1978; Bishop of Kokstad 1981; Archbishop of Durban 1992–; Vice-Pres. S African Catholic Bishops' Conf. 1984, Pres. 1987–92, First Vice-Pres. 1994–; cr. Cardinal 2001. *Leisure interests:* gardening, tennis, golf, DIY mechanics, fishing. *Address:* Archbishop's House, 154 Gordon Road, Durban 4001; PO Box 47489, Greyville 4023, South Africa. *Telephone:* (31) 3031417. *Fax:* (31) 231848. *E-mail:* chancery@durban-archdiocese.co.za (office).

NAPOLI, Jacopo; Italian composer; b. 25 Aug. 1911; ed S. Pietro a Majella Conservatoire of Music, Naples; obtained diplomas in Composition, Organ and Piano; Chair. of Counterpoint and Fugue at Cagliari Conservatoire and at Naples Conservatoire; Dir S. Pietro a Majella Conservatoire of Music, Naples 1955, 1962; Dir Giuseppe Verdi Conservatoire of Music, Milan –1972, then Dir St Cecilia Conservatory, Rome; Dir Scarlatti Arts Soc. 1955–; works performed in Germany, Spain and on Italian radio. *Works include:* operas: Il Malato Immaginario 1939, Miseria e Nobiltà 1946, Un curioso accidente 1950, Masaniello 1953, I Pescatori 1954, Il Tesoro 1958; oratorios: The Passion of Christ, Il Rosario 1962, Il Povero Diavolo 1963, Piccola Cantata del Venerdì Santo 1964; orchestral works: Overture to Love's Labours Lost 1935, Preludio di Caccia 1935, La Festa di Anacapri 1940. *Address:* 55 Via Andrea da Isernia, 80122 Naples, Italy.

NAPOLITANO, Giorgio; Italian politician and head of state; *President;* b. 29 June 1925, Naples; m. Clio Maria Bittoni; ed Univ. of Naples Frederico II; joined Italian Communist Party (PCI) 1945, mem. Nat. Cttee, subsequently responsible for Comm. for Southern Italy 1956, then Sec. for Naples and Caserta, coordinator of Party Sec.'s Office and Political Office 1966–69, responsible for culture and later econ. policy and int. relations during 1970s and 80s; joined Democratic Party of the Left (later Democrats of the Left) following dissolution of PCI, 1981; elected to Chamber of Deputies 1953, Pres. 1992–94; Minister of the Interior 1996–98; MEP 1999–2004; Senator for Life 2005–; Pres. of Italy 2006–; Dr hc (Università degli Studi di Bari) 2004. *Publications:* Movimento Operaio e Industria di Stato 1962, Intervista sul PCI (jtly) 1975, In Mezzo al Guado 1979, Oltre i Vecchi Confini 1988, Europa e America dopo l'89 1992, Dove va la Repubblica - Una Transizione Incompiuta 1994, Europa Politica 2002, Dal PCI al Socialismo Europeo: Un 'Autobiografia Politica 2005. *Address:* Office of the President, Palazzo del Quirinale, 00187 Rome, Italy (office). *Telephone:* (06) 46991 (office). *Fax:* (06) 46993125 (office). *E-mail:* presidenza.repubblica@quirinale.it (office). *Website:* www.quirinale.it (office).

NAPOLITANO, Janet Ann, BS, JD; American lawyer, government official and fmr state official; *Secretary of Homeland Security;* b. 29 Nov. 1957, New York City; d. of Leonard Michael Napolitano and Jane Marie Napolitano (née Winer); ed Univ. of Santa Clara, Univ. of Virginia Law School; Assoc. Lewis & Roca (law firm), Phoenix 1984–89, Pnr 1989–93, attorney 1997–98; US Attorney, Phoenix 1993–97; Attorney-Gen. of Ariz. 1999–2002; Gov. of Ariz. 2003–09; Sec. of Homeland Security, Washington, DC 2009–; mem. Ariz. Bar Asscn, Maricopa Co. Bar Asscn, American Judicature Soc., Ariz. Women Lawyers' Asscn, Ariz. Women's Forum, Charter 100; Fellow, Ariz. Bar Foundation; Democrat; Leader of Distinction, Anti-Defamation League, Woman of Distinction, Crohns and Colitis Disease Foundation, Women Making History Award, Nat. Museum of Women's History. *Publications:* numerous contribs. to legal journals. *Leisure interests:* hiking, trekking, travel, reading, film, sports. *Address:* Department of Homeland Security, 1600 Pennsylvania Avenue, NW, Washington, DC 20528, USA (office). *Telephone:* (202) 282-8000 (office). *Website:* www.dhs.gov (office).

NAQI, Abbas Ali, BComm; Kuwaiti government official and international organization official; *Secretary General, Organization of Arab Petroleum Exporting Countries;* b. 1947; ed Kuwait Univ., Univ. of Southern California, USA; Financial Accountant, State Budget, Ministry of Finance and Oil 1971–75, Controller, Oil and Gas Marketing, Ministry of Oil 1975–81, Controller, Int. Relations and Orgs Dept 1981–84, Dir Econ. Planning and Analysis Dept 1984–89, Dir Oil Accounting and Financial Analysis Dept 1989–94, Asst Under-Sec. for Econ. Affairs 1994–2007, Under-Sec. 2007–08; Sec. Gen. Org. of Arab Petroleum Exporting Countries 2008–, mem. Exec. Bd representing Kuwait 2000–08; Chair. Kuwaiti Nat. Cttee for UN Convention on Climate Change 1994–; Vice Pres. representing Asia, Second UN Convention on Climate Change 1996; Head of Jt Exec. Cttee, Aramco Overseas Co. 2000–02; mem. Bd of Dirs Arab Maritime Petroleum Transport Co. 1977–96, Kuwait Nat. Petroleum Co. 1995–98, Kuwait Oil Co. 1998–2002, Arab Petroleum Investments Corpn 1996–, Kuwait Gulf Oil Co. 2004–07, Kuwait Nat. Petroleum Corpn 2007–; mem. UN Cttee for Sustainable Devt, Kuwait

Accountant Soc. *Address:* Organization of Arab Petroleum Exporting Countries, POB 20501, Safat 13066, Kuwait (office). *Telephone:* 24959000 (office). *Fax:* 24959755 (office). *E-mail:* oateefa@oapecorg.org (office). *Website:* www.oapecorg.org (office).

NARASIMHAM, Maidavolu; Indian government official; b. 3 June 1927, Bangalore; s. of M. Seshachelapati; m. Shanthy Sundaresan; one s.; ed Presidency Coll., Madras and St John's Coll. Cambridge; joined Reserve Bank of India, Bombay 1950, Sec. 1967, Gov. 1977; Chief of S. Asia Div., IMF 1960–63, Exec. Dir of IMF for India, Bangladesh and Sri Lanka 1980–82; Exec. Dir IBRD 1978–80; Additional Sec. Ministry of Finance 1972, Sec. Banking Dept 1976–78, Sec. Dept of Econ. Affairs 1982; Finance Sec., Govt of India 1983; Prin. Admin. Staff Coll. of India, Hyderabad 1983–85, Chair. 1991–; Vice-Pres. Asian Devt Bank, Manila 1985–88; Norton Prize (Madras Univ.), Padma Vibhushan 2000, Telugu Talli Award 2001, Lifetime Achievement Award 2001. *Publications include:* World Economic Environment and Prospects for India 1988, Economic Reforms: Development and Finance 2002, From Reserve Bank to Finance Ministry and Beyond: Some Reminiscences 2002. *Leisure interests:* reading, music. *Address:* 'Sukruti', 8-2-681/7, Road No. 12, Banjara Hills, Hyderabad 500 034, India (home). *Telephone:* (40) 23310994 (office); (40) 23396511 (home). *Fax:* (40) 23310994 (office); (40) 23312954.

NARASIMHAN, Ekkadu Srinivasan Lakshmi, BSc, LLB, MA; Indian lawyer, diplomatist and politician; *Governor of Chhattisgarh;* m. Vimala Narasimhan; ed Madras Univ., Madras Law Univ., Nat. Defence Coll., Delhi; joined Indian Police Service in 1968, served in various capacities in Police and Intelligence Bureau services, Head of Intelligence Bureau –2006; served in Ministry of External Affairs, first Sec., Embassy in Moscow 1981–84; fmr Dir-Gen. of Police in Chhattisgarh; Gov. of Chhattisgarh 2007–. *Address:* Governor's House, Civil Line, Raipur 492 001, Chhattisgarh, India (office). *Telephone:* (771) 2331101 (office). *Fax:* (771) 2331104 (office). *E-mail:* info@chhattisgarh.nic.in (office). *Website:* chhattisgarh.nic.in (office).

NARASIMHAN, Mudumbai Seshachalu, PhD, FRS; Indian mathematician and academic; *Honorary Fellow, Tata Institute of Fundamental Research;* b. 1932, Thandarai, Tamiladu; ed Univ. of Bombay; fmr Prof. at Tata Inst. of Fundamental Research, Mumbai mid-1960s–1992, now Hon. Fellow; Head of Research Group in Math., Int. Centre for Theoretical Physics, Trieste 1992; pioneer of study of moduli spaces of holomorphic vector bundles on projective varieties; Bhatnagar Prize for Math. 1975, Third World Acad. Award for Math. 1987, Padma Bhushan 1990, King Faisal Int. Prize for Science, King Faisal Foundation (co-recipient) 2006. *Address:* c/o Tata Institute of Fundamental Research, Homi Bhabha Road, Mumbai 400 005, India. *Telephone:* (22) 22782000. *Fax:* (22) 22804610. *E-mail:* webmaster@tifr.res.in. *Website:* www.tifr.res.in.

NARAYANAN, M.K., BA (Econs); Indian government official; *National Security Adviser to the Prime Minister;* b. 10 March 1934, New Delhi; s. of the late C.B. Nair and M.K. Kallianikvity Amma; m. Padmini Narayanan; one s. one d.; fmr Head, Indian Intelligence Bureau; Special Adviser to Prime Minister Manmohan Singh with rank of Minister of State 2004–; Nat. Security Adviser to the Prime Minister 2005–; Padmashree Award 1992. *Address:* c/o Prime Minister's Office, South Block, New Delhi 110 011 (office); 10 Teen Murti Lane, New Delhi 110 011, India (home). *Telephone:* (11) 23019227 (office); (11) 23015890 (office); (11) 23019856 (home). *Fax:* (11) 23017990 (office); (11) 23018788 (home). *E-mail:* mk.narayanan@pmo.nic.in (office). *Website:* www.pmindia.nic.in (office).

NARDELLI, Robert L., BS, MBA; American business executive; *Chairman and CEO, Chrysler LLC;* b. 17 May 1948, Old Forge, Pa; m. Sue Nardelli 1971; four c.; ed Western Ill. Univ., Univ. of Louisville (Ky); with Gen. Electric (GE) Corpn 1971–88; Exec. Vice Pres. and Gen. Man. Case Corpn, Racine, Wis. 1988–91; returned to GE and served in various exec. positions including CEO Canadian Appliance Mfg Co., Toronto 1991–92, GE Transportation Systems, Erie, Pa 1992–95, GE Power Systems 1995–2000, Sr Vice-Pres. GE and mem. Bd of Dirs GE Capital Corpn; Pres. Home Depot Inc. 2000–02, Pres. and Chair. 2002–07 (resgnd); Chair. and CEO Chrysler LLC, Auburn Hills, Mich. 2007–; mem. Bd of Dirs The Coca-Cola Co. 2002–05; mem. Pres. 's Council on Service and Civic Participation 2003; mem. Advisory Bd Univ. of Louisville Grad. School of Business; Dr hc (Univ. of Louisville) 2001, (Siena Coll.) 2001, (Western Ill. Univ.) 2002. *Address:* Chrysler LLC, 1000 Chrysler Drive, Auburn Hills, MI 48326-2766, USA (office). *Telephone:* (248) 576-5741 (office). *Fax:* (248) 512-2912 (office). *Website:* www.chrysler.com (office).

NARIMAN, Fali Sam, BA; Indian lawyer and politician; *President, Bar Association of India;* b. 10 Jan. 1929, Rangoon, Burma (now Myanmar); m. Bapsi F. Nariman 1955; one s. one d.; ed St Xavier's Coll., Bombay, Government Law Coll., Bombay; advocate, High Court of Bombay 1950; Sr Advocate, Supreme Court of India 1971–; Additional Solicitor Gen. of India 1972–75; mem. Rajya Sabha (Parl.) 1999– (mem. Rules Cttee, Ethics Cttee, Consultative Cttee for Ministry of External Affairs, Standing Cttee of Parl. on External Affairs); Founder Chair. Law Asscn for Asia and the Pacific (LAWASIA) Standing Cttee on Human Rights 1979, Pres. LAWASIA 1985–87; Pres. Bar Asscn of India 1991–, Int. Council for Commercial Arbitration 1994–; Chair. Exec. Cttee Int. Comm. of Jurists, Geneva 1995–97; Co-Chair. Int. Bar Asscn Human Rights Inst.; Vice-Chair. Int. Court of Arbitration of the ICC, Paris 1989–; mem. London Court of Int. Arbitration 1988–, Press Comm. of India, Advisory Bd of UNCTAD, Governing Council Body of Nat. Law School Univ., Bangalore, Gen. Council of West Bengal Nat. Univ. of Judicial Sciences, Kolkata; Founding mem. PUCL (People's Union for Civil Liberties); Leader, Indian Del. of Lawyers to 59th Int. Law Asscn Conf., Belgrade, Serbia and to Int. Bar Asscn Conf., Berlin, Germany; Padma Bhushan; several nat. and int. awards including Kinlock Forbes Gold Medal and Prize for Roman Law and Jurisprudence 1950, named a Living Legend of the Law by the Int. Bar Asscn 1995, Peter Gruber Foundation Justice Prize 2002. *Publications:* numerous articles on politics, religion, the constitution and human rights. *Address:* Bar Association of India, 93 Lawyers Chambers, Supreme Court of India, New Delhi 110 001, India (office). *Telephone:* (11) 3385902 (office). *Fax:* (11) 3329273 (office).

NARITA, Yoriaki, DJur; Japanese professor of law; *President, Japan Energy Law Institute;* b. 20 Jan. 1928, Tokyo; s. of Masaji Narita and Masako Narita; m. Akiko Narita 1956; two d.; ed Tokyo Univ.; Lecturer, Faculty of Econs, Yokohama Nat. Univ. 1929, Asst Prof. 1933, Prof. 1943, Dean of Econs 1982–86, Dir and Prof., Grad. School of Int. and Business Law 1990–93; Pres. Japan Energy Law Inst. 1993–. *Publications:* Introduction to Modern Administrative Law, Legal Theories and Reform of Local Self-government, Land Policy and Law. *Leisure interest:* gardening. *Address:* Japan Energy Law Institute, Tanakayama Bldg, 7F, 4-1-20, Toranomon Minato-ku, Tokyo 105-0001, Japan (office). *Telephone:* (3) 3434-7701 (office). *Fax:* (3) 3434-7703 (office). *Website:* www.jeli.gr.jp (office).

NARITA, Yutaka; Japanese advertising executive; b. 19 Sept. 1929; Sr Man. Dir Dentsu Inc. (advertising agency) –2000, Pres. 2001–02, Chair. and CEO 2002–07; mem. Bd of Dirs Japan Advertising Agencies Asscn (JAAA) 2001; mem. Supervisory Bd Publicis Groupe SA 2002–. *Address:* c/o Dentsu Incorporated, 1-8-1 Higashi-shimbashi, Minato-ku, Tokyo, Japan (office).

NARLIKAR, Jayant Vishnu, PhD, ScD; Indian scientist; *Founder Director, Inter-University Centre for Astronomy and Astrophysics (IUCAA);* b. 19 July 1938, Kolhapur; s. of Prof. and Mrs V. V. Narlikar; m. Mangala S. Rajwade 1966; three d.; ed Banaras Hindu Univ. and Fitzwilliam Coll. Cambridge; Berry Ramsey Fellow, King's Coll. Cambridge 1963–69; Grad. Staff Mem., Inst. of Theoretical Astronomy, Cambridge 1966–72; Sr Research Fellow, King's Coll. 1969–72; Jawaharlal Nehru Fellow 1973–75; mem. Science Advisory Council to the Prime Minister 1986–90; Founder Dir Inter-Univ. Centre for Astronomy and Astrophysics (IUCAA), Pune 1988–; Hon. Prof. Jawaharlal Nehru Centre for Advanced Scientific Research; Homi Bhabha Prof. 1998–; Pres. Cosmology Comm. of Int. Astronomical Union 1994–97; Fellow, Indian Nat. Science Acad. (INSA), Assoc. Royal Astronomical Soc., London; Hon. DSc (Calcutta) 2000; awarded Padma Bhushan by the Indian Govt 1965, S. S. Bhatnagar Award 1978, Rashtrabhushan Award of FIE Foundation 1981, Rathindra Award 1985, INSA Vainu Bappu Award 1988, INSA Indira Gandhi Award for Science Popularization 1990, UNESCO Kalniga Award 1996, Padma Vibhushan 2004. *Publications:* articles on cosmology, general relativity and gravitation, quantum theory, astrophysics etc. in the Proceedings of the Royal Soc., London, The Monthly Notices of the Royal Astronomical Soc., London, The Astrophysical Journal, Nature, Observatory and scientific articles in various magazines; Action at a Distance in Physics and Cosmology (with Sir F. Hoyle) 1974, The Structure of the Universe 1977, General Relativity and Cosmology 1978, The Physics Astronomy Frontier (with Sir F. Hoyle) 1980, Violent Phenomena in the Universe 1982, The Lighter Side of Gravity 1982, Introduction to Cosmology 1983, From Black Clouds to Black Holes 1985, Gravity Gauge Theories and Quantum Cosmology (with T. Padmanabhan) 1986, The Primeval Universe 1988. *Address:* IUCAA, Post Bag 4, Ganeshkhind, Pune 411007, India (office). *Telephone:* (20) 351414 (office); (20) 5651414 (office). *Fax:* (20) 5656417 (office). *Website:* www.iucaa.ernet.in (office).

NARRO ROBLES, José, MD; Mexican physician, government official and university administrator; *Rector, Universidad Nacional Autónoma de México;* b. 5 Dec. 1948, Saltillo, Coahuila; ed Universidad Nacional Autónoma de México, Univ. of Birmingham, UK; fmr Gen. Dir of Health Services of Mexico City; fmr Sec.-Gen. Mexican Inst. of Social Security; fmr Under-Sec. of Migratory Services and Population, Ministry of the Interior (Secretaría de Gobernación), later Under-Sec. of Health, Fed. Secr. of Health; Dir Faculty of Medicine, Universidad Nacional Autónoma de México 2003–07, Rector Universidad Nacional Autónoma de México 2007–; Adviser to WHO; mem. Academia Nacional de Medicina (Nat. Acad. of Medicine). *Address:* Office of the Rector, Universidad Nacional Autónoma de México, Ciudad Universitaria, Del. Coyoacán, 04510 México DF, Mexico (office). *Telephone:* (55) 5622-0958 (office). *Fax:* (55) 5616-0245 (office). *Website:* www.dgi.unam.mx/rector (office).

NARS, Kari, DrSc; Finnish banker; m.; two c.; ed Univ. of Helsinki, Helsinki Swedish School of Econs; economist, Bank of Finland 1964–66, Sec. of Bank 1967, Head Foreign Exchange Policy Dept 1972–75, Dir (Int.) 1977–83; Exec. Man. Dir Bank of Helsinki 1984–85; Economist, IMF, Washington, DC 1967–71; Dir Council of Econ. Orgs 1975–76; Dir of Finance, Ministry of Finance 1986–91, 1994; Exec. Dir EBRD, London 1991–94; Chair Admin. Cttee, Social Devt Fund of Council of Europe 1993, fmrly Pres. Governing Bd, Council of Europe Devt Bank; Alt. Gov. for Finland, IMF 1981–82; mem. Bd Nordic Investment Bank 1989–91; Co-Chair. Govt Borrowers' Forum 1988–91. *Publications include:* Corporate Foreign Exchange Strategies 1980, Foreign Financing and Foreign Exchange Strategy (co-author) 1981, Financial Sector Study on Mozambique – A World Bank Study (co-author) 1992, Cross Currency Swaps (contrib.) 1992; numerous articles and speeches. *Address:* c/o Ministry of Finance, Snellmaninkatu 1A, 00170 Helsinki, Finland.

NARUHITO, Crown Prince, MA; Japanese; b. 23 Feb. 1960, Tokyo; s. of Emperor Akihito (q.v.) and Empress Michiko; m. Masako Owada (now Crown Princess Masako) 1993; one d.; ed Gakushuin Univ., Merton Coll., Oxford, UK. *Leisure interests:* music, playing viola and violin, mountaineering, tennis. *Address:* The Imperial Palace, 1-1 Chiyoda, Chiyoda-ku, Tokyo 100, Japan. *Telephone:* (3) 32131111.

NARVEKAR, Prabhakar R.; American (b. Indian) international civil servant; *Vice-Chairman, Centennial Group of Consultants;* b. 5 Jan. 1932, Mumbai; s. of Ramkrishna Manjunath Narvekar and Indira Narvekar; m. (wife deceased); one s. one d.; ed Bombay, Columbia and Oxford Univs; Research Asst IMF 1953; subsequently held various positions in Asian and European Depts of IMF; Dir Asian Dept, IMF 1986–91, Special Advisor to Man. Dir 1991–94, Deputy Man. Dir 1994–97; Special Adviser to Pres. of Indonesia 1998; Sr Adviser to the Pres. Nikko Securities, Japan 1997–2000; Vice-Chair. Centennial Group of Consultants. *Leisure interest:* reading. *Address:* Centennial Group, 2600 Virginia Avenue, Washington, DC 20037 (office). *Telephone:* (202) 393-6663 (office). *Fax:* (202) 393-6556 (office). *E-mail:* narvekarpr@yahoo.com (home).

NARYSHKIN, Sergei Yevgenyevich; Russian engineer and government official; *Head of Presidential Administration;* b. 27 Oct. 1954, Leningrad; ed Leningrad Inst. of Mechanics, Petersburg International Management Institute; Head Foreign Investments Dept, Promstroybank 1995–97; with Leningrad Regional Govt, positions including Head Investments Dept, Head Int. Affairs Cttee 1997–98; Chair. Cttee for External Economic and Int. Relations, Leningrad Regional Govt 1998–2004; Deputy Head of the Govt Staff, Russian Fed. 2004, Chief of Staff 2004–07, Deputy Prime Minister responsible for external econ. activity 2007–08; Head, Presidential Admin. 2008–. *Address:* Office of the President, 103132 Moscow, Staraya pl. 4, Russia (office). *Telephone:* (495) 925-35-81 (office). *Fax:* (495) 206-07-66 (office). *E-mail:* president@gov.ru (office). *Website:* www.kremlin.ru (office).

NASCIMENTO, Lopo Fortunato Ferreira do; Angolan politician; *Chairman, National Centre for Social and Development Studies;* b. 10 July 1940, Luanda; s. of Vaz I. do Nascimento and Arminda F. do Nascimento; m. Maria do Carmo Assis 1969; two s. one d.; ed Commercial Inst., Luanda; mem. Presidential Collegiate in transitional govt before independence from Portugal Jan.–Nov. 1975; Prime Minister of Angola 1975–78; Minister of Internal Trade 1977–78, of Foreign Trade 1979–82, of Planning 1980–86; Deputy Exec. Sec. UN ECA, Addis Ababa 1979; Head Fifth Mil. Region 1986–90; Gov. Huila Prov. 1986–90; Presidential Adviser for Special Political Affairs 1990; Head Govt Del. at negotiations on a peace agreement for Angola 1991; Minister of Territorial Admin. 1991; Sec.-Gen. Movimento Popular de Libertação de Angola (MPLA) –1993; Deputy Speaker of Parl.; currently MP and Chair. Nat. Centre for Social and Devt Studies. *Leisure interests:* music, writing, walking. *Address:* 93 Amilcar Cabral Street, First Floor, Luanda; 47 Ambuíla Street, PO Box 136, Luanda, Angola. *Telephone:* (2) 399640 (office); (2) 444229 (home); (24491) 205732. *Fax:* (2) 399639 (office); (2) 2442-328451 (home); (2) 443088. *E-mail:* mcir@netangola.com (office); mcir@snet.co.ao (home); nascimento@post.com (home).

NASCIMENTO, Milton; Brazilian singer, songwriter, composer and musician (piano, accordion, guitar, bass guitar); b. 26 Oct. 1942, Rio de Janeiro; one s.; DJ, announcer, dir, Rádio Três Pontas, early 1960s; composer 1963–; played Carnegie Hall 1994; collaborations with Art Blakey, Laudir De Oliviera, Deodato, João Gilberto, Herbie Hancock, Airto Moreira, Flora Purim, Charlie Rouse, Wayne Shorter, Roberto Silva; Chevalier, Ordre des Arts et des Lettres 1984, Ordem do Rio Branco 1985; Dr hc (Universidade Federal de Ouro Preto) 2000; Festival of Brazilian Popular Music Best Performer 1965, Villa-Lobos Prize 1977, Santos Dumont Medal 1998, Sisac Gold Medal, Chile 2000, Latin Grammy Awards for Best Brazilian song (for Tristesse) 2004, (for A Festa) 2005, Gold Medal, Acad. des Arts, Sciences et Belles-Lettres, France 2006. *Recordings:* albums: Milton Nascimento (aka Travessia) 1967, Courage 1968, Milton Nascimento 1969, Milton 1970, Clube Da Esquina–Milton Nascimento E Lo Borges 1972, Milagre Dos Peixes 1973, Milagre Dos Peixes–Gravado Ao Vivo–Milton Nascimento E Som Imaginário 1974, Native Dancer 1974, Minas 1975, Geraes 1976, Clube Da Esquina Dois 1978, Journey To Dawn 1979, Sentinela 1980, Caçador De Mim 1981, Missa Dos Quilombos 1982, Anima 1982, Milton Nascimento Ao Vivo 1983, Encontros E Despedidas 1985, A Barca Dos Amantes 1986, Yauarete 1987, Miltons 1988, Txai 1990, O Planeta Blue Na Estrada Do Sol 1991, Ângelus 1993, Amigo 1995, Nascimento (Grammy Award for Best World Music Record of the Year 1998) 1997, Tambores De Minas–Ao Vivo 1998, Crooner (Latin Grammy Award for Best Brazilian Contemporary Pop Album 2000) 1999, Gil E Milton (with Gilberto Gil) 2001, Pietá 2002, Bossas Novas (with Jobim Trio) 2008. *Address:* Tribo Produções Artísticas, Avenida Armando Lombardi 800, gr 225, Barra da Tijuca, 22640-000 Rio de Janeiro, RJ, Brazil (office). *Telephone:* (21) 3154-8200 (office). *Fax:* (21) 3154-8220 (office). *E-mail:* miltonnascimento@triboproducoes.com.br (office). *Website:* www.triboproducoes.com.br (office); www2.uol.com.br/miltonnascimento.

NASH, Charles; Irish fmr professional boxer; b. 10 May 1951, Londonderry, Northern Ireland; s. of Alexander Nash and of the late Bridget Nash; m. Elizabeth Nash; one s. one d.; ed St Joseph's Secondary School, Londonderry; five times Irish amateur lightweight champion; boxed for Ireland in Olympic Games and European championships; won Irish title in first professional contest Oct. 1975; won vacant British lightweight title v. Johnny Claydon Feb. 1978; won vacant European title v. Andre Holyk June 1979, retained title v. Ken Buchanan Dec. 1979; relinquished British and European titles Jan. 1980 to challenge, unsuccessfully, for world title v. Jim Watt, Glasgow March 1980; regained European title from Francisco Leon Dec. 1980; 25 fights, 23 wins. *Leisure interests:* football, snooker, table tennis, coaching amateur boxers.

NASH, David, OBE, RA; British sculptor; b. 14 Nov. 1945, Surrey; s. of Lt-Col W. C. E. Nash and Dora Nash (née Vickery); m. Claire Langdown 1972; two s.; ed Brighton Coll., Kingston Art School and Chelsea School of Art; has exhibited widely in Britain, Europe, USA and Japan; first exhbn Briefly Cooked Apples, York Festival 1973; works in over 100 public collections including Tate Gallery and Guggenheim Museum; Research Fellow, Dept of Visual and Performing Arts, Univ. of Northumbria 1999–2002; Hon. Fellow, Univ. of Wales (Cardiff) 2003; Dr hc (Kingston) 1999; Hon. DH (Glamorgan) 2002. *Publications:* Forms into Time 1996, The Sculpture of David Nash 1996, Twmps 2000, Black and Light 2001, The Return of Art to Nature 2003, Pyramids Rise, Spheres Turn, Cubes Stay Still, David Nash 2008. *Address:* Capel Rhiw, Blaenau Ffestiniog, Gwynedd, LL41 3NT, Wales; c/o Annely Juda Fine Art, 23 Dering Street, London, W1S 1AW, England. *Telephone:* (20) 7629-7578 (London). *Fax:* (1766) 831179 (Blaenau Ffestiniog); (20) 7491-2139 (London).

NASH, John Forbes, Jr, MS, PhD; American mathematician, economist and academic; *Senior Research Mathematician, Department of Mathematics, Princeton University;* b. 13 June 1928, Bluefield, W Va; s. of John F. Nash and Margaret Virginia Martin Nash; m. Alicia Larde 1957; one s.; ed Carnegie Mellon Univ., Princeton Univ.; Research Asst, Instructor, Princeton Univ. 1950–51; Moore Instructor, MIT 1951–53, Asst Prof. 1953–57, Assoc. Prof. 1957–59, Research Assoc. in Math. 1966–67; Sr Research Mathematician, Princeton Univ. 1959–, Visiting mem. Inst. of Advanced Study 1956–57, 1961–62, 1963–64; mem. NAS 1996; Fellow, Econometric Soc., Sloan Fellow, NSF Fellow, Westinghouse Scholar; Hon. ScD (Carnegie-Mellon) 1999; Hon. PhD (Athens) 2000; Dr hc (Naples) 2003, (Charleston) 2003; Von Neumann Medal, Operations Research Soc. of America, shared Nobel Prize for Econs for pioneering work on game theory 1994, Business Week Award, Erasmus Univ., Rotterdam 1998, Leroy P. Steele Prize, American Mathematical Soc. 1999. *Publications:* Essays on Game Theory, The Essential John Nash; articles on econometric and math. theory. *Address:* Department of Mathematics, Fine Hall, Room 910, Princeton University, Washington Road, Princeton, NJ 08544-1000, USA (office). *Fax:* (609)-258-1367 (office). *Website:* www.math.princeton.edu (office).

NASH, Steve, BA; Canadian professional basketball player; b. 7 Feb. 1974, Johannesburg, SA; s. of John Nash and Jean Nash; m. Alejandra Nash (née Amarilla); two d.; ed St Michael's Univ. School, Santa Clara Univ., USA; plays point guard; selected 15th overall in 1996 Nat. Basketball Assen (NBA) draft by Phoenix Suns, played with Suns 1996–98, moved to Dallas Mavericks 1998–2004, returned to Phoenix Suns 2004–; Capt. Canadian Men's Basketball Team, Sydney Olympics 2000, qualifying stages of Athens Olympics 2004; f. Steve Nash Foundation 2001; Order of British Columbia 2006; NBA West Conference Player of the Year 1995, 1996; NBA Most Valuable Player Award 2005, 2006; All-Star 2002, 2003, 2005, 2006, 2007, 2008; All-NBA First Team 2005, 2006, 2007, Third Team 2002, 2003; Lou Marsh Trophy 2005, Lionel Conacher Award 2005, 2006, Canada's Most Influential Sports Figure, The Globe and Mail 2006. *Address:* Phoenix Suns, 201 East Jefferson Street, Phoenix, AZ 85004; Steve Nash Foundation, 3921 East 86th Avenue, Anchorage, Alaska 99507, USA. *Telephone:* (602) 379-7900. *Fax:* (602) 379-7990. *Website:* www.nba.com/suns; www.stevenash.org.

NASHASHIBI, Nassiriddin; Palestinian journalist; b. 1924; ed American Univ. of Beirut; Arab Office, Jerusalem 1945–47; Chief Chamberlain, Amman, Jordan 1951; Dir Gen. Hashemite Broadcasting 1952; Ed. Akhbar al Youm, Cairo; Chief Ed. Al-Gumhuriyah, 1959–65; Rep. of the Arab League 1965–67; Diplomatic Ed. Al-Ahram; freelance journalist in Europe and the Middle East; Diplomatic Commentator, Jordanian, Israeli and other Middle Eastern TV stations; Order of Independence, Jordan; Order of the Jordanian Star. *Publications:* What Happened in the Middle East 1958, Political Short Stories 1959, Return Ticket to Palestine 1960, Some Sand 1962, An Arab in China 1964, Roving Ambassador 1970, The Ink is Very Black 1976 and 40 other books. *Address:* 55 Avenue de Champel, Geneva, Switzerland; PO Box 1897 Jerusalem 91017, Israel; 26 Lowndes Street, London, SW1, England. *Telephone:* (22) 3463763 (Geneva) (office); (20) 7235-1427 (London) (office).

NASHEED, Mohamed, (Anni), BSc; Maldivian journalist, political activist and head of state; *President;* b. 17 May 1967, Malé; m. Laila Ali; two d.; ed Overseas School of Colombo, Sri Lanka, Dauntsey's School, Wilts. and John Moores Univ., Liverpool, UK; fmr journalist for Sangu magazine; arrested several times for political reasons, adopted as prisoner of conscience by Amnesty Int. 1991; arrested and sentenced several times for criticism of the govt; Dir Safari Tours Maldives 1994–98; mem. Parl. 1999–2001; Dir Oriental Acad. Centre 2001–; Co-founder and mem. Gen. Council, Maldivian Democratic Party 2003, fmr Chair.; Pres. of the Maldives 2008–; commonly known in the Maldives as Anni; Hon. mem. Int. PEN. *Publications:* Dhagadu Dhahanan: Internal Feuding and Anglo-Dhivehi Relations 1800–1900 1995, Maldives: Historical Overview of Dhivehi Policy, Hithaa Hithuge Gulhuu. *Leisure interests:* tennis, music, reading, writing. *Address:* President's Office, Boduthakurufaanu Magu, Malé 20-05 (office); Maldivian Democratic Party, H. Sharaashaa, 1st Floor, Sosun Magu, Malé 20059 (office); G. Canaray-ge, Malé, Maldives (home). *Telephone:* 3320701 (office); 3340044 (office); 3342776 (home). *Fax:* 3325500 (office); 3322960 (office). *E-mail:* info@presidencymaldives.gov.mv (office); secretariat@mdp.org.mv (office). *Website:* www.presidencymaldives.gov.mv (office); www.mdp.org.mv (office).

NASHID, Ahmed; Maldivian business executive; Chair. Horizon Fisheries Pvt. Ltd. *Address:* Horizon Fisheries Private Ltd, 3rd Floor, No. 12, Boduthkurufaanu Magu, Malé, Maldives (office). *Telephone:* 3328855 (office). *Fax:* 3324455 (office). *E-mail:* info@horizonfisheries.com (office). *Website:* www.horizonfisheries.com (office).

NASIM, Anwar, PhD; Pakistani professor of genetics; *Science Adviser, OIC Standing Committee on Scientific and Technological Cooperation (COMSTECH);* b. 7 Dec. 1935, Pasrur; ed Univ. of the Punjab, Univ. of Edinburgh; lecturer, Govt Coll., Multan and Lahore 1957–62; Research Officer, Atomic Energy of Canada Ltd, Chalk River, Canada 1966–73; Sr Research Officer, Nat. Research Council of Canada 1973–89; Adjunct Prof. Carleton Univ.,

Ottawa 1984–89, Univ. of Ottawa 1983–89; Prin. Scientist and Head, Molecular Genetics Group, Biology and Medical Research Dept, King Faisal Specialist Hosp. and Research Centre, Riyadh 1989–93; Exec. Sec. Pakistan Acad. of Sciences 1994–96; Adviser (Science) COMSTECH 1996–; Fellow, Third World Acad. of Sciences 1987, Islamic Acad. of Sciences 1998, Pakistan Acad. of Medical Sciences 2000; Foreign Fellow, Pakistan Acad. of Sciences 1988; Civil Award Prime of Performance in Molecular Genetics 1995, Award for Outstanding Service (Overseas Pakistanis Inst.) 1995, Sitara-e-Imtiaz Civil Award in Molecular Genetics 1999 Gold Medal, MSc (Punjab). *Publications:* Repairable Lesions in Microorganisms (with A. Hurst) 1984, Recombinant DNA Methodology (with J. R. Dillon and E. R. Nestmann) 1985, Molecular Biology of the Fission Yeast (with P. Young and B. F. Johnson) 1989, Genetic Engineering and Biotechnology (with V. L. Chopra) 1990, Genetic Engineering – State of the Art (monograph) 1992, Biotechnology for Sustainable Development (with A. Malik Kauser and M. Khalid Ahmed) 1995; more than 100 scientific papers published in int. journals since 1965. *Leisure Interests:* reading literature, music. *Address:* COMSTECH Secretariat, 3 Constitution Avenue, G-5, Islamabad 44000, Pakistan (office); 237, Street 23, F-11/2, Islamabad (home). *Telephone:* (51) 9226813 (office); (51) 2299838 (home). *Fax:* (51) 9221115/92220265. *E-mail:* advisersc@comstech.org.pk (office); comstech@isb.comsats.net.pk (office); anwar_nasim@yahoo.com (home); comstech@isb.apollo.net.pk (office). *Website:* www.comstech.org.pk (office).

NASIR, Agha, MA; Pakistani television executive and playwright; *Executive Director, Geo TV Network;* b. 9 Feb. 1937, Meerut, UP, India; s. of Ali Ahmad Khan and Ghafari Begum; m. Safia Sultana 1957; one s. two d.; ed Karachi Univ.; Programmes Man. Pakistani TV 1967–68, Additional Gen. Man. 1967, Gen. Man. 1969–72, Dir Programmes Admin. 1972–86, Deputy Man. Dir 1986–87, Man. Dir 1987–88; Man. Dir Nat. Film Devt Corpn 1979; Dir-Gen. Pakistan Broadcasting Corpn 1989–92; Chief Exec. Shalimar Recording and Broadcasting Co. 1992–97; media consultant 1997–; Exec. Dir Geo TV Network 1998–; recipient of numerous awards for radio and TV plays; Pride of Performance Award from Pres. of Pakistan for services in field of broadcasting 1993. *Radio:* has written numerous features and plays for radio and produced more than 500 programmes. *Television:* has written more than 20 plays for TV and has produced about 100. *Publications:* Saat Dramay (plays), Television Dramey (TV plays), Gumshuda Log (collection of articles), Gulshan-e-Yaad, Hum Jeetay Jee Masroof Rahey (collection and comments on poet Faiz Ahmad Faiz). *Leisure interests:* reading, walking. *Address:* Geo TV Network, 40 Blue Area, Fazal-ul-huq Road, Islamabad (office); House No. 23, Street No. 3, F-8/3, Islamabad, Pakistan (home). *Telephone:* (51) 2263685 (home); (51) 2852619 (home). *Fax:* (51) 2827396 (office); (51) 2263685 (home). *E-mail:* agha.nasir@geo.tv (office). *Website:* www.geo.tv (office).

NASR, Farouk Mahmoud Sayf an-; Egyptian politician; b. Dec. 1922; fmr Pres. Supreme Constitutional Court; Dir Tech. Office, Ministry of Justice; worked on the preparation of laws, on Nationalist Councils; Minister of Justice 1987–2004. *Address:* c/o Ministry of Justice, Justice and Finance Building, Sharia Majlis ash-Sha'ab, Lazoughli Square, Cairo, Egypt.

NASR, Seyyed Hossein, MS, PhD; Iranian academic; *University Professor of Islamic Studies, George Washington University;* b. 7 April 1933, Tehran; s. of Valiallah Nasr and Ashraf Kia; m. Soussan Daneshvari 1958; one s. one d.; ed Mass. Inst. of Tech. and Harvard Univ.; Teaching Asst Harvard Univ. 1955–58, Visiting Prof. 1962, 1965; Assoc. Prof. of History of Science and Philosophy, Tehran Univ. 1958–63, Prof. 1963–79, Dean, Faculty of Letters 1968–72, Vice-Chancellor 1970–71; Chancellor (Pres.) Aryamehr Univ. 1972–75; First Prof. of Islamic Studies, American Univ. of Beirut 1964–65; Prof. of Islamic Studies, Temple Univ. 1979–84; Univ. Prof. of Islamic Studies, George Washington Univ. 1984–; Visiting Prof., Harvard Univ. 1962, 1965, Princeton Univ. 1975, Univ. of Utah 1979; A. D. White Prof.-at-Large, Cornell Univ. 1991–98; Founder and first Pres. Iranian Acad. of Philosophy 1974–79; mem. Inst. Int. de Philosophie, Greek Acad. of Philosophy, Royal Acad. of Jordan; Dr hc (Uppsala) 1977, (Lehigh) 1996. *Publications:* more than 30 books and 300 articles in Persian, Arabic, English and French in leading int. journals. *Leisure interests:* classical music (both Western and Eastern), tennis, hiking. *Address:* 709R Gelman Library, The George Washington University, Washington, DC 20052, USA (office). *Telephone:* (202) 994-5704 (office). *Fax:* (202) 994-4571 (office). *E-mail:* zsirat@gwu.edu (office). *Website:* www.nasrfoundation.org/default.html (office).

NASRALLAH, Sheikh Hasan; Lebanese ecclesiastic and political leader; *Secretary-General, Hezbollah;* b. 31 Aug. 1960, Beirut; m. Fatima Yassin; five c. (one deceased); at age 15 joined Amal movt, Bassouriyeh, 1975, then moved to Najaf, Iraq to study at Hawza (Islamic Seminary); forced to leave Iraq and returned to Lebanon to study with Amal leader Sheikh Abbas al-Musawi; elected Amal political del. Biqaa; resgnd from Amal and joined Hezbollah 1982, chief exec. and mem. Consultative Council, Beirut 1987–89, moved to Qom, Iran to resume studies 1989; returned briefly to Lebanon then back to Tehran to represent Hezbollah 1989; Sec.-Gen. Hezbollah 1992–. *E-mail:* hizbollahmedia@hizbollah.org. *Website:* www.moqawama.org/english; www.hizbollah.org.

NASREDDIN, Mahmoud; Lebanese international organization executive and academic; currently Dir-Gen. Arab Atomic Energy Agency. *Address:* Arab Atomic Energy Agency, PO Box 402, 7, rue Fatma El Fehria, Mutuelle Ville, al-Manzah 1004, 1004 Tunis, Tunisia (office). *Telephone:* (71) 800099 (office). *Fax:* (71) 781820 (office). *E-mail:* aaea@gnet.tn (office).

NASREEN, Taslima; Bangladeshi feminist, writer and doctor; b. 25 Aug. 1962, Mymensingh, E Pakistan (now Bangladesh); d. of Royab Ali; m. 3rd (divorced); ed Mymensingh Medical Coll., Dhaka Univ.; practised as a gynaecologist 1986–93; columnist Ajker Kagoj 1989; books banned in Bangladesh and Indian state of W Bengal, fatwa (death threat) pronounced against her 1993; left Bangladesh to live in self-imposed exile in Sweden 1994, later in Germany, USA, France and India; conducting research into women's rights in Islamic countries Harvard Univ. 2003–04; has published 16 books; Dr hc (Ghent Univ., Belgium) 1995, (American Univ. in Paris) 2005; Ananda Puroshkar, India 1992, Kurt Tukholsky Prize, Sweden 1994, Feminist of the Year, USA 1994, Human Rights Award, French Govt 1994, Edit de Nantes Award, France 1994, Monismanien Prize, Sweden 1995, Sakharov Prize, European Parl. 1995, Int. Humanist Award, Int. Humanist and Ethical Union 1996, Erwin Fischer Award 2002, UNESCO Prixe 2004, Grand Prix International Condorcet-Aron 2005, Prix Simone de Beauvoir 2008. *Publications include:* Shikore Bipul Khudha 1986, Nirbashito bahire Ontore 1989, Amar Kichu Jay Ashe Ne 1990, Atole Ontorin 1991, Nirbachito Kolam 1991, Nosto meyer nosto goddo 1992, Oporpokkho 1992, Shodh 1992, Balikar Gollachut 1992, Nimontron 1993, Laija (novel) 1993, Phera 1993, Choto choto dukkho kotha (selected columns) 1994, Bhromor koio gia 1994, Nirbashito Narir Kobita 1996, Amar Meyebela 1999, Jolopodyo 2000, Utal Hawa 2002, Forashi Premik 2002, Dwihkandita 2003, Ko 2003, Sei Sob Ondhokar 2004, Khali Khali Lage 2004, Kicchukhan Thako 2005, Ami bhalo nei, tumi bhalo theko prio desh 2006, Narir Kono Desh Nei 2007. *Address:* c/o Penguin Books India Pvt. Ltd, #11 Community Centre, Panchsheel Park, New Delhi 110 017, India (office). *E-mail:* taslima.web@gmail.com (office). *Website:* taslimanasrin.com.

NASSER, Jacques A. (Jac), AO; Australian business executive; *Chairman, Polaroid Holding Company;* b. 12 Dec. 1947, Lebanon; m.; ed Royal Melbourne Inst. of Tech.; with Ford of Australia 1968–73, mem. financial staff N American Truck operations, Ford Motor Co. 1973, profit analysis, product programming Ford Motor Co., Australia 1973–75, various positions, Int. Automotive Operations, Ford Motor Co. 1975–87, Dir, Vice-Pres. Finance and Admin., Autolatina jt venture, Brazil and Argentina 1987–90, Pres., CEO Ford of Australia 1990–93, Chair. Ford of Europe 1993–96, Vice-Pres. Ford Motor Co. 1993–96, CEO 1999–2001, Chair. Ford of Europe, Pres. Ford Automotive Operations, Exec. Vice-Pres. 1996–2002; Sr Partner, One Equity Partners LLC (JPMorgan Chase & Co.) 2002–; Chair. (non-exec.), Polaroid Holding Co. 2002–; Dir (non-Exec.) Brambles Industries 2004–; mem. Int. Advisory Bd Allianz AG; mem. Bd of Dirs BSkyB, Brambles (non-exec.); Order of the Cedar (Lebanon). *Leisure interest:* opera. *Address:* Polaroid Holding Company, 1265 Main Street, Waltham, MA 02451 (office); One Equity Partners LLC, 320 Park Avenue, 18th Floor, New York, NY 10022; 100 Bloomfield Hills Parkway, Suite 175, Bloomfield Hills, MI 48304, USA (home). *Telephone:* (781) 386-2000 (office). *Fax:* (781) 386-8588 (office). *Website:* www.polaroid.com (office).

NASSOUR, Gen. Mahamat Ali Abdallah; Chadian army officer and politician; fmr Minister of Territorial Admin; State Minister and Minister of Mines and Energy 2006–08; Minister of Nat. Defence Feb.–March 2008. *Address:* c/o Ministry of National Defence, BP 916, N'Djamena, Chad (office).

NĂSTASE, Adrian, LLM, PhD; Romanian academic and politician; b. 22 June 1950, Bucharest; s. of Marin Năstase and Elena Năstase; m. Daniela Miculescu 1985; two s.; ed Bucharest Univ.; Research Fellow, Inst. of Legal Research, Bucharest 1973–90; Prof. of Public Int. Law, Bucharest Univ. 1990–, Titu Maiorescu, Dimitrie Cantemir and Nicolae Titulescu pvt. univs 1992–; Assoc. Prof. of Public Int. Law, Paris-Panthéon Sorborne I 1994–; Minister of Foreign Affairs 1990–92; Speaker Chamber of Deputies 1992–96, Deputy Speaker 1996–; Exec. Pres. Social Democracy Party of Romania 1992–97, First Vice-Pres. 1997–2000, Pres. 2001–06 (resgnd); Prime Minister of Romania 2000–04; Vice-Chair. Camera Deputaţilor (Chamber of Deputies) 1996–2000, Chair. 2004–06 (resgnd); apptd mem. Romanian Parl. Del. to Parl. Asscn Council of Europe 1996; Vice-Pres. Asscn of Int. Law and Int. Relations, Bucharest 1977–; Dir of Studies, Int. Inst. of Human Rights, Strasbourg 1984; Pres. Titulescu European Foundation 1990–92 (Hon. Pres. 1992–); Exec. Pres. Euro-Atlantic Centre, Bucharest 1991–92; mem. Bd of Dirs Inst. for East-West Studies, New York 1991–97; mem. Human Rights Information and Documentation System; mem. French Soc. of Int. Law 1984–, American Soc. of Int. Law 1995–; indicted by Romanian prosecutors on corruption charges Jan. 2009; Order of Diplomatic Service Merit 1991, Gwanghwa Medal, Repub. of Korea 1991, Grande Croix de Mérite, Sovereign Order of Malta 1992; Nicolae Titulescu Prize, Romanian Acad. 1994, The Political Man of 1995, Turkish Businessmen's Asscn, Global Leader for Tomorrow Prize 1993. *Publications include:* Human Rights: An End-of-the-Century Religion 1992, International Law: Achievements and Prospects (co-author) 1992, Human Rights, Civil Society, Parliamentary Diplomacy 1994, Public International Law (co-author) 1995, Nicolae Titulescu – Our Contemporary 1995, Parliamentary Humour 1996, International Economic Law II 1996, Romania and the New World Architecture 1996, Documenta universales I (with law documents) 1997, 1998, The Treaties of Romania (1990–1997) 1998, Documenta universales II: The Rights of Persons Belonging to National Minorities 1998, Battle for the Future 2000, Contemporary International Law-Essential Texts 2001; more than 240 articles and papers. *Leisure interests:* hunting, music, modern art, collecting antiques, gardening, tennis. *Address:* c/o Social Democratic Party (SDP) (Partidul Social Democrat) (PSD), 71271 Bucharest 2, Str. Kiseleff 10, Romania (office). *Website:* www.adriannastase.ro.

NĂSTASE, Ilie; Romanian fmr professional tennis player; b. 19 July 1946, Bucharest; m. 1st; one d.; m. 2nd Alexandra King 1984; nat. champion (13–14 age group) 1959, (15–16 age group) 1961, (17–18 age group) 1963, 1964; won the Masters Singles Event, Paris 1971, Barcelona 1972, Boston 1973, Stockholm 1975; winner of singles at Cannes 1967, Travemünde 1967, 1969, Gauhati 1968, Madras 1968, 1969, New Delhi 1968, 1969, Viareggio 1968,

Barranquilla 1969, Coruna 1969, Budapest 1969, Denver 1969, Salisbury 1970, Rome 1970, 1973, Omaha 1971, 1972, Richmond 1971, Hampton 1971, Nice 1971, 1972, Monte Carlo 1971, 1972, Baastad 1971, Wembley 1971, Stockholm 1971, Istanbul 1971, Forest Hills 1972, Baltimore 1972, Madrid 1972, Toronto 1972, South Orange 1972, Seattle 1972, Roland Garros 1973, US Open 1973; winner of doubles at Roland Garros (with Ion Ţiriac) 1970, Wimbledon (with Rosemary Casals) 1970, 1972, (with Jimmy Connors q.v.) 1975; winner of ILTF Grand Prix 1972, 1973; won 108 pro titles in his career; played 130 matches for the Romanian team in the Davis Cup; elected to Nat. Council of Romania's Social Democracy Party (Partidul Social Democrat—PSD) 1995; PSD cand. in elections for Mayor of Bucharest 1996; Pres. Romanian Tennis Fed.; currently competes on Delta Tour of Champions; Best Romanian Sportsman of the Year 1969, 1970, 1971, 1973, Int. Tennis Hall of Fame 1991, mem. Laureus World Sports Acad. *Publication:* Breakpoint 1986. *Address:* Clubul sportiv Steaua, Calea Plevnei 114, Bucharest, Romania.

NATADZE, Nodar; Georgian politician and academic; *Chairman, People's Front of Georgia;* b. 27 May 1929, Tbilisi; s. of Revas Natadze and Tina Natadze (née Tatiana); m. Nana Gadyatska 1968; two s.; Philologist and Head Dept, Inst. of Philosophy, Georgian Acad. of Sciences; Leader Popular Front of Georgia (now People's Front of Georgia) 1989–, Nat. Cttee of United Republican Party of Georgia; mem. Supreme Council (Parl.) of Georgia 1989–90, 1990–91, 1992–95. *Leisure interests:* mountaineering, skiing, literary criticism. *Address:* People's Front of Georgia Pushkin 5, Tbilisi, Georgia. *Telephone:* (32) 93-17-10.

NATAPEI, Edward; Ni-Vanuatu politician; *Prime Minister;* b. 17 July 1954, Futuna Island; ed Fiji Inst. of Tech. and Malapoa Coll., Vanuatu; mem. Parl. for Port Vila 1983–; Minister of Health 1987; fmr Minister of Public Works, of Civil Aviation, of Meteorology, of Posts and Telecommunications and Tourism and of Foreign Affairs; Speaker of Parl. 1996–99; Pres. (acting) of Vanuatu March 1999; Leader of Opposition 2000; Prime Minister of Vanuatu 2001–04; Deputy Prime Minister and Minister of Infrastructure and Public Utilities 2007–08, Prime Minister 2008–; Pres. Vanua'aku Pati (Our Land Party). *Address:* Prime Minister's Office, PMB 053, Port Vila (office); Vanuaaku Pati (Our Land Party), POB 472, Port Vila, Vanuatu (office). *Telephone:* 22413 (office); 22584 (office). *Fax:* 22863 (office). *Website:* www.vanuatugovernment .gov.vu (office).

NATH, Indira, MD, FRCPath, FAMS, FNASc, FASc; Indian immunologist and academic; *Director, LEPRA-Blue Peter Research Centre;* b. 14 Jan. 1938; m.; one d.; studied leprosy and immunology at MRC Lab., UK; Indian Nat. Science Acad. Sr Scientist, Dept of Biotechnology, All India Inst. of Medical Sciences, New Delhi –2003; Dean, Medical School, Asian Inst. of Medicine, Science and Tech. 2003; currently Dir LEPRA-Blue Peter Research Centre, Hyderabad; Country Rep. to UN Comm. on Science and Tech. for Devt (UNCSTD) 2003–05; served on several ICSU cttees including the Cttee on Science and Social Responsibility 2003, Scoping Group on Health 2006–07; Fellow, Indian Acad. of Sciences 1988– (mem. Council 1992–94, Vice-Pres. 2001–03), Indian Nat. Science Acad., Nat. Acad. of Sciences (India), Nat. Acad. of Medical Sciences (India), Acad. of Sciences for the Developing World (TWAS), Royal Coll. of Pathologists (UK); Chevalier, Ordre nat. du Mérite 2004; Hon. DSc (Pierre and Marie Curie Univ., Paris) 2003; S.S. Bhatnagar Award, Council for Scientific and Industrial Research 1983, Shri Om Prakash Bhasin Foundation Award 1990, Padma Shri (India) 1999, L'Oréal-UNESCO For Women in Science Award 2002. *Publications:* numerous articles in scientific and medical journals on leprosy. *Address:* Blue Peter Research Centre, Near TEC Building, Cherlapally, Hyderabad 501 301 (office); 3F, Shangrila Apartments, Road No.2, Banjara Hills, Hyderabad 500034, India. *Telephone:* (40) 27264547 (office). *E-mail:* indiranath@gmail.com; indiran@hotmail.com. *Website:* www.leprasociety.org (office).

NATH, Kamal, BCom; Indian politician; *Minister of Commerce and Industry;* b. Nov. 1946, Kanpur; m.; two s.; ed Doon School, Dehra Dun, St Xavier's Coll.; joined Indian Nat. Congress 1968 as youth worker; first elected to Parl. for Chhindwara 1980, re-elected 1985, 1989, 1991, 1998, 1999, 2004; mem. Del. to UN Gen. Ass. 1982–83; apptd Minister of Environment and Forests 1991, later Minister of Textiles; Minister of Commerce and Industry 2004–; Sec.-Gen. Indian Nat. Congress; mem. Congress Working Cttee; Pres. Bd Govs Inst. of Man. Tech.; Chair. Madhya Pradesh Devt Council. *Address:* Ministry of Commerce and Industry, Udyog Bhavan, New Delhi 110 011 (office); No. 1 Tughlak Road, New Delhi 110 011, India (home). *Telephone:* (11) 23016664 (office); (11) 23792233 (home). *Fax:* (11) 23014335 (office); (11) 23793396 (home). *E-mail:* cim@ub.nic.in (office); knath@knath.com (home). *Website:* www.commin.nic.in (office).

NATHAN, S(ellapan) R(amanathan); Singaporean head of state; *President;* b. (Sellapan Ramanathan), 3 July 1924; s. of V. Sellapan and Mdm Abirami; m. Urmila (Umi) Nandey; one s. one d.; ed Victoria School and Univ. of Malaya, Singapore; almoner, Medical Dept, Gen. Hosp. 1955–56; Seaman's Welfare Officer, Ministry of Labour 1956–62; Asst Dir, Labour Research Unit 1962–63, Dir 1964–66; Asst Sec., Ministry of Foreign Affairs Feb.–June 1966, Prin. Asst Sec. 1966–67, Deputy Sec. 1967–71; Dir, Security and Intelligence Div., Ministry of Defence 1971–79; First Perm. Sec., Ministry of Foreign Affairs 1979–82; Exec. Chair., The Straits Times Press 1982–88; High Commr in Malaysia 1988–90; Amb. to USA 1990–96; Amb.-at-Large, Ministry of Foreign Affairs 1996–99; Dir, Inst. of Defence and Strategic Studies, Nanyang Technological Univ. 1996–99; Pres. of Singapore 1999–; Pro-Chancellor, Nat. Univ. of Singapore; Chair., Hindu Endowments Bd, Mitsubishi Singapore Heavy Industries (Pte) Ltd; mem. Bd of Trustees, NTUC Research Unit, Singapore Indian Devt Asscn; Dir, Singapore Nat. Oil Co. (Pte) Ltd, New Nation Publishing Berhad, Times Publishing Berhad, Singapore Press Holdings Ltd, Marshall Cavendish Ltd, Singapore Mint (Pte) Ltd,

Singapore Int. Media (Pte) Ltd; mem. Bd of Govs, Civil Service Coll.; Friend of Labour Award 1962, Public Service Star 1964, Public Admin Medal (Silver) 1967, Meritorious Service Medal 1974, NTUC May Day Meritorious Service Award 1984. *Leisure interests:* walking, reading. *Address:* President's Office, Istana, Orchard Road, Singapore 238823 (office). *Telephone:* 67375522 (office). *Website:* www.istana.gov.sg (office).

NATOCHIN, Yury Viktorovich, DSc; Russian physiologist and academic; *Head of Laboratory, Sechenov Institute of Evolutionary Physiology and Biochemistry, Russian Academy of Sciences;* b. 6 Dec. 1932, Kharkov, USSR (now Ukraine); s. of Victor Natochin and Frida Kohan; m. 1957; one s. one d.; ed Novosibirsk High Medical School; Jr, then Sr Researcher, Sechenov Inst. of Evolutionary Physiology and Biochemistry, St Petersburg 1959–64, Head of Lab. 1964–; Dean, Medical Faculty, St Petersburg State Univ. 1995–2002, Prof. of Physiology 1996–; Corresp. mem. USSR (now Russian) Acad. of Sciences 1987, mem. 1992, Acad.-Sec. Dept of Physiology 1996–2002; Ed.-in-Chief Russian Journal of Physiology 1995–; main research in physiology of kidney, functional nephrology, molecular physiology; mem. Int. Acad. of Astronautics, Academia Europaea; Hon. mem. Hungarian Physiology Soc. 1984, Hon. Prof. (Univ. of St Petersburg); L. A. Orbeli Prize 1980, Jan Parkinje Gold Medal 1982, S. Rach Medal 1986, S. Korolev Medal 1992, Science Prize of Govt of Russia 1997, I. Pavlov Gold Medal 2001. *Publications include:* Ion-Regulating Function of Kidney 1976, Physiology of Kidney 1982, Problems of Evolutional Physiology of Water-Salt Balance 1984, Kidney 1997, Fluid and Electrolyte Regulation in Spaceflight 1998. *Leisure interests:* photography, poetry, travelling. *Address:* Sechenov Institute of Evolutionary Physiology and Biochemistry, 44 M. Thorez prospekt, 194223 St Petersburg (office); 8/2 Vernosty str., Apt 25, St Petersburg, Russia (home). *Telephone:* (812) 552-30-86 (office). *Fax:* (812) 552-30-86 (office). *E-mail:* natochin@iephb.ru (office). *Website:* www.iephb.ru (office).

NATSUKI, Shizuko, Japanese novelist; b. (Shizuko Idemitsu), 21 Dec. 1938, Tokyo; m. Yoshihide Idemitsu 1963; one s. one d.; ed Keio Univ.; screenplay for Only I Know (Japanese TV); followed by numerous novels, short stories and screenplays; Mystery Writers of Japan Prize 1973, Prix du Roman d'Aventures (France) 1989, Nishinippon Shinsbeen Cultural Award 1999, Fukuoka Prefecture Cultural Award 2001. *Films:* Tragedy of W 1984. *Plays:* novels adapted for the stage: Tragedy of W 1993, Actress X 1994. *Works adapted for television include:* The Angel Vanishes 1972 and more than 200 others. *Publications:* 39 novels including The Angel Vanishes 1970, Disappearance 1973, Murder at Mt. Fuji 1984, Dome 1986, The Third Lady 1987, The Obituary arrives at Two O'Clock 1988, Portal of the Wind 1990, Marianne 1997, Mariko 1999, The Punishment 2001, and about 240 novelettes and short stories. *Leisure interests:* golf, go (started own go tournament using go stone she developed herself). *Address:* 2-6-1 Ooike, Minami-ku, Fukuoka-shi 815-0073, Japan. *Telephone:* (92) 553-1893. *Fax:* (92) 552-0181.

NATTIEZ, Jean-Jacques, OC, LèsL, MèsL, PhD; Canadian (b. French) musicologist and academic; *Titular Professor of Musicology, Faculty of Music, University of Montreal;* b. 30 Dec. 1945, Amiens, France; ed Amiens Conservatoire, Université d'Aix-en-Province, Université de Paris VIII-Vincennes, France; naturalized Canadian 1975; Prof., Depts of Linguistics and French Studies, Univ. of Montreal 1970–72, Prof. of Musicology, Faculty of Music 1972–; Co-Ed. first six issues of CUMR 1980–85; fmr Ed. Circuit periodical; pioneer in br. of musicology known as musical semiology (analysis of music dealing with musical meaning, sometimes inspired by structural linguistics); Co-Ed. series Musique/Passé/Présent, Christian Bourgois publishing house, Paris 1981; Musical Dir Joliette-Lanaudière Symphony Orchestra 1984–87; currently Gen. Ed. five-volume Encyclopedia of Music; contrib. to EMC; in field of ethnomusicology, has produced several recordings of Inuit (Canada), Ainu (Japan) and Baganda (Uganda) music; mem. RSC 1988–; Ordre nat. du Québec 2001; Killam Research Fellowship 1988–90, Dent Medal, Royal Musical Asscn (England) for his complete works 1988, Prix André-Laurendeau pour les sciences humaines, Asscn canadienne française pour l'avancement des sciences 1989, Molson Prize 1990, Prix Léon-Gérin pour les sciences sociales du Gouvernement du Québec 1994, Prize for Teaching Excellence, Univ. of Montreal in 2004, Killam Prize (Humanities), Canada Council for the Arts 2004. *Recordings include:* Inuit Games and Songs (UNESCO's Musical Sources series) (Grand prix du disque de l'Acad. Charles-Cros 1979) 1978, Jeux vocaux des Inuit (Inuit du Caribou, Netsilik et Igloolik); contributed to Chants des Aïnou 1982, LP edn of oral music recordings made by Romanian ethnomusicologist Constantin Brailoïu in the 1950s, under the title Collection universelle de musique populaire enregistrée (Grand prix Charles-Cros 1987) 1985. *Publications:* Fondements d'une sémiologie de la musique 1975, Tétralogies 1983, Proust musicien 1984, Music and Discourse 1987, Wagner androgyne 1990; has edited texts by composer Pierre Boulez and published several major articles on the composer; Opera (novel); has published three collections of articles: De la sémiologie à la musique 1988, Le combat de Chronos et d'Orphée and La musique, la recherche et la vie; more than 150 papers. *Address:* Faculté de musique, Université de Montréal, 200 avenue Vincent-d'Indy, CP 6128, succursale Centre-ville, Montréal, PQ H3C 3J7, Canada (office). *Telephone:* (514) 343-6427 (office). *Fax:* (514) 343-5727 (office). *E-mail:* musique@umontreal.ca (office). *Website:* www.musique .umontreal.ca (office).

NATTRASS, E. M. B. (Sue), AO, FAIM, FAIAM; Australian arts administrator, director and trustee; b. 15 Sept. 1941, Horsham, Vic.; d. of John Elliott Nattrass and Elizabeth Claven Saul; ed Univ. of Melbourne and Melbourne Business School; Stage Man., Lighting Designer and Production Dir 1963–79; Gen. Man. J. C. Williamson Productions Ltd 1980–83; Dir Playbox Theatre Co. 1981–84; Theatre Operations Man., Victorian Arts Centre 1983–88, Deputy Gen. Man. 1988–89, Gen. Man. 1989–96; Artistic Dir Melbourne Int. Festival of the Arts 1998–; Exec. Dir Producer Services Millmaine Entertainment 2000–04; CEO Artistic Dir Adelaide Festival 2002; owner The Yarts Consulting 2004–; numerous public appts. including mem. Drama Advisory Panel, Vic. Ministry for the Arts 1983–85, 1987–88, mem. Bicentennial Arts and Entertainment Cttee 1987–88; mem. Ministerial Advisory Cttee, Queen Victoria Women's Centre 1993–94, Patron 1994–2001; Pres. Australian Entertainment Industry Assn 1994–2003; Councillor Victorian Coll. of Arts 1989–2004, Deputy Pres. 1992–2002, Pres. 2002–04; Dir John Truscott Design Foundation 1994–, Leadership Vic. 1996–2003, Theatre Royal Hobart 2000–08, Fed. Square Pty Ltd 2000–08, Harold Mitchell Foundation 2000–; mem. Melbourne and Olympics Parks Trust 2000–, Sydney Opera House Trust, Brian Stacey Foundation, Australian Int. Cultural Council; Chair. Collections Council of Australia, City of Melbourne Cultural Devt Bd; Patron Victorian Theatres Trust, The Song Room Inc.; George Fairfax Fellow, Deakin Univ.; Premier Award, The AGE Performing Arts Awards, St Michael's Medal 1996, Vic. Day Award for Community and Public Service 1999, Centenary Medal, The Green Room Award for Lifetime Achievement, J.C. Williamson Award for outstanding contribution to Australian live performance industry, Dame Elisabeth Murdoch Cultural Leadership Award. *Leisure interests:* cooking, walking, staring at trees, the bush. *Address:* The Yarts Consulting, 19 Myross Avenue, Ascot Vale, Vic. 3032, Australia (home). *Telephone:* (3) 9370-7062 (home). *E-mail:* sue@theyarts.com.au (home).

NAUGHTIE, (Alexander) James, MA; British journalist; b. 9 Aug. 1951, Aberdeen, Scotland; s. of Alexander Naughtie and Isabella Naughtie; m. Eleanor Updale 1986; one s. two d.; ed Univ. of Aberdeen and Univ. of Syracuse, NY, USA; journalist, The Scotsman (newspaper) 1977–84, The Guardian 1984–88, also Chief Political Corresp.; Presenter The World at One, BBC Radio 1988–94, The Proms, BBC Radio and TV 1991–, Today, BBC Radio 4 1994–, Book Club BBC Radio 4 1998–; mem. Council Gresham Coll. 1997–; Hon. LLD (Aberdeen), (St Andrews); Hon. DUniv (Stirling). *Publications:* The Rivals 2001, The Accidental American: Tony Blair and the Presidency 2004, The Making of Music: A Journey with Notes 2007. *Leisure interests:* books, opera. *Address:* BBC News Centre, London, W12 8QT, England. *Telephone:* (20) 8624-9644. *Website:* www.bbc.co.uk/radio4/today.

NAUMAN, Bruce, MFA; American artist; b. 6 Dec. 1941, Fort Wayne, IN; ed Univ. of Wisconsin, Madison and Univ. of Calif. at Davis, studied with Italo Scango, William Wiley, Robert Arneson, Frank Owen, Stephen Kaltenbach; Instructor San Francisco Art Inst. 1966–68, Univ. of Calif. at Irvine 1970; has participated in numerous group exhbns in USA and Europe; work in many perm. collections, including Whitney Museum, LA County Museum of Art, Tate Modern (London); first solo exhibition 1966; Dr hc (San Francisco Art Inst.) 1989; Artist Fellowship Award, Nat. Endowment for the Arts 1968, Max Beckmann Prize (Frankfurt) 1990, Wolf Prize 1993, Aldrich Prize 1995; ranked ninth in ArtReview magazine's Power 100 list 2005. *Publications:* Pictures of Sculptures in a Room 1966, Clear Sky 1968, Burning Small Fires 1968, Bruce Naumann 1988, Bruce Naumann Prints 1989. *Address:* c/o Sperone Westwater, 415 W 13 Street, New York, NY 10014, USA. *Telephone:* (212) 999-7337. *Fax:* (212) 999-7338. *E-mail:* info@speronewestwater.com. *Website:* www.speronewestwater.com.

NAUMANN, Gen. Klaus, OBE; German army officer (retd); b. 25 May 1939, Munich; m. Barbara Linke; one s. one d.; joined Bundeswehr 1958, Col staff of German Mil. Rep., NATO Mil. Cttee, Brussels 1981–84; Brigade Commdr Armoured Infantry Brigade, Ellwangen 1984–86; Brig. Dept Head of Force Planning, Gen. Staff, Ministry of Defence 1986–88; Maj.-Gen., Head of Defence Policy and Operations staff 1988–90; adviser in two-plus-four negotiations on German Unification 1990; Lt-Gen., Commdr first German corps April–Oct. 1991; Insp.-Gen. of the Bundeswehr 1991; Chair. NATO Mil. Cttee 1996–99; mem. Int. Advisory Bd Worldsecuritynetwork.com; Great Distinguished Service Cross 1993; Commdr Legion of Merit 1993, Grand Officer, Légion d'honneur 1994, Grosses Bundesverdienstkreuz mit Stern 1998, Commdr's Cross of the Merit of FRG, Gold Cross of Honour of the Federal Armed Forces, Gran Cruz de la Orden del Mérito Militar con Distintivo Blanco (Spain), Knight Commdr of the Order of the British Empire (mil) (United Kingdom), Grootofficier in de Kroonorde (Belgium), Commdr's Cross of the Legion of Merit (US), Grand Cross 2nd Class of the Order of Merit of the Republic of Austria, Kommandor m/Stjerne av den Kongelige Norske Fortjenstorden (Norway), Defence Medal, 1st class (Hungary), Grand Officier de l'Ordre de Leopold (mil) (Belgium), Grootofficier in de orde van Oranje-Nassau (Netherlands), Commdr's Grand Cross of the order of the Lion of Finland. *Publication:* Die Bundeswehr in einer Welt im Umbruch; numerous articles in newspapers and journals. *Leisure interests:* politics, history, art, photography, Latin American culture. *Address:* c/o World Security Network Foundation, 945 Fifth Avenue, New York, NY 10021, USA.

NAUMANN, Michael, DPhil; German publisher; b. 8 Dec. 1941, Köthen; s. of Eduard Naumann and Ursula Naumann (née Schönfeld); m. Christa Wessel 1969 (divorced); one s. one d.; ed Univ. of Munich and Queen's Coll., Oxford, UK; Asst Prof., Univ. of Bochum 1971–76; Florey Scholar, Queen's Coll. Oxford 1976–78; Ed., Foreign Corresp. Die Zeit, Hamburg 1978–82; Sr Foreign Ed. Der Spiegel, Hamburg 1982–84; Publr Rowohlt Verlag, Reinbek 1984–95; Pres. and CEO Henry Holt and Co., New York 1996–98; Minister of State for Culture 1998–2000; Chief Ed. and Publisher, Die Zeit 2001–07; SPD cand. for Hamburg mayoral elections 2008; Commdr Légion d'honneur. *Publications:* Der Abbau einer Verkehrten Welt 1969, Amerika liegt in Kalifornien 1983, Strukturwandel des Heroismus 1984, Die Geschichte ist offen 1990, Die schönste Form der Freiheit 2001. *Leisure interests:* books, motor-cycling, sailing. *Address:* Kurt-Schumacher-Allee 10, 20097 Hamburg, Germany (office). *Telephone:* (40) 2808480 (office). *Fax:* (40) 28084818 (office). *Website:* www.naumann-hamburg.de (office).

NAUMI, Najeeb an-, PhD; Qatari lawyer and politician; b. 21 March 1954, Doha; m.; four s. one d.; ed Alexandria Univ., Egypt, Univ. of Dundee, UK; legal adviser, Qatar Gas and Petrochemical Co. 1981–88, Diwan Amiri 1988–92; Minister and Legal Adviser, Office of HH The Heir Apparent and Minister of Defence 1992–95; Minister of Justice 1995–97; advocate and legal consultant 1997–. *Publication:* International Legal Issues Arising under the United Nations Decade of International Law 1995. *Leisure interests:* boating, Internet, reading, writing. *Address:* PO Box 9952, Doha, Qatar (office). *Telephone:* (974) 675374 (office). *Fax:* (974) 675378.

NAUMOV, Vladimir Naumovich; Russian film director and screenwriter; *CEO, Soyuz-Navona Film Production Company;* b. 6 Dec. 1927, Leningrad (now St. Petersburg); m. Natalia Belokhvostikova; one s. one d.; ed Dept of Directing, State Inst. of Cinematography (under I. A. Savchenko); Artistic Dir workshop unit at Mosfilm 1961–89 (with A. Alov until 1983); Chair. Bd Mosfilm Studios Co. 1989–; Prof. VGIK 1980–; currently CEO Soyuz-Navona film production company; Head of Dept, Nesterova Univ.; Pres. Nat. Film Acad.; Sec. Nat. Union of Cinematographers; Academician European Film Acad.; mem. Bd Mosfilm Cinema Concern; Order of Honour 1971, Order of the Red banner of Labour 1972, Order of the Friendship of Peoples 1987, Order of Merit for the Country 1997, Golden Cross for the Resurrection of Russia 2004; Meritorious Art worker 1965, People's Artist of the RSFSR 1974, People's Artist of USSR 1983, USSR State Prize 1984, First Degree Peacemaker Award for charity work 2007, Second Degree Merit Award for outstanding contribution to cinema art 2007, Golden Eagle Award for outstanding contribution to cinematography 2008. *Films include:* (in collaboration with Alov to 1983) Uneasy Youth 1955, Pavel Korchagin (based on Ostrovsky's novel How the Steel Was Tempered) 1957, Wind 1959, Peace to Him Who Enters (two prizes at 22nd Venice Film Festival) 1961, A Nasty Story (based on Dostoevsky) 1966 (banned, shown 1989), Flight (based on M. Bulgakov's play) 1971, How the Steel Was Tempered (TV series) 1974, Legend about Til (three prizes at All-Union Festival, First Prize Int. Festival Haugesunde, Norway, Int. Festival Brussels) 1976, Tehran-43 (Golden Prize at 12th Int. Film Festival, Moscow, Golden Prize All-Union Festival) 1981, The Shore (First Prize at 17th Int. Film Festival, Kiev) 1984, The Choice 1987, The Law 1989, Ten Years of Confinement 1990, The White Holiday (two prizes Int. Film Festival Rimini 1995) 1994, Nardo's Mystery (aka White Dog's Dream) (Moscow Film Festival Prize 1998) 1998, Clock Without Hands (Russian 'Window to Europe' Film Festival Prize 2000, Grand Gold Pegasus Prize from the Moscow Film Festival 2001, Moscow Mayor's Prize 2001) 2000, Joconda on Asphalt 2007. *Address:* 123056 Moscow, Bolshaya Gruzinskaya 39, Apt. 214, Russia. *Telephone:* (495) 147-23-10 (office); (495) 253-87-32. *Fax:* (495) 938-20-88.

NAUR, Peter, Mag. Scient., DrPhil; Danish computer scientist and academic; b. 25 Oct. 1928, Frederiksberg; ed Copenhagen Univ. Astronomical Observatory; began career as astronomer; employed at Regnecentralen (Danish computing inst.) 1959–69; Lecturer, Niels Bohr Inst. and Danmarks Tekniske Højskole (Tech. Univ. of Denmark) 1959–69; Prof. of Datalogi (Computer Science), Copenhagen Univ. 1969–98; currently developing theory of human thinking called Synapse-State Theory of Mental Life; A.M. Turing Award, Association for Computing Machinery for his work on defining the ALGOL 60 programming language 2005. *Achievements include:* last name is the N in BNF notation (Backus-Naur form), attributed to him by Donald Knuth, used in description of syntax for most programming languages; contributed to creation of ALGOL 60 programming language. *Publications:* Computing: A Human Activity 1992, Report on the Algorithmic Language ALGOL 60 (ed.), Antiphilosophical Dictionary 2001, Psykologi i videnskabelig rekonstruktion 2002; large number of articles and chapters on astronomy, computer science, issues in society, classical music, psychology and educ. *Address:* c/o Universitetsparken 13, 2100 Copenhagen Ø, Denmark. *Telephone:* 35-37-11-33. *E-mail:* naturfag@unibog.dk; info@naur.com. *Website:* www.naur.com.

NAVA-CARRILLO, Germán, DR.; Venezuelan diplomatist and politician; b. 21 Aug. 1930, Maracaibo; m.; two c.; ed Universidad Central de Venezuela; joined Ministry of Foreign Affairs 1955; Minister Plenipotentiary, Chargé d'affaires, London; Asst Dir-Gen. of Int. Politics and Chief Div. of Inter-American Affairs, Ministry of Foreign Affairs; Minister-Counsellor, Perm. Mission at UN 1967–69; Amb. and Deputy Perm. Rep. to UN 1969–70; Amb. to Egypt, also accred to Ethiopia 1970–72; Dir of Protocol, Ministry of Foreign Affairs 1972–74; Amb. to Costa Rica 1974–75; Dir of Int. Politics, Ministry of Foreign Affairs 1975–78, Gen. Dir of Int. Politics and Vice-Minister 1978–79; Perm. Rep. to UN 1979–81; Vice-Minister, Ministry of Foreign Affairs 1984–88, Minister of Foreign Affairs 1988–89; Rep. of Venezuela to several UN and other int. confs; Prof., Int. Studies School, Cen. Univ. of Venezuela 1981. *Address:* c/o Ministry of Foreign Affairs, Casa Amarilla, Biblioteca Central, esq. Principal, Caracas 1010, Venezuela.

NAVARETTE CORTÉS, HE Cardinal Urbano, SJ; Spanish canon lawyer, editor and ecclesiastic; b. 25 May 1920, Camarena de la Sierra; ed Pontifical Gregorian Univ., Rome; entered Society of Jesus (Jesuits) 1937, ordained priest 1952; taught canon law at and served several terms as Dean of the Canon Law Faculty, Pontifical Gregorian Univ., Rector 1980–86, retd as Dean 1995, ed. univ.'s journal on canon law, morality and liturgy 1995–2002; cr. Cardinal 2007; continues to publish and to advise Congregation for Divine Worship and Sacraments, Pontifical Council for Legis. Texts, Supreme Court of the Apostolic Signature. *Address:* c/o Society of Jesus, Borgo S. Spirito 4, CP 6139, 00195 Rome -Prati, Italy. *Telephone:* (06) 689771. *Fax:* (06) 6868214. *E-mail:* info@jesuit.org. *Website:* www.jesuit.org.

NAVARETTE LÓPEZ, Jorge Eduardo; Mexican economist, diplomatist and academic; *Head of Research on International Affairs, National Autonomous University of Mexico;* b. 29 April 1940, Mexico City; m. Martha L. López; one s.; ed Nat. Autonomous Univ. of Mexico (UNAM); Prof., Nat. School of

Econs and Nat. School of Political and Social Sciences, UNAM 1964–71, Head of Research on Int. Affairs, 2004–; various positions with Foreign Trade Nat. Bank 1966–72; Ed. Comercio Exterior; with Secr. of Finance and Public Credit –1972; Amb. to Venezuela 1972–75, to Austria 1975–77, to Yugoslavia 1977–78, to UK 1986–89, to People's Repub. of China 1989–93, to Chile 1993–95, to Brazil 1997–2001, to Germany 2002–04; Rep. of Mexico at Int. Conf. for Co-operation and Devt, Paris 1976–77; Deputy Perm. Rep. to UN and Vice-Pres. Econ. and Social Council 1978–79, Perm. Rep. to UN 2001–02; Under-Sec. for Econ. Affairs, Secr. of Foreign Relations 1979–86; Under-Sec. for Policy and Devt, Secr. of Energy 1995–97; fmr consultant for Inter-American Bank and UNDP; fmr Perm. Rep. to UNIDO; fmr mem. Bd of Govs IAEA; fmr mem. South Comm. *Publications include:* The International Transference of Technology: The Mexican Case (with Gerardo Bueno and Miguel Wionczek) 1969, Mexico: The Economic Policy of the New Government 1971, The Latin American External Debt 1986. *Address:* National Autonomous University of Mexico, Ciudad Universitaria, Del. Coyoacán, 04510, Mexico (office). *Telephone:* (55) 5623-0264 (office). *Fax:* (55) 1107-6963 (office). *E-mail:* joredune@servidor.unam.mx (office). *Website:* www.unam.mx (office).

NAVARRO, Samuel Lewis; Panamanian politician; *First Vice-President and Minister of Foreign Affairs;* b. 1958, Panama City; s. of Gabriel Lewis Galindo; m.; several c.; ed Georgetown and American Univs, Washington, DC, USA; worked in pvt. sector; Founder, Partido de Solidaridad 1993, est. alliance with Partido Revolucionario Democrático 1999, left to serve as running mate to presidential cand. Martín Torrijos 2004; Vice-Pres. of Panama and Minister of Foreign Affairs 2004–; Pres. and Dir Empaques de Colón 1985–2001, Grupo ELE 1985–2001, Northsound Corpn, Inc. 1985–2001; mem. Bd of Dirs Panama Canal Authority 1997–2001; fmr mem. Bd of Dirs Distribuidora de Productos de Papel, Inmobiliaria Costa Azul, Cervecería Nacional, Red Crown Corpn. *Address:* Ministry of Foreign Affairs, Altos de Ancón, Complejo Narciso Garay, Panamá 4, Panama (office). *Telephone:* 227-0013 (office). *Fax:* 227-4725 (office). *E-mail:* prensa@mire.gob.pa (office). *Website:* www.mire.gob.pa (office).

NAVARRO BERMÚDEZ, Leopoldo, PhD; Nicaraguan politician; *President, Partido Liberal Constitucionalista;* Vice-Pres. of Nicaragua 2000–01; Pres. Partido Liberal Constitucionalista (PLC); mem. Asamblea Nacional. *Address:* Colonial Los Robles 211, Managua, Nicaragua (office). *Telephone:* (2) 78-8705 (office). *Fax:* (2) 78-1800 (office).

NAVARRO NAVARRO, Miguel; Spanish sculptor; b. 29 Sept. 1945, Mislata, Valencia; s. of Vicente Navarro Lopez and Valentina-Francisca Navarro Hernandez; ed Escuela Superior de Bellas Artes de San Carlos, Valencia; began career as a painter; from 1972 devoted himself mainly to sculpture; works in public spaces include: public fountains Valencia 1984, Turis (Valencia) 1986, Minerva Paranoica (sculpture), Castellón 1989, Torre del Sonido (sculpture), Universidad Carlos III, Getafe 1990, Fraternitat (sculpture), Barcelona 1992, Boca de Luna (fountain), Brussels 1994, Casco Industrial (sculpture) Bilbao 1999, Vigía (sculpture) Las Palmas 2000, Cabeza con Luna Menguante, Mislata 2001, La Mirada (sculpture) Vitoria-Gasteiz 2002, Palera (sculpture), Malaga 2002, Palas Fundición (sculpture) Ceuti, Murcia 2003, El Parotet, Valencia 2003; works in public collections including: Guggenheim Museum, New York, Fundació Caixa de Pensions, Barcelona, Instituto Valenciano de Arte Moderno, Valencia, Museo Nacional Centro de Arte Reina Sofía, Madrid, Fondation Lambert, Brussels, Diputación Prov. de Valencia, Centre Georges Pompidou, Paris, Museu d'Art Contemporani, Barcelona, Colección Argentaria, Madrid, Colección Banco de España, Madrid, Fundación Coca Cola España, Madrid, Fundazion I.C.O., Madrid, Universidad Politécnica de Valencia, Museo de Arte Contemporáneo Sofía Imbert, Caracas, Mie Prefectural Art Museum, Japan; Premio Nacional de Artes Plásticas 1986, Premio Alfons Roig, Valencia 1987, Premio CEOE a las Artes 1990, Premio Nacional de la Asociación de Críticos de Arte ARCO 95 1995, Premio Valencianos para el Siglo XXI 2001, Distinción de la Generalidad Valenciana al Merito Cultural 2002. *Leisure interests:* cooking, countryside. *Address:* c/o San Martín 13, 46920 Mislata, Valencia, Spain. *Telephone:* (6) 3792624.

NAVASKY, Victor Saul, AB, LLB; American writer, editor and academic; *Publisher Emeritus, The Nation;* b. 5 July 1932, New York; s. of Macy Navasky and Esther Goldberg; m. Anne Landey Strongin 1966; one s. two d.; ed Swarthmore Coll., Yale Univ. Law School; Special Asst to Gov. G. Mennen Williams, Mich. 1959–60; Founding Ed. and Publr Monocle quarterly 1961–65; Ed. New York Times Magazine 1970–72, wrote monthly column (In Cold Print) for The New York Times Book Review; Ed.-in-Chief The Nation magazine 1978–94, Editorial Dir and Publr 1995–2007, Publr Emer. 2007–; George Delacorte Prof. of Magazine Journalism, Grad. School of Journalism, Columbia Univ. 1999–, Dir Delacorte Center of Magazines, Chair. Columbia Journalism Review; Visiting Scholar, Russell Sage Foundation 1975–76; Ferris Visiting Prof. of Journalism, Princeton Univ. 1976–77; Visiting Prof. of Social Change, Swarthmore Coll. 1982; Fellow, John F. Kennedy School of Govt, Harvard Univ. 1994, Freedom Forum Media Studies Center 1995; has taught at numerous colls and univs; mem. Man. Bd Swarthmore Coll. 1991–94; fmr mem. Bd Authors' Guild, Cttee to Protect Journalists, Bd of Govs New School for Social Research; fmr Vice-Pres. PEN; mem. American Acad. of Arts and Sciences; numerous hon. degrees; Guggenheim Fellow 1975–76, Carey McWilliams Award, American Political Science Asscn 2001. *Play:* Starr's Last Tape (with Richard R. Lingeman) 1999. *Publications include:* Kennedy Justice, Naming Names (Nat. Book Award), The Experts Speak: The Definitive Compendium of Authoritative Misinformation, A Matter of Opinion (George Polk Book Award 2005, Ann M. Sperber Prize 2006) 2005, Mission Accomplished: The Experts Speak About Iraq (with Christopher Cerf) 2008; numerous articles and reviews published in magazines and journals of opinion. *Address:* The Nation, 33 Irving Place, 8th Floor, New York, NY 10003 (office); 33 W 67th Street, New York, NY 10023, USA (home). *Telephone:* (212) 209-5411 (office). *Fax:* (212) 982-9000 (office). *E-mail:* vic@thenation.com (office). *Website:* thenation.com (office).

NAVICKAS, Vytas, PhD; Lithuanian economist and politician; *Minister of the Economy;* b. 14 March 1952, Lazdijai Dist; m.; two d.; ed Vilnius Univ.; Research Fellow, Inst. of Econs, Lithuanian Acad. of Sciences 1975–89; Lecturer, Vilnius Univ., Vilnius Pedagogical Univ. and Vilnius Gediminas Tech. Univ. 1983–90, 1997–2004; Head of Div. for Econ. Reforms, Council of Ministers 1989; Minister of the Economy 1990–91, 1995–96, 2007–, Deputy Minister 1991–95; Dir UAB Draudos Asistavimas 1996–2004; Pres. Vilnius Chamber of Commerce, Industry and Crafts 2001–05; mem. Lithuanian Peasant Nationalists' Union. *Address:* Ministry of the Economy, Gedimino pr. 38/2, Vilnius 01104, Lithuania (office). *Telephone:* (5) 262-3863 (office). *Fax:* (5) 262-3974 (office). *E-mail:* kanc@ukmin.lt (office). *Website:* www.ukmin.lt (office).

NAVON, Yitzhak; Israeli fmr head of state and teacher; b. 9 April 1921, Jerusalem; s. of Yosef Navon and Miriam Ben-Atar; m. Ofira Reznikov-Erez; one s. one d.; ed Hebrew Univ. of Jerusalem; Dir Hagana Arabic Dept, Jerusalem 1946–49; Second Sec., Israel Legation in Uruguay and Argentina 1949–51; Political Sec. to Foreign Minister 1951–52; Head of Bureau of Prime Minister 1952–63; Head, Dept of Culture, Ministry of Educ. and Culture 1963–65; mem. Knesset (Parl.) 1965–78; fmr Deputy Speaker; fmr Chair. Knesset Defence and Foreign Affairs Cttee; Chair. World Zionist Council 1973–78; Pres. of Israel 1978–83; Vice-Premier and Minister of Educ. and Culture 1984–90; mem. Mapai Party 1951–65, Rafi 1965–68, Israel Labour Party 1968–; Chair. Acad. of Music and Dance, Nat. Authority of Ladino, Neot Kedumim (Biblical Gardens). *Television:* Out of Spain – series of five programmes on the history of the Jews in Spain. *Play:* The Sephardic Orchard. *Publications:* Romancero Sephardi, Six Days and Seven Gates; collection of articles on Ben Gurion. *Leisure interests:* theatre, folklore, cantorial music. *Address:* 31 Hanevi'im Street, Jerusalem (office); 39 Jabotinsky Street, Jerusalem, Israel (home). *Telephone:* (2) 623-63-53 (office); (2) 563-85-66 (home). *Fax:* (2) 623-63-55 (office). *E-mail:* fpnavon@netvision.net.il (office).

NAVRATILOVA, Martina; American/Czech professional tennis player; b. 18 Oct. 1956, Prague; d. of Miroslav Navratil and Jana Navratilova; professional since 1975, the year she defected to USA; ranked No. 1 1982–85; Wimbledon singles champion 1978, 1979, 1982, 1983, 1984, 1985, 1986, 1987, 1990, finalist 1988, 1989, 1994; (doubles 1976, 1979, 1982, 1983, 1984, 1985); French champion 1982, 1984; Australian champion 1981, 1983, 1985; Avon champion 1978, 1979, 1981; US Open champion 1983, 1984, 1986, 1987; 57 Grand Slam titles (18 singles, 37 women's doubles, 2 mixed doubles); won 167 singles and 173 doubles titles (more than any other player, male or female); World No. 1 for 332 weeks at retirement (Nov. 1994); 19 Wimbledon titles (1995); set professional women's record for consecutive victories 1984; won 100th tournament of career 1985; only player to win 100 matches at Wimbledon 1991; record of 158 wins (Feb. 1992) in singles beating the record of Chris Evert Lloyd; Pres. Women's Tennis Asscn 1979–80, 1983–84, 1994–95; World Champion 1980; played Federation Cup for Czechoslovakia 1973, 1974, 1975; 1,400 victories (Oct. 1993); designer own fashion wear; made comeback (in doubles only) 2000; winner Mixed Doubles, Australian Open 2003, Wimbledon 2003 (at age 46 year and 6 months, oldest winner of a Grand Slam title); rep. USA in Federation Cup 2003; Dr hc (George Washington) 1996; Female Athlete of the Decade for the 1980s, Nat. Sports Review, Sportswomen of the Year 1982–84, Women's Sports Foundation, Int. Tennis Hall of Fame 2000. *Publications:* Being Myself (autobiog.) 1985, The Total Zone (novel with Liz Nickles) 1994, The Breaking Point (with Liz Nickles) 1996, Killer Instinct (with Liz Nickles) 1998, Shape Yourself 2006. *Leisure interests:* golf, snowboarding, skiing, basketball. *Address:* IMG, 1360 E 9th Street, Cleveland, OH 44114, USA (office). *Website:* www.martinanavratilova.com (office).

NAWAR, Ahmed, PhD; Egyptian arts administrator; b. 3 June 1945, el-Shin, Gharbia district; s. of Mohamed Ismail Nawar and Fakiha Karam Mostafa Ghali; m. Wafaa Mossallem 1969; three d.; ed Cairo Univ. and St Fernando Acad., Madrid, Spain; Prof. of Graphics, Faculty of Fine Art, Helwan Univ. 1967–; founder and Dean, Faculty of Fine Art, Menia Univ. 1983–88; Head Nat. Centre for Fine Arts, Ministry of Culture 1988–; Head Museums Service, Higher Council for Antiquities 1994–99; Gen. Supervisor Nubia Savings Fund 1996–98; Adviser to People's Ass. 1999–; Nobel Gold Medal 1986; State Order of Arts and Sciences, First Class 1979, Order of Merit (Spain) 1992, Officier, Ordre des Arts et des Sciences. *Address:* 78, el-Shishiny Street, off Al-Mariyoutiyah Canal Street, Al-Hram, Giza (studio); 54 Dimashk Street, Madinat al-Mohandeseen, Flat 16, Giza, Egypt (home). *Telephone:* (2) 7448336. *E-mail:* a-nawar@a-nawar.com. *Website:* www.a-nawar.com.

NAWAWI AYOB, Ahmad, PhD; Malaysian professor of botany and university vice-chancellor; *Professor Emeritus, Institute of Biological Sciences, University of Malaya;* b. 11 Feb. 1937, Perak; m.; two c.; ed Queen's Univ., Belfast; Demonstrator in Botany, Mycology and Plant Pathology, Queen's Univ., Belfast 1963–65; botanist and plant pathologist Ministry of Agric., Malaysia 1966–67; Post-doctoral Research Fellow Wageningen Agricultural Univ., Netherlands 1970, Queen's Univ. Belfast 1971–72; Lecturer in Botany, Univ. of Malaya 1967–74, Assoc. Prof. 1974–78, now Emer., Head Dept of Botany 1974–75, Prof. of Botany 1978, Dean Faculty of Sciences 1976–78, Acting Deputy Vice-Chancellor 1977, Deputy Vice-Chancellor for Finance and Devt 1983–86, Acting Vice-Chancellor 1986, Deputy Vice-Chancellor 1991; Pres. Malaysian Soc. for Microbiology 1986–87; Pres. Malaysian Soc. for Microbiology 1986–87; fmr Pres. Malaysian Soc. Applied Biology; mem. Council Malaysian Agricultural Research and Devt Inst., Malaysian Nat. Science

Council 1981–, Man. Cttee Nat. Scientific Research and Devt Trust Fund 1981–; mem. Council Nat. Inst. of Public Admin.; Fellow Islamic Acad. of Sciences, Malaysian Acad. of Sciences; mem. Acad. of Sciences Malaysia; Hon. DSc (Portsmouth), (Belfast) 1995; Johan Mangku Negara 1982, Datuk Paduka Cura Si Manja Kini 1986, Dato Paduka Cura Simanja Kini (D.P.C.M.). *Publications:* over 60 specialized publs. *Address:* Institute Of Research Management and Consultancy, IPS Building, University Of Malaya, 50603 Kuala Lumpur, Malaysia (office). *Telephone:* (3) 79674370 (office). *Fax:* (3) 79674178 (office). *E-mail:* nawawi@um.edu.my (office). *Website:* www.ippp .um.edu.my (office).

NAYLOR, David, OC, MD, DPhil, FRSC; Canadian university administrator and medical researcher; *President, University of Toronto;* b. 1954, Woodstock, Ont.; m. Ilse Treurnicht; ed Univ. of Toronto, Univ. of Oxford, UK; fmr Sr Scientist, Medical Research Council of Canada (MRC); mem. Faculty Univ. of Toronto 1987–, Dean of Medicine and Vice-Provost, Relations with Health Care Insts 1999–2005, Pres. Univ. of Toronto 2005–; Founding CEO Inst. for Clinical Evaluative Sciences 1991–98; Co-Founder Cardiac Care Network, Ont.; Chair. Nat. Advisory Cttee on SARS and Public Health 2003; fmr Gov. Canadian Insts of Health Research (CIHR); fmr mem. Bd Mount Sinai Hosp., St Michael's Hosp., Univ. Health Network, Sunnybrook and Women's Coll. Health Sciences Centre, Toronto Rehabilitation Inst.; Foreign Assoc., US Inst. of Medicine 2005; Royal Australasian Coll. of Physicians John Dinham Cottrell Medal 1996, Royal Coll. of Physicians and Surgeons of Canada G. Malcolm Brown Award 1996, Medical Research Council of Canada Michael Smith Award 1999, Canadian Cardiovascular Soc. Research Achievement Award 2002, R. D. Defries Award, Canadian Public Health Asscn 2005. *Publications:* more than 300 scholarly works. *Leisure interests:* music, golf. *Address:* Office of the President, University of Toronto, Room 206, 27 King's College Circle, Toronto, ON M5S 1A1, Canada (office). *Telephone:* (416) 987-2121 (office). *Fax:* (416) 971-1360 (office). *E-mail:* president@utoronto.ca (office). *Website:* www.utoronto.ca/president (office).

NAYLOR, Sir Robert, Kt, BSc; British health services executive; *CEO, University College London Hospitals;* b. 1950, Manchester; ed Univ. of Greenwich; began career as graduate trainee, later Hosp. Admin. Nat. Hosp., Queen Square, London; CEO Birmingham Heartlands & Solihull NHS Trust 1985–2000; CEO Univ. Coll. London Hosps (UCLH) 2000–; Sr Assoc. Fellow, Univ. of Warwick Inst. of Governance and Public Man. *Leisure interests:* football (Manchester United), opera, scuba diving. *Address:* UCLH, 250 Euston Road, London, NW1 2PG, England (office). *Website:* www.uclh.nhs.uk (office).

NAZARBAYEV, Nursultan Abishevich, DSc; Kazakhstani politician and head of state; *President;* b. 6 July 1940, Chemolgan, Kaskelen Dist, Almaty Oblast; s. of Abish Nazarbayev and Aizhan Nazarbayeva; m. Sara Alplisovna Kounakayeva 1962; three d.; ed Higher Tech. Course at Karaganda Metallurgical Combine, Russian Acad. of Management and Higher Party School of Cen. Cttee CPSU; mem. CPSU 1962–91; worked for Karaganda Metallurgical Plant 1960–64, 1965–69; Sec. Temirtau City Cttee of Kazakh CP 1969–84; Sec. party Cttee of Karaganda Metallurgical Combine 1973–77; Second, then First Sec. Karaganda Dist Cttee of Kazakh CP 1977–79; Sec. Cen. Cttee of Kazakh CP 1979–84; Chair. Council of Ministers of Kazakh SSR 1984–89; USSR People's Deputy 1989–91; First Sec. Cen. Cttee of Kazakh CP 1989–91, Socialist Party 1991–; Chair. Kazakh Supreme Soviet 1989–90; Exec. Pres. Kazakh SSR 1990–91; Pres. Repub. of Kazakhstan 1991–; Chair. World Kazakh Union 1992–; mem. Int. Eng Acad. 1993, Acad. of Social Sciences of the Russian Fed. 1994, Nat. Acad. of Sciences of the Repub. of Kazakhstan 1995; Hon. Citizen of Temirtau 1991, Duluth, USA 1991, Almaty 1995; Diploma of Freeman of Municipality of Bucharest 1998; Hon. Prof., Al-Farabi Kazakh State Nat. Univ., M.V. Lomonosov Moscow State Univ. 1996; Hon. mem. Belarusian Acad. of Sciences 1996, Nat. Acad. of Applied Sciences of Russia 1997; Order of the Red Banner of Labour, Badge of Honour 1972, Order of Saint Lord-and-Master Prince Daniil of Moscow, First Class 1996, Order of Yaroslav Mudryi (Ukraine) 1997, Order of Big Cross Holder with Ribbon (Italy) 1998, Order of Holy Apostole Andrei Pervosvannyi 1998, Ismoili Samoni Order (Tajikistan) 2000, Pi Order (Vatican) 2001; Dr hc (Kazakh Inst. of Man., Economy and Forecasting) 1995, (Bilkent Univ., Ankara) 1998; Capri Award (Italy) 1992, Rukhaniyat Man of the Year 1993, Gold Medal of Guild of Econ. Devt and Marketing of the City of Nurnberg (FRG) 1993, Award of Crans-Montana Int. Forum 1996, star No. Perseus RA 3h 23v Osd 40* 43 named after him 1997, Medal No. 1 of Al-Farabi Kazakh State Nat. Univ. 1998, Award for Int. Understanding, Indian Fund Unity International 1998, Award For Service to Turkish World 1998, Gold Medal and Diploma for Special Contrib. to Devt of CIS Aviation, Int. Aviation Comm. 1998, Peace Dove Prize, UNESCO Club of Dodecanese Islands (Greece) 1999, Man of the Century Award, Abylai Khan Int. Fund 2000, Grand Star of Respect for Merits (Austria) 2000. *Publications:* Steel Profile of Kazakhstan, With Neither the Right nor the Left, Strategy of Resource Saving and Market Transition, Strategy of Formation and Development of Kazakhstan as a Sovereign State, Market and Social-and-Economic Development, On the Threshold of the XXIst Century, Eurasian Union: Ideas, Practice, Prospects 1994–1997, In the Flood of History, The Epicenter of Peace, and others; numerous scientific articles and articles on econs. *Leisure interests:* tennis, water-skiing, horses, reading history books. *Address:* Office of the President, 010000 Astana, Beibitshilik 11, Kazakhstan (office). *Telephone:* (7172) 32-13-99 (office). *Fax:* (7172) 32-61-72 (office). *Website:* www.akorda.kz (office).

NAZARBAYEVA, Dariga Nursultanova, Dr rer. pol; Kazakhstani politician and media executive; b. 7 May 1963, Temirtau, Kazakh SSR, USSR; d. of Pres. Nursultan Nazarbayev; m. Rakhat Aliyev (divorced 2007); two s. one d.; ed Moscow M.V. Lomonosov State Univ., S.M. Kirov State Univ., Russian

Presidential Acad. of Public Service; Vice-Pres. Khabar Broadcasting Agency 1994–95, Gen. Dir 1995–98, Pres. 1998–2001, Chair. Council of Dirs 2001–03; Founder and Chair. Mutual Help Republican Party (Asar, later Fatherland Republican Political Party, Otan' Respublikalyk Sayasi Partiyasy, following merger) 2003–06, Chair. Light of the Fatherland People's Democratic Party 2006–; Chair. Eurasian Media Forum; Leader, Congress of Journalists of Kazakhstan; Chair., Supervisory Bd of Int. Inst. for Modern Politics, Kazakhstan; mem. Bd Int. TV Acad., New York; Pres. Eurasian Centre for Strategic Studies, Russia; Vice-Pres. Eurasian TV Acad., Russia; Co-Chair. Eurasian TV Forum Organizing Cttee; Assoc. mem. Int. Econ. Acad. Eurasia; Vice-Pres. Children's Charitable Fund Bobek 1992–94; mem. Nat. Comm. of Repub. of Kazakhstan for UNESCO; fmr Pres. Sports Gymnastics Fed. of Repub. of Kazakhstan; jury mem., second season of SuperStar KZ. *Publications:* Democratization of Political Systems in the Commonwealth of Independent States 1997, The Eurasian Commonwealth 2000, From the Union Towards the Commonwealth (ed. and co-author) 2001, Ten Years of the Commonwealth of Independent States: Experience, Problems, Future Prospects (co-author) 2001. *Leisure interest:* amateur opera singer. *Address:* Light of the Fatherland People's Democratic Party ('Nur Otan' Khalyktyk Demokratiyalyk Partiyasy), 050000 Almaty, Abylai khana 79, Kazakhstan (office). *Telephone:* (727) 279-78-00 (office). *Fax:* (727) 279-40-66 (office). *E-mail:* partyotan@nursat.kz (office). *Website:* www.ndp-nurotan.kz (office).

NAZARENKO, Tatyana Georgievna; Russian painter; b. 24 June 1944, Moscow; m.; two s.; ed Moscow Surikov State Fine Arts Inst.; worked Studio of USSR Acad. of Fine Arts 1969–72; mem. USSR (now Russian) Union of Painters 1969; solo exhbns in France, USA, Spain, Russia, Germany and other countries 1987–; Assoc. Russian Acad. of Fine Arts 1998, Full mem. and mem. Bd of Dirs 2001–; Acad. of Arts Silver Medal 1987, Russian State Prize 1993, Moscow Govt Prize 1999, Honored Artist of Russia 2003, Triumph Prize 2009. *Address:* c/o Volga Art Gallery, 125009 Moscow, Bolshoi Gnezdnikovsky per. 10, Russia. *Telephone:* (495) 921-51-88. *E-mail:* tatyana@nazarenko-art.ru. *Website:* www.nazarenko-art.ru.

NAZAREWICZ, Witold (Witek), MSc, PhD, Dr hab., FInstP; American (b. Polish) physicist and academic; *Professor of Physics, University of Tennessee;* b. 26 Dec. 1954, Warsaw, Poland; s. of Ryszard Nazarewicz and Hanna Blonska; m. Krystyna Nazarewicz; one s. one d.; ed Warsaw Univ. of Tech., Inst. for Nuclear Research, Warsaw, Warsaw Univ.; Teaching Asst, Warsaw Univ. of Tech. 1977–81; Asst Prof., Warsaw Univ. 1981–88, Assoc. Prof. 1988–91, Prof. 1994–; Visiting Research Fellow, Lund Univ., Sweden 1982–84, Visiting Prof. 1990; Visiting Research Fellow, Niels Bohr Inst., Copenhagen, Denmark 1984–85; Visiting Prof., Jt Inst. for Heavy Ion Research, Oak Ridge, TN, USA 1985–86, 1991–95, Scientific Dir, Oak Ridge Nat. Lab. Holifield Radioactive Ion Beam Facility 1996–; Visiting Prof., Florida State Univ. 1986, 1991, Cologne Univ., Germany 1987, KTH (Royal Inst. of Tech.), Stockholm, Sweden 1988; Visiting Sr Lecturer, Univ. of Liverpool, UK 1988–89; Visiting Prof., Univ. of Lund, Sweden 1990, Kyoto Univ., Japan 1992, Univ. of Liverpool 1995; Prof. of Physics, Univ. of Tennessee, Knoxville 1995–; Carnegie Centenary Prof., Scotland, UK 2006; mem. Editorial Bd Physical Review C 1994–96, Reports on Progress in Physics 2001–06, Reviews of Modern Physics 2006–, European Physical Journal A 2006–; mem. numerous expert panels; mem. Bd of Physics and Astronomy, Nat. Research Council 1996–99, Nat. Advisory Cttee, Inst. for Nuclear Theory, Seattle 1996–98; Co-Chair., later Chair. RIA Steering Group 2000–04; mem. and Chair. RIA Users Organization Exec. Cttee 2004–05; mem. Bd Mazurian Lakes Confs on Physics, Warsaw 2006, Steering Cttee Japan US Theory Inst. for Physics with Exotic Nuclei 2006–, Jefferson Lab. Program Advisory Cttee 2007–; Chair. Bd Zdzisław Szymanski Prize, Warsaw Univ. 2002–; Scientific Expert, Scientific Advisory Bd for the Finnish Centre of Excellence in Nuclear and Accelerator Based Physics, Univ. of Jyvaskyla 2006–; organizer numerous Int. confs; mem. European Physical Soc. 1992–95, Polish Physical Soc.; Fellow, American Physical Soc. 1994, Inst. of Physics 2004; Carnegie Centenary Prof. (Scotland, UK) 2008; hon. DUniv (Univ. of the West of Scotland) 2009; Individual Scientific Award, Polish Ministry of Educ. 1982, 1987, 1989, Individual Scientific Award, Polish Nuclear Energy Comm. 1983, Individual Scientific Award, Polish Physical Soc. 1986, Lockheed Martin Tech. Achievement Award 1999, Univ. of Tennessee Battelle Tech. Achievement Award 2000, Coll. of Arts and Sciences Sr Research/Creative Achievement Award 2001, Univ. of Tennessee Research and Creative Achievement Award 2002. *Publications:* author of editor of four books and more than 450 research papers on theoretical nuclear physics, nuclear structure, and the many-body problem, listed by ISI among the most highly cited in physics. *Leisure interest:* map collecting. *Address:* Department of Physics and Astronomy, University of Tennessee, 401 Nielsen Physics Building, Knoxville, TN 37996-1200, USA (office). *Telephone:* (865) 574-4580 (office). *Fax:* (865) 974-4375 (office). *E-mail:* witek@utk.edu (office). *Website:* www.phys.utk.edu/faculty_nazarewicz.htm (office).

NAZARIAN, Karen; Armenian diplomatist; *Ambassador to Iran;* b. 29 Nov. 1966, Yerevan; m.; two c.; ed Faculty of Oriental Studies, Yerevan State Univ.; worked in Dept on Mil.-Political Problems, Ministry of Foreign Affairs 1991–92, at Embassy of Armenia, Moscow 1992–94; Chief of Secr., Ministry of Foreign Affairs 1994–96; Amb. to UN, Geneva 1996, Resident Rep. to UN, Geneva –2002; Adviser to Minister of Foreign Affairs 2002–05; Amb. to Iran 2005–; fmr mem. Armenian-American Inter-Governmental Comm. *Address:* Embassy of Armenia, 1 Ostad Shahriar St., Razi Street, Jomhouri Islami Avenue, Tehran 11337, Iran (office). *Telephone:* (21) 66704833 (office). *Fax:* (21) 66700657 (office). *E-mail:* emarteh@yahoo.com (office).

NAZAROV, Talbak Nazarovich, DEconSc; Tajikistani politician and academic; b. 15 March 1938, Danghara, Kulyab District; s. of Khojaev Nazar and

Ismailova Hanifa; m. Tatyana Grigorievna Teodorovich 1959; one s. one d.; ed Leningrad (now St Petersburg) Inst. of Finance and Econs; Asst, then Deputy Dean of Econs Faculty, Tajik State Univ. 1960–62, Head of Dept, Dean 1965–80, Rector 1982–88; Chair Supreme Soviet Tajik SSR 1986–88; Minister of Public Educ. 1988–90; USSR People's Deputy 1989–92; First Deputy Chair. Tajikistan Council of Ministers, Chair. State Planning Cttee 1990–91; Minister of Foreign Affairs 1994–2006, Amb.-at-Large 2006–; mem. Tajikistan Acad. of Sciences 1980–, currently Vice-Pres.; Merited Worker of Science and many other awards and medals. *Publications:* books and articles on Tajikistan's economy and external policies. *Leisure interests:* reading fiction and political literature. *Address:* c/o Ministry of Foreign Affairs, 734051 Dushanbe, pr. Rudaki 42, Tajikistan (office).

NAZDRATENKO, Yevgeny Ivanovich; Russian politician; b. 16 Feb. 1949, Severo-Kurilsk, Sakhalin Region; m.; two s.; ed Far East Inst. of Tech.; served with Pacific Fleet; Head of sector Bor Co.; mechanic, Vice-Pres., Pres. Primorsk Mining Co., Vostok 1980–93; Peoples' Deputy of Russian Fed. 1990–93; Head of Admin. Primorsk Territory 1993–95, Gov. 1995–2001; mem. Council of Fed. of Russia 1996–2001; Chair. State Cttee for Fisheries 2001–03; Deputy Sec. Russian Security Council 2004–; Dr hc (St Petersburg Mining Univ., Seoul Univ.); Order for Personal Courage 1994, Hon. Citizen of Russia 1995. *Address:* Security Council, 103132 Moscow, Ipat'yevski per. 4/10, Russia.

NAZER, Sheikh Hisham Mohi ed-Din; Saudi Arabian politician; b. 1932; ed Univ. of California; legal adviser 1958; assisted in foundation of OPEC 1960; Deputy Minister of Petroleum 1962–68; with Ministry of Planning 1975–, Acting Minister of Planning 1986–91; Minister of Petroleum and Mineral Resources 1986–95; Pres. Cen. Org. for Planning 1968–; mem. Supreme Council for Petroleum and Minerals 1968–; Chair. SAMAREC, Saudi Arabian Oil Co. *Address:* c/o Ministry of Petroleum and Mineral Resources, PO Box 247, Riyadh 11191, Saudi Arabia.

NAZIF, Ahmad Mahmoud Muhammad, BSc, MA, PhD; Egyptian computer engineer and government official; *Prime Minister;* b. 8 July 1952, Alexandria; m.; two s.; ed Cairo Univ., McGill Univ., Canada; Prof. of Computer Eng, Cairo Univ. 1994; Exec. Man. IDSC 1989–95; apptd Minister for Communications and Technology 1999; Prime Minister 2004–; First Order Medal of Science and Art. *Address:* 2 Magles El Shaab Street, Kasr El Aini St., Cairo; Office of the Prime Minister, Sharia Majlis ash-Sha'ab, Cairo, Egypt (office). *Telephone:* (2) 7935000 (office), (2) 7958014 (office). *Fax:* (2) 7958016 (office), (2) 7958048 (office). *E-mail:* questions@cabinet.gov.eg (office). *Website:* www.cabinet.gov.eg (office).

NAZIR-ALI, Rt Rev. Michael James, BA, MLitt, ThD, DHLitt, DD; British/Pakistani ecclesiastic; *Bishop of Rochester;* b. 19 Aug. 1949, Karachi; s. of James Nazir-Ali and Patience Nazir-Ali; m. Valerie Cree 1972; two s.; ed St Paul's High School, Karachi, St Patrick's Coll., Karachi, Univ. of Karachi, Fitzwilliam Coll. Cambridge, Ridley Hall, Cambridge, St Edmund Hall, Oxford, Australian Coll. of Theology with assistance from the Centre for World Religions, Harvard etc.; Tutorial Supervisor in Theology, Univ. of Cambridge 1974–76; Asst Curate, Holy Sepulchre, Cambridge 1964–76; Tutor then Sr Tutor, Karachi Theological Coll. 1976–81; Assoc. Priest Holy Trinity Cathedral, Karachi 1976–79; Priest-in-Charge St Andrew's Akhtar Colony, Karachi 1979–81; Provost Lahore Cathedral 1981–84; Bishop of Raiwind 1984–86; fmr Visiting Lecturer, Selly Oak Colls, Birmingham; Asst to Archbishop of Canterbury; Co-ordinator of Studies for 1988 Lambeth Conf. 1986–89; Gen. Sec. Church Mission Soc. 1989–94; Asst Bishop, Diocese of Southwark 1990–94; Canon Theologian, Leicester Cathedral 1992–94; Bishop of Rochester 1994–; mem. House of Lords 1999–; Chair. Mission Theological Advisory Group 1992–2001, Chair. Governing Council, Trinity Coll. Bristol 1996–; Dir Oxford Centre for Mission Studies, Christian Aid; mem. Design Group for 1998 Lambeth Conf., Anglican Roman Catholic Int. Comm. 1991–, Bd of Mission Gen. Synod, Church of England 1992–94, 1996–, Human Fertilization and Embryology Authority 1998–2003 (Chair. of Ethics and Law Cttee); Fellow, St Edmund Hall, Oxford 1998–; Fellow, Fitzwilliam Coll., Cambridge; Visiting Prof. of Theological and Religious Studies, Univ. of Greenwich 1996–; mem. Archbishop's Council 2001–, House of Bishops' Standing Cttee 2001–, Anglican-Roman Catholic Jt Working Group 2001–, Chair. Working Party on Women in the Episcopate, Chair. House of Bishops' Theological Group, Lecturer Royal Coll. of Defence Studies; Hon. DLitt (Bath), (Greenwich); Hon. DD (Kent) 2004; Radio Pakistan Prize for English Language and Literature 1964, Burney Award (Cambridge) 1973, 1975, Oxford Soc. Award for Grads 1973, Langham Scholarship 1974. *Publications:* Islam, a Christian Perspective 1982, Frontiers in Christian–Muslim Encounter 1985, Martyrs and Magistrates: Toleration and Trial in Islam 1989, The Roots of Islamic Tolerance: Origin and Development 1990, From Everywhere to Everywhere 1991, Mission and Dialogue 1995, The Mystery of Faith 1995, Citizens and Exiles 1998, Shapes of the Church to Come 2001, Understanding My Muslim Neighbour 2002, Conviction and Conflict 2006, The Unique and Universal Christ 2008; numerous articles on Islam, Christianity, mission, inter-faith dialogue, Anglican and ecumenical affairs. *Leisure interests:* cricket, hockey, table tennis, reading and writing poetry. *Address:* House of Lords, Westminster, London, SW1A 0PW (office); Bishopscourt, Rochester, Kent, ME1 1TS, England (home). *Telephone:* (1634) 842721 (home). *Fax:* (1634) 831136 (home). *E-mail:* bishops.secretary@rochester.anglican.org (home).

NAZRUL-ISLAM, Jamal, PhD; Bangladeshi professor of mathematics; *Director, Centre for Mathematics and Physical Sciences, University of Chittagong;* b. 24 Jan. 1939, Jhenidah, Jessore; ed Trinity Coll. Cambridge, UK and Calcutta Univ., India; Postdoctoral Fellow, Dept of Physics and Astronomy, Univ. of Maryland, USA 1963–65; staff mem. Inst. of Theoretical

Astronomy, Univ. of Cambridge 1967–71; Visiting Assoc. in Physics, Calif. Inst. of Tech. 1971–72; Sr Research Assoc., Dept of Astronomy, Univ. of Wash. 1972–73; Lecturer in Applied Math., King's Coll., London 1973–74; Science Research Council Fellow, Univ. Coll. Cardiff 1975–78; Lecturer and Reader, Dept of Math., City Univ., London 1978–84: Prof. Math., Founder and Dir Centre for Math. and Physical Sciences, Univ. of Chittagong; Fellow, Third World Acad. of Sciences, Cambridge Philosophical Soc., Royal Astronomical Soc., Bangladesh Acad. of Sciences, Islamic Acad. of Sciences; mem. Bd. of Trustees Gono Bishwabidyalay University; Gold Medal, Bangladesh Acad. of Sciences for Physical Sciences, Sr Group 1985. *Address:* Department of Mathematics, University of Chittagong, 4331 Chittagong, Bangladesh (office). *Telephone:* (31) 210133 (office). *Fax:* (31) 210141 (office).

NCUBE, Most Rev. Pius Alick, LTh; Zimbabwean ecclesiastic; b. (Mvundla Ncube), 1 Jan. 1947, Mtshabezi, Gwanda; s. of Amos Ncube and Ivy Mkwananzi; ed Chishawasha Major Seminary, Harare, Lateran Univ., Rome, Italy; ordained Priest, Bulawayo 1973, Parish Priest, St Patrick's 1986–90, St Mary's Cathedral 1990–1995; Vicar Gen., Bulawayo Archdiocese 1995–98, Archbishop of Bulawayo 1998–2007 (resgnd); Human Rights Award, Lawyers Cttee for Human Rights, New York 2003. *Radio:* one week per month of morning and evening prayers on nat. radio 1990–98; interviews on human rights issues. *Publications include:* Imfundiso. Yebandla. Elikhatholike (Catholic catechism). *Leisure interests:* reading, writing articles. *Address:* 73 Marigold Road, North Trenance, Bulawayo, Zimbabwe (home). *Telephone:* (9) 204951 (home); (23) 226932 (mobile) (home).

NCUBE, Welshman, MPhil, LLB; Zimbabwean politician, academic and judge; b. 7 July 1961, Gweru; ; m. Thobekile Ncube; five c.; ed Univ. of Zimbabwe; Prof. of Law, Univ. of Zimbabwe 1992–; serves as Advocate of the High Court and Supreme Court of Zimbabwe; Sec.-Gen. Movt for Democratic Change (MDC) 1999–, Co-leader pro-Senate faction of MDC 2006–; mem. of House of Ass. of Zimbabwe for Bulawayo North East 2000–, Chair. Parl. Legal Cttee; charged with high treason over alleged plot to assassinate Pres. Robert Mugabe 2002, found not guilty; mem. Bd of Trustees, Amani Trust; mem. Advisory Bd, ZimRights; mem. Zimbabwe Lawyers for Human Rights; Dr hc (Oslo) 2005. *Publications:* numerous books and articles on family law, women's law, human rights law and constitutional law. *Address:* Movement for Democratic Change, 6th Floor, cnr Angwa Street and Nelson Mandela Avenue, Harare, Zimbabwe (office). *Website:* www.mdczimbabwe.org (office).

NDAYIZEYE, Domitien; Burundian politician and fmr head of state; Sec.-Gen. opposition pro-Hutu party Front pour la démocratie au Burundi (FRODEBU); Vice-Pres. of Burundi responsible for Political and Admin. Affairs 2001–03; Pres. of Burundi 2003–05. *Address:* c/o Office of the President, Bujumbura, Burundi (office).

NDEBELE, Njabulo Simakahle, PhD; South African academic, writer and university administrator; *Vice-Chancellor and Principal, University of Cape Town;* b. 4 July 1948, Johannesburg; m. Kathleen Mpho; one s. two d.; ed Univs of Botswana, Lesotho and Swaziland, Univ. of Cambridge, UK, Univ. of Denver, USA; Head of Dept, Nat. Univ. of Lesotho, Dean of Humanities Faculty 1987, Pro-Vice-Chancellor 1988; Chair. and Head of Dept of African Literature, Wits Univ.; Vice-Rector, Univ. of the Western Cape; Vice-Chancellor and Prin. Univ. of the North, Scholar in Residence, Ford Foundation; Vice-Chancellor and Prin. Univ. of Cape Town 2000–; Chair. S African Broadcasting Policy Project, Ministry of Post, Telecommunications and Broadcasting, S African Univs Vice-Chancellors' Asscn –2000; mem. Exec. Bd AA4, AC4; Dr hc (Natal Univ., Chicago State Univ., Vrije Univ. Amsterdam, Soka Univ. Japan, Wesleyan Univ., Univ. of Cambridge, Univ. Coll. London); Lincoln Univ. President's Award, Nat. Univ. of Lesotho Fiftieth Anniversary Distinguished Service Award, NOMA Award for Publishing in Africa 1984, Sanlam Award for Outstanding Fiction, Pringle Prize for Outstanding Criticism. *Publications:* Fools and Other Stories 1983, Bonolo and the Peach Tree 1991, Rediscovery of the Ordinary 1991, The Prophetess 1992, Sarah, Rings and I 1993, South African Literature and Culture: Rediscovery of the Ordinary 1994, Death of a Son 1996, The Cry of Winnie Mandela (novel) 2004, Telling Tales (contrib. to charity anthology) 2004, Fine Lines from the Box 2007. *Leisure interests:* bird watching, computer simulation games. *Address:* University of Cape Town, Private Bag, Rondebosch 7701, Cape Town (office); Glenara, Burg Road, Rondebosch 7700, Cape Town, South Africa (home). *Telephone:* (21) 6502105 (office); (21) 6502106 (office). *Fax:* (21) 6505100 (office). *E-mail:* vc@uct.ac.za (office). *Website:* www.uct.ac.za (office).

NDEREBA, Catherine; Kenyan athlete; b. 21 July 1972, Nyeri; m. Anthony Maina 1996; one d.; ed Ngorano Secondary School, Nairobi; long distance and marathon runner; rep. Kenya at women's relay race in Seoul, S Korea 1995; won individual bronze and team gold medals at World Half-Marathon Championships 1999; ran world's fastest times at 5,000m (15:09), 12,000m (38:37), 15,000m (48:52) and 10 miles (53:07) 1999; marathon debut in Boston Marathon, finishing sixth 1999; runner-up, New York Marathon 1999, 2003; won both Boston and Chicago Marathons 2000, 2001; gold medal, World Championships Marathon 2003 (Championship Record time of 2 hours, 23 minutes, 55 seconds); silver medal, Olympic Games marathon, Athens 2004, Beijing 2008; set the then women's world marathon record time of 2 hours, 18 minutes, 47 seconds in Chicago Marathon Oct. 2001; ranked No. 1 by Runner's World for three consecutive years; works as telephone operator at a Kenyan prison; Runner's World magazine Road Runner of the Year 1996, 1998, Running Times Road Racer of the Year 1996, 1998, 1999, IAAF Athlete of the Year 2001, Asscn of Int. Marathon and Road Races (AIMS)/ASICS Golden Shoe World Athlete of the Year Award 2001. *Address:* c/o Association of International Marathons and Road Races, PMPR, Windsor House, 15 Kirklee Terrace, Kelvinside, Glasgow, Scotland. *Telephone:* (141) 357-2516. *Fax:* (141) 357-2516.

N'DIAYE, Babacar; Senegalese banker; b. 11 June 1936, Conakry, Guinea; joined African Devt Bank 1965, subsequently Group Dir of Finance, then Vice-Pres. for Finance, Pres. 1985–95, now Hon. Pres.; Chair. African Business Round Table; LLD (Clark Atlanta Univ., Ga) 1992, (Lincoln Univ., Pa) 1993. *Address:* c/o African Development Bank, 01 BP 1387, Abidjan 01, Côte d'Ivoire.

NDIAYE, Souleymane Ndéné, LLM; Senegalese politician; *Prime Minister;* b. 6 Aug. 1958, Kaolack; m.; four c.; Mayor of Guinguinéo 2002–; Minister of Civil Service, Labour, Employment and Professional Orgs March–Aug. 2005; Dir of Cabinet, Office of the Pres. Aug. 2005–07; mem. Nat. Ass. 2007–; Minister of State for the Environment and Protection of Nature June–July 2007, for Maritime Economy July 2007–09; Prime Minister of Senegal 2009–. *Address:* Office of the Prime Minister, Bldg Administratif, ave Léopold Sédar Senghor, BP 4029, Dakar, Senegal (office). *Telephone:* 33-889-6969 (office). *Fax:* 33-823-4479 (office). *Website:* www.gouv.sn (office).

NDIMIRA, Pascal-Firmin; Burundian politician; b. 1956; fmr univ. rector, IBRD official; fmr Minister of Agric.; Prime Minister of Burundi 1996–98; mem. Union pour le progrès national (UPRONA). *Address:* c/o Union pour le progrès national (UPRONA), BP 1810, Bujumbura, Burundi. *Telephone:* 2225028.

NDOLOU, Brig. Gen. Jacques Yvon; Republic of the Congo army officer; Minister-Del. at the Presidency, responsible for Nat. Defence 2002–. *Address:* Office of the Minister-Delegate of the Presidency, responsible for National Defence, Brazzaville, Republic of the Congo (office). *Telephone:* 81-22-31 (office).

NDONG, Jean Eyéghé; Gabonese politician; *Prime Minister and Head of Government;* b. 12 Feb. 1946, Libreville; ed Ecole des Hautes Études en Sciences Sociales, Paris, Université de Paris X Nanterre, France; elected mem. Nat. Ass. 1996; Sec. of State for Finance 1996, later Minister-Del. to Minister of State, Minister of Economy, Finance, Budget and Privatisation; Prime Minister and Head of Govt 2006–; mem. Gabonese Democratic Party. *Address:* Office of the Prime Minister, BP 546, Libreville, Gabon (office). *Telephone:* 77-89-81 (office).

N'DONG, Léon; Gabonese diplomatist; b. 15 Feb. 1935, Libreville; s. of the late Jean-Martin Bikègne and of Marthe Kemeboune; m. Chantal Annette Bekale 1971; four s. one d.; ed School of Law and Econ. Sciences, Rennes, France; Under-Sec.-Gen. of Ministry of Foreign Affairs, later Sec.-Gen.; Teacher, Nat. School of Admin. 1969–72; Amb. to Cen. African Repub. and Sudan 1972–73, to Morocco 1973–74, to UN Office at Geneva 1974–76, to UN 1976–80, to UK 1980–86, to FRG 1986–90 (also accred to Norway, Denmark, Finland and Sweden); Amb. du Gabon, Diplomatic Adviser to Prime Minister 1990–99; High Commr, Office of Prime Minister 1997–; Commdr de l'Etoile Equatoriale, Grand Cordon of Order of the Brilliant Star (China), Commdr, Order of Devotion (Malta), Commdr Nat. Order of Dahomey, Order of Nile (Sudan), Ordre Nat. du Mérite (Gabon), Diplomatic Order of Repub. of Korea, Ordre de la Pléïade (France), Grand Officier Etoile Equatoriale, Grand Officier Ordre du Mérite, Officier Courtoisie française. *Leisure interests:* swimming, walking, music, reading, fishing, gardening. *Address:* B.P. 848, Libreville, Gábon (home). *Telephone:* (241) 263175 (home); (241) 071952.

N'DOUR, Youssou; Senegalese singer and songwriter; b. 1959, Dakar; mem., Sine Dramatic 1972, Orchestre Diamono 1975, The Star Band (house band of Dakar nightclub, the Miami Club) 1976–79; formed band Etoile de Dakar (changed name to Super Etoile 1982) 1979–; has performed with Peter Gabriel, Paul Simon, Bob Dylan, Branford Marsalis; sings in English, French, Fulani, Serer and native Wolof; Goodwill Amb. to UN, UNICEF, Int. Bureau of Work; owner, Jololi Records recording studio, radio station, Thoissane nightclub, Dakar; Best African Artist 1996, African Artist of the Century 1999, MOBO Award for Best African Act 2005. *Recordings include:* albums: A Abijan 1980, Xalis 1980, Tabaski 1981, Thiapathioly 1983, Absa Gueye 1983, Immigrès 1984, Nelson Mandela 1985, Inedits (1984–1985) 1988, The Lion 1989, African Editions Vols 5–14 1990, Africa Deebeub 1990, Jamm La Prix 1990, Kocc Barma 1990, Set 1990, Hey You: The Essential Collection 1988–90, Eyes Open 1992, The Best of Youssou N'Dour 1994, The Guide 1994, Gainde-Voices From The Heart Of Africa (with Yande Codou Sene) 1996, Lii 1996, Immigrès/Bitim Rew 1997, St Louis 1997, Best of the 80s 1998, Special Fin D'annee Plus Djamil 1999, Rewmi 1999, Joko: From Village to Town 2000, Le Grand Bal, Bercy 2000, Le Grand Bal 1 & 2 2001, Batay 2001, Birth of a Star 2001, Nothing's In Vain (Coono Du Réér) 2002, Et Ses Amis 2002, Sant Allah (Homage to God) 2003, Egypt (BBC Radio 3 World Music Award for Album of the Year 2005) 2004, Hey You! The Essential Collection 2005, Rokku Mi Rokka 2007. *Film roles include:* Picc Mi 1992, Amazing Grace 2006. *Leisure interest:* football. *Address:* Youssou N'Dour Head Office, 8 Route des Almadies Parcelle, BP 1310, Dakar, Senegal (office). *Telephone:* 865-1039 (office). *Fax:* 865-1068 (office). *E-mail:* yncontact@yahoo.fr (office). *Website:* www.youssou .com (office).

N'DOURO, Issifou Kogui, PhD; Benin government official; *Minister of National Defence;* b. Bembereke; ed Université Louis Pasteur, Strasbourg, France; consultant to UNSO Tree Planting Project, FAO 1979; fmr Finance Dir Organisation Internationale de la Francophonie; fmr Dir Office of Minister of Rural Devt; Minister of Nat. Defence 2006–. *Address:* Ministry of National Defence, BP 2493, Cotonou, Benin (office). *Telephone:* 21-30-08-90 (office). *Fax:* 21-30-18-21 (office). *E-mail:* sgm@defense.gouv.bj (office). *Website:* www.defense.gouv.bj (office).

NDULU, Benno J., PhD; Tanzanian economist and central banker; *Governor, Bank of Tanzania;* ed Northwestern Univ., USA; began career as econs teacher; Research Dir, later Exec. Dir African Econ. Research Consortium,

Nairobi; African Country Dir, World Bank, Dar es Salaam; Deputy Gov., Bank of Tanzania (Benki Kuu Ya Tanzania) –2008, Gov. 2008–; fmr Chair. Tanzania Revenue Authority; Dr hc (Int. Inst. of Social Studies, The Hague). *Publications include:* Agenda for Africa's Economic Renewal 1996 (jt author), New Directions in Development Economics 1996, Regional Integration and Trade Liberalization in Africa 1999 (jt author), Challenges of African Growth 2007 (jt author); numerous articles in The Journal of Development Studies. *Address:* Bank of Tanzania, 10 Mirambo Street, POB 2939, Dar es Salaam, Tanzania (office). *Telephone:* (22) 2110946 (office). *Fax:* (22) 2113325 (office). *E-mail:* info@hq.bot-tz.org (office). *Website:* www.bot-tz.org (office).

NDUNGANE, Most Rev. Njongonkulu Winston Hugh, MTh, DD, AFTS; South African ecclesiastic; *Anglican Archbishop of Cape Town;* b. 2 April 1941, Kokstad; s. of Foster Ndungane and Tingaza Ndungane; m. 1st Nosipo Ngcelwane 1972 (died 1986); 2nd Nomahlubi Vokwana 1987; one step-s. one step-d.; ed Lovedale High School, Univ. of Cape Town, Fed. Theological Seminary and King's Coll. London, UK; Rector St Nicholas Church, Matroosfontein, Cape Town 1980–81; Prov. Liaison Officer, Johannesburg 1982–84; Prin., St Bede's Theological Coll. Umtata 1985–86; Exec. Officer, Church of the Prov. of Southern Africa (Anglican) 1987–91; Bishop of Kimberley and Kuruman 1991–96; Archbishop of Cape Town 1996–; mem. Bd SABC, Johannesburg 1992–96; Chair. Hearings into Poverty in S Africa; Patron Jubilee 2000 1998–; Hon. DD (Rhodes) 1997, (Protestant Episcopal Theological Seminary, Virginia) 2000; Hon. DHumLitt (Worcester State Coll., Mass) 2000; Hon. DScS (Natal) 2001. *Publications:* The Commuter Population for Claremont, Cape 1973, Human Rights and the Christian Doctrine of Man 1979, A World with a Human Face: A Voice from Africa 2003. *Leisure interests:* music, walking. *Address:* Bishopscourt, 20 Bishopscourt Drive, Claremont 7708, South Africa. *Telephone:* (21) 761-2531. *Fax:* (21) 761-4193. *E-mail:* archbish@bishopscourt-cpsa.org.za (home).

NDUWIMANA, Martin, MD; Burundi politician and physician; b. Mugamba, Prov. of Bururi; currently Prof. of Paediatrics, Univ. of Burundi; fmr Dir Nat. Centre for Public Health; fmr MP for Bururi Prov.; First Vice-Pres. of Burundi in charge of Political and Admin. Affairs 2005–07 (resgnd); mem. Union pour le progresse nationale (Uprona). *Address:* University of Burundi, Faculty of Medicine, BP 1020, Bujumbura, Burundi (office). *Telephone:* (257) 232074 (office). *Fax:* (257) 232267 (office). *E-mail:* m.nduwim@medecine.ub.edu.bi (office). *Website:* www.ub.edu.bi (office).

NEAL, Sir Eric James, Kt, AC, CVO, CEng, FIGasE, FIEAust, FAIM, FAICD; Australian state governor, business executive and chartered engineer; *Chancellor, The Flinders University of South Australia;* b. 3 June 1924, London, UK; s. of James Neal and May Neal (née Johnson); m. Thelma Joan Bowden 1950; two s.; ed South Australian School of Mines; Dir Boral Ltd 1972–92, Chief Exec. 1973–82, Man. Dir 1982–87; Dir Oil Co. of Australia NL 1982–87, Chair. 1984–87; Dir Westpac Banking Corpn 1985–92, Chair. 1989–92; Dir Atlas Copco Australia Ltd 1987–96, Chair. 1990–96; Dir Metal Manufactures Ltd 1987–96, Chair. 1990–96; Dir Wormald Int. Ltd 1978–85, John Fairfax Ltd 1987–88, Cola-Cola Amatil Ltd 1987–96, BHP 1988–94; Gov. S Australia 1996–2001; Chancellor The Flinders Univ. of S Australia 2002–; mem. Gen. Motors Australia Advisory Council 1987–94; Chief Commr Council of City of Sydney 1987–88; Int. Trustee, The Duke of Edinburgh's Award Int. Foundation 1987–97; Chair. of Trustees, Sir David Martin Foundation 1991–94; Nat. Pres. Australian Inst. of Co. Dirs 1990–93; KStJ; Hon. DEng (Sydney) 1989; Hon. DUniv (S Australia) 2001, (Flinders) 2001; numerous awards and medals. *Leisure interests:* reading, walking, motor boating, sailing, naval and eng history, opera. *Address:* Office of the Chancellor, The Flinders University of South Australia, GPO Box 2100, Adelaide 5001 (office); 82/52 Brougham Place, North Adelaide 5006, South Australia (home). *Telephone:* (8) 8201-2721 (office); (8) 8361-7014 (home). *Fax:* (8) 8201-3988 (office); (8) 8267-1715 (home). *E-mail:* chancellor@flinders.edu.au (office). *Website:* www.flinders.edu.au (office).

NEAL, Patricia; American actress; b. 20 Jan. 1926, Packard, Ky; d. of William Burdette Neal and Eura Mildred Petrey; m. Roald Dahl 1953 (divorced 1983, died 1990); one s. three d. (and one d. deceased); ed Northwestern Univ., Ill.; illustrious film and stage career; numerous TV appearances; public lectures in America and abroad; Hon. degrees from Simmons Coll., Rockford Coll., Univ. of Mass, Niagara Univ., Northwestern Univ.; Antoinette Perry Award (Tony) 1946. *Stage appearances include:* The Voice of the Turtle 1945, Another Part of the Forest (NY Critic's Award, Tony Award 1946) 1946, The Children's Hour 1953, A Roomful of Roses 1954, Suddenly Last Summer 1958, The Miracle Worker 1959. *Films:* John Loves Mary 1949, The Hasty Heart 1949, The Fountainhead 1949, The Breaking Point 1950, Three Secrets 1950, Raton Pass 1951, The Day the Earth Stood Still 1951, Diplomatic Courier 1952, Something for the Birds 1953, A Face in the Crowd 1957, Breakfast at Tiffany's 1961, Hud (Acad. Award, British Acad. Award 1963) 1963, The Third Secret 1964, In Harms Way (British Acad. Award 1965) 1965, The Subject was Roses (Acad. Award nomination 1968) 1968, The Road Builder 1970, The Night Digger 1971, The Boy 1972, Happy Mother's Day, Love George 1973, Baxter! 1973, B Must Die 1975, Widow's Nest 1977, The Passage 1979, Ghost Story 1981, An Unremarkable Life 1989, Cookie's Fortune 1999, For the Love of May 2000. *Television includes:* The Homecoming: A Christmas Story (Golden Globe Award, Best TV Actress) 1971, Things in their Season 1974, Eric 1975, The American Woman: Portraits of Courage (narrator) 1976, Tail Gunner Joe 1977, Including Me 1977, A Love Affair: The Eleanor and Lou Gehrig Story 1978, The Bastard 1978, All Quiet on the Western Front 1979, The Way They Were 1981, Little House on the Prairie 1981, Glitter 1984, Shattered Vows 1984, Love Leads the Way 1984, Murder She Wrote 1990, Caroline? 1990, A Mother's Right: The Elizabeth Morgan Story 1992, Heidi 1993, Days and Nights of Beebee Fenstermaker

(BBC), The Country Girl (BBC). *Publication:* As I Am (autobiog.) 1988. *Leisure interests:* needlepoint, gardening, cooking. *Address:* 45 East End Avenue, New York, NY 10028, USA. *Telephone:* (212) 772-1268.

NEAME, Ronald, CBE; British film director; b. 23 April 1911, London; s. of Elwin Neame and Ivy Close; m. 1st Beryl Heanly 1933; one s.; m. 2nd Donna Friedberg 1993; messenger and tea boy, British Int. Film Studios 1927, became Dir of Photography 1932; with Sir David Lean and Anthony Havelock-Allan, formed Cineguild and produced Great Expectations 1946, Oliver Twist 1947 and The Passionate Friends 1948; film dir 1950–, The Poseidon Adventure; teacher of film direction, UCLA 1992–96; Founder Mem. and fmr Chair., British Film Acad. (later Soc. of Film and TV, later still BAFTA); Lifetime Gov. BAFTA; Founder Mem. Asscn of Cine Technicians, British Soc. of Cinematographers; BAFTA Lifetime Achievement Award. *Films photographed include:* Happy 1933, Give Her a Ring 1934, Girls Will Be Boys 1934, Once In a Million 1935, Honours Easy 1935, Invitation to the Waltz 1935, Joy Ride 1935, Music Hath Charms 1935, Drake of England 1935, The Crimes of Stephen Hawke 1936, The Improper Duchess 1936, King of the Castle 1936, Radio Lover 1936, A Star Fell From Heaven 1936, Against the Tide 1937, Brief Ecstasy 1937, Cafe Colette 1937, Catch As Catch Can 1937, Feather Your Nest 1937, Keep Fit 1937, Member of the Jury 1937, Strange Experiment 1937, I See Ice 1938, It's in the Air 1938, Murder in the Family 1938, Penny Paradise 1938, Second Thoughts 1938, Who Goes Next? 1938, The Gaunt Stranger 1938, The Ware Case 1938, Let's Be Famous 1939, Trouble Brewing 1939, The Four Just Men, Saloon Bar 1940, Let George Do It 1940, Return to Yesterday 1940, Young Man's Fancy 1940, Come on George! 1939, Cheer Boys Cheer 1939, Major Barbara 1941, One of Our Aircraft is Missing 1942, In Which We Serve 1942, This Happy Breed 1944, Blithe Spirit 1945. *Films directed include:* Take My Life 1947, The Golden Salamander 1950, The Card 1950, The Million Pound Note 1953, The Man Who Never Was 1956, The Seventh Sin 1957, Windom's Way 1957, The Horse's Mouth 1958, Tunes of Glory 1960, Escape from Zahrain 1962, I Could Go On Singing 1963, The Chalk Garden 1964, Mister Moses 1965, A Man Could Get Killed 1966, Gambit 1966, Prudence and the Pill 1968, The Prime of Miss Jean Brodie 1969, Hello-Goodbye (uncredited) 1970, Scrooge 1970, The Poseidon Adventure 1972, The Odessa File 1974, Meteor 1979, Hopscotch 1980, First Monday in October 1981, Foreign Body 1986, The Magic Balloon 1990. *Publication:* Auto Bio – Straight From the Horse's Mouth 2004. *Leisure interests:* painting, photography, stereo and hi-fi equipment. *Address:* 2317 Kimridge Road, Beverly Hills, CA 90210, USA. *Fax:* (310) 271-3044. *E-mail:* rnfilm@aol.com (home).

NÉAOUTIYNE, Paul; New Caledonian politician; b. 1952, St Michel Village; ed Univ. of Lyon; teacher of econs at secondary coll. in Nouméa until 1980; jailed for participation in pro-independence demonstration 1980; reinstated as teacher 1983; Aide to Jean-Marie Tjibaou (Pres. Northern Regional Council) 1985; Leader, Party of Kanak Liberation (Palika); Mayor of Poindimie; mem. Northern Provincial Govt; currently Leader Parti de Libération Kanak (PALIKA) (merged with Kanak Socialist Nat. Liberation Front 1984). *Address:* Kanak Socialist National Liberation Front, Nouméa, New Caledonia. *Telephone:* 272599.

NEARY, J. Peter, DPhil, FBA; Irish economist and academic; *Professor of Economics and Professorial Fellow, Merton College, University of Oxford;* b. 11 Feb. 1950, Drogheda; s. of Peter Neary and Anne Loughran; m. 1st Frances Ruane 1972 (divorced); two s.; m. 2nd Mairéad Hanrahan 1997; two d.; ed Clongowes Wood Coll., Co. Kildare, Univ. Coll. Dublin, Univ. of Oxford; Jr Lecturer, Trinity Coll. Dublin 1972–74, Lecturer 1978–80; Heyworth Research Fellow, Nuffield Coll. Oxford 1976–78; Prof. of Political Economy, Univ. Coll. Dublin 1980–2006; Prof. of Econs, Univ. of Oxford and Professorial Fellow, Merton Coll. 2006–; Visiting Prof., Princeton Univ. 1980, Univ. of California, Berkeley 1982, Queen's Univ., Ont. 1986–88, Univ. of Ulster at Jordanstown 1992–93; Research Assoc. Centre for Econ. Performance, LSE 1993–2003; Dir de Recherche, Ecole Polytechnique, Paris 1999–2000; mem. Council Royal Econ. Soc. 1984–89, European Econ. Asscn 1985–92, Econometric Soc. 1994–99; Co-Ed. Journal of International Economics 1980–83; Assoc. Ed. Economic Journal 1981–85, Econometrica 1984–87, Review of Economic Studies 1984–93, Economica 1996–2000; Ed. European Economic Review 1986–90; Pres. Irish Econ. Asscn 1990–92, Int. Trade and Finance Soc. 1999–2000, European Econ. Asscn 2002, Econs Section, BAAS 2005; Fellow, Centre for Econ. Policy Research, London 1983–, Econometric Soc. 1987–, European Econ. Asscn 2004–; mem. Academia Europaea 1989–, Royal Irish Acad. 1997–; Royal Irish Acad. Gold Medal in the Social Sciences 2006. *Publications:* Measuring the Restrictiveness of International Trade Policy (with J. E. Anderson) 2005, three edited books and more than 100 publs on econs, especially int. econs. *Leisure interests:* family, travel, reading, music. *Address:* Department of Economics, University of Oxford, Manor Road Building, Manor Road, Oxford, OX1 3UQ, England (office). *Telephone:* (1865) 271085 (office). *Fax:* (1865) 271094 (office). *E-mail:* peter.neary@economics.ox.ac.uk (office). *Website:* www.economics.ox.ac.uk/members/peter.neary/neary.htm (office).

NEARY, Martin Gerard James, LVO, MA, FRCO; British conductor and organist; b. 28 March 1940; s. of the late Leonard W. Neary and of Jeanne M. Thébault; m. Penelope J. Warren 1967; one s. two d.; ed City of London School and Gonville & Caius Coll. Cambridge; Asst Organist, St Margaret's Westminster 1963–65, Organist and Master of Music 1965–71; Prof. of Organ, Trinity Coll. London 1963–72; Organist and Master of Music, Winchester Cathedral 1972–87; Organist and Master of Choristers, Westminster Abbey 1988–98; has led Westminster Abbey Choir on tours to France, Germany, Switzerland, Hungary, USA, Russia, Ukraine; Founder and Conductor Martin Neary Singers 1972–; Chair. Church Services Cttee, Musicians Benevolent Fund 1993–, Herbert Howells Soc. 1993–; Conductor Waynflete Singers 1972–87; Pres. Cathedral Organists Asscn 1985–88; Pres. Royal Coll. of Organists 1988–90, 1996–98; Guest Conductor Australian Youth Choir 1999–; Visiting Artistic Dir Paulist Boy Choristers of Calif. 1999–2000; many organ recitals and broadcasts in UK, Europe, USA, Canada, the Far East and Australia; many choral premières; guest conductor English Chamber Orchestra, London Symphony Orchestra; numerous recordings; Hon. RAM; Hon. F.T.C.L.; Hon. Fellow Royal School of Church Music. *Publications:* editions of early organ music, contribs to organ journals. *Leisure interest:* watching cricket. *Address:* 71 Clancarty Road, Fulham, London, SW6 3BB, England. *Telephone:* (20) 7736-5268. *Fax:* (20) 7610-6995. *E-mail:* mgjneary@btinternet.com.

NEČAS, Petr, DrScNat; Czech politician; *Deputy Prime Minister and Minister for Labour and Social Affairs;* b. 19 Nov. 1964, Uherské Hradiště; m. Radka Nečas; two s. two d.; ed Univ. Brno; research engineer, Tesla Rožnov 1988–92; mem. Civic Democratic Party 1991–, Jt Vice-Chair. 1999–2004, First Deputy Chair. 2004–; mem. Parl. for Zlin 1992–; mem. Parl. Cttee for Foreign Affairs 1992–96; Deputy Minister of Defence 1995–96; Chair. Parl. Cttee for Defence and Security 1996–2002; Vice-Chair. Parl. Cttee for European Affairs 2002–06; Deputy Prime Minister 2007–, Minister for Labour and Social Affairs 2007–. *Leisure interest:* history. *Address:* Ministry of Labour and Social Affairs, Na poříčním právu 1, 128 01 Prague 2, Czech Republic (office). *Telephone:* 221921111 (office). *Fax:* 221922664 (office). *E-mail:* posta@mpsv.cz (office). *Website:* www.mpsv.cz (office).

NECHAEV, Andrey Alekseevich, PhD; Russian politician, economist, banker and journalist; *President, Russian Financial Corporation;* b. 2 Feb. 1953, Moscow; s. of Aleksey Nechaev and Marseliesa Nechaev; m. 1st Elena Belyanova 1975; one d.; m. 2nd Margarita Kitova 1986; m. 3rd Svetlana Sergienko 1997; ed Moscow State Univ.; Researcher, USSR Acad. of Sciences 1979–90, Deputy Dir Inst. of Econ. Policy, Acad. of Nat. Economy 1990–91; First Deputy Minister of Economy and Finance of Russia 1991–92; Minister of Economy 1992–93; Pres. Russian Financial Corpn 1993–, Moscow Finance Club 1994–; mem. Political Consultative Council under Pres. of Russia 1996–2000, Scientific Council under Security Council of Russia 1997–2002; mem. Expert Council under Chair. Financial Control Chamber of Russian Fed., Nat. Econ. Council; Prof., Russian Acad. of Econs; mem. Acad. of Nat. Sciences, Int. Acad. of Informatization, Acad. of Security and Defence, Advisory Bd RBC-TV; mem. Russian Union of Journalists, Council 'Union of Right Forces' (political party); Order of State Statistical Comm. 2002, Order of Ministry of Internal Affairs 2003, Leader of Russian Economy 2003, 2005, Public Order Glory of Russia 2003; State Medal 1997, 2003, Public Recognition Prize 2001, Honour Staff of Ministry of Economy and Trade 2003, Best Pen of Russia Prize. *Radio:* author and presenter of Financial Club programme, econ. analyst on Russian radio. *Television:* author and presenter of Money Matter programme. *Publications:* 250 publs on econs and econ. policy. *Leisure interests:* journalism, publicity, politics, history, theatre, travelling, tennis, gardening. *Address:* Russian Financial Corporation, Georgievsky per. 1, 125009 Moscow, Russia (office). *Telephone:* (495) 692-74-82 (office). *Fax:* (495) 692-35-62 (office). *E-mail:* rfc@rusfincorp.ru (office); nechaev@rusfincorp.ru (home). *Website:* www.rusfincorp.ru (office).

NEDERKOORN, Erik Jan; Dutch business executive; b. 22 Aug. 1943, Haarlem; m.; two s. one d.; Vice-Pres. Fokker (aircraft mfrs) 1988–91, Chair. Bd of Man. and CEO 1991–94; mem. Bd Deutsche Telekom 1996–. *Address:* c/o Deutsche Telekom, PO Box 2000, 53105 Bonn, Germany.

NEDERLANDER, James Morton; American impresario; *Chairman, Nederlander Producing Company Of America, Inc.;* b. 31 March 1922, Detroit, Mich.; s. of David T. Nederlander and Sarah L. Applebaum; m. Charlene Saunders 1969; one s. two d.; ed Pontiac Sr High School and Detroit Inst. of Tech.; former usher, box-office asst and press agent for father's Schubert-Lafayette Theatre; served in USAF during World War II; Man. Lyceum Theatre, Minneapolis for eight years; returned to Detroit to assist in devt of Nederlander theatre chain in Detroit and Chicago in 1950s; chain expanded to Broadway with purchase of Palace Theatre 1965; now Chair. Bd Nederlander Org. (now Nederlander Producing Co. Of America, Inc. 1966–, owners and operators of largest chain of theatres in world including 11 Broadway theatres and Adelphi and Aldwych theatres, London and producers and backers of maj. Broadway musicals such as Annie, La Cage aux Folles and Will Roger Follies; est. Nederlander TV and Film Production (creating films, mini-series, etc. for TV) in 1980s. *Address:* Nederlander Producing Company Of America, Inc., 1450 Broadway, Floor 6, New York, NY 10018, USA. *Telephone:* (212) 840-5577. *Website:* www.nederlander.org.

NEDVED, Pavel; Czech professional footballer; b. 30 Aug. 1972, Cheb; s. of Vaclav Nedved and Ana Nedved; midfielder; teams played for include Dukla Prague (19 league appearances, 3 goals) 1991–92, Sparta Prague (98 league appearances, 23 goals) 1992–96, Lazio, Italy (138 appearances, 33 goals) 1996–2001, Juventus, Italy (91 appearances, 19 goals) 2001–; 83 caps and 17 goals for Czech Repub. (debut 1994, retd from int. football after European Championships 2004); won Czechoslovakian Championship with Sparta Prague 1993, won further Czech Repub. titles with Sparta 1994, 1995, won Czech Repub. Cup with Sparta 1996, won Italian Cups with Lazio 1998, 2000, won Super Cup and European Cup Winner's Cup with Lazio 1999, won Serie A with Lazio 2000 and with Juventus 2002, 2003; five-times winner of Czech Player of the Year, Czech Athlete of the Year 2003, World Soccer Magazine Player of the Year 2003, European Footballer of the Year 2003. *Address:* Juventus Football Club SpA, C.so Galileo Ferraris 32, 10128 Torino, Italy (office). *Telephone:* (011) 7380081 (office). *Website:* www.juventus.com (office).

NEEDLEMAN, Jacob, PhD; American academic; *Professor of Philosophy, San Francisco State University;* b. 6 Oct. 1934, Philadelphia; s. of Benjamin

Needleman and Ida Needleman; m. 1st Carla Satzman 1959 (divorced 1989); one s. one d.; m. 2nd Gail Anderson 1990; ed Research Assoc., Rockefeller Inst., New York 1960–61, Harvard Coll., Yale Univ.; Assoc. Prof. of Philosophy, San Francisco State Univ. 1962–66, Prof. 1967–; Dir Center for the Study of New Religions, Grad. Theological Union, Berkeley, Calif. 1977–83; Vice-Pres. Audio Literature Co. 1987–; Rockefeller Humanities Fellow, Fulbright Scholar. *Publications:* The New Religions 1970, A Sense of the Cosmos 1975, Lost Christianity 1980, The Heart of Philosophy 1982, The Way of the Physician 1985, Sorcerers 1986, Money and the Meaning of Life 1991, A Little Book on Love 1996, Time and the Soul 1998, The American Soul 2002, The Wisdom of Love 2005, Why Can't We Be Good 2007. *Address:* San Francisco State University, Department of Philosophy, 1600 Holloway Avenue, San Francisco, CA 94132, USA (office). *Telephone:* (415) 338-1596 (office). *E-mail:* jneedle@sfsu.edu (office). *Website:* www.jacobneedleman.com (office).

NEEMAN, Yaakov, LLB, LLM, JSD; Israeli politician and lawyer; *Founding Partner, Herzog, Fox & Neeman;* b. 1939, Tel-Aviv; m.; six c.; ed Hebrew Univ. of Jerusalem, New York Univ. Law School; mem. Israeli Bar Asscn 1966–; Founding and Sr Pnr Herzog Fox & Neeman (law firm) 1972– (with two-year interruption); Visiting Prof. of Law, Univ. of Calif. at LA, USA 1976, Tel-Aviv Univ. 1977–79, New York Univ. 1989–90, Hebrew Univ. of Jerusalem 1990, 1994; Dir-Gen. Ministry of Finance 1979–81; Chair. Cttee of Inquiry into Inter-Relation between Tax Laws and Foreign Currency Restrictions 1977–78, Public Cttee on Allocation of Distributions by Ministry of Interior 1991–92, Nat. Cttee Committee for the Identification of Fallen Soldiers in Times of Emergency 1991, Cttee for the Conversion Law 1997-98, Public Cttee Committee on Privatisation Issues of El Al, Public Cttee on Educational Centres 2000, Public Cttee apptd by the Cabinet for the Drafting of the Constitution 2002-2003, Exec. Cttee, Bar Ilan Univ. 2000–; mem. Investigation Cttee on Temple Mount Affair 1991; mem. Bd of Govs Bank of Israel 1992–96, 2003–; mem. Cen. Cttee of World Bank, 1979–81, mem. Cttee for Atomic Energy 1979-1981, Public Committee appointed by the Speaker of the Parl. to determine salaries and other payments to cabinet members, Knesset members, judges, and other govt officials 2000–02; mem. Bd of Dirs El Al Ltd 1979–81, Israel Aircraft Industries Ltd 1979–81; Minister of Justice 1996, of Finance 1997. *Publications:* seven books and over 30 articles on taxation, corpn and securities law. *Address:* Herzog, Fox & Neeman, Asia House, 4 Weizmann Street, 64239 Tel-Aviv, Israel (office). *Telephone:* 3-6922032 (office). *Fax:* 3-6966464 (office). *E-mail:* neeman@hfn.co.il (office). *Website:* www.hfn.co.il (office).

NEESON, Liam, OBE; British actor; b. 7 June 1952, Ballymena, Co. Antrim, Northern Ireland; m. Natasha Richardson 1994 (died 2009); two s.; ed St Mary's Teachers' Coll., London, Queen's Univ., Belfast; worked as forklift operator, then as architect's asst; acting debut with Lyric Players' Theatre, Belfast, in The Risen 1976. *Theatre includes:* Of Mice and Men (Abbey Theatre Co., Dublin), The Informer (Dublin Theatre Festival), Translations (Nat. Theatre, London), The Plough and the Stars (Royal Exchange, Manchester), The Judas Kiss. *Films include:* Excalibur 1981, Krull 1983, The Bounty 1984, The Innocent 1985, Lamb 1986, The Mission 1986, Duet for One 1986, A Prayer for the Dying 1987, Suspect 1987, Satisfaction 1988, High Spirits 1988, The Dead Pool 1988, The Good Mother 1988, Next of Kin 1989, Darkman 1990, The Big Man 1990, Under Suspicion 1991, Husbands and Wives 1992, Leap of Faith 1993, Ethan Frome 1993, Ruby Cairo 1993, Schindler's List 1993, Nell 1994, Rob Roy 1995, Before and After 1996, Michael Collins (Best Actor Evening Standard Award 1997) 1996, Les Misérables 1998, The Haunting 1999, Star Wars: Episode 1 – The Phantom Menace 1999, Gun Shy 2000, Reflections of Evil (voice, uncredited) 2002, K-19: The Widowmaker 2002, Gangs of New York 2002, Love Actually 2003, Kinsey (Best Actor, Los Angeles Film Critics' Asscn) 2004, Kingdom of Heaven 2005, Batman Begins 2005, The Proposition 2005, Breakfast on Pluto 2005, The Chronicles of Narnia: The Lion, the Witch and the Wardrobe (voice) 2005, Seraphim Falls 2006, Taken 2008, The Other Man 2008, The Chronicles of Narnia: Prince Caspian (voice) 2008, Gake no ue no Ponyo (aka Ponyo on the Cliff) (voice: English version) 2008, Fallout 3 (video game) 2008, Five Minutes of Heaven 2009. *Television includes:* An Audience with Mel Brooks 1983, A Woman of Substance 1983, Ellis Island (mini-series) 1984, Arthur the King 1985, If Tomorrow Comes (mini-series) 1986, Hold the Dream 1986, Sweet As You Are 1987, Sworn to Silence 1987, The American Film Institute Salute to Steven Spielberg 1995, Out of Ireland (voice) 1995, Riverdance: The New Show (video) 1996, Kiss Me Goodnight, The Great War and the Shaping of the 20th Century (mini-series) (voice) 1996, Comic Relief VIII 1998, Empires: The Greeks – Crucible of Civilization (narrator) 2000, The Endurance: Shackleton's Legendary Antarctic Expedition (voice) 2000, Inside the Space Station (voice) 2000, The Man Who Came to Dinner 2000, The Greeks (mini-series) (voice) 2001, Revenge of the Whale 2001, Nobel Peace Prize Concert (host) 2001, Uncovering the Real Gangs of New York 2002, The Maze (voice) 2002, Inside the Playboy Mansion (uncredited) 2002, Martin Luther (voice) 2002, Evolution (mini-series) (narrator) 2002, Liberty's Kids: Est. 1776 (series) (voice) 2002, Happy Birthday Oscar Wilde 2004, Patrick (voice) 2004. *Address:* c/o Ed Limato, ICM, 8942 Wilshire Boulevard, Beverly Hills, CA 90211-1934, USA (office). *Telephone:* (310) 550-4000 (office). *Website:* www.icmtalent.com (office).

NEEWOOR, Anund Priyay, BA; Mauritian diplomatist and international organization official; *Secretary for Foreign Affairs;* b. 26 June 1940; m. Chandranee Neewoor 1971; two s. one d.; ed Delhi Univ., Makerere Univ., Uganda; teacher, Prin. Northern Coll. (secondary school), Mauritius 1964–67; joined Ministry of External Affairs, Tourism and Emigration (in charge of UN affairs and West Asia affairs) 1970; Admin. Asst, Civil Service 1972; Second Sec., High Comm., London 1973–75; First Sec., High Comm., New Delhi 1975–81; Minister-Counsellor, Embassy, Washington, DC 1982; Amb. to Pakistan 1983, to USA 1993–96; High. Commr to India 1983–93; Amb. in

Ministry of External Affairs in charge of Multilateral Econ. Affairs 1996; Sec. for Foreign Affairs 1996–99, 2005–; Amb. and Perm. Rep. to UN, New York 1999–2001; Commdr of the Order of the Star and Key of the Indian Ocean — C.S.K. 2003. *Leisure interests:* reading, sports. *Address:* c/o Ministry of Foreign Affairs, International Trade and Co-operation, New Government Centre, Level 5, Port Louis; 17 Avenue des Dodos, Sodnac, Quatre Bornes, Mauritius (home). *Telephone:* (230) 2112692 (office). *Fax:* (230) 2088087 (office). *E-mail:* apneewoor@hotmail.com (office). *Website:* foreign.gov.mu (office).

NEFEDOV, Oleg Matveyevich, DSc; Russian chemist; *Head of Laboratory, N. D. Zelinksky Institute of Organic Chemistry, Russian Academy of Sciences;* b. 25 Nov. 1931, Dmitrov, Moscow region; s. of Matvey Kondrat'evich Nefedov and Mariya Adolfovna Teodorovich; m. Galina Gimelfarb 1954; one s. one d.; ed D. I. Mendeleev Inst. of Chem. and Tech.; worked as jr then sr researcher; Head, Lab. N. D. Zelinsky Inst. of Organic Chem., USSR (now Russian) Acad. of Sciences 1968–; Corresp. mem. USSR (now Russian) Acad. of Sciences (RAS) 1979–87, mem. 1987–, Academic Sec. Div. of Gen. and Applied Chem. 1988–91, Vice-Pres. RAS 1988–2001, Rector Higher Chemical Coll. 1990–, Counsellor, RAS 2001–; Ed.-in-Chief Mendeleev Communications 1990–, Russian Chemical Bulletin 1991–, Russian Chemical Reviews 1995–; Chair. Nat. Cttee of Russian Chemists 1996–; mem. IUPAC Bureau and Exec. Cttee 1999–; Pres. Mendeleev Congresses on Gen. and Applied Chem., Tashkent 1989, Minsk 1993, St Petersburg 1998, Kazan 2003; USSR People's Deputy 1989–91; USSR State Prize 1983, 1990, ND Zelinsky Prize 1987, Prize of USSR and Hungarian Acads 1988, N. Semyonov Prize 1991, A. Karpinsky Prize 1993, D. I. Mendeleev Gold Medal 1998, Russian Fed. State Prize in Science and Tech. 2002. *Publications:* The Structure of Cyclopropane Derivatives 1986, Chemistry of Carbenes and Small-sized Cyclic Compounds (ed.) 1989, Carbenes Chemistry 1990; more than 700 articles and 201 patents. *Leisure interests:* sport, gathering mushrooms. *Address:* N.D. Zelinsky Institute of Organic Chemistry, GSP-1, Leninsky prospekt 47, Moscow, Russia (office). *Telephone:* (495) 938-18-73 (office). *Fax:* (495) 135-63-90 (office). *E-mail:* nefedov@ras.ru (office).

NEGISHI, Takashi, PhD; Japanese economist and academic; *Emeritus Professor, Tokyo University;* b. 2 April 1933, Tokyo; s. of Setsuko Negishi and Suteta Negishi; m. Aiko Mori 1964; one d.; ed Univ. of Tokyo; Research Asst, then Research Assoc., Stanford Univ., Calif. 1958–60; Research Asst, Univ. of Tokyo 1963–65, Assoc. Prof. 1965–76, Prof. 1976–94, Prof. Emer. 1994–, also Dean, Faculty of Econs 1990–92; Prof., Aoyama Gakuin Univ. 1994–2002, Toyo Eiwa Univ. 2002–06; Fellow Econometric Soc. 1966–, Vice-Pres. 1992–93, Pres. 1994; Pres. Japan Asscn of Econs and Econometrics 1985; Pres. The Soc. for the History of Econ. Thought, Japan 1997–99; mem. Exec. Cttee Int. Econ. Asscn 1989–92, Science Council of Japan 1985–88, Japan Acad. 1998–; Foreign Hon. mem. American Econ. Asscn 1989; Distinguished Fellow, History of Econs Soc. 2005; Japan Acad. Prize 1993. *Television:* Introduction to History of Economic Thought, Univ. of the Air, Japan 2001. *Publications:* General Equilibrium Theory and International Trade 1972, Microeconomic Foundations of Keynesian Macro Economics 1979, Economic Theories of a Non-Walrasian Tradition 1985, History of Economic Theory 1989, The Collected Essays of Takashi Negishi 1994, 2000. *Address:* 1-3-1-2003, Motoazabu, Minato-ku, Tokyo 106-0046, Japan. *Telephone:* 3440-0630. *E-mail:* tnegishi@bk9.so-net.ne.jp.

NEGMATULLAEV, Sabit, DTechSc; Tajikistani physicist; b. 16 Sept. 1937, Ura-Tube; ed Tajik Polytech. Inst.; mem. CPSU 1966–91; jr researcher, Tajik Inst. of Seismic Resistance, Construction and Seismology of Seismology, Tajik Acad. of Sciences, Scientific Sec. 1964–65, Vice-Dir 1965–69, Dir 1969, now Hon. Dir; mem. Tajik Acad. of Sciences 1987–, Pres. 1988–95; Chair. Scientific-Publishing Council of Acad. of Sciences; mem. Cen. Cttee CPSU 1990–91. *Address:* c/o Academy of Sciences of Tajikistan, Rudaki Prospect 33, 734025 Dushanbe, Tajikistan. *Telephone:* (3772) 27-91-61. *E-mail:* pmp_international@yahoo.com.

NEGRI, Barjas; Brazilian politician; *Mayor of Piracicaba;* b. 8 Dec. 1950, Santo Amaro, São Paulo; s. of Affonso Negri Neto and Hirce Rodrigues Negri; m. Sandra Regina Bonsi; one s. two d.; ed Methodist Univ. of Piracicaba; Prof. of Econs, Univ. of Piracicaba 1974–95; researcher and lecturer UNIVCAMP Univ. 1986–; Sec. of Educ., São Paulo State Parl. 1979–82, Sec. of Planning 1993–94; Sec. Dept of Educ., Fed. Govt 1995–96; Sec. Dept of Health 1997–2001, Minister for Health 2002; Mayor of Piracicaba 2005–. *Address:* Prédio da Prefeitura Municipal, Rua Amadeu Amaral, 255, 13380 Piracicaba São Paulo, Brazil (office). *Website:* www.piracicaba.sp.gov.br (office).

NEGRITOIU, Misu, MS, PhD; Romanian politician, economist and banker; *General Manager, ING Bank Romania;* b. 25 May 1950, Dăbuleni, Dolj Co.; s. of Marin Negritoiu and Floarea Negritoiu; m. Paulina Urzica 1977; one s. one d.; ed Bucharest Acad. of Econ. Studies, Law School, Bucharest Univ., HDS Hertfordshire Univ.; foreign trade economist and then foreign trade co. dir 1973–90; Minister-Counsellor, Embassy, Washington; Pres. Romanian Devt Agency 1990–92; Deputy Prime Minister, Chair. Council for Strategy and Econ. Reform Co-ordination 1993; Chief Econ. Adviser to Pres. of Romania 1994–96; mem. Parl. 1996–; Exec. Dir Wholesale Banking, ING Bank Romania 1997–2006, Gen. Man. and Pres. Country Platform 2006–; Prof. Acad. of Econ. Studies, School of Political Studies and Public Admin., Bucharest; Chair. Bd Dirs Grad. School of Man., MBA Canadian Programme; Pres. Forum for European Integration; mem. Romanian Econ. Soc. (SOREC), Romanian Soc. for Club of Rome, Romanian Asscn for Energy Policy (APER), American Asscn for Arbitration, Centre for European Policy Studies, Econ. Policy Forum, Faculty for Int. Econs and Business, Business Advisory Council – South-East European Co-operation Initiative/Stability Pact; Banker of the Year, Bucharest Business Week magazine 2004, Banker of the Year, Piata

Financiara magazine 2006. *Publications:* Jumping Ahead – Economic Development and FDI 1996, International Finance (textbook) 1994, Management in International Trade 1997; numerous studies and articles on int. and domestic econ. issues, presentations to int. and domestic conferences and seminaries. *Leisure interest:* golf. *Address:* ING Building, 11–13 Kiseleff Boulevard, Bucharest 1 (office); 16 Dionisie Fotino Street, Apt 3, Bucharest 1, Romania (home). *Telephone:* (21) 2091103 (office). *Fax:* (21) 2229385 (office). *E-mail:* misu.negritoiu@ingromania.ro (office). *Website:* www.ingromania.ro (office).

NEGROPONTE, John Dimitri, BA; American diplomatist; *Deputy Secretary of State;* b. 21 July 1939, London, England; s. of Dimitri J. Negroponte and Catherine C. Negroponte; m. Diana Mary Villiers 1976; two s. three d.; ed Phillips Exeter Acad., NH, Yale Univ., New Haven, Conn.; entered Foreign Service 1960, Amb. to Honduras 1981–85; Asst Sec. of State for Oceans and Int. Environmental and Scientific Affairs 1985–87; Deputy Asst to Pres. for Nat. Security Affairs 1987–89; Amb. to Mexico 1989–93, to the Philippines 1993–95; Special Co-ordinator for post-1999 US Presence in Panama 1996–97; Exec. Vice-Pres. Global Markets McGraw-Hill 1997–2001; Perm. Rep. to UN 2001–04; Amb. to Iraq 2004–05; Dir of Nat. Intelligence 2005–07; Deputy Sec. of State 2007–; Chair. French-American Foundation 1998–; mem. Council on Foreign Relations, American Acad. of Diplomacy. *Leisure interests:* swimming, skiing, reading, history. *Address:* Office of the Deputy Secretary, Department of State, 2201 C Street, NW, Washington, DC 20520 (office); 4936 Lowell Street, NW, Washington, DC 20016, USA (home). *Telephone:* (202) 647-4000 (office). *Fax:* (202) 647-6738 (office). *Website:* www.state.gov (office).

NEHER, Erwin; German research scientist and academic; b. 20 March 1944, Landsberg; s. of Franz Xaver Neher and Elisabeth Neher; m. Dr Eva-Maria Neher 1978; three s. two d.; ed Tech. Univ. Munich, Univ. of Wisconsin-Madison, USA; Research Assoc., Max-Planck-Institut für Psychiatrie, Munich 1970–72, Max-Planck-Institut für biophysikalische Chemie, Göttingen 1972–75, 1976–83, Research Dir 1983–; Research Assoc., Yale Univ., New Haven, Conn., USA 1975–76; Fairchild Scholar, California Inst. of Tech. 1988–89; shared Nobel Prize for Medicine 1991; several nat. and int. scientific awards; Bundesverdienstkreuz mit Stern und Schulterband 1998. *Publications:* Elektronische Messtechnik in der Physiologie 1974, Single Channel Recording (ed.) 1983. *Address:* Max-Planck-Institut für biophysikelische Chemie, Am Fassberg 11, 37077 Göttingen (office); Domäne 11, 37120 Bovenden, Germany (home). *Telephone:* (551) 2011630 (office); (5594) 93135 (home). *Fax:* (551) 2011688 (office). *E-mail:* eneher@gwdg.de (office). *Website:* www.mpibpc.gwdg.de (office).

NEI, Masatoshi, BS, MS, PhD; American (b. Japanese) biologist and academic; *Evan Pugh Professor of Biology and Director, Institute of Molecular Evolutionary Genetics, Pennsylvania State University;* b. 2 Jan. 1931, Miyazaki; m. Nobuko Nei; one s. one d.; ed Miyazaki and Kyoto Univs, Univ. of California, Davis and North Carolina State Univ., USA; Asst Prof., Kyoto Univ. 1958–62; Geneticist, Nat. Inst. of Radiological Sciences, Chiba 1962–65, Head, Population Genetics Lab. 1965–69; Assoc. Prof. of Biology, Brown Univ., Providence, RI 1969–71, Prof. of Biology 1971–72; Prof. of Population Genetics, Center for Demographic and Population Genetics, Univ. of Texas at Houston 1972–90, Acting Dir 1978–80; Distinguished Prof. of Biology, Pennsylvania State Univ. 1990–94, Dir Inst. of Molecular Evolutionary Genetics 1990–, Evan Pugh Prof. of Biology 1994–; Visiting Prof. of Biology, Tokyo Inst. of Tech. 2001; Ed. Molecular Biology and Evolution 1983–93; mem. Editorial Bd, Proceedings of the National Academy of Sciences, USA 2003–; mem. Bd of Overseers, Harvard Univ. 1988–94; mem. Advisory Bd Gene: Evolutionary Genomics 2004–; mem. NAS (USA) 2003– (mem. Nat. Research Council Cttee 1994–96), American Genetic Asscn (Pres. 1999), Soc. for Molecular Biology and Evolution (Pres. 1994); Hon. Mem. Genetics Soc. of Japan 1989, Japan Soc. of Human Genetics 1996, Japan Soc. for Histocompatibility and Immunogenetics 2000, Japan Soc. of Animal Genetics and Breeding 2001; Dr hc (Miyazaki Univ.) 2002; Japan Soc. of Human Genetics Award 1977, Kihara Prize, Genetics Soc. of Japan 1990, P.R. Krishnaiah Memorial Lecture, Pennsylvania State Univ. 1999, Masatoshi Nei Annual Lecture, est. for the Soc. for Molecular Biology and Evolution 2000, Certificate of Award 'Highly Cited Researchers', Inst. for Scientific Information 2000, Wilhelmine E. Key Invitational Lecture, Annual Meeting of American Genetic Asscn 2001, Int. Prize for Biology, Japan Soc. for the Promotion of Sciences 2002, Barbara Bowman Award, Texas Geneticist Soc. 2003, Thomas Hunt Morgan Medal, Genetics Soc. of America 2006, Masatoshi Nei Legacy Symposium held at the Molecular Biology and Evolution Soc. meeting, Tempe, Ariz. 2006. *Publications:* more than 260 articles in scientific journals. *Address:* Institute of Molecular Evolutionary Genetics, Pennsylvania State University, Department of Biology, 328 Mueller Laboratory, University Park, PA 16802, USA (office). *Telephone:* (814) 863-7334 (office). *Fax:* (814) 863-7336 (office). *E-mail:* nxm2@psu.edu (office). *Website:* www.bio.psu.edu/people/faculty/nei/lab (office).

NEIL, Andrew Ferguson, MA, FRSA; British publisher, broadcaster and editor; *Publisher, Press Holdings Media Group;* b. 21 May 1949, Scotland; s. of James Neil and Mary Ferguson; ed Paisley Grammar School, Univ. of Glasgow; with Conservative Party Research Dept 1971–73; with The Economist 1973–83, Ulster Political then Industrial Corresp. 1973–79, American Corresp. 1979–82, UK Ed. 1982–83; Ed. The Sunday Times 1983–94; Exec. Ed. Fox TV News, USA 1994; Exec. Chair. Sky TV 1988–90; Publr The Scotsman, Scotland on Sunday, Edinburgh Evening News 1996–2006; Publr, The Business 1999–2007; regular anchorman and TV commentator UK and USA; anchorman, The Daily Politics (BBC 2) and This Week (BBC 1), Straight Talk with Andrew Neil (BBC News Channel), Contrib. Ed. Vanity Fair, New York 1994–; Chief Exec., The Spectator magazine, Chair. 2008–, also Spectator Business; Chief Exec., Apollo magazine 2004–; Chair. World Media Rights (WMR) 2005–, ITP Magazines (Dubai) 2005–, Peters Fraser & Dunlop (talent agency) 2008–; Lord Rector Univ. of St Andrews 1999–2002; Hon. DLit (Napier Univ.) 1998; Hon. DUniv (Paisley) 2001; Hon. LLD (St Andrews) 2002. *Publications:* The Cable Revolution 1982, Britain's Free Press: Does It Have One? 1989, Full Disclosure 1996, British Excellence 1999, 2000, 2001. *Leisure interests:* dining out in New York, London, Dubai and Côte d'Azur. *Address:* Glenburn Enterprises, Flat 3, 53 Onslow Gardens, London, SW7 3QY, England (office); c/o 22 Old Queen Street, London, SW1H 9HP, England (office). *Telephone:* (20) 7244-9968 (office); (20) 7961-0002 (office). *E-mail:* afneil@aol.com (office); afneil@aol.com (office).

NEILAND, Brendan Robert, MA, RA; British artist and professor of painting; b. 23 Oct. 1941, Lichfield; s. of Arthur Neiland and Joan Whiley; m. Hilary Salter 1970; two d.; ed St Philip's Grammar School, Birmingham, St Augustine's Seminary, Ireland, Birmingham School of Art and Royal Coll. of Art; painter and printmaker; gallery artist, Angela Flowers Gallery 1970–78, Fischer Fine Art 1978–92, Redfern Gallery 1992–; one-man shows and group shows throughout Europe, Middle East, America and Australia; Lecturer in Fine Art, Univ. of Brighton 1983–96, Prof. of Painting 1996–98; Keeper of the Royal Acad. 1998–2004; Visiting Prof. of Fine Art, Univ. of Loughborough 1999; Daler Rowney Award, Royal Acad. Summer Exhbn 1989. *Publication:* Upon Reflection 1997. *Leisure interests:* cricket, golf, fine wines. *Address:* c/o Redfern Gallery, 20 Cork Street, London, W1S 3HL (office); 2 Granard Road, London, SW12 8UL, England (home); Crepe, La Grévé sur Mignon, 17170 Courcon, France. *Telephone:* (20) 8673-4597 (home); (5) 46-01-62-97 (France). *Website:* www.redfern-gallery.com (office).

NEILD, Robert Ralph; British economist, academic and writer; *Professor Emeritus of Economics, University of Cambridge;* b. 10 Sept. 1924, Peterborough; s. of Ralph Neild and Josephine Neild; m. 1st Nora Clemens Sayre (divorced 1961); m. 2nd Elizabeth W. Griffiths 1962 (divorced 1986); one s. four d.; m. 3rd Virginia Meagher 2004; ed Charterhouse and Trinity Coll. Cambridge; RAF 1943–44, Operational Research, RAF, 1944–45; Secr., UN Econ. Comm. for Europe, Geneva 1947–51; Econ. Section, Cabinet Office (later Treasury) 1951–56; Lecturer in Econs, Fellow and Steward of Trinity Coll. Cambridge 1956–58; Nat. Inst. of Econ. and Social Research 1958–64; Econ. Adviser to Treasury 1964–67; mem. Fulton Cttee on the Civil Service 1966–68; Dir Stockholm Int. Peace Research Inst. 1967–71, mem. Governing Bd 1972–82; Prof. of Econs, Cambridge Univ. 1971–84, Prof. Emer. 1984–; mem. Governing Body Queen Elizabeth Coll. Oxford 1978–87; Fellow, Trinity Coll. 1971–. *Publications:* Pricing and Employment in the Trade Cycle 1964, The Measurement and Reform of Budgetary Policy (with T. S. Ward) 1978, How to Make up your Mind about the Bomb 1981, An Essay on Strategy 1990, The Foundations of Defensive Defence (ed. with A. Boserup) 1990, The English, the French and the Oyster 1995, Public Corruption: The Dark Side of Social Evolution 2002. *Leisure interests:* painting, oysters. *Address:* Trinity College, Cambridge, CB2 1TQ, England (office). *Telephone:* (1223) 338400 (office); (1223) 338444 (home). *E-mail:* RRN20@cam.ac.uk (office).

NEILL, Rt Hon. Sir Brian (Thomas) Neill, Kt, PC, MA; British judge and arbitrator; b. 2 Aug. 1923; s. of Sir Thomas Neill and Lady (Annie Strachan) Neill (née Bishop); m. Sally Margaret Backus 1956; three s.; ed Highgate School, Corpus Christi Coll., Oxford, Notre Dame Law School, London; served with Rifle Brigade 1942–46; called to Bar, Inner Temple 1949, Bencher 1976; in practice at jr Bar specialising in media law and in drafting banking and other documents for financial institutions 1949–68; QC 1968; a Recorder of the Crown Court 1972–78; a Judge of the High Court, Queen's Bench Div. 1978–84; a Lord Justice of Appeal 1985–96 (retd), sitting occasionally as retd Lord Justice in Court of Appeal and Judicial Cttee of Privy Council 1997–98; Justice of Court of Appeal, Gibraltar 1997–, Pres. 1998–; fmr Pres. Soc. for Computers and Law; first Chair. Information Tech. and the Courts Cttee (ITAC); mem. Departmental Cttee to examine operation of Section 2 of Official Secrets Act 1971; Chair. Advisory Cttee on Rhodesia Travel Restrictions 1973–78; mem. Court of Assistants 1972– (Master 1980–81), Lord Chancellor's Dept's Civil Justice IT Strategy Devt Group, City Disputes Panel, London Court of Int. Arbitration; mem. Worshipful Co. of Turners; Certified Mediator in Alternative Dispute Resolution 2000; Hon. Fellow, Corpus Christi Coll., Oxford 1986–. *Publication:* Defamation (with Colin Duncan) 1978. *Address:* 20 Essex Street, London, WC2, England (office); ADR Chambers UK & Europe, Equity House, Blackbrook Park Avenue, Taunton, TA1 2PX, Somerset. *E-mail:* mail@adrchambers.co.uk. *Website:* www.adrchambers.co.uk.

NEILL, Sam, OBE; New Zealand (b. British) actor; b. 14 Sept. 1947, Omagh, Co. Tyrone, Northern Ireland; m. Noriko Watanabe; one d.; one s. by Lisa Harrow; ed Univ. of Canterbury; toured for one year with Players Drama Quintet; appeared with Amamus Theatre in roles including Macbeth and Pentheus in The Bacchae; joined NZ Nat. Film Unit playing leading part in three films 1974–78; moved to Australia 1978, to England 1980. *Films:* Sleeping Dogs 1977, The Journalist, My Brilliant Career, Just Out of Reach, Attack Force Z, The Final Conflict (Omen III), Possession, Enigma, Le Sang des Autres, Robbery Under Arms, Plenty, For Love Alone, The Good Wife, A Cry in the Dark, Dead Calm, The French Revolution, The Hunt for Red October, Until the End of the World, Hostage, Memoirs of an Invisible Man, Death in Brunswick, Jurassic Park, The Piano, Sirens, Country Life, Restoration, Victory, In the Month of Madness, Event Horizon, The Horse Whisperer, My Mother Frank, Molokai: The Story of Father Damien, Bicentennial Man, The Dish 2000, Monticello, The Zookeeper 2001, Jurassic Park III 2001, Dirty Deeds 2002, Perfect Strangers 2002, Yes 2004, Wimbledon 2004, Little Fish 2005, Irresistible 2006, Angel 2006, Dean Spanley 2008. *Television appearances include:* From a Far Country, Ivanhoe, The Country Girls, Reilly: Ace of Spies, Kane and Abel (mini-series), Submerged (film) 2001, Framed (film) 2002, Dr Zhivago (mini-series) 2002,

Stiff 2004, Jessica (mini-series) 2004, To the Ends of the Earth (mini-series) 2005, Mary Bryant (mini-series) 2005, The Triangle (mini-series) 2005, Merlin's Apprentice (mini-series) 2006. *Address:* c/o ICM, 8942 Wilshire Boulevard, Beverly Hills, CA 90211, USA. *Website:* www.samneill.com (office).

NEILL OF BLADEN, Baron (Life Peer), cr. 1997, of Briantspuddle in the County of Dorset; **Francis Patrick Neill,** Kt, QC; British lawyer; b. 8 Aug. 1926; s. of the late Sir Thomas Neill and of Annie Strachan Neill (née Bishop); m. Caroline Susan Debenham 1954; three s. two d. (and one s. deceased); ed Highgate School and Magdalen Coll. Oxford; served with Rifle Brigade 1944–47; GSO III (Training), British Troops Egypt 1947; called to the Bar, Gray's Inn 1951; Recorder of the Crown Court 1975–78; Judge of the Court of Appeal of Jersey and Guernsey 1977–94; Fellow of All Souls Coll., Oxford 1950–77, Sub-Warden 1972–74, Warden 1977–95; Vice-Chancellor Oxford Univ. 1985–89; Chair., Justice–All Souls Cttee for Review of Admin. Law 1978–87, Press Council 1978–83, Council for Securities Industry 1978–85; mem. DTI Cttee of Inquiry into Regulatory Arrangements at Lloyds 1986–87; Bencher, Gray's Inn 1971, Vice-Treasurer 1989, Treasurer 1990; mem. Bar Council 1967–71, Vice-Chair. 1973–74, Chair. 1974–75; Chair. Senate of the Inns of Court and the Bar 1974–75; Chair. Cttee on Standards in Public Life 1997–2001; Dir Times Newspapers Holdings Ltd 1988–97; Hon. Fellow Magdalen Coll. Oxford 1988; Hon. Prof. of Legal Ethics, Birmingham Univ. 1983–84; mem. Hon. Soc. of Gray's Inn, Gen. Council of the Bar, American Law Inst., British Inst. of Int. and Comparative Law, Int. Law Assn; Hon. DCL (Oxford) 1987; Hon. LLD (Hull) 1978, (Buckingham) 1994. *Publication:* Administrative Justice: Some Necessary Reforms 1988. *Leisure interests:* music, forestry. *Address:* Serle Court, 6 New Square, Lincoln's Inn, London, WC2A 3QS (office); House of Lords, London, SW1A 0PW (office); 1 Hare Court, Temple, London, EC4Y 7BE, England. *Telephone:* (20) 7242-6105 (office). *Fax:* (20) 7405-4004 (office). *E-mail:* pneill@serlecourt.co.uk (office). *Website:* www .serlecourt.co.uk (office).

NEILSON, Kerr; Australian investment fund manager; *Managing Director, Platinum Asset Management Ltd;* b. South Africa; m.Judith Neilson; two c.; early career as stockbroker in London; with Banker's Trust, South Africa, moved to Australia 1984 to work for Banker's Trust Asset Man. Div.; Founder and Man. Dir Platinum International Fund 1994–. *Address:* Platinum Asset Management Ltd, Level 8, 7 Macquarie Place, Sydney, NSW 2000, Australia (office). *Telephone:* (2) 9254-5590 (office). *Website:* www.platinum.com.au (office).

NEIMAN, LeRoy; American artist; b. 8 June 1921, St Paul, Minn.; s. of Charles Runquist and Lydia Runquist (née Serline); m. Janet Byrne 1957; ed Art Inst., Chicago, Univ. of Illinois and DePaul Univ.; Instructor, Art Inst., Chicago 1950–60, Saugatuck (Mich.) Summer School of Painting 1957–58, 1963, School of Arts and Crafts, Winston-Salem, NC 1963; Instructor in painting Atlanta Youth Council for Poverty Program 1968–69; contrib. to features Playboy magazine 1956–; graphics printmaker 1971–; artist Olympic Games, Munich, ABC TV 1971, official artist Olympic Games, Montréal, ABC TV 1976, US Olympics 1980, 1984; computer artist Superbowl, New Orleans CBS TV 1978; official artist for Goodwill Games, Moscow, CNN TV 1986, for Ryder Cup 2008, World Equestrian Games, Kentucky 2010, Winter Olympic Games, Vancouver 2010; first official artist Kentucky Derby, Louisville 1997; rep. in perm. collections Minneapolis Inst. of Arts, State Museum, Springfield, Joslyn Museum, Omaha, Wadham Coll. Oxford, Nat. Art Museum Sport, New York, Museo de Bellas Artes, Caracas, Hermitage Museum, St Petersburg, The Armand Hammer Collection, Los Angeles, The Art Inst. of Chicago, Whitney Museum, New York; work commissioned for Baseball Hall of Fame, Coca-Cola, Gen. Mills, Gen. Motors, Kentucky Derby, Los Angeles Dodgers 100th Anniversary, Nat. Football League, Newport Jazz Festival, Rocky II, III, IV and V films; executed murals at Merchant Nat. Bank, Hammond, Ind., Continental Hotel, Chicago, Swedish Lloyd ship SS Patricia, Stockholm, Sportsmans Park, Chicago; donor and mem. advisory cttee, LeRoy Neiman Center for Print Studies, School of the Arts, Columbia Univ. 1995, LeRoy Neiman Center for Study of American Soc. and Culture, UCLA; mem. advisory Cttee New York Comm. for Cultural Affairs 1995; numerous hon. doctorates including Franklin Pierce Coll. 1976, St Francis Coll. 1998, St Bonaventure Univ. 1999, Art Inst. of Chicago 2006; numerous prizes including Gold Medal, Salon d'Art Moderne, Paris 1961, Award of Merit, Outstanding Sports Artist, AAU 1976, Gold Plate Award, American Acad. of Achievement 1977, Olympic Artist of Century Award 1979, Gold Medal Award, St John's Univ. 1985, Hofstra Univ. 1998, Ellis Island Medal of Honor 2004, Lifetime Achievement Award, Univ. of Southern California 2008. *Publications include:* Art and Lifestyle 1974, Illustrations for new edn of Moby Dick 1975, Horses 1979, Posters 1980, Carnaval 1981, Winners 1983, Monte Carlo Chase 1988, Big Time Golf 1992, An American in Paris 1994, LeRoy Neiman on Safari 1997, The Prints of LeRoy Neiman 1991–2000, Casey at the Bat 2001, LeRoy Neiman: Five Decades 2003, LeRoy Neiman Sketchbook 1964, Liston vs Clay 1965, Ali vs Liston 2004, Femlin 2007. *Address:* Hammer Galleries, 33 West 57th Street, New York, NY 10019; Knoedler Publishing, 19 East 70th Street, New York, NY 10021; LeRoy Neiman Inc., 1 West 67th Street, New York, NY 10023, USA. *Telephone:* (212) 644-4400 (Hammer Galleries); (212) 794-0571 (Knoedler Publishing).

NEISS, Hubert; Austrian international finance official; *Chairman, Deutsche Bank Asia;* b. 1935; ed Hochschule für Welthandel and Univ. of Kansas, USA; Economist, European Dept IMF 1967; Chief, S Pacific Div. 1973; Resident Rep. of IMF in Indonesia; Deputy Dir Asian Dept 1980–91; Dir Asian Regional Dept IMF 1991–2000; Chair. Deutsche Bank Asia 2001.

NEIZVESTNY, Ernst Iosifovich; Russian artist and sculptor; b. 9 April 1925, Sverdlovsk; ed V. I. Surikov State Inst. of Arts (M. G. Maniser's studio); Soviet Army 1942–45; sculptor at studios of USSR Agricultural Exhbn (later Econ. Achievements of USSR Exhbn) 1953–54; mem. Artists' Union of USSR 1955–57; granted permission to emigrate to Geneva 1976; moved to New York 1977; Soviet citizenship restored 1990; mem. Royal Acad. of Fine Arts, Sweden, New York Acad. of Sciences 1986, European Acad. of Arts, Sciences and Humanities, Paris, Swedish Acad. of Sciences, Latvian Acad. of Sciences 1997, Int. Soc. for Human Rights; Guest Prof., Columbia Univ., New York Univ., Harvard Univ., Yale Univ., Univ. of Calif., Berkeley; fmr American Asscn for the Advancement of Slavic Studies and Humanist in Residence, Univ. of Ore.; Order of Red Star for heroism on the Second Ukrainian front 1945, Russian State Award for Merit 1995, Order of Honour 2000; Dr hc (Moscow State Univ. for Humanic Studies) 1996; Russian Govt Award for Achievement in the Arts 1996, Lifetime Achievement Award, Nat. Children's Leukemia Foundation 1997, Russian Medal of Honor for Artistic Achievements 2000. *Television:* Monumental Statues 1998, Cold War Postscript, CNN 1999. *Main works:* Kremlin Builder, First Wings, The Youth, Mother, series: War – is. . .; Robots and Semi-robots, Great Mistakes, Nikita Krushchev Memorial, Lotus Blossom, Aswan Dam, Egypt 1968, Monument to the Golden Child, Odessa, Ukraine 1995, Monument to Victims of Stalinism, Magadan, Russia 1990–96, Bust of Boris Yeltsin 1996, Monument to the Kalmykia Deportation 1996, The Great Centaur, Palace of Nations, Geneva 1997; illustrations to works of Dante, Beckett and Dostoyevsky. *Publications:* Space, Time and Synthesis in Art 1990, Artist's Fate 1992. *Leisure interests:* building sculpture garden on Shelter Island, New York. *Address:* Ernst Neizvestny Studio, 81 Grand Street, New York, NY 10013, USA. *Telephone:* (212) 226-2677 (office). *Fax:* (212) 226-2603. *E-mail:* enstudio@yahoo.com (office). *Website:* www.enstudio.com (office).

NEJAD-HOSSEINIAN, Seyed Mohammad Hadi, MS; Iranian diplomatist and politician; *Deputy Oil Minister;* b. 2 Feb. 1947, Karbala; s. of Hossein Nejad Hosseinian and Razie Haj Tarkhani; m. Fatemeh Tadbir; two s. two d.; ed Tehran Univ., George Washington Univ., Washington, DC; Deputy, Plan and Budget Org. 1980–81; Minister for Road and Transportation 1981–85; Deputy Minister of Oil 1985–89, 1994–97; Minister for Heavy Industry 1989–94; apptd Amb. and Perm. Rep. to UN 1998; currently Deputy Oil Minister, Ministry of Oil. *Address:* Ministry of Oil, Hafez St, Taleghani Avenue, Tehran, Iran (office). *Telephone:* (21) 6152738 (office). *Fax:* (21) 6152823 (office). *E-mail:* webmaster@nioc.org (office). *Website:* www.nioc.org (office).

NEKIPELOV, Alexander Dmitriyevich, DrEcon; Russian economist and academic; *Director, Moscow School of Economics, Lomonosov Moscow State University;* b. 16 Nov. 1951, Moscow; m.; one d.; ed Moscow State Univ.; jr researcher, sr researcher, Head of Sector, Deputy Dir, Inst. of. Int. Econ. and Political Studies, Russian Acad. of Sciences 1973–98, Dir 1998–; Dir Moscow School of Econs, Lomonosov Moscow State Univ. 2004–; mem. Russian Acad. of Sciences 1997, currently Vice-Pres.; also currently Co-Chair. Bd of Trustees Nat. Investment Council; Medal of Order for Service to Motherland. *Publications:* numerous scientific publs including monograph Essays on Economics of Postcommunism 1996. *Leisure interest:* chess. *Address:* Moscow School of Economics, 1, Building 44, Leninskie Gory, M.V. Lomonosov MSU, 119992 Moscow, Russia (office). *Telephone:* (495) 939-45-00 (office). *Website:* www.mse -msu.ru (office).

NEKROŠIUS, Eimuntas; Lithuanian theatre director and actor; b. 21 Nov. 1952, Pažobris; s. of Petras Nekrošius and Elena Nekrošienė; m. Nadezhda Gultyaeva 1976; two s.; ed State Inst. of Theatre Art in Moscow; Theatre Dir Kaunas Drama Theatre 1978–79; Theatre Dir Youth Theatre Lithuanian SSR (now Lithuania), Vilnius 1979–91, Dir LIFE Int. Theatre Festival 1993–97; f. Meno Fortas Theatre Studio; Order of Grand Duke Gediminas; USSR State Prize 1987, Award of European Theatre Union 1991, Baltic Ass. Award 1994, Nat. Culture and Art Award. *Productions include:* A Taste of Honey 1976, Duokishkis Ballad 1978, Ivanov 1978, Square 1980, Pirosmani 1981, Love and Death in Verona 1982, The Day Lasts More Than Ages 1983, Uncle Vanya 1986, Mozart and Salieri, Don Juan, Plague 1994, Three Sisters 1995, Hamlet 1997, Macbeth 1999, Othello 2001, Ivanov 2002, Veridi's Macbeth 2002, The Seasons 2003. *Film roles include:* Girenas in Flight Through Atlantics 1983, Father in Lessons of Hatred 1984, Minister in Team 1985. *Address:* Bernardinų 8/8, 2000 Vilnius, Lithuania. *Telephone:* (52) 685816. *Fax:* (52) 685817 (office). *E-mail:* info@menofortas.lt (office). *Website:* www.menofortas .lt (office).

NEKVASIL, Lt-Gen. Jiří; Czech army officer and diplomatist; *Ambassador to Mongolia;* b. 24 April 1948, Benešov; m. 1st Jaroslava Papeová; m. 2nd Danuše Kadlečková; two s. two d.; m. 3rd Nanuli Kobaladze; two s. three d.; ed Tech. Inst. Liptovský Mikuláš, Mil. Acad., Kalinin, Acad. of Gen. Staff of Mil. Forces, Moscow, NATO Defence Coll., Rome; 2nd in Command Czech AF and Anti-Air Defence System 1990–92; Commdr of Gen. Staff 1993–98; Adviser to Ministry of Defence 1998–99; Amb. to Georgia 2000–04, to Mongolia 2004–; Order of Red Star (Czechoslovakia) 1985, Commdr, Legion of Merit 1996, Legion d'honneur 1996, Bundeswehr Gold Cross (Germany) 1998, Gold Cross (Austria) 1998. *Leisure interests:* mushrooming, tennis, gardening, photography. *Address:* Embassy of the Czech Republic, PO Box 665, Olimpiin Gudamj 14, Ulan Bator, Mongolia (office). *Telephone:* (11) 321886 (office); (11) 327969 (home). *Fax:* (11) 323791 (office). *E-mail:* czechemb@magicnet.mn (office); jirinekva@seznam.cz (home). *Website:* www.mzv.cz/ulaanbaatar (office).

NELDER, John Ashworth, MA, DSc, FRS; British statistician; b. 8 Oct. 1924, Dulverton, Somerset; s. of Reginald Charles Nelder and Edith May Ashworth (née Briggs); m. Mary Hawkes 1955; one s. one d.; ed Blundell's School, Tiverton, Sidney Sussex Coll., Cambridge Univ.; Head of Statistics Section, Nat. Vegetable Research Station, Wellesbourne 1950–68; Head of Statistics Dept, Rothamsted Experimental Station, Harpenden 1968–84; Sr Research

Fellow London Business School 1984–87; Originator statistical computer programs Genstat and GLIM; Visiting Prof. Imperial Coll., London 1971–; fmr Pres. Int. Biometric Soc.; Pres. Royal Statistical Soc. 1985–86; Guy Medal (Silver) of Royal Statistical Soc. *Publications:* Generalized Linear Models (with P. McCullagh), Computers in Biology; more than 150 papers in scientific journals. *Leisure interests:* ornithology, music (especially playing piano). *Address:* Cumberland Cottage, 33 Crown Street, Redbourn, St Albans, Herts., AL3 7JX, England. *Telephone:* (1582) 792907. *E-mail:* jnelder@imperial.ac.uk (office); jnelder@ntlworld.com (home).

NELISSEN, Roelof J., MA; Dutch politician and banker; b. 4 April 1931, Hoofdplaat, Zeeland Prov.; m. A. M. van der Kelen; three s. one d.; ed grammar school at Dongen and Faculty of Law, Catholic Univ. of Nijmegen; various posts in employers' asscns, Amsterdam and The Hague 1956–69; mem. Second Chamber, States-Gen. (Parl.) 1963–70; Minister of Econ. Affairs 1970–71; First Deputy Prime Minister, Minister of Finance 1971–73; mem. Bd of Man. Dirs Amsterdam-Rotterdam Bank NV 1974–, Vice-Chair. 1979–82, Chair. 1983–92; Chair. Bd of Man. Dirs ABN-AMRO Holding NV 1990–92. *Address:* PO Box 552, 1250 AN Laren, Netherlands.

NELLIGAN, Kate; Canadian actress; b. 16 March 1950, London, Ont.; d. of Patrick Joseph Nelligan and Alice (née Dier) Nelligan; one s.; ed St Martin's Catholic School, London, Ont., York Univ., Toronto and Cen. School of Speech and Drama, London, England; professional stage debut as Corrie in Barefoot in the Park, Little Theatre, Bristol 1972; other parts there and at Theatre Royal for Bristol Old Vic 1972–73 include: Hypatia in Misalliance, Stella Kowalski in A Streetcar Named Desire, Pegeen Mike in The Playboy of the Western World, Grace Harkaway in London Assurance, title role in Lulu, Sybil Chase in Private Lives; London debut as Jenny in Knuckle, Comedy Theatre 1974; joined Nat. Theatre Co. at Old Vic 1975 to play Ellie Dunn in Heartbreak House, also in Plenty and Moon for the Misbegotten 1984; As You Like It for RSC, Stratford; Serious Money, Broadway 1988, Spoils of War 1988, Eleni; Evening Standard Best Actress Award 1978. *Films include:* The Count of Monte Cristo, The Romantic Englishwoman 1975, Dracula 1979, Mr. Patman 1980, Agent 1980, Eye of the Needle 1981, Without a Trace 1983, Eleni 1985, Il Giorno prima 1987, White Room 1990, The Prince of Tides 1991, Frankie and Johnny 1991, Shadows and Fog 1992, Fatal Instinct 1993, Wolf 1994, Margaret's Museum 1995, How to Make An American Quilt 1995, Up Close and Personal 1996, U.S. Marshals 1998, Stolen Moments (voice), Boy Meets Girl 1998, The Cider House Rules 1999, Blessed Stranger 2000, Premonition 2007. *Television includes:* The Onedin Line (series) 1971, The Arcata Promise 1974, Count of Monte Cristo 1975, The Lady of the Camellias 1976, Bethune 1977, Measure for Measure 1979, Licking Hitler, Thérèse Raquin (mini-series) 1980, Forgive our Foolish Ways 1980, Victims 1982, Kojak: The Price of Justice 1987, Love and Hate: The Story of Colin and Joanne Thatcher 1989, Golden Fiddles (min-series) 1990, Three Hotels 1991, Old Times 1991, Terror Stalks the Class Reunion 1992, The Diamond Fleece 1992, Liar, Liar 1992; Shattered Trust: The Shari Karney Story 1993, Spoils of War 1994, Million Dollar Babes 1994, A Mother's Prayer 1995, Captive Heart: The James Mink Story 1996, Calm at Sunset 1996, Love is Strange 1999, Swing Vote 1999, Blessed Stranger: After Flight 111 2000, Walter and Henry 2001, A Wrinkle in Time (mini-series) 2003, Human Cargo (mini-series) 2004, In From the Night 2005,. *Leisure interests:* reading, cooking. *Address:* Innovative Artists, 235 Park Ave South, Suite 7, New York, NY 10003, USA (office). *Telephone:* (212) 253-6900.

NELSON, Bill, JD; American politician; *Senator from Florida;* b. 29 Sept. 1942, Miami, Fla; s. of C. W. Nelson and Nannie Nelson; m. Grace H. Cavert 1972; one s. one d.; ed Yale Univ., Univ. of Va; with US Army Reserves 1965–75, Army 1968–70, rank of Capt.; admitted to Bar, Fla; pvt. law practice Melbourne, Fla 1970–79; mem. House of Reps, Fla 1972–78, US Congress 1979–91, Chair. Space Sub-Cttee of the Science, Space and Tech. Cttee (flew with crew on 24th flight of NASA Space Shuttle); State Treas., Insurance Commr and Fire Marshall, Fla 1995–2000, Senator from Fla 2000–, mem. Senate Foreign Relations, Armed Services, Budget and Commerce Cttees, Sub-Cttee on Int. Operations and Terrorism. *Address:* 716 Hart Senate Building, Washington, DC 20510, USA (office). *Telephone:* (202) 224-5274 (office). *Fax:* (202) 228-2183 (office). *Website:* billnelson.senate.gov (office).

NELSON, Brendan; Australian physician and politician; b. 19 Aug. 1958, Melbourne; m. Gillian Nelson; three c.; ed Flinders Univ.; gen. practitioner Hobart, Tasmania 1985–95; Dir Hobart and Launceston After Hours Medical Services 1987–91; Tasmanian State Pres. Australian Medical Asscn 1990–92, Fed. Vice-Pres. 1991–93, Fed. Pres. 1993–95; MP for Bradfield (Liberal) 1996–, Chair. House of Reps Standing Cttee on Employment, Educ. and Workplace Relations 1998; Chair. Sydney Airport Community Forum –2000; Parl. Sec. to Minister for Defence 2000–01; Minister for Educ., Science and Training 2001–06, for Defence 2006–07; Fed. Parl. Leader, Liberal Party of Australia 2007–08; Hon. Fellow, Royal Australasian RACP; AMA Gold Medal for Distinguished Service to Medicine and Humanity 1995, Sydney Univ. John Lowenthal Medal. *Leisure interests:* music, motorcycles, tennis. *Address:* Liberal Party of Australia, Federal Secretariat, cnr Blackall and Macquarie Streets, Barton, ACT 2600 (office); PO Box 6022, House of Representatives, Parliament House, Canberra, ACT 2600 (office); Suite 8, 12 Tryon Road, Lindfield, NSW 2070, Australia (office). *Telephone:* (2) 6273-2564 (Liberal Party); (2) 6277-7800 (Canberra) (office); (2) 9465-3950 (office). *Fax:* (2) 6273-1534 (Liberal Party) (office); (2) 6273-4118 (Canberra) (office); (2) 9465-3999 (office). *E-mail:* libadm@liberal.org.au (office). *Website:* www.liberal.org.au (office); www.brendannelson.com.au.

NELSON, E. Benjamin (Ben), MA, JD; American politician and lawyer; *Senator from Nebraska;* b. 17 May 1941, McCook, Neb.; s. of Benjamin E. Nelson and Birdella Nelson; m. Diane Nelson (née Gleason); two s. two d. from previous marriage; one step-s. one step-d.; ed Univ. of Nebraska; Instructor Dept of Philosophy, Univ. of Neb. 1963–65; Dir of Compliance Neb. Dept of Insurance 1965–72, Dir 1975–76; admitted to Neb. Bar 1970; Gen. Counsel, Cen. Nat. Insurance Group of Omaha 1972–74, Exec. Vice-Pres. 1977, Pres. 1978–79, Pres. and CEO 1980–81; Attorney of Counsel Kennedy, Holland DeLacy and Svoboda, Omaha 1985–90; Gov. of Nebraska 1990–98, Senator from Nebraska Jan. 2001–; mem. of counsel Lumson, Dugan and Murray 1999; Exec. Vice-Pres. Nat. Asscn of Insurance Commrs 1982–85; Chair. Nat. Educ. Goals Panel 1992–94, Govs' Ethanol Coalition (also f.) 1991, 1994, Midwestern Govs' Conf. 1994; fmr Chair. Interstate Oil and Gas Compact Comm., Western Govs' Asscn and Co-Lead Gov. on Int. Trade; Pres. Council of State Govts 1994; Chair. Nat. Resources Cttee and Co-Lead Gov. on Federalism, Nat. Govs' Asscn; Co-Chair. Nat. Summit on Federalism 1995; fmr Vice-Chair. Democratic Govs' Asscn; Hon. LLD (Creighton Univ.) 1992, (Peru State Coll.) 1993; Hon. DHumLitt (Coll. of St Mary) 1995; numerous awards. *Leisure interests:* spending time with my family, hunting and fishing, reading and collecting clocks. *Address:* 720 Hart Senate Office Building, Washington, DC 20510 (office); Lamson, Dugan and Murray, 10306 Regency Parkway Drive, Omaha, NE 68114, USA (office). *Telephone:* (202) 224-6551 (office). *Website:* bennelson.senate.gov (office).

NELSON, Judith, BA; American singer (soprano); b. 10 Sept. 1939; d. of Virgil D. Nelson and Genevieve W. Manes; m. Alan H. Nelson 1961; one s. one d.; ed St Olaf Coll., Northfield, Minn.; Alfred Hertz Memorial Fellowship, Univ. of Calif., Berkeley 1972–73; European debut 1972; specializes in baroque repertoire; has appeared with most of the major baroque orchestras in USA and Europe including Acad. of Ancient Music, Tafelmusik, Toronto, Philharmonia, San Francisco; has performed with San Francisco, St Louis, Baltimore and Washington Nat. Symphony Orchestras and Los Angeles Philharmonic; has appeared in opera in Boston, LA, Brussels, Innsbruck, Venice, Turin and Rome and at Maryland Handel Festival; masterclasses at UCLA, Univ. of Chicago, Bath Summer School, Bruges Festival, Jerusalem Music Center; Hon. DFA (St Olaf Coll.) 1979. *Leisure interests:* languages, support of local arts orgs, local politics. *Address:* 2600 Buena Vista Way, Berkeley, CA 94708, USA. *Telephone:* (415) 848-1992.

NELSON, M. Bruce, BBA; American business executive; b. 1945; m. La Vaun Nelson; one s. one d.; ed ID State Univ.; man. positions with Boise Cascade, BT Office Products USA; Pres. and CEO Viking Inc. –1998; Pres. and CEO Viking Office Products (following merger of Viking and Office Depot 1998) 1998–2000, Pres. Office Depot Int. Inc. 1998–2000, CEO Office Depot Inc. 2000–04 (resgnd); mem. Advisory Council Ida State Univ., Exec.-in-Residence 2001; Distinguished Alumnus Award, ID State Univ. 2001; FL Atlantic Univ. Entrepreneur Business Leader of the Year 2001. *Address:* c/o Office Depot Incorporated, 2200 Old Germantown Road, Delray Beach, FL 33445, USA (office).

NELSON, Marilyn Carlson; American business executive; *Chairperson, Carlson Companies;* b. 1940, Minneapolis; m. Glen Nelson; ed Smith Coll., Mass, Univ. of the Sorbonne, Paris, France and Inst. des Hautes Etudes Economiques Politiques, Geneva, Switzerland; began career as Securities Analyst with PaineWebber; Dir of Community Relations, Carlson Cos Inc. 1968–88, Sr Vice-Pres. 1989–91, COO 1997–2003, Chair. and CEO 1998–2008, Chair. 2008–; Co-founder and mem. Minn. Women's Econ. Roundtable 1974–; mem. Bd of Dirs First Bank System 1978–97, Nat. Tourism Org. 1996–98, Exxon Mobil Corpn 1991–, US West Inc., Mayo Foundation 2001–, Singapore Tourism Bureau 1999–, Travel Industry Asscn of America 2000–, Juran Center for Leadership in Quality 1999–2005, Univ. of Minnesota Foundation 1999–; Chair. Nat. Women's Business Council 2002–05, Pres.'s Cttee on Trade and Industry 2002; mem. Minn. Orchestral Asscn 1972–, Business Roundtable 2004–, Int. Business Council, World Travel and Tourism Council 1997–, World Econ. Forum 2000–; Co-Chair. Annual Meeting, Davos, Switzerland 2004, mem. Cttee to Encourage Corp. Philanthropy 2004–; mem. Bd of Overseers Curtis L. Carlson School of Man. 1999–; Del., White House Conf. on Tourism 1996; fmr Pres. United Way of Minneapolis; fmr mem. Bd United Way of America 1984–90; fmr Chair. New Sweden '88; Leader Gov.'s Task Force to bring 1992 Super Bowl to Minnesota; fmr Chair. Scandinavia Today celebration in USA; Distinguished Visiting Prof., Johnson & Wales Univ.; Royal Order of the North Star (First Class) (Sweden), Order of the White Rose (Finland); Hon. DBA (Johnson & Wales Univ.); Hon. DHumLitt (Coll. of St Catherine, Gustavus Adolphus Coll.); Outstanding Business Leader 1996, ranked by Travel Agent magazine as The Most Powerful Woman in Travel 1997–2004, Woodrow Wilson Award for Corp. Citizenship, Woodrow Wilson Int. Center 2000, Penn State Hotel and Restaurant Soc. Hospitality Exec. of the Year 2000, FIRST magazine Responsible Capitalism Award, London, UK 2001, Businesswoman of the World, Business Women's Network 2001, American Hotel & Lodging Asscn Cutting Edge Award 2001, Int. Hotel Investment Forum Lifetime Achievement Award, Berlin, Germany 2002, Great Swedish Heritage Award, Swedish Council of America 2002, inducted into Travel Industry Asscn of America's Hall of Fame 2003, inducted into Sales and Marketing Execs Int. Hall of Fame 2003, Swedish-American of the Year, King Carl XVI Gustaf and Queen Silvia of Sweden 2003, ranked by Fortune magazine amongst 50 Most Powerful Women in Business in the US (40th) 2002, (45th) 2003, (46th) 2004, ranked by Forbes magazine amongst 100 Most Powerful Women (82nd) 2004, (79th) 2005, (64th) 2006, (78th) 2007, ranked by Business Week as one of Top 25 Executives in Business, Athena Award 2004, Businesswoman of the Year, US Commerce Dept's Small Business Admin 2005, 18th Annual Lucia Trade Award, Swedish-American Chamber of Commerce 2005. *Leisure interests:* skiing, skating. *Address:* Carlson Companies, 701 Carlson Parkway, Minnetonka, MN 55305-8212, USA (office). *Telephone:* (763) 212-5000 (office). *Fax:* (763) 212-2219 (office). *Website:* www.carlson.com (office).

NELSON, Ralph Alfred, MD, PhD, FACP; American physician and academic; *Director of Medical Research, Carle Foundation Hospital;* b. 19 June 1927, Minneapolis; s. of Alfred Walter Nelson and Lydia Nelson (née Johnson); m. Rosemarie Pokela 1954; three s. two d.; ed Univ. of Minnesota; Pathology Residency, Univ. of Minnesota 1954–55; Fellowship in Physiology, Mayo Grad. School, Mayo Clinic, Rochester 1957–60, Resident Internal Medicine 1976–78; Asst Prof. of Nutrition, Cornell Univ. 1961–62; Assoc. Prof. of Physiology, Assoc. Prof. of Nutrition, Mayo Medical School, Rochester 1967–78; Prof. of Nutrition, Dept of Medicine, Univ. of Ill. 1979–2002, Prof. Emer. 2002–, Prof. of Medicine, Food Science, Prof. of Physiology, Univ. of Ill. 1979–84, Exec. Head, Dept of Internal Medicine, Univ. of Ill. Coll. of Medicine at teaching sites of Urbana-Champaign, Chicago, Ill., Rockford, Ill. and Peoria, Ill. 1986–2002, Head, Dept of Medicine 1989–2002; Consultant for Nutritional Support Service, Danville Veterans Admin. Hosp.; Dir of Medical Research, Carle Foundation Hosp., Urbana 1979–; mem. American Physiological Soc., American Inst. of Nutrition, American Soc. of Clinical Nutrition, American Soc. of Gastroenterology; Mayo Clinic Alumni Award for Outstanding Research 1959, Fulbright Scholar 1988, Lifetime Achievement Award, Carle Foundation Hosp. 2004. *Publications:* Mayo Clinic Renal Diet Cook Book 1974, numerous learned papers, including over 140 on the metabolism of bears and clinical nutrition. *Leisure interests:* walking, bicycling, canoeing, mountain hiking. *Address:* Carle Foundation Hospital, Department of Medical Research, 611 West Park Street, Urbana, IL 61801 (office); 2 Illinois Circle, Urbana, IL 61801, USA (home). *Telephone:* (217) 383-3036 (office); (217) 344-4676 (home). *Fax:* (217) 383-3993 (office). *E-mail:* ralph.nelson@carle.com (office). *Website:* www.med.uiuc.edu/departments/internalMed (office).

NELSON, Ronald L., BA, MBA; American car rental industry executive; *Chairman and CEO, Avis Budget Group, Inc.;* ed Univ. of Calif., Berkeley, UCLA; Exec. Vice-Pres., Chief Financial Officer and mem. Bd of Dirs, Paramount Communications, Inc. (fmrly Gulf & Western Industries, Inc.) 1987–94; Co-COO DreamWorks SKG 1994–2003; Pres., Chief Financial Officer and mem. Bd of Dirs, Cendant Corpn (now Avis Budget Group, Inc.) 2003–06, Chair. and CEO 2006–. *Address:* Avis Budget Group Inc., 6 Sylvan Way, Parsippany, NJ 07054, USA (office). *Telephone:* (973) 496-3500 (office). *Fax:* (888) 304-2315 (office). *Website:* www.avisbudgetgroup.com (office).

NELSON, Willie Hugh; American country and western singer, musician and songwriter; b. 30 April 1933, Abbott, TX; m. Annie Marie Nelson; three s. four d.; ed Baylor Univ.; fmr salesman, announcer, host and DJ, country music shows in Texas; bass player, Ray Price's band; formed own band; appearances at Grand Ole Opry, Nashville and throughout USA 1964–; tours to New Zealand, Australia, USA, Canada, Europe, Japan; annual Fourth of July picnics throughout USA 1972–; performed with Frank Sinatra, Neil Young, Dolly Parton, Linda Ronstadt, ZZ Top, Waylon Jennings, Ray Charles, Santana, Joni Mitchell, Kris Kristofferson, Bob Dylan, Patsy Cline; six Grammy (NARAS) Awards, eight CMA Awards, Nashville Songwriters' Asscn Hall of Fame 1973, Nat. Acad. of Popular Music Lifetime Achievement Award 1983, three ACM Awards, Tex Ritter Songwriting Award (with Kris Kristofferson) 1984. *Film appearances:* Electric Horseman 1980, Honeysuckle Rose 1980. *Compositions include:* Crazy (performed by Patsy Cline), Hello Walls (performed by Faron Young). *Recordings include:* albums: The Sound In Your Mind 1976, The Troublemaker 1976, Willie Nelson And His Friends 1976, To Lefty From Willie 1977, Willie Before His Time 1978, Wanted/The Outlaw 1978, The Willie Way 1978, Stardust 1978, One For The Road 1979, Willie And Family Live 1979, Pretty Paper 1979, Willie Sings Kristofferson 1979, San Antonio Rose 1980, Honeysuckle Rose 1980, Family Bible 1980, Tougher Than Leather 1983, City Of New Orleans 1984, Me And Paul 1985, Highwayman 1985, The Promised Land 1986, Partners 1986, Island In The Sea 1987, Seashores Of Old Mexico 1987, What A Wonderful World 1988, A Horse Called Music 1989, Highwayman II 1990, Born For Trouble 1990, Clean Shirt Waylon And Willie 1991, Across The Borderline 1993, Six Hours At Pedernales 1994, Healing Hands Of Time 1994, Just One Love 1995, Spirit 1996, How Great Thou Art 1996, Christmas With Willie Nelson 1997, Hill Country Christmas 1997, Teatro 1998, Nashville Was The Roughest 1998, Night And Day 1999, Forever Gold 2000, Me And The Drummer 2000, Milk Cow Blues 2000, Rainbow Connection 2001, Joy 2001, The Great Divide 2002, All The Songs I've Loved Before 2002, Crazy: the Demo Sessions 2003, Picture In A Frame (with Kimmie Rhodes) 2003, It Always Will Be 2004, Countryman 2005, Songbird 2006, Last of the Breed (with Merle Haggard and Ray Price) 2007, Moment of Forever 2008, Two Men with the Blues (with Wynton Marsalis) 2008, Willie and the Wheel (with Asleep at the Wheel) 2009. *Address:* Mark Rothbaum and Associates Inc., PO Box 2689, Danbury, CT 06813-2689, USA (office). *Website:* www.willienelson.com.

NEMBANG, Subas Chandra, BA, BL; Nepalese barrister and politician; *Chairperson, Constituent Assembly;* b. 11 March 1953; m.; fmr Minister of Law, Justice and Parl. Affairs; fmr mem. Standing Cttee; Leader of Communist Party of Nepal (Unifed Marxist-Leninist—UML), mem. Cen. Cttee; Sr Most Advocate, Supreme Court of Nepal; Speaker of the Interim Parl. ('Legislature-Parl.') –2008, Chair. Security Special Cttee, House of Reps Proclamation Implementation Special Cttee, Business Man. Advisory Cttee, Chair. Constituent Ass. 2008–. *Address:* Office of the Chairperson, Constituent Assembly of Nepal, Kathmandu (office); Suntalabari-2, Ilam Constituency No. 2, Nepal (office). *Telephone:* (1) 4228459 (constituency) (office). *Fax:* (1) 4222923 (constituency (office). *E-mail:* nparl@ntc.net.np (office); parliament@ntc.net.np (office). *Website:* www.parliament.gov.np (office).

NĚMEC, Jaroslav, DrTech, DrSc; Czech engineer and metallurgist (retd); *Consultant, Czech Academy of Sciences;* b. 15 March 1921, Horaždovice, Klatovy Dist; s. of Karel Němec and Bohuslava Němcová; m. Zdenka Němcová 1944 (died 1996); ed Eng Faculty, Tech. Univ. of Prague (ČVUT); design engineer 1942–45; Dir of Research and Devt, ČKD Sokolovo 1945–53; Prof., Coll. of Transport (VŠD), Dean 1953–55, Deputy Rector 1955–59; Prof., Head of Materials Dept, Faculty of Nuclear and Physical Eng, ČVUT 1969–86, Deputy Dean 1967–74, Deputy Rector 1973–79; Corresp. mem. Czechoslovak (now Czech) Acad. of Sciences (ČSAV) 1972–75, mem. ČSAV 1975–, mem. Presidium 1979–87, Dir Acad. Inst. of Theoretical and Applied Mechanics, Prague 1979–87, Consultant 1991–; mem. Czechoslovak Atomic Comm.; Expert Adviser, Skoda Works, ČKD and others; mem. various foreign scientific and eng socs; Hon. mem. Int. Conf. on Fracture, Nat. Tech. Museum; Dr hc (Pardubice Univ.) 1999; All States Prize of Sciences 1965, 1974, Kaplan Medal 1968, Felber Medal 1971, Křížík Medal 1976, Order of Labour 1981, Nat. Prize 1985, Komensky Medal 1986, Medal of Sciences and Humanities, Acad. of Sciences 1986 and many others. *Publications:* over 400 original papers on mechanics, material eng and strength; 24 books including: Strength of Pressure Vessels under Different Operational Conditions, Toughness and Strength of Steel Parts, Failure of Strength of Plastics (with Acad. Serensen, Moscow), Shape and Strength of Metal Bodies (with Prof. Puchner), New Methods of Calculations of Rigidity and Strength of Machines (with Prof. Valenta), Fracture Dynamics, Dynamics and Reliability of Locomotive Parts, The Problem of Nuclear Equipment, with Special Reference to Reliability and Safety, Endurance of Mechanical Structures (with Dr Drexler), Strength and Lifetime of Gas Pipes (jtly); subject of book 'Five Minutes to Crash... Call Prof. Němec' 1998. *Leisure interest:* painting. *Address:* UTAM, Czech Academy of Sciences, Prosecka 74, Prague 9 (office); Letohradská 60, 7 Prague 17000, Czech Republic (home). *Telephone:* (2) 86882121 (office); (2) 33376423 (home). *Fax:* (2) 86884634 (office). *E-mail:* gajdos@itam.cas.cz (office). *Website:* www.itam.cas.cz (office).

NÉMETH, János, PhD; Hungarian academic and lawyer; *Senior Partner, Békés-Németh-Vékás & Company, and Chairman, Editorial Board, European Law;* b. 31 July 1933, Újpest; s. of János Németh and Erzsébet Németh (née Nemes); m. Izabella Vass 1959, two d.; ed Eötvös Loránd Univ. of Budapest; jr legal official in law firm 1957, teacher at Dept of Civil Procedural Law at Eötvös Loránd Univ. 1982–97, Vice-Chancellor 1993–97, Head of Dept, Prof. 1994–2003, Prof. Emer. 2004–; Ed. Hungarian Law (journal) 1991–; Chief Ed. Pres. Comm. for Hungarian Lawyers Asscn; Chair. Editorial Bd European Law (review) 2001–, Jog Ok (Lawyer's Training) 2005–; mem. of Nat. Legal Comm. of Hungarian Acad. of Sciences, Nat. Legal Cttee of Experts for Doctorates at Hungarian Acad. of Sciences; Sr Pnr Békés-Németh-Vékás and Co. law firm; Chair. of Nat. Electoral Cttee 1990–97; judge, Constitutional Court of Hungary 1997–98, Pres. 1998–2003; Arbitrator Arbitration Court attached to Hungarian Chamber of Commerce and Industry; Cross of Honours with Spurs of Hungarian Repub. 1995, Order of the Rising Sun (Japan) 2002, Grand Cross of Honours of Hungarian Repub. 2003, Grand Gold Honours on Sash for Service to Repub. of Austria 2004. *Publications:* more than 100 legal publs. *Leisure interest:* hunting. *Address:* ELTE Polgári Eljárásjogi Tanszék, 1053 Budapest, Egyetem tér 1-3 (office); Brassó köz 8, 1112 Budapest, Hungary (home). *Telephone:* (1) 411-6522 (office). *Fax:* (1) 411-6522 (office). *E-mail:* nemethj@ajk.elte.hu (office).

NÉMETH, Miklós; Hungarian politician; b. 24 Jan. 1948, Monok; s. of András Németh and Margit Németh (née Stajz); m. Erzsébet Szilágyi 1971; two s.; ed Karl Marx Univ. of Budapest; Lecturer in Political Economy, Karl Marx Univ. 1971–77; Deputy Section Head, Nat. Planning Office 1977–81; worked on staff, later as deputy leader, of HSWP Cen. Cttee Dept of Political Economy, Dept Leader 1987–88; mem. of Cen. Cttee, Secr. 1987–88; mem. Political Cttee 1987–88; mem. Parl. 1988–90; Prime Minister of Hungary 1988–90; apptd to four-mem. Presidium of HSWP 1989; mem. Presidium, HSP Oct.–Dec. 1989 (resgnd); Vice-Pres. (Personnel and Admin) EBRD, London, UK 1991–2000; returned to Hungary and attempted to become PM-designate of opposition socialist party, but was unsuccessful. *Leisure interests:* sailing, tennis, classical music. *Address:* c/o Keszi u. 7, 1029 Budapest II, Hungary.

NÉMETH, Zsolt; Hungarian politician; *Chairman of the Foreign Affairs and Hungarian Minorities Abroad Committee, Hungarian National Assembly;* b. 14 Oct. 1963, Budapest; m.; three c.; ed Radnóti Miklós Grammar School, Budapest, Karl Marx Univ. of Economics (MKKE), Univ. of Oxford, UK; trainee, Inst. for Hungarian Studies 1987–90; resident educator, Széchenyi István Coll., MKKE 1987–90; Founding mem. Alliance of Free Democrats (FIDESZ), Party Spokesman 1988–89, mem. Nat. Cttee 1989–93, Vice-Pres. 1993–2003, Deputy Faction Leader 2003–; Pres. Széchenyi Coll. Asscn 1992–95; Chief Trustee, then Hon. Chief Trustee, Transylvanian (Calvinist) Church 1995–; mem. Kts of St John 1999–; mem. Nat. Ass. 1990–; mem. Council of Europe Parl. Ass. 1994–98; State Sec., Ministry of Foreign Affairs 1998–2002; Deputy Leader, Hungarian Delegation to Council of Europe 2002–; Chair. Foreign Affairs Cttee, Nat. Ass. 2002–06, Foreign Affairs and Hungarian Minorities Abroad Committee 2006–. *Address:* Hungarian National Assembly, 1357 Budapest, Kossuth tér 1–3, Hungary. *Telephone:* (1) 441-4000 (office); (1) 441-4626 (office). *Fax:* (1) 441-4816 (office). *Website:* www.parlament.hu (office).

NEMITSAS, Takis; Greek-Cypriot fmr politician and industrialist; *Executive Chairman, Nemitsas Group of Companies;* b. 2 June 1930, Limassol; s. of Xanthos Nemitsas and Vassiliki Nemitsa; m. 1st Daisy Petrou 1958 (died 1983); three d.; m. 2nd Louki Loucaides 1986; mem. House of Reps 1976–81; fmr Pres. Parl. Cttee on Commerce and Industry; Minister of Commerce and Industry 1988–93; Exec. Chair. and Man. Dir Nemitsas Group 1993–95, Chair. Bd of Dirs 1995–; fmr mem. Bd Bank of Cyprus, Cyprus Employers' and Industrialists' Fed., Chamber of Commerce and Industry, Cyprus Tourism Org.; fmr Deputy Chair. Woolworth Cyprus; Grand Cross of Leopold II (Belgium), Grand Officer Kt of the Order of Merit (Italy). *Publications:*

Environmental policy and the EU, Recycling of Scrap Metal in Cyprus. *Leisure interest:* swimming. *Address:* 153 Franklin Roosevelt Avenue, Limassol (office); Nemitsas Ltd, PO Box 50124, 3601 Limassol, Cyprus. *Telephone:* (25) 569222 (office); (25) 636844 (home). *Fax:* (25) 569275 (office); (25) 636050 (home). *E-mail:* central@nemitsas.com (office). *Website:* www.nemitsas.com (office).

NEMTSOV, Boris Yefimovich, CTechSc; Russian politician; b. 9 Oct. 1959, Sochi; m.; one s. three d.; ed Gorkii (now Nizhnyi Novgorod) State Univ.; researcher then sr researcher, Research Inst. of Radiophysics 1981–91; elected to Supreme Soviet of the Russian Fed. 1990; rep. of Pres. of Russia in Nizhnyi Novgorod Oblast 1991; Gov. of Nizhny Novgorod Oblast 1991–97; People's Deputy of Russia 1990–93; mem. Federation Council 1993–97; First Deputy Chair. Russian Govt 1997–98 (resgnd); Minister of Fuel and Power Eng March–Nov. 1997; f. Young Russia Movt; joined pre-election coalition Pravoye delo (The Right Thing) 1999; mem. State Duma (Parl.) 1999–2003, Deputy Chair. Feb.–June 2000; Leader Union of Rightist Forces faction 2000–01; mem. Fed. Political Council Union of Rightist Forces (Chair. 2001–03, resgnd) 2004–07; co-founder and mem. Cttee Free Choice 2008 for democratic elections 2004; Chair. Bd of Dirs Neftyanoi 2004–05 (resgnd); apptd adviser to Pres. of Ukraine 2005; regular participant in various Russian TV programmes; Order of Prince Yaroslav the Wise (Ukraine) 2007. *Publications:* The Provincial 1997, The Provinical in Moscow 1999. *Leisure interests:* tennis, windsurfing, fishing. *Address:* Malaya Ordynka 3–8, 119017, Moscow (home); Union of Rightist Forces (Soyuz pravykh sil), 109544, Moscow, ul. M. Andronyevskaya 15, Russia (office). *Telephone:* (495) 729-29-79 (home); (495) 232-04-05 (office); (985) 920-08-16 (office). *E-mail:* pomnem@list.ru (office). *Website:* www.nemtsov.ru (home).

NEMYRYA, Hryhoriy, BA, PhD; Ukrainian academic and politician; *Deputy Prime Minister for European and International Integration;* b. 5 April 1960, Donetsk; m.; one s.; ed Donetsk State Univ., Kiev Shevchenko Univ.; began career as Lecturer, Dept of History, Donetsk State Univ., becoming Head Centre for Political Research 1992–96; Nat. Forum Foundation Fellow, Centre for Strategic and Int. Studies, Washington DC, USA 1994; Dean, Mohyla Acad., Kiev 1996–98; fmr Deputy Head European Integration Faculty, Nat. Acad. of Public Admin; fmr Head Centre for European and Int. Studies, Shevchenko Univ.; Chair. George Soros Int. Renaissance Foundation, Kiev 2002; fmr Ed. Noval Bezpeka (New Security); mem. Tymoshenko Bloc, Adviser to Yuliya Tymoshenko 2005–; mem. Verkhovna Rada (Supreme Council, Parl.) 2006–; Deputy Prime Minister for European and Int. Integration 2007–; mem. Socialist Group, Council of Europe 2006–. *Address:* Verkhovna Rada, Grushevsky 5, 01008 Kiev, Ukraine (office). *Telephone:* (44) 253-32-17 (office). *Fax:* (44) 253-32-17 (office). *E-mail:* Nemyria.Hrihorii@rada.gov.ua (office). *Website:* www.kmu.gov.ua/control (office).

NEOH, Anthony Francis, LLB, QC, JP; Chinese lawyer; b. 9 Nov. 1946, Hong Kong; ed Univ. of London, UK; teacher 1964–66; Hong Kong Civil Service 1966–79; pvt. practice, Hong Kong Bar 1979–95, Calif. Bar 1984–95; Hong Kong public service in educ., health etc. 1985–; People's Repub. of China public service in teaching, Govt advisory work etc., including Chief Adviser to China Securities Regulatory Comm. 1998; Visiting Scholar, Harvard Univ., USA 1990–91; fmr Chair. Securities and Futures Comm. Hong Kong; Chair. IOSCO Tech. Cttee 1996–98; Nomura Visiting Prof. of Int. Financial Systems, Harvard Law School, USA 2004; Vice-Chair. Exec. Cttee, School of Law, Chinese Univ. of Hong Kong 2005–. *Leisure interests:* reading, music. *Address:* 12th Floor, The Landmark, 15 Queen's Road Central, Hong Kong Special Administrative Region, People's Republic of China. *Telephone:* 28409201. *Fax:* 28101872.

NEPAL, Madhav Kumar; Nepalese politician; b. Rautahat Dist; ed Thakur Ram Campus, Birgunj; Deputy Prime Minister 1995; mem. Communist Party of Nepal (Unified Marxist Leninist—UML), Gen. Sec. –2008, Head of Foreign Dept 2008–, mem. Standing Cttee. *Address:* Communist Party of Nepal (UML), PO Box 5471, Madan Nagar, Balkhu, Kathmandu, Nepal (office). *Telephone:* (1) 278081 (office). *Fax:* (1) 278084 (office). *E-mail:* uml@ntc.net.np (office). *Website:* www.cpnuml.org (office).

NEPTUNE, Yvon; Haitian politician and architect; b. 8 Nov. 1946, Cavaillon; m.; two c.; ed Brothers of the Christian Instruction, Coll. Philippe Guerrier of Cayes, Port-au-Prince Lycée Alexandre Petion, Univ. of State of Haiti Faculty of Science, New York Inst. of Tech., USA; architect with Emery Roth and Sons, New York, USA; political activist, opponent of coup d'etat in Haiti 1991, produced radio broadcasts and helped org. of exiles, adviser to Bertrand Aristide, returned to Haiti 1994; mem. Lavalas Party, also Spokesman and Rep.; elected to Senate 2002, fmr Pres.; Prime Minister of Haiti 2002–04; held in prison 204–06 on charges relating to killing of opponents of Aristide. *Address:* c/o Office of the Prime Minister, Villa d'Accueil, Delmas 60, Musseau, Port-au-Prince, Haiti (office).

NERI, Romulo L., MBA; Philippine government official and business executive; *Director-General, National Economic and Development Authority;* ed Ateneo de Manila, Coll. of Business Admin, Univ. of the Philippines, Grad. School of Man., UCLA, USA; fmr Eugenio Lopez Assoc. Prof. for Corp. Financial Man., Asian Inst. of Man.; fmr Corp. Planning and Finance Officer, Canlubang Sugar Estate, Canlubang Pulp and Manufacturing Corpn, C-J Yulo and Sons Inc., Philippine Nat. Oil Co., Luzon Stevedoring Corpn, Mobil Oil Philippines Inc.; Dir-Gen. Nat. Econ. and Devt Authority (NEDA) –2005; Dir-Gen. House of Reps Congressional and Budget Office –2005; Sec. of the Budget and Man. 2005–07; Dir-Gen. Nat. Econ. and Devt Authority 2007–. *Address:* National Economic and Development Authority (NEDA), NEDA-sa-Pasig Building, 12 St Josemaria Escriva Street, Pasig City, 1605 Metro, Manila, Philippines (office). *Telephone:* (2) 6313747 (office). *Fax:* (2) 6313282 (office). *E-mail:* info@neda.gov.ph (office). *Website:* www.neda.gov.ph (office).

NERLOVE, Marc L., MA, PhD; American academic; *Professor of Agricultural and Resource Economics, University of Maryland;* b. 12 Oct. 1933, Chicago; s. of Samuel Henry Nerlove and Evelyn Nerlove (née Andelman); two d.; ed Univ. of Chicago and Johns Hopkins Univ.; Analytical Statistician, US Dept of Agric., Washington, DC 1956–57; Assoc. Prof., Univ. of Minn., Minneapolis 1959–60; Prof., Stanford Univ. 1960–65, Yale Univ. 1965–69; Prof. of Econs, Univ. of Chicago 1969–74; F. W. Taussig Research Prof., Harvard Univ. 1967–68; Visiting Prof., Northwestern Univ., 1973–74, Cook Prof. 1974–82; Prof. of Econs, Univ. of Pennsylvania 1982–86, Univ. Prof. 1986–93; Prof. of Agric. and Resource Econs, Univ. of Maryland, Coll. Park 1993–; mem. NAS 1979; Fellow and Past Pres. Econometric Soc.; Fellow, American Statistical Asscn 1964; Distinguished Fellow, American Agricultural Econ. Asscn 1993; John Bates Clark Medal 1969, P. C. Mahalinobis Medal 1975. *Publications:* Dynamics of Supply 1958, Distributed Lags and Demand Analysis 1958, Estimation and Identification of Cobb-Douglas Production Functions 1965, Analysis of Economic Time Series: A Synthesis 1979, Household and Economy: Welfare Economics of Endogenous Fertility 1987; numerous articles. *Address:* Department of Agricultural and Research Economics, 2105 Symons Hall, University of Maryland, College Park, MD 20742, USA. *Telephone:* (301) 405-1388 (office). *E-mail:* mnerlove@arec.umd.edu (office). *Website:* www.arec.umd.edu (office).

NERO, Franco; Italian actor; b. (Francesco Sparanero), 23 Nov. 1941, Parma; m. Vanessa Redgrave (q.v.). *Films:* The Bible 1966, Ojango, Camelot, The Hired Killer, The Wild, Wild Planet, The Brute and the Beast, The Day of the Owl, Sardinia, Mafia, Vendetta, Companeros, Detective Belli, The Mercenary, A Quiet Place in the Country, Tristana, The Virgin and the Gypsy, Battle of the Neretva, Confessions of a Police Captain, The Vacation, Pope Joan, Deaf Smith and Johnny Ears, The Last Days of Mussolini, Force Ten from Navarone, The Roses of the Danzig, Mimi, The Man With Bogart's Face, Enter the Ninja, Mexico in Flames, Querelle, Kamikaze '89, The Salamander, Wagner, Victory March, The Day of the Cobra, Ten Days That Shook the World, Der Falke, The Repenter, The Forester's Sons, Garibaldi: The General, The Girl, Sweet Country, Die Hard 2, Brothers and Sisters, A Breath of Life, Jonathan of the Bears, Conflict of Interest, The Dragon's Ring, Talk of Angels, The Innocent Sleep, The King and Me, White Smoke 2002, Cattive inclinazioni 2003. *Television includes:* The Last Days of Pompeii, Moyles: The Legend of Valentino, 21 Hours at Munich, The Pirate, Young Catherine, The Versace Murder, Das Babylon Komplott, The Uncrowned Heart 2003.

NESTERENKO, Evgeni, DipEng; Russian/Austrian singer (bass) and teacher; b. 8 Jan. 1938, Moscow; s. of Evgeni Nesterenko and Velta Baumann; m. Ekaterina Alexeyeva 1963; one s.; ed Leningrad Eng Inst. and Leningrad Conservatory with V. Lukanin; debut as General Ermolov in War and Peace, Maly Theatre, Leningrad 1963; soloist with Leningrad Maly Opera and Ballet Theatre 1963–67; soloist with Kirov Opera 1967–71; teacher of solo singing, Leningrad Conservatory 1967–72, Moscow Conservatory 1975–93, Konservatorium Wien 1993–2003; soloist with Bolshoi 1971–; mem. staff, Moscow Musical Pedagogical Inst. 1972–74; Chair. of Singing at Moscow Conservatoire 1975–93, Prof. 1981–93; USSR People's Deputy 1989–91; seasons at Vienna Staatsoper 1975, Metropolitan Opera 1975, Teatro Colón, Buenos Aires 1975, La Scala, Milan 1978, Covent Garden 1978, Verona Festival 1978, Munich 1978, Japan 1983, Barcelona 1984, Bregenz Festival 1986, Savonlinna Festival 1987, Hamburg 1986, Orange Festival 1990, Antwerp 1993, Hong Kong 2002, São Paulo 2006, Estonia 2008; mem. Int. Acad. of Creative Endeavours, Moscow 1991; People's Artist of the USSR 1976, Viotti d'Oro Prize, City of Vercelli (Italy) 1981, Lenin Prize 1982, Melodia Golden Disc, USSR 1984, Giovanni Zenatello Prize, Verona (Italy) 1986, Hero of Labour 1988, Chaliapin Prize 1992, Wilhelm Furtwängler Prize (Germany) 1992, Austrian Kammersänger 1992, Casta Diva Prize 2001, Golden Pegasus Theatre Prize (Poland) 2004, Centaur with Gold Flower 2009. *Roles include:* roles include Boris Godunov, Dosifey (Khovanshchina), Khan Konchak (Prince Igor), Mephistopheles (Faust), Grigori (Quiet Flows the Don), General Ermolov (War and Peace), Kutuzov (War and Peace), Filippo II (Don Carlo), Attila, Zaccaria (Nabucco), Don Pasquale, Sarastro (Magic Flute), Bluebeard, Gremin (Eugene Onegin), Ivan Susanin, Old Convict (Lady Macbeth), Don Basilio, Enrico VIII, Moses, Ivan Khovansky, Water-Sprite (Rusalka), Don Bartolo. *Recordings:* Glinka's Ruslan and Lyudmila and Ivan Susanin, Tchaikovsky's Mazeppa, Iolanta and Eugene Onegin, Rachmaninov's Francesca da Rimini and Aleko, Songs by Shostakovich and Mussorgsky, Suite on Poems of Michelangelo and 14th Symphony by Shostakovich, Verdi Requiem, Nabucco, Attila and Trovatore, Gounod's Faust, Dvořák's Rusalka, Donizetti's Don Pasquale and L'Elisir d'amore, Bela Bartók's Bluebeard's Castle; videos: Verdi's Attila, Rachmaninov's Aleko, Mussorgsky's Boris Godunov and Khovanshtchina, Glinka's A Life for the Tsar. *Publications:* Evgeni Nesterenko, Thoughts on my Profession 1985, Evgeni Nesterenko, Memoirs of a Russian Bass 2009. *Leisure interests:* tea collecting and testing.

NESTERIKHIN, Yuri Yefremovich; Russian nuclear physicist; *Head, Synchrotron and Applied Electronics Divisions, Kurchatov Institute;* b. 10 Oct. 1930, Ivanovo; s. of Yefrem Nesterikhin and Maria Morozova; m. 1954; one s. one d.; ed Moscow Lomonosov State Univ.; mem. CPSU 1960–91; Jr Researcher, Inst. of Atomic Energy 1954–61; Sector Head and Head of Lab., Inst. of Nuclear Physics (Siberian Br.) 1961–65; Prof. 1970; Corresp. mem., USSR (now Russian) Acad. of Sciences 1970, Full mem. 1981–; Dir, Inst. of Automation and Electrometrics, Siberian Br. of Acad. of Sciences 1967–87; Head of Synchrotron and Applied Electronics Divs, Kurchatov Inst., Moscow 1987–; Dir Multimedia Centre, Acad. of Nat. Economy 1992–; mem. Bd Ranet (jt stock co.) 1992–95; Chair. Moscow Physics and Tech. Inst. 2001–; Deputy Chair. Scientific Council for Cybernetics; most important works on plasma physics and thermonuclear synthesis; USSR Council of Ministers Prize. *Publications:* Methods of Speed Measurements in Geodynamics and Plasma Physics 1967; several other works on nuclear physics and automation of research. *Leisure interest:* sauna. *Address:* Kurchatov Institute, Kurchatova ploshchad 46, R-123182 Moscow (office); Leninski Prosp. 13, Apt. 93, 117071 Moscow, Russia. *Telephone:* (495) 196-97-79 (office); (495) 237-43-47 (home). *Fax:* (495) 420-22-66.

NESTEROVA, Natalia Igorevna; Russian painter; b. 23 April 1944, Moscow; one s.; ed Moscow Surikov State Fine Arts Inst.; mem. USSR (now Russian) Union of Painters; Stage Designer, Bolshoi Theatre 1958; participated in over 170 exhbns including solo exhbns Russia, Europe, N America 1988– (Moscow 1997); Prof., Russian Acad. of Theatre Art 1992–; works in collections of Tretyakov Gallery, Moscow, Ludwig Collection, Germany, Guggenheim Museum, New York; State Prize of Russia 1998. *Address:* c/o Moscow Artists Union, 101000 Moscow, Starosadsky per. 5, Russia. *Telephone:* (495) 921-51-88.

NESTEROVA, Natalya Vasilyevna; Russian academic; *Rector, Moscow Centre for Education;* b. 1952; ed Moscow State Univ., Moscow Pedagogical Inst.; worked in several higher educ. insts in Moscow; Founder and Rector, Moscow Centre of Educ. 1990–; Founder Humanitarian Gymnasium of N. Nesterova 1991–; Founder and Rector, New Humanitarian Univ. and Acad. of Dance N. Nesterova 1992–; Founder Acad. of Painting 1994–. *Address:* Moscow Centre of Education, 115 230 Moscow, Varshavskoye shosse 38, Russia (office). *Telephone:* (495) 753-80-00 (office). *Fax:* (495) 111-51-18 (office). *Website:* www.nesterova.ru (office).

NETANYAHU, Benjamin, MSc; Israeli politician and diplomatist; *Prime Minister;* b. 21 Oct. 1949, Tel-Aviv; m.; three c.; ed Massachusetts Inst. of Tech., USA; Man. Consultant, Boston Consulting Group 1976–78; Exec. Dir Jonathan Inst. Jerusalem 1978–80; Sr Man. Rim Industries, Jerusalem 1980–82; Deputy Chief of Mission, Israeli Embassy, Washington, DC 1982–84; Perm. Rep. to UN 1984–88; Deputy Minister of Foreign Affairs 1988–91; Deputy Minister, Prime Minister's Office 1991–92; Prime Minister of Israel, Minister of Housing and Construction 1996–99; Leader Likud 1993–99, 2005–; Minister of Foreign Affairs 2002–03, of Finance 2003–05; Prime Minister of Israel 2009–; mem. Knesset 1988–. *Publications:* Yoni's Letters (ed.) 1978, Terror: Challenge and Reaction (ed.) 1980, Terrorism: How the West Can Win (ed.) 1986, International Terrorism: Challenge and Response (ed.) 1991, A Place Among the Nations: Israel and the World 1993, Fighting Terrorism: How Democracies Can Defeat Domestic and International Terrorism 1995, A Durable Peace 2000. *Address:* Office of the Prime Minister, POB 187, 3 Kaplan St, Kiryat Ben-Gurion, Jerusalem 91950 (office); Likud (Consolidation), 38 Rehov King George, Tel-Aviv 61231, Israel (office). *Telephone:* 2-6705555 (PM) (office); 3-5630666 (Likud) (office). *Fax:* 2-5664838 (PM) (office); 3-5282901 (Likud) (office). *E-mail:* pm_eng@pmo.gov.il (office); likud@likud.org.il (office). *Website:* www.pmo.gov.il (office); www.likud.org.il (office).

NETREBKO, Anna; Austrian (b. Russian) singer (soprano); b. 1971, Krasnodar, Russia; ed Rimsky-Korsakov Conservatory; debut at Mariinsky Opera Theatre, St Petersburg 1994, as Susanna; roles include Glinka's Ludmila with Kirov Opera, Gilda in Rigoletto and Kundry in Parsifal at St Petersburg; first appearance at Salzburg Festival 1998; tours with Kirov Opera as Pamina and Bizet's Micaela; sang Gilda at Washington 1999 and New York, Mimi at San Francisco 1999–2000 and New York; concerts with Rotterdam Philharmonic Orchestra include London Proms and Teresa in Benvenuto Cellini, Royal Festival Hall 1999; sang Natasha in War and Peace at St Petersburg and London 2000; other roles include Zerlina and Louisa in Prokovfiev's Betrothal in a Monastery at San Francisco, Rosina, Pamina and Xenia in Boris Godunov, Mozart's Servilia at Covent Garden 2002, Donna Anna in Don Giovanni at Salzburg 2003 and Covent Garden 2007, Violetta in La Traviata at Salzburg 2005, Norina in Don Pasquale in New York 2005, and Elvira in I Puritani 2006; first prize All-Russian Glinka Vocal Competition, Moscow 1993, third prize Rimsky-Korsakov Int. Competition of young opera singers St Petersburg 1996, Costa Diva prize 1998, Golden Sophit prize St Petersburg 1999, Classical BRIT Award for Singer of the Year 2007, named as one of 100 People Who Shape Our World, Time magazine 2007, Musician of the Year, Musical America Awards 2008. *Recordings include:* Glinka's Ruslan and Ludmila, Mozart Album 2006, Souvenirs 2008. *Address:* IMG Artists, The Light Box, 111 Power Road, London, W4 5PY, England (office). *Telephone:* (20) 7957-5843 (office). *Fax:* (20) 8742-8758 (office). *E-mail:* jvanderveen@imgartists.com (office). *Website:* www.imgartists.com (office); www.annanetrebko.com.

NEUBER, Friedel; German banker; *Chairman of the Supervisory Board, RWE AG;* b. 10 July 1935, Rheinhessen; Chair. Man. Bd, Westdeutsche Landesbank Girozentrale (WestLB), Düsseldorf/Münster 1981–2001; Chair. Supervisory Bd Preussag AG, Hanover/Berlin, Deutsche Babcock AG, Oberhausen, LTU Lufttransport Unternehmen GmbH & Co. KG, Düsseldorf, LTU Touristik GmbH, Düsseldorf, WestLB (Europa) AG, Düsseldorf, RWE AG; mem. Supervisory Bd Deutsche Bahn AG, Frankfurt, Douglas Holding AG, Hagen, Friedr. Krupp AG Hoesch-Krupp, Essen, KD Cologne-Düsseldorfer Deutsche Rheinschiffahrt AG, Düsseldorf, Essen, STEAG, Essen, VIAG AG, Munich, Bank Austria, Vienna, UAP SA, Paris; Chair. Bd, Verband öffentlicher Banken e.V., Bonn/Bad Godesberg; Pres. Handelshochschule Leipzig 1997–; mem. Bd of Dirs Deutsche Girozentrale-Deutsche Kommunalbank, Frankfurt and of numerous other bds; Hon. DUniv (Duisburg). *Address:* RWE Aktiengesellschaft, Opernplatz 1, 45128 Essen, Germany (office). *Telephone:* 201-12-00 (office). *Fax:* 201-12-15199 (office). *Website:* www.rwe.com (office).

NEUBERGER, Baroness (Life Peer), cr. 2004; **Rabbi Julia Babette Sarah,** DBE, MA; British rabbi, public health official, writer, politician and broadcaster; b. 27 Feb. 1950, London; d. of the late Walter Schwab and Alice Schwab; m. Anthony John Neuberger 1973; one s. one d.; ed South Hampstead High School, Newnham Coll. Cambridge and Leo Baeck Coll. London; Rabbi, S London Liberal Synagogue 1977–89; Lecturer and Assoc. Fellow, Leo Baeck Coll. 1979–97; Assoc. Newnham Coll. Cambridge 1983–96; Sec. and Chief Exec. The King's Fund 1997–2004; Chancellor Univ. of Ulster 1994–2000; Chair. Rabbinic Conf. Union of Liberal and Progressive Synagogues 1983–85; Camden and Islington Community Health Services NHS Trust 1993–97; mem. Policy Planning Group, Inst. of Jewish Affairs 1986–90, NHS Complaints Review 1993–94, Gen. Medical Council 1993–2001, Council, Univ. Coll. London 1993–97, MRC 1995–2000, Council, Save the Children Fund 1995–96; Visiting Fellow, King's Fund Inst. 1989–91; Chair. Patients Asscn 1988–91, Royal Coll. of Nursing Comm. on Health Service; mem. Nat. Cttee Social Democratic Party 1982–88, Funding Review of BBC 1999, Cttee on Standards in Public Life 2001–04; Civil Service Commr 2001–02; mem. Bd of Visitors, Memorial Church, Harvard Univ. 1994–2000, Bloomberg Prof. of Philanthropy and Public Policy, Divinity School 2006; Trustee Runnymede Trust 1990–97, Imperial War Museum 1999–, British Council, Booker Prize Foundation; other public and charitable appointments; Harkness Fellow, Commonwealth Fund of New York; Visiting Fellow, Harvard Medical School 1991–92; Hon. Fellow, City and Guilds Inst., Mansfield Coll. Oxford; Hon. FRCP 2004; Hon. Fellow, Royal Coll. of Gen. Practioners; Dr hc (Open Univ., City Univ. London, Humberside, Ulster, Stirling, Oxford Brookes, Teesside, Nottingham, Queen's Belfast, Aberdeen). *Television:* Presenter, Choices (BBC) 1986, 1987. *Publications:* The Story of Judaism 1986, Days of Decision (ed., four vols) 1987, Caring for Dying Patients of Different Faiths 1987, Whatever's Happening to Women? 1991, A Necessary End (co-ed. with John White) 1991, Ethics and Healthcare: The Role of Research Ethics Committees in the UK 1992, The Things That Matter 1993, On Being Jewish 1995, Dying Well: A Health Professional's Guide to Enabling a Better Death 1999, Hidden Assets: Values and Decision-Making in the NHS Today (co-ed. with Bill New) 2002, The Moral State We're In 2005, Not Dead Yet: A Manifesto for Old Age 2008; contribs to various books on cultural, religious and ethical factors in nursing; contribs journals and newspapers, including Nursing Times, Jewish Chronicle, Times, Irish Times, The Independent, Guardian, Telegraph, Sunday Express, Mail on Sunday, Evening Standard. *Leisure interests:* riding, sailing, Irish life, opera, setting up the old girls' network, children. *Address:* House of Lords, Westminster, London, SW1 0PW (office). *Telephone:* (1206) 503130 (PA Paola Churchill) (office); (20) 7428-9895 (home); 7711-386974 (mobile). *Fax:* (1206) 503130 (office); (20) 7813-2030 (home). *E-mail:* paolachurchill@hotmail.com (office); jneuberger@blueyonder.co.uk (home).

NEUBERGER, Michael S., PhD, FRS, FMedSci; British research scientist; *Joint Head, Division of Protein and Nucleic Acid Chemistry, Medical Research Council Laboratory of Molecular Biology;* b. 2 Nov. 1953, London; s. of the late Albert Neuberger and of Lilian Neuberger (née Dreyfus); m. Gillian A. Pyman 1991; two s. two d.; ed Westminster School, Trinity Coll. Cambridge, Imperial Coll. London; Sr mem. scientific staff MRC Lab. of Molecular Biology, Cambridge 1980–, Jt Head of Div. of Protein and Nucleic Acid Chem. 2002–; mem. European Molecular Biology Org.; Int. Research Scholar, Howard Hughes Medical Inst.; Hon. Prof., Univ. of Cambridge 2002; Novartis Medal, Biochemical Soc. 2002, William Hardy Bate Prize, Cambridge Philiosophical Soc. 2002, Prix J-P Lecocq (Institut de France) 2002, GlaxoSmithKline Medal, Royal Soc. 2003, Danny-Heinemann Prize, Akad. der Wissenschaft zu Göttingen 2003. *Publications:* papers on molecular immunology in learned journals. *Address:* MRC Laboratory of Molecular Biology, Hills Road, Cambridge, CB2 2QH, England (office). *Telephone:* (1223) 248011 (office). *Fax:* (1223) 412178 (office). *Website:* www2.mrc-lmb.cam.ac.uk/PNAC (office).

NEUHARTH, Allen H.; American journalist and business executive; *Senior Advisory Chairman, The Freedom Forum;* b. 22 March 1924, Eureka, S Dakota; s. of Daniel J. Neuharth and Christina Neuharth; m. 1st Loretta F. Helgeland 1946 (divorced 1972); one s. one d.; m. 2nd Lori Wilson 1973 (divorced 1982); m. 3rd Rachel Fornes 1993; two adopted s. four adopted d.; ed Univ. of S Dakota; reporter, The Associated Press, Sioux Falls, S Dakota 1950–52; launched weekly tabloid SoDak Sports 1952; reporter, rising to Asst Man. Ed., Miami Herald 1954–60; Asst Exec. Ed. Detroit (Mich.) Free Press 1960–63; joined Gannett (newspaper and communications group) 1963, Exec. Vice-Pres. 1966, Pres. and COO 1970, Pres. and CEO 1973, Chair., Pres. and CEO 1979, Chair. and CEO 1984–86, Chair. 1986–89; Dir Starcraft Corpn; Founder and Chair. The Freedom Forum 1991–97, Trustee 1991–98, Sr Advisory Chair. 1998–; Founder Florida Today 1966, USA Today 1982; Chair. and Pres. American Newspaper Publishers' Asscn 1979, 1980; currently writes weekly column for US and int. editions of USA Today; 14 hon. degrees; numerous awards including Katharine Graham Lifetime Achievement Award, Newspaper Asscn of America 2004. *Publication:* Confessions of an S.O.B. 1989. *Address:* c/o Freedom Forum, 1101 Wilson Boulevard, Suite 2300, Arlington, VA 22209, USA. *Website:* www.freedomforum.org.

NEUHAUSER, Duncan von Briesen, PhD, MBA, MHA; American professor of epidemiology and biostatistics; *The Charles Elton Blanchard MD Professor of Health Management, Medical School, Case Western Reserve University;* b. 20 June 1939, Philadelphia, Pa; s. of Edward B. D. Neuhauser and Gernda von Briesen Neuhauser; m. Elinor Toaz Neuhauser 1965; one s. one d.; ed Harvard Univ. and Univs of Michigan and Chicago; Research Assoc. (Instructor), Center for Health Admin. Studies, Univ. of Chicago 1965–70; Asst Prof., then Assoc. Prof., Harvard School of Public Health 1970–79; Assoc. Chair., Program for Health Systems Man., Harvard Business School 1972–79; Consultant in Medicine, Massachusetts Gen. Hosp. 1975–80; Prof. of Epidemiology and Biostatistics, Case Western Reserve Univ. 1979–, Prof. of Organizational Behavior 1979–, Prof. of Medicine 1981–, Keck Foundation Sr Research Scholar 1982–, Prof. of Family Medicine 1990–, Charles Elton Blanchard MD Prof. of Health Man. 1995–; Adjunct Prof. of Nursing, Vanderbilt Univ. 1998–; mem. bioscientific medical staff, Cleveland Metropolitan Gen. Hosp. 1981–; Adjunct mem., Medical Staff, Cleveland Clinic Foundation 1984–99; Co-Dir Health Systems Man. Centre, Case Western Reserve Univ. 1985–; Ed. Medical Care 1983–97, Health Matrix 1982–90; mem. Inst. of Medicine (NAS) 1983–; Visiting Prof. of Health Man., Karolinska Inst., Stockholm, Sweden 2002–; Festschrift Issue of Medical Care, Aug. 1998, The Duncan Neuhauser PhD Endowed Chair in Community Health Improvement created at Case Western Reserve Univ. 2003. *Publications:* (co-author) Health Services in the US 1976, The Efficient Organization 1977, The Physician and Cost Control 1979, Clinical Decision Analysis 1980, Competition, Co-operation or Regulation 1981, The New Epidemiology 1982, Coming of Age 1984, 1995, Clinical CQI 1995, Health Services Management 1997; numerous scientific papers in professional journals. *Leisure interests:* sailing, curling. *Address:* Department of Epidemiology and Biostatistics, Medical School, Case Western Reserve University, 10900 Euclid Avenue, Cleveland, OH 44106-4945 (office); 2655 North Park Boulevard, Cleveland Heights, OH 44106-3622(Winter) (home); Parker Point Road, PO Box 932, Blue Hill, ME 04614, USA (Summer) (home). *Telephone:* (216) 368-3726 (office); (216) 321-1327 (Cleveland Heights) (home); (207) 374-5325 (Blue Hill) (home). *Fax:* (216) 368-3970 (office). *E-mail:* dvn@case.edu (office).

NEUHOFF, Eric; French writer and journalist; b. 1956, *Publications:* Des gens impossibles 1986, Lettre ouverte à François Truffaut 1987, Les Hanches de Laetitia 1989, Actualités françaises 1992, Comme hier 1993, Pas trop près de l'écran 1993, Michel Déon 1994, Barbe à Papa 1996, La Petite française (Prix Interallié) 1997, Champagne! 1998, La Séance du mercredi à 14 heures 1998, Précautions d'usage 2001, Un Bien fou (Grand Prix du Roman) 2001, Rendez-vous à Samarra 2005, Folie dans la famille 2005, Histoire de Franck 2005. *Address:* c/o Albin Michel, 22 rue Huyghers, 75680 Paris Cédex 14, France.

NEUKIRCHEN, Karl Josef, Dr rer. pol; German business executive; b. 17 March 1942, Bonn; Chair. Man. Bd Klöckner-Humboldt-Deutz AG, Cologne –1988, Hösch AG, Dortmund 1991–92; Chair. Supervisory Bd Klöckner-Werke AG Duisburg 1992–95, Dynamit Nobel AG 1994–, FAG Kugelfischer Georg Schäfer AG, Vossloh AG, Sixt AG; CEO Metallgesellschaft AG 1993–2004; ind. consultant to EnBW AG and mem. Supervisory Bd of subsidiary Stadtwerke Düsseldorf AG. *Address:* c/o Supervisory Board, Stadtwerke Düsseldorf AG, Höherweg 100, 40233 Düsseldorf, Germany (office). *Website:* www.swd-ag.de (office).

NEUMANN, Ronald E., BA, MA; American diplomatist; b. 30 Sept. 1944, Washington, DC; s. of Robert G. Neumann; ed Univ. of Calif., Riverside; served as infantry officer, Vietnam 1969–70; entered Foreign Service 1970; tour in Senegal 1971–73; Vice Consul Tabriz, Iran 1973–74, Prin. Officer 1974–76; worked in Office of Southern European Affairs 1976–77; Staff Asst to Asst Sec. for Near Eastern and S Asian Affairs 1977–78; Desk Officer, Jordan 1978–81; Deputy Chief of Mission, Yemen 1981–83; Deputy Dir Bureau of Near Eastern Affairs, Office of Arabian Peninsula Affairs 1983–87; Deputy Chief of Mission in UAE 1987–90; Dir Office of Northern Gulf Affairs (Iran and Iraq) 1991–94; Amb. to Algeria 1994–97; Deputy Asst Sec. of State for Near Eastern Affairs 1997–2000; Amb. to Bahrain 2000–04; political adviser in Iraq 2004; Amb. to Afghanistan 2005–07. *Address:* c/o Department of State, 2201 C Street, NW, Washington, DC 20520, USA (office).

NEUMEIER, John, BA; American choreographer and ballet director; *Chief Choreographer, Ballet Director and Ballettintendant, The Hamburg Ballet;* b. 1942, Milwaukee, Wis.; s. of Albert Neumeier and Lucille Neumeier; ed Marquette Univ., Milwaukee; dance training in Milwaukee, Chicago, Royal Ballet School, London and in Copenhagen with Vera Volkova; soloist, The Stuttgart Ballet 1963; Ballet Dir Frankfurt 1969; Ballet Dir and Chief Choreographer, Hamburg Ballet 1973–, Balletintendant 1997–; Prof., City of Hamburg 1987; f. John Neumeier ballet centre, Hamburg 1989; noted for his creation of new works and original interpretations of well-known ballets; f. a ballet training school in Hamburg 1978; appears as soloist, notably in The Chairs with Marcia Haydée, a ballet cr. for them by M. Béjart; dances lead role of St Matthew Passion 1981–; Hon. mem. Semper Oper, Germany 2002; Bundesverdienstkreuz; Chevalier de la Légion d'honneur, Ordre des Arts et Lettres; Medal of the Kt's Cross of the Danebrog in Gold 2000; Hon. DFA (Marquette); Golden Camera Award for TV series of his Ballet Workshops 1978, Dance Magazine Award 1983, Deutscher Tanzpreis 1988, Diaghilev Prize 1988, Benois de la Danse 1992, Medal of Honour (City of Tokyo) 1994, Carina-Ari Gold Medal (Sweden) 1994, Nijinsky Medal (Polish Ministry of Culture) 1996, Min-On Int. Award for Arts (Tokyo) 1997, European Prince Henrik of Denmark Award 2000, Danza Magazine Award for production of Messiah 2001, Bayerischers Theaterpreis for production of Nijinsky 2001, Gold Mask (Russia) 2002, Wilhelm Hausen Prize (Denmark) 2002, Medal for Art and Science, Hamburg 2003. *Works choreographed include:* A Midsummer Night's Dream (Mendelssohn/Ligeti), ballets to the Mahler symphonies, Le Sacre (Stravinsky), The Lady of the Camellias (Chopin), Bach's St Matthew Passion, A Streetcar Named Desire (Prokofiev/Schnittke), Messiah (Handel/Pärt), Nijinsky (Chopin/Rimsky-Korsakov/Shostakovich), Giselle (Adam), Sounds of Empty Pages (Schnittke), Voice of the Night (Britten), Winterreise (Schubert/Zender), The Seagull (Shostakovich), Glennie (Tchaikovsky/Scriabin), Préludes CV (Auerbach), Death in Venice (Bach/Wagner). *Films:* The Lady of the Camellias, Illusions Like Swan Lake (DVD). *Television:* Wendung:

String Quintet in C Major by Franz Schubert, Legend of Joseph, The Chairs (WDR), Third Symphony of Gustav Mahler (ZDF), Othello (ZDF), Scenes of Childhood (NDR3). *Publications:* John Neumeier Unterwegs 1972, John Neumeier und das Hamburg Ballett 1977, Matthäus-Passion 1983, John Neumeier Traumwege 1980, 10 Jahre – John Neumeier und das Hamburg Ballett 1983, 20 Jahre – John Neumeier und das Hamburg Ballett 1993, My Favourite Pictures for John 1998, John Neumeier 2004. *Address:* Hamburg Ballet, Ballettzentrum Hamburg, Caspar-Voght-Str. 54, 20535 Hamburg, Germany (office). *Telephone:* (40) 211188-11 (office). *Fax:* (40) 211188-18 (office). *E-mail:* presse@hamburgballett.de (office). *Website:* www.hamburgballett.de (office).

NEURRISSE, André, DenD, DèsScEcon; French historian and economist; b. 21 April 1916, Pomarez; m. Louise Marie Verdier 1942; two d.; ed Univs of Bordeaux and Paris; civil servant, Ministry of Finance 1941–58; Treas.-Paymaster Gen. 1958–82; Consultant to IMF, World Bank and UN 1982–; Man. Dir Soc. d'Etudes et des Participations 1984–89; Man. Dir Banque Internationale de Financement et de Négociation 1985–91; Pres., Dir-Gen. Union Commerciale de crédit multiservices 1989–91; Officier des Palmes académiques 1964, de la Légion d'honneur 1970; Commdr, Ordre Nat. du Mérite 1980; Médaille d'Or de L'Educ. Physique et des Sports 1958, Lauréat de l'Inst. (Prix Joseph Dutens) 1964. *Publications:* Précis de droit budgétaire 1961, La comptabilité économique française 1963, Les règlements internationaux 1972, Histoire du Franc 1974, Les jeux de casino 1977, Histoire de l'impôt 1978, L'économie sociale 1983, Le Trésorier-Payeur Général 1986, Le Franc C.F.A. 1987, Les jeux d'argent et de hasard 1990, Deux mille ans d'impôts 1994, Histoire de la Fiscalité en France 1996; contribs. to collective works and numerous articles in La Revue du trésor. *Address:* 9 rue Docteur Blanche, 75016 Paris, France. *Telephone:* 1-45-25-89-32. *Fax:* 1-45-25-89-32.

NEUVILLE, Colette Jeannine Michelle Claude, LenD; French organization executive and economist; *President, l'Association de défense des actionnaires minoritaires (Adam);* b. 21 Jan. 1937, Coutances (Manche); d. of Pierre Wacongne and Suzanne Wacongne (née Piquot); m. Christian Neuville 1961; one s. four d.; ed Lycée de jeunes filles et Ecole Saint-Julien, Le Mans, Faculté de droits, Caen, Faculté de droit et de sciences économiques, Paris; economist with Kléber Colombes group 1959–60; with NATO 1960–63; with Nat. Office of Irrigation, Rabat, Morocco 1963–68; with Financial Agency, Loire Bretagne 1968–69; Founder-Pres. l'Asscn de défense des actionnaires minoritaires (Adam) 1991–; mem. Supervisory Council Paribas 1995–2000; non-Exec. Dir Eurotunnel plc 2005–, mem. Jt Bd Eurotunnel 2005–, Dir Eurotunnel SA 2007–. *Leisure interests:* music, walking in the mountains. *Address:* Adam, 4 rue Montescot, BP 208, 28004 Chartres cedex, France.

NEUVO, Yrjö A., PhD, FIEEE; Finnish electronics engineer and academic; *Technology Advisor, Nokia Corporation;* b. 21 July 1943, Turku; s. of Olavi Neuvo and Aune Neuvo (née Vaisala); m. Tuula Halsas 1968; two s. one d.; ed Cornell Univ., NY, USA and Helsinki Univ. of Tech.; Acting Prof., Helsinki Univ. of Tech. 1975–76; Prof. of Electronics, Tampere Univ. of Tech. 1976–92; Sr Vice-Pres., Tech. and Chief Tech. Officer Nokia Corpn 1993–; Sr Research Fellow Acad. of Finland 1979–80, Research Prof. 1984–; Visiting Prof., Univ. of California 1981–82; Commdr Order of Lion of Finland 1992; Hon. MD (Tampere Univ. of Tech.) 1992; IEEE Bicentennial Award 1986, Asscn in Finland Hon. Prize 1988, Nokia Prize 1989. *Publications:* more than 300 scientific publs on computer eng and new technologies. *Address:* Nokia Corporation, Keilalahdentie 4, 00045 Espoo, Finland (office). *Telephone:* (0) 18071 (office). *Fax:* (0) 176015 (office). *Website:* www.nokia.com (office).

NEVANLINNA, (Eero) Olavi, DipEng, DTech; Finnish academic; *Professor of Mathematics, Institute of Mathematics, Helsinki University of Technology;* b. 17 April 1948, Helsinki; m. Marja Lähdesmäki 1968; three s. one d.; ed Helsinki Univ. of Technology; Asst Prof. of Math., Helsinki Univ. of Tech. 1971–74, Prof. 1980–, Vice-Rector 2003–05; Sr Researcher Acad. of Finland 1975–77; Assoc. Prof. of Applied Math., Oulu Univ. 1978–79; Research Prof., Acad. of Finland 1986–92; Visiting Prof. at several US univs and at ETH, Zürich; Chair. Rolf Nevanlinna Inst. 1989–90; Chair. Supervisory Bd Suomi Mutual Life Assurance Co. 1996–98; Pres. Int. Council for Industrial and Applied Math. 1999–2003, Past Pres. 2003–05; mem. Bd Pohjola Insurance Co. Ltd 1997–99; mem. Editorial Bd BIT, Finnish Acad. of Tech. Sciences 1984, Finnish Acad. of Sciences and Letters 1986, Nat. Cttee in Math. 1984–. *Publications:* Convergence of Iterations for Linear Equations 1993, Meromorphic Functions and Linear Algebra 2003. *Address:* Institute of Mathematics, Helsinki University of Technology, PO Box 1100, 02015 HUT, Helsinki, Finland (office). *Telephone:* (9) 4513034 (office). *Fax:* (9) 4513016 (office). *Website:* www.tkk.fi (office).

NEVES, José Maria Pereira, BA; Cape Verde politician; *Prime Minister;* b. 28 March 1960, Santa Catarina; three s.; ed São Paulo School of Business and Admin; consultant in organizational devt and human resources man., Cape Verde 1987–96; Dir Nat. Public Admin Training Centre 1988–89; Coordinator Admin Reform and Modernization Projects 1987–88; mem. Parl. 1996–; Mayor of Santa Catarina 2000–01; Chair. Partido Africano da Independência de Cabo Verde 2000–; Prime Minister of Cape Verde 2001–; Asst Prof. of Man., Higher Educ. Inst.; Marechal Floriana Peixoto Merit Award, Brazil 2005, Patrons of Century Ruby Cross 2006. *Leisure interests:* reading, walking, music. *Address:* Office of the Prime Minister, Palácio do Governo, Várzea, CP 16, Praia, Santiago, Cape Verde (office). *Telephone:* 2610411 (office). *Fax:* 2613099 (office). *E-mail:* gab.imprensa@gpm.gov.cv (office). *Website:* www.primeiroministro.cv (office).

NEVES DA CUNHA, Aécio; Brazilian politician; *Governor of Minas Gerais;* b. 10 March 1960, Belo Horizonte; s. of Aécio Ferreira da Cunha and Inês

Maria Neves; grand s. of fmr Brazilian Pres. Tancredo Neves; m. (divorced); one d.; ed Pontifícia Universidade Católica de Minas Gerais; Sec. to Tancredo Neves 1980–85; Fed. Deputy for Minas Gerais 1986–2002; Co-f. PSDB (Partido da Social Democracia Brasileira) 1988, Leader in Chamber of Deputies 1997–2001, Pres. Chamber of Deputies 2001–02; Governor of Minas Gerais 2002–. *Address:* Palácio dos Despachos, Praça José Mendes Júnior, Funcionários, 30140-912 Belo Horizonte, Minas Gerais, Brazil (office). *Telephone:* (31) 3250 6011 (office). *Fax:* (31) 3250 6339 (office). *Website:* www.mg.gov.br (office).

NEVILLE, John, OBE; British actor and theatre director; b. 2 May 1925, Willesden, London; s. of Reginald D. Neville and Mabel L. Fry; m. Caroline Hooper 1949; three s. three d.; ed Chiswick Co. Grammar School and Royal Acad. of Dramatic Art, London; with Bristol Old Vic Co., London 1953, played Othello, Iago, Hamlet, Aguecheek and Richard II; mem. Chichester Theatre Co. 1962; created part of Alfie (Alfie by Bill Naughton), London 1963; Dir Nottingham Playhouse 1963–68, Newcastle Playhouse 1967; Drama Adviser to Howard and Wyndham Ltd; in musical Mr & Mrs 1968; series of TV plays 1968; presented four plays at Fortune Theatre, London with the Park Theatre Co.; appeared in the Apple Cart, Mermaid Theatre, London 1970, The Beggar's Opera, Chichester 1972, Happy Days, Nat. Theatre, London 1977, The School for Scandal, Nat. Theatre 1990, The Dance of Death, Almeida 1995, Beethoven's Tenth, Chichester 1996, Krapp's Last Tape, Nottingham Playhouse 1999; went to Canada 1973; staged The Rivals, Nat. Arts Theatre, Ottawa; Dir opera Don Giovanni, Festival Canada, Ottawa; played Prospero (The Tempest), Judge Brack (Hedda Gabler), Sir George Croft (Mrs. Warren's Profession), in Sherlock Holmes, New York 1975; Artistic Dir of Citadel Theatre, Edmonton, Alberta 1973–78; Artistic Dir Neptune Theatre, Halifax, Nova Scotia 1978–83; with Stratford Festival Theatre, Ont. 1983–89, Artistic Dir 1985–89; Dir Hamlet 1986, Mother Courage, Othello 1987, Three Sisters 1989; film (in title role) Adventures of Baron Munchausen 1987–88; acted in School for Scandal, Nat. Theatre 1990; Hon. Prof. of Drama, Nottingham Univ. 1967–; Hon. Dr Dramatic Arts (Lethbridge Univ., Alberta) 1979; Hon. DFA (Nova Scotia Coll. of Art and Design) 1981; Dr hc (Ryerson Univ.) 1999. *Films acted in include:* Mr Topaz, Oscar Wilde, Billy Budd, A Study in Terror, Adventures of Baron Munchausen. *Leisure interests:* watching football, listening to music (all kinds), thinking about gardening. *Address:* 24 Wellesley Street West, #511, Toronto, Ont., M4Y 2X6, Canada.

NEVO, Ruth, PhD; Israeli painter and fmr professor of English literature; b. 8 July 1924, Johannesburg, SA; d. of Benjamin Weinbren and Henrietta Weinbren (née Goldsmith); m. Natan Nevo 1952; three s.; ed Univ. of the Witwatersrand, Johannesburg and Hebrew Univ., Jerusalem; tutor, Dept of English, Hebrew Univ. 1952, Prof. 1973; Renee Lang Prof. of Humanities 1982–87; full-time painter 1987–; nine solo exhbns 1987–2005; mem. Israel Acad. 1985–, Israel Asscn of Painters and Sculptors 1989–. *Publications:* The Dial of Virtue 1963, Tragic Form in Shakespeare 1972, Comic Transformations in Shakespeare 1980, Shakespeare's Other Language 1987; trans. Selected Poems by Bialik 1981, Travels by Amichai 1986, The Challenge of Poetry 2008. *Address:* Hehalutz 22, Jerusalem (home); c/o Department of English, Hebrew University, Mount Scopus, Jerusalem, Israel. *Telephone:* (2) 6523752 (home). *E-mail:* rnevo@cc.huji.ac.il (home). *Website:* www.intopoetry.com (home).

NEWALL, James Edward Malcolm (Ted), OC, BComm; Canadian business executive; *Chairman, NOVA Chemicals Corporation;* b. 20 Aug. 1935, Holden, Alberta; m. Margaret Elizabeth Lick; ed Prince Albert Coll. Inst., Univ. of Saskatchewan; joined Du Pont Canada Inc. 1957, various posts in marketing and gen. man. in fibres business, leading to Dir Fibres Group 1972, Vice-Pres., Corp. Devt 1974, Marketing 1975, Exec. Vice-Pres. 1975, Dir 1976, Pres. and CEO 1978–89, Chair. 1979, Chair. and CEO du Pont Canada –1994 and responsible for E.I. du Pont's int. businesses outside Canada and USA 1989–91, Sr Vice-Pres. E.I. du Pont de Nemours Agricultural Products 1989–91; Vice-Chair., CEO and Dir NOVA Chemicals Corpn 1991–98, Chair. 1998–; Chair. Canadian Pacific Railway Ltd, Maritime Transport Services 1994–, Newall & Assocs 1998–; Chair. Business Council on Nat. Issues; Dir Alcan Inc., BCE Inc., The Molson Cos Ltd, Pratt & Whitney Canada Inc., The Royal Bank of Canada; Chair. Business Council on Nat. Issues; fmr Chair. and Dir Conf. Bd of Canada; mem. Advisory Group to Prime Minister on exec. compensation in the public service. *Address:* NOVA Chemicals Corporation, 645 Seventh Avenue, SW, POB 2518, Calgary, Alberta T2P 5; Canadian Pacific Railway, Gulf Canada Square, 401-9th Avenue, SW, Calgary, Alberta T2P 4Z4; Newall & Associates, 2015 Bankers Hall, 855 2nd Street, SW, Calgary, Alberta, T2P 4J7, Canada (office).

NEWBERY, David Michael Garrood, PhD, ScD, FBA; British economist and academic; *Professor of Applied Economics, University of Cambridge;* b. 1 June 1943, Bucks.; m. Terri E. Apter 1975; two d.; ed Portsmouth Grammar School, Trinity Coll. Cambridge; Economist, Treasury of Tanzanian Govt 1965–66; Asst Lecturer, Faculty of Econs and Politics, Univ. of Cambridge 1966–71, Lecturer 1971–86, Reader in Econs 1986–88, Prof. of Applied Econs 1988–, Dir Dept of Applied Econs 1988–2003, Fellow, Churchill Coll. 1966–; Div. Chief, World Bank 1981–83; Fellow, Econometric Soc. 1989; Vice-Pres. European Econ. Asscn 1994–95, Pres. 1996; hon. degree (Antwerp) 2004; Frisch Medal, Econometric Soc. 1990, Harry Johnson Prize (jtly), Canadian Econ. Asscn 1993, Int. Asscn for Energy Econs 2002 Outstanding Contribs to the Profession Award 2003. *Publications:* Project Appraisal in Practice (co-author) 1976, The Theory of Commodity Price Stabilization: A Study in the Economics of Risk (with J. E. Stiglitz) 1981, The Theory of Taxation for Developing Countries (with N. H. Stern) 1987, Hungary: An Economy in Transition (with I. Székely) 1993, Tax and Benefit Reform in Central and Eastern Europe 1995, A European Market for Electricity? (co-author) 1999, Privatization, Restructuring and Regulation of Network Utilities 2000; numerous articles. *Address:* Faculty of Economics, Sidgwick Avenue, Cambridge, CB3 9DE (office); 9 Huntingdon Road, Cambridge, CB3 0HH, England (home). *Telephone:* (1223) 335248 (office). *Fax:* (1223) 335299 (office). *E-mail:* david.newbery@econ.cam.ac.uk (office). *Website:* www.econ.cam.ac.uk/dae/people/newbery/index.html (office).

NEWBIGGING, David Kennedy, OBE; British business executive; *Chairman, Cancer Research UK;* b. 19 Jan. 1934, Tientsin, China; s. of the late D. L. Newbigging and of L. M. Newbigging; m. Carolyn S. Band 1968; one s. two d.; ed Oundle School; joined Jardine, Matheson & Co., Ltd 1954, Dir 1967, Man. Dir 1970, Chair. and Sr Man. Dir 1975–83; Chair. Hong Kong & Kowloon Wharf & Godown Co., Ltd 1970–80; Chair. and Man. Dir Hong Kong Land Co., Ltd 1975–83; Dir Hong Kong & Shanghai Banking Corpn 1975–83; Dir Hong Kong Electric Holdings Ltd 1975–83, Chair. 1982–83; Dir Hong Kong Telephone Co., Ltd 1975–83; Chair. Jardine, Fleming & Co., Ltd 1975–83; Dir Rennies Consolidated Holdings Ltd 1975–83, Safmarine and Rennies Holdings Ltd 1984–85, Provincial Insurance PLC 1984–86 (Deputy Chair. Provincial Group PLC 1985–91); Deputy Chair. Ivory & Sime PLC 1990–95, Chair. 1992–95 (Dir 1987–95); Dir NM UK (Chair. 1990–93), Rentokil Group PLC 1986–94 (Chair. 1987–94), PACCAR (UK) Ltd 1986–97, Mason Best Int. Ltd 1986–90 (Chair. 1987–90), Int. Financial Markets Trading Ltd 1986–93, United Meridian Corpn 1987–97, Thai Holdings Ltd 1989–91, Merrill Lynch Inc., USA 1997–, Ocean Energy Inc., USA 1998–, PACCAR Inc., USA 1999–; Deputy Chair. Benchmark Group PLC 1996–2004; Chair. Redfearn PLC March–Dec. 1988, Faupel PLC 1994–2005 (Dir 1989–2005), London Capital Holdings PLC March–Dec. 1994, Talbot Holdings Ltd 2003–07; Dir Wah Kwong Shipping Holdings Ltd 1992–99, Lloyd's Market Bd 1993–95, Friends' Provident Life Office 1993–2001 (Deputy Chair. 1996–98, Chair. 1998–2001, Chair. Friends Provident PLC 2001–05); Chair. Equitas Holdings Ltd 1995–98, Maritime Transport Services Ltd 1993–95; Trustee Cancer Research UK 2001–, Deputy Chair. Council of Trustees 2002–04, Chair. 2004–; Trustee, King Mahendra UK Trust for Nature Conservation 1988–; Chair. of Trustees, Wilts Community Foundation 1991–97; Chair. of Council, Mission to Seafarers (fmrly Mission to Seaman) 1993–; mem. Legis. Council of Hong Kong 1978–82, mem. Exec. Council 1980–84; mem. Int. Council, Morgan Guaranty Trust Co. of New York 1977–85, Supervisory Bd DAF Trucks NV 1997–99; mem. British Coal Corpn (fmrly Nat. Coal Bd) 1984–87, CIN Man. 1985–87; Deputy Lt of Wiltshire 1994–, High Sheriff of Wiltshire 2003–04. *Leisure interests:* most outdoor sports, Chinese art. *Address:* Cancer Research UK, 61 Lincoln's Inn Fields, London, WC2A 3PX, England (office). *Telephone:* (20) 7061-8178 (office). *E-mail:* david.newbigging@cancer.org.uk (office).

NEWBY, Sir Howard Joseph, KCB, CBE, BA, PhD, AcSS, FRSA; British sociologist, academic and university vice-chancellor; *Vice-Chancellor, University of Liverpool;* b. 10 Dec. 1947, Derby; s. of Alfred J. Newby and Constance A. Potts; Lecturer in Sociology, Univ. of Essex 1972–75, Sr Lecturer 1975–79; Prof. of Sociology, Univ. of Wis. 1979–83, Univ. of Essex 1983–88; Chair. Econ. & Social Research Council 1988–94, Chief Exec. 1994;; Vice-Chancellor, Univ. of Southampton 1994–2001; mem. Rural Devt Comm. 1991–99, S. & W. Regional Health Authority 1994–96, European Sciences and Technology Asscn 1997–; Chair. Centre for Exploitation of Science and Tech. 1995, Cttee of Vice-Chancellors and Prins 1999–2001; Pres. British Asscn for the Advancement of Science 2001–02; Chief Exec. Higher Educ. Funding Council for England 2001–06; Vice-Chancellor Univ. of the West of England 2006–07, of Univ. of Liverpool 2008–; visiting appointments include Univs of New South Wales 1976, Sydney, Australia 1976, Wisconsin, USA 1977–78, Newcastle-upon-Tyne 1983–84; ten hon. degrees. *Publications include:* Community Studies (jtly) 1971, The Deferential Worker 1977, Property, Paternalism and Power (jtly) 1978, Green and Pleasant Land? 1979, The Problem of Sociology (jtly) 1983, Country Life 1987, The Countryside in Question 1988, Social Class in Modern Britain 1988 (jtly), The National Trust: The Next 100 Years 1995. *Leisure interests:* family life, gardening, Derby County, railway enthusiasms. *Address:* Office of the Vice-Chancellor, University of Liverpool, Liverpool, L69 3BX, England (office). *Telephone:* (151) 794-2000 (office). *E-mail:* Howard.Newby@liverpool.ac.uk (office). *Website:* www.liv.ac.uk (office).

NEWCOMBE, John David, AO, OBE; Australian fmr professional tennis player; b. 23 May 1944, Sydney; s. of George Ernest Newcombe and Lillian Newcombe; m. Angelika Pfannenberg (fmr German pro tennis player) 1966; one s. two d.; ed Sydney Church of England Grammar School; winner of Wimbledon Singles Championship 1967 (last amateur), 1970, 1971, US Singles Championship 1967, 1973, Australia Singles Championship 1973, 1975, World Championship Tennis Crown 1974, Wimbledon Doubles Championship 1965–66, 1968–70, 1974; won 73 pro titles; played with Australian Davis Cup Team 1963–67, 1973–76, Capt. (non-playing) 1994–2000; set up a tennis camp, the John Newcombe Tennis Ranch, in Texas in 1968; Pres. Asscn of Tennis Professionals (Int.) 1976–78, Nat. Australia Day Council 1981–91; Chair. Player Devt Bd Tennis Australia 1985–94; Hon. Life mem. Australian Wheelchair Tennis Asscn; mem. Bd McDonald's System of Australia; Dr hc (Bond, Queensland) 1999; inducted Int. Tennis Hall of Fame 1986. *Television:* has appeared as a commentator for various networks on numerous tennis tournaments in Australia, America and the UK. *Publications:* The Family Tennis Book 1975, The Young Tennis Player 1981, Bedside Tennis 1983, Newk 2002. *Leisure interests:* skiing, waterskiing, golf, fishing. *Address:* c/o Tennis Australia, Batman Avenue, Melbourne, Vic. 3000, Australia.

NEWELL, Frances Mary, FRSA, FCSD; British design consultant; *Founder, The Sorrell Foundation;* b. 19 Jan. 1947, Surrey; d. of the late Alexander C. Newell and of Julie S. Newell; m. John William Sorrell 1974; two s. one d.; Founder and Chair. Newell & Sorrell (identity & design consultants, merged with Interbrand 1997) 1976–97; apptd Group Creative Dir Interbrand Newell and Sorrell 1997; Chair. City & Guilds Nat. Advisory Cttee on Art, Craft and Design 1994–96, mem. Colour Group 1996–, City & Guilds Sr Awards Cttee 1996–; f. The Sorrell Foundation 1999; Bd Dir Royal Acad. Enterprises 1996–99; mem. Exec. Cttee Mencap Blue Sky Appeal 1996–98, Advisory Bd of Nat. Museum of Photography, Film and TV; 11 DBA Design Effectiveness Awards, 5 Silver D&ADs, 5 Clios, 1 Grand Award for British Airways Corp. Identity and 5 Gold Awards in New York Festivals, 2 Art Directors' Club of Europe Awards. *Publications:* joinedupdesignforschools (with John Sorrell) 2005. *Leisure interests:* art, travel, gardening. *Address:* The Sorrell Foundation, Somerset House, The Strand, London, WC2R 1LA, England. *Website:* www.thesorrellfoundation.com.

NEWELL, Mike; British film director; b. 1942, St Albans, Herts.; s. of Terence William Newell and Mollie Louise Newell; m. Bernice Stegers 1979; one s. one d.; ed Univ. of Cambridge; trainee Dir Granada TV 1963; Dir European premiere of Tennessee Williams' The Kingdom of the Earth, Bristol Old Vic. *Films as director:* The Man in the Iron Mask 1976, The Awakening 1979, Bad Blood 1980, Dance with a Stranger (Prix de la Jeunesse, Cannes) 1984, The Good Father 1985, Amazing Grace and Chuck 1986, Soursweet 1987, Common Ground 1990, Enchanted April 1991, Into the West 1992, Four Weddings and a Funeral (BAFTA Award for Best Film and Best Achievement in Direction 1995, Cesar Award for Foreign Film) 1994, An Awfully Big Adventure 1994, Donnie Brasco 1997, Pushing Tin 1998, Mona Lisa Smile 2003, Harry Potter and the Goblet of Fire 2005, Love in the Time of Cholera 2007. *Films as executive producer:* Photographing Fairies 1997, 200 Cigarettes 1999, Best Laid Plans 1999, High Fidelity 2000, Traffic 2000, I Capture the Castle 2003. *TV Films:* Ready when you are, Mr McGill, Tales out of School, Birth of a Nation (Prix Futura, Berlin), The Melancholy Hussar, Lost Your Tongue, Baa Baa Black Sheep, Common Ground (for CBS), Blood Feud (for Fox) 1983. *TV work includes:* Mr and Mrs Bureaucrat, Destiny, The Gift of Friendship, Brassneck (play), Just your Luck (play). *Leisure interests:* reading (anything but fiction), walking. *Address:* c/o ICM, Oxford House, 76 Oxford Street, London, W1N 0AX, England.

NEWHOUSE, Samuel I., Jr; American publishing executive; *Chairman and CEO, Advance Publications, Inc.;* b. 8 Nov. 1927; s. of the late Samuel Irving Newhouse and Mitzi Newhouse (née Epstein); m. 1st Jane Franke (divorced); three c.; m. 2nd Victoria Newhouse; took over father's Staten Island Advance co. 1922 and built newspaper and magazine chain; Publr Vogue magazine 1964; Chair. Condé Nast Publs Inc., New York 1975–, also Chair. and CEO Advance Publs Inc., New York 1979–; fmr mem. Bd NY Museum of Modern Art; Henry Johnson Fisher Award, Magazine Publishers' Asscn 1985. *Address:* Advance Publications, Inc. 950 Fingerboard Road, Staten Island, NY 10305, USA (office). *Telephone:* (212) 286-2860 (office). *Fax:* (212) 981-1456 (office). *Website:* www.advance.net (office).

NEWLAND, Martin, BA (Hist), MA (Theol); British newspaper editor; *Editor-in-Chief, The National;* b. 1961, Nigeria; m.; four c.; ed Univ. of London; reporter The Catholic Herald 1986–89; night reporter The Daily Telegraph 1989, News Ed. mid-1990s, Ed. 2003–05; Deputy Ed. The National Post, Canada 1998–2003; founder and Ed.-in-Chief, The National newspaper, UAE 2008–. *Leisure interest:* working out in the gym. *Website:* thenational.ae (office).

NEWMAN, Edwin Harold; American journalist; b. 25 Jan. 1919, New York; s. of Myron Newman and Rose Parker Newman; m. Rigel Grell 1944; one d.; ed Univ. of Wisconsin, Louisiana State Univ.; Washington Bureau, Int. News Service 1941, United Press 1941–42, 1945–46; USN 1942–45; CBS News, Washington, DC 1947–49; freelance, London 1949–52; NBC News, London Bureau 1952–, Rome Bureau 1957–58, Paris Bureau 1958–61; Corresp. and Commentator, NBC News, New York 1961–83; Moderator of Presidential Cand. debates Ford-Carter 1976, Reagan-Mondale 1984; Columnist, King Features Syndicate 1984–89; freelance journalist and lecturer; appeared as self in numerous TV comedy series and films including The Pelican Brief and Spies Like Us; Chevalier, Légion d'honneur and other decorations; Peabody Award, Overseas Press Club Award, Emmy Award, Univ. of Mo. School of Journalism Award. *Publications:* Strictly Speaking 1974, A Civil Tongue 1976, Sunday Punch 1979, I Must Say 1988; articles for Punch, Esquire, Atlantic, Harper's, New York Times, Saturday Review, Chicago Tribune, TV Guide, Sports Illustrated. *Leisure interests:* music, reading. *Address:* c/o Richard Fulton Inc., 66 Richfield Street, Plainview, NY 11803, USA.

NEWMAN, Frank, BA; American banker; *Vice-Chairman, The Broad Center for the Management of School Systems;* b. 20 April 1942, Quincy, Mass; m. Lizabeth Newman; one s.; ed Harvard Univ.; Man. Peat Marwick Livingston & Co. 1966–69; Vice-Pres. Citicorp 1969–73; Exec. Vice-Pres., Chief Financial Officer Wells Fargo Bank 1973–86; Vice-Chair., Chief Financial Officer Bank America Corp. 1986–93; Under-Sec., Deputy Sec. Treasury Dept 1993–95; Sr Vice-Chair. Bankers Trust Co. 1995–, Chair., CEO, Pres. 1996–99, resgnd as Chair., now Chair. Emer.; currently Vice-Chair. The Broad Center for Man. of School Systems, LA; mem. Bd Deutsche Bank 1999, Dow Jones & Co., Korea First Bank, GUS; Alexander Hamilton Award (US Treasury Dept). *Address:* The Broad Center for the Management of School Systems, 10900 Wilshire Boulevard, Los Angeles, CA 90024, USA (office). *Telephone:* (310) 954-5080 (office). *Fax:* (310) 954-5081 (office). *Website:* www.broadcenter.org.

NEWMAN, Jocelyn Margaret, LLB; Australian public official and fmr politician; b. 8 July 1937; ed Melbourne Univ.; Senator (Liberal Party) for Tasmania 1986–2002; Shadow Minister for Defence, Science and Personnel 1988–92, Veterans' Affairs 1990–92; Shadow Minister Assisting Leader on Status of Women 1989–93; Shadow Minister for the Aged and Veterans' Affairs 1992–93; Shadow Minister for Family Health, Shadow Minister Assisting Leader on Family Matters, Chair. Health, Welfare and Veterans' Affairs Group 1993–94; Shadow Minister for Defence 1994–96; Minister for Social Security and Minister Assisting Prime Minister on Status of Women 1996–98, for Family and Community Services and Minister Assisting Prime Minister on Status of Women 1998–2001; mem. Bd Australian Strategic Policy Inst. 2001–; mem. Australian War Memorial Council 2002–. *Address:* Australian Strategic Policy Institute, Level 2, Arts House, 40 Macquarie Street, Barton ACT 2600, Australia (office); POB 146, Red Hill, ACT 2063, Australia. *Website:* www.aspi.otr.au (office).

NEWMAN, Sir Kenneth (Leslie), Kt, GBE, QPM, LLB, FIBM; British police officer and academic; b. 15 Aug. 1926; s. of John William and Florence Newman; m. Eileen Lilian Newman 1949; one s. one d.; ed Univ. of London; with RAF 1942–46; mem. Palestine Police 1946–48; with Metropolitan Police, London 1948–73, Commdr New Scotland Yard 1972; with Royal Ulster Constabulary 1973–79, Sr Deputy Chief Constable 1973, Chief Constable 1976–79; Commandant, Police Staff Coll. 1980–82; Insp. of Constabulary 1980–82; Commr Metropolitan Police 1982–87 (retd); Prof. of Law, Bristol Univ. 1987–88; Registrar Imperial Soc. of Kts Bachelor 1991–98; Dir Control Risks 1987–92; Chair. Disciplinary Cttee, Security Systems Inspectorate, British Security Industry Asscn 1987–95, Asscn for Prevention of Theft in Shops 1987–91; Pres. Asscn of Police and Public Security Suppliers 1993–2000; Vice-Pres. Defence Mfrs Asscn 1987–2000; Trustee Community Action Trust 1987–99, World Humanity Action Trust 1993–98; CIMgt 1977; Patron, The Police Foundation; Queen's Police Medal 1982, COTY Award, British Asscn of Communicators in Business 1984, numerous foreign decorations. *Leisure interests:* bridge, walking. *Address:* c/o The Police Foundation, First Floor, Park Place, 12 Lawn Lane, London, SW8 1UD, England.

NEWMAN, Kevin, BA; Canadian broadcast journalist; *Anchor and Executive Editor, Global National with Kevin Newman;* b. Toronto; m. Cathy; one s. one d.; ed Univ. of Western Ont.; Corresp., Global News, Global TV Network, Toronto, Parl. Bureau, Ottawa 1983–87; later with CTV Nat. News, CBC The National, CBC Midday; joined ABC (American Broadcasting Corpn) News, New York 1994, positions including Substitute Anchor and Corresp., World News Tonight with Peter Jennings, Sr Corresp., Nightline, Co-Host, Good Morning America; Anchor and Exec. Ed., Global National with Kevin Newman, Global TV Network, BC 2001–; fmr Instructor in Broadcast Journalism, Ryerson Univ. School of Journalism; Rogers Communication Lecturer, Univ. of Western Ont. 1999; Emmy Award for Outstanding News and Documentary Program Achievement 2000, Emmy Award for Outstanding Coverage of a Breaking News Story 2000, George Foster Peabody Award for ABC 2000 Millennium Coverage 2000, Women's Sport Foundation Award for Outstanding Network TV Journalism 2000, Leo Award for Best Anchor 2002, 2003, Canadian Radio and TV News Dirs Asscn Best Breaking News Coverage Award 2001, Best Continuing Coverage Award 2001. *Address:* Global National with Kevin Newman, Global Television Network, 7850 Enterprise Street, Burnaby, BC V5A 1V7, Canada (office). *Telephone:* (604) 420-2288 (office). *Fax:* (604) 422-6427 (office). *Website:* www.canada.com/globaltv (office).

NEWMAN, Maurice Lionel, AM; Australian banker and business executive; *Chairman, Australian Stock Exchange;* b. 20 March 1938, Ilford, England; s. of J. Newman; m. 1st 1963 (divorced); two s.; m. 2nd Jeanette Newman 1994; ed Univ. of Sydney; Partner, Bain and Co. 1966–73, Man. Dir Bain and Co. Group 1983–85; Exec. Chair. Deutsche Bank Australia Group (fmrly Deutsche Morgan Grenfell Group) 1985–; Chair. Australian Stock Exchange Ltd 1994–, Australian-Taiwan Business Council 1995–, E Asian and Oceanic Stock Exchanges Fed. 1995–96, Axiom Funds Man. Ltd 1997–, Benchmark Securities Man. Ltd 1997–, Commercial Investment Trust 1998–, Financial Sector, Advisory Council 1998–; Dir Financial Futures Market 1990–, Securities Industry Research Centre Australia; mem. Australian Inst. of Co. Dirs; Trustee Stock Exchange Superannuation and Accumulation Fund 1990–; mem. Bd of Dirs Australian Broadcasting Corpn —2004. *Leisure interests:* cycling, horse riding, tennis. *Address:* Australian Stock Exchange Ltd, Level 9, 20 Bridge Street, Sydney, NSW 2001 (office); 35 Burran Avenue, Mosman, NSW 2088, Australia (home). *Telephone:* (2) 9321-4000 (office). *Fax:* (2) 9235-0056 (office). *Website:* www.asx.com.au.

NEWMAN, Nanette; British actress and writer; b. Northampton; d. of Sidney Newman and Ruby Newman; m. Bryan Forbes (q.v.) 1955; two d.; ed Sternhold Coll., London, Italia Conti Stage School, Royal Acad. of Dramatic Art. *Film appearances include:* The L-Shaped Room 1962, The Wrong Arm of the Law 1962, Seance on a Wet Afternoon 1963, The Wrong Box 1965, The Whisperers 1966, The Madwoman of Chaillot 1968, The Raging Moon (Variety Club Best Actress Award) 1971, The Stepford Wives 1974, International Velvet 1978. *Television appearances include:* The Fun Food Factory, London Scene, Stay with Me Till Morning, Jessie, Let There Be Love, Late Expectations, The Endless Game 1988, Ideal Home Cooks, Newman Meets (series), Celebrations (series). *Publications:* God Bless Love 1972, Lots of Love 1973, All Our Love 1978, Fun Food Factory 1976, The Root Children 1978, Amy Rainbow 1980, That Dog 1980, Reflections 1981, Dog Lovers Coffee Table Book 1982, Cat Lovers Coffee Table Book 1983, My Granny was a Frightful Bore 1983, 2004, Christmas Cookbook 1984, Cat and Mouse Love Story 1984, The Best of Love 1985, Pigalev 1985, Archie 1986, The Summer Cookbook 1986, Small Beginnings 1987, Bad Baby 1988, Entertaining with Nanette Newman 1988, Charlie the Noisy Caterpillar 1989, Sharing 1989, ABC 1990, 123 1991, Cooking for Friends 1991, Spider, The Horrible Cat 1992, There's a Bear in the Bath 1993, There's a Bear in the Classroom 1996, Take 3 Cooks 1996, Up to the Skies and Down Again 1999, To You with Love 1999, Bad Baby Good Baby 2002, Small Talk 2004, Ben's Book 2005, Eating In 2005. *Leisure interests:* needlepoint, china painting. *Address:* c/o Chatto & Linnit Ltd, 123A King's Road, London, SW3 4PL, England (office).

NEWMAN, Peter Charles, CC, CD; Canadian author and journalist; b. 10 May 1929, Vienna, Austria; s. of Oscar Newman and Wanda Newman; m. 1st Christina McCall (divorced); m. 2nd Camilla J. Turner 1978; two d.; m. 3rd Alvy Björklund 1992; ed Upper Canada Coll., Toronto, Univ. of Toronto and McGill Univ.; Asst Ed. The Financial Post 1951–55; Ottawa Ed. Maclean's 1955–64; Ottawa Ed. Toronto Daily Star 1964–69, Ed.-in-Chief 1969–71; Ed.-in-Chief, Maclean's 1971–82, Sr Contributing Ed. 1982–; Dir Maclean Hunter Ltd 1972–83, Key Radio Ltd 1983–; Prof. Creative Writing, Univ. of Victoria 1985–90; Prof. Creative Writing, Univ. of British Columbia; several honours and awards including Kt Commdr Order of St Lazarus; Hon. LLD (Brock) 1974, (Wilfrid Laurier) 1983, (Royal Mil. Coll.) 1986, (Queens) 1986; Hon. DLitt (York) 1975, (British Columbia) 1998. *Publications:* Flame of Power 1959, Renegade in Power 1963, The Distemper of Our Times 1968, Home Country 1973, The Canadian Establishment: Vol. I 1975, Bronfman Dynasty 1978, The Acquisitors – The Canadian Establishment: Vol. II 1981, The Establishment Man 1982, True North – Not Strong and Free 1983, Debrett's Illustrated Guide to the Canadian Establishment 1983, Company of Adventurers 1985, Caesars of the Wilderness 1987, Sometimes A Great Nation 1988, Empire of Bay 1989, Merchant Princes 1991, The Canadian Revolution 1995, Defining Moments 1996, Titans: How the New Canadian Establishment Seized Power 1998, Sometimes a Great Nation – Will Canada belong to the 21st Century? 1998, Here be Dragons: Telling Tales of People, Passion and Power 2004, The Secret Mulroney Tapes: Unguarded Confessions of a Prime Minister 2005. *Leisure interest:* sailing. *Address:* One Mount Pleasant Road, Toronto, M4Y 2Y5, Canada. *Telephone:* (604) 222-8274 (office); (604) 222-8274 (home). *Fax:* (604) 222-8275 (office). *E-mail:* petercnewman@home.com (home).

NEWMAN, Thomas Montgomery, MMus; American composer; b. 29 Oct. 1955, Los Angeles, CA; s. of Alfred Newman; m. Ann Marie Zirbes; three c.; ed Univ. of Southern California, Yale Univ.; mem. BMI; BAFTA, American Beauty; Grammy Awards, American Beauty. *Compositions for film:* Summer's End 1984, Reckless 1984, Revenge of the Nerds 1984, Grandview, USA 1984, Desperately Seeking Susan 1985, Girls Just Want to Have Fun 1985, The Man with One Red Shoe 1985, Real Genius 1985, Gung Ho 1986, Jumpin' Jack Flash 1986, Light of Day 1987, The Lost Boys 1987, Less Than Zero 1987, The Great Outdoors 1988, The Prince of Pennsylvania 1988, Cookie 1989, Men Don't Leave 1990, Welcome Home, Roxy Carmichael 1990, Career Opportunities 1991, Naked Tango 1991, The Rapture 1991, Deceived 1991, The Linguini Incident 1991, Fried Green Tomatoes 1991, The Player 1992, Whispers in the Dark 1992, Scent of a Woman 1992, Flesh and Bone 1993, Josh and S.A.M. 1993, Threesome 1994, The Favor 1994, Corrina, Corrina 1994, The Shawshank Redemption 1994, The War 1994, Little Women 1994, Unstrung Heroes 1995, How to Make an American Quilt 1995, Up Close & Personal 1996, Phenomenon 1996, American Buffalo 1996, The People vs Larry Flynt 1996, Mad City 1997, Red Corner 1997, Oscar and Lucinda 1997, The Horse Whisperer 1998, Meet Joe Black 1998, American Beauty 1999, The Green Mile 1999, Erin Brockovich 2000, My Khmer Heart 2000, Pay It Forward 2000, In the Bedroom 2001, The Execution of Wanda Jean 2002, The Salton Sea 2002, Road to Perdition 2002, White Oleander 2002, Finding Nemo 2003, Lemony Snicket's A Series of Unfortunate Events 2004, Cinderella Man 2005, Jarhead 2005, Little Children 2006, The Good German 2006, Nothing is Private 2007, Wall-E 2008, Revolutionary Road 2009. *Compositions for television:* The Paper Chase (series) 1978, The Seduction of Gina (film) 1984, Amazing Stories (episode 'Santa '85) 1985, Heat Wave (film) 1990, Against the Law (series) 1990, Those Secrets (film) 1992, Citizen Cohn (film) 1992, Arli$$ (series) 1996, Boston Public (series theme) 2000, Six Feet Under (series theme) 2001, Angels in America (mini series) 2003, Katedralen 1.z 2004. *Address:* Gorfaine/Schwartz Agency Inc, 13245 Riverside Drive, Suite 450, Sherman Oaks, CA 91423, USA (office). *Website:* www.gsamusic.com (office).

NEWMARCH, Michael George, BSc (Econs); British insurance executive; b. 19 May 1938, London; s. of George Langdon Newmarch and Phillis Georgina Newmarch; m. Audrey Ann Clarke 1959; one s. two d.; ed Tottenham Co. Grammar School, Univ. of London; joined Econ. Intelligence Dept, Prudential Assurance Co. Ltd 1955; Exec. Dir Prudential Corpn 1985, CEO Prudential Financial Services 1987, Chair. Prudential Holborn 1986–89, CEO and Deputy Chair. Prudential Portfolio Man. Ltd 1980–90, CEO Prudential Corpn 1990–95; Dir (non-exec.) Celltech plc 1996–2004; Chair. Weston Medical Ltd 1999–2004; Consultant, Price Waterhouse 1997–99; Chair. Bourne End Properties plc 1997–2001, Transacsys plc 2000–03; Trustee Princess Royal Trust for Carers 1994– (Chair. 2004–), Berkshire Community Foundation 1996–2003 (Chair. 1998–2003); mem. Advisory Council, Orchestra of the Age of Enlightenment 1994–, Council Univ. of Reading 1997–. *Leisure interests:* salmon fishing, fly-tying, bridge, music, theatre, cinema, travel, grandchildren. *Address:* 7 The Bromptons, Rose Square, London, SW3 6RS (home); Craven View, Craven Hill, Hamstead Marshall, nr Newbury, Berks., RG20 0JG, England (home).

NEWSOME, William T., III, BS, PhD; American neuroscientist and academic; *Professor, Department of Neurobiology, Stanford University;* ed Stetson Univ., Calif. Inst. of Tech.; Postdoctoral Researcher, Nat. Eye Inst.; fmr mem. faculty, State Univ. of New York at Stony Brook; Prof., Dept of Neurobiology, Stanford Univ. School of Medicine 1988–; Investigator, Howard Hughes Medical Inst., Chevy Chase, Md; mem. NAS; Rank Prize in Optoelectronics, Spencer Award, Columbia Univ. Coll. of Physicians and Surgeons, Distinguished Scientific Contrib. Award, American Psychological Asscn 2002, Dan David Prize (Brain Sciences), Dan David Foundation and Tel-Aviv Univ. 2004. *Publications:* numerous scientific papers in professional journals on the neural mechanisms underlying visual perception, visually based decision-making, and related issues in cognitive neuroscience. *Address:* Department of Neurobiology, Fairchild Building, Room D209, Stanford University School of Medicine, Stanford, CA 94305-2130, USA (office). *Telephone:* (650) 725-5814 (office). *Fax:* (650) 725-3958 (office). *E-mail:* bill@monkeybiz.stanford.edu (office). *Website:* monkeybiz.stanford.edu (office).

NEWSOM, Gavin, BA; American politician; *Mayor of San Francisco;* b. 10 Oct. 1967, San Francisco; s. William Newsom and Tessa Newsom; ed Santa Clara Univ., Calif.; opened first business, PlumpJack Wine Shop 1992; gen. partner in several business including Squaw Valley Inn, PlumpJack Man. Group; Pres. Parking and Traffic Comm., San Francisco 1996, mem. Bd of Supervisors 1996–2003; mem. Democratic Party; Mayor of San Francisco 2004–. *Address:* Office of the Mayor, City Hall, 1 Dr Carlton B. Goodlett Place, San Francisco, CA 94102, USA (office). *Telephone:* (415) 554-6141 (office). *Fax:* (415) 554–6160 (office). *E-mail:* gavin.newsom@sfgov.org (office). *Website:* www.sfgov.org (office).

NEWSON, Marc, RDI; Australian designer; b. 20 Oct. 1963, Sydney; ed Sydney Coll. of the Arts; staged first exhbn at Rosyln Oxley Galery, Sydney 1986; designed first of pod series of watches 1986; designer Idée Co., Tokyo, Japan 1987–91; set up studio in Paris, France 1991; began to work for Flos for Lighting, Cappellini and Moroso 1991; est. Ikepod Watch Co. (jt venture) 1991; designed Shiseido Men's Toiletries Range, Paris 1992; Visiting Prof. European Inst. of Design, Milan, Italy 1992, Vitra Design Museum Summer Workshop, Germany 1992; designed Gluon Chair and TV Chair for Moroso 1993, Helice Lamp for Flos 1993, Gello Table for 3 Suisses 1994; co-f. Ikepod, Switzerland (with Oliver Ike) 1994; set up Marc Newson Ltd, London 1997; designed Walter Van Beirendonck's Streetwear Label W&LT 1997, Dishdoctor and Rock Doorstep for Magis 1997, Lo Table for B&B Italia 1998, Glassware for Iittala, Finland 1998, MNO1 Aluminium Bicycle for Biomega, Denmark 1999, O21C Concept Car for Ford Motor Co. 1999, Hair Care Products for Vidal Sassoon, NY 2000; design work for Nike, Idée-Sputnik 2000; est. Partnership with Syn to develop products for Japanese market 2000; Royal Designer for Industry (UK); Australian Arts Council Grant 1986, Visual Arts Bd Grant, Australia Council 1988, Créateur de l'année, Salon du Meuble, Paris 1993. *Designs include:* Lockheed Lounge 1984, Orgone Lounge, Charlotte Chair, Sugar Guppy Lamp 1987, Black Hole Table and Felt Chair 1988, Wood Chair for House of Fiction Exhbn, Sydney 1988, Embryo Chair for Powerhouse Museum, Sydney 1988, Andoni Shop Interior, Sydney 1988, Pod Bar Interior, Tokyo 1989, Orgone Fiberglass Chair and Lounge, Sydney 1989, Carbon Fibre Mystery Clock 1990, Event Horizon Table 1991, Interiors of Hysterie and Skoda Boutiques, Germany 1992, Seaslug Watch 1994, Interior of Coast Restaurant, London 1995, Hemipode Watch 1996, Interior of Syn Recording Studio, Tokyo 1996, Interior of Komed Restaurant, Cologne 1996, Falcon 900B Business Jet, London 1999, Llama Apartments Project, Brisbane 2000, Interior of Lever Bar, New York 2000, Miniature Lockheed Lounge 2000. *Museum Collections:* Art Gallery of S Australia, Adelaide, Carnegie Museum, Pittsburgh, Design Museum, London, Musee des Arts Decoratifs, Paris, Powerhouse Museum, Sydney, San Francisco Museum of Modern Art, Vitra Design Museum, Weil am Rhein (Germany). *Publications:* Marc Newson 1999. *Address:* Marc Newson Ltd, 175–185 Gray's Inn Road, London, WC1X 8UP, England (office). *Telephone:* (20) 7287-9388 (office). *Fax:* (20) 7287-9347 (office). *E-mail:* pod@marc-newson.com (office). *Website:* www.marcnewson .com (office).

NEWTON, Sir (Charles) Wilfrid, Kt, CBE, CA (SA), FRSA, CCIM; British business executive; *Chairman, Mountcity Investments Ltd;* b. 11 Dec. 1928, Johannesburg, South Africa; s. of the late Gore M. Newton and of Catherine K. Newton; m. Felicity Mary Lynn 1954; two s. two d.; ed Highlands North High School, Johannesburg, Univ. of Witwatersrand; Territory Accounting and Finance Man., Mobil Oil Corpn of South Africa 1955–62; Controller, Mobil Sekiyu KK, Tokyo 1962–63, Finance Dir 1965–68; Financial Man. and Deputy Gen. Man., Mobil Oil East Africa Ltd 1963–65; Chief Financial Officer, Mobil Interests Japan 1965–68; Finance Dir, Turner and Newall Ltd 1968–74, Man. Dir Finance and Planning 1974–76, Man. Dir Plastics, Chemicals and Mining Divs 1976–79, Group Man. Dir 1979–82, CEO 1982–; Chair. Mass Transit Railway Corpn, Hong Kong 1983–89, Hong Kong Futures Exchange Ltd 1987–89, Chair. Jacobs Holdings PLC 1994–2002, Raglan Properties PLC 1994–99, G. Maunsell Int. Ltd 1996–98; Chair. and CEO London Regional Transport 1989–94, London Underground Ltd 1989–93; Dir (non-exec.) Hong Kong and Shanghai Banking Corpn 1986–92, Sketchley PLC 1990–99, HSBC Holdings PLC 1990–99, Midland Bank PLC 1992–99, Mountcity Investments Ltd 1994–; mem. Inst. of Chartered Accountants of South Africa; Fellow, Hong Kong Man. Asscn; Hon. FREng; Hon. Fellow, Hong Kong Inst. of Engineers. *Leisure interests:* sailing, reading, current affairs, economics. *Address:* Newtons Gate, Ramley Road, Pennington, Lymington, Hants., SO4 8GQ, England. *Telephone:* (20) 7629-1339 (office); (1590) 679750 (home). *Fax:* (20) 7629-0728 (office); (1590) 677440 (home). *E-mail:* wandf.newton@btinternet .com (home).

NEWTON, Christopher, OC, CM, BA, MA, FRCM; Canadian actor, director and author; *Artistic Director Emeritus, The Shaw Festival;* b. 11 June 1936, Deal, Kent; s. of Albert E. Newton and Gwladys M. Emes; ed Sir Roger Manwood's School, Sandwich, Kent, UK, Univ. of Leeds, UK and Illinois and Purdue Univs, USA; actor, Stratford Festival, New York; Founding Artistic Dir Theatre Calgary, Calgary, Alberta 1968–71; Artistic Dir Vancouver Playhouse and Founder (with the late Powys Thomas), The Playhouse Acting School 1973–79; Artistic Dir The Shaw Festival, Niagara-on-the-Lake 1979–2002, Artistic Dir Emer. 2002–; Hon. Fellow, Ryerson Univ., Royal Conservatory; Hon. LLD (Brock Univ., Guelph, Toronto); Hon. DLitt (Wilfrid Laurier Univ.); Hon. DHL (State Univ. of NY at Buffalo); Gov.-Gen.'s Award, Molson Prize, Gascon-Thomas Award, Chalmers Award. *Plays directed include:* (for the Shaw Festival) Heartbreak House, Cavalcade, Man and Superman, Pygmalion, The Importance of Being Earnest, Easy Virtue, The Doctor's Dilemma,

Lady Windermere's Fan, Caesar and Cleopatra, The Return of the Prodigal, (for Melbourne Theatre Co.) Misalliance, (for Vancouver Playhouse) She Stoops to Conquer, Hamlet, Julius Caesar, Taming of the Shrew, (for Theatre Calgary) An Inspector Calls, (for YPT) Great Expectations. *Operas directed include:* (for Canadian Opera Co.) Madama Butterfly, Patria I, The Turn of the Screw, Albert Herring, (for Nat. Arts Centre and Vancouver Opera) The Barber of Seville, (for Opera Hamilton) I due Foscari. *Publications:* plays: You Two Stay Here the Rest Come with Me, Slow Train to St Ives, Trip, The Sound of Distant Thunder, The Lost Letter (adaptation). *Leisure interest:* landscape architecture. *Address:* c/o Shaw Festival, Box 774, Niagara-on-the-Lake, ON L0S 1J0 (office); 22 Prideaux Street, PO Box 609, Niagara-on-the-Lake, ON L0S 1J0, Canada (home). *Telephone:* (905) 468-2153 (office); (905) 468-4169 (home). *E-mail:* c_newton@sympatico.ca (home). *Website:* www.shawfest.com (office).

NEWTON, John Oswald, MA, PhD, DSc, FAA; Australian/British nuclear physicist and academic; *Professor Emeritus and Visiting Fellow, Department of Nuclear Physics, Australian National University;* b. 12 Feb. 1924, Birmingham; s. of O.J. Newton and R.K. Newton; m. 2nd Silva Dusan Sablich 1964; two s. one d.; ed Bishop Vesey's Grammar School, Sutton Coldfield, St Catharine's Coll. Cambridge, Cavendish Lab., Cambridge; Jr Scientific Officer, Telecommunications Research Establishment, Great Malvern 1943–46; Harwell Fellow 1951–54; Prin. Scientific Officer, AERE Harwell 1954–59; Sr Lecturer, Univ. of Manchester 1959–67, Reader 1967–70; Prof. of Nuclear Physics, ANU 1970–89, Head of Dept of Nuclear Physics, Inst. of Advanced Studies 1970–88, Prof. Emer. and Visiting Fellow in Dept of Nuclear Physics 1990–; Visiting Physicist, Lawrence Berkeley Lab. (several times since 1956); Visiting Prof., Univ. of Manchester 1985–86; Centenary Medal 2003. *Publications:* more than 100 publs in nuclear physics and several book chapters. *Leisure interests:* painting, chess, music, walking, tennis. *Address:* Department of Nuclear Physics, IAS, Australian National University, Canberra, ACT 0200 (office); 8 Mackenzie Street, Hackett, ACT 2602, Australia (home). *Telephone:* (2) 6125-2074 (office). *Fax:* (2) 6125-0748 (office). *E-mail:* jon@nuc.anu.edu.au (office). *Website:* wwwrsphysse.anu.edu .au/nuclear (office).

NEWTON, Thandie; British actress; b. 6 Nov. 1972, Zambia; d. of Nick Newton and Nyasha Newton; m. Oliver Parker 1998; ed Downing Coll. Cambridge. *Films include:* Flirting 1991, The Young Americans 1993, Interview with a Vampire 1994, Loaded 1994, Jefferson in Paris 1995, The Journey of August King 1995, The Leading Man 1996, Gridlock'd 1997, Besieged 1998, Beloved 1998, Mission: Impossible II 2000, It Was an Accident 2000, The Truth About Charlie 2002, Shade 2003, The Chronicles of Riddick 2004, Crash (BAFTA Award for Best Actress in a Supporting Role 2006) 2005, The Pursuit of Happyness 2006, Norbit 2007, Run, Fat Boy, Run 2007, RocknRolla 2008, How to Lose Friends & Alienate People 2008, W. 2008. *Television includes:* Pirate Prince 1991, In Your Dreams 1997, ER (series) 2003–05. *Address:* c/o William Morris Agency, One William Morris Place, Beverly Hills, CA 90212, USA.

NEWTON, Sir Wilfrid (see NEWTON, Sir (Charles) Wilfrid).

NEWTON-JOHN, Olivia, OBE; British singer and actress; b. 26 Sept. 1948, Cambridge; d. of Brin Newton-John and Irene Born; m. Matt Lattanzi 1984; one d.; co-owner Koala Blue 1982–; UNEP Goodwill Amb. 1989–; Humanitarian Award US Red Cross 1999 and numerous other awards. *Albums include:* If Not For You 1971, Let Me Be There 1974, Music Makes My Day 1974, Long Live Love 1974, If You Love Me Let Me Know (No. 1, USA) 1974, Have You Ever Never Been Mellow 1975, Clearly Love 1975, Come On Over 1976, Don't Stop Believin' 1976, Making A Good Thing Better 1977, Greatest Hits 1978, Grease (film soundtrack) 1978, Totally Hot 1979, Xanadu (film soundtrack) 1980, Physical 1981, 20 Greatest Hits 1982, Olivia's Greatest Hits Vol. 2 1983, Two of a Kind 1984, Soul Kiss 1986, The Rumour 1988, Warm and Tender 1990, Back To Basics: The Essential Collection 1971–92 1992, Gaia – One Woman's Journey 1995, More than Physical 1995, Greatest Hits 1996, Olivia 1998, Back with a Heart 1998, Highlights from the Main Event 1999, Greatest Hits: First Impressions 1999, Country Girl 1999, Best of Olivia Newton John 1999, Love Songs: A Collection: One Woman's Live Journey 2000, Grace and Gratitude 2007. *Film appearances include:* Grease 1978, Xanadu 1980, Two of a Kind 1983, It's My Party 1995, Sordid Wives 1999. *Television appearances:* numerous, including It's Cliff Richard (BBC series). *Leisure interests:* horse riding, songwriting, cycling, astrology, conservation, animals. *Address:* MCA, 70 Universal City Plaza, North Hollywood, CA 91608 (office); PO Box 2710, Malibu, CA 90265, USA (home). *Website:* www .onlyolivia.com (office).

NEWTON OF BRAINTREE, Baron (Life Peer), cr. 1997, of Coggeshall in the County of Essex; **Antony Harold (Tony) Newton,** OBE, PC; British politician; b. 29 Aug. 1937; m. 1st Janet Huxley 1962 (divorced 1986); two d.; m. 2nd Patricia Gilthorpe 1986; one step-s. two step-d.; ed Friends' School, Saffron Walden, Trinity Coll., Oxford; Pres. Oxford Union 1959; fmr Sec. and Research Sec. Bow Group; Head Econ. Section, Conservative Research Dept 1965–70, Asst Dir 1970–74; Parl. Cand. for Sheffield, Brightside 1970; MP for Braintree 1974–97; Asst Govt Whip 1979–81; Lord Commr, Treasury 1981–82; Parl. Under-Sec. for Social Security 1982–84 and Minister for the Disabled 1983–84, Minister of State 1984–86, Minister of State (Health) and Chair. Nat. Health Service Man. Bd 1986–88; Chancellor Duchy of Lancaster 1988–89; Sec. of State for Social Security 1989–92; Lord Pres. of the Council and Leader of the House of Commons 1992–97; Chair. NE Essex Mental Health Nat. Health Service Trust 1997–, E Anglia's Children's Hospices 1998–; Professional Standards Dir, Inst. of Dirs 1998–; mem. Further Educ. Funding Council 1998–; Chair. Council on Tribunals 1999–, Cttee of Privy Counsellors to review operation of Anti-Terrorism, Crime and Security Act 2001–03. *Address:* House of Lords, Westminster, London, SW1A 0PW, England. *Telephone:* (20) 7219-5878.

NEY, Edward Noonan, BA; American advertising executive; *Chairman Emeritus, Young & Rubicam Brands;* b. 26 May 1925, St Paul, Minn.; s. of John Ney and Marie Noonan Ney; m. 1st Suzanne Hayes 1950 (divorced 1974); one s. two d.; m. 2nd Judith I. Lasky 1974; ed Amherst Coll.; Account Exec., Young & Rubicam Inc. (now Young & Rubicam Brands) 1951, Vice-Pres. 1959–63, Sr Vice-Pres. 1963–67, Exec. Vice-Pres. 1967–68, Pres. Int. Div. 1968–70, Pres. and CEO 1970–72, Pres., CEO and Chair. 1972–83, Chair. and CEO 1983–85, Chair. 1985–86 (now Chair. Emer.), Chair. PaineWebber/ Young Rubicam Ventures 1987–89, Young and Rubicam Ventures 1989, Vice-Chair. PaineWebber 1987–89; Chair. Bd of Advisers Burton-Marsteller 1992–98; Amb. to Canada 1989–92; Vice-Chair. The Advertising Council 1984–87, Chair. 1987–88 (now Chair. Emer.); mem. Bd Int. Broadcasting 1984–, Bd of Govs Foreign Policy Assen 1980– (Vice-Chair. 1984–87); Dir Center for Communications 1986–; Chair. Manteller Advertising 1996–98; Trustee, Nat. Urban League 1974–, Amherst Coll. 1979–, New York Univ. Medical Center 1979–, Museum of Broadcasting 1982–; mem. Council on Foreign Relations 1974; mem. Bd Advisory Council, Center for Strategic and Int. Studies 1986–. *Leisure interests:* tennis, paddle tennis, reading. *Address:* c/o Young & Rubicam Brands, 285 Madison Avenue, New York, NY 10017, USA (office).

NEYELOVA, Marina Mstislavovna; Russian actress; b. 8 Jan. 1947; m. Kyrill Gevorgyan; one d.; ed Leningrad Inst. of Theatre, Music and Cinema; actress, Moscow Theatre Studio of Film Actors 1968–71, Mossoviet Theatre 1971–74, Sovremennik 1974–; prin. roles in classical and contemporary repertoire including Chekhov's plays; debut in cinema 1968; Order Friendship of Peoples 1996; People's Artist Russian Fed. 1980; USSR State Prize 1990, Prize Nika (film I Have Only You) 1994, State Prize of Russia 2000. *Films include:* Prison Romance, Old, Old Tale 1970, Monologue 1973, With You and Without You 1974, Speech for the Defence 1976, Enemies 1977, Errors of Youth 1978, Autumn Marathon 1979 (State Prize of Russia), Ladies Invite Gentlemen 1980, We Are Cheerful, Happy, Talented! 1986, Dear Yelena Sergeyevna 1988, Scar-Free 1989, You Are My Only Love 1993, Side by Side 1994, The First Love 1995, Inspector 1996, The Barber of Siberia 1998, Azazel' (TV) 2002, Probka 2009. *Address:* 117333 Moscow, Potapovsky per. 12, Apt 24, Russia (home).

NEZVAL, Jiří; Czech automobile executive; b. 5 April 1941, Brno; s. of František Nezval and Květa Nezvalová; m. Silva Moltašová 1963; two d.; ed Railway Coll. Žilina and Polytechnic Inst. Brno; designer and design office man. in automation of rail transport, Prague; involved in Czechoslovak Scientific and Tech. Soc., Peace Movt; Fed. Minister of Transport 1990–92; mem. Civic Movt Party 1991–93, Free Democrats Party 1993– (merged with Liberal Nat. Social Party 1995); Dir Denzel Praha Co. 1992–; Chair. Union of Motor Car Importers 1995–; Exclusive Mitsubishi dealership in Czech Repub. 1997–. *Leisure interests:* computer art, man. systems, reading books, sports (skiing, cycling, volleyball). *Address:* Denzel Praha s.r.o., Revoluční 2, Prague 1, Czech Republic. *Telephone:* (2) 24810836 (office). *Fax:* (2) 22315926 (office).

NFUBEA, Ricardo Mangue Obama; Equatorial Guinean politician; mem. Democratic Party of Equatorial Guinea (PDGE); fmr State Minister for Labor and Social Security; Deputy Prime Minister 2004–06, Prime Minister 2006–08 (resgnd). *Address:* Office of the Prime Minister, Malabo, Equatorial Guinea.

NG, Daniel; Chinese business executive, entrepreneur and arts administrator; *Chairman, Board of Directors, Arts4All Ltd;* fmr Chair. McDonald's Restaurants (Hong Kong Special Admin. Region); Chair. Bd Dirs Arts4All Ltd, New York 2000–. *Address:* Arts 4All Ltd, 2 West 45 Street, Suite 500, New York, NY 10036, USA (office). *E-mail:* info@arts4all.com (office). *Website:* www .arts4all.com (office).

NG, Teng Fong; Singaporean real estate executive; *Chairman, Far East Organization;* b. 1930; m. Tan Kim Choo; six c.; began career in real estate 1962; currently Chair. Far East Org., related cos include Orchard Parade Holdings, Sino Group, Sino Land Co., Sino Hotels; holds majority stake in Tsim Sha Tsui Properties; extensive property interests in Singapore and Hong Kong. *Address:* Far East Organization, 14 Scotts Road, #06-00 Far East Plaza, Singapore 228213, Singapore (office). *Telephone:* 62352411 (office). *Fax:* 62353316 (office). *Website:* www.fareast.com.sg (office).

NGAPO Ngawang–Jigme (see NGAPOI Ngawang Jigme).

NGAPOI, Lt-Gen. Ngawang Jigme; Chinese politician; *Vice-Chairman, National Committee, 10th Chinese People's Political Consultative Conference;* b. Feb. 1910, nr Lhasa, Tibet; joined Tibet Noble Children's Cantonment 1934; forage officer, civil judge, auditor and fourth ranking official, Tibet Local Govt and Gov., Qamdo (Tibetan Mil. Region) 1936–50; captured by Communist troops, Qamdo 1950; Vice-Chair. Qamdo Liberation Cttee 1950; Del. Leader, Tibet Local Govt 1951, First Deputy Commdr Tibet Mil. Region 1952, rank of Lt-Gen. 1955; Vice-Chair. and Sec. Gen. 1959; Deputy for Tibet, 1st NPC 1954; mem. Nat. Defence Council 1954–Cultural Revolution; Sec.-Gen. Preparatory Cttee for Establishment of Tibet Autonomous Region 1956, Vice-Chair. and later Acting Chair. 1959–64; Deputy for Tibet, 2nd NPC 1959; Vice-Chair. Standing Cttee, 3rd CPPCC 1959–64; Head, Cadre School, Lhasa 1961; Vice-Chair. Standing Cttee, 3rd NPC 1965–75, 4th NPC 1975–78, 5th NPC 1978–86, 6th NPC 1983–87, 7th NPC 1988–93; Chair. Tibet Autonomous Region 1965; Vice-Chair. Tibet Autonomous Regional Revolutionary Cttee 1968–78; Chair. People's Congress, Tibet Autonomous Region 1979–91; Exec. Chair. Presidium 6th NPC 1986; Chair. Tibet Autonomous Region 5th People's Congress 1988–93; Chair. Nationalities Cttee, NPC 1979–83; Chair. China-Tibet Devt Fund 1987–, Vice-Chair. CPPCC 8th Nat. Cttee 1993–98,

9th Nat. Cttee 1998–2003, 10th Nat. Cttee 2003–08, 11th Nat. Cttee 2008–; mem. Govt Del., Macao Hand-Over Ceremony, Macao Special Admin. Region Preparatory Cttee 1999; Hon. Pres. Asscn for Well-Known Chinese Figures 1993–; First Class Liberation Medal 1955. *Publication:* Tibet (jtly). *Address:* National Committee of Chinese People's Political Consultative Conference, 23 Taipingqiao Street, Beijing, People's Republic of China (office).

NGEMA, Mbongeni; South African writer, producer and composer; b. 1955, Hlabisa; m. Leleti Khumalo (separated); mem. Gibson Kente's acting co., f. Cttee Artists; est. S African struggle theatre on London and New York stages 1981. *Plays:* Woza Albert! (with Percy Mtwa and Barney Simon) 1981, Asinamali 1986, Sarafina! 1987, Township Fever 1989, Sarafina 2! 1996, The Zulu 2000. *Recordings:* Sarafina! 1990, Time to Unite 1990, Woza My Fohlaza 1998, AmaNyida 2002, Best of Mbongeni Ngema 2002. *Publications:* Voices of Sarafina! Songs of Hope and Freedom 1988; contrib. to Woza Afrika!: A Collection of South African Plays 1986, Where is the Way: Song and Struggle in South Africa 1990. *Address:* c/o Skotaville Publishers, PO Box 32483, Braamfontein, South Africa.

NGENZEBUHORO, Frederic; Burundian politician; mem. Union pour le progrès nat. (Uprona, main Tutsi party); Minister of Information, then of Communication, then of Sports and Culture, then of Transport 1987–93; Deputy Pres. Nat. Ass. 1998–2004; Vice-Pres. of Burundi 2004–05. *Address:* c/o Union pour le progrès national, BP 1810, Bujumbura, Burundi (office).

NGHIMTINA, Erikki; Namibian politician; fmr Man. Dir Prin. Bank for Devt and Agricultural Credit; Minister of Defence 1997–2005. *Address:* c/o Ministry of Defence, PMB 13307, Windhoek, Namibia (office).

NGO, Quang Xuan; Vietnamese diplomatist; *Permanent Representative, United Nations, Geneva;* b. 1 Jan. 1951, Nghe An; s. of Ngo Tri Tai and Dau Thi Nghiem; m. Le Thi Hoa 1975; two d.; ed Inst. of Int. Relations, Hanoi, Inst. des Hautes Etudes Internationales, Geneva, Diplomatic Acad. of Moscow; Deputy Gen. Dir Dept for Multilateral Econ. and Cultural Co-operation, Foreign Ministry 1988–91, Deputy Dir Int. Orgs Dept 1992–93, Dir of Ministry 1995–; Nat. Rep. to Francophone Community 1990–93; Acting Perm. Rep. to UN 1993–95, Perm. Rep. 1995–2000; currently Perm. Rep., UN, Geneva; Medal for Diplomatic Service. *Leisure interests:* classical music, tennis. *Address:* Vietnam Mission to United Nations and International Organizations, Chemin des Corbillettes 30, 1218 Grand-Saconnex, Geneva, Switzerland (office). *Telephone:* 227982485 (office). *Fax:* 227980724 (office). *E-mail:* mission.vietnam@ties.itu.int (office). *Website:* www.unog.ch.

NGOUBEYOU, François Xavier; Cameroonian politician; b. 1937; mem. Rassemblement Démocratique du Peuple Camerounais (RDPC); fmr Perm. Rep. to UN, Geneva; Minister of State in charge of External Relations 2001–04. *Address:* c/o Ministry of External Relations, Yaoundé, Cameroon (office).

NGOUPANDE, Jean-Paul; Central African Republic politician and fmr diplomatist; b. 6 Dec. 1948, Dekoa; m.; three s. three d.; Dean Faculty of Letters Univ. de Bangui 1982–85; Minister of Educ. 1985–87; fmr Amb. to France and to Côte d'Ivoire; Prime Minister of Cen. African Repub. 1996–97; mem. Parl. 1998–; Leader Parti pour l'union nationale; Minister of Foreign and Francophone Affairs and Regional Integration 2006; Commdr Meritorious Order of Cen. African Rep., Commdr Ordre de Palmes Académiques, Grand Officier Ordre Nat. de Côte d'Ivoire. *Publications include:* Racines historiques et culturelles de la crise africaine 1994, Chronique de la crise centrafricaine 1997. *Leisure interests:* reading, music. *Address:* National Assembly of Central African Republic, Bangui (office); PO Box 179, Bangui, Central African Republic (home). *Telephone:* 61-82-96. *Fax:* 61-78-66 (home).

NGOWENUBUSA, Dieudonné; Burundi politician; *Minister of Finance;* b. 8 Sept. 1964, Ngagara; Minister of Finance 2005–; mem. Conseil nat. pour la defense de la democratie–Forces pour la defense de la democratie (CNDD-FDD). *Address:* Ministry of Finance, BP 1830, Bujumbura, Burundi (office). *Telephone:* 225142 (office). *Fax:* 223128 (office). *E-mail:* minifin@usan.bu.net (office).

NGUBANE, Ben, MB, ChB; South African politician and doctor; *Minister of Arts, Culture, Science and Technology;* b. 22 Oct. 1941, Camperdown; m. Sheila Buthelezi; four c.; ed St Francis Coll., Marrianhill, Durban Medical School, Univ. of Witwatesrand, Natal Medical School; fmr Latin teacher; mem. Inkatha Freedom Party Cen. Cttee Exec. 1977–; mem. KwaZulu Legis. Ass. 1978–; led KwaZulu Govt del. to Constitutional negotiations; Minister of Health, KwaZulu Govt 1991–94, Premier 1997–99; Minister of Arts, Culture, Science and Tech. 1994–96, 1999–; mem. S African Red Cross Soc. 1977–; Regional Counsellor 1978–; mem. Council Univ. of Zululand; mem. Nat. Boxing Bd of Control 1991–. *Leisure interests:* tennis, reading, photography. *Address:* Ministry of Arts, Culture, Science and Technology, Oranje Nassau Building, 188 Schoeman Street, Pretoria 0002 (office); Empangeni, KwaZulu-Natal, South Africa (home). *Telephone:* (12) 3378378 (office); (12) 3242687. *E-mail:* frans@dacsts.pwv.gov.za (office). *Website:* www.dacst.gov.za (office); www.gov.za (home).

N'GUESSAN, Pascal Affi; Côte d'Ivoirian politician; *President, Front populaire ivoirien (FPI);* b. 1953, Bouadikro; ed Lycée Moderne de Dimbokro, Lycée Technique d'Abidjan; Dir of Studies and Work Placements, École Nat. Supérieure des Postes et Télécommunications 1989–1993; Vice-Pres. Union des villes et commune de Côte d'Ivoire (UVICOCI) 1990–95; mem. nat. directorate, Front populaire ivoirien—FPI (Ivorian Popular Front) 1990–, Pres. 2001–; Special Adviser to the Regional Dir, Ci-Télécom, Bouaké 1993–97; Head Dept of Resources and Standards, Côte d'Ivoire Télécom 1997–2000; Campaign Man. for Laurent Gbagbo in presidential elections 2000; Minister of Industry and Tourism 2000; Prime Minister of Côte d'Ivoire

2000–03; Minister for Planning and Devt 2000–03; Officier du mérite sportif 1995. *Address:* Front populaire ivoirien (FPI), 22 BP 302, Abidjan 22, Côte d'Ivoire (office). *Telephone:* 21-24-36-76 (office). *Fax:* 21-35-35-50 (office). *E-mail:* president@fpi-ci.org. *Website:* www.fpi-ci.org.

NGUM, Alieu M.; Gambian government official; *Secretary of State for Trade, Industry and Employment;* Amb. to Belgium and Head of Mission to the EC 2001; fmr Sec.-Gen., Office of the Pres.; fmr Sec.-Gen., Head of Civil Service; Sec. of State for Finance and Econ. Affairs –2005, for Trade, Industry and Employment Nov. 2005–. *Address:* Department of State for Trade, Industry and Employment, Central Bank Bldg, Independence Drive, Banjul, The Gambia (office). *Telephone:* 4228868 (office). *Fax:* 4227756 (office).

NGWENYA, Sindiso, BSc, MSc; Zimbabwean international organization official; *Secretary General, Common Market for Eastern and Southern Africa;* b. 16 April 1951; m.; three c.; ed Middlesex Polytechnic, Univ. of Birmingham, UK; Corp. Planning Officer, Ethiopia Airlines 1979–80; Planning Officer, Nat. Railways of Zimbabwe 1980–83; Sr Transport Expert, Common Market for Eastern and Southern Africa (COMESA) 1994–98, Asst Sec. Gen., in charge of Programming 1998–2008, Sec. Gen. 2008–; mem. Interim Cttee Food, Agric. and Natural Resources Policy Analysis Network 2007. *Address:* COMESA Secretariat, Ben Bella Road, POB 30051, 101101 Lusaka, Zambia (office). *Telephone:* (1) 229725 (office). *Fax:* (1) 225107 (office). *E-mail:* comesa@comesa.int (office). *Website:* www.comesa.int (office).

NHASSÉ, Alamara; Guinea-Bissau politician; b. 1957; Pres. Partido para a Renovação Social (PRS); Minister of Internal Admin. 2001; Prime Minister of Guinea-Bissau 2001–02. *Address:* c/o Office of the Prime Minister, Avda Unidade Africana, CP 137 Bissau, Guinea-Bissau.

NHIEK, Bun Chhay; Cambodian politician; *Deputy Prime Minister;* b. 7 Feb. 1956; Second Vice-Pres. of the Senate 1999–2004; Acting Head of State July 2004; Deputy Prime Minister 2004–; Minister of Defence 2004–06; Sec.-Gen. United Nat. Front for an Ind., Neutral, Peaceful and Co-operative Cambodia Party (Funcinpec) 2006–. *Address:* Funcinpec, 11 boulevard Monivong (93), Sangkat Sras Chak, Khan Daun Penh, BP 1444, Phnom-Penh, Cambodia (office). *Telephone:* (23) 428864 (office). *Fax:* (23) 218547 (office). *E-mail:* funcinpec@funcinpec.org (office). *Website:* www.funcinpec.org (office).

NHLAPO, Welile Witness Augustine; South African diplomatist; *Ambassador to USA;* b. Alexandra Township, Johannesburg; m. Sissy Nhlapo; one s. two d.; active in SA Students Org.; banning order served 1973, went into exile to Botswana 1974; joined ANC 1974 and served various positions, including Deputy Ed. Sechaba (official ANC publ.), London 1978–81, Head, ANC Youth Section 1982–87, mem. Regional ANC Political Cttee –1990, ANC Chief Rep. in Botswana 1991–93, Head, Political Section in ANC Sec.-Gen. office in Shell House 1993, then joined ANC Int. Affairs Dept; joined SA Dept of Foreign Affairs 1994, mem. SA del. to UN Gen. Ass., New York when SA was readmitted 1994; Amb. to Ethiopia (also accred. to Djibouti, Eritrea and Sudan), also Perm. Rep. to Org. of African Unity and UN Econ. Comm. for Africa 1995; Special Envoy for Burundi 1996; fmr Deputy Dir. Gen. for Africa, fmr Dir. Gen. Presidential Support Unit, Ministry of Foreign Affairs; fmr Dir. Africa Div., UN Dept of Political Affairs; Amb. to USA 2007–. *Address:* Embassy of South Africa, 3051 Massachusetts Avenue, NW, Washington, DC 20008, USA (office). *Telephone:* (202) 232-4400 (office). *Fax:* (202) 265-1607 (office). *E-mail:* ambassador.washington@foreign.gov.za (office); info@saembassy.org (office). *Website:* www.saembassy.org (office).

NHUSSI, Filipe Jacinto; Mozambican engineer and politician; *Minister of National Defence;* b. 1959, Namau; ed Univ. of Manchester, UK; Exec. Dir CMF-Norte, Mozambique Ports and Railways 1995–2007, mem. Bd of Dirs 2007–; Minister of Nat. Defence 2007–; Pres. Clube Ferroviário de Nampula (football club) 1993–2002; Fellow, Africa Leadership Initiative. *Address:* Ministry of National Defence, Av. Mártires de Mueda 280, 3216 Maputo, Mozambique (office). *Telephone:* 21492081 (office). *Fax:* 21491619 (office).

NI, Runfeng; Chinese business executive; b. 1944, Rongcheng, Shandong Prov.; ed Dalian Eng Coll.; Dir, later Gen. Man., later Chair. Bd Changhong Machinery Factory, Sichuan Prov. 1985, Gen. Man. Changhong Electronics Corpn 1995–2000, Chair. Bd 1996–2004; mem. CCP; Del., 14th CCP Nat. Congress 1992–97; Deputy, 8th NPC 1993–98; Alt. mem. 15th CCP Cen. Cttee 1997–2002; named Prof.-grade Sr Engineer, named Most Outstanding Man. by All-China Fed. of Trade Unions 1990, winner of Nat. Wuyi Labour Medal 1990, Awarded Special Governmental Subsidy 1991, named amongst Ten Most Outstanding Persons of Sichuan 1993, named amongst 5th Nat. Most Outstanding Entrepreneurs 1994, Nat. Model Worker, State Council 1995, chosen as one of 1995 Ten Men of the Moment in Chinese Business Circles 1996, Nikkei Asian Prize 1998, named amongst Ten Most Outstanding Operators of Industrial Enterprises of People's Repub. of China 1998, honoured as Man. Guru by Int. Statistics Conf. 1998, named amonst Ten Most Outstanding Entrepreneurs 1998, Most Outstanding Entrepreneurs of Sichuan Prov. 1998, Award for Achievement of Asian Entrepreneurs 1998, named on List of China's Richest People of the Moment 1999. *Address:* c/o Changhong Electronics Corporation, Chengdu, Sichuan Province, People's Republic of China (office).

NI, Zhifu; Chinese party official; b. 1933, Chuansha Co., Shanghai; ed elementary school 1945–48; errand boy for Mobil Oil Corpn 1944; apprentice, a Shanghai printing machine factory 1948, Detai Mould Plant 1950–53; joined trades union 1950; mechanic, Yongding Machine Tool Factory, Beijing 1953; joined CCP 1958; promoted engineer 1962, then deputy chief engineer, acting chief engineer, chief engineer 1965–; Chair. Municipal Trade Union Council, Beijing 1973; Second Sec. CCP Cttee, Beijing 1973–78; Vice-Chair. Municipal Revolutionary Cttee, Beijing 1974–78; Second Sec. CCP Cttee, Shanghai

1976–78; First Vice-Chair. Municipal Revolutionary Cttee, Shanghai 1976–78; Pres. All-China Fed. of Trade Unions 1978–93; Vice-Minister State Machine-Building Industry Comm. 1979; Sec. Tianjin Municipal Cttee of CCP 1984–87; mem. 9th Cen. Cttee CCP 1967–72, Alt. mem. Politburo 10th Cen. Cttee CCP 1972–77, mem. Politburo 11th Cen. Cttee CCP 1977–82, mem. Politburo 12th CCP Cen. Cttee 1982–87, mem. 13th CCP Cen. Cttee 1987–92, 14th CCP Cen. Cttee 1992–97, 15th CCP Cen. Cttee 1997–2002; Vice-Chair. Standing Cttee 7th NPC 1988–93, Standing Cttee 8th NPC 1993–98; fourth Chair. China Invention Asscn 2000, Hon. Chair. 2005–; Hon. Chair. Bd Dirs Beijing Science and Eng Univ. 1995–; Nat. Outstanding Workers Award 1959, Nat. Invention Award, State Science and Tech. Comm. 1964, Gold Medal and Certificate for co-authoring a book on his drill bit, UN World Intellectual Property Org. 1966. *Achievement:* inventor of Ni Zhifu drill bit, also known as three-point multi-fork twist drill bit. *Address:* 10 Fuxingmenwai Street, Beijing, People's Republic of China.

NI Chih-Fu (see NI Zhifu).

NÍ DHOMHNAILL, Nuala, BA; Irish poet; b. 16 Feb. 1952, St Helens, Lancs., England; d. of Séamus Ó Dhomhnaill and Eibhlín Ní Fhiannachta; m. Dogan Leflef 1973; one s. three d.; ed Laurel Hill Convent, Limerick and Univ. Coll., Cork; travel overseas 1973–80; writer-in-residence Univ. Coll., Cork 1992–93; Visiting Prof. New York Univ., 1998, Villanova Univ. 2001; Ireland Prof. of Poetry 2002–04; mem. Aosdána, Irish Writers' Union, Poetry Ireland; Oireachtas Poetry Awards, 1982, 1989, 1990, 1998; Irish Arts Council Awards, 1985, 1988; Irish American O'Shaughnessy Award 1988, Ireland Fund Literary Prize 1991. *Publications:* An Dealg Droighinn 1981, Feár Suaithinseach 1984, Raven Introductions (with others) 1984, Selected Poems/ Rogha Danta 1986, Pharoah's Daughter 1990, Feís 1991, The Astrakhan Cloak 1992, Jumping Off Shadows: Selected Contemporary Irish Poets (ed. with Greg Delanty) 1995, Cead Aighnis 1998, In the Heart of Europe: Poems for Bosnia 1998, The Water Horse 1999, The Fifty Minute Mermaid: Poems in Irish 2007; contribs to many anthologies and magazines. *Leisure interests:* swimming, mountain walks, reading. *Website:* www.nualanidhomhnaill.com.

NIANG, Souleymane, PhD; Senegalese mathematician, academic and university administrator; *President, L'Académie des Sciences et Techniques du Sénégal (ASTS);* b. Dec. 1929, Matam; ed Univ. of Toulouse; teacher, Lycée Fermat, Toulouse, William Ponty Teachers' School, Daker 1956–60; Lecturer, Faculty of Sciences, Univ. of Dakar 1960, Sr Lecturer 1964, Prof. 1969–; Dir Research Inst. on the Teaching of Math., Physics and Tech. 1970; Rector and Pres. Univ. Cheikh Anta Diop 1986, currently Prof. Dept of Math.; Pres. L'Académie des Sciences et Techniques du Sénégal (ASTS); fmr Pres. Scientific Section, UNESCO Nat. Comm., Nat. Cttee of Int. Comm. for Teaching Math.; Pres. Math. and Physics Section, Africa and Mauritius Advisory Cttee on Higher Educ.; mem. Office of African Comm. for Teaching Math., Scientific Council, OAU; Officer, Ordre Nat. du Lion, Ordre Nat. du Mérite, Chevalier, Ordre des Palmes Académiques Sénégalaises, Commdr. Ordre des Palmes Académiques; Zoa D. Shilling Award, Western Mich. Univ. 2002. *Address:* L'Académie des Sciences et Techniques du Sénégal (ASTS), 61, Avenue Djily Mbaye, BP 4344, RP Dakar (office); Université Cheikh Anta Diop, BP 5005, Dakar-Fann, Senegal. *Telephone:* 849-10-99 (office). *Fax:* 849-10-96 (office). *E-mail:* Academ.sc@sentoo.sn (office). *Website:* www.ucad.sn (office).

NIASSE, Cheikh Moustapha; Senegalese politician, UN official and company director; *Special Envoy to the Democratic Republic of the Congo, United Nations;* b. 4 Nov. 1939; ed Lycée Faidherbe, St Louis, Univs of Dakar and Paris, Nat. School of Admin, Dakar; Dir for Information and Press Affairs, Ministry of Information 1968–69; Dir de Cabinet at Presidency 1970–78; Minister of Town Planning, Housing and Environment March–Sept. 1978, of Foreign Affairs 1978–84; Minister of Foreign Affairs of the Confed. of Senegambia 1982–84; fmr Minister of State, Minister of Foreign Affairs and Senegalese Abroad; Presidential cand. 2000; Prime Minister of Senegal April 2000–01; UN Special Envoy to Peace Process of the Democratic Repub. of the Congo June 2002–; Political Sec. Union Progressiste Sénégalaise until 1984; Founder and Leader Alliance des forces de progrès (AFP) 1999–; mem. Bd Dirs several pvt.-sector cos world-wide. *Address:* Alliance des forces de progrès, BP 5825, Dakar, Senegal (office); Special Envoy to the Democratic Republic of the Congo, United Nations, New York, NY 10017, USA (office). *Telephone:* 825-40-21 (office). *Fax:* 825-77-70 (office). *E-mail:* admin@afp-senegal.org (office). *Website:* www.afp-senegal.org (office).

NIBBERING, Nicolaas Martinus Maria, PhD; Dutch scientist and academic; *Professor Emeritus of Chemical Mass Spectrometry, University of Amsterdam;* b. 29 May 1938, Zaandam; s. of Dirk Nibbering and Hendrika Clijnk; m. Christina A. de Waart 1964; three s. one d.; ed Gymnasium B Zaanlands Lyceum Zaandam and Univ. of Amsterdam; mem. Faculty, Univ. of Amsterdam 1967–75, Assoc. Prof. 1975–80, Prof. of Organic Mass Spectrometry 1980–88, Prof. of Chemical Mass Spectrometry 1988–2000, Prof. Emer. 2000–, Scientific Dir Inst. of Mass Spectrometry 1988–2000; Visiting Faculty mem. Cornell Univ. 1974; Guest Prof., Univ. of Colorado 1980, Univ. of Rome 'La Sapienza' 2002; Chair. 12th Int. Mass Spectrometry Conf., Amsterdam 1991; Chair. European Soc. for Mass Spectrometry 1993–97, Pres. 1997–2000; Treas. Int. Mass Spectrometry Soc. 1997–2000, Pres. 2000–03; Co-Ed. Scientific Journal of Mass Spectrometry Reviews 1991–2000; Ed. Scientific Journal of Mass Spectrometry 1995–2000; mem. Royal Netherlands Acad., New York Acad. of Sciences; Hon. mem. Netherlands Soc. for Mass Spectrometry 1999; Hon. Life mem. British Mass Spectrometry Soc. 1999, Indian Soc. for Mass Spectrometry 2000, Mass Spectrometry Soc. of Japan 2003; Unilever Chem. Prize 1964, Shell Research Chem. Prize 1968, J. J. Thomson Award 1991, Joannes Marcus Marci Award 1992. *Publications:* Encyclopedia of Mass Spectrometry Vol. 4 (ed.) 2004; articles in books and journals. *Leisure interests:* motorbike races, classical music, opera, musicals, travelling, history. *Address:* Laser Centre and Chemistry Department, Vrije Universiteit, De Boelelaan 1083, 1081 HV Amsterdam (office); Janshof 39, 1391 XK Abcoude, Netherlands (home). *Telephone:* (20) 5987646 (office); (294) 283211 (home). *Fax:* (20) 5987643 (office); (294) 283211 (home). *E-mail:* nibberin@chem.vu.nl (office).

NIBLETT, Robin, MA, PhD; British academic; *Director, Chatham House;* b. 1962; ed Univ. of Oxford; Politics Lecturer, Univ. of Oxford 1985–88; Research Assoc., Political-Mil. Studies Program, Center for Strategic and Int. Studies (CSIS) 1988–92, European Rep. 1992–97, Dir Strategic Planning 1997–2001, Exec. Vice-Pres. 2001–07, Dir Europe Program 2004–07; Dir Chatham House 2007–. *Publications:* Rethinking European Order (with William Wallace) 2000; numerous contributions to CSIS publications including The Atlantic Alliance Transformed 1992, From Shadows to Substance: An Action Plan for Transatlantic Defense Cooperation 1995; contrib. to Euro-Focus, Washington Quarterly, International Herald Tribune, NPR, CNN, Fox News, BBC World News. *Address:* Office of the Director, Chatham House, 10 St James's Square, London, SW1Y 4LE, England (office). *Telephone:* (20) 7314-2798 (office). *Fax:* (20) 7957-5710 (office). *E-mail:* kburnet@chathamhouse.org.uk (office). *Website:* www.chathamhouse.org.uk (office).

NIBLOCK, Robert A., BA; American accountant and business executive; *Chairman and CEO, Lowe's Companies Inc.;* b. 1963, Fla; m. Melanie Niblock; two c.; ed Univ. of North Carolina at Charlotte; certified public accountant; began career with Ernst & Young 1984–93; joined Lowe's Companies Inc. as Dir of Taxation 1993, Vice Pres. and Treas. 1997–99, Sr Vice Pres. 1999–2000, Sr Vice Pres. and Chief Financial Officer 2000–01, Exec. Vice-Pres. and Chief Financial Officer 2001–03, Pres. 2003–06, Chair. and CEO 2005–; mem. Bd of Dirs Retail Industry Leaders Asscn. *Address:* Lowe's Companies Inc., 1000 Lowe's Boulevard, Mooresville, NC 28117, USA (office). *Telephone:* (704) 758-1000 (office). *Fax:* (336) 658-4766 (office). *E-mail:* info@lowes.com (office). *Website:* www.lowes.com (office).

NICA, Dan, PhD; Romanian telecommunications engineer and politician; *Deputy Prime Minister and Minister of the Interior and Administrative Reform;* b. 2 July 1960, Panciu, Vrancea Co.; m.; one c.; ed Faculty of Electronics and Telecommunications, Iasi, secializations in man. and communications in France, Sweden, Austria and Canada; various positions at Galati Co. Telecommunications Directorate 1985–96, Dir Galati Co. Telecommunications Directorate 1991–96; Assoc. Prof., Univ. 'Lower Danube' for Telecommunications and Data Transmission 1993–96; mem. Partidul Social Democrat (PSD—Social Democratic Party) Cen. Exec. Bureau 1999–2004, Pres. Galati Municipal PSD Org. 1997–2003, First Vice-Pres. PSD Galati Co. Org. 1999–2003, Pres. 2003–, mem. PSD Co-ordinating Bureau 2004–05, Vice-Pres. PSD and Pres. Dept of Transportation and Communications 21 April 2005, Vice-Pres. PSD and Co-ordinator Dept of Transport and Communications 2006–; mem. Chamber of Deputies (Partidul Democraţiei Sociale din România) for Galati Electoral Ward 1996– (re-elected for PSD 2000, 2004), mem. Parl. Comm. for Industries and Services, mem. Parl. Groups of Friendship with Egypt, Syria and Sweden, mem. Parl. Comm. for Public Admin, Territory Man. and Ecological Balance 2000–04, Vice-Pres. Comm. for Communication and Information Tech. 2004–08; Minister of Communication and Information Tech. 2000–04; Deputy Prime Minister and Minister of the Interior and Admin. Reform 2008–; Pres. Romania-Bavaria Governmental Comm. 2001–04; mem. UN Information and Communication Technologies Task Force 2002–04, Nat. Council for Science and Tech. Policy; Kt, Steaua României Nat. Order (Order of the Star of Romania) 2002; Prize for Excellence for the promotion of Romanian IT industry abroad, CHIP Review 2002, Prize for Excellence for the promotion and development of e-governance and transparency, ARIES 2003, 'Ion Irimescu – 100' Homage Medal, Ministry of Culture and Denominations 2003, Personalitatea anului (Personality of the Year) Prize, eFinance Review 2004. *Publications:* Government, Citizen, IT Society 2001, Le Gouvernement électronique (Concepts Appliqués en Roumanie) (Tudor Tanasescu Prize, Romanian Acad. 2007) 2005. *Address:* Ministry of the Interior and Administrative Reform, 010086 Bucharest, Piaţa Revoluţiei 1A, Sector 1, Romania (office). *Telephone:* (21) 3037080 (office). *Fax:* (21) 3103072 (office). *E-mail:* petitii@mai.gov.ro (office); dcrp@mira.gov.ro. *Website:* www.mai.gov.ro (office).

NICHOLAS, Sir David, Kt, CBE; British television executive and editor; b. 25 Jan. 1930, Tregaron; m. Juliet Davies 1952; one s. one d.; ed Neath Grammar School, Univ. Coll. of Wales, Aberystwyth; Nat. Service 1951–53; journalist with Yorkshire Post, Daily Telegraph, Observer; joined ITN (Ind. TV News) 1960, Deputy Ed., Ed. 1963–77, Ed. and CEO 1977–89, Chair. 1989–91; Dir (non-exec.) Channel 4 TV 1992–97; Chair. Sports News TV 1996–2003; Visiting Ed. 10 US Schools of Journalism 1992–99; Hon. LLD (Univ. Coll. of Wales, Aberystwyth); Hon. DHumLitt (Univ. of Southern Illinois). *Leisure interests:* walking, sailing, golf. *Address:* Lodge Stables, 2F Kidbrooke Park Road, London, SE3 0LW, England (home). *Telephone:* (20) 8319-2823 (home). *E-mail:* dnicholas1@btinternet.com (home).

NICHOLAS, Nicholas John, Jr, AB, MBA; American communications industry executive; b. 3 Sept. 1939, Portsmouth, NH; s. of Nicholas John Nicholas; brother of Peter M. Nicholas (q.v.); m. Llewellyn Jones 1972; two s. three d.; ed Princeton Univ and Harvard Business School; Dir of Financial Analysis, Time Inc., New York 1964–69, Asst to Pres. 1970, Asst Treas. 1971–73, Vice-Pres. 1975–86, Pres. and COO 1986–90, Co-CEO Time Warner Inc. 1990–92; Pres. Manhattan Cable TV 1973–76; Pres. Home Box Office, New York 1976–80, Chair. 1979–82; mem. Bd of Dirs Boston Scientific Corpn, Xerox Corpn, Time Warner Cable Inc.; fmr Dir Turner Broadcasting; Trustee Environmental Defense; mem. Council on Foreign Relations; fmr mem. Pres.'s Advisory Cttee for Trade Policy and Negotiations, Pres.'s Comm. on Environmental Quality. *Address:* c/o Board of Directors, Boston Scientific, Corporate Headquarters, One Boston Scientific Place, Natick, MA 01760-1537, USA.

NICHOLAS, Peter M., MSc; American medical device industry executive; *Chairman, Boston Scientific Corporation;* s. of Nicholas John Nicholas; brother of Nicholas John Nicholas, Jr; m.; three c.; ed Duke Univ., Durham, NC, Univ. of Pa Wharton School; Founder, Chair. and CEO Boston Scientific 1979–99, Chair. 1999–. *Address:* Boston Scientific Corporation, 1 Boston Scientific Place, Natick, MA 01760-1537, USA (office). *Telephone:* (508) 650-8000 (office). *Fax:* (508) 647-2393 (office). *Website:* www.bostonscientific.com (office).

NICHOLLS OF BIRKENHEAD, Baron (Life Peer), cr. 1994, of Stoke D'Abernon in the County of Surrey; **Donald James Nicholls,** PC, MA, LLB; British judge; b. 25 Jan. 1933, Bebington, Cheshire; s. of the late William Greenhow Nicholls and of Eleanor J. Nicholls; m. Jennifer Mary Thomas 1960; two s. one d.; ed Birkenhead School, Univ. of Liverpool and Trinity Hall, Cambridge; Nat. service 1951–53 (2nd Lt, Royal Army Pay Corps); called to Bar, Middle Temple 1958; in practice at Chancery Bar, London 1958–83; QC 1974; Judge, High Court of Justice, Chancery Div. 1983–86; Lord Justice of Appeal 1986–91; Vice-Chancellor, Supreme Court 1991–94; a Lord of Appeal in Ordinary 1994–2007, Second Sr Lord of Appeal 2002–07; Chair. Lord Chancellor's Advisory Cttee on Legal Educ. and Conduct 1996–97, Jt Cttee on Parl. Privilege 1997–99; a non-perm. Judge, Hong Kong Court of Final Appeal 1998–2004; Hon. Fellow, Trinity Hall, Cambridge 1986; Treas. Middle Temple 1997; Hon. LLD (Liverpool) 1987. *Leisure interests:* history, music, walking. *Address:* House of Lords, Westminster, London, SW1A 0PW, England (office). *Telephone:* (20) 7219-3143 (office).

NICHOLS, Mike; American director and producer; b. (Michael Igor Peschowsky), 6 Nov. 1931, Berlin, Germany; s. of Paul Nikolaievich Peschowsky and Brigitte Landauer; m. 1st Patricia Scot 1957 (divorced); m. 2nd Margot Callas 1974 (divorced); one d.; m. 3rd Annabel Nichols (divorced); m. 4th Diane Sawyer 1988; ed pvt. schools and Univ. of Chicago; started Playwrights Theatre Club, Chicago which became the Compass Players and later Second City; formed improvised nightclub double-act with Elaine May, touring for two years and recording TV programmes and record albums; appeared in An Evening with Mike Nichols and Elaine May, New York 1961–62; acted in Shaw's St Joan and directed The Importance of Being Earnest, Vancouver; Antoinette Perry (Tony) Awards for Direction: Barefoot in the Park, Luv, The Odd Couple, Plaza Suite, The Real Thing; Acad. Award for The Graduate; Emmy Award for TV programme Julie and Carol at Carnegie Hall; Nat Asscn Theatre Owners' Achievement Award for Direction for Who's Afraid of Virginia Woolf?. *Shows:* Barefoot in the Park, New York 1963, The Knack 1964, Luv 1964, The Odd Couple 1965, The Apple Tree 1966, The Little Foxes 1967, Plaza Suite 1968. *Films:* Who's Afraid of Virginia Woolf? 1966, The Graduate 1967, Catch-22 1969, Carnal Knowledge 1971, Day of the Dolphin 1973, The Fortune 1975, Gilda Live 1980, Silkwood 1983, Heartburn 1985, Biloxi Blues 1987, Working Girl 1988, Postcards From the Edge 1990, Regarding Henry (also producer) 1991, Wolf 1994 (co-producer), Mike Nichols 1995, The Birdcage (co-producer), Primary Colors 1998, What Planet Are You From? (also producer) 2000, Closer (also producer) 2004, Charlie Wilson's War 2007. *Television:* Wit (dir, producer and writer) 2001, Angels in America (dir and producer) 2003. *Plays:* Streamers 1976, Comedians 1976, The Gin Game 1978, Lunch Hour 1980, The Real Thing 1984, Hurlyburly 1984, Waiting for Godot 1988, Death and the Maiden 1992, Blue Murder 1995, The Seagull 2001, Spamalot (Tony Awards for Best Musical, Best Dir) 2005; Producer: Annie (New York) 1977. *Leisure interest:* Arabian horse breeding. *Address:* c/o CAA, 9830 Wilshire Boulevard, Beverly Hills, CA 90212, USA.

NICHOLS, Peter Richard, FRSL; British playwright; b. 31 July 1927, Bristol; s. of the late Richard G. Nichols and of Violet A. Poole; m. Thelma Reed 1960; one s. two d. (and one d. deceased); ed Bristol Grammar School, Bristol Old Vic School and Trent Park Training Coll.; actor, mostly in repertory 1950–55; schoolteacher 1958–60; mem. Arts Council Drama Panel 1973–75; Playwright-in-Residence, Guthrie Theatre, Minneapolis; Visiting Writer, Nanyang Coll., Singapore 1994; directed revivals of Joe Egg and Forget-me-not Lane (Greenwich), National Health (Guthrie, Minneapolis) and first productions of Born in the Gardens (Bristol), A Piece of My Mind (Southampton), Blue Murder (Bristol), Nicholodeon (Bristol); Tony Award, New York 1985; several SWET and four Evening Standard Drama Awards, Ivor Novello Award for Best Musical 1977. *Plays:* A Day in the Death of Joe Egg 1967, The National Health 1969, Forget-me-not Lane 1971, Chez Nous 1973, The Freeway 1974, Privates on Parade 1977, Born in the Gardens 1979, Passion Play 1980, Poppy (musical) 1982, A Piece of My Mind 1986, Blue Murder 1995, So Long Life 2000, Nicholodeon 2000. *Films:* Catch Us If You Can 1965, Georgy Girl 1967, Joe Egg 1971, The National Health 1973, Privates on Parade 1983. *Television:* plays include Walk on the Grass 1959, Promenade 1960, Ben Spray 1961, The Reception 1961, The Big Boys 1961, Continuity Man 1963, Ben Again 1963, The Heart of the Country 1963, The Hooded Terror 1963, When the Wind Blows 1964, The Brick Umbrella 1968, Daddy Kiss It Better 1968, The Gorge 1968, Hearts and Flowers 1971, The Common 1973 and Greeks Bearing Gifts (in the Inspector Morse series). *Publications:* Feeling You're Behind (memoirs) 1984, Nichols: Plays One and Two 1991, Diary 1969–71, Diary Selection 2000; all listed plays published separately; archive now available in Manuscripts Dept, British Library. *Leisure interests:* listening to jazz, looking at cities. *Address:* Alan Brodie Representation, Fairgate House, 6th Floor, 78 New Oxford Street, London, WC1A 1HB, England (office); 22 Belsize Park Gardens, London, NW3 4LH, England. *Telephone:* (20) 7079-7990 (office). *E-mail:* info@alanbrodie.com (office).

NICHOLS, Most Rev. Vincent Gerard, STL, PhL, MA, MEd; British ecclesiastic; *Archbishop of Westminster;* b. 8 Nov. 1945, Crosby; s. of Henry Joseph Nichols and Mary Russell; ed St Mary's Coll., Crosby, Gregorian Univ., Rome, Manchester Univ. and Loyola Univ., Chicago; Chaplain St John Rigby VI Form Coll., Wigan 1972–77; Priest in inner city of Liverpool 1978–81; Dir Upholland Northern Inst., Lancs. 1981–84; Gen. Sec. Catholic Bishops' Conf. of England and Wales 1984–91; Auxiliary Bishop of Westminster 1992–2000; Archbishop of Birmingham 2000–09; Archbishop of Westminster 2009–; Adviser to HE Cardinal Hume and Archbishop Worlock at the Int. Synods of Bishops 1980, 1983, 1985, 1987, 1990, 1991; Del. of Bishops' Conf. to Synod of Bishops 1994, 1999. *Publication:* Promise of Future Glory – Reflections on the Mass 1997, Missioners. *Address:* Archbishop's House, Ambrosden Avenue, London SW1P 1QJ, England (office). *Telephone:* (20) 7798-9033 (office). *E-mail:* abhreception@rcdow.org.uk (office). *Website:* www.rcdow.org.uk/archbishop (office).

NICHOLSON, Sir Bryan Hubert, Kt, GBE, MA, FRSA, CBIM, FCIM; British business executive; *Trustee, International Accounting Standards Committee Foundation;* b. 6 June 1932, Rainham, Essex; s. of the late Reginald H. Nicholson and of Clara Nicholson; m. Mary E. Harrison 1956; one s. one d. (and one s. deceased); ed Palmers School, Grays and Oriel Coll. Oxford; man. trainee, Unilever 1955–58; Dist Man. Van den Berghs 1958–59; Sales Man. Three Hands/Jeyes Group 1960–64; joined Sperry Rand 1964, Sales Dir UK Remington Div. 1964–66, Gen. Man. Australia, Remington Div. 1966–69, Man. Dir UK and France, Remington Div. 1969–72; Dir Operations, Rank Xerox (UK) 1972–76, Dir Overseas Subsidiaries 1976, Exec. Dir 1976–84, Chair. Rank Xerox (UK) and Rank Xerox GmbH 1979–84; Chair. Manpower Services Comm. 1984–87, The Post Office 1987–92; Chair. BUPA 1992–2001, Varity Holdings Ltd (now Varity Europe Ltd) 1993–96, Cookson Group PLC 1998–2003; Pres. Involvement and Participation Asscn 1990–94; Chair. CBI Vocational Educ. and Training Task Force 1988–89, CNAA 1988–91, Nat. Council for Vocational Qualifications 1990–93, CBI Educ. and Training Affairs Cttee 1990–93, Industrial Soc. 1990–93, Deputy Pres. CBI 1993–94, Pres. 1994–96; Non-exec. Dir GKN 1990–2000, Varity Corpn, USA 1993–96, LucasVarity 1996–99, Equitas Holdings Ltd 1996–2005, Newsquest PLC 1997–99, Action Centre for Europe Ltd 1997–2004, Accountancy Foundation 2000–04; mem. Nat. Econ. Devt Council 1985–92; Pres. Oriel Soc. 1988–92; Vice-Pres. Nat. Children's Home 1990–2002, Industrial Trust 1999–; Deputy Chair. Educ. Devt Int. 2003–04, Chair. 2004–05; Chancellor Sheffield Hallam Univ. 1992–2001; Pro-Chancellor and Chair. Council The Open Univ. 1996–2004; Chair. United Oxford and Cambridge Univ. Club 1995–97, Financial Reporting Council 2001–05, Goal PLC 2001–02; mem. Int. Advisory Bd Active Int. 2001–; EU Observer, Public Interest Oversight Bd, Int. Fed. of Accountants; Trustee Int. Accounting Standards Cttee Foundation 2006–; Pres. Nat. Centre for Young People with Epilepsy; Hon. FCGI 1988; Hon. Fellow Oriel Coll. Oxford 1989, Manchester Metropolitan Univ. 1990, Scottish Vocational Ed. Council 1994, Scottish Qualifications Authority 1997; Hon. Companion Inst. of Personnel and Devt 1994; Hon. DEd (CNAA) 1994; Dr hc (Open Univ.) 1994, (Sheffield Hallam) 2001; Hon. DLitt (Glasgow Caledonian) 2000. *Leisure interests:* tennis, bridge, opera, political history. *Address:* Point Piper, Lilley Drive, Kingswood, Surrey, KT20 6JA, England. *Telephone:* (1737) 832208. *Fax:* (1737) 833208. *E-mail:* bryannicholson@aol.com (office).

NICHOLSON, Rev. Ernest Wilson, PhD, DD, FBA; British fmr university administrator; b. 26 Sept. 1938, Northern Ireland; s. of Ernest Tedford Nicholson and Veronica Muriel Nicholson; m. Hazel Jackson 1962; one s. three d.; ed Trinity Coll. Dublin, Univ. of Glasgow; Lecturer in Semitic Languages, Trinity Coll. Dublin 1962–67; Lecturer in Divinity, Cambridge Univ. 1967–79, Fellow, Univ. Coll. (now Wolfson Coll.) Cambridge 1967–69, Fellow and Chaplain, Pembroke Coll. Cambridge 1969–79, Dean 1973–79; Oriel Prof. of The Interpretation of Holy Scripture, Oxford Univ. 1979–90, Provost of Oriel Coll. 1990–2003; Pro-Vice-Chancellor, Univ. of Oxford 1993–2003; Chair., Jardine Foundation 1993–2000; mem. Bd Govs, English Speaking Union 1998–2004; Hon. Fellow, Trinity Coll. Dublin, Wolfson Coll. Cambridge, St Peter's Coll. Oxford, Oriel Coll. Oxford; Commdr, Order of Merit, Italy. *Publications:* Deuteronomy and Tradition 1967, Preaching to the Exiles 1970, Exodus and Sinai in History and Tradition 1973, The Book of Jeremiah 1–25 1973, Kimchi's Commentary on Psalms 120–150 1973, The Book of Jeremiah 26–52 1974, God and His People 1986, The Pentateuch in the Twentieth Century 1998, A Century of Theological and Religious Studies in Britain (ed.) 2003. *Leisure interests:* country walking, music. *Address:* 39A Blenheim Drive, Oxford, OX2 8DJ, England. *Telephone:* (1865) 515826.

NICHOLSON, Jack; American actor and film director; b. 22 April 1937, Neptune, NJ; s. of John Nicholson and Ethel May Nicholson; m. Sandra Knight 1961 (divorced 1966); two d.; f. Proteus Films Inc. (production co.); Commdr des Arts et des Lettres; American Film Inst. Lifetime Achievement Award 1994, Cecil B. De Mille Award 1999, Kennedy Center Honor 2001. *Films include:* Cry-Baby Killer 1958, The Wild Ride 1960, Too Soon to Love 1960, The Little Shop of Horrors 1960, Studs Lonigan 1960, The Broken Land 1962, The Raven 1963, The Terror 1963, Ensign Pulver 1964, Flight to Fury 1964, Back Door to Hell 1964, Ride the Whirlwind (wrote, produced and acted) 1965, The Shooting (produced and acted) 1967, Hell's Angels on Wheels 1967, The Trip (wrote screenplay) 1967, Head (co-scripted, co-produced) 1968, Psych-Out 1968, Easy Rider 1969 (Acad. Award for Best Supporting Actor), The Rebel Rousers 1970, On a Clear Day You Can See Forever 1970, Five Easy Pieces 1971, Drive, He Said (dir) 1971, A Safe Place 1971, Carnal Knowledge 1971, The King of Marvin Gardens 1972, The Last Detail 1973, Chinatown 1974, The Passenger 1974, Tommy 1974, The Fortune 1975, The Missouri Breaks 1975, One Flew over the Cuckoo's Nest 1975 (Acad. Award for Best Actor 1976), The Last Tycoon 1976, Goin' South (actor, dir) 1978, The Shining 1980, The Postman Always Rings Twice 1981, Reds 1981, The Border 1982,

Terms of Endearment 1984 (Acad. Award for Best Supporting Actor), Prizzi's Honor 1984, Heartburn 1985, The Witches of Eastwick 1986, Ironweed 1987, Batman 1989, The Two Jakes (actor, dir) 1989, Man Trouble 1992, A Few Good Men 1992, Hoffa 1993, Wolf 1994, The Crossing Guard 1995, Mars Attacks! 1996, The Evening Star 1996, Blood and Wine 1996, As Good As It Gets 1997, The Pledge 2001, About Schmidt (Golden Globe for Best Dramatic Actor 2003) 2002, Anger Management 2003, Something's Gotta Give 2003, The Departed 2006, The Bucket List 2007. *Address:* Bresler Kelly and Associates, 11500 West Olympic Boulevard, Suite 510, Los Angeles, CA 90064, USA (office).

NICHOLSON, Jim; American diplomatist, business executive and fmr government official; b. 4 Feb. 1938, Struble, Iowa; m.; three c.; ed West Point, Columbia Univ., Univ. of Denver; US Army ranger, paratrooper, army reserve, retd with rank of Col; pnr in pvt. law practice; founder Nicholson Enterprises, Inc. 1978–; Pres. Renaissance Homes, Denver 1987–; mem. for Colo Republican Nat. Cttee 1986–2000, Vice-Chair. 1993–97, Chair. 1997–2000; Amb. to the Holy See 2001–04; Sec. of Veterans Affairs 2004–07 (resgnd); Kt, Sovereign Military Order of Malta; Dr hc (Regis, Denver) 2001; Bronze Star Medal, Combat Infantry Badge, Meritorious Service Medal, Vietnamese Cross for Gallantry, two Air Medals, Horatio Alger Award. *Address:* c/o Department of Veterans Affairs, 810 Vermont Avenue, NW, Washington, DC 20420, USA (office).

NICHOLSON, Pamela M., BA; American business executive; *President and Chief Operating Officer, Enterprise Rent-a-Car Company;* b. St Louis, Mo.; ed Univ. of Missouri; joined Enterprise Rent-a-Car co. as man. trainee in St Louis 1981, Asst Br. Man. 1982, transferred to Southern California group 1982, rose through ranks to become Regional Vice-Pres. 1994, returned to St Louis to become Corp. Vice-Pres. 1994–97, Gen. Man. Enterprise's New York group 1997–99, Sr Vice-Pres., North American operations 1999–2003, Exec. Vice-Pres. and COO Enterprise Rent-a-Car Co. 2003–08, Pres. and COO 2008–, mem. Bd of Dirs Crawford Group (parent co.), Dir Enterprise Rent-A-Car Foundation; mem. Bd of Dirs Energizer Holdings, Inc.; mem. Bd of Dirs Humane Soc. of Missouri; mem. Bd Trustees St Louis Regional Chamber and Growth Asscn; fmr mem. Bd United Way of Bergen Co., NJ, Bd INROADS, St Louis; ranked by Fortune magazine amongst 50 Most Powerful Women in Business in the US (44th) 2007, ranked by Forbes magazine amongst 100 Most Powerful Women (92nd) 2008. *Address:* Enterprise Rent-a-Car Company, 600 Corporate Park Drive, St Louis, MO 63105, USA (office). *Telephone:* (314) 512-5000 (office). *Fax:* (314) 512-4706 (office). *E-mail:* info@enterprise.com (office). *Website:* www.enterprise.com (office); www.erac.com (office).

NICHOLSON, Robert Douglas, BA; Canadian lawyer and politician; *Minister of Justice and Attorney-General of Canada;* b. 1952, Niagara Falls; m. Arlene Nicholson; three c.; ed Queen's Univ., Univ. of Windsor; fmr Niagara Regional Councillor, Conservation Authority Dir, Niagara Escarpment Commr; elected MP 1984, 1988, 2004, 2006; Parl. Sec. to the Leader of the Govt in the House of Commons 1989–90, to the Attorney-Gen. 1989–93; Minister for Science and Minister responsible for Small Business 1993; fmr Transport Critic; Chief Opposition Whip 2005; Leader of the Govt in the House of Commons and Minister for Democratic Reform 2006–07; Minister of Justice and Attorney-Gen. of Canada 2007–; mem. Upper Canada Law Soc. *Address:* Department of Justice Canada, East Memorial Bldg, 284 Wellington Street, Ottawa, ON K1A 0H8, Canada (office). *Telephone:* (613) 957-4222 (office). *Fax:* (613) 954-0811 (office). *E-mail:* webadmin@justice.gc.ca (office). *Website:* www.canada.justice.gc.ca (office); www.robnicholson.ca.

NICHOLSON, Robin, CBE, MA (Cantab.), MSc (Lon), RIBA, FRSA; British architect; *Senior Member, Edward Cullinan Architects;* b. 27 July 1944, Hertford; s. of Gerald Nicholson and Margaret Hanbury; m. Fiona Mary Bird; three s.; ed Eton Coll., Magdalene Coll. Cambridge, Bartlett School, Univ. Coll., London; worked for James Stirling Chartered Architects, London 1969–76; Boza Lührs Muzard, Santiago, Chile 1973; Polytechnic of North London 1976–79; Partner, Edward Cullinan Architects 1980–90, Dir 1989–, now Sr Mem.; Vice-Pres. RIBA 1992–94; CABE (Comm. for Architecture and the Built Environment) Commr 2002–, Jt Deputy Chair. 2008–; Dir Nat. House-Building Council (NHBC) 2007–; Chair. Dept for Children, Schools and Families (DCSF) Zero Carbon (Schools) Task Force; Hon. Fellow, Inst. of Structural Eng; RIBA Student Design Prize 1969. *Publications:* Innovations in Healthcare Design 1995, The Cost of Bad Design 2006. *Leisure interests:* gardening, making things. *Address:* Edward Cullinan Architects, 1 Baldwin Terrace, London, N1 7RU, England (office). *Telephone:* (20) 7704-1975 (office). *Fax:* (20) 7354-2739 (office). *E-mail:* eca@ecarch.co.uk (office). *Website:* www.edwardcullinanarchitects.com (office).

NICHOLSON, Sir Robin Buchanan, Kt, BA, MA, PhD, FRS, FREng, FIM, MInstP; British metallurgist; b. 12 Aug. 1934, Sutton Coldfield; s. of the late Carroll Nicholson and of Nancy Nicholson; m. 1st Elizabeth Mary Caffyn 1958 (died 1988); one s. two d.; m. 2nd Yvonne Appleby 1991; ed Oundle School and St Catharine's Coll., Cambridge; Demonstrator in Metallurgy, Univ of Cambridge 1960–64, lecturer 1964–66, Fellow of Christ's Coll. 1962–66; Prof. of Metallurgy, Univ. of Manchester 1966–72; Dir of Research Lab., Inco Europe Ltd 1972–76, Dir 1975–81, Man. Dir 1976–81; Co.-Chair. Biogen NV 1979–81; Chief Scientist, Cen. Policy Review Staff 1981–83; Chief Scientific Adviser, Cabinet Office 1983–86; Chief. Exec., Chair. Electro-Optical Div., Pilkington PLC 1986–96, Dir Pilkington PLC (fmrly Pilkington Bros PLC) 1986–96, Pilkington Optronics Ltd 1991–98; Dir Rolls-Royce 1986–2005, BP PLC 1987–2005; Chair. Centre for Exploitation of Science and Tech. 1987–90, Advisory Council on Science and Tech. 1990–93; Pres. Inst. of Materials 1997–98; Fellow, Royal Acad. of Eng, Royal Soc. (mem. Council 1983–85); mem. Council for Science and Tech. 1993–2000; fmr Pro Chancellor UMIST; Hon. DSc (Cranfield, Aston) 1983, (Manchester) 1985, (Nottingham) 2000; Hon. DMet (Sheffield) 1984; Hon. DEng (Birmingham) 1986; Rosenhain

Medal, Inst. of Metals 1971, Platinum Medal, Metals Soc. 1981. *Publications:* Precipitation Hardening (with A. Kelly) 1962, Electron Microscopy of Thin Crystals (with Sir P. Hirsch and others) 1965, Strengthening Methods in Crystals (ed. and contrib. with A. Kelly) 1971. *Leisure interests:* family life, gardening, music. *Address:* Penson Farm, Diptford, Totnes, Devon, TQ9 7NN, England.

NIČIĆ, Radovan; Serbian politician; *Speaker, 'Assembly of the Union of Municipalities of Kosovo and Metohija';* b. 1971, Čaglavica; ed Univ. of Prishtina; worked at Inst. for the Protection of Cultural Monuments, City of Prishtina 1990s; mem. Nat. Ass. (Serbian Radical Party); Speaker, 'Ass. of the Union of Municipalities of Kosovo and Metohija', Mitrovica 2008–; Pres. 'Municipal Ass. of Prishtina' 2008–. *Address:* Srpska Radikalna Stranka, 11080 Belgrade, Zemun, Magistratski trg 3, Serbia (office). *Telephone:* (11) 3164621 (office). *E-mail:* info@srs.org.yu (office). *Website:* www.srs.org.yu (office).

NICKELL, Stephen John, CBE, BA, MSc, FBA, FES; British economist and academic; *Warden, Nuffield College Oxford;* b. 25 April 1944; s. of John Edward Hilary Nickell and Phyllis Nickell; m. Susan Elizabeth Pegden; one s. one d.; ed Merchant Taylors' School, Pembroke Coll., Cambridge, London School of Econs; math. teacher, Hendon Co. School 1965–68; Lecturer, LSE 1970–77, Reader 1977–79, Prof. of Econs 1979–84, 1998–2005; Dir Inst. of Econs and Statistics, Prof. of Econs and Fellow, Nuffield Coll., Oxford 1984–98, Warden Nuffield Coll. 2006–; mem. Academic Panel, HM Treasury 1981–89, Council of Royal Econ. Soc. 1984–94 (Pres. Royal Econ. Soc. 2001–04), Econ. and Social Research Council 1990–94; external mem. Monetary Policy Cttee Bank of England 2000–06; Fellow, Econometric Soc. 1980; Hon. mem. American Econ. Asscn 1997, American Acad. of Arts and Sciences; Hon. Fellow, Nuffield Coll. Oxford 2003. *Publications:* The Investment Decisions of Firms (jtly) 1978, The Performance of the British Economy (jtly) 1988, Unemployment (jtly) 1991, The Unemployment Crisis 1994, The Performance of Companies 1995; numerous articles in learned journals. *Leisure interests:* reading, riding, cooking. *Address:* Nuffield College, New Road, Oxford, OX1 1NF, England (office). *Telephone:* (1865) 278520 (office). *Fax:* (1865) 278621 (office). *E-mail:* wardens.secretary@nuffield.ox.ac.uk (office). *Website:* www.nuffield.ox.ac.uk (office).

NICKLAM, Jimmy; Ni-Vanuatu politician; mem. Vanua'aku Pati (VP); MP for Tanna; Minister of Finance 2004. *Address:* c/o Ministry of Finance, PMB 058, Port Vila, Vanuatu (office).

NICKLAUS, Jack William; American professional golfer; b. 21 Jan. 1940, Columbus, Ohio; s. of L. Charles Nicklaus and Nicklaus Helen (née Schoener); m. Barbara Bash 1960; four s. one d.; ed Ohio State Univ.; professional golfer 1961–; won US Amateur Championship 1959, 1961; US Open Championship 1962, 1967, 1972, 1980, US Masters 1963, 1965, 1966, 1972, 1975, 1986, US PGA Championship 1963, 1971, 1973, 1975, 1980, British Open Championship 1966, 1970, 1978; by 1973 had won more major championship titles (totals now: 18 as professional, two as amateur) than any other player; Australian Open Champion six times, World Series winner five times, record three times individual winner World Cup, six times on winning team; rep. USA in six Ryder Cup matches; 97 tournament victories, 76 official tour victories, 58 times second, 36 times third; joined Seniors Tour 1990; won US Sr Open; 136 tournament appearances 1996; played in 154 consecutive majors 1999; has also designed over 100 golf courses in 26 countries; Co-Chair. The First Tee's Capital Campaign, More Than A Game 2000; Capt. US team. Pres.'s Cup 2003; f. Nicklaus Design (golf course design co.); founder and Chair. Nicklaus Children's Health Care Foundation; Hon. LLD (St Andrews) 1984; five times US PGA Player of the Year; Golfer of the Century 1988; Athlete of the Decade Award 1970s; Golf World's Golf Course Architect of the Year 1993, Presidential Medal of Freedom 2005. *Publications:* My Story 1997 and numerous books about golf. *Leisure Interests:* fishing, hunting, tennis. *Address:* Nicklaus Design, 11780 US Highway 1, Suite 500, North Palm Beach, FL 33408, USA (office). *Telephone:* (561) 227-0300 (office). *Fax:* (561) 227-0548 (office). *Website:* www.nicklaus.com (office).

NICKLES, Don; American business executive and fmr politician; *Chairman and CEO, Nickles Group LLC;* b. 6 Dec. 1948, Ponca City, Okla; s. of Robert Nickles and Coeweene Nickles; m. Linda Morrison 1968; one s. three d.; mem. Nat. Guard 1971–76; mem. Okla State Senate 1978–80, US Senator from Oklahoma (Republican) 1981–2005; Asst Majority Leader, US Senate; Founder, Chair. and CEO Nickles Group LLC (lobbyist firm), Washington, DC 2005–; Vice-Pres., Gen. Man. Nickles Machine Co. 1972–80; mem. Bd of Dirs Fortress America Acquisition Corpn 2005–, Chesapeake Energy Corpn 2005–. *Address:* Nickles Group LLC, 601 13th Street, NW, Suite 250 North, Washington, DC 20005, USA (office). *Telephone:* (202) 637-0214 (office). *E-mail:* mail@nicklesgroup.com (office). *Website:* www.nicklesgroup.com (office).

NICKS, Stephanie (Stevie); American singer and songwriter; b. 26 May 1948, Phoenix, AZ; m. Kim Anderson 1983 (divorced 1984); fmr mem., Fritz (with Lindsey Buckingham); mem. duo, Buckingham Nicks (with Lindsey Buckingham) 1971–74; mem., Fleetwood Mac 1975–93, 1997–; solo artist 1978–; numerous world-wide tours and concert appearances; American Music Award for Favorite Pop/Rock Group 1978, Billboard Award for Group of the Year 1977, BRIT Award for Outstanding Contribution 1998. *Recordings:* albums: with Lindsey Buckingham: Buckingham Nicks 1973; with Fleetwood Mac: Fleetwood Mac 1975, Rumours (Billboard Award for Album of the Year 1977, American Music Award for Favorite Pop/Rock Album 1978, Grammy Award for Album of the Year 1978) 1977, Tusk 1979, Fleetwood Mac Live 1980, Mirage 1982, Tango In The Night 1987, Behind The Mask 1990, The Dance 1997, Say You Will 2003, Pious Bird Of Good Omen 2004; solo: Bella

Donna 1981, The Wild Heart 1983, Rock A Little 1985, The Other Side Of The Mirror 1989, Street Angel 1994, Maybe Love Will Change Your Mind 1994, Trouble In Shangri-La 2001, The Divine 2001. *Address:* Sanctuary Artist Management, 15301 Ventura Boulevard, Building B, Suite 400, Sherman Oaks, CA 91403, USA (office); PO Box 112083, Carrolton, TX 75011-2083, USA (office). *Telephone:* (818) 286-4800 (office). *Fax:* (818) 286-4833 (office). *E-mail:* blain.clausen@sanctuarygroup.com (office). *Website:* www.sanctuarygroup.com (office); www.nicksfix.com; www.fleetwoodmac.com.

NICKSON, Baron (Life Peer), cr. 1994, of Renagour in the District of Stirling; **David Wigley Nickson,** CBE, KBE, FRSE; British business executive (retd); b. 27 Nov. 1929, Eton; s. of Geoffrey W. Nickson and Janet M. Nickson; m. Helen L. Cockcraft 1952; three d.; ed Eton and Royal Mil. Acad. Sandhurst; man. trainee, Wm. Collins, Publrs Glasgow 1954, Dir 1961, Jt Man. Dir 1967, Vice-Chair. 1976, Vice-Chair. and Group Man. Dir 1979–82, Non-exec. Dir 1982–85; Non-exec. Dir Scottish & Newcastle Breweries PLC 1981–95, Deputy Chair. 1982, Chair. 1983–89; Chair. Atlantic Salmon Trust 1989–96 (Vice-Chair. 1985–88), Sec. of State for Scotland's Atlantic Salmon Task Force 1996, Scottish Devt Agency 1989–90, Scottish Enterprise 1990–92; Deputy Chair. Clydesdale Bank PLC 1989–91, (Chair. 1991–98), Gen. Accident 1993–98; Dir (non-exec.) Gen. Accident Fire & Life Assurance Corpn PLC, Edin. Investment Trust PLC 1983–94; Pres. CBI 1986–88; Chair. Top Salaries Review Body 1989–95; Chancellor Glasgow Caledonian Univ. 1993–2002; Vice-Lord-Lt of Stirling and Falkirk 1997–2004; Hon. DL; Hon. DUniv (Stirling) 1986, (Glasgow) 1993; Hon. DBA (Napier) 1990, (Paisley) 1991. *Leisure interests:* fishing, birdwatching, shooting, the countryside. *Address:* The River House, Doune, Perthshire, FK16 6DA, Scotland (home). *Telephone:* (1876) 841614 (home). *Fax:* (1876) 841062 (home).

NICODIM, Ion; Romanian painter, engraver and sculptor; b. 26 March 1932, Constanţa; ed Coll. of Fine Arts, Bucharest; mem. of the Romanian Artists' Union; exhbns Bucharest, Cluj, Venice, Turin, Rome, São Paulo, Cagnes-sur-Mer, Yugoslavia, Vienna, Warsaw, Prague, Paris, Baden-Baden, Copenhagen; Prize of the Romanian Artists' Union 1964, 1977; Prize of the Romanian Acad. 1975, Gottfried von Herder Prize, Vienna 1992. *Works:* frescoes, mosaics, tapestries including Praise to Man, at the UN headquarters in New York, painting, graphics, glass, furniture, design, engravings, monumental decorative designs. *Publication:* La Surface et le Cri 1986. *Address:* Str. E. Broeşeanu nr. 17, Bucharest, Romania; 60 rue de Domrémy, 75013 Paris, France. *Telephone:* 45-70-87-04 (Paris); (1) 2111398 (Bucharest).

NICOL, Peter Franz, MBE; British professional squash player; b. 5 April 1974, Inverurie, Scotland; s. of Patrick Nicol; professional debut 1992; achieved world number 1 ranking Feb. 1998, current world number 1 (at Dec. 2003); major singles titles include US Open 1994, Canadian Open 1995, Mahindra International 1995, 1996, 1997, Al-Ahram International 1997, 2000, 2001, Kuwait Open 1997, British Open 1998, 2002, Commonwealth Games 1998 (silver medal 2002), PSA Super Series Final 1999, 2000, 2001, Hong Kong Open 1999, 2000, 2002, World Open 1999, 2001, Flanders Open 2000, Irish Open 2000, 2001, PSA Masters 2000, Tournament of Champions 2001, 2003, Scottish Open 2001, Qatar Classic 2001, 2003, YMG Capital Classic 2001, Memorial US Open 2002, British National Championship 2003; 67 appearances for Scotland (66 wins, 1 defeat); switched allegiance from Scotland to England in 2001 (qualified for England in May 2002); doubles gold for England (with Lee Beachill) Commonwealth Games 2002; winner (with England team) European Team Championships 2003; Dr hc in Law (Robert Gordon Univ., Aberdeen). *Leisure interests:* golf, shopping. *Website:* www.pnsquash.com.

NICOLAOU, Kyriacos C., BSc, PhD; Cypriot chemist and academic; *Aline W. and L. S. Skaggs Professor of Chemical Biology, Scripps Research Institute;* b. 5 July 1946; ed Bedford Coll., Univ. of London, England, Univ. Coll., London; Research Assoc., Columbia Univ., USA 1972–73; Research Assoc., Harvard Univ. 1973–76; Asst Prof. of Chemistry, Univ. of Pa 1976–80, Assoc. Prof. 1980–81, Prof. 1981–88, Rhodes-Thompson Prof. of Chemistry 1988–89; Prof. of Chemistry, Univ. of Calif., San Diego 1989–; Chair. Dept of Chemistry and Darlene Shiley Chair. in Chemistry, Scripps Research Inst., La Jolla, CA 1989–, also Aline W. and L. S. Skaggs Prof. of Chemical Biology 1996–; Fellow, American Acad. of Arts and Sciences 1993–, AAAS 1999–; mem. NAS 1996–, ACS, German Chemical Soc., European Chemical Soc.; mem. Editorial Bd numerous journals; Hon. mem. Pharmaceutical Soc. of Japan 1996–; Order of the Commdr of Honour (Greece) 1998; Hon. MA (Univ. of Pa) 1980, Hon. DSc (Univ. Coll., London) 1994, Hon. PhD (Univ. of Athens 1995, Univ. of Thessaloniki 1996, Univ. of Cyprus 1997, Univ. of Crete 1998, Univ. of Alcala 1998, Agric. Univ. of Athens 2000); numerous awards including Alexander von Humboldt Foundation US Sr Scientist Award 1987, ACS Award for Creative Work in Synthetic Organic Chemistry 1993, Royal Soc. of Chemistry Rhone-Poulenc Medal 1995, Harvard Univ. Max Tischler Prize 2000, Royal Soc. of Chemistry Centenary Medal 2000, Ernst Schering Prize 2001. *Address:* Department of Chemistry, Scripps Research Institute, 10550 North Torrey Pines Road, La Jolla, CA 92037, USA (office). *Telephone:* (858) 784-2400 (office). *Fax:* (858) 784- 2469 (office). *E-mail:* kcn@scripps.edu (office). *Website:* www.scripps.edu/chem/nicolaou (office).

NICOLAS, Alrich; Haitian diplomatist and politician; *Minister of Foreign Affairs;* fmr Chief, Strategy and Policy Unit, Haiti, UNDP; fmr Amb. to Germany (also accred to Denmark); Minister of Foreign Affairs 2008–. *Address:* Ministry of Foreign Affairs, boulevard Harry S Truman, Cité de l'Exposition, Port-au-Prince, Haiti (office). *Telephone:* 222-8482 (office). *Fax:* 223-1668 (office). *E-mail:* webmaster@maehaitiinfo.org (office).

NICOLAS, Gwenael, MA; French interior designer and product designer; *President, Curiosity Inc.;* b. 6 June 1966, Rosporden; ed Ecole supérieure d'art graphique et d'architecture d'intérieure, Royal Coll. of Art, London; Pres. Curiosity Inc.; Nintendo Game Boy Advance Design Consultant 2000; American Inst. of Architecture Citation 1998, I.D. Magazine Distinction 1999, 2000, I.F. Design Award 2003, Japan Display Design Award 2005. *Achievements:* Tag Heuer Shops, Tokyo, New York, London, Sony LCD TV 'Capujo', Sony Showroom, Tokyo 2003, Nissan Booth, Tokyo Motor Show 2004, 2005. *Publication:* Curiosity 2002. *Address:* Curiosity Inc., 2-13-16, Tomigaya, Shibuya-ku, Tokyo 151-0063, Japan (office). *Telephone:* (3) 5452-0095 (office). *Fax:* (3) 5454-9691 (office). *E-mail:* nicolas@curiosity.jp (office). *Website:* www.curiosity.jp (office).

NICOLET, Claude; French historian and academic; *Professor Emeritus, University of Paris, Sorbonne;* b. 15 Sept. 1930, Marseilles; s. of Edmond Nicolet and Suzanne Nicolet; m. 1st Michelle Brousset 1956 (divorced, deceased); one s.; m. 2nd Hélène Pierre 1963; three s.; ed Ecole Normale Supérieure and Ecole Française de Rome; served on Staff of Minister of State Pierre Mendès-France 1956; Editorial Sec., Cahiers de la République 1956–57; mem. Ecole Française de Rome 1957–59; Lecturer, Univ. of Tunis 1959–61; Lecturer and Prof., Univ. of Caen 1961–69; Prof. of Roman History, Univ. of Paris, Sorbonne 1969–92, Emer. Prof. 1992–; Dir of Studies, Ecole Pratique des Hautes Etudes (Section IV) 1969–; mem. Inst. for Advanced Studies, Princeton 1966–67, 1972; Prof., Univ. Paris I 1971–; Dir Era 757, CNRS 1978–91; Dir, Centre Gustav Glotz 1981–92, Ecole Française de Rome 1992–95; Pres., Soc. for Latin Studies 1983, Conseil scientifique du Centre d'études et des prévisions du Ministère de l'Interiéur 1998; mem. Acad. des Inscriptions et Belles Lettres (Inst. de France); Assoc. mem. Accad. dei Lincei; Corresp. Fellow, British Acad. 1987; Officier, Légion d'honneur; Officier des Palmes académiques; Prix Galileo Galilei des Rotary italiens 1994, Grand Prix Nat. (histoire) 1996, Prix des Cultori di Roma 1997. *Publications include:* Le radicalisme 1957, Pierre Mendès France ou le métier de Cassandre 1959, Cicéron 1961, Les idées politiques à Rome sous la République 1964, L'ordre équestre à l'époque républicaine Vol. I 1966, Vol. II 1978, Les Gracques, crise agraire et révolution à Rome 1967, Le métier de citoyen dans la Rome républicaine 1976, Rome et la conquête du monde méditerranéen 1977, L'idée républicaine en France 1982, Des ordres à Rome 1984, L'inventaire du monde: Géographie et politique aux origines de l'Empire romain 1988, Rendre à César 1988, La République en France: état des lieux 1992, Nation, Histoire, République 2000, Censeurs et Publicains 2000, La fabrique d'une nation: La France entre Rome et les Germains 2003. *Address:* Université Paris-Sorbonne (Paris IV), 1 rue Victor Cousin, 75005 Paris (office); Institut de France, 23 quai Conti, 75006 Paris; 2 rue de Paradis, 75010 Paris, France. *Telephone:* 1-47-70-02-91. *Website:* www.paris4.sorbonne.fr/en/sommaire.php3 (office).

NICOLI, Eric Luciano, CBE, BSc; British business executive; b. 5 Aug. 1950, Pulham Market, Norfolk; s. of Virgilio Nicoli and Ida Nicoli; m. Rosalind West 1977; one s. one d.; ed Diss Grammar School, Norfolk, King's Coll. London; worked briefly in market research, then various positions with Rowntree Marketing Dept 1972–80; Sr Marketing Controller Biscuit Div., United Biscuits 1980–81, Marketing Dir Biscuits 1981–84, and Confectionery 1982–84; UK Business Planning Dir 1984, Man. Dir UB Frozen Foods 1985, UB Brands 1986–89, apptd. to Bd of UB (Holdings) PLC 1989, CEO European Operations 1989–90, Group CEO United Biscuits (Holdings) PLC 1991–99, Acting Chair. 2001; Non-Exec. Dir EMI Group PLC 1993–99, Exec. Dir and Chair. 1999–2007, CEO Jan.–Aug. 2007; Deputy Chair. Business in the Community 1991–2003; Chair. (non-exec.) HMV Media Group PLC 2001–04, Tussauds Group Ltd 2001–, Vue Entertainment 2006–, R&R Music 2008–; Chair. Per Cent Club 1993–, EMI Music Sound Foundation 2003–07; advisor, Nick Stewart and Assocs 2008–. *Leisure interests:* all sports (especially golf), music, food. *Address:* Vue Entertainment, 10 Chiswick Park, 566 Chiswick High Road, London, W4 5XS, England (office). *Telephone:* (20) 8396-0100 (office). *Fax:* (20) 8396-2009 (office). *Website:* www.myvue.com (office).

NICOLIN, Curt René; Swedish business executive; b. 10 March 1921, Stockholm; s. of Felix Nicolin and Anna-Lisa Nicolin; m. Ulla Sandén 1946 (died 1999); three s. two d.; ed Royal Inst. of Tech., Stockholm; with STAL Finspong 1945–61; Interim Pres. Scandinavian Airlines System (SAS) 1961–62; Swedish Chair. SAS 1973–91; Pres. ASEA AB, Västerås 1961–76, Chair. of Bd 1976–91, Incentive AB 1991–92; Co-Chair. ABB Asea Brown Boveri 1988–91; Hon. Chair. ASEA AB 1991; Hon. DTech 1974; Hon. LLD 1991; Hon. DEcon 1994; Lucia Trade Award 1996; Commdr, Order of Vasa, First Class 1974, Medal, Order of Seraphim 1991. *Publications:* Private Industry in a Public World 1973, New Strategy for Sweden 1996, Ethics in Society, Business and Management 1989–99. *Leisure interests:* tennis, sailing.

NICOLL, Roger, BA, MD; American neuroscientist and academic; *Professor of Cellular and Molecular Pharmacology, University of California, San Francisco;* b. 15 Jan. 1941, Camden, NJ; m.; one c.; ed Lawrence Univ., Wis., Univ. of Rochester Medical School, Nat. Insts of Health; Research Fellow, Public Health Service, Nat. Inst. of Mental Health Lab. of Neuropharmcology, Bethesda, Md 1965–66, Research Assoc. (Mil.) 1969–73; Intern in Medicine, Univ. of Chicago Hosps and Clinic 1968–69; Research Assoc. Prof., State Univ. of NY, Lab. of Neurobiology, Buffalo 1973–75; Asst Prof., Depts of Pharmacology and Physiology, Univ. of California, San Francisco 1975–76, Assoc. Prof. 1977–80, Prof. 1980–, currently Prof. of Cellular and Molecular Pharmacology, Interim Dept Chair. 1991–93; Visiting Assoc. Prof., Salk Inst. for Biological Studies 1976; mem. Editorial Bd Current Opinion in Neurobiology 1991–, Hippocampus 1993–, Molecular and Cellular Neurobiology 1996–, Physiological Reviews 1998–; mem. NAS 1994–, American Acad. of Arts and Sciences 1999–; numerous awards including Gruber Neuroscience Prize, The Peter and Patricia Gruber Foundation (co-recipient) 2006. *Publications:* numerous scientific papers in professional journals on the cellular and molecular mechanisms underlying learning and memory in the mammalian brain. *Address:* Department of Cellular and Molecular Pharmacology, University of California, San Francisco, Genentech Hall, 600 16th Street, Box 2140, San Francisco, CA 94143-2140, USA (office). *Telephone:* (415) 476-2018 (office). *E-mail:* nicoll@phy.ucsf.edu (office). *Website:* keck.ucsf.edu/neurograd/faculty/nicoll.html (office).

NICORA, HE Cardinal Attilio; Italian ecclesiastic; *President, Patrimony of the Apostolic See, Roman Curia;* b. 16 March 1937, Varese; ed Pontifical Gregorian Univ., Rome, Theological Faculty, Milan; ordained priest 1964; Prof. of Canon Law, Theological Seminary of Venegano 1964–77; Auxiliary Bishop of Milan and Titular Bishop of Furnos Minor 1977–92; Bishop of Verona 1992–97, Bishop Emer. 1997–; Bishop of Roman Curia 1997–2002; Pres. Patrimony of the Apostolic See, Roman Curia 2002–2 April 2005, 21 April 2005–; cr. Cardinal (Cardinal-Deacon of S. Filippo Neri in Eurosia) 2003; oversaw revision of Concordat between Italy and the Vatican 1984; participated in Papal conclave that elected Pope Benedict XVI 2005. *Address:* Administration of the Patrimony of the Holy See, Palazzo Apostolico, 00120 Città del Vaticano, Italy (office). *Telephone:* (06) 69883247 (office). *Fax:* (06) 69885512 (office). *E-mail:* segreteria.presidenza@aosa.va (office).

NICULESCU, Alexandru A.; Romanian diplomatist and international organization official; b. 1 Jan. 1941, Bucharest; s. of Alexandru Niculescu and Elisabeth Niculescu; m.; three c.; ed Polytechnical Inst. and Univ. of Law, Bucharest; Chargé d'affaires, Perm. Mission to UN, Geneva 1990–91, Deputy Perm. Rep. 1991–95; Dir Div. for UN and Specialized Agencies, Ministry of Foreign Affairs, Bucharest 1995–98; Deputy Perm. Rep. to UN, New York 1999–2000, Perm. Rep. 2000–03. *Publications:* essays and articles on world econ. relations, globalization and UN system's activities. *Leisure interests:* music, economic literature (on globalization), art. *Address:* 13A, Dumbrava Rosie Street, Ap. 6, Sector 2, Bucharest, Romania (home). *Telephone:* (1) 2117877 (home).

NIE, Lt-Col Haisheng; Chinese astronaut; b. Sept. 1964, Zaoyang, Hubei Prov.; m. Nie Jielin; one d.; served as fighter pilot in PLA Air Force; attained rank of Lt-Col; selected to be astronaut, Shenzhou Program 1998; support crew for Shenzhou 5, (China's first manned space mission) 2003; debut space flight on board Shenzhou 6, with astronaut Fei Junlong (q.v.), launched from Jiuquan Satellite Launch Centre, Gobi Desert (China's second space mission) 12 Oct. 2005. *Address:* China National Space Administration, c/o State Commission of Science, Technology and Industry for National Defence, 2a Guang'anmennan Jie, Xuanwu Qu, Beijing 100053, People's Republic of China. *Website:* www.cnsa.gov.cn.

NIE, Lt-Gen. Li (Lili); Chinese public official; b. 1930; d. of the late Marshal Nie Rongzhen; m. Ding Henggao; joined CCP 1950; Vice-Chair. of Scientific and Tech. Cttee under Comm. of Science, Tech. and Industry for Nat. Defence 1982–85; rank of Maj.-Gen. PLA 1988; Vice-Chair. Nat. Examination Cttee for Science Award; Deputy, 6th NPC 1983–88, 7th NPC 1988–93, mem. Standing Cttee 8th NPC 1993–98 (mem. Internal and Judicial Affairs Cttee 1994–98), mem. Standing Cttee 9th NPC 1998–2003; rank of Lt-Gen. 1993–; Vice-Pres. All-China Women's Fed. 1993–98. *Address:* National Examination Committee for Science Award, Sanlihe, Beijing, People's Republic of China (office).

NIEDERAUER, Duncan L., BA, MBA; American business executive; *CEO, NYSE Euronext Inc.;* b. 7 Sept. 1959; m.; three c.; ed Colgate Univ., Emory Univ.; joined Goldman Sachs and Co. 1985, joined Equities Div. 1987, relocated to HQ of Spear, Leeds & Kellogg (subsidiary) 2000, Man. Dir and Co-Head, Equities Div. Execution Services, Goldman Sachs and Co. –2007; Pres. and Co-COO New York Stock Exchange (now NYSE Euronext Inc.) and Head, US Cash Markets April–Nov. 2007–, CEO Nov. 2007–, mem. NYSE Euronext Man. Cttee April 2007–; mem.Colgate Univ. Alumni Corpn Bd of Dirs, also Alumni Trustee 2006–; fmr mem. Bd of Mans Archipelago Holdings LLC; fmr mem. Bd of Dirs EzeCastle Software. *Address:* NYSE Euronext Inc., 11 Wall Street, New York, NY 10005, USA (office). *Telephone:* (212) 656-3000 (office). *Fax:* (212) 656-2126 (office). *Website:* www.nyse.com (office).

NIEDERHUBER, John Edward, MD; American surgeon, academic, researcher and institute director; *Director, National Cancer Institute;* b. 21 June 1938, Steubenville, Ohio; s. of William Henry Niederhuber and Helen (Smittle) Niederhuber; one s.; ed Bethany Coll., W Va, Ohio State Univ. School of Medicine; NIH Academic Trainee in Surgery, Univ. of Michigan 1969–70, completed his training in surgery 1973, mem. Faculty 1973–87, apptd Prof. of Microbiology/Immunology and Prof. of Surgery 1980; Visiting Fellow, Div. of Immunology, Karolinska Inst., Stockholm, Sweden 1970–71; Visiting Prof., Dept of Molecular Biology and Genetics, Johns Hopkins Univ. School of Medicine, Baltimore, Md 1986–87, Prof. of Surgery, Oncology, and Molecular Biology and Genetics 1987–91; Emile Holman Prof. of Surgery, Prof. of Microbiology and Immunology, and Chair. Dept of Surgery, Stanford Univ. 1991–97; Prof. of Surgery and Oncology, Univ. of Wisconsin School of Medicine 1997–2002, Dir Univ. of Wisconsin Comprehensive Cancer Center 1997–2002; Chair. Nat. Cancer Advisory Bd (NCAB) 2002–05; COO and Deputy Dir for Translational and Clinical Sciences, Nat. Cancer Inst. (NCI) 2005–, Dir NCI 2006–, external adviser to NCI, mem. NCI Cancer Centers Review Cttee 1984–86, mem. NCI Div. of Cancer Treatment's Bd of Scientific Counselors 1986–91 (Chair. 1987–91), mem. NCAB's Sub-cttee to Evaluate the Nat. Cancer Program (Cttee to Assess Measures of Progress Against Cancer) and Chair. Molecular Medicine Panel 1993–95, Lab. Investigator supported by NCI and NIH, Leader, Lab. of Tumor and Stem Cell Biology (part of Cell and Cancer Biology Br. of NCI's Center for Cancer Research); holds clinical appointment on NIH Clinical Center Medical Staff; mem. Bd C-Change; mem. CEO Roundtable, fmr Co-Chair. Task Force to develop a plan for future oncology devt; Pres. Asscn of American Cancer Insts 2001–03; Founding mem. and Exec. Cttee mem. American Coll. of Surgeons Oncology Cooperative Group; mem. American Coll. of Surgeons Comm. on Cancer 1983–95, Chair. 1989–90, General Motors Cancer Research Foundation Kettering Prize Selection Cttee 1988–89, GMCRF Awards Assembly 1988–92, 1998–2002, Burroughs-Wellcome Foundation Translational Research Advisory Cttee 1999–2006; Chair. American Soc. of Clinical Oncology Surgical Oncology Task Force Strategic Planning Process 2001–02, ASCO Public Policy and Practice Cttee 2002, 2003; mem. 10 scientific journal editorial bds, including Journal of Clinical Oncology 1993–95; mem. Soc. of Surgical Oncology 1978 (Pres. 2001–02); mem. NAS Inst. of Medicine 2008; hon. DSc (Bethany Coll.) 2007numerous hon. professorships; US Public Health Service Career Devt Award, Nat. Inst. of Allergy and Infectious Diseases, Distinguished Faculty Service Award, Univ. of Michigan, Alumni Achievement Award, Ohio State Univ. Coll. of Medicine 1989, Distinguished Alumni Award in Medicine, Bethany Coll. 1995, Professional Achievement Award, Ohio State Univ. 2007. *Achievements include:* recognized for pioneering work in hepatic artery infusion chemotherapy and was first to demonstrate feasibility of totally implantable vascular access devices. *Publications:* editor of four books, including Clinical Oncology; author or co-author of more than 180 publs. *Address:* National Cancer Institute, NCI Public Inquiries Office, 6116 Executive Boulevard, Room 3036A, Bethesda, MD 20892-8322, USA (office). *Telephone:* (301) 496-5615 (office). *Fax:* (301) 402-0338 (home). *E-mail:* niederj@mail.nih.gov (office). *Website:* www.cancer.gov (office).

NIELSEN, Jakob, PhD; American (b. Danish) software designer; *Principal, Nielsen Norman Group;* b. 1957, Copenhagen; s. of Gerhard Nielsen and Helle Nielsen; m. Hannah Kain; ed Tech. Univ. of Denmark; fmr software designer, Bellcore, IBM; Sr Researcher Sun Microsystems 1988; Co-Founder and Prin., Nielsen Norman Group; mem. editorial bd several professional journals including Morgan Kaufmann Publishers, ACM Interactions, Behaviour & Information Technology, Personal and Ubiquitous Computing. *Achievements include:* holder of more than 70 US patents. *Publications:* Usability Engineering 1994, Multimedia and Hypertext: The Internet and Beyond 1995, Designing Web Usability: The Practice of Simplicity 2000, Homepage Usability: 50 Websites Deconstructed 2001, Prioritizing Web Usability 2006, Eyetracking Web Usability 2008; author of monthly newsletter on web design. *Address:* Nielsen Norman Group, 48105 Warm Springs Boulevard, Fremont, CA 94539, USA (office). *Telephone:* (415) 682-0688 (office). *E-mail:* nielsen@nngroup.com (office). *Website:* www.nngroup.com (office).

NIELSON, Poul, MSc; Danish civil servant, academic and fmr politician; *Adjunct Professor, Department of History, International and Social Studies, University of Aalborg;* b. 1943, Copenhagen; m. Anne-Marie Nielson 1967; three c.; ed Univ. of Århus; Chair. Nat. Social Democratic Students Org. 1966–67; mem. Social Democratic Foreign Affairs Cttee 1965–79 (Chair. 1974–79); mem. Parl. 1971–73, 1977–84, 1986–99; Head of Section, Ministry of Foreign Affairs 1974–79, 1984–85; Chair. Danish European Movt 1977–79; Chair. Parl. Commerce Cttee 1979; Minister of Energy 1979–82; Asst Prof., Danish School of Public Admin. 1985–86; CEO LD-Energy Inc. 1988–94; Minister for Devt Co-operation 1994–99; EU Commr for Devt and Humanitarian Aid 1999–2004; Adjunct Prof., Dept of History, Int. and Social Studies, Univ. of Aalborg 2005–. *Publications:* Power Play and Security 1969, The Wage Earners and the Company Act 1974, Politicians and Civil Servants 1987. *Address:* University of Aalborg, Department of History, International and Social Studies, Fibigerstræde 2, 9220 Aalborg East, Denmark (office).

NIEMCZYCKI, Zbigniew; Polish business executive; b. 23 Jan. 1947, Nisko; m. Katarzyna Frank; one d. three s.; ed Warsaw Univ. of Tech.; Owner and Chair. Curtis Group; Founder and Chair. Polish Eagles Aviation Foundation; Pres. Bd Polish Business Roundtable; Vice-Pres. Main Council Business Centre Club; mem. Council of European Integration affiliated to Prime Minister's Office, Council to the Rector of Warsaw Univ.; Kt's Cross, Order of Polonia Restituta, St Gregory Cross, Pope John Paul II, Heart Oscar, Cardiosurgery Devt Foundation; Businessman of the Year 1992, Leader of Polish Business 1992. *Leisure interests:* piloting helicopters and planes, tennis. *Address:* Curtis Group, ul. Wołoska 18, 02-675 Warsaw, Poland (office). *Telephone:* (22) 848-65-53 (office). *Website:* www.curtisgroup.pl (office).

NIEMEYER, Oscar; Brazilian architect; b. 15 Dec. 1907, Rio de Janeiro; s. of Oscar Niemeyer Soares; m. 1st Anita Baldo (died 2004); one d.; m. 2nd Vera Lucia Cabreira; ed Escola Nacional de Belas Artes, Rio de Janeiro; in office of Lúcio Costa 1935; designed Ministry of Educ. and Health Bldg, Rio de Janeiro 1937–43, Brazilian Pavilion, New York World Fair 1939, with others designed UN Bldg, New York 1947; Dir of Architecture for new capital of Brasília and given a free hand in design of public and other bldgs 1957–; designs include Bienal Exhbn Hall, São Paulo, urban area of Grasse (near Nice) 1966, French CP Bldg, Paris 1966, Palace of Arches (for Foreign Ministry) Brasília, Sambódromo, Rio de Janeiro 1984; f. Fundação Oscar Niemeyer, Brasilia 1988, Museum of Contemporary Art, Niterói 1996, Oscar Niemeyer Museum, Curitiba 2003, Caminho Niemeyer, Niterói 2007, Niemeyer Cultural Centre, Avilés, Spain 2007; Commdr, Légion d'Honneur 2007; Lenin Peace Prize 1963, Prix Int. de l'Architecture d'aujourd'hui 1966, shared Pritzker Prize 1988, Prince of the Asturias Prize for the Arts 1989, RIBA Gold Medal for Architecture 1998, Praemium Imperiale 2004. *Publication:* Curves of Time: The Memoirs of Oscar Niemeyer 2000. *Address:* Fundação Oscar Niemeyer, Rua Conde Lages, 25 - Glória, Rio de Janeiro, RJ; 3940 avenida Atlântica, Rio de Janeiro, RJ, Brazil. *Telephone:* (21) 2509-1844. *E-mail:* fundacao@niemeyer.org.br. *Website:* www.niemeyer.org.br.

NIEMI, Irmeli, DPhil; Finnish fmr civil servant and university professor; b. 3 Feb. 1931, Helsinki; d. of Taneli Kuusisto and Kyllikki Valtonen; m. Mikko Niemi 1953; one s. two d.; ed Univ. of Helsinki; freelance translator, literature and theatre critic; Ed. 1950–68; Jr Research Fellow, Acad. of Finland 1968–69; Assoc. Prof. of Comparative Literature and Drama, Univ. of Turku 1970–78,

Prof. 1978–81, 1984–90; Dir-Gen. Dept of Culture, Ministry of Educ. 1990–96; Sr Teacher, Theatre Acad. Helsinki 1964–96; Research Prof., Acad. of Finland 1981–84; Chair. Finnish Research Council for the Humanities 1986–88, Arts Council of Finland 1989–90, Bd of Finnish Nat. Opera 1996–2001, Finland Festivals 1998–2006; Council of the Finnish Inst. in London 1996–2003; mem. Science Policy Council of Finland 1986–90. *Publications:* Maria Jotunin näytelmät 1964, Nykydraaman ihmiskuva 1969, Nykyteatterin juuret 1975, The Role of the Spectator 1984, Suomalainen alueteatteri 1978–82 1984, Arki ja tunteet Maria Jotunin elämä ja kirjailijantyö 2001. *Leisure interests:* modern music, forest walks, travel. *Address:* Vähäpellontie 5 A1, 21570 Sauvo, Finland (home). *Telephone:* (50) 5286050 (home). *E-mail:* irniemi@saunalahti.fi (home).

NIEN, Nguyen Dy; Vietnamese politician; b. 9 Dec. 1935, Thanh Hoa; m.; three d.; ed Banaras Hindu Univ., India; mem. Nat. Liberation Movt 1951; joined Ministry of Foreign Affairs 1954, Deputy Dir, then Dir 1980–83, Asst Minister 1984–86, Deputy 1987–2000, Minister of Foreign Affairs 2000–06; elected mem. Cen. Cttee Communist Party of Viet Nam 1991–; Pres. Viet Nam Nat. Comm. for UNESCO 1987; Pres. Nat. Cttee for Overseas Vietnamese 1995; retd 2007. *Address:* c/o Ministry of Foreign Affairs, 1 Ton That Dam, Ba Dinh District, Hanoi, Viet Nam (office).

NIETO GALLO, Gratiniano; Spanish art official; b. 6 March 1917, La Aguilera, Burgos; s. of Francisco Nieto Gallo and Genoveva Nieto Gallo; m. María de Mergelina Cano-Manuel; one s. one d.; ed Institución Teresiana, Instituto Ramiro de Maeztu and Univ. de Madrid; Prof., Univ. de Valladolid 1940–52; Dir Colegio Mayor Santa Cruz de Valladolid 1943–52; Sec. School of Art and Archaeology, Univ. de Valladolid 1940–52; Dir Colegio Mayor Nebrija, Univ. de Madrid 1952–56; Tech. Sec.-Gen. Directorate of Archives and Libraries 1956–61; attached to Univ. de Murcia 1959–61; Dir-Gen. of Fine Arts 1961–68; Dir Cen. Inst. for Conservation and Restoration of Works of Art 1968–; Prof. Univ. Madrid 1968–; Pres. Univ. Autónoma de Madrid 1973; decorations from Spain, Portugal, Malta, FRG, Italy, France and Peru. *Publications:* La Necrópolis Ibérica del Cabecico del Tesoro 1940, 1944, 1947, Las tablas flamencas de la Igl. del Salvador de Valladolid 1941, Criterio de Reconstrucción de Objetos Arqueológicos 1941, El Oppidum de Iruña 1949, Guía Artística de Valladolid 1954, Historia de los Monumentos de Lerma 1959, La cueva artificial del Bronco I de Alguazas 1959, Tendencias Actuales de la Arqueología 1959, Guía de la Exposición Conmemorativa de la Paz de los Pirineos 1963, Las Bellas Artes en España 1963, Conservación del Patrimonio Artístico 1968, Museos de Artes y Costumbres Populares 1968, Conservación de Objetos Arqueológicos 1969, Panorama de los Museos Españoles y cuestiones museológicas 1971, Reflexiones sobre la Universidad 1973. *Leisure interests:* swimming, rowing, mountaineering. *Address:* c/o Universidad Autónoma de Madrid, Km. 15 Carretera de Colmenar Viejo, Canto Blanco, 28049 Madrid, Spain.

NIGHTINGALE, Anthony J. L.; British business executive; *Chairman and Managing Director, Jardine Matheson Ltd;* joined Jardine Matheson Group 1969, served in several exec. positions, mem. Bd of Dirs Jardine Matheson Holdings 1994–, Man. Dir 2006–, Chair. and Man. Dir Jardine Matheson Ltd 2006–, Chair. Jardine Cycle & Carriage, Jardine Motors Group, Jardine Pacific; Man. Dir Dairy Farm, Hongkong Land, Jardine Strategic, Mandarin Oriental; Chair. Business Facilitation Advisory Cttee est. by Financial Sec. in Hong Kong; mem. Council of Hong Kong Trade Devt Council; Hong Kong Rep. to APEC Business Advisory Council; mem. Greater Pearl River Delta Business Council; Commr of Astra. *Address:* Jardine Matheson Holdings Ltd, 48th Floor, Jardine House, Hong Kong Special Administrative Region, People's Republic of China (office); Matheson & Co. Ltd, 3 Lombard Street, London, EC3V 9AQ, England (office). *Telephone:* (20) 7816-8100 (UK) (office). *Fax:* (20) 7623-5024 (UK) (office). *E-mail:* jml@jardines.com (office). *Website:* www.jardines.com (office).

NIGHTINGALE, (William) Benedict Herbert, BA; British writer and theatre critic; b. 14 May 1939, London; s. of R. E. Nightingale and Hon. Mrs Nightingale (née Gardner); m. Anne B. Redmon 1964; two s. one d.; ed Charterhouse School, Magdalene Coll., Cambridge and Univ. of Pennsylvania; gen. writer, The Guardian 1963–66; Literary Ed. New Society 1966–67; Theatre Critic, New Statesman 1968–86; Prof. of English, Theatre and Drama Univ. of Mich. 1986–89; Chief Drama Critic The Times 1990–; Sunday Theatre Critic, New York Times 1983–84. *Publications:* Charities 1972, Fifty British Plays 1982, Fifth Row Center 1986, The Future of the Theatre 1998; numerous articles on cultural and theatrical matters in British and American journals. *Leisure interests:* music, literature, watching soccer. *Address:* 40 Broomhouse Road, London, SW6 3QX, England.

NIGHY, Bill; British actor; b. 12 Dec. 1949, Caterham, Surrey; s. of Alfred Nighy and Catherine Whittaker; partner Diana Quick; one d.; ed John Fisher Grammar, Purley; Theatre Managers Best Actor 1996, Barclays Best Actor Award 2004. *Stage appearances include:* Arcadia, Rosencrantz & Guildenstern, Entertaining Mr Sloane, Speak Now, Under New Management, Freedom of the City, Comings and Goings, Illuminations, Map of the World, The Seagull, Skylight, Blue Orange, Mean Tears, King Lear, Pravda, Betrayal, Skylight (Best Actor, Barclays Theatre Award 1996), A Kind of Alaska, Blue/Orange, The Vertical Hour 2006. *Film appearances include:* The Bitch (uncredited) 1979, The Girl in the Cafe, Underworld: Evolution, Flushed Away, The Constant Gardener, The Threepenny Opera, The Bass Player, Eye of the Needle 1981, Curse of the Pink Panther 1983, The Little Drummer Girl 1984, The Phantom of the Opera 1989, Mack the Knife 1990, Being Human 1993, True Blue 1996, Indian Summer 1996, Fairy Tale – A True Story 1997, The Canterbury Tales (voice) 1998, Still Crazy (Best Comedy Performance, Evening Standard Peter Sellers Award 1998) 1998, Guest House Paradiso 1999, The Magic of Vincent 2000, Blow Dry 2001, The Lawless Heart (Best Supporting Actor, LA Critics' Circle Award 2004) 2001, Lucky Break 2001, AKA 2002, I Capture the Castle (Best Supporting Actor, LA Critics' Circle Award 2004) 2003, Love Actually (London Film Critics' Award 2004, Best Supporting Actor, LA Critics' Circle Award 2004, BAFTA Award for Best Actor in a Supporting Role 2004) 2003, Underworld 2003, Shaun of the Dead 2004, Enduring Love 2004, The Magic Roundabout (voice) 2005, The Hitchhiker's Guide to the Galaxy 2005, The Constant Gardener 2005, Underworld Evolution 2006, Pirates of the Caribbean: Dead Man's Chest 2006, Stormbreaker 2006, Flushed Away (voice) 2006, Notes on a Scandal 2006, Hot Fuzz 2007, Pirates of the Caribbean: At World's End 2007. *Radio:* Lord of the Rings, No Commitments, Bleak House, numerous others. *Television appearances include:* Auf Wiedersehen Pet, Insiders, Kavanagh Series III, Wycliffe, Peak Practice, Bergerac, Antonia and Jane 1991, The Cat Bought It In, South of the Border, Under the Skin, Dreams of Leaving, Soldiers Talking Cleanly, Fat, Standing in for Henry; Agony (series) 1979), Fox 1980, Easter 2016 1982, Reilly: The Ace of Spies (mini-series) 1983, The Last Place on Earth (mini-series) 1985, Hitler's S.S.: Portrait in Evil 1985, Thirteen at Dinner (film) 1985, Making News (series) 1989, Absolute Hell 1991, The Men's Room (mini-series) 1991, A Masculine Ending 1992, Eye of the Storm (mini-series) 1993, Unnatural Causes 1993, Don't Leave Me This Way 1993, The Maitlands 1993, Kiss Me Kate (series episode) 1998, Longitude 2000, The Inspector Lynley Mysteries: Well Schooled in Murder 2002, Ready When You Are Mr. McGill 2003, The Lost Prince (Best Actor, Broadcasting Press Guild Award 2003) 2003, State of Play (series) (Best Actor, Broadcasting Press Guild Award 2003, BAFTA Award for Best Actor in a Television Drama 2004) 2003, The Canterbury Tales (mini-series, The Wife of Bath's Tale) 2003, The Young Visiters (sic) (Best Actor, Broadcasting Press Guild Award 2003) 2003, Life Beyond the Box: Norman Stanley Fletcher (narrator) 2003, He Knew He Was Right (mini-series) 2004, Gideon's Daughter (Golden Globe Award for Best Actor in a mini-series or film made for TV 2007) 2005, The Girl in the Café 2005, The Armstrongs (series) 2006. *Leisure Interests:* reading, rhythm and blues. *Address:* c/o Markham & Froggatt Ltd Personal Management, 4 Windmill Street, London, W1T 2HZ, England (office). *Telephone:* (20) 7636-4412 (office). *Fax:* (20) 7637-5233 (office). *Website:* www.markhamfroggatt.com (office).

NIGMATULIN, Robert I., MS, PhD, DrSc; Russian mechanical engineer and academic; *Director, P.P. Shirsov Institute of Oceanology, Russian Academy of Sciences;* b. 17 June 1940; m. 1968; two c.; ed Bauman Technical Univ., Lomonosov Univ., Moscow; Jr Researcher, Inst. of Mechanics, Lomonosov Univ., Moscow 1963–70, Sr Researcher 1970–74, Prof. and Scientific Chief of Lab. 1974–86, currently Prof.; Vice-Dir, Inst. of North Devt Problems and Inst. of Thermophysics, Siberian Br. of Russian Acad. of Sciences, Tyumen 1986–90, Dir Tyumen Inst. of Mechanics of Multiphase Systems 1990–95; Prof. and Chair., Dept of Mechanics, Tyumen Univ. 1986–93; Deputy in State Duma 1999–2003, Chair. Highest Ecology Council; Pres. Ufa (Bashkortostan) Br., Russian Acad. of Sciences 1993–2006, Scientific Chief, Inst. of Mechanics, Ufa Br. 2006–; mem. Presidium Russian Acad. of Sciences 2006–; Dir P.P. Shirsov Inst. of Oceanology, Moscow 2006–; Visiting Scholar and Prof., Center for Multiphase Research, Rensselaer Polytechnic Inst. 1993–2006; Academician Russian Acad. of Sciences 1991–, Bashkortostan Academy of Sciences 1991–; mem. Russian Nat. Cttee of Theoretical and Applied Mechanics 1976–, Cen. Asia Acad., Uzbekistan 1993–, Int. Eastern Petroleum Acad., Azerbaijan 1993–; Hon. Mem., Acad. of Natural Sciences of Russian Fed. 1995, Acad. of Sciences of Tatarstan 2007; Order of Honor (Decree of the President of Russia 2000; Lenin Komsomol Prize 1973, USSR State Prize 1983, Gold Medal, Nat. Econ. Achievements Exhibition 1989, First Prize, Siberian Br. of Russian Acad. of Sciences 1990, Makeev Medal, Russian Fed. of Astronautica 1996, Tsiolkovski Gold Medal, Russian Fed. of Astronautica 2000. *Achievements include:* holds 13 patents. *Publications include:* eight books, 200 papers and 20 preprints. *Address:* P.P. Shirsov Institute of Oceanology, 36, Nahimovski prospect, 117997 Moscow, Russia (office). *Telephone:* (495) 124-59-96 (office). *Fax:* (495) 124-59-83 (office). *Website:* www.ocean.ru (office); www.nigmatulin.ru.

NIGO; Japanese fashion designer and music producer; b. (Tomoaki Nagao), ed Bunka Fashion Coll., Tokyo; fashion student, magazine stylist, DJ early 1990s; began making T-shirts and selling them at parties and DJ shows; opened store Nowhere with Jun Takahashi 1993; set up A Bathing Ape fashion label 1993, label now has stores across Japan and in Hong Kong, Taiwan, London, New York; built Ape Sounds the studio and f. The Bapesounds music label; f. A Bathing Ape fashion label in 1993 with stores across Japan and in Hong Kong and London, opened New York store 2005; also has interests in music, art, cafés, hairstyling; f. Bapesta!!Wrestling (professional wrestling), Bape Gallery; Best Producer Award Tokyo Art Directors Club (ACD) 2002, one of 30 Best Asian Heroes, Time Asia 2004. *Television:* Nigoldeneye (MTV Japan). *Broadcasts:* (B)ape TV, live show Bape Heads Show. *Recordings include:* Ape Sounds 2000, Return of the Ape Sounds.

NIILUS, Leopoldo Juan (Leopold Johannes); Argentine lawyer and international human rights consultant; b. 19 Jan. 1930, Tallinn, Estonia; s. of the late Jaan Eduard Niilus and Meta Kiris; m. Malle Reet Veerus 1961; one d.; ed Faculty of Law, Univ. Buenos Aires, Argentina, Southern Methodist Univ., Dallas, Tex., USA; left Estonia 1944; fmrly practising lawyer, Buenos Aires; fmr Chair. Argentine Student Christian Movt; fmr mem. World Student Christian Fed. (WSCF); Dir Argentine Dept River Plate Centre of Christian Studies 1966–67; Gen. Sec. ISAL (Comm. for Church and Soc. in Latin America) 1968–69; Dir Comm. of the Churches on Int. Affairs of WCC, Geneva 1969–81; Dir Int. Ecumenical Relations, Middle East Council of Churches (MECC) 1982–95; Consultant on int. affairs and human rights, Lutheran World Fed. 1988–95; ind. political consultant 1996–; participated in mediation for Sudan peace negotiations 1972, Guatemala peace negotiations, signed as witness, Oslo accords on Guatemala 1990; Order of Two Niles, 1st Grade (Sudan). *Publications:* On Penal Law (essays); numerous articles and essays in ecumenical publs on peace, disarmament, North–South relations, Middle East, Central America. *Address:* 7 chemin du Champ d'Anier, 1209 Geneva, Switzerland (home). *Telephone:* (22) 7983259 (home). *Fax:* (22) 7884448 (home). *E-mail:* leopoldo_niilus@compuserve.com (home).

NIINILUOTO, Ilkka, BSc, MSc, PhD; Finnish philosopher, mathematician, academic and university administrator; *Rector, Helsinki University;* b. 12 March 1946, Helsinki; m. Ritva Pelkonen; three c.; ed Univ. of Helsinki, Stanford Univ., USA; Teaching Asst, Dept of Philosophy, Univ. of Helsinki 1969–71, Acting Assoc. Prof. of Math. 1973–75, Docent of Philosophical Theory 1974–81, Acting Prof. of Theoretical Philosophy 1977–81, Prof. 1981–, Chair. Dept of Philosophy 1983–88, 1992, 1995–2000, Vice Dean, Faculty of Arts 1988–89, 1991, 1995–98, Dean 1990, 1993–94, Vice Rector Univ. of Helsinki 1998–2003, Rector 2003–; Research Asst, Dept of Philosophy, Acad. of Finland 1971–73; Chair. Finnish Cultural Foundation 1993–94, Helsinki Inst. of Physics 1998–; Pres. Philosophical Soc. of Finland 1975–, Finnish Soc. for Science Studies 1985–86; mem. Finnish Acad. of Science 1985–, British Soc. for the Philosophy of Science. *Publications:* Truthlikeness 1987, Critical Scientific Realism 2002; numerous journal articles. *Address:* Chancellor's Office, PO Box 33, Yliopistonkatu 4, 00014 Helsinki, Finland (office). *Telephone:* (9) 19122206 (office). *E-mail:* ilkka.niiniluoto@helsinki.fi (office). *Website:* www.helsinki.fi/administration/chancellor.htm (office).

NIINISTÖ SAULI, Väinämö; Finnish politician and lawyer; b. 24 Aug. 1948, Salo; m. (wife deceased); two s.; own law office in Salo 1978–88; Sr Sec. Turku Court of Appeal 1976; mem. Salo City Council 1977–, Chair. 1989–92, mem. City Bd 1977–88; mem. Nat. Coalition Party (KOK) Council 1979–81, Party Chair. 1994; mem. Parl. 1987–; Chair. Constitutional Cttee of Parl. 1993–95; Deputy Prime Minister 1995–2001; Minister of Justice 1995–96; Minister of Finance 1996–2003; Chair. European Democratic Union (EDU) 1998; Gov. for Finland, World Bank 2001. *Address:* c/o Ministry of Finance, PO Box 28, 00023 Government, Finland (office).

NIKAI, Toshihiro; Japanese politician; *Minister of Economy, Trade and Industry;* b. 17 Feb. 1939; ed Faculty of Law, Chuo Univ.; Sec. to Saburo Endo 1961; mem. Wakayama Prefectural Ass. 1975; mem. House of Reps (Wakayama 3rd Dist; elected eight times) 1983–, Chair. Standing Cttee on Construction 1997, Special Cttee on Postal Privatization 2005; State Sec. of Transportation 1990, 1993; Dir Election Div., New Frontier Party 1995; Minister of Transport and Dir-Gen. Hokkaido Devt Agency 1999, 2000; Sec.-Gen. and Rep. New Conservative Party 2002; joined Liberal Democratic Party (LDP) 2003, Chair. Special Cttee on Tourism, Dir-Gen. Election Bureau 2004–05, Chair. Diet Affairs Cttee 2006, Chair. Gen. Council 2007–; Minister of Economy, Trade and Industry 2005–06, 2008–. *Address:* Ministry of Economy, Trade and Industry, 1-3-1, Kasumigaseki, Chiyoda-ku, Tokyo 100-8901, Japan (office). *Telephone:* (3) 3501-1511 (office). *Fax:* (3) 3501-6942 (office). *E-mail:* webmail@meti.go.jp (office). *Website:* www.meti.go.jp (office).

NIKITIN, Nikolai F.; Russian mechanical engineer and aviation engineer; *Director-General, Russian Aviation Production Corporation MIG;* b. 1 Jan. 1950, Orudyevo, Moscow region; ed Moscow State Aviation Inst.; worked for OKB Sukhoi 1973–91; Deputy Dir-Gen. 1991–97, Dir-Gen., mem. Bd of Dirs 1997–99; First Deputy Dir-Gen. ABPK Sukhoi 1999; Dir-Gen. Russian Aviation Production Corporation MIG 1999–; gen. constructor of SU-27M, S-80, SU-35, SU-37MP; USSR State Prize for aviation complex SU-27 1991. *Address:* Russian Aviation Production Corporation MIG, 1 Botkinsky proyezd 7, Moscow 125040, Russia (office). *Telephone:* (495) 207-04-75 (office); (495) 207-07-57 (office). *Website:* www.migavia.ru (office).

NIKOLAYEV, Army Gen. Andrei Ivanovich; Russian politician and fmr army officer; b. 21 April 1949, Moscow; m. Tatyana Yuryevna Nikolayeva; two s.; ed Moscow Gen. Troops Commdg School of RSFSR Supreme Soviet, M. Frunze Mil. Acad., Gen. Staff Acad.; commdr of platoon, co., regt; First Deputy Head Main Admin. of Gen. HQ of USSR Armed Forces; First Deputy Head of Gen. HQ of Russian Army 1992–94; C-in-C of Border troops of Russian Fed. 1994–; Head of Fed. Border Troops Service 1995–97; mem. State Duma (Parl.) 1998–2003; Chair. Cttee of Defence 2000–03; Adviser to the Pres. on Military and Naval Matters 2004; f. Union of People's Power and Labour 1998. *Leisure interests:* theatre, organ music. *Address:* c/o Office of the President, 103132 Moscow, Staraya pl. 4, Russia (office).

NIKOLAYEV, Mikhail Yefimovich; Russian/Yakut politician; b. 13 Nov. 1937, Ordzhonikidze Region, Yakutia; m.; three c.; ed Omsk Veterinary Inst., Higher CP School; worked as veterinarian, then Sec. Zhigan Regional Comsomol Cttee, First Sec. Yakut Comsomol Cttee, Sec., then First Sec. Verkhneviluysk Regional CP Cttee 1971–75; Deputy Chair. Council of Ministers Yakut ASSR 1975–79; Minister of Agric. 1979–85; Sec. Yakut Regional CP Cttee 1985–89; Chair. Presidium of Supreme Soviet Yakut ASSR 1989–91; Pres. Repub. of Sakha (Yakutia) 1991–2001; mem. Council of Fed. of Russia 1993–, Rep. Sakha-Yakutia Rep. In Council of Fed. 2001–, Deputy Chair. 2002–; Order of Red Banner of Labour, Order of Friendship, Order for Prominent Services to the Fatherland and other honours. *Publications include:* My People are My Republic 1992, The Arctic: The Pain and Hope of Russia 1994, The Arctic. XXI Century 1999. *Address:* Council of Federation, Bolshaya Dmitorvka 26, 103426 Moscow, Russia; House of Government, Kirova str. 11, 677022 Yakutsk, Russia. *Telephone:* (4112) 43-50-50 (office). *Fax:* (4112) 24-06-24 (office).

NIKOLSKY, Boris Vassilyevich; Russian politician; *Moscow Representative to Council of Federation;* b. 1 May 1937, Moscow; m.; two c.; ed Moscow Inst. of Agric. Eng, Higher School Cen. Cttee CPSU; master, chief engineer in a factory; Deputy Chair. Moscow Municipal Exec. Cttee on problems of energy and eng 1976–82; Sec. Moscow City CP Cttee 1982–84; Sec., then Second Sec. Cen. Cttee of Georgian CP 1984–; First Deputy Chair. Moscow City Planning Cttee 1989–; First Deputy Chair. Moscow City Construction Cttee 1990–91; Deputy Prime Minister Moscow Govt 1991–92, First Deputy Chair. 1992–2002; Moscow Rep. to Council of Fed. 2002–. *Address:* Moscow Government, Tverskaya str. 13, 103032 Moscow, Russia (office). *Telephone:* (495) 229-24-24 (office). *Fax:* (495) 230-20-69. *E-mail:* mayor@mos.ru (office).

NIKONENKO, Sergey Petrovich; Russian actor, film director and scriptwriter; b. 16 April 1941, Moscow; s. of Peter Nikonenko and Nina Nikonenko; m. Yekaterina Voronina-Nikonenko; one s.; ed All-Union Inst. of Cinematography; mem. Union of Cinematographers 1968–; f. Yesenin Cultural Foundation 1994–; Order of Honour 1971; Comsomol Prize 1976, A. Dovzhenko Medal 1988, Grand Prix. Int. Film Festival in Oberhausen (Germany), People's Artist of Russia 1991. *Film appearances include:* War and Peace 1965–67, Wings 1966, They are Ringing, Open the Door 1966, Strange People 1969, Journalist, I Have Come This Way, Crime and Punishment, White Explosion 1969, Sing a Song, Poet 1971, Inspector of Road Police 1982, Unfinished Piece for a Mechanical Piano 1976, Winter Evening in Gagry 1986, Tomorrow was War 1987, The Red Wine of Victory 1990, Family Man 1991, Unwilling to Marry 1992, Time of the Dancer 1996, Kids of Monday 1997, Sinful Love 1997, Chinese Service 1999, Classic 1998, Istinnyye proishestviya (True Stories) 2002, Interesnyye muzhchiny (Interesting Men) 2003. *Films directed include:* Gypsy's Happiness, Birds Above the Town, Love, Wait, Lyonya, I Want Your Husband. *Television appearances include:* Kamenskaya 2000, Igry v podkidnogo" (Tricky Games) 2001, Nevozmozhnye zelyonye glaza 2002, In the Service of My Country 2003. *Leisure interests:* classical literature and music, opera music, painting. *Address:* Sivcev-Vrasheu 44/14, 119002 Moscow (office); Sivtsev Vrazhek str. 44, Apt. 20, 121002 Moscow, Russia (home). *Telephone:* (495) 244-03-44 (office); (495) 241-78-72 (home).

NIKONOV, Vyacheslav Alekseyevich, DrHis; Russian politician and academic; *President, Unity for Russia Foundation;* b. 5 June 1956, Moscow; s. of Aleksey Dmitrievich Nikonov and Svetlana Vyacheslavovna Molotova; grandson of Vyacheslav Molotov; m. 1st Viktoria Makarovna Kostyuk 1976; m. 2nd Olga Mikhailovna Rozhkova 1987; three s.; ed Moscow State Univ.; researcher, Moscow State Univ.; on staff Admin. Cen. Cttee CPSU 1989–90; on staff of Pres. Gorbachev 1990–91; Asst to Chair. USSR State Security Cttee (KGB) 1991–92; counsellor, Dept of Political Problems, Int. Foundation of Econ. and Social Reforms (Foundation Reforma) 1992–93; mem. State Duma (Parl.); Chair. Sub-cttee on Int. Security and Arms Control 1994–95; Deputy Chair. Cttee to Re-elect the Pres. 1996; Dean of History and Political Science Moscow Int. Univ. 2001; Deputy Chair. Editorial Bd Russia in Global Affairs 2002; Pres. Unity for Russia Foundation 2003–; Head, Int. Cooperation and Public Diplomacy Cttee, Public Council of the Russian Fed. 2006–; Ed.-in-Chief Strategy for Russia Journal 2003–. *Publications:* Republicans: From Eisenhower to Nixon 1984, Iran-Contra Affair 1988, Republicans: From Nixon to Reagan 1989, The Age of Change: Russia in the 90s as Viewed by a Conservative 1999, Contemporary Russian Politics (ed.) 2003, 2005, Agenda for Russia 2004 (ed.), Russia in Contemporary Politics 2005 (ed.), Agenda for Russia 2005 (ed.), Molotov: Youth 2005. *Leisure interests:* reading, gardening. *Address:* Politika Foundation, Zlatoustinsky per. 8/7, 101000 Moscow, Russia (office). *Telephone:* (495) 206-81-49 (office). *Fax:* (495) 206-86-61 (office). *E-mail:* info@polity.ru (office). *Website:* www.polity.ru (office).

NILEKANI, Nandan M., BEng, BTech; Indian business executive; *Co-Chair, Infosys;* b. 2 June 1955, Bangalore; m. Rohini Nilekani; two c.; ed Indian Inst. of Tech.; Co-Founder, Dir Infosys 1981–, later Man. Dir, Pres. and COO, CEO, Pres. and Man. Dir 2002–07, Co-Chair. 2007–; Co-Founder India's Nat. Asscn of Software and Service Cos (NASSCOM), Bangalore Chapter of The IndUS Entrepreneurs (TiE); mem. Asia Pacific Regional Advisory Bd, London Business School, Global Advisory Council, The Conf. Bd; Co-Chair. Business Leaders Dialogue, Initiative for Social Innovation Through Business, Aspen Inst.; Co-Chair. Advisory Bd, IIT Bombay Heritage Fund; Chair. Govt of India's IT for the Power Sector task force, Bangalore Agenda task force; Alumnus Award, Indian Inst. of Tech. 1999, Corporate Citizen of the Year, Fortune Asian Businessman of the Year 2003, Asia Business Leaders Awards 2004. *Publication:* Imagining India: Ideas for the New Century 2009. *Address:* Infosys, Plot No. 44&97A, Electronics City, Hosur Road, Bangalore 560 100 (office); 856, 13th Main, III Block, Koramangala, Bangalore 560 034, India (home). *Telephone:* (80) 8520261 (office); (80) 25536150 (home). *Fax:* (80) 8520362 (office); (80) 25534654 (home). *E-mail:* nandan_mn@infosys.com (office). *Website:* www.infosys.com (office).

NILES, Thomas Michael Tolliver, MA; American diplomatist; *Vice Chairman, United States Council for International Business;* b. 22 Sept. 1939, Lexington, Ky; s. of John Jacob Niles and Rena Niles (née Lipetz); m. Carroll C. Ehringhaus 1967; one s. one d.; ed Harvard Univ. and Univ. of Kentucky; Foreign Service Officer, Dept of State 1962; posts in Moscow, Belgrade and Brussels; Amb. to Canada 1985–89, to Greece 1993–97; Perm. Rep. to the EEC, Brussels 1989; Vice-Pres. Nat. Defense Univ. 1997–98 (retd); Pres. US Council for Int. Business 1998–2005, Vice Chair. 2005–; mem. Bd of Dirs Jacobs Eng Group Inc., Internet Corpn for Assigned Names and Numbers (ICANN) 2003–05; Superior Honor Award, Dept of State 1982, 1985. *Address:* United States Council for International Business, 1212 Avenue of the Americas, New York, NY 10036, USA (office). *Telephone:* (212) 354-4480 (office). *Fax:* (212) 575-0327 (office). *E-mail:* info@uscib.org (office). *Website:* www.uscib.org (office).

NIMATALLAH, Yusuf A., PhD; Saudi Arabian economist; b. 1936; ed American Univ., Beirut and Univ. of Mass., USA; with Banque de l'Indochine 1952–57; Teaching Asst in Econs, Univ. of Mass. 1963–65; Prof. Monetary and Int. Econs, Univ. of Riyadh (King Saud Univ. 1982–) 1965 (on leave 1973);

Adviser to Minister of Finance on Money and Banking, Oil Finance and Planning 1967–73; Adviser to Sultan of Oman on Oil, Finance, Money and Banking; Deputy Chair. and Pres. Cen. Bank of Oman 1975–78; Deputy Chair. UBAF Arab American Bank, New York 1976–78; Exec. Dir Fund for Saudi Arabia 1979–89; currently Head Injaz Money Exchange Co. (Yousuf Abdul Wahab Niamatullah Co.) Jeddah. *Address:* Injaz Money Exchange Company, POB 7039, Behind Al Shoalah Centre 88, Moh Taweel Street, 21462 Jeddah, Saudi Arabia. *Telephone:* (2) 667-6025. *Fax:* (2) 665-8858.

NIMETZ, Matthew, LLB, MA; American diplomatist, lawyer and business executive; *Managing Director, General Atlantic LLC;* b. 17 June 1939, Brooklyn, New York; m. Gloria S. Lorch; one d. one s.; ed Williams Coll., Balliol Coll. Oxford, UK, Harvard Univ.; called to Bar, NY 1966, DC 1968; Law clerk to Justice John M. Harlan, Supreme Court 1965–67; Staff Asst to Pres. Johnson 1967–69; Assoc. with Simpson Thatcher and Bartlett LLC, New York 1969–74, Pnr 1974–77; Pnr Paul, Weiss, Rifkind, Wharton and Garrison LLC 1981–2000; Man. Dir Gen. Atlantic Pnrs (now Gen. Atlantic) LLC, Greenwich, Conn. 2000–; Counsellor Dept of State 1977–80, Acting Co-ordinator Refugee Affairs 1979–80; Presidential Envoy to Greece–Macedonian Negotiations 1994–95, Chair. 1997, Personal Envoy of UN Sec.-Gen. for Greece-FYROM Talks Dec. 1999; Commr Port Authority NY and NJ 1975–77; Dir and Chair. World Resources Inst. 1982–94; Trustee William Coll. 1981–96; Chair. UN Devt Corpn 1986–94, Carnegie Forum in USA, Greece and Turkey 1996–98, Centre for Democracy and Reconciliation in SE Europe 1997–; mem. Bd Dirs. Charles H. Revson Foundation 1990–98, NY State Nature Conservancy 1997–; Dir Inst. Public Admin. 1999–; mem. NY State Advisory Council on State Productivity 1990–92; mem. Bd of Trustees, Cen. European Univ., Budapest, Hungary 1998–, Asscn of Bar of City of NY, Council on Foreign Relations; Rhodes Scholar, Balliol Coll. Oxford, UK 1962; Hon. LLD (Williams Coll.) 1979. *Address:* General Atlantic LLC, 3 Pickwick Plaza, Greenwich, CT 06830-5538, USA (office). *Website:* www.generalatlantic.com.

NIMLEY, Thomas Yaya; Liberian politician; Minister of Foreign Affairs 2003–06; Chair. Movt for Democracy in Liberia (MODEL). *Address:* Ministry of Foreign Affairs, Mamba Point, POB 10-9002, 1000 Monrovia 10, Liberia (office).

NIMOY, Leonard; American actor and director; b. 26 March 1931, Boston; s. of Max Nimoy and Dora Nimoy (née Spinner); m. 1st Sandi Zober 1954 (divorced); one s. one d.; m. 2nd Susan Bay 1988; ed Boston Coll. and Antioch Univ.; served in US Army 1954–56; trained at the Pasadena Playhouse, Calif. 1960-63; numerous stage appearances. *Films include:* Queen for a Day, Rhubarb 1951, Kid Monk Baron, Francis Goes to West Point 1952, Old Overland Trail 1953, Satan's Satellites 1958, The Balcony 1963, Deathwatch 1966, Valley of Mystery (co-producer) 1967, Catlow (co-producer) 1971, Invasion of the Bodysnatchers (co-producer) 1978, Star Trek: The Motion Picture (also co-producer) 1979, Star Trek: The Wrath of Khan (also co-producer) 1982, Star Trek III: The Search for Spock (also dir) 1984, Star Trek IV: The Voyage Home (also dir) 1986, Star Trek V: The Final Frontier 1989, Star Trek VI: The Undiscovered Country 1991, The Pagemaster (voice) 1994, Carpati: 50 Miles, 50 Years (narrator) 1996, A Life Apart: Hasidism in America (narrator) 1997, Sinbad: Beyond the Veil of Mists 2000, Atlantis: The Lost Empire (voice) 2001; also directed Three Men and A Baby 1987, The Good Mother 1988, Body Wars 1989, Funny About Love 1990, Holy Matrimony 1994. *Television includes:* Star Trek 1966–69, Eleventh Hour, The Virginian, Rawhide, Dr Kildare, Never Forget 1991, Bonanza: Under Attack 1995, David 1997, Brave New World 1998, Invasion America (series) (voice) 1998, Ultimate Trek: Star Trek's Greatest Moments (archive footage) 1999, The 100 Greatest TV Characters (archive footage) 2001; also directed Night Gallery (series) 1970, T.J. Hooker (series episode, The Decoy) 1982, The Powers of Matthew Star (series) 1982, Deadly Games (series) 1995. *Publications:* I Am Not Spock (autobiog.) 1975, We Are All Children 1977, Come Be With Me 1979. *Address:* c/o Gersh Agency Inc., 232 North Cannon Drive, Beverly Hills, CA 90210, USA.

NIMR, Nabih an-; Jordanian diplomatist; b. 26 Oct. 1931, Tubas; m. Rabab Al-Nimr 1961; one s. one d.; ed Alexandria Univ.; Amb. to Syria 1974–78, to FRG (also accred to Sweden, Denmark, Norway and Luxembourg) 1978–81, to Tunisia and Perm. Rep. to the Arab League 1981–85, to UK 1985–87, (also accred to Ireland 1986–87), to Egypt 1988; Sec. Gen. Ministry of Foreign Affairs 1987–88. *Address:* c/o Ministry of Foreign Affairs POB 35217, Amman 11180, Jordan.

NIMROD, Elvin, MA, DJur; Grenadian politician; b. Carriacou; ed Brooklyn Coll., John Jay Coll. of Criminal Justice, NY, New York Law School, USA, Hugh Wooding Law School, Port-of-Spain, Trinidad and Tobago; teacher Mt. Pleasant Govt Primary School, Carriacou; called to the Bar, Grenada 1993; Minister of Labour 1999, of Foreign Affairs and Int. Trade and of Carriacou and Petit Martinique Affairs 1999–2008, and of Legal Affairs 1999–2007; fmr Attorney-Gen. of Grenada; currently Chair. New National Party (NNP). *Address:* New National Party (NNP), Upper Lucas Street, St George's, Grenada (office). *Telephone:* 440-1875 (office). *Fax:* 440-1876 (office). *E-mail:* nnpadmin@spiceisle.com (office). *Website:* nnpnews.com (office).

NIN NOVOA, Rodolfo; Uruguayan politician; *Vice-President of Uruguay and President, Chamber of Senators;* b. 25 Jan. 1948; m.; three s. one d.; active in Agricultural Soc. of Cerro Largo and Fed. of Rural Uruguay during 1970s; elected Nat. Party rep. for Cerro Largo 1982; Mayor of Cerro Largo 1985–95; left Nat. Party 1994; Co-founder Encuentro Progresista party 1994, Vice-Pres. Encuentro Progresista–Frente Amplio 1995; Founder Alianza Progresista 738 political alliance 1999, currently Leader; Senator 2000–05, mem. various senate cttees including Budget Cttee (Vice-Chair. 2002) 2000–04, Livestock, Agric. and Fisheries (Vice-Chair. 2002) 2000–04, Admin. Affairs (Vice-Chair. 2002) 2000–04; Vice-Pres. of Uruguay and Pres., Chamber of Senators 2005–. *Address:* c/o Alianza Progresista 738, Col. 1831, Montevideo, Uruguay (office). *Telephone:* (2) 4016365 (office). *E-mail:* rnin@parlamento.gub.uy (office); a738@alianza738.org.uy (office). *Website:* www.alianza738.org.uy (office).

NINAGAWA, Yukio; Japanese theatre director; b. 15 Oct. 1935, Kawaguchi, Saitama Prefecture; known for his direction of Western classic plays, especially Shakespeare, in a Japanese style; his co. appeared at Edin. Festival with samurai-style Macbeth 1985, Suicide of Love, Nat. Theatre, London 1989, Medea, Suicide for Love and a Noh-inspired version of The Tempest, Barbican Theatre, London 1992; also Dir Tango at the End of Winter, King Lear 1999; Dr hc (Edinburgh) 1992. *E-mail:* ninagawa@my-pro.co.jp. *Website:* www.my-pro.co.jp/ninagawa.

NINEHAM, Rev. Canon Dennis Eric, MA, DD; British professor of theology and ecclesiastic (retd); b. 27 Sept. 1921, Southampton; s. of Stanley Martin Nineham and Bessie Edith Gain; m. Ruth Corfield Miller 1946; two s. two d. (one d. deceased); ed King Edward VI School, Southampton, Queen's Coll., Oxford and Lincoln Theological Coll.; Chaplain Queen's Coll. Oxford 1944–54, Fellow 1946–54; Prof. of Biblical and Historical Theology, Univ. of London 1954–58, Prof. of Divinity 1958–64; Regius Prof. of Divinity, Univ. of Cambridge 1964–69; Fellow, Emmanuel Coll. 1964–69; Warden Keble Coll. Oxford 1969–79; Prof. of Theology, Univ. of Bristol 1980–86; Visiting Prof., Rikkyo Univ., Tokyo 1994; Fellow, King's Coll. London; Hon. Canon Emer. Bristol Cathedral; Hon. Fellow, Keble Coll. Oxford, Queen's Coll. Oxford; Hon. DD (Yale) 1965, (Birmingham) 1972. *Publications:* The Gospel of St Mark 1963, The Use and Abuse of the Bible 1976, Explorations in Theology 1977, Christianity Medieval and Modern: A Study in Religious Change 1993. *Leisure interests:* walking and reading. *Address:* 9 Fitzherbert Close, Iffley, Oxford, OX4 4EN, England (home). *Telephone:* (1865) 715941 (home).

NING, Frank Gaoning, BA, MBA; Chinese business executive; *Chairman, China National Cereals, Oils and Foodstuffs Corporation (COFCO);* b. 1958, Shandong Prov.; m.; one d.; ed Shandong Univ., Univ. of Pittsburgh, USA; previous positions include Gen. Man. China Resources Enterprise Ltd 1990–99, Chair. 1999–2004; fmr Chair. China Resources Land Ltd, Vice-Chair. and Pres. China Resources (Holdings) Co. Ltd, China Resources National Corpn; Chair. China Nat. Cereals, Oils and Foodstuffs Corpn (COFCO) 2005–; mem. Bd of Dirs HIT Investments Ltd, SAB Miller; mem. Asia Business Council; named by Sixth Chinese Business Leaders Annual Meeting as one of the 25 most influential business leaders 2007. *Address:* China National Cereals, Oils and Foodstuffs Corporation, COFCO Plaza, Tower A, 11th Floor, No. 8, Jian Guo Men Nei Avenue, Beijing 100005, People's Republic of China (office). *Telephone:* (10) 65268888 (office). *Fax:* (10) 65276028 (office). *E-mail:* info@cofco.com.cn (office). *Website:* www.cofco.com.cn (office).

NINH, Vu Van, MBA; Vietnamese government official; *Minister of Finance;* b. 23 Feb. 1955, Hai Duong Prov.; ed Hanoi Univ. of Finance and Accountancy; mem. staff, Ministry of Finance 1977–82, Head of Economy Div. 1982–90, Deputy Dir of State Budget Dept 1990–93, Dir 1993–99; Vice-Minister of Finance 1999–2003, Minister of Finance 2006–; Vice-Chair. Hanoi People's Cttee 2003–06; mem. CP of Viet Nam Central Cttee (CPVCC). *Address:* Ministry of Finance, 8 Phan Huy Chu, Hoan Kiem District, Hanoi, Viet Nam (office). *Telephone:* (4) 8264872 (office). *Fax:* (4) 8262266 (office). *E-mail:* support@mof.gov.vn (office). *Website:* www.mof.gov.vn (office).

NINN-HANSEN, Erik, LLD; Danish politician; b. 12 April 1922, Skørpinge, Western Zealand; s. of Christian Hansen; in pvt. law practice 1955–; mem. Folketing (Parl.) 1953–94; Minister of Defence 1968–71, of Finance 1971, of Justice 1982–89; Pres. of the Folketing Jan.–Oct. 1989; Nat. Chair. Conservative Youth 1948–50. *Publication:* Syv år for VKR 1974, Fra Christmas til Baunsgaard 1985, Ret Færd mellem jura og politik 1990, Christmas Møller, En stridsmand i dansk politik 1991, Vaerelse 28 Dansk politik 1974–94 (1997). *Address:* Bregnegårdsvej 11, 2920 Charlottenlund, Denmark.

NIRENBERG, Louis, PhD; American mathematician and academic; b. 28 Feb. 1925, Hamilton, Ont., Canada; s. of Zuzie Nirenberg and Bina Katz; m. Susan Blank 1948 (deceased); one s. one d.; ed McGill and New York Univs; Instructor, New York Univ. 1949–51, Asst Prof. 1951–54, Assoc. Prof. 1954–57, Prof. 1957–; Dir Courant Inst. of Mathematical Sciences 1970–72; mem. NAS, American Acad. of Arts and Sciences, American Philosophical Soc., Accad. dei Lincei, Acad. des Sciences, France, Istituto Lombardo Accad. di Scienze e Lettere, Italy; Honorable Mem. European Acad. of Sciences 2004; Hon. Prof. Nankai Univ., Zhejiang Univ.; Hon. DSc (McGill Univ., Univ. of Pisa, Univ. of Paris, Dauphine, McMaster Univ.); Bôcher Prize and Steele Prize of American Mathematical Soc, Crafoord Prize (Royal Swedish Acad. of Sciences) 1982. *Publications:* various papers in mathematical journals. *Leisure interests:* classical music, reading, cinema, walking. *Address:* 221 West 82nd Street, New York, NY 10024, USA (home). *Telephone:* (212) 998-3192 (office); (212) 724-1069 (home). *Fax:* (212) 995-4121 (office); (212) 724-1069 (home). *E-mail:* nirenl@cims.nyu.edu (office).

NIRENBERG, Marshall Warren, PhD; American biochemist; *Chief, Laboratory of Biomedical Genetics, National Heart, Lung and Blood Institute;* b. 10 April 1927; s. of Harry Edward Nirenberg and Minerva Nirenberg (née Bykowsky); m. Perola Zaltzman 1961; ed Univ. of Florida and Univ. of Michigan; Postdoctoral Fellow, American Cancer Soc., NIH 1957–59, US Public Health Service, NIH 1959–60; mem. staff, NIH 1960–, research biochemist 1961–62; research biochemist, Head of Section for Biochemical Genetics, Nat. Heart Inst. 1962–66; Chief, Lab. of Biochemical Genetics, Nat. Heart, Lung and Blood Inst. 1962–; has researched on mechanism of protein synthesis, genetic code, nucleic acids, regulatory mechanism in synthetic macromolecules; mem. New York Acad. of Sciences, AAAS, NAS, Pontifical

Acad. of Sciences 1974, Deutsche Leopoldina Akad. der Naturforscher; Foreign Assoc. Acad. des Sciences (France) 1989; Hon. mem. Harvey Soc.; Molecular Biology Award, NAS 1962; Medal from Dept of Health, Educ. and Welfare 1963, Modern Medicine Award 1964, Nat. Medal for Science, Pres. Johnson 1965, Nobel Prize for Medicine (with Holley and Khorana) for interpreting the genetic code and its function in protein synthesis 1968, Louisa Gross Horwitz Prize for Biochem. 1968. *Address:* Laboratory of Biochemical Genetics, National Heart, Lung and Blood Institute, 10 Center Drive, Building 10, Room 7N315, Bethesda, MD 20892, USA (office). *Telephone:* (301) 496-0098 (office). *Website:* dir.nhlbi.nih.gov/labs/lbg/index.asp (office).

NISBET, Robin George Murdoch, MA, FBA; British classical scholar; b. 21 May 1925, Glasgow; s. of Robert George Nisbet and Agnes Thomson Husband; m. Anne Wood 1969 (died 2004); ed Glasgow Acad., Glasgow Univ. and Balliol Coll. Oxford; Fellow and Tutor in Classics, Corpus Christi Coll. Oxford 1952–70, Prof. of Latin 1970–92; Hon. Fellow, Balliol Coll. 1989, Corpus Christi Coll. 1992; Kenyon Medal, British Acad. 1997. *Publications:* Commentary on Cicero, In Pisonem 1961, Horace, Odes I, II (with M. Hubbard) 1970, 1978, III (with N. Rudd) 2004, Collected Papers on Latin Literature 1995. *Address:* 80 Abingdon Road, Cumnor, Oxon., OX2 9QW, England (home). *Telephone:* (1865) 862482 (home).

NISHANI, Bujar; Albanian politician; *Minister of the Interior;* b. 29 Sept. 1966, Durrës; ed Univ. of Tirana, Univ. of Texas at San Antonio, USA; Lecturer, Ushtarake Skënderbej Mil. Acad. 1988–93; with Foreign Relations Dept, Ministry of Defence 1993–94; with NATO Relations Dept, Ministry of Foreign Affairs 1994–96; mem. Cabinet of Ministry of Defence 1996–97; Freelance Chair. European-Atlantic Mil. Forum 1997–99; mem. Democratic Party of Albania (Partia Demokratike e Shqipërisë), Sec.-Gen., Tirana br. 2001–03, mem. Nat. Council 2004–, mem. Chairmanship 2005–; mem. Municipal Council of Tirana 2004–; Minister of the Interior 2007–. *Address:* Ministry of the Interior, Sheshi Skënderbej 3, Tirana, Albania (office). *Telephone:* (4) 247155 (office). *E-mail:* mb@moi.gov.al (office). *Website:* www.moi.gov.al (office); www.bujarnishani.com (office).

NISHIDA, Atsutoshi, MA; Japanese electronics industry executive; *President and CEO, Toshiba Corporation;* ed Tokyo Univ.; joined Toshiba Corpn 1978, Sr Vice-Pres. Toshiba Europe 1984, Pres. Toshiba America Information Systems Inc. 1992, Gen. Man. Personal Computer Div. 1995, Vice-Pres., Deputy Group Exec. Information Equipment Group 1997, Vice-Chair. Toshiba America Inc., Pres. Toshiba America Information Systems Inc. 1997–99, Corp. Vice-Pres., Exec. Vice-Pres. Digital Media Equipment & Services Co. 1998–2000, Gen. Man. Corp. Devt Center, Electronic Commerce Strategy Planning Div. 2000–01, Corp. Sr Vice-Pres. 2000–03, Pres. and CEO Digital Media Network Co. 2001–03, CEO Digital Products Group 2003, Pres. and CEO Personal Computer and Network Co., Dir, Corp. Exec. Vice-Pres. 2003–05, Pres. and CEO Toshiba Corpn 2005–. *Address:* Toshiba Corporation, 1-1, Shibaura 1-chome, Minato-ku, Tokyo, 105-8001, Japan (office). *Telephone:* (3) 3457-4511 (office). *Fax:* (3) 3455-1631 (office). *E-mail:* info@toshiba.co.jp (office). *Website:* www.toshiba.co.jp (office).

NISHIDA, Mamoru; Japanese politician; b. Ehime Pref.; mem. LDP; mem. for Shikoku, House of Reps; fmr Dir-Gen. Nat. Land Agency; Minister of Home Affairs 1998–99; Chair. Nat. Public Safety Comm. 2000. *Address:* c/o Ministry of Home Affairs, 2-1-2, Kasumigaseki, Chiyoda-ku, Tokyo 100, Japan.

NISHIHARA, Haruo, LLD; Japanese professor of law and academic administrator; *Chairman of the Executive Board, Kokushikan University;* b. 13 March 1928, Tokyo; s. of Keiichi Nishihara and Makoto Tateyama Nishihara; m.; one s.; ed Waseda Univ.; Asst, School of Law, Waseda Univ. 1953–59, Asst Prof. 1959–63, Assoc. Prof. 1963–67, Prof. 1967–, Dean School of Law and mem. Bd of Trustees 1972–76, Exec. Dir 1978–80, Vice-Pres. 1980–82, Pres. and mem. Bd of Trustees 1982–95; currently Chair. Exec. Bd; Hon. LLD (Korea Univ.) 1985, (Earlham Coll.) 1988; Hon. DUniv (Sydney) 1989; Educational Man. Prize (De La Salle Univ.) 1988. *Publications:* On the Theory of 'mittelbare Täterschaft' 1962, Traffic Accidents and the Principle of Trust 1962, Particular Aspects of Criminal Law 1974, 1983, General Aspects of Criminal Law 1977, What Governs the Criminal Law? 1979. *Leisure interests:* swimming, skiing. *Address:* Kokushikan University, 4-28-1 Setagaya, Setagaya-ku, Tokyo 154-8515 (office); 619-18 Nohgaya-cho, Machida-shi, Tokyo, Japan. *Telephone:* (3) 5481-3112 (office). *Fax:* (3) 3413-7420 (office). *E-mail:* wwwadmin@kiss.kokushikan.ac.jp (office). *Website:* www.kokushikan.ac.jp (office).

NISHIKAWA, Yoshifumi; Japanese financial executive; b. 1939; ed Osaka Univ.; Pres. Sumitomo Bank –2001; Pres. and CEO Sumitomo Mitsui Financial Group (Sumitomo Mitsui Banking Corpn) 2001–05; Chair. Nat. Banking Asscn 2003–05. *Leisure interest:* supporting Hanshin Tigers baseball team. *Address:* c/o Sumitomo Mitsui Financial Group Inc., 3-2 Marunouchi 1-chome, Chiyoda-ku, Tokyo, Japan (office).

NISHIMATSU, Chikara, BSME; Japanese business executive; b. 3 Nov. 1931, Osaka; m. Michiko Yamada 1959; two s. one d.; ed Pratt Inst.; joined Itochu Co., Ltd 1959, mem. Bd Dirs 1984–91, Gen. Man. Itochu Asian Operations 1985, Man. Dir 1986, Gen. Man. Itochu Europe and Africa Operation 1989–91; Pres. and CEO Matsubo Co. Ltd (fmrly. known as Matsuzaka Co. Ltd) 1992–98, Chair. and CEO 1998–2000, Adviser 2000–02; CEO The Mirai Creative Co. Inc. *Address:* 3-21-6, Katsuta-Dai, Yachiyo City, Chiba-ken 276-0023, Japan (home). *Telephone:* (47) 480-1436 (home). *Fax:* (47) 480-1436 (home). *E-mail:* chik-ni@ma.kcom.ne.jp (home).

NISHIMATSU, Haruka; Japanese airline industry executive; *President and CEO, ;* b. 5 Jan. 1948, Hamamatsu, Shizuoka Pref.; m.; one s. one d.; ed Tokyo Univ.; joined Japan Airlines 1972, assigned to Flight Crew Training Dept in charge of preparing schedules for pilot trainees; moved to Finance Dept 1974 and held several positions in finance and investor relations –1980, Traffic Div., Admin in charge of budgets for airport offices 1980–83, worked in Corp. Planning 1983–87, Admin Man., Frankfurt, Germany 1987–91, returned to Finance Dept 1991, Dir 1999–2001, Exec. Officer, Finance and Investor Relations 2003–05, Sr Vice-Pres., Finance and Investor Relations 2005–06, Sr Man. Dir, Finance and Investor Relations 2006, Pres. and CEO 2006–. *Leisure interests:* golf, reading. *Address:* Japan Airlines Corpn, 4-11, Higashi-shinagawa 2-chome, Shinagawa-ku, Tokyo 140-8605, Japan (office). *Telephone:* (3) 5769-6098 (office). *E-mail:* info@jal.com (office). *Website:* www.jal.com (office).

NISHIMI, Toru; Japanese retail industry executive; *President, The Daiei Inc.;* Corporate Sr Vice-Pres. Marubeni Corpn –2006, mem. Bd of Dirs Marubeni-Itochu Steel Inc. 2006–; Pres. The Daiei Inc. retail group 2006–. *Address:* The Daiei Inc., 4-1-1, Minatojima Nakamachi, Chuo-ku, Kobe 650-0046, Japan (office). *Telephone:* (78) 302-5001 (office). *Fax:* (3) 3433-9226 (office). *Website:* www.daiei.co.jp (office).

NISHIMURA, Hidetoshi; Japanese business executive; *President and Co-CEO, Nissho Iwai-Nichimen Holdings Corporation;* Sr Man. Exec. Officer Nissho Iwai Corpn –2002, Pres. 2002, Pres. and CEO 2002–03, Pres. and Co-CEO Nisho Iwai-Nichimen Holdings Corpn (est. as holding corpn of Nichimen Corpn and Nissho Iwai Corpn 2003) 2003–; fmr Gov. Ehime Prefecture, also Vice-Gov. in charge of Educ. and Foreign Affairs. *Address:* Nissho Iwai-Nichimen Holdings Corporation, 1-23 Shiba 4-chome, Minato-ku, Tokyo 108-8408, Japan (office). *Telephone:* (3) 5446-3600 (office). *Fax:* (3) 5446-1542 (office). *Website:* www.nn-holdings.com (office).

NISHIMURA, Hiroshi; Japanese insurance executive; *President, Mitsui Mutual Life Insurance Company;* currently Pres. Mitsui Mutual Life Insurance Co., negotiated jt pension man. venture and marketing collaborations with Sumitomo Life 2001. *Address:* Mitsui Mutual Life Insurance Company, 1-2-3 Ohtemachi, Chiyoda-ku, Tokyo 100-8123, Japan (office). *Telephone:* (3) 3211-6111 (office). *Fax:* (3) 3215-1580 (office). *Website:* www.mitsui-seimei.co.jp (office).

NISHIMURA, Kiyohiko G., PhD; Japanese economist and central banker; *Deputy Governor, Bank of Japan;* b. 30 March 1953, Tokyo; s. of Giichi Nishimura and Sumiko Otsuka; m. Yukiko Kurihata 1979; two d.; ed Univ. of Tokyo, Yale Univ., USA; Arthur Okun Research Fellow, Brookings Inst., USA 1981–82; Assoc. Prof. of Econs, Univ. of Tokyo 1983–94, Prof. 1994–2005; Assoc. Ed. Economic Studies Quarterly 1989–93; Research Assoc. US-Japan Center, New York Univ. 1989–; Dir Tokyo Centre for Econ. Research 1990–91; Visiting Scholar, MIT, USA 1991–92; Visiting Research Fellow, Inst. for Int. Econ. Studies, Sweden 1993; Visiting Prof., Louis Pasteur Univ. 1994, Århus Univ., Denmark 1996; Special mem. Econ. Council, Japanese Govt 1994–98; mem. Regulatory Reform Cttee, Japanese Govt 1999–2001, Council Japanese Econ. Asscn 1999–2005, Statistic Council, Japanese Govt 2003–05, Financial System Council, Japanese Govt 2003–05; mem. Policy Bd Bank of Japan 2005–08, Deputy Gov. 2008–; Co-Ed. Journal of Industry, Competition and Trade 2000–; Sr Advisor, Asian Econ. Panel 2001–; Exec. Research Fellow, Cabinet Office, Japanese Govt 2003–05; Fellow, East Asian Econ. Asscn 2005; Nikkei Prize 1993, Japan Economist's Prize 1997, Nakahara Prize, Japanese Econ. Asscn 1998, Prize of the Japan Asscn for Real Estate Sciences 2005, Telecom Social Science Award, 2006. *Publications:* Stock and Land Prices in Japan (in Japanese) 1990, The Distribution System in Japan (ed., in Japanese) 1991, Imperfect Competition, Differential Information and Microfoundations of Macroeconomics 1992, Macroeconomics of Price Revolution 1996, The Grief of a Prairie Dog (socioeconomic essays) 1998, The Distribution in Japan 2002, The Japanese Economy: Inconspicuous Structural Transformation 2004, Advancement of Information and Communication Technology and Its Impacts on the Japanese Economy 2004, Socially-Oriented Investment Trusts – Beyond Private Finance Initiative 2004. *Leisure interest:* photography. *Address:* 2-1-1, Nihonbashi-Hongokucho, Chuo-ku, Tokyo 103-8660 (office). *Telephone:* (3) 3279-1111 (office). *Fax:* (3) 5255-6785 (office).

NISHIMURO, Taizo, BEcons; Japanese electronics industry executive; *Adviser, Toshiba Corporation;* b. 19 Dec. 1935, Yamanashi; ed Faculty of Econs, Keio Univ.; joined Toshiba Corpn 1961, Dir Industrial Mfg Div., Iwate Prefectural Office 1984–86, Gen. Man. Semiconductor Marketing & Sales Div. 1986–90, Gen. Man. Overseas Operations Promotion Div. 1990–92, Vice-Pres. and Dir 1992–94, Sr Vice-Pres. and Dir 1994–95, Exec. Vice-Pres. and Dir 1995–96, Pres. and CEO 1996–2000, Chair. 2000–05, Adviser 2005–; Chair. Tokyo Stock Exchange Inc. June–Dec. 2005, Pres. and CEO 2006–07; Chair. Japan–US Business Council 2002; Vice-Chair. Japan Business Fed. 2003. *Address:* Toshiba Corporation, 1-1 Shibaura 1-chome, Minato-ku, Tokyo 105-8001, Japan (office). *Telephone:* (3) 3457-4511 (office). *Fax:* (3) 3455-1631 (office). *Website:* www.toshiba.com (office).

NISHIO, Shinji; Japanese petroleum industry executive; *President and Representative Director, Nippon Oil Corporation;* joined Nippon Oil Co. 1964, Exec. Vice-Pres. and Chief Financial Officer Nippon Oil Corpn –2005, Pres. 2005–, currently also Rep. Dir. *Address:* Nippon Oil Corpn, 3-12 Nishi Shimbashi 1-chome, Minato-ku, Tokyo 105-8412, Japan (office). *Telephone:* (3) 3502-1131 (office). *Fax:* (3) 3502-9352 (office). *E-mail:* info@eneos.co.jp (office). *Website:* www.eneos.co.jp (office).

NISHIOKA, Takashi; Japanese manufacturing executive; *Chairman, Mitsubishi Motors Corporation;* b. 5 March 1936; joined Mitsubishi Heavy Industries Ltd 1959, mem. Bd 1992–, Man.-Dir 1995–98, Exec. Vice-Pres. 1998–99, Pres. 1999–2003, Chair. 2003–08, Sr Adviser 2008–, also mem. Bd Mitsubishi Motors Corpn 2003–, Chair. 2006–, led negotiations with Caterpillar Inc. to est. jt venture Shin Caterpillar Mitsubishi Ltd 2003. *Address:* Mitsubishi Motors Corpn, 2-16-4 Konan, Minato-ku, Tokyo 108-8410, Japan (office). *Telephone:* (3) 6719-2111 (office). *Fax:* (3) 6719-0059 (office). *E-mail:* info@mitsubishi-motors.co.jp (office). *Website:* www.mitsubishi-motors.co.jp (office).

NISHIZAWA, Jun-ichi, BS, DEng, FIEE; Japanese electrical engineer, academic and university administrator; *President, Tokyo Metropolitan University;* b. 12 Sept. 1926, Sendai; s. of Kyosuke Nishizawa and Akiko (née Ishii) Nishizawa; m. Takeko Hayakawa 1956; one s. two d.; ed Tohoku Univ.; Research Asst, Electrical Communication Research Inst., Tohoku Univ. 1953–54, Asst Prof. 1954–62, Prof. 1962–90, Dir 1983–86, 1989–90, Pres. of Univ. 1990–96; Dir Semiconductor Research Inst., Sendai 1968–2004; Pres. Iwate Prefectural Univ. 1998–2005; Chair. Japan Atomic Industrial Forum (JAIF) 2000–06, Eng Acad. of Japan (EAJ); Pres. Tokyo Metropolitan Univ. 2005–; approx. 615 patents in Japan, 345 patents abroad; mem. Japan Acad.; Foreign mem. Polish Acad. of Sciences, Russian Acad. of Sciences, Korea Acad. of Science and Tech., Yugoslav Acad. of Engineering; Life Mem. IEEE; Dr hc (Humboldt Univ., Berlin) 1989; Dirs Award of Japanese Science and Tech. Agency 1965, 1970, Invention Prize by the Emperor 1966, Matsunaga Memorial Award 1969, Okochi Memorial Tech. Prize 1971, Japan Acad. Prize 1974, Science and Tech. Merits Award 1975, Purple Ribbon Medal conferred from Japanese Govt 1975, Achievement Award from Inst. of Electronics and Communication Engineers of Japan 1975, Dir Award of Patent Agency 1980, Okochi Memorial Tech. Prize 1980, IEEE Jack A. Morton Award 1984, Honda Prize 1986, Laudise Prize of Int. Org. of Crystal Growth 1989, Power Conversion and Intelligent Motion (PCIM) Award 1989, Kenneth J. Button Prize 1993, Harushige Inoue Award 1993, The Okawa Prize 1996, IEEE Edison Medal 2000; Hon. Citizen of Sendai City 1984, First Hon. Citizen of Miyagi Prefecture 1990; Person of Cultural Merits (Bunka-Korosha), conferred from Japanese Government 1983, Order of Cultural Merits from the Japanese Emperor 1989. *Publications:* Semiconductor Devices 1961, Semiconductor Materials 1968, Optoelectronics 1977. *Leisure interests:* classical music, reading, pottery, pictures (especially Impressionist school). *Address:* Tokyo Metropolitan University, Minami-Osawa 1-1, Hachioji-shi, Tokyo 192-0397, Japan (office). *Telephone:* (426) 77-1111 (office). *Fax:* (426) 77-2009 (office). *Website:* www.tmu.ac.jp (office); .

NISHIZAWA, Ryue; Japanese architect; b. 1966, Tokyo; has worked with Kazuyo Sejima at their architects' office SANAA in Tokyo since 1995; their architecture has been described as "translucent minimalism", in which glass walls and thin, white textiles divide interior from exterior; Rolf Schock Prize in the Visual Arts, Royal Swedish Acad. of Sciences (co-recipient) 2005. *Works include:* Gifu Kitagata Apartment Bldg, Motosu 1994–98, N-Museum, Nakahechi 1995–97, O-Museum, Iida 1995–99, K Bldg, Hitachi 1996–97, M-House, Tokyo 1996–97, Park Café, Koga 1996–98, Multi-Media Workshop, Oogaki 1996–97, Weekend House, Usui-gun 1997–98, New Campus Center for Illinois Inst. of Tech., Chicago 1997–98, Museum für Zeitgenössische Kunst, Sydney 1997–2001, Day Care Centre for the Elderly, Yokohama 1997–2000, S-House, Okayama 1997, Centre for the Contemporary Arts, Rome 1998–99, Stadstheater, Almere 1998, Renovation of the Antique Quarter, Salerno 1998, pvt. residence, Kamakura 1999–2001, Contemporary Art Museum, Kanazawa 1999, Wochenendhaus, Japan 2000, Christian Dior Shop, Tokyo-Minato-ku 2004, Museum of Contemporary Art, Kanazawa 2004, new bldg for The New Museum, New York 2006. *Address:* Sanaa Ltd/Kazuyo Sejima, Ryue Nishizawa & Associates, 7-A Shinagawa-Soko, 2-2-35-6B, Higashi-Shinagawa, Shinagawa-ku, Tokyo 140-0002, Japan (office). *Telephone:* (3) 34500117 (office). *Fax:* (3) 34501757 (office). *E-mail:* sanaa@sanaa.co.jp (office); office@ryuenishizawa.com (office). *Website:* www.sanaa.co.jp (office); www.ryuenishizawa.com (office).

NISKALA, Markku, MPA; Finnish international organization executive; *Secretary General, International Federation of Red Cross and Red Crescent Societies;* b. 5 Dec. 1945; m.; began career as Dist Sec., Red Cross 1970; various positions in Red Cross Soc. of Finland 1970–78; Rep. of League of Red Cross and Red Crescent Socs, Zambia, Tanzania and Zimbabwe 1978–81, oversaw implementation of S African Programme –1985; Head of Europe Dept, Int. Fed. of Red Cross and Red Crescent Socs (IFRC) Secr., Geneva 1985–87; missions to Tanzania, Zambia, Zimbabwe and Ethiopia IFRC 1987–88; Sec. Gen. Finnish Red Cross 1988–2003; Chair. Comm. of the Financing of Int. Cttee of Red Cross 1992–; Acting Sec. Gen. IFRC July–Nov. 2003, Sec. Gen. Nov. 2003–. *Address:* International Federation of Red Cross and Red Crescent Societies, PO Box 372, 1211 Geneva 19, Switzerland. *Telephone:* 227304222. *Fax:* 227330395. *E-mail:* secretariat@ifrc.org. *Website:* www.ifrc.org.

NISSIM, Moshe, LLB, MJ; Israeli politician and lawyer; *Head of Law Office, Moshe Nissim, Rinkor, Senderovitch;* b. 1935, Jerusalem; s. of Isaac Nissim (Chief Rabbi of Israel) and Victoria Nissim; m.; five c.; ed Hebrew Univ. of Jerusalem; elected to Knesset (Parl.) (youngest-ever member) 1959–96 (as rep. of Union of Gen. Zionists 1959, subsequently as rep. of Gahal faction of the Liberal Party, then of the Likud Bloc); has served on Defence, Foreign Affairs and Security, Constitution Law and Legislation, Labour and Housing Cttees in the Knesset; Co-Chair. Likud Group 1975–79; Chair. Exec. Cttee, Likud 1978–; Minister without Portfolio 1978–80, 1988–89; Minister of Justice 1980–86, of Finance 1986–88, of Trade and Industry 1989–92; Deputy Prime Minister 1990–92; Head of Law Office Moshe Nissim, Rinkov, Senderovitch; Dr hc (Ben-Gurion Univ.). *Address:* 3A Jabotinsky Street, Haya'lom Tower, Ramat-Gan 52520 (office); 6 Shlom Aleichem Street, Jerusalem 92148, Israel (home). *Telephone:* 3-6133333 (office). 2-5619414 (home). *Fax:* 3-6133334 (office); 2-5617155 (home). *E-mail:* nrs@nrs-law.com (office).

NISSINEN, Mikko; Finnish artistic director, teacher, ballet dancer and choreographer; *Artistic Director, Boston Ballet;* b. 1962, Helsinki; ed Stanford Univ., USA; began dance training at Finnish Nat. Ballet School 1973; began performing as soloist 1977; joined Kirov Ballet School 1979; performer with Dutch Nat. Ballet and Basel Ballet; Prin. Dancer, San Francisco Ballet, USA 1986–96; guest artist at numerous int. galas; Artistic Dir, Marin Ballet, San Rafael, Calif., USA 1996–98, Alberta Ballet, Calgary, Canada 1998–2001; Artistic Dir, Boston Ballet and Boston Ballet Center for Dance Educ. 2001–; mem. Artistic Cttee, New York Choreographic Inst.; mem. Advisory Bd, Albert Schweitzer Fellowship, Armitage Gone! Dance; First Prize, Nat. Ballet Competition, Kuopio 1978, UN Asscn of Greater Boston Leadership Award 2007, Finlandia Foundation Arts and Letters Award 2008. *Dance:* as choreographer: The Nutcracker, Alberta and Boston Ballets 2003, Swan Lake, Boston Ballet 2004, Raymonde (Act III), Alberta and Boston Ballets. *Address:* Boston Ballet, 19 Clarendon Street, Boston, MA 02116-6100, USA (office). *Telephone:* (617) 695-6950 (office). *Fax:* (617) 695-6995 (office). *Website:* www.bostonballet.org (office).

NITTVE, Lars; Swedish museum director and writer; *Director, Moderna Museet;* b. 17 Sept. 1953, Stockholm; m. Shideh Shaygan; one c. from previous m.; fmr Stockholm newspaper critic; fmr journalist for Artforum; Sr Curator Moderna Museet (nat. contemporary art museum) 1986–89, Dir 2001–, also Deputy Chair. Bd Dirs; Dir Rooseum, Malmö 1990–95, Louisiana Museum of Modern Art, Humlebæk, Denmark 1995–98, Tate Modern, London 1998–2001. *Address:* Moderna Museet, Box 16382, 103 27 Stockholm, Sweden (office). *Telephone:* (8) 5195-62-59 (office). *Fax:* (8) 5195-62-84 (office). *E-mail:* l.nittve@modernamuseet.se (office). *Website:* www.modernamuseet.se (office).

NIU, Han; Chinese poet; b. (Shi Chenghan), 23 Oct. 1923, Dingxiang, Shanxi Prov.; s. of Niu Yingfeng and Shi Buchan; m. Wu Ping; one s. one d.; ed Northwest Univ.; fmrly Sec. Research Dept Renmin Univ.; Dir Cultural and Educational Office, Political Dept of Northeast Air Force; Exec. Assoc. Chief Ed. Chinese Literature; Chief Ed. Historical Records of New Literature Movt; Dir Editorial Office of May 4th Literature; Sr Ed. People's Publishing House; mem. Nat. Cttee, Chinese Writers' Asscn; Creative Literary Works Award 1981–82, Literary Stick Prize for Nation's Best New Poem (Macedonia) 2003, China Central TV Poet of the Year 2006. *Publications:* Motherland, In Front of the Motherland, Coloured Life, Hot Spring, Love and Songs, Earthworm and Feather, Selected Lyric Poems of Niu Han, Notes Taken While Learning to Write Poems, A Sonambulist's Talk on Poetry 2001, Spaciousness Afar-off 2005. *Leisure interests:* fine arts, Chinese calligraphy. *Address:* 203 Gate 6 Building 309 Balizhuang Beili, Beijing 100025 (home); People's Literature Publishing House, 166 Chaoyangmen Nei Dajie, Beijing 100705, People's Republic of China (office). *Telephone:* (10) 85836410 (home); (10) 65138394 (office). *Fax:* (10) 65138394 (office). *E-mail:* fangjia2001@yahoo.com.cn (home).

NIU, Maosheng; Chinese government official; b. 1939, Beijing; ed Beijing Agricultural Inst.; joined CCP 1961; sent to the countryside 1963–65; Sec., later Deputy Dir Office, Bureau for Water Resources and Meteorology, Beijing 1965–73 (mem. CCP Party Cttee), Dir Water Conservancy Man. Div.; Deputy Dir Water Conservancy Bureau, Beijing 1973–82 (Deputy Sec. CCP Party Cttee); Sec. CCP Miyun Co. Cttee, Beijing 1982–85; Vice-Chair. and Gen. Man. China Water Resources Devt Corpn 1980s; First Deputy Dir, later Dir Yellow River Man. Cttee, Ministry of Water Resources 1980s; mem. CCP Beijing Municipal Cttee 1982–85; Sec.-Gen. State Flood Control and Drought Relief HQ 1985–88, Deputy Head 1993–98; Vice-Minister of Water Resources 1988–93, Minister 1993–98; Head, Leading Group, Construction Comm. for Diverting Water from the South to the North Project 1998; Vice-Gov. Hebei Prov. 1998, Acting Gov. 1998–99, Gov. 1999–2002; mem. 15th CCP Cen. Cttee 1997–2002, 16th CCP Cen. Cttee 2002–07; mem. Standing Cttee 10th CPPCC Nat. Cttee 2003–, Chair. CPPCC Sub-cttee of Ethnic and Religious Affairs 2003–. *Address:* Chinese Communist Party Provincial Committee, Shijiazhuang City, Hebei Province, People's Republic of China (office).

NIU, Qun; Chinese actor; b. Dec. 1949, Tianjin; joined PLA 1971; actor Zhanyou Art Troupe of PLA Beijing Mil. Command 1974–93; actor China Broadcasting Art Troupe 1993–; performs comic dialogues with Feng Gong; Vice-Mayor Mengcheng Co., Anhui Prov. 2001–; numerous prizes. *Publications:* In Various Ingenious Names (five cassettes of comic dialogues). *Address:* China Broadcasting Art Troupe, Beijing, People's Republic of China (office).

NIVERT, Marianne; Swedish business executive; *Chairman, Posten AB;* participated in Televerket's (Swedish telecom admin) telecom engineer programme 1961, joined Televerket AB 1963, Admin. Man. Teli (Telverket's Industrial Div.) 1976–77, Telecom Dir for Stockholm 1977–82, Man. Gothenburg Telecom Area 1982–92, Man. Telia Region East 1992–93, Dir Human Resources, Telia Group 1993, Exec. Vice-Pres. and mem. Group Exec. Man. Telia AB 1997–98, Head of Network Services 1998–2000, Pres. and CEO Telia Group (now TeliaSonera following merger with Sonera of Finland) 2000–02; Dir Posten AB 2002–, Chair. 2003–; fmr Chair. Save the Children Sweden; mem. Bd of Dirs SSAB Svenskt Stal 2002–, Beijer Alma AB 2002–, Wallenstams Byggnads AB, Systembolaget AB, Swedish Corp. Governance Bd; Assar Gabrielsson Guest Prof., School of Econs and Commercial Law, Göteburg Univ. 2004; selected by The Wall Street Journal Europe as among Europe's most influential businesswomen 2001, ranked fourth by Fortune magazine amongst 50 Most Powerful Women in Business outside the US 2001. *Address:* Posten Sverige AB, Kundtjänst Företag/Private Box 1840, 171 29 Solna, Sweden (office). *Telephone:* (8) 232220 (office). *Website:* www.posten.se (office).

NIWA, Uichiro; Japanese business executive; *Chairman, Itochu Corporation;* ed Nagoya Univ.; joined Itochu Corpn (gen. trading co. involved in aerospace, electronic, multimedia, chemicals, energy, finance, automobile and textiles industries) 1966, Pres. and CEO 2000–04, Chair. 2004–; Pres. Keidanren Cttee on Agric. Policy 2000–. *Address:* ITOCHU Corpn, 5-1 Kita-

Aoyama 2-chome, Minato-ku, Tokyo 107-8077, Japan (office). *Telephone:* (3) 3497-2121 (office). *Fax:* (3) 3497-4141 (office). *E-mail:* info@itochu.co.jp (office). *Website:* www.itochu.co.jp (office).

NIWA, Yuya; Japanese politician; mem. House of Reps; fmr Parl. Vice-Minister for Health and Welfare; fmr Health and Welfare Minister; fmr Chair. LDP Policy Research Council; Minister for Health and Welfare 1999–2000. *Address:* Ministry of Health and Welfare, 1-2-2, Kasumigaseki, Chiyoda-ku, Tokyo 100-0013, Japan (office). *Telephone:* (3) 3503-1771 (office). *Fax:* (3) 3501-2532 (office). *E-mail:* www-admin@mhw.ho.jp (office).

NIWANO, Nichiko; Japanese religious leader; *President, Rissho Kosei-kai;* b. 1938; s. of Nikkyo Niwano; ed Rissho Univ.; entered Rissho Kosei-kai 1968, later Head, Dissemination Dept, later Pres. Rissho Kosei-kai Seminary, Pres. Rissho Kosei-kai 1991–; Pres. Niwano Peace Foundation, World Conf. on Religion and Peace, Asian Conf. on Religion and Peace; Vice-Chair. Shinshuren. *Publications:* Modern Meditations – The Inward Path; My Father, My Teacher. *Address:* Rissho Kosei-kai, 2-11-1, Wada Suginami-ku, Tokyo 166-8537, Japan (office). *Telephone:* (3) 3380-5185 (office). *Fax:* (3) 3381-9792 (office). *E-mail:* info@rk-world.org (office). *Website:* www.rk-world.org (office).

NIXON, Gordon M., BComm; Canadian banking executive; *President and CEO, Royal Bank of Canada Financial Group;* b. 1957, Montreal; m.; three c.; ed Queen's Univ., Kingston, Ont.; began investment banking career with Dominion Securities, 1979, with Fixed Income and Govt Finance Divs 1979–86, Head of Operations, Japan 1986–89, Man. Dir Investment Banking, Royal Bank of Canada (following RBC's acquisition of Dominion) 1989–95, Head of Global Investment Banking 1995–98, Head of Banking RBC Financial Group 1998–99, CEO RBC Dominion Securities 1999–2001, mem. Exec. Cttee RBC Financial Group 1999–, Pres. and CEO RBC Financial Group 2001–; Dir RBC and Chair. Group Man. Cttee; Chair. United Way of Greater Toronto 2002 Campaign; mem. Bd The Hosp for Sick Children, Branksome Hall, Canadian Council for Chief Execs, Inst. of Int. Finance; Hon. LLD (Queen's Univ.); Rotary Foundation Paul Harris Fellowship, Queen's Golden Jubilee Medal. *Address:* Royal Bank of Canada, 123 Front Street West, Suite 600, Toronto, M5J 2M2, Canada (office). *Telephone:* (416) 955-7802 (office). *Fax:* (416) 955-7800 (office). *E-mail:* info@rbc.com (office). *Website:* www.rbc.com (office).

NIXON, Jeremiah (Jay) W., BA, JD; American lawyer and politician; *Governor of Missouri;* b. 13 Feb. 1956, DeSoto, Mo.; m. Georganne Wheeler Nixon; two s.; ed Univ. of Missouri; Pnr, Nixon, Nixon Breeze and Roberts (law firm) 1981–86; mem. Mo. State Senate from Dist 22 1986–93; Attorney-Gen. for State of Mo. 1992–2009; Gov. of Missouri 2009–; Democrat. *Address:* Office of the Governor, Room 216, State Capitol Building, Jefferson City, MO 65101, USA (office). *Telephone:* (573) 751-3222 (office). *Website:* governor.mo.gov (office).

NIXON, John Forster, PhD, DSc, FRS, FRSA; British scientist and academic; *Research Professor, Department of Chemistry, University of Sussex;* b. 27 Jan. 1937, Whitehaven, Cumberland (now Cumbria); s. of Edward Forster Nixon, MBE and Mary Nixon (née Lytton); m. 'Kim' Smith 1960; one s. one d.; ed Univs of Manchester and Cambridge; Research Assoc. in Chem., Univ. of Southern California, LA 1960–62; ICI Fellow, Inorganic Chem. Dept, Univ. of Cambridge 1962–64; Lecturer in Inorganic Chem., Univ. of St Andrews 1964–66; Lecturer in Chem., Univ. of Sussex 1966, Reader 1976, Subject Chair. in Chem. 1981–84, Prof. of Chem. 1986–, now Research Prof., Dean School of Chem. and Molecular Sciences 1989–92; Visiting Assoc. Prof. of Chem., Univ. of Victoria, BC 1970–71; Visiting Prof., Simon Fraser Univ., Vancouver BC 1975; Chair. Downland Section, Chemical Soc. 1973–74; mem. Int. Cttee on Phosphorus Chem. 1983–, Inorganic Chem. Panel Science and Eng Research Council Cttee 1986–89, Int. Cttee Inorganic Ring Systems (IRIS) 2002–06, Main Group Element Council 2002–06; elected Titular mem. IUPAC Comm., Inorganic Nomenclature 1985; Royal Soc.-Leverhulme Sr Research Fellow 1993; Visiting Prof. Indian Inst. of Science, Bangalore 2002, 2005–06; Visiting Fellow, ANU, Canberra 2004; Corday-Morgan Medal and Prize, Royal Soc. of Chem. (RSC) 1973, RSC Main Group Element Prize 1985, RSC Tilden Lectureship 1991–92, RSC Ludwig Mond Lectureship and Prize 2003, Alexander von Humbold Prize Winner 2001–02, Geza Zemplen Medal, Budapest Inst. of Tech. 2003. *Publications:* Phosphorus: The Carbon Copy (co-author) 1998 and over 370 publs in chemical journals and invited lectures to int. chemical socs. *Leisure interests:* walking, theatre, music, watching cricket, playing tennis and squash. *Address:* Chemistry Department, School of Life Sciences, Chichester Building 3R515, University of Sussex, Brighton, Sussex, BN1 9QJ (office); Juggs Barn, The Street, Kingston, Lewes, Sussex, BN7 3PB, England (home). *Telephone:* (1273) 678536 (office); (1273) 483993 (home). *Fax:* (1273) 677196 (office). *E-mail:* j.nixon@sussex.ac.uk (office). *Website:* www.sussex.ac.uk/chemistry/profile1954 (office).

NIXON, Patrick Michael, CMG, OBE; British diplomatist (retd); b. 1 Aug. 1944, Reading, Berks.; s. of the late John Moylett Gerard Nixon and Hilary Mary Paterson; m. Elizabeth Carlton 1968; four s.; ed Downside School, Magdalene Coll., Cambridge; joined Diplomatic Service 1965, served Middle East Centre for Arab Studies, Lebanon, Cairo, Lima, Tripoli, British Information Services, New York 1980–83; Asst, later Head Near East and N Africa Dept, FCO 1983–87; Amb. to Qatar 1987–90; Counsellor, FCO 1990–93; High Commr in Zambia 1994–97; Dir FCO 1997–98; Amb. to UAE 1998–2003; Coordinator Coalition Provision Authority, Southern Iraq 2004; Gov., All Hallows School 1993– (Chair. 2005–), Downside School 2005–.

NIYOYANKANA, Lt-Gen. Germain; Burundian politician; *Minister of National Defence and War Veterans;* commdr during civil war; Armed Forces Chief of Staff, Nat. Defence Force 2004–05; Minister of Nat. Defence and War Veterans 2005–; mem. Union pour le progresse nationale (Uprona). *Address:* Ministry of National Defence, Bujumbura, Burundi (office). *Telephone:* 2222148 (office).

NIYUNGEKO, Vincent; Burundian politician; Minister of Defence 2002–05. *Address:* c/o Ministry of Defence, Bujumbura, Burundi (office).

NIZAMI, Farhan Ahmad, CBE, DPhil; Indian/British academic; *Director, Oxford Centre for Islamic Studies;* b. 25 Dec. 1956; s. of the late Khaliq Nizami and Razia Nizami; m. Farah Deba Ahmad 1983; one s., one d.; ed Aligarh Muslim Univ. and Wadham Coll., Oxford; founding Dir Oxford Centre for Islamic Studies 1985–; Prince of Wales Fellow Magdalen Coll. Oxford 1997–, mem. Faculties of Modern History and Oriental Studies; Founder Ed. Journal of Islamic Studies 1990–; Series Ed., Makers of Islamic Civilization 2004–; Rothman's Fellow in Muslim History, St Cross College, Oxford 1983–85, Fellow 1985–97, Emer. Fellow 1997–; f. Ed. Journal of Islamic Studies 1990–; Series Ed. Makers of Islamic Civilization 2004–; Sec. Bd of Trustees The Islamic Trust 1985–; Sec. Bd of Dirs Oxford Trust for Islamic Studies 1998–; Dir Oxford Inspires 2002–03; Chair. Oxford Endeavours 2003–; mem. Council Al-Falah Programme, Univ. of Calif., Berkeley 1997–2004, Advisory Bd Duke Univ. Islamic Studies Centre, Acad. Council of Wilton Park 2000–04 (Chair. 2004–), Court of Oxford Brookes Univ. 2000–, Advisory Bd Dialogues Project World Policy Inst. New School Univ., NY 2003–, Archbishop of Canterbury's Reference Group for Christian-Muslim Relations 2002–04; Scholar Consultant to the Christian-Muslim Forum 2005–; mem. Academic Consultative Cttee, Cumberland Lodge 2003–, Steering Cttee C-100, World Econ. Forum, Davos 2003–, Int. Advisory Panel, OIC Business Forum, Malaysia 2004–; Patron Oxford Amnesty Lectures 2003–; Order of the Crown of Brunei (Class IV) 1992. *Leisure interests:* reading, cricket. *Address:* Oxford Centre for Islamic Studies, George Street, Oxford, OX1 2AR, England. *Telephone:* (1865) 278731 (office). *Fax:* (1865) 248942 (office).

NIZIGAMA, Clotilde; Burundian politician; *Minister of Finance;* fmr Dir-Gen. Office Nat. Pharmaceutique (ONAPHA); Minister of the Economy, Finance and Co-operation and Devt 2007–; mem. Conseil national pour la défense de la démocratie—Force pour la défense de la démocratie (CNDD—FDD). *Address:* Ministry of Finance, BP 1830, Bujumbura, Burundi (office). *Telephone:* 22225142 (office). *Fax:* 22223128 (office).

NJIE-SAIDY, Isatou, MSc; Gambian teacher and politician; *Vice-President and Secretary of State for Women's Affairs;* b. 5 March 1952, Kuntaya, N Bank Div.; m.; four c.; ed Yundum Teacher's Training Coll., Univ. Coll. of Swansea, Univ. of Wales, UK; schoolteacher 1970–76; Sr Business Advisory and Training Officer, Indigenous Business Advisory Services 1976–83; Deputy Exec. Sec., Women's Bureau (exec. arm of Nation's Women's Council) 1983–89; Minister of Health, Social Welfare and Women's Affairs 1996–, Vice-Pres. and Sec. of State for Women's Affairs 1997–. *Address:* Office of the Vice-President, State House, Banjul, The Gambia (office). *Telephone:* 227605 (office). *Fax:* 224012 (office). *E-mail:* vicepresident@statehouse.gm (office).

NJOJO, Rt Rev. Patrice Byankya; Democratic Republic of the Congo ecclesiastic; *Bishop of Boga and Honorary Archbishop of the Province of the Congo;* b. 1935, Boga; m. Kamanyoho Njojo; seven c.; ed teachers' coll., schools' inspector training, Univ. of Montreal, Canada; teacher, schools inspector, priest, currently Bishop of Boga; Archbishop of the Prov. of the Congo 1992–2002; Bronze Medal 1968, Gold Medal 1972. *Leisure interests:* cattle breeding, music. *Address:* PO Box 25586, Kampala, Uganda (office); Bishop's Residence, CAC-Boga, PO Box 25586, Kampala, Uganda (home). *Telephone:* 78321454 (office); 77847365 (home). *E-mail:* eac-mags@infocom.co.ug (office); njojob2000@yahoo.com (office).

NJUE, HE Cardinal John, MA; Kenyan ecclesiastic; *Archbishop of Nairobi;* b. 1944, Kiriari Village, Mukangu Sub-Ngandori, Embu Dist; s. of Joseph Nyaga Kibariki and Monica Ngima Nyaga; ed Nguviu Intermediate School, Kyaweru, Nkubu Jr Seminary, Pontifical Urbanian Univ. and Pontifical Lateran Univ., Rome; ordained priest of Embu 1973; served in Kariakomu Parish, Meru South Dist, Meru Diocese 1973–75; apptd Prof. of Philosophy and Dean of Students at St Augustine Sr Seminary, Mabanga, Bungoma 1975, Rector 1978–82; went to USA and undertook spiritual renewal programme course for six months; appointed Father-in-Charge of Chuka Parish (first African priest to be assigned in the parish as Parish Priest after Consolata Missionaries left) 1982; Rector St Joseph's Philosophicum Seminary, Nairobi 1985–86; Bishop of Embu 1986–2002; Coadjutor Archbishop of Nyeri 2002–07; Apostolic Admin. of Vicariate of Isiolo –2006; Archbishop of Nairobi 2007–; currently Apostolic Admin. of Catholic Diocese of Muranga; cr. Cardinal 2007; Chair. Seminary Episcopal Comm. for Major Seminaries in Kenya 1987–91, Kenya Episcopal Conf. 1997–2003, Kenya Episcopal Conf. Justice and Peace Comm., Devt and Social Services Dept of Kenya Catholic Secr. *Address:* Archdiocese of Nairobi, PO Box 14231, Nairobi, Kenya (office). *Telephone:* (2) 441919 (office). *Fax:* (2) 447027 (office).

NKATE, Jacob, LLB; Botswana politician and lawyer; *Minister of Education;* ed Univ. of Botswana, Univ. of Edin., UK; Attorney at Law, Magistrate Grade I, Francistown and Palapye 1986–88; Attorney at Law and pvt. practitioner 1988–95; mem. of Parl. 1994–; Asst Minister of Finance and Devt Planning 1997–99; Minister of Lands, Housing and Environment 1999–2002; Minister of Trade and Industry 2002–05, of Education 2005–; del. to numerous int. and multilateral confs including Commonwealth and Trade Conf., UK and S Korea, IPU and UNESCO Conf. in Educ. Science, UNEP Governing Council, Malmo; Chair. Parl. Law Reform; mem. Presidential Task Force on Vision 2016; Gov. and Chair. African Devt Bank. *Address:* Ministry of Education, Private Bag 005, Gaborone, Botswana (office). *Telephone:* 3655400 (office). *Fax:* 3655458 (office). *E-mail:* moe.webmaster@gov.bw (office). *Website:* www.moe.gov.bw/moe/index.html (office).

NKOMO, John Landa; Zimbabwean politician; *Minister for Special Affairs in the President's Office;* b. 22 Aug. 1934; s. of Lufele Nkomo; m. Georgina Nkomo 1963; five s. one d.; school teacher 1957–64; mem. Cen. Cttee Zimbabwe African People's Union (ZAPU) 1975–89, mem. Political Bureau Zimbabwe African Nat. Union-Patriotic Front (ZANU-PF) and Cen. Cttee 1989–; MP for Bulawayo Constituency 1980–; Deputy Minister of Industry 1981–82; Minister of State, Prime Minister's Office 1982–84; Minister of Labour, Manpower Planning and Social Welfare 1988; Pres. Int. Labour Conf. 1989–; Minister of Local Govt and Nat. Housing –2001; Minister of Home Affairs 2001–02; Minister for Special Affairs in the Pres.'s Office responsible for Lands, Land Reform and Resettlement 2002–; mem. Public Accounts Cttee 1980–81; Chair. Cttee of Estimates of Expenditure 1985–87, African Regional Labour Centre; Exec. mem. Southern Rhodesia Teachers' Asscn; Trustee Devt Trust of Zimbabwe, The Pres. Fund; Hon. Life Pres. Matebeleland Turf Club; mem. Highlanders Football Club, Bulawayo Club; Zimbabwe Gold Liberation Medal. *Leisure interest:* reading. *Address:* Office of the President, Munhumu-tapa Building, Samora Machel Ave, Private Bag 7700, Causeway, Harare, Zimbabwe (office). *Telephone:* (4) 707091 (office).

NKURUNZIZA, Pierre, BA; Burundi politician and head of state; *President;* b. Dec. 1963, Mwumba, Ngozi Prov.; s. of the late Eustache Ngabisha; m.; three s.; ed Gitega Secondary School, Univ. of Burundi, Bujumbura; began career as sports teacher, Vugizo and Muramvya Secondary Schools 1991; fmr Asst Lecturer, Faculty of Physical Educ. and Sports, Univ. of Burundi and ISCAM Mil. Acad. of Burundi; coached Army Football Team, Muzinga, and Union Sporting (first div. football team); forced into exile following inter-ethnic clashes 1995; joined Hutu rebellion CNDD-FDD (Force for the Defence of Democracy) 1995, elected Leader of CNDD-FDD 2001; signed ceasefire accord with Govt Nov. 2003; Minister of State for Good Governance 2004–05; Pres. of Burundi 2005–. *Address:* Office of the President of Burundi, Bujumbura, Burundi. *Telephone:* 22226063. *E-mail:* ikiyago@burundi-gov.bi (office). *Website:* presidence.burundi-gov.bi (office).

NOAH, Harold Julius, MA, PhD; American academic; *Gardner Cowles Professor Emeritus of Economics and Education, Teachers College, Columbia University;* b. 21 Jan. 1925, London, England; s. of Abraham Noah and Sophia Cohen; m. 1st Norma Mestel 1945 (divorced 1966); m. 2nd Helen Claire Chisnall 1966; two s. two d.; ed Stratford Grammar School, London School of Econs, King's Coll. London, Teachers Coll. Columbia Univ., New York; Asst Master then Head of Econs, Henry Thornton School, London 1949–60; Asst, later Assoc. and Gardner Cowles Prof. of Econs and Educ., Teachers Coll., Columbia Univ., New York 1964–87, now Prof. Emer., also Dean 1976–81; Prof. of Educ., State Univ. of New York, Buffalo 1987–91; has received numerous academic honours and awards. *Publications include:* Educational Financing and Policy Goals for Primary Schools: General Report (with Joel Sherman) 1979, The National Case Study: An Empirical Comparative Study of Twenty-one Educational Systems (with Harry Passow and others) 1976, Canada: Review of National Policies for Education 1976, International Study of Business/Industry Involvement in Education 1987, Secondary School Examinations: International Perspectives on Policies and Practice 1993, Doing Comparative Education: Three Decades of Collaboration (with Max Eckstein) 1998, Fraud in Education: The Worm in the Apple 2001. *Address:* Teachers College, Columbia University, Box 211, New York, NY 10027, USA (office). *E-mail:* hjn9@columbia.edu (office).

NOAKES, Michael; British painter; b. 28 Oct. 1933, Brighton, Sussex; s. of the late Basil Noakes and Mary Noakes; m. Vivien Langley 1960; two s. one d.; ed Downside, Reigate School of Art, The Royal Acad. Schools; mil. service 1954–56; has painted numerous portraits of mems. of Royal Family including Queen Elizabeth II, Queen Elizabeth The Queen Mother, Prince of Wales, Prince Philip, the Duke and Duchess of York, the Princess Royal, Princess Margaret, The Duchess of Kent, Princess Alice Countess of Athlone and of other leading figures, including Earl Mountbatten, Earl of Snowdon, Lady Thatcher as Prime Minister, Pres. Clinton, Archbishop Hope when Bishop of London, Duke of Norfolk, HE Cardinal Hume, Lord Aberconway, Princess Ashraf of Iran, Lord Charteris, Lord Denning, Sir Alec Guinness, Haham Dr. Solomon Gaon, Gen. Sir John Hackett, Robert Hardy, Cliff Michelmore, Robert Morley, Malcolm Muggeridge, Airey Neave, Valerie Hobson Profumo, Sir Ralph Richardson, Lord Runcie when Archbishop of Canterbury, Dame Margaret Rutherford, Dennis Wheatley, Sir Mortimer Wheeler, etc.; exhbns internationally, including Royal Acad., Royal Inst. of Oil Painters, Royal Soc. of British Artists, of Marine Artists, of Portrait Painters, Nat. Soc. etc.; represented in perm. collections, The Queen, The Prince of Wales, The British Museum, Nat. Portrait Gallery, House of Commons, Frank Sinatra, etc.; mem. Royal Inst. of Oil Painters 1964, Vice-Pres. 1968–72, Pres. 1972–78, Hon. mem. Council 1978–; mem. Royal Soc. of Portrait Painters 1967–, served Council, 1969–71, 1972–74, 1978–80, 1993–95; Gov. Fed. of British Artists 1972–83, a Dir 1981–83; Liveryman Co. of Woolmen; fmr Chair. Contempor-ary Portrait Soc.; designed Crown Piece (£5 coin) as a mark of 50th Birthday of Prince of Wales and the work of the Prince's Trust 1998; throughout 1999 illustrated The Daily Life of The Queen: An Artist's Diary; has broadcast frequently in UK and also in USA on art subjects; Freeman City of London; Hon. mem. numerous socs including Nat. Soc., United Soc.; Platinum Disc Award for record sleeve, Portrait of Sinatra 1977. *Publications:* A Professional Approach to Oil Painting 1968, The Daily Hope of the Queen 2000, numerous contribs to art journals and books on art. *Leisure interest:* idling. *Address:* 146 Hamilton Terrace, St John's Wood, London, NW8 9UX, England. *Telephone:* (20) 7328-6754. *Fax:* (20) 7625-1220. *E-mail:* mail@michael-noakes.co.uk (office). *Website:* www.michael-noakes.co.uk (office).

NOAKES, Baroness (Life Peer), cr. 2000, of Goudhurst in the County of Kent; **Sheila (Valerie) Masters,** DBE, LLB, FCA; British business executive; d. of

Albert Frederick Masters and Iris Sheila Ratcliffe; m. Colin Barry Noakes 1985; ed Univ. of Bristol; joined Peat Marwick Mitchell & Co. 1970; seconded to HM Treasury 1979–81; Pnr, KPMG (fmrly Peat Marwick Mitchell & Co., then KPMG Peat Marwick) 1983–2000; seconded to Dept of Health as Dir of Finance, Nat. Health Service Man. Exec. 1988–91; Dir Bank of England 1994–2001, Chair. Cttee of Non-Exec. Dirs 1998–2001; mem. Council, Inst. of Chartered Accountants in England and Wales 1987–2002 (Pres. 1999–2000), Inland Revenue Man. Bd 1992–99, Chancellor of Exchequer's Pvt. Finance Panel 1993–97; Dir (non-exec.) Hanson PLC 2001–, Carpetright PLC 2001–, Three PLC 2001–, John Laing PLC 2002–; Assoc. Inst. of Taxation; Trustee Reuters Founders Share Co. 1998–; Dir Social Market Foundation 2002–; mem. Bd ENO 2000–; Gov. London Business School 1998–2001, Eastbourne Coll. 2000–, Marlborough Coll. 2000–02; Hon. LLD (Bristol) 2000; Hon. DSc (Buckingham) 2001; Hon. DBA (London Guildhall) 1999. *Leisure interests:* opera, early classical music, horse racing, skiing. *Address:* House of Lords, Westminster, London, SW1A 0PW, England (office). *Telephone:* (20) 7219-5230 (office). *Fax:* (20) 7219-4215 (office). *E-mail:* noakess@parliament.uk (office).

NOAM, Eli M., BA, MA, PhD, JD; American economist, lawyer, academic and author; *Professor of Finance and Economics, Columbia Business School and Director, Institute for Tele-Information, Columbia University;* b. 1946; m. Nadine Strossen 1980; ed Harvard Univ. and Harvard Law School; mil. service in Israel 1966–68, 1973; Visiting Asst Prof., Princeton Univ. 1975–76; Prof. of Econs and Finance, Columbia Business School, Columbia Univ. 1976–, Founder and Dir Inst. for Tele-Information 1983–87, 1991–, faculty mem. School of Public and Int. Affairs, has also taught at Columbia Law School; Commr New York State Public Service Comm. 1987–90; Virtual Visiting Prof., Univ. of St Gallen, Switzerland 1998–2002; mem. numerous panels including NAS Cttee on Future of Broadband Communications, Comm. on the Status of Women in Computing, NY Gov.'s Task Force on New Media and the Internet; mem. numerous bds and advisory bds including Electronic Privacy Informa-tion Center (EPIC), European Inst. on the Media, France Telecom Scientific Advisory Bd, Intek Corpn, Minority Media Telecommunications Council, Oxford Internet Inst.; Trustee, Jones Int. Univ. (online coll.); mem. editorial bds The Communications Review, Information Law Series, New Media, Telecommunications Policy, Telematics, Transborder Data Report, Utility Policy, Communications and Strategies, International Journal of Media Management, Info: The International Journal of Information; columnist for Financial Times online edn; Dr hc (Munich) 2004. *Publications:* Telecommu-nications Regulation: Today and Tomorrow (ed.) 1982, Video Media Compe-tition: Regulation, Economics, and Technology (ed.) 1985, Services in Transition: The Impact of Information Technologies on the Service Sector (co-ed.) 1986, Law of International Telecommunications in the United States (co-ed.) 1988, The Cost of Libel (co-ed.) 1989, Technologies without Boundaries (ed.) 1990, Television in Europe 1991, Telecommunications in Europe 1992, The Telecommunications Revolution (co-ed.) 1992, The International Market for Film and Television (co-ed.) 1992, Asymmetric Deregulation (co-ed.) 1992, Privacy in Telecommunications: Markets, Rights, and Regulations 1994, Telecommunications in the Pacific Basin (co-ed.) 1994, Private Networks and Public Objectives (co-ed.) 1996, Globalism and Localism in Telecommunica-tions (co-ed.) 1997, Telecommunications in Western Asia 1997, Public Television in America 1998, Telecommunications in Latin America 1998, Telecommunications in Africa 1999, The New Investment Theory of Real Options and its Implication for Telecommunications Economics (co-ed.) 1999, Interconnecting the Network of Networks 2001, Internet Television (co-ed.) 2004, Competition for the Mobile Internet (co-ed.) 2004, Telecommunications Meltdown (co-author) 2005, Mobile Media: Content and Services for Wireless Communications (co-ed.) 2006, Media Ownership and Concentration in America 2007; Gen. Ed. Business, Govt and Soc., Columbia Univ. Press Book series; over 400 articles in econ., legal, communications and other journals. *Address:* Columbia Institute for Tele-Information, Graduate School of Business, Uris Hall, Suite 1A, 3022 Broadway, Columbia University, New York, NY 10027 (office); Riverside Drive, Apt 51, New York, NY 10027, USA (home). *Telephone:* (212) 854-8332 (office); (212) 864-3776 (home). *Fax:* (212) 854-1471 (office); (212) 851-1846 (home). *E-mail:* noam@columbia.edu (office). *Website:* www.citi.columbia.edu (office).

NOBILO, Mario, MA, PhD; Croatian diplomatist; *Ambassador to Slovenia;* b. 15 June 1952, Lumbarda, Korcula Island; s. of Donko I. Nobilo and Frana Mušić; m. Marijana Kujundzić; two s. one d.; ed Univ. of Zagreb; Research Assoc. Dept of Political and Strategic Studies, Inst. for Int. Relations, Zagreb 1979–89; Guest Prof. in USA, Germany and Spain 1985–90; Co-Founder and Vice-Pres. Croatian Council of European Movt 1990–92; Spokesman and Foreign Policy Adviser to Pres. of Croatia 1991–92; Perm. Rep. of Croatia to UN 1992–96, to OSCE 1996; currently Amb. to Slovenia; Decoration of Homeland War 1993. *Publications:* Western Sahara 1984, Namibia 1985, South Africa 1986, Atlas 1989, War Against Croatia 1992, Croatian Phoenix 2000. *Leisure interests:* diving, fishing, sailing, do-it-yourself skills. *Address:* Croatian Embassy, Gruberjevo nabrežje 6, 1000 Ljubljana, Slovenia (office). *Telephone:* (1) 4256220 (office). *Fax:* (1) 4258106 (office). *E-mail:* croemb .slovenia@siol.net (office).

NOBLE, Adrian Keith, BA; British theatre director; b. 19 July 1950; s. of the late William John Noble and Violet Ena Noble (née Wells); m. Joanne Pearce 1991; one d. one s.; ed Chichester High School for Boys, Univ. of Bristol, London Drama Centre; Resident Dir then Assoc. Dir Bristol Old Vic 1976–79; Resident Dir RSC 1980–82, Assoc. Dir 1982–90, Artistic Dir 1991–2003; Guest Dir Royal Exchange Theatre, Man. 1980–81; Visiting Prof. London Inst. 2001; Hon. Bencher Middle Temple; Hon. DLitt (Birmingham) 1994, (Bristol) 1996, (Exeter) 1999, (Warwick) 2001. *Film directed:* A Midsummer Night's Dream 1995. *Stage productions include:* Ubu Rex 1977, A Man's a Man 1977, A View from a Bridge 1978, Titus Adronicus 1978, The Changeling 1978, Love for Love 1979, Timon of Athens 1979, Recruiting Officer 1979, The Duchess of Malfi (Best Dir, Plays and Players) 1980, Dr Faustus 1981, The Forest (Best Revival, Drama Awards) 1981, A Doll's House (Best Dir, Best Revival, Critics' Awards) 1981, King Lear 1982, Antony and Cleopatra 1982, A New Way to Pay Old Debts 1983, Comedy of Errors 1983, Measure for Measure 1983, Henry V 1984, The Winter's Tale 1984, As You Like It 1985, Mephisto 1986, The Art of Success 1986, Macbeth 1986, Kiss Me Kate 1987, The Plantagenets 1989, The Master Builder 1989, The Fairy Queen (Aix-en-Provence), The Three Sisters 1990, Henry IV Parts 1 and 2 1991, The Thebans 1991, Hamlet, Winter's Tale 1992, Travesties, King Lear, Macbeth 1993, A Midsummer Night's Dream 1994, Romeo and Juliet 1995, The Cherry Orchard 1995, Little Eyolf 1996, Cymbeline 1997, Twelfth Night 1997, The Tempest 1998, The Lion, the Witch and the Wardrobe 1998, The Seagull, The Family Reunion 2000, The Return of Ulysses (Aix-en-Provence) (Grand Prix des Critiques) 2000, The Secret Garden 2000–01, Chitty Chitty Bang Bang 2002, Pericles 2002, Brand 2003, A Woman of No Importance 2003, The Home Place (Dublin and London) 2005; opera: Don Giovanni (Kent Opera) 1983, The Faery Queen (Aix-en-Provence Festival) (Grand Prix des Critiques) 1989, Falstaff (Gothenburg Opera) 2005, Cosi fan Tutti (Opera de Lyons) 2006, Marriage of Figaro (Opera de Lyons) 2007, Macbeth (Metropolitan Opera) 2007. *Address:* c/o Independent, Oxford House, 76 Oxford Street, London, W1D 1BS, England (office). *Telephone:* (20) 7636-6565 (office). *Website:* www.independenttalent .com (office).

NOBLE, Denis, CBE, PhD, FRS; British scientist and academic; *Director of Computational Physiology, University of Oxford;* b. 16 Nov. 1936, London; s. of George Noble and Ethel Rutherford; m. Susan Jennifer Barfield 1965; one s. (adopted) one d.; ed Emanuel School and Univ. Coll. London; Asst Lecturer, Univ. Coll. London 1961–63; Fellow, Lecturer and Tutor in Physiology, Balliol Coll. Oxford 1963–84, Praefectus, Balliol Grad. Centre 1971–89, Burdon Sanderson Prof. of Cardiovascular Physiology, Univ. of Oxford 1984–2004, Professorial Fellow 1984–2004, currently Dir of Computational Physiology, Univ. of Oxford; Visiting Prof., Univ. of Alberta 1969–70; Ed., Progress in Biophysics 1967–; Founder Dir, Oxsoft Ltd 1984–, Physiome Sciences Inc. 1994–; Chair., Jt Dental Cttee 1984–90; Pres. Medical Section, British Asscn 1992; Gen.-Sec., Int. Union of Physiological Sciences 1993–2001; Hon. Sec., Physiological Soc. 1974–80, Foreign Sec. 1986–92; Fellow, University Coll. London 1986; Founder Fellow, Acad. of Medical Sciences 1998; Adjunct Prof., Xi'an Jiaotong Univ., China 2003–07; Visiting Prof., Osaka Univ., Japan 2006; Hon. FRCP; Hon. mem. Acad. de Medécine de Belgique, American Physiological Soc., Academia Europaea 1989, Japanese Physiological Soc. 1998, The Physiological Soc. 1999; Hon. DSc (Sheffield) 2004, (Warwick) 2008, Dr hc (Bordeaux) 2005; Darwin Lecturer, British Asscn 1966, Scientific Medal, Zoological Soc. 1970, Nahum Lecturer, Yale Univ. 1977, British Heart Foundation Gold Medal and Prize 1985, Lloyd Roberts Lecturer 1987, Bowden Lecturer 1988, Alderdale Wyld Lecturer 1988, Pierre Rijlant Prize, Belgian Royal Acad. 1991, Baly Medal, Royal Coll. of Physicians 1993, Pavlov Medal, Russian Acad. of Science 2004, Hodgkin-Huxley-Katz Prize, Physiological Soc. 2004, Mackenzie Prize, British Cardiac Soc. 2005. *Publications:* Initiation of the Heartbeat 1975, Electric Current Flow in Excitable Cells 1975, Electrophysiology of Single Cardiac Cells 1987, Goals, No Goals and Own Goals 1989, Sodium-Calcium Exchange 1989, Logic of Life 1993, Ionic Channels and the Effect of Taurine on the Heart 1993, Ethics of Life 1997, The Music of Life 2006; scientific papers mostly in Journal of Physiology. *Leisure interests:* Occitan language and music, Indian and French cooking, classical guitar. *Address:* University Laboratory of Physiology, Parks Road, Oxford, OX1 3PT (office); 49 Old Road, Oxford, OX3 7JZ, England (home). *Telephone:* (1865) 272533 (office); (1865) 762237 (home). *Fax:* (1865) 272554 (office). *E-mail:* denis.noble@physiol.ox.ac.uk (office). *Website:* www.physiol.ox.ac.uk (office).

NOBLE, Ronald Kenneth, BA, JD; American law enforcement executive; *Secretary-General, International Criminal Police Organization (INTERPOL);* ed Univ. of New Hampshire, Stanford Univ. Law School; fmr Asst to US Attorney, then Deputy Asst to Attorney-Gen., Dept of Justice; Pres. Financial Action Task Force (26 mem. multi-nat. org. est. to fight money-laundering by G7) 1989; Chief Law Enforcement Officer, US Treasury Dept 1989–96, responsible for The Secret Service, Customs Service, Bureau of Alcohol, Tobacco and Firearms, Fed. Law Enforcement Training Center, Financial Crimes Enforcement Network, Office of Foreign Assets Control and Criminal Investigation Div. of Internal Revenue Service; Prof. of Law, New York Univ. School of Law; fmr mem. Exec. Cttee INTERPOL, Sec.-Gen. 2000–. *Address:* International Criminal Police Organization (INTERPOL), 200 quai Charles de Gaulle, 69006 Lyon, France (office). *Telephone:* 4-72-44-70-00 (office). *Fax:* 4-72-44-71-63 (office). *E-mail:* cp@interpol.int. *Website:* www.interpol.int (office).

NOBOA BEJARANO, Gustavo, PhD; Ecuadorean politician and academic; b. 21 Aug. 1939, Guayaquil; m. Marta Baquerizo; six c.; teacher of social sciences and politics 1962–; fmr Rector of Catholic Univ. of Guayaquil; fmr Rector of Public Univ. of Guayaquil; Gov. of Guayas Province 1983; mem. of peace comm. on border dispute with Peru 1996; Vice-Pres. of Ecuador 1998–2000, Pres. 2000–02; investigated for allegedly mishandling $126 million in govt. bonds to bail out state-run banks during his Presidency; granted asylum by govt. of Dominican Republic 2003; Order of St Sylvester, Commdr. State of the Vatican.

NOBOA PONTÓN, Alvaro Fernando; Ecuadorean business executive and politician; *President, Noboa Corporation; Leader, Partido Renovador Institucional de Acción Nacional (PRIAN);* b. 21 Nov. 1950, Guayaquil; s. of Luis Noboa Naranjo; m. Anabella Azín; three s.; ed Le Rosey School, Switzerland, State Universidad de Guayaquil; est. first business Promandato Global SA

1973; f. La Verdad (monthly magazine) 1986; f. Banco del Litoral 1990; f. Global Financing Co. and other investment cos 1992, joined these companies with Banco del Litoral to form Grupo de Empresas Ab. Alvaro Noboa P. 1994; inherited portion of Noboa Corpn following death of father 1994, Pres. Noboa Corpn (controls 105 cos in Ecuador, Europe, USA and New Zealand with interests in coffee, bananas, real estate and flour) 1995–, cos include Bonita Bananas (largest banana co. in Ecuador), four shipping cos, one bank, two insurance cos, La nica (edible oils), Valdez (sugar refinery), Los Álamos and 14 other banana plantations, mines, media cos and other Ecuadorean businesses; Pres. Monetary Bd 1996; presidential cand. for Partido Roldosista Ecuatoriano (PRE) 1998, for Partido Renovador Institucional Acción Nacional (PRIAN) 2002, 2006 (also founder and Leader); f. Fundación Cruzada Nueva Humanidad (charity) 1977. *Address:* Corporacion Noboa, El Oro y La Ria, Guayaquil (office); Partido Renovador Institucional de Acción Nacional (PRIAN), Quito, Ecuador. *Website:* www.alvaronoboa.com (office); www .prian.org.ec.

NOBRE CABRAL, Maria da Conceição; Guinea-Bissau politician; m. Alfredo Lopes Cabral; three c.; Minister of Foreign Affairs, Int. Co-operation and Communities 2007–09. *Address:* c/o Ministry of Foreign Affairs, International Co-operation and Communities, Rua Gen. Omar Torrijo, Bissau, Guinea-Bissau (office).

NÓBREGA SUÁREZ, Tobías, DEcon; Venezuelan economist and politician; b. 30 Jan. 1961, Puerto Cabello, Carabobo; ed Univ. Central de Venezuela, Univ. Complutense de Madrid, Spain; Lecturer, Dept of Econs, Univ. Central de Venezuela 1986–97; Chief Economist, Central Hipotecaria 1988, Asociácion Bancaria de Venezuela 1995–97, Asociácion de Gobernadores de Venezuela 1993–98; Ind. Financial Consultant 1986–, also Financial Adviser to Nat. Govt and several regional govts; Dir Oficina de Asesoría Económica del Parlamento Nacional (OAEF) 2000; adviser to numerous parl. cttees including Parl. Finance Sub-Cttee 2000; Minister of Finance 2002–04. *Publications:* numerous articles in econ. journals. *Address:* c/o Ministry of Finance, esq. de Carmelitas, Avda Urdaneta, Caracas, Venezuela.

NOBS, Claude; Swiss festival administrator; *Founder, Montreux Jazz Festival;* b. Feb. 1936, Territet; worked as chef at station buffet in Spiez; apprentice at Schweizerhof, Basle; account with Dist Tourist Office; Co-founded and organized concerts for Montreux Youth Org.; Founder Montreux Jazz Festival 1967; Dir WEA (Warner, Elektra and Atlantic) in Switzerland 1973–; Commdr, Ordre des Arts et des Lettres 2006; Dr hc (Swiss Inst. of Tech.) 2007; award-winning chef. *Address:* Montreux Jazz Festival Foundation Press Office, Sentier de Collonge 3, PO Box 126, 1820 Montreux-Territet, Switzerland (office). *Telephone:* (21) 966-44-44 (office). *Fax:* (21) 966-44-33 (office). *E-mail:* info@mjf.ch (office). *Website:* www.montreuxjazz.com (office); www.claudenobs.com.

NODA, Seiko; Japanese politician; *Minister of State for Science and Technology Policy and Food Safety, Consumer Affairs, Space Policy;* b. 3 Sept. 1960, Kitakyushu, Fukuoka; m. Yosuke Tsuruho 2001; ed Futaba Acad. Secondary School, Tokyo, Jonesville High School, Michigan, USA, Sophia Univ.; mem. staff Imperial Hotel 1983–87; elected mem. Gifu Prefectural Ass. 1987; mem. LDP; mem. for Gifu No. 1 Dist, House of Rep. 1993–; Parl. Vice-Minister of Posts and Telecommunications, Minister 1998–99; Minister of State for Science and Tech. Policy and Food Safety, Consumer Affairs, Space Policy 2008–; adviser to Sake Mfrs Asscn; Pres. Sake-Loving Female Diet Members Club. *Publications:* (in Japanese): I am Seeing 1987, Under the Pretext of Reform 1994, Things I Want to Get Across to the People – Politics Spoken with Sincerity 1996, Japan Will Win the Post-IT Era! – Proposals of Seven Leading Figures (co-author) 2001, I Want to Give Birth 2004, Who is Taking Away Our Future – Fighting the Declining Birthrate 2005, Easy-to-understand Guide to the Revised Child Prostitution/Pornography Law (co-author) 2005. *Leisure interests:* reading, watching movies, karaoke, using the computer. *Address:* Cabinet Office, 1-6-1, Nagata-cho, Chiyoda-ku, Tokyo 100-8914, Japan (office). *Telephone:* (3) 5253-2111 (office). *E-mail:* info@cao.go.jp (office). *Website:* www.cao.go.jp (office).

NODA, Takeshi; Japanese politician; mem. House of Reps, constituency Kumamoto-1; Chair. LDP Nat. Campaign HQ, Cttee on Commerce and Industry House of Reps; fmr Construction Minister, LDP Deputy Sec. Gen.; Dir Gen. Econ. Planning Agency (State Minister) 1991–92; Minister for Home Affairs Jan.–Oct. 1999, 2000. *Address:* c/o Ministry of Home Affairs, 2-1-2 Kasumigaseki, Chiyoda-ku, Tokyo 100, Japan.

NODA, Tetsuya, MA; Japanese printmaker and academic; *Professor Emeritus, Tokyo National University of Fine Arts and Music;* b. 5 March 1940, Kumamoto Pref.; s. of Tesshin Noda and Sakae Noda; m. Dorit Bartur; one s. one d.; ed Tokyo Nat. Univ. of Fine Arts and Music; Visiting Artist, Alberta Univ., Canada 1984, Betzalel Art Acad., Israel 1985, Canberra Art School, Australia 1990, Columbia Univ., USA 1998; Prof., Tokyo Nat. Univ. of Fine Arts and Music 1990–2007, Prof. Emer. 2007–; mem. Int. Jury for the British Int. Print Biennale 1976, Korean Int. Print Biennale 1996, Space Int. Print Biennale, Seoul 2002, First Int. Print Biennale, Istanbul 2008, Edmonton Print Int. 2008, 2nd Bangkok Triennale Int. Print and Drawing Exhbn 2008; Hon. DLitt (London Metropolitan Univ.); prizes include Int. Grand Prize (Tokyo Int. Print Biennale) 1968, Grand Prize (Ljubljana Int. Print Biennale) 1977 and Grand Prize of Honour 1987, Grand Prize (Norwegian Int. Print Biennale) 1978, Friends of Bradford Art Galleries and Museum Prize (British Int. Print Biennale) 1986, Gen Yamaguchi Memorial Grand Prize, City of Numazu 1993; Medal of Purple Ribbon (Japanese Govt). *Publications:* Tetsuya Noda – The Works III 1992–2000 2001. *Leisure interest:* gardening. *Address:* 2-12-4 Kikkodai, Kashiwa-shi, Chiba-ken, 277-0031, Japan (home).

Telephone: (471) 63-5332 (home). *Fax:* (471) 63-5332 (home). *E-mail:* tetsuyanoda@hotmail.com (home).

NODDLE, Jeffrey (Jeff), BA; American retail executive; *Chairman and CEO, Supervalu Inc.;* ed Univ. of Iowa; began career as Dir of Retail Operations, JM Jones Div., Supervalu Inc. 1976, held various positions including Merchandising Dir, Vice-Pres. Marketing JM Jones Div. –1982, Pres. Fargo and Miami Divs 1982–85, Corp. Vice-Pres. Merchandising, Supervalu Inc. 1985–88, Sr Vice-Pres. Marketing 1988–92, Corp. Exec. Vice-Pres. Marketing 1992–93, Corp. Exec. Vice-Pres. and Pres. 1993–95, COO Distribution Food Cos 1995–2000, Pres. and COO 2000–01, Pres. and CEO 2001–02, Chair. and CEO Supervalu Inc. 2002–, Chair. Exec. Cttee and mem. Finance Cttee; mem. Bd Donaldson Co. Inc., Gen. Cable Corpn; Vice-Chair. and mem. Exec. Cttee Food Marketing Inst. (FMI); mem. Bd Ind. Grocers Alliance Inc. (IGA), Bd Sarah W. Stedman Center for Nutritional Studies, Duke Univ. Medical Center, Exec. Cttee Minneapolis Business Partnership, Bd of Overseers Univ. of Minnesota Carlson School of Man.; fmr Chair. Greater Twin Cities United Way. *Address:* Supervalu Inc., 11840 Valley View Road, Eden Prairie, MN 55344, USA (office). *Telephone:* (952) 828-4000 (office). *Fax:* (952) 828-8998 (office). *E-mail:* info@supervalu.com (office). *Website:* www.supervalu.com (office).

NOE PINO, Hugo, PhD; Honduran economist, diplomatist and politician; b. 11 Jan. 1955, Tegucigalpa; s. of Roberto Noe and Elidia Pino; m. Vivian Bustamante; two s. one d.; ed Universidad Nacional Autonoma de Honduras (UNAH), Univ. of Texas at Austin, USA; fmr teaching Asst, Dept of Econs, Univ. of Tex.; Pres. Cen. Bank of Honduras 1994–97; Dir Master's Programme in Econs for Cen. American and Caribbean Region, UNAH; Pres. Asscn of Economists of Honduras; mem. Editorial Council of various magazines published in Honduras; Spokesman of Shadow Cabinet 1993; Amb. to USA –1999; mem. Partido Liberal (PL), campaign man. for successful presidential cand. José Manuel (Mel) Zelaya Rosales 2005; Minister of Finance Jan.–July 2006;. *Publications:* An Assessment of the Campesino Associative Enterprise of Isletas 1987, Honduras: Structural Adjustment and Agrarian Reform 1992. *Leisure interests:* reading, music. *Address:* Partido Liberal (PL), Col. Miramonte, Tegucigalpa, Honduras. *Telephone:* 232-0520. *Fax:* 232-0797. *Website:* www.partidoliberal.net.

NOELLE, Elisabeth, DPhil; German academic; *Professor of Communications Research, University of Mainz;* b. 19 Dec. 1916, Berlin; d. of Dr Ernst Noelle and Eva Schaper; m. 1st Erich P. Neumann 1946 (died 1973); m. 2nd Heinz Maier-Leibnitz 1979 (died 2000); ed Univs. of Königsberg and Munich, School of Journalism, Univ. of Missouri, Univ. of Berlin; Founder and Dir Inst. für Demoskopie Allensbach (first German survey research inst.) 1947–; Lecturer in Communications Research, Free Univ. of Berlin 1961–64; Prof. of Communications Research, Univ. of Mainz 1964–, also Dir Inst. für Publizistik (until 1983); f. Allensbach Foundation for Public Opinion Research 1996; Public Opinion Analyst, Frankfurter Allgemeine Zeitung (newspaper) 1978–; Visiting Prof., Dept of Political Science, Univ. of Chicago 1978–91, Univ. of Munich 1993–94; Co-Ed. Int. Journal of Public Opinion Research; Hon. Citizen of Allensbach 1977; Hon. Prof. Moscow External Univ. of the Humanities; Hon. mem. German Univ. Asscn 2000; Grosses Bundesverdienstkreuz 1976; Order of Merit, Baden-Württemberg 1990; Hon. DrOec (St Gallen); Alexander Rüstow Medal 1978, Nürnberger Trichter Award 1985, Viktor Matajy Medal 1987, Helen Dinerman Award 1990, Boveri Award 1997, Schleyer Foundation Award 1999. *Publications include:* Allensbacher Jahrbücher der Demoskopie (11 vols) (ed.) 1947–2002, The Germans, (Vol. I) 1967, (Vol. II) 1980, Fischer Lexikon Publizistik–Massenkommunikation (co-ed.) 1971, 1989, 1994, 1998, 2002, Umfragen in der Massengesellschaft: Einführung in die Methoden der Demoskopie 1963, revised edn, Alle, nicht jeder: Einführung in die Methoden der Demoskopie (with T. Petersen) 1996, 1998, 2000, Öffentlichkeit als Bedrohung 1977, 1979, Die Schweigespirale: Öffentliche Meinung—unsere soziale Haut 1980, 2001, Eine demoskopische Deutschstunde 1983, Macht Arbeit krank? Macht Arbeit glücklich? 1984 (with B. Strümpel), Die verletzte Nation (with R. Köcher) 1987, Öffentliche Meinung: Die Entdeckung der Schweigespirale 1989, 1991, 1996, Demoskopische Geschichtsstunde 1991, Kampa: Meinungsklima und Medienwirkung im Bundestagwahlkampf 1998, 1999, Die soziale Natur des Menschen 2002. *Leisure interests:* painting, strolling by Lake Constance. *Address:* Institut für Demoskopie Allensbach, Radolfzeller Str. 8, 78476 Allensbach am Bodensee, Germany (office). *Telephone:* (7533) 8050 (home). *Fax:* (7533) 805-108 (office); (7533) 3048 (home). *E-mail:* enoelle@ifd-allensbach.de (office). *Website:* www.ifd-allensbach.de (office).

NOFAL, María Beatriz, MA, PhD; Argentine economist, politician and academic; *President, National Agency for Investment Development;* b. 7 Oct. 1952, Mendoza; ed Universidad Nacional de Cuyo, Inst. of Social Studies, Netherlands, Univ. of Paris, France, Johns Hopkins Univ., Baltimore, Md, USA; Assoc. Prof., Johns Hopkins Univ. 1983–84, MIT 1985; Prof., Univ. of Bologna based in Buenos Aires 1999; Visiting Prof., Univ. of Toronto, Canada 2004; Prof., Universidad Católica Argentina 2005; Under-Sec. of Industrial Devt, Industry and Foreign Trade Secr., Ministry of Economy 1986–89; Pres. of ECO-AXIS, SA consultants 1993–99, 2002–06; Congresswoman (Unión Cívica Radical) 1999–2002; Pres. Nat. Agency for Investment Devt (ANDI) 2006–; Dir, Arthur D. Little (consultancy firm), Argentina 1999–2000; mem. Bd of Dirs (non-exec.) Nobleza Piccardo/British American Tobacco 2006; mem. Interamerican Dialogue (US-based think tank) 2001–; adviser to Argentine Council for Int. Relations (CARI); Ed. and Prin. Author Mercosur Journal 1995–99. *Publications include:* Absentee Entrepreneurship and the Dynamics of the Motor Vehicle Industry in Argentina 1989; numerous articles in newspapers, magazines and professional journals. *Address:* c/o Ministry of Economy and Production, Hipólito Yrigoyen 250, C1086AAB, Buenos Aires, Argentina (office); c/o Inter-American Dialogue, 1211 Connecticut Avenue, NW, Suite 510, Washington, DC 20036, USA. *Telephone:* (11) 4349-5000 (Buenos Aires) (office); (202) 822-9002 (Washington, DC). *Fax:* (202) 822-9553 (Washington, DC). *E-mail:* sagpya@mecon.gov.ar (office). *Website:* www.mecon.gov.ar (office); www.thedialogue.org.

NOGAMI, Tomoyuki, PhD; Japanese educationalist, university administrator and academic; *President, Kobe University;* b. 1946; ed Hiroshima Univ.; Research Assoc., Faculty of Educ., Hiroshima Univ. 1979–80; Lecturer, Faculty of Home Econs, Hiroshima Women's Univ. 1980–83, Assoc. Prof. 1983–86; Visiting Scholar, Teachers' Coll., Columbia Univ., New York 1986–88; Assoc. Prof., Faculty of Educ., Kobe Univ. 1988–92, Prof., Faculty of Human Devt 1992–94, Dir Research Centre for Human Science 1994–96, Prin. Kindergarten/Akashi Elementary School/Akashi Jr High School attached to Faculty of Human Devt 1996–98, Dean Faculty of Human Devt 1998–2001, Dean Grad. School of Cultural Studies and Human Science 2001, Pres. Kobe Univ. 2001–; mem. Japanese Nat. Comm. for UNESCO 2003–. *Address:* Office of the President, Kobe University, 1-1, Rokkodai-cho, Nada-ku Kobe 657-8501, Hyogo, Japan (office). *Telephone:* (78) 881-5040 (office). *E-mail:* intl-plan@office.kobe-u.ac.jp (office). *Website:* www.kobe-u.ac.jp (office).

NOGAMI, Yoshiji; Japanese diplomatist; b. 1942; m. Geraldine Nogami; three s.; ed Tokyo Univ.; joined Ministry of Foreign Affairs 1966, held positions as Dir-Gen. Econ. Affairs Bureau, Deputy Minister, later Vice-Minister for Foreign Affairs 2001, Consul-Gen. to Hong Kong, Amb. to OECD, Paris, to UK 2004–08; Sr Visiting Fellow, Chatham House (fmrly Royal Inst. of Int. Affairs) 2002–. *Address:* Ministry of Foreign Affairs, 2-11-1, Shiba-Koen, Minato-ku, Tokyo 105-8519, Japan (office). *Telephone:* (3) 3580-3311 (office). *Fax:* (3) 3581-2667 (office). *E-mail:* webmaster@mofa.go.jp (office). *Website:* www.mofa.go.jp (office).

NOGHAIDELI, Zurab; Georgian business executive, academic and politician; b. 22 Oct. 1964, Kobuleti, Ajara; s. of Nazi Katamadze; m. Nino Tsintsabadze; one s.; ed Moscow M.V. Lomonosov State Univ., USSR (now Russian Fed.); Asst, Inst. of Geography, Acad. of Sciences of Georgia, Batumi 1988–89; Guest Researcher, Inst. of Geology, Acad. of Sciences of Estonia, Tallinn 1989–91; Sr Researcher and Head of Lab., Niko Berzenishvili Research Inst., Acad. of Sciences of Georgia, Batumi 1989–92; Exec. Sec. Georgia Greens 1992–93; mem. Parl., Chair. Cttee of Environment Protection and Natural Resources 1992–95, Chair. Cttee of Tax and Revenue 1999–2000; Co-ordinator Office of the Chair. 1995–99; Int. Sec., Citizens' Union of Georgia 1995–98; mem. Supreme Council, Adjara Autonomous Rep. 1996–98; Minister of Finance 2000–02, 2004–05; Prime Minister of Georgia 2005–07 (resgnd); mem. Bd People's Bank of Georgia 2002–03; Partner, Solidary Responsibilities Soc. Damenia, Varshalomidze, Noghaideli and Kavtaradze April–Nov. 2003; Chair. Kala Capital (investment co.) 2007–; Chair. Int. School of Econs Business Council, Tbilisi State Univ. 2008–. *Address:* Kala Capital 4A, 1st Drive, I. Chavchavadze, 0179 Tbilisi, Georgia (office). *Telephone:* (32) 91-92-22.

NOGOYBAYEV, Bolotbek, CandJur; Kyrgyzstani politician; *Minister of Internal Affairs;* b. 10 Nov. 1955, Telman village, Panfilov Dist; m. Mariya Boronbayevna Nogoybayeva; two s. one d.; ed Kyrgyz State Univ.; served in Soviet Army 1973–75; served in various policing roles including police officer, Inspector and Head, Criminal Investigation Dept, Dept of Transport Pishpek office 1976–85, Head, Transport Police Div. 1987–90; Dir Internal Affairs Dept, Sverdlov region 1990–95; Deputy Head of Internal Affairs, Talas Dist 1995–96; Head, Criminal Investigation Dept, Ministry of Internal Affairs 1996–98; Head of Internal Affairs, Osh Dist 1998–99; Deputy Minister of Internal Affairs 1999–2001, 2002–05; Chief Inspector, Kyrgyz Security Council Feb.–Aug. 2005; Dir Kyrgyz Drug Control Agency 2005–07; Minister of Internal Affairs 2007–. *Publications:* Narcotics: Theory and Practice of Counteraction; numerous articles on drug control. *Address:* Ministry of Internal Affairs, 720040 Bishkek, Frunze 469, Kyrgyzstan (office). *Telephone:* (312) 66-24-50 (office). *Fax:* (312) 68-20-44 (office). *E-mail:* mail@mvd.bishkek.gov.kg (office). *Website:* www.mvd.kg (office).

NOGUCHI, Teruhisa, PhD; Japanese business executive; b. 22 Oct. 1924, Chiba Pref.; m.; one s. three d.; ed Schools of Medicine, Kanazawa and Tokyo Univs; with Nihon Soda Co. 1949–72; with Teijin Ltd 1972–79, Dir 1973, Dir Teijin Inst. for Biomedical Research 1976; with Suntory Ltd 1979–92, Dir 1979, Exec. Man. Pharmaceutical Div. 1981, Sr Man. Dir 1987–, Chief Exec. 1991; Exec. Vice-Pres. Yamanouchi Pharmaceutical Co. Ltd 1992–; Adjunct Prof., The Rockefeller Univ. 1984–; Fellow American Acad. of Microbiology; several prizes and awards. *Publications include:* Biochemistry of Interferons 1982, New Trends in Neuro-Science 1984. *Leisure interests:* fine arts, golf. *Address:* 2-18-11, Kugenuma Kaigan, Fujisawa City, Kanagawa Prefecture 251, Japan.

NØJGAARD, Morten, DPhil; Danish academic; *Romance Editor, Orbis Litterarum;* b. 28 July 1934, Holbaek; s. of Niels Nøjgaard and Annie Nøjgaard (née Bay); m. Stina Lund 1962; two s. two d.; secondary school teacher, Roedovre Statskole 1960–63; Research Scholar, Univ. of Copenhagen 1963–65; Prof. of Romance Philology, Univ. of Southern Denmark, Odense 1966–2004; Chief Ed. Orbis Litterarum 1968–99, Romance Ed. 1999–; Pres. Asscn of French Prof. 1962–63, Alliance Française, Odense 1970–; mem. Soc. of Letters (Lund, Sweden) 1978, Royal Danish Acad. of Science 1982, Royal Norwegian Acad. of Science 1991, Royal Swedish Acad. of Antiquities 1997; Ordre du Mérite 1980; Fnske Bladfond Research Award 1975. *Publications:* La Fable Antique, (Vols I–II) 1964–67, Elévation et Expansion. Les deux dimensions de Baudelaire 1973, An Introduction to Literary Analysis 1975, Romain-Gary-Emile Ajar, Homo Duplex 1986, Les Adverbes français, Vol. I

1992, Vol. II 1993, Vol. III 1995, Plaisir et vérité, Le paradoxe de l'évaluation littéraire 1993, Le Temps de la littérature. Sur Paul Ricoeur et les paradoxes du temps raconté 1999, Temps, réalisme et description – Essais de théorie littéraire 2004; numerous scientific articles. *Address:* Odense University, Campusvej 55, 5230 Odense M (office); Åløkken 48, 5250 Odense SV, Denmark (home). *Telephone:* 65-50-10-00 (office); 65-96-18-06 (home). *Fax:* 65-93-51-41 (office); 65-93-51-49 (home). *E-mail:* mno@litcul.sdu.dk (office). *Website:* www .humaniora.sdu.dk/institut.html?vis=3⟨=en (office).

NOJI, Kunio; Japanese business executive; *President and CEO, Komatsu Ltd;* b. 17 Nov. 1946, Fukui Pref.; m.; two d.; ed School of Eng Science, Osaka Univ.; joined Komatsu Ltd 1969, Gen. Man. Production Control Dept, Tech. Div. 1993–95, Plant Man. Chattanooga Manufacturing Operation, Komatsu Dresser Co. (currently Komatsu America Corpn) 1995–97, Gen. Man. Information Systems Div. 1997–99, Dir June 1997, Exec. 1999–2000, Exec. Officer and Pres. Production Div. and Vice-Pres. e-Komatsu Tech. Centre April–June 2000, Sr Exec. Officer, Pres. Production Div. and Vice-Pres. e-Komatsu Tech. Centre 2000–01, Man. Dir and Pres. Production Div. and e-Komatsu Tech. Centre 2001–03, Dir and Sr Exec. Officer, Pres. of Construction and Mining Equipment Marketing Div. 2003–05, Dir and Sr Exec. Officer, Supervising Construction and Mining Equipment Business and e-Komatsu Tech. Centre 2005–06, Dir and Sr Exec. Officer, Supervising Construction and Mining Equipment Business, e-Komatsu Tech. Centre and Komatsu Way April–July 2006, Dir and Sr Exec. Officer, Gen. Man. of Komatsu Way Dept, Supervising Construction and Mining Equipment Business and e-Komatsu Tech. Centre 2006–07, Dir and Sr Exec. Officer, Pres. of Production Div. and Gen. Man. Komatsu Way Dept, Supervising Construction and Mining Equipment Business and e-Komatsu Tech. Centre Jan.–June 2007, Pres. and CEO Komatsu Ltd 2007–. *Leisure interests:* golfing, mountain climbing. *Address:* Komatsu Ltd, 2-3-6, Akasaka, Minato-ku, Tokyo 107-8414, Japan (office). *Telephone:* (3) 5561-2616 (office); (3) 5561-2687 (office). *Fax:* (3) 3505-9662 (office). *E-mail:* info@komatsu.com (office). *Website:* www.komatsu.com (office).

NOJIMA, Hideo; Japanese retail executive; *Chairman, AEON Co. Ltd;* fmrly with Okadaya Corpn; fmr Man. Dir AEON Co. Ltd, later Sr Man. Dir, Chair. and Rep. Dir 2006–. *Address:* AEON Co. Ltd, 1-5-1 Nakase, Mihama-ku, Chiba-shi, Chiba 261-8515, Japan (office). *Telephone:* (43)-212-6000 (office). *Fax:* (43)-212-6849 (office). *Website:* www.aeon.info/en (office).

NOLAN, Christopher Jonathan James; British/American director, writer and producer; b. 30 July 1970, London; s. of an English father and American mother; m. Emma Thomas 1997; three c.; ed Haileybury Coll., Herts., UK, Univ. Coll., London; filmed several short films in his univ. film soc., London; short film Tarantella shown on Image Union, an ind. film and video showcase featured on PBS 1989; short film Larceny shown during Cambridge Film Festival in 1996; Visionary Award, Palm Springs Int. Film Festival 2003. *Films directed:* Doodlebug (as Chris Nolan; also writer, cinematographer, ed. and set designer) 1997, Following (also writer, producer, cinematographer and ed.) (Silver Hitchcock, Dinard British Film Festival 1999, Best Dir Award, Newport Int. Film Festival 1999, Tiger Award, Rotterdam Int. Film Festival 1999, Black & White Award, Slamdance Film Festival 1999) 1998, Memento (also screenplay) (CinéLive Award, Critics' Award and Jury Special Prize, Deauville Film Festival 2000, Prize of the Catalan Screenwriter's Critic and Writer's Asscn, Sitges-Catalonian Int. Film Festival 2000, Boston Soc. of Film Critics' Award for Best Screenplay 2001, ALFS Award for British Screenwriter of the Year, London Critics' Circle Film Awards 2001, Los Angeles Film Critics' Asscn Award for Best Screenplay 2001, SEFCA Award for Best Original Screenplay, Southeastern Film Critics' Asscn Awards 2001, Waldo Salt Screenwriting Award, Sundance Film Festival 2001, Toronto Film Critics' Asscn Award for Best Screenplay 2001, AFI Screenwriter of the Year 2002, Bram Stoker Award for Best Screenplay 2002, Critics' Choice Award for Best Screenplay, Broadcast Film Critics' Asscn Awards 2002, Chicago Film Critics' Asscn Award for Best Screenplay 2002, Chlotrudis Award for Best Dir 2002, Russell Smith Award, Dallas-Fort Worth Film Critics' Asscn Awards 2002, Edgar for Best Motion Picture, Edgar Allan Poe Awards 2002, Florida Film Critics' Circle Award for Best Screenplay 2002, Independent Spirit Awards for Best Dir and Best Screenplay 2002, Sierra Award for Best Screenplay, Las Vegas Film Critics' Soc. Awards 2002, MTV Movie Award for Best New Filmmaker 2002, Online Film Critics' Soc. Award for Best Breakthrough Filmmaker 2002, Phoenix Film Critics' Soc. Awards for Best Newcomer and Best Original Screenplay 2002) 2000, Insomnia (ALFS Award for British Dir of the Year, London Critics' Circle Film Awards 2003) 2002, Cinema16: British Short Films (video) 2003, Batman Begins (also screenplay) (Saturn Award for Best Writing, Academy of Science Fiction, Fantasy & Horror Films, USA 2006) 2005, The Prestige (also screenplay and producer) (Empire Award for Best Dir 2007) 2006, The Dark Knight (also story and producer) 2008. *Address:* c/o Creative Artists Agency, 9830 Wilshire Blvd, Beverly Hills, CA 90212-1825, USA (office). *Telephone:* (310) 288-4545 (office). *Fax:* (310) 288-4800 (office). *Website:* www.caa.com (office).

NOLAN, Philip, MBA, PhD; British telecommunications executive; *Chief Executive Officer, Eircom plc;* b. Enniskillen, NI; ed Queens Univ., Belfast, London Business School; fmr Lecturer of Geology, Univ. of Ulster; with British Petroleum (BP) Exploration –1996, numerous roles including Man. of Acquisitions and Disposals; Dir Transco East Area, BG Group 1996–97, Man. Dir Transco 1997–, CEO 1999–2000, mem. Bd BG Group 1998–2000; CEO Lattice Group (fmrly part of the BG Group) 2000–02; CEO Eircom 2002–. *Address:* Eircom plc, 114 St Stephen's Green, Dublin 2, Ireland (office). *Website:* www.eircom.ie.

NOLAN, William (Bill) C., Jr; American lawyer and business executive; *Chairman, Murphy Oil Corporation;* ed Yale Univ. and Yale Law School;

worked in Law Dept of Murphy Oil Corpn –1969, left to found Nolan & Alderson (law firm), El Dorado, Ark., currently Pnr; mem. Bd of Dirs Murphy Oil Corpn 1977–, Chair. 2002–, Chair. Exec. Cttee; Pres. and CEO Noalmark Broadcasting Corpn. *Leisure interests:* running (has run more than 70 marathons). *Address:* Murphy Oil Corpn, PO Box 7000, El Dorado, AR 71731-7000 (office); Murphy Oil Corpn, 200 Peach Street, El Dorado, AR 71730, USA (office). *Telephone:* (870) 862-6411 (office). *Fax:* (870) 864-6373 (office). *E-mail:* info@murphyoilcorp.com (office). *Website:* www .murphyoilcorp.com (office).

NOLAND, Kenneth Clifton; American artist; b. 10 April 1924, Asheville, NC; s. of Harry C. Noland and Bessie (née Elkins) Noland; m. 1st Cornelia Langel (divorced); one s. two d.; m. 2nd Stephanie Gordon 1967; m. 3rd Peggy Schiffer (divorced); one s.; m. 4th Paige Rense 1994; ed Black Mountain Coll., North Carolina and Paris; teacher, Inst. of Contemporary Arts 1950–52, Catholic Univ. 1951–60, Bennington Coll. 1968; work in perm. collections in Museum of Modern Art, Guggenheim Museum, Whitney Museum, Tate Gallery, London, Stedelijk Museum, Amsterdam, Zürich Kunsthaus and others; North Carolina Medal of Arts 1995. *Address:* c/o Ameringer & Yohe Fine Art, New York, 20 West 57th Street, New York, NY 10022; North Bennington, VT 05257, USA.

NOLL, João Gilberto, BA; Brazilian writer; b. 15 April 1946, Porto Alegre; s. of João Noll and Ecila Noll; columnist, Folha de São Paulo newspaper; Writer-in-Residence, Univ. of Calif., Berkeley, also teaching Brazilian Literature 1996, 1997, 1998; Guggenheim Fellowship 1999–2000; residency Center for the Study of Brazilian Culture and Soc., King's Coll. London 2004; Prêmio Jabuti on five occasions; Prize for Fiction, Brazilian Academy of Letters 2004. *Play:* Quero Sim 1992. *Publications:* (short stories) O cego e a dançarina; (novels) A fúria do corpo, Bandoleiros, Hotel Atlântico, Harmada, A céu aberto, Canoas e marolas, Rastros do verão, O quieto animal da esquina, Lorde, Mínimas Múltiplos Comuns. *Leisure interests:* music, travelling. *Address:* Rua José do Patrocínio 557/306, 90050-003 Porto Alegre, RS, Brazil. *Telephone:* (50) 224-8766. *Fax:* (50) 224-8766. *E-mail:* jgnoll@via-rs.net. *Website:* www.joaogilbertonoll.com.br.

NOLTE, Nick; American film actor; b. 8 Feb. 1941, Omaha; m. Rebecca Linger 1984 (divorced 1995); one s.; pnr Clytie Lane; one d.; ed Pasadena City Coll., Phoenix City Coll.; stage appearance in The Last Pad 1973; TV films 1974–75 and drama mini-series Rich Man, Poor Man 1976; f. Kingsgate Films Inc. (production co.). *Films:* Return to Macon County 1975, The Deep 1977, Who'll Stop the Rain 1978, North Dallas Forty 1979, Heartbeat 1980, Cannery Row 1982, 48 Hours 1982, Under Fire 1983, The Ultimate Solution of Grace Quigley 1984, Teachers 1984, Down and Out in Beverly Hills 1986, Weeds 1987, Extreme Prejudice 1987, Farewell to the King 1989, New York Stories 1989, Three Fugitives, Everybody Wins, Q & A 1990, Prince of Tides 1990, Cape Fear 1991, Lorenzo's Oil 1992, Blue Chips 1994, I'll Do Anything 1994, Love Trouble 1994, Jefferson in Paris 1994, Mulholland Falls 1996, Mother Night 1996, Afterglow 1997, Affliction 1998, U-Turn, Breakfast of Champions 1998, The Thin Red Line 1998, Trixie 2000, The Golden Bowl 2000, Investigating Sex 2001, Double Down 2001, The Good Thief 2003, Hotel Rwanda 2004, Neverwas 2005, Over the Hedge (voice) 2006, Paris, je t'aime 2006, A Few Days in September 2006, Off the Black 2006, Peaceful Warrior 2006, The Spiderwick Chronicles 2007, Tropic Thunder 2008. *Address:* Kingsgate Films, Inc., 18954 West Pico, 2nd Floor, Los Angeles, CA 90035; Creative Artists Agency, Inc., 9830 Wilshire Blvd, Beverly Hills, CA 90212-1825; 6153 Bonsall Drive, Malibu, CA 90265, USA. *Telephone:* (310) 288-4545 (CAA). *Fax:* (310) 288-4800 (CAA).

NOMA, Sawako; Japanese publishing executive; *President and CEO, Kodansha Ltd;* granddaughter of Seiji Noma, founder of Kodansha; m. (widowed 1987); one s.; Pres. and CEO Kodansha (largest publishing co. in Japan) Ltd 1987–; ranked by Fortune magazine amongst 50 Most Powerful Women in Business outside the US (27th) 2002, (33rd) 2003, (31st) 2004, (31st) 2005, (43rd) 2006, (45th) 2007, UNESCO Mahatma Gandhi Silver Medal in honour of the Noma Literacy Award 2004. *Films produced:* Akira (exec. producer) 1988, Debiruman: Kaichou shireinyu hen (Devil Man. Volume 2: Demon Bird) (producer) 1990. *Address:* Kodansha Ltd, 2-12-21 Otowa, Bunkyo-ku, Tokyo 112-8001, Japan (office). *Telephone:* (3) 3946-6201 (office). *Fax:* (3) 3944-9915 (office). *Website:* www.kodansha.co.jp (office).

NOMAKUCHI, Tamotsu, PhD; Japanese electronics executive; *Chairman, Mitsubishi Electric Corporation;* joined Mitsubishi Electric Corpn 1965, various positions including researcher Cen. Research Laboratory, Dir Mitsubishi Information Tech. Research and Devt Centre 1996–97, mem. Bd of Dirs 1997–, Sr Vice-Pres. and Vice-Pres. of Corp. Research and Devt 1997–2001, Exec. Vice-Pres. and Vice-Pres. of Information Systems & Network Services 2001–02, Pres. and CEO Mitsubishi Electric Corpn 2002–06, Chair. 2006–; Chair. Echonet Consortium. *Address:* Mitsubishi Electric Corpn, Tokyo Building, 2-7-3, Marunouchi, Chiyoda-ku, Tokyo 100-8310, Japan (office). *Telephone:* (3) 3218-2111 (office). *Fax:* (3) 3218-2185 (office). *E-mail:* Minoru.ueda2@hg.melco.co.jp (office). *Website:* global .mitsubishielectric.com (office).

NOMIYAMA, Akihiko, LLB; Japanese business executive; *Special Adviser, Nippon Mining Holdings Incorporated;* b. 15 June 1934, Fukuoka Pref.; one s. one d.; ed Tokyo Univ.; joined Nippon Mining Co. 1957, assignments in budget control, corp. financing, Gen. Man. Admin. Dept, Petroleum Operation 1981–92, Man. Dir Japan Energy Corpn (formed from merger with Kyodo Oil Co.) 1992–96, apptd Pres., CEO and Dir 1996, Chair. and Rep. Dir Nippon Mining Holdings Inc. –2006, Special Adviser 2006–; Vice-Chair. Petroleum Asscn of Japan. *Leisure interests:* golf, classical music. *Address:* Nippon Mining Holdings Incorporated, 2-10-1, Toranomon, Minato-ku, Tokyo 105-

0001, Japan (office). *Telephone:* (3) 5573-5123 (office). *Fax:* (3) 5573-6784 (office). *Website:* www.shinnikko-hd.co.jp (office).

NOMURA, Issei; Japanese diplomatist; b. 20 May 1940; ed Tokyo Univ.; First Sec., Embassy in London 1974, in Moscow 1976; fmr Dir USSR Div. Ministry of Foreign Affairs; fmr Dir-Gen. European and Oceanian Affairs; Amb. to Germany 2001, to Russian Fed. 2002–06; Grand Master, Imperial Household Agency 2006–. *Address:* Imperial Household Agency, 1-1, Chiyoda, Chiyoda-ku, Tokyo 100-8111, Japan (office). *Telephone:* (3) 3213-1111 (office). *Fax:* (3) 3282-1407 (office). *E-mail:* information@kunaicho.go.jp (office). *Website:* www.kunaicho.go.jp (office).

NOMURA, Masayasu, PhD, FAAS; American molecular biologist and academic; *Grace Bell Professor of Biological Chemistry, Department of Biological Chemistry, University of California, Irvine;* b. 27 April 1927, Hyogo-Ken, Japan; s. of Hiromichi Nomura and Yaeko Nomura; m. Junko Hamashima 1957; one s. one d.; ed Univ. of Tokyo; Research Assoc., Prof. S. Spiegelman's Lab., Univ. of Ill. and Prof. J. D. Watson's Lab., Harvard Univ. 1957–59; Prof. S. Benzer's Lab., Purdue Univ. 1959–60; Asst Prof., Inst. for Protein Research, Osaka Univ. 1960–63; Assoc. Prof., Dept of Genetics, Univ. of Wis. 1963–66, Prof. 1966–70; Elvehjem Prof. of Life Sciences, Inst. for Enzyme Research, with jt appointments in Depts of Genetics and Biochem. 1970–84; Grace Bell Prof. of Biological Chem., Univ. of Calif., Irvine 1984–; mem. American Acad. of Arts and Sciences, NAS; Foreign mem. Royal Danish Acad. of Sciences and Letters, Royal Netherlands Acad. of Arts and Sciences; US Steel Award in Molecular Biology (NAS) 1971, Japan Acad. Award 1972, Y. D. Mattia Award (Roche Inst.). *Leisure interests:* hiking, reading. *Address:* University of California, Department of Biological Chemistry, 109 Plumwood House, Irvine, CA 92697-1700 (office); 74 Whitman Court, Irvine, CA 92612, USA (home). *Telephone:* (949) 824-4673 (office); (949) 854-3482 (home). *Fax:* (949) 824-3201 (office). *E-mail:* mnomura@uci.edu (office). *Website:* www.ucihs.uci.edu/biochem/faculty/nrmura.html (office).

NOMURA, Tetsuya; Japanese construction industry executive; *Chairman and Representative Director, Shimizu Corporation;* joined Shimizu Corpn (contractor in eng and construction projects) 1961, served in various exec. roles including Man. of Kyushu Office, Man. Dir, Sr Man. Dir and Vice Pres., Pres. and CEO –2007, Chair. and Rep. Dir 2007–, led negotiations with NTT Data Corpn to est. jtly funded corpn NTT Data Billing Service 2002; Dir Global Industrial and Social Progress Research Inst. (GISPRI) 2003–, Japan Productivity Centre for Socio-Econ. Devt (JPC-SED) 2003–. *Address:* Shimizu Corporation, Seavans South, 1-2-3 Shibaura, Minato-ku, Tokyo 105-8007, Japan (office). *Telephone:* (3) 5441-1111 (office). *Fax:* (3) 5441-0526 (office). *Website:* www.shimz.co.jp (office).

NOMURA, Yoshihiro; Japanese legal scholar and academic; *Professor of Civil Law, Faculty of Law, Meiji-Gakuin University;* b. 3 Jan. 1941, Nagoya City; s. of Akio Nomura and Michiko Nomura; m. 1966; three s. one d.; ed Univ. of Tokyo; Asst Researcher in Law, Univ. of Tokyo 1963; Lecturer, Tokyo Metropolitan Univ. 1966, Assoc. Prof. 1967, Prof. of Civil and Environmental Law 1977; currently Prof. of Civil Law, Meiji-Gakuin University. *Publication:* Automobile Accident Damages 1970, Environmental Law 1981. *Leisure interest:* nature watching. *Address:* Faculty of Law, Meiji-Gakuin University, 1-2-37 Shirokanedai, Minato-ku, Tokyo 108-8636, Japan (office). *Telephone:* (35) 421-5209 (office). *Fax:* (35) 421-5692 (office). *Website:* www.meijigakuin.ac.jp/~law/english (office).

NONAKA, Tomoyo, BA, MA; Japanese television journalist and business executive; *Chairman, Gaia Initiative;* b. 18 June 1954; ed Sophia Univ., Tokyo, Univ. of Missouri at Columbia, USA; worked as TV anchor on Japan Broadcasting Corpn (NHK) programme International News Weekly (Kaigai Weekly) 1979–92; main newscaster for TV Tokyo's World Business Satellite programme 1992–96; has served as mem. of many advisory and discussion councils, including at Ministry of Finance, Ministry of Posts and Telecommunications (now Ministry of Public Man., Home Affairs, Posts and Telecommunications), and Ministry of Educ. and Science and Tech. Agency (now the Ministry of Educ., Culture, Sports, Science and Tech.); mem. Council on the Financial System, Ministry of Finance, Council on Science and Tech.; mem. Bd of Dirs Sanyo Electric Co. Ltd 2002–07 Chair. and CEO 2005–06, Chair. 2006–07; Founder and Chair. Gaia Initiative (non-profit org.) 2007–; mem. Bd of Dirs Asahi Breweries 2002–07; Exec. mem. Advisory Bd Mitsui Fudosan Co. Ltd 2001–; ranked by Fortune magazine amongst 50 Most Powerful Women in Business outside the US (fifth) 2005, (24th) 2006. *Publications include:* Ganbare, Jibun! (Do the Best for Yourself!), Iron John no Kokoro (The Shadow of Iron John) (trans.). *Address:* Gaia Initiative, 3-4-8-202 Minamiaoyama, Minato-ku, Tokyo 107-0062, Japan (office). *Telephone:* (3) 5411-4422 (office). *Fax:* (3) 3222-6204 (office). *E-mail:* info@gaiainitiative.org (office). *Website:* www.gaiainitiative.org (office).

NOOR, Dato' Mohamad Yusof, MA, PhD; Malaysian politician and teacher; b. 5 Feb. 1941, Raja, Terangganu; m.; two c.; ed Islamic Coll., Klang, Selangor, Al Azhar Univ., Ein Shams Univ. and Univ. of Cairo; secondary school teacher 1969–70; Insp. of Secondary Schools, Terengganu State 1970; Prin., Sultan Zainal Abidin Secondary Religious School 1970; Lecturer and Head of Coll., Nat. Univ. of Malaysia 1974, Dean, Faculty of Islamic Studies 1975–79, Deputy Vice-Chancellor for Student Affairs 1980–84; mem. Senate 1984; Deputy Minister responsible for Islamic Affairs, Prime Minister's Dept 1984; mem. House of Reps 1987–; mem. Supreme Council, United Malays Nat. Org. (UMNO) 1987–; Minister, Prime Minister's Dept 1987; Chair. Religious Council for Fed. Territory; many other appointments in Islamic and religious field. *Publications:* numerous articles in fields of educ. and Islamic affairs. *Address:* c/o House of Representatives, Parliament Building, Kuala Lumpur, Malaysia.

NOOR AL-HUSSEIN, HM Queen, BA; Jordanian public servant and international humanitarian activist; *United Nations Expert Adviser;* b. (Lisa Najeeb Halaby), 23 Aug. 1951, USA; d. of the late Najeeb Halaby; m. King Hussein I of Jordan 1978 (died 1999); two s.: HRH Prince Hamzah (b. 29 March 1980), HRH Prince Hashim (b. 10 June 1981) two d.: HRH Princess Iman (b. 24 April 1983), HRH Princess Raiyah (b. 9 February 1986); ed attended schools in Los Angeles, Washington, DC and New York City, Concord Acad., Mass, Princeton Univ., USA; architectural and urban planning projects in Australia, Iran and Jordan 1974–78; f. in Jordan: Royal Endowment for Culture and Educ. 1979, annual Arab Children's Congress 1980, annual int. Jerash Festival for Culture and Arts 1981 (also Chair.), Noor Al-Hussein Foundation 1985 (also Chair.), King Hussein Foundation (also Chair.) 1999; Chair. UN Univ. Int. Leadership Inst. (UNU/ILI), Amman; UN Expert Adviser; Founding mem. Int. Comm. on Peace and Food 1992; Pres. United World Colls 1995; mem. Int. Eye Foundation, Int. Council Near East Foundation, Int. Comm. on Missing Persons, The Mentor Foundation, Hunger Project; Trustee Refugees Int., Conservation Int., WWF Int., Aspen Inst. 2004–; Adviser, Women Waging Peace and Seeds of Peace; Patron Royal Soc. for the Conservation of Nature, World Conservation Union 1988, Int. Campaign to Ban Landmines, Landmine Survivors Network (also Chair.) 1998, Int. Alert's Women and Peace-building Campaign, Council of Women World Leaders' Advisory Group 2004–; Hon. Pres. Jordan Red Crescent, Birdlife Int. 1996–2004 (Hon. Pres. Emer. 2004–); Hon. Chair. Petra Nat. Trust, SOS Children's Asscn, McGill Middle East Program in Civil Society and Peace Building; numerous hon. doctorates, numerous int. awards and decorations for the promotion educ., culture, women and children's welfare, sustainable community devt, environmental conservation, human rights, conflict resolution, cross-cultural understanding and world peace, ranked 83rd by Forbes magazine amongst 100 Most Powerful Women 2004. *Publication:* Leap of Faith: Memoirs of an Unexpected Life 2002. *Leisure interests:* skiing, water skiing, tennis, horse riding, reading, gardening, photography, biking, sailing. *Address:* Office of Her Majesty Queen Noor, Bab Al Salam Palace, Amman, Jordan. *Telephone:* (6) 551-5191. *Fax:* (6) 464-7961. *E-mail:* noor@queennoor.jo. *Website:* www.noor.gov.jo.

NOOTEBOOM, Cornelis (Cees) Johannes Jacobus Maria; Dutch writer and poet; b. 31 July 1933, The Hague; hon. mem. Modern Language Asscn, USA 1997; Chevalier, Légion d'honneur 1991; Hon. DLitt (Katholieke Universiteit Brussel) 1998; Prijs van de dagbladjournalistiek 1969, Cestodaprijs 1982, Preis zum 3 Oktober 1990, Constantijn Huygensprijs 1992, Hugo Ball Preis 1993, Aristeion Prijs 1993, Premio Grinzane Cavour 1994, Dirk Martens-prijs 1994, Goethe-prijs 2002, Oostenrijkse staatsprijs 2002, P. C. Hooftprijs 2004. *Publications:* fiction: Philip en de anderen (Anne Frank-prijs 1957) 1954, De verliefde gevangene 1958, De koning is dood 1961, De ridder is gestorven (Lucy B. en C. W. van der Hoogtprijs 1963) 1963, Rituelen (F. Bordewijkprijs 1981, Mobil Pegasus Literatuurprijs 1982) 1980, Een lied van schijn en wezen 1981, Mokusei 1982, In Nederland (Multatuliprijs 1985) 1984, De Boeddha achter de schutting. Aan de oever van de Chaophraya 1986, Ina Rilke 1991, Allerzielen 1998, Paradijs Verloren 2004, Nachts kommen die Füchse 2009; plays: De zwanen van de Theems (ANV-Visser Neerlandia-prijs 1960) 1959, Gyges en Kandaules. Een koningsdrama 1982; poetry: De doden zoeben een huis 1956, Koude gedichten 1959, Het zwarte gedicht 1960, Ibicenzer gedicht (Poëzieprijs van de gemeente Amsterdam) 1960, Gesloten gedichten (Poëzieprijs van de gemeente Amsterdam 1965) 1964, Gemaakte gedichten 1970, Open als een schelp – dicht als een steen (Jan Campertprijs 1978) 1978, Aas 1982, Vuurtijd, Ijstijd. Gedichten 1955–1983 1984, Het gezicht van het oog 1989, Zo kon het zijn (Gedichtendagprijzen 2000) 1999, Bitterzoet, honderd gedichten van vroeger en zeventien nieuwe 2000, Die schlafenden Götter 2005; non-fiction: Een middag in Bruay 1963, Een nacht in Tunesië 1965, Een ochtend in Bahia 1968, De Parijse beroerte 1968, Bitter Bolivia, Maanland Mali 1971, Een avond in Isfahan 1978, Waar je gevallen bent, blijf je 1983, De zucht naar het Westen 1985, De wereld een reiziger 1989, Berlijnse notities 1990, Vreemd water 1991, Het volgende verhaal 1991, De omweg naar Santiago (Preis für Reiseliteratur des Landes Tirol 1996) 1992, Zurbarán̈k 1992, De ontvoering van Europa (essay) 1993, De koning van Suriname 1993, Van de lente de dauw. Oosterse reizen 1995, De filosoof zonder ogen: Europese reizen 1997, Terugkeer naar Berlijn 1997. *Address:* c/o Arbeiderspers, Herengracht 370-372, 1016 CH Amsterdam, The Netherlands.

NOOYI, Indra K., BS, MBA; Indian/American business executive; *Chairman and CEO, PepsiCo Inc.;* b. 28 Oct. 1955, Madras, India; m. Rajkishan Nooyi; two d.; ed Madras Christian Coll., Indian Inst. of Man., Calcutta, Yale School of Man.; spent six years at Boston Consulting Group; fmr Pres. and Dir of Corp. Strategy and Planning, Motorola; Sr Vice-Pres. of Strategic Planning and Strategic Markets, Asea Brown Boveri –1994; Sr Vice-Pres. PepsiCo Inc. 1994–2001, Chief Financial Officer 2000–06, Pres. 2001–06, CEO 2006–, Chair. 2007–; mem. Bd of Dirs PepsiCo, PepsiCo Foundation, Motorola, Fed. Reserve Bank of New York, Int. Rescue Cttee, Lincoln Center for the Performing Arts, New York; mem. Pres.'s Council on Int. Activities, Yale Univ.; Successor Trustee, The Yale Corpn 2002; ranked by Fortune magazine amongst 50 Most Powerful Women in Business in the US (fourth) 2002, (eighth) 2003, (12th) 2004, (11th) 2005, (first) 2006, (first) 2007, ranked by Forbes magazine amongst 100 Most Powerful Women (29th) 2004, (28th) 2005, (fourth) 2006, (fifth) 2007, (third) 2008, named by The Wall Street Journal as one of 50 Women to Watch in 2005. *Address:* PepsiCo Inc., 700 Anderson Hill Road, Purchase, NY 10577-1444, USA (office). *Telephone:* (914) 253-2000 (office). *Fax:* (914) 253-2070 (office). *Website:* www.pepsico.com (office).

NORBU, Lyonpo Wangdi, BA; Bhutanese politician and civil servant; *Minister of Finance;* b. 1954, Galing, Trashigang Dist; m. Aum Pem Zangmo; one s. one d.; ed Scotch Coll., Australia, Univ. of Western Australia; various posts within Ministry of Finance since 1977 including Dir Dept of Budget and Accounts, Auditor Gen. Royal Audit Authority, Finance Sec.; Minister of Finance 2003–07 (resgnd), 2008–; mem. Nat. Ass. from Bartsham-Shongphu constituency, Trashigang; fmr Chair. Royal Monetary Authority. *Address:* Ministry of Finance, Tashichhodzong, PO Box 117, Thimphu, Bhutan (office). *Telephone:* (2) 322223 (office). *Fax:* (2) 323154 (office). *E-mail:* yanki@mof.gov.bt (office).

NORDAL, Jóhannes, PhD; Icelandic economist and banker; b. 11 May 1924, Reykjavik; s. of Prof. Sigurdur Nordal and Olöf Jónsdóttir; m. Dóra Gudjónsdóttir 1953; one s. five d.; ed Reykjavik Grammar School and London School of Econs, UK; Chief Economist, Nat. Bank of Iceland 1954–59, Gen. Man. 1959–61; Gov., Cen. Bank of Iceland (Sedlabanki Islands) 1961–93, (Chair. Bd of Govs 1964–93); Chair. of Bd Nat. Power Co. (Landsvirkjun) 1965–96; Gov. IMF for Iceland 1965–93; Ed. Fjármálatíáindi (Financial Review) 1954–94; Co.-Ed. Nýtt Helgafell (literary periodical) 1955–59; Chair. Humanities Div. of Science Fund for Iceland 1958–87, Icelandic Council of Science 1987–94, Nat. Library Bd 1994–; mem. Soc. Scientiarum Islandica 1959–; Overseas Advisory Trustee, American-Scandinavian Foundation; mem. Bd of Dirs Scandinavia-Japan Sasakawa Foundation; Grand Kt Order of Falcon 1966. *Publications:* Iceland 1966, 1974, 1986, Iceland: The Republic (co-ed.) 1996. *Leisure Interests:* fly-fishing, books. *Address:* Laugarásvegur 11, Reykjavik (home); Sedlabanki Islands, Kalkofnsvegur 1, 150 Reykjavik, Iceland (office). *Telephone:* 5699600 (office); 5533350 (home). *Fax:* 5699609 (office). *E-mail:* j.nordal@mmedia.is (home).

NORDENBERG, Mark A., BA, JD; American teacher, university administrator and academic; *Chancellor and CEO, University of Pittsburgh;* b. Duluth, Minn.; m. Dr Nikki Pirillo Nordenberg; two s. one d.; ed Thiel Coll., Univ. of Wisconsin Law School; joined Law Faculty, Univ. of Pittsburgh 1977, Dean School of Law 1985–1993, Interim Provost and Sr Vice-Chancellor for Academic Affairs 1993–94, Distinguished Service Prof. of Law 1994–, Interim Chancellor 1995, Chancellor and CEO Univ. of Pittsburgh 1996–; Chair. Citizens' Advisory Cttee on Efficiency and Effectiveness of City-County Govt; fmr mem. US Advisory Cttee on Civil Rules, Pa Civil Procedural Rules Cttee; Founding mem. Technology Collaborative, Pittsburgh Life Sciences Greenhouse (Co-Chair. both bds); mem. Assn of American Univs, Pa Assn of Colls and Univs, Univ. of Pittsburgh Medical Center, Allegheny Conf. on Community Devt, Pittsburgh Council on Higher Educ., Mellon Financial Corpn, Pittsburgh Post-Gazette Dapper Dan Charities, Pittsburgh-Wuhan Friendship Cttee Inc.; first recipient Univ. of Pittsburgh School of Law's Excellence-in-Teaching Award (first recipient) 1984, Chancellor's Distinguished Teaching Award 1985, Vectors Pittsburgh Person of the Year in Educ. 1997, selected by Vectors Pittsburgh as Pittsburgh's Overall Person of the Year 1998, named by Pittsburgh magazine as a Pittsburgher of the Year 1999, Pittsburgh magazine's Pittsburgher of the Year Award (co-recipient) 2001, Person of Vision Award, Pittsburgh Vision Services 2003, endowed Chancellor Mark A. Nordenberg Univ. Chair (est. to honour his 10 years of leadership) 2005, Chief Exec. Leadership Award, Council for Advancement and Support of Educ., District II 2006, Nellie Leadership Award, Three Rivers Youth 2006, Kesher Award, Edward and Rose Berman Hillel Jewish Univ. Center (co-recipient) 2006. *Publications:* has published books, articles and reports on civil litigation. *Address:* Office of the Chancellor, University of Pittsburgh, CL 107, Pittsburgh, PA 15260, USA (office). *Telephone:* (412) 624-4200 (office). *Fax:* (412) 624-7539 (office). *E-mail:* norden@pitt.edu (office). *Website:* www.pitt.edu (office).

NORDH, Sture, BPA; Swedish trade union official; *President, Swedish Confederation of Professional Employees;* b. 3 June 1952, Skellefteå; m. Gudrun Nordh (née Nygren); one d. one s.; ed Univ. of Umeå; Union Sec. Swedish Union of Local Govt Employees (SKTF) 1975–79, Gen.-Sec. 1979–83, Pres. 1983–96; State Sec. Ministry of Labour 1996–98; Deputy Dir-Gen. Nat. Inst. of Working Life 1999; Pres. Swedish Confed. of Professional Employees (TCO) 1999–. *Publication:* Future of the Welfare State (co-author with Bengt Westerberg). *Leisure interests:* skiing, literature. *Address:* Tjänstemännens Centralorganisation (TCO), Linnégt. 14, 114 94 Stockholm (office); Gyllenstiernsg. 10, 115 26 Stockholm, Sweden (home). *Telephone:* 87-82-91-00 (office); 86-61-34-23 (home). *Fax:* 87-82-91-15 (office); 86-62-16-75 (home). *E-mail:* ordforande@tco.se (office); sture.nordh@telia.com (home). *Website:* www.tco.se (office).

NORDHAGEN, Per Jonas, DPhil; Norwegian professor of history of art; b. 30 Oct. 1929, Bergen; s. of Rolf Nordhagen and Elisabeth M. Myhre; m. Inger K. Noss 1978; one s. four d.; ed Univ. of Oslo; Lecturer, Univ. of Oslo 1962; Assoc. Prof., Univ. of Bergen 1969; Dir Norwegian Inst. Rome 1973; Sr Lecturer, Univ. of Oslo 1977; Prof. of History of Art, Univ. of Bergen 1986–2000; mem. Norwegian Acad. of Sciences. *Publications:* The Frescoes of John VII (705–707 AD) in S. Maria Antiqua, Rome 1968, Frescoes of the Seventh Century 1978, The Capri Papers (novel) 1986, Collected Papers in the History of Byzantine and Early Medieval Art 1990, Bergen – Guide and Handbook 1992, The Wooden Architecture of Bergen 1994, The Technique of Early Christian and Byzantine Mosaics 1997, Art and Architecture of Norway: an Outline 1997. *Leisure interests:* skiing, hiking, books, botany. *Address:* c/o Institute of Art History, University of Bergen, Parkv. 22B, 5014 Bergen, Norway.

NORDHEIM, Arne; Norwegian composer; b. 20 June 1931, Larvik; m. 1st 1956; m. 2nd 1981; two c.; ed Oslo Conservatory of Music and electronic music studies in Utrecht, Warsaw and Stockholm; began to compose 1950; first maj. work Stringquartett 1956; since composed several works for orchestra and solo instruments and symphonic music, voice or electronic sound and one ballet score; worked as music critic for several daily newspapers 1959–67; critic Dagbladet, Oslo 1960–68; fmr Prof. of Electronic Music; mem. Royal Swedish Acad. of Music; Hon. mem. Int. Soc. for Contemporary Music 1996–; Commdr Order of St Olav 1997, Order al Merito (Italy) 1998, Orderu Zasługi Rzeczy pos Politej Polskie (Poland) 1999; Nordic Council Music Prize 1972, Prix Italia 1980, awarded Norwegian State Residence of Honour 1982, Steffens Prize 1993. *Music:* approx. 200 works including Epitaffio, Canzona, Floating, Wirklicher Wald, The Tempest (ballet) and solo concertos for cello, oboe and accordion. *Publications:* Alt Skal Synge (All Singing) 1991, Klingende Ord, Conversations with Arne Nordheim 2001. *Address:* Wergelandsveien 2, 0167 Oslo, Norway (home). *Telephone:* 22-11-28-27 (home).

NORDLI, Odvar; Norwegian politician; b. 3 Nov. 1927, Stange, Hedmark; ed in business admin; asst, Baerum Municipal Auditor's Office 1948–49; Chief Clerk, Hedmark County Auditor's Office 1949–57; Dist Auditor, Vang and Löten 1957–61; mem. Storting (Parl.) 1961; mem. and Deputy Chair. Stange Municipal Council 1952; Chair. Municipal Cttee of Hedmark Labour Party 1960–; Deputy mem. Cen. Cttee of Labour Party 1965, Chair. Hedmark Labour Party 1968; Chair. Trade Union and Labour Party Tax Cttee 1967–68; Vice-Chair. Parl. Municipal Cttee 1965–69; Chair. Parl. Social Welfare Cttee 1969–71; Minister of Labour and Municipal Affairs 1971–72; Chair. Comm. of Defence 1974–75; Prime Minister 1976–81; Vice-Pres. Parl. 1981; Leader Parl. Labour Party 1973–76.

NORDLING, Carl, PhD; Swedish physicist and academic; *Professor Emeritus of Atomic and Molecular Physics, University of Uppsala;* b. 6 Feb. 1931, Edmonton, Canada; s. of Jarl Nordling and Karin Thorén; m. Gunhild Söderström 1954; two s. one d.; ed Univ. of Uppsala; Asst Prof., Univ. of Uppsala 1959–61, Lecturer 1962–64, Assoc. Prof. 1965–69, Prof. of Atomic and Molecular Physics 1970–95, Prof. Emer. 1996–; Sec.-Gen. Swedish Nat. Science Research Council 1987–93; Chair. Nobel Cttee for Physics 1992–96. *Publications:* ESCA-Atomic, Molecular and Solid State Structure Studied by Means of Electron Spectroscopy (co-author) 1967, ESCA Applied to Free Molecules (co-author) 1969, Physics Handbook (co-author) 1982; 150 scientific papers on electron, X-ray and laser spectroscopy. *Address:* Department of Physics, University of Uppsala, Box 530, 751 21 Uppsala (office); Malma Ringv. 45B, 756 45 Uppsala, Sweden (home). *Telephone:* (18) 471-35-45 (office); (18) 30-22-21 (home). *Fax:* (18) 51-22-27 (office). *E-mail:* carl.nordling@fysik.uu.se (office). *Website:* www.fysik.uu.se/english (office).

NORDLUND, Roger; Åland Islands politician; *Chairman (Lantråd) of the Landskapsregering;* b. 19 Nov. 1957; mem. Lagting (Åland Parl.) 1983–87, Ålands landskapsstyrelse, sedan 2004; Chair. Äländsk Ungcenter 1979–85, Äländsk Center (Åland Centre Party) 1986–87, 1997–; Minister of Educ. and Culture 1991–95; Deputy Chair. Landskapsregering (Deputy Premier—Vicelantråd) 1995–99, Chair. (Premier—Lantråd) 1999–. *Address:* Pb 1060, 22111 Mariehamn, Åland Islands, Gulf of Bothnia, Finland (office). *Telephone:* (18) 25370 (office). *Fax:* (18) 19155 (office). *E-mail:* roger.nordlund@regeringen.ax (office). *Website:* www.regeringen.ax (office).

NORDSTRÖM, Anders, MD; Swedish physician and international organization official; m.; two c.; ed Karolinska Institut; worked with Swedish Red Cross in Cambodia and Int. Cttee of the Red Cross in Iran; worked for Swedish Int. Devt Co-operation Agency (SIDA) for 12 years, including three years as Regional Advisor, Zambia and four years as Head, Health Div., Stockholm; Interim Exec. Dir Global Fund to Fight AIDS, Tuberculosis and Malaria 2002; Asst Dir-Gen. for Gen. Man., WHO 2003-06, Acting Dir-Gen. 2006–07. *Address:* c/o World Health Organization (WHO), Ave Appia 20, 1211 Geneva 27, Switzerland (office).

NORDSTRÖM, Lars G.; Swedish financial services executive; b. 1943; ed Uppsala Univ.; with Skandinaviska Enskilda Banken 1970–93, Exec. Vice-Pres. 1989–93; Exec. Vice-Pres. and mem. Group Exec. Man., Nordbanken 1993–98, CEO 1998–2000, Exec. Vice-Pres. and mem. Group Exec. Bd, MeritaNordbanken 1998–99; Exec. Vice-Pres. and mem. Group Exec. Cttee, Nordic Baltic Holding 1999–2000; Exec. Vice-Pres. and Head of Retail Banking, Nordea 2000–02, mem. Group Exec. Man. 2000–02, Pres. and Group CEO 2002–07 (retd). *Address:* c/o Nordea AB, Hamngatan 10, 105 71 Stockholm, Sweden (office).

NORÉN, Lars; Swedish playwright and director; b. 9 May 1944, Stockholm; s. of Matti Norén and Britt Norén; m. 1st Titti Mörk 1979; m. 2nd Charlott Neuhauser 1993; two d.; started career as a poet; wrote first play 1968; has written 55 plays, performed world-wide; De Nio's Pris 1985, Expressens Reviewers' Prize 1993, Pilot Prize 1994 and many other prizes and awards. *Plays include:* Courage to Kill 1978, Munich-Athens 1981, Night is Day's Mother 1982, Comedians 1985, Hebriana 1987, Autumn and Winter 1987, And Give Us the Shadows 1988, Trick or Treat 1989, Lost and Found 1991, The Shadow Boys 1991, Leaves in Vallombrosa 1992, Blood 1994, Some Kind of Hades 1994, The Clinic 1995, Personkrets 3:1 1997, 7:3 1998, Autumn and Winter 1997, Blood 2003, War 2008. *Leisure interests:* fishing, hunting. *Address:* Östermalmsgatan 33, S-11426 Stockholm, Sweden, (home).

NØRGAARD, Carl Aage, DJur; Danish professor of law; b. 15 Sept. 1924; s. of Edvard Nørgaard and Jensine Kristine Kristensen; m. Hedvig Hauberg 1951; one d.; ed Univ. of Århus, Univ. of Cambridge, UK and Univ. of Geneva, Switzerland; Asst, Faculty of Law, Univ. of Århus 1955–58, Lecturer 1958–64, Prof. 1964–89, Head of Inst. of Public Law 1964–86; Rockefeller Fellowship, Univ. of Geneva 1959–60; mem. European Comm. of Human Rights 1973–95, Second Vice-Pres. 1976–81, Pres. 1981–95, Ind. Legal Adviser for UN concerning the release of political prisoners in Namibia 1989–90; Legal Adviser to S African Truth and Reconciliation Comm. 1994–98; German Grand Order of Merit with Star and Sash 1995, Danish Grand Cross 1996; Hon. DJur (Lund) 1994; Prix de la Tolérance and Prix Marcel Rudloff, Strasbourg 1998. *Publications:* The Position of the Individual in International Law 1962, Forvaltningsret-Sagsbehandling 1972, 1981, 1987, 1995, 2001, 2007, Administration og Borger (with Claus Haagen Jensen) 1972, 1984, 1988;

contrib. articles to legal periodicals. *Leisure interests:* rowing, gardening. *Address:* Skjoldsbjergvej 2A, Skórring, 8464 Galten, Denmark. *Telephone:* 89-42-11-33 (office); 86-94-40-47 (home).

NORMAN, Archie John, MA, MBA; British business executive and politician; *Chairman, Energis;* b. 1 May 1954, London; s. of Archibald Percy Norman and Aleida Elizabeth Norman; m. Vanessa Peet 1982; one d.; ed Univ. of Minnesota, Emmanuel Coll. Cambridge, Harvard Business School; with Citibank N.A. 1975–77; Partner, McKinsey & Co. Inc. 1979–86; Group Finance Dir Kingfisher PLC 1986–91; Chief Exec. Asda Group PLC 1991–96, Chair. 1996–97; Chair. (non-exec.) French PLC 1999–2001; MP for Tunbridge Wells 1997–; Vice-Chair. Conservative Party 1997–98; Chief Exec. and Deputy Chair. Conservative Party 1998–99; Shadow Foreign Affairs Post 1999–2000; Shadow Spokesman on Environment, Transport and the Regions 2000–01; Dir (non-exec.) Geest 1988–91, British Rail 1992–94, Railtrack 1994–2000, Holmes Place 2003–; Chair. Energis 2002–; Sr Adviser, Lazard 2004–. *Leisure interests:* farming, music, opera, tennis, football. *Address:* House of Commons, Westminster, London, SW1A 0AA, England (office). *Telephone:* (20) 7219-5156 (office). *Fax:* (020) 7219-5050 (office). *E-mail:* kyriakoub@parliament.uk (office).

NORMAN, Barry Leslie, CBE; British writer and broadcaster; b. 21 Aug. 1933, London; s. of Leslie Norman and Elizabeth Norman; m. Diana Narracott 1957; two d.; ed Highgate School, London; Entertainment Ed. Daily Mail, London 1969–71; weekly columnist The Guardian 1971–80; Writer and Presenter of BBC 1 Film 1973–81, 1983–98, The Hollywood Greats 1977–79, 1984, The British Greats 1980, Omnibus 1982, Film Greats 1985, Talking Pictures 1988, Barry Norman's Film Night, BSkyB 1998–2001, Radio 4 Today 1974–76, Going Places 1977–81, Breakaway 1979–80; Barry Norman's Film Night, Sky 1998–2001; Hon. DLitt (E Anglia) 1991, (Herts.) 1996; Richard Dimbleby Award, BAFTA 1981, Columnist of the Year Award 1990. *Publications:* Novels: The Matter of Mandrake 1967, The Hounds of Sparta 1968, End Product 1975, A Series of Defeats 1977, To Nick a Good Body 1978, Have a Nice Day 1981, Sticky Wicket 1984, The Birddog Tape 1992, The Mickey Mouse Affair 1995, Death on Sunset 1998; non-fiction: Tales of the Redundance Kid 1975, The Hollywood Greats 1979, The Movie Greats 1981, The Film Greats 1985, Talking Pictures 1987, The Good Night In Guide 1992, 100 Best Films of the Century 1992, And Why Not? (autobiog.) 2002. *Leisure interest:* cricket. *Address:* c/o Curtis Brown Group Ltd, Haymarket House, 28–29 Haymarket, London, SW1Y 4SP, England (office). *Telephone:* (20) 7396-4400 (office). *Fax:* (20) 7393-4401 (office). *E-mail:* presenters@curtisbrown.co.uk (office). *Website:* www.curtisbrown.co.uk (office).

NORMAN, Donald (Don) A., BS, MS, PhD; American psychologist, computer scientist, academic and industrial consultant; *Professor of Electrical Engineering and Computer Science, of Psychology, and of Cognitive Science, Northwestern University;* b. New York, NY; m. Julie J. Norman; two s. one d.; ed Massachusetts Inst. of Tech., Univ. of Pennsylvania; Jr Faculty mem. Harvard Univ.'s Center for Cognitive Studies for four years; joined Dept of Psychology, Univ. of California, San Diego, fmr Chair. Dept of Psychology and Dept of Cognitive Science, now Prof. Emer. of Cognitive Science; acted as consultant on Three Mile Island nuclear accident, realized his unique combination of eng and psychology could be combined in study of design; research moved to study of aviation safety and computers, then to everyday items; Exec. at Apple Computer (Vice-Pres. Advanced Tech. Group), Hewlett-Packard and Cardean Learning Systems, UNext; currently Co-Dir MMM Man. and Design Program, Co-Dir Segal Design Inst., Breed Univ. Prof. and Prof. of Electrical Eng and Computer Science, of Psychology, and of Cognitive Science, Northwestern Univ., Evanston, Ill.; Co-founder and Prin. Nielsen Norman Group, Palo Alto, Calif.; mem. Editorial Bd Encyclopædia Britannica; Fellow, American Acad. of Arts and Sciences, Asscn for Computational Machinery, American Psychological Asscn; Founding mem. and Fellow, Cognitive Science Soc.; Charter Fellow, American Psychological Soc.; hon. degrees (Univ. of Padua, Technical Univ. of Delft); Franklin V. Taylor Award, American Psychological Asscn, Presidential Citation and Lifetime Achievement Award, ACM Human-Computer Interaction Group, Benjamin Franklin Medal in Computer and Cognitive Science, The Franklin Inst. 2006. *Publications include:* Human Information Processing: An Introduction to Psychology (co-author) 1975, Memory and Attention 1977, Learning and Memory 1982, Direct Manipulation Interfaces (co-author) 1985, User Centered System Design: New Perspectives on Human-Computer Interaction (co-ed) 1986, The Design of Everyday Things (originally under the title The Psychology of Everyday Things) 1988, Turn Signals Are the Facial Expressions of Automobiles 1992, Things That Make Us Smart: Defending Human Attributes in the Age of the Machine 1993, The Invisible Computer: Why Good Products Can Fail, the Personal Computer Is So Complex and Information Appliances Are the Solution 1999, Emotional Design 2003, The Design of Future Things. *Address:* MMM Program, Northwestern University, Ford 1-325, 2133 Sheridan Road, Evanston, IL 60208, USA (office). *E-mail:* don@jnd.org (home). *Website:* www.jnd.org (office).

NORMAN, Gregory (Greg) John, AO; Australian professional golfer; *Chairman and CEO, Great White Shark Enterprises, Inc.;* b. 10 Feb. 1955, Queensland; s. of M. Norman; m. Laura Andrassy 1981 (divorced 2006); one s. one d.; m. Chris Evert 2008; ed Townsville Grammar School, High School, Aspley, Queensland; turned professional 1976; won West Lake Classic, Australia 1976, Martini Int., Kuzuhz Int., Japan 1977, NSW Open, South Seas Classic, Fiji 1978, Martini Int., Hong Kong Open 1979, Australian Open, French Open, Scandinavian Open 1980, Australian Masters, Martini Int., Dunlop Masters 1981, Dunlop Masters, State Express Classic, Benson & Hedges Int. 1982, Australian Masters, Nat. Panasonic NSW Open, Hong Kong Open, Cannes Invitational, Suntory World Match Play Championship 1983, Canadian Open, Victorian Open, Australian Masters, Toshiba Australian PGA Championship 1984, Toshiba Australian PGA Championship, Nat. Panasonic Australian Open 1985, European Open, British Open, Suntory World Matchplay Championship, Panasonic-Las Vegas Invitational, Kemper Open 1986, Australian Masters, Nat. Panasonic Australian Open 1987, Palm Meadows Cup, Australia, PGA Nat. Tournament Players Championship, Australia, Panasonic NSW Open, Lancia Italian Open 1988, Australian Masters, PGA Nat. Tournament Players Championship 1989, Australian Masters, The Memorial Tournament 1990, Canadian Open 1992, British Open, Taiheyo Masters, Japan 1993, Johnnie Walker Asian Classic, The Players Championship 1994, Australian Open, Memorial Tournament, Canon Greater Hartford Open 1995, Doral-Ryder Open, S African Open 1996, World Championship, FedEx St Jude Classic 1997, Greg Norman Holden Int. 1998, Franklin Templeton Shootout 1998, Skins Game 2001; Chair. and CEO Great White Shark Enterprises, Inc.; apptd Australian Amb. for Sport by Prime Minister 1998; inducted into World Golf Hall of Fame 2001. *Publications:* My Story 1983, Shark Attack 1988, Greg Norman's Instant Lessons 1993, Greg Norman's Better Golf 1994. *Leisure interests:* family, fishing, hunting, scuba diving. *Address:* Great White Shark Enterprise Inc., 2041 Vista Parkway, Level 2, West Palm Beach, FL 33411, USA. *Telephone:* (561) 640-7000 (office). *Website:* www.shark.com (office).

NORMAN, Jessye, MMus; American singer (soprano); b. 15 Sept. 1945, Augusta, Ga; d. of Silas Norman and Janie Norman (née King); ed Howard Univ., Washington, DC, Peabody Conservatory, Univ. of Michigan; Vocal Winner, Int. Musikwettbewerb, Bayerischer Rundfunk, Munich, Fed. Repub. of Germany 1968; operatic début Deutsche Oper Berlin 1969; début La Scala, Milan 1972, Royal Opera House, Covent Garden 1972; American operatic début, Hollywood Bowl 1972; performer Lincoln Centre 1973–; tours in N and S America, Europe, Middle East, Australia; int. festivals including Aix-en-Provence, Aldeburgh, Berliner Festwochen, Edin., Flanders, Helsinki, Lucerne, Salzburg, Tanglewood, Spoleto, Hollywood Bowl, Ravinia; with leading orchestras from USA, UK, Israel, Australia; recent performances include La Voix Humaine, Orchestre nat. de Lyon 2002; Founder and Pres. L'Orchidee Inc.; mem. Bd of Dirs Ms. Foundation, New York Botanical Garden, Nat. Music Foundation, City-Meals-on-Wheels (New York City); Trustee, Paine Coll., Augusta, Ga; spokesperson Partnership for the Homeless; Fellow, American Acad. of Arts and Sciences; Commdr, Ordre des Arts et des Lettres 1984; Hon. MusDoc (Howard) 1982, (Univ. of the South, Sewance) 1984, (Univ. of Mich.) 1987, (Edin.) 1989; Hon. DMus (Cambridge) 1989; Grand Prix du Disque (Acad. du Disque Français) 1973, 1976, 1977, 1982; Deutsche Schallplatten Preis für Euryanthe 1975; Cigale d'Or (Aix-en-Provence Festival) 1977; Grammy Award 1980, 1982, 1985, Musician of the Year (Musical America) 1982, IRCAM Record Award 1982, Alumna Award (Univ. of Michigan) 1982, Edison Award for Lifetime Achievement, Amsterdam 2006. *Leisure interests:* reading, cooking, houseplant growing, fashion designing. *Address:* 244 Mount Airy Road West, Croton On Hudson, NY 10520-3311; Philips Records Polygram, 825 8th Avenue, New York, NY 10019, USA.

NORMAN, Marsha, BA, MAT; American playwright and writer; b. 21 Sept. 1947, Louisville, KY; d. of Billie Williams and Bertha Conley; m. 1st Michael Norman (divorced 1974); m. 2nd Dann C. Byck Jr 1978 (divorced); m. 3rd Timothy Dykman; one s. one d.; ed Agnes Scott Coll. and Univ. of Louisville; Rockefeller playwright-in-residence grantee 1979–80; American Acad. and Inst. for Arts and Letters grantee; Pulitzer Prize for Drama 1983; Tony Award 1991; many other awards and prizes. *Plays:* Getting Out 1977, Third and Oak 1978, Circus Valentine 1979, Merry Christmas 1979, The Holdup 1980, 'Night, Mother 1982, Traveler in the Dark 1984, The Fortune Teller 1987, Sarah and Abraham 1987, The Secret Garden (musical) 1991, D. Boone 1991–92, Loving Daniel Boone 1992, The Red Shoes 1992, Trudy Blues 1995, Love's Fire 1998, 140 1998, Last Dance 2003, The Color Purple 2005. *Television plays:* It's the Willingness 1978, In Trouble at Fifteen 1980, The Laundromat 1985, The Pool Hall 1989, Face of a Stranger 1991. *Publications:* The Fortune Teller (novel) 1987; books of lyrics; plays. *Address:* The Gersh Agency, 41 Madison Avenue, 33rd Floor, New York, NY 10010, USA (office). *Telephone:* (212) 997-1818 (office). *Fax:* (212) 997-1818 (office). *E-mail:* info@gershla.com (office). *Website:* www.gershagency.com (office).

NORMURODOV, Mamarizo Berdimurodovich; Uzbekistan politician; Minister of Finance 2000–04. *Address:* c/o Ministry of Finance, Mustaqillik maydoni 5, 100008 Tashkent, Uzbekistan (office). *Telephone:* (71) 133-70-73 (office). *Fax:* (71) 144-56-43 (office).

NORODOM RANARIDDH, Prince; Cambodian politician; b. 2 Jan. 1944; s. of King Norodom Sihanouk; m. 1968; two s. one d.; ed Univ. of Aix-Marseilles, France; worked with resistance leaders during early 1970s, arrested, acquitted on charges of engaging in terrorism 1971, returned to France in mid-1970s to teach at alma mater; Supreme Commander ANS 1985, C-in-C and Chief of Staff 1986; Pres. United Nat. Front for an Ind., Neutral, Peaceful and Co-operative Cambodia (FUNCINPEC); Co-Chair. Provisional Nat. Govt of Cambodia, also Minister of Nat. Defence, Interior and Nat. Security June–Sept. 1993; mem. Nat. Ass. 1993 (fmr Pres.); Co-Prime Minister and mem. Throne Council Sept.–Oct. 1993; First Prime Minister of Royal Govt of Cambodia 1993–97; Chair. Nat. Devt Council 1993–97; found guilty of conspiracy with Khmer Rouges to overthrow the Govt, sentenced to 30 years imprisonment; in exile; returned from exile May 1998; Prof. of Public Law. *Leisure interest:* aviation.

NORODOM SIHAMONI, HM King of Cambodia; b. 14 May 1953, Phnom Penh; s. of HM King Norodom Sihanouk and HM Queen Norodom Monineath Sihanouk; ed Norodom School, Descartes High School, Phnom Penh, Prague High School, Nat. Conservatory of Prague, Acad. of Musical Art, Prague,

Czechoslovakia (now Czech Repub.); studied dance, music, theatre and cinematography; Prof. of Classical Dance and Artistic Pedagogy, Marius Petipa Conservatory, Gabriel Faure Conservatory, W. A. Mozart Conservatory, Paris 1981–2004; Pres. Khmer Dance Asscn, France 1984–2004; Dir-Gen. and Artistic Dir Deva Ballet Group 1984–2004; Dir-Gen. and Artistic Dir Khmer Cinematographic Soc.'Khemara Pictures' 1990–2004; Perm. Rep. to UN 1992–2004; Amb. to UNESCO 1993–2004; elevated to rank of Sdech Krom Khun (Great Prince) 1994; crowned King of Cambodia Oct. 2004; Grand Collier de L'Ordre National de l'Independence, Grand Cross of the Royal Order of Monisaraphon, Grand Cross of the Légion d'honneur, Grand Cross of the Royal Order of Cambodia. *Address:* Royal Palace, Phnom Penh, Cambodia. *E-mail:* cabinet@norodomsihanouk.info.

NORODOM SIHANOUK, fmr King of Cambodia Samdech Preah; b. 31 Oct. 1922, Phnom Penh; s. of the late King Norodom Suramarit and Queen Kossamak Nearireath; m. Queen Norodom Monineath Sihanouk; fourteen c. (six deceased); ed Chasseloup-Labaut High School, Saigon (now Ho Chi Minh City), Viet Nam, School of Instruction, Army Cavalry and Armoured Div., Saumur, France; mil. training in Saumur, France; elected King by Council of the Crown April 1941, claimed and obtained independence of Cambodia from France 1952–53, abdicated in favour of his father HM Norodom Suramarit March 1955, granted rank of Samdech and title of Upayuvareach of Cambodia; f. Sangkum Reastr Niyum (People's Socialist Community) 1955, (Leader 1955–70), won 82% of vote at legislative elections 1955; Prime Minister and Minister of Foreign Affairs Oct. 1955, March 1956, Sept. 1956, April 1957; Co-Founder Movt of Non-aligned Countries 1956; Perm. Rep. to UN Feb.–Sept. 1956; elected Head of State after death of his father 1960, took oath of fidelity to vacant throne 1960, deposed while on official visit to Soviet Union by forces of Lon Nol and Siri Matak March 1970; became Pres. Cambodian Resistance (FUNC –Nat. United Front of Cambodia) March 1970; resided in Peking (now Beijing), People's Repub. of China; est. Royal Govt of Nat. Union of Cambodia (GRUNC) May 1970; restored as Head of State (Pres.) of Democratic Kampuchea when FUNC forces overthrew Khmer Repub. April 1975, resgnd April 1976; Special Envoy of Khmer Rouge to UN 1979; f. Nat. United Front for an Ind., Neutral, Peaceful Co-operative Kampuchea 1981–89; Head of State in exile of Govt of Democratic Kampuchea and Head Cambodian Nat. Resistance 1982–88, 1989–90; in exile 13 years, returned to Cambodia Oct. 1991; Chair. Supreme Nat. Council 1991–93; Pres. of Cambodia 1991–93; crowned King of Cambodia Sept. 1993–2004 (abdicated); C-in-C of Armed Forces June 1993–; musician and composer; producer of films including Le Petit Prince. *Publications:* L'Indochine vue de Pékin (with Jean Lacouture) 1972, My War With the C.I.A. (with Wilfred Burchett) 1973, War and Hope: The Case for Cambodia 1980, Souvenirs doux et amers 1981, Prisonnier des Khmers Rouges 1986, Charisme et Leadership 1989. *Leisure interests:* badminton, film making in DPR Korea, French style cooking in Beijing. *Address:* Khemarindra Palace, Phnom Penh, Cambodia.

NORONHA NASCIMENTO, Luís António; Portuguese judge; *President, Supreme Court of Justice;* b. 1943, Porto; early career as Asst to Public Prosecutor for Comarcas de Paredes, Pombal e Santo Tirso; Judge for Trancoso, Marco de Canavezes, Vila Nova de Famalicão, Vila Nova de Gaia and Porto; Judge Court of Appeal, Lisbon –1994; mem. Superior Council of Magistrates 1989–90, Vice-Pres. 2001–; Judge Supreme Court of Justice 1994–98, Vice-Pres. 1998–2006, Pres. 2006–; mem. Portuguese Asscn of Judges 1984–88, Pres. 1992–96. *Address:* Supremo Tribunal da Justiça, Praça do Comércio, 1149-012 Lisbon, Portugal (office). *Telephone:* (213) 477449 (office). *Fax:* (213) 430300 (office). *E-mail:* gabinete.presidente@stj.pt (office). *Website:* www.stj.pt (office).

NOROV, Vladimir Imamovich, PhD; Uzbekistani diplomatist and government official; *Minister of Foreign Affairs;* b. 31 Aug. 1955, Buxoro; m.; three c.; ed Buxoro State Pedagogical Inst., Moscow Acad. of Internal Affairs; school teacher 1976; mil. service 1976–77; worked in Dept of Internal Affairs, Buxoro 1978–88, Head of Criminal Investigation Dept 1990–93; consultant on admin. and legal issues, Pres.'s Office 1993–95, State Adviser for Foreign Relations 1996–98; Deputy Minister of Foreign Affairs 1995–96, First Deputy Minister of Foreign Affairs 2003–04, Minister of Foreign Affairs 2006–; Amb. to Germany 1998–2003 (also accred to Switzerland and Poland 2002–03); Amb. to Belgium and Chief of Missions to EU and NATO, Brussels 2004–06. *Address:* Ministry of Foreign Affairs, 100029 Tashkent, O'zbekiston shoh ko'ch. 9, Uzbekistan (office). *Telephone:* (71) 233-64-75 (office). *Fax:* (71) 239-15-17 (office). *E-mail:* letter@mfa.uz (office). *Website:* www.mfa.uz (office).

NORRBACK, Johan Ole; Finnish diplomatist and politician; *Ambassador for Baltic Sea Issues, Ministry of Foreign Affairs;* b. 18 March 1941, Övermark; m. Vivi-Anna Lindqvist 1959; two c.; teacher 1966–67; Dist Sec. Swedish People's Party in Ostrobothnia 1967–71; Exec. Man. Prov. Union of Swedish Ostrobothnia 1971–91; Political Sec. to Minister of Communications 1976–77; mem. Parl. 1979–87, 1991–99; mem. Exec. Cttee Svenska Folkpartiet (SFP) (Swedish People's Party) 1983–89, Chair. 1990–99; Minister of Defence 1987–90, of Educ. and Science 1990–91, of Transport and Communications 1991–95, for Europe and Foreign Trade 1995–99; Amb. to Norway 1999–2003, to Greece 2003–07; Amb. for Baltic Sea Issues, Ministry for Foreign Affairs 2007–, Special Adviser to the Prime Minister on border obstacles between Nordic countries 2007–. *Address:* Ministry for Foreign Affairs, Maringatan 22H, 00161 Helsingfors, Finland (office); c/o Svenska Folkpartiet (SFP), Simonsgatan 8A, 00100 Helsinki, Finland. *Telephone:* (9) 16055438 (office). *Fax:* (9) 16055653 (office). *E-mail:* ole.norrback@formin.fi (office).

NORRINGTON, Sir Roger Arthur Carver, Kt, CBE; British conductor; b. 16 March 1934; s. of Sir Arthur Norrington and Edith Joyce Carver; m. 1st Susan Elizabeth McLean May 1964 (divorced 1982); one s. one d.; m. 2nd Karalyn Mary Lawrence 1986; one s.; ed Dragon School, Oxford, Westminster School, Clare Coll. Cambridge, Royal Coll. of Music; freelance singer 1962–72; Prin. Conductor, Kent Opera 1966–84; Guest Conductor with many British and European orchestras, appearances BBC Promenade Concerts and City of London, Bath, Aldeburgh, Edin. and Harrogate festivals; regular broadcasts UK, Europe, USA; Prin. Conductor Bournemouth Sinfonietta 1985–89; Assoc. Chief Guest Conductor London Philharmonic Orchestra 1993–; Chief Conductor South German Radio Orchestra 1997–, Camerata Academica Salzburg 1997–2007; conductor Radio Sinfonie Orchester, Stuttgart 1998–; Musical Dir London Classical Players 1978–97, London Baroque Players 1975–, Schütz Choir of London 1962, Orchestra of St Lukes, NY 1990–94; Co.-Dir Early Opera Project 1984–, Historic Arts 1986–; many gramophone recordings; Hon. DMus (Kent) 1994; Cavaliere, Ordine al Merito della Repubblica Italiana, Ehrenkreuz Erster Klasse (Austia) 1999. *Leisure interests:* reading, walking, sailing. *Telephone:* (1635) 37231. *Fax:* (1635) 34681. *E-mail:* kay@norrington.info.

NORRIS, David Owen, MA, FRAM, FRCO; British pianist and broadcaster; *Professor, Royal College of Music;* b. 16 June 1953, Northampton; s. of Albert Norris and Margaret Norris; two s.; ed Keble Coll. Oxford, Royal Acad. of Music, and privately in Paris; Prof., RAM 1977–89; Dir Petworth Festival 1986–92; Artistic Dir Cardiff Festival 1992–95; Chair. Steans Inst. for Singers, Chicago 1992–98; Gresham Prof. of Music, London 1993–97; Prof., Royal Coll. of Music 2000–; Lecturer in Music and Head of Keyboard, Univ. of Southampton 2000–07, Prof. of Musical Performance 2007–; Fellow, Worshipful Co. of Musicians 2005; Hon. Fellow, Keble Coll., Oxford 2006; First Gilmore Artist Award 1991. *Recordings:* Complete piano music of Elgar, Dyson, Quilter and the World's First Piano Concertos. *Achievements:* gave world premières of Schubert's First Song Cycle and Elgar's Piano Concerto (also on CD). *Leisure interests:* naval and detective fiction. *Address:* Ikon Arts, Suite 111, Office E, Business Design Centre, 52 Upper Street, London N1 0QH, England (office); 17 Manor Road, Andover, Hants., SP10 3JS, England (home). *Telephone:* (20) 7354-9199 (office); (1264) 355409 (home). *Fax:* (20) 7281-9687 (office). *E-mail:* info@ikonarts.com (office); info@davidowennorris.com (home). *Website:* www.ikonarts.com (office); davidowennorris.com.

NORRIS, Elwood (Woody); American inventor and engineer; *Chairman, American Technology Corporation;* b. Barrelville, Cumberland, MD; m.; eleven c.; ed Univ. of New Mexico; joined USAF 1956, trained as Nuclear Weapons Specialist, Monzano Base, New Mexico; cameraman, American Broadcasting Corpn (ABC) TV network, Albuquerque 1958; joined Tech. Staff, Univ. of Wash. 1959, Dir Eng Experiment Station –1970; worked for Heath Technic Corpn 1970s; f. American Tech. Corpn, San Diego 1980, currently Chair.; commercial contracts with automobile cos, supermarket chains, museums, airports and US Dept of Defense; inventions include Transcutaneous Doppler System (precursor to sonogram) 1967, tone arm, unidirectional microphone, virtual speaker, electrostatic transducer, holographic transparent speaker, magnetic film, ear-mounted speaker/microphone device (designed for NASA astronaut helmets, now used for cell phone headsets), Flashback®, HyperSonic Sound®, AirScooter® ultralight helicopter, hydrogen-poweres automobiles, artificial hip alarm; holds 47 US patents and over 300 patents worldwide; licensed pilot; Lemelson-MIT Inventor of the Year Award 2005. *Leisure interests:* flying airplanes. *Address:* American Technology Corporation, 13114 Evening Creek Drive South, San Diego, CA 92128, USA (office). *Telephone:* (858) 679-2114 (office). *Fax:* (858) 679-0545 (office). *E-mail:* info@atcsd.com (office). *Website:* www.atcsd.com (office).

NORRIS, Ralph James; New Zealand banking executive; *Managing Director and CEO, Commonwealth Bank of Australia;* b. Auckland; ed Lynfield Coll.; began career as commercial cadet, Mobil Oil NZ 1967–69; joined Auckland Savings Bank (ASB) Ltd 1969, Man. Dir and CEO 1991–2001; Head of Int. Financial Services, Commonwealth Bank of Australia 1999–2001, Man. Dir and CEO 2005–; mem. Bd of Dirs Air New Zealand Ltd 1998–2005, Man. Dir and CEO 2002–05; fmr Chair. NZ Bankers Asscn, Business Roundtable, Hosting Cttee of Asia–Pacific Econ. Council CEO Summit; mem. Bd of Dirs Fletcher Building Ltd 2001–05, Team NZ Defence 2003; fmr mem. Prime Minister's Enterprise Council, Prime Minister's Y2K Task Force, Pacific Basin Econ. Council; Fellow, NZ Inst. of Man., NZ Computer Soc.; mem. Starship Foundation Trust, Knowledge Wave Trust, Northern Lifeguard Services Trust; Distinguished Companion, NZ Order of Merit 2006; NZ Exec. of the Year Award 1997, 2004. *Address:* Commonwealth Bank of Australia, Level 7, 48 Martin Place, Sydney 1155, Australia (office). *Telephone:* (2) 9378-2000 (office). *Fax:* (2) 9378-3317 (office). *E-mail:* info@commbank.com.au (office). *Website:* www.commbank.com.au (office).

NORRIS, Steve; British film producer; fmrly with Rank Org.; fmr exec. Columbia Pictures, Warner Brothers, Enigma, USA; fmr Vice-Pres. Producers' Alliance for Cinema and TV, Chair. Film Cttee; British Film Commr 1998–2000; several awards, including Golden Globe for The Burning Season. *Films include:* Memphis Belle, Being Human, War of the Buttons, The Burning Season, Le Confessionnal, My Life So Far.

NORRIS, Steven, MA; British politician and business executive; *Executive Chairman, Jarvis plc;* b. 24 May 1945, Liverpool; s. of John Francis Birkett and Eileen Winifred Walsh; m. 1st Peta Veronica Cecil-Gibson 1969 (divorced); two s.; m. 2nd Emma Courtney 2000; one s.; ed Liverpool Inst. High School, Worcester Coll., Oxford; Berks. Co. Councillor 1977–85; various man. positions in industry –1983; MP for Oxford E 1983–87, for Epping Forest 1988–97; Parl. Pvt. Sec. to William Waldegrave, Minister of State, Dept of Environment 1985–87, to Nicholas Ridley, Sec. of State for Trade and Industry 1990, to Kenneth Baker, Home Sec. 1991–92; Minister for Transport in London 1992–96; Dir-Gen. Road Haulage Asscn 1997–99; Conservative cand. for Mayoralty of London 2000, 2004; Vice-Chair. Conservative Party 2000–01; mem. Bd Transport for London –2001; Sr Partner, Park Place

Communications 2003–; Exec. Chair. Jarvis plc 2004–; Chair. AMT-Sybex Ltd; Sr Ind. Dir ITIS Holdings plc; Chair. East Side Young Leaders Acad., British Urological Foundation; Companion Inst. of Civil Engineers; Trustee London Action Trust; Freeman of the City of London; Liveryman of the Worshipful Co. of Coachmakers and Coach Harness Makers, Worshipful Co. of Carmen; Craftowning Freeman of Co. of Watchmen and Lightermen of City of London. *Publication:* Changing Train 1996. *Leisure interests:* football, opera, reading. *Address:* Jarvis plc, Meridian House, The Crescent, York, YO24 1AW, England (office). *Telephone:* (1904) 712712 (office). *Website:* www.jarvis -uk.com (office).

NORSHTEIN, Yuri Borisovich; Russian film director, animator and scriptwriter; b. 15 Sept. 1941, Andreyevka, Penza Region; s. of Berko Leibovich Norshtein and Basya Girshevna Krichevskaya; m. Francesca Alfredovna Yarbusova; one s. one d.; ed Soyuzmultfilmstudio courses; debut as film dir The 25th is the First Day 1968 (co-dir with Arkady Tyurin); cutout film Battle at Kerzhenets 1971 (co-dir with I. Ivanov-Vano); later with his wife (art dir Yarbusova): Fox and Hare 1973, Heron and Crane 1974, Hedgehog in Mist 1975, The Tale of Tales 1979, Great Coat 2002; Tale of Tales voted best animated film of all time 1984 in int. survey, LA Animation Olympiad; Tarkovsky Prize 1989; Grand Prix Zagreb Animation Festival 1980; USSR State Prize 1979, Triumph Prize 1995. *Address:* Butlerov str. 4, korp. 2, Apt. 88, 117485 Moscow, Russia (home). *Telephone:* (495) 335-08-21 (home).

NORTEN, Enrique, BArch, MArch; Mexican architect and teacher; *Principal, TEN Arquitectos (Taller de Enrique Norten Arquitectos, SC);* b. 27 Feb. 1954, Mexico City; ed Universidad Iberoamericana, Mexico City, Cornell Univ., USA; Pnr, Albin y Norten Arquitectos SC, Mexico City 1981; f. TEN Arquitectos (Taller de Enrique Norten Arquitectos, SC) 1986, currently Prin.; involved in projects of different types and scales, including furniture design, single-family apartments and houses, residential, commercial and cultural bldgs, parks, urban design and redevelopment projects; Prof. of Architecture, Universidad Iberoamericana, Mexico City 1980–90; currently holds Miller Chair, Univ. of Pennsylvania, Phila; fmr holder of O'Neal Ford Chair in Architecture, Univ. of Texas at Austin; fmr Lorch Prof. of Architecture, Univ. of Michigan; fmr Eero Saarinen Visiting Prof. of Architectural Design, Yale School of Architecture; fmr Visiting Prof., UCLA Dept of Architecture and Urban Design, Cornell Univ., Parsons School of Design, Pratt Inst., Sci-Arc, Rice Univ., Columbia Univ.; fmr Elliot Noyes Visiting Design Critic, Harvard Univ.; has participated in several int. exhbns, int. juries and award cttees, including World Trade Center Site Memorial Competition, New York, Holcim Foundation for Sustainable Construction; mem. Bd Trustees Deutsche Bank 2006–; Hon. FAIA 1999; Mies van der Rohe Award 1998, Nat. Creator System Grant 2000, Gold Medal, Soc. of American Registered Architects 2003, Design Award, Boston Soc. of Architects 2004, 2005, Certificate of Merit, Municipal Art Soc. of New York 2004, 'Leonardo da Vinci' World Award of Arts, World Cultural Council 2005, 'Legacy Award', Smithsonian Inst. 2007. *Projects include:* Nat. School of Theater at Nat. Center of the Arts, Churubusco, Mexico City, Televisa Mixed Use Bldg, Mexico City (First Prize 'Mies van der Rohe Pavilion' of Latin American Architecture, Barcelona 1998), House RR, Mexico City (Design Excellence in Housing, Boston Soc. of Architects 2004), Hotel HABITA (Latin American Bldg of the Year, World Architecture Awards/RIBA, London 2002, Business Week/ Architectural Record Awards and AIA New York Chapter Award 2003), Educare in Zapopan, Jalisco (Hon. Mention at VII Mexican Architecture Biennial, First Prize of Int. Design, XIII Bienal de Arquitectura de Quito, Ecuador, AIA New York Chapter Award 2003), Princeton Parking Garage Structure (Gold Medal, AIA/New Jersey Design Awards 2002), Parque España Residential Bldg, Colonia Condesa, Mexico City (Design Excellence in Housing, Boston Soc. of Architects 2004, Guggenheim Museum, Guadalajara (AIA New York Chapter Design Awards Citation 2006) 2005. *Address:* TEN Arquitectos, 22 West 19th Street, 7th Floor, New York, NY 10011, USA (office); TEN Arquitectos, Cuernavaca 114/PB, Colonia Condesa, 06140 Mexico City DF, Mexico (office). *Telephone:* (212) 620-0794 (New York) (office); (55) 5211-8004 (Mexico City) (office). *Fax:* (212) 620-0798 (New York) (office); (55) 5286-1735 (Mexico City) (office). *E-mail:* ten@ten-arquitectos.com (office). *Website:* www.ten-arquitectos.com (office).

NORTH, Alastair Macarthur, OBE, PhD, DSc; British professor of chemistry (retd); b. 2 April 1932, Aberdeen; s. of Norman R. North and Anne North; m. Charlotte Muriel Begg 1957; two s. two d.; ed Univs of Aberdeen and Birmingham; Lecturer, Dept of Inorganic, Physical and Industrial Chem., Univ. of Liverpool; apptd to Burmah Chair of Physical Chem., Univ. of Strathclyde 1967, subsequently Dean of School of Chemical and Materials Science, then Vice-Prin. of the Univ.; Pres., Asian Inst. of Tech. 1983–96; mem. several nat. cttees on formation of science policy; Commdr des Palmes académiques; Commdr, Order of King Leopold II (Belgium); Prasidda Prabala Gorkha Dakshin Bahu (Nepal); Hon. ScD (Politechnika Lodzka), Hon. PhD (Ramkhamhaeng Univ.), Hon. DUniv (Strathclyde), Hon. DTech (AIT), Hon. LLD (Aberdeen), Dr hc (Inst. Nat. Polytechnique de Toulouse). *Leisure interest:* gardening. *Address:* 79/78 Soi 7/1 Mooban Tararom, Ramkhamhaeng Soi 150, Sapansoong, Bangkok 10240, Thailand. *Telephone:* (2) 373-2818 (home). *Fax:* (2) 373-3052 (home).

NORTH, Douglass Cecil, PhD; American economist and academic; *Spencer T. Olin Professor in Arts and Sciences, Department of Economics, Washington University;* b. 5 Nov. 1920, Cambridge, Mass; s. of Henry North and Edith Saitta; m. Elisabeth Willard Case 1972; three s. by previous m.; ed Univ. of Calif. at Berkeley; Asst Prof., Univ. of Washington 1950–56, Assoc. Prof. 1957–60, Prof. of Econs 1960–63, Prof. Emer. 1983–, Chair. Dept of Econs 1967–79; Dir Inst. of Econ. Research 1960–66, Nat. Bureau of Econ. Research 1967–87; Pitt Prof. of American History and Inst., Univ. of Cambridge, UK 1981–82; Luce Prof. of Law and Liberty, Prof. of Econs, Washington Univ., St Louis 1983–, Spencer T. Olin Prof. in Arts and Sciences 1996–; Bartlett Burnap Sr Fellow, Hoover Inst. 2000–; mem. Bradley Foundation 1986–; Fellow, Center for Advanced Study on Behavioral Sciences 1987–88; Guggenheim Fellow 1972–73; Fellow, American Acad. of Arts and Sciences; mem. American Econ. Asscn, Econ. History Asscn; Hon. Dr rer. pol (Cologne) 1988, (Zürich) 1993, (Stockholm School of Econs) 1994, (Prague School of Econs) 1995; shared Nobel Prize for Econs 1993. *Publications:* The Economic Growth of the US 1790–1860 1961, Growth and Welfare in the American Past 1971, Institutional Change and American Economic Growth (with L. Davis) 1971, The Economics of Public Issues (with R. Miller) 1971, The Rise of the Western World (with R. Thomas) 1973, Structure and Change in Economic History 1981, Institutions, Institutional Change and Economic Performance 1990, Understanding the Process of Economic Change 2004. *Address:* Department of Economics, Eliot 305, Washington University, Campus Box 1208, St Louis, MO 63130, USA (office). *Telephone:* (314) 935-5809 (office); (314) 935-5670 (office). *Fax:* (314) 935-4156 (office). *E-mail:* north@economics .wustl.edu (office). *Website:* economics.wustl.edu (office).

NORTH, Oliver L.; American radio show host and fmr marine officer; b. 7 Oct. 1943, San Antonio, Tex.; s. of Oliver Clay North and Ann North; m.; c.; ed US Naval Acad., Annapolis; served 22 years with US Marines, platoon Commdr Viet Nam; marine instructor 1969; leader marine mission, Turkey 1980; mem. Nat. Security Council staff as Deputy Dir for Political Mil. Affairs 1981–86; dismissed Nov. 1986 because of involvement with secret operation to sell arms to Iran and the diversion of proceeds from the sales to aid anti-govt 'Contra' guerrillas in Nicaragua; rank of Lt-Col 1983, retd from Marines 1988; found guilty on three counts May 1989, appeal court reversed one count 1990, three convictions set aside 1990; cleared of all charges 1991; f. Freedom Alliance 1990, now Hon. Chair.; radio show host 1995–; TV host War Stories with Oliver North; Dr hc (Liberty Univ.) 1988. *Publication:* Under Fire: An American Story 1991. *Address:* c/o Freedom Alliance, 22570 Markey Court, Suite 240, Dulles, VA 20166, USA. *Telephone:* (703) 444-7940. *Fax:* (703) 444-9893. *Website:* www.freedomalliance.org.

NORTH, Sir Peter Machin, Kt, CBE, QC, MA, DCL, FBA; British academic; *Chairman, Finance Committee, Oxford University Press;* b. 30 Aug. 1936, Nottingham; s. of Geoffrey Machin North and Freda Brunt North (née Smith); m. Stephanie Mary Chadwick 1960; two s. one d.; ed Oakham School, Rutland, Keble Coll., Oxford; Teaching Assoc., Northwestern Univ. Law School, Chicago 1960–61; Lecturer, Univ. Coll. of Wales, Aberystwyth 1961–63, Univ. of Nottingham 1964–65; Fellow and Tutor in Law, Keble Coll. Oxford 1965–76; Chair. Faculty of Law, Univ. of Oxford 1971–75; Prin. Jesus Coll., Oxford 1984–; Pro-Vice-Chancellor Univ. of Oxford 1988–93, 1997–, Vice-Chancellor 1993–97; Ed. Oxford Journal of Legal Studies 1987–92; Law Commr for England and Wales 1976–84; mem. Lord Chancellor's Advisory Cttee on Legal Educ. 1973–75, Council of Man., British Inst. of Int. and Comparative Law 1976–, Econ. and Social Research Council Cttees 1982–87, Council, Univ. of Reading 1986–89, Finance Cttee, Oxford Univ. Press 1993– (Chair. 2005–), Sr Salaries Review Body 2004–, Accountancy Investigation and Discipline Bd Tribunal 2005–, Academic Council and Int. Advisory Bd, Univ. Canada West 2004–; Chair. Conciliation Advisory Cttee 1985–88, Road Traffic Law Review 1985–88, Ind. Review of Parades and Marches in Northern Ireland 1996–97, Ind. Cttee for Supervision of Standards of Telephone Information Services 1999–; mem. Inst. de droit int.; Visitor, Ashmolean Museum, Oxford 2004–; Hon. Bencher, Inner Temple; Hon. Fellow, Keble Coll. Oxford, Jesus Coll. Oxford, Univ. Coll. of N Wales, Bangor, Trinity Coll., Carmarthen, Univ. of Wales, Aberystwyth; Hon. LLD (Reading) 1992, (Nottingham) 1996, (Aberdeen) 1997, (New Brunswick) 2002; Hon. DHumLitt (Arizona) 2005. *Publications:* Occupier's Liability 1971, Modern Law of Animals 1972, Chitty on Contracts (ed.) 1968–89, Private International Law of Matrimonial Causes 1977, Contract Conflicts (ed.) 1982, Cases and Materials on Private International Law (with J. H. C. Morris) 1984, Cheshire and North's Private International Law (ed.) 1970–99, Private International Law Problems in Common Law Jurisdictions 1993, Essays in Private International Law 1993. *Address:* Oxford University Press, Great Clarendon Street, Oxford, OX2 6DP, England (office). *Telephone:* (1865) 556767 (office); (1865) 557011 (home). *E-mail:* peter.north@oup.com (office). *Website:* www.oup.com (office).

NORTH, Richard; British business executive; *Chairman, Woolworths Group PLC;* b. 1950; Group Finance Dir Bass PLC 1994, Chief Exec., Hotels Div. 2002; CEO InterContinental Hotels Group PLC 2002–04; mem. Bd of Dirs Woolworths Group PLC 2006–, Chair. 2007–; mem. Bd of Dirs Mecom Group PLC 2007–, Majid al Futteim Group LLC; fmr Chair. Britvic Soft Drinks, The Burton Group PLC; fmr mem. Bd of Dirs (non-exec.) Asda Group PLC, Leeds United PLC, Logica PLC, Six Continents Ltd, Mitchells & Butlers PLC, Orchid Drinks Ltd; fmr mem. Exec. Cttee World Travel and Tourism Council. *Address:* Woolworths Group PLC, Woolworth House, 242-246 Marylebone Road, London, NW1 6JL, England (office). *Telephone:* (20) 7262-1222 (office). *Fax:* (20) 7706-5416 (office). *Website:* www.woolworthsgroupplc.com (office).

NORTHFLEET, Ellen Gracie; Brazilian judge; b. 16 Feb. 1948, Rio de Janeiro; d. of José Barros Northfleet and Helena Northfleet; m. (divorced); one d.; ed Universidade do Estado da Guanabara, Universidade Federal do Rio Grande do Sul; Public Prosecutor (1st Level) 1980–89; Prof. of Law, Universidade Federal do Rio Grande do Sul 1983–87, Universidade do Vale do Rio dos Sinos 1987–; mem. Fed. Public Ministry 1973–1989; mem. Regional Electoral Tribune, Rio Grande do Sul 1989–2000, Pres. 1997–2000; Minister for Supreme Fed. Tribunal 2000–2004, Vice Pres. 2004–06, Pres. 2006–08; Pres., Nat. Justice Council 2006–08; Fulbright Scholar, American Univ., Washington DC 1991–92; mem. Fulbright Alumni Asscn of Brazil; Jurist in

Residence, Library of Congress, USA 1992; Hon. mem. Federal Judiciary of the United States 2006; Santos Dumont Medal 1977, Grand Official of the Order of Merit 2001, Grand Cross of the Order of Rio Branco 2006, numerous other decorations. *Publications:* numerous articles in professional journals. *Address:* c/o Supremo Tribunal Federal, Praça dos Três Poderes, 70175-900 Brasília, DF, Brazil (office).

NORTON, Edward, BA; American actor; b. 18 Aug. 1969, Boston, Mass.; s. of Edward Norton and the late Robin Norton (née Rouse); ed Wilde Lake High School, Md, Yale Univ., Columbia School for Theatrical Arts, Md; fmr consultant Enterprise Foundation, Osaka, Japan, currently mem. Nat. Bd; mem. Signature Theatre Repertory Co. 1994–, performed in the premiere of Edward Albee's Fragments, mem. Bd 1996–; Co-founder Class 5 Films (production co.). *Plays:* Burn This (Obie Award). *Films include:* Primal Fear (Golden Globe, Best Supporting Actor) 1996, Everyone Says I Love You 1996, The People vs. Larry Flynt 1996, American History X 1998, Rounders 1998, Fight Club 1999, Keeping the Faith (also dir and producer), The Score, Death to Smoochy, Red Dragon 2002, The 25th Hour 2001, Frida 2002 (also co-wrote screenplay), The Italian Job 2003, Down in the Valley 2004, Kingdom of Heaven 2005, The Illusionist 2006, The Painted Veil 2006, Pride and Glory 2007, The Incredible Hulk 2008. *Television includes:* host, National Geographic's Strange Days on Planet Earth. *Address:* c/o Endeavor Talent Agency, 9701 Wiltshire Boulevard, 10th Floor, Beverly Hills, CA 90210, USA (office).

NORTON, Gale Ann, BA, JD; American lawyer and fmr government official; *General Counsel, Shell Exploration and Production, Unconventional Resources, Royal Dutch Shell PLC;* b. 11 March 1954, Wichita, Kan.; d. of Dale Bentsen Norton and Anna Jacqueline Norton (née Lansdowne); m. John Goethe Hughes 1990; ed Univ. of Denver; lawyer, Colo 1978, US Supreme Court 1981; judicial clerk, Colo Court of Appeals 1978–79, Sr Attorney, Mountain States Legal Foundation 1979–83; Nat. Fellow, Hoover Inst., Stanford Univ. 1983–84; Asst to Deputy Sec., US Dept of Agric., Washington, DC 1984–85; Assoc. Solicitor, US Dept of Interior 1985–87; pvt. law practice 1987–90; Attorney-Gen., Colo 1991–99; attorney, Brownstein, Hyatt & Farber, PC, Sr Counsel 1999–2001; US Sec. of the Interior, Washington, DC 2001–06; Gen. Counsel, Royal Dutch Shell 2006–; Transportation Law Program Dir, Univ. of Denver 1978–79, Lecturer, Univ. of Denver Law School 1989; Past Chair. Nat. Asscn of Attorneys Environmental Cttee; Co-Chair. Nat. Policy Forum Environmental Council; Chair. Environmental Comm. of Republican Nat. Lawyers Asscn; Policy Analyst, Presidential Council on Environmental Quality 1985–88; Young Lawyer of the Year 1991, Mary Trailblazer Award, Colo Women's Bar Asscn 1999. *Leisure interest:* skiing. *Address:* 6645 South Quemoy Circle, Aurora, CO 80016-2686; Shell Exploration and Production, Unconventional Resources, Denver Tech Center, 10333 East Dry Creek Road, Englewood, CO 80112, USA (office).

NORTON, Hugh Edward, BA; British business executive; b. 23 June 1936, London; s. of Lt-Gen. Edward F. Norton and I. Joyce Norton; m. 1st Janet M. Johnson 1965 (died 1993); one s.; m. 2nd F. Joy Harcup 1998; ed Winchester Coll., Trinity Coll. Oxford; joined British Petroleum Co. 1959, Exploration Dept 1960, in Abu Dhabi, Lebanon and Libya 1962–70, subsequently held appointments in Supply, Cen. Planning, Policy Planning, Regional Director-ate Middle East and Int. and Govt Affairs Depts; Man. Dir BP's assoc. cos., Singapore, Malaysia, Hong Kong 1978–81, Dir of Planning 1981–83, Regional Dir for Near East, Middle East and Indian sub-continent 1981–86, Dir of Admin. 1983–86, Man. Dir and CEO BP Exploration Co. 1986–89, Chair. 1989–95, Man. Dir The British Petroleum Co. PLC 1989–95; Chair. BP Asia Pacific Pvt. Co. Ltd 1991–95; Dir Inchcape PLC 1995–, Standard Chartered PLC 1995–, Lasmo PLC 1997–; mem. Council Royal Inst. of Econ. Affairs 1991–. *Leisure interests:* painting, ornithology, tennis, travel. *Address:* c/o BP Asia Pacific Pte Ltd, BP Tower, 25th Storey, 396 Alexandra Road, Singapore 0511.

NORVIK, Harald, MS; Norwegian business executive; b. 21 June 1946, Vadsø; ed Norwegian School of Econs and Business Admin., Bergen; Adviser, Nat. Inst. of Tech. 1971–73; Group Sec. for Industrial and Financial Affairs 1973–75; trainee course, Ministry of Foreign Affairs 1975–76; Personal Sec. to Prime Minister 1976–79; Minister of Petroleum and Energy 1979–81; Dir of Finance Aker mek. Verksted A/S 1981–85, Sr Exec. Vice-Pres. 1985–86; Pres. Astrup Hoyer A/S 1986–87; now Pres. and Chair. Exec. Bd Statoil Group; alternating Chair. Bd of Dirs SAS Norge ASA, Scandinavian Airlines System (SAS); Chair. Supervisory Bd Den Norske Bank; mem. Bd Orkla Borregaard AS, Supervisory Council Nycomed ASA; mem. Advisory Bd OILspace; Commdr Order of the Lion of Finland (1st Class), Grosses Bundesverdienstk-reuz. *Address:* c/o Board of Advisors, OILspace, Aurora House, 5-6 Carlos Place, London, W1K 3AP, England.

NORWICH, 2nd Viscount, cr. 1952, of Aldwick; **John Julius (Cooper),** CVO, FRSL, FRGS; British author and broadcaster; b. 15 Sept. 1929, London; s. of 1st Viscount Norwich, PC, GCMG, DSO and of the late Lady Diana Cooper; m. 1st Anne Clifford 1952 (divorced 1985); one s. one d.; m. 2nd Mollie Philipps 1989; ed Upper Canada Coll. Toronto, Eton Coll., Univ. of Strasbourg, France and New Coll., Oxford; entered Foreign Office 1952; Third Sec. Belgrade 1955–57; Second Sec. Beirut 1957–60; Foreign Office and British del. to Disarmament Conf. Geneva 1960–64; Chair. British Theatre Museum 1966–71, Venice in Peril Fund 1970–99, World Monuments Fund in Britain 1994–; mem. Exec. Cttee Nat. Trust 1969–95; mem. Franco-British Council 1972–79; mem. Bd ENO 1977–81; Ed. New Shell Guides to Britain 1987–91; Dir Robclif Productions Ltd 1991–94; has made over 30 documentary films for TV, mainly on history and architecture; mem. Soc. of Authors, fellow; Commendatore, Ordine al Merito della Repubblica Italiana; Commendatore della Solidarità Italiana; Hadrian Award, World Monuments Fund, New York 2005.

Television: has made some 30 documentary films for TV, mainly on history and architecture. *Publications:* as John Julius Norwich: Mount Athos (with R. Sitwell) 1966, The Normans in the South 1967, Sahara 1968, The Kingdom in the Sun 1970, Great Architecture of the World (ed.) 1975, A History of Venice Vol. I 1977, Vol. II 1981, Christmas Crackers 1970–79 1980, Britain's Heritage (ed.) 1982, The Italian World (ed.) 1983, Fifty Years of Glyndebourne 1985, A Taste for Travel (anthology) 1985, The Architecture of Southern England 1985, Byzantium, the Early Centuries 1988, More Christmas Crackers 1980–89 1990, Venice: a Traveller's Companion 1990, The Oxford Illustrated Encyclopaedia of the Arts, Vol. V (ed.) 1990, Byzantium: The Apogee 1991, Byzantium: Decline and Fall 1995, The Twelve Days of Christmas 1998, Shakespeare's Kings 1999, Still More Christmas Crackers 1990–99 2000, Paradise of Cities 2003, The Middle Sea 2007. *Leisure interests:* sight-seeing, walking at night through Venice, night-club piano. *Address:* 24 Blomfield Road, London, W9 1AD, England. *Telephone:* (20) 7286-5050. *Fax:* (20) 7266-2561. *E-mail:* jjnorwich@dial.pipex.com (home).

NORWOOD, Mandi; British magazine editor; b. 9 Oct. 1963, Oldham, Lancs.; m. Martin Kelly 1995; two d.; ed Lord Lawson Comprehensive School, Park View Grammar School, Darlington Coll. of Tech. and London Coll. of Fashion; Sub-Ed. then Deputy Chief Sub-Ed. Look Now magazine 1984–86; freelance journalist 1986–87; Features Ed. Clothes Show magazine Aug.–Oct. 1987; Deputy Ed. More! magazine 1987–89; Ed. Looks magazine 1989–90, Company magazine 1990–95, Cosmopolitan 1995–2000; Ed.-in-Chief Mademoiselle, New York 2000–01; Founding Ed.-in-Chief SHOP Etc. (shopping magazine) 2004–06; mem. British Soc. of Magazine Eds 1990; mem. Periodical Publrs Asscn Editorial Cttee; Women's Magazine Ed. of the Year Award, British Soc. of Magazine Eds 1993, 1999. *Publications:* Sex & the Married Girl: From Clicking to Climaxing – The Complete Truth About Modern Marriage 2003, The Hitched Chick's Guide to Modern Marriage – Essential Advice for Staying Single Minded and Happily Married 2003, Michelle Style: Celebrating the First Lady of Fashion 2009. *Address:* 312 East 69th Street, New York, NY 10021, USA (home). *Telephone:* (212) 585-0668 (home). *E-mail:* mnk63@msn.com (home).

NOSIGLIA, Enrique; Argentine politician; b. 28 May 1949, Posadas; m. Nina Ciarlotti; four c.; ed Universidad Nacional de Buenos Aires; joined Unión Cívica Radical 1972; mem. Nat. Exec. Movimiento de Renovación y Cambio 1975–80; Sec. Comité de la Capital (Wealth) 1983–87, Pres. 1987; Under-Sec. for Health and Social Affairs, Ministry of Health and Social Affairs 1983–85; Sec. Exec. Comm. Programa Alimentario Nacional (PAN) 1983–85; mem. Consejo para la Consolidación de la Democracia 1986; Minister of the Interior 1987–89; Sec. for Institutional Relations, Unión Cívica Radical.

NOSSAL, Sir Gustav Joseph Victor, AC, CBE, MB, BS, PhD, FRS, FRCP, FRACP, FRCPA, FRCPath, FRSE, FTSE, FAA; Australian medical research scientist; *Professor Emeritus, University of Melbourne;* b. 4 June 1931, Bad Ischl, Austria; s. of R. I. Nossal and I. M. C. Lowenthal; m. Lyn B. Dunnicliff 1955; two s. two d.; ed St Aloysius Coll., Sydney, Univs of Sydney and Melbourne; Jr and Sr Resident Officer, Royal Prince Alfred Hosp., Sydney 1955–56; Research Fellow, The Walter and Eliza Hall Inst. of Medical Research, Melbourne 1957–59, Deputy Dir (Immunology) 1961–65, Dir 1965–96; Asst Prof., Dept of Genetics, Stanford Univ. School of Medicine, Calif., USA 1959–61; Prof. of Medical Biology, Univ. of Melbourne 1965–96, Prof. Emer. 1996–; Chair. WHO Global Programme for Vaccines and Immunization 1992–2002; Partner, Foursight Assocs Pty Ltd 1996–; Dir, CRA Ltd 1977–97; Pres. Australian Acad. of Science 1994–98; Foreign Assoc. NAS; mem. or hon. mem. many other nat. and foreign acads and learned socs; Hon. FRACOG; Hon. LLD (Monash, Melbourne); Hon. MD (Mainz, Newcastle, Leeds, Univ. of Western Australia); Hon. DSc (Sydney, Queensland, ANU, Univ. of NSW, La Trobe, McMaster, Oxford); Robert Koch Gold Medal, Albert Einstein World Award of Science, Emil von Behring Prize, Rabbi Shai Shacknai Prize, Australian of the Year 2000, Australia Post 6th Annual Australian Legends Award and many other awards and prizes. *Publications:* Antibodies and Immunity 1968, Antigens, Lymphoid Cells and Immune Response 1971, Medical Science and Human Goals 1975, Nature's Defences (1978 Boyer Lectures), Reshaping Life: Key Issues in Genetic Engineering 1984; 500 publs on immunology. *Leisure interests:* golf, literature. *Address:* Department of Pathology, University of Melbourne, Melbourne, Vic. 3010 (office); 46 Fellows Street, Kew, Vic. 3101, Australia (home). *Telephone:* (3) 8344-6946 (office). *Fax:* (3) 9347-5242 (office).

NOSSOL, Most Rev. Archbishop Alfons, PhD; Polish ecclesiastic and professor of theology; *Archbishop ad personam of Opole;* b. 8 Aug. 1932, Brożec, Opole Prov.; ed Higher Ecclesiastic Seminary in Opole Silesia, Catholic Univ. of Lublin (KUL); ordained priest, Opole 1957; Lecturer, Higher Ecclesiastic Seminary, Opole Silesia 1962–; Lecturer, Catholic Univ. of Lublin 1968, Asst Prof. 1976, Head, Second Dept of Dogmatic Theology 1977, Prof. 1981, Head Ecumenical Inst. 1983; Prof., Theological Dept, Jan Gutenberg Univ., Mainz 1977; Prof., Pontifical Theology Dept, Wrocław 1978; Prof., Diocesan Theology and Pastoral Inst., Opole 1981; Bishop of Opole 1977–; Archbishop ad personam of Opole 1999–; High Chancellor and Prof., Opole Univ. Theological Dept 1994–; mem. Main Council Polish Episcopate; mem. Scientific Council of the Episcopate of Poland; Chair. Episcopate Cttee for Ecumenism; Vice-Leader Episcopate Cttee for Catholic Learning; mem. Christian Unity Pontifical Council, int. cttees for theological dialogue with the Orthodox Church and the Lutheran Church; mem. European Acad. of Science and Art, Salzburg; Dr hc (Munster) 1991, (Mainz) 1992, (Opole) 1995, (Christian Acad. of Theology, Warsaw) 1997, (Bamberg) 1998, (Olomuniec) 2000; Augsburger Friedenspreis 1997, Kulturpreis Schlesien des Landes Niedersachsen 2001. *Publications:* Theology for the Service of Faith 1968, Cognito Dei experimentalis 1974, Karol Barth Christology 1979, Truth and Love 1982, Towards a Civilization of Love 1984, Theology Closer to Life 1984,

Der Mensch braucht Theologie 1986, Love the Victor of Truth 1987, Gelebte Theologie Heute 1991, By Truth to Love 1994, Love Rejoices Together with Truth 1996, Ecumenism as Imperative of Christian Conscience 2001, Brücken bauen Wege zu einem christlichen Europa von Morgen 2002. *Leisure interests:* classical literature, philosophy, the history of art. *Address:* Kuria Diecezjalna, ul. Książąt Opolskich 19, 45-005 Opole, Poland (office). *Telephone:* (77) 454-38-37 (home). *Fax:* (77) 453-79-61 (office). *E-mail:* kuria@diecezja.opole.pl. *Website:* www.diecezja.opole.pl (office).

NOTE, Kessai H.; Marshall Islands politician and fmr head of state; b. 7 Aug. 1950, Ailinglablab Atoll; m. Mary Note; five c.; fmr Speaker of Nitijela (Parl.) and Senator from Jabot; mem. United Democratic Party (UDP); Pres. of the Marshall Islands 2000–08. *Address:* c/o Office of the President, PO Box 2, Majuro, MH 96960, Marshall Islands.

NOTEBAERT, Richard C. (Dick), BA, MBA; American business executive; m. Peggy Notebaert; two c.; ed Univ. of WI; began career with Amitech Corpn 1969, various positions including Pres. Amitech Mobile Communications 1986–89, Pres. IN Bell 1989–92, Pres. Amitech Services 1992–93, Pres. and COO Amitech Corpn 1993–94, Pres. and CEO 1994, Chair. and CEO 1994–99; Pres. and CEO Tellabs 2000–02; Chair. and CEO Qwest Communications Int. Inc. 2002–07 (retd); mem. Bd Dirs AON Corpn, Cardinal Health Inc., Denver Center for Performing Arts, Qwest Communications Int. Inc., Univ. of Notre Dame; mem. Business Council, Reliability and Interoperability Council, Nat. Security Telecommunications Advisory Cttee (NSTAC), US Dept of State 2003–; fmr Vice-Chair. Civic Cttee of Commercial Club of Chicago; fmr Co-Chair. Alexis de Tocqueville Soc., United Way; mem. Bd Execs Club of Chicago; Trustee Univ. of Notre Dame; Distinguished Alumni Award, Univ. of Wisconsin 1999. *Address:* c/o Qwest Communications International Inc., 1801 California Street, Denver, CO 80202, USA (office).

NÖTH, Heinrich, Dr rer. nat; German scientist and academic; *Professor Emeritus of Inorganic Chemistry, University of Munich;* b. 20 June 1928, Munich; s. of Hans Nöth and Eugenie Nöth; m. 1951; two d.; ed Univ. of Munich; Scientific Asst, Univ. of Munich 1952–55, 1957–62, Research Officer 1956, Lecturer 1962–64, Assoc. Prof. 1964–65, Prof. 1965–, Prof. Emer. 1997–, Head Inst. of Inorganic Chem. 1969–97; Pres. German Chemical Soc. 1988–89, 1991–92, Hon. mem.; Pres. Bavarian Acad. of Sciences 1998–2005; Foreign mem. Russian Acad. of Sciences, Mexican Acad. of Sciences; Corresp. mem. Acad. of Sciences, Göttingen, Austrian Acad. of Sciences; mem. Academia Europaea; Hon. mem. Austrian Chemical Soc., Royal Soc. of Chem.; Bavarian Order of Maximilian for Science and Art; Dr hc (Marburg); Hon. DSc (Leeds); Alfred Stock Medal, IMEBORON Award, Bavarian Constitutional Medal in Gold. *Publications:* Nuclear Magnetic Resonance of Boron Compounds 1973, Cluster Compounds of Main Group Elements 2004 and more than 780 original research papers. *Leisure interests:* hiking, gardening, music. *Address:* Department of Inorganic Chemistry, Office D1.036, University of Munich, Butenandtstr. 5-13, 81377 Munich (office); Eichleite 25A, 82031 Grünwald, Germany. *Telephone:* (89) 21807454 (office). *Fax:* (89) 21807455 (office). *E-mail:* H.Noeth@lrz.uni-muenchen.de (office). *Website:* www.cup.uni-muenchen.de/ac/noeth (office).

NOTT, Rt Hon. Sir John William Frederic, KCB, PC, BA; British fmr politician and business executive; b. 1 Feb. 1932; s. of Richard Nott and Phyllis Nott (née Francis); m. Miloska Sekol 1959; two s. one d.; ed Bradfield Coll. and Trinity Coll., Cambridge; Lt with 2nd Gurkha Rifles, (regular officer) 1952–56; Pres. Cambridge Union 1959; called to the Bar, Inner Temple 1959; MP for St Ives, Cornwall 1966–83; Minister of State at Treasury 1972–74; Sec. of State for Trade 1979–81, for Defence 1981–83; Man. Dir, Lazard Brothers 1983–90, Chair. and CEO 1985–90; Chair., Hillsdown Holdings PLC 1993–99 (Dir 1991–), Maple Leaf Foods Inc., Toronto 1993–95; Deputy Chair., Royal Insurance PLC 1986–89; Chair. (non-exec.), Etam 1991–95; Dir, Apax Partners & Co. Capital 1996–. *Publications:* Here Today, Gone Tomorrow, Mr Wonderful Takes a Cruise 2004. *Leisure interests:* farming, fishing, golf. *Address:* 31 Walpole Street, London, SW3 4QS, England. *Telephone:* (20) 7730-2351. *Fax:* (20) 7730-9859.

NOTT, Rt Rev. Peter John, MA; British ecclesiastic; b. 30 Dec. 1933, Belfast; s. of Cecil Frederick Wilder Nott and Rosina Mabel Nott; m. Elizabeth May Maingot 1961; one s. three d.; ed Bristol Grammar School, Dulwich Coll., London, RMA, Sandhurst and Fitzwilliam House and Westcott House, Cambridge; served in regular army, commissioned RA 1951–55; Curate of Harpenden 1961–64; Chaplain and Fellow of Fitzwilliam Coll. Cambridge 1966–69, Hon. Fellow 1993; Chaplain of New Hall, Cambridge 1966–69; Rector of Beaconsfield 1969–77; Bishop of Taunton 1977–85; Bishop of Norwich 1985–99; Asst Bishop, Diocese of Oxford 1999–; Archbishop's Adviser to HMC 1980–85; Vice-Chair. Archbishops' Comm. on Rural Areas 1988–90; Pres. SW Region of Mencap 1978–84, Somerset Rural Music School 1981–85, Royal Norfolk Agricultural Assn 1996; Council of Nat. Army Museum 2001; Dean of the Priory of England, Order of St John 1999–2003; KStJ 1999. *Publication:* Bishop Peter's Pilgrimage: His Diary and Sketchbook 1996. *Leisure interests:* gardening, sketching, fishing. *Address:* Westcot House, Westcot, Wantage, OX12 9QA, England. *Telephone:* (1993) 850688.

NOTTEBOHM, Fernando, BA, PhD; American (b. Argentine) neuroscientist and academic; *Dorothea L. Leonhardt Professor, Head of the Laboratory of Animal Behavior and Director, Field Research Center for Ecology and Ethology, The Rockefeller University;* b. Buenos Aires, Argentina; ed Univ. of California, Berkeley; joined faculty, The Rockefeller Univ., New York 1967, currently Dorothea L. Leonhardt Prof., Head of Lab. of Animal Behavior and Dir Field Research Center for Ecology and Ethology; mem. NAS, Soc. for Neuroscience, American Philosophical Soc.; Fellow, American Acad. of Arts and Sciences, AAAS; Kenneth Caik Research Award, St John's Coll., Cambridge 1983, Karl Spencer Lashley Award (co-recipient) 1983, Charles A. Dana Award (co-recipient) 1983, Lewis S. Rosensteil Award for Distinguished Work in the Basic Medical Sciences (co-recipient) 2004, French Fondation Ipsen Neuronal Plasticity Prize 2004, MERIT Award, Nat. Insts of Mental Health 2004, Pattison Award for Distinguished Research in the Neurosciences 2004, Benjamin Franklin Medal in Life Science, The Franklin Inst. 2006, Sven Berggren Lecture and Prize, Royal Physiographic Soc., Lund 2006. *Achievement:* most famous for providing definitive proof that neurogenesis occurs in the vertebrate brain. *Publications:* more than 135 scientific papers in professional journals. *Address:* Laboratory of Animal Behavior, The Rockefeller University, 1230 York Avenue, New York, NY 10065, USA (office). *Telephone:* (212) 327-8000 (office). *E-mail:* nottebo@rockefeller.edu (office). *Website:* www.rockefeller.edu/labheads/nottebohm/nottebohm-lab.php (office).

NOURISSIER, François; French writer and journalist; b. 18 May 1927, Paris; s. of Paul E. E. Nourissier and Renée Heens; m. 1st Marie-Thérèse Sobesky 1949; two s.; m. 2nd Cécile Muhlstein 1962; one d.; ed Lycée St Louis, Lycée Louis-le-Grand, Paris, Ecole libre des Sciences Politiques, Paris and Faculté de Droit, Paris; mem. staff Secours Catholique Int. and worked with Int. Refugee Org. 1949–51; Dir Chalet Int. des Etudiants, Combloux (World Univ. Service) 1951–52; Sec.-Gen. Editions Denoël 1952–56; Ed.-in-Chief La Parisienne (review) 1956–58; Literary Adviser to Editions Grasset 1958–95; Literary Dir Vogue (French) 1964–66, Contributing Ed. Vogue (American) 1964–; Literary Critic Les Nouvelles littéraires 1963–72; Cinema Critic L'Express 1970–72; Literary Critic Le Point 1972–, Le Figaro 1975–, Figaro-Magazine 1978–; mem. l'Acad. Goncourt 1977–2008, Sec.-Gen. 1983–96, Pres. 1996–2002; Commdr, Légion d'honneur, Commdr, Ordre nat. du Mérite, Commdr des Arts et des Lettres; Prix Prince Pierre de Monaco 1975, Grand Prix de la Ville de Paris 1987, Prix Jean Giono, Prix Mondial Cino Del Duca 2002. *Publications:* L'eau grise (novel) 1951 (Prix Félix Fénéon), Lorca (essay) 1955, Les orphelins d'Auteuil (novel) 1956, Le corps de Diane (novel) 1957, Portrait d'un indifférent 1957, Bleu comme la nuit 1958, Un petit bourgeois 1964, Une histoire française 1966 (Grand Prix de la Guilde du Livre, Grand Prix du Roman de l'Acad. française), Les Français (essay) 1967, Le maître de maison 1968 (plume d'or du Figaro littéraire), The French (trans. of Les Français) 1970, Cartier-Bresson's France 1971, La crève (novel) 1970 (Prix Fémina), Allemande (novel) 1973, Lettre à mon chien (essay) 1975, Lettre ouverte à Jacques Chirac (essay) 1977, Le musée de l'homme (essay) 1979, L'empire des nuages (novel) 1981, La fête des pères (novel) 1986, En avant, calme et droit (novel) 1987, Bratislava (essay) 1990, Autos Graphie (essay) 1990, Le Gardien des ruines (novel) 1992, Mauvais genre (essay) 1994, Le Bar de l'escadrille (novel) 1997, Les Plus belles histoires d'amour (anthology) 1997, A défaut de génie (autobiog.) 2000, Prince des berlingots 2003, La maison Mélancolie 2005. *Leisure interests:* walking, dogs. *Address:* c/o Editions Grasset, 61 rue des Saints-Pères, 75006 Paris (office); Gallimard, 5 rue Sébastien Bottin, 75007 Paris, France.

NOUVEL, Jean; French architect; b. 12 Aug. 1945, Fumel, Lot-et-Garonne; s. of Roger Nouvel and Renée Barlangue; m. Catherine Richard 1992; one d. two s. by Odil Fillion; ed Ecole des Beaux Arts, Paris; first major bldg, medical centre, Bezons; began Nemausus housing projects, Nîmes 1985; built Institut d Monde Arabe, Paris 1987; Hon. Prof. Univ. of Buenos Aires; in 1992 completed designs for La Tour Sans Fins, a 1,400 ft (425m) glass tower to be built in Paris, completed Opéra Lyon, opened 1993, Fondation Cartier, opened 1994, Galeries Lafayette Berlin, opened 1996, Centre de Culture et de Congrès de Lucerne, Switzerland, opened 1998, Musée de la Publicité au Louvre, opened 1999; commissioned to design extension to Museum of Modern Art, New York 2007; curator César: An Anthology, Fondation Cartier, Paris 2008; mem. Acad. d'Architecture 2002; Chevalier ordre nat. du Mérite, des Arts et des Lettres; Grand Prix de l'Architecture for Arab cultural centre, Paris 1987, Praemium Imperiale Award, Japan Art Assn 2001, Francesco Borromini Int. Architecture Prize 2001, Wolf Prize in the Arts 2005, Pritzker Prize 2008. *Address:* Architectures Jean Nouvel, 10 Cité d'Angoulême, 75011 Paris, France (office). *Telephone:* 1-49-23-83-83 (office). *Fax:* 1-43-14-81-10 (office). *E-mail:* info@jeannouvel.fr (office). *Website:* www.jeannouvel.com (office).

NOVÁK, Jiří, LLD; Czech politician and lawyer; b. 11 April 1950, Hranice, Přerov Dist; m.; one s. one d.; ed J.E. Purkyně (now Masaryk) Univ., Brno; lawyer 1976–89; mem. Standing Comm. of the Presidium of Czech Nat. Council for Prison System Issues 1989–92; Deputy to Czech Nat. Council Feb.–June 1990; mem. Presidium, Czech Nat. Council 1990–92; Chair. Cttee on Law and Constitution of Czech Nat. Council 1990–92; Minister of Justice, Czech Repub. 1992–96; Chair. Legis. Council of Govt of Czech Repub. Feb.–July 1992; mem. Parl. 1996–98; Chair. Parl. Cttee for Petitions 1996–98; Vice-Chair. Interdepartmental Antidrug Comm. 1996; mem. Civic Democratic Party 1991–98; advocate 1998–. *Address:* Sokolská 60, 120 00 Prague 2 (office); nám. T.G. Masaryka 15, Lipník/Bečvou, Czech Republic (home). *Telephone:* (2) 22494146. *E-mail:* advokati@broz-sokol.cz.

NOVAK, Michael, BT, MA; American theologian and writer; *George Frederick Jewett Scholar in Religion, Philosophy and Public Policy, American Enterprise Institute;* b. 9 Sept. 1933, Johnstown, Pa; s. of Michael J. Novak and Irene Sakmar; m. Karen R. Laub 1963; one s. two d.; ed Stonehill Coll., North Easton, Mass. and Gregorian Univ., Rome; Teaching Fellow, Harvard Univ. 1961–63; Asst Prof. of Humanities, Stanford Univ. 1965–68; Assoc. Prof. of Philosophy and Religious Studies, State Univ. of NY, Old Westbury 1969–71; Assoc. Dir Humanities, Rockefeller Foundation 1973–74; Ledden-Watson Distinguished Prof. of Religion, Syracuse Univ. 1976–78; Resident Scholar American Enterprise Inst. 1978–, George Frederick Jewett Prof. of Religion, Philosophy, and Public Policy 1983–, Dir Social and Political Studies 1987–; Visiting Prof., Univ. of Notre Dame 1987–88; columnist, The Nat. Review

1979–86, Forbes Magazine 1989–; f., Publr Crisis 1982–95, Ed.-in-Chief 1993–95; mem. Bd for Int. Broadcasting 1983; Judge, Nat. Book Awards, DuPont Awards in Broadcast Journalism; Head, US Del. to UN Human Rights Comm., Geneva 1981, 1982, to CSCE, Berne 1996; other public appointments; Kt of Malta; several hon. degrees; Freedom Award, Coalition for a Democratic Majority 1979, George Washington Honor Medal, Freedom Foundation 1984, Angel Award 1985, Ellis Island Medal of Honor 1986, Templeton Prize 1994, Bratislava Medal 1998, Boyer Award 1999, Masaryk Medal 2000, Econs Medal, Inst. of Italian Mans and Entrepreneurs 2000. *Publications include:* Belief and Unbelief 1965, The Rise of the Unmeltable Ethnics 1972, Choosing Our King 1974, The Spirit of Democratic Capitalism 1982, Freedom with Justice: Catholic Social Thought and Liberal Institutions 1984, Taking Glasnost Seriously 1988, Free Persons and the Common Good 1989, This Hemisphere of Liberty 1990, The Catholic Ethic and the Spirit of Capitalism 1993, Business as a Calling 1996, The Experience of Nothingness 1998, Tell Me Why 1998, On Cultivating Liberty 1999, A Free Society Reader (ed.) 2000, Three in One 2001, On Two Wings 2002, The Universal Hunger for Liberty 2004, Washington's God 2006 and more than 500 articles in journals. *Address:* American Enterprise Institute, 1150 17th Street, NW, Washington, DC 20036, USA. *Telephone:* (202) 862-5839. *Fax:* (202) 862-5821 (office). *E-mail:* mnovak@aei.org (office). *Website:* www.aei.org (office).

NOVELLI, Hervé; French politician; *Minister of State for Commerce, Arts and Crafts, Small and Medium Businesses, Tourism and Services;* b. 6 March 1949, Paris; ed Univ. of Paris-Dauphine; began his career at Chambre Syndicale de la Sidérurgie Française (French Steel Industry Employers' Asscn); Chair. and Man. Dir family-owned prosthesis and orthesis maker based in Richelieu (commune in Indre-et-Loire Dist) 1982–2006; Head of Minister's Office, Ministry of Industry, the Post Office and Tourism 1986–90; apptd Gen. Sec. Republican Party 1990, subsequently became mem. Exec. Bureau; elected Deputy to Nat. Ass. for Indre-et-Loire Dist 1993, re-elected for UMP party 2002, sat on Finance Cttee, re-elected 2007; joined Audace Pour l'Emploi group made up of 50 mems Parl. with entrepreneurial backgrounds 1993; elected to Conseil Général (deliberative ass.) as Rep. of Richelieu canton 1997, Vice-Pres. Conseil Général 1998; Co-founder and first Gen. Del. Démocratie Libérale party 1998; elected mem. European Parl. 1999; Deputy Mayor of Richelieu 2001; elected mem. Conseil Régional (governing body) of Centre region 2004 (resigned when appointed to Govt); Pres. Les Réformateurs (asscn formed under aegis of UMP) 2002–; Co-founder Euro 92 Inst. to prepare French businesses for European Single Market 1988; charged with interministerial mission to find ways to promote creation of jobs in SMEs 1993; successively rapporteur of comm. of enquiry into employment aid and rapporteur of mission to brief Nat. Ass. on application of five-year employment act; special rapporteur for industrial appropriations and chair. special cttee apptd to examine Economic Initiative Bill 2002; reported on Nat. Ass. cttee on 35-hour working week 2003–04; Minister of State for Businesses and Foreign Trade 2007–08, for Commerce, Arts and Crafts, Small and Medium Businesses, Tourism and Services, Ministry of the Economy, Industry and Employment 2008–. *Address:* Ministry of the Economy, Industry and Employment, 139 rue de Bercy, 75572 Paris Cedex 12, France (office). *Telephone:* 1-40-04-04-04 (office). *Fax:* 1-43-43-75-97 (office). *E-mail:* info@herve-novelli.com (office). *Website:* www.minefi.gouv.fr (office); www.herve-novelli.com.

NOVELLO, Antonia Coello, MD, MPH, DPhil; American paediatrician and public health official; b. 23 Aug. 1944, Fajardo, Puerto Rico; m. Joseph Novello 1970; ed Univ. of Michigan, Univ. of Puerto Rico, Johns Hopkins Univ.; intern, Mott Children's Hosp., Univ. of Mich., Ann Arbor 1970–71; Univ. of Mich. Medical Center 1971–73; postgrad. training in nephrology, Dept of Internal Medicine, Univ. of Mich. Medical Center 1973–74, Dept of Pediatrics, Georgetown Univ. 1974–75; pvt. practice in pediatrics, Springfield, Va 1976–78; entered US Public Health Service 1978; various posts at NIH, Bethesda, Md 1978–90, Deputy Dir Nat. Inst. of Child Health and Human Devt 1986–90; Clinical Prof. of Pediatrics, Georgetown Univ. Hospital, Washington, DC 1986, 1989–, Uniformed Services Univ. of the Health Services, Bethesda, Md 1989–; Adjunct Prof. of Pediatrics and Communicable Diseases, Univ. of Mich., of Int. Health, Johns Hopkins School of Public Health; Surgeon-Gen., US Public Health Service (first woman and first Hispanic) 1990–93; UNICEF Special Rep. for Health and Nutrition 1993–96; Visiting Prof. of Health Policy and Man., Johns Hopkins Univ. School of Hygiene and Public Health 1996–99 (also Special Dir for Community Health Policy); New York State Commr of Health 1999–2007, Pres. Health Research, Inc.; mem. Alpha Omega Alpha, American Soc. of Nephrology, American Soc. of Pediatric Nephrology, American Pediatrics Soc., Soc. for Pediatric Research; Fellow, American Acad. of Pediatrics; numerous professional appointments, memberships and affiliations; 50 hon. doctorates; recipient of numerous awards including Surgeon Gen.'s Exemplary Service Medallion and Medal, USPHS Distinguished Service Medal, US Army Legion of Merit, US Coast Guard Meritorious Medal, US Dept of the Navy Distinguished Public Service Award, American Medical Asscn Nathan B. Davis Award, Congressional Hispanic Caucus Medal, Johns Hopkins Soc. of Scholars Award and Univ. Alumni Asscn's Woodrow Wilson Award for Distinguished Govt Service, Elizabeth Blackwell Award, Univ. of Michigan Medical Center Alumni Award and Alumna Council Athena Award, Public Health Service Commissioned Officer's Asscn Health Leader of the Year Award, Ellis Island Medal of Honor, Elizabeth Ann Seton Award, Charles C. Shepard Science Award for Scientific Excellence, American Medical Women's Asscn Leadership Award, Nat. Council of La Raza Pres.'s Award, Nat. Council of Alcohol and Drug Dependency Golden Key Award, American Acad. of Pediatrics Excellence in Public Service Award, Healthy American Fitness Leaders Award, Nat. Women's Hall of Fame, Ronald McDonald Children's Charities Award of Excellence, Hispanic Hero Award, Miami Children's Hosp. Int. Hall of Fame; Women at Work Science Award.Award for Leadership, Hispanic Heritage Awards 1998, James Smithson Bicentennial Medal.2002. *Leisure interest:* collecting antique furniture. *Address:* 5438 Coral Ridge Drive, Grand Blanc, MI 48439, USA (home). *Telephone:* (518) 429-7694 (office). *E-mail:* novello .antonia@gmail.com (office).

NOVIKOV, Arkady; Russian restaurateur; *Owner, Yolki-Palki (restaurant chain);* fmr mem. CP; opened Sirena fish restaurant 1992, followed by White Sun of the Desert; Founder and Owner Yolki-Palki chain of over 60 restaurants 1996–; est. Vogue Café in jt venture with Condé Nast; opened Gallery restaurant 2004, Cantinetta Antinori 2004; f. Rodnik NT to open and operate chain of grocery stores in Moscow 2004. *Address:* Vogue Café, 7/9 Ulitsa Kuznetsky Most, Moscow, Russia (office). *Telephone:* (495) 923-17-01 (office).

NOVIKOV, Sergey Petrovich; Russian mathematician and academic; *Distinguished University Professor, Department of Mathematics, University of Maryland;* b. 20 March 1938, Gorky (now Nizhniy Novgorod); s. Petr Novikov and Ludmila Keldysh; m. Eleonora Tsoi 1962; one s. two d.; ed Moscow Univ., Steklov Math. Inst.; Prof., Moscow Univ. 1966–; Head, Dept, Landau Inst. for Theoretical Physics 1975–, Chair. Dept of Geometry and Topology, Moscow Univ. 1984–; Head, Dept, Steklov Math. Inst. 1983–; Distinguished Univ. Prof., Univ. of Maryland, USA 1997–; Corresp. mem. USSR (now Russian) Acad. of Sciences 1966–, mem. 1981–; Hon. mem. London Math. Soc. 1987, Serbian Acad. of Art and Science 1988, Academia Europaea 1993, Pontifical Acad. of Sciences 1996, Foreign mem. Acad. dei Lincei 1991, Foreign Assoc. NAS 1994, European Acad. of Sciences 2003; Dr hc (Athens) 1989, (Tel-Aviv) 1999; Moscow Math. Soc. Prize 1964, Lenin Prize 1967, Field's Medal, Int. Math. Union 1970, Lobachevsky Int. Prize, USSR Acad. of Sciences 1981, Wolf Foundation Prize in Math. 2005. *Publications:* Algebraic and Differential Topology 1960, General Relativity 1971–75, Theory of Solitons 1974, Topological Phenomena in Physics 1981, Riemannian Geometry and Poisson Structures 1983. *Leisure interest:* history. *Address:* University of Maryland, College Park, IPST, MD 20742, USA (office); Landau Institute for Theoretical Physics, Kosygina 2, 117334 Moscow, Russia (office). *Telephone:* (301) 405-5133 (USA) (office); (495) 137-32-44 (Russia) (office); (495) 135-12-24 (Russia) (home); (301) 779-7472 (USA) (home). *Fax:* (301) 314-9363 (USA) (office). *E-mail:* novikov@ipst.umd.edu (office). *Website:* www.ipst .umd.edu/Faculty/novikov.htm (office).

NOVITSKY, Gennady; Belarusian politician and construction engineer; *Chairman, Council of the Republic, National Assembly;* b. 2 Jan. 1949, Mogilev; m.; two s.; ed Belarus State Polytechnic Inst. Acad. of Social Sciences; foreman, supervising foreman, Head of Construction Div., Mogilev Construction Trust No. 12 1971–77; worked in econ. man. and as a party exec. 1977–94, Chief Engineer of Mogilev Region Agricultural Construction Enterprise, Instructor and Head of Construction Dept at Mogilev Region CP Cttee, Head of Mogilev Agricultural Construction Enterprise Bd; Minister of Architecture and Construction 1994–97; Deputy, later Acting Prime Minister 1997–2001; Prime Minister 2001–03; Chair. Council of the Repub., Nat. Ass. of Repub. of Belarus 2003–; Certificate of Honour, Council Ministers, Repub. of Belarus. *Leisure interests:* simple sports like jogging. *Address:* 4 Krasnoarmeyskaya str., 220016 Minsk, Belarus (office). *Telephone:* (17) 222-67-65 (office). *Fax:* (17) 222-66-94 (office). *E-mail:* cr@sovrep.gov.by (office). *Website:* www.sovrep .gov.by (office).

NOVODVORSKAYA, Valeria Ilyinichna; Russian politician; b. 17 May 1950; ed Krupskaya Moscow Region Pedagogical Inst.; in dissident movt since late 1960s, arrested as student on charge of organizing underground anti-Soviet group 1969; trans., Second Moscow Medicine Inst. 1975–90; organized political action against invasion of Czechoslovakia Dec. 1969; arrested, discharged 1972; initiator and participant of anti-Soviet meetings; was arrested 17 times 1985–91; imprisoned for anti-Soviet activities 1978, 1985, 1986, 1991; mem. Co-ordination Council of Democratic Union, participated in political seminar Democracy and Humanism 1988; Leader Party of Democratic Union 1992; political reviewer, Khozyain 1993–95, Stolitsa 1995–96. *Publications:* articles in newspapers and magazines. *Leisure interests:* reading, mountain climbing, swimming. *Address:* Democratic Union, Onezhskaya str. 4, Apt 113, Moscow, Russia. *Telephone:* (495) 453-37-76.

NOVOTNÝ, Petr; Czech actor, writer and producer; b. 6 Aug. 1947, Olomouc; m. Miroslava Novotný; four c.; ed Charles Univ., Prague; mem. Laterna Magika Theatre, Prague; owner of Firma 6P and Amfora Football Club. *Awards:* Best Comedian and Best Programme (Novotný), TYTY Awards 1999, Most Popular Male Actor, TYTY Awards 2000. *Theatre productions directed:* Sugar (Some Like It Hot), Gypsies Go to Heaven, Libuse (opera) 1995, Hello Dolly! 1996, My Fair Lady, Evita 1999, Pokuseni sv. Antonina 2001. *Television includes:* Big Ear; writer and presenter of numerous programmes. *Leisure interests:* football, cooking. *Address:* Firma 6P—Petr Novotný, s.r.o, Koterovská 833, 15500 Prague 5, Czech Republic (office). *Telephone:* (2) 57960560 (office). *Fax:* (2) 57960562 (office). *E-mail:* firma6p@decent3000.cz (office). *Website:* www.firma6p.cz (office); www.petr-novotny.cz.

NOVOZHILOV, Genrikh Vasilievich; Russian mechanical engineer and aircraft designer; b. 27 Oct. 1925, Moscow; m.; one s.; ed Moscow Aviation Inst.; mem. CPSU 1951–91; constructor, constructing engineer, leading engineer, Sec. CP Cttee aviation plant 1948–57; Deputy Constructor-in-Chief, Chief Constructor, Constructor-Gen. USSR Ministry of Aviation Industry 1958–86; simultaneously First Deputy Constructor-Gen. Moscow Ilyushin Machine Constructing Plant 1964–, Constructor-Gen. 1976–2000, Adviser and Gen. Designer Illushin Design Bureau 2000–; Deputy to USSR Supreme Soviet 1974–89, USSR People's Deputy, 1989–91; mem. Cen. CPSU

Cttee 1986–91; Head of Production of IL76T, IL86 and IL96-300 aircraft; Hero of Socialist Labour (twice), Lenin Prize and other awards and decorations. *Publications:* works in the field of new samples of aviation tech., including Theory and Practice of Designing Passenger Aircraft 1976, Design, Testing and Production of Wide-Fuselage Passenger Aircraft 1980, essays on History of Constructions and Systems of Aircraft 1983. *Leisure interests:* tennis, photography. *Address:* Ilyushin Design Bureau, Leningradsky prospekt 45G, 125190 Moscow, Russia (home). *Telephone:* (495) 943-81-16 (home); (495) 212-21-32 (home). *E-mail:* ilyushin@online.ru (home).

NOWAK, Rev. Arkadiusz; Polish ecclesiastic and charity worker; b. 28 Nov. 1966, Rybnik; ed Pontifical Faculty of Theology, Warsaw, Szczecin Univ.; mem. Camillian Order (Ordo Clericorum Regularium Ministrantium Infirmis–OSCam.) 1985–; opened first AIDS hospice in Poland; Dir Centre of Re-adaptation Ministry of Health, Konstancin (brs in Piastów and Anielin) 1990–; ordained priest 1993; Co-Founder Polish Humanitarian Aid Foundation Res Humanae 1993–; Adviser on Issues of AIDS and Drugs to Minister of Health 1995–2001, Plenipotentiary 2001; Order of the Smile 1995; numerous prizes include Medal of St Georges (Tygodnik Powszechny Award) 1993, Award for Acting Against Intolerance, Xenophobia and Racialism (Finland), Global Leader for Tomorrow, World Econ. Forum 2000, UN Award for Breaking the Silence on HIV/AIDS 2000. *Address:* National Aids Centre, ul. Samsonowska 1, 02-829 Warsaw, Poland (office). *Telephone:* (22) 6418301 (office). *Fax:* (22) 6412190 (office). *E-mail:* arknowak@poczta.onet.pl (office).

NOWELL, Peter C., MD, FAAS; American pathologist and academic; *Gaylord P. and Mary Louise Harnwell Professor of Pathology and Laboratory Medicine, University of Pennsylvania School of Medicine;* ed Wesleyan Univ., Middletown, Conn., Univ. of Pennsylvania School of Medicine; Rotating Internship, Philadelphia Gen. Hosp. 1952–53, Clinical Asst, Lab. Service 1956–70, Consultant, Lab. Service, Philadelphia Gen. Hosp. and Philadelphia Veterans' Admin Hospital 1970–77; Resident in Pathology, Presbyterian Hosp., Philadelphia (Trainee of Nat. Cancer Inst.) 1953–54; Lt, Medical Corps, USNR (Pathologist for US Naval Radiological Defense Lab., San Francisco, Calif.) 1954–56; Sr Research Fellowship, US Public Health Service 1956–61; Instructor to Prof. of Pathology, Univ. of Pennsylvania School of Medicine 1956–64, Prof. of Pathology 1964–, Chair. of Pathology 1967–73, Dir Univ. of Pennsylvania Cancer Center 1973–75, Deputy Dir 1975–, Academic Coordinator, Dept of Pathology and Lab. Medicine 1980–87, Gaylord P. and Mary Louise Harnwell Prof. of Pathology and Lab. Medicine 1990–; Consultant in Pathology, Children's Hosp. of Philadelphia 1974–; mem. Nat. Cancer Inst. DCBD Bd of Scientific Counselors 1982–86, American Cancer Soc. Advisory Bd on Institutional Grants 1982–84, Leukemia Soc. of America Grants Review Bd 1987–90, Advisory Cttee to Dir NIH 1990–94; mem. NAS 1976, Inst. of Medicine 1991, American Soc. for Experimental Pathology (mem. Council 1967–71, Pres. 1970–71), American Asscn for Cancer Research (Dir 1970–73, 1990–93) Pathological Soc. of Philadelphia, Coll. of Physicians of Philadelphia, American Soc. for Investigative Pathology, American Asscn of Immunologists, Acad. of Clinical Lab. Physicians and Scientists; mem. Editorial Bd Cancer Research 1973–76, 1982–85, 1990–93, Journal of Immunology 1977–80, American Journal of Pathology 1980–, Cancer Genetics and Cytogenetics 1980–, Cancer Reviews 1985–, Cancer and Metastasis Reviews 1985–, Hematological Oncology 1987–89, Genes, Chromosomes and Cancer 1989–, International Review of Experimental Pathology 1990–; Hon. mem. Asscn of American Physicians 1992; Research Career Devt Award, US Public Health Service 1961–64, Research Career Award, US Public Health Service 1964–67, Parke Davis Award in Experimental Pathology 1965, Lindback Distinguished Teaching Award 1967, Distinguished Alumnus Award, Wesleyan Univ. 1968, Gerhardt Medal, Philadelphia Pathological Soc. 1974, American Cancer Soc. (Phila) Scientific Award 1976, Shubitz Prize, Univ. of Chicago 1980, La Madonnina Award, Milan 1982, Passano Foundation Award 1984, Rous-Whipple Award, American Asscn of Pathologists 1986, NIH Outstanding Investigator Grant 1986, Robert de Villiers Award, Leukemia Soc. of America 1987, Cotlove Award, Acad. of Clinical Lab. Physicians and Scientists 1987, Philip Levine Award, American Soc. of Clinical Pathologists 1989, Fred W. Stewart Award, Memorial Sloan-Kettering Cancer Center 1989, Mott Prize, General Motors Cancer Research Foundation 1989, Distinguished Graduate Award, Univ. of Pennsylvania School of Medicine 1992, 3M Life Sciences Award, Fed. of American Socs for Experimental Biology 1993, American Philosophical Soc. 1993, Leukemia Soc. of America Award (Eastern Pennsylvania Chapter) 1995, Gold-Headed Cane Award, American Soc. for Investigative Pathology 1997, Albert Lasker Award for Clinical Medical Research (jt recipient) 1998. *Publications:* numerous articles in medical journals. *Address:* University of Pennsylvania School of Medicine, Department of Pathology, M163 John Morgan/6082, Philadelphia, PA 19104, USA (office). *E-mail:* nowell@mail.med.upenn.edu (office). *Website:* www.med.upenn.edu (office).

NOWINA-KONOPKA, Piotr Maria, MSc (Econs), PhD; Polish politician, economist, publicist and scholar; b. 27 May 1949, Chorzów; s. of Mikołaj Nowina-Konopka and Anna Nowina-Konopka; m. Wanda Nowina-Konopka 1975; two d.; ed Higher School of Econs, Sopot and Gdańsk Univ. 1972; Asst Gdańsk Tech. Univ. 1972–74; Deputy Head, Centre of Revocatory Maritime Chamber, Gdynia 1977–79; Lecturer, Foreign Trade Econs Inst. of Gdańsk Univ. 1979–; Co-Founder and Sec. Catholic Intelligentsia Club in Gdańsk 1980–81; mem. Solidarity Independent Self-governing Trade Union 1980–1990, Press Spokesman 1988–89, Chief of Press 1989; mem. Civic Cttee attached to Lech Wałęsa (q.v.) 1988–91; Lecturer, Gdańsk Theology Inst. 1988–; Minister of State in Chancellery of Pres. of Poland 1989–90; Sec.-Gen. Democratic Union 1990–94; Union for Freedom Sec. for Foreign Affairs 1994–98; Deputy to Sejm (Parl.) 1991–2001, Vice-Chair. Cttee for the European Treaty 1992–97; Sec. of State Office of the Cttee for European

Integration 1998; Sec. of State in Chancellery of Prime Minister 1998–99; Deputy Chair. Jt Parl. Cttee Poland-European Parl. 1993–97; mem. Foreign Affairs Comm. 1991–2001; Pres. Polish Robert Schuman Foundation 1996–; Vice-Rector Coll. of Europe, Bruges/Warsaw 1999–2004; Deputy Chief Negotiator for negotiations with EU 1998–99; Chevalier Ordre du Mérite Verdienstkreuz Erste Klasse des Verdienstordens. *Publicatons:* weekly columnist in Wprost, political articles in different books/periodicals. *Leisure interests:* family life, reading, social sciences, yachting, riding, skiing. *Address:* c/o College of Europe, Rezydencja Natolin, ul. Nowoursynowska 84, Box 120, 02-797 Warsaw, Poland (office). *Fax:* (22) 750-9000 (home). *E-mail:* pnk@omet.pl (home).

NOWRA, Louis; Australian writer and scriptwriter; b. 12 Dec. 1950; m. Mandy Sayer; Dr hc (Griffiths University) 1996; Literature Board Grants 1975, 1977, 1979, 1980, 1981, 1982; Prix Italia 1990, NSW Premier's Literary Prize 1992, Victoria Premier's Prize 1994, Australian Literary Soc. Gold Medal 1994, The Australia/Canada Award 1994, The Green Room Award for Best New Play 1995, Courier-Mail Book of the Year 2000. *Radio:* Albert Names Edward 1975, The Song Room 1980, The Widows 1984, Summer of the Aliens 1989, Sydney 1993, Moon of the Exploding Trees 1995, The Divine Hammer 2001, Jez 2006. *Publications:* The Misery of Beauty 1976, The Cheated 1978, Albert Names Edward 1975, Inner Voices 1978, Visions 1979, Inside The Island/The Precious Woman 1981, The Song Room 1982, Sunrise 1983, The Golden Age 1985, Palu 1987, Capricornia 1988, The Watchtower 1992, Summer of the Aliens 1992, Cosi 1992, Radiance 1993, The Temple 1993, Crow 1994, The Incorruptible 1995, Cosi (Australian Film Inst. Award for Best Adapted Screenplay 1996) 1996, Red Nights 1997, The Jungle 1998, Language of the Gods 1999, The Twelfth of Never 1999, Byzantine Flowers 2000, Radiance 2000, In the Gutter... Looking at the Stars (anthology, co-ed.) 2000, Abaza 2001, Warne's World 2002, Walkabout 2003, Shooting the Moon 2004, Chihuahuas, Women and Me 2005, Bad Dreaming 2007, The Boyce Trilogy Includes: The Woman with Dog's Eyes, The Marvellous Boy, The Emperor of Sydney 2007, Ice 2008. *Leisure interests:* cricket, mycology. *Address:* HLA Management, PO Box 1536, Strawberry Hills, NSW 2012, Australia (office). *E-mail:* hla@hlamgt.com.au (office). *Website:* www.hlamgt.com.au (office). *Telephone:* (2) 9310-4948 (home). *Fax:* (2) 9310-4113 (home).

NOYCE, Phillip; Australian film director; b. 29 April 1950, Griffith, NSW; ed Univ. of Sydney, Australian Film and Television School. *Films directed include:* That's Showbiz 1973, Castor and Pollux (Rouben Mamoulien Award, Sydney Film Festival) 1974, God Knows Why But It Works 1975, Backroads (writer, dir and producer) 1977, Newsfront 1978, Heatwave 1982, Echoes of Paradise (1987), Dead Calm 1989, Blind Fury (1989), Patriot Games 1992, Sliver 1993, Clear and Present Danger 1994, The Saint 1997, The Bone Collector 1999, Rabbit Proof Fence (dir and producer) 2002, The Quiet American 2002. *Television includes:* The Dismissal (mini series) 1983, Cowra Breakout (mini series) 1984, The Hitchhiker (various episodes) 1983, Tru Calling (series pilot) 2003. *Address:* c/o Endeavor Talent Agency, 9701 Wiltshire Boulevard, #1000, Beverly Hills, CA 90212, USA (office); c/o The Cameron Creswell Agency Pty Ltd., 5/2 New McLean Street, Edgcliff, NSW 2027, Australia.

NOYER, Christian; French banker and civil servant; *Governor, Banque de France;* b. 6 Oct. 1950, Soisy; ed Univs of Rennes and Paris, Inst. of Political Science, Ecole Nat. d'Admin; mil. service as naval officer 1972; joined French Treasury 1976, Chief of Banking Office, then of Export Credit Office 1982–85, Deputy Dir in charge of Int. Multilateral Issues 1988–90, then of Debt Man., Monetary and Banking Issues 1990–92, Dir of Dept responsible for public holdings and public financing 1992–93, Dir of Treasury 1993–95; financial attaché, French Del. to EC, Brussels 1980–82; Econ. Adviser to Minister for Econ. Affairs and Finance, Edouard Balladur (q.v.) 1986–88, Chief of Staff to E. Alphandéry 1993, to Jean Arthuis (q.v.) 1995–97; Dir, Ministry for Econ. Affairs, Finance and Industry 1997–98; Alt. Gov., IMF and World Bank 1993–95; Vice-Pres., European Cen. Bank 1998–2002; Gov., Banque de France 2003–; Alt. mem., European Monetary Cttee 1988–90, mem. 1993–95, 1998; Alt. mem., G7 and G10 1993–95; mem. Working Party No. 3 OECD 1993–95; Chair., Paris Club of Creditor Countries 1993–97; mem. European Econ. and Financial Cttee 1999–2002; Officier Légion d'honneur, Chevalier Ordre nat. du Mérite, Commdr Nat. Order of the Lion, Senegal; Grand Cross, Orden del Mérito, Spain. *Publications:* Banks: The Rules of the Game 1990; various articles. *Leisure interest:* sailing. *Address:* Banque de France, 3 rue de la Vrillière, 75001 Paris, France (office). *Telephone:* 1-42-92-20-01 (office). *E-mail:* secretariat.gouv@banque-france.fr (office).

NOYORI, Ryoji, MEng, PhD; Japanese scientist and academic; *President, RIKEN;* b. 3 Sept. 1938, Kobe; m. Hiroko Oshima; two s.; ed Kyoto Univ.; Research Assoc. Dept of Industrial Chem., Kyoto Univ. 1963–68; Assoc. Prof., Dept of Chem., Nagoya Univ. 1968–72, Prof. 1972–2003, Dir Chemical Instrument Center 1979–91, Dean Grad. School of Science 1997–99, Dir Research Center for Materials Science 2000–03; Pres. RIKEN (scientific research inst.) 2003–; Dir ERATO Molecular Catalysis Project, Research Devt Corpn of Japan 1991–96; Science Adviser, Ministry of Educ., Science and Culture 1992–96, mem. Scientific Council 1996–2003; Prof. Inst. for Fundamental Research on Organic Chem., Kyushu Univ. 1993–96; Cttee Chair. Research for the Future Program on Advanced Processes, Japan Soc. for the Promotion of Science 1996–2002; Pres. Soc. of Synthetic Organic Chem. 1997–99; mem. numerous professional bodies including Chemical Soc. of Japan, Pharmaceutical Soc. of Japan, ACS, Royal Soc. of Chem. (UK); Visiting Prof. at numerous int. univs; mem. editorial bd of 30 learned journals; numerous hon. degrees; numerous awards and prizes, including Chemical Soc. of Japan Award 1985, Japan Acad. Prize 1995, Wolf Prize (jtly) 2001, Nobel Prize in Chem. (jt recipient) 2001 and several ACS awards. *Address:*

RIKEN, 2-1, Hirosawa, Wako, Saitama 351-0198 (office); Department of Chemistry, Graduate School of Science, Nagoya University, Furo-cho, Chikusa, Nagoya, Aichi, 464-8602 (office); 1105 Luxembourg House, 8-9, Yonban-cho, Chiyoda, Tokyo 102-0081, Japan (home). *Telephone:* (48) 463-9900 (RIKEN) (office); (52) 789-2956 (Nagoya University) (office). *Fax:* (48) 462-4604 (RIKEN) (office); (52) 783-4177 (Nagoya University) (office). *E-mail:* noyori@riken.jp (office); noyori@chem3.chem.nagoya-u.ac.jp (office). *Website:* www.riken.jp/engn/index.html (office); www.nagoya-u.ac.jp/en/ (office).

NOZARI, Gholamhossein, BS, MA; Iranian petroleum industry executive; *Minister of Petroleum;* b. 1954; responsible for air defence in southern Iran during Iran-Iraq war; fmr Head of Security, Nat. Iranian South Oil Co.; fmr mem. Cen. Council, Islamic Republic Party; fmr Deputy Chair. Majlis Energy Comm., fmr mem. Majlis Devt Comm.; fmr Man. Dir Nat. Iranian Cen. Oil Co., then Man. Dir Nat. Iranian Oil Co. –2007; Minister of Petroleum 2007–. *Address:* Ministry of Petroleum, Hafez Crossing, Taleghani Avenue, Tehran, Iran (office). *Telephone:* (21) 66152606 (office). *Fax:* (21) 66154977 (office). *E-mail:* public-relations@mop.ir (office). *Website:* www.mop.ir (office).

NOZIÈRES, Philippe Pierre Gaston François; French physicist; b. 12 April 1932, Paris; s. of Henri Nozières and Alice Noël; m. Catherine Michel 1982; one d. (one s. and one d. by previous m.); ed Ecole Normale Supérieure and Princeton Univ., USA; Prof. of Physics, Univ. of Paris 1961–72; Physicist, Laue-Langevin Inst. 1972–76; Prof. of Physics, Grenoble Univ. 1976–83; Prof. of Statistical Physics, Coll. de France 1983–2001; mem. Acad. des Sciences (Inst. de France); Foreign Assoc. NAS; Holweck Prize 1976, Prix du CEA (Acad. des Sciences) 1979, Wolf Prize 1985, Gold Medal CNRS 1988, Feenberg Medal 2000. *Publications:* papers on theoretical and statistical physics. *Address:* ILL, BP 156, 38042 Grenoble Cedex (office); 15 route de Saint Nizier, 38180 Seyssins, France (home). *Telephone:* (4) 76-20-72-74 (office); (4) 76-21-60-28 (home). *Fax:* (4) 76-88-24-16 (office). *E-mail:* nozieres@ill.fr (office).

NOZOE, Kuniaki, BA; Japanese business executive; *President and Representative Director, Fujitsu Limited;* ed Waseda Univ.; joined Fujitsu Ltd 1971, has held several exec. positions including Corp. Sr Vice-Pres. Fujitsu Ltd –2007, Corp. Vice-Pres., Group Support, and Corp. First Sr Vice-Pres. 2007–, Corp. Sr Exec. Vice-Pres. April–June 2008, Pres. and Rep. Dir Fujitsu Ltd June 2008–; mem. Bd of Dirs Fujitsu Frontech Ltd, Asscn of Radio Industries and Businesses. *Address:* Fujitsu Headquarters, Shiodome City Center, 1-5-2 Higashi-Shimbashi, Minato-ku, Tokyo 105-7123, Japan (office). *Telephone:* (3) 6252-2220 (office). *Fax:* (3) 6252-2783 (office). *E-mail:* info@fujitsu.com (office). *Website:* www.fujitsu.com (office).

NQAKULA, Charles; South African politician; *Minister of Defence;* b. 13 Sept. 1942; m.; ed Cradock, Lovedale; fmr waiter, wine steward; fmr clerk, Dept of Bantu Educ.; journalist, Midland News 1966; Political Reporter, Imvo Zabantsundu 1973; with Daily Dispatch, London 1976; placed under banning order 1981, declared prohibited immigrant, forbidden to enter S Africa 1982; est. Veritas News Agency, Zwelitsha 1982; Publicity Sec. United Democratic Front (UDF) 1983; fmr underground operative African Nat. Congress (ANC), mem. Nat. Exec. Cttee 1994; granted amnesty 1991; mem. S African Communist Party (SACP), Deputy Gen. Sec. 1991, later Gen. Sec., currently Chair.; Parl. Counsellor to Pres. –2001; Deputy Minister of Home Affairs 2001–02; Minister of Safety and Security 2002–08, of Defence 2008–; mem. Union of Black Journalists, Vice-Pres. 1976; Vice-Pres. Writers' Asscn of S Africa (later Media Workers' Asscn of S Africa) 1979. *Leisure interests:* composing choral music, writing poetry. *Address:* Ministry of Defence, Armscor Building, Block 5, Nossob Street, Erasmusrand 0181 Private Bag X161, Pretoria 0001, South Africa (office). *Telephone:* (12) 3556321 (office). *Fax:* (12) 3556398 (office). *E-mail:* info@mil.za (office). *Website:* www.dod.mil.za (office).

NSEKELA, Amon James, MA, DipEd, FIBA; Tanzanian fmr diplomatist, civil servant and banker; b. 4 Jan. 1930, Lupepo, Rungwe; s. of the late Ngonile Reuben Nsekela and of Anyambilile Nsekela (née Kalinga); m. Christina Matilda Kyusa 1957; two s.; ed Rungwe Dist School, Malangali Secondary School, Tabora Govt Sr Secondary School, Makerere Univ. Coll. and Univ. of the Pacific, Calif., USA; teacher 1955–59; Admin. Officer 1960–62; Perm./Prin. Sec. Ministries of External Affairs and Defence, Industries, Mineral Resources and Power and Treasury 1963–67; Chair. and Man. Dir Nat. Bank of Commerce 1967–74, 1981–91; Chair. Nat. Insurance Corpn of Tanzania 1967–69, Tanzania Investment Bank 1981–91, Inst. of Devt Man., Mzumbe, Morogoro 1982–91; High Commr in UK 1974–81 (also accred to Ireland) 1980–81; Dir Tanzania-Zambia Railway Authority 1982–, Computers & Telecoms Systems 1993–; Chair., Council, Univ. of Dar es Salaam 1970–74, Pensioners' Union of Tanzania 1992–; Vice-Pres. Britain–Tanzania Soc.; Hon. DLit (Dar es Salaam) 1990; African Insurance Org. Award 1982; Order of the United Republic of Tanzania. *Publications:* Minara ya Historia ya Tanganyika: Tanganyika hadi Tanzania, Demokrasi Tanzania, Socialism and Social Accountability in a Developing Nation, The Development of Health Services in Mainland Tanzania: Tumetoka Mbali (with Dr. A. L. Nhonoli), Towards National Alternatives 1984, A Time to Act 1984. *Leisure interests:* swimming, darts, reading and writing. *Address:* 9 Lupa Way, P.O. Box 722, Mbeya, Tanzania. *Telephone:* (65) 3487. *Fax:* (65) 2541.

NSEREKO, Daniel David Ntanda, LLB, MCJ, LLM, JSD; Ugandan judge; *Judge, International Criminal Court;* m.; ed Univ. of East Africa, Dar es Salaam, Tanzania, Howard Univ. School of Law, Washington, DC, USA, The Hague Acad., Netherlands, New York Univ. School of Law, USA; pupil advocate with Kiwanuka & Co., Advocates, Kampala 1968; Advocate, High Court of Uganda 1972–, included on List of Counsel eligible for appointment to represent accused or victims before Int. Criminal Court 2007; Lecturer in Law, Makerere Univ., Kampala 1971–75, Sr Lecturer in Law 1975–78; full-

time pvt. law practice, Kampala 1978–82; expert consultant, Crime Prevention and Criminal Justice Br. of UN Centre for Social Devt and Humanitarian Affairs, New York, USA 1983–84, Social Affairs Officer, UN Centre for Social Devt and Humanitarian Affairs 1983; Sr Lecturer in Law, Univ. of Botswana, Gaborone 1984–92, Head of Dept of Law 1985–93, Assoc. Prof. of Law 1992–96, Prof. of Law 1996–; Walter S. Owen Visiting Prof. of Law, Univ. of British Columbia, Canada 1993–94; Visiting Scholar, Max Planck Inst. for Foreign and Int. Criminal Law, Freiburg, Germany 1995, 2006; Judge (Trial Div.), Int. Criminal Court 2008–; served as Amnesty International Trial Observer to Swaziland 1990, Amnesty International mission to Swaziland to investigate allegations of human rights abuses and to inspect prison conditions 1991, Amnesty International Trial Observer to Ethiopia 1996, Head of an Amnesty International del. to Lesotho to investigate allegations of human rights and humanitarian law violations and inspecting prison conditions following S African and Botswana mil. intervention 1998; mem. Exec. Cttee Uganda Red Cross Soc. 1975–80, Bd Int. Soc. for Reform of Criminal Law, Vancouver, Canada 1988–, Advisory Exec. War Crimes Research Office, American Univ., Washington, DC 2006–; mem. Editorial Council Journal of Church and State 1985–, Editorial Bd Journal Violence, Aggression and Terrorism 1986–90, Criminal Law Forum: An International Journal 1990–, University of Botswana Law Journal 2005–; mem. Int. Advisory Bd Int. Doctorate School of Excellence, Univ. of Cologne, Germany 2006–; mem. Uganda Law Soc. 1972– (mem. Law Council (Exec. Cttee) 1975–80), East African Law Soc. 2004–; Fellow, Inst. of Int. Law and Int. Relations Research, The Hague Acad. of Int. Law 1982; Medal of Int. Soc. for Reform of Criminal Law 1996. *Publications:* Police Powers and the Rights of the Individual in Uganda 1973, The International Protection of Refugees (doctoral dissertation) 1975, Antigone: A Greek Play by Sophocles (trans. into the Luganda language) 1989, English–Luganda Law Dictionary 1993, Eddembe Lyaffe (Our Rights; treatise written in the Luganda language) 1995, Criminal Law and Procedure in Uganda (in, International Encyclopaedia of Laws) 1996, Criminal Procedure in Botswana: Cases and Materials (third edn) 2002, Constitutional Law in Botswana (in, International Encyclopaedia of Laws) 2002, Legal Ethics in Botswana: Cases and Materials (with K. Solo) 2004, Criminal Law and Procedure in Botswana 2007; several book chapters and reviews and numerous articles in professional journals. *Address:* International Criminal Court, PO Box 19519, 2500 CM The Hague, The Netherlands (office). *Telephone:* (70) 515-8515 (office). *Fax:* (70) 515-8555 (office). *E-mail:* info@icc-cpi.int (office). *Website:* www.icc-cpi.int (office).

NSHUTI, Paul Manasseh, PhD; Rwandan government official and academic; Minister of Commerce, Industry, Investment, Tourism and Co-operation –2005, of Finance and Econ. Planning 2005–06. *Address:* c/o Ministry of Finance and Economic Planning, BP 158, Kigali, Rwanda (office).

NSIMBAMBI, Apollo; Ugandan politician; *Prime Minister;* fmr Minister of Educ. and Sports; Prime Minister of Uganda 1999–; mem. Nat. Resistance Movt. *Address:* Office of the Prime Minister, PO Box 341, Kampala, Uganda (office). *Telephone:* (41) 259518 (office). *Fax:* (41) 242341 (office).

N'SINGA UDJUU ONGWABEKI UNTUBE, Joseph; Democratic Republic of the Congo politician; *President, Union chrétienen pour le renouveau et la justice;* b. (Joseph N'Singa Udjuu), 29 Oct. 1934, Nsontin, Bandundu Prov.; s. of Nshue O. N'singa and Monkaju Medji; m. Mbu Modiri Marie; four s. four d.; ed Kokoro and Kabue Seminaries, Bandundu Prov., Univ. of Lovanium (now Kinshasa); Juridical adviser of the provisional Govt, Inongo, Bandundu Prov. 1963; Provincial Minister of the Interior (Home Affairs) and Information 1963–64; elected Nat. Deputy 1964; Vice-Minister of the Interior (Home Affairs) 1965, of Justice 1965; Minister of Justice 1966–69; Minister of State for Home Affairs 1968; Minister of State at the Presidency Sept. 1970; Chair. Nat. Inst. of Social Security 1975–80; Co-founder and mem. Cen. Cttee, Mouvement Populaire de la Révolution (MPR) 1980–83 (Exec. Sec. 1981–83), First Vice-Pres. 1980–83; Chair. 1990–91; Prime Minister (first State Commissary) 1981; Pres. Judiciary Council 1987–90; mem. Sovereign Nat. Conf. and elected Counsellor of the Repub. during Nat. Conf.; mem. transition Parl.; Minister of Transportation 1994–95, of Justice 1995–96, of Reconstruction and Planning 1997; participant at nat. consultation assizes conf., Kinshasa 2000; mem. Jt Comm. Cttee in charge of Law Review 2001; Founder and Pres. own political party Union chrétienen pour le renouveau et la justice (UCRJ); Grand Cordon of the Leopard Nat. Order, Commdr of the Belgian King Leopold II Cross, Commdr of the Cen. African Repub. Order of Merit. *Leisure interests:* walking, jogging. *Address:* 68 Avenue Uvira, #5 Commune de Gombe, Kinshasa, Democratic Republic of the Congo (home). *E-mail:* nsinga5@hotmail.com.

N'TCHAMA, Caetano; Guinea-Bissau politician; b. 1955; Prime Minister of Guinea-Bissau 2000–01 (dismissed from post by Pres. Kumba Yala). *Address:* c/o Office of the Prime Minister, Avda Unidade Africana, CP 137, Bissau, Guinea-Bissau (office).

NTETURUYE, Marc; Burundian diplomatist; b. 23 Nov. 1954, Murambi; m.; six c.; ed Univ. of Burundi, Inst. Int. d'Admin. Publique, Paris; taught history in a Jesuit secondary school 1978–81; Dir of secondary school 1981–82; Adviser to Pres. of Repub. on press and information matters 1982–85; First Counsellor, Embassy in Tanzania 1981–87; Amb. to Kenya 1987–91 (also accred to Somalia and Namibia and to Rwanda 1991–93); Perm. Rep. to UNEP and UN Habitat 1990–91; Diplomatic and Political Adviser to Prime Minister 1994–95; Dir Office of Prime Minister 1995–96; Dir External Intelligence 1997–98; Perm. Rep. to UN (also accred to Cuba) 1999–2008. *Publications:* A Study of the Problem of Energy in the Rural Villages of Burundi 1978, A Study on the Role of Sorghum in the Socio-Culture of Burundi. *Address:* c/o Ministry of External Relations, Bujumbura, Burundi (office); 16 Murray Hill Road, Scarsdale, NY 10583, USA (home). *Telephone:* (914) 722-0915 (home).

NTIBANTUNGANYA, Sylvestre; Burundian politician; b. 8 May 1956, Nyamutobo; m. Eusebie Ntibantunganya (deceased); ed Nat. Audiovisual Inst. Paris; worked for Burundi State TV and Radio for two years; joined Nat. Secr. Unity for Nat. Progress (UPRONA); in exile in Rwanda 1979–83; Founding mem. Sahwanya-Frodebu Party, mem. Exec. Cttee 1991, Leader 1993–; Chief Ed. Aube de la Démocratie (Frodebu Party newspaper) until 1993; Deputy for Gitega 1993; Minister for External Relations 1993; fmr Speaker of Parl.; Pres. of Burundi 1994–96; Chair. Nat. Security Council 1996. *Address:* National Security Council, Bujumbura, Burundi.

NTISEZERANA, Gabriel; Burundian economist, central banker and politician; *Second Vice-President;* m.; three c.; Customers Officer, Credit Dept, Interbank Burundi s.a. in charge of business portfolio 1993–99, Man. Cen. Market Br. 1999–2000, Head of Asian Area br. Jan.–Aug. 2001; Chair. Banque nationale de développement économique (Nat. Bank for Econ. Devt) –2006; Gov. Cen. Bank 2006–07, Gov. for Burundi, IMF 2006; mem. Conseil nat. pour la défense de la démocratie-Forces pour la défense de la démocratie (CNDD-FDD— Nat. Council for the Defence of Democracy-Forces for the Defence of Democracy); Second Vice-Pres. of Burundi 2007–. *Address:* Office of the Second Vice-President, Bujumbura, Burundi (office). *Website:* presidence .burundi-gov.bi (office).

NTOUTOUME EMANE, Jean-François; Gabonese politician; b. 6 Oct. 1939; Minister of State, Minister of Land Registry, Town Planning and Housing and Minister for State Control, Decentralization, Territorial Admin and Regional Integration 1997–99; Prime Minister of Gabon and Head of Govt 1999–2006, also fmrly Minister of Housing and Urbanization. *Address:* c/o Office of the Prime Minister, BP 546, Libreville, Gabon (office).

NUAIMI, Ali ibn Ibrahim an-, MS; Saudi Arabian government official and fmr oil industry executive; *Minister of Petroleum and Mineral Resources;* b. 1935, Eastern Prov.; m. 1962; four c.; ed Int. Coll. Beirut, American Univ., Beirut and Lehigh Univ., Pennsylvania and Stanford Univ., USA; Asst Geologist, Exploration Dept, Aramco 1953, Hydrologist and Geologist 1963–67, worked in Econs and Public Relations Dept 1967–69, Vice-Pres. Aramco 1975, Sr Vice-Pres. 1978, Dir 1980, Exec. Vice-Pres., Operations 1982, Pres. 1984, CEO 1988; Minister of Petroleum and Mineral Resources 1995–. *Leisure interests:* hunting, hiking. *Address:* Ministry of Petroleum and Mineral Resources, PO Box 247, King Abd al-Aziz Road, Riyadh 11191, Saudi Arabia. *Telephone:* (1) 478-1661. *Fax:* (1) 478-1980.

NUAIMI, HH Sheikh Humaid bin Rashid an-, (Ruler of Ajman); United Arab Emirates Ruler of Ajman 1981–; mem. Supreme Council of UAE 1981–; Patron, Sheikh Humaid bin Rashid Prizes for Culture and Science 1983–. *Address:* Ruler's Palace, PO Box 1, Ajman, United Arab Emirates.

NUAIMI, Rashid Abdullah an-; United Arab Emirates politician; Acting Minister of Foreign Affairs 1980–90, Minister of Foreign Affairs 1990–2006. *Address:* c/o Ministry of Foreign Affairs, PO Box 1, Abu Dhabi, United Arab Emirates (office).

NUDER, Pär, BL; Swedish politician; b. 1963; m.; two d.; mem. Österåker Municipal Exec. Cttee 1982–94; Chair. Stockholm co. br. Swedish Social Democratic Youth League 1986–89, mem. Nat. Exec. Cttee 1989–90; Political Adviser to Minister for Justice 1986–87, to Prime Minister's Office 1988–91, to Prime Minister 1994–96, 1996–97; Alt. mem. Riksdag 1988–94, mem. 1994–, mem. Parl. Cttee on Justice 1994–97; Political Sec. Social Democratic Parl. Party Group 1992–94, mem. Exec. Cttee, Stockholm county br. Social Democratic Party 1992–94; Exec. mem. Prime Minister's Advisory Council for Baltic Sea Cooperation 1996–2000; Chair. Task Force on Organized Crime in the Baltic Sea Area 1996–2000; State Sec. Prime Minister's Office 1997–2002, Minister for Policy Coordination 2002–04, for Finance 2004–06; Chair. Vasallen AB 2001–02; mem. Bd Vin & Sprit AB 2001–02; Vice-Pres. Bd Nat. Swedish Art Museums 1995–97. *Address:* c/o Sveriges Socialdemokratiska Arbetareparti (SAP) (Swedish Social Democratic Party), Sveavägen 68, 105 60 Stockholm, Sweden.

NUGIS, Ülo; Estonian politician and business executive; b. 28 April 1944, Tallinn; ed Minsk Polytechnical Inst.; Chief Engineer, Tegur Factory 1970–73; Dir Ehitusdetail (experimental factory) 1974–80; Dir Dunamo (ski mfg factory) 1980–86; Dir-Gen. Production Asscn Estoplast 1986–1990; mem. Congress of Estonia and Speaker Supreme Soviet of Estonian Repub. 1990–92; mem. Republican Coalition Party (now People's Party of Republicans and Conservatives) 1990–; Chair. Riigikogu (State Ass.) 1992–95, mem. 1995–2005, Deputy Chair. Foreign Affairs Cttee. *Address:* c/o Riigikogu, Lossi-plats 1A, 15165 Tallinn, Estonia. *Telephone:* (6) 31-63-50.

NUJOMA, Sam; Namibian fmr head of state; *Founding President of the Republic of Namibia and Founding Father of the Namibian Nation;* b. (Samuel Shafiihuma Nujoma), 12 May 1929, Etunda Village, Ongandjera Dist; s. of the late Daniel Uutoni Nujoma and of Helvi Mpingana Kondombolo; m. Kovambo Theopoldine Katjimune 1956; three s. one d.; ed Okahaol Finnish Mission School, St Barnabas School, Windhoek; with State Railways until 1957; Municipal Clerk, Windhoek 1957; clerk in wholesale store 1957–59; elected Leader of Ovamboland People's Org. (OPO) 1959; arrested Dec. 1959; went into exile 1960; Founder, with Herman Toivo ja Toivo (q.v.) and Pres. SWAPO (SW Africa People's Org.) April 1960–2007; appeared before UN Cttee on SW Africa June 1960; set up SWAPO provisional HQ in Dar es Salaam, Tanzania March 1961; arrested on return to Windhoek and formally ordered out of the country March 1966; turned to armed struggle after rejection by Int. Court of Justice of SWAPO complaint against S Africa Aug. 1966; gave evidence at UN Security Council Oct. 1971; led SWAPO negotiations at numerous int. negotiations culminating in implementation in March 1989 of UN Resolution 435 providing for independence of Namibia; returned to Namibia Sept. 1989; mem. Constituent Ass. 1989–90; Pres. of Namibia 1990–2005, also Minister of Home Affairs 1995–96; Fellow, Inst. of Governance and Social Research – Jos, Plateau State, Nigeria 2003–; Grand Master, Order of Merit Grand Cruz (Brazil), Companion of the Order of Star of Ghana 2004; Hon. LLD (Ahmadu Bello Univ., Nigeria) 1982, (Lincoln Univ., USA) 1990, (Ohio Cen. State Univ., USA) 1993, (State Univ. of NJ, USA) 1997; Hon. DTech (Fed. Univ. of Tech., Minna) 1992, Hon. DEd (Univ. of Namibia) 1993; Hon. DSc (Abubakar Tafawa Balewa Univ., Nigeria) 2003; Dr hc (Academic Council, Russian Econ. Acad.) 1998, (People's Friendship Univ. of Russia); Lenin Peace Prize 1973, Frederic Joliot Curie Gold Medal 1980, Ho Chi Minh Peace Award 1988, Indira Gandhi Peace Prize 1990, Africa Prize for Leadership for Sustainable End to Hunger, New York 1995, Order of Friendship Award (Viet Nam) 2000; numerous honours and awards. *Publications:* To Free Namibia 1994, Where Others Wavered – My Life in SWAPO and My Participation in the Liberation Struggle of Namibia (autobiog.) 2001. *Address:* The Sam Nujoma Foundation, Private Bag 13220, Robert Mugabe Avenue, Windhoek, Namibia (office). *Telephone:* (61) 377700 (office). *Fax:* (61) 253098 (office). *E-mail:* jnauta@iway.na (office).

NUKAGA, Fukushiro; Japanese politician and fmr journalist; b. 1944; ed Waseda Univ.; fmr political and econ. reporter for Sankei Shimbun; fmr mem. Ibaraki Prefectural Ass.; mem. LDP; mem. for Ibaraki, House of Reps; fmr Deputy Chief Cabinet Sec.; Dir-Gen. Defence Agency 1998–2000, of Econ. Planning Agency 2000–01; Minister of State for Defence 2005–06; Minister of Finance 2007–08; fmr Chair. Policy Research Council, Liberal-Democratic Party–LDP (Jiyu-Minshuto). *Address:* Liberal-Democratic Party, 1-11-23, Nagata-cho, Chiyoda-ku, Tokyo 100-8910, Japan (office). *Telephone:* (3) 3581-6211 (office). *E-mail:* koho@ldp.jimin.or.jp (office). *Website:* www.jimin.jp (office).

NUMAN, Yasin Said; Yemeni politician; fmr Deputy Prime Minister and Minister of Fisheries; Prime Minister of Democratic Republic of Yemen 1986–90, Minister of Labour and Civil Service 1986.

NUMATA, Sadaaki; Japanese diplomatist; b. 1943, Hyogo Prefecture; m. Kyoko Numata; one s. one d.; ed Tokyo Univ., Univ. Coll., Oxford, UK; served in Embassy in London 1968–70; positions at Ministry of Foreign Affairs, Tokyo dealing with econ. cooperation, then N American affairs 1970–76; served in Embassy in Jakarta, Indonesia 1976–78; Politico-Mil. Officer, Embassy in Washington DC 1978–82; Dir, First Int. Orgs (GATT) Div., Econ. Affairs Bureau, Tokyo 1982–84; Dir Japan-US Security Div., N American Affairs Bureau 1984–85, Dir First N America Div. 1985–87; Deputy Japanese Rep. to Conf. on Disarmament, Geneva 1987–88; Deputy Head of Mission, Embassy in Canberra, Australia 1989–91; Deputy Spokesman of Foreign Ministry, Tokyo 1991–94; Deputy Head of Mission, Embassy in London 1994–98; Foreign Ministry Spokesman and Dir Gen. for Press and Public Information, Tokyo 1998–2000; Amb. to Pakistan 2000–02; Amb. in Charge of Okinawan Affairs 2003–04; Amb. to Canada 2005–07; Exec. Dir Center for Global Partnership, Japan Foundation 2007–. *Leisure interests:* singing folk songs, fly fishing, skiing. *Address:* Center for Global Partnership, 4-4-1 Yotsuya, Shinjuku-ku, Tokyo 160-0004, Japan (office). *Telephone:* (03) 5369-6072 (office). *Fax:* (03) 5369-6042 (office). *Website:* www.cgp.org (office).

NUNEZ-TESHEIRA, Karen, MBA; Trinidad and Tobago lawyer, politician, educator and writer; *Minister of Finance;* m. (deceased); two c.; ed St Joseph's Convent, San Fernando and Port of Spain, Univ. of the West Indies; fmr Sr Lecturer and Vice-Prin. Hugh Wooding Law School; currently MP (People's Nat. Movt) for D'Abadie/O'Meara; Minister of Finance 2007–. *Publications:* Non-Contentious Probate Practice in the English-Speaking Caribbean 2001, The Legal Profession in the English-Speaking Caribbean 2004, Non-Contentious Probate Cases in the English-Speaking Caribbean 2005. *Address:* Ministry of Finance, Eric Williams Finance Bldg, Independence Square, Port of Spain, Trinidad and Tobago (office). *Telephone:* 627-9700 (office). *Fax:* 627-5882 (office). *E-mail:* mofcmu@tstt.net.tt (office). *Website:* www.finance.gov.tt (office).

NUNGESSER, Roland, LenD; French politician; b. 9 Oct. 1925, Nogent-sur-Marne; s. of Léon Nungesser and Aline Sanguinolenti; m. 1st Michèle Jeanne Elizabeth Selignac 1957 (divorced 1981); three d.; m. 2nd Marie-Christine Ventrillon 1981; ed Ecole Libre des Sciences Politiques, Paris Law Faculty; Commissaire-général du Salon Nautique Int. 1957–62; Vice-Pres. Chambre Syndicale des Industries Nautiques; Pres. Conseil Nat. de la Navigation de Plaisance 1961–67; Regional Chair. 1962; Deputy for Seine 1958–67, Val-de-Marne 1967–95; Sec. Nat. Ass. 1958–60; Sec. of State for Housing 1966–67; Sec. of State at Ministry of Economy and Finance 1967–68; Minister of Youth and Sports May–July 1968; Mayor of Nogent-sur-Marne 1959–95; Pres. Franco-Soviet (then Franco-Russian 1992) Chamber of Commerce 1969–98, Liaison Cttee for Local Councillors 1971, Union of Parisian Region Mayors 1983, Soc. for Protection of Animals (SPA) 1984–88 (Hon. Pres. 1988–); Vice-Pres. Nat. Ass. 1969–74; Pres. Conseil Général du Val de Marne 1970–76; Vice-Pres. Movt Nat. des élus Iocaus 1976–95; Pres. Carrefour du Gaullisme 1979–, Asscn des Maires de l'Ile-de France 1983–95, now Hon. Pres.; mem. RPR; mem. various socs and asscns; Commdr Légion d'honneur. *Publications:* Le Chevalier du ciel, La Revolution qu'il faut faire. *Leisure interests:* motor yachting, athletics. *Address:* c/o Association des Maires de l'Ile-de-France, 26 rue du Renard, 75004 Paris (office); 18 avenue Duvelleroy, 94130 Nogent-sur-Marne, France. *Telephone:* 1-48-77-76-76. *Fax:* 1-48-77-99-16 (home).

NUNN, Sam, LLB; American fmr politician and lawyer; *Co-Chairman and CEO, Nuclear Threat Initiative;* b. 8 Sept. 1938, Macon, Ga; s. of Samuel Augustus Nunn and Elizabeth Cannon Nunn; m. Colleen O'Brien 1965; one s. one d.; ed Georgia Inst. of Tech., Emory Univ. and Emory Univ. Law School, Atlanta; pvt. law practice 1964–72; mem. Georgia House of Reps 1968–72; US

Senator from Georgia (Democrat) 1972–96, mem. Armed Services Cttee, Govt Affairs Cttee, Small Business Cttee; Sr Partner, King & Spalding, Atlanta 1997 (now retd); currently Co-Chair. and CEO Nuclear Threat Initiative, Washington; also currently Distinguished Prof., Sam Nunn School of Int., Georgia Inst. of Tech.; also currently Chair. Bd of Trustees Center for Strategic and Int. Studies, Washington; mem. Bd Dirs ChevronTexaco Corpn, The Coca-Cola Co., Dell Inc., General Electric Co., Internet Security Systems. Inc., Scientific-Atlanta Inc. *Leisure interests:* golf, reading. *Address:* Nuclear Threat Initiative (NTI), 1747 Pennsylvania Avenue, NW, 7th Floor, Washington, DC 20006 (office); Center for Strategic and International Studies, 1800 K Street, NW, Suite 400, Washington, DC 20006, USA (office). *Telephone:* (202) 296-4810 (NTI) (office); (404) 385-6544 (Georgia Tech) (office). *Fax:* (202) 296-4811 (NTI) (office). *Website:* www.nti.org (office); www.inta.gatech.edu/~sam_nunn (office); www.csis.org/experts/4nunn.htm (office).

NUNN, Sir Trevor Robert, Kt, CBE; British theatre director; *Director Emeritus, Royal Shakespeare Company;* b. 14 Jan. 1940, Ipswich; s. of Robert Alexander Nunn and Dorothy May Nunn (née Piper); m. 1st Janet Suzman (q.v.) 1969 (divorced 1986); one s.; m. 2nd Sharon Lee Hill 1986 (divorced 1991); two d.; m. 3rd Imogen Stubbs 1994; one s. one d.; ed Northgate Grammar School, Ipswich and Downing Coll. Cambridge; Trainee Dir Belgrade Theatre, Coventry; Assoc. Dir Royal Shakespeare Co. 1964–86, Artistic Dir 1968–78, CEO 1968–86, Jt Artistic Dir 1978–86, Dir Emer. 1986–; f. Homevale Ltd and Awayvale Ltd; Artistic Dir Royal Nat. Theatre 1996–2001; toured USA, Australia with own version of Hedda Gabler 1975; mem. Arts Council of England 1994–; Hon. LittD (Warwick) 1982; Hon. MA (Newcastle-upon-Tyne) 1982; Hon. DLitt (Suffolk) 1997. *Productions:* Tango 1965, The Revenger's Tragedy (London Theatre Critics' Best Dir Award) 1965, 1969, The Taming of the Shrew, The Relapse, The Winter's Tale (London Theatre Critics' Best Dir Award) 1969, Hamlet 1970, Henry VIII 1970, Roman Season: Antony and Cleopatra (Soc. of Film and TV Arts Award 1975), Coriolanus, Julius Caesar, Titus Andronicus 1970, Macbeth 1974, 1976, Hedda Gabler (own version) 1975, Romeo and Juliet 1976, The Comedy of Errors (Ivor Novello Award for Best British Musical of 1976 (Lyrics), Soc. of West End Theatre Award for Best Musical of the Year 1977) 1976, Winter's Tale (co-dir) 1976, King Lear (co-dir) 1976, Macbeth 1976, The Alchemist 1977, As You Like It 1977, Every Good Boy Deserves Favour 1977, Three Sisters 1978, The Merry Wives of Windsor 1979, Once in a Lifetime (Plays and Players Award 1978, 1979 for Best Production (Dir), Sydney Edwards Award for Best Dir, Evening Standard Drama Awards 1978, 1979) 1979, Juno and the Paycock 1980, The Life and Adventures of Nicholas Nickleby (Soc. of West End Theatres Awards, including Best Dir, Best New Play, Evening Standard Award, Best Dir, Drama Award for Best Dir, Mr. Abbott Award (Broadway) 1980 (with John Caird) (New York 1981), Cats 1981, All's Well That Ends Well 1981, Henry IV (Parts I & II) 1981, 1982, Peter Pan (with John Caird) 1982, Starlight Express 1984, Les Misérables (with John Caird) 1985, Chess 1986, The Fair Maid of the West 1986, Aspects of Love 1989, Othello 1989, The Baker's Wife 1989, Timon of Athens 1991, The Blue Angel 1991, Measure for Measure 1991, Heartbreak House 1992, Arcadia 1993, Sunset Boulevard 1993, Enemy of The People 1997, Mutabilitie 1997, Not About Nightingales 1998, Oklahoma! 1998, Betrayal 1998, Troilus and Cressida 1999, The Merchant of Venice 1999, Summerfolk 1999, Love's Labour's Lost 2002, We Happy Few 2004, The Woman in White 2004, Acorn Antiques 2005, Katya Kabanova 2007. *Television:* Antony and Cleopatra 1975, Comedy of Errors 1976, Every Good Boy Deserves Favour 1978, Macbeth 1978, Shakespeare Workshops Word of Mouth (written and directed by T. Nunn) 1979, The Three Sisters, Othello 1989, Porgy and Bess 1992, Oklahoma! 1999. *Films:* Hedda (own scripted version), Lady Jane 1985, Twelfth Night 1996. *Operas:* Idomeneo 1982, Porgy and Bess 1986, Così fan tutte 1991, Peter Grimes 1992, Katya Kabanova 1994, Sophie's Choice 2002, Porgy and Bess 2006. *Publication:* British Theatre Design 1989. *Address:* c/o Royal Shakespeare Company, Royal Shakespeare Theatre, Waterside, Stratford-upon-Avon, Warwicks., CV37 6BB, England.

NURBERDIYEVA, Akja Tajiyevna; Turkmenistani politician; *Chairman, Majlis;* mem. Majlis (Parl.), Vice-Chair. 2003–06, Acting Chair. 2006–07, Chair. 2007–. *Address:* Majlis, 744000 Aşgabat, ul. Bitarap Türkmenistan 17, Turkmenistan (office). *Telephone:* (12) 35-31-25 (office). *Fax:* (12) 35-31-47 (office).

NURGALIYEV, Col-Gen. Rashid Gumarovich, PhD; Russian politician and security officer; *Minister of Internal Affairs;* b. 8 Oct. 1956, Zhetygar, Kazakh SSR; m.; two c.; ed Kuusinen State Univ.; ethnic Tatar; physics teacher, Nadvoitsy 1979–81; with KGB, and its successor, since 1981, Head of Anti-Terrorist Dept, Karelian Republican KGB 1991–95, Chief Inspector, Fed. Counterespionage Service (FSB) 1995–98, Head, Office for Drug Trafficking Control, Dept of Econ. Security 1999–2000, Deputy Dir, Head of Inspectors Admin 2000–02; First Deputy Minister of Internal Affairs 2002–04, Head of Criminal Militia Service 2002–04, Minister of Internal Affairs 2004–. *Address:* Ministry of Internal Affairs, 119049 Moscow, ul. Zhitnaya 16, Russia (office). *Telephone:* (495) 239-69-71 (office). *Fax:* (495) 293-59-98 (office). *E-mail:* mvd12@mvdrf.ru (office). *Website:* www.mvd.ru (office).

NUROWSKI, Piotr, LLB; Polish business executive and fmr diplomatist; *President of the Management Board, Elektrim SA;* b. 1948; ed Warsaw Univ.; Pres., Polish Athletics Asscn 1973–80; joined Ministry of Foreign Affairs 1981, First Sec., Polish Embassy, Moscow, Russia 1981–84, Ministry of Foreign Affairs Asia, Africa and Australia Dept, Warsaw 1984–86, Counsellor, Polish Embassy, Rabat, Morocco 1986–91; Dir, PZ SOLPOL 1991–92; mem. Man. Bd, Polska Telewizja Satelitarna Polsat SA (later Telewizja Polsat SA) 1992–98, mem. Supervisory Bd 1998–; Vice-Pres., Children and Youth Sport Asscn 1998–; currently mem. Supervisory Bd and Pres., Man. Bd, Elektrim SA; consultant, LP Piotr Nurowski. *Address:* Elektrim SA, Pańska 77/79, 00–834 Warsaw, Poland (office). *Website:* www.elektrim.pl (office).

NURSE, Sir Paul Maxime, Kt, MA, PhD, FRS; British university president and scientist; *President, Rockefeller University;* b. 25 Jan. 1949, Norfolk; s. of Maxime Nurse and Cissie Nurse (née White); m. Anne Teresa Talbott 1971; two d.; ed Harrow County Grammar School, Univ. of Birmingham, Univ. of East Anglia; Research Fellow, Dept of Zoology, Univ. of Edin. 1974–78; Sr Research Fellow, School of Biology, Univ. of Sussex 1980–84; Head Cell Cycle Control Lab., Imperial Cancer Research Fund (ICRF), London 1984–87; Iveagh Prof. of Microbiology, Univ. of Oxford 1987–91, Napier Research Prof. of Royal Soc. 1991–93; Dir of Research (Labs) and Head Cell Cycle Lab., ICRF 1993–96, Dir-Gen. ICRF 1996–2002, Dir-Gen. (Science) and CEO Cancer Research UK 2002–03; Pres. Rockefeller Univ., NY 2003–; Fleming Lecturer, Soc. of Gen. Microbiology 1984; Florey Lecturer, Royal Soc. 1990; Marjory Stephenson Lecturer, Soc. of Gen. Microbiology 1990; mem. EMBO 1987–; Pres. Genetical Soc. 1990–93; mem. Academia Europaea 1991; Foreign Assoc. NAS 1995–; Hon. FRCP; Hon. FRCPath 2000; Feldberg Prize for Medical Research (UK/Germany) 1991, CIBA Medal (Biochemical Soc.) 1991, Louis Jeantet Prize for Medicine in Europe, Switzerland 1992, Gairdner Foundation Int. Award, Canada 1992, Royal Soc. Wellcome Medal 1993, Jiménez Díaz Memorial Award and Medal (Spain) 1993, Purkyne Medal, Czech Acad. 1994, Pezcoller Award for Oncology Research (Italy) 1995, Royal Soc. Medal 1995, Dr Josef Steiner Prize, Switzerland 1996, Dr H.P. Heineken Prize for Biochemistry and Biophysics (Netherlands) 1996, Alfred P. Sloan, Jr Prize and Medal, General Motors Cancer Research Foundation 1997, Berkan Judd Award (USA) 1998, Albert Lasker Award (USA) 1998, Nobel Prize for Physiology or Medicine 2001. *Publications:* numerous articles in scientific journals concerned with cell and molecular biology. *Leisure interests:* hang gliding, motorcycling, running, astronomy, talking. *Address:* Rockefeller University, 1230 York Avenue, New York, NY 10021, USA (office). *Telephone:* (212) 327-8000 (office). *Fax:* (212) 327-7974 (office). *E-mail:* pubinfo@rockefeller.edu (office). *Website:* www.rockefeller.edu (office).

NUSSBAUM, Martha Craven, MA, PhD; American academic; *Ernst Freund Distinguished Service Professor of Law and Ethics, University of Chicago;* b. 6 May 1947, New York, NY; d. of George Craven and Betty Craven; m. Alan J. Nussbaum 1969 (divorced 1987); one d.; ed New York and Harvard Univs.; Jr Fellow, Soc. of Fellows, Harvard Univ. 1972–75, Asst Prof. of Philosophy and Classics 1975–80, Assoc. Prof. 1980–83; Assoc. Prof. of Philosophy and Classics, Brown Univ. 1984–85, Prof. of Philosophy, Classics and Comparative Literature 1985–87, David Benedict Prof. 1987–89, Prof. 1989–95; Visiting Prof. of Law, Univ. of Chicago 1994, Prof. of Law and Ethics 1995–96, Prof. of Philosophy 1995–, Prof. of Divinity 1995–, Ernst Freund Prof. of Law and Ethics 1996–, Assoc. mem. Classics Dept 1996–, Assoc. mem. Dept of Political Science 2003–, Founder and Coordinator, Center for Comparative Constitutionalism 2002–; Visiting Prof. Jawaharlal Nehru Univ., New Delhi, India 2004; Fellow, American Acad. of Arts and Science; mem. American Philosophical Asscn (Chair. Cttee on Status of Women 1994–97); Brandeis Creative Arts Award 1990, PEN Spielvogel-Diamondstein Award 1991, NY Univ. Distinguished Alumni Award 2000, Grawwmeyer Award in Educ. 2002, Barnard Medal of Distinction 2003; many other awards. *Publications:* Aristotle's De Motu Animalium 1978, Language and Logic (ed.) 1983, The Fragility of Goodness 1986, Love's Knowledge 1990, Essays on Aristotle's De Anima (ed. with A. Rorty) 1992, The Therapy of Desire 1994, The Quality of Life (ed. with A. Sen) 1993, Passions and Perceptions (ed. with J. Brunschwig) 1993, Women, Culture and Development (ed. with J. Glover) 1995, Poetic Justice 1996, For Love of Country 1996, Cultivating Humanity 1997, Sex and Social Justice 1998, Hiding from Humanity: Disgust, Shame and the Law 2004, Liberty of Conscience 2008. *Leisure interests:* music, running, hiking. *Address:* 520 Law Quad, Law School, University of Chicago, 1111 East 60th Street, Chicago, IL 60637, USA (office). *Telephone:* (773) 702-3470 (office). *Fax:* (773) 702-0730 (office). *E-mail:* martha_nussbaum@law.uchicago.edu (office). *Website:* www.law.uchicago.edu/faculty/nussbaum (office).

NUSSLE, James (Jim) Allen, BA, JD; American lawyer, politician and fmr government official; b. 27 June 1960, Des Moines, Ia; m. 1st Leslie Jeanne Harbison 1986 (divorced 1996); one s. one d.; m. 2nd Karen Chiccehitto 2001; ed Luther Coll., Drake Univ.; called to the Bar, Iowa 1985, States Attorney for Delaware Co., Ia 1986–90; mem. US House of Reps (Ia 2nd Dist) 1991–2006 (retd), Chair. House Budget Cttee 2001–06; ran unsucessfully for Gov. of Ia 2006; Dir Office of Man. and Budget 2007–09; Republican.

NÜSSLEIN-VOLHARD, Christiane, PhD, FRS; German scientist and academic; b. 20 Oct. 1942, Magdeburg; d. of Rolf Volhard and Brigitte Volhard (née Haas); ed Univ. of Tübingen; Research Assoc., Lab. of Dr Schaller, Max-Planck-Inst. für Virusforschung, Tübingen 1972–74; Postdoctoral Fellow (EMBO Fellowship), Lab. of Prof. Dr W. Gehring, Biozentrum Basel, Switzerland 1975–76, Lab. of Prof. Dr K. Sander, Univ. of Freiburg 1977; Head of Group, European Molecular Biology Lab. (EMBL), Heidelberg 1978–80; Group Leader, Friedrich-Miescher-Laboratorium, Max-Planck-Gesellschaft, Tübingen 1981–85, Scientific mem. Max-Planck-Gesellschaft and Dir Max-Planck-Institut für Entwicklungsbiologie, Tübingen 1985–90, Dir Dept of Genetics 1990–; f. Christiane Nüsslein-Volhard Stiftung 1994; mem. NAS; Hon. ScD (Yale) 1990, (Oxford) 2005; Dr hc (Utrecht) 1991, (Princeton) 1991, (Harvard) 1993; Albert Lasker Medical Research Award, New York 1991, Prix Louis Jeantet de Médicine, Geneva 1992, Ernst Schering Prize, Berlin 1993, Nobel Prize in Medicine 1995, Grosses Verdienstkreuz mit Stern 1996, Ordre pour le Mérite 1997. *Publications:* 135 Zebra Fish: A Practical Approach 2002; numerous scientific articles. *Address:* Max-Planck-Institut für Entwicklungsbiologie, Spemannstrasse 35, 72076 Tübingen,

Germany. *Telephone:* (7071) 601487. *Fax:* (7071) 601384 (office). *E-mail:* christiane.nuesslein-volhard@tuebingen.mpg.de (office). *Website:* www.cnv -stiftung.de; www.eb.tuebingen.mpg.de/departments/3-genetics/christiane -nusslein-volhard (office).

NUTT, Jim, BFA; American artist; b. 28 Nov. 1938, Pittsfield, Mass.; s. of Frank E. Nutt and Ruth Tureman Nutt; m. Gladys Nilsson 1961; ed School of Art Inst. of Chicago, Washington Univ. and Univ. of Pennsylvania; Prof. of Art, Calif. State Univ., Sacramento 1968–75, School of Art Inst. of Chicago 1990; Cassandra Foundation Award 1969, Nat. Endowment for the Arts Award 1975, 1990. *Address:* c/o Phyllis Kind Gallery, 136 Greene Street, New York, NY 10012, USA.

NUWEIR, Abd as-Salam Ahmad; Libyan government official; currently Sec. for Economy. *Address:* c/o General Secretariat of the General People's Congress, Tripoli, Libya.

NYAKYI, Anthony Balthazar, BA; Tanzanian diplomatist; b. 8 June 1936, Moshi; m. Margaret Mariki 1969; two s. two d.; ed Umbwe Secondary School, Moshi, Holy Ghost Secondary School, Pugu, Makerere Univ. Coll., Kampala, Uganda; Dir Political Div., Ministry of Foreign Affairs 1966–68; Amb. to Netherlands 1968–70, to FRG (also accred to the Holy See 1970 and Romania 1972) 1970–72; Prin. Sec. Ministry of Foreign Affairs 1972–78, Ministry of Defence and Nat. Service 1978–80; High Commr in Zimbabwe 1980–81, in UK 1981–89; Perm. Rep. to UN 1989–94; UN Special Rep. for Liberia 1994–98; apptd. Amb. to Burundi 1998. *Address:* c/o Ministry of Foreign Affairs and International Co-operation, POB 9000, Dar es Salaam, Tanzania.

NYAMDORJ, Tsendiin, LLB, PhD; Mongolian lawyer and politician; *Minister of Justice and Home Affairs;* b. 1956, Aimag Uws; ed Leningrad Univ.; Div. Prosecutor and Head of Div., State Gen. Authority of Prosecutor 1981–88; First Deputy, Gen. Prosecutor's Office of Mil Affairs 1988–90; First Deputy Minister of Justice 1990–92; mem. People's Grand Hural (Parl.) 1992–, Chair. (Speaker) 2005–07; Minister of Justice and Home Affairs 2000–05, 2008–; mem. Mongolian People's Revolutionary Party. *Address:* Ministry of Justice and Home Affairs, Government Bldg 5, Khudaldaany Gudamj 6/1, Chingeltei District, Ulan Bator, Mongolia (office). *Telephone:* (11) 267014 (office). *Fax:* (11) 325225 (office). *E-mail:* admin@mojha.gov.mn (office). *Website:* www .mojha.gov.mn (office).

NYAN WIN, Maj.-Gen.; Myanma government official; *Minister of Foreign Affairs;* fmr mem. of staff, Office of Strategic Studies (OSS); Vice-Chief of Defence Services Training –2004; Minister of Foreign Affairs 2004–; mem. Nat. Convention Convening Comm. *Address:* Ministry of Foreign Affairs, Pyay Road, Dagon Township, Yangon, Myanmar (office). *Telephone:* (1) 222844 (office). *Fax:* (1) 222950 (office). *E-mail:* mofa.aung@mptmail.net.mm (office). *Website:* www.mofa.gov.mm (office).

NYANDA, Gen. Siphiwe, (Gebhuza), BA; South African army officer (retd); b. 22 May 1950, Soweto; s. of Henry Nyanda and Betsy Nyanda; two s. five d.; ed Orlando High School, Soweto, Univ. of S Africa, Univ. of London, UK; fmrly sports journalist; trained in fmr GDR and USSR as platoon commdr, artilleryman and in intelligence; mem. African Nat. Congress (ANC), fmrly guerrilla fighter for ANC, Commissar of Transvaal Region 1979–86, mem. Nat. Exec. Cttee 1991–96; Deputy Chief, S African Nat. Defence Force 1997–98, Chief 1998–2005; Chief of Staff Mkhonto we Sizwe 1992–94; Chevalier, Légion d'honneur and other decorations; Mil. Merit Medal 1995, Gold Star of South Africa 1998, American Legion of Honor, Star of South Africa. *Leisure interests:* reading, watching soccer, playing golf, aerobics. *Address:* Private Bag X414, Pretoria 0001 (office); 15 Westminster Avenue, Bryanstown; c/o Ministry of Defence, Armscor Building, Block 5, Nossob Street, Erasmusrand 0181, South Africa. *Telephone:* (11) 4632778 (home). *Fax:* (11) 4632847. *E-mail:* s.nyanda@mweb.co.za.

NYE, Erle, BEng, LLB; American energy executive; *Chairman, TXU Corporation;* m. Alice Nye; five c.; ed TX A&M Univ., Southern Methodist Univ. (SMU); joined Enserch/Lone Star Gas 1959, various positions in eng, finance, regulation, operations and legal depts, Chief Financial Officer presiding over mergers that formed TXU 1997, CEO TXU Corpn 2001–04, Chair. 2001–(05), also Chair. TXU Energy, Oncor Electric Delivery, TXU Gas and TXU Australia; Chair. Electric Inst., N American Electric Reliability Council, Electric Reliability Council of Texas, Nuclear Energy Inst.; mem. Pres.'s Nat. Infrastructure Advisory Council; mem. Bd Dallas Citizens Council, Boys & Girls Clubs of America (BGCA), State Fair of Texas, North Texas Public Broadcasting, Dallas Cttee on Foreign Relations, Salvation Army Dallas County Advisory Bd, Dallas Symphony, Dallas Center for the Performing Arts Foundation; mem. Bd Regents Texas A&M Univ. 1997–, Chair. 2001–; mem. Devt Council Univ. of Texas at Dallas; mem. Exec. Bd Cox Schools of Business and Law, Maguire Center for Ethics and Public Responsibility; mem. Gov.'s Business Council; mem. local, state and nat. bar asscns; Dr hc (Baylor Coll. of Dentistry); Distinguished Citizen Award, Longhorn Council of Boy Scouts of America 1998, Humanitarian of the Year Award, American Jewish Cttee 1999, Russell H. Perry Free Enterprise Award 2000, Conn Distinguished New Venture Leader, Texas A&M Univ. 2001, SMU Robert G. Storey Award 2002, Nasher Award, Dallas Business Cttee for the Arts 2002, Distinguished Leader Award, Texas Asscn of Business 2002, Bernard H. Falk Award, Nat. Electric Mfrs Asscn 2002, Corp. Social Responsibility Award, Mexican-American Legal Defense and Educ. Fund 2002. *Address:* TXU Corporation, Energy Plaza, 1601 Bryan Street, 33rd Floor, Dallas, TX 75201-3411, USA (office). *Telephone:* (214) 812-4600 (office). *Fax:* (214) 812-7077 (office). *Website:* www.txucorp.com (office).

NYE, John Frederick, MA, PhD, FRS, FInstP; British physicist and academic; *Professor Emeritus of Physics, University of Bristol;* b. 26 Feb. 1923, Hove,

Sussex; s. of Haydn Percival Nye and Jessie Mary Nye (née Hague); brother of Peter Hague Nye; m. Georgiana Wiebenson 1953; one s. two d.; ed Stowe School, King's Coll., Cambridge; Demonstrator, Dept of Mineralogy and Petrology, Univ. of Cambridge 1949–51; mem. of Tech. Staff, Bell Telephone Labs, NJ 1952–53; Lecturer in Physics, Univ. of Bristol 1953–65, Reader 1965–69, Prof. 1969–88, Prof. Emer. 1988–; Pres. Int. Glaciological Soc. 1966–69, Int. Comm. of Snow and Ice 1971–75; Foreign mem. Royal Swedish Acad. of Sciences 1977; glacier in Palmer Peninsula, Antarctica officially named Nye Glacier 1963; Seligman Crystal Int. Glaciological Soc. 1969, Antarctic Service Medal (USA) 1974, Charles Chree Medal and Prize, Inst. of Physics 1989. *Publications:* Physical Properties of Crystals 1957, Natural Focusing and Fine Structure of Light 1999; numerous papers in scientific journals on glaciers, physics of ice, waves and math. catastrophes. *Leisure interest:* gardening. *Address:* University of Bristol, H. H. Wills Physics Laboratory, Royal Fort, Tyndall Avenue, Bristol, BS8 ITL (office); 45 Canynge Road, Bristol, BS8 3LH, England (home). *Telephone:* (117) 928-8727 (office); (117) 973-3769 (home). *E-mail:* john.nye@bristol.ac.uk (office). *Website:* www .phy.bris.ac.uk (office).

NYE, Joseph Samuel, Jr, BA, PhD; American political scientist, academic and fmr government official; *University Distinguished Service Professor and Sultan of Oman Professor of International Relations, Harvard University;* b. 19 Jan. 1937; s. of Joseph Nye and Else Ashwell; m. Molly Harding 1961; three s.; ed Princeton and Harvard Univs, Univ. of Oxford, UK; Prof. of Govt, Harvard Univ. 1969–, also Dir Centre for Int. Affairs 1989–93, Dean and Don K. Price Prof. of Public Policy, John F. Kennedy School of Govt 1995–2004, Univ. Distinguished Service Prof. and Sultan of Oman Prof. of Int. Relations 2004–; Deputy Under-Sec. Dept of State, Washington, DC 1977–79, Chair. Nat. Intelligence Council 1992–; Asst Sec. of Defense for Int. Security Affairs 1994–95; mem. Trilateral Comm.; mem. Council, Int. Inst. of Strategic Studies; mem. Council on Foreign Relations; Fellow, American Acad. of Arts and Sciences, Aspen Inst.; Dept of State Distinguished Honor Award 1979, Intelligence Distinguished Service Award 1994, Dept of Defense Distinguished Service Medal 1995, Charles E. Merriman Award, American Political Science Asscn 2003, Woodrow Wilson Award, Princeton Univ. 2004. *Publications:* Power and Independence (co-author) 1977, The Making of America's Soviet Policy (ed. and co-author) 1984, Hawks, Doves and Owls (co-author and ed.) 1985, Nuclear Ethics 1986, Fateful Visions (co-ed.) 1988, Bound to Lead: The Changing Nature of American Power (co-ed.) 1990, Understanding International Conflicts: An Introduction to Theory and History 1993 (fourth edn) 2002, Governance in a Globalizing World 2000, The Paradox of American Power 2002, Soft Power: The Means to Success in World Politics 2004, Power in a Global Information Age 2004, The Power Game (novel) 2004, The Powers to Lead 2008. *Leisure interests:* fly-fishing, skiing, hiking, squash, gardening. *Address:* Harvard University, John F. Kennedy School of Government, Mailbox 53, 79 John F. Kennedy Street, Cambridge, MA 02138-5801, USA (office). *Telephone:* (617) 495-1123 (office). *Fax:* (617) 495-8963 (office). *E-mail:* joseph_nye@harvard.edu (office). *Website:* ksgfaculty.harvard.edu/ Joseph_Nye (office).

NYE, Robert, FRSL; British poet, novelist and critic; b. 15 March 1939, London; s. of Oswald William Nye and Frances Dorothy Weller; m. 1st Judith Pratt 1959 (divorced 1967); three s.; m. 2nd Aileen Campbell 1968; one d. one step-s. one step-d.; ed Southend High School; freelance writer 1961–; contributes critical articles and reviews to British periodicals, including The Times and The Scotsman; Poetry Critic, The Times 1971–96; Eric Gregory Award 1963, Guardian Fiction Prize 1976, Hawthornden Prize 1977, Soc. of Authors Travelling Scholarship 1991, Authors' Foundation Award 2003, 2007, Cholmondeley Award 2007. *Publications include:* (poetry) Juvenilia 1 1961, Juvenilia 2 1963, Darker Ends 1969, Agnus Dei 1973, Two Prayers 1974, Five Dreams 1974, Divisions on a Ground 1976, A Collection of Poems 1955–1988 1989, 14 Poems 1994, Henry James and Other Poems 1995, Collected Poems 1995, 1998, The Rain and the Glass: 99 Poems, New and Selected 2005, Sixteen Poems 2005; (novels) Doubtfire 1967, Falstaff 1976, Merlin 1978, Faust 1980, The Voyage of the Destiny 1982, The Facts of Life and Other Fictions 1983, The Memoirs of Lord Byron 1989, The Life and Death of My Lord Gilles de Rais 1990, Mrs. Shakespeare: The Complete Works 1993, The Late Mr. Shakespeare 1998, and several children's books; plays: ed.: A Choice of Sir Walter Ralegh's Verse 1972, William Barnes of Dorset: A Selection of his Poems 1973, A Choice of Swinburne's Verse 1973, The English Sermon 1750–1850 1976, The Faber Book of Sonnets 1976, PEN New Poetry I 1986, First Awakenings: The Early Poems of Laura Riding (co-ed.) 1992, A Selection of the Poems of Laura Riding 1993, Some Poems by Ernest Dowson 2006. *Address:* c/o Curtis Brown Ltd, 28–29 Haymarket, London, SW1Y 4SP, England (office). *Telephone:* (20) 7393-4400 (office). *Fax:* (20) 7393-4401 (office). *E-mail:* cb@curtisbrown.co.uk (office). *Website:* www.curtisbrown.co .uk (office).

NYEMBO SHABANI, DSc (Econs); Democratic Republic of the Congo politician and professor of economics; b. 5 Aug. 1937, Kayanza; ed Inst. Saint Boniface, Elisabethville (now Lubumbashi) and Univ. Catholique de Louvain, Belgium; Dir, Bureau of Econ. Co-operation attached to the Prime Minister's Office 1964–65; Research in Econs, Univ. Catholique de Louvain 1967–76; Prof. Faculty of Econ. Science, Nat. Univ. of Zaire Oct. 1976; State Commr for Nat. Econ. and Industry Feb.–Aug. 1977, for Nat. Econ. 1977–78, for the State Portfolio (Investments) 1978–80, for Agric. and Rural Devt 1980–81, 1983–84, for Econ., Industry and Foreign Trade 1982–83, for Finance and Budget 1986–88, for Agric. 1988–89; Pres. Gécamines Holdings 1985. *Publications:* L'industrie du cuivre dans le monde, Le progrès économique du Copperbelt Africain, Bruxelles, La Renaissance du Livre 1975. *Address:* B.P. 3. 824, Kinshasa 1, Democratic Republic of the Congo (home).

NYMAN, Michael, CBE; British composer; b. 23 March 1944, London; ed Royal Acad. of Music, King's Coll. London; composer, writer and music critic 1968–78; lecturer 1976–80; established MN Records label 2005–; Hon. DLitt. *Film and television soundtracks:* Peter Greenaway films: 5 Postcards from Capital Cities 1967, Vertical Features Remake 1976, Goole by Numbers 1976, A Walk Through H: The Reincarnation of an Ornithologist 1978, 1–100 1978, The Falls 1980, Act of God 1980, Terence Conran 1981, The Draughtsman's Contract 1982, The Coastline 1983, Making a Splash 1984, A Zed and Two Noughts 1985, Inside Rooms: 26 Bathrooms, London & Oxfordshire 1985, Drowning by Numbers 1988, Fear of Drowning 1988, Death in the Seine 1988, The Cook, The Thief, His Wife and Her Lover 1989, Hubert Bals Handshake 1989, Prospero's Books 1991; other films: Keep it Downstairs 1976, Tom Phillips 1977, Brimstone and Treacle 1982, Nelly's Version 1983, Frozen Music 1983, The Cold Room 1984, Fairly Secret Army 1984, The Kiss 1985, L'Ange frénétique 1985, I'll Stake My Cremona to a Jew's Trump 1985, The Disputation 1986, Ballet Méchanique 1986, Le Miraculé 1987, The Man Who Mistook His Wife for a Hat 1987, Monsieur Hire 1989, Out of the Ruins 1989, Le Mari de la coiffeuse 1990, Men of Steel 1990, Les Enfants Volants 1990, Not Mozart: Letters, Riddles and Writs 1991, The Final Score 1992, The Fall of Icarus 1992, The Piano 1993, Ryori no tetsujin 1993, Mesmer 1994, A La Folie (Six Days, Six Nights) 1994, Carrington 1995, Anne no nikki (The Diary of Anne Frank) 1995, Der Unhold (The Ogre) 1996, Enemy Zero 1996, Gattaca 1997, Titch 1998, Ravenous 1999, How to Make Dhyrak: A Dramatic Work for Three Players and Camera, Truncated with Only Two Players 1999, Wonderland 1999, Nabbie no koi (Nabbie's Love) 1999, The End of the Affair 1999, The Claim 2000, Act Without Words I 2000, That Sinking Feeling 2000, La Stanza del figlio 2001, Subterrain 2001, 24 heures de la vie d'une femme 2002, The Man with a Movie Camera 2002, The Actors 2003, Nathalie... 2003, Charged 2003, Ident (Channel 5) 2004, Man on Wire 2007. *Other compositions:* orchestral: A Handsom, Smooth, Sweet, Smart, Clear Stroke: Or Else Play Not At All 1983, Taking a Line for a Second Walk 1986, L'Orgie Parisienne 1989, Six Celan Songs 1990, Where the Bee Dances 1991, Self Laudatory Hymn of Inanna and Her Omnipotence 1992, The Upside-Down Violin 1992, MGV (Musique à Grande Vitesse) 1993, On the Fiddle 1993, Concerto for Harpsichord and Strings 1995, Concerto for Trombone 1995, Double Concerto 1996, Strong on Oaks, Strong on the Causes of Oaks 1997, Cycle of Disquietude 1998, a dance he little thinks of 2001, The Draughtsman's Contract for Orchestra 2001, Dance of the Engines 2002, Gattaca for Orchestra 2003, The Claim for Orchestra 2003, The Piano: Concert Suite 2003, Violin Concerto 2003; chamber music: First Waltz in D, Bell Set No. 1 1974, 1–100 1976, Waltz in F 1976, Think Slow, Act Fast 1981, 2 Violins 1981, Four Saxes (Real Slow Drag) 1982, I'll Stake My Cremona to a Jew's Crump 1983, Time's Up 1983, Child's Play 1985, String Quartet No. 1 1985, Taking a Line for a Second Walk 1986, String Quartet No. 2 1988, String Quartet No. 3 1990, In Re Don Giovanni 1991, Masque Arias 1991, Time Will Pronounce 1992, Songs for Tony 1993, Three Quartets 1994, H.R.T. 1995, String Quartet No. 4 1995, Free for All 2001, Five who Figured Four Years Ago 2002, Mapping 2002, Yellow Beach 2002, 24 Hour Sax Quartet 2004, For John Peel 2004; instrumental: Shaping the Curve 1990, Six Celan Songs 1990, Flugelhorn and Piano 1991, For John Cage 1992, The Convertibility of Lute Strings 1992, Here to There 1993, Yamamoto Perpetuo 1993, On the Fiddle 1993, To Morrow 1994, Tango for Tim 1994, Elisabeth Gets her Way 1995, Viola and Piano 1995, Titch 1997, Fourths, Mostly (for organ) 2001; dramatic works: Strange Attractors, The Princess of Milan, A Broken Set of Rules 1984, Basic Black 1984, Portraits in Reflection 1985, And Do They Do 1986, The Man Who Mistook His Wife for a Hat 1986, Miniatures/Configurations 1988, Letters, Riddles and Writs 1991, Noises, Sounds and Sweet Airs 1994, Facing Goya 2000, Man and Boy: Dada (opera) 2003, Love Counts 2004; vocal: A Neat Slice of Time 1980, The Abbess of Andouillets 1984, Out of the Ruins 1989, Polish Love Song 1990, Shaping the Curve 1991, Anne de Lucy Songs 1992, Mozart on Mortality 1992, Grounded 1995, The Waltz Song 1995, The Ballad of Kastriot Rexhepi 2001, Mosè 2001, A Child's View of Colour 2003, Acts of Beauty 2004; with Michael Nyman Band: In Re Don Giovanni 1977, The Masterwork/Award-Winning Fishknife 1979, Bird List Song 1979, Five Orchestral Pieces Opus Tree 1981, Bird Anthem 1981, M-Work 1981, Love is Certainly, at Least Alphabetically Speaking 1983, Bird Work 1984, The Fall of Icarus 1989, La Traversée de Paris 1989, The Final Score 1992, AET (After Extra Time) 1996, De Granada a la Luna 1998, Orfeu 1998, The Commissar Vanishes 1999, Man with a Movie Camera 2001, Compiling the Colours (Samhitha) 2003, Three Ways of Describing Rain (Sawan; Rang; Dhyan) 2003, Zeit und Ziel 1814–2002, Manhatta 2003; dance: Flicker 2005. *Recordings include:* film soundtracks, The Piano Sings 2005. *Publications:* Libretto for Birtwistle's Dramatic Pastoral, Down by the Greenwood Side 1968–69, Experimental Music: Cage and Beyond 1974; contrib. critical articles to journals, including The Spectator. *Address:* Michael Nyman Ltd, 5 Milner Place, London, N1 1TN, England (office). *Telephone:* (20) 7226-3188 (office). *Fax:* (20) 7689-0824 (office). *E-mail:* office@michaelnyman.com (office). *Website:* www.michaelnyman.com (office).

NYRUP RASMUSSEN, Poul; Danish politician; *President, Party of European Socialists (PES);* b. 15 June 1943, Esbjerg, Western Jutland; s. of Olof Nyrup Rasmussen and Vera Nyrup Rasmussen; m. 1st (divorced); m. 2nd (divorced); m. 3rd Lone Dybkjar; one c. (deceased); ed Esbjerg Statsskole and Univ. of Copenhagen; worked for Danish Trade Union Council in Brussels for a year; Chief Economist, Danish Trade Union Council 1981; Man. Dir Employees' Capital Pension Fund 1986–88; Deputy Chair. Social Democratic Party 1987–92, Chair. 1992–2002; mem. Folketing (Parl.) 1988–2004; Prime Minister of Denmark 1993–2001; MEP 2004–, Pres. Party of European Socialists (PES) 2004–. *Leisure interests:* music, spending time with his wife and grandchild. *Address:* Office 11, G 130, European-Parliament, Rue Wiertz, 1047, Brussels, Belgium (office). *Telephone:* (2) 284-54-63 (office). *Fax:* (2) 284-94-63 (office). *E-mail:* pnrasmussen@europarl.europa.eu (office). *Website:* www.nyrup.dk.

NZAMBIMANA, Lt-Col Edouard; Burundian politician and army officer; *Chairman, Union Commerciale d'Assurances et de Réassurance;* Minister of Public Works, Transport and Equipment 1974–76; participated in coup which overthrew Pres. Micombero Nov. 1976; Prime Minister 1976–78 and Minister of Planning 1976–78, of Agric., Livestock and Rural Devt 1978, of Foreign Affairs and Co-operation 1978–82; currently Chair. Union Commerciale d'Assurances et de Réassurance (UCAR). *Address:* Union Commerciale d'Assurances et de Réassurance, B.P. 3012, Bujumbura, Burundi. *Telephone:* 223638. *Fax:* 223695.

NZOMUKUNDA, Alice; Burundi politician; b. 12 April 1966; trained as accountant; elected mem. Parl. for Bujumbura; Second Vice-Pres. of Burundi in charge of Econ. and Social Affairs 2005–06 (resgnd); mem. Conseil nat. pour la defense de la democratie–Forces pour la defense de la democratie (CNDD-FDD). *Address:* c/o Office of the Vice-President, Bujumbura, Burundi (office).

O

Ó MÓRÁIN, Dónall; Irish public official; b. 6 Sept. 1923, Co. Kerry; s. of Mícheál Ó Móráin and Eibhlín Ní Loingsigh; m. Maire Beaumont 1949; three s. two d.; ed Coláiste Muire, Dublin, Univ. Coll., Dublin and King's Inns, Dublin; called to the Bar 1946; Man. Ed. of Retail Food Trade Journal 1946–50; Gen. Man., printing and publishing firm 1951–63; Founder, Gael-Linn (voluntary nat. cultural and social asscn) 1953, Chair. 1953–63, Dir-Gen. 1963–88, Chair. and Life mem. of Bd 1988–; Chair. Convocation of Nat. Univ. of Ireland 1955–84; Chair. Inisfree Handknits Group 1965–; mem. Radio Telefis Éireann Authority 1965–70, Chair. 1970–72, 1973–76; mem. Language Consultative Council, Dept of Finance 1965–75; Dir Glens of Antrim Tweed Co. Ltd 1967–79; mem. Irish Comm. for UNESCO 1966–, Irish Film Industry Comm. 1967–69; Chair. Consultative Council to Radio na Gaeltachta (first local radio service in Ireland) 1971–76; Founder and Man. Dir Anois, Sunday newspaper 1984–96; Man. Dir Gael-Linn Educational Publications 1996–; Hon. LLD (Nat. Univ. of Ireland) 1979. *Leisure interests:* fowling, salmon fishing. *Address:* 32 Sydney Avenue, Blackrock, Dublin, Ireland. *Telephone:* (1) 2880541. *Fax:* (1) 6767030.

OAKLEY, Ann, BA, MA, PhD; British sociologist, academic and writer; *Professor of Social Policy and Founding Director, Social Science Research Unit, Institute of Education, University of London;* b. 17 Jan. 1944; d. of the late Richard Titmus and Kay Titmus; m. Robin Oakley (divorced); three c.; ed Chiswick Polytechnic and Somerville Coll., Oxford; Research Fellow, Bedford Coll., Univ. of London 1974–79, Univ. of Oxford 1979–84; Deputy Dir Thomas Coram Research Unit, Univ. of London 1985–90; Prof. of Social Policy and Dir Social Science Research Unit, Inst. of Educ., Univ. of London 1991–2005, Founding Dir Social Science Research Unit 2005–; Hon. Prof., Univ. Coll. London 1996–; Hon. Fellow, Somerville Coll., Oxford 2001–; Hon. DLitt (Salford) 1995. *Publications include:* novels: The Men's Room (adapted for TV 1991) 1988; as Rosamund Clay: Only Angels Forget 1990; as Ann Oakley: Matilda's Mistake 1991, The Secret Lives of Eleanor Jenkinson 1992, Scenes Orginating in the Garden of Eden 1993, A Proper Holiday 1996, Overheads 1999; two short stories; non-fiction: Sex, Gender and Society 1972, Housewife 1974, The Sociology of Housework 1974, The Rights and Wrongs of Women (co-ed. with J. Mitchell) 1976, Becoming a Mother (also published as From Here to Maternity 1981) 1979, Women Confined: Towards a Sociology of Childbirth 1980, Subject Women 1981, Miscarriage (with A. McPherson and H. Roberts) 1984, The Captured Womb: A History of the Medical Care of Pregnant Women 1984, Taking it Like a Woman 1984, What is Feminism? (co-ed. with J. Mitchell) 1986, Telling the Truth About Jerusalem: Selected Essays 1986, Helpers in Childbirth: Midwifery Today (with S. Houd) 1990, Social Support and Motherhood: The Natural History of a Research Project 1992, Essays on Women, Medicine and Health 1993, Young People, Health and Family Life (with others) 1994, The Politics of the Welfare State (co-ed. with A.S. Williams) 1994, Evaluating Social Interventions: A Report on Two Workshops (co-ed. with H. Roberts) 1996, Man and Wife: Richard and Kay Titmus, My Parents' Early Years 1996, Who's Afraid of Feminism? (co-ed. with J. Mitchell) 1997, The Gift Relationship: From Human Blood to Social Policy (co-ed. with J. Ashton) 1997, Welfare Research: A Critical Review (co-ed. with F. Williams and J. Popay) 1998, Experiments in Knowing: Gender and Method in the Social Sciences 2000, Welfare and Being: Richard Titmuss's Contribution to Social Policy (co-ed. with P. Alcock and H. Glennerster) 2001, Gender on Planet Earth 2002, The Ann Oakley Reader 2005. *Leisure interests:* cycling, grandchildren. *Address:* Social Science Research Unit, Institute of Education, University of London, Room 102, 18 Woburn Square, London, WC1H 0NR (office); c/o Tessa Sayle Agency, Bickerton House, 25–27 Bickerton Road, London, N19 5JT, England. *Telephone:* (20) 7612-6380 (Inst. of Educ.) (office). *Fax:* (20) 7612-6400 (Inst. of Educ.) (office). *E-mail:* a.oakley@ioe.ac.uk (office). *Website:* www.ioe.ac.uk/SSRU (office); www.annoakley.co.uk (home).

OATES, Joyce Carol, (Rosamond Smith), MA; American writer, poet, publisher and academic; *Roger S. Berlind '52 Professor in the Humanities, Princeton University;* b. 16 June 1938, Lockport, NY; d. of Frederic J. Oates and Caroline Bush; m. Raymond J. Smith 1961; ed Syracuse Univ. and Univ. of Wis.; instructor 1961–65, Univ. of Detroit, Asst Prof. of English 1965–67; faculty mem. Dept of English, Univ. of Windsor, Ont. 1967–78; publr (with Raymond Joseph Smith), Ontario Review 1974–; Writer-in-Residence, Princeton Univ. 1978–81, Prof. 1987–, currently Roger S. Berlind '52 Prof. in the Humanities; mem. American Acad., Inst. of Arts and Letters; Guggenheim Fellow 1967–68; O. Henry Prize Story Award 1967, 1968, Rea Award for Short Story 1990, Elmer Holmes Bukst Award 1990. *Plays:* Three Plays: Ontological Proof of My Existence, Miracle Play, The Triumph of the Spider Monkey 1980, Twelve Plays 1991, The Perfectionist and Other Plays 1995. *Publications:* novels: With Shuddering Fall 1964, A Garden of Earthly Delights 1967, Expensive People 1968, Them 1969, Wonderland 1971, Do With Me What You Will 1973, The Assassins: A Book of Hours 1975, Childworld 1976, Son of the Morning 1978, Unholy Loves 1979, Cybele 1979, Bellefleur 1980, A Sentimental Education 1981, Angel of Light 1981, A Bloodsmoor Romance 1982, Mysteries of Winterthurn 1984, Solstice 1985, Marya: A Life 1986, You Must Remember This 1987, American Appetites 1989, Because it is Bitter and Because it is my Heart 1990, Black Water 1992, Foxfire 1993, What I Lived For 1994, Zombie 1995, First Love: A Gothic Tale 1996, We Were the Mulvaneys 1996, Man Crazy 1997, My Heart Laid Bare 1998, Come Meet Muffin 1998, The Collector of Hearts 1999, Broke Heart Blues 1999, Blonde: A Novel 2000, Middle Age: A Romance 2002, I'll Take You There 2002, Big Mouth and Ugly Girl 2002, The Tattooed Girl 2004, Rape: A Love Story 2004, I Am No One You Know 2004, The Falls 2004, Mother, Missing 2005, The Gravedigger's Daughter 2007, My Sister, My Love: The Intimate Story of Skyler Rampike 2008; short story collections: By the North Gate 1963, Upon the Sweeping Flood and Other Stories 1966, The Wheel of Love 1970, Cupid and Psyche 1970, Marriages and Infidelities 1972, A Posthumous Sketch 1973, The Girl 1974, Plagiarized Material 1974, The Goddess and Other Women 1974, Where Are You Going, Where Have You Been?: Stories of Young America 1974, The Hungry Ghosts: Seven Allusive Comedies 1974, The Seduction and Other Stories 1975, The Poisoned Kiss and Other Stories from the Portuguese 1975, The Triumph of the Spider Monkey 1976, Crossing the Border 1976, Night-Side 1977, The Step-Father 1978, All the Good People I've Left Behind 1979, Queen of the Night 1979, The Lamb of Abyssalia 1979, A Middle-Class Education 1980, A Sentimental Education 1980, Last Day 1984, Wild Saturday and Other Stories 1984, Wild Nights 1985, Raven's Wing 1986, The Assignation 1988, Heat and Other Stories 1991, Where Is Here? 1992, Haunted Tales of the Grotesque 1994, Faithless: Tales of Transgression 2001, The Female of the Species 2006, High Lonesome: New & Selected Stories 1966–2006 2006, Wild Nights! 2008, Museum of Doctor Moses 2008; poetry: Women in Love and Other Poems 1968, Anonymous Sins and Other Poems 1969, Them (Nat. Book Award 1970) 1969, Love and its Derangements 1970, Wooded Forms 1972, Angel Fire 1973, Dreaming America and Other Poems 1973, The Fabulous Beasts 1975, Seasons of Peril 1977, Women Whose Lives are Food, Men Whose Lives are Money 1978, Celestial Timepiece 1980, Nightless Nights: Nine Poems 1981, Invisible Women: New and Selected Poems 1970–1982 1982, Luxury of Sin 1984, The Time Traveller: Poems 1983–1989 1989; non-fiction: The Edge of Impossibility: Tragic Forms in Literature 1972, The Hostile Sun: The Poetry of D. H. Lawrence 1973, New Heaven, New Earth: The Visionary Experience in Literature 1974, The Stone Orchard 1980, Contraries: Essays 1981, The Profane Art: Essays and Reviews 1983, Funland 1983, On Boxing 1987, (Woman) Writer: Occasions and Opportunities 1988, George Bellows: American Artist (biog.) 1995, The Faith of a Writer: Life, Craft, Art 2004, Black Girl/White Girl 2006, The Journals of Joyce Carol Oates, 1973–1982 2007; editor: Scenes from American Life: Contemporary Short Fiction 1973, The Best American Short Stories 1979 (with Shannon Ravenel) 1979, Night Walks: A Bedside Companion 1982, First Person Singular: Writers on Their Craft 1983, Story: Fictions Past and Present (with Boyd Litzinger) 1985, Reading the Fights (with Daniel Halpern) 1988, The Oxford Book of American Short Stories 1993, The Best American Mystery Stories 2006; as Rosamond Smith: The Lives of the Twins 1987, Kindred Passions 1988, Soul-Mate 1989, Nemesis 1990, Snake Eyes 1992, You Can't Catch Me 1995, Double Delight 1997, Starr Bright Will Be With You Soon 1999, The Barrens 2001, Beasts 2003; fiction in nat. magazines. *Address:* Department of Creative Writing, Princeton University, 185 Nassau Street, Princeton, NJ 08544 (office); c/o John Hawkins, 71 West 23rd Street, Suite 1600, New York, NY 10010, USA. *Website:* www.princeton.edu/~visarts/cwr.

OBAID, Thoraya Ahmed, BA, MA, PhD; Saudi Arabian UN official; *Executive Director, United Nations Population Fund;* b. 2 March 1945, Baghdad, Iraq; m. Mahmoud Saleh; two d.; ed Mills Coll., Oakland, Calif., Wayne State Univ., Detroit, Mich., USA; mem. League of Arab States working group for formulating the Arab Strategy for Social Devt 1984–85; mem. Editorial Bd Journal of Arab Women 1984–90; mem. Int. Women's Advisory Panel, Int. Planned Parenthood Fed. 1993; Chair. UN Inter-agency Task Force on Gender, Amman 1996; mem. UN Inter-agency Gender Mission to Afghanistan Nov. 1997; mem. UN Strategic Framework Mission to Afghanistan 1997; Assoc. Social Affairs Officer (Women and Devt), Econ. and Social Comm. for W Africa (ESCWA) Social Devt and Population Div. (SDPD) 1975–81, Women and Devt Programme Man. ESCWA SDPD 1981–92, Chief ESCWA SDPD 1992–93, Deputy Exec. Sec. ESCWA 1993–98; Dir Div. for Arab States and Europe, UN Population Fund (UNFPA) 1998–2000, Exec. Dir and Under-Sec. Gen. UNFPA 2001–; mem. Middle East Studies Asscn, Al-Nahdha Women's Philanthropic Asscn; Dr hc of Law (Mills Coll.) 2002; George P. Younger Award, UN Cttee of Religious NGOs 2002, Medal and Key to the City of Managua, Nicaragua 2003, Pedro Joaquin Chamorro Award, Nicaragua 2003, Second Century Award for Excellence in Health Care, Columbia Univ. 2003. *Address:* UN Population Fund, 220 East 42nd Street, 19th Floor, New York, NY 10017, USA (office). *Telephone:* (212) 297-5020 (office); (212) 297-5111 (office). *Fax:* (212) 297-4911 (office). *E-mail:* obaid@unfpa.org (office). *Website:* www.unfpa.org (office).

OBAMA, Barack Hussein, Jr, BA, JD; American lawyer, politician and head of state; *President;* b. 4 Aug. 1961, Honolulu, Hawaii; s. of the late Barack Obama and Ann Dunham; m. Michelle Obama 1992; two d.; ed Punahou School, Hawaii, Occidental Coll., Columbia Univ., Harvard Law School; family lived in Hawaii and Indonesia; Ed.-in-Chief Harvard Law Review (first African-American) and mem. Exec. Bd Black Law Students Asscn, Harvard Univ.; writer and financial analyst, Business Int. Corpn 1984–85; Dir Developing Communities Project, Chicago 1985–88; worked for Bill Clinton's presidential election campaign as Dir Ill. Project Vote 1992; Assoc., Miner, Barnhill & Galland, PC (law firm), Chicago 1993–96, Of Counsel 1996–2004; Sr Lecturer, Univ. of Chicago Law School 1993–2004; Ill. State Senator (13th Senate Dist, S Chicago) 1996–2004, Chair. Public Health and Welfare Cttee, mem. Judiciary Cttee, Revenue Cttee; lost Democratic primary run for US House of Reps to incumbent Congressman Bobby Rush 2000; Senator from Ill. (only third-ever African-American mem. of Senate) 2005–08; Pres. of USA 2009–; Chair. Chicago Lawyers Cttee for Civil Rights under the Law; fmr Chair. Chicago Annenberg Challenge; mem. Ill. Bar Asscn, Cook Co. Bar

Asscn; Democrat; Hon. DJur (New South Hampshire Univ.) 2007; Grammy Award for Best Spoken Word Album (for audio-book version of The Audacity of Hope) 2008, named by Time magazine as its Person of the Year 2008. *Publications:* Dreams from My Father 1995, The Audacity of Hope 2006. *Address:* The White House, 1600 Pennsylvania Avenue, NW, Washington, DC 20500, USA (office). *Telephone:* (202) 456-1414 (office). *Fax:* (202) 456-2461 (office). *E-mail:* president@whitehouse.gov (office). *Website:* www.whitehouse.gov (office).

OBAMA, Michelle LaVaughn Robinson, BA, JD; American lawyer; *First Lady;* b. 17 Jan. 1964, Chicago; d. of Fraser Robinson III and Marian Shields Robinson; m. Barack Obama 1992; two d.; ed Whitney Young High School, Chicago, Princeton Univ., Harvard Law School; Assoc., Sidley Austin (law firm), Chicago 1988–91; Asst to Chicago Mayor Richard M. Daley 1991–93, also Asst Commr of Planning and Devt; Exec. Dir Public Allies, Chicago 1993–96; Assoc. Dean of Student Services, Univ. of Chicago 1996–2002; Exec. Dir for Community Affairs, Univ. of Chicago Hosps 2002–05, Vice-Pres. for Community and External Affairs 2005–09; First Lady of USA 2009–; mem. Bd of Dirs Chicago Council on Global Affairs. *Address:* The White House, 1600 Pennsylvania Avenue, NW, Washington, DC 20500, USA (office). *Telephone:* (202) 456-1414 (office). *Fax:* (202) 456-2461 (office). *Website:* www.whitehouse.gov/administration/michelle_obama (office).

OBANDO Y BRAVO, HE Cardinal Miguel; Nicaraguan ecclesiastic; *Archbishop of Managua;* b. 2 Feb. 1926, La Libertad (Chontales), Juigalpa; ordained priest 1958; consecrated Bishop (Titular Church of Puzia di Bizacena) 1968–, Archbishop of Managua 1970–; cr. Cardinal 1985; Chair. Nat. Reconciliation Comm. for Nicaragua 1987; currently Pres. Nicaragua Bishops' Conf. *Address:* Conferencia Episcopal de Nicaragua, Ferretería Long 1c al. Norte, 1c al. Este, Zona 3, Las Piedrecitas, Apdo 2407, Managua (office); Arzobispado, Apartado 3058, Managua, Nicaragua. *Telephone:* (2) 66-6292 (office); (2) 277-1754. *Fax:* (2) 66-8089 (office); (2) 276-0130. *E-mail:* cen@tmx.com.ni (office).

OBASANJO, Gen. Olusegun; Nigerian politician, fmr army officer and fmr head of state; b. 5 March 1937, Abeokuta, Ogun State; m. 1st Oluremi Akinbwon; two s. four d.; m. 2nd Stella Abebe (died 2005); ed Abeokuta Baptist High School and Mons Officers' Cadet School, UK; joined Nigerian Army 1958, commissioned 1959; served in Congo (now Democratic Repub. of the Congo) 1960; promoted Capt. 1963, Maj. 1965, Lt-Col 1967, Col 1969, Brig. 1972, Lt-Gen. 1976, Gen. 1979; Commdr Eng Corps 1963, later Commdr 2nd Div. (Rear), Ibadan; GOC 3rd Infantry Div. 1969; Commdr 3rd Marine Commando Div. during Nigerian Civil War, accepted surrender of Biafran forces Jan. 1970; Commdr Eng Corps 1970–75; Fed. Commr for Works and Housing Jan.–July 1975; Chief of Staff, Supreme HQ 1975–76; mem. Supreme Mil. Council 1975–79; Head of Fed. Mil. Govt and C-in-C of Armed Forces 1976–79; mem. Advisory Council of State 1979; farmer 1979–; arrested March 1995, interned 1995; Pres. of Nigeria and C-in-C of Armed Forces 1999–2007; Chair. Bd of Trustees, People's Democratic Party (PDP) 2007–; UN Special Envoy for the Democratic Repub. of the Congo 2008–; fmr Chair. African Union; Fellow, Univ. of Ibadan 1979–81; mem. Ind. Comm. on Disarmament and Security 1980, mem. Exec. Cttee Inter Action Council of fmr Heads of Govt; Chair. Africa Leadership Forum and Foundation; Co-Chair. Eminent Persons Group on S Africa (EPG) 1985; Grand Commdr Fed. Repub. of Nigeria 1980; Hon. DHumLitt (Howard); Hon. LLD (Maiduguri) 1980, (Ahmadu Bello Univ., Zaria) 1985, (Ibada) 1988. *Publications:* My Command 1980, Africa in Perspective 'Myths and Realities' 1987, Nzeogwu 1987, Africa Embattled 1988, Constitution for National Integration and Development 1989, Not My Will 1990, Elements of Development 1992, Elements of Democracy 1993, Africa: Rise to Challenge 1993, Hope for Africa 1993, This Animal Called Man 1999, Exemplary Youth in a Difficult World 2002, I See Hope 2002. *Leisure interests:* table tennis, squash, reading, writing. *Address:* Olusegun Obasanjo Presidential Library Foundation, Presidential Boulevard, Oke-Mosan Abeokuta, Ogun, Nigeria (office). *Telephone:* (9) 245821 (office); (9) 245690 (office). *E-mail:* info@ooplibrary.org (office). *Website:* www.ooplibrary.org (office).

OBAYASHI, Takeo, MS; Japanese construction industry executive; *Chairman, Obayashi Corporation;* s. of the late Yoshiro Obayashi; m.; ed Keio Univ., Stanford Univ., Calif., USA; trained as civil engineer; joined Obayashi Corpn 1977, apptd Dir 1983, Vice-Pres. 1997, Vice-Chair., then Chair. 2003–; Chair. Obayashi Foundation; Man.-Dir Kansei Asscn of Corp. Execs; mem. Bd Kansei Econ. Fed., Bd of Councillors, Int. Inst. for Advanced Studies Foundation, Bd of Visitors, Stanford Inst. for Int. Studies, Research Governance Cttee, Stanford Japan Center, Int. Council, Tate Gallery, London, UK; Trustee and mem. Council, Museum of Modern Art. *Address:* Obayashi Corporation, Shinagawa Intercity Tower B, 2-15-2 Konan, Minato-ku, Tokyo 108-8502, Japan (office). *Telephone:* (3) 5769-1906 (office). *Fax:* (3) 5769-1910 (office). *Website:* www.obayashi.co.jp (office).

OBEID, Atif Muhammad, MA, PhD; Egyptian politician; m.; two c.; ed Faculty of Commerce, Cairo Univ. and Univ. of Illinois; mem. Arab League Media Policy Co-ordinating Cttee 1970; fmr Prof. of Business Admin, Faculty of Commerce, Cairo Univ. and Pres. Int. Man. Centre; Minister of Cabinet Affairs and Minister of State for Admin. Devt 1985–93, Minister of the Public Enterprise Sector 1993–99; Prime Minister of Egypt 1999–2004 (resgnd). *Address:* c/o Sharia Majlis ash-Sha'ab, Lazoughli Square, Cairo, Egypt.

OBEID, Jean, BA; Lebanese politician; b. 8 May 1939, Alma, Zghorta; m. Loubna Emile El-Boustani; two s. three d.; ed Collège de Frères-Pères Carmélites-Lycée Officiel, Tripoli, St Joseph's Univ., Beirut; journalist, Magazine and Isbouh El Arabi 1959–62, Lissan Al Hal 1960–63, Al Nahar 1963–66, Assayad 1963–66, Ed. Assayad 1966–72; began political career 1973; adviser to Pres. Elias Sarkis of Lebanon 1973; counsellor and presidential del. to Summit of Non-Aligned States, New Delhi, India 1983; participated in Inter-Lebanese Nat. Reconciliation Conf., Geneva, Switzerland; Deputy of the Chouf 1991; Deputy for Tripoli, N Lebanon 1992; Minister of State 1993; Deputy for N Lebanon 1996–2004; Minister of Nat. Educ., Sports and Youth 1996–2003, of Foreign Affairs and Emigrants 2003–04; unsuccessful cand. for Pres. of Lebanon 2007. *Address:* c/o Ministry of Foreign Affairs and Emigrants, rue Sursock, Achrafieh, Beirut, Lebanon (office).

OBEIDAT, Ahmad Abdul-Majeed; Jordanian politician; b. 1938, Hartha, Irbid; m.; five c.; ed Salahiyah School and Univ. of Baghdad; teacher, Minister of Educ. 1957; Customs Officer 1961; First Lt-Gen. Security Service 1962–64; Asst Dir Gen. Intelligence Service 1964–74, Dir 1974–82; Minister of the Interior 1982–84; Prime Minister of Jordan and Minister of Defence 1984–85; Partner, Law and Arbitration Centre 1985–; fmr Deputy Speaker of the Senate; Pres. Jordan Environment Soc.; Chair. Bd of Trustees Nat. Centre for Human Rights. *Address:* Law and Arbitration Centre, PO Box 926544, Amman, Jordan. *Telephone:* 672222.

OBENG, Letitia Eva, BA, MSc, PhD, FRSA; Ghanaian scientist, research director and environmental manager; b. (Takyibea Asihene), 10 Jan. 1925, Anum; d. of Rev. E. V. Asihene and Dora Asihene; m. George A. Obeng 1953; two s. one d.; ed Achimota Coll., Ghana, Univs of Birmingham and Liverpool, UK; Lecturer, Coll. of Science and Tech. Kumasi 1952–59; Research Scientist, Nat. Research Council, Ghana 1960–62; research staff, Ghana Acad. of Sciences 1963–65; built and served as first Dir Inst. of Aquatic Biology, Council for Scientific and Industrial Research, Ghana 1965–74; Project Co-Man., Ghana Govt/UNDP Volta Lake Research Project; Sr Programme Officer and Chair. Soil and Water Task Force, UNEP, Nairobi 1974–80; Regional Dir and Rep. of UNEP to Africa 1980–85; Dir Environmental Man. Services 1986; Distinguished Int. Visitor, Radcliffe Coll., Cambridge, Mass., USA 1992; mem. Exec. Council, Africa Leadership Forum 1991, Bd of Stockholm Environment Inst., PANOS etc. 1986–95; Trustee, Bd of Int. Rice Research Inst., Int. Irrigation Man. Inst., Human Ecology Foundation; Affiliate mem. Africa Leadership Forum, Royal Soc. (UK), New York Acad. of Sciences 1995, Int. Rice Research Inst., Int. Irrigation Man. Inst., Stockholm Environment Inst.; Fellow, Ghana Acad. of Arts and Sciences (Pres. 2006–); Star of Ghana 2006; Silver Medal, Royal Soc. of Arts, Ghana Council for Scientific and Industrial Research (CSIR) Award 1997, Ghana Govt Award for Biological Sciences 1998, CSIR Bldg named The Letitia Obeng Block 1998; featured on nat. commemorative postage stamp. *Publications:* Man-made Lakes (ed.) 1969, Environment and the Responsibility of the Privileged, Environment and Population, The Right to Health in Tropical Agriculture; Parasites: The Sly and Sneaky Enemies Inside You 1997, Ephraim Amu – A Portrait of Cultured Patriotism, Kwame Mkrumah and the Sciences 2005; scientific articles; book chapters. *Leisure interests:* poetry, painting flowers, Akan culture and traditions. *Address:* PO Box C223, Accra, Ghana.

OBENG, Lt-Gen. Seth Kofi, MSc; Ghanaian army officer; b. 26 Jan. 1945, Lagos, Nigeria; s. of Nicholas Emmanuel Obeng and Dina Kwaley Obeng; ed US Command and Staff Coll., Fort Leavenworth, Kansas, London School of Econs, UK, Nat. Defence Coll., Delhi, India; commissioned into Ghanaian Army as artillery officer 1965, various sr command and staff appointments including Commdt Mil. Acad. and Training School and Ghana Armed Forces Command and Staff College as well as Chief of Staff/Gen. HQ; Defence Adviser, Ghana High Comm., London 1984–88; Chief Staff Officer, Army HQ 1988–89; Man. Dir State Housing Corpn (now State Housing Co. 1989–92, 1992–93; Deputy Force Commdr Econ. Community of W African States (ECOWAS) Monitoring Group in Liberia 1994–96; Force Commdr UN Observer Mission to Angola 1998–99; Force Commdr UN Interim Force in Lebanon (UNIFIL) 1999–2001; Chief of Defence Staff 2001–05; Chair. ECOWAS Defence and Security Comm., mem. ECOWAS Council of the Wise 2006–, mem. Bd of Govs Small Arms and Light Weapons Contol Programme; Under-Sec. Gen., UN Secr. 2006–, mem. Follow Up Cttee of the Greentree Agreement of 12th June 2006; Special Adviser on Mil. Affairs to AU Chair. 2007; Commdr Nat. Legion of Cedars (Lebanon) 2001; Officer Nat. Order of Côte d'Ivoire 2002, Meritorious Service Medal (USA) 2004, Order of the Star of Ghana 2006; ECOWAS Award 1996, Int Officer Hall of Fame (USA) 2004. *Leisure interests:* reading, keeping fit, football, hockey, volleyball.

OBERMANN, René; German business executive; *CEO, Deutsche Telekom AG;* b. March 1963, Düsseldorf; m.; two d.; ed Univ. of Muenster; traineeship with BMW AG 1984–86; f. ABC Telekom (subsequently Hutchison Mobilfunk), Muenster 1986, Man. Partner 1991, Chair. Man. Bd 1994–98; Man. Dir of Sales, T-Mobile Deutschland 1998–2000, CEO T-Mobile Int. AG (holding co. for Deutsche Telekom AG mobile operations) 2000–02, mem. Man. Bd responsible for European operations 2001–02, responsible for mobile operations 2002–06, also responsible for mobile communications strategic business area, CEO Deutsche Telekom AG 2006–; Chair. VAM – Verband der Anbieter von Mobilfunkdiensten (Asscn of Mobile Communications Service Providers) 1995–96; Presidium mem. BITKOM German industry asscn 2007–. *Address:* Deutsche Telekom AG, Friedrich-Ebert-Allee 140, 53113 Bonn, Germany (office). *Telephone:* (228) 1814949 (office). *Fax:* (228) 18194004 (office). *E-mail:* info@deutschetelekom.com (office). *Website:* www.deutschetelekom.com (office).

OBERMEIER, Georg, DPhil; German business executive; b. 21 July 1941, Munich; m.; Knorr-Bremse GmbH 1964–72; Bayernwerk AG, Munich, latterly Dir of Finance and Org. 1973–89; mem. Man. Bd VIAG AG 1989–, Chair. 1995–98; Chair. Supervisory Bd Isar-Amperwerke AG, Munich, Rheinhold & Mahla AG, Munich, SKW Trostberg AG, Trostberg; Vice-Chair. and mem. Supervisory Bd Kühne & Nagel Int. AG; mem. Supervisory Bd Bayernwerk AG, Munich, Didier-Werke AG, Wiesbaden, Gerresheimer Glas AG, Düsseldorf, Klöckner & Co. AG, Duisburg, Schindellegi, Mobil Oil AG, Hamburg,

Schmalbach-Lubeca AG, Brunswick, Thomassen & Drijver Verblifa NV, Deventer, Thyssengas GmbH, Duisburg, VAW Aluminium AG, Berlin/Bonn. *Address:* c/o VIAG AG, Nymphenburger Strasse 37, 80335 Munich, Germany.

OBERWETTER, James C., BA; American business executive and fmr diplomatist; b. 3 Nov. 1944, Cuero; m. Anita Oberwetter; three d.; ed Univ. of Texas; joined Hunt Consolidated, Inc. 1974, later serving as Sr Vice-Pres. of Governmental and Political Affairs –2003; Amb. to Saudi Arabia 2003–07; fmr Press Sec. for Congressman George W. Bush; fmr Special Asst to Admin. Environmental Protection Agency; Chair. Tex. Comm. on Alcohol and Drug Abuse 1996–2001; Lifetime Achievement Award, Tex. Parent-Teachers Asscn. *Address:* c/o Department of State, 2201 C Street, NW, Washington, DC 20520, USA.

OBETSEBI-LAMPTEY, Jake; Ghanaian politician and advertising executive; b. 4 Feb. 1946, Accra; scriptwriter, commentator and TV and radio presenter, Ghana Broadcasting Corpn 1966–69; Account Exec. and radio and TV producer Lintas West African advertising agency 1969, Client Service Man., Ghana 1971, wrote, co-ordinated and executed Ghana Nat. Family Planning Programme motivation campaign, Gen. Man. Lintas Ghana Ltd 1974–84; devised operation manuals and presentations for WHO and SOMARC Futures Group 1984–99; Nat. Campaign Man. for New Patriotic Party, presidential elections 2000; Minister of Information and Presidential Affairs and Chief of Staff 2001, Minister of Tourism and the Modernization of the Capital City –2007; fmr Pres. Advertising Asscn of Ghana. *Publications:* Using Commercial Resources in Family Planning Programmes: the International Experience, The Handbook for AIDS Prevention in Africa. *Address:* c/o Ministry of Tourism and the Modernization of the Capital City, POB 4386, Accra, Ghana (office).

OBI, Onyeabo C., LLB, FCIArb; Nigerian international business lawyer; b. 20 Nov. 1938, Ogidi; s. of Chief Z. C. Obi; m. Evelyn Nnenna Obioha 1967; two s. three d.; ed London School of Econs, UK; admitted to Bar (Gray's Inn) 1962; in pvt. practice as barrister and solicitor of Supreme Court of Nigeria 1963–; Dir Nigerian Rubber Bd 1977–79; Senator, Fed. Repub. of Nigeria 1979–83; mem. of Council (and Vice-Chair. Cttee on Procedures for Settling Disputes), Section on Business Law, Int. Bar Asscn 1986–92; mem. Advisory Cttee on Rules of the Supreme Court of Nigeria (by appointment of Hon. Chief Justice) 1986–92. *Leisure interest:* short walks. *Address:* Western House (13th Floor), 8–10 Broad Street, PO Box 4040, Lagos, Nigeria (office). *Telephone:* (1) 263-0843 (office); (1) 743-2365 (office); (1) 263-4604 (office). *Fax:* (1) 263-7609 (office). *E-mail:* abobi@hyperia.com (office).

OBIALA, Edmund, MESc; Polish/Australian civil and structural engineer; *Operations Director, Bovis Lend Lease Ltd;* b. 9 Feb. 1946, Poland; m. Grażyna Guth; ed Poznań Univ. of Technology, Bydgoszcz Univ. Technology; geodesist Pomeranian Mil. Dist 1966–72; construction designer, head of designer team, Eltor, Bydgoszcz 1972–78; research worker, Ibmer Warsaw, constructed works in Bydgoszcz 1977–80; mem. staff, Civil and Civic Pty Ltd, Sydney 1982–88, Multiplex Constructions Pty Ltd 1988–2000; Operations Dir Bovis Lend Lease Ltd 2000–; Award for Excellence, Concrete Inst. of Australia 1999, Grand Award for Excellence in Arboriculture, Nat. Arborist Asscn 1999, British Construction Award for Olympic Stadium in Sydney 2000, Structural Special Award 2000, Green Apple Award 2004. *Works:* constructions designed include Nat. Bank of Australia, Sydney 1982–85, sports stadium Parramatta and football stadium, Sydney 1985–88, Chiefley Tower, Coles Myer Centre and re-building of Chelsea football team stadium, London 1988–2000. *Achievements:* project director on major constructions including Olympic Stadium, Sydney 1994–99, Wembley Stadium 1999–2001, Chelsea Stadium 1999–2001, Munich City Tower 2001–02, Everton Stadium, Liverpool 2002–03, Chapelfield Shopping Centre, Norwich 2003–. *Leisure interests:* cinema, literature, tennis, volleyball. *Address:* Bovis Lend Lease Ltd, Bovis House, Northolt Road, Harrow, Middx, HA2 OEE (office); 42 Wherry Road, Norwich, NR1 1WS, England (home). *Telephone:* (20) 8271-8000 (office); (1603) 285050 (office); (1603) 766584 (home). *E-mail:* Edmund.Obiala@eu.bovislendlease.com (office); eobiala@onetel.com (home); gguth@onetel.net (home).

OBRAZTSOVA, Elena Vasilyevna; Russian singer (mezzo-soprano); *Director, Elena Obraztsova Cultural Centre, St Petersburg;* b. 7 July 1939, Leningrad (now St Petersburg); d. of Vasily Alekseevich Obraztsov and Nataliya Ivanovna Obraztsova (née Bychkova); m. 1st Vyacheslav Makarov (divorced 1983); one d.; m. 2nd Algis Žiuraitis 1983 (died 1998); ed Leningrad Conservatoire (under tuition of Prof. Grigoriyeva); Prof., Moscow Conservatoire 1973–94; mem. and Prin. Soloist Bolshoi Theatre, Moscow 1964–; Dir St Petersburg Elena Obraztsova Cultural Center 1999–, Mikhailovsky Opera, St Petersburg 2007–; has appeared at most leading opera houses of Europe and America, including Vienna State Opera 1975, Metropolitan Opera New York 1976, La Scala Milan 1976, Salzburg 1978, Covent Garden, London 1981 and has toured extensively in Russia and throughout world; gives masterclasses in Europe and Japan; judge of int. vocal competitions; est. Int. Elena Obraztsova Competition for young opera singers, St Petersburg 1999, Elena Obraztsova Int. Competition for young vocalists, St Petersburg 2006 and for chamber music singers, Moscow 2000; Academician Acad. of Russian Art 1999–; Hon. mem. Pushkin Acad. 1995–, Russian Acad. of Art Critics and Musical Performance 1999–; Order for Services to the Fatherland 1999 and other decorations; gold medals at competitions Helsinki 1962, Moscow 1962, 1970, Barcelona 1970, Medal of Granados 1971, Gold Pen of Critics, Wiesbaden 1972, Award of Merit, San Francisco 1977, Gold Verdi, Italy 1978, Bartók Memorial Medal, Hungary 1982, State Prize of Russia 1974, Lenin Prize 1976, People's Artist of USSR 1976, Gold Star-Hero of Labour 1990. *Roles include:* Marina Mniszek in Boris Godunov (debut, Bolshoi 1963), Countess in Queen of Spades, Konchakovna in Prince Igor, Marfa in Khovanshchina, Lyubasha in The Tsar's Bride, Helene Bezukhova in War and Peace, Frosia in Semionkotko, Princess de Bouillon in Adriana Lecouvreur, Jocasta in Oedipus Rex, Oberon in A Midsummer Night's Dream, Eudosya in La Fiamma, Giovanna Seymour in Anna Bolena, Herodiade, Amneris in Aida, Azucena in Il Trovatore, Eboli in Don Carlos, Santuzza in Cavelleria Rusticana, Ulrica in Un Ballo in Maschera, Adalgiza in Norma, Orfeo in Orfeo ed Euridice, Neris in Medea, Leonora in La Favorita, Aunt Princess in Suor Angelica, Frederica in Louise Miller, Carmen, Charlotte in Werther, Delilah in Samson and Delilah, Judith in Duke Bluebeard's Castle, Granny in The Gambler, the Countess in The Queen of Spades and others; recital repertoire includes works by more than 100 composers; staged Werther at Bolshoi Theatre 1986. *Film:* Cavalleria Rusticana 1981. *Recordings:* over 50 recordings for Melodia, Polydor, DG, EMI, CBS, Philips etc. including operas, oratorios, cantatas, solo discs of arias and chamber music. *Play:* Amalia in Antonia von Elba 1999. *Television includes:* My Carmen 1977, And My Image Will Rise Before You 1979, The Merry Widow 1984, Higher Than The Love 1991, Elena The Great 1995, People, Years, Life 2007. *Publication:* Bolshoi (poetry) 2001. *Leisure interests:* dogs, horses, fishing, mushrooms. *Address:* Bolshoi Theatre, Teatralnaya pl. 1, 125009 Moscow (office). *Telephone:* (495) 692-31-08 (office); (495) 692-06-58 (office); (495) 692-66-90 (office). *Fax:* (495) 692-66-90 (office). *E-mail:* admin@elenaobraztsova.ru (office). *Website:* www.elenaobraztsova.ru (office).

O'BRIEN, David P., BA, BCL; Canadian business executive; *Chairman, Royal Bank of Canada;* b. 9 Sept. 1941, Montreal; s. of John Lewis and Ethel O'Brien (née Cox); m. Gail Baxter Cornell 1968; two s. one d.; ed Loyola Coll., McGill Univ.; Assoc. Ogilvy Renault 1967, later Pnr; joined Petro-Canada 1978, positions including Exec. Vice-Pres. 1985–89; Pres. and CEO Noverco Inc. 1989; with PanCanadian Petroleum 1990–95, Chair., Pres. and CEO –1995; Pres. and COO Canadian Pacific Ltd 1995–96, Chair., Pres. and CEO 1996–2001; Chair. and CEO PanCanadian Energy Corpn 2001–02, Chair. EnCana Corpn (following merger of PanCanadian Energy Corpn and Alberta Energy Co.) 2002–; mem. Bd Dirs Royal Bank of Canada 1996–, Chair. 2004–; mem. Bd Dirs Fairmont Hotel and Resorts, Inco Ltd, TransCanada Pipelines Ltd, Molson Inc., C. D. Howe Inst.; Hon. DCL (Bishops Univ.) 1998, Hon. BA (Mount Royal Coll.) 2000. *Address:* Royal Bank of Canada, 200 Bay Street, Toronto, ON M5J 2J5, Canada (office). *Telephone:* (416) 974-5151 (office). *Fax:* (416) 955-7800 (office). *E-mail:* info@rbc.com (office). *Website:* www.rbc.com (office).

O'BRIEN, Edna; Irish writer; b. Tuamgraney, Co. Clare; d. of Michael O'Brien and Lena Cleary; m. Ernest Gébler 1954 (divorced 1964); two s.; ed convents, Pharmaceutical Coll. of Ireland; engaged in writing from an early age; Hon. DLitt (Queen's) 1999; Yorkshire Post Novel Award 1971, Kingsley Amis Award, Writers' Guild of GB Award 1993, European Prize for Literature 1995, American Nat. Arts Gold Medal, Bob Hughes Lifetime Achievement Award, Irish Book Awards 2009. *Publications include:* The Country Girls 1960 (film 1983), The Lonely Girl 1962, Girls in Their Married Bliss 1963, August is a Wicked Month 1964, Casualties of Peace 1966, The Love Object 1968, A Pagan Place 1970 (play 1971), Night 1972, A Scandalous Woman (short stories) 1974, Mother Ireland 1976, Johnny I Hardly Knew You (novel) 1977, Arabian Days 1977, Mrs. Reinhardt and other stories 1978, Virginia (play) 1979, Mrs. Reinhardt (adapted for TV) 1981, The Dazzle (children's book), Returning: A Collection of New Tales 1982, A Christmas Treat 1982, A Fanatic Heart (Selected Stories) 1985, Madame Bovary (play) 1987, Vanishing Ireland 1987, Tales for the Telling (children's book) 1987, The High Road (novel) 1988, On the Bone (poetry) 1989, Scandalous Woman and Other Stories 1990, Lantern Slides (stories) 1990, Time and Tide (novel) 1992, House of Splendid Isolation (novel) 1994, Down By the River (novel) 1997, Maud Gonne (screenplay) 1996, James Joyce 1999, Wild Decembers 1999, In the Forest (novel) 2002, Iphigenia (play) 2003, Triptych (play) 2004, The Light of Evening (novel) 2006, Byron in Love (biography) 2009. *Leisure interests:* reading, walking, meditating. *Address:* c/o David Godwin Associates, 55 Monmouth Street, London, WC2H 9DG, England. *Telephone:* (20) 7240-9992.

O'BRIEN, Gregory Michael St Lawrence, PhD; American academic and university chancellor; b. 7 Oct. 1944, New York; s. of Henry J. O'Brien and Mary A. McGoldrick; m. Mary K. McLaughlin 1968; two d.; ed Lehigh Univ., Pa and Boston Univ.; Dean and Prof. School of Social Welfare, Univ. of Wisconsin-Milwaukee 1974–78; Provost and Prof. of Psychology, Univ. of Mich.-Flint 1978–80; Prof. of Psychology, Univ. of S Fla 1980–87, also Prof. of Social Work 1980–87, Prof. of Man. 1986–87, Vice-Pres. for Academic Affairs 1980–87, Univ. Provost 1983–87; Chancellor, Univ. of New Orleans 1987–2003; Chair. Metro Council Govts Metrovision 1992–; Vice-Chair. State of LA Film and Video Comm. 1993–94 (mem. 1994–); Supt New Orleans Public Schools 1999–2000; mem. Kellogg Comm. on Future of Land Grant Colls and State Univs 1996–; Gambit Weekly's New Orleanian of the Year 1999. *Address:* c/o Office of the Chancellor, University of New Orleans, Lakefront, New Orleans, LA 70148 (office); 2468 Lark Street, New Orleans, LA 70122, USA (home).

O'BRIEN, HE Cardinal Keith Michael Patrick, KM, GCHS, BSc, DipEd; British ecclesiastic; *Roman Catholic Archbishop of St Andrews and Edinburgh;* b. 17 March 1938, Ballycastle, Co. Antrim, Northern Ireland; s. of Mark Joseph O'Brien and Alice Mary Moriarty; ed St Patrick's High School, Dumbarton, Holy Cross Acad., Edin., Univ. of Edin., St Andrew's Coll., Drygrange and Moray House Coll. of Educ.; ordained to priesthood 1965, asst priest, Holy Cross, Edin. 1965–66, St Bride, Cowdenbeath 1966–71; Chaplain and teacher, St Columba's High School, Dunfermline 1966–71; asst priest, St Patrick's, Kilsyth 1972–75, St Mary's, Bathgate 1975–78; Spiritual Dir St Andrew's Coll., Drygrange 1978–80; Rector St Mary's Coll., Blairs 1980–85; RC Archbishop of St Andrews and Edin. 1985–; Apostolic Admin. Diocese of

Argyll and the Isles 1996–99; cr. Cardinal-Priest of Ss Giachino e Anna ad Tusculanum 2003; Grand Cross Conventual Chaplain of Sovereign Mil. Order of Malta 1985, Grand Prior of Scottish Lieutenancy of Equestrian Order of Holy Sepulchre of Jerusalem 2001, Kt Grand Cross 2003, Bailiff Grand Cross of Honour and Devotion, Sovereign Mil. Order of Malta 2005; Hon. LLD (Univ. of St Francis Xavier, Antigonish, Nova Scotia) 2004; Hon. DD (Univ. of St Andrews) 2004, (Univ. of Edin.) 2004. *Address:* The Archbishop's House, 42 Greenhill Gardens, Edinburgh, EH10 4BJ, Scotland (home). *Telephone:* (131) 447-3337 (home). *Fax:* (131) 447-0816 (home). *E-mail:* cardinal@staned.org.uk (home). *Website:* www.archdiocese-edinburgh.org.uk (office).

O'BRIEN, (Michael) Vincent; Irish fmr race horse trainer; b. 9 April 1917, Cork; s. of Daniel P. O'Brien and Kathleen O'Brien (née Toomey); m. Jacqueline Wittenoom 1951; two s. three d.; ed Mungret Coll., Limerick; started training in Co. Cork 1944, moved to Co. Tipperary 1951; won all principal English and Irish steeplechases, including three consecutive Champion Hurdles, three consecutive Grand Nationals and four Gold Cups; concentrated on flat racing from 1959; trained winners of 16 English classics, including six Derbys; trained Nijinsky, first Triple Crown winner since 1935, also trained winners of 27 Irish Classics (including six Irish Derbys); other major training triumphs include the French Derby, Prix de l'Arc de Triomphe (three), King George VI and Queen Elizabeth Diamond Stakes (two), Washington Int., Breeders' Cup Mile; Hon. LLD (Nat. Univ. Ireland) 1983; Dr hc (Ulster) 1995. *Publication:* Vincent O'Brien: The Man and the Legend. *Leisure interests:* golf, fishing. *Address:* Ballydoyle House, Cashel, Co. Tipperary, Ireland. *Telephone:* (62) 61222. *Fax:* (62) 61677.

O'BRIEN, Patricia, BA, MA, BL, LLB; Irish lawyer; *Under-Secretary-General for Legal Affairs and Legal Counsel, United Nations;* b. 8 Feb. 1957; m.; three c.; ed Trinity Coll., Dublin, Kings Inns, Dublin, Univ. of Ottawa, Canada; lawyer, Irish Bar 1979–88; called to Bar of England and Wales 1986; fmr lawyer, Bar of BC, Canada; Lecturer, Dept of Law, Univ. of British Columbia 1989–92; fmr Sr Legal Adviser to Irish Attorney-Gen.; fmr Legal Counsellor, Irish Perm. Representation to EU, Brussels; Legal Adviser, Dept of Foreign Affairs, Dublin 2003–08; Under-Sec.-Gen. for Legal Affairs and Legal Counsel, UN 2008–; Fellow, Soc. for Advanced Legal Studies, Inst. of Advanced Legal Studies, London. *Address:* Office of Legal Affairs, United Nations Headquarters, Room No. 3427A, New York, NY 10017, USA (office). *Fax:* (212) 963-6430 (office). *Website:* untreaty.un.org/ola (office).

O'BRIEN, Patrick Karl, BSc (Econ), MA, DPhil, FRSA, FRHistS, FBA; British historian and academic; *Centennial Professor of Economic History, London School of Economics;* b. 12 Aug. 1932, London; s. of William O'Brien and Elizabeth O'Brien Stockhausen; m. Cassy Cobham 1959; one s. two d.; ed London School of Econs, Nuffield Coll. Oxford; Lecturer, SOAS, Univ. of London 1963–70; Reader in Econs and Econ. History, Univ. of London 1967–70; Univ. Lecturer in Econ. History and Faculty Fellow, St Antony's Coll. Oxford 1970–84, Univ. Reader in Econ. History and Professorial Fellow 1984–90; Prof. of Econ. History, Univ. of London 1990–98; Sr Research Fellow and Convener of Programme in Global History, Inst. of Historical Research, Univ. of London 1998– (now Dir); Centennial Prof. of Econ. History, LSE 1999–; Fellow, Academia Europaea; Dr hc (Carlos III Univ., Madrid) 1999, (Uppsala) 2000. *Publications:* The Revolution in Egypt's Economic System 1966, The New Economic History of Railways 1977, Two Paths to the 20th Century: Economic Growth in Britain and France 1978, The Economic Effects of the Civil War 1988. *Leisure interests:* theatre, Western art, foreign travel. *Address:* Department of Economic History, Room E488, London School of Economics, Houghton Street, Aldwych, London, WC2A 2AE (office); 66 St Bernard's Road, Oxford, OX2 6EJ, England (home). *Telephone:* (20) 7955-6586 (office); (1865) 512004 (home). *Fax:* (20) 7955-7730 (office). *E-mail:* p.o'brien@lse.ac.uk (office). *Website:* www.lse.ac.uk (home).

O'BRIEN, Vincent (see O'BRIEN, Michael Vincent).

O'BRIEN QUINN, James Aiden, BA, LLB, QC; Irish lawyer; b. 3 Jan. 1932, Tipperary; s. of the late William Patrick Quinn and Helen Mary Quinn (née Walshe); m. Christel Mary Tyner 1960; two s. one d.; ed Presentation Coll., Bray, Univ. Coll. Dublin and King's Inns, Dublin; studied banking, Nat. City Bank, Dublin 1949–53; Crown Counsel and Acting Sr Crown Counsel, Nyasaland (Malawi) 1960–64; Asst Attorney-Gen. and Acting Attorney-Gen., West Cameroon 1964–66, Attorney-Gen. 1966–68; Avocat-Général près la Cour Fédérale de Justice, Cameroon 1966–68; Conseiller à la Cour Fédérale de Justice, Yaoundé, Cameroon 1968–72; Président du Tribunal Administratif du Cameroon Occidental 1968–72; Conseiller Technique (Harmonisation des Lois), Yaoundé, Cameroon 1968–72; Attorney-Gen. of Seychelles and British Indian Ocean Territory 1972–76; Chief Justice of Seychelles 1976–77; Acted as Deputy Gov. of Seychelles for a period during 1974; mem. Seychelles dels on self-govt and independence constitutions 1975, 1976; Chief Justice of Gilbert Islands (later Kiribati), Pacific Ocean 1977–81; Judge of High Court of Solomon Islands 1977–81; Special Prosecutor, Falkland Is. 1980; Chief Justice of Botswana 1981–87; Chair. of Judicial Service Comm., Botswana 1981; Adjudicator Immigrations Appeals 1990–96; Vice-Pres. Immigration Appeal Tribunal 1996–; BESO Adviser, Dominica 1992; Third Place, Inst. of Bankers in Ireland 1950; QC, Seychelles 1973; Kiribati Independence Medal 1979; Chevalier de l'Ordre National de la Valeur, Cameroon 1967. *Publications:* Ed. W Cameroon Law Reports 1961–68 and Gilbert Islands Law Reports, Kiribati Law Reports 1977–79; Magistrates' Courts' Handbook, W Cameroon 1968, Magistrates' Courts' Handbook, Kiribati 1979. *Leisure interests:* swimming, reading, languages, travel. *Address:* Field House, 15–25 Bream's Buildings, London, EC4A 1DZ (office); 9 Lorane Court, Langley Road, Watford, Herts., WD1 3LZ, England. *Telephone:* (1923) 232861.

OBUKHOV, Alexei Aleksandrovich, PhD; Russian diplomatist (retd); b. 12 Nov. 1937, Moscow; s. of Alexander Obukhov and Klaudia Obukhov; m. Olga Obukhov; two s.; ed Moscow Inst. of Int. Relations and Univ. of Chicago; joined Ministry of Foreign Affairs 1965; served in Embassy in Thailand; took part in Soviet-American Strategic Arms Limitation Talks on Threshold Test Ban Treaty (TTBT), Moscow 1974; Deputy Dir US Dept, Ministry of Foreign Affairs 1980–86; mem. Soviet negotiating team in arms control talks, responsible for negotiations on long-range strategic weapons, subsequently for negotiations on medium-range nuclear weapons, Geneva 1985; Deputy Head Soviet Del., Nuclear and Space Talks, Geneva 1987, Head 1988; Head, Dept of USA and Canada, Ministry of Foreign Affairs 1989–90; Deputy Minister of Foreign Affairs 1990–91; Amb. to Denmark 1992–96; Amb.-at-Large 1996–2002; Head of Del. to Russian-Lithuanian talks on border issues 1996–2005; Head of Del. to Joint Russian-Lithuanian Comm. on Demarcation 2005–; Chair. Cttee of Sr Officers (CSO) of the Barents Euro/Arctic Council 2000–01, CSO of the Council of Baltic Sea States 2001–02; Order of the Red Banner 1988; Harold Weill Medal for Outstanding Contrib. to Peace and Understanding through the Rule of Law, New York Univ. 1988, Medal of Merit, Russian Acad. of Arts 2006. *Publications:* Russia and Denmark: Painters of the Royal Courts from Catherine the Great to Margrethe II and numerous texts on diplomatic affairs. *Address:* 117049 Moscow, 40/7/71 Bolshaya Yakimanka str. (home); Ministry of Foreign Affairs, 119200 Moscow, Smolenskaya-Sennaya pl. 32/34, Russian Federation (office). *Telephone:* (495) 238-00-48 (home); (495) 244-16-06 (office). *Fax:* (495) 238-00-48 (home); (495) 230-21-30 (office). *E-mail:* moscowsuper@mtu-net.ru (home). *Website:* www.mid.ru (office).

OCAMPO, José Antonio, PhD; Colombian UN official; b. 20 Dec. 1952; m. Ana Lucia Ocampo; three c.; ed Univ. of Notre Dame, Yale Univ., USA; researcher, Centre for Devt Studies, Univ. de los Andes 1976–80, Dir 1980–82; at Foundation for Higher Educ. and Devt 1983–93, Deputy Dir 1983–84, Exec. Dir 1984–88, Sr Researcher and mem. Bd of Dirs; Minister of Agric. 1993–94, of Planning 1994–96, of Finance and Public Credit 1996–97; Exec. Sec. UN Econ. Comm. for Latin America and the Caribbean 1998–2003; UN Under-Sec.-Gen. for Econ. and Social Affairs 2003–07; Nat. Dir Employment Mission 1985–86; Adviser, Colombian Foreign Trade Bd 1990–91; Adviser, Colombian Nat. Council of Entrepreneurial Asscn; mem. Tech. Comm. on Coffee Affairs, Public Expenditure Comm., Advisory Comm. for Fiscal Reform, Mission on Intergovernmental Finance; consultant to IBRD, IDB and UN; mem. Colombian Acad. of Econ. Science 1987; Visiting Fellow, Univ. of Oxford, England, Yale Univ.; Nat. Science Prize 1988. *Address:* c/o Office of the Under Secretary-General for Economic and Social Affairs, United Nations, Room DC2–2320, New York, NY 10017, USA.

O'CATHAIN, Baroness, cr. 1991 (Life Peer), of The Barbican in the City of London; **Detta O'Cathain,** OBE, BA, FCIM; British economist and business executive; b. 3 Feb. 1938, Cork, Ireland; d. of Caoimhghin O'Cathain and Margaret Prior; m. William Ernest John Bishop 1968 (died 2001); ed Loreto School, Rathfarnham, Co. Dublin, Laurel Hill, Limerick, Univ. Coll. Dublin; Asst Economist, Aer Lingus 1961–66; Group Economist, Tarmac Ltd 1966–69; Econ. Adviser, Rootes Motors Ltd 1969–72; Sr Economist, Carrington Viyella 1972; Market Planning Dir, British Leyland 1973–76; Corp. Planning Exec., Unigate PLC 1976–81; Head of Strategic Planning, Milk Marketing Bd 1981–83, Dir and Gen. Man. 1983, Man. Dir Milk Marketing 1984–88; Man. Dir Barbican Centre, London 1990–95; Dir (non-exec.) Midland Bank PLC 1984–93, Tesco PLC 1985–2000, Sears PLC 1987–94, British Airways 1993–2004, BET PLC 1994–96, BNP Paribas (UK) PLC 1995–2005, Thistle Hotels 1996–2003; Pres. Chartered Inst. of Marketing 1998–2001, Southeast Water PLC 1998, Allders PLC 2000–03, William Baird PLC 2000–02. *Leisure interests:* music, reading, swimming, gardening. *Address:* House of Lords, Westminster, London, SW1A 0PW (office). *Telephone:* (20) 7219-0662 (office). *Fax:* (20) 7219-0785. *E-mail:* ocathaind@parliament.uk (office).

OCCHETTO, Achille; Italian politician; b. 3 March 1936, Turin; joined Italian Communist Party (PCI) and Young Communists' Fed. 1953, apptd Nat. Sec. Young Communists 1962; Sec. PCI Palermo 1969, subsequently Regional Sec. for Sicily; moved to Rome, held succession of party posts 1976; Deputy Leader PCI (name changed to Partito Democratico della Sinistra 1991) 1987–88, Gen.-Sec. 1988–94; Senator 2001–, Alternate Chair. Cttee on Rules of Procedure and Immunities, Cttee on Migration, Refugees and Population. *Address:* Senato della Repubblica, Piazza S. Eustachio 83, 00186 Rome, Italy. *E-mail:* achille@achilleocchetto.it (office). *Website:* www.achilleocchetto.it (office).

OCHIRBAT, Punsalmaagin, DSc; Mongolian politician; *President, Ochirbat Fund;* b. 23 Jan. 1942, Tudevtei Dist, Zavkhan Prov.; s. of Gonsiin Gendenjav and Tsogtiin Punsalmaa; m. Sharaviin Tsevelmaa 1965; two d.; ed Mining Inst. of USSR; apptd official at Ministry of Industry 1966, Chief Engineer, Sharyn Gol coal mine 1967, Deputy Minister, Ministry of Fuel and Power Industry and Geology 1972–76, Minister 1976; Chair. State Cttee External Econ. Relations 1985–87, Minister 1987; elected mem. Mongolian People's Revolutionary Party (MPRP) Cen. Cttee 17th, 18th and 19th Party Congresses and at 1990 Extraordinary Congress; resgnd from MPRP 1991; elected Deputy to Great People's Hural 9th, 10th and 11th elections, Chair. 1990; Pres. of Mongolia 1990–97, C-in-C of the Armed Forces 1993–97; Pres. Ochirbat Fund 1997–; Altan Gadas 1972, Mu Gung Hwa (Repub. of Korea) 1991, Liberty Award (USA) 1995. *Publications:* Black Gold, Art of Management, Organisation and Management of Fuel and Energy Complex, Heavenly Hour, Without the Right to Mistakes, Ecolog-Steady Development. *Address:* Tengeriin Tsag Co. Head Office, Olympic Street 14, Ulan Bator, Mongolia (office). *Telephone:* (11) 327215 (office). *Fax:* (11) 327233 (office). *E-mail:* pobmongolia@magicnet.mn (office).

OCHMAN, Wiesław; Polish tenor, producer and painter; b. 6 Feb. 1937, Warsaw; s. of Jan Ochman and Bronisława Ochman; m. Krystyna Ochman 1963; one s. one d.; ed Acad. of Mining and Metallurgy, Kraków 1960, studied with Prof. Gustaw Serafin, Kraków and with Prof. Maria Szłapak, Jerzy Gaczek and Sergiusz Nadgryzowski; début Silesian Opera, Bytom 1960; soloist, Silesian Opera, Bytom 1960–63, Opera in Kraków 1963–64, Great Theatre, Warsaw 1964–75, Deutsche Staatsoper 1967, Hamburgische Staatsoper 1967–, Metropolitan Opera, New York 1975–, La Scala, Milan 1981; festivals at Glyndebourne, Salzburg, Orange; guest performances in operas in Paris, Munich, Frankfurt am Main, San Francisco, Miami, Chicago, Geneva, Budapest, Washington, Staatsoper in Vienna, Grand Theatre in Moscow, Staatsoper and Deutsche Oper in W Berlin, Teatro Colón in Buenos Aires, Gran Teatre del Liceu in Barcelona, Accademia Santa Cecila in Rome, Carnegie Hall in New York, Teatro de la Maestranza in Seville; participation in TV films including Eugene Onegin, Tcharevitch, Salome, Don Giovanni; numerous recordings; mem. Pres. Council for Culture 1992–95; Goodwill Amb. for UNICEF 1996; Commdr's Cross with Star, Order of Polonia Restituta 2001; Minister of Culture and Art Prize 1973, The City of Warsaw Prize 1976, Pres. of Radio and TV Cttee Prize (1st Class) 1976, Prime Minister Prize (1st Class) 1979, Minister of Foreign Affairs Diploma 1977, 1986, Medal Maecenas of Art 1976, The City of Kraków Gold Award, Medal of Merit for Nat. Culture 1986. *Operatic roles include:* Faust, Don Carlos, Cavaradossi in Tosca, Don José in Carmen, Dimitri in Boris Godunov, Edgardo in Lucia di Lammermoor, Arrigo in I vespri siciliani, Alfredo in La Traviata, Don Carlos in Don Carlos, Stefan in The Hunted Manor, Turiddu in Cavalleria Rusticana, Lensky in Eugene Onegin, Herman in Pique Dame, Tamino in Der Zauberflöte, Idomeneo in Idomeneo, Titus in La clemenza di Tito, Eric in Der Fliegende Holländer, Florestan in Fidelio, Shepherd in King Roger, Les pêcheurs de perles, Herod in Salome, Prince Golitsyn in Khovanshchina, Jontek in Halka, Laca in Jenůfa, Prince in Rigoletto, Don Ottavio in Don Giovanni. *Operas directed:* Mozart's Don Giovanni, Verdi's La Traviata 2000, Lehar's Tcharevitch 2001, Tchaikovsky's Eugene Onegin 2002. *Recordings:* Jenůfa 1995, 2002, Halka 1995, Bruckner Masses 1996, Armida 1996, Stabat Mater/Legends 1997, Rusalka 1998, King Roger 1999, Great Operas of Richard Strauss 2001, Orchestral & Choral Works 2002, Te Deum/Lachrimosa 2003, Prokofiev: 50th Anniversary Edn – Limited Edn 2003, Cantatas 2004. *Leisure interests:* painting, collecting objects of art. *Address:* ul. Miączyńska 46B, 02-637 Warsaw, Poland (office). *Telephone:* 603-640-845 (office).

OCHOJSKA-OKOŃSKA, Janina; Polish charity administrator; *Chairman, Polska Akcja Humanitarna;* b. 12 March 1955, Gdańsk; m. Michał Okoński; ed Nicolaus Copernicus Univ., Toruń; Asst Astrophysics Lab. of Astronomy Centre of Polish Acad. of Sciences (PAN), Toruń 1980–92; co-f. EquiLibre Foundation 1989, Dir (and Co-Founder) Warsaw br. 1992–94; Co-Founder and Chair. Polska Akcja Humanitarna (Polish Humanitarian Org.) 1994–; The Order of the Smile awarded by Polish children 1995; EU Woman of Europe 1994 Feliks Civic Prize, Gazeta Wyborcza 1994, St George Medal, Tygodnik Powszechny magazine 1994, Pax Christi Int. Peace Award 1995, Woman of the Year, Poland 1995, Atsushi Nakata Memorial, Japan 1996, Romers' Foundation Award, Canada 1997, European German Culture Award 1999, Life Guide Award, Lublin Archdiocese's Youth Council 2000, Jt Winner, Twój Styl Magazine poll for the 50 Most Influential Woman in Poland 2000, 2001, Gold Medal of Voluntary Fire Brigades of Poland, Winner, first Jan Karski Freedom Award for Valour and Compassion, American Center of Polish Culture, Washington, DC 2002. *Leisure interests:* music, books, cooking. *Address:* Polska Akcja Humanitarna, 00-031 Warsaw, ul. Szpitalna 5 lok. 3, Poland (office). *Telephone:* (22) 8288882 (office). *Fax:* (22) 8319938 (office). *E-mail:* pah@pah.org.pl (office). *Website:* www.pah.org.pl (office).

OCKRENT, Christine; Belgian journalist; *Editor-in-Chief and Presenter, France Europe Express;* b. 24 April 1944, Brussels, Belgium; d. of Roger Ockrent and Greta Bastenie; m. Bernard Kouchner (q.v.); one s.; ed Collège Sévigné, Paris, Cambridge Univ., England and Institut d'Etudes Politiques de Paris; journalist, Information Office, EEC 1965–66; researcher, NBC News, USA 1967–68; producer and journalist, CBS News, USA 1968–77; journalist and producer, FR3, France 1976–80; Ed. and Anchor, news programme on Antenne 2 1980–85; Chief Ed. RTL 1985–86; Deputy Dir-Gen. TF1 1986–87; Ed., anchor and producer, news programmes on Antenne 2 1988–92, on France 3 1992–95; Chief Ed. L'Express 1995–96; Deputy Dir BFM 1996–2000; Ed.-in-Chief Dimanche Soir programme France 3 1996–98; Ed.-in-Chief and Presenter France Europe Express 1997–; Pres. BFMbiz.com; columnist La Provence, Dimanche CH; Chevalier de la Légion d'honneur 2000. *Publications:* Dans le secret des princes 1986, Duel 1988, Les uns et les autres 1993, Portraits d'ici et d'ailleurs 1994, La Mémoire du cœur 1997, Les Grands patrons (jtly) 1998, L'Europe racontée à mon fils, de Jules César à l'euro 1999, La double vie d'Hillary Clinton 2000, Françoise 2003. *Leisure interests:* riding, skiing, tennis. *Address:* France 3, 7 esplanade Henri de France, 75907 Paris cedex 15, France. *Website:* www.bfmbiz.com.

O'CONNELL, Brian; American musician (bass guitar); b. Queens, NY; m. Ayesha Alam; one d.; ed State Univ. of New York; mem., Junoon (with Ali Azmat and Salman Ahmad) 1992–2005, banned by Pakistani authorities for criticism of govt corruption early 1990s; upon invitation of UN Sec.-Gen., Kofi Annan, performed at UN Gen. Ass. (first band to play at Gen. Ass.); tours throughout Asia, N America, Middle East and Europe; Jazbe-e-Junoon selected as official song of cricket world cup, hosted by Pakistan 1996; Channel V Music Award for Int. Group 1998, UNESCO Award for Outstanding Achievement in Music and Peace 1999, BBC Asia Award 1999. *Recordings include:* albums: Junoon 1990, Talaash 1993, Inquilaab 1995, Khashmakash 1996, Azaadi 1997, Parvaaz 1999, Andaz 2001, The Millennium Edition (compilation) 2000, Daur-e-Junoon 2002, Dewaar 2003.

O'CONNELL, Robert J., MA; American insurance executive; *Chairman, President and CEO, MassMutual Life Insurance;* b. 1943; ed Univ. of Pennsylvania; with American Int. Group Inc. (AIG) 1989–98; joined MassMutual Life Insurance 1998, Pres. and CEO 1999–2000, Chair., Pres. and CEO 2000–; mem. Bd Dirs Oppenheimer Acquisition Corpn, DLB Acquisition Corpn, American Council of Life Insurance, Life Office Man. Asscn, US Chamber of Commerce. *Address:* Massachusetts Mutual Life Insurance Company, 1295 State Street, Springfield, MA 0111-0001, USA (office). *Telephone:* (413) 788-8411 (office). *Fax:* (413) 744-6005 (office). *Website:* www.massmutual.com (office).

O'CONNOR, Gordon, BSc, BA; Canadian politician and military officer (retd); *Minister of State and Chief Government Whip;* b. 18 May 1939, Toronto; m.; two c.; ed Concordia and York Univs; fmr mil. officer, Second Lt Armour Br., later Brig. Gen.; fmr Sr Assoc., Hill and Knowlton Canada; MP 2004–, mem. Standing Cttee on Nat. Defence and Veterans Affairs, Subcttee on Veterans Affairs; fmr Official Opposition Critic for Nat. Defence; Minister of Nat. Defence 2006–07, of Nat. Revenue 2007–08; Minister of State and Chief Govt Whip 2008–. *Address:* c/o Office of the Prime Minister, Langevin Block, 80 Wellington Street, Ottawa, ON K1A 0A2, Canada (office). *Telephone:* (613) 941-6888 (office). *Fax:* (613) 941-6900 (office). *E-mail:* OConnor.G@parl.gc.ca (office). *Website:* www.pm.gc.ca (office); www.gordonoconnor.ca (home).

O'CONNOR, Sandra Day, BA, LLB; American judge and university administrator; *Chancellor, College of William and Mary;* b. 26 March 1930, El Paso, Tex.; d. of Harry A. Day and Ada Mae Day (née Wilkey); m. John Jay O'Connor III 1952; three s.; ed Stanford Univ.; pvt. law practice, Phoenix, Ariz. 1959–65; served in Ariz. Senate 1969–74, Majority Leader 1973–74; elected Superior Court Judge, Ariz. 1975, Judge of Appeals 1979–81; Assoc. Justice, US Supreme Court 1981–2005; mem. Nat. Bd, Smithsonian Assocs 1981–, Exec. Bd, Cen. European and Eurasian Law Initiative (ABA) 1990–; Chancellor Coll. of William and Mary 2005–; mem. Bd of Trustees Rockefeller Foundation; mem. American Bar Asscn, State Bar of Ariz., State Bar of Calif., Maricopa Co. Bar Asscn, Ariz. Judges' Asscn, Nat. Asscn of Women Judges, Ariz. Women Lawyers' Asscn; mem. Iraq Study Group, US Inst. of Peace 2006; Harry Rathbun Visiting Fellow, Office for Religious Life, Stanford Univ. 2008; f. ourcourts.org web site 2009; 25 hon. degrees; numerous awards including Service to Democracy Award, American Ass. 1982, Fordham-Stein Prize, Fordham Univ. 1992, Award of Merit, Stanford Law School 1990, Nat. Women's Hall of Fame, Seneca Falls, NY 1995, ABA Medal 1997, Sylvanus Thayer Award, US Mil. Acad. 2005, Harry F. Byrd Jr. '35 Public Service Award, Virginia Mil. Inst. 2008, ranked by Forbes magazine amongst 100 Most Powerful Women (sixth) 2004, (36th) 2005. *Publication:* Finding Susie (children's book) 2009. *Address:* Office of the Chancellor, College of William and Mary, PO Box 8795, Williamsburg, VA 23187-8795, USA (office). *Telephone:* (757) 221-4000 (office). *Website:* www.wm.edu/chancellor (office); ourcourts.org.

O'CONNOR, Sinéad; Irish singer; b. 8 Dec. 1967, Dublin; d. of John O'Connor and the late Marie O'Connor; m. 1st John Reynolds (divorced); one d. (by John Waters); m. 2nd Nick Sommerland; ed Dublin Coll. of Music; mem., Ton Ton Macoute 1985–87; refused to accept Grammy Award for Best Alternative Album 1991; now Tridentine priest Sister Bernadette; MTV Award for Best Video, MTV Award for Best Single (both for Nothing Compares 2 U) 1990, MTV Award for Best Female Singer 1990, Rolling Stone Artist of the Year Award 1991, BRIT Award for Best Int. Solo Artist 1991. *Recordings include:* albums: The Lion and the Cobra 1987, I Do Not Want What I Have Not Got (Grammy Award for Best Alternative Album 1991) 1990, Am I Not Your Girl? 1992, Universal Mother 1994, Gospeloak 1997, Sean-Nós Nua 2002, Throw Down Your Arms 2005, Theology 2007. *Video films:* Value of Ignorance 1989, The Year of the Horse 1991. *Television:* Hush-a-Bye-Baby. *Address:* c/o Rubyworks, 6 Park Road, Dun Laoghaire, Co. Dublin, Ireland (office). *E-mail:* info@rubyworks.com. *Website:* www.sineadoconnor.com.

ODA, Beverley J., BA; Canadian politician and broadcasting executive; *Minister of International Co-operation;* b. 27 July 1944, Thunder Bay, Ont.; ed Univ. of Toronto; joined TVO 1973; various positions in broadcasting industry; Commr CRTC 1987–93; Sr Vice-Pres., Industry Affairs, CTV Inc. 1999; fmr Chair. Lakeridge Health Hosp. Network, Co-Chair. Task Force on Diversity on Canadian TV; MP 2004–; Minister of Canadian Heritage and Status of Women 2006–07, of Int. Co-operation 2007–; Queen's Golden Jubilee Medal 2002, Canadian Broadcasters Hall of Fame 2003. *Address:* House of Commons, Ottawa, ON K1A 0A6, Canada (office). *Telephone:* (613) 992-2792 (office). *Fax:* (613) 992-2794 (office). *E-mail:* Oda.B@parl.gc.ca (office). *Website:* www.parl.gc.ca (office); www.bevoda.ca (home).

ODA, Shigeru, LLM, JSD, LLD; Japanese international judge, lawyer and academic; *Professor Emeritus, Tôhoku University;* b. 22 Oct. 1924; s. of Toshio and Mioko Oda; m. Noriko Sugimura 1950; one s. one d.; ed Univ. of Tokyo, Yale Univ.; Research Fellow, Univ. of Tokyo 1947–49; Asst Prof. Tôhoku Univ. 1950–53, Assoc. Prof. 1953–59, Prof. 1959–76, Prof. Emer. 1985–; Tech. Adviser, Atomic Energy Comm. 1961–64; Special Asst to Minister for Foreign Affairs 1973–76; mem. Science Council of Ministry of Educ. 1969–76, of Council for Ocean Devt in Prime Minister's Office 1971–76, Advisory Cttee for Co-operation with UN Univ. 1971–76; Judge, Int. Court of Justice 1976–85, 1985–94, 1994–2003, (Vice-Pres. 1991–94); del. to UN Confs on Law of the Sea 1958, 1960, 1973–75; Rep. at 6th Gen. Conf. of Inter-Governmental Oceanographic Comm., UNESCO 1969; consultative positions with bodies concerned with marine questions; Counsel for FRG before Int. Court of Justice 1968; Ed.-in-Chief, Japanese Annual of International Law 1973–77; Assoc. Inst. de Droit Int. 1969 (mem. 1979, Hon. mem. 2003); mem. Curatorium, Hague Acad. of Int. Law 1989–2004, fmr. mem. Bd Dirs, Int. Devt Law Inst., Rome, Int. Council of Arbitration for Sport, Lausanne 1994–2006; mem. Japan

Acad. 1994–; Hon. mem. American Soc. of Int. Law 1975, Inst. of Int. Law 2001; Hon. Citizen of the City of Sendai 2004; Grand Order of the Sacred Treasure (by the Emperor of Japan); Hon. DJur (Bhopal) 1980, (New York Law School) 1981. *Publications:* in Japanese: International Law of the Sea 1956–85 (eight vols), International Law and Maritime Resources 1971–75, Judicial Decisions relating to International Law before Japanese Courts 1978; in English: International Control of Sea Resources 1962, The International Law of Ocean Development (four vols) 1972–79, The Law of the Sea in Our Times (two vols) 1977, The Practice of Japan in International Law 1961–70 1982, The International Court of Justice 1987, 1993, Fifty Years of the Law of the Sea 2002; various articles. *Address:* c/o Japan Academy, Ueno Koen 7-32, Taito-ku, Tokyo, 110-0007 (office); Akashicho 8-2-704, Chuo-ku, Tokyo 104-0044, Japan (home). *Telephone:* (3) 3822-2101 (office); (3) 5550-6666 (home). *Fax:* (3) 3822-2105 (office); (3) 5550-6694 (home). *E-mail:* oda.icj@bma.biglobe .ne.jp (home).

ODDSSON, David; Icelandic politician and central banker; *Governor, Central Bank of Iceland;* b. 17 Jan. 1948, Reykjavik; s. of Oddur Ólafsson and Ingibjörg Kristín Lúðvíksdóttir; m. 1st Ástríður Thorarensen 1951; one s.; m. 2nd Þorsteinn Davíðsson 1971; ed Reykjavik Coll., Univ. of Iceland; Chief Clerk Reykjavik Theatre 1970–72; parl. reporter for Morgunbladid newspaper 1973–74; worked for Almenna bokafelagid publishing co. 1975–76; Office Man., Reykjavik Health Insurance Fund 1976–78, Man. Dir 1978–82; mem. Reykjavik City Council 1974–99; Mayor of Reykjavik 1982–91; Vice-Chair. Independence Party 1989–91, Chair. 1991–; mem. Parl. 1991–; Prime Minister of Iceland 1991–2004; Minister of the Statistical Bureau of Iceland; Minister of Foreign Affairs 2004–05; Gov. Cen. Bank of Iceland 2005–; Chair. of Exec. Cttee Reykjavik Arts Festival 1976–78; Hon. LLD (Univ. of Manitoba) 2000. *Publications:* plays: For My Country's Benefit (Nat. Theatre 1974–75), Icelandic Confabulations (Reykjavik Theatre 1975–76); TV dramas: Robert Eliasson Returns From Abroad 1977, Stains on the White Collar 1981; short stories: A Couple of Days Without Gudny 1997, Stolen from the Author of the Alphabet 2002; essay The Independence Movement 1981; trans. A Small Nation Under the Yoke of a Foreign Power by Anders Küng-Estonia 1973. *Leisure interests:* bridge, salmon fishing, forestry. *Address:* Central Bank of Iceland, Kalkofnsvegi 1, 150 Reykjavik, Iceland (office). *Telephone:* 5699600 (office). *Fax:* 5699605 (office). *E-mail:* sedlabanki@sedlabanki.is (office). *Website:* www.sedlabanki.is (office).

O'DEA, Willie, LLM, CA; Irish politician; *Minister for Defence;* b. Nov. 1952, Limerick; m. Geraldine Kennedy; ed Patrician Brothers Coll., Ballyfin, Co. Laois, Univ. Coll. Dublin (UCD), Kings Inns, Inst. of Certified Accountants; fmr barrister and accountant; fmr Lecturer, UCD and Univ. of Limerick; TD 1982–, Minister of State at Dept of Justice 1992–93, at Depts of Justice and Health 1993–94, at Dept of Educ. 1997–2002, at Dept of Justice, Equality and Law Reform with special responsibility for Equality Issues 2002–04, Minister for Defence 2004–; regular columnist, Sunday Independent and other nat. newspapers. *Address:* Department of Defence, Parkgate, Infirmary Road, Dublin 7, Ireland (office). *Telephone:* (1) 8042000 (office). *Fax:* (1) 6703399 (office). *E-mail:* webmaster@defence.irlgov.ie (office). *Website:* www.defence.ie (office); www.willieodea.ie (office).

ØDEGÅRD, Knut, LittD; Norwegian poet, writer, critic and diplomatist; *Norwegian Consul General, Republic of Macedonia;* b. 6 Nov. 1945, Molde; m. Thorgerdur Ingólfsdóttir 1981; two d.; ed Univ. of Oslo; poetry critic Aftenposten newspaper 1968–; Man. Dir Scandinavian Centre, Nordens Hus, Reykjavík 1984–89; Pres. Norwegian Festival of Int. Literature 1992–; Consul Republic of Slovakia 1995–97; Consul Gen. Republic of Macedonia 1997–; Pres. Bjornstjerne Bjornson Acad., Norwegian Acad. of Literature and Freedom of Expression 2003–; mem. Acad. of Norwegian Language, Icelandic Soc. of Authors, Literary Acad. of Romania, Norwegian Soc. of Authors, European Acad. of Poetry; Norwegian State Scholar for Life 1989–; knighted by Pres. of Iceland 1987, Grand Kt Commdr, Order of the Icelandic Falcon 1993, Int. Order of Merit 1993, Kt, Norwegian Order of Literature 1995, knighted by King of Norway 1998. *Publications include:* poetry: Bee-buzz, Salmon Leap 1968, Cinema Operator 1991, Ventriloquy 1994, Selected Poems 1995, Missa 1998, The Stephensen House 2003; books of prose and essays, a play, and two non-fiction books about Iceland 1992, 1998. *Address:* c/o J. W. Cappelen, Oslo, Norway (office); Postboks 326, 6401 Molde, Norway. *Telephone:* 71-21-59-91 (office). *E-mail:* knut.odegard@moldenett.no.

ODEH, Ayman, LLM; Jordanian lawyer and politician; *Minister of Justice;* b. 1961; ed Univ. of Jordan, Miami Univ., USA; practising lawyer 1985–; mem. various legal cttees including Jordan First Comm. Anti-Corruption Cttee, We Are All Jordan Cttee; Minister of Justice 2007–. *Address:* Ministry of Justice, POB 6040, Amman 11118, Jordan (office). *Telephone:* (6) 4603630 (office). *Fax:* (6) 4643197 (office). *E-mail:* moj@moj.gov.jo (office). *Website:* www.moj.gov.jo (office).

ODENBERG, Mikael; Swedish politician; b. 1953, Stockholm; m. Catherine Odenberg; two s. two d.; ed Östra Real Upper Secondary School, Stockholm, Stockholm Univ., Stockholm School of Econs, Reserve Officer Training, Nat. Defence Coll.; Maj. (reserve) in Swedish Marines; Local Govt Ombudsman, Swedish Young Conservatives and Moderate Party, Nacka 1972–73; Sec. Moderate Youth (MUF) 1978; Deputy Sec. to Stockholm City Commr (real estate, town-planning and highways depts) and Sec. to Moderate City Council Group 1979–85; self-employed 1985–2004; mem. Riksdag (Parl.) 1987, 1990, 1991–2006, mem. Cttee on Housing 1991–94, Cttee on Industry and Trade 1994–98, Cttee on Labour Market and Cttee on EU Affairs 1998–2002, Deputy Chair. Cttee on Industry and Trade 2002–03, mem. War Del. 2003–; Leader Moderate Party Parl. Group 2003–06, Deputy Chair. Cttee on Finance 2003–06, mem. Advisory Council on Foreign Affairs 2003–06, mem. Riksdag Bd 2003–06, mem. Parl. Review Comm. 2003–06; Minister for Defence 2006–07; Leader Moderate Party's group on healthcare matters, Stockholm Co. Council 1988–91. *Address:* Moderata Samlingspartiet (Moderate Party), Stord Nygatan 30, PO Box 2080, 103 12 Stockholm, Sweden (office). *Telephone:* (8) 676-80-00 (office). *Fax:* (8) 21-61-23 (office). *E-mail:* info@ moderat.se (office). *Website:* www.moderat.se (office).

ODENT, Michel; French obstetrician and writer; developed and led maternity unit, Pithiviers 1962–86; commissioned by WHO to report on planned home birth in industrialized countries 1986–90; moved to London 1990; f. Primal Health Research Centre, London, for study of long-term consequences of early experiences; Contributing Ed. Midwifery Today, USA. *Publications:* 11 books, published in 22 languages, including Birth Reborn 1984, Primal Health 1986, The Scientification of Love 2001, The Farmer and the Obstetrician 2002, The Caesarean 2004, The Functions of the Orgasms 2009; numerous medical articles. *Address:* 72, Savernake Road, London, NW3 2JR, England (office). *Telephone:* (20) 7485-0095 (office). *Fax:* (20) 7267-5123 (office). *E-mail:* modent@aol.com (home). *Website:* www.wombecology.com (home); www.primalhealthresearch.com (home).

ODGERS, Sir Graeme David William, Kt, MA, MBA; British business executive; *Chairman, Kent Economic Board;* b. 10 March 1934, Johannesburg, SA; s. of the late William Arthur Odgers and of Elizabeth Minty (née Rennie); m. Diana Patricia Berge 1957; one s. three d. (one deceased); ed St John's Coll., Johannesburg, Gonville and Caius Coll., Cambridge, Harvard Business School, USA; Investment Officer, IFC, Washington DC 1959–62; Man. Consultant, Urwick Orr & Partners Ltd 1962–64; Investment Exec., Hambros Bank Ltd 1964–65; Dir, Keith Shipton Ltd 1965–72, C.T. Bowring (Insurance) Holdings Ltd 1972–74; Chair., Odgers & Co. Ltd (Man. Consultants) 1970–74; Dir, Industrial Devt Unit, Dept of Industry 1974–77; Assoc. Dir (Finance), Gen. Electric Co. 1977–78; Group Finance Dir, Tarmac PLC 1979–86, Group Man. Dir 1983–86, Dir (non-exec.) 1986–87; Dir (non-exec.), Dalgety PLC 1987–93; part-time Bd mem., British Telecommunications PLC 1983–86, Govt Dir 1984–86, Deputy Chair. and Chief Finance Officer 1986–87, Group Man. Dir 1987–89; Chief Exec., Alfred McAlpine 1990–93; Chair., Monopolies and Mergers Comm. 1993–97; Dir (non-exec.), Southern Electric PLC 1998–; Dir, Scottish and Southern Energy PLC 1999–; Chair., Locate in Kent Ltd 1998–2005, Kent Econ. Bd 2001–; DL, Co. of Kent 2002–; Hon. LLD (Greenwich) 2004, (Kent) 2005. *Leisure interest:* golf. *Address:* 5 The Coach House, Springwood Park, Tonbridge, TN11 9LZ, England.

ODIERNO, Lt-Gen. Raymond T., BSc, MS, MA; American army officer; *Commander, Multi-National Force—Iraq;* b. 1953, Rockaway, NJ; s. of Ray and Helen Odierno; m. Linda Burkarth; two s. one d.; ed US Mil. Acad., West Point, NC State Univ., Naval War Coll.; began army career with US Army Europe and US Seventh Army, Germany, becoming Platoon Leader and Survey Officer, 1st Bn, US 41st Field Artillery Brigade, 56th Field Artillery Brigade, and Aide-de-Camp to Commanding Gen.; Exec. Officer, 2nd Bn, 3rd Field Artillery and later Div. Artillery, 3rd Armored Div., Operation Desert Storm 1990–91; fmr Chief of Staff, US States V Corps, US Army Europe; Commdr, US 4th Infantry Div. (4th ID) 2001–04; Asst to Chair. of Jt Chiefs of Staff and Sr Mil. Adviser to Sec. of State, Washington DC 2004–06; Commanding Gen., US III Corps., Iraq, also Commanding Gen. Multi-National Force – Iraq, Baghdad 2008–; numerous medals including Army Distinguished Service Medal, Defense Superior Service Medal, Legion of Merit, Bronze Star. *Address:* Multi-National Force—Iraq, 7115 South Boundary Boulevard, MacDill AFB, Tampa, FL 33621, USA (office). *E-mail:* mnfi.webmaster@iraq.centcom.mil (office). *Website:* www.mnf-iraq.com (office).

ODINGA, Raila Amollo, MSc; Kenyan politician; *Prime Minister;* b. 7 Jan. 1945, Nyanza; s. of Jaramogi Odinga and Mary Emma Odinga; m. Ida Anyango Oyoo; four c.; ed Herder Inst., Leipzig, Otto von Guericke Tech. Univ., Magdeburg, Germany; Asst Lecturer, Dept of Mechanical Eng, Univ. of Nairobi 1971–72; f. Spectre Ltd (later East African Spectre Ltd) eng co. 1971; Group Standards Man. Kenya Bureau of Standards 1974–78, Deputy Dir 1978–82; detained without trial following coup attempt by Kenya Air Force personnel 1982–88, re-arrested and detained 1988, 1990, spent four months in political asylum in Norway 1991; Co-founder Forum for the Restoration of Democracy 1991; elected mem. Parl. for Langata 1992, joined NDP (Nat. Devt Party) 1996; finished third in presidential election 1997; Minister for Energy 2001–02; joined LDP (Liberal Democratic Party) 2002; Minister for Roads and Public Works 2002–05; Co-founder Orange Democratic Movt 2005, Leader 2007–; Prime Minister 2008–. *Address:* Orange Democratic Movement–Kenya, Orange House, Vanga Road, POB 2478, 00202 Nairobi, Kenya (office). *E-mail:* odmk2007@yahoo.com (office); contact@raila07.com (office). *Website:* odmk.org (office); www.raila2007.com (office).

ODIO BENITO, Elizabeth; Costa Rican politician, lawyer and international arbitrator; *Judge, International Criminal Court;* ed Univ. of Costa Rica, Univ. of Buenos Aires; Minister of Justice and Attorney-Gen. 1978–82, Minister of Justice 1990–94, Second Vice-Pres. of Costa Rica and Minister of Environment and Energy 1998–2002; Perm. Rep. to UN, Geneva 1993; mem. Sub-Comm. for the Prevention of Discrimination and Minorities Protection, Human Rights Comm., UN 1980–83, Special Rapporteur, Sub-Comm. on Discrimination and Intolerance Based on Religion or Creed 1983–86, Vice-Pres. of the Criminal Tribunal for the Fmr Yugoslavia 1993–95, mem. Admin. Tribunal of the Inter-American Devt Bank 1997–98, mem. and Vice-Pres. Bd of Dirs Univ. para la Paz, UNESCO 1999–, Pres. Working Group on Optional Protocol for the Int. Convention against Torture 1998, Judge, Int. Tribunal for the fmr Yugoslavia 1993–98, mem. Costa Rican Nat. Group to the Perm. Court of Arbitration 2000–03, Judge, Int. Criminal Court 2003–; Visiting Prof. Univs of Strasbourg, France 1986, Utrecht, Netherlands 1995, Zaragoza, Spain 1996, Leiden, The Netherlands 1998, Barcelona, Spain 1998; Prof. Univ. of Costa

Rica 1986–94, Vice-Pres. of Academic Affairs 1988–90, Prof. Emer. 1994–; Prof. Inter-American Inst. of Human Rights, Costa Rica 1992–; mem. Costa Rican Law Asscn, Steering Cttee Asser Inst., The Hague, Bd Dirs Inter-American Inst. of Human Rights, Int. Comm. of Jurists. *Address:* International Criminal Court (ICC), Maanweg 174, 2516 AB, The Hague, Netherlands (office); PO Box 2292/1000, San José, Costa Rica. *Telephone:* (70) 5158515 (office); (506) 2809654 (home). *Fax:* (70) 5158555 (office); (506) 253-6984 (home). *E-mail:* pio@icc-cpi.int (office); eodio@racsa.co.cr (home). *Website:* www.icc-cpi.int (office).

ODJIG, Daphne, CM; Canadian artist and muralist; b. 11 Sept. 1919, Wikwemikong, Manitoulin Island, Ont.; d. of Dominic Odjig and Joyce Emily Odjig (née Peachey); m. Chester Beavon 1963; two s. two step-s. one step-d.; mem. Odawa Tribe; numerous solo exhbns Canada 1967–; numerous group exhbns in Canada, also London, UK 1976, São Paulo, Brazil 1977, Okla, USA 1978; commissions include: Earthmother, for Canadian Pavilion, Expo 1970, Osaka, Japan; mural depicting Indian legend, Creation of the World, Museum of Man 1972, From Mother Earth Flows the River of Life, Cultural Devt Div., Ministry of Indian and Northern Affairs 1974; The Indian in Transition, for Nat. Museum of Man. 1978; works in collections of Winnipeg Art Gallery, Ministry of Indian and Northern Affairs, Winnipeg, Nat. Museum of Man, Man. Indian Brotherhood, Canadian Council Art Bank, McMichael Canadian Coll., Kleinberg, Ont., Tom Thompson Gallery, Sir Wilfrid Laurier Univ., Govt of Israel, Jerusalem and other; Founding mem. Professional Native Indian Artists' Asscn Inc. 1973–; Co-founder Warehouse Gallery, Winnipeg 1974; mem. Royal Canadian Acad. of Art 1989; Hon. LLD (Laurentian Univ.) 1982, (Toronto) 1985; Hon. DEd (Nipissing Univ., Ont.) 1996; Swedish Brucebo Foundation Scholarship 1973, Man. Arts Council Bursary 1973, Canadian Silver Jubilee Medal 1977, Eagle Feather presented by Chief Wakageshig, Wikwemikong Reserve in recognition of artistic accomplishments 1978, Commemorative Medal, 125th Anniversary of Confed. of Canada 1992, Nat. Aboriginal Achievement Award, Toronto 1998. *Publications:* Nanabush Indian Legends for Children (author and illustrator; 10 books) 1971, A Paintbrush in my Hand 1992, The Art of Daphne Odjig 2001. *Address:* 101–102 Forest Brook Place, Penticton, BC V2A 7N4, Canada. *Telephone:* (250) 493-7475 (home).

ODLAND, Steve, BBA, MM; American business executive; *Chairman and CEO, Office Depot Inc.;* ed Univ. of Notre Dame, Northwestern Univ.; with Quaker Oats Co. 1981–96; Sr Vice-Pres., Gen. Man. Snacks Div., Sara Lee 1996–98, Pres. Foodservice Div. 1997–98; Exec. Ahold USA 1998–2000; Chair., CEO, Pres. and Dir AutoZone Inc. 2001–05; Chair. and CEO Office Depot Inc. 2005–; mem. Bd of Dirs General Mills Inc. *Address:* Office Depot Inc., 2200 Old Germantown Road, Delray Beach, FL 33445, USA (office). *Telephone:* (561) 438-4800 (office). *Fax:* (561) 438-4001 (office). *Website:* www.officedepot.com (office).

ODLING-SMEE, John Charles, CMG, MA; British economist (retd); b. 13 April 1943; s. of the late Rev. Charles William Odling-Smee and Katherine Hamilton Odling-Smee (née Aitchison); m. Carmela Veneroso 1996; ed Durham School, St John's Coll. Cambridge; Jr Research Officer, Dept of Applied Econs, Cambridge 1964–65; Asst Research Officer, Inst. of Econs and Statistics, Oxford 1968–71, 1972–73; Econ. Research Officer, Govt of Ghana 1971–72; Sr Research Officer, Centre for Urban Econs LSE 1973–75; Econ. Adviser, Cen. Policy Review Staff, Cabinet Office 1975–77; Sr Econ. Adviser, HM Treasury 1977–80; Sr Economist, IMF 1981–82; Under-Sec., HM Treasury 1982–89; Deputy Chief Econ. Adviser, HM Treasury 1989–90; Sr Adviser, IMF 1990–91, Dir IMF European II Dept 1992–2003 (dept dissolved), retd 2004. *Publications:* Housing Rent Costs and Subsidies 1978, British Economic Growth 1856–1973 1982; various articles in books and learned journals. *Address:* 3506 Garfield Street, NW, Washington, DC 20007, USA (home).

ODOKI, Hon. Benjamin Joses, LLB; Ugandan lawyer; *Chief Justice of Uganda;* b. 23 March 1943, Busia; m. Veronica Odoki; three s. one d.; ed Kings Coll. Budo, Kampala, Univ. of Dar-es-Salaam; State Attorney 1969–72; Advocate, High Court of Uganda 1970; Dir Law Devt Centre 1974–78; Judge, High Court of Uganda 1978–81, Dir Public Prosecution 1981–84; Judge, Supreme Court 1986–2001; Chair. Uganda Constitutional Comm. 1989–93; Chair. Judicial Service Comm. 1996–2000; Chief Justice of Uganda 2001–; Gen. Ed. Uganda Law Focus 1974–78, Ed.-in-Chief Uganda Law Reports 1974–78; mem. Editorial Advisory Bd Commonwealth Law Bulletin 2005–; Independence Medal 1974, Order of Merit, Uganda Law Soc. 1998, Distinguished Jurist Award (Nigeria) 2002. *Publications include:* A Guide to Criminal Procedure in Uganda 1990, An Introduction to Juridicial Conduct and Practice 1992, A Guide to the Legal Profession in Uganda 1992, Criminal Investigation and Prosecutions 1999. *Leisure interests:* music, fine art, drama. *Address:* Chambers of the Chief Justice, Courts of Judicature, POB 7085, Kampala (office); Plot 4 Philip Road, Kololo, Kampala, Uganda (home). *Telephone:* (41) 231727 (office); (41) 343576 (home). *Fax:* (41) 343971 (office). *E-mail:* bodoki2000@yahoo.com (home). *Website:* www.judicature.go.ug (office).

O'DONNELL, Sir Augustine Thomas (Gus), Kt, KCB, CB, BA, MPhil; British economist and civil servant; *Secretary to the Cabinet and Head of the Home Civil Service;* b. 1 Oct. 1952, London; s. of James O'Donnell and Helen O'Donnell (née McLean); m. Melanie Timmis 1979; one d.; ed Salesian Coll., Battersea, Univ. of Warwick and Nuffield Coll., Oxford; Lecturer, Dept of Political Economy, Univ. of Glasgow 1975–79; economist, HM Treasury 1979–85; First Sec. (Econ.) Embassyin Washington, DC 1985–88; Sr Econ. Adviser, HM Treasury 1988–89, Press Sec. to Chancellor of the Exchequer 1989–90; Press Sec. to Prime Minister John Major 1990–94; Under-Sec. (monetary group) HM Treasury 1994–95, Deputy Dir Macroeconomic Policy

and Prospects Directorate 1995–96, Minister (Econs), Embassy in Washington, DC; Exec. Dir IMF, World Bank 1997–98, Man. Dir Macroeconomic Policy and Prospects Directorate 1998–2002; Head of Govt Econ. Service, HM Treasury 1998–2002, Perm. Sec. (with responsibility for Euro entry tests) 2002–05; Sec. to Cabinet and Head of Home Civil Service 2005–. *Publications:* The O'Donnell Review of the Revenue Departments, Reforming Britain's Economic and Financial Policy (ed.), Microeconomic Reform in Britain (ed.); various articles in econ. journals. *Leisure interests:* football, cricket, tennis. *Address:* Cabinet Office, 70 Whitehall, London, SW1A 2AS, England (office). *Telephone:* (20) 7276-0101 (office). *E-mail:* mst@cabinet-office.x.gsi.gov.uk (office). *Website:* www.cabinetoffice.gov.uk (office).

O'DONNELL, Chris; American actor; b. 26 June 1970, Winnetka, Ill.; m. Caroline Fentress 1997; f. George Street Pictures (production co.). *Films include:* Men Don't Leave 1990, Fried Green Tomatoes 1991, Scent of a Woman 1992, School Ties 1992, The Three Musketeers 1993, Blue Sky 1994, Circle of Friends 1995, Mad Love 1995, Batman Forever 1995, The Chamber, In Love and War, Batman and Robin, Cookie's Fortune 1998, The Bachelor (producer and actor) 1999, Vertical Limit 2000, 29 Palms 2002, Kinsey 2004, The Sisters 2005, Max Payne 2008. *Television includes:* The Practice (series) 2003, The Amazing Westerbergs (2004), Head Cases (series) 2005, Grey's Anatomy (series) 2006. *Address:* George Street Pictures, 4000 Warner Blvd., Bldg. 81, Room 203, Burbank, CA 91522; c/o Josh Lieberman, CAA, 9830 Wilshire Boulevard, Beverly Hills, CA 90212, USA. *Telephone:* (818) 954-4361 (George Street).

O'DONNELL, Daniel, MBE; Irish singer; b. 12 Dec. 1961, Kincasslagh, Co. Donegal; m. Majella McLennan 2002; backing vocalist for sister Margo O'Donnell, early 1980s; tours of UK and Ireland 1985–, Australia and NZ 1993–, USA 2003–; numerous live appearances. *Radio:* numerous interviews in Ireland, UK, USA and Australia. *Television:* series, Ireland, Pledges (PBS TV, USA). *Recordings include:* albums: Two Sides Of Daniel O'Donnell 1985, I Need You 1986, Don't Forget To Remember 1987, The Boy From Donegal 1987, Love Songs 1988, From The Heart 1988, Thoughts Of Home 1989, Favourites 1990, The Last Waltz 1990, The Very Best Of... 1991, Follow Your Dream 1992, Christmas With Daniel 1994, Especially For You 1994, The Classic Collection 1995, Irish Collection 1996, Timeless (with Mary Duff) 1996, Songs Of Inspiration 1996, Country Collection 1997, This is Daniel O'Donnell 1997, I Believe 1997, Love Hope & Faith 1998, Greatest Hits 1999, Faith and Inspiration 2000, Live Laugh Love 2001, Heartbreakers 2002, Songs of Love 2002, Irish Album 2002, Yesterday's Memories 2002, Dreaming 2002, The Daniel O'Donnell Show 2003, Welcome to North America 2003, Date With (live) 2003, Daniel In Blue Jeans 2003, Daniel O'Donnell and Friends (live) 2003, At The End Of The Day 2003, The Jukebox Years 2004, Welcome To My World 2004, Until the Next Time 2006. *Videos include:* Daniel O'Donnell Live In Concert 1988, Thoughts Of Home 1989, TV Show Favourites 1990, An Evening With Daniel O'Donnell 1990, Follow Your Dream 1992, Daniel And Friends Live 1993, Just For You 1994, The Classic Concert 1995, Christmas With Daniel 1996, The Gospel Show, Live At The Point 1997, Give A Little Love 1998, Peaceful Waters 1999, Faith And Inspiration 2000, Live Laugh Love 2001, The Daniel O'Donnell Show 2001, Shades of Green 2002, Songs of Faith 2003. *Publications:* My Story (autobiography) 2000, Daniel O'Donnell: My Pictures and Places 2004. *Address:* Brockwell Ltd, Unit 6, 90B Lagan Road, Dublin Industrial Estate, Glasnevin, Dublin 11, Ireland (office). *Telephone:* (1) 830 1707 (office). *Fax:* (1) 830 1981 (office). *E-mail:* srmanagement@eircom.net (office). *Website:* www.daniel-site.com.

O'DONOGHUE, John, BCL, LLB; Irish politician; *Minister for Arts, Sport and Tourism;* b. 28 May 1956, Cahirciveen, Co. Kerry; m. Kate Ann Murphy; two s. one d.; ed Christian Brothers' Secondary School, Cahirciveen, Univ. Coll., Cork, Inc. Law Soc. of Ireland; fmrly solicitor; mem. Dáil Éireann Feb. 1987–; Minister of State Dept of Finance 1991–92; fmr Fianna Fáil Spokesperson on Justice; Minister of Justice, Equality and Law Reform June 1997–2002, for Arts, Sport and Tourism 2002–; mem. Kerry Co. Council (Chair. 1990–91), mem. Kerry Co. Library Cttee, Kerry Fisheries and Coastal Man. Cttee, Southern Health Bd Psychiatric Services Cttee, Caherciveen Social Services Cttee, British–Irish Parl. Body. *Leisure interests:* English literature, history, Gaelic games, horse racing. *Address:* Department of Arts, Sport and Tourism, Kildare Street, Dublin 2 (office); Garranearagh, Cahirciveen, Co. Kerry, Ireland (home). *Telephone:* (1) 6789181 (office); (66) 72413 (home). *Fax:* (1) 6785906 (office); (66) 72667 (home). *E-mail:* ministersoffice@dast.gov.ie (office). *Website:* www.gov.ie/arts-sport-tourism (office).

O'DRISCOLL, Patricia, FRSA; British (b. Zimbabwe) business executive; *Operational Managing Director, Terra Firma Captial Partners Ltd;* b. 1959; ed Univ. of Exeter; trainee chartered accountant, Price Waterhouse; buyer and store man., Marks & Spencer grad. programme; buying controller, later food broker, Tesco PLC 1987–94; Dir Business Unit responsible for alcoholic drinks and tobacco, Safeway PLC 1994–97; Global Strategy Vice-Pres., Shell Retail International 1997, Retail Vice-Pres. Shell Europe 2003–04; CEO Northern Foods PLC 2004–07; Head of EVP People, Restructuring and Change, EMI Group 2008–09; Operational Man. Dir, Terra Firma Capital Partners Ltd 2009–; fmr Ind. Dir (non-exec.) Assa Abloy AB, Sweden; mem. Investor Bd EMI Group 2007–; ranked by the Financial Times amongst Top 25 Businesswomen in Europe (13th) 2005, (22nd) 2006. *Address:* Terra Firma Capital Partners Ltd, 2 More London Riverside, London, SE1 2AP, England (office). *Telephone:* (20) 7015-9500 (office). *Website:* www.terrafirma.com (office).

ODROWĄŻ-PIENIĄŻEK, Janusz, MA; Polish writer, literary historian and museum director; *Director, Adam Mickiewicz Museum of Literature;* b. 2 July 1931, Opatowice; m. Izabella Romanowska; one s.; ed Warsaw Univ., Lublin

Catholic Univ.; scientific worker, Inst. of Literary Research, Polish Acad. of Science, Warsaw 1956–72; Dir Adam Mickiewicz Museum of Literature, Warsaw 1972–; Ed.-in-Chief Muzealnictwo (journal) 1981–; mem. Asscn of Friends of Books 1958–, Adam Mickiewicz Literature Asscn 1952–, Soc. of Authors ZAiKS 1962–, Pen Club 1969–, Accad. di Storia e Letteratura Polacca e Slava 'Adamo Mickiewicz', Bologna 1976–, Deutsche Schillergesellschaft (Marbach am Neckar) 1995–, mem. Polish Nat. Cttee, ICOM 1972–, Vice-Chair. 2002–; Pres. Int. Cttee Museum of Literature ICOM 1995–2001; mem. Man. Bd SEC 1975–; Vice-Chair. Polish Writers' Asscn 1996–99, Chair. 1999–2002; Golden Cross of Merit 1974, Kt's Cross, Order of Polonia Restituta 1988, Commdr's Cross 1999; Diploma of Merit, Acad. Internationale des Sciences de l'Homme du Canada 1982, Warsaw Award 1983, Editor's Award, Polish Pen Club 1998, Minister of Culture Award 2003, Zygmunt Gloger Award 2004, Gloria Artis Medal 2005. Publications: short stories: Opowiadania paryskie 1963, Ucieczka z ciepłych krajów 1968, Wielki romans w Bucharze 1984, Bulwar Wilshire 2004; poetical prose: Teoria fal 1964, Głos z szuflady 2002; novels: Małżeństwo z Lyndą Winters 1971, Mit Marii Chapdelaine 1985; essays: Polonika zbierane po świecie 1992, Mickiewicziana zbierane po świecie 1998; Paul Cazin, diariste, epistolier, traducteur (co-author) 1997; numerous works on literary history in scientific journals. Leisure interest: travelling. Address: Adam Mickiewicz Museum of Literature, Rynek Starego Miasta 20, 00-272 Warsaw (office); Uniwersytecka 1 Apt. 2, 02-036 Warsaw, Poland (home). Telephone: (22) 8314061 (office); (22) 8225913 (home). Fax: (22) 8317692 (office); (22) 8225913 (home). E-mail: muzeum .literatury@poczta.wp.pl (office).

ODUBER, Nelson Orlando; Dutch politician; Prime Minister of Aruba; b. 7 Feb. 1947; m. Glenda Oduber; three s.; ed St Antonius Coll., Santa Cruz, Administrative Acad. of Brabant, Tilburg, Univ. of Utrecht; Teacher, Governmental Org. and mem. Exams Preparatory Cttee 1973–75; mem. Cttee of the Kingdom to prepare the independence of Suriname 1973–75; Deputy in charge of Dept for Legislative and Constitutional Affairs 1975–85; Vice-Pres. Consultative Cttee for Independence of Aruba 1978–85; mem. Kingdom Cttee for political restructuring of Antilles 1978–80; Leader Movimento Electoral di Pueblo (MEP) (People's Electoral Movt); Prime Minister of Aruba 1989–; Minister of Gen. Affairs 1989–94, 2001–; Ordén Francisco de Miranda (Venezuela) 1989, Order of the Liberatador First Class (Venezuela) 1991, Kt in the Order of Orange Nassau 1995; Man of the Year (Diario) 1980, Gold Award for contributing to educ. of Aruba 1983, Politician of the Year by readers of Extra 1990, Man of the Year (MEP) 1993, Man of the Year 2001. Leisure interests: swimming, gardening, keeping fit. Address: L. G. Smith Boulevard 76, Oranjestad (office); Nayostraat 5, Oranjestad (home); MEP, Nayostraat 5, Oranjestad, Aruba. Telephone: (297) 5880300 (office); (297) 5824206 (home). Fax: (297) 5880024 (office).

ODUMEGWU-OJUKWU, Gen. Chukwuemeka; Nigerian politician and army officer; b. 4 Nov. 1933, Zungeru; s. of Sir Odumegwu Ojukwu, KBE and Grace Ojukwu; m. Bianca Olivia Odinaka Onoh 1994; ed CMS Grammar School and King's Coll., Lagos, Epsom Coll., UK, Lincoln Coll., Oxford, Eaton Hall Officer Cadet School, UK and Joint Services Staff Coll., UK; Admin. Officer, Nigerian Public Service 1956–57; joined Nigerian Army 1957; at Nigerian Army Depot, Zaria 1957; army training in UK 1957–58; joined 5th Bn Nigerian Army 1958; Instructor, Royal West African Frontier Force Training School, Teshie 1958–61; returned to 5th Bn Nigerian Army 1961; Maj., Army HQ 1961; Deputy Asst Adjutant and Quartermaster-Gen. Kaduna Brigade HQ 1961; Congo Emergency Force 1962; Lt-Col and Quartermaster-Gen. 1963–64; Commdr 5th Bn, Kano 1964–66; Mil. Gov. of E Nigeria 1966–67; Head of State of Repub. of Biafra (E Region of Nigeria) 1967–70; sought political asylum in Ivory Coast 1970–82; returned to Nigeria 1982; joined Nat. Party of Nigeria 1983–84; imprisoned Jan.–Oct. 1984; then released; disqualified from presidential candidacy Feb. 1993; left SDP May 1993; unsuccessful cand. for presidency 2003. Publications: Biafra: Random Thoughts 1969, Because I am Involved 1982. Leisure interests: sports, music, art, photography, poetry. Address: Villaska, 29 Queen's Drive, Ikoyi, Lagos, Nigeria.

ODUNTON, Nii Allotey, MS; Ghanaian mining engineer, administrative officer and international organization official; Secretary-General, International Seabed Authority; b. 14 June 1951; m. Nijama Odunton; four c.; ed Achimeta Secondary School, Accra; Henry Krumb School of Mines, Columbia Univ., USA; Mine Planning Officer, Bethlehem Steel Corpn, Morgantown, Pa 1974–75; Econ. Affairs Officer, Dept of Int. Econ. Social Affairs, UN Secr., New York 1980–83; held several other UN positions 1984–88 including Chief of Mineral Resources Section and Ocean Econs and Tech. Br., First Officer in Charge, UN Office for Law of the Sea, Kingston, Jamaica 1988–; Adviser to Minerals Comm. of Govt of Ghana 1984–87; Interim Dir-Gen. and Programme Coordinator, Int. Seabed Authority 1996–2008, Head of Office of Resources and Environmental Monitoring 2008, Deputy to Sec.-Gen. 2008, Sec.-Gen. 2009–; mem. American Inst. of Mining, Metallurgical and Petroleum Engineers, Ghana Inst. of Engineers; African Scholarship Programme of American Univs Award 1969, 1969–72, Henry Krumb Research Fellow 1972, Henry Krumb Fellow 1974–75. Address: International Seabed Authority, 14–20 Port Royal Street, Kingston, Jamaica (office). Telephone: 922-9105 (office). Fax: 922-0195 (office). Website: www.isa.org.jm (office).

ŌE, Kenzaburō, BA; Japanese writer; b. 31 Jan. 1935, Ehime, Shikoku; m. Yukari Itami 1960; two s. one d.; ed Tokyo Univ.; first stories published 1957; first full-length novel Pluck The Flowers, Gun The Kids 1958; represented young Japanese writers at Peking (now Beijing) 1960; travelled to Russia and Western Europe writing a series of essays on Youth in the West 1961; Commdr, Légion d'Honneur 2002; Hon. DLit (Harvard) 2000; Shinchosha Literary Prize 1964, Tanizaka Prize 1967, Europelia Arts Festival Literary

Prize 1989, Nobel Prize for Literature 1994. Publications: fiction: Shisha no ogori (trans. as The Catch) (Japanese Soc. for the Promotion of Literature Akutagawa Prize) 1958, Memushiri kouchi (trans. as Nip the Buds, Shoot the Kids) 1958, Miru mae ni tobe 1958, Our Age (in trans.) 1959, Screams (in trans.) 1962, The Perverts (in trans.) 1963, Nichijo seikatsu no boken 1963, Kojinteki na taiken (trans. as A Personal Matter) 1964, Adventures in Daily Life (in trans.) 1964, Man'en gannen no futtoburu (trans. as The Silent Cry) 1967, Football in The First Year of Mannen (in trans.) 1967, Pinchi ranna chosho (trans. as The Pinch Runner Memorandum) 1976, Warera no kyoki o iki nobiru michi o 1969, Shosetsu no hoho 1978, Natsukashii toshi e no tegami 1986, M/T to mori no fushigi no monogatari 1986, A Healing Family (in trans.) 1996, A Quiet Life (in trans.) 1998, Rouse Up, O Young Men of the New Age (in trans.) 2002, Somersault (in trans.) 2003, Telling Tales (contrib. to charity anthology) 2004, Torikaeko (trans. as Changeling) 2000, Jibun no Ki'no Sitade (trans. as Under My Tree) 2000, Sakokushiteha Naranai 2001, Iigataki Nagekimote 2001, Ureigao no Douij 2002, Bouryoku ni Sakaratte kaku (trans. as Writing Against Violence) 2003, Atarasii hito' no houe 2003, Nihyakunen no kodomo 2003, Sayounara, Watashi no Hon yo! 2005; non-fiction: Hiroshima noto (trans. as Hiroshima Notes) 1963, Okinawa noto 1970, Chiryo noto 1990, Japan, the Ambiguous and Myself (the Nobel Prize speech and other lectures) 1995. Address: Marion Boyars Publishers Ltd, 24 Lacy Road, London, SW15 1NL, England (office); 585 Seijo-machi, Setagaya-ku, Tokyo, Japan (home). Telephone: 482-7192 (home). E-mail: catheryn@marionboyars.com (office). Website: www.marionboyars.co.uk (office).

OELZE, Christiane; German singer (soprano); b. 9 Oct. 1963, Cologne; m. Bodo Primus; one d.; ed studied with Klesie Kelly-Moog and Erna Westenberger; began singing in opera 1990; recital tours USA, S. America, Japan; has worked with many maj. int. conductors and has appeared on all important European concert stages and at int. festivals, including Salzburg Festival; roles include Despina (Ottawa), Pamina (Leipzig, Lyon, Hamburg, Munich), Konstanze (Salzburg, Zürich), Anne Trulove (Glyndebourne), Regina (in Mathis der Maler, Covent Garden), Zdenka (Covent Garden), Zerlina (Covent Garden), Ännchen (in Der Freischütz, Covent Garden), Mélisande (Glyndebourne), Servilia (in La Clemenza di Tito, Covent Garden), Susanna (Salzburg), Ilia (in Idomeneo, Glyndebourne), Igluno (Palestina, Covent Garden), Sophie (in Rosenkavalier, Hamburg); winner, several Lieder competitions including Hugo-Wolf-Wettbewerb 1987, Hochschule Wettbewerb für Lied-Duo 1988. Recordings include: several solo recitals, concert arias, Mass in C minor (Mozart), Christmas Oratorio, St John and St Matthew Passions, Webern songs and cantatas, Le Nozze di Figaro and many others. Television: Pelléas et Mélisande, Glyndebourne 1999. Address: Michael Kocyan Artists Management, Alt-Moabit 104a, 10559 Berlin, Germany (office). Telephone: (30) 31004940 (office). Fax: (30) 31004984 (office). E-mail: oleze@kocyan.de (office). Website: www.kocyan.de (office); www .christianeoelze.com.

OESTERHELT, Jürgen, LLD, MCL; German diplomatist (retd); Trustee, Anglo-German Foundation; b. 19 Aug. 1935, Munich; s. of Dr Egon Oesterhelt and Trude Pfohl; m. Katharina Galeiski 1964; one s. one d.; ed Univ. of Munich and Columbia Univ.; int. lawyer, Paris 1963–64; entered diplomatic service, Bonn 1964; served Moscow 1964–65, New York (UN) 1966–71, Sofia 1971–74, Athens 1977–80; Ministry of Foreign Affairs 1980–92; Amb. to Turkey 1992–95, to UK 1995–97, to the Holy See 1997–2000; Trustee, Anglo-German Foundation; Grosses Bundesverdienstkreuz and decorations from Greece, Finland, Austria. Leisure interests: reading, music, sports. Address: Auf der Königsbitze, 4, 53639 Königswinter, Germany. Telephone: (2223) 27109 (home). Fax: (2223) 904075 (home). E-mail: juergen@oesterhelt.de (home).

OESTREICHER, Rev. Canon Paul, MA; British/New Zealand/German clergyman and journalist; b. 29 Sept. 1931, Meiningen, Germany; s. of Paul Oestreicher, MD and Emma Oestreicher (née Schnaus); m. 1st Lore Feind 1958 (died 2000); two s. (one deceased) two d.; m. 2nd Dr Barbara Einhorn 2002; ed Otago and Victoria Univs, NZ, Bonn Univ., FRG, Lincoln Theological Coll., UK; emigrated to NZ with parents 1939; Ed. Critic student newspaper, Otago Univ. 1952–53; Humboldt Research Fellow, Bonn Univ. 1955, Berlin 1992; studied industrial mission (Opel, Gen. Motors), Rüsselsheim 1958–59; ordained in Church of England 1959; freelance journalist and broadcaster in FRG and UK 1959–; Curate in Dalston, London 1959–61; Programme Producer, Religious Dept, BBC Radio 1961–64; Assoc. Sec., Dept of Int. Affairs, British Council of Churches, with special responsibility for East–West relations 1964–69, Hon. Sec. East–West Relations Cttee 1969–81, Asst Gen. Sec. and Div. Sec. for Int. Affairs 1981–86; Vicar, Church of the Ascension, Blackheath, London 1968–81; Dir of Lay Training, Diocese of Southwark 1969–72; mem. Gen. Synod of Church of England 1970–86, 1996–97, Int. Affairs Cttee. 1965–2001; mem. Exec. Council Amnesty Int. (UK Section) 1969–80, Chair. 1974–79; Founder and Trustee, Christian Inst. (of Southern Africa) Fund 1974–94, Chair. Trustees 1983–94; Hon. Chaplain to Bishop of Southwark 1975–80; Hon. Canon of Southwark Cathedral 1978–83, Canon Emer. 1983–86; Public Preacher, Diocese of Southwark 1981–86; Dir Int. Ministry of Coventry Cathedral 1986–97, Canon Residentiary 1986–97, Canon Emer. 1998–; int. consultant 1997–2000; Chair. Christians Aware 1999–2000; mem. Council Keston Coll. 1975–83; mem. Nat. Council Campaign for Nuclear Disarmament 1980–82, Vice-Chair. 1983–85, Vice-Pres. 1985–; mem. Religious Soc. of Friends (Quakers) 1982, Quaker Chaplain Univ. of Sussex 1994–; Hon. Citizen of Meiningen 1995; Bundesverdienstkreuz (Cross of Merit First Class), Germany 1995, Verdienstorden of Free State of Saxony 2004; Hon. DLitt (Coventry); Hon. LLD (Sussex); Wartburg Prize for Promotion of European Unity 1997, City of Coventry Distinguished Citizen Award 2002. Publications: Ed.: Gollwitzer: The Demands of Freedom (English edn) 1965, The Christian Marxist Dialogue 1969, (with J. Klugmann) What Kind of Revolution 1969, The Church and the Bomb (co-author) 1983, The

Double Cross 1986; trans. Schulz: Conversion to the World 1967; contrib. to British Council of Churches working party reports on Eastern Europe and Southern Africa. *Address:* 97 Furze Croft, Furze Hill, Brighton, BN3 1PE, England (home). *Telephone:* (1273) 728033 (home). *E-mail:* paulo@reconcile .org.uk (home).

O'FARRELL, Anthony Gilbert, PhD, MRIA; Irish mathematician and academic; *Professor of Mathematics, National University of Ireland, Maynooth;* b. 28 May 1947, Dublin; s. of Patrick O'Farrell and Sheila O'Farrell, née Curtis; m. Lise Pothin 1972; three s. one d.; ed Univ. Coll. Dublin, Brown Univ., USA; Meteorological Officer, Irish Meteorological Service 1967–68; Fellow and Teaching Asst, Brown Univ., Providence, RI, USA 1970–73; Asst Prof., Univ. of Calif., LA 1973–75; Prof. of Math., Maynooth Coll. (now Nat. Univ. of Ireland, Maynooth) 1975–, now also Head of Dept, Head of Computer Science 1992–95; Research Assoc., Dublin Inst. for Advanced Studies 1979–; mem. Irish Math. Soc. (Pres. 1982–84, Sec. 1984–85, 1987–89), London Math. Soc., Soc. Mathématique de France, American Math. Soc., Math. Asscn of America, Irish Meteorological Soc.; Fellow, Inst. of Math. and its Applications; Nat. Univ. Travelling Studentship 1969. *Publications:* numerous research papers. *Leisure interests:* literature, walking, music. *Address:* Department of Mathematics, National University of Ireland, Maynooth, Co. Kildare, Ireland (office). *Telephone:* (1) 7083914 (office). *Fax:* (1) 7083913 (office). *E-mail:* admin@maths.nuim.ie (office). *Website:* www.maths.nuim.ie/staff/aof (office).

OFFICER, David Adrian, MA, FRSA; British artist, art lecturer, television presenter and producer; b. 24 Aug. 1938, Belfast, Northern Ireland; s. of Adrian Charles Officer and Eileen Officer (née Sterritt); ed Hutcheson's Grammar School, Glasgow, Univ. of Durham and Moray House Coll. of Educ. Edinburgh; Head of Art Dept Rhyl Grammar School, lecturer in Fine Art, Harrow School 1970–71; Lecturer in Art Educ., W Australian Inst. of Tech. (now Curtin Univ.) Perth 1972–78; ABC TV lecturer, Melbourne and Sydney 1973–78; Festival Artist, Perth 1974; Art Consultant, Whittaker (USA), Tabuk Mil. Hosp. Saudi Arabia 1979–83; Lecturer in Art and Design, United Coll. of Educ. Zimbabwe 1983–85; weekly art and design programmes, ZTV Television, Zimbabwe 1985–87; Lecturer in Fine Art, Hillside Teacher's Coll. Bulawayo 1985–87; Lecturer in Fine Art and World Art History, Univ. of Anatolia, Turkey 1987–89; Visiting Examiner in Art, Cambridge Univ. 1991–; freelance artist, display artist, art educator, exhbn organizer; exhbns in most major European cities and in Sydney, Adelaide, Melbourne and Perth. *Publications:* articles in Liverpool Gazette, festival magazines etc. *Leisure interests:* fine arts, drawing, painting, calligraphy, typography, stained glass, rugby, cricket. *Address:* 86 London Road, Plaistow, London, E13, England.

OFFORD, Robin Ewart, MA, PhD; British medical scientist, biochemist and academic; *Executive Director, Mintaka Foundation for Medical Research;* b. 28 June 1940, Stondon, Beds.; s. of Frank Offord and Eileen Offord; m. Valerie Wheatley 1963; one s. two d.; ed Dame Alice Owen's School, London, Peterhouse Coll., Cambridge; scientific staff (part-time), UKAEA 1959–62; grad. student, MRC Lab. for Molecular Biology 1962–65, on scientific staff 1965–66; scientific staff, Lab. of Molecular Biophysics, Oxford 1966–72; Fellow, Univ. Coll., Oxford 1968–73, Univ. Lecturer in Molecular Biophysics, Univ. of Oxford 1972–80, Tutor in Biochemistry and Official Fellow, Christ Church Coll., Oxford 1973–80; Prof., Dir Dept of Medical Biochemistry, Univ. of Geneva 1980–2005, Pres. Pre-Clinical Medicine 1994–2000; Dir Geneva Bioinformatics SA 1999–2000; Pres. and Exec. Vice-Chair. GeneProt Inc. 2000–01; Chair. Scentific and Econ. Advisory Bd Eclosion SA 2003–; Co-founder and Exec. Dir Mintaka Foundation for Medical Research 2005–; Agefi Man. of the Year Award (Switzerland) 2002, Makineni Award, American Peptide Soc. 2005, Tribune de Genève 'Personality of the Year-Society' 2008. *Publications:* author, co-author or ed. six scientific books; author or co-author more than 180 articles in scientific journals. *Leisure interests:* scuba diving (PADI Instructor), windsurfing, cross-country skiing, comparative linguistics. *Address:* Mintaka Foundation, 31 route Pré-Marais, 1233 Bernex, Switzerland (office). *Telephone:* (79) 293-5781 (office). *E-mail:* Robin.Offord@ medecine.unige.ch (office). *Website:* www.mintakafoundation.org (office).

OFILI, Chris, MA; British artist; b. 1968, Manchester; ed Chelsea School of Art, Royal Coll. of Art, Hochschule der Kunst, Berlin; has exhibited as solo artist in Southampton and at Serpentine Gallery, London, Manchester City Art Gallery, Venice Biennale 2003; winner Whitworth Young Contemporaries Exhbn, Turner Prize 1998. *Address:* c/o Victoria Miro Gallery, 21 Cork Street, London, W1X 1HB, England. *Telephone:* (20) 7734-5082. *Fax:* (20) 7494-1787.

OGATA, Sadako, PhD; Japanese international organization official; *President, Japan International Co-operation Agency;* b. 1927; one s. one d.; ed Univ. of Sacred Heart, Tokyo, Georgetown Univ., Univ. of Calif., Berkeley; Minister, Japan's Mission to UN 1978–79; UN special emissary investigating problems of Cambodian refugees on Thai-Cambodian border; rep. of Japan on UN Comm. for Human Rights 1982–85; fmr Chair. Exec. Bd UNICEF; fmr Dir Inst. of Int. Relations, Sophia Univ. Tokyo; Dean, Faculty of Foreign Studies, Sophia Univ. until 1990; UN High Commr for Refugees 1991–2000; Co-Chair. Comm. for Human Security 2001–03; Prime Minister's Special Rep. for Afghanistan 2002–04; mem. UN High Level Panel on Threat, Challenges and Change 2003–04, Chair. Advisory Bd on Human Security 2003–; Pres. Japan Int. Co-operation Agency 2003–; Ford Foundation Scholar-in-Residence 2002; Dr hc (Harvard) 1994; Hon. DCL (Oxford) 1998; UNESCO Houphouët-Boigny Peace Prize 1996, Ramon Magsaysay Award for Int. Understanding 1997, Seoul Peace Prize 2000, Delta Prize for Global Understanding 2002, J. William Fulbright Prize for Int. Understanding 2002, Eleanor Roosevelt Val-Kill Medal 2002, Indira Gandhi Prize 2002, Great Negotiator Award, Harvard 2005, Woodrow Wilson Award for Public Service 2007. *Publications:* The Turbulent Decade: Confronting the Refugee Crises of the 1990s 2005, Defiance in Manchuria: the Making of Japanese Foreign Policy, 1931–1932.

Address: Shinjuku Maynds Tower, 1-1 Yoyogi 2chome, Shibuya-ku, Tokyo 151-8558, Japan (office).

OGATA, Shijuro, CBE, MA; Japanese fmr central banker; b. 16 Nov. 1927, Tokyo; s. of Taketora Ogata and Koto Ogata; m. Sadako Nakamura 1961; one s. one d.; ed Seikei Higher School, Tokyo, Univ. of Tokyo and Fletcher School of Law and Diplomacy; joined Bank of Japan 1950, Asst Rep. in London 1962–64, Rep. in New York 1975–78, Adviser to Gov. 1978–79, Dir Foreign Dept 1979–81, Exec. Dir 1981–84, Deputy Gov. for Int. Relations 1984–86; Deputy Gov. The Japan Devt Bank 1986–91; Dir Barclays Bank 1991–95, Fuji Xerox 1991–2001, Horiba Ltd 1995–2006; Auditor Fuji Xerox 2001–02; Adviser Swire Group 1991–98, Yamaichi Securities 1991–97; Chair. Barclays Trust & Banking Co. (Japan) Ltd 1993–97; Co-Chair. Study Group on UN Financing 1992–93; Japan Soc. Award 1992. *Publications:* International Financial Integration: The Policy Challenges (co-author) 1989, The Yen and the Bank of Japan 1996; several articles on int. monetary issues. *Leisure interests:* reading, writing. *Address:* 3-29-18 Denenchofu, Ota-ku, Tokyo 145-0071, Japan (home).

OGAWA, Seiji, BS, PhD; Japanese neuroscientist; *Director, Ogawa Laboratories for Brain Function Research;* b. 19 Jan. 1934; ed Univ. of Tokyo, Stanford Univ., Calif., USA; pioneer in devt of nuclear magnetic resonance (NMR) and functional magnetic resonance imaging (fMRI) of brain; Research Assoc., Radiation Research Labs, Mellon Inst., Pittsburgh, USA 1962–64; Postdoctoral Fellow, Stanford Univ. 1967–68; mem. Tech. Staff, Biophysics Research (later Biological Computation Research) Dept, Bell Labs, AT&T, Murray Hill, NJ 1968–80, Distinguished Mem. of Tech. Staff and Prin. Investigator, Biophysics Research 1984–96; Distinguished Mem. of Tech. Staff and Prin. Investigator, Bell Labs, Lucent Technologies 1996–2001; Visiting Prof., Dept of Biophysics and Physiology, Albert Einstein Coll. of Medicine, Yeshiva Univ., Bronx, NY 2001; Dir Ogawa Labs for Brain Function Research, Hamano Life Science Research Foundation, Tokyo 2001–; Fellow, Int. Soc. for Magnetic Resonance in Medicine 1997; mem. Inst. of Medicine, NAS 2000, Soc. for Neuroscience; Hon. mem. Japanese Soc. of Magnetic Resonance in Medicine 2004, Japanese Soc. of Nuclear Magnetic Resonance 2004; Eastman Kodak Award in Chem. 1967, Gold Medal Award, Soc. of Magnetic Resonance in Medicine 1995, Biological Physics Prize, American Physical Soc. 1996, Nakayama Prize, Nakayama Foundation for Human Science 1998, Asahi Prize, Asahi-Shinbun Cultural Foundation 1999, Japan Int. Prize, Japan Foundation for Science and Tech. 2003, Gairnder Int. Award, Gairdner Foundation, Canada 2003. *Publications:* numerous articles in scientific journals. *Address:* Ogawa Laboratories for Brain Function Research, Hamano Life Science Research Foundation, 12 Daikyo-cho, Shinjuku-ku, Tokyo 160-0015, Japan (office). *Telephone:* (3) 5919-3991 (office). *Fax:* (3) 5919-3993 (office). *E-mail:* info@hlsrf.or.jp (office). *Website:* www.hlsrf.or.fp (office).

OGAWA, Tadashi, LLB; Japanese tobacco industry executive; *Chairman, Japan Tobacco Inc.;* b. 1940, Tokyo; ed Faculty of Law, Univ. of Tokyo; began career with Ministry of Finance, held positions successively as Dir-Gen. of Tax Bureau, Commr of Nat. Tax Agency, and Admin. Vice Minister of Finance –1997; Visiting Prof., Research Centre for Advanced Science and Tech., Univ. of Tokyo 1997–2001; Chair. and Rep. Dir Japan Tobacco Inc. 2001–; mem. Bd of Dirs AEON Co. Ltd. *Publications:* Detailed Explanation of the Tobacco Consumption Tax (co-author). *Address:* Japan Tobacco Inc., 2-1 Toranomon 2-chome, Minato-ku, Tokyo 105-8422, Japan (office). *Telephone:* (3) 3582-3111 (office). *Fax:* (3) 5572-1441 (office). *Website:* www.jti.co.jp (office).

OGI, Adolf; Swiss fmr head of state, politician and international consultant; b. 18 July 1942, Kandersteg; s. of Adolf Ogi and Anna Ogi; m.; two c.; ed Ecole Supérieure de Commerce, La Neuveville, Swiss Mercantile School, London; Man. Soc. for the Devt and Improvement of Meiringen and the Hasli Valley 1963–64; joined Swiss Ski Asscn 1964, Tech. Dir 1969–74, Dir 1975–81; Maj. in Army 1981–83, Staff Liaison Officer 1984–87; mem. Swiss People's Party 1978–, Chair. 1984–87; mem. Parl. 1979–; mem. Fed. Council 1987, Vice-Pres. 1999; Head Fed. Dept of Transport, Communications and Energy 1988–95; Pres. of Switzerland Jan.–Dec. 1993, Jan.–Dec. 2000; Special Adviser to UN Sec.-Gen. on Sport for Devt and Peace 2001–07; Head Fed. Mil. Dept 1995–97, Fed. Dept of Defence, Civil Protection and Sports 1998–2002; Chair. Candidature Cttee for Winter Olympic Games Sion 2006 1998–99; Vice-Chair. Int. and European Cttee, Int. Ski Fed. 1971–83; Dir-Gen. and mem. of Bd Intersport Schweiz Holding AG 1981–; Hon. Pres. Swiss Olympic Asscn; Citizen of Honour, Kandersteg 1992, Fraubrunnen 1999, Sion 2000, Crans Montana, Gondo; Dr hc (Univ. of Berne, Int. Univ. in Geneva, Geneva School of Diplomacy and Int. Relations, American Coll. of Greece); European Solar Prize, Human Rights Prize (Switzerland). *Address:* Bureau Ogi, Schürmatt-strasse 6, 3073, Gümligen, Switzerland (office). *Telephone:* (31) 952-54-77. *E-mail:* info@adolfogi.ch (office).

OGI, Chikage; Japanese politician; b. (Hiroko Hayashi), 10 May 1933, Hyogo; m. Nakamura Ganjiro; ed Kobe High School; fmr actress of all-female Takarazuka Revue theatre group, also fmr singer and broadcaster; mem. House of Councillors 1977–89, 1993–, Speaker 2004–07; apptd Minister of State, Dir-Gen. Nat. Land Agency 2000; Minister of Construction 2000, of Land, Infrastructure and Transport 2001–03; mem. LDP –1994, Head of Hoshuto (New Conservative Party) 2000–01; returned to LDP 2003. *Address:* c/o House of Councillors, Nagatacho 1-7-1, Chiyoda-ku, Tokyo, Japan (office).

OGILVIE, Dame Bridget Margaret, DBE, ScD, FRS, FIBiol, FRCPath, FMedSci; Australian scientist; *Visiting Professor, University College London;* b. 24 March 1938, Glen Innes, NSW; d. of the late John Mylne Ogilvie and Margaret Beryl McRae; ed New England Girls School, Armidale, NSW, Univ. of New England, NSW, Univ. of Cambridge; Fellow, Wellcome Animal Health Trust 1963–66; mem. scientific staff MRC 1966–81; mem. staff of The Wellcome

Trust (various capacities) 1979–, Dir 1991–98; Visiting Prof., Univ. Coll. London 1997–; Dir (non-exec.) Lloyds Bank 1995–96, Lloyds TSB Group PLC 1996–2000, Zeneca Group PLC 1997, AstraZeneca 1999–2006; mem. UK Council for Science and Tech. 1993–2000, Advisory Council for Chem., Univ. of Oxford 1997–2001, Australian Health and Medical Research Strategic Review 1998; Trustee Nat. Museum of Science and Industry 1992–2002, Royal Coll. of Veterinary Surgeons Trust Fund 1998–2001, Nat. Endowment for Science and Tech. and the Arts 1998–2002, Cancer Research Campaign 2000–02, Research UK 2002–; Chair. Governing Body, Inst. for Animal Health 1997–2003, Cttee on the Public Understanding of Sciences 1998–2002, British Library Advisory Cttee for Science and Business 1999–2002; High Steward Univ. of Cambridge 2002–; Chair. Asscn of Medical Research Charities 2002–; Chair. Medicines for Malaria Venture 1999–2006, Lister Inst. Governing Body 2002–; Ian McMaster Fellow 1971–72; Vice-Chair. Sense About Science; Hon. mem. British and American Socs of Parasitology, British Veterinary Asscn; Hon. MRCP; Hon. FRCP; Hon. Assoc. Royal Coll. of Veterinary Surgeons; Hon. Fellow. Univ. Coll. London, Girton Coll. Cambridge, St Edmunds Coll. Cambridge, Royal Australasian Coll. of Physicians, Inst. of Biology, Royal Soc. of Medicine; Foundation Hon. Fellow Royal Veterinary Coll.; Hon. MD (Newcastle); Hon. DSc (Nottingham, Salford, Westminster, Bristol, Glasgow, ANU, Buckingham, Dublin, Nottingham Trent, Oxford Brookes, Greenwich, Auckland, Durham, Kent, Exeter, London, Leicester, Manchester, St Andrews, Wollongong); Hon. LLD Trinity Coll., Dundee; Dr hc (Edin.); Univ. Medal (Univ. of New England); Inaugural Distinguished Alumni Award (Univ. of New England); Lloyd of Kilgerran Prize 1994, Wooldridge Memorial Medal 1998, Australian Soc. of Medical Research Medal 2000, Kilby Award 2003, Duncan Davies Memorial Medal 2004. *Publications:* various scientific papers, reviews, book chapters on the immune response to parasitic infections of man and animals 1964–84. *Leisure interests:* the company of friends, looking at landscape, swimming, walking, music, gardening. *Address:* c/o Medical Administration, University College London, Gower Street, London, WC1E 6BT, England. *Telephone:* (20) 7679-6939. *Fax:* (20) 7383-2462. *E-mail:* rachel.chapman@ucl.ac.uk (office).

OGILVIE THOMPSON, Julian, MA; South African business executive (retd); b. 27 Jan. 1934, Cape Town; s. of the late the Hon. Newton Ogilvie Thompson and Eve Ogilvie Thompson; m. the Hon. Tessa M. Brand 1956; two s. two d.; ed Diocesan Coll., Rondebosch and Worcester Coll., Oxford; Dir (non-exec.) De Beers Consolidated Mines Ltd 1966–, Chair. 1985–97, Deputy Chair. 1998–2001; Chair. Mineral and Resources Corpn 1982–99; Deputy Chair. Anglo-American Corpn of South Africa Ltd 1983–90, Chair. 1990–2002, Chair. Anglo-American PLC 1999–2002; Dir Anglogold Ltd 1998–2004, Nat. Business Initiative; Rhodes Trustee 2002–; Trustee Mandela-Rhodes Foundation 2003–; Commdr, Order of Leopold (Belgium), Grand Official, Order of Bernardo O'Higgins (Chile), Presidential Order of Honour (Botswana); Hon. LLD (Rhodes Univ.); Rhodes Scholar 1953. *Leisure interests:* golf, fishing, shooting. *Address:* PO Box 61631, Marshalltown 2107 (office); Froome, Froome Street, Athol Ext. 3, Sandton, Gauteng, South Africa (home). *Telephone:* (11) 274-2040 (office); 884-3925 (home). *Fax:* (11) 643-2720 (office).

OGILVY, HRH Princess Alexandra, the Hon. Lady, KG, GCVO; b. 25 Dec. 1936; d. of the late Duke of Kent (fourth s. of King George V) and Princess Marina (d. of the late Prince Nicholas of Greece); m. Hon. Angus James Bruce Ogilvy (second s. of the late 12th Earl of Airlie, KT, GCVO, MC) 1963 (died 2004); one s. one d.; ed Heathfield School, Ascot; Chancellor, Univ. of Lancaster 1964–2004; Col-in-Chief, the King's Own Royal Border Regt –2006, The Queen's Own Rifles of Canada and the Canadian Scottish Regt (Princess Mary's); Col-in-Chief, The Light Infantry –2007; Deputy Col-in-Chief, Queen's Royal Lancers 1993–; Patron and Air Chief Commdt, Princess Mary's Royal Air Force Nursing Service; Patron, Queen Alexandra's Royal Naval Nursing Service; Pres. or Patron of many charitable and social welfare orgs; rep. HM Queen Elizabeth II at independence celebrations of Nigeria 1960 and St Lucia 1979, 150th anniversary celebrations, Singapore 1969; Hon. Royal Col The Royal Yeomanry (Territorial Army Voluntary Reserves); Hon. Liverywoman, Worshipful Co. of Clothworkers; Royal Hon. Freeman, Worshipful Co. of Barbers; Hon. Freeman, City of Lancaster, City of London; Hon. Fellow, Royal Coll. of Physicians and Surgeons of Glasgow, Royal Coll. of Anaesthetists, Royal Coll. of Obstetricians and Gynaecologists, Royal Coll. of Physicians; decorations from Mexico, Peru, Chile, Brazil, Japan, Finland, Luxembourg, Netherlands, Canada; hon. degrees (Queensland, Hong Kong, Mauritius, Liverpool). *Leisure interests:* music, reading, tapestry, outdoor recreations including swimming, skiing, riding. *Address:* Buckingham Palace, London, SW1A 1AA, England. *Telephone:* (20) 7024-4270.

OGRIS, Werner, DIur; Austrian academic; *Professor Emeritus of Law, University of Vienna;* b. 9 July 1935, Vienna; s. of Alfred Ogris and Maria Erber; m. Eva Scolik 1963; two s.; ed Univ. of Vienna; Asst, Inst. für Deutsches Recht, Vienna 1958–61; Prof., Freie Univ. Berlin 1962, Univ. of Vienna 1966, now Prof. Emer.; Prof. Bratislava School of Law 2004, Dean 2005–07; mem. Austrian Acad. of Sciences; Corresp. mem. Saxon Acad.; Foreign mem. Royal Netherlands Acad.; Großes Silbernes Ehrenzeichen für Verdienste um die Republik Österreich 2003; Hon. DrIur (Prague, Bratislava); Theodor-Körner-Stiftung Prize 1961, Brothers Grimm Prize, Univ. of Marburg 1997. *Publications:* Der mittelalterliche Leibrentenvertrag 1961, Der Entwicklungsgang der österreichischen Privatrechtswissenschaft im 19. Jahrhundert 1968, Die Rechtsentwicklung in Österreich 1848–1918 1975, Personenstandsrecht 1977, Recht und Macht bei Maria Theresia 1980, Goethe—amtlich und politisch 1982, Jacob Grimm. Ein politisches Gelehrtenleben 1986, Friedrich der Grosse und das Recht 1987, Joseph von Sonnenfels als Rechtsreformer 1988, Zur Entwicklung des Versicherungsaufsichtsrechts und des Versicherungsvertragsrechts in Österreich von 1850 bis 1918 1988, Deutsche und österreichische Rechtsgeschichte in Japan 1991, Tatort Rechtsgeschichte

1994, Vom Galgenberg zum Ringtheaterbrand 1997, Tatort Rechtsgeschichte 2 1998, Mozart im Familien und Erbrecht seiner Zeit 1999, Die Universitätsreform des Ministers Leo Graf Thun-Hohenstein 1999, Joseph von Sonnenfels (Grundsätze) 2003, Elemente europäischer Rechskultur 2003, Die Zensur in der Ära Metternich 2006, Ubi sponsa ibi sponsalia 2006, Einige Aspekte der Beziehungen Böhmens zum Reichshofrat (with Eva Ortlieb) 2006. *Address:* c/o Österreichische Akademie der Wissenschaften, Dr Ignaz Seipel-Platz 2, 1010 Vienna (office); Mariahilferstrasse 71/21, 1060 Vienna, Austria (home). *Telephone:* (1) 515-81-2446 (office); (1) 586-41-57 (home). *Fax:* (1) 515-81-2400 (office). *E-mail:* werner.ogris@oeaw.ac.at (office). *Website:* www.oeaw.ac.at/krgoe (office).

O'HALI, Abdulaziz A., PhD; Saudi Arabian business executive; b. 1935; one s. three d.; ed Univ. of Puget Sound, Tacoma, Wash. and Claremont Grad. School, Calif.; entered govt service 1957, held various posts, including Mil. Advisory Dir, Prime Minister's Office, Acting Dir of Planning and Budgeting, Dir Cultural and Educ. Directorate, Ministry of Defense and Aviation; retd with rank of Col 1979; founding shareholder United Saudi Commercial Bank, Nat. Industrialization Co. 1983; Chair. Saudi Investment Bank; Man. Dir Gulf Center Man. Consultants; mem. Jt Econ. and Tech. Comm. of Saudi Arabia and USA, of Saudi Arabia and Germany. *Address:* Saudi Investment Bank, PO Box 3533, Riyadh 11481 (office); Gulf Center Management Consultants, PO Box 397, Riyadh 11411, Saudi Arabia (office). *Telephone:* 476-0287 (office). *Fax:* 478-1557 (office).

OHANIAN, Col.-Gen. Seyran; Armenian government official and fmr army officer; *Minister of Defence;* b. 1 July 1962, Shushi (Şuşa), Nagorno-Karabakh Autonomous Oblast, Azerbaijan SSR; m.; three s. one d.; ed Baku Higher Jt Command Coll.; began mil. service serving as Platoon Commdr with USSR motorized rifle platoon, Germany 1987–88, Co. Commdr 1987–88; Co. Commdr, 366th motorized rifle regt, Stepanakert 1988–89, Battalion Deputy Commdr 1989–90, Battalion Commdr 1990–92; Chief of Staff of Self-Defence Forces, 'Repub. of Nagornyi-Karabakh' 1992–94, First Deputy Commdr of Defence Army 1994–98; Commdr 5th Army Corps of Armenia 1998–99; rank of Maj.-Gen. 1995, Lt-Gen. 2000, Col.-Gen. 2007; Minister of Defence, 'Repub. of Nagornyi-Karabakh' 1999–2000, Minister of Defence and Commdr of Defence Army 2000–07; Chief of Staff, Armenian Armed Forces 2007–08; Minister of Defence 2008–; 70th Anniversary of USSR Armed Forces, For Perfect Service, For Excellency, Soviet Union Marshal Zhukov (all from USSR); Hero of Artsakh, Golden Eagle, Combat Cross 1st degree, For the Liberation of Shushi (Nagornyi-Karabakh); Combat Cross 1st degree, Tigranes the Great, For the Service to the Motherland, For Perfect Service 1st and 2nd Degrees, Drastamat Kanayan, Marshal Baghramyan, For the Strengthening of Co-operation, Maternal Gratitude, Coat of Arms. *Address:* Ministry of Defence, 0044 Yerevan, Bagrevand 5, Armenia (office). *Telephone:* (10) 29-45-29 (office). *Fax:* (10) 29-45-31 (office). *E-mail:* press@mil.am (office). *Website:* www.mil .am (office).

O'HANLON, Rory, MB, BCh, BAO, DCH; Irish politician and physician; b. 7 Feb. 1934, Dublin; s. of Michael O'Hanlon and Anna Mary O'Hanlon; m. Teresa Ward 1962; four s. two d.; ed Blackrock Coll. Dublin and Univ. Coll. Dublin; mem. Dáil 1977–; mem. Monaghan Co. Council 1979–87; Minister of State, Dept of Health and Social Welfare Oct.–Dec. 1982; Minister of Health 1987–91, for the Environment 1991–92; Chair. Fianna Fáil Parl. Party 1994–2002; Deputy Speaker of Dáil 1997–2002, Ceann Comhairle (Speaker) 2002–07; Fellow, Royal Acad. of Medicine; mem. British-Irish Parl. Group 1992–2002, Jt Cttee on Foreign Affairs 1993–97. *Leisure interests:* swimming, reading, walking, computers. *Address:* Dáil Éireann, Dublin 2 (office); Mullinary, Carrickmacross, Co. Monaghan, Ireland (home). *Telephone:* (1) 6183457 (office); (42) 9661530 (home). *Fax:* (1) 6184111 (office); (42) 9663220 (home). *E-mail:* rory.ohanlon@oireachtas.irlgov.ie (office). *Website:* www .roryohanlon.ie (office).

O'HARA, Michael John, MA, PhD, FRS, FRSE; British scientist (retd); b. 22 Feb. 1933, Sydney, Australia; s. of the late Michael Patrick O'Hara and Dorothy Winifred Avis; m. 1st Janet Prudence Tibbits 1962 (divorced 1977); one s. two d.; m. 2nd Susan Howells 1977; two s. one d.; ed Dulwich Coll. Prep., London, Cranleigh School, Surrey and Peterhouse, Cambridge; Univ. of Edin., Grant Inst. of Geology 1958–78, Reader 1967, Prof. 1971–78; Research Fellow, Carnegie Inst. of Washington Geophysical Lab. 1962–63; Prof., Univ. Coll. Aberystwyth, Dept of Geology 1978–88, Head of Dept 1978–87, Prof., Inst. of Earth Sciences 1988–93; Distinguished Research Prof., Earth Sciences Dept, Univ. of Cardiff 1994–2003; Sherman-Fairchild Distinguished Visiting Scholar, Calif. Inst. of Tech. 1984–85; Visiting Prof., Dept of Earth Sciences, Harvard Univ. 1986; Prof. and Head of Dept, Sultan Qaboos Univ., Oman 1988–90; Visiting Prof., North West Univ., Xi'an, People's Repub. of China 2004; Concurrent Prof., Nanjing Univ., People's Repub. of China 2004; mem. Natural Environment Research Council 1986–88; mem. Univ. Grants Cttee 1987–89, Chair. Univ. Grants Cttee, Earth Sciences Review; Geochemistry Fellow, jt geochemical socs of America and Europe 1997; Fellow, American Geophysical Union 2004; Hon. Prof., Aberystwyth Univ. 2004, China Univ. of Geosciences, Beijing 2004, Univ. of Durham 2005; Hon. mem. Geological Soc. France; Geological Soc. of London Murchison Medal 1983, American Geophysical Union Bowen Award 1984. *Publications:* over 100 articles in scientific journals 1961–2004. *Leisure interests:* mountaineering, hill walking. *Address:* Golwg-y-Mor, Talybont, Ceredigion, SY24 5EQ, Wales (home). *Telephone:* (1970) 832460 (home). *E-mail:* mio@aber.ac.uk (home).

O'HARE, Joseph Aloysius, MA, PhL, STL, PhD; American priest, editor and fmr university president; *Associate Editor, America Magazine;* b. 12 Feb. 1931, New York; ed Berchmans Coll., Cebu City, Philippines, Woodstock Coll., Md and Fordham Univ., New York; Instructor in Humanities, Ateneo de Manila Univ. 1955–58, Assoc. Prof. in Philosophy 1967–72; Assoc. Ed.

America Magazine, New York 1972–75, 2003–, Ed.-in-Chief 1975–84; Pres. Fordham Univ. 1984–2003 (retd); Chair. NY City Campaign Financial Bd; numerous hon. degrees. *Leisure interests:* contemporary fiction, Irish folk music. *Address:* America Magazine, 106 West 56th Street, New York, NY 10019-3803, USA (office). *Telephone:* (212) 581-4640 (office). *Fax:* (212) 399-3596 (office). *Website:* www.americamagazine.org (office).

OHASHI, Nobuo; Japanese business executive; *Chairman and Executive Director, Mitsui & Company Ltd;* Sr Man.-Dir Kawasaki Steel Corpn 1990; Pres. Techno-Research Corpn (subsidiary of Kawasaki Steel Corpn) 1991; mem. Bd Dirs (Dir, Gen. Man. Seoul Br.) 1994–97, Rep. Dir, Exec. Man. Dir, COO Foods Unit 1997–99, Rep. Dir, Sr Exec. Man. Dir, Gen. Man. Corp. Planning Div. 1999–2000, Rep. Dir, Exec. Vice-Pres. 2000–02, Rep. Dir, Exec. Vice-Pres., Group Pres. Consumer Products and Services Group 2002, Rep. Dir, Chair. and Exec. Dir 2002–04, Chair. and Dir 2004–; Chair. Japan-India Business Cooperation Cttee; mem. Exec. Cttee Japan-US Business Council 2004; mem. Bd of Dirs The Angel Foundation 2002. *Address:* Mitsui & Company Ltd, 2-1 Ohtemachi 1-chome, Chiyoda-ku, Tokyo 100-0004, Japan (office). *Telephone:* (3) 3285-1111 (office). *Fax:* (3) 3285-9819 (office). *E-mail:* info@mitsui.co.jp (office). *Website:* www.mitsui.co.jp (office).

OHENE, Elizabeth Akua, BA; Ghanaian journalist and politician; *Minister of State in charge of Tertiary Education;* b. 24 Jan. 1945; ed Mawuli High School, Univ. of Ghana, Univ. of Indiana, USA; work experience with newspapers in USA; Reporter, Staff Writer, Columnist, Leader Writer then Ed. The Daily Graphic and Mirror 1967–82; f. Talking Drum Publications 1986, Publr and Ed.; joined BBC, London, UK 1986, worked successively as Producer of Radio Programmes, Presenter, Sr Producer World Service and BBC Domestic Radio, Researcher and Columnist Focus on Africa Magazine, Deputy Ed. African Service for English Daily Programmes, Ed. Focus on Africa Programme, Dir Operational Budget, Corresp. 1993–94; conducted training programmes for BBC in SA, Nigeria, Liberia, Senegal, Sierra Leone, Kenya, Ethiopia and Somalia; Minister of State for Media Relations 2001–02; Govt Spokesperson 2002–03; Minister of State in charge of Tertiary Educ. 2003–; mem. Int. Women Media Foundation, Bd Int. Comm. of Investigative Journalists, CNN Africa Journalist of the Year Competition 1997–. *Address:* Ministry of Education, Youth and Sports, POB M45, Accra, Ghana (office). *Telephone:* (21) 665421 (office). *Fax:* (21) 664067 (office). *Website:* www.ghana .edu.gh (office).

OHGA, Norio, BMus; Japanese business executive; *Honorary Chairman, Sony Corporation;* b. 29 Jan. 1930, Numazu, Shizuoka Pref.; s. of Shoichi Ohga and Toshi Mizuno; m. Midori Matsubara 1957; ed Tokyo Nat. Univ. of Art, Kunst Universität, Berlin; joined Tokyo Tsushin Kogyo KK (Tokyo Telecom-munications Eng Corpn) as Consultant and Adviser 1953, co. name changed to Sony Corpn 1958; Gen. Man. Tape Recorder Div. and Product Planning (also in charge of Industrial Design) 1959, Dir 1964; Sr Man. Dir CBS/Sony Inc. 1968, Pres. 1970; Man. Dir Sony Corpn 1972, Sr Man. Dir 1974, Deputy Pres. 1976, Pres. 1982–95, Chair. 1995–2003, Rep. Dir 1999–2000, Chair. Bd of Dirs 2000–03, Hon. Chair. 2003–; Chair. CBS/Sony Group Inc. 1980–90; Chair. Sony USA Inc. 1988–2003, CEO Sony Corpn 1989–2003, Pres. 1989–95, Chair. Sony Software Corpn 1991–2003, Hon. Chair. Sony Corpn 2003–; Vice-Chair. Tokyo Chamber of Commerce and Industry 1989–97; Chair. Cttee on New Business, Keidanren 1994–98; Chair. Electronic Industries Asscn of Japan 1995–97; Vice-Chair. Keidanren 1998–2002, Chair. Housing and Building Land Council 1998–2001, The Japan Intellectual Property Asscn 1999–2001; Pres. Tokyo Philharmonic Orchestra 1999–2001, Chair. 2001–; Commdr's Cross First Class of the Order of Merit (Austria) 1987; Medal of Honour with Blue Ribbon (Japan) 1988; Commdr's Cross Order of Merit (Germany) 1994, Grande Ufficiale dell' Ordine Al Merito (Italy) 1998, Grand Decoration of Honour in Silver with Star (Austria) 1999, Order of Panglima Jasa Negara (Malaysia) 1999, Knight Commdr's Cross (Badge and Star), FRG 2001, First Class Order of the Sacred Treasure (Japan) 2001; Dr hc in Music (Rochester) 1996, (McGill) 1999; Int. CEO of the Year (George Washington Univ.) 1994, Nat. Day Award for Public Service (Singapore) 2002. *Leisure interests:* yachting and flying. *Address:* c/o Sony Corporation, 6-7-35 Kita Shinagawa 6-chome, Shinagawa-ku, Tokyo 141-0001, Japan.

OHKUCHI, Shunichi; Japanese business executive; b. 15 Jan. 1918, Tokyo; s. of Tatsuzo and Takae Ohkuchi; m. Kazuko Ohkuchi 1948; two s.; ed Tokyo Imperial Univ.; Ministry of Agric. and Forestry 1941; mil. service 1942–48; Chief, Import Planning Div., Food Agency, Ministry of Agric. and Forestry; First Sec. Embassy, London 1956–59; Dir Overseas Fishery Dept, Fishery Agency, Ministry of Agric. and Forestry 1961–64; Deputy Vice-Minister of Agric. and Forestry 1965, Vice-Minister 1968–69; Dir-Gen. Food Agency, Ministry of Agric. and Forestry 1966–68; retd from Govt service 1969; Adviser, Nippon Suisan Kaisha Ltd 1970, Man. Dir, Sr Man. Dir, then Vice-Pres. 1971–75, Exec. Vice-Pres. 1975–80, Pres. 1980–86, apptd Chair. 1986. *Leisure interests:* golf, audio (classical music), billiards. *Address:* c/o Nippon Suisan Kaisha Ltd, 2-6-2, Otemachi, Chiyoda-ku, Tokyo 100-8686, Japan.

OHLSSON, Garrick; American pianist; b. 3 April 1948, White Plains, NY; ed Westchester Conservatory, Juilliard School with Sascha Gorodnitsky, studied with Olga Barabini, Rosina Lhevinne and Claudio Arrau; appears regularly with major orchestras, including New York Philharmonic, Chicago Symphony, Boston Symphony, Philadelphia Orchestra, Los Angeles Philharmonic and with orchestras and in recital series throughout the world; complete cycle of Beethoven piano sonatas at the Verbier, Tanglewood and Ravinia festivals; prizewinner at Busoni Piano Competition, Italy 1966, Chopin Int. Piano Competition, Warsaw 1970, Montreal Int. Piano Competition 1970, Avery Fisher Prize 1994, Grammy Award for Best Instrumental Soloist Performance 2008. *Recordings include:* Complete Solo Works of Chopin and numerous other recordings. *Address:* Opus 3 Artists, 470 Park Avenue South, 9th Floor North, New York, NY 10016, USA (office). *Telephone:* (212) 584-7500 (office). *Fax:* (646) 300-8200 (office). *E-mail:* info@opus3artists.com (office). *Website:* www.opus3artists.com (office).

OHLSSON, Per Evald Torbjörn; Swedish journalist and author; *Senior Columnist, Sydvenska Dagbladet;* b. 3 March 1958, Malmö; s. of Ulla Ohlsson and Torsten Ohlsson; m. Maria Rydqvist-Ohlsson 1989; one s.; ed Univ. of Lund; Ed. Lundagard 1980–81; editorial writer, Expressen, Stockholm 1981–85; New York Corresp., Sydvenska Dagbladet 1985–88, Ed.-in-Chief 1990–2005, Sr Columnist 2005–; Soderberg Foundation Prize for Journalism 1998. *Publications:* Over There – Banden Över Atlanten 1992, Gudarnas Ö 1993, 100 År Av Tillväxt 1994. *Leisure interests:* music, literature, sports. *Address:* Sydvenska Dagbladet, 205 05 Malmö, Sweden (office). *Telephone:* 40-28-12-00 (office). *Fax:* 40-28-13-86 (office). *E-mail:* per.t.ohlsson@sydsvenskan .se (office).

OHNISHI, Minoru; Japanese business executive; *Chairman, Fuji Photo Film Company Ltd;* b. 28 Oct. 1925, Hyogo Pref.; s. of Sokichi and Mitsu Ohnishi; m. Yaeko Yui 1951; two s.; ed School of Econs, Tokyo Univ.; joined Fuji Photo Film Co. Ltd 1948, Man. Tokyo Sales Dept of Consumer Products Div. 1957–61, Sales Dept of Industrial Products Div. 1961–62, Fukuoka Br. Office 1962–64, Exec. Vice-Pres. Fuji Photo Film USA Inc. 1964–68, Man. Export Sales Div. Fuji Photo Film Co. Ltd 1968–76, Dir 1972–, Man. Dir 1976–79, Sr Man. Dir 1979–80, Pres. 1980–96, Chair. 1996–; Pres. Photo-Sensitized Materials Mfrs Asscn of Japan 1980–96; mem. Photography Soc. of Japan (Chair. 1997–). *Leisure interests:* golf, reading. *Address:* Fuji Photo Film Company Ltd, 26-30 Nishiazabu, Minato-ku, Tokyo 106-8620, Japan. *Telephone:* (3) 3406-2111. *Fax:* (3) 3406-2193. *Website:* www.home.fujifilm .com (office).

OHNO, Shigeru; Japanese energy industry executive; *Chairman, Kyushu Electric Power Company Inc.;* Dir Japan Nuclear Fuel Ltd 1997; currently Chair. Kyushu Electric Power Co. Inc.; Chair. Fukuoka Venture Market Asscn; fmr Chair. Kyushu Industrial Tech. Centre; mem. Kyushu Economy Int.; Auditor Nisseki Plasto Co. Ltd 2002; Hon. mem. Bd of Dirs Asian-Pacific Children's Convention (APCC), Fukuoka 2003–. *Address:* Kyushu Electric Power Company Inc., 1-82 Watanabe-dori, 2-chome, Chuo-ku, Fukuoka 810-8720, Japan (office). *Telephone:* (9) 2761-3031 (office). *Fax:* (9) 2733-1435 (office). *Website:* www.kyuden.co.jp (office).

OHNO, Yoshinori; Japanese politician; *Chairman, Research Commission on the Finance and Banking Systems, Liberal Democratic Party (LDP);* b. 16 Oct. 1935; ed Univ. of Tokyo, Univ. of Pennsylvania, USA (Fulbright Exchange Student); joined Ministry of Finance 1958, First Sec., Perm. Del. of Japan, Geneva, Switzerland 1971–75, Dir Int. Orgs Section, Int. Finance Bureau 1976; mem. House of Reps 1986–, Chair. Standing Cttee on Transport 1997, Standing Cttee on Rules and Admin 2002, Research Comm. on the Annuities System 2003; Parl. Vice-Minister of Posts and Telecommunications 1990; Dir Nat. Defence Div., LDP 1994; Sr State Sec. for Finance 1999–2000, for Science and Tech. 2000–01; Sr Vice-Minister of Educ., Culture, Sports, Science and Tech. 2001–04; Minister of State for Defence 2004–05; Chair. Research Comm. on the Finance and Banking Systems, LDP, Deputy Chair. Research Comm. on the Tax System; Order of Merit of Duarte, Sanchez and Mella. *Publication:* Warm Heart etc. *Address:* Room #432, 1st Members' Office Building, 2-2-1, Nagata-cho, Chiyoda-ku, Tokyo 100-8981, Japan (office). *Telephone:* (3) 3508-7132 (office). *Fax:* (3) 3502-5870 (office). *Website:* www.e-ohno.com (office).

OHRYZKO, Volodymyr Stanislavovych, PhD; Ukrainian diplomatist; *First Deputy Secretary, National Security and Defence Council;* b. 1 April 1956, Kyiv; m.; one s. two d.; ed Kyiv Taras Shevchenko Univ.; joined Ukrainian SSR Ministry of Foreign Affairs 1978; Attaché, Press Dept 1978–80, Third Sec. 1980–81, 1983–85 (mil. service 1981–83), Second Sec. 1985–88; First Sec., Prin. Counselor's Dept 1988–91, Counselor June–July 1991; Counselor Political Analysis and Co-ordination Dept July 1991–March 1992; Counselor, Embassy in FRG 1992–93, 1994–96; Minister, Embassy in Vienna 1993–94; Head, Foreign Policy Dept and Head, Main Foreign Policy Dept of the Presidential Admin 1996–99; Chair. External Policy Dept 1996–99; Amb. to Austria and Perm. Rep. to Int. Orgs, Vienna 1999–2004; Amb.-at-Large, Dept of Euro-Atlantic Co-operation 2004–05; First Deputy Minister of Foreign Affairs 2005–07; Acting Minister of Foreign Affairs Jan.–March 2007, Minister of Foreign Affairs 2007–09; First Deputy Sec. Nat. Security and Defence Council 2009–. *Address:* National Security and Defence Council, 01601 Kiev, Domandarma Kameneva Str. 8, Ukraine (office). *Telephone:* (44) 255-05-36 (office). *Fax:* (44) 255-05-36 (office). *Website:* www .rainbow.gov.ua (office).

OHTA, Tomoko Harada, PhD; Japanese geneticist and academic; *Professor Emerita, National Institute of Genetics;* b. 7 Sept. 1933, Aichi-Ken; d. of Mamoru Harada and Hatsu Harada; m. Yasuo Ohta 1960 (divorced 1972); one d.; ed Tokyo Univ., N Carolina State Univ.; researcher Kihara Inst. for Biological Research 1958–62; Postdoctoral Fellow Nat. Inst. of Genetics 1967–69, Researcher 1969–76, Assoc. Prof. 1976–84, Prof. 1984–97, Prof. Emer. 1997–, Head Dept of Population Genetics 1988–97; Vice-Pres. Soc. for the Study of Evolution 1994; Fellow, AAAS 2000; Foreign Assoc. NAS 2002; Foreign Hon. mem. American Acad. of Arts and Sciences 1984; Saruhashi Prize 1981, Japan Acad. Prize 1985, Weldon Memorial Prize, Oxford Univ. 1986, Person of Cultural Merit 2002. *Publications:* Evolution and Variation of Multigene Families, Lecture Notes in Biomathematics Vol. 37 1980. *Leisure interest:* reading. *Address:* 20-20 Hatsunedai, Mishima-shi, Shizuoka-ken 411-0018 (home); National Institute of Genetics, Mishima 411-8540, Japan (office). *Telephone:* (55) 972-4638 (home); (55) 981-6779 (office). *Website:* www .nig.ac.jp (office).

OHTANI, Ichiji; Japanese textile industry executive; *Honorary Senior Advisor, Toyobo Company Ltd;* b. 31 Aug. 1912, Kobe; s. of Kyosuke Ohtani and Tama Ohtani; m. Atsuko Suzuki 1943; two s. one d.; ed Kobe Univ.; Dir Toyobo Co. Ltd 1964–68, Man. Dir 1968–72, Sr Man. Dir 1972–74, Deputy Pres. 1974, Pres. 1974–78, Chair. 1978–83, Counsellor 1983–92, Hon. Sr Adviser 1992–; Dir Toyobo Petcord Co. Ltd 1969–83, Chair. Toyobo Co. Ltd 1978–83, Counsellor 1983–; Vice-Pres. Industrias Unidas, SA 1973–79; Exec. Dir Fed. of Econ. Orgs. 1976–83; Chair. Japan Spinners' Asscn 1976–79, Diafibres Co. Ltd 1977–88; Vice-Pres. Japan Textile Fed. 1976–79; Jr Vice-Pres. Int. Textile Mfrs Fed. 1976–78, Sr Vice-Pres. 1978–80, Pres. 1980–82, Hon. Life mem. 1982–; Blue Ribbon Medal 1979; Order of the Rising Sun (Second Class) 1984. *Leisure interest:* sports. *Address:* 7-18 Yamate-cho, Ashiya-shi 659 (home); c/o Toyobo Co. Ltd, 2-8 Dojima Hama 2-chome, Kita-ku, Osaka 530, Japan (office).

OHTANI, Monshu Koshin, MA; Japanese ecclesiastic; *Monshu (Ecclesiastic Patriarch);* b. 12 Aug. 1945, Kyoto; s. of Kosho Ohtani and Yoshiko Ohtani; m. Noriko Tanaka 1974; two s. two d.; ed Tokyo Univ. and Ryukoku Univ.; ordained Priest of Jodo Shinshu Hongwanji-ha Aug. 1960, Monshu (Ecclesiastic Patriarch) Apparent 1970–1977, Monshu 1977–; Pres. All-Japanese Buddhist Fed. 1978–80, 1988–90, 2002–04. *Leisure interests:* classical music, skiing. *Address:* Horikawa-dori, Hanayacho-sagaru, Shimogyo-ku, Kyoto 600-8501, Japan. *Telephone:* (75) 371-5181 (office). *Fax:* (75) 351-1211 (office). *Website:* www.hongwanji.or.jp (office).

OHTSUBO, Fumio, MA; Japanese business executive; *President and Representative Director, Panasonic Corporation;* ed Kansai Univ., Osaka; joined Matsushita Electric Industrial Co. in 1971, mem. Bd Dirs and Vice-Pres. Audio and Video Sector (now Panasonic AVC Networks Co.) 1998–2000, Man. Dir 2000–03, Pres. Panasonic AVC Networks Co., Business Group Exec. AVC Network Business Group, and in Charge of Storage Device Business Jan.–June 2003, Sr Man. Dir Matsushita Electric Industrial Co. Ltd –2006, Pres. and Rep. Dir Matsushita Electric Industrial Co. Ltd 2006– (renamed Panasonic Corpn Oct. 2008). *Address:* Panasonic Corpn, Corporate Headquarters, 1006 Oaza Kadoma, Kadoma-shi, Osaka 571-8501, Japan (office). *Telephone:* (6) 6908-1121 (office). *Fax:* (6) 6908-2351 (office). *E-mail:* info@panasonic.net (office). *Website:* panasonic.net (office).

OHURUOGU, Christine Ijeoma, MBE; British athlete; b. 17 May 1984, Newham, East London; ed Univ. Coll., London (UCL); sprinter; specializes in 400m, Commonwealth, World and Olympic Champion; has run personal bests of 49.61 for 400m in 2007 and 22.94 for 200m in 2008; Bronze Medal, 400m, European Jr Championships 2003; AAA Champion in 400m 2004; semi-finalist in 400m, Olympic Games, Athens 2004, also took part in 4×400m relay team that finished 4th; Silver Medal, 400m and 4×400m relay, European Under 23 Championships 2005; semi-finalist in 400m, World Championships, Helsinki 2005, Bronze Medal, 4×400m relay; Gold Medal, 400m, Commonwealth Games, Melbourne 2006; banned from athletics for one year for missing three out-of-competition drugs tests 2006, also banned by British Olympic Asscn from competing at future Olympic Games for GB, appealed to Court of Arbitration for Sport, original decision upheld, appealed against her Olympic ban which was overturned Nov. 2007; Gold Medal, World Championships, Osaka 2007, Olympic Games, Beijing 2008; Bronze Medal, 4×400m relay, World Championships, Osaka 2007; mem. Newham and Essex Beagles Athletics Club. *Address:* c/o British Athletics Federation, 10 Harborne Road, Edgbaston, Birmingham, B15 3AA, England. *Telephone:* (870) 998-6800. *Fax:* (870) 998-6752. *E-mail:* information@ukathletics.org.uk. *Website:* www.ukathletics.net.

OIKE, Kazuo, BSc, DSc; Japanese geophysicist and university administrator; b. 1940, Tokyo; ed Kyoto Univ.; Research Assoc., Disaster Prevention Research Inst., Kyoto Univ. 1963–73, Assoc. Prof. 1973–88, Prof. of Seismology, Grad. School of Science 1988–2003, Dean Grad. School of Science 1997–99, Dir Fmr Research Centre for Sports Science 2001–03, Vice-Pres. Kyoto Univ. 2001–03, Pres. 2003–08; f. observation network of microearthquakes in Inner Zone of southwestern Japan to study stress field. *Publications:* numerous scientific papers in professional journals. *Address:* Kyoto University, Yoshida-Honmachi, Sakyo-ku, Kyoto 606-8501, Japan (office). *Telephone:* (75) 753-7531 (office). *Fax:* (774) 334598 (home). *E-mail:* koryu52@mail.adm.kyoto-u.ac.jp (office); konamazu@infoseek.to (office). *Website:* www.kyoto-u.ac.jp (office); homepage2.nifty.com/cat-fish.

OISHI, Katsuro; Japanese insurance industry executive; *President and CEO, Taiyo Life Insurance Company;* Dir and Gen. Man. Investment Planning Dept, Taiyo Mutual Life Insurance Co. 1999; currently Pres. and CEO Taiyo Life Insurance Co.; Dir T & D Holdings Inc. 2004–. *Address:* Taiyo Life Insurance Company, 11-2 Nihonbashi 2-chome, Chuo-ku, Tokyo 103-0027, Japan (office). *Telephone:* (3) 3272-6211 (office). *Fax:* (3) 3271-1259 (office). *Website:* www.taiyo-seimei.co.jp (office).

OIZERMAN, Teodor Ilyich; Russian philosopher; b. 14 May 1914, Petroverovka; s. of Ilya Davidovich Oizerman and Yelizaveta Abramovna Nemirovskaya; m. Genrietta Kasavina; two s. one d.; ed Moscow Inst. of History, Philosophy and Literature; industrial worker 1930–33; post grad. 1938–41; army service 1941–46; Asst Prof., Moscow Inst. of Econs 1946–47; Asst Prof., Prof. Moscow Univ. 1952–54, Head of Chair 1954–68; Corresp. mem. USSR (now Russian) Acad. of Sciences 1966–81, mem. 1981–; Foreign mem. Acad. of Sciences, GDR 1981–90; mem. Int. Inst. of Philosophy 1982–; Head Dept of History of Philosophy, Inst. of Philosophy of Acad. of Sciences 1971–87, Adviser to Acad. of Sciences 1987–; Vice-Pres. USSR (now Russian) Philosophical Soc. 1982–95; Order of the Red Star 1944, Order of the Patriotic War 1945, 1985, Order of the Badge of Honour 1961, Order of the Red Banner 1974, Order of the October Revolution 1984, Order of Friendship 2004; Dr hc (Jena); Lomonosov Prize 1965, Plekhanov Prize 1981, State Prize 1983. *Publications:* (works have been translated into German, French, English and more than 10 other foreign languages), Development of Marxist Theory in Experience of the Revolution of 1848 1955, Philosophie Hegels 1959, The Making of Marxist Philosophy 1962, 1974, 1986, On the History of pre-Marxist Philosophy 1961, Alienation as an Historical Category 1965, Problems of Historical-Philosophical Science 1969, Principal Philosophical Trends 1971, Crisis of Contemporary Idealism 1973, Problems of the History of Philosophy 1973, Philosophy of Kant 1974, Dialectic Materialism and the History of Philosophy 1982, Principles of the Theory of the Historical Process in Philosophy 1986, The Main Trends in Philosophy 1988, Philosophical and Scientific World Outlook of Marxism 1989, Kant's Theory of Knowledge 1991, Philosophy as a History of Philosophy 1999, Marxism and Utopism 2003, Justification of Revisionism 2005, Problems: Sociopolitical and Philosophical Essays 2006; and over 550 articles on philosophical problems, including more than 220 articles in foreign languages. *Leisure interest:* walking. *Address:* Institute of Philosophy, Russian Academy of Sciences, Volchonka str. 14, Moscow (office); Mendeleyev str. 1, Apt 168, 117234 Moscow, Russia (home). *Telephone:* (495) 203-91-98 (office); (495) 939-01-37 (home).

OJEDA PAULLADA, Pedro; Mexican lawyer; b. 19 Jan. 1934, México, DF; s. of Manuel Ojeda Lacroix and Adela Paullada de Ojeda; m. Olga Cárdenas de Ojeda 1959; two s. three d.; ed Univ. Nacional Autónoma de México (UNAM); Head of Personnel and lawyer, Técnica y Fundación, SA de CV 1955, Sub-Man. 1955–57; Gen. Man. Industria Química de Plásticos SA 1957–58; Deputy Dir-Gen. Juntas Federales de Mejoras Materiales 1959–65; Dir-Gen. of Legal Affairs, SCT 1966–70; Sec.-Gen. Presidential Secr. 1970–71; Attorney-Gen. 1971–76; Sec. of Labour and Social Welfare 1976–81; Minister of Fisheries 1982–88; Gen. Coordinator Nat. Food Comm. 1988–91; Pres. Fed. Court of Conciliation and Arbitrage 1995–; Prof. of Law and Economics, UNAM, Prof. of Social Security; rep. Mexico on many int. and regional comms etc., including Pres. Perm. Conf. of Political Parties of Latin America (COPPAL) 1981–82, Chair. World Conf. of Int. Women's Year 1975, 64th Int. Conf. of ILO 1978, World Conf. on Fishing Devt (FAO) 1984; Fed. Congressman 1991–94; Pres. Energy Comm. of the Mexican Congress 1991–94, Nat. Fed. of Lawyers in the Service of Mexico (FENASEM) 1992–, Tech. Comm. of Foreign Relations of Fundación Mexicana Luis Donaldo Colosio, AC 1992–94, Mexican Coll. of Lawyers 1994–, Mexican Acad. of Law and Econs 1995–; Mexican Soc. of Geography and Statistics, 1994–97; mem. Institutional Revolutionary Party (PRI) 1951–, Pres. Nat. Exec. Cttee 1981–82; mem. Nat. Acad. of History and Geography, American Law and Econs Asscn 1991–; Order of Merit (Italy), Gran Cruz al Mérito (Italy), Orden de Isabel la Católica (Spain) and other decorations. *Leisure interests:* art, dominoes, reading, tennis. *Address:* Avenida del IMAN 660, 3° piso, Col Pedregal del Maurel, CP 04720, Del. Coyoacan, Mexico, DF, Mexico. *Telephone:* (5) 568-1878; (5) 606-8881. *Fax:* (5) 606-9070.

OJEDA Y EISELEY, Jaime de, LLB; Spanish diplomatist; *Ambassador-in-Residence, Shenandoah University;* b. 5 Aug. 1933; ed Univ. of Madrid, Int. Acad. of The Hague, Naval War Coll. of Madrid and Sr Center for Nat. Defence Studies (CESEDEN), Madrid; Prof. of Political Law, Complutense Univ. of Madrid 1958; joined diplomatic service 1958; served Washington, DC 1962–69; Minister-Counsellor, Beijing 1973–76; Consul-Gen. of Spain in Hong Kong and Macao 1976–79; Fellow Center for Int. Relations, Harvard Univ. 1979–80; Deputy Perm. Rep. to North Atlantic Council 1982–83, Perm. Rep. to NATO 1983–90; Amb. to USA 1990–97; Pres. Sr Council on Foreign Affairs 1997–98; Amb.-in-Residence Shenandoah Univ. 1998–; Great Cross, Mil. Merit, Great Cross Civil Merit; Kt Order of Carlos III. *Publications:* El 98 en el Congreso y en la Prensa de los Estados Unidos 1999; trans. Alice in Wonderland (Lewis Carroll) 1971, Through the Looking Glass (Lewis Carroll) 1974, Spain and America: The Past and the Future 1994. *Leisure interests:* music, botany, sailing. *Address:* 1460 University Drive, Winchester, VA 22643 (office); 3770 Leed's Manor Road, Markham, VA 22643, USA (home). *Telephone:* (540) 665-4696 (office); (540) 364-2275 (home). *Fax:* (540) 665-4698 (office); (540) 364-9281 (home). *E-mail:* wsherdow@su.edu (office).

OJO, Bayo, LLM; Nigerian lawyer and politician; ed Univ. of Lagos, Royal Inst. of Public Admin, London, LSE, London; began career as civil servant, fmr Kwara State; called to Nigerian Bar 1978; fmr State Counsel, Ministry of Justice, Kwara State; Head of Chambers, Oniyangi & Co. 1983–86; Prin. Pnr, Bayo Ojo & Co. (law firm) 1986–; Minister of Justice and Attorney-Gen. 2005–07; Solicitor of Supreme Court of England and Wales; Fellow, Chartered Inst. of Arbitrators, UK; Chair. Nigeria Legal Aid Council; fmr Pres. Nigeria Bar Asscn, also mem. Nat. Exec. Cttee; Sr Advocate of Nigeria (SAN). *Address:* c/o Ministry of Justice, New Federal Secretariat Complex, Shehu Shagari Way, Central Area District, Abuja, Nigeria (office).

OJUKWU, Gen. Chukwuemeka Odumegwu- (see Odumegwu-Ojukwu, Gen. Chukwuemeka).

OJULAND, Kristiina; Estonian politician; *Deputy Speaker of Parliament;* b. 17 Dec. 1966, Kohtla-Jarve; m.; ed Tartu Univ., Estonian School of Diplomacy; specialist, Dept of Draft Legislation, Ministry of Justice 1990–92; First Sec. Political Dept, Ministry of Foreign Affairs 1992–94, Rep. to Council of Europe; Man. Dir Estonian Broadcasting Asscn 1994–96; mem. Riigikogu (Parl.) 1994–2001; Euro-Integration Dir Concordia Int. Univ. 1997–2001; mem. Tallinn City Council 1996–2001; Vice-Pres. of Parl. Ass., Council of Europe 1996–2002, Pres. LDR Group, Parl. Ass., Council of Europe 1999–2002; Minister of Foreign Affairs 2002–05 (dismissed from office); Deputy Speaker of Parl. 2007–. *Leisure interests:* tennis, reading. *Address:* Estonian Parliament, Lossi plats 1a, 15165 Tallinn, Estonia (office). *Telephone:* 631-6331 (office). *Fax:* 631-6314 (office). *E-mail:* riigikogu@riigikogu.ee (office). *Website:* www.riigikogu.ee (office).

OKA, Motoyuki; Japanese business executive; *Chairman, Sumitomo Corporation;* joined Sumitomo Corpn (gen. trading co.) 1966, served as Gen. Man. Tubular Products Import and Export Dept No. 1 and Gen. Man., Sumitomo Corpn of America, Houston Office, Dir and Gen. Man. Iron and Steel Div. No. 3 and Gen. Man. Planning and Co-ordination Div. 1994–98, Man. Dir and Gen. Man. Planning and Co-ordination Div., Responsible for Personnel Div., C&C System Div. 1998–2001, Sr Man. Dir Responsible for Legal Div., Personnel and Gen. Affairs Div., Planning and Co-ordination Div. April–June 2001, Pres. and CEO Sumitomo Corpn 2001–07, Chair. 2007–; Chair. Int. Market Cttee, Japan Foreign Trade Council 2001–. *Address:* Sumitomo Corpn, 8-11 Harumi 1-chome, Chuo-ku, Tokyo 104-8610, Japan (office). *Telephone:* (3) 5166-5000 (office). *Fax:* (3) 5166-6292 (office). *E-mail:* info@sumitomocorp.co.jp (office). *Website:* www.sumitomocorp.co.jp (office).

OKA, Takeshi, PhD, FRS, FRSC; Canadian/American (b. Japanese) scientist and academic; *Robert A. Millikan Distinguished Professor Emeritus of Chemistry, Astronomy and Astrophysics, Enrico Fermi Institute, University of Chicago;* b. 10 June 1932, Tokyo, Japan; s. of Shumpei Oka and Chiyoko Oka; m. Keiko Nukui 1960; two s. two d.; ed Univ. of Tokyo; Fellow, Japan Soc. for the Promotion of Science 1960–63; Postdoctoral Fellow, Nat. Research Council of Canada 1963–65; Research Physicist, Herzberg Inst. of Astrophysics 1965–81; Prof. of Chem. and Astronomy and Astrophysics, Enrico Fermi Inst., Univ. of Chicago, USA 1981–, Robert A. Millikan Distinguished Service Prof. 1989–2003, Prof. Emer. 2003–; Fellow, American Acad. of Arts and Sciences, American Physical Soc., Optical Soc. of America; Hon. DSc (Waterloo) 2001, (Univ. Coll. London) 2004; Steacie Prize 1972, Plyler Prize 1982; Meggers Award 1997, Lippincott Award 1998, Wilson Award 2002, Davy Medal 2004. *Leisure interest:* history of science. *Address:* Department of Chemistry, Astronomy and Astrophysics, University of Chicago, 5735 S Ellis Avenue, Chicago, IL 60637 (office). *Telephone:* (773) 702-7070 (office). *Fax:* (773) 702-0805 (office). *E-mail:* t-oka@uchicago.edu (office). *Website:* www.fermi.uchicago.edu (office).

OKABE, Hiromu, BSc; Japanese business executive and economist; *Chairman, Denso Corporation;* ed Faculty of Econs, Nagoya Univ., Aichi; joined Denso Corpn 1960, held various positions in Accounting Dept and Corp. Planning Dept, Head of Planning Centre No. 2 (Electrical Products), Head of Corp. Planning 1989–95, apptd mem. Bd of Dirs 1989, Man.-Dir in charge of Engine Electrical Systems Product Div. 1995–96, Pres. and CEO 1996–2003, Vice-Chair. 2003–04, Chair. 2004–; Japanese Prime Minister's Award for a Treatise on Econs 1971. *Leisure interests:* reading, writing, playing the traditional board game "Go". *Address:* Denso Corporation, 1-1 Showa-cho, Kariya, Aichi 448-8661, Japan (office). *Telephone:* (5) 6625-5511 (office). *Fax:* (5) 6625-4509 (office). *Website:* www.denso.co.jp (office).

OKABE, Keiichiro; Japanese oil industry executive; *Chairman, Cosmo Oil Company Limited;* b. 1946; fmr Pres. AOC Holdings; Pres. and CEO Cosmo Oil Co. Ltd –2004, Chair. 2004–; Chair. Japan Oil Asscn 2000, Petroleum Asscn of Japan 2002–; Pres. Qatar Petroleum Devt Co.; mem. Business Leaders' Inter-Forum for Environment 2002; mem. Bd Auditors Tokyo Broadcasting System Inc. (TBS) 2003–; mem. Bd of Dirs Japan Cooperative Centre for the Middle East. *Address:* Cosmo Oil Co. Ltd, 1-1-1, Shibaura, Minato-ku, Tokyo 105-8528, Japan (office). *Telephone:* (3) 3798-3211 (office). *Fax:* (3) 3798-3237 (office). *E-mail:* info@cosmo-oil.co.jp (office). *Website:* www.cosmo-oil.co.jp (office).

OKABE, Masahiko; Japanese business executive; *Chairman, Nippon Express Company Ltd;* joined Nippon Express Co. Ltd 1961, various positions within Corp. Admin and Human Resources Depts, Gen.-Man. Chugoku Regional Br. Office 1995–97, Man.-Dir Nippon Express Co. Ltd 1997–99, Pres. 1999–2001, Pres. and CEO 2001–05, Chair. 2005–; Co-Chair. Cttee on Transportation, Nippon Keidanren 2003–. *Address:* Nippon Express Company Ltd, 1-9-3 Higashi-Shimbashi, Minato-ku, Tokyo 105-8322, Japan (office). *Telephone:* (3) 6251-1111 (office). *Website:* www.nittsu.co.jp (office).

OKADA, Akashige; Japanese banking executive; Pres. Sakura Bank –2001; Chair. Sumitomo Mitsui Banking Corpn 2001–05; Chair. and Rep. Dir Sumitomo Mitsui Financial Group Inc. 2004–05; Dir Sony Corpn 2002– (also Chair. Compensation Cttee 2004–), Mitsui & Co. Ltd, Kao Corpn 2002–; mem. Japan Cttee, Pacific Basin Econ. Council; Auditor Toray Science Foundation. *Address:* c/o Sumitomo Mitsui Financial Group Inc., 1-2 Yurakucho 1-chome, Chiyoda-ku, Tokyo 100-0006, Japan (office).

OKADA, Katsuya; Japanese politician; *Vice-President, Democratic Party of Japan;* b. 14 July 1953; ed Univ. of Tokyo and Harvard Univ., USA; entered Ministry of Int. Trade and Industry; joined Takeshita faction of LDP; joined Shinsheito 1993; later mem. Shinshinto and Taiyo Party, then Minseito, finally Democratic Party of Japan following merger with Minseito 1998–, Pres. 2004–05 (resgnd), Vice-Pres. 2006–; mem. House of Reps for Mie Pref. *Address:* Democratic Party of Japan, 1-11-1, Nagata-cho, Chiyoda-ku, Tokyo 100-0014, Japan (office). *Telephone:* (3) 3595-9960 (office). *Fax:* (3) 3595-7318 (office). *E-mail:* dpjenews@dpj.or.jp (office). *Website:* www.dpj.or.jp (office).

OKADA, Motoya, MBA; Japanese retail executive; *President and CEO, AEON Company Limited;* ed Babson Coll., Boston; mem. Bd Dirs Jusco Co. Ltd (retail co.) 1990–92, Man. Dir 1992–95, Sr Man. Dir 1995–97, Pres. and CEO 1997– (renamed AEON Co. Ltd 2001), Pres. Talbots Japan Co. Ltd (subsidiary of AEON) 1990–97, mem. Bd Dirs AEON Co. (Malaysia) Berhad, The Talbots, Inc. 1993–; Chair. Mycal; mem. Bd of Dirs CIES – The Food Business Forum 2000–. *Address:* AEON Co. Ltd, 1-5-1 Nakase, Mihama-ku, Chiba-shi, Chiba 261-8515, Japan (office). *Telephone:* (4) 3212-6042 (office). *Fax:* (4) 3212-6849 (office). *E-mail:* info@aeon.info (office). *Website:* www.aeon.info (office).

OKALIK, Paul, BA, LLB; Canadian politician; *Premier of Nunavut, Minister of Executive and Intergovernmental Affairs, Minister of Justice, and Minister Responsible for Aboriginal Affairs;* b. 1964, Pangnirtung, NWT; s. of Auyaluk; m.; 2 c.; ed Carleton Univ., Univ. of Ottawa; first Inuit law grad.; called to the Bar 1999; mem. Nunavut Ass. 1999–; first Premier of Nunavut, Minister of Exec. and Intergovernmental Affairs and Minister of Justice 1999–. *Leisure interests:* hunting, fishing, golf. *Address:* Office of the Premier, Government of Nunavut, PO Box 2410, 2nd Floor Legislative Building, Iqaluit, Nunavut X0A 0H0, Canada (office). *Telephone:* (867) 975-5050 (office). *Fax:* (867) 975-5051 (office). *E-mail:* premier@gov.nu.ca (office). *Website:* www.gov.nu.ca (office).

OKAMOTO, Kunie; Japanese insurance company executive; *President, Nippon Life Insurance;* ed Univ. of Tokyo; joined Nippon Life Insurance 1969, Sr Man. Dir 2002–05, Pres. 2005–; Corp. Auditor Sapporo Holdings Ltd, Mitsubishi Financial UFJ Group 2005–; Vice-Chair. Life Insurance Asscn of Japan. *Address:* Nippon Life Insurance, 3-5-12, Imabashi, Chuo-ku, Osaka 541-8501, Japan (office). *Telephone:* (6) 6209-5525 (office). *E-mail:* info@nissay.co.jp (office). *Website:* www.nissay.co.jp (office).

OKAMURA, Tadashi, LLB; Japanese electronics industry executive; *Chairman, Toshiba Corporation;* ed Univ. of Tokyo; joined Toshiba Corpn 1962, Gen.-Man. Marketing Planning Div. 1989–93, Group Exec. Information Processing and Control Systems Group 1993–94, Dir 1994–, Vice-Pres. 1994–96, Sr Vice-Pres. 1996–2000, Pres. and CEO Toshiba Corpn 2000–05, Chair. 2005–. *Address:* Toshiba Corporation, 1-1 Shibaura 1-chome, Minato-ku, Tokyo 105-8001, Japan (office). *Telephone:* (3) 3457-4511 (office). *Fax:* (3) 3455-1631 (office). *Website:* www.toshiba.com (office).

O'KANE, Dene Philip; New Zealand professional snooker player; b. 24 Feb. 1963, Christchurch; s. of Robert John O'Kane and Lesley Joan Marshall; ed Northcote Coll.; NZ Under-21 Champion 1977; youngest-ever NZ Champion 1980; turned professional 1984; tournament record includes Embassy World Championship Quarter Final 1987, World Cup Runner Up (Rest of World Team) 1989, Hong Kong Open runner up 1989; retd 2001; NZ Seniors Champion 2004, IBSF World Seniors Championship 2004, Bob Hawke AC Australian Open Snooker Championship 2005; Chair. NZ Confed. of Billiard Sports; Overseas (non-British) Player of the Year 1987. *Leisure interests:* golf, skin-diving, Formula One motor-racing, wine, clothes. *Address:* c/o Speakers New Zealand, POB 51 266, Auckland 1730, New Zealand.

O'KANE, Maggie, BA; Irish journalist; *Editorial Director, Guardian Films;* b. 8 June 1962, Ardglas, Co. Down, Northern Ireland; d. of Peter O'Kane and Maura McNeil; m. John Mullin 1995; one s.; ed Loreto Convent (Balbriggan, Co. Dublin), Univ. Coll. Dublin, Coll. de Journalistes en Europe, Paris and Coll. of Commerce, Dublin; reporter on Irish TV 1982–84, for Sunday Tribune newspaper 1984–87; reporter, TV Producer and Presenter 1987–89; Foreign Corresp. and Feature Writer, The Guardian 1989–2003; has reported from world trouble spots: Eastern Europe 1989–91, Baghdad 1991, Kurdistan 1991–92, Yugoslavia 1992–94, Bosnia, Haiti, Cuba 1994–96, Afghanistan, Cambodia, Kosovo, Yugoslavia 2000, etc.; Editorial Dir, Guardian Films 2003–; writer and presenter various TV documentaries; Journalist of the Year 1992, Foreign Corresp. of the Year 1992, Reporter of the Year (commended) (jt award) 1994, Amnesty Int. Foreign Corresp. of the Year 1993, James Cameron Award for Journalism 1996, European Journalist of the Year 2002, 2003. *Films:* (documentaries) Milosevic: Puppet Master of the Balkans (Channel 4) (Royal TV Soc. Documentary of the Year 1993), Bloody Bosnia (Royal TV Soc. Documentary of the Year 1994), Looking for Karadzic (Guardian Films) (European Journalist of the Year 2002). *Publications:* A Woman's World: Beyond the Headlines 1996, Mozambique. *Leisure interests:* swimming, cooking, triathlon training in Co. Mayo. *Address:* The Guardian, 119 Farringdon Road, London, EC1R 3ER, England (office). *Telephone:* (20) 7886-9799 (office). *Fax:* (20) 7713-4033 (office). *E-mail:* maggie.okane@guardian.co.uk (office). *Website:* www.guardian.co.uk/guardianfilms (office).

OKANLA, Moussa, PhD; Benin politician; b. 2 Sept. 1950; m.; ed Univ. of Michigan, USA; Prof. of Law, Univ. of Benin; Minister of Foreign Affairs, African Integration, Francophonie and Beninese Diaspora 2007–08; Chair. Group of Least Developed Countries, UNDP. *Address:* c/o Ministry of Foreign Affairs, Zone Résidentielle, route de l'Aéroport, 06 BP 318, Cotonou, Benin (office).

OKASHA, Sarwat Mahmoud Fahmy, DèsSc; Egyptian author, fmr diplomatist and politician; *President, Egypt–France Association;* b. 18 Feb. 1921, Cairo; s. of Mahmoud Okasha and Saneya Okasha; m. Islah Abdel Fattah Lotfi 1943; two s. one d.; ed Military Coll., Cairo Univ. and Univ. of Paris; Cavalry Officer 1939; took part in Palestine war 1948–49, Egyptian Revolt 1952: Mil. Attaché, Berne 1953–54, Paris 1954–56; Counsellor in Presidency of Repub. 1956–57; Egyptian Amb. to Italy 1957–58; UAR Minister of Culture and Nat. Guidance 1958–62; Chair. and Man. Dir Nat. Bank 1962–66; Deputy Prime Minister and Minister of Culture 1966–67; Minister of Culture 1967–71; Asst to the Pres. 1971–72; Visiting Prof. Coll. de France 1973; Pres. of Supreme Council for Literature, Art and Social Sciences; Pres. Egypt–France Asscn 1965–; mem. Exec. Bd UNESCO 1962–70 (masterminded int. campaign to save temples of Abu Simbel, etc. from the rising waters of the Aswan Dam); Pres. Consultative Cttee, Inst. du Monde Arabe (Paris) 1990–93; Corresp. Fellow British Acad.; Hon. DHumLitt (American Univ., Cairo) 1995; Commdr des Arts et des Lettres 1964, Légion d'honneur 1968; numerous other awards including UNESCO Gold Medal 1970 and State Award for the Arts 1988. *Publications:* 55 works (including trans): Ovid's Metamorphoses and Ars Amatoria, Khalil Gibran's works, Etienne Drioton's Le Théâtre Egyptien, studies of the works of Wagner, The Development of European Music (in Arabic), History of Art (25 vols), The Muslim Painter and the Divine 1979, Ramsès Recouronné, The Renaissance 1996, The Baroque 1997, The Rococo

1998, Indian Art 2000, Chinese Art 2001, Japanese Art 2001, Egypt in the Eyes of Foreigners 2001. *Leisure interests:* horse-riding, golf, music. *Address:* 34 Street 14, Villa 34, Maadi, Cairo, Egypt. *Telephone:* 3585075.

OKAWA, Ryuho; Japanese religious leader; *Leader, Kofuku-no-Kagaku;* b. 7 July 1956, Tokushima Pref.; ed Univ. of Tokyo, Graduate Center, City Univ. of New York, USA; attained enlightenment 23 March 1981, realized his identity as El Cantare, saviour of humanity; f. Kofuku-no-Kagaku (Inst. for Research in Human Happiness) 1986; holds numerous open lecture sessions with large audiences that are broadcast by satellite throughout Japan. *Publications:* more than 400 books including The Starting Point of Happiness – A Practical and Intuitive Guide to Discovering Love, Wisdom, and Faith, Love, Nurture, and Forgive – A Handbook on Adding New Richness in Your Life, An Unshakeable Mind – How to Cope with Life's Difficulties and Turn Them into Food for Your Soul 2002, A Revolution of Happiness – The Power of Thought to Change the Future, The 'Inability to Attain Happiness' Syndrome – Say Good-bye to a Life of Gloom, Work and Love – Become a True Leader in the Business World, Invincible Thinking – Become a Master of Your Own Destiny. *Address:* Kofuku-no-Kagaku, 1–2–38 Higashi Gotanda, Shinagawa-ku, Tokyo, 141-0022, Japan (office). *Telephone:* (3) 5437-2777 (office). *Fax:* (3) 5437-2806 (office). *E-mail:* inquiry@happy-science.org (office). *Website:* www.kofuku-no-kagaku.or.jp (office).

OKAYAMA, Norio; Japanese electronics industry executive; *Chairman, Sumitomo Electric Industries;* fmrly with Juki Corpn; Pres. Sumitomo Electric Industries Ltd 1999, now Chair.; mem. Bd of Dirs Dunlop Co. 2000–, Optoelectronic Industry and Tech. Devt Asscn (OITDA); Acting Pres. Int. Cablemakers Fed. 2006. *Address:* Sumitomo Electric Industries Ltd, 5-33 Kitahama 4-chome, Chuo-ku, Osaka 541-0041, Japan (office). *Telephone:* (6) 6220-4141 (office). *Fax:* (6) 6222-3380 (office). *Website:* www.sei.co.jp (office).

OKAYO, Margaret; Kenyan runner; b. 30 May 1976, Masaba, Nyanza Province; ed Itierio Secondary School, Kisii; distance runner; ran in Kenyan Nat. Championships then joined Fila Race Club, Italy 1997; won three Italian half-marathons in three weeks in 1998, won Prato, Trieste and Rio half-marathons in 1999; second place Chicago marathon 1999; won three half-marathons in 2000 then won first marathon Diego, also finished second in New York marathon; won San Diego, Calif. and New York marathons in course record times 2001; won Boston marathon 2002, becoming first woman in eight years to hold Boston and New York marathon titles; won Milan and NY marathons (both in course record times) 2003; won London marathon 2004; employed and sponsored by Kenya's Prison Service. *Address:* c/o Athletics Kenya, Riadha House, POB 46722, 00100, Nairobi, Kenya.

OKAZAKI, Tuneko, PhD; Japanese biologist and academic; *Guest Professor, Division of Artificial Chromosome Project, Institute for Comprehensive Medical Science, Fujita Health University;* ed Univ. of Nagoya; has spent much of her career at Univ. of Nagoya; currently Guest Prof., Div. of Artificial Chromosome Project, Inst. for Comprehensive Medical Science, Fujita Health Univ., Aichi; L'Oréal-UNESCO For Women in Science Award 2000. *Achievements include:* co-discoverer of Okazaki fragments of DNA. *Publications:* numerous articles in scientific journals on mechanisms of DNA replication. *Address:* Institute for Comprehensive Medical Science, Fujita Health University, 1-98 Dengakugakubo, Kutsukake-cho, Toyoake-shi, Aichi 470-1192, Japan (office). *Telephone:* (562) 932640 (office). *Fax:* (562) 935382 (office). *E-mail:* okazaki@fujita-hu.ac.jp (office). *Website:* www.fujita-hu.ac.jp/english/university (office). hp.fujita-hu.ac.jp/ICMS (office).

OKAZAKI, Yoichiro; Japanese engineering executive; *Chairman, President and CEO, Mitsubishi Motors Corporation;* b. 1943; joined Mitsubishi Heavy Industries Ltd 1965, Deputy Gen. Man., Sagamihara Machinery Works 1995–97, Chief Engineer, Gen. Machinery & Components HQ 1997, Pres. Mitsubishi Caterpillar Forklift America Inc. 1997–2001, Dir and Chief Coordinator, Gen. Machinery & Components HQ 1999–2000, Gen. Machinery & Special Vehicle HQ 2000–01, Dir, Gen. Man. then Man.-Dir 2001–04; Chair., Pres. and CEO Mitsubishi Motors Corpn 2004–; Dir Shin Caterpillar Mitsubishi Ltd 2001, Mitsubishi Heavy Industries Ltd 2004–; mem. Hon. Cttee FISITSA. *Address:* Mitsubishi Motors Corporation, 2-16-4 Konan, Minato-ku, Tokyo 108-8410, Japan (office). *Telephone:* (3) 6719-2111 (office). *Fax:* (3) 6719-0014 (office). *Website:* www.mistubishi-motors.co.jp (office).

OKE, Timothy R., OC, FRSC, PhD; Canadian/British geographer and academic; *Professor Emeritus of Geography, University of British Columbia;* b. 22 Nov. 1941, Kingsbridge, Devon; s. of late Leslie and Kathleen Oke; m. Margaret 1967; one s. one d.; ed Lord Wandsworth Coll., Univ. of Bristol and McMaster Univ.; Asst Prof., McGill Univ. 1967–70; Asst Prof., Univ. of British Col 1970–71, Assoc. Prof. 1971–78, Prof. of Geography 1978–, now Prof. Emer., also Head, Dept of Geography 1991–96; Ed.-in-Chief, Atmosphere-Ocean 1977–80; Hooker Distinguished Visiting Prof., McMaster Univ. 1987; Visiting Fellow, Keble Coll. Oxford 1990–91; Research Scholar (Rockefeller Foundation) Bellagio, Italy 1991; consultant to WMO and other orgs; Pres. Int. Asscn for Urban Climate 2000–03; Fellow, Royal Canadian Geographical Soc., Canadian Meteorological and Oceanographic Soc. 2003, American Meteorological Soc. 2004;; Dr hc (Łódź) 2005; Pres.'s Prize, Canadian Meteorological Soc. 1972, Killam Prize 1988, Award for Scholarly Distinction, Canadian Asscn of Geographers 1986, Guggenheim Fellow 1990, American Meteorological Soc. Outstanding Achievement in Biometeorology Award 2002, Patterson Medal, Meteorological Service of Canada, Environment Canada 2002, Luke Howard Award, Int. Asscn for Urban Climate 2004, Massey Medal, Royal Canadian Geog Soc. 2005, Helmut E. Landsberg Award, American Meteorological Soc. 2006. *Publications:* Boundary Layer Climates 1978, Vancouver and its Region 1992, The Surface Climates of Canada 1997; almost 200 articles on climate of cities. *Leisure interests:* golf, music, walking,

art. *Address:* Department of Geography, University of British Columbia, 1984 West Mall, Vancouver, BC, V6T 1Z2, Canada (office). *Telephone:* (604) 822-2900 (office). *Fax:* (604) 822-6150 (office). *Website:* www.geog.ubc.ca/~toke (office).

O'KEEFE, Sean; American space research administration official and fmr university administrator; b. 1956, Louisiana; m. Laura McCarthy O'Keefe; three c.; fmr staff dir and professional staff mem. Defense Subcttee. of Senate Appropriations Cttee; Comptroller, Dept of Defense 1989, Sec. of the Navy 1992–93; Prof. of Business Admin., Sr Vice-Pres. for Research, Dean of Grad. School Pennsylvania State Univ. 1993–96; Louis A. Bantle Prof. of Business and Govt Policy, Maxwell Grad. School of Citizenship and Public Affairs, Syracuse Univ., New York 1996–2001, Dir Nat. Security Studies, Syracuse Univ. and Johns Hopkins Univ. 1996–2001; Deputy Dir Office of Man. and Budget March–Dec. 2001; Admin. NASA Dec. 2001–05 (resgnd); Chancellor Louisiana State Univ. 2005–08; Fellow, Nat. Acad. of Public Admin., Int. Acad. of Astronautics; mem. Naval Postgraduate School Bd of Advisors; Hon. Engineer of the Year Award, Engineer's Council 2005; Distinguished Public Service Award 1993, Syracuse Univ. Chancellor's Award for Public Service 1999, Dept of the Navy Public Service Award 2000, Navigator Award, Potomac Inst. for Policy Studies 2005; inducted into Louisiana Political Hall of Fame 2007. *Address:* c/o Office of the Chancellor, Louisiana State University, 156 Thomas Boyd Hall, Baton Rouge, LA 70803, USA (office).

O'KENNEDY, Michael, MA; Irish politician; b. 21 Feb. 1936, Nenagh, Co. Tipperary; s. of Éamonn O'Kennedy and Helena (Slattery) O'Kennedy; m. Breda Heavey 1965; one s. two d.; ed St Flannan's Coll., Ennis, Univ. Coll. Dublin, King's Inns, Dublin; practised as barrister 1961–70, as Sr Counsel 1973–77, 1982–; mem. Senate 1965–69, 1993–, Front Bench Spokesman on Educ. and Justice, Senate Statutory Instruments Cttee on the Constitution until 1967; mem. Dáil for N Tipperary 1969–80, 1982–93, 1997–2002; presidential cand. 1997; Parl. Sec. to Minister of Educ. 1970–72, Minister without Portfolio 1972–73, Minister for Transport and Power 1973; Opposition Spokesman on Foreign Affairs 1973–77; Minister for Foreign Affairs 1977–79, of Finance 1979–80; mem. Comm. of European Communities 1980–82; Commr for Personnel, Consumer Affairs, Environment 1981–82; Opposition Spokesman for Finance 1982–87, Minister of Agric. 1987–92; mem. All-Parties Cttee on Irish Relations, Chair. 1973–80; mem. Informal Cttee on Reform of Dáil Procedure until 1972, Dáil and Senate Joint Cttee on Secondary Legislation of EEC 1973–80, Anglo-Irish Parl. Body 1993– (Co-Chair. 1997–); mem. Inter-Parl. Union, mem. Exec. of Irish Council of European Movt; Pres. EEC Council of Ministers July–Dec. 1979; Pres. EC Council of Agric. Ministers Jan.–June 1990; Pres. Re-negotiation EEC/ACP at 2nd Lomé Convention 1979; Nat. Trustee Fianna Fáil. *Leisure interests:* reading, philosophy, history, politics, drama, music, sports. *Address:* Gortlandroe, Nenagh, Co. Tipperary, Ireland. *Telephone:* (67) 31366 (home).

OKETA, Gazmend; Albanian engineer and politician; *Minister of Defence;* b. 14 Dec. 1968, Durrës; s. of Nuri Oketa; m.; two c.; ed General High School 'Gjergj Kastrioti', Durrës, Faculty of Civil Eng, Tirana Polytechnic Univ., Siegen Univ., Germany; Prof., Faculty of Civil Eng, Tirana 1994–95; Specialist of World Bank project on water supply rehabilitation, Durrës 1995–97; designing engineer and pvt. admin. in pvt. construction enterprises 1997–2003; adviser to Voith Siemens (Austria), project on Bistrica hydroelectric power station rehabilitation 2003–04; mem. Democratic Party of Albania (Partia Demokratike e Shqipërisë), Deputy Head of DPA, Durrës Br. 2004, Head of DPA and Spokesman Nov. 2005; mem. Durrës Municipal Council 2003–05; mem. Parl. for Durrës City, Zone No. 29 2005–, mem. Parl. Comm. for Legal Issues, Public Admin and Human Rights; Successive Pres. Cen. European Initiative Parl. Dimension Jan. 2006; Deputy Prime Minister 2007–08; Minister of Defence 2008–. *Address:* Ministry of Defence, Bulevardi Dëshmorët e Kombit, PO Box 2031, Tirana, Albania (office). *Telephone:* (4) 225726 (office). *E-mail:* kontakt@mod.gov.al (office). *Website:* www.mod.gov.al (office).

OKHOTNIKOV, Nikolai Petrovich; Russian singer (bass); b. 5 July 1937, Glubokoye, Kazakh Repub.; s. of P.Y. Okhotnikov and K.A. Okhotnikov; m. Larkina Tamara 1973; two s.; ed Leningrad Conservatoire with I.I. Pleshakov; mem. CPSU 1974–90; soloist with Leningrad Concert Union; with Maly Theatre, Leningrad 1967–71, with Kirov (now Mariinsky) Opera 1971–; teacher of singing at Leningrad (later St Petersburg) Conservatoire 1976–; Grand Prix, Barcelona 1972, People's Artist of USSR 1983, USSR State Prize 1985. *Major roles include:* Kochubey in Mazeppa, René in Iolanta, the Miller in Rusalka, Susanin in Glinka's Ivan Susanin, Dosifey in Mussorgsky's Khovanshchina, Kutuzov in Prokofiev's War and Peace, Philip II in Don Carlos, Heinrich in Lohengrin, Gremin in Eugene Onegin, Boris Godunov and Pimen in Boris Godunov, Don Basilio in The Barber of Seville. *Leisure interests:* fishing, photography. *Address:* Canal Griboedova 109, Apt 13, 190068 St Petersburg, Russia (home).

OKINAGA, Shoichi, MD, PhD; Japanese physician, academic and university president; *Professor of Medicine, Teikyo University;* b. 29 June 1933, Tokyo; s. of Shobei Okinaga and Kin Ino-Okinaga; m. Yoko Ishida 1968; two s.; ed Univ. of Tokyo; Prin. Teikyo Commercial and Eng Sr High School 1961–71; Founder and Pres. Teikyo Women's Jr Coll. 1965–; Founder and Pres. Teikyo Univ. 1966–2002, Prof. of Medicine 1971–; pvt. practice in obstetrics and gynaecology 1971–; Pres. Teikyo Special School of Medical Tech. 1969–; f. Teikyo Univ. of Tech. 1987; Chair. Bd of Trustees, Teikyo Univ. Foundation 1987–; Chair. Judo Fed. of Tokyo 1987–; f. Teikyo School UK 1989, Nishi-Tokyo Univ. 1990; Chair. Salem-Teikyo Univ., USA 1990–, Teikyo-Loretto Heights Univ., USA 1990–, Teikyo Westmar Univ., USA 1990, Teikyo Marycrest Univ., USA 1991–, Teikyo Post Univ., USA 1991–; Fellow, Wadham Coll. Oxford 1991, St Edmund's Coll. Cambridge 1991. *Publication:* Hitasura

No Michi (autobiog.) 1984. *Leisure interest:* judo. *Address:* Teikyo University, 2-11-1, Kaga, Itabashi-ku, Tokyo 173, Japan (office). *Telephone:* (42) 678-3237 (office). *Fax:* (42) 678-3544 (office). *E-mail:* t-sac@main.teikyo-u.ac.jp (office). *Website:* www.teikyo-u.ac.jp (office).

OKOGIE, HE Cardinal Anthony Olubunmi, STL, DD; Nigerian ecclesiastic; *Archbishop of Lagos;* b. 16 June 1936, Lagos; s. of Prince Michael Okogie and Lucy Okogie; ed St Gregory's Coll., Lagos, St Theresa Minor Seminary, Ibadan, St Peter and St Paul's Seminary, Ibadan, Urban Univ., Rome; ordained priest 1966; Acting Parish Priest, St Patrick's Church, Idumagbo, Lagos; Asst Priest, Holy Cross Cathedral, Lagos; Religious Instructor, King's Coll., Lagos; Dir of Vocations, Archdiocese of Lagos; Man. Holy Cross Group of Schools, Lagos; Master of Ceremonies, Holy Cross Cathedral; broadcaster of religious programmes, NBC-TV; Auxiliary Bishop of Oyo Diocese 1971–72; Auxiliary Bishop to the Apostolic Admin., Archdiocese of Lagos 1972–73; Archbishop of Lagos 1973–; cr. Cardinal-Priest of Beata Vergine Maria del Monte Carmelo a Mostacciano 2003; Vice-Pres. Catholic Bishops' Conf. of Nigeria 1985–88, Pres. 1988–94; Nat. Pres. Christian Asscn of Nigeria 1988–96; mem. Prerogative of Mercy, Religious Advisory Council; Commdr, Order of the Niger 1999. *Leisure interests:* reading, watching films, table tennis. *Address:* Archdiocese of Lagos, 19 Catholic Mission Street, PO Box 8, Lagos, Nigeria (office). *Telephone:* (1) 2633841 (office); (1) 2635729 (home). *Fax:* (1) 2633841 (office). *E-mail:* arclagos@yahoo.com (office).

OKONJO-IWEALA, Ngozi, AB, PhD; Nigerian economist, politician and international organization official; *Managing Director, World Bank Group;* b. 13 June 1954; m.; four c.; ed Harvard Univ., Massachusetts Inst. of Tech., USA; joined World Bank (IBRD) 1982, various positions including Economist, Country Dir in E Asia Region responsible for Malaysia, Cambodia, Laos and Mongolia 1997–99, Dir of Operations Middle East Region 2001–02, Vice-Pres. and Corp. Sec., World Bank Group 2002–03, Man. Dir 2007–; Adviser on Econ. Issues to Pres. of Nigeria 2000; Minister of Finance and Economy (first woman) 2003–06, of Foreign Affairs (first woman) June–Aug. 2006 (resgnd); Distinguished Visiting Fellow in the Global Economy and Devt Program, Brookings Inst., Washington, DC 2007; Founder NOI-Gallup polls; Co-founder African Inst. for Applied Econs, Enugu (currently Chair.), Makeda Fund; mem. bd several NGOs and think-tanks, including DATA, World Resources Inst., Clinton Global Initiative, Nelson Mandela Inst. and African Insts of Science and Tech., Mo Ibrahim Foundation Governance Prize Cttee, Friends of the Global Fund Africa; adviser to World Bank on the Stolen Assets Recovery (STAR) initiative; fmr mem. Malan Cttee on Bank-Fund collaboration; Hon. LLD (Brown Univ.) 2006, (Colby Coll.) 2007; Hon. DHumLitt (Northern Caribbean Univ., Jamaica); Dr hc (Trinity Coll., Dublin); Euromarket Forum Award for Vision and Courage 2003, Time Magazine European Hero 2004, This Day Nigeria Minister of the Year 2004, 2005, Euromoney Magazine Global Finance Minister of the Year 2005, Financial Times/The Banker African Finance Minister of the Year 2005, ranked 62nd by Forbes magazine amongst 100 Most Powerful Women 2006. *Publications include:* The Debt Trap in Nigeria: Towards a Sustainable Debt Strategy (co-ed.); several papers in devt journals. *Address:* World Bank Group, 1818 H Street, NW, Washington, DC 20433, USA (office). *Telephone:* (202) 473-1000 (office). *Fax:* (202) 477-6391 (office). *E-mail:* pic@worldbank.org (office). *Website:* www.worldbank.org (office).

OKOUNKOV, Andrei Yurovich, PhD; Russian mathematician and academic; *Professor, Princeton University;* b. 1969, Moscow; two d.; ed Moscow State Univ.; fmr Research Fellow, Dobrushin Math. Lab., Inst. for Problems of Information Transmission, Russian Acad. of Sciences; has taught at Inst. for Advanced Study in Princeton and Univ. of Chicago; Asst Prof., Univ. of Calif., Berkeley –2002; Prof., Princeton Univ. 2002–; Sloan Research Fellowship 2000, Packard Fellowship 2001; European Math. Society Prize 2004, Fields Medal (co-recipient) 2006. *Publications:* numerous papers in professional journals on probability, representation theory, algebraic geometry and math. physics. *Leisure interests:* cooking, playing football and ping-pong, reading. *Address:* Princeton University, Department of Mathematics, Fine 701, Fine Hall, Washington Road, Princeton, NJ 08544, USA (office). *Telephone:* (609) 258-4200 (office). *Fax:* (609) 258-1367 (office). *E-mail:* okounkov@math.princeton.edu (office). *Website:* www.math.princeton.edu/~okounkov (office).

OKOUR, Abdul Rahim, BA; Jordanian politician; *Minister of State for Parliamentary Affairs;* b. 1939; ed Univ. of Damascus; fmr secondary school teacher; fmr Lecturer, Howwara Coll., Yarmouk Univ.; served 22 years in various civil service positions; fmr mem. House of Reps, Majlis al-Umma; fmr mem. Consultative Council Irbid Governorate; fmr mem. Islamic Action Front (IAF); Minister of State for Parl. Affairs 2007–. *Address:* Ministry of Parliamentary Affairs, Amman 11118, Jordan (office).

OKPAKO, David Tinakpoevwan, PhD, CBiol, FIBiol, FNIBiol, FAAS, FAS, FRPharmS; Nigerian pharmacologist and pharmacist; b. 22 Nov. 1936, Owahwa, Delta; s. of the late Okun Okoro-Okpako Tsere and Obien Rebayi-Tsere; m. Kathleen Gweneth Jones-Williams 1967; one s. one d.; ed Urhobo Coll. Effurun, Nigerian Coll. of Arts, Science & Tech. Ibadan, Univ. of Bradford and Univ. Coll. London; Visiting Fellow, Corpus Christi Coll. Cambridge 1973–74, 1983–84; Prof. and Head, Dept of Pharmacology and Therapeutics, Univ. of Ibadan 1978–81, 1986–87, Dean, Faculty of Pharmacy 1987–91; Pres. W African Soc. for Pharmacology 1987–90; Foundation Pres. Nigeria Inst. of Biology 1990–92; Chair. Council, Nigerian Field Soc. 1991–2000; Visiting Prof. Univ. of the Western Cape, SA 1995–96; Visiting Fellow, Humanities Research Centre, ANU, Canberra 1996, Fitzwilliam Coll. Cambridge 1997; Visiting Scientist, Research Inst. Hosp. for Sick Children, Univ. of Toronto; now working as consultant pharmacist and pharmacologist. *Publications:* Principles of Pharmacology – A Tropical Approach 1991, 2001, Pharmacological Methods in Phytotherapy Research, Vol. 1. Selection, Preparation and Pharmacological Evaluation of Plant Material (with E.M. Williamson and F.J. Evans) 1996; articles in professional journals; book chapters. *Leisure interests:* golf, tennis, reading, fishing. *Address:* PO Box 20334, University of Ibadan Post Office, Oyo Road, Ibadan; 22 Sankore Avenue, University of Ibadan, Ibadan, Nigeria. *Telephone:* (234) 28107602 (home). *E-mail:* dpc@skannet.com.ng (office).

OKREPILOV, Vladimir V., DrEcon; Russian economist; *Director-General, TEST-St Petersburg;* b. 23 Feb. 1944, Leningrad; m.; two s.; ed Leningrad State Inst. of Mechanics; engineer, sr engineer-constructor, Leningrad factory of radiotechnology equipment 1965–70; Komsomol and CP service 1970–79; Chief Engineer, Research-Production Co. Mendeleyev VNIIM 1979–86; Dir Leningrad Centre of Standardization and Metrology of USSR State Cttee of Standards 1986–90; Dir-Gen. TEST-St Petersburg 1986–; Prof., Head of Chair, St Petersburg Univ. of Econs and Finance; Pres. St Petersburg Br. of Acad. of Quality Problems; mem. Presidium Russian Acad. of Sciences 2003–, Acad. of Electrotechnological Sciences, St Petersburg Acad. of Eng, Int. Acad. of Ecological Sciences, Security of Man and Nature; Corresp. mem. Russian Acad. of Sciences 2000–; Merited Worker of Science and Tech. of Russian Fed., Order of Friendship of Peoples 1988, Order for Merits to the Fatherland, Fourth Grade 1997; hon. prize for merits in standardization 1984, State Prize of Russian Fed. 1997, Prize of Pres. of Russian Fed. for Educ. 2002. *Publications include:* more than 200 scientific publs. *Address:* TEST-St Petersburg, Kurlyandskaya str. 1, St Petersburg 190103, Russia Federation (office). *Telephone:* (812) 251-39-50 (office). *Fax:* (812) 251-41-08 (office). *E-mail:* letter@rustest.spb.ru (office).

OKRI, Ben, OBE, FRSL, FRSA; Nigerian/British author and poet; b. 15 March 1959, Minna; s. of Silver Okri and Grace Okri; ed John Donne's School, Peckham, London, Children's Home School, Sapele, Nigeria, Christ High School, Ibadan, Urhobo Coll., Warri and Univ. of Essex, UK; staff writer and librarian, Afriscope magazine 1978; Poetry Ed. West Africa magazine 1983–86; broadcaster with BBC 1983–85; Fellow Commoner in Creative Arts, Trinity Coll. Cambridge 1991–93; mem. Int. PEN, a Vice-Pres. English Centre of Int. PEN 1997–; mem. Bd Royal Nat. Theatre of GB 1999–2006; mem. Soc. of Authors, RSL (mem. of Council 1999–2004); Hon. DLitt (Westminster) 1997, (Essex) 2002, (Exeter) 2004; Commonwealth Prize for Africa 1987, Paris Review Aga Khan Prize for Fiction 1987, Premio Letterario Internazionale, Chianti Ruffino-Antico Fattore 1992, Premio Grinzane Cavour 1994, The Crystal Award (World Econ. Forum, Switzerland) 1995, Premio Palmi 2000, Grinzane for Africa Mainstream Prize 2008. *Play:* In Exilus (The Studio, Royal Nat. Theatre of GB) 2001. *Television:* Great Railway Journey: London to Arcadia 1996. *Publications:* Flowers and Shadows 1980, The Landscapes Within 1982, Incidents at the Shrine 1986, Stars of the New Curfew 1988, The Famished Road (Booker Prize) 1991, An African Elegy (vol. of poems) 1992, Songs of Enchantment 1993, Astonishing the Gods 1995, Birds of Heaven (essays) 1996, Dangerous Love (novel) 1996, A Way of Being Free (non-fiction) 1997, Infinite Riches (novel) 1998, Mental Fight (epic poem) 1999, In Arcadia (novel) 2002, Starbook (novel) 2007, Tales of Freedom 2009; poems, essays, short stories. *Leisure interests:* chess, music, travel, theatre, cinema, art, walking, good conversation, silence. *Address:* c/o Orion Books, Orion House, 5 Upper St Martin's Lane, London, WC2H 9EA, England.

OKRUASHVILI, Irakli; Georgian lawyer and politician; b. 6 Nov. 1973, Tskhinvali; s. of Koba Okruashvili and Eter Giguashvili; m. Irina Gordeladze; one d.; ed Tbilisi State Univ.; leading specialist, Elections Cen. Comm. 1995; consultant, TACIS project, State Service Div. 1996; lawyer, Korzadze, Svanidze & Okruashvili, Okruashvili & Partners 1996–2000; Lecturer in Int. Trade Law, Tbilisi State Univ. 1997–2001; Deputy Minister of Justice 2000–01; mem. Tbilisi Sakrebulo (City Ass.) 2002–, Head of Revision Comm. Nov. 2002; Pres.'s plenipotentiary in Shida Kartli Mkhare Nov. 2003; Gen. Prosecutor Jan.–June 2004; Minister of Internal Affairs June–Dec. 2004, of Defence Dec. 2004–06, of Econ. Devt Nov. 2006; f. Movt for a United Georgia 2007; mem. Georgian Young Lawyers' Asscn, World Lawyers' Asscn, Lawyers' Int. Asscn; sentenced in absentia to 11 years imprisonment on corruption charges March 2008; granted asylum in France April 2008. *Leisure interest:* hunting.

OKU, Masayuki; Japanese banking executive; *Chairman and Representative Director, Sumitomo Mitsui Financial Group, Inc.;* Deputy Pres. Sumitomo Mitsui Banking Corpn and Sr Man. Dir Sumitomo Mitsui Financial Group Inc. –2005, Pres. and Rep. Dir Sumitomo Mitsui Banking Corpn and Chair. and Rep. Dir Sumitomo Mitsui Financial Group 2005–. *Address:* Sumitomo Mitsui Financial Group, Inc., 1-2, Yurakucho 1-Chome, Chiyoda-ku, Tokyo 100-0006, Japan (office). *Telephone:* (3) 5512-3411 (office). *Fax:* (3) 5512-4429 (office). *E-mail:* info@smfg.co.gp (office). *Website:* www.smfg.co.jp (office).

OKUDA, Hiroshi; Japanese automotive industry executive; *Senior Adviser, Toyota Motor Corporation;* b. 29 Dec. 1932; ed Hitotsubashi Univ.; fmr Exec. Dir Toyota Motor Corpn, Pres. 1995, Chair. –2006, now Sr Adviser; Chair. Nippon Keidanren (business fed.) –2006, Japan Business Fed. –2006. *Leisure interests:* reading, watching films. *Address:* Toyota Motor Corporation, 1 Toyota-cho, Toyota, Aichi 471-8571, Japan (office). *Telephone:* (565) 28-2121 (office). *Fax:* (565) 23-5800 (office). *Website:* www.global.toyota.com (office).

OKUI, Isao; Japanese business executive; *Chairman and Representative Director, Sekisui House Ltd;* currently Chair. and Rep. Dir Sekisui House Ltd; Chair. Kansai Employers' Asscn; Vice-Chair. Nippon Keidanren 2002, Japan Fed. of Employers' Asscns (Nikkeiren) 2002; mem. Advisory Cttee, Ritsumeikan Asia-Pacific Univ. (APU); mem. Cttee, The 3rd World Water Forum. *Address:* Sekisui House Ltd, 1-1-88 Oyodonaka, Kita-ku, Osaka 531-0076, Japan (office). *Telephone:* (6) 6440-3111 (office). *Fax:* (6) 6440-3331 (office). *Website:* www.sekisuihouse.co.jp (office).

OKULOV, Valery Mikhailovich; Russian business executive and pilot; *Chairman of the Managing Board and General Director, Aeroflot;* b. 22 April 1952, Kirov; m. Yelena Yeltsin (d. of fmr Pres. Boris Yeltsin); one s. two d.; ed Acad. of Civil Aviation; navigator, instructor, Sverdlovsk aviation team 1976–85; leading navigator, First Deputy Gen. Dir Aviation Co. Aeroflot (now Aeroflot Russian Airlines JSC) 1996–97, Gen. Dir 1997–, also Chair. of Man. Bd. *Leisure interest:* boating. *Address:* Aeroflot, Leningradsky prosp. 37, korp. 9, 125167 Moscow, Russia (office). *Telephone:* (495) 155-6648 (office). *Fax:* (495) 752-9016 (office). *Website:* www.aeroflot.ru (office).

OKUN, Lev Borisovich; Russian theoretical physicist; *Head of Laboratory, A.I. Alikhanov Institute of Theoretical and Experimental Physics;* b. 7 July 1929, Sukhinichi, Kaluga Dist; s. of B. G. Okun and B. R. Ginzburg; m. Erica Gulyaeva 1954; one s. two d.; ed Moscow Physics and Eng Inst.; mem. of staff, A.I. Alikhanov Inst. of Experimental and Theoretical Physics, now Head of Lab. 1954–; Prof., Moscow Inst. of Physics and Tech. 1967–; main work has been on the theory of elementary particles; Corresp. mem. of USSR (now Russian) Acad. of Sciences 1966–90, mem. 1990–, mem. Bureau Nuclear Physics Div., mem. Bureau Div. of Physical Sciences 2002–; mem. Science Policy Cttee CERN, Geneva, Switzerland 1981–86, Super Conducting Super Collider Lab., Dallas, Tex., USA 1989–93; mem. Extended Scientific Council of Deutsches Elektronen-Synchrotron (DESY) 1992–98, Bd Int. Science Foundation 1993–97, Council of Scientists of Int. Asscn for the Promotion of Co-operation with Scientists from the Ind. States of the Fmr Soviet Union (INTAS), Brussels 1993–97; mem. Academia Europaea 1991; Loeb Lecturer, Harvard Univ. 1989; Regents Prof., Univ. Calif., Berkeley 1990; Buhl Lecturer, Carnegie Mellon Univ. 1991; Visiting Prof., CERN 1992; Fermi Lecturer, Scuola Normale Superiore, Pisa 1993; Schrödinger Professorship, Univ. of Vienna, Austria 1994; AUI Distinguished Lecturer, Brookhaven Nat. Lab., USA 1995; Henry Primakoff Lecturer, Univ. of Pennsylvania 2001; invited lecturer at numerous major int. confs on high energy physics; Hon. Life mem. New York Acad. of Sciences 1993; Matteucci Prize (Italy) 1988, Lee Page Prize, Yale Univ. 1989, Karpinsky Prize, F.V.S. Foundation (FRG) 1990, Humboldt Research Award 1993, Bruno Pontecorvo Prize (Jt Inst. for Nuclear Research, Dubna) 1996, Open Soc. Inst. Prize 1997, L.D. Landau Gold Medal, Russian Acad. of Sciences 2003. *Achievements:* formulation of the theoretical model of strongly interacting particles based on three fundamental fermions 1957, coining of the term hadron 1961, notion of vacuum domains and unstable vacuum 1974. *Publications include:* The Weak Interaction of Elementary Particles 1963, Leptons and Quarks 1981, Particle Physics: The Quest for the Substance of Substance 1984, A Primer in Particle Physics 1987, The Relations of Particles 1991; more than 200 research and review articles in leading physics journals. *Address:* A.I. Alikhanov Institute of Theoretical and Experimental Physics, B. Cheremushkinskaya 25, 117218 Moscow, Russia (office). *Telephone:* (495) 123-31-92 (office); (495) 124-19-41 (home). *Fax:* (495) 127-08-33. *E-mail:* okun@itep.ru (office). *Website:* www.itep.ru (office).

OLAFSSON, Thröstur; Icelandic government official and business consultant; *General Manager, Iceland Symphony Orchestra;* b. 4 Oct. 1939, Husavík; m. 1st Monika Büttner 1966 (divorced); m. 2nd Thorunn Klemenzdóttir 1975; three s. one d. (and one s. deceased); ed Akureyri Gymnasium, Free Univ. of Berlin, Ruhr Univ., Bochum, Germany; economist, Nat. Bank of Iceland 1968–69, Civil Servants' Org. 1969–71; specialist adviser to Minister of Industry 1971–73; Man. Dir Mál og Menning (publishing co.) 1973–80; Asst to Minister of Finance 1980–83; Man. Dir Gen. Workers and Transport Union 1983–88; Exec. Dir Mikligarður Ltd 1989–90; Political Asst to Minister of Foreign Affairs 1991–95; Chair. Bd of Dirs Cen. Bank of Iceland 1994–98; Sec.-Gen. Social Democratic Party's Parl. Group 1995–97; consultant 1997–98; Chair. Bd Icemarkt Ltd 1989–, Icelandic Int. Devt Agency 1991–95, Social Housing Co. Felagsbustadir Ltd; Gen. Man. Iceland Symphony Orchestra 1998–; mem. Bd Edda Ltd (publishing co.); mem. Admin. Council of Europe Devt Bank 1995–2004. *Publications:* numerous articles on Icelandic econs and politics. *Leisure interests:* music, literature, skiing, forestry. *Address:* Brædraborgarstígur 21B, 101 Reykjavik, Iceland (home); Háskólabíó v. Hagetorg 107, Reykjavik (office). *Telephone:* 5452500 (office); 5519698 (home). *Fax:* 5624475 (office). *E-mail:* throl@sinfonia.is (office).

OLAH, George Andrew, PhD; American chemist and academic; *Distinguished Professor and Director, Donald P. and Katherine B. Loker Hydrocarbon Research Institute and Department of Chemistry, University of Southern California;* b. 22 May 1927, Budapest, Hungary; s. of Julius Olah and Magda Krasznai; m. Judith Lengyel 1949; two s.; ed Tech. Univ. Budapest; mem. Faculty, Tech. Univ. Budapest 1949–54; Assoc. Dir Centre for Chemical Research, Hungarian Acad. of Sciences 1954–56; research scientist, Dow Chemical Canada Ltd 1957–64, Dow Chemical Co. Framingham, Mass 1964–65; Prof. of Chem., Case Western Reserve Univ. 1965–69, C. F. Mabery Research Prof. 1969–77; Distinguished Prof. and Dir, Donald P. and Katherine B. Loker Hydrocarbon Research Inst. and Dept of Chem., Univ. of S California, LA 1977–; consultant to industry; numerous visiting professorships; mem. NAS, Accad. dei Lincei, Hungarian Acad. of Sciences, European Acad. of Arts, Sciences and Humanities; Foreign Fellow, Royal Soc. (UK), Canadian Royal Soc.; Hon. mem. Royal Soc. of Chem., German Chemical Soc. etc.; Grand Cordon, Order of the Rising Sun (Japan) 2003, Hungarian Order of Merit 2006; Dr hc (Durham) 1988, (Budapest) 1989, (Munich) 1990, (Crete) 1994, (Southern Calif., Case Western, Szeged, Veszprem) 1995, (Montpellier) 1996, (NY State Univ.) 1998, (Pecs, Debrecen, Hungary) 2003; Alexander von Humboldt Sr US Scientist Award 1979; Pioneer of Chem. Award, American Inst. of Chemists 1993; Nobel Prize for Chem. 1994, Priestley Medal (ACS) 2005. *Publications:* Friedel-Crafts Reactions (Vols I–IV) 1963–64, Carbonium Ions (Vols I–V) 1969–76 (with P. Schleyer), Friedel-Crafts Chemistry 1973, Carbocations and Electrophilic Reactions 1973, Halonium Ions 1975, Superacids (with G. K. S. Prakash and J. Somer) 1984, Hypercarbon Chemistry (with others) 1987, Nitration (with R. Malhotra and S. C. Narang) 1989, Cage Hydrocarbons 1990, Electron Deficient Boron and Carbon Clusters (with K. Wade and R. E. Williams) 1991, Synthetic Fluorine Chemistry (with Chambers and Prakash) 1992, Hydrocarbon Chemistry 1995, Onium Ions (jtly) 1998, A Life of Magic Chemistry 2001, Across Conventional Lines (selected papers with commentary, with Prakash) 2003, Beyond Oil and Gas: The Methanol Economy (with Goeppert and Prakash) 2006, Super-electrophiles and Their Chemistry (with Klumpp) 2007; several book chapters, 1,300 scientific papers and 140 patents. *Leisure interests:* reading, swimming. *Address:* Loker Hydrocarbon Research Inst., University of Southern California, Los Angeles, CA 90007 (office); 2252 Gloaming Way, Beverly Hills, CA 90210, USA (home). *Telephone:* (213) 740-5976 (office). *Fax:* (213) 740-5087 (office). *E-mail:* olah@usc.edu (office). *Website:* chem.usc.edu/faculty/Olah.html (office).

OLARREAGA, Manuel; Uruguayan academic; *Professor of International Marketing, Catholic University of Uruguay;* b. 1 June 1937, Salto; s. of Manuel Olarreaga and Hilda Leguisamo; m. Marina Rico 1966; three s.; ed Univ. of Paris; Minister-Counsellor, Uruguay's Perm. Del. to GATT 1982–87; First Exec. Sec. Latin American and Caribbean Program of Commercial Information to Support Foreign Trade 1988–91; Co-ordinator, Admin. Secr. of MERCOSUR 1991–96, Head Regulations Div. 1997–2003, Ed. Official Bulletin of MERCOSUR 1997–2003; Prof. of Int. Marketing, Catholic Univ. of Uruguay 1993–; Chair. Cttee of Countries Participating in Protocol Relating to Trade between Developing Countries, GATT; Deputy Chair. 18th, 19th and 20th Consultative Groups, UNCTAD–GATT Int. Trade Centre. *Publications:* several publs on int. trade. *Leisure interests:* reading, collecting antique keys. *Address:* avenue 8 de octubre 2738, CP 11600, Montevideo (office); Tomás Diago 769, Ap. 601, CP 11300, Montevideo, Uruguay (home). *Telephone:* (2) 487-27-17 (office); (2) 710-24-33 (home). *Fax:* (2) 487-32-27 (office). *E-mail:* molarrea@ucu.edu.uy (office); olarreaga@hotmail.com (home). *Website:* www.ucu.edu.uy (office).

ÓLASON, Vésteinn, PhD; Icelandic academic and university administrator; *Director, Árni Magnússon Institute;* b. 14 Feb. 1939, Höfn; s. of Óli K. Gudbrandsson and Adalbjörg Gudmundsdóttir; m. Unnur Alexandra Jónsdóttir 1960; one s. one d.; ed Menntaskólinn Laugarvatni, Univ. of Iceland; Lecturer in Icelandic Language and Literature Univ. of Copenhagen 1968–72, in Comparative Literature Univ. of Iceland 1972–80, docent Icelandic Literature 1980–85; Prof. of Icelandic Univ. of Oslo 1985–91; Prof. of Icelandic Literature Univ. of Iceland 1991–99, Dean Faculty of Arts 1993–95, Prorektor 1993–94; mem. Icelandic Soc. for Sciences 1983–, Norwegian Acad. of Sciences 1994–, Icelandic Research Council 1994–, Royal Gustaf Adolfs Acad. of Letters 1999–, Royal Norwegian Soc. of Sciences and Letters 2000–; Dir Árni Magnússon Inst. 1999–; Hon. Mem. Soc. of Antiquaries of London 2005; Iceland Literary Prize for Non-Fiction 1993. *Publications:* Sagnadansar: Edition and Study 1979, The Traditional Ballads of Iceland 1982, Islensk Bókmenntasaga I–II (History of Icelandic Literature 870–1720) 1992–93, Dialogues with the Viking Age: Narration and Representation in the Sagas of the Icelanders 1998; more than 100 articles in professional publs. *Address:* Árni Magnússon Institute, Reykjavik (office); Nylendugata 43, 101 Reykjavik, Iceland (home). *Telephone:* 5254011 (office); 5521792 (home). *Fax:* 5254035 (office). *E-mail:* vesteinn@hi.is (office).

OLAYAN, Khaled S.; Saudi Arabian business executive; *Chairman, Olayan Group;* s. of Suliman Saleh Olayan; Chair. Olayan Group 2002–. *Address:* c/o Olayan Financing Co., POB 8772, Riyadh, Saudi Arabia (office). *Telephone:* (1) 477-8740 (office). *Fax:* (1) 478-0988 (office). *Website:* www.olayangroup.com (office).

OLAYAN, Lubna S., BSc, MBA; Saudi Arabian business executive; *CEO and Deputy Chairperson, Olayan Financing Co.;* d. of the late Suliman Saleh Olayan; sister of Khaled S. Olayan; m. John Xefos; three d.; ed Cornell and Indiana Univs, USA; CEO and Deputy Chair. Olayan Financing Co. 1986–, mem. Bd of Dirs Olayan Investments Co. Establishment; Co-Chair. Arab World Competitiveness Forum, Geneva, Switzerland 2002; Dir (non-exec.) WPP 2005–; mem. Bd Chelsfield Plc (UK) 1996–2004, Saudi Hollandi Bank 2004–; mem. Int. Council of Institut Européen d'Admin des Affaires (INSEAD) 1997– (mem. Bd of Dirs INSEAD 2006–), Arab Business Council of World Econ. Forum, Int. Business Council of World Econ. Forum 2005–, Int. Advisory Bd of Council on Foreign Relations 2005–; spokesperson for women's rights in the Middle East, first woman to speak at a 'mixed' conf. in Saudi Arabia, Jeddah Econ. Conf. 2004; Co-Chair. World Econ. Forum, Davos, Switzerland 2005; ranked by Fortune magazine amongst 50 Most Powerful Women in Business outside the US (40th) 2003, (37th) 2004, (35th) 2005, (33rd) 2006, (29th) 2007, Middle East Award for Distinguished Businesswoman (UAE) 2003, Pioneer Achievement Award, Ninth Forum for Investment and Arab Capital Markets, Business and Economics, Beirut 2003, named Female Executive of the Year, Arabian Business Achievement Awards 2004, Arab Bankers Asscn of North America Achievement Award 2004, Distinguished Arabic Woman Award in the Businesswomen Sector in the Arab World, Sec.-Gen. Arab League, Cairo 2004, listed by Time magazine as one of the top 100 Most Influential People 2005, ranked by Forbes magazine amongst 100 Most Powerful Women (97th) 2005, (97th) 2006. *Address:* Olayan Financing Co., PO Box 8772, Riyadh, Saudi Arabia (office). *Telephone:* (1) 477-9000 (office). *Fax:* (1) 478-9207 (office). *Website:* www.olayan.com (office).

OLAZABAL, José María; Spanish professional golfer; b. 5 Feb. 1966, Fuenterrabía, Spain; s. of Gaspar Olazabal and Julia Olazabal; won Italian Open, Spanish Open and British Boys' Amateur Championships 1983, Belgian Int. Youth Championship 1984, Spanish Open Amateur Championship 1984, British Youths' Amateur Championship 1985; turned professional 1985; winner World Series of Golf 1990, 1994, The Int. (USA) 1991, US Masters

1994, 1999, Dubai Desert Classic 1998, Benson and Hedges Int. Open 2000, French Open 2001, Buick Invitational 2002; mem. European Ryder Cup Team 1987, 1989, 1991, 1993, 1997, 1999; golf-course designer (15 designed). *Leisure interests:* cinema, music, hunting, wildlife, ecology. *Address:* c/o PGA, 100 Avenue of Champions, Palm Beach Gardens, FL 33418, USA.

OLBRYCHSKI, Daniel; Polish actor; b. 27 Feb. 1945, Łowicz; m.; one s. one d.; ed State Higher School of Drama, Warsaw; actor, Nat. Theatre 1969–77; mem. Polish Film Union; Officier Ordre des Arts et Lettres; State Prize (2nd Class) 1974; numerous awards at Polish and foreign film festivals. *Roles include:* Koral in Wounded in the Forest 1964, Rafał Olbromski in Ashes 1965, boxer in Boxer 1966, Marek in Jowita 1967, Daniel in All for Sale 1968, Azja in Michael Wołodyjowski 1969, Angel of Death in Agnus Dei 1970, Tadeusz in Landscape After Battle 1970, Bolesław in The Birch Wood 1971, Wit in Family Life 1971, Pan Młody in The Wedding 1972, Mateusz in Pilatus und Andere 1972, Kmicic in The Deluge 1974, Karol Borowiecki in The Promised Land 1975, Przybyszewski in Dagny 1976, Wiktor in The Maids of Wilko 1978, Jan in Little Tin Drum 1978, Saint-Genis in The Trout 1982, Pisarz in Flash-Back 1983, Love in Germany 1983, I'm Against 1985, Leon in Rosa Luxemburg 1986, Scope in Ga-ga 1986, Michał Kątny in Siekierezada 1986, Pitt in Tiger's Fight 1987, The Unbearable Lightness of Being 1988, Borys in Pestka 1995, Old Tuchajbej in With Fire and Sword 1998, Gerwazy in Last Foray in Lithuania 1999, Seweryn in It's Me, the Thief 2000, Szymon Gajowiec in The Spring to Come 2001, Prince of Elfs in The Hexer 2001, Konrad Sachs in Gebürtig (2002) 2002, Dyndalski in The Revenge 2002, Piastun in Stara basn. Kiedy slonce bylo bogiem 2003, Nitschewo 2003, Break Point 2004, Milady (TV) 2004, Anthony Zimmer 2005. *Stage appearances:* Hamlet 1970, Rhett in Gone With the Wind, Rodric in Cyd 1985, Cześnik in Revenge 1998. *Television:* Raskolnikow in Crime and Punishment 1980, Chello 1985, Kean 1993. *Leisure interests:* tennis, horses, family life.

OLDENBURG, Claes Thure, BA; American (b. Swedish) artist; b. 28 Jan. 1929, Stockholm, Sweden; s. of Gösta Oldenburg and Sigrid E. Oldenburg (née Lindforss); brother of Richard Oldenburg (q.v.); m. Patricia Joan Muschinski 1960 (divorced 1970); m. Coosje van Bruggen 1977; ed Yale Coll. and Art Inst. of Chicago; arrived in USA 1929 (naturalized 1953); moved to New York City 1956; took up fabrication on large scale 1969; has worked in partnership with Coosje van Bruggen 1976–; mem. American Acad. Inst. of Arts and Letters, American Acad. of Arts and Sciences; Dr hc (Oberlin Coll.) 1970, (Art Inst. of Chicago) 1979, (Bard Coll.) 1995, (RCA) 1996, (Nova Scotia Coll. of Art and Design—NSCAD Univ.) 2005; Skowhegan Medal for Sculpture 1972, Brandeis Univ. Sculpture Award 1976, Art Inst. of Chicago Sculpture Award 1976, Medal American Inst. of Architects 1977, Wilhelm Lehmbruck Sculpture Award 1981, Wolf Foundation Prize for the Arts 1989, Brandeis Univ. Creative Arts Award for Lifetime Artistic Achievement 1993, Lifetime Achievement Award, Int. Sculpture Center, New York 1994, Distinction in Sculpture, New York 1994, Rolf Schock Foundation Stockholm 1995, Nathaniel S. Saltonstall Award, Boston 1996, National Medal of Arts, Washington, DC 2000, Pnrs in Educ. Award, Solomon R. Guggenheim Museum 2002, Medal Award, School of the Museum of Fine Arts, Boston 2004. *Numerous public sculptures with Coosje van Bruggen include:* Trowel I, Rijkmuseum Kröller-Müller, Otterlo, The Netherlands 1971–76, Crusoe Umbrella, Nollen Plaza, Civic Center of Greater Des Moines, Iowa 1979, Balancing Tools, Vitra Int. AG, Weil am Rhin, Germany 1984, Spoonbridge and Cherry, Minneapolis Sculpture Garden, Wlker Art Center, Minn., Bicyclette Ensevelie Parc de la Villette, Paris 1990, Bottle of Notes, Central Gardens, Middlesbrough, England 1993, Shuttlecocks, Nelson-Atkins Museum of Art, Kansas City, MO 1994, Saw Sawing, Tokyo Int. Exhbn Centre, Tokyo, Japan 1996, Soft Shuttlecocks, Guggenheim Foundation 1996, Ago, Filo e Nodo, Piazzale Cadorna, Milan, Italy 2000, Flying Pins, Eindhoven, The Netherlands 2000, Dropped Clone, Neumarkt Galerie, Cologne, Germany 2001, Cupid's Span, San Francisco 2002, Big Sweep, Denver, CO 2006. *Publications include:* Store Days 1967, Notes in Hand 1971, Raw Notes 1973, Multiples in Retrospect 1991; with Coosje van Bruggen: Claes Oldenburg: Sketches and Blottings Toward the European Desk Top 1990, Large Scale Projects 1994, Claes Oldenburg Coosje van Bruggen 1999, Down Liquidambar Lane: Sculpture in the Park 2001,Images á la Carte 2004. *Address:* 556 Broome Street, New York, NY 10013-1517, USA (office). *Telephone:* (212) 966-2290 (office). *Fax:* (212) 226-4315 (office). *E-mail:* office@oldenburgvanbruggen.com (office). *Website:* www .oldenburgvanbruggen.com (office).

OLDENBURG, Richard Erik, AB; American museum director; b. 21 Sept. 1933, Stockholm, Sweden; s. of Gösta Oldenburg and Sigrid E Lindfors; brother of Claes Oldenburg (q.v.); m. 1st Harriet L. Turnure 1960 (died 1998); m. 2nd Mary Ellen Meehan 2003; ed Harvard Coll.; Man. Ed., Macmillan Co. 1964–69; Dir of Publs, Museum of Modern Art, New York 1969–71, Acting Dir Jan.–June 1972, Dir 1972–94, Dir Emer. and Hon. Trustee 1995–; Chair. Sotheby's N and S America 1995–2000, Hon. Chair. 2000–06, Consultant 2006–. *Leisure interest:* reading. *Address:* Sotheby's Inc., 1134 York Avenue, New York, NY 10021 (office); 447 East 57th Street, New York, NY 10022, USA (home).

OLDFIELD, Bruce, OBE; British fashion designer; b. 14 July 1950, brought up in Dr Barnardo's charity home, Ripon; ed Ripon Grammar School, Sheffield City Polytechnic, Ravensbourne Coll. of Art and St Martin's Coll. of Art; est. own fashion house, producing designer collections 1975; began making couture clothes for individual clients 1981; opened retail shop selling couture and ready-to-wear 1984; designed for films Jackpot 1974, The Sentinel 1976; Vice-Pres. Barnardo's 1998; Trustee Royal Acad. 2000–02; Gov. London Inst. 1999–2001; Hon. Fellow Sheffield Polytechnic 1987, RCA 1990, Univ. of Durham 1991; Hon. DCL (Northumbria) 2001; Hon. DUniv (Univ. of Cen. England) 2005. *Publications:* Seasons 1987, Rootless (autobiog.) 2004. *Leisure interests:* music, reading, gardening, working, cooking. *Address:* 27 Beauchamp Place, London, SW3 1NJ, England. *Telephone:* (20) 7584-1363. *Fax:* (20) 7761-0351. *E-mail:* hq@bruceoldfield.com (office). *Website:* www .bruceoldfield.com.

OLDMAN, Gary; British actor; b. 21 March 1958, New Cross, S London; m. 1st Lesley Manville; one s.; m. 2nd Uma Thurman (q.v.) 1991 (divorced 1992); m. 3rd Donya Fiorentino (separated 2001); two c.; m. 4th Alexandra Edenborough 2008; ed Rose Bruford Drama Coll.; studied with Greenwich Young People's Theatre; acted with Theatre Royal, York and then with touring co.; appeared at Glasgow Citizens Theatre in Massacre at Paris, Chinchilla, Desperado Corner, A Waste of Time; London stage appearances: Minnesota Moon, Summit Conference, Real Dreams, The Desert Air (RSC), War Play I, II, III (RSC), Serious Money (Royal Court), Women Beware Women (Royal Court), The Pope's Wedding; appeared in The Country Wife, Royal Exchange Theatre, Manchester; Co-founder SE8 Group (production co.) 1995. *Films:* Sid and Nancy 1986, Prick Up Your Ears 1987, Track 29 1988, Criminal Law 1988, We Think The World of You 1988, Chattahoochee 1989, State of Grace 1990, Rosencrantz and Guildenstern are Dead 1990, JFK 1991, Dracula 1992, True Romance 1993, Romeo is Bleeding 1993, Léon 1994, Immortal Beloved 1994, Murder in the First 1995, The Scarlet Letter 1995, Basquiat 1996, Nil by Mouth (producer, BAFTA Award) 1997, The Fifth Element 1997, Air Force One 1997, Lost in Space 1998, Anasazie Moon 1999, Plunkett & Macleane (exec. producer) 1999, The Contender (also exec. producer) 2000, Nobody's Baby 2001, Hannibal 2001, Interstate 60 2002, The Hire: Beat the Devil 2002, Tiptoes 2003, Sin 2003, Harry Potter and the Prisoner of Azkaban 2004, Who's Kyle? 2004, Dead Fish 2004, Batman Begins 2005, Harry Potter and the Goblet of Fire 2005, BackWoods 2006, The Legend of Spyro: A New Beginning (voice) 2006, Harry Potter and the Order of the Phoenix 2007, Legend of Spyro: The Eternal Night (voice) 2007, The Dark Knight 2008. *Television appearances include:* Remembrance, Meantime (Channel 4); Honest, Decent and True (BBC); Rat in the Skull (Central), The Firm, Heading Home, Fallen Angels. *Address:* c/o Douglas Urbanski, Douglas Management Inc., 515 North Robertson Boulevard, Los Angeles, CA 90048, USA; SE8 Group, 12 Great James Street, Camden, London, WC1N 3DR, England.

OLDSTONE, Michael B. A., MD, PhD; American neuropharmacologist and academic; *Head, Division of Virology, Department of Neuropharmacology, Scripps Research Institute;* ed Univ. of Maryland School of Medicine and Johns Hopkins McCullom Pratt Inst. of Biochemistry; Postdoctoral Fellow, Dept of Experimental Pathology, Scripps Research Inst. 1966, Assoc. mem. Dept of Immunopathology 1972–78, mem. Dept of Immunology 1978–89, Head, Div. of Virology and mem. Dept of Neuropharmacology 1989–; mem. Nat. Advisory Cttee, PEW Scholars Program in the Biomedical Sciences, WHO Cttee for the Eradication of Poliomyelitis and Measles Virus; Ed. Virology; mem. Editorial Bd Current Topics in Microbiology and Immunology, Journal of Experimental Medicine, Immunity; mem. Inst. of Medicine of NAS, American Asscn of Physicians, American Soc. for Clinical Investigation, Scandinavian Soc. of Immunology; Fellow, American Acad. of Microbiology; Burroughs Wellcome Professorship Award, Cotzias Award 1986, Abraham Flexner Award 1988, Rous-Whipple Award 1993, Biomedical Science Award, Karolinska Inst. (Sweden) 1994, J. Allyn Taylor Int. Prize in Medicine 1997, R. E. Dyer Lectureship and Directors Award, NIH 2000. *Publications:* HIV and Dementia 1995, Transgenic Models of Human Viral and Immunology Disease 1995, Arenaviruses I: The Epidemiology, Molecular and Cell Biology of Arenaviruses 2002, Arenaviruses II: The Molecular Pathogenesis of Arenavirus Infections 2002; numerous articles in scientific journals. *Address:* Scripps Research Institute, Department of Neuropharmacology, 10550 North Torrey Pines Road, La Jolla, CA 92037, USA (office). *Telephone:* (858) 785-1000 (office). *Website:* www.scripps.edu (office).

OLE-MOIYOI, Onesmo K.; Kenyan molecular biologist and immunologist; *Chairman, Council, Kenyatta University;* b. Tanzania; ed Harvard Coll. (Aga Khan Scholar) and Harvard Medical School, USA; looked after Maasai village cattle herd of 800 cows as a boy; Head of Biochemistry and Molecular Biology Lab. and Leader in Program on Pathophysiology and Genetics, Int. Lab. for Research on Animal Diseases, Int. Livestock Research Inst., Nairobi 1987–2001; est. Inst. of Molecular and Cell Biology, Nairobi; Dir of Research and Partnerships, Int. Centre of Insect Physiology and Ecology (now African Insect Science for Food and Health—ICIPE), Nairobi 2001–07; fmr Asst Prof. and Capps' Scholar, Harvard Medical School; fmr Visiting Prof., Harvard School of Public Health; mem. Science Council for the Consultative Group of Int. Agricultural Research, Steering Cttees of HUGO (Human Genome Org.), among other appointments; Chair. Kenyatta Univ. Council in Kenya 2007–; Elder of the Order of the Burning Spear; Dr hc (Soka Univ., Japan); Kilby Int. Award 2003. *Address:* Kenyatta University, PO Box 43844-00100, Nairobi 30772, Kenya (office). *Telephone:* (20) 810901 (office). *Fax:* (20) 811575 (office). *E-mail:* info@ku.ac.ke (office). *Website:* www.ku.ac.ke (office).

O'LEARY, Hazel, BA, JD; American lawyer, academic administrator and fmr government official; *President, Fisk University;* b. 17 May 1937, Newport News, Va; d. of Russell Reid and Hazel Palleman; m. John F. O'Leary 1980 (deceased); one s.; ed High School of Fine and Performing Arts, Newark, NJ, Fisk Univ., Rutgers Univ. Law School; fmr prosecutor, then an Asst Attorney-Gen., NJ; fmr mem. staff US Dept of Energy and Fed. Energy Admin.; Vice-Pres. and Gen. Counsel, O'Leary Assocs (consultants on energy econs and planning) 1981–89, 1997–2000; joined Northern States Power Co., Minn. 1989, subsequently Exec. Vice-Pres.; US Sec. of Energy 1993–97; COO Blaylock & Pnrs (investment banking firm), New York 2001–02; Pres. Fisk Univ., Nashville 2004–. *Address:* Office of the President, Fisk University, 1000

Seventeenth Avenue North, Nashville, TN 37208-3051 (office); 4215 Harding Pike, Apt 301, Nashville, TN 37205-2029, USA. *Telephone:* (615) 329-8500 (office). *Website:* www.fisk.edu (office).

O'LEARY, Michael; Irish airline industry executive; *CEO, Ryanair Holdings PLC;* b. 1961; m. Anita Farrall 2003; ed Clongowes Wood Coll., Trinity Coll. Dublin; tax consultant, KPMG 1984–86; Dublin property developer and financial adviser to Tony Ryan; Dir Ryanair Holdings PLC 1988–91, Deputy CEO 1991–93, COO 1993–94, CEO 1994–; European Businessman of the Year, Fortune Magazine 2001. *Leisure interests:* horse riding, farming, watching rugby. *Address:* Ryanair Holdings PLC, Dublin Airport, Dublin, Ireland (office). *Telephone:* (1) 812-1212 (office). *Fax:* (1) 812-1213 (office). *Website:* www.ryanair.ie (office).

OLECHNOWICZ, Paweł, BEcons, PhD; Polish business executive; *Chairman, President and CEO, Grupa LOTOS SA;* b. 2 Jan. 1952, Puszcza Obalska; s. of Leon Olechnowicz and Janina Olechnowicz (née Rodziewicz); m. Krystyna Olechnowicz 1975; one s.; ed Acad. of Mining and Metallurgy, Krakow, INSEAD, Fontainebleau, France, Tech. Univ., Gdansk; Technologist, Zamech Mechanical Works, Elblag 1976–77, Foreman, Metallurgical Dept, 1977–80, Man. 1980–90, Gen. Man. Elzam and Zamech 1990, CEO ABB Zamech Ltd 1990–96, Dir Power Generation Div. 1993–96, Vice-Pres. Cen. and E Europe Power Generation Div. 1996–98; Vice-Pres. and Deputy CEO, ZML Kęty SA 1999–2000; Dir Pawel Olechnowicz Consulting 2001; Chair., Pres. and CEO Grupa Lotos SA (fmrly Rafineria Gdanska), Gdansk 2002–; mem. Polish Tech. Cttee, Det Norske Veritas Classification AS, Norway 1993–; Chair. Supervisory Bd Rekoenergo, Warsaw 1991; mem. Polish Council for Econ. Devt, Warsaw 1993; Dir Business Forum, Polish Higher Educ.; mem. Polish Centre Club, Int. Inst. of Man. Devt. *Leisure interests:* chess, sports, playing guitar and piano. *Address:* Grupa Lotos SA, ul. Elbląska 135, 80–718 Gdansk, Poland (office). *Telephone:* (58) 3087111 (office). *Fax:* (58) 3018838 (office). *E-mail:* lotos@grupalotos.pl (office). *Website:* www.lotos.pl (office).

OLECHOWSKI, Andrzej, MA, PhD; Polish politician, economist and writer; *European Deputy Chairman, Trilateral Commission;* b. 9 Sept. 1947, Kraków; m. Irena Olechowska 1971; two s.; ed Cen. School of Planning and Statistics, Warsaw; Assoc. Econ. Affairs Officer, UNCTAD Multilateral Trade Negotiations Project, Geneva 1973–78; Head, Dept of Analysis and Projections, Foreign Trade Research Inst. Warsaw 1978–82; Econ. Affairs Officer, UNCTAD, Geneva 1982–84; Economist, IBRD, Washington, DC 1985–87; Adviser to Gov. Nat. Bank of Poland 1987; Dir World Bank Cooperation Bureau, Nat. Bank of Poland 1988; Dept Dir Ministry of Foreign Econ. Relations 1988–89; Deputy Gov. Nat. Bank of Poland 1989–91; Sec. of State, Ministry of Foreign Econ. Relations and Chief Negotiator of Asscn Treaty with EU and Cen. European Free Trade Agreement 1991–92; Minister of Finance Feb.–May 1992; Sr Adviser, EBRD 1992–93; Econ. Adviser to Pres. of Repub. 1992–93, 1995; Minister of Foreign Affairs 1993–95; Chair. Bd Dirs Bank Handlowy w Warszawie SA 1991–96, 1998–2000, Cen. Europe Trust 1996–2000; Chair. Civic Platform (Platforma Obywatelska—PO, a centrist political movt) 2001–04, Pres. Program Council; presidential cand. 2000; Commr US–Poland Action Comm.; currently European Deputy Chair. Trilateral Comm.; mem. Advisory Bd Baltic Devt Forum; mem. Bd Globe Theatre Group. *Publications include:* Wygrac przyszlosc; publs on int. trade and foreign policy. *Address:* The Trilateral Commission, 5 rue de Téhéran, 75008 Paris, France (office); ul. Emilii Plater 53, (WFC XXI), 00-113 Warsaw, Poland. *Telephone:* 1-45-61-42-80 (office). *Fax:* 1-45-61-42-80 (office). *E-mail:* trilateral.europe@wanadoo.fr (office). *Website:* www.trilateral.org (office).

OLEKAS, Juozas; Lithuanian physician and politician; b. 30 Oct. 1955, Krasnojarsk Kraj, Siberia; m. Aurelija Olekas; one s. two d.; ed Kaunas Medical Inst., Vilnius Univ.; worked at hosp. in Vilnius 1980–90; physician and sr researcher, Vilnius Univ. Microsurgery Centre 1982–89; particiated in Sàjûdis activity, elected mem. Sàjûdis Seimas 1988, People's Deputy of USSR 1989; mem. Lithuanian Del., Supreme Council of USSR 1989–91; Minister of Health 1990–92 (resgnd), 2003–04; surgeon, Vilnius Ambulance Univ. Hosp. 1993–94; Chief Physician, Vilnius Univ. Hosp. 1994; staff mem. Stomatology Clinic, Medical Faculty, Vilnius Univ. Hosp. 1994–99; mem. Social Democratic Party 1989–, mem. Seimas 1996–; Minister of Nat. Defence 2006–08; mem. Org. Comm., European Regional Bureau of WHO 1992–93; Chair. Lithuanian Trade Union Centre 1997; Medal of Independence 2000; Nat. Award of Lithuania 1998. *Publications:* over 100 scientific articles. *Leisure interests:* gardening, sport, dancing, theatre. *Address:* c/o Lithuanian Social Democratic Party (Lietuvos Socialdemokratų Partija), Barboros Radvilaites g. 1, Vilnius 01124, Lithuania. *Telephone:* (5) 261-3907. *Fax:* (5) 261-5420. *E-mail:* info@lsdp.lt. *Website:* www.lsdp.lt.

OLEKSY, Józef, DEcon; Polish politician and economist; b. 22 June 1946, Nowy Sącz; s. of Józef Oleksy and Michalina Oleksy; m. Maria Oleksy 1983; one s. one d.; ed Warsaw School of Econs, European Faculty of Comparative Law, Strasbourg; researcher, Faculty of Foreign Trade, Vice-Dir Int. Law Dept, Warsaw School of Econs (SGH) 1969–; Founder-Pres. Movt of Young Scientists in Poland 1969–72; Minister, mem. of Council of Ministers 1989; mem. Polish Group of IPU; Deputy to Sejm (Parl.) 1989–2005, Marshal (Speaker) of Sejm 1993–95, 2004–05 (resgnd), Chair. European Cttee 2001–04; Prime Minister of Poland 1995–96; fmr Deputy Prime Minister and Minister for Internal Affairs; mem. Polish United Workers' Party (PZPR) 1968–90, First Sec. Voivodship Cttee 1987–89; mem. Parl. Asscn of OSCE 1989–93; mem. Governing Bd of the Council for Social Democracy of the Repub. of Poland (SDRP) 1990–, Vice-Chair. 1992–96, Chair. 1996–97; Pres. Polish Council of Young Scientists 1969–76; participant, Historical Compromise in Poland Round Table 1989; mem. Cttee on Foreign Affairs and Cttee on European Integration; Rep. EU–Poland Jt Parliamentary Cttee 1997, Co-Chair. 2001–04. *Publications:* numerous articles on econ. and int. affairs. *Leisure interests:* walking, hunting, history, futurology, parapsychology, cosmology. *Address:* c/o Sejm RP, ul. Wiejska 4/6/8, 00-902 Warsaw, Poland (office).

OLESEN, Poul; Danish physicist and academic; *Professor of Theoretical Physics, Niels Bohr Institute, University of Copenhagen;* b. 28 April 1939, Ålborg; s. of Viktor Olesen and Herdis Olesen; m. Birgitte Sode-Mogensen 1984; ed Univ. of Copenhagen; Research Assoc., Univ. of Rochester, New York 1967–69; Research Assoc., CERN, Geneva 1969–71, Visiting Fellow 1985; Assoc. Prof. of Theoretical Physics, The Niels Bohr Inst., Copenhagen 1971–97, Prof. 1997–, Chair. Research Cttee 1993–95, 2005–08, mem. Governing Body 1996–99; mem. Faculty of Science Council, Univ. of Copenhagen 1989–2005, Exec. Cttee 1990–93, Research Cttee 1998–; mem. Royal Danish Acad.; Hermer Prize. *Publications:* articles in int. journals on particle physics. *Address:* The Niels Bohr Institute, Blegdamsvej 17, 2100 Copenhagen Ø (office); Malmmosevej 1, 2840 Holte, Denmark (home). *Telephone:* 31-42-16-16 (office). *E-mail:* polesen@nbi.dk (office). *Website:* www.nbi.dk (office).

OLEVAR, Blanca; Paraguayan politician; b. 2 Sept. 1957; Minister of Educ. –2007; selected as cand. for 2008 presidential election by Asociación Nacional Republicana—Partido Colorado (National Republican Association—Colorado Party). *Address:* Asociación Nacional Republicana—Partido Colorado (National Republican Association—Colorado Party), Casa de los Colorados, 25 de Mayo 842, Asunción, Paraguay (office). *Telephone:* (21) 44-4137 (home). *Fax:* (21) 49-7857 (office). *Website:* www.anr.org.py (office).

OLHAYE, Roble; Djibouti diplomatist; *Ambassador to USA and Dean of the Diplomatic Corps; Permanent Representative, United Nations;* b. 24 April 1944; m.; five c.; ed Commercial School of Addis Ababa; worked in area of financial and admin. man. in various orgs in Ethiopia engaged in communication, printing, export trade, insurance and mfg 1964–73; regional accountant, TAW Int. Leasing Corpn Nairobi 1973, Financial Dir 1975; ind. consultant 1980–82; Hon. Consul of Djibouti to Kenya 1980–85; f. (as jt venture with Middle East Bank of Dubai) Banque de Djibouti et du Moyen Orient, SA 1982; Perm. Rep. to UNEP and UN Centre for Human Settlements (Habitat), Nairobi 1986–88; Amb. to USA 1988– (also accred to Canada 1989–), Perm. Rep. to UN 1988–, Dean of the Diplomatic Corps; Pres. of Council 1994, Chair. of Sanctions Cttee 1994, mem. Security Council Mission to Mozambique 1994, Dean of African Diplomatic Corps 1999, Chair. Second Cttee (Econ. and Social) 1999–; Fellow, Asscn of Int. Accountants, UK; mem. British Inst. of Man. *Address:* Embassy of Djibouti, 1156 15th Street, NW, Suite 515, Washington, DC 20005 (office); Permanent Mission of Djibouti to the United Nations, 866 United Nations Plaza, Suite 4011, New York, NY 10017, USA. *Telephone:* (202) 331-0270 (Washington, DC) (office); (212) 753-3163 (New York) (office). *Fax:* (202) 331-0302 (Washington, DC) (office); (212) 223-1276 (New York) (office). *E-mail:* djibouti@nyct.net (office).

OLI, K. P. Sharma; Nepalese politician; b. 22 Feb. 1952; m.; mem. CP of Nepal 1970–, mem. Area Cttee 1970, Dist Cttee 1971, Head, Jhapa Movt Organizing Cttee 1972; imprisoned 1973–87; mem. CP Cen. Cttee 1987, head of Lumbini zone –1990; mem. Standing Cttee and Head of Foreign Dept 1992–; Founder and Pres. Nat. Democratic Youth Fed. 1990; Head, Dept of Publicity and Propaganda 1993; Head, Parl. Affairs 1995–, Deputy Leader 1999–2002, Head, Party School 2004–; mem. House of Reps for Jhapa Dist 1991–2002, 2006–; Minister for Home Affairs, 1994–95; Deputy Prime Minister and Minister for Foreign Affairs 2006–07; led comm. investigating Dasdhunga jeep accident 1993; mem. Presidium of Afro-Asian Peoples' Solidarity Org. (AAPSO) in Nepal 1994–2000, Pres. 2000–. *Address:* Parliament of Nepal, Singha Durbar, Kathmandu, Nepal (office). *Telephone:* 4227480 (office). *Fax:* 4222923 (office). *E-mail:* nparl@ntc.net.np (office). *Website:* www.parliament.gov.np (office).

OLINS, Wallace (Wally), CBE, MA, FCSD; British business executive; *Chairman, Saffron Brand Consultants;* b. 19 Dec. 1930; s. of Alfred Olins and Rachel Olins (née Muscovitch); m. 1st Renate Steinart 1957 (divorced 1989); two s. one d.; m. 2nd Dornie Watts 1990; one d.; ed Highgate School, St Peter's Coll., Oxford; nat. service with army in Germany 1950–51; with S.H. Benson Ltd, London 1954–57; with Benson, India 1957–62; with Caps Design Group, London 1962–65; co-f. Wolff Olins 1965, Chair. –1997; Vice-Pres. SIAD 1982–85; visiting lecturer Design Man. London Business School 1984–89; Visiting Prof. Man. School Imperial Coll., London 1987–89, Lancaster Univ. 1992–, Copenhagen Business School 1993–, Duxx, Centro de Excelencia Empresarial, Mexico 1992–2001, Said Business School, Oxford 2001–; Chair. Design Dimension Educ. Trust 1987–93, Saffron Brand Consultants 2001–; Trustee Design Museum 1988–93; mem. Council RSA 1989–95; mem. Devt Trust Royal Philharmonic Orchestra 1994–2000; Dir Glasgow 1999; Dir Health Educ. Authority 1996–99; mem. Master's Council St Peter's Coll., Oxford 1995–; RSA Bicentenary Medal 2000, D & AD President's Award 2003. *Publications:* The Corporate Personality 1978, The Wolff Olins Guide to Corporate Identity 1983, The Wolff Olins Guide to Design Management 1985, Corporate Identity 1989, International Identity 1995, New Guide to Identity 1996, Trading Identitites 1999, Wally Olins on Brand 2003, numerous articles in design and man. publs. *Leisure interests:* looking at buildings, shopping for books, theatre, old cars. *Address:* 3 Jacob's Well Mews, London, W1U 3DU (office). *Telephone:* (20) 7190-3500 (office). *Fax:* (20) 7190-3501 (office). *E-mail:* wally@wallyolins.com. *Website:* www.wallyolins.com.

OLIPHANT, Patrick (Pat), DHumLitt; American political cartoonist, artist and sculptor; b. 24 July 1935, Adelaide, Australia; copyboy, press artist, Adelaide Advertiser 1953–55, cartoonist 1955–64; cartoonist, Denver Post 1964–75, Washington Star 1975–81; ind. cartoonist syndicated through Universal Press Syndicate 1980–; Hon. LHD (Dartmouth Coll.) 1981; Pulitzer

Prize 1967, Reuben Award 1968, 1972, Nat. Cartoonist of Year Award 1971, 1973, 1974, 1984, 1989, 1990, 1991, Washington Journalism Review 'Best in the Business' Award 1985, Thomas Nast Prize (Germany), Premio Satira Politica of Italy. *Publications:* The Oliphant Book 1969, Four More Years 1973, An Informal Gathering 1978, Oliphant, A Cartoon Collection 1980, The Jellybean Society 1981, Ban This Book 1982, But Seriously Folks 1983, The Year of Living Perilously 1984, Make My Day! 1985, Between Rock and a Hard Place 1986, Up to Here in Alligators 1987, Nothing Basically Wrong 1988, What Those People Need is a Puppy 1989, Oliphant's Presidents: Twenty-Five Years of Caricature 1990, Fashions for the New World Order 1991, Just Say No 1992, Waiting for the Other Shoe to Drop 1994, Off to the Revolution 1995, Maintain the Status Quo 1996, So That's Where They Came From 1997, Are We There Yet? 1999, Now We'll Have to Spray for Politicians! 2000, When We Can't See The Forest For The Bushes 2001, Leadership: Cartoon and Sculptures from the Bush Years 2008. *Address:* Universal Press Syndicate, 4520 Main Street, Suite 700, Kansas City, MO 64112; c/o Susan Conway Gallery, 1214 Thirtieth Street, NW, Washington DC 20007, USA. *Telephone:* (505) 670-6266 (office). *E-mail:* sconwaygly@aol.com (office). *Website:* www.ucomics.com/patoliphant.

OLIVA, L. Jay, PhD; American university president; *Chairman and Executive Producer, Skirball Center for the Performing Arts, New York University;* b. 23 Sept. 1933, Walden, NY; s. of Lawrence Oliva and Catherine Mooney; m. Mary E. Nolan 1961; two s.; ed Manhattan Coll. and Univs. of Freiburg and Paris; Univ. Fellow, Syracuse Univ. 1955–57, Research Assoc. 1957–58, Univ. Research Inst. 1959–60; Instr., Assoc. Prof. of History, New York Univ. (NYU) 1960–69, Prof. of History 1969–, Deputy Vice-Chancellor 1970–75, Vice-Pres. for Academic Planning and Service 1975–77, Vice-Pres. for Academic Affairs 1977–80, Provost and Exec. Vice-Pres. for Academic Affairs 1980–83, Chancellor and Exec. Vice-Pres. for Academic Affairs 1983–91, Pres. 1991–2002, now Pres. Emer., currently Chair. and Exec. Producer Skirball Center for the Performing Arts, NYU; mem. Council on Foreign Relations 1992–2002; other academic and professional appointments: Hon. DHumLi t (Manhattan Coll.) 1987, (Hebrew Union Coll.) 1992; Hon. LLD (St Thomas Aquinas Coll.); Hon. DLit (Univ. Coll. Dublin) 1993; Medal of the Sorbonne 1992. *Publications include:* Misalliance: A Study of French Policy in Russia During the Seven Years War 1964, Russia and the West from Peter to Kruschev (ed.) 1965, Russia in the Era of Peter the Great 1969, Peter the Great (ed.) 1970, Catherine the Great (ed.) 1971. *Leisure interests:* athletics, music, reading. *Address:* Jack H. Skirball Center for the Performing Arts, New York University, Kimmel Center for University Life, 60 Washington Square South, Suite 503, New York, NY 10012, USA (home). *Telephone:* (212) 992-8484 (office). *Website:* www.skirballcenter.nyu.edu (office).

OLIVE, David Ian, CBE, MA, PhD, FRS; British theoretical physicist and academic (retd); *Professor Emeritus of Physics, University of Wales, Swansea;* b. 16 April 1937, Staines; m. Jenifer Tutton 1963; two d.; ed Royal High School, Edinburgh and Univs of Edinburgh and Cambridge; Fellow, Churchill Coll., Cambridge 1963–70; Asst Lecturer, Lecturer, Univ. of Cambridge 1965–71; staff mem. CERN Theory Div. 1971–77; Lecturer, Reader, Blackett Lab. Imperial Coll., London 1977–84, Prof. of Theoretical Physics 1984–92; Research Prof. in Physics, Univ. of Wales, Swansea 1992–2004, Prof. Emer. 2004–; Dirac Medal and Prize (Italy) 1997. *Publications:* The Analytic S-Matrix (co-author) 1965; many scientific papers and articles on the theory of elementary particles and their symmetries. *Leisure interests:* golf, listening to music. *Address:* Department of Physics, University of Wales Swansea, Singleton Park, Swansea, SA2 8PP (office); 4 Havergal Close, Caswell, Swansea, SA3 4RL, Wales (home). *Telephone:* (1792) 295842 (office). *E-mail:* d.i.olive@swansea.ac.uk (office). *Website:* physics.swan.ac.uk (office).

OLIVEIRA, Manoel de; Portuguese film director and screenwriter; b. 11 Dec. 1908, Oporto; s. of Francisco José de Oliveira; m. Maria Isabel Brandão Carvalhais de Oliveira. *Films include:* Douro, Faina Fluvial 1931, Aniki-Bóbó 1942, O Pinto e a Cidade 1956, O Pão 1959, O Acto da Primavera 1963, A Caça 1964, O Passado e Presente 1972, Benilde ou A Virgem Mãe 1975, Amor de Perdição 1979, Francisca 1981, Visita ou Memórias e Confissões 1982, Nice: À propos de Jean Vigo 1983, Lisboa Cultural 1983, Le Soulier de satin 1985, Mon cas 1986, Os Canibais 1988, Non', ou A Vã Glória de Mandar 1990, A Divina Comédia 1991, O Dia do Desespero 1992, Vale Abraão 1993, A Caixa 1994, O Convento 1995, Party 1996, Viagem ao Princípio do Mundo 1997, Inquietude 1998, La Lettre 1999, Palavra e Utopia 2000, Je rentre à la maison 2001, Porto da Minha Infância 2001, O Princípio da Incerteza 2002, Um Filme Falado 2003, O Quinto Império: Ontem Como Hoje 2004, O Espelho Mágico 2005, Belle Toujours 2006, Os Invisíveis 2006. *Address:* c/o Madragoa Filmes, Rua da Palmeira, 6, 1200-313 Lisbon, Portugal. *E-mail:* geral.madragoa@madragoafilmes.com. *Website:* www.madragoafilmes.pt/manoeloliveira.

OLIVER, Jamie, MBE; British chef; b. May 1975; m. Jools Oliver 2000; two d.; ed Westminster Catering Coll.; began cooking at parents' pub/restaurant The Cricketers, Cambridge; fmr Head Pastry Chef, The Neal Street Restaurant; fmr Chef, The River Café; Presenter, The Naked Chef (Optomen TV), Jamie's Kitchen, Jamie's School Dinners (Channel 4 TV UK and internationally) 2005, Jamie at Home 2007, Jamie's Ministry of Food 2008; advertising contract with Sainsbury's Co.; cookery show tour The Happy Days Tour, UK, New Zealand and Australia 2001; designed range of cooking and tableware for Royal Worcester; Consultant Chef, Monte's Restaurant, London; est. restaurant Fifteen, London 2003; Food Ed. GQ magazine (UK), Marie Claire magazine (UK); contrib. to Saturday Times Magazine; British Book Awards Outstanding Achievement Award 2006. *Publications include:* The Naked Chef (three cookery books), Jamie's Kitchen 2002, Jamie's Dinners 2004, Jamie's Italy 2005, Cook With Jamie 2006, Jamie at Home 2007, Jamie's Ministry of Food 2008. *Address:* Fifteen, Westland Place, London, N1 7LP, England (office).

Telephone: (20) 7251-3909 (office). *Fax:* (20) 7251-2749 (office). *Website:* www.jamieoliver.net (office).

OLIVER, Roland Anthony, PhD, FBA; British writer and Africanist; b. 30 March 1923, Srinagar, Kashmir; s. of Douglas Gifford Oliver and Lorimer Janet Donaldson; m. 1st Caroline Linehan 1947 (died 1983); one d.; m. 2nd Suzanne Miers 1990; ed Univ. of Cambridge; Lecturer, SOAS, Univ. of London 1948–49, 1950–57, Reader 1958–63, Prof. of African History 1963–86, Hon. Fellow 1992; organized first confs on history and archaeology of Africa, London Univ. 1953, 1957, 1961; gounder and Ed. Journal of African History 1960–73; Pres. British Inst. in E Africa 1981–93; Chair. Minority Rights Group 1976–92; Distinguished Africanist Award, American African Studies Asscn 1989, African Studies Asscn of the UK 2004. *Publications:* The Missionary Factor in East Africa 1952, Sir Harry Johnston and the Scramble for Africa 1957, The Dawn of African History 1961, Short History of Africa (with J. D. Fage) 1962, History of East Africa (with G. Mathew) 1963, Africa Since 1800 (with A. Atmore) 1967, Africa in the Iron Age (with B. M. Fagan) 1975, The African Middle Ages 1400–1800 (with A. Atmore) 1980, The African Experience 1991, The Realms of Gold 1997, Medieval Africa (with A. Atmore) 2001; Gen. Ed. Cambridge History of Africa (eight vols) 1975–86. *Address:* Frilsham Woodhouse, near Thatcham, Berkshire RG18 9XB, England. *Telephone:* (1635) 201407. *Fax:* (1635) 202716.

OLLIER, Patrick; French politician; *Mayor of Rueil-Malmaison;* b. 17 Dec. 1944, Périgueux, Dordogne; m. (divorced) one s.; pnr, Michèle Alliot-Marie (q.v.); Founding mem. Union des jeunes pour le progrès 1965; participated in presidential campaign of Jacques Chaban-Delmas 1974; attached to Mayor of Rueil-Malmaison (Hauts-de-Seine) 1983–89; Deputy (RPR) for Hautes-Alpes 1988–2002; Mayor of La Salle les Alpes (Hautes-Alpes) 1989–2001; mem. Conseil général, Hautes-Alpes 1992–2001; Deputy (Union pour un Mouvement Populaire) for Hauts-de-Seine, 7è conscription 2002–, Pres. Cttee on Econ. Affairs, the Environment, and Territory, Head of French-Libyan Friendship Group; Mayor of Rueil-Malmaison, Hauts-de-Seine 2004–; Hon. Mem. Rotary-Club of Rueil-Malmaison. *Address:* Assemblée nationale, 126 rue de l'Université, 75355 Paris 07 SP, France (office). *Telephone:* 1-40-63-60-00 (office). *Fax:* 1-45-55-75-23 (office). *E-mail:* infos@patrick-ollier.com (office). *Website:* www.patrick-ollier.com (office).

OLLILA, Esko Juhani, LLM; Finnish bank executive; b. 14 July 1940, Rovaniemi; s. of Heikki Armas Ollila and Lempi Maria Ollila (née Häggman); m. Riitta Leena, née Huhtala 1963; two s.; Man. Dir Rovaniemi Savings Bank 1971–75; Man. Dir and Chair. Bd Regional Devt Fund of Finland 1975–79; mem. Bd Skopbank 1979–83; Minister of Trade and Industry 1982–83; Minister of Finance 1986–87; mem. Bd Bank of Finland 1983–2000; Chair. Finnish Nat. Fund for Research and Devt (SITRA) 1991–95, mem. 1995–; mem. Supervisory Bd Finnish Guarantee Bd 1995–; Chair. Advisory Bd Baltic Investment Fund 1995–; mem. Wise Men Assembly (group promoting cooperation between Finland and Estonia).

OLLILA, Jorma Jaakko, MPolSci, MSc (Econs), MSc (Eng); Finnish business executive; *Chairman, Nokia Corporation; ; Royal Dutch Shell plc;* b. 15 Aug. 1950, Seinäjoki; m. Liisa Annikki (née Metsola); two s. one d.; ed Univ. of Helsinki, London School of Econs, UK and Helsinki Univ. of Tech.; rank of Sr Lt; Account Man., Corporate Bank, Citibank N-A, London UK 1978–80; Account Officer, Citibank Oy 1980–82, mem. Bd of Man. 1983–85; Vice-Pres. Int. Operations, Nokia 1985–86, mem. Group Exec. Bd 1986–, Sr Vice-Pres. Finance 1986–89, Deputy mem. Bd of Dirs 1989–90, Pres. Nokia Mobile Phones 1990–92, Pres. and CEO Nokia 1992–99, Chair. Group Exec. Bd 1992–2006, mem. Bd Nokia Corpn 1995–2006, Chair. and CEO 1999–2006, Chair. 2006–; Chair. Royal Dutch Shell plc 2006–; Chair. Bd MTV Oy 1993–97; mem. Bd Dirs Oy Dipoli Ab 1990–94, ICI PLC 1992–2000, Otava Books and Magazines Group Ltd 1996–, UPM-Kymmene 1997–; Dir (non-exec.) Ford Motor Co. 2000–; mem. Supervisory Bd, Oy Rastor AB 1992–93, Tietotehdas Oy 1992–95, Industrial Mutual Insurance Co., Pohjola Insurance Co. Ltd 1992–97, NKF Holding NV 1992–99, Pension-Varma Mutual Insurance Co. 1993–98, Sampo Insurance Co. Ltd 1993–2000, Merita Bank Ltd (fmr Union Bank of Finland Ltd) 1994–2000; Chair. Nat. Union of Finnish Students 1973–74; mem. Planning Bd for Defence Economy 1992–96; mem. Bd and Exec. Cttee Confed. of Finnish Industries and Employers 1992–2002, Deputy Chair. Bd 1995–2002; Chair. Supervisory Bd Finnish Foreign Trade Asscn 1993–98; Chair. Bd Dirs and Supervisory Bd Finnish Business and Policy Forum 2004–, Research Inst. of the Finnish Economy 2004–; Vice-Chair. Bd, Finnish Section, Int. Chamber of Commerce 1993–97, Advisory Cttee Helsinki Univ. of Tech. 1993–95 (Chair. 1996–); mem. Bd Econ. Information Bureau 1993–97; mem. Exec. Bd Asscn for the Finnish Cultural Foundation 1993–99; mem. Council, Centre for Finnish Business and Policy Studies 1993–2001, Helsinki School of Econs and Business Admin 1993–98; mem. Supervisory Bd Foundation for Pediatric Research 1993–98, WWF Finland 1995–97; mem. Science and Tech. Policy Council of Finland 1993–2002; mem. Council of Supervisors, Research Institute of the Finnish Economy 1993–2000; mem. Dean's Council, John F. Kennedy School of Govt, Harvard Tech. 1995–; Overseas Advisory Trustee The American-Scandinavian Foundation 1994–; mem. Int. Bd United World Coll. 1995–; mem. European Round Table of Industrialists 1997–, GBDe Business Steering Cttee 1999–; Hon. Citizen of Beijing 2002; Hon. Fellow, LSE 2003; Hon. mem. IEEE 2003; Kt, Order of White Rose of Finland, First Class 1991; Commdr, Order of Orange-Nassau 1995, Order of White Star (Estonia) 1995, Officer's Cross, Order of Merit (Hungary) 1996; Commdr's Cross, Order of Merit (Germany) 1997, Order of Merit (Poland) 1999; Hon. PhD (Helsinki) 1995; Hon. DSc (Helsinki Univ. of Tech.) 1998. *Address:* Nokia Corporation, Keilalahdentie 4, Espoo 00045, Finland (office); Royal Dutch Shell plc, Carel van Bylandtlaan 30, 2596 HR The Hague, Netherlands (office). *Telephone:* 7180-08000 (Finland) (office); (70)

3779111 (Netherlands) (office). *Fax:* 7180-38226 (Finland) (office); (70) 3773115 (Netherlands) (office). *Website:* www.nokia.com (office); www.shell.com (office).

OLMERT, Ehud, BA, LLB; Israeli politician and lawyer; b. 1945, Binyamina; m.; four c.; ed Hebrew Univ. of Jerusalem; served in Israeli Defence Force (IDF) as combat infantry unit officer; mil. corresp. for IDF journal *Bamachane;* mem. Likud Party; mem. Knesset 1973–98, 2003–, mem. Foreign Affairs and Security Cttee 1981–88; Minister without Portfolio responsible for Minority Affairs 1988–90; Minister of Health 1990–92; Mayor of Jerusalem 1993–2003; Vice-Prime Minister and Minister of Industry, Trade, Labor and Communications 2003–05, Vice-Premier and Minister of Finance 2005–06; left Likud party to join newly formed Kadima party Dec. 2005; Acting Chair. of Kadima Jan.–April 2006, Chair. April 2006–08; Acting Prime Minister Jan.–April 2006, Prime Minister and Minister for Social Affairs April 2006–08 (resgnd), Minister of Finance April–July 2007. *Address:* Kadima, Petach Tikva, Tel-Aviv, Israel. *Telephone:* 3-9788000 (office). *Fax:* 3-9788020 (office). *Website:* www.kadima.org.il (office).

OLMI, Ermanno; Italian film director; b. 24 July 1931, Bergamo; fmr clerk, Edison-Volta electric plant; later dir and producer sponsored documentary films; made first feature film 1959, f. production co. 22 December SpA 1961 and helped found Hypothesis Cinema. *Films include:* Il Tempo si è Fermato 1959, Il Posto 1961, I Fidanzati 1963, E Venne un Uomo 1965, Un Certo Giorno 1969, I Recuperanti 1970, Durante l'Estate 1971, La Circostanza 1974, L'Albero degli Zoccoli (Palme d'Or, Cannes) 1978, Legend of a Holy Drinker 1988, Il Segreto Del Bosco Vecchio, The Profession of Arms 2001, Tickets (with others) 2005.

OLOVSSON, Ivar (Olov Göte), DrSc; Swedish chemist and academic; *Professor Emeritus of Inorganic Chemistry, University of Uppsala;* b. 15 Oct. 1928, Rödön; s. of Erik Olovsson and Anna Andersson; m. Kristina Jonsson 1950; three s. one d.; ed Univ. of Uppsala; Teaching Asst, Univ. of Uppsala 1953–57, Asst Prof. 1961–64, Assoc. Prof. 1965–69, Prof. of Inorganic Chem. 1969–93, Prof. Emer. 1993–; Research Assoc., Univ. of Calif., Berkeley 1957–59, 1964–65, Visiting Miller Prof. 2002; Guest Prof., Lab. de Cristallographie, Grenoble 1977–78, Univ. of Konstanz 1982–83, 1999; mem. Royal Soc. of Sciences 1970 (Pres. 1996–97), Royal Acad. of Sciences of Sweden 1974; Kt of Northern Star 1975; Chevalier des Palmes académiques 1981; Gold Medal, Royal Acad. of Sciences of Sweden 1961, Gold Medal, Swedish Chem. Soc. 1965, María Sklodowska-Curie Medal, Polish Chem. Soc. 2003. *Publications:* about 90 scientific papers, mainly in field of structural chem. *Leisure interests:* outdoor life, mountaineering, skiing, music. *Address:* Ångström Laboratory, Materials Chemistry, PO Box 538, 751 21 Uppsala (office); Murklevägen 27, 756 46 Uppsala, Sweden (home). *Telephone:* (18) 471-37-21 (office); (18) 30-22-76 (home). *Fax:* (18) 51-35-48 (office). *E-mail:* ivar.olovsson@mkem.uu.se (office). *Website:* www.mkem.uu.se (office).

OLSEN, Olaf, PhD; Danish archaeologist, historian and fmr museum director; b. 7 June 1928, Copenhagen; s. of the late Prof. Albert Olsen and of Agnete Bing; m. 1st Jean Catherine Dennistoun Sword; one s; m. 2nd Rikke Agnete Clausen 1971; ed Copenhagen Univ.; Asst, Medieval Dept, Nat. Museum 1950–58, Asst Keeper 1958–71, State Antiquary and Dir Nat. Museum 1981–95; Prof. of Medieval Archaeology, Århus Univ. 1971–81; Dir Hielmstierne-Rosencrone Foundation 1979–; Vice-Pres. Det kgl. nordiske Oldskriftselskab 1981–95, Royal Danish Acad. of Sciences and Letters 1983–89; Founding mem. Academia Europaea 1988; dir numerous archaeological excavations, mainly of Viking ships and fortresses and medieval churches and monasteries; Hon. Fellow, Soc. of Antiquaries; Dr hc (St Petersburg Univ.) 1994; GEC Gad Foundation Prize 1966, 1992, Hartmann Prize 1995, Westerby Prize 2002. *Publications:* numerous books and papers on history and medieval archaeology. *Address:* Strevelshovedvej 2, Alrø, 8300 Odder, Denmark (home). *Telephone:* 86-55-21-28 (home). *Fax:* 86-55-21-28 (home). *E-mail:* olaf.olsen@rikkeslyst.dk (home).

OLSEN, Ole Wøhlers; Danish diplomatist and administrator; *Ambassador to Tunisia;* fmr Amb. to Saudi Arabia, Amb. to Syria 1999–2003, to Tunisia 2007–; Regional Co-ordinator of Basra Province 2003–07. *Address:* Embassy of Denmark, 5 rue de Mauritanie, BP 254, Belvédère, 1002, Tunis, Tunisia (office). *Telephone:* (71) 792-600 (office). *Fax:* (71) 790-797 (office). *E-mail:* dannebrog@planet.tn (office); oleols@um.dk (office).

OLSON, Lyndon L., Jr; American insurance executive, politician and diplomatist; *Consultant, Citigroup Inc.;* b. 7 March 1947, Waco, Texas; m. Kay Woodward Olson 1982; ed Baylor Univ., Baylor Law School, Tex.; mem. Texas State House of Reps 1973–78; Chair. Cttee on Higher Educ., House Standing Cttee on Local Govt; Chair. Texas State Bd of Insurance 1979–81, 1983–87; fmr. CEO Nat. Group of Insurance Cos 1987; helped negotiate US–Israeli Free Trade Agreement; led Trade Del. on Financial Services to Russia and China 1985; Amb. to Sweden 1997–2001; currently consultant Citigroup Inc.; Pres. Nat. Asscn of Insurance Commrs 1982; Pres. and CEO Travellers Insurance Holdings Inc. 1990–98, Assoc. Madison Cos Inc.; Elder Cen. Pres. Church, Texas; Gates of Jerusalem Award (Israel), Baylor Young Outstanding Alumni Award, Distinguished Public Official (Texas Medical Asscn). *Address:* Citigroup Inc., 399 Park Avenue, New York, NY 10043, USA (office). *Telephone:* (212) 559-1000 (office). *Fax:* (212) 793-3946 (office). *Website:* www.citigroup.com (office).

OLSON, Maynard V., BS, PhD; American chemist, geneticist and academic; *Professor of Genome Sciences and of Medicine and Adjunct Professor of Computer Science and Engineering, University of Washington;* ed California Inst. of Tech., Stanford Univ.; chemist at Dartmouth Coll. 1970–74; Visiting Scholar and Research Assoc., Dept of Genetics, Univ. of Washington 1974–79, rejoined Dept of Molecular Biotechnology 1992–, currently Prof. of Genome Sciences and of Medicine and Adjunct Prof. of Computer Science and Eng; joined faculty, Washington Univ. in St Louis 1979; fmr Investigator, Howard Hughes Medical Inst.; mem. NAS 1994–; Genetics Soc. of America Medal 1992, Gairdner Foundation Int. Award 2002, Gruber Genetics Prize, The Peter and Patricia Gruber Foundation 2007. *Achievements include:* one of main architects of Human Genome Project; created a method to break the yeast genome into manageable pieces for analysis; his pioneering work paved way for analysis of entire human genome. *Publications:* numerous scientific papers in professional journals. *Address:* Fluke Hall 316, University of Washington, Box 352145, Seattle, WA 98195, USA (office). *Telephone:* (206) 685-7346 (office). *Fax:* (206) 543-0754 (office). *E-mail:* mvo@u.washington.edu (office). *Website:* www.genome.washington.edu/UWGC (office).

OLSON, Peter, AB, MBA, JD; American publishing executive; b. 1 May 1950, Chicago, Ill.; m. 1st (divorced); three c.; m. 2nd Candice Carpenter 2001; ed Harvard Univ., Cambridge, Mass, Harvard Business School, Harvard Law School; Assoc. Attorney, Baker & Botts (law firm), Washington, DC 1976–77; Assoc. Attorney, Hamada & Matsumoto (law firm), Tokyo, Japan 1977–79; Officer, Int. Div. Dresdner Bank, Frankfurt am Main, Germany 1979–81, Deputy Man. Corp. Business Dept, Tokyo Br. 1981–84, Man. Credit Dept, Tokyo Br. 1984–87, Vice-Pres. Planning Dept, Treasury Div., Frankfurt 1987–88; Man. Bertelsmann AG Corp. Office, Gütersloh, Germany 1988–89; Sr Vice-Pres. Doubleday Book & Music Clubs, Inc., Garden City, NY, USA 1989–90, Pres. Bertelsmann, Inc., New York, USA 1990–92; Exec. Vice-Pres. and Chief Financial Officer Bantam Doubleday Dell Publishing Group, New York 1992–94; Chair. and CEO Bertelsmann Book Group North America, New York 1994–98 (mem. Bertelsmann Book AG Exec. Bd); Chair. and CEO Random House, Inc., New York 1998–2008 (mem. Bertelsmann Book AG Exec. Bd), mem. Bd Bertelsmann AG 2001–; Detur Prize; Phi Beta Kappa. *Leisure interest:* reading. *Address:* c/o Random House, Inc., 1745 Broadway, New York, NY 10019, USA (office).

OLSSON, Christian; Swedish athlete; b. 25 Jan. 1980, Gothenburg; competes in triple jump; Programme Seller, World Championships, Gothenburg Stadium 1995; coached by Viljo Nousiainen 1995–99, Yannick Tregaro 1999–; professional debut 1999; equalled world record at World Indoor Championships 2004; winner Gold Medal for triple jump, Grand Prix, Athens 2002, World Athletics Final, St Denis 2002, Monaco 2003, World Championships, St Denis 2003, World Indoor Championships, Birmingham 2003, Budapest 2004, Super Grand Prix, Gateshead 2003, 2004, Stockholm 2003, 2004, Olympic Games, Athens 2004, Golden League, Monaco 2002, Bergen 2004, Rome 2004, Zurich 2004, St Denis 2004; winner Silver Medal for triple jump, Grand Prix, Stockholm 2001, 2002, Golden League, Oslo 2002, St Denis 2002, Brussels 2002, World Championships, Edmonton 2003; winner Bronze Medal for triple jump, Golden League, Zurich 2002; mem. Örgryte IS Club; Best Sports Achievement of the Year, Swedish Sports Awards 2001, European Athletic Asscn Athlete of the Year 2003. *Leisure interests:* cars, reading, computer games, music. *Address:* c/o Svenska Friidrottsförbundet, Box 11, 171 18 Solna, Sweden (office).

OLSSON, Curt G., BScEcon; Swedish banker; b. 20 Aug. 1927, Mjällby; s. of N. E. Olsson and Anna Olsson (née Nilsson); m. Asta Olsson 1954; two d.; Man. Dir Swedish Bank Giro Centre 1959; Deputy Man. and Head of Marketing, Skandinaviska Banken, Stockholm 1964, Man. and Head of Cen. Man. Group 1966, Man. Dir (Stockholm Group) 1970; Man. Dir Skandinaviska Enskilda Banken, Stockholm Group 1972; Man. Dir and Chief Exec. Head Office, Stockholm 1976–82, 1st Deputy Chair. of Bd 1982–84, Chair. 1984–96; mem. Royal Swedish Acad. of Eng Sciences; Consul Gen. hc for Finland 1990–99; Kt, Order of Vasa; Commdr Royal Norwegian Order of Merit, Order of the Lion of Finland; Hon. DEcon; HM King Carl XVI Gustaf's Gold Medal. *Address:* c/o Skandinaviska Enskilda Banken, Kungsträdgårdsgt. 8, 106 40 Stockholm, Sweden.

OLSSON, Hans-Olov, MBA; Swedish automobile industry executive; *Senior Vice-President and Chief Marketing Officer, Ford Motor Company;* b. 1941, Amal; m. Monica Olsson; two d.; ed Univ. of Gothenburg, Harvard Univ., Vevey, Switzerland; joined Volvo Corpn 1966, systems engineer responsible for production control, logistics and procurement 1966–69, Man. of Material and Production Control 1969–72, Production Man. of Final Ass. Plant, Volvo Truck Corpn, Gothenburg 1972–74, Project Man., Chesapeake Plant, Volvo Car Corpn, VA 1974–77, Gen. Plant Man., Component Supply, Volvo Daisland Plant 1977–80, Dir of Area Overseas, Global Sales and Marketing Div. 1984–87, Vice-Pres. of Div. 1987–89, est. Volvo Business Univ. 1989, Pres. of Volvo Japan, Tokyo 1990–96, Pres. of Volvo Cars Market Area Europe, Brussels, Belgium 1996–98, Pres. and CEO Volvo Cars N America, Rockleigh, NJ 1998–2000, Pres. and CEO Volvo Car Corpn 2000, Chair. of Bd –2005, Chair. (non-exec.) 2005–; Sr Vice-Pres. and Chief Marketing Officer, Ford Motor Co. 2005–. *Leisure interests:* jogging, golf, gardening, skiing. *Address:* Ford Motor Company, 1 American Road, Dearborn, MI 48126-2798, USA (office). *Telephone:* (313) 322-3000 (office). *Fax:* (313) 845-6073 (office). *Website:* www.ford.com (office).

OLSSON, Karl Erik; Swedish politician and farmer; *Member, Executive Board, Global Crop Diversity Trust, Food and Agriculture Organization, Rome;* b. 23 Feb. 1938, Häglinge, Kristianstad; m. Sonja Olsson; three c.; ed Colls of Agric.; farmer, Nygård Farm 1963–; Chair. Nat. Centre Party Youth League 1971–74; mem. Centre Party Nat. Bd 1981–92, Asst Vice-Chair. 1986–87, Vice-Chair. 1987–92; mem. Parl. 1976–79, 1985–95; mem. Bd Nuclear Power Inspectorate 1977–91, Foundation for the Promotion of Literature 1980–91, Swedish Univ. of Agric. Sciences 1986–91; Chair. Standing Cttee on Agric. 1985–91; Minister of Agric. 1991–94; MEP 1995–2004; mem. European Liberal, Democrat and Reform Party Group (ELDR), Bureau European Parl., Cttee on Agric. and Rural Devt, Cttee on

Fisheries, Substitute Cttee on Environment, Public Health and Consumer Policy, mem. Del. to EU–Czech Repub. Jt Parl. Cttee, Substitute Del. to EU–Bulgaria Jt Parl. Cttee; Chair. Häglinge Church Council, Swedish Mutual Guarantee Asscn 2004–; mem. ELDR Group Bureau; mem. Royal Swedish Acad. for Agric. and Forestry 1999–; mem. Exec. Bd Global Crop Diversity Trust, FAO, Rome; Chair. Swedish Asscn for Sr Citicens 2008–; Hon. DrAgr. *Publications:* Bonde i lokalsamhället 1973, Tankar 1978, Naturresurserna och framtiden 1984, Sverige behöver en Livskraftig Landsbygd 1985, Europeiskt jordbruk i battre takt med naturen 1998, Jordbruk, Handel och Utreckling 2006. *Address:* Nygård 2116, 280 10 Sösdala, Sweden (home). *Telephone:* (451) 63091 (home). *Fax:* (451) 63275 (home). *E-mail:* karl.erik.olsson@hotmail.com (home). *Website:* www.haglingenygard.se (home).

OLSZEWSKI, Jan Ferdynand; Polish politician and lawyer; *Leader, Movement for the Reconstruction of Poland;* b. 20 Aug. 1930, Warsaw; m.; ed Warsaw Univ.; mem. underground Boy Scouts WWII; Research Asst Legal Sciences Dept Polish Acad. of Sciences 1954–56; journalist Po prostu 1956–57; banned from working as a journalist 1957; mem. Crooked Circle Club 1956–62; Trial Lawyer 1962–68; suspended from the Bar by Justice Minister for defending students involved in anti-Communist demonstrations 1968; returned to work as Attorney 1970; Defence Counsel for anti-Communist Ruch Organization 1972; Co-Founder, Leader Polish Independence Alliance 1975–80; Co-Founder Workers' Defence Cttee (KOR) 1976–77; drafted (jtly) Statute of the Free Trade Union of Coast Workers 1980; Adviser Solidarity Nat. Comm. 1980–; Legal Adviser Secretariat of Polish Episcopate; Plenipotentiary to family of Father Jerzy Popiełuszko during trial of his murderers; Rep. Solidarity opposition in sub-comm. on legal and judicial reform 1989; mem. Pres. Lech Wałęsa's Advisory Cttee Jan.–Nov. 1991; Deputy to Sejm (Parl.) 1991–93, 1997–; Prime Minister of Poland 1991–92; Co-founder and Pres. Movt for the Repub. 1992–94; Co-Founder and Leader Movt for the Reconstruction of Poland (Ruchu Odbudowy Polski—ROP) 1995–; Leader Homeland Patriotic Movt 1997; Founder-mem. Civic Inst. and Atlantic Club. *Address:* Ruchu Odbudowy Polski, ul. Piękna 22 Lok. 7, 00-549 Warsaw, Poland. *Telephone:* (22) 6253282 (office). *Fax:* (22) 6253501 (office). *E-mail:* jan.olszewski@sejm.gov.pl (office). *Website:* www.rop.sky.pl (office).

OLTEANU, Bogdan, MBA; Romanian politician; *Chairman, Camera Deputaţilor (Chamber of Deputies);* b. 29 Oct. 1971, Bucharest; m.; two c.; ed Univ. of Bucharest, Romanian Banking Inst. and City Univ., Seattle, USA; mem. Nat. Liberal Party (Partidul Naţional Liberal—PNL) 1991–, Pres. Youth Section 1998–2000, Alt. mem. Standing Bureau 2001–02, Chair. Court of Honour and Arbitration 2002–; Sec.-Gen. Org. of Liberal Students 1993–96; Adviser to State Minister, Ministry of Industry and Commerce 1997; lawyer, Bogdan Olteanu Law Firm 1998–; Govt Minister responsible for relations with Parl. 2004–06; mem. Camera Deputaţilor (Chamber of Deputies) 2004–, Chair. 2007–, mem. Culture, Arts, Mass Information Means Cttee (Chair. 2004–05) 2004–06, Investigation of Abuses, Corrupt Practices and Petitions Cttee 2006–07, Defence, Public Order and Nat. Security Cttee 2007–. *Address:* Office of the Chairman, 050563 Bucharest 5, Palatul Parlamentului, Str. Izvor 2–4, Romania (office). *Telephone:* (21) 4021444 (office). *Fax:* (21) 4022149 (office). *E-mail:* bogdan.olteanu@cdep.ro (office). *Website:* www.cdep.ro (office).

OLVASÓ, Árpád, DipEng, PhD, MBA; Hungarian business executive; *CEO and Deputy Chairman, TVK Rt.;* b. 18 Aug. 1959; m.; two c.; ed Veszprém Chemical Univ., SZÁMALK (School of Econ. Studies), Budapest, Coll. of Petroleum and Energy Studies, Brunel Univ., UK; joined Dunai Kőolajipari Vállalat 1983, various posts including Plant Engineer, Operator, Shift Man., Asst Plant Man. 1983–92; Plant Man. and later Project Man., MOL Rt. Dunai Finomító 1992–95; Sr Consultant and Project Man., Oracle Hungary 1995–97; Man., Pnr Relations, MOL Group 1997, Head of Chemical Div. 1999, also Dir, Chemical Portfolio Man. 2001, Dir, Tiszai Vegyi Kombinát (TVK) 2000–, Chair. 2000–02, CEO and Deputy Chair. 2003–; mem. Bd, Hungarian Chemical Asscn 1997– (Chair. 2004–). *Address:* Tiszai Vegyi Kombinát (TVK), TVK Industrial Site, 3581 Tiszaújváros, Hungary (office). *Telephone:* (49) 522-222 (office). *Fax:* (49) 5221-322 (office). *E-mail:* tvkinfo@tvk.hu (office). *Website:* www.tvk.hu (office).

OLVER, Richard (Dick) L., BCE, FREng; British engineer and business executive; *Non-Executive Chairman, BAE Systems plc;* b. 1947; m.; two d.; joined British Petroleum (BP) 1973, apptd Vice-Pres. BP Pipelines Inc., BP North America 1979, Div. Man. of Corp. Planning 1985, Gen. Man. Gas, BP Exploration Europe 1988, Chief of Staff to Chair., Head of Corp. Strategy 1990, CEO BP Exploration USA 1992, Deputy CEO BP Exploration 1995, CEO BP Exploration and Production Div. 1998–2002, apptd Deputy Group CEO BP plc 2003–04; Chair. (non-exec.) BAE Systems plc 2004–; Dir (non-exec.) Thomson Reuters PLC 1997–, mem. Remuneration Cttee; Guardian of New Hall School; mem. Trilateral Comm.; Fellow, Royal Acad. of Eng 2005– (mem. Council); mem. ICE; Hon. DSc (City Univ.) 2004, (Cranfield Univ.) 2006. *Leisure interests:* grandchildren, education, sailing, skiing, ballet, fine arts. *Address:* BAE Systems plc, 6 Carlton Gardens, London, SW1Y 5AD, England (office). *Telephone:* (1252) 373232 (office). *Fax:* (1252) 383000 (office). *E-mail:* info@baesystems.com (office). *Website:* www.baesystems.com (office).

O'MAHONY, W. I. (Liam), BE, BL, MBA, FIEI; Irish business executive; *Chairman, Smurfit Kappa Group plc;* b. 1947; began career as civil engineer in Repub. of Ireland and UK; joined CRH plc 1971, worked in Middle E, Africa and USA for CRH Cos, sr man. positions include COO of US Operations, Man.-Dir Repub. of Ireland and UK Group Cos 1991–94, mem. Bd of Dirs 1992–, Chief Exec. Oldcastle Inc., USA 1994–2000, Dir 2000–, Group Chief Exec. 2000–08; mem. Bd of Dirs Smurfit Kappa Group plc 2007–, Chair. 2008–; mem. The Irish Man. Inst. Council, Harvard Business School European Advisory Bd, USA. *Address:* Smurfit Kappa Group Beech Hill, Clonskeagh, Dublin 4, Ireland (office). *Telephone:* (1) 202 7000 (office). *Website:* www.smurfitkappa.com (office).

O'MALLEY, Bert W., MD; American biologist and academic; *Chair, Department of Molecular and Cellular Biology, Baylor College of Medicine;* b. Pittsburgh; ed Univ. of Pittsburgh School of Medicine; Resident, Duke Univ. 1963–65; Clinical Assoc., NIH, Bethesda, Md 1965–67, Head of Molecular Biology Section 1967–69; Luscious Birch Prof. and Dir Reproductive Biology Center, Vanderbilt Univ. 1969–73; Tom Thompson Distinguished Service Prof. of Molecular and Cellular Biology, Baylor Coll. of Medicine 1973–, also Chair. Dept of Molecular and Cellular Biology; Fellow AAAS, American Acad. of Arts and Sciences, American Acad. of Microbiology; mem. NAS, Inst. of Medicine, Endocrine Soc. (Pres. 1985); several hon. doctorates (Karolinska Inst., New York Univ., Nat. Univ. of Ireland, Univ. of Maryland); Ernst Oppenheimer Award, British Endocrine Soc. Award, Carl G. Hartman Award 2007, Nat. Medal of Science 2007. *Publications:* more than 600 publs; holder of 19 patents. *Address:* Baylor College of Medicine, Interdepartmental Program in Cell and Molecular Biology, One Baylor Plaza, Room N204Q, Houston, TX 77030, USA (office). *Telephone:* (713) 798-6205 (office). *Fax:* (713) 798-5599 (office). *E-mail:* berto@bcm.edu (office). *Website:* www.bcm.edu (office).

O'MALLEY, Desmond Joseph, BCL; Irish politician, solicitor and banker; *Alternate Director for Denmark, Ireland, Lithuania and Macedonia, European Bank for Reconstruction and Development;* b. 2 Feb. 1939, Limerick; s. of Desmond J. O'Malley and Una O'Malley; m. Patricia McAleer 1965; two s. four d.; ed Crescent Coll., Limerick, Nat. Univ. of Ireland; practised as solicitor 1962; mem. Dáil (House of Reps) for Limerick East 1968–2002; mem. Limerick Corpn 1974–77; Parl. Sec. to Taoiseach (Prime Minister) and to Minister for Defence 1969–70; Minister for Justice 1970–73; Opposition Spokesman on Health 1973–75, on Industry and Commerce 1975–77; Minister for Industry and Commerce 1977–81, 1989–92, for Energy 1977–79; Opposition Spokesman on Industry and Commerce 1981–82; Minister for Trade, Commerce and Tourism 1982; Opposition Spokesman on Energy 1983–84; fmrly Fianna Fáil (expelled 1984); Co-Founder and Leader of Progressive Democrats Party 1985–93; Chair. Foreign Affairs Cttee, Irish Parl. 1997–2002; Alt. Dir for Denmark, Ireland, Lithuania and Macedonia, EBRD 2003–; Hon. LLD (Univ. of Limerick) 2003. *Leisure interests:* golf, horse racing. *Address:* European Bank for Reconstruction and Development, 1 Exchange Square, London, EC2A 2JN, England (office). *Telephone:* (20) 7338-6508 (office). *Fax:* (20) 7338-6489 (office). *E-mail:* omalleyd@ebrd.com (home). *Website:* www.ebrd.com (office).

O'MALLEY, Martin Joseph, JD; American lawyer, politician and state official; *Governor of Maryland;* b. 18 Jan. 1963, Washington, DC; m. Catherine Curran (Katie) O'Malley 1990; two s. two d.; ed Gonzaga Coll. High School, Catholic Univ. of America, Univ. of Maryland School of Law; worked for Gary Hart for President campaign; named by US Congresswoman Barbara Mikulski as her state field dir for her primary and gen. election campaigns for US Senate 1986, served as Legis. Fellow in Senator Mikulski's office 1987–88; Asst State's Attorney for City of Baltimore 1988–90; cand. for Maryland State Senate in 43rd Dist 1990; mem. Baltimore City Council for 3rd Dist 1991–99, served as Chair. Legis. Investigations Cttee, Taxation and Finance Cttee; Mayor of Baltimore 1999–2006; Gov. of Maryland 2007–; Democrat; named by Esquire Magazine "The Best Young Mayor in the Country" 2002, named by Time Magazine one of America's "Top 5 Big City Mayors" 2005, named by Business Week Magazine Online as one of five "New Faces" in the Democratic Party 2005. *Film:* appeared as himself, then-Mayor of Baltimore City, in film Ladder 49. *Address:* Office of the Governor, State House, Annapolis, MD 21401-1925, USA (office). *Telephone:* (410) 974-3901 (office). *Fax:* (410) 974-3275 (office). *Website:* www.gov.state.md.us (office); www.martinomalley.com.

O'MALLEY, The Most Rev. Sean P.; American ecclesiastic; *Archbishop of Boston;* b. 29 June 1944, Cleveland, OH; ordained priest 1970; mem. Capuchin Order; ordained bishop 1984; apptd co-adjutator Bishop of the Diocese of St Thomas in VI 1984; apptd diocesan bishop of the Caribbean diocese 1985; Bishop of Fall River, Mass 1992–2002; Bishop of Palm Beach, Fla 2002–03; Archbishop of Boston 2003–. *Address:* Cardinal's Residence, 2121 Commonwealth Avenue, Boston, MA 02135-3192, USA (office). *Telephone:* (617) 782-2544 (office). *Fax:* (617) 782-8358 (office). *Website:* www.rcab.org (office).

OMAND, Sir David Bruce, Kt, KCB, GCB, BA; British civil servant (retd); b. 15 April 1947, Glasgow, Scotland; s. of the late J. Bruce Omand and Esther Omand; m. Elizabeth Wales 1971; one s. one d.; ed Glasgow Acad., Corpus Christi Coll., Cambridge; Asst Prin., Ministry of Defence 1970, Pvt. Sec. to Chief Exec. (Procurement Exec.) 1973, Asst Pvt. Sec. to Sec. of State 1973–75, 1979–80, Prin. 1975, Asst Sec. 1981, Pvt. Sec. to Sec. of State 1981–82; Asst UnderSec. of State (Man. Strategy) 1988–91, Deputy UnderSec. of State (Policy) Ministry of Defence 1993–96, Dir Govt Communications HQ 1996–97; Perm. UnderSec. of State Home Office 1998–2001; Defence Counsellor FCO UK Del. to NATO, Brussels 1985–88; Chair. Centre for Man. and Policy Studies, Cabinet Office 2001–02, Perm. Sec. Cabinet Office, also Security and Intelligence Co-ordinator 2002–05 (retd); Visiting Prof., King's Coll. London.2005–; Deputy Chair. Windsor Leadership Trust; mem. Bd The Natural History Museum 2006–; British Soc. for History and Math. Prize 2003. *Leisure interests:* opera, walking. *Address:* c/o Windsor Leadership Trust, Gainsborough House, 59-60 Thames Street, Windsor, Berks., SL4 1TX, England (office).

OMAR, Dato Abu Hassan Bin Haj, MA; Malaysian politician; b. 15 Sept. 1940, Bukit Belimbing, Kuala Selangor; m. Datin Wan Noor bint Haj Daud; five c.; ed Univ. of Hull; fmr Deputy State Sec. State of Selangor and Deputy Sec.-Gen. Ministry of Land and Fed. Devt; mem. Parl. 1978–; Parl. Sec.

Ministry of Commerce and Industry 1978–80; Deputy Minister of Defence 1980–81, of Transport 1981–84; Minister of Welfare Services 1984–86, of Fed. Territory 1986–87, of Foreign Affairs 1987–91, of Domestic Trade and Consumer Affairs 1991–97; Menteri Besar of Selangor 1997–2000; mem. (for Permatang) Selangor State Ass. 1997–; mem. UMNO Supreme Council 1978–; Hon. DSc; recipient of several awards. *Leisure interests:* gardening, photography. *Address:* c/o Ministry of Domestic Trade and Consumer Affairs, Tingat 19, 22–24 and 40, Menara Maybank, 100 Jalan Tun Perak, 50050 Kuala Lumpur, Malaysia.

OMAR, Chamassi Said; Comoran politician; fmr naval officer; Prime Minister of Comoros 1998–99.

OMAR, Ibrahim Amin, BA; Egyptian civil servant; b. 1 Dec. 1936, Kfr El-Moseillha; s. of Amin Ebraim Omar; m. Afaf Ghazy 1971; three d.; ed Cairo Univ.; mem. Nat. Guards 1953; Gen. Sec. War Civilian's Gen. Cttee 1969; Bd mem. Menufia Governorate 1967, Giza Prov. Council 1981; served as Mayor Hurghada, Safaga, Al-Areish, Al-Salam 1981–96; Head, Safag Port 1982, Areesh City 1990; Sec.-Gen. Al Aswan Governorate 1995–; Sec., Head Cttee of Interior Front 1969; mem. Nat. Democratic Party 1981; mem. Red Sea Ports Corpn Council 1983–84; Head of Salam District, Nasser suburb 1992; State Prize, Science Day 1957, Gen. Syndicate of Engineers Medal for efforts in reconstructing Sinai and other awards. *Publication:* Planning and Developing Education Policy in Egypt. *Leisure interests:* reading, swimming, shooting. *Address:* 28 Abdel Aziz Fahmay Street, Kafr El Mosselha, Menufia; Shebin El-Kom, POB 173, Menofiya Governorate, Egypt (home). *Telephone:* 329944.

OMAR, Mullah Mohammad; Afghan fmr guerrilla leader and politician; b. 1959, Uruzgan Prov.; m. Guljana Omar 1995; two other wives; five c. (one s. died 2001); studied in several Islamic schools; joined jihad (Islamic holy war) against Soviet occupation in 1980s, became a deputy chief commdr Mujahidin guerrilla movt fighting Soviet occupation forces; helped form, recruit for and consolidate the Taliban regime (with Osama bin Laden q.v.) 1994; declared Afghanistan a 'complete' Islamic State (Islamic Emirate of Afghanistan); Leader Taliban-apptd Interim Council of Ministers 1996–2001, given title Emir al-Mo'menein (Commdr of the Faithful); went into hiding during US-led mil. action against Taliban and al-Qa'ida targets in Afghanistan, following suspected al-Qa'ida terrorist attacks in USA Sept. 2001.

OMAR, Tan Sri Dato' Napsiah binti, MSc; Malaysian politician and regional organization official; b. 21 April 1943; m. (husband deceased); ed Australian Nat. Univ., Canberra and Cornell Univ., New York; Admin. Officer, Fed. Land Devt Authority, Kuala Lumpur 1967–69; started Women's and Family Devt Programme 1967; lecturer, Agricultural Coll. Malaya Serdang 1972; Co-ordinator, Food Tech., Home and Food Tech. Div. Agricultural Univ. 1972–73, Deputy Head, Dept of Home Tech. 1973–76, Head, Dept of Human Devt Studies 1978–80, Warden, Fourth Residential Coll. 1974–82; Assoc. Prof. Dept of Human Devt Studies 1981; Deputy Minister of Housing and Local Govt 1981–87; Minister of Public Enterprises 1988–90; mem. Barisan Nasional—UMNO party, mem. Exec. Cttee UMNO Women Malaysia and Chair. of Unity Bureau, UMNO Malaysia 1987–90; Chair. Econ. Bureau, UMNO 1986–88; Senator; Treas. Asian Forum of Parliamentarians on Population and Devt (AFPPD). *Address:* c/o United Malays National Organization (Pertubuhan Kebangsaan Melayu Bersatu), Menara Dato' Onn, 38th Floor, Jalan Tun Ismail, 50480 Kuala Lumpur, Malaysia. *Telephone:* (3) 40429511. *Fax:* (3) 40412358. *E-mail:* email@umno.net.my. *Website:* www.umno-online.com.

O'MEARA, Mark Francis; American professional golfer; b. 13 Jan. 1957, Goldsboro, NC; m. Alicia O'Meara; one s. one d.; ed Long Beach State Univ.; professional golfer 1980–; mem. Ryder Cup team 1985, 1989, 1991, 1997, 1999; won US Amateur Championship 1979, Greater Milwaukee Open 1984, Bing Crosby Pro-Am 1985, Hawaiian Open 1985, Fuji Sankei Classic 1985, Australian Masters 1986, Lawrence Batley Int. 1987, AT&T Pebble Beach Nat. Pro-Am 1989, 1990, 1992, 1997, H-E-B Tex. Open 1990, Walt Disney World/Oldsmobile Classic 1991, Tokia Classic 1992, Argentine Open 1994, Honda Classic 1995, Bell Canada Open 1995, Mercedes Championships 1996, Greater Greensboro Open 1996, Buick Invitational 1997, US Masters 1998, British Open 1998, World Matchplay 1998; best finish 2002, 2nd in Buick Invitational and 2nd in Buick Open; All-American Rookie of Year, Long Beach State Univ. 1981; PGA Tour Player of the Year 1998. *Leisure interests:* golf course consulting, hunting, fishing. *Address:* c/o IMG Golf, IMG Center, 1360 East 9th Street, Suite 100, Cleveland, OH 44114, USA.

OMI, Koji; Japanese politician; b. 14 Dec. 1932, Gunma Pref.; ed Faculty of Commercial Science, Hitotsubashi Univ.; joined Ministry of Int. Trade and Industry (MITI) 1956, Consul, Consulate Gen., New York 1970–74, Dir S Asia and Eastern Europe Div., Trade Policy Bureau 1974, Dir Small Enterprise Policy Div., Small and Medium Enterprise Agency (SMEA) 1978, Dir Admin. Div., Science and Tech. Agency 1979–81, Dir-Gen. Guidance Dept, SMEA 1981–82 (retd from MITI); mem. House of Reps 1983–, Parl. Vice-Minister for Finance 1990, Dir-Gen. Research and Investigation Bureau, LDP 1991–92, Dir-Gen. Commerce and Industry Policy Bureau, LDP 1992–93, Dir-Gen. Science and Tech. Policy Bureau, LDP 1993–94, LDP Deputy Sec.-Gen. 1994–95, Chair. House Standing Cttee on Finance 1995, Sec.-Gen. Research Council for Promotion of Science and Tech.-oriented Nation, LDP 1996, Dir Special Cttee on Taxation System Problems and Relatives Matters 1996, mem. Standing Cttee on Budget 1996, Deputy Chair. Policy Research Council, LDP 1996–97, Minister of State for Econ. Planning 1997–98, Dir-Gen. Election Bureau, LDP 1998–99, Dir Interest Group Policy Div., LDP 1999–2000, Acting Chair. Party Org. HQ, LDP 1999–2000, Acting Sec.-Gen., LDP 2000–01, Minister of State for Okinawa and Northern Territories Affairs and Minister of State for Science and Tech. Policy 2001, Chair. LDP Research Comm. to Promote Research and Establish a Nation of Innovative Science and Tech. 2002, Deputy Chair. LDP Gen. Council 2004, Chair. LDP Research Comm. on Oil, Resources and Energy 2005, Minister of Finance 2006–07. *Address:* Liberal-Democratic Party (Jiyu-Minshuto), 1-11-23, Nagata-cho, Chiyoda-ku, Tokyo 100-8910, Japan (office). *Telephone:* (3) 3581-6211 (office). *E-mail:* koho@ldp.jimin.or.jp (office). *Website:* www.jimin.jp (office).

OMI, Shigeru, MD, PhD; Japanese molecular biologist and international organization executive; *Director, Regional Office for the Western Pacific, World Health Organization;* b. 11 June 1949, Tokyo; m.; one s. one d.; ed American Field Service scholarship to Potsdam Central High School, New York, Keio Univ., Jichi Medical School; Medical Officer, Div. of Medical Affairs, Bureau of Public Health, Tokyo Metropolitan Govt (assigned as sole doctor on remote Pacific islands) 1978–87; Researcher, Div. of Immunology, Jichi Medical School 1987–89; Deputy Dir Office of Medical Guidance and Inspection, Bureau of Health Insurance, Ministry of Health and Welfare 1989–90; Medical Officer and Regional Adviser, Expanded Programme on Immunization, WHO Regional Office for the Western Pacific 1990–95, Dir Div. of Communicable Disease Prevention and Control 1995–98, Dir WHO Regional Office for Western Pacific 1999–; Prof. of Public Health, Jichi Medical School and Tech. Adviser, Ministry of Health and Welfare 1998; Exec. Ed. Polio Eradication in the Western Pacific Region 2002; Hon. Fellow, Hong Kong Coll. of Community Medicine 2002; Hon. Mem. Keio Univ. 2004; Dr hc (Mongolian Nat. Medical Univ.) 2002; 37th Kojima Award 2001. *Publication:* SARS: How a Global Epidemic Was Stopped (ed.) 2006. *Address:* World Health Organization Regional Office for the Western Pacific, PO Box 2932, 1000 Manila, Philippines (office). *Telephone:* (2) 528-9991 (office). *Fax:* (2) 521-1036 (office); (2) 526-0279 (office). *E-mail:* pio@wpro.who.int (office). *Website:* www.wpro.who.int (office).

OMIDYAR, Pierre M., BS; French/American internet executive; *Chairman, eBay Incorporated;* b. Paris; m.; ed Tufts Univ., Mass; family moved to Washington, DC, when he was a child; joined Claris (Apple Computer subsidiary) and wrote MacDraw application 1988–91; co-f. Ink Development (later renamed eShop and acquired by Microsoft) 1991; software engineer, General Magic 1991–96; Founder and Chair. eBay 1995–; Founder Omidyar Network (charity), now Chair. and CEO; est. (with Tufts Univ.) Univ. Coll. of Citizenship and Public Service; mem. Bd of Trustees Tufts Univ., Santa Fe Inst.; Co-founder Peer News Inc. (operating as Ginx) 2008. *Address:* Omidyar Network, 1991 Broadway, Suite 200, Redwood City, CA 94063; eBay Inc., 2145 Hamilton Avenue, San Jose, CA 95125, USA (office). *Telephone:* (408) 376-7400 (office). *Fax:* (408) 376-7401 (office). *Website:* www.ebay.com (office); www.omidyar.net.

OMIYA, Hideaki; Japanese business executive; *President, Mitsubishi Heavy Industries;* joined Mitsubishi Heavy Industries in 1969, served in several exec. positions including Deputy Head of Industrial Machinery Div. and Head of Air Conditioning and Refrigeration Systems Div., Sr Exec. Vice-Pres. 2007–08, Pres. Mitsubishi Heavy Industries 2008–. *Address:* Mitsubishi Heavy Industries, 16-5, Konan 2-chome, Minato-ku, Tokyo 108-8215, Japan (office). *Telephone:* (3) 6716-3111 (office). *Fax:* (3) 6716-5800 (office). *E-mail:* info@mhi.co.jp (office). *Website:* www.mhi.co.jp (office).

OMIYI, Basil; Nigerian oil industry executive; *Managing Director, Shell Petroleum Development Company of Nigeria Ltd;* joined Shell Petroleum Devt Co. of Nigeria Ltd (SPDC) as petroleum engineer 1970, worked in Nigeria, UK and the Netherlands, apptd to Bd of SPDC as Gen. Man. Relations and Environment 1996–99, External Affairs Dir 1999–2002, Production Dir 2002–04, Man. Dir Shell Petroleum Devt Co. of Nigeria Ltd (first Nigerian) 2004–. *Address:* Shell Petroleum Development Company of Nigeria Ltd, Freeman House, 21/22 Marina, PMB 2418, Lagos, Nigeria (office). *Telephone:* (1) 2602600 (office). *Website:* www.shell.com/home/Framework?siteId=nigeria (office).

OMOROGBE, Oluyinka Osayame, LLB, LLM, BL, MCIArB; Nigerian academic, legal practitioner and energy consultant; *Professor and Dean, Department of Public and International Law, University of Ibadan;* b. (Oluyinka Osayame Ighodaro), 21 Sept. 1957, Ibadan; d. of Samuel O Ighodaro and Irene E. B. Ighodaro; m. Allan Omorogbe 1984; one s. two d.; ed Univ. of Ife and London School of Econs; Nat. Youth Service 1979–80; Pvt. Legal Practitioner 1980–81; Lecturer, Dept of Jurisprudence and Int. Law, Univ. of Benin 1983–90, Head of Dept 1988–89; Sr Lecturer, Univ. of Lagos 1990–; Dir Centre for Petroleum, Environment and Devt Studies, Lagos 1996–; E-Publisher and Consultant 2001–; Prof. and Dean Dept of Public and Int. Law, Ibadan Univ. 2002–; mem. Exec. Cttee Petroleum Energy and Mining Law Asscn of Nigeria 1986–; mem. Acad. Advisory Group, Section on Energy and Natural Resources Law, Int. Bar Asscn, African Soc. of Int. and Comparative Law; mem. Oil and Gas Sector Reform Implementation Cttee (OGIC) 1999–; Treas. Nigerian Soc. of Int. Law 1994–97, Gen. Sec. 1997–. *Publications:* The Oil and Gas Industry: Exploration and Production Contracts 1997, Oil and Gas Law in Nigeria 2000; numerous articles on petroleum and energy law and int. econ. law in int. journals and books. *Leisure interests:* cooking, baking, handicrafts. *Address:* Faculty of Law, University of Ibadan, Ibadan, Oyo State (office); PO Box 9261, Ikeja, Lagos, Nigeria. *Telephone:* (1) 3203461 (office). *Fax:* (1) 3203461 (office); (1) 2693737. *E-mail:* law@ui.edu.ng; yomorogbe@hotmail.com (home). *Website:* www.ui.edu.ng; petrojournal.com (office).

OMRANA, Abderrahim, PhD; Moroccan economist and banker; *Adviser to the President, Islamic Development Bank;* b. 1947, Quezane; m.; three c.; with Govt Gen. Inspection Dept 1970; Head of Mission, Treasury Dept, Ministry of Finance 1973; Asst Lecturer, Univ. of Rabat 1974, Sr Lecturer 1975–78; Exec. Attaché, Banque Nationale pour le Développement Economique 1975–78; Lecturer, Univ. of Dakar, Senegal 1978–79; Deputy Dir Gen. African Centre for Monetary Studies and Fed. of African Cen. Banks 1978–87; Dir Gen. ICOMA and NASCOTEX 1989–95; Bank Sec., Islamic Devt Bank 1996–2001, 2003–, Dir Gen. Fund for Municipal Equipments 2001–03, currently Adviser to Bank Pres. *Publications:* three books on finance, accountancy and modern econs and more than 100 articles on econs and finance. *Address:* c/o Islamic Development Bank, PO Box 5925, Jeddah 21432, Saudi Arabia (office). *Telephone:* (2) 644-2432 (office). *Fax:* (2) 644-2432 (office). *E-mail:* aomrana@isdb.org (office). *Website:* www.isdb.org (office).

OMURA, Satoshi, MS, PhD; Japanese biochemist and academic; *Professor and President, The Kitasato Institute;* b. 12 July 1935; ed Yamanashi Univ., Tokyo Univ. of Science, Univ. of Tokyo; Research Assoc., Yamanashi Univ. 1963–65; Researcher, Kitasato Inst. 1965–71, Prof. and Exec. Vice-Pres. 1984–90, Prof. and Pres. 1990–, Assoc. Prof., School of Pharmaceutical Sciences, Kitasato Univ. 1968–75, Prof. 1975–84, Dir, Kitasato Univ. 1985–, Prof., Kitasato Inst. for Life Sciences, Kitasato Univ. 2001–02, also Prof., Graduate School of Infection Control Sciences 2002–; foreign mem., Académie des sciences (France) 2002–Ed.; Naranishi Prize 2000. *Publications:* over 600 research papers; The Search for Bioactive Compounds from Microorganisms (Ed.) 1992, MacRolide Antibiotics: Chemistry, Biology and Practice (Ed.). *Address:* Kitasato Institute for Life Sciences, Kitasato University, 9-1, Shirokane 5-chome, Minato-ku, Tokyo 108-8642, Japan (office). *Telephone:* (3) 5791-6101 (office). *Fax:* (3) 444-8360 (office). *E-mail:* omura-s@kitasato.or.jp (office). *Website:* www.kitasato.or.jp (office).

OMURA, Yukiko, BA (Econs), MA; Japanese banker; *Executive Vice-President, Multilateral Investment Guarantee Agency (MIGA), World Bank Group;* b. Paris, France; ed in Japan, Geneva, Switzerland and Univ. of London, UK and at Boston Univ., USA; began career as project economist with IDB; spent ten years with J.P. Morgan, Tokyo, New York and London; fmrly Head of Emerging Markets, Asia, Lehman Brothers, Head of Credit Business, Asia; fmrly Head of Global Fixed Income and Derivatives UBS Japan; fmrly Head of Global Markets and Global Debt, Dresdner Bank, Japan; Founder, CEO and Exec. Dir AIDS Prevention Fund, London 2002–04; Exec. Vice-Pres. Multilateral Investment Guarantee Agency (MIGA), World Bank Group 2004–. *Address:* Multilateral Investment Guarantee Agency, World Bank Group, 1818 H Street NW, Washington, DC 20433, USA (office). *Telephone:* (202) 473-1000 (office). *Fax:* (202) 522-2630 (office). *E-mail:* agentile@worldbank.org (office). *Website:* www.miga.org (office).

ONDAATJE, Michael, OC, BA, MA; Canadian (b. Sri Lankan) writer, poet and filmmaker; b. 12 Sept. 1943, Colombo, Sri Lanka; s. of Philip Mervyn Ondaatje and Enid Doris Gratiaen; m. Linda Spalding; two s.; ed Dulwich Coll. London, Bishop's Univ., Queen's Univ. and Univ. of Toronto; has taught at Univ. of Western Ontario, York Univ., Univ. of Hawaii at Manoa, Brown Univ., Univ. of Toronto; Founding Trustee, Griffin Trust For Excellence In Poetry; Foreign Hon. Member, American Acad. of Arts and Letters. *Films include:* Sons of Captain Poetry 1970, Carry on Crime and Punishment 1970, The Clinton Special: A Film About The Farm Show 1974. *Publications include:* poetry: The Dainty Monsters 1967, The Man with Seven Toes 1968, The Collected Works of Billy the Kid (Gov.-Gen.'s Award) 1970, There's a Trick with a Knife I'm Learning to Do (Gov.-Gen.'s Award) 1979, Secular Love 1984, The Cinnamon Peeler 1991, Handwriting 1998; fiction: The Collected Works of Billy the Kid, Coming Through Slaughter, Running in the Family, In the Skin of a Lion (City of Toronto Book Award) 1988, The English Patient (shared the Booker Prize for Fiction, Gov.-Gen's Award) 1992, Anil's Ghost (Prix Medicis, Giller Prize. Gov.-Gen.'s Award, Kiriyama Pacific Rim Book Prize) 2000, The Story 2005, Divisadero (Gov.-Gen.'s Literary Award) 2007. *Address:* c/o Trident Media Group LLC, 41 Madison Avenue, 36th Floor, New York, NY 10010, USA; 2275 Bayview Avenue, Toronto, ON N4N 3M6, Canada.

ONDAATJE, Sir (Philip) Christopher, Kt, CBE, OC, FRGS, FRSL; Canadian/British financier and author; *Chairman, The Ondaatje Foundation;* b. 22 Feb. 1933; s. of Philip Mervyn Ondaatje and Enid Doris Gratiaen; m. Valda Bulins 1959; one s. two d.; ed Blundell's School, UK; Nat. and Grindlays Bank, London 1951–55; Burns Bros & Denton, Toronto 1955–56; Montrealer Magazine and Canada Month Magazine 1956–57; Maclean-Hunter Publishing Co. Ltd, Montreal 1957–62; Financial Post, Toronto 1963–65; Pitfield Mackay, Ross & Co. Ltd, Toronto 1965–69; Founder Pagurian Corpn Ltd 1967–89, Loewen, Ondaatje, McCutcheon & Co. Ltd 1970–88; Chair. The Ondaatje Foundation 1975–; major donor to Ondaatje Wing, Nat. Portrait Gallery, London 2000 and to the Ondaatje Theatre, Royal Geographical Soc.; mem. Advisory Bd Royal Soc. of Portrait Painters; Patron Somerset Co. Cricket Club; Trustee Nat. Portrait Gallery 2002–; mem. Canadian Bobsled Team 1964; Hon. Vice-Pres. Royal Geographical Soc. Hon. LLD (Dalhousie) 1994; Hon. DLit (Buckingham) 2003, (Exeter) 2003. *Publications:* Olympic Victory 1964, The Prime Ministers of Canada (1867–1985) 1985, Leopard in the Afternoon 1989, The Man-Eater of Punanai 1992, Sindh Revisited 1996, Journey to the Source of the Nile 1998, Hemingway in Africa 2003, Woolf in Ceylon 2005, The Power of Paper 2007, The Glenthorne Cat 2008. *Leisure interests:* golf, tennis, adventure, writing, photography. *Address:* Glenthorne, Countisbury, nr Lynton, N Devon, EX35 6NQ, England (home). *Website:* www.ondaatje.com.

ONDEKANE, Jean-Pierre; Democratic Republic of the Congo politician; fmr leader rebel forces; Minister of Defence, Demobilization and War Veterans' Affairs 2003–05. *Address:* c/o Ministry of Defence, Demobilization and War Veterans' Affairs, BP 4111, Kinshasa-Gombe, Democratic Republic of the Congo (office).

ONDETTI, Miguel A., PhD; Argentine chemist; b. 14 May 1930, Buenos Aires; ed Univ. of Buenos Aires; bookkeeper 1948–57; Prof. of Organic Chem., Catholic Inst. for Teachers 1957–60; Instructor in Organic Chem., Univ. of

Buenos Aires 1957–60; Sr Research Chemist, The Squibb Inst. for Medical Research, Argentina 1957–60; Sr Research Chemist, New Brunswick, NJ 1960–66, Research Group Leader, Peptide Synthesis, Princeton, NJ 1966–73, Section Head, Peptides, Steroids and Antibiotic Research 1973–76, Dir Dept of Biological Chem. 1976–80, Assoc. Dir Chemical and Microbiological Research 1980–81, Vice-Pres. Basic Research 1981–83, Vice-Pres. Research, Cardiopulmonary Diseases 1984–89, Sr Vice-Pres. Research, Cardiovascular Diseases 1989–90, Sr Vice-Pres. Cardiovascular and Metabolic Diseases 1990–91, retd 1991; mem. ACS, American Heart Asscn, Council on High Blood Pressure, American Soc. for Biological Chemists, American Soc. of Hypertension, Pharmaceutical Manufacturers' Asscn; Hon. mem. American Soc. of Peptide Chem.; ACS Alfred Burger Award in Medicinal Chem. 1981, Thomas Alva Edison Patent Award, Research and Devt Council, New Jersey 1983, Ciba Award for Hypertension Research, American Heart Asscn, Council on High Blood Pressure Research 1983, Chairmanís Edward Robinson Squibb Award, E. R. Squibb & Sons, Inc. 1986, Award for Contribs to Medical Science, Pharmaceutical Manufacturers' Asscn and Nat. Health Council 1988, Inventor of the Year Award, New Jersey Inventors' Congress 1988, Perkin Medal, Soc. of Chemical Industry (American Section) 1991, Warren Alpert Foundation Prize, Harvard Medical School 1991, ACS Award for Creative Invention 1992, Herman Bloch Award for Scientific Excellence in Industry, Univ. of Chicago 1992, Albert Lasker Award for Clinical Medical Research 1999. *Publications:* Peptide Synthesis (co-author) 1966, Peptide Synthesis (Interscience Monographs on Organic Chemistry); inventor or co-inventor in 122 US patents related to isolation and/or synthesis of biologically active peptides and amino-acid derivatives; more than 100 articles in scientific journals. *Address:* c/o Bristol-Myers Squibb Institute for Medical Research, Princeton, NJ USA (office).

O'NEAL, E. Stanley, BS, MBA; American business executive; b. 7 Oct. 1951, Roanoke, Ala; m. Nancy A. Garvey; two c.; ed Kettering Univ., Harvard Univ.; joined treasury Dept, Gen. Motors 1978; Dir of Investment Banking, Merrill Lynch 1986–91, Man. Dir of High Yield Finance and Restructuring 1991–95, Head of Capital Markets Group 1995–98, Exec. Vice-Pres. and Co-Head of Corp. and Institutional Client Group 1997–99, Pres. US Pvt. Client Group 1999–2001, COO, mem. Bd Dirs and Exec. Man. Cttee Merrill Lynch 2001–07, CEO 2002–07, Chair. 2003–07 (retd); Co-Head CICG 1997–, CFO 1998–2000, Pres. 2000–; Vice-Chair. Securities Industry Asscn; mem. Advisory Cttee New York Stock Exchange; mem. Bd of Dirs Nasdaq Stock Market, General Motors Corpn 2001–06; mem. Bd Nat. Urban League, McDonald House of New York, Catalyst, Buckley School; mem. Advisory Council, Bronx Preparatory Charter School; named among Most Influential Black Americans, Ebony magazine 2006. *Address:* c/o Merrill Lynch & Company, Inc., 4 World Financial Center, New York, NY 10080, USA (office).

O'NEAL, Hon. Ralph T., OBE; British Virgin Islands politician and business executive; *Chief Minister and Minister of Finance;* b. 1933; m. Edris O'Neal; Leader Virgin Islands Party; fmr civil servant and mem. of govt in various capacities; Deputy Chief Minister –1995; Chief Minister and Minister of Finance 1995–2003, 2007–; fmr Dir British Virgin Islands Red Cross; founding mem. Rotary Club, Tortola. *Leisure interest:* watching cricket. *Address:* Office of the Chief Minister, 33 Admin Drive, Wickham's Cay 1, Tortola VG1110, The British Virgin Islands (office). *Telephone:* 468-3701 (office). *Fax:* 468-4435 (office). *E-mail:* cmo@surfbvi.com (office). *Website:* www.bvigazette.org (office).

O'NEAL, Rodney, MEng; American business executive; *President and CEO, Delphi Corporation;* b. 1953; ed Kettering Univ., Stanford Univ.; joined General Motors (GM) 1971, Inland Div. 1976–91, Dir of Industrial Eng, Chevrolet-Pontiac-GM of Canada Group 1991–92, Dir of Mfg, Delphi Corpn (GM subsidiary spun off from parent 1999) 1992–94, Gen. Dir of Warehousing & Distribution, GM Service Parts Operations 1994–97, Vice-Pres. GM 1997, also Gen. Man. Delphi Interior Systems 1997–98, Vice-Pres. Delphi 1998–2000, also Pres. Delphi Interior Systems 1998–2000, Exec. Vice-Pres. Safety, Thermal & Electrical Architecture Sector 2000–03, Pres. Dynamics, Propulsion, and Thermal Sector 2003–05, mem. Bd of Dirs, Pres. and COO Delphi Corpn 2005–07, Pres. and CEO 2007–; mem. Bd of Dirs Goodyear Tire & Rubber Co., Sprint/Nextel; fmr mem. Bd of Dirs Inroads Inc., Michigan Mfrs Asscn, Woodward Governor Co.; mem. Advisory Bd Focus: HOPE (charity); mem. Exec. Leadership Council. *Address:* Delphi Corpn, 5725 Delphi Drive, Troy, MI 48098-2815, USA (office). *Telephone:* (248) 813-2000 (office). *Fax:* (248) 813-2673 (office). *E-mail:* info@delphi.com (office). *Website:* www.delphi.com (office).

O'NEAL, Ryan; American actor; b. 20 April 1941, Los Angeles; s. of Charles O'Neal and Patricia O'Neal (née Callaghan); m. 1st Joanna Moore 1963 (divorced 1967), one s. one d. Tatum O'Neal (q.v.); m. 2nd Leigh Taylor-Young 1967, one s.; one s. by Farrah Fawcett; ed US Army High School, Munich, Germany. *Television includes:* Dobie Gillis, Two Faces West, Perry Mason, The Virginian, This is the Life, The Untouchables, My Three Sons, Bachelor Father, Empire, Peyton Place, Epoch 2000, Miss Match (series) 2003. *Films include:* The Big Bounce 1969, Love Story 1970, The Wild Rovers 1971, What's Up, Doc? 1972, The Thief Who Came to Dinner 1973, Paper Moon 1973, Oliver's Story 1978, The Main Event 1979, So Fine 1981, Partners 1982, Irreconcilable Differences 1983, Fever Pitch 1985, Tough Guys Don't Dance 1986, Chances Are 1989, Faithful 1996, Hacks 1997, Burn Hollywood Burn 1997, Zero Effect 1998, Coming Soon 1999, The List 2000, Gentleman B. 2000, People I Know 2002, Malibu's Most Wanted 2003. *Address:* 21368 Pacific Coast Highway, Malibu, CA 90265, USA.

O'NEAL, Shaquille Rashaun, BA, MBA; American professional basketball player; b. 6 March 1972, Newark, NJ; s. of Philip A. Harrison and Lucille O'Neal; m. Shaunie Nelson 2002; four c.; two c. from previous relationships; ed

Louisiana State Univ., Univ. of Phoenix; center; drafted in first round (first overall) by Orlando Magic 1992, played 1992–96; signed as free agent LA Lakers 1996, played 1996–2004; traded to Miami Heat 2004–08, traded to Phoenix Suns 2008–; mem. four Nat. Basketball Asscn (NBA) championship teams (with Lakers 2000, 2001, 2002, with Heat 2006); Most Valuable Player in NBA Finals 2000, 2001, 2002; NBA Most Valuable Player 2000; 14-time NBA All-Star team 1993–98, 2000–07; NBA Rookie of the Year 1993; NBA scoring champion 1995, 2000; mem. gold-medal winning World Championship team 1994, US Olympic team, Atlanta 1996; Hon. US Deputy Marshal 2006; named one of 50 Greatest Players in NBA History 1996. *Films:* Blue Chips 1994, Kazaam 1996, Steel 1997, Freddy Got Fingered 2001, The Wash 2001, The Kid & I 2005, Scary Movie 4 2006. *Music:* has released five rap albums; owns record label Twism. *Publications:* Shaq Talks Back: The Uncensored Word on My Life and Winning in the NBA 2001. *Address:* c/o Suns Legacy Partners, LLC, 201 East Jefferson Street, Phoenix, AZ 85004, USA. *Telephone:* (602) 379-7900. *Fax:* (602) 379-7990. *Website:* www.nba.com/ suns; www.nba.com/playerfile/shaquille_oneal.

O'NEAL, Tatum; American actress; b. 5 Nov. 1963, Los Angeles; d. of Ryan O'Neal (q.v.) and Joanna Moore; m. John McEnroe (q.v.) 1986 (divorced 1994); two s. one d. *Film appearances include:* Paper Moon (Acad. Award for Best Supporting Actress) 1973, The Bad News Bears 1976, Nickelodeon 1976, International Velvet 1978, Little Darlings 1980, Circle of Two 1980, Prisoners 1981, Certain Fury 1985, 15 and Getting Straight (TV) 1989, Little Noises 1991, Woman on The Run: The Lawrencia Bembenek Story (TV) 1993, Basquiat 1996, The Scoundrel's Wife 2002, The Technical Writer 2003, My Brother 2005. *Achievements include:* youngest person to ever win a competitive Acad. Award (1973). *Publication:* A Paper Life 2004. *Address:* c/o Innovative Artists, 1999 Avenue of the Stars, Suite 2850, Century City, CA 90067, USA.

O'NEIL, William Andrew, CMG, CM, BASc, FRSA, FREng, PEng; Canadian international public servant and engineer; b. 6 June 1927, Ottawa; s. of Thomas Wilson O'Neil and Margaret O'Neil (née Swan); m. Dorothy Muir 1950; one s. two d.; ed Univ. of Toronto; engineer, Fed. Dept of Transport, Ottawa 1949–53, Resident Engineer, Special Projects Br. 1954; Div. Engineer, St Lawrence Seaway Authority 1955–59, Regional Dir 1960–63, Dir of Construction 1964–70; Deputy Admin., Marine Services, Canadian Marine Transportation Admin. 1970–79; Commr, Canadian Coast Guard and Deputy Admin., Marine Admin. 1975–89; Pres. St Lawrence Seaway Authority 1980–89; Chair. Council Int. Maritime Org. 1980–89, Sec.-Gen. 1990–2003; mem. Bd of Govs. World Maritime Univ. 1983–; Chair. Governing Bd, Int. Maritime Law Inst., Malta 1991–2004; Canadian del. to Perm. Int. Asscn of Navigation Congresses 1984–90; Chair. Canadian Cttee Lloyd's Register of Shipping 1987–88; Chancellor World Maritime Univ. 1991–2004; Dir Canarctic Shipping Co.; Pres. Seaway Authority, Int. Bridge Corpn; Pres. Inst. of Chartered Shipbrokers 2004–; Pres. Videotel 2004–; mem. Bd of the Thousand Islands Bridge Authority 1980–90; mem. Asscn of Professional Engineers of Ont., American Soc. of Civil Engineers; Foreign mem. Royal Acad. of Eng (UK); Hon. Commodore, Canadian Coast Guard; Hon. mem. Canadian Maritime Law Asscn, Honourable Co. of Master Mariners, UK, Int. Maritime Pilots Asscn, Int. Fed. of Shipmasters' Asscns, NUMAST (Nat. Union of Marine Aviation and Shipping Transport Officers) (UK), Soc. of Naval Architects and Marine Engineers (USA), Singapore, Int. Asscn of Lighthouse Authorities, Co. of Master Mariners, India 1998; Hon. Fellow The Nautical Inst., UK 1996, Royal Inst. of Naval Architects 1998, Royal Inst. of Navigation; Hon. Titular mem. Comité Maritime Int.; Commdr, Ordre Nat. des Cèdres (Lebanon) 1995, Grand Cross, Orden Vasco Núñez de Balboa (Panama) 1998; Hon. Dip. Canadian Coast Guard Coll.; Hon. LLD (Malta) 1993, (Memorial Univ. of Newfoundland) 1996; Hon. DSc (Nottingham Trent) 1994 (World Maritime Univ.) 2004; Eng Medal, Asscn of Professional Engineers of Ont. 1972, Distinguished Public Service Award, US Govt, Admirals' Medal 1994, Seatrade Personality of the Year Award 1995, NUMAST Award (UK) 1995, Professional Engineers Ont. Gold Medal 1995, mem. Eng Alumni Hall of Distinction, Univ. of Toronto 1996, Silver Bell Award, Seamen's Church Inst. New York 1997, Vice Adm. Jerry Land Medal, Soc. of Naval Architects and Marine Engineers, USA 1999, Cdre Award, Conn. Maritime Asscn 1998, Dioscun Prize, Lega Navale Italiana (Italy) 1998, Halert C. Shepheard Award (USA) 2000, Medal for Distinguished Services to the Directorate Gen. for Maritime Affairs, Colombia 2001, CITIS Lifetime Achievement Award UK 2002, Freeman of the Worshipful Company of Shipwrights (hc) UK 2002, Golden Jubilee Medal, Canada 2002, "15 November 1817 Medal", Uruguay 2002. *Leisure interests:* reading, swimming, golf. *Address:* 2 Dean Wood Close, Woodcote, RG8 0PW, England (home). *Telephone:* (1491) 682897 (home). *Fax:* (1491) 682625 (home). *E-mail:* bill .oneil@imo.org (home).

O'NEILL, Brendan, MA, PhD, FCMA; British business executive; b. 6 Dec. 1948; s. of John Christopher O'Neill and Doris Monk; m. Margaret Maude O'Neill 1979; one s. two d.; ed Churchill Coll., Cambridge, Univ. of E Anglia; with Ford Motor Co. 1973–75, British Leyland 1975–81, BICC PLC 1981–83; Group Financial Controller Midland Bank 1983–87; Dir of Financial Control Guinness PLC 1987, Finance Dir 1988–90, Man. Dir Int. Regulation, United Distillers 1990–92, Guinness Brewing Worldwide 1993–97, CEO Guinness Diageo PLC 1997–98; COO ICI PLC 1998–99, CEO 1999–2003, Dir 1998–2003; Dir EMAP PLC 1995–, Diageo 1997–98, Endurance Specialty Holdings Ltd 2005–, Tyco Int. Ltd 2003–, Rank Group PLC; Life Gov. Imperial Cancer Research Fund 1994–2002; Trustee Cancer Reserch UK 2002–; Fellow, Chartered Inst. of Man. Accountants. *Leisure interests:* music, reading. *Address:* c/o Board of Directors, Tyco International Ltd, 90 Pitts Bay Road, 2nd Floor, Pembroke HM 08, Bermuda (office).

O'NEILL, Paul H., MPA; American business executive and fmr government official; *Principal, Value Capture;* b. 4 Dec. 1935, St Louis, Mo.; s. of John Paul O'Neill and Gayland Elsie Irvin; m. Nancy Jo Wolfe 1955; one s. three d.; ed Fresno State Coll., Indiana Univ., Claremont Grad. School and George Washington Univ.; computer systems analyst, US Veterans Admin.; later engineer, Morris-Knudsen, Anchorage, Alaska; mem. staff, Office of Man. and Budget 1967–77, Deputy Dir 1974–77; Vice-Pres. Planning, Int. Paper Co. 1977, Sr Vice-Pres. Planning and Finance 1981, Sr Vice-Pres. paperboard and packaging Div. 1983, Pres. 1985–87; Chair., CEO Aluminum Co. of America (Alcoa) 1987–99, Chair. 1999–2000; Sec. of Treasury 2001–02; co-founder and CEO Pittsburgh Regional Healthcare Initiative 2002–05, mem. Bd of Dirs 2002–; founder and principal Value Capture (hospital consulting firm) 2005–; fmr Dir Manpower Demonstration Research Group, Alcoa, Lucent Technologies, Eastman Kodak Co., RAND Corpn (fmr Chair.), American Enterprise Inst.; Dr hc (Clarkson Univ.) 1993. *Address:* c/o Board of Directors, Pittsburgh Regional Healthcare Initiative, 650 Smithfield Street, Centre City Tower, Suite 2400, Pittsburgh, PA 15222, USA.

O'NEILL, Robert John, AO, MA, BE, DPhil, FASSA; Australian historian, academic and army officer (retd); b. 5 Nov. 1936, Melbourne; s. of Joseph Henry O'Neill and Janet Gibbon O'Neill; m. Sally Margaret Burnard 1965; two d.; ed Scotch Coll. Melbourne, Royal Mil. Coll. of Australia, Melbourne Univ., Brasenose Coll. Oxford; served in Australian army 1955–68, Fifth Bn Royal Australian Regt, Vietnam (despatches) 1966–67, Maj. 1967–68 (resgnd); Rhodes scholar, Vic. 1961; Official Australian Historian for the Korean War 1969–82; Head of Strategic and Defence Studies Centre, ANU 1971–82; Dir IISS, London 1982–87, Chair. Council 1996–2001; Chichele Prof. of the History of War, Univ. of Oxford 1987–2001; Dir Grad. Studies Modern History Faculty, Oxford 1990–92; Fellow, All Souls Coll. Oxford 1987; Sr Fellow in Int. Relations, ANU 1969–77, Professorial Fellow 1977–82; Trustee Imperial War Museum 1990–, Deputy Chair. 1996–98, Chair. 1998–2001; Gov. Ditchley Foundation 1989–, Int. Peace Acad. 1990–; Chair. Bd Centre for Defence Studies and Bd Centre for Australian Studies, Univ. of London 1990–95; Chair. Council of Australian Strategic Policy Inst. 2001–05; Deputy Chair., Grad. School of Govt, Univ. of Sydney 2001–05; Dir The Shell Transport and Trading Co. 1992– and two mutual funds of Capital Group, LA 1992–, The Lowy Inst. 2001–; mem. Advisory Bd Investment Co. of America 1988–; mem. Commonwealth War Graves Comm. 1990, The Rhodes Trust 1995–; Hon. Fellow, Brasenose Coll. Oxford; Hon. Col 5th (V) Bn, The Royal Greenjackets 1993–99; Hon. DL (ANU) 2001. *Publications:* The German Army and the Nazi Party 1933–39 1966, Vietnam Task 1966, General Giap: politician and strategist 1969, (ed.) The Strategic Nuclear Balance 1975, (ed.) The Defence of Australia: fundamental new aspects 1977, (ed.) Insecurity: the spread of weapons in the Indian and Pacific Oceans 1978, (co-ed.) Australian Dictionary of Biography Vols 7–12, 1891–1939, 1979–91, (co-ed.) New Directions in Strategic Thinking 1981, Australia in the Korean War 1950–53: Vol. I Strategy and Diplomacy 1981, Vol. II Combat Operations 1985, (co-ed.) Australian Defence Policy for the 1980s 1982, (ed.) Security in East Asia 1984, (ed.) The Conduct of East–West Relations in the 1980s 1985, (ed.) New Technology and Western Security Policy 1985, (ed.) Doctrine, the Alliance and Arms Control 1986, (ed.) East Asia, the West and International Security 1987, (ed.) Security in the Mediterranean 1989, (co-ed.) The West and the Third World 1990, (co-ed.) Securing Peace in Europe 1945–62 1992, (co-ed.) War, Strategy and International Politics 1992, Alternative Nuclear Futures 1999; articles in numerous journals. *Leisure interests:* local history, walking. *Address:* c/o The Lowy Institute for International Affairs, 31 Bligh Street, Sydney, NSW 2000, Australia (office). *E-mail:* director@lowyinstitute.org (office). *Website:* www.lowyinstitute.org (office).

O'NEILL, Terence (Terry) Patrick; British photographer; b. 30 July 1938, London; s. of Leonard Victor O'Neill and Josephine Mary O'Neill; m. 1st Vera Day; one s. one d.; m. 2nd Faye Dunaway (q.v.) 1981; one s.; ed Gunnersbury Grammar School; fmr modern jazz drummer in leading London jazz clubs; army service as physical training instructor; subsequently took up photography, took first photographs of Beatles and Rolling Stones early 1960s; went to Hollywood 1962; has photographed leading actors and actresses, rock and classical musicians, political and sports personalities, mems. of British and other royal families; work published in The Sunday Times, Time, Life, Newsweek, Tatler, Elle, Paris Match, Stern etc. and other newspapers and magazines, in 52 countries and used on about 500 front covers worldwide a year. *Publication:* Legend S. *Leisure interests:* music, food, wine, art in all forms, literature.

O'NEILL OF BENGARVE, Baroness (Life Peer), cr. 1999, of The Braid in the County of Antrim; **Onora Sylvia O'Neill,** CBE, PhD, FBA, FMedSci; British philosopher; b. 23 Aug. 1941, Aughafatten, Northern Ireland; d. of the late Sir Con O'Neill and of Lady Garvey (née Rosemary Pritchard); m. Edward Nell 1963 (divorced 1976); two s.; ed St Paul's Girls' School, London, Somerville Coll., Oxford, Harvard Univ., USA; Asst Prof., Barnard Coll., Columbia Univ. 1970–76, Assoc. Prof. 1976–77; Lecturer, Univ. of Essex 1977–78, Sr Lecturer 1978–82, Reader 1982–87, Prof. 1987–92; Prin., Newnham Coll., Cambridge 1992–2006; Chair. Nuffield Foundation 1998–, Human Genetics Advisory Comm. 1997–99; Fellow, Wissenschaftskolleg, Berlin 1989–90; Foreign Corresp. mem. Österreichischen Akad. der Wissenschaften 2002; Foreign mem. American Philosophical Soc. 2003, Leopoldina 2004, Norwegian Acad. of Sciences 2006; Foreign Hon. mem. American Acad. of Arts and Sciences 1993; Hon. Bencher of Gray's Inn 2002; Hon. MRIA 2003; Hon. FRCP; Dr hc (E Anglia) 1995, (Essex) 1996, (Nottingham) 1999, (Aberdeen) 2001, (Dublin) 2002, (Oxford) 2003, (Ulster) 2003, London (2003), (Bath) 2004, (Stirling) 2005, (Queen's Univ. Belfast) 2005. *Radio:* The Reith Lectures 2002. *Publications:* Faces of Hunger: An Essay on Poverty, Development and Justice 1986, Constructions of Reason: Explorations of Kant's Practical

Philosophy 1989, Towards Justice and Virtue: A Constructive Account of Practical Reasoning 1996, Bounds of Justice 2000, Autonomy and Trust in Bioethics 2002, A Question of Trust 2002. *Leisure interests:* walking, talking. *Address:* House of Lords, London, SW1A 0PW; c/o British Academy, 10 Carlton House Terrace, London, SW1Y 5AH, England (office). *Telephone:* (20) 7219-5353.

ONG, Beng Seng; Singaporean hotel industry executive; *Owner and Managing Director, Hotel Properties Ltd;* m. Christina Ong; Owner and Man. Dir, Hotel Properties Ltd with 18 hotels in nine countries in Asia, Australia and Europe; acquired NatSteel through 98 Holdings consortium 2003. *Address:* Hotel Properties Ltd, 50 Cuscaden Road, #08-01, HPL House, 249724 Singapore (office). *Telephone:* 6734-5250 (office). *Fax:* 6732-0347 (office). *Website:* www.hplhotels.com (office).

ONG, John Doyle, LLB, MA; American diplomatist and business executive; b. 29 Sept. 1933, Uhrichsville, OH; s. of Louis Brosee and Mary Ellen Ong (née Liggett); m. Mary Lee Schupp 1957; two s. one d.; ed Ohio State Univ., Harvard Univ.; admitted to Ohio Bar 1958; Asst Counsel B. F. Goodrich Co., Akron 1961–66, Group Vice-Pres. 1972–73, Exec. Vice-Pres. 1973–74, Vice-Chair. 1974–75, Pres. 1975–84, Dir 1975–77, COO 1978–79, Chair., Pres. and CEO 1979–84, Chair. 1984–97, CEO 1984–96, Chair. Emer. 1997–; Amb. to Norway 2002–05; Asst to Pres. Int. B. F. Goodrich Co., Akron 1966–69, Vice-Pres. 1969–70, Pres. 1970–72; Dir Cooper Industries, The Kroger Co., Ameritech Corpn; Chair. Ohio Business Roundtable 1994–97; mem. Bd Dirs Nat. Alliance for Business; Pres. Bd of Trustees, Western Reserve Acad., Hudson 1977–95; Trustee John S. and James L. Knight Foundation 1995–, Univ. of Chicago 1991–, Ohio Historical Soc. 1998–; Dr hc (Ohio State Univ., Kent State Univ., Univ. of Akron, South Dakota State University); Humanities Award of Distinction, Ohio State Univ., Alumni Medal, Ohio State Univ. *Leisure interests:* fishing, hunting. *Address:* 230 Aurora Street, Hudson, OH 44236, USA (home).

ONG, Keng Sen; Singaporean theatre director; *Artistic Director, Theatre-Works (Singapore) Ltd;* ed Nat. Univ. of Singapore, Tisch Schools of the Arts, New York Univ.; trained as lawyer;; Artistic Dir TheatreWorks, Singapore 1988–; f. Arts Networks Asia 1999; Co-Artistic Dir 'In Transit' Arts Festival (annual three-week festival) Berlin 2002–03; mem. Int. Council of The Asia Soc. of New York; Artist-in-Residence, New York Univ. Asian Pacific and American Studies Programme/Inst. 2002, Vienna Schauspielhaus 2003, Leverhulme Artist-in-Residence, Inst. for Advanced Studies in the Humanities, Univ. of Edinburgh.2008; Singapore Young Artist Award 1992, Singapore Cultural Medallion Award 2003, Int. Soc. of Performing Arts Distinguished Artist Award 2003, Excellence for Singapore Award, Singapore Totalisator Bd 2003. *Productions include:* A Language of Their Own, New York Shakespeare Festival 1995, Lear, Tokyo 1997, The Silver River, Spoleto Festival, Charleston, 2000, The Continuum: Beyond the Killing Fields, Int. Festival of Arts and Ideas, Yale Univ. and Singapore 2001, The Myths of Memory, Vienna 2003. *Theatre includes:* Continuum: Beyond the Killing Fields, Yale Univ., USA and Singapore 2001. *Address:* TheatreWorks (Singapore) Ltd, 72-13 Mohamed Sultan Road, Singapore 239007 (office). *Telephone:* 6737 7213 (office). *Fax:* 67377013 (office). *E-mail:* tworks@singnet .com.sg (office). *Website:* www.theatreworks.org.sg (office).

ONG, Keng Yong, LLB; Singaporean international organization official and diplomatist; b. 6 Jan. 1954; m. Irene Tan Lee Chen; ed Univ. of Singapore, Georgetown Univ., Washington, DC, USA; Chargé d'affaires, Embassy in Riyadh 1984–88; Counsellor, High Comm. in Kuala Lumpur 1989–91; Minister Counsellor and Deputy Chief of Mission, Embassy in Washington, DC 1991–94; Press Sec. to Minister of Foreign Affairs and Ministry Spokesperson 1994–95; High Commr to India and Amb. to Nepal 1996–98; Press Sec. to Prime Minister 1998–2002; Deputy Sec. Ministry of Information, Communication and the Arts 1998; Chief Exec. Dir The People's Asscn 1999–2002; Sec.-Gen. ASEAN 2003–08; Amb. at Large, Ministry of Foreign Affairs 2008–; Public Admin Medal, Long Service Medal. *Address:* Ministry of Foreign Affairs, MFA Building, Tanglin, off Napier Road, Singapore 248163 (office). *Telephone:* 63798000 (office). *Fax:* 64747885 (office). *E-mail:* ongkengyong@ gmail.com. *Website:* www.mfa.gov.sg (office).

ONG, Tan Sri Haji Omar Yoke-Lin; Malaysian politician and diplomatist; b. 23 July 1917, Kuala Lumpur; m. Toh Puan Datin (Dr) Hajjah Aishah 1974; three s. one d.; mem. Kuala Lumpur Municipal Council 1952–55; co-founder Alliance Party; mem. Fed. Legis. Council 1954; Malayan Minister of Posts and Telecommunications 1955–56, of Transport 1956–57, of Labour and Social Welfare 1957–59, of Health and Social Welfare 1959–72; MP 1959–72; Vice-Pres. Commonwealth Parl. Asscn 1961; Amb. to UN 1962–64, to USA 1962–72, also accred to Canada 1966–72 and Brazil 1967–72; Minister without Portfolio 1964–73; Pres. of the Senate 1973–80; Chair. Asian Int. Merchant Bankers Bhd., Malaysian Oxygen Bhd., Omariff Holdings Sdn. Bhd., Syarikat Ong Yoke Lin Sdn. Bhd., OYL Industries Sdn. Bhd., Raza Sdn. Bhd.; Dir Esso Malaysia Berhad, Hume Industries (Malaysia) Berhad, Malayan Flour Mills Bhd., United Chemical Industries Bhd.; Pro-Chancellor Nat. Univ. of Malaysia 1987; Council mem. Inst. of Strategic Studies, Malaysia; Vice-Pres. UN Malaysia Asscn; Hon. LLD (Hanyang Univ. Seoul) 1978, Hon. PhD (Malaysia); SSM 1979; Panglima Mangku Neyara (Malaysia) 1959; Order of First Homayon (Iran) 1969, Grand Cross (1st Class), FRG; Order of Civil Merit (1st Class), Rep. of Korea, Commdr Ordre nat. du Mérite. *Leisure interests:* golf, photography, swimming. *Address:* 44 Pesiaran Duta, Kuala Lumpur, Malaysia (home).

ONG, Romualdo Añover, BSc; Philippine diplomatist; *Director, Foreign Service Institute;* b. 25 April 1939, Manila; s. of the late Juan Salido Ong and of Adelaida Añover; m. 1st Cecilia Hidalgo 1964 (deceased); m. 2nd Farita Aguilucho 1994; two s. two d.; ed Ateneo de Manila and Univ. of the Philippines; joined Ministry of Foreign Affairs 1968; served Bonn 1972–75, Geneva 1975–79, Minister Counsellor, Beijing 1979–82; Special Asst to Deputy Minister for Foreign Affairs 1983; Asst Minister for ASEAN Affairs 1984–85; Sr Econ. Consultant, Tech. Secr. for Int. Econ. Relations/Bd. of Overseas Econ. Promotion 1985; Amb. to Australia (also accred to Vanuatu) 1986–89; Asst Sec. for Asian and Pacific Affairs, Dept of Foreign Affairs, Manila 1990–93; Amb. to Russia 1993–94, to People's Repub. of China 1994–2000; Dir Foreign Service Inst. 2000–. *Leisure interests:* reading, car driving, basketball, hiking, movies, listening to music. *Address:* Foreign Service Institute, 5th Floor, DFA Building, 2330 Roxas Blvd, 1300 Pasay City, Metro Manila, The Philippines (office). *E-mail:* afsd@fsi.gov.ph (office). *Website:* www.info.com.ph/~fsi (office).

O'NIONS, Sir Robert Keith, Kt, MA, PhD, FRS; British geochemist and academic; *Director General of Research Councils, Office of Science and Technology, Department of Trade and Industry; Chief Scientific Adviser, Ministry of Defence;* b. 26 Sept. 1944, Birmingham; s. of William Henry O'Nions and Eva Stagg; m. Rita Bill 1967; three d.; ed Univ. of Nottingham, Univ. of Alberta; Postdoctoral Fellow, Univ. of Alberta, Canada 1969–70; Unger Vetlesen Postdoctoral Fellow, Univ. of Oslo, Norway 1970–71; Demonstrator in Petrology, Univ. of Oxford 1971–72, Lecturer in Geochemistry 1972–75; Assoc. Prof. and Prof. of Geology, Columbia Univ., New York, USA 1975–79; Royal Soc. Research Prof., Univ. of Cambridge 1979–95; Fellow Clare Hall Cambridge 1980–95; Prof. of Physics and Chem. of Minerals, Univ. of Oxford 1995–2003; Chief Scientific Adviser, Ministry of Defence 2000–; Dir Gen. Research Councils 2004–; Fellow St Hugh's Coll. Oxford 1995–2003; Fellow American Geophysical Union; Foreign Fellow Indian Nat. Science Acad.; mem. Norwegian Acad. of Sciences; Foreign mem. India Acad. of Sciences; Hon. Fellow, Univ. of Cardiff; J. B. Macelwane Award 1979, Bigsby Medal 1983, Holmes Medal 1995, Lyell Medal 1995, Urey Medal 2001. *Publications:* numerous publs in scientific journals on geochemistry. *Address:* Office of Science and Technology, Department of Trade and Industry, Victoria Street, London, SW1H 0ET, England (office). *Telephone:* (20) 7215-3803 (office). *Fax:* (20) 7215-0054 (office). *E-mail:* keith.oonions@dti.gsi.gov.uk (office). *Website:* www.ost.gov.uk (office).

ONKELINX, Laurette, BL; Belgian politician; *Deputy Prime Minister and Minister of Social Affairs and Public Health;* b. 2 Oct. 1958, Ougrée; Lecturer in Admin. Sciences 1982–85; barrister, Liège 1981–; Parti Socialiste (PS) Deputy for Liège 1988; Chair. Interfederal Comm. of Socialist Women; Vice-Chair. Socialist Group, House of Reps; mem. PS Party Office 1988; Chair. Justice Cttee, House of Reps; Vice-Pres. House of Reps; Minister for Social Integration, Health and Environment 1992–93; Minister-Pres. in Govt of Communauté française in charge of Civil Service, Childhood and Promotion of Health 1993–95, Minister-Pres. in charge of Educ., Audio-visual, Youth Help and Promotion of Health 1995–99; apptd. Deputy Prime Minister and Minister for Employment (later Employment and Equal Opportunities) 1999, then also Minister of Mobility and Transport 2003; Deputy Prime Minister and Minister for Justice 2003–07; Minister of Social Affairs and Public Health 2007 (resgnd), reappointed Dec. 2007, resgnd March 2008, Deputy Prime Minister and Minister of Social Affairs and Public Health March–Dec. 2008 (resgnd), reappointed Dec. 2008–. *Publications:* Continuons le débat, Théâtre du jeune public. *Address:* Rue du Commerce, 76–80, 1040 Brussels (office); c/o Parti Socialiste (PS), Maison du PS, 13 blvd de l'Empereur, 1000 Brussels (office). *Telephone:* (2) 233-51-11 (office); (2) 548-32-11 (office). *Fax:* (2) 230-10-67 (home); (2) 548-33-80 (office). *E-mail:* info@ laurette-onkelinx.be (office); secretariat@ps.be (office). *Website:* www.laurette -onkelinx.be (home); www.ps.be (office).

ONODERA, Tadashi, BEng; Japanese business executive; *Chairman and President, KDDI Corporation;* b. 3 Feb. 1948; ed Tohuko Univ.; began career as electronic engineer Microwave Div., Nippon Telegraph and Telephone Public Corpn 1970; joined DDI Corpn 1984, Dir and Gen. Man. Microwave Eng Dept, Network Communications Group and Mobile Communications Group 1989–95, Man. Dir and Sr Gen. Man. Eng Group 1995–97, Exec. Vice-Pres. and Sr Gen. Man. Eng Group 1997–98, Exec. Vice-Pres., Chief Engineer and Sr Gen. Man. Mobile Communications Group 1998–2000, Exec. Vice-Pres. and Deputy Operating Officer Mobile Communications Sector 2000–01, Pres. KDDI Corpn (following merger of DDI Corpn, KDD Corpn and IDO Corpn 2000) 2001–, Chair. 2005–. *Address:* KDDI Corpn, Garden Air Tower, 3-10-10, Iidabashi, Chiyoda-ku, Tokyo 102-8460, Japan (office). *Telephone:* (3) 6678-0692 (office). *Fax:* (3) 6678-0305 (office). *E-mail:* info@kddi.com (office). *Website:* www.kddi.com (office).

ONORIO, Teima, MA; I-Kiribati politician; *Vice-President and Minister for Education, Youth and Sport Development;* MP 1998–; Vice-Pres. of Kiribati, Minister for Educ., Youth and Sport Devt 2003–. *Address:* Ministry of Education, Youth and Sport Development, POB 263, Bikenibeu, Tarawa, Kiribati (office). *Telephone:* 28091/28033 (office). *Fax:* 28222 (office).

ONWUMECHILI, Ozo Ochendo Cyril Agodi, PhD, DSc; Nigerian professor of physics and administrator; b. 20 Jan. 1932, Inyi; s. of Nwaime Onwumechili and Akuviro Onwumechili (née Orji); m. Cecilia Bedeaka (née Anyadibe) 1958; two s. one d.; ed King's Coll., Lagos, Univ. Coll., Ibadan and Univ. of London; Prof. 1962–; Dir of chain of observatories 1960–66; Dean, Faculty of Science, Univ. of Ibadan 1965–66; Prof. and Head of Dept, Univ. of Nigeria 1966–73, 1976–78, Dean, Faculty of Science 1970–71, Dean, Faculty of Physical Sciences 1973–76, 1978; Visiting Prof. of Geophysics, Univ. of Alaska 1971–72; Consultant, Inst. for Space Research, Nat. Research Council of Brazil 1972; Vice-Chancellor, Univ. of Ife, Ile-Ife 1979–82; Deputy Pres. Anambra State Univ. of Tech., Enugu 1983–84, Pres. 1984–85, Vice-Chancellor 1985–86; Consultant UN Econ. Comm. for Africa 1987, Commonwealth Science Council 1988; Vice-Chair. Div. II Int. Asscn of Geomagnetism and Aeronomy 1987–91, Chair. Interdivisional Comm. 1991–95; mem. Int. Scientific Programmes Cttee, Int. Symposia on Equatorial Aeronomy 1972–, UN Advisory Cttee on Science and Tech. for Devt 1981–83; Chair. Man. Cttee UNESCO African Network of Scientific and Technological Insts (ANSTI) 1985–90; Vice-Pres. Asscn of African Univs 1984–89, Consultant 1990–2002, Chair. Scientific Cttee 1993–; mem. American Geophysical Union, Soc. for Terrestrial Magnetism and Electricity of Japan; Fellow UK and Nigerian Inst. of Physics 1969; Foundation Ed.-in-Chief Nigerian Journal of Science 1964–67; Visiting Prof. of Physics, Univ. of Wales at Cardiff 1987–88; Foundation Fellow and Former Pres. Nigerian Acad. of Science; UK Chartered Physicist 1986; Fellow African Acad. of Sciences 1987, Third World Acad. of Sciences 1989; Foundation Fellow, Science Asscn of Nigeria 1974; Hon. DSc (Ife) 1977, (Enugu State Univ.) 1992, (Univ. of Nigeria) 2001. *Publications:* Geomagnetic Variations in the Equatorial Zone 1967, University Administration in Nigeria: the Anambra State University of Technology Approach I 1991, Cost Effectiveness and Efficiency in African Universities 1993, The Equatorial Electrojet 1997, Igho Enwe Eze?: The 2000 Ahiajoku Lecture; numerous scientific articles. *Leisure interests:* swimming, table tennis, lawn tennis. *Address:* 4813 Lackawanna Street, College Park, MD 20740, USA (home); 69 Lansdowne Drive, Hackney, London, E8 3EP, England; P.O. Box 9059, Uwani, Enugu, Nigeria. *Telephone:* (301) 446-0312 (home); (20) 7249-3260 (London); (42) 254987 (Enugu). *Fax:* (212) 829-0146 (home). *E-mail:* cagodionwumechili@yahoo.com (home).

ONYSZKIEWICZ, Janusz, DMath; Polish government official and mathematician; *Senior Fellow, Center for International Relations;* b. 18 Dec. 1937, Lvov, s. of Stanislaw Onyszkiewicz and Franciszka Onyszkiewicz; m. 1st Witoslawa Boretti (died 1967); m. 2nd Alison Chadwick (died 1978); m. 3rd Joanna Jaraczewska 1983; two s. three d.; ed Warsaw Univ.; Asst. Math. Engines Inst., Polish Acad. of Sciences, Warsaw 1958–61; Asst. later Sr Asst, Faculty of Math., Informatics and Mechanics, Math. Inst., Warsaw Univ. 1963–67, Lecturer 1967–75, now Sr Lecturer; Lecturer, Univ. of Leeds, UK 1976–79; lectured at many univs abroad; mem. Polish Teachers' Union (ZNP) 1969-80, Ind. Self-governing Trade Union of Science, Tech. and Educ. Workers 1980, Deputy Chair. Br. at Warsaw Univ. Sept.–Oct. 1980; adviser to Interfactory Founding Cttee of Solidarity Ind. Self-governing Trade Union–Mazovia Region, subsequently mem. Presidium of Nat. Comm. of Solidarity Trade Union, Bd and Press Spokesman of Mazovia Region of Solidarity Trade Union; Press Spokesman Nat. Understanding Comm. and First Nat. Congress of Solidarity Trade Union 1980–81; interned 1981–82; arrested April 1983, released under amnesty July 1983; sentenced to six weeks' confinement May 1988; Press Spokesman Nat. Exec. Comm., Solidarity Trade Union; mem. Civic Cttee attached to Lech Wałęsa (q.v.) 1988–91; participant Round Table debates, mem. team for mass media and opposition press spokesman Feb.–April 1989; Deputy to Sejm (Parl.) 1989–2001; Vice-Minister of Nat. Defence 1990–92, Minister 1992–93, 1997–2000; Chair. Defence Cttee, Council of Ministers 1997–99; mem. Democratic Union Parl. 1991–94, Freedom Union Parl. 1994–; Vice-Pres. Polish Asia-Pacific Council 1996–; mem. Nat. Council Freedom Union 1996; mem. Euro-Atlantic Asscn 1994– (Pres. 1994–98); currently Sr Fellow Center for Int. Relations; Pres. Polish Mountaineering Fed. 2001–; mountaineer and speleologist, participant mountaineering expeditions in Himalayas, Hindu Kush, Karakoram, Pamir; Great Cross of Gedymin (Lithuania), Great Cross of King Leopold II (Belgium); Hon. DSc (Leeds) 1991; Gold Medal (For Outstanding Sporting Achievements), Manfred Wörner Medal. *Publications:* 15 works on foundations of math., including Complete Abstract Logics 1979; co-author Zdobycie Gasherbrumów 1977. *Leisure interests:* climbing, caving, tourism, classical music. *Address:* Center for International Relations, ul. Emilii Plater, 00-688 Warsaw, Poland (office). *Telephone:* (22) 6465267 (office). *Fax:* (22) 6465258 (office). *E-mail:* onyszkiewicz@csm.org.pl (office); janusz.onyszkiewicz@n17.waw.pl (home). *Website:* www.csm.org.pl (office).

OOKA, Makoto; Japanese poet, writer and academic; b. 16 Feb. 1931, Mishima City; s. of Hiroshi Ooka and Ayako Ooka; m. Kaneko Aizawa 1957; one s. one d.; ed Tokyo Nat. Univ.; journalist with Yomiuri (newspaper), foreign news section 1953–63; Asst Prof., Meiji Univ., Tokyo 1965–70, Prof. 1970–87; Pres. Japan Poets' Asscn 1979–81; Prof., Nat. Univ. for Fine Arts and Music 1988–93; Soshitsu Sen XV Distinguished Lecturer in Japanese Culture and Visiting Fellow, Donald Keene Center of Japanese Culture, Columbia Univ. 2000; Pres. Japan PEN Club 1989–93; mem. Int. Advisory Bd of Poetry Int., Rotterdam; mem. Japan Art Acad. 1995–; Officier des Arts et Lettres; Order of Cultural Merit 2003; Yomiuri Prize for Literature, Kikuchi Kan Prize, Hanatsubaki Prize for Poetry, Golden Wreath Prize, Struga Poetry Evenings Macedonia 1996, Asahi Prize 1996, Japanese Art Acad. Imperial Award 1996, Person of Cultural Merit 1997, Japan Foundation Prize 2002. *Publications:* poetry: Memories and the Present 1956, For a Girl in Springtime 1978, City of Water 1981, Odes to the Waters of my Hometown 1989, The Afternoon in the Earthly Paradise 1992, The Last Will of Fire 1995; Criticism: The Banquet and the Solitary Mind, Aesthetics of Japanese Poetry 1978; English translations: Japanese Poetry; Past and Present, A Poet's Anthology 1979–, an anthological series for the newspaper Asahi, A String Around Autumn 1982, A Play of Mirrors: Eight Major Poets of Modern Japan (co-ed) 1987, Elegy and Benediction 1991, The Colours of Poetry – Essays on Classic Japanese Verse 1991, What the Kite Thinks, a linked poem with three American poets 1994, The Range of Japanese Poetry 1994, Beneath the Sleepless Tossing of the Planets 1995, The Poetry and Poetics of Ancient Japan 1997, Love Songs from the Man'yoshu: Selections from a Japanese Classic 2000; French translations: Poèmes de tous les jours 1993, Propos sur le vent et autres poèmes 1995, Poésie et Poétique du Japon Ancien 1995, Dans

l'Océan du Silence 1998, Citadelle de Lumière 2002. *Address:* 2-18-1-2606, Iidabashi, Chiyoda-ku, Tokyo 102-0072, Japan.

OPERTTI BADDAN, Didier, PhD; Uruguayan lawyer, politician and international organization official; b. 1937, Montevideo; m.; four c.; ed Univ. of Uruguay; fmr Asst Prof. of Int. Pvt. Law, Univ. of Uruguay, Prof. of Int. Relations 1986; Dir Office of Codification and Devt of Int. Law, Gen. Secr., OAS 1979–81, Perm. Rep. to OAS 1988–93, Pres. OAS Perm. Council's Comm. of Juridical and Political Matters 1989, Pres. OAS Perm. Council 1990; Dir Diplomatic Law Advisory Council, Ministry of Foreign Affairs 1985–88; Prof. of Int. Pvt. Law, Int. Law Acad., The Hague; Prof. of Int. Pvt. Law, Catholic Univ. of Uruguay 1994; Minister of the Interior 1995–98, of Foreign Affairs 1998, 2000–05; Sec.-Gen., Latin-American Integration Asscn (Asociación Latinoamericana de Integración—ALADI) 2005–08; Pres. 53rd Session of UN Gen. Ass. 1998–2000; Special Counsellor for MERCOSUR issues to IDB and Inst. for Integration of Latin America and the Caribbean 1993–94; mem. UN Law Comm.; fmr mem. Uruguayan Nat. Group of Perm. Court of Arbitration; Founder and Bd mem. Int. Law Asscn of Uruguay; mem. and Dir Uruguayan Comparative Law Inst.; mem. Lawyers Asscn of Uruguay, Portuguese-Spanish American Int. Law Inst., Int. Law Asscn of Argentina, Int. and Comparative Law Acad. of Brazil. *Address:* c/o Asociación Latinoamericana de Integración, Cebollati 1461, Casilla 577, CP 11200, Montevideo, Uruguay. *Telephone:* (2) 410-1121.

OPIE, Julian Gilbert, BA; British artist; b. 12 Dec. 1958, London; s. of Roger G. Opie and Norma Opie; m. Lisa K. Milroy 1984; ed Magdalen Coll. School, Oxford, Chelsea School of Art, London and Goldsmiths' School of Art, London; exhibited Young Blood, Riverside Studios, London 1983, Sculpture 1983, Rotterdam 1983, The Sculpture Show, Hayward Gallery, London 1983, Making Sculpture, Tate Gallery, London 1983, Perspective, Basel Art Fair, Basel 1984, Home and Abroad, Serpentine Gallery, London 1984, Myth and Symbol, Tokyo Museum of Modern Art 1984, The British Show touring Australia 1984, Paris Biennale, Paris 1985, Anniotanta, Ravenna 1985, British Sculpture Louisiana Museum, Denmark 1986, De Sculptura, Vienna 1986, Correspondence Europe, Stedelijk Museum, Amsterdam 1986, Prospect 86, Frankfurt 1986; works in the collections of The British Council, The Contemporary Arts Soc., Tate Gallery, Cincinnati Museum of Modern Art, Documenta 8, Kassel 1987, Stedelijk Museum, Amsterdam. *Publications:* Julian Opie, Kunstverein Cologne: Catalogue of Works 1984, Julian Opie Drawings, ICA, London, Julian Opie New Works, Lisson Gallery. *Leisure interests:* art, music, films, books, architecture, travel, a 1981 Chevrolet Caprice Classic, supermarkets, fast food restaurants, hotel lobbies, petrol stations. *Address:* Lisson Gallery, 66–68 Bell Street, London, NW1 6SP, England. *Telephone:* (20) 7262-1539.

OPIE, Lionel Henry, MD, PhD, MRCP, FACC, FRSSA; South African cardiologist and academic; *Professor Emeritus of Medicine, Hatter Institute for Cardiology Research, Cape Heart Group, University of Cape Town;* b. 6 May 1933, Hanover, SA; s. of Prof. William Henry Opie and Marie Opie (née Le Roux); m. Carol June Sancroft Baker 1969; two d.; ed Diocesan Coll., Rondebosch, Cape Town, Univ. of Cape Town, Univ. of Oxford, UK; Intern, Groote Schuur Hosp. 1956; Sr House Officer, Dept of Neurology, Radcliffe Infirmary, Oxford 1957–59; House Physician (Endocrinology), Hammersmith Hosp., London 1959; Asst in Medicine, Peter Bent Brigham Hosp., Boston, Mass, USA, Samuel A. Levine Fellow in Cardiology, Harvard Medical School 1960–61; Asst Resident in Medicine, Toronto Gen. Hosp., Canada 1961–62; Consultant Physician, Karl Bremer Hosp. and Univ. of Stellenbosch, SA; Out-Patient Asst Physician, Radcliffe Infirmary, Wellcome Research Fellow, Dept of Biochemistry, Univ. of Oxford 1964–66; Part-Time Registrar, Hammersmith Hosp., London 1966–67; Research Fellow, Dept of Biochemistry, Imperial Coll., London 1966–68; Sr Registrar in Medicine (Cardiology), Hammersmith Hosp. 1967–69, Consultant in Medicine 1969; Sr Specialist Physician, Groote Schuur Hosp. 1971; Assoc. Prof. of Medicine, Univ. of Cape Town 1975, Dir MRC Research Unit for Ischaemic Heart Disease (now Hatter Inst., Cape Heart Centre) 1976, Personal Chair in Medicine, Prof. of Medicine 1980, now Prof. Emer., Dir Hypertension Clinic 1979; Visiting Prof., Div. of Cardiovascular Medicine, Stanford Univ. School of Medicine, Calif., USA 1991–94; British Heart Foundation Sr Fellow and Visiting Prof. St Thomas' Hosp., London 1992; Pres. Southern Africa Cardiac Soc. 1980–82; Chair. Council on Cardiac Metabolism, Int. Soc. and Fed. of Cardiology 1980; Pres. Southern Africa Hypertension Soc. 1986; Chair. Cttee Cardiovascular Drugs, Int. Soc. and Fed. Cardiology 1990; mem. British Cardiac Soc., Physiological Soc. (UK), SA Socs of Cardiology, Pharmacology, Biochemistry and Hypertension, Int. Hypertension Soc. *Publications:* over 300. *Address:* Hatter Institute for Cardiology Research, Cape Heart Centre, Faculty of Health Sciences, University of Cape Town, 7925 Observatory (office); 66A Dean Street, Newlands 7700, South Africa (home). *Telephone:* 471250; 6853855 (home). *Website:* web.uct.ac.za/depts/chc/hatter/intro.htm.

OPPENHEIM, Dennis A., MFA, BFA; American artist; b. 6 Sept. 1938, Electric City, Wash.; s. of David Oppenheim and Katherine Belknap; m. Karen Cackett (divorced); one s. two d.; ed School of Arts and Crafts, Oakland, Calif., Stanford Univ.; Prof. of Art, Yale Univ. 1969, State Univ. of NY at Stony Brook 1969; Guggenheim Foundation Sculpture Grant 1972; Nat. Endowment for the Arts Sculpture Grant 1974; numerous individual and group exhbns at galleries in USA and Europe since 1968; works in many public collections including Museum of Modern Art, New York, Tate Gallery, London, Stedelijk Museum, Amsterdam and Musée d'Art Moderne, Paris. *Publications:* Indentations 1974, Proposals 1967–1974 1975; articles in journals. *Leisure interest:* films. *Address:* 54 Franklin Street, 6th Floor, New York, NY 10013, USA (office). *Telephone:* (212) 962-0178 (office). *Fax:* (212) 587-3314 (office). *E-mail:*

dennisoppenheim@earthlink.net (office). *Website:* dennisoppenheim.com (office); dennisoppenheim.net (home).

OPPENHEIMER, Nicholas Frank, MA; South African business executive; *Chairman, De Beers;* b. 8 June 1945, Johannesburg; s. of Harry F. Oppenheimer; m. Orcillia M. L. Lasch 1968; one s.; ed Harrow School, UK and Christ Church, Oxford, UK; Chair. De Beers Consolidated Mines Ltd 1998–, The Diamond Trading Co. Ltd; Exec. Chair. De Beers Centenary AG; Dir De Beers Industrial Corpn Ltd, E. Oppenheimer & Son (Pty) Ltd; Dir (non-exec.) Anglo-American Corpn of South Africa Ltd; Hon. DTech (Technikon Witwatersrand) 2003. *Leisure interests:* squash, golf, cricket, flying. *Address:* PO Box 61631, Marshalltown 2107, South Africa. *E-mail:* www.debeersgroup .com (office).

OPPENLÄNDER, Karl Heinrich, DEcon; German economist; b. 17 Jan. 1932, Dörzbach; m. Cäcilie Oppenländer 1958; one s. one d.; ed Univ. of Munich; entered IFO Inst. for Econ. Research 1958, Head of Dept 1966, mem. Exec. Cttee 1972, Pres. (Prof.) 1976–99; Lecturer, Univ. of Tübingen 1975, Univ. of Munich 1976–, Univ. of Augsburg 1980–83. *Publications:* Die moderne Wachstumstheorie 1963, Der investitionsinduzierte technische Fortschritt 1976.

OPREA, Gabriel, DIur; Romanian politician; *Minister of Administration and Interior;* b. 1 Jan. 1961, Fundulea; m.; two c.; ed Univ. of Bucharest, Nat. Coll. of Defence; officer, Ministry of Defence 1983–90; Vice-Pres. Nat. Coll. of Defence 2000, Deputy Dir 2000–01, Prof. 2001; Sec. of State and Pres. Nat. Admin of State Reserves 2001–02; Prefect, Bucharest 2002–03; Del. Minister of Public Admin 2003–04; mem. Chamber of Deputies 2004–; mem. Democrat Party (PSD), Pres. PSD Ilfov 2004–, PSD Defence Dept 2006–; Minister of Admin and Interior 2008–; Prof., Nat. Intelligence Acad. 2008–; Kt, Nat. Order of the Star of Romania 2000, Nat. Order of Faithful Service 2001. *Address:* Ministry of the Interior and Administrative Reform, 010086 Bucharest, Piaţa Revoluţiei 1a, Sector 1, Romania (office). *Telephone:* (21) 3037080 (office). *Fax:* (21) 3103072 (office). *E-mail:* drp@mai.gov.ro (office). *Website:* www.mai.gov.ro (office).

OPRESCU, Sorin Mircea; Romanian physician and politician; *Mayor of Bucharest;* b. 7 Nov. 1951, Bucharest; m. (divorced); one c.; ed Faculty of Medicine, Univ. of Bucharest; surgical intern 1975–78; physician, M. Kogălniceanu Int. Airport, Constanţa 1978–79; Trainee Univ. Ass, Surgery Clinic of Brancovenian Clinic Hosp. 1978, Univ. Asst 1982; Surgeon, Bucharest Univ. Hosp.1985–90, Primary Surgeon, Clinic for Higher Digestive Surgery 1990–94, Dir Bucharest Univ. Hosp. 1994–; Lecturer, Carol Davila Univ. of Medicine and Pharmacy 1996–2000, Univ. Prof. and Chair. of Surgery 2000–; Adviser to Minister of Health 1993–94; Adviser to Gen. Council of Bucharest City Hall 1996–2000; Deputy Mayor of Bucharest 2000; mem. Senatul (The Senate) 2000–08 (resgnd) fmr mem. Social Democrat Party, Pres. Bucharest br. 2006–08; Mayor of Bucharest (ind.) 2008–. *Address:* 050013 Bucharest 5, Bd. Regina Elisabeta 47, Romania (office). *Telephone:* (21) 3055500 (office). *Fax:* (21) 3120030 (office). *E-mail:* sorin.oprescu@ bucuresti-primaria.ro (office). *Website:* www.pmb.ro (office); www .sorinoprescu.ro.

ORANGE, The Prince of; Willem-Alexander Claus George Ferdinand, MA; Dutch; b. 27 April 1967, Utrecht; s. of HM Queen Beatrix and Prince Claus; m. Máxima Zorreguieta 2002; three d.; ed Baarns Lyceum, Eerste Vrijzinnig Christelijk Lyceum, The Hague, Atlantic Coll. Llantwit Major, Wales, Leiden Univ.; mil. service in Royal Netherlands Navy 1985–87, gained Mil. Pilot's Licence 1993, attended Netherlands Defence Coll. 1994, currently holds ranks of Commodore Navy Reserve and Air Force Reserve, Brig.-Gen. Army Reserve and Royal Mil. Constabulary Reserve, Aide-de-Camp Extraordinary to HM The Queen; Patron Global Water Partnership 1998; fully-qualified pvt, commercial and airline pilot, volunteer pilot African Medical Research and Educ. Foundation 1989, Kenya Wildlife Service 1991; mem. founding cttee World Water Vision 1999–2000; Chair. Second World Water Forum, The Hague 2000; mem. Panel of Eminent Persons, UN conf. on sustainable devt, Johannesburg 2002; Chair. Integrated Water Man. Comm. 2002–04; Chair. Water Advisory Cttee 2004–; mem. IOC 1998–; Patron Orange Fund; hon. mem. Royal Naval Yacht Club, Royal Dutch Yachting and Rowing Asscn; Officers' Long Service Decoration 2001. *Address:* Noordeinde Palace, Postbus 30412, The Hague 2500 GK, The Netherlands (office). *Website:* www.koninklijkhuis.nl.

ORAYEVSKY, Victor Nikolayevich, DPhysMathSc; Russian physicist; b. 9 March 1935, Poltava, Ukraine; ed Kharkov State Univ.; Jr researcher Inst. of Nuclear Physics, USSR Acad. of Sciences (Siberian br.) 1958–65, Head of Div. Inst. of Earth Magnetism, Ionosphere and Radiowaves Propagation (IZMIRAN) 1979–89, Dir 1989–, Head of int. Sputnik projects; Sr Researcher Inst. of Physics, Ukrainian Acad. of Sciences 1965–70, Head of Div. Inst. of Nuclear Studies 1970–74; Head of Scientific Production Div., Energia Co. 1974–79, Head of Lab., Head of Dept 1979–89; mem. Int. Acad. of Astronautics, NY Acad. of Sciences, Russian Acad. of Sciences, Int. Acad. of Informatics; State Prize of Ukrainian SSR, USSR State Prize 1987, Merited Worker of Science, Russian Fed. 1996. *Address:* IZMIRAN, 142092 Troitsk, Moscow, Russia (office). *Telephone:* (495) 334-01-20 (office).

ORAZBAY, Askhat T.; Kazakhstani international organization official; Sec.-Gen. Econ. Co-operation Org. 2004–06. *Address:* c/o Economic Co-operation Organization, 1 Golbou Alley, Kamranieh Street, POB 14155-6176, Tehran, Iran (office).

ORAZMUKHAMEDOV, Nury Orazovich; Turkmenistani politician and diplomatist; b. 1949, Mary; ed Turkmenistan Polytech. Inst.; master, engineer, chief engineer Turkmencentrstroi 1971–; head of Ashkhabad construction

units; Deputy Chair. State Construction Cttee 1990–91; Minister of Construction of Turkmenistan 1991–94; Minister of Construction and Architecture 1994–95; Head of Admin. Khikim Ashkhabad Feb. 1995; Amb. to Russian Fed. 1996–2000, to Moldova 2000. *Address:* c/o Ministry of Foreign Affairs, Ashgabat, Turkmenistan (office).

ORBAN, Leonard; Romanian engineer and politician; *Commissioner for Multilingualism, European Commission;* b. 28 June 1961, Braşov; m.; one c.; ed Faculty of Mechanical Eng, Univ. of Braşov, Faculty of Man., Acad. of Econ. Studies, Bucharest; engineer, Inst. of Research for Machine Mfg Tech., Bucharest, Enterprise for Special Industrial Constructions, Bucharest, Tractor Mfg Co. Miercurea Ciuc 1986–93; Parl. Counsellor on European and Int. affairs, Chamber of Deputies, Romanian Parl. 1993–2001; Deputy Chief Negotiator for accession to EU 2001–04, Chief Negotiator 2004–05; State Sec., Ministry of European Integration 2005–06; Head of Romanian del. for negotiating accession to European Econ. Area 2006–; nominated as Romania's cand. for EC Oct. 2006, European Commr for Multilingualism 2007–; Coordinator Elaboration of Romanian Post Accession Strategy for 2007–2013; mem. several governmental cttees related to Romania's EU accession negotiations, including European Integration Exec. Cttee, State Aid Cttee, Cttee for the Man. of EU Funds, Romanian Steel Sector Restructuring); mem. Romanian Social and Econ. Council; Kt of 'Steaua Romaniei' Nat. Order (Star of Romania) 2002. *Publications:* articles and analyses in nat. and foreign newspapers and magazines on European integration and European affairs 2001–. *Leisure interests:* foreign policy, classical music, reading, cinema. *Address:* Ministry of European Integration, Apolodor 17 latura Nord, sector 5, 050741 Bucharest, Romania (office). *Telephone:* (21) 3011656 (office). *Fax:* (21) 3353495 (office). *Website:* europa.eu (office).

ORBÁN, Viktor, LLD, PhD; Hungarian politician and lawyer; *Vice-President, Christian Democrat and People's Parties International;* b. 31 May 1963, Székesfehérvár; s. of Győző Orbán; m.; two s. three d.; ed Eötvös Loránd Univ., Budapest and Pembroke Coll., Oxford, UK; worked as sociologist for Man. Training Inst., Ministry of Agric. and Food 1987–88; researcher, Middle Europe Research Group 1989–91; co-f. Hungarian opposition group Fed. of Young Democrats (FIDESZ) 1988, Spokesman 1989, Pres. Fidesz–Hungarian Civic Union 2003–; represented FIDESZ political Sub-cttee of Opposition Round Table Discussion 1989; mem. Parl., Leader FIDESZ Parl. Group 1990–94; Prime Minister 1998–2002; Chair. Parl. Cttee on European Integration Affairs 1994–98; Pres. FIDESZ 1993–2000, New Atlantic Initiative Hungarian Cttee 1996–98; Vice-Pres. Liberal Int. 1992–2000, mem. Bureau 1993–2002; Vice-Pres. Christian Democrat and People's Parties Int. 2001–, European People's Party 2002–; Hon. Senator, European Acad. of Sciences and Arts 2000; Grande Croix de l'ordre nat. du Mérite (France) 2001, Papal Grand Cross of the Order of St Gregory the Great 2004; Freedom Prize, American Enterprises Inst. and the New Atlantic Initiative 2001, Vesek and Maria Polák Prize 2001, Franz Josef Strauss Prize 2001, Capo Circeo Prize 2001, Förderpreis Soziale Marktwirtschaft, German Club of Econs 2002, Mérite Européen Prize, European Peoples's Party 2004. *Publication:* National Policy 1988–1998. *Leisure interest:* playing soccer. *Address:* Christian Democrat and People's Parties International, CDI Headquarters, rue d'Arlon 67, 1040 Brussels, Belgium (office). *Telephone:* (2) 285-41-60 (office). *Fax:* (2) 285-42-66 (office). *E-mail:* idc@idc-cdi.org (office). *Website:* www.orbanviktor.hu (office).

ORDE, Hugh Stephen Roden, BA, KBE, OBE; British police officer; *President, Association of Chief Police Officers;* b. 27 Aug. 1958; s. of Thomas Orde and Stella Orde; m. Kathleen Helen Orde; one s.; ed Univ. of Kent; joined London Metropolitan Police 1977, apptd Sergeant, Brixton 1982, Police Staff Coll. 1983, Insp., Greenwich 1984–90, Chief Insp., Deputy Asst Commdr SW London 1990, Chief Insp., Hounslow 1991–93, Supt Territorial Support 1993–95, Commdr (Community Safety and Partnership) 1997–98, Commdr (Crime), S London 1998–99, Deputy Asst Commr attached to Commr's Pvt. Office, New Scotland Yard 1999–2002; Chief Constable Police Service Northern Ireland (PSNI) 2002–09; Pres. Asscn of Chief Police Officers 2009–. *Leisure interests:* marathon running, wine, gardening. *Address:* Association of Chief Police Officers, 1st Floor, 10 Victoria Street, London, SW1H 0NN, England (office). *Telephone:* (20) 7084-8950 (office). *Website:* www .acpo.police.uk (office).

ORDJONIKIDZE, Iosif Nikolaevich; Georgian engineer and politician; b. 9 Feb. 1948, Borjomi; m.; two c.; ed Georgian Polytechnic Inst.; engineer Tbilisi Aviation plant 1971–73, Sec. Komsomol cttee 1973–76; First Sec. Regional Komsomol Cttee of Georgia 1976–83; Sec. USSR Cen. Komsomol Cttee 1983–90; Chair. Union of Innovation Enterprises 1990–91; Deputy Premier for Int. and External Econ. Relations, Govt of Moscow 1991-2001, Deputy Mayor 2001–; Order of the Red Banner of Labour, Order of Friendship of Nations, Badge of Honour. *Address:* Moscow Government, Tverskaya str. 13, 103032 Moscow, Russia (office). *Telephone:* (095) 229-63-90 (office); (095) 230-28-56 (office).

ORDZHONIKIDZE, Sergei Alexandrovitch; Russian diplomatist and UN official; *Director-General, United Nations, Geneva;* b. 14 March 1946, Moscow; m.; two s.; ed Moscow State Inst. of Int. Relations, Diplomatic Acad., Moscow; mem. staff USSR Ministry of Foreign Affairs –1991; Deputy Perm. Rep. to UN, New York 1991–96; Head Dept of Int. Orgs, Ministry of Foreign Affairs 1996–99, Deputy Minister of Foreign Affairs 1999–2002; Under-Sec.-Gen. UN and Dir-Gen. UN Office, Geneva 2002–, Sec. Gen., Conf. on Disarmament and Personal Rep. of Sec.-Gen. to the Conf.; numerous state awards. *Publications:* numerous publs on int. and legal affairs, in particular on UN problems. *Leisure interests:* tennis, skiing, cycling. *Address:* United Nations Office at Geneva, Palais des Nations, 1211 Geneva 10, Switzerland (office). *Telephone:* (22) 9172100 (office). *Fax:* (22) 9170002 (office). *Website:* www.unog.ch (office).

OREFFICE, Paul F(austo), BS; American business executive; *Chairman, National Parkinson Foundation Inc.;* b. 29 Nov. 1927, Venice, Italy; s. of Max Oreffice and Elena Oreffice (née Friedenberg); m. Franca Giuseppina Ruffini 1956; one s. one d.; ed Purdue Univ.; joined Dow Chemical Int., Midland, Mich. 1953, Mediterranean Area Sales Man., Milan, Italy 1955–56, Man. Dow Quimica do Brazil, São Paulo 1956–63, Gen. Man. Dow. Int., Spain 1963–65, Gen. Man. Dow Chemical Latin America 1965–67, Pres. Dow Chemical Inter-American Ltd 1967–69, Financial Vice-Pres. The Dow Chemical Co. 1969–75, Dir Dow Chemical Co. 1971–, Pres. Dow Chemical USA 1975–78, Chair. Exec. Cttee Dow Chemical Co. 1978–87, Pres. and CEO 1978–86, Chair., Pres. and CEO 1986–87, Chair. Bd 1987–92; Dir Cigna Corpn, Northern Telecom Ltd 1983, The Coca-Cola Company 1985, Morgan Stanley Group Inc. 1987; Chair. American Enterprise Inst., Bd of Overseers Inst. for Civil Justice; mem. Bd of Govs Nat. Parkinson Foundation, now Chair.; mem. The Business Council; Hon. DEng (Purdue) 1976; Hon. Dr Industrial Man. (Lawrence Inst. of Tech.); Hon. DSc (Saginaw Valley State Coll.), Business Admin. (Tri-State Univ.); Encomienda del Mérito Civil (Spain) 1966. *Leisure interests:* tennis, bridge, golf, various other sports. *Address:* c/o National Parkinson Foundation Inc., 1501 NW 9th Avenue, Bob Hope Road, Miami, FL, 33136-1494, USA (office). *Website:* www.parkinson.org (office).

O'REGAN, (Andrew) Brendan, CBE; Irish business executive; b. 15 May 1917, Co. Clare; s. of James O'Regan and Norah O'Regan; m. (Rita) Margaret Barrow 1950; two s. three d.; ed Blackrock Coll., Dublin; Comptroller, Sales and Catering, Shannon Airport 1943–73; Chair. Bord Fáilte Eireann 1957–73, Shannon Free Airport Devt Co. 1959–78; Jt Pres., State Agencies Devt Co-operation Org. (DEVCO) 1974–79, 1988–89; Chair. Co-operation North 1979–82, Pres. 1982–; Pres. Co-operation Ireland Inc. (NY) 1982–90; Chair. Irish Peace Inst. 1984–90, Pres. 1990–; Chair. Shannon Centre for Int. Co-operation 1987–90, Pres. 1990–; Founder mem. OBAIR Enterprise, New-market-on-Fergus 1993; Fellow, Inst. of Engineers of Ireland 1977, Irish Hotel and Catering Inst. 1977; Freeman of City of Limerick 1995; Hon. LLD (Nat. Univ. of Ireland) 1978, (Queen's Univ., Belfast) 1999, (Univ. of Limerick) 2001; United Dominions Trust Endeavour Award for Tourism 1973, American Soc. of Travel Agents—Hall of Fame 1977, British Airways Tourism Endeavour Award 1980, Clareman of the Year 1983, Rotary's Paul Harris Award, Duty Free News Int. and Möet et Chandon Lifetime Achievement Award 1999, Co-Operation Ireland 'Peace Dove' Award 2000, Morton Deutsch Conflict Resolution Award, American Psychological Asscn 2004. *Publications:* numer-ous speeches and articles on peace through managed co-operation. *Leisure interests:* reading, walking. *Address:* 12 The Sycamores, Grove Road, Malahide, Co., Dublin, Ireland. *Telephone:* (61) 368408 (office); (1) 8454523 (home). *Fax:* (61) 368717 (office). *E-mail:* obairnewmarket@eirom.net (office).

O'REILLY, Sir Anthony (John Francis), Kt, BCL; Irish business executive; *CEO, Independent News and Media PLC;* b. 7 May 1936, Dublin; s. of John Patrick O'Reilly and Aileen O'Reilly (née O'Connor); m. 1st Susan Cameron 1962 (divorced); three s. three d.; m. 2nd Chryss Goulandris 1991; ed Belvedere Coll., Dublin, Univ. Coll., Dublin; qualified as solicitor 1958; Demonstrator and Lecturer, Univ. Coll., Cork 1960–62; Personal Asst to Chair., Suttons Ltd, Cork 1960–62; Dir Robert McCowen & Sons Ltd, Tralee 1961–62; Gen. Man. Bord Bainne (Irish Dairy Bd) 1962–66; Man. Dir and CEO, Comhlucht Siuicre Eireann Teo. (Irish Sugar Co.) 1966–69; Jt Man. Dir Heinz-Erin Ltd 1967–70, Man. Dir H. J. Heinz Co. Ltd, UK 1969–71, Sr Vice-Pres. N America and Pacific, H. J. Heinz Co. 1971–72, Exec. Vice-Pres. and COO 1972–73, Pres. and COO 1973–79, Chair. 1978–2000, Pres. 1979–90, CEO 1979–98; Chair. Ind. Newspapers PLC 1980–, Chair. and CEO Ind. News and Media PLC 2000–2004, CEO 2004–; Chair. Waterford Wedgwood PLC 1993–2009 (resgnd); Chair. European Advisory Bd Bankers Trust 1992–, Fitzwilton PLC, Atlantic Resources, Dublin, Eircom PLC 2001–; numerous other commercial appointments; Fellow, BIM, RSA; Dr hc (Bradford) 1991; Hon. LLD (Leicester) 1992. *Publications:* Prospect 1962, Developing Creative Management 1970, The Conservative Consumer 1971, Food for Thought 1972. *Leisure interests:* tennis, rugby. *Address:* Independent News and Media, Independent House, 2023 Bianconi Avenue, Citywest Business Park, City-west Business Campus, Naas Road, Dublin 2 (office); Castlemartin, Kilcullen, Co. Kildare, Ireland (home). *Telephone:* (1) 4663200 (office). *Fax:* (1) 4663222 (office). *Website:* www.independentnewsmedia.com (office).

O'REILLY, David J., BEng; American/Irish petroleum company executive; *Chairman and CEO, Chevron Corporation;* b. Jan. 1947, Dublin, Ireland; ed Univ. Coll., Dublin; joined Chevron Research Co. 1968, Sr Vice-Pres. and COO Chevron Chemical Co. 1989–91, Vice-Pres. Chevron 1991–98, Pres. Chevron Products Co. 1994–98, mem. Bd Dirs Chevron Corpn 1998–, Vice-Chair. Chevron Corpn 1998–99, Chair. and CEO 2000–; mem. American Petroleum Inst., Peterson Inst. for Int. Econs, The Business Council, The Business Roundtable, JPMorgan Int. Council, World Econ. Forum's Int. Business Council, Nat. Petroleum Council, American Soc. of Corp. Execs, Bd of Trustees Eisenhower Fellowships, King Fahd Univ. of Petroleum, Minerals Int. Advisory Bd. *Address:* Chevron Corporation, 6001 Bollinger Canyon Road, San Ramon, CA 94583, USA (office). *Telephone:* (925) 842-1000 (office). *Fax:* (925) 842-3530 (office). *E-mail:* comment@chevron.com (office). *Website:* www .chevron.com (office).

O'REILLY, Francis Joseph, BA, BAI, LLD, MRIA; Irish university chancellor (retd) and fmr banker; b. 15 Nov. 1922, Dublin; s. of Lt-Col C. J. O'Reilly and Dorothy Mary Martin; m. Teresa Williams 1950; three s. seven d.; ed Ampleforth Coll. and Trinity Coll. Dublin; Chair. Irish Distillers Group 1966–83; Dir Ulster Bank 1961–90, Chair. 1982–89; Dir Nat. Westminster Bank 1982–89; Chair. Coll. des Irlandais, Paris 1988–2000; Chancellor, Univ. of Dublin 1985–98; mem. Inst. of Royal Engineers; Hon. LLD (Dublin) 1978, (Nat. Univ. of Ireland) 1986, Hon. Fellow (Trinity Coll. Dublin) 1999; Grand

Cross, Order of St Lazarus of Jerusalem 1982, Knight Commdr, Order of St Gregory the Great 2002. *Leisure interests:* racing, gardening, reading. *Address:* Rathmore, Naas, Co. Kildare, Ireland (home). *Telephone:* (45) 862136 (home). *Fax:* (45) 862012 (home).

OREJA AGUIRRE, Marcelino, LLD; Spanish diplomatist and government official; b. 13 Feb. 1935; m. Silvia Arburua 1967; two s.; ed Univ. of Madrid; entered diplomatic service 1958; Dir Tech. Office of Minister of Foreign Affairs 1962; fmr Asst Dir, Prof. of Foreign Affairs at Escuela Diplomática; mem. dels to UN, IMF, IDB, OECD; mem. interministerial cttee drafting bill for religious freedom; Dir of Int. Relations, Banco de España 1971–74; Under-Sec. for Information and Tourism 1974, for Foreign Affairs Dec. 1975; Minister of Foreign Affairs 1976–80; elected Deputy for Guipúzcoa and Alava in 1979 and 1982; Govt Rep. in Basque Country 1980–82; Sec. Gen. Council of Europe 1984–89; EC Commr for Energy, Euratom Supply Agency and Transport 1994–95, for Relations with European Parl., with mem. States, Culture and Public Affairs 1995–99; Senator by royal appointment 1977. *Address:* The Senate, Madrid, Spain (office); 81 Núñez de Balboa, 28006 Madrid, Spain. *Telephone:* (91) 5759101.

OREKHOV, Ruslan Gennadyevich; Russian politician; b. 14 Oct. 1963, Kalinin (now Tver); m.; two c.; ed Kazakh State Univ.; engineer-researcher Kazakh State Univ. 1985–87; Head of Div., Alma-Ata Dist Exec. Cttee 1987–88; instructor Moscow Dist Exec. Cttee 1989–90; expert USSR Union of Lawyers 1990; leading expert Cttee on Law Supreme Soviet of Russian Fed. 1990–91; Head Div. of Service of State Counsellors Russian Fed. 1991–93; Head State Dept of Law; Russian Presidency 1993–94; Co-Chair. Expert Council on Law, Russian Presidency 1994–96; Deputy Head of Admin. Russian Presidency, Head Dept of State Law 1996–2000, Pres. World Bank Group for Russia 2001. *Address:* The World Bank, Sadovo-Kudrinskaya str. 3, 123242 Moscow, Russia (office). *Telephone:* (495) 745-70-00 (office). *Fax:* (495) 253-06-12.

ORELLANA, José Roberto, MS; Salvadorean economist and banker; b. 20 Jan. 1944, San Salvador; s. of Roberto Orellana and Aida Milla; m. Julia Raquel Aguilar 1977; four c.; ed Trinity Coll., Conn., USA, Stanford Univ.; Vice-Pres., Gen. Man. Banco Cuscatlán 1971–81; Dir Fundación Salvadoreña para el Desarrollo Económico y Social (FUSADES) 1984–89; fmr Pres. Banco Cen. de Reserva de El Salvador; Alt. Gov. Interamerican Devt Bank 1989–95, IMF, World Bank, Banco Centroamericano de Integración Económica. *Address:* c/o Banco Central de Reserva de El Salvador, Alameda Juan Pablo II y 17 Avenida Norte, San Salvador, El Salvador.

ORELLANA MERCADO, Angel Edmundo, DJur; Honduran diplomatist and legal executive; *Minister of National Defence;* b. 20 Oct. 1948, Honduras; m.; ed Universidad Autónoma de Honduras, Univ. of Bologna, Italy; Asst to Legal Counsel of Nat. Housing Inst. 1968; Legal Counsel of Tech. Secr. of Council for Econ. Planning 1976–79; Dir Honduran Pre-Investment Fund 1980–84; Dir-Gen. Admin. Reform of the State Secr. for Planning, Co-ordination and Budget 1985–88; Pty Magistrate of Court of Appeals, Admin. Jurisdiction 1989–94; Attorney-Gen. 1994–99; Perm. Rep. to UN, New York 1999–; mem. Faculty of Law and Social Sciences, Universidad Nacional Autónoma de Honduras 1976–; Hon. Consul in Genoa, Italy 1974–75; mem. Admin. Law Comm., Honduran Bar Asscn 1980–91; Vice-Chair. for Co-ordination, Comm. on Judicial Reform 1988–93; Co-ordinator Cttee on Admin. Oversight of the Judiciary 1988–93; Minister of the Interior 2007–08, for Foreign Affairs 2008–09, of Nat. Defence 2009–. *Publications include:* numerous articles and books; participated in promulgation of several bills. *Address:* Ministry of National Defence, 5a Avda, 4a Calle, Tegucigalpa, Honduras (office). *Telephone:* 238-3427 (office). *Fax:* 238-0238 (office).

ORESHARSKI, Plamen, PhD; Bulgarian politician; *Minister of Finance;* b. 21 Feb. 1960, Dupnitsa; m.; ed Univ. of Nat. and World Economy; Vice-Dean Finance Dept, Univ. of Nat. and World Economy 1992–93, Vice-Chancellor and Prof., Teaching on Finance Man., Investments, Investment Analysis 2003–; Dir State Treasury and Debt Directorate, Ministry of Finance 1993–97, Deputy Minister 1997–2001, Minister of Finance 2005–; Pres. Man. Bd Sofiabank 1996–96; mem. Man. Bd Bulgarian Stock Exchange 1995–99, State Saving Bank 1996–97, Bulbank 1997–2000, Bulgarian Consolidation Co. 1997–2000; mem. Union of Democratic Forces (UDF), Deputy Chair. and mem. UDF Nat. Exec. Bd –2003 (resgnd), UDF nominee for Mayor of Sofia at 2003 elections, candidature withdrawn; Emerging Markets magazine Finance Minister of the Year Award 2007. *Publications:* Investment Analysis, Finance; more than 100 articles, reviews and comments. *Address:* Ministry of Finance, 1000 Sofia, ul. G.S. Rakovski 102, Bulgaria (office). *Telephone:* (2) 985-920-00 (office). *Fax:* (2) 987-05-81 (office). *E-mail:* feedback@minfin.bg (office). *Website:* www.minfin.bg (office).

ORGAN, (Harold) Bryan; British artist; b. 31 Aug. 1935, Leicester; s. of the late Harold Victor Organ and Helen Dorothy Organ; m. 2nd Sandra Mary Mills 1982; ed Loughborough Coll. of Art; Royal Acad. Schools, London; Lecturer in Drawing and Painting, Loughborough 1959–65; represented: Kunsthalle, Darmstadt 1968, Mostra Mercatao d'Arte Contemporanea, Florence 1969, 3rd Int. Exhbns of Drawing Germany 1970, São Paulo Museum of Art, Brazil; works in pvt. and public collections in England, France, Germany, Italy, Switzerland, USA, Canada, Brazil; Hon. MA (Loughborough) 1974; Hon. DLitt (Leicester) 1985. *Portraits include:* Sir Michael Tippett 1966, David Hicks 1968, Mary Quant 1969, Princess Margaret 1970, Elton John 1973, Viscount Stockton 1980, HRH The Prince of Wales 1980, The Princess of Wales 1981, Lord Denning 1982, Sir James Callaghan 1982, HRH The Duke of Edinburgh 1983. *Leisure interest:* cricket. *Address:* c/o Redfern Gallery, 20 Cork Street, London, W1X 2HL; The Stables,

Marston Trussell, nr Market Harborough, Leics., LE16 9TX, England. *Telephone:* (20) 7734-1732 (London).

O'RIORDAN, Timothy, MA, PhD, FRSA, FBA; British academic; *Emeritus Professor of Environmental Sciences, University of East Anglia;* b. 21 Feb. 1942, Edinburgh; s. of the late Kevin O'Riordan and Norah O'Riordan; m. Ann Philip 1968 (died 1992); two d.; ed Univs of Edinburgh and Cambridge, Cornell Univ., USA; Asst Prof., Dept of Geography, Simon Fraser Univ. Vancouver, BC 1967–74; Visiting Lecturer, Univ. of Canterbury, NZ 1970; Visiting Assoc. Prof., Clark Univ., Worcester, Mass, USA 1972; Reader, Univ. of East Anglia 1974, Prof. of Environmental Sciences 1980–2005, Emer. Prof. 2005–; Chair. Environment Cttee Broads Authority 1989–99, Environment Science and Soc. Programme, European Science Foundation 1989–; Adviser, Environmental Research Directorate 1996–97; Trustee, Soil Asscn 2005–; mem. Environmental Advisory Council, Dow Chemical 1992–97, Eastern Group PLC 1995–98; Fellow, British Acad. 1999; mem. UK Sustainable Devt Comm. 2000–07; DL, Co. of Norfolk 1998; Sheriff, City of Norwich 2009; Gill Memorial Prize, Royal Geographical Soc. *Publications:* Environmentalism 1976, Countryside Conflicts 1986, Sizewell B: An Anatomy of the Inquiry 1987, The Greening of the Machinery of Government 1990; ed. Interpreting the Precautionary Principle 1994, The Politics of Climate Change in Europe 1996, Ecotaxation 1996, The Transition to Sustainability in Europe 1998, Environmental Science for Environmental Management 2000, Globalism, Localism and Identity 2001, Reinterpreting the Precautionary Principle 2001, Biodiversity, Sustainability and Human Communities 2002. *Leisure interests:* classical double bass playing, jogging, cycling, swimming, intuition. *Address:* Wheatlands, Hethersett Lane, Colney, Norwich, NR4 7TT, England (office). *Telephone:* (1603) 810534 (home). *Fax:* (1603) 593739 (home). *E-mail:* t.oriordan@uea.ac.uk (office). *Website:* www.uea.ac.uk/env (office).

ORITA, Masaki, LLB; Japanese diplomatist; *Special Envoy (Europe) for United Nations Reform, Ministry of Foreign Affairs;* b. 29 July 1942, Tokyo; s. of Saburo Orita and Saeko Orita; m. Masako Orita; one s.; ed Univ. of Tokyo, St Catherine's Coll., Oxford, UK; diplomatic postings to UK 1967, USSR 1975–77, OECD, Paris 1977–79, Washington, DC 1984–87; Exec. Asst to Prime Minister 1989–1992; Consul-Gen., Hong Kong 1992–94, Dir Gen. Treaties Bureau and N American Affairs Bureau, Ministry of Foreign Affairs 1994–97, Amb. to Denmark 1997–2001, Insp. Gen., Ministry of Foreign Affairs 2001, Amb. to UK 2001–04, Special Envoy (Europe) for UN Reform, Ministry of Foreign Affairs 2005–; Commdr, Order of Orange (Netherlands) 1991; Grand Cross, Order of the Dannebrog (Denmark) 1998. *Address:* Ministry of Foreign Affairs, Kasumigaseki 2-2-1, Chiyoda-ku, Tokyo 100-8919, Japan (office). *Telephone:* (3) 3580-3311 (office). *Website:* www.mofa.go.jp (office).

ORLOV, Viktor Petrovich, CandGeolSc, DEconSc; Russian politician and geologist; b. 23 March 1940, Chernogorsk, Krasnoyarsk Region; s. of Petr Orlov and Eva Orlova; m.; three d.; ed Tomsk State Univ., Acad. of Nat. Econ. at USSR Council of Ministers; geologist, Chief Geologist, Team Leader, W Siberian Geological Survey 1968–75; Chief Engineer Geological Exploration, Iran 1975–78; Chief Geologist, Deputy Head Geological Div., Amalgamation Tsentrgeologiya 1979–81, Dir Gen. 1986–90; Deputy Head Geology and Production Depts, Ministry of Geology Russian Fed. 1981–84, 1986–; Deputy Minister of Geology USSR 1990–91; First Deputy Chair. State Cttee on Geology Russian Fed. 1991–92; Chair. Cttee on Geology and Use of Mineral Resources Russian Fed. 1992–96; Minister of Natural Resources Russian Fed. 1996–98, 1998–99; Pres. Russian Geological Soc. 2000–01; mem. Council of Fed., Fed. Ass. of the Russian Fed., Rep., Admin, Koryak Autonomous Area 2001–; Laureate, RF State Prize in Science and Eng 2001; Honoured Geologist of Russia 1990, Order for Services to the Native Land, IVth degree, 2001. *Publications:* Geological Forecasting 1991, Iron-Ore Base of Russia 1998, Mineral Resources and Geological Service of Russia during the Economic Reforms 1999, Reforms in Geology 2000; more than 200 scientific articles. *Leisure interests:* fishing, hunting. *Address:* Russian Geological Society, Zvenigorodskoye Shosse 9, 123022 Moscow, Russia (office); Council of Federation, Bolshaya Dmitrovka str. 26, Moscow (office); Palana, Portova str. 22, 684620 Kamchatka region, Karyak autonomous district, Russia (office). *Telephone:* (495) 292-75-43 (Geological Soc.) (office); (495) 926-69-53 (Council of Fed.) (office); (8415-43) 3-13-80 (Palana) (office); (495) 259-79-53. *Fax:* (495) 292-75-43. *E-mail:* VPOrlov@council.gov.ru (office).

ORMESSON, Comte Jean d'; French writer, journalist and international official; b. 16 June 1925; s. of Marquis d'Ormesson; nephew of late Comte Wladimir d'Ormesson; m. Françoise Béghin 1962; one d.; ed Ecole Normale Supérieure; Deputy Sec.-Gen. Int. Council for Philosophy and Humanistic studies (UNESCO) 1950–71, Sec.-Gen. 1971; staff of various Govt ministers 1958–66; Deputy Ed. Diogène (int. journal) 1952–72, mem. Man. Cttee 1971–; mem. Council ORTF 1960–62, Programme Cttee 1973; mem. Control Comm. of Cinema 1962–69; mem. Editorial Cttee Editions Gallimard 1972–74; Ed.-in-Chief, Columnist, Le Figaro 1974–77, Dir-Gen. 1976, leader writer, columnist 1977–; mem. Acad. Française 1973; Pres., Soc. des amis de Jules Romains 1974–; Officier, Légion d'honneur, Commdr des Arts et Lettres, Officier, Ordre nat. du Mérite, Chevalier des Palmes académiques. *Publications:* L'amour est un plaisir 1956, Du côté de chez Jean 1959, Un amour pour rien 1960, Au revoir et merci 1966, Les illusions de la mer 1968, La gloire de l'empire (Grand Prix du Roman (Acad. Française) 1971, Au plaisir de Dieu 1974, Le vagabond qui passe sous une ombrelle trouée 1978, Dieu, sa vie, son oeuvre 1981, Mon dernier rêve sera pour vous 1982, Jean qui grogne et Jean qui rit 1984, Le vent du soir 1985, Tous les hommes en sont fous 1985, Bonheur à San Miniato 1987, Garçon de quoi écrire (jtly.) 1989 (prix de Mémorial 1990), Histoire du juif errant 1991, Tant que vous penserez à moi, entretien avec Emmanuel Berl 1992, La Douane de mer 1994, Presque rien sur presque tout 1996, Casimir mène la grande vie 1997, Une autre histoire de la littérature française 1997,

Le rapport Gabriel (Prix Jean Giono) 1999, Voyez comme on danse 2001, C'était bien 2003, Une Fête en Larmes 2005; numerous articles in Le Figaro, Le Monde, France-Soir, Paris Match, etc. *Leisure interests:* skiing, sailing. *Address:* c/o Le Figaro, 37 rue du Louvre, Paris 75001 (office); 1 rue Miollis, 75015 Paris (office); 10 avenue du Parc-Saint-James, 92200 Neuilly-sur-Seine, France (home).

ORMOND, Julia; British actress; b. 4 Jan. 1965, Epsom, Surrey; m. Rory Edwards (divorced); ed Guildford High School, Cranleigh School, Farnham Art School and Webber Douglas Acad.; worked in repertory, Crucible Theatre, Sheffield, Everyman Theatre, Cheltenham and on tour with Royal Exchange Theatre, Manchester; appeared in Faith, Hope and Charity (Lyric, Hammersmith), Treats (Hampstead Theatre); West End debut in Anouilh's The Rehearsal (Almeida), My Zinc Bed (Royal Court) 2000; Founding Chair. and Co-Chair. FilmAid Int., mem. UK Bd of Trustees; Crystal Award, World Econ. Forum 2003. *Films include:* The Baby of Mâcon 1993, Nostradamus 1994, Captives 1994, Legends of the Fall 1994, First Knight 1995, Sabrina 1995, Calling the Ghosts (producer) 1996, Smilla's Sense of Snow 1997, The Barber of Siberia 1998, The Prime Gig 2000, Resistance 2003, Inland Empire 2006, I Know Who Killed Me 2007, Surveillance 2008, The Argentine 2008, Kit Kittredge: An American Girl 2008, La Conjura de El Escorial 2008, The Curious Case of Benjamin Button 2008. *Television appearances:* Traffik (Channel 4 mini-series) 1989, Capital City (series) 1989, Ruth Rendell Mysteries: The Best Man to Die 1990, Young Catherine 1991, Stalin 1992, Animal Farm (voice) 1999, Varian's War 2001, Iron Jawed Angels 2004. *Address:* c/o FilmAid International UK, Flat 2, 9 Colville Terrace, London W11 2BE; c/o Marmont Management, Langham House, 302/8 Regent Street, London, W1R 5AL, England. *Telephone:* (20) 7727-1030 (FilmAid). *Website:* www.filmaidinternational.org.

ORMOND, Richard Louis, CBE, MA; British museum director and art historian; b. 16 Jan. 1939, Bath; s. of Conrad E. Ormond and Dorothea Gibbons; m. Leonée Ormond 1963; two s.; ed Marlborough Coll., Brown Univ., USA and Christ Church, Oxford; Asst Keeper, Nat. Portrait Gallery 1965–75, Deputy Dir 1975–83; Head of Picture Dept Nat. Maritime Museum 1983–86; Dir Nat. Maritime Museum 1986–2000; Dir J. S. Sargent Catalogue Raisonné project. *Publications:* J. S. Sargent 1970, Catalogue of Early Victorian Portraits in the National Portrait Gallery 1973, Lord Leighton 1975, Sir Edwin Landseer 1982, The Great Age of Sail 1986, F.X. Winterhalter and the Courts of Europe 1987, Frederic, Lord Leighton (co-author) 1996, Sargent Abroad (co-author) 1997, John Singer Sargent: The Early Portraits (co-author) 1998, John Singer Sargent (co-author) 1998, Sargent (co-author) 1998, Sargent e l'Italia (co-author) 2001, John Singer Sargent: Portraits of the 1890s (co-author) 2002, John Singer Sargent: The Later Portraits (co-author) 2004, John Singer Sargent: Figures and Landscapes (co-author) 2006. *Leisure interests:* opera, theatre, cycling. *Address:* Crusader House, Pall Mall, London SW1Y 5LU (office); 8 Holly Terrace, London, N6 6LX, England (home). *Telephone:* (20) 7839-3125. *E-mail:* rormond@ceoexpress.com (office).

ORMOS, Mária, DSc; Hungarian historian and academic; b. 1 Oct. 1930, Debrecen; d. of János Ormos and Elza Förster; one s. one d.; ed Kossuth Lajos Univ., Debrecen; Asst Lecturer, Historic Science Inst. 1963; Univ. Prof., Eötvös Loránd Univ., Budapest 1982; Prof. of History then Prof. Emer., Janus Pannonius Univ. (now Univ. of Pécs), Rector 1984–92, f. Foundation of the Univ. of Pécs 1992; mem. Nat. Cttee of Historians; Pres. Italian-Hungarian Mixed Cttee of Historians; Vice-Pres. Asscn d'histoire des relations internationales; mem. Hungarian Acad. of Sciences 1993 (mem. of Presidium), European Acad. of Arts, Sciences and Humanities; Széczhenyi Prize 1995, Szentgyörgyi Prize 1995, Leo Sziliard Prize 2000, Deák Ferenc Prize 2000, Pulitzer Prize 2000. *Publications:* Franciaország és a keleti biztonság 1931–36 (France and the Eastern Security) 1969, Europai Fasizmusok 1919–1939 (co-author) 1976, Merénylet Marseille-Ben (Assassination in Marseille) 1984, Mussolini: Politikai eletrajz (Mussolini: A Political Portrait) 1987, Nacizmus, Fasizmus (Nazism and Fascism) 1987, Never as Long as I Shall Live 1989, Civitas fidelissima 1921 1990, From Padua to the Trianon 1918–1920 1991, Hitler 1993, Documents Diplomatiques Francais Sur L'Histoire Du Bassin Des Carpates 1918–1932: Août 1919–Juin 1920 (co-author) 1995, Magyarország a világháborúk korában 1914–45 (Hungary in the Age of the World Wars 1914–45) 1997, Európa a nemzetközi Küzdőtéren. Felemelkedés és hanyatlás 1814–1945 (Europe in the International Arena. Rise and Decline) (co-author) 1998, Hitler–Sztálin (Hitler-Stalin) (co-author 1999), Documents Diplomatiques Francais Sur L'histoire Du Bassin Des Carpates: 1918–1932 (co-author) 1999, Kozma Miklós, Egy magyar Médiavezér (Nikolaus Kozma, Life of Hungarian Media Leader) 2000, Hungary Governments and Politics 1848–2000 (co-ed.) 2001, Gazdasagi Vilagvalsag Magyar Visszhangja: 1929-1936 2004, Hungary in the Age of the Two World Wars: 1914-1945 2008. *Leisure interests:* music, books, theatre. *Address:* Department of History, University of Pécs, 7633 Pécs, Szántó Kovács János u. 1/B, Hungary (office).

ORNSTEIN, Donald Samuel, PhD; American mathematician and academic; *Professor of Mathematics, Stanford University;* b. 30 July 1934; s. of Harry Ornstein and Rose Ornstein (née Wisner); m. Shari Richman 1964; two s. one d.; ed Swarthmore Coll. and Univ. of Chicago; mem. Inst. for Advanced Study, Princeton 1956–58; Instructor, Univ. of Wis. 1958–60; Asst Prof., Stanford Univ. 1960–63, Sloan Fellow and Assoc. Prof. 1963–65, Assoc. Prof. 1965–66, Prof. of Math. 1966–; Visiting Prof., Cornell Univ. and New York Univ. (Courant Inst.) 1967–68, Hebrew Univ., Jerusalem 1975–76, Math. Sciences Research Inst., Berkeley 1983–84;; mem. NAS 1981, American Acad. of Arts and Sciences 1991; Bocher Prize 1974. *Publications:* Ergodic Theory Randomness and Dynamical Systems 1974; mathematical papers in many journals since 1959. *Address:* Department of Mathematics, Stanford University, 450 Serra Mall, Building 380, Stanford, CA 94305-2125 (office); 857

Tolman Drive, Stanford, CA 94305, USA (home). *Fax:* (415) 725-4066 (office). *E-mail:* ornstein@math.stanford.edu (office). *Website:* math.stanford.edu (office).

OROZCO, Esther, PhD; Mexican biologist and academic; *Investigator and Professor of Experimental Pathology, Center for Research and Advanced Studies, National Polytechnic Institute (Cinvestav-IPN);* b. 25 April 1945, Est. Pascual Orozco, Chihuahua; m. Tomás Sánchez; one s. one d.; ed Universidad Autónoma de Chihuahua, Center for Research and Advanced Studies, Nat. Polytechnic Inst. (Cinvestav-IPN); conducted postdoctoral research for short periods at MRC, London and Netherlands Cancer Inst., Amsterdam; fmr Visiting Prof., Harvard School of Public Health; Assoc. Prof., Dept of Genetics and Molecular Biology, Center for Research and Advanced Studies, Nat. Polytechnic Inst. (Cinvestav-IPN), now Investigator and Prof. of Experimental Pathology, est. Multidisciplinary Program of Molecular Biomedicine; Howard Hughes Medical Inst. Int. Research Scholar 1991–96, currently Howard Hughes Medical Inst. Foreign Prof.; mem. Mexican Acad. of Sciences, Instituto de las Mujeres, Nat. Researcher System (Level E); unsuccessful cand. (Revolutionary Democratic Party–PRD) for Gov. of Chihuahua (first woman) 1998; Dir Inst. for Science and Tech., Mexico City; Premio Nacional Miguel Otero, Secr. of Health 1985, Pasteur Medal, Institut Pasteur and UNESCO, L'Oreal/UNESCO Award for Women in Science (Latin American) for discovery of mechanisms and control of infections by amoebae in the tropics 2006, Medal for Scientific Merit, Asamblea Legislativa, Mexico City. *Publications:* numerous scientific papers in professional journals. *Leisure interests:* writing, reading, theatre. *Address:* Centro de Investigación y de Estudios Avanzados del IPN, Av. Instituto Politécnico Nacional, 2508 Col. San Pedro, Apartado Postal 14-740, 07000 Mexico City, DF, Mexico (office). *Telephone:* (52) 5061-3800 ext 5650 (office). *Fax:* (52) 5061-7108 (office). *E-mail:* esther@cinvestav.mx (office). *Website:* www.cinvestav.mx (office).

OROZCO, Gabriel; Mexican artist; b. 1962, Jalapa, Veracruz; ed Escuela Nacional de Arte Plasticas, Mexico City, Circulo de Bellas Artes, Madrid, Spain; works include Black Kites, Oval Billiard Table, Horses Running Endlessly, Pinched Ball; numerous photographs, sculptures and installations; terra-cotta ceramics featured at Documenta XI 2002; lives and works in New York, Paris, and Mexico City.

ORR, Christopher John, MBE, MA, RCA, RA; British artist; *Emeritus Professor of Printmaking, Royal College of Art;* b. 8 April 1943, London; s. of Ronald Orr and Violet Townley; m. Catherine Terris 1985; one s. one d.; ed Royal Coll. of Art; worked as artist and teacher, latterly as a tutor and Visiting Lecturer, RCA 1976–, Prof. and Course Dir of Printmaking 1998–2008, Prof. Emer. 2008–; solo touring exhbns The Complete Chris Orr 1976, Many Mansions 1990; numerous exhbns world-wide; Fellow, Royal Soc. of Painters and Printmakers; elected Royal Academician 1995. *Publications:* Many Mansions 1990, The Small Titanic 1994, Happy Days 1999, Semi-antics 2001, The Disguise Factory 2003, City of Holy Dreams 2006, The Multitude Diaries 2008. *Telephone:* (020) 7738-1203 (home). *E-mail:* info@chrisorr-ra.com (office). *Website:* www.chrisorr-ra.com (office).

ORREGO VICUÑA, Francisco, PhD; Chilean lawyer and professor; *Professor of International Law, University of Chile;* b. 12 April 1942, Santiago; m. Soledad Bauza; three c.; ed schools in Chile, Argentina, Spain and Egypt, Univ. of Chile and London School of Econs; fmr Dir Inst. of Int. Studies Univ. of Chile; fmr Visiting Prof., Stanford Univ., Univ. of Paris II Law School, Univ. of Miami Law School; participated in projects for Acad. of Int. Law, The Hague, UNITAR and various studies and projects undertaken by univs in Europe, USA, Asia and Latin America; fmr legal adviser to OAS; fmr del. to Law of Sea Conf.; fmr int. corresp., El Mercurio (daily newspaper); Amb. to UK 1983–85; Prof. of Int. Law, Inst. of Int. Studies, Law School, Univ. of Chile 1985–; Pres. Chilean Council on Foreign Relations 1989–2000, Chilean Acad. of Social Sciences 1995–2000; mem. Chilean-US Comm. for Settlement of Disputes; mem. Advisory Cttee on Foreign Policy, Ministry of Foreign Affairs; Conciliator and Arbitrator of ICSID 1995–; Judge and Vice-Pres. Admin. Tribunal of IBRD, Pres. 2001–2004; Commr UN Compensation Comm. 1998–2000; Arbitrator Int. Chamber of Commerce, London Court of Int. Arbitration; mem. Inst. of Int. Law; arbitrator, 20 Essex Street Chambers (Barristers), London; Judge ad-hoc Int. Court of Justice, The Hague; Nat. Award for the Humanities and Social Sciences 2001, Medal of Merit, Univ. of Heidelberg. *Publications:* Antarctic Resources Policy 1983, Antarctic Mineral Exploitation 1988, The Exclusive Economic Zone 1989, The Changing International Law of High Seas Fisheries 1999, International Dispute Settlement in a Global 2004, and other books and articles. *Address:* Francisco Orrego Vicuña y Cia., Avenida El Golf No. 40, Sixth Floor, Santiago 755-0107, Chile (office). *Telephone:* (2) 4416326 (office). *Fax:* (2) 4416399 (office). *E-mail:* forrego@uchile.cl (office). *Website:* francisco.orrego.googlepages.com.

ORRELL-JONES, Keith, MA, CInstM; British business executive; b. 15 July 1937; s. of Francis George Orrell-Jones and Elsie Orrell-Jones; m. Hilary Kathleen Orrell-Jones (née Pegram) 1961; four s.; ed The High School, Newcastle-under-Lyme, St John's Coll., Cambridge; Chief Exec. ARC Ltd 1986–89; Dir Consolidated Gold Fields PLC 1989; Dir Blue Circle Industries PLC 1990, Chief Exec. 1992–99; Chair. FKI PLC 1999–2004; Dir (non-exec.) Smiths Group PLC 1990, Chair. 1998–2004 (retd). *Leisure interests:* music (particularly opera), field sports, art, walking.

ORSENNA, Erik (see Arnoult, Erik).

ORSZAG, Peter Richard, AB, MS, PhD; American economist and government official; *Director, Office of Management and Budget;* b. 16 Dec. 1968, Boston; two c.; ed Princeton Univ., London School of Econs, UK; Research Officer, Centre for Econ. Performance, London School of Econs 1992–93, mem. Professional Research Staff 1994–95; Econ. Adviser, Macroeconomic and Fiscal Unit, Ministry of Finance, Russian Fed., Moscow 1993; Staff Economist, Council of Econ. Advisers, Washington, DC 1993–94; Sr Adviser 1996; Sr Economic Advisor, Nat. Econ. Council 1997, Special Asst to Pres. Clinton for Econ. Policy 1998; consultant, McKinsey & Co. 1998; Pres. Sebago Assocs Inc. 1998–2007, Sr Dir 2002–07; Dir Congressional Budget Office, Washington, DC 2007–08; Dir Office of Man. and Budget 2009–; Dir Competition Policy Assocs Inc. 2003–07; Sr Fellow in Economic Studies, Brookings Inst. 2001–07, Joseph A. Pechman Fellow in Tax and Fiscal Policy 2001–07, Co-Dir Tax Policy Center 2003–07, Dir The Hamilton Project 2005–07, Deputy Dir of Econ. Studies 2006–07; Dir Retirement Security Project, Pew Charitable Trust 2004–07; Lecturer, Univ. of California, Berkeley 1999–2000; Research Prof., Georgetown Univ. 2005–07; mem. Inst. of Medicine. *Publications:* American Economic Policy in the 1990s (co-ed.) 2002, Protecting the American Homeland: A Preliminary Analysis (co-author) 2002, Protecting the American Homeland: One Year On (co-author) 2003, Saving Social Security: A Balanced Approach (co-author) 2005, Aging Gracefully: Ideas to Improve Retirement Security in America (co-author) 2006, Protecting the Homeland 2006/7 (co-author) 2006; numerous articles. *Address:* Office of Management and Budget, 725 17th Street, NW, Washington, DC 20503, USA (office). *Telephone:* (202) 395-3888 (office). *Fax:* (202) 395-3080 (office). *Website:* www.whitehouse.gov/omb (office).

ORSZULIK, Most Rev. Alojzy; Polish ecclesiastic; b. 21 June 1928, Baranowice Śląskie; ed Catholic Univ. of Lublin; ordained priest, Soc. of the Catholic Apostolate 1957; Lecturer, Higher Ecclesiastic Seminar, Ołtarzew 1962–89; mem. staff, Secr. of Episcopate of Poland 1962–68, Head, Press Bureau 1968–93, Deputy Sec. 1989–94, Chair. Comm. for Social Communications 1984–94; Adviser, Pontifical Council for Social Communications 1974–2000; Sec. Jt Comm. of Gov. and Episcopate of Poland 1980–; mem. Working Group for Legis. Affairs 1981–83, 1987–89; Legis. Council of Episcopate of Poland 1993–; rep. of Catholic Church during Round Table Talks 1989; Auxiliary Bishop of Siedlce, Titular Bishop of Vissalsa and Curate-Gen. 1989–92; Bishop of Łowicz 1992–2004; del. of the Holy See for negotiations with Polish Govt about the concordat 1990–93. *Publications:* numerous articles on canon law. *Address:* c/o Bishops Curie, Stary Rynek 20, 99-400 Łowicz, Poland (office). *Telephone:* (46) 837-66-15 (office). *Fax:* (46) 837-43-49 (office). *Website:* www.diecezja.lowicz.pl (office).

ORTEGA GAONA, Amancio; Spanish retail executive; *Chairman, Industria de Diseño Textil, SA;* b. March 1936, León; fmr shop assistant; f. Confecciones Goa (mfrs of bathrobes) 1963, f. Zara (chain of fashion stores, 700 outlets world-wide) 1975, now majority shareholder and Chair. Inditex group (Industrias de Diseño Textil SA), including Zara, Massimo Dutti and Pull and Bear and other brands; also Chair. Capital Energy (renewable energy co.). *Address:* Industria de Diseño Textil, SA, Avenida de la Diputación, 15142 Arteixo, A Coruña, Spain (office). *Telephone:* (98) 1185400 (office). *Fax:* (98) 1185544 (office). *Website:* www.inditex.com (office).

ORTEGA SAAVEDRA, José Daniel; Nicaraguan politician, fmr resistance leader and head of state; *President;* b. 11 Nov. 1945, La Libertad, Chontales; s. of Daniel Ortega and Lidia Saavedra; m. Rosario Murillo; seven c.; ed Univ. Centroamericano, Managua; joined Frente Sandinista 1963; active in various underground resistance movts against regime of Anastasio Somoza from 1959 and was several times imprisoned and tortured for revolutionary activities; ed. El Estudiante, official publ of Frente Estudiantil Revolucionaria and directed org. of Comités Cívicos Populares in Managua 1965; mem. Nat. Directorate of FSLN (Sandinista Liberation Front) 1966–67; imprisoned 1967–74; resumed position with FSLN and with José Benito Escobar became involved in further revolutionary activities; fought on front in two-year mil. offensive which overthrew Somoza regime 1979; mem. Junta of Nat. Reconstruction Govt 1979, Co-ordinator of Junta 1981–85, Pres. of Nicaragua 1985–90, 2006–; presidential cand. 2001; Gen. Sec. FSLN. *Address:* c/o Oficina del Presidente, Managua, Nicaragua. *Telephone:* (2) 28-9090. *E-mail:* Presidente@presidencia.gob.ni (office). *Website:* www.presidencia.gob.ni (office).

ORTEGA Y ALAMINO, HE Cardinal Jaime Lucas; Cuban ecclesiastic; *Archbishop of San Cristóbal de la Habana;* b. 18 Oct. 1936, Jagüey Grande, Matanzas; ed Arturo Echemendía School, Matanzas, Advanced Inst. for Secondary Studies of Matanzas, Diocesan Seminary of San Alberto Magno, Seminary of Foreign Mission in Quebec, Canada; ordained priest 1964; Coadjutor Vicar of Cárdenas 1964, detained in work camp 1966, released 1967; Parish Priest of Jagüey Grande 1967 and also of Cathedral of Matanzas, also responsible for Parish of Pueblo Nuevo in city and another two churches outside it; Pres. Diocesan Comm. for Catechesis; taught moral theology part-time at Sts Charles and Ambrose Interdiocesan Seminary, Havana; Bishop of Pinar del Rio 1979; Archbishop of San Cristobal de La Habana 1981–; Pres. Cuban Conf. of Catholic Bishops 1988–98, 2001–, took part in fourth Gen. Conf. Latin-American Bishops, Santo Domingo; Founder Caritas Cuba 1991; Vice-Pres. Latin American Episcopal Council 1995–99; cr. Cardinal Priest of SS Aquila e Priscilla 1994; attended Special Ass. for America of World Synod of Bishops, Vatican City 1997; Special Papal Envoy to Nat. Eucharistic Congress of El Salvador, San Salvador 2000; Dr hc (St John's Univ., New York); hon. degrees from Barry and St Thomas Univs, Fla, Univ. of San Francisco, Calif., Providence Coll., RI, Boston Coll., Mass 2001. *Address:* Apartado 594, Calle Habana 152, Havana 10100, Cuba (office). *Telephone:* (7) 624000 (office). *Fax:* (7) 338109 (office).

ORTIZ, Cristina; Brazilian pianist; b. 17 April 1950, Bahia; d. of Silverio M. Ortiz and Moema F. Ortiz; m. Jasper W. Parrott 1974; two d.; ed Conservatório Brasileiro de Música, Rio de Janeiro, Acad. Int. de Piano (with Magda Tagliaferro), Paris and Curtis Inst. of Music, Philadelphia (with Rudolf Serkin); New York recital debut 1971; London debut with LSO and André

Previn 1973; has appeared in concerts with the Vienna Philharmonic, Berlin Philharmonic, the Concertgebouw, Chicago Symphony, New York Philharmonic, Israel Philharmonic, Los Angeles Philharmonic, leading British orchestras and has undertaken many tours of North and South America, the Far East, New Zealand and Japan; appeared with NHK Symphony, the Bergen Philharmonic and Philharmonia under Janowski 1997; played with conductors including Previn, Mehta, Kondrashin, Ashkenazy, Leinsdorf, Chailly, Masur, Salonen, Colin Davis, Janssons, Fedoseyev, Zinman, Rattle, Järvi and Fürst; first prize Van Cliburn Int. Competition, Texas 1969. *Leisure interests:* tennis, swimming, reading, hiking, holidaying, horse riding. *E-mail:* mscristinaortiz@gmail.com (office). *Website:* www.cristina.ortiz.name.

ORTIZ, Francis Vincent, MS, LLD; American diplomatist (retd); b. 14 March 1926, Santa Fe, NM; s. of Frank V. Ortiz and Margaret Delgado Ortiz; m. Mary Dolores Duke 1953; three s. one d.; ed Georgetown, George Washington, New Mexico, Madrid Univs and American Univ. of Beirut, Lebanon; diplomatic posts in Ethiopia and Mexico 1953–57; Special Asst to Under-Sec. of State 1957–60, to Amb. to Mexico 1961–63; Country Dir for Spain and Portugal 1963–67, for Argentina, Uruguay and Paraguay 1973–75; Head, Political Section and Chargé d'Affaires, Peru and Uruguay 1967–73; Deputy Exec. Sec. of State 1975–77; Amb. to Barbados, Grenada, St Lucia and Dominica 1977–79, to Guatemala 1979–80, to Peru 1981–83, to Argentina 1983–86; Diplomat in Residence, Latin American Inst., New Mexico Univ. 1986–88; Special Asst to Under-Sec. of State for Man. 1988–90; Political Adviser, C-in-C, Southern Command 1980–81; Regent, Museum of New Mexico 1999–; mem. American Foreign Service Asscn; Kt Grand Cross of Civil Merit of Spain; Order of the Kts of Malta; Grand Cross Order of Mayo (Argentina) and others; Hon. DrIur (New Mexico); Superior Service Award, Meritorious Honor Award, Presidential Chamizal Medal (Mexico). *Leisure interests:* history, tennis. *Address:* 663 Garcia Street, Santa Fe, NM 87505, USA. *Telephone:* (505) 984-2586. *Fax:* (505) 984-2741. *E-mail:* f.ortiz453@comcast.net (home).

ORTIZ BOSCH, Milagros María; Dominican Republic politician; b. 23 Aug. 1936, Santo Domingo; one s.; niece of fmr Pres. Juan Bosch Gaviño; ed Univ. of Santo Domingo; Adviser, Chamber of Deputies 1982–90; mem. Senate 1990–2000; Vice-Pres. of the Dominican Republic 2000–04; Sec. of State for Educ. 2000–04; mem. Partido Revolucionario Dominicano, fmr Vice-Pres. *Address:* c/o Partido Revolucionario Dominicano, Avda Dr Comandante Enrique Jiménez Moya 14, Bella Vista, Santo Domingo, DN, Dominican Republic. *Telephone:* 687-2193. *Fax:* . *E-mail:* prensa_tribunalp.r.d@hotmail.com. *Website:* www.prd.partidos.com.

ORTIZ DE LA CADENA, Fausto, MBA; Ecuadorean economist and government official; ed Universidad Católica de Guayaquil; served as State Treasurer 2005, Sub-Sec. of Public Credit 2005; Deputy Minister of Economy 2005–07, Minister of the Economy and Finance 2007–08 (resgnd); mem. Alianza País. *Address:* Alianza País, Of. 501, Edif. Torres Whimper, Diego de Almagro 32-27 y Whimper, Quito, Ecuador (office). *Telephone:* (2) 600-0630 (office). *Fax:* (2) 600-1029 (office). *E-mail:* info@rafaelcorrea.com (office). *Website:* www.rafaelcorrea.com (office).

ORTIZ DE ROZAS, Carlos; Argentine diplomatist, lawyer and academic; *Professor of International Relations, University of Belgrano;* b. 26 April 1926, Buenos Aires; s. of the late Alfredo Ortiz de Rozas and Susana del Valle; m. Carmen Sarobe 1952; ed Univ. de Buenos Aires School of Diplomacy; entered foreign service 1948; Chargé d'Affaires, Bulgaria 1952–54; Sec. Greece 1954–56; mem. Cabinet, Argentine Ministry of Foreign Affairs 1958–59; Counsellor, Argentine Mission at UN 1959–61; subsequently Dir-Gen. Policy Dept, Ministry of Foreign Affairs and later Minister at embassies in UAR and UK; Amb. to Austria 1967–70; Chief Rep. to Conf. of Cttee on Disarmament, Geneva 1969 (Chair. of Cttee 1979); Perm. Rep. to UN 1970–77; Amb. to UK 1980–82, to France 1984–89, to USA 1991–93; Under-Sec. of State for Foreign Relations 1990; Head of Argentine Special Mission to Holy See 1982–83; Pres. UN Security Council 1971, 1972; mem. Advisory Bd to Sec.-Gen. on Disarmament 1978–92; Prof. of Int. Relations, Univ. of Belgrano, Buenos Aires 1995–; Dir and Pres. Del. of Conf. on Law of the Sea 1973; Chair. First (Political and Security) Cttee of the 29th General Ass. 1974; has held several teaching posts including Prof. of Public Law and Int. Relations, Univ. del Salvador, Buenos Aires (now mem. Bd Dirs); Pres. Bunge and Born Foundation 1994–99, Alliance Française de Buenos Aires 1999–2001; mem. Exec. Bd Argentine Council for Int. Relations 1994–; mem. Nat. Acad. of Social and Political Sciences, Buenos Aires 2005; decorations from Italy, Chile, Brazil, Greece, Japan, Peru, Thailand, Egypt, Austria, Nicaragua, the Republic of Korea, Spain, Holy See and France; Personality of the Year in Int. Relations, Rotary Club, Buenos Aires 1995. *Publications:* Paths to Peace – The UN Security Council and its Presidency 1981, La reunion de Palm Beach – J.F. Kennedy – A. Frondizi 1994, Contribuciones Argentinas a las Naciones Unidas 1995. *Address:* Avenida Gelly y Obes 2263, 1425 Buenos Aires, Argentina (home). *Telephone:* (11) 4803-3630 (home). *Fax:* (11) 4804-6791 (home). *E-mail:* corzas@yahoo.com (home).

ORTIZ MARTÍNEZ, Guillermo, PhD; Mexican central banker and economist; *Governor, Banco de México;* ed Universidad Nacional Autónoma de México, Stanford Univ., USA; economist, Ministry of the Presidency of Mexico 1971–72; Deputy Man., Man. Econ. Research Bureau, Banco de México 1977–84; Exec. Dir IMF 1984–88; Undersec. of Finance and Public Credit 1988–94; Sec. of Telecommunications and Transportation –1994, of Finance and Public Credit 1994–97; Gov. Banco de México (BANXICO) 1998–; fmr teacher, univs in Mexico and USA; mem. Group of Thirty. *Publications:* two books, several papers. *Address:* Banco de México, Avenida 5 de Mayo 2, Col. Centro, Del. Cuauhtémoc, 06059 México, DF, Mexico (office). *Telephone:* (55) 5237-2000 (office). *Fax:* (55) 5237-2070 (office). *E-mail:* comsoc@banxico.org.mx (office). *Website:* www.banxico.org.mx (office).

OSBALDESTON, Hon. Gordon Francis, PC, CC, BComm, MBA, LLD; Canadian academic and fmr government official; b. 29 April 1930, Hamilton, Ont.; s. of John E. Osbaldeston and Margaret Osbaldeston (née Hanley); m. Geraldine M. Keller 1953; three s. one d.; ed St Jerome's Coll., Kitchener, Ont. and Univs of Toronto and W Ontario; Sec. Treasury Bd 1973–76; Deputy Minister, Dept of Industry, Trade and Commerce 1976–78; Sec. Ministry of State for Econ. Devt 1978–82; Under-Sec. of State for External Affairs 1982; Clerk of Privy Council and Sec. to Cabinet 1982–86; Sr Fellow, School of Business Admin., Univ. of W Ontario 1986–95, Prof. Emer., Ivey School of Business 1995–; Dir Great West Lifeco Inc., London Life Insurance Co.; Hon. DrIur (W Ont.), (Carleton), (Dalhousie); Vanier Medal, Inst. of Public Admin. of Canada 1990. *Publications:* Keeping Deputy Ministers Accountable 1989, Organizing to Govern 1992. *Leisure interests:* golf, stamp collecting. *Address:* 1353 Corley Drive, London, ON N6G 4L4, Canada (home). *Telephone:* (519) 438-9772 (home). *Fax:* (519) 433-7605 (home). *E-mail:* gordon5304@aol.com (home).

OSBORN, Frederic (Derek) Adrian, CB, BA, BPhil; British government official; b. 14 Jan. 1941, Dorset; s. of the late Rev. George Osborn and Betty Osborn; m. Caroline Niebuhr Tod 1971; one s. one d.; ed Leys School, Cambridge and Balliol Coll., Oxford; with Ministry of Housing and Local Govt 1965–70, Dept of Transport 1975–77, Dept of Environment 1977–95, Dir-Gen. (Deputy Sec.) 1990–95; Chair. European Environment Agency 1995–99; Chair. UNED, UK (name changed to Stakeholder Forum for Our Common Future 2002, renamed Stakeholder Forum for a Sustainable Future 2004) 1996–, Earth Centre 1996– (mem. Bd 1996–), Joseph Rowntree Foundation Steering Group on Reconciling Environmental and Social Objectives 1998–, UK Round Table on Sustainable Devt 1999–; mem. Bd England and Wales Environment Agency 1996–98, Severn Trent PLC 1998–; Special Adviser House of Commons Environmental Audit Cttee 1998–99; Chair. Jupiter Global Green Investment Trust 2001–; mem. Royal Soc. for Protection of Birds 1996–; mem. Bd of Trustees Green Alliance; Visiting Fellow Green Coll., Oxford 1996–97; Visiting Prof., School of Public Policy, Univ. Coll., London 1998–. *Publications:* Earth Summit II 1998, contribs. to Journal of Environmental Law etc. *Leisure interests:* music, reading. *Address:* Stakeholder Forum for a Sustainable Future, 33 Bloomsbury Place, London WC1A 2QL, England (office). *Telephone:* (20) 7580-6912 (office). *Website:* www.stakeholderforum.org (office).

OSBORN, Mary, PhD; British biologist and academic; *Professor, Max Planck Institute for Biophysical Chemistry;* lab. work in USA; Prof., Max Planck Inst. for Biophysical Chem. (Karl Friedrich Bonhoeffer Inst.), Göttingen 1978–, also Hon. Prof. in the Medical Faculty, Georgia Augusta Univ.; Pres. Exec. Cttee Int. Union of Biochemistry and Molecular Biology 2003–06; Chair. European Tech. Assessment Network expert working group on gender balance in research policy 1998; mem. Editorial Advisory Bd Encyclopedia of Human Biology; mem. Helmholtz Soc. Senate, European Strategy Forum on Research Infrastructures Group A, Descartes Prize Grand Jury of the EC; fmr Trustee Swedish Foundation on the Environment; Dr hc (Pomerian Medical Acad., Sczeczin, Poland); L'Oréal-UNESCO For Women in Science Award 2002, Meyenburg Prize. *Publications:* numerous articles in scientific journals. *Address:* Max-Planck-Institut für biophysikalische Chemie, Am Faßberg 11, 37077 Göttingen, Germany (office). *Telephone:* (551) 201-1477 (office). *Fax:* (551) 201-1578 (office). *E-mail:* mosborn@gwdg.de (office). *Website:* www.mpibpc.gwdg.de (office).

OSBORNE, George; British politician; *Shadow Chancellor of the Exchequer;* b. 23 May 1971, London; m. Frances Osborne; two c.; ed St Paul's School, London, Magdalen Coll., Oxford; fmr Jt Ed. Isis (Univ. of Oxford magazine); Dean Rusk Scholar (for a semester), Davidson Coll., N Carolina, USA; worked briefly as freelance journalist; joined Conservative Research Dept in 1994, later Head of Political Section; Special Adviser, Minister of Agric., Fisheries and Food 1995–97; worked in Political Office, No. 10 Downing Street, Political Sec. to Leader of the Opposition and Sec. to Shadow Cabinet 1997–2001; MP for Tatton, Cheshire 2001–, Shadow Chief Sec. to the Treasury 2004, fmr Opposition Whip, fmr Shadow Work and Pensions Minister and Shadow Econ. Sec., Chair. David Cameron's leadership election campaign 2005, fmr mem. Public Accounts Cttee, Transport Select Cttee, Shadow Chancellor of the Exchequer 2005–; Vice-Pres. East Cheshire Hospice; Trustee Arts and Business; Conservative; Hon. Pres. The British Youth Council; Macmillan Cancer Relief Champion 2005. *Address:* House of Commons, Westminster, London, SW1A 0AA, England (office). *Telephone:* (20) 7219-8214 (office); (1565) 632181 (office); (1565) 873037 (constituency office) (office). *Fax:* (1565) 632182 (office). *E-mail:* contact@georgeosborne.co.uk (office). *Website:* www.georgeosborne.co.uk (office).

OSBORNE, John A.; Montserratian politician; *Leader, New People's Liberation Movement;* Leader People's Liberation Movt 1978–96, People's Progressive Alliance 1996–2001, New People's Liberation Movt 2001–; Chief Minister of Montserrat 1978–91, 2001–06 (also Minister of Finance, Economic Devt, Trade, Tourism and Media). *Address:* New People's Liberation Movement, Montserrat.

OSBORNE, Ronald Walter, BA, FCA; Canadian (b. British) chartered accountant and business executive; *Chairman, Sun Life Financial Inc.;* b. 1946; m. Grace Osborne (neé Snead); two s. one d.; ed Univ. of Cambridge, UK; fmr Partner, Arthur Young, Clarkson Gordon and Co., Rio de Janeiro, 1976–79, Clarkson Gordon, Toronto 1979–81; Vice-Pres. and Chief Financial Officer, Maclean Hunter Ltd 1981–82, Vice-Pres. of Broadcasting 1982–84, Pres. and COO 1984–86, Pres. and CEO 1986–95, Exec. Vice-Pres. and CFO

1995–96; Pres. BCE Inc. 1996–97, CEO and Pres. Bell Canada Inc. 1997–98; CEO and Pres. Ont. Power Generation Inc. 1998–2003; mem. Bd of Dirs Sun Life Financial Inc. and Sun Life Assurance Co. of Canada 1989–, Chair. 2005–; mem. Bd of Dirs St Lawrence Cement Group, Shell Canada Ltd, Four Seasons Hotels, Torstar Corpn, Nortel Networks Corpn, Nortel Networks Ltd, Air Canada 1999–2004; Hon. DJur (Ryerson Polytechnic Univ.). *Address:* Sun Life Financial Inc., 150 King Street West, Toronto, ON M5H 1J9, Canada (office). *Telephone:* (416) 979-9966 (office). *Fax:* (416) 597-9108 (office). *E-mail:* boarddirectors@sunlife.com (office). *Website:* www.sunlife.com (office).

OSBOURNE, John (Ozzy); British musician and singer; b. 3 Dec. 1948, Aston, Warwicks.; m. 1st Thelma; two d.; m. 2nd Sharon Arden 1982; two d. one s.; mem. and lead singer, Black Sabbath (fmrly Polka Tulk, then Earth) 1967–77 (reunion tour 1998–99); solo artist with backing group Blizzard of Ozz 1979–; cr. annual touring festival Ozzfest 1996–; numerous live performances and festival appearances; Grammy Awards 1994, 2000, Nordoff-Robbins O2 Silver Clef Award (with Sharon Osborne) 2006. *Television series:* The Osbournes (MTV) 2001–05. *Recordings include:* albums: with Black Sabbath: Black Sabbath 1969, Paranoid 1970, Master Of Reality 1971, Black Sabbath Vol. 4 1972, Sabbath Bloody Sabbath 1973, Sabotage 1975, Technical Ecstasy 1976, Never Say Die! 1978, Reunion 1998; solo: Blizzard of Ozz 1980, Diary of a Madman 1981, Speak of the Devil 1982, Bark at the Moon 1983, The Ultimate Sin 1986, Tribute 1987, No Rest for the Wicked 1988, Just Say Ozzy 1990, No More Tears 1991, Live & Loud 1993, Ozzmosis 1995, The Ozzman Cometh 1997, OzzFest Vol. 1 1997, Down To Earth 2001, Live At Budokan 2002, X-Posed 2002, Under Cover 2005, Black Rain 2007. *Address:* Sharon Osbourne Management, POB 15397, Beverly Hills, CA 90209, USA (office). *Website:* www.ozzy.com.

OSCARSSON, Per Oscar Heinrich; Swedish actor; b. 28 Jan. 1927, Stockholm; s. of Ing Einar Oscarsson and Theresia Küppers; m. Bärbel Krämer 1960; one s. two d.; ed Royal Dramatic School; Royal Dramatic Theatre 1947–52, Gothenburg Town Theatre 1953–59, TV-Theatre 1966–67; now works mainly as freelance film actor; Best Actor Award, Cannes 1966; New York Critics Award for Best Actor 1968; Silver Hugo Best Actor Award, Chicago Int. Film Festival 1969. *Films include:* The Doll 1962, My Sister My Love 1965, Hunger 1965, Ole Dole Doff 1967, It's Up to You 1968, Close to the Wind (also writer) 1969, The Last Valley 1971, Salem Comes to Supper 1971, Secrets 1971, Endless Night 1971, The New Land 1972, The Blockhouse 1973, Dream Town 1973, Ebon Lundin (also writer, producer and dir) 1973, A Stranger Came by Train 1974, Metamorphosis 1976, Dagny 1977, The Assigment 1977, The Brothers Lionheart 1977, Victor Frankenstein 1977, The Adventures of Picasso 1978, Chez nous 1978, Christopher's House 1979, Charlotte Löwensköld 1979, Hello Sweden (also writer) 1979, Tvingad att leva 1980, Outrage 1980, Sweden for the Swedes (also writer, producer and dir) 1980, Montenegro 1980, The Sleep of Death 1981, Who Pulled the Plug? 1981, Historien om lilla och stora kanin (voice) 1982, Henrietta 1983, Ronia, the Robber's Daughter 1984, Da Capo 1985, Nattseilere 1986, Vilde, the Wild One 1986, Venus 90 1988, 1939 1989, Kurt Olsson – The Film About My Life as Myself 1990, Bulan 1990, House of Angels 1993, Dreaming of Rita 1993, Cross My Heart and Hope to Die 1994, Harry och Sonja 1996, Christmas Oratorio 1997, The Last Viking 1997, Rika barn leka bäst 1997, Ogginoggen 1997, Forbudt for børn 1998, Jubilee, the Darkest Hour 1998, Järngänget 2000, Send More Candy 2001, Midsummer 2003, Manden bag døren 2003. *Television includes:* Inferno 1973, Das Blaue Hotel 1974, Julius Julskötare (mini-series) 1978, Kallocain (mini-series) 1981, Polisen som vägrade svara (mini-series) 1981, Hans-Christian och sällskapet 1981, Mäster Olof (mini-series) 1983, Vargen 1984, Polisen som vägrade ge upp (mini-series) 1984, Bröderna Lejonhjärta (mini-series) 1985, Flykten (mini-series) 1986, Ondskans år 1987, Oväder 1988, Polisen som vägrade ta semester 1988, Kråsnålen (mini-series) 1988, Nattseilere (mini-series) 1988, Fasadklättraren 1991, Kejsarn av Portugallien 1992, Polisen och domarmordet (mini-series) 1993, Håll huvet kallt (series) 1994, Kan du vissla Johanna 1994, Polisen och pyromanen (mini-series) 1996, Stormen 1998, Lukas 8:18 (series) 1999, Herr von Hancken (mini-series) 2000, Anderssons älskarinna (mini-series) 2001, Kaspar i Nudådalen (series) 2001, Stora teatern (mini-series) 2002, Dieselråttor och sjömansmöss (series) 2002, Att sörja Linnea 2004, Unge Andersen (mini-series) 2005, Skattejakten (mini-series) 2005. *Stage appearances include:* Hamlet 1953, Candida 1961, Waiting for Godot 1963. *Leisure interests:* reading, riding.

OSEI, Isaac, BSc, MA; Ghanaian economist, diplomatist, politician and business executive; b. 29 March 1951; s. of Nana Osei Nkwantabisa I and Rosina Eunice Osei (née Inkumsah); m. Marian Osei; two s. two d.; ed Achimota School, Univ. of Ghana, Legon, American Econ. Asscn Econ. Inst., Univ. of Colo, USA, Williams Coll., Mass, USA; Asst Econ. Planning Officer, Ministry of Finance and Econ. Planning 1970s; Founder and Man. Consultant, Ghanexim Econ. Consultants Ltd; fmr consultant to numerous official orgs. including Govt of Ghana, USAID, World Bank, UNCTAD, Japan Int. Cooperation Agency, Dept for Int. Devt; Man. Dir Intravenous Infusions Limited, Koforidua; fmr Chief, Commercial Operations Dept, Ghana Tourist Devt Co. Ltd; High Commr to UK 2001–06; Chair. Bd of Govs Commonwealth Secr. 2003–05; Chief Exec. Ghana Cocoa Bd (COCOBOD) 2006–08; MP for Subin constituency 2009–; Officer, Order of the Volta. *Leisure interest:* football (from a distance). *Address:* Parliament House, Accra, (office); PO Box OS 1402, Accra, Ghana (office). *Telephone:* (21) 777625 (office). *E-mail:* ikeosei@email .com (office).

OSEI-ADJEI, Akwasi, MSc; Ghanaian politician; b. 29 Dec. 1949, Onwe, Ashanti Region; m.; five c.; ed De Montfort Univ., UK; trained and qualified as an accountant, worked at Ozze Ghana Ltd; mem. Parl. for Ejisu/Juabeng constituency; fmr Deputy Minister of Foreign Affairs, Regional Integration

and New Partnership for Africa's Devt (NEPAD), Minister of Foreign Affairs, Regional Integration and NEPAD 2007–09; mem. New Patriotic Party. *Address:* c/o New Patriotic Party, C912/2 Duade St, Kokomlemle, POB 3456, Accra, Ghana (office). *Telephone:* (21) 227951 (office). *Fax:* (21) 224418 (office). *E-mail:* npp@africanonline.com.gh (office).

O'SHEA, Sir Timothy Michael Martin, Kt, PhD; British university principal and professor of computer science; *Principal and Vice-Chancellor, University of Edinburgh;* b. 28 March 1949, Hamburg, Germany; s. of John Patrick O'Shea and Elisabeth Hedwig Oberhof; m. Eileen Scanlon 1982; two s. two d.; ed Royal Liberty School Havering, Univ. of Sussex, Univ. of Leeds; Research Fellow, Dept of Artificial Intelligence, Univs of Texas at Austin and Edin. 1974–78; joined Open Univ. 1978–, f. Computer Assisted Learning Research Group 1978, Lecturer, Inst. of Educational Tech. 1980–82, Sr Lecturer 1983–87, Prof. of Information Tech. and Educ. 1987–97, Pro-Vice-Chancellor of Quality Assurance and Research 1994–97, Visiting Research Prof. in Computer Supported Collaborative Learning 1997–; Master Birkbeck Coll. and Chair in Information and Communication Tech., Univ. of London 1998–2002, Gov. City Literary Inst. 1998–2000, Gov. SOAS 1998–2002, Curator School of Advanced Study 1999–2002, Gov. St George's Medical School 2000–02, Provost Gresham Coll. 2000–02, Pro-Vice-Chancellor Univ. of London 2001–02; Prin., Univ. of Edin. 2002–; Visiting Scientist, Xerox PARC, Palo Alto, Calif., USA 1986–87; Visiting Scholar, Univ. of California, Berkeley 1986–87; Chair. Advanced Educational Tech. Programme, NATO 1988–90; Chair. Artificial Intelligence Soc. of Britain 1979–82, London Metropolitan Network Ltd 1999–2002, Information Systems Sectory Group, CVCP 1999–, Higher Educ. and Research Opportunities Ltd (HERO) 2000–; Dir Edexcel Foundation 1998–2001 (mem. Exec. Cttee 1998–2001), Univs and Colls Staff Devt Agency 1999–2000; mem. HEFCE Cttee on Equal Opportunities, Access and Lifelong Learning 1998–, Jt Information Systems Cttee 2000–; mem. Bd UUK 2001–; Pres. Pyschology Section, BAAS 1991–92; Trustee Eduserv 1999–2000; mem. Council Royal Coll. of Music 2001–. *Television:* The Learning Machine (series-presenter and author) 1985. *Publications include:* Self-Improving Teaching Systems 1979, Learning and Teaching with Computers (co-author) 1983, Artificial Intelligence: Tools, Techniques and Applications (co-author) 1984, Advances in Artificial Intelligence (ed.) 1985, Intelligent Knowledge-based Systems: An Introduction (co-ed.) 1987, Educational Computing (co-ed.) 1987, New Directions in Educational Tech. (co-ed.) 1992. *Address:* Office of the Principal, University of Edinburgh, Old College, South Bridge, Edinburgh, EH8 9YL, Scotland (office). *Telephone:* (131) 650-2150 (office). *Fax:* (131) 650-6519 (office). *E-mail:* principal@ed.ac.uk. *Website:* www.ed.ac.uk (office).

OSHEROFF, Douglas Dean, PhD; American physicist and researcher; b. 1 Aug. 1945, Aberdeen, Wash.; s. of William Osheroff and Bessie Anne Osheroff (née Ondov); m. Phyllis S.K. Liu 1970; ed California Inst. of Tech., Cornell Univ.; mem. tech. staff, Bell Labs, Murray Hill, NY 1972–82, Head Solid State and Low Temperature Physics Research Dept 1982–87; Prof., Stanford Univ., Calif. 1987–, J.G. Jackson and C.J. Wood Prof. of Physics 1992–, Chair. Physics 1993–96; co-discoverer superfluidity in liquid^{3}He 1971, nuclear antiferromagnetic resonance in solid^{3}He 1980; Fellow, American Physical Soc., American Acad. of Arts and Sciences, NAA; co-recipient Simon Memorial Prize, British Inst. of Physics 1976, Oliver E. Buckley Solid State Physics Prize 1981, John D. and Catherine T. MacArthur Prize Fellow 1981, shared Nobel Prize for Physics 1996. *Address:* Department of Physics, Stanford University, Stanford, CA 94305-4060, USA.

OSHII, Mamoru; Japanese film director; b. 8 Aug. 1951, Tokyo; ed Fine Arts School, Dept of Educ., Tokyo Liberal Arts Univ. (Tokyo Gakugei Daigaku); involved in anti-ANPO (US–Japan Security Treaty) student movt 1970s; began directing short films 1976; joined Tatsunoko Productions 1977; made film On the Roof using permeable light filming process; worked for Studio Pierrot under supervision of Nagayuki Toriumi 1980–84; joined Headgear as writer and dir 1980s; cr. Patlabor franchise with Masami Yuuki, Kenji Kawaï and Akemi Tadaka. *Films directed include:* Darossu 1983, Urusei Yatsura 1: Only You 1983, Urusei Yatsura 2: Beautiful Dreamer 1984, Angel's Egg 1985, The Red Spectacles 1987, Twilight Q Episode 2: Meikyu Bukken File 538 1987, Mobile Police Patlabor 1988, Patlabor: The Movie 1989, Stray Dogs: Kerberos Panzer Cops 1991, Talking Head 1992, Patlabor 2: The Movie 1993, Ghost in the Shell 1995, Avalon 2001, Innocence 2004, Tachiguishi retsuden 2006. *Films written include:* Urusei Yatsura 1: Only You 1983, Urusei Yatsura 2: Beautiful Dreamer 1984, When All's Said and Done 1984, Angel's Egg 1985, The Red Spectacles 1987, In the Aftermath 1988, Legend of a Wolf—Dog 1988, Stray Dogs: Kerberos Panzer Cops 1991, Talking Head 1992, Seraphim 1995, Jin Roth: The Wolf Brigade 1998, Innocence 2004, Tachiguishi retsuden 2006. *Television series:* The Wonderful Adventures of Nils 1980, Urusei Yatsura (Those Obnoxious Aliens) 1981–84, Mrs Pepperpot 1983, Mini-Pato 2002. *Website:* www.oshiimamoru.com.

OSHIMA, Kenzo; Japanese diplomatist; b. 1943; ed Tokyo Univ.; served in diplomatic posts in Australia, France, India, USA and at Perm. Mission to UN; Dir-Gen. Econ. Co-operation Bureau, Ministry of Foreign Affairs; Sec.-Gen. Secr. for Int. Peace Co-operation HQ, Office of the Prime Minister –2000; UN Under-Sec.-Gen. for Humanitarian Affairs and Emergency Relief Co-ordinator 2001–03; Amb. to Australia 2003; Perm. Rep. to UN 2004–07; Senior Vice Pres. Japan Int. Cooperation Agency 2007–. *Address:* Japan International Cooperation Agency, 6th–13th floors, Shinjuku Maynds Tower 2-1-1 Yoyogi, Shibuya-ku, Tokyo 151-8558, Japan (office). *Telephone:* (3) 5352-5311 (office). *Website:* www.jica.go.jp (office).

OSHIMA, Nagisa; Japanese film director; b. 31 March 1932, Kyoto; m. Akiko Koyama 1960; two s.; ed Kyoto Univ.; with Shochiku Co. 1954–59; formed own film co. 1959; Pres. Dirs' Guild of Japan 1980–; has also directed TV films.

Films: Ai To Kibo No Machi (A Town of Love and Hope) 1959, Seishun Zankoku Monogatari (Cruel Story of Youth) 1960, Taiyo No Hakaba (The Sun's Burial) 1960, Nihon No Yoru To Kiri (Night and Fog in Japan) 1960, Shiiku (The Catch) 1961, Amakusa Shiro Tokisada (The Rebel) 1962, Etsuraku (The Pleasures of the Flesh) 1965, Yunbogi No Nikki (Yunbogi's Diary) 1965, Hakuchu No Torima (Violence at Noon) 1966, Ninja Bugeicho (Band of Ninja) 1967, Nihon Shunka-ko (A Treatise on Japanese Bawdy Song) 1967, Muri Shinju Nihon No Natsu (Japanese Summer: Double Suicide) 1967, Koshikei (Death By Hanging) 1968, Kaettekita Yopparai (Three Resurrected Drunkards) 1968, Shinjuku Dorobo Nikki (Diary of a Shinjuku Thief) 1968, Shonen (Boy) 1969, Tokyo Senso Sengo Hiwa (He Died After the War, or The Man Who Left His Will on Film) 1970, Gishiki (The Ceremony) 1971, Natsu No Imooto (Dear Summer Sister) 1972, Ai no Corrida (In the Realm of the Senses) 1976, Ai no Borei (Empire of Passion) 1978, Merry Christmas, Mr. Lawrence 1982, Max, mon amour 1985, Kyoto, My Mother's Place 1991, Gohatto 1999.

OSHIMA, Shotaro; Japanese diplomatist; *Ambassador to South Korea;* b. 20 Sept. 1943; ed Univ. of Tokyo; joined Ministry of Foreign Affairs 1968; fmr positions include Foreign Service Officer, First Sec., Embassy in Washington DC, Counsellor, Embassy in Israel; Dir in charge of First SE Asia Div., Asian Affairs Bureau, Ministry of Foreign Affairs 1985–87, Dir of Policy Planning Div., Information Analysis-Research-Planning Bureau 1987–89, Dir of Overseas Establishment Div. 1989–91; Minister, Embassy in Moscow 1991–94, Embassy in Washington, DC 1994–97; Dir-Gen., Econ. Affairs Bureau 1997–2000; Amb. to Saudi Arabia 2000–01; Deputy Minister for Foreign Affairs, Ministry of Foreign Affairs 2001–02; Perm. Rep. to UN, Geneva 2002–05; Amb. to South Korea 2005–07; mem. Appellate Body, WTO 2008–. *Address:* World Trade Organization, rue de Lausanne 154, 1211 Geneva, Switzerland (office). *Telephone:* 227395111 (office). *Fax:* 227314206 (office). *E-mail:* enquiries@wto.org (office). *Website:* www.wto.org (office).

OSHIOMHOLE, Adams; Nigerian trade union official; *President, Nigeria Labour Congress;* b. 1953; five c.; ed Ruskin Coll., Oxford, UK and Nat. Inst. for Policy and Strategic Studies, Kuru; began career as shop steward at textile factory; Pres. Nigeria Labour Congress; Chair. Governing Bd Nigerian Social Insurance Trust Fund Scheme. *Address:* Nigeria Labour Congress, 29 Olajuwon Street, off Ojuelegba Road, PO Box 620, Yaba, Lagos, Nigeria (office). *Telephone:* (1) 7743988 (office); (1) 5840288 (office). *Fax:* (1) 5840288 (office). *Website:* www.nlcng.org (office).

OSHO, Pierre, MA; Benin politician; b. 5 May 1945, Porto Novo; m.; six c.; ed Acad. of Grenoble, Univ. of Dakar, Univ. of Aix-en-Provence, France; Prof. of History and Geography, Coll. Père Aupiais, Cotonou 1968–70, Coll. d'Enseignement Moyen Général de Gbégamey, Cotonou 1970–73; Dir of Information and Propaganda (MISON) 1976–78; mem. Cen. Cttee, Party of Popular Revolution (PRPB) 1979–90; Chief of Dist of Klouékanmey, Prov. of Mono 1978–84; Peoples' Commr, Nat. Ass. 1980–90; Pres. Comm. on Govt and Ass. Relations 1980–84; Dir Nat. Centre of Revolutionary Educ. 1982–84; Sec.-Gen. Perm. Cttee of Nat. Ass. 1984–89; Pres. Comm. on Constitutional Affairs 1989–90; Dir Cabinet of Pres. of Benin 1989–91; with Dept of Research of Human and Social Sciences 1991–96; Minister of Foreign Affairs and Cooperation 1996–98; Minister to Pres. of Benin 1998–2001; Minister of Nat. Defence 2001–06 (resgnd); del. to int. and multilateral confs. *Address:* c/o Ministry of National Defence, BP 2493 Cotonou, Benin (office).

OSIPOV, Victor Ivanovich; Russian engineer, geologist and hydrogeologist; *Director, Sergeev Institute of Environmental Geoscience, Russian Academy of Sciences;* b. 15 April 1937, Bashkortostan; ed Moscow State Univ.; Dir scientific station 1959–61; Lecturer, Prof., Moscow State Univ. 1964–90; Deputy Dir Inst. of Lithosphere 1990; Dir Centre of Eng Geology and Geoecology (now Sergeev Inst. of Environmental Geoscience), Russian Acad. of Sciences; Corresp. mem., USSR (now Russian) Acad. of Sciences 1987, mem. 1991–; main research in eng geology, environmental protection; State Prize 1988. *Publications:* more than 500 articles in scientific journals. *Leisure interests:* travelling, sports (skiing), gardening, fishing. *Address:* Sergeev Institute of Environmental Geoscience, PO Box 145, Ulansky per. 13, Building 2, 101000 Moscow, Russia (office). *Telephone:* (495) 623-31-11 (office). *Fax:* (495) 623-18-86 (office). *E-mail:* direct@geoenv.ru (office). *Website:* www.geoenv.ru (office).

OSIPOV, Yuri Sergeyevich, DPhys-MathSc; Russian mathematician and technician; *President, Russian Academy of Sciences;* b. 7 July 1936, Tobolsk; m.; one d.; ed Urals State Univ.; Corresp. mem. USSR (now Russian) Acad. of Sciences 1984, mem. 1987, Pres. 1991–; staff mem., Inst. of Mechanics and Math., Urals Scientific Cen. Acad. of Sciences 1959, Dir 1990–93; Prof., Urals Univ. 1961–70; fmr Head of Chair of Moscow State Univ.; Dir Steklov Math. Inst. 1993–; mem. American Math. Soc., American Acad. of Sciences, Mongolian Acad. of Sciences, Armenian Acad. of Sciences, Santiago Univ., Chile; Dr hc (Bar-Ilan Univ., Israel), (Santiago Univ., Chile); Lenin Prize 1976, USSR State Prize. *Publications:* more than 150 works on the theory of math., differential equations and their application. *Address:* Russian Academy of Sciences, Leninsky prospekt 14, 119991 GSP-1, Moscow; Steklov Mathematical Institute, 42 Vavilov Street, 117966 Moscow, Russia. *Telephone:* (495) 954-35-06 (Acad.); (495) 135-22-91 (Inst.). *Website:* www.ras.ru.

OSKANIAN, Vardan, BS, MSc, MA; Armenian diplomatist; *Minister of Foreign Affairs;* b. 7 Feb. 1955, Syria; m. Dr Nani Oskanian; two s.; ed Yerevan Polytechnic Inst., Tufts Univ., Mass, Harvard Univ., Fletcher School of Law and Diplomacy, USA; Founder and Ed. Armenian Int. Magazine 1990; on staff, Armenian Ministry of Foreign Affairs 1992–; Deputy Head, Middle East Dept, Head, Dept of N America 1992–94; prin. negotiator in Misk process on Nagorno-Karabakh conflict 1994–97; Visiting Asst Prof. of Int. Relations, American Univ. of Armenia 1994–96; Deputy Foreign Minister 1994–96, First Deputy Foreign Minister 1996–98, Minister of Foreign Affairs 1998–. *Address:* Ministry of Foreign Affairs, 0010 Yerevan, Republic Sq., Govt House 2, Armenia (office). *Telephone:* (10) 52-35-31 (office). *Fax:* (10) 54-39-25 (office). *E-mail:* oskanian@mfa.am (office). *Website:* www.armeniaforeignministry.com (office).

OSKARSON, Peter, (Dhyan Manyu); Swedish theatre director and actor; b. 13 June 1951, Stockholm; s. of Per-Otto Oskarson and Margareta Du Rietz; m. 1st Kajsa Reingardt 1979; m. 2nd Gunilla Kindstrand 1983 (divorced 2002); one s. four d.; m. 3rd Sofie Livebrant 2004; one d.; ed Swedish Actors' School, Stockholm; Artistic Dir Skånska Teatern Landskrona 1973–82, Folkteatern Gävleborg 1982–90; Head, Helsingegården, inst. for theatre and popular arts, N Scandinavia 1990–2004; Artistic Dir Orion Theatre 1993–2000; Gen. Man. Folkteatern Gävleborg 1997–2006; Artistic Adviser, Peking Opera, Anhui, Hefei, China 1996–2000; Artistic Dir World Theatre Project 1999–; plays produced also at Royal Opera House and at Royal Dramatic Theatre, Stockholm, Drottningholm Theatre, Staatsoper, Stuttgart, Intiman, Seattle, USA, Oper der Stadt, Bonn, Festwochen, Vienna, Schwetzingen Festspiele, Swedish TV, Nationaltheater Mannheim etc.; mem. Swedish Theatre Acad. 1993–, Swedish World Culture Forum 1998–2001, Framtidens Kultur 2003–06; Alf Sjöberg Prize, Swedish Acad. Theatre Prize, Svenska Dagbladet Thalia Prize, Expressen Theatre Prize, Gävle and Gävleborg Culture Prize, Malmö Thalia Prize, Gefledagblad Culture Prize, Olof Hogberg Prize. *Address:* Köpmangatan 7, 111 31 Stockholm, Sweden (office). *Telephone:* (8) 201313 (office). *E-mail:* peter@oskarson.se (office).

OSLON, Alexander A., Cand.Tech. sciences; Russian engineer; *President, All-Russian Foundation for Public Opinion;* b. 19 March 1952, Zlatoust, Chelyabinsk region; m.; one d.; ed Tula State Polytech. Inst.; worked as engineer, then chief constructor GSKTB 1974–87; researcher All-Union Centre of Public Opinion Studies 1988–90, Deputy Dir 1990–92; Pres. All-Russian Foundation for Public Opinion 1992–. *Publications include:* numerous articles in the press on results of public pools of population and methodical problems of sociological studies. *Address:* All-Russian Foundation for Public Opinion, Obrucheva str. 26, bldg 2, Moscow, Russia (office). *Telephone:* (495) 745-87-65 (office). *Website:* www.fom.ru (office).

OSMAN, Ahmed, LLM; Moroccan politician and diplomatist; *Leader, Rassemblement national des indépendants;* b. 3 Jan. 1930, Oujda; m. HRH Princess Lalla Nezha (sister of King Hassan II) 1965; one s.; ed Royal High School, Rabat, Univ. of Rabat and Univ. of Bordeaux, France; Head of the Legal Section, Royal Cabinet 1956; joined Ministry of Foreign Affairs 1957; Sec.-Gen. Ministry of Nat. Defence 1959–61; Amb. to FRG 1961–62; Under-Sec.-of-State for Industry and Mines 1963–64; Pres. and Gen. Man. Moroccan Navigation Co. 1964–67; Amb. to USA, Canada and Mexico 1967–70; Minister of Admin. Affairs 1970–71; Dir of Royal Cabinet 1971–72; Prime Minister 1972–79; Parl. Rep. for Oujda 1977–; Leader Rassemblement nat. des indépendants 1978–; mem. Nat. Defence Council 1979–; Minister of State 1983; Pres. Chamber of Reps. 1984; participated in UN sessions 1957, 1958, 1960, 1961, 1968, Conf. on Maritime law 1958, Conf. of the League of Arab States 1961. *Leisure interests:* bridge, sports, reading, swimming. *Address:* Rassemblement national des indépendants, 6 rue Laos, avenue Hassan II, Rabat, Morocco. *Telephone:* (3) 7721420. *Fax:* (3) 7733824.

OSMAN, Salih Mahmoud; Sudanese lawyer and human rights activist; b. Darfur; m.; for 20 years has defended people who were allegedly arbitrarily detained and tortured by Sudanese govt; Lawyer, Sudanese Org. Against Torture 2003–, also works with Amal Center for Rehabilitation of Torture Victims, Nyala; imprisoned Feb.–Sept. 2004; mem. Parl., Nat. Democratic Alliance 2006–; mem. Bd of Dirs Darfur Peace and Devt Org.; Human Rights Defender Award, Human Rights Watch 2005, International Human Rights Award 2006, Sakharov Prize 2007.

OSMANI, S. R.; Bangladeshi business executive; Dir of Finance Petrobangla, Bangladesh Oil, Gas and Mineral Corpn, Acting Chair., then Chair. 2003–06. *Address:* c/o Petrocenter Bhaban, 3 Kawran Bazar C/A, POB 849, Dhaka, 1215, Bangladesh (office).

OSMOND, Charles Barry, PhD, FRS, FAA; Australian biologist and academic; *Honorary Visiting Fellow, School of Biochemistry and Molecular Biology and Photo Bioenergetics Group, Australian National University;* b. 20 Sept. 1939; s. of Edward Charles Osmond and Joyce Daphne Osmond (née Krauss); m. 1st Suzanne Ward 1962 (divorced 1983); one s. one d.; m. 2nd Cornelia Gauhl 1983; ed Morisset Central and Wyong High Schools and Univs of New England and Adelaide; Postdoctoral Fellow, UCLA 1965–66, Univ. of Cambridge 1966–67; Research Fellow, Dept of Environmental Biology, Research School of Biological Sciences, ANU 1967, subsequently Fellow, Sr Research Fellow, Prof. of Biology 1978–87, Dir 1991–98, Dir Research School of Biol. Sciences 1991–98, Prof., Photo Bioenergetics Group 1998–2001, currently Hon. Visiting Fellow, School of Biochemistry and Molecular Biology and Photo Bioenergetics Group; Exec. Dir Biological Science Center, Desert Research Inst., Univ. of Nevada 1982–86; Arts and Sciences Distinguished Prof., Dept of Botany, Duke Univ. 1987–91; Pres. and CEO Biosphere 2 Center, Columbia Univ. 2001–03; Sr Fulbright Fellowship, Univ. of Calif., Santa Cruz 1973–74; Guest Prof., Technical Univ., Munich 1974; Overseas Fellow, Churchill Coll., Cambridge 1980; mem. Australian Nat. Comm. for UNESCO 1980–82; mem. Council, Australian Acad. of Sciences 1982–85, Deutsche Akad. der Naturforscher, Leopoldina (German Acad. of Sciences) 2001; Treas. Int. Soc. Photosynthesis Research 2004–; Research Prize, Alexander von Humboldt Foundation, Univs of Darmstadt and Göttingen 1997–2000. *Publications:* numerous publs on plant physiology. *Address:* PO Box 3252, Weston Creek, ACT 2611, Australia (home). *Telephone:* (2) 6287-1487 (home). *E-mail:* barry.osmond@anu.edu.au (office).

OSMOND, Donald (Donny) Clark; American singer; b. 9 Dec. 1957, Ogden, UT; m. Debra Glenn 1978; three c.; ed Brigham Young Univ.; singer with The Osmonds 1963–80; solo artist 1971–78, 1988–; also duo with sister Marie; head of own TV production co., Night Star 1980s, also satellite TV entrepreneur; Georgie Award for Best Vocal Team (with Marie Osmond) 1978. *Television:* Donny and Marie (show) 1976–79, Osmond Family (show) 1980. *Film:* Goin' Coconuts 1978, College Road Trip 2008. *Theatre:* Joseph and his Amazing Technicolour Dreamcoat, Toronto, Canada 1992–93, Beauty and the Beast, New York 2006. *Recordings include:* albums: with The Osmonds: Homemade 1971, Osmonds 1971, Crazy Horses 1972, Phase-III 1972, The Osmonds Live 1972, The Plan 1973, Love Me For A Reason 1974, Around The World: Live In Concert 1975, The Proud One 1975, Brainstorm 1976, The Osmond Christmas Album 1976, Osmond Family Christmas 1991; solo: The Donny Osmond Album 1971, To You With Love, Donny 1971, Portrait of Donny 1972, Too Young 1972, My Best To You 1972, A Time For Us 1973, Alone Together 1973, Donny Osmond Superstar 1973, Donny 1974, I'm Leaving It All Up To You (with Marie Osmond) 1974, Love Me For A Reason 1974, Make The World Go Away (with Marie Osmond) 1975, Donny and Marie – Featuring Songs From Their Television Show (with Marie Osmond) 1976, Donny and Marie: New Season (with Marie Osmond) 1976, Deep Purple (with Marie Osmond) 1976, Disco Train 1976, Donald Clark Osmond 1977, Goin' Coconuts (with Marie Osmond) 1978, Winning Combination 1978, Donny Osmond 1989, Eyes Don't Lie 1990, Christmas At Home 1998, This Is The Moment 2001, Somewhere In Time 2002, What I Meant To Say 2004, Love Songs of the '70s 2007, From Donny with Love 2008. *Publication:* Life is Just What You Make of It (autobiog.) 2005. *Address:* William Morris Agency, 1 William Morris Place, Beverly Hills, CA 90212; 51 W Center Street, Suite 424, Orem, UT 84057, USA (office). *Website:* www.donny.com.

OSMONOV, Kurmanbek Ergeshovich; Kyrgyzstani politician and lawyer; *Chairman of the Supreme Court;* b. 1 March 1953, Kara-Kulja; m.; two s. two d.; ed Kyrgyz State Univ.; Deputy Minister for Justice, subsequently First Deputy Minister 1991–94; Judge Constitutional Court 1994–2000; mem. Jogorku Kenesh (parl.) 2000–02; First Deputy Prime Minister of Kyrgyzstan and Minister of Justice 2002–04; Chair. of the Supreme Court 2004–; Honoured Lawyer of Kyrgyz Repub.; Dank Medal (highest nat. award). *Publications:* several books on development and court reform in Kyrgyzstan. *Leisure Interests:* music, chess, cars. *Address:* 37 Orozbekova Street, Bishkek (office); 26 Keldibek Karboz Uulu Street, Orto-sai, Bishkek, Kyrgyzstan (home). *Telephone:* (312) 66-33-18 (office), (312) 55-01-37 (home). *Fax:* (312) 66-29-46 (office). *E-mail:* scourt@bishkek.gov.kg (office); aziz0002@mail.ru (office). *Website:* www.gov.kg (office).

OSPEL, Marcel; Swiss banker; b. 8 Feb. 1950; ed Higher School of Econs and Man., Basel; joined Dept of Planning and Marketing Swiss Bank Corpn (SBC) 1977, with SBC Capital Markets, London, New York 1980, Dir 1987, mem. Enlargement Group 1990, CEO Capital Markets and Treasury 1992, SBC Warburg 1995, Group Pres. 1996; Pres. and Group CEO Swiss Bank Corpn (SBC) 1996–98; Group CEO UBS AG 1999–2001, Chair. 2001–08 (resgnd); Dr hc (Univ. of Rochester) 2005. *Address:* c/o UBS AG, Bahnhofstrasse 45, 8098 Zürich, Switzerland (office).

OSPINA BERNAL, Camilo; Colombian government official and lawyer; ed Colegio Mayor de Nuestra Señora del Rosario; Vice-Dean Faculty of Law, Colegio Mayor de Nuestra Señora del Rosario 1990–91; Legal Adviser Ministry of Finance and Public Credit 1991–92, Sec.-Gen. Budget Directorate 1992–94; Consultant UNDP 1994–95; Legal Adviser to Pres. 2002–05; Minister of Nat. Defence 2005–06; Founding Pnr and mem. Soc. of Constitutional Rights, Sec. 1997–99. *Address:* c/o Ministry of National Defence, Centro Administrativo Nacional (CAN), 2°, Avda El Dorado, Santafé de Bogotá, Colombia (office).

OST, Friedhelm; German politician; b. 15 June 1942, Castrop-Rauxel; s. of Franz Ost and Barbara Ost; m. Erika Herrmann 1968; three s. two d.; ed Univs of Freiburg and Cologne; bank employee 1966–69; Adviser, Bundesverband Deutscher Banken 1969–72; Econ. Ed., moderator and commentator, Zweites Deutsches Fernsehen (ZDF) 1973–85; State Sec. and Head, Govt Press and Information Dept 1985–89; Econ. and Political Adviser to German Fed. Chancellor and freelance journalist and public relations consultant 1989–90; Gen. Man. Wirtschaftsvereinigung Bergbau –1990; mem. CDU 1980–; mem. Bundestag 1990–, Chair. Econ. Cttee; Adviser Frankfurter Rothschild GmbH 1997–; now Gen. Rep. Deutsche Vermögensberatungs AG; mem. Russian Acad. of Sciences. *Leisure interests:* football, tennis. *Address:* Deutsche Vermögensberatungs AG, Querstr. 1, 60322 Frankfurt-am-Main, Germany (office).

OSTAPCIUC, Eugenia; Moldovan politician and engineer; *Chairperson of Parliament;* b. 19 Oct. 1947, Fintinitsa, Soroka region; m.; two s.; ed Chişinău Trade Higher School, Moscow Inst. of Nat. Econs; engineer, Deputy Dir, then Dir Dietary Dept 1966–87; Dir-Gen. Dept of Trade Soroka 1988–95; Deputy Dir Asscn Logos, Chişinău 1995–98; Sec. Parl. faction, Party of Communists of Repub. of Moldova; mem. Perm. Comm. on Social Protection, Public Health and Family 1998–2001; Chair. Parl. of Moldova 2001–. *Address:* House of Parliament, Stefan cel Mare avenue, 105, 2073 Chişinău, Moldova (office). *Telephone:* (2) 23-75-86 (office). *Fax:* (2) 54-65-79 (office). *Website:* www.parlament.md (office).

OSTEN, Suzanne Carlota; Swedish playwright and theatre and film director; b. 20 June 1944, Stockholm; d. of Carl Otto Osten and Gud Osten; m.; one d.; ed Lund Univ.; started directing while a student 1963; ran Fickteatern fringe theatre group performing in schools, prisons, public areas, etc. 1967–71; joined City Theatre, Stockholm 1971; f. and Artistic Dir, Unga Klara Stadsteatern ind. repertory co. 1975–; has written and directed over 30

plays, numerous radio and TV productions; began directing films 1980; Prof. of Directing, Dramatic Inst., Stockholm 1995–; Nat. Theatre Critics Prize 1982, Paris-Creteil Prize 1993, Expressens Theatre Prize 2002, Assitej Int. Prize 2002, Berns Prize, Swedish PEN 2002, numerous other awards and prizes. *Plays:* as writer and dir: Medea's Children 1975, The Haga-Princesses 1976, The Hunt for Snores 1976, Lazarillo 1977, Prince Carefree 1977, The Children from Mount Frostmo 1978, The Pork Horses 1981, The Frontier 2000; as dir: The Vampire 1975, The Sweaty Tiger 1978, Unga Klara tells Life 1982, The Smile of Hades 1982, A Clean Girl 1983, Hitler's Childhood 1 1984, Hitler's Childhood 2 1984, The Danton Affair 1986, Everybody - But Me 1987, The Toad Aquarium 1988, In the Summer House 1988, R 1990, The Piggle 1991, The Dolphin 1992, Preparation for Suicide 1994, Mirad 1994, Money 1994, Lilacs 1914 1996, Irina's New Life 1996, The Girl, the Mother and the Trash 1998, Difficult People 1999, Time of Darkness 2002, The Main Thing 2002. *Films include:* Ei inspelat, Mamma 1982, Bröderna Mozart (Guldbagge Award for Direction 1986) 1986, Livsfarlig film 1988, Skyddsängeln 1990, Tala det är så mörkt 1992, Bara du och jag 1994, Bengbulan 1996, Besvärliga Människor 2001. *Address:* Unga Klara, Stockholms Stadsteater, Box 16412, 103 27 Stockholm, Sweden (office). *Telephone:* (8) 506-20-100 (office). *E-mail:* maja .svae@stadsteatern.stockholm.se (office). *Website:* www.stadsteatern .stockholm.se (office); www.suzanneosten.nu.

OSTERWALDER, Konrad, PhD; Swiss physicist and university administrator; *Rector, United Nations University;* b. 3 June 1942, Frauenfeld, Thurgau; m.; three c.; ed Eidgenössische Technische Hochschule (ETH) Zürich, Univ. of Zürich, Harvard Grad. School for Higher Educ., USA; Asst Prof. of Math. Physics, Harvard Univ. 1973–76, Assoc. Prof. 1976–78; Prof. of Math. Physics, ETH Zürich 1977–, Head Dept of Math. 1986–90, Head, Planning Cttee 1990–95, Rector 1995–2007; Guest Prof., Univ. of Austin, Tex., Univ. of Cambridge, UK, IHES, Bures-sur-Yvette, France, Max-Planck-Institut für Physik und Astrophysik, Munich, Università La Sapienza, Rome, Università di Napoli, Tokyo Univ., Weitzmann Inst., Rehovot, Israel; Rector UN Univ., Tokyo 2007–; Founder and Pres. UNITECH Int.; Chair. Univ. Council, Tech. Univ., Darmstadt, Germany; mem. Admin. Cttee, Ecole Polytechnique de France, Educ. Cttee, Ecole des Mines, Paris, Conseil d'Orientation Statégique, ParisTech, Consiglio dell'Università della Svizzera, Italy, Academic Council, Int. Council on Systems Eng; mem. Swiss Acad. of Tech. Sciences 2000; Fellow, Alfred P. Sloan Foundation 1974–78; Hon. mem. Riga Tech. Univ. 2002; Dr hc (Tech. Univ., Helsinki) 2003; J. Bauer Prize 1959, 1960, ETH Medaille, Kern Prize 1970. *Address:* United Nations University Centre, 53–70, Jingumae 5-chome, Shibuya-ku, Tokyo 150-8925, Japan (office). *Telephone:* (3) 3499-2811 (office). *Fax:* (3) 3499-2828 (office). *E-mail:* mbox@hq.unu.edu (office). *Website:* www.unu.edu (office).

ÖSTLING, Leif, MEng, BEcons; Swedish business executive; *Chairman, AB SKF;* b. 1945, Luleå; ed Chalmers Univ. of Tech., Göteborg Univ.; joined Scania 1972, Head of Strategic Planning 1977–81, Marketing Man., Scania Nederland BV 1981–83, Pres. Scania Nederland 1983–88, Man. Scania Div. (part of Saab-Scania) 1988, Pres. and CEO Scania AB 1994–; Chair. ISS A/S 2005; Dir SKF AB 2005–, Vice-Chair. 2006–08, Chair. 2008–; mem. Bd Confed. of Swedish Enterprise, Asscn of Swedish Eng Industries. *Address:* AB SKF, Hornsgatan 1, 415 50 Göteborg, Sweden (office). *Telephone:* (31) 337-10-00 (office). *Fax:* (31) 337-28-32 (office). *E-mail:* info@skf.com (office). *Website:* www.skf.com (office).

ÖSTMAN, Arnold; Swedish conductor; b. 1939, Malmö; m. Kristina Modig; ed Univs of Paris and Stockholm; fmr Lecturer, State Acad. of Music and Drama, Stockholm; Artistic Dir Vadstena Acad. 1969, f. Norrlands Operan 1974, Gen. Admin. and Artistic Dir Drottningholm Court Theatre 1979–92; has conducted at opera houses including Covent Garden, Parma, Paris Bastille, Paris Garnier, Trieste, Cologne, Bonn, Toulouse, Nice, Vienna Staatsoper, Vienna Volksoper, Wexford, Washington, Lausanne, Gothenburg Opera, Graz Opera; symphonic conductor with orchestras including German radio orchestras of Hamburg, Cologne, Stuttgart and Baden-Baden, Stuttgart Philharmonic, Orchestre nat. de France, de Lille, orchestra of La Fenice, Venice, Adelaide Symphony Orchestra, Orchestra Sinfonia Siciliana, Scottish Chamber Orchestra, Acad. of Ancient Music, London, Royal Concertgebouw Orchestra, Amsterdam, Oslo Philharmonic Orchestra, Minneapolis Symphony Orchestra, Sydney Symphony Orchestra, Melbourne Symphony Orchestra, Rotterdam Philharmonic, Gothenburg Symphony Orchestra, Swedish Radio Orchestra; works regularly with Netherlands Radio Chamber Orchestra (symphonic and operatic); mem. Royal Swedish Acad. of Music; Chevalier, Légion d'honneur; Hon. PhD. *Recordings include:* Così fan tutte, Le Nozze di Figaro, Don Giovanni, Die Zauberflöte (Diapason d'Or and Deutsche Schallplattenpreis), Gluck's Alceste for Naxos; co-producer two TV films: Christina the Winter Queen, Gustav III (both winners of Prix d'Italia). *Address:* c/o Haydn Rawstron Ltd, 29a High Street, First Floor, West Wickham, Kent, BR4 0LP, England (office). *Telephone:* (20) 8777-6070 (office). *Fax:* (20) 8777-4073 (office). *Website:* www.haydnrawstron.com (office).

OSTRIKER, Jeremiah (Paul), PhD, FAAS; American astronomer, astrophysicist and academic; *Director, Princeton Institute for Computational Science and Engineering;* b. 13 April 1937, New York; s. of Martin Ostriker and Jeanne Sumpf; m. Alicia S. Suskin 1958; one s. two d.; ed Harvard Univ. and Univ. of Chicago; Postdoctoral Fellow, Univ. of Cambridge, UK 1964–65; Research Assoc. and Lecturer, Princeton Univ. 1965–66, Asst Prof. 1966–68, Assoc. Prof. 1968–71, Prof. 1971–, Chair. Dept of Astrophysical Sciences and Dir Observatory 1979–95, Charles A. Young Prof. of Astronomy 1982–2002, Provost, Princeton Univ. 1995–2001, Dir, Princeton Inst. for Computational Science and Eng 2005–; Plumian Prof. of Astronomy and Experimental Physics, Inst. of Astronomy, Univ. of Cambridge 2001–04; mem. Editorial Bd and Trustee Princeton Univ. Press 1982–84, 1986; Visiting Prof., Harvard

Univ. and Regents Fellow, Smithsonian Inst. 1984–85, 1987; mem. NAS 1974–, mem. Council 1992–95, mem. Bd of Govs 1993–95; mem. American Acad. of Arts and Sciences 1975–, American Astronomical Soc., Int. Astronomical Union, American Philosophical Soc. 1994–; Assoc. mem. Royal Astronomical Soc. 1994–; Foreign mem. Royal Netherlands Acad. of Arts and Sciences; NSF 1960–65; Alfred P. Sloan Fellowship 1970–72; Sherman Fairchild Fellowship of CalTech 1977; Trustee American Museum of Nat. History 1997–; Hon. FRAS 1994; Hon. DSc (Univ. of Chicago) 1992; Helen B. Warner Prize (American Astronomical Soc.) 1972, Henry Norris Russell Prize 1980; Vainu Bappu Memorial Award (Indian Nat. Science Acad.) 1993, Karl Schwarzschild Medal, Astronomische Gesellschaft (Germany) 1999, US Nat. Medal of Science 2000, American Acad. of Achievement Golden Plate Award 2001, Royal Astronomical Soc. Gold Medal 2004. *Leisure interest:* squash. *Address:* Department of Astrophysical Sciences, Peyton Hall, Ivy Lane, Princeton University, Princeton, NJ 08544-1001 (office); 33 Philip Drive, Princeton, NJ 08540, USA (home). *Telephone:* (609) 258-4267 (office); (609) 924-5737 (home). *Fax:* (609) 258-1020 (office). *E-mail:* ostriker@astro.princeton.edu (office). *Website:* www.astro.princeton.edu/faculty/webpages/jpo (office).

OSTROUMOVA, Olga Mikhailovna; Russian actress; b. 21 Sept. 1947, Buguruslan; ed Moscow Inst. of Theatre Arts; actress Moscow Theatre of Young Spectators until 1973, Moscow Theatre on Malaya Bronnaya 1973–83, Moscow Mossoviet Theatre 1983–; Silver Nymph Prize, Sorrento and Naples 1973, USSR Official State Prize 1979, RSFSR Merited Actress 1982, Golden Dovzhenko Medal 1982, Peoples' Actress of Russian Fed. 1993. *Films include:* Garage, Stop Kidding, Fate, Snake's Spring, We'll Live up to Monday 1969, Dawns Here Are Quiet 1972, Destiny 1977, Garazh 1979, Earthly Love, Vassily and Vassilisa 1981, There Was No Sorrow 1982, Ya sdelal vsyo, chto mog 1986, The Time of Sons 1986, The Spy 1987, Tower 1987, The Charming Traveller 1990, Very Faithful Wife 1992, Zmeiny istochnik 1997, Ne valyai duraka 1997, Novogodnie priklyucheniya 2002, Photo 2003, Syn 2004, Admiral 2008. *Television includes:* Whilom at California 1978, Engineer Barkasov's Crazy Day 1983, My Sister Lucy 1985, Days and Years of Nikolai Batygin (mini-series) 1987, Zhenshchiny, kotorym povezlo (mini-series) 1989, Po tu storonu volkov (mini-series) 2002, Zachem tebe alibi? (mini-series) 2003, Bednaya Nastya (mini-series) 2003, Zhenshchiny v igre bez pravil (mini-series) 2004, Karusel (series) 2005. *Music:* (CDs) Tribute to Vladimir Visotsky 2000, A Song about Earth, A Novel about Girls 2002. *Theatre includes:* White Guard, Madame Bovary, At the Threshold of the Tsardom, Cherry Orchard 2001, A Husband, a Wife and a Lover, The Eternal Husband (Dostoevsky) 2003. *Leisure interest:* travelling. *Address:* 121002 Moscow, Arboit str. 17, 4, Apt 9 (home); Moscow Mossoviet Theatre, 103050 Moscow, B. Sadovaya str. 16, Russia (office). *Telephone:* (495) 202-01-88 (home); (495) 299-33-77 (office).

OSTROVSKY, Mikhail Arkadievich, DBiolSc; Russian physiologist, biophysicist and academic; b. 22 Feb. 1935, Leningrad; m. Raisa Brook; two s.; ed Moscow State Univ.; jr then sr researcher, Inst. of Higher Nervous Activity and Neurophysiology 1959–70, Head of Sensory Reception Lab., Inst. of Biochemical Physics USSR (now Russian) Acad. of Sciences 1970–; Prof. Moscow State Univ. 1977–; Visiting Prof., Univ. of Md at Coll. Park 1994–; Corresp. mem. USSR (now Russian) Acad. of Sciences 1990, mem. 1994; Ed. Russian Sensory Systems 1987–; Chair. Expert Comm. on Physiology and Medicine of Russian Foundation for Basic Research 1992–; mem. Int. Brain Research Organization 1980, Russian Pavlov Physiological Soc. 1976, Int. Eye Research Asscn 1989; mem. Bd and Chair. Cttee for Relations with E European Neuroscience Asscns. *Publications:* more than 100 articles and papers on photoreception, visual pigments, phototransduction, eye screening pigments, light damage to eye structures; patents for devices and methods in biochem., medicine and optics; invented UV blue light-absorbing intraocular lenses. *Address:* ul. Kosygina 4, 119991 Moscow, Russia. *Telephone:* (495) 135-70-73 (office); (495) 939-73-57 (lab.); (495) 434-15-35 (home). *Fax:* (495) 137-41-01. *E-mail:* ostrovsky@sky.chph.ras.ru (office); ostrovsky@eye.phys.msu.su (home).

OSTROWSKI, Hartmut; German business executive; *Chairman and CEO, Bertelsmann AG;* b. 25 Feb. 1958, Bielefeld; m.; one s. one d.; ed Univ. of Bielefeld; Asst to Bd of Dirs, Bertelsmann Distribution GmbH, Gütersloh, Germany 1982–83, Dept Head 1983–86, Exec. Dept Head 1986–88, Head of Business Unit, 1990–92, Man. Dir 1992–95, Chair. 1995–96, mem. Exec. Bd Bertelsmann Industrie AG (now Bertelsmann Arvato AG) 1996–2002, Chair. 2002–07, Deputy mem. Exec. Bd Bertelsmann AG, Gütersloh 2001–02, mem. 2002–, Chair. and CEO 2008–; Man. Dir Security Pacific Eurofinance, Inc., Munich 1988–90. *Address:* Bertelsmann AG, Carl-Bertelsmann-Strasse 270, 33311 Gütersloh, Germany (office). *Telephone:* 5241800 (office). *Fax:* 5241809662 (office). *E-mail:* info@bertelsmann.de (office). *Website:* www.bertelsmann.de (office).

OSTRY, Sylvia, CC, PhD, FRSC, OC; Canadian economist and academic; *Distinguished Research Fellow in International Studies, University of Toronto;* b. (Sylvia Knelman), Winnipeg; d. of Morris J. Knelman and B. Knelman (née Stoller); m. Bernard Ostry; two s.; ed McGill Univ. and Univ. of Cambridge, UK; Chief Statistician, Statistics Canada 1972–75; Deputy Minister of Consumer and Corp. Affairs and Deputy Registrar Gen. 1975–78; Chair. Econ. Council of Canada 1978–79; Head, Econ. and Statistics Dept, OECD 1979–83; Deputy Minister (Int. Trade) and Co-ordinator for Int. Econ. Relations, Dept of External Affairs 1984–85; Amb., Multilateral Trade Negotiations and Personal Rep. of the Prime Minister, Econ. Summit, Dept of External Affairs 1985–88; Per Jacobsson Foundation Lecture, Washington 1987; Sr Research Fellow, Univ. of Toronto 1989–90; Volvo Distinguished Visiting Fellow, Council on Foreign Relations, New York 1989; Chair. Centre for Int. Studies, Univ. of Toronto 1990–97, Distinguished Research Fellow 1997–; Chancellor, Univ. of Waterloo 1991–97; Western Co-Chair. Blue Ribbon Comm. for Hungary's Econ. Devt 1990–94; Chair. Council Canadian Inst. for Int. Affairs 1990–94; mem. Int. American Dialogue, Advisory Bd Inst. of Int. Econs, Washington, DC, Academic Advisory Council of Deputy Minister for Int. Trade; Founding mem. Pacific Council on Int. Policy; mem. several learned socs and professional orgs; Fellow American Statistical Asscn; Sylvia Ostry Foundation annual lecture series launched 1992; 19 hon. degrees; Outstanding Achievement Award, Govt of Canada 1987, Career Achievement Award, Canadian Policy Research 2000. *Publications include:* International Economic Policy Co-ordination (with Michael Artis) 1986, Governments and Corporations in a Shrinking World: The Search for Stability 1990, The Threat of Managed Trade to Transforming Economies 1993, Rethinking Federalism: Citizens, Markets and Governments in a Changing World (jtly) 1995, The Halifax G7 Summit: Issues on the Table (ed. with Gilbert Winham) 1995, Who's On First? The Post Coldwar Trading System 1997, The Future of the World Trading System 1999, Business, Trade and the Environment 2000, The Changing Scenario in International Governance 2000, The World Trading System: In Dire Need of Reform 2003, Global Integration: Currents and Counter Currents (in The World Trade Organization: Legal, Economic and Political Analysis) 2005, The WTO and Global Governance 2008, Economic Integration in the Americas 2008, The World Trade Organization: System Under Stress 2008; articles on labour econs, demography, productivity, competition policy. *Leisure interests:* films, theatre, contemporary reading. *Address:* Munk Centre for International Studies, University of Toronto, 1 Devonshire Place, Toronto, Ont., M5S 3K7, Canada (office). *Telephone:* (416) 946-8927 (office); (416) 946-8839 (office). *Fax:* (416) 946-8915 (office). *E-mail:* sylvia.ostry@utoronto.ca (office). *Website:* www.utoronto.ca/cis/ostry (office).

O'SULLEVAN, Sir Peter John, Kt, CBE; British racing correspondent and fmr commentator; b. 3 March 1918; s. of the late Col John Joseph O'Sullevan and Vera O'Sullevan; m. Patricia Duckworth 1951; ed Hawtreys, Charterhouse and Collège Alpin, Switzerland; attached to Chelsea Rescue Services 1939–45; then editorial work and manuscripts reading with Bodley Head Publr; Racing Corresp., Press Asscn 1945–50, Daily Express 1950–86, Today 1986–87; race-broadcaster 1946–98 (from Australia, S Africa, Italy, France, USA etc.); first regular TV (BBC) horse-racing commentator to work without a race-reader; commentator on first televised Grand National 1960, world's first televised electronic horse race from Atlas computer at London Univ. (transmitted by BBC) 1967, first horse race transmitted live via satellite from New York 1980; Dir Int. Racing Bureau 1979–93, Racing Post Ltd 1985–95; mem. Jockey Club 1986–; Chair. Osborne Studio Gallery 1999–; numerous awards for services to horse-racing include Derby Award for Racing Journalist of the Year (with the late Clive Graham) 1971, Racehorse Owner of the Year Award, Horserace Writers' Asscn 1974, Sport on TV Award, Daily Telegraph 1994, Services to Racing Award, Daily Star 1995, Lester's Award, Jockeys' Asscn 1996, Special Award, TV and Radio Industries Club 1998. *Publication:* Calling the Horses: A Racing Autobiography 1989. *Leisure interests:* travel, reading, art, food and wine. *Address:* 37 Cranmer Court, London, SW3 3HW, England. *Telephone:* (20) 7584-2781.

O'SULLIVAN, David, BA; Irish international civil servant; *Director-General for Trade, European Commission;* b. 1 March 1953, Dublin; s. of Gerald O'Sullivan and Philomena Boland; m. Agnes O'Hare; one s. one d.; ed Trinity Coll. Dublin, Collège d'Europe, Bruges; Dept of Foreign Affairs, Dublin 1976–79; mem. staff External Relations, EC 1979–81, First Sec. (Econ. and Commercial), Del. of EC in Japan 1981–85; mem. Cabinet of Commr P. Sutherland 1985–89; Head of Unit (Educ. and Youth, Training) 1989–92; mem. Cabinet of Commr P. Flynn 1993–96, Deputy Head 1994–96; Dir Social Affairs, European Social Fund 1996–98, Social Affairs, Man. of Resources 1998–99; Dir-Gen. DGXXII (Educ., Training and Youth) 1999; Head of Cabinet of Pres. of Comm. 1999–2000; Sec.-Gen. European Comm. 2000–05, Dir-Gen. Trade 2005–; Dr hc (Dublin Inst. of Tech.) 2005; European of the Year, Irish Council of the European Movt 1999. *Leisure interests:* tennis, fitness, cinema, music, scuba-diving, yoga. *Address:* Directorate General for Trade, European Commission, 1049 Brussels (office); 87 rue Langeveld, 1180 Brussels, Belgium (home). *Telephone:* (2) 295-09-48 (office); (2) 372-32-55 (home). *Fax:* (2) 299-05-87 (office). *E-mail:* david.o'sullivan@ec.europa.eu (office). *Website:* ec.europa.eu/trade/index_en.htm (office).

O'SULLIVAN, John, OBE, BA; British editor and journalist; b. 25 April 1942, Liverpool; s. of Alfred M. O'Sullivan and Margaret (née Corner) O'Sullivan; ed Univ. of London; jr tutor, Swinton Conservative Coll. 1965–67, Sr Tutor 1967–69; Ed. Swinton Journal 1967–69; London Corresp. Irish Radio and TV 1970–72; editorial writer and parl. sketchwriter, Daily Telegraph 1972–79; Ed. Policy Review 1979–83; Asst Ed. Daily Telegraph 1983–84; columnist, The Times 1984–86, Assoc. Ed. 1986–87; Editorial Page Ed. New York Post 1984–86; Ed. Nat. Review 1988–97, Ed.-at-Large 1998–; columnist, Sunday Telegraph 1988–; Dir of Studies Heritage Foundation 1979–83; Special Adviser to the Prime Minister 1987–88; Founder, Co-Chair. The New Atlantic Initiative 1996–; Conservative parl. cand. 1970; mem. Exec. Advisory Bd Margaret Thatcher Foundation, Advisory Council Social Affairs Unit, Hon. Bd Civic Inst., Prague; Fellow Inst. of Politics, Harvard Univ. 1983. *Leisure interests:* reading, cinema, theatre, dining out. *Address:* National Review, 215 Lexington Avenue, New York, NY 10016, USA. *Telephone:* (212) 679-7330.

O'SULLIVAN, Ronnie; British professional snooker player and business executive; b. 5 Dec. 1975, Chigwell, Essex; commenced professional career 1992; winner of 13 ranking titles: UK Championship 1993, 1997, 2001, British Open 1994, Asian Classic 1996, German Open 1996, Regal Scottish 1998, 2000, China Open 1999, 2000, Embassy World Championship 2001, 2004, European Open 2003, Irish Masters 2003, Welsh Open 2004; winner Nations Cup (with England) 2000; became youngest winner of a ranking title 1993 (aged 17); career prize money: £4,238,510; world ranked No. 1; has made a record six maximum (147) breaks, including the five fastest (fastest was 5 minutes, 20 seconds 1997); f. and owns Viva la Diva lingerie shop in London 2003. *Publications:* The Autobiography of Ronnie O'Sullivan 2003.

O'SULLIVAN, Sonia; Irish/Australian athlete; b. 28 Nov. 1969, Cóbh, Co. Cork; d. of John O'Sullivan and Mary O'Sullivan; pnr Nick Bedeau; two d.; ed Villanova Univ., USA; gold medal, 1,500m, silver medal, 3,000m, World Student Games 1991; holds seven nat. (Irish) records; set new world record (her first) in 2,000m TSB Challenge, Edinburgh 1994, new European record in 3,000m, TSB Games London 1994, gold medal in 3,000m, European Athletic Championships, Helsinki 1994; winner, Grand Prix 3,000m, second overall 1993; silver medal, 1,500m, World Championships, Stuttgart 1993; gold medal, 5,000m, World Championships, Gothenburg 1995; gold medal, World Cross Country Championships 4km, 8km 1998; gold medal, European Championships 5,000m, 10,000m 1998; silver medal, 5,000m Olympic Games, Sydney 2000; silver medal, 5,000m, 10,000m European Championships, Munich 2002; winner BUPA Great South Run, Portsmouth 2002 (new world 10-mile record); winner Great BUPA Ireland Run, Dublin 2003; silver medal (with Ireland team), European Cross Country Championships 2003; ran London Marathon for the first time 2005, finished 8th in personal best time of 2hrs 29mins 01sec; chosen for the Australian team for the 5000m in Commonwealth Games, Melbourne 2006, unable to compete due to a hamstring injury; Female Athlete of the Year 1995, Texaco Sports Star of the Year (Athletics) 2002. *Publication:* Running to Stand Still. *Leisure interests:* mountain biking, reading, films, cooking, playing with children. *Address:* c/o Kim McDonald, 201 High Street, Hampton Hill, Middx, TW12 1NL, England. *Telephone:* (20) 8941-9732. *Fax:* (20) 8979-8325. *E-mail:* sonia@osullivan.net (home). *Website:* www.soniaosullivan.com.

OSWALD, Sir (John) Julian (Robertson), GCB, FRSA; British naval officer and company director; b. 11 Aug. 1933, Selkirk, Scotland; s. of George Oswald and Margaret Oswald (née Robertson); m. Veronica Thompson 1958; two s. three d.; ed Beaudesert Park, Minchinhampton, Britannia Royal Naval Coll., Royal Coll. of Defence Studies; joined RN 1947; served in HM ships Devonshire, Vanguard, Verulam, Newfoundland, Jewel, Victorious, Naiad; specialised in Gunnery 1960; commanded HMS Yarnton 1962–63, HMS Bacchante 1971–72, HMS Newcastle 1977–79; Ministry of Defence 1972–75; RN Presentation Team 1979–80; Capt. Britannia, RN Coll. 1980–82; Asst Chief of Defence Staff (Programmes) 1982–84, (Policy and Nuclear) 1985; Flag Officer, Third Flotilla, Commdr Anti-Submarine Warfare, Striking Fleet 1985–87; C-in-C, Fleet, Allied C-in-C, Channel and C-in-C, E Atlantic Area 1987–89; First Sea Lord and Chief of Naval Staff 1989–93; First and Prin. Aide-de-Camp to HM the Queen 1989–93; Chair. Aerosystems Int. 1995–; Dir Sema Group PLC 1993–2001 (Chair. 1999–2001), BAe Sema 1995–98, James Fisher & Sons 1993–2001, Marine and Gen. Mutual Life Assurance 1994–; Chair. Maritime Trust 1994–, Nat. Historic Ships Cttee 1995–, Ends of the Earth 1996–, Naval Review 1999–; Pres. Sea Cadet Asscn 1994–; Gov. Portsmouth Univ. 1994–99; Hon. DBA (CNAA) 1992, Hon. LLD (Portsmouth) 2000. *Publications:* The Royal Navy Today and Tomorrow 1993; defence and strategy articles in specialized journals, book reviews. *Leisure interests:* gliding, travel, stamp collecting, music, tennis. *Address:* Aerosystems International, Alvington, Yeovil, Somerset, BA22 8UZ; c/o Naval Secretary, Victory Building, HM Naval Base, Portsmouth, PO1 3LS, England. *Telephone:* (1935) 443116 (office). *Fax:* (1935) 443169 (home).

OSWALD, Peter J., LLM, MBA; Austrian business executive; *CEO, Mondi Packaging;* b. 29 Oct. 1962, Braunau/Inn; s. of Peter Oswald and Elfriede Oswald (née Lehbrunner); m. Regina M. Deimel 1983; two s. one d.; ed Univ. of Vienna; Man. Dir Univ. Publishing House WUV-Universitätsverlag, Vienna 1986–89; intern, Deutsche Bank, Germany 1989–90; Purchasing and Logistics Man. KTM, Mattighofen 1990–91; Corp. Controller, Frantschach Packaging (later part of Mondi Packaging), Austria 1992–93; Man. Dir Bates Cepro, Netherlands 1994, Gen. Man. Frantschach Packaging Converting and mem., Man. Bd 1995–2001, Deputy CEO Frantschach Group 2000–04, also CEO (following merger), Mondi Packaging 2002–; Pres. Frapack Iberica, Barcelona, Spain, Franfin, Milan, Italy 1995–; Dir Roxxo, Bates, Brussels, Behn, Krefeld, Franconia, Karlstadt, Germany. *Publications:* articles in professional journals. *Address:* Mondi Packaging Paper Świecie SA, ul. Bydgoska 1, 86–100 Świecie, Poland (office). *Telephone:* (52) 3321000 (office). *Fax:* (52) 3321910 (office). *Website:* www.mondipackaging.com (office).

OSYKA, Sergey Grigorovich, CandJur; Ukrainian politician; b. 27 March 1955; m.; one s.; ed Kiev State Univ.; worked as researcher and teacher Kiev State Univ., then chief consultant Comm. of Foreign Affairs Verkhovna Rada (Parl.) of Ukraine 1991–92; adviser to Prime Minister Kuchma 1992–93; Deputy, First Deputy Minister of External Econ. Relations 1993–94, Minister of Foreign Econ. Relations and Trade 1994–99, Deputy Prime Minister Jan.–July 1995. *Address:* c/o Ministry of External Economic Relations, Lvivska pl. 8, 252053 Kiev, Ukraine. *Telephone:* (44) 226-27-33.

OSZKÓ, Péter, PhD; Hungarian lawyer, management consultant and government official; *Minister of Finance;* b. 22 March 1973; ed Eötvös Loránd Univ.; Marketing Dir and Chair. Bd of Trustees, ELTE Student Foundation 1995–97; Man. Dir HÖOK Kht 1997–99, Vice-Pres. Asscn of Student Councils 1997–99; Man. Dir Agora Universitatis Kht 1997–99; adviser to KPMG Hungary 1996–2000, Tax Man. 2000, Man. KPMG, London 2000–01; Sr Attorney and Head of Tax Group, Freshfields Bruckhaus Deringer Budapest 2001–04; Tax Pnr, Deloitte Hungary Inc. 2004–06, Head of Tax Dept 2006–07, Chair. and CEO 2007–09; Minister of Finance 2009–; mem. Bd of Trustees Pro Facultati Iuridica Foundation 1997–; Bd mem. American Chamber of Commerce 2007–, Jt Venture Asscn 2008–. *Address:* Ministry of Finance, 1051 Budapest, József Nádor tér 2–4, Hungary (office). *Telephone:* (1) 318-

2066 (office). *Fax:* (1) 318-2570 (office). *E-mail:* kommunikacio@pm.gov.hu (office). *Website:* www1.pm.gov.hu (office).

OTA, Hiroji; Japanese energy industry executive; *Chairman, Chubu Economic Federation;* Chair. Chubu Electric Power Co. Inc. –2004; Chair. Chubu Econ. Fed. *Address:* c/o Chubu Electruc Power Company Inc., 1 Higashi-shincho, Higashi-ku, Nagoya 461-8680, Japan (office). *Telephone:* (5) 2951-8211 (office). *Fax:* (5) 2962-4624 (office). *Website:* www.chuden.co.jp/english/ (office).

OTA, Hiroko; Japanese economist, academic and government official; b. 2 Feb. 1954; ed Faculty of Social Sciences, Hitotsubashi Univ.; with Mikimoto Corpn 1976–81; Research Fellow, Japan Inst. of Life Insurance 1981–93; Guest Lectuer, Econs Dept, Osaka Univ. 1993–96; Assoc. Prof., Grad. School of Political Science, Saitama Univ. 1996–97; Assoc. Prof. Nat. Grad. Inst. for Policy Studies 1997–2001, Prof. of Econs 2001–; Dir of Policy Analysis, Cabinet Office 2002–03, Deputy Dir Gen. for Econ. Research 2003–04, Dir Gen. for Econ. Research 2004–05; Minister of State for Econ. and Fiscal Policy 2006–08 (resgnd). *Address:* c/o Ministry of Economy, Trade and Industry, 1-3-1, Kasumigaseki, Chiyoda-ku, Tokyo 100-8901, Japan (office).

OTA, Seiichi, PhD; Japanese economist, academic and politician; *Minister of Agriculture, Forestry and Fisheries;* b. 30 Oct. 1945, Fukuoka Pref.; ed Grad. School of Econs, Keio Univ.; Assoc. Prof., Faculty of Econs, Fukuoka Univ. 1976–77; Visiting Assoc. Prof., Faculty of Econs, Brown Univ., USA (specialized in econs — gen. equilibrium and optimum control theory of econ. and business growth) 1977–80; mem. House of Reps (Fukuoka Pref. 3rd Dist; elected eight times) 1980–; Dir-Gen. Man. and Coordination Agency (State Minister) 1998–99, State Minister in Charge of Admin. Reform and Chief of Youth Devt HQ 1998–2008; Minister of Agric., Forestry and Fisheries 2008–; mem. Shinshinto 1994–95. *Address:* Ministry of Agriculture, Forestry and Fisheries, 1-2-1, Kasumigaseki, Chiyoda-ku, Tokyo 100-8950, Japan (office). *Telephone:* (3) 3502-8111 (office). *Fax:* (3) 3592-7697 (office). *E-mail:* info@maff.go.jp (office). *Website:* www.maff.go.jp (office).

OTAKA, Tadaaki; Japanese conductor; b. 8 Nov. 1947, Kamakura; s. of Hisatada Otaka and Misaoko Otaka; m. Yukiko Otaka 1978; ed Toho Music School, Toho Music Acad., Vienna Acad., Austria; began studying violin 1951; apptd. Chief Conductor Tokyo Philharmonic Orchestra 1971–, Conductor Laureate 1991–; Chief Conductor Sapporo Symphony 1981–86, Prin. Conductor 1998–; Prin. Conductor BBC Welsh Symphony Orchestra (now BBC Nat. Orchestra of Wales) 1987–95, Conductor Laureate 1996–; Chief Conductor Yomiuri Nippon Symphony Orchestra 1992–98; Music Adviser and Prin. Conductor Kioi Sinfonietta (Tokyo) 1995–; Dir Britten Pears Orchestra 1998–2001; has conducted BBC Proms, and orchestras including City of Birmingham Symphony, Royal Liverpool Philharmonic, Royal Scottish National, Bournemouth Symphony, BBC Symphony, London Symphony, London Philharmonic, Rotterdam Philharmonic, Bamberg Symphony, Strasbourg Philharmonic, Bergen Philharmonic and Singapore Symphony; Hon. Fellowship (Welsh Coll. of Music and Drama) 1993; Hon. CBE 1997; Dr hc (Univ. of Wales) 1993; 2nd Prize Min-On Conductors' Competition 1969, Suntory Music Award 1992, Elgar Medal 2000. *Music:* many recordings with BBC Nat. Orchestra of Wales including works by Takemitsu and Franck, and Britten's Peter Grimes with Yomiuri Nippon. *Leisure interests:* fishing, tennis, cooking. *Address:* c/o Askonas Holt, Lincoln House, 300 High Holborn, London, WC1V 7JH, England (office). *Telephone:* (20) 7400-1700 (office). *Fax:* (20) 7400-1799 (office). *E-mail:* info@askonasholt.co.uk (office). *Website:* www .askonasholt.co.uk (office).

OTARI, Muhammad Naji al-; Syrian politician; *Prime Minister;* b. 1944, Aleppo; Head of Aleppo City Council 1983–87; fmr Gov. of Hums; mem. Baath Party Central Cttee 2000–, mem. Regional Command 2000–; Deputy Prime Minister for Services Affairs 2000–03; Speaker of the People's Ass. (Parl.) 2003; Prime Minister of Syria 2003–. *Address:* Office of the Prime Minister, rue Chahbandar, Damascus, Syria (office). *Telephone:* (11) 2226000 (office).

OTČENÁŠEK, Most Rev. Karel, Th.Lic.; Czech ecclesiastic; b. 13 April 1920, České Meziříčí nr Opočno; s. of František Otčenášek and Žofie Otčenášková (née Šolcová); ed Papal Lateran Univ., Rome; ordained priest 1945; secretly Apostolic Admin. of Hradec Králové Diocese and Titular Bishop of Chersonesus, Creta without approval from communist authorities 1950; sentenced to 13 years' imprisonment by communist regime 1954; pardoned 1962; labourer 1962–65; ecclesiastical admin. 1965–89; Bishop of Hradec Králové Diocese 1989–98, Archbishop *ad personam* 1998–; Scout Orders of Lily of Honour and of Silver Wolf; Order of T. G. Masaryk 1996; Dr hc (Pedagogical Univ. Hradec Králové) 1996; Golden Medal of Honour, Charles Univ. Prague 1995, František Ulrich Prize, Hradec Králové 1998. *Leisure interests:* scouting, travelling, social service. *Address:* Biskupství Královéhradecké, Velké náměstí 35, 500 01 Hradec Králové, Czech Republic (office). *Telephone:* (49) 506-36-11 (office). *Fax:* (49) 551-28-50 (office). *Website:* www.diecezehk.cz (office).

OTCHAKOVSKY-LAURENS, Paul, LenD; French publisher; b. 10 Oct. 1944, Valreas, Vaucluse; s. of Zelman Otchakovsky and Odette Labaume; adopted s. of Berthe Laurens; m. Monique Pierret 1970; one s. one d.; ed Coll. and Lycée de Sablé sur Sarthe, Coll. Montalembert de Courbevoie, Coll. St Croix de Neuilly and Faculté de Droit, Paris; Reader, Editions Christian Bourgois 1969–70; Dir of Collection, Editions Flammarion 1970–77; Dir of Collections, then Dir of Dept Editions Hachette 1977–82; Pres. Dir-Gen. Editions P.O.L. 1983–; Commdr Ordre des Arts et des Lettres, Chevalier Légion d'honneur. *Address:* Editions P.O.L., 33 rue Saint-André-des-Arts, 75006 Paris, France. *Telephone:* 1-43-54-21-20. *E-mail:* otchakov@pol-editeur .fr (office).

OTELLINI, Paul S., BA, MBA; American business executive; *President and CEO, Intel Corporation;* b. 2 Oct. 1950, San Francisco; m.; two c.; ed Univ. of San Francisco, Univ. of Calif., Berkeley; joined Intel Corpn 1974, Man. business with IBM Corpn 1980–85, Gen. Man. Peripheral Components Operations 1985–87, Folsom Microcomputer Div. 1987–89, Vice-Pres. Operating Group 1988, Asst to Pres. 1989, Gen. Man. Microprocessor Products Group 1990, Corp. Officer 1991, Exec. Vice-Pres. Sales and Marketing 1992–98, Sr Vice-Pres. 1993–96, Exec. Vice-Pres. 1996–2002, Exec. Vice-Pres. and Gen. Man. Architecture Group 1998–2002, Pres. and COO Intel Corpn 2002–05, mem. Bd of Dirs 2002–, Pres. and CEO 2005–; mem. Bd of Dirs Google Inc. *Address:* Intel Corporation, 2200 Mission College Boulevard, Santa Clara, CA 95052-8119, USA (office). *Telephone:* (408) 765-8080 (office). *Fax:* (408) 765-9904 (office). *E-mail:* info@intel.com (office). *Website:* www.intel.com (office).

OTHMAN BIN WOK; Singaporean company director, fmr journalist and politician; b. 8 Oct. 1924; m. Asnah Bte Suhaimi (now called Lina Binte Abdullah) 1975; one s. two d.; ed Telok Saga Malay School, Raffles Inst. and London School of Journalism; worked on Utusan Melayu as reporter, News Ed. then Deputy Ed. 1946–63; mem. People's Action Party 1954–; MP for Pasir Panjang Constituency 1963–81; Minister for Social Affairs 1963–77; Amb. to Indonesia (also accred to Papua New Guinea) 1977–80; Dir Overseas Investment Pte Ltd 1981–, Overseas Trustees Ltd 1982–, Overseas Investment Nominees Pte Ltd 1982–, Biohealth Int. (S) Pte Ltd 1983–99, Autologous Blood Bank (S) Pte Ltd 1987–99, Sembawang Eng Pte Ltd 1989–97, Utusan Melayu (S) Pte Ltd 1988–2001, Gainall Pte Ltd 1992–, Property Services Int. 1993–99, Hale Medical Clinic (Concourse) Pte Ltd 1995–, Bright Steel Pte Ltd 1996–, Genesis School for Special Educ. 1998–; The Hale Medical Group 2001–, Dimas (S) Pte Ltd 2001–, Ms Twilight Pte Ltd 2001–02, Chair. Lion Asiapac Ltd 1996–, Mainstream Techs Pte Ltd 2000–, Mindsets Pte Ltd 2000–, d'Oz International Pte Ltd; Perm. mem. Presidential Council for Minority Rights 1981–; mem. Singapore Tourist Promotion Bd 1981–94, Sentosa Devt Corpn 1981–97 Singapore Professional Execs Co-operative Ltd 2000–, Ang Mo Kio Community Hosp. 2002; Hon. Consul Principality of Monaco 1996–99; Jasa Utama Star for Outstanding Services (Indonesia) 1980, Order of Nila Utama for Distinguished Service 1983. *Leisure interests:* reading, music, keep-fit exercise, golf. *Address:* Overseas Investment Pte Ltd, 300 Beach Road, #02-01, The Concourse, Singapore 199555 (office); "Wisma Bahagia", 35 Carmen Street, Singapore 459756, Singapore (home). *Telephone:* (65) 63929881 (home). *Fax:* (65) 63929901 (office). *E-mail:* mindsets@pacific.net.sg (office).

OTI, Paterson; Solomon Islands politician; mem. Parl. for Temotu and Nende 1997–; Deputy Speaker Nat. Parl. Feb.–Dec. 2005; Minister for Foreign Affairs 1997–2000, 2006–07; Minister of Communications, Aviation and Meteorology 2004–05; Deputy Prime Minister Nov.–Dec. 2007; mem. Solomon Islands Alliance for Change. *Address:* National Parliament, P.O. Box G19, Honiara, Solomon Islands (office). *Telephone:* 28520 (office). *Fax:* 24272 (office). *Website:* www.parliament.gov.sb (office).

OTMAN ASSED, Mohamed; Libyan politician; b. Oct. 1922, Fezzan; s. of Ahmed al-Badawi Assed and Fatima Nuweir; m. Lola Seif 1959; nine s.; ed Libyan religious and Arabic schools; teacher 1942–43; in Liberation Movt; Head of Fezzan Del. in Legis. Ass. 1950–51; Rep. for Fezzan, UN Council for Libya 1951; Deputy 1952–64; Minister of Health, Fed. Govt 1951–58, of Econ. Affairs Feb.–Oct. 1960; Prime Minister 1960–63; pvt. business 1964–; emigrated to Morocco 1969; Order of Independence 1954; Order of Independence (Tunisia) 1957; Order of the Throne (Morocco) 1962; Muhammad Ali al-Sanoussi Medal 1964. *Address:* Villa Rissani, Route Oued Akrach, Souissi, Rabat, Morocco. *Telephone:* 75-16-25; 75-11-83.

OTOMO, Katsuhiro; Japanese animator and manga artist; b. 14 April 1954, Tome-gun, Miyagi Pref.; m. Yoko Otomo; ed Sanuma High School; following high school, moved to Tokyo to work in manga industry, wrote short strips for Action comics, including Prosper Merimee's short novel Mateo Falcone (retitled A Gun Report) 1973; began Fireball series (unfinished) introducing themes that later became his trademark 1979; serialization of Domu (A Child's Dream) graphic novel was his first major success, selling over half a million copies 1980–82, won Science Fiction Grand Prix 1983 (first ever manga recipient); began work on his masterpiece Akira which took 10 years and over 2,000 pages to complete, animated film version released in 1988 (greatest box office success in Japan that year). *Films:* genre filmography: Koko Erotopia: Akai seifuku (scriptwriter) 1979, Shuffle (comic strip Run) 1981, Jiyu o warera (dir) 1982, Crusher Joe (special character designer) 1983, Harmagedon: Genam taisen (Armageddon: The Great Battle with Genma) (animator, character designer) 1983, Meikyu monogatari (Labyrinth Tales) (segment scriptwriter, dir and character designer) 1987, Roboto kanibauru (segment dir) 1987, Akira (scriptwriter, dir) 1988, Akira Production Report (performed as himself) 1988, Fushigi monogatari: Hachi neko wa yoku asagata kaette kuru (scriptwriter) 1988, Rojin Z (Oldman Z) (scriptwriter) 1991, Warudo apaatoment hora (World Apartment Horror) (dir) 1991, Memories (exec. producer, scriptwriter, dir, art dir) 1995, Perfect Blue (supervisor) 1997, Spriggan (gen. supervisor) 1998, Metoroporisu (Metropolis) (scriptwriter, storyboard artist) 2001, Animax Special: The Making of Metropolis (performed as himself) 2002, Steamboy (dir) 2004, Mushishi (scriptwriter and dir) 2006; non-genre filmography: Give Us Guns (dir) 1981, So What (scriptwriter) 1988. *Address:* c/o Toho Co. Ltd, 1-2-1 Yurako-cho, Chiyoda-ku, Tokyo 100-8415, Japan (office).

O'TOOLE, Peter Seamus; Irish actor; b. 2 Aug. 1932, Connemara, Co. Galway; s. of Patrick Joseph O'Toole; m. 1st Siân Phillips (q.v.) 1960 (divorced 1979); two d.; m. 2nd Karen Brown 1983 (divorced); one s.; ed Royal Acad. of Dramatic Art; office boy, later reporter for Yorkshire Evening News; Nat. Service as signalman, RN; joined Bristol Old Vic Theatre Co., playing 73 parts 1955–58; West End debut in musical play Oh, My Papa 1957; toured England in play The Holiday; appeared in The Long, the Short and the Tall 1959; Stratford season 1960, playing Shylock, Petruchio and Thersites; stage appearances in Pictures in the Hallway 1962, Baal 1963, Ride a Cock Horse, Waiting for Godot 1971, Dead Eyed Dicks 1976, Present Laughter 1978; Bristol Old Vic Theatre Season 1973; inaugurated Britain's Nat. Theatre Co.; appeared with Abbey Theatre Co. in Waiting for Godot, Man and Superman 1976; fmr Assoc. Dir Old Vic Theatre Co.; Artistic Dir North American Tour of Royal Alexandra Theatre Co. playing Present Laughter and Uncle Vanya 1978; Macbeth, Old Vic 1980; Man and Superman 1982–83, Pygmalion 1984, 1987, The Apple Cart 1986, Jeffrey Bernard is Unwell 1989, 1991, 1999, Our Song 1992; Commdr des Arts et Lettres 1988; Outstanding Achievement Award 1999; Hon. Acad. Award for Lifetime Achievement 2003. *Films include:* Kidnapped 1959, The Day They Robbed the Bank of England 1959, Lawrence of Arabia 1960, Becket 1963, Lord Jim 1964, The Bible 1966, What's New Pussycat? 1965, How to Steal a Million 1966, Night of the Generals 1967, Great Catherine 1967, The Lion in Winter 1968, Goodbye Mr. Chips 1969, Brotherly Love 1970, Country Dance 1970, Murphy's War 1971, Under Milk Wood 1972, The Ruling Class 1972, Man of La Mancha 1972, Rosebud 1974, Man Friday 1975, Foxtrot 1975, Caligula 1977, Power Play 1978, Stuntman 1978, Zulu Dawn 1978, The Antagonists 1981, My Favourite Year 1981, Supergirl 1984, Club Paradise 1986, The Last Emperor 1986, High Spirits 1988, On a Moonlit Night 1989, Creator 1990, King Ralph 1990, Wings of Fame 1991, Rebecca's Daughters 1992, Our Song 1992, Fairytale: A True Story 1997, Phantoms 1998, The Manor 1999, Molokai: The Story of Father Damien 1999, Global Heresy 2002, The Final Curtain 2002, Bright Young Things 2003, Troy 2004, Lassie 2005, One Night with the King 2006, Romeo and Me 2006, Venus 2006, One Night with the King 2006, Ratatouille (voice) 2007, Stardust 2007. *Television includes:* Rogue Male 1976, Masada 1981, Svengali 1982, Banshee 1986, The Dark Angel 1989, Civies 1992, Coming Home 1998, Joan of Arc 1999, Jeffrey Bernard Is Unwell 1999, Hitler: The Rise of Evil 2003, Imperium: Augustus 2003, Casanova (mini-series, BBC) 2005, The Tudors 2007. *Publications:* Loitering with Intent 1992, Loitering with Intent 2: The Apprentice 1996. *Address:* c/o Steve Kenis & Co, Royalty House, 72-74 Dean Street, London, W1D 3SG (office); Guyon House, Hampstead High Street, London, NW3, England.

O'TOOLE, Shane, BArch, FRIAI, RIBA; Irish architect and critic; b. 5 July 1955, Dublin; s. of James Patrick O'Toole and Caroline Louise O'Toole (née Hannan); m. Maeve O'Neill 1984; one s. one d.; ed Franciscan Coll., Gormanston, Co. Meath, Univ. Coll., Dublin (UCD); Lynch O'Toole Walsh Architects, Dublin 1979–86; Project Man. Energy Research Group, UCD 1986–92; Co-Founder and Dir urban design consortium Group 91 Architects 1990–99; Shane O'Toole Architect 1991–97; Co. Architect Tegral Bldg Products Ltd 1994–2008; architecture critic, The Sunday Times 1999–; Pres. Architectural Asscn of Ireland 1982–83; Vice-Pres. Royal Inst. of the Architects of Ireland 1988, 1997; Founder and Convenor, Docomomo Ireland 1990–; Dir Irish Architectural Archive 2003–; inaugural Curator and Dir Irish Architecture Foundation 2005–06; mem. CICA (Int. Cttee of Architectural Critics) 2008–; Adviser to Mies van der Rohe Award for European Architecture 1992–, to Nation Building (TV series on architecture in Ireland 1922–2000) 2000, to Veronica Rudge Green Prize in Urban Design (Harvard Prize in Urbanism), Harvard Univ. Grad. School of Design 2000–04, to biennial New Trends of Architecture in Europe and Asia-Pacific Exhbn 2002–07, to Art and Architecture of Ireland research project, Royal Irish Acad. 2008–(14); Hon. mem. Architectural Asscn of Ireland 1995–; Silver Medal Sofia Biennale 1987, Grand Prix Kraków Biennale 1989, Irish Bldg of the Year Award 1996, Architectural Asscn of Ireland Downes Medal 1996, European Architectural Award (RIBA) 1997, Int. Union of Architects Sir Patrick Abercrombie Prize for Town Planning and Territorial Devt 2002, Gold Medal Commendation, Royal Inst. of the Architects of Ireland 2003, Int. Bldg Press Architectural Critic of the Year 2008, and other prizes and awards. *Achievements:* Co-Dir Architectural Framework Plan for Regeneration of Temple Bar, Dublin 1992–2000; Co-Designer The Ark, Europe's first cultural centre for children 1992–95; represented in architecture exhbns including 40 Under 40: Emerging British Architects, UK and USA 1988–89, The New Breed, Sydney 1988, Making a Modern Street, Zurich 1991, 20 Young Architects of the World, London 1993, Presenting Architecture, Dublin 2005, Collection Building, Dublin 2006, Group 91: 15 Years On, Belfast 2006; cr. exhbns, The Pillar Project, Dublin 1988, Tales from Two Cities: Emerging Architects in Dublin and Edinburgh (Edin., Dublin, Berlin, London) 1994, Master of All the Muses: Michael Scott 1905–2005 (Cork, Dublin) 2005; Irish Commr, Venice Biennale 2004, 2006; North by Northwest: Liam McCormick 1916-1996 (Dublin, Belfast, Letterkenny, Greencastle) 2008. *Publications:* Collaboration: The Pillar Project 1988, The Architect and the Drawing 1989, Tales from Two Cities 1994, Transformation of an Institution 2004, SubUrban to SuperRural 2006; Co-Ed.: Kevin Roche Architect 1983, Aldo Rossi 1983, Making a Modern Street 1991, North by Northwest 2008. *Leisure interests:* family, football, films, food, good buildings, a glass of wine. *Address:* 68 Irishtown Road, Dublin 4, Ireland (home). *Telephone:* (1) 6609843 (home). *E-mail:* shane_otoole@hotmail.com (home). *Website:* www.irish-architecture.com/tesserae (office).

OTSASON, Rein, DEconSc; Estonian economist; b. 24 May 1931, Tartu; s. of August Otsason and Marta Otsason; m. Valentina Otsason 1979; one s.; Dir Inst. of Econ., Acad. of Sciences of Estonia 1984–88; Chair. State Planning Cttee and Deputy Chair. Council of Ministers of Estonian SSR (now Estonia) 1988–89; Pres. Eesti Bank (Bank of Estonia) 1989–91, Eesti Krediidipank 1992–. *Publications:* works on monetary policy and currency reforms. *Address:* Eesti Krediidipank, Narva Mnt. 4, 15014 Tallinn, Estonia (office). *Telephone:* 669-0900 (office). *Fax:* 661-6037 (office). *E-mail:* reino@ekp.ee (office).

OTSUJI, Hidehisa; Japanese politician; mem. (LDP) House of Councilors; fmr Sr Vice-Minister of Finance; Minister of Health, Labour and Welfare 2004–05. *Address:* c/o Ministry of Health, Labour and Welfare, 1-2-2, Kasumigaseki, Chiyoda-ku, Tokyo 100-8916, Japan.

OTSUKA, Mutsutake; Japanese transport industry executive; *Chairman, East Japan Railway Company;* b. 5 Jan. 1932, Beijing, China; ed Tokyo Univ.; began career with Japanese Nat. Railways 1965, various positions 1965–87; Man. Dir E Japan Railway Co. 1987–97, Vice Pres. 1997–2000, Pres. and CEO JR East (formed during privatisation of railways) 2000–06, Chair. E Japan Railway Co. 2006–. *Leisure interests:* music, golf. *Address:* East Japan Railway Co., 2-2 Yoyogi 2-chome, Shibuya-ku, Tokyo 151-8578, Japan (office). *Telephone:* (3) 5334-1310 (office). *Fax:* (3) 5334-1297 (office). *Website:* www.jreast.co.jp (office).

OTT, Hans Rudolf, PhD; Swiss physicist and academic; *Professor, Eidgenössische Technische Hochschule, Zürich;* b. 4 July 1940, Berne; m. Marie-Louise Ott (née Gruaz); one s.; ed Eidgenössische Technische Hochschule (ETH), Zürich; Asst, ETH, Zürich 1971, Admin. Dir, Dept of Physics 1976–88, Prof. of Physics 1986–, Deputy Chair., Dept of Physics 1999–2001, Chair. 2001–05, also Head, Inst. for Solid State Physics 1990–93, 1998–99; Head of Research, Paul Scherrer Inst. (PSI), Villigen 1988–91, also Dir and Chair. of Research Cttee 1991–; Vice-Chair., Comm. C5, IUPAP 1996–2002; Pres. Physikalische Gesellschaft, Zürich 1994–97; Sec. of Comm., Int. Inst. of Refrigeration 1976–86; mem. Council European Physical Soc. 1993–96 (mem. Cttee for Low Temperature Physics, IUPAP 1987–92, Chair. Condensed Matter Div. 1998–2005); Co-Ed. Physica C 1988–2004; Assoc. Ed. Reviews of Modern Physics 1994–99; Ed.-in-Chief European Physical Journal B 2004–; mem. Research Council, Swiss Nat. Science Foundation 1997–; Foreign mem. Finnish Acad. of Sciences 2005–; Fellow, American Physical Soc. 1989–, World Innovation Foundation 2004–; Hon. Mem. Swiss Physical Soc. 2005–; European Physical Soc. Hewlett-Packard Europhysics Prize 1989, American Physical Soc. Int. Prize for New Materials 1990. *Publications:* several books and more than 500 articles in scientific journals. *Address:* Laboratorium für Festkörperphysik, ETH Hönggerberg Office, HPF F 4, 8093 Zürich, Switzerland (office). *Telephone:* (1) 633-2311 (office). *Fax:* (1) 633-1077 (office). *E-mail:* ott@phys.ethz.ch (office). *Website:* www.solid.phys.ethz.ch/ott/staff/ott.html (office).

OTTER, Clement Leroy (Butch), BA; American business executive and state official; *Governor of Idaho;* b. 3 May 1942, Caldwell, Ida; m. 1st Gay Simplot 1964 (m. annulled 1992); four c.; m. 2nd Lori Easley 2006; ed St Teresa's Acad. (now Bishop Kelly High School), Boise, Boise Junior Coll. (now Boise State Univ.), Coll. of Idaho (now Albertson Coll. of Idaho); served in Ida Army Nat. Guard's 116th Armored Cavalry 1968–73, received specialized training at Fort Knox, Ky; mem. Bd of Dirs J.R. Simplot Co., later Dir Food Products Div., later Pres. Simplot Livestock, Pres. Simplot Int. –1993; mem. Ida State House of Reps from Canyon Co. 1973–76, served as Deputy Majority Whip; cand. for Gov. of Ida 1978; remained active in Ida Republican Party, including its Cen. Cttee, served as Chair. Canyon Co. Republican Party; Lt-Gov. of Ida 1987–2001; mem. US House of Reps for Ida First Congressional Dist 2001–06; Gov. of Ida 2007–; mem. Nat. Rifle Asscn, Maple Grove State Grange, Ida Cowboys Asscn, American Legion, Idaho 4-H Million Dollar Club; Grand Slam mem. Ducks Unlimited; Lifetime mem. Safari Club International; Republican; Dr hc (Mindanao State Univ., Philippines, Albertson Coll. of Ida). *Address:* Office of the Governor, PO Box 83720, Boise, ID 83720, USA (office). *Telephone:* (208) 334-2100 (office). *Fax:* (208) 334-2438 (office). *Website:* www.state.id.us (office).

OTTEWILL, Ronald Harry, OBE, MA, PhD, FRS, FRSC; British scientist and academic; *Professor Emeritus of Physical Chemistry, University of Bristol;* b. 8 Feb. 1927, Southall, Middx; s. of Harry A. Ottewill and Violet D. Ottewill (née Bucklee); m. Ingrid G. Roe 1952; one s. one d.; ed Southall County School, Queen Mary Coll., London and Fitzwilliam Coll., Cambridge; Asst Lecturer, Queen Elizabeth Coll., London 1951–52; Nuffield Fellowship, Dept of Colloid Science, Univ. of Cambridge 1952–55, Sr Asst in Research 1955–58, Asst Dir of Research 1958–63; Lecturer in Physical Chem., Univ. of Bristol 1964–66, Reader in Colloid Science 1966–71, Prof. of Colloid Science 1971–82, Leverhulme Prof. of Physical Chem. 1982–92, Prof. Emer. of Physical Chem. 1992–, Dean, Faculty of Science 1988–90, Head of School of Chem. 1990–92; Sr Research Fellow Univ. of Bristol 1996; mem. NATO Research Grants Cttee 1980–84, Chair. 1984; mem. Science Bd SERC 1982–85, Chair. Neutron Beam Cttee 1982–85; mem. Scientific Council Inst. Laue Langevin 1981–86; mem. Council Faraday Soc. (now Faraday Div. of Royal Soc. of Chem. — RSC) 1981–99, Hon. Treas. 1985–89, Vice-Pres. 1986–89, 1991–99, Pres. 1989–91; Monsanto Lecturer 1979, Alexander Lecturer, Royal Australian Chem. Inst. 1982; RSC Liversidge Lecturer 1985–86; Founders Lecturer, Soc. of Chemical Industry 1985; Xerox Lecturer, Canada 1987; RSC Rideal Lecture 1990; Dunning Lecture, Univ. of Bristol 1992; Yamada Lecturer, Kyoto 1984, ACS Langmuir Lecturer 1988; Orica Lecture, Melbourne Univ. 1998; Chemical Soc. Medal 1974, Wolfgang Ostwald Prize, Kolloid Gesellschaft 1979, Bude Medal, Collège de France 1981, RSC Liversidge Medal 1985, Presidential Medal, Faraday Div., RSC 1991, Faraday Soc. CISG Medal 1993. *Publications:* more than 300 papers in scientific journals; ed. 10 books. *Leisure interests:* gardening, walking, music. *Address:* The Glen House, Holt Close, Wickham, Hants., PO17 5EY, England (home). *Telephone:* (1329) 834745 (home). *Fax:* (1329) 834745 (home). *E-mail:* ingrid@ottewill02.wanadoo.co.uk (home).

OTTEY, Merlene, BA; Jamaican athlete; b. 10 May 1960, Pondside, Cold Springs; d. of Hubert and Joan Ottey; m. Nathaniel Page 1984; ed Univ. of Nebraska, USA; set 200m indoor record (21.87) 1993; winner 100m finals 57 consecutive times from Sept. 1987 to Aug. 1991; winner 200m finals 36 consecutive times from May 1989 to Aug. 1991; winner eight Olympic medals; tested positive for nandrolone 1999, one-year ban lifted after IAAF ruled that Swiss lab. had mishandled sample; co-owner TMG Co., Slovenia; Roving Amb. for Jamaica; granted citizenship of Slovenia 2002; IAAF Patron for the Year of Women in Athletics 1998. *Publication:* Merlene Ottey: Unyielding Spirit (autobiog.). *Address:* c/o Slovenian Athletic Federation, Letališka cesta 33c, 1122 Ljubljana, SloveniaE-pošta:. *E-mail:* info@atletska-zveza.si; www.atletska-zveza.si.

OTTO, Frei, PhD; German architect and engineer; b. 1925, Siegmar, Saxony; ed Tech. Univ., Berlin, Univ. of Va, USA; served as pilot with Luftwaffe 1943–45; taken prisoner and served as architect, builder and repairman for POW camp, France 1945–47; freelance architect, inventor, author and designer 1952–; led revival of tent as feature of modern architecture 1950s; f. Centre of Devt for Lightweight Structures, Berlin 1957; Founding Dir Inst. for Lightweight Structures, Univ. of Stuttgart 1964–90; f. Wide-Spanned Lightweight Structures Special Research Unit, Deutschen Forschungsgemeinschaft 1969; fmr Prof., Tech. Univ., Berlin; fmr Visiting Prof. at Yale, Wash., Harvard Univs, Univ. of Calif., Berkeley, MIT; Hon. mem. AIA 1968, RIBA 1981; Hon. Citizen of the City of Leonberg 2000; Dr hc Tech. Univ., Munich; Berlin Prize for Architecture 1967, Thomas Jefferson Medal in Architecture, Univ. of Va 1974, Aga Khan Award for Architecture 1980, 1998, Honda Prize for Architecture and Nature (Japan) 1990, Grand Prize, German Architects and Engineers Asscn 1996, Wolf Prize in Architecture 1997, Lifetime Achievement Special Prize, VII Int. Biennial for Architecture, Buenos Aires 2000, RIBA Royal Gold Medal 2005. *Architectural works include:* Music Pavilion, Fed. Garden Exhbn, Kassel 1955, Entrance Arch, Fed. Garden Exhbn, Cologne 1957, Snow and Rocks Pavilion, Swiss Nat. Exhbn, Lausanne 1964, W German Pavilion, Montreal Exposition, Canada 1967, Intercontinental Hotel and Conf. Centre, Mecca, Saudi Arabia 1968–72, Sport Structures Roofs, Olympic Park, Munich 1972, Multihall Complex, Mannheim 1975, Bird House, Hellabrunn Zoo 1980, Cultural Centre, Tuwaiq Palace, Riad, Saudi Arabia 1985, Ecological Houses in Berlin 1990, Stuttgart Train Station Project 2000, Japanese Pavilion for Hannover Exposition 2000. *Publications:* Natürliche Konstruktionen 1981, Gestaltwerdung. Zur Formentstehung in Nature, Technik und Baukunst 1988, Das hängende Dach 1990; various articles on tensile and pneumatic structures. *Address:* c/o Institute for Lightweight Structures, University of Stuttgart, Pfaffenwaldring 7, 70569 Stuttgart, Germany (office). *Website:* www.uni-stuttgart.de/ilek (office).

OTTO, Michael, Dr rer. pol; German business executive; *Chairman of the Supervisory Board, Otto Group;* b. 12 April 1943; joined Otto Group 1971, mem. Exec. Bd Merchandise 1971–81, Chair. Exec. Bd and CEO 1981–2007, Chair. Supervisory Bd 2007–; mem. Bd of Dirs Axel Springer Verlag AG, Berlin, Gerling-Konzern Versicherungs-Beteiligungs-AG, Cologne; Vice-Pres. Hamburg Chamber of Commerce; Chair. Council WWF Deutschland; Chair. Bd of Trustees Soc. for Politics and Industry, Werner Otto Foundation for Medical Research; Founder and Chair. Bd of Trustees Michael Otto Foundation for Environmental Protection, Foundation for Sustainable Agriculture and Forestry (FSAF); Hon. Senator, Univs of Hamburg and Greifswald 2000; Bundesverdienstkreuz mit Stern 2006; Manager of the Year 1986, 2001, Hamburg Senate Alfred Töpfer Medal 1996, German Environment Award 1997, Corp. Ethics Award 2000, German Business Ethics Network Business Ethics Award, Sustainability Leadership Award 2002, Jewish Museum Berlin Prize for Understanding and Tolerance 2004, BAUM Sustainability Special Award 2005, Vernon A. Walters Award, Atlantik-Brücke 2005, German Incorporaters Prize (for life's work) 2006, Int. Lifetime award 2006. *Address:* Otto GmbH & Co. KG, Wandsbeker Strasse 3–7, 22179 Hamburg, Germany (office). *Telephone:* (40) 64610 (office). *Fax:* (40) 64618571 (office). *E-mail:* info@ottogroup.com (office). *Website:* www.ottogroup.com (office).

OTUNBAYEVA, Roza Isakovna, CPhilSc; Kyrgyzstani diplomatist and politician; *Co-Chairman, Banner (Asaba) Party of National Revival;* b. 23 Aug. 1950; m.; one s. one d.; ed Moscow State Univ.; sr teacher, Head of Chair Kyrgyz Univ. 1975–81; Second Sec. Regional CP Cttee in Frunze (now Bishkek), Sec. City CP Cttee 1979–86; Vice-Chair. Council of Ministers, Minister of Foreign Affairs of Kyrgyz SSR 1986–89; Exec. Sec. USSR Comm. on UNESCO 1989–90, Chair. 1990–91; Amb. of USSR to Malaysia 1991–92; Vice-Prime Minister and Minister of Foreign Affairs of Repub. of Kyrgyzstan Feb.–May 1992; Amb. of Kyrgyzstan to USA 1992–94 (also accred to Canada); Minister of Foreign Affairs 1994–97; Amb. to UK 1997–2002; apptd Deputy Special Rep. of UN Sec.-Gen. for Georgia (to regulate conflict between Georgia and Abkhazia) 2002; Chair. Ata-Jurt party 2004–06, key leader of Tulip Revolution that led to overthrow of Pres. Akayev 2005, Acting Minister of Foreign Affairs 2005; Co-Chair. Banner (Asaba) Party of Nat. Revival 2006–; mem. Advisory Bd (Moscow Br.), Carnegie Endowment for Int. Peace. *Address:* Banner (Asaba) Party of National Revival, 720000 Bishkek, pr. Chui 26, Kyrgyzstan (office). *Telephone:* (312) 43-04-45 (office). *Fax:* (312) 28-53-64 (office).

OTUNNU, Olara; Ugandan diplomatist and fmr UN official; *President, LBL Foundation for Children;* b. Sept. 1950, Mucwini, northern Uganda; guardian of six c.; ed Makerere Univ., Univ. of Oxford, UK, Harvard Law School, USA; practised law in USA; Asst Prof. of Law, Albany Law School, USA; participated in resistance activities against regime of Idi Amin; Perm. Rep. to UN 1980–85, Pres. Security Council 1981, Vice-Pres. Gen. Ass. 1982–83; Minister of Foreign Affairs 1985–86; Pres. Int. Peace Acad. 1990–97; Special Rep. of UN Sec.-Gen. for Children and Armed Conflict 1997–2005, UN Under-Sec.-Gen. for Children and Armed Conflict 1998–2005; Founder and Pres. LBL Foundation for Children, New York 2005–; mem. Bd of Dirs Carnegie Endowment for Int. Peace, Aspen Inst., Aspen France, Carnegie Corpn of New York; mem. Int. Selection Comm. of the Phila Liberty Medal, Jury for Hilton

Humanitarian Prize; German Africa Prize 2002, Sydney Peace Prize 2005. *Address:* c/o Carnegie Corporation of New York, 437 Madison Avenue, New York, NY 10022, USA (office).

OU, Francisco H. L., BA; Taiwanese diplomatist and politician; *Minister of Foreign Affairs;* b. 5 Jan. 1940; ed Nat. Cheng-chi Univ.; Officer, Dept of Cen. and S American Affairs, Ministry of Foreign Affairs 1964–67; Third Sec., Embassy in Peru 1967–71, Second Sec. 1971; Section Chief, Dept of Cen. and S American Affairs, Ministry of Foreign Affairs 1971–73, Deputy Dir-Gen. 1973–75, Dir-Gen. 1981–84; Dir Far E Commercial Office, Santiago, Chile 1975–81; Amb. to Nicaragua 1984–85, to Guatemala 1990–96, 2003–08; Dir Commercial Office, Argentina 1986–90; Vice Minister of Foreign Affairs 1996–2000; Rep. Taipei Econ. and Cultural Office, Spain 2000–03; Minister of Foreign Affairs 2008–. *Address:* Ministry of Foreign Affairs, 2 Kaitakeland Boulevard, Taipei 10048, Taiwan (office). *Telephone:* (2) 23482999 (office). *Fax:* (2) 23812703 (office). *E-mail:* eyes@mofa.gov.tw (office). *Website:* www.mofa.gov.tw (office).

OU, Jinping; Chinese engineer and university administrator; *President, Dalian University of Technology;* Prof., Dept of Civil Eng, Dalian Univ. of Tech., also currently Univ. Pres.; Deputy, 11th NPC 2008; mem. Chinese Acad. of Eng; winner of first Feng Kang Prize for Scientific Computing. *Address:* Office of the President, Dalian University of Technology, Dalian 116024, Liaoning Province, People's Republic of China (office). *Telephone:* (411) 84708114 (office). *Fax:* (411) 84708116 (office). *E-mail:* oujinping@dlut.edu.cn (office). *Website:* www.dlut.edu.cn (office).

OUAIDOU GUELENGDOUKSIA, Nassour; Chadian politician; fmrly Sec.-Gen. in Office of the Pres.; Prime Minister of Chad 1997–99. *Address:* c/o Office of the Prime Minister, N'Djamena, Chad.

OUALALOU, Fathallah, DèsSc; Moroccan economist and politician; b. 1942, Rabat; m.; four c.; ed Lycée Moulay Youssef, Univ. of Rabat, Univ. of Paris; began career as Research Asst, Centre Universitaire de Recherche Scientifique, also Pres. Union Nationale des Etudiants (UNEM); Lecturer, Law Dept, Univs of Rabat, Casablanca and Ecole Nat. d'Admin 1968; mem. Groupe de Rabat; co-founder Socialist Union of Popular Forces (USFP) 1972, mem. Political Bureau 1989–, Leader Parl. Group 1984–98; Minister of Economy, Finance, Privatization and Tourism 1998–2002, of Finance and Privatization 2002–07; mem. Nat. Bureau, Syndicat Nat. de l'Enseignement Supérieur (SNESUP); co-founder Asscn des économistes marocains 1972, Pres. 1982–; Pres. Union des économistes Arabes; mem. Chambre des Représentants. *Publications:* numerous articles on econ. theory and Maghreb economies. *Address:* Union socialiste des forces populaires (USFP), 9 ave al-Araâr, Hay Riad, Rabat, Morocco (office). *Telephone:* (3) 7565511 (office). *Fax:* (3) 7565510 (office). *E-mail:* webmaster@usfp.ma (office). *Website:* www.usfp.ma (office).

OUANE, Moktar, MA; Malian diplomatist; *Minister of Foreign Affairs and International Co-operation;* b. 11 Oct. 1955, Bidi; m.; two c.; ed Univ. of Dakar, Senegal; with Gen. Secr. of Govt 1982–86, Chief Div. of Int. Agreements and Conventions, Foreign Ministry March–June 1986, Diplomatic Counsellor, Office of the Prime Minister 1986–88, Prin. Pvt. Sec. to Minister Sec.-Gen., Office of the Pres. and Diplomatic Counsellor to the Pres. 1988–91; mem. del. to UN Gen. Ass. 1988–91, 1993, mediation del., Senegal–Mauritania and Liberian conflicts; Diplomatic Counsellor, Office of the Head of State 1991–92, Office of the Prime Minister June–Oct. 1992, Tech. Counsellor, Political and Diplomatic Affairs, Foreign Ministry 1994–95; Perm. Rep. to the UN 1995–2004; Minister of Foreign Affairs May 2004–; Founder and Pres. Democracy and Repub. Club, Mali. *Address:* Ministry of Foreign Affairs and International Co-operation, Koulouba, Bamako, Mali (office). *Telephone:* 222-83-14 (office). *Fax:* 222-52-26 (office). *E-mail:* info@maliensdelexterieur.gov.ml. *Website:* www.maliensdelexterieur.gov.ml.

OUATTARA, Alassane Dramane, DSc; Côte d'Ivoirian politician and financial official; *President, Rassemblement des républicains (RDR);* b. 1 Jan. 1942, Dimbokro; s. of Dramane Ouattara and Nabintou Cissé; m.; four c.; ed Drexel Inst. of Tech., Phila and Univ. of Pennsylvania, USA; Economist, IMF 1968–73; sr staff mem. in charge of missions Banque Centrale des Etats de l'Afrique de l'Ouest (BCEAO) 1973–75, Special Adviser to the Gov. and Dir of Research 1975–82, Vice-Gov. 1983–84, Gov. 1988–90; Dir African Dept, IMF 1984–88, Counsellor to Man. Dir 1987–88; Prime Minister of Côte d'Ivoire and Minister of Economy and Finance 1990–93; Deputy Man. Dir IMF 1994–99; Pres. UNCTAD 1979–80; mem. Bd of Dirs Global Econ. Action Inst.; Expert Adviser Comm. on Transnat.Corpns; Hon. Gov. BCEAO; Pres. Rassemblement des républicains (RDR) 1999–; in exile in Gabon; being also a citizen of Burkina Faso he was barred from standing in 2000 presidential elections of Côte d'Ivoire; granted Côte d'Ivorian citizenship 2002; Commdr Ordre du Lion du Sénégal, Ordre du Mono du Togo, Ordre Nat. du Niger, Grand Officier Ordre Nat. de Côte d'Ivoire. *Address:* Rassemblement des républicains (RDR), 8 rue Lepic, Cocody, 06 BP 1440, Abidjan, Côte d'Ivoire (office). *Telephone:* 22-44-33-51 (office). *E-mail:* rdrci@rdrci.org (office). *Website:* www.rdrci.org (office); www.ado.ci (home).

OUCHI, Tsutomu, DEcon; Japanese professor of economics; *Emeritus Professor of Economics, University of Tokyo;* b. 19 June 1918, Tokyo; s. of Hyoe Ouchi; m. Setsuko Otsuka 1944; one s. one d.; ed The Daiichi Kotogakko and Tokyo Imperial Univ.; researcher Japan Inst. of Agric. 1942–46; Assoc. Prof. Univ. of Tokyo 1947–60, Prof. 1960–79, Prof. Emer. 1979–; Prof. Shinshu Univ. 1979–84, Prof. Emer. 1984–; Prof. Daito Bunka Univ. 1987–91; Dean Faculty of Econs, Univ. of Tokyo 1968–69; Vice-Pres. Univ. of Tokyo 1972–73; Dir Nat. Fed. of Univ. Co-operative Asscns 1988–99; Dir Nat. Fed. of Co-operatives of Aged People of Japan 2001–; Chair. Cen. Cttee for Security of Employment 1976–88, Employment Cttee, Ministry of Labour 1988–96; mem. Japan Acad. 1981–; Mainichi Press Prize, Nasu Prize, Nihon Keizai Press Prize. *Publications:* Agricultural Crisis 1954, American Agriculture 1965, State Monopolistic Capitalism 1970, American Agriculture in the 1960s 1975, Japanese Agriculture 1978, Methodology of Economics 1980, Principles of Economics (2 vols) 1981–82, Imperialism (2 vols) 1984–85, World Economy 1991, Japanese Economy 2000. *Leisure interests:* skiing, trekking. *Address:* 26-19 Hyakunin-cho II, Shinjuku-ku, Tokyo 169 0073, Japan. *Telephone:* (3) 3371-3760.

OUEDRAOGO, Ablassé, DEcon; Burkinabè international organization official; *Regional Adviser for Africa, African Development Bank;* b. 30 June 1953, Burkina Faso; ed Univ. of Nice, France; Deputy Resident Rep. of UNDP, Kinshasa 1991–93; Head of Regional Office for E Africa of UN Sudano-Sahélienne Office (also accred to OAU, ECA, UNEP) 1993–94; Minister of Foreign Affairs 1994–99; Special Adviser to Pres. of Burkina Faso 1999; Jt Deputy Dir-Gen. WTO 1999–2000; Regional Adviser for Africa, African Devt Bank 2006–; Officer of Nat. Order of Burkina Faso 1997; Officer of Equatorial Order of Gabon 2000. *Publications:* Réflexions sur la crise industrielle en France 1979, Les firmes multinationales et l'industrialisation des pays en voie de développement 1981. *Address:* African Development Bank, Rue Joseph Anoma 1, BP 1387, Abidjan 01, Cote d'Ivoire.

OUÉDRAOGO, Gérard Kango; Burkinabè politician; b. 19 Sept. 1925, Ouahigouya; s. of Jean Ouédraogo and Christine Ouédraogo; m. 1947; Rep. to French West African Fed. 1952; Deputy to French Nat. Ass. 1956–59; Co-Founder Mouvement Démocratique Voltaïque; mem. Parl. 1957–65; Minister of Finance 1958–59; Amb. to UK 1961–66; Adviser, Ministry of Foreign Affairs; Pres. Union Démocratique Voltaïque 1970–74, now Commr; Prime Minister 1971–74; Pres. Nat. Ass. 1978–80; Jr Pres. ACP/EEC Lomé Convention 1970–80; fmr Leader Rassemblement Démocratique Africain (RDA); Deputy and Pres. Parl. Group RDA, Assemblée des Députés du Peuple; Grand Officier Ordre Nat. Burkina Faso; Grand Officier du Mérite Français; Grand Officier Légion d'honneur; several other decorations. *Address:* ADF-RDA, 01 BP 2061, Ouagadougou, Burkina Faso. *Telephone:* 31-15-15.

OUEDRAOGO, Idrissa; Burkinabè film director and screenwriter; b. 21 Jan. 1954; ed film school in Burkina Faso; Grand Jury Prize, Cannes Film Festival 1990. *Films include:* Poko 1981, Les Écuelles 1983, Les Funérailles du Larle Naba 1984, Ouagadougou, ouaga deux roues 1985, Issa le tisserand 1985, Yam Daabo (The Choice) 1986, Yaaba, Tilaï (Etalon de Yenenga (Grand Prix), Pan-African Film Festival) 1990, Obi 1991, Karim and Sala 1991, Samba Traore 1993, Afrique, mon Afrique... 1995, Lumiè et Compagnie 1995, Kini and Adams 1997, Les Parias du cinéma 1997, Scenarios from the Sahel 2001, 11'09"01 – September 11 (segment) 2002, La Colère des dieux (Anger of the Gods) 2003. *Address:* FEPACI, 01 BP 2524, Ouagadougou, Burkina Faso.

OUEDRAOGO, Kadré Désiré; Burkinabè politician, economist and banker; *Ambassador to the European Union;* m. Solange Ouedraogo; ed Haute Ecole, Paris, Université Paris I (Sorbonne); fmr Deputy Exec. Sec. ECOWAS in charge of Econ. Affairs; fmr Gov. of Cen. Bank of West African States; Prime Minister of Burkina Faso 1996–2000; currently Amb. to the EU (also accred to Belgium, Luxembourg, Netherlands and UK); Grand Officier de l'Ordre National du Burkina Faso 1996. *Address:* Mission of Burkina Faso to the European Union, 16 place Guy d'Arezzo, 1180 Brussels, Belgium (office); 01 BP 3474, Ouagadougou 01, Burkina Faso (home). *Telephone:* (322) 3459912 (office). *Fax:* (322) 3450612 (office). *E-mail:* ambassade.burkina@skynet.be (office). *Website:* www.ambassadeduburkina.be (office).

OUÉDRAOGO, Youssouf, PhD; Burkinabè politician; b. 25 Dec. 1952, Tikaré, Bam Prov.; m.; two c.; ed Univ. of Dijon and Univ. of Clermont-Ferrand, France; Head of Business Admin Course, Univ. of Dijon, France 1979–82; Prof. of Admin, Univ. of Ouagadougou 1983–84; Minister of Planning and Population Devt 1984–87, of Planning and Co-operation 1987–89; Pres. Social and Econ. Council 1989–92; Deputy, Nat. Ass. (Parl.) 1992–; Prime Minister 1992–94; Amb. to Belgium, the Netherlands, Luxembourg, the UK and EU 1994–99; Minister of State, Ministry of Foreign Affairs 1999–2002; State Minister and Minister of Foreign Affairs and Regional Co-operation 2002–07; Gov. Islamic Bank for Devt, World Bank and African Bank for Devt 1987–89; Silver Medal of the Torch of the Revolution 1986, Grand Officier of the Nat. Order 1994, Grand Cordon, Order of the Shining Star, Taiwan 2002, Grand Officier, Order of the Crown, Belgium 2005. *Address:* c/o Ministry of Foreign Affairs, rue 988, blvd de Faso, 03 BP 7038, Ouagadougou 03, Burkina Faso (office).

OUELLET, Hon. André, PC, BA, LLL; Canadian fmr politician and lawyer; b. 6 April 1939, St-Pascal, Québec; s. of Dr Albert Ouellet and Rita Turgeon; m. Edith Pagé 1965; two s. two d.; ed Pensionnat St-Louis de Gonzague, Québec Seminary, Ottawa and Sherbrooke Univs; MP for Papineau 1967–93; Parl. Sec. to Minister for External Affairs 1970, to Minister for Nat. Health and Welfare 1971; Postmaster Gen. 1972–74; Minister for Consumer and Corp. Affairs 1974–76, 1980–84, for Urban Affairs 1976–79, for Public Works 1978–79, for Canada Post Corpn 1980–83, for Labour 1983, for Regional Econ. Devt 1983–84; Pres. Privy Council 1984; Govt Leader of Commons 1984; Opposition Transport Critic 1984; Opposition External Affairs Critic 1987; Opposition Critic for Fed. Provincial Relations 1990; Minister for Foreign Affairs 1993–96; Chair. Canada Post Corpn 1996–99, Pres. and CEO 1999–2004. *Leisure interests:* tennis, swimming, squash, skiing, reading and collecting works of art. *Address:* c/o Canada Post Corporation, 2701 Riverside Drive, Suite N1250, Ottawa, Ont., K1A 0B1, Canada.

OUELLET, HE Cardinal Marc, PSS; Canadian ecclesiastic; *Archbishop of Quebec City;* b. 8 June 1944, Lamotte; ed Collège de Berthier, Ecole Normale of Amos, Univ. of Laval, Major Seminary of Montreal, Pontifical Univ. San Tommaso d'Aquino, Pontifical Gregorian Univ., Rome, Italy; ordained priest 1968; entered Soc. of Priests of St Sulpice 1972, held several teaching positions in Colombia, Montreal and Edmonton; Prof., John Paul II Inst. for Studies on Marriage and the Family 1997–2001; apptd to Pontifical Council for Promoting Christian Unity 2001; consecrated Bishop of Titular See of Agropoli, Rome 2001; Archbishop of Quebec City 2002–; cr. Cardinal Priest of Santa Maria in Traspontina 2003; Consultor, Congregation for the Doctrine of Faith, Congregation for Divine Worship; Sec. Comm. for Religious Relations with Jews; mem. Perm. Interdiscasteral Comm. for the Eastern Churches in Europe, Pontifical Acad. of Theology; mem. Editorial Bd Rivista Internazionale Communio (N American edn); mem. XIth Gen. Ordinary Ass. of Synod of Bishops 2005, Vatican City. *Address:* Archdiocese of Quebec, 1073 boulevard René-Lévesque Ouest, Québec, PQ G1S 4R5, Canada (office). *Telephone:* (418) 688-1211 (office). *Fax:* (418) 688-1399 (office). *E-mail:* diocese@diocesequebec.qc.ca (office). *Website:* www.diocesequebec.qc.ca (office).

OULD AHMED WAGHF, Yahya; Mauritanian economist and politician; fmr Prof. of Econs, Univ. of Nouakchott; fmr Minister Sec.-Gen. of the Presidency; Chair. Nat. Pact for Devt and Democracy (PNDD-ADIL); Prime Minister 2008 (ousted in coup). *Address:* c/o Office of the Prime Minister, BP 237, Nouakchott, Mauritania.

OULD BEN HMEIDA, Abdallahi; Mauritanian diplomatist and politician; b. 1954; fmr Amb. to Libya; Minister of Foreign Affairs and Co-operation 2008. *Address:* c/o Ministry of Foreign Affairs and Co-operation, BP 230, Nouakchott, Mauritania (office).

OULD TAH, Sidi, PhD; Mauritanian economist and politician; fmrly with Islamic Devt Bank; fmr econ. advisor to Prime Minister; Minister of Economy and Finance 2008. *Address:* c/o Ministry of Finance, BP 181, Nouakchott, Mauritania (office).

OUMAROU, Mamane; Niger politician and diplomatist; *Ambassador to Saudi Arabia;* b. 1945; m.; Prime Minister of Niger Jan.–Nov. 1983, 1988–90; mem. Mouvement Nat. de la coc. de développement (MNSD); currently Amb. to Saudi Arabia. *Address:* PO Box 94334, Riyadh 11693, Saudi Arabia (office). *Telephone:* (1) 464-2931 (office). *Fax:* (1) 464-2931 (office).

OUMAROU, Seyni; Niger politician; *Prime Minister;* b. 9 Aug. 1950, Tillabéri; m.; six c.; mem. Mouvement national pour la société de développement, Pres. Tillabéry regional council; apptd Special Adviser to Prime Minister 1995; Minister of Trade and Industry 1999–2004; Minister of State for Equipment 2004–07; Prime Minister 2007–. *Address:* Office of the Prime Minister, BP 893, Niamey, Niger (office). *Telephone:* 20-72-26-99 (office). *Fax:* 20-73-58-59 (office).

OURISSON, Guy, DrSc, PhD; French chemist and academic; *Professor of Chemistry, Centre de Neurochimie, Université Louis Pasteur;* b. 26 March 1926, Boulogne-sur-Seine; s. of Jacques Ourisson and Colette Ourisson (née de Bosredon); m. 1st Paula Baylis 1950 (deceased 1958); m. 2nd Nicole Heiligenstein 1959 (died 2004); one s. two d. from previous m.; ed Ecole Normale Supérieure, Paris, Harvard Univ.; Maître de Conférences, Université Louis Pasteur, Strasbourg 1955–58, Prof. of Chem. 1958–, Pres. of Université Louis Pasteur 1971–75; Dir of Univ. Studies, Ministry of Educ. Nat. 1981–82; Dir Inst. of Chem. of Natural Products, CNRS, Gif/Yvette 1984–89; Chair. Scientific Council, Rhône-Poulenc 1988–92, Compagnie Générale des Eaux 1998–2000; Pres. of many scientific cttees in France; Chair. Publications Cttee, IUPAC 1973–77, Sec.-Gen. 1975–83; Regional Ed. Tetrahedron Letters 1965–2003; Vice-Pres. Acad. of Sciences 1997–99, Pres. 1999–2001; Pres. Fondation Alfred Kastler; mem. Acad. Leopoldina (Halle), European Acad. of Arts and Sciences, American Acad. of Arts and Sciences, Danish, Swedish, Indian, Rheinland-Westphalia, Serbian and French Acads of Sciences; Hon. mem. Chemical Socs of Belgium, UK, Switzerland; Commdr, Légion d'honneur; Grand Officier, Ordre nat. du Mérite; Commdr des Palmes académiques; Order of Sacred Treasure (Japan); awards from Chemical Socs of France, FRG, Belgium, UK, USA. *Publications:* more than 400 publs on chem. and on ethics of science. *Address:* Centre de Neurochimie, Université Louis Pasteur, 5 rue Blaise Pascal, 67084 Strasbourg (office); 10 rue Geiler, 67000 Strasbourg, France (home). *Telephone:* (3) 88-60-05-13 (office). *Fax:* (3) 88-60-76-20 (office). *E-mail:* ourisson@chimie.u-strasbg.fr (office). *Website:* www-ulp.u-strasbg.fr (office).

OUSELEY, Baron (Life Peer) cr. 2001 Herman (George), Kt; British civil servant and race relations adviser; various public service posts 1963–86; Race Relations Adviser Lambeth Borough Council 1979–81, GLC 1981–84; Dir of Educ. ILEA 1986–88, Chief Exec. 1988–90; Chief Exec. London Borough of Lambeth 1990–93; Chair. Comm. for Racial Equality 1993–2000; Man. Dir Different Realities Partnership Ltd 2000–; Dir Focus Consultancy Ltd 2000–; mem. Council Policy Studies Inst. 1988–, Inst. of Race Relations 1990–, Inst. of Educ., Univ. of London 1995–; mem. Advisory Council Prince's Youth Business Trust 1993–; Chair. Uniting Britain Charitable Trust 1997–, Presentation Educ. and Employment Charitable Trust 1997–; Patron Presentation Housing Asscn 1990–; Dr hc (Edin.) 1999. *Publications:* The System 1981, pamphlets and articles on local govt, public services, employment, training and race equality issues. *Address:* House of Lords, London, SW1A 0PW, England (office).

OUTRAM, Dorinda, MA, PhD; British historian and academic; *Professor and Gladys I. and Franklin W. Clark Chair in History, University of Rochester;* b. 11 Dec. 1949, Leicester; d. of Albert Ernest Outram and Rosemary Elenor Collins; m. 1976 (divorced 1980); one s.; ed Univ. of Cambridge; Research Fellowship British Acad. 1974, Univ. of Reading 1975; Lectureship and Research Fellowships, Univ. of London 1977–81; Asst Prof. Univ. of Montreal 1981–82; Research Fellowship, Girton Coll., Cambridge 1982–84; Lecturer in Modern History, Univ. Coll., Cork 1984–98; Clark Chair and Prof. of History, Univ. of Rochester, NY 1998–; Visiting Prof. Griffith Univ., Australia 1990; Landon Clay Visiting Assoc. Prof. Harvard Univ. 1991–92; Editorial Dir, Comité int. pour l'édition de la correspondance de Georges Cuvier 1983–; mem. Editorial panel, Dictionary of Irish Biography 1984–; Ed. Bulletin of the Irish Asscn for Research in Women's History 1987–88; Trustee, British Soc. for History of Science; Hon. Sec. Irish Nat. Cttee for Research in Women's History 1988–; Vellacott Historical Essay Prize, Cambridge 1971, Royal Soc. of London Research Award 1982, CNRS Research Award, Paris 1982. *Publications:* Science, Vocation and Authority in Post-Revolutionary France; Georges Cuvier 1984, Uneasy Careers and Intimate Lives: Women in Science 1987, The Body and the French Revolution 1989, The Enlightenment 1994, Panorama of the Enlightenment 2007; numerous articles. *Leisure interests:* walking, talking, learning languages, visiting France, Italy and Germany. *Address:* 369A Rush Rhees Library, University of Rochester, Rochester, NY 14627-0070, USA. *Telephone:* (585) 275-4097 (office). *Fax:* (585) 756-4425 (office). *E-mail:* otrm@mail.rochester.edu (office). *Website:* www.rochester.edu/College/HIS/index.php (office).

OUVRIEU, Jean-Bernard; French diplomatist; b. 13 March 1939; m. Arabella Cruse 1968; one s. two d.; ed Ecole Nat. d'Admin; Head of Mission, Office of Prime Minister 1968–69; served in Perm. Mission to European Communities, Brussels 1971–74, Baghdad 1975–77, Washington, DC 1977–79; Deputy Dir, Office of Minister of Foreign Affairs 1979–80; Rep. to Governing Council of IAEA 1981–85; Amb. to Repub. of Korea 1985–87; Dir of Econ. and Financial Affairs, Ministry of Foreign Affairs 1987–89; Amb. to Brazil 1989–93, to Japan 1993–98; Personal Rep. of Minister of Defence 1998–2002; mem. Bd of Dirs CS Communication & Systèmes; Counselor, Association Pasteur Japon; Officier, Légion d'honneur, Officier, Ordre nat. du Mérite. *Address:* c/o Board of Directors, CS Communication & Systèmes, 22, avenue Galilée, 92350 Le Plessis Robinson, France (office).

OUYAHIA, Ahmed; Algerian politician and diplomatist; *Prime Minister;* b. 2 July 1952, Bouadnane; m.; two c.; Sec., Ministry of Foreign Affairs 1975–81; Counsellor, Embassy in Abidjan 1981–84; Counsellor, Perm. Mission to UN, New York 1984–89, Deputy Rep. to Security Council 1988–89; Counsellor, Office of the Minister of Foreign Affairs 1989–90, Dir Gen. Dept of African Affairs, Ministry of Foreign Affairs 1990–91; Amb. to Mali 1992–93; Sec. of State for Cooperation and N African Affairs 1993–94; Dir of Cabinet to the Presidency 1994–95; Prime Minister of Algeria 1995–98, 2003–06 (resgnd), 2008–; Deputy, Nat. Ass. 1997–; Minister of Justice 2000–02; Minister of State, Personal Rep. of the Pres. of the Repub. 2002–03; Sec.-Gen. Rassemblement nat. démocratique (RND) 1999–. *Address:* Office of the Prime Minister, rue Docteur Saâdane, Algiers (office); Rassemblement national démocratique (RND), Cité des Asphodèles, BP 10, Ben Aknoun, Algiers, Algeria (office). *Telephone:* (21) 73-23-40 (office); (21) 91-64-10 (office). *Fax:* (21) 71-79-27 (office); (21) 91-47-40 (office). *E-mail:* rnd@rnd-dz.org (office). *Website:* www.cg.gov.dz (office); www.rnd-dz.org (office).

OUYANG, Ziyuan, MSc; Chinese scientist; *President, Chinese Society of Mineralogy, Petrology and Geochemistry;* b. Oct. 1935, Jian City, Jiangxi Prov.; ed Beijing Coll. of Geology, Inst. of Geology, Beijing, Univ. of Science and Tech., Beijing, Inst. of Atomic Energy; Asst Prof., Inst. of Geology Chinese Acad. of Sciences 1960–66, Assoc. Prof., Inst. of Geochemistry 1966–78, Prof., Vice-Dir then Dir 1978–94, Prof. 1994–, Dir Bureau of Resources and Environmental Sciences 1991–93; Vice-Pres. People's Congress of Guizhou Prov. 1993–; Chair. Asscn for Science and Tech. Guizhou Prov. 1993–; Pres. Chinese Soc. of Mineralogy, Petrology and Geochemistry 1994–; Guest Prof., Beijing, Nanjing and other univs 1993–; Standing Vice-Pres. Chinese Soc. of Mineralogy, Petrology and Geochemistry 1976–94; Vice-Pres. Chinese Soc. of Space Sciences; Chair. Cttee of Space Chem. and Space Geology, Assoc. Ed.-in-Chief Journal of Space Science, Chinese Journal of Geochemistry 1980–; Ed.-in-Chief Journal of Environmental Science, Journal of Geology-Geochemistry, Bulletin of Mineralogy, Petrology and Geochemistry 1985–; Vice-Pres. Chinese Soc. of Geology 1992–96; Academician, Chinese Acad. of Sciences 1991–; First-Class Award of Natural Science Prize, Chinese Acad. of Sciences Nat. Science Conf. Prize. *Publications:* Progress of Selenology Research, Space Chemistry, Progress of Geology and Geochemistry during the 1980s, Progress of Mineralogy, Petrology and Geochemistry Research in China, Riddle of Dinosaur Depopulation, Formation and Evolution of the Planets and the Earth. *Leisure interests:* music, literature, tourism, photography. *Address:* Chinese Society for Mineralogy, Petrology and Geochemistry, 73 Guanshui Road, Guiyang 550002, Guizhou Province (office); Institute of Geochemistry, China Academy of Sciences, Guiyang City, Guizhou Province, People's Republic of China. *Telephone:* (851) 5895328 (office); (851) 5891338 (office). *Fax:* (851) 5891923 (office); (851) 5891379 (home). *E-mail:* ouyangziyuan@ms.gyig.ac.cn (home); kydhtb@263.net (home). *Website:* (office).

OVCHINIKOV, Vladimir Pavlovich; Russian pianist; b. 1 Jan. 1958, Beleby, Urals; ed studied with Anna Artobolevskaya and at Moscow Conservatoire with Alexey Nasedkin; London debut, Barbican Hall 1987; has since given recitals in UK, Europe, USA, Canada and Japan and appeared with BBC Symphony, Royal Liverpool Philharmonic, Netherlands Philharmonic, Moscow Philharmonic and other major orchestras; Lecturer in Keyboard Studies, Royal Northern Coll. of Music 1994–; silver medal (jtly with Peter Donohoe) Moscow Tchaikovsky Competition 1982, first prize Leeds Int. Piano Competition 1987.

OVCHINNIKOV, Col-Gen. Vyacheslav Victorovich; Russian army officer; b. 25 Oct. 1946, Tambov Region; m.; two s.; ed Leningrad Artillery Higher School, Kalinin Mil. Artillery Acad.; various posts in internal troops; service in Dept of Internal Affairs; fmr Deputy Head of Gen. Staff, Ministry of Internal Affairs, Head Dept of Punishments 1989–99, Deputy Minister of Internal Affairs 1999; Commdt of Stepanakert during Karabakh Conflict 1992, of N Osetia during Osetia-Ingush Conflict, of Grozny during mil. operations in

Chechnya; First Deputy C-in-C Internal Troops, Ministry of Internal Affairs 1999, C-in-C 1999–2000, Adviser to Dir-Gen. Rosoboronexport Co. 2001; Order for Personal Courage, Order for Service to Motherland and numerous other medals. *Address:* Rosoboronexport, Gogolevski Blvd 21, 119865 Moscow, Russia (office). *Telephone:* (495) 239-52-66 (office).

OVENDEN, Graham Stuart, MA, ARCA, ARCM; British art historian, artist and poet; b. 11 Feb. 1943, Alresford, Hants.; s. of the late Henry Ovenden and Gwendoline D. Hill; m. Ann. D. Gilmore 1969; one s. one d.; ed Alresford Dames School, Itchen Grammar School, Southampton, Southampton Coll. of Art, Royal Coll. of Music and Royal Coll. of Art; corresp. and critic, Architecture Design Magazine; Founder mem. South West Acad. of Fine and Applied Art. *Publications:* Illustrators of Alice 1971, Victorian Children 1972, Clementina, Lady Harwarden 1973, Pre-Raphaelite Photography 1972, Victorian Erotic Photography 1973, Aspects of Lolita 1975, A Victorian Album (with Lord David Cecil) 1976, Satirical Poems and Others 1983, The Marble Mirror (poems) 1984, Lewis Carroll Photographer 1984; Graham Ovenden... A Monograph with Essays by Laurie Lee, etc. 1987, Sold With All Faults (poems) 1991; photographs: Alphonse Mucha 1973, Hill & Adamson 1973, Graham Ovenden – Childhood Streets (Photographs 1956–64) 1998; contribs on art to numerous journals. *Leisure interests:* music (very seriously indeed), architecture, social science. *Address:* Barleysplatt Chapel, Panters Bridge, Mount, nr Bodmin, Cornwall PL30 3DP, England (home).

OVERBEEK, Jan Theodoor Gerard, DrsChem, PhD; Dutch chemist and academic; b. 5 Jan. 1911, Groningen; s. of Dr A.A. Overbeek and J.C. (van Ryssel) Overbeek; m. Johanna Clasina Edie 1936; four d.; ed Univ. of Utrecht; Asst at Univ. of Ghent, Belgium 1935–36, Univ. of Utrecht 1936–41; Scientific Officer, NV Philips, Eindhoven 1941–46; Prof. of Physical Chem., Univ. of Utrecht 1946–81, Vice-Pres. of Univ. 1971–76; Visiting Prof., MIT, Cambridge, Mass, USA 1952–53, 1966–67, 1969–81, 1984–88, Columbia Univ., New York 1956, Univ. of Southern Calif., LA 1959–60; Ed. Advances in Colloid Interface Science –1967, Ed. Emer. 1990–; mem. Bd Verenigde Bedrijven Bredero, Utrecht 1963–83; mem. Royal Netherlands Acad. of Arts and Sciences 1953–; mem. Emer. ACS; Foreign mem. Royal Flemish Acad. of Sciences (Belgium) 1957–; Hon. mem. Royal Netherlands Chem. Soc. 1993–, Kolloid-Gesellschaft 1993–; Foreign Hon. mem. American Acad. of Arts and Sciences 1969–; Hon. FRSC (London) 1983; Kt, Order of Netherlands Lion 1971; Hon. DSc (Clarkson Coll. of Tech., Potsdam, NY) 1967, (Univ. of Bristol) 1984; Wolfgang-Ostwald-Preis (Kolloid-Gesellschaft) 1989. *Publications:* Theory of Stability of Lyophobic Colloids (with E.J.W. Verwey) 1948, Colloid Science (with H.R. Kruyt) Vol. I 1952, Vol. II 1949, The Electrical Double Layer (with A.L. Loeb, P.H. Wiersema) 1960; An Introduction to Physical Chemistry (with H.R. Kruyt) 1954, Colloid and Surface Chemistry Vols I–IV 1971–74, Electrochemistry Vols I, II & III 1981; numerous articles and study guides on colloid and surface science. *Leisure interests:* outdoor activities, hiking, photography. *Address:* Zweerslaan 35, 3723 HN Bilthoven, Netherlands (home). *Telephone:* (30) 2282882 (home).

OVERHAUSER, Albert Warner, PhD; American physicist and academic; *Stuart Distinguished Professor Emeritus of Physics, Purdue University;* b. 17 Aug. 1925, San Diego; s. of Clarence Albert Overhauser and Gertrude Irene (Pehrson) Overhauser; m. Margaret Mary Casey 1951; four s. four d.; ed Univ. of California, Berkeley; service with USNR 1944–46; Research Assoc., Univ. of Ill. 1951–53; Asst Prof. of Physics, Cornell Univ. 1953–56, Assoc. Prof. 1956–58; Supervisor, Solid State Physics, Ford Motor Co., Dearborn, Mich. 1958–62, Man. Theoretical Sciences 1962–69, Asst Dir of Physical Sciences 1969–72, Dir 1972–73; Prof. of Physics, Purdue Univ., West Lafayette, Ind. 1973–74, Stuart Distinguished Prof. of Physics 1974–, now Emer.; Fellow, American Physics Soc., American Acad. of Arts and Sciences; mem. NAS; Hon. DSc (Chicago) 1979, (Purdue) 2004; Hon. LLD (Simon Fraser Univ., Canada) 1998; Oliver E. Buckley Solid State Physics Prize (American Physical Soc.) 1975, Alexander von Humboldt Sr US Scientist Award 1979, Nat. Medal of Science 1994. *Address:* Department of Physics, Purdue University, West Lafayette, IN 47907 (office); 236 Pawnee Drive, West Lafayette, IN 47906, USA (home). *Telephone:* (765) 494-3037 (office). *Fax:* (765) 494-0706 (office). *E-mail:* awo@physics.purdue.edu (office). *Website:* www.physics.purdue.edu (office).

OVERY, Richard James, PhD, FRHistS, FBA, FRSA; British historian and academic; *Professor of History, University of Exeter;* b. 23 Dec. 1947, London; s. of James Herbert Overy and Margaret Grace Overy (née Sutherland); m. 1st Tessa Coles 1969 (divorced 1976); m. 2nd Jane Giddens 1979 (divorced 1992); m. 3rd Kim Turner 1992 (divorced 2004); one s. four d.; ed Sexey's Blackford Grammar School, Somerset, Gonville and Caius Coll., Cambridge; Research Fellow, Churchill Coll., Cambridge 1972–73; Fellow and Coll. Lecturer, Queen's Coll., Cambridge 1973–79; Asst Univ. Lecturer, Univ. of Cambridge 1976–79; Lecturer in History, King's Coll., London 1980–88, Reader in History 1988–92, Prof. of Modern History 1992–2004, Fellow 2003–; Prof. of History, Univ. of Exeter 2004–; T.S. Ashton Prize 1983, Cass Prize for Business History 1987, Samuel Eliot Morison Prize for lifetime contrib. to mil. history, Soc. for Mil. History 2001. *Publications:* William Morris, Viscount Nuffield 1976, The Air War 1939–1945 1980, The Nazi Economic Recovery 1982, Goering: The Iron Man 1984, The Origins of the Second World War 1987, The Road to War 1989, War and Economy in the Third Reich 1994, The Interwar Crisis 1919–1939 1994, Why the Allies Won 1995, The Penguin Atlas of the Third Reich 1996, The Times Atlas of the Twentieth Century 1996, Bomber Command 1939–1945 1997, Russia's War 1998, The Times History of the World (Gen. Ed.) 1999, The Battle 2000, Interrogations: The Nazi Elite in Allied Lands 1945 2001, The Dictators: Hitler's Germany and Stalin's Russia (Second Prize, Wolfson Prize for History 2004, Hessell-Tiltman Prize for History (jtly) 2005) 2004, What Britain Has Done: September 1939–May 1945

A Selection of Outstanding Facts and Figures 2007; contrib. to scholarly books and professional journals. *Leisure interests:* opera, art, football. *Address:* School of Humanities and Social Science, Amory Building, Rennes Drive, Exeter, Devon, EX4 4RJ, England (office). *Fax:* (1392) 263291 (office). *E-mail:* R.Overy@ex.ac.uk (office). *Website:* www.ex.ac.uk/shipss/history/index.php (office).

OVETT, Stephen Michael (Steve), OBE; British fmr athlete; b. 9 Oct. 1955, Brighton, Sussex; m. Rachel Waller 1981; ed Brighton College of Art; European Jr Champion at 800m 1973; European Champion at 1500m 1978 and silver medallist at 800m 1974 and 1978; competed Olympic Games, Montreal 1976, finished 5th in 800m, reached semi-final of 1,500m; Moscow 1980, won gold medal at 800m and bronze medal at 1,500m; set four world records; holder of record for greatest number of mile/1,500m victories (45 to 1980); also winner of major titles at 5,000m. *Publication:* Ovett: An Autobiography. *Leisure interest:* art.

OVITZ, Michael, BA; American entertainment industry executive; *Principal, CKE Associates;* b. Dec. 1946, Chicago; m. Judy Reich 1969; three c.; ed Birmingham High School and UCLA; tour guide at Universal Studios while at coll.; joined William Morris Agency, Beverly Hills 1968; with three others formed Creative Artists Agency (CAA) 1975, Pres. 1975–95; Pres. Walt Disney Co. 1995–97; private investor 1997–98; Head Livent Inc. Toronto 1998–99; Founder, CEO Artists Man. Group 1998–2002; Principal, CKE Assocs 2002–; mem. Bd of Dirs D.A.R.E. America; Chair. Exec. Bd of UCLA Hosp. and Medical Center; Trustee Museum of Modern Art, NY; mem. Bd of Advisors UCLA School of Theater, Film and Television; mem. Council on Foreign Relations. *Address:* c/o Board of Advisors, UCLA School of Theater, Film and Television, 102 East Melnitz Hall, Box 951622, Los Angeles, CA 90095-1622, USA.

OWADA, Hisashi, LLB; Japanese judge and academic; *Judge, International Court of Justice;* b. 18 Sept. 1932, Niigata; s. of Takeo Owada and Shizuka Tamura; m. Yumiko Egashira 1962; three d.; (one d. Masako; m. Crown Prince Naruhito of Japan); ed Univs of Tokyo and Cambridge; Pvt. Sec. to Prime Minister 1976–78; Minister-Plenipotentiary, USSR 1981–84; Dir-Gen. Treaties Bureau and Office for Law of the Sea 1984–87; Deputy Vice-Minister, Ministry of Foreign Affairs 1987–88; Amb. to OECD 1988–89; Deputy Minister, Ministry of Foreign Affairs 1989–91, Vice-Minister for Foreign Affairs 1991–93; Adviser to Minister for Foreign Affairs 1993–94, 1999–2003; Amb. and Perm. Rep. to UN 1994–98; Sr Adviser to Pres. World Bank 1999–2003; Adjunct Prof., Tokyo Univ. 1963–88, Colo Law School 1994–98; Visiting Prof., Harvard Univ. 1979–81, 1987, 1989, 1999–2002, NY Univ. Law School 1994–; Prof., Waseda Univ. 1999–2003; Pres. Japan Inst. of Int. Affairs 1999–2003; Judge, Int. Court of Justice 2003–; Associé de l'Institut de Droit Int; Hon. LLD. *Publications:* US–Japan Economic Interaction in an Independent World 1981, Japanese Perspectives on Asian Security 1982, Practice of Japan in International Law 1984, From Involvement to Engagement: A New Course for Japanese Foreign Policy 1994, Diplomacy 1997, A Treatise on International Relations 2003. *Leisure interests:* music, skiing, mountain walking. *Address:* International Court of Justice, Carnegieplein 2 (Peace Palace), 2517 KJ, The Hague, Netherlands (office). *Telephone:* (70) 3022323 (office). *Fax:* (70) 3022409 (office). *E-mail:* mail@icj-cij.org (office). *Website:* www.icj-cij.org (office).

OWEN, Clive; British actor; b. 3 Oct. 1964, Keresley, Warwicks.; m. Sarah-Jane Fenton; ed Royal Acad. of Dramatic Arts. *Film appearances include:* Vroom 1988, Close My Eyes 1991, Century 1993, The Turnaround 1994, The Rich Man's Wife 1996, Bent 1997, Croupier 1998, Greenfingers 2000, The Hire: Ambush 2001, The Hire: Chosen 2001, The Hire: The Follow 2001, The Hire: Star 2001, The Hire: Powder Keg 2001, Gosford Park 2001, A Day in the Death of Joe Egg 2001, Beyond Borders 2002, The Bourne Identity 2002, The Hire: Hostage 2002, The Hire: Beat the Devil 2002, The Hire: Ticker 2002, I'll Sleep When I'm Dead 2003, Beyond Borders 2003, King Arthur 2004, Closer (Best Supporting Actor, Golden Globe Awards 2005, Best Actor in a Supporting Role, BAFTA Awards 2005) 2004, Sin City 2005, Derailed 2005, Inside Man 2006, Children of Men 2006, Shoot 'Em Up 2007, Elizabeth: The Golden Age 2007. *Television appearances include:* Precious Bane 1989, Capital City (series) 1989, Lorna Doone 1990, Chancer (series) 1990, The Magician 1993, Class of '61 1993, Nobody's Children 1994, An Evening with Gary Lineker 1994, Doomsday Gun 1994, The Return of the Native 1994, Bad Boy Blues 1995, Sharman (series) 1996, The Echo 1998, Split Second 1999, Second Sight 1999, Second Sight: Parasomnia 2000, Second Sight: Kingdom of the Blind 2000, Second Sight II: Hide and Seek 2000. *Other work includes:* Privateer 2: The Darkening (video game). *Stage appearances include:* Design for Living 1994, Closer 1997. *Address:* c/o Creative Artists Agency, 9830 Wilshire Blvd, Beverly Hills, CA 90212-1825, USA. *Telephone:* (310) 288-4545. *Fax:* (310) 288-4800. *Website:* www.caa.com.

OWEN, Baron (Life Peer), cr. 1992, of the City of Plymouth; **David Anthony Llewellyn Owen,** CH, PC, MA, MB, BChir, FRCP; British politician and business executive; b. 2 July 1938, Plymouth; s. of Dr John William Morris Owen and Mary Llewellyn; m. Deborah Schabert 1968; two s. one d.; ed Bradfield Coll., Sidney Sussex Coll., Cambridge, St Thomas' Hosp.; house appointments, St Thomas' Hosp. 1962–64; Neurological and Psychiatric Registrar 1964–66; Research Fellow, Medical Unit 1966–68; MP for Sutton Div. of Plymouth 1966–74, for Devonport Div. of Plymouth 1974–92; Parl. Pvt. Sec. to Minister of Defence, Admin. 1967; Parl. Under-Sec. of State for Defence, RN 1968–70; Opposition Defence Spokesman 1970–72, resgnd over party policy on EEC 1972; Parl. Under-Sec. of State, Dept of Health and Social Security (DHSS) March–July 1974; Minister of State, DHSS 1974–76, FCO 1976–77; Sec. of State for Foreign and Commonwealth Affairs 1977–79; Opposition Spokesman for Energy 1979–80; co-f. Social Democratic Party (SDP) 1981; Chair. Parl.

Cttee 1981–82; Deputy Leader SDP 1982–83, Leader 1983–87, 1988–92; now Ind. Social Democrat; Chair. Decision Tech. Int. 1970–72, Palme Comm. on Disarmament and Security Issues 1980–89, Ind. Comm. on Int. Humanitarian Issues 1983–88; EC Co-Chair. Int. Conf. on fmr Yugoslavia 1992–95, Carnegie Comm. on Preventing Deadly Conflict 1994–2000; Chair. Global Natural Energy 1996–2006, New Europe 1999–2005, Europe Steel 2000–, Yukos Int. 2002–05; Dir (non-exec.) Coats Viyella 1994–2001, Intelligent Energy 2003–05; Dir Abbott Laboratories 1996–; Chancellor Univ. of Liverpool 1996–; Dir Center for Int. Health and Co-operation; Freeman, City of Plymouth 2000. *Publications:* Ed.: A Unified Health Service 1968; contrib.: Social Services for All 1968; author: The Politics of Defence 1972, In Sickness and in Health –The Politics of Medicine 1976, Human Rights 1978, Face the Future 1981, A Future that Will Work 1984, A United Kingdom 1986, Personally Speaking to Kenneth Harris 1987, Our NHS 1988, Time to Declare (autobiography) 1991, Seven Ages (poetry) 1992, Balkan Odyssey 1995, The Hubris Syndrome: Bush, Blair and the Intoxication of Power 2007, In Sickness and in Power 2008; articles in The Lancet, Neurology and Clinical Science. *Leisure interest:* sailing. *Address:* House of Lords, Westminster, London, SW1A 0PW (office); 78 Narrow Street, Limehouse, London, E14 8BP, England (home). *Telephone:* (1442) 872617 (office); (20) 7987-5441 (home). *Fax:* (1442) 876108 (home). *E-mail:* lordowen@gotadsl.co.uk (home).

OWEN, Sir Geoffrey David, Kt, MA; British newspaper editor and academic; b. 16 April 1934; s. of L. G. Owen; m. 1st Dorothy J. Owen 1961 (died 1991); two s. one d.; m. 2nd Miriam Marianna Gross 1993; ed Rugby School and Balliol Coll., Oxford; joined Financial Times as feature writer and Industrial Corresp. 1958, US Corresp. 1961, industrial 1967; Exec. Industrial Reorganization Corpn 1967–69; Dir of Admin, Overseas Div. of British Leyland Int. 1969, Dir of Personnel and Admin 1972; Deputy Ed. Financial Times 1974–80, Ed. 1981–90; Dir Business Policy Programme, Centre for Econ. Performance, LSE 1991–98, Sr Fellow Inter-disciplinary Inst. of Man. 1998–; mem. Council Foundation for Mfg and Industries 1993–; Chair. Wincott Foundation 1998–; Dir Laird Group 2000–. *Publications:* Industry in the USA 1966, From Empire to Europe 1999. *Address:* London School of Economics and Political Science, Houghton Street, London, WC2A 2AE, England. *Telephone:* (20) 7405-7686. *Fax:* (20) 7242-0392. *Website:* www.lse.ac.uk (office).

OWEN, Michael James; British professional football player; b. 14 Dec. 1979, Chester; s. of Terence Owen and Jeanette Owen; m. Louise Bonsall; one d.; ed Idsall High School; player with Liverpool Football Club since High School, scored during debut against Wimbledon May 1997 (youngest ever Liverpool player to score); player for England nat. team 1998–, scored hat-trick in 5–1 victory over Germany in World Cup qualifier 2001; 21 goals for Liverpool in European competition (club record) and 28 goals in 66 int. matches for England; signed for Real Madrid, Spain 2004, for Newcastle United 2005; Professional Footballers' Asscn Young Player of the Year 1997, BBC Sports Personality of the Year 1998, European Footballer of the Year 2001. *Film appearance:* Goal II: Living the Dream 2006. *Publication:* Michael Owen: Off the Record 2004. *Leisure interests:* golf, table-tennis, snooker. *Address:* Newcastle United Football Club Ltd., St. James Park, Newcastle upon Tyne, NE1 4ST, England (office). *Telephone:* (191) 201-8400. *Fax:* (191) 201-8600. *Website:* www.nufc.premiumtv.co.uk.

OWEN, Ray David, PhD, ScD; American biologist and academic; *Professor Emeritus, Division of Biology, California Institute of Technology;* b. 30 Oct. 1915, Genesee, Wis.; s. of Dave Owen and Ida Hoeft Owen; m. June Johanna Weissenberg 1939; one s.; ed Carroll Coll., Wis., Univ. of Wisconsin; Research Fellow, Wisconsin 1941–43, Asst Prof. of Genetics and Zoology 1943–47; Gosney Fellow, Calif. Inst. of Tech. 1946–47, Assoc. Prof. 1947–53, Prof. 1953–83, Chair. Div. of Biology 1961–68, Vice-Pres. for Student Affairs and Dean of Students 1975–80, Prof. Emer. 1983–; Research Participant, Oak Ridge Nat. Lab. 1957–58; mem. Genetics Soc. of America (Treas. 1957–60, Vice-Pres. 1961, Pres. 1962), NAS, American Acad. of Arts and Sciences, American Philosophical Soc., Soc. for the Study of Evolution, American Asscn of Immunologists (Excellence in Mentoring Award 1999); served on numerous scientific cttees; Mendel Award, Czechoslovak Acad. of Sciences 1965, Morgan Award, Genetics Soc. of America 1995, Medawar Award, Transplantation Soc. 2000. *Publications:* General Genetics (with Srb and Edgar) 1952, 1965; numerous research papers. *Address:* Division of Biology, 156-29, California Institute of Technology, Pasadena, CA 91125, USA (office). *Telephone:* (626) 395-4960 (office). *Fax:* (626) 449-0756. *Website:* www.biology.caltech.edu (office).

OWEN, Robert John Richard, MA; British financial industry official; *Chairman, International Securities Consultancy Ltd;* b. 11 Feb. 1940, London; s. of Thomas R. Owen and Margaret Fletcher; m. Beatrice M. Voelker 1962 (divorced); two s. one d.; ed Repton School and Oriel Coll., Oxford; Foreign Office 1961–68, served in British Embassy, Washington, DC 1964–68; HM Treasury 1968–70; Morgan Grenfell & Co. Ltd 1970–79, Dir 1973; Dir Merchant Banking Div. Lloyds Bank Int., Ltd 1979–82, Dir Far East Div. 1982–84; Dir of Investment Banking, Lloyds Bank PLC and Chair. Lloyds Merchant Bank, Ltd 1984–88; Adviser to Hong Kong Govt on implementation of Securities Review Cttee Report 1988–89; Chair. Securities and Futures Comm. of Hong Kong 1989–92; Dir European Capital Co. Ltd 1992–, Regulatory Bd and Council of Lloyd's of London 1993–95; Deputy Chair. Nomura Int. Ltd, Hong Kong 1993– (now Sr Adviser), Capital Ltd, Crosby Ltd; mem. Bd of Dirs Singapore Stock Exchange, IB Daiwa Corpn, Yaohan Int. Holdings 1993–, Int. Securities Consultancy Ltd 1995– (now Chair.), Regent Pacific Group Ltd 1998–, ECK and Partners Ltd 1999–, TechPacific Ltd 1999–; Gov. Repton School; mem. Regulatory Council, Dubai Int. Financial Centre 2002–. *Leisure interests:* mountain walking, collecting oriental paintings and carvings. *Address:* International Securities Consultancy Ltd, 9A, Carfield

Commercial Building, 75-77 Wyndham Street, Central, Hong Kong Special Administrative Region (office). *Telephone:* 28773417 (office). *Fax:* 28770914 (office). *Website:* www.isc-global.com (office); www.crosby.com.

OWEN-JONES, Sir Lindsay, KBE, BA; British business executive; *Chairman L'Oréal;* b. 17 March 1946, Wallasey; s. of Hugh A. Owen-Jones and Esmee Owen-Jones (née Lindsay); m. 1st; one d.; m. 2nd Cristina Furno 1994; ed Univ. of Oxford and European Inst. of Business Admin (INSEAD); Product Man. L'Oréal 1969, Head, Public Products Div., Belgium 1971–74, Man. SCAD (L'Oréal subsidiary), Paris 1974–76, Marketing Man. Public Products Div., Paris 1976–78, Gen. Man. SAIPO (L'Oréal subsidiary, Italy) 1978–81, Chair. 1991–, Pres. COSMAIR Inc. (exclusive L'Oréal agent) USA 1981–83, Vice-Pres. L'Oréal Man. Cttee 1984, mem. Bd of Dirs 1984, Pres. and COO 1984–88, Chair. and CEO 1988–2006, Chair. 2006–; mem. Bd of Dirs Banque Nat. de Paris 1989–, Lafarge 1993–2001, Air Liquide 1994–; Officier, Légion d'honneur; Hon. DSc (Cranfield School of Man.); named by Futuro magazine as Best European Manager 2002, Challenges magazine Best Manager of the Last 20 Years 2002, Le Nouvel Economiste magazine Manager of the Year 2002. *Leisure interest:* sailing. *Address:* L'Oréal, 41 rue Martre, 92117 Clichy Cedex, France (office). *Telephone:* 1-47-56-70-00 (office). *Fax:* 1-47-56-80-02 (office). *E-mail:* info@loreal.com (office). *Website:* www.loreal.com (office).

OWENS, Bill, BA, MPA; American business executive and fmr state official; *Vice Chairman, RBS Greenwich Capital Markets, Inc;* b. 22 Oct. 1950, Fort Worth, Tex.; m. Frances Owens; two s. one d.; ed Austin State Univ., LBJ School of Public Affairs Univ. of Texas; fmrly with Touche Ross & Co., Gates Corpn; State Treas., Colorado 1994–99; Gov. of Colorado 1999–2007; Vice Chair. RBS Greenwich Capital Markets, Inc., Greenwich, Conn. 2007–; fmrly guest host Mike Rosen, Ken Hamblin and Chuck Baker talk shows; Republican. *Publications:* contrib. to professional journals. *Address:* RBS Greenwich Capital Markets, Inc, 600 Steamboat Road, Greenwich, CT 06830, USA (office). *Telephone:* (203) 625-2700 (office). *Website:* www.rbsgc.com (office).

OWENS, James W., PhD; American business executive; *Chairman and CEO, Caterpillar Inc.;* b. Elizabeth City, NC; ed N Carolina State Univ.; Corp. Economist, Caterpillar Inc. 1972–75, Chief Economist, Caterpillar Overseas SA, Geneva 1975–80, Man. Accounting and Product Source Planning Dept, Peoria, Ill. 1980–87, Man. Dir, P. T. Natra Raya, Indonesia 1987–90, Corp. Vice Pres. 1990, also Pres., Solar Turbines Inc., San Diego 1990, Vice Pres. and Chief Financial Officer, Caterpillar Corp. Services Div., Peoria 1993–95, Group Pres. Caterpillar Inc. 1995–2004, Chair. and CEO 2004–; Dir Inst. for Int. Econs, Washington, DC, FM Global Insurance Co., IBM, Johnston, RI, Black & Veatch Holding Co., Overland Park, Kan.; Trustee, Manufacturers Alliance/MAPI, Arlington, Va; mem. Council on Foreign Relations, New York, The Business Roundtable, Washington, DC, Global Advisory Council to The Conf. Bd, New York, Community Advisory Bd, St Francis Medical Center, Peoria. *Address:* Caterpillar Inc., 100 NE Adams Street, Peoria, IL 61629, USA (office). *Telephone:* (309) 675-1000 (office). *Fax:* (309) 675-1182 (office). *E-mail:* info@cat.com (office). *Website:* www.cat.com (office).

OWONO EDU, Marcelino; Equatorial Guinean politician; *Minister of Minister of Mines, Industry and Energy;* Minister of Finance and of the Budget 2003–08, of Mines, Industry and Energy 2008; Alternate Gov. for Equatorial Guinea of the ADB Group. *Address:* Ministry of Mines, Industry and Energy, Calle 12 de Octubre s/n, Malabo, Equatorial Guinea (office). *Telephone:* (09) 35-67 (office). *Fax:* (09) 33-53 (office). *E-mail:* d.shaw@ecqc .com (office). *Website:* www.equatorialoil.com (office).

OWUSU-AGYEMANG, Hackman, MSc; Ghanaian politician and economist; b. 22 Nov. 1941, Effiduase-Koforidua; ed St Augustine's Coll., Cape Coast, Kwame Nkrumah Univ. of Science and Tech., Kumasi, Inst. of Social Studies, The Hague, Netherlands, Wye Coll., Univ. of London, UK; economist, Ministry of Agric. 1965–68, Sr Agricultural Economist 1968–70; economist, Econ. Analysis Div., FAO, Rome, Field Programme Officer, FAO-Regional Co-operation and Liaison Officer for Africa 1970–84; FAO Rep. in Zambia, Trinidad and Tobago 1979–84; Chief FAO Regional Bureau for Africa, Italy 1984; mem. New Patriotic Party (NPP) 1982–; mem. Parl. for New Juaben 1996–; Shadow Minister of Foreign Affairs 2000–01, Minister 2001–03; Minister of the Interior 2003–05, for Water Resources, Works and Housing 2005–07. *Address:* c/o New Patriotic Party (NPP), C912/2 Duade Street, Kokomlemle, POB 3456, Accra-North, Ghana. *Telephone:* (21) 227951. *Fax:* (21) 224418. *E-mail:* npp@africanonline.com.gh. *Website:* www.nppghana.org.

OXBURGH, Baron (Life Peer), cr. 1999, of Liverpool in the County of Merseyside; **Ernest Ronald Oxburgh,** Kt, KBE, PhD, FRS; British geologist; *Chairman, Shell Transport and Trading Company;* b. 2 Nov. 1934, Liverpool; s. of Ernest Oxburgh and Violet Bugden; m. Ursula Mary Brown 1934; one s. two d.; ed Liverpool Inst., Univ. of Oxford and Univ. of Princeton, USA; Departmental Demonstrator, Univ. of Oxford 1960–61, Lecturer in Geology 1962–78, Fellow, St Edmund Hall 1964–78, Emer. Fellow 1978, Hon. Fellow 1986; Prof. of Mineralogy and Petrology, Univ. of Cambridge 1978–91, Head of Dept of Earth Sciences 1980–88; Chief Scientific Adviser, Ministry of Defence 1988–93; Rector Imperial Coll. of Science, Tech. and Medicine 1993–2001; Fellow, Trinity Hall Cambridge 1978–82, Hon. Fellow 1983; Pres. Queens' Coll. Cambridge 1982–89, Hon. Fellow 1989; Dir Shell Transport and Trading Co. 1996– (Chair. 2004–); Nirex 1996–97; Sherman Fairchild Distinguished Scholar, Calif. Inst. of Tech. 1985–86; Pres. European Union of Geosciences 1985–87; mem. Nat. Cttee of Inquiry into Higher Educ. (Dearing Cttee) 1996–97; Trustee Natural History Museum 1993–2002, Chair. of Trustees

1999–2002; Chair. House of Lords Select Cttee on Science and Tech. 2001–04; Chair. SETNET 2001–; Foreign mem. Venezuelan Acad. of Sciences 1992, Deutsche Acad. der Naturforscher Leopoldina 1994; Hon. mem. Geologists' Asscn; Hon. Fellow Univ. Coll., Oxford 1983; Hon. FREng 2002; Hon. DSc (Paris) 1986, (Leicester) 1990, (Loughborough) 1991, (Edin.) 1994, (Birmingham, Liverpool) 1996, (Southampton) 2003; Bigsby Medal, Geological Soc. of London 1979. *Publications:* The Geology of the Eastern Alps (ed. and contrib.) 1968, Structural, Metamorphic and Geochronological Studies in the Eastern Alps 1971 and contribs to Nature, Journal of Geophysical Research, Tectonophysics, Journal of the Geological Soc. of London and other learned journals. *Leisure interests:* reading, various sports. *Address:* House of Lords, Westminster, London, SW1A 0PW (office); Shell Centre, London, SE1 7NA, England (office). *Telephone:* (20) 7219-4341 (House of Lords) (office). *E-mail:* oxburghe@parliament.uk (office).

ØYE, Harald Arnljot, DTech; Norwegian chemist and academic; *Professor Emeritus, Norwegian University of Science and Technology;* b. 1 Feb. 1935, Oslo; s. of Leiv C. Øye and Ingrid H. Øye; m. Tove Stiegler 1963; two s. one d.; ed Norwegian Inst. of Tech.; Postdoctoral Fellow, Argonne Nat. Lab., Ill., USA 1963–64; Assoc. Prof., Inst. of Inorganic Chem., Norwegian Inst. of Tech. 1965–72, Prof. and Head of Inst., Norwegian Univ. of Science and Tech. (fmrly Norwegian Inst. of Tech.) 1973–90, 1992–98, Prof., Chem. Dept, later Dept of Materials Tech. 1999–2006, Prof. Emer. 2006–; Pres. Norwegian Acad. of Tech. Sciences 1985–92, Hon. Fellow 1993–; guest scientist at various insts in Germany, Italy, USA, France, NZ, Switzerland, UK; Brotherton Distinguished Prof., Univ. of Leeds 1985; Hon. Prof. North-Eastern Univ., Shenyang, People's Repub. of China; Kt First Class, Royal Norwegian Order of St Olav; Prize for Outstanding Research, Research Council of Norway 1997, Guldberg-Waage Medal, Norwegian Chemical Soc. 1998, Max Bredig Award, Electrochemical Soc., USA 1998, Royal Norwegian Soc. of Sciences and Letters Gunnerus Gold Medal 2004. *Publications:* Cathodes in Aluminium Electrolysis (with M. Sørlie) 1991; more than 350 publs on electrowinning of aluminium and magnesium, characterization of silicon, carbon technology, transport properties, molten salt chem., spectroscopy and thermodynamics of high temperature systems. *Leisure interests:* reading, outdoor activities. *Address:* Department of Materials Technology, Norwegian University of Science and Technology, 7491 Trondheim (office); Steinhaugen 5, 7049 Trondheim, Norway (home). *Telephone:* 73-59-40-16 (office); 73-93-75-58 (home). *Fax:* 73-59-39-92 (office). *E-mail:* oye@material.ntnu.no (office). *Website:* (office).

OYÉ-MBA, Casimir, LLD; Gabonese banker and politician; *Senior Minister of Mining, Oil, Energy and Water;* b. 20 April 1942, Nzamaligue Village, Libreville; s. of Ange Mba and Marie-Jeanne Nse; m. Marie-Françoise Razafimbelo 1963; three s. three d.; ed Univs of Rennes and Paris, France; trainee, Banque Centrale, Libreville 1967–69, Asst Dir 1969–70, Dir 1970–73; Nat. Dir Banque pour le Gabon 1973–76; Asst Dir-Gen. Banque Centrale 1977–78; Gov. Banque des Etats de l'Afrique Centrale 1978–90; Prime Minister of Gabon 1990–94; Minister of Foreign Affairs and Co-operation 1994–99; fmr Minister of State for Planning and Devt; Sr Minister of Mining, Oil, Energy and Water 2007–; Alt. Gov. IMF for Gabon 1969–76; apptd Pres. Asscn des Banques Centrales Africaines 1987; elected mem. Parl. for Komo-Mondah dist 1990, re-elected 1996, 2001, 2006; mem. political bureau, Gabonese Democratic Party 1991; Campaign Man. for Pres. Omar Bongo 1993; Gabon mem. Bd of Govs of World Bank 1999–; mem. Ntoum City Council; Chevalier, Légion d'honneur; Gabon, Cameroon, Congo, Equatorial Guinea and Cen. African Repub. decorations. *Leisure interests:* football, tennis, cinema, reading. *Address:* BP 874, Libreville (office); Ministry of Mining, Libreville (office); BP 13016, Libreville, Gabon (home). *Telephone:* 72-47-83. *Fax:* 72-49-90 (office).

OYELOWO, David Oyetokunbo; British actor, writer and director; *Co-Director, Inservice Productions;* b. 1 April 1976, Oxford; m. Jessica Oyelowo; two s.; ed Model Coll., Lagos, Nigeria, Highbury Grove Boys, Islington Sixth Form Centre, London Acad. of Music and Dramatic Art; left drama school early to do work on BBC TV series Maisie Raine 1998; joined the RSC 1999, played Henry VI 2000, first black actor to play an English King at the RSC, mem. Bd Dirs RSC 2005–; Amb. for the Prince's Trust 2003–; Co-Dir Inservice Productions; London Acad. of Music and Dramatic Art (LAMDA) Scholarship of Excellence, Ian Charleson Award for Best Newcomer 2001, Gold Award for Achievement beyond Further Educ., GAB (Gathering of Africa's Best) Award for Excellence. *Plays:* The Suppliants (Gate Theatre, London) 1998; Oroonoko, Volpone, Antony and Cleopatra (RSC) 1999; Henry VI Parts 1, 2, 3 (RSC) 2001, Richard III, The Godbrothers (Bush Theatre London), Prometheus Bound (Sound Theatre, London, Classic Stage Co., New York); Dir: The Man of Mode (Pavilion Theatre), The White Devil (Pavilion Theatre). *Films:* Dog Eat Dog 2000, A Sound of Thunder 2004, Spice of Life 2005, Derailed 2005, The Best Man 2006, The Last King of Scotland 2006, As You Like It 2006. *Television:* Maisie Raine 1998, Brothers and Sisters 1998, Spooks 2002, 2003, 2004, Tomorrow La Scala (film) 2002, Shoot the Messenger, As Time Goes By; writer: Graham & Alice (BBC). *Radio:* The Faerie Queen (BBC), Man Talk, Woman Talk (BBC), Oroonoko (BBC), The Word (BBC). *Publications:* Actors on Shakespeare: Henry VI 2003. *Leisure interests:* drawing, film, tennis, football, travel, writing. *Address:* Hamilton Hodell Management, 66–68 Margaret Street, London, W1W 8SR, England (office). *Telephone:* (20) 7636-1221 (office). *Fax:* (20) 7636-1226 (office).

ÖYMEN, Onur Basaran, PhD; Turkish diplomatist and politician; *Deputy Leader, Cumhuriyet Halk Partisi (CHP) (Republican People's Party);* b. 1940, Istanbul; s. of Münir Raşit Öymen and Nebahat Öymen; m. Nedret Gürsel 1971; one s. one d.; ed Galatasay Lisesi, Istanbul, Univ. of Ankara; joined Ministry of Foreign Affairs 1964; mil. service 1964–66; Second Sec. NATO Dept, Ministry of Foreign Affairs 1966–68, First Sec. Perm. Del. to Council of Europe, Strasbourg 1968–72, Chief of Section, Policy Planning Dept, Ministry of Foreign Affairs 1972–74, Counsellor Turkish Embassy, Nicosia 1974–78; Special Adviser to Minister of Foreign Affairs 1978–80; Counsellor, Turkish Embassy, Prague 1980–82, Madrid 1982–84; Head Policy Planning Dept, Ministry of Foreign Affairs 1984–88; Amb. to Denmark 1988–90, to Germany 1990–95; Under-Sec. Ministry of Foreign Affairs 1995–97; Perm. Rep. to NATO 1997–2002; currently Deputy Leader, Cumhuriyet Halk Partisi (CHP) (Republican People's Party); Bureaucrat of the Year, Nokta Review 1995, Diplomat of the Year, Asscn of Turkish Industrialists and Business 1995, 1996, 1997; Abdi Ipekçi Special Peace Award, Milliyet newspaper 1997. *Publications:* Türkiye 'nin Gücü (Turkish Strength) 1998, trans. into Turkish of Science and Common Sense by Oppenheimer. *Address:* Cumhuriyet Halk Partisi (CHP) (Republican People's Party), Çevre Sok. 38, Ankara, Turkey (office). *Telephone:* (312) 4685969 (office). *Fax:* (312) 4685969 (office). *E-mail:* chpbim@chp.org.tr (office). *Website:* www.chp.org.tr (office).

OYUUN, Sanjaasurengin, DPhil; Mongolian politician; *Minister of Foreign Affairs;* b. 1964, Ulan Bator; ed Univ. of Cambridge, UK; worked as exploration geologist on surveys in Mongolia and for Rio Tinto-Zinc; Founder and Chair. Civil Courage Party ('Irgenii Zorig Nam') 2000–; Minister of Foreign Affairs 2007–. *Address:* Ministry of Foreign Affairs, Enkh Taivny Örgön Chölöö 7A, Sükhbaatar District, Ulan Bator (office); Civil Courage Party ('Irgenii Zorig Nam'), PO Box 49, Ulan Bator (office); Ulan Bator 13, PO Box 37, Mongolia; Ulan Bator 13, Sukhbaatar District, 2-28-6 (home). *Telephone:* (11) 311311 (office); (11) 323645 (office); (91) 913964 (home). *Fax:* (11) 322127 (office); (11) 322866 (office). *E-mail:* mongmer@magicnet.mn (office); oyuna@mail.parl.gov.mn (office). *Website:* www.pmis.gov.mn (office); www.zorigfoundation.org.mn (office).

OZ, Amos, BA; Israeli writer; b. 4 May 1939, Jerusalem; m. Nily Zuckermann 1960; one s. two d.; ed Hebrew Univ. Jerusalem; Kibbutz Hulda 1957–86; teacher of literature and philosophy, Hulda High School and Givat Brenner Regional High School 1963–86; Visiting Fellow, St Cross Coll. Oxford 1969–70; Writer-in-residence Hebrew Univ. Jerusalem 1975; Visiting Prof. Univ. of Calif. at LA (Berkeley); Writer-in-Residence and Prof. of Literature Colorado Coll., Colorado Springs 1984–85; Prof. of Hebrew Literature, Ben Gurion Univ. 1987–, Agnon Chair in Modern Hebrew 1990–; Visiting Prof. of Literature, Writer in Residence, Boston Univ. 1987; Writer-in-Residence, Hebrew Univ. 1990– and Prof of Literature, Princeton Univ. 1997, Weidenfeld Visiting Prof. of European Comparative Literature St Anne's Coll., Oxford 1998; Officier, Ordre des Arts et des Lettres; Kt's Cross, Légion d'honneur 1997; Dr hc (Hebrew Union Coll., Cincinnati, OH and Jerusalem) 1988, (Western New England Coll.) 1988, (Tel-Aviv) 1992; Holon Prize 1965, Brenner Prize 1976, Zeev Award for Children's Books 1978, Bernstein Prize 1983, Bialik Prize 1986, Wingate Prize, London 1988, Prix Femina, Paris 1989 (for novel Black Box), German Publrs' Int. Peace Prize 1992, Luchs Prize for Children's Books (Germany) 1993, Hamore Prize 1993, Israeli Prize for Literature 1998, Freedom of Speech Prize, Writers' Union of Norway 2002, Int. Medal of Tolerance, Polish Ecumenical Council 2002, Goethe Cultural Prize, Frankfurt, Germany 2005, Premio Príncipe de Asturias (for literature) 2007, Dan David Prize 2008. *Publications:* novels: Elsewhere, Perhaps 1966, My Michael 1968, Touch the Water, Touch the Wind 1973, A Perfect Peace 1982, Black Box 1987, To Know a Woman 1989, The Third Condition (Fima) 1991, The Same Sea 1991, Don't Call It Night 1994, Panther in the Basement 1995, The Same Sea 1999, The Silence of Heaven 2000, Suddenly in the Depths of the Forest 2005, Rhyming Life and Death 2007; novellas and short stories: Where the Jackals Howl 1965, Unto Death 1971, Different People (selected anthology) 1974, The Hill of Evil Counsel 1976, Soumchi (children's story) 1978, Telling Tales (contrib. to charity anthology) 2004; essays: Under this Blazing Light 1979, In the Land of Israel 1983, The Slopes of Lebanon 1987, Report of the Situation (in German) 1992, Israel, Palestine and Peace 1994, A Story Begins 1996, All Our Hopes 1998, But These Are Two Different Wars 2002, How to Cure a Fanatic 2006; other: A Tale of Love and Darkness (memoir) (The Jewish Quarterly Wingate Literary Prize for non-fiction 2005) 2002. *Address:* Ben Gurion University of the Negev, PO Box 653, Beersheva 84105, Israel. *Telephone:* (8) 6461111. *Fax:* (8) 6237682. *E-mail:* acsec@bgumail.bgu.ac.il (office). *Website:* www.bgu.ac.il (office).

OZAL, Kurkut; Turkish engineer, administrator and politician; b. 29 May 1929, Malatya; m.; five c.; ed Istanbul Tech. Univ.; chief engineer, Water Works Dept, Malatya Region 1951–55; Regional Dir Water Works Dept, Euphrates and Tigris River Basins 1957–60; Instructor, then Asst Prof., then Assoc. Prof., Middle East Tech. Univ., Ankara 1960–67, Prof. 1967–71; Chair., CEO Turkish State Petroleum Corpn; Prof., Bosphorus Univ., Consultant Shell Group 1972–73; mem. Nat. Ass.; Minister of Agric., of the Interior 1973–80; CEO of cos dealing in Islamic banking, construction and int. oil trade 1981–85; fmr Dir Islamic Research and Training Inst., Islamic Devt Bank; Founding Fellow Islamic Acad. of Sciences 1986. *Address:* c/o Islamic Academy of Sciences, PO Box 830036, Amman, Jordan (office). *Telephone:* 5523385 (office). *Fax:* 5511803 (office). *E-mail:* secretariat@ias-worldwide.org (office). *Website:* www.ias-worldwide.org (office).

OZAWA, Ichiro, BA; Japanese politician; *President, Democratic Party of Japan;* b. 24 May 1942, Mizusawa, Iwate Pref.; s. of Saeki Ozawa and Michi Ozawa; m. Kazuko Fukuda 1973; three s.; ed Keio Univ.; mem. House of Reps representing Iwate Prefecture 1967–; Minister of Home Affairs 1985–87; fmr Deputy Chief Cabinet Sec.; fmr Dir-Gen. Liberal-Democratic Party (LDP) Election Bureau; Sec.-Gen. LDP 1989–91; Chair. Cttee on Rules and Admin.; left LDP 1993; Co-Founder and Sec.-Gen. Shinseito (Japan Renewal Party) 1993–94; Sec.-Gen. Shinshinto (New Frontier Party) 1994–95, Pres. 1995–97; Founder and Pres. Jiyuto (Liberal Party) 1998–2003 (resgnd), Acting Pres.

Democratic Party of Japan (DPJ) (after merger with Liberal Party) 2003–04, Vice-Pres. 2004–05, Pres. 2006–. *Publication:* Blueprint for a New Japan 1993. *Leisure interests:* fishing, Go. *Address:* Democratic Party of Japan (DPJ), 1-11-1, Nagata-cho, Chiyoda-ku, Tokyo, 100-0014 (office); 2-38 Fukuro-machi, Mizusawa-shi, Iwate-ken 023-0814, Japan (home). *Telephone:* (3) 3595-9960 (office). *Fax:* (3) 3595-7318 (office). *E-mail:* dpjenews@dpj.or.jp (office). *Website:* www.dpj.or.jp (office).

OZAWA, Seiji; Japanese conductor; *Artistic Director, Tokyo Opera Nomori;* b. 1 Sept. 1935, Shenyang, China; m. 1st Kyoko Edo; m. 2nd Vera Ilyan; one s. one d.; ed Toho School of Music, Tokyo with Prof. Hideo Saito, Tanglewood, USA and in West Berlin under Herbert von Karajan; Asst Conductor (under Leonard Bernstein), New York Philharmonic 1961–62 (including tour of Japan 1961); Guest Conductor, San Francisco Symphony, Detroit Symphony, Montréal, Minneapolis, Toronto and London Symphony Orchestras 1961–65; Music Dir Ravinia Festival, Chicago 1964–68; Music Dir Toronto Symphony Orchestra 1965–69, San Francisco Symphony Orchestra 1970–76, Boston Symphony Orchestra 1973–2002, Vienna State Opera 2002–(10); co-founder and Artistic Dir Tokyo Opera Nomori 2005–; toured Europe conducting many of the major orchestras 1966–67; Salzburg Festival 1969; toured USA, France, FRG, China 1979, Austria, UK 1981, Japan 1981, 1986, toured England, Netherlands, France, Germany, Austria and Belgium 1988; opened music acad., Geneva 2005–; makes frequent guest appearances with leading orchestras of America, Europe and Japan; has conducted opera at Salzburg, Covent Garden, La Scala, Vienna Staatsoper and Paris Opera; conducted world premiere, Messiaen's St Francis of Assisi, Paris 1983; Hon. mem., Vienna Staatsoper 2007; Hon. DMus (Univ. of Mass., New England Conservatory, Wheaton Coll., Norton, Mass.); First Prize, Int. Competition of Orchestra Conductors, France 1959, Koussevitsky Prize for outstanding student conductor 1960, Laureate, Fondation du Japon 1988. *Leisure interests:* golf, tennis, skiing. *Address:* c/o Ronald A. Wilford, Columbia Artists Management Inc., Conductors Division, 165 W 57th Street, New York, NY, USA (office); c/o Harold Holt Ltd, 31 Sinclair Road, London, W14 0NS, England (office); Tokyo Opera Nomori Committee Office, Jimbo-cho Mitsui Building 17F, Kanda Jimbo-cho 1-105, Chiyoda-ku, Tokyo 101-0051, Japan. *Website:* www.tokyo-opera-nomori.com.

ÖZAYDINLI, F. Bülend; Turkish business executive; *CEO, Koç Holding AS;* b. 1949, Eskişehir; ed Izmir Maarif Coll., American Univ. of Beirut, Lebanon; Asst Man. Oyak 1972–76; Regional Man. Motorlu Araçlar Tic. AS 1976–79; Asst Gen. Man. Oyak 1979–87; Investments Co-ordinator, Migros Türk TAS 1987–88; Asst Gen. Man. Maret AS 1988–90; Gen. Man. Migros Türk TAS 1990–2001; Deputy CEO Koç Holding AS 2001, CEO 2002–, mem. Bd of Dirs 2002–; Pres. Fiat Group 2001. *Address:* Koç Holding AS, Nakkastepe, Azizbey Sok. No. 1, Kuzguncuk, 34674 Istanbul, Turkey (office). *Telephone:* (216) 5310277 (office). *Fax:* (216) 5311947 (office). *Website:* www.koc.com.tr (office).

OZBEK, (Ibrahim Mehmet) Rifat, BA; Turkish/British couturier; b. 8 Nov. 1953, Istanbul; s. of Melike Osbek and Abdulazim Mehmet Ismet; ed St Martin's School of Art, London; worked with Walter Albini for Trell; designer Monsoon Co.; launched O for Ozbek (now Future Ozbek) 1987; presented first collection 1984; began presenting collections for Pollini 2004–; British Fashion Council Designer of the Year 1988, 1992. *Address:* c/o Pollini SpA, via Erbosa, 2–B, 47030 Gatteo, Italy; 18 Haunch of Venison Yard, London, W1Y 1AF, England. *Telephone:* (20) 7408-0625. *Fax:* (20) 7629-1586.

OZDAS, Mehmet Nimet, DipEng, PhD; Turkish professor of engineering and administrator; b. 6 March 1921, Istanbul; m.; two c.; ed Istanbul Tech. Univ., Univ. of London, UK; Visiting Prof., Case Western Reserve Univ., Ohio, USA 1953–59; Research Fellow, MIT 1955–56; Prof., Istanbul Tech. Univ. 1961; Founding Dir Computer Centre 1961; Founding Sec.-Gen. Turkish Scientific Council (TUBITAK) 1964–66, mem. Science Bd 1968–72; Founding Dir Marmara Scientific and Industrial Research; Pres. NATO Science Cttee 1973–79; mem. Bd Von Karman Inst. and Steering Cttee AGARD 1973; Minister of State for Science and Tech. 1980–83; Prof. Dept of Mechanical and Control Eng, Istanbul Tech. Univ. 1983–; Fellow Islamic Acad. of Sciences; Pres. Turkish Org. for Automatic Control. *Address:* Department of Mechanical and Control Engineering, Istanbul Technical University, Ayazaga, Istanbul 80626, Turkey (office). *Telephone:* (212) 2853000 (office). *Fax:* (212) 2852916 (office). *Website:* www.mkn.itu.edu.tr (office).

OZICK, Cynthia, MA; American writer and poet; b. 17 April 1928, New York, NY; d. of William Ozick and Celia Regelson; m. Bernard Hallote 1952; one d.; ed New York Univ. and Ohio State Univ.; mem. PEN, Authors' League, American Acad. of Arts and Sciences, American Acad. of Arts and Letters; Founder mem. Acad. Universelle des Cultures; Guggenheim Fellow 1982; Hon. degrees (Yeshiva) 1984, (Hebrew Union Coll.) 1984, (Williams Coll.) 1986, (Hunter Coll.) 1987, (Jewish Theological Seminary) 1988, (Adelphi) 1988, (State Univ. of NY) 1989, (Brandeis) 1990, (Bard Coll.) 1991, (Spertus Coll.) 1991, (Seton Hall Univ.) 1999, (Rutgers Univ.) 1999, (Asheville) 2000, (New York) 2001, (Bar-Ilan) 2002, (Baltimore Hebrew Univ.) 2004, (Georgetown) 2007; Mildred and Harold Strauss Living Award, American Acad. of Arts and Letters 1983; Rea Award for short story 1986, PEN/Spiegel-Diamonstein Award for the Art of the Essay 1997, Harold Washington Literary Award, City of Chicago 1997, John Cheever Award 1999, Lotos Club Medal of Merit 2000, Lannan Foundation Award 2000, Nat. Critics' Circle Award for Criticism 2001, Koret Foundation Award for Literary Studies 2001, Mary McCarthy Award, Bard Coll. 2007, Nat. Humanities Medal 2007, PEN/Malamud Prize 2008, PEN/Nabokov Prize 2008. *Publications:* Trust 1966, The

Pagan Rabbi and Other Stories 1971, Bloodshed and Three Novellas 1976, Levitation: Five Fictions 1982, Art & Ardor: Essays 1983, The Cannibal Galaxy 1983, The Messiah of Stockholm 1987, Metaphor & Memory: Essays 1989, The Shawl 1989, Epodes: First Poems 1992, What Henry James Knew, and Other Essays on Writers 1993, Blue Light (play) 1994, Portrait of the Artist as a Bad Character and Other Essays on Writing 1995, The Shawl (novel) 1996, Fame & Folly: Essays 1996, The Puttermesser Papers (novel) 1997, The Best American Essays (ed.) 1998, Quarrel & Quandary (essays) 2000, Heir to the Glimmering World (novel published as The Bear Boy in UK) 2004, Collected Stories 2006, A Din in the Head: Essays 2006, Dictation: A Quartet 2008; contrib. fiction to numerous periodicals and anthologies including New Criterion, New Yorker, Harper's, Partisan Review, Yale Review, New York Times Magazine, Best American Short Stories, O. Henry Prize Stories, Best American Essays, The Oxford Book of Jewish Short Stories, The Norton Anthology of Jewish American Literature. *Fax:* (914) 654-6583.

OZIM, Igor; Slovenian violinist; b. 9 May 1931, Ljubljana; s. of Rudolf Ozim and Marija Kodric; m. Dr Breda Volovsek 1963; one s. one d.; ed Akad. za glasbo Ljubljana, Royal Coll. of Music; studied with Prof. Max Rostal; Prof. of Violin, Akad. za glasbo Ljubljana 1960–63, Staatliche Hochschule für Musik, Cologne 1963–96, Berne Conservatoire 1985–96, Hochschule für Musik, Vienna 1996–, Universität Mozarteum Salzburg; mem trio with Walter Grimmer and Ilse Dorati-von Alpenheim which performed and recorded all of Mozart's and Schubert's works –1995; concerts throughout Europe; First Prize, Int. Carl-Flesch Competition, London 1951, Munich 1953; Pres. Cen. Cttee European String Teachers' Asscn. *Leisure interests:* photography, table tennis. *Address:* Department of Strings, Universität Mozarteum, Mirabellplatz 1, 5020 Salzburg, Austria (office). *Telephone:* (662) 61-98-0 (office). *E-mail:* igor.ozim@moz.ac.at (office). *Website:* www.moz.ac.at (office).

ÖZKÖK, Gen. Hilmi; Turkish army officer; b. 1940, Turgutlu, Manisa; m. Özenç Özkök; two c.; ed Işıklar Mil. High School, Turkish Mil. Acad., Field Artillery School, Army War Coll., NATO Defence Coll.; Artillery 3rd Lt 1959; Platoon Leader and Anti-Aircraft Battery Commdr 1972; Chief of Operations and Training Br., 15th Training Brigade; Staff Officer, Plan and Policy Dept of Shape, HQ; Chief of Defence Research Section, Plan and Policy Dept of Shape, HQ; Dir Exec. Office of Sec.-Gen. of Nat. Security Council; Commdr Cadet Regiment, Turkish Mil. Acad.; rank of Brig.-Gen. 1984; Chief of Planning and Operations Dept, Turkish Gen. Staff (TGS) 1984–86; Commdr 70th Infantry Brigade 1986–88; rank of Maj.-Gen. 1988; Commdr 28th Infantry Div. 1988–90; Chief of Personnel, Dept of TGS 1990–92; rank of Lt-Gen. 1992; Chief of Turkish Mil. Del. to NATO, Brussels 1992–95; Commdr 7th Corps 1995–96; rank of Gen. 1996; Command of Allied Land Forces South-Eastern Europe 1996–98; Deputy Chief of TGS 1998–99; 1st Army Commdr 1999–2000; Commdr of Turkish Army 2000–02; Chief of the Gen. Staff 2002–06; fmr mem. NATO Mil. Cttee; Turkish Armed Forces Medal of Honour, Turkish Armed Forces Medal of Distinguished Service, Medal of Distinguished Service and Self-Sacrifice, Chevalier, Ordre nat. du Mérite, Legion of Merit (USA), Medal of Nishan-i-Imtiaz (Pakistan), Great Cross for Military Merit (Spain), Tong-II Medal (Repub. of Korea), Eagle Golden Medal (Albania). *Address:* c/o Ministry of National Defence, Milli Savunma Bakanlığı, 06100 Ankara, Turkey (office).

OZPETEK, Ferzan; Turkish film director and screenwriter; b. 3 Feb. 1959, Istanbul. *Films directed:* Hamam (Hamam: The Turkish Bath, UK) (also screenplay) 1997, Harem Suare' (also screenplay) 1999, Le fate ignoranti (The Ignorant Fairies) (also screenplay) 2001, La finestra di fronte (The Window Opposite) (also screenplay) (David di Donatello Award 2003, also won awards for Best Leading Actor and Actress) 2003, Cuore sacro (also screenplay) 2005; otherfilms include Scusate il ritardo 1982 (first asst dir) 1982, Son contento (first asst dir) 1983, Il tenente dei carabinieri (asst dir) 1986, Noi uomini duri (asst dir) 1987, Il volpone (The Big Fox) (asst dir) 1988, Il maestro del terrore (The Prince of Terror) (TV) (asst dir) 1988, La scorta (The Escort) (asst dir) 1993, Il branco (The Pack) (asst dir) 1994, Anche i commercialisti hanno un'anima (asst dir) 1994.

OZSOYLU, Sinasi, (Nasih), MD; Turkish physician; *Professor of Paediatrics and Haematology, Fatih University, Ankara;* b. 29 July 1927, Erzurum; s. of Ahmet Fazil Ozsoylu and Azime Ozsoylu; m. Selma Ozsoylu; two s. one d.; ed Istanbul Univ.; paediatrician, Washington Univ. Medical School, St Louis, USA 1960; haematologist, Harvard Univ. Medical School, Boston, Mass 1963; Assoc. Prof. of Paediatrics, Hacettepe Univ., Ankara 1964–69, Prof. 1969–94, Head of Haematology 1970–94, of Paediatrics 1976–77; Prof. of Paediatrics and Haematology, Fatih Univ., Ankara 1996–; Visiting Prof., Md Univ. Medical School, Baltimore 1972; mem. Turkish Medical Soc. 1953–, Turkish Paediatrics Soc. 1958–, Turkish Haematology Soc. 1974–, Int. Paediatrics Soc. 1974–; Pres. European Soc. of Haematology and Immunology 1991–93; Fellow Islamic Acad. of Sciences 1989–; Ed. Turkish Journal of Medical Sciences 1989–94, Hon. Ed. 1994–; Ed. Yeni Tip Dergisi 1994–; invited to speak at numerous specialist congresses; Hon. mem. American Pediatric Soc. 1992–; Hon. Fellow American Acad. of Pediatrics 1995–; numerous awards and prizes including Exceptional Scientific Achievement Award, Hacettepe Univ. 1991. *Publications:* several hundred papers on paediatrics, haematology, liver disorders, etc. *Leisure interests:* gardening, music. *Address:* Kenedi Cad. No. 148/14, GOP 06700, Ankara, Turkey (home); Fatih University, Medical School Hospital, Alpaslan Turkes Cad. No. 57, Emek. 06510, Ankara (office). *Telephone:* (312) 2126262 (office), (312) 2121804 (office), (312) 4280975 (home). *Fax:* (312) 2213276 (office). *E-mail:* sinasi.ozsoylu@hotmail.com (office).

OZZIE, Raymond (Ray) E., BS; American software industry executive; *Chief Software Architect, Microsoft Corporation;* b. 20 Nov. 1955, Chicago; m. Dawna Bousquet 1982; one s. one d.; ed Main Township High School South, Park Ridge, Ill., Univ. of Ill.; Programmer, Protection Mutual Insurance Co. 1972–73; Technician, Dept of Nuclear Eng, Univ. of Ill. 1974, System Programmer, PLATO project, 1974–79; Co-founder Urbana Software Enterprises 1998–79; with Data Gen. Corpn 1979–81; Co-founder Microcosm Corpn 1981; with Software Arts 1981–82; with Lotus Devt 1982–84, led team that developed Lotus Symphony; Founder and Pres. Iris Assocs (back by Lotus), developed Lotus Notes 1984–97; Founder, Chair. and CEO Groove Networks Inc. (provider of collaboration software for the virtual office), Beverly, Mass 1997–2005, Chief Tech. Officer, Microsoft Corpn, Redmond, Wash. (after acquisition of Groove Networks by Microsoft) 2005–06, Chief Software Architect 2006–; mem. Nat. Acad. of Eng, Nat. Research Council; mem. and Gov. for IT and Telecommunications, World Econ. Forum; mem. Int. Council, John F. Kennedy School of Govt, Harvard Univ.; Person of the Year, PC Magazine 1995, W. Wallace McDowell Award, IEEE Computer Society 2000; named one of seven Windows Pioneers by Microsoft; inducted into Computer Museum Industry Hall of Fame and InfoWorld Hall of Fame. *Address:* Microsoft Corporation, 1 Microsoft Way, Redmond, WA 98052-6399, USA (office). *Telephone:* (425) 882-8080 (office). *Fax:* (425) 936-7329 (office). *Website:* www.microsoft.com (office).

P

PÄÄBO, Svante, PhD; Swedish biologist and academic; *Director, Max Planck Institute, Leipzig;* b. 1955, Stockholm; ed Uppsala Univ.; School of Interpreters, Swedish Defense Forces 1975–76; Researcher, Dept of Biochemistry, Univ. of Calif., Berkeley, USA 1987–90; Docent in Medical Genetics, Univ. of Uppsala 1990; Prof. of Gen. Biology, Univ. of Munich 1990–98; Founding Dir Max Planck Inst. for Evolutionary Anthropology, Leipzig, Germany 1997–; pioneer in study of ancient DNA; mem. Academia Europaea, Swedish Royal Acad. of Sciences, Deutsche Akademie der Naturforscher Leopoldina, Halle, Saxonian Acad. of Sciences, Leipzig; Foreign mem. Finnish Soc. of Sciences and Letters, NAS; Hon. Prof. of Genetics and Evolutionary Biology, Univ. of Leipzig 1999–; Dr hc (Zurich, Helsinki); Leibniz Prize German Science Foundation 1992, Max Delbrück Medal, Berlin, Germany 1998, Carus Medal and Prize, Halle and Schweinfurt, Germany 1999, Rudbeck Prize, Uppsala, Sweden 2000, Leipzig Science Prize 2003, Ernst Schering Prize, Berlin 2003, Louis-Jeantet Prize for Medicine 2005. *Publications:* numerous book chapters and articles and papers in scientific journals. *Address:* Max Planck Institute, Deutscher Platz 6, 04103 Leipzig, Germany (office). *Telephone:* (341) 3550501 (office). *Fax:* (341) 3550555 (office). *E-mail:* paaboeva@mpg.de (office). *Website:* www.mpg.de (office).

PAAR, Vladimir, DSc; Croatian physicist; *Professor of Physics, Zagreb University;* b. 11 May 1942, Zagreb; s. of Vladimir Paar and Elvira Paar; m. Nada Paar-Pandur 1968; three s. one d.; ed Zagreb Univ.; Research Assoc., Zagreb Univ. 1973–76, Prof. 1981–; Visiting Prof. in Copenhagen, Julich, Paris, Moscow, Munich, Amsterdam, Livermore (Calif.) and Rio de Janeiro; participation in numerous int. confs; mem. Croatian Acad. of Arts and Sciences, Croatian Physical Soc., European Physical Soc. *Television:* Deterministic Chaos, Energy Crisis, Physics in Educ. *Publications:* author and ed. of several books and more than 300 papers on atomic nucleus structure, symmetry, supersymmetry and deterministic chaos, energetics and scientific econ. devt. *Leisure interests:* soccer, tennis, presenting science in the media. *Address:* Theoretical Physics Department, Faculty of Science, University of Zagreb, Bijenicka 32, 10000 Zagreb (office); Croatian Academy of Sciences and Arts, Zrinski trg 11, 10000 Zagreb, Croatia. *Telephone:* (1) 4605555 (office). *Fax:* (1) 4680336 (office). *E-mail:* paar@hazu.hr (office); vpaar@phy.hr (office). *Website:* www.hazu.hr/~paar (office).

PAASIO, Pertti Kullervo, MSc; Finnish politician and organization official; *Chairman, Finland Society;* b. 2 April 1939, Helsinki; s. of Rafael Paasio and Mary Wahlman; m. Kirsti Johansson 1967; two s. two d.; ed Turku Univ.; regional organizer, Nuoret Kotkat (Young Falcons) 1963–66; mem. Turku City Council 1965–91; Sec. for Tourism, City of Turku 1967–73; Political Sec. Ministry of Finance 1972; Head of Turku Labour Exchange 1973–87; Vice-Pres. Int. Falcon Movt 1975–81; Chair. Young Falcons Fed. 1978–81; Political Sec. to Prime Minister 1975; mem. Parl. 1975–79, 1982–96; mem. Exec. Cttee Social Democratic Party of Finland 1978–91; mem. Presidential Electoral Coll. 1978, 1982, 1988; Leader, Social Democratic Parl. Group 1984–87; Chair. Social Democratic Party 1987–91; Deputy Prime Minister, Minister for Foreign Affairs 1989–91; Chair. Parl. Cttee for Foreign Affairs 1991–96; mem. European Parl. 1996–99 Quaestor 1997–; currently Chair. Finland Soc. *Leisure interests:* photography, caravanning. *Address:* Finland Society, Mariankatu 8, 00170 Helsinki (office); Eerikinkatu 30, 20100 Turku, Finland. *Telephone:* (9) 6841210 (office). *Fax:* (9) 68412140 (office). *Website:* www.suomi-seura.fi (office).

PABLO ROSSO, Pedro, MD; Chilean paediatrician, academic and university administrator; *Rector, Pontificia Universidad Católica de Chile;* b. 27 Aug. 1941, Spotorno, Italy; s. of José Pablo Rosso and Laura Pablo Rosso; m. Mary Rose Streeter, two s. one d.; ed Scuola Italiana de Valparaíso, Scuola Italiana de Santiago, Pontificia Universidad Católica de Chile; Paediatrician, Roberto del Río Hosp., Santiago 1966–69; Paediatrician, Weill Cornell Medical Coll., Cornell Univ., NY 1970–72; Asst Prof. and Researcher, Coll. of Physicians and Surgeons, Columbia Univ., New York 1972–75, Assoc. Prof. of Paediatrics 1978, Dir Growth and Devt Div. 1982–84; Prof., Faculty of Medicine, Pontificia Universidad Católica de Chile 1984–, f. Centro de Investigaciones Médicas 1990, Dean, Faculty of Medicine 1991, Rector, Pontificia Universidad Católica 2000–; fmr Visiting Prof., Universidad de Puerto Rico, Universidad de San Marcos, Lima; Pres., Asscn of Chilean Medical Faculties 1996–2000; Vice-Pres. Federación Internacional de Escuelas de Medicina de Universidades Católicas 1994–96; mem. Academia Chilena de Medicina 1999–; Cavalier, Order of Merit of Repub. of Italy 2008; US March of Dimes/Birth Defect Foundation Agnes Higgins Prize. *Publications:* more than 120 publs. *Address:* Office of the Rector, Pontificia Universidad Católica de Chile, 8320000 Santiago, Chile (office). *Telephone:* (2) 354-2000 (office). *Website:* www.puc.cl (office).

PABRIKS, Artis, PhD; Latvian politician and political scientist; b. 22 March 1966, Jūrmala; ed Univ. of Latvia, Univ. of Århus, Denmark; Research Asst, Acad. of Sciences 1988–90; External Lecturer, Univ. of Århus, Denmark 1994; Lecturer, Univ. of Latvia 1995–99; First Rector, Vidzeme Univ. Coll. 1996–97, Asst Prof. 1996–2001, Assoc. Prof. 2001–; Policy Analyst, Latvian Centre for Human Rights and Ethnic Studies 2001–03, Political Educ. Foundation 2003–04; mem. Saeima (Parl.) 2004–, Chair. Foreign Affairs Comm.; Parl. Sec., Ministry of Foreign Affairs 2004, Minister of Foreign Affairs 2004–07; Deputy mem. for Latvia, European Comm. against Racism and Intolerance, Council of Europe 2002–; mem. Editorial Bd, Baltic Review magazine 2002–; Great Commdr, Order of Duke Gediminas. *Leisure interest:* karate (black belt). *Address:* Saeima (Parliament), Jekaba iela 11, Rīga 1811, Latvia (office). *Telephone:* 6708-7111 (office). *Fax:* 6708-7100 (office). *E-mail:* web@saeima.lv (office). *Website:* www.saeima.lv (office).

PACARI VEGA, Nina, BA, JD; Ecuadorean lawyer and politician; b. (María Estela Vega), 9 Oct. 1960, Imbabura-Cotopaxi; ed Universidad Cen. del Ecuador; Legal Advisor, Confed. of Indigenous Nationalities of Ecuador (CONAIE) 1989; elected mem. Nat. Ass. 1998, Vice-Pres. (first native Quécha-Indian in position) 1999–2000, Acting Pres. 2000–03; Minister of Foreign Affairs 2003 (resgnd); mem. Inter-American Dialogue; mem. UN Perm. Forum on Indigenous Issues 2005–07; Best Congresswoman of the Year, TC Television 1998. *Address:* c/o Movimiento de Unidad Pluriacional Pachakútik Nuevo País (Pachakútik), Calle Lugo 13-04 y Avda Ladrón de Guevara, La Floresta, Quito, Ecuador (office).

PACE, Gen. Peter, MBA; American management consultant and military officer (retd); *President and CEO, SM&A Strategic Advisors Inc.;* b. 5 Nov. 1945, Brooklyn, NY; m.; one s. one d.; ed US Naval Acad., George Washington Univ., Harvard Univ., Nat. War Coll.; Rifle Platoon Leader, then Asst Operations Officer, 1st Marine Div. in Vietnam 1968–69; various positions 1969–71, including Head, Infantry Writer Unit, Marine Corps Inst., White House Social Aide; CO, Marine Corps Recruiting Station, Buffalo, NY 1980–83, 2nd Battalion, 1st Marines 1983–85; assigned to Combined/Jt Staff, Seoul 1986, served as Chief, Ground Forces Br., then Exec. Officer to the Asst Chief of Staff; Chief of Staff, 2nd Marine Div., Camp Lejeune 1991–92, Asst Div. Commdr 1992; Pres. Marine Corps Univ., Commanding Gen. Marine Corps Schools, Marine Corps Combat Devt Command, Quantico, Va 1992; Deputy Commdr Marine Forces, Somalia 1992–93, Deputy Commdr Jt Task Force 1993–94; Deputy Commdr/Chief of Staff, US Forces, Japan 1994–96; Dir for Operations, Jt Staff, Washington, DC 1996–97; Commdr US Marine Corps Forces, Atlantic/Europe/South 1997–2000; C-in-C US Southern Command 2000–01; Vice-Chair. Jt Chiefs of Staff 2001–05, Chair. 2005–07; Pres. and CEO SM&A Strategic Advisors Inc. (man. consultancy) 2008–, mem. Bd of Dirs SM&A 2008–; mem. Bd of Dirs Marine Corps Law Enforcement Foundation; promoted to Capt. 1971, Maj. 1977, Lt-Col 1982, Col 1988, Brig.-Gen. 1992, Maj.-Gen. 1994, Lt-Gen. 1996, Gen. 2000; Legion of Merit, Combat Action Ribbon; Defense Distinguished Service Medal, Defense Superior Service Medal, Bronze Star Medal with Combat V, Defense Meritorious Service Medal, Meritorious Service Medal with Gold Star, Navy Commendation Medal with Combat V, Navy Achievement Medal with Gold Star. *Address:* SM&A Strategic Advisors Inc., 4695 Macarthur Court, 8th Floor, Newport Beach, CA 92660, USA (office). *Telephone:* (949) 975-1550 (office). *Fax:* (949) 975-1624 (office). *Website:* www.smawins.com (office).

PAČES, Vaclav, DrSc; Czech biochemist and academic; *Chairman, Academy of Sciences of the Czech Republic;* b. 2 Feb. 1941, Prague; m. Magdalena Tomková Pačes 1966; two s.; ed Charles Univ., Czechoslovak Acad. of Sciences; joined Inst. of Molecular Genetics 1977, Head of Lab. 1986, Docent 1992–95, Full Prof. 1995, Dir 1999–2005; Chair. Czech Acad. of Sciences 2005–; at Yale Univ. 1990–91, has also conducted research at Univs of Chicago, Seville, Bristol and Japan; mem. Czech Soc. of Arts and Sciences (SVU), Fellow 2004–; mem. European Acad. of Sciences and Arts, European Molecular Biology Org. (EMBO); recipient of several prizes including State Prize for Science 1989, Prize for Popularization of Science 1992. *Publications:* Molecular Biology of the Gene 1982, Molecular Genetics 1983, Antibiotics: Mechanism of Action and Resistance (co-author) 1987, Highlights of Modern Biochemistry 1989; more than 100 original papers. *Address:* The Academy of Sciences of the Czech Republic, Narodni 3, 11720 Prague 1, Czech Republic (office). *Telephone:* (224) 229610 (office). *Fax:* (224) 240512 (office). *E-mail:* paces@kav.cas.cz (office). *Website:* www.cas.cz (office).

PACHACHI, Adnan, PhD; Iraqi politician and diplomatist; *Founder and President, Independent Democratic Movement;* b. (Adnan Muzahim al-Pachachi), 14 May 1923, Baghdad; m. Selwa Pachachi 1946; three d.; ed Victoria Coll., Alexandria, Egypt, American Univ., Beirut, Lebanon, Georgetown Univ, Washington, DC, USA; Perm. Rep. to UN 1959–65, 1967–69; Minister of Foreign Affairs 1965–67; left Iraq to settle in UAE 1971, returned 2003; Founder and Pres. Ind. Democratic Movt 2003–; led Iraqi del. to UN Security Council July 2003; mem. Iraq Governing Council 2003–04, Pres. Jan. 2004; mem. Parl. 2005–; decorations from Italy and Morocco. *Publications:* Muzahim Pachachi – Political Career (in Arabic) 1990, Voice of Iraq in the UN 1959–1969 – Personal Record 1991. *Leisure interests:* music, swimming, theatre, visiting art galleries and exhibitions. *Address:* Independent Democratic Movement, Baghdad, Iraq (office). *E-mail:* adnan@pachachi.org (office).

PACHAURI, Rajendra Kumar, MS, DEcon, DEng; Indian economist, research director and international organization official; *Chairman, Intergovernmental Panel on Climate Change;* b. 20 Aug. 1940, Nainital; s. of A. R. Pachauri; m. Saroj Pachauri; three d.; ed N Carolina State Univ., USA; Asst Prof. NC State Univ. 1974–75; mem. Sr Faculty, Admin. Staff Coll. of India 1975–79, Dir Consulting and Applied Research Div. 1979–81; Dir Tata Energy Research Inst. New Delhi 1981–2001, Dir-Gen. 2001–; Visiting Prof. W Va Univ. 1981–82; Visiting Fellow, Energy Dept, IBRD 1990; Pres. Int. Asscn for Energy Econs 1988, Chair. 1988–90; Pres. Asian Energy Inst. 1992–; mem. World Energy Council 1990–93; Adviser on Energy and Sustainable Man. of Natural Resources to the Admin., UNDP 1994–99; Vice-Chair. Intergovernmental Panel on Climate Change (IPCC) 1997, Chair. 2002–; Dir-Gen. Energy and Resources Inst., New Delhi; Chancellor TERI Univ.; mem. Bd of Dirs Inst. for Global Environmental Strategies 1999, Indian Oil Corpn Ltd 1999–2003, Nat. Thermal Power Corpn Ltd 2002–, GAIL (India) Ltd 2003–; McCluskey

Fellow, Yale Univ., USA Sept.–Dec. 2000; Padma Bhushan 2001; Millennium Pioneer Award 2000, Padma Bhushan 2001, Intergovernmental Panel on Climate Change awarded Nobel Peace Prize (shared with Al Gore) 2007. *Publications:* The Dynamics of Electrical Energy Supply and Demand 1975, Energy and Economic Development in India 1977, International Energy Studies 1980, Energy Policy for India: An Interdisciplinary Analysis 1980, The Political Economy of Global Energy 1985, Global Energy Interactions 1986, Contemporary India 1992, Climate Change in Asia and Brazil: The Role of Technology Transfer (co-ed. with Preety Bhandari) 1994, Population, Environment and Development (ed. with Lubina F. Qureshy) 1997; Energy in the Indian Sub-Continent (co-ed. with Gurneeta Vasudeva) 2000; scientific papers and newspaper articles. *Leisure interests:* cricket, flying, golf. *Address:* Intergovernmental Panel on Climate Change, World Meteorological Organization, 7 bis, ave de la Paix, CP 2300, 1211 Geneva 2, Switzerland (office); 160 Golf Links, New Delhi 110003, India (home). *Telephone:* (11) 4634663 (home). *E-mail:* IPCC-Media@wmo.int (office). *Website:* www.ipcc.ch (office).

PACHE, Bernard; French business executive and engineer; b. 13 Oct. 1934, Sallanches; s. of Joseph Pache and Sabine Pache (née Minjoz); m. Yvette Vitaly 1959; three s. (two deceased); ed Ecole Polytechnique de Paris and Ecole des Mines de Paris; mining engineer 1957–; Asst to Dir of Mines 1963–65; Tech. Adviser to Minister of Industry 1965–67; Chief Mining Engineer 1967; joined Compagnie Pechiney 1967, Asst to Dir, Uranium and Nuclear Activity Dept, then Dir of Mines Div., Nuclear Branch of Pechiney Ugine Kuhlmann 1969–73; Gen.-Man. Soc. des Electrodes et Refractaires Savoie 1972–73; Chair. Cie Générale d'Electrolyse du Palais 1972–76; Gen.-Man. Soc. Cefilac 1973–74; Dir and Gen. Man. Soc. Française d'Electrométallurgie 1974–79; Dir of Industrial Policy, Pechiney Ugine Kuhlmann Group 1979–83, Deputy Dir of Pechiney 1983–84, Chair. and CEO 1985–86, Hon. Pres. 1986–; Dir-Gen. Charbonnages de France 1986, Chair. and CEO 1987–92, Hon. Pres. 1992–; Pres., Dir-Gen. Cie des Machines Bull 1992–93, Hon. Pres. 1993–; Pres. Directoire de l'Entreprise minière et chimique 1994–99, Hon. Pres. 1999–; Chair. la Fondation Georges Besse 1994–99; Chair. NOVATEC 1999–2003; Ind. Dir on Bd of European cos; Officier, Légion d'honneur, Officier, Ordre nat. du Mérite. *Address:* 7 Résidence de l'Observatoire, 8 rue Bel Air, 92190 Meudon, France (home). *Telephone:* 1-46-26-32-90 (home).

PACHECO, Abel; Costa Rican fmr head of state, psychiatrist and writer; b. (Abel Pacheco de la Espriella), 22 Dec. 1933, San José; ed Nat. Autonomous Univ. of Mexico, Louisiana State Univ., USA; fmr TV commentator and producer of documentaries; Pres. Partido Unidad Social Cristiana (PUSC); Pres. of Costa Rica 2002–06. *Publications:* series of novels, six books on Costa Rica and several popular songs. *Address:* c/o Partido Unidad Social Cristiana (PUSC), Del Restaurante Kentucky Fried Chicken 75 metros al sur, frente a la Embajada de España, Paseo Colón, Apdo 10.095, 1000 San José, Costa Rica (office).

PACHECO, Máximo, MBA; Chilean economist and business executive; *President, International Paper-Brazil;* b. 12 Feb. 1953, Santiago; s. of Máximo Pacheco and Adriana Matte; m. Soledad Flanagan 1976; four d.; ed Univ. of Chile; Man. Banco Osorno; Man. Planning, Banco Talca; Gen. Man. Leasing Andino 1983–90; Exec. Dir Cabildo SA 1982–90, Jucosa 1987–90; Pres. Chilean Leasing Asscn 1984–90; Faculty mem. Univ. de Chile; COO Codelco-Chile; Exec. Vice-Pres. for Chile and Latin America, Carter Holt Harvey 1994–; Pres. International Paper-Latinamerica 2000–04, International Paper-Brazil 2004–, SVP International Paper Co. 2004–. *Address:* Avenida Paulista 37, 14th Floor, 01311-902 São Paulo SP, Brazil (office). *Telephone:* (11) 3797-5787 (office). *Fax:* (11) 3797-5791 (office). *E-mail:* maximo.pacheco@ipaperbr.com (office). *Website:* www.ipaper.com (office).

PACINO, Al (Alfredo James); American actor; b. 25 April 1940, New York; s. of Salvatore Pacino and Rosa Pacino; ed High School for the Performing Arts, New York, The Actors Studio; worked as messenger and cinema usher; Co-artistic Dir The Actors Studio, Inc., New York 1982–83; mem. Artistic Directorate Globe Theatre 1997–; Broadway début in Does a Tiger Wear a Necktie? 1969; appeared with Lincoln Center Repertory Co. as Kilroy in Camino Real 1970; other New York appearances include The Connection, Hello Out There, Tiger at the Gates and The Basic Training of Pavlo Hummel 1977, American Buffalo 1981 (UK 1984), Julius Caesar 1988, Salome 1992; appearances at Charles Playhouse, Boston, include: Richard III 1973 (repeated on Broadway 1979), Arturo Ui 1975, Rats (director) 1970; f. Chal Productions (production co.); Nat. Soc. of Film Critics Award (for The Godfather), British Film Award (for The Godfather Part II) Tony Award 1996, American Film Inst. Lifetime Achievement Award 2007. *Films include:* Me, Natalie 1969, Panic in Needle Park 1971, The Godfather 1972, Scarecrow 1973, Serpico 1974, The Godfather Part II 1974, Dog Day Afternoon 1975, Bobby Deerfield 1977, And Justice For All 1979, Cruising 1980, Author! Author! 1982, Scarface 1983, Revolution 1985, Sea of Love 1990, Dick Tracy 1991, The Godfather Part III 1990, Frankie and Johnny 1991, Glengarry Glen Ross 1992, Scent of a Woman (Acad. Award for Best Actor 1993) 1992, Carlito's Way 1994, City Hall 1995, Heat 1995, Donny Brasco 1996, Looking for Richard 1996 (also producer, Dir), Devil's Advocate 1997, The Insider 1999, Chinese Coffee 1999, Man of the People 1999, Any Given Sunday 1999, People I Know 2002, Insomnia 2002, Simone 2002, The Recruit 2003, The Merchant of Venice 2004, Two for the Money 2005, 88 Minutes 2007, Ocean's Thirteen 2007, Righteous Kill 2008. *Television:* Angels in America (Golden Globe for Best Actor in a Miniseries or TV Movie 2004, Screen Actors Guild Award for Best Actor in a Miniseries 2004, Emmy Award for Outstanding Lead Actor in a Miniseries 2004) 2003. *Address:* c/o Rick Nicita, CAA, 9830 Wilshire Boulevard, Beverly Hills, CA 90212, USA (office); Chal Productions, 301 West 57th Street, Suite 49A, New York, NY 10017, USA (office). *Telephone:* (212) 247-0227.

PACKER, James Douglas; Australian media company executive; *Executive Chairman, Consolidated Media Holdings Ltd;* b. 8 Sept. 1967; s. of the late Kerry Francis Packer and Roslyn Packer; m. 1st Jodie Meaves 1999; m. 2nd Erica Baxter2007; ed Cranbrook School, Sydney; worked as a 'jackeroo' on a family-owned cattle station, Newcastle Walters; joined family business as magazine sales rep.; Dir Publishing & Broadcasting Ltd (PBL) 1991–, Man. Dir 1996–98, Exec. Chair. 1998–, inherited co. after father's death and split into two public cos., Consolidated Media Holdings Ltd and Crown Ltd, Dir Australian Consolidated Press Group Ltd 1991–, Gen. Man. 1993–, currently Jt CEO Consolidated Press Holdings Ltd, Chair. Crown Ltd; Chair. Burswood Ltd; Dir Nine Network Australia Ltd 1992–, Huntsman Corpn (Utah) 1994–, Optus Vision Pty Ltd 1995–, Valassas Inserts, USA, Ecorp Ltd 1999–, Challenger Int. 1999–, Crown Ltd 1999–, Hoytes Cinemas Ltd 1999–, Qantas Ltd –2007, Foxtel. *Address:* Consolidated Media Holdings Ltd, 2nd Floor, 54 Park Street, Sydney, NSW 1028, Australia (office). *Telephone:* (2) 9282-8000 (office). *Fax:* (2) 9282-8828 (office). *Website:* www.pbl.com.au (office).

PACKER, Sir Richard John, KCB, MSc; British former government official and business executive; b. 18 Aug. 1944, Bexley, England; s. of the late George Packer and Dorothy Packer; m. 1st Alison Sellwood; two s. one d.; m. 2nd Lucy Neville-Rolfe; four s.; ed City of London School and Univ. of Manchester; joined Ministry of Agric., Fisheries and Food (MAFF) 1967; on secondment, First Sec., Office of Perm. Representation to EEC 1973–76; Prin. Pvt. Sec. to Minister, MAFF 1977–78, Asst Sec. 1979–85, Under-Sec. 1985–89, Deputy Sec. 1989–93, Perm. Sec. 1993–2000; Dir (non-exec.) Express Foods (later Arla Foods) PLC 2002–07. *Publication:* The Politics of BSE 2006. *Leisure interests:* philosophy, history, arts, sport. *Address:* 113 St George's Road, London, SE1 6HY, England (home).

PACKER, William John; British artist, art critic and teacher; b. 19 Aug. 1940, Birmingham; s. of Rex Packer and Molly Wornham; m. Clare Winn 1965; three d.; ed Windsor Grammar School, Wimbledon School of Art; Nat. Diploma in Design (Painting); secondary school teacher 1964–67; part-time art school lecturer 1967–77; art critic, Art & Artists 1969–74, Financial Times 1974–2004; first exhibited Royal Acad. 1963; mem. Fine Art Bd of Council for Nat. Academic Awards and Specialist Adviser 1976–83, Specialist Adviser 1983–87; mem. Advisory Cttee to Govt Art Collection 1977–84, Crafts Council 1980–87; sole selector first British Art Show (Arts Council) 1979–80; external examiner at various art schools 1980–2000; mem. New English Art Club 2006; Hon. Fellow, RCA; Hon. RBA; Hon. RBS; Inaugural Henry Moore Memorial Lecturer, Florence 1986. *Publications:* Fashion Drawing in Vogue 1983, Henry Moore 1985. *Leisure interests:* France, books. *Address:* 60 Trinity Gardens, London, SW9 8DR, England (home). *Telephone:* (20) 7733-4012 (home). *E-mail:* williampacker@hotmail.com (home).

PACQUEMENT, Alfred; French museum administrator; *Director, Musée National d'Art Moderne, Centre Pompidou;* Curator, Centre Nat. d'Art Contemporain 1971–72, with Ministry of Cultural Affairs 1973, Exhbns Dir, Musée National d'Art Moderne (MNAM) 1974–81, Curator 1982–87, Attached to Ministry of Culture 1987–89, Dir, Galerie Nat. du Jeu de Paume 1990–93, Dir for 'Arts plastiques', Ministry of Culture 1993–96, Dir, École Nationale Supérieure des Beaux-Arts 1996–2000, Dir MNAM, Centre Pompidou 2000–. *Address:* Musée National d'Art Moderne, Centre Pompidou, 75191 Paris, Cedex 04, France (office). *Telephone:* (1) 44784640 (office). *Fax:* (1) 44781677 (office). *Website:* www.centrepompidou.fr (office).

PADAR, Ivari, BA; Estonian politician; *Minister of Finance;* b. 12 March 1965, Navi, Võru Prov.; m.; one s. one d.; ed Tartu Univ.; began career as transport worker, Võru Dairy Factory 1984–88; carpenter, Võru Dept of Repairs and Construction 1988–90; teacher, Võru School 1990–92; Deputy Mayor of Võru 1993–94; Chair. Võru Farmers' Union 1994–95; Asst to Chancellor of the Exchequer 1995–97; Dir-Gen. AS HT Hulgi (customs warehouse) 1997–99; Minister of Agric. 1999–2002, of Finance 2007–; Chair. Võru City Council 2002–03; Advisor AS Tallink Duty Free 2002–03; mem. Parl. 2002–; mem. Estonian Social Democratic Party 1999– (Chair. 2003–); mem. Bd Govs Estonian Univ. of Life Sciences; Hon. Pres. Estonian Asscn of Equestrian Sports. *Address:* Ministry of Finance, Suur-Ameerika 1, Tallinn 15006, Estonia (office). *Telephone:* 611-3558 (office). *Fax:* 696-6810 (office). *E-mail:* info@fin.ee (office). *Website:* www.fin.ee (office).

PADGAONKAR, Dileep, PhD; Indian journalist; *Consulting Editor and Columnist, Times of India;* b. 1 May 1944, Pune; s. of Vasant Padgaonkar and Shakuntala Padgaonkar (née Kattakar); m. Latika Tawadey 1968; two s.; ed Fergusson Coll., Pune, Institut des Hautes Etudes Cinématographiques, Sorbonne, France; Paris Corresp., The Times of India 1968–73, Asst Ed., Bombay and Delhi 1973–78, Assoc. Ed. and Exec. Ed. The Times of India Group 1986–88, Ed. 1988–94, Dir (Corp.) and Exec. Man. Ed. 1998–2002, Consulting Ed. and Columnist 2002–; f. Asia Pacific Communication Assocs 1994; Information Chief for Asia and Pacific, UNESCO 1978–81; Deputy Dir Office of Public Information, Paris 1981–85, Acting Dir 1985–86, Acting Dir Communication Sector 1986; Presenter Question Time India, BBC World; Chevalier, Legion d'honneur 2001. *Television:* presenter, BBC World's Question Time India panel discussion programme. *Publication:* When Bombay Burned (ed.) 1993. *Leisure interests:* reading, classical music, contemporary art, cooking. *Address:* The Times of India, Times House, 7 Bahadur Shah Zafar Marg, New Delhi 110002 (office); C-313, Defence Colony, New Delhi 110024, India (home). *Telephone:* (11) 3312277 (office); (11) 4697949 (home). *Fax:* (11) 3323346. *Website:* www.timesofindia.com (office).

PADILLA, James J., MEconSc; American automobile industry executive (retd); b. 1947, Detroit; ed Univ. of Detroit; joined Ford Motor Co. as Quality Control Engineer 1966; held various man. positions in product eng and manufacturing including manufacturing operations man. for Ford Escort and

Mercury Tracer, Ford Contour and Mercury Mystique, Ford Taurus and Mercury Sable car lines 1976–92, Dir of Eng and Manufacturing, Jaguar Cars 1992–94, Dir of performance luxury vehicle lines 1994–96, Pres. S American Operations 1996–98, Group Vice Pres. for Global Manufacturing 1999, for Quality 2001, Group Vice Pres. N America 2001–02, Pres. N American Operations 2002, then Exec. Vice Pres. and Pres. the Americas, COO and Chair. Automotive Operations 2004, Pres. and COO Ford Motor Co. 2004–06 (retd); mem. US Dept of Commerce Manufacturing Council; Fellow, Nat. Acad. of Eng; Ohtli Award (Mexico) 2004. *Address:* c/o Ford Motor Company, 1 American Road, Dearborn, MI 48126–2798, USA (office).

PADILLA ARANCIBIA, Gen. David; Bolivian army officer and fmr head of state; career officer with regional commands; Pres. of Bolivia and C-in-C of the Armed Forces 1978–79.

PADMANABAN, A., MA; Indian civil servant and writer; b. 14 Dec. 1928, Pinji, Ranipet, Tamil Nadu; m. Seetha Padmanaban 1961; two s. one d.; fmrly with Indian Admin. Service; Chief Sec. Govt of Tamil Nadu 1986–87, adviser to Gov. 1988–89; mem. Union Public Service Comm. 1989–93; Gov. of Mizoram 1998–2000; Indian Ed. Poet Int.; Pres. Authors' Guild of India; Vice-Pres. World Acad. of Arts and Culture, USA; Gov. Indian Council for Cultural Affairs; Eminent Poet Award, Int. Acad., India, Nat. Integration Award 1994, Michael Madhusudan Award. *Publications:* (biographical sketches) Dalits at the Cross-Roads: Their Struggle Past and Present 1996, (poetry) Rain Drops 1986, Light a Candle 1987, Buddha 1987, Untouchable's Journey 1991, My Dream 1992, Cosmic Accident 1995. *Leisure interests:* freelance writing, social work. *Address:* c/o Ananda Illam 14, 9th Cross Street, Shastri Nagar, Chennai 600020, India.

PADOA-SCHIOPPA, Tommaso, MSc (Econs); Italian banker, economist and government official; *Chairman, International Monetary and Financial Committee, International Monetary Fund;* b. 23 July 1940, Belluno; s. of Fabio Padoa and Stella Schwarz; m. Fiorella Kostoris 1966; one s. two d.; ed Università Commerciale Luigi Bocconi, Milan, Massachusetts Inst. of Tech., USA; with insurance co., Bremen, FRG 1959–60, C. & A. Brenninkmeyer 1966–68; Economist, Research Dept, Banca d'Italia, Rome 1970–79, Head, Money Market Dept 1975–79, Direttore Centrale for Econ. Research 1983–84, Deputy Dir-Gen. 1984–97; Economic Adviser, the Treasury 1978–79; Dir-Gen. Econ. and Financial Affairs, Comm. of EC 1979–83; mem. Group of Thirty; Chair. Banking Advisory Cttee, Comm. of EC 1988–91, Cen. Bank's Working Group on EC Payment Systems 1991–95, Group of Ten Basel Cttee on Banking Supervision, BIS 1993–97; mem. Exec. Bd European Cen. Bank 1998–2005; Minister of Economy and Finance 2006–08; Chair. Int. Monetary and Financial Cttee, IMF 2007–; Hon. Prof. Univ. of Frankfurt am Main 1999; Dr hc (Trieste) 1999. *Publications include:* The Management of an Open Economy with One Hundred Per Cent Plus Wage Indexation (with F. Modigliani, in Essays in International Finance) 1978, Money, Economic Policy and Europe 1985, The Road to Monetary Union in Europe 1994, Il governo dell'economia 1997, Che cosa ci ha insegnato l'avventura europea 1998. *Address:* International Monetary Fund, 700 19th Street, Washington, DC 20431, USA. *Telephone:* (202) 623-7000 (office). *Fax:* (202) 623-4661 (office). *Website:* www.imf.org (office).

PADOAN, Pier Carlo; Italian economist, international organization executive and academic; *Deputy Secretary-General, Organisation for Economic Co-operation and Development;* ed Univ. of Rome; has held various academic positions in Italian and foreign univs including at Univ. of Rome, College of Europe (Bruges), Université Libre de Bruxelles, Univ. of Urbino, Universidad de La Plata and Univ. of Tokyo; Italian Exec. Dir at IMF, Washington, DC, with competence also for Greece, Portugal, San Marino, Albania and Timor Leste, served as mem. Bd and chaired several Bd Cttees, was also in charge of European Coordination; Econ. Adviser to Prime Ministers Massimo D'Alema and Giuliano Amato, in charge of int. econ. policies 1998–2001; Pres. of Econs, Univ. La Sapienza, Rome and Dir Fondazione Italianieuropei (policy think-tank) 2001–07; Deputy Sec.-Gen. OECD 2007–, in charge of relations with other int. orgs. *Address:* OECD, 2 rue André Pascal, 75775 Paris Cedex 16, France (office). *Telephone:* 1-45-24-82-00 (office). *Fax:* 1-45-24-85-00 (office). *E-mail:* webmaster@oecd.org (office). *Website:* www.oecd.org (office).

PADVA, Genrikh Pavlovich; Russian lawyer; *Managing Partner, Padva & Partners;* b. 20 Feb. 1931, Moscow; s. of Pavel Padva and Eva Rappoport; ed Moscow Inst. of Law; Kalinin Pedagogical Inst.; mem. Kalinin Bar 1953, Presidium 1965–71, of Moscow Bar 1971–, of the Presidium 1986, Dir Research Inst. of Bar; one of founders of the USSR (now Russian) Union of Barristers, Deputy-Chair. of the Exec. Board 1990; Vice-Pres. of the Int. Asscn of Lawyers 1990, acted as a barrister on major political and economic trials in 1970s, was a lawyer for many dissidents, rendered legal advice to the families of Andrei Sakharov, singer Vladimir Vysotsky, Pavel Borodin; represented Mikhail Khodorkovsky in criminal proceedings; investigated some major econ. and criminal cases in late 1980s–1990s, a founder and Dir-Gen. of Russian-American Int. Lawyers Co.; Man. Partner Padva & Partners, Attorneys at Law; Honoured Barrister of Russian Fed., F.N. Plevako Gold Medal. *Publications:* articles in specialized journals and newspapers on legal problems. *Address:* Padva & Partners, Bolshoi Golovin 6, Moscow 107045, Russia (office). *Telephone:* (495) 737-43-03 (office). *Fax:* (495) 737-43-08 (office). *E-mail:* padva@col.ru (office). *Website:* www.padva..ru (office).

PAE, Chong-yeul; South Korean electronics industry executive; began career as jr economist, Research Dept, Bank of Korea 1969–76; Asst Adviser on Econ. Policy, Office of Pres. of Repub. of Korea 1973–75; Man. Planning Dept, Samsung Corpn 1976–83, Pres. Samsung Pacific Int. Inc., LA, USA 1983, Pres. Samsung America Inc., NY 1983–87, Sr Exec. Man.-Dir Sales and Marketing, Semiconductor Div., Samsung Electronics Co. Ltd 1988–90, Vice-

Pres., Office of Chair., Samsung Group 1991–93, Pres. and CEO Samsung Corpn Ltd 2001; Exec. Vice-Pres. Joong-ang Daily News 1994–98; Pres. and CEO Cheil Communications Inc. 1998–2001. *Address:* c/o Samsung Corporation, Samsung Plaza, 263 Seohyeon-dong, Bundang-gu, Songnam, Kyonggi 463-721, Republic of Korea.

PAENIU, Rt Hon Bikenibeu, BAgr, MSc; Tuvaluan politician and economist; b. 10 May 1956, Bikenibeu, Tarawa; m. Foketi Paeniu; two s. two d.; ed King George V School, Tarawa, Univ. of S Pacific, Suva and Univ. of Hawaii; worked in Agric. Div. Tuvalu; later Asst Economist, South Pacific Comm. Nouméa; returned to Tuvalu 1988; Prime Minister of Tuvalu 1989–93, 1996–99; Minister for Finance and Econ. Planning and Industries –2006. *Address:* c/o Ministry of Finance, Economic Planning and Industries PMB, Vaiaku, Funafuti (office); Nukulaezae, Tuvalu (home).

PAET, Urmas; Estonian journalist and politician; *Minister of Foreign Affairs;* b. 20 April 1974, Tallinn; m. Tiina Paet; two d.; ed Univ. of Tartu; Ed. Chief Editorial Office for Int. News, Estonian Radio 1991–92, Ed. News Editorial Office 1993–94; reporter, News Editorial Office, AS Postimees 1994–98, Sr Ed. and Political Journalist 1998–99; Adviser Estonian Reform Party 1999; Dist Elder, Nõmme city 1999–2003; Minister of Culture 2003–05, of Foreign Affairs 2005–. *Address:* Ministry of Foreign Affairs, Islandi Väljak 1, Tallinn 15049, Estonia (office). *Telephone:* 637-7092 (office). *Fax:* 637-7099 (office). *E-mail:* vminfo@vm.ee (office). *Website:* www.vm.ee (office).

PAFFRATH, Hans-Georg; German art dealer; b. 12 April 1922, Düsseldorf; s. of Hans Paffrath and Eleonore Paffrath (née Theegarten); m. Helena née Baroness Åkerhielm 1958; two s. three d.; ed Gymnasium; war service 1941–45; art dealer 1945–2000; fmr Royal Swedish Consul-Gen. for North Rhine Westphalia; Commdr Nordstjerne Orden, Verdienstorden des Landes Nordrhein-Westfalen, Medalj för förtjänster om utrikes förvaltningen. *Leisure interest:* riding. *Address:* Königsallee 46, 40212 Düsseldorf, Germany. *Telephone:* (211) 323128 (home). *Fax:* (211) 320216.

PAGAN, Adrian Rodney, BEcons, PhD, FASSA; Australian economist and academic; *Professor of Economics, Queensland University of Technology;* b. 12 Jan. 1947, Mungindi, Queensland; m.; two c.; ed Queensland Univ., ANU; Visiting Research Fellow, Princeton Univ., USA 1973; Lecturer, then Sr Lecturer, ANU, 1974–80, Sr Research Fellow 1980–83, Sr Fellow 1983–88, Adjunct Prof. 1989–90, Prof. of Econs, Research School of Social Sciences 1992–2006; Prof. of Econs, Univ. of Rochester, USA 1986–90, 1992–95, Wilson Prof. of Econs 1990–92; Prof. of Econs, Queensland Univ. of Tech. 2005–; currently also Prof. of Econs, Australian School of Business, Univ. of New South Wales; Visiting Prof., Inst. of Advanced Studies, Vienna 1982, Yale Univ. 1985, Johns Hopkins Univ. 1996, 2000–, UCLA 1997; mem. Bd Reserve Bank of Australia 1995–2000; Professorial Assoc., Univ. of Melbourne 1996–99; Professorial Fellow, Nuffield College and Visiting Prof. of Econs, Univ. of Oxford, UK 2000–02; numerous assoc. editorships and editorial bd memberships; Fellow, Centre of Operations Research and Econometrics 1977–78, Econometric Soc. 1985, Journal of Econometrics 1990; University of Queensland Scholarship, Esso Prize in Accounting, Brinds Prize in Econs, Univ. Medal (Queensland), Medallist Fellow and Socio-Econ. Systems Medal, Modelling and Simulation Soc. of Australia 1997, Distinguished Fellow Award, Econ. Soc. of Australia 1999, Centenary Medal 2003. *Publications include:* The Theory of Economic Policy (with A. J. Preston) 1982, The Effects of Inflation (co-ed. with P. K. Trivedi) 1983, Non-Parametric Econometrics (with A. Ullah) 1999; numerous journal articles on macro-econ. modelling and its uses in policy analysis and for the explanation of business cycles. *Address:* School of Economics and Finance, Queensland University of Technology, 2 George Street, Brisbane 4001 (office); Room 459, West Wing 4th Floor, Australian School of Business Building, School of Economics, University of New South Wales, Kensington, NSW 2052, Australia (office). *Telephone:* (7) 3138-1031 (Brisbane) (office); (2) 9385-3319 (Kensington) (office). *Fax:* (7) 3138-1500 (Brisbane) (office); (2) 9313-6337 (Kensington) (office). *E-mail:* a.pagan@qut.edu.au (office); a.pagan@unsw.edu.au (office). *Website:* www.bus .qut.edu.au/adrianpagan (office); www2.economics.unsw.edu.au (office); www .economics.unsw.edu.au/AdrianPagan (office).

PAGBALHA, Geleg Namgyai; Chinese administrator; *Vice-Chairman of National Committee, 11th Chinese People's Political Consultative Congress;* b. 1940, Litang Co., Sichuan Prov.; was confirmed by the Qangdin Lamasery as 11th incarnation of a living Buddha 1942; Vice-Chair. Qamdo Prefectural People's Liberation Cttee, Tibet Autonomous Region 1950; Vice-Chair. Tibet Autonomous Regional Preparatory Cttee 1956, Vice-Chair. Religious Affairs Cttee, Chair. Ethnic Affairs Cttee; sent to do manual labour 1966–76; Vice-Chair. People's Govt of Tibet Autonomous Region 1979–83; Acting Chair., Tibet Autonomous Region People's Congress 1983–86; Vice-Chair. Tibet Autonomous Region Cttee of CPPCC and Vice Chair. Standing Cttee of Tibetan Autonomous Regional People's Congress 1983–88; Vice-Chair. 3rd CPPCC Nat. Cttee 1959–64, 4th CPPCC Nat. Cttee 1964–78, mem. Presidium 4th NPC 1975–78, Vice-Chair. 5th CPPCC Nat. Cttee 1978–83, mem. Presidium 5th NPC 1978–83, Exec. Chair. 6th CPPCC 1983–88, Vice-Chair. 7th CPPCC Nat. Cttee 1988–92, 10th CPPCC Nat. Cttee 2003–08, 11th CPPCC Nat. Cttee 2008–; Deputy, 2nd NPC 1959, 3rd NPC 1964, 4th NPC 1975, 5th NPC 1978, Vice-Chair. Standing Cttee 8th NPC 1993–98, 9th NPC 1998–2003; Chair. CPPCC, Tibetan Autonomous Region 1993–; Vice-Pres. Buddhist Asscn of China 1993–2002, Hon. Pres. 2002–; Pres. China Tibet Devt Foundation. *Address:* Standing Committee of National People's Congress, Beijing, People's Republic of China (office).

PAGE, Ashley, OBE; British classical dancer, choreographer and artistic director; b. 9 Aug. 1956, Rochester, Kent; s. of John H. Laverty and Sheila R. Medhurst; m. Nicola J. Roberts; one s. one d.; ed St Andrew's, Rochester, Royal

Ballet, Lower and Upper Schools; joined Royal Ballet Co. 1975, soloist 1980, Prin. 1984, House Choreographer; leading roles in classical and modern repertoire; cr. numerous roles for MacMillan, Ashton and other leading choreographers; Choreographer Royal Opera House 1984; with numerous cos in London, Europe; Artistic Dir Scottish Ballet 2002–; Frederick Ashton Choreographer Award 1982, Frederick Ashton Memorial Comm. Award 1990, Time Out Dance Award 1994, Olivier Award for Best New Dance Production 1995. *Productions include:* 19 works for the Royal Ballet, 2 for the Dutch Nat. Ballet, 3 for the Rambert Dance Co. and several for Dance Umbrella, West Australian Ballet and other cos . *Films:* (all dance) Savage Water (Channel 4) 1989, Soldat (BBC) 1990; (art films) Pull-Dance for the Camera 1998. *Leisure interests:* fine arts, driving, film, music, reading, theatre, travel, photography, family, friends. *Address:* Scottish Ballet, 261 West Princes Street, Glasgow, G4 9EE, England. *Telephone:* (141) 331-6263 (office). *Fax:* (141) 331-2629 (office). *E-mail:* ashley.page@scottishballet.co.uk (home).

PAGE, Bruce; British journalist; b. 1 Dec. 1936, London; s. of Roger Page and Amy B. Page; m. 1st Anne Gillison 1964 (divorced 1969); m. 2nd Anne L. Darnborough 1969; one s. one d.; ed Melbourne High School and Melbourne Univ., Australia; trained as journalist, Melbourne Herald 1956–60; Evening Standard, London 1960–62; Daily Herald, London 1962–64; various exec. posts, Sunday Times, London 1964–76; Assoc. Ed. Daily Express 1977; Ed. New Statesman 1978–82; Dir Direct Image Systems and Communications 1992–95; various awards for journalism; British Newspaper Hall of Fame 2005. *Publications:* co-author: Philby, the Spy who Betrayed a Generation, An American Melodrama, Do You Sincerely Want to be Rich?, Destination Disaster, Ulster (contrib.), The Yom Kippur War, The British Press; author: The Murdoch Archipelago 2003. *Leisure interests:* reading, sailing, computers. *Address:* c/o PFD Limited, Drury House, 34–43 Russell Street, London WC2B 5HA (office); Beach House, Shingle Streeet, Shottisham, Suffolk, IP12 3BE, England (home). *Telephone:* (1394) 411427 (home); (7771) 641018 (mobile). *E-mail:* bruce@pages2.ads24.co.uk (office).

PAGE, Geneviève, (pseudonym of Geneviève Bonjean); French actress; b. 13 Dec. 1927, Paris; d. of Jacques Bonjean and Germaine Lipmann; m. Jean-Claude Bujard 1959; one s. one d.; ed Lycée Racine, Paris, Sorbonne, Paris, Conservatoire nat. d'art dramatique, École du Louvre; prin. actress in the Comédie Française, the Jean-Louis Barrault company and TNP Jean Vilar; has appeared in many famous classical and tragic stage roles, including Les larmes amères de Petra von Kant (Critics' Prize for Best Actress 1980), La nuit des rois, L'aigle à deux têtes, Angelo, tyran de Padoue 1984, Perséphone 1988, Mère Courage 1988, Le balcon 1991, Paroles de poètes 1992, La peste 1992, La femme sur le lit 1994 (Colombe Prix, Plaisir du Théâtre Best Actress), Les grandes forêts 1997, Delicate Balance 1998, Le martyre de Saint Sébastien 2005; Chevalier de la Légion d'honneur, du Mérite sportif, du Cèdre du Liban, Officier des Arts et des Lettres 2006. *Films include:* Ce siècle a cinquante ans, Pas de pitié pour les femmes, Fanfan la tulipe, Lettre ouverte, Plaisirs de Paris, Nuits andalouses, L'étrange désir de M. Bard, Cherchez la femme, L'homme sans passé, Foreign Intrigue, The Silken Affair, Michael Strogoff, Un amour de poche, Song Without End, Le bal des adieux, El Cid, Les égarements, Le jour et l'heure, L'honorable correspondence, Youngblood Hawke, Le majordome, Les corsaires, Trois chambres à Manhattan, Grand Prix, Belle de jour, Mayerling, A Talent for Loving, The Private Life of Sherlock Holmes, Les Gémeaux, Décembre, Buffet froid, Beyond Therapy 1987, Les bois noirs 1991, Lovers 1999, Last Night 1999, Eye of the Beholder 2000, Eye 2000, Rien que du bonheur 2002. *Television includes:* La nuit des rois 1962 (Best Actress TV, Quatre Siècles de Théâtre français 2002), La chambre 1964, La chasse aux hommes 1976, Athalie 1980, Les gens ne sont pas forcément ignobles 1990, Mémoire en fuite 2001. *Music includes:* Jeanne au Boucher-Persephone, Le Martyre de St-Sebastien, Oedipus Rex, Histoire du Soldat. *Publications include:* Pour l'amour du Grec, Les Femmes et l'Amour. *Leisure interests:* ancient artefacts, skiing, tennis, riding, skin diving. *Address:* 52 rue de Vaugirard, 75006 Paris, France.

PAGE, Lawrence (Larry) E., BSc; American internet industry executive; *Co-Founder and President, Products, Google Inc.;* b. Ann Arbor, Mich.; s. of Carl Victor and Gloria Page; m. Lucy Southworth 2007; ed Univ. of Mich.; co-f. Google Inc. with Sergey Brin, fmr CEO, currently Pres., Products; mem. Nat. Advisory Cttee, Univ. of Mich. Coll. of Eng; mem. Nat. Acad. of Eng (NAE); Marconi Prize (with Sergey Brin) 2004, Economist Innovation Award (with Sergey Brin) 2005; named one of the World's Most Influential People by Time Magazine 2005. *Address:* Google Inc., 2400 Bayshore Parkway, Mountain View, CA 94043, USA (office). *Telephone:* (650) 623-4000 (office). *Fax:* (650) 618-1499 (office). *Website:* www.google.com (office).

PAGLIA, Camille, BA, MPhil, PhD; American academic and writer; *University Professor of Humanities and Media Studies, University of the Arts;* b. 2 April 1947, Endicott, NY; d. of Pasquale Paglia and Lydia Paglia; ed State Univ. of New York at Binghamton, Yale Univ.; Faculty mem., Bennington Coll. 1972–80; Visiting Lecturer, Wesleyan Univ. 1980, Yale Univ. 1980–84; Asst Prof., Philadelphia Coll. of Performing Arts (now Univ. of the Arts) 1984–87, Assoc. Prof. 1987–91, Prof. of Humanities 1991–2000; Univ. Prof. of Humanities and Media Studies 2000–; columnist, Salon.com 1995–2001, 2007–; Contributing Ed. Interview magazine 2001–. *Publications:* Sexual Personae: Art and Decadence from Nefertiti to Emily Dickinson 1990, Sex, Art and American Culture: Essays 1992, Vamps and Tramps: New Essays 1994, Alfred Hitchcock's The Birds 1998, Break, Blow, Burn: Camille Paglia Reads Forty-Three of the World's Best Poems 2005. *Address:* University of the Arts, 320 South Broad Street, Philadelphia, PA 19102, USA (office). *Telephone:* (212) 421-1700 (agent) (office); (215) 717-6265 (office). *Fax:* (212) 980-3671 (agent). *Website:* www.uarts.edu (office).

PĄGOWSKI, Andrzej; Polish graphic designer; b. 19 April 1953, Warsaw; ed Academy of Fine Arts, Poznań; est. own graphic studio 1990–; illustrator of books, covers of compact discs; designer of posters, TV and film billboards, TV programme credits, satirical drawings; has designed over 1,000 posters including Husband and Wife and series highlighting dangers of alcohol, tobacco and drug abuse; Art Dir Polish edn of Playboy 1992–; works in numerous pvt. and public collections including Metropolitan Museum, New York; numerous awards include: Silver Medal, Biennale Polish Poster 1983, 1993, First Prize Int. Competition for the Best Film and TV Poster, Los Angeles 1980–1993, Silver Hugon, Golden and Silver Badge (twice), Int. Competition Film Poster, Chicago 1982–1987, Annual Award of Hollywood Reporters for film posters 1986, Clio Poland Award 1993. *Address:* Andrzej Pągowski Studio P, ul. Balaton 8, 01-981 Warsaw, Poland (office). *Telephone:* (22) 8649293 (office). *Fax:* (22) 8649290 (office). *E-mail:* pagowski.a@studio-p.pl (office).

PAHAD, Aziz Goolam Hoosein, MA; South African politician; *Deputy Minister of Foreign Affairs;* b. 25 Dec. 1940, Schweizer-Reneke, Western Transvaal; s. of Goolam Hoosein Ismail Pahad and Amina Pahad; m. Sandra Pahad 1994; two s. one d.; ed Cen. Indian High School, Johannesburg, Univ. of Witwatersrand, Univ. Coll., London, and Univ. of Sussex, UK; in exile 1964–90; worked in London office of African Nat. Congress (ANC) from 1968, later mem. ANC Revolutionary Council until its dissolution in 1983; rep. of ANC Revolutionary Council in Angola and Zambia; mem. ANC Nat. Exec. Cttee 1985–; Deputy Head, ANC Dept of Int. Affairs 1991; mem. Nat. Peace Exec. Cttee 1991–92; mem. Sub-Council on Foreign Affairs of Transitional Exec. Council 1993–94; MP 1994–; Deputy Minister of Foreign Affairs 1994–. *Leisure interests:* listening to music, watching sport, reading. *Address:* Room 1725, 120 Plein Street, Cape Town (office); Room 283, East Wing, Union Buildings, Pretoria, South Africa (office). *Telephone:* (21) 4643711 (Cape Town) (office); (12) 3510105 (Pretoria) (office). *Fax:* (21) 4618090 (Cape Town) (office); (12) 3510259 (Pretoria) (office). *E-mail:* dmpahad@foreign.gov.za (office). *Website:* www.dfa.gov.za (office).

PAHANG, HRH The Sultan of; Haji Ahmad Shah al-Musta'in Billah ibni al-Marhum Sultan Abu Bakar Ri'ayatuddin al-Mu'adzam Shah, DKP; Malaysian; b. 24 Oct. 1930, Istana Mangga Tunggal, Pekan; m. Tengku Hajjah Afzan binti Tengku Muhammad 1954; ed Malay Coll. Kuala Kangsar, Worcester Coll., Oxford and Univ. Coll., Exeter, UK; Tengku Mahkota (Crown Prince) 1944; Capt. 4th Battalion, Royal Malay Regt 1954; Commdr of 12th Infantry Battalion of Territorial Army 1963–65, Lt-Col; mem. State Council 1955; Regent 1956, 1959, 1965; succeeded as Sultan 1974; Timbalan Yang di Pertuan Agong (Deputy Supreme Head of State of Malaysia) 1975–79, Yang di Pertuan Agong (Supreme Head of State) 1979–84, 1985; Constitutional Head of Int. Islamic Univ. 1988; Hon. DLitt (Malaya) 1988; Hon. LLD (Northrop, USA) 1993. *Address:* Istana Abu Bakar, Pekan, Pahang, Malaysia.

PAHLAVI, Farah Diba, fmr Empress of Iran; b. 14 Oct. 1938; d. of Sohrab and Farida Diba; m. HIM Shah Mohammed Reza Pahlavi 1959 (died 1980); two s. two d.; ed Jeanne d'Arc School and Razi School, Tehran and Ecole Spéciale d'Architecture, Paris; Foreign Assoc. mem. Fine Arts Acad., France 1974; fmr Patron, Farah Pahlavi Asscn (admin. of Social Educ. Asscn), Iran Cultural Foundation and 34 other educational, health and cultural orgs; left Iran 1979, living in Egypt 1980–. *E-mail:* fpahlavi@hotmail.com. *Website:* www.farahpahlavi.org.

PAHOR, Borut, BA; Slovenian politician; *Prime Minister;* b. 2 Nov. 1963, Postojna; m. Tanja Pečar; one s.; ed Faculty of Sociology, Political Sciences and Journalism; Deputy to Nat. Ass. 1992–2004, mem. Comms for EU Affairs and the Supervision of Intelligence and Security Services 1992–96, Cttee on Defence 1992–96, Vice-Pres. Cttee on Int. Relations 1996–97, Chair. Slovenian Del. to the Parl. Ass. of the Council of Europe 1996–97, mem. Constitutional Comm 1996–97, Exec. Cttee of Inter-Parl. Union 1996–97, Pres. Nat. Ass. 2000–04; Deputy Leader United List of Social Democrats (renamed Social Democrats 2005) 1993–97, Leader 1997–; mem. European Parl. (Socialist Group) 2004–08, Vice-Chair. of Del. to EU-Croatia Jt Parl. Cttee, mem. Cttee Budgetary Control, on Constitutional Affairs; Prime Minister of Slovenia 2008–. *Leisure interest:* sport. *Address:* Office of the Prime Minister, 1000 Ljubljana, Gregorčičeva 20, Slovenia (office). *Telephone:* (1) 4781000 (office). *Fax:* (1) 4781721 (office). *E-mail:* gp.kpv@gov.si (office). *Website:* www.kpv.gov.si (office).

PAHR, Willibald P., DrIur; Austrian diplomatist and politician; *Chairman of the Advisory Board, International Centre for Migration Policy Development;* b. 5 June 1930, Vienna; m. Ingeborg Varga 1960; one s. one d.; ed Univ. of Vienna and Coll. of Europe, Bruges, Belgium; Asst in Inst. of Int. Law and Int. Relations, Univ. of Vienna 1952–55; served in Fed. Chancellery 1955–76, Head of Section 1968, Head of Dept 1973, Dir-Gen. 1975–76; Fed. Minister for Foreign Affairs 1976–83; Amb. to FRG 1983–85; Sec.-Gen. World Tourism Org. 1986–88; Special Commr for Refugees and Migration, Austrian Ministry of the Interior 1990–95; fmr Chair. Int. Centre for Migration Policy Devt (ICMPD), now Chair. Advisory Bd. *Publications:* Der österreichische Status der dauernden Neutralität 1967, several articles in Revue des Droits de l'Homme, numerous articles on current int. problems in various periodicals; co-ed. Grundrechte, die Rechtsprechung in Europa (journal). *Address:* ICMPD, Möllwaldplatz 4, 1040 Vienna, Austria. *E-mail:* Willibald.Pahr@icmpd.org.

PAIGE, Elaine, OBE; British singer and actress; b. (Elaine Bickerstaff), 5 March 1948, Barnet, England; d. of Eric Bickerstaff and Irene Bickerstaff; ed Aida Foster Stage school; Variety Club Award for Showbusiness Personality of the Year and Recording Artist of the Year 1986, BASCA Award 1993, Lifetime Achievement Award, Nat. Operatic and Dramatic Assn 1999. *Theatre:* West

End, London appearances in Hair 1968, Jesus Christ Superstar 1973, Grease (played Sandy) 1973, Billy (played Rita) 1974, Evita (created role of Eva Perón) (Soc. of West End Theatre Award for Best Actress in a Musical 1978) 1978, Cats (created role of Grizabella) 1981, Abbacadabra (played Carabosse) 1983, Chess (played Florence) 1986, Anything Goes (played Reno Sweeney) 1989, Piaf 1993–94, Sunset Boulevard (played Norma Desmond) 1995–96, The Misanthrope (played Célimène) 1998, The King and I (played Anna) 2000, The Drowsy Chaperone (Novello Theatre, London) 2007. *Recordings include:* albums: Sitting Pretty 1978, Elaine Paige 1981, Stages 1983, Cinema 1984, Love Hurts 1985, Christmas 1986, Memories: The Best Of Elaine Paige 1987, The Queen Album 1988, Elaine Paige: The Collection 1990, Love Can Do That 1991, An Evening With Elaine Paige 1991, Elaine Paige And Barbara Dickson 'Together' 1992, Romance And The Stage 1993, Piaf 1994, Encore 1995, Performance 1996, From A Distance 1997, On Reflection 1998, Centre Stage: The Best of Elaine Paige 2004; contributions to soundtrack recordings, including Nine, Anything Goes, Chess, Cats, Evita, Billy, The King And I; appears on: Tim Rice Collection: Stage and Screen Classics 1996, Christmas with the Stars Vol. 2 1999. *Leisure interests:* antiques, gardening, skiing, tennis. *Address:* Sanctuary Artist Management, Sanctuary House, 45–53 Sinclair Road, London, W14 0NS, England. *Telephone:* (20) 7602-6351. *Fax:* (20) 7300-6650. *E-mail:* liz.gould@sanctuarygroup.com. *Website:* www .elainepaige.com.

PAIGE, Roderick (Rod), PhD; American educational administrator and fmr government official; *Public Policy Scholar, Woodrow Wilson International Center for Education;* b. Monticello, Miss.; ed Jackson State Univ., Indiana Univ.; mem. Bd of Educ., Houston Ind. School Dist 1989, Pres. 1992; Supt of Schools 1994; Dean Coll. of Educ. Texas Southern Univ.; US Sec. of Educ. 2001–05; Public Policy Scholar, Woodrow Wilson Int. Center for Scholars 2005–; mem. Bd of Trustees Thomas B. Fordham Foundation 2005–; mem. Houston Job Training Partnership Council; Community Advisory Bd of Texas Commerce Bank, NAACP; consultant, Greater New Orleans Educ. Foundation; Sec.-Treas. Council of the Great City Schools; Richard R. Green Award 1998, Outstanding Urban Educator Award 1999, McGraw Prize in Educ. 2000, Supt of the Year Award 2000, 2001. *Address:* Woodrow Wilson International Center for Scholars, Ronald Reagan Building and International Trade Center, One Woodrow Wilson Plaza, 1300 Pennsylvania Avenue, NW, Washington, DC 20004-3027, USA (office). *Telephone:* (202) 691-4000 (office). *Website:* wwics.si.edu (office).

PAIHAMA, Gen. Kundi; Angolan politician and army general; *Minister of National Defence;* b. 1958; with Angolan armed forces, also seconded to the Portuguese army; fmr Councillor of Benguela; fmr Minister of the Interior; Gov. of Huíla Prov. 1992–99, also of the City of Luanda; Minister of State Security 1998; elected to Congress (MPLA) 1998; Minister of Nat. Defence 1999–. *Address:* Ministry of National Defence, Rua 17 de Settembro, Luanda, Angola (office). *Telephone:* 222337530 (office). *Fax:* 222334276 (office). *E-mail:* mindenl@ebonet.net (office).

PAIK, Kun-woo; South Korean pianist; b. 10 March 1946; ed Juilliard School, New York and in London and Italy; interpreter of piano works of Ravel, Liszt, Scriabin and Prokofiev; has played with orchestras throughout N America and Europe, notably Indianapolis Symphony, Rotterdam Philharmonic, Royal Philharmonic, London Symphony, BBC Symphony (soloist, Last Night of the Proms 1987), Orchestre Nat. de France, Polish Radio Nat. Symphony; lives in Paris; recitals at all maj. European music festivals; three Diapason d'Or awards. *E-mail:* kw@kunwoopaik.com (office). *Website:* www .kunwoopaik.com.

PAIN, Emil Abramovich, PhD; Russian sociologist; *Director-General, Center of Ethnopolitical and Regional Studies (CEPRS);* b. 6 Dec. 1948, Kiev; m.; one s.; ed Voronezh State Univ., Moscow State Univ.; researcher on problems of regional sociology and ethnology, problems of nat. conflicts, Voronezh State Univ. and Inst. of Ethnography USSR (now Russian) Acad. of Sciences 1974–91; during perestroika was expert of Deputies' Comm. on Deported Peoples and Problems of Crimea Tartars 1989–91; Chief Adviser Int. Asscn of Foreign Policy 1991–92; Dir-Gen. Cen. Ethnopolitical and Regional Studies (CEPRS) 1993–; mem. Pres.'s Council 1993–97; mem. Expert-Analytical Dept of Pres. of Russia 1994–98; Adviser to Pres. 1996–99; Prof. Inst. of Int. Relations 1992–99, Moscow Univ. 1999–, Inst. of Sociology, Russian Acad. of Sciences; fmr Galina Starovoitova Fellow, Kennan Inst. for Advanced Russian Studies. *Publications:* Russia between the Nation and Empire 2004; numerous articles on relations between nations, prevention of social conflicts, sociology and ethnology. *Address:* CEPRS, Krzhizhanovskogo str. 24/35 Korp. 5, Suite 522, 117259 Moscow, Russia. *Telephone:* (495) 128-56-51 (office); (495) 431-56-07 (home). *Fax:* (495) 128-56-51 (office); (495) 431-56-07 (home).

PAINTAL, Autar Singh, MD, PhD, FRCP, FRS, FRSE; Indian physiologist, medical researcher and academic; *Programme Director, DST Centre for Visceral Mechanisms, Vallabhbhai Patel Chest Institute, University of Delhi;* b. 24 Sept. 1925; s. of Dr Man Singh and Rajwans Kaur; one s. two d.; ed Forman Christian Coll., Lahore, Lucknow and Edinburgh Univs; lecturer, King George's Medical Coll. Lucknow Univ. 1949; Rockefeller Fellow 1950; lecturer, Univ. of Edin. 1951; Control Officer, Tech. Devt Establishment Labs., Ministry of Defence, Kampur 1952–54; Prof. of Physiology, All India Inst. of Med. Sciences, Delhi 1958–64; Prof. of Physiology Delhi Univ. 1964–, Dir Vallabhbhai Patel Chest Inst., 1964–90, now Programme Director, DST Centre for Visceral Mechanisms; fmr Dir-Gen. Indian Council of Medical Research; Dean Faculty of Med. Sciences, Delhi Univ. 1966–77; Fellow, Indian Acad. of Medical Sciences, Indian Nat. Science Acad. (Pres. 1987–88), and other learned socs; Pres. Nat. Coll. of Chest Physicians 1981–86, Indian Science Congress 1984–85; numerous awards and distinctions including R. D. Birla Award 1982, Nehru Science Award 1983, Acharya J.C. Bose Medal

1985, CV Raman Medal 1995; Hon. DSc (Benares Hindu Univ.) 1982, (Delhi) 1984, (Aligarh Muslim Univ.) 1986, other hon. degrees. *Publications:* articles in professional journals. *Leisure interests:* swimming, rowing, bird watching. *Address:* DST Centre for Visceral Mechanisms, Vallabhbhai Patel Chest Institute, Delhi University, PO Box 2101, Delhi 110007, India (office). *Telephone:* (11) 7257749 (office). *E-mail:* visc.mechs@mail.com (office). *Website:* www.vpci.org.in (office).

PAISLEY, Rev. Ian Richard Kyle, DD, FRGS; British politician; b. 6 April 1926; s. of Rev. J. Kyle Paisley and Isabella Paisley; m. Eileen E Cassells 1956; two s. (twins) three d.; ed Ballymena Model School, Ballymena Tech. High School and S Wales Bible Coll. and Reformed Presbyterian Theological Coll., Belfast; ordained 1946; Minister, Martyrs Memorial Free Presbyterian Church 1946–; Moderator, Free Presbyterian Church of Ulster 1951–2008; f. The Protestant Telegraph 1966; MP (Democratic Unionist) 1974– (Protestant Unionist 1970–74) resgnd seat Dec. 1985 in protest against Anglo-Irish Agreement; re-elected Jan. 1986; MP (Protestant Unionist) for Bannside, Co. Antrim, Parl. of Northern Ireland (Stormont) 1970–72, Leader of the Opposition 1972, Chair. Public Accounts Cttee 1972; mem. NI Ass. 1973–74, elected to Second NI Ass. 1982; MEP 1979–; MP for Antrim N, NI Ass. 1998–2000; First Minister of NI Ass. 2007–08; mem. Constitutional Convention 1975–76; Leader (co-founder) of Democratic Unionist Party 1972–2008; Chair. Agric. Cttee and Cttee of Privileges 1983; Pres. Whitefield Coll. of the Bible, Laurencetown, Co. Down 1979–; Co-Chair. World Congress of Fundamentalists 1978; mem. Political Cttee European Parl., NI Ass. 1998–; mem. Int. Cultural Soc. of Korea 1977. *Publications include:* History of the 1859 Revival 1959, Christian Foundations 1960, Ravenhill Pulpit Vol. I 1966, Vol. II 1967, Exposition of the Epistle to the Romans 1968, Billy Graham and the Church of Rome 1970, The Massacre of Saint Bartholomew 1972, Paisley, the Man and his Message 1976, America's Debt to Ulster 1976, Ulster – The Facts 1981 (jtly), No Pope Here 1982, Dr. Kidd 1982, Those Flaming Tennents 1983, Crown Rights of Jesus Christ 1985, Be Sure: 7 Rules for Public Speaking 1986, Paisley's Pocket Preacher 1986, Jonathan Edwards, The Theologian of Revival 1987, Union with Rome 1989, The Soul of the Question 1990, The Revised English Bible: An Exposure 1990, What a Friend We Have in Jesus 1994, Understanding Events in Northern Ireland: An Introduction for Americans 1995, My Plea for the Old Sword 1997, The Rent Veils at Calvary 1997, A Text a Day Keeps the Devil Away 1997. *Address:* c/o Democratic Unionist Party, 91 Dundela Avenue, Belfast, BT4 3BU, Northern Ireland (office). *Telephone:* (28) 9052-1323 (office). *Fax:* (28) 9052-1289((office). *E-mail:* info@dup.org.uk (office). *Website:* www.dup.org.uk (office).

PAJAZITI, Zenun; Kosovo politician; *Minister of Internal Affairs;* b. 12 Sept. 1966, Gjilan; m.; two s. one d.; ed Tech. Faculty, Univ. of Prishtina, Prishtina School of Politics, completed Int. Visitor Leadership Programme course on Accountability and Ethics in Govt and Business, sponsored by US Dept of State/US Office, Prishtina; served with Emergency Cttee of Kosovo in Prishtina with responsibility for displaced persons; worked as Programme Devt Co-ordinator with Int. Medical Corps 1999–2000; mem. Advisory Bd for Kosovo Action Together 2000–, Exec. Dir 2005–08; Jt Head, Dept of Sports within Jt Interim Admin. Structure (highest level advisory body to UN Interim Admin Mission in Kosovo—UNMIK) March–Nov. 2000, Head Nov. 2000–04; entered Govt of Kosovo 2004, served in Office of the Prime Minister as Head of Govt Liaison Office with UNMIK and Special Rep. of Sec.-Gen. and Co-ordinator for Standards; consultant, Public Administration International 2005–07, engaged in Support for European Integration and Standards Process (UK Dept for Int. Devt-funded project); Minister of Internal Affairs 2008–; mem. Partia Demokratike e Kosovës (Democratic Party of Kosovo); Pres. Bd of Volleyball Fed. of Kosovo; Vice-Pres. Olympic Cttee of Kosovo; has participated in int. seminars in Albania, Italy, Turkey and other countries. *Address:* Ministry of Internal Affairs, 10000 Prishtina, Bulevardi 'Nëna Terezë' p.n. Objekti i Qeverisë, kati IX, Kosovo (office). *Telephone:* (38) 213307 (office); (38) 20019024 (office). *E-mail:* merita.vidishiqi@ks-gov.net (office). *Website:* www.mpb-ks.org (office).

PAK, Gil-yon; North Korean diplomatist; m.; three c.; ed Univ. of Int. Relations; joined Ministry of Foreign Affairs 1964, served as Officer, Consul in Singapore and Myanmar, Section Chief, Deputy Dir, Dir of Ministry 1978–1983, Vice-Minister 1983–84, 1996–; Perm. Rep. to UN, New York 1984–96, 2001–08; Kim Il Sung Order. *Address:* c/o Ministry of Foreign Affairs, Pyongyang, Democratic People's Republic of Korea (office).

PAK, Pong-ju; North Korean politician; Minister of Chemical Industry –2003; Prime Minister of Democratic People's Repub. of Korea 2003–07. *Address:* c/o Office of the Premier, Pyongyang, Democratic People's Republic of Korea (office).

PAK, Se Ri; South Korean golfer; b. 28 Sept. 1977, Daejeon, Repub. of Korea; won 30 tournaments in Repub. of Korea as amateur; turned professional 1996; moved to USA 1997; became youngest player to capture four major tournments; 22 other Ladies Professional Golf Asscn (LPGA) victories; finished second in LPGA prize money 1998, 2001–2003; first woman in 58 years to make cut in men's golf tournament, SBS Super Tournament on Korean tour (finished tenth overall); Rolex Rookie of the Year 1998, Golf Writers Asscn of America Player of the Year 1998, Repub. of Korea Order of Merit 1998, Vare Trophy 2003, LPGA Heather Farr Award 2006, inducted into World Golf Hall of Fame 2007. *Leisure interests:* playing video games, watching television, shopping. *Address:* c/o IMG Golf Client Management, 1360 East 9th St., Suite 100, Cleveland, OH 44114-1730, USA.

PAK, Ui-chun; North Korean diplomatist; *Minister of Foreign Affairs;* began diplomatic career at Embassy in Cameroon 1972; fmr Amb. to Algeria, Syria and Lebanon; Amb. to Russian Fed. 1998–2006; Minister of Foreign Affairs

2007–. *Address:* Ministry of Foreign Affairs, Pyongyang, Democratic People's Republic of Korea (office).

PAKENHAM, Hon. Sir Michael, Kt, KBE, CMG, MA; British financial consultant and fmr diplomatist; *Senior Adviser, Access Industries; Chairman, Droege & Co.;* b. 3 Nov. 1943, Oxford; s. of the late Earl of Longford and Elizabeth Pakenham, Countess of Longford; brother of Antonia Fraser (q.v.); m. Mimi Doak; two d.; ed Ampleforth Coll., N Yorks., Trinity Coll. Cambridge, Rice Univ., Tex., USA; joined FCO 1965, served in Warsaw, New Delhi, Paris, Washington, DC; seconded to Cabinet Office 1971–74; Counsellor British Representation to EU 1987–91; Amb. to Luxembourg 1991–94; Deputy Sec. to Cabinet, Chair. Jt Intelligence Cttee and Intelligence Co-ordinator 1997–2000; Amb. to Poland 2000–03; Sr Adviser Access Industries 2004–, Signet Asset Management 2004–, Droege & Co. (Dusseldorf) 2006–; European Security Project Consultant Thales International 2004–06. *Leisure interests:* golf, tennis, museums, military history. *Address:* Cope House, 15B Kensington Palace Gardens, London, W8 4QG, England (office). *Telephone:* (20) 7908-9966 (office). *E-mail:* mpakenham@accind.co.uk (office). *Website:* www.accessindustries.com (office).

TUHEITIA, Te Arikinui; New Zealand Maori king; b. 21 April 1955; eldest son of the late Whatumoana Paki and Te Arikinui Dame Te Atairangikaahu (previous monarch); m. Atawhai; three c.; ed Rakaumanga School, Huntly, St Stephen's Coll., Bombay (now Mumbai), India; fmr univ. man. and Tainui cultural adviser to Te Wananga o Aotearoa, Huntly; chosen as king at secret meeting and crowned following his mother's funeral 21 Aug. 2006. *Address:* Tūrongo House, Tūrangawaewae marae, Ngaruawahia, Waikato, New Zealand.

PAKSAS, Rolandas; Lithuanian politician, engineer and fmr head of state; *Chairman, Order and Justice Party;* b. 10 June 1956, Telšiai; s. of Feliksas Paksas and Elena Paksienė; m. Laima Paksienė; one s. one d.; ed Žemaitės Secondary School, Telšiai, Vilnius Inst. of Civil Eng, Leningrad Inst. of Civil Aviation; flight instructor –1984; Chair. Vilnius Darius ir Girenas Aero Club, Aviation Dept, Voluntary Nat. Defence Service 1985–92; Pres. Construction Co. Restako 1992–97; elected to Vilnius City Council, Mayor of Vilnius 1997–99, 2000; Prime Minister of Lithuania 1999–2000 (resgnd), 2000–01; Adviser Pres. of Lithuania and Plenipotentiary of Pres. for Special Assignments 1999–2000; elected Chair. newly founded Liberal Democratic Party 2002– (now renamed Order and Justice Party); Pres. of Lithuania 2003–04, charged with violating the constitution and his oath of office March 2004, impeached April 2004; fmr Chair. Lithuanian Liberal Union. *Leisure interest:* aviation. *Address:* Order and Justice Party, Gedimino Ave. 10/1, Vilnius 01103 (office). *Telephone:* (5) 269-1618 (home). *Fax:* (5) 269-1618 (office). *E-mail:* tt@tvarka.lt (office). *Website:* www.tvarka.lt (office).

PÁL, László; Hungarian politician and electrical engineer; b. 5 Sept. 1942, Budapest; m.; two c.; ed Inst. of Energetics, Moscow, Political Acad., Budapest; Research Inst. for Electrical Eng 1966–69; mem. Nat. Cttee for Technological Devt 1969–89; State Sec. Ministry of Industry 1989–90; mem. of Parl. 1990–97; Minister for Industry and Trade 1994–95; Chair. Bd Hungarian Oil and Gas Co.; fmr Chief Exec. Magyar Villamos Müvek Reszvenytarsag (MVM— nat. electricity co.); Lóránd Eötvös Award 1986, János Neumann Award 1988. *Address:* Okt. 23. str. 18, 1117 Budapest, Hungary. *Telephone:* (1) 209-0101. *Fax:* (1) 209-0051.

PÁL, Lénárd; Hungarian physicist; b. 7 Nov. 1925, Gyoma; s. of Imre Pál and Erzsébet Varga; m. Angela Danóci 1963; one d.; ed Budapest and Moscow Univs; Dept Head, Cen. Research Inst. for Physics, Budapest 1953–56, Deputy Dir 1956–69, Dir 1970–74, Dir-Gen 1974–78; Prof. of Nuclear Physics, Eötvös Lóránd Univ., Budapest 1961–77, 1989–98; Pres. State Office for Tech. Devt 1978–80, 1984–85, Nat. Atomic Energy Comm. 1978–80, 1984–85; mem. Science Policy Cttee, Council of Ministers 1978–85; Sec. Cen. Cttee Hungarian Socialist Workers' Party 1985–88; fmr Vice-Pres. IUPAP; Corresp. mem. Hungarian Acad. of Sciences 1961–73, mem. 1973, Gen. Sec. 1980–84, Pres. Intercosmos Council 1980–84; Foreign mem. Acad. of Sciences of the USSR 1976, of GDR 1982, of Czechoslovakia 1983, Russian Acad. of Sciences 1996; mem. Leibniz Soc. eV 1994; Gold Medal, Order of Labour 1956, 1968, Red Banner Order of Labour (USSR) 1975, Red Banner of Work 1985; Kossuth Prize 1962, Memorial Medal 25th Anniversary of the Liberation 1970, Kurtchatov Memory Medal (USSR) 1970, Gold Medal of the Hungarian Acad. of Sciences 1975, Eötvös Lóránd Physical Soc. Medal 1976, Wigner's Award 2001. *Publications:* Science and Technical Development 1987, Science and Technology Policies in Finland and Hungary 1985, Foundation of Probability Calculus and Statistics 1995, Elements of the Probability Theory and Mathematical Statistics 1995; approx. 275 articles in Hungarian and foreign scientific journals. *Leisure interests:* hunting, angling. *Address:* Széher út 21/a, 1021 Budapest II, Hungary. *Telephone:* (1) 275-0725; (1) 167-7890. *Fax:* (1) 275-0725. *E-mail:* lpal@rmki.kfki.hu (office).

PAL, Shri Satyabrata; Indian diplomatist; *High Commissioner to Pakistan;* m.; Deputy Perm. Rep., UN, New York 1979–93, 1997–2002; Deputy Sec. and Dir, Ministry of External Affairs 1983–88; Deputy High Commr, Dhaka 1988–91; High Commr Gaborone, Botswana 1991–94; Jt Sec. Ministry of External Affairs 1994–97; Deputy High Commr, London 2002–05; High Commr to South Africa 2005–06, to Pakistan 2006–. *Address:* High Commission of India, G-5, Diplomatic Enclave, Islamabad, Pakistan (office). *Telephone:* (51) 2828375 (office). *Fax:* (51) 2823102 (office). *E-mail:* hicomind@isb.compol.com (office).

PAL SINGH, Krishna; Indian politician; b. 2 Aug. 1922, V. Birhuli, Shahdol Dist, Madhya Pradesh; politically active at school and in higher educ.; Pres. Students' Union, Rewa, organized students' congress and congress volunteer corps; worked with Sindhi refugees during communal riots of 1947–48; became follower of Bhai Paramanandji 1942, joined Quit India Movt, arrested and served prison sentence; after independence became trades union leader, continuing to campaign for causes of students, kisans, colliery workers and other labourers; Vice-Pres. MP Unit of All India Trades Union Congress; joined Socialist Party 1946 and became Pres. of party in fmr Vindya Pradesh and Pres. Samyukta Socialist Party, MP; joined Congress Party 1965; mem. AICC and MPCC, later Gen. Sec. and Vice-Pres. MPCC and special invitee AIC Working Cttee; MP Vidhan Sabha 1962–90; served five times as Minister with many different portfolios, finance, law, etc., becoming Deputy Leader; fmr Gov. of Gujarat; party and political observer gen. and party elections in Indian states; Pres. Friends of Soviet Union, India-China Soc., MP Unit of Nepal Friendship Soc., India-Africa Friendship Asscn and Gen. Sec. All India Indo-Arab Friendship Soc.

PALACIO, Alfredo, MD; Ecuadorean politician, cardiologist and fmr head of state; b. 22 Jan. 1939, Guayaquil; ed Colegio San José La Salle, Universidad de Guayaquil; worked at various hosps in USA 1969–74, including Mount Sinai Hosp., Cleveland, OH 1969–71, Veterans Admin. Hosp., Missouri 1971–72, Barnes Hosp., Washington Univ. 1972–74; Dir Nat. Inst. of Cardiology 1980–; Prin. Prof. of Cardiology, Faculty of Medicine, Univ. of Guayaquil 1989–2003, Prof. of Public Health 2001–2003; Minister of Public Health 1994–96; Vice-Pres. of Ecuador 2003–05, Pres. 2005–07; fmr Regional Dir Ecuador Inst. of Social Security (IESS); Fellow, American Coll. of Cardiology, American Coll. of Chest Physicians, American Coll. of Physicians; mem. American Acad. of Sciences, Ecuador Acad. of Medicine, and numerous other medical socs; Dr hc (John Hopkins, USA) 2007; Commdr, Al Mérito Atahualpha, Ministry of Nat. Defence 1995, Recognition of Merit, Ecuador Nat. Civil Defence 1996, Recognition of Merit, Gran Cruz, Pres. of Ecuador 1996; American Medical Asscn Award 1976, Eugenio Espejo Award, Quito Municipality 1982, Scientific Merit Award, Guayaquil Municipality 1982, 1987. *Publications include:* Atlas de Ecocardiografía Bidimensional 1981, Atlas of 2D Echocardiography 1983, Cardiopatía Isquémica (ed.) 1985, Estudio Guayaquil 1991, Hacia un Humanisco Científico 1997. *Address:* c/o Office of the President, Palacio Nacional, García Moreno 1043, Quito, Ecuador (office).

PALACIO VALLELERSUNDI, Ana; Spanish lawyer, politician and international organization official; *Senior Vice-President and General Counsel, World Bank Group;* b. 22 Aug. 1948, Madrid; ed Complutense Univ., Madrid; early career as lawyer in pvt. practice, held numerous sr positions in Madrid Bar; MEP (PPE, PP) 1994–2002, mem. Cttee on Transport and Tourism, on the Rules of Procedure, on the Verification of Credentials and Immunities, Del. for Relations with SE Europe; Chair. Cttee on Legal Affairs and the Internal Market, European Parl. 1994–2002, Justice and Home Affairs Cttee 1994–2002, Conf. of Cttee Chairs 1994–2002; Minister of Foreign Affairs 2002–04; mem. Parl. 2002–06, Chair. Jt Parl. Cttee for European Affairs 2004–06; Sr Vice-Pres. and General Counsel, World Bank Group, Washington, DC 2006–, also Sec.-Gen. Int. Centre for the Settlement of Investment Disputes; First Vice-Pres., later Pres.-elect, Council of Bars and Law Societies of the European Union, Brussels; Pres. Acad. of European Law; Trustee, Carnegie Corpn, New York; mem. Bd Council on Foreign Relations, Fundación para el Análisis y los Estudios Sociales, Fundacion para las Relaciones Internacionales y el Diálogo Exterior, CSIS Initiative for Renewed Transatlantic Partnership, Transatlantic Policy Network; mem. Bd of Govs Law Soc. of Madrid; Hon. mem. Bar of England and Wales (including the Inner Temple); Ramer Award for Diplomatic Excellence, American Jewish Cttee 2004. *Address:* The World Bank, 1818 H Street, NW, Washington, DC 20433, USA (office); Palacio & Partners SC, Plaza de las Salesas, 3, 28004 Madrid, Spain. *Telephone:* (202) 473-1000 (office). *Fax:* (202) 477-6391 (office). *Website:* www.worldbank.org (office).

PALAITIS, Raimundas, BSc; Lithuanian politician; *Minister of the Interior;* b. 21 Dec. 1957, Palanga; m.; three c.; ed Vilnius Univ.; programmer, Kaunas Inst. of Cardiology 1980–89; Founder and Dir Klaipėdos Securities 1997–2000; mem. Lithuanian Liberal Union 1994–2003, Liberal and Central Union 2003; mem. Palanga City Municipality Bd, Mayor of Palanga 2000; mem. Seimas (Parl.) 2000–08; Minister of the Interior 2008–. *Leisure interests:* music, sport. *Address:* Ministry of the Interior, Šventaragio 2, Vilnius 01510 (office); Gedimino pr. 53, Vilnius, Lithuania. *Telephone:* (5) 271-7130 (office). *Fax:* (5) 271-8551 (office). *E-mail:* korespondencija@vrm.lt (office); Raimundas.Palaitis@lrs.lt. *Website:* www.vrm.lt (office); www.palaitis.lt.

PALAU, Luis; American evangelist and writer; b. 27 Nov. 1934, Buenos Aires, Argentina; s. of Luis Palau Sr; m. Patricia Marilyn Scofield 1961; four s.; ed St Alban's Coll., Buenos Aires, Multnomah School of the Bible, Portland, Ore., USA; mem. staff Bank of London, Buenos Aires and Cordoba 1952–59; moved to USA 1960; worked as interpreter for Billy Graham 1962; began Spanish radio broadcasts as missionary in Colombia 1967; began evangelistic ministry as part of Overseas Crusades 1968; made crusade broadcasts to all Latin America 1975; named Pres. Overseas Crusades 1976; f. Luis Palau Evangelistic Asscn 1978; first major crusade in USA, San Diego 1981; Dr hc (Talbot Theological Seminary) 1977, (Wheaton Coll.) 1985. *Publications:* Heart After God 1978, My Response 1985, Time To Stop Pretending 1985, So You Want To Grow 1986, Calling America and the Nations to Christ 1994; 26 books and booklets in Spanish; works have been transl. into 30 languages. *Leisure interest:* family. *Address:* Luis Palua Evangelistic Association, POB 50, Beaverton, OR 97207, USA (office). *Telephone:* (503) 614-1500 (office). *Fax:* (503) 614-1599 (office). *E-mail:* info@palau.org (office). *Website:* www.palau.org (office).

PALECKIS, Justas Vincas; Lithuanian diplomatist and politician; b. 1 Jan. 1942, Samara (Kuibyshev), Russia; s. of Justas Paleckis and Genovaite Paleckiene; m. Laima Paleckienė; two s. one d.; ed Univ. of Vilnius, Diplomatic

Univ. of the Ministry of Foreign Affairs, USSR; contrib. Komjaunimo Tiesa (daily), Head of Dept 1960, 1963–66; Third Sec. USSR Embassy to Switzerland; Second, First Sec., Counsellor, USSR Embassy to GDR 1969–83; Deputy Dir, Dir of sector Lithuanian CP Cen. Cttee 1983–89; Sec., Ind. Lithuanian CP Cen. Cttee 1989–90; Deputy Chair. Foreign Affairs Cttee, Lithuanian Repub. Supreme Council (Parl.) 1990–92; Lecturer, Inst. of Journalism, Vilnius State Univ. 1990–93; Lecturer, Inst. of Int. Relations and Political Science, Vilnius State Univ. 1993–95; adviser on Foreign Affairs to Lithuanian Pres. 1993–96; rank of Amb. 1993–; Amb. to UK 1996–2001 (also accred to Portugal and Ireland 1997–2001); Deputy Minister of Foreign Affairs 2002–04; mem. European Parl. (Socialist Group) 2004–, Vice-Chair. Sub-cttee on Security and Defence, mem. Cttee on Foreign Affairs, Substitute mem. Cttee on the Environment, Public Health and Food Safety, Temporary Cttee on Climate Change, Del. to EU-Russia Parl. Cooperation Cttee, Del. to EU-Fmr Yugoslav Repub. of Macedonia Jt Parl. Cttee, Del. to EU-Bulgaria Jt Parl. Cttee; Kt, Royal Swedish Order of the Northern Star 1994, Lithuanian Independence Medal 2000, Commdr, Order of Merit (Lithuania) 2003. *Publications:* Swiss Pyramids 1974, At the Foot of Swiss Pyramids 1985, Life in a Triangle. Vilnius-Brussels-Strasbourg 2007. *Leisure interests:* reading, theatre, gardening, tennis, swimming. *Address:* European Parliament, Bâtiment Altiero Spinelli, ASP 13G158, 60 rue Wiertz, 1047 Brussels, Belgium (office); Europos Parlamento nario Justo Paleckio bíuras, Pylimo g. 12-10, 01118 Vilnius; K. Donelaicio 20-5, 2000 Vilnius, Lithuania (home). *Telephone:* (2) 284-79-21 (office); (5) 2635445 (home). *Fax:* (2) 284-99-21 (office). *E-mail:* justasvincas .paleckis@europarl.europa.eu (office); biuras@paleckis.lt (office). *Website:* www.europarl.europa.eu (office); www.paleckis.lt (office).

PALECZNY, Piotr; Polish pianist and academic; *Artistic Director, International Chopin Festival;* b. 10 May 1946, Rybnik; m.; one s.; ed State Higher School of Music, Warsaw (studied under Prof. Jan Ekier); f. master courses in music, Bordeaux, Amsterdam, Paris, Buenos Aires, Tokyo, Lugano, Warsaw; soloist with orchestras including Warsaw Nat. Philharmonic Orchestra, Polish Radio Nat. Symphony Orchestra, Chicago Symphony, American Symphony, Royal Philharmonic, Concertgebouw, BBC London Orchestra, Yomiuri Nippon, Tonhalle Zurich, RAI Roma, Santa Cecilia, Mexico Nat., Buenos Aires Nat., Gewandhaus, Nat. Orchestra Madrid; has performed major concert halls, including Carnegie Hall, Avery Fisher Hall and Alice Tully Hall, New York, Orchestra Hall, Chicago, Suntory Hall, Tokyo, Teatro Colon, Buenos Aires, Gewandhaus, Leipzig, Concertgebouw, Amsterdam, Royal Festival Hall, London; Artistic Dir, Int. Chopin Festival, Duszniki Zdrój 1993–; Prof. of Piano Performance, Frederick Chopin Acad. of Music, Warsaw; judge, int. music competitions in Warsaw, Paris, Santander, Tokyo, Hamamatsu, Prague, Taipei, Cleveland, London; Kt's Cross, Order of Polonia Restituta, Gold Cross of Merit; granted title of Prof. by Pres. of Poland 1998; winner, competitions in Sofia 1968, Munich 1969, Warsaw 1970, Pleven 1971, Bordeaux 1972, Grand Prix VIII Chopin Competition 1970. *Recordings include:* K. Szymanowski Concert Symphony No. 4, complete Ballads, Sonatas, and Concertos by Chopin, The Best of Fryderyk Chopin ('Fryderyk 1999' Award, Polish Phonographic Acad.), works by Paderewski, Szymanowski, Lutosławski. *Address:* International Chopin Festival, 57-340 Duszniki-Zdrój, Rynek 10, Poland (office). *Telephone:* (74) 8669280 (office). *E-mail:* chopin@festival.pl (office). *Website:* www.chopin.festival.pl (office).

PALIN, Michael Edward, CBE, BA; British actor, writer and traveller; b. 5 May 1943, Sheffield, Yorks.; s. of the late Edward Palin and Mary Palin; m. Helen M. Gibbins 1966; two s. one d.; ed Birkdale School, Sheffield, Shrewsbury School, Brasenose Coll. Oxford; Pres. Transport 2000; Dr hc (Sheffield) 1992, (Queen's, Belfast) 2000; Michael Balcon Award for outstanding contrib. to cinema (with Monty Python), BAFTA 1987, Travel Writer of the Year, British Book Awards 1993, Lifetime Achievement Award, British Comedy Awards 2002, BCA Illustrated Book of the Year Award 2002, BAFTA Special Award for Outstanding Contrib. to TV 2005, British Book Award for Outstanding Achievement 2009. *Television:* actor and writer: Monty Python's Flying Circus, BBC TV 1969–74, Ripping Yarns, BBC TV 1976–79; actor: Three Men in a Boat, BBC 1975: writer: East of Ipswich, BBC TV 1987, Number 27, BBC TV, The Weekend (play for stage) 1994; TV series: contrib. to Great Railway Journeys of the World, BBC TV 1980, 1993; presenter Around the World in 80 Days 1989, Pole to Pole 1992, Palin's Column 1994, Full Circle 1997, Michael Palin's Hemingway Adventure 1999, Sahara 2002, Himalaya with Michael Palin 2004, Michael Palin's New Europe 2007; art documentaries (presenter): Palin on Redpath 1997, The Bright Side of Life 2000, The Ladies Who Loved Matisse 2003, Michael Palin and the Mystery of Hammershoi 2005. *Musical theatre:* Monty Python's Spamalot 2006. *Films:* actor and co-author: And Now for Something Completely Different 1970, Monty Python and the Holy Grail 1974, Monty Python's Life of Brian 1979, Time Bandits 1980, Monty Python's 'The Meaning of Life' 1982; actor, writer and co-producer: The Missionary 1982; actor, co-scriptwriter: American Friends 1991; actor: Jabberwocky 1976, A Private Function 1984, Brazil 1985, A Fish Called Wanda 1988 (Best Supporting Film Actor, BAFTA Award 1988), GBH (Channel 4 TV) 1991, Fierce Creatures 1997. *Publications include:* Monty Python's Big Red Book 1970, Monty Python's Brand New Book 1973, Montypythonscrapbook 1979, Dr Fegg's Encyclopaedia of All World Knowledge 1984, Limericks 1985, Around the World in 80 Days 1989, Pole to Pole 1992, Hemingway's Chair 1995, Full Circle 1997, Michael Palin's Hemingway Adventure 1999, Sahara 2002, The Pythons Autobiography (co-author) 2003, Himalaya (British Book Award for TV & Film Book of the Year 2005) 2004, Diaries 1969–1979: The Python Years 2006, New Europe 2007; for children: Small Harry and the Toothache Pills 1981, The Mirrorstone 1986, The Cyril Stories 1986. *Leisure interests:* reading, running, railways. *Address:* Mayday Management, 34 Tavistock Street, London, WC2E 7PB, England (office). *Telephone:* (20) 7497-1100 (office). *Fax:* (20) 7497-1133 (office).

PALIN, Sarah, BS; American politician and state official; *Governor of Alaska;* b. 11 Feb. 1964, Sandpoint, Idaho; m. Todd Palin; five c.; ed Wasilla High School and Univ. of Idaho; worked briefly as journalist in media and utility industry 1992; mem. Wasilla, Alaska City Council 1992–96; Mayor and Man. of Wasilla 1996–2002; cand. for Lt-Gov. of Alaska 2002; Chair. Alaska Oil and Gas Conservation Comm. 2003–04 (resgnd); fmr Pres. Alaska Conf. of Mayors; also served on Interstate Oil and Gas Compact Comm.; Gov. of Alaska 2006– (youngest gov. in state's history and first woman to hold the office); Republican nominee for Vice-Pres. of US 2008; mem. Bd Valley Hosp., Iditarod Parent-Teacher Asscn; fmr mem. American Man. Asscn, Alaska Outdoor Council, Alaska Miner's Asscn, Alaska Resource Devt Council, Youth Court Steering Cttee, Salvation Army Bd; Lifetime mem. Nat. Rifle Asscn; fmr coach, Valley Youth Sports, hockey team man.; Hon. mem. Rotary; named Miss Wasila (beauty pageant) 1984, State Chamber 'Top 40 Under 40' Award, American Public Works Asscn Alaska Chapter Person of the Year. *Leisure interests:* hunting, fishing, snowmachining, running, Alaskan history. *Address:* Office of the Governor, PO Box 110001, Juneau, AK 99811-0001, USA (office). *Telephone:* (907) 465-3500 (office). *Fax:* (907) 465-3532 (office). *E-mail:* governor@gov.state.ak.us (office). *Website:* www.gov.state.ak.us (office); www .sarahpac.com.

PALIS, Jacob, PhD; Brazilian mathematician and academic; *Director Emeritus, Instituto de Matemática Pura e Aplicada (IMPA);* b. 15 March 1940, Uberaba; s. of Jacob Palis and Sames Palis; m.; three c.; ed Fed. Univ. of Rio de Janeiro, Univ. of California, Berkeley, USA; Prof., Instituto de Matemática Pura e Aplicada (IMPA), Rio de Janeiro 1971–, Dir 1993–2003, Dir Emer. 2003–; Visiting Prof. Univ. of Warwick, Inst. des Hautes Etudes Scientifiques, France, Univ. of Dijon, Ecole Polytechnique, Paris, City Univ. of New York, Steklov Inst., Moscow, ETH-Zurich, Univs of Nagoya, Tokyo, Kyoto, Toulouse, Rome, Paris-Orsay, Nice, Collège de France 1969–94; Chair. Int. Center for Theoretical Council (ICTP), Trieste, Italy 2003–05, mem. Scientific Cttee 1993–2005; mem. Exec. Bd Int. Math. Union 1982–91, Sec. 1991–99, Pres. 1999–2002; mem. Exec. Bd Int. Council for Science 1993–96, Vice-Pres. 1996–99; mem. Scientific Advisory Cttee, ETH, Zürich 1990–2006, Scientific and Strategic Council, Collège de France 2003–(08); Founding Mem. Latin American and Caribean Math. Union 1995; Guggenheim Fellow 1993; mem. Brazilian Acad. of Sciences 1970 (Vice-Pres. 2004–07), Third World Acad. of Sciences (now Acad. of Sciences for the Developing World) 1991 (Sec.-Gen. 2004–06), Indian Acad. of Sciences 1995, Chilean Acad. of Sciences 1997, Mexican Acad. of Sciences 2001, US Nat. Acad. of Sciences 2002, French Acad. of Sciences 2002, European Acad. of Sciences 2004, Norwegian Acad. of Sciences 2005, Russian Acad. of Sciences 2006; Hon. mem. Peruvian Math. Soc.,; Chevalier de la Légion d'honneur 2005; Dr hc (State Univ. of Rio de Janeiro) 1993, (Univ. of Chile) 1996, (Univ. of Warwick) 2000, (Univ. of Santiago de Chile) 2000, (Universidad de la Habana) 2001, (Universidad de Ingenieria, Peru) 2003; Prize Moinho Santista 1976, Math. Prize, Third World Acad. of Sciences 1988, Grand-Croix National Order of Scientific Merit, Brazil, 1994, Nat. Prize for Science and Tech., Brazil 1990, Inter-American Prize for Science, OAS 1995, Prize Mexico for Science and Technology 2001, Trieste Science Prize in Math. (co-winner with C.S. Seshadri) 2006; honoured for contribution to science by Brazil UNESCO in its 60th annniversary 2006. *Publications:* Geometric Theory of Dynamical Systems (with W. de Melo) 1982, Hyperbolicity and Sensitive-Chaotic Dynamics and Homoclinic Bifurcations, Fractal Dimensions and Infinitely Many Attractors (with F. Takens) 1994; numerous scientific papers. *Address:* Instituto Matemática Pura e Aplicada, Estrada Dona Castorina 110, Jardim Botânico, 22460-320 Rio de Janeiro, RJ, Brazil (office). *Telephone:* (21) 2529-5270 (office). *Fax:* (21) 512-4112 (office). *E-mail:* jpalis@impa.br (office). *Website:* w3.impa.br/~jpalis (office).

PALLANT, John, BA; British advertising executive; *European Creative Director, Saatchi & Saatchi;* b. 10 Aug. 1955; s. of Dennis Pallant and Doreen Pallant (née Hirst); ed St John's Coll., Southsea, Univ. of Reading; copywriter, Griffin & George Ltd 1977, Acroyd Westwood Assocs 1977, Collett Dickenson Pearce 1980, Gold Greenless Trott 1982, Boase Massimi Politt 1978, copywriter and creative group head 1983; copywriter, Saatchi & Saatchi 1988, Group Head 1991, Deputy Creative Dir and Exec. Bd Dir 1995, Creative Dir 1996–97, Jt Exec. Creative Dir 1997–98, Deputy Exec. Creative Dir 1999–; European Creative Dir 2003–; numerous awards. *Address:* Saatchi & Saatchi, 80 Charlotte Street, London, W1A 1AQ, England (office). *Telephone:* (20) 7636-5060 (office). *Fax:* (20) 7637-8489 (office). *Website:* www.saatchi.com (office).

PALLASMAA, Juhani Uolevi; Finnish architect and academic; *Principal, Juhani Pallasmaa Architects;* b. 14 Sept. 1936, Hämeenlinna; s. of Harry Alexander Pallasmaa and Aili Pallasmaa (née Kannisto); m. 1st 1957; two d.; m. 2nd Hannele Jäämeri 1980; one s. one d.; ed Helsinki Univ. of Tech.; Dir Exhbn Dept, Museum of Finnish Architecture, Helsinki 1968–72, 1974–83, Dir of Museum 1978–83; Rector Coll. of Crafts and Design, Helsinki 1970–72; Assoc. Prof., Haile Selassie Univ., Addis Ababa, Ethiopia 1972–74; Prin. own architectural practice, Juhani Pallasmaa Architects, Helsinki 1983–; State Artist Prof., Helsinki 1983–88; Prof., Faculty of Architecture, Univ. of Tech., Helsinki 1991–97; Eero Saarinen Visiting Prof., Yale Univ., New Haven, Conn., USA 1993; Raymond E. Maritz Visiting Prof. of Architecture, Washington Univ., St Louis, Mo., USA 1999–2004; participant in numerous exhbns of architecture and visual arts, designer numerous nat. and int. exhbns of architecture and visual arts, on town planning, architecture, design and visual arts; Dr hc (Helsinki Univ. of Industrial Arts) 1993, (Helsinki Univ. of Tech.) 1998, (Estonian Art Acad.) 2004; Kt, Order of White Rose 1988, Commdr, Order of the White Rose 1997; Finnish State Award for Architecture 1992, Helsinki City Culture Award 1993, Russian Fed. Architecture Award 1996, Fritz Schumacher Prize for Architecture, Germany 1997, Int. Union of Architects Jean Tschumi Prize for Architectural Criticism 1999, Finland

Award 2000. *Publications:* Language of Wood 1987, Animal Architecture 1995, The Melnikov House 1996, The Eyes of the Skin: Architecture and the Senses 1996, 2005, Alvar Aalto, Villa Mairea 1938–39 1998, Architecture of Image: Existential Space in Cinema 2001, Sensuous Minimalism 2002, Encounters: Architectural Essays 2005, The Thinking Hand: Embodied and Existential Wisdom in Architecture 2009. *Leisure interests:* philosophy and psychology of artistic phenomena. *Address:* Tehtaankatu 13 B 28, 00140 Helsinki (office); Huvilakatu 14 A 8, 00150 Helsinki, Finland (home). *Telephone:* (9) 669740 (office); (9) 666625 (home). *Fax:* (9) 669741 (office). *E-mail:* juhani.pallasmaa@pallasmaa.fi (office); office@pallasmaa.fi (office). *Website:* www.pallasmaa.fi (office).

PALLISER, Rt Hon. Sir (Arthur) Michael, GCMG, PC, MA, FRSA; British diplomatist; *Vice-Chairman, Salzburg Global Seminar;* b. 9 April 1922, Reigate, Surrey; s. of the late Admiral Sir Arthur Palliser, KCB, DSC and of Lady Palliser (née Margaret E. King-Salter); m. Marie M. Spaak (d. of the late Paul-Henri Spaak) 1948 (died 2000); three s.; ed Wellington Coll. and Merton Coll., Oxford; war service in Coldstream Guards (mentioned in despatches) 1942–46; entered diplomatic service 1947; Foreign Office 1947–49, 1951–56; posted to Athens 1949–51, Paris 1956–60; Head of Chancery, Dakar 1960–62; Counsellor and seconded to Imperial Defence Coll. 1963; Head of Planning Staff, Foreign Office 1964; a Pvt. Sec. to Prime Minister 1966–69; Minister, Paris 1969–71; Amb. and Head, UK Del. to EEC 1971–72; Amb. and UK Perm. Rep. to EC 1973–75; Perm. Under-Sec., Head of Diplomatic Service 1975–82; Chair. Council, Int. Inst. for Strategic Studies 1983–90; Deputy Chair. Midland Bank PLC 1987–91; Deputy Chair. Midland Montagu (Holdings) 1987–93; Vice-Chair. Samuel Montagu and Co. Ltd 1983–84, 1993–96 (Chair. 1984–85, 1986–93); Dir Arbor Acres Farm Inc., Booker PLC, BAT Industries PLC, Eagle Star (Holdings), Shell Transport and Trading Co. PLC 1983–92, United Biscuits PLC 1983–89; Pres. China-Britain Trade Group 1992–96; Deputy Chair. British Invisible Exports Council 1987–95; Dir XCL Ltd 1994–2000; Chair. Major Projects Asscn 1994–98; Vice-Chair. Salzburg Global Seminar 1996–; Pres. Int. Social Service (UK) 1982–96; Chair. City and E London Confed. of Medicine and Dentistry 1989–95; Gov. Wellington Coll. 1982–92; mem. Security Comm. 1983–92; mem. Bd Royal Nat. Theatre 1988–96; Assoc. Fellow, Centre for Int. Affairs, Harvard Univ. 1982; Hon. Fellow, Merton Coll. Oxford 1986, Queen Mary Coll. London 1990; Chevalier, Order of Orange-Nassau 1944; Chevalier, Légion d'honneur 1957, Commdr 1996. *Leisure interests:* travel, theatre. *Address:* 12B Wedderburn Road, London, NW3 5QG, England (home). *Telephone:* (20) 7794-0440 (home). *Fax:* (20) 7916-2163 (home).

PALMER, Andrew Clennel, PhD, FRS, FREng, FICE; British civil engineer and academic; *Managing Director, Bold Island Engineering Ltd;* b. 26 May 1938, Colchester; s. of Gerald Basil Coote Palmer and Muriel Gertrude Palmer (née Howes); m. Jane Rhiannon Evans 1963; one d.; ed Cambridge Univ., Brown Univ., USA; lecturer, Univ. of Liverpool 1965–67, Univ. of Cambridge 1968–75; Chief Pipeline Engineer, R. J. Brown & Assocs 1975–79, Vice-Pres. Eng 1982–85; Prof. of Civil Eng, UMIST 1979–82; Man. Dir and Tech. Dir Andrew Palmer & Assocs 1985–96; Research Prof. of Petroleum Eng, Cambridge Univ. 1996–2005; Fellow Churchill Coll., Cambridge 1996–. *Publications:* Structural Mechanics 1976, Subsea Pipeline Engineering (with R. A. King) 2004; papers in learned journals. *Leisure interests:* travel, languages, glassblowing. *Address:* 49 Ashley Gardens, Ambrosden Avenue, London SW1P 1QF, England. *Telephone:* (20) 7828-8843 (office). *E-mail:* acp24@eng.cam.ac.uk (office). *Website:* www.eng.cam.ac.uk (office).

PALMER, Arnold Daniel; American professional golfer and business executive; b. 10 Sept. 1929, Latrobe, Pa; s. of Milfred J. Palmer and Doris Palmer; m. 1st Winifred Walzer 1954 (died 1999); two d.; m. 2nd Kathleen Gawthrop 2005; ed Wake Forest Univ., NC; US Coast Guard 1950–53; US Amateur Golf Champion 1954; professional golfer 1954–; winner of 92 professional titles, including British Open 1961, 1962, US Open 1960, US Masters 1958, 1960, 1962, 1964, Canadian PGA 1980, US Srs Championship 1981; mem. US Ryder Cup team 1961, 1963, 1965, 1967, 1971, 1973, Captain 1963, 1975; joined Seniors (Champions) Tour 1980, finished first 10 times; Pres. Arnold Palmer Enterprises, one automobile agency, Latrobe Country Club, Bay Hill Club; Chair. Latrobe Area Hospital Charitable Foundation; Hon. Nat. Chair. Nat. Foundation March of Dimes 1971–90; consultant Golf Channel; mem. of numerous golf clubs including Royal and Ancient and Hon. Life mem. Carnoustie, Royal Birkdale, Royal Troon; designer numerous golf courses; Hon. LLD (Wake Forest, Nat. Coll. of Educ.); Hon. DH (Thiel Coll.); Hon. DHL (Fla Southern Coll., St Vincent Coll.); Athlete of Decade, Associated Press 1970; Sportsman of the Year, Sports Illustrated 1960; Hickok Belt, Professional Athlete of Year 1960. *Publications:* My Game and Yours 1965, Situation Golf 1970, Go for Broke 1973, Arnold Palmer's Best 54 Golf Holes 1977, Arnold Palmer's Complete Book of Putting 1986, Play Great Golf 1987, Arnold Palmer: A Personal Journey (with Thomas Hauser) 1994, A Golfer's Life (with James Dodson) 1999, Playing by the Rules 2002, Memories, Stories and Memorabilia 2004. *Leisure interests:* bridge, occasional hunting, fishing, aviation, business, clubmaking. *Address:* PO Box 52, Youngstown, PA 15696, USA (Home and Office). *Telephone:* (724) 537-7751 (office); (724) 537-7751 (home). *Fax:* (724) 537-9355 (office). *Website:* www.arnoldpalmer.com.

PALMER, Frank Robert, MA, DLitt, FBA; British academic; *Professor Emeritus of Linguistic Science, University of Reading;* b. 9 April 1922, Westerleigh, Glos.; s. of George Samuel Palmer and Gertrude Lilian Palmer (née Newman); m. Jean Elisabeth Moore 1948; three s. two d.; ed Bristol Grammar School, New Coll., Oxford, Merton Coll., Oxford; Lecturer in Linguistics, SOAS, Univ. of London 1950–60; Prof. of Linguistics, Univ. Coll. of North Wales, Bangor 1960–65; Prof. of Linguistic Science, Univ. of Reading 1965–87, Dean, Faculty of Letters and Social Sciences 1969–72, Prof. Emer. 1987–; Vice-Pres., Philological Soc.; Chair. Linguistics Asscn (GB) 1965–68, Ed. Journal of Linguistics 1969–79, Linguistic Soc. of America Prof., Buffalo, USA 1971; Distinguished Visiting Prof. Univ. of Delaware, Newark, USA 1982; mem. Academia Europaea 1992; Hon. DLitt 1997. *Publications:* The Morphology of the Tigre Noun 1962, A Linguistic Study of the English Verb 1965, Selected Papers of J. R. Firth (1951–58) (ed.) 1968, Prosodic Analysis (ed.) 1970, Grammar 1971, 1984, The English Verb 1974, 1987, Semantics 1976, 1981, Modality and the English Modals 1979, 1990, Mood and Modality 1986, 2001, Studies in the History of Western Linguistics in Honour of R. H. Robins (co-ed.) 1986, Grammatical Roles and Relations 1994, Grammar and Meaning: Essays in Honour of Sir John Lyons (ed.) 1995, Modality in Contemporary English (co-ed.) 2003, English Modality in Perspective (co-ed.) 2004. *Leisure interests:* gardening, crosswords. *Address:* 'Whitethorns', Roundabout Lane, Winnersh, Wokingham, Berks., RG41 5AD, England (home). *Telephone:* (118) 978-6214 (home). *E-mail:* llspalmf@reading.ac.uk (home).

PALMER, Geoff (Godfrey) Henry Oliver, DSc, PhD OBE, FRSA; British (b. Jamaican) academic; *Professor of Brewing, Heriot-Watt University;* b. 1940, St Elizabeth, Jamaica; m.; three c.; ed Kingston Senior School, Leicester Univ., Heriot-Watt Univ.; researcher and later Sr Scientist, Brewing Research Foundation, British Brewing Soc., Surrey 1968–77; Lecturer, Heriot-Watt Univ. 1977–, Prof. of Brewing 1989–; visiting Prof., Kyoto Univ., Japan; mem. Exec. and Hon. Pres., Edinburgh and Lothian Racial Equality Council; fellow, numerous learned socs; American Soc. of Brewing Chemists Award 1998, Good Citizen of Edinburgh Award 2002. *Publications:* Mr White and the Ravens; over 150 scientific papers. *Leisure interests:* reading, pop music, travel. *Address:* School of Life Sciences, Heriot-Watt University, Riccarton, Edinburgh, EH14 4AS, Scotland (office). *Telephone:* (131) 451-3461 (office). *Fax:* (131) 451-3009. *E-mail:* g.h.palmer@hw.ac.uk. *Website:* www.bio.hw.ac.uk.

PALMER, Rt Hon. Sir Geoffrey Winston Russell, KCMG, PC, AC, BA, LLB, JD; New Zealand fmr politician, academic and lawyer; *President, New Zealand Law Commission;* b. 21 April 1942, Nelson; s. of Leonard R. Palmer and Jessie P. Palmer; m. Margaret E. Hinchcliff 1963; one s. one d.; ed Nelson Coll., Victoria Univ. of Wellington and Univ. of Chicago; solicitor, Wellington 1964–66; Lecturer in Political Science, Vic. Univ. 1968–69; Prof. of Law, Univ. of Iowa and Univ. of Va, USA 1969–73; Prof. of English and New Zealand Law, Victoria Univ. 1974–79, Prof. of Law 1991–95; Prin. Asst to Australian Nat. Comm. of Inquiry on Rehabilitation and Compensation 1973; Visiting Fellow, Wolfson Coll., Oxford 1978; MP for Christchurch Cen. 1979–90; Deputy Leader, NZ Labour Party 1983–89; Deputy Prime Minister, Minister of Justice and Attorney-Gen. 1984–89; Minister for the Environment 1987–90; Prime Minister of NZ 1989–90; Minister in Charge of NZ Security Intelligence; Prof. of Law, Victoria Univ. 1991–95; Prof. of Law, Univ. of Iowa 1991–95, Ida Beam Distinguished Visiting Prof. of Law 1991; Partner, Chen, Palmer & Partners, Wellington 1994–2005; Pres. NZ Law Comm. 2005–; Dr hc (Victoria Univ. of Wellington, Washington Univ. St Louis, Hofstra Univ.) UNEP Global 500 Laureate 1991. *Publications:* Unbridled Power?: An Interpretation of New Zealand's Constitution and Government 1979, Compensation for Incapacity: A Study of Law and Social Change in Australia and New Zealand 1979, Environmental Politics: A Greenprint for New Zealand 1990, New Zealand's Constitution in Crisis 1992, Public Law in New Zealand (with Mai Chen) 1993, Environment: The International Challenge 1995, Bridled Power 1997. *Leisure interests:* cricket, golf, playing the trumpet, fishing. *Address:* 63 Roxburgh Street, Mount Victoria, Wellington (home); Law Commission, PO Box 2590, Level 10, 89 The Terrace, Wellington, New Zealand (office). *Telephone:* (4) 8015185 (home); (4) 9144815 (office). *Fax:* (4) 4710959 (office). *E-mail:* geoffrey.palmer@xtra.co.nz (home); gpalmer@lawcom.govt.nz (office). *Website:* www.lawcom.govt.nz (office).

PALMER, Thomas Joseph, CBE, MA; British business executive; b. 11 Sept. 1931, Cheddar; m. Hilary Westrup 1955; two s. two d.; ed King's School, Bruton and Trinity Coll. Cambridge; Gen. Man. (Admin.), Legal & General Group PLC 1972–78, Gen. Man. (Int.) 1978–84, Group Chief Exec. 1984–91, Dir 1972–91; Chair. Asscn of British Insurers 1989–91, Laser Richmount Ltd 1991–93, Personal Investment Authority 1993–2000; fmr Chair. Springman Tipper Campbell Partnership (now STC Partners Ltd); Dir Nat. Power PLC 1991–96, SIB, Halifax Bldg Soc. 1991–93, Sedgwick Group PLC, Investors Compensation Scheme 1992–93; Hon. Fellow, London Business School. *Leisure interests:* mountain walking, langlauf, gardening, reading.

PALMISANO, Samuel J.; American business executive; *Chairman, President and CEO, International Business Machines Corporation (IBM);* ed Johns Hopkins Univ., Baltimore, Md; joined Int. Business Machines Corpn (IBM), Baltimore, Md 1973, subsequently Sr Man. Dir of Operations, IBM Japan, Pres., CEO ISSC (IBM subsidiary) 1993, mem. Worldwide Man. Council IBM 1994, in charge of IBM's strategic outsourcing business 1995, Sr Vice-Pres. and Group Exec. Enterprise Systems Group, IBM Global Services, Personal Systems Group, mem. Corp. Exec. Cttee 1998, Pres. and COO 2000–02, Chair., Pres. and CEO IBM Corpn 2002–; mem. Bd of Dirs Gannett Co. Inc. *Address:* International Business Machines Corporation, 1 New Orchard Road, Armonk, NY 10504-1722, USA (office). *Telephone:* (914) 499-1900 (office). *Fax:* (914) 765-7382 (office). *E-mail:* info@ibm.com (office). *Website:* www.ibm.com (office).

PALOCCI, António Filho; Brazilian politician and physician; b. 4 Oct. 1960; s. of António Palocci and Antonia de Castro Palocci; m. Margareth Rose Silva Palocci; one s. two d.; ed Univ. of São Paulo; physician specializing in preventive medicine; mem. Partido dos Trabalhadores 1980–, Municipal Party Exec. 1988–89, Regional Party Directorate 1990–91 (Pres. 1997–99), Nat. Party Directorate 1996–97, Deputy Leader 2000; Pres. Rocha Lima Centre,

Univ. of São Paulo 1981; Regional Dir DCE Alexandre Vanucci Leme, Univ. of São Paulo 1982; Pres. Ass. Resident Physicians of Ribeirão Pret 1984–85; Regional Dir SIMESP 1985; Pres. Regional CUT Ribeirão Preto 1985; Regional Dir Sanitary Monitoring Service São Paulo 1986–88; Mayor of Ribeirão Preto 1993–96, 2001–02; Fed. Deputy 1999–2000, 2007–; Co-ordinator Govt transition team Oct.–Dec. 2002; Minister of Finance 2003–06; Pres. Conselho Monetário Nacional 2003–06; UNICEF Child and Peace Prize 1995, Juscelino Kubitschek Prize, Serviço Brasileiro de Apoio às Micro e Pequenas Empresas–SEBRAE 1996. *Publications include:* Saúde do trabalhador (Health of the Worker) 1994, A reforma do Estado e os municípios: a experiência de Ribeirão Preto (State and City Reform: The Experience of Ribeirão Preto) 1996, Sobre Formigas e Cigarras (autobiography) 2007. *Address:* Gabinete 548, Anexo IV, Câmara dos Deputados, Praça dos Três Poderes, 70160-900, Brasília, DF, Brazil (office). *Telephone:* (61) 3215-5548 (office). *Fax:* (61) 3215-2548 (office). *E-mail:* dep.antoniopalocci@camara.gov.br (office). *Website:* www.camara.gov.br (office).

PALOUŠ, Radim, PhD; Czech university rector (retd); b. 6 Nov. 1924, Prague; s. of Jan A. Palouš and Marie Paloušová; m. Anna Štausová 1949; two s.; ed Charles Univ. of Prague, Pedagogical Univ.; mem. student anti-Nazi resistance movt; Lecturer in Analytical Chem., Faculty of Natural Sciences 1957–59, Inst. of Univ. Studies, Tech. Univ. of Prague; after 1959 suffered intermittent persecution from Communist regime; Chair. Educ. Techniques Dept, Faculty of Pedagogics, Prague 1968–69; Charter 77 spokesman; Rector Charles Univ. 1990–94; Vice-Chair. Czechoslovak Asscn of the Roman Club 1991–; mem. numerous acads and orgs; Dr hc (Pittsburgh) 1990, (Omaha) 1990, (Int. Acad. for Philosophy) 1991, (Cracow) 1991, (Moravian Coll., USA) 1991, (York) 1992, Seoul 1993, (Edin.) 1993, (Pardubice) 2008; Czechoslovak Acad. of Sciences Prize 1990, mem. Pontificum Concilium de Kultura (awarded by Pope John Paul II) 1990–2003, Comenius Scheidegger Prize, Netherlands 1992, T.G. Masaryk Order 1997. *Publications include:* Die Schule den Alten 1979, The Time of Education 1983, The Czech Experience 1994, Das Weltzeitalter 1993, Totalism and Holism 1995, Letters to Godchildren of the Present Age 2001, Ars docenti (The Art of Teaching) 2004, Globalization 2005, Adventure of My Life 2006, Heretic School 2008. *Address:* Charles University, Ovocný trh 3-5, 116 36 Prague 1, Czech Republic (office). *E-mail:* rpalous@ruk.cuni.cz (office).

PALSSON, Gunnar, PhD; Icelandic diplomatist; *Ambassador to India;* b. 25 Jan. 1955; m. Elín Snorradóttir; four c.; ed Univ. Coll. Dublin, Ireland, Karl Eberhardt Univ., Tübingen, Germany, State Univ. of New York, Buffalo, USA; First Sec., Ministry of Foreign Affairs, Reykjavík 1984-86, officer, Div. of Political Affairs, NATO Int. Staff, Brussels 1986–88, Counsellor, Ministry of Foreign Affairs 1988–90, Amb. to CSCE, Negotiations on Confidence and Security-Building Measures and Negotiations on Conventional Forces in Europe, Vienna 1991–92, Deputy Perm. Under-Sec. for Political Affairs, Ministry of Foreign Affairs 1992–94, Dir Dept of Natural Resources and Environmental Affairs –1996, Amb. and Perm. Rep. to UN, New York 1994–98, to NATO and WEU, Brussels and the Org. for the Prohibition of Chemical Weapons (OPCW), The Hague 1998–2002, Chair. Senior Arctic Officials, Arctic Council 2002–04, Amb. to India Jan. 2007– (also accred to Singapore Sept. 2007–). *Address:* Embassy of Iceland, 11 Aurangzeb Road, New Delhi 110011, India (office). *Telephone:* (11) 4353-0300 (office). *Fax:* (11) 4240-3001 (office). *E-mail:* emb.newdelhi@mfa.is (office); gunnar.palsson@utn.stjr.is (office). *Website:* www.mfa.is (office).

PÁLSSON, Thorsteinn; Icelandic politician and diplomatist; *Co-Editor, Fréttablaðið;* b. 29 Oct. 1947; m. Ingibjörg Rafnar; three c.; ed Commercial Coll., Reykjavik and Univ. of Iceland; Chair. Vaka (student's union) 1969–70; Ed. Vísir 1975; Dir Confed. of Icelandic Employers 1979–83; mem. Parl. 1983–99; Chair. Independence Party 1983–91; Minister of Finance 1985–87, Prime Minister of Iceland 1987–88, Minister of Fisheries 1991–99, of Justice 1991–99, also of Ecclesiastical Affairs –1999; Amb. to UK 1999–2002, to Denmark 2003–05; co-Ed. Fréttablaðið (daily newspaper) 2006–. *Address:* Fréttablaðið (The Newspaper), Útgáfufélagið Frétt ehf, Suðurgata 10, 101 Reykjavík, Iceland (office). *Telephone:* 5157500 (office). *E-mail:* ristjorn@frettabladid.is (office). *Website:* www.frettabladid.is (office).

PALTRIDGE, Garth William, PhD, FAA; Australian research scientist; b. 24 April 1940, Brisbane; s. of T. B. Paltridge and A. T. Savage; m. Kay L. Petty 1965; one s. one d.; ed Brisbane Boys' Coll. and Queensland and Melbourne Univs; Postdoctoral Fellow, New Mexico Tech. 1965; Sr Scientific Officer RSRS, UK 1966; research scientist, CSIRO Div. of Meteorological Physics 1967; Exec. Dir PIECE of Australian Inst. of Petroleum 1980; Chief Research Scientist, CSIRO Div. of Atmospheric Research 1981–89; Dir Co-operative Research Centre for Antarctic and Southern Ocean Environment, Univ. of Tasmania 1991–2002; WMO Research Prize. *Publications:* Radiative Processes in Meteorology and Climatology; 100 research papers on environmental topics. *Leisure interests:* golf, history, furniture and cabinet making. *Address:* c/o Inst. of Antarctic and Southern Ocean Studies, University of Tasmania, GPO 252-80, Hobart, Tasmania 7001 (office); 9 Waymouth Avenue, Sandy Bay, Tasmania 7005, Australia (home).

PALTROW, Gwyneth; American actress; b. 28 Sept. 1972, Los Angeles; d. of the late Bruce Paltrow and of Blythe Danner; m. Chris Martin 2003; one d. one s.; ed Spence School, New York and Univ. of California, Santa Barbara. *Films include:* Flesh and Bone 1993, Hook, Moonlight and Valentino, The Pallbearer, Seven, Emma 1996, Sydney 1996, Kilronan, Great Expectations 1998, Sliding Doors 1998, Hush 1998, A Perfect Murder 1998, Shakespeare in Love (Acad. Award for Best Actress) 1998, The Talented Mr Ripley 1999, Duets 2000, Bounce 2000, The Intern 2000, The Anniversary Party 2001, The Royal Tennenbaums 2001, Shallow Hal 2001, Austin Powers in Goldmember (cameo) 2002, Possession 2002, View from the Top 2003, Sylvia 2003, Sky Captain and the World of Tomorrow 2004, Proof 2005, Love and Other Disasters 2006, Running with Scissors 2006, The Good Night 2007, Iron Man 2008. *Play:* Proof (Donmar Warehouse, London) 2002. *Address:* c/o Rick Kurtzman, CAA, 9830 Wilshire Boulevard, Beverly Hills, CA 90212; Screen Actors Guild, 5757 Wilshire Boulevard, Los Angeles, CA 90036, USA.

PALTSEV, Mikhail Alexandrovich, DrMed; Russian pathologist; *Rector and Head of Pathology Department, Moscow Sechenov Academy of Medicine;* b. 9 Nov. 1949, Russia; m.; one d.; ed 1st Moscow Sechenov Inst. of Medicine; Prof., Moscow Sechenov Acad. of Medicine; active as pathology anatomist and organizer of medical sciences; mem. Presidium Russian Acad. of Sciences; Pres. Asscn of Medical and Pharmaceutical Educ.; Ed.-in-Chief Molecular Medicine, Pathology Archives; mem. Int. Acad. of Pathology, Exec. Cttee European Soc. of Pathology; Rector and Head of Pathology Dept, Moscow Sechenov Acad. of Medicine; Order of Friendship Between Peoples, USSR State Prize 1991, Order for Service to the Fatherland, Rank IV 1999; Russian Govt's Prize 2000, 2006. *Publications:* Pathological Anatomy (with N. Anichkov) 2001, 2005, Pathology (textbook, co-author) 2002, Intercellular Interactions (co-author) 2003. *Address:* Moscow Sechenov Academy of Medicine, Trubetskaya str. 8–2, 119991 Moscow, Russia (office). *Telephone:* (495) 248-05-53 (office). *Fax:* (495) 248-02-14 (office). *E-mail:* mma-sechenov@mtu-net.ru. *Website:* www.mma.ru (office).

PALUMBO, Baron (Life Peer), cr. 1991, of Walbrook in the City of London; **Peter Garth Palumbo,** MA; British property developer; b. 20 July 1935, London; s. of Rudolph Palumbo and Elsie Palumbo; m. 1st Denia Wigram 1959 (died 1986), one s. two d.; m. 2nd Hayat Morowa 1986, one s. two d.; ed Eton Coll. and Worcester Coll., Oxford; Gov. LSE 1976–94; Hon. mem. Emmanuel Coll., Cambridge 1994–; Trustee, Mies van der Rohe Archive 1977–, The Tate Gallery 1978–85, Whitechapel Art Gallery Foundation 1981–87; Trustee and Hon. Treas. Writers and Scholars Educational Trust 1984–99; Chair. The Tate Gallery Foundation 1986–87, Painshill Park Trust Appeal 1986–96; Chair. The Arts Council of GB 1989–94; Chair. Pritzker Architecture Prize Jury 2004–; Chancellor Univ. of Portsmouth 1992–; mem. bd and Dir Andy Warhol Foundation for the Arts 1994–97; Trustee Natural History Museum 1994–2007, Design Museum 1995–2005; mem. Council, Royal Albert Hall 1995–99; Gov. RSC 1995–2000, Whitgift School 2002–; Hon. FRIBA 1986; Hon. Fellow Inst. of Structural Eng 1994; mem. Livery, Salters' Co. 1965; Dr hc (Portsmouth) 1993; Nat. Order of Southern Cross, Brazil; Cranbrook Patronage of the Arts Award, Detroit, USA 2002. *Leisure interests:* music, travel, gardening, reading. *Address:* 2 Astell Street, London, SW3 3RU, England (home). *Telephone:* (20) 7351-7371 (home). *Fax:* (20) 7352-5660 (home).

PAMFILOVA, Ella Aleksandrovna; Russian politician; *Chairperson, Presidential Council for Assisting the Development of Civil Society and Human Rights Institutions;* b. 12 Sept. 1953, Tashkent Region, Uzbekistan; d. of Aleksandr Lekomtsev and Polina Lekomtseva; m. 1st Nikita Leonidovich Pamfilov 1976 (divorced 1993); one d.; m. 2nd; ed Moscow Inst. of Power Eng; foreman at cen. factory Mosenergo, Chair. of trade union at factory 1981–89; USSR People's Deputy 1989–91; Sec. Comm. of Supreme Soviet on Privileges Jan.–Nov. 1991; Russian Fed. Minister for Social Security 1991–94; mem. State Duma (Parl.) 1993–99, mem. Cttee on Security 1995–98; Chair. Council on Social Policy under Presidential Admin. 1994; Founder and Head Movt for Healthy Russia (later Movt for Civic Dignity) 1996; Chair. Presidential Comm. on Human Rights 2002–08; Chair. Council for Assisting the Devt of Civil Society and Human Rights Insts 2009–; Pres. Acad. Revival. *Leisure interest:* gardening. *Address:* Civil Society Institutions and Human Rights Council, 103132 Moscow, 4, Staraya Square, Russia (office). *Telephone:* (495) 606-49-14 (office). *E-mail:* sovetpamfilova@yandex.ru (office).

PAMPURO, José Juan Bautista, MD; Argentine politician and physician; *Provisional President of the Senate;* b. 28 Dec. 1949, Buenos Aires; m.; three d.; ed Univ. of Buenos Aires; Sec. of Health, Lanús Municipality 1983–87; elected Nat. Deputy for Justice, Buenos Aires Prov. 1987–91; Minister of Health and Social Action, Buenos Aires Prov. 1991–92; in pvt. medical practice 1992–95; Gov. of Buenos Aires 1995–99; re-elected Nat. Deputy 1999–2002; Gen. Coordinator for Pres. Eduardo Duhalde 2002; Sec.-Gen. of the Nat. Presidency 2002–04; Minister of Defence 2004–05; Provisional Pres. of the Senate 2006–. *Address:* Senate, 1328 Buenos Aires, Argentina (office). *E-mail:* jose.pampuro@senado.gov.ar (office). *Website:* www.senado.gov.ar (office).

PAMUK, Orhan; Turkish novelist; b. 7 June 1952, Istanbul; m. Aylin Turegen 1982 (divorced 2001); one d.; ed Robert Coll., Istanbul Technical Univ., Inst. of Journalism at Istanbul Univ.; jury mem. Cannes Film Festival 2007; mem. American Acad. of Arts and Sciences 2008–, Chinese Acad. for Social Sciences 2008–; Dr hc (American Univ. of Beirut) 2003, (Georgetown Univ.) 2007, Bogaziçi Univ.) 2007, (Tilburg Univ.) 2007, (Free Univ. of Berlin) 2007, (Univ. of Bucharest) 2008, (Madrid Univ.) 2008; Milliyet Press Novel Contest, first prize 1979, Orhan Kemal Novel Prize 1983, Prix de la Découverte Européenne 1991, Ricardo-Huch Prize 2005, Nobel Prize in Literature 2006, Distinguished Humanist Award, Washington Univ. 2006, Puterbaugh Award 2006, Ovid Award 2008. *Publications:* Cevdet Bey ve Ogullari (Cevdet Bey and His Sons) 1983, Sessiz Ev (The Quiet House) (Madarali Novel Prize, Turkey 1984) 1983, Beyaz Kale (trans. as The White Castle) (Independent Foreign Fiction Prize 1990) 1985, Kara Kitap (trans. as The Black Book) (Prix France Culture 1995) 1990, Gizli Yuz (screenplay of Kara Kitap) 1992, Yeni Hayat (trans. as The New Life) 1995, My Name is Red (trans.) (Prix du Meilleur Livre Etranger, France 2002, Premio Grinzane Cavour, Italy 2002, Int. IMPAC Dublin Literary Award 2003) 2000, Istanbul 2003, Snow (trans.) (Prix Médicis Etranger, France 2005) 2004, Istanbul: Memories of a City 2006, Istanbul: City of a Hundred Names 2007, Other Colours (essays) 2007, Masumiyet Müzesi (trans. as The Museum of

Innocence) 2008; contrib. to various newspapers and magazines. *Address:* c/o Iletisim Yayinlari, Binbirdirek Meydanı Sok., Iletisim Han 7/2, 34122 Cağaloğlu, Istanbul, Turkey (office). *E-mail:* iletisim@iletisim.com.tr (office). *Website:* www.iletisim.com.tr (office); www.orhanpamuk.net.

PAN, Hong; Chinese film actress; b. 4 Nov. 1954, Shanghai; m. Mi Jingshan (divorced 1990); ed Shanghai Drama Acad. 1973–76; actress, Shanghai Film Studio, Shanghai 1977–80, Omei Film Studio, Chengdu 1980–; mem. 5th Nat. Cttee, Fed. of Literary and Art Circles 1988–; mem. CPPCC Nat. Cttee; mem. Jury 5th Shanghai Int. Film Festival 2001. *Films include:* Troubled Laughter 1979, Sunray Through Clouds 1980, At Middle Age (3rd Golden Rooster Best Actress Award 1983) 1982, The Last Empress 1985, The Trouble-shooters 1988, Well (8th Golden Rooster Best Actress 1988), The Last Aristocrats 1989, The Single Woman 1991, Woman-TAXI-Woman 1991, Shanghai Fever 1994, Up For the Raising Sun 1997, Destination – 9th Heaven 1997. *Television includes:* Secret Murder, Amazing Cases 2003, Beijing My Love 2005, Qing Tian Ya Men 2006, Embroiderer Lan Xin 2007, Ancestral Temple 2008. *Address:* Omei Film Studio, Tonghui Menwai, Chengdu City, Sichuan Province, People's Republic of China (office). *Telephone:* (28) 22991 (office).

PAN, Marta; French (b. Hungarian) sculptor; b. 12 June 1923, Budapest, Hungary; d. of Zsigmond Pan and Maria Pan (née Piltzer); m. André Wogenscky 1952; ed School of Fine Art, Budapest and Paris; one-woman exhbns and numerous nat. and int. group shows in Paris, San Francisco, New York, Los Angeles, Amsterdam, Brussels, Basle, Budapest, Vienna, Tokyo, Osaka and Sapporo 1952–; numerous public sculptures, fountains and monuments in Japan, USA, Saudi Arabia, Lebanon, Italy, Netherlands, France, Luxembourg, Germany, UK, etc.; cr. fountains for the Champs Elysées and Place des Fêtes, Paris; Commdr des Arts et des Lettres 1994; Chevalier, Légion d'honneur 1997; Médaille des Arts Plastiques, Acad. d'Architecture 1986, Prix Int. de l'Eau, de la Création et des Arts UNESCO 2001, Praemium Imperiale (Japan) 2001. *Major works include:* Sculpture flottante, Musée Kröller-Müller 1961, Patio and Fountain, 26 Champs Elysées, Paris 1982, Perspective, St Quentin-en-Yvelques, France 1986–97, Les Lacs, Brest, France 1988, Floating Sculpture, Santomato di Pistoia, Italy 1990, Signe infini, nr Lyon 1994, Jardin de la ligne blanche, Osaka 1994, Fragment de paysage, Tokyo 1994, Floating Sculpture 3 Islands, Luxembourg 1999, Monument, Atami, Japan 2000, Fragment of a Landscape, nr London 2001, Gateway, Taipei, Taiwan 2004, Sculpture 500, Brussels 2005, 'Amphitheatre' for the Kröller-Müller Museum, Otterlo, Netherlands 2007. *Leisure interests:* swimming, ornithology, music, gardening. *Address:* 80 avenue du Général Leclerc, 78470 Saint-Rémy-les-Chevreuse, France (home).

PAN, Rongwen, MD; Chinese physician; b. 1 July 1931, Jiangsu Prov.; d. of Pan Yu Qi and Pan Cao Shi; m. Lu Shi Cai 1960; one s. one d.; Alt. mem. 12th CCP Cen. Cttee 1982–87; Physician-in-Charge, Changzheng Hosp. 1982, Vice-Pres. 1983–, Prof. 1986–. *Address:* Changzheng Hospital, 428 Feng Yang Road, Shanghai 200003, People's Republic of China (office). *Telephone:* (21) 3275997 (office).

PAN, Wenent P., BS, PhD; Taiwanese oil industry executive; *Chairman, CPC Corporation;* ed Nat. Taiwan Normal Univ., Univ. of Wyoming, USA; fmrly with ACE Chemical Co. and Fluid Properties Research Inst.; joined CPC Corpn, Taiwan (fmrly Chinese Petroleum Corpn), held various roles including Man. of Process Research, Dir of Corp. Planning, Vice-Pres. then Pres. 1996–2004, Chair. 2006–, also Vice-Chair. Kuo Kuang Power Co. (subsidiary co.) 1997–2004, Chair. 2004–; Chair. ROC-Australia Business Council; fmr Pres. Chinese Asscn for Energy Econs. *Address:* CPC Corpn, No. 3, Songren Road, Sinyi District, Taipei City 110, Taiwan (office). *Telephone:* (2) 8789-8989 (office). *Fax:* (2) 8789-9000 (office). *E-mail:* ir@cpc.com.tw (office). *Website:* www.cpc.com.tw (office).

PAN, Xia; Chinese film director; b. Aug. 1937, Yidu, Shandong Prov.; ed Tongji Univ. Shanghai; Ed. and Dir Literature and Arts Dept, Chinese People's Cen. Radio Station 1959–75; Dir TV Drama Troupe, Cen. Broadcasting Art Co. 1975–83; Dir China TV Drama Centre 1984–; mem. Standing Cttee 8th CPPCC Nat. Cttee 1993–98, Standing Cttee 9th CPPCC Nat. Cttee 1998–2003; Best TV Drama Award 1980, Flying Apsaras Award 1982, several Gold Eagle Awards; awarded the titles of Nat. Jinguo Pacesetter for Meritorious Service 1991 and Nat. Sanba Standard-Bearer 1992. *Television:* The Sacred Mission, Multi-Prism, Walking into the Storm, Xiang Jingyu, The Pioneers' Footsteps, Madame Sun Yatsen and Her Sisters. *Publications:* over 20 research papers. *Address:* China Television Drama Centre, Beijing, People's Republic of China (office).

PANAFIEU, HE Cardinal Bernard Louis Auguste Paul; French ecclesiastic; *Metropolitan Archbishop of Marseille;* b. 26 Jan. 1931, Châtellerault; s. of Andre Panafieu and Madeleine Doussière; ed Grand Seminary of Albi, Seminary of Issy-les-Moulineaux; ordained priest 1956; Vicar of Saint-Sauveur-de-Mazamet and Chaplain of lyceum La Perouse, Aibi 1962; chaplain of univ. parish and responsible for chaplaincy of public educ.; Student Chaplain, Toulouse 1967–70; curé-doyen of Brassac 1971–74; Sec.-Gen. Presbyteral Council 1973–74; Titular Bishop of Tibili and Auxiliary Bishop of Annecy 1974; Archbishop of Aix 1978; Coadjutor Archbishop of Marseille 1994–95, Archbishop of Marseille 1995–2002, Metropolitan Archbishop of Marseille 2002–; cr. Cardinal (Cardinal Priest of St Gregory Barbarigo alle Tre Fontane) 2003. *Address:* Archdiocese of Marseille, 14 place du Colonel-Edon, 13284 Marseille, France (office). *Telephone:* (4) 91-52-38-23 (office). *Fax:* (4) 91-52-45-19 (office). *Website:* catholique-marseille.cef.fr (office).

PANAYIDES CHRISTOU, Tasos, MA, MPA, GCVO; Cypriot diplomatist; *President, ENESEL SA;* b. 9 April 1934, Ktima-Paphos; s. of Christos Panayi and Efrosini Savva; m. Pandora Constantinides 1969; two s. one d.; ed Paphos Gymnasium, Cyprus Teacher's Training Coll., Univ. of London and Univ. of

Indiana; Teacher, Cyprus 1954–59; First Sec. to Pres. (Archbishop Makarios), then Dir President's Office 1960–69; Amb. to Fed. Repub. of Germany (also to Austria and Switzerland) 1969–79; Sec. and Dean, Commonwealth Group, Bonn 1976–79; High Commr in UK (also Amb. to Denmark, Iceland, Norway and Sweden) 1979–90; Perm. Sec. of Ministry of Foreign Affairs and Amb. to Iceland 1990–94; Amb. to Sweden 1994–96 (also to Denmark, Finland, Iceland, Norway, Latvia, Lithuania and Estonia); Chair. AVRA Shipmanagement SA 1997–2002; Chair. Commonwealth Foundation Grants Cttee 1985–88, Commonwealth Fund for Tech. Co-operation (CFTC) 1986–89, Finance Cttee of Commonwealth Secr. 1988–90, SCOSO (Commonwealth Steering Cttee of Senior Officials) 1994–95; First Vice Chair., Cyprus Union of Shipowners 2007–; Rep. to IAEA 1976–79; Fellow, Ealing Coll.; Pres. ENESEL SA 2003–; Hon. LLD (Birmingham) 1991; Grand Cross (with Star and Sash) of Fed. Repub. of Germany, Grand Cross (with Star and Sash) of Austria, Thyateira Archbishopric Grand Cross (in Gold), Grand Cross (in Gold) of the Patriarchate of Antioch 1984, Freeman of City of London 1984; Hon. GCVO 1990. *Leisure interests:* history, swimming, reading. *Address:* ENESEL SA, Kolonaki Int. Center, 23A Vas. Sofias Avenue, Athens 10 674, Greece (office). *Telephone:* (210) 7260500. *Fax:* (210) 7260550.

PANDAY, Basdeo, BLL, BSc (Econs); Trinidad and Tobago politician; *Leader, United National Congress;* b. 25 May 1933, Prince's Town; m. 1st Norma Mohammed (died 1981); one d.; m. 2nd Oma Ramkisson; three d.; ed Lincoln's Inn, Univ. of London, UK; entered politics as mem. of Workers' and Farmers' Party 1966; trade union legal adviser; Pres.-Gen. All Trinidad Sugar and Gen. Workers' Trade Union 1973, Sugar Industry Staff Asscn 1975; founder mem. United Labour Front (ULF); Leader of the Opposition 1976–86; Minister of Foreign Affairs 1986–91; mem. Nat. Alliance for Reconciliation (NAR), expelled 1988; Founder and Leader, United Nat. Congress (UNC); Prime Minister of Trinidad and Tobago 1995–2001. *Address:* United National Congress, Rienzi Complex, 78–81 Southern Main Road, Couva; La Fantasie Gardens, St Ann's, Port of Spain, Trinidad and Tobago (home).

PANDE, Arvind, MA; Indian business executive; b. 7 Sept. 1942; ed Allahabad Univ., Univ. of Cambridge, UK; Adviser to Exec. Dir for India, Bangladesh and Sri Lanka, IBRD 1971–74; Dept of Econ. Affairs, Ministry of Finance 1974–78; Special Sec., Govt of Madhya Pradesh 1978–81; Jt Sec. to Prime Minister of India 1981–86; Dir (Corp. Planning) Steel Authority of India Ltd (SAIL) 1986–90, (Personnel and Corp. Planning) 1990–93, Vice-Chair. 1993–97, Chair. (CEO) 1997–2002; Chair. Indian Iron and Steel Co. Ltd; Dir HDFC Bank Ltd (ADR); Pres. Nat. HRD Network; Council mem. Indian Inst. of Metals, Confed. of Indian Industry; mem. Bd of Govs Int. Man. Inst.; Dir Int. Iron and Steel Inst., Belgium; mem. Bureau of Indian Standards. *Address:* B-249, Asian Games Village, New Delhi 110 049, India (home). *Telephone:* 6493167 (home).

PANDE, Kabinga; Zambian politician; *Minister of Foreign Affairs;* fmr Head Public Relations, Zambian Cen. Bank; fmr Pres. Africa Travel Asscn; Minister of Science, Tech. and Vocational Training 2005, of Tourism, Environment and Natural Resources 2005–07, of Foreign Affairs 2007–; Deputy Chair. Movt for Multi-party Democracy. *Address:* Ministry of Foreign Affairs, POB RW50069, Lusaka, Zambia (office). *Telephone:* (1) 213822 (office). *Fax:* (1) 222440 (office).

PANDEY, Ramesh Nath; Nepalese politician; b. Feb. 1944; fmr Minister of Population and Devt, Information, Communication and Gen. Admin; fmr Minister for Industry and Communication; fmr Minister of State for Tourism, Labour and Social Welfare; fmr Govt Spokesman; mem. Parl.; Minister of Foreign Affairs 2005–06. *Address:* c/o Ministry of Foreign Affairs, Shital Niwas, Maharajganj, Kathmandu, Nepal (office).

PANDIT, Jasraj, DMus; Indian musician; b. 28 Jan. 1930, Hissar, Hariyana; s. of Motiram Pandit and Krishnabai Pandit; m. Madhura Pandit 1962; one s. one d.; studied under elder brother Maniram Pandit; belongs to Mewati Gharana (school of music); has conducted extensive research in Haveli Sangeet and presented the original Pure Haveli Sangeet with its devotional content intact; has est. an Ashram Motiram Sangeet Natale Acad. with main object of propagating Indian classical music by teaching students free of charge; mem. advisory bds of radio and TV; numerous awards and honours, including Rajiv Gandhi Award for professional excellence, Padma Bhushan 1990 and Sangeet Martand. *Works include:* compositions for opera, ballet and short films etc., including Kan Khani Sunyo Kare, Geet Govindam, Sur, Laya Aur Chhanda. *Publication:* Sangeet Saurabh. *Leisure interests:* teaching, travel, sport. *Address:* G-2, Trishul B-1. Raheja Complex, 7 Bungalows, Versova, Andheri (W) Mumbai 400061, India (office). *Telephone:* (22) 6343520 (office). *E-mail:* panditjasraj@panditjasraj.com (office). *Website:* www .panditjasraj.com.

PANDIT, Vikram S., BS, MS, PhD; American (b. Indian) banking executive; *CEO, Citigroup Inc.;* b. 14 Jan. 1957, Nagpur, Maharashtra, India; s. of Shankar Pandit; m. Swati Pandit; two c.; ed Dadar Parsee Youths Assembly High School, Mumbai, Columbia Univ., New York; moved to USA to study aged 16; Prof., Indiana Univ., Bloomington 1986–90; worked 20 years with Morgan Stanley & Co., becoming Man. Dir 1990–94, Head of Equity Derivatives 1994–2000, also Man. Dir 1997–2000, Co-Pres. and COO Institutional Securities Div. 2000–03, Pres. and COO Institutional Securities & Investment Banking Group 2003–05; Founder and Chair. Old Lane LP (hedge fund) 2005–07; Chair. and CEO Citigroup Alternative Investments 2007, Chair. and CEO Institutional Clients Group 2007, mem. Bd of Dirs and CEO Citigroup Inc. 2007–; mem. Bd of Dirs Columbia Univ., Columbia Business School, Indian School of Business, Trinity School, NASDAQ 2000–03; fmr mem. Bd of Dirs NY City Investment Fund, American India Foundation; Padma Bhushan 2008. *Address:* Citigroup Inc., 399 Park Avenue, New York,

NY 10043, USA (office). *Telephone:* (212) 559-1000 (office). *Fax:* (212) 793-3946 (office). *Website:* www.citigroup.com (office).

PANDOLFI, Filippo Maria, PhD; Italian politician; b. 1 Nov. 1927, Bergamo; fmr company Dir; mem. Chamber of Deputies for Brescia-Bergamo 1968; mem. Comm. on Finance and the Treasury; fmr Under-Sec. of State in Ministry of the Budget; Minister of Finance 1976–78, of the Treasury 1978–80, of Industry 1980–81, 1982–83, of Agric. 1983–88; EEC Commr for Science, Research, Telecommunications and Information Tech. 1989–92; Christian Democrat.

PANETTA, Leon E., BA, JD; American lawyer, academic, government official and fmr politician; *Director, Central Intelligence Agency;* b. 28 June 1938, Monterey, Calif.; s. of Carmelo Panetta and Carmelina Panetta; m. Sylvia Varni 1962; three s.; ed Santa Clara Univ.; served US Army 1964–66; Legis. Asst to Senator Thomas Kuchel, Washington 1966–69; Dir US Office of Civil Rights 1969–70; Exec. Asst to Mayor of New York 1970–71; Pnr, Panetta, Thompson and Panetta (law firm), Monterey 1971–76; mem. US House of Reps 1977–93, mem., House Agric. Cttee 1977–93, Budget Cttee 1979–85 (Chair. 1989–92), Vice Chair. New Mem. Caucus 1977, Caucus of Vietnam Era Veterans in Congress; and a member of the president's Commission on Foreign Language and International Studies; Head of US Office of Man. and Budget 1993–94; Chief of Staff to Pres. Clinton 1994–97;; Founder and Co-Dir Leon and Sylvia Panetta Inst., Calif. State Univ., Monterey Bay 1998–, also Distinguished Scholar to the Chancellor, Calif. State Univ. System, Presidential Prof., Santa Clara Univ.; Dir CIA, Langley, Va 2009–; est. Leon Panetta Lecture Series; Chair. Pew Oceans Comm., Co-Chair. Jt Ocean Cttee Initiative; Co-Chair. Calif. Council on Base Support and Retention, Calif. Forward Leadership Council; mem. Iraq Study Group, US Inst. of Peace 2006; mem. Independent Task Force on Immigration and America's Future; mem. Bd of Dirs Blue Shield, Zenith, Nat. Marine Sanctuary Foundation, Bread for the World, Close Up, BP America's Public Policy Inst. of Calif.; mem. Bd of Visitors Santa Clara Univ. School of Law; mem. Advisory Bd Fleishman-Hillard Int.; Trustee Monterey Bay Aquarium; Democrat; numerous awards including John H. Chafee Coastal Stewardship Award, Julius A. Stratton Award for Coastal Leadership and Distinguished Public Service Medal, Center for the Study of the Presidency, Army Commendation Medal, NEA Lincoln Award, A. Philip Randolph Award, Smithsonian Inst. Nat. Portrait Gallery Paul Peck Presidential Award, Nat. Marine Sanctuary Foundation Lifetime Achievement Award, Natural Resources Defense Council Forces for Nature, Nat. Hospice Foundation Silver Anniversary Honouree. *Publication:* Bring Us Together 1971. *Address:* Central Intelligence Agency, Office of Public Affairs, Washington, DC 20505 (office); Panetta Institute, California State University at Monterey, 100 Campus Centre, Building 86E, Seaside, CA 93955, USA (office). *Telephone:* (703) 482-0623 (office). *Fax:* (703) 482-1739 (office). *Website:* www.cia.gov (office); www.panettainstitute.org (office).

PANFILOV, Gleb Anatolyevich; Russian film director; b. 21 Dec. 1934, Magnitogorsk; m. Inna Mikhailovna Churikova (q.v.); one s.; grad. Sverdlovsk Polytechnic Inst. as chemical engineer and Mosfilm Studios (course in directing); work as Dir in Sverdlovsk, Leningrad (now St Petersburg), Moscow 1976–; RSFSR People's Artist 1984, RSFSR State Prize 1985. *Films include:* No Ford in the Fire (scenario: Yevgeniy Gabrilovich) 1968 (Grand Prix Locarno 1969), Début 1970, both starring Inna Churikova, I Wish to Speak 1975, Valentina 1981, Vassa Zheleznova 1983, The Theme 1986, The Mother 1989, Hamlet 1989, The Romanovs: An Imperial Family 2000; stage productions at Lenkom Theatre include Hamlet 1986, Sorry (A. Galin) 1992, The Romanovs: An Imperial Family 2000. *Address:* Universitetski Prosp. 6, Korp. 4, Apt 68, 117333 Moscow, Russia. *Telephone:* (495) 137-89-67.

PANGALOS, Theodoros, PhD; Greek politician, economist and lawyer; b. 17 Aug. 1938, Elefsis; m.; three s. two d.; ed Athens and Sorbonne Univs; a founder of the Grigoris Lambrakis Youth Movt; stood as EDA cand. in 1964 election; active in dissident Movt during mil. dictatorship; deprived of Greek citizenship by junta 1968; Lecturer and Researcher specializing in Econ. Devt, Programming and Town and Country Planning, Sorbonne, Paris and Head of Econ. Devt Inst. 1969–78; practises as lawyer in Athens; legal adviser to trade unions; active in Movt to protect environment; Socialist MP for Attica 1981–; Deputy Minister of Commerce 1982–84, of Foreign Affairs 1984–89, 1993–94; Minister of Transport and Communications 1994, of Foreign Affairs 1996–99, of Culture 2000; currently mem. of Greek Del. WEU Ass. and Council of Europe; mem. Political Council and Head of Int. Affairs and Defence section, PASOK; 17 awards or honours from various countries. *Publications:* several works on econs, sociology and philosophy. *Address:* 16–18 Pireos Street, 104 31 Athens, Greece (home). *Telephone:* (1) 5231142 (home). *Fax:* (1) 5231178 (home). *E-mail:* pangalos@otenet.gr (office). *Website:* www.pangalos.gr (office).

PANGGABEAN, Gen. Maraden Saur Halomoan; Indonesian politician and army officer; b. 29 June 1922, Tarutung, N Sumatra; s. of M. Patuan Natoras and Katharina Panjaitan; m. Meida Seimima Matiur Tambunan; one s. three d.; studied mil. affairs in various mil. acads including the Advanced Infantry Officer Course, USA; mil. posts include C-in-C of the Army 1968, Vice-Commdr Armed Forces 1969–73, C-in-C 1973–78; Deputy Commdr for Restoration of Security and Order 1968, Commdr 1969–73, Exec. Officer Command 1973–78; Minister of State for Defense and Security 1969–73, Minister 1973–78; Acting Minister of Home Affairs 1973; Minister Co-ordinator for Political and Security Affairs 1978–83; Acting Foreign Minister 1978–83; Chair. Bd of Guidance, GOLKAR 1973–78, Vice-Chair. 1978–83; Chair. Exec. Presidium, Bd of Guidance, GOLKAR 1978–83; mem. People's Consultative Ass. 1973–78, 1978–83, 1983–; War of Independence Medal, Service Award Medal, Best Son of the Nation Medal, Rep. of Indonesia Medal and numerous other medals and awards. *Leisure interests:* golf, jogging, gymnastics, hunting, reading. *Address:* Jalan Teuku Umar 21, Jakarta, Indonesia. *Telephone:* 378012.

PANHOFER, Walter; Austrian concert pianist; b. 3 Jan. 1910, Vienna; s. of Josef and Maria Panhofer; m. Gertraut Schmied 1956; two s.; ed Akad. für Musik und darstellende Kunst, Hochschule für Musik und darstellende Kunst, Vienna; concerts in Austria, Germany, England, Switzerland, Italy and Yugoslavia; performed with Vienna Philharmonic and Vienna Symphony Orchestras and Royal Philharmonic and London Chamber Orchestras, England; has toured with and made records with Vienna Octet; masterclasses in Brussels, Vienna and in Italy; has adjudicated many times at Int. Beethoven piano competition, Vienna; Ehrenkreuz für Wissenschaft und Kunst. *Leisure interests:* mountains, books. *Address:* Erdbergstrasse 35/9, 1030 Vienna, Austria. *Telephone:* 7147902 (home). *Fax:* 7147902 (home).

PANIČ, Milan; Serbian business executive and fmr politician; *Owner, MP Global Enterprises;* b. 20 Dec. 1929, Belgrade; one s. two d.; ed Univ. of Belgrade, Univ. of South Carolina, USA, and Heidelberg Univ., Germany; emigrated to USA 1956; Founder and Chair. ICN Pharmaceuticals Inc. 1960–2002; returned to Yugoslavia 1991; Prime Minister of Yugoslavia July–Dec. 1992; cand. for Presidency of Serbia 1992; Founder and Owner of MP Global Enterprises 2003–; Dir Galenica Co., Belgrade and Moscow; mem. Bd Fund for Interdisciplinary Scientific Research (ISRF); Corresp. mem. California Inst. of Tech.; mem. American Nuclear Soc., Swiss Chemical Soc., Int. Soc. of Haemotherapy; mem. Bd Freedoms Foundation of Valley Forge; Wall Street Journal European of the Year. *Leisure interests:* tennis, cycling (fmr Yugoslav Champion). *Address:* MP Global Enterprises, 650 Town Center Drive, No. 660, Costa Mesa, CA 92626 (office); 1050 Arden Road, Pasadena, CA 91106, USA (home). *Telephone:* (714) 384-4000 (office). *Fax:* (714) 384-4010 (office). *Website:* www.milanpanic.com (office).

PANICHAS, George Andrew, FRSA, MA, PhD, LittD; American writer and academic; *Professor Emeritus of English, University of Maryland;* b. 21 May 1930, Springfield, Mass; s. of Andrew Panichas and Fannie Dracouli Panichas; ed Springfield Classical High School, American Int. Coll., Trinity Coll. and Nottingham Univ., England; Instructor in English, Univ. of Maryland 1962, Asst Prof. 1963, Assoc. Prof. 1966, Prof. 1968–92, now Prof. Emer.; Co-Dir of Conf. "Irving Babbitt: Fifty Years Later" 1983; mem. Richard M. Weaver Fellowship Awards Cttee 1983–88; Academic Bd Nat. Humanities Inst. 1985–, Advisory Bd Humanitas 1993–; Editorial Adviser, Modern Age: A Quarterly Review 1972–77, Assoc. Ed. 1978–83, Ed. 1984–2007; mem. Advisory Bd Continuity: A Journal of History 1984; Ingersoll Prizes Jury Panel 1986; Earhart Foundation Award 1982, Henry Regnery Award 2003. *Publications:* Adventure in Consciousness: The Meaning of D.H. Lawrence's Religious Quest 1964, Renaissance and Modern Essays: Presented to Vivian de Sola Pinto in Celebration of his Seventieth Birthday (ed. with G. R. Hibbard and A. Rodway) 1966, Epicurus 1967, Mansions of the Spirit: Essays in Literature and Religion (ed.) 1967, Promise of Greatness: The War of 1914–1918 (ed.) 1968, The Politics of Twentieth-Century Novelists (ed.) 1971, The Reverent Discipline: Essays in Literary Criticism and Culture 1974, The Burden of Vision: Dostoevsky's Spiritual Art 1977, The Simone Weil Reader (ed.) 1977, Irving Babbitt: Representative Writings (ed.) 1981, The Courage of Judgment: Essays in Criticism, Culture and Society 1982, Irving Babbitt in Our Time (ed. with C. G. Ryn) 1986, Modern Age: The First Twenty-Five Years. A Selection (ed.) 1988, The Critic as Conservator: Essays in Literature, Society and Culture 1992, In Continuity: The Last Essays of Austin Warren (ed.) 1996, The Critical Legacy of Irving Babbitt: An Appreciation 1999, Growing Wings to Overcome Gravity: Criticism as the Pursuit of Virtue 1999, Joseph Conrad: His Moral Vision 2005, The Essential Russell Kirk: Selected Essays (ed.) 2007; also numerous articles, trans. and reviews for books and journals published in USA and Europe. *Leisure interests:* hiking, playing racquetball, keeping physically fit, listening to music. *Address:* 4313 Knox Road, Apartment 402, College Park, MD 20740, USA (home). *Telephone:* (301) 779-1436 (office).

PANINA, Yelena Vladimirovna, CandEconSci; Russian civil servant; *Deputy Chairwoman, State Duma Committee for Economic Policy, Entrepreneurship and Tourism;* b. 29 April 1948, Smolensk Region; m. Aleksandr Andreyevich Panin; one d.; ed Moscow Inst. of Finance, Higher School of Econs; on staff Control-Audit Dept Ministry of Finance, Russian Fed. 1970–75; Head of Dept, Deputy Dir-Gen. Production Union 1975–86; Sec. Dist CP Cttee Moscow Region 1986–88; Head of Dept Moscow CP City Cttee 1988–91; Dir-Gen. USSR Trade Chamber 1991–92; mem. Exec. Bd Russian Union of Businessmen 1992–; Chair. Russian Zemsvto Movt 1993–; Deputy Head World Russian People's Sobor 1995–; Co-Chair., Co-ordinator Moscow Confed. of Businessmen 1992–; Chair. Moscow Confed. of Industrialists and Entrepreneurs 2000–; Dir-Gen. Centre of Business Projects (Interbusinessproekt) 1992–97; mem. State Duma 1997–99, currently Deputy Chair. State Duma Cttee for Econ. Policy, Entrepreneurship and Tourism; Chair. Russian United Industrialists Party 2002–. *Address:* State Duma, 103265 Moscow, Okhotnyi ryad 1; Moscow Confederation of Industrialists and Entrepreneurs, Novy Arbat 21, Moscow, Russia (office). *Telephone:* (495) 291-98-74 (office).

PANITCHPAKDI, Supachai, MA, PhD; Thai banker, fmr government official and international organization official; *Secretary-General, United Nations Conference on Trade and Development (UNCTAD);* b. 30 May 1946, Bangkok; m. Mrs Sasai; one s. one d.; ed St Gabriel's Coll. and Trium Udom School, Bangkok, Netherlands School of Econs (now Erasmus Univ.), Rotterdam, and in UK; worked in Research Dept, Int. Finance Div., and Financial Insts Supervision Dept, Bank of Thailand 1974–86; elected mem. Thai Parl. 1986, Deputy Minister of Finance 1986–88; Dir and Adviser, then Pres. Thai Military Bank 1988–92; apptd Senator 1992, then Deputy Prime Minister of Thailand 1992–95, Deputy Prime Minister and Minister of Commerce 1997–99; Dir-Gen. WTO 2002–05; Sec.-Gen. UNCTAD 2005–; Visiting Prof.,

Int. Inst. for Man. Devt, Lausanne 2001; Knight Grand Cordon (Special Class) of the Most Exalted Order of the White Elephant. *Publications include:* Globalization and Trade in the New Millennium 2001, China and WTO: Changing China Changing WTO (with Mark Clifford) 2002. *Address:* United Nations Conference on Trade and Development (UNCTAD), Palais des Nations 8-14, Avenue de la Paix, 1211 Geneva 10, Switzerland (office). *Telephone:* (22) 9175806 (office). *Fax:* (22) 9170042 (office). *E-mail:* sgo@unctad.org (office). *Website:* www.unctad.org (office).

PANKE, Helmut, PhD; German business executive; b. 1946; Head of Corp. Strategy and Co-ordination, Bayerische Motoren Werke (BMW) AG 1990–93, Chair. and CEO BMW (US) Holding Corpn 1993–96, mem. Bd of Man. (Personnel and Information Tech.) 1996–99, mem. Bd of Man. (Finance) 1999–2002, Chair. Bd of Man. BMW AG 2002–06. *Address:* c/o Board of Management, BMW AG, Petuelring 130, 80788 Munich, Germany (office).

PANKIN, Boris Dmitriyevich; Russian diplomatist (retd) and essayist; b. 20 Feb. 1931, Frunze (now Bishkek); m.; two s. one d.; ed Moscow State Univ.; journalist and literary critic 1957–; Ed. Komsomolskaya Pravda 1965–73; Chair. Bd USSR Copyright Agency 1973–82; USSR Amb. to Sweden 1982–90, to Czechoslovakia 1990–91; Foreign Minister Aug.–Dec. 1991; Russian Amb. to UK 1991–94; now living in Sweden; USSR State Prize 1982. *Publications:* Severe Literature, Time and Word, Boundaries and Books, The Last 100 Days of the Soviet Union, Four I of Konstantin Simonov. *Telephone:* (46) 880-7871.

PANNENBERG, Wolfhart Ulrich, DTheol, FBA; German academic; *Professor Emeritus, University of Munich;* b. 2 Oct. 1928, Stettin; s. of Kurt B.S. Pannenberg and Irmgard Pannenberg; m. Hilke Sabine Schütte 1954; ed Univ. of Heidelberg; ordained as Lutheran Minister 1956; Privatdozent, Heidelberg 1955–58; Prof. of Systematic Theology, Univ. of Wuppertal 1958–61; Prof., Univ. of Mainz 1961–67; Prof., Univ. of Munich 1967–94, Prof. Emer. 1994–, fmr Head, Inst. of Ecumenical Theology; mem. Bavarian Acad. of Sciences; Hon. DD (Glasgow) 1972, (Manchester) 1977, (Trinity Coll. Dublin) 1979, (St Andrews) 1993, (Cambridge) 1997, (Comillas, Madrid) 1999. *Publications:* Offenbarung als Geschichte (translated as Revelation as History) 1961, Was ist der Mensch?: Die Anthropologie der Gegenwart im Lichte der Theologie (translated as What is Man?) 1962, Grundzüge der Christologie (translated as Jesus: God and Man) 1964, Grundfragen systematischer Theologie (two vols, translated as Basic Questions in Theology) 1967, 1980, Theology and the Kingdom of God 1969, Spirit, Faith and Church (with Carl E. Braaten and Avery Dulles) 1970, Thesen zur Theologie der Kirche 1970, Das Glaubensbekenntnis (translated as The Apostles' Creed in the Light of Today's Questions) 1972, Gottesgedanke und menschliche Freiheit (translated as The Idea of God and Human Freedom) 1972, Wissenschaftstheorie und Theologie (translated as Theology and the Philosophy of Science) 1973, Glaube und Wirklichkeit (translated as Faith and Reality) 1975, Ethik und Ekklesiologie 1977, Human Nature, Election and History 1977, Anthropologie in Theologischer Perspektive (translated as Anthropology in Theological Perspective) 1983, Christian Spirituality 1983, Christentum in Einer Säkularisierten Welt (translated as Christianity in a Secularized World) 1988, Systematische Theologie (three vols, translated as Systematic Theology) 1988–93, Metaphysik und Gottesgedanke (translated as Metaphysics and the Idea of God) 1988, An Introduction to Systematic Theology 1991, Toward a Theology of Nature: Essays on Science and Faith 1993, Grundlagen der Ethik 1996, Theologie und Philosophie 1996, Problemgeschichte der neueren Evangelischen Theologie in Deutschland 1997, Beiträge zur systematischen Theologie (three vols) 1999–2000, Beiträge zur Ethik 2004, Analogie und Offenbarung 2007. *Leisure interests:* history, music, philosophy. *Telephone:* (89) 21803482 (office); (89) 855915 (home).

PANNI, Marcello; Italian conductor and composer; *Artistic Director, Accademia Filarmonica Romana;* b. 24 Jan. 1940, Rome; s. of Arnaldo Panni and Adriana Cortini; m. Jeanne Colombier 1970; one d.; ed Accad. di Santa Cecilia, Rome under Goffredo Petrassi and Conservatoire Nat. Supérieur, Paris under Manuel Rosenthal; conducting debut, Festival of Contemporary Music, Venice 1969; has since achieved renown in field of avant-garde music conducting first performances of works by Berio, Bussotti, Cage, Feldman, Donatoni, Clementi, Sciarrino, and others at all major European festivals and for Italian Radio; regular guest conductor for Accademia di Santa Cecilia, the Italian radio orchestras and other European orchestras performing full range of baroque, classical and modern works; Musical Dir Bonn Opera House 1994–97, Nice Opera House 1997–2001; Artistic Dir San Carlo Opera House, Naples 2001–02; Artistic Dir Accademia Filarmonica Romana 2001–04, 2007–09; opera début with The Barber of Seville, Hamburg 1977 and has since conducted opera in all the principal opera houses in Europe; American debut with Elisir d'amore, Metropolitan Opera, New York 1988; conducted world premiere of Bussotti's Cristallo di Rocca (opera) at La Scala 1983; Bolshoi debut with Macbeth, Moscow 2003; Milhaud Prof. of Composition and Conducting, Mills Coll., Oakland, Calif. 1980–84; mem. Accademia di Santa Cecilia 2003–. *Works include* symphonic and chamber music and music for experimental theatrical works; operas: Hanjo (one act) 1994, Il giudizio di Paride (one act) 1996, The Banquet (one act) 1998, Garibaldi en Sicile (two acts) 2005. *Leisure interests:* arts, sport. *Address:* 3 Piazza Borghese, 00186 Rome, Italy. *Telephone:* (06) 6873617. *E-mail:* info@filarmonicaromana.org (office). *Website:* www.filarmonicaromana.org (office).

PANNICK, David Philip, QC, BCL, MA; British barrister; b. 7 March 1956, London; s. of Maurice A. Pannick and Rita L. Pannick; m. Denise Sloam 1978 (died 1999); two s. one d.; m. Nathalie Trager-Lewis 2003; one d.; ed Bancroft's School, Essex and Hertford Coll. Oxford; called to the Bar 1979, QC 1992; Fellow, All Souls Coll. Oxford 1978–; Jr Counsel to the Crown (Common Law) 1988–92; columnist on law, The Times 1991–; Bencher of Gray's Inn 2001; Hon. Fellow, Hertford Coll. Oxford; Hon. LLD (Hertfordshire) 1998. *Publications:* Sex Discrimination Law 1985, Judges 1987, Advocates 1992, Human Rights Law and Practice (co-author with Lord Lester of Herne Hill) 1999, 2004. *Leisure interests:* theatre, cinema, jogging. *Address:* Blackstone Chambers, Temple, London, EC4Y 7BH, England (office). *Telephone:* (20) 7583-1770 (office). *Fax:* (20) 7822-7222 (office).

PANNONE, Rodger John, DL, FRSA; British solicitor; b. 20 April 1943, Minehead, Somerset; s. of Cyril Pannone and Violet Weeks; m. Patricia Todd 1966; two s. one d.; ed St Brendan's Coll. Bristol and Coll. of Law, London and Manchester Polytechnic; articled clerk, Casson & Co. Salford; joined W.H. Thompson 1969, later partner; joined Conn Goldberg (now Pannone & Partners) 1973, Sr Partner 1991–2003, consultant 2003–; lecturer and broadcaster on legal affairs; mem. Lord Chancellor's Advisory Cttee on Civil Justice; fmr mem. Supreme Court Rule Cttee; Chair. Forensic Science Service; Chair. Gov. Coll. of Law, Council Manchester Univ.; Fellow, Manchester Metropolitan Univ.; mem. Council Law Soc. of England and Wales, Pres. 1993–94; DL Greater Manchester; Hon. Mem. Canadian Bar Asscn; Hon. Fellow, Soc. of Chiropodists, Univ. of Birmingham 1998; Hon. DLitt (Salford); Hon. LLD (Nottingham Trent); Hon. LittD (Manchester). *Publications:* legal articles. *Leisure interests:* walking slowly, food and drink. *Address:* Pannone & Partners, 123 Deansgate, Manchester, M3 2BU, England. *Telephone:* (161) 909-3000. *Fax:* (161) 909-4444. *E-mail:* law@pannone.co.uk (office). *Website:* www.pannone.com (office).

PANOV, Alexander Nikolayevich, CandHistSc; Russian diplomatist; *Ambassador to Norway;* b. 6 July 1944, Moscow; m. 1967; one d.; ed Moscow Inst. of Int. Relations; diplomatic service 1968–; trans., attaché Embassy in Tokyo 1968–71; teacher, Asst Prof., Moscow Inst. of Int. Relations 1971–77; Third, Second Sec., Perm. Mission to UN, New York 1977–82; First Sec., Second Far East Dept USSR Ministry of Foreign Affairs 1982–83; First Sec., Counsellor, Embassy in Tokyo 1983–88; Deputy Chief, Chief of Div., Deputy Chief, Dept of Countries of Pacific Ocean and SE Asia, USSR Ministry of Foreign Affairs 1988–90, Chief 1990–92; Amb. to Repub. of Korean 1992–94; Deputy Minister of Foreign Affairs 1994–96; Amb. to Japan 1996–2003, to Norway 2004–; Order of Merit. *Publications:* Postwar Reforms in Japan 1945–52, Japanese Diplomatic Service, Beyond Distrust to Trust; articles in periodicals. *Leisure interest:* photography. *Address:* Embassy of the Russian Federation, Drammensvn 74, 0244 Oslo, Norway (office). *Telephone:* 22-55-32-78 (office). *Fax:* 22-55-00-70 (office). *E-mail:* rembassy@online.no (office). *Website:* www.norway.mid.ru (office).

PANSA CEDRONIO, Paolo, LLD, LicPolSc; Italian diplomatist; b. 15 Nov. 1915, Naples; s. of Ciro Pansa Cedronio and Elina Stammelluti; ed Univs of Naples and Florence; entered Italian diplomatic service 1940; Sec., Italian Embassy, Washington 1945–49; Sec., Italian Del. to NATO, London and Paris 1951–55; Head of Service, Ministry of Foreign Affairs, Rome 1955–61; Minister, Italian Embassy, London 1961–66; Amb. to Chile 1966–70, to Canada 1970–71; Deputy Sec.-Gen. NATO 1971–78; Amb. to USA 1978–81; mem. Cttee of Patrons, Atlantic Treaty Asscn, Brussels; fmr alt. Pres. NATO Appeals Bd, Brussels; fmr mem. Consiglio del Contenzioso Diplomatico, Ministry of Foreign Affairs, Rome; mem. Bd Comitato Atlantico; mem. Centro Conciliazione Internazionale, Circolo Studi Diplomatici, Rome; Croce di Guerra, Cavaliere di Gran Croce al Merito della Repubblica Italiana, Gran-Cruz Orden al Mérito de Chile, Officier, Légion d'honneur, etc. *Leisure interests:* golf, horse riding, sailing. *Address:* Palazzo Borghese, Largo Fontanella Borghese 19, 00186 Rome, Italy. *Telephone:* (06) 6876128.

PANT, Krishna Chandra, MSc; Indian politician; b. 10 Aug. 1931, Bhowali, Nainital Dist; s. of the late Pandit Govind Ballabh Pant; m. Ila Pant 1957; two s.; ed St Joseph's Coll., Nainital, Univ. of Lucknow; mem. Lok Sabha for Nainital 1962–77, 1978–; Minister of Finance 1967–69, of Steel and Heavy Eng 1969–70, of Home Affairs and Head, Depts of Science, Electronics and Atomic Energy 1970–73; Minister of Irrigation and Power 1973–74, of Energy 1974–77, 1979–80, of Educ. Jan.–Sept. 1985, of Steel and Mines 1985–87, of Defence 1987–89; Chair. Advisory Bd on Energy 1983–84; First Vice-Pres. Human Rights Comm. 1966; Leader Del. to Int. Conf. on Human Rights, Tehran 1968; Deputy Chair. Planning Comm.; del. to various other int. confs; mem. Nat. Integration Council; Hon. Fellow Inst. of Engineers; Hon. DSc (Udaipur). *Leisure interests:* welfare work, reading, travelling, sports. *Address:* Yojana Bhavan, Sansad Marg, New Delhi 110001, India (office); 22 Dakshineshwar, 10 Hailey Road, New Delhi 110001. *Telephone:* (11) 3716354 (office); (11) 3012618. *Fax:* (11) 3717681 (office).

PANTÓ, György; Hungarian geochemist and academic; *Research Professor, Institute for Geochemical Research;* b. 1936, Budapest; s. of Endre Pantó and Ilona Botár; m. Márta Juhász; one s. one d.; ed Loránd Eötvös Univ.; mine geologist, Hungarian Mineral and Ore Mines 1959–62; postgraduate scholarship, Hungarian Acad. of Sciences 1962–65, Sr Researcher, Lab. for Geochemical Research 1965–76, Dir 1976–2000, now Research Prof.; Dir-Gen. Hungarian Acad. of Sciences Research Centre for Earth Sciences 1998–2004; mem. Hungarian Acad. of Sciences, Pres. Earth Sciences Section 1999–2005; Foreign mem. Serbian Acad. of Arts and Sciences; mem. Editorial Bd Acta Geologica Hungarica; Szèchenyi Prize 2000. *Publications:* numerous articles, books and contribs on geochemistry. *Leisure interests:* gardening, tourism. *Address:* Hungarian Academy of Sciences, Institute for Geochemical Research, Budaörsi út 45, 1112 Budapest, Hungary (office). *Telephone:* (1) 319-3145 (office). *Fax:* (1) 319-3145 (office). *E-mail:* panto@sparc.core.hu (office). *Website:* www.geochem.hu/people/panto_hu.html (office).

PANTON, Seymour; Jamaican judge; *President, Court of Appeal;* called to the Bar, Lincoln's Inn, London 1968; held posts in Jamaica including Deputy Clerk of Courts, Clerk of Courts, Crown Counsel (Acting) in Dir of Public Prosecutions Office, Resident Magistrate, Puisne Judge; fmr Legal Asst to

Attorney Gen., Sr Counsel and Judge of Grand Court, Cayman Islands; Appeal Judge, Court of Appeal, Jamaica 1999–, Pres. 2007–; fmr mem. Bench and Bar Consultative Cttee, Asscn of Resident Magistrates (Vice-Pres.), Commonwealth Magistrates and Judges Asscn; Assoc. Tutor, Norman Manley Law School 1986–93; Examiner, Deputy Clerk of Courts Qualifying Exams 1986–96; Fulbright Grant 1990, Outstanding Service Awards from Rusea's Old Students' Asscn 1990, Cornwall Bar Asscn 1995, Jamaican Govt 2006. *Address:* Supreme Court of Jamaica, Public Building E, 134 Tower Street, Kingston, Jamaica (office). *Telephone:* 922-8300 (office). *E-mail:* justice .srpanton@sc.gov.jm (office). *Website:* www.sc.gov.jm (office).

PANULA, Jorma; Finnish conductor, composer and academic; b. 10 Aug. 1930, Kauhajoki; ed Sibelius Acad., Helsinki; Artistic Dir and Chief Conductor, Turku Philharmonic Orchestra 1963–65, Helsinki Philharmonic 1965–72, Aarhus Symphony, Denmark 1970–73; Prof. of Orchestral Conducting, Sibelius Acad., Helsinki 1973–94; trains conductors in USA, France, Netherlands, Russia, Sweden, Italy, Australia and UK; fmr Visiting Prof. Music, Stockholm Royal Acad. of Music and Copenhagen Royal Acad. of Music, Yale Univ., Bartók Seminar, Hungary; Music Prize, Royal Swedish Acad. of Science 1997. *Music:* (operas) Jaakko Ilkka, The River Opera; musicals, church music, a violin concerto, a jazz capriccio and vocal music. *Address:* Jorma Panula Foundation, c/o Taco Kooistra, Sloterweg 1188, 1066 Amsterdam, Netherlands (office). *E-mail:* tckooistra@zonnet.nl (office). *Website:* www .jormapanula.com.

PANYARACHUN, Anand, KBE; Thai business executive and fmr politician; *Director, Siam Commercial Bank;* b. 9 Aug. 1932, Bangkok; s. of Maha Ammat Tri Phya Prichanusat (Sern Panyarachun) and Khunying Prichanusat (Pruek Chotikasathien); m. R. R. Sodsee Chakrabandh; two d.; ed Bangkok Christian Coll., Dulwich Coll., Univ. of Cambridge, UK; joined Ministry of Foreign Affairs 1955; Sec. to Foreign Minister 1959; First Sec. Perm. Mission of Thailand to UN 1964, Counsellor 1966; concurrently Amb. to Canada and Acting Perm. Rep. to UN 1967–72 (Perm. Rep. 1972–76), concurrently Amb. to USA 1972–76; Amb. to FRG 1978–79; Head, Ministry of Foreign Affairs 1976; accused of being a Communist after coup, suspended but exonerated and reinstated; fmr Exec. Chair. Saha-Union Group (industrial conglomerate); fmr Chair. Fed. of Thai Industries 1990; Prime Minister of Thailand 1991–92; elected mem. Constitution Drafting Ass. 1997, Chair. Drafting Cttee; Chair. UN High-Level Panel on Threats, Challenges and Change, Steering Cttee Asia Pacific Leadership Forum on HIV/AIDS and Devt; mem. Advisory Group Anti-Corruption Issues for the East Asia and Pacific Region, World Bank; UNICEF Amb. 1996–; Dir Sime Darby Berhad 1982–98, Siam Commercial Bank 1984– (Chair. Compensation Cttee, Nomination and Corp. Governance Cttee); Chair. Thailand Devt Research Inst., Council of Trustees Thailand Environment Inst., Council of Asian Univ. of Science and Tech., Bd of Trustees of Asian Inst. of Tech.; mem. Int. Advisory Bd American Int. Group, Unocal Asia Pacific Ventures, Toyota Motor Corpn; mem. Asian advisory bd The Carlyle Group –2004; Kt Grand Cordon (Special Class) of the Most Noble Order of the Crown of Thailand, Kt Grand Cordon (Special Class) of the Most Exalted Order of the White Elephant, Kt Grand Commdr (Second Class, higher grade) of the Most Illustrious Order of Chula Chom Klao, Order of Diplomatic Service Merit, Repub. of Korea, Ringtang Jasa (First Class) Indonesia, Grand Officier de l'Ordre de la Couronne (2nd class) Belgium, Grand Cordon of the Order of the Rising Sun, Japan; 20 hon. degrees from univs in Thailand, Canada, Hong Kong and Japan; Royal Cypher Medal (Third Class), Ramon Magsaysay Award for Government Service 1997. *Address:* c/o Board of Directors, Siam Commercial Bank PCL, 9 Ratchadaphisek Road, SCP Park, Chatuchak, Bangkok 10900, Thailand. *Telephone:* (2) 544-1111. *Fax:* (2) 937-7754. *Website:* www.scb.co.th/html/eng/ cg_org_board_anand.shtml.

PANZA di BIUMO, Count Giuseppe, DJur; Italian art collector; b. 23 March 1923, Milan; s. of Ernesto Panza di Biumo and Maria Mantegazza; m. Rosa G. Magnifico 1955; four s. one d.; ed self-taught in art history; 80 works of art acquired by Museum of Contemporary Art, LA 1984; 220 works of art acquired by Guggenheim Museum 1990; 150 works of art in gift to Guggenheim Museum, 200 to Museo Cantonale d'Arte, Lugano, 70 to Museum of Contemporary Art, LA, 51 to Palazzo Ducale–Sassuolo, 217 works of art and the 18th century villa in Biumo. *Publications:* Art of the Sixties and Seventies 1988, Panza di Biumo: The Eighties and Nineties from the Collection 1992, The Panza Collection 2002. *Address:* P.O. Box 6218, 6901 Lugano; Sentiero Vinorum 2, 6900 Massagno, Switzerland. *Telephone:* (91) 9676021; (91) 9682353. *Fax:* (91) 9676125. *E-mail:* info@panzacollection.org (office).

PAOLILLO, Felipe; Uruguayan diplomatist and lawyer; *Vice-President, Assembly of States Parties, International Criminal Court;* b. 8 Oct. 1931; Prof. of Int. Public Law, Univ. of Uruguay 1967–74, 1985–87; Assoc. Prof. New York Univ. School of Law 1977–84; Perm. Rep. to UN 1987–90, 2000–01, 2003, to Holy See and FAO 1996–2000; Chair. UN Gen. Ass. Credentials Cttee 2002; currently Vice-Pres. Ass. of States Parties, Int. Criminal Court, The Hague; mem. Inst. of Int. Law; mem. Interamerican Judicial Council. *Address:* Secretariat of the Assembly of States Parties, International Criminal Court, Maanweg 174, 2516 AB The Hague, Netherlands (office). *Telephone:* (70) 5158097 (office). *Fax:* (70) 5158376 (office). *E-mail:* asp@asp.icc-cpi.int (office). *Website:* www.icc-cpi.int/asp.html (office).

PAOLINELLI, Alysson; Brazilian agronomist and academic; b. 1936, Bambuí, Minas Gerais; ed Fed. Agricultural Univ. of Lavras; Prof. of Agric., Fed. Agricultural Univ. of Lavras 1960–67, Dean 1967–71; Sec. of Agric. for Minas Gerais 1971–74; Minister of Agric. for Brazil 1974–79; currently consultant in agribusiness; Pres. Brazilian Asscn for Agricultural Educ. 1970–71; Personality of the Year in Agrobusiness, Ministry of Agriculture 2006, World Food Prize 2006. *Address:* c/o Brazilian Agribusiness Association,

Avenida Paulista 1754, 14° andar, Conj. 147–148, 01310-920 São Paulo, Brazil.

PAOLUCCI, Antonio; Italian art historian and museum director; *Director, Vatican Museums;* b. 1939, Rimini; ed student of Roberto Longhi; began his career at Soprintendenza per i Beni Culturali for Venice Region 1969–80; fmr Supt Polo Museale Fiorentino; worked for Mantova-Brescia-Cremona Region 1984–86; Dir Office of Hard Stones and the restoration laboratory in Florence 1986–88, Dept of Artistic Affairs of Tuscany 1988; Minister of Culture 1995–96; supervised comm. in charge of restoration of Basilica of St Francis of Assissi after the earthquake in 1997; was at centre of controversy concerning restoration of Michelangelo's David in Florence 2003; Dir Museums in Florence 2004–06, Vatican Museums 2007–; Pres. Accad. Carrara, Bergamo. *Publications:* more than 300 articles in various journals, including Paragone, Bollettino d'Arte, and of monographic studies on Palmezzano, Signorelli, as well as other Florentine artists and monuments. *Address:* Musei Vaticani, Città del Vaticano, 00120 Città del Vaticano, Rome, Italy (office). *E-mail:* info@mv.vatican.va (office). *Website:* mv.vatican.va (office).

PAPACOSTAS, Costas; Cypriot fmr police officer and politician; *Minister of Defence;* b. 12 Nov. 1939, Agia Triada of Yialousa, Famagusta District; m. Chryso Mammidou; one s. one d.; ed War Coll. and Nat. Defence Coll. of Greece, attended further special police training in crisis nan. and int. terrorism matters in Germany and USA; served in Cyprus Army and Nat. Guard for 18 years, reaching rank of Col; seconded to Auxiliary Police Force to fight against illegal activities of EOKA B' 1973, participated in resistance against coup of 15 July 1974; seconded again to Police Force to establish and command Mobile Immediate Action Unit to fight terrorism and organized crime 1974; transferred to Police Force with rank of Chief Supt 1984, attained rank of Deputy Chief of Police, resgnd comm. in protest at state of affairs in the Force 1996; elected mem. House of Reps (AKEL-Left-New Forces) for Famagusta 1996–, Chair. House Standing Cttee on Crime and on the Fight against Drugs and Addictive Substances, Deputy Chair. House Standing Cttee on Refugees-Enclaved-Missing-Adversely Affected Persons. mem. House Standing Cttee on Defence Affairs, House Standing Cttee on Legal Affairs; Minister of Defence 2008–; Hon. Diploma and Resistance Medal for his actions towards the defence of the Repub. and the defence of law and order against the coup of 15 July 1974, Govt of Cyprus 2004, Hon. Diploma and Medal for his participation in the liberation struggle of EOKA 1955–1959, Govt of Cyprus 2006. *Publications:* two extended essays, 'The Legal and Historical Truth on the Cyprus Problem' 1985, and 'Today's Turkey-trends and Prospects' (in Greek). *Address:* Ministry of Defence, 4 Emmanuel Roides Avenuw, 1432 Nicosia, Cyprus (office). *Telephone:* 22807622 (office). *Fax:* 22676182 (office). *E-mail:* defense@mod.gov.cy (office). *Website:* www.mod.gov .cy (office).

PAPACOSTEA, Serban, DHist; Romanian historian and academic; b. 25 June 1928, Bucharest; s. of Petre G. Papacostea and Josefina Papacostea; ed Univ. of Bucharest; scientific researcher and Dir 'Nicolae Iorga' Inst. of History, Bucharest; mem. editorial Bd Revue Roumaine d'Histoire, Studii si materiale de istorie medie (Studies and Materials of Medieval History), Il Mar Nero (Rome); Corresp. mem. Romanian Acad., Accad. Ligure di Scienze e Lettere; Prize of the Roman Acad. 1971. *Publications:* Istoria României (The History of Romania) (in collaboration) 1964, 1998, 2002, Istoria poporului român (History of the Romanian People) (in collaboration) 1970, Nochmals Wittenberg und Byzanz: die Moldau im Zeitalter der Reformation 1970, Oltenia sub stăpânirea austriacă, 1718–1739 (Oltenia under Austrian Rule, 1718–1739) 1971, Venise et les Pays Roumains au Moyen Age, in Venezia e il Levante fino al secolo XV, 1973, Stephan der Grosse, Fürst der Moldau 1975, Kilia et la politique orientale de Sigismond de Luxembourg 1976, Die politischen Voraussetzungen für die wirtschaftliche Vorherrschaft des Osmanischen Reiches im Schwarzmeergebiet 1453–1484 1978, La fondation de la Valachie et de la Moldavie et les Roumains de Transylvanie 1978, 'Quod non iretur ad Tanam': Un aspect fondamental de la politique génoise dans la Mer Noire au XIVe siècle 1979, Inceputurile politicii comerciale a Tării Românești și Moldovei (The Beginnings of Trade Policy in Wallachia and Moldavia) 1983, La fin de la domination génoise à Licostomo 1985, La Valachie et la crise de structure de l'Empire Ottoman (1402–1413) 1986, La Mer Noire: du monopole byzantin à la domination des Latins aux Détroits 1988, La première crise des rapports byzantino-génois après Nymphaion: le complot de Guglielmo Guercio (1264) 1988, Geneza statului in Evul mediu Rómánesc (The Formation of the Medieval Romanian State) 1988, Gênes, Venise et la Mer Noire à la fin du XIIIe siècle 1990, Byzance et la Croisade au Bas-Danube à la fin du XIVe siècle 1991, Jews in the Romanian Principalities during the Middle Ages 1993, Romanii in Secolul XIII intre Cruciata și Imperial Mongol 1993, Une révolte antigénoise en Mer Noire et la riposte de Gênes (1432–1434) 1994, Captive Clio: Romanian Historiography under Communist Rule 1996, Un tournant de la politique génoise en Mer Noire au XIVᵉsiècle 1997, Gênes, Venise et la Croisade de Varna 1997, Between the Crusades and the Mongol Empire 1998, Evul Mediu românesc (The Romanian Middle Ages) 2001, Welthandel und Weltpolitik im Spätmittelalter 2001, Byzance et les Detroits sous les Premiers Paléologues 2003, Les Génois et la Horde d'Or: le tournant de 1313 2004. *Leisure interest:* pre-classical music. *Address:* Institutul de Istorie 'Nicolae Iorga', Blvd Aviatorilor 1, Bucharest (office); Caragea Vodă 19, 71149 Bucharest, Romania (home). *Telephone:* (21) 6509045 (office); (21) 2114455 (home). *E-mail:* spap@b.astral.ro (home).

PAPADEMOS, Lucas D., PhD; Greek economist and banker; *Vice-President, European Central Bank;* b. 11 Oct. 1947, Athens; ed Athens Coll., MIT, USA; Prof. of Econs Columbia Univ., NY 1975–84, Univ. of Athens 1988–; Sr Economist Fed. Reserve Bank of Boston; Econ. Adviser Bank of Greece 1985–93, Head of Econ. Research Dept 1988–92, Deputy Gov. 1993–94, Gov.

1994–2002; Vice-Pres. ECB 2002–; mem. Cttee of Alts of Govs of EC Cen. Banks 1985–93, Council of Econ. Advisers 1985–88, 1991–94, EMI and various bds; Grand Commdr, Order of Honour 1999. *Address:* European Central Bank, Kaiserstrasse 29, Postfach 160319, 60066 Frankfurt am Main, Germany (office). *Telephone:* (69) 13440 (office). *Fax:* (69) 13446000 (office). *E-mail:* info@ecb.europa.eu (office). *Website:* www.ecb.europa.eu (office).

PAPADIMITRIOU, George, DJur; Greek academic and lawyer; *Professor of Constitutional Law, University of Athens;* b. 1944, Thessaloniki; s. of Alexandros Papadimitriou and Argiri Papadimitriou; m. Anna Papadimitriou Tsatsou 1976; one s.; ed Univs of Thessaloniki, Heidelberg and Paris I; Research Fellow, Inst. für Int. Recht, Kiel 1971–72, Max Planck Inst. of Foreign, Public and Int. Law, Heidelberg 1972–74; lecturer, Thessaloniki Univ. Law School 1975–79; Prof. of Constitutional Law, Thrace Univ. 1979–84, Univ. of Athens 1984–; Dean, Dept of Political Science and Public Admin. Univ. of Athens 1993; Legal Adviser to Prime Minister 1996–2004; mem. several nat. and foreign learned socs. *Publications include:* Die Stellung der allgemeinen Regeln des Voelkerrechts im innerstaatlichen Recht 1972, The Dispute of the Aegean Shelf and the Cyprus Problem 1975, Constitutional Law. The Electorate 1981, The European Parliament: Problems, Realities and Perspectives 1984, Constitutional Problems 1989–91, Democracy and European Integration 1993, Constitutional Problems 1992–93 1995, The Charter of Fundamental Rights. *Address:* 30 Sina Street, Athens 10672 (office); 8 Izodotou Street, Athens 10675, Greece (home). *Telephone:* (210) 3635137 (office); (210) 3617443 (office); (210) 7245851 (home). *Fax:* (210) 7216307 (home). *E-mail:* gpapdim@ath.forthnet.gr (office).

PAPADONGONAS, Alexandros; Greek politician and naval officer; b. 11 July 1931, Tripolis; s. of Dionisios Papadongonas and Vasiliki Papadongonas; m. Niki Maidonis 1976; one s. one d.; ed Greek Naval Acad., Naval War Coll., US Naval Schools, NATO Defence Coll.; has served on Greek fleet vessels and submarines and has held staff positions; organized with other Navy officers Movt of Navy against the dictatorship; arrested May 1973 and removed from service; returned to Navy July–Nov. 1974; MP 1974–93; Minister of Merchant Shipping 1974–77, of Communications 1977–80; Deputy Minister of Defence 1990–91, Minister of Merchant Shipping 1992–93; mem. Council of Europe 1982–89, 1991; Pres. Greek Del. to Parl. Ass. of OSCE 1993–; mem. North Atlantic Ass.; New Democracy Party; Medal of Mil. Valour, Commdr Order of the Phoenix, Officer Order of George I. *Leisure interests:* sailing, scuba diving, underwater archaeology. *Address:* 11 Nikis Street, Athens 105 57, Greece. *Telephone:* (1) 3255150.

PAPAIOANNOU, Miltiades; Greek politician and lawyer; b. 1946, Kalavryta, Achaia; ed Panteio Univ., Law Faculty of Athens; Panhellenic Socialist Movt (PASOK) MP; Deputy Minister, Ministry of Internal Affairs 1982–85, Minister of Justice 1985, Deputy Minister, Prime Minister's Dept and Govt Spokesman 1985–86, Gen. Sec. Ministry of Nat. Economy 1993–96; Minister of Labour and Social Security 1998–2000; Minister of State 2000–02; mem. Exec. Bureau and Cen. Cttee PASOK. *Publications:* numerous articles on politics, econs, public admin, local govt and regional devt. *Address:* c/o Ministry of Labour and Social Security, Odos Pireos 40, 104 37 Athens, Greece.

PAPALOIZOU, John Christopher Baillie, DPhil, FRS; British theoretical physicist and academic; *Professor, Department of Applied Mathematics and Theoretical Physics, University of Cambridge;* b. 1947; ed Queen Mary Coll., Univ. of London, Univ. of Sussex, Brighton; fmr Prof. of Math. and Astronomy and Dir Astronomy Unit, Queen Mary, Univ. of London; currently Prof., Dept of Applied Math. and Theoretical Physics, Univ. of Cambridge; Brouwer Award Winner 2004, asteroid 17063 Papaloizou named after him. *Achievements include:* co-discovered, with Jim E. Pringle, the Papaloizou-Pringle instability 1984. *Publications:* numerous scientific papers in professional journals on the theory of accretion disks, with particular application to the formation of planets, radial-orbit instability, toroidal modes in stars and different instabilities in accretion disks. *Address:* Department of Applied Mathematics and Theoretical Physics, Centre for Mathematical Sciences, Wilberforce Road, Cambridge, CB3 0WA, England (office). *Telephone:* (1223) 760390 (office). *Fax:* (1223) 765900 (office). *E-mail:* jcbp2@cam.ac.uk (office). *Website:* damtp.cam.ac.uk (office).

PAPANDREOU, Georgios A., MSc; Greek politician; *Leader, Panhellenic Socialist Movement—PASOK;* b. 16 June 1952, St Paul, Minn., USA; m. Ada Papandreou; one s. one d.; ed Athens Coll., Amherst Coll., Mass, USA, Stockholm Univ., Sweden, London School of Econs, UK; mem. Parl. (Panhellenic Socialist Movt —PASOK) for Achaia (Patras) 1981–96, for First Dist. of Athens 1996–; Under-Sec. for Cultural Affairs 1985–87; Minister of Educ. and Religious Affairs 1988–89, 1994–96; Deputy Minister of Foreign Affairs 1993–94; Alt. Foreign Minister 1996–99, Foreign Minister 1999–2004; unsuccessful presidential cand. 2004; mem. Cen. Cttee PASOK 1984–, Exec. Cttee 1987–88, mem. Exec. Office and Political Bureau 1996–, elected Leader PASOK Feb. 2004–; Govt Co-ordinator for 2004 Athens Olympic bid 1997; mem. Socialist Int. (Vice-Pres. 2005–06, Pres. 2006–); mem. Bd Foundation of Mediterranean Studies, for Research and Self-Educ., Cambridge Foundation for Peace; Fellow, Center for Int. Affairs, Harvard Univ. 1992–93; decorations from numerous countries including Grand Commdr, Order of the Polish Repub. 1996, Grand Cross, Order of Civil Merit (Spain) 1998, Grand Cross, Order of Merit (Germany) 2000, (Italy) 2003, El Sol de Peru 2003, Grand Commdr, Order of Merit (Hungary) 2003; Botsis Foundation for Promotion of Journalism Award 1988, SOS against Racism Award 1996, Abdi İpekçi Special Award for Peace and Friendship (Turkey) 1997, Statesman of the Year Award, Eastwest Inst. (USA) 2000. *Address:* Panhellenic Socialist Movement (Panellinion Socialistikon Kinima), Odos Charilaou Trikoupi 50, 106 80 Athens, Greece (office). *Telephone:* (210) 3665380 (office). *Fax:* (210) 3665092

(office). *E-mail:* pasok@pasok.gr (office). *Website:* www.pasok.gr (office); www.papandreou.gr.

PAPANDREOU, Vasiliki (Vasso), PhD; Greek politician; b. 1944, Valimitika nr Aeghiou; ed School of Econ. and Trade Sciences, Univ. of Athens, Univs of London and Reading, UK; Lecturer, Univ. of Athens; Research Asst, Univs of Exeter and Oxford, UK; Dir Hellenic Org. of Small and Medium-sized Businesses, Athens 1981–85; Founder-mem. Panhellenic Socialist Party (PASOK) 1974, mem. Cen. Cttee Exec. Bureau 1984–88, 1996–; MP 1985–89, 1993–; Deputy Minister for Industry, Energy and Tech. 1985–89, Alt. Minister 1986–87; Alt. Minister for Trade 1988–89; Commr for Social Affairs, Employment, Educ., Comm. of European Communities 1989–92; Head of Greek Del. Council of Europe Parl. Ass. 1993–96, Vice-Pres. 1995–96; Minister for Devt 1996–99, of the Interior, Public Admin and Decentralization 1999–2001, of the Environment, Physical Planning and Public Works 2001–04; Chevalier Légion d'honneur, France 1993, Grand-Croix, Belgium 1993, Great Cross of the Order of the North Star 1999; Hon. LittD (Sheffield) 1992; Dr hc (CNAA, London) 1992, (P. Sabatier, Toulouse) 1993. *Publications:* Multinational Companies and Less Developed Countries: The Case of Greece 1981; numerous papers on politics and econs. *Address:* c/o Ministry of the Environment, Physical Planning and Public Works, Odos Amaliados 17, 115 23 Athens; 15 Omirou Street, 10672 Athens, Greece. *Telephone:* (210) 6431461 (office). *Fax:* (210) 6432589 (office).

PAPANTONIOU, Ioannis, PhD; Greek politician; b. 1949, Paris, France; m.; two s. one d.; ed Univs of Athens, Wisconsin, USA, Paris, France and Cambridge, UK; Lecturer, Dept of Econs, Univ. of Athens, Researcher Centre of Planning and Econ. Research 1977–78; staff mem. Econs Dept OECD, Paris 1978–81; Panhellenic Socialist Movt (PASOK) MEP 1981–84; Special Adviser to Prime Minister on EC Affairs; Deputy Minister for Nat. Economy 1985–89, Minister of Trade 1989; mem. Parl. for first Dist of Athens 1989–; Deputy Minister for Nat. Economy 1985–86, 1987–89; Minister for Commerce 1993–94; Minister for Nat. Economy 1994–96, for Nat. Economy and Econs 1996–2001, of Nat. Defence 2001–04. *Address:* c/o Ministry of National Defence, Stratopedo Papagou, Holargos, Athens, Greece.

PAPATHANASIOU, Yannis; Greek business executive and politician; *Minister of Economy and Finance;* b. 1 Jan. 1954, Athens; m. Ileana Iliopoulou; two d.; ed Tech. Univ. of Athens; Pres. and Man. Dir J.D. Papathanassiou SA –2002; mem. Bd of Dirs Athens Chamber of Commerce and Industry 1982–88, Sec.-Gen. 1988–93, Pres. 1994–2000; adviser to Minister of Commerce, Industry and Energy 1991–92; Vice-Pres. DEPA (Public Gas Enterprises) 1992–93; mem. Vouli (Parl.) 2000–; Deputy Minister of Devt 2004–07, of Economy and Finance 2007–09, Minister of Economy and Finance 2009–. *Address:* Ministry of Economy and Finance, Odos Nikis 5–7, 101 80 Athens, Greece (office). *Telephone:* (210) 3332000 (office). *E-mail:* ypetho@mnec.gr (office); info@papathanassiou.gr. *Website:* www.mnec.gr (office); www.papathanassiou.gr.

PAPAZIAN, Vahan; Armenian politician, diplomatist, historian and orientalist; *Professor of Political Sciences, Yerevan State University;* b. 26 Jan. 1957, Yerevan; s. of Hagop Papazian and Ophelia Papazian; m. Anahit Papazian; two s.; ed Yerevan State Univ.; researcher, Inst. of History, Armenian Acad. of Sciences 1980–91; Counsellor to Pres. of Armenia 1991–92; Chargé d'Affaires of Armenia to France 1992–93; Minister of Foreign Affairs 1993–96; on staff, Acad. of Sciences 1996–98; Amb. to France 1997–98; Prof. of Political Sciences, Yerevan State Univ. 1998–. *Publications:* works on history of Armenian-Iranian relations and trade routes in Middle Ages, politics. *Address:* Yerevan State University, 1 Alek Manukian, 375025 Yerevan (office); 1st Pass, Av. Baghramian 1, Apt 30, Yerevan, Armenia (home). *Telephone:* (10) 551804 (office); (10) 542980 (home). *E-mail:* vahanpapazian@yahoo.com (home).

PAPIERNIK-BERKHAUER, Emile, DenM, FRCOG; French obstetrician, gynaecologist and academic; b. 14 Feb. 1936, Paris; s. of Motel Papiernik and Pesa Bonk; m. Martine Czermichow 1961; two s. one d.; ed Univ. of Paris; Asst Prof., Faculté de Médecine René Descartes, Paris and Maternité de Port-Royal, Paris 1966–, now Emer. Prof.; Prof. of Obstetrics and Gynaecology, Univ. of Paris-Orsay and Chair. Dept of Obstetrics and Gynaecology, Hôpital Béclère, Clamart 1972–90; Dir Research Unit 187, Inst. de la santé et de la recherche médicale (INSERM) (Physiology and Psychology of Human Reproduction) 1979–; mem. Bd of Dirs Collège nat. des gynécologues-accouchers; Fellow, American Acad. of Pediatrics, Royal Coll. of Obstetricians and Gynaecologists; Chevalier, Légion d'honneur. *Publication:* Le prix de la vie 1988, Le Guide Papiernik de la grossesse (jtly) 1991, Le passeur de vie, entretien avec Emile Papiernik (jtly) 1998. *Leisure interest:* collector of contemporary painting. *Address:* Maternité de Port Royal Baudeloque, 123 blvd de Port Royal, 75674 Paris cedex 14 (office); 35 rue Imbergeres, 92330 Sceaux, France (home).

PAPOULIAS, George Dimitrios; Greek diplomatist (retd); b. 19 May 1927; s. of Dimitrios G. Papoulias and Caterina Kontopoulou; m. Emily Pilavachi 1974; one d.; ed Univ. of Athens; entered diplomatic service 1955; served Athens, New Delhi, Bonn; Deputy Perm. Del. to UN and int. orgs Geneva 1964–69; Dir Political Affairs, Ministry of Northern Greece 1969–70; Minister, Paris and Perm. Rep. to UNESCO 1971–74; mem. Bd of Dirs Resettlement Fund, Council of Europe 1971–74; Perm. Rep. to UN, New York 1975–79; Amb. to Turkey 1979–83, to USA 1983–89; Alt. Minister and Minister for Foreign Affairs 1989, 1990; Amb. to UK (also accred to Iceland) 1990–93; mem. Bd of Dirs Constantin Karamanlis Inst. for Democracy 1995–; mem. Inst. for Mediterranean Political Studies, Club de Monaco 2002–; Commdr Order of the Phoenix, Order of George I (Greece); several foreign orders and decorations including Grand Officier de l'Ordre du Mérite (France) 1975.

Leisure interests: archaeology, history. *Address:* Rigillis 16, 106 74 Athens, Greece. *Telephone:* (1) 7229888 (office). *Fax:* (1) 7236798 (office).

PAPOULIAS, Karolos, PhD; Greek politician, lawyer and head of state; *President;* b. 4 June 1929, Ioannina, Epirus; s. of the late Maj.-Gen. Gregorios Papoulias; m. May Panou Papoulias; three d.; ed Univs of Athens, Madrid and Cologne; fmr practising lawyer in Athens; lived in Germany 1962–74; founding mem. Socialist Democratic Union which mobilized Greeks living in W Europe against the military coup 1967; worked for Greek radio programme of Deutsche Welle; mem. Greek democratic del. at Gen. Ass. of Council of Europe during period of mil. dictatorship in Greece; mem. Parl. 1977–2004; mem. Cen. Cttee Panhellenic Socialist Movt (PASOK); Sec.-Gen. Centre for Mediterranean Studies, Athens; Deputy Minister for Foreign Affairs 1981–84, Alt. Minister 1984–85, Minister of Foreign Affairs 1985, 1993–96; Alt. Minister for Defence 1989–90; Pres. of Greece 2005–; Founder and fmr Pres. Asscn for Greek Linguistic Heritage; fmr Pres. Ethnikos athletic union. *Address:* Office of the President, Odos Vassileos Georgiou 2, 100 28 Athens, Greece (office). *Telephone:* (210) 7283111 (office). *Fax:* (210) 7248938 (office). *E-mail:* publicrelationsoffice@presidency.gr (office). *Website:* www.presidency.gr (office).

PAPOUTSIS, Christos; Greek politician and economist; b. 11 April 1953, Larissa; m.; one d.; ed Univ. of Athens; Pres. Greek Nat. Union of Students 1978–80; Special Adviser on Public Admin, Ministry of Presidency of Govt 1981–84; mem. Exec. Bureau Pan-Hellenic Socialist Movt (PASOK), Leader PASOK Del. to European Parl., mem. Political Council for Foreign Affairs, Security and Defence Policy; mem. European Parl. 1984–95, Vice-Pres. Socialist Group 1987–89; mem. Presidium, Party of European Socialists 1988–; Commr for Energy and Euratom Supply Agency, Small and Medium Enterprises (SME) and Tourism, European Comm. 1995–99; Minister of Mercantile Marine 2000–01; mem. Parl. 2000, 2004; Highest Mark of Distinction with Cross (Austria), Gran Official, Orden Libertador Bernardo O'Higgins (Chile). *Publications:* European Journeys 1994, The Colour of the Future 1998, For Europe in the 21st Century 1999. *Address:* Lykavittou 5, 10672 Athens, Greece (office). *Telephone:* (210) 3387700 (office). *Fax:* (210) 3387709 (office). *E-mail:* papoutsi@otenet.gr (office). *Website:* www.cpapoutsis.gr (office).

PAPPANO, Antonio; American conductor and pianist; *Music Director, The Royal Opera, Covent Garden;* b. 30 Dec. 1959, Epping, London; m. Pam Bullock 1995; ed studied in USA with Norma Verrilli, Arnold Franchetti and Gustav Meier; Répétiteur and Asst Conductor New York City Opera, Gran Teatro del Liceo, Barcelona, Frankfurt Opera, Lyric Opera of Chicago early to mid-1980s; asst to Daniel Barenboim for Tristan und Isolde, Parsifal and the Ring cycle at Bayreuth Festival 1986; opera conducting debut with Norwegian Opera, Oslo 1987; Music Dir, Norwegian Opera 1990–92; Covent Garden debut conducting La Bohème 1990; Vienna Staatsoper debut conducting new production of Wagner's Siegfried 1993; season 1996 included the original Don Carlos in Brussels and at the Paris Théâtre du Châtelet; season 1997 Salome at Chicago and Eugene Onegin at the Metropolitan; Prin. Guest Conductor Israel Philharmonic Orchestra 1997–2000; seasons 1999–2001 Lohengrin at Bayreuth; has conducted many world-class orchestras, including Berlin Philharmonic Orchestra, Boston Symphony Orchestra, Chicago Symphony Orchestra, Cleveland Orchestra, London Symphony Orchestra, Los Angeles Philharmonic Orchestra, Orchestre de Paris, Oslo Philharmonic Orchestra, Munich Philharmonic Orchestra; Music Dir Théâtre Royal de la Monnaie, Brussels 1992–2002, conducting a wide variety of titles; Music Dir Royal Opera, Covent Garden 2002–; new productions of Ariadne auf Naxos, Wozzeck, Madama Butterfly and Pagliacci, revival of Falstaff 2002–03; Don Giovanni, Aida, Lady Macbeth of Mtsensk, Faust and Peter Grimes in 2003–04; Das Rheingold and Die Walküre 2005; Music Dir Orchestra of the Nat. Acad. of Santa Cecilia, Rome 2005–; Royal Philharmonic Soc. Award for best conductor 2005, Assoc. Naz. Critici Musicali Premio Abbiati Prize for Conductor 2006. *Recordings include:* Puccini's La Rondine (Gramophone Award for Best Opera Recording and Record of the Year 1997), Il Trittico 1999, Britten's The Turn of the Screw (Théâtre Royal de la Monnaie production) (Choc du Monde de la Musique, Prix de l'Acad. du Disque Lyrique Grand Prix Int., Orphée d'Or) 1999, Werther 1999, Manon Gramophone Award for Best Opera Recording 2001; many recordings as conductor including Rachmaninov's Piano Concertos 1 & 2 2005; recordings as pianist with Rockwell Blake, Barbara Bonney and Han-Na Chang. *Address:* c/o Peter Wiggins, IMG Artists, 31–33 rue du Temple, 75004 Paris, France (office); c/o Royal Opera House, Covent Garden, London, WC2E 9DD, England. *Telephone:* 1-44-31-00-10 (office). *Fax:* 1-44-31-44-40 (office). *E-mail:* pwiggins@imgartists.com (office). *Website:* www.imgartists.com (office); www.roh.org.uk.

PAPPAS, Spyros; Greek lawyer, civil servant and EU official; b. 1 Jan. 1953, Athens; m. Frady Karkanis; one s. one d.; ed Univ. of Athens, Panteios School of Econ. and Political Studies, Univ. of Paris, Directorate for European Affairs, INSEAD; fmr naval Petty Officer; barrister, Athens 1976; Auditor Council of State 1978, Counsel 1983; Special Adviser in Prime Minister's Legal Office 1981; mem. Cen. Comm. for Drafting of Laws 1982; est. Nat. Centre of Public Admin., Sec.-Gen. 1985; est. Inst. of Permanent Training 1985; Assoc. Prof., European Inst. of Public Admin, Maastricht 1988, Dir of Faculty 1989, Dir-Gen. 1990, Prof. of European Law 1992; Dir-Gen. for Consumer Policy, EC 1995, for Information, Communication, Culture and Audiovisual Media 1997–99; Chair. Bd of Govs Int. East–West Acad.; mem. Supreme Council Church of Greece 1984, Comm. of Information on National Affairs, Inst. for Admin. Studies, Asscn of the Judges of the Council of State, Inst. of Public Admin., Cttee for Drafting of the Encyclopedia of Admin., Centre for European Policy Studies Int. Advisory Council, Scientific Council of Academia Istropolitana Bratislava Inst. of Advanced Studies, Foundation for Hellenic Culture; assoc. mem. Asscn of European Magistrates for Democracy and Liberty (MEDEL); substitute bd mem. Open Univ., Athens; cr. European Centre of Judges and Lawyers 1992; Hon. State Scholar 1970–73, Scholar of Council of Europe 1977; Officer Order of Merit, Luxembourg 1994; First Prize Michel Stassinopoulos Foundation for Admin. Law 1976. *Publications:* La constitution de la Grèce de 1975 1976, Le régime de planification en Grèce 1977, Le Tribunal de Première Instance 1990, Tendances actuelles et évolution de la jurisprudence de la cour de justice des Communautés européennes: suivi annuel (ed.) Vol. I 1993, Vol. II 1995, Procédures administratives nationales: préparation et mise en oeuvre des décisions communautaires: études comparatives (ed.) 1994, EC Competition Law: Financial Aspects (Co-Ed.) 1994, The Changing Role of Parliaments in the European Union (co-ed.) 1995, The European Union's Common Foreign and Security Policy: The Challenges of the Future 1996, Politiques publiques dans l'Union européenne 1996.

PAPUC, Gheorghe; Moldovan politician and military officer; *Minister of Internal Affairs;* b. 6 May 1954, Frăsineşti; m.; three c.; ed Inst. of Econs and Law, Moscow, Legal Inst., Ministry of Internal Affairs of Russian Fed.; various military positions in Soviet and Moldovan armed forces to brigade command level 1973–97; Head of Advanced Courses, Ministry of the Interior, fmr USSR 1989–92; Minister of Internal Affairs 2002–. *Address:* Ministry of Internal Affairs, 2012 Chişinău, bd Ştefan cel Mare 75, Moldova (office). *Telephone:* (22) 22-45-47 (office). *Fax:* (22) 22-27-43 (office). *E-mail:* mai@mai.md (office). *Website:* www.mai.md (office).

PAQUET-SEVIGNY, Thérèse, PhD; Canadian UN official, sociologist and academic; *Director, UNESCO Chair in Communication and International Development and Professor of Communications, Québec University;* b. 3 Feb. 1934, Sherbrooke, Québec; d. of René Paquet and Marie-Reine Cloutier; m. Robert Sévigny 1956; one s. one d.; ed Sorbonne-Paris Univ. and Univ. of Montreal; journalism and communications research for La Tribune and L'Actualité, Montreal and for Montreal and Laval Univs 1952–61; Man. Dir for Consumer Research, Steinberg Limitée 1961–66; various appointments at Communications Depts Montreal Univ., McGill Univ. and Ecole des Hautes Etudes Commerciales, Montreal 1969–76; Vice-Pres. for Research and Planning, BCP Publicité Limitée 1969–71, Vice-Pres. and Man. Dir 1974–81, Pres. and Chief of Operations 1981–83; Vice-Pres. RSGL Publicité Limitée 1971–74; Vice-Pres. for Communications, Canadian Broadcasting Corpn (CBC) 1983–87; Under-Sec.-Gen. for Public Information, United Nations 1987; Prof. of Communications, Québec Univ., Montreal (UQAM) 1993–; Dir, UNESCO Chair in Communication and Int. Devt 1993–; Int. Consultant 1993–; Sec.-Gen. Orbicom (Int. Network of UNESCO Chairs in Communications) 1993–98, Sr Adviser 1999–; Dr hc (Sherbrooke, Bishop's Univ.) 1991. *Publications:* articles in books and journals. *Leisure interests:* reading, films, walking, friends. *Address:* PO Box 8888, Downtown Station, Montreal, Québec, H3C 3P8 (office); 1509 Sherbrooke Street, West, Apartment 29, Montreal, Québec, H3G 1M1, Canada.

PARADIS, Christian; Canadian politician; *Minister of Public Works and Government Services;* b. 1 Jan. 1974, Thetford Mines, Québec; MP Parl. for Mégantic—L'Érable 2006–; Parl. Sec. to Minister of Natural Resources 2006–07; Sec. of State for Agric. and Agri-food 2007–08; Minister of Public Works and Govt Services 2008–; mem. Conservative Party of Canada. *Address:* Public Works and Government Services Canada, 102 Corporate Communications, 16a1, Portage III, Gatineau, PQ K1A 0S5, Canada (office). *Telephone:* (819) 956-3115 (office). *Fax:* (819) 956-9062 (office). *E-mail:* questions@pwgsc.gc.ca (office). *Website:* www.pwgsc.gc.ca (office).

PARAMONOVA, Tatyana Vladimirovna, CandSci; Russian banker; *First Deputy Chairperson, Central Bank of the Russian Federation;* b. 24 Oct. 1950; one s.; ed G. V. Plekhanov Inst. of Nat. Economy, Moscow; economist, later Head of Div., USSR State Bank 1972–92; Deputy Chair. Cen. Bank of Russian Fed. 1992–94, 1995–97, Acting Chair. 1994–95, First Deputy Chair. 1998–, mem. Bd of Dirs 2002–, also IMF Alt. Gov. for Russian Fed. 2000–; worked in various Moscow commercial banks 1992, 1997–98; Dr hc (G. V. Plekhanov Inst. of Nat. Economy); Order of Merit 2000; Merited Economist of the Russian Fed. 1999. *Publications:* more than 120 research papers on economics. *Address:* Central Bank of Russian Federation, Neglinnaya str. 12, 107016 Moscow, Russia (office). *Telephone:* (495) 771-91-00 (office). *Fax:* (495) 921-64-65 (office). *Website:* www.cbr.ru (office).

PARAS BIR BIKRAM SHAH DEV; Nepalese royal; b. 30 Dec. 1971, Kathmandu; s. of King Gyanendra Bir Bikram Shah Dev and Queen Komal Rajya Laxmi Devi Shah; m. Himani Rajya Laxmi Devi Shah 2000; one s. two d.; ed St Joseph's Coll., Darjeeling, India, Budhanilkantha School, Schiller Int. Univ., UK; proclaimed Crown Prince of Nepal 26 Oct. 2001, heir-apparent to throne of Nepal until monarchy was abolished and replaced by secular fed. repub. May 2008; Chair. Council of Royal Reps during state visits; Coordinator, Zoo Devt Cttee, King Mahendra Trust for Nature Conservation –2001, Chair. King Mahendra Trust for Nature Conservation 2001–; conferred title of Grand Master of all Orders of the Kingdom of Nepal 2006; Shubha Rajyabhisheka Padaka 1975, Gaddi Aarohan Ko Rajat Mahotsav Padaka, 2028–2053 B.S. 1997, Vishista Seva Padaka 1999, Birendra-Aishwarya Seva Padaka 2001, Suprasiddha Prabala Gorkha Dakshina Bahu 2001, Daivi Prakopa Piditoddhara Padaka 2003, Maha Ujjvala Keertimaya Nepal-Shreepada (First Class) 2004, Birendra-Mala 2006, Ati Maha Gauravamaya Supradeepta Birendra Prajatantra Bhaskara 2006. *Leisure interests:* horse riding, music, composing poems.

PARASKEVA, Janet, BA, JP; British civil servant; *First Civil Service Commissioner;* b. 28 May 1946; d. of Antonis Paraskeva and Doris Paraskeva (née Fowler); m. Alan Hunt 1967 (divorced 1983); two d., two step s.; ed

Worcester Coll. of Educ., Open Univ., UK; teacher 1967–71; self-employed toy maker 1970–73; several positions in youth work 1972–78; Head of Youth Work Unit, Nat. Youth Bureau 1978–81; HM Insp. of Schools Dept of Educ. and Science (now Dept for Educ. and Employment) 1983–88; Dir Nat. Youth Bureau 1988–91; CEO Nat. Youth Agency 1991–95; Dir Nat. Lotteries Charities Bd, England 1995–2000; CEO Law Soc. of England and Wales 2000–06; First Civil Service Commr 2006–; Chair. Olympic Lottery Distributor 2006–; Chair. Child Maintenance and Enforcement Comm. 2007–; mem. Bd of Dirs Serious Organised Crime Agency, Asset Recovery Agency; mem. Consumer Council for Water; mem. Fosse Community Nat. Health Service Trust 1992–2000, Council of Leicester Univ. 1998–2000. *Leisure interests:* golf, riding, gardening. *Address:* Office of Civil Service Commissioners, 3rd Floor, 35 Great Smith Street, London, SW1P 3BQ, England (office). *Telephone:* (20) 7276-2617 (office). *E-mail:* info@civilservicecommissioners.org (office). *Website:* www.civilservicecommissioners.org (office).

PARAVAĆ, Borislav; Bosnia and Herzegovina politician; b. 18 Feb. 1943, Kostajnica; m.; two c.; ed Univ. of Zagreb; certified accountant and financial auditor; fmr Mayor of Doboj; mem. Republika Srpska Parl. 1996–2002; First Deputy Chair. Parl. House of Reps 2002; Serb mem. Presidency (tripartite) of Bosnia and Herzegovina 2003–06, Chair. April–June 2003, Oct. 2004–June 2005. *Address:* c/o Social Democratic Party of Bosnia and Herzegovina (SDP BiH) (Socijaldemokratska Partija BiH), 71000 Sarajevo, Alipašina 41, Bosnia and Herzegovina.

PARAYRE, Jean-Paul-Christophe; French building and civil engineering executive; b. 5 July 1937, Lorient; s. of Louis Parayre and Jeanne (Malarde) Parayre; m. Marie-Françoise Chaufour 1962; two s. two d.; ed Lycées in Casablanca (Morocco) and Versailles, Ecole Polytechnique, Paris, Ecole Nat. des Ponts et Chaussées; Engineer, Dept of Highways 1963–67; Tech. Adviser, Ministry of Social Affairs 1967, Ministry of Econ. and Finance 1968; Dir of Mech. Industries at Ministry of Industry and Research 1970–74; Chief Adviser to Pres. and Gen. Man. Banque Vernes et Commerciale 1974; Man. of Planning, Automobile Div. of Peugeot 1975; Man. Automobile Div. of Peugeot-Citroën 1976, Chair. Bd of Dirs Peugeot SA 1977–84, mem. advisory Bd 1984; mem. Supervisory Bd Soc. Dumez 1977–84 (Dir-Gen. 1984, Chair. 1988–90, Pres. 1991–92); Pres., Dir-Gen. Fided Financière (affil. to Dumez) 1985; Vice-Pres., Dir-Gen. Lyonnaise des Eaux-Dumez 1990–92, Vice-Pres. 1990–93; Pres. Supervisory Bd Razel 1991; Pres. Bolloré Technologies Jan.–Sept. 1994, Scac-Delmas-Vieljeux 1994, Pres. Saga 1996–99; Vice-Pres. Bolloré Group 1994–99; Dir Bolloré Investissement 1994, Carillion PLC 1999, Stena UK 1999; Chair. Advisory Bd Vallourec 2000; Officier, Légion d'honneur, Commdr Ordre nat. du Mérite. *Leisure interests:* golf, tennis. *Address:* 31/32 Ennismore Gardens, London, SW7 1AE, England (home). *Fax:* (20) 7581-1707 (home).

PARDEE, Arthur Beck, BS, MA, PhD; American biochemist and academic; *Professor Emeritus of Biological Chemistry and Molecular Pharmacology, Harvard Medical School;* b. 13 July 1921, Chicago, Ill.; s. of Charles A. Pardee and Elizabeth Beck; m. Ruth Sager (died 1997); three s. from previous m.; m. Ann Goodman; ed Univ. of California, Berkeley, California Inst. of Tech.; Postdoctoral Fellow, Univ. of Wisconsin 1947–49; Instructor, Asst and Assoc. Prof., Univ. of Calif., Berkeley 1949–61; Sr Postdoctoral Fellow, Pasteur Inst. 1957–58; Prof. of Biochemical Sciences and Donner Prof. of Science, Princeton Univ. 1961–75; Prof. of Biological Chem. and Molecular Pharmacology, Harvard Medical School, Boston 1975–97, Prof. Emer. 1997–; Prof. Emer., Harvard Univ. 1998–; Chief, Div. Cell Growth and Regulation, Dana Farber Cancer Inst. 1975–98; mem. ACS, American Soc. of Biological Chemists (Treasurer 1964–70, Pres. 1980), American Asscn for Cancer Research (Pres. 1985), American Acad. of Arts and Sciences, American Soc. of Microbiologists, Japanese Biochemical Soc.; mem. Council American Cancer Soc. 1967–71; Fellow, Int. Inst. for Advanced Studies Nara, Japan 1999, American Philosophical Soc. 2001; Hon. Faculty mem. Nanjing Univ. 1999; Dr hc (Paris) 1993; ACS Paul Lewis Award 1960, Krebs Medal, Fed. of European Biochemical Socs 1973, Rosensteil Award, Brandeis Univ. 1975, Princess Takamatsee Award (Japan) 1990, Boehringer Bioanalytica Award 1998, Ludwig Award 2002, and numerous other honours and awards. *Publications:* Experiments in Biochemical Research Techniques (co-author) 1957; more than 500 articles on subjects including bacterial physiology and enzymology in synchronous cultures, cell division cycle events, growth regulation in cancer and normal cells, enzymology of DNA synthesis, repair of damaged DNA . *Leisure interests:* music, tennis, travel, art. *Address:* Dana Farber Cancer Institute, 44 Binney Street, Boston, MA 02115 (office); 987 Memorial Drive, Unit 271, Cambridge, MA 02138 (home). *Telephone:* (617) 632-3372 (office). *Fax:* (617) 632-4680 (office). *E-mail:* arthur-pardee@fci.harvard.edu (office). *Website:* hms.harvard.edu/hms/home.asp (office).

PARED PÉREZ, Rear-Adm. Sigfrido; Dominican Republic government official and military officer; fmr Head Nat. Investigations Directorate; Sec. of State for Armed Forces 2004–. *Address:* Secretariat of State for the Armed Forces, Plaza de la Independencia, Avda 27 de Febrero, esq. Luperón, Santo Domingo, DN, Dominican Republic (office). *Telephone:* 530-5149 (office). *Fax:* 531-1309 (office). *Website:* www.secffaa.mil.do (office).

PAREDES RANGEL, Beatriz Elena; Mexican politician; *President, Partido Revolucionario Institucional (PRI);* b. 18 Aug. 1953, Tlaxcala; ed Nat. Autonomous Univ. of Mexico (UNAM); Tlaxcala state deputy (Partido Revolucionario Institucional—PRI) 1974–77; adviser to Gov. of Tlaxcala 1978–80; Under-Sec. for Agrarian Reform 1982; Gov. of Tlaxcala (first woman) 1987–92; Amb. to Cuba 1993; unsuccessful cand. for presidency of PRI 2002; unsuccessful campaign for mayoralty of Mexico City, representing alliance of PRI and Partido Verde Ecologista de Mexico (PVEM) 2006; Pres. PRI Nat. Exec. Cttee 2007–; fmr mem. Chamber of Deputies and Senate; fmr Pres. Nat. Comm. of Integral Devt and Social Justice for Indigenous Peoples; fmr Pres.

Colosio Trust Fund; Vice-Pres. Socialist Int.; fmr Pres. Parlatino (Latin American Parl.), currently mem. Consulting Council; Orden de la Solidaridad (Cuba) 1994, Gran Cruz, Orden del Soberano Congreso Nacional de Guatemala 2001, Gran Cruz de Isabel la Católica (Spain) 2002, Ordem Nacional do Cruzeiro do Sul (Brazil) 2003. *Music:* two CDs: El Loco Afán, Corazón Gemelo. *Publications:* Acaso la Palabra, Con la Cabeza Descubierta; regular contrib. to journal El Universal. *Leisure interests:* music and poetry. *Address:* Partido Revolucionario Institucional (PRI), Insurgentes Norte 59, Col. Buenavista, Del. Cuauhtémoc, CP 06359, México, DF, Mexico (office). *Telephone:* (55) 55-41-91-22 (office). *Fax:* (55) 55-41-91-34 (office). *E-mail:* beatrizparedes@pri.org.mx (office). *Website:* www.pri.org.mx (office).

PARET, Peter, PhD, DLit, LittD, DH; American historian and academic; *Andrew W. Mellon Professor Emeritus in the Humanities, Institute for Advanced Study;* b. 13 April 1924, Berlin, Germany; s. of Dr Hans Paret and Suzanne Aimée Cassirer; m. Isabel Harris 1961; one s. one d.; ed Univ. of Calif. and Univ. of London; Research Assoc. Center of Int. Studies, Princeton Univ. 1960–62; Visiting Asst Prof., Univ. of Calif., Davis 1962–63, Assoc. Prof. 1963–66, Prof. of History 1966–69; Prof. of History, Stanford Univ. 1969–77, Raymond A. Spruance Prof. in Int. History 1977–86; Andrew W. Mellon Prof. in the Humanities, Inst. for Advanced Study, Princeton 1986–97, Andrew W Mellon Prof. Emer. 1997–; Lees Knowles Lecturer, Univ. Cambridge 2008; mem. American Philosophical Soc., Historische Kommission zu Berlin; Fellow, American Acad. of Arts and Sciences, Royal Historical Soc., Leo Baeck Inst.; Hon. Fellow LSE, Clausewitz Gesellschaft; Officer's Cross, German Order of Merit; four hon. degrees; Thomas Jefferson Medal, Samuel Eliot Morison Medal, Moncado Prizes. *Publications:* Guerrillas in the 1960s (with John Shy) 1961, French Revolutionary Warfare 1964, Yorck and the Era of Prussian Reform 1966, The Berlin Secession 1980, Makers of Modern Strategy (ed.) 1986, Art as History 1988, Carl von Clausewitz: On War (ed. and trans. with Michael Howard) 1976, 1984, Clausewitz and the State 1985, Carl von Clausewitz, Historical and Political Writings (ed. and trans.) 1991, Understanding War 1992, Persuasive Images (with Beth Lewis and Paul Paret) 1992, Sammler, Stifter und Museen (ed. with Ekkehard Mai) 1993, Imagined Battles 1997, German Encounters with Modernism 2001, An Artist against the Third Reich: Ernst Barlach, 1933–38 2003, 1806: The Cognitive Challenge of War 2009. *Address:* School of Historical Studies, Institute for Advanced Study, Einstein Drive, Princeton, NJ 08540, USA (office). *Telephone:* (609) 734-8344 (home). *Fax:* (609) 924-8399 (home). *E-mail:* paret@ias .edu (office). *Website:* www.hs.ias.edu (office).

PARETSKY, Sara N., MBA, PhD; American writer; b. 8 June 1947, Ames, IA; d. of David Paretsky and Mary E. Edwards; m. S. Courtenay Wright 1976; three c.; ed Univs of Kansas and Chicago; Man. Urban Research Center, Chicago 1971–74; CNA Insurance Co., Chicago 1977–85; writer of crime novels 1985–; Pres. Sisters in Crime, Chicago 1986–88; Dir Nat. Abortion Rights Action League, Ill. 1987–90; mem. Crime Writers' Asscn; four hon. degrees; Ms Magazine Woman of the Year 1987, CWA Silver Dagger Award 1988, Diamond Dagger for Lifetime Achievement, British Crime Writers Asscn 2002. *Publications include:* Indemnity Only 1982, Deadlock (Friends of American Writers Prize 1985) 1984, Killing Orders 1986, Bitter Medicine 1987, Toxic Shock (British Crime Writers Asscn Silver Dagger for Fiction 1988) 1987, Blood Shot 1988, Burn Marks 1990, Guardian Angel 1992, A Woman's Eye (ed.) 1992, Tunnel Vision 1994, Women on the Case 1997, Hard Time 2000, Total Recall 2002, Blacklist 2003 (British Crime Writers Asscn Gold Dagger for Fiction 2004), Fire Sale 2006, Writing in an Age of Silence 2007, Bleeding Kansas 2008; numerous short stories and articles. *Leisure interests:* walking, singing, making the perfect cappuccino. *Address:* c/o Dominick Abel Literary Agency, Inc., 146 West 82nd Street, 1B, New York, NY 12546, USA (office); 146 W 82nd Street, Apartment 18, New York, NY 10024, USA (office). *Telephone:* (212) 877-0710 (office). *E-mail:* dominick@ dalainc.com (office); viwarshawski@mindspring.com (office). *Website:* www .saraparetsky.com.

PARFIT, Derek, MA, FBA; British academic; *Senior Research Fellow, All Souls College, University of Oxford;* b. 11 Dec. 1942, Chengtu, China; s. of Norman Parfit and Jessie Browne; ed Oxford Univ.; Fellow All Souls Coll., Oxford 1967–; Sr Research Fellow 1984–; Visiting Prof. Dept of Philosophy, Harvard, Princeton and New York Univs; Fellow American Acad. of Arts and Sciences. *Publication:* Reasons and Persons 1984. *Leisure interest:* architectural photography. *Address:* All Souls College, Oxford, OX1 4AL, England. *Telephone:* (1865) 279282. *Fax:* (1865) 279299.

PARFITT, David; British film producer; b. 8 July 1958; s. of the late William Parfitt and of Maureen Collinson; m. 1st Susan Coates (divorced 1993); one s.; m. 2nd Elizabeth Barron 1996; two s.; ed Bede Grammar School, Sunderland, Barbara Speake Stage School, London; actor 1970–88; producer 1985–; Man. Dir Renaissance Theatre Co. 1987–, Trademark Films 1999–; mem. Bd Chicken Shed Theatre Trust 1997–; mem. Council BAFTA 2000–06, mem. Bd of Trustees 2006–, Chair. of Film 2004–07, Deputy Chair. BAFTA 2007–08, Chair. 2008–; Dr hc (Sunderland) 2000, Hon. Dr Drama (Royal Scottish Acad. of Music and Drama) 2001. *Films include:* Henry V 1989, Peter's Friends 1992, Swan Song 1992, Much Ado About Nothing 1993, Mary Shelley's Frankenstein 1994, The Madness of King George (BAFTA Best British Film 1995) 1994, Twelfth Night: Or What You WIll 1996, The Wings of the Dove 1997, Shakespeare in Love (BAFTA Best Film 1998, Golden Globe Award for Best Musical or Comedy 1998, Academy Award for Best Film 1998) 1998, Gangs of New York (production consultant), I Capture the Castle 2003, Chasing Liberty 2004, A Bunch of Amateurs 2008. *Plays (as producer):* Public Enemy, John Sessions' Napoleon, Twelfth Night, Much Ado About Nothing, Hamlet, As You Like It, Scenes from a Marriage, A Midsummer Night's Dream, King Lear, Travelling Tales, Uncle Vanya, Coriolanus, Les Liaisons Dangereuses, Elling.

Television (as producer): Twelfth Night 1988, Look Back in Anger 1989. *Address:* Trademark Films, Phoenix Theatre, 110 Charing Cross Road, London, WC2H 0JP, England (office). *Telephone:* (20) 7240-5585 (office). *E-mail:* mail@trademarkfilms.co.uk (office).

PARISI, Arturo; Italian politician and academic; b. 13 Sept. 1940, San Mango Piemonte; ed Nunziatella Mil. School, Univ. of Sassari; worked as forester and teacher at training centre for industrial workers while attending univ.; Sec., then Nat. Vice-Pres. Youth Dept, Azione Cattolica, also mem., Exec. Cttee, Int. Fed. of Catholic Youth Movt 1963–68; academic posts have included Asst Lecturer of Statistics, Univ. of Sassari, Researcher, Cattaneo Inst., Bologna 1968, Asst Prof. of Ecclesiastical Law, Univ. of Parma, Asst Prof. of History of Religious Insts, Univ. of Firenze; First Prof. of Sociology of Religions, then full Prof. of Sociology of Political Phenomena, Cattaneo Inst., Bologna 1971–, also currently Dir Cattaneo Inst.; mem. Chamber of Deputies 1999–; mem. Partito Democratico 2007–; Minister of Defence 2006–08; political adviser to Romani Prodi; Under-Sec., Presidency of Council of Ministers 1996; active in I Democratici movt 1999; Co-founder and Nat. Vice-Pres. Democrazia è Libertà – La Margherita 2001, Pres. of party in Fed. Ass. 2004–07; Vice-Pres. Il Mulino Asscn, also ed. of journal; fmr Pres. Italian Soc. of Electoral Studies; served as expert to govt cttee and parl. comm. on domestic terrorism 1987–88; active in movt for Institutional Reforms and Ulivo movt. *Address:* Partito Democratico, Piazza Saint'Anastasia 7, 00186 Rome, Italy (office). *Telephone:* (06) 675471 (office). *Fax:* (06) 67547319 (office). *E-mail:* info@partitodemocratico.it (office). *Website:* www.partitodemocratico.it (office).

PARISOT, Laurence; French business executive; *President, Medef, le Mouvement des Entreprises de France;* b. 31 Aug. 1959, Luxeuil-les-Bains; d. of Michel Parisot and Janine Parisot; ed l'Institut d'études politiques de Paris, Univ. of Nancy 11, Sciences Po, Paris; inherited Optimum (France's leading maker of cupboard doors) from her grandfather; Asst to Alain Lancelot, Pres. of CEVIPOF (Centre d'Etudes de la Vie Politique Française) 1983–85; Dir Gen. Louis Harris France (polling co.) 1986–90; CEO IFOP (polling co.) 2000–; mem. Exec. Council Medef, le Mouvement des Entreprises de France 2003, Pres. 2005–; mem. Bd of Dirs Euro Disney SCA, Ernst and Young; Chevalier l'Ordre nat. de la Légion d'honneur, l'Ordre nat. du Mérite. *Address:* IFOP, 6-8, rue Eugène Oudiné, 75013 Paris (home); Medef, 55 avenue Bosquet, 75330 Paris Cedex 07, France (office). *Telephone:* 1-45-84-14-44 (IFOP) (office); 1-53-59-19-19 (Medef) (office). *Fax:* 1-45-84-93-36 (IFOP) (office); 1-45-51-20-44 (Medef) (office). *Website:* www.ifop.com (office); www.medef.fr (office).

PARIVODIĆ, Milan, LLM, PhD; Serbian lawyer, academic and politician; b. 1966, Belgrade; m. Alexandra Parivodić; two d.; ed Faculty of Law, Univ. of Belgrade, University College London, UK; Lecturer in Civil Law and Property Law, Faculty of Law, Univ. of Belgrade 1991–2004; pvt. law practice 2004–06; Minister of Int. Econ. Relations 2006, Co-ordinator Ministry of Finance 2006; mem. Editorial Advisory Bd Journal of International Franchising; Sec. Gen. Serbian chapter of Association Internationale pour la Protection de la Propriété Intellectuelle— Int. Asscn for Protection of Intellectual Property; mem. Democratic Party of Serbia. *Publications:* Exclusive Distribution in the Laws of Yugoslavia and the European Community 1996, Law of International Franchising 2003; numerous articles on int. trade law, contract law, intellectual property law, competition law, distribution law in professional journals. *Address:* c/o Ministry of International Economic Relations, 11000 Belgrade, Gračanička 8, Serbia (office).

PARIZEAU, Jacques, PhD; Canadian fmr politician; b. 9 Aug. 1930, Montreal; s. of Gérard Parizeau and Germaine Parizeau (née Biron); m. 1st Alicja Poznanska 1956, one s. one d.; m. 2nd Lisette Lapointe 1992; ed Ecole des Hautes Etudes Commerciales, Montreal, Institut d'Etudes Politiques, Paris, London School of Econs, UK; Adviser to Govt of Québec 1961–65; elected Deputy for Assomption, Montreal 1976–84, 1989–; fmr Minister of Finance, Prov. of Québec (resgnd 1985); mem. Exec. Cttee Parti Québecois 1969, Pres. 1988–96; Premier of Québec 1994–95 (resgnd). *Publications:* The Terms of Trade of Canada 1966, Initiation à l'économie du Québec 1975, Pour un Québec souverain 1997, numerous articles. *Leisure interests:* reading, music.

PARK, Chan-wook; South Korean filmmaker; b. 23 Aug. 1963, *Films directed:* Simpan (Judgement) (also screenplay) 1999, Gongdong gyeongbi guyeok JSA (Joint Security Area) (also screenplay) 2000, Boksuneun naui geot (Sympathy for Mr Vengeance) (also screenplay) 2002, Yeoseot gae ui siseon (If You Were Me) (also screenplay) 2003, Oldboy (also screenplay) (Grand Prix, Cannes Film Festival 2004) 2003, Three... Extremes (also screenplay) 2004, Chinjeolhan Geumja-ssi (Sympathy for Lady Vengeance) (Bangkok Film Festival Golden Kinaree Award for Best Director 2006) 2005, I'm A Cyborg 2006. *Film screenplays:* Anarchists 2000, The Humanist 2001.

PARK, Charles Rawlinson, AB, MD; American biochemist and academic; *Adjunct Professor of Biochemistry, Meharry Medical College;* b. 2 March 1916, Baltimore, Md; s. of Edwards A. Park and Agnes Bevan Park; m. Jane Harting 1953; one s.; ed Harvard Coll. and Johns Hopkins School of Medicine; Intern in Medicine, Johns Hopkins 1942; Asst Resident then Chief Resident, Harvard 1943–44; US Army 1944–47; Welch Fellow in Biochemistry, Wash. Univ. 1947–52; Prof. of Physiology and Chair. of Dept, Vanderbilt School of Medicine 1952–84, Prof. of Molecular Physiology and Biophysics, Emer. 1984–; Adjunct Prof. Biochemistry, Meharry Medical Coll. 1993–; mem. Bd, Life Insurance Fund, Howard Hughes Medical Inst. 1964–84, Juvenile Diabetes Foundation, Int. Inst of Cellular and Molecular Pathology, Nat. Inst. of Heart, Lung and Blood (Nat. Insts of Health); mem. Editorial Bd, Journal of Biological Chem.; mem. American Physiological Soc., American Soc. of Biological Chemists, American Soc. of Clinical Investigation (Vice-Pres. 1961), Asscn of American Physicians, NAS; Banting Medal for Research, American Diabetes Asscn, Nat. Acad. of Sciences. *Publications:* approx. 120 scientific papers in journals of biochemistry and physiology 1942–; major topics concern action of hormones, diabetes, metabolic regulation, sugar and fat transport into mammalian cells. *Leisure interests:* music, reading, outdoor sports. *Address:* Oxford House 212, Vanderbilt School of Medicine, Nashville, TN 37232 (office); 5325 Stanford Drive, Nashville, TN 37215, USA (home). *Telephone:* (615) 936-0721 (office); (615) 665-1228 (home). *Fax:* (615) 936-3027 (office); (615) 322-7236. *E-mail:* charles.park@vanderbilt.edu (office). *Website:* www.mmc.edu (office).

PARK, Geun-hye; South Korean politician; b. 2 Feb. 1952, Gumi, northern Gyeongsang Prov.; d. of Park Chung-Hee (Pres. of Repub. of Korea 1961–79); ed Sogang Univ.; worked for Yukyoung Foundation and Saemaeum Hosp.; served as dir in sr citizen welfare centre; Dir Korean Cultural Foundation 1993; Dir Jeongsu Scholarship Fund 1994; mem. Grand Nat. Party (GNP) 1998–2002, 2003–, Vice-Pres. 2000–02, Chair. 2004–06; mem. Nat. Ass. for Daegu 1998–; Chair. Preparatory Cttee Korean Coalition for the Future 2001, Leader 2002– (merged with GNP 2003); mem. Korean Literature Asscn 1994; Hon. Pres. Korean Girl Scouts 1974. *Publications include:* four books on family and literature. *Address:* National Assembly, 1 Yeouido-dong, Yeongdeungpo-gu, Seoul (office); Grand National Party, 17-7, Yeouido-dong, Yeongdeungpo-gu, Seoul 150-010, Republic of Korea. *Telephone:* (2) 3786-3373. *Fax:* (2) 3786-3610. *E-mail:* pgh545@parkgeunhye.or.kr. *Website:* www.hannara.or.kr; www.parkgeunhye.or.kr.

PARK, Nicholas (Nick) W., CBE, BA; British animated film director; b. 6 Dec. 1958, Preston, Lancs.; ed Sheffield Art School and Nat. Film and TV School, Beaconsfield; joined Aardman Animations 1985, partner 1995–. *Films include:* Wallace & Gromit: A Grand Day Out (BAFTA Awards for Best Short Animated Film) 1989, Creature Comforts (Acad. Award for Best Animated Short Film) 1990, Wallace & Gromit: The Wrong Trousers (Acad. Award for Best Animated Short Film) 1993, Wallace & Gromit: A Close Shave (Acad. Award for Best Animated Short Film) 1995, Chicken Run (co-dir) 2000, Wallace & Gromit: The Curse of the Were-Rabbit (BAFTA Best British Film 2006, Acad. Award for Best Animated Feature Film 2006) 2005. *Address:* Aardman Animations Ltd, Gas Ferry Road, Bristol, BS1 6UN, England. *Telephone:* (117) 984-8485. *Fax:* (117) 984-8486. *Website:* www.aardman.com.

PARK, Seung, PhD; South Korean central banker, economist and academic; b. 16 Feb. 1936; ed Seoul Nat. Univ. and State Univ. of New York, USA; economist at Bank of Korea 1961–76, Gov. 2002–07, fmr mem. Monetary Bd; Assoc. Prof., Chung-Ang Univ. 1976, Prof. 1982–88, 1990–, Dean Coll. of Politics and Econs 1984–87, Dean Grad. School 1988; Sr Sec. for Econs, Presidential Secr. 1988; Minister of Construction 1988–89; Chief Dir Korea Nat. Housing Corpn 1993–96; Chief Dir Korea Transport Inst. 1997; Chair. Korea Econ. Asscn 1999; Head, Public Funds Man. Cttee –2002; Pres. Korea Int. Econ. Asscn 1986. *Address:* c/o Bank of Korea, 110, 3-ga, Namdaemun-no, Jung-gu, Seoul 100-794, Republic of Korea (office).

PARK, Won-jin, BA; South Korean business executive; *President and CEO, Hyundai Corporation;* ed Korea Univ.; Sr Exec. Vice-Pres. Hyundai Corpn 2000–01, Pres. Hyundai Petrochemical Co. Ltd 2001–02, Pres., CEO and Dir Hyundai Corpn 2002–, est. Miyocen (micro-brewery restaurant), Seoul 2003; Vice-Chair. Korea–Russia Business Council (CIS); mem. Fed. of Korean Industries (FKI) China Forum 2003. *Address:* Hyundai Corporation, 140-2 Kye-dong, Chongro-ku, Seoul 110-793, Republic of Korea (office). *Telephone:* (2) 746-1114 (office). *Fax:* (2) 741-2341 (office). *E-mail:* webmaster@hyundaicorp.com (office). *Website:* www.hyundaicorp.com (office).

PARK, Yong-sung, MBA; South Korean business executive and international organization official; *Chairman, Doosan Heavy Industries and Construction Company;* b. 11 Sept. 1940, Seoul; ed School of Commerce, Seoul Nat. Univ., Leonard N. Stern School of Business, NY Univ., USA; fmr mem. Exec. Bd ICC 1998–2003, Vice-Chair. 2003–05, Chair. 2005–06; currently Chair. Doosan Heavy Industries and Construction Co.; Chair. Korean Chamber of Commerce and Industry (KCCI), hosted World Chambers Congress 2001; mem. Int. Olympic Cttee 2002–; Pres. Int. Judo Fed. *Address:* Doosan Heavy Industries and Construction Company, 1303–22 Seocho-Dong, Seocho-Gu, Seoul 137-920, South Korea (office). *Telephone:* (2) 513-6114 (office). *Fax:* (2) 513-6200 (office). *Website:* www.doosanheavy.com.

PARK OF MONMOUTH, Baroness (Life Peer), cr. 1990, of Broadway in the County of Hereford and Worcester; **Daphne Margaret Sybil Désirée Park,** CMG, OBE; British fmr diplomatist and college principal; b. 1 Sept. 1921; ed Rosa Bassett School and Somerville Coll. Oxford; WTS (Field Aid Nursing Yeomanry) 1943–47; entered Foreign Office 1948; served UK Del. to NATO 1952, Moscow 1954, Léopoldville 1959, Lusaka 1964, Consul-Gen. Hanoi 1969–70, Chargé d'Affaires a.i. Ulan Bator 1972, FCO 1973–79, retd; Hon. Research Fellow, Univ. of Kent 1971–72; Prin. Somerville Coll. Oxford 1980–89, Pro-Vice-Chancellor, Univ. of Oxford 1985–89; Chair. Royal Comm. on Historical Monuments of England 1989–94; Vice Patron Atlantic Council Appeal 2001–; mem. Thatcher Foundation 1992–; other public appointments; Hon. LLD (Bristol) 1988. *Leisure interests:* good talk, politics, difficult places. *Address:* House of Lords, London, SW1A 0PW, England. *Telephone:* (20) 7219-5353. *Fax:* (20) 7219-5979. *E-mail:* parkd@parliament.uk.

PARKANOVÁ, Vlasta, JUDr; Czech lawyer and politician; *Minister of Defence;* b. 21 Nov. 1951, Prague; m. Zdeněk Parkan; one d.; ed Charles Univ.; began legal career specialising in commercial law 1975–88; co-f. Civic Forum, Tábor 1989; mem. Fed. Ass. 1990–93; various positions within Ministry of Foreign Affairs and Ministry of Interior 1992–96; mem. Parl. 1996–; Minister of Justice 1997–98, Deputy Chair. Cttee on Defence and Security 1998–2002, Minister of Defence 2007–; Vice-Chair. Constitution and

Legal Cttee 1998–2002, Chair. 2003–06; mem. Perm. Del. of Parl. of Czech Repub. to NATO 1998–2006; mem. Civic Democratic Alliance (ODA) 1991–98; mem. Christian Democratic Party (KDU-ČSL) 2001–. *Address:* Ministry of Defence, Tychonova 1, 160 01 Prague 6, Czech Republic (office). *Telephone:* 973201111 (office). *Fax:* 973200149 (office). *E-mail:* info@army.cz (office). *Website:* www.army.cz (office).

PARKER, Sir Alan William, Kt, CBE; British film director and writer; b. 14 Feb. 1944, London; s. of William Parker and Elsie Parker; m. Annie Inglis 1966 (divorced 1992); three s. one d.; ed Owen's School, Islington, London; Advertising Copywriter 1965–67; TV Commercials Dir 1968–78; wrote screenplay Melody 1969; Chair. Dirs Guild of GB 1982–86, British Film Inst. 1998–99; Chair. Film Council 1999–; mem. British Screen Advisory Council 1985–; BAFTA Michael Balcon Award for Outstanding Contrib. to British Film, Dirs' Guild of Great Britain Lifetime Achievement Award; Officier, Ordre des Arts et des Lettres 2005. *Wrote and directed:* No Hard Feelings 1972, Our Cissy 1973, Footsteps 1973, Bugsy Malone 1975, Angel Heart 1987, A Turnip Head's Guide to the British Cinema, Come See the Paradise 1989, The Road to Wellville 1994, Angela's Ashes 1999. *Directed:* The Evacuees 1974, Midnight Express 1977, Fame 1979, Shoot the Moon 1981, The Wall 1982, Birdy 1984, Mississippi Burning (Nat. Review Bd Best Dir Award) 1988, The Commitments (BAFTA Award for Best Dir) 1991, Evita 1996, The Life of David Gale 2003. *Publications:* (novels) Bugsy Malone 1976, Puddles in the Lane 1977, The Sucker's Kiss 2003; (cartoon) Hares in the Gate 1983; Making Movies 1998. *Leisure interest:* cartooning. *Address:* c/o Creative Artists' Agency, 9830 Wilshire Boulevard, Beverly Hills, CA 90212, USA.

PARKER, Cornelia, BA, MFA; British artist; b. 1956, Cheshire; ed Gloucestershire Coll. of Art and Design, Wolverhampton Polytechnic, Univ. of Reading; Artist-in-Residence, Crewe and Alsager Coll., Cheshire 1979–80; Artist-in-School Project, Walsall, West Midlands 1984, Rugby, West Midlands 1985; Sr Fellow in Fine Art, Cardiff Inst. 1995; Int. Artist in Residence, ArtPace Foundation for Contemporary Art, San Antonio, Tex., USA 1997; Koopman Chair, Jose Loff Gallery, Hartford Art School, USA 1997; Artist in Residence, Science Museum, London 1998–99; best known for several large-scale installations including Cold Dark Matter: An Exploded View 1991 and The Maybe (collaboration with actress Tilda Swinton), Serpentine Gallery, London 1995; ongoing series of smaller objects including Avoided Object, Chapter Arts Centre, Cardiff 1996, working in collaboration with HM Customs & Excise, The Royal Armouries and Madame Tussauds; comms include sculpture for Nat. Garden Festival, Stoke 1986, Siteworks Project, Southwark, London 1986, installation for St Peter's Church, Kettle's Yard, Cambridge 1988, 'Left Luggage', Platform 6, St Pancras Street, London 1990, 'Inhaled Roof', Newcastle, 'Exhaled Schoolhouse', Glasgow 1990, installation at Union Station, Los Angeles, Calif. 1992, installation 'Reading Matter' at Victoria & Albert Museum, London 1992, Tate Gallery Christmas Tree, London 1995, 'City Space' for European City of Culture, Copenhagen 1996, 'Cassette Brushes with fame, seven little frictions', Audio Arts, London 1997, 'Avoided Object', 5 Artists' Inserts, Nature –int. weekly Journal of Science, Vol. 389, Issues 6648–6652, perm. installation for British Galleries, Victoria & Albert Museum 2001; works in Tate Collection, The Arts Council of England, British Council, Contemporary Arts Soc., Glaxo Wellcome Collection, Govt Art Collection, Leicestershire Council, MAG Collection, British Museum, Milwaukee Art Museum and numerous public and pvt. collections in Europe and USA; Dr hc (Univ. of Wolverhampton) 2000; First Prize for 'Midland View', Stoke City Art Gallery touring exhbn 1980, Southern Arts Award 1983, Greater London Arts Award 1985, British School at Rome Award 1989, Henry Moore Scholarship, Wimbledon School of Art 1991–92, Int. Asscn of Art Critics Prize, 'Best Show by an Emerging Artist', for 'Mass: Colder Darker Matter', Deitch Projects, New York 1998–99. *Publications:* Lost Volume: A Catalogue of Disasters 1992. *Address:* c/o Frith Street Gallery, 59–60 Frith Street, London, W1D 3JJ, England (office). *Telephone:* (20) 7494-1550 (office). *Fax:* (20) 7287-3733 (office). *E-mail:* info@frithstreetgallery.com (office). *Website:* www.frithstreetgallery.com (office).

PARKER, Sir Eric Wilson, Kt, FCA; British business executive; *Owner, Crimbourne Stud Farm;* b. 8 June 1933, Shrewsbury; s. of Wilson Parker and Gladys Edith Wellings; m. Marlene Teresa Neale 1955; two s. two d.; ed The Priory Grammar School for Boys, Shrewsbury; articled clerk with Wheeler, Whittingham & Kent, Shrewsbury 1950–55; nat. service, Pay Corps 1956–58; Taylor Woodrow Group 1958–64; joined Trafalgar House Group 1965, Finance/Admin. Dir 1969, Deputy Man. Dir 1973, Group Man. Dir 1977, Group Chief Exec. 1983–92, Deputy Chair. 1988–93; Chair. Caradon PLC 1998–99; Pres. Racehorse Owners Asscn 1998–2001; Dir (non-exec.) Int. Real Estates 1997–, Ministry of Defence Quartermaster Gen. Bd 1997–2000, British Borneo PLC 1998–2000, European Real Estates, Sweden 1998–2000, British Horseracing Bd 1999–, Horserace Betting Levy Bd 2000, Job Partners 2000–02; Dir Kvaerner Trustees (Keps) Ltd 2001–, Kvaerner Trustees (KPF) Ltd 2002–, Horserace Totalisator Bd 2002–, Albert Goodwin PLC 2003–; Cttee mem. Teenage Cancer Trust; owner Crimbourne Stud Farm. *Leisure interests:* golf, horse racing, wines. *Address:* Crimbourne Stud Farm, Crimbourne Lane, Wisborough Green, nr Billingshurst, West Sussex, RH14 0HR, England (home). *Telephone:* (1403) 700400. *Fax:* (1403) 700776. *E-mail:* crimbournestud@ecosse.com (office).

PARKER, Eugene N., PhD; American physicist (retd); b. 10 June 1927, Houghton, Mich.; s. of Glenn H. Parker and Helen M. Parker; m. Niesje Meuter 1954; one s. one d.; ed Michigan State Univ. and California Inst. of Tech.; Instructor, Dept of Math. and Astronomy, Univ. of Utah 1951–53, Asst Prof., Dept of Physics 1953–55; at Univ. of Chicago 1955–, Prof., Dept of Physics 1962–95, Prof., Dept of Astronomy 1967–95; mem. NAS 1967–, Norwegian Acad. of Sciences 1988–; Hon. DSc (Michigan State Univ.) 1975; Dr

hc (Utrecht) 1986; Space Science Award, AIAA 1964, John Adam Fleming Award, American Geophysical Union 1968, Henryk Arctowski Medal, NAS 1969, Henry Norris Russell Lecture, American Astronomical Soc. 1969, George Ellery Hale Award, Solar Physics Div. American Astronomical Soc. 1978, Sydney Chapman Medal, Royal Astronomical Soc. 1979, Distinguished Alumnus Award, Calif. Inst. of Tech. 1980, James Arthur Prize Lecture, Harvard Smithsonian Center for Astrophysics 1986, US Nat. Medal of Science 1989, William Bowie Medal, American Geophysical Union 1990, Karl Schwarzschild Medal (FRG) 1990, Gold Medal, Royal Astronomical Soc. 1992, Bruce Medal, Astronomical Soc. of the Pacific 1997, ADION Medal, Observatoire de Nice 1997, James Clark Maxwell Prize, American Physical Soc. 2003, Kyoto Prize, Inamori Foundation 2003, Outstanding Alumni Award, Michigan State Univ. 2004. *Publications:* Interplanetary Dynamical Processes 1963, Cosmical Magnetic Fields 1979, Spontaneous Current Sheets in Magnetic Fields 1994. *Leisure interests:* hiking, history, wood-carving. *Address:* 1323 Evergreen Road, Homewood, IL 60430, USA (home). *Telephone:* (708) 798-3497 (home).

PARKER, Franklin, BA, MS, EdD; American writer and educationalist; b. 2 June 1921, New York; m. Betty June Parker 1950; ed Berea Coll., Ky, Univ. of Illinois, Peabody Coll. Vanderbilt Univ., Nashville, Tenn.; Librarian and Speech Teacher, Ferrum Coll., Va 1950–52; Belmont Coll., Nashville, Tenn. 1952–54, Peabody Coll. Vanderbilt Univ. 1955–56; Assoc. Prof. of Educ., State Univ. Coll., New Paltz, NY 1956–57, Univ. of Tex. 1957–64; Prof., Univ. of Okla 1964–68; Claude Worthington Benedum Prof. of Educ., West Va Univ., Morgantown 1968–86; Distinguished Prof. Emer., Center for Excellence in Educ. 1986–89; Visiting Distinguished Prof. Western Carolina Univ. 1989–94; Consultant Macmillan Merrill (Publrs), Teachers Coll. Press, William C. Brown 1988–; several visiting professorships; Sr Fulbright Research Scholar, Zambia 1961–62; Distinguished Alumnus Award, Peabody Coll., Vanderbilt Univ. 1970, Berea Coll., Kentucky 1989. *Publications include:* African Development and Education in Southern Rhodesia 1960, Government Policy and International Education 1965, Church and State in Education 1966, Strategies for Curriculum Change: Cases from 13 Nations 1968, International Education: Understandings and Misunderstandings 1969, George Peabody, A Biography 1971, American Dissertations on Foreign Education: Abstracts of Doctoral Dissertations (20 Vols) 1971–91, What We Can Learn From China's Schools 1977, Education in Puerto Rico and of Puerto Ricans in the USA Vol. 1 1978, Vol. 2 1984, British Schools and Ours 1979, Women's Education (2 Vols) 1979–81, US Higher Education: Guide to Information Sources 1980, Education in the People's Republic of China, Past and Present: Annotated Bibliography 1986, Education in England and Wales: Annotated Bibliography 1991, Academic Profiles in Higher Education 1993, Tennessee Encyclopaedia of History and Culture (mem. editorial bd) 1998, many articles, contribs. to encyclopaedias.

PARKER, Mark G., BS; American business executive; *President and CEO, NIKE, Inc.;* b. Poughkeepsie, New York; ed Pa State Univ.; Designer and Devt Man., NIKE, Inc., Exeter, NH 1979–80, Man. Advanced Product Design, Exeter 1980–81, Dir Design Concepts and Eng 1981–82, Dir Footwear Design 1982–83, Man. Running and Fitness Footwear Marketing 1983–85, Head Special Design Project Teams 1985–87, Divisional Vice-Pres. Footwear Research, Design and Devt 1987–88, Corporate Vice-Pres. Research, Design and Devt 1988–93, Vice-Pres. Consumer Product Marketing 1993–98, Vice-Pres. and Gen. Man. Global Footwear 1998–2001, Pres. Nike Brand 2001–06, CEO and Pres. NIKE Inc. 2006–. *Address:* NIKE, Inc., 1 Bowerman Drive, Beaverton, OR 97005-6453, USA (office). *Telephone:* (503) 671-6453 (office). *Fax:* (503) 671-6300 (office). *Website:* www.nikebiz.com (office).

PARKER, Michael D., CBE, BChemEng, MBA; American/British business executive; *CEO, British Nuclear Fuels plc;* m. Noreen Parker; one s. one d.; ed Univ. of Manchester and Manchester Business School, UK; joined Dow Chemical Co. 1968, later served with Dow Int. Research and Devt, Freeport, TX, field sales post, Birmingham, UK 1972, Dist Sales Man. 1975, Product Marketing Man. for Epoxy Resins, Dow Europe, later Dir Marketing for Inorganic Chemicals, then Dir Marketing for Organic Chemicals, Commercial Dir Functional Products Dept, Dow Europe 1983, Gen. Man. Specialty Chemicals Dept, Dow USA, Midland, MI 1984, Commercial Vice-Pres. Dow Pacific, Hong Kong 1987, Pres. 1988–93, Group Vice-Pres. (Chemicals and Hydrocarbons) 1993–95, Pres. Dow N America 1995–96, mem. Bd of Dirs 1995–, mem. Exec. Cttee Bd, Chair. Corp. Operating Bd, Exec. Vice-Pres. 1996–2000, Pres. and CEO 2000–02, also mem. Bd of Dirs and Exec. Cttee Dow Corning Corpn 2000–02, mem. Mems Cttee of Dow Agrosciences; CEO, British Nuclear Fuels plc 2003–; Dir Univation Technologies, LLC 2001–; Dir Nat. Legal Center for the Public Interest; mem. Exec. Cttee American Chem. Council; mem. Exec. Cttee, Soc. of Chemical Industry-American Section 2001–. *Address:* British Nuclear Fuels plc, 1100 Daresbury Park, Warrington, WA4 4GB, England (office). *Website:* www.bnfl.com (office).

PARKER, Robert Brown, PhD; American writer; b. 17 Sept. 1932, Springfield, Mass.; s. of Carroll Snow Parker and Mary Pauline (née Murphy) Parker; m. Joan Hall 1956; two s.; ed Colby Coll., Boston Univ.; served with US Army 1954–56; Co-Chair. Parker-Farman Co. 1960-62; lecturer Boston Univ. 1962–64; mem. faculty Lowell State Coll., Mass. 1964–66; lecturer Suffolk Univ. 1965–66; mem. faculty Bridgewater State Coll. 1966–68; Asst Prof. of English Northeastern Univ., Boston 1968–73, Assoc. Prof. 1973–76, Prof. 1976–79; screenwriter with Joan Parker 1985–; mem. Writers Guild of America; Hon. DLitt (Northeastern Univ.) 1987. *Screenwriting includes:* Spenser: For Hire 1985–88 (series), Blues for Buder 1988, High Rise 1988, A Man Called Hawk (series) 1989–90, Spenser: Ceremony 1993, Spenser: Pale Kings and Princes 1993, Spencer: Small Vices 1999. *Publications include:* Small Vices, Widow's Walk, The Godwulf Manuscript 1974, God Save the

Child 1974, Mortal Stakes 1975, Promised Land 1976 (Edgar Allan Poe Award for Best Novel, Mystery Writers of America 1976), Three Weeks in Spring (with Joan Parker) 1978, Wilderness 1979, Looking for Rachel Wallace 1980, Early Autumn 1980, A Savage Place 1982, Surrogate: A Spenser Short Story 1982, Ceremony 1982, The Judas Goat 1983, Love and Glory 1983, The Widening Gyre 1983, Parker on Writing 1985, A Catskill Eagle 1985, Taming a Seahorse 1986, Valediction 1987, Pale Kings and Princes 1987, Crimson Joy 1988, Poodle Springs (with Raymond Chandler) 1989, Playmates 1989, A Year at the Races 1990, Perchance to Dream 1991, Pastime 1991, Stardust 1992, Double Deuce 1992, Paper Doll 1994, All Our Yesterdays 1994, Spenser's Boston 1994, Walking Shadow 1994, Thin Air 1995, Chance 1996, Small Vices 1997, Night Passage 1997, Sudden Mischief 1998, Family Honor 1999, Trouble in Paradise 2000, Perish Twice 2000, Hush Money 2000, Hugger Mugger 2000, Death in Paradise 2001, Gunman's Rhapsody 2001, Potshot 2001, Shrink Rap 2002, Stone Cold 2003, Back Story 2003, Melancholy Baby 2004, Bad Business 2004, Appaloosa 2005, Double Play 2005, School Days 2005, Cold Service 2005, Sea Change 2006, Dream Girl 2006, Blue Screen 2006, Hundred Dollar Baby 2006, High Profile 2007, Edenville Owls 2007, Now and Then 2007, Spare Change 2007, Stranger in Paradise 2008, Resolution 2008, Rough Weather 2008, Chasing the Bear 2009, Night and Day 2009, Brimstone 2009. *Address:* Penguin Group (USA) Inc., c/o Putnam's Publicity, 375 Hudson Street, New York, NY 10014, USA (office). *Website:* www.robertbparker.net.

PARKER, Robert M., Jr, BA, LLB; American writer and wine critic; *Publisher, The Wine Advocate;* b. 23 July 1947, Baltimore, Md; m. Patricia Parker 1969; one d.; ed Univ. of Maryland; attorney, Sr Attorney and later Asst Gen. Counsel for Farm Credits, Bank of Baltimore 1973–84; Founder, Writer and Publr The Wine Advocate 1978–; Contributing Ed. Food and Wine Magazine; wine critic for L'Express magazine (first non-French holder of post); Hon. Citizen of Châteauneuf du Pape 1995; Chevalier, Ordre nat. du Mérite 1993, Chevalier, Légion d'honneur 1999; Loyola Coll. Marylander of the Year Award 1992, James Beard Foundation Wine and Spirits Professional of 1997. *Publications include:* Bordeaux (Glenfiddich Award 1986, Int. Asscn of Cooking Professionals Award for second edn 1992, Goldene Feder Award (Germany) for third edn 1993, Moët-Hennessy Wine and Vine Communication Award for French edn 1993) 1985, Parker's Wine Buyer's Guide 1987, The Wines of the Rhône Valley and Provence (Tastemaker's Award, USA 1989, Wine Guild's Wine Book of the Year Award, UK 1989) 1987, Burgundy (Moët-Hennessy Wine and Vine Communication Award for French edn 1993) 1990; contribs to The Field. *Address:* The Wine Advocate, Inc., PO Box 311, Monkton, MD 21111, USA (office). *Telephone:* (410) 329-6477 (office). *Fax:* (410) 357-4504 (office). *E-mail:* wineadvocate@erobertparker.com (office). *Website:* www.erobertparker.com (office).

PARKER, Sarah Jessica; American actress; b. 25 March 1965, Nelsonville, Ohio; m. Matthew Broderick (q.v.) 1997; one s. *Stage appearances include:* The Innocents 1976, The Sound of Music 1977, Annie 1978, The War Brides 1981, The Death of a Miner 1982, To Gillian on Her 37th Birthday 1983–84, Terry Neal's Future 1986, The Heidi Chronicles 1989, How To Succeed in Business Without Really Trying 1996, Once Upon A Mattress 1996, Wonder of the World 2001. *Television appearances include:* Equal Justice 1990–91, Sex and the City (Golden Globe for Best Actress in a TV series 2001, 2004, Emmy Award for Outstanding Lead Actress in a Comedy 2004) 1998–2004, Sex and the Matrix 2000. *Film appearances include:* Rich Kids 1979, Somewhere Tomorrow 1983, Firstborn 1984, Footloose 1984, Girls Just Want to Have Fun 1985, Flight of the Navigator 1986, LA Story 1991, Honeymoon in Vegas 1992, Hocus Pocus 1993, Striking Distance 1993, Ed Wood 1994, Miami Rhapsody 1995, If Lucy Fell 1996, Mars Attacks! 1996, The First Wives Club 1996, Extreme Measures 1996, A Life Apart: Hasidism in America 1997, 'Til There Was You 1997, Isn't She Great 1999, Dudley Do-Right 1999, State and Main 2000, Life Without Dick 2001, Strangers with Candy 2005, Family Stone 2005, Failure to Launch 2006, Smart People 2007, Slammer 2007, Sex and the City: The Movie 2008. *Address:* c/o Jane Berliner, Creative Artists Agency, 9830 Wilshire Boulevard, Beverly Hills, CA 90212, USA.

PARKER, Sir (Thomas) John, Kt, DSc (Eng), ScD, FREng; British business executive; *Chairman, National Grid PLC;* b. 8 April 1942, Downpatrick, Northern Ireland; s. of Robert Parker and Margaret Elizabeth Parker (née Bell); m. Emma Elizabeth Blair 1967; one s. one d.; ed Belfast Coll. of Tech., Queen's Univ., Belfast; Ship Design Staff, Harland and Wolff PLC 1963–69, Ship Production Man. 1969–71, Production Drawing Office Man. 1971–72, Sales and Projects Dept Gen. Man. 1972–74; Man. Dir Austin & Pickersgill 1974–78; mem. Bd for Shipbuilding (Marketing and Operations), British Shipbuilders 1978–80, Corpn Deputy Chief Exec. 1980–83; Chair. and CEO Harland and Wolff Holdings PLC 1983–93, Dir (non-exec.) 1993–94; Chair. Harland-MAN Engines 1983–93; mem. Industrial Devt Bd for NI 1983–87; mem. Gen. Cttee Lloyds Register of Shipping 1983– (Chair. Tech. Cttee 1996–); mem. Bd QUBIS 1984–93, British Coal 1986–93; Deputy Chair. Babcock Int. Group PLC 1993–94, Chief Exec. 1993–2000, Chair. 1994–2001; Jt Chair. (non-exec.) Mondi Group (following its demerger from Anglo American plc); Deputy Chair. Port and Free World Zone (Dubai); Chair. (non-exec.) Lattice Group PLC (merged with Nat. Grid Group to become Nat. Grid Transco PLC 2002, renamed Nat. Grid PLC 2005) 2000–, Firth Rixson PLC 2001–04; Chair. RMC 2002–05; Sr Dir (non-exec.), Bank of England 2005–; Dir (non-exec.) GKN PLC 1993–2008, BG PLC 1997–2000, Carnival PLC and Carnival Inc. 2003–, P&O Princess Cruises PLC (Chair. P&O Group PLC 2005–08); fmr Dir (non-exec.) British Coal Corpn Brambles Industries plc; Vice-Pres. Royal Inst. of Naval Architects 1985–93, Pres. 1996–99; Chair. Council of European Shipbuilders Asscn 1993; Chancellor Univ. of South-ampton; Fellow, Royal Inst. of Naval Architects, Inst. of Marine Engineers; Hon. DSc (Trinity Coll. Dublin, Ulster, Abertay); Man. of the Year Award,

Ireland 1986, Inst. of Energy Melchett Medal 2003, and other awards. *Publications:* A Profile of British Shipbuilders 1979, British Shipbuilders – A Period of Constructive Change (Marintec Conf., Shanghai) 1981, The Challenge of Change in Shipbuilding Today (ICCAS '85 Conf., Trieste) 1985. *Leisure interests:* reading, music, ships, sailing. *Address:* National Grid PLC, 1–3 The Strand, London, WC2N 5EH, England (office). *Telephone:* (20) 7004-3000 (office). *Fax:* (20) 7004-3004 (office). *E-mail:* info@nationalgrid.com (office). *Website:* www.nationalgrid.com (office).

PARKHOMENKO, Sergey Borisovich; Russian journalist; b. 13 March 1964, Moscow; m.; two s.; ed Moscow State Univ.; Head of Div. Teatre (magazine) 1985–90; political observer Nezavisimaya Gazeta 1990–92; mem. Bd Segodnya (newspaper) 1993–95; co-founder Moscow Charter for Journalists 1994; Ed.-in-Chief Itogi (magazine) 1996–2001, IT Weekly (journal) 2002, Real Itogi 2002, now ind. journalist.

PARKIN, Stuart S. P., MA, PhD, FRS; British physicist; *IBM Fellow, IBM Almaden Research Center;* b. Watford; ed Univ. of Cambridge; Research Student, Cavendish Lab., Cambridge 1977; Research Fellow, Trinity Coll., Cambridge 1979–85; Royal Soc. European Exchange Fellowship, Univ. Paris-Sud, Lab. de Physique des Solides, France 1980–81, Visiting Prof. 1988; IBM World Trade Fellowship, IBM Research Lab., Almaden Research Center, San José, Calif., USA 1982, Adjunct Research Staff Mem. 1983, Research Staff Mem. 1984, mem. IBM Acad. of Tech. 1997–, IBM Fellow 1999–; Consulting Prof., Dept of Applied Physics, Stanford Univ. 1997–, Nat. Taiwan Univ. 2007; Visiting Chair Prof., Taipei, Taiwan 2007; Distinguished Visiting Prof., Dept of Electrical and Computer Eng, Nat. Univ. of Singapore 2007; Distinguished Research Chair Prof., Nat. Yunlin Univ. of Science and Tech., Douliou, Taiwan; Distinguished Visiting Prof., Eindhoven Univ. of Tech. 2008–; mem. Advisory Bd Journal of Physics: Condensed Matter 1993–96; Assoc. Ed. Materials Letters 1993–; mem. numerous scientific cttees; Fellow, American Physical Soc., Cambridge Philosophical Soc., Inst. of Physics, London, Materials Research Soc., IEEE, AAAS; mem. NAS 2008–; Dr hc (RWTH Aachen Univ.) 2007, (Eindhoven Univ. of Tech.) 2008; numerous IBM Patent Achievement Awards; Inst. of Physics Charles Vernon Boys Prize 1991, American Physical Soc. Int. Prize for New Materials 1994, European Physical Soc. Hewlett-Packard Europhysics Prize 1997, American Inst. of Physics Prize for Industrial Application of Physics 1999–2000, R&D Magazine's first Innovator of the Year 2001, Economist Magazine's 'No Boundaries' Award for Innovation 2007, IEEE Daniel E. Noble Award 2008, Johannes Gutenberg Research Award 2008. *Address:* IBM Almaden Research Center, Room D1-306, 650 Harry Road, San José, CA 95120-6099, USA (office). *Telephone:* (408) 927-2390 (office). *Fax:* (845) 489-9710 (office). *E-mail:* parkin@almaden.ibm .com (office). *Website:* www.almaden.ibm.com/spinaps (office).

PARKINSON, Bradford W., BS, SM, PhD; American engineer, inventor and academic; *Edward C. Wells Professor of Aeronautics and Astronautics, Stanford University;* b. 1935, Wis.; m. Virginia Parkinson; ed US Naval Acad., MIT, Stanford Univ.; served in USAF 1957–78, retiring with rank of Col; instructor, Air Foce Test Pilot School, Edwards Air Force Base, Calif.; Head, Dept of Astronautics and Computer Science, USAF Acad. Colo; cr. and managed NAVSTAR GPS Jt Program Office 1972–78; Edward C. Wells Prof. of Aeronautics and Astronautics, W. W. Hansen Experimental Physics Lab., Stanford Univ. 1984–; fmr Prof., Colo State Univ.; Chair. Bd of Trustees The Aerospace Corpn; co-Chair. JPL Advisory Council; mem. AAAS, IEEE, Pres. Comm. on Air Safety and Security, Royal Inst. of Navigation (RION); Legion of Merit; Defense Dept Superior Performance Award for Best Program Dir in USAF 1977, Discover Innovation Award, NASA Distinguished Public Service Medal, IEEE Simon Ramo Award, Von Karman Lectureship and Aerospace Contrib. to Soc. Medal, AIAA, Thurlow Award ION, Gold Medal RION, Draper Prize (jtly) 2003. *Invention:* Global Positioning System (GPS) (co-inventor). *Address:* W. W. Hansen Experimental Physics Laboratory, Stanford University, Stanford, CA 94305-4085, USA (home). *Website:* einstein.stanford.edu.

PARKINSON, Baron (Life Peer), cr. 1992, of Carnforth in the County of Lancashire; **Cecil Edward Parkinson,** PC, MA; British politician and chartered accountant; b. 1 Sept. 1931; s. of Sidney Parkinson; m. Ann Mary Jarvis 1957; three d.; one d. by Sarah Keays; ed Royal Lancaster Grammar School and Emmanuel Coll., Cambridge; joined Metal Box Co. as man. trainee; joined West, Wake, Price & Co. (chartered accountants) as articled clerk 1956, Partner 1961–71; f. Parkinson Hart Securities Ltd 1967, Chair. 1967–79, Dir 1967–79, 1984–; Dir several other cos 1967–79; Branch Treas. Hemel Hempstead Conservative Asscn 1961–64, Constituency Chair. 1965–66, Chair. and ex-officio mem. all cttees 1966–69; Chair. Herts. 100 Club 1968–69; Pres. Hemel Hempstead Young Conservatives 1968–71, North-ampton Young Conservatives 1969–71; contested Northampton, Gen. Election 1970; MP for Enfield West 1970–74, for Hertfordshire South 1974–83, for Hertsmere 1983–92; Sec. Conservative Backbench Finance Cttee 1971–72; Parl. Pvt. Sec. to Minister for Aerospace and Shipping 1972–74; Asst Govt Whip 1974, Opposition Whip 1974–76; Opposition Spokesman on Trade 1976–79; Minister of State for Trade 1979–81; Paymaster-Gen. 1981–83; Chair. Conservative Party 1981–83, 1997–98; Sec. of State for Trade and Industry June–Oct. 1983, for Energy 1987–89, for Transport 1989–90; Chair. Conservative Way Forward Group 1991–; Chancellor of the Duchy of Lancaster 1982–83; Leader, Inst. of Dirs. Parl. Panel 1972–79; Sec. Anglo-Swiss Parl. Group 1972–79, Chair. 1979–82; Chair. Anglo-Polish Conservative Soc. 1986–98, Chemical Dependency Centre Ltd 1986–, Jarvis (Harpenden) Holdings, Usborne 1991–, Midland Expressway Ltd 1993–, Dartford River Crossing Ltd 1993–; Dir Babcock Int. 1984–87, Sports Aid Foundation, Save and Prosper 1984–87, Tarmac 1984–87, Sears PLC 1984–87. *Publication:* An Autobiography: Right at the Centre 1992. *Leisure interests:* skiing, reading, golf. *Address:* House of Lords, London, SW1A 0PW, England. *Telephone:* (20) 7219-5353.

PARKINSON, Mark Vincent, BA, JD; American lawyer and politician; *Governor of Kansas;* b. 24 June 1957, Wichita; m. Stacy Parkinson 1983; three c.; ed Wichita State Univ., Univ. of Kansas; Assoc., Payne and Jones (law firm), Olathe, Kan. 1984–86; Co-founder and Pnr, Parkinson, Foth and Reynolds (law firm) 1986–96; mem. Kan. State House of Reps 1990–92, Kan. State Senate 1992–96; Chair. Kan. Republican Party 1999–2003; became mem. Democratic party 2006; Lt-Gov. of Kan. 2007–09, Gov. of Kan. 2009–; Chair. Shawnee Area Chamber of Commerce 2004; mem. Kan. Bar Asscn; mem. ABA, Johnson Co. Bar Foundation (fmr Pres.), Kan. Bar Asscn, Kan. Mentors Leadership Council. *Address:* Office of the Governor, Capitol, 300 SW 10th Avenue, Suite 212S, Topeka, KS 66612-1590, USA (office). *Telephone:* (785) 296-3232 (office). *Website:* governor.ks.gov (office).

PARKINSON, Sir Michael, Kt, CBE; British television and radio presenter and writer; b. 28 March 1935, Barnsley; m. Mary Heneghan 1959; three s.; ed Barnsley Grammar School; began career as journalist with local paper, then worked on The Guardian, Daily Express, Sunday Times, Punch, The Listener etc.; joined Granada TV as interviewer/reporter 1965; joined 24 Hours (BBC) as reporter; Exec. Producer and Presenter, London Weekend TV 1968; Presenter Cinema 1969–70, Tea Break, Where in the World 1971, host own chat show 'Parkinson' 1971–82, 1998–2004, The Boys of '66 1981, Presenter TV-AM 1983–84, Give Us a Clue 1984–92, All Star Secrets 1984–86, The Skag Kids 1985, Desert Island Discs (BBC Radio 4) 1986–88, The Help Squad 1991–92, Ghostwatch 1992, Parkinson on Sport (BBC Radio 5) 1994–97, Going for a Song 1995–99, A League Apart, 100 Years of Rugby League (BBC 2) 1995, Parkinson: The Interviews 1995–97, Parkinson's Sunday Supplement (BBC Radio 2) 1996–2007, Auntie's All-Time Greats 1997, Parkinson's Choice (BBC Radio 2) 1999–2004; columnist for Daily Mirror 1986–90, for Daily Telegraph 1991–2007; Parkinson One-to-One 1987–88; Parkinson (ITV) 2004–07; Ed. Catalyst 1988–; has worked extensively on Australian TV; founder and Dir Pavilion Books 1980–97; Dr hc (Lincs. and Humberside) 1999; Sports Feature Writer of the Year, British Sports Journalism Awards 1995, 1998, Fellow, BFI for contrib. to TV 1997, Yorks. Man of the Year 1998, Sony Radio Award 1998, Sports Writer of the Year, British Press Award 1998, BAFTA Award for Best Light Entertainment (for 'Parkinson') 1999, Media Soc. Award for Distinguished Contrib. to Media 2000. *Publications:* Football Daft 1968, Cricket Mad 1969, Sporting Fever 1974, George Best: An Intimate Biography 1975, A–Z of Soccer (Jt author) 1975, Bats in the Pavilion 1977, The Woofits 1980, Parkinson's Lore 1981, The Best of Parkinson 1982, Sporting Lives 1992, Sporting Profiles 1995, Michael Parkinson on Golf 1999, Michael Parkinson on Football 2001, Parky: My Autobiography 2008. *Leisure interests:* cricket, golf. *Address:* PFD, Drury House, 34–43 Russell Street, London, WC2B 5HA, England (office). *Telephone:* (20) 7344-1010 (office). *Fax:* (20) 7836-9544 (office). *Website:* www.pfd.co.uk (office); www.michaelparkinson.tv.

PARKS, Suzan-Lori, BA; American playwright; b. 10 May 1963, Fort Knox, Ky; m. Paul Oscher; ed John Carroll School, Mount Holyoke Coll.; Guggenheim Foundation Fellow 2000; Master Writer Chair., Public Theater, New York 2008–; Visiting Arts Prof., Tisch School of the Arts, New York Univ. 2008–; MacArthur Foundation Award 2001, Eugene McDermott Award in the Arts, Council for the Arts at MIT 2006. *Plays include:* The Sinner's Place 1984, Imperceptible Mutabilities in the Third Kingdom (OBIE Award for Best New American Play) 1989, Betting on the Dust Commander 1990, The Death of the Last Black Man in the Whole Entire World 1990, Devotees in the Garden of Love 1992, The America Play 1994, Venus 1996, In the Blood 1999, Fucking A 2000, Topdog/Underdog (Pulitzer Prize for Drama 2002) 2001, 365 Days/365 Plays 2006, Ray Charles Live! A New Musical 2007. *Plays for radio:* Pickling 1990, Third Kingdom 1990, Locomotive 1991. *Screenplays:* Girl 6 1996, Their Eyes Were Watching God 2005, The Great Debaters (co-writer) 2007. *Publication:* Getting Mother's Body: A Novel 2003. *Address:* The Public Theater, 425 Lafayette Street, New York, NY 10003, USA (office). *Telephone:* (212) 539-8500 (home). *E-mail:* press@publictheater.org (office). *Website:* www.publictheater.org (office).

PARMIGGIANI, Claudio; Italian artist; b. 1 March 1943, Lussara, Reggio Emilia; ed Istituto Statale di Belle Arti, Modena; first solo exhbn at Libreria Feltrinelli, Bologna 1965; progression from conceptual works, including installations, photo-works and books, towards use of assemblage; first Delocazioni appear 1970, works realized with use of powder, fire and smoke; realized series of works using plaster models of ancient works of art early 1960s; among the more significant later works are the Iconostasi of statues and veiled canvases 1980s (presented for the first time at Galleria Stein, Milan 1989); realized Il faro d'Islanda (perm. work) in most deserted part of Iceland 2000; realized Teatro dell'arte e della guerra in Teatro Farnese in Parma (labyrinth of shattered crystals) 2006; most recent work includes Ex-voto at Louvre Museum; lives and works in Bologna. *Address:* c/o Galerie Serge Leborgne, 108 rue Vieille-du-Temple, Paris - 3, France (office). *Telephone:* 1-42-74-53-57 (office).

PARODI, Anton Gaetano; Italian journalist and playwright; b. 19 May 1923, Castanzaro Lido (Calabria); s. of Luigi Parodi and Grazia Scicchitano; m. Piera Somino 1952; two c.; ed Università degli Studi, Turin and Genoa; journalist 1945–; professional journalist 1947–; corresp. of Unità, Budapest 1964–; Premio nazionale di teatro Riccione 1959, 1965, Premio nazionale di teatro dei giovani 1947 and numerous other prizes. *Plays include:* Il gatto, Il nostro scandalo quotidiano, L'ex-maggiore Hermann Grotz, Adolfo o della nagia, Filippo l'Impostore, Una corda per il figlio di Abele, Quel pomeriggio di domenica, Dialoghi intorno ad un'uovo, Una storia della notte, Pioggia d'estate, Cielo di pietra, I giorni dell'Arca, Quello che dicono.

PAROUBEK, Jiří, MA; Czech politician; *Chairman, Czech Social Democratic Party;* b. 21 Aug. 1952, Olomouc; m. Zuzana Paroubek; one s.; ed Prague School of Econs; economist, pvt. sector 1976–90; Sec.-Gen. Czechoslovak Social Democrats 1990; financial consultant 1991–98; various positions in the Czech Social Democratic Party (CSSD) Prague Regional Exec. 1993–95, Vice-Chair. 2001–03; Deputy Mayor for Finance, Prague 1998–2004; Minister of Regional Devt 2004–05; Prime Minister of Czech Repub. 2005–06; Vice-Chair. CSSD 2005–06, Chair. 2006–; Chair. Editorial Bd, Trend; contrib. to several daily newspapers. *Address:* Czech Social Democratic Party (Česká strana sociálně demokratická), Lidový dům, Hybernská 7, 110 00 Prague 1, Czech Republic (office). *Telephone:* 296522218 (office). *Fax:* 224222190 (office). *E-mail:* jparoubek@socdem.cz (office). *Website:* www.socdem.cz (office); www.paroubek.cz (home).

PARR, Robert Ghormley, AB, PhD; American theoretical chemist and academic; *Research Professor of Chemical Physics, University of North Carolina;* b. 22 Sept. 1921, Chicago, Ill.; s. of Leland Wilbur Parr and Grace Ghormley; m. Jane Bolstad 1944; one s. two d.; ed Western High School, Washington, DC, Brown Univ., Univ. of Minnesota; Asst Prof. of Chem., Univ. of Minn. 1947–48; Asst Prof. to Prof. of Chem., Carnegie Inst. of Tech. 1948–62, Chair. of Gen. Faculty 1960–61; Prof. of Chem., Johns Hopkins Univ. 1962–74, Chair. of Dept of Chem. 1969–72; William R. Kenan, Jr Prof. of Theoretical Chem., Univ. of NC 1974–90, Wassily Hoeffding Prof. of Chemical Physics 1990–2000, Research Prof. 2000–; Guggenheim Fellow and Fulbright Scholar, Univ. of Cambridge 1953–54; Sloan Fellow 1956–60; Visiting Prof., Univ. of Ill. 1962, State Univ. of New York at Buffalo and Pa State Univ. 1967, Japan Soc. for Promotion of Sciences 1968, 1979; Firth Prof., Univ. of Sheffield 1976; Visiting Prof., Univ. of Berlin 1977, Duke Univ. 1996–97; Fellow, Univ. of Chicago 1949, Research Assoc. 1957; NSF Sr Postdoctoral Fellow, Univ. of Oxford and CSIRO, Melbourne 1967–68; fmr mem. editorial bd of numerous specialist magazines and reviews; mem. of numerous academic and scientific socs including AAAS, American Physical Soc., ACS, NAS, American Acad. of Arts and Sciences, Int. Acad. of Quantum Molecular Science (Vice-Pres. 1973–79, Pres. 1991–97); Trustee, Inst. for Fundamental Chem., Kyoto 1988–2000; Dr hc (Louvain) 1986, (Jagiellonian) 1996; NC Inst. of Chemists Distinguished Chemists Award 1982, Langmuir Award in Chemical Physics, ACS 1994, North Carolina Award in Science 1999, Nat. Acad. of Sciences Award in Chemical Sciences 2004, ACS Award in Theoretical Chem. 2009. *Publications:* The Quantum Theory of Molecular Electronic Structure 1963; Density: Functional Theory of Atoms and Molecules 1989; more than 200 scientific articles in specialist publs. *Address:* Department of Chemistry, Kenan Laboratory C440, University of North Carolina, Chapel Hill, NC 27599-3290 (office); 701 Kenmore Road, Chapel Hill, NC 27514, USA (home). *Telephone:* (919) 962-1577 (office); (919) 929-2609 (home). *Fax:* (919) 962-2388 (office). *E-mail:* rgparr@email.unc.edu (office). *Website:* www.chem.unc.edu/people/faculty/parrrg/rgpindex.html (office).

PARRA, Nicanor; Chilean poet; b. 5 Sept. 1914, San Fabián; s. of Nicanor P. Parra and Clara S. Navarrete; m. 1st Ana Troncoso 1948; m. 2nd Inga Palmen; seven c.; ed Univ. de Chile, Brown Univ., USA and Oxford; Prof. of Theoretical Mechanics, Univ. de Chile 1964–; has given poetry readings in LA, Moscow, Leningrad, Havana, Lima, Ayacucho, Cuzco; Premio Municipal de Poesía, Santiago 1937, 1954, Premio Nacional de Literatura 1969. *Publications:* poetry: Cancionero sin nombre 1937, Poemas y antipoemas 1954, La cueca larga 1958, Antipoems 1958, Versos de salón 1962, Discursos (with Pablo Neruda) 1962, Manifiesto 1963, Deux Poèmes (bilingual) 1964, Antología (also in Russian) 1965, Antología de la Poesía Soviética Rusa (bilingual) 1965, Canciones Rusas 1967, Defensa de Violeta Parra 1967, Artefactos 1972, Sermones y prédicas del Cristo de Elqui 1977, Nuevos sermones y prédicas del Cristo de Elqui 1979, El anti-Lázaro 1981, Poema y antipoema de Eduardo Frei 1982, Cachureos, ecopoemas, guatapiques, últimas prédicas 1983, Chistes para desorientar a la policía 1983, Coplas de Navidad 1983, Poesía política 1983, Hojas de Parra 1985, Poemas para combatir la calvicie 1993, Páginas en blanco 2001, Lear Rey & Mendigo 2004, Discursos de Sobremesa 2006; scientific works: La Evolución del Concepto de Masa 1958, Fundamentos de la Física (trans. of Foundation of Physics by Profs Lindsay and Margenau) 1967, Obra Gruesa 1969, Los profesores, 1971. *Address:* Julia Bernstein, Parcela 272, Lareina, Santiago, Chile. *Website:* www.nicanorparra.uchile.cl.

PARRA-ARANGUREN, Gonzalo; Venezuelan judge; b. 5 Dec. 1928, Caracas; ed Cen. Univ. of Venezuela, Inter-American Law Inst., Univ. of New York, USA, Ludwig-Maximilians Univ., Munich, Germany; Prof., Cen. Univ. of Venezuela, Caracas 1956, Andrés Bello Catholic Univ., Caracas 1957; Judge, Second Court of First Instance (commercial matters), Fed. Dist and State of Miranda, Caracas 1958–71; First Assoc. Judge, Chamber of Cassation (civil, commercial and labour matters) of Supreme Court of Justice 1988–92, elected Alt. Judge 1992; mem. nat. group for Venezuela, Perm. Court of Arbitration, The Hague 1985–; Judge, Int. Court of Justice 1991–96; has acted as arbitrator in Venezuela and abroad on pvt. commercial matters; mem. Legal Advisory Cttee of Ministry of Foreign Affairs 1984–96, of Nat. Congress 1990–96; mem. Acad. of Political and Social Sciences of Caracas 1966– (Pres. 1993–95), Inst. of Int. Law 1979–; rep. Venezuela at several sessions of The Hague Conf. on Pvt. Int. Law. *Publications:* several books and numerous articles in Venezuelan and foreign journals on law of nationality, pvt. int. law and int. civil procedural law. *Address:* International Court of Justice, Peace Palace, Carnegieplein 2, 2517 KJ The Hague, Netherlands (office). *Telephone:* (70) 3022323 (office). *Fax:* (70) 3022409 (office). *E-mail:* information@icj-cij.org (office). *Website:* www.icj-cij.org (office).

PARRA GIL, Antonio; Ecuadorean politician; Minister of Foreign Affairs 2004–05. *Address:* c/o Ministry of Foreign Affairs, Avda 10 de Agosto y Carrión, Quito, Ecuador (office).

PARRATT, James Roy, DSc, DSc (Med), PhD, FESC, FRCPath, FRSE; British professor of cardiovascular pharmacology; *Professor Emeritus, University of Strathclyde;* b. 19 Aug. 1933, London; s. of James J. Parratt and Eunice E. King; m. Pamela J. Lyndon 1957; two s. one d.; ed St Clement Danes Holborn Estate Grammar School, London and Univ. of London; Nigerian School of Pharmacy 1958–61; Dept of Physiology, Univ. Coll. Ibadan, Nigeria 1961–67; Univ. of Strathclyde, Glasgow 1967–, Reader 1970, Personal Prof. 1975, Prof. of Cardiovascular Pharmacology 1983–, now Prof. Emer., Head, Dept of Physiology and Pharmacology 1986–90, Chair. School of Pharmacy and Pharmacology 1988; Visiting Prof. Albert-Szent-Györgyi Medical Univ., Szeged 1995–; Vice-Pres. European Shock Soc.; Fellow Royal Pharm. Soc., Inst. of Biology; mem. Council, Int. Soc. for Heart Research (European Section); Emeritus Fellow Leverhulme Trust 2002–03; Szent-Györgyi Research Fellow, Szeged Univ. 2003–; Hon. mem. Hungarian Pharmacological Soc., Slovak Medical and Cardiological Socs, Czech Cardiological Soc.; Hon. MD (Albert-Szent-Gyorgyi Univ. Medical School); Gold Medal, Univ. of Szeged, Hungary, Gold J.E. Purkyne Medal, Acad. of Sciences of the Czech Repub. *Leisure interests:* active within Baptist denomination in Scotland and in Christian mission, music. *Address:* Department of Physiology and Pharmacology, University of Strathclyde, Strathclyde Institute for Biomedical Sciences, 27 Taylor Street, Glasgow, G4 0NR; 16 Russell Drive, Bearsden, Glasgow, G61 3BD, Scotland. *Telephone:* (141) 548-2858 (office); (141) 942-7164 (home). *Fax:* (141) 552-2562. *E-mail:* j.r.parratt@strath.ac.uk (office). *Website:* spider.science.strath.ac.uk/physpharm (office).

PARRIKAR, Manohar, BTech; Indian politician and industrialist; *Leader of the Opposition, Goa Legislative Assembly;* b. 13 Dec. 1955; m. Medha Parrikar; two s.; ed Indian Inst. of Tech., Bombay (now Mumbai); started industrial unit in specialized hydraulic eng; Leader of the Opposition, Goa Legis. Ass. June–Nov. 1999, 2005–; Chief Minister of Goa 2000–05; instrumental in setting up perm. centre for Int. Film Festival of India in Goa; started unique Cyberage scheme for providing computers to students in Goa, initiated and implemented various devt schemes in Goa. *Address:* H. No. 157, Opp. Pharmacy College, 18th June Road, Panaji, Goa 403 001 (home); Next to ICICI Bank, AB Road, Panaji, Goa, India (office). *Telephone:* (832) 2250905 (home); 6511211 (office). *E-mail:* manohar.parrikar@gmail.com (office).

PARRIS, Matthew, BA, MA; British writer and broadcaster; b. 7 Aug. 1949, Johannesburg, S Africa; s. of Leslie F. Parris and Theresa E. Parris (née Littler); civil partnership with Julian Glover; ed Waterford School, Swaziland, Clare Coll., Cambridge and Yale Univ.; FCO 1974–76; with Conservative Research Dept 1976–79; MP (Conservative) for W Derbyshire 1979–86; presenter Weekend World 1986–88; Parl. Sketch Writer for The Times 1988–2001; columnist for The Times 1988–, for The Spectator 1992–; mem. Broadcasting Standards Council 1992–97; various awards for writing and journalism. *Publications:* Chance Witness (memoir) 2001, A Castle in Spain 2005, Mission Accomplished (with Phil Mason) 2007; various books about travel, politics, insult, abuse and scandal. *Address:* The Spout, Gratton, Bakewell, Derbyshire, DE45 1LN, England; c/o The Times, Pennington Street, London, E1 9XN. *Telephone:* (20) 7219-4078 (office). *E-mail:* wrighte@parliament.uk (office).

PARROTT, Andrew Haden, BA; British conductor and scholar; b. 10 March 1947, Walsall; s. of R. C. Parrott and E. D. Parrott; m. 1st Emma Kirkby 1971; m. 2nd Emily Van Evera 1986; one d.; ed Queen Mary's Grammar School, Walsall, Merton Coll., Oxford; Dir of Music Merton Coll., Oxford 1969–71; Founder, Conductor and Dir, Taverner Choir, Taverner Consort and Taverner Players 1973–; Music Dir and Prin. Conductor London Mozart Players 2000–06; Music Dir New York Collegium 2002–; BBC Promenade Concerts début 1977; fmr musical asst to Sir Michael Tippett; freelance orchestral and operatic conductor; occasional writer, lecturer and continuo player; Open Postmastership, Merton Coll. 1966–69; Leverhulme Fellowship 1984–85; Hon. Research Fellow, Royal Holloway, Univ. of London 1995–; Hon. Sr Research Fellow, Univ. of Birmingham 2000–. *Recordings include:* medieval, renaissance and music, Monteverdi, Purcell, Vivaldi, Bach, Handel, Mozart, Beethoven. *Publications include:* New Oxford Book of Carols (co-ed.) 1992, The Essential Bach Choir 2000 (German edn. 2003); articles in Early Music and other journals. *Address:* c/o Allied Artists, 42 Montpelier Square, London SW7 1JZ, England (office). *Telephone:* (20) 7589-6243 (office). *Fax:* (20) 7581-5269 (office). *E-mail:* info@alliedartists.co.uk (office). *Website:* www.alliedartists.co.uk (office).

PARROTT, Jasper William, BA; British impresario and agent; b. 8 Sept. 1944, Stockholm, Sweden; s. of the late Prof. Sir Cecil Parrott and of Lady Parrott; m. Cristina Ortiz; two d.; ed Tonbridge School, Peterhouse Cambridge; joined Ibbs and Tillett Ltd 1965–69; f. Harrison Parrott Ltd 1969, Chair. and Man. Dir 1987–; Dir Japan Festival 1991, Swiss Festival in UK 1991; Dir Rambert Dance Co. 1993–98; Hon. Trustee Kew Foundation, Royal Botanical Gardens 1991–; Co-Dir Simdi Now, Turkish Festival of Arts, Berlin 2004; Int. Adviser, Sakip Sabanci Museum, Istanbul 2005–07; Dir Polyarts UK 2004–; consultant, The Icelandic Nat. Concert and Conf. Centre 2007–. *Publication:* Beyond Frontiers: Vladimir Ashkenazy. *Leisure interests:* reading, theatre, history, tennis, landscape and water gardening, languages. *Address:* Harrison Parrott, 5–6 Albion Court, Albion Place, London, W6 0QT, England (office). *Telephone:* (20) 7229-9166 (office). *Fax:* (20) 7221-5042 (office). *E-mail:* info@harrisonparrott.co.uk (office). *Website:* www .harrisonparrott.com (office).

PARRY, Eric Owen, RA, MA, RIBA; British architect; *Principal, Eric Parry Architects;* b. 24 March 1952, Kuwait; s. of the late Eric Parry and of Marion Parry; m. Jane Anne Parry (née Saunders); one d.; ed Univ. of Newcastle upon Tyne, Royal Coll. of Art, London, Architectural Asscn, London; Founder and Prin. Eric Parry Architects 1983–, est. Eric Parry Assocs 1983, including Eric Parry Architects Ltd 1990; Lecturer, Univ. of Cambridge 1983–97, Harvard Univ. Grad. School of Design 1988, Univ. of Houston 1988, 1990, Tokyo Inst. of Tech. 1996; mem. RIBA Awards Group 2001–04, Chair. 2002–04; mem. Arts Council of England (ACE) Architecture Unit 1991–2003, ACE Lottery Architecture Advisory Cttee 1991–99, ACE Visual Arts Panel 1996–2003; mem. Council Architectural Asscn 1995– (Pres. 2005–07); External Examiner, Univ. of Kent at Canterbury, John Moore's Univ., Univ. of Cardiff and Univ. Coll., London; Hon. Librarian Architectural Asscn. *Architectural works include:* Artists' Studio, London 1986–88, Stockley Park Office Bldg W3, London 1989–91, Foundress Court, Pembroke Coll. Cambridge (RIBA Award 1998) 1993–98, Damai Suria Luxury Apartments, Kuala Lumpur 1996–97, Southwark Information Centre, London Bridge (RIBA Award 1999) 1997–99, Mandarin Oriental, Hyde Park, London (FX Int. Interior Award for the Spa 2001) 1997–2000, 30 Finsbury Square, London 1999–2002, King Edward Court, Paternoster Square (HQ for London Stock Exchange) 2000–03, St Martin-in-the-Fields, London 2002–08. *Publications include:* On Certain Possibilities of the Irrational Embellishment of a Town (co-author with Peter Carl) 1999, Eric Parry Architects Vol. 1 2002. *Leisure interests:* walking, drawing, general cultural pursuits. *Address:* Eric Parry Architects Ltd, 28-42 Banner Street, London, EC1Y 8QE, England (office). *Telephone:* (20) 7608-9600 (office). *Fax:* (20) 7608-9601 (office). *E-mail:* eric.p@ericparryarchitects .co.uk (office). *Website:* www.ericparryarchitects.co.uk (office).

PARRY, Martin, OBE, PhD; British environmentalist and academic; *Climate Scientist, Met Office;* b. 12 Dec. 1945; s. of John Fyson Parry and Frances Joan Stewart; m. Cynthia Jane Mueller 1968; two d.; ed Durham and West Indies Univs; Prof. of Environmental Man. and Dir Oxford Univ. Environmental Change Unit 1991–94; Prof. of Environmental Man., Dept of Geography, Univ. Coll. London 1996–99; apptd Prof. of Environmental Sciences and Dir Jackson Environment Inst., Univ. of East Anglia 1996; later Climate Scientist with Met Office; Co-Chair. Working Group II, Intergovernmental Panel on Climate Change (IPCC) 2002–08; fmrly with Univ. of Birmingham; Chair. UK Climate Change Review Group; Royal Geographical Soc. Peek Award 1991, WMO Gerbier-Mumm Int. Award 1993. *Publications:* Climatic Change, Agric. and Settlement 1976, Climate Change and World Agriculture 1990, Economic Implications of Climate Change in Britain 1995. *Leisure interests:* riding, sailing. *Address:* Technical Support Unit, Hadley Centre, Met Office, Fitzroy Road, Exeter, EX1 3PB, England (office). *Telephone:* (1392) 886695 (office). *Fax:* (1392) 885681 (office). *E-mail:* martin.parry@metoffice.gov.uk (office); parryml@aol.com. *Website:* www.metoffice.gov.uk (office).

PÄRSON, Anja; Swedish professional skier; b. 25 April 1981, Umeå; d. of Anders Pärson and Madeleine Pärson; coached by her father who also trained nat. team; won Jr World Giant Slalom title in 1998, Europa Cup Giant Slalom 1998; Gold Medal, Slalom, World Championships, St Anton, Austria 2001, Giant Slalom, St Moritz, Switzerland 2003; Bronze Medal, Giant Slalom, World Championships, St Anton, 2001; Gold Medal, Slalom, Winter Olympic Games, Turin, Italy 2006; Silver Medal, Giant Slalom, Winter Olympic Games, Salt Lake City, USA 2002; Bronze Medal, Slalom, Winter Olympic Games, Salt Lake City 2002, Downhill, Turin 2006, Combined, Turin 2006; World Cup Ranking (Gen.) 8th 2000, 11th 2001, 5th 2002, 3rd 2003, 1st 2004, 2005; 22 World Cup wins (15 Slalom, 7 Giant Slalom). *Leisure interests:* music, especially rhythm and blues, plays guitar. *Address:* c/o Tik Fjällvinden, Grenvägen 2, 920 64 Tärnaby, Sweden. *E-mail:* info@anjapaerson.com. *Website:* www.anjapaersson.com.

PARSONS, Charles Dacre, PhD; American philosopher and academic; *Professor Emeritus of Philosophy, Harvard University;* b. 13 April 1933, Cambridge, Mass; s. of Talcott Parsons and Helen Walker Parsons; m. Marjorie Louise Wood 1968; one s. one d.; ed Harvard Coll., King's Coll., Cambridge, UK, Harvard Univ.; Jr Fellow, Soc. of Fellows, Harvard Univ. 1958–61; Asst Prof. of Philosophy, Cornell Univ. 1961–62, Harvard Univ. 1962–65; Assoc. Prof. of Philosophy, Columbia Univ. 1965–69, Prof. 1969–89, Chair. Dept of Philosophy 1976–79, 1985–89; Prof. of Philosophy, Harvard Univ. 1989–91, Edgar Pierce Prof. of Philosophy 1991–2005, Prof. Emer. 2005–; Visiting Prof. of Philosophy, UCLA 2002, 2005, 2007; Ed. The Journal of Philosophy 1966–90, Consulting Ed. 1990–; Sec. Asscn for Symbolic Logic 1971–76, Vice-Pres. 1986–89, Pres. 1989–92; Santayana Fellow, Harvard 1964–65, NEH Fellow 1979–80, Guggenheim Fellow 1986–87; Fellow, Center for Advanced Study in The Behavioral Sciences 1994–95; Foreign mem. Norwegian Acad. of Science and Letters 2002–; Fellow, American Acad. of Arts and Sciences 1982–. *Publications:* Mathematics in Philosophy 1983, Kurt Gödel, Collected Works, Vols III–V (co-ed. with Solomon Feferman *et al.*) 1995, 2003, Mathematical Thought and its Objects 2008; articles on logic and philosophy. *Address:* Department of Philosophy, Emerson Hall, Harvard University, Cambridge, MA 02138 (office); 22 Hancock Street, Cambridge, MA 02139, USA (home). *Telephone:* (617) 495-2191 (office). *E-mail:* parsons2@fas .harvard.edu (office). *Website:* www.fas.harvard.edu/~phildept (office).

PARSONS, Nigel; British media executive; *Managing Director, Al Jazeera English;* m. Zoulfia Parsons; four c.; previous roles at BBC Radios 1–4, BBC World Service Radio and WTN (Worldwide Television News), also managed TV start-up news network teams, EBC in Switzerland and Telecampione in Italy; Regional Exec. (Eastern European and fmr USSR markets), WTN, then Vice-Pres. Europe; Dir of Associated Press TV News (APTN, cr. when Associated Press bought WTN); Man. Dir Al Jazeera English, Doha, Qatar 2004–. *Address:* Al Jazeera English, PO Box 23127, Doha, Qatar (office). *Telephone:* (7768) 728234 (office). *E-mail:* nigel.parsons@gmail.com (home). *Website:* www.aljazeera.net/english (office).

PARSONS, Peter John, MA, FBA; British academic; b. 24 Sept. 1936, Surbiton, Surrey; s. of Robert John Parsons and Ethel Ada Parsons (née Frary); m. Barbara Montagna Macleod 2006; ed Raynes Park County

Grammar School and Christ Church, Oxford; Lecturer in Documentary Papyrology, Oxford Univ. 1960–65, Lecturer in Papyrology 1965–89, Regius Prof. of Greek 1989–2003; Student (Fellow), Christ Church Oxford 1964–2003; J. H. Gray Lecturer, Cambridge Univ. 1982; Hon. PhD (Berne) 1985, (Athens) 1995; Hon. DLitt (Milan) 1994. *Publications:* The Oxyrhynchus Papyri (jtly) Vols XXXI 1966, XXXIII and XXXIV 1968, LIV 1987, LIX 1992, LX 1994, LXVI 1999, LXVIII 2003, (solely) Vol. XLII 1973, Supplementum Hellenisticum (with H. Lloyd-Jones) 1983, City of the Sharp-nosed Fish 2007; articles in learned journals. *Leisure interests:* music, cinema, cooking, eating. *Address:* Christ Church, Oxford, OX1 1DP, England. *Telephone:* (1865) 422132. *E-mail:* peter.parsons@classics.ox.ac.uk (office).

PARSONS, Richard (Dick) D.; American lawyer and entertainment industry executive; *Chairman, Citigroup Inc.;* b. 4 April 1948, Queens, NY; m. Laura Bush; three c.; ed Univ. of Hawaii, Albany Law School, Union Univ.; began career with various positions in state and fed. service, including counsel for NY Gov. Nelson Rockefeller and Sr White House aide under Pres. Gerald Ford; Founder and Man. Partner, Patterson, Belknap, Webb & Tyler 1979–88; COO Dime Bancorp Inc. 1988–90, Chair. 1990–94; joined Time Warner Inc., mem. Bd of Dirs 1991–2008, apptd Pres. 1995, Co-COO –2002, CEO 2002–07, Chair. 2003–08; mem. Bd of Dirs Citigroup Inc. 1996–, Lead Dir and Chair. Nomination and Governance Cttee –2009, Chair. 2009–; mem. Bd of Dirs Citigroup, Estée Lauder; Co-Chair. Pres.'s Comm. to Strengthen Social Security 2001–, Mayor's Comm. on Econ. Opportunity in New York; Chair. Emer. Partnership for New York City; Chair. Apollo Theatre Foundation; mem. Bd Howard Univ., Museum of Modern Art, American Museum of Natural History; econ. advisor on Pres. Barack Obama's transition team 2008–09. *Address:* Citigroup Inc., 399 Park Avenue, New York, NY 10043, USA (office). *Telephone:* (212) 559-1000 (office). *Fax:* (212) 793-3946 (office). *Website:* www.citigroup.com (office).

PARSONS, Roger, PhD, DSc, FRS; British chemist and academic; *Professor Emeritus of Chemistry, University of Southampton;* b. 31 Oct. 1926, London; s. of Robert H. A. Parsons and Ethel Fenton; m. Ruby M. Turner 1953; three s. one d.; ed King Alfred School, London, Strathcona High School, Edmonton, Alberta, Canada and Imperial Coll., London; Asst Lecturer, Imperial Coll. London 1948–51; Deedes Fellow, Univ. Coll., Dundee 1951–54; Lecturer, Univ. of Bristol 1954–63, Reader 1963–79; Dir Lab. d'Electrochimie Interfaciale du CNRS, Meudon, France 1977–84; Prof. of Chem., Univ. of Southampton 1985–92, Prof. Emer. 1992–; Pres. Faraday Div., Royal Soc. of Chem. 1991–93; Hon. DUniv (Buenos Aires) 1997; Prix Pascal, Palladium Medal, Breyer Medal, Galvani Medal, Frumkin Memorial Medal, Royal Soc. Davy Medal 2003. *Publications:* Electrochemical Data 1956, Electrical Properties of Interfaces (with J. Lyklema), Standard Potentials in Aqueous Solution (co-ed.) 1985, Electrochemistry in Research and Development 1985; more than 200 scientific papers. *Leisure interests:* listening to music, going to the opera. *Address:* 16 Thornhill Road, Bassett, Southampton, SO16 7AT, England (home). *Telephone:* (23) 8079-0143 (home). *E-mail:* roger.parsons@care4free.net (home).

PARSURAMAN, Armoogum (Dassen), BA; Mauritian politician; b. 30 June 1951; m.; ed Univ. of Mauritius; mem. Legis. Ass. 1982–; Minister of Educ., Arts and Culture 1983–92, of Educ. and Science 1992–95; Chair. Parti Socialiste Mauricien (PSM); Vice-Pres. MSM 1986–; mem. MSM/PMSD/Labour Party Govt –1990, MSM/MMM Govt 1990–; Chair. Public Accounts Cttee 1982–83, Mauritius Ex-Servicemen Welfare Fund; mem. Local Govt Comm., Select Cttee on Industrial Relations Act. *Address:* c/o Ministry of Education, Science and Technology, Government Centre, Port Louis, Mauritius.

PÄRT, Arvo; Estonian composer; b. 11 Sept. 1935, Paide; ed Tallinn Conservatory with Heino Eller; worked as sound producer for Estonian radio 1957–67; teacher at Tallinn Conservatory 1967–78; emigrated to Berlin 1980; Hon. DMus (Sydney) 1996; Hon. Dr (Tartu) 1998, (Durham) 2002; Triumph Award (Russia) 1997, Culture Prize 1998, Herder Award (Germany) 2000, Commandeur de l'Ordre des Arts et des Lettres de la République Française (France) 2001, C. A. Segizzi Composition Trophy (Italy) 2003, Musical America Composer of the Year 2005. *Compositions include:* orchestral music: four symphonies 1963, 1966, 1971, 2009, Collage über B-A-C-H 1964, Cantus in Memory of Benjamin Britten 1977, Tabula Rasa 1977, Psalom, 1985, 1991, 1995, Festina lente 1988, Trisagion 1992, 1994, Orient and Occident 1999, Lamentate 2002; vocal music: Our Garden 1959 (rev. 2003), Credo 1968, An den Wassern zu Babel sassen wir und weinten… 1976, 1984 and other versions, Summa 1977, several other versions, Missa Syllabica 1977, 1995, 1996, Passio 1982, Te Deum 1984–85, 1992, Stabat Mater 1985, Magnificat 1989, Miserere 1989, Berliner Messe 1990, 1997, Litany 1994, Kanon Pokajanen 1997, Triodion 1998, Como anhela la cierva 1999, Cecilia 2000, Littlemore Tractus 2001, Most Holy Mother of God 2003, In principio 2003; chamber music: Für Alina 1976, Pari intervallo 1976, Fratres 1977 (several other versions), Passacaglia 2003; music for film: The Banishment (with Andrey Dergatchev) 2007. *Address:* c/o Universal Edition Ltd, Karlplatz 6, A-1010 Vienna, Austria (office). *Telephone:* (1) 337-23-0 (office). *Fax:* (1) 337-23-400 (office). *E-mail:* office@universaledition.com (office). *Website:* www.universaledition.com (office).

PARTON, Dolly Rebecca; American singer and songwriter; b. 19 Jan. 1946, Sevier County, Tenn.; d. of Robert Lee Parton and Avie Lee Parton (née Owens); m. Carl Dean 1966; owner of the Dollywood Entertainment Complex, including Dollywood Theme Park; CMA Vocal Group of the Year (with Porter Wagoner) 1968, Vocal Duo of the Year 1970, 1971, Female Vocalist of the Year 1975, 1976, Country Star of the Year 1978, Nashville Metronome Award 1979, People's Choice 1980, ACM Female Vocalist of the Year 1980, ACM Vocal Event of the Year and Video of the Year (both for When I Get Where I'm Going,

with Brad Paisley) 2006, Kennedy Center Honor 2006, US Songwriters' Hall of Fame Johnny Mercer Award 2007. *Films include:* Nine to Five 1980, The Best Little Whorehouse in Texas 1982, Rhinestone 1984, Steel Magnolias 1989, Straight Talk 1991, The Beverly Hillbillies 1993, Frank McKlusky, C.I. 2002, Miss Congeniality 2: Armed and Fabulous 2005. *Stage:* as score writer: Nine to Five: The Musical, Broadway 2009. *Recordings include:* albums: Here You Come Again (Grammy Award 1978), Real Love 1985, Just the Way I Am 1986, Heartbreaker, Great Balls of Fire, Rainbow 1988, White Limozeen 1989, Home for Christmas 1990, Eagle When She Flies 1991, Slow Dancing with the Moon 1993, Honky Tonk Angels 1994, The Essential Dolly Parton 1995, Just the Way I Am 1996, Super Hits 1996, I Will Always Love You and Other Greatest Hits (with others) 1996, Hungary Again 1998, Grass is Blue 1999, Best of the Best-Porter 2 Doll 1999, Halos and Horns 2002, Those Were The Days 2006, Backwoods Barbie 2008. *Composed numerous songs including:* Nine to Five (Grammy Award 1981). *Radio includes:* Grand Ole Opry, WSM Radio, Cass Walker Program. *Publication:* Dolly: My Life and Other Unfinished Business 1994. *Address:* c/o Sugar Hill Records, 120 31st Avenue North, Nashville, TN 37203, USA. *Telephone:* (615) 297-6890. *E-mail:* info@sugarhillrecords.com. *Website:* www.dollypartonmusic.net.

PARTRIDGE, Frank David Peregrine; British art dealer; b. 14 Sept. 1955, London; s. of John A. Partridge and The Hon. Caroline M. Cust; m. Susan A. Hince 1982; three d.; ed Elstree and Harrow Schools; Dir Partridge Fine Arts PLC 1981–2004. *Leisure interests:* shooting, tennis, skiing, golf, bridge. *Address:* 7 Thurloe Square, London, SW7 2TA, England. *Telephone:* (20) 7629-0834 (office). *Fax:* (20) 7495-6266 (office).

PARTRIDGE, John Albert, CBE, RA, FRIBA; British architect; b. 26 Aug. 1924, London; s. of George Partridge and Gladys Partridge; m. Doris Foreman 1953 (died 2000); one s. one d.; ed Shooter's Hill Grammar School, Woolwich and Polytechnic School of Architecture, London; London County Council Housing Architects' Dept 1951–59; Sr and Founding Partner, Howell, Killick, Partridge & Amis (HKPA) 1959–95; John Partridge Consultancy 1995–; Vice-Pres. RIBA 1977–79, Concrete Soc. 1979–81; RIBA Hon. Librarian 1977–81; Chair. RIBA Architectural Research Steering Cttee 1978–84, Clients Advisory Steering Cttee 1990–94; Gov. Building Centre, London 1981–96; Chair. Trustees Eric Lyons Memorial Fund 1982–; Chair. Asscn of Consultant Architects 1983–85; mem. NEDO Construction Research Strategy Cttee 1983–86; Architect mem. FCO Advisory Bd on the Diplomatic Estate 1985–94; External Examiner in Architecture, Univ. of Bath 1975–78, 1992, Thames Polytechnic 1978–86, Univ. of Cambridge 1979–81, Univ. of Manchester 1982–, South Bank Polytechnic (London) 1981–86, Brighton Polytechnic 1987–91, Royal Coll. of Art 1991–94; Asscn of Consultant Architects Award 2005. *Major works include:* Wolfson Rayne and Gatehouse Bldg, St Anne's Coll., Oxford, New Hall and Common Room, St Antony's Coll., Oxford, Weston Rise Housing, Islington, Wells Hall, Univ. of Reading, Middlesex Polytechnic Coll. of Art, Cat Hill, Medway Magistrates Court, The Albany, Deptford, Hall of Justice, Trinidad & Tobago, in Asscn with ACLP, Trinidad; Warrington Crown Courthouse, Basildon Courthouse, Haywards Heath Magistrates Courthouse, Chaucer Coll., Univ. of Kent; exhbns of HKPA work at Heinz Gallery, London 1983, Puck Bldg, New York 1983; 35 Nat. Design Awards for HKPA 1965–93. *Publications:* articles in the tech. press and architectural papers to conferences. *Leisure interests:* looking at buildings and gardens, travel, sketching, taking photographs, listening to music. *Address:* Cudham Court, Cudham, nr Sevenoaks, Kent, TN14 7QF, England (home). *Telephone:* (1959) 571294 (home). *Fax:* (1959) 570478 (home). *E-mail:* john.partridge1@btinternet.com (home).

PARTRIDGE, Linda, BA, DPhil, FRS, FRSE, CBE; British biometrist; *Research Professor, Biotechnology and Biological Sciences Research Council;* b. 18 March 1950, Bath; d. of George Albert Partridge and Ida Partridge (née Tucker); m. 1st Vernon French (divorced 1989); m. 2nd Michael John Morgan 1996; ed Convent of Sacred Heart, Tunbridge Wells, Univ. of Oxford; Demonstrator then Lecturer, Reader, Prof. of Evolutionary Biology Univ. of Edinburgh 1976–1993; Weldon Prof. of Biometry Univ. Coll. London 1994–; NERC Research Prof. 1997–2002, Biotechnology and Biological Sciences Research Council, Research Prof. 2002–; London Zoological Soc. Frink Medal 2000, American Soc. of Naturalists Sewall Wright Award 2002, Longevity Prize of the Fondation IPSEN. *Leisure interests:* sailing, gardening, tennis, natural history. *Address:* Department of Biology, University College London, Darwin Building, Gower Street, London, WC1E 6BT, England (office). *Telephone:* (20) 7679-2983 (office). *Fax:* (20) 7679-7096 (office). *Website:* www.ucl.ac.uk/~ucbtcee/cee/index.html (office).

PARTRIDGE, Sir Michael John Anthony, Kt, KCB, MA; British civil servant; b. 29 Sept. 1935, Stourbridge, Worcs.; s. of Dr John Henry Partridge and Ethel Green; m. Joan Elizabeth Hughes 1968; two s. one d.; ed Merchant Taylors' School, St John's Coll., Oxford Univ.; joined Home Civil Service (Ministry of Pensions and National Insurance—MPNI) 1960, Pvt. Sec. to Perm. Sec. 1962–64, Prin. MPNI 1964–71, Asst Sec. 1971–76, UnderSec. 1976–81, Deputy Sec. 1981–83; Deputy Under-Sec. of State, Home Office 1983–87; Second Perm. Sec. Dept of Health and Social Security 1987–88; Perm. Sec. Dept of Social Security 1988–95; Sr Treas. Methodist Church Finance Div. 1980–96; Hon. Fellow St John's Coll. Oxford 1991–; Dir (non-exec.) Methodist Ministers' Pensions Trust 1992–, Epworth Investment Man. 1995–, Commercial Gen. and Norwich Union 1996–2003, Stationery Office 1997–99; Gov. Middx Univ. 1992–, Chair. Bd of Govs 1996–2002, Pro-Chancellor 2001–; Vice-Chair. Harefield Research Foundation 2001–; mem. Council Sheffield Univ. 2001–03; Gov. Merchant Taylors' School 1992–99; Chair. Stationery Office Pension Scheme 2002–, Bd of Govs Heathfield School 2004–; Pres. Old Merchant Taylors' Soc. 2002–03; Trustee Harefield Hosp. Heart Transplant Trust 1992–2003; Liveryman Merchant Taylors' Co. 1987. *Leisure interests:*

do-it-yourself, Greece, reading, skiing. *Address:* 27 High View, Pinner, Middx, HA5 3NZ, England. *Telephone:* 020) 8868-0657. *Fax:* 020) 8429-4532.

PARTS, Juhan, BL; Estonian politician; *Minister of Economic Affairs and Communications;* b. 27 Aug. 1966, Tallinn; m.; one s. one d.; ed Tallina First Secondary School, Univ. of Tartu; Deputy Sec.-Gen., Ministry of Justice 1992–98; Auditor Gen. 1998–2002; Chair. Res Publica Party 2002–05; Prime Minister of Estonia 2003–05 (resgnd); Minister of Econ. Affairs and Communications 2007–. *Leisure interest:* football (mem. FC Toompea). *Address:* Ministry of Economic Affairs and Communications, Harju 11, Tallinn 15072 (office); Res Publica, Narva mnt. 7, Tallinn 10117, Estonia (office). *Telephone:* 625-6342 (Ministry) (office); 610-9244 (Res Publica) (office). *Fax:* 631-3660 (Ministry) (office); 610-9243 (Res Publica) (office). *E-mail:* juhan.parts@mkm.ee (office); respublica@respublica.ee (office). *Website:* www.mkm.ee (office); www.respublica.ee (office).

PARVANOV, Georgi, MA, PhD; Bulgarian historian and head of state; *President;* b. 28 June 1957, Sirishnik, Pernik Dist; m. Zorka Parvanova; two s.; ed mathematics college in Pernik, Sofia Univ. St Kliment Ohridski; researcher, Inst. of History, Bulgarian CP (BCP—became Bulgarian Socialist Party—BSP 1990) 1981–91, conducted research on the nat. question and history of social democracy in Bulgaria, Sr Research Assoc. 1989–92, Dir Centre for History and Policy Studies with the Supreme Council of the Bulgarian Socialist Party (BSP) 1992–96; joined BCP 1981 first party post 1991, Deputy Chair. Supreme Council 1994–96, Chair. 1996–2001; mem. Narodno Sobraniye (Parl.) for Kurdjali (Southern Bulgaria) 1994–2001, Chair. Parl. Group for Friendship with Greece and mem. Parl. Cttee on Radio and Television 1994–97, Parl. Group of the Democratic Left, Parl. Group of Coalition for Bulgaria 1997–2001; Pres. of Bulgaria 2002–; fmr Chair. Parl. Group on Friendship between Bulgaria and Greece; Grand Gold Medal, Tomáš Garrigue Masaryk Univ., Brno, Czech Republic; Dr hc (Prešov Univ.), (Baku Univ.), (Yerevan State Univ.). *Publications:* numerous scientific articles, monographs and books, including Dimitar Blagoev and the Bulgarian National Problem 1879–1917 1988, From Bouzloudja to the Corona Theatre–An Attempt at a New Reading of Pages from the BSP's Social Democratic Period 1995, The Bulgarian Social Democracy and the Macedonian Issue at the End of the 19th Century up to 1918 1997, November 10: Before and After 2001. *Address:* Office of the President, 1123 Sofia, bul. Dondukov 2, Bulgaria (office). *Telephone:* (2) 923-93-33 (office). *E-mail:* press@president.bg (office). *Website:* www.president.bg (office).

PARVEEN, Abida; Pakistani singer; b. 1954, Larkana, Sindh; d. of Ghulam Haider; m. Ghulam Hussain Sheikh (deceased); one s. two d.; ed attended father's music school; studied classical music with Salamat Ali Khan; debut on Hyderabad Radio Station; repertoire includes classical music, ghazals, traditional Sufiana kalaam and Punjabi folk music; worldwide tours and performances before heads of state; made recordings of original works of Sufi poets; President's Award for Pride of Performance 1982, Sitara-i-Imtiaz Award 2005. *Recordings include:* Iere Ishq Nachaya, Ho Jamalo, Raqs-e-Bismil, Pakistani Sufi Songs 1995, The Best of Abida Parveen 1997, Songs of the Mystics 2000, Faiz by Abida, Jahan E. Khusrau 2001, Visal – The Meeting Mystic Poets from the Hind & Mind 2002, Baba Bulleh Shah 2003.

PASANELLA, Giovanni, FAIA; American architect; b. 13 Jan. 1931, New York; two s.; ed Cooper Union, New York, Yale Univ.; designer, Edward L. Barnes, New York 1959–64; Prin. Giovanni Pasanella, New York 1964–76; co-owner Pasanella & Klein, New York 1976–; Architecture Critic, Univ. of Ky, Lexington 1963, Yale Univ. 1964; Adjunct Prof. of Architecture, Columbia Univ. 1965–87, Project Dir Inst. of Urban Environment 1965–68; Visiting Fellow Urban Studies, Inst. of Architecture 1975; Consultant Architect to Chair. New York City Planning Comm. 1967; mem. Bd of Trustees Il Piccolo Teatro dell'Opera, Brooklyn, New York 1986; Yale Univ. Travelling Fellow 1958–59; mem. Soc. of Architectural Historians; Architecture Award, Architectural Record 1974, 1975. *Address:* 115 South Street, New York, NY 10038, USA (home); Villa Cannizzaro, via Fondi Camaiore, Lucca, Italy. *Telephone:* (584) 989297 (office); (212) 566-2352 (home). *Fax:* (212) 566-2481 (home). *E-mail:* marcopasanella@verizon.net (home).

PASCAL, Amy; American film industry executive; *Chairman, Sony Pictures Entertainment Motion Picture Group and Co-Chairman, Sony Pictures Entertainment;* b. Los Angeles, Calif.; m. Bernard Weinraub; ed Univ. of Calif., Los Angeles; worked for producer Tony Garnett at Kestral Films (affiliated to Warner Bros); Vice-Pres. of Production, 20th Century Fox 1986–87; Studio Exec., Columbia Pictures 1987–94, Pres. 1996–99, Chair. 1999–2003, Vice-Chair. Sony Pictures Entertainment 2002–06, Chair. Sony Pictures Entertainment Motion Picture Group 2003–, Co-Chair. Sony Pictures Entertainment 2006–; Pres. of Production, Turner Pictures 1994–96; mem. Exec. Bd UCLA School of Theater, Film and Television; Trustee RAND Corpn, American Film Inst.; named by The Hollywood Reporter No. 1 on Power 100 List in Women in Entertainment 2003, Hollywood Leadership Award™ Honoree 2003, ranked by Fortune magazine amongst 50 Most Powerful Women in Business in the US (21st) 2004, (42nd) 2005, (41st) 2006, (46th) 2007, ranked by Forbes magazine amongst 100 Most Powerful Women (66th) 2004, (50th) 2005, (59th) 2006, (35th) 2007, (54th) 2008. *Films:* appeared in Intimate Portrait: Jennifer Lopez (TV documentary) 2002; Peter Pan (co-producer) 2003. *Address:* Sony Pictures Entertainment, 10202 W Washington Boulevard, Culver City, CA 90232, USA (office). *Telephone:* (310) 244-4000 (office). *Fax:* (310) 244-2626 (office). *Website:* www.sonypictures.com (office).

PASCAL, Jean-Baptiste Lucien, LenD; French banker; b. 26 Nov. 1930, Bordeaux; s. of Ernest Pascal and Paule de Battisti; m. Christiane Gardelle 1962; three s. (one deceased); ed Univ. of Paris; attached to Banque Nat. pour le Commerce et l'Industrie 1954; Head of Supplies Mission for the Devt of Algeria and Jt Govt Commr for Crédit Populaire de France in Algeria 1959; Head of Bureau for Financial Co-operation to Sec. of State for Algerian Affairs 1963; mem. Crédit Commercial de France (CCF) 1965, Deputy Dir Cen. Admin. CCF 1967, Dir-Gen. d'Interbail 1971, Dir Cen. Admin. 1973–, Admin. Dir-Gen. 1974, Vice-Pres. Dir-Gen. d'Interbail 1978–96; Dir Crédit Commercial de France 1977; Pres. Dir-Gen. Banque Hervet 1986–89; Pres. Admin. Council SOFEC 1991; Pres. GOBTP 1993–97, Pres. Conseil de Surveillance du GOBTP 1997–99, Interbail 1996– (Chair. Bd of Dirs 1996–97); Dir French Asscn of Financial Cos, Vice-Pres. 1995–97; Chevalier, Légion d'honneur. *Publication:* La Décolonisation de l'Europe: Querelle des Continents 1964. *Leisure interests:* alpinism, hunting. *Address:* 14 rue Jules Claretie, 75116 Paris, France (home).

PASCHKE, Fritz, DTechSc; Austrian electrical engineer; *Professor Emeritus, Technical University of Vienna;* b. 2 March 1929, Graz/Goesting; s. of late Eduard Paschke and Stefanie Mittellehner; m. Gertrud P. Kutschera 1955; two d.; ed Tech. Univs of Graz and Vienna; Asst, Tech. Univ. Vienna 1953–55; consultant, New York 1955–56; mem. tech. staff, RCA David Sarnoff Research Center 1956–61; Components Div. Siemens AG, Munich 1961–66; Prof. of Gen. Electronics, Tech. Univ. Vienna 1965–97, Prof. Emer. 1997–, Dean, School of Electrical Eng 1970–71, Rector/Pro-Rector 1971–76, Head, Inst. für Allgemeine Elektrotechnik und Elektronik 1980–97; Vice-Pres. Austrian Nat. Science Foundation 1974–82; Dr hc (Budapest) 1974; Ludwig Boltzmann Award 1977, HE Cardinal Innitzer Award 1984, Erwin Schrödinger Award (Austrian Acad.) 1988, City of Vienna Award for Science and Tech. 1988, SEFI (European Soc. for Eng. Educ.) Leonardo da Vinci Medal 1996. *Leisure interests:* art, hiking, swimming. *Address:* Technical University of Vienna, Karlsplatz 13, 1040 Vienna, Austria (office). *Telephone:* (1) 58801-36653 (office). *Fax:* (1) 58801-36699 (office). *E-mail:* fritz.paschke@tuwien.ac.at (office); fritz.paschke@chello.at (home). *Website:* www.isas.tuwien.ac.at (office).

PASCHKE, Karl Theodor; German diplomatist; b. 12 Nov. 1935, Berlin; s. of Adolf Paschke and Adele Cornill; m. Pia-Irene Schwerber 1963; one s. one d.; ed Univs of Munich and Bonn; Consul, New Orleans, La, USA 1964–68; Deputy Chief of Mission, Kinshasa 1968–71; Dean, Foreign Office Training School, Bonn 1972–77; Press Counsellor, Washington, DC 1977–80; Spokesman, German Foreign Office, Bonn 1980–84; Amb. to UN Orgs Vienna 1984–86; Minister, Washington, DC 1987–90; Dir-Gen. for Personnel and Man., Foreign Office, Bonn 1990–94; Under-Sec.-Gen. for Internal Oversight Services, UN, New York 1994–99; Special Insp., Foreign Office 2000; currently Chair. Cttee on Budget and Finance, Ass. of States Parties to Rome Statute of Int. Criminal Court. *Publication:* Reform der Attache-Ausbildung 1975. *Leisure interest:* music, especially jazz. *Address:* International Criminal Court, POB 19519, 2500 CM, The Hague, Netherlands (office); Denglerstrasse 46, 53173 Bonn, Germany (home). *Telephone:* (228) 9562032 (home). *Fax:* (228) 9562083 (home). *Website:* www.icc-cpi.int (office).

PASCO, Richard Edward, CBE; British actor; b. 18 July 1926, Barnes; s. of Cecil George Pasco and Phyllis (née Widdison) Pasco; m. 1st Greta Watson 1956 (divorced 1964); one s.; m. 2nd Barbara Leigh-Hunt 1967; ed Colet Court and King's Coll. School, Wimbledon, Cen. School of Speech and Drama; first appearance on stage, Q Theatre 1943; served in HM forces 1944–48; Old Vic Co. 1950–52; Birmingham Repertory Co. 1952–55; played Fortinbras in Hamlet (Moscow and London) 1955; English Stage Co. 1957, played in The Member of the Wedding, Look Back in Anger, The Entertainer, Man from Bellac and The Chairs; toured USA and Europe 1967 (with RSC), Japan, Australia 1970, Japan 1972; joined RSC 1969, Nat. Theatre 1987; now Hon. Assoc. Artist RSC; has made broadcasts and recordings of plays and verse, including complete sonnets of Shakespeare. *Roles include:* The Entertainer (New York) 1958, Moscow Youth Festival in Look Back in Anger 1959, Teresa of Avila (Dublin Theatre Festival and Vaudeville) 1961, Henry V, Love's Labour's Lost (Bristol Old Vic, Old Vic and tour to Europe) 1964; Hamlet, Bristol Old Vic, 1965, Measure for Measure, Peer Gynt, Man and Superman, Hamlet 1966, Polixenes in The Winter's Tale, Proteus in The Two Gentlemen of Verona, Buckingham in Henry VIII 1969, Major Barbara, Richard II, Duchess of Malfi 1971, Becket in Murder in the Catherdral, Medraut in the Island of the Mighty 1972, Richard and Bolingbroke in Richard II 1973–74; The Marrying of Ann Leete 1975, Jack Tanner in Man and Superman 1977, Trigorin in The Seagull 1978, Timon in Timon of Athens 1980, Clarence in Richard III 1980, Arkady Schatslivtses in The Forest 1981, La Ronde 1982, Father in Six Characters in Search of an Author 1987, Pavel in Fathers and Sons 1987, Charlie Southwark in Racing Demon, Sir Peter Edgcombe in Murmuring Judges, Mr Birling in An Inspector Calls, Malcolm Pryce in Absence of War, Boss Findley in Sweet Bird of Youth 1994, Sorin in The Seagull, Stratford, Barbican 2000. *Television appearances include:* Henry Irving, The Three Musketeers, Savages, As You Like It, Julius Caesar, British in Love, Trouble with Gregory, Philby, The House Boy, Number 10—Disraeli, The Plot to Murder Lloyd George, Let's Run Away to Africa, Sorrell and Son, Drummonds, etc. *Films include:* Room at the Top, Yesterday's Enemy, The Gorgon, Rasputin, Watcher in the Woods, Wagner, Arch of Triumph, Inspector Morse, etc. *Publications:* Time and Concord: Aldeburgh Festival Recollections (contrib.) 1997, Acting in Stratford (contrib.) 1997. *Leisure interests:* music, gardening, preservation of rural England. *Address:* c/o Michael Whitehall Ltd, 10 Lower Common South, London, SW15 1BP, England.

PASCOE, B. Lynn, MA; American diplomatist and UN official; *Under-Secretary-General, United Nations Department for Political Affairs;* b. 1943, Mo.; m. Diana Pascoe; two d.; ed Univ. of Kansas, Columbia Univ.; served on Soviet and China Desks; postings to Moscow, Hong Kong, Bangkok, Beijing (twice) and Taiwan; Prin. Deputy Asst Sec., East Asian and Pacific Bureau, State Dept; Deputy Chief of Mission, American Embassy, Beijing; Deputy Exec. Sec., Dept of State; Special Asst to Deputy Sec. of State; Dir American Inst., Taiwan 1993–96; Sr Adviser, Bureau of East African and Pacific Affairs and at US Mission to the UN; Special Negotiator for Nagorno-Karabakh and Regional Conflicts; Co-Chair. OSCE Minsk Group; apptd Amb. to Malaysia 1999; Deputy Asst Sec. for European and Eurasian Affairs, US Dept of State 2001–04; Amb. to Indonesia 2004–07; Under-Sec.-Gen., UN Dept for Political Affairs 2007–. *Address:* Department of Political Affairs, United Nations, New York, NY 10017, USA (office). *Telephone:* (212) 963-1234 (office). *Fax:* (212) 963-4879 (office). *Website:* www.un.org/Depts/dpa (office).

PASCUAL, Ramon, DSc; Spanish academic; *Professor of Theoretical Physics, Universitad Autónoma de Barcelona;* b. 4 Feb. 1942, Barcelona; s. of Josep Montserrat; m. Maria Lluisa Roca 1966; two s. one d.; Junta de Energía Nuclear, Madrid 1963–64; Teaching Asst Univ. of Valencia 1964–67; Asst Prof. of Quantum Mechanics, Univ. Complutense de Madrid 1967–70; Prof. of Mathematical Physics, Univ. of Zaragoza Jan.–Sept. 1970; Prof. Univ. Autónoma de Madrid 1970–71; Prof. of Theoretical Physics, Univ. Autónoma de Barcelona 1971–, Dean, Faculty of Science 1976–79, Vice-Rector for Academic Affairs 1979–80, Rector 1986–90; Visiting Scientist, CERN, Geneva, 1969, 1970, 1977, 1978, 1981, 1983, 1986, Faculty of Science, Paris (Orsay) 1972, 1975, Rutherford Appleton Lab. Oxford 1975; Chair. Exec. Cttee of the Synchrotron Light Source Alba; mem. Real Sociedad Española de Física y Química, European Physical Soc., Real Acad. Ciencias y Artes de Barcelona. *Publications:* over 40 articles in scientific journals etc. *Address:* Universitat Autónoma de Barcelona, Edificio C, 08193 Bellaterra, Barcelona, Spain. *Telephone:* (3) 5811307. *Fax:* (3) 5813213. *E-mail:* pascual@ifae.es (office). *Website:* www.ifae.es (office).

PASHIN, Valentin Mikhailovich, DSc, CEng, FIMarEST; Russian naval engineer; *Science Principal and Director, Krylov Shipbuilding Research Institute;* b. 25 July 1937, Saratov Region; m.; two c.; ed St Petersburg State Marine Tech. Univ.; on staff A.N. Krylov Research Inst. 1960; Jr, Sr Researcher, Head of Dept, Tech. Dir; Science Prin. and Dir Krylov Shipbuilding Research Inst. 1990–; Corresp. mem. Russian Acad. of Sciences 1991, mem. 1997; USSR State Prize 1985, Gold Star Medal of Hero of the Russian Fed. and several other awards. *Publications:* monographs, scientific articles and reports. *Address:* Krylov Shipbuilding Research Institute, Moskovskoye shosse 44, 196158 St Petersburg (office); Sofiyskaya ulitsa 30, Bldg 2, Flat 69, 192236 St Petersburg, Russia (home). *Telephone:* (812) 373-54-82 (office); (812) 123-66-23 (office). *Fax:* (812) 127-95-95 (office). *E-mail:* krylov@krylov.spb.ru (office); pashin@krylov.spb.ru (office). *Website:* www.krylov.com.ru (office).

PASHTUN, Yousef, BSc; Afghan politician; *Minister of Urban Development and Housing;* b. 1947, Kandahar; ed American Univ. of Beirut, Lebanon; fmr Lecturer, Kabul Univ.; Minister of Urban Affairs 2002–03; Gov. of Qandahar Prov. 2003–04; Minister of Urban Development and Housing 2004–. *Address:* Ministry of Urban Development and Housing, Micro-rayon 3, Kabul, Afghanistan (office).

PASIARDIS, Christodoulos; Cypriot politician and diplomatist; b. 31 Jan. 1944, Tseri; m. Ava Pasiardis; two c.; ed Pancyprian Gymnasium and Univ. of Athens; worked in Political Affairs Dept, Ministry of Foreign Affairs 1974–75, 1978–84; Dir Office of the Minister of Foreign Affairs 1975–78, 1992–93; Diplomatic Adviser to the Pres. 1984–88; First Counsellor and Chargé d'Affaires, Embassy in Athens 1989–92; High Commr to Australia 1994–96; Political Dir, Ministry of Foreign Affairs 1996–98; Amb. to Greece (also accred to Bulgaria and Romania) 1998–2001; Perm. Sec., Ministry of Foreign Affairs 2001–03; Deputy Minister to the Pres. and Govt Spokesperson 2003–07; Minister of Defence 2007–08. *Address:* c/o Ministry of Defence, 4 Emmanuel Roides Avenue, 1432, Nicosia, Cyprus (office).

PASINETTI, Luigi Lodovico, MA, PhD; Italian economist and academic; *Professor Emeritus of Economics, Università Cattolica del Sacro Cuore, Milan;* b. 12 Sept. 1930, Bergamo; s. of Giovanni Pasinetti and Romilda Arzuffi; m. Carmela Colombo 1966; one s.; ed Univ. Cattolica del Sacro Cuore, Milan, Univ. of Cambridge, UK, Harvard Univ., USA; Research Fellow, Nuffield Coll., Oxford 1960–61; Fellow and Lecturer in Econs, King's Coll., Cambridge 1961–73; Lecturer, then Reader in Econs, Univ. of Cambridge 1961–76; Prof. of Econs, Università Cattolica del Sacro Cuore 1976–2007, Prof. Emer. 2007–, Chair. 1980–83; Wesley Clair Mitchell Visiting Research Prof. of Econs, Columbia Univ., New York 1971, 1975; Visiting Research Prof., Indian Statistical Inst., Calcutta and New Delhi 1979; Visiting Prof. of Econs, Univ. of Ottawa, Carleton Univ. 1981, Kyoto Univ. 1984, Univ. of Southern California 1985; Visiting Fellow, Gonville and Caius Coll., Cambridge 1989; McDonnell Distinguished Scholars Fellow, WIDER, the UN Univ., Helsinki 1991, 1992; Visiting Prof., Univ. of Sydney 1993; Visiting Fellow, Trinity Coll. Cambridge 1997, 1999; mem. Council and Exec. Cttee Int. Econ. Assen 1980–99, Hon. Pres. 2005; Pres. Italian Econ. Assen 1986–89, Confed. of European Econ. Assens 1992–93, European Soc. for the History of Econ. Thought 1995–97; Fellow, Econometric Soc. 1978–; mem. Accad. Lincei, Rome 1986–, Inst. Lombardo Accad. di Scienze e Lettere, Milan 1995–; Hon. Fellow, Gonville and Caius Coll., Cambridge 1999–; Hon. Pres. European Assen for Evolutionary Political Economy 1989, European Soc. for the History of Economic Thought 2003–, Int. Econ. Assen 2005–; Dr hc (Fribourg) 1986; St Vincent Prize for Econs 1979, 2002, Gold Medal (First Class) for Educ., Culture and Arts 1982, 'La Madonnina' Int. Prize (Econs section), Milan 1987, Special Prize for Culture (Econs section), Presidency of the Council of Ministers 1996, Invernizzi Prize for Econs 1997. *Publications:* Growth and Income Distribution 1974, Lectures on the Theory of Production 1977, Structural Change and Economic Growth 1981, Structural Change and Adjustment in the World Economy (with P. Lloyd) 1987, Structural Economic Dynamics 1993, Economic Growth and the Structure of Long-Term Development (with R. M. Solow) 1994, The Impact of Keynes in the 20th Century (with B. Schefold) 1999, Keynes and the Cambridge Keynesians 2007; numerous articles on income distribution, capital theory, econ. growth and structural econ. dynamics. *Leisure interests:* tennis, climbing, music. *Address:* Faculty of Economics, Università Cattolica del Sacro Cuore, Largo A. Gemelli 1, 20123 Milan, Italy (office). *Telephone:* (02) 72342470 (office). *Fax:* (02) 72342406 (office). *E-mail:* llp@unicatt.it (office). *Website:* www.unicatt.it/docenti/pasinetti (office).

PAŠKA, Pavol, BA; Slovak politician; *Speaker, Národná Rada Slovenskej Republiky (Parliament);* b. 23 Feb. 1958, Košice; m.; two s.; ed Comenius Univ., Bratislava; several roles at State Company Zdroj, Educ. and Culture Centre, Self-Admin Office and Municipal Dist. Admin KVP, Košice; Co-founder Direction (later Direction-Social Democracy) 1999, Vice-Pres. 2003–; mem. Národná Rada Slovenskej Republiky (Parl.) 2002–, Speaker 2006–, Chair. Foreign Relations Cttee 2004–06, mem. Health Care Cttee 2002–04, Special Oversight Cttee for the SIS 2002–04; Chair. Conf. of Speakers of EU Parls 2006. *Address:* Office of the Speaker, Národná Rada Slovenskej Republiky, nám. Alexandra Dubčeka 1, 812 80 Bratislava, Slovakia (office). *Telephone:* (2) 5972-1111 (office). *Fax:* (2) 5441-9529 (office). *E-mail:* info@nrsr.sk (office). *Website:* www.nrsr.sk (office).

PASKAI, HE Cardinal László, OFM; Hungarian ecclesiastic; *Archbishop Emeritus of Esztergom-Budapest;* b. 8 May 1927, Szeged; joined Minor Franciscan Order, professed his vows 1949; assumed diocesan service 1950; ordained priest 1951; Episcopal liturgist 1952–55, Szeged; Prof. of Philosophy, Theological Acad., Szeged 1955–65, simultaneously Prefect 1955–62, Spiritual 1962–65; Spiritual Prefect, Central Seminary of Budapest 1965–69; commissioned lecturer 1965–67, leading Prof. of Philosophy, Theological Academy, Budapest 1967–78; Rector of Seminary 1973–78; apptd Titular Bishop of Bavagaliana and Apostolic Gov. of Veszprém 1978; Diocesan Bishop of Veszprém 1979, Coadjutor Archbishop of Kalocsa-Kecskemét 1982; Archbishop of Esztergom (now Esztergom-Budapest) and Primate of Hungary 1987–2002, Archbishop Emer. 2002–; cr. Cardinal (Cardinal-Priest of S. Teresa al Corso d'Italia) 1988; Chair. Hungarian Episcopal Conf. 1986–90. *Address:* Primasi es Erseki Hivatal, Mindszenty hercegprimas ter 2, Pf. 25, 2501 Esztergom; Úri u. 62, 1014 Budapest, Hungary. *Telephone:* (1) 202-5611. *Fax:* (1) 202-5458.

PASQUA, Charles Victor; French politician; b. 18 April 1927, Grasse; s. of André Pasqua and Françoise Rinaldi; m. Jeanne Joly 1947; one s.; ed College de Grasse, Inst. d'Etudes Juridiques, Nice and Faculté de Droit, Aix-en-Provence; Rep. Société Ricard 1952, Insp. 1955, Regional Dir 1960, Dir French Sales 1962, Dir-Gen. French Sales and Export 1963; Pres.-Dir-Gen. Société Euralim 1967–71; Commercial Consultant 1972–; Deputy to Nat. Ass. (UDR) 1968–73; Sec.-Gen. UDR 1974–76; Senator, Hauts de Seine 1977–86, 1988–93, 1995–99, 2004–; Pres. RPR Group in Senate 1981–86, 1988–93; Minister of the Interior and Administration 1986–88, 1993–95; Political adviser Exec. Comm. of RPR 1998–99; Co-founder and Pres Rassemblement pour la France et l'Indépendance de l'Europe 1999–; mem. European Parl. 1999–2004; Chevalier, Légion d'honneur; Médaille de la France libre. *Publications:* La libre entreprise – un état d'esprit 1964, L'ardeur nouvelle 1985, Que demande le peuple 1992, Demain, la France (Vol. I): la priorité sociale (jtly) 1992, Tous pour la France 1999. *Address:* Le Rassemblement pour la France et L'Indépendance de l'Europe, 129 avenue Charles de Gaulle, 92521 Neuilly-sur-Seine Cedex; Conseil Général, Hôtel du Département, 2–16 Blvd Soufflot, 92015 Nanterre Cedex, France. *Telephone:* 1-55-62-24-24 (office). *Fax:* 1-55-62-24-44 (office). *E-mail:* infos@charles-pasqua.com (office). *Website:* www.rpfie.org (office).

PASQUAL, Lluís; Spanish theatre and opera director; b. 5 June 1951, Reus, Catalonia; ed Universitat Autònoma de Barcelona, Institut del Teatre, Barcelona; founder and Dir Lliure Theatre, Barcelona 1976, co-Dir 1998–2000; worked in Poland; Asst to Giorgio Strehler, Italy 1978; Dir Centro Dramático Nacional, Teatro María Guerrero, Madrid 1983–89; Dir Odéon, Théâtre de l'Europe, Paris 1990–96; Dir Venice Theatre Biennale 1995–96; Commr Projecte Ciutat del Teatre, Barcelona City Council 1997–99; Officier des Arts et des Lettres; Nat. Theatre and Dance Prize 1984, Ciutat de Barcelona Prize 1985, Generalitat de Catalunya Prize 1988, Nat. Theatre Prize, Spanish Ministry of Culture 1991, Paris Chamber of Commerce Prize 1995, Egyptian Ministry of Culture's Hon. CIFET Prize 1995, Comunidad de Madrid Prize 2002, Max de Teatro Award 2003. *Plays directed include:* Luces de Bohemia (Valle Inclán) 1984, Sans Titre (Lorca) 1990, Le Balcon (Genet) 1991, Tirano Banderas (Valle Inclán) 1992; Le Chevalier d'Olmédo (Lope de Vega) 1992, El Público (Lorca) 1986. *Operas directed include:* (Teatro de la Zarzuela, Madrid); Samson et Dalila (Saint-Saëns) 1982, Falstaff (Verdi) 1983, Don Carlo (Verdi) 1985, Il Trittico (Puccini) 1987, Il Turco in Italia (Rossini) 1990; La Vera Storia (Berio), Paris 1985, Maggio Musicale, Florence 1986, Falstaff, Bologna 1987. *Address:* c/o Teatre Lliure, plaça margarida xirgu, 1, 08004 Barcelona, Spain; c/o Matthias Vogt Artistic Management, 211 Gough Street, Suite 115, San Francisco, CA 94102, USA.

PASSACANTANDO, Franco, DEcon; Italian economist; *Central Manager, Central Banking and Markets, Payment Systems and Treasury, Banca d'Italia (Bank of Italy);* b. 7 Aug. 1947, Rome; m. Miriam Veronesi 1987; three s. one d.; ed Rome and Stanford Univs; Head, Money Market Div., Research Dept, Banca d'Italia (Bank of Italy) 1981–85, Task Force on the Reform of the Italian Payment System 1986–89, Dir Monetary and Financial Sector, Research Dept 1990–95, Head Asset Man. Dept 2003–06, Cen. Man., Cen. Banking and Markets, Payment Systems and Treasury 2006–; Exec. Dir World Bank Group 1995–2003, Chair. Budget Cttee, Audit Cttee, Steering Cttee; mem. PSSC,

ECB; mem. CPSS, BIS; Fulbright, Einaudi and Stringher fellowships. *Publications:* White Paper on the Payment System in Italy 1988, Le Banche e il Finanziamento delle Imprese 1997, Governance Reforms at the World Bank 2002, Building an International Framework for Monetary Stability: The Case of Italy 1979–1994 1996, The Loss of Confidence in Bank Money in the Great Depression; and articles on monetary policy in professional journals. *Leisure interests:* making movies, art. *Address:* Banca d'Italia, Via Nazionale, 91, 00184 Rome, Italy (office). *Telephone:* (6) 47923515 (office). *Fax:* (6) 47923883 (office). *E-mail:* email@bancaditalia.it (office). *Website:* www .bancaditalia.it (office).

PASSERA, Corrado, MBA; Italian banking executive; *Managing Director and CEO, Intesa Sanpaolo SpA;* b. 30 Dec. 1954, Como; m. Cecilia Canepa; one s. one d.; ed Bocconi Univ., Milan, Wharton School, Univ. of Pa; Sr Engagement Man., McKinsey & Co., Milan 1980–85; with CIR SpA, Milan 1985–66, COO 1988–90; Deputy Chair. Credito Romagnolo 1988–95; COO Arnoldo Mondadori Editore SpA 1990–91; Deputy Chair. and CEO Gruppo Espresso–Repubblica, Rome 1991–92; Man. Dir and Co-CEO Olivetti SpA, Ivrea 1992–96; Man. Dir and CEO Banco Ambrosiano Veneto 1996–98; Man. Dir and CEO Poste Italiane 1998–2002; Man. Dir and CEO Banca Intesa SpA (fmrly IntesaBci) 2002–06, Man. Dir and CEO Intesa Sanpaolo (following merger between Banca Intesa and Sanpaolo IMI) 2007–; Dir RCS MediaGroup, Bocconi Univ.; Dir and mem. Exec. Cttee Italian Bankers' Asscn (ABI); mem. Advisory Bd Scuola Normale, Pisa, Int. Advisory Bd Wharton School, Gen. Council Fondazione Giorgio Cini. *Address:* Intesa Sanpaolo SpA, Via Monte di Pietà 8, 20121 Milan, Italy (office). *Telephone:* (02) 87963705 (office). *Fax:* (02) 87963837 (office). *E-mail:* segreteriaceo@intesasanpaolo.com (office). *Website:* www.intesasanpaolo.com (office).

PASSY, Solomon Isaac, MS, PhD; Bulgarian politician and academic; *Chairman, Foreign Affairs Committee, Bulgarian National Assembly;* b. 22 Dec. 1956, Plovdiv; m.; two s. one d.; ed Sofia Univ. 'St Kliment Ohridski'; in opposition to anti-Muslim repressive policy of the Communist regime 1985–89; Asst Prof. of Math. Logic and Computer Science, Sofia Univ. 'St Kliment Ohridski' and at Bulgarian Acad. of Sciences 1984–94; participant in Nat. Round Table for transition to democracy 1989–90; activist of Ecoglasnost opposition movt 1989; Co-founder and mem. Coordinating Council of UDF 1990–91; Founding Pres. and CEO Atlantic Club of Bulgaria (first pro-Atlantic NGO ever founded in a non-NATO mem. state) 1991–2001; Founder and Spokesman, Green Party of Bulgaria 1989; Mem. Grand Nat. Ass. (Green Party, Union of Democratic Forces—UDF) 1990–91, (Nat. Movt Simeon II) 2005–, Chair. Foreign Affairs, Defence and Security Cttee, 39th Nat. Ass. July 2001, Foreign Affairs Cttee, 40th Nat. Ass. 2005–, Bulgaria–USA caucus, 40th Nat. Ass. 2005–; Minister of Foreign Affairs 2001–05; Chair. Ad hoc Cttee on Transparency and Accountability, Parl. Ass. OSCE 2006–; Vice-Pres. Nat. Movt Simeon II 2005, mem. Political Council 2002–05; Special Adviser on NATO accession to Govt of Macedonia 2007–; mem. 2nd, 3rd, 4th and 13th Bulgarian Antarctic Expeditions to Livingston Island, Antarctica 1993–2005; Chair. Host Cttee for the Dalai Lama's visit to Sofia 1991; Leader Bulgarian Del. for the Audience with His Holiness Pope John Paul II 1994; Vice-Chair. Atlantic Treaty Asscn, Paris 1996–99; Co-Chair. Host Cttee for the visit of Pres. Bill Clinton to Bulgaria 1999; Hon. Citizen of Nedelino 2003, of State of Tex., USA 2004; Orden Infante Don Enrique (Grã-Cruz) (Portugal) 2002; Orden del Mérito Civil (Gran Cruz) (Spain) 2003; Order of Léopold II (Grand Cross) (Belgium) 2004; Ordine della Stella della Solidarieta' Italiana (I classe) (Italy) 2006; Orden de Isabel la Catolica (Gran Cruz) (Spain) 2006; Dr hc (South-West Univ. of Bulgaria) 2005; Balkan Peace Award 2004. *Publications:* numerous scientific articles on math. logic and computer science. *Address:* Foreign Affairs Committee, Bulgarian National Assembly, 1 Al. Battenberg Square, 1169 Sofia (office); National Movement Simeon II, 23 Vrabcha Street, 1000 Sofia, Bulgaria. *Telephone:* (2) 9861133 (office). *Fax:* (2) 9818568 (office). *E-mail:* kvp@parliament.bg; ndsv@ndsv.bg. *Website:* www.parliament.bg/kvp (office).

PASTORELLI, Jean, LenD; Monegasque civil servant, diplomatist and politician; *Ambassador to France;* m.; two c.; ed Institut d'Etudes Politiques and Ecole Nationale d'Admin (Fonctionnaire Etranger), Paris; joined Secr., Dept of Finance and Economy 1969; Dir Budget and Treasury 1978–88; Govt Counsellor for Finance and the Economy 1988–95; Pres. Radio Monte Carlo 1995–2000, Monaco Telecom 1997–99; Perm. Del. to Posteurop 1995–; Perm. Del. to ITU, UPU 1995–2004; Pres. Tele Monte Carlo 1995–, Monte Carlo Radiodiffusion (MCR) 1995–; Minister Plenipotentiary 1995; Perm. Del. to UNESCO 2003, to French-speaking community 2003; Perm. Rep. at IAEA 2003; Nat. Authority for Principality of Monaco to Org. for Prohibition of Chemical Weapons 2003, Perm. Rep. 2003–; Pres. EUTELSAT Ass. of Parties 2001–04, INTELSAT Ass. of Parties (ITSO) 2002–04; Amb. to Belgium, the Netherlands and Grand Duchy of Luxembourg 2003–07; Head of Mission to European Communities 2003–07, Observer within Int. Criminal Court 2003–; Govt Counsellor for External Relations 2007–08; Amb. to France 2008–; Commdr, Ordre de Saint-Charles. *Address:* Embassy of Monaco, 22 boulevard Suchet, 75116 Paris, France (office). *Telephone:* 1-45-04-74-54 (office). *Fax:* 1-45-04-45-16 (office). *E-mail:* ambassade.en.france@gouv.mc (office).

PASTRANA ARANGO, Andrés, LLD; Colombian diplomatist and fmr head of state; b. 17 Aug. 1954, Bogotá; s. of Misael Pastrana Borrero (fmr Pres. of Colombia) and María Cristina Arango de Pastrana; m. Nohra Puyana Bickenbach; one s. two d.; ed Colegio San Carlos de Bogotá, Colegio Mayor de Nuestra Señora del Rosario Law School, Harvard Univ.; Man. Dir Revista Guión (publ.) 1978–79; Man. Dir Datos y Mensajes SA News Broadcasting Co. 1979–80; Dir TV Hoy News 1980–87; Councillor Bogotá City Council 1982–86, Chair. Jan.–April 1983, 1984–85; Mayor of Bogotá 1988–90; Senator 1991–93; founder and Presidential Cand. of Nueva Fuerza Democrática 1994; Pres. of

Colombia 1998–2002; Amb. to USA 2005–06 (resgnd); mem. Int. Union of Local Authorities, Exec. Cttee 1989, Pres. Latin American Chapter 1988–89; Vice-Pres. Latin American Union of Capital Cities; Co-Dir World Mayors' Conf. on Drug Addiction, New York 1989, Madrid 1990; Sec. Gen. Union of Latin American Parties 1992–; Adviser to UN Univ., Tokyo 1994; Dir and f. UN Leadership Acad., Jordan; fmr Chair. Bogotá Telephone Co., Bogotá Aqueduct and Sewerage Co., Electricity and Public Utilities Co. of Bogotá, Inst. for Urban Devt, Dist Planning; Nat. Police Distinguished Service Order, UNESCO Order, Grand Cross, Civilian Order of Merit 1988, Order of Merit, Colombian Publishing Industry 1988, Civilian Defence Order 1989, Order of Santa Bárbara, Colombian Navy 1990, José María Córdova Order of Mil. Merit 1990; Colombian Jr Chamber Exec. of the Year 1981, King of Spain Int. Journalism Award 1985, Simón Bolívar Nat. Journalism Award 1987, King of Spain Nat. Journalism Award 1987, Bogotá Circle of Journalists Nat. Award 1987. *Publication:* Hacia la formulación de un derecho ecológico (Towards the formulation of an ecological law). *Address:* c/o Ministry of Foreign Affairs, Palacio de San Carlos, Calle 10a, No 5-51, Bogotá, DC, Colombia.

PASTUKHOV, Boris Nikolayevich; Russian politician; b. 10 Oct. 1933, Moscow; m. Janna Pastukhova; two d.; ed Bauman Higher Tech. Coll., Moscow; mem. CPSU 1959–91; First Sec. Bauman Regional Komsomol Cttee, Moscow 1959–61; Second Sec. Moscow City Komsomol Cttee 1961–62, First Sec. 1962–64; Second Sec. All-Union Komsomol Cttee 1964–77, First Sec. 1977–82; Chair. USSR State Cttee for Publishing, Printing and Bookselling, USSR Goskomizdat 1982–86; mem. Presidium, Supreme Soviet of the USSR 1978–83; USSR Amb. to Denmark 1986–89, to Afghanistan 1989–92; Deputy Foreign Minister of Russia 1989–96; First Deputy Foreign Minister 1996–98; mediator in negotiations between Georgia and Abkhazia; Minister for CIS Affairs 1998–99; Chair. Govt Cttee on CIS; mem. State Duma (Otechestvo) 1999–, re-elected 2003 (United Russia); mem. Cttee on Connections with Compatriots 2000–. *Address:* State Duma, Okhotny Ryad 1, 103265, Moscow, Russia. *Telephone:* (495) 292-59-95. *Fax:* (495) 292-41-90.

PASTUSIAK, Longin, PhD; Polish politician and professor of international affairs; *Professor, Financial Academy, Warsaw;* b. 22 Aug. 1935, Łódź; s. of Josef Pastusiak and Sabina Pastusiak; m. Anna Ochab; one s. one d.; ed Warsaw Univ., American Univ., Washington DC, Univ. of Virginia; Prof. and Head Dept, Polish Inst. of Int. Affairs 1963–93; Deputy to Sejm (Parl.) 1991–2001, Vice-Chair. Foreign Affairs Cttee 1993–2001; Head, Polish Del. to WEU Ass. 1993–; Head, Polish Del. to NATO Parl. Ass. 1993–, Vice-Pres. 2002–; Senator 2001–05, Pres. of the Senate 2001–05; Prof. of Int. Relations, Gdansk Univ. 1994–2005; Prof., Financial Acad., Warsaw 2005–, Higher School of Communications and Mass Media, Warsaw 2005–; Visiting Prof. Appalachian State Univ., USA; Silver Cross of Merit 1972, Kt's Cross 1985, Order of Merit (Lithuania) 2004, Grand Commdr's Cross (Lithuania) 2004; Dr hc (Naval Mil. Acad. Gdynia, Poland) 2003, Hon. DHumLitt (Appalachian State Univ.) 2004; Parliamentarian of the Year 1997, numerous scholarly awards. *Television:* various programmes on Polish public television. *Publications:* more than 70 books including Poland–Canada 1945–1961 1994, United States Diplomacy, 18th and 19th Century 1997, Chicago: Portrait of the City 1997, Will the World Come to an End? 1999, From the Secrets of the Diplomatic Archives: Polish–American Relations 1948–1954 1999, Ladies of the White House 2000, Presidents of the USA 2002; 600 scholarly publs and more than 3,000 articles in daily and weekly journals on American history and foreign policy, German studies, East–West relations, Polish foreign policy, Polish–American relations and theoretical aspects of int. relations. *Leisure interest:* tennis. *Address:* al. Niepodleglosci 151, Apt 21, 02-555 Warsaw, Poland (home). *Telephone:* (22) 8495044 (home). *Fax:* (22) 8495044 (home). *E-mail:* longin.pastusiak@mac.com (home).

PASUGSWAD, Suwan, MA; Thai international civil servant; b. 19 March 1937, Songkhla; s. of Dam Pasugswad and Kate Pasugswad; m. 1973; two d.; ed Thammasat Univ. of Bangkok and Queen's Univ. Ont., Canada; Asst to Exec. Dir IBRD and affiliates 1975–78; Alt. Exec. Dir Asian Devt Bank, Manila 1985–87, Exec. Dir 1987–89; Deputy Dir-Gen. Fiscal Policy Office, Ministry of Finance 1992–94; Exec. Dir IBRD and affiliates 1994–97. *Leisure interests:* swimming, gardening. *Address:* 123/4 Soi Bangkrabue, Samsen Road, Dusit, Bangkok, Thailand. *Telephone:* (2) 669-0340. *Fax:* (2) 669-0340.

PASWAN, Ram Vilas, BL, MA; Indian politician; *Minister of Chemicals and Fertilizers and of Steel;* b. 5 July 1946, Shaharbanni, Bihar; s. of the late Jamun Paswan and Siya Devi; m. Reena Paswan; one s. three d.; ed Kosi Coll., Khagaria, Patna Univ.; mem. Bihar Legis. Ass. 1969; Gen. Sec. Lok Dal, Bihar 1974; mem. Lok Sabha 1977–, Leader of the House 1996; Gen. Sec. Janata Party 1987–88, Janata Dal 1988–90; Sec. Nat. Front 1988–90; Minister of Labour and Welfare 1989–90, of Railways 1996–98, of Communications 1999–2001, of Coal and Mines 2001–02, of Chemicals and Fertilizers and of Steel 2004–; Pres. Lok Jan Shakti Party. *Address:* Ministry of Chemicals and Fertilizers, Shastri Bhavan, New Delhi 110 001, India (office). *Telephone:* (11) 23386519 (office). *Fax:* (11) 23015477 (office). *Website:* chemicals.nic.in (office).

PATAIL, Abdul Gani; Malaysian lawyer; *Attorney-General;* b. 1955; involved in numerous high-profile cases; led the prosecution of fmr Deputy Prime Minister Anwar Ibrahim in trials involving corruption and sodomy 1998; Sr Public Prosecutor in Chambers of Attorney-Gen. –2001, Attorney-Gen. Jan. 2002–. *Address:* Attorney-General's Chambers, c/o Federal Court of Malaysia, Bangunan Sultan Abdul Samad, Salan Raja, 50506 Kuala Lumpur, Malaysia (office).

PATAKI, George E., BA, JD; American lawyer, politician and fmr state official; *Counsel, Chadbourne & Parke LLP;* b. 24 June 1945, Peekskill, NY; m. Elizabeth Rowland; two s. two d.; ed Yale Univ., Columbia Univ. Law School; Assoc. Dewey Ballantine PC (law firm), New York 1970–74; Pnr, Plunkett &

Jaffee PC (law firm), White Plains and New York; Co-Owner, Pataki's Farm, Peekskill, NY; Mayor of Peekskill 1981–84; mem. New York State Ass. 1985–92; mem. New York State Senate 1993–94; Gov. of New York State 1994–2007; Counsel, Chadbourne & Parke LLP (law firm), New York 2007–; Republican. *Address:* Chadbourne & Parke LLP, 30 Rockefeller Plaza, New York, NY 10112, USA (office). *Telephone:* (212) 408-5145 (office). *E-mail:* gpataki@chadbourne.com (office). *Website:* www.chadbourne.com (office).

PATASSÉ, Ange-Félix; Central African Republic politician; b. 25 Jan. 1937, Paoua; ed Higher Acad. of Tropical Agric., Nogent-sur-Marne, France; Agricultural inspector 1959–65; Dir of Agric. 1965; Minister of Devt 1965; Minister of State for Transport and Power 1969–70, concurrently Minister of State for Devt and Tourism 1969–70; Minister of State for Agric., Stock-breeding, Waters and Forests, Hunting, Tourism, Transport and Power Feb.–June 1970; Minister of State for Devt June–Aug. 1970; Minister of State for Transport and Commerce 1970–72, for Rural Devt 1972–73, of Health and Social Affairs 1973–74; Minister of State for Tourism, Waters, Fishing and Hunting 1974–76, Prime Minister 1976–78, also Keeper of the Seals Sept.–Dec. 1976; Vice-Pres. Council of the Cen. African Revolution Sept.–Dec. 1976; Leader Mouvement pour la libération du peuple centrafricain; under house arrest Oct. 1979, escaped, recaptured and detained Nov. 1979; Cand. in Pres. Election March 1981; took refuge in French Embassy March 1982, fled to Togo April 1982; lived in France, returned to Cen. African Repub.; Pres. of Cen. African Repub. 1993–2003 (overthrown in coup while on visit to Niger); in exile in Togo March 2003–.

PATCHETT, Ann, BA, MFA; American writer; b. 2 Dec. 1963, Los Angeles; ed Sarah Lawrence Coll. and Univ. of Iowa Writers' Workshop; writer-in-residence Allegheny Coll. 1989–90; Yaddo Fellow 1990; Millay Fellow 1990; Resident Fellow, Fine Arts Work Center, Provincetown 1990–91; Visiting Asst Prof. Murray State Univ. 1992; Bunting Fellow, Mary Ingram Bunting Inst., Radcliffe Coll. 1993; Guggenheim Fellowship 1994; Nashville Banner Tenn. Writer of the Year Award 1994. *Publications:* The Patron Saint of Liars (Univ. of Iowa James A. Michener/Copernicus Award for a book in progress 1989, American Library Asscn Notable Book 1992) 1992, Taft (Janet Heidinger Kafka Prize) 1994, The Magician's Assistant 1997, Bel Canto (PEN/Faulkner Award 2002, Orange Prize 2002) 2001, Truth and Beauty (biog.) 2004, Run 2007; contrib. to anthologies and to periodicals, including The New York Times Magazine, Chicago Tribune, Boston Globe, Vogue, GQ, Elle, Gourmet. *Address:* c/o Carol Fass Ivy Publishing, 201 East 50th Street, New York, NY 10022, USA (office). *Website:* www.annpatchett.com (office).

PATE, John Stewart, PhD, FAA, FRS; British scientist and academic; *Emeritus Professor of Botany, University of Western Australia;* b. 15 Jan. 1932; s. of H. S. Pate and M. M. Pate; m. Elizabeth L. Sloan 1959; three s.; ed Campbell Coll. Belfast and Queen's Univ. Belfast; lecturer in Botany, Univ. of Sydney 1957–60; lecturer in Botany, Queen's Univ. Belfast 1960–65, then Reader, Personal Chair. in Plant Physiology 1970–83; Prof. of Botany, Univ. of W Australia 1974–2001, Emer. Prof. 2001–; Australian Minerals and Energy Research Foundation Award 1999, Commonwealth Centenary Medal 2003. *Publications:* Restionaceae and Allied Families of Australia 1999 (co.-ed.); over 350 books, research articles, reviews, chapters for textbooks and conf. proceedings. *Leisure interests:* music, reading, nature study, committed Christian. *Address:* Department of Botany, University of Western Australia, Nedlands, WA 6009 (office); RMB 1452, Denmark, WA 6333, Australia. *Telephone:* (9) 848-1096.

PATEL, A. K., MB; Indian politician and medical practitioner; b. 1 July 1931, Vadu, Mehsana Dist, Gujarat; s. of Kalidas Patel; m.; two s. one d.; ed B.J. Medical Coll., Ahmedabad; mem. Gujarat Legis. Ass. –1984; mem. for Mehsana, Lok Sabha 1984–, Minister of State for Chemicals and Fertilizers 1998–99; Pres. Bharatiya Janata Party, Gujarat 1982–85; mem. Rajya Sabha; Man. Trustee SRST Gen. Hosp., Vijapur, Asha Educ. Trust, Girls' Coll., Vijapur; Trustee St Joseph Public School, Vijapur. *Leisure interests:* reading, swimming, riding, sports. *Address:* 30 Canning Lane, New Delhi, 110001 (office); nr T.B. Hospital, Bhavsor, Vijapur, District Mahesaona, Gujarat, India. *Telephone:* (11) 3722922.

PATEL, Indraprasad Gordhanbhai, PhD; Indian economist; b. 11 Nov. 1924, Sunav; s. of Gordhanbhai Patel and Kashiben Patel; m. Alaknanda Dasgupta 1958; one d.; ed Baroda Coll., Bombay Univ., King's Coll., Cambridge and Harvard Univ.; Prof. of Econs and Principal Baroda Coll., Maharaja Sayajirao Univ., Baroda 1949–50; Economist and Asst Chief, Financial Problems and Policies Div., IMF 1950–54; Deputy Econ. Adviser, Indian Ministry of Finance 1954–58; Alt. Exec. Dir for India, IMF 1958–61; Chief Econ. Adviser, Ministry of Finance, India 1961–63, 1965–67, Econ. Adviser Planning Comm. 1961–63; Special Sec. Ministry of Finance 1968–69, Sec. 1970–72; Deputy Admin., UN Devt Programme 1972–77; Gov. Reserve Bank of India 1977–82; Dir Indian Inst. of Man., Ahmedabad, India 1982–84; Dir LSE 1984–90; Chair. Indian Council for Research on Int. Econ. Relations, Delhi 1997–, Hindustan Gil Exploration Ltd 1999–; mem. Bd of Dirs State Bank of India 1996–; Visiting Prof., Delhi School of Econs, Delhi Univ. 1964; Hon. Fellow King's Coll., Cambridge 1986, LSE 1990; Hon. DLitt (Sardar Patel Univ.) 1980, (MS Univ. of Baroda) 1993, (Univ. of Roorkee) 1997, (Banaras Hindu University) 2004; Hon. Dr Civil Laws (Univ. of Mauritius) 1990; Hon. KBE 1990; Padmavibhushan 1990. *Publications:* On the Economics of Development 1986, Essays in Economic Policy and Economic Growth 1986, Economic Reform and Global Change 1998, Glimpses of Indian Economic Policy 2002, An Encounter With Higher Education: My Years at LSE 2003, and articles on inflation and econ. devt, monetary and credit policy, etc. *Leisure interests:* reading, music. *Address:* 12 Amee Co-operative Housing Society, Diwali Pura, Old Padra Road, Vadodara 390015, India. *Telephone:* (265) 2339026. *Fax:* (265) 2333918.

PATEL, Lilian; Malawi politician; b. 21 Feb. 1951; four d.; ed Malawi Polytechnic, Univ. of New Delhi, India; sec. 1970–80; Man. Dir Holiday Motel and Budu Estate, Mangochi 1981; Ward Counsellor Mangochi Town Council 1989–92, Chair. (acting) 1991–92; elected MP for Mangochi South 1994; Sec. Women's Parl. Caucus 1995–99; Minister of Gender, Youth and Community Services 1996–99, of Health and Population 1999–2000, of Foreign Affairs and Int. Co-operation 2000–04, of Labour and Vocational Training 2004–05; Chair. Cabinet Cttee on Gender, Youth and Persons with Disabilities 1999; mem. United Democratic Front (UDF). *Address:* c/o United Democratic Front (UDF), POB 5446, Limbe, Malawi (office). *Website:* www.udf.malawi.net.

PATEL, Praful Raojibhai Chaturbhai; British campaigner and business executive; *Chairman, Asia Fund Limited;* b. 7 March 1939, Jinja, Uganda; s. of Raojibhai Chaturbhai Patel and Maniben Jivabhai Lalaji Patel; ed Govt Secondary School and London Inst. of World Affairs, Univ. Coll., London; Gen. Sec. Uganda Students' Union 1956–58; Del. to Int. Youth Ass., New Delhi 1958; arrived in UK as student, then commenced commercial and financial services activities 1962; Pres. Nava Kala India Socio-Cultural Centre, London 1962–75; Hon. Sec. All-Party Parl. Cttee on UK Citizenship 1968–82; Founder and Council mem. UK Immigration Advisory Service 1970–82; Chair. Bd of Trustees, Swaminarayan Hindu Mission, UK 1970–76; mem. Uganda Resettlement Bd 1972–74; Hon. Sec. Uganda Evacuees Resettlement Advisory Trust 1974–2000; Jt Convener Asian Action Cttee 1976; mem. Indian Govt Consultative Cttee on Non-Resident Indian Investments 1986–91; adviser to His Holiness Pramukh Swami Maharaj on NGO activities, continues to support the activities of Worldwide Swaminarayan Fellowship; initiator of many inter-faith dialogues with spiritual leaders in India and abroad, including organizing many recitations of Hindu scriptures; fmr Gov. City Lit Coll., London; cand. (Labour) for Brent N constituency 1986; organized historic trip of His Holiness Sant Shri Morari Bapu to Kailas Manasarovar, Tibet, China in 1997; Dir Indo-British Cultural Exchange 2002–; involved in industrial, cultural and educational projects affecting immigrants in UK; spokesman for Asians in UK following restrictions of immigration resulting from Commonwealth Immigrants Act 1968; active campaigner for civil and human rights issues, co-operation between Third World countries and investments in India; mem. British Labour Party, Charter '88 Movt, UK Democratic Audit; UK Del. to Indo-British Conf. on Democracy and Human Rights organized by Rajiv Gandhi Foundation, New Delhi; specialist on immigration, citizenship and race-relation issues; Chair. Asia Fund Ltd; Chair. and Trustee, Manava Trust 1979–; Trustee and Gen. Sec. Int. Ayurveda Foundation, UK 2002–; Trustee, The Charutar Arogya Mandal Trust, UK 1980, India Overseas Trust 2002–, Kailas Manasarovar Trust 2002–; Queen's Scout 1956, Asian Times Award for achievement 1986, Neasden Swaminarayan Mandir Award. *Dance:* Nritya Natika Ramayana (producer) 1982. *Film:* Kailas Manasarovar Yatra (producer). *Publications:* numerous articles in newspapers and journals on political, immigration, race relations and business related issues. *Leisure interests:* cricket, campaigning and lobbying, current affairs, promoting traditional Ayurveda medicines, inter-faith co-operation, passionate about his unique collection of more than 2,500 Ganesh Murtis (idols) and Hindu artifacts. *Address:* 60 Bedford Court Mansions, Bedford Avenue, London, WC1B 3AD, England (home); Praful Patel Associates, Readymoney Mansion, 3rd Floor, 43 Veer Nariman Road, Mumbai, 400023 India. *Telephone:* (20) 7580-0897 (London) (home); (22) 22049248 (India) (office). *Fax:* (20) 7436-2418 (London) (office); (22) 22048938 (India) (office). *E-mail:* prcpatel@vsnl.com. *Website:* www.prafulpatel.co.uk (office).

PATERSON, David Alexander, BA, JD; American politician and academic; *Governor of New York;* b. 20 May 1954, Brooklyn; s. of Basil Paterson; m. Michelle Paige Paterson; one s. one step-d.; ed Hempstead High School, Columbia Univ., New York, Hofstra Law School; born legally blind; worked for Queens Dist Attorney's Office (failed NY Bar examination); Adjunct Prof., School for Int. and Public Affairs, Columbia Univ.; joined campaign staff of David Dinkins for Manhattan Borough Pres. 1985; won selection process to serve remainder of term in NY State Senate for 30th Senate Dist following death of Senator Bogues 1985, youngest senator when elected aged 31, won seat for first full term representing 29th Dist 1986–2007; ran in Democratic primary for office of New York Public Advocate 1993; elected by Democratic Caucus of Senate as Minority Leader (first non-white state legis. leader and highest-ranking black elected official in history of NY State) 2002; mem. Democratic Nat. Cttee, Bd Democratic Legis. Campaign Cttee; selected as running mate by NY Attorney Gen. and Democratic Party nominee Eliot Spitzer in NY gubernatorial election 2006; Lt-Gov. NY 2006–08, Gov. of NY 2008–; mem. Bd of Dirs Achilles Track Club; mem. American Foundation for the Blind. *Achievement:* ran New York City Marathon 1999. *Leisure interests:* playing basketball, fan of New York sports teams. *Address:* State Capitol, Albany, NY 12224 -0341, USA (office). *E-mail:* info@www.ny.gov (office). *Website:* www.ny.gov/ltgov (office).

PATERSON, Sir Dennis Craig, Kt, MB, BS, MD, FRCS, FRACS; Australian orthopaedic surgeon; b. 14 Oct. 1930, Adelaide; s. of Gilbert Charles Paterson and Thelma Drysdale Paterson; m. Mary Mansell Hardy 1955 (deceased 2004); one s. three d.; m. Katalin Clara Maria Line 2006; ed Collegiate School of St Peter, Adelaide, Univ. of Adelaide; Resident Medical Officer, Royal Adelaide Hosp. 1954, Adelaide Children's Hosp. 1956; Registrar, Robert Jones and Agnes Hunt Orthopaedic Hosp., Oswestry, Shropshire, England 1958–60; Sr Registrar, Royal Adelaide Hosp. 1960–62; Consultant Orthopaedic Surgeon, Repatriation Gen. Hosp., Adelaide 1962–70; Asst Hon. Orthopaedic Surgeon, Adelaide Children's Hosp. 1964–66, Sr Hon. Orthopaedic Surgeon 1966–70, Dir and Chief Orthopaedic Surgeon 1970–95, mem. Bd of Man., Chair. Medical Advisory Cttee, Medical Staff Cttee 1976–84; Sr Hon. Orthopaedic Surgeon, Queen Victoria and Modbury Hosps, Adelaide

1970–95; Sr Visiting Consultant Orthopaedic Surgeon, Royal Adelaide Hosp. 1962–85; Clinical Assoc. Prof. Orthopaedic Surgery Univ. of Adelaide 1990–; mem. Bd of Orthopaedic Surgery, RACS 1974–82, 1984–87, Chair. 1977–82, mem. Court of Examiners 1974–84; Censor-in-Chief, Australian Orthopaedic Asscn 1976–80, Dir Continuing Educ. 1982–86; Pres. Crippled Children's Asscn of S. Australia 1970–84; Pres. Int. Soc. of Orthopaedic Surgery and Traumatology (SICOT) 1987–90; Chair. S Australia Road Safety Consultative Council 1994–99, Trauma Systems Cttee of S Australia 1994–2000; mem. Bd Man. McLaren Vale and Fleurian Visitor Centre 1995–2001, Chair. 1998–2001; Chair. Southern Partnership 1997–2000; mem. Archbishops' Appeal Cttee 1993–2005, Cttee of the Commonwealth Club of South Australia, Probus Club of Glen Osmond, South Australian Cricket Asscn, Royal Adelaide Golf Club; Queen's Jubilee Medal 1977, L.O. Betts Medal in Orthopaedic Surgery 1980. *Publications:* Electrical Stimulation and Osteogenesis (Thesis) 1982; over 80 articles in refereed scientific journals. *Leisure interests:* golf, tennis, gardening. *Address:* 26 Queen Street, Glenunga, SA 5064, Australia (home). *Telephone:* (8) 8379-2669 (home). *Fax:* (8) 8379-6449 (home). *E-mail:* paterson@awam.com.au (home).

PATERSON, Rt Rev. John Campbell, BA, LTh; New Zealand ecclesiastic; *Bishop of Auckland;* b. 4 Jan. 1945, Auckland; s. of Thomas Paterson and Mary Paterson; m. Marion Reid Anderson 1968; two d.; ed King's Coll., Univ. of Auckland, St John's Coll.; asst curate, Whangarei 1969–71; vicar, Waimate N Maori pastorate 1971–76; Priest-in-Charge, Hokianga 1973–74, Bay of Islands 1974–75; Chaplain, Queen Victoria School 1976–82; Asst Priest, Maori Mission 1976–82; Sec. Bishopric of Aotearoa 1978–87; Prov. Sec. 1986–92; mem. Anglican Consultative Council 1990–96, Chair. 2002; Gen. Sec. of Anglican Church, Aotearoa, Polynesia and NZ 1992–95, Presiding Bishop and Primate of Anglican Church, Aotearoa, Polynesia and NZ 1998–2004; Bishop of Auckland 1995–; Outstanding Old Collegian Award King's Coll. 2000, Univ. of Auckland Distinguished Alumni Award 2004. *Publications:* He Toenga Whatiwhatinga 1984. *Leisure interests:* literature, music. *Address:* Bishopscourt, PO Box 37242, Parnell 1033, New Zealand (home). *Telephone:* (9) 302-7202 (home). *Fax:* (9) 377-6962 (home). *E-mail:* bishop.auckland@xtra.co.nz (office).

PATERSON, Mervyn Silas, FAA, ScD; Australian geophysicist; *Visiting Fellow and Emeritus Professor, Research School of Earth Sciences, Australian National University;* b. 7 March 1925, South Australia; s. of Charles Paterson and Edith M. Michael; m. Katalin Sarosy 1952; one s. one d.; ed Adelaide Technical High School, Univs of Adelaide and Cambridge; research, Aeronautical Research Labs, Melbourne 1945–53; ANU, Canberra 1953–, Prof. Research School of Earth Sciences 1987–90, Visiting Fellow and Emer. Prof. 1990–; Consultant Australian Scientific Instruments Pty Ltd; Fellow American Mineralogical Soc., American Geophysical Union; Hon. Fellow Geological Soc. of America 1987, Walter H Bucher medal of American Geophysical Union 2004. *Publications:* Experimental Rock Deformation: The Brittle Field 1978; about 110 research papers in rock deformation and materials science. *Leisure interests:* walking, reading. *Address:* Research School of Earth Sciences, Australian National University, Canberra 0200, Australia. *Telephone:* (2) 6125-2497 (office). *Fax:* (2) 6125-0738.

PATERSON, William Edgar, OBE, MSc, PhD, FRSE, FRSA; British academic; *Director, Institute for German Studies, University of Birmingham;* b. 26 Sept. 1941, Blair Atholl, Scotland; s. of William Edgar Paterson and Winnie Paterson (née McIntyre); m. 1st Jacqueline Cramb 1964 (died 1974); two s.; m. 2nd Phyllis MacDowell 1979; one d. one step-s. one step-d.; ed Morrison's Acad., Univ. of St Andrews, London School of Econs; Lecturer in Int. Relations, Univ. of Aberdeen 1967–70; Volkswagen Lecturer in German Politics, Univ. of Warwick 1970–75, Sr Lecturer 1975–82, Reader 1982–89, Prof. and Chair. of Dept 1989–90; Salvesen Prof. and Dir of Europa Inst., Univ. of Edin. 1990–94; Dir Inst. for German Studies, Univ. of Birmingham 1994–; Chair. Asscn for the Study of German Politics 1974–76, Univ. Asscn for Contemporary European Studies 1989–94; Vice-Chair. German-British Forum 1996, Chair. 2005–; mem. Econ. and Social Research Council Research Priorities Bd 1994–99, British Königswinter Cttee 1995–, Kuratorium Allianz Kulturstiftung 2001–04; Co-Ed. German Politics 1991–2001, Journal of Common Market Studies 2003–; Academician, Acad. of Learned Socs in Social Sciences 2000; Bundesverdienstkreuz (Germany) 1999; Lifetime Award, Asscn for the Study of German Politics 2004, Lifetime Award, Univ. Asscn for Contemporary European Studies 2007. *Publications include:* The Federal Republic of Germany and the European Community (with Simon Bulmer) 1987, Government and the Chemical Industry (with Wyn Grant) 1988, Developments in German Politics II 1996, The Kohl Chancellorship (with Clay Clemens) 1998, The Future of the German Economy (with Rebecca Harding) 2000, Developments in German Politics 3 2003, Governance in Contemporary Germany: The Semisovereign State Revisited (co-ed.) with Simon Green) 2005; 20 other books and over 100 articles in learned journals. *Leisure interest:* walking. *Address:* 220 Myton Road, Warwick, CV34 6PS, England (home). *Fax:* (1926) 492492 (home). *E-mail:* williampaterson@btconnect.com (home); w.paterson@aston.ac.uk (office).

PATIASHVILI, Dzhumber Ilich; Georgian politician; *Leader, Unity Alliance (Ertoba);* b. 5 Jan. 1940, Lagodekhi, Kakheti Oblast; m.; two c.; ed Tbilisi Agricultural Inst.; worked for the Komsomol (V. I. Lenin Young Communist League) from 1966, subsequently for Communist Party; Dir Land Inst. of Georgia 1980–2000; apptd First Sec. Communist Party of Georgian SSR 1985–89 (resgnd after Soviet troops killed demonstrators in Tbilisi); cand. for presidency 1995, 2000; Founder and Leader of Unity Alliance (Ertoba) social-democratic party which contested gen. election as part of Dzhumber Patiashvili-Unity bloc 2003. *Address:* Unity Alliance (Ertoba), Svobodi pl.,

Tbilisi, Georgia (office). *Telephone:* (32) 92-30-65 (office). *Fax:* (32) 93-46-94 (office). *E-mail:* ertoba@post.com (office).

PATIL, Pratibha Devisingh, LLB, MA; Indian politician and head of state; *President;* b. 19 Dec. 1934, Jalgaon, Mahar; d. of Narayanrao and Gangaji Patil; m. D. R. Shekhawat; one s. one d.; mem. Mahar Ass. 1962–85, Deputy Minister 1967–72, Cabinet Minister for Social Welfare 1972–74, for Public Health and Social Welfare 1974–75, for Prohibition, Rehabilitation and Cultural Affairs 1975–76, for Educ. 1977–78, for Urban Devt and Housing 1982–83; Deputy Chair. Rajya Sabha (Council of States, Parl.) 1986–88; mem. Lok Sabha 1991; Gov. of Rajasthan 2004–07; Pres. of India 2007–; Vice-Chair. Nat. Fed. for Co-op Urban Banks and Credit Soc.; Chair. Bhartiya Granin Mahila Sangh, Mahar; Organizer Women Home Guards, Jalgaon Dist 1962; mem. Standing Cttee, All India Women's Council; Convener first Women's Conf., Delhi. *Address:* Office of the President, Rashtrapati Bhavan, New Delhi 110 004 (office); 57 New Congress Nagar, Opp. Govt. Milk Scheme, Amravati, Maharashtra, India (home). *Telephone:* (11) 23015321 (office). *Fax:* (11) 23017290 (office). *E-mail:* presidentofindia@rb.nic.in (office). *Website:* www .presidentofindia.nic.in (office).

PATIL, Shivraj V.; Indian politician; b. 12 Oct. 1935, Chakur, Maharashtra; ed Osmania Univ., Univ. of Bombay (now Mumbai); Pres. Latur Municipality 1967–69, 1971–72; mem. Maharashtra Legis. Ass. 1972–79; mem. Lok Sabha 1980, Speaker of 10th Lok Sabha 1991–96; Minister of State, including Defence, Commerce, Science and Tech., Space and Tourism portfolios 1980–89; Minister of Home Affairs 2004–08 (resgnd); mem. Indian Nat. Congress. *Address:* Indian National Congress, 24 Akbar Road, New Delhi 110 011, India (office). *Telephone:* (11) 23019080 (office). *Fax:* (11) 23017047 (office). *E-mail:* aicc@congress.org.in (office). *Website:* www.congress.org.in (office).

PATIÑO AROCA, Ricardo Armando, PhD; Ecuadorean economist and politician; *Co-ordinating Minister for Politics;* b. 1955, Guayaquil; m. Miriam Alcívar; one d.; ed Autonomous Metropolitan Univ. of Iztalapa, Mexico, Univ. of Guayaquil and Int. Univ., Andalucía, Spain; Head, Econ. Planning Dept Nat. Agrarian Reform Inst. in southern Nicaragua 1980–81; mem. Econs Dept, Univ. of Guayaquil; fmr Coordinator Inter-Ministerial Comm. on Employment; fmr consultant ILO; Deputy Minister of the Economy 2005–07, Minister of the Economy and Finance 2007, of Coastal Affairs 2007, Co-ordinating Minister for Politics 2007–; Dir Acción Política del Movimiento Patria Altiva y Soberana (PAÍS) 2006. *Address:* c/o Office of the President, Palacio Nacional, García Moreno 1043 Quito, Ecuador (office). *Telephone:* (2) 221-6300 (office). *Website:* www.presidencia.gov.ec (office).

PATKAR, Medha, BSc, MSW; Indian activist and social scientist; *Founder, Narmada Bachao Andolan;* b. 1 Dec. 1954, Bombay; ed Tata Inst. of Social Sciences; held position on faculty of Tata Inst.; worked with voluntary orgs in Bombay slums for five years as well as tribal dists of NE Gujarat for two years; left faculty position and unfinished PhD to found Narmada Bachao Andolan (NBA, people's movt organized to stop construction of series of dams planned for River Narmada), organized peaceful marches and rallies against project 1985, arrested by police, almost died during 22-day hunger strike 1991, undertook two more long protest fasts 1993, 1994, NBA office ransacked 1994, Patkar arrested for refusing to leave village of Manibeli which was about to be flooded 1994; as a result, World Bank reviewed project and concluded it was ill-conceived, Indian Govt cancelled final instalment of Bank's loan and was forced to review project 1993; NBA took case to Supreme Court May 1994, court put stay on further construction while trying to reconcile state and cen. govts Jan 1995; mass protests continued, Patkar arrested once again 1996, protests on other dam sites continued forcing state govt review of project by ind. task force 1997; Patkar est. Nat. Alliance of People's Movts (network of activists across India); Deena Nath Mangeshkar Award, Mahatma Phule Award, Right Livelihood Award, Goldman Environmental Prize 1992, BBC Green Ribbon Award for Best Int. Political Campaigner, Amnesty International Human Rights Defender's Award. *Publication:* River Linking: A Millennium Folly? 2004; contrib. numerous articles. *Address:* c/o B13 Shivam Flats, Ellora Park, Vadodara 390 023, Gujarat, India (office). *Telephone:* (265) 2282232 (office). *E-mail:* medha@narmada.org (office).

PATNAIK, Janaki Ballav, MA; Indian politician; *Leader of the Opposition, Orissa Legislative Assembly, Bhubaneswar;* b. 3 Jan. 1927, Khurda District, Orissa; s. of Gokulanand Devi and Rambha Devi; m. Jayanti Patnaik; one s. two d.; ed Banaras and Utkal Univs; Sub-Ed. Eastern Times 1949, Jt Ed. 1950, Ed. (also for Prajatantra) 1952–67; Ed. Paurusha; led tenants' agitation in Madhupur, Cuttack District 1953; mem. Sahitya Akademi, Orissa 1956–57; Lok Sabha 1971–77; Minister of State for Defence, Govt of India 1973–77; Minister of Tourism, Civil Aviation and Labour Jan.–Dec. 1980; Chief Minister of Orissa State 1980–89, 1995–99; Pres. Pradesh Congress Cttee, Orissa 1978–80, 1992–98, 1999–2001, Jan.–June 2004; Leader of the Opposition, Orissa Legislative Ass., Bhubaneswar 2004; Hon. PhD (Jagannath Sanskrit Univ.), Hon. DLitt (Tirupati Sanskrit Univ.); Orissa Sahitya Akademi Puraskar Award, Bankim Chandra Sahitya Samman. *Publications:* Life History of the Lord Buddha; collections of poems and essays: Gautama Buddha, Swapna O'Sankalpa, Sindhu Upatyaka, Mahabharat, Ramayana, Niti Sataka, Srungar Sataka, Bairagya Staka, Gokulananda Granthavali, Novels of Bankimchandra, Prabandha Sankalan, Srimad Bhagabat, Swadhinata Sangramara Smruti. *Leisure interests:* reading, writing creative literature. *Address:* Qrs. No. S.G.O.-5, Type–VIII, Unit-6, Bhubaneswar, Orissa (office); 201, Forest Park, Bhubaneswar, Orissa, India (home). *Telephone:* (674) 2536878 (office); (674) 2536789 (office). *Fax:* (674) 2536653 (office); (674) 2536957 (home).

PATNAIK, Naveen, BA; Indian politician; *Chief Minister of Orissa;* b. 16 Oct. 1946; s. of the late Biju Patnaik; ed Delhi Univ.; mem. Lok Sabha 1997–; State Minister of Steel and Mines 1998–99, of Mines and Minerals 1999–2000, of Water Resources, Information and Tech. 2000–02, of Home, Agric. and Admin 2000–, of Works, Parl. Affairs, Housing, Health, Families and Rural Devt 2001–02, of Finance, Planning and Co-ordination 2002–, mem. Library Cttee, Standing Cttee on Commerce, Gen. Purpose Cttee; Chief Minister of Orissa 2000–; Founder and Pres. Pres. Biju Janata Dal; Founding mem. Indian Nat. Trust for Art and Cultural Heritage. *Publications:* A Second Paradise, A Desert Kingdom, The Garden of Life. *Leisure interests:* reading, watching programmes on culture, history and environment. *Address:* Office of the Chief Minister, Government of Orissa, Bhubaneswar, Orissa (office); Naveen Nivas, Aerodrome Road, Bhubaneswar, District Khurda, 751001, Orissa, India (home). *Telephone:* (674) 2590299 (home); (674) 2531100 (office). *E-mail:* cmo@ori.nic.in (office). *Website:* orissagov.nic.in (office).

PATON, Boris Yevgenovich, DTechSc; Ukrainian metallurgist; b. 27 Nov. 1918, Kiev; s. of Evgen Oskarovich Paton and Natalya Viktirovna Paton; m. Olga Borisivna Milovanova 1948; one d.; ed Kiev Polytechnic Inst.; Dir E. O. Paton Electric Welding Institute of Ukrainian SSR (now Ukraine) Acad. of Sciences 1953–; Corresp. mem. Ukrainian SSR (now Ukraine) Acad. of Sciences 1951–58, mem. 1958–, Pres. 1962–; mem. USSR (now Russian) Acad. of Sciences 1962, mem. Presidium 1963–91; Pres. Int. Engineering Acad. 1991–; mem. CPSU 1952–91, cand. mem. Cen. Cttee of CPSU 1961–1966, mem. 1966–91; mem. Central Cttee of CP of Ukraine 1960–91; Deputy to USSR Supreme Soviet 1962–89; Vice-Chair. Soviet of the Union USSR Supreme Soviet 1966–89; Deputy to Ukrainian SSR Supreme Soviet 1959–90, mem. of Pres. 1963–80; People's Deputy of the USSR 1989–91; mem. of editorial bd and ed.-in-chief of several scientific and tech. journals; Foreign mem. of Acads of Science of 10 countries; author of over 1000 patents 1942–2004; Honoured Scientist of Ukrainian SSR 1968; Honoured Inventor of USSR 1983; over 10 hon. doctorates; State Prize of the USSR 1950, Lenin Prize 1957, State Prize of the Ukraine 2004; numerous other awards. *Publications:* numerous books and articles in professional journals. *Leisure interest:* swimming. *Address:* E. O. Paton Electric Welding Institute, 11 Bozhenko Street, Kiev 150 03680, Ukraine. *Telephone:* (44) 287-31-83. *Fax:* (44) 528-04-86. *E-mail:* office@paton.kiev.ua. *Website:* www.paton.kiev.ua (home).

PATRICIU, Dan Costache (Dinu), MA; Romanian architect, academic, politician and business executive; *Chairman and CEO, Rompetrol Group NV;* b. 1950; m.; two d.; ed Bucharest Inst. of Architecture; Prof., Bucharest Inst. of Architecture 1975–; fmr Chair. Investment Cttee, Romania and Moldova Direct Fund LP (pvt. equity investment fund); mem. Parl. and Leader, Romanian Liberal Party Parl. Group 1990–96, 2000–03; led investor buyout of Rompetrol SA 1998, mem. Supervisory Bd 1998–, Chair. and CEO 2001–; f. Free Initiative Foundation; shareholder in several real estate cos and investment funds; First Prize, Abu Dhabi City Centre Architecture Contest 1984, Runner up, Nat. Contest for Urban Dwellings, Romania. *Achievements:* has designed more than 40 residential and commercial projects in Romania and more than 25 residential complexes, offices and hotels in UAE. *Address:* Rompetrol Building, 222 Calea Victoriei, 010099 Bucharest, Romania (office). *Telephone:* (21) 3030800 (office). *Fax:* (21) 3122490 (office). *E-mail:* office@rompetrol.com (office). *Website:* www.rompetrol.ro (office).

PATRICK, Deval Laurdine, JD; American lawyer, business executive, politician and state official; *Governor of Massachusetts;* b. 31 July 1956, Chicago, Ill.; s. of Pat Patrick and Emily Patrick; m. Diane Bemus; two d.; ed Milton Acad., Harvard Coll., Harvard Law School; worked with UN in Africa 1978; Pres. Legal Aid Bureau, Harvard Law School; worked as law clerk for Judge Stephen Reinhardt, US Court of Appeals for the Ninth Circuit; attorney for Nat. Asscn for the Advancement of Colored People (NAACP) Legal Defense and Educational Fund, New York City; attorney, Hill & Barlow 1986–90, Pnr 1990; apptd Asst Attorney Gen. for Civil Rights 1994; adviser to post-apartheid S Africa and helped to create their civil rights laws; attorney, Day, Berry & Howard 1997; apptd by Fed. Dist Court to serve as Chair. Task Force to oversee implementation of terms of race discrimination settlement at Texaco, apptd Vice-Pres. and Gen. Counsel, Texaco, New York City; Exec. Vice-Pres., Gen. Counsel and Corp. Sec. Coca-Cola Co., Atlanta 2000–04 (resgnd); Gov. of Commonwealth of Massachusetts 2007– (first African-American state gov. and only second in US history); mem. Bd of Dirs United Airlines 2004–06; Democrat. *Address:* Office of the Governor, Room 360, State House, Boston, MA 02133, USA (office). *Telephone:* (617) 725-4005 (office). *Fax:* (617) 727-9725 (office). *Website:* www.mass.gov (office); www.devalpatrick.com.

PATRIOTA, Antonio de Aguiar; Brazilian diplomatist; *Ambassador to USA;* b. 27 April 1954, Rio de Janeiro; m. Tania Cooper Patriota; two s.; ed Univ. of Geneva, Switzerland, Rio Branco Inst.; mem. staff, Perm. Mission to UN and other Int. Orgs, Geneva 1983–86; Political Counselor, Embassy in Beijing 1987–88; Head of Econ. Section, Embassy in Caracas 1988–90; Advisor to Sec. Gen. for Political Affairs, Ministry of Foreign Relations 1990–92; Deputy Diplomatic Advisor to fmr Pres. Itamar Franco 1992–94; Political Counselor, Perm. Mission to UN, New York 1995–99; Deputy Perm. Rep. to WTO, Geneva 2001–03; Sec. for Diplomatic Planning, Office of Minister of Foreign Relations 2003–05, Chief of Staff to Minister of Foreign Relations 2004–05; Under-Sec. Gen. for Political Affairs, Ministry of Foreign Relations 2005–06; Amb. to USA 2007–. *Address:* Embassy of Brazil, 3006 Massachusetts Avenue, NW, Washington, DC 20008, USA (office). *Telephone:* (202) 238-2700 (office). *Fax:* (202) 238-2827 (office). *E-mail:* webmaster@brasilemb.org (office). *Website:* www.brasilemb.org (office).

PATRUSHEV, Col.-Gen. Nikolai Platonovich, PhD; Russian government security official; *Secretary of the Security Council;* b. 11 July 1951, Leningrad (now St Petersburg); m.; two s.; ed Leningrad Inst. of Vessel Construction (now the State Marine Tech. Univ. of St Petersburg); on staff KGB, Kareliyan ASSR 1974; in Leningrad Oblast 1974–92; Minister of Security, Repub. of Kareliya 1992–94; Head Dept of Self-Security, Fed. Security Service 1994–98, Deputy Dir, then Head, Dept of Econs 1998–99, Dir 1999–; Head of Presidential Control Dept May–Aug. 1998; Deputy Head Admin. of Russian Presidency Aug.–Oct. 1998; Deputy Dir Fed. Security Service of Russia (FSB), Head of Econ. Security Dept 1998, First Deputy Dir April–Aug. 1999, Dir Aug. 1999–2008; Sec. Security Council of Russian Fed. 2008–; Hero of the Russian Fed., Honour of the Mil. Merits and seven other medals. *Achievement:* joined expedition of polar explorer, Arthur Chilingarov, that flew on two helicopters to Antarctica and visited S Pole and Amundsen-Scott station Jan. 2007. *Address:* Security Council of Russian Federation, 103132 Moscow, Ipatyevskii per. 4/10, Russia (office). *Telephone:* (495) 206-35-96 (office). *Website:* www.scrf.gov.ru (office).

PATRY, Gilles G., MASc, PhD; Canadian engineer, academic and university administrator; *President and Vice-Chancellor, University of Ottawa;* ed Univ. of Ottawa, Univ. of Calif., Davis; began career as consulting engineer 1971–78; Prof. of Civil Eng, École Polytechnique de Montréal 1978–83; Prof. of Civil Eng, McMaster Univ. 1983–93; f. Hydromantis Inc. 1985; Dean, Faculty of Eng, Univ. of Ottawa 1993, Vice-Pres. (Academic) 1997, Pres. and Vice-Chancellor 2001–; Assoc. Ed. Journal of Environmental Engineering and Science 2001–05; Fellow, Canadian Acad. of Eng 2002–; Dir Univ. of Ottawa Heart Inst., Ottawa Centre for Research and Innovation (OCRI), Nat. Research Council of Canada. *Publications:* more than 125 journal and conf. papers. *Address:* Office of the President, University of Ottawa, 550 Cumberland Street, Ottawa, Ont., K1N 6N5, Canada (office). *Telephone:* (613) 562-5809 (office). *Fax:* (613) 562-5103 (office). *E-mail:* president@uottawa.ca (office). *Website:* www.president.uottawa.ca (office).

PATSEV, Aleksander Konstantinovich; Russian fmr diplomatist; b. 29 June 1936, Moscow; m.; two c.; ed Moscow State Inst. of History and Archives, Higher Diplomatic School at Ministry of Foreign Affairs; Komsomol functionary 1959–66; mem. staff Ministry of Foreign Affairs 1966–69; Head of Sector, Dept of Information 1985–87, Deputy Head Gen. Secr. 1987–89; Amb. to Oman 1990–96, to Uzbekistan 1997–99, Amb. to Finland 1999–2003. *Address:* c/o Ministry of Foreign Affairs, Smolenskaya-Sennaya pl. 32/34, 119200 Moscow, Russian Federation (office).

PATTAKOS, Stylianos; Greek politician; b. 8 Nov. 1912, Crete; s. of George and Maria Pattakos; m. Dimitra Nickolaidou 1940; two d.; ed high school, cadet school, War Coll. and Nat. Defence Acad.; commissioned 1937, promoted Maj.-Gen. 1967, retd; Minister of the Interior 1967–73, Deputy Premier Dec. 1967; First Deputy Premier 1971–73; arrested Oct. 1974, sentenced to death for high treason and insurrection Aug. 1975 (sentence commuted to life imprisonment).

PATTAMA, Noppadon, LLB (Hons), BA, LLM, MA; Thai lawyer and politician; b. 23 April 1961, Nakorn Rachasima; ed Thammasat Univ., Univs of Oxford and London, UK; practised as barrister in Bangkok 1983–; called to the Bar, Lincoln's Inn, London 1991; Sec. to Leader of the Opposition Chuan Leekpai 1995–96; mem. Parl. (Democrat Party) 1996–2000, mem. Standing Cttee on Foreign Affairs, House of Reps 1996–2000; Parl. Sec. to Minister of Foreign Affairs 1999–2001; defected to Thai Rak Thai party 2006; Vice-Minister of Natural Resources and Environment 2006; legal adviser to fmr Prime Minister Thaksin Shinawatra (deposed in mil. coup Sept. 2006) Nov. 2006; mem. People's Power Party (successor to Thai Rak Thai); Minister of Foreign Affairs 2008; Pres. Thai Students' Asscn in UK (Samaggi Samagom) 1988–89; participant in The Ship for Southeast Asian Youth Programme 1981; Fulbright Scholarship to study in USA 1982, Ananda Mahidol Scholarship to study law in UK, King of Thailand 1984. *Address:* People's Power Party (Palang Prachachan), 1770 Thanon Petchaburi Tat Mai, Bang Gapi, Huay Kwang, Bangkok 10310, Thailand (office). *Telephone:* (2) 686–7000 (office). *Website:* www.ppp.or.th (office).

PATTEN, Brian, FRSL; British poet and author; b. 7 Feb. 1946, Liverpool; s. of Ireen Stella Bevan; Regents Lecturer, Univ. of California at San Diego; performance work and lectures worldwide for British Council; Freedom of City of Liverpool 2000; Hon. Fellow, John Moores Univ. 2002; Cholmondeley Award for Poetry 2002. *Radio:* History of 20th-Century Poetry for Children, BBC Radio 2000, The Dittisham Nativity, BBC Radio 2005. *Publications include:* poetry: The Mersey Sound 1967, Little Johnny's Confession 1967, The Home Coming 1969, Notes to the Hurrying Man 1969, At Four O'Clock in the Morning 1971, Walking Out: The Early Poems of Brian Patten 1971, Love Poems 1981, New Volume 1983, Gargling With Jelly 1985, Storm Damage 1988, Grinning Jack: Selected Poems 1990, Thawing Frozen Frogs 1990, Armada 1996; (ed) Clare's Countryside: A Book of John Clare 1981; children's: Grizzelda Frizzle and Other Stories 1992, The Magic Bicycle 1993, Impossible Parents 1994, Frognapped! and Other Stories 1994, The Utter Nutters 1995, The Blue and Green Ark 1999, Juggling with Gerbils 2000, Little Hotchpotch 2000, Impossible Parents Go Green; (ed) The Puffin Book of 20th Century Children's Verse 1991, The Story Giant 2001, Ben's Magic Telescope 2003, Selected Poems 2007, New Collected Love Poems 2007. *Leisure interests:* river cruising. *Address:* c/o Rogers, Coleridge & White Literary Agency, 20 Powis Mews, London, W11 1JN, England (office). *Telephone:* (20) 7221-3717 (office). *Fax:* (20) 7229-9084 (office). *Website:* www.rcwlitagency.co.uk (office).

PATTEN OF BARNES, Baron (Life Peer), cr. 2005, of Barnes in the London Borough of Richmond; **Christopher Francis Patten,** CH, PC; British politician; *Chancellor, University of Oxford;* b. 12 May 1944; s. of the late

Francis Joseph Patten and Joan McCarthy; m. Mary Lavender Thornton 1971; three d.; ed St Benedict's School, Ealing, Balliol Coll., Oxford; worked in Conservative Party Research Dept 1966–70, Dir 1974–79; seconded to Cabinet Office 1970; at Home Office, then personal asst to Lord Carrington, Party Chair. 1972–74; MP for Bath 1979–92; Parl. Pvt. Sec. (PPS) to Leader of the House 1979–81, to Social Services Sec. 1981–83; Parl. Under-Sec. for Northern Ireland 1983–85; Minister of State for Educ. 1985–86; Overseas Devt Minister 1986–89; Sec. of State for the Environment 1989–90; Chancellor of the Duchy of Lancaster and Chair. of the Conservative Party 1990–92; Gov. of Hong Kong 1992–97; Chair. Comm. charged with reform of Royal Ulster Constabulary 1998–99; Chancellor Newcastle Univ. 1999–, Univ. of Oxford 2003–; EU Commr for External Relations 1999–2004; Dir Ind. Newspapers 1998–99; Hon. FRCP (Edin.) 1994; Hon. Fellow Balliol Coll., Oxford 1999; Hon. DCL (Newcastle) 1999; Coolidge Travelling Scholarship, USA 1965. *Publications:* The Tory Case 1983, East and West 1998, Not Quite the Diplomat: Home Truths About World Affairs 2005, What Next? Surviving the 21st Century 2008. *Leisure interests:* reading, tennis, gardening. *Address:* House of Lords, London, SW1A 0PW, England. *Telephone:* (20) 7219-3000.

PATTERSON, Henry (Harry), (Martin Fallon, James Graham, Jack Higgins, Hugh Marlowe), BSc (Soc.), FRSA; British/Irish novelist; b. 27 July 1929, Newcastle upon Tyne; s. of Henry Patterson and Rita Higgins Bell; m. 1st Amy Margaret Hewitt 1958 (divorced 1984); one s. three d.; m. 2nd Denise Leslie Ann Palmer 1985; ed Roundhay School, Leeds, Beckett Park Coll. for Teachers, London School of Econs; NCO, The Blues 1947–50, tried numerous jobs including clerk and circus tent hand 1950–58; schoolmaster, lecturer in liberal studies, Leeds Polytechnic, Sr Lecturer in Educ., James Graham Coll. and Tutor in School Practice, Leeds Univ. 1958–72; full-time writer from age of 41; Hon. DUniv (Leeds Metropolitan Univ.) 1995. *Publications:* as Martin Fallon: The Testament of Caspar Schultz 1962, Year of the Tiger 1963, The Keys to Hell 1965, Midnight Never Comes 1966, Dark Side of the Street 1967, A Fine Night for Dying 1969, Day of Judgement 1979; as Hugh Marlowe: Seven Pillars to Hell 1963, Passage by Night 1964, A Candle for the Dead (aka The Violent Enemy) 1966; as James Graham: A Game for Heroes 1970, The Wrath of God 1971, The Khufra Run 1972, The Run to Morning 1974; as Harry Patterson: Sad Wind from the Sea 1959, Cry of the Hunter 1960, The Thousand Faces of Night 1961, Comes the Dark Stranger 1962, Wrath of the Lion 1963, Pay the Devil 1963, The Dark Side of the Island 1963, A Phoenix in Blood 1964, Thunder at Noon (aka Dillinger) 1964, The Graveyard Shift 1965, Iron Tiger 1966, Brought in Dead 1967, Hell is Always Today 1968, Toll for the Brave 1971, To Catch a King (aka The Judas Gate) 1979; as Jack Higgins: East of Desolation 1968, In the Hour Before Midnight 1969, Night Judgement at Sinos 1970, The Last Place God Made 1971, The Savage Day 1972, The Eagle has Landed 1975, Storm Warning 1976, The Valhalla Exchange 1976, A Prayer for the Dying 1977, Solo (aka The Cretan Lover) 1980, Luciano's Luck 1981, Touch the Devil 1982, Exocet 1983, Confessional 1985, Night of the Fox 1986, Walking Wounded (play) 1987, Memoirs of a Dance Hall Romeo 1989, A Season in Hell 1989, Cold Harbour 1989, The Eagle Has Flown 1990, Eye of the Storm (aka Midnight Man) 1992, Thunder Point 1993, On Dangerous Ground 1994, Angel of Death 1995, Sheba 1995, Drink With the Devil 1996, The President's Daughter 1996, The Violent Enemy 1997, Flight of Eagles 1998, The White House Connection 1999, Day of Reckoning 1999, Midnight Runner 2001, Edge of Danger 2001, The Keys of Hell 2002, Bad Company 2003, Without Mercy 2005, Death Run (with Justin Richards) 2007, Sure Fire (juvenile, with Justin Richards) 2007, The Killing Ground. *Leisure interests:* tennis, old movies. *Address:* Ed Victor Ltd, 6 Bayley Street, London, WC1B 3HB, England (office).

PATTERSON, James, BA, MA; American writer and fmr advertising executive; b. 22 March 1947, Newburgh, NY; m.; one s.; ed Manhattan Coll., Vanderbilt Univ.; wrote first novel 1976; joined J. Walter Thompson as jr copywriter 1971, subsequently Exec. Creative Dir, CEO, Chair. 1990–96. *Publications:* The Thomas Berryman Number (MWA Edgar Award) 1976, The Season of the Machete 1977, The Jericho Commandment (aka See How They Run) 1979, Virgin 1980, Black Market 1986, The Midnight Club 1989, The Day America Told the Truth: What People Really Believe About Everything that Matters (non-fiction, with Peter Kim) 1991, Along Came a Spider 1993, The Second American Revolution 1994, Kiss the Girls 1995, Hide & Seek 1996, Jack & Jill 1996, Miracle on the 17th Green (with Peter de Jonge) 1996, Cat & Mouse 1997, When the Wind Blows 1998, Pop Goes the Weasel 1999, Cradle and All (revised version of Virgin) 2000, Roses are Red 2000, Suzanne's Diary for Nicholas 2001, 1st to Die 2001, Violets are Blue 2001, 2nd Chance (with Andrew Gross) 2002, Four Blind Mice 2002, The Beach House (with Peter de Jonge) 2002, The Jester 2003, The Lake House 2003, The Big Bad Wolf 2003, 3rd Degree 2003, Sam's Letters to Jennifer 2004, London Bridges 2004, Honeymoon 2005, 4th of July 2005, Mary Mary 2005, Maximum Ride: The Angel 2005, The 5th Horseman (with Maxine Paetro) 2006, Judge and Jury 2006, Lifeguard (with Andrew Gross) 2006, Thriller (short stories) (ed) 2006, Maximum Ride: School's Out Forever (with Peter De Jonge) 2006, Cross 2006, Step on a Crack (with Michael Ledwidge) 2007, The Beach Road (with Peter De Jonge) 2007, The 6th Target (with Maxine Paetro) 2007, Maximum Ride: Saving the World and Other Extreme Sports (children's fiction) 2007, The Quickie (with Michael Ledwidge) 2007, Double Cross 2007, You've Been Warned 2007, 7th Heaven 2008, Maximum Ride: The Final Warning 2008, Sundays at Tiffany's 2008, Sail 2008, The Dangerous Days of Daniel X 2008, Against All Odds (non-fiction), Cross Country 2008, 8th Confession 2009, Max: A Maximum Ride Novel 2009, The 8th Confession (with Maxine Paetro) 2009. *Address:* c/o Little, Brown and Company, 1271 Avenue of the Americas, New York, NY 10020, USA (office). *Website:* www.jamespatterson.com.

PATTERSON, The Most Hon. Percival James, ON, PC, QC, MP; Jamaican politician and lawyer; b. 10 April 1935, Cross Road, St Andrew; s. of Henry Patterson and Ina James; m. (divorced); one s. one d.; ed Univ. of West Indies, London School of Econs; called to Bar, Middle Temple 1963, Jamaican Bar 1963; nominated to Senate 1967; Leader of Opposition Business in Senate 1969–70; mem. House of Reps for S.E.Westmoreland 1970–80, 1989–2006; Minister for Industry, Foreign Trade and Tourism 1972–77, Deputy Prime Minister and Minister for Foreign Trade 1978–80, Deputy Prime Minister and Minister for Devt, Planning and Production 1989–90, for Finance and Planning 1990–91, of Defence 1993–2006; Prime Minister 1992–2006; QC, Inner Bar 1984; Adviser to Gov't of Belize 1982; Pursell Trust Scholarship, Leverhulme Scholarship; Gran Cruz Placa De Oro, Order of Francisco Morazán, Honduras 1990, Order of Aguila Aztec, Mexico 1990, Order of San Martí, Argentina 1992, Great Cross of the Order of Bernado O'Higgins, Chile 1992, Order of the Liberator Simon Bolivar, Venezuela 1992, Order of the Volta, Ghana 1999, Gran Cruz Placa, Order Juan Mora Fernández, Costa Rico 2001, Grand Cross, Nat. Order of Civil Merit, Spain 2006, Order of Excellence, Guyana 2006, Order of Belize 2006, Grand Cross, Order of Cruzeiro do Sul, Brazil 2006; Hon. DLitt (Northeastern, Boston), Hon. LLD (Brown, RI); FAO Agricola Medal 2001. *Leisure interests:* jazz, Jamaican music, spectator sports including cricket, boxing, track and field events, tennis. *Address:* HEISCONSULTS, Sagicor Life Jamaica Centre, 28-48 Barbados Avenue, Kingston 5, Jamaica.

PATTERSON, Walter Cram, MSc; Canadian/British energy analyst and writer; *Associate Fellow, Chatham House;* b. 4 Nov. 1936, Winnipeg; s. of Walter Thomas Patterson and Thirza Helen Cram; m. Cleone Susan Davis 1966; two d.; ed Kelvin High School, Winnipeg, Univ. of Manitoba; Ed. Your Environment 1970–73, European Ed. Bulletin of the Atomic Scientists 1979–81; First 'Energy Campaigner' Friends of the Earth 1972–78; ind. analyst, writer 1978–93; with Gorleben Int. Review 1978–79; course tutor, Open Univ. 1981–91; series adviser, BBC TV Drama Edge of Darkness 1984–85; specialist adviser, House of Commons Select Cttee on Environment 1985–86, on Energy 1991–92; Assoc. Fellow, Energy and Environmental Programme, Royal Inst. of Int. Affairs (now Chatham House) 1991–93, Sr Research Fellow 1993–2000, Assoc. Fellow 2001–; Fellow, Energy Inst.; Companion, Inst. of Energy 1991; Melchett Medal, Inst. of Energy 2000, Scientific American 50 Energy Policy Leader 2004. *Publications:* Nuclear Power 1976–86, The Fissile Society 1977, Coming to a Boil 1978, The Plutonium Business 1984, Going Critical 1985, Advanced Coal-Use Technology 1987, The Energy Alternative 1990, Coal-Use Technology in a Changing Environment 1990, Coal-Use Technology: New Challenges, New Responses 1993, Power from Plants 1994, Rebuilding Romania: Energy, Efficiency and the Economic Transition 1994, Electric Futures 1997, Transforming Electricity 1999, Keeping The Lights On 2007. *Leisure interests:* baseball, beer, computers, languages, music, orchids, playing with the family, travel. *Address:* Little Rushmoor, High Bois Lane, Chesham Bois, Bucks., HP6 6DQ, England (home); Chatham House, St James's Square, London, SW1Y 4LE, England (office). *Telephone:* (1494) 726748 (home); (7971) 840036 (mobile) (office). *E-mail:* waltpattersn@gn.apc.org (home); walt@waltpatterson.org (home). *Website:* www.waltpatterson.org (home); www.chathamhouse.org.uk (office).

PATTISON, Jim, OC; Canadian business executive; *Managing Director, Chairman and CEO, The Jim Pattison Group;* b. Luseland, Sask.; m.; three c.; ed Univ. of BC; paid univ. tuition fees washing cars and selling cars to fellow students; bought General Motors automobile dealership 1961, Owner, Man. Dir, Chair. and CEO The Jim Pattison Group 1961–; bought CJOR radio station 1965; Owner Ripley's Believe It or Not!, Overwaitea Food Group (including Save-On-Foods) and Buy-Low Foods grocery stores, Canadian Fishing Co., News Group; Dir The Toronto Dominion Bank, Canadian Pacific Ltd, Livent Inc.; Chair. and Pres. Vancouver EXPO '86; mem. Bd Trustees Ronald Reagan Presidential Foundation; Order of British Columbia 1990; Gov. Gen.'s Commemorative Medal 1992; inducted into Canadian Business Hall of Fame 1996, one of eight inaugural laureates of Canadian Professional Sales Asscn Sales Hall of Fame. *Leisure interests:* playing the piano, organ and trumpet. *Address:* The Jim Pattison Group, 1055 W. Hastings Street, Suite 1600, Vancouver, BC V6E 2H2, Canada (office). *Telephone:* (604) 688-6764 (office). *Fax:* (604) 687-2601 (office). *Website:* www.jimpattison.com (office).

PATTISON, Sir John Ridley, Kt, BSc, MA, DM, FRCPath, FMedSci; British medical scientist (retd); b. 1 Aug. 1942; s. of Tom Frederick Pattison and Elizabeth Pattison; m. Pauline Evans 1965; one s. two d.; ed Barnard Castle School, Univ. Coll. Oxford, Middlesex Hosp. Medical School; Asst Lecturer in Pathology, later Lecturer in Virology, Middx Hosp. Medical School 1970–75; Lecturer, later Sr Lecturer in Virology, St Bartholomew's and London Hosp. Medical Colls 1976–77; Prof. of Medical Microbiology, King's Coll. Hosp. Medical School 1977–84, Univ. Coll. London 1984–2004, Dean 1990–98, Vice-Provost 1994–99; Dir of Research and Devt, Dept of Health and Nat. Health Service 1999–2004; mem. MRC 1992–2004, Sr Medical Advisor 1996–99; mem. Spongiform Encephalopathy Advisory Cttee 1994–95, Chair. 1995–99; mem. Council, Int. Journal of Experimental Pathology 1979–2001, Soc. of Gen. Microbiology 1981–87; mem. Bd Inst. of Child Health 1992–96, Inst. of Neurology 1995–97; mem. Man. Cttee King's Fund 1993–, Deputy Chair. 1994–99; Founder-Fellow, Acad. of Medical Science 1998; Ed.-in-Chief Epidemiology and Infection 1980–94; Hon. Fellow, Imperial Coll. London, Univ. Coll. London; hon. degrees (Middlesex, Southampton, Durham). *Publications:* Principles and Practice of Clinical Virology (co-ed.) 1987–, Practical Guide to Clinical Virology (co-ed.) 1989, Practical Guide to Clinical Bacteriology (co-ed.) 1995; numerous papers on medical virology. *Address:* 17 Broadwater Lane, Towcester, Northants., NN12 6YF, England (home). *Telephone:* (1327) 352116 (home). *E-mail:* portsea200@btopenworld.com (home).

PATTISON, Seamus, DipSocEconSc; Irish trade union official and politician (retd); b. 19 April 1936, Kilkenny; s. of James Pattison and Ellen Fogarty; ed St Kieran's Coll., Kilkenny, Univ. Coll., Dublin; mem. Dáil Eireann 1961–2007; MEP 1981–83; Minister of State Dept of Social Welfare 1983–87; mem. British–Irish Parl. Body 1991–97; Chair. Select Cttee on Social Affairs 1993–97; Speaker Dáil Eireann 1997–2002, Father of the Dáil 1995–2007, Deputy Speaker 2002–07; fmr Labour Party spokesman on Educ. 1963–67, on Justice 1967–72, 1991–92, on Lands 1972–73, on Defence and Marine Affairs 1987, on Energy and Forestry 1989–91; mem. Parl. Ass. of Council of Europe 1989–90, 1996–97; mem. Kilkenny Co. Council 1964–97 (Chair. 1975–76 and 1980–81); Alderman Kilkenny Corpn 1964–97; Mayor of Kilkenny 1967–68, 1976–77, 1992–93; mem. Kilkenny Vocational Educ. Cttee 1964–97 (Vice-Chair. 1990–97), South Eastern Health Bd 1971–84. *Leisure interests:* reading, theatre, travel and sport. *Address:* 6 Upper New Street, Kilkenny, Ireland (home). *Telephone:* (56) 7721295 (home). *Fax:* (56) 7752533 (home).

PATTON, Paul E., BEng; American politician and government official; b. Fallsburg; ed Univ. of Ky; with coal co. –1979, Deputy Sec. for Transportation; Judge Exec., Pike Co. 1981; Lt-Gov., Sec. for Econ. Devt, Pres. State of Ky 1991–95; Gov. of Ky 1995–2003; Chair. Ky Democrats 1981–83; served numerous terms Pike Co. Democrats Exec. Comm.; mem. Bd Overseers Bellarmine Coll., Bd Trustees Pikeville Coll. *Address:* c/o Office of the Governor, State Capitol, 700 Capitol Avenue, Frankfort, KY 40601, USA (office).

PATTULLO, Sir (David) Bruce, Kt, CBE, BA, FCIBS, FRSE; British banker (retd); b. 2 Jan. 1938, Edinburgh; s. of late Colin Pattullo and Elizabeth Bruce; m. Fiona Nicholson 1962; three s. one d.; ed Rugby School and Hertford Coll. Oxford; Gen. Man. Bank of Scotland Finance Co. Ltd 1973–77; Dir British Linen Bank Ltd 1977–98, Chief Exec. 1977–78; Deputy Treas. Bank of Scotland 1978, Treas. and Gen. Man. (Chief Exec.) 1979–88, Dir 1980–98, Group Chief Exec. 1988–96, Deputy Gov. 1988–91, Gov. 1991–98; Chair. Cttee of Scottish Clearing Bankers 1981–83, 1987–89; three hon. degrees; Bilsland Prize, Inst. of Bankers in Scotland 1964. *Leisure interests:* tennis, hill walking. *Telephone:* (131) 339-6012 (home).

PATZAICHIN, Ivan; Romanian fmr canoeist; b. 26 Nov. 1949, Mila, Tulcea Co.; m.; one d.; ed Coll. for Physical Educ. and Sport, Bucharest; world champion: simple canoe 1,000m (Tampere 1973, Sofia 1977) and 10,000m (Belgrade 1978, 1982); double canoe 500m (Duisburg 1979) and 1,000m (Copenhagen 1970, Nottingham 1981, Tampere 1983); Olympic champion simple canoe 500m (Munich 1972) and double canoe 1,000m (Mexico City 1968, Moscow 1980, Los Angeles 1984); numerous silver and bronze medals at world and Olympic championships; 25 times nat. champion of Romania. *Address:* Clubul Sportiv Unirea Tricolor, Soseaua Stefan cel Mare nr 9, Bucharest, Romania.

PATZIG, Günther, DPhil; German philosopher and academic; *Professor Emeritus, Philosophisches Seminar, Universität Göttingen;* b. 28 Sept. 1926, Kiel; s. of Admiral Conrad Patzig and Gertrud Patzig (née Thomsen); m. Christiane Köhn 1948; one s. one d.; ed Gymnasiums in Kiel and Berlin-Steglitz, Univs of Göttingen and Hamburg; Asst, Philosophisches Seminar, Göttingen 1953–60, Privatdozent 1958–60, Prof. of Philosophy 1963–91, now Emer.; Prof. of Philosophy, Univ. of Hamburg 1960–63; Christian-Wolff Prof., Univ. of Halle-Wittenberg 2002; UNESCO Fellowship in Philosophy 1951–52; mem. Göttingen Acad. of Sciences 1971– (Pres. 1986–90), Wissenschaftskolleg, Berlin 1984–85, J. Jungius-Gesellschaft, Hamburg 1989–, Oslo Acad. of Sciences 1997–; Hon. DPhil (Saarbrücken) 2003; Howison Memorial Lecturer, Berkeley 1971, Lower Saxony Prize for Science 1983, Keeling Lecturer, London 1992, Heisenberg Medal 1998, Ernst-Hellmut-Vits-Preis 2000. *Publications:* Die aristotelische Syllogistik 1959, Sprache und Logik 1970, Ethik ohne Metaphysik 1971, Tatsachen, Normen, Sätze 1980, Aristoteles Metaphysik Z: Text, Übersetzung, Kommentar (with M. Frede) 1988, Gesammelte Schriften Vols I–IV 1993–96, Die Rationalität der Moral 1996, Gottlob Frege: Logische Untersuchungen (Hrsg.) 2003, Wie geht man mit bioethischen Grundkonflikten um? In: Kaminsky/Hallich. Verantwortung für die Zukunft 2006. *Address:* Philosophisches Seminar, Universität Göttingen, Humboldtallee 19, 37073 Göttingen (office); Otfried-Müller-Weg 6, 37075 Göttingen, Germany (home). *Telephone:* (551) 394742 (office); (551) 42929 (home). *Fax:* (551) 399607 (home). *E-mail:* ikaraku@gwdg.de (office). *Website:* www.uni-goettingen.de/de/70432.html (office).

PAU, Louis-François, DSc, MBA, PhD; French communications industry executive; *Chief Technology Officer, Ericsson Network Systems Division;* b. 29 May 1948, Copenhagen, Denmark; s. of Louis Pau and Marie-Louise Von Jessen; m. 1st Miki Miyamoto 1983 (divorced 1990); one d.; m. 2nd Maria Joukovskaia; one d.; ed Ecole Nat. Supérieure de l'Aéronautique et de l'Espace, Paris Univ., Inst. d'Etudes Politiques, Paris; dancer, Royal Ballet, Copenhagen 1957–66; served in Air Force 1970–72; Asst Prof., Tech. Univ., Denmark 1972–74; Prof. and Dept Head, Ecole Nat. Supérieure Télécommunications, Paris 1974–82; Assoc. Prof., MIT, USA 1977–78; Science and Tech. Counsellor, French Embassy, Washington, DC 1979–82; Professorial Lecturer, Univ. of Maryland, College Park, Md 1980–82; Sr Scientist, Battelle Memorial Inst. 1982–86; Research Prof., Tech. Univ., Denmark 1986–90; CSK Prof., Univ. of Tokyo 1988–90; Tech. Dir, Digital Equipment Corpn (Europe) 1990–95; Chief Tech. Officer, Ericsson Network Systems Div., Sweden 1995–; Prof. Mobile Commerce, Rotterdam School of Man. 2001–; Adjunct Prof., Copenhagen Business School 2003–; mem. Bd of Dirs SCF Technologies A/S 2006–, Kamala Estate Ltd 2008–; consultant to several int. corpns; adviser to several govts and govt agencies in USA, Asia and Europe; mem. review bds, Singapore, Hong Kong, EEC, USA; Vice-Pres. (Tech.) Int. Fed. of Automatic Control 1982–86; Fellow, IEEE, Japan Soc. of Promotion Sciences, British Computer Soc.; many awards and prizes. *Publications:* author of 10 books and editor of 12 books, more than 350 papers on computers and communications, management science, aerospace tech. and financial/econ. models. *Leisure interests:* ballet, flying, travel. *Address:* Ericsson, PO Box 1505, 12525 Älvsjö, Sweden (office); T-9, Rotterdam School of Management, PO Box 1738, Rotterdam, NL 3000, Netherlands (office). *Telephone:* (8) 727-30-00 (Sweden) (office); (10) 590-13-39 (Netherlands) (office); 6-79-57-10-59 (France) (home). *Fax:* (8) 647-82-76 (Sweden) (office). *E-mail:* lfp.inf@cbs.dk (office). *Website:* www.ericsson.com (office).

PAUGET, Georges, PhD; French banking executive; *CEO, Crédit Agricole SA;* b. 1947; joined Groupe Crédit Agricole SA 1973, early man. positions with Aude Regional Bank and Caisse Nationale de Crédit Agricole, then internal auditor and then project leader in Group Control and Audit, Cen. Sec. then Sr Gen. Man. Unicrédit; CEO Haute Saône et du Territoire de Belfort Regional Bank 1985–87, Pyrénées-Atlantique 1987–92, Pyrénées-Gascogne Regional Bank 1992–2002; Deputy CEO Crédit Agricole SA 2003–05, CEO 2005–; Chair. Crédit Lyonnais 2003–; mem. Exec. Cttee Fédération Bancaire Française. *Address:* Crédit Agricole SA, 91–93 Boulevard Pasteur, 75015 Paris, France (office). *Telephone:* 1-43-23-52-02 (office). *Fax:* 1-43-23-34-48 (office). *E-mail:* info@credit-agricole-sa.fr (office). *Website:* www.credit-agricole-sa.fr (office).

PAUK, György; British violinist; b. 26 Oct. 1936, Budapest, Hungary; m. Susan Mautner 1959; one s. one d.; ed Franz Liszt Acad. of Music, Budapest under Zathureczky, Leo Weiner and Zoltán Kodály; concerts all over East Europe 1952–58 and the rest of the world; settled in Western Europe 1958, The Netherlands 1958–61, England 1961–; Prof. of Violin, Royal Acad. of Music 1987–; Artistic Dir Mozart Bicentenary Festival, London 1991; Prof. of violin, Winterthur-Zürich Konservatorium of Music 1994–; jury mem. Int. violin competitions; Hon. mem. and Prof. Guildhall School of Music and Drama, London 1987; Hon. RAM 1990; highest civilian award, Hungarian Govt 1998; Paganini Prize 1956, Sonata Competition Prize, Munich 1957, Jacques Thibaud Prize 1959, Grand Prix for Bartók Records (Ovation Magazine, USA) 1982, Best Record of 1983 (Gramophone Magazine). *Recordings include:* numerous concertos, the complete violin/piano music of Mozart and Schubert, Handel and Brahms sonatas, Mozart string quintets, all Bartok's music for solo, duo and sonatas; first performances of Penderecki's violin concerto, UK, Japan, Sir Michael Tippett's Triple Concerto, London 1980, Lutoslawski's Chain 2, UK, Netherlands, Hungary, with composer conducting, Sir Peter Maxwell Davies' violin concerto, Switzerland, Germany, William Mathias violin concerto, England. *Leisure interests:* football, tennis, theatre, reading, swimming, grandchildren. *Address:* Royal Academy of Music, Marylebone Road, London, NW1 5HT, England (office). *Telephone:* (20) 7873-7395 (office). *E-mail:* strings@ram.ac.uk (office). *Website:* www.ram.ac.uk (office).

PAUL, Robert Cameron, CBE, MEng, FREng, FIChemE; British chemical engineer; b. 7 July 1935, Uxbridge; m. 1st Diana Kathleen Bruce 1965 (died 2001); two d.; m. 2nd Catherine Frances Young 2003; ed Rugby School and Corpus Christi Coll., Cambridge; Nat. Service (2nd Lt in Royal Engineers) 1953–55; Imperial Chemical Industries (ICI) 1959–86; Deputy Chair. ICI Mond Div. 1979–86; Deputy Chair. and Man. Dir Albright and Wilson 1986–95, Chief Exec. 1995–97; Dir (non-exec.) Courtaulds PLC 1994–98; Pres. Chemical Industries Asscn 1995–97; Hon. DEng; Soc. of Chemical Industry Centenary Medal 1990. *Leisure interests:* music (piano), astronomy. *Address:* 2 Devonshire Place, Kensington, London, W8 5UD, England (home).

PAUL, Baron (Life Peer), cr. 1996, of Marylebone in the City of Westminster; **Swraj Paul,** MSc, FRSA; British business executive; *Deputy Speaker, House of Lords;* b. 18 Feb. 1931, India; s. of Payare Paul and Mongwati Paul; m. Aruna Vij 1956; three s. one d. (and one d. deceased); ed Punjab Univ., Massachusetts Inst. of Tech., USA; joined family-owned Apeejay Surrendra Group as Partner 1953; moved to UK and est. Natural Gas Tubes Ltd 1966; Founder-Chair. Caparo Group Ltd 1978–, Caparo Industries PLC 1981–; Chair. Caparo Inc., USA 1988–, Armstrong Equipment Ltd 1989–, CREMSA, Spain 1989–, ENSA, Spain 1989–; Founder-Chair. Indo-British Asscn 1975–; Pres. Family Service Unit 1997–; Chancellor, Univ. of Wolverhampton 1999–; Trustee Police Foundation 1997–; Deputy Speaker, House of Lords 2008–; Hon. PhD (American Coll. of Switzerland, Leysin) 1986; Hon. DSc (Econ.) (Hull) 1992; Hon. DLitt (Westminster) 1996; Hon. DHL (Chapman) 1996; Hon. DUniv (Bradford) 1997, (Cen. England) 1999; Hon. DSc (Buckingham) 1999; Corp. Leadership Award, MIT 1987; Padma Bhushan 1983. *Publications:* Indira Gandhi 1984, Beyond Boundaries 1998. *Address:* House of Lords, London SW1A 0PW, England (office). *Telephone:* (20) 7219-5016 (office). *Website:* www.parliament.uk (office).

PAUL, Vivek, BE, MBA; American (b. Indian) business executive; *Managing Director, Texas Pacific Ventures;* b. 1958; m.; ed BITS, Pilani, Univ. of Mass; fmrly with Pepsi and Bain & Co.; joined Gen. Electric (GE) 1989, Pres. and CEO medical equipment joint venture in India, then global head Computerized Tomography business 1995–99; Vice-Chair. Wipro, Bangalore, India 1999–2005, Pres. and CEO global IT, product engineering, and business process services; pnr Texas Pacific Group (TPG), Man. Dir Ventures 2005–. *Address:* TPG Ventures, Inc., 2882 Sand Hill Road, Suite 106, Menlo Park, CA 94025, USA (office). *Telephone:* (650) 289-5800. *Fax:* (650) 289-5801. *Website:* www.tpgventures.com.

PAULA, Alejandro Felippe "Jandi"; Netherlands Antilles politician and librarian; Govt Librarian 1973–93; Prime Minister of Netherlands Antilles 1993–94. *Address:* c/o Office of the Prime Minister, Curaçao, Netherlands Antilles.

PAULA GUTIÉRREZ, Francisco de, MA, PhD; Costa Rican economist and former politician; *President, Banco Central de Costa Rica;* ed Univ. of Costa Rica, Univ. of Pa, USA; lecturer in Econs, Univ. of Costa Rica 1972–86; Economist, Banco Centroamericano de Integración Ecónomico, Tegulcigalpa, Honduras 1973–74; Adviser to Pres. of Costa Rica 1974–76, to Exec. Cttee, Banco Central de Costa Rica 1974–76; Economist, Wharton Econometric Forecasting Associates, Philadelphia, PA 1981–84; Dir Consejeros Económicos y Financieros SA (CEFSA) 1984; mem. Comisión Internacional para la Reconstrucción y el Desarrollo de Centroamérica 1987–89; Minister of Finance 1996–98; Dir Banco Central de Costa Rica 1989–90, 1996–98, becoming Pres.; Prof. of Econs, INCAE Business School 1986–; Pres. Grupo Financiero SAMA 1998–; Dir Banco de Fomento Agrícola 1985–87, Productos de Concreto 1985–86, RICALIT SA 1986–96, Atlas Eléctrica 1990–96, ACORDE 1993–95, FUNDES 1993–96, Banco de COFISA 1993–96, Corporación INCSA 1998–, El Financiero (periodical) 1998–. *Publications:* numerous specialist papers on economics. *Address:* Banco Central de Costa Rica, Avdas Central y Primera, Calles 2 y 4, Apdo 10.058, 1000 San José, Costa Rica (office). *Telephone:* 255-0867 (office). *Fax:* 235-5930 (office). *E-mail:* gutierrf@mail.incae.ac.dr (office). *Website:* www.bccr.fi.cr (office).

PAULAUSKAS, Artūras; Lithuanian politician; b. 23 Aug. 1963; m. Jolanta Paulauskienė; one s. one d. (and two s. from previous m.); ed Vilnius State Univ.; Deputy Prosecutor, Kaisiadoris 1979–82; Prosecutor, Varena 1982–87; instructor, Cen. Cttee CP 1987; Deputy Prosecutor-Gen. of Lithuania 1987–90, Prosecutor-Gen. 1990–95; barrister 1997–2000; cand. in presidential elections 1997, 1998; est. The New Union (Social Liberals) Party, Leader 2006–; mem. Seimas (Parl.) of Lithuania 2000–08, Speaker 2000–06; Acting Pres. of Lithuania 6 April–12 July 2004; Minister of Environment Jan.–Nov. 2008. *Leisure interests:* sport, reading. *Address:* New Union (Social Liberals), Gedimino pr. 10/1, Vilnius 01103, Lithuania (office). *Telephone:* (5) 210-7600 (office). *Fax:* (5) 210-7602 (office). *E-mail:* arturas.paulauskas@lrs.lt (office); centras@nsajunga.lt (office). *Website:* www.nsajunga.lt (office); www.paulauskas.lt.

PAULIN, Pierre; French designer; b. 1927, Paris; ed Ecole Camondo; first exhbn of furniture in section entitled Le Foyer d'aujourd'hui, Salon des Arts ménagers 1953; influenced by Scandinavian furniture and American productions of Charles Eames and Florence Knoll; first revealed to general public in article by New York Times 1967; recognized by Museum of Modern Art, New York as world-class designer; commissioned by French Govt to redesign Pres. Georges Pompidou's pvt. apartments 1968; participates in devt of Denon Wing of Louvre Museum 1968–72; also asked by Pres. François Mitterrand to design his furniture 1984; participated in devt of Airbus aircraft 1986; works in collections of Museum of Modern Art, New York, Fonds nat. d'art contemporain, Centre Nat. d'art et de culture Georges-Pompidou, Musée des Arts Décoratifs, Paris, Victoria and Albert Museum, London, etc.; Chicago Design Award for the Ribbon Chair 1969, Grand Prix Nat. de la Création industrielle 1987. *Address:* c/o Gallerie des Gobelins, 42 avenue des Gobelins, Paris - 13, France. *Telephone:* 1-44-08-53-49.

PAULIN, Thomas (Tom) Neilson, BA, BLitt; British poet, critic and academic; *G. M. Young Lecturer in English Literature, Hertford College, University of Oxford;* b. 25 Jan. 1949, Leeds, Yorkshire; m. Munjiet Kaut Khosa 1973; two s.; ed Univ. of Hull, Lincoln Coll., Oxford; Lecturer, Univ. of Nottingham 1972–89, Reader in Poetry 1989–94; G. M. Young Lecturer in English Literature, Hertford Coll., Univ. of Oxford 1994–; Fellow, Hertford Coll., Oxford 1994–; Co-founder Field Day Theatre Co., Derry; Eric Gregory Award 1978, Faber Memorial Prize 1982, Fulbright Scholarship 1983–84. *Television:* panel mem. Newsnight Review (BBC 2). *Publications:* poetry: Theoretical Locations 1975, A State of Justice (Somerset Maugham Award 1978) 1977, Personal Column 1978, The Strange Museum 1980, The Book of Juniper 1981, Liberty Tree 1983, The Argument at Great Tew 1985, Fivemiletown 1987, Selected Poems 1972–90 1993, Walking a Line 1994, The Wind Dog 1999, The Invasion Handbook 2002, The Road to Inver 2004; non-fiction: Thomas Hardy: The Poetry of Perception 1975, Ireland and the English Crisis 1984, The Faber Book of Political Verse (ed.) 1986, Hard Lines 3 (co-ed.) 1987, Minotaur: Poetry and the Nation State 1992, Writing to the Moment: Selected Critical Essays 1996, The Day Star of Liberty: William Hazlitt's Radical Style (biog.) 1998, Crusoe's Secret: The Aesthetics of Dissent 2005, The Secret Life of Poems 2008. *Address:* Hertford College, Catte Street, Oxford, OX1 3BW (office); c/o Faber and Faber, Bloomsbury House, 74–77 Great Russell Street, London, WC1B 3DA, England (office). *Website:* www.faber.co.uk (office).

PAULS, Raymond; Latvian composer and jazz pianist; b. 12 Jan. 1936, Riga; ed Latvian Conservatory; Artistic Dir and Chief Conductor of Latvian State Radio and TV 1985–88; Chair. Latvian State Cttee for Culture, later Minister of Culture 1988–93 (first non-communist minister in USSR since 1920s); Counsellor to Pres. 1993–97; mem. Parl. (Saeima) 1998–; Latvian State Prize 1979, USSR People's Artist 1985. *Compositions include:* musicals Sister Kerry, Sherlock Holmes; many popular songs, jazz pieces. *Recordings include:* Cinema 1982, U morya zhizn' moya 1995, Na Rozhdestvo 1995, Izbrannoe 1995, Nostal'giya. Instrumental'naya muzika 1996, Dva maestro 1997. *Address:* Veidenbaum Str. 41/43, Apt 26, 6001 Rīga, Latvia. *Telephone:* 6227-5588.

PAULSON, Henry (Hank) Merritt, Jr, BA, MBA; American investment banker and fmr government official; *Distinguished Visiting Scholar, Paul H. Nitze School of Advanced International Studies, Johns Hopkins University;* b. 28 March 1946, Palm Beach, Fla; s. of Henry Merritt and Marianna Paulson (née Gallaeur); m. Wendy Judge 1969; one s. one d.; ed Dartmouth Coll., Harvard Univ. Business School; Staff Asst to Asst Sec. of Defense (Comptroller), Pentagon, Washington, DC 1970–72; Staff Asst to Pres.'s Domestic Council, The White House, Washington, DC 1972–73; Assoc. Goldman Sachs & Co., Chicago 1974–77, Vice-Pres. 1977–82, Pnr, Investment Banking Dept 1982–, pnr in charge of investment banking, Midwest Region 1984–90, Man. Cttee Co-Head Investment Banking Div., Vice-Chair., COO 1990–99, CEO and Chair. 1999–2006; US Sec. of the Treasury 2006–09; Distinguished Visiting Scholar, Johns Hopkins School of Advanced Int. Studies, Washington, DC 2009–, Fellow, Bernard Schwartz Forum on Constructive Capitalism; Trustee Chicago Symphony Orchestra; Dir The Peregrine Fund Inc.; Vice-Chair. Nature Conservancy and co-Chair. of Nature Conservancy Asia-Pacific Council. *Leisure interests:* skiing, fishing, canoeing, tennis, visiting wildlife habitats. *Address:* Paul H. Nitze School of Advanced International Studies, The Johns Hopkins University, 1740 Massachusetts Avenue, NW, Washington, DC 20036 (office); 101 West 67th Street, Apt 50A, New York, NY 10023, USA (home). *Telephone:* (202) 663-5600 (office). *Fax:* (202) 663-5656 (office). *Website:* www.sais-jhu.edu (office).

PAULY, Daniel, PhD; French marine biologist and academic; b. 2 May 1946, Paris; ed Univ. of Kiel, Germany; currently Prof., Univ. of British Columbia, Vancouver, Project Leader of Sea Around Us Project, Dir Fisheries Centre 2003–08; mem. Bd of Oceana; earned place in Scientific American 50 2003, labelled by New York Times as an "iconoclast" 2003, Int. Cosmos Prize 2005, Volvo Environment Prize, Volvo Environment Foundation (co-recipient) 2006, ECI Prize 2007, Ted Danson Ocean Hero Award 2007, Ramon Margalef Prize in Ecology 2008. *Achievements include:* early in his career, worked in tropics and developed new methods for estimating fish populations; developed concept of shifting baselines in 1995; published seminal paper on Fishing Down Marine Food Webs in Science 1998; developed important models and tools, including the Marine Trophic Index, Ecopath Modelling Model, and global database FishBase. *Publications:* author of several books and more than 500 scientific papers in professional journals on studies of human impacts on global fisheries. *Address:* AERL Room 333, Fisheries Centre, Aquatic Ecosystems Research Laboratory, University of British Columbia, 2202 Main Mall, Vancouver, BC V6T 1Z4, Canada (office). *Telephone:* (604) 822-1201 (office). *E-mail:* d.pauly@fisheries.ubc.ca (office). *Website:* www.fisheries.ubc.ca (office).

PAVIĆ, Milorad, DPhil; Serbian poet, novelist and historian; b. 15 Oct. 1929, Belgrade; m. 1st Branka Pavić; one s. one d.; m. 2nd Jasmina Mihailović; ed Belgrade Univ. and Univ. of Zagreb; journalist, Radio Belgrade 1958–63, Prosveta Publrs 1963–74; Prof., Dean, Faculty of Philosophy, Novy Sad Univ. 1974–82; Prof., Belgrade Univ. 1982–94; Lecturer, Univ. of Paris (Sorbonne); works trans. into 30 languages; Theatre performances in France, USA, Russia, Germany, Italy, Slovenia and Serbia; mem. Serbian Acad. of Sciences and Arts; Beli orao (White Eagle) 2006; Hon. Prof., Natalia Nesterovoj Univ., Moscow 2006; Zepter Int. Award for Literature, Warsaw 2005. *Plays:* adaptation of the novel Dictionary of the Khazars, Forever and a Day 1993, Triple Bed, Glass Snail 2002, Three Interactive plays 2005. *Publications:* Vojislav Ilic (1860–1894) 1961, Vojislav Ilic, njegovo vreme i delo (non-fiction) 1962, Palimpsesti (poems) 1967, Istorija srpske knjizevnosti baroknog doba (non-fiction) 1970, Mesecev kamen (poems) 1971, Vojislav Ilic i evropsko pesnistvo 1971, Gavril Stefanovic Venclovic 1972, Gvozdena zavesa (short stories, trans. as The Iron Curtain) 1973, Jezicko pamcenje i pesnicki oblik 1976, Konji svetoga Marka (short stories, trans. as St Mark's Horses) 1976, Istorija srpske knjizevnosti klasicizma i predromantizma 1979, Ruski hrt/Borzoi (short stories, trans. as Borzoi) 1979, Nove beogradske price 1981, Duse se kupaju poslednji put 1982, Radjanje nove srpske knjizevnosti (non-fiction) 1983, Hazarski recnik (novel, trans. as Dictionary of the Khazars) 1984, Istorija, stalez i stil 1985, Izabrana dela 1985, Predeo slikan cajem (novel, trans. as Landscape Painted with Tea) 1988, Izvrnuta rukavica (short stories, trans. as The Inverted Glove) 1989, Kratka istorija Beograda 1990, Unutrasnja strana vetra ili roman o Heri i Leandru (novel, trans. as The Inner Side of the Wind) 1991, Istorija srpske knjizevnosti 1991, Pozorisni jelovnik za uvek i dan vise (trans. as Forever and a Day) 1993, Poslednja ljubav u Carigradu (novel, trans. as The Last Love in Constantinople) 1994, Sesir od riblje koze 1996, Stakleni puz 1998, Zvezdani plast (novel) 2001, Sedam smrtnih grehova (novel) 2002, Nevidljivo ogledalo - Sareni hleb (children's novel, trans. as Invisible Mirror and Multicoloured Bread) 2002, Unikat (novel, trans. as Unique Item) 2004, Plava sveska (catalogue of endings to accompany Unikat) 2004, Interaktivne drame (collection of plays) 2004, Love Story in Two Tales (with Jasmina Mihajlović) 2004, Prica koja jeubila Emiliju Knor (trans. as The Tale that Killed Emily Knorr), Roman Kaodrzava i drugi ogledi 2005, Svadba u kupatilu vesela igra u sedam slika 2005, Drugo telo (Second Body) 2006, Pozorište od hartije (Paper Theater) 2007, Sve priče (All stories) 2008; contrib. numerous articles and essays. *Address:* Brace Baruh 2, Belgrade, Serbia. *E-mail:* mpavic@eunet.yu. *Website:* www.khazars.com.

PAVLE, Patriarch (secular name Gojko Stojcevic); Serbian ecclesiastic; *Patriarch of Serbia;* b. 11 Sept. 1914, Kućanci, Slavonia; s. of Stefan Stojcevic and Ann Stojcevic; ed Fourth Male Gymnasium, Belgrade, Orthodox Theological Faculty, Belgrade and Theological Faculty, Athens; worked as catechist of refugee children at Holy Trinity Monastery, Ovcar during World War II; took monastic vows, ordained deacon 1948; mem. Raca Monastery 1949–55; teacher, Theological Seminary, Prizren, Kosovo 1950–51; ordained priest 1954; Bishop, Raska-Prizren Diocese/Kosovo-Metohija 1957–90; 44th Patriarch of Serbia 1990–, Archbishop of Péc, Metropolitan of Belgrade-Karlovac; Dr hc (Theological Faculty, Belgrade) 1992, (St Vladimir Theological Seminary, New York) 1992. *Publications:* Some Questions Concerning Our Faith; ed. of liturgical books in Serbian and in Old Church Slavonic; articles in liturgics in monthly journal Glasnik. *Address:* Kralja Petra 5, PO Box 182, 11001 Belgrade, Serbia (office). *Telephone:* (11) 3283997 (office); (11)

3282527, ext. 55 (office). *Fax:* (11) 3283997 (office). *E-mail:* kabinetspc@beotel.yu (office). *Website:* www.spc.yu (office).

PAVLOVSKY, Gleb Olegovich; Russian journalist and historian; b. 5 March 1951, Odessa; m.; one s. four d.; ed Odessa State Univ.; with Samizdat 1972–86; co-f., mem. Bd Poiski (magazine) 1978–80; Chair. Bd of Dirs Postfactum (information agency) 1988–93; mem. ed. bd Obshchaya Gazeta 1993–; Ed.-in-Chief Twentieth Century and World; Co.-Publr Sreda (Russian-European review) 1993–95; took part in election campaign of Pres. Vladimir Putin 2000; Founder and Pres. Fund of Efficient Policy 1995–. *Address:* Fund of Efficient Policy, Zubovsky blvd 4 entr. 8, 119021 Moscow, Russia (office). *Telephone:* (495) 745-52-25 (office).

PAVLYCHKO, Dmytro Vasylovych; Ukrainian poet and politician; *President, Ukrainian World Coordinating Council;* b. 28 Sept. 1929, Ivano-Frankivsk; s. of Vasyl Pavlychko and Paraska Bojchuk; ed Lviv Univ.; started publishing in early 1950s; mem. CPSU 1954–88; keen advocate of de-Stalinization from 1962; f. Taras Shevchenko Ukrainian Language Soc. 1988, for protection of language; Chair. Inaugural Congress of the Popular Movt of the Ukraine for Perestroika (Rukh); Deputy to Ukrainian Supreme Soviet 1990–95; Chair., Parl. Cttee for Int. Affairs 1991–95; Amb. to Slovakia 1995–98, to Poland 1999–2003; Pres., Ukrainian World Coordinating Council 2006–. *Publications include:* poems: My Land 1955, The Day 1960, Bread and Banner 1968, Sonnets 1978, Turned to the Future 1986, Repentance Psalms 1994, Nostalgia 1998, Thimble 2002, Memory 2004, Three Verses 2007, Autodaphe 2008; trans.: C. Baudelaire, Poems 2001, José Martí, Poesías 2001, W. Shakespeare, Sonnets 2001; contrib. to anthologies. *Address:* c/o Ministry of Foreign Affairs, pl. Mykhailivska 1, 01018 Kiev (office); Khreshchatyk str. 13, Apt 42, 01001 Kiev, Ukraine (home). *Telephone:* (44) 287-22-41 (office); (44) 278-79-75 (home). *Fax:* (44) 287-22-41 (office). *E-mail:* uvkr@ipteleocm.net.ua (office). *Website:* www.uvkr.ua (office).

PAWAR, Sharadchandra Govindrao, BCom; Indian politician; *Minister of Agriculture and of Consumer Affairs, Food and Public Distribution; President, Nationalist Congress Party;* b. 12 Dec. 1940, Katychiwadi, Pune; s. of Govindrao Jijaba Pawar; m. Pratibha Pawar 1967; one d.; Head, State Level Youth Congress; Gen. Sec. Maharashtra Pradesh Congress Cttee; elected to State Legis. 1967, held Portfolios of Home and Publicity and Rehabilitation; Minister of State and Educ. and Youth Welfare, Home, Agric. and Industries and Labour; Chief Minister of Maharashtra 1978–80, 1988–91; Minister of Defence 1991–92; Minister of Agric. and of Consumer Affairs, Food and Public Distribution 2004–; Pres. Nat. Congress (opposition) 1981–86; rejoined Congress (I) 1986; fmr Pres. Congress Forum for Socialistic Action; Sec. Defence Cttee; mem. Lok Sabha 1996–; Leader of Opposition 1998–99; Pres. Nationalist Congress Party 1999–; Pres. Maharashtra Kabbadi Asscn, Maharashtra Olympic Asscn, Agricultural Devt Foundation, Mumbai Cricket Asscn. *Address:* Ministry of Agriculture, Krishi Bhavan, Dr Rajendra Prasad Road, New Delhi 110 001 (office); Nationalist Congress Party, 10 Dr Bishambhar Das Marg, New Delhi 110 001 (office); Ramalayan, 44-A Pedder Road, Mumbai 400026, India (home). *Telephone:* (11) 23383370 (office); (11) 23359218 (office); (22) 23659191 (home). *Fax:* (11) 23384129 (office); (11) 23352112 (office).

PAWLAK, Waldemar, MSc; Polish politician and business executive; *Deputy Prime Minister and Minister of the Economy;* b. 5 Sept. 1959, Pacyna, Płock Prov.; m.; two s. one d.; ed Warsaw Univ. of Tech.; farm man. 1984–; mem. United Peasant Party (ZSL) 1984–90; Deputy to Sejm (Parl.) 1989–; mem. Polish Peasant Party (PSL) 1992– (Chair. 1992–97); Chair. Council of Ministers (Prime Minister) of Poland June–July 1992, 1993–95; Chair. Union of Volunteer Fire Brigades 1992–; Pres. Warszawska Gielda Towarowa Spolka Akcyjna (WGT) S.A. (commodity exchange) Warsaw 2001–05; Deputy Prime Minister and Minister of the Economy 2007–. *Leisure interests:* philosophy, information science, computers. *Address:* Ministry of the Economy, pl. Trzech Krzyży 3/5, 00-507 Warsaw, Poland (office). *Telephone:* (22) 6935000 (office). *Fax:* (22) 6934048 (office). *E-mail:* bpi@mgip.gov.pl (office). *Website:* www.mgip.gov.pl (office).

PAWLENTY, Tim, BA; American state official; *Governor of Minnesota;* b. 1960, South St. Paul; m. Mary Pawlenty; two d.; ed South St Paul High School, Univ. of Minn.; fmr prosecutor Hennepin County; mem. Egan City Council –1992; elected mem. Minn. House of Reps 1992, Majority Leader 1998–2002; Gov. of Minn. 2003–; Republican. *Address:* Office of the Governor, 130 State Capitol Building, 75 Rev. Dr. Martin Luther King Jr. Blvd., St Paul, MN 55155, USA (office). *Telephone:* (651) 296-3391 (office). *Fax:* (651) 296-2089 (office). *E-mail:* tim.pawlenty@state.mn.us (office). *Website:* www.governor.state.mn.us (office).

PAWLIK, Kurt, PhD, PrivDoz; academic; *Professor of Psychology, University of Hamburg;* b. 16 March 1934, Vienna; ed Univ. of Vienna; Prof. of Psychology and Dept Dir, Univ. of Hamburg, Germany 1966–; Founder and Ed.-in-Chief European Psychologist journal; Ed. Methods of Psychology monograph series; Co-Ed. Research Texts in Psychology monograph series (more than 60 vols) and several scientific journals including American Psychologist; Pres. German Soc. of Psychology 1972–74, Int. Social Science Council 1998–2000, J. Jungius Soc. of Science 1999–; Sec.-Gen. Int. Union of Psychological Science 1984–92, Pres. 1992–96, 2000–02; Hon. mem. German Soc. of Psychology 2002–; Fellow, Chinese Psychological Soc. 2004– Austrian Cross of Honours (First Class) in Science and Arts 1999. *Publications include:* International Handbook of Psychology (co-ed.) 2000; 12 books and more than 180 research papers. *Leisure interests:* music, theatre, skiing. *Address:* University of Hamburg, Department of Psychology, Von Melle Park 11, 20146 Hamburg, Germany (office). *Telephone:* (40) 428384722 (office); (40) 6072210 (home). *Fax:* (40) 428386591 (office); (40) 6072334 (home). *E-mail:* pawlik@uni-hamburg.de (office); kfpawlik@aol.com (home).

PAWSON, Anthony James, OC, PhD, FRS, FRSC; British/Canadian molecular biologist; *Research Director, Samuel Lunenfeld Research Institute, Mount Sinai Hospital (Toronto);* b. 18 Oct. 1952, Maidstone; s. of Henry Anthony Pawson and Hilarie Anne Pawson (née Bassett); m. Margaret Ann Luman 1975; two s. one d.; ed London Univ., Cambridge Univ.; Asst Prof., Dept of Microbiology, Univ. of British Columbia 1981–85; Sr Scientist, Samuel Lunenfeld Research Inst., Mount Sinai Hosp., Toronto 1985–, Head of Programme in Molecular Biology and Cancer 1994–, Research Dir 2002–; Assoc. Prof., Dept of Medical Genetics, Univ. of Toronto 1985-88, Prof. 1989–; Gairdner Foundation Int. Award 1994, Dr H. P. Heineken Prize for Biochemistry and Biophysics, Royal Netherlands Acad. of Arts and Sciences 1998, American Asscn for Cancer Research-Pezcoller Foundation Award for Cancer Research 1998, Flavelle Medal of the Royal Soc. of Canada 1998, Distinguished Scientist of the Medical Research Council of Canada 1998; Izaak Walton Killam Memorial Prize 2000, J. Allyn Taylor Int. Prize 2000, Ont. Platinum Research Medal 2002, Prix Galien Canada 2002, Michael Smith Prize for health research 2002, Wolf Foundation Prize in Medicine, 2005, Kyoto Prize 2008. *Publications:* over 275 papers in various scientific journals. *Leisure interests:* reading, theatre, fly-fishing. *Address:* Samuel Lunenfeld Research Institute, Mount Sinai Hospital, 600 University Avenue, Room 1084, Toronto, Ont. M5G 1X5, Canada. *Telephone:* (416) 586-8262. *Fax:* (416) 586-8869. *E-mail:* pawson@mshri.on.ca (office). *Website:* pawson.mshri.on.ca.

PAWSON, John; British architect; b. 6 May 1949; s. of the late Jim Pawson and Winifred Ward; m. Catherine Berning 1989; two s.; ed Eton; lived three years in Japan before studying architecture; pvt. architectural practice 1981–; pvt. bldgs designed include Neundorf House, Majorca, Klein Apartment, NY; commercial bldgs designed include Calvin Klein Store, Madison Avenue, NY, Jigsaw clothes store, Bond St, London, Cathay Pacific Lounges, Chek Lap Kok Airport, Hong Kong, Novy Dvur Monastery, Czech Rep., Sackler Crossing, Royal Botanic Gardens, Kew. *Publications:* Minimum 1996, Living and Eating (with Annie Bell) 2001, Themes and Projects 2002. *Address:* Unit B, 70–78 York Way, London, N1 9AG, England. *Telephone:* (20) 7837-2929. *Fax:* (20) 7837-4949. *E-mail:* email@johnpawson.co.uk (office).

PAXMAN, Jeremy Dickson, MA; British broadcast journalist and writer; *Presenter, Newsnight;* b. 11 May 1950, Leeds; s. of Arthur Keith Paxman and Joan McKay Dickson; one s. two d.; ed Malvern Coll., St Catharine's Coll., Cambridge; journalist, Northern Ireland 1973–77; reporter, BBC TV Tonight and Panorama programmes 1977–85, presenter BBC TV Breakfast Time 1986–89, Newsnight 1989–, Univ. Challenge 1994–, Start the Week, Radio 4, 1998–2002; Fellow St Edmund Hall, Oxford, St Catharine's Coll. Cambridge 2001; Vice-Pres. The Wild Trout Trust (WTT) 2004–; Dr hc (Leeds, Bradford) 1999, (Open Univ.) 2006 TV Soc. Award for Int. Reporting, Richard Dimbleby Award, BAFTA 1996, 2000, Interview of the Year, Royal TV Soc. 1997, 1998, 2001, Voice of the Viewer and Listener Presenter of the Year 1994, 1997, 2005, Variety Club Media Personality of the Year 1999, Royal TV Soc. Presenter of the ear 2007. *Publications:* A Higher Form of Killing (co-author) 1982, Through the Volcanoes 1985, Friends in High Places 1990, Fish, Fishing and the Meaning of Life 1994, The Compleat Angler 1996, The English 1998, The Political Animal 2002, On Royalty 2006; numerous articles in newspapers and magazines. *Leisure interests:* fly-fishing, daydreaming. *Address:* c/o Capel & Land, 29 Wardour Street, London, W1V 6PS, England. *Website:* news.bbc.co.uk/1/hi/programmes/newsnight.

PAYÁ SARDIÑAS, Oswaldo José; Cuban human rights activist; *Leader, Movimiento Cristiano Liberación;* b. 29 Feb. 1952; m. Ofelia Acevedo Maura Payá Sardiñas 1986; three c.; ed Maristas Brothers Catholic School and Univ. of Havana; sentenced to hard labour in Isla de Pinos and Camagüey Prov. for openly criticizing communist regime 1969–72; later forced to abandon his teaching post for refusing to join Cuban Communist Party (PCC); specialist in electronic medical equipment for Public Health Dept 1980s–; del. of Havana Diocese at Church Nat. Meeting, presented document 'Faith and Justice' defending right of Catholics to practise their religion 1986; f. 'La Peña del Pensamiento Cubano'; prohibited from publishing 'Peña Cristiana' by Bishop of Havana 1988; f. Movimiento Cristiano Liberación (MCL) 1988; detained and interrogated by State Security 1990; drafted Transitory Program 1992, collected signatures for referendum on Transitory Program 1993; Co-Organizer of Cuban Council 1995; drafted Varela Project to secure referendum on guaranteeing basic human rights 1996–97, collected required number of signatures under Cuban Constitution to make Varela Project become a bill of law May 2002; move blocked when ordinary session of Nat. Ass. suspended by Fidel Castro July 2002; Homo Homini Prize 1999, European Parl. Sakharov Award for Human Rights and Freedom of Thought 2002. *Publications include:* Pueblo de Dios (God's Nation) 1987, Todos Unidos (All Together) 1999. *Address:* Buró de Información del Movimiento Cubano de Derechos Humanos, 999 South Brickell Bay Drive, 1704 Miami, FL 33131 (office); c/o Cuba Free Press, P.O. Box 652035, Miami, FL 33265-2035, USA; Movimiento Cristiano Liberación, Havana, Cuba. *Website:* www.infoburo.org; www.cubaproyectovarela.org.

PAYE, Jean-Claude; French diplomatist and attorney; *Counsel, Gide Loyrette Nouel;* b. 26 Aug. 1934, Longué; s. of Lucien Paye and Suzanne Paye (née Guignard); m. Laurence Jeanneney 1963; two s. two d.; ed Inst. d'Etudes Politiques and Ecole Nat. d'Admin; Head, pvt. office of Mayor of Constantine 1961–62; Sec. of Embassy, Algiers 1962–63; Ministry of Foreign Affairs 1963–65; special adviser, Office of Sec. of State for Scientific Research 1965, Office of Minister for Social Affairs 1966; Head of pvt. office of M. Barre (Vice-Pres. of Comm. of European Communities) 1967–73; Counsellor, Bonn

1973–74; Deputy Head, Office of Minister for Foreign Affairs 1974–76; Counsellor to Prime Minister Raymond Barre 1976–79; Sec.-Gen. Interministerial Cttee for European Econ. Co-operation questions 1977–79; Dir Econ. and Financial Affairs, Ministry for External Relations 1979–84; Sec.-Gen. OECD 1984–96; Conseiller d'Etat en Service Extraordinaire 1996–2000; counsel with legal firm Gide Loyrette Nouel 2001–; Chair. Fondation pour l'innovation politique 2005–; mem. Bd Renault 2000–, Transparency International-France 2000–, Fondation Nat. des Sciences Politiques 2002–; Chevalier, Légion d'honneur, Commdr, Ordre nat. du Mérite. *Address:* Cabinet d'Avocats Gide Loyrette Nouel, 26 Cours Albert Ier, 75008 Paris (office); Fondation pour l'innovation politique, 137 rue de l'Université, 75007, Paris; 1 place Alphonse Deville, 75006 Paris, France (home). *Telephone:* 1-40-75-35-86 (office); 1-45-49-20-30 (home). *Fax:* 1-45-49-20-06 (home). *E-mail:* paye@gide.fr (office).

PAYNE, Alexander, BA, MFA; American film director and screenwriter; b. 1961, Omaha, Neb.; m. Sandra Oh 2003; ed Stanford Univ. and UCLA; began making films aged six; employee Universal Pictures; completed several shorts for Propaganda Films and screened on Playboy Channel; feature film debut with Citizen Ruth (co-wrote screenplay with Jim Taylor) 1996. *Films include:* The Passion of Martin (thesis film, dir) 1989, Inside Out (dir and screenwriter) 1992, Citizen Ruth (dir and screenwriter) (First Prize, Munich Film Festival) 1996, Election (dir and co-screenwriter with Jim Taylor) (Best Screenplay Award: WGA, New York Film Critics' Circle and Ind. Spirit, Best Film and Best Dir, Ind. Spirit Awards) 1999, Jurassic Park III (screenplay) 2001, About Schmidt (dir and co-screenwriter with Jim Taylor) (Best Movie of the Year, Los Angeles Film Critics' Asscn 2002, Golden Globe for Best Screenplay 2003) 2002, Sideways (dir) (Los Angeles Film Critics' Asscn Best Movie of the Year, Golden Globe Award for Best Screenplay 2005, BAFTA Award for Best Adapted Screenplay 2005, Writers' Guild of America Award for best adapted screenplay 2005, Acad. Award for Best Adapted Screenplay 2005, Independent Spirit Awards for Best Dir, Best Screenplay 2005) 2004, Paris, je t'aime (segment) 2006, I Now Pronounce You Chuck and Larry (co-screenwriter) 2007. *Address:* c/o New Line Cinema Corporation, 116 North Robertson Boulevard, Los Angeles, CA 90048, USA (office).

PAYNE, Anthony Edward, BA, FRCM; British composer; b. 2 Aug. 1936, London; s. of the late Edward Alexander Payne and (Muriel) Margaret Payne; m. Jane Manning (q.v.) 1966; ed Dulwich Coll., London and Durham Univ.; freelance musical journalist, musicologist, lecturer, etc. with various publs and BBC Radio, active in promoting "new music", serving on Cttee of Macnaghten Concerts (Chair. 1967) and Soc. for the Promotion of New Music (Chair. 1969–71), composed part-time 1962–73; full-time composer 1973–; tutor in Composition, London Coll. of Music 1983–85, Sydney Conservatorium 1986, Univ. of W Australia 1996; Milhaud Prof., Mills Coll., Oakland, Calif. 1983; Artistic Dir Spitalfields Festival; Composition Tutor Univ. of Western Australia 1996; Contrib. Daily Telegraph 1964–, The Times 1964–, The Independent 1986–, Country Life 1995–; Creative Arts Fellow Royal Coll. of Music 2007–08; mem. Cttee Asscn Frank Bridge Trust, RVW Trust, MBF Awards and Trusts; Hon. DMus (Birmingham) 2000, (Kingston) 2002, (Durham) 2007; Radcliffe Award 1975, South Bank Show Award 1998, Evening Standard Classical Music Award 1998, New York Critics' Circle Nat. Public Radio Award 1999, Classical CD Award 1999. *Compositions:* Paraphrases and Cadenzas 1969, Paean for solo piano 1971, Phoenix Mass 1972, The Spirits Harvest for full orchestra 1972, Concerto for Orchestra (Int. Jury Choice for Int. Soc. for Contemporary Music Festival 1976) 1974, The World's Winter for soprano and ensemble 1976, String Quartet 1978, The Stones and Lonely Places Sing (septet) 1979, Song of the Clouds for oboe and orchestra 1980, A Day in the Life of a Mayfly (sextet) 1981, Evening Land for soprano and piano 1981, Spring's Shining Wake for orchestra 1981, Songs and Seascapes for strings 1984, The Song Streams in the Firmament (sextet) 1986, Fanfares and Processional 1986, Half Heard in the Stillness for orchestra 1987, Consort Music for string quintet 1987, Sea Change (septet) 1988, Time's Arrow for orchestra 1990, The Enchantress Plays bassoon and piano 1990, Symphonies of Wind and Rain for chamber ensemble 1991, A Hidden Music 1992, Orchestral Variations: The Seeds Long Hidden 1993, Empty Landscape–Heart's Ease (sextet) 1995, Break, Break, Break for unaccompanied chorus 1996, Elgar's Third Symphony (commissioned by Elgar Trust to complete Elgar's sketches) 1997, Piano Trio 1998, Scenes from The Woodlanders for soprano and ensemble 1999, Of Knots and Skeins for violin and piano 2000, Betwixt Heaven and Charing Cross for unaccompanied chorus 2001, Visions and Journeys for orchestra (British Composers Award 2003) 2001, Poems of Edward Thomas for soprano and piano quartet 2003, Horn Trio 2005, Elgar's Sixth Pomp & Circumstance March (commissioned by Elgar Trust to complete Elgar's sketches) 2006, Windows on Eternity 2007, Piano Quintet 2007, Out of the Depths Comes Song for cello and piano 2008, From a Mouthful of Air for quintet 2009. *Recordings include:* The Music of Anthony Payne (Gramophone Critics' Choice) 1977, Time's Arrow 1996, A Day in the Life of a Mayfly 1998, The Stones and Lonely Places Sing 2007. *Publications:* Schoenberg 1968, The Music of Frank Bridge 1984, Elgar's Third Symphony: The Story of the Reconstruction 1998; contrib. to Musical Times, Tempo, Music and Musicians, The Listener, Daily Telegraph, The Times, The Independent, Country Life. *Leisure interests:* English countryside, cinema. *Address:* 2 Wilton Square, London, N1 3DL (office); c/o Boosey & Hawkes, 295 Regent Street, London, W1B 2JH, England (office). *Telephone:* (20) 7359-1593 (office). *Fax:* (20) 7226-4369 (office).

PAYNE, Julien David, OC, CM, LSM, QC, LLD, FRSC; Canadian/British lawyer; *President, Danreb Incorporated;* b. 4 Feb. 1934, Nottingham; s. of Frederick Payne and Kathleen Payne (née Maltby); m. Marilyn Ann Payne; five c.; ed Univ. of London; Asst Lecturer, Queens Univ., Belfast 1956–60; Prof. of Law in various Canadian univs 1960–2001; admitted as solicitor and barrister,

Prov. of Ont. 1965; served as advocate, mediator and arbitrator of family law disputes across Canada (pioneer of no-fault divorce and Unified Family Courts); adviser to fed. and prov. govts on family and law reform 1966–; Dir Family Law Project, Law Reform Comm. of Canada 1972–75; Prof., Common Law Section, Univ. of Ottawa 1974–99; Chair. Law Foundation of Saskatchewan 1999–2001; Pres. Danreb Inc. 1985–; Founding mem. Int. Soc. on Family Law 1972; visiting univ. fellowships or chairs include Manchester, Santa Clara, Calif., Victoria, British Columbia, Hong Kong Univ., City Univ. of Hong Kong, Saskatchewan; Hon. Life Mem. Bd of Dirs, Ont. Asscn of Family Mediation, Ottawa 1992; Hon. Life Fellow, Canadian Inst. for Conflict Resolution, St Paul's Univ., Ottawa; Simon Sr Fellowship, Univ. of Manchester 1968; Law Soc. of Upper Canada, Medal for Contribs to Legal Profession 2002. *Publications include:* Power on Divorce 1964, Conceptual Analysis of Unified Family Courts, Law Reform Commission of Canada 1973, Payne on Divorce 1996, Child Support Guidelines in Canada 2004, Canadian Family Law 2006. *Address:* 1188 Morrison Drive, Ottawa, ON K2H 7L3, Canada (home). *Telephone:* (613) 829-1905 (home). *E-mail:* j_d_payne@sympatico.ca (office); julien.payne@gmail.com (home).

PAYNE, Nicholas; British opera company director; *Director, Opera Europa;* b. 4 Jan. 1945, Bromley, Kent, England; m. Linda Jane Adamson 1986; two s.; ed Eton Coll. and Trinity Coll. Cambridge; worked for Paterson Concert Management 1967; Arts Council administration course 1967–68; joined finance dept Royal Opera House, Covent Garden 1968–70; Subsidy Officer, Arts Council 1970–76; Financial Controller, Welsh Nat. Opera 1976–82; Gen. Admin. Opera North 1982–93; Dir of Opera, Royal Opera House 1993–98; Gen. Dir ENO 1998–2002; Dir Opera Europa 2003–; Hon. mem. Guildhall School of Music and Drama, Royal Northern College of Music; Dr hc (Leeds Metropolitan Univ.). *Address:* Opera Europa, 23 rue Léopold, 1000 Brussels, Belgium (office). *Telephone:* (2) 217-67-05 (office). *E-mail:* nicholas.payne@opera-europa.org (office). *Website:* www.opera-europa.org (office).

PAYNE-BANFIELD, Gloria M., OBE, BSc, MScS; Grenadian politician; *Leader, Grenada United Labour Party;* ed Wesley Hall School, Anglican High School, Univ. of the W Indies, Long Island Univ., New York; served in various positions in civil service as Chargé d'Affaires Grenada Mission to UN, Perm. Mission of Grenada to UN, New York, Acting Perm. Rep. to OAS; Perm. Sec., Ministry of External Affairs and Sec. to the Cabinet 1995–98; fmr Head of Public Sector Reform Devt Programme; Leader, Grenada United Labour Party 2003–; Dir Port Cullis Ltd; Chair. Nat. Org. of Women; Queen's Silver Jubilee Medal 1977, Grenada Nat. Arts Festival Award, Univ. of the W Indies 50th Anniversary Celebration Distinguished Grad. Award. *Address:* Grenada United Labour Party, St George's, Grenada. *Website:* www.gulpstar.org.

PAZ, George, BS; American business executive; *Chairman, President and CEO, Express Scripts Inc.;* b. 27 Aug. 1955, St Louis, Mo.; s. of Geronimo Paz and Collen May Hart; m. Georgene Marie Wade 1974; three c.; ed Univ. of Missouri; Jr Accountant, Gen. Am. 1980–82, Sr Accountant 1982–83, Accounting Admin. 1983–85, Tax Planning Analyst 1985–87, Dir of Tax Planning 1987–, mem. Bd of Dirs Gen. Am. Employees Fed. Credit Union 1985–; Partner, Coopers & Lybrand 1988–93, 1996–98; Exec. Vice-Pres. and Chief Financial Officer, Life Partners Group 1993–95; Sr Vice-Pres. and Chief Financial Officer, Express Scripts Inc. 1998–2003, Pres. 2003–, CEO 2005–, Chair. 2006–; mem. Pharmaceutical Care Man. Asscn; Fellow, Life Office Man. Asscn. *Leisure interests:* golf, running, softball. *Address:* Express Scripts Inc., 13900 Riverport Drive, Maryland Heights, MO 63043, USA (office). *Telephone:* (314) 770-1666 (office). *Fax:* (314) 702-7037 (office). *E-mail:* info@express-scripts.com (office). *Website:* www.express-scripts.com (office).

PAZ ZAMORA, Jaime; Bolivian politician, academic and fmr head of state; b. 15 April 1939, Cochabamba; ed Colegio Jesuita, Sucre, Seminario Mayor de Villa Allende en Córdoba, Argentina and Catholic Univ. of Louvain, Belgium; Pres. de la Fed. de Estudiantes Latino-Americanos (Belgium); Prof. of Sociology, Univ. Mayor de San Andrés; Prof. of Int. Relations, Dir Univ. Extension; f. Movimiento de la Izquierda Revolucionaria; cand. Vice-Pres. 1978 and 1980; first Vice-Pres. of the Andean Parl.; Vice-Pres. Repub. of Bolivia and Pres. Nat. Congress 1982–84; Pres. Repub. of Bolivia 1989–93; presidential cand. 2002; mem. Exec. Cttee of the Assoc. Latino-Americana de Derechos Humanos; mem. Movimiento de la Izquierda Revolucionaria (MIR). *Address:* Movimiento de la Izquierda Revolucionaria, Avda América 119, 2°, La Paz, Bolivia (office). *E-mail:* mir@coibo.entelnet.bo (office); jpazamora@mail.megalinks.com (home). *Website:* www.cibergallo.org (office); www.jaimepazamora.com (home).

PAZNIAK, Zianon Stanislavavich; Belarusian politician; *Chairman, Conservative Christian Party of the Belarusian Popular Front;* b. 24 April 1944; fmr anti-Communist dissident; founder mem. Belorussian Popular Front (BPF) Oct. 1988, Leader 1989–99, Chair. Conservative Christian Party of the BPF (breakaway faction) 1999–; elected to Supreme Soviet as mem. Belorussian Democratic Bloc 1990–; cand. in presidential elections 1994; lives in Warsaw. *Address:* c/o Conservative Christian Party of the BPF, PO Box 208, 220040 Minsk, Belarus.

PEACE, John W., FRSA; British retail executive; *CEO, GUS PLC;* b. 2 March 1949; m. Christine Peace (née Blakemore); three d.; ed Royal Mil. Acad., Sandhurst; joined Great Universal Stores (now GUS) PLC 1970, held several sr IT man. positions 1970–80, Co-founder CCN (market information services co.) 1980, CEO CCN 1991–2000, mem. Bd GUS PLC 1997–, Group CEO 2000–; apptd Chair. Burberry Group PLC 2002; Chair. Bd Govs Nottingham Trent Univ.; mem. Bd Companions of the Chartered Man. Inst. *Leisure interests:* horseriding, golf, watching Manchester United. *Address:* GUS PLC, One Stanhope Gate, London, W1K 1AF, England (office). *Telephone:* (20) 7495-

0070 (office). *Fax:* (20) 7318-6244 (office). *E-mail:* johnpeace@gusplc.com (office). *Website:* www.gusplc.co.uk (office).

PEACOCK, Sir Alan, Kt, DSC, MA, FBA, FRSE; British economist and academic; *Research Professor in Public Finance, Heriot-Watt University;* b. 26 June 1922, Ryton-on-Tyne; s. of Alexander D. Peacock and Clara M. Peacock; m. Margaret Martha Astell-Burt 1944; two s. one d.; ed Grove Acad., Dundee High School, Univ. of St Andrews; RN 1942–45; Lecturer in Econs, Univ. of St Andrews 1947–48; lecturer in Econs, LSE 1948–51, Reader in Public Finance 1951–56; Prof. of Econ. Science, Univ. of Edinburgh 1956–62; Prof. of Econs, Univ. of York 1962–78; Prof. of Econs and Prin. Univ. Coll. at Buckingham 1980–83, Vice-Chancellor 1983–84, Prof. Emer. 1985–; Research Prof. in Public Finance, Heriot-Watt Univ. 1987–; Chief Econ. Adviser, Dept of Trade and Industry 1973–76; Pres. Int. Inst. of Public Finance 1966–69, Hon. Pres. 1975–; mem. Royal Comm. on Constitution 1970–73, Social Science Research Council 1971–72; Trustee, Inst. of Econ. Affairs; mem. Council, London Philharmonic Orchestra 1975–79; Chair. Arts Council Enquiry into Orchestral Resources 1969–70, Cttee on Financing the BBC 1985–86, Scottish Arts Council 1986–92; mem. Bd of Dirs English Music Theatre Ltd 1975–77; Chair. Hebrides Ensemble 1994–2000; mem. Council of Man., Nat. Inst. of Econ. and Social Research 1977–86; non-exec. Dir Economist Intelligence Unit 1977–84; Exec. Dir David Hume Inst. 1985–90, Hon. Pres. 2002–(05); non-exec. Dir Caledonian Bank PLC 1989–96; Hon. mem. Royal Soc. of Musicians 1999–; Hon. Pres. Atlantic Econ. Soc. 1981–82; Hon. Fellow LSE 1980–; Foreign mem. Accademia Naz. dei Lincei, Rome 1996–; Keynes Lecturer, British Acad. 1994; Dr hc (Stirling) 1974, (Catania) 1991, (Brunel) 1989, (York) 1997, (Lisbon) 2000, (Turin) 2001; Hon. DEcon (Zürich) 1984; Hon. DSc (Buckingham) 1986; Hon. DSocSc (Edinburgh) 1990; Hon. LLD (St Andrews, Dundee) 1990; Scottish Free Enterprise Award 1987, Royal Soc. of Edinburgh 2002 (Royal Medal). *Publications:* Economics of National Insurance 1952, Growth of Public Expenditure in United Kingdom (with J. Wiseman) 1961, Economic Theory of Fiscal Policy (with G. K. Shaw) 1971, The Composer in the Market Place (with R. Weir) 1975, Welfare Economics: A Liberal Reinterpretation (with Charles Rowley), The Credibility of Liberal Economics 1977, The Economic Analysis of Government 1979, The Political Economy of Taxation (ed. with Francesco Forte) 1980, The Regulation Game (ed.) 1984, Public Expenditure and Government Growth (ed. with F. Forte) 1985, Corporate Takeovers and the Public Interest (with G. Bannock) 1991, Public Choice Analysis in Historical Perspective 1991, Paying the Piper: Culture, Music and Money 1993, Cultural Economics and Cultural Policies (ed. with Ilde Rizzo), The Political Economy of Economic Freedom 1997, The Political Economy of Heritage (ed.) 1998, What Price Civil Justice (with B. Main) 2000, Calling the Tune 2001, The Enigmatic Sailor 2003, The Political Economy of Sustainable Development 2003, Public Service Broadcasting without the BBC? 2004; and numerous articles in professional journals on economics, public finance and public policy. *Leisure interest:* trying to write music, wine spotting. *Address:* David Hume Institute, 25 Buccleuch Place, Edinburgh, EH8 9LD (office); 5/24 Oswald Road, Edinburgh, EH9 2HE, Scotland (home). *Telephone:* (131) 667-9609 (office); (131) 667-5677 (home). *Fax:* (131) 667-9609 (office). *E-mail:* hume.institute@ed.ac.uk (office); peacock@ebs.hw.ac.uk (home). *Website:* www.ed.ac.uk/~hume/ (office).

PEACOCK, Hon. Andrew Sharp, AC, LLB, MP; Australian diplomatist and fmr politician; b. 13 Feb. 1939, Melbourne; s. of the late A. S. Peacock and Iris Peacock; m. 1st Susan Peacock (divorced), three d.; m. 2nd Margaret Peacock 1983 (divorced); ed Scotch Coll., Univ. of Melbourne; Pres., Victorian Liberal Party 1965–66; mem. House of Rep. for Kooyong, Vic. 1966–94; fmr partner Rigby and Fielding, solicitors; fmr Chair. Peacock & Smith Pty Ltd, engineers; Minister for the Army and Minister Assisting the Prime Minister 1969–71, Assisting the Treas. 1971–72; Minister for External Territories 1972; mem. Opposition Exec. 1973–75, Spokesman on Foreign Affairs 1973–75; Minister for Foreign Affairs 1975–80, for the Environment Nov.–Dec. 1975, for Industrial Relations 1980–81, for Industry and Commerce 1982–83; Leader Parl. Liberal Party 1983–85; Opposition Spokesman on Foreign Affairs 1985–87; Deputy Leader of the Opposition and Shadow Treas. 1987–89; Leader of the Opposition 1989–90; Shadow Attorney-Gen. and Shadow Minister for Justice 1990–92; Shadow Minister for Trade 1992–93, for Foreign Affairs 1993–94; Chair. Parl. Political Strategy Cttee 1994; Amb. to USA 1997–2000; Chair. Int. Democrat Union 1989–92, Australian Horse Council 1996. *Leisure interests:* horse racing, Australian Rules Football, surfing, reading. *Address:* 19 Queens Road, Melbourne, Vic. 3004, Australia (home).

PEACOCK, William James, AC, PhD, FRS, FAA, FAIAS, FTSE; Australian research scientist; *Fellow, Commonwealth Scientific and Industrial Research Organisation (CSIRO);* b. 14 Dec. 1937, Leura, NSW; s. of William Edward Peacock and Evelyn Alison Peacock; m. Margaret Constance Woodward 1961; one s. two d.; ed Univ. of Sydney; Visiting Research Scientist, Genetics, CSIRO, Canberra 1963; Fellow, Dept of Biology, Univ. of Oregon 1963–64, Visiting Assoc. Prof. 1964–65; Research Consultant, Biology Div., Oak Ridge Nat. Lab., USA 1965; Sr Research Scientist, Div. of Plant Industry, CSIRO, Canberra 1965–69, Prin. Research Scientist 1969–73, Sr Prin. Research Scientist 1973–77, Chief Research Scientist 1977–78, Chief 1978–2003, currently Fellow; Pres. Australian Acad. of Science 2002–06; Chief Scientist of Australia 2006–08; Adjunct Prof. of Biology, Univ. of Calif., San Diego 1969–70; Visiting Prof. of Biochem., Stanford Univ. 1970–71; Visiting Distinguished Prof. of Molecular Biology, UCLA 1977; Scientific Adviser, Australian Genetic Eng Ltd; Foreign Fellow, Indian Nat. Science Acad. 1990; Foreign Assoc., NAS 1990; Hon. DSc (Charles Sturt Univ., Wagga Wagga) 1996, (Ghent) 2004, (Sydney) 2008, Hon. DSc Ag (Sydney) 2002; Edgeworth David Medal, Royal Soc. of NSW 1967, Lemberg Medal, Australian Biochemical Soc. 1978, N.I. Vavilov Medal 1987, BHP Bicentennial Prize 1988, Burnet Medal, Australian Acad. of Science 1989, CSIRO Medal 1989, Farrer

Memorial Medal 1999, Prime Minister's Prize for Science 2000. *Publications:* 350 research papers on molecular biology, cytogenetics and evolution; ed. of six books. *Leisure interests:* bush-walking. *Address:* 16 Brassey Street, Deakin, ACT 2600, Australia (home). *Telephone:* (2) 6246-5250 (office); (2) 6281-4485 (home). *Fax:* (2) 6246-4866 (home). *E-mail:* jim.peacock@csiro.au (office).

PEACOCKE, Christopher Arthur Bruce, DPhil, FBA; British academic; *Professor of Philosophy, Columbia University;* b. 22 May 1950, Birmingham; s. of Arthur Peacocke and Rosemary Peacocke; m. Teresa Rosen 1980; one s. one d.; ed Magdalen Coll. School, Exeter Coll., Oxford and Harvard Univ. (Kennedy Scholar), USA; Sr Scholar, Merton Coll. Oxford 1972–73; Jr Research Fellow, Queen's Coll. Oxford 1973–76; Visiting Lecturer, Univ. of Calif., Berkeley 1975–76; Prize Fellow, All Souls Coll. Oxford 1975–79; Visiting Prof., Univ. of Mich. 1978; Fellow, New Coll., Oxford and Common Univ. Fund Lecturer in Philosophy, Univ. of Oxford 1979–85; Visiting Prof., UCLA 1981; Visiting Fellow, ANU, Canberra 1981, 1998; Fellow, Center for Advanced Study in Behavioural Sciences, Stanford 1983–84; Susan Stebbing Prof. of Philosophy, King's Coll. London 1985–88; Pres. Mind Asscn 1986; Waynflete Prof. of Metaphysical Philosophy, Univ. of Oxford and Fellow Magdalen Coll. Oxford 1989–2000; Leverhulme Research Professorship 1996–2000; Visiting Prof., New York Univ. 1996–2000, Prof. of Philosophy 2000–04; Prof. of Philosophy, Columbia Univ. 2004–; Richard Wollheim Chair of Philosophy, University Coll. London 2007–; Hon. DLit (Warwick) 2007; Wilde Prize 1971, Webb-Medley Prize 1971, John Locke Prize 1972; Whitehead Lecturer, Harvard Univ. 2001, Immanuel Kant Lecturer, Stanford Univ. 2003. *Publications:* Holistic Explanation: Action, Space, Interpretation 1979, Sense and Content 1983, Thoughts: An Essay on Content 1986, A Study of Concepts 1992, Being Known 1999, The Realm of Reason 2004, Truly Understood 2008; papers in Mind, Philosophical Review, Journal of Philosophy etc. *Leisure interests:* music, visual arts. *Address:* Department of Philosophy, MC 4971, Columbia University, 1150 Amsterdam Avenue, New York, NY 10027, USA (office). *Telephone:* (212) 854-3384 (office). *Fax:* (212) 854-4986 (office). *E-mail:* cp2161@columbia.edu (office). *Website:* www .columbia.edu/cu/philosophy/fac-bios/peacocke/faculty.html (office); www .columbia.edu/~cp2161/Online_Papers (office).

PEARCE, Sir (Daniel Norton) Idris, Kt, CBE, TD, DL, FRICS; British chartered surveyor; b. 28 Nov. 1933, Neath; s. of Lemeul George Douglas Pearce and Evelyn Mary Pearce; m. Ursula Helene Langley 1963 (divorced 1997); two d.; ed West Buckland School, Coll. of Estate Man.; joined Richard Ellis 1959, Partner 1961–92, Man. Partner 1981–87, Consultant 1992–2000; Chair. English Estates 1989–94; Chair. Higher Educ. Funding Council for Wales 1992–96; mem. Advisory Panel for Institutional Finance in New Towns 1974–80; mem. Property Services Agency Advisory Bd 1981–86; Property Adviser to Nat. Health Service Man. Bd 1985–90; mem. FCO Advisory Panel on Diplomatic Estate 1982–90, Financial Reporting Review Panel 1991–92, UFC 1991–93; Vice-Chair. Greater London TA & VRA 1991–94; mem. Gen. Council The Royal Inst. of Chartered Surveyors 1989–95, mem. Exec. Cttee 1984–91, Pres. 1990–91, Chair. Int. Assets Valuation Standards Cttee 1981–86; mem. Higher Educ. Funding Council for England 1992–96; Deputy Chair. Urban Regeneration Agency 1993–2000; Dir (non-exec.) Swan Hill 1993–2002, Nat. Mortgage Bank 1992–97, Innisfree Man. Ltd 1996–, Redburgh Ltd 1996–98, Millennium and Copthorne Hotels PLC 1996–; Gov. Peabody Trust 1992–2003; Pro-Chancellor Univ. of Surrey 1994–2003, Chair. Council 1997–2000, Pro-Chancellor Emer. 2003–; Hon. Fellow, Coll. of Estate Man., Univ. of Wales, Cardiff 1997; Hon. Col, 135 Independent Topographic Squadron Royal Engineers (V); Hon. DSc (City Univ., London, Salford, Oxford Polytechnic); Hon. DTechSc (Univ. of E London); Hon. DEng (Bristol, Univ. of W of England); Hon. DUniv (Surrey); Thames Polytechnic, Centenary Fellowship 1991. *Publications:* Profession of the Land – A Future; articles on valuation and property matters. *Leisure interests:* reading, opera, ballet, travel.

PEARCE, Reynold, MA; British fashion designer; ed Nottingham Trent Univ., Cen. St Martin's Coll. of Art and Design; worked for John Galliano (q.v.); design asst for Roland Klein; launched Pearce Fionda collection with Andrew Fionda (q.v.) 1994; with Andrew Fionda received British Apparel Export Award for Best New Designer 1994, New Generation Award Lloyds Bank British Fashion Award 1995, Int. Apparel Fed. World Young Designers Award 1996, Glamour Category Award (British Fashion Awards) 1997. *Address:* Pearce Fionda, The Loft, 27 Horsell Road, Highbury, London, N5 1XL, England. *Telephone:* (20) 7609-6470. *Fax:* (20) 7609-6470. *E-mail:* pearce@dircon.co.uk.

PEARL, Valerie Louise, DPhil, FRHistS, FSA; British professor of history and college president; b. 31 Dec. 1926, Newport, Mon.; d. of the late C. R. Bence, MP and F. Bowler; m. Morris L. Pearl 1949; one d.; ed King Edward VI High School, Birmingham and St Anne's Coll. Oxford; Sr Research Studentship, Westfield Coll. London 1962; Leverhulme Research Award 1962; Graham Research Fellow, lecturer in History, Somerville Coll. Oxford 1965–68; Reader in History of London, Univ. Coll. London 1968–76, Prof. 1976–81; Pres. New Hall, Cambridge 1981–1995; Founder and Ed.-in-Chief, The London Journal 1973–77; McBride Visiting Prof. Bryn Mawr Coll. Pennsylvania 1974; Woodward Lecturer, Yale Univ. 1974; Literary Dir Royal Historical Soc. 1975–77; Gov. Museum of London 1978–92; Stow Commemorative Lecturer 1979; Ford Special Lecturer, Oxford 1980; Syndic, Cambridge Univ. Library, Cambridge Univ. Press 1982–92; Commr Royal Comm. on Historical Manuscripts 1983–92; Hon. Fellow St Anne's Coll. Oxford 1992. *Publications:* London and the Outbreak of the Puritan Revolution 1625–43 1961, contrib. to The Interregnum; Puritans and Revolutionaries, co-ed. and contrib. to History and Imagination (vol. in honour of Hugh Trevor-Roper) 1981, Stow's Survey of

London (ed.) 1985, Change and Continuity in 17th-Century London 1981 (Japanese edn 1992); articles and contribs to books, encyclopedias and learned journals. *Leisure interests:* walking, gardening, swimming. *Address:* c/o New Hall, Cambridge, CB3 0DF, England. *Telephone:* (1223) 350709 (home); (1223) 351721.

PEARLSTEIN, Philip, MA; American artist; b. 24 May 1924, Pittsburgh; s. of David Pearlstein and Libbie Kalser; m. Dorothy Cantor 1950; one s. two d.; ed Carnegie Inst. of Tech. and New York Univ.; Instructor Pratt Inst. 1959–63; visiting critic, Yale 1962–63; Asst Prof. then Prof., Art Dept Brooklyn Coll. 1963–82, now Distinguished Prof. Emer.; participant in numerous group exhbns at Whitney Museum of American Art and elsewhere; work in perm. collections including Whitney Museum and Museum of Modern Art, New York; mem. American Acad. of Arts and Letters; Fulbright Fellow 1958–59; Guggenheim Fellow 1971–72. *Address:* c/o Forum Gallery, New York, 745 Fifth Avenue, New York, NY 10151, USA.

PEARLSTINE, Norman, LLB; American journalist and organization official; *President and CEO, The American Academy in Berlin; Chief Content Officer, Bloomberg L.P.;* b. 4 Oct. 1942, Philadelphia; s. of Raymond Pearlstine and Gladys Pearlstine (née Cohen); m. Nancy Colbert Friday 1988; ed Haverford Coll., Univ. of Pennsylvania; staff reporter, Wall Street Journal, Dallas, Detroit, LA 1968–73, Tokyo Bureau Chief 1973–76, Man. Ed. Asian Wall Street Journal, Hong Kong 1976–78; Exec. Ed. Forbes Magazine, LA 1978–80; Nat. News Ed. Wall Street Journal, New York 1980–82, Ed. and Publr Wall Street Journal Europe, Brussels 1982–83, Man. Ed. and Vice-Pres. Wall Street Journal, New York 1983–91, Exec. Ed. 1991–92; Pres. and CEO Friday Holdings L.P., New York 1993–94; Ed.-in-Chief Time Inc. 1995–2006, now Sr Advisor to Time Warner; Sr Advisor to global telecommunications and media team, The Carlyle Group 2006–; Pres. and CEO The American Acad. in Berlin 2007–; Chief Content Officer, Bloomberg L.P. 2008–; mem. New York Historical Soc., Council on Foreign Relations; Ed. of Year Award, Nat. Press Foundation 1989, American Soc. of Magazine Editors Lifetime Achievement Award. *Publication:* Off the Record 2007. *Address:* The American Academy in Berlin, Hans Arnhold Center, Am Sandwerder 17-19, 14109 Berlin, Germany (office); Bloomberg L.P., 731 Lexington Avenue, New York, NY 10022, USA (office). *Telephone:* (30) 804830 (Berlin) (office); (212) 318-2000 (New York) (office). *Fax:* (30) 80483111 (Berlin) (office); 917-369-5000 (New York) (office). *E-mail:* mailbox@americanacademy.de (office). *Website:* www.americanacademy.de (office); www.bloomberg.com (office).

PEARSE, Sir Brian, Kt, FCIB; British banker; b. 23 Aug. 1933; s. of Francis and Eileen Pearse; m. Patricia M. Callaghan 1959; one s. two d.; ed St Edward's Coll., Liverpool; joined Martin's Bank Ltd 1950; joined Barclays Bank 1969, Local Dir, Birmingham 1972, Gen. Man. 1977, CEO, N America 1983, Finance Dir Barclays Bank PLC 1987–91; Chief Exec. Midland Bank 1991–94; Pres. Chartered Inst. of Bankers 1993–94; Chair. Housing Corpn 1994–97, British Invisibles 1994–97, Lucas Industries PLC 1994–96, LucasVarity PLC 1996–98; Dir British American Chamber of Commerce 1987–98; Dir (non-exec.) Smith & Nephew 1993–; Dir British Overseas Trade Board 1994–97; Gov. Univ. of Plymouth 1997– (Vice-Chair. 1999–); Deputy Chair. Britannic Assurance PLC 1997–; mem. Bd of Banking Supervision 1998–. *Leisure interests:* rugby, opera. *Address:* Flat 7, 14 Gloucester Street, London, SW1V 2DN, England (home).

PEARSON, Ralph Gottfried, PhD; American chemist and academic; *Professor Emeritus of Chemistry, University of California, Santa Barbara;* b. 12 Jan. 1919, Chicago, Ill.; s. of Gottfried Pearson and Kerstin Pearson (née Larson); m. Lenore Johnson 1941 (died 1982); two s. one d.; ed Lewis Inst., Northwestern Univ.; First Lt USAF 1944–46; Asst Prof. Chem. Dept, Northwestern Univ. 1946–52, Assoc. Prof. 1952–57, Prof. 1957–76; Prof. of Chem. Univ. of Calif., Santa Barbara 1976–89, Prof. Emer. 1989–; mem. NAS 1974–; fmr Guggenheim Fellow; Inorganic Award, American Chemical Soc., Chemical Pioneer Award, American Inst. of Chemists 1995. *Publications:* Kinetics and Mechanism 1953, Mechanisms of Inorganic Reactions 1958, Hard and Soft Acids and Bases 1974, Symmetry Rules for Chemical Reactions 1976, Chemical Hardness 1997. *Leisure interest:* classical music. *Address:* c/o Chemistry Department, University of California, Santa Barbara, CA 93106 (office); 715 Grove Lane, Santa Barbara, CA 93105, USA (home). *Telephone:* (805) 893-3745 (office); (805) 687-7890 (home). *Fax:* (805) 893-4120 (office).

PEARSON, W. Robert, BA, LLB; American diplomatist; b. 28 June 1943; ed Vanderbilt Univ., Univ. of Virginia; served in USN Judge Advocate Gen.'s Corps 1969–73; posted to New Zealand 1976–78, China 1981–83, NATO, Brussels 1987–90, 1993–97, Paris 1997–2000; Amb. to Turkey 2000–03; Deputy Exec. Sec. Nat. Security Council 1985–87; Exec. Sec. Dept of State 1991–93, Dir-Gen. Foreign Service and Dir Human Resources 2003–06 (retd); mem. IISS, London. *Leisure interest:* golf. *Address:* c/o US Department of State, 2201 C Street, NW, Washington, DC 20520, USA (office).

PEART, Sir (William) Stanley, Kt, MB, BS, MD, FRCP, FRS; British academic and physician; *Professor Emeritus of Medicine, St Mary's Hospital, London;* b. 31 March 1922, South Shields; s. of J. G. Peart and M. Peart; m. Peggy Parkes 1947 (died 2002); one s. one d.; ed King's Coll. School, Wimbledon and St Mary's Hosp. Medical School, London; Lecturer in Medicine, St Mary's Hosp., London 1950–56, Prof. of Medicine 1956–87, Prof. Emer. 1987–; Master, Hunterian Inst. Royal Coll. of Surgeons 1988–92; Chair. Medical Research Soc. 1968, Beit Trust Advisory Bd 1980, Northwick Park Inst. for Medical Research 1994–; mem. Medical Research Council 1969; mem. Advisory Bd for the Research Councils 1973; Trustee Wellcome Trust 1975–94 (Deputy Chair. 1991–94, Consultant 1994–99); Councillor, Royal Coll. of Physicians 1977; Stouffer Prize 1968, Buchanan Medal, Royal Soc. 2000. *Publications:* Clinical Atlas of Hypertension 1991; articles in The Biochemical Journal, Journal of Physiology, The Lancet; chapters in textbooks on renal disease and high blood pressure. *Leisure interests:* reading, photography, astronomy. *Address:* 17 Highgate Close, London, N6 4SD, England (home). *Telephone:* (20) 8341-3111 (home). *E-mail:* stanleypeart@aol.com (home).

PÉBEREAU, Georges Alexandre; French engineer and business executive; b. 20 July 1931, Digne, Basses-Alpes; s. of Alexandre Pébereau and Yvonne Raybaud; m. Bernadette Potier 1954; three d.; ed Lycées Buffon, Saint-Louis, Paris, Ecole Polytechnique; engineer of roads and bridges in various wards 1955–64; Pres. Asscn des ingénieurs des ponts et chaussées 1964; teacher of Urban Man. École nat. des ponts et chaussées 1964; Chief-Eng, Dept Seine-St-Denis 1965, Tech. Counsellor to Ministry of Equipment 1966, Dir Office Ministry of Equipment and Housing 1967–68; Dir Land and Urban Man. 1966–68; Vice-Pres. Cttee action concertée Urbanisation 1967–68; at Cie industrielle des télécommunications (Cit) 1968–70, Jt Dir-Gen. 1968–69, Dir-Gen. 1969–70; Admin.-Dir-Gen. Cie industrielle des télécommunications (Cit-Alcatel) 1970–83, Pres., Dir-Gen. 1982–86, Hon. Pres. 1986–; at Cie Gén d'électricité 1970–86, Dir then Jt Dir-Gen. 1970–72, Admin. 1971, Dir-Gen. 1972, then Chair., Pres. and CEO Admin., Dir –1986; Hon. Pres. 1986; Co-owner Cie Privée de Banque 1987; Founder and Chair. Marceau Investissements 1997–, Indra Finance 1987–95; Pres. Délia Finance 1997–; mem. Cttee de direction et de conseil d'admin 1970–; mem. conseil d'admin de la Soc. des sucreries de Bourbon 1995–, of Musée du Louvre 1996; Commdr Légion d'honneur, Commdr, Ordre nat. du Mérite. *Address:* Marceau Investissements, 10–12 Avenue de Mesine, 75008 Paris (office); 19 avenue Charles Floquet, 75007 Paris, France (home). *Telephone:* 1-40-74-25-06 (office). *Fax:* 1-40-74-25-10 (office). *E-mail:* contact@marceau-finance.fr (office). *Website:* www.marceau-finance.fr (office).

PÉBEREAU, Michel Jean Denis; French banker; *Chairman, BNP Paribas;* b. 23 Jan. 1942, Paris; s. of Alexandre Pébereau and Yvonne Raybaud; m. Agnès Faure 1962; two s. two d.; ed Lycées Buffon and Louis-le-Grand, Paris, Ecole Polytechnique and Ecole Nat. d'Admin; various appointments in Ministry of Economy and Finance 1970–81; Man. Dir Crédit Commercial de France 1982–87, Chair. and CEO 1987–93; Chair. and CEO Banque Nationale de Paris (BNP) 1993–2000; apptd Chair. Paribas 1999, Chair. BNP Paribas 2006–; Dir BNP, Cie Européenne de Publication, SA des Galeries Lafayette, Lafarge Coppée, Saint-Gobain, Lagardère Groupe, Rhône Poulenc, Elf, UAP, Renault, Financière BNP, Cie d'Investissements de Paris, Banque Pour l'Expansion Industrielle, BNP UK Holdings Ltd; Chair. Banking Operations Comm. of Asscn Française des Banques; Deputy Chair. Comm. for Control of Cinema Films 1981–85, Comm. for Selective Aid for Film Distribution 1987–88; Lecturer, Inst. d'Etudes Politiques Paris 1967–78, Prof. 1980–, mem. Man. Cttee 1984–; Lecturer, Ecole Nat. de Statistiques et d'Admin Economique 1968–79; Inspecteur Général des Finances; mem. Supervisory Bd Axa-UAP 1997–, Dresdner Bank 1997–; mem. Int. Capital Markets Advisory Cttee Fed. Reserve Bank, New York 1998; Pres. Comm. d'exploitation bancaire de l'Asscn française des banques 2000; Commdr, Légion d'honneur; Commdr, Ordre nat. du Mérite. *Publications:* La politique économique de la France (3 vols); science fiction book reviews for scientific magazine La Recherche 1983–. *Leisure interest:* piano. *Address:* BNP Paribas, 3 rue d'Antin, 75002 Paris (office); 40 rue du Bac, 75007 Paris, France. *Telephone:* 1-40-14-45-46 (office). *Fax:* 1-55-77-50-51 (office). *Website:* www.bnpparibas.com (office).

PECCERELLI, Fredy, BA; Guatemalan forensic anthropologist; *Executive Director, Guatemalan Forensic Anthropology Foundation;* b. 1971; m.; several c.; ed Brooklyn Coll., City Univ. of New York, USA and Univ. of Bournemouth, UK; went into exile with his family to New York aged nine; led forensic archeological investgations of war crimes in Bosnia and Herzegovina for Int. Criminal Tribunal for the Fmr Yugoslavia; founding mem. Fundación de Antropología Forense de Guatemala (FAFG–Guatemalan Forensic Anthropology Foundation) 1996, responsible for investigating human right's abuses committed during 36-year civil war, now Exec. Dir FAFG; currently studying for MSc degree in UK; chosen by Time magazine as one of 50 Latin American Leaders for the New Millennium 1999, named by Guatemalan Youth Comm. an Icon for Youth of Guatemala 1999. *Address:* c/o AAAS Science and Human Rights Program, 1200 New York Avenue, NW, Washington, DC 20005, USA (office).

PECKER, David J., CPA; American publishing executive; *Chairman and CEO, American Media, Inc.;* b. 24 Sept. 1951; m. Karen Balan 1987; ed Pace and New York Univs; fmrly Sr Auditor Price Waterhouse & Co.; fmrly Man. Financial Reporting Diamandis Communications Inc., also Dir Financial Reporting, Dir Accounting, Asst Controller; Exec. Vice-Pres. Hachette Magazines Inc. 1990–91, Pres. 1991–92, Pres., CEO 1992–99, Chair. and CEO American Media Inc. 1999–; mem. Fashion Group's Int. Advisory Bd, NY City Partnership Cttee, American Man. Asscn; mem. Bd Dirs Pace Univ., Drug Enforcement Agents Foundation 1995–. *Address:* American Media Inc., 1000 American Media Way, Boca Raton, FL 33431-1000, USA (office). *Telephone:* (561) 997-7733 (office). *Fax:* (561) 272-8411 (office). *Website:* www.nationalenquirer.com (office).

PECKER, Jean-Claude, (Jean-Claude Pradel); French astronomer; *Honorary Professor, Collège de France;* b. 10 May 1923, Reims; s. of Victor-Noel Pecker and Nelly Catherine Herrmann; m. 2nd Annie A. Vormser 1974 (died 2002); one s. two d. (by previous m.); ed Lycée de Bordeaux, Univs of Grenoble and Paris (Sorbonne) and Ecole Normale Supérieure; Research Asst, CNRS 1946–52; Assoc. Prof., Univ. of Clermont-Ferrand 1952–55; Assoc. Astronomer, Paris Observatory 1955–62, Astronomer 1962–65; Dir Nice Observatory 1962–69; Dir Inst. of Astrophysics, Paris 1972–79; Prof., Coll. de France 1963–89, Hon. Prof. 1989–; Asst Gen. Sec. Int. Astronomical Union 1961–63, Gen. Sec. 1964–67; Pres. Comité Nat. Français d'Astronomie 1970–73; Dir

Inst. Astrophysique, Paris 1971–78; Pres. Soc. Astronomique de France 1973–76; Pres. French Asscn for Advancement of Science 1978; Chair. Orientation Cttee, Sciences-Industries Museum, La Villette 1983–85; Chair. Nat. Cttee Scientific and Tech. Culture 1985–87; Vice-Chair. French Comm. for UNESCO 1991–96; Perm. Rep. to UNESCO of Int. Humanist and Ethical Union; Vice-Chair. Scientific Cttee Musées de France 1988–; Pres. Asscn française d'information scientifique 1999–2001; Assoc. Royal Soc. of Science, Liège 1967; Corresp., Bureau des Longitudes 1968; Assoc. Royal Astronomical Soc. 1968; Corresp. mem. Acad. des Sciences, France 1969, mem. 1977; mem. Acad. Nat. Bordeaux 1977, Acad. Royale Belgique 1979, Acad. European of Science, Arts and Letters 1982, Int. Acad. of Humanism 1983 (Sec.), Acad. Europaea 1988 (Council mem., Vice-Pres. 1989–92; Commdr, Légion d'honneur, des Palmes académiques, Grand Croix, Ordre nat. du Mérite; Prix Forthuny, Inst. de France, Prix Stroobant Acad. des Sciences de Belgique 1965, Prix Manley-Bendall de l'Acad. de Bordeaux 1966, Prix des Trois Physiciens 1969, Janssen Medal Astronomical Soc., France 1967, Prix Jean Perrin, Soc. Française de Physique 1973, Medal Univ. de Nice 1972, Adion Medal 1981, Prix Union Rationaliste 1983, Personnalité de l'année 1984, Janssen Medal, Photographic Soc. of France 1989, Lodén Prize, Royal Astronomical Soc. of Sweden 1996. *Radio includes:* many programmes on popular astronomy 1957–. *Television includes:* many programmes on popular science. *Publications include:* L'astronomie au jour le jour (with P. Couderc and E. Schatzman) 1954, Astrophysique générale (with E. Schatzman) 1959, Le ciel 1959, L'astronomie expérimentale 1969, Les laboratoires spatiaux 1969, Papa, dis-moi: L'astronomie, qu'est-ce que c'est? 1971, L'astronomie nouvelle (ed.) 1971, Clefs pour l'astronomie 1981, Sous l'étoile soleil 1984, Astronomie (ed.) 1985, Pour comprendre l'univers (with Delsemme and Reeves) 1988, L'avenir du soleil 1990, Le promeneur du ciel 1992, Le soleil est une étoile 1992, Débat sur les phénomènes paranormaux 1997, Understanding the Universe 2001, L'Univers exploré, peu à peu expliqué 2003, La photographie astronomique 2003, Lalanduana I (with S. Dumont) 2007. *Leisure interests:* painting, poetry, swimming. *Address:* Annexe du Collège de France, 3 rue d'Ulm, 75005 Paris (office); Pusat-Tasek, Les Corbeaux, 85350 L'Ile d'Yeu, France (home). *Telephone:* 1-44-27-16-95 (office); 2-51-58-58-27 (home). *E-mail:* j.c.pecker@wanadoo.fr (home).

PECKHAM, Sir Michael John, Kt, MA, MD, FRCP, FRCPath, FRCR, FRCS; British physician and academic; b. 2 Aug. 1935, Panteg, Wales; s. of William Stuart Peckham and Gladys Mary Peckham (née Harris); m. Catherine Stevenson King 1958; three s.; ed St Catharine's Coll. Cambridge, Univ. Coll. Hosp. Medical School; Sr Lecturer, Inst. of Cancer Research 1972–74, Prof. and Hon. Consultant, Inst. of Cancer Research and Royal Marsden Hosp. 1974–86, Dean Inst. of Cancer Research 1984–86; Dir British Post grad. Medical Fed. 1986–90; Ed.-in-Chief European Journal of Cancer 1990–95; Dir of Research and Devt, Dept of Health 1991–95; Dir School of Public Policy, Univ. Coll. London 1996–2000; Vice-Chair. Imperial Cancer Research Fund 1987–90; Chair. Office of Science and Tech. Healthcare Foresight Programme 1999–2000, Nat. Educational Research Forum 2000, Devt Forum 2000; Founding Pres. British Oncological Asscn 1986–88; Pres. Fed. of European Cancer Socs 1989–91, European Soc. for Therapeutic Radiology and Oncology 1983–85; Foreign Assoc. mem. NAS Inst. of Medicine 1994–; Hon. Fellow, St Catharine's Coll., Cambridge 1998; Dr hc (Besançon), (Catholic Univ. of Louvain) 1993; Hon. DSc (Loughborough), (Exeter) 1996. *Publications:* Oxford Textbook of Oncology (co-author) 1995, Clinical Futures 1999, A Model for Health: Innovation and the Future of Health Services 2000. *Address:* 6 Crescent Place, London, SW3 2EA, England (home). *E-mail:* michael.peckham@yahoo.com (home).

PECKOVÁ, Dagmar; Czech singer (mezzo-soprano); b. 4 April 1961, Chrudim; m. 1st J. Vejvoda; m. 2nd Aleš Kaspřík 1997; one s.; m. 3rd Klaus Schiesser; one d.; ed Prague Conservatory; soloist at Karlín Musical Theatre, Prague 1982–85; soloist with numerous cos including Czech Philharmonic 1985–, with Semper Opera, Dresden 1985–88, with State Opera Berlin 1989–92; guest appearances in Tokyo, Paris 1992, Bregenz Festival, Austria 1992, 1993, Hamburg 1993, Salzburg Festival 1993, 1995, 1996, Basel 1994, Zürich 1994, London 1995, Tel-Aviv 1996, La Corona Festival, Spain 1996, San Sebastien Festival, Spain 1996, Prague Spring Festival 1996, Frankfurt 1996; concert tours Austria, Switzerland, Germany, UK 1993, France, Japan 1990, 1994, USA 1997–99; charity concerts after floods in Czech Repub. 2002; roles include Leonora (Basel), Cherubino in The Marriage of Figaro (London), Rosina in The Barber of Seville (Berlin, Dresden), Carmen (Prague), Varvara in Katya Kabanova (Salzburg, Barcelona); First Prize, Antonin Dvořák Competition 1982, Second Prize, Brno Vocal Competition 1985, Czech Music Fund Award (for role of Liza Doolittle in My Fair Lady) 1985, First Prize, Prague Spring Vocal Competition 1986, Berlin Critics' Prize (for role of Dorabella in Così fan tutte) 1989, European Foundation for Music Prize 1993, Thalia Prize (for Carmen) 2000. *Recordings include:* Martinů—Nipponari 1991, Mozart—Che Bella 1994, Janáček—Moravian Folk Poetry in Song 1994, Mahler—Adagietto, Kindertotenlieder 1996, Songs of Mahler and Berio 1997, Janáček—Kátă Kabanová 1997, Janáček—Diary of One Who Disappeared 1999, recital of music by Wagner, Schoenberg, Zemlinsky and Brahms 2000, Lieder by Strauss, Schoeck, Berg 2001, Lieder by Dvořák 2001, Arias (live) 2002. *Leisure interests:* reading, driving. *Address:* c/o Supraphon Music a. s., Palackého 1 / 740, 112 99 Prague; Okrouhlo 45, 254 01 Prague, Czech Republic (office). *E-mail:* yaga@telecom.cz (office).

PECRESSE, Valerie; French politician; *Minister of Higher Education and Research;* m.; two s. one d.; ed Haute École de Commerce, École Nat. d'Admin; auditor, Conseil d'État 1992–98; adviser, French Presidency 1998; currently Deputy for Yvelines, Nat. Ass., mem. Comm. on Cultural, Family and Social Affairs, Rapporteur, Mission of Information on the Family and the Rights of Children, Pres. Study Group on the Applications of Biotechnologies in Genetics and Ethical Problems, Vice-Pres. Study Group on the Internet, Information Technologies and of Communication and e-Commerce, mem. Del. on the Rights of Women and Gender Equality, Organizer, Union pour un Mouvement Populaire (UMP) Working Group on the Family; Spokesman for UMP; Councillor, Île-de-France; Minister of Higher Educ. and Research 2007–. *Address:* Ministry of Higher Education and Research, 1 rue Descartes. 75231 Paris Cedex 05, France (office). *Telephone:* 1-55-55-90-90 (office). *E-mail:* secretariat-communication@recherche.gouv.fr (office). *Website:* www.enseignementsup-recherche.gouv.fr (office); www.valeriepecresse.net.

PEDDER, Anthony P. (Tony), MSc; British company director and fmr steel industry executive; *Chairman, Sheffield Forgemasters International Ltd;* b. 1949; m.; two. s.; ed London Univ.; joined steel industry 1972; several sr man. positions in British Steel (now Corus), Man. Dir Stainless Steel business 1986, Man. Dir Gen. Steels business 1989, Head of procurement and logistics operations 1991, mem. bd British Steel 1992, mem. bd Corus Group (after merger with British Steel) 1999, CEO 2001–03; Chair. Sheffield Forgemasters Int. Ltd 2005–; mem. Bd of Dirs (non-exec.) Sheperd Group Ltd 2004–, Metalysis Ltd 2005–, JSW Ltd 2005–, Bone Group Ltd 2006–, Hatch Corporate Finance Ltd 2006–; Chair. Sheffield NHS Primary Care Trust 2006–; Deputy Lt, South Yorkshire 2007. *Address:* Sheffield Forgemasters International Ltd, POB 286, Brightside Lane, Sheffield, S9 2RW, England (office). *Website:* www.sheffieldforgemasters.com (office).

PEDERSEN, Helga; Norwegian politician; *Minister of Fisheries and Coastal Affairs;* b. 13 Jan. 1973; ed Univ. of Tromsø, Univ. of Bergen; teacher, Boftsa School, Tana 1992–93; Civil Servant, Econ. Devt and Transport Dept, Finnmark County 1998–2000, County Council Rep. 1999–2005, Chair. County Council 2003–05; Political Adviser to Minister of Trade and Industry 2001; part-time project worker, UNEP/GRID, Arendal 2001–02; Head of Project to Promote Econ. and Cultural Devt, Tanafjord Area 2002–03; Minister of Fisheries and Coastal Affairs 2005–; mem. Det norske Arbeiderparti (Norwegian Labour Party). *Address:* Ministry of Fisheries and Coastal Affairs, Grubbegt. 1, POB 8118 Dep., 0032 Oslo, Norway (office). *Telephone:* 22-24-90-90 (office). *Fax:* 22-24-95-85 (office). *E-mail:* postmottak@fkd.dep.no (office). *Website:* www.odin.dep.no/fkd (office).

PEDERSEN, K. George, OC, PhD,; Canadian professor and university president (retd); b. 13 June 1931, Peace River, Alberta; s. of Hjalmar Pedersen and Anna Jensen; m. 1st Joan Vanderwarher 1953 (died 1988), 2nd Penny Jones 1988; one s. one d.; ed Chilliwack Sr High School and Univs of BC, Washington and Chicago; school teacher, N Vancouver school system 1952–56; Vice-Prin., North Star Elementary School 1956–59; Prin. Carisbrooke Elementary School 1959–61; Vice-Prin., Handsworth Secondary School 1961–63; Prin., Balmoral Secondary School 1963–65; Research Assoc. Univ. of Chicago 1965–68; Asst Prof. Ont. Inst. for Studies in Educ. and Univ. of Toronto 1968–70; Assoc. Dir Midwest Admin. Center, Univ. of Chicago 1970–72; Dean, Faculty of Educ. Univ. of Vic. 1972–75, Vice-Pres. (Academic) 1975–78; Pres. and Vice-Chancellor Simon Fraser Univ. 1979–83, Univ. of BC 1983–85, Univ. of Western Ont. 1985–94, Univ. of Northern BC 1995–2004, Royal Roads Univ. 1995–96; Chancellor Univ. of Northern BC 1998–2004; Fellow, Canadian Coll. of Teachers, Royal Soc. for Encouragement of Arts; Univ. of Chicago Scholarships 1965–68, Canada Council Scholarships 1966–68; Ford Foundation Fellowship 1967–68; Hon. LLD (McMaster) 1996, (Simon Fraser Univ.) 2003; Hon. DLitt (Emily Carr Inst. of Art and Design) 2003; Commemorative Medal 1992, Order of Canada 1993, Queen's Jubilee Medal 2002, Order of Ontario 1994, Order of British Columbia 2002. *Publications:* The Itinerant Schoolmaster 1973; book chapters and numerous articles. *Leisure interests:* fishing, golf, gardening, cooking, carving. *Address:* 2232 Spruce Street, Vancouver, BC, V6H 2P3, Canada. *Telephone:* (604) 733-2400. *Fax:* (604) 733-2430. *E-mail:* pedersen@sfu.ca (home).

PEDERSEN, Roger A., PhD; American embryologist and academic; *Professor of Regenerative Medicine, Department of Surgery, School of Clinical Medicine and Director, Cambridge Stem Cell Institute, University of Cambridge;* Prof., Univ. of California, San Francisco –2001, Prof. Emer. 2001–; Prof. of Regenerative Medicine, Dept of Surgery, Univ. of Cambridge School of Clinical Medicine 2001–, Dir Cambridge Stem Cell Inst. (fmrly Cambridge Centre for Stem Cell Biology and Medicine) 2004–, Prin. Collaborator, Cambridge Inst. of Medical Research 2004–. *Publications:* Experimental Approaches to Mammalian Embryonic Development 1988, Current Topics in Developmental Biology 1998, Embryonic Stem Cells for Medicine: A Scientific American article 2002, Handbook of Stem Cells –Vol. 1: Embryonic Stem Cells, Vol. 2: Adult and Fetal Stem Cells 2004; numerous articles in medical and scientific journals on stem cell research. *Address:* Cambridge Stem Cell Institute, University of Cambridge, Cambridge, CB2 2XY (office); University of Cambridge School of Clinical Medicine, Department of Surgery, Box 202, Level 9, Addenbrooke's Hospital, Hills Road, Cambridge, CB2 2QQ, England (office). *Telephone:* (1223) 763236 (Inst.) (office); (1223) 336978 (Addenbrooke's) (office). *Fax:* (1223) 410772 (Addenbrooke's (office). *E-mail:* ralp2@cam.ac.uk (office). *Website:* stemcells.cimr.cam.ac.uk (office); www.medschl.cam.ac.uk (office).

PEDERSEN, Thor; Danish politician; *President of the Folketing;* b. 14 June 1945, Gentofte; s. of Laurits Pedersen; ed Copenhagen Univ.; fmr mem. staff, Assessments Div.; fmr Man. Dir of a construction co., North Zealand; fmr Mayor of Helsinge; mem. Folketing (Parl.) 1985–, Pres. 2007–; Minister of Housing 1986–87, of the Interior 1987–93, of Nordic Affairs 1988, of Econ. Affairs 1992–93, of Finance 2001–07. *Address:* Graudebjerggaard, Nakke Øst Vej 49, 4500 Nykøbing Sjælland, Denmark (office). *E-mail:* thor.pedersen@ft.dk (office). *Website:* www.folketinget.dk (office).

PEDLEY, Timothy John, ScD, FRS; British academic; *G. I. Taylor Professor of Fluid Mechanics, University of Cambridge;* b. 23 March 1942, Leicester; s. of Richard Rodman Pedley and Jeanie Mary Mudie Pedley; m. Avril Jennifer Martin Uden 1965; two s.; ed Rugby School, Trinity Coll., Cambridge; Postdoctoral Fellow, Johns Hopkins Univ., USA 1966–68; Research Assoc. and lecturer, Imperial Coll. London 1968–73; Lecturer, Dept of Applied Math. and Theoretical Physics, Univ. of Cambridge 1973–89, Reader in Biological Fluid Dynamics 1989, G. I. Taylor Prof. of Fluid Mechanics 1996–, Head, Dept of Applied Math. and Theoretical Physics 2000–05; Fellow, Gonville & Caius Coll. Cambridge 1973–89, 1996–; Prof. of Applied Math., Univ. of Leeds 1990–96; Ed. Journal of Fluid Mechanics 2000–; Foreign Assoc. Nat. Acad. of Eng (USA) 1999–; Pres. Inst. of Math. and its Applications 2004–05; Chair. World Council for Biomechanics 2002–; Fellow, American Inst. of Medical and Biological Eng 2001, American Physical Soc. 2005; Adams Prize, Univ. of Cambridge 1977. *Publications:* The Mechanics of the Circulation (co-author) 1978, Scale Effects in Animal Locomotion (ed.) 1977, The Fluid Mechanics of Large Blood Vessels 1980, Biological Fluid Dynamics (co-ed.) 1995. *Leisure interests:* bird-watching, running, reading. *Address:* Department of Applied Mathematics and Theoretical Physics (DAMTP), Centre for Mathematical Sciences, University of Cambridge, Wilberforce Road, Cambridge, CB3 0WA (office); Oakhurst Farm, 375 Shadwell Lane, Leeds, LS17 8AH, England (home). *Telephone:* (1223) 339842 (office); (113) 266-2854 (home). *Fax:* (1223) 760497 (office). *E-mail:* t.j.pedley@damtp.cam.ac.uk (office). *Website:* www.damtp.cam.ac.uk (office).

PEDNYCYA, Kazys; Lithuanian lawyer; b. 16 Nov. 1949, Plaskunai, Kaisiadoriai Region, Lithuania; m. Viktorija Pednycienė; two s.; ed Vilnius State Univ.; interrogator, Kedainai Regional Public Prosecutor's Office 1972–76; Asst Public Prosecutor, Panevezys City 1976–84; Supervision Prosecutor, Lithuanian Repub. Reformatories 1984–91; Judge, Lithuanian Repub. Supreme Court 1991–92; Sr Customs Official, Lithuanian Repub. 1992–93; Asst Dir-Gen. Lithuanian Nat. Security Dept 1993–97; Gen. Public Prosecutor 1997–2001. *Address:* Justiniskiu 36-20, 2000 Vilnius, Lithuania (home). *Telephone:* (2) 22-83-38 (home).

PEDRAZA RODRÍGUEZ, Lina, BSc; Cuban politician; *Minister of Finance and Pricing;* Deputy, Nat. Ass. of People's Power; mem. Central Cttee, Communist Party of Cuba, Head of Econs Div. 2006–09; mem. Communist Party Secr. 2006–09; Minister of Auditing and Control 2001–06, of Finance and Planning 2009–. *Address:* Ministry of Finance and Prices, Calle Obispo 211, esq. Cuba, Habana Vieja, Havana, Cuba (office). *Telephone:* (7) 867-1920 (office). *Fax:* (7) 33-8050 (office). *E-mail:* bhcifip@mfp.gov.cu (office). *Website:* www.mfp.cu (office).

PEDROSO, Ivan; Cuban athlete; b. 17 Dec. 1972, Havana; long jumper; gold medallist, World Indoor Championships 1993, 1995, 1997, 1999, 2001; gold medallist, 1995, 1997, 1999, 2001; gold medallist, Olympic Games 2000; voted Best Cuban Sportsman 1998. *Address:* c/o Cubadeportes SA, 710 Calle 20 no. 710 e/ 7ma y 9na, Miramar, Havana, Cuba.

PEEBLES, Phillip James E., BS, PhD, FRS, FRSC; American (b. Canadian) cosmologist and academic; *Albert Einstein Professor Emeritus of Science, Princeton University;* b. 25 April 1935, Winnipeg, Man.; m. Alison Peebles; one s. two d.; ed Univ. of Manitoba, Princeton Univ.; Instructor, Princeton Univ. 1961–62, Research Assoc. 1962–64, Research Staff mem. 1964–65, faculty mem. Physics Dept 1965–, Asst Prof. to Prof. 1965–84, Albert Einstein Prof. of Science 1984–2000, Albert Einstein Prof. Emer. of Science 2000–; Fellow, American Acad. of Arts and Sciences, American Physical Soc., American Philosophical Soc.; mem. NAS (Foreign Assen), American Astronomical Soc., AAAS, Int. Astronomical Union; Hon. DSc (Toronto) 1986, (Chicago) 1986, (McMaster) 1989, (Manitoba) 1989, (Newcastle-upon-Tyne, Catholic Univ. of Louvain); numerous hon. lectureships including Henry Norris Russell Lectureship (American Astronomical Soc.), Silliman Lectureship (Yale Univ.), de Vaucouleurs Lectureship (Univ. of TX), Jansky Lectureship (Nat. Radio Astronomy Observatory, NRAO), Feshbach Lectureship (MIT), McPherson Lectureship (McGill Univ.), Klein Lectureship (Univ. of Stockholm); Danz Prof., Univ. of Washington; New York Acad. of Sciences A.C. Morrison Award in Nat. Science 1977, Royal Astronomical Soc. Eddington Medal 1981, Gold Medal 1998, American Astronomical Soc. Heineman Prize 1982, Univ. of Newcastle Robinson Prize, Astronomical Soc. of the Pacific Bruce Medal 1995, Université catholique de Louvain Lemaitre Award, Peter Gruber Foundation Cosmology Prize 2000, ADION Medal (France) 2003, Shaw Prize in Astronomy (Hong Kong) 2004, Royal Swedish Acad. of Sciences Crafoord Prize 2005. *Publications:* Physical Cosmology 1971; numerous scientific papers in professional journals. *Leisure interest:* gardening. *Address:* Department of Physics, Princeton University, 216 Jadwin Hall, Princeton, NJ 08544-0001, USA (office). *Telephone:* (609) 258-4386 (office). *Fax:* (609) 258-6853 (office). *E-mail:* pjep@princeton.edu (office); pjep@pupgg.princeton.edu (office). *Website:* www.phy.princeton.edu/cosmology (office); www.physics.princeton.edu (office).

PEERS, Most Rev. Michael Geoffrey, BA, zert.dolm., LTh; Canadian ecclesiastic (retd); b. 31 July 1934, Vancouver, BC; s. of Geoffrey H. Peers and Dorothy E. Mantle; m. Dorothy E. Bradley 1963; two s. one d.; ed Univs of British Columbia and Heidelberg and Trinity Coll. Toronto; ordained priest 1960; Curate, Ottawa 1959–65; Univ. Chaplain, Diocese of Ottawa 1961–66; Rector, St Bede's, Winnipeg 1966–72, St Martin's, Winnipeg with St Paul's Middlechurch 1972–74; Archdeacon of Winnipeg 1969–74; Rector, St Paul's Cathedral, Regina 1974–77; Dean of Qu'Appelle 1974–77; Bishop of Qu'Appelle 1977–82; Archbishop of Qu'Appelle and Metropolitan of Rupert's Land 1982–86; Primate, Anglican Church of Canada 1986–2004; Ecumenist-in-Residence, Toronto School of Theology 2004–06; mem. Cen. Cttee World Council of Churches (WCC) 1991–98, Jt Standing Cttee of Anglican Communion 1994–2003, WCC Special Comm. on relations with Orthodox Churches 1999–2006; Hon. DD (Trinity Coll. Toronto) 1978, (Wycliffe Coll. Toronto) 1981, (St John's Coll. Winnipeg) 1981, (Univ. of Kent) 1988, (Montreal Diocesan Coll.) 1989, (Coll. of Emmanuel and St Chad, Saskatoon) 1990, (Thorneloe Univ. Sudbury) 1993, (Huron Coll., London, Ont.) 1998, (Huron Univ. Coll.) 1998, (Lutheran Theological Seminary Saskatoon) 2001, (Episcopal Divinity School, Cambridge USA) 2004; Hon. DCL (Bishop's Univ., Lennoxville) 1993. *Publications:* Grace Notes: Journeying with the Primate 1995–2004 2005. *Address:* 195 Westminster Avenue, Toronto, Ont., M6R 1N9, Canada. *Telephone:* (416) 531-8958. *E-mail:* mpeers@sympatico.ca.

PEERTHUM, Satteeanund; Mauritian diplomatist; b. 15 March 1941; m.; three c.; ed People's Friendship Univ., Moscow; Sr Research Fellow Inst. of Oriental Studies, Moscow 1973–74; Head History Dept, Bhojoharry Coll., Mauritius several times between 1975 and 1987; Sr Research Fellow School of Mauritian Asian and African Studies, Mahatma Gandhi Inst. 1985–87; Founding mem. Mouvement Socialiste Militant; mem. Mauritian Parl. and Minister of Labour and Industrial Relations 1982–83; Chair. Sugar Industry Devt Fund Boards of Mauritius 1984–87; Perm. Rep. to UN 1987–96; Chair. Nat. Steering Cttee for the Teaching of Mauritian History; mem. Advisory Cttee African Cultural Centre of Mauritius 1986–87; fmr mem. Court Nat. Univ. of Mauritius. *Address:* c/o Ministry of Foreign Affairs, International and Regional Co-operation, Level 5, New Government Centre, Port Louis, Mauritius.

PEFANIS, Harry N.; American petroleum industry executive; *President and Chief Operating Officer, Plains All American Pipeline LP;* b. 1957, Buffalo, NY; ed Univ. of Oklahoma; has worked with Plains All American Pipeline LP and its predecessors since 1983, Special Asst for Corp. Planning, Plains Resources 1983–87, Products Marketing Man. 1987–88, Vice-Pres. Products Marketing 1988–96, Sr Vice-Pres. 1996–98, Exec. Vice-Pres., Midstream of Plains Resources 1998–2001, Pres. and COO Plains All American Pipeline LP 1998–; mem. Bd of Dirs PAA/Vulcan. *Address:* Plains All American Pipeline LP, 333 Clay Street, Suite 1600, Houston, TX 77002, USA (office). *Telephone:* (713) 646-4100 (office). *Fax:* (713) 646-4572 (office). *E-mail:* info@paalp.com (office). *Website:* www.paalp.com (office).

PEI, I(eoh) M(ing), MArch, FAIA, RIBA; American architect; b. 26 April 1917, Canton, China; s. of Tsu Yee Pei and Lien Kwun Chwong; m. Eileen Loo 1942; three s. one d.; ed Shanghai, MIT and Harvard Univ.; moved to USA 1935–; naturalized citizen 1954; est. architectural practice 1939; Nat. Defense Research Cttee 1943–45; Asst Prof. Harvard Graduate School of Design 1945–48; Webb and Knapp Inc. 1948–55, Pei, Cobb, Freed & Pnrs (fmrly I. M. Pei & Pnrs) 1955–90; Wheelwright Traveling Fellowship, Harvard Univ. 1951; MIT Traveling Fellowship 1940; Fellow AIA; mem. Nat. Council on the Humanities 1966–70, American Acad. of Arts and Sciences, Nat. Acad. of Design, American Acad. of Arts and Letters (Chancellor 1978–80), Nat. Council on the Arts 1981–84, RIBA, Urban Design Council (New York), Corpn of MIT 1972–77, 1978–83, American Philosophical Soc., Institut de France (Foreign Assoc.); Commdr, Ordre des Arts et des Lettres, Officier, Légion d'honneur 1988; Hon. DFA (Pennsylvania) 1970, (Rensselaer Polytechnic Inst.) 1978, (Northeastern Univ.) 1979, (Univs of Mass., Rochester, Brown) 1982, (New York Univ.) 1983; Hon. LLD (Chinese Univ. of Hong Kong) 1970, Hon. DHL (Columbia Univ., Univs of Colorado, Rochester, Hong Kong, American Univ. of Paris); Hon. Prof. Tonji Univ., Shanghai 1985; Brunner Award, Nat. Inst. of Arts and Letters 1961; Medal of Honor NY Chapter AIA 1963, The Thomas Jefferson Memorial Medal for Architecture 1976, Gold Medal (American Acad. of Arts and Letters) 1979, Gold Medal (American Inst. of Architects) 1979, La Grande Medaille d'Or (Académie d'Architecture) 1981, Pritzker Architecture Prize 1983, Asia Soc. Award 1984, Medal of Liberty 1986, Nat. Medal of Arts 1988, Praemium Imperiale (Japan Art Assen) 1989, Univ. of Calif. Gold Medal 1990, Calbert Award for Excellence 1991, Presidential Medal of Freedom 1992, Edward MacDowell Medal 1998, BZ Kulturpreis (Germany) 1999, Historic Landmarks Preservation Center, New York Cultural Laureate 1999. *Projects include:* Mile High Center, Denver; MIT Earth Science Bldg, Cambridge, Mass.; US Embassy Bldg, Montevideo; East–West Center, Univ. of Hawaii; Nat. Center for Atmospheric Research, Boulder, Colo; Grave of Robert F. Kennedy; Nat. Airlines Terminal, Kennedy Int. Airport; Washington Square East, Phila, Everson Museum of Art, Syracuse, New York; Nat. Gallery of Art East Bldg, Washington, DC; Wilmington Tower, Wilmington, Del.; John Fitzgerald Kennedy Library Complex, Boston; Canadian Imperial Bd of Commerce Complex, Toronto; Des Moines Art Center Addition; Cleo Rogers Memorial County Library, Columbus, Ind.; Master Plan Columbia Univ., NY 1970; Dallas Municipal Bldg; Raffles City, Singapore; Overseas-Chinese Banking Corpn Centre, Singapore; Herbert F. Johnson Museum of Art, Ithaca, New York; New West Wing, Museum of Fine Arts, Boston; Mellon Art Center, The Choate School, Wallingford, Conn.; Sunning Plaza, Hong Kong; Fragrant Hills Hotel, Beijing; Javits Convention Center, New York, Texas Commerce Tower, Houston; Meyerson Symphony Center, IBM, Purchase, New York; Le Grand Louvre, Paris; Bank of China, Hong Kong; Luce Chapel, Taiwan; Rock-and-Roll Hall of Fame, Cleveland 1995; Museum of Modern Art, Athens; Bilbao Estuary Project; Four Seasons Hotel, New York; Musee Miko, Kyoto 1998; Buck Institute for Age Research, Marin Co., Calif. 1999; Musée d'Art Moderne, Kitchberg, Luxembourg; Museum of Islamic Art, Qatar. *Address:* I. M. Pei Architect, 88 Pine Street, New York, NY 10005, USA (office). *Telephone:* (212) 872-4010 (office). *Fax:* (212) 872-4222 (office). *E-mail:* information@pcf-p.com (office). *Website:* www.pcf-p.com (office).

PEI, Yanling; Chinese actress; b. Aug. 1947, Shuning Co., Hebei Prov.; Vice-Chair. Hebei Fed. of Literary and Art Circles 1993–, China Fed. of Literary and Art Circles 2001–; Chair. Hebei Professional Dramatists' Assen; Dir Pei

Yanling Co. of Hebei Prov. Peking Opera Theatre; mem. 7th CPPCC 1987–92, 8th CPPCC 1992–97; Excellent Performing Artist Award, Ministry of Culture 1992, Plum Blossom Award. *Performances include:* The Man and the Ghost, Lotus Lantern, Ren gui qing (Woman-Demon-Human) 1987 and others. *Address:* Hebei Federation of Literary and Art Circles, Shijiazhuang City, People's Republic of China (office).

PEICHL, Gustav; Austrian architect and caricaturist; b. 18 March 1928, Vienna; Prof. Acad. of Fine Arts, Vienna; major works include Austrian Broadcasting Stations in Salzburg, Linz, Innsbrück, Dornbirn 1970–72, Graz 1979–80, Eisenstadt 1981–83; EFA Radio Satellite Station, Aflenz 1976–79; PEA-Phosphate Elimination Plant, Berlin-Tegel; design for Papal visit to Vienna 1984; art and exhbn centre, Bonn 1986–92; extension to Städel Museum, Frankfurt am Main; ÖMV-Center, Vienna 1991–; rehearsal stage of Burgtheater, Vienna 1991–93; co-founder Peichl & Pnr ZT GmbH 2002; caricaturist under alias Ironimus; Award of City of Vienna for Architecture, Austrian State Award, Reynolds Memorial Award, Styria Award for Architecture, Mies van der Rohe Award, Berlin Architectural Award; Verleihung der Grossen Verdienst-kreuzes des Verdienstordens 1996. *Address:* Peichl & Partner, Opernring 4/2/20, 1010 Vienna, Austria (office). *Telephone:* 512-25-00 (office). *Fax:* 512-25-00-5 (office). *E-mail:* office@peichl-partner.at (office). *Website:* www.peichl-partner.at (office).

PEIMBERT, Manuel, PhD; Mexican astronomer; *Professor, Instituto de Astronomía, Universidad Nacional Autónoma de México;* b. 9 June 1941, Mexico City; s. of Gonzalo Peimbert and Catalina Sierra; m. Silvia Torres-Peimbert 1962; one s. one d.; ed Universidad Nacional Autónoma de México (UNAM) and Univ. of Calif., Berkeley; Research Asst, Instituto de Astronomía, UNAM 1960–63; Research Asst, Univ. of Calif., Berkeley 1963–64, Postdoctoral Fellow 1967–68; Prof. Faculty of Sciences, UNAM 1968–, Instituto de Astronomía 1970–; on sabbatical leave at Univ. Coll. London 1976, Tokyo Astronomical Observatory 1986; Vice-Pres. Int. Astronomical Union 1982–88; Foreign Assoc. NAS; Fellow, Third World Acad. of Sciences (Vice-Pres. 1998–2002); Assoc. Royal Astronomical Soc.; Science Prize, Acad. de la Investigación Científica 1971; Guillaume Budé Medal, Coll. de France 1974; Investigador ad Honorem, F. J. Duarte Center for Astronomy, Venezuela 1981; Mexican Nat. Prize in Science and Arts 1981; UNAM Science Prize 1988. *Publications:* more than 170 research papers in int. journals of astronomy and astrophysics. *Address:* Instituto de Astronomía, Universidad Nacional Autónoma de México, Apartado Postal 70-264, México DF, Mexico 04510. *Telephone:* (5) 622-3906. *Fax:* (5) 616-0653.

PEINEMANN, Edith; German concert violinist; b. 3 March 1939, Mainz; d. of Robert Peinemann and Hildegard (née Rohde) Peinemann; ed studied under her father and later with Heinz Stauske and Max Rostal; has performed with leading orchestras and conductors worldwide; orchestral debut, Carnegie Hall 1965; performed at Salzburg, Lucerne, Ravinia, Mozart, Marlboro Chamber Music Festivals; Prof. of Violin, Hochschule für Musik, Frankfurt 1976–; Int. Pres., European String Teachers' Asscn 2005–; First Prize, ARD competition, Munich 1956, Plaquette Eugène Ysaye 1858–1958. *Leisure interests:* art, hiking, cooking, cross-country skiing. *Address:* Oberlindau 15, 60323 Frankfurt, Germany (office). *E-mail:* info@esta-int.com (office). *Website:* www.esta-int.com (office).

PEIRANO, Miguel Gustavo; Argentine economist and government official; *Minister of Economy and Production;* ed Universidad de Buenos Aires; began career at Banco Sudameris 1989; worked for Techint Group 1990–92; various posts at Argentine Industrial Union (UIA) 1993–2004; Prof. of Political Economy, Colegio Nacional de Buenos Aires 1995–97; served as econ. adviser to Dir-Gen. of Industry of the City of Buenos Aires, Bd of Bank of the Province of Buenos Aires, Nat. Sub-secretariat of Small and Medium Enterprise and Regional Devt; fmr Pres. Econs Dept, Buenos Aires City Industrial Union; fmr Sr Vice-Pres. Bank of Investment and Foreign Trade (BICE); Sec. of Industry, Commerce and Small and Medium Enterprises –2007; Minister of Economy and Production 2007–. *Address:* Ministry of Economy and Production, Hipólito Yrigoyen 250, C1086AAB Buenos Aires, Argentina (office). *Telephone:* (11) 4349-5000 (office). *E-mail:* sagpya@mecon.gov.ar (office). *Website:* www.mecon .gov.ar (office).

PEIRIS, Gamini Lakshman, DPhil, PhD; Sri Lankan politician and academic; *Minister of Export Development and International Trade;* b. 13 Aug. 1946, Colombo; s. of Glanville S. Peiris and Lakshmi C. Salgado; m. Savitri N. Amarasuriya 1971; one d.; ed St Thomas' Coll., Mount Lavinia, Univ. of Ceylon and New Coll., Oxford, UK; Prof. of Law, Univ. of Colombo 1979, Dean, Faculty of Law 1982–88; Vice-Chancellor, Univ. of Colombo –1994; Dir Nat. Film Corpn of Sri Lanka 1973–88; Commr Law Comm. of Sri Lanka 1986–; mem. Inc. Soc. of Legal Educ. 1986–; Visiting Fellow, All Souls Coll. Oxford 1980–81; Butterworths Visiting Fellow, Inst. of Advanced Legal Studies, Univ. of London 1984; Distinguished Visiting Fellow, Christ's Coll. Cambridge, UK 1985–86; Smuts Visiting Fellow in Commonwealth Studies, Univ. of Cambridge 1985–86; Chair. Cttee of Vice-Chancellors of the Univs of Sri Lanka; Minister of Justice, Constitutional Affairs, Ethnic Affairs and Nat. Integration and Deputy Minister of Finance 1994–99; Minister of Enterprise Devt, Industrial Policy and Investment Promotion and of Constitutional Affairs 1999–2004, of Export Devt and Int. Trade 2007–; mem. United People's Freedom Alliance (UPFA) 2007–; Vice-Chair. Janasaviya Trust Fund; mem. Securities Council of Sri Lanka 1987–; mem. Pres. Comm. on Youth Unrest 1989; mem. Nat. Educ. Comm., Exec. Cttee of Asscn of Teachers and Researchers in Intellectual Property Law, Bd Govs Inst. of Fundamental Studies; Assoc. mem. Int. Acad. of Comparative Law; Presidential Award 1987. *Publications:* Law of Unjust Enrichment in South Africa and Ceylon 1971, General Principles of Criminal Liability in Ceylon 1972, Offences Under the Penal Code of Sri Lanka 1973, The Law of Evidence in Sri Lanka 1974,

Criminal Procedure in Sri Lanka 1975, The Law of Property in Sri Lanka 1976, Landlord and Tenant in Sri Lanka 1977; numerous articles on comparative and admin. law and law of evidence. *Leisure interest:* walking. *Address:* Ministry of Export Development and International Trade, 'Rakshana Mandiraya', 21 Vauxhall Street, Colombo, Sri Lanka (office); No. 37, Kirula Place, Off Kirula Road, Colombo 05, (home).

PEIROTES, Yves Jean-Marie, MSc; French business executive; b. 7 Nov. 1940, Epinal, Vosges; s. of Marcel Georges Peirotes and Germaine Eugénie Schaeffer; m. 1st Victoria Longacre 1968 (divorced 1981); two s.; m. 2nd Viviane France Bastiani 1987; ed Lycée de Belfort, Lycée Kleber, Strasbourg, Ecole Polytechnique, Paris, Ecole Nat. Supérieure du Génie Maritime, Paris, Univ. of Calif., Berkeley; prin. engineer, Maritime Eng, Del. Ministérielle pour l'Armement 1966–70; Head of Logistics, Strafor, Strasbourg 1971–72, Tech. and Industrial Devt Dir 1972–77; Gen. Man. Industrial Equipment Div., Forges de Strasbourg 1997–81; Man. Dir Air Industrie 1981–84; Chair., Man. Dir Sofiltra Poelman 1981–84; Deputy Man. Dir Cie Industrielle et Financière de Pompey 1984–85; Gen. Man. White Goods Div. Electrolux France 1985–90, White Goods & Floor Care Appliances Div. 1990–94, Man. Dir Electrolux France SA 1995–97, Chair. and Man. Dir 1997–; Chair. Usines et Fonderies Arthur Martin 1985–; Pres. Bureau Départemental d'Industrialisation des Ardennes 1987–91; mem. Advisory Bd Senlis branch, Banque de France 1995–; Chevalier, Ordre nat. du Mérite. *Leisure interests:* skiing, jogging, swimming. *Address:* Electrolux France SA, 43 ave. Félix Louat, BP 20139, 60300 Senlis (office); 6 place Winston Churchill, 92200 Neuilly sur Seine, France (home). *Telephone:* (3) 44-62-28-00 (office). *Fax:* (3) 44-62-21-89 (office). *E-mail:* yves.peirotes@notes.electrolux.fr (office).

PEISACH, Max, PhD, DSc, FRSSA, FRPSL; South African nuclear analytical chemist; b. 3 Aug. 1926, Birzai, Lithuania; s. of Hyman Peisach and Sonia Kantor; m. Eunice Sheila Glick 1950; one s. three d.; ed Boys' High School, Worcester, SA, Univ. of Cape Town; demonstrator, Univ. of Cape Town 1948–49, Jr lecturer 1949–50, lecturer 1950–53; Research Officer, Nat. Chemical Research Lab., S African Council for Scientific and Industrial Research 1953–57, Sr Research Officer 1957–60; Head, Isotope Production, Israel Atomic Energy Comm. 1960–63; Head Chem. Div., Southern Univs Nuclear Inst. 1963–83; Head Nuclear Analytical Chem. Div., Nat. Accelerator Centre 1983–91, Chief Specialist Researcher 1986–91; mem. Int. Cttee on Modern Trends in Activation Analysis 1969–91, Hon. Life mem. 1994–; Nat. Rep., IUPAC Comm. on Radiochemistry 1985–96; Research Consultant, Witwatersrand Chem. Ion-Beam Analysis Group 1992–98; Research Fellow, Solid State and Materials, Nat. Accelerator Centre 1994; Research Adviser, Dept of Materials and Interfaces, Weizmann Inst., Rehovot, Israel 1995–2004; Assoc. Royal Soc. of Chem. (London) 1951–61, Fellow 1962–86; Fellow Royal Soc. of SA 1984–, Royal Philatelic Soc. London 1966–; mem. S African Chemical Inst. 1952–96, Sr mem. 1996–98, Life mem. 1998–; AE & CI Gold Medal 1965, Roll of Distinguished Philatelists (SA) 1966, Int. Hevesy Medal 1981, SA Chemical Inst. Gold Medal 1986; Hon. Citizen, State of Tenn., USA 1965, Order of the Postal Stone (SA) 1988. *Publications:* Elemental Analysis by Particle Accelerators; many scientific papers; research papers on nuclear analytical chem.; book chapters on specialized analytical topics; research articles on philately of South Africa and Israel. *Leisure interests:* philately, numismatics, judging philatelic exhbns. *Address:* Sderot Ye'elim 30/4, Beersheba 84739 (home); PO Box 3581, Beersheba 84135, Israel. *Telephone:* 8-6442232. *E-mail:* mpeisach@bezeqint.net (home).

PEKHTIN, Vladimir Alekseyevich, DrTechSci; Russian politician and engineer; *Deputy Chairman, State Duma;* b. 9 Dec. 1950, Leningrad; m.; one s.; ed Leningrad Polytech. Inst.; engineer in Kolymagestroi, then Kolymaenergo 1974–97; Chair. Magadan Regional Duma 1994; Chair. Council of Feds of Russia 1997–; mem. State Duma (Parl.) 1999–, Head Cttee on Property; Head Yedinstvo faction in State Duma (Parl.) 2001–, currently Deputy Chair.; mem. Co-ordination Council of Centrist Parties 2001–; Order, Friendship of Peoples, Merited Constructor of Russia. *Leisure interests:* hunting, shooting (Master of Sports). *Address:* State Duma of Russian Federation, Okhotny Ryad 1, 103265 Moscow, Russia (office). *Telephone:* (495) 292-83-01 (office). *Fax:* (495) 292-34-76 (office). *Website:* www.duma.ru (office).

PEKKANEN, Raimo Oskari, LLD; Finnish judge; *Chairman, Sub-Committee on Medical Research Ethics, National Advisory Board on Health Care Ethics;* b. 29 July 1927, Kivennapa; m. Eeva Niittyla 1953; two s.; ed Univ. of Helsinki; State Admin. 1950–60; researcher and teacher, Helsinki School of Econ. and Univ. of Tampere 1961–67; Acting Prof. in Labour Law, Univ. of Helsinki 1967–68; Justice, Supreme Admin. Court of Finland 1969–90; Sec.-Gen. Ministry of Justice (on leave of absence from Supreme Admin. Court) 1982–90; Judge, European Court of Human Rights 1990–98; Chair. Sub-Cttee on Medical Research Ethics, Nat. Advisory Bd on Health Care Ethics 2000–; Commdr Order of Finnish Lion, Commdr Order of Finnish White Rose. *Publications:* Mixed Type Contracts of Employment 1966, On the Commencement and Termination of Employment Relationships 1968, On Participation in Water System Regulation 1968; articles in legal publs. *Leisure interests:* fly-fishing, skiing. *Address:* Nyyrikinte 8, 02100 Espoo, Finland (home). *Telephone:* (9) 4554557 (home). *E-mail:* raimo.pekkanen@ppl .inet.fi (home).

PEKKARINEN, Mauri, MSc; Finnish politician; *Minister of Economic Affairs;* b. 6 Oct. 1947, Kinnula; m. Raija Kaarina Pekkarinen 1979; four c.; ed Univ. of Jyväskylä; mem. Jyväskylä Town Council 1977–2004; mem. Parl. (Finnish Centre Party) 1979–, Vice-Pres. Finnish Centre Party Parl. Group 1987–91, Chair. 1999–2003, Chair. Finance Cttee 1995–99; Political Sec. Ministry of Labour 1976–77, Ministry of the Interior 1978–79; Minister of the Interior 1991–95, of Trade and Industry 2003–07, of Econ. Affairs 2008–; Chair. Cen. Finland 1999–2002, Cen. Finnish Sports Fed. 1995–2002, Asscn of

Finnish Local Councils 1997–2001; Vice-Pres. Biathlon Asscn 2006–; mem. Cen. Finland Regional Planning Asscn of the Fed. Govt 1981–84; mem. Supervisory Bd Export Credit Agency 1982–86; mem. Supervisory Bd State Guarantee Fund 1995–96; mem. Supervisory Bd Finnish Broadcasting Company YLE 1982–91, Chair. 1987–91; Bd mem. Cen. Prov. of Finland 1985–90; Chair. Cen. Finland Centre Party constituency 1987–1991; mem. Parliamentary Supervisory Bd, Bank of Finland 1995–2003, Chair. 2003; DSc hc (Lappeenranta) 2008. *Leisure interests:* music, sport. *Address:* Ministry of Employment and the Economy, Aleksanterinkatu 4, 00170 Helsinki, Finland (office). *Telephone:* (0) 106063500 (office). *Fax:* (9) 16062155 (office). *E-mail:* mauri.pekkarinen@tem.fi (office). *Website:* www.tem.fi (office).

PELÉ; Brazilian writer and fmr professional football player; b. (Edson Arantes do Nascimento), 23 Oct. 1940, Três Corações, Minas Gerais State; s. of João Ramos do Nascimento and Celeste Arantes; m. 1st Rosemeri Cholbi 1966 (divorced 1978); one s. two d.; m. 2nd Assiria Lemos 1994; ed Santos Univ.; first played football at Baurú, São Paulo; mem. Baurú Atlético Clube; joined Santos Football Club 1955, Dir 1993–; first int. game v. Argentina; played in World Cup 1958, 1962, 1966, 1970; finished career with New York Cosmos; Chair. Pelé Soccer Camps 1978–82; Special Minister for Sports, Govt of Brazil 1994–98; Dir Soccer Clinics; three World Cup winners' medals; two World Club Championship medals; 110 int. caps, 97 goals for Brazil; 1,114 appearances for Santos, 1,088 goals; career total 1,282 goals in 1,364 games, nine league championship medals, four Brazil cup medals; most goals in season 53 (1958); has appeared in several films, including Escape to Victory 1981, A Minor Miracle 1983, Hot Shot 1986; has composed numerous songs in Samba style; Goodwill Amb. for 1992, UN Conf. on Environment and Devt, Rio de Janeiro; Hans Christian Andersen Amb. 2003–; Hon. KBE 1997; Int. Peace Award 1978, Athlete of the Century 1980, WHO Medal 1989; FIFA World Footballer of the Century 2000, BBC Sports Personality of the Year Lifetime Achievement Award 2005. *Publications:* Eu Sou Pelé 1962, Jogando com Pelé 1974, My Life and the Beautiful Game 1977, Pelé Soccer Training Program 1982, The World Cup Murders (novel) 1988, Pelé: The Autobiography 2006. *Address:* 75 Rockefeller Plaza, New York, NY 10019, USA.

PELEVIN, Viktor Olegovich; Russian writer; b. 27 Nov. 1962, Moscow; ed Moscow Power Engineering Inst., Gorky Inst. of Literature, Moscow; army service; corresp. Face-to-Face journal 1989–90; journal Science and Religion; author of numerous novels and stories; Wanderer Prize 1995, Nonino Literary Prize 2001, Robert Schönefeld Prize 2000, 2001, Grigoriev Prize 2004. *Publications include:* (most in trans.) Omon Ra (novel) 1996, Vera Pavlovna's Ninth Dream, Reconstructor, Prince of Gosplan, The Yellow Arrow (novella) 1996, Ivan Kublakhanov, Generation, Babylon, The Blue Lantern (short stories) (Russian Booker Prize 1997), The Life of Insects 1998, Crystal World, A Werewolf Problem in Central Russia (short stories) 1998, Chapayev and Pustota (Buddha's Little Finger, aka Babylon) 2000, The Clay Machine-Gun (novel), Generation P 1999, Homo Zapiens (aka Generation P) 2002, Dialectic for the Transitional Phase From Nowhere to Nowhere 2003, The Sacred Book of Werewolf 2006. *Address:* c/o Aragi Inc., 143 West 27th Street, #4F, New York, NY 10001, USA (office). *E-mail:* queries@aragi.net (office).

PELHAM, Hugh Reginald Brentnall, MA, PhD, FRS; British research scientist and institute director; *Director, MRC Laboratory of Molecular Biology;* b. 26 Aug. 1954, Shawford; s. of the late Reginald Arthur Pelham and Pauline Mary Pelham; m. Mariann Bienz; one s. one d.; ed Marlborough Coll. and Christ's Coll., Cambridge; Research Fellow, Christ's Coll., Cambridge 1978–84; Postdoctoral Fellow, Carnegie Inst. of Washington, Baltimore, Md 1979–81; mem. Scientific Staff, MRC Lab. of Molecular Biology, Cambridge 1981–, Head Cell Biology Div. 1995–2006, Deputy Dir 1996–2006, Dir 2006–; mem. European Molecular Biology Org. 1985, Academia Europaea 1990, Acad. of Medical Sciences 1998; Colworth Medal 1988, European Molecular Biology Org. Medal 1989, Louis Jeantet Prize for Medicine 1991, King Faisal Int. Prize for Science 1996, Royal Soc. Croonian Medal 1999. *Publications:* articles on molecular and cell biology in scientific journals. *Address:* MRC Laboratory of Molecular Biology, Hills Road, Cambridge, CB2 0QH, England (office). *Telephone:* (1223) 402216 (office). *Fax:* (1223) 249565 (office). *Website:* www.mrc-lmb.cam.ac.uk (office).

PELIZA, Maj. Sir Robert John, KBE, ED, MHA; British soldier, business executive and politician; b. 16 Nov. 1920, Gibraltar; s. of Robert Peliza and Emily Victory; m. Irma Risso 1950; three s. four d.; ed Christian Brothers' Coll., Gibraltar; served in Royal Gibraltar Reg. 1939–61, Hon. Col 1993–98; co. dir 1962–; City Councillor 1945–48; Leader, Integration with Britain Party 1967; elected mem. House of Ass. 1969–84; Chief Minister of Gibraltar 1969–1972; Leader of the Opposition 1972; Speaker, House of Assembly 1989–96; Founder Gibraltar branch of European Movt 1976– (Patron 1995–); Pres. Gibraltar branch, Commonwealth Parl. Asscn 1989–96; Freeman of Gibraltar 1998. *Leisure interests:* painting, writing, swimming, walking and sports in general. *Address:* 125 Beverley Drive, Edgware, Middx HA8 5NH, England (home); 203 Water Gardens, Gibraltar. *Telephone:* (20) 8952-1712 (England); 78387 (Gibraltar). *E-mail:* rjpeliza@pelizar.freeserve.co.uk; rjpeliza@gibrynet.gi.

PELL, HE Cardinal George, AC, STL, MEd, DPhil (Oxon.), DD, FACE; Australian ecclesiastic; *Roman Catholic Metropolitan Archbishop of Sydney;* b. 8 June 1941, Ballarat; s. of George Arthur Pell and Margaret Lillian Burke; ed Loreto Convent and St Patrick's Coll., Ballarat, Corpus Christi Coll., Werribee, Propaganda Fide Coll. and Urban Univ., Rome, Italy, Univ. of Oxford, UK, Monash Univ., Vic.; signed to play professional Australian Rules Football with Richmond Football Club, Melbourne 1959 (currently Vice-Patron), chose to study for priesthood; fmr sports coach in soccer, Aussie Rules and rowing; ordained priest 1966; Asst Priest, Swan Hill 1971–72, Ballarat East 1973–83; Episcopal Vicar for Educ., Diocese of Ballarat 1973–84; Dir Aquinas Campus,

Inst. of Catholic Educ. 1974–84, Prin., Inst. of Catholic Educ. (now merged into Australian Catholic Univ.) 1981–84; Admin. Bungaree Parish 1984; Rector Corpus Christi Seminary 1985–87; Parish Priest, Mentone and Bishop for the Southern Region of Melbourne 1987–96; Auxiliary Bishop of Melbourne and Titular Bishop of Scala 1987; Apostolic Visitor on behalf of the Congregation for Evangelization of Peoples to the seminaries of NZ 1994, Papua New Guinea and the Solomon Islands 1995, the Pacific 1996, Irian Jaya and Sulawesi 1998; Metropolitan Archbishop of Melbourne 1996; Metropolitan Archbishop of Sydney 2001–; cr. Cardinal (Cardinal Priest of Santa Maria Dominica Mazzarello) 2003; participated in Conclave of Cardinal Electors 18–19 April 2005; Founding mem. Catholic Educ. Comm. of Victoria 1973–84; Ed. Light magazine 1979–84; fmr mem. Acad. Bd State Coll. of Victoria, Council, State Coll. of Victoria-Ballarat, Ballarat Coll. of Advanced Educ., Signadou Coll., Canberra; mem. Nat. Catholic Educ. Comm. 1988–97; Sec. Bishops' Cttee for Educ. 1994–97, 2000–03 (Chair. 2003–06), Council of Cardinals for the Study of Admin. and Econ. Problems of the Holy See 2007–; Chair. Caritas Australia 1988–97; Chair. cttee charged with setting up the new Australian Catholic Univ. 1989, served as Univ.'s Foundation Pro-Chancellor 1991–95, Pres. Univ.'s Bd of Owners 1996–, assisted in establishment of the new city campus of the Univ. in Melbourne 1999–2000; currently Chair. Australian Catholic Bishops' Cttee for Doctrine and Morals; mem. Bishops' Cttee for Justice Devt and Peace 1987–97, Pontifical Council for Justice and Peace 1990–95, 2002–, Vatican Congregation for the Doctrine of the Faith 1990–2000, Vatican Council of the Synod of Bishops 2001–05, 2006–, Supreme Cttee of the Pontifical Missions Socs 2005–, Congregation for Divine Worship 2005–; fmr Consultor to Pontifical Council for the Family, apptd to Presidential Cttee of the Council 2002; Pres. Vox Clara Cttee to advise the Congregation for Divine Worship on English trans of liturgical texts; Visiting Scholar, Campion Hall, Oxford 1979, St Edmund's Coll., Cambridge, UK 1983; Patron Campion Coll. Australia's capital appeal 2003; weekly columnist for Sunday Telegraph, Sydney 2001–; has lectured throughout Australia and in USA, UK, Ireland, NZ and Croatia; Hon. Fellow, St Edmund's Coll., Cambridge 2003–; Grand Prior Equestrian Order of the Holy Sepulchre of Jerusalem, Australian Lieutenancy-Southern 1998–2001, Grand Prior for the Order in NSW 2001, Kt Grand Cross 2003, Grand Cross of Merit of the Order of St Lazarus, Nat. Chaplain 2001–07, Ecclesiastic Grand Cross of St Lazarus 2003, Bailiff Grand Cross of Honour and Devotion, Sovereign Mil. Order of Malta 2007; Centenary Medal 2003. *Publications:* Issues of Faith and Morals 1996, The Sisters of St Joseph in Swan Hill 1922–72 1972, Catholicism in Australia 1988, Rerum Novarum – One Hundred Years Later 1992, Catholicism and the Architecture of Freedom 1999, Be Not Afraid 2004, God and Caesar: Selected Essays on Religion, Politics and Society 2007. *Leisure interests:* reading, writing, football. *Address:* Archdiocese of Sydney, Polding Centre, 133 Liverpool Street, Sydney, NSW 2000, Australia (office). *Telephone:* (2) 9390-5100 (office). *Fax:* (2) 9261-8312 (office). *E-mail:* cardinal@ado .syd.catholic.org.au (office). *Website:* www.sydney.catholic.org.au (office).

PELLEGRINO, Edmund Daniel, MD; American medical scientist and academic; *Professor Emeritus of Medicine and Medical Ethics, Georgetown University;* b. 22 June 1920, Newark, NJ; m. Clementine Coakley; two s. four d.; ed Xavier High School, New York, St John's Univ., Jamaica and New York; Prof. and Chair. Dept of Medicine, Univ. of Ky Medical Center 1959–66; Vice-Pres. for Health Sciences, Dean of School of Medicine, Dir of Health Services Center and Prof. of Medicine, State Univ. of New York 1966–73; Chancellor and Vice-Pres. for Health Affairs, Univ. of Tenn. and Prof. of Medicine and Medical Humanities, Univ. of Tenn. Center for Health Sciences 1973–75; Pres. and Chair. Bd of Dirs Yale-New Haven Medical Center and Prof. of Medicine, Yale Univ. 1975–78; Pres. and Prof. of Philosophy and Biology, Catholic Univ. of America, Washington, DC, concurrently Prof. of Clinical Medicine and Community Medicine, Georgetown Univ. Medical School 1978–82; John Carroll Prof. of Medicine and Medical Ethics, Georgetown Univ. Medical Center 1982–, now Prof. Emer., Dir Kennedy Inst. of Ethics 1983–88, Dir Centre for Advanced Study Ethics 1988–94, founder and Dir Center for Clinical Bioethics 1991–99, Chief (a.i.) Div. of Gen. Internal Medicine 1993–94, also currently Adjunct Prof. of Philosophy; Ed. Journal of Medicine and Philosophy 1983–; Fellow or mem. of 20 scientific, professional and honorary socs including Inst. of Medicine of NAS; mem. numerous nat. cttees and bds; Kt of Malta; Kt Order St Gregory the Great, Kts of the Holy Sepulchre;; recipient of 44 hon. degrees; Pres. Medal Georgetown Univ. 1990, Distinction in Bioethics Award 1993, Abraham Flexner Award 1997, Lifetime Achievement Award 1998 and many other honours and awards. *Publications:* ten books and more than 500 research papers in learned journals. *Leisure interests:* music, cooking, reading. *Address:* Center for Clinical Bioethics, Georgetown University, Box 571409, Washington, DC 20057-1409 (office); 5610 Wisconsin Avenue, Apt 17A, Chevy Chase, MD 20815, USA (home). *Telephone:* (202) 687-5397 (home). *Fax:* (202) 687-8955 (office). *Website:* clinicalbioethics.georgetown.edu (office).

PELLI, César, MArch; American architect and academic; b. 12 Oct. 1926, Tucumán, Argentina; s. of Victor Vicente Pelli and Teresa S. Pelli (née Suppa); m. Diana Balmori 1950; two s.; ed Univs of Tucumán, Illinois at Urbana Champaign; Project Designer Eero Saarinen Offices, Mich., Conn. 1954–64; Dir of Design Daniel, Mann, Johnson and Medenhall (DMJM) 1964–68; Partner in Charge of Design Gruen Assocs 1968–77; Prof. of Architecture 1977–, Dean Yale School of Architecture 1977–84; Prin. César Pelli and Assocs 1977–; mem. American Acad. of Arts and Letters; Fellow AIA; numerous awards and prizes including UN City Competition First Prize, Vienna 1969, Arnold W. Brunner Prize Nat. Inst. Arts and Letters 1978, AIA Honor Award for Fed. Office Bldg, Lawndale, San Bernardino City Hall, Calif., Arnold M. Brunner Memorial Prize Nat. Acad. of Design 1991, AIA Honor Award 1994; AIA Firm Award 1989, Gold Medal 1995. *Buildings include:* Pacific Design

Centre, LA, Calif. 1973, US Embassy, Tokyo, Japan 1975, Museum of Modern Art, New York 1984, Herring Hall, Rice Univ. 1984, World Financial Centre, New York 1985–87, Canary Wharf Tower, London 1990, Carnegie Hall Tower, New York 1991, Cincinnati Arts Theatre 1995, New Terminal, Wash. Nat. Airport 1998 (Design Award AIA 1998, Design for Transportation Award 2000). *Publications:* César Pelli (monograph) 1991, César Pelli, in The Master Architect series 1993; various articles in specialist journals. *Address:* César Pelli and Associates, 1056 Chapel Street, New Haven, CT 06510, USA (office). *Telephone:* (203) 777-2515 (office). *Fax:* (203) 787-2856 (office). *E-mail:* mailroom@cesar-pelli.com (office). *Website:* www.cesar-pelli.com (office).

PËLLUMBI, Servet, PhD; Albanian politician; b. 14 Dec. 1936, Korçë; s. of Ismail Pëllumbi and Hazize Pëllumbi; ed State Univ. of St Petersburg; Prof. of Philosophy 1960–74; Univ. Prof. of Philosophy 1974–91; Vice-Chair. Socialist Party of Albania 1991–96; mem. Parl. 1992–2003; Speaker of Parl. of Albania 2002–05; Academic Dir Inst. of Political and Social Studies; Dir Publishing Bd Policy & Society magazine. *Publications include:* Think Differently, Transition in its Light-Shade, Endeavour in Political Sociology, Sociology Tracing, Dictionary of Philosophy 1974, 1982; univ. text books and numerous articles on policy and society. *Leisure interests:* sports, reading, books, music, community devt activities, writing memories. *Address:* Rruga "Brigada e tetë", Pallati Havari, shk. 2, Ap. 7/1, Tirana, (home); c/o Socialist Party of Albania (SPA) (Partia Socialiste e Shqipërisë) (PSSh), Tirana, Albania. *Telephone:* (5) 4271500 (home).

PELLY, Derek (Derk) Roland, MA, AIB; British banker; b. 12 June 1929, Welwyn Garden City; s. of the late Arthur Roland Pelly and Phyllis Elsie Henderson; m. Susan Roberts 1953; one s. two d.; ed Marlborough Coll. and Trinity Coll., Cambridge; joined Barclays Bank Ltd (various positions) 1952, Local Dir, Chelmsford 1959, Sr Local Dir, Luton 1969; Vice-Chair. Barclays Bank Int. Ltd 1977, full-time Vice-Chair. 1979; Group Vice-Chair. Barclays Bank PLC 1985, Group Deputy Chair. and Chair. Barclays Int. Ltd 1986–88; Gov. London House for Overseas Grads 1985–91; Dir The Pvt. Bank and Trust Co. 1989–94. *Leisure interest:* painting. *Address:* Kenbank, St John's Town of Dalry, Kircudbrightshire, DG7 3TX, Scotland. *Telephone:* (1644) 430424.

PELOSI, Nancy; American politician; *Speaker, House of Representatives;* b. Baltimore, Md; d. of Thomas D'Alesandro, Jr; m. Paul Pelosi; one s. four d.; ed Trinity Coll., Washington, DC; Democratic Nat. Committeewoman 1976–96, Chair. Democratic Nat. Convention Host Cttee 1984, Chief Fundraiser for Nat. Democratic Senatorial Campaign Cttee 1986, State and Northern Chair. Calif. Democratic Party –1987; Rep. (Democrat) 8th Congressional Dist of Calif. 1987–, mem. House Perm. Select Cttee on Intelligence, House Democratic Whip 2001–03, Democratic Minority Leader 2002–07 (first woman to lead a major party in Congress), Speaker 2007–; sr mem. House Appropriations Cttee, mem. Appropriations Sub-cttee on Labor, Health and Human Services and Educ.; Chair. Congressional Working Group on China; Co-Chair. AIDS Task Force of House Democratic Caucus, Bio-Medical Research Caucus; fmr Ranking Democrat on Appropriations Sub-cttee on Foreign Operations and Export Financing; fmr mem. House Cttee on Standards of Official Conduct (Ethics); ranked by Forbes magazine amongst 100 Most Powerful Women (11th) 2004, (76th) 2005, (48th) 2006, (26th) 2007, (35th) 2008. *Address:* Office of the Speaker, H-232, US Capitol, Washington, DC 20515 (office); 235 Cannon HOB, Washington, DC 20515, USA (office). *Telephone:* (202) 225-0100 (office); (202) 225-4965 (office). *E-mail:* americanvoices@mail.house.gov (office). *Website:* speaker.gov (office); www.house.gov/pelosi (office).

PELPOLA, Daya; Sri Lankan lawyer, politician and business executive; fmr sports sub-ed., Ceylon Daily News; fmr mem. Parl.; Vice-Chair. United Nat. Party, also legal adviser to party leader Ranil Wickramasinghe; Chair. Sri Lankan Airlines Ltd 2002–08; judge, Miss Tourism Int. competition 2002. *Leisure interests:* sports, especially hockey and rugby. *Address:* c/o Head Office, Sri Lankan Airlines Ltd, Level 22, East Tower, World Trade Centre, Echelon Square, Colombo 1, Sri Lanka. *Telephone:* (19) 7335555. *Fax:* (19) 7335122. *E-mail:* ulweb@srilankan.aero. *Website:* www.srilankan.aero.

PELTASON, Jack W., PhD; American university president (retd); *President Emeritus, University of California;* b. 29 Aug. 1923, St Louis, Mo.; s. of Walter Peltason and Emma Hartman; m. Suzanne Toll 1945; one s. two d.; ed Univ. of Missouri and Princeton Univ.; Asst Prof. Smith Coll. 1947–51; Asst Prof. of Political Science, Univ. of Ill., Urbana-Champaign 1951–52, Assoc. Prof. 1953–59, Dean Coll. of Liberal Arts and Sciences 1960–64, Chancellor 1967–77; Vice-Chancellor Univ. of Calif. Irvine 1964–67, Chancellor 1984–92, Chancellor Emer. 1992–; Pres. Univ. of Calif. 1992–95, Pres. Emer. 1995–; Pres. American Council on Educ. 1977–84, Bren Foundation 1997–; mem. numerous bds, cttees etc.; Fellow, American Acad. of Arts and Sciences; 22 hon. degrees and other awards. *Publications include:* Federal Courts in the Political Process 1955, Fifty-Eight Lonely Men: Southern Federal Judges and School Desegregation 1961, Understanding the Constitution 1997, Government by the People; co-author of several other books; articles in journals and encyclopedias and book chapters etc. *Leisure interests:* reading, writing, family. *Address:* University of California, 5295 Social Sciences Plaza B, Mail Code: 5100, Irvine, CA 92697 (office); 18 Whistler Court, Irvine, CA 92612, USA (home). *Telephone:* (949) 824-3938. *Fax:* (949) 824-3960. *E-mail:* jwpeltas@uci.edu (office); jwpeltason@aol.com (home); jwpeltason@uci.edu. *Website:* www.faculty.uci.edu/profile.cfm?faculty_id=2462 (office).

PELTOLA, Timo Veikko, MSc; Finnish petroleum industry executive; *Chairman, Managing Board, Neste Oil Oyj;* b. 19 April 1946, Lieto; m. Katariina Helena Toivonen; three c.; Product Man. Huhtamäki Corpn 1971–75, Marketing Dir 1975–81, Pres. Polarcup Div. 1981–83, Corp. Vice-Pres. 1984–86, Exec. Vice-Pres. 1987–89, CEO 1989–2004; Chair. Neste Oil

Oyj 2005–; Chair. AW-Energy Oy; Chair. Supervisory Bd Ilmarinen Mutual Pension Insurance Co.; Vice-Chair. Nordea AB; mem. Bd of Dirs TeliaSonera AB, SAS AB; mem. Supervisory Bd Finnish Fair Corpn Co-operative; mem. Advisory Bd CVC Capital Pnrs; Hon. DEcon. *Address:* Neste Oil Oyj, Keilaranta 8, PO Box 95, 00095 Espoo, Finland (office). *Telephone:* (10) 45811 (office). *Fax:* (10) 4584442 (office). *Website:* www.nesteoil.com (office).

PEÑA, Federico, LLB; American lawyer, business executive, fmr politician and fmr government official; *Managing Director, Vestar Capital Partners;* b. 15 March 1947, Laredo, Tex.; m. Ellen Hart 1988; two d.; ed Univ. of Tex.; fmr Pnr, Pena & Pena (law firm); mem. Colo Legis. 1979–83; Mayor of Denver, Colo 1983–91; f. Pena Investment Advisors Inc. 1991; apptd part-time legal consultant, Brownstein Hyatt Farber & Strickland (law firm), Denver 1992; US Sec. of Transportation 1993–97, of Energy 1997–98; Sr Advisor, Vestar Capital Pnrs (pvt. equity firm), Denver 1998–2000, Man. Dir 2000–; mem. Bd of Dirs Marsico Capital Man., Prin. Financial Group, Sonic Corpn, Valor Telecommunications; mem. Toyota North American Diversity Advisory Bd; Assoc., Harvard Univ. Centre for Law and Educ. *Address:* Vestar Capital Partners, Seventeenth Street Plaza, 1225 17th Street, Suite 1660, Denver, CO 80202 USA. *Telephone:* (303) 294-1826. *Website:* www.vestarcapital.com.

PEÑA, Paco; Spanish flamenco guitarist; b. 1 June 1942, Córdoba; s. of Antonio Peña and Rosario Pérez; m. Karin Vaessen 1982; two d.; int. concert artist since 1968; f. Paco Peña Flamenco Co. 1970, Centro Flamenco Paco Peña, Córdoba 1981; Prof. of Flamenco, Rotterdam Conservatory, Netherlands 1985; composed Misa Flamenca 1991; produced Musa Gitana 1999, Voces y Ecos 2002; composed Flamenco Requiem 2004; Ramón Montoya Prize 1983, Oficial de la Cruz de la Orden del Mérito Civil, Spain. *Address:* MPM London, 1 Prince of Wales Road, Suite 20, London, NW5 3LW, England (office). *Telephone:* (20) 7681-7475 (office). *Fax:* (20) 7681-7476 (office). *E-mail:* mpm@pacopena.com (office). *Website:* www.pacopena.com.

PEÑALOSA, Antonio; Spanish international organization official; *Secretary-General, International Organization of Employers;* ed Univ. of Santiago, Coll. of Europe, Brussels, Belgium; staff mem. Industrial Policy Directorate, EC 1977–78; Asst to Sec.-Gen. of Int. Org. of Employers 1978–1983, Exec. Sec. 1983–94, Deputy Sec.-Gen. 1993–99, Sec.-Gen. 1999–. *Address:* International Organization of Employers, 26 Chemin de Joinville, Cointrin, 1216 Geneva, Switzerland (office). *Telephone:* (22) 9290000 (office). *Fax:* (22) 9290001 (office). *E-mail:* penalosa@ioe-emp.org (office). *Website:* www.ioe-emp.org (office).

PEÑALOSA LONDONO, Enrique; Colombian politician and accountant; ed Duke Univ., NC, USA; Pres. of the Instituto Colombiano de Ahorro y Vivienda (ICAV); Econ. Sec. Pres. of Colombia 1986; Mayor of Bogotá 1998–2000; currently Visiting Scholar, New York Univ.; Eisenhower Fellowship, Nat. Simon Bolivar Prize for Journalism, Soc. of Economists of Bogotá and Cundinamarca Prize. *Publications:* Capitalism: The Better Option 1989, Democracy and Capitalism: The Challenges of the Next Century 1990, Cerros de Bogotá 2003; numerous articles on econ. issues. *Address:* Acaldía de Bogotá, Bogotá, Colombia (office). *E-mail:* enrpenalosa@hotmail.com.

PENCHAS, Shmuel, MD, DIC, MSc; Israeli professor of health administration; *Consultant, Hadassah Medical Organization;* b. 12 Feb. 1939, Romania; s. of Nathan Penchas and Liuba Penchas; four s.; ed Hebrew Univ. Hadassah Medical School, Haifa Technion Grad. School, Imperial Coll., Univ. Coll. London, Harvard Univ.; Lecturer in Medicine, Hebrew Univ-Hadassah Medical School, Jerusalem 1975, Sr Lecturer 1978; Research Fellow, Harvard Univ Medical School, USA 1978; Assoc Prof, Internal Medicine, Hebrew Univ-Hadassah Medical School, 1984, Prof Health Care Admin 1993; Physician, Hadassah Univ. Hosp., Jerusalem 1967–76, Dir of Computing 1977–78; Deputy Dir-Gen. Hadassah Medical Org. 1978, Dir-Gen. 1981–98, now Consultant; Chair. Israel Asscn of Hosp. Dirs 1984–91, Foreign Assoc. Inst. of Medicine of NAS (USA); Consultant to Hadassah (Women's Zionist Org. of America); mem. Romanian Nat. Acad. of Science; Hon. DrSc, Hon. PhD. *Publications:* articles in professional journals. *Address:* Hadassah Mt Scopus Hospital, PO Box 24035, Jerusalem 91240, Israel (office). *Telephone:* 25844200 (office). *Fax:* 25844750 (office). *E-mail:* penchas@netvision.net.il (office).

PENDERECKI, Krzysztof; Polish composer and conductor; b. 23 Nov. 1933, Dębica, Cracow Prov.; s. of Tadeusz Penderecki and Zofia Penderecka; m. Elżbieta Solecka 1965; one s. two d.; ed Jagiellonian Univ., Cracow and State Higher Music School, Cracow; studied composition first with Skołyszewski, later with Malawski and Wiechowicz, Cracow; graduated from State Higher Music School, Cracow 1958; Lecturer in Composition, State Higher Music School (now Music Acad.), Cracow 1958–66, Prof. Extraordinary 1972–75, Prof. 1975–; Rector Cracow Conservatory 1972–87; Prof. of Composition, Folkwang Hochschule für Musik, Essen 1966–68; Musical Adviser, Vienna Radio 1970–71; Prof. of Composition, Yale Univ., USA 1973–78; Music Dir, Casals Festival, Puerto Rico 1992–2002; Music Man. Sinfonia Varsovia Orchestra 1997–; Guest Conductor China Philharmonic Orchestra 2000–; mem. Presidential Council of Culture 1992–; Corresp. mem. Arts Acad. of GDR, Berlin 1975, Academia Nacional de Bellas Artes, Buenos Aires 1982; Extraordinary mem. Arts Acad. of W Berlin 1975; mem. Royal Acad. of Music, Stockholm 1976, Acad. Nat. de Sciences, Belles-Lettres et Arts, Bordeaux, American Acad. of Arts and Letters 1999, Hong Kong Acad. for the Performing Arts 2001, etc.; Fellow Royal Irish Acad. of Music; Hon. mem. RAM, London 1974, Accad. Nazionale di Santa Cecilia, Rome 1976, Acad. Int. de Philosophie et de l'Art, Berne 1987, Musikkreis der Stadt, Duisburg 1999, Gesellschaft der Musikfreunds, Vienna 2000, Hon. Prof. Moscow Conservatory 1997, Cen. Beijing Conservatory 1998, St Petersburg Conservatory 2003; Officier, Ordre de Saint-Georges de Bourgogne (Belgium) 1990, Grand Cross Order of Merit (Fed. Repub. of Germany) 1990, Commdr Ordre des Arts et des Lettres 1996,

Ordine al Merito della Repub. Italiana 2000, Commdr of the Three Star Order Riga (Latvia) 2006, Order of the White Eagle (Poland) 2006; Dr hc (Univ. of Rochester, NY) 1972, (St Olaf Coll., Northfield, Minn.) 1977, (Katholieke Univ., Leuven) 1979, (Univ. of Bordeaux) 1979, (Georgetown Univ., Washington, DC) 1984, (Univ. of Belgrade) 1985, (Univ. Autónoma, Madrid) 1987; Hon. DMus (Glasgow) 1995, (Jagiellonian Univ., Cracow) 1998, (Ukrainian Nat. Tchaikovsky Acad. of Music) 1999, (Pittsburgh) 1999, (Lucerne) 2000, Univ. of St Petersburg, Yale Univ., Univ. of Leipzig 2003, and many others; Fitelberg Prize for Threnody for the Victims of Hiroshima 1960, also UNESCO award 1959, Polish Minister of Culture and Art Prize 1961, (First Class) 1981, Cracow Composition Prize for Canon 1962, North Rhine-Westphalia Grand Prize for St Luke's Passion 1966, also Pax Prize (Poland) 1966, Alfred Jurzykowski Foundation Award, Polish Inst. of Arts and Sciences in America 1966, Prix Italia 1967/68, State Prize (1st Class) 1968, Gustav Charpentier Prize 1971, Gottfried von Herder Prize 1977, Prix Arthur Honegger for Magnificat 1978, Grand Medal of Paris 1981, Sibelius Prize (Wihouri Foundation, Finland) 1983, Order of Banner of Labour (1st Class) 1983, Premio Lorenzo il Magnifico (Italy) 1985, Wolf Foundation Award 1987, Grammy Award Nat. Acad. of Recording Arts and Sciences (for Best Contemporary Composition) 1988 (for Best Instrumental Soloist Performance with Orchestra) 1999, (for Best Choral Composition) 2001, Grawemeyer Award for Music Composition 1992, City of Strasbourg Medal 1995, Crystal Award, World Econ. Forum, Davos 1997, Business Center Club Special Award, Warsaw 1998, AFIM Indie Award 1999, Köhler-Osbahr-Siftung Music Award 1999, Best Living Composer Award, Midem Classic Cannes 2000, Príncipe de Asturias Award 2001, Roman Guardini Prize, Catholic Acad. of Music 2002, North Rhine-Westphalia Award 2003, Praemium Imperiale 2004. *Works include:* Psalms of David (for choir and percussion) 1958, Emanations (for 2 string orchestras) 1958, Strophes (for soprano, speaker and ten instruments) 1959, Anaklasis (for strings and percussion) 1959–60, Dimensions of Time and Silence (for 40-part mixed choir and chamber ensemble) 1959–60, String Quartet no. 1 1960, no. 2 1968, Threnody for the Victims of Hiroshima (for 52 strings) 1960, Polymorphia (for strings) 1961, Psalms (for tape) 1961, Fluorescences (for large orchestra) 1961, Sonata for Cello and Orchestra 1964, St Luke's Passion 1965–66, Capriccio per oboe e 11 archi 1965, De natura sonoris (for large orchestra) 1966, Dies irae (for soprano, tenor, bass, chorus and large orchestra) 1967, The Devils of Loudun (opera) 1968–69, Cosmogony 1970, De natura sonoris II (for wind instruments, percussion and strings) 1970, Russian Mass Utrenja 1971, Partita (for harpsichord, guitars, harp, double bass and chamber orchestra) 1972, Symphony no. 1 1972–73, Canticum Canticorum Salomonis (for 16 voices and chamber orchestra) 1970–73, Magnificat (for bass solo, voice ensemble, double choir, boys' voices and orchestra) 1973–74, When Jacob Awoke (for orchestra) 1974, Violin Concerto 1967–77, Paradise Lost (opera) 1976–78, Christmas Symphony No. 2 1979–80, Te Deum 1979–80, Lacrimosa 1980, Cello Concerto no. 2 1982, Viola Concerto 1983, Polish Requiem 1980–84, Black Mask (opera) 1984–86, Der unterbrochene Gedanke (for string quartet) 1988, Adagio (for orchestra) 1989, Symphony No. 4 (Adagio for orchestra) 1989, Sinfonietta (for orchestra) 1990–91, Symphony No. 5 (for orchestra) 1991–92, Partita (for orchestra, rev. ed.) 1991, Ubu Rex (opera) 1991, Benedicamus Domine 1992, Benedictus 1992, Flute Concerto 1992–93, Quartet for Clarinet and String Trio 1993, Violin Concerto No. 2 1992–95, Divertimento (for cello solo) 1994, Symphony No. 3 1995, Agnus Dei from Versöhnung Messe (a cappella choir) 1995, Seven Gates of Jerusalem (oratorio) 1995–96, Passacaglia (chamber music) 1995–96, Larghetto (chamber music) 1997, Credo 1997–98, Sonata for Violin and Piano 2000, Sextet for Violin, Viola, Cello, Piano, Clarinet and French Horn 2000, Concerto Grosso for Three Cellos 2001, Benedictus 2002, Resurrection Piano Concerto 2002, Largo for violoncello and orchestra 2003, Symphony No. 8 2005–07. *Leisure interest:* dendrology. *Address:* Schott Musik International, Weihergarten 5, 55116 Mainz, Germany (office). *Telephone:* (6131) 246812 (office). *Fax:* (6131) 246250 (office). *E-mail:* katja.riepl@schott-music.com (office). *Website:* www.penderecki.de.

PENDRY, Sir John Brian, Kt, BA, MA, PhD, FRS, FInstP; British physicist and academic; *Professor of Theoretical Solid State Physics, Imperial College London;* b. 4 July 1943; ed Downing Coll., Cambridge; Research Fellowship in Physics, Downing Coll., Cambridge 1969–73, Fellow in Physics and Praelector 1973–75; ICI Post-doctoral Fellow 1969–71; mem. tech. staff, Theoretical Physics Dept, Bell Labs, Murray Hill, NJ, USA 1972–73; Sr Asst in Research, Cavendish Lab., Cambridge 1973–75; Sr Prin. Scientific Officer: Head of Theory Group, Science and Eng Research Council (SERC) Daresbury Lab. 1975–81; Prof. of Theoretical Solid State Physics, Imperial Coll. of Science and Tech. and Head of Condensed Matter Theory Group 1981–, Head of Experimental Solid State Physics Group 1983–85, Assoc. Head of Physics Dept 1984–92, Head of Physics Dept 1998–2001, Prin., Faculty of Physical Sciences 2001–02; mem. SERC Science Bd, SERC Nuclear Physics Bd 1992–93, Council, Royal Soc. 1992–94, Particle Physics and Astronomy Research Council 1998–2002; Dean, Royal Coll. of Science 1993–96; Ed. Proceedings A of the Royal Society 1996–2002; Leverhulme Trust Sr Research Fellowship 1996–97; Eng and Physical Sciences Research Council (EPSRC) Sr Research Five-Year Fellowship 1997–98 (resgnd), 2003–; Commonwealth Scholarships Commr 1998–2000; Chair. Physics sub-panel of Research Assessment Exercise (RAE 2008) 2005–; Fellow, Optical Soc. of America 2005; British Vacuum Council Prize and Medal 1994, Dirac Medal and Prize, Inst. of Physics 1996, Int. Surface Structure Prize 1996, Appleton Lecturer 2003, Celsius Lecturer, Univ. of Uppsala, Sweden 2004, Bakerian Lecturer, Royal Soc. 2005, Larmor Lecturer, Queen's Univ. Belfast 2005, Fröhlich Lecturer, Univ. of Liverpool 2005, EU Decartes Prize for "extending electromagnetism through novel artificial materials" 2005, Royal Medal, Royal Soc. 2006. *Publications:* numerous scientific papers in professional journals on condensed matter theory. *Address:* Room 808 Blackett, Department of Physics, Imperial College London, Prince Consort Road, London, SW7 2AZ, England (office). *Telephone:* (20) 7594-7606 (office). *Fax:* (20) 7594-7604 (office). *E-mail:* j.pendry@imperial.ac.uk (office). *Website:* www.cmth.ph.ic.ac.uk/photonics/Newphotonics (office).

PENG, Bo; Chinese diver; b. 18 Jan. 1981, Jiangxi Prov.; competes in 3m springboard dive; began training at Nanchang City Sport School, Jiangxi Prov. 1987; joined Jiangxi prov. team 1991; joined nat. team 1998; Silver Medal, World Championships 2003; Gold Medal, Athens Olympics 2004. *Leisure interests:* personal computer and video games. *Address:* c/o China Swimming Association, 5 Tiyuguan Road, Chongwen District, Beijing 100763, China. *Telephone:* (10) 67020332. *Fax:* (10) 67020320.

PENG, Chong; Chinese politician; b. 1909, Zhangzhou, Fujian; joined CCP 1933; Political Commissar, Regt of New 4th Army 1938; Deputy Sec.-Gen. Prov. People's Govt, Fujian 1950; Mayor of Nanjing 1955–59; First Sec. Municipal CCP Cttee, Nanjing 1955-60; Deputy for Jiangsu, 2nd NPC 1958; Alt. Second Sec. CCP Cttee, Jiangsu 1960; Political Commissar Nanjing militia 1960; First Sec. Municipal CCP Cttee, Nanjing 1962–68; Second Sec. CCP Cttee, Jiangsu 1965–68; Vice-Chair. Prov. Revolutionary Cttee, Jiangsu 1968–74; alt. mem. 9th Cen. Cttee CCP 1969; Sec. CCP Cttee, Jiangsu 1970–74; alt. mem. 10th Cen. Cttee CCP 1973; Chair. Prov. Revolutionary Cttee, Jiangsu 1974–76; Second Political Commissar, PLA Nanjing Mil. Region 1975–80; Third Sec. CCP Cttee, Shanghai 1976–79; Second Vice-Chair. Municipal Revolutionary Cttee, Shanghai 1976–79; Chair. Municipal CPPCC Cttee, Shanghai 1977–79; mem. 11th Cen. Cttee CCP 1977; Head, Group in Charge of Snail Fever Prevention, Cen. Cttee CCP 1978–; Deputy for Shanghai, 5th NPC 1978; Vice-Chair. Nat. Cttee, 5th CPPCC 1978–80; First Sec. CCP Cttee, Shanghai 1979–80; Chair. Municipal Revolutionary Cttee, Shanghai 1979–80; Mayor of Shanghai 1980; Sec. 11th Cen. Cttee CCP 1980–82; Vice-Chair. Standing Cttee, 5th NPC 1980–83; mem. 12th Cen. Cttee CCP 1982–87; Vice-Chair. Standing Cttee, 6th NPC 1983–88; mem. Presidium 6th NPC 1986–88; Chair. Law Cttee, NPC 1983–87; Vice-Chair. 7th NPC 1988–93; mem. Presidium of 14th CCP Nat. Congress Oct. 1992; Pres. China Int. Cultural Exchange Centre 1984–; Exec. mem. China Welfare Inst. 1978–; Hon. Pres. Gymnastics Asscn 1983–, Soc. for Industry and Commerce Admin. 1991–; China Foundation for Heroism Awards. *Address:* Standing Committee, National People's Congress, Tian'anmen Square, Beijing, People's Republic of China (office).

PENG, Dixian; Chinese politician and economist; b. 1908, Meishan Co., Sichuan Prov.; ed in Japan; joined China Democratic League 1947, Vice-Chair. 1988; joined CCP 1984; Perm. mem. 8th Nat. Cttee CPPCC 1993–98.

PENG, Liyuan; Chinese singer; b. Nov. 1952, Yuncheng, Shandong Prov.; m. Xi Jinping 1987; one d.; ed Shandong Acad. of Arts, China Acad. of Music; solo singer, Qianwei Song and Dance Troupe of Ji'nan Mil. Command 1980–84; solo singer, Song and Dance Troupe, PLA Gen. Political Dept 1984–; mem. 11th CPPCC Nat. Cttee; several awards including Plum Blossom Award, Nat. Cultural Projects Award, China Golden Records Award. *Works include:* People from our Village, Mount Everest, On the Plains of Hope, Mu Lang Poems. *Operas include:* White Haired Girl, The Daughter of the Party, Melancholy Dawn, Poems of Mulan. *Television:* appears every year on CCTV New Year Gala. *Address:* Song and Dance Troupe, People's Liberation Army General Political Department, Beijing, People's Republic of China (office).

PENG, Ming-Min; Taiwanese politician; b. 1923; ed in Japan and Nat. Taiwan Univ.; lost left arm during US bombing raid on Nagasaki; fmr Chair. Political Science Dept, Nat. Taiwan Univ.; arrested for activities supporting self-determination for Taiwan 1964 and sentenced to eight years' imprisonment; sentence commuted to house arrest; escaped into exile in USA; returned home 1992; joined Democratic Progressive Party (DDP) 1995; DDP cand., presidential elections March 1996. *Address:* Democratic Progressive Party, 14th Floor, 128 Ming Sheng East Road, Sec. 3, Taipei, Taiwan.

PENG, Peiyun; Chinese administrator; *President, Red Cross Society of China;* b. 1929, Liuyang Co., Hunan Prov.; ed Tsinghua Univ., Beijing; joined CCP Communist Youth League 1945, CCP 1946; Sec.-Gen. CCP Party Br., Tsinghua Univ. 1949–78 (also Deputy Sec. CCP Party Cttee); Vice-Chair. CCP Revolutionary Cttee, Beijing Chemical Eng Inst., Beijing 1949–78; Head, 1st Bureau, State Science and Tech. Comm., 1978–79; Vice-Minister of Educ. 1982–88, State Educ. Comm. 1982–88; Sec. CCP Party Cttee, Chinese Univ. of Science and Tech., Anhui Prov. 1982–88; mem. Central Comm. for Discipline Inspection, CCP Cen. Cttee 1982–92; Minister of State Family Planning Comm. 1988–98; State Councillor 1988–98; Del., 12th CCP Nat. Congress 1982–87, 13th CCP Nat. Congress 1987–92; mem. 14th CCP Cen. Cttee 1992–97, 15th CCP Cen. Cttee 1997–2002; Chair. Coordination Cttee for the Handicapped (State Council) 1993–; Chair. Nat. Cttee for Patriotic Public Health Campaign 1994–, Women and Children's Work Cttee of the State Council; Vice-Chair. Standing Cttee of 9th NPC 1998–2003; Pres. Chinese Asscn for Promotion of the Population Culture 1993, Soc. of Population 1994, Exec. Cttee All-China Women's Fed. 1998–2003, Hon. Pres. 2003–; Pres. Red Cross Soc. of China 1999–; ranked 47th by Forbes magazine amongst 100 Most Powerful Women 2004. *Address:* Red Cross Society of China, No 8 Beixinqioa, Santiao, Dongcheng District, Beijing 100007, People's Republic of China (office).

PENGO, HE Cardinal Polycarp, DTheol; Tanzanian ecclesiastic; *Archbishop of Dar es Salaam and Pro-Vice-President of Tanzania Episcopal Conference;* b. 5 Aug. 1944, Mwazye; ed Kipapala Major Seminary, Tabora, Makerere Univ., Pontifical Lateran Univ.; ordained priest 1971; sec. to Bishop of Sumbawanga 1971–73; Rector Segerea Major Seminary 1977–90; Bishop of Nachingwea 1984–87, of Tunduru-Massai 1987–90; Archbishop Coadjutor of

Dar es Salaam 1990–92, Archbishop 1992–; Cardinal 1998–; Pro-Vice-Pres. Tanzania Episcopal Conf. *Address:* Archbishop's House, PO Box 167, Dar es Salaam, Tanzania. *Telephone:* (22) 2113223 (office). *Fax:* (22) 2125751 (office). *E-mail:* nyumba@cats-net.com (office). *Website:* www.rc.net/tanzania/tec/dsmweb/contents.htm (office).

PENJOR, Rinzin, BCom, LLB, LLM; Bhutanese lawyer and government official; *Attorney-General;* b. Kazhi geog, Wangduephodrang; ed Shri Ram Coll. of Commerce, New Delhi and Delhi Univ., India, Lord Dalhousie Law Coll., Canada; began career with High Court 1989, has served as Drangpoen in Tsirang, Sarpang and Punakha Dist Courts; militia officer with Royal Bhutan Army 1990–95; Attorney-Gen. 2008–; Patang. *Address:* Office of the Attorney General, Cabinet Secretariat, Tashichhodzong, Thimphu, Bhutan (office). *Telephone:* (2) 321437 (office). *Fax:* (2) 321438 (office). *E-mail:* cabinet@druknet.bt (office). *Website:* www.bhutan.gov.bt (office).

PENN, Arthur; American theatre and film director; b. 27 Sept. 1922, Philadelphia; m. Peggy Maurer 1955; one s. one d.; joined Army theatre company during World War II; worked in television 1951–53; directed plays for Broadway theatre including The Miracle Worker (Tony Award for Best Director 1960), All the Way Home, Toys in the Attic, Two for the Seesaw, Wait Until Dark, Sly Fox, Monday after the Miracle, Golden Boy, Hunting Cockroaches; Lifetime Achievement Award, Berlin Film Festival 2007. *Films directed include:* The Left-Handed Gun 1957, The Miracle Worker 1962, Mickey One 1964, The Chase 1965, Bonnie and Clyde 1967, Alice's Restaurant 1969 (also screenwriter), Little Big Man 1971, Visions of Eight (segment) 1973, Night Moves 1975, The Missouri Breaks 1976, Four Friends 1981, Target 1985, Dead of Winter 1987, Penn and Teller Get Killed 1989, The Portrait 1993, Lumière and Company 1995. *Television:* Philco Television Playhouse (multiple episodes) 1948, Goodyear Television Playhouse (multiple episodes) 1951, Playwrights 56 1955, Flesh and Blood 1968, The Portrait 1993, Inside 1996; exec. producer Law & Order (series) 2000-2001. *Address:* c/o Bell and Co., 535 Fifth Avenue, 21st Floor, New York, NY 10017, USA.

PENN, Sean; American actor; b. 17 Aug. 1960, Burbank, Calif.; s. of Leo Penn and Eileen Penn (née Ryan); m. 1st Madonna (q.v.) 1985 (divorced); m. 2nd Robin Wright 1996; two c.; f. Clyde is Hungry Films (production co.); Chair. Cannes Film Festival jury 2008; Modern Master Award, Santa Barbara Int. Film Festival 2002, Donostia Lifetime Achievement Award, San Sebastian Film Festival 2003, John Steinbeck Award 2004, Christopher Reeve First Amendment Award 2006. *Theatre appearances include:* Heartland (Broadway debut), Slab Boys, Hurlyburly 1988. *Films include:* Taps 1981, Fast Times at Ridgemont High 1982, Bad Boys 1983, Crackers 1984, Racing with the Moon 1984, The Falcon and the Snowman 1985, At Close Range 1986, Shanghai Surprise 1986, Colors 1988, Judgement in Berlin 1988, Casualties of War 1989, We're No Angels 1989, State of Grace 1990, Carlito's Way 1993, Dead Man Walking 1996 (Best Actor Award Berlin Film Festival 1996), U Turn 1997, She's So Lovely 1997, Hurlyburly 1998, As I Lay Dying 1998, Up at the Villa 1998, The Thin Red Line 1998, Sweet and Lowdown 1999, The Pledge 2000, Up at the Villa 2000, Before Night Falls 2000, The Weight of Water 2000, I am Sam 2001, It's All About Love 2003, Mystic River (Golden Globe Award, Best Dramatic Actor 2004, Critics' Choice Award Best Actor 2004, Acad. Award, Best Actor 2004) 2003, 21 Grams (Venice Film Festival Best Actor Award 2003) 2003, The Assassination of Richard Nixon 2005, The Interpreter 2005, All the King's Men 2006, Persepolis 2007, What Just Happened? 2007, Milk 2008 (Acad. Award for Best Actor 2009); dir and writer The Indian Runner 1991, The Crossing Guard 1995, The Pledge 2001, Into the Wild 2007. *Address:* 2049 Century Park East, Suite 2500, Los Angeles, CA 90067-3101, USA (office).

PENNANEACH, Biova-Soumi, MSc; Togolese diplomatist; b. 5 Oct. 1941, Lomé; m. 1972; two s. four d.; ed State Univ. of Moscow, USSR and Laval Univ., Québec, Canada; active trade unionist since 1966; Head, Soils Analysis Labs 1966–74, 1976–80; Dir Agricultural and Land Legislation Service 1980–82; Prefect of Tchaoudjo and the Lakes and Tech. Adviser, Nat. Science Inst. 1982–87; Dir Office of Minister of Rural Devt 1987–90; Under-Sec.-Gen. Nat. Confed. of Workers of Togo 1988–90; Perm. Rep. to UN 1990–96; Vice-Pres. 46th session of UN Gen. Ass. 1991. *Publications:* numerous, on conservation and environment protection. *Address:* c/o Ministry of Foreign Affairs and Cooperation, Place du Monument aux Morts, Lomé, Togo.

PENNANT-REA, Rupert Lascelles, MA; British business executive and journalist; *Chairman, Henderson Group plc;* b. 23 Jan. 1948, Harare, Zimbabwe; s. of Peter A. Pennant-Rea and Pauline E. Pennant-Rea; m. several times; two s. one d.; ed Peterhouse, Zimbabwe, Trinity Coll. Dublin and Univ. of Manchester; with Confed. of Irish Industry 1970–71, Gen. and Municipal Workers' Union 1972–73, Bank of England 1973–77; with The Economist 1977–93, Ed. 1986–93; Deputy Gov. of Bank of England 1993–95; Chair. TSO (The Stationery Office) 1996–, PGI 1997–, Henderson Group plc 2005–; numerous other appointments; Wincott Prize for Journalism 1984. *Publications:* Gold Foil 1979, Who Runs the Economy? (co-author) 1980, The Pocket Economist (co-author) 1983, The Economist Economics (co-author) 1986. *Leisure interests:* music, tennis, fishing, golf, family. *Address:* Henderson Group plc, 4 Broadgate, London, EC2M 2DA, England (office). *Telephone:* (20) 7818-4142 (office). *Fax:* (20) 7818-4143 (office). *E-mail:* rpr@henderson.com (office). *Website:* www.henderson.com (office).

PENNER, Stanford S. 'Sol', PhD; American chemical engineer and academic; *Distinguished Professor of Engineering Physics Emeritus, University of California, San Diego;* ed Univ. of Wisconsin; worked during World War II at Allegany Ballistics Lab. on solid rocket propulsion systems; Research Engineer, Jet Propulsion Lab., Pasadena, Calif. 1946–50; Prof. of Jet Propulsion, California Inst. of Tech. (Caltech) 1950–62; Dir Research and

Eng Div., Inst. for Defense Analyses, Washington, DC 1962–64; Founding Chair. Dept of Aerospace and Mechanical Eng Sciences, Univ. of California, San Diego 1964, has also held positions of Vice-Chancellor for Academic Affairs, Dir Inst. for Pure and Applied Physical Sciences, and Founding Dir Energy Center (later named Center for Energy and Combustion Research) 1972–90, now Distinguished Prof. of Eng Physics Emer.; Founding Ed. The Journal of Quantitative Spectroscopy and Radiative Transfer 1960–92, Energy – The International Journal 1974–98, (classified) Journal of Defense Research; mem. Nat. Acad. of Eng, Int. Acad. of Astronautics; Fellow, American Acad. of Arts and Sciences, and of seven learned socs; numerous hon. degrees; numerous nat. and int. awards, including Distinguished Assoc. Award, US Dept of Energy, Edward Teller Award for the Defense of Freedom 1998, three different awards from AIAA for combustion research, thermophysics, and energy-system studies, Founders Award, Nat. Acad. of Eng 2007. *Publications:* Chemistry Problems in Jet Propulsion (textbook) 1954; numerous scientific papers in professional journals on thermophysics, applied spectroscopy, combustion, propulsion, and energy. *Address:* Irwin & Joan Jacobs School of Engineering, University of California, San Diego, EBU II 559, 9500 Gilman Drive, La Jolla, CA 92093-0403, USA (office). *Telephone:* (858) 534-4284 (office). *E-mail:* spenner@ucsd.edu (office). *Website:* www.jacobsschool.ucsd.edu (office).

PENNIE, Michael William, ARCA; British sculptor; b. 23 Oct. 1936, Wallasey, Cheshire; s. of George A. Pennie and Isabel Duff; m. 1st Norah Kimmit 1959 (divorced 1977); m. 2nd Marlene Stride 1985; two s. one d.; ed Bede Collegiate for Boys, Sunderland, Sunderland Coll. of Art and Royal Coll. of Art; Visiting Lecturer, Bath Acad. of Art, Winchester and Wimbledon Schools of Art, Norwich Coll. of Art and Brighton Polytechnic 1962–82; Sr Lecturer, Bath Spa, Univ. Coll. 1985–2001, now Prof.; Co-Organizer, Sculpture in the City, Bath 1986; Consultant, Goodwill Art Service 1992–; Chair. Bath Area Network for Artists 2001–03; Consultant, Horniman Museum and Gardens, Bath Spa Sculpture Garden, Bath Spa Univ. 2005–; 12 research trips to W Africa 1994–2000; Rome Scholar 1962, Gregynog Fellow, Univ. of Wales 1971. *Publications:* Where Shall We Put This One? 1987, Smoke of the Savannah 1989, African Assortment: African Art in Museums in England and Scotland 1991, Friday's Rain Takes a Long Time to Stop 1994, Some Sculptors and African Art 1995, Marriage Poles of the Lobi 1996, Adventures with Lobi – an abc 1998, West African Journeys 2001, Lobi Notes 2002, Across the Board and 2 Other Sculptures 2007. *Leisure interest:* African music. *Address:* 117 Bradford Road, Atworth, Melksham, Wilts., SN12 8HY, England (home). *Telephone:* (1225) 705409 (home). *Fax:* (1225) 705409 (home). *E-mail:* michael.pennie@btinternet.com (home). *Website:* www.michaelpennie.net (home).

PENNINGER, Josef Martin, PhD; Austrian biologist and academic; *Scientific and Administrative Director, IMBA, Institute for Molecular Biotechnology, Austrian Academy of Sciences;* b. 5 Sept. 1964, Gurten; m. Liqun Zhang 1997; one s. two d.; ed Humanistic Gymnasium, Ried, Univ. of Innsbruck; Post-doctoral Fellow, Ont. Cancer Inst., Princess Margaret Hosp., Toronto, Canada 1990–94, Assoc. Scientist, Dept of Molecular and Cellular Biology 1994–; Prin. Investigator, Amgen Inst., Toronto 1994–; Asst Prof., Depts of Immunology and Medical Biophysics, Univ. of Toronto 1994–99, Full mem. School of Grad. Studies 1998–, Assoc. Prof., Depts of Immunology and Medical Biophysics 1999–2002, Full Prof. 2002–, Adjunct Prof., Depts of Immunology and Medical Biophysics 2004–; Assoc. Prof. (Dozent), Dept of Experimental and Gen. Pathology, Univ. of Innsbruck 1998–; Scientific and Admin. Dir IMBA, Inst. for Molecular Biotechnology of the Austrian Acad. of Sciences, Vienna 2002–; Corresp. mem. Austrian Acad. of Sciences 2002, mem. 2007; mem. Deutsche Akad. der Naturforscher Leopoldina 2004; Hon. Prof. of Genetics, Univ. of Vienna 2004–; Hon. Prof., Peking Union Medical Coll., Beijing; Hon. mem. Golden Key Soc. 2002; Special fellowship from Austrian Ministry for Arts and Science 1987, Scholarship from European Fed. of Immunological Societies 1988, 'Highest Talented' Award, Rotary Club, Innsbruck 1990, Anton von Eiselsberg Prize for best medical related scientific work in Austria 1991, Erwin Schroedinger Fellowship, Austrian Fonds zür Foerderung der Wissenschaftlichen Forschung 1990–92, Austrotransplant-Biotest Prize, Austrian Soc. of Transplantation, Transfusion and Genetics 1993, Talentefoerderpraemie (talent prize for science and culture), Prov. of Upper Austria 1994, The William E. Rawls Prize, Nat. Cancer Inst. of Canada 1999, included in 'Celebration of Canadian Healthcare Research' of leading historical and contemporary medical scientists in Canada during 20th century selected by Asscn of Canadian Medical Colls, Asscn of Canadian Teaching Hosps, Alumni and Friends of the Medical Research Council and Partners in Research 2000, selected as a 'Young Leader in Medicine in Canada' by the Globe and Mail, Univ. of Toronto 2000, named One of Canada's Top 40 under 40 2001, CIAR Young Canadian Explorer Award 2002, listed among the 10 most promising scientists in all fields in the world by Esquire magazine 2002, Culture Prize for Science, Prov. of Upper Austria 2003, Int. Research Prize in Bone Research 2003, Austrian Scientist of the Year Award 2003, Austria04 Award: Austrian of the Year (in science), Die Presse newspaper 2004, Young Global Leader appointed by World Econ. Forum 2004, Descartes Prize for Research, European Comm. 2007, Ernst Jung Prize, Jung-Stiftung für Wissenschaft und Forschung (co-recipient) 2007, Carus Medal, German Academy of Sciences Leopoldina 2007, Wellenreiter Prize, Austrian Man. Club 2007. *Publications:* numerous scientific papers in professional journals. *Address:* IMBA, Institute of Molecular Biotechnology of the Austrian Academy of Sciences, Dr Bohrgasse 3–5, 1030 Vienna (office); Himmelhofgasse 62, 1130 Vienna, Austria (home). *Telephone:* (1) 79730 ext. 454 (office). *Fax:* (1) 79730-459 (office). *E-mail:* josef.penninger@imba.oeaw.ac.at (office). *Website:* www.imba.oeaw.ac.at (office).

PENNINGTON, Thomas Hugh, MB, PhD, FRCPath, FRCP, FRSE, FMedSci; British microbiologist; *Governor, Moredun Research Institute;* b. 19 April

1938, Edgware; m.; two d.; ed Royal Grammar School, Lancaster, St Thomas's Medical School, Univ. of London; house appointments, St Thomas's Hosp. 1962–63, Asst Lecturer in Medical Microbiology, St Thomas's Hosp. Medical School 1963–67; Postdoctoral Fellow, Univ. of Wisconsin 1967–68; lecturer then sr lecturer in Virology, Univ. of Glasgow 1969–79; Prof. of Bacteriology, Univ. of Aberdeen 1979–2003, Dean of Medicine, 1987–92; Gov. Rowett Research Inst. 1980–88, 1996–; Gov. Moredun Research Inst. 2003–; Chair. Expert Group on 1996 E. Coli Outbreak in Cen. Scotland; Vice-Chair. Broadcasting Council for Scotland; Vice-Pres. Chartered Inst. of Environmental Health; mem. Scottish Food Advisory Cttee, Food Standards Agency; Pres. Soc. for General Microbiology; Hon. DSc (Lancaster) 1999, (Strathclyde) 2001, (Aberdeen) 2003; Caroline Walker Trust Consumer Advocate Award 1997, John Kershaw Memorial Prize for Notable Services to Public Health 1998, Royal Scottish Soc. of Arts Silver Medal 1999, Thomas Graham Medal, Royal Glasgow Philosophical Soc. 2001, Burgess of Guild, City of Aberdeen 2002. *Publications:* When Food Kills 2003; many papers, articles and book chapters on viruses and bacteria and on food safety. *Leisure interest:* collecting old books. *Address:* Department of Medical Microbiology, Medical School, University of Aberdeen, Foresterhill, Aberdeen, AB25 2ZD (office); 13 Carlton Place, Aberdeen, AB15 4BR, Scotland (home). *Telephone:* (1224) 55863 (office); (1224) 645136 (home). *Fax:* (1224) 685604 (office). *E-mail:* mmb036@abdn.ac.uk (office). *Website:* www.abdn.ac.uk/mmb/theme/penn.htl (office).

PENNY, Gareth, MA; South African business executive; *Managing Director, De Beers Group;* b. 1962; m. Kate Penny; two c.; ed Diocesan Coll. (Bishops), Cape Town, Eton Coll., Univ. of Oxford, UK; joined Anglo American Corpn 1988, becoming Man. Anglo American/De Beers Small Business Initiative, SA, Personal Asst to Chair. of Anglo American/De Beers, Dir of Sales and Marketing, Diamond Trading Co. 2001–04, Dir De Beers 2003–, Group Man. Dir and Chair. Exec. Cttee, De Beers Group 2005–; mem. Bd Julius Baer Holding Ltd; Hon. Life mem. London Diamond Bourse & Club. *Address:* De Beers Group, Private Bag X01, Southdale 2135, South Africa (office). *Telephone:* (11) 374-7000 (office). *Website:* www.debeersgroup.com (office).

PENNY, Nicholas, PhD; British art historian, gallery director and academic; *Director, National Gallery, London;* b. 21 Dec. 1949; m. Mary Crettier; ed Shrewsbury School, St Catharine's Coll., Cambridge, Courtauld Inst. of Art, London; academic career began with a research fellowship at Clare Hall, Cambridge; taught art history at Univ. of Manchester 1975–82; Slade Prof. of Fine Art, Univ. of Oxford 1980–81; Sr Research Fellow, King's Coll., Cambridge 1982–84; Keeper of Dept of Western Art, Ashmolean Museum, Oxford 1984–89; Clore Curator of Renaissance Painting, Nat. Gallery, London 1990–2000, identified the Madonna of the Pinks belonging to the Duke of Northumberland as a genuine Raphael, and not a copy of a lost original, as was previously supposed 1991, Keeper 1998–2002, made unsuccessful bid for directorship of Nat. Gallery 2002, Dir 2007–; Andrew W. Mellon Prof., Center for Advanced Study in the Visual Arts, Nat. Gallery of Art, Washington, DC, USA 2000–07, Sr Curator of Sculpture, Nat. Gallery of Art 2002–07. *Publications include:* Church Monuments in Romantic England 1977, Taste and the Antique (co-author, with Francis Haskell) 1981, Raphael (co-author) 1987, Ruskin's Drawings (Ashmolean Handbooks) 1988, Alfred and Winifred Turner: Exhibition Catalogue 1988, Giotto to Dürer: Early Renaissance Painting in The National Gallery (co-author) 1991, three-volume scholarly catalogue of European sculpture in the Ashmolean Museum 1992, The Materials of Sculpture 1993, Tradition and Revolution in French Art, 1700–1880: Paintings and Drawings from Lille 1993, Making and Meaning: the Young Michelangelo: The Artist in Rome, 1496–1501 (Making & Meaning Series) (co-author) 1994, Frames 1997, Saints (National Gallery Pocket Guides) 2000, Dürer to Veronese: Sixteenth-century Painting in the National Gallery (co-author) 2002, Titian (National Gallery Catalogues) 2003, Desiderio Da Settignano: Sculpture of Renaissance Florence (co-author) 2007; regular contrib. to The Burlington Magazine and London Review of Books. *Address:* The National Gallery, Trafalgar Square, London, WC2N 5DN, England (office). *Telephone:* (20) 7747-2885 (office). *Fax:* (20) 7747-2423 (office). *E-mail:* information@ng-london.org.uk (office). *Website:* www.nationalgallery.org.uk (office).

PENROSE, Oliver, PhD, FRS, FRSE; British mathematician and academic; *Professor Emeritus, Heriot-Watt University;* b. 6 June 1929, London; s. of Lionel S. Penrose and Margaret Leathes; m. Joan L. Dilley 1953; three s. (one deceased) one d.; ed Central Collegiate Inst. London, Canada, Univ. Coll. London and King's Coll. Cambridge; Mathematical Physicist, English Electric Co. Luton 1952–55; Research Asst Yale Univ. 1955–56; lecturer, Reader, Imperial Coll. London 1956–69; Prof. of Math. Open Univ. 1969–86, Heriot-Watt Univ. 1986–94, Prof. Emer. 1994–. *Publications:* Foundations of Statistical Mechanics 1969; about 80 papers in scientific journals. *Leisure interests:* music, chess. *Address:* Dept of Mathematics, Heriot-Watt University, Riccarton, Edinburgh, EH14 4AS (office); 29 Frederick Street, Edinburgh, EH2 2ND, Scotland (home). *Telephone:* (131) 451-3225 (office); (131) 225-5879 (home). *E-mail:* oliver@ma.hw.ac.uk (office). *Website:* www.ma.hw.ac.uk/~oliver (office).

PENROSE, Sir Roger, Kt, OM, PhD, FRS; British mathematician and academic; *Professor Emeritus of Mathematics, University of Oxford;* b. 8 Aug. 1931, Colchester; s. of Lionel Sharples Penrose; m. 1st Joan Wedge 1959 (divorced 1981), three s.; m. 2nd Vanessa Thomas 1988; one s.; ed Univ. Coll. School, Univ. Coll. London and St John's Coll. Cambridge; Asst Lecturer, Bedford Coll. London 1956–57; Research Fellow, St John's Coll. Cambridge 1957–60; NATO Research Fellow, Princeton and Syracuse Univs 1959–61; Research Assoc., King's Coll. London 1961–63; Visiting Assoc. Prof., Univ. of Tex. Austin 1963–64; Reader, Birkbeck Coll. London 1964–66, Prof. of Applied Math. 1966–73; Rouse Ball Prof. of Math., Univ. of Oxford 1973–98, Prof. Emer. 1998–, Emer. Fellow, Wadham Coll.; Gresham Prof. of Geometry, Gresham Coll. 1998–2001; Fellow, Univ. Coll. London 1975; Visiting Prof. Yeshiva, Princeton and Cornell Univs 1966–67, 1969; Lovett Prof. Rice Univ. Houston 1983–87; Distinguished Prof. of Physics and Math. Syracuse Univ. 1987–93, Francis and Helen Pentz Distinguished Prof. of Physics and Math., Pa State Univ. 1993–; mem. London Math. Soc., Cambridge Philosophical Soc., Inst. for Math. and its Applications, Int. Soc. for Gen. Relativity and Gravitation; Fellow, Birkbeck Coll. 1998, Inst. of Physics 1999; Foreign mem. Polish Acad. of Science, Accademia Nazionale dei Lincei; Foreign Assoc. Nat. Acad. of Sciences, USA 1998; Hon. mem. Royal Irish Acad. of Science 2001; Dr hc, (New Brunswick) 1992, (Surrey) 1993, (Bath) 1994, (London) 1995, (Glasgow) 1996, (Essex) 1996, (St Andrew's) 1997, (Santiniketon) 1998, Hon. DUniv (Open Univ.) 1998, (Southampton) 2002, (Waterloo, Ontario) 2003, (Leiden) 2004, (Athens) 2005, (York) 2006; Hon. Fellow, St John's Coll. Cambridge 1987; Adams Prize (Cambridge Univ.) 1966–67, Dannie Heinemann Prize (American Physics Soc. and American Inst. of Physics) 1971, Eddington Medal (with S. W. Hawking) (Royal Astronomical Soc.) 1975, Royal Medal (Royal Soc.) 1985, Wolf Foundation Prize for Physics (with S. W. Hawking) 1988, Dirac Medal and Prize, Inst. of Physics 1989, Einstein Medal 1990, Science Book Prize 1990, Naylor Prize, London Math. Soc. 1991, DeMorgan Medal 2004, Copley Medal 2008. *Publications:* Techniques of Differential Topology in Relativity 1973, Spinors and Space-time (with W. Rindler), (Vol. I) 1984, (Vol. II) 1986, The Emperor's New Mind 1989, The Nature of Space and Time (with S. W. Hawking) 1996, The Large, the Small and the Human Mind 1997, White Mars (with B. Aldiss) 1999, The Road to Reality: A Complete Guide to the Laws of the Universe 2004; articles in scientific journals. *Leisure interests:* three-dimensional puzzles, doodling at the piano. *Address:* Mathematical Institute, 24–29 St Giles', Oxford, OX1 3LB, England (office). *Telephone:* (1865) 273525 (office). *Fax:* (1865) 273583 (office). *E-mail:* rouse@maths.ox.ac.uk (office). *Website:* www.maths.ox.ac.uk (office).

PENSKE, Roger S., ; American motor racing team owner, business executive and fmr racing driver; *Chairman, Penske Corporation;* b. 20 Feb. 1937, Shaker Heights, Ohio; ed Lehigh Univ.; early career buying, racing and selling race cars, f. Penske Racing 1958–, launched Team Penske 1966; co-f. Championship Auto Racing Teams (CART); Penske Racing has won 12 Indianapolis 500s and 9 CART points titles; Nat. Sports Car Driving Champion 1964; founding Chair. Penske Corpn 1969–; Chair. Penske Truck Leasing Business 1982–; Chair. Bd United Auto Group 1999–; mem. Bd of Dirs Home Depot, Inc., Universal Technical Inst. Inc., Detroit Renaissance, Inc.; Chair. Detroit Super Bowl XL Host Cttee 2004–06; Chair. Downtown Detroit Partnership 2006–; mem. Business Council; Sports Illustrated Driver of the Year 1960, New York Times Driver of the Year 1962, inducted into Int. Motorsports Hall of Fame 1998. *Address:* Penske Corporation, 2550 Telegraph Road, Bloomfield Hills, MI 48302, USA (office). *Telephone:* (248) 648-2000 (office). *Fax:* (248) 648-2005 (office). *Website:* www.penske.com (office).

PENZIAS, Arno Allan, PhD; American astrophysicist; *Venture Partner, New Enterprise Associates;* b. 26 April 1933, Munich, Germany; s. of Karl Penzias and Justine Penzias; m. 1st Anne Barras Penzias 1954; one s. two d.; m. 2nd Sherry Chamovelevit 1996; ed City Coll. of New York, Columbia Univ.; mem. tech. staff Bell Laboratories, Holmdel, NJ 1961–72, Head Radiophysics Research Dept 1972–76, Dir Radio Research Lab. 1976–79, Exec. Dir Research, Communications Sciences Div. 1979–81, Exec. Dir Research, Bell Labs, Murray Hill, NJ 1979–81, Vice-Pres. Research 1981–95, Vice-Pres., Chief Scientist 1995–96; Vice-Pres., Chief Scientist Bell Labs Innovations 1996–98; Venture Partner, New Enterprise Assocs 1998–; Sr Tech Adviser Lucent Technologies 1998–; Lecturer, Princeton Univ. 1967–72, Visiting Prof. Astrophysical Sciences Dept 1972–85; Harvard Coll. Observatory Research Assoc. 1968–80; Adjunct Prof., State Univ. of New York (SUNY) at Stony Brook 1974–84; discovered cosmic microwave background radiation 1965; Assoc. Ed. Astrophysical Journal 1978–82; mem. Editorial Bd Annual Review of Astronomy and Astrophysics 1974–78, AT & TBL Tech. Journal 1978–84 (Chair. 1981–84); mem. Bd of Trustees of Trenton State Coll. 1977–79, Visiting Cttee of Calif. Inst. of Tech. 1977–79; mem. Astronomy Advisory Panel of NSF 1978–79, Industrial Panel on Science and Tech. 1982–, Bd of Overseers, School of Eng and Applied Science, Univ. of Pa 1983–86; mem. Max Planck Inst. Fachbeirat 1978–85 (Chair. 1981–83); mem. Council on Competitiveness 1989–; Vice-Chair. Cttee Concerned Scientists; mem. NAS, Nat. Acad. Eng, American Astronomical Soc., World Acad. Art and Science; Fellow AAAS, American Physical Soc.; numerous hon. degrees; Nobel Prize for Physics 1978; Henry Draper Medal, NAS 1977; Herschel Medal, Royal Astronomical Soc. 1977, Pender Award 1992, Int. Eng Consortium Fellow Award 1997 and numerous other prizes, awards, lectureships. *Publications:* Ideas and Information 1989, Digital Harmony 1995; over 100 scientific papers in various journals. *Leisure interests:* swimming, jogging, skiing. *Address:* New Enterprise Associates, 2490 Sand Hill Road, Menlo Park, CA 94025, USA (office). *Telephone:* (650) 854-9499 (office). *Fax:* (415) 544-0833. *E-mail:* apenzias@nea.com (office). *Website:* www.nea.com (office).

PEPPER, Sir David Edwin, Kt, KCMG, MA, DPhil; British civil servant; *Director, Government Communications Headquarters;* b. 1947; m.; two s.; ed St John's Coll., Oxford; joined Govt Communications HQ (GCHQ) 1972, various positions in operational intelligence work, Dir of Personnel 1995–98, Head Corp. Devt Directorate Home Office 1998–2000, Dir of Finance GCHQ 2000–03, Dir GCHQ 2003–(08). *Leisure interests:* music, reading, walking, cooking. *Address:* GCHQ, A3A, Hubble Road, Cheltenham, Glos., GL51 0EX, England (office). *Telephone:* (1242) 221491 (office). *E-mail:* david.pepper@gchq.gsi.gov.uk (office). *Website:* www.gchq.gov.uk (office).

PEPPER, John Ennis Jr; American business executive; *Chairman, The Walt Disney Company;* b. 2 Aug. 1938, Pottsville, Pa; s. of John Ennis Pepper,

Sr and Irma O'Connor; m. Frances Graham Garber 1967; three s. one d.; ed Yale Univ.; with Procter & Gamble Co. 1963–, Gen. Man. Italian subsidiary 1974–77, Vice-Pres. and Gen. Man. packaged soap div. 1977–80, Group Vice-Pres. 1980–84, mem. Bd Dirs 1984–2003, Exec. Vice-Pres. 1984–86, Pres. 1986–95, Chair. and CEO 1995–99, Chair. 2000–02, Chair. Exec. Cttee of the Bd 2000–03 (retd); Vice-Pres. for Finance and Admin, Yale Univ. 2004–05; Chair. The Walt Disney Co. 2007–; mem. Bd Dirs Boston Scientific Corpn; Co-Chair. Gov.'s Educ. Council of State of Ohio; fmr CEO Nat. Underground Railroad Freedom Center, currently Co-Chair.; mem. Advisory Council Yale School of Man., Exec. Cttee Cincinnati Youth Collaborative. *Address:* The Walt Disney Co., 500 South Buena Vista Street, Burbank, CA 91521-9722, USA (office). *Telephone:* (818) 560-1000 (office). *Fax:* (818) 560-1930 (office). *E-mail:* TWDC.Corp.Communications@disney.com (office). *Website:* disney.go .com (office); corporate.disney.go.com (office).

PEPPER, Sir Michael, Kt, ScD, PhD, FRS, FInstP; British physicist, academic and business executive; *Professor of Nanoelectronics, University College, London;* b. 10 Aug. 1942, London; s. of Morris Pepper and Ruby Pepper; m. Dr Jeannette D. Josse 1973; two d.; ed St Marylebone Grammar School, London, Reading Univ.; physicist, Mullard Research Lab. 1967–69; physicist engaged in solid state device research, Allen Clark Research Centre, Plessey Co. 1969–73; research at Cavendish Lab., Cambridge 1973–, Prof. of Physics, Univ. of Cambridge 1987–2009; Pender Chair of Nanoelectronics, Univ. Coll., London 2009–; Jt Man. Dir Toshiba Research Europe Ltd 1991–2007; Co-founder and Dir TeraView Ltd 2001; Warren Research Fellow, Royal Soc. 1978–86; Sr Research Fellow, Trinity Coll., Cambridge 1982–87, Professorial Fellow 1987–; Sr Research Fellow, GEC Hirst Research Centre 1982–87; Visiting Prof., Bar-Ilan Univ., Israel 1984; Fellow, American Physical Soc.; Hon. DSc (Bar-Ilan) 1993, (Linköping) 1997; Guthrie Prize and Medal, Inst. of Physics 1985, Hewlett-Packard Prize, European Physical Soc. 1985, Hughes Medal, Royal Soc. 1987, Mott Prize, Inst. of Physics 2000, Bakerian Lecturer, Royal Soc. 2004 and various other named lectures, Royal Medal, Royal Soc. 2005. *Publications:* numerous papers on solid state physics and semiconduct-ors in scientific journals. *Leisure interests:* travel, music, whisky tasting. *Address:* Dept. of Electronic and Electrical Engineering, University College, Torrington Place, London, WC1E 6BT, England (office). *Telephone:* (20) 7679-3978 (office). *E-mail:* m.pepper@ee.ucl.ac.uk (office).

PEPY, Guillaume; French transport industry executive; *Chairman, Société Nationale des Chemins de Fer Français (SNCF);* b. 26 May 1958, Neuilly-sur-Seine (Hauts-de-Seine); ed Alsace School, Paris, Inst. of Political Studies, Paris, Ecole Nat. d'Admin; began career as magistrate Conseil d'Etat (French Admin. Court); Chief of Staff to Chair., Soc. Nat. des Chemins de Fer Français (SNCF–French Nat. Railways) 1988–93, Dir of Strategy 1993–98, apptd mem. Exec. Cttee 1998, Vice-Pres. –2003, CEO 2003–08, Chair. 2008–; Chair. Eurostar Group 2002–; Asscn pour le Développement du Mécénat Industriel et Commerciel (Admical) 2008–; Vice-Chair. Keolis Group; Chevalier, Légion d'honneur. *Address:* Société Nationale des Chemins de Fer Français (SNCF), 34 rue du Commandant Mouchotte, 75699 Paris Cedex 14, France (office). *Telephone:* 1-53-25-62-02 (office). *Fax:* 1-53-25-62-25 (office). *E-mail:* guillaume.pepy@sncf.fr (office). *Website:* www.sncf.fr (office).

PEPYS, Mark Brian, PhD, MD, FRCP, FRCPath, FMedSci, FRS; British physician and academic; *Professor and Head of Medicine, Royal Free and University College Medical School;* b. 18 Sept. 1944, Cape Town, South Africa; s. of Jack Pepys and Rhoda Pepys; m. Elizabeth Olga Winternitz 1971; one s. one d.; ed Trinity Coll., Cambridge, Univ. Coll. Hosp. Medical School, London, Harvard Medical School; house officer, Univ. Coll. Hosp., London 1968–69; Sr House Officer, Hammersmith Hosp. 1969–70, Asst Lecturer/Hon. Sr Registrar 1974–76, Head of Immunological Medicine and Hon. Consultant Physician 1977–79, Sr Lecturer 1977–81, Reader 1981–84; Prof. of Immunological Medicine 1984–99; MRC Jr Research Fellowship, Cambridge Univ., Research Scholar 1970–73, Fellow (Title A) Trinity Coll. Cambridge 1973–79, Registrar 1973–74; Sr Lecturer/Hon. Consultant and Head of Immunology Dept Royal Free Hosp. School of Medicine, London 1976–77, Prof. and Head of Medicine 1999–, Hon. Consultant Physician 1999–; Royal Coll. of Physicians Goul-stonian Lecturer 1982, Lumleian Lecturer 1998; Moxon Trust Medal 1999; Royal Coll. of Pathologists Kohn Lecturer; Royal Coll. of Surgeons of England Sir Arthur Sims Commonwealth Travelling Professorship 1991; Fellow Royal Soc. 1998; Acad. of Medical Sciences Founder Fellow 1998; Fellow Univ. Coll. London 2003. *Publications:* Samter's Immunologic Diseases (contrib.) 2001, Oxford Textbook of Medicine (contrib.) 2003; numerous research papers in learned journals. *Leisure interests:* tennis, surfing, skiing, wine. *Address:* Centre for Amyloidosis and Acute Phase Proteins, Department of Medicine, Royal Free and University College Medical School, Rowland Hill Street, London, NW3 2PF (office); 22 Wildwood Road, London, NW11 6TE, England (home). *Telephone:* (20) 7433-2802 (office). *Fax:* (20) 7433-2803 (office). *E-mail:* m.pepys@rfc.ucl.ac.uk (office). *Website:* www.ucl.ac.uk/medicine/amyloidosis (office).

PERA, Marcello; Italian politician and professor of philosophy; b. 28 Jan. 1943, Lucca, Tuscany; ed Univ. of Pisa; Full Prof. of Theoretical Philosophy, Univ. of Catania 1989–92; Full Prof. of Philosophy of Science, Univ. of Pisa 1992; Visiting Fellow, Univ. of Pittsburgh, USA 1984, Van Leer Foundation, Jerusalem 1987, MIT Dept of Linguistics and Philosophy, Cambridge, Mass 1990; mem. Steering Cttee Forza Italia Party, Deputy Leader Forza Italia Parl. Group 1996–2001; Head, Judiciary Dept, Nat. Co-ordinator Convention for Liberal Reform; Senator (Forza Italia) 1996–2006, Pres. of Senate 2001–06; mem. Cttee on Justice, Cttee on Educ. and Culture, Jt Cttee on Constitutional Reforms 1996–2001; mem. Advisory Panel Physis – Rivista internazionale di storia della scienza, Epistemologia, Perspectives on Science, Philosophical, Historical, Social; Fellow, Center for the Study of Science in Soc., Univ. of Virginia, USA; mem. Accademia Lucchese di Lettere, Scienze e Arti. *Publications include:* The Ambiguous Frog – The Galvani-Volta Controversy on Animal Electricity 1991, The Discourses of Science 1994; Senza radici (with Cardinal Joseph Ratzinger); ed. or co-ed. several books including Rational Changes in Science 1987, Persuading Science – The Art of Scientific Rhetoric 1991, Scientific Controversies 2000, Without Roots (with Pope Benedict XVI) 2006; numerous articles and essays in learned journals. *Leisure interests:* reading essays and novels. *Address:* c/o Office of the President, Senato della Repubblica, 00186 Rome, Italy (office).

PERAHIA, Murray; American pianist and conductor; b. 19 April 1947, New York, NY; s. of David Perahia and Flora Perahia; m. Naomi (Ninette) Shohet 1980; two s.; ed High School of Performing Arts, Mannes Coll. of Music, studied with Jeanette Haien, Arthur Balsam, Mieczyslaw Horszowski; debut, Carnegie Hall 1968; won Leeds Int. Piano Competition 1972; has appeared with many of world's leading orchestras and with Amadeus, Budapest, Guarneri and Galimir string quartets; regular recital tours N America, Europe, Japan; Co-Artistic Dir Aldeburgh Festival 1983–89; numerous recordings including complete Mozart Piano Concertos; prin. guest conductor, Acad. of St Martin-in-the-Fields; Dr hc (Univ. of Leeds), Hon. FRCM, FRAM; Kosciusko Chopin Prize 1965, Avery Fisher Award 1975, Gramophone Record Award 1997, Grammy Award 1999; Hon. KBE 2004. *Recordings include:* Bach Partitas Nos 2, 3, 4 (Midem Classical Award for Solo Instrument Recording 2009) 2008. *Address:* Askonas Holt, Lincoln House, 300 High Holborn, London, WC1V 7JH, England (office); IMG Artists, Carnegie Hall Tower, 152 W. 57th Street, 5th Floor, New York, NY 10019, USA (office). *Telephone:* (20) 7400-1700 (office); (212) 994-3500 (office). *Fax:* (20) 7400-1799 (office); (212) 994-3550 (office). *E-mail:* info@askonasholt.co.uk (office); info@imgartists.com (office). *Website:* www.askonasholt.co.uk (office); www.imgartists.com (office); www.murrayperahia.com.

PERAK, HRH The Sultan of; Tuanku Azlan Muhibuddin Shah ibni al-Marhum Sultan Yusuf Izuddin Ghafarullah Shah; Malaysian; b. 19 April 1928, Batu Gajah; m. Tuanku Bainun Mohamed Ali 1954; two s. three d.; ed Govt English School (now Sultan Yussuf School), Malay Coll. and Univ. of Nottingham, UK; called to Bar, Lincoln's Inn; Magistrate, Kuala Lumpur; Asst State Sec., Perak; Deputy Public Prosecutor; Pres. Sessions Court, Seremban and Taiping; State Legal Adviser, Pahang and Johore; Fed. Court Judge 1973; Chief Justice of Malaysia 1979; Lord Pres. 1982–83; Raja Kechil Bongsu (sixth-in-line) 1962, Raja Muda (second-in-line to the throne) 1983; Sultan of Perak Jan. 1984–; Yang di-Pertuan Agong (Supreme Head of State) 1989–94; Pro-Chancellor Univ. Saina Malaysia 1971, Chancellor Univ. of Malaya 1986; Hon. Col-in-Chief Malaysian Armed Forces' Engineers Corps; Man. Malaysian Hockey Team 1972; Pres. Malaysian Hockey Fed., Asian Hockey Fed.; Vice-Pres. Int. Hockey Fed., Olympic Council of Malaysia.

PERBEN, Dominique; French politician and civil servant; b. 11 Aug. 1945, Lyon; s. of Jacques Perben and Agnès Berthier; m. 1st Annick Demoustier 1968; m. 2nd Corinne Garnier 1996; one s. two d. from previous m.; ed Univ. of Paris, Inst. of Political Studies, Paris; Pvt. Sec. to Maine-et-Loire Prefect 1972–75, to Norbert Ségard (Sec. of State for Postal Services and Telecom-munications) 1977; Sec.-Gen. Territoire de Belfort 1975–76; Head of Mission Del. of Devt of Belfort Region 1977, Pres.'s Office Regional Council at Rhône-Alpes 1983–86; Admin. Télédiffusion de France 1980; with Ministry of the Interior 1981; Mayor of Chalon-sur-Saône 1983–2002, Deputy Mayor 2002–04; Vice-Pres. Regional Council Saône-et-Loire 1985–88, RPR Deputy 1986–93, 1997–; mem. Regional Council Bourgogne 1992–93; Vice-Pres. Regional Council Rhône 2004–08; RPR Nat. Sec. of Local Elections 1984–86, of General Elections 1986–88, of Communication 1988–89, Asst Sec.-Gen. 1990–93; Minister of Overseas Territories 1993–95, for the Civil Service, Admin. Reform and Decentralization 1995–97; Keeper of the Seals and Minister of Justice 2002–05, Minister of Transport, Capital Works, Tourism and the Sea 2005–07; Chevalier du Mérite agricole. *Leisure interests:* skiing, tennis. *Address:* Assemblée nationale, 126 rue de l'Université, 75355 Paris Cedex 07 (office); Mairie, BP 92, Place de l'Hôtel de Ville, 71321 Chalon-sur-Saône Cedex, France (office).

PERCOVICH ROCA, Luis; Peruvian politician; b. 14 July 1931, Yungay, Ancash; s. of Alfredo Pércovich Jaramillo and Rosa Roca de Pércovich; m. Haydée Bambarén de Pércovich 1961; two s. one d.; Nat. Deputy 1963–68; Vice-Dean Chemical Pharmaceutical School of Peru 1967–68; Pres. Chamber of Deputies 1981–82; Minister of Fisheries Jan.–April 1983, Minister of the Interior 1983–84; Prime Minister of Peru and Minister of Foreign Affairs 1984–85; mem. Acción Popular (AP); Nat. Org. Sec. and Vice-Nat. Sec. Gen. Acción Popular, 1983–85; Acción Popular Del. Frente Democrático de Perú gen. election 1990. *Leisure interests:* nat. and int. econ. devt, sport. *Address:* Los Eucaliptos 355-13A, San Isidro, Lima 27, Peru. *Telephone:* 440-1705. *Fax:* 440-4624.

PERCY, Charles Harting; American fmr politician and business executive; b. 27 Sept. 1919, Pensacola, Fla; s. of Edward H. Percy and Elisabeth Percy; m. Loraine Diane Guyer 1950; two s. two d.; ed Univ. of Chicago; Lt Sr Grade US Naval Air Corps 1943–45; sales trainee, apprentice, Bell & Howell 1938, Man., War Co-ordinating Dept 1941–43, Asst Sec. 1943–46, Corpn Sec. 1948–49, Pres., CEO 1949–63, Chair. Bd 1961–66; Senator from Illinois 1967–85; Pres. Charles Percy and Assocs Inc. 1985–; Chair. Foreign Relations Cttee 1981–85; Chair. Inst. of Int. Educ. 1985–89; Chair. and Pres. Hariri Foundation 1985–; Chair. US Int. Cultural and Trade Center Pres. Comm. 1988–; Founding Chair. Kennedy Center for Performing Arts; Republican; Hon. LLD (Kent Coll. of Law) and various other hon. degrees. *Publications:* Growing Old In the Country of the Young 1974, I Want To Know about the United States Senate 1976. *Leisure interests:* reading, travel, swimming, tennis, skiing. *Address:* 1691 34th Street, NW, Washington, DC 20007, USA (home). *Telephone:* (202)

337-1558 (office); (202) 337-1691 (home). *Fax:* (202) 337-5101 (office); (202) 337-5101 (home). *E-mail:* percycharles@ls.com (office); percycharles@ls.com (home).

PERDOMO, Carlos; Belizean fmr teacher and politician; *Minister of National Security;* m.; five c.; fmr Pres. St John's Coll; fmr Gen. Man. Centre for Employment Training; fmr Cabinet Sec. and Perm. Sec.; mem. United Democratic Party; Minister of Nat. Security 2008–. *Address:* Ministry of National Security, New Administration Building, Belmopan, Belize (office). *Telephone:* 822-1039 (office). *Fax:* 822-0433 (office). *E-mail:* min_defencehousing@yahoo.com (office). *Website:* www.governmentofbelize.gov.bz/ministry_details.php?ministry_id=11 (office).

PERDUE, Beverly Eaves, BA, MEd, PhD; American politician; *Governor of North Carolina;* b. 14 Jan. 1948, Grundy, Va; m.; two c.; ed Univ. of Kentucky, Univ. of Florida; Pres. The Perdue Co., 1985–; mem. N Carolina State Gen. Ass. Reps 1986–90, North Carolina State Senate 1990–2001; Lt Gov. of North Carolina 2001–09, Gov. of North Carolina 2009–; Democrat. *Address:* Office of the Governor, 20301 Mail Service Center, Raleigh, NC 27699-0301, USA (office). *Telephone:* (919) 733-4240 (office). *Fax:* (919) 715-3175 (office). *Website:* www.governor.state.nc.us (office).

PERDUE, Sonny; American state official; *Governor of Georgia;* b. 20 Dec. 1946, Perry, Ga; s. of Ervin Perdue; m. Mary Ruff; four c.; ed Warner Robbins High School, Univ. of Ga; with USAF 1971–74; fmr veterinarian, Raleigh, NC; Propr Houston Fertilizer and Grain, Agrowstar Inc.; began public service 1980s serving on Houston County Planning and Zoning Bd; Democratic mem. of State Senate, Ga 1991–1998, Pres. Pro Tempore 1997, re-elected as Republican cand. 1998–2002; Gov. of Ga 2003–. *Leisure interest:* flying. *Address:* Office of the Governor, State Capitol, Atlanta, GA 30334 (office); POB 698, Bonaire, GA 31005, USA (home). *Telephone:* (404) 656-1776 (office). *Website:* www.gov.state.ga.us (office).

PEREIRA, Aristides Maria; Cape Verde politician; b. 17 Nov. 1923, Boa Vista; s. of Porfírio Pereira Tavares and Maria das Neves Crus Silva; m. Carlina Fortes 1959; one s. two d.; ed Lycée du Cap-Vert; began career as radio-telegraphist; Head, Telecommunications Services, Bissau, Portuguese Guinea (now Guinea-Bissau); f. Partido Africano da Independência da Guiné e Cabo Verde (PAIGC) with the late Amílcar Cabral 1956; mem. Political Bureau, Cen. Cttee, PAIGC 1956–70; fled to Repub. of Guinea 1960; Asst Sec.-Gen. PAIGC 1964–73, Sec.-Gen. 1973–81; Sec.-Gen. Partido Africano da Independência de Cabo Verde (PAICV) 1981; mem. Perm. Comm. of Exec. Cttee for Struggle in charge of Security, Control and Foreign Affairs 1970; Pres. Repub. of Cape Verde 1975–91; Dr hc (Univs. of Rhode Island, Sacred Heart of Bridport, USA, Coimbra, Portugal, Usmane Danfodyo Univ., Sokoto, Nigeria); mem. Orders of Santiago of the Sword and Infante Dom Henrique (Portugal), Médaille, Ordre du Lyon (Senegal), Médaille Amílcar Cabral (Guinea-Bissau), Médaille de Fidélité au Peuple (Repub. of Guinea), Grand Cordon of Nat. Order of Southern Cross (Brazil), Agostinho Neto Medal, First Class (Angola), Amílcar Cabral Medal, First Class (Cape Verde). *Publications:* Uma luta, um Partido, dois país. *Leisure interests:* swimming, tennis, music. *Address:* c/o Prainha, PO Box 172, Praia, Cape Verde. *Telephone:* 612461 (office); 617747 (home). *Fax:* 614302 (office). *E-mail:* a-pereira@cvtelecom.cv (office).

PEREIRA, Raimundo; Guinea Bissau lawyer and politician; b. 1956; mem. African Party for Independence of Guinea and Cape Verde (PAIGC); mem. Assembléia Nacional Popular (Parl.) 2008–, Speaker 2008–; Pres. (interim) of Guinea Bissau 2009–. *Address:* c/o Office of the Prime Minister, Av. Unidade Africana, CP 137, Bissau, Guinea-Bissau (office).

PEREIRA PUCHY, Gonzalo; Chilean lawyer, academic and international organization official; *Secretary-General, Permanent Commission of the South Pacific;* b. 1967; ed Inst. of Int. Studies, Univ. of Chile; participated in numerous courses, seminars and meetings organized or sponsored by Cepal, FAO, Int. Whaling Comm., Int. Fund for Animal Welfare, Inst. of Int. Studies, Univ. of Chile and other Chilean univs on Law of the Sea, fishing legislation and environment; represented Chile at int. meeting of operating countries of ships of fishing and oceanographic investigation, Barcelona, Spain 1997; visited Spain and Portugal to observe insts and examine fishing legislation 2001; mem. Chilean del. to XXV Ordinary Meeting of Comision Permanente del Pacifico Sur Quito, Ecuador 2001, Chilean del. to VIII Ronda de Negociaciones Chile, EU to obtain Agreement on Free Trade, Brussels, Belgium 2002, Chilean del. to X Round of Chile Negotiations EU 2002; Prof. of Environmental Law, Univ. of the Sea, Valparaiso, Chile 2001–02; worked at Legal Div. of Under-Sec.'s Office of Fishing, Ministry of Economy 1995–98; Head of Legal Dept, Nat. Fishing Service, Ministry of Economy 1998–2002; Under-Sec. Comision Permanente del Pacifico Sur (Perm. Comm. of the South Pacific) 2002–06, Sec.-Gen. 2006–10. *Address:* Comision Permanente del Pacifico Sur, Av. Carlos Julio Arosemena, KM 3 Ed. Classic, 2 piso, Guayaquil, Ecuador (office). *Telephone:* (4) 222-12-02 (ext. 111) (office). *E-mail:* gpereira@cpps-int.org (office). *Website:* www.cpps-int.org (office).

PEREK, Luboš, RNDr, DrSc; Czech astronomer (retd); b. 26 July 1919, Prague; s. of Zdeněk Perek and Vilemina (née Trapp) Perek; m. Vlasta Straková 1945 (died 2007); ed Masaryk Univ., Brno and Charles Univ., Prague; Asst Astronomical Inst., Masaryk Univ., Brno 1946, Head 1953; Head, Stellar Dept, Astronomical Inst. of Czechoslovak Acad. of Sciences, Prague 1956, Dir Astronomical Inst. 1968–75; Vice-Pres. Comm. of the Galactic Structure and Dynamics, Int. Astronomical Union 1961–64, Asst Gen. Sec., Int. Astronomical Union 1964–67, Gen. Sec. 1967–70; Chief, Outer Space Affairs Division, UN Secr. 1975–80; Visiting Prof., Dearborn Observatory, Evanston, Ill. 1964; mem. Czechoslovak Astronomical Soc., Exec. Cttee Int. Council of Scientific Unions 1967–70, Vice-Pres. 1968–70; Chair. Int. Astronautical Fed. 1980–82; mem. Leopoldina Acad., Int. Acad. of Astronautics, Int. Inst. of Space Law, Nat. Acad. of the Air and Space, Toulouse, Czech Learned Soc. 1999; Assoc. mem. Royal Astronomical Soc.; Dr hc (Masaryk Univ., Brno) 1999; Silver Plaque for services to science 1969, Gold Plaque 1989, Janssen Medal, Paris 1992. *Publications include:* Catalogue of Galactic Planetary Nebulae (with L. Kohoutek) 1967, about 80 articles on geostationary orbits, definition of space, space debris and environment of space. *Leisure interest:* collecting seashells. *Address:* Astronomical Institute, Bočni II 1401, 141 31 Prague 4 (office); Kouřimská 28, 130 00 Prague 3, Czech Republic (home). *Telephone:* (267) 103068 (office); (272) 744780 (home). *Fax:* (272) 769023 (office). *E-mail:* perek@ig.cas.cz (office). *Website:* www.galaxy.ig.cas.cz (office); www.asu.cas.cz (home).

PERELLA, Joseph (Joe) Robert, MBA, CPA; American investment banker; *Chairman and CEO, Perella Weinberg Partners LP;* b. 20 Sept. 1941, Newark; s. of Dominic Perella and Agnes Perella; m. Amy Gralnick 1974; ed Lehigh Univ. and Harvard Business School; public accountant, Haskins & Sells, New York 1964–70; consultant, IBRD, Washington, DC 1971; Assoc. The First Boston Corpn New York 1972–74, Asst Vice-Pres. 1974–75, Vice-Pres. 1975–78, Man. Dir 1978–88; Chair. Wasserstein, Perella & Co. New York 1988–93; head of mergers and acquisitions then Chair. Institutional Securities and Investment Banking Group, mem. operating Cttee Morgan Stanley 1993–2005; co-f. Perella Weinberg Pnrs LP (investment banking firm), New York, Chair. and CEO 2006–. *Address:* Perella Weinberg Partners LP, 767 Fifth Avenue, New York, NY 10153, USA (office); Perella Weinberg Partners UK LLP, 20 Grafton Street, London, W1S 4DZ, England (office). *Telephone:* (212) 287-3300 (NY) (office); (20) 7268-2800 (London) (office). *Fax:* (212) 287-3201 (NY) (office); (20) 7268-2900 (London) (office). *Website:* www.pwpartners.com (office).

PERELMAN, Grigori Yakovlevich, CandSci; Russian mathematician; b. 13 June 1966, Leningrad (now St Petersburg); ed Leningrad Secondary School #239, Leningrad State Univ.; worked under Aleksandr Danilovich Aleksandrov and Yuri Dmitrievich Burago at Leningrad Dept of Steklov Math. Inst. of USSR (now Russian) Acad. of Sciences –2003; held posts at several univs in USA late 1980s–early 1990s; invited to spend a semester each at New York Univ. and State Univ. of NY at Stony Brook 1992; held fellowship at Univ. of Calif., Berkeley 1993–95; returned to Steklov Math. Inst. 1995; accepted invitation to visit and give series of talks on his work at MIT, Princeton Univ., State Univ. of NY at Stony Brook, Columbia Univ. and Harvard Univ. 2003; solved affirmatively the famous Poincaré conjecture, posed in 1904, and regarded as one of the most important and difficult open problems in math.; won Gold Medal as mem. USSR team competing in Int. Math. Olympiad 1982, Fields Medal (co-recipient) for "his contributions to geometry and his revolutionary insights into the analytical and geometric structure of the Ricci flow" (declined to accept the award or appear at the congress) 2006. *Publications:* numerous papers in professional journals. *Address:* c/o Steklov Mathematical Institute, Gubkina str. 8, 119991 Moscow, Russian Federation. *Telephone:* (495) 135-22-91. *Fax:* (495) 135-05-55. *E-mail:* steklov@mi.ras.ru. *Website:* www.mi.ras.ru.

PERELMAN, Ronald Owen, MBA; American business executive; *Chairman, Revlon, Inc.;* b. 1944, Greensboro, NC; s. of Raymond Perelman and Claudia (née Cohen) Perelman; m. 1st Faith Golding (divorced); four c.; m. 2nd Claudia Cohen (divorced); one d.; m. 3rd Patricia Duff (divorced); one d.; m. 4th Ellen Barkin (q.v.) 2000 (divorced 2006); ed Univ. of Pennsylvania and Wharton School of Finance; with Belmont Industries Inc. 1966–78; Dir, Chair. and CEO MacAndrews & Forbes Group, Inc., New York City 1978–; Dir, Chair. and CEO Revlon Group, Inc. (later Revlon, Inc.), New York City 1985–; Chair., CEO and Man. REV Holdings LLC; Chair. and CEO MacAndrews & Forbes Holdings, Inc.; Andrews Group Inc., New York 1985–; Chair. Nat. Health Labs, La Jolla, Calif. 1985–; Chair. Technicolor Inc., Hollywood, Calif.; Co-Chair. and CEO Panavision Inc.; Pres. Solomon R. Guggenheim Museum, NY 1995–; Dir Four Star Int. Inc., Compact Video Inc., M&F Worldwide Corpn, Scientific Games Corpn. *Address:* Revlon Inc., 237 Park Avenue, New York, NY 10017 (office); Solomark Guggenheim Museum, 1071 5th Avenue, New York, NY 10128, USA. *Telephone:* (212) 527-4000 (office). *Fax:* (212) 527-4995 (office). *Website:* www.revloninc.com (office).

PERENCHIO, A. Jerrold, BA; American media executive; *Chairman and CEO, Univision Communications Inc.;* b. Fresno, Calif.; m.; three c.; ed UCLA; boxing promoter and talent agent 1960s; pioneer of pay-TV; co-f. Embassy Communications 1974, sold to Coca-Cola 1985; bought Spanish-language broadcaster Univision 1992, floated 1996, added second Spanish-language network Telefutura 2003, currently Chair. and CEO Univision Communications Inc. *Address:* Univision Communications Inc., 1999 Avenue of the Stars, Suite 3050, Los Angeles, CA 90067, USA (office). *Telephone:* (310) 556-7676 (office). *Fax:* (310) 556-7615 (office). *Website:* www.univision.com (office).

PERÉNYI, Miklós; Hungarian cellist and composer; ed Music Acad. of Budapest; studied with Enrico Meinardi in Rome and Ede Bande in Budapest; started playing cello aged five, first public recital aged nine, Budapest; Violoncello Teacher, Franz Liszt Acad. of Music, Budapest 1974–, Prof. 1980–; appearances at int. music festivals including Edinburgh, Lucerne, Prague, Salzburg, Vienna, Hohenems, Warsaw, Berlin, also cello festivals in Kronberg, Wintherthur and Manchester, Festival Pablo Casals, Prades, France, as well as in Japan, China and USA; collaborates with pianist András Schiff, including concerts at Schubertiade Festival, Austria, Wigmore Hall, London, Edinburgh and Ruhr Festivals; performs regularly with Keller Quartet; prizewinner, Int. Pablo Casals Cello Competition, Budapest 1963, Liszt Prize 1970, Kossuth Prize 1980, Bartòk-Pasztory Prize 1987. *Recordings include:* works of Ernö Dohnányi, Ferenc Farkas, Zoltán Kodály, György Ligeti, András Mihály and Sàndor Veress (with Dénes Várjon), complete

Beethoven Sonatas (with András Schiff), Hungarian Cello Music, Beethoven: Complete Music for Piano and Violoncello (with András Schiff) (Cannes Classical Award 2005). *Leisure interests:* swimming, cycling. *Address:* c/o Impresariat Simmenauer, Bornstrasse 12, 20146 Hamburg, Germany (office). *Telephone:* (40) 42313111 (office). *Fax:* (40) 42313113 (office). *E-mail:* andreea.butucariu@impresariat-simmenauer.de (office). *Website:* www.impresariat-simmenauer.de (office).

PERERA, Air Chief Marshal G. Donald; Sri Lankan air force officer; *Chief of Defence Staff;* s. of the late G. Victor Perera and W. Somawathi Perera; ed Nat. Defence Coll., India, Air Command and Staff Coll., Air Univ., Maxwell Air Force Base, Ala, USA; participated in Air Operations in North and East since 1983, Chief of Staff 1998–2002, Commdr Sri Lanka Air Force 2002–06, Chief of Defence Staff 2006–; Vishista Seva Vibhushanaya, Utthama Seva Padakkama, Repub. of Sri Lanka Armed Services Medal, Sri Lanka Air Force 50th Anniversary Medal, Sri Lanka Armed Services Long Service Medal, Presidential Inauguration Medal, 50th Independence Anniversary Commemoration Medal, North and East Operations Medal, Purna Bhumi Padakkama, Vadamarachchi Operations Medal, Riviresa Campaign Service Medal. *Address:* c/o Group Capt. N. H. V. Gunaratne, Commanding Officer, Sri Lanka Air Force, Colombo, Sri Lanka (office). *Telephone:* (11) 2441044 (office). *E-mail:* info@airforce.lk (office). *Website:* www.airforce.lk (office).

PERES, Shimon; Israeli politician and head of state; *President;* b. 1923, Poland; s. of Isaac Persky and Sara Persky; m. Sonia Gelman; two s. one d.; ed New York Univ., Harvard Univ.; immigrated to Palestine 1934; fmr Sec. Hano'ar Ha'oved Movt; mem. Haganah Movt 1947; Israel Naval Service, Ministry of Defence 1948; Head of Defence Mission in USA; Deputy Dir-Gen. of Ministry of Defence 1952–53, Dir-Gen. 1953–59, Deputy Minister of Defence 1959–65; mem. Knesset 1959–; mem. Mapai Party 1941–65, founder mem. and Sec.-Gen. Rafi Party 1965, mem. Labour Party after merger 1968, Chair. 1977–92, 1995–97, 2003–05, resgnd from party Nov. 2005; Minister for Econ. Devt in the Administered Areas and for Immigrant Absorption 1969–70, of Transport and Communications 1970–74, of Information March–June 1974, of Defence 1974–77, of Foreign Affairs 1992–95; Acting Prime Minister April–May 1977; Leader of the Opposition 1977–84, 1996–97; Prime Minister of Israel 1984–86, 1995–96; Minister of the Interior and of Religious Affairs 1984–85, of Defence 1995–96; Vice-Premier and Minister of Foreign Affairs 1986–88, Vice-Premier and Finance Minister 1988–90, Minister of Regional Co-operation –2001, of Foreign Affairs 2001–02; Vice-Premier –2005; Vice-Premier and Minister for Devt of the Negev and Galillee 2006–07; Pres. of Israel 2007–; shared Nobel Prize for Peace 1994; Int. Council of Christians and Jews Interfaith Gold Medallion 1997. *Publications:* The Next Step 1965, David's Sling 1970, Tomorrow is Now 1978, From These Men 1979, Witness (autobiog.) 1993, The New Middle East 1993, Battling for Peace 1995 and numerous political articles in Israeli and foreign publs. *Address:* Office of the President, 3 Hanassi Street, Jerusalem 92188, Israel (office). *Telephone:* 2-6707211 (office). *Fax:* 2-5611033 (office). *E-mail:* president@president.gov.il (office). *Website:* www.president.gov.il (office).

PERESYPKIN, Oleg Gerasimovich, (Oleg Gerasimov), DHist, MSc (Econ); Russian diplomatist and orientalist; b. 12 Aug. 1935, Baku; s. of Gerasim Peresypkin and Anna Kochergina; m. Natalia Ushakova 1957; one d.; ed Moscow Inst. of Int. Relations; Counsellor, Embassy, Yemen Arab Repub. 1971–76; Adviser, Near Eastern Countries Dept, USSR Ministry of Foreign Affairs 1976–80; Amb. to Yemen Arab Repub. 1980–84, to Libya 1984–86; mem. Collegium of Foreign Ministry 1985–; Rector Diplomatic Acad. 1986–93; Chief Adviser on Near Eastern and N African Countries, Ministry of Foreign Affairs 1993–96; Amb. to Lebanon 1996–2000; Pres. Imperial Orthodox Palestine Soc. 1989–2000; Pres. Russian Soc. for Friendship and Cultural Co-operation with Lebanon 2001–; Vice-Pres. Russian Soc. for Friendship with Yemen; Honoured worker of Russian diplomatic corps 2001; Order of Friendship 1995. *Publications:* Iraqi Oil 1969, Yemen Revolution 1979, On the New East Crossroads 1979, Fifth Season 1991, Oriental Patterns 1993, Informal Notes 1997, Yemen and Yemenites – Memoirs of a Russian Diplomat 2005. *Leisure interests:* travelling, reading. *Address:* PO Box 103, 121069 Moscow; Vosdvijenka 14, 103885 Moscow, Russia. *Telephone:* (495) 243-68-35. *Fax:* (495) 243-68-35. *E-mail:* hmbperesypkin@mail.ru.

PERETSMAN, Nancy B., MPPM; American investment banker; *Executive Vice-President and Managing Director, Allen & Co. LLC;* m.; one d.; ed Woodrow Wilson School, Princeton Univ., Yale School of Man.; joined Salomon Brothers in 1983, Man. Dir 1990–95; Exec. Vice-Pres. and Man. Dir Allen & Co. LLC (fmrly Allen & Co. Inc.) 1995–; mem. Bd Dirs Charter Communications Inc. –2004, Priceline.com 1999–, several privately held cos; mem. Advisory Bd Narad Networks; Vice-Chair. Bd The New School; mem. Bd Teach for America; Trustee Inst. of Advanced Study, Princeton Univ. (Emer.); named by Money magazine one of Smartest Women in the Money Business, Financial Women's Asscn Private Sector Woman of the Year 2001, ranked by Fortune magazine amongst 50 Most Powerful Women in Business in the US 1999–2001, (31st) 2002, (36th) 2003, (37th) 2004, (38th) 2005, (47th) 2006, ranked 44th by The Hollywood Reporter amongst Women in Entertainment Power 100 2003. *Address:* 9 East 79th Street, New York, NY 10075; Allen & Co. LLC, 711 5th Avenue, 9th Floor, New York, NY 10022, USA (office). *Telephone:* (212) 832-80000 (office). *Fax:* (212) 832-8023 (office).

PERETZ, Amir; Israeli politician and fmr trade union official; b. (Armand Peretz), 1952, Morocco; m. Ahlama; four c.; emigrated to Israel at age of four; fmr Munitions Officer, Paratroopers Div., Israeli Army; fmr farmer; elected Mayor of Sderot 1983; mem. Knesset 1988–; CEO Histadrut Haovdim Haleumit 1995–2005; founder and Leader Am Ehad (One Nation) 1999–2004 (until merger with Israel Labour Party); Chair. Israel Labour Party 2005–07; Deputy Prime Minister and Minister of Defence 2006–07; mem. Peace Now. *Address:* Israel Labour Party, POB 62033, Tel-Aviv 61620, Israel (office). *Telephone:* 3-6899444 (office); 3-6899431 (office). *Fax:* 3-6899420 (office); 3-6899430 (office). *E-mail:* inter@havoda.org.il (office). *Website:* www.havoda.org.il (office).

PERETZ, David Lindsay Corbett, CB, MA; British international finance official; b. 29 May 1943; s. of Michael Peretz and April Peretz; m. Jane Wildman 1966; one s. one d.; ed The Leys School Cambridge and Exeter Coll. Oxford; Asst Prin. Ministry of Tech. 1965–69; Head of Public Policy and Institutional Studies, Int. Bank Research Org. 1969–76; Prin. HM Treasury 1976–80, Asst Sec. External Finance 1980–84, Prin. Pvt. Sec. to Chancellor of Exchequer 1984–85, Under-Sec. (Home Finance) 1985–86, (Monetary Group, Public Finance) 1986–90; UK Exec. Dir IMF and IBRD and Econ. Minister, Washington, DC 1990–94; Deputy Dir Int. Finance, HM Treasury 1994–99; UK G7 Financial Sherpa 1994–98; Sr Adviser, World Bank Group 1999–, Exec. Sec. World Bank Joint Task Force on Small States 2001; currently consultant Ind. Evaluation Office of the IMF, Washington, DC; Chair. UK UK Advisory Cttee on Devt Effectiveness. *Leisure interests:* walking, sailing, listening to music. *Address:* Independent Evaluation Office of the International Monetary Fund, 700 19th Street, NW, Washington, DC 20431, USA (office). *Telephone:* (202) 623-7312 (office). *Fax:* (202) 623-9990 (office). *E-mail:* dperetz@imf.org (office); dlcperetz@yahoo.co.uk (office). *Website:* www.ieo-imf.org (office); www.iacdi.independent.gov.uk/ (office).

PEREZ, Antonio M.; Spanish business executive; *Chairman and CEO, Eastman Kodak Company;* ed Madrid Univ.; fmrly with Hewlett-Packard Co., positions including Corp. Vice-Pres., Pres. Consumer Business, mem. Exec. Council; Pres. and CEO Gemplus Int. 2000–01; COO Eastman Kodak Co. 2003–05, Pres. 2003–06, CEO 2005–, Chair. 2006–, mem. Bd of Dirs; mem. Bd of Dirs Freescale Semiconductor Inc.; mem. Business Roundtable. *Address:* Eastman Kodak Company, 343 State Street, Rochester, NY 14650, USA (office). *Fax:* (585) 724-1089 (office). *Website:* www.kodak.com (office).

PÉREZ, Jésus Arnaldo; Venezuelan diplomatist and politician; *Ambassador to Canada;* Amb. to France –2004; Minister of Foreign Affairs 2004; Amb. to Canada 2005–. *Address:* Embassy of Venezuela, 32 Range Road, Ottawa, ON K1N 8J4, Canada (office). *Telephone:* (613) 235-5151 (office). *Fax:* (613) 235-3205 (office). *E-mail:* info.canada@misionvenezuela.org (office). *Website:* www.misionvenezuela.org (office).

PEREZ, Vincent; Swiss actor; b. 10 June 1962, Lausanne; ed Conservatoire, Paris. *Film appearances include:* Cyrano de Bergerac 1990, Indochine 1992, La Reine Margot 1994, The Crow: City of Angels 1996, Swept from the Sea 1997, Le Bossu 1997, Shot Through the Heart (TV) 1998, The Treat 1998, Talk of Angels 1998, Those Who Love Me Can Take the Train 1999, Time Regained 1999, Marry Me 2000, The Libertine 2000, I Dreamed of Africa 2000, Love Bites 2001, Bride of the Wind 2001, Queen of the Damned 2002, The Pharmacist 2003, Happiness Costs Nothing 2003, Fanfan la tulipe 2003, Je reste! 2003, Les clefs de bagnole 2003, New France 2004.

PEREZ, William (Bill) D., BA; American business executive; *President and CEO, Wm. Wrigley Jr. Company;* b. 1947, Akron, Ohio; m. Catherine A. Perez; two c.; ed Cornell Univ., American Grad. School of Int. Man.; joined S.C. Johnson & Son Inc. 1970, fmr positions include Gen. Man. S.C. Johnson Spain, S.C. Johnson Iberia, Vice-Pres. and Regional Dir of Consumer Products, Latin America, Vice-Pres. Home Care business, Exec. Vice-Pres. of Consumer Products, N America, Pres. and COO Worldwide Consumer Products 1993–96, Pres. and CEO S.C. Johnson & Son Inc. 1996–2004; Pres. and CEO Nike Inc. 2004–06 (resgnd), mem. Bd of Dirs –2006; Pres. and CEO Wm. Wrigley Jr. Co., Chicago 2006–; mem. Bd of Dirs Kellogg Co. (mem. Audit Cttee, Consumer Marketing Cttee) 1999–, Hallmark Cards Inc., Grocery Manufacturers of America. *Leisure interests:* running. *Address:* Wm. Wrigley Jr. Company, 410 North Michigan Avenue, Chicago, IL 60611, USA (office). *Telephone:* (312) 644-2121 (office). *Fax:* (312) 644-0097 (office). *Website:* www.wrigley.com (office).

PÉREZ BALLADARES, Ernesto, MBA; Panamanian fmr head of state; b. 29 June 1946, Panama City; s. of Ernesto Pérez Balladares Sr and María Enriqueta González Revilla; m. Dora Boyd; two s. three d.; ed Univs of Notre Dame and Pennsylvania; Dir, Corp. Credit Official for Cen. America and Panama, Citibank 1971–75; Minister of Finance and the Treasury 1976–81, of Planning and Econ. Policy 1981–82; founding mem. Partido Revolucionario Democrático (PRD) 1979, Sec.-Gen. 1982, 1992; Dir-Gen. Instituto de Recursos Hidráulicos y Electrificación (IRHE) 1983; Pres. of Panama 1994–99; Pres. Golden Fruit, SA, Inversionista el Torreón, SA; mem. Legislation Comm., PRD Political Comm.; Order of Sacred Treasure (1st class) (Japan) 1980, Orden Aguila Azteca en Grado de Bando (Mexico) 1981. *Address:* c/o Office of the President, Palacio Presidencial, Valija 50, Panamá 1, Panama.

PÉREZ DE BRICIO OLARIAGA, Carlos; Spanish oil industry executive; b. 31 Dec. 1927, Madrid; Vice-Pres. Comm. of Basic Industries of Iron and Steel 1968; Chair. Sub-Cttee on Iron and Steel, OECD 1969; Chief of Directorate of Naval and Iron and Steel Industries 1969–74; Minister of Industry 1975–76, 1976–77; Pres. Sodiex 1981–83; Dir Compañía Española de Petróleos SA (CEPSA) 1991–2008, Exec. Vice-Pres. 1996, Chair. and CEO 1996–2008; Head of Ministry of Public Works 1997; Pres. Union of Iron and Steel Cos (UNESID) 1968; Founder and Pres. Spanish Confed. of Metal Cos (CONFEMETAL) 1978–; Vice-Pres. Spanish Confed. of Enterprise Orgs (CEOE) 1981–98, European Org. of Metallurgical Industries 1990; fmr mem. Advisory Bd Macosa, Carburos Metálicos, Acerinox; mem. Bd Dirs Compañía Logistica de Hidrocarburos CLH SA 2004.

PÉREZ DE CUÉLLAR, Javier; Peruvian politician and diplomatist (retd); b. 19 Jan. 1920, Lima; m. Marcela Temple; two c.; ed Catholic Univ., Lima; joined Foreign Ministry 1940, diplomatic service 1944; served as Sec. in embassies in France, UK, Bolivia, Brazil (later Counsellor); Dir Legal and Personnel Dept, Dir of Admin., of Protocol and of Political Affairs, Ministry of External Relations 1961–63; Amb. to Switzerland 1964–66; Perm. UnderSec. and Sec.-Gen. Foreign Office 1966–69, Amb. to USSR (concurrently to Poland) 1969–71, to Venezuela 1978; Perm. Rep. to UN 1971–75; mem. UN Security Council 1973–74, Pres. 1974; Special Rep. of UN Sec.-Gen. in Cyprus 1975–77; UN Under-Sec.-Gen. for Special Political Affairs 1979–81; UN Sec.-Gen. 1982–91; Prime Minister of Peru 2000–01; Amb. to France 2001–04; Pres. World Comm. on Culture and Devt UN/UNESCO 1992–, Int. Disability Foundation 1992–, Fondation de l'Arche de la Fraternité 1993–; Dir Repub. Nat. Bank of New York 1992–; Pres. Cand. in 1995 Elections; fmr Prof. of Diplomatic Law, Acad. Diplomática del Perú and Prof. of Int. Relations, Acad. de Guerra Aérea del Perú; del. to First UN Gen. Ass. 1946–47 and other int. confs; Montague Burton Visiting Prof. of Int. Relations, Univ. of Edinburgh 1985; mem. Acad. Mexicana de Derecho Int. 1988–; Dr hc (Univ. of Nice) 1983, (Jagiellonian, Charles and Sofia Univs, Univ. of San Marcos and Vrije Univ., Brussels) 1984, (Carleton Univ., Ottawa, Sorbonne Univ., Paris) 1985, (Osnabruck) 1986, (Univs of Mich., Coimbra, Mongolian State, Humbolt, Moscow State) 1987, (Univ. of Leiden) 1988, (Cambridge) 1989, (Univ. of Kuwait) 1993, (Oxford) 1993; Olaf Palme Prize for Public Service 1989, Prince of Asturias Prize for Ibero-American Co-operation, Alexander Onassis Foundation Prize 1990, Four Freedoms Award (Franklin Delano Roosevelt Inst.) 1992. *Publication:* Manual de Derecho Diplomático 1964, Anarchy or Order 1992, Pilgrimage for Peace 1997. *Address:* c/o Ministry of Foreign Affairs, Jirón Lampa 535, Lima 1; Avenida A. Miro Quesada, 1071 Lima, Peru.

PÉREZ ESQUIVEL, Adolfo; Argentine human rights leader, architect and sculptor; b. 26 Nov. 1931, Buenos Aires; m. Amanda Pérez 1956; three s.; ed Nat. School of Fine Arts, Buenos Aires; trained as architect and sculptor; Prof. of Art, Manuel Belgrano Nat. School of Fine Arts, Buenos Aires 1956–71; Prof. Faculty of Architecture and Urban Studies; Univ. Nacional de la Plata; gave up teaching to concentrate on non-violent human rights movt; f. Servicio Paz y Justicia en America Latina, Buenos Aires 1973, Sec.-Gen. 1974–86, Hon. Pres. 1986–; co-founder Ecumenical Movt for Human Rights, Argentina; Pres. Perm. Ass. for Human Rights; arrested 1977, released May 1978; visited Europe 1980; Pres. Int. League for Human Rights and Liberation of Peoples 1987; fmr Rector UN Univ. for Peace; Hon. Citizen of Assisi 1982; Nobel Prize for Peace 1980. *Publication:* Caminando Junto al Pueblo (Walking Together with the People) 1995. *Address:* Servicio Paz y Justicia, Piedras 730, CP 1070, Buenos Aires, Argentina.

PÉREZ-LLORCA, José Pedro; Spanish politician and lawyer; *Partner, Pérez-Llorca law firm;* b. 30 Nov. 1940, Cadiz; s. of José Pérez-Llorca and Carmen Pérez-Llorca; m. Carmen Zamora Bonilla 1965; one s. one d.; ed Madrid Central (Complutense) Univ., Univs of Freiburg and Munich; entered diplomatic service 1964; adviser, Spanish del. to 21st and 22nd Gen. Ass. of UN and 5th extraordinary emergency session; Legal Adviser to Parl. 1968; Higher Council for Foreign Affairs 1970; practised law, Madrid 1970–, pvt. law practice 1983–; mem. Cortes 1977–82; fmr Parl. Leader Unión de Centro Democrático (UCD); mem. Comm. for drawing up Constitution 1978; Minister of the Presidency 1979–80, for Relations with Parl. Jan.–May 1980, for Territorial Admin. May–Oct. 1980, for Foreign Affairs 1980–82; Chair. AEG-Ibérica SA, Urquiso Leasing SA; Dir Robert Bosch Española SA; Prof. of Constitutional Law, School of Diplomacy; Iberian Law Firm of the Year, Chambers Global Awards 2006. *Address:* Alcalá 61, 28014 Madrid, Spain (office). *Telephone:* (914) 360420 (office). *Fax:* (914) 360430 (office). *E-mail:* ppl@perezllorca.com (office). *Website:* www.perezllorca.com (office).

PÉREZ MOLINA, Gen. Otto; Guatemalan army officer (retd) and politician; *Secretary-General, Partido Patriota;* b. 1 Dec. 1950, Guatemala City; ed School of the Americas (now Western Hemisphere Inst. for Security Cooperation), Fort Benning, Columbus, Ga and Inter-American Defense Coll., Washington, DC, USA; served as Dir of Mil. Intelligence and Insp.-Gen. of the Army, member of group of army officers who backed Defence Minister Óscar Mejía's coup d'état against de facto Pres. Efraín Ríos Montt 1983, also instrumental in restoring normality in aftermath of Pres. Jorge Serrano Elías's abortive 'self-coup' 1993; apptd by incoming Pres. Ramiro de León Carpio as Head of Presidential Gen. Staff (EMP) 1993–95; also represented mil. in negotiations that led to 1996 Peace Accords, ending Guatemala's 30-year-long civil war; represented Guatemala on Inter-American Defense Bd 1998–2000; retd from active mil. duty in Jan. 2000; f. Partido Patriota (Patriotic Party) 2001; elected to Congress 2003–; cand. in presidential election 2007. *Address:* Partido Patriota, 11 Calle 11-54, Zona 1, Guatemala City, Guatemala (office). *Telephone:* 2230-5068 (office). *Fax:* 2230-6227 (office). *E-mail:* comunicacion@partidopatriota.org (office). *Website:* www.partidopatriota.com (office).

PÉREZ-REVERTE, Arturo; Spanish journalist and writer; b. 1951, Cartagena; fmr journalist, war corresp., Pueblo; war corresp., Spanish nat. TV; elected to Spanish Royal Acad. 2003; Chevalier, Ordre des Arts et des Lettres (France) 1998, Gran Cruz del Mérito Naval 2005, Chevalier, Ordre Nat. du Mérite (France) 2008; Grand Prix for Detective Literature (France) 1993, Asturias Prize for Journalism for his coverage of the war in the fmr Yugoslavia for TV 1993, Ondas Prize for Radio de España's La Ley de la Calle 1993. *Films:* El Maestro de Esgrima 1992, La Tabla de Flandes 1994, Cachito 1995, Territorio Comanche 1997, La Novena Puerta 1999, Gitano 2000, Alatriste 2006, La Carta Esférica 2007. *Publications:* El Húsar 1986, El maestro de esgrima (trans. as The Fencing Master) 1988, La tabla de Flandes (trans. as The Flanders Panel) 1990, El club Dumas (trans. as The Dumas

Club) 1993, La sombra del águila 1993, Territorio comanche 1994, Un asunto de honor 1995, Obra breve 1995, La piel del tambor (trans. as The Seville Communion; Jean Monnet Prize for European Literature 1997) 1995, El capitán Alatriste (trans. as Captain Alatriste) 1996, Limpieza de sangre (trans. as Purity of Blood) 1997, El sol de Breda (trans. as The Sun Over Breda) 1998, Patente de corso 1998, La carta esférica (trans. as The Nautical Chart) (Prix Beau Livre de l'Académie de Marine Française) 2000, El oro del rey (trans. as The King's Gold) 2000, Con ánimo de ofender 2001, La Reina del Sur (translated as The Queen of the South) 2002, El caballero del jubón amarillo (trans. as The Man in the Yellow Doublet) 2003, Cabo Trafalgar 2004, No me cogeréis vivo 2005, El pintor de batallas (trans. as The Painter of Battles) (Premio Vallombrosa - Gregor von Rezzori 2008) 2006, Corsarios de Levante 2006, Un Día de Cólera 2007, Ojos Azules 2009; contrib. to Spanish periodicals, including XL Semanal (weekly article). *Address:* c/o RDC Agencia Literaria, Fernando VI 13–15, 3° derecha, 28004 Madrid, Spain (office). *Telephone:* (91) 3085585 (office). *Fax:* (91) 3085600 (office). *E-mail:* rdc@rdclitera.com (office); RDCprom@rdclitera.com (office). *Website:* www.capitanalatriste.com; www.perez-reverte.com.

PÉREZ RODRÍGUEZ, Carlos Andrés; Venezuelan fmr head of state; b. 27 Oct. 1922, Rubio; m. Blanca Rodríguez de Pérez; one s. five d.; ed Univ. Cen. de Venezuela; Pvt. Sec. to Pres. Rómulo Betancourt 1945; mem. Chamber of Deputies 1947–48, 1958–74; in exile 1949–58; Chief Ed. La República, San José 1953–58; Minister of the Interior 1963–64; Sec.-Gen. Acción Democrática 1968; Pres. of Venezuela 1974–79, 1989–93; suspended, to stand trial on embezzlement charges; barred from returning to office Sept. 1993; found guilty of misappropriation of public funds May 1996 and sentenced to two years and four months' imprisonment, served as house arrest owing to age.

PÉREZ RODRÍGUEZ, Florentino; Spanish civil engineer and construction industry executive; *Chairman and CEO, ACS Group;* b. 1947; served in various public admin posts 1976–82, including Del. for Sanitation and Environment, Madrid City Council, Gen. Sub-Dir of Promotion, Centre for Devt of Industrial Tech., Ministry of Industry and Energy, Gen. Man. Transport Infrastructures, Ministry for Transport, Chair. IRYDA, Ministry of Agric.; joined Construcciones Padrós SA as CEO 1983; Chair. OCP Construcciones SA 1993–97; mem. Bd Dirs ACS Group (Actividades de Construcción y Servicios SA) 1989–, Chair. and CEO 1993–; Vice-Chair. Abertis Infraestructuras; mem. Bd Dirs Sanef. *Address:* ACS, Actividades de Construcción y Servicios SA, Avenida Pío XII 102, Madrid 28036, Spain (office). *Telephone:* (91) 3439200 (office). *Fax:* (91) 3439456 (office). *E-mail:* info@grupoacs.com (office). *Website:* www.grupoacs.com (office).

PEREZ ROQUE, Felipe Ramón; Cuban politician; *Minister of Foreign Affairs;* b. 28 March 1965, Havana; m.; two c.; ed Superior Politécnico José A. Echeverría; head univ. students union 1988; fmr electronics engineer; involved with biotechnology complex 1960; mem. Cen. Cttee CP of Cuba 1991–; mem. Nat. Ass. 1986–, State Council 1993–; Pvt. Sec. to Fidel Castro; Minister of Foreign Affairs 1999–; José A. Echeverría Medal. *Address:* Ministry of Foreign Affairs, Calzada 360, Vedado, Havana, Cuba (office). *Telephone:* (7) 55-3537 (office). *Fax:* (7) 33-3460 (office). *E-mail:* cubaminrex@minrex.gov.cu (office). *Website:* www.cubaminrex.cu (office).

PÉREZ VERA, Víctor L., MSc; Chilean engineer, university administrator and academic; *Rector, University of Chile;* b. Rancagua; ed liceo Manuel Barros Borgoño de Santiago and studies with Prof. Elisa Gayán, Faculty of Physical Sciences and Math., Univ. of Chile, Univ. of Michigan, USA; Dir Polytechnic Inst. of Santiago 1967–69; Investigator and Prof., Dept of Industrial Eng, Universidad de Chile 1969, Titular Prof. 1986, Dir Dept of Industrial Eng 1980–84, 1988–90, Vice-Dean Faculty 1984–85, mem. Comm. of Academic Evaluation 1991–92, Pro-Rector Universidad de Chile 1993, Dean Faculty of Physical Sciences and Math. 1994–2002, mem. Special Univ. Senate Comm. 2002–05, Rector Universidad de Chile 2006–; Visiting Prof. at several nat. and Latin American univs; mem. Editorial Cttee Information and Management journal; Coordinator Higher Educ. Comm.; mem. Inst. of Engineers of Chile; Premio 'Profesor Enrique Silva a la Trayectoria Docente', Dept of Industrial Eng, Universidad de Chile 1994, Premio 'Ingeniero Civil Industrial del Año', Especialidad Civil Industrial, Coll. of Engineers of Chile, AG 1994, Premio 'Raúl Devés Jullián', Inst. of Engineers of Chile 2001, Premio 'Al Ingeniero por Acciones Distinguidas' 2003. *Publications:* author or co-author of seven books; numerous scientific papers in professional journals on information systems and financial analysis; articles on higher educ. in El Mercurio, La Segunda, El Mostrador, La Tercera. *Address:* Office of the Rector, Universidad de Chile, Avda Libertador Bernardo O'Higgins 1058, Casilla 10-D, Santiago, Chile (office). *Telephone:* (2) 9782000 (office). *Fax:* (2) 6781012 (office). *Website:* ww.uchile.cl (office).

PERHAM, Richard Nelson, MA, PhD, ScD, FRS, FRSA, FMedSci; British biochemist and academic; *Professor Emeritus of Structural Biochemistry, University of Cambridge;* b. 27 April 1937, London; s. of Cyril Perham and Helen Thornton; m. Nancy Lane 1969; one s. one d.; ed Latymer Upper School, London and St John's Coll., Cambridge; MRC Scholar, MRC Lab. of Molecular Biology, Cambridge 1961–64; Helen Hay Whitney Fellow, Dept of Molecular Biophysics, Yale Univ. 1966–67; Univ. Lecturer in Biochemistry, Univ. of Cambridge 1969–77, Reader in Biochemistry of Macromolecular Structures 1977–89, Prof. of Structural Biochemistry 1989–2004, Head Dept of Biochemistry 1985–96, Prof. Emer. 2004–; Fellow, St John's Coll., Cambridge 1964–2004, 2007–, Pres. 1983–87, Master 2004–07; Fogarty Int. Scholar, NIH, USA 1990–93; Chair. Editorial Bd FEBS Journal 1998–; Chair. Bd Govs Latymer Upper School 2004–; Chair. Scientific Advisory Bd Max-Planck-Institut fur Molekulare Physiologie, Dortmund 2002–; Deputy Pres. Science Cttee, Fondation Louis-Jeantet de Medecine, Geneva 2005–; mem. Biochemical Soc., Royal Inst. of GB; Fellow Academia Europaea, European Molecular

Biology Org.; Max Planck Prize 1993, Novartis Medal and Prize 1998, Silver Medal Italian Biochemical Soc. 2000, Int. Asscn of Protein Structure and Proteomics Pehr Edman Award 2008. *Publications:* Instrumentation in Amino Acid Sequence Analysis; more than 250 papers and articles in learned journals. *Leisure interests:* gardening, theatre, opera, rowing, antiques (18th century). *Address:* St John's College, Cambridge, CB2 1TP, England (office). *Telephone:* (1223) 337724 (office). *Fax:* (1223) 337720 (office). *E-mail:* rnp1@cam.ac.uk (office). *Website:* www.joh.cam.ac.uk (office); www.bioc.cam.ac.uk (office).

PERIGOT, François; French business executive; b. 12 May 1926, Lyons; s. of Jean-Paul Perigot and Marguerite de la Tour; m. 2nd Isabelle Paque 1986; one s. one d. from fmr marriage; ed Lycée de Bastia, Faculté de Droit, Paris and Inst. d'Etudes Politiques, Paris; joined Unilever group (France) 1955, Head of Personnel 1966; Pres.-Dir-Gen. Thibaud Gibbs et Cie 1968–70; Dir Unilever (Spain) 1971–75; Pres.-Dir-Gen. Unilever (France) 1976–86; Pres. Campagnie de Plâtre 1987–98; mem. Bd of Sodexho, OENEO, CDC lxis Pvt. Equity, Lever, Astra; mem. Exec. Council, Conseil Nat. du Patronat Français (CNPF) 1981–86, Pres. 1986–94; Vice-Pres. Union des confédérations de l'industrie et des employeurs d'Europe (UNICE) 1988–92, Pres. 1994; mem. Social and Econ. Council (CES) 1989–99; Pres. MEDEF Int. (Int. Br. of French Employers' Asscn) 1997–2005, Hon. Pres. 2005–; Pres. Org. Int. des Employeurs (OIE), Geneva 2001–06, Hon. Pres. 2006–; mem. Bd of Dirs Sodexho; mem. World Comm. on the Social Dimension of Globalization; Commdr, Légion d'honneur; numerous foreign decorations. *Leisure interest:* golf. *Address:* Organisation Internationale des Employeurs, Geneva, Switzerland (office); 9 Avenue Fréderic le Ploy, 75007 Paris, France (home). *Telephone:* 1-53-59-16-12 (office). *Fax:* 1-45-55-03-77 (office). *E-mail:* ioe@ioe-emp.org (office). *Website:* www.ioe-emp.org (office).

PERIN, François; Belgian politician, legal scholar, academic and writer; *Professor Emeritus of Constitutional Law, University of Liège;* b. 31 Jan. 1921, Liège; ed Univ. of Liège; mem. of Socialist Party 1943–64; Asst Chef de Cabinet to Minister of Interior 1954–57; Asst to Prof. of Public Law 1954–58; Dir of Studies, Faculty of Law, Univ. of Liège 1958, Prof. of Constitutional Law 1967–86, Prof. Emer. 1986–; Deputy to Nat. Ass. 1965–; Pres. Rassemblement Wallon 1968–74; Minister of Institutional Reforms 1974–76; mem. co-founders Parti Réformateur Libéral (PRL) 1976–; author of Les invités du Dr. Klaust, staged Théâtre Arlequin, Liège 1998–99 and of Double jeu. Drame à Liège 1632–1637, staged Théâtre Arlequin 2002. *Publications:* La démocratie enrayée—essai sur le régime parlementaire belge de 1918 à 1958 1960, La Belgique au défi: Flamands Wallons à la recherche d'un état 1962, La décision politique en Belgique (co-author) 1965, Le régionalisme dans l'intégration européenne 1969, Germes et bois morts dans la société politique contemporaine 1981, Histoire d'une nation introuvable 1988, Franc parler: témoignage sur la double crise du Christianisme et du Rationalisme 1996, Tabous-chemins croisés (co-author) 2001. *Leisure interests:* music, concerts, history of religions, philosophy and science. *Address:* 10 rue Chevaufosse, 4000 Liège, Belgium. *Telephone:* (4) 223-67-82.

PERINETTI, André Louis; French administrator and theatre director; *Honorary President, International Theatre Institute;* b. 7 Aug. 1933, Asnières; m. Fatiha Bel-el-Abbas 1974; two s. one d.; ed Collège Turgot, Law Faculty of Paris, Univ. of Theatre of Nations; theatre dir 1965–83; Gen. Man. Théâtre Cité Universitaire 1968–72, Nat. Theatre of Strasbourg 1972–75, Nat. Theatre of Chaillot, Paris 1974–81; Consultant, UNESCO 1974, Ministry of Culture 1982–83; Sec.-Gen. Int. Theatre Inst. (UNESCO) 1984–2004, Hon. Pres. 2004–; Chevalier, Légion d'honneur, des Arts et Lettres; Dr hc (Bratislava). *Leisure interests:* theatre, music, tennis. *Address:* International Theatre Institute—ITI, Maison de l'UNESCO, 1 rue Miollis, 75732 Paris Cedex 15 (office); 109 avenue Charles de Gaulle, 92200 Neuilly, France. *Telephone:* 1-45-68-48-80 (office). *Fax:* 1-45-66-50-40 (office). *E-mail:* iti@iti-worldwide.org (office). *Website:* iti-worldwide.org (office).

PERINO, Dana Marie, BA; American journalist, consultant and fmr government official; *Chief Issues Counselor, Burson-Marsteller;* b. 9 May 1972, Evanston, Wy.; d. of Leo Perino and Jan Perino; m. Peter McMahon; ed Ponderosa High School, Parker, Colo, Univ. of Southern Colorado, Univ. of Illinois at Springfield; while attending univ. worked with KTSC (Univ. of Southern Colorado radio station), also host Capitol Journal, weekly TV summary of Colo politics and producer Standoff, a weekly TV public affairs program; worked as daily reporter covering Springfield, Ill. for WCIA-TV; early career in Washington, DC as Staff Asst for US Congressman Scott McInnis of Colo 1995, then Press Sec. for US Congressman Dan Schaefer of Colo; worked in high-tech public affairs, San Diego, Calif.; Spokesperson US Dept of Justice, Washington, DC 2001, then Dir of Communications, White House Council on Environmental Quality; Deputy Asst to the Pres. and Deputy White House Press Sec. 2006–07, White House Press Sec. 2007–09; Chief Issues Counselor, Burson-Marsteller, Washington, DC 2009–. *Address:* Burson-Marsteller, 1110 Vermont Avenue, NW, Suite 1200, Washington, DC 20005-3554, USA (office). *Telephone:* (202) 530-0400 (office). *Fax:* (202) 530-4500 (office). *Website:* www.burson-marsteller.com (office).

PERIŠIC, Zoran; Serbian film director, writer, producer and visual effects supervisor; b. 16 March 1940, Zemun; Dir Sky Bandits/Gunbus (film) 1986; Producer-Dir The Phoenix and the Magic Carpet 1995; Dir-Writer Captain Cook's Travels (TV, animated series), Magic Fountain (TV, animated series), In Search of the Real Dracula (documentary), etc.; cr. visual and/or special effects for 2001 – A Space Odyssey 1968, Land of the Minotaur 1976, Superman I 1978, Superman II 1980, Superman III 1983, Return to Oz 1985, Sky Bandits 1986, Cliffhanger and other films; several patents, including ZOPTIC front-projection system and 3D cinematography; Acad. Award (Oscar) for Outstanding Achievement in Visual Effects (for Superman – the Movie), BAFTA Award for Outstanding Contrib. to the Cinema, American Acad. Tech. Achievement Award for the invention and devt of the ZOPTIC dual-zoom front-projection system. *Publications:* Special Optical Effects, The Animation Stand, Photoguide to Shooting Animation, Visual Effects Cinematography 2000. *Leisure interest:* flying (pvt. pilot's licence). *E-mail:* zoptic@hotmail.com (office); zoran@zoptic.force9.co.uk (home). *Website:* www.zoptic.com (office).

PERISSICH, Riccardo; Italian international civil servant; b. 24 Jan. 1942, Milan; m. Anne Treca 1989; one c.; writer on foreign policy for Il Punto (Rome weekly) 1962; with Italconsult SpA (consulting engineers) 1962–64; Head of EC Studies, Istituto Affari Internazionali, Rome 1966–70; joined Comm. of EC, Brussels 1970; Chef de Cabinet of Altiero Spinelli 1970–76, Cesidio Guazzaroni 1976; Dir Directorate A (energy savings and energy forecasts) 1977–81; Chef de Cabinet of Antonio Giolitti (regional policy) 1981–84, of Carlo Ripa di Meana (institutional affairs) 1985–86; Dir, later Deputy Dir-Gen. Directorate-Gen. for Industry 1986, Dir-Gen. 1990–94; Bd mem. and Dir Public and Econ. Affairs Pirelli SpA 1994–2001, Co-ordinator of Institutional Affairs 2001–; Dir Public and Econ. Affairs Telecom Italia Group 2001–; Chair. Seat Pagine Gialle 2002–; Vice-Chair. Assolombarda 1995–, Unione Industriali di Roma, ASSONIME (Italian Cos Asscns); Bd mem. European Inst. of Oncology; mem. Int. Inst. for Strategic Studies (London), Istituto Affari Internazionali, Aspen Inst. Italia. *Publications:* Gli eurocrati fra realtà e mitologia 1969, Europa America: materiali per un dibattito (with S. Silvestri) 1970. *Address:* Telecom Italia, Corso d'Italia 41, 00198 Rome, Italy.

PERISSINOTTO, Giovanni, BEcons; Italian insurance executive; *Joint Managing Director, Assicurazioni Generali SpA;* b. 1953, Conselice; ed Univ. of Trieste; joined Generali Assicurazioni SpA, Trieste 1980, Cen. Dept of parent co. 1988–89, Deputy Man. responsible for the Italian and foreign market 1989–92, responsible for Admin. Office 1992–93, responsible for co-ordination of corp. assets at Admin and Finance Dept 1993–95, Jt Man. responsible for Accounting and Finance Dept 1995–96, Deputy Gen. Man. with responsibilities a.i. for Admin and Finance Dept 1996–98, Gen. Man. 1998–2001, Jt Man. Dir 2001–, also Chair. Banca Generali, Generali Properties SpA, Supervisory Bd Generali Investments SpA, Deputy Chair. Banca della Svizzera Italiana SA (BSI SA); mem. Bd Dirs Participatie Maatschappij Graafscap Holland NV, Transocean Holding Corpn, Generali France Holding, Generali Espana Holding de Entidades de Seguros, INA Assitalia SpA, Alleanza Assicurazioni SpA, Generali Property Investments Sgr, Toro Assicurazioni SpA, Pirelli & Co. SpA 2003–; mem. Supervisory Bd Participatie Maatschappij Transhol BV, Man. Cttee Intesa San Paolo, Advisory Bd SDA Bocconi School of Man., Consiglio Direttivo (Exec. Bd) Assonime, Exec. Cttee ANIA; Cavaliere del Lavoro 2007. *Publications include:* articles on econs including The Creation of Value through a Specialized Distribution Network 2003. *Address:* Assicurazioni Generali SpA, Piazza Duca degli Abruzzi 2, 34132 Trieste, Italy (office). *Telephone:* (40) 6711 (office). *Fax:* (40) 671600 (office). *E-mail:* info@generali.com (office). *Website:* www.generali.com (office).

PERISSOL, Pierre-André Daniel; French politician and engineer; b. 30 April 1947, Nice; s. of Louis Perissol and Aline Cardiec; ed Lycée Massena, Nice, Ecole Polytechnique, Ecole Nat. des Ponts et Chaussées; Dir of Planning, Saint-Quentin-en-Yvelines new town 1972–74; Adviser to Sec. of State for Housing 1974–76; Chief Eng Ecole Nat. des Ponts et Chaussées 1986; Dir-Gen. Soc. Centrale de Crédit Immobilier 1977–91, Pres., Dir-Gen. 1991–92, Pres. 1993–95; Founder and Dir.–Gen. Groupe Arcade 1980–91, Pres. 1991–95; Pres. Coopérer pour Habiter 1982, Aiguillon Construction 1987, Fed. Nat. (now Chambre Syndicale) des Sociétés de Crédit Immobilier 1988, Caisse Centrale de Crédit Immobilier 1990–93; Regional Councillor, Ile-de-France 1983–86; Councillor, Paris 1983–95; Deputy Mayor of Paris responsible for Educ. 1989–93; RPR Deputy to Nat. Ass. 1993–95; Minister of Housing May–Nov. 1995, Deputy Minister 1995–97; Mayor of Moulins 1995–; Vice-Pres. Regional Council of Auvergne 1998–; UMP Deputy to Nat. Ass. 2002–; Officier, Légion d'honneur, Ordre Nat. du Mérite. *Publications:* Le défi social 1985, En mal de toit 1995, A bonne école 2002. *Leisure interests:* travel, tennis. *Address:* Assemblée Nationale, 126 rue de l'Université, 75007 Paris, France (office). *Telephone:* 4-70-48-50-21 (office). *Fax:* 4-70-48-50-84 (office). *E-mail:* paperissol@asemblee.nationale.fr (office).

PERKIN, James Russell Conway, DPhil; British/Canadian university president; b. 19 Aug. 1928, Northants.; s. of William Perkin and Lily Drage; m. Dorothy Bentley 1953; two s. one d.; ed Daventry Grammar School, Northants. and Univ. of Oxford; Minister, Altrincham Baptist Church, Cheshire 1955–62; lecturer in New Testament Greek, New Coll. Edinburgh 1963–65; Assoc. Prof. of New Testament Interpretation, McMaster Divinity Coll. Hamilton, Ont. 1965–69; Prof. of Religious Studies and Head of Dept Acadia Univ. NS 1969–77, Dean of Arts 1977–80, Vice-Pres. (Academic) 1980–81, Acting Pres. 1981–82, Pres. 1982–93; mem. Soc. for New Testament Studies, Canadian Soc. for Study of Religion; Hon. DD (McMaster) 1986; Hon. DLitt (Acadia) 1995; Canada 125th Medal 1992. *Publications:* Such is Our Story (with E. A. Payne) 1955, Study Notes on Romans 1957, Resurrection in Theology and Life 1966, Handbook for Biblical Studies 1973, Scripture Then and Now 1975, In Season 1978, With Mind and Heart 1979, Crucial Questions 1980, Seedtime and Harvest 1982, Arrows in the Mind 1984, Morning in his Heart: Life and Writings of Watson Kirkconnell (with J. Snelson) 1986, Morning in his Heart: a Biographical Sketch of Watson Kirkconnell 1987, Commonplace Book 1986, Reflections and Insights 1993, Ordinary Magic 1995, Devotional Diary 1998; book chapters, essays, articles and reviews. *Leisure interests:* reading, gardening, sailing, classical music. *Address:* 10 Harris Place, Wolfville, NS B4P 1T2, Canada (home). *Telephone:* (902) 542-5501 (home).

PERKINS, Alice Elizabeth, BA, CB; British business executive; *Non-Executive Director, Taylor Nelson Sofres;* b. 24 May 1949; d. of Derrick Leslie John Perkins and Elsa Rose Perkins (née Rink); m. Jack (John Whitaker) Straw) 1978; one s. one d.; ed N London Collegiate School for Girls and St Anne's Coll., Oxford; joined Civil Service in Dept of Health and Social Security (DHSS) 1971, Prin. 1976–84, Asst Sec. DHSS, then Dept of Social Security (DSS) 1984–90, Dir of Personnel 1990–93; Under-Sec. Defence Policy and Material Group, HM Treasury 1993–95, Deputy Dir of Public Spending 1995–98; Dir of Corp. Man., Dept of Health 1998–2000; Head of Civil Service Human Resources and Corp. Devt, Cabinet Office 2000–05; Trustee Whitehall and Industry Group 1993–98; Dir (non-exec.) Littlewoods Org. 1997–2000, Taylor Nelson Sofres 2005–, BAA 2006; Exec. Coach JCA Group 2006–; External mem. Oxford Univ. Council 2006; Hon. Fellow, St Anne's Coll., Oxford 2006. *Leisure interests:* gardening, travelling, looking at paintings. *Address:* Taylor Nelson Sofres, Westgate, London, W5 1UA, England (office).

PERKINS, Donald H., CBE, MA, PhD, FRS; British physicist and academic; *Professor Emeritus of Physics, University of Oxford;* b. 15 Oct. 1925, Hull; s. of G. W. Perkins and G. Perkins; m. Dorothy M. Maloney 1955; two d.; ed Imperial Coll. London; Sr 1851 Scholar, Univ. of Bristol 1949–52, G. A. Wills Research Assoc. 1952–55; Visiting Scientist, Univ. of Calif. 1955–56; Lecturer, then Reader in Physics, Univ. of Bristol 1956–65; Prof. of Elementary Particle Physics, Univ. of Oxford 1965–93, now Emer., Fellow St Catherine's Coll. 1965–; mem. SERC 1985–89; Hon. DSc (Sheffield) 1982, (Bristol) 1995; Guthrie Medal, Inst. of Physics 1979, Holweck Medal (Société française de physique) 1992, Royal Medal, Royal Soc. of London 1997, High-Energy Physics Prize, European Physical Soc. 2001. *Publications:* Study of Elementary Particles by the Photographic Method (with C. F. Powell and P. H. Fowler) 1959, Introduction to High Energy Physics 1972, Particle Astrophysics 2002. *Leisure interests:* squash, skiing, lepidoptera. *Address:* 37 Redan Street, London, W14 0AB, England (home). *Telephone:* (20) 7348-0028 (home). *E-mail:* d.perkins1@physics.ox.ac.uk (office).

PERKINS, Edward J., DPA; American diplomatist and academic; *Professor Emeritus, University of Oklahoma;* b. 8 June 1928, Sterlington, La; s. of Edward Joseph Perkins Sr and Tiny Estella Noble Holmes; m. Lucy Cheng-mei Liu; two d.; ed Univ. of Maryland and Univ. of Southern California; Chief of Personnel, Army and Air Force Exchange Service, Taiwan 1958–62; Deputy Chief, Okinawa, Japan 1962–64, Chief of Personnel and Admin. 1964–66; Asst Gen. Services Officer, Far East Bureau, AID 1967–69, Man. Analyst 1969–70; Deputy Dir Man. US Operations, Mission to Thailand 1970–72; Staff Asst Office of Dir-Gen. of Foreign Service 1972; Personnel Officer 1972–74; Admin. Officer, Bureau of Near Eastern and South Asian Affairs 1974–75; Man. Analysis Officer, Office of Man. Operations, Dept of State 1975–78; Counsellor for Political Affairs, Accra 1978–81; Deputy Chief of Mission, Monrovia 1981–83; Dir Office of W African Affairs, Dept of State 1983–85; Amb. to Liberia 1985–86, to S Africa 1986–89; Dir-Gen. Foreign Service, Washington 1989–92; Perm. Rep. to UN 1992–93; Amb. to Australia 1993–96; William J. Crowe Chair Prof. of Geopolitics and Exec. Dir Int. Programs Center, Univ. of Okla 1996–2007, Prof. Emer. 2007–; Bd Dir Asscn for Diplomatic Studies and Training 1998–; Trustee Lewis and Clark Coll. 1994–, Asia Soc. 1997–2000, Inst. of Int. Educ. 1997–2000; Gov. Jt Center for Political and Econ. Studies 1996–2002; mem. Advisory Council Univ. Office of Int. Programs Pa State Univ. 1997–; mem. Advisory Bd Inst. of Int. Public Policy 1997–; Trustee Woodrow Wilson Fellowship Foundation 1999–; Bd of Visitors, Nat. Defense Univ. 2002–; mem. Pres.'s Advisory Cttee on Trade Policy ad Negotiation 2003–; Distinguished Alumni Award, Univ. of Southern Calif. 1991, Distinguished Honor Award, Dept of State 1992, Statesman of the Year Award, George Washington Univ. 1992, Dept of State Dir-Gen. Cup 2001 and numerous other awards. *Publications include:* Preparing America's Foreign Policy for the 21st Century (ed. with David L. Boren) 1999, Palestinian Refugees: Traditional Positions and New Solutions (ed. with Joseph Ginat) 1999, Democracy, Morality and the Search for Peace in America's Foreign Policy (ed. with David L. Boren) 2002, Middle East Peace Process: Vision versus Reality (ed. with Joseph Ginat and Edwin G. Corr) 2002; contribs to specialized journals and reviews. *Leisure interests:* art, jazz. *Address:* Room 105, 729 Elm Avenue, Norman, OK 73019, USA (office). *Telephone:* (405) 325-1584 (office). *Fax:* (405) 325-7738 (office).

PERKINS, Frederick J., MSc; British business executive; *Chairman, Public Policy Forum;* b. 2 March 1948, Glasgow; ed Univ. of Strathclyde, Univ. of Sussex; fmr Vice-Pres. Europe, McGraw-Hill; Chief Exec. The Stationery Office (fmrly Her Majesty's Stationery Office) 1996–2003; Group Dir The Financial Times; Chair. Electronic Publrs Forum 1998–, Public Policy Forum 2001–. *Address:* Public Policy Forum, InsightExec, Sift Group Ltd., Bristol, BS1 6HZ, England (office). *Telephone:* (0800) 400-414 (office). *E-mail:* service@insightexec.com (office). *Website:* ppf.insightexec.com (office).

PERKINS, Kieren John, OA; Australian fmr swimmer; b. 14 Aug. 1973, Brisbane; s. of Kevin Perkins and Gloria Perkins; m. Symantha Liu 1997; one s. one d.; ed Brisbane Boys' Coll., Univ. of Queensland; gold medal Olympic Games, Barcelona 1992 for 1,500m freestyle (world record), gold medal Olympic Games, Atlanta 1996 for 1,500m (first swimmer to hold Olympic, World, Commonwealth and Pan Pacific titles simultaneously), two gold medals World Championships, Rome 1994 (world and Commonwealth records for 400m freestyle), four gold medals Commonwealth Games, Canada 1994 (world and Commonwealth records for 800m and 1,500m freestyle); set 10 Australian, 11 Queensland and 10 Brisbane records and two Commonwealth and one Australian standard time records; silver medal 1500m freestyle Olympic Games, Sydney 2000; retd; World Oceania Award, LA Amateur Athletic Foundation Award 1992, Australian Sports and Tourism Amb., Australia Tourist Comm. 1993, Advance Australia Award 1993, World Male Swimmer of the Year 1994, FINA Award 1994, Australian flag-bearer Commonwealth Games 1998. *Leisure interests:* music, motorcycling, horse riding, reading, surfing, boating, fishing, jetskiing. *Address:* c/o Swimming Australia, 12/7 Beissel Street, Belconnen, ACT 2617, Australia.

PERKINS, Lawrence Bradford, Jr., BA, BArch, MBA, FAIA, MRAIC, AICP; American architect; b. 13 Jan. 1943, Chicago, Ill.; s. of Lawrence B. Perkins and Margery Perkins; m. Phyllis Friedman 1966; three d.; ed Cornell and Stanford Univs and City Coll. of New York; President, Omnidata Services 1971–73; Man. Pnr, Llewellyn-Davies Assocs 1973–77; Sr Vice-Pres., Pnr, Perkins and Will 1977–81; Pnr Attia & Perkins 1981–83; Pres. Perkins Eastman Architects 1983–; Dir Settlement Housing Fund 1991–, Helen Keller Int. 1993–; Dir New York City AIA, NY Foundation for Architecture; Fellow, American Inst. of Architects, Epsilon Asscn (Pres. 1993–96); various design awards. *Publications:* articles in professional journals and chapters for professional textbooks. *Address:* Perkins Eastman Architects, 115 Fifth Avenue, New York, NY 10003 (office); 4 Rectory Lane, Scarsdale, NY 10583, USA (home). *Telephone:* (212) 353-7200 (office); (914) 723-8875 (home). *Fax:* (212) 353-7676 (office). *Website:* www.perkinseastman.com (office).

PERL, Martin Lewis, PhD; American research physicist, academic and engineer; *Professor of Physics, Stanford Linear Accelerator Center (SLAC), Stanford University;* b. 24 June 1927, New York; three s. one d.; ed Polytechnic Inst. of New York and Columbia Univ.; Chemical Engineer, General Electric Co. 1948–50; Asst, then Assoc. Prof. of Physics, Univ. of Mich. 1955–63; Prof. of Physics, Stanford Linear Accelerator Center, Stanford Univ. 1963–, Prof. of Physics, Stanford Univ. 1970–; research in experimental elementary particle physics 1955–, small drop technology 1995–; discovered the elementary particle tau lepton 1975–78; Hon. DSc (Chicago) 1990, (Polytechnic Univ.) 1997; Wolf Prize in Physics 1982, Nobel Prize in Physics (jtly) 1995. *Publications:* High Energy Hadron Physics 1974, Reflections on Experimental Science 1996, articles on science and soc. issues and on physics educ. *Leisure interests:* mechanical antiques, gardening. *Address:* SLAC National Accelerator Laboratory, 2575 Sand Hill Road, Menlo Park, CA 94025 (office); 3737 El Centro Avenue, Palo Alto, CA 94306, USA (home). *Telephone:* (650) 926-4286 (office). *Fax:* (650) 926-4001 (office). *E-mail:* martin@SLAC.Stanford.edu (office). *Website:* www.slac.stanford.edu (office).

PERLE, Richard Norman, BA, MA; American business executive and fmr government official; *Resident Fellow, American Enterprise Institute;* b. 16 Sept. 1941, New York, NY; s. of Jack and Martha Perle; m. Leslie Barr; one s.; ed Univ. of S California, Princeton Univ.; Asst Sec. US Dept of Defense, Int. Security Policy 1981–88; fmr foreign policy adviser; mem. Defense Policy Bd 2001–04, Chair. 2001–03 (resgnd); fmr Dir GeoBiotics; Dir Hollinger Int. Inc. 1994–2005; Resident Fellow, American Enterprise Inst. for Public Policy Research 1987–; Patron, Henry Jackson Soc. *Television:* produced The Gulf Crisis: The Road to War for PBS 1992. *Publications:* Reshaping Western Security (ed.) 1991, Hard Line 1992, An End to Evil (with David Frum) 2004. *Address:* American Enterprise Institute for Public Policy Research, 1150 17th Street, NW, Washington, DC 20036, USA (office). *Telephone:* (301) 656-0390 (office). *Fax:* (202) 862-7177 (office). *E-mail:* rperle@aei.org (office). *Website:* www.aei.org (office).

PERLIS, HRH The Raja of; Tuanku Syed Sirajuddin ibni al-Marhum Syed Putra Jamalullail; Malaysian ruler; b. 1943; m.; one s. one d.; ed Sandhurst Mil. Acad., UK; fmr army officer; Raja of Perlis 2000–; elected as twelfth Yang di-Pertuan Agong (Supreme Head of State) 13 Dec. 2001–06.

PERLMAN, Itzhak; Israeli violinist and conductor; b. 31 Aug. 1945, Tel-Aviv; s. of Chaim Perlman and Shoshana Perlman; m. Toby Lynn Friedlander 1967; two s. three d.; ed Shulamit High School, Tel-Aviv, Tel-Aviv Acad. of Music and Juilliard School, USA, studied with Ivan Galamian and Dorothy De Lay; gave recitals on radio at the age of 10; went to USA 1958; first recital at Carnegie Hall 1963; has played with maj. American orchestras 1964–; has toured Europe regularly and played with maj. European orchestras 1966–; debut in UK with London Symphony Orchestra 1968; toured Poland, Hungary, Far East; played with Israel Philharmonic Orchestra in fmr Soviet Union; appearances at Israel Festival and most European Festivals; Prin. Guest Conductor Detroit Symphony Orchestra 2001–; numerous recordings; Hon. DMus (Univ. of S Carolina) 1982, Dr hc (Yale, Harvard and Yeshivah Univs); several Grammy awards, EMI Artist of the Year 1995, Royal Philharmonic Soc. gold medal 1996; Medal of Liberty 1986, Nat. Medal of Arts 2001. *Leisure interest:* cooking. *Address:* c/o IMG Artists, Carnegie Hall Tower, 152 West 57th Street, 5th Floor, New York, NY 10019, USA (office). *Telephone:* (212) 994-3500 (office). *Fax:* (212) 994-3550 (office). *E-mail:* esobol@imgartists.com (office). *Website:* www.imgartists.com (office).

PERLMUTTER, Saul, BS, PhD; American physicist and academic; *Professor, University of California, Berkeley;* b. 1959; ed Harvard Univ., Univ. of California, Berkeley; currently astrophysicist, Lawrence Berkeley Nat. Lab. and Leader of int. Supernova Cosmology Project; Prof., Physics Dept, Univ. of California, Berkeley 2004–; Fellow, Ameican Acad. of Arts and Sciences; Henri Chretien Award, American Astronomical Soc. 1996, Lawrence Award in Physics, US Dept of Energy 2002, Calif. Scientist of Year 2003, John Scott Award 2005, Padua Prize 2005, Feltrinelli International Prize, Lincei Acad., Rome 2006, Shaw Prize in Astronomy (co-recipient) 2006, Gruber Cosmology Prize (co-recipient) 2007. *Achievements include:* discovery through the study of distant supernovae that the expansion of the universe is speeding up rather than slowing down. *Television:* has appeared in Public Broadcasting System and BBC TV documentaries on astronomy and cosmology. *Publications:* numerous scientific papers in professional journals; has also written popular articles for Sky and Telescope magazine. *Address:* 429 Old LeConte Hall, Department of Physics, University of California, Berkeley, CA 94720, USA (office). *Telephone:* (510) 642-3596 (office). *Fax:* (510) 643-8497 (office). *E-mail:* saul@lbl.gov (office). *Website:* www.physics.berkeley.edu/research/faculty/perlmutter.html (office); supernova.lbl.gov/~saul/home.html (office).

PERMAN, Finley S.; Micronesian auditor and government official; *Secretary, Department of Finance and Administration;* ed Hawaii Pacific Coll.; previous positions include Devt Specialist, Pohnpei Small Business Guarantee and Finance Corpn, Sr Service Asst, Bank of Hawaii, Pohnpei br.; Dir Pohnpei State Dept of Treasury and Admin 2005–07; Sec. Dept of Finance and Admin 2007–. *Address:* Department of Finance and Administration, PS158, Palikir 96941, Pohnpei State, Federated States of Micronesia (office). *Telephone:* (691) 320-2640 (office). *Fax:* (691) 320-2380 (office). *E-mail:* fsmpio.fm (office). *Website:* www.fsmgov.org (office).

PERNG, Fai-Nan, MA; Taiwanese central banker and economist; *Governor, Central Bank of China;* b. 2 Jan. 1939; m.; two s.; ed Nat. Chung Hsing Univ., Univ. of Minn., USA and Int. Monetary Fund Inst.; with Bank of Taiwan 1969; Asst Specialist, Cen. Bank of China (CBC), later Deputy Div. Chief, Div. Chief, Econ. Research Dept 1971–78, Asst Dir-Gen. and Div. Chief, Econ. Research Dept 1978–80, Deputy Dir-Gen. 1980–85, Dir-Gen. 1986–89, Dir-Gen. Foreign Exchange Dept 1989–94, Deputy Gov. CBC 1994–95, mem. Bd of Dirs 1995–, Gov. 1998–, also mem. Exec. Yuan (cabinet); Chair. Cen. Trust of China 1995–97, Int. Commercial Bank of China 1997–98; Gov. for Taiwan, Asian Devt Bank 1998–, Cen. American Bank for Econ. Integration 1998–; Adjunct Prof., Nat. Chung Hsing Univ. 1986–89; Office of the Pres. Best Employee Award 1975, Cen. Bank of China Best Essay Award 1982, Excellence Magazine Outstanding Govt Official 1998, Nat. Chung Hsing Univ. Outstanding Alumnus Award 1999, Univ. of Minn. Outstanding Achievement Award 2000, Global Finance Top Central Banker Award 2000. *Publications include:* Possible Methods for the Liberalization of Foreign Exchange Control 1985, Asian Financial Crisis 1998; numerous articles. *Address:* Central Bank of China, 2 Roosevelt Road, Sec. 1, Taipei 100, Taiwan (office). *Telephone:* (2) 2393-6161 (office). *Fax:* (2) 2357-1974 (office). *E-mail:* adminrol@mail.cbc.gov.tw (office). *Website:* www.cbc.gov.tw (office).

PÉROL, François; French civil servant; *Deputy General Secretary, Office of the President;* b. 1963; ed HEC School of Man., Institut d'études politiques, École nationale d'administration, Paris; served as rapporteur and later Asst Sec.-Gen., Comite Interministeriel de Restructuration Industrielle 1994–96; Head, Office of Financial Markets, Treasury 1996–99, Asst Dir of Financial Support and Devt 2001–02; Sec.-Gen., Club de Paris 1999–2001; served as Deputy Chief of Staff to ministers François Mer and Nicolas Sarkozy, Ministry of Economy 2002–05; Gen. Pnr, Rothschild Bank 2005–; Deputy Gen. Sec., Office of the Pres. 2007–. *Address:* Palais de l'Elysée, 55 rue du faubourg Saint-Honoré, 75008 Paris, France (office). *Telephone:* 1-42-92-81-00 (office). *Website:* www.elysee.fr (office).

PERÓN, María Estela (Isabelita) (see Martínez de Perón).

PEROT, (Henry) Ross; American business executive; *Chairman, Perot Systems Corporation;* b. 27 June 1930, Texarkana, Tex.; s. of Gabriel Ross Perot; m. Margot Birmingham 1956; five c.; ed US Naval Acad.; USN 1953–57; with IBM Corpn 1957–62; formed Electronic Data Systems Corpn 1962, Chair. of Bd and CEO 1982–86; Dir Perot Group, Dallas 1986–; f. Perot Systems Corpn, Washington 1988–, Chair. 1988–92, 1992–, mem. Bd 1988–; Chair. Bd of Visitors US Naval Acad. 1970–; cand. for Presidency of USA 1992, 1996, f. Reform Party 1995, Chair. 1995–99. *Publications:* Not For Sale at Any Price 1993, Intensive Care 1995. *Leisure interest:* horses. *Address:* Perot Systems Corporation, 2300 West Plano Parkway, Plano, TX 75075-8427, USA (office). *Telephone:* (972) 577-0000 (office). *Fax:* (972) 340-6100 (office). *Website:* www.perotsystems.com (office).

PERPIÑA-ROBERT, Fernando; Spanish diplomatist; b. 17 April 1937, San Sebastián; s. of Benito Perpiña and Cármen Peyra; m. Alba Navarro Feussier 1964; two s. two d.; ed Univ. of Barcelona; joined Diplomatic Service 1965, Consul Gen. Boston, USA 1978, Minister Counsellor, Bonn 1982, Under-Sec. of State, Ministry of Foreign Affairs, Madrid 1985, Sec.-Gen. Foreign Affairs, Madrid 1988, Amb. to Germany 1991–96; numerous Spanish and foreign decorations. *Leisure interest:* bridge. *Address:* c/o Ministerio de Asuntos Exteriores, Plaza de la Provincia 1, 28071 Madrid, Spain.

PERRAULT, Dominique; French architect; b. 9 April 1953, Clermont-Ferrand; s. of Jean Perrault and Thérèse Souchon; m. Aude Lauriot-dit-Prévost 1986; three c.; ed Univ. of Paris, Ecole Nat. des Ponts et Chaussées, Ecole des Hautes Etudes en Sciences Sociales; f. architectural practice, Paris 1981; opened offices in Berlin 1992, Luxembourg 2000, Barcelona 2001; major works include Electronic Engineers Acad. Marne-la-Vallée, Bibliothèque de France (received Prix Mies Van Der Röhe 1997), Olympic swimming pool, Berlin, re-devt of town centre, Tremblay-en-France 1995, Town Hall, Innsbruck, Austria 1997, Montiagalá Stadium 1998, European Court of Justice Luxembourg (2007), tennis stadium Madrid (2012); consultant to city of Nantes 1990, Bordeaux 1992, Barcelona 2000–; Pres. Institut français d'architecture 1998–2001; mem. Salzburg Urban Cttee 1994–; Hon. mem. Royal Inst. of British Architects; Grand prix nat. d'architecture 1993; Chevalier, Légion d'honneur; numerous architectural awards and prizes. *Publication:* An Atmosphere of Falling Meteors, Perrault Architecte (monograph) Italy 2000, 2004, El Croquis 2001, Mesh A+U 2003, Dominique Perrault by Gilles de Bure 2004. *Address:* Perrault Architecte, 26 rue Bruneseau, 75629 Paris Cedex 13, France (office). *Telephone:* 1-44-06-00-00 (office). *Fax:* 1-44-06-00-01 (office). *E-mail:* dominique.perrault@perraultarchitecte.com (office). *Website:* www.perraultarchitecte.com (office).

PERREIN, Michèle Marie-Claude; French writer; b. 30 Oct. 1929, La Réole; d. of Roger Barbe and Anne-Blanche Perrein; m. Jacques Laurent (divorced); ed Univ. of Bordeaux, Centre de Formation des Journalistes; literary contrib. to periodicals Arts-Spectacles, La Parisienne, Marie-Claire, La vie judiciaire, Votre beauté, Le point, F. magazine, Les nouvelles littéraires. *Plays:* L'Hôtel Racine 1966, a+b+c = la Clinique d'anticipation 1971, L'alter-auto 1971; film collaborator La vérité 1959. *Publications:* La sensitive 1956, Le soleil dans l'oeil 1957, Barbastre 1960, La flemme 1961, Le cercle 1962, Le petit Jules 1965, M'oiselle S, la Chineuse 1970, La partie de plaisir 1971, Le buveur de Garonne 1973, Le mâle aimant 1975, Gemma lapidaire 1976, Entre chienne et louve 1978, Comme une fourmi cavalière 1980, Ave Caesar 1982, Les cotonniers de Bassalane 1984, La Margagne 1989. *Leisure interests:* tapestry, swimming, skating. *Address:* c/o Grasset et Fasqualle, 61 rue des Saints-pères, 75006 Paris, France (office).

PERRY, Grayson, BA; British artist; b. 1960, Chelmsford; m.; one d.; ed Portsmouth Polytechnic; Turner Prize 2003. *Works include:* Mother of All Battles 1996, Growing Up As a Boy, Strangely Familiar, Golden Ghosts 2001. *Publication:* Portrait of the Artist as a Young Girl (with Wendy Jones) 2006. *Address:* c/o Tate Britain, Millbank, London, SW1P 4RG, England.

PERRY, John Richard, PhD; American professor of philosophy; *Henry Waldgrave Stuart Professor of Philosophy, Stanford University;* b. 16 Jan. 1943, Lincoln, Neb.; s. of Ralph R. Perry and Ann Roscow Perry; m. Louise E. French 1962; two s. one d.; ed Doane Coll., Crete, Neb. and Cornell Univ.; Asst Prof. of Philosophy, UCLA 1968–72, Assoc. Prof. 1972–74; Assoc. Prof. of Philosophy, Stanford Univ. 1974–77, Prof. of Philosophy 1977–85, Henry Waldgrave Stuart Prof. of Philosophy 1985–, Chair. Dept of Philosophy 1976–82, 1990–91, Dir Center for Language and Information 1982–83, 1985–86, 1993–99; Pres. American Philosophical Asscn 1993–94; Hon. DLitt (Doane Coll.) 1982, Dr hc (Univ. of the Basque Country) 2002; Woodrow Wilson Fellow 1964, Danforth Fellow 1964–68, Guggenheim Fellow 1975–76, NEH Fellow 1980–81, Dinkelspiel Teaching Award 1989, Humboldt Prize 1998, Nicod Prize 1999. *Publications:* A Dialogue on Personal Identity and Immortality 1978, Situations and Attitudes (with J. Barwise) 1983, The Problem of the Essential Indexical and Other Essays 1993, A Dialogue on Good, Evil and the Existence of God 1999, Knowledge, Possibility and Consciousness 2000, Reference and Reflexivity 2001, Identity, Personal Identity and the Self 2002. *Leisure interests:* reading, walking, grandchildren. *Address:* Department of Philosophy, 450 Serra Mall, Building 90, Stanford University, Stanford, CA 94305-2155, USA (office). *Telephone:* (650) 723-1619 (office). *Fax:* (650) 723-0985 (office). *E-mail:* john@csli.stanford.edu (office). *Website:* www-csli.stanford.edu/~/john/ (office).

PERRY, Matthew Langford; American/Canadian actor; b. 19 Aug. 1969, Williamstown, Mass; s. of John Bennett Perry and Suzanne Perry; ed Ashbury Coll., Ottawa, Canada; mem. Bd of Dirs Ron Clark Acad. *Films:* A Night in the Life of Jimmy Reardon 1988, She's Out of Control 1989, Getting In 1994, Fools Rush In 1997, Almost Heroes 1998, Three To Tango 1999, Imagining Emily (writer) 1999, The Whole Nine Yards 2000, Serving Sara 2002, The Whole Ten Yards 2004, Numb 2007. *Television includes:* Friends (series) 1994–2004, The West Wing (series) 2003, The Ron Clark Story 2006, Studio 60 on the Sunset Strip (series) 2006. *Play:* Sexual Perversity in Chicago, Comedy Theatre, London 2003. *Leisure interests:* ice hockey, softball. *Address:* c/o CAA, 9830 Wilshire Blvd, Beverly Hills, CA 90212-1825, USA (office). *Telephone:* (310) 288-4545. *Fax:* (310) 288-4800.

PERRY, Sir Michael Sydney, Kt, GBE, MA; British business executive; b. 26 Feb. 1934, Eastbourne; s. of Sydney Albert Perry and Jessie Kate Perry (née Brooker); m. Joan Mary Stallard 1958; one s. two d.; ed King William's Coll., Isle of Man, St John's Coll., Oxford; Chair. Lever Brothers (Thailand) Ltd 1973–77, Centrica 1997–2004, Nippon Lever (Japan) 1981–83, UAC Int. Ltd 1985–87, Unilever PLC 1992–96, Dunlop Slazenger Group 1996–2002; Pres. Lever y Asociados (Argentina) 1977–81; Dir Unilever NV 1985–96 (Vice-Chair. 1992–96), Bass PLC 1991–2001 (Deputy Chair. 1996–2001); Dir (non-exec.) British Gas 1994–97, Marks & Spencer 1996–2001; Pres. Liverpool School of Tropical Medicine 1997–2002; Pres. Advertising Asscn 1993–96; Chair. Leverhulme Trust 2008–; Trustee Shakespeare Globe Trust 1987– (Chair. 1993–2006), Glyndebourne Arts Trust 1996–2004, Dyson Perrins Museum Trust 2000–, Inst. of Public Policy Research 2003–07, Three Choirs Festival Asscn 2007–; Commdr, Order of Oranje Nassau. *Leisure interest:* music. *Address:* Bridges Stone Mill, Alfrick, Worcester, WR6 5HR, England (home).

PERRY, Rick (James Richard); American state official and rancher; *Governor of Texas;* b. 4 March 1950, Paint Creek, Tex.; s. of Ray Perry and Amelia Perry; m. Anita Perry; one s. one d.; ed Texas A&M Univ.; served USAF 1972–77; farmer and rancher 1977–90; mem. Tex. House of Reps 1985–90; Tex. Commr of Agric. 1991–98; Lt-Gov. of Tex. 1999–2000, Gov. 2000–; Republican; Border Texan of the Year 2001, Govt Leadership Award, Nat. Comm. Against Drunk Driving 2001, Top Cowboy of the Year Award 2001. *Address:* Office of the Governor, POB 12428, Austin, TX 78711-2428, USA (office). *Telephone:* (512) 463-2000 (office). *Fax:* (512) 463-1849 (office). *Website:* www.governor.state.tx.us (office).

PERRY, Robert Palese, PhD; American molecular biologist and academic; *Stanley Reimann Chair in Research, Institute for Cancer Research, Fox Chase Cancer Center;* b. 10 Jan. 1931, Chicago; s. of Robert P. Perry, Sr and Gertrude Hyman; m. Zoila Figueroa 1957; one s. two d.; ed Univ. of Chicago and Northwestern Univ.; Postdoctoral Fellow, Oak Ridge Nat. Lab. 1956–57, Univ. of Pennsylvania 1957–59, Univ. of Brussels 1959–60; Staff mem. Inst. for Cancer Research, Fox Chase Cancer Center 1960–, Sr mem. 1969–, Stanley Reimann Chair in Research 1994–; Prof. of Biophysics, Univ. of Pennsylvania 1973–95; UNESCO Tech. Asst Expert, Univ. of Belgrade 1965; Chair. Exec. Cttee Int. Cell Research Org. (UNESCO) 1982–85; mem. NAS; Dr hc (Univ. of

Paris VII); Guggenheim Fellow, Univ. of Paris 1974–75. *Publications:* more than 100 articles in int. scientific journals. *Address:* Institute for Cancer Research, Fox Chase Cancer Center, 333 Cottman Avenue, Philadelphia, PA 19111 (office); 1808 Bustleton Pike, Churchville, PA 18966, USA (home). *Telephone:* (215) 728-3606 (office); (215) 357-0272 (home). *Fax:* (215) 728-2412 (office). *E-mail:* rp_perry@fccc.edu (office). *Website:* www.fccc.edu/research/pid/perry/index.html (office).

PERRY, Simon Frank, CBE, BA; British film producer; b. 5 Aug. 1943, Farnham; s. of Frank Horace Perry and Brenda Mary Dorothea Perry; ed Eton Coll., King's Coll.; worked in theatre production (RSC, Bristol Old Vic, London West End) 1965–69, TV production (Anglia TV, Yorkshire TV) 1969–74; independent filmmaker 1974–77; entertainment trade journalist (Variety Magazine etc.) 1978–80; Admin. Nat. Film Devt Fund 1980–82; feature film producer 1982–; Chief Exec. British Screen Finance 1991–2000; Chevalier des Arts et Lettres. *Films include:* Knots 1975, Loose Connections 1983, Another Time, Another Place 1983, Nineteen Eighty-Four 1984, Hôtel du paradis 1986, Nanou 1986, White Mischief 1987, The Favour, the Watch and the Very Big Fish 1991, The Playboys 1992, Innocent Lies 1995. *Leisure interests:* cinema-going, cycling, European travel. *Address:* Studio C, Chelsea Studios, 416 Fulham Road, London, SW6 1EB, England. *Telephone:* (20) 7386-5119. *Fax:* (20) 7386-0017.

PERRY, William J., BS, MS, PhD; American academic and fmr government official; *Michael and Barbara Berberian Professor, Freeman Spogli Institute for International Studies, Center for International Security and Cooperation, Stanford University;* b. 11 Oct. 1927, Vandergift, Pa; s. of Edward Martin Perry and Mabelle Estelle Dunlop; m. Leonilla Mary Green 1947; three s. two d.; ed Stanford Univ., Pennsylvania State Univ.; served in US Army Corps of Engineers 1946–47, Reserve Officer Training Corps 1948–55; laboratory dir General Telephone and Electronics 1954–64; f. and served as Pres. ESL, Inc. 1964–77; Exec. Vice-Pres. Hambrecht & Quist, Inc. 1981–85; f. and served as Chair. Tech. Strategies & Alliances 1985–93; Prof. (half-time) Stanford Univ. 1988–93, also Co-Dir Center for Int. Security and Arms Control; Under-Sec. of Defense for Research and Eng 1976–81; Mil. Tech. Adviser to Pres. Clinton 1993; Deputy Sec. of Defense 1993–94, Sec. of Defense 1994–97; Sr Fellow, Stanford Univ. 1997–, now also Sr Fellow, Freeman Spogli Inst. for Int. Studies (FSI) and Michael and Barbara Berberian Prof. (FSI and School of Eng), Stanford Univ., also Co-Dir Preventive Defense Project; Chair. Global Tech. Pnrs; mem. Bd of Dirs United Techs Corpn, FMC Corpn, Sylvania/General Telephone's Electronic Defense Labs, Space Foundation, Thomas Jefferson Program in Public Policy, Concord Coalition, Strategic Partnerships LLC, Center for the Study of the Presidency; mem. Pres.'s Foreign Intelligence Advisory Bd, Sec. of State's Arms Control and Nonproliferation Advisory Bd, FBI Dir's Advisory Bd, Iraq Study Group, US Inst. of Peace 2006; fmr Chair. Bd of Visitors, US Naval Acad.; fmr Co-Chair. Pres. Comm. on Intelligence Capabilities of the US Regarding Weapons of Mass Destruction; mem. Nat. Acad. of Eng, NAS Cttee on Int. Security and Arms Control; Fellow, American Acad. of Arts and Sciences; Trustee MITRE Corpn, Carnegie Endowment for Int. Peace; fmr Fellow, Inst. of Politics, Harvard Univ., Marshall Wythe School of Law, Coll. of William and Mary; several nat. and int. honours including Outstanding Civilian Service Medals from the Army 1962, 1997, Air Force 1997, Navy (1997, Defense Intelligence Agency 1977, 1997, NASA 1981, Coast Guard 1997; Dept of Defense Distinguished Service Medal 1980, 1981, American Electronic Asscn Medal of Achievement 1980, Forrestal Medal 1994, Henry Stimson Medal 1994, Arthur Bueche Medal 1996, Eisenhower Award 1996, Marshall Award 1997, Presidential Medal of Freedom 1997. *Address:* CISAC, Encina Hall, Stanford University, Stanford, CA 94305-6165, USA (office). *Telephone:* (650) 725-6501 (office). *Fax:* (650) 725-0920 (office). *E-mail:* dcgordon@stanford.edu (office). *Website:* cisac.stanford.edu (office).

PERRY OF SOUTHWARK, Baroness (Life Peer), cr. 1991, of Charlbury in the County of Oxfordshire; **Pauline Perry,** MA, FRSA, CIMgt; British university administrator; b. (Pauline Welch), 15 Oct. 1931, Wolverhampton; d. of John Welch and Elizabeth Welch (née Cowan); m. George W. Perry 1952 (died 2008); three s. one d.; ed Girton Coll., Cambridge; Univ. Lecturer in Philosophy, Univs of Manitoba, Canada, Massachusetts, USA, Exeter and Oxford 1956–59, 1961–63, 1966–70; HM Insp. 1970, Staff Insp. 1975, HM Chief Insp. of Schools 1981–86; Vice-Chancellor South Bank Univ. (fmrly South Bank Polytechnic) 1987–93; Pres. Lucy Cavendish Coll., Cambridge 1994–2001; Pro-Chancellor Univ. of Surrey 2001–06; Chair. Dept of Trade and Industry Export Group for Educ. and Training Sector 1993–98; Vice-Pres. City and Guilds of London Inst. 1994–99, Chair. City and Guilds Quality and Standards Cttee 2005–; Co-Chair. All-Party Univs Group; mem. House of Lords Select Cttee on Sciences and Tech. 1992–95, 2004–, on Scrutiny of Delegated Powers 1995–98, on Cen. and Local Govt Relations 1995–96, on Religious Offences 2002–03; mem. Prime Minister's Advisory Group on the Citizen's Charter 1993–97, Jt Select Cttee on Human Rights 2001–03; Chair. Judges Panel on Citizen's Charter 1997–2003, Church of England Review of the Gown Appointments Comm. 1999–2001, Nuffield Council on Bio-Ethics Inquiry into Animals in Scientific Experiments 2003–05; Co-Chair. Conservative Party Policy Comm. on Public Services; mem. Bd of Patrons Royal Soc. Appeal 1995–2001; Trustee Cambridge Univ. Foundation 1997–2006; Liveryman, Worshipful Co. of Bakers, Hon. Freeman, Worshipful Co. of Fishmongers, Freeman City of London, Hon. Fellow, Coll. of Preceptors, City and Guilds, Girton Coll. Cambridge, Roehampton Univ., Lucy Cavendish Coll. Cambridge, Hon. Fellow, Swedish Acad. of Sciences (Pedagogy); Hon. LLD (Aberdeen, Bath), Hon. DLitt (Sussex, South Bank, City Univ.), Hon. DUniv (Surrey); Hon. DEd (Wolverhampton). *Publications:* The Womb in Which I Lay 2003; four books, several chapters and numerous articles. *Leisure interests:* music, power walking. *Address:* House of Lords, Westminster, London, SW1A 0PW, England (office). *Telephone:* (20) 7219-5474 (office). *Fax:* (20) 7738-2911 (office). *E-mail:* perryp@parliament.uk (office).

PERSSON, Göran; Swedish politician; b. 20 Jan. 1949, Vingaker; m. Gunnel Persson (divorced); two c.; m. Anitra Steen; ed Orebro Univ.; Org. Sec. Swedish Social Democratic Youth League Sörmland 1971; Studies Sec. Workers' Educ. Asscn Sörmland, 1974–76; Chair. Katrineholm Educ. Authority 1977–79; mem. Parl. 1979–84; Councillor, Chair. Municipal Exec. Bd Katrineholm 1985–89; Minister with special responsibility for schools and adult educ., Ministry of Educ. and Cultural Affairs 1989–91, of Finance 1994–96; Prime Minister of Sweden 1996–2006; Chair. Sveriges Socialdemokratiska Arbetareparti (SAP) (Swedish Social Democratic Party) 1996–07; Vice-Chair. Bd Oppunda Savings Bank 1976–89, Nordic Museum 1983–89; Chair. Sörmland Co-operative Consumers' Asscn 1976–89; Chair. Sörmland Co. Bd of Educ. 1982–89; Nat. Auditor, Swedish Co-operative Wholesale Soc. 1988–89. *Address:* c/o Sveriges Socialdemokratiska Arbetareparti (SAP) (Swedish Social Democratic Party), Sveavägen 68, 105 60 Stockholm, Sweden. *Telephone:* (8) 700-26-00. *Fax:* (8) 21-93-31. *E-mail:* info@sap.se. *Website:* www.socialdemokraterna.se.

PERSSON, Jörgen; Swedish director of photography; b. 10 Sept. 1936, Helsingborg; s. of Erik W. Persson and Thyra Liljeroth; m. Anne von Sydow 1969; two s.; ed High School and Swedish Film School; Dir of Photography (Features) 1965–; Felix Award, Paris 1989 and Swedish awards. *Films include:* Elvira Madigan 1967, Ådalen-31 1969, My Life as a Dog 1986, Pelle the Conqueror 1988, Best Intentions 1991, Sofi 1991, Young Indy, The House of the Spirits 1993, Jerusalem 1995, Smilla's Sense of Snow 1996, Digging to China 1996, Les Misérables 1997, Faithless 2000, A Song for Martin 2001, Wolf 2008. *Leisure interests:* off-road sport, classic cars. *Address:* Rydbolundsvagen 7, 18531 Vaxholm, Sweden.

PERSSON, Stefan; Swedish retail executive; *Chairman, H&M Hennes & Mauritz AB;* b. 4 Oct. 1947; s. of the late Erling Persson; m.; three c.; ed Univ. of Stockholm; started working for family-controlled H&M Hennes & Mauritz AB 1973, Man. Dir 1982–98, Chair. (succeeded on death of his father) 1998–; Deputy Bd of Dirs Stockholm School of Econs, mem. Bd of Dirs AB Electrolux, Investor AB, Atlas Copco, ABB, Ingha Holding, Mentor Foundation (charitable foundation), Stockholm School of Entrepreneurship. *Address:* H&M Hennes & Mauritz AB, Norrlandsgatan 15, Box 1421, 111 84 Stockholm, Sweden (office). *Telephone:* (8) 796-55-00 (office). *Fax:* (8) 20-99-19 (office). *Website:* www.hm.com (office).

PERT, Geoffrey James, PhD, FRS, FInstP, CPhys; British physicist and academic; *Professor of Computational Physics, University of York;* b. 15 Aug. 1941, Market Harborough, Leics.; s. of Norman James Pert and Grace W. Pert; m. Janice Ann Alexander 1967; one d.; ed Norwich School, Imperial Coll., Univ. of London; Asst Prof., Univ. of Alberta 1967–70; Lecturer, Univ. of Hull 1970–76, Sr Lecturer, Reader 1976–82, Prof. 1982–87; Prof. of Computational Physics, Univ. of York 1987–. *Publications:* numerous scientific papers. *Leisure interests:* hill-walking, gardening. *Address:* Department of Physics, University of York, Heslington, York, YO10 5DD, England. *Telephone:* (1904) 432250 (office). *Fax:* (1904) 432214 (office). *E-mail:* gjp1@york.ac.uk (office). *Website:* www.york.ac.uk/depts/phys (office).

PERVYSHIN, Erlen Kirikovich; Russian industrial manager; b. 25 June 1932, Russia; ed Moscow Electrotechnical Inst. of Communications; mem. Int. Engineer Acad.; engineer 1955–, then Head of Ass. Section, Deputy Chief Engineer, Head of Admin., Manager of Design and Ass. Trust, Dir-Gen. All-Union Scientific production Asscn; Deputy USSR Minister of Radio Industry 1970–74, Minister of Communications Equipment Mfg 1974–89, of Communications 1989–91; Chair. Telecom (now Mirtelecom Corpn) 1991–; Pres. ORB & TEL Co., Andrew Int. Corpn 1997–; Pres. Mirtelecom Asscn 1999–. *Address:* Mirtelecom, Gubkina str. 8, Moscow 17966, Russia. *Telephone:* (495) 748-00-01. *Fax:* (495) 748-00-02.

PESCATORE, Pierre, DIur; Luxembourg diplomatist and professor of law; b. 20 Nov. 1919, Luxembourg; s. of Ferdinand Pescatore and Cunégonde Heuertz; m. Rosalie Margue 1948; three s. one d.; Ministry of Foreign Affairs 1946–67, Sec., later mem., Del. to UN Gen. Ass. 1946–52; Legal Adviser, Min. of Foreign Affairs 1950–58; Dir for Political Affairs, Min. of Foreign Affairs 1958–64; Minister Plenipotentiary 1959; Sec.-Gen. Ministry of Foreign Affairs 1964–67; Judge, Court of Justice of the European Communities 1967–86, Perm. Court of Arbitration 1969, Pres. Luxembourg Nat. Group; fmr mem. Admin. Tribunal ILO; served on several GATT Panels 1989–; Prof. Law Faculty and Inst. for European Legal Studies, Univ. of Liège; Lectured Hague Acad. of Int. Law 1961; mem. Inst. de Droit Int. 1965–; Dr hc (Nancy, Geneva, Tübingen, Leiden, Neuchâtel Univs). *Publications:* complete bibliography to 1987 appears in Liber Amicorum Pierre Pescatore 1987; Handbook of GATT Dispute Settlement (loose-leaf) 1991–. *Address:* 16 rue de la Fontaine, 1532 Luxembourg. *Telephone:* 46-07-97 (office); 22-40-44 (home). *Fax:* 46-61-42.

PESCI, Joe; American film actor; b. 9 Feb. 1943, Newark, NJ. *Films include:* Death Collector 1976, Raging Bull 1980, I'm Dancing as Fast as I Can 1982, Easy Money 1983, Dear Mr Wonderful 1983, Eureka 1983, Once Upon a Time in America 1984, Tutti Dentro 1984, Man On Fire 1987, Moonwalker 1988, Backtrack 1988, Lethal Weapon 2 1989, Betsy's Wedding 1990, Goodfellas (Acad. Award for Best Supporting Actor) 1991, Home Alone 1990, The Super 1991, JFK 1991, Lethal Weapon 3 1992, Home Alone II 1992, The Public Eye 1992, My Cousin Vinny 1992, A Bronx Tale 1993, With Honours 1994, Jimmy Hollywood 1994, Casino 1995, 8 Heads in a Duffel Bag 1997, Gone Fishing 1997, Lethal Weapon 4 1998, The Good Shepherd 2006. *Address:* c/o Fred Specktor, Creative Artists Agency, Inc., 9830 Wilshire Blvd, Beverly Hills, CA 90212-1825, USA. *Telephone:* (310) 288-4545. *Fax:* (310) 288-4800. *Website:* www.caa.com.

PESCUCCI, Gabriella; Italian costume designer; b. Castiglioncello, Tuscany; ed Accademia di Belle Arti, Florence; worked as Asst to Piero Tosi on set of Luchino Visconti's films Death in Venice and Ludwig; solo debut designing costumes for Charlotte Rampling in Italian film adaptation of 'Tis Pity She's a Whore 1971; designed costumes for Maria Callas in Medea, for Sean Connery in The Name of the Rose, Montserrat Caballé in Norma at La Scala, Milan; prizes and awards include two Donatello Davids from Italian Acad. of Cinema and two BAFTA Awards. *Films as costume designer include:* I Sette fratelli Cervi 1967, Uomini contro 1970, Addio, fratello crudele 1971, Fatti di gente per bene 1974, Identikit 1974, Divina creatura 1976, L' Eredità Ferramonti 1976, Prova d'orchestra 1978, La Città delle donne 1980, Tre fratelli 1981, Passione d'amore 1981, La Nuit de Varennes 1982, Once Upon a Time in America 1984, Il Trovatore 1985, Orfeo 1985, The Name of the Rose 1986, La Famiglia 1987, The Adventures of Baron Munchausen 1988, Haunted Summer 1988, Splendor 1989, Che ora è? 1989, Indochine 1992, Per amore, solo per amore 1993, The Age of Innocence (Acad. Award for Best Costume Design 1994) 1993, The Scarlet Letter 1995, Albergo Roma 1996, Dangerous Beauty 1998, Les Misérables 1998, Cousin Bette 1998, Le Temps retrouvé 1999,A Midsummer Night's Dream 1999, Perduto amor 2003, Secret Passage 2004, Van Helsing 2004, Charlie and the Chocolate Factory 2005, The Brothers Grimm 2005, Beowulf 2007.

PEŠEK, Libor; Czech conductor; b. 22 June 1933, Prague; ed Prague Acad. of Musical Arts; studied conducting with Karel Ancerl, Vaclav Neumann and Václav Smetáček; f. Prague Chamber Harmony 1958; Chief Conductor Slovak Philharmonic 1980–81; Conductor-in-Residence Czech Philharmonic Orchestra 1982–, Germany tour 1998; Prin. Conductor and Artistic Adviser Royal Liverpool Philharmonic Orchestra 1982–97, Hon. Conductor 1997–; Visiting Conductor Prague Symphony Orchestra 1989–; Pres. Prague Spring Festival 1994–; mem. Bd of Supervisors OPS Prague European City of Culture 1999–; conducted Royal Liverpool Philharmonic Orchestra, Prague Spring Festival 2000; has conducted Philharmonia, London Symphony, Royal Philharmonic, BBC Philharmonic, Hallé, Oslo Philharmonic, Danish Radio, Los Angeles Philharmonic and Cincinnati, Dallas, Minnesota, Pittsburgh, Cleveland, Montreal, Indianapolis and Philadelphia orchestras, Orchestra of La Scala, Milan and Orchestre de Paris; charity concerts after floods in Czech Repub. 2002; Hon. mem. Preston Univ. 1997; Hon. Fellow, Univ. of Cen. Lancashire 1997; Hon. KBE; Classic Prize for Extraordinary Merit in Musical Culture (Czech Repub.) 1997, Journal Harmonie Lifelong Contrib. to Czech Culture 2002. *Recordings include:* works by Dvořák, Suk, Janáček, Martinů and Britten. *Leisure interests:* physics, Eastern philosophy, literature. *Address:* IMG Artists, The Light Box, 111 Power Road, London, W4 5PY, England (office). *Telephone:* (20) 7957-5800 (office). *Fax:* (20) 7957-5801 (office). *E-mail:* labrahams@imgartists.com (office). *Website:* www.imgartists.com (office).

PESIĆ, Dragiša, MSc(Econ); Montenegrin fmr head of state and business executive; b. 8 Aug. 1954, Danilovgrad; s. of Lazar Pesić and Andja Pesić; m. Lela Savović; one s. one d.; ed Sarajevo Univ.; worked as financial expert; fmr Chair. Exec. Bd Municipal Ass. of Podgorica (twice); Deputy to Fed. Ass., Chair. Budget Cttee, Chamber of Citizens; Minister of Finance 1998–2001; Prime Minister of Serbia and Montenegro (fmr Fed. Repub. of Yugoslavia) 2001–03, Pres. 2003–04; mem. Socialist Nat. Party of Montenegro. *Leisure interests:* music, literature, sports. *Address:* c/o Office of the Federal Government, Belgrade, Serbia (office).

PEŠIĆ, Vesna, BA, MA, PhD; Serbian lawyer, diplomatist and politician; b. 6 May 1940, Groska; ed Belgrade Univ.; on staff, Inst. of Social Sciences 1964–72; Sr Researcher, Inst. of Social Policy 1972–78; Prof., Higher School for Social Workers 1978–91; Sr Researcher, Inst. of Philosophy and Social Theory, Belgrade 1991–2001; Co-f. Union for Yugoslavian Democratic Initiative (IZDI) 1991, Helsinki Cttee for Serbia, Belgrade 1985; Founder and Pres. Center of Peace and Democracy Devt (fmrly Cen. for Antiwar Action); mem. Cttee for Freedom of Speech and Self-Expression; fmr Pres. Civil Alliance of Serbia (now merged into Liberal Democratic Party), currently Pres. Political Council of Liberal Democratic Party; Amb. to Mexico 2001–05; mem. Narodna skupština (Parl.) 2007–; Int. Policy Fellowship 2006–07; Award for Democracy Nat. Foundation of Democracy, Washington, DC 1993, Andrej Sakharov Freedom Price, Norwegian Sakharov Freedom Fund 1997, W. Averell Harriman Democracy Award, Nat. Democratic Inst. 1997. *Publications include:* Social Traditions and Style of Life 1977, Ethnomethodology and Sociology 1985, Social Deviations: Criticism of Social Pathology (with I. Jancović) 1981, Brief Course of Equality 1988, Theory of Changes and Parsons Concept of Contemporary Soc. 1990, Yugoslavian Military Crisis and World Movement 1992, Nationalism, War and Disintegration of Communist Federation 1993; articles in scientific journals and periodicals. *Address:* Narodna skupština Republike Srbije (National Assembly of the Republic of Serbia), 11000 Belgrade, Kralja Milana 14, Serbia (office). *Telephone:* (11) 3222001 (office). *E-mail:* vpesic@policy.hu; webmaster@parlament.sr.gov.yu (office). *Website:* www.parlament.sr.gov.yu (office).

PESONEN, Jussi, MSc; Finnish paper production industry executive; *President and CEO, UPM-Kymmene Corporation;* b. 1960; ed Univ. of Oulu; joined UPM-Kymmene Corpn 1987, various positions including Production Man. Jämsänkoski Mill, Production Unit Dir Kajaani, Kaukas and Shotton Mills, Vice-Pres. Newsprint Product Group, Publ. Papers Div. 2001, Group Sr Exec. Vice-Pres. and COO 2001–04, Pres. and CEO 2004–; mem. Bd Asscn of European Publ. Paper Producers (CEPIPRINT), Finnish Forest Industries Fed. *Address:* UPM-Kymmene Corporation, Eteläesplanadi 2, POB 380, 00101 Helsinki, Finland (office). *Telephone:* (8) 204-15-111 (office). *Fax:* (8) 204-15-110 (office). *E-mail:* jussi.h.pesonen@upm-kymmene.com (office). *Website:* www.upm-kymmene.com (office).

PESSINA, Stefano; Italian engineer and pharmaceutical industry executive; *Executive Chairman, Alliance Boots plc;* m.; two c.; ed Univ. of Milan; trained as nuclear engineer; fmr Lecturer, Univ. of Milan; Consultant, AC Nielsen 1973–76; f. Gruppo Alliance Santé 1977 (merged with UniChem PLC to form Alliance UniChem Plc 1997), apptd to Bd 1997, Exec. Deputy Chair. 2004–06 (merged with Boots PLC to form Alliance Boots plc), Exec. Deputy Chair. 2006–07, Exec. Chair. 2007–; Dir (non-exec.) Galenica; mem. Council Int. Fed. of Pharmaceutical Wholesalers (IFPW) 1999–, Chair. 2000–02. *Leisure interest:* yachting. *Address:* Alliance Boots plc, 4th Floor, Sedley Place, 361 Oxford Street, London, W1C 2JL, England (office); Alliance Boots GmbH, Baarerstrasse 78, 6300 Zug, Switzerland. *Telephone:* (115) 950-6111 (Nottingham) (office). *Fax:* (20) 7491-0149 (London) (office). *E-mail:* enquiries@allianceboots.com (office). *Website:* www.allianceboots.com (office).

PESSOA PEREIRA DA SILVA PINTO, Ana Maria; Timor-Leste politician; *Prosecutor General;* m. José Ramos-Horta (divorced); one s.; mem. Nat. Political Comm. of Timorese Resistance 1998–2000; mem. Transitional Cabinet for Internal Admin 2000–01; Minister of Justice 2001–03; Deputy Prime Minister and Minister of State and Minister of the Presidency of the Council of Ministers 2003–05; Minister for State and Internal Admin 2005–07, Sr Minister of State 2006; unsuccessful cand. for Prime Minister 2006; mem. Nat. Parl. 2007–; Prosecutor Gen. 2009–; mem. FRETILIN (Frente Revolucionaria do Timor-Leste Independente). *Address:* Ministry of Justice, Av. Jacinto Candido, Dili, Timor-Leste (office). *Telephone:* 3331160 (office). *E-mail:* mj@mj.gov.tl (office). *Website:* www.mj.gov.tl (office).

PESTILLO, Peter J., BEcons, LLB; American automotive executive; b. 22 March 1938, Bristol, Conn.; ed Fairfield Univ., Georgetown Univ., Harvard Business School; admitted to Bar, Washington, DC; began career in industrial relations, Gen. Electric (GE) Co.; Vice-Pres. Corp. and Employee Relations, B.F. Goodrich –1980; Vice-Pres. Labour Relations Ford Motor Co. 1980–85, Vice-Pres. Employee Relations 1985–86, Vice-Pres. Employee Relations and External Affairs 1986–90, Vice-Pres. Corp. Relations and Diversified Businesses 1990–93, apptd Exec. Vice-Pres. Corp. Relations 1993, Vice-Chair. and Chief of Staff –1999; Chair. and CEO Visteon 2000–2004, Chair. –2005; mem. Bd of Dirs Rouge Industries, Mich. Mfrs Asscn, Nat. Asscn of Mfrs and Sentry Insurance. *Address:* c/o Visteon Corporation, 17000 Rotunda Drive, Dearborn, MI 48120, USA (office).

PESTKA, Sidney, BA, MD; American (b. Polish) molecular geneticist and academic; *Chairman and Professor, Department of Molecular Genetics, Microbiology and Immunology, Robert Wood Johnson Medical School, University of Medicine and Dentistry of New Jersey;* b. 1936; ed Princeton Univ., Univ. of Pennsylvania School of Medicine; worked as intern in medicine and paediatrics; worked at NIH, later at NIH Nat. Cancer Inst. 1966–69; mem. staff, Roche Inst. of Molecular Biology, Nutley, NJ 1969; currently Chair. and Prof., Dept of Molecular Genetics, Microbiology and Immunology, Robert Wood Johnson Medical School, Univ. of Medicine and Dentistry of New Jersey; Founder and Chief Scientific Officer, Pestka Biomedical Laboratories (PBL) 1990; Sec. Int. Soc. for Interferon and Cytokine Research 1989–93, 1996–2005, Vice-Pres. 1992–93, Pres. 1994–95; known as the "father of interferon" for work developing antiviral treatments for chronic hepatitis B and C, multiple sclerosis and cancers; Hon. DSc (Rider Univ.) 1987; Mayer Lecturer in the Life Sciences, MIT 1986, Nat. Medal of Tech., Pres. George W. Bush 2001, Warren Alpert Foundation Prize, Harvard Univ. 2004, Lemelson-MIT Lifetime Achievement Award 2006. *Publications:* more than 270 US and foreign patents; ed five books; more than 400 papers on protein biosynthesis and interferons. *Address:* Department of Molecular Genetics, Microbiology and Immunology, Robert Wood Johnson Medical School, University of Medicine and Dentistry of New Jersey, RWJMS 736, 675 Hoes Lane, Piscataway, NJ 08854-5635, USA (office). *Telephone:* (732) 235-4567 (office). *Fax:* (732) 235-5223 (office). *E-mail:* pestka@umdnj.edu (office). *Website:* www2.umdnj.edu/mgenmweb (office).

PETERLE, Lojze; Slovenian politician; b. 5 July 1948, Čužnja Vas, Trebnje; ed Ljubljana Univ.; Researcher Urban Planning Inst. 1975–84; environmental protection adviser Social Planning Inst. 1985–89; mem. Nat. Ass. 1990–; Pres. Slovenian Christian Democrats (SKD) 1989–2000 (merged to form Slovenian People's Party 2000); Prime Minister of Slovenia 1990–92; Minister of Foreign Affairs 1993–94, 2000; Chair. Parl. Cttee on European Affairs 1997–; First Vice-Pres. European Union of Christian Democrats 1996–99; Observer European Parl. 2003–04, mem. European Parl. 2004–, mem. Cttee on Foreign Affairs, Subcttee on Human Rights, delegation for relations with countries of Southeast Asia and ASEAN; unsuccessful cand. of Pres. of Slovenia 2007; mem. Praesidium of the Convention on the Future of Europe 2002–03; Vice-Pres. Union of European Federalists 2004–; mem. State Legis. Leaders Foundation 1989; Kt Grand Cross, Papal Order 1993. *Address:* Cankarjeva 11, 1000 Ljubljana, Slovenia; European Parliament, Bât. Altiero Spinelli, 05F366 60, rue Wiertz 60, 1047 Brussels, Belgium (office). *Telephone:* (1) 4223585; (2) 2845638 (Brussels) (office). *Fax:* (1) 4261092; (2) 2849638 (Brussels) (office). *E-mail:* press@peterle.si; alojz.peterle@europarl.europa .eu (office). *Website:* www.peterle.si.

PETERS, Janis; Latvian diplomatist, writer and poet; b. 30 June 1939, Liepāja Region; s. of Janis Peters and Zelma Peters; m. Baiba Kalniņa 1969; one s.; started as journalist in Latvian newspapers, later freelance; Chair. Bd of Latvian Writers' Union 1985–89; participant democratic movt for independence; Chair. Org. Cttee People's Front of Latvia 1988; USSR People's Deputy 1989–90; Perm. Rep. of Council of Ministers of Latvia to Russia 1990–91, then Amb. to Russian Fed. 1991–97; mem. govt del. to negotiations with Russia 1992–; Hon. mem. Latvian Acad. of Sciences 1990–, Latvian Univ. 1991–; Cavaliere di San Marco 1993. *Publications:* more than 30 books of poetry, prose and essays in Latvian, Russian and English. *Leisure interests:*

gardening, driving. *Address:* Vesetas Str. 8, Apt 12, 1013 Rīga, Latvia; c/o Latvijas vestnieciba (Embassy of Latvia in Russia), Ul. Chapligina 3, Moscow 103062, Russia. *Telephone:* (095) 925-27-07 (Moscow); 6237-0774 (Rīga); 6733-9350 (Rīga). *Fax:* (095) 923-9295 (Moscow).

PETERS, Lenrie Leopold Wilfred, MA, FRCS; Gambian physician and writer; *Surgeon Specialist, Westfield Clinic;* b. 1 Sept. 1932, Banjul; s. of Lenrie Peters and Keria Peters; m. (divorced); ed Boys' High School, Banjul, Prince of Wales Secondary School, Freetown, Sierra Leone, Trinity Coll., Cambridge, UK, Univ. Coll. Hospital, London; surgeon specialist, Westfield Clinic, Banjul 1972–; farmer, Chair. and Chief Exec. Farato Farms Export Ltd 1981–99; Chair. Colloquium Cttee, Lagos 1977, Bd of Govs Gambia Coll. 1979–87, W African Examinations Council 1988–91, Nat. Consultative Cttee The Gambia 1995–; Fellow Int. Coll. of Surgeons 1992; Distinguished Friend of W African Examinations Council; Officer of Repub. of The Gambia. *Publications:* Poems 1964, The Second Round (novel) 1965, Satellites (poems) 1967, Katchikali (poems) 1971, Selected Poetry 1981; contrib. to many anthologies. *Leisure interests:* tennis, music, reading. *Address:* PO Box 142, Banjul, Gambia (home). *Telephone:* 392219 (office); 495419 (home). *Fax:* 495419.

PETERS, Mary E., BA; American fmr government official; m. Terry Peters; three c.; ed Univ. of Phoenix; joined Ariz. Dept of Transportation 1985, served in several positions including Contract Admin., Deputy Dir for Admin, Deputy Dir –1998, Dir 1998–2001; US Fed. Highway Admin. 2001–05; Nat. Dir for Transportation Policy and Consulting, HDR, Inc., Phoenix 2005–06; US Sec. of Transportation 2006–09; fmr Chair. Standing Cttee on Planning and Asset Man. Task Force, American Asscn of State Highway Officials; Nat. Woman of the Year Award, Women's Transportation Seminar 2004, ARTBA Award, American Road and Transportation Builders Asscn 2005. *Address:* c/o Department of Transportation, 400 Seventh Street, SW, Washington, DC 20590, USA.

PETERS, Wallace, MD, DSc, FRCP; British professor of parasitology; *Professor Emeritus of Medical Protozoology, London School of Hygiene and Tropical Medicine;* b. 1 April 1924, London; s. of Henry Peters and Fanny Peters; m. Ruth Scheidegger-Frehner 1954; ed Haberdashers Aske's Hampstead School, St Bartholomew's Hosp. Medical Coll., Univ. of London; Physician West and East Africa, including RAMC 1947–53; Scientist-Entomologist and Malariologist, WHO, in Liberia and Nepal 1953–55; Malariologist, Territory of Papua and New Guinea 1956–61; Research Assoc., CIBA Pharmaceutical Co., Basel 1961–66; Prof. of Parasitology, Liverpool School of Tropical Medicine 1966–79, Dean 1975–78; Prof. of Medical Protozoology, London School of Hygiene and Tropical Medicine 1979–89, now Prof. Emer.; Hon. Consultant in Parasitology, Camden Area Health Authority 1978–89, on malariology, to Army 1986–89; Jt Dir Public Health Lab. Service Malaria Reference Centre 1979–89; Dir Centre for Tropical Antiprotozoal Chemotherapy, Northwick Park Inst. for Medical Research 1999–2004; Hon. Research Fellow Int. Inst. of Parasitology (IIP) (then CABI Bioscience) 1992–99; Pres. Royal Soc. of Tropical Medicine and Hygiene 1987–88 (Vice-Pres. 1982–83, 1985–87); mem. Expert Advisory Panel on Malaria of WHO 1967–2004; Hon. Fellow Royal Soc. of Tropical Medicine and Hygiene; Hon. mem. American Soc. of Tropical Medicine and Parasitology; Dr hc (Univ. René Descartes, Paris) 1992; King Faisal Int. Prize, Medicine 1983, Rudolf Leuckart Medallist, German Soc. of Parasitology 1980, Le Prince Medallist, American Soc. of Tropical Medicine and Hygiene 1994, Emile Brumpt Prize, Société de Pathologie Exotique 1998. *Publications:* Checklist of Ethiopian Butterflies 1952, Chemotherapy and Drug Resistance in Malaria 1970, 1987, Rodent Malaria (co-ed.) 1978, Atlas of Tropical Medicine and Parasitology (with H. M. Gilles) 1977, 1995, Pharmacology of Antimalarials (2 Vols) (co-ed.) 1984, Leishmaniases in Biology and Medicine (co-ed.) 1987, Atlas of Arthropods in Clinical Medicine 1992, Tropical Medicine and Parasitology (with G. Pasvol) 2001. *Leisure interests:* photography, entomology, writing. *Address:* c/o Northwick Park Institute for Medical Research, Watford Road, HA1 3UJ, England (office). *Fax:* (20) 8422-7136 (office); (144) 284-3044 (home). *E-mail:* w.peters@imperial.ac.uk (office); wallacepeters2@aol.com (home).

PETERS, Rt Hon Winston R.; New Zealand politician and lawyer; *Leader, New Zealand First Party;* b. 11 April 1945; MP for Tauranga; fmr Minister of Maori Affairs, Minister in charge of the Iwi Transition Agency, Chair. Cabinet Cttee on Treaty of Waitangi Issues 1990–91; independent MP 1993–, now New Zealand First Party; Leader New Zealand First Party 1993–; Deputy Prime Minister and Treas. 1996–98; Minister of Foreign Affairs and for Racing 2005–08. *Address:* New Zealand First Party, Parliament Buildings, Wellington, New Zealand. *Telephone:* (4) 471-9292 (office). *Fax:* (4) 472-8557 (office). *E-mail:* info@nzfirst.org.nz (office). *Website:* www.nzfirst.org.nz (office).

PETERSEN, George Bouet, MSc, MA, DPhil, DSc, FNZIC, FRSNZ; New Zealand scientist and academic; *Professor Emeritus of Biochemistry, University of Otago;* b. 5 Sept. 1933, Palmerston North, NZ; s. of George C. Petersen and Elizabeth S. Petersen; m. Patricia J.E. Caughey 1960; four d.; ed Univ. of Otago and Univ. of Oxford, UK; scientist, Dept of Scientific and Industrial Research Plant Chem. Div., Palmerston North 1959–60, 1963–67; Departmental Demonstrator in Biochemistry, Univ. of Oxford 1961–63; Head Dept of Biochemistry, Univ. of Otago 1968–91, Prof. of Biochemistry 1968–99, Prof. Emer. 1999–; Deputy Dean, Otago Medical School 1991–95; Pres. Acad. Council Royal Soc. of NZ 1997–2000; Visiting Research Fellow, Harvard Univ., USA 1964; Royal Soc. Commonwealth Bursar, MRC Lab. of Molecular Biology, Cambridge, UK 1973–74, 1981; Carnegie Corpn of New York Travel Grantee 1964; Officer, NZ Order of Merit 1997; Hon. DSc (Otago) 2000; Marsden Medal, NZ Asscn of Scientists 1995, Rutherford Medal, Royal Soc. of NZ 2003. *Publications:* numerous papers on aspects of nucleic acid chemistry and biochemistry in various scientific journals. *Leisure interests:* music,

literature, book collecting. *Address:* Department of Biochemistry, University of Otago, PO Box 56, Dunedin, New Zealand (office). *Telephone:* (3) 479-7846 (office). *Fax:* (3) 479-7866 (office). *E-mail:* george.petersen@otago.ac.nz (office).

PETERSEN, Jan, LLB; Norwegian politician; b. 11 June 1946, Oslo; m.; two c.; with Norwegian Consumers' Asscn, Norwegian Agency for Devt Co-operation (NORAD); Chair. Young Conservatives 1971–73; Mayor of Oppegård 1976–81; mem. Stortinget (Parl.) 1981–; mem. Standing Cttee on Local Govt and Environment 1981–84, Standing Cttee on Foreign Affairs 1984– (Chair. 1985–86, later Deputy Chair.); Leader Akershus Conservative Party 1992–94, Conservative Party (Høyre) 1994–; Chair. Political Cttee of N Atlantic Ass. 1996–2001; Minister of Foreign Affairs 2001–05. *Address:* c/o Ministry of Foreign Affairs, 7 juri pl. 1, PO Box 8114 Dep., 0032 Oslo; Høyre, Stortingst. 20, PO Box 1536 Vika, 0117 Oslo, Norway.

PETERSEN, Niels Helveg, LLD; Danish politician; b. 17 Jan. 1939, Odense; s. of Kristen Helveg Petersen and Lilly Helveg Petersen; ed Copenhagen Univ. and Stanford Univ., Calif., USA; mem. Folketing (Parl.) 1966–74, 1977–; Chef de Cabinet to Danish Commr for the European Communities 1974–77; mem. Parl. Foreign Affairs Cttee 1968–74, Market Cttee 1972–74, 1977–78, 1982–88, 1990–93, Parl. Politico-Econ. Cttee 1982–84; Social Liberal Party Spokesman on Political Affairs 1968–74, 1977–78, Chair. Parl. Group 1978–88; Minister for Econ. Affairs 1988–90, for Foreign Affairs 1993–2000. *leisure interests:* football, tennis, chess. *Address:* Folketinget, Christiansborg, 1240 Copenhagen K, Denmark (office); Drosselvej 72, 2000 F Frederiksberg, Denmark (home). *Telephone:* 33-37-47-10 (office). *E-mail:* niels.helveg .petersen@ft.dk (office).

PETERSEN, Wolfgang; German film director and producer; b. 14 March 1941, Emden; ed German Film and TV Acad.; Asst Stage Dir Ernst Deutsch Theatre, Hamburg. *Films include:* Smog (Prix Futura Award 1975), For Your Love Only, Scene of the Crime, The Consequence 1977, Black and White Like Day and Night 1978, Das Boot 1981, The Neverending Story 1984, Enemy Mine 1985, Shattered 1991, In the Line of Fire 1993, Outbreak 1995, Air Force One, The Red Corner 1997, The Perfect Storm 2000, Troy 2004. *Address:* c/o Rand Halstan, CAA, 9830 Wilshire Boulevard, Beverly Hills, CA 90212, USA.

PETERSON, David Robert, BA, PC, LLD, QC,; Canadian lawyer, business executive and fmr politician; *Senior Partner, Cassels Brock & Blackwell LLP;* b. 28 Dec. 1943, Toronto; s. of Clarence Peterson; m. Shelley Matthews 1974; two s. one d.; ed Univ. of Western Ont., Univ. of Toronto; called to the Bar 1969; MP for London Centre 1975, re-elected 1977, 1981; elected Leader Ont. Liberal Party 1982, won election for Liberal Party 1985; Premier of Ont. 1985–90; currently Chair. and Sr Pnr, Cassels Brock & Blackwell LLP; Chancellor Univ. of Toronto 2006–; numerous directorships; Founding Chair. Toronto Raptors Basketball Club, Chapters Inc.; Dir Young Pres.' Org., Council for Canadian Unity, etc; Adjunct Prof., York Univ.; Liberal; Chevalier, Légion d'honneur 1994, Commdr of the Order of St John of Jeruselem, Order of Ontario 2009; several hon. degrees; Ordre de la Pléiade, Int. Ass. of French-speaking Parliamentarians 1995. *Leisure interests:* golf, riding, reading, gardening, skiing. *Address:* Cassels Brock, 2100 Scotia Plaza, 40 King Street West, Toronto, ON M5H 3C2 (office); 8 Gibson Avenue, Toronto, ON M5R 1T5, Canada (home). *Telephone:* (416) 869-5451 (office); (416) 925-0460 (home). *Fax:* (416) 350-6961 (office). *E-mail:* dpeterson@casselsbrock.com (office). *Website:* www.casselsbrock.com (office).

PETERSON, G. P. (Bud), BS, MS, PhD; American engineer, academic and university administrator; *Chancellor, University of Colorado at Boulder;* b. Prairie Village, Kan.; m. Val Peterson; four c.; ed Kansas State Univ., Texas A&M Univ.; Visiting Research Scientist, NASA Johnson Space Center 1981–82; Lecturer and Researcher, Dept of Mechanical Eng, Texas A&M Univ. 1985–90, Halliburton Prof. of Mechanical Eng 1990, also Tenneco Prof., Coll. of Eng 1991, Head of Dept of Mechanical Eng 1993–96, Exec. Assoc. Dean, Coll. of Eng, also Assoc. Vice Chancellor for Eng 1996; Provost Rensselaer Polytechnic Inst. 2000–06; Chancellor Univ. of Colorado, Boulder 2006–; Program Dir Thermal Transport and Thermal Processing Div., Nat. Science Foundation 1993; mem. Nat. Science Bd 2008–; mem. American Asscn of Colls and Univs, Middle States Comm. on Higher Educ., New England Asscn of Schools and Colls; Fellow, American Soc. of Mechanical Engineers (ASME), American Inst. of Aeronautics and Astronautics (AIAA); Ralph James and the O. L. "Andy" Lewis Awards, ASME, Pi Tau Sigma Gustus L. Larson Memorial Award, ASME, AIAA Thermophysics Award, ASME Memorial Award, AIAA Sustained Service Award, NSF Award for Outstanding Man., Int. Astronautical Fed. Frank J. Malina Astronautics Medal 2005. *Publications:* author or co-author of 14 books or book chapters, 165 refereed journal articles and more than 140 conference publications. *Address:* Office of the Chancellor, University of Colorado, 914 Broadway, Boulder, CO 80309, USA (office). *Telephone:* (303) 492-8908 (office). *E-mail:* chanchat@colorado .edu (office). *Website:* www.cu.edu (office).

PETERSON, James Scott, DCL, LLM; Canadian politician; b. 1941, Ottawa; m. Heather Peterson; ed McGill Univ., Columbia Univ., USA, Univ. of W Ont., Acad. de Droit Int., The Hague, The Netherlands, La Sorbonne, Paris, France; mem Faculty of Law, Univ. of Toronto 1974–79; pvt. practice, int. tax and business law 1970–80; Chair. Cambridge Acceptance Corpn Ltd 1984–87; MP for Willowdale 1980, re-elected 1988, 1993, 1997; fmr Liberal Party Industry Critic, Treasury Bd Critic, Parl. Sec. to Minister of State for Econ. Devt, Science and Tech. and to Minister of Justice; Chair. Parl. Task Force on Regulatory Reform; Chair Standing Cttee on Finance 1993–97, Sec. of State (Int. Financial Insts) 1997–2002, Minister of Int. Trade Dec. 2003–06; fmr legal counsel and consultant to UN on jt ventures and major devt projects; Sr Res. Massey Coll., Munk Centre for Int. Studies, Univ. of Toronto 2002–; mem. numerous bds including Nat. Ballet of Canada, George R. Gardiner Museum of Ceramic Art, Candian Soc. for Yad Vashem, Streethaven (charity). *Publications:* numerous works on int. taxation and int. jt business ventures. *Address:* c/o International Trade Canada, Lester B. Pearson Building, 125 Sussex Drive, Ottawa, Ont. K1A 0G2, Canada (office).

PETERSON, Paul E., PhD; American political scientist and academic; *Director, Program on Education Policy and Governance, Kennedy School of Government, Harvard University;* b. 16 Sept. 1940, Montevideo, Minn.; s. of Alvin C. Peterson and Josephine M. Telkamp; m. Carol D. Schnell 1963; two s. one d.; ed Concordia Coll., Moorhead, Minn. and Univ. of Chicago; Asst Prof., then Assoc. Prof. and Prof., Depts of Political Science and Educ., Univ. of Chicago 1967–83, Chair. Cttee on Public Policy Studies 1981–83; Dir Governmental Studies, The Brookings Inst., Washington, DC 1983–87; Benjamin H. Griswold III Prof. of Public Policy, Dept of Political Science, Johns Hopkins Univ. 1987–88; Prof. Dept of Govt, Harvard Univ. 1988–89, Henry Lee Shattuck Prof. of Govt 1989, Dir Centre for American Political Studies 1989–2000, Dir Program on Educ. Policy and Governance 1996–; Acad. Visitor, Dept of Govt, LSE, England 1977–78; John Simon Guggenheim Fellowship, German Marshall Fund of the US Fellowship 1977–78; mem. Nat. Acad. of Educ., American Acad. of Arts and Sciences. *Publications:* School Politics Chicago Style 1976 (Gladys Kammerer Award), City Limits 1981 (Woodrow Wilson Foundation Award), The Politics of School Reform, 1870–1940 1985, The New Urban Reality (Ed.) 1985, The New Direction in American Politics (Ed. with J. Chubb) 1985, When Federalism Works (with B. Rabe and K. Wong) 1987, Political Institutions and Effective Government, Can the Government Govern? 1989, Welfare Magnets (with Mark Rom) 1991, The Urban Underclass (with C. Jencks) 1991, The President, the Congress and the Making of Foreign Policy 1994, The Price of Federalism 1995 (Aaron Wildavsky Award 1996), Classifying by Race 1995, The New American Democracy (with M. Fiorina) 2001, Learning from School Choice (Ed. with B. Hassel) 1998, Earning and Learning (Ed. with S. Mayer), Charters, Vouchers and Public Education (Ed. with David E. Campbell) 2001, The Education Gap: Vouchers and Urban Schools (with William G. Howell) 2002. *Leisure interests:* tennis, piano. *Address:* Kennedy School of Government, Harvard University, 79 JFK Street, T306, Cambridge, MA 02138, USA (office). *Fax:* (617) 496-4428. *E-mail:* ppeterson@latte.harvard.edu (office). *Website:* www.ksg.harvard/pcpg (office).

PETERSON, Peter G., MBA; American business executive and fmr government official; *Chairman, The Blackstone Group L.P.;* b. 5 June 1926, Kearney, Neb.; s. of George Peterson and Venetia Peterson (née Paul); m. 1st Sally Hornbogen 1953 (divorced 1979); four s. one d.; m. 2nd Joan Ganz Cooney 1980; ed MIT, Northwestern Univ. and Univ. of Chicago; Market Analyst, Market Facts Inc., Chicago 1947–49, Assoc. Dir 1949–51, Exec. Vice-Pres. 1951–53; Dir of Marketing Services, McCann-Erickson (advertising firm) 1953, Vice-Pres. 1954–58, Gen. Man. Chicago Office 1955–57, Dir, Asst to Pres. co-ordinating services regional offices 1957–58; Exec. Vice-Pres. and Dir Bell & Howell 1958–61, Pres. 1961–63, CEO 1963–71, Chair. of Bd 1968–71; Asst to Pres. of USA for Int. Econ. Affairs 1971–72, also Exec. Dir Council on Int. Econ. Policy; Sec. of Commerce 1972–73; Chair. Bd Lehman Bros Kuhn Loeb Inc. (fmrly Lehman Bros Inc.), New York 1973–83; Chair. The Blackstone Group 1985–; mem. Ind. Comm. on Int. Devt Issues, Trilateral Comm.; Pres. Clinton's Bipartisan Comm. on Entitlement Reform 1994; nominated as Amb. to Viet Nam May 1996; Dir Minnesota Mining and Mfg Co., Rockefeller Center Properties Inc.; fmr Dir Federated Dept Stores, Black and Decker Mfg Co., Gen. Foods Corpn, RCA, Continental Group, Cities Service; mem. Inst. of Int. Econs (Chair Bd); Trustee, Museum of Modern Art, New York; Per Jacobsson Lecture 1984; Man of Vision Award 1994. *Publications:* Facing Up: How to Rescue the Economy from Crushing Debt and Restore the American Dream, On Borrowed Time (co-author), Readings in Market Organization and Price Policies (ed.). *Address:* The Blackstone Group L.P., 345 Park Avenue, Suite 3101, New York, NY 10154 (office); 435 E 52nd Street, Apartment 11G, New York, NY 10022, USA (home). *Telephone:* (212) 583-5000 (office). *Fax:* (212) 583-5712 (home). *Website:* www.blackstone.com (office).

PETERSON, Russell Wilbur, PhD; American politician, conservationist, scientist and industrial executive; b. 3 Oct. 1916, Portage, Wis.; s. of John Anton Peterson and Emma Marie Anthony; m. 1st Eva Lillian Turner 1937; two s. two d.; m. 2nd June Bigelow-Jenkins 1995; ed Portage High School and Univ. of Wisconsin; with Du Pont Company for 26 years, various research, sales and man. assignments to Dir Research and Devt Div. of Devt Dept 1968; Vice-Pres. Nat. Municipal League 1968–78; Gov. of Delaware 1969–73; Chair. Cttee on Law Enforcement, Justice and Public Safety, Nat. Govs Conf. 1971, Mid-Atlantic Govs Conf. 1971; Vice-Chair. Council of State Govts 1971; Chair. President's Nat. Advisory Comm. on Criminal Justice Standards and Goals 1971–72; Chair. of Bd, Textile Inst.; Chair. Exec. Cttee, Comm. on Critical Choices for Americans 1973; Chair. Council on Environmental Quality 1973–76; Pres. and CEO of New Directions, citizens' action org. focused on global problems 1976–77; Special Adviser to Aspen Inst. for Humanistic Studies 1976–77; Dir AAAS 1977–82, US Asscn of Club of Rome 1975–80, Population Crisis Cttee (now called Population Action Int.) 1973–98, World Wildlife Fund 1976–82, Office of Tech. Assessment, US Congress 1978–79, Global Tomorrow Coalition 1981–91; Pres. Nat. Audubon Soc. 1979–85 (Pres. Emer. 1985–), Better World Soc. 1985–87; Chair. Advisory Bd Solar Energy Research Inst. 1979–81; mem. President's Three Mile Island Comm. 1979; Regional Councillor, Int. Union for the Conservation of Nature (IUCN) 1981–88, Vice-Pres. 1984–88; mem. World Environment Prize Cttee, UNEP 1989–2003; Pres. Int. Council for Bird Preservation 1982–90, Pres. Emer. 1990–; Chair. Earth Lobby 1992–97, Stand up for What's Right and Just 2000–; Visiting Prof. Dartmouth Coll. 1985, Carleton Coll. 1986, Univ. of Wisconsin-Madison 1987; mem. Linnaean Soc., American Ornithologists' Union; Democrat 1996– (fmrly Republican); Hon. DSc (Williams Coll., Butler Univ., Alma Coll., Fairleigh Dickinson) 1976, (State Univ. of NY) 1981, (Univ. of Delaware) 2006, Hon. Dr Humanics (Springfield Coll.), Hon. DEng (Stevens Inst. of Tech.), Hon. LLD (Gettysburg Coll.), (Univ. of Wis.) 1984, (Monmouth Coll.) 1982, (Salisbury State Univ.) 1988, Hon. LHD (Ohio State Univ., Northland Coll.); Hon. DHumLitt (Meadville/Lombard Theological School) 1992, (Colby Sawyer Coll.) 2000;Distinguished Policy Fellow, Univ. of Delaware 2001, Paul Harris Fellow, Rotary Int. 2002; Vrooman Award 1964, Nat. Conf. of Christians and Jews 1966 Citizenship and Brotherhood Award, Josiah Marvel Cup for Humanitarian and Civic Work, Commercial Devt Asscn Honor Award 1971, Gold Medal Award World Wildlife Fund 1971, Golden Plate Award American Acad. of Achievement 1971, Conservationist of the Year, Nat. Wildlife Fed. 1971, Parsons Award, American Chemical Soc. 1974, Nat. Audubon Soc. Medal 1977, Swedish American of the Year 1982, Robert Marshal Award of The Wilderness Soc. 1984, Environmental Law Inst. Award 1990, Lifetime Achievement Award, Global Tomorrow Coalition 1994, Lifetime Achievement Award, League of Conservation Voters 1996, Liberty Bell Award, Del. Bar Asscn 1998, New Century Award, Resource Renewal Inst. 1999, Russell W. Peterson Wildlife Refuge Naming 2000, Bronze Statue, Wilmington, Delaware Riverfront 2002, Delaware State Univ. Presidential Medal of Honor 2003, Wisconsin Conservation Hall of Fame 2007, Top Man Award, 2008; Order of the Golden Ark (Netherlands) 1985. *Publications:* Rebel with a Conscience (memoirs) 1999, We Can Save the Earth (CD-Rom) 2000. Patriots, Stand Up! 2004; various articles on autoxidation, new product developments, crime reduction, environmental quality, conservation and population. *Leisure interests:* nature study, reading. *Address:* 11 E Mozart Drive, Wilmington, DE 19807, USA. *Telephone:* (302) 995-0736. *Fax:* (302) 995-9137.

PETERSON, Thage G.; Swedish politician; *Senior Adviser, Expandum AB;* b. 1933, Berg, Kronoberg; ed Inst. of Social Studies, Lund; Municipal Treas. Community Centre Asscn 1957–59, head 1967–71; Sec. and Vice-Chair. Social Democratic Youth Union 1964–67; elected to Parl. 1970; Under-Sec. of State to Cabinet 1971–75; Chair. Stockholm County br. of Socialdemokratiska Arbetarepartiet (Social Democratic Labour Party—SDLP) 1974–89; mem. SDLP Exec. Cttee 1975–90; Minister without Portfolio 1975–76; SDLP spokesman for Industrial Policy 1976–82; mem. SDLP Parl. Group Exec. and Head of Research Div.; Minister of Industry 1982–88, of Justice 1988, of Defence 1994–97, Minister in the Prime Minister's Office 1997; Speaker of Parl. 1988–91; Chair. Standing Cttee on the Constitution 1991–94; Sr Adviser Expandum AB. *Address:* Expandum AB, Box 840, 982 28 Gällivare, Sweden (office). *Telephone:* (970) 641-60 (office). *Fax:* (970) 641-05 (office). *E-mail:* info@expandum.se (office). *Website:* www.expandum.se (office).

PETERSSON, Lars-Eric Gustav, BSc (Econ); Swedish business executive; b. 21 June 1950, Mönsterås; m.; two s.; Exec. Vice-Pres. Sparbanken/Svenska Sparbanksförmingen 1984–90; Pres., later Pres. and Chair. Pronator 1990–93; with Skandia Insurance Co. Ltd as mem. Man. Group, Head Business Control/Business Devt, Exec. Vice-Pres., mem. Exec. Man., Head Int. Direct Insurance and Reinsurance (IDR), Acting Head Skandia Investment Man., Deputy Chief Exec. 1993–97, Pres. and CEO Skandia Insurance Co. Ltd 1997–2003. *Address:* c/o Skandia Insurance Co. Ltd, Sveavägen 44, Stockholm 103 50, Sweden (office).

PETHICA, John B., BA, PhD, FRS; British physicist and academic; *Director, Centre for Research on Adaptive Nanostructures and Nanodevices (CRANN), Trinity College, Dublin;* ed St Ambrose Coll., Altrincham, Cambridge Univ.; Staff Scientist, Brown Boveri Corp. Research Centre, Baden, Switzerland 1980–82; Oppenheimer Fellow, Cambridge Univ. 1982–84; Guest Scientist, ABB Research Centre, Baden, Switzerland 1983–87; Royal Soc. Univ. Research Fellow, Cavendish Lab., Cambridge 1984–87; Guest Scientist, Oak Ridge Nat. Lab., TN, USA 1985–89; Univ. Lecturer in Physics of Materials and Fellow of St Cross Coll., Oxford 1987–96, Prof. of Materials Science 1996–2003; Visiting Prof., Univ. of Konstanz, Germany 1990; Visiting Prof., Univ. of Nijmegen, Netherlands 1992; Sabbatical Chair., Sony Corpn, Yokohama, Japan 1993–94; Visiting Fellow, Australian Nuclear Science and Tech. Org. (ANSTO), Menai, Australia 1994; Prin. Investigator, Trinity Coll., Dublin Nanoscience Research Lab. and Dir CRANN (Centre for Research on Adaptive Nanostructures and Nanodevices) 2003–; Founder and Dir, Nano Instruments Inc., Knoxville, TN, USA 1984–88; consultant for several cos.; Inst. of Materials Rosenhain Medal and Prize 1997, Royal Soc. Hughes Medal 2001, Sociéte Française de Physique Holweck Medal 2002. *Address:* Department of Physics, Trinity College, Dublin 2, Ireland (office). *Telephone:* (1) 607–3200 (office). *E-mail:* john.pethica@tcd.ie (office). *Website:* www.tcd.ie/Physics/Crann (office).

PETHRICK, Richard Arthur, PhD, CChem, FRSC, FRSE, FRSA; British scientist and academic; *Burmah Professor of Chemistry, University of Strathclyde;* b. 26 Oct. 1942, Yate; s. of A. T. A. Pethrick and L. M. Pethrick; m. J. Hume 1975; one s.; ed Univs of London and Salford; Lecturer, Dept of Pure and Applied Chem., Univ. of Strathclyde 1970, Sr Lecturer 1978, Reader 1981, Prof. of Chem. 1983–, Head of Dept 1992–95, 1999–2005, Burmah Prof. of Chem. 2005–; mem. Editorial Bd British Polymer Journal 1979–93, Int. Journal of Polymeric Materials 1990–, Polymer News 1991–, Trends in Polymer Science 1992–, Polymer Int. 1993–; Ed. Polymer Yearbook 1983–; Visiting Prof., Univ. of Punjab 1979; British Council Visiting Lecturer, Australia 1985, 1989; Royal Soc. Visiting Lecturer, UK-China Del., Beijing 1992; mem. Int. Swedish Tech. Review Cttee for Polymer Science 1988, Int. Danish Tech. Review Cttee for Polymer Science 2003, Polymers and Composites Cttee Science and Eng Research Council 1993–, Large Area Displays Cttee Eng and Physical Sciences Research Council 1994–, IRC Review Cttee 1995–; Chair. Science Sector Scottish Vocational Awards Council 1995–2001;

mem. Royal Soc. of Chem. (RSC) Accreditation Cttee 1996–2002, RSC Educ. Cttee 2005–, NSF Polymers Cttee 2009; elected mem. Hon. Craft of Weavers of Glasgow 1991; Elder, Merrylea Church, Church of Scotland 1995; Fellow, Inst. of Materials, Minerals and Mining. *Publications:* Molecular Motion in High Polymers 1979, Modern Methods of Polymer Characterization 1999, Polymer Characterization – Physical Techniques 2000, Techniques for Polymer Organization and Morphological Characterization 2003, Polymer Structure Characterization 2007; more than 460 scientific papers and numerous book chapters and review articles. *Leisure interests:* walking, painting, photography. *Address:* Department of Pure and Applied Chemistry, University of Strathclyde, Thomas Building, 295 Cathedral Street, Glasgow, G1 1XL, Scotland (office). *Telephone:* (141) 548-4760 (office); (141) 548-2795 (office). *Fax:* (141) 548-4822 (office). *E-mail:* r.a.pethrick@strath.ac.uk (office).

PETIT, Christine, MD, PhD; French geneticist, biochemist and academic; *Director, Unité de Génétique des Déficits Sensoriels, Institut Pasteur;* ed Université Paris V (Medicine), Université Paris XI-Orsay (Sciences); researcher, Immunochemistry Lab., Institut Pasteur 1970s, Dir Sensory Deficit Genetics Unit 1985–; postdoctoral researcher, Basel, Switzerland; researcher, CNRS Molecular Genetics Centre, Gif-sur-Yvette; Prof. of Genetics and Cellular Physiology, Collège de France, Paris; mem. Acad. des sciences 2002, European Molecular Biology Org. 1996, Accad. Europae 1998; Chevalier, Légion d'honneur 2002; Prix de thèse de médecine 1974, Prix Janine Courrier de l'Académie des sciences 1992, Charles-Léopold Meyer Award 1999, Ernst Jung für Wissenschaft und Forschung: Medizin Award 2001, Leçon Inaugurale, Collège de France 2002, L'Oréal-UNESCO For Women in Science Award 2004, Rechercher Medecine, ISS 2004, Freedom to Discover in Neuroscience Prize (Bristol-Myers Squibb Inst.) 2005, Prix Louis-Jeantet de Médecine 2006. *Publications:* numerous articles in medical journals on genetic basis of sensory disorders and pathophysiology. *Address:* Unité de Génétique des Déficits Sensoriels, INSERM U587, Institut Pasteur, 25 rue du Dr Roux, 75724 Paris Cedex 15, France (office). *Telephone:* 1-45-68-80-90 (office). *Fax:* 1-45-67-69-78 (office). *E-mail:* cpetit@pasteur.fr (office). *Website:* (office).

PETIT, Roland; French dancer and choreographer; b. 13 Jan. 1924, Villemomble; s. of Edmond and Victoria (née Repetto) Petit; m. Zizi Jeanmaire (q.v.) 1954; one s.; ed Paris Opera Ballet School; Premier Danseur Paris Opera 1940–44; f. Les Vendredis de la Danse 1944, Les Ballets de Champs-Elysées 1945, Les Ballets de Paris 1948; Dir Paris Opera Ballet 1970; f. Les Ballets de Marseilles 1972, Marseille Nat. Dance School 1992; Officier, Légion d'honneur; Officier des Arts et des Lettres, Ordre nat. du Mérite; French Nat. Prize for Dance 1979, Benois Prize, Moscow 1993. *Works include:* Le rossignol et la rose, Le jeune homme et la mort, Les demoiselles de la nuit, Deuil en vingt-quatre heures, Le loup, Cyrano de Bergerac, Carmen, Les forains, La belle au bois dormant, Hans Christian Andersen, Folies Bergères, L'éloge de la folie, Paradise Lost, Pelléas et Mélisande, Les intermittences du coeur 1975, La symphonie fantastique 1975, Die Fledermaus 1980, Soirée Debussy, Le mariage du ciel et de l'enfer 1985, Fantôme de l'opéra, Charlot danse avec vous, Pink Floyd Ballet, Marcel et la belle excentrique 1992, La chauve-souris 1993, Camera obscura 1994, Passcaille 1994, Clavigo 1999. *Films as choreographer include:* Alice in Wonderland 1949, Hans Christian Andersen 1952, The Glass Slipper 1955, Daddy Long Legs 1955, Anything Goes 1956, Folies-Bergère 1956, Charmants garçons 1957, 1-2-3-4 ou Les Collants noirs 1960, Roland Petit Ballet Company in Paris 1965, Carmen (TV) 1980, Les Intermittences du coeur (TV) 1981, White Nights 1985, Le Chat botté (TV) 1986, Le Diable amoureux (TV) 1991, Notre-Dame de Paris (TV) 1996, Roland Petit à Marseille (TV) 1997, Clavigo (TV) 1999, Il Pipistrello (TV) 2003. *Address:* 20 boulevard Gabes, 13008 Marseille, France.

PETKOFF MALEC, Teodoro, BEcons; Venezuelan politician, journalist and economist; *President, TalCual newspaper;* b. 3 Jan. 1932, Maracaibo, Zulia; ed Central Univ. of Venezuela; father was Bulgarian emigrant and mother a Pole; Prof., Central Univ. of Venezuela for 14 years; joined CP of Venezuela (PCV) and formed part of student resistance against dictatorship of Marcos Pérez Jiménez 1950s; served as guerrilla commdr under Douglas Bravo, operating under codenames 'Roberto' and 'Reodulo Perdomo' against govt of Rómulo Betancourt 1960s; escaped from San Carlos prison via tunnel 1967; accepted govt's peace offer 1969; left PCV along with other dissidents; f. Movimiento al Socialismo (MAS) 1971; mem. Congress (MAS) 1974–94; cand. for presidency 1983, 1988; Minister of Central Office of Coordination and Planning (Cordiplan) 1996–99; quit MAS after party's support of candidacy of Hugo Chávez 1998; Dir El Mundo newspaper 1999–2001; Founder and Dir TalCual (evening paper) 2001–; intended to run as ind. cand. in presidential elections Dec. 2006 but dropped out of race to support Manuel Rosales Aug. 2006. *Publications:* Checoslovaquia: El Socialismo como problema 1969, ¿Socialismo para Venezuela? 1970, Razón y pasión del socialismo: el tema socialista en Venezuela 1973, Proceso a la izquierda: O de la falsa conducta revolucionaria 1976, Del optimismo de la voluntad: Escritos políticos 1987, Por qué hago lo que hago 1997, Venezuela en la encrucijada (co-author) 1998, Una segunda opinión: La Venezuela de Chávez: un libro hablado con Ibsen Martínez y Elías Pino Iturrieta 2000, Hugo Chávez, tal cual 2000, Las Dos Izquierdas (The Two Lefts) 2005. *Address:* TalCual, Edif. Menegrande, 5°, Of. 51, Avda Francisco de Miranda, Caracas, Venezuela (office). *Telephone:* (212) 286-7446 (office). *Fax:* (212) 232-7446 (office). *E-mail:* tpetkoff@talcualdigital.com (office). *Website:* www.talcualdigital.com (office).

PETKOV, Petko Danev; Bulgarian politician; b. 2 March 1942, Dobrotich; ed Higher Naval School, Varna; joined Dimitrov Young Communist League 1956, Bulgarian Communist Party (BCP) 1973; worked for 1st Coast Artillery Regt, Varna, radio mechanic for Navigation Maritime Bulgare Shipping Co., designer at Resprom Plant, Varna, Deputy Man., then Man. of Radio Navigation Equipment Works, Varna, Man. Dir of Cherno More Research and Industry Combined Works; First Sec., BCP Municipal Cttee, Varna Sept. 1987–; Alt. mem., BCP Cen. Cttee; Alt. mem., Political Bureau 1989–. *Address:* Bulgarian Communist Party, Sofia, Bulgaria.

PETKOVSKI, Tito; Macedonian politician; b. 23 Jan. 1945, Psacha, Kriva Palanka; m. Tanja Petkovska; two d.; ed Kriva Palanka High School, Skopje Univ.; worked in Municipal court Kriva Palanka, Repub. Bureau on Urban Planning and Communal Issues; political career started as deputy in Karposh Communal Ass., deputy City Ass. Skopje; later Vice-Pres. Exec. Council City Ass. Skopje; Sec. Cen. Cttee League of Communists of Macedonia—Party for Democratic Prosperity; mem. Cttee on Constitutional Problems, Ass. Repub. of Macedonia; Vice-Pres. first multi-party Ass. of Macedonia 1994–96; co-ordinator Parl. Group Social-Democratic Union of Macedonia; mem. Council of Inter-Parl. Union; Pres. Ass. (Sobranje) Repub. of Macedonia 1996–98, Pres. Standing Inquiry Cttee for Protection of Citizens' Freedoms and Rights 1998–; cand. in presidential elections 1999. *Publications include:* legal articles on housing policy, town planning and land devt. *Address:* 11 Oktombri blvd, 91000 Skopje, Macedonia. *Telephone:* (91) 112255. *Fax:* (91) 237947 (office).

PETO, Sir Richard, Kt, MSc, MA, FRS; British epidemiologist; *Professor of Medical Statistics and Epidemiology, University of Oxford;* b. 14 May 1943; s. of Leonard Huntley Peto and Carrie Clarinda Peto; m. 1st Sallie Messum 1970 (divorced); two s.; partner Gale Mead (deceased); two s.; ed Trinity Coll., Cambridge, Imperial Coll., London; Research Officer, MRC 1967–69; with Univ. of Oxford 1969–, Lecturer 1972–75, Reader in Cancer Studies 1975–92, Prof. of Medical Statistics and Epidemiology 1992–; Charles S. Mott Prize 2002, King Faisal Int. Prize (co-winner) 2005. *Publications include:* Natural History of Chronic Bronchitis and Emphysema 1976, Quantification of Occupational Cancer 1981, The Causes of Cancer 1983, Diet, Lifestyle and Mortality in China 1990, Mortality from Smoking in Developed Countries 1950–2000 1994, Emerging Tobacco Hazards in China 1998, Tobacco: The Growing Epidemic 2000, Geographic Study of Mortality, Biochemistry, Diet and Lifestyle in Rural China 2006; more than 500 papers. *Leisure interests:* science, children. *Address:* Clinical Trial Service Unit and Epidemiological Studies Unit (CTSU), Nuffield Department of Clinical Medicine, Richard Doll Building, Old Campus Road, Oxford, OX3 7LF (office); 62 Great Clarendon Street, Oxford, OX2 6AX, England (home). *Telephone:* (1865) 743801 (office). *Fax:* (1865) 743985 (office). *E-mail:* secretary@ctsu.ox.ac.uk (office). *Website:* www.ctsu.ox.ac.uk (office).

PETRAEUS, Gen. David Howell, BS, MPA, PhD; American military officer; *Commander, US Central Command;* b. 7 Nov. 1952, Cornwall-on-Hudson, NY; m. Holly Knowlton 1974; two c.; ed West Point Mil. Acad., Princeton Univ.; commissioned second lt 1974, assigned to 509th Airborne Infantry Bn, Vicenza, Italy, served in various leadership posts in airborne, mechanized and air assault infantry units in Europe and USA including Operations Officer, 3rd Infantry Div. (Mechanized) 1st Bn 1978–79, command of 101st Airborne Div. (Air Assault) 3rd Bn 1991–93, command of 82nd Airborne Div. 1st Brigade 1995–97; staff posts have included Aide to Chief of Staff of the Army, Mil. Asst to Supreme Allied Commdr —Europe, Chief Mil. Operations Officer, UN Mission, Haiti 1995, Exec. Asst to Dir of Jt Staff and subsequently Chair. Jt Chiefs of Staff, Pentagon 1997–99; promoted to Brig.-Gen. 1999; Asst Div. Commdr for Operations, 82nd Airborne Div., Fort Bragg, NC 1999–2000; Chief of Staff, XVIII Airborne Corps 2000–01; promoted to Maj.-Gen. 2001; Asst Chief of Staff for Operations, NATO Stabilization Force and Deputy Commdr, US Jt Interagency Counter-Terrorism Task Force, Bosnia 2001–02; commanded 101st Airborne Div. during Operation Iraqi Freedom, Iraq 2003; promoted to Lt-Gen. 2004; Commdr, Multi-Nat. Security Transition Command and NATO Training Mission, Iraq 2004–05; Commanding Gen. US Army Combined Arms Center and Fort Leavenworth 2005–07; promoted to Gen. 2007; Commdr Multi-Nat. Force—Iraq, overseeing all coalition forces 2007–08; Commdr US Cen. Command 2008–; Gen. George C. Marshall Award 1983, Combat Action Badge, Army Achievement Medal, Defense Distinguished Service Medal, two Distinguished Service Medals, two Defense Superior Service Medals, four Legion of Merit awards, Bronze Star Medal for Valor, State Dept Superior Honor Award, NATO Meritorious Service Medal, Gold Award of the Iraqi Order of the Date Palm. *Publication:* US Army Counterinsurgency Field Manual (co-author). *Address:* US Central Command, 7115 South Boundary Boulevard, MacDill AFB, Tampa, FL 33621-5101, USA (office). *Telephone:* (813) 827-5895 (office). *Fax:* (813) 827-2211 (office). *E-mail:* pao@centcom.mil (office). *Website:* www.centcom.mil (office).

PETRAKOV, Nikolai Yakovlevich, D.ECON.SC.; Russian economist; *Director, Institute for Market Problems;* b. 1 March 1937; m. Tat'yana Aleksandrovna; one s. one d.; ed Moscow Univ.; mem. CPSU 1964–90; mem. staff Inst. of Tech.-Econ. Research 1959–61, Econ. Inst. 1961–65, then Head of Lab.; Deputy Dir, Cen. Mathematics-Econ. Inst., USSR Acad. of Sciences 1965–91; corresp. mem. USSR (now Russian) Acad. of Sciences 1984–90, mem. 1990–; USSR People's Deputy 1989–91; Dir Inst. for Market Problems 1991–; Adviser to Pres. Yeltsin 1994; mem. Political Consultative Council 1991; mem. State Duma (Parl.) 1993–95; Chair. Bd Savings Investment Bank 1996–. *Publications:* papers and articles on the problems of pricing policies and on socialist econs. *Address:* Institute for Market Problems, Krasikova Str. 32, 117418 Moscow (office); Acad. Zelinski Str. 38, korp. 8, Apt 40, 117334 Moscow, Russia (home). *Telephone:* (495) 129-10-00 (office); (495) 135-14-46 (home).

PETRÁŇOVÁ, Ludmila; Czech business executive; *CEO, Lumen Energy a.s.;* ed Faculty of Nuclear and Physical Eng, Czech Tech. Univ., Prague; Chair. and CEO ČEPS a.s. (state-owned transmission grid) 2002–06; mem. Bd Electricity Market Operator (OTE) 2006–09; CEO Lumen Energy a.s. 2009–; ranked by Fortune magazine amongst 50 Most Powerful Women in Business outside the US (50th) 2004. *Address:* Lumen Energy a.s., Tylovická 372/16, 155 21 Prague 5, Czech Republic (office). *Telephone:* (2) 272655855 (office). *Fax:* (office). *E-mail:* ludmila.petranova@lumen-energy.com (office). *Website:* www.lumen-energy.cz (office).

PETRE, Zoe, PhD; Romanian historian, academic and politician; *Vice-President, Actiunea Populara (Popular Action);* b. 23 Aug. 1940, Bucharest; m. (husband deceased); two s.; ed Univ. of Bucharest; Prof., Head of Dept of Ancient History and Archaeology and fmr Dean, History Faculty, Univ. of Bucharest 1990–96; worked on presidential campaign of Emil Constantinescu 1996, after election served as Sr Adviser to the Pres. and co-ordinator Dept of Public Policy –2000; Founding mem. and Vice-Pres. Actiunea Populara (Popular Action) 2003–; Assoc. Prof., École des Hautes Études en Sciences Sociales, Centre de Recherches Comparées sur les Sociétés anciennes, Paris 1982, 1991, 1993; mem. Romanian socs of Classical Studies, Historical Sciences and Anthropology, Asscn pour l'encouragement des études grecques, France, East-West Inst., New York; Order of the Dannebrog, Commdr Légion d'honneur; Timotei Ciparius Award of the Romanian Acad., Nicolae Jorga Award, Romanian Ministry of Culture and several other honours and awards. *Publications:* Commentaire aux 'Sept contre Thèbes' d'Eschyle (with Liana Lupas) 1981, Civilizaţia greacă şi originile democratiei 1993–, Virsta de Bronz 2000, Cetatea greacă, între real şi imaginar 2000; and articles in scientific journals specializing in ancient history, culture, philology. *Leisure interests:* literature, music. *Address:* Actiunea Populara (Popular Action), 050093 Bucharest 5, Splaiul Independenţei 17/101 (office); Universitatea Bucureşti, Bd. Regina Elisabeta 4-12, sala 301, 70609 Bucharest Romania. *Telephone:* (21) 3160293 (office). *Fax:* (21) 3160399 (office). *E-mail:* office@actiunea.ro (office). *Website:* www.actiunea.ro (home).

PETRENKO, Aleksey Vasilyevich; Ukranian actor; b. 26 March 1938, Tchernigov; ed Kharkov Theatre Inst.; acted with various prov. cos in the USSR, including Lensovet Theatre 1967–81, Moscow Art Theatre 1978–83, Moscow Taganka Theatre, Russia 1985–; actor Cen. M. Gorki film studio 1983–; RSFSR People's Artist 1988, United Russia and Belarus Prize for Devt of Russia 1998, Russian Govt Prize 2001. *Films include:* King Lear 1971, Peter the First (title role) 1975, Marriage 1978, Agony (role of Grigoriy Rasputin) 1981, A Cruel Romance 1984, 20 Days Out of War 1987, The Servant 1989, Balthazar's Feasts or The Night with Stalin 1990, The Small Bees 1995, The Barber of Siberia 1998, Fortune 1999, Listen! Isn't it Raining? 2000, Collectioner 2002, Belle occasion 2003, Idiot 2003, Casus belli 2003, The Chess Player 2004, Dr Zhivago 2005, Comrade Chief 2 2005, Not Only With Bread 2005, Wedding. Case. Death 2005, 12 Angry Men 2006, and many others. *Address:* Nikitsky Blvd 9, Apt 39, 121019 Moscow, Russia. *Telephone:* 291-48-51.

PETRESKI, Dušan; Macedonian association executive; b. 19 Jan. 1948, Mavrovo; m. Liliana Mirchevska 1973; two s.; ed Skopje Univ.; Sec. and mem. Exec. Bd Econ. Chamber of Macedonia 1984–87, Vice-Pres. 1987–90, Pres. 1990–2005; Vice-Pres. Asscn of Balkan Chambers 1997–98, Pres. 1998; many state and other decorations and awards. *Publications:* professional articles in many magazines and journals. *Leisure interests:* social activities, sport, walking. *Address:* c/o Economic Chamber of Macedonia, Dimitrie Čupovski 13, 1000 Skopje (office); Meksička 7, 1000 Skopje, Macedonia (home).

PETRI, Michala; Danish musician (recorder player); b. 7 July 1958, Copenhagen; d. of Kanny Sambleben and Hanne Petri; m. Lars Hannibal 1992; two d.; ed Staatliche Hochschule für Musik und Theater, Hanover; debut aged five, Danish Radio 1964; soloist with Orchestra Tivoli, Copenhagen 1969; over 4,000 concerts in Europe, USA, Japan, China, Korea, Mexico, Canada and Australia; numerous appearances at festivals, performances on TV and radio; performs frequently world-wide as duo with lutenist and guitarist, Lars Hannibal; has inspired and initiated various contemporary compositions by Malcolm Arnold, Vagn Holmboe, Per Norgaard, Thomas Koppel, Daniel Boertz, Gary Kulesha, Stephen Stucky, Joan Albert Amargos, Chen Yi and others; mem. of presidium, UNICEF Denmark; bd mem., Wilhelm Hansen Foundation; Vice-Pres., Cancer Asscn, Denmark; Jacob Gade Prize 1969, 1975, Critics' Prize of Honour 1976, Nording Radio Prize 1977, Niels Prize 1980, Tagea Brandts Prize 1980, Maarum Prize 1981, Schroder Prize 1982, Deutscher Schallplattenpreis 1997, 2002, Sonning Music Prize 2000, H. C. Lumbye Prize 2000, European Soloist Pirze 'Pro Europa' 2005; Knight of Dannebrog 1995. *Recordings:* more than 50 albums, including 12 with the Acad. of St Martin-in-the-Fields, Bach Sonatas and Handel Sonatas with Keith Jarrett, Vivaldi Concertos with Heinz Holliger, Henryk Szeryng, contemporary concerts with English Chamber Orchestra and Danish Nat. Symphony Orchestra, four albums with Lars Hannibal, albums with Chen Yue, Kremerata Baltica. *Publications:* ed. of several works for Wilhelm Hansen and Moeck; Sheet Music Now. *Address:* Nordskraenten 3, 2980 Kokkedal, Denmark (office). *Telephone:* 45-86-25-77 (office). *Fax:* 45-86-56-77 (office). *E-mail:* mail@michalapetri.com (office). *Website:* www.michalapetri .com.

PETRIC, Ernest, PhD; Slovenian diplomatist and academic; *Ambassador to Austria;* b. 18 Nov. 1936, Trzic; s. of Joze Petric and Angela Godnov; m. Silvestra Rogelj; three d.; ed Univ. of Ljubljana, Univ. of Vienna; Research Asst, Inst. for Ethnic Studies, Ljubljana 1961–65; Asst Prof. of Int. Law, Univ. of Ljubljana 1965–67, Prof. 1972–83; mem. Exec. Council of Slovenia, Minister of Science and Tech. 1967–72; Prof., Univ. of Addis Ababa, Ethiopia 1983–86; Dean Faculty of Social Science, Univ. of Ljubljana 1986–89; Amb. of Yugoslavia to India (also accred to Nepal) 1989–91; Amb. to USA (also accred to Mexico) 1991–97; State Sec. Ministry of Foreign Affairs 1997–2000; Perm. Rep. to UN, New York (also Amb. to Brazil) 2000–02; Amb. to Austria, also Perm. Rep. to UN, Vienna and to OSCE 2002–; Kidric Award 1979, Yugoslav Silver Medal for Achievement 1986, Colorado Meritorious Service Medal, USA 1997. *Publications:* International Legal Protection of Minorities 1977, The International Legal Position of the Slovenian Minority in Italy 1981, The Right to Self-Determination 1984, From Emperor to Leader 1987. *Leisure interests:* literature, skiing, tennis. *Address:* Embassy of Slovenia, Nibelungengasse 13/3, 1010 Vienna, Austria (office). *Telephone:* (1) 586-13-09 (office). *Fax:* (1) 586-12-65 (office). *E-mail:* vdu@gov.si (office).

PETRIDES, Paul; Greek historian and academic; *Professor, Thessaloniki University;* b. 19 Aug. 1947, Thessaloniki; m. Lina Voreopoulou; ed Thessaloniki and Vienna Univs; Prof., Thessaloniki Univ. 1982–; Visiting Prof., Panteion Univ.; Chair. Hellenic Lyric Stage 1989–93; Vice-Chair. G. Papandreou Cultural Foundation, Kapodistrias Foundation; Chair. Cultural Cttee of Law Faculty, Thessaloniki Univ.; Chair. Macedonian News Agency; recipient of several awards and prizes. *Publications include:* The Diplomatic Action of John Kapodistrias for Greeks 1974, Die Jonische Frage auf den Wiener Kongress, Griechenland und Grossmaechte, Political and Social History of Greece, Contemporary Political History of Greece. *Leisure interests:* painting, music. *Address:* 5 P. Mela Street, 552 36 Panorama, Thessaloniki, Greece. *Telephone:* (31) 341-682.

PETRIE, Sir Peter (Charles), 5th Bt, cr. 1918, of Carrowcarden, CMG; British diplomatist; b. 7 March 1932, London; s. of Sir Charles Petrie, Bt, CBE and Lady Petrie; m. Countess Lydwine von Oberndorff 1958; two s. one d.; ed Westminster School and Christ Church, Oxford; Second Sec. UK del. to NATO 1958–62; First Sec. New Delhi 1961–63; Chargé d'affaires, Kathmandu 1963–64; Cabinet Office, London 1965–67; FCO 1967–69; First Sec. later Counsellor, UK Perm. Mission at UN, New York 1969–73; Counsellor, Bonn 1973–76; FCO 1976–79; Minister, Paris 1979–85; Amb. to Belgium 1985–89; Adviser to Gov. of Bank of England on European and Parl. Affairs 1989–2003; mem. Franco-British Council 1995, Chair. British Section 1997–2002; Acad. de Compatibilité (Paris) 1997–; mem. Council, City Univ. 1997–2002. *Leisure interests:* gardening, golf, shooting. *Address:* 16a Cambridge Street, London, SW1V 4QH, England (home); 40 rue Lauriston, 75116 Paris, France (home); 4 Hameau du Jardin, 50310 Lestre, France (home). *Telephone:* (20) 7834-0801 (home). *E-mail:* lydwinep@aol.com (home).

PETRIN, Tea, MEconSc, PhD; Slovenian economist, academic, politician and diplomatist; *Ambassador to the Netherlands;* b. 9 July 1944, Celje; ed Univ. of Ljubljana, Louisiana State Univ., USA; Visiting Prof., Univ. of Massachusetts at Amherst, USA 1988–89, the Haas School of Business, Univ. of Calif., Berkeley 1992; Head, Research Centre and Centre for Continuous Educ., Faculty of Econs, Univ. of Ljubljana 1989–92, f. Postgrad. Studies in Entrepreneurship Programme 1990; Adviser to Cttee for Small Business Devt, Govt of Slovenia 1987–90, to Agency for Restructuring and Privatization Fund 1990–91, to Govt on Real Sector Structuring 1992–93; Adviser on Devt of Entrepreneurship in Rural Areas, to Foreign Affairs Office (FAO) Regional Office for Europe 1990–93, mem. staff 1994–97; involved in assessment of financial entrepreneurs in Slovenia, World Bank (IBRD) 1993; mem. working group World Bank, UNDP/UNIDO 1988–92, FAO Investment Centre 1996–97, EU Enterprise Enlargement Unit 2000; Minister for Econ. Affairs 1999–2000, of the Economy 2001–04; Amb. to Netherlands 2004–; mem. Editorial Bd Review of Industrial Org. 1994–; mem. Int. Small Business Council 1992–, Econ. Council of Govt of Slovenia 1992, European Small Business Council 1994–96, European Asscn for Industrial Econs Research 1998–, Bd of Advisors of The Competitiveness Inst.; Fulbright Scholar, Inst. of Int. Studies, Univ. of Calif., Berkeley 1993–94, Univ. of Massachusetts, Lowell 1994. *Publications include:* over 200 books, monographs and articles in professional journals in fields of industrial policy, competition policy, restructuring of enterprises and entrepreneurship. *Address:* Embassy of the Republic of Slovenia, Anna Paulownastraat 11, 2518 BA, The Hague, Netherlands (office). *Telephone:* (70) 3108690 (office). *Fax:* (70) 3626608 (office). *E-mail:* vhg@mzz-dkp.gov.si (office). *Website:* www.gov.si/mzz/dkp/vhg/eng (office).

PETRINI, Carlo; Italian journalist, political activist and academic; *Founder, Slow Food Movement;* b. 22 June 1949, commune of Bra, Prov. of Cuneo; ed studied Sociology in Trento; began writing about food and wine in major Italian periodicals and newspapers 1977; first came to prominence for taking part in campaign against McDonald's fast food chain opening nr Spanish Steps, Rome 1980s; f. Slow Food Movt 1989, Bra, Piedmont 1989, Int. Slow Food Movt, Paris 1989; organised festival of traditional music (Canté j'euv); est. Free and Deserving Asscn of the Friends of Barolo (original group that gave rise to Arcigola, the Wine and Food League of the Arci org.) 1986; now edits numerous publs through publishing house Slow Food Editore 1990–; responsible for publication of Guide to the Wines of the World (published in Italian, English, German, French, Spanish) and magazine Slow; Co-founder and Co-ed., with Daniele Cernilli, Vini d'Italia (guide to wines of Italy); columnist, L'Unità daily newspaper, La Stampa newspaper 1999–; est. Int. Slow Food Prize; f. Univ. of Gastronomic Science, Pollenzo, Bra and Colorno, Parma 2004; Communicator of the Year Trophy, Int. Wine and Spirit Competition 2000, Sicco Mansholt Prize 2002, named by TIME magazine as one of its Heroes of the Environment 2004. *Publications:* Slow Food: The Case for Taste (Arts & Traditions of the Table: Perspectives on Culinary History) 2003, Slow Food Revolution: A New Culture for Dining and Living (in conversation with Gigi Padovani) 2006, Slow Food Nation: Why Our Food Should Be Good, Clean, and Fair 2007. *Address:* Slow Food International, Piazza XX Settembre 5, 12042 Bra (Cuneo), Italy (office). *Telephone:* (0172) 419611 (office). *Fax:* (0172) 421293 (office). *E-mail:* international@slowfood .com (office). *Website:* www.slowfood.com (office).

PETRITSCH, Wolfgang, PhD; Austrian diplomatist; *Permanent Representative, Organisation for Economic Co-operation and Development;* b. 26 Aug. 1947, Klagenfurt; ed Univs of Vienna and Southern California, USA; Adviser,

Press Sec. of Austrian Fed. Chancellor 1977–83; mem. Austrian Mission to OECD, Paris 1983–84; Head Austrian Press and Information Service, NY 1984–92; Acting Head Dept for Multilateral Econ. Co-operation, Ministry of Foreign Affairs 1992–94; Head Dept for Information on European Affairs, Fed. Chancellery 1994; Head Dept for Int. Relations, City of Vienna 1995–97; Amb. to Yugoslavia 1997–99; EU Special Envoy for Kosovo 1998–99, EU Chief Negotiator at Kosovo peace talks, France Feb.–March 1999; High Rep. of the Int. Community in Bosnia and Herzegovina 1999–2002; Perm. Rep. to UN, WTO, Geneva 2002–08, to OECD 2008–; Pres. Mine Ban Convention's First Review Conference (Nairobi Summit) 2004; Chair. Vienna Cluster Munitions Conf. 2007; mem. Bd European Cultural Foundation, Int. Advisory Bd Esterhazy Foundation (Amsterdam Chair.), Paul Lazarsfeld Soc. for Social Research (Eisenstadt Chair.), Centre for European Integration Strategies, Geneva-Vienna-Sarajevo (Vienna Chair.), Bd Sigmund Freud Soc., Vienna, Bd Bruno Kreisky Forum for Int. Dialogue, Vienna; Person of the Year, Bosnia and Herzegovina 2002, Friedrich Torberg Medal for Human Rights 2002, Strasbourg Bruno Kreisky Award for the Political Book 2004, European Award for Human Rights 2006. *Publications include:* Kosovo-Kosova. Mythen, Daten, Fakten, Bosnien und Herzegowina fünf Jahre nach Dayton – Hat der Friede eine Chance?. *Address:* Permanent Mission of Austria, 2 rue André Pascal, 75775 Paris Cedex 16, France (office). *Telephone:* 1-45-2-82-00 (office). *Fax:* 1-45-24-85-00 (office). *E-mail:* wolfgang.petritsch@bka.gv.at (office).

PETROV, Aleksander Aleksandrovich; Russian scientist; *Head of Division, Dorodnicyn Computing Centre, Russian Academy of Sciences;* b. 3 Feb. 1934, Orekchovo-Zuyevo, Moscow Region; s. of late Alexander Vasilyevich Petrov and Evgenia Nikolaevna Petrova; ed Moscow Inst. of Physics and Eng; Head of Div., Dorodnicyn Computation Centre, Russian Acad. of Sciences 1975–; Corresp. mem. Russian Acad. of Sciences 1991, mem. 1997–; main research in problems of evolution of econ. systems and methods of estimating potential possibilities of Econs, math. modelling of complex systems; USSR State Prize 1980, Nat. Peter The Great Prize and Medal 2000, Order of Friendship. *Publications include:* From Gosplan to Market Economy: Mathematics Analysis of the Evolution of the Russian Economic Structures 1999. *Leisure interests:* tennis, music. *Address:* Dorodnicyn Computing Centre, Russian Academy of Sciences, Vavilov str. 40, 119333, Moscow, Russia (office). *Telephone:* (495) 135-30-23 (office). *Fax:* (495) 135-61-59 (office). *E-mail:* petrov@ccas.ru (office).

PETROV, Andrei Borisovich; Russian ballet dancer and choreographer; *Artistic Director, Kremlin Ballet Theatre;* b. 27 Dec. 1945, Moscow; s. of Boris Kholfin and Olga Petrova; m. Olga Polyanskaya; ed Moscow Higher School of Choreography, Moscow Inst. of Theatre Arts; ballet dancer Bolshoi Theatre 1965–86, head of ballet troupe 1987–89, choreographer 1989–90; Founder and Artistic Dir Kremlin Ballet Theatre 1990–; juror and Chair. Organizing Cttee Moscow Int. Ballet Competition; juror Maya (St Petersburg), Benoit de la Dance (UNESCO); Chair. Theatre Artists' League Choreography Cttee; Order of the Great Services to the Native Land, Order of Saint Prince Daniyl of Moscow RSFSR People's Artist 1985. *Ballets include:* Don Quixote, Swan Lake, Fountain of Bakhchisarai, Raimonda, Romeo and Juliet; *Ballets directed include:* Red Snowball-Tree, Wooden Prince, Sketches, Knight of a Sorrowful Look, Ruslan and Ludmila, Swan Lake, Nutcracker, Zeus, Napoleon Bonaparte, Nevsky Prospect, Tom Sawyer, Fantastic Symphony, Coppelia. *Address:* Kremlin Ballet Theatre, Kremlin, Palace of Congresses, 03073 Moscow (office); Academician Zelensky str. 6, 41, Moscow, Russia (home). *Telephone:* (495) 917-23-36 (office); (495) 419-44-49 (home). *Fax:* (495) 928-52-32 (office). *Website:* www.kremlin-gkd.ru/index.htm (office).

PETROV, Nikolai Arnoldovich; Russian pianist and academic; *President, Academy of Russian Art;* b. 14 April 1943, Moscow; m. Larisa Petrova; one d.; ed Moscow Conservatory (pupil of Yakov Zak); debut in Moscow 1962; soloist of Moscow Philharmonic 1966–; toured many countries of Europe and America as soloist and with maj. conductors and orchestras; took part in music festivals; first performer of music by contemporary Russian composers, including Rodion Shchedrin, first performances in Russia of works by Bach, Beethoven, Mozart, Debussy, Ravel, Liszt; Prof. Moscow Conservatoire 1994–; Founder and Pres. Acad. of Russian Art 1995–; Vice-Pres. Int. Asscn The World of Culture 1993; State Prize of Russia 1993; People's Artist of Russia, Musician of the Year (Musikalnaya Zhizn journal) 1994. *Address:* c/o Sovinart, Murmansky proezd 18, apt 77, 129075 Moscow; Ostozhenka 22, apt 2, 119034 Moscow, Russia (home). *Telephone:* (495) 215-7571 (office); (495) 992-8333 (home). *Fax:* (495) 215-2274 (office). *E-mail:* soninart.mos@g23.relcom.ru (office); npetrov@mail.ru (home). *Website:* www.nbcf.ru.

PETROV, Rem Viktorovich, DrMedSc; Russian immunologist; b. 22 March 1930, Serafimovitch; s. of Victor Ivanovich Petrov and Kutniak Evdokia Emelianovna; m. 1st Tatiana Kuk 1960 (died 1970); m. 2nd Natalia Yemetz 1978; one s. one d.; ed Voronezh Medical Inst.; mem. CPSU 1956–91; research work at various grades in USSR (now Russian) Ministry of Health Inst. of Bio-Physics 1959–83, Head of Lab. 1983–; Pres. USSR (now Russian) Immunology Soc. 1983–; Dir of USSR (now Russian) Ministry of Health Inst. of Immunology 1983–88; mem. of Acad. of Medical Sciences 1978–; concurrently Head of Dept of Immunology of Second Moscow Inst. of Medicine 1974–; mem. Int. Scientific Advisory Bd of UNESCO 1996–; mem. USSR (now Russian) Acad. of Sciences 1984–, Vice-Pres. 1988–; mem. Acad. of Agric. 1991–; Ed. Sciences in Russia 1989; mem. World Acad. of Art and Sciences 1989–, New York Acad. of Sciences 1992–, Washington Acad. of Sciences 1993–, Norwegian Acad. of Sciences 1999–; Dr hc (Bar-Ilan Univ.) 1990, (Madrid Polytechnic Univ.) 1995; L. Mechnikov Gold Medal and Prize, Acad. of Sciences 1987; Hero of Labour 1990, Order of Lenin 1990, Achievements for the Fatherland, Third Degree 1999, State Prize in Science and Tech. 2001. *Publications:* Essays on the New Immunology 1976, Immunology and Immunogenetics 1981, Immunology 1982, Me or Not Me 1983, Suppressor B-lymphocytes 1988, Myelopeptides 1999, Scientific Publicistics 2000. *Leisure interests:* fishing, hunting, woodwork. *Address:* Russian Academy of Sciences, Leninsky pr. 14, 117901 Moscow (office); 38-8-86 Zelinskogo St, 117334 Moscow, Russia (home). *Telephone:* (495) 954-32-76 (office); (495) 135-10-63 (home). *Fax:* (495) 954-32-26 (office). *E-mail:* petrov@pran.ru (office).

PETROVICS, Emil; Hungarian composer; b. 9 Feb. 1930, Nagybecskerek (now Zrenjanin, Yugoslavia); s. of Jovan Petrovics and Erzsébet Weninger; one d.; studied at Conservatory, graduated from Music Acad. of Budapest; Musical Dir Petöfi Theatre 1960–64; Lecturer Coll. of Dramatic and Cinematographic Arts 1964–; Prof. of Composition Music Acad., Budapest; Dir Hungarian State Opera 1986–90, Gen. Music Dir 2002–05; mem. Hungarian Parl. 1967–85; mem. Széchenyi Acad. of Arts, Budapest 1991–, Serbian Acad. of Sciences and Arts, Belgrade 1993–, Hungarian PEN Club 2003–; Medal of Merit (Hungary); Erkel Prize 1960, 1963, Kossuth Prize 1966, 2006, holder of titles Merited Artist 1975, Eminent Artist 1982. *Compositions for musical stage:* C'est la guerre (single act) 1961; Crime and Punishment 1969; Book of Jonah (oratorio) 1965; Lysistrate (comic opera for concert performance) 1962 (all performed in Czechoslovakia, Finland, France, FRG, Hungary and Yugoslavia); Salome (ballet) 1984; Cantatas I-IX: There Let Me Die 1972, Fanny's Posthumous Papers 1978, We All Must Go 1980, Letters from Turkey 1981, 6th Cantata: We Take a Rest, Pygmalion 1995, Lament and Solace (based on Lorincz Szabo work), At the Danube (based on poem by Attila Jozsef), String Quartet I, II, III, Symphony I, II Piano Concerto I, Rhapsody I and II for Violin and Cello, Passamezzo and Saltarello for Solo Violin and Percussion 2000. *Instrumental music:* Concerto for Flute 1957, String Quartet 1959, Symphony for Strings 1964, Quintet for Winds 1966, Rhapsody No. 1 and No. 2 for Violin and Viola Solo 1982, 1983, Concertino for Trumpet and Orchestra 1990, 2nd String Quartet 1991, Rhapsody No. 2 for Violoncello Solo 1991, Vörösmarty – Overture for Orchestra 1993, Cantata No. 7: Pygmalion, for Mixed Chorus, Narrator and Orchestra 1994–95, Lament and Consolation (three poems for tenor voice and piano) 1996, Piangendo e Meditando, for String Orchestra 1997, Cantata No. 9: By the Danube 1998, Concerto for Piano and Orchestra 1999, Symphony No. 2 for Orchestra 2001; score for 60 feature films, 30 stage plays, 15 radio plays, 12 TV productions. *Publication:* Ravel 1959, Selfportrait: without a mask (memoirs), Vol. I 2007, Vol. II 2008. *Address:* Attila utca 39, 1013 Budapest, Hungary (home). *Telephone:* (1) 375-6032 (home). *Fax:* (1) 375-6032 (home). *E-mail:* petrovics.emil@chello.hu (home).

PETROVSKY, Artur Vladimirovich, PhD; Russian academic; *Professor of Psychology, RAE University;* b. 14 May 1924, Sevastopol; s. of Vladimir Vasilievich Petrovskay and Alexandra Abramovna Petrovskaya; m. Ivetta Sinelnikova; one s., one d.; ed Moscow Pedagogical Inst.; teacher, sr teacher, Vologda Pedagogical Inst. 1947–58; Asst Prof., Moscow State Pedagogical Inst., Prof. 1952–66; Chair. Psychology Dept 1966–92; Prof. RAE Univ. 1998–, Head of Theory and History of Psychology Lab.; Corresp. mem. USSR Acad. of Pedagogical Sciences 1968, mem. 1971; Academician-Sec. Dept of Psychology and Age Physiology 1968–76, 1997–, Vice-Pres. 1976–79, Pres. 1992–97; mem. Russian Acad. of Educ. 1991; Consultant Russian Acad. of Educ. Univ.; Honoured Scientist, Govt Prize of Russian Fed. 1998, Order of Honour 1999. *Publications:* History of Soviet Psychology 1967, General Psychology 1970, 1976–86, Problems of History and Theory of Psychology: selected works 1984. Essays on Psychology 1985, Psychology in USSR 1990, Psychology of Each of Us 1992, History of Psychology (co-author Yaroshevsky) 1994, Foundations of Theoretical Psychology 1996–98, Psychology in Russia: 20th Century 2001, Theoretical Psychology (co-author Yaroshevsky) 2001, Memories of a Psychologist 2001. *Leisure interest:* collecting books of fiction. *Address:* RAE University, Bolshaya Polyanka Str. 58, 119180 Moscow (office); Str. Chernyakhovskogo 4, Apt. 11, 125319 Moscow, Russia (home). *Telephone:* (495) 237-31-51 (office); (045) 151-98-63 (home). *Fax:* (495) 237-45-61 (office). *E-mail:* boris@urao.edu.

PETROVSKY, Vladimir Fyodorovich, DHist; Russian diplomatist; *Senior Research Fellow, United Nations Institute for Training and Research (UNITAR);* b. 29 April 1933, Volgograd; s. of Fyodor Petrovsky and Anna Khritinina; m. Myra Mukhina; one d.; ed Moscow Inst. of Int. Relations; with USSR (now Russian) Ministry of Foreign Affairs 1957–; staff mem. USSR Mission to UN 1957–61, mem. Office of the Foreign Minister, USSR Ministry of Foreign Affairs 1961–64; mem. UN Secr. 1964–71; with dept of planning of int. policy, USSR Ministry of Foreign Affairs 1971–78, Head of Dept 1978–79, Head Dept of Int. Orgs 1979–86, Deputy Minister 1986–91, First Deputy Minister Aug.–Dec. 1991; Exec. Sec. CSCE Conf. on Human Dimension 1991; UN Under-Sec.-Gen. for Political Affairs 1992; Dir-Gen. UN Office, Geneva 1993–2002; Sec.-Gen. Conf. on Disarmament 1994–2002; Sr Research Fellow, UN Inst. for Training and Research (UNITAR) 2002–; Chair. Asscn for Comprehensive Dialogue Among Civilizations 2003–; mem. Acad. of Natural Sciences of Russian Fed., Mil. Acad. of Russian Fed., Russian Acad. of Outer Space, Int. Acad. of Information; Order of Merit (Russia) 1976, Order of Labour Red Banner 1983, Polish Order of Merit 2001. *Publications:* The Foreign Service of Great Britain 1958, The Diplomacy of 10 Downing Street 1964, US Foreign Policy Thinking: Theories and Concepts 1976, The Doctrine of National Security in US Global Strategy 1980, Disarmament: Concept, Problems, Mechanisms 1983, Security in the Era of Nuclear and Outer Space Technology 1985, The Triad of Strategic Security in the Global Society 2005, The Triad of Strategic Security in the New Global Community 2006. *Leisure interests:* art, memoirs. *Address:* Maly Kozhinsky Perelok 4, Apt 12, 123001 Moscow, Russia (home); c/o Ministry of Foreign Affairs, Smolenskaya-Sennaya pl. 32/34, 119200 Moscow, Russia (office). *Telephone:* (495) 650-78-12 (home). *E-mail:* vpetrovs@yandex.ru (home).

PETRUCCIOLI, Claudio; Italian journalist, broadcasting executive, politician, writer and essayist; *President, Radiotelevisione Italiana SpA (RAI);* b. 22 March 1941, Terni, Umbria; obtained degree in political science and moved to Rome to become a professional journalist; mem. Partito Comunista Italiano (Italian Communist Party—PCI) 1960s, Municipal and Regional Sec., Terni and Regional Vice-Sec. in Umbria, Pres. Italian Communist Youth Fed. 1966–69, Nat. Dir PCI 1987; contributed to definition of first major reform of broadcasting system, implemented by Law 103 1975; Dir L'Unità 1980–83; elected to Lower House for Democratici di Sinistra (Democrats of the Left— DS) 1992–94; apptd by Parl. Cttee for Supervision of Broadcasting to post of Pres. Radiotelevisione Italiana SpA (RAI) 2005–. *Publications:* Rendi conto 2001, Quale Futuro per Il Servizio Pubblico Radiotelevisivo: Una [i.E. Un] Dibattito a Partire Dal Documento Per Una Discussione Su Televisione E Servizio Pubblico. Dentro E Fuori La Rai Di Claudio Petruccioli 2006. *Address:* Radiotelevisione Italiana SpA, Viale Mazzini 14, 00195 Rome, Italy (office). *Telephone:* (06) 38781 (office). *E-mail:* info@rai.it (office). *Website:* www.rai.it (office).

PETRUSHEVSKAYA, Liudmila Stefanovna; Russian author, playwright and poet; b. 26 May 1938, Moscow; d. of Stefan Antonovitsh Petrushevskij and Valentina Nikolaevna Jakovleva; m. 1st Evgenij Kharatian; one s.; m. 2nd Boris Pavlov; one s. one d.; ed Moscow Univ.; newspaper and radio journalist 1957–73; started writing short stories 1968, plays and folk tales 1971; stage productions and publ. of works were forbidden for many years; first underground performance 1975, first official performance, Tallinn 1979; mem. Bayerische Akad. der Schönen Kunste 1997; Int. A. Pushkin Prize (Germany) 1991, Triumph Award for Lifetime Achievement 2002, Russian State Prize for Arts 2004, Stanislavsky Award 2005; prizes for the best short story of the year from Ogoniok 1988, 1989 and Oktiabr 1993, 1996, Grand Prize for play The Time: Night, Annual All-Russian Theatre Festival of Solo Theatre, Perm 1995, Moscow-Penne Prize (Russia/Italy) 1996. *Plays include:* Two Windows 1971, Music Lessons 1973, Cinzano 1973, Love 1974, The Landing 1974, Andante 1975, The Execution, A Glass of Water, Smirnova's Birthday 1977–78, Three Girls in Blue 1980, Colombina's Flat 1981, Moscow Choir 1984, The Golden Goddess 1986, The Wedding Night 1990, The Men's Quarters 1992; co-author of screenplay Tale of Tales (prize for best animated film of all time, Los Angeles 1980). *Publications:* Immortal Love 1988, Songs of the 20th Century 1988, On the Way to the God Eros 1993, The Mystery of the House 1993; (children's books) Vasilli's Treatment 1991, Once Upon a Time There Was a Trrrr! 1994, Real Fairy Tales 1997, The Alphabet's Tale 1997, Complete Works (5 vols) 1996, The Girl's House 1998, Find Me, My Dream 2000. *Leisure interest:* watercolour painting. *Address:* 107113 Moscow, Staroslobodsky per. 2A, Apt 20, Russia. *Telephone:* (495) 269-74-48. *Fax:* (495) 269-74-48.

PETRY, Heinz, Dipl Ing; German industrial executive; b. 12 Jan. 1919, Rheinhausen; s. of Heinrich Petry and Elise Petry (née Maas); m. Liselotte Petry (née Gebauer) 1945; two s. one d.; ed Berlin Tech. Coll., Stuttgart Univ.; construction engineer in dredger mfg, Krupp Industrie und Stahlbau, Rheinhausen 1946, Deputy Head of Dept 1950, given proxy of firm 1961, Head of Dept 1962, Deputy mem. of Man. Bd 1965, mem. 1966, Spokesman 1973; mem. Man. Bd, Friedrich Krupp GmbH, Essen 1974–, Deputy Chair. 1975–76, Chair. 1976–80; mem. Supervisory Bd AG Weser, Bremen, Krupp-Koppers GmbH, Essen. *Leisure interests:* hunting, golf, films. *Address:* Kaiserstrasse 238, 47800 Krefeld, Germany.

PETTENGILL, Gordon Hemenway, PhD; American physicist and academic; *Professor Emeritus of Planetary Physics, Center for Space Research, Massachusetts Institute of Technology;* b. 10 Feb. 1926, Providence, RI; s. of Rodney G. Pettengill and Frances Pettengill (née Hemenway); m. Pamela Wolfenden 1967; one s. one d.; ed MIT and Univ. of California at Berkeley; staff mem., MIT Lincoln Lab. 1954–68, Assoc. Leader, Haystack Observatory 1965–68; Dir Arecibo Observatory, Puerto Rico (operated by Cornell Univ.) 1968–70; Prof. of Planetary Physics, Dept of Earth and Planetary Sciences, MIT 1970–2001, Prof. Emer. 2001–; Dir MIT Center for Space Research 1984–90; involved in the study of the solar system using radar and radio techniques; discovered 3/2 spin-orbit resonance of Mercury 1965; pioneered delay-doppler radar mapping of planets; prin. investigator of Pioneer Venus Radar Mapper 1978–81, Magellan Venus Radar Mapper 1990–93; mem. NAS, American Acad. of Arts and Sciences, AAAS, American Physical Soc., American Astronomical Soc., Int. Radio Science Union; Fellow, American Geophysical Union, Guggenheim Fellow 1980–81, Magellan Premium, American Philosophical Soc. 1994, Charles A. Whitten Medal, American Geophysical Union 1997. *Leisure interests:* ornithology, genealogy. *Address:* MIT Center for Space Research, Room 37-582d, Massachusetts Institute of Technology, 77 Massachusetts Avenue, Cambridge, MA 02139, USA (office). *Telephone:* (617) 253-4281 (office). *Fax:* (617) 253-0861 (office). *E-mail:* ghp@space.mit.edu (office). *Website:* space.mit.edu (office).

PETTIGREW, Pierre S., BA, MPhil; Canadian politician; b. 18 April 1951; ed Univ. du Québec à Trois-Rivières, Balliol Coll., Oxford, UK; Dir Political Cttee NATO Ass., Brussels 1976–78; Exec. Asst to Leader of Québec Liberal Party 1978–81; Foreign Policy Adviser to Prime Minister, Privy Council Office 1981–84; Vice-Pres. Samson Belair Deloitte and Touche Int. (Montreal) 1985–95; elected MP 1996, re-elected 1997; Minister for Int. Co-operation and Minister with special responsibility for La Francophonie 1996–97, Minister of Human Resources Devt 1997–99, of Int. Trade 1999–2003, of Health, of Intergovernmental Affairs, responsible for Official Languages 2003–04, of Foreign Affairs 2004–06; Co-Chair. First Nat. Forum on Canada's Int. Relations 1994. *Publication:* The New Politics of Confidence 1999. *Address:* c/o Liberal Party of Canada, 81 Metcalfe Street, Suite 400, Ottawa, ON K1P 6M8, Canada (office). *E-mail:* pettigrew.p@parl.gc.ca (office).

PETTIT, Philip Noel, PhD; Irish/Australian philosopher and academic; *L. S. Rockefeller University Professor of Politics and Human Values, Princeton University;* b. 20 Dec. 1945, Ballinasloe, Ireland; s. of Michael A. Pettit and Bridget C. Molony; m. Victoria McGeer; two s.; ed Maynooth Coll., Nat. Univ. of Ireland, Queen's Univ. Belfast, Northern Ireland; Lecturer, Univ. Coll. Dublin 1968–72, 1975–77; Research Fellow, Trinity Hall Cambridge, UK 1972–75; Prof. of Philosophy, Univ. of Bradford, UK 1977–83; Professorial Fellow, Research School of Social Sciences, ANU, Canberra, Australia 1983–89, Prof. of Social and Political Theory 1989–2002; Visiting Prof. of Philosophy, Columbia Univ., New York, USA 1997–2001; William Nelson Cromwell Prof. of Politics, Princeton Univ., USA 2002, currently L. S. Rockefeller Univ. Prof. of Politics and Human Values; Assoc. Faculty Mem. Dept of Philosophy; Fellow, Acad. of Social Sciences, Australia, Australian Acad. of Humanities; Hon. mem. Italian Soc. for Analytical Philosophy; Hon. DLitt (Nat. Univ. of Ireland) 2000, (Queen's Univ., Belfast), Hon. PhD (Univ. of Crete) 2005, (Univ. of Montreal); Univ. Medal, Univ. of Helsinki 1992. *Publications:* Concept of Structuralism 1975, Judging Justice 1980, Semantics and Social Science (with G. Macdonald) 1981, Not Just Deserts: A Republican Theory of Criminal Justice (with J. Braithwaite) 1990, The Common Mind: An Essay on Psychology, Society and Politics 1992, Republicanism: A Theory of Freedom and Government 1997, A Theory of Freedom: From the Psychology to the Politics of Agency 2001, Rules, Reasons and Norms: Selected Essays 2002, Penser en Société 2003, Mind, Morality, and Explanation: Selected Collaborations (co-author) 2004, The Economy of Esteem (with Geoffrey Brennan) 2004, Made with Words: Hobbes on Language, Thought and Mind 2008, Examen a Zapatero 2008. *Leisure interests:* walking, tennis. *Address:* UCHV, 308 Marx Hall, Princeton University, Princeton, NJ 08544-1012 (office); 16 College Road, Princeton, NJ 08540, USA (home). *Telephone:* (609) 258-4759 (office); (609) 924-3664 (home). *E-mail:* ppettit@princeton.edu (office). *Website:* www .princeton.edu/~ppettit (office).

PETTY, Richard; American fmr racing driver; b. 2 July 1937, Level Cross, NC; s. of Lee Petty Lee; m. Lynda Owens Petty; one s. three d.; stock car racing driver 1958–92; Winston Cup Rookie of the Year 1959; total of 200 Career NASCAR Winston Cup Victories, NASCAR Winston Cup Champion 1964, 1967, 1971, 1972, 1974, 1975, 1979; winner Daytona 500 1964, 1966, 1971, 1973, 1974, 1979, 1981; 27 victories in one season 1967; sport's first million-dollar driver; last race in 1992; f. Petty Enterprises LLC (complete stock car racing operation); est. Richard Petty Museum 1988; Most Popular Winston Cup Driver 1962, 1964, 1968, 1970, 1974, 1975, 1976, 1977, 1978; Nat. Motorsports Press Asscn (NMPA) Myers Brothers Award 1964, 1967, 1971, 1992, NMPA Driver of the Year 1974, 1975; Nat. NC Athletic Hall of Fame 1973, Int. Motorsports Hall of Fame 1997, Automotive Hall of Fame 2002; Medal of Freedom 1992; American Auto Racing Writers & Broadcasters Asscn (AARWBA) Man of the Year 1995. *Address:* Petty Enterprises LLC, 311 Branson Mill Road, Randleman, NC 27317-8008, USA. *Telephone:* (336) 498-3745. *Website:* www.pettyracing.com (office).

PETTY, Tom; American singer, songwriter and musician (guitar); b. 20 Oct. 1953, Gainesville, Fla; guitarist with local groups, Sundowners, Epics, Mudcrutch; founder mem., Tom Petty and The Heartbreakers 1975–; mem., The Traveling Wilburys 1988–; regular US and int. tours, concert and festival appearances; MTV Music Video Award (for Don't Come Around Here No More) 1985, Billboard Century Award 2005. *Film appearances:* FM 1978, Made in Heaven 1987, The Postman 1997. *Recordings include:* albums: with the Heartbreakers: Tom Petty and The Heartbreakers 1976, You Gonna Get It! 1978, Damn The Torpedoes 1979, Hard Promises 1981, Long After Dark 1982, Southern Accents 1985, Pack Up The Plantation 1986, Let Me Up (I've Had Enough) 1987, Full Moon Fever 1989, Into The Great Wide Open 1991, Greatest Hits 1993, Take The Highway 1994, She's The One (OST) 1996, Echo 1999, Anthology: Through The Years 2000, The Last DJ 2002; with The Traveling Wilburys: Traveling Wilburys 1988, Vol. 2 1989, Vol. 3 1990; solo: Wildflowers 1994, Highway Companion 2006; with Mudcrutch: Mudcrutch 2008. *Address:* East End Management, 8209 Melrose Avenue, Second Floor, Los Angeles, CA 90046, USA (office). *Website:* www.tompetty.com; www .mudcrutchmusic.com.

PEUGEOT, Patrick; French insurance executive; *Chairman, Comité Intermouvements auprès des Évacués;* b. 3 Aug. 1937, Paris; s. of Jacques Peugeot and Edith Peugeot (née Genoyer); m. Catherine Dupont 1963; three s.; ed Lycée Hoche, Ecole Sainte-Geneviève à Versailles, Ecole polytechnique, Ecole nat. d'admin.; auditor, Cour des comptes 1965, Commissariat au plan (Public Enterprises Cttee) 1966–70; Sec.-Gen. Librairie Hachette 1972–74; Sec.-Gen. Groupe des Assurances générals de France (AGF) 1975–83, Dir-Gen. AGF-Réassurance 1979–83; tech. consultant to Ministry of Economy and Finances 1981–83; Dir-Gen. Caisse centrale de réassurance 1983–84, Pres. Advisory Bd 1984–85, Hon. Pres. 1985–; Pres. Dir-Gen. Société commerciale de réassurance (Scor) 1983–94, Hon. Pres. and Dir. 1994–; Vice-Pres. Dir-Gen. La Mondiale 1995, Chair. and CEO 1996–2005; Pres. Groupement des assurances des personnes (Gap) 1997–99; Pres. Réunion des organismes d'assurance mutuelle 1999–2005; Chair. Asscn Int. des Socs d'Assurance Mutelle 2004–, Comité Intermouvements auprès des Évacués (CIMADE) 2005–; Chevalier, Ordre nat. du Mérite. *Address:* CIMADE, 64 rue Clisson, 75013 Paris (office); 82 rue Notre-Dame-des-Champs, 75006 Paris, France (home). *Telephone:* 1-44-18-60-50 (office). *Fax:* 1-45-56-08-59 (office). *E-mail:* infos@cimade.org (office). *Website:* www.cimade.org (office).

PEUGEOT, Roland; French automotive industry executive; b. 20 March 1926, Valentigney; s. of Jean-Pierre and Colette (née Boillat-Japy) Peugeot; m. Colette Mayesky 1949; two s.; ed Lycées Janson-de-Sailly and Saint-Louis, Paris and Harvard Business School, Mass., USA; Pres. Etablissements Peugeot Frères 1959–; Pres. du Conseil de Surveillance de Peugeot SA

1972–98, advisor to Supervisory Bd 2001–07; mem. Bd Automobiles Peugeot 1982–; Pres. Peugeot Talbot Belgique 1985; Dir of subsidiaries and other cos including L'Union et Le Phénix Espagnol 1974–, Champagne Laurent Perrier 1992–; Officier, Légion d'honneur, Officier, Ordre des Arts et des Lettres 2002. *Address:* 75 avenue de la Grande Armée, 75116 Paris (office); 170 avenue Victor-Hugo, 75116 Paris, France (home).

PEUGEOT, Thierry; French automotive industry executive; *Chairman, Supervisory Board, PSA Peugeot Citroën S.A.;* b. 19 Aug. 1957; s. of Pierre Peugeot (died 2002); early career as Export Man. for Middle East, Marrel Group, then Dir of American subsidiary; joined Peugeot 1988, fmrly Regional SE Asia Man., Peugeot, Man. Dir Peugeot do Brasil, Man. Dir SLICA, Vice-Pres. Citroën Large Int. Accounts, Citroën Services and Spare Parts, Chair. Peugeot SA 2002–03, Chair. Supervisory Bd PSA Peugeot Citroën SA 2003–. *Address:* PSA Peugeot Citroën SA, 75 Avenue de la Grande-Armée, 75116 Paris, France (office). *Telephone:* 1-40-66-55-11 (office). *Fax:* 1-40-66-54-14 (office). *Website:* www.psa-peugeot-citroen.com (office).

PEVTSOV, Dmitry Anatlyevich; Russian actor; b. 8 July 1963, Moscow; m. Olga Drozdova; ed Moscow State Inst. of Theatre Arts; actor Taganka Theatre 1985–91; Moscow Theatre of Leninsky Komsomol (LENKOM) 1991–; European Prize Felix (Glasgow). *Films include:* Mother 1989, The Witches Cave 1989, His Nickname is Beast 1990, I Hope for You 1992, The Possessed 1992, Alice and the Bookseller 1992, The Mafia is Immortal 1993, Line of Life 1996, Queen Margo 1996, The Countess of Monsoreau 1998. *Plays include:* The Marriage of Figaro, The Seagull. *Address:* Teplichny per. 5, Apt 139, 123298 Moscow, Russia (home). *Telephone:* (495) 198-77-69 (home).

PEYRAT, Jérôme, LenD; French civil servant; *Director of Cabinet, Secretariat of State for Cooperation and Francophony;* b. 28 Nov. 1962, Sarlat, Dordogne; m.; three c.; ed Institut d'études politiques de Paris, École nationale d'administration, Institut des Hautes Etudes de la Défense Nationale; served as intern in Embassy in Turkey; joined Dept of Int. Relations, Mayor of Paris 1990; served as foreign press adviser and asst spokesperson to Pres. Jacques Chirac; Dir of Communications to Mayor of Paris 1998–2000; Dir of Communications and Dir of Cabinet to Michèle Alliot-Marie, Pres. Rassemblement pour la République 2000–02; Political Adviser to Minister of Interior, Nicolas Sarkozy 2005–07, to Pres. Nicolas Sarkozy 2007–09; mem. Union pour un Mouvement Populaire (UMP) 2002–09; unsuccessful UMP cand. for parl. elections in Dordogne; currently Mayor, La Roque-Gageac; Dir of Cabinet to Alain Joyandet, Minister of State for Cooperation and Francophony 2009–; Pres. Communauté de Communes du Périgord Noir; Chevalier, Ordre Nat. du Mérite. *Publications:* Les Petits matins: essai sur la pensée politique (with Nathalie Kosciusko-Morizet) 2002. *Leisure interests:* mountaineering, skiing, hiking. *Address:* Mairie, 24250 La Roque-Gageac (office); Secrétariat d'État à la Coopération et à la Francophonie, 20 Rue Monsieur, 75007 Paris, France (office). *Telephone:* 1-53-69-40-02 (office). *Fax:* 1-53-69-43-73 (office). *E-mail:* jerome.peyrat@diplomatie.gouv.fr (office). *Website:* www.jeromepeyrat.org (home); www.diplomatie.gouv.fr (office).

PEYRELEVADE, Jean; French business executive; *Partner, Toulouse et Associés;* b. 24 Oct. 1939, Marseille; s. of Paul Peyrelevade and Nadia Benveniste; m. Anne Chavy 1962; three s. one d.; ed Faculté de droit de Paris, Ecole Nat. de l'aviation civile; fmr armaments and aviation engineer; Dir Dept of Foreign Business, Crédit Lyonnais 1973–82; Asst Dir Cabinet of M. Pierre Mauroy 1982; Pres. Cie Financière de Suez 1983–86; Pres. Banque Stern 1986–88; Chair. Union des Assurances de Paris 1988–93; Dir Bouygues 1994–; Chair. Crédit Lyonnais 1993–2003 (resgnd after bank's acquistion by Crédit Agricole); Govt Rep. on Bd of Renault 1996–2000; mem. Econ. and Social Council 1994–; Partner Toulouse et Assocs 2004–; mem. Supervisory Bd CMA-CGM 2005–; mem. Bd of Dirs Suez. *Publications:* La mort du dollar 1974, L'economie de spéculation 1978, Economie de l'entreprise 1989, Pour un capitalisme intelligent 1993, Le gouvernement d'entreprise 1999. *Leisure interests:* skiing, golf. *Address:* Conseil de surveillance, CMA-CGM Marseille Siège Social 4, quai d'Arenc, 13235 Maresille Cedex 02, France (office). *Telephone:* 4-88-91-90-00 (office). *Fax:* 4-88-91-90-95 (office). *E-mail:* media@cma-cgm.com (office). *Website:* www.cma-cgm.com (office).

PEZANT, Jean-Louis; French lawyer and politician; *Member, Conseil Constitutionnel;* b. 5 Oct. 1938, Dun-le-Palestel (Creuse); ed Institut d'études politiques de Paris; several positions while serving as mem. Assemblée nationale, including Admin. Service Comm 1966–77, Admin. for Meeting 1977–78, Head Secretariat of Cttee on Legislation 1978–86, Adviser, in charge of transport, Gen Admin. Affairs 1986–88, Dir of Communications Service 1988–90, Chief of the Meeting 1990–93, Chief Legislative Services 1993–2002, Sec. Gen. of Assemblée nationale and the Presidency 2002–03; Assoc. Prof., Univ. de Paris-I Panthéon-Sorbonne 1997–2000; mem. Editorial Bd Pouvoirs (journal); Mem. Conseil Constitutionnel 2004–; Officier de la Légion d'honneur 1999. *Address:* Conseil Constitutionnel, 2 rue de Montpensier, 75001 Paris, France (office). *Telephone:* 1-40-15-30-00 (office). *Fax:* 1-40-20-93-27 (office). *E-mail:* relations-exterieures@conseil-constitutionnel.fr (office). *Website:* www.conseil-constitutionnel.fr (office).

PFAFF, Judy, BFA, MFA; American artist; b. 22 Sept. 1946, London, England; ed Wayne State Univ., Detroit, Southern Illinois Univ., Univ. of Washington and Yale Univ.; numerous visiting faculty positions since 1971 including Calif. Inst. of Arts, Yale Univ. Rhode Island School of Design, Oberlin Coll., Princeton Univ.; mem. of grad. faculty School of Visual Arts, New York 1986–91; Prof. of Visual Arts, Columbia Univ. 1992–94; Guggenheim Fellowship for Sculpture, MacArthur Fellow 2004; mem. American Acad. of Arts and Letters 2009–. *Address:* c/o Bob Kornstein, Bellas Artes Gallery, 653 Canyon Road, Santa Fe, NM 87501, USA (office). *Telephone:* (505) 983-2745 (office). *E-mail:* bc@bellasartesgallery.com (office). *Website:* www.bellasartesgallery.com.

PFAFF, William; American writer and journalist; *Columnist, Tribune Media Services, The Tribune Company;* m. Carolyn Cleary; two c.; ed Univ. of Notre Dame, Ind.; Asst Ed. Commonweal magazine, New York 1949–55; Writer, ABC News 1955–57; Exec. Free Europe Cttee 1957–61; Sr Mem. Hudson Inst., New York 1961–75, Deputy Dir Hudson Research Europe, Paris 1971–78; freelance writer 1978–; syndicated columnist International Herald Tribune 1978–; Contrib. New Yorker magazine 1971–92, also New York Review of Books, Harper's Magazine, Foreign Affairs, The National Interest, The Observer, London, Commentaire, Paris, etc; Rockefeller Foundation Grant 1962; Hon. LLD (Univ. of Notre Dame) 1992 Prix de l'Annuaire Français de Relations Internationales 2004. *Publications include:* The New Politics (with Edmund Stillman) 1960, The Politics of Hysteria (with Edmund Stillman) 1964, Power and Impotence (with Edmund Stillman) 1966, Condemned to Freedom 1971; published in Best American Essays: The Lay Intellectual (autobiog. essay) 1987, Barbarian Sentiments: How the American Century Ends (Prix Jean-Jacques Rousseau, Geneva) 1989, The Wrath of Nations 1993, Barbarian Sentiments: America in the New Century 2000, Fear Anger and Failure 2004, The Bullet's Song: Romantic Violence and Utopia 2004. *Address:* 23/25 Rue de Lisbonne, 7608 Paris Cedex, France (office). *Telephone:* 1-43-59-05-66 (office). *Fax:* 1-43-59-09-98 (office). *E-mail:* wpfaff@wanadoo.fr (office). *Website:* www.williampfaff.com (office).

PFEFFER, Philip Maurice, MA; American business executive; *President and CEO, Treemont Capital;* b. 20 Jan. 1945, St Louis; s. of Philip McRae and Jeanne (Kaufman) Pfeffer; m. Pamela Jean Korte 1965; three s.; ed South Illinois Univ., Vanderbilt Univ.; joined Genesco Inc., Nashville 1968, Pres. Genesco Export co. 1970–75; Dir Financial Planning, Ingram Distribution Group Inc., Nashville 1976–77, Vice-Pres. Finance and Admin. 1977–78, Exec. Vice-Pres. 1978, Pres. and CEO 1978–81, Dir 1978–95, Chair. of Bd and CEO 1981–95, Exec. Vice-Pres. Ingram Industries Inc. 1981–95, Dir 1981–95; Pres. and COO Random House 1996–98; CEO Borders Group 1999 (resgnd); f. Treemont Capital, Pres. and CEO 1999–; also currently Chair. Mailnet Services Inc.; mem. Bd of Dirs King Pharmaceuticals, PureWorks Inc., The City Paper (Nashville), Publishing Group of America, Casual Furniture Repair and Sales; Instructor in Finance and Econs, Univ. of Tenn., Nashville 1968–77; lecturer in Corp. Finance, Vanderbilt Univ. 1972–77. *Leisure interests:* scouting, sailing, water sports, landscaping. *Address:* 836 Treemont Court, Nashville, TN 37220 (home); Mailnet Services Inc., 800 Crescent Centre Drive, Suite 450, Franklin, TN 37067, USA (office).

PFEIFFER, Didier-Bernard, LenD; French business executive; *President of the Supervisory Board, Fonds de Garantie des Assurances de Personnes (FGAP);* b. 3 Nov. 1938, Paris; s. of Jacques Pfeiffer and Denise Pontzen; m. Maryse Bloch 1961; three c.; ed Lycée Pasteur, Neuilly, Univ. de Paris, Inst. d'études politiques de Paris, Ecole Nat. d'Admin; civil servant Treasury Dept, Ministry of Economy and Finance 1966–68, Head of Dept Office of Minister of Econ. and Finance 1968–71; Financial Attaché French Embassy, Washington 1971; a Deputy Dir World Bank 1972; Dir Financial Operations l'Union des Assurances de Paris (UAP) 1973, Dir of Investments 1976–84, Man. Dir 1984–91, Dir 1991–94, Vice-Pres. and Man. Dir 1994–96; Pres., Groupe des Assurances Nationales (GAN) 1996–98; Vice-Pres. Exec. Cttee Groupama GAN 1998–99; Pres. Supervisory Bd Fonds de Garantie des Assurances de Personnes (FGAP) 1999–, Comité Européen des Assurances; Vice-Pres. Supervisory Bd Eurazeo 2002–; Pres. Comité des Entreprises d'Assurance; Officier, Légion d'honneur, Officier, Ordre nat. du Mérite. *Address:* FGAP, 51 rue Saint-Georges, 75009 Paris, Cédex 08 (office); 68 rue des Belles Feuilles, 75116 Paris, France (home). *Telephone:* 1-40-22-03-09 (office); 1-45-53-98-11 (home). *Fax:* 1-40-22-98-73 (office).

PFEIFFER, Michelle; American actress; b. 29 April 1957, Santa Ana, Calif.; d. of Dick Pfeiffer and Donna Pfeiffer; m. 1st Peter Horton (divorced 1987); one adopted d.; m. 2nd David E. Kelley 1993; one s.; ed Fountain Valley High School, Golden West Coll., Whitley Coll. *Films include:* Grease 2, Into the Night, The Witches of Eastwick, Sweet Liberty, Married to the Mob, Tequila Sunrise 1989, Dangerous Liaisons 1989, The Fabulous Baker Boys 1989, The Russia House 1989, Love Field, Frankie and Johnny 1991, Batman Returns 1992, The Age of Innocence 1993, Wolf 1994, My Posse Don't Do Homework 1994, Dangerous Minds, Up Close and Personal, To Gillian on Her 37th Birthday, One Fine Day 1997, A Thousand Acres 1997, Privacy 1997, The Prince of Egypt (voice) 1998, The Story of Us 1999, The Deep End of the Ocean 1999, A Midsummer Night's Dream 1999, Being John Malkovich 1999, What Lies Beneath 2000, I am Sam 2001, White Oleander 2002, Sinbad: Legend of the Seven Seas (voice) 2003, I Could Never Be Your Woman 2007, Hairspray 2007, Stardust 2007, Personal Effects 2008. *Address:* ICM, 8492 Wilshire Blvd, Beverly Hills, CA 90211-1934, USA (office). *Telephone:* (310) 550-4000 (office). *Website:* www.icmtalent.com (office).

PFISTER, Bruno, LLM, MBA; Swiss business executive; *Group CEO, Swiss Life Holding;* b. 1959; ed Univ. of Geneva, Grad. School of Man., Univ. of California, Los Angeles, USA; called to the Bar, Geneva; worked for Chase Manhattan Bank in London and Geneva; Man. Consultant, McKinsey & Co. 1988–96; Chief of Staff of Pvt. Banking Div., Liechtenstein Global Trust 1996–98, Chief Financial Officer LGT Group and LGT Bank, Liechtenstein 1998–99; mem. Credit Suisse Group Exec. Bd, Head of Customer Segment Man. and Product Man., Credit Suisse 1999–2002; Chief Financial Officer Swiss Life Group 2002–06, CEO Swiss Life Group International 2006–08, Group CEO Swiss Life Holding 2008–; mem. Bd of Dirs Gottex Fund Man. Holdings Ltd, St Peter Port, Guernsey, Swiss Insurance Assen; Vice-Chair. Admission Bd and Exec. Cttee of Admission Bd of SWX Swiss Exchange. *Address:* Swiss Life Holding, General Guisan-Quai 40, 8022 Zürich, Switzerland (office). *Telephone:* (4) 32843253 (office). *Fax:* (4) 33383253 (office). *E-mail:* info@swisslife.ch (office). *Website:* www.swisslife.com (office).

PFLIMLIN, Etienne Alphonse Marie Georges; French banking executive and fmr civil servant; *Chairman of the Supervisory Board, CIC Crédit Industriel & Commercial SA;* b. 16 Oct. 1941, Thonon les Bains, Haute Savoie; s. of Pierre Pflimlin and Marie-Odile Pflimlin (née Heinrich); m. Marie-Sophie Nehlil; two s.; ed Ecole Polytechnique, Ecole Nat. d'Admin, Institut d'Etudes Politiques, Paris; fmr teacher, Univ. Paris-IX Dauphine, Institut d'Etudes Politiques de Paris; Commr, Ministry of Finance 1964–67; Dir of Cabinet, Pref. of Finistère 1968; Counsellor, Cour des Comptes (Nat. Audit Office) 1970–84; with Ministry of Culture 1973–78; Counsellor, Ministry of Budget 1978–79; Dir of Cabinet Ministry of Commerce and Handicrafts 1979–81; joined Crédit Mutuel 1984, became Pres. Banque Fédérative du Crédit Mutuel 1985, Pres. Crédit Mutuel Centre Est Europe 1985, Pres. Confédération Nationale du Crédit Mutuel 1987, Pres. Supervisory Bd Banque de l'Economie du Commerce et de la Monetique 1992, Chair. CIC Crédit Industriel et Commercial SA 1998–; Pres. Groupe L'Alsace 1988–, Le Monde Enterprises 1988–, European Co-operative Bank Group 2002–; Pres. European Cttee Int. Co-operative Banking Asscn; Chevalier, Order nat. du Mèrite, Officier, Légion d'honneur, des Palmes académiques. *Address:* CIC Crédit Industriel & Commercial SA, 6 avenue de Provence, 75452 Paris 9, France (office). *Telephone:* 1-45-96-96-96 (office). *Fax:* 1-45-96-96-66 (office). *E-mail:* filbass@cic.fr (office). *Website:* www.cic.fr/en (office).

PHAM MINH MÁN, HE Cardinal Jean-Baptiste, MEd; Vietnamese ecclesiastic; *Archbishop of Thành-Phô Hô Chí Minh;* b. 31 Dec. 1934, Ca Mau; ed Minor Seminary of Cantho, St Joseph's Major Seminary, Saigon (now Ho Chi Minh City, and in USA; ordained priest 1965; Prof., Minor Seminary of Cantho; further studies in USA 1968–71; returned to Viet Nam and again named Prof. at Minor Seminary of Cantho until Communist invasion in 1975; Rector Major Seminary of Can Tho for three dioceses of Can Tho, Vinh Long and Long Xuyen 1989–93; Coadjutor Bishop of My Tho 1993–98; Archbishop of Thành-Phô Hô Chí Minh 1998–; attended Xth Ordinary Ass. of World Synod of Bishops, Vatican City 2001; cr. Cardinal (Cardinal Priest of San Giustino) 2003. *Address:* Archdiocese of Thành-Phô Hô Chí Minh, Toa Tong Muc, 180 Nguyen Dink Chieu, Q. 3, Thành-Phô Hô Chí Minh City, Viet Nam (office). *Telephone:* (8) 930-3828 (office). *Fax:* (8) 930-0598 (office).

PHANSTIEL, Howard G., MA; American healthcare industry executive; *Chairman, President and CEO, PacifiCare Health Systems Inc.;* ed Syracuse Univ., NY; various exec. and man. positions with Prudential Bache Int. Bank, Marine Midland Bank, Student Loan Marketing Asscn (Sallie Mae), US Dept of Health, Educ. and Welfare, Health Care Financing Administration (HCFA), Citibank, Ill. Bureau of Budget, WI Bureau of Planning and Budget; fmr Exec. Vice-Pres. Finance and Information Services, WellPoint Health Networks Inc., Calif.; Chair. and CEO ARV Assisted Living Inc., Calif. –2000, Exec. Vice-Pres. and Chief Financial Officer, PacifiCare Health Systems July–Oct. 2000, Pres. and CEO Oct. 2000–. *Address:* PacifiCare Health Systems Inc., 5995 Plaza Drive, Cypress, CA 90630, USA (office). *Telephone:* (714) 952-1121 (office). *Fax:* (714) 226-3581 (office). *Website:* www.pacificare.com (office).

PHANTOG; Chinese mountaineer; b. Aug. 1939, Xigazê, Tibet; d. of Cirhen Phantog and Cijiu Phantog; m. Jia-shang Deng 1963; one s. two d.; ed Cen. Coll. of Nationalities; first Chinese woman to climb Everest 1975; Deputy Dir Wuxi Sports and Physical Culture Comm. 1981–. *Leisure interests:* table tennis, badminton. *Address:* Wuxi Sports and Physical Culture Commission, Jiangsu, People's Republic of China (office). *Telephone:* 225810 (office).

PHARAON, Ghaith Rashad, MBA, PhD; Saudi Arabian business executive; b. 7 Sept. 1940, Riyadh; ed Stanford and Harvard Univs, USA; Founder Saudi Arabia Research and Devt Corpn (Redec) 1965, now Chair. of Bd and Dir-Gen.; Chair. Bd Saudi Arabian Parsons Ltd, Saudi Automotive Industries Ltd, Redec Daelim Ltd, Interstal, Saudi Chemical Processors Ltd, Arabian Maritime Co., Saudi Inland Transport, etc.; Vice-Chair. Jezirah Bank Ltd, Saudi Light Industries Ltd, Arabian Chemical Industries Ltd; mem. Bd Okaz Publications, Tihama; Commendatore (Italy); King Abdul Aziz Award. *Address:* PO Box 1935, Jeddah (office); Ghaith Pharaon Residence, Ruwais, Jeddah, Saudi Arabia (home). *Website:* www.pharaon.com (office).

PHELAN, John Joseph, Jr, BBA; American fmr stock exchange executive and company director; b. 7 May 1931, New York; ed Adelphi Univ., New York; with Nash and Co. stockbrokers, New York 1955–62, partner 1957–62; Man. partner Phelan and Co., New York 1962–72; Sr partner Phelan, Silver, Vesce, Barry and Co., New York 1977–80; Pres. New York Stock Exchange 1980–84, Chair. and CEO 1984–1991; Chair. New York Futures Exchange 1979–85, Presidential Bd of Advisors on Pvt. Sector Initiatives 1986–; Pres. Int. Fed. of Stock Exchanges 1990–92; Chair., Bd of Trustee Adelphi Univ. 1980–84; Sr Adviser Boston Consulting Group 1991–2002; mem. Bd Dirs Avon Products 1992–95, Eastman Kodak 1988–2001, Met Life, Merrill Lynch, Sonat Inc. 1991–2000; mem. Securities Industries Asscn (mem. Governing Bd 1978–79, Exec. Cttee 1979–80); mem. Bd of Trustees Aspen Inst. 1990–2001, Council on Foreign Relations; Kt Sovereign Mil. Order of Malta, Holy Sepulchre, Jerusalem; Chevalier, Ordre des Arts et Lettres 1987 and other decorations; Hon. LLD (Adelphi) 1987, (Hamilton Coll.) 1980, (Niagara) 1985; Dr hc (Notre Dame Univ.) 1986, (Tuslawe Univ.), (Fairfield Univ.). *Address:* 108 Forest Avenue, Locust Valley, New York, NY 11560, USA.

PHELPS, Edmund Strother, PhD; American economist and academic; *Professor of Political Economics and Director of Center on Capitalism and Society, Columbia University;* b. 26 July 1933, Evanston, Ill.; s. of Edmund S. Phelps and Florence Stone Phelps; m. Viviana Montdor 1974; ed Amherst Coll. and Yale Univ.; Research Economist, RAND Corpn 1959–60; taught Yale Univ. 1960–66; Prof., Univ. of Pennsylvania 1966–71; Prof., Columbia Univ. 1971–78, 1979–82, McVickar Prof. of Political Econs 1982–, also Dir, Center on Capitalism and Soc.; Prof., New York Univ. 1977–78; Sr Adviser Brookings Inst. 1976–; Econ. Adviser EBRD 1991–94; mem. NAS 1982; mem. Econ. Policy Panel, Observatoire Français des Conjonctures Economiques 1991–; Sr Adviser Consiglio Nazionale delle Ricerche 1997–2000; Distinguished Fellow, American Econ. Asscn 2000; several hon. professorships; Hon. DH (Amherst Coll.) 1985, (Univ. of Mannheim) 2001, (Univ. Tor Vergata, Rome) 2001; Chevalier, Légion d'Honneur (France) 2008; Kenan Enterprise Award 1996, Nobel Prize in Econ. Science 2006, Premio Pico della Mirandola for humanism 2008, Kiel Global Economy Prize 2008. *Publications:* Golden Rules of Economic Growth 1966, Microeconomic Foundations of Employment and Inflation Theory (ed.) 1970, Studies in Macroeconomic Theory: Vols 1, 2 1979, 1980, Political Economy: An Introductory Text 1985, The Slump in Europe 1988, Seven Schools of Macroeconomic Thought 1990, Structural Slumps 1994, Rewarding Work 1997. *Leisure interest:* music. *Address:* Department of Economics, Columbia University, 1004 International Affairs Building, MC 3308, 420 West 118th Street, New York, NY 10027, USA (office). *Telephone:* (212) 854-2060 (office). *Fax:* (212) 854-3735 (office). *E-mail:* esp2@columbia.edu (office). *Website:* www.columbia.edu/~esp2 (office).

PHELPS, Michael; American swimmer; b. 30 June 1985, Baltimore, Md; s. of Fred Phelps and Debbie Davisson Phelps; ed Towson High School, Univ. of Michigan, Ann Arbor; Olympic Games, Sydney 2000: 5th 200m butterfly; World Championships 2001: gold medal 200m butterfly (world record); World Championships 2003: gold medal 200m butterfly (world record), gold medal 200m individual medley (world record), gold medal 400m individual medley (world record), silver medal 100m butterfly (broke world record in semi-final, subsequently broken by gold-medallist Ian Crocker), silver medal 4×200m free relay; youngest male Olympian since 1932, Olympic Games, Sydney 2000; Olympic Games, Athens 2004: gold medal 400m individual medley, 200m butterfly, 4×200m free relay, 200m individual relay, 100m butterfly, 4×100m medley relay, bronze medal 4×100m freestyle relay, 200m freestyle; first in 200m freestyle, World Short Course Championships 2004; five gold medals, World Championships 2005; three gold medals, US Nat. Championships 2005; three gold medals, Pan Pacific Games 2006; six medals, US Nat. Championships 2006; Olympic Games, Beijing 2008: gold medal, 200m freestyle, 100m butterfly, 200m butterfly, 200m individual medley, 400m individual medley, 4×100m freestyle relay, 4×200m freestyle relay, 4×100m medley relay (five gold medals won in individual events, tying record for individual gold medals at a single Games originally set by Eric Heiden in 1980 Winter Olympics and equalled by Vitaly Scherbo at 1992 Summer Games); eight medals in 2004 Athens Olympics and in 2008 Beijing Olympics tie with 1980 USSR gymnast Alexandr Dityatin for most medals by an athlete at a single Olympics (only athlete to win eight in a non-boycotted Olympics); 14 Olympic gold medals (the most by any Olympian); ranks second in total career Olympic medals, after Soviet gymnast Larissa Latynina, who won a total of 18 medals (nine gold) spanning three Olympic Games; only man to win five US Nat. titles at the same Championships, only swimmer to win US Nat. titles in three different strokes at the same Championships 2003; seven medals (five world records), World Championships, Melbourne 2007; set seven world records and one Olympic record at Beijing Olympics 2008 (only swimmer to break seven world records at one tournament); has won total of 48 career medals to date (Aug. 2008): 40 gold, six silver, two bronze from Olympics, World Championships, and Pan Pacific Championships; coach Bob Bowman, swims for North Baltimore Aquatic Club; American Swimmer of the Year Award 2001, 2002, 2003, 2004, 2006, 2007, FINA Trophy 2003 (best swimmer, World Championships 2003), Sullivan Award 2003, World Swimmer of the Year 2003, 2004, 2006, 2007, Sports Illustrated Sportsman of the Year 2008. *Address:* c/o Melissa Gagnon, Octagon, 2 Union Street, Portland, ME 04101, USA (office); PO Box 1734, Olney, MD 20830-1734, USA. *Telephone:* (207) 775-1500 (office). *E-mail:* melissa.gagnon@octagon.com (office); media@michaelphelps.com. *Website:* www.octagon.com (office); www.michaelphelps.com.

PHELPS DE CISNEROS, Patricia; Venezuelan art collector; *Chairman, Fundación Cisneros;* m. Gustavo Cisneros; began collecting art works from 1970, Co-founder (with husband and brother-in-law, Ricardo Cisneros, in asscn with Cisneros Group of Cos) and Chair. Fundación Cisneros (pvt. philanthropic org. based in Caracas, Venezuela). *Address:* Colección Patricia Phelps de Cisneros, Fundación Cisneros, Quinta Centro Mozarteum, Final Avenida La Salle, Colina de los Caobos, Caracas 1050, Venezuela (office). *Telephone:* (212) 708-96-97 (office). *E-mail:* info@coleccioncisneros.org (office). *Website:* www.coleccioncisneros.org (office).

PHIEU, Gen. Le Kha; Vietnamese army officer and politician; b. 27 Dec. 1931, Dong Khe Commune, Dong Son Dist, Thanh Hoa Prov.; ed Vietnam Mil. Coll.; joined CP 1949; several positions 1964–93 including Regiment's Political Commissar and Commdr of the Regiment, Deputy Chief Army Political Dept of Second Army Corps, Deputy Political Commissar and Chief Political Dept of Ninth Mil. Zone, Maj.-Gen., Chief of Political Dept and Deputy Political Commdr of 719 Front, Lt-Gen., Deputy Chief and then Sr Lt-Gen. and Chief Gen. Political Dept Vietnamese People's Army; Sec.-Gen. CP of Viet Nam 1997–2001; mem. Politburo, Politburo Standing Bd. *Address:* Communist Party of Viet Nam, 1 Hoang Van Thu, Hanoi, Viet Nam.

PHILAKONE, Phiane, LLB; Laotian diplomatist and fmr banker; *Ambassador to USA;* b. 6 July 1947, Muang Khong Dist, Champasak Prov.; m. Somchit Philakone; three c.; ed Int. Inst. for Public Admin, Paris, Inst. Royal de Droit et d'Admin, Vientiane; Dir of Admin, Lao Devt Bank 1973–75; Research Dir Bank of Lao People's Democratic Repub. (cen. bank) 1976–89, Deputy Gov. 1996–99; Man. Dir Banque pour le Commerce Extérieur 1990–93; Pres. Jt Devt Bank 1990–93; Amb. to Philippines 2001–07, to USA (also accred to Canada and Mexico) 2007–. *Leisure interests:* golf, painting.

Address: Embassy of the Lao People's Democratic Republic, 2222 S Street, NW, Washington, DC 20008, USA (office). *Telephone:* (202) 332-6416 (office). *Fax:* (202) 332-4923 (office). *E-mail:* laoemb@verizon.net (office). *Website:* www.laoembassy.com (office).

PHILARET, (Kyrill Varfolomeyevich Vakhromeyev); Russian/Belarusian ecclesiastic; *Patriarchal Exarch of All Byelorussia;* b. 21 March 1935, Moscow; s. of Varfolomey and Aleksandra V. Vakhromeyev; ed Moscow Theological Seminary and Moscow Theological Acad.; became monk 1959, ordained as a priest 1961; lecturer, Asst Prof., Moscow Theological Acad. 1961–65, Rector 1966–73; Bishop of Tikhvin 1965, of Dmitrov 1966; Vice-Chair. Dept of External Church Relations, Moscow Patriarchate 1968–71, Chair. 1981–; Archbishop 1971; Archbishop of Berlin and Middle Europe 1973–78; Metropolitan 1975, of Minsk and Byelorussia 1978, of Minsk and Grodno (later Minsk and Slutsk 1992), Patriarchal Exarch of All Byelorussia 1989; Perm. mem. Holy Synod of Russian Orthodox Church 1981–, Chair. Foreign Relations Dept 1987–89, Theological Comm. 1993–; Dean, Theological Faculty of St Methodius & Cyril, European Humanities Univ. 1993–2005; Rector, Theological Inst. of St Methodius & Cyril, Byelorussian State Univ. 2005–; Chair. Editorial Bd Theological Studies 2001–; Hon. mem. Moscow and St Petersburg Theological Acads; Order of St Vladimir 1969, Order of St Sergey of Radonezh 1981, Order of Friendship of the Peoples 1985, 2005, Order of Daniil of Moscow 1990, Order of Fatherland 1998, Cross of St Euphrosyne of Polotsk 1998, Order of St Seraphim of Sarov 2005; DTheol hc (St Vladimir Seminary, New York), (St Sergey Orthodox Theological Inst., Paris) Medal of Frantsysk Skorina 1995. *Publications:* Russian Orthodox Church Relations to Western Non-Orthodox Churches, St Cyril and Methodius' Works in the Territory of The Russian State in Russian Historical Literature, Patriotic Character of Patriarch Aleksiy, Theology of Neighbourhood 2002, The Vital Way of Life 2004, The Search for the Kingdom 2005; contrib.: Studies of the Minsk Theological Acad. *Address:* 220004 Minsk, 10 Osvobozdeniya Street, Belarus (home). *Telephone:* (172) 03-73-48 (office); (172) 09-42-99 (office). *Fax:* (172) 00-11-19 (office). *E-mail:* press-service@church.by (office). *Website:* www.church.by (office).

PHILBIN, Ann, BA, MA; American museum curator; *Director, UCLA Hammer Museum of Art and Cultural Center;* b. 21 March 1952, Boston; ed Univ. of New Hampshire, New York Univ.; Researcher, Frick Art Reference Library, New York 1977–79; Program Coordinator, Artists Space 1979–80; Asst Curatorial Coordinator, The New Musuem 1980–81; Curator The Ian Woodner Family Collection 1981–83; Asst Dir Grace Borgenicht Gallery 1983–85; Dir Curt Marcus Gallery 1985–88; Dir The Drawing Center, New York 1989–98; Dir UCLA Hammer Museum of Art and Cultural Center 1999–; mem. Bd Dirs several arts and non-profit orgs, including Vera List Center for Art and Politics at The New School for Social Research, Etant Donne (grant-making agency promoting French-American cultural exchange), Streb/Ringside dance co., HIV Law Project, New York. *Address:* Hammer Museum, 10899 Wilshire Blvd, Los Angeles, CA 90024, USA (office). *Telephone:* (310) 443-7032 (office). *E-mail:* info@hammer.ucla.edu (office). *Website:* www.hammer.ucla.edu (office).

PHILEMON, Bart; Papua New Guinea politician; Minister for Transport and Civil Aviation –2000, Minister for Foreign Affairs and Bougainville Affairs 2000–02; Caretaker Gov., Minister for Treasury, Finance, Privatisation and Agric. 2002; Minister for Finance and Treasury 2002–06; Gov. World Bank for Papua New Guinea. *Address:* c/o Ministry for Finance and Treasury, POB 710, Vulpindi Haus, Waigani NCD, Papua New Guinea (office).

PHILIPPE, HRH Crown Prince (Duke of Brabant), MA; Belgian; b. 15 April 1960; s. of King Albert II and Queen Paola; m. Mathilde d'Udekem d'Acoz 1999; one d. two s.; ed Royal Mil. Acad., Trinity Coll., Oxford, England and Stanford Univ., USA; apptd Second Lt Belgian armed forces 1980, subsequently obtained fighter pilot's wings and certificates as parachutist and commando, attended Royal Higher Defence Inst. 1989, apptd Col 1989, apptd Maj.-Gen. and Rear-Adm. 2001; Royal Household established 1992; Pres. Nat. Sustainable Devt Council 1993–97; apptd Senator 1994; Founder Le Fonds Prince Philippe 1998–; Hon. Pres. Bd of Dirs Foreign Trade Office 1993–, Fed. Sustainable Devt Council 1997–. *Address:* Royal Palace, 16 rue Bréderode, Brussels 1000, Belgium (office). *Telephone:* (2) 5512020 (office). *Fax:* (2) 5023949 (office). *Website:* www.monarchie.be.

PHILIPPE, Guy; Haitian rebel leader; *Secretary-General, Front de Reconstruction Nationale;* b. 29 Feb. 1968; m.; ed law degree from Ecuador and studied medicine in Mexico for a year; fmr mem. FAD'H (Haitian Army); trained by US Special Forces in Ecuador 1991–94; sr security official under Pres. René Preval 1995; when FAD'H was dissolved in early 1995, Philippe incorporated into new Nat. Police Force, served as police chief in Port-au-Prince suburb of Delmas 1997–99, in Cap-Haitien 1999–2000; accused of organizing coup attempt, fled to Ecuador then to Dominican Repub. 2002, remained there until rebellion against Pres. Aristide Feb. 2004; named commdr of rebel army by Buteur Metayer; Sec.-Gen. Front de Réconstruction Nationale 2004–. *Address:* Front de Réconstruction Nationale, Genaïres, Haiti (office).

PHILIPPOU, Andreas N., PhD; Cypriot politician and university professor; *Member, Republic of Cyprus Tax Tribunal;* b. 15 July 1944, Katokopia; s. of Nicholas Philippou and Maria G. Protopapa; m. Athina Roustani 1984; three d.; ed Pancyprian Gymnasium, Athens Univ., Greece, Univ. of Wisconsin, USA; Teaching and Research Asst, Univ. of Wis., Asst Prof. of Math., Univ. of Tex., El Paso; Asst then Assoc. Prof. of Math., American Univ. of Beirut, Lebanon; Prof. of Business Admin., Beirut Univ. Coll.; Visiting Prof. of Applied Math., subsequently Prof. of Probability and Statistics, Pres. of Math. Dept and Vice-Rector, Univ. of Patras, Greece; Minister of Educ. 1988–90; Pres. Preparatory Cttee for establishment of Univ. of Cyprus, then first Pres. Interim Governing Bd of Univ. 1988–90; mem. House of Reps 1991–2001, mem. House Cttees. on Educ. and the Budget, Council of IPU, Rapporteur for Kosovo 1998, for the Middle East 1991–2001; Founding mem. Cen. Cttee, Social Democratic Movt (EDEK) 2000–; mem., Tax Tribunal 2004–; fmr Vice-Pres. Hellenic Aerospace Industry; Hon. Pres. Math. Asscn of Cyprus 1988; Grande Ufficiale Repub. of Italy. *Publications:* 65 research papers; ed seven books. *Leisure interests:* swimming, sailing. *Address:* Tax Tribunal, 9 Stasandrou, 1648 Nicosia (office); 26 Atlantis Street, 2107 Nicosia, Cyprus (home). *Telephone:* (22) 803405 (office); (22) 336360 (also fax) (home). *Fax:* (22) 803450 (office).

PHILIPS, Luc; Belgian financial executive; *Managing Director, Almanij NV;* b. 1952; ed Coll. of Man. and Commercial Sciences, Brussels; joined KBC Bank 1971, various positions in Credit Dept and Int. Credit Div., with NY Br., 1981–87, Man.-Dir NY Br. 1987–91, Head of Cen. Man. –Multinationals Div. 1991–93, Gen.-Man. Investment Banking Directorate 1993–97, Man.-Dir and mem. Exec. Cttee KBC Bank and KBC Bank and Insurance Holding Co. 1998–2003; Man.-Dir and mem. Exec. Cttee Kredietbank 1997–98; Man.-Dir and mem. Exec. Cttee Almanij NV 2003–; mem. Bd Dirs KBC Bank, KBC Bank and Insurance Holding Co. *Address:* Almanij NV, Snyderhuis, Keizerstraat 8, 2000 Antwerp, Belgium (office). *Telephone:* (3) 202-87-00 (office). *Fax:* (3) 202-87-05 (office). *E-mail:* info@almanij.be (office). *Website:* www.almanij.be (office).

PHILIPSON, Lennart Carl, MD, DrMedSci; Swedish microbiologist and academic; *Professor Emeritus, Department of Cell and Molecular Biology, Karolinska Institutet;* b. 16 July 1929, Stockholm; s. of the late Carl Philipson and Greta Svanstrom; m. Malin Jondal 1954; three s.; ed Univ. of Uppsala; Asst Prof., Inst. of Virology, Univ. of Uppsala 1958–59, Asst Prof., Assoc. Prof. Swedish Medical Research Council 1961–68, Founder and Dir Wallenberg Lab. 1967–76, Prof. and Chair. Dept of Microbiology 1968–82, Prof. Emer. 1998–; Dir-Gen. European Molecular Biology Lab., Heidelberg 1982–93; Dir Skirball Inst. of Biomolecular Medicine, New York Univ. Medical Center 1993–97; Hon. Prof., Heidelberg Univ. 1985; Dr hc (Turku) 1987, (Umeå) 1994, Karol Inst. 1999. *Publications:* over 300 scientific publs in fields of virology, microbiology, immunology, molecular biology and biochemistry. *Leisure interests:* sailing, golf. *Address:* Karolinska Institutet, Department of Cell and Molecular Biology, Program in Cell Biology, PO Box 285, 171 77, Stockholm (office); Grev Turegatan 47, 11438 Stockholm, Sweden (home). *Telephone:* (8) 52487333 (office); (8) 218797 (home). *Fax:* (8) 348135 (office). *E-mail:* lennart.philipson@ki.se (office). *Website:* www.cmb.ki.se/projektdokument/philipson1.htm (office).

PHILLIPPE, Ryan; American actor; b. 10 Sept. 1974, New Castle, Del.; m. Reese Witherspoon 1999 (divorced 2007); one s. one d. *Films include:* Crimson Tide 1995, Invader 1996, White Squall 1996, Nowhere 1997, I Know What You Did Last Summer 1997, Little Boy Blue 1997, Homegrown 1998, 54 1998, Playing by Heart 1998, Cruel Intentions 1999, Company Man 2000, The Way of the Gun 2000, Antitrust 2001, Igby Goes Down 2002, Gosford Park 2002, The I Inside 2003, Crash 2004, Five Fingers 2005, Chaos 2005, Flags of Our Fathers 2006, Breach 2007, Stop-Loss 2008. *Television includes:* One Life to Live 1992, The Secrets of Lake Success (mini-series) 1993, Natural Enemies 1993, A Perry Mason Mystery: The Case of the Grimacing Governor 1994, Deadly Invasion: The Killer Bee Nightmare 1995. *Address:* c/o Paradigm Talent Agency, 10100 Santa Monica Blvd, #2500, Los Angeles, CA 90067; c/o CAA, 9830 Wilshire Blvd, Beverly Hills, CA 90212, USA. *Website:* www.ryan-phillippe.com (office).

PHILLIPS, Caryl, BA, FRSL; British/Saint Christopher and Nevis writer and academic; *Professor of English, Yale University;* b. 13 March 1958, St Kitts, West Indies; ed The Queen's Coll., Oxford; Writer-in-Residence, The Factory Arts Centre, London 1980–82, Univ. of Mysore, India 1987, Univ. of Stockholm 1989; visiting writer, Amherst Coll., Mass., USA 1990–92, Writer-in-Residence and Co-Dir Creative Writing Center 1992–94, Prof. of English 1994–97, Prof. of English and Writer-in-Residence 1997–98; Prof. of English and Henry R. Luce Prof. of Migration and Social Order, Barnard Coll., Columbia Univ., New York 1998–2005, Dir of Initiatives in the Humanities 2003–05; Prof. of English, Yale Univ. 2005–; writing instructor, Arvon Foundation, UK 1983–; Visiting Prof. of Humanities, Univ. of W Indies, Barbados 1999–2000; Exec. Sec., N American Network of Cities of Asylum 2005–; Consultant Ed. Faber Inc., Boston 1992–94; Contributing Ed. Bomb Magazine, New York 1993–; Consultant Ed. Graywolf Press, Minneapolis 1994–; Dir Heartland Productions Ltd 1994–2000; Advisory Ed. Wasifiri Magazine, London 1995–; Series Ed. Faber and Faber, London 1996–2000; mem. Arts Council of GB Drama Panel 1982–85, British Film Inst. Production Bd 1985–88, Bd, The Bush Theatre, London 1985–89; mem. English PEN 1997, Writers' Guild (UK) 1997, American PEN, council mem. 1998; Hon. Sr mem. Univ. of Kent 1988–; Fellow New York Public Library 2002–03; Hon. AM (Amherst Coll.) 1995; Hon. DUniv (Leeds Metropolitan) 1997, (York) 2003; Hon. DLitt (Leeds) 2003; Hon. MA (Yale) 2006; British Council 50th Anniversary Fellowship 1984, Guggenheim Fellowship 1992; Lannan Literary Award 1994. *Films:* Playing Away 1986, The Mystic Masseur 2001. *Plays:* Strange Fruit 1980, Where There is Darkness 1982, The Shelter 1983. *Radio:* plays: The Wasted Years (BBC Giles Cooper Award for Best Radio Play of the Year) 1984, Crossing the River 1985, The Prince of Africa 1987, Writing Fiction 1991, A Kind of Home 2004, Hotel Cristobel 2005; several documentaries. *Television:* The Final Passage (Channel 4) 1996. *Publications:* fiction: The Final Passage (Malcolm X Prize for Literature) 1985, A State of Independence 1986, Higher Ground 1989, Cambridge (Sunday Times Young Writer of the Year Award) 1991, Crossing the River (James Tait Black Memorial Prize) 1993, The Nature of Blood 1997, A Distant Shore (Commonwealth Writers Prize 2004) 2003, Dancing in the Dark 2005; non-fiction: The European Tribe (Martin Luther King Memorial Prize) 1987, The Atlantic Sound 2000, A New World Order: Selected Essays 2001, Foreigners: three English lives 2007; editor: Extravagant Strangers 1997, The Right Set: A Tennis Anthology 1999. *Leisure interests:* golf, running. *Address:* c/o Georgia Garrett, A.P. Watt Ltd, 20 John Street, London, WC1N 2DR, England (office). *Telephone:* (20) 7282-3106 (office). *Fax:* (20) 7282-3142 (office). *E-mail:* apw@apwatt.co.uk (office). *Website:* www.carylphillips.com.

PHILLIPS, Charles E., Jr, BS, MBA, JD; American business executive; *President, Oracle Corporation;* ed USAF Acad., Hampton Univ., New York Law School; served as Capt. in US Marine Corps; with Morgan Stanley –2003; joined Oracle in 2003, currently mem. Bd of Dirs and Pres. Oracle Corpn, responsible for global field operations, including consulting, marketing, sales, alliances and channels, and customer programmes; mem. Bd of Dirs Jazz at Lincoln Center, New York City, American Museum of Natural History, New York Law School, Viacom Inc., Morgan Stanley. *Address:* Oracle Corpn, 500 Oracle Parkway, Redwood City, CA 94065-1675, USA (office). *Telephone:* (650) 506-7000 (office). *Fax:* (650) 506-7200 (office). *E-mail:* info@oracle.com (office). *Website:* www.oracle.com (office).

PHILLIPS, David, OBE, PhD, FRSC; British scientist and academic; *Hofmann Professor Chemistry, Imperial College, London;* b. 3 Dec. 1939, Kendal, Westmorland (now Cumbria); s. of Stanley Phillips and Daphne Ivy Phillips (née Harris); m. Caroline L. Scoble 1970; one d.; ed South Shields Grammar Tech. School and Univ. of Birmingham; Postdoctoral Fellow and Fulbright Scholar, Univ. of Tex., USA 1964–66; Visiting Scientist, Acad. of Sciences of USSR 1966–67; Lecturer, Dept of Chem., Univ. of Southampton 1967–73, Sr Lecturer 1973–76, Reader 1976–80; Wolfson Prof. of Natural Philosophy, Royal Institution of GB 1980–89, Acting Dir 1986, Deputy Dir 1986–89; Prof. of Physical Chem., Imperial Coll. of Science, Tech. and Medicine 1989–, Head Dept of Chem. 1992–2002, Hofmann Prof. of Chem. 1999–, Dean of Life Sciences and Physical Sciences faculties 2002–05, Sr Dean 2005–; Spinks Lecturer, Univ. of Sask. 1979; Wilsmore Fellow, Univ. of Melbourne 1983–90; Vice-Pres. and Gen. Sec. BAAS 1987–89, Nyholm Lecturer, Royal Soc. of Chem. 1994, Chair. London Gifted and Talented 2004–; Faraday Award for Public Understanding of Science, Royal Soc. 1997. *Publications:* Time-Correlated Single-Photon Counting 1984, Polymer Photophysics 1985, Time-Resolved Laser Raman Spectroscopy 1987, Jet Spectroscopy and Dynamics 1994. *Leisure interests:* music, theatre, popularization of science. *Address:* Department of Chemistry, Imperial College, Exhibition Road, London, SW7 2AZ (office); 195 Barnett Wood Lane, Ashtead, Surrey, KT21 2LP, England (home). *Telephone:* (20) 7594-5716 (office); (1372) 274385 (home). *E-mail:* d.phillips@imperial.ac.uk (office); dclphillips@tecres.net (office). *Website:* www.ch.ic.ac.uk (office).

PHILLIPS, Dwight; American track and field athlete; b. 1 Oct. 1977, Decatur, Ga; m. Valerie Phillips 2004; ed Univ. of Ky, Ariz. State Univ.; started out in triple jump before switching to long jump; gold medal World Indoor and Outdoor Championships 2003; gold medal Athens Olympics 2004; gold medal World Outdoor Championships 2005. *Address:* c/o USA Track and Field, One RCA Dome, Suite 140, Indianapolis, IN 46225, USA.

PHILLIPS, Sir Fred Albert, Kt, CVO, MCL, QC; Saint Vincent and the Grenadines barrister; b. 14 May 1918; s. of Wilbert A. Phillips; ed London Univ., McGill Univ.; called to Bar, Middle Temple 1956; legal clerk to Attorney-Gen. of St Vincent 1942–45; Prin. Officer, Secr. 1945–47; Chief Clerk, Gov.'s Office, Windward Island 1948–49, Distr. Officer/Magistrate of District III 1949–53; magistrate, Grenada and Commr of Carriacou 1953–56; Asst Admin. and mem. Exec. Council, Grenada 1957–58; Sr Asst Sec., Secr. Fed. of W Indies 1958–60, Perm. Sec. (Sec. to Cabinet) 1960–62; Acting Admin. of Montserrat 1961–62; Sr lecturer Univ. of W Indies and Sr resident tutor, Dept of Extramural Studies, Barbados 1962–63; Sr Asst Registrar Coll. of Arts and Science, Univ. of W Indies 1963–64; Sr research fellow, Faculty of Law and Centre for Developing Area Studies, McGill Univ. 1964–65; Admin. of St Christopher 1966–67, Gov. St Christopher and Nevis 1967–69; Chief Legal Adviser and Special Rep. of Cable & Wireless in the Caribbean 1969–97; Hon. LLD (W Indies) 1989. *Publications:* Freedom in the Caribbean: A Study in Constitutional Change 1977, The Evolving Legal Profession in the Commonwealth 1978, West Indian Constitutions: Post-Independence Reforms 1985, Caribbean Life and Culture: A Citizen Reflects 1991, Commonwealth Caribbean Constitutional Law 2002, Ethics of the Legal Profession 2004; numerous papers in journals. *Leisure interests:* bridge, reading, legal writing. *Address:* PO Box 3298, St John's, Antigua. *Telephone:* 461-3683 (office); 461-3683 (home). *Fax:* 463-0350 (office); 463-0350 (home). *E-mail:* fredp@candw.ag (home).

PHILLIPS, John Harber, AC, LLB; Australian judge, author and professor of law; *Provost, Sir Zelman Cowen Centre, Victoria University;* b. 18 Oct. 1933, Melbourne; s. of Anthony Phillips and I. Muriel Phillips; m. Helen Rogers 1962; two s. one d.; ed Presentation Convent, De La Salle Coll. and Univ. of Melbourne; mem. Bar of Victoria 1959–84; QC 1975; Judge, Supreme Court of Victoria 1984–90; Judge, Fed. Court of Australia 1990–91; Chief Justice of Supreme Court of Victoria 1991–2003; Provost Sir Zelman Cowen Centre, Victoria Univ. 2004–; Chair. Nat. Inst. of Forensic Science, Attorney-Gen.'s Council of Law Reform, Victoria Police Forensic Centre Advisory Group, Community Grants Council; Pres. French Australian Lawyers' Asscn; Hellenic Distinction 1992, 2000; Hon. LLD (VUT). *Publications:* Forensic Science and the Expert Witness (jtly), Advocacy with Honour, The Trial of Ned Kelly; plays: By a Simple Majority – The Trial of Socrates, Conference with Counsel, The Cab-Rank Rule, The Eureka Advocates, Starry Night with Cypresses – the Last Hours of Vincent Van Gogh 2003; poetry: Wounds 2000, Lament for an Advocate 2005; play: Starry Night with Cypresses, The Last Hours of Vincent Van Gogh 2003. *Address:* Sir Zelman Cowen Centre, Victoria University, Level 2, 295 Queen Street, Melbourne 3000, Australia (office). *Telephone:* (3) 9919-1818 (office). *Fax:* (3) 9919-1817 (office). *E-mail:* cowen.centre@vu.edu.au (office). *Website:* www.vu.edu.au/szcc (office).

PHILLIPS, Leon Francis, PhD, ScD; New Zealand scientist, academic and novelist; *Professor of Chemistry, University of Canterbury;* b. 14 July 1935; m. Pamela A. Johnstone 1959; two s.; ed Westport Tech. Coll., Christchurch Boys' High School, Univs of Canterbury (NZ) and Cambridge Univ.; Upper Atmosphere Chem. Group, McGill Univ. 1961; lecturer, Univ. of Canterbury 1962, Prof. of Chem. 1966–; Pres. NZ Inst. of Chemistry 2001; Visiting Prof. Univ. of Washington 1968, Monash Univ. 1969, Univ. of Perugia 2000; Visiting Fellow, Balliol Coll. Oxford 1975, Japan Soc. for Promotion of Science 1984; Visiting Scholar, Rice Univ., Houston 1987; SERC Research Fellow Univ. Birmingham 1989; Harkness Fellow 1968; Fulbright Award 1980; Corday-Morgan Medal (Royal Soc. of Chem.), Hector Medal, (Royal Soc. of NZ), Easterfield and ICI prizes (NZ Inst. of Chem.), Univ. of Canterbury Research Medal 1999. *Publications:* Basic Quantum Chemistry, Electronics for Experimenters, Chemistry of the Atmosphere (with M. J. McEwan), First Year Chemistry (with J. M. Coxon and J. E. Fergusson); over 200 scientific papers; novels: Fire in His Hand 1978, The Phoenix Reaction 1979, Ritual Fire Dance 1980. *Leisure interests:* sailing, skiing, reading, writing. *Address:* University of Canterbury, Private Bag 4800, Christchurch 1 (office); 12 Maidstone Road, Christchurch 4, New Zealand (home). *Telephone:* 366-7001. *Fax:* 364-2999. *E-mail:* enquiries@regy.canterbury.ac.nz (office). *Website:* www.canterbury.ac.nz (office).

PHILLIPS, Leslie Samuel, OBE, CBE; British actor, producer and director; b. 20 April 1924, Tottenham, London; m. four c.; ed Chingford School; early career as child actor; fmr army officer; Vice-Pres. Royal Theatrical Fund, Disabled Living Foundation; Evening Standard Lifetime Achievement in Films Award 1997, Dilys Powell Award, London Film Critics' Circle Awards 2007. *Theatre includes:* Falstaff in The Merry Wives of Windsor (RSC), On the Whole Life's Been Jolly Good (Edin. Festival), Love for Love, Naked Justice, For Better or Worse, Ghosts of Albion, Charley's Aunt, Camino Real, Deadly Game, Diary of a Nobody, Man Most Likely To..., Passion Play, Naked Justice. *Films include:* Lassie From Lancashire (uncredited) 1938, The Citadel (uncredited) 1938, Train of Events 1949, The Woman with No Name 1950, Pool of London 1951, The Galloping Major (uncredited) 1951, The Sound Barrier 1952, Time Bomb (uncredited) 1953, The Fake 1953, The Limping Man 1953, You Know What Sailors Are 1954, Value for Money 1955, As Long as They're Happy 1955, High Flight 1956, The Gamma People 1956, Just My Luck 1957, The Barretts of Wimpole Street 1957, Brothers in Law 1957, Les Girls 1957, The Smallest Show on Earth 1957, I Was Monty's Double 1958, The Big Money 1958, This Other Eden 1959, Please Turn Over 1959, The Night We Dropped a Clanger 1959, The Navy Lark 1959, The Man Who Liked Funerals 1959, The Angry Hills 1959, Carry on Nurse 1959, Carry on Teacher 1959, Ferdinando I. re di Napoli (Ferdinand I: King of Naples) 1959, Watch Your Stern 1960, No Kidding 1960, Inn for Trouble 1960, Carry on Constable 1960, Doctor in Love 1960, Raising the Wind 1961, In the Doghouse 1961, Very Important Person 1961, A Weekend with Lulu 1962, Crooks Anonymous 1962, The Fast Lady 1962, Father Came Too! 1963, You Mus Be Joking! 1965, Doctor in Clover 1966, Maroc 7 (also producer) 1967, Some Will, Some Won't 1969, Doctor in Trouble 1970, The Magnificent Seven Deadly Sins 1971, Don't Just Lie There, Say Something 1973, Not Now Darling 1973, Not Now, Comrade 1976, Spanish Fly 1976, Out of Africa 1985, Empire of the Sun 1987, Scandal 1989, Mountains of the Moon 1990, King Ralph 1991, Carry on Columbus 1992, August 1996, Caught in the Act (video) 1997, The Jackal 1997, Gex: Enter the Gecko (video game; voice) 1998, The Orgasm Raygun 1998, Saving Grace 2000, Lara Croft – Tomb Raider 2001, Harry Potter and the Philosopher's Stone (voice) 2001, Arthur's Amazing Things 2002, Thunderpants 2002, Harry Potter and the Chamber of Secrets (voice) 2002, Collusion 2003, Doctor in Trouble, Pool of London, Churchill: The Hollywood Years 2004, Colour Me Kubrick 2005, With Shadows, Venus 2006. *Radio:* numerous plays including Navy Lark, Les Miserables, Tales From the Backbench, Round the World in 80 Days, Wind in the Willows. *Television includes:* Impasse 1963, Our Man at St. Mark's (series) 1963, The Time and Motion Man 1965, Foreign Affairs (series) 1966, The Suit 1969, The Culture Vultures (series) 1970, Casanova '73 (series) 1973, Monte Carlo 1986, Reluctant Debutante, A Very Fine Line, Casanova 74 (series), You'll Never See Me Again, Rumpole, Summer's Lease (mini-series) 1989, Chancer (series) 1990, The Trials of Oz 1991, Royal Celebration 1993, Two Golden Balls 1994, The Changeling 1994, Bermuda Grace 1994, Honey for Tea (series) 1994, Lovejoy, Boon, The House of Windsor (series) 1994, Love on the Branch Line (mini-series) 1994, Vanity Dies Hard 1995, The Canterville Ghost 1996, Die Katze von Kensington 1996, Das Karussell des Todes 1996, Der Blinde 1996, The Pale Horse 1997, Dalziel and Pascoe: Recalled to Life 1999, Cinderella 2000, Take a Girl Like You 2000, Sword of Honour 2001, Ghosts of Abion: Legacy (voice) 2003, Revolver (series) 2004, Into the Void, Tales of the Crypt, Who Bombed Birmingham?, Holby City, Midsomer Murders, Where the Heart Is, Heartbeat, Marple: By the Pricking of My Thumbs 2006. *Publication:* Hello: The Autobiography 2006. *Leisure interests:* restoring property, chess, poker, racing, gardening. *Address:* c/o Jonathan Lloyd, Curtis Brown Ltd, Haymarket House, 28–29 Haymarket, London, SW1Y 4SP, England (office); Hobson's International, 62 Chiswick High Road, London, W4 1SY, England (office); 78 Maida Vale, London, W9 1PR, England (home). *Telephone:* (20) 7393-4400 (office); (20) 8995-3628 (office); (20) 7624-5975 (home). *Fax:* (20) 7393-4401 (office); (20) 8995-5350 (office); (20) 7624-1250 (home). *E-mail:* info@curtisbrown.co.uk (office). *Website:* www.curtisbrown.co.uk (office); www.hobsons-international.com (office).

PHILLIPS, (Mark) Trevor, OBE, BSc, ARCS, FRSA; British journalist, broadcaster and public servant; *Chair, Equality and Human Rights Commission;* b. 31 Dec. 1953; s. of George Milton Phillips and Marjorie Eileen Canzius; m. Asha Bhownagary 1981; two d.; ed Queens' Coll., Georgetown, Guyana, Imperial Coll., London; Pres. Nat. Union of Students 1978–80; researcher London Weekend TV 1980–81, producer Black on Black, The Making of Britain 1981–86, Ed. London Programme 1987–92 (presenter 1987–2000), Head of Current Affairs 1992–94; reporter This Week, Thames TV 1986–87; presenter, Crosstalk 1994–2000, The Material World 1998–2000; Dir Pepper Productions 1994–; mem. and Chair. London Ass., GLA 2000–03; columnist, The Independent 1997–99; Chair. Runnymede Trust 1993–98, Hampstead Theatre 1993–97, London Arts Bd 1997–2000; Chair. or Deputy Chair. London Ass. 2000–03; Chair. Comm. for Racial Equality 2003–06, Equality and Human Rights Comm. 2006–; Hon. DLitt (Westminster, South Bank, Warwick, York, City Univ., Luton, Open Univ.); Hon. MU (London Metropolitan); Journalism Award, Royal TV Soc. 1988, 1993, 1998. *Television:* several series and productions including The London Programme, Windrush. *Publication:* Windrush: The Irresistible Rise of Multi-Racial Britain 1998, Britian's Slave Trade 1999. *Leisure interests:* music, reading, running, crosswords. *Address:* Equality and Human Rights Commission, 3 More London, Riverside, Tooley Street, London, SE1 2RG, England (office). *Telephone:* (20) 3117-0235 (office). *Fax:* (20) 7407-7557 (office). *E-mail:* chair@equalityhumanrights.com (office). *Website:* www.equalityhumanrights.com (office).

PHILLIPS, Owen Martin, PhD, FRS; American scientist, engineer and academic; *Decker Professor Emeritus of Science and Engineering and Research Professor, Department of Earth and Planetary Sciences, Johns Hopkins University;* b. 30 Dec. 1930, Parramatta, NSW, Australia; s. of Richard Keith Phillips and Madeline Constance (Lofts); m. Merle Winifred Simons 1953; two s. two d.; ed Univ. of Sydney, Australia and Univ. of Cambridge; ICI Fellow, Univ. of Cambridge 1955–57, Fellow, St John's Coll. 1957–60; Assoc. Prof., Johns Hopkins Univ., Baltimore, Md, USA 1960–63; Asst Dir of Research, Cambridge Univ. 1961–64; Prof. of Geophysical Mechanics and Geophysics, Johns Hopkins Univ. 1963–75, Chair. Dept of Earth and Planetary Sciences 1968–78, Decker Prof. of Science and Eng 1978–98, Decker Prof. Emer. and Research Prof. 1998–; Assoc. Ed., Journal of Fluid Mechanics 1964–95; mem. US Nat. Acad. of Eng; Hon. Fellow Trinity Coll. Cambridge, England 1997; Adams Prize, Cambridge Univ. 1965, Sverdrup Gold Medal, American Meteorological Soc. 1974. *Publications:* The Dynamics of the Upper Ocean 1966 (Russian edns 1969, 1979), The Heart of the Earth 1968, The Last Chance Energy Book 1979, Wave Dynamics and Radio Probing of the Ocean Surface (Ed.) 1985, Flow and Reactions in Permeable Rocks 1991; many research publs in the tech. literature. *Leisure interest:* sailing. *Address:* Department of Earth and Planetary Sciences, Johns Hopkins University, 126 Olin Hall, 34th and North Charles Streets, Baltimore, MD 21218; 23 Merrymount Road, Baltimore, MD 21210, USA. *Telephone:* (410) 516-7036 (office); (410) 433-7195 (home). *Fax:* (410) 516-7933. *E-mail:* omphil@aol.com (office). *Website:* www.jhu.edu/~eps/faculty/phillips/index.html (office).

PHILLIPS, Peter David, BSc, MSc, PhD; Jamaican economist, politician and academic; b. 28 Dec. 1949, Kingston; s. of Prof. Aubrey and Mrs Thelma Phillips; m. Sandra Minott; two s.; ed Univ. of the West Indies, State Univ. of NewYork, Binghampton, USA; Lecturer, Univ. of the West Indies 1981–89; Gen. Sec. People's Nat. Party 1991–94, Vice-Pres. 1998–2008; elected MP (People's Nat. Party) 1994 (re-elected 1997, 2002, 2007); Minister without Portfolio, Office of the Prime Minister 1993–94, Minister of Special Projects 1994–95, of Health 1995–97, of Transport and Works 1998–2001, of Nat. Security 2001–07, also Minister of Electoral Matters; Leader, House of Reps 1995–2007, Leader of Opposition Business 2007–08; mem. Electoral Advisory Cttee, Jt Select Cttee on Constitutional Reform. *Publications:* numerous works on Caribbean devt issues. *Address:* Belleville Consultants Limited, 26 Trafalgar Road, Kingston 10, Jamaica (office). *Telephone:* 926-2345 (office). *Fax:* 960-1944 (office). *E-mail:* belleconsults@gmail.com (office).

PHILLIPS, Ronald L., BS, MS, PhD; American scientist and academic; *Regents Professor and McKnight Presidential Chair in Genomics, University of Minnesota;* ed Purdue Univ., Univ. of Minn., Cornell Univ.; Prof., Univ. of Minn. 1967–, currently Regents Prof. and McKnight Presidential Chair in Genomics, fmr Dir Plant Molecular Genetics Inst. and Center for Microbial and Plant Genomics; specializes in plant biotechnology and genetics related to agric.; Chief Scientist, US Dept of Agric. 1996–98; fmr Pres. Crop Science Soc. of America; mem. NAS 1991, fmr Chair. Section on Plant, Soil and Microbial Sciences; mem. Scientific Advisory Bd Donald Danforth Plant Science Center; mem. Bd of Trustees, Int. Rice Research Inst. of the Philippines; Fellow (non-resident), Noble Foundation; Dr hc (Purdue Univ.); Purdue Univ. Agric. Distinguished Alumni Award, Dekalb Genetics Crop Science Distinguished Career Award, Wolf Foundation Prize in Agriculture 2007. *Publications:* over 70 chapters, 130 refereed journal articles and 300 abstracts. *Address:* Department of Agronomy and Plant Genetics, University of Minnesota, 411 Borlaug Hall, 1991 Upper Buford Circle, St Paul, MN 55108-6026, USA. *Telephone:* (612) 625-1213 (office). *Fax:* (612) 625-1268 (office). *E-mail:* phill005@umn.edu (office). *Website:* www.umn.edu (office).

PHILLIPS, Siân, CBE, FRSA, BA; British actress; b. 14 May 1934, Bettws, Carmarthenshire, Wales; d. of D. Phillips and Sally Phillips; m. 1st D. H. Roy 1954; m. 2nd Peter O'Toole (q.v.) 1960 (divorced 1979); two d.; m. 3rd Robin Sachs 1979 (divorced 1992); ed Pontardawe Grammar School, Univ. of Wales (Cardiff Coll.), RADA; child actress at BBC Radio Wales and BBC TV Wales; newsreader and announcer and mem. BBC repertory co. 1953–55; toured for Welsh Arts Council with Nat. Theatre Co. 1953–55; Arts Council Bursary to study drama outside Wales 1955; Royal TV Soc. annual televised lecture 1992; Vice-Pres. Welsh Coll. of Music and Drama; mem. Gorsedd of Bards (for services to drama in Wales) 1960; mem. Arts Council Drama Cttee for 5 years; Gov. St David's Trust; fmr Gov. Welsh Coll. of Music and Drama; Fellow Royal Soc. of Arts; Vice-Pres. Actors Benevolent Fund; Hon. Fellow, Univ. of Cardiff 1981, Polytechnic of Wales 1988, Univ. of Wales, Swansea 1998, Trinity Coll., Carmarthen; Hon. DLitt (Wales) 1984; many awards for work in cinema, theatre and on TV including BAFTA Wales Lifetime Achievement Award 2001. *Stage appearances include:* Hedda Gabler 1959, Ondine and The Duchess of Malfi 1960–61 (first RSC season at Aldwych), The Lizard on the Rock 1961, Gentle Jack, Maxibules and the Night of the Iguana 1964, Ride a Cock Horse 1965, Man and Superman and Man of Destiny 1966, The Burglar 1967, Epitaph for George Dillon 1972, A Nightingale in Bloomsbury Square 1973, The Gay Lord Quex 1975, Spinechiller 1978, You Never Can Tell, Lyric, Hammersmith 1979, Pal Joey, Half Moon and Albery Theatres 1980 and 1981, Dear Liar 1982, Major Barbara, Nat. Theatre 1982, Peg (musical) 1984, Love Affair 1984, Gigi 1986, Thursday's Ladies 1987, Brel (musical) 1987–88, Paris Match 1989, Vanilla 1990, The Manchurian Candidate 1991, Painting Churches 1992, Ghosts (Cardiff and touring, Wales) 1993, The Lion in Winter 1994, Marlene, An Inspector Calls, Broadway 1995, A Little Night Music, Royal Nat. Theatre 1995–96, Marlene 1996–97, int. tour 1998, concert tour Middle East 1999, Marlene, Broadway 1999, Lettice and Lovage 2001, Divas at The Donmar Season 2001, My Old Lady, Doolittle Theatre, Los Angeles 2002, Promenade Theatre, New York 2002–03, Nat. Tour The Old Ladies 2003, The Dark, Donmar, London 2004, Falling in Love Again, Cabaret, London, Europe, Israel, New York, continuing UK Tour. *Films include:* Becket 1963, Goodbye Mr. Chips (Critics' Circle Award, New York Critics' Award and Famous Seven Critics' Award 1969), Laughter in the Dark 1968, Murphy's War 1970, Under Milk Wood 1971, The Clash of the Titans 1979, Dune 1983, Ewok II, The Two Mrs Grenvilles, "Siân" (Cineclaire), Valmont 1988, Dark River 1990, The Age of Innocence 1993, House of America 1997, Coming and Going 2001, The Gigolos 2006. *Television appearances include:* Shoulder to Shoulder 1974, How Green was my Valley (BAFTA Award) 1975, I, Claudius (Royal Television Soc. Award and BAFTA Award 1978) 1976, Boudicca, Off to Philadelphia in the Morning 1977, The Oresteia of Aeschylus 1978, Crime and Punishment 1979, Tinker, Tailor, Soldier, Spy 1979, Sean O'Casey (RTE) 1980, Churchill: The Wilderness Years 1981, How Many Miles to Babylon 1982, Smiley's People 1982, George Borrow 1983, A Painful Case (RTE), Beyond All Reason, Murder on the Exchange, The Shadow of the Noose (BBC series) 1988, Snow Spider (HTV serial) 1988, Freddie & Max, Emlyn's Moon, Perfect Scoundrels 1990, Heidi 1992, The Borrowers (series) 1992, 1993, The Chestnut Soldier 1992, Huw Weldon TV Lecture 1993, Summer Silence (HTV musical), The Vacillations of Poppy Carew (BBC), Mind to Kill (TV film series), Ivanhoe (mini-series) 1997, The Scold's Bridle 1998, The Aristocrats (series) 1998, Alice Through the Looking Glass (feature film) 1998, Aristocrats (mini-series) 1999, Nikita 1999, The Magician's House 1999, 2000, Cinderella 2000, Attila (mini-series) 2001, The Last Detective, The Murder Room. *Recordings include:* Bewitched, Bothered and Bewildered, Pal Joey, Peg, I Remember Mama, Gigi, A Little Night Music 1990, A Little Night Music (2) 1995, Marlene 1996, Both Sides Now 2002. *Radio work includes:* Phédre, Oedipus, Henry VIII, Antony and Cleopatra, Bequest to a Nation, The Maids, Henry VIII, All's Well That Ends Well, Leopard in Autumn, Bridge of San Luis Rey, Ghosts, Dance to the Music of Time, Private Lives, The Visits. *Publication:* Needlepoint 1987, Private Faces (autobiog. vol. I) 1999, Public Places (autobiog. vol. II) 2001 (UK), 2003 (USA). *Leisure interests:* travelling, drawing. *Address:* c/o L. King, PDF, Drury House, 34–43 Russell Street, London, WC2B 5HA, England. *Telephone:* (20) 7344-1010 (office). *E-mail:* sianphillips@dircon.co.uk (home).

PHILLIPS, Tom, CBE, MA, NDD, RA, RE; British artist, writer and composer; b. 24 May 1937, London; s. of David John Phillips and Margaret Agnes Arnold; m. 1st Jill Purdy 1961 (divorced 1988), one s. one d.; m. 2nd Fiona Maddocks 1995, two step-d.; ed St Catherine's Coll., Oxford and Camberwell School of Art; one-man exhbns: A1A Galleries, Angela Flowers Gallery, Marlborough Fine Art and Waddingtons, London, Galerie Ba Ma, Paris; touring retrospective exhbn Serpentine Gallery, London, Gemeente Museum, The Hague, Kunsthalle, Basel 1975; 50 years of Tom Phillips, Angela Flowers Gallery, Mappin Art Gallery, Sheffield 1987, British Council Touring Exhibition Nat. Gallery, Australia 1988; retrospective exhbns: Nat. Portrait Gallery, London 1989, NC Museum of Art, USA 1990, Royal Acad., London 1992, Victoria & Albert Museum, London 1992, Univ. of Pennsylvania 1993, Yale Centre for British Art, USA 1994, Dulwich Picture Gallery 1998, South London Gallery 1998, Modern Art Museum, Forth Worth 2001, Flowers East 2004; publ. music scores 1965–; first performance opera IRMA, York Univ. 1973, revival ICA, London 1983 (CD 1986); collaborations with Jean-Yves Bosseur and John Tilbury on music works/performances 1970–84, Retrospective Concert ICA 1992; Music Works CD 1996, Six of Hearts CD 1997; worked with Peter Greenaway on TV version of Dante's Inferno, as published, translated and illustrated by the artist, broadcast 1990 (1st Prize Montreal TV Festival 1990, Italia Prize 1991); Curator exhbn "Africa: The Art of a Continent", Royal Acad. London, Gropius Bau, Berlin, Guggenheim Museum, New York 1995–96; stage design for A Winter's Tale 1997, Otello 1998, The Entertainer 2003; Vice-Chair. Copyright Council 1985–89; Trustee Nat. Portrait Gallery 1998, British Museum 2000; Chair. Royal Acad. Library, Frua Foundation 1997–2002; Chair. Exhbns Royal Acad; Pres. Heatherley's School of Fine Art 2004; Slade Prof. of Fine Art, Oxford Univ. 2005–06; mem. Royal Soc. of Painter-Etchers and Engravers; Hon. mem. Royal Soc. of Portrait Painters 1999, Pastel Soc. 2001, Hon. Fellow, The London Inst. 1999, St Catherine's Coll., Oxford, Leeds Univ. (Bretton Hall); John Moores Prize 1969, Frances Williams Memorial Prize, Victoria and Albert Museum 1983;. *Publications:* Trailer 1971, A Humument 1973, Works and Texts to 1974 1975, Dante's Inferno 1983, Heart of a Humument 1985, Where are They Now? The Class of

'47 1990, Works and Texts II 1992, Merely Connect (with Salman Rushdie) 1994, Africa: The Art of a Continent 1995, Aspects of Art 1997, Music in Art 1997, The Postcard Century 2000, We Are The People 2004, A Humument 2005, Merry Meetings 2005. *Leisure interests:* opera, ping pong. *Telephone:* (20) 7701-3978. *Fax:* (20) 7703-2800. *E-mail:* tom@tomphillips.co.uk (home). *Website:* www.tomphillips.co.uk (home).

PHILLIPS, Warren Henry, BA; American publisher and newspaper executive; b. 28 June 1926, New York City; s. of Abraham and Juliette Phillips; m. Barbara Anne Thomas 1951; three d.; ed Queens Coll.; Copyreader Wall Street Journal 1947–48, Foreign Corresp., Germany 1949–50, Chief, London Bureau 1950–51, Foreign Ed. 1951–53, News Ed. 1953–54, Man. Ed. Midwest Edition 1954–57, Man. Ed. Wall Street Journal 1957–65, Publr 1975–88; Exec. Ed. Dow Jones & Co. 1965–70; Vice-Pres. and Gen. Man. Dow Jones & Co. Inc. 1970–71, Editorial Dir 1971–88, Exec. Vice-Pres. 1972, Pres. 1972–79, CEO 1975–90, Chair. 1978–91, mem. Bd of Dirs 1972–97, Dir Emer. 1997–; Pres. American Council on Educ. for Journalism 1971–73; Co-Publr Bridge Works Publishing Co. 1992–; mem. Bd of Dirs Public Broadcasting Service 1991–97; Pres. American Soc. of Newspaper Eds 1975–76; mem. Pulitzer Prizes Bd 1977–87; Trustee, Columbia Univ. 1980–93, Trustee Emer. 1993–; mem. Visitors' Cttee Kennedy School of Govt, Harvard Univ. 1984–90, 1992–97; mem. Corp. Advisory Bd Queens Coll. 1986–90, Foundation Bd of Trustees 1990–97; Hon. LHD (Pace) 1982, (Queens Coll.) 1987, (Long Island) 1987; Hon. JD (Portland) 1973. *Publication:* China: Behind the Mask (with Robert Keatley) 1973. *Address:* Bridge Works Publishing, PO Box 1798, Bridge-hampton, NY 11932, USA (office). *Telephone:* (631) 537-3418. *Fax:* (631) 537-5092.

PHILLIPS, William D., BS, PhD; American physicist and academic; *Physicist, National Institute of Standards and Technology;* b. 5 Nov. 1948, Wilkes-Barre, Pa; s. of William Cornelius Phillips and Mary Catherine Phillips (née Savine); m. Jane Van Wynen 1970; two d.; ed Juniata Coll., Huntington, Massachusetts Inst. of Tech.; mem. tech. staff, Nat. Inst. of Standards and Tech., Gaithersburg, Md 1978–; Distinguished Univ. Prof., Univ. of Maryland 2001–06, Fellow, Jt Quantum Inst. 2006–; Eastman Prof., Univ. of Oxford, UK 2002–03; mem. NAS; Fellow, American Physical Soc., American Acad. of Arts and Sciences; Fellow and Hon. Mem. Optical Soc. of America; Hon. DSc (Williams Coll.) 1998, (Juniata Coll.) 1999, Dr hc (Universidad de Buenos Aires) 1998; shared Nobel Prize for Physics for developing methods of cooling matter to very low temperatures using lasers 1997, Schawlow Prize in Laser Sciences 1998, Pennsylvania Soc. Gold Medal 1999, Service to America Medal, Career Achievement Award 2006. *Publications:* Laser Cooling and Trapping of Neutral Atoms (Nobel Lecture, published in Reviews of Modern Physics, Vol. 70, pp. 721–741 1998); numerous scientific papers in professional journals. *Address:* National Institute of Standards and Technology, 100 Bureau Drive, Stop 8424, Gaithersburg, MD 20899, USA (office). *Telephone:* (301) 975-6554 (office). *E-mail:* william.phillips@nist.gov (office); william.phillips@physics.umd.edu (office). *Website:* www.physics.umd.edu/amo (office); www.nist.gov (office).

PHILLIPS, Zara Anne Elizabeth, MBE; British professional equestrian; b. 15 May 1981, London; d. of Capt. Mark Phillips and HRH The Princess Anne, Princess Royal; grand-daughter of HRH Queen Elizabeth II; ed Exeter Univ.; victories include Individual Gold Medal, European Eventing Championship 2005, Gold Team Medal; Individual Gold Medal, World Equestrian Games 2006, Silver Team Medal, named Eventing World Champion (third rider in historym to hold both European and World titles simultaneously); rides horse ToyTown; fmr Pres. Club 16-24, Cheltenham Racetrack; Eventing European Champion 2005, Sunday Times Sportswoman of the Year Award 2005, Eventing World Champion 2006, BBC Sports Personality of the Year Award 2006, Equestrian Olympic Athlete of the Year 2006, British Equestrian Writers' Asscn Personality of the Year 2006. *Address:* Gatcombe Park, Minchinhampton, Stroud, Glos., GL6 9AT, England.

PHILLIPS OF WORTH MATRAVERS, Baron (cr. 1999) of Belsize Park in the London Borough of Camden; **Nicholas Addison Phillips,** Kt, MA, PC; British judge; *Lord Chief Justice of England and Wales;* b. 21 Jan. 1938; s. of Michael Pennington Phillips and Dora Hassid; m. Christylle Marie-Therese Rouffiac 1972; two d. one step-d. one step-s.; ed Bryanston School, King's Coll. Cambridge; called to the Bar 1962; in practice 1962–87; Jr Counsel to Ministry of Defence and Treasury 1973–78; QC 1978; Recorder 1982–87; Judge, Queen's Bench Div., High Court of Justice 1987–95; Lord Justice of Appeal 1995–98; Chair. BSE Inquiry 1998–2000; Lord of Appeal in Ordinary 1999–2000; Master of the Rolls 2000–05; Lord Chief Justice of England and Wales 2005–; Chair. Law Advisory Cttee, British Council 1991–97; Chair. Council of Legal Educ. 1992–97; Vice-Pres. British Maritime Law Asscn 1993–; Gov. Bryanston School 1975–, Chair. of Govs 1981–; Hon. Fellow, Soc. for Advanced Legal Studies 1999, American Coll. of Trial Lawyers 2002–; King's Coll. Cambridge 2003; Hon. LLD (Exeter) 1998, (Birmingham) 2003, (London) 2004; Hon. DCL (City Univ.) 2003. *Leisure interests:* sea, mountains. *Address:* Royal Courts of Justice, The Strand, London, WC2A 2Ll, England (office). *Telephone:* (20) 7947-6776 (office). *Website:* www.parliament.uk/about_lords/about_lords.cfm (office).

PHILLIS, Sir Robert Weston, Kt, BA, FRSA, FRTS; British media executive; b. 3 Dec. 1945, Croydon; s. of Francis W. Phillis and Gertrude G. Phillis; m. Jean Derham 1966; three s.; ed John Ruskin Grammar School and Univ. of Nottingham; apprentice, printing industry 1961–65; Thomson Regional Newspapers Ltd 1968–69; British Printing Corpn Ltd 1969–71; lecturer in industrial relations, Univ. of Edin. and Scottish Business School 1971–75; Visiting Fellow, Univ. of Nairobi 1974; Personnel Dir, later Man. Dir Sun Printers Ltd 1976–79; Man. Dir Independent TV Publs Ltd 1979–82; Man. Dir Cen. Independent TV PLC 1981–87, Dir (non-exec.) 1987–91; Group Man. Dir Carlton Communications PLC 1987–91; Chief Exec. Independent TV News (ITN) 1991–93; Man. Dir BBC World Service 1993–94, Deputy Dir-Gen. BBC 1993–97, Chair. BBC Worldwide 1994–97; Chief Exec. Guardian Media Group 1997–2006, Non-Exec. Dir 2006–; Chair. ITV Network Programming Cttee 1984–86, ITV Film Purchase Group 1985–87, Zenith Productions 1984–91, Trader Media Group Ltd 2001–, All3 Media 2004–; Dir (non-exec.) ITN Ltd 1982–87, ITV 2005–07; Dir and Trustee TV Trust for the Environment, Teaching Awards Trust 2001–; Vice-Chair. (Int.), Int. Council, Nat. Acad. of TV Arts and Sciences 1994–97 (Life Fellow), (Dir 1985–93); Vice-Pres. European Broadcasting Union 1996–97; Hon. Prof. Univ. of Stirling 1997; Fellow Royal Television Soc. 1993 (Chair. 1989–92, Vice-Pres. 1994, currently Pres.); Trustee Nat. Film and TV School Foundation; Hon. DLitt (Salford Univ.) 1999; Hon. DLit (City Univ.) 2000; Hon. DLitt (Nottingham Univ.) 2003. *Leisure interests:* news, skiing, golf, military and political history. *Address:* c/o Guardian Media Group, 75 Farringdon Road, London, England (office). *E-mail:* bob.phillis@gmgplc.co.uk (office).

PHILO, Phoebe; British fashion designer; *Creative Director, Celine;* b. 1973, Paris, France; m. Max Wigram; two c.; ed Central St Martin's Fashion Coll.; grew up in London suburb; invited to work at Chloé, Paris (part of Swiss-based Richemont Group) working as Asst to Stella McCartney 1997–2001, Creative Dir 2001–06 (resgnd); presented first collection for Spring/Summer 2002; Creative Dir, Celine 2008–; Designer of the Year, British Fashion Awards 2004. *Address:* c/o Celine, 23–25 rue du Pont Neuf, 75001 Paris, France (office). *Telephone:* 1-55-80-12-12 (office). *Website:* www.celine.com (office).

PHOENIX, Joaqin Rafael; American actor; b. 27 Oct. 1974, Puerto Rico; s. of John Bottom Amram and Arlyn Dunitz Jochebed; brother of the late River Phoenix. *Films include:* SpaceCamp 1986, Russkies 1987, Parenthood 1989, Walking the Dog 1991, To Die For 1995, Inventing the Abbotts 1997, U Turn 1997, Return to Paradise 1998, Clay Pigeons 1998, 8MM 1999, The Yards 2000, Gladiator 2000, Quills 2000, Buffalo Soldiers 2001, Signs 2002, It's All About Love 2003, Brother Bear 2003, The Village 2004, Hotel Rwanda 2004, Ladder 49 2004, Walk the Line 2005 (Golden Globe Award for Best Performance by Actor in a Musical or Comedy 2006), We Own the Night 2007, Reservation Road 2007. *Television includes:* Backwards: The Riddle of Dyslexia 1984, Kids Don't Tell 1985, Morningstar/Eveningstar 1986, Secret Witness 1988. *Address:* c/o The Endeavour Agency, 9601 Wilshire Blvd, 10th Floor, Beverly Hills, CA, USA. *Telephone:* (310) 248-2000 (office). *Fax:* (310) 248-2020 (office).

PHOMMAHAXAY, Phanthong; Laotian diplomatist; b. 2 March 1941, Vientiane; m. Amphanh Phommahaxay (née Luangrath); three s. one d.; ed Nat. Centre for Political Studies, Vientiane; joined Ministry of Foreign Affairs 1962, Head Passport and Political Sections 1968–73, Dir NGO Section, Dept for Int. Orgs 1978–80, Deputy Dir-Gen., then Dir-Gen. Press Dept 1984–90, Dir-Gen. Asia Pacific and Africa Dept 1994–95; Attaché in Beijing, People's Repub. of China 1965–68; Second Sec., First Sec. then Chargé d'affaires in Paris, France 1974–78; First Sec., then Deputy Head of Mission to Thailand, Bangkok 1980–84; Amb. to Indonesia 1990–94, to Australia and New Zealand 1995–98, to Germany, The Netherlands, Switzerland and Austria 1998–2001, to USA 2002–07. *Leisure interests:* reading, golf. *Address:* c/o Ministry of Foreign Affairs, rue That Luang 01004, Ban Phonxay, Vientiane, Laos. *Telephone:* (21) 413148. *Fax:* (21) 414009. *E-mail:* cabinet@mofa.gov.la. *Website:* www.mofa.gov.la.

PHOSA, Nakedi Mathews, LLB; South African lawyer, business executive and politician; *Treasurer, African National Congress (ANC);* b. 1 Sept. 1952, Mbombela township, Nelspruit; m. Pinkie Phosa; three c.; ed Univ. of the North (Turfloop); articled clerk Godfrey Rabin Attorneys 1979–81; f. Nelspruit (first black-owned legal firm) 1981, Pnr 1981–85 (went into exile); fmr Nat. Organiser Black Lawyers' Asscn; fmr Head Legal Div., African Nat. Congress (ANC) Dept of Constitutional and Legal Affairs, mem. ANC Nat. Exec. Cttee 1999–, Treasurer ANC 2007–; fmr mem. Nat. Negotiations Comm.; Premier Mpumalanga regional govt 1994–99; Chair. (non-exec.) EOH 2003–; fmr Chair. (non-exec.) Atos KPMG Consulting; Chair. Vuka Alliance (Pty) Ltd, Ruslyn Mining and Plant Hire (Pty) Ltd, African Legalnetwork (Pty) Ltd, Du Toit-Smuts & Phosa (attorneys), Zero Pollution (Pty) Ltd, BMW (Nelspruit dealership), Value Logistics Ltd, Technikon Southern Africa Council, SA Golden Leaf, Hans Merensky Holdings, Command Holdings Ltd, ABSA (Mpumalanga Region); Chair. Council Univ. of SA, Afrikaanse Handelsinstituut, Special Olympics SA; Acting Chancellor Mgwenya Training Coll. 1993, later Chancellor; Pres. Chambers of Commerce and Industry SA; Hon. PhD (Boston). *Address:* African National Congress, 54 Sauer Street, Johannesburg 201, South Africa (office). *Telephone:* (11) 3761000 (office). *Fax:* (11) 3761134 (office). *E-mail:* nmtyelwa@anc.org.za (office). *Website:* www.anc.org.za (office).

PHOSIKHAM, Chansy; Laotian politician; *Governor of Vientiane Province;* fmr Gov. Prov. of Luang Prabang; Gov. State Bank –2003; Minister of Finance 2003–07; Gov. Vientiane Prov. 2007–; mem. Seventh Party Cen. Cttee. *Address:* c/o Ministry of Finance, rue That Luang, Ban Phonxay, Vientiane, Laos (office).

PHOUPHET, Khamphounvong; Laotian central banker; *Governor, Bank of the Lao PDR;* Alt. Gov. for Laos, IFAD 2003, Asian Devt Bank –2007; Deputy Gov., then Gov. Bank of the Lao PDR 2006–. *Address:* Bank of the Lao PDR, rue Yonnet, BP 19, Vientiane, Laos (office). *Telephone:* (21) 213109 (office). *Fax:* (21) 213108 (office). *E-mail:* bol@pan-laos.net.la (office). *Website:* www.bol.gov.la (office).

PIANO, Renzo; Italian architect; b. 14 Sept. 1937, Genoa; s. of Carlo Piano and Rosa Odone; m. 1st Magda Ardnino 1962; two s. one d.; m. 2nd Emilia Rossato 1992; ed Milan Polytechnic School of Architecture; worked with Louis

I. Kahn, Phila, USA, Z.S. Makowsky, London 1965–70, with Richard Rogers (as Piano & Rogers) 1977–, with Peter Rice (as Atelier Piano & Rice) 1977–; currently has offices in Genoa, Paris, Berlin (Renzo Piano Bldg Workshop); Hon. Fellow Union Int. des Architectes 1978, AIA, 1981, RIBA, 1985, American Acad. of Arts and Letters 1994; Dr hc (Stuttgart) 1990, (Delft) 1992; Compasso d'Oro Award, Milan 1981, RIBA Gold Medal 1989, Kyoto Prize, Japan 1990, Neutra Prize, Pomona, Calif. 1991, Goodwill Amb. of UNESCO for Architecture 1994, Premio Michelangelo 1994, Art Prize of Akademie der Künste, Berlin 1995, Praemium Imperiale, Tokyo 1995, Erasmus Prize, Amsterdam 1995, The Pritzker Architecture Prize, Washington, DC 1998 and other prizes and awards; Commdr des Arts et des Lettres, Légion d'honneur, Cavaliere di Gran Croce, Officer, Ordre Nat. du Mérite. *Completed projects include:* office bldg for B&B, Como 1973, Georges Pompidou Centre, Paris 1977, IRCAM Inst. for Acoustic Research, Paris 1977, housing, Rigo Dist, Perugia 1982, office bldg for Olivetti, Naples 1984, office bldg for Lowara, Vicenza 1985, museum for Menil Collection, Houston, USA 1988, HQ for Light Metals Experimental Inst., Novara 1988, S. Nicola Football Stadium, Bari 1989, Underground stations for Ansaldo, Genoa 1990, Bercy commercial centre, Paris 1990, cruise ships for P&O 1991, housing, Paris 1991, Thomson factories, Guyancourt, France 1991, HQ for Credito Industriale Sardo, Cagliari 1992, Lingotto congress and concert hall, Turin 1994, Kansai Int. Airport, Osaka, Japan 1994, Meridien Hotel, Lingotto and Business Centre, Turin 1995, Harbour Authorities HQ, Genoa 1995, cinema, offices, contemporary art gallery, conf. centre, landscaping, Cité Int., Lyon 1996, Ushibuka Bridge, Kumamoto, Japan 1996, Museum of Science and Tech., Amsterdam 1997, Museum of Beyeler Foundation, Basel 1997, Debis Bldg HQ, Daimler Benz, Berlin 1997, Cultural Centre J.-M. Tjibao, Nouméa, New Caledonia 1998, Mercedes-Benz Design Centre, Stuttgart 1998, Daimler-Benz Potsdamer Platz project including Imax theatre, offices, housing, shops, Berlin 1998, Lodi Bank HQ, Milan 1998, Rome Auditorium 2003, Morgan Library extension, NY 2006, Broad Contemporary Art Museum, Los Angeles 2008. *Projects in progress include:* contemporary art gallery, Varnamö, Sweden, office block, Sydney, Australia, PTT Telecom office tower, Rotterdam, Harvard Univ. Art Gallery master plan, renovation and extension, HQ newspaper Il Sole/24 Ore, Milan Padre Pio Basilica Church, Puglia, Italy; work shown at exhbns Europe, USA, Australia, Japan 1967–, contracted for NY Times Bldg, Manhattan 2000, Whitney Museum; numerous lectures worldwide. *Publications:* author or co-author of 12 books on architecture. *Leisure interest:* sailing. *Address:* Renzo Piano Building Workshop, Via Rubens 29, 16158 Genoa, Italy; 34, rue des Archives, 75004 Paris, France. *Telephone:* (010) 61711 (Genoa). *Fax:* (010) 6171350 (Genoa).

PIĄTAS, Gen. Czesław; Polish army officer and politician; *Secretary of State, Ministry of National Defence;* b. 20 March 1946, Germany; m. Danuta Piątas; two c.; ed Armour Officer's School, Acad. of Gen. Staff, USSR, US Nat. War Coll., USA; began career in Polish Armed Forces 1968; served in variety of command and staff positions in armour units 1970s; Chief of Staff, Deputy Commdr of 10th Armoured Div. and Commdr of tank regiment 1980–82; apptd G-3 Dir Silesian Mil. Dist HQ 1982; Commdr 4th Mechanized Div.; Staff Position Silesian Mil. Dist. HQ 1993–94; Chief of Staff DCG, Warsaw Mil. Dist 1995–96; Chief of Operational and Strategic Div., Gen. Staff 1996–99; Deputy Chief of Gen. Staff of Polish Armed Forces 1999–2000, Chief of Gen. Staff Sept. 2000–06; Sec. of State, Ministry of Defence 2008–; apptd Brig.-Gen. 1992, Maj.-Gen. 1999, Lt-Gen. 2000, Gen. 2000. *Leisure interests:* mil. history, tennis. *Address:* Ministry of National Defence, ul. Klonowa 1, 00-909 Warsaw, Poland (office). *Telephone:* (22) 6280031 (office). *Fax:* (22) 8455378 (office). *E-mail:* bpimon@wp.mil.pl (office). *Website:* www.wp.mil.pl (office).

PIBULSONGGRAM, Nitya, MA; Thai diplomatist; b. 30 June 1941; s. of Field Marshal Pibul Songgram and Lady La-iad Bhandhukran; m. Pacharin Pibulsonggram 1965; ed Dartmouth Coll. and Brown Univ.; entered Foreign Service as Third Sec. Foreign News Div. Information Dept June 1968; served in fmr SEATO Div., Thailand's Int. Org. Dept 1969–72; Office of Sec. to Minister of Foreign Affairs 1973, Office of Under-Sec. of State, Policy Planning Div. 1974; Head Southeast Asia Div., Political Dept 1975; First Sec. Perm. Mission to UN 1976–79, Deputy Perm. Rep. 1979–80, Perm. Rep. 1988–96; Deputy Dir-Gen. Information Dept, Foreign Ministry 1980, Political Dept 1981; Amb.-at-Large 1982; Dir-Gen. Dept of Int. Org. 1983–88; Amb. to USA 1996–2001; Adviser and Special Envoy of the Minister of Foreign Affairs, 2002–06, Chief Negotiator for US-Thai Free Trade Agreement 2002–06, Minister of Foreign Affairs 2006–08; Chair. Thailand–US Educational Foundation (TUSEF); Trustee Kenan Inst. Asia; Knight Grand Cross, Order of White Elephant 1984, Special Grand Cordam, Order of Crown of Thailand 1988, Kt Commdr Order of Chula Chom Klao 2000. *Leisure interests:* tennis, golf, skiing. *Address:* c/o Ministry of Foreign Affairs, Thanon Sri Ayudhya, Bankok, Thailand (office).

PICADO, Sonia, LicenD; Costa Rican lawyer, international organization official, academic and fmr politician; *President, Inter-American Institute of Human Rights;* b. 20 Dec. 1936; d. of Antonio de Picado and Odile Sotela; m. (divorced); one s. one d.; ed Univ. of Costa Rica; Prof., Faculty of Law, Univ. of Costa Rica 1972–2003, Dean, Faculty of Law 1980–84, Cathedratical Chair. 1984; Co-Chair. Int. Comm. for Central American Recovery and Devt 1987–89; mem. Cttee of Jurists, World Conf. on Refugees, UNHCR, Geneva 1988–89; Prof., Inter-American Inst. of Human Rights 1985–, Exec. Dir 1988–94, currently Pres.; Vice-Pres. Inter-American Court of Human Rights 1988–94; Co-Chair. Inter-American Dialogue, Washington, DC 1993–94; Amb. to USA 1994–98; Head of UN Comm. of Inquiry on East Timor 1999–2000; mem. Legislative Ass. for San José 1999–2001; Pres. Nat. Liberation Party 1999–2001; mem. Legislative Ass. for San José; mem. Comm. on Human Security; Pres. UN Voluntary Fund for Victims of Torture; Trustee Equal Rights Trust; Dr hc (Elmhurst Coll., Chicago) 2000, (Univ. of Miami) 2002, (Colby Coll.) 2003; Max Planck/Humboldt Award (Germany) 1991, Leonidas Proaño Award (Ecuador) 1991, UN Prize in Human Rights 1993, UNDP Award 1995. *Publications:* Women and Human Rights 1986, Philosophical Fundamentals of Human Rights in Latin America 1987, Religion, Tolerance and Liberty: A Human Rights Perspective 1989, Peace, Development and Human Rights 1989. *Address:* Inter-American Institute of Human Rights, PO Box 10.081-1000, San José, Costa Rica (office). *Telephone:* 234-0404 (office). *Fax:* 234-0955 (office). *E-mail:* instituto@iidh.ed.cr (office). *Website:* www.iidh.ed.cr (office).

PICARD, Dennis J.; American business executive; *Chairman Emeritus, Raytheon Company;* b. 1932; m. Dolores M. Petit; five c.; ed Northeastern Univ.; Sr Vice-Pres., Gen. Man. Missile Systems Div. Raytheon Co., Lexington, Mass., 1985–89, Pres. 1989–90, Chair. 1990–99, CEO 1990–99 (also mem. Bd Dirs), Chair. Emer. 1999–; Pres. American Inst. of Aeronautics and Astronautics, Va 2001; mem. Defence Policy Advisory Cttee on Trade, Pres.'s Export Council; US Army's Order of Santa Barbara 1991; Nat. Security Industrial Asscn's Environmental Achievement Award 1996, Navy League of the United States Fleet Admiral Chester W. Nimitz Award 1997, Intrepid Museum Foundation's Intrepid Salute Award 1997, USAF Asscn John R. Allison Award 1997, Asscn of the US Army John W. Dixon Medal 1997, New England Council "New Englander of the Year" 1997, Ralph Lowell Distinguished Citizen Award, Boston Minuteman Council, Boy Scouts of America 1997, Nat. Defense Industrial Asscn Industrial Leadership Award 1998, Marine Corps Scholarship Foundation Semper Fidelis Award 1998, Navy League (New York Council) Rear Admiral John J. Bergen Leadership Medal for Industry 1998. *Address:* 1373 Monument Street, Concord, MA 01742, USA (home).

PICASSO, Paloma; French designer; b. 19 April 1949, Paris; d. of the late Pablo Ruiz-Picasso and Françoise Gilot; m. Rafael Lopez-Cambil (Lopez-Sanchez) 1978 (divorced 1998); m. 2nd Eric Thevennet 1999; ed Univ. of Paris, Sorbonne; studied jewellery design and manufacture; fashion jewellery for Yves St Laurent 1969; jewellery for Zolotas 1971, costumes and sets for Parisian theatre productions, L'Interprétation 1975, Succès 1978; created Paloma Picasso brand; creations designed by her for the Paloma Picasso brand include jewellery for Tiffany & Co. 1980, fragrance (Paloma Picasso 1984, Minotaure 1992, Tentations 1996) and cosmetics for L'Oréal, eyewear for Metzler Optik Partner AG, bone china, crystal, silverware and tiles for Villeroy & Boch, home linens for KBC, fabrics and wall coverings for Motif; pieces in perm. collections of Smithsonian Inst. (Washington, DC), Musée des Arts Décoratifs (Paris) and Die Neue Zamlang (Munich); f. Paloma Picasso Foundation, Lausanne, Switzerland; Council of Fashion Design of America (CFDA) Accessory Award 1989. *Film:* Contes immoraux 1974. *Address:* Paloma Picasso Foundation, c/o Piaget & De Mitri SA, Avenue Mon-Repos 14, 1000, Lausanne, Switzerland.

PICCOLI, Michel; French actor; b. 27 Dec. 1925, Paris; s. of Henri Piccoli; m. 1st Juliette Gréco 1966; m. 3rd Ludivine Clerc 1978; one s. from fmr m.; ed Collège d'Annel, Collège Sainte Barbe, Paris; Man. of the Théâtre de Babylone for two years before joining the Madeleine Renaud and Jean-Louis Barrault Theatre Co.; appeared in Phèdre at the Théâtre Nationale Populaire; jury mem. Cannes Film Festival 2007; Best Actor, Cannes 1980 (for Salto nel Vuoto), European Prize, Taormina Theatre, Sicily 2001; Chevalier Légion d'honneur, Ordre nationale du Mérite. *Films include:* Le point du jour 1946, Parfum de la dame en noire 1949, French Cancan 1955, The Witches of Salem 1956, Le mépris 1963, Diary of a Chambermaid 1964, De l'amour 1965, Lady L 1965, La curée 1965, Les demoiselles de Rochefort 1967, Un homme de trop 1967, Belle de jour 1967, Dillinger is Dead 1968, The Milky Way 1969, Topaz 1969, The Discreet Charm of the Bourgeoisie 1972, Themroc 1972, Blow-out 1973, The Infernal Trio 1974, Le fantôme de la liberté 1974, La faille 1975, Léonar 1975, Sept morts sur ordonnance 1976, La dernière femme 1976, Savage State 1978, Le divorcement 1979, Le saut dans le vide 1979, Le mors aux dents 1979, La città delle donne 1980, Salto nel Vuoto 1980, La passante du sans-souci 1982, Adieu Bonaparte 1985, The Night is Young 1986, L'homme voilé, Maladie d'amour, La rumba 1987, Y a bon les blancs, Blanc de Chine 1988, Milou en mai 1990, Martha et moi 1991, La belle noiseuse 1991, Les equilibristes, Le voleur d'enfants 1991, Le bal des cassepieds 1992, Archipel 1993, Rupture(s) 1993, L'Ange noir 1994, Les cent et une nuits 1995, 2 × 50 Years of French Cinema 1995, Compagna di Viaggio 1996, Beaumarchais l'insolent 1996, Généalogies d'un crime 1997, Alors voilà (dir) 1997, Rien sur Robert 1999, Compagne de voyage 2000, Les acteurs 2000, Je rentre à la maison 2001, La Plague noire 2001, Ce Jour-là 2003, Belle Toujours 2006, Jardins en Automne 2006. *Publication:* Dialogues égoistes 1976. *Leisure interests:* riding, flying. *Address:* 11 rue des Lions Saint-Paul, 75004 Paris, France.

PICEK, Lt-Gen. Vlastimil; Czech military officer; *Chief of General Staff;* b. 25 Oct. 1956, Turnov; m. Dagmar Picková; two c.; ed Mil. Acad., Brno, Czech Tech. Univ.; sr radio operator 1975–78; Deputy Battalion Commdr for Tech. Issues 1983–86, Sr Officer, Nat. Air Defence HQ 1986–89; Chief of Signal Br, Fourth Air Defence Corps HQ 1993–94; Section Chief Signal Br, Armed Forces Gen. Staff 1994–95, Deputy Chief 1995–96, Chief of Signal Br 1996–97, Chief of Operational-Tactical C2 Systems Dept 1997–2000, Chief of Command and Control Div. 2000–03; Security Dir, Ministry of Defence 2001–03; promoted to Brig. 2001; Chief of Mil. Office of Pres. 2003–07; promoted to Maj. Gen. 2003; promoted to Lt Gen. 2006; Chief of Gen. Staff 2007–; Cross of Merit of the Minister of Defence Third Grade, ACR Medal Third Grade, Nat. Service Medal, Hon. Commemorative Badge for Service in Peace Operation in the Balkans, NATO 50th Anniversary Medal. *Leisure interests:* tennis, skiing. *Address:* Office of the Chief of General Staff, Generální štáb AČR, Vítězné nám. 5, 160 01 Prague, Czech Republic (office). *Telephone:* 973216027 (office).

Fax: 973216084 (office). *E-mail:* kangs@army.cz (office). *Website:* www.army.cz (office).

PICHLER, Joseph A., PhD; American business executive; b. 3 Oct. 1939, St Louis, Mo.; s. of late Anton Pichler and Anita Pichler; m. Susan Eyerly 1962; two s. two d.; ed Notre Dame Univ. of Chicago, Univ. of Chicago; Dean Univ. of Kan. 1974–80; Exec. Vice-Pres. Dillon Companies Inc. 1980–82, Pres. 1982–84, Pres. and CEO 1984–86, CEO 1986–88; Exec. Vice-Pres. The Kroger Co. 1985–86, Pres. and COO 1986–90, Pres. and CEO 1990–2003, Chair. of Bd 1990–2004; Woodrow Wilson Fellow 1961, Ford Foundation Doctoral Fellow 1962–64, Standard Oil Industrial Relations Fellow 1964; mem. Cin. Business Comm. 1991–, Chair. 1997–98; Performance Award, US Dept of Labor Manpower Admin. 1969, William Booth Award, The Salvation Army 1998, Horatio Alger Award 1999, Distinguished Service Award, Nat. Conf. Cttee of Justice 2000. *Publications:* Inequality: The Poor and the Rich in America (with Joseph W. McGuire) 1969, Ethics, Free Enterprise and Public Policy (with Richard T. De George) 1978. *Leisure interests:* fly-fishing, music, reading. *Address:* c/o The Kroger Co., 1014 Vine Street, Cincinnati, OH 45202, USA (office).

PICKARD, Sir (John) Michael, Kt, FCA, CIMgt; British business executive; *Deputy Chairman, Epsom Downs Racecourse Ltd;* b. 29 July 1932, Banstead, Surrey; s. of the late John Stanley Pickard and of Winifred Joan Pickard; m. Penelope Jane Catterall 1959; one d. three s.; ed Oundle School; Finance Dir British Printing Corpn 1965–68, Man. Dir Trusthouses Ltd 1968–70, Trusthouse Forte Ltd 1970–71; Chair. Happy Eater Ltd 1972–86, Grattan PLC 1978–84, Courage Ltd and Imperial Brewing & Leisure Ltd 1981–86; CEO Sears PLC 1986–92; Chair. Freemans PLC 1988–92, Bullough PLC 1996–2002 (Dir 1995–), London Docklands Devt Corpn 1992–98, Servus Holdings Ltd 1997–2001, Nat. House-Building Council 1998–2002, London First Centre 1998–2001; Dir (non-exec) Brown Shipley Holdings PLC 1986–93, Electra Investment Trust PLC 1989–2002, Nationwide Bldg Soc. 1991–94, Pinnacle Clubs Ltd 1992–99, Bentalls PLC 1993–2001, United Racecourses (Holdings) Ltd 1995–02; mem. Bd London First 1992–2002 (Deputy Chair. 1998–03), Epsom Downs Racecourse Ltd (Deputy Chair. 2002–); mem. Cttee The Automobile Asscn 1994–99; Chair. Roedean School Council 1980–90, The Housing Forum 1999–2002, Freeport PLC 2001–03; Gov. Oundle School 1987–2000, Chair. Bd Govs 2004–; Hon. LLD (East London) 1997. *Leisure interests:* sport, education. *Address:* Kingsbarn, Tothill, Headley, Surrey, KT18 6PU, England (home). *Telephone:* (1372) 377331 (office). *Fax:* (1372) 363350 (home).

PICKENS, Thomas Boone, Jr, BS; American business executive; *Chairman and CEO, BP Capital Management LP;* b. 22 May 1928, Holdenville, Okla; s. of Thomas Boone Pickens and Grace Molonson Pickens; m. Beatrice L. Carr 1972 (divorced); m. Madeleine Pickens; ed Oklahoma State Univ.; geologist, Phillips Petroleum Co. 1951–55; Founder, Pres., Chair. Bd Mesa Petroleum Co., Amarillo, Tex. 1956–1996; Gen. Pnr, Mesa Inc. 1985–; Founder, Chair. and CEO BP Capital Man. LP (pvt. investment firm) 1997–; f. Pickens Fuel Corpn (now Clean Energy) 1997; mem. Nat. Petroleum Council 1970–; Founder and Chair. United Shareholders Asscn Washington 1986–93. *Publication:* Boone 1987. *Address:* BP Capital Management, LP, 8117 Preston Road, Suite 260, Dallas TX 75225, USA (office). *Telephone:* (214) 265-4165 (office). *Fax:* (214) 750-0216 (office). *E-mail:* info@bpcap.net (office). *Website:* www.bpcap.net (office).

PICKERING, Thomas Reeve, MA; American diplomatist and business executive; *Vice-Chairman, Hills and Company;* b. 5 Nov. 1931, Orange, NJ; s. of Hamilton Reeve Pickering and Sarah P. Chasteney; m. Alice Jean Stover 1955; one s. one d.; ed Bowdoin Coll., Brunswick, Maine, Fletcher School of Law and Diplomacy, Medford, Mass., Univ. of Melbourne, Australia; Lt Commdr USNR 1956–64; joined Dept of State 1959, Intelligence Research Specialist 1960, Foreign Affairs Officer 1961, Arms Control and Disarmament Agency 1961–62; mem. US Del. to Disarmament Conf., Geneva 1962–64; Prin. Officer, Zanzibar 1965–67; Deputy Chief of Mission, Dar es Salaam 1967–69; Deputy Dir Bureau of Politico-Mil. Affairs 1969–73; Exec. Sec. Dept of State, Special Asst to Sec. of State 1973–74; Amb. to Jordan 1974–78; Asst Sec. of State, Bureau of Oceans, Environment and Science 1978–81; Amb. to Nigeria 1981–83; Amb. to El Salvador 1983–85, to Israel 1985–88; Perm. Rep. to UN 1989–92, Amb. to India 1992–93, to Russia 1993–96; Under-Sec. of State for Political Affairs 1997–2000; named Career Amb.; Pres. Eurasia Foundation 1996–97; fmr Sr Vice-Pres. Int. Relations, The Boeing Co., now consultant; Vice-Chair. Hills and Co. 2006–. *Leisure interests:* archaeology, scuba, photography, carpentry. *Address:* Hills and Company, 901 15th Street, NW, Washington, DC 20006 (office); 2318 Kimbro Street, Alexandria, VA 22307-1822, USA (home). *Telephone:* (202) 822-4912 (office); (903) 660-8929 (home).

PICKETT, John Anthony, CBE, PhD, DSc, CChem, FRS, FRSC, FRES; British research chemist; *Head of Biological Chemistry Division, Rothamsted Research;* b. 21 April 1945, Leicester; s. of Samuel Victor Pickett and Lilian Frances Hoar; m. Ulla Birgitta Skålén 1970; one s. one d.; ed King Edward VII Grammar School, Coalville, Univ. of Surrey; Postdoctoral Fellowship, UMIST (organic chem.) 1970–72; Sr Scientist, Chem. Dept, Brewing Research Foundation, Surrey 1972–76; Prin. Scientific Officer, Dept of Insecticides and Fungicides, Rothamsted Experimental Station 1976–83, Individual Merit (Grade 2) and Head Dept Insecticides and Fungicides, (now Biological Chem. Div.), Inst. of Arable Crops Research (now Rothamsted Research) 1984–; Special Prof., Univ. of Nottingham 1991–; Pres. Int. Soc. of Chemical Ecology (ISCE) 1995; mem. Deutsche Akad. der Naturforscher Leopoldina 2001; Foreign mem. Royal Swedish Acad. of Agriculture and Forestry 2005; Hon. mem. Academic Staff Univ. of Reading 1995; Rank Prize for Nutrition and Crop Husbandry 1995, ISCE Medal 2002. *Research:* chemical ecology and insect pheromones in particular. *Publications:* over 300 papers, including patents. *Leisure interest:* jazz trumpet playing. *Address:* Biological Chemistry Division, Rothamsted Research, Harpenden, Herts., AL5 2JQ (office); 53 Parkfield Crescent, Kimpton, nr Hitchin, Herts., SG4 8EQ, England (home). *Telephone:* (1582) 763133 (ext. 2321) (office); (1438) 832832 (home). *Fax:* (1582) 762595. *E-mail:* john.pickett@bbsrc.ac.uk (office). *Website:* www.rothamsted.bbsrc.ac.uk (office).

PICKETT-HEAPS, Jeremy David, BA, PhD, FAA, FRS; Australian botanist and academic; *Professorial Fellow of Botany, University of Melbourne;* b. 5 June 1940, Bombay, India; m. 1st Charmian Scott 1964; one s. one d.; m. 2nd Julianne Francis 1978; two s.; ed Univ. of Cambridge; Prof., Dept of Molecular, Cellular and Developmental Biology, Univ. of Colo, Boulder, USA 1970–88; Prof. of Botany, Univ. of Melbourne 1988–, Professorial Fellow 2003–. *Publication:* Green Algae 1975; 180 research publs in refereed journals. *Address:* School of Botany, University of Melbourne, Parkville, Vic. 3052 (office); PO Box 1113, Carlton, Vic. 3053, Australia (home). *Telephone:* (3) 8344-4519 (office); (3) 9654-0300 (home). *Fax:* (3) 9349-3268 (office). *E-mail:* jeremyph@unimelb.edu.au (office). *Website:* www.cytographics.com (office).

PICULA, Tonino; Croatian politician and historian; b. 31 Aug. 1961, Mali Losinj; ed Zagreb Univ.; Assoc. Prof. and Sec. Kulturni Radnik (magazine), Cultural and Educ. Ass. 1987–89; mem. Exec. Cttee, Int. Sec. SDP of Croatia 1993–; Counsellor, SDP Co. Ass. of Zagreb, mem. Cttee for Int. Co-operation for Local Self-Govt Devt, Pres. City Org. SDP for Velika Gorica 1997–2000; mem. Croatian Parl. 2000–; Minister of Foreign Affairs 2000–03. *Address:* c/o Ministry of Foreign Affairs, trg. Nikole Šubića Zrinskog 7-8, 10000 Zagreb, Croatia (office).

PIEBALGS, Andris; Latvian EU official, politician and diplomatist; *Commissioner for Energy, European Union;* b. 17 Sept. 1957, Valmiera; m.; three c.; ed Univ. of Latvia; teacher, Headmaster, Secondary School No. 1, Valmiera 1980–88; desk officer, Head of Dept, Ministry of Educ. 1988–90; Minister of Educ. 1990–93; mem. Parl. 1993–94, Chair. Budget and Finance Cttee; Minister of Finance 1994–95; Amb. to Estonia 1995–97; Perm. Rep. of Latvia to EU 1998–2003; Deputy Sec. of State, Ministry of Foreign Affairs, responsible for relations with EU 2003–04; Head of Cabinet of Commr Kalniete 2004; EU Commr for Energy 2004–. *Address:* European Commission, 200 Rue de la Loi, 1049 Brussels, Belgium (office). *Telephone:* (2) 299-11-11 (office). *Fax:* (2) 295-01-38 (office). *E-mail:* cab-piebalgs-archives@ec.europa.eu (office). *Website:* ec.europa.eu/commission_barroso/piebalgs (office).

PIËCH, Ferdinand; Austrian automotive executive; *Chairman of the Supervisory Board, Volkswagen AG;* b. 17 April 1937, Vienna; ed Eidgenössische Technische Hochschule (ETH), Zürich; joined Porsche KG in engine testing 1963, Tech. Man. 1971; joined Audi NSU Auto Union AG 1972, Divisional Man. Gen. Testing 1973, mem. Bd of Man. 1975, Vice-Chair. Bd of Man. 1983, Chair. Bd of Man. Audi AG 1988; Chair. Bd Dirs Volkswagen AG 1993–2002, Dir, Head of Research and Devt 1995–2000, responsible for Production Optimisation and Purchasing 1996–2001, Chair. Supervisory Bd 2002–; Chair. Supervisory Bd MAN AG; Pres. Asscn of European Automobile Mfrs 1999–2000; Chair. Scania 2000–02; Hon. DTech (Tech. Univ. Vienna) 1984; Dr hc (Ben Gurion Univ.) 1997, (ETH, Zurich) 1999, Hon. Prof. (Tech. Univ. Vienna) 2002; Distinguished Service Medal (1st Class) 1984, Automobile Business Manager of the Century 1999. *Address:* Volkswagen AG, Brieffach 1848-2, 38436 Wolfsburg, Germany (office). *Telephone:* (53) 6190 (office). *Fax:* (53) 61928282 (office). *Website:* www.volkswagen.de (office).

PIEDRABUENA, Guillermo; Chilean lawyer; *National Public Prosecutor;* b. 18 Jan. 1937, Viña del Mar; m. Isabel Keymer; six c.; ed Saint George's Coll., Santiago, School of Law, Universidad de Chile, Santiago; lawyer, Consejo de Defensa del Estado 1963–76, Lawyer Counsellor 1976–96, Pres. 1990–93; Sub-Sec. Justice Dept 1970; mem. Appeal Court, Santiago 1997, Special Tribunal of Industrial Property 1993–2000; Nat. Public Prosecutor of Chile 2000–. *Publications include:* Breves comentarios a la reforma procesal penal 1998, El Recurso de apelación y la consulta 1999, Introducción a la reforma procesal penal 2000. *Address:* Fiscalia Nacional del Ministerio Publico, Almirante Lorenzo Gotuzzo 124, Piso 11, 650 10 61 Santiago, Chile (office). *Telephone:* (2) 690-9101 (office). *Fax:* (2) 690-9108 (office). *E-mail:* gpiedrabuena@minpublico.cl (office). *Website:* www.ministeriopublico.cl (office).

PIENAAR, Jacobus François, LLB; South African rugby player; b. 2 Jan. 1967, Vereeniging; s. of Johan Pienaar and Valerie Du Toit; m. Nerene Pienaar 1996; ed Patriot High School and Rand Afrikaans Univ.; capped for S African Schools 1985, S African Under 20 1987, S African Barbarians 1990; Capt. Transvaal; Capt. S African Rugby Team 1993–96, World Cup winners 1995; holds record for most tests as Capt. of SA (29); played for British club Saracens, then Chief Exec.; motivational speaker; Int. Rugby Player of Year 1994; British Rugby Writers' Lifetime Achievement Award 1995. *Publication:* Rainbow Warrior (autobiog.). *Leisure interests:* golf, spending time at home. *Address:* c/o South African Rugby Football Union, PO Box 99, Newlands 7725, South Africa. *Telephone:* (21) 6853038. *Fax:* (21) 6856771.

PIENE, Otto Ludwig Wilhelm Hermann Leonhard; German artist and academic; *Director Emeritus, Center for Advanced Visual Studies, Massachusetts Institute of Technology;* b. 18 April 1928, Laasphe, Westphalia; s. of Otto and Anne (Niemeyer) Piene; m. Elizabeth Olson 1988; one s. three d.; ed Acad. of Fine Arts, Munich and Düsseldorf and Univ. of Cologne; organized Night Exhbns, f. Group Zero, Düsseldorf, with Heinz Mack 1957–66; Visiting Prof., Graduate School of Art, Univ. of Pa 1964; Prof. of Environmental Art, School of Architecture, MIT 1972–, Dir Center for Advanced Visual Studies, MIT 1974–94, Acting Dir 1993–94, Dir Emer. 1994–; Prof. Emer. MIT 1993–; Founder and Dir Sky Art Conf. 1981–; one-man exhbns include: Galerie Heseler, Munich 1971, 1972, 1975, 1977–79, 1981, 1983, Galerie Heimeshoff, Essen 1974, 1977, 1983, 1988, Galerie Schoeller, Düsseldorf 1976, 1977, 1980,

1984, 1987, 1991, 1995, 2000, Galerie Löhrl, Mönchengladbach 1986, 1988, 1991, 1996, Gallery 360°, Tokyo 1991, 1992; retrospective exhbn Museum am Ostwall, Dortmund 1967, Hayden Gallery, MIT 1975, Karlsruhe 1988, Städt. Kunstmuseum, Düsseldorf 1996, City Gallery, Prague 2002; group exhbns. include: Tate Gallery 1964, Düsseldorf 1973, Antwerp 1979, Paris 1983, London, Berlin 1987, New York 1988–89, Copenhagen 1992; performed works include Olympic Rainbow 1972, Sky Events, SAC 1981, 1982, 1983, 1986, Sky Dance, Guggenheim 1984, Dialogue de Têtes, Reims 1990; Les fleurs du mal, Québec 1996; works in museums in many countries; DFA hc (Univ. of Md) 1995; North Rhine-Westphalia Medal of Merit, American Acad. of Arts and Letters Sculpture Prize, Leonardo da Vinci Prize 2003. *Publications:* (with Heinz Mack) Zero 1, Zero 2 1958, Zero 3 1961; More Sky 1973; author and ed. Zero 1973, Art Transition 1975–76, Centerbeam 1980, Sky Art Conference Catalog 1981, 1982, 1983, 1986, Lightsorot 1988, Feuerbilder und Texte 1988, Überblick 1991. *Address:* Center for Advanced Visual Studies, Massachusetts Institute of Technology, N52-373g, 265 Massachusetts Avenue, Cambridge, MA 02139-4307 (office); 383 Old Ayer Road, Groton, MA 01450, USA (Home and Studio); Hüttenstr. 104, Atelier 40215 Düsseldorf, Germany (Studio). *Telephone:* (617) 253-4415 (office); (978) 448-5240 (Home and Studio). *Fax:* (617) 253-1660 (office); (978) 448-6716 (Home and Studio). *Website:* web.mit.edu/cavs/people/piene/piene.html (office).

PIERANTOZZI, Sandra Sumang, BEd; Palauan politician and business executive; b. 9 Aug. 1953, Koror; d. of the late Yechadrechemai Sumang Demei and of Mitsko Wong Sumang; m. Marcello Pierantozzi; ed Palau Mission Acad., Union Coll., Lincoln, Neb., USA, Univ. of Hawaii; teacher, Micronesian Occupational Coll. 1974–79; Journal Clerk, First Palau Constitutional Convention 1979; Office Man. Koror Wholesalers 1980; owner pvt. business including MVP Construction & Realty, Belau Business Services, SPACO Finance 1980–; newscaster WALU-TV 1980–82; Clerk of the Senate 1981–91; Minister of Admin. 1991–92; Special Consultant, Nat. Congress 1992–93; Senator, Floor Leader, Chair. Cttee on Health and Social Welfare 1997–2000; Minister of Health 2001–04; Vice-Pres. of Palau 2001–04; mem. Bd of Dirs Palau Chamber of Commerce; Gov. and Dir Pacific Islands Devt Bank; Senate Rep., Bd of Dirs Asscn Pacific Island Legislatures; Sec. Center for Asia-Pacific Women in Politics; Founding Dir Palau Conservation Soc.; f. Sumang Demei Memorial Scholarship Award 1992. *Leisure interests:* philately, numismatics, environmental conservation, travel. *Address:* c/o Office of the Vice-President, PO Box 100, Koror, PW 96940, Palau (office).

PIERCE, Mary; French (b. Canadian) professional tennis player; b. 15 Jan. 1975, Montréal, Canada; d. of Jim Pierce and Yannick Pierce; turned professional 1989; moved to France 1990; first career title, Palermo 1991; runner-up French Open 1994; winner Australian Open 1995, Tokyo Nichirei 1995; semi-finalist Italian Open, Canadian Open 1996; finalist Australian Open singles 1997, doubles (with Martina Hingis q.v.), 2000; won singles and doubles (with Martina Hingis) French Open 2000; highest singles ranking No. three; winner of doubles (with Martina Hingis q.v.), Pan Pacific; French Fed. Cup team 1990–92, 1994–97; French Olympic team 1992, 1996; 26 WTA Tour singles and doubles titles; France's (rising star) Burgeon Award 1992, WTA Tour Comeback Player of the Year 1997. *Leisure interests:* hiking, jet skiing, boating, shopping, reading, yoga. *Address:* c/o WTA, 133 First Street NE, St Petersburg, FL 33701, USA. *Website:* www.wtatour.com.

PIERCY, Marge, MA; American novelist, poet and essayist; b. 31 March 1936, Detroit, Mich.; d. of Robert Douglas Piercy and Bert Bernice Piercy (née Bunnin); m. Ira Wood 1982; ed Univ. of Mich. and Northwestern Univ.; instructor, Gary Extension, Indiana Univ. 1960–62; Poet-in-Residence, Univ. of Kansas 1971; Distinguished Visiting Lecturer, Thomas Jefferson Coll., Grand Valley State Coll. 1975, 1976, 1978, 1980; mem. staff, Fine Arts Work Center, Provincetown, Mass 1976–77; Visiting Faculty, Women's Writers' Conf., Cazenovia, NY 1976, 1978, 1980; Fiction Writer-in-Residence, Holy Cross Univ., Worcester, Mass 1976; Purdue Univ. Summer Write-In 1977; Butler Chair of Letters, State Univ. of NY at Buffalo 1977; poetry and fiction workshops at Writers' Conf., Univ. of Indiana, Bloomington 1977, 1980; poetry, Writers' Conf., Vanderbilt Univ., Nashville, Tenn. 1981; Visiting Faculty, Women's Writers' Conf., Hartwick Coll. 1979, 1981, 1984; poetry and fiction, Lake Superior Writers' Conf. 1984; Fiction Writer-in Residence, Ohio State Univ. 1986; Elliston Poetry Fellow, Univ. of Cincinnati 1986; master-class in poetry, Omega Inst. for Holistic Studies 1990, 1991, 1994; DeRoy Distinguished Visiting Prof., Univ. of Michigan 1992; Thunder Bay Writers' Conf. 1994; Univ. of N Dakota Writers' Conf. 1995; Florida Suncoast Writers' Conf. 1996; Hassayampa Summer Inst. for Creative Writing, Prescott, Ariz. 1998, 2000, 2002, 2004, 2006; Washington Library Association Conf., Spokane, Wash. 2001; Bilgray Scholar-in-Residence, Temple Emmanuel Residency, Univ. of Arizona 2001; Residency and Silver Memorial Lecture, Temple Israel, Duluth, Minn. 2002; mini-residency, Trinity Coll., San Antonio, Tex. 2003; Writers in Residence, World Fellowship Center, Conway, NH 2005; mem. Advisory Bd Eastern Massachusetts Abortion Fund 1999–, Advisory Bd FEMSPEC: An Interdisciplinary Feminist Journal 1998–2004, Advisory Bd The Poetry Center at Passaic Co. Community Coll. 2004–, Advisory Bd Carrie A. Seaman Animal Shelter 2005–, Artists Grants Panel in Poetry 2006; Ed. Leapfrog Press 1997–; Poetry Ed. Lilith 2000–; Fiction Ed. Seattle Review 2003–; Honorary Doctor of Letters, Lesley College; Honorary Doctor of Letters, Bridgewater State College; Honorary Degree of Doctorate of Humane Letters, Eastern Connecticut State University, 2005; Doctor of Human Letters, honoris causa Hebrew Union College, 2004; Rhode Island School of Design Faculty Asscn Medal, Borestone Mountain Poetry Award (twice), Avery Hopwood Contest, Orion Scott Award in Humanities, Lucinda Goodrich Downs Scholar, James B. Angell Scholar, Sheaffer-PEN/New England Award for Literary Excellence, Calapooya Coll. 1986, 1990, Carolyn Kizer Poetry Prize, Literary Award, Gov. of Mass Comm. on Status of Women

1974, Nat. Endowment for the Arts Award 1978, Golden Rose Poetry Prize 1990, The Golden Rose, New England Poetry Club 1990, May Sarton Award, New England Poetry Club 1991, Barbara Bradley Award, New England Poetry Club 1992, Brit ha-Dorot Award, The Shalom Center 1992, Arthur C. Clarke Award for Best Science Fiction Novel published in UK 1993, American Library Asscn Notable Book Award 1997, Notable Book Award 1997, Paterson Poetry Prize 2000, Paterson Award for Literary Achievement 2004. *Recording:* Louder We Can't Hear You (Yet!): The Political Poems of Marge Piercy 2004. *Publications:* Breaking Camp 1968, Hard Loving 1969, Going Down Fast 1969, Dance the Eagle to Sleep 1970, Small Changes 1973, To Be of Use 1973, Living in the Open 1976, Woman on the Edge of Time 1976, The High Cost of Living 1978, Vida 1980, The Moon is Always Female 1980, Braided Lives 1982, Circles on the Water 1982, Stone, Paper, Knife 1983, My Mother's Body 1985, Gone to Soldiers 1988, Available Light 1988 (May Sarton Award 1991), Summer People 1989, He, She and It 1991, Body of Glass 1991 (Arthur C. Clarke Award 1993), Mars and Her Children 1992, The Longings of Women 1994, Eight Chambers of the Heart 1995, City of Darkness, City of Light 1996, What Are Big Girls Made Of? 1997, Storm Tide 1998, Early Grrrl 1999, The Art of Blessing the Day 1999, Three Women 1999, So You Want to Write: How to Master the Craft of Writing Fiction and the Personal Narrative (with Ira Wood) 2001, 2005, Sleeping with Cats, A Memoir 2002, The Third Child 2003, Colors Passing Through Us 2003, Sex Wars 2005, The Crooked Inheritance 2006, Pesach for the Rest of Us 2007. *Address:* PO Box 1473, Wellfleet, MA 02667, USA (home). *Telephone:* (508) 349-3163 (office). *E-mail:* hagolem@c4.net (office). *Website:* www.margepiercy.com (office).

PIERONEK, Most Rev. Tadeusz; Polish ecclesiastic and professor of theology and canon law; *Auxiliary Bishop Emeritus of Sosnowiec;* b. 24 Oct. 1934, Radziechowy n. Żywiec; ed Jagiellonian Univ., Kraków, Higher Ecclesiastic Seminary, Kraków, Catholic Univ. of Lublin, Lateral Univ., Rome; ordained priest, Kraków 1957; notary, Metropolitan Curia, Kraków; prefect, Higher Ecclesiastic Seminary, Kraków; Lecturer, Catholic Theology Acad., Warsaw 1967–76, Asst Prof. 1975; Lecturer and Head of Dept of Canon Law, Pontifical Acad. of Theology, Kraków 1965–, Prof. 1985; Visiting Prof., Santa Croce Univ., Rome 1985–; Titular Bishop of Cufruta 1992; Auxiliary Bishop of Sosnowiec 1992–98, Auxiliary Bishop Emer. 1998–; Deputy Gen. Sec. Polish Episcopate 1992–93; Gen. Sec. Polish Episcopate Conf. 1993–98; Gen. Sec. Second Plenary Synod, Poland 1987; Rector Pontifical Acad. of Theology, Kraków 1998–. *Publications:* The Church Is Not Afraid of Freedom 1998, and over 100 articles. *Leisure interests:* Polish poetry, landscape tourism, cooking, classical music, painting, folklore. *Address:* Diocese of Sosnowiec, ul. Wawel 19, 41-200 Sosnowiec (office); Papieska Akademia Teologiczna, ul. Kanonicza 25, 31-002 Kraków, Poland. *Telephone:* (32) 293-51-51 (office). *Fax:* (32) 293-51-88 (office). *Website:* www.kuria.sosnowiec.pl (office).

PIEROTH, Elmar; German politician and viticulturist; b. 9 Nov. 1934, Bad Kreuznach; s. of Philip Pieroth; m. Hannelore Ribow 1957; six c.; ed Stefan Georg Gymnasium, Bingen and Univs of Mainz and Munich; has run Weingut Ferdinand Pieroth GmbH since 1955; creator of Pieroth-Modell; devt work in Togo 1960; initiator Bad Kreuznach talks; mem. Bundestag 1969–81; mem. Berlin Chamber of Deputies 1981–; Senator for Economy and Labour, Berlin 1981–89, 1995–98, for Finance, Berlin 1991–95; Rep. for Eastern Europe, Fed. State of Berlin 1999–2001; mem. CDU. *Publications:* Die Union in der Opposition (with G. Golter) 1970, Chancen der Betriebe durch Umweltschutz (with L. Wicke) 1988. *Address:* 105 Martin-Luther-Strasse, 10825 Berlin, Germany.

PIERRE, D. B. C. (Dirty But Clean); British novelist; b. (Peter Finlay), 1961, Australia; James Joyce Award, Literary & Historical Soc., Univ. Coll., Dublin 2005. *Television:* Imagine, with Alan Yentob (biographical; BBC) 2004, The Last Aztec (Channel 4 two-hour special on the Spanish conquest of Mexico) 2006. *Publications:* Vernon God Little (Man Booker Prize, Bollinger Everyman Woodhouse Award, Whitbread Prize for first novel) 2003, Ludmila's Broken English 2006. *Leisure interests:* travel, music, cricket. *Address:* c/o Conville & Walsh Ltd, 2 Ganton Street, London, W1F 7QL, England (office); c/o Faber and Faber Ltd, Bloomsbury House, 74–77 Great Russell Street, London, WC1B 3DA, England (office). *Telephone:* (20) 7287-3030 (office); (20) 7927-3800 (office). *Fax:* (20) 7287-4545 (office); (20) 7927-3801 (office). *E-mail:* info@convilleandwalsh.com (office). *Website:* www.convilleandwalsh.com (office); www.faber.co.uk (office).

PIERRE-BROSSOLETTE, Claude, LenD; French civil servant; b. 5 March 1928, Paris; s. of Pierre Brossolette and Gilberte (née Bruel); m. Sabine Goldet 1953; two d.; ed Lycée Henri-IV, Faculty of Law of Paris Univ., Ecole nat. d'admin; Inspecteur adjoint des Finances 1952, Insp. 1955; served under two successive Ministers in Office of Minister of Econ. and Financial Affairs 1956; Asst to Financial Adviser, Embassy in USA 1957; served Direction des Finances Extérieures 1958; Tech. Adviser, Office of Minister of Finance 1960–62, Asst Dir of Office 1962, Deputy Dir 1963; Asst Dir of External Financial Affairs in Direction du Trésor 1964, later Chef de Service 1966; Sec.-Gen. Conseil nat. du Crédit 1967–71; served in office of Valéry Giscard d'Estaing, Minister of Econ. and Financial Affairs 1969–71; Dir du Trésor, Ministry of Econ. and Financial Affairs 1971; Censeur, Banque de France, Crédit nat. 1971; Vice-Chair. Caisse nat. des Télécommunications 1971–74; Dir SNCF (Nat. Railways Bd) 1971–74, Air France 1971–74; Sec.-Gen. of Presidency of the Repub. 1974–76; Chair. Crédit Lyonnais 1976–82, Omnium financier pour l'Industrie nat. (OFINA) 1976, Europartners Securities Corpn, Banque Stern 1982–86 (Vice-Chair. 1986); Assoc. Man. Worms et Cie 1986–92; Admin. Crédit Nat. 1976–81; Pres. Démachy et Assocs 1987; mem. Conseil nat. du Crédit 1976–81, Conseil de Surveillance de la Cie Bancaire 1976, Dir Société Air-liquide, Crédit Foncier de France 1978–82, Générale Occidentale

1979–82, Péchiney Ugine Kuhlmann 1980–82, Lyonnaise des Eaux 1980, BSN 1981, Norsolor 1988; Pres. Supervisory Council Câbles Pirelli 1992–; Vice-Pres. Eurofin 1992–95, Pres. 1995–96; Pres. Caisse de refinancement hypothécaire 1995; Adviser to Pres. of Merrill Lynch Int. 1993–97, Chair. Supervisory Bd Merrill Lynch France 1997–99; fmr Dir GTM-Enterpose; Chair. Bd of Dirs Caisse de Refinancement de l'Habitat SA 1994–2007; Officier, Légion d'honneur, Commdr de l'Ordre nat. du Mérite, Chevalier, Ordre des Palmes académiques; Médaille de la Résistance. *Address:* c/o Caisse de Refinancement de l'Habitat, 35 rue la Boetie, 75008 Paris (office); 37 avenue d'Iéna, 75116 Paris, France (home).

PIERRE-LOUIS, Michèle, MEconSc, DH; Haitian politician; *Prime Minister;* b. 5 Oct. 1947, Jeremie; ed Queens Coll., City Univ. of New York, St Michael's Coll., USA; Operations and Credit Officer, Bank of Nova Scotia 1976–79; Asst Dir Gen. Nat. Airport Authority 1979–82; Admin. Dir Société Financière Haïtienne de Développement (SOFIHDES) 1983–84; Nat. Trainer, Mission Alpha (nat. literacy program) 1986–88; Consultant to Pres. Jean-Bertrand Aristide on land reform 1991; Exec. Dir Knowledge and Freedom Foundation 1995–; Prime Minister of Haiti 2008–; fmr Dir Karl Leveque Inst., Man. Consultant Haitian Devt Foundation. *Address:* Office of the Prime Minister, Villa d'Accueil, Delmas 60, Musseau, Port-au-Prince, Haiti (office). *Telephone:* 245-0007 (office). *Fax:* 245-1624 (office).

PIERRET, Alain Marie, BA; French diplomatist (retd); *President, Comité interministériel de l'agriculture et de l'alimentation;* b. 16 July 1930, Mourmelon; s. of Henri Pierret and Yvonne Delhumeau; m. Jacqueline Nanta 1958; three d. (one deceased); ed Faculties of Arts (Sorbonne) and Law, Paris and Ecole Nat. de la France d'Outre-Mer; reserve officer (navy) in Vietnam 1953–55; District Commr Togo 1955–59, Sahara (S. Algeria) 1959–61; Sec. of Embassy, Sierra Leone 1961–63, South Africa 1963–66; Africa Div. Ministry of Foreign Affairs 1966–69; Counsellor, Moscow 1969–72; Head, Soviet Affairs Bureau, Ministry of Foreign Affairs 1972; mem. French Del. to Conf. on Security and Co-operation in Europe Helsinki 1972–75; Counsellor, Belgrade 1975–80; Amb. to Niger 1980–82; Asst Sec. of State for UN Affairs and Int. Orgs 1983–86; Amb. to Israel 1986–91, to Belgium 1991–93, to the Holy See 1993–95; Pres. Interministerial Cttee for Agric. and Food (CIAA) 1996–; mem. study mission into the spoliation of Jews in France during Second World War 1997–2000; Del. to Conf. on Nazi Gold, London 1997, to Conf. on Holocaust-era Assets, Washington, DC 1998; Officier, Légion d'honneur, Croix de Guerre (Vietnam), Grand Cross Order Pius IX (Holy See). *Publications include:* Ambassadeur en Israel, 1986–1991 1999. *Address:* Comité interministériel de l'agriculture et de l'alimentation, Carré Austerlitz 2, Boulevard Diderot, 75572 Paris (office); i 117, 26 rue du Cdt Mouchotte, 75014 Paris, France (home). *Telephone:* 1-44-87-16-00 (office); 1-43-20-53-71 (home). *Fax:* 1-44-87-16-04 (office); 1-43-20-53-71 (home). *E-mail:* ajpierret@free.fr (home).

PIERRET, Christian; French politician, economist and lawyer; *Mayor of St-Dié-des-Vosges;* b. 12 March 1946, Bar-le-Duc; s. of Jean Pierret and Anne Radet; m. Marie-Odile Schibler 1978; one d. (and three d. from previous marriages); ed Faculty of Law and Econs, Paris, Inst. d'Etudes Politiques de Paris, Ecole Nat. d'Administration; civil servant, Ministry for the Economy and Finance, then Cour des Comptes 1972–78; fmr Lorraine regional councillor and mem. Vosges Gen. Council; Nat. Ass. Deputy for Vosges 1978–93, 1997–; Minister of State attached to Minister for the Economy, Finance and Industry, with responsibility for Industry 1997–2002; Mayor of St-Dié-des-Vosges 1989–97, 2002–, Deputy Mayor 1997–2002; Chair. Caisse Nat. d'Epargne 1986–93; Vice-Chair. Accor Hotels group 1993–96; Chair. Parl. Study Group on Textile and Clothing industry 1988–, France–Israel Parl. Friendship Group 1988–; Vice-Chair. France–Great Britain Parl. Friendship Group 1988–; Regional councillor of Vosges (Saint Dié Est) 1979–89, of Lorraine 1978–88, 1998–2001; mem. Comité pour l'union monétaire de l'Europe (CUME); lawyer, Paris Bar 2003–. *Publications:* Plan et autogestion, Socialisme et multinationales; many articles in various publs. *Address:* Hôtel de Ville, BP 275, 88100 St-Dié, France. *Telephone:* 3-29-52-66-66. *Fax:* 3-29-52-66-89. *E-mail:* contact@christianpierret.net (home). *Website:* www.christianpierret.net.

PIETERS, Bruno; Belgian fashion designer; *Artistic Director, Hugo Boss;* ed Royal Acad. of Antwerp; began career as an asst designer for Martin Margiela, Josephus Thimister and Christian Lacroix Haute Couture 1999; also worked as freelance designer for cos such as New York Industry, Milan and Antonio Pernas, Madrid; presented his first couture collection entitled 'Part I: Daywear. The Suit' during the Paris couture week in 2001; launched his first complete ready-to-wear collection March 2002; Artistic Dir for Hugo Boss 2007–; Swiss Textiles Award 2006. *Address:* c/o MO Communications, 33 avenue de l'Opera, 75002 Paris, France (office). *Telephone:* 1-44-77-93-60 (office). *Fax:* 1-44-77-93-70 (office). *E-mail:* presse@mocommunications.com (office). *Website:* www.mocommunications.com (office); www.brunopieters.com (office).

PIETRUSKI, John Michael, BS; American business executive; b. 12 March 1933, Sayreville, NJ; s. of the late John M. Pietruski, Sr and Lillian Christensen Pietruski; m. Roberta Jeanne Talbot 1954; two s. one d.; ed Sayreville High School and Rutgers Univ.; First Lt US Army 1955–57; Mfg Man., Industrial Eng Man., Procter & Gamble Co. 1954–63; Pres. Medical Products and Hosp. Divs, C.R. Bard, Inc. 1963–77; Pres. Pharmaceutical Group, Sterling Drug Inc. 1977–81, Corp. Exec. Vice-Pres. 1981–83, Pres. and COO 1983–85, Chair. and CEO 1985–88, mem. Bd of Dirs 1977–88; Pres. Dansara Co. 1988–; Chair. Bd Encysive Pharmaceuticals Inc. (fmrly Texas Biotech Corp.) 1990–2008; mem. Bd of Dirs Irving Bank Corpn 1985–89, Associated Dry Goods Corpn 1985–88, Hershey Foods Corpn 1987–2003, Cytogen Corpn 1989–94, Gen. Public Utilities Corpn 1989–2001, Lincoln Nat. Corpn 1989–2003, McKesson Corpn 1990–99, PDI Inc. 1998–, FirstEnergy Corpn 2001–04, Xylos Corpn 2001–, Trial Card Inc.; mem. Pharmaceutical Mfrs Asscn 1985–88; Trustee Rutgers Univ. Foundation 1985–94; Regent, Concordia Coll. 1993–2003, 2005–; Hon. LLD 1993. *Leisure interests:* boating, fishing, travelling, athletics. *Address:* Suite 3408, One Penn Plaza, New York, NY 10119; 27 Paddock Lane, Colts Neck, NJ 07722, USA (home). *Telephone:* (212) 268-5510 (office). *Fax:* (212) 268-5765 (office).

PIGEAT, Henri Michel; French civil administrator and publisher; *President and CEO, Editions de l'Ilissos;* b. 13 Nov. 1939, Montluçon; s. of Eugène Pigeat and Odette Micard; m. Passerose Cyprienne Rueff 1976; one d.; ed Inst. des Sciences Politiques, Paris and Ecole Nat. d'Admin; Civil Servant Office of Gen. Admin. and Public Service 1965–69; Head Office of Sec. of State for Public Service 1969–71, Tech. Adviser 1971–72; Head of Information Services, Office of Sec. of State for Public Service and Information 1973; Sec.-Gen. Interministerial Cttee for Information 1973–74; Asst Gen. Dir Information, Gen. Office of Information 1974, Dir 1975–76; Dir Information and Broadcasing Service 1976–; Deputy Man. Dir Agence France-Presse 1976–79, Chair. and Man. Dir 1979–86; Chair. and Man. Dir IBIS SA: Prof. Univ. of Paris II; Prof. Inst. d'Etudes Politiques de Paris 1986–92; Dir Soc. nat. des entreprises de presse 1974–76; Dir Soc. financière de radiodiffusion (Sofirad) 1972–76; fmr Dir E1, RMC, Sud Radio, SNEP, TDF, Europe 1, Radio Monte Carlo; Maître de conférances, Inst. d'études politiques, Paris 1966–73, Ecole nat. d'admin. 1967–69, Inst. int. d'admin publique 1966–73; CEO Burson Marsteller 1987–89; Pres. Quicom SA; mem. Exec. Cttee Int. Inst. of Communications, London, fmr Pres. of French section; Pres. and Dir Gen. L & A Editions 2000–; Pres. and CEO Editions de l'Ilissos 2002–; mem. Int. Press Inst.; Chevalier, Ordre nat. du Mérite; Commdr Nat. Order of FRG. *Publications:* La France contemporaine, L'Europe contemporaine (both jointly) 1966–70, Saint Ecran ou la télévision par câbles 1974, Du téléphone à la télématique, La télévision par cable commence demain 1983, Le nouveau désordre mondial de l'information 1987, Les agences de presse 1997, Médias et déontologie 1997, Tendences Economiques Internationales de la Presse 2002. *Leisure interest:* tennis. *Address:* Editions de l'Ilissos, 14 rue de la Sourdière, 75001 Paris (office); 23 quai Antatole France, 75007 Paris, France (home). *Telephone:* 1-42-60-11-03 (office); 1-45-51-70-01 (home). *E-mail:* edesc@wanadoo.fr (home).

PIGGOTT, Arnold A., BBA; Trinidad and Tobago diplomatist and politician; *Minister of Agriculture, Land and Marine Resources;* m. Allison Wendy Kitson-Piggott; two s. one d.; ed St Francis Coll., Brooklyn, New York; fmr banker; pvt. consultant in electronic banking –2001; Senator and Minister of Works and Transport 2001–02; High Commr to Canada 2003–06; Minister of Foreign Affairs and Govt Senator 2006–07, Minister of Agriculture, Land and Marine Resources 2007–; Chair. Bd of Man., Bishop Anstey Jr School 1992–97. *Address:* Ministry of Agriculture, Land and Marine Resources, St Clair Circle, St Clair, Port of Spain, Trinidad and Tobago (office). *Telephone:* 622-1221 (home). *Fax:* 622-8202 (office). *E-mail:* apdmalmr@trinidad.net (office). *Website:* www.agriculture.gov.tt (office).

PIGGOTT, Lester Keith; British fmr jockey and trainer; b. 5 Nov. 1935; s. of Keith Piggott and Iris Rickaby; m. Susan Armstrong 1960; two d.; rode over 100 winners per year in UK alone in several seasons since 1955; rode 3,000th winner in UK 27 July 1974; Champion Jockey 11 times (1960, 1964–71); frequently rode in France; equalled record of 21 classic victories 1975; retd Oct. 1985; races won include: the Derby (nine times): 1954 (on Never Say Die), 1957 (on Crepello), 1960 (on St Paddy), 1968 (on Sir Ivor), 1970 (on Nijinsky), 1972 (on Roberto), 1976 (on Empery), 1977 (on The Minstrel), 1983 (on Teenoso); St Leger (eight times); Prix de l'Arc de Triomphe (three times): 1973 (on Rheingold), 1977 and 1978 (on Alleged); Washington, DC Int. 1968 (on Sir Ivor, first time since 1922 an English Derby winner raced in USA), 1969 (on Karabas), 1980 (on Argument); trainer 1985–87; sentenced to three years' imprisonment for tax fraud Oct. 1987, released after 12 months, returned to racing Oct. 1990; retd as jockey 1995; achieved a record of 30 classic wins; 4,493 winners in total. *Leisure interests:* swimming, water skiing, golf. *Address:* Florizel, Newmarket, Suffolk, CB8 0NY, England. *Telephone:* (1683) 662584 (office).

PIGOTT, Mark C., OBE, BA, BS, MS; American business executive; *Chairman and CEO, PACCAR Inc.;* b. 1954; s. of Charles McGee Pigott and Yvonne Flood; ed Stanford Univ.; Internal Auditor PACCAR Inc. 1977–88, Vice-Pres. 1988–90, Sr Vice-Pres. 1990–93, Exec. Vice-Pres. 1993–95, mem. Bd of Dirs 1994–, Vice-Chair. 1995–96, Chair. and CEO 1997–; Chair. PACCAR Foundation Europe; mem. Business Council, Washington, DC, Washington State Roundtable, World Econ. Forum, Switzerland. *Address:* PACCAR Inc., 777 106th Avenue NE, Bellvue, WA 98004, USA (office). *Telephone:* (425) 468-7400 (office). *Fax:* (425) 468-8216 (office). *Website:* www.paccar.com (office).

PIGOTT-SMITH, Tim; British actor and director; b. 13 May 1946, Rugby; s. of Harry Pigott-Smith and Margaret Pigott-Smith; m. Pamela Miles 1972; one s.; ed Bristol Univ., Bristol Old Vic Theatre School; began stage career at Bristol Old Vic; mem. RSC 1972–75; Dir Company by Samuel Beckett, Edinburgh Fringe Festival 1988; Artistic Dir Compass Theatre 1989; Dir The Royal Hunt of the Sun 1989, Playing the Wife 1992, Hamlet, Regent's Park 1994; Hon. DLitt (Leicester) 2002; BAFTA Award for Best TV Actor 1984, Broadcasting Press Guild Award for Best TV Actor 1984, TV Times Award for Best Actor on TV 1984. *Stage appearances include:* As You Like it, Major Barbara, Benefactors, Sherlock Holmes 1973, Broadway 1974, Bengal Lancer 1985, Antony and Cleopatra, Coming into Land 1987, Entertaining Strangers, Cymbeline, The Winter's Tale, The Tempest 1988, Julius Caesar 1990, Amadeus 1991, Old Times, Jane Eyre 1993, The Picture of Dorian Gray 1994, Retreat, The Letter 1995, Mary Stuart 1996, The Alchemist, Heritage 1997, The Iceman Cometh 1998, Broadway 1999, Five Kinds of Silence 2000, Julius Caesar 2001, Christmas Carol 2002, Mourning Becomes Electra 2003. *TV appearances include:* Hamlet, Antony and Cleopatra, Glittering Prizes,

Wings, Eustace and Hilda, Lost Boys, Measure for Measure, Fame is the Spur, The Hunchback of Notre Dame, The Jewel in the Crown, Dead Man's Folly, Life Story 1990, The Chief 1990, 1991, 1992, The Adventures of Christopher Columbus, Bullion Boys 1993, The Shadowy Third, Calcutta Chronicles 1995, Innocents 2000, The Vice 2001, Kavanagh QC 2001, Dr. Terrible's House of Horrible 2001, Bloody Sunday 2002, Inspector Lynley Mysteries, Pompeii: the Last Day, Peter Ackroyd's London, Eroica 2003, North and South 2004. *Film appearances include:* Aces High 1975, Joseph Andrews 1977, Sweet William, Richard's Things 1978, The Day Christ Died 1979, Clash of the Titans 1981, Escape to Victory, State of Emergency, Life Story 1986, The Remains of the Day 1993, Four Feathers 2001, Laissez Passer 2001, Bloody Sunday 2002, Johnny English 2003, V for Vendetta 2006, Quantum of Solace 2008. *Publication:* Out of India 1986. *Leisure interests:* music, reading. *Address:* c/o Actual Management, 7 Great Russell Street, London, WC1B 3NH, England. *Telephone:* (20) 7631-4422 (office).

PIGOZZI, Jean, BA; Italian photographer and investor; *Owner, Contemporary African Art Collection;* b. 1952, Paris, France; s. of founder of French car manufacturer Simca; ed lycée in Paris, Harvard Univ., USA; sold supermarket carts for uncle in France 1974; worked in Accounting Dept at Gaumont Film Co., Paris and at Fox Studios, Los Angeles, USA 1975–80; venture capital investor, mainly in USA and UK 1981–; est. Contemporary African Art Collection 1992, world's largest collection of contemporary African Art; recently est. Liquid Jungle Lab in Panama working on high-tech ecological research with Smithsonian Tropical Research Inst., Woods Hole Oceanographic Inst., Royal Botanical Garden of Madrid, Yale School of Forestry. *Address:* The Contemporary African Art Collection, Geneva, Switzerland (office). *E-mail:* caacart-contact@cogitel-forum.com (office). *Website:* www.caacart.com (office).

PIHL, Jüri; Estonian lawyer and politician; *Minister of the Interior;* b. 17 March 1954, Kuressaare; m.; one d. from previous m.; ed Faculty of Law, Univ. of Tartu; served as Criminal Investigation Inspector, Tallinn 1975–86, Head, Criminal Investigation Dept 1986–88, 1990–91; Head, Võru Police 1988–90; Dir of Security, Estonian Police Bd's Security Police 1991–93, Dir-Gen. 1993–2003; Attorney-Gen. of Estonia 2003–05; Sec.-Gen. Ministry of Justice 2005–07; Minister of the Interior 2007–; Order of the Cross of the Eagle (Third Class), Order of the White Star (Fourth Class), Police Cross of Merit (First Class), Grand Duke Gediminas' Order of the Cross of Commdr, Lithuania, Police Golden Cross of Merit, Finland, Cross of Recognition (Second Class), Latvia. *Address:* Ministry of the Interior, Pikk 61, Tallinn 15065, Estonia (office). *Telephone:* 612-5001 (office). *Fax:* 612-5010 (office). *E-mail:* jyri.pihl@siseministeerium.ee (office). *Website:* www.siseministeerium.ee (office).

PIKE, Edward Roy, PhD, FRS, CPhys, CMath, FInstP, FIMA; British physicist and academic; *Clerk Maxwell Professor of Theoretical Physics, King's College London;* b. 4 Dec. 1929, Perth, Western Australia; s. of Anthony Pike and Rosalind Irene Davies; m. Pamela Sawtell 1955; one s. two d.; ed Southfield Grammar School, Oxford, Univ. Coll., Cardiff; Royal Corps of Signals 1948–50; Instructor, Physics Faculty, MIT 1958–60; Sr Scientific Officer, Royal Signals and Radar Establishment Physics Group 1960, Prin. Scientific Officer 1967, Deputy Chief Scientific Officer 1973, Chief Scientific Officer 1984–91; Visiting Prof. of Math., Imperial Coll. London 1985–86; Clerk Maxwell Prof. of Theoretical Physics, King's Coll. London 1986–, Head, School of Physical Sciences and Eng 1991–94; fmr Fulbright Scholar; Chair. Oval (114) Ltd 1984–85; Vice-Pres. for Publs, Inst. of Physics 1981–85; Chair. Adam Hilger Ltd 1981–85; Dir (non-exec.) Richard Clay plc 1985–86; Chair. Stilo Tech. Ltd 1996–2002; Chair. (non-exec.) Stilo Int. PLC 2000–02, Dir (non-exec.) 2002–04; Dir (non-exec.) Phonologica Ltd 2004–05; Royal Soc. Charles Parsons Medal and Lecture 1975, MacRobert Award (jtly) and Lecture 1977, Worshipful Co. of Scientific Instrument Makers Annual Achievement Award (jtly) 1978, Civil Service Award to Inventors 1980, Guthrie Medal and Prize, Inst. of Physics 1996. *Publications:* The Quantum Theory of Radiation (co-author) 1995, Light Scattering and Photon Correlation Spectroscopy (co-author) 1997, Scattering (co-author) 2002; Jt-Ed.: Photon Correlation and Light-Beating Spectroscopy 1974, High Power Gas Lasers 1975, Photon Correlation Spectroscopy and Velocimetry 1977, Frontiers in Quantum Optics 1986, Fractals, Noise and Chaos 1987, Quantum Measurement and Chaos 1987, Squeezed and Non-classical Light 1988, Photons and Quantum Fluctuations 1988, Inverse Problems in Scattering and Imaging 1992; numerous papers in scientific journals. *Leisure interests:* music, languages, woodwork. *Address:* Physics Department, King's College, Strand, London, WC2R 2LS (office); 3A Golborne Mews, North Kensington, London, W10 5SB, England (home). *Telephone:* (20) 7848-2043 (office). *Fax:* (20) 7848-2420 (office). *E-mail:* roy.pike@kcl.ac.uk (office). *Website:* kcl.ac.uk/schools/pse/physics/people/roypike.html (office).

PIKE, Jimmy; Australian artist; m. Pat Lowe 1987; aboriginal artist; began painting and printmaking while serving prison sentence for murder 1980–86; work is represented in nat. and state galleries of Australia and in pvt. collections in Europe and America; comms from Australian Museum, Sydney, Art Gallery of NSW, Sydney, Art Gallery of South Australia, Adelaide, Art Gallery of Western Australia, Perth, Flinders Univ. Art Museum, Adelaide, Gold Coast City Art Gallery, Surfers Paradise, Queensland, Museum and Art Gallery of the Northern Territory, Darwin, Nat. Gallery of Australia, Canberra, Nat. Gallery of Vic., Melbourne, Nat . Maritime Museum, Darwin Harbour, Sydney, Parl. House Art Collection, Canberra, Queensland Art Gallery, Brisbane, The Holmes à Court Collection, Perth. *Address:* c/o Wendy Awart, Backroom Press, POB 1870, Broome, WA 6725, Australia (office).

PIKHOYA, Rudolf Germanovich, D.HIST.SC.; Russian historian; b. 27 Jan. 1947, Polevskoe, Sverdlovsk Region; m.; one s.; ed Ural Univ.; with Ural Univ. 1971–, Sr researcher Ural Scientific Centre, USSR Acad. of Sciences 1981–86; Pro-rector Ural Univ. 1986–90; Chair. Cttee on problems of archives, Council of Ministers of Russian Fed. 1990–, Chief, Archive Service of Russia 1992–96; participated in movt for making secret documents of the Communist period public; Vice-Pres. Int. Fund for Democracy, Dir of Research Programmes 1996–98; Prof. and Chair. Acad. of State Service 1998–. *Leisure interest:* music. *Address:* Academy of State Service, Vernadskogo prospekt 84, 117606 Moscow, Russia. *Telephone:* (495) 436-98-14.

PIKIS, Georghios M., LLB; Cypriot judge; *Judge, International Criminal Court;* b. 22 Jan. 1939, Larnaca; s. of Michael I. Pikis and Erini M. Pikis; m. Maria G. Pikis (née Papaneophytou); two s. one d.; ed Univ. of London, UK; called to the Bar, Gray's Inn, London 1961; Advocate of the Cyprus Bar 1961–66; Dist Judge 1966–72; Pres. Dist Court 1972–81; Justice of Supreme Court of Cyprus 1981–95, Pres. Supreme Court 1995–2004; Judge, Int. Criminal Court (ICC), The Hague 2003–, full-time mem. 2004–; ad hoc judge European Court of Human Rights 1993, 1997; mem. UN Cttee against Torture 1996–98; mem. Bd of Dirs Int. Assen of Supreme Admin. Jurisdictions 1999–2004; mem. Circle of Pres of Conf. of European Constitutional Courts 1999–2004, Pres. 2002–04. *Publications:* books: Criminal Procedure in Cyprus (in English, co-author) 1975, Sentencing in Cyprus (in English) 1978, The Common Law and Principles of Equity and Their Application in Cyprus (in Greek) 1981, Basic Aspects of Cyprus Law (in Greek) 2003, Constitutionalism – Human Rights – Separation of Powers, The Cyprus Precedent (in English) 2006; numerous lectures, speeches and reports (including reports to Int., European and Commonwealth Judicial Confs and Asscns) on human rights, constitutional law and the judiciary. *Address:* International Criminal Court, Maanweg 174, 2516 AB The Hague, The Netherlands (office). *Telephone:* (70) 5158216 (office). *Fax:* (70) 5158789 (office). *E-mail:* georghios.pikis@icc-cpi.int (office). *Website:* www.icc-cpi.int (office).

PĪKS, Rihards; Latvian politician; b. 31 Dec. 1941, Rīga; m.; four c.; ed All-Union Cinematography Inst.; film dir, producer, cameraman, Riga Film Studio –1987, Studio Dir 1987–1990; Founder-Dir Nat. Cinematography Centre 1991–93, SIA Baltic Cinema 1993–95; Founder-Pres. Baltic Films asscn 1991–93; Founder, lecturer Cinematography Dept, Latvian Acad. of Culture 1993–95; Deputy Chair. Nat. Radio and TV Council 1995–96; Minister for Culture 1996–97; Pres. SIA Audiovizuālie Multimediji Baltija 1997–98; mem. Parl. 1998–, Deputy Speaker 1999–2002, Chair. Foreign Affairs Cttee Feb.–March 2004; Minister of Foreign Affairs 2004; mem. People's Party. *Address:* c/o Ministry of Foreign Affairs, Brīvības bulv. 36, Rīga 1395, Latvia (office).

PILARCZYK, Most Rev. Daniel Edward, MA, PhD, STD; American ecclesiastic; *Archbishop of Cincinnati;* b. 12 Aug. 1934, Dayton, Ohio; s. of Daniel J. Pilarczyk and Frieda S. Hilgefort; ed St Gregory Seminary, Ohio, Pontifical Urban Univ. Rome, Xavier Univ. Cincinnati and Univ. of Cincinnati; ordained Roman Catholic priest 1959; Asst Chancellor, Archdiocese of Cincinnati 1961–63; Faculty, Athenaeum of Ohio (St Gregory Seminary) 1963–74, Vice-Pres. 1968–74, Trustee 1974–; Rector, St Gregory Seminary 1968–74; Synodal Judge, Archdiocesan Tribunal 1971–82; Dir of Archdiocesan Educ. Services 1974–82; Auxiliary Bishop of Cincinnati 1974–82, Archbishop 1982–, pleaded no contest on behalf of the Archdiocese to five misdemeanor counts of failing to report a crime during period 1978–82 2003; Vice-Pres. Nat. Conf. of Catholic Bishops 1986–89; Pres. Nat. Conf. of Catholic Bishops 1989–92; mem. Episcopal Bd Int. Comm. on English in Liturgy 1987–97; mem. Jt Cttee of Orthodox and Catholic Bishops 2002; numerous professional appts; Hon. LLD (Xavier Univ.) 1975, (Calumet Coll.) 1982, (Univ. of Dayton) 1990, (Marquette Univ.) 1990, (Thomas More Coll.) 1991, (Coll. of Mount St Joseph) 1994, (Hebrew Union Coll./Jewish Inst. of Religion) 1997. *Publications:* Twelve Tough Issues 1988, We Believe 1989, Living in the Lord 1990, The Parish: Where God's People Live 1991, Forgiveness 1992, What Must I Do? 1993, Our Priests: Who They Are and What They Do 1994, Lenten Lunches 1995, Bringing Forth Justice 1996, Thinking Catholic 1997, Practicing Catholic 1998, Believing Catholic 2000, Live Letters 2001, Twelve Tough Issues and More 2002, Being Catholic 2006, When God Speaks 2006; numerous articles in newspapers and journals. *Address:* 100 East Eighth Street, Cincinnati, OH 45202, USA (home). *Telephone:* (513) 421-3131.

PILGER, John Richard; Australian journalist, filmmaker and writer; b. Sydney, NSW; s. of Claude Pilger and Elsie Pilger (née Marheine); m. (divorced); one s. one d.; ed Sydney High School, Journalism Cadet Training, Australian Consolidated Press; journalist, Sydney Daily/Sunday Telegraph 1958–62, Reuters, London 1962; feature writer, columnist and Foreign Corresp. (latterly Chief Foreign Corresp.), Daily Mirror, London 1963–86; columnist, New Statesman, London 1991–; freelance contrib., The Guardian, London, The Independent, London, New York Times, Melbourne Age, The Nation, New York, South China Morning Post, Hong Kong, Aftonbladet, Sweden; documentary filmmaker, Granada TV, UK 1969–71, Associated Television 1972–80, Central/Carlton/Granada Television, UK 1980–; credited with alerting much of int. community to horrors of Pol Pot régime in Cambodia, also occupation of Timor-Leste; Visiting Fellow, Deakin Univ., Australia 1995; Frank H. T. Rhodes Visiting Prof., Cornell Univ., USA 2003–; Hon. DLitt (Staffordshire Univ.) 1994; Hon. PhD (Dublin City Univ.) 1995, (Kingston) 1999, (Open Univ.); Hon. DArts (Oxford Brookes Univ.) 1997; Hon. DrIur (St Andrews) 1999; Hon. DUniv (Open Univ.) 2001; Descriptive Writer of the Year, UK 1966, Journalist of the Year, UK 1967, 1979, Int. Reporter of the Year, UK 1970, Reporter of the Year, UK 1974, BAFTA Richard Dimbleby Award 1991, US Acad. Award (Emmy) 1991, Reporteurs sans frontières, France 1993, George Foster Peabody Award, USA 1992, Sophie Prize for Human Rights 2003, Royal TV Soc. Award 2005. *Feature film:* The Last Day 1983. *Documentary films include:* Cambodia: Year Zero 1979 (and four other films on Cambodia), The Quiet Mutiny 1970, Japan Behind the Mask 1986,

The Last Dream 1988, Death of a Nation 1994, Flying the Flag: Arming the World 1994, Inside Burma 1996, Breaking The Mirror: The Murdoch Effect 1997, Apartheid Did Not Die 1998, Welcome to Australia 1999, Paying the Price: Killing the Children of Iraq 2000, The New Rulers of the World 2001, Palestine Is Still The Issue 2002, Breaking the Silence: Truth and Lies in the War on Terror 2003, Stealing a Nation 2004, The War on Democracy 2007. *Publications:* The Last Day 1975, Aftermath: The Struggle of Cambodia and Vietnam 1981, The Outsiders 1983, Heroes 1986, A Secret Country 1989, Distant Voices 1992, Hidden Agendas 1998, Reporting the World: John Pilger's Great Eyewitness Photographers 2001, The New Rulers of the World 2002, Tell Me No Lies: Investigative Journalism and its Triumphs (ed) 2004, Freedom Next Time 2006. *Leisure interests:* swimming, running, reading, sunning, mulling. *Address:* 57 Hambalt Road, London, SW4 9EQ, England (home). *Telephone:* (20) 8673-2848 (home). *Fax:* (20) 8772-0235 (home). *E-mail:* jpmarheine@hotmail.com (home). *Website:* www.johnpilger.com.

PILIKIAN, Hovhanness Israel, BSc, MA; British theatre director, writer, composer, academic and filmmaker; *Group Executive Director, SHE Management;* b. 15 April 1942, Nineveh-Mosul, Iraq; s. of Israel and Tefarik Pilikian; m. 1st Gail Rademacher (divorced 1992, died 2000); two s. one d.; m. 2nd Clarice Stephens 1993; one s. two d.; ed Univ. of Munich, Univ. of London, Royal Acad. of Dramatic Art, Open Univ., American Univ. of Beirut; has directed more than 40 plays (specializing in classical Greek drama); cr. Hanano Mask Theatre Co. 1970, Cervantes Players (first all-black actors' co. in Europe), London 1971; f. Spice of Life Theatre Club 1980, Bloomsbury Theatre Club 1982; Consultant, Cheltenham Int. Guitar Music Festival 2001; mem. Acad. Bd City Lit Inst. 2000–; Group Exec. Dir SHE Management, London 2004–; Fellow, Royal Anthropological Inst., Deutscher Akademischer Austauschdienst; life mem. Swedenborg Soc. of GB, Univ. of London Convocation Governing Bd; mem. Turner Soc.; Visiting Prof., State Univ. of Yerevan, Dutch Drama Center, Slade School of Art, Cen. School of Art and Design, Yerevan Inst. of Literature, Armenian Acad. of Sciences; regular columnist, Gibrahayer weekly internet magazine 2005–; Adamian Award for Lifetime Achievement, Ministry of Culture of Armenian SSR 1985, Calouste Gulbenkian Foundation Scholar (LSE) 1990, Wandsworth Council Business Award 2004. *Films:* The New Supremes in London 1986, A King of Arabia 1987. *Plays directed include:* Euripides' Electra (Greenwich Theatre, London) 1971, Euripides' Medea (Yvonne Arnaud Theatre) 1971, William Alfred's Agamemnon (McCarthur Theater, Princeton Univ.) 1973, Sophocles' Oedipus Tyrannus (Chichester Festival Theatre) 1974, Schiller's Die Räuber (Roundhouse) 1975, King Lear (Nat. Theatre of Iceland) 1977, Fat Hamlet (Shaw Theatre, London) 1993. *Music:* Clarice de Lune 2003, Katya's Baby Or Lenin's Revolution 2005. *Achievements:* organized and produced first ever season of Armenian Cinema for the Nat. Film Theatre, London 1981; Armenian Cinema weeks in Venice 1983, Paris 1986, Montreal 2000. *Publications include:* My Hamlet 1961, An Armenian Symphony and Other Poems 1980, Armenian Cinema, A Source Book 1981, Flower of Japanese Theatre 1984, Aspects of Armenian History 1986; contrib. to Society Matters (Open Univ. newspaper), Encyclopedia Britannica. *Leisure interests:* book mad –pvt. library of 10,000 books and expanding. *E-mail:* profpilikian@hotmail.com. *Website:* pilikian .blogspot.com.

PILLAY, Navanethem, BA, LLM, SJD, LLB; South African judge and UN official; *High Commissioner for Human Rights, United Nations Office of the High Commissioner for Human Rights;* b. 23 Sept. 1941, Durban; m. (deceased); two d.; ed Natal Univ., Harvard Univ., USA; first woman to start a law practice in Natal Prov. 1967, Sr Pnr 1967–95; first black woman apptd Acting Judge High Court of SA 1995; Judge, UN Int. Criminal Tribunal for Rwanda 1995–2003, Pres. 1999–2003; Judge, Int. Criminal Court 2003–08; UN High Commr for Human Rights, Geneva 2008–; Chair. Equality Now 1990–95, Hon. Chair. 1995–; Pres. Advice Desk for Abused Women 1989–99, Women Lawyers' Asscn 1995–98; Vice-Chair. of Council, Univ. of Durban-Westville 1995–98; Lecturer, Dept of Public Law, Natal Univ. 1980; Trustee, Legal Resources Centre 1995–98, Lawyers for Human Rights 1998–2001; mem. Women's Nat. Coalition 1992–93, Black Lawyers' Asscn 1995–98, UN Expert Groups on Refugees and on Gender Persecution 1997, Rules Bd for Courts 1997–98, Expert Group on African Perspectives on Universal Jurisdiction, Cairo and Arusha 2001–02; currently mem. Int. Criminal Law Network, Advisory Bd Journal of Int. Criminal Justice, Bd Harvard-South Africa Scholarship Cttee, Bd Dirs Nozala Investments (women's component of Nat. Econ. Initiative); Hon. mem. American Soc. of Int. Law; Unifem and Noel Foundation Life Award (Los Angeles), Award for Leadership in the Fight for Human Rights, California Legislative Assembly, Dr Edgar Brookes Award, Natal Univ., Award for Outstanding Contrib. in Raising Awareness of Women's Rights and Domestic Violence, Advice Desk for Abused Women, Award for Dedication to Human Rights, Equality Now, New York, One Hundred Heroines Award, Washington DC, Human Rights Award, Int. Asscn of Women Judges, Award for High Achievement by a Woman in the Legal Profession, Center for Human Rights and Univ. of Pretoria; further awards from Asscn of Law Soc. of SA, Black Lawyers' Asscn, Feminist Majority Foundation, Int. Bar Asscn, Peter Gruber Foundation. *Publications:* contrib.: Civilians in War 2001, Essays in Memory of Judge Cassese 2003. *Address:* Office of the High Commissioner for Human Rights, Palais Wilson 52 rue des Pâquis, 1201 Geneva, Switzerland (home); 16 Lavery Crescent, Durban 4091, South Africa (home). *Telephone:* (22) 917-9011 (office). *E-mail:* InfoDesk@ ohchr.org (office). *Website:* www.ohchr.org (office).

PILLAY, Patrick, MA; Seychelles politician; *Minister of Foreign Affairs;* two s. (one adopted) one d.; fmr Minister of Educ., of Youth and Culture, of Industries and Int. Business, of Health; Minister of Foreign Affairs 2005–; fmr Seychelles Gov. to African Devt Bank; fmr Pres. Seychelles Nat. Comm. for UNESCO. *Address:* Ministry of Foreign Affairs, Maison Queau de Quincy, POB 656, Mont Fleuri, Seychelles (office). *Telephone:* 283500 (office). *Fax:* 225398 (office). *E-mail:* hope@seychelles.net (home); mfapesey@seychelles.net (office); dazemia@mfa.gov.sc (office). *Website:* www.mfa.gov.sc (office).

PILLINGER, Colin Trevor, CBE, BSc, PhD, FRS, FRAS, FRGS; British space scientist and academic; *Professor of Planetary Sciences, Open University;* b. 9 May 1943, Bristol; s. of Alfred Pillinger and Florence Honour; m. Judith Mary Hay 1975; one s. one d.; ed Kingswood Grammar School, Univ. Coll., Swansea, Univ. of Wales; Postdoctoral Fellow, Dept of Chem., Univ. of Bristol 1968–72, BSC Fellow 1972–74, Research Assoc. 1974–76; Research Assoc. and Sr Research Assoc., Dept of Earth Science, Univ. of Cambridge 1976–84; Sr Research Fellow, Dept of Earth Science, Open Univ. 1984–90, Prof. of Planetary Sciences 1990–, Head of Planetary Science and Space Research Inst. 1997–2005; Prin. Investigator, ESA Inc., Rosetta Cometary Mission 1994–2000, Gresham Prof. of Astronomy 1996–2000; Lead Scientist,Beagle 2 project, Lander element of ESA's Mars Express Mission 1997–; mem. British Mass Spectrometry Soc.; Fellow, Meteoritical Soc. 1986, Int. Astronomical Union (IAU) 1993; Hon. Fellow, (Univ. Coll. Swansea 2003; Hon. DSc (Bristol) 1985; asteroid 15614 named 'Pillinger' by IAU 2004. *Publications:* Beagle: From Sailing Ship to Mars Spacecraft, The Guide to Beagle 2 (with M. R. Simms and J. Clemmet); more than 1,000 refereed papers, conf. proceedings, abstracts, reports and scientific journalism. *Leisure interests:* animals, farming, football. *Address:* Planetary and Space Sciences Research Institute, Open University, Milton Keynes, MK7 6AA, England (office). *Telephone:* (1908) 655169 (office). *Fax:* (1908) 655910 (office). *E-mail:* psrg@open.ac.uk (office). *Website:* pssri.open.ac.uk (office).

PILLSBURY, Edmund Pennington, PhD; American museum director; b. 28 April 1943, San Francisco, Calif.; s. of Edmund P. Pillsbury and Priscilla K. (Giesen) Pillsbury; m. Mireille Marie-Christine Bernard 1969; one s. one d.; ed Yale Univ. and Univ. of London; David E. Finley Fellow, Nat. Gallery of Art, Washington, DC 1967–70; Ford Foundation Fellow, Cleveland Museum of Art 1970–71; Curator, European Art, Yale Univ. Gallery and Lecturer, History of Art, Yale Univ. 1972–76; Dir Yale Center, British Art and Adjunct Prof. of History of Art Yale Univ. 1976–80; CEO Paul Mellon Centre, Studies in British Art, London 1976–80; Dir Kimbell Art Museum and Vice-Pres. Kimbell Art Foundation 1980–98; CEO Pillsbury & Peters Fine Art Ltd, Dallas, 1999–2003; Dir Meadows Museum, Southern Methodist Univ. 2003–05; mem. Presidential Task Force on Arts and Humanities 1981, The Century Asscn 1991; Adjunct Prof. Tex. Christian Univ. 1985; Chevalier, Ordre des Arts et des Lettres. *Publications:* Florence and the Arts 1971, David Hockney: Travels with Pen, Pencil and Ink 1977, The Graphic Art of Federico Barocci 1978. *Leisure interests:* skiing, running, reading. *Address:* c/o Meadows Museum of Fine Art, 5900 Bishop Blvd, Southern Methodist University, Dallas, TX 75275-0357 (office); 1110 Broad Avenue, Fort Worth, TX 76107, USA (home).

PILON, Jean-Guy, OC, LLB, CQ; Canadian poet; b. 12 Nov. 1930, St Polycarpe; s. of Arthur Pilon and Alida Besner; m. 2nd Denise Viens 1988; two s. from 1st marriage; ed Univ. de Montreal; founded Liberté (review) 1959, Ed. 1959–79; Head of Cultural Programmes and Producer Radio-Canada 1970–88; Les Ecrits (literary review); mem. Académie des lettres du Québec 1982, Royal Soc. of Canada 1967–; Prix de Poésie du Québec 1956, Louise Labé (Paris) 1969, France-Canada 1969, van Lerberghe (Paris) 1969, du Gouverneur gén. du Canada 1970, Athanase-David 1984, Prix littéraire int. de la Paix (PEN Club Quebec) 1991; Ordre du Canada 1986, Chevalier Ordre Nat. du Québec 1987, Officier Ordre des Arts et des Lettres (France) 1992. *Publications (poems):* La fiancée du matin 1953, Les cloîtres de l'été 1954, L'homme et le jour 1957, La mouette et le large 1960, Recours au pays 1961, Pour saluer une ville 1963, Comme eau retenue 1969 (enlarged edn 1985), Saisons pour la continuelle 1969, Silences pour une souveraine 1972. *Address:* 5724 Côte St-Antoine, Montreal, PQ, H4A 1R9, Canada.

PILSWORTH, Michael John, MA; British television executive; b. 1 April 1951, Leeds; s. of Alwyne Pilsworth and Catherine Pilsworth (née Silverwood); m. Stella Frances Pilsworth (née Hore) 1972; one s. one d.; ed King Edward VI Grammar School, Retford, Univ. of Manchester; Research Asst Inst. of Advanced Studies, Manchester Polytechnic 1972–73; Research Associate Univ. of Manchester 1973–75, lecturer 1973–77; Research Fellow, Centre for TV Research 1977–79, Univ. of Leeds 1979–81; researcher, London Weekend 1982–83; Head of Programme Devt TV South 1984–86, Controller Corp. Devt 1987–88; Chief Exec. MGMM Communications Ltd 1988–89; Man. Dir Alomo Productions Ltd 1990–92, Selec TV PLC 1992–93; Chief Exec. Chrysalis TV Group Ltd 1993; now mem. Advisory Bd MediaWin & Partners. *Publications:* co-author Broadcasting in the Third World 1977. *Leisure interests:* reading, cinema, gardening. *Address:* MediaWin & Partners, 100 Pall Mall, St. James, London SW1 5HP (office); 1 Church Lane, Eaton Bray, Beds., LU6 2DJ, England. *Telephone:* (20) 7664-8770 (office). *Fax:* (20) 7664-8775 (office). *Website:* www.mediawinpartners.com (office).

PIMENTA, HE Cardinal Simon Ignatius, DCL; Indian ecclesiastic; b. 1 March 1920, Bombay (now Mumbai); s. of Joseph Pimenta and Rosie Pimenta; ordained priest 949, elected to the titular Church of Bocconia 1971, consecrated bishop 1971, coadjutor bishop 1977, Archbishop of Bombay 1978–97 (retd); cr. Cardinal 1988. *Publications:* Priest for Ever 1999, Memoirs and Milestones 2000, Cardinal Valerian Gracias 2002. *Address:* Archbishop's House, 21 Nathalal Parekh Marg, Mumbai 400 001, India. *Telephone:* (22) 2202-1093 (office); (22) 2204-9696 (home). *Fax:* (22) 2285-3872 (office). *E-mail:* bombaydiocese@usrl.com (office); cardsp@vsnl.net (home).

PINA-CABRAL, Prof. João de, BA, DPhil Hab; Portuguese social anthropologist and academic; *Research Coordinator, Institute of Social Sciences, University of Lisbon;* b. 9 May 1954; s. of Daniel de Pina Cabral and Ana A. de

Pina Cabral; m. Monica Chan; ed Univ. of Witwatersrand, Johannesburg, Univ. of Oxford, Univ. of Lisbon; Auxiliary Prof., Dept of Social Anthropology, ISCTE, Lisbon 1982–84, Assoc. Prof. 1988–; Gulbenkian Fellow in Portuguese Studies, Univ of Southampton 1984–86; Research Fellow, Inst. of Social Sciences, Univ. of Lisbon 1986–92, Sr Research Fellow 1992–2004, Research Coordinator 2004–, Pres. Scientific Bd 1998–2004; Pres. European Asscn of Social Anthropologists 2003–05; mem. Portuguese Acad. of Sciences 2004–; Corresp. mem. Real Academia de Ciencias Morales y Politicas; Hon. mem. Royal Anthropological Inst.; Malinowski Memorial Lecturer 1992. *Publications:* over 80 papers in refereed journals; books: Death in Portugal (co-ed.) 1983, Sons of Adam, Daughters of Eve 1986, Os Contextos da Antropologia 1991, Europe Observed (co-ed.) 1992, Aromas de Urze e de Lama 1993, Em Terra de Tufões 1993, Elites: Choice, Leadership and Succession (co-ed.) 2000, Between China and Europe 2002, O Homem na Família 2003, A persistência da história: Passado e contemporaneidade em África (co-ed.) 2004, Nomes: Género, Etnicidade e Familia (co-ed.) 2007, On the margins of Religion (co-ed.) 2008. *Address:* Institute of Social Sciences, University of Lisbon, Avenida A. Bettencourt 9, 1600-189 Lisbon, Portugal (office). *Telephone:* (21) 7804700 (office). *Fax:* (21) 7940274 (office). *E-mail:* pina.cabral@ics.ul.pt (office). *Website:* www.ics.ul.pt (office).

PINA TORIBIO, César, PhD; Dominican Republic politician; *Secretary of State for the Presidency;* fmr Juridical Consultant of the Presidency; Sec. of State for the Presidency 2008–; mem. Partido de la Liberación Dominicana (PLD), also PLD del. to Cen. Electoral Bd. *Address:* Office of the President, Palacio Nacional, Avda México, esq. Dr Delgado, Santo Domingo, The Dominican Republic (office). *Telephone:* 695-8000 (office). *Website:* www .presidencia.gov.do (office).

PINARD, Hon. Yvon, BA, LLL; Canadian politician and lawyer; *Judge of the Federal Court;* b. 10 Oct. 1940, Drummondville, Québec; s. of Jean-Jacques Pinard and Cécile Chassé; m. Renée Chaput 1964; two d.; ed Immaculate Conception School, Drummondville, Nicolet Seminary, Sherbrooke Univ.; Pres. Sherbrooke Univ. Law Faculty 1963; admitted to Québec Bar 1964; Pres. and founder Drummond Caisse d'Entraide Economique; Pres. Drummond Liberal Asscn 1968–70; mem. Admin. Council Centre Communautaire d'Aide Juridique Mauricie-Bois-Francs region; mem. Commonwealth Parl. Asscn and Canadian Del. Interparl. Union; mem. House of Commons 1974–84; Parl. Sec. to Pres. of Privy Council Oct. 1977; Pres. of HM the Queen's Privy Council for Canada 1980–84; Judge Federal Court of Canada, Trial Div. Judge 1984–; mem. ex-officio Fed. Court of Appeal 1984–, Judge of Federal Court 2003–; Liberal. *Address:* Federal Court of Canada, Ottawa, Ont. K1A 0H9, Canada (office). *Website:* www.fct-cf.gc.ca (office).

PINAULT, François-Henri; French business executive; *Chairman and CEO, PPR SA;* b. 21 Aug. 1936, Champs Géraux, Côtes-du-Nord; s. of François Pinault and Eugénie Gabillard; m. Mary Campbell 1970; two s. two d.; ed Coll. Saint-Martin, Rennes; worked in father's timber co. aged 16; f. Société Pinault, Rennes 1963, Président-Directeur Général 1970; Pres. Co. française de l'Afrique occidentale (CFAO) 1990–91; Vice-Pres. Supervisory Bd Groupe Pinault-Printemps (now PPR SA) 1992, CEO and Chair. 2005–; Founder, Président-Directeur Général Artémis SA (family holding co.) 1992; Head, Christie's UK 1998–; leading modern art collector, owns vineyard Château Latour, Vail ski resort in Colo, luggage mfrs Samsonite and majority shareholding in French real estate investment co. Sefimeg; Officier, Légion d'honneur, Croix de la Valeur Militaire. *Leisure interests:* cinema, theatre, art collecting, cycling, walking. *Address:* PPR SA, 10 avenue Hoche, 75381 Paris, France (office); Christie's International PLC, 8 King Street, London, SW1, England (office). *Telephone:* 1-45-64-61-00 (Paris) (office). *Fax:* 1-44-90-62-25 (Paris) (office). *E-mail:* info@ppr.com (office). *Website:* www.ppr.com (office).

PINCAY, Laffit, Jr; Panamanian fmr jockey; b. 29 Dec. 1946, Panama City; m. 1st Linda Pincay 1967 (died 1985), one s. one d.; m. 2nd Jeanine Pincay, one s.; rode first winner 1964, first US winner 1966, 3,000th winner 1975; Winner Belmont Stakes 1982, 1983, 1984, Ky Derby 1984; rode 6,000th winner 1985; broke Willie Shoemaker's record with 8,834 wins 1999; first jockey to reach 9,000 wins; seven Breeders' Cup wins; 9,530 wins in total; Eclipse Award 1971, 1973, 1974, 1979, 1985.

PINCHUK, Viktor Mykhaylovych, PhD; Ukrainian business executive and philanthropist; m. 1st Elena Arshava (divorced); m. 2nd Elena Leonidivna Franchuk (d. of fmr Pres. of Ukraine, Leonid Kuchma); ed Dnipropetrovsk Metallurgical Inst.; f. Interpipe Corpn (industrial conglomerate) 1990, Pres. 1997–98, fmr Chair. of Bd; owner of a wide range of businesses including Int. Commercial TV (first nat. commercial TV network in Ukraine), New Channel TV, STB TV channel, UkroBank, Fakty newspaper, Nizhnyodniprovsky Pipe Mill and other cos; f. EastOne investment and consulting group; mem. Verkhovna Rada (Supreme Council) 1998–2006; mem. Working Ukraine Party (Trudova Ukraina); f. Victor Pinchuk Foundation 2006. *Address:* 42–44 Shovkovychnaya str., Kiev, Ukraine (office). *Telephone:* (44) 4904880 (office). *Fax:* (44) 4904880 (office). *E-mail:* press@pinchukfund.org (office). *Website:* www.pinchukfund.org (office).

PINCOTT, Leslie Rundell, CBE, FCA; British company director (retd); b. 27 March 1923, London; s. of Hubert George and Gertrude Elizabeth (Rundell) Pincott; m. 1st Mary Mae Tuffin 1944 (died 1996); two s. one d.; m. 2nd Elaine Sunderland 1997; ed Mercers School, Holborn, London, Harvard Business School, USA; Lt in RNVR 1942–46; qualified as chartered accountant; worked for Exxon 1950–1978, Man. Dir 1970–78; Chair. Oxford Univ. Business Summer School 1975–78; Vice-Chair. Remploy Ltd 1979–87 (Dir 1975–79); Dir British Railways Southern Bd 1977–86, Chair. 1986–89; Pres. Dist Heating Asscn 1977–79; Chair. Canada Perm. Trust (UK) Ltd 1978–80, Dir in Toronto; Dir George Wimpey PLC 1978–85, Brown & Root-Wimpey Highlands Fabricators Ltd 1984–91; Deputy Chair., Chair. Price Comm. 1978–80; Chair. Stone-Platt Industries Ltd 1980–82, Edman Communications Group PLC 1982–87, Printing Industries Econ. Devt Cttee 1982–88; mem. Investment Cttee, London Devt Capital Devt Fund 1984–99; Chair. The Hurlingham Club 1989–92, Trustee 1996–98; mem. bd Wandle Housing Asscn 1996, Chair. 1997–99; Chair. Hurlingham Court Ltd 1999–2003. *Leisure interests:* walking, travel, swimming, painting, bowls. *Address:* 53 Hurlingham Court, Ranelagh Gardens, London, SW6 3UP, England (home). *Telephone:* (20) 7736-1440 (home). *Fax:* (20) 7736-1440 (home).

PINDA, Mizengo Kayanza Peter; Tanzanian politician; *Prime Minister;* b. 12 Aug. 1948, Rukwa Region; ed Univ. of Dar es Salaam; State Attorney, Ministry of Justice and Constitutional Affairs 1974–78; State House Security Officer, Pres.'s Office 1978–82; Asst Pvt. Sec. to the Pres. 1982–92; State House Clerk to the Cabinet 1996–2000; MP for Mpanda East 2000–05, for Mpanda Mashariki 2005–; Deputy Minister in Prime Minister's Office for Regional Admin and Local Govt 2000–05; Minister of State for Regional Admin and Local Govt 2006–08; Prime Minister 2008–. *Address:* Office of the Prime Minister, PO Box 980, Dodoma, Tanzania (office). *Telephone:* (26) 233201 (office). *Website:* www.tanzania.go.tz/pmoffice.htm (office).

PINE, Courtney Fitzgerald, CBE; British jazz musician (saxophone) and composer; b. 18 March 1964, London; m. June Guishard 1997; one s. three d.; founder mem. Jazz Warriors 1985–, The Abiba Jazz Arts 1985–; tours internationally with reggae and acoustic jazz bands; Musical Dir Windrush Gala Concert, BBC TV 1998; organizes free workshops for young people in many countries; regular presenter of radio shows (BBC); bandleader at concerts worldwide; Fellow Leeds Coll. of Music, MOBO for Best Jazz Act 1996, BBC Jazz Award for Best Jazz Act 2001, Acad. of Composers and Songwriters Gold Badge 2002, Urban Music Award for Best Jazz Act 2005, Ronnie Scott Award for Int. Saxophonist 2007. *Recordings include:* albums: Journey to the Urge Within 1986, Destiny's Song and The Image of Pursuance 1988, The Vision's Tale 1989, Closer to Home 1990, Within the Realm of Our Dreams 1991, To the Eyes of Creation 1993, Modern Day Jazz Stories (Mercury Music Prize for Best Album of the Year 1996) 1996, Underground 1997, Another Story 1998, History is Made at Night (soundtrack) 1999, Back in the Day 2000, Devotion 2003. *Television:* soundtrack to BBC documentary Mandela: Living Legend 2002. *Radio:* presented BBC Radio 2 series Millennium Jazz 1999, five series of BBC Radio 2 Jazz Crusade 1999–2004, UK Black 2003, Jazz Makers, weekly show on digital station The Jazz 2007–. *Address:* c/o 33 Montpelier Street, Brighton, BN1 3DI (office); Collaboration, 33 Montpelier Street, Brighton, BN1 3DI, England. *Telephone:* (1273) 730744 (office). *Fax:* (1273) 775135 (office). *E-mail:* nikki@collaborationuk.com (office). *Website:* www.courtney-pine.com (office).

PINEAU-VALENCIENNE, Didier; French company director; b. 21 March 1931, Paris; s. of Maurice and Madeleine (née Dubigeon) Pineau-Valencienne; m. Guillemette Rident 1964; one s. three d.; ed Lycée Janson-de-Sailly, Paris, Hautes Etudes Commerciales, Paris, Dartmouth Univ. (USA) and Harvard Business School,; Man. Asst Banque Parisienne pour l'Industrie 1958, Prin. Man. Asst 1962, Dir 1964–67, Dir-Gen. 1969 and Admin. 1971; Pres. and Dir-Gen. Carbonisation et Charbons Actifs (CECA) 1972–74, Société Resogil 1975–76; Dir-Gen. Société Celogil 1975–76; Admin. Isorel 1976; Dir of Admin. and Strategy and Planning Rhone-Poulenc SA 1976–77, Dir-Gen. (Polymer Div.) 1978; Admin. Quartz et Silice; Admin., Vice–Pres., Dir-Gen. Schneider SA 1980–81, Pres.-Dir-Gen. 1981–98; Pres.-Dir-Gen. Jeumont-Schneider 1987–89, Pres. Schneider Industries Services Int. 1991–92, Schneider Electric SA 1993–98; Asst Admin. Société Electrorail SA 1980–; Dir Merlin-Gérin 1981–, Pres.-Dir-Gen. 1989–; Chair. Empain-Schneider Group 1981–, Société Parisienne d'Etudes et de Participations 1982–; Chair. and Man. Dir Creusot-Loire 1982–84; Vice-Chair. Crédit Suisse First Boston, London 1999–; Dir Paribas 1989–98, Whirlpool Corpn 1992–; Pres. Admin. Council, Tech. Univ. of Compiègne 1992–96; Pres. Inst. de L'Entreprise 1993–96, Hon. Pres. 1996–; Pres. Asscn française des entreprises privées 1999–; Vice-Pres. and Pres. Comm. Sociale du Conseil nat. du patronat français (CNPF) 1997; Chair. Advisory Bd Sisie 1997–98; fmr teacher Ecole des Hautes Etudes Commerciales; Officier, Légion d'honneur, Officier Ordre nat. du Mérite; Chair. and Partner SAGARD; Senior Advisor Crédit Suisse First Boston (Europe) Ltd; Manager of the Year (Le Nouvel Economiste) 1991, Falk Award (USA) 1998, Man of the Year (Franco-American Chamber of Commerce). *Leisure interests:* tennis, skiing, collecting books. *Address:* Crédit Suisse First Boston, 1 Cabot Square, London, E14, England (office); Schneider Electric, 64 rue de Miromesnil, 75008 Paris, France (office). *Telephone:* 1-42-56-02-88 (office); 1-42-56-60-33 (office). *Fax:* 1-42-56-59-48 (office). *E-mail:* d-pineau -valencienne@wanadoo.fr (office).

PINES, Alexander, BSc, PhD, FRS; American chemist and academic; *Glenn T. Seaborg Professor of Chemistry, University of California, Berkeley;* b. 1945; ed Hebrew Univ. of Jerusalem, MIT; joined Dept of Physics, Univ. of Calif., Berkeley 1972, becoming Faculty Sr Scientist, Lawrence Berkeley Nat. Lab., also Chancellor's Research Prof. in Chemistry and Glenn T. Seaborg Prof. of Chemistry; mem. NAS 1988–, American Acad. of Arts and Sciences 1999; fmr Pres. Int. Soc. of Magnetic Resonance; numerous hon. lectureships, including Loeb Lecturer, Harvard Univ., Joliot-Curie Prof., Ecole Superieure de Physique et Chemie, Paris 1987, Hinshelwood Prof., Oxford Univ. 1990, Centenary Lecturer and Medal, Royal Soc. of Chemistry 1994, Lord Todd Prof., Cambridge Univ. 1999; Dr hc (Paris VI) 1999 ACS Baekeland Award in Pure Chemistry 1985, Univ. of Calif. Distinguished Teaching Award 1986, ACS Nobel Signature Award for Graduate Education, Pittsburgh Spectroscopy Award 1989, ACS Harrison Howe Award 1991, Royal Soc. of Chemistry Bourke Medal, ACS Langmuir Award, Wolf Prize in Chemistry 1991, Baylor Univ. Robert Foster Cherry Great Teacher Award 1995, Dept of Energy

Ernest O. Lawrence Award 1997, ACS Irving Langmuir Award in Chemical Physics 1998, F. A. Cotton Medal for Excellence in Chemical Research 1998, ACS Remsen Award 2000, Carnegie Mellon Univ. Dickson Prize in Science, Seaborg Medal 2003. *Address:* Department of Chemistry, Room 419, Latimer Hall, University of California, Berkeley, CA 94720-1460, USA (office). *Telephone:* (510) 642-1220 (office). *Fax:* (510) 486-5744 (office). *E-mail:* pines@cchem.berkeley.edu (office). *Website:* chem.berkeley.edu/people/faculty/pines/pines.html (office).

PINES-PAZ, Ophir, BA, MA; Israeli politician; *Minister of Culture and Sport;* b. 1961, Rishon LeZion; m.; two c.; ed Hebrew Univ. of Jerusalem, Tel Aviv Univ.; Staff Sergeant in Israeli mil.;; previous exec. positions include Deputy Dir-Gen. Immigration and Absorption Dept, Jewish Agency, Chair. Authority for Rehabilitation of Prisoners; fmr Sec.-Gen. Israeli Labour Party; mem. Knesset 1996–, fmr mem. Constitution, Law and Justice, State Control, Science and Tech. Cttees; Minister of the Interior 2005–06, of Culture and Sport 2006–. *Address:* Ministry of Education, Culture and Sport, POB 292, 34 Shivtei Israel Street, Jerusalem, 91911 (office); The Knesset, HaKiryah, Jerusalem, 91950, Israel (office). *Telephone:* 2-5602222 (office); 2-6753333 (office). *Fax:* 2-5602752 (office). *E-mail:* info@education.gov.il (office); pinespaz@knesset.gov.il (office). *Website:* www.education.gov.il (office).

PING, Jean, PhD; Gabonese economist, politician and international organization official; *Chairman, Commission of the African Union;* b. 24 Nov. 1942, Omboué; m.; c.; ed Univ. of Paris I (Panthéon-Sorbonne); began career 1972 at UNESCO, Sector for External Relations and Cooperation, Paris; Perm. Rep. to UNESCO 1978–84; Dir Cabinet of the Pres. of Gabon 1984–90; Minister of Information 1990, then Minister of Mines, Energy and Water Resources and Deputy Minister, Ministry of Finance, Economy, Budget and Privatization, then Minister of Planning, Environment and Tourism –1999, Vice-Prime Minister, Minister of Foreign Affairs, Co-operation, Francophonie and Regional Integration 1999–2008; Chair. Comm. of the African Union 2008–; Pres. 59th session of UN Gen. Ass. 2004–05; mem. French Nat. Asscn of Doctors of Econs; Commdr of the Equatorial Star, Grand Officer of the Equatorial Star, Commdr of the Maritime Merit Order, Commdr of the Gabonese Nat. Order of Merit, Commdr Légion d'honneur, Officer of the Order of the Pleiad and the Order of la Francophonie, Grand Cross of the Order of Merit (Portugal); Dr hc (Inst. of Diplomacy of China), (Inst. of African Studies, Russian Acad. of Sciences). *Address:* African Union (AU), PO Box 3243, Addis Ababa, Ethiopia (office). *Telephone:* (11) 5517700 (office). *Fax:* (11) 5517844 (office). *E-mail:* webmaster@africa-union.org (office). *Website:* www.africa-union.org (office).

PINHEIRO FARINHA, João de Deus; Portuguese judge; b. 8 March 1919, Redondo; s. of Simão Martins Pereira and Isabel Gapete (Pinheiro) Farinha; m. Maria das Dores Pombinho 1947; ed Liceu Nacional André da Gouveia and Univ. of Lisbon; Deputy Public Prosecutor 1943–50; Insp. of Prison Services 1944–49; Judge, Leiria Industrial Court 1950–51; Judge in lower courts 1951–66; Asst Public Prosecutor 1957–58; Pres. Corregitor (3rd Civil Chamber) 1966–70; Judge, Coimbra and Lisbon Appeal Courts 1970–74; Attorney-Gen. 1974; Minister of Justice 1975–76, of Foreign Affairs 1991–92; Commr of the European Communities (now European Comm.) for Openness, Communication and Culture 1993–95, for Relations with African, Caribbean and Pacific Countries, S Africa, the Lomé Convention 1995–99; mem. Perm. Court of Arbitration 1975; Pres. Court of Accounts 1977–91; Judge, European Court of Human Rights 1977–98, Supreme Court of Justice 1978–99; Vice-Pres. Int. Comm. on Civil Status 1977–79, Pres. 1980; Hon. DEng (Birmingham) 1992; Gold Medal of Penitentiary Social Merit (Spain), Medal of Council of Europe. *Publications:* many legal publications. *Leisure interests:* travel, philosophy, religion. *Address:* Avenida Dr Baraona 14, 7170 Lisbon (home); c/o Supremo Tribunal de Justiça, Praça do Comércio, 1149-012 Lisbon, Portugal.

PINKAYAN, Subin, MEng, PhD; Thai business executive and engineer; *Chairman, Seatec Group;* b. 16 June 1934, Chiang Mai; m. Boonsri Pinkayan; one s. one d.; ed Chulalongkorn Univ., Asian Inst. of Tech. and Univ. of Colo, USA; civil engineer, Port Authority of Thailand, Bangkok 1958–60; hydrologist, Royal Irrigation Dept 1967–69; Assoc. Prof. Asian Inst. of Tech. 1969–74; mem. Parl. for Chiang Mai 1983–91; Deputy Leader Social Action Party 1986–91, mem. Exec. Cttee 1981–91, Registrar 1981–86, Deputy Sec.-Gen. 1979–80; Deputy Minister of Finance 1986, Minister of Univ. Affairs 1986–88, Minister of Commerce 1988–90, Minister of Foreign Affairs 1990; Chair. Seatec Group 1991–; Kt Grand Cordon, Most Exalted Order of the White Elephant. *Leisure interests:* golf, travel, gardening. *Address:* Seatec Group, 281 Soi Phanit Anan 7, Preedee Phanomyong 42, Sukhumvit 71, Bangkok 10110, Thailand (office). *Telephone:* (2) 7133888 (office). *Fax:* (2) 7133889 (office). *E-mail:* seatec@seatecgroup.com (office). *Website:* www.seatecgroup.com (office).

PINKER, Robert Arthur, CBE, MSc (Econ); British academic; *Professor Emeritus of Social Administration, London School of Economics;* b. 27 May 1931; s. of Dora Elizabeth Pinker and Joseph Pinker; m. Jennifer Farrington Boulton 1955 (died 1994); two d.; ed Holloway Co. School, London School of Econs; Head Sociology Dept, Goldsmiths Coll., London Univ. 1964–72, Lewisham Prof. of Social Admin., Goldsmiths Coll. and Bedford Coll. 1972–74; Prof. of Social Studies, Chelsea Coll. 1974–78; Prof. of Social Work Studies, LSE 1978–93, Pro-Dir LSE 1985–88, Prof. of Social Admin. 1993–96, Prof. Emer. 1996–; Pro-Vice-Chancellor for Social Sciences, Univ. of London 1989–90; Chair. Editorial Bd Journal of Social Policy 1981–86; Chair. British Library Project on Family and Social Research 1983–86; Acting Chair. Press Complaints Comm. 2002; mem. Council, Advertising Standards Authority 1988–95, Press Complaints Comm. 1991– (Privacy Commr 1994–2004, Acting Chair. 2002–03), Council, Direct Mail Accreditation and Recognition Centre 1995–97 (Int. Consultant 2002–), Bd of Man. London School of Hygiene and Tropical Medicine 1990–94; Chair. Govs Centre for Policy on Ageing 1988–94; Fellow, Soc. of Editors 2004–; Hon. Fellow, Goldsmiths Coll., Univ. of London 1999–. *Publications:* English Hospital Statistics 1861–1938 1964, Social Theory and Social Policy 1971, The Idea of Welfare 1979, Social Work in an Enterprise Society 1990. *Leisure interests:* reading, writing, travel, unskilled gardening. *Address:* Press Complaints Commission, 1 Salisbury Square, London, EC4Y 8JB (office); 76 Coleraine Road, Blackheath, London, SE3 7PE, England (home). *Telephone:* (20) 7955-7358 (office); (20) 8858-5320 (home). *Fax:* (20) 8293-4770 (home). *E-mail:* rpinker@freenetname.co.uk (home).

PINKER, Steven, BA, PhD; American psychologist, scientist, writer and academic; *Johnstone Family Professor of Psychology, Harvard University;* b. 18 Sept. 1954, Montreal, Canada; s. of Harry Pinker and Roslyn Pinker; m. Ilavenil Subbiah 1995; ed McGill Univ., Canada, Harvard Univ.; Asst Prof., Harvard Univ. 1980–81, Johnstone Family Prof. of Psychology 2003–; Asst Prof., Stanford Univ. 1981–82; Asst Prof., MIT 1982–85, Assoc. Prof., Dept of Brain and Cognitive Sciences 1985–89, Prof. 1989–, Peter de Florez Prof. 2000–03, Margaret MacVicar Fellow 2000–, Co-Dir Center for Cognitive Science 1985–94, Dir McDonnell-Pew Center for Cognitive Neuroscience 1994–99; Assoc. Ed. Cognition; Hon. DSc (McGill) 1999; Hon. DPhil (Tel-Aviv) 2003; Hon. DUniv (Surrey) 2003; Distinguished Scientific Award for Early Career Contribution to Psychology, American Psychological Asscn 1984, Boyd R. McCandless Young Scientist Award, Div. of Developmental Psychology, American Psychological Asscn 1986, Troland Research Award NAS 1993, Linguistics, Language and the Public Interest Award, Linguistics Soc. of America 1997, Los Angeles Times Book Prize in Science and Technology 1998, Golden Plate Award, American Acad. of Achievement 1999, Humanist Laureate Int. Acad. of Humanism 2001. *Publications include:* Language Learnability and Language Development 1984, Visual Cognition (ed.) 1985, Connections and Symbols (ed. with J. Mehler) 1988, Learnability and Cognition: The Acquisition of Argument Structure 1989, The Language Instinct 1994 (William James Book Prize, American Psychological Asscn 1995), How the Mind Works 1997 (William James Book Prize, American Psychological Asscn 1999), Words and Rules: The Ingredients of Language 1999, The Blank Slate: The Modern Denial of Human Nature 2002, The Stuff of Thought: Language as a Window into Human Nature 2007, Seven Words You Can't Say on Television 2008; contribs to Animal Learning and Behavior, Annals of the New York Academy of Sciences, Behavioral and Brain Sciences, Canadian Journal of Psychology, Child Development, Cognition, Cognitive Psychology, Cognitive Science, Communication and Cognition, Journal of Child Language, Journal of Cognitive Neuroscience, Journal of Experimental Psychology, Journal of Mental Imagery, Journal of Psycholinguistic Research, Journal of Verbal Learning and Verbal Behavior, Language and Cognitive Processes, Language, Lingua, Memory and Cognition, Monographs of the Society for Research in Child Development, Nature, New York Times, The New Yorker, Papers and Reports in Child Language, Psychological Science, Science, Slate, Time, Trends in Cognitive Science, Trends in Neurosciences, Visual Cognition. *Leisure interests:* bicycling, photography. *Address:* The Lavin Agency, 872 Massachusetts Avenue, Cambridge, MA 02139, USA (office); Department of Psychology, Harvard University, William James Hall, 33 Kirkland Street, Cambridge, MA 02138, USA (office). *Website:* pinker.wjh.harvard.edu (office).

PINNOCK, Trevor David, CBE, ARCM, FRAM; British harpsichordist and conductor; b. 16 Dec. 1946, Canterbury; s. of Kenneth and Joyce Pinnock; ed Canterbury Cathedral School, Royal Coll. of Music, London; Jt F. Galliard Harpsichord Trio, début, London 1966, solo début, London 1968, Dir The English Concert 1973–2003; Artistic Dir, Prin. Conductor Nat. Arts Centre Orchestra, Ottawa 1991–96, Artistic Adviser 1996–; f. European Brandenburg Ensemble 2006–, numerous tours and recordings; has toured Western Europe, USA, South America, Canada, Australia, Japan with The English Concert, as solo harpsichordist and as orchestral/opera conductor; début Metropolitan Opera, New York 1988; has worked with Opera Australia, Freiburg Baroque Orchestra, Salzburg Camerata, Deutsche Kammerphilharmonie Bremen, Deutsche Symfonie Orchester Berlin, Amsterdam Concertgebouw Orchestra; Gramophone Award for Bach Partitas BWV 825-30 2001. *Recordings include:* Rameau, Pièces de Clavicin (with Jonathan Manson, J. S. Bach, Sonatas for viola da gamba and obligato harpsichord, and works by Handel, C. P. E. Bach, Vivaldi, Scarlatti, 16th-, 17th- and 18th-century harpsichord music and most of the standard baroque orchestral/concerto/choral repertoire, Brandenburg Concertos (with European Brandenburg Ensemble) (Gramophone Award for Best Baroque Instrumental Recording 2008). *Address:* Askonas Holt Ltd, Lincoln House, 300 High Holborn, London, WC1V 7JH, England (office). *Telephone:* (20) 7400-1700 (office). *Fax:* (20) 7400-1799 (office). *E-mail:* info@askonasholt.co.uk (office). *Website:* www.askonasholt.co.uk (office).

PINÓS, Carmen; Spanish architect; b. 23 June 1954, Barcelona; ed Escuela Superior de Arquitectura de Barcelona, Int. Lab. of Architecture with Urban Design (ILAUD), Urbino, Columbia Univ.; visiting Prof. at the Univs of Illinois at Urbana-Champaign 1994–95, the Kunstakademie in Dusseldorf 1994–98, Columbia Univ. 1999, the École Polytechnique Federale de Lausanne 2001–02, the ETSAV in Barcelona 2002, the Università degli Studi di Sassari, Alghero, Italy 2002, 2004, Harvard Univ. Graduate School of Design 2003; FAD Prize at the La Llauna School, FAD Prize for the Igualada Cemetery, The City of Barcelona Prize for the archery range building for the 1992 Olympic Games, Spanish Nat. Architecture Prize for the boarding school of Morella 1995, the Inst. of Architects form the Valencia Govt for the public spaces of the Waterfront Juan Aparicio in Torrevieja 2001. *Major works:* El Croquis 1986, Arte Cemento 1987, Baumeister 1989. *Publications:* Carme Pinós: Some Projects (since 1991) 1998, Carme Pinós: An Architecture of Overlay (Ana Maria Torres) 2004. *Address:* Diagonal 490, 3-2, 08006 Barcelona, Spain (office). *Telephone:* (3) 4160372 (office). *Fax:* (3) 2781473 (office). *E-mail:* info@cpinos.com (office). *Website:* www.cpinos.com (office).

PINSENT, Sir Matthew Clive, Kt, CBE, BA; British fmr oarsman; b. 10 Oct. 1970, Norfolk; s. of Rev. Ewen Pinsent and Jean Pinsent; m. Demetra Pinsent 2002; two s.; ed Eton Coll. and Univ. of Oxford; first rep. UK at Jr World Championships 1987, 1988, Gold Medal in Coxless Pairs (with Tim Foster) 1988; competed three times in University Boat Race for Oxford 1990, 1991, 1993, winning twice; Gold Medal, Coxless Pairs (with Steve Redgrave q.v.) World Championships 1991, 1993, 1994, 1995, Olympic Games, Barcelona 1992, Atlanta 1996; Gold Medal, Coxless Fours (with Steve Redgrave, Tim Foster and James Cracknell) World Championships 1997, 1998, 1999, Olympic Games, Sydney 2000; Gold Medal, Coxless Pairs (with James Cracknell) World Championships 2001, 2002 (new world record); Gold Medal, Coxless Fours (with Cracknell, Coode and Williams) Olympic Games, Athens 2004; mem. Int. Olympic Cttee 2002–04; announced retirement Nov. 2004; Int. Rowing Fed. Male Rower of the Year, mem. BBC Sports Team of the Year 2004. *Publication:* A Lifetime in a Race 2004. *Leisure interests:* golf, flying. *Address:* c/o Chris Evans-Pollard, Professional Sports Partnerships Ltd, The Town House, 63 The High Street, Chobham, GU24 8AF, England. *Telephone:* (1276) 858930; (1276) 858930 (office). *Fax:* (1276) 856974. *E-mail:* enquiries@matthewpinsent.co.uk (office); contact@profsports.com. *Website:* www.matthewpinsent.com (office); www.profsports.com.

PINSKY, Robert Neal, PhD; American poet and academic; *Professor of Creative Writing, Boston University;* b. 20 Oct. 1940, Long Branch, NJ; s. of Milford Simon Pinsky and Sylvia Pinsky (née Eisenberg); m. Ellen Jane Bailey 1961; three d.; ed Rutgers Univ., Stanford Univ.; taught English at Univ. of Chicago 1967–68, Wellesley Coll. 1968–80; Prof. of English, Univ. of Calif., Berkeley 1980–89; Prof., Boston Univ. 1980–89, Prof. of Creative Writing 1989–; Poet Laureate of USA 1997–2000; f. Favorite Poem Project; Visiting Lecturer, Harvard Univ.; Hurst Prof., Washington Univ., St Louis; Poetry Ed. New Republic magazine 1978, Slate Magazine 1994–; Guggenheim Fellow 1980; mem. AAAL (Sec. 2003–06); Chancellor, Acad. of American Poets; Artist's Award, American Acad. of Arts and Letters 1979, Saxifrage Prize 1980, William Carlos Williams Prize 1984, Shelley Memorial Award 1996, Harold Washington Literary Award 1999, Manhae Foundation Prize 2006, Jewish Cultural Foundation Achievement Award 2006, Theodore Roethke Prize 2008. *Publications:* Landor's Poetry 1968, Sadness and Happiness 1975, The Situation of Poetry 1977, An Explanation of America 1980, History of My Heart 1980, Poetry and the World 1988, The Want Bone 1990, The Inferno of Dante (trans.; Howard Morton Landon Translation Prize) 1994, The Figured Wheel: New and Collected Poems 1966–96 (Lenore Marshall Award, Amb. Book Award, English Speaking Union) 1996, The Sounds of Poetry 1998, The Handbook of Heartbreak 1998, Americans' Favorite Poems (co-ed.) 1999, Jersey Rain 2000, Democracy, Culture, and the Voice of Poetry 2002, Poems to Read (co-ed.) 2002, Invitation to Poetry (co-ed.) 2004, First Things to Hand 2006, Gulf Music 2007, Thousands of Broadways: Dreams and Nightmares of the American Small Town 2009. *Address:* Steven Barclay Agency, 12 Western Avenue, Petaluma, CA 94952, USA (office); Department of English, Boston University, 236 Bay State Road, Boston, MA 02215, USA (office). *Telephone:* (707) 773-0654 (office); (617) 353-2506 (office). *Fax:* (707) 778-1868 (office). *E-mail:* steven@barclayagency.com (office); rpinsky@bu.edu (office). *Website:* www.barclayagency.com (office); www.bu.edu/english (office).

PINTAT SANTOLÀRIA, Albert, Lic en Sc économiques; Andorran diplomatist and politician; *Cap de Govern (Head of Government);* b. 23 June 1943; m.; three c.; ed Catholic Univ. of Friburg, Switzerland; Asst Consul, Sant Julià, Andorra 1982–83; Sec. to Josep Pintat, Head of Govt 1984–85; Counsellor-Gen. 1986–91; Amb. to Benelux countries and EU 1995–97; Minister of Foreign Affairs 1997–2001; Amb. to Switzerland and UK 2001–04; Cap de Govern (Head of Govt) 2005–; mem. Liberal Party of Andorra (PLA). *Address:* Office of the Head of Government, Govern d'Andorra, Carrer Prat de la Creu 62–64, Edif. Administratiu, Andorra la Vella AD500, Andorra (office). *Telephone:* 875700 (office). *Fax:* 822882 (office). *E-mail:* comunicacio.gov@andorra.ad (office). *Website:* www.presidencia.ad (office).

PINTER, Frances Mercedes Judith, PhD; American/British publisher; *Publisher, Bloomsbury Academic;* b. 13 June 1949, Venezuela; d. of George Pinter and Vera Hirschenhauser Pinter; m. David Percy 1985; ed Univ. Coll., London; Research Officer, Centre for Criminological Research, Univ. of Oxford, UK 1976–79; Man. Dir Pinter Publrs 1979–94; Chair. Ind. Publrs Guild 1979–82, Publrs Asscn E European Task Force 1990–; Man. Dir Cen. European Univ. Press 1994–96; Chair. Bd of Trustees, Int. House 2001, CEO Int. House Trust 2002–06; Deputy Chair. Book Devt Council 1985–89; Publisher, Bloomsbury Academic 2008–; mem. Bd UK Publrs Asscn 1987–92, IBIS Information Services 1988–90, Libra Books 1991–; Exec. Dir Centre for Publishing Devt 1994–, Open Soc. Inst. 1994–99; Visiting Fellow, LSE 2000–01, 2006–. *Leisure interests:* reading, travelling, hiking. *Address:* 1 Belsize Avenue, London, NW3 4BL, England (home). *Telephone:* (20) 7431-7849 (office). *E-mail:* frances@pinter.org.uk (office). *Website:* www.pinter.org.uk.

PINTILIE, Lucian; Romanian director; b. 9 Nov. 1933, Tarutino (Bessarabia); s. of Victor Pintilie and Amelia Pintilie; ed Bucharest Theatrical and Cinematographic Art Inst.; career at Lucia Sturdza Bulandra Theatre, directing The Cherry Orchard by Chekhov, D'ale carnavalului by I.L. Caragiale, The Inspector General by Gogol; staged several plays by Chekhov, Gorki, Ibsen, Eugène Ionesco, Pirandello and Strindberg abroad; also operas such as Rigoletto, Carmen, The Magic Flute etc.; worked for TV, doing reporting and theatrical programs 1956–59; debut as film dir 1965; Commdr des Arts et des Lettres 2001. *Films:* Duminică la ora 6 (At Six O'Clock on Sunday), Reconstituirea (The Reconstruction) 1969, Salonul nr 6 (Ward No. 6) 1973 (Yugoslavia), De ce trag clopotele Mitică? (What Do The Bells Toll For Mitică?) 1980, Balanţa (The Oak) 1992, O Vară de Neuitat (An Unforgettable Summer) 1994, Prea tirziu (Too Late) 1996, Terminus Paradis (Last Stop Paradise) (Jury's Special Award, Venice Film Festival 1998) 1998, Dupăamiaza unui torţionar (A Torturer's Afternoon) 2001, Niki et Flo (Niki and Flo) 2003, Tertium Nom Datur 2006. *Publications:* Bricabrac 2004. *Address:* 44 Mihail Kogălniceanu Blvd, Bucharest, Romania. *Telephone:* 3154715; 2320644.

PINTO, Rossano Maranhão, MEconSc; Brazilian banking executive; *Chairman and President, Banco do Brasil SA;* b. 17 July 1957, São Luís, Maranhão; m.; one s. two d.; ed Univ. of Ill., USA, Univ. of Brasília; joined Banco do Brasil 1976, served as Man. Dir for Int. Div., CEO BB Leasing Co., Vice-Pres. for Int. Businesses and Wholesale 2001–04, Pres. 2004–, mem. Bd of Dirs 2005–, Chair. 2006–; fmr Prof. Instituto Brasileiro de Mercado de Capitais–Ibmec and Universidade Católica de Brasília. *Address:* Banco do Brasil SA, SBS Qd. 01 Bloco C - Edifício Sede III, 24th Floor, Brasília DF 70073-901, Brazil (office). *Telephone:* (61) 3310-3400 (office). *Fax:* (61) 3310-3735 (office). *E-mail:* presidencia@bb.com.br (office). *Website:* www.bb.com.br (office).

PINTO BALSEMÃO, Francisco José Pereira; Portuguese politician, lawyer and journalist; *Chairman and CEO, Impresa SGPS;* b. 1 Sept. 1937, Lisbon; s. of Henrique Pinto Balsemão and Maria Adelaide C. P. Pinto Balsemão; m. Mercedes Presas Pinto Balsemão 1975; three s. two d.; Ed.-in-Chief review Mais Alto 1961–63; Sec. to Man. Bd Diário Popular, later Man. –1971; f. weekly Expresso 1973; mem. Nat. Ass. during govt of Dr Marcello Caetano; f. Popular Democratic Party (PPD), later renamed Social Democratic Party (PSD), with the late Dr Sá Carneiro and Joaquim Magalhães Mota May 1974; Vice-Pres. Constituent Ass. 1975; Opposition Spokesman on Foreign Affairs 1977; mem. Ass. of the Repub. 1979; Minister Without Portfolio and Deputy Prime Minister 1980; Prime Minister of Portugal 1981–83; Pres. Instituto Progresso Social e Democracia, Francisco dá Carneiro 1983–; Chair. Int. Relations Cttee and mem. Political Cttee PSD, party leader 1980–83; Pres. Sociedad Independente de Comunicação (SIC); Pres. European Inst. for the Media 1990; Chair. Sojornal and Controjornal (Media) Groups; Chair. and CEO Impresa SGPS; Chair. European Publrs Council; Pres. Companhia de Seguros Allianz Portugal SA; Prof. of Communication Science, New Univ., Lisbon; Rafael Calvo Serer Prize, Spain 2007. *Address:* Impresa SGPS SA, Rua Ribeiro Sanches 65, 1200-787 Lisbon, Portugal (office). *Telephone:* (213) 929780 (office). *Fax:* (213) 929787 (office). *Website:* www.impresa.pt (office).

PINTO COELHO SERRA, João António, BEcon; Cape Verde politician; b. 25 Jan. 1961, Praia, Santiago; fmr Sec. of State for Finance; fmr Pres. Admin Council, Instituto Nacional da Previdência Social; fmr Man. Dir Instituto do Emprego e Formação Profissional; fmr Dir Projecto de Promoção de Microempresas; Minister of Finance and Public Admin 2005, of Finance, Planning and Devt 2006. *Address:* c/o Ministry of Finance and Public Administration, 107 Avda Amílcar Cabral, CP 30, Praia, Santiago, Cape Verde (office).

PINTO MONTEIRO, Fernando José; Portuguese lawyer and judge; *Chief Public Prosecutor;* b. 5 April 1942, Porto de Ovelha, Almeida; s. of Amílcar Monteiro and Lurdes Monteiro; ed Univ. of Coimbra; Public Prosecutor, Idanha-a-Nova, Anadia, Porto and Lisbon 1966; Judge, Ponta do Sol, Alcácer do Sal, Loures, Torres Vedras and Lisboa; fmr Asst High Commr Higher Authority Against Corruption; Judge Court of Appeals 1990–98; Judge Supreme Court of Justice 1998–2006; Chief Public Prosecutor 2006–; Visiting Prof. of Law, Autonomous Univ. of Lisbon 1992–2006; Pres. Disciplinary Council, Portuguese Football Asscn 1995–97; fmr Sec. Gen. Portuguese Asscn of Judges. *Address:* Procuradoria-Geral da República, Rua da Escola Politécnica, 140, 1269-269 Lisbon, Portugal (office). *Telephone:* (213) 921900 (office). *Fax:* (213) 975255 (office). *Website:* www.pgr.pt (office).

PINTO RUBIANES, Pedro Alfredo; Ecuadorean politician and industrialist; b. 31 Jan. 1931, Quito; ed Univ. Cen. del Ecuador, Vanderbilt Univ.; Gen. Man. Textile San Pedro SA 1967–82, 1984–97, Pres. 1997; Pres. Asscn of Textile Mfrs 1968–70; Dean Faculty of Admin, Univ. Cen. del Ecuador 1970–72; Pres. Chamber of Mfrs of Pichincha 1971–73, Fed. of Industrialists of Ecuador 1972–73; town councillor, Quito 1973–77; Dir Corporación Financiera Ecuatoriana (COFIEC) 1976–82; Minister of Finance and Public Credit 1982–84; Gov. for Ecuador, Banco Interamericano de Desarrollo (BID), IBRD 1983–84; Dir CORDES 1988, Bank of Pichincha 1993–98, Chamber of Mfrs of Pichincha 1997–98; Deputy for Pichincha 1998; apptd Vice-Pres. of Ecuador 2001. *Address:* c/o Office of the Vice-President, Manuel Larrea y Arenas, Edif. Conseyo Provincial de Pichincha, 21°, Quito, Ecuador (office).

PIOT, Baron; **Peter,** MD, PhD, FRCP; Belgian international development and public health official; *Professor and Director, Institute of Global Health, Imperial College, London;* b. 17 Feb. 1949, Leuven; m. Greet Kimzeke 1975; two c.; ed Univs of Ghent and Antwerp, Belgium, and Washington, USA; Asst in Microbiology, Inst. of Tropical Medicine, Antwerp 1974–78, Prof., Head Dept of Microbiology 1981–92; NATO Fellow 1978–79; Sr Fellow, Microbiology and Infectious Diseases, Washington Univ. 1978–79; Researcher, Nairobi Univ., STD/AIDS Project, Kenya 1981–92; Supervisor, Project SIDA, Kinshasa 1985–91; Asst Prof. of Public Health, Free Univ. Brussels 1989–94; Assoc. Dir Global Program AIDS, WHO 1995, Exec. Dir Jt UN Program on HIV/AIDS (UNAIDS), Geneva 1995–2008, Under-Sec.-Gen. UN 1995–2008; currently Prof. and Dir, Inst. of Global Health, Imperial Coll. London; Dir WHO Collaborating Centre on AIDS, Antwerp; Chair. King Baudouin Foundation, Brussels; mem. Royal Acad. of Medicine, Int. AIDS Soc. (Pres. 1992–), Inst. of Medicine, Washington DC, AAAS, and numerous other socs in Europe, USA and Africa; cr. baron by King Albert II 1995; numerous decorations including Officier, Ordre Nat. du Léopard (Zaïre) 1977, Ordre du Lion (Senegal), Nat. Order, Burkina Faso, Madagascar, Vietnam, Grand Official, Order of the Infante Don Enrique (Portugal) 2005, Commandeur, Ordre Nat., Mali 2008; various hon. doctorates; numerous awards including De Kerkheer Prize for Medicine 1989, Health Research Award (Belgium) 1989, Public Health Award, Flemish Community 1990, AMICOM Award for Medicine 1991, H. Breurs Prize 1992, A. Jaunioux Prize 1992, van Thiel Award 1993, Glaxo award for infectious diseases 1995, Nelson Mandela Award 2001, Royal Acad. of Arts and Sciences Gold Medal, Belgium 2002, E. Calderone Medal, Columbia Univ. 2003, Outstanding Physician AMA Chicago, Vlerick Award, Belgium 2004, Congressional Award of Achievement, Philippines 2005, Mother Theresa Award, New Delhi, 2007, Person of the Year, Knack Magazine, Belgium 2008. *Publications:* author and co-author of 16 books and over 500 scientific papers on women's health, AIDS and other sexually transmitted diseases. *Address:* Institute of Global Health, Imperial College, 30 Guilford Street, London WC1N 1EH, England (office). *Telephone:* (20) 7905-2122 (office). *E-mail:* p.piot@imperial.ac.uk (office). *Website:* http://www.ucl.ac.uk/global-health (office).

PIOTROVSKY, Mikhail Borisovich, DHist; Russian art researcher; *Director, State Hermitage;* b. 9 Dec. 1944, Yerevan, Armenia; s. of Boris Piotrovsky; m. Irina Leonidovna Piotrovskaya; one s. one d.; ed Leningrad State Univ., Cairo Univ.; researcher Leningrad Inst. of Oriental Studies USSR Acad. of Sciences 1967–91; First Deputy Dir State Hermitage, St Petersburg 1991–92, Dir. 1992–; Corresp. mem. Russian Acad. of Sciences 1997–; mem. Acad. of Humanitarian Sciences; mem. Presidium, Cttee on State Prizes of Russian Presidency, Presidium, Russian Cttee of UNESCO; mem. Int. Council of Museums; consultant to European Parl.; main research in ancient and medieval history of Near E, Muslim art in archaeology. *Publications:* over 150 scientific works. *Address:* State Hermitage, Dvortsovaya nab. 34, 191186 St Petersburg, Russia (office). *Telephone:* (812) 110-96-01. *Fax:* (812) 311-90-09. *E-mail:* haltunen@hermitage.ru.

PIOVANELLI, HE Cardinal Silvano; Italian ecclesiastic; b. 21 Feb. 1924; ordained priest 1947; consecrated Bishop (Titular Church of Tubune, Mauritania) 1982; Archbishop of Florence 1983–2001, Archbishop Emer. 2001–; cr. Cardinal-Priest S. Maria delle Grazie a Via Tionfale 1985. *Address:* Arcivescovado, Piazza S. Giovanni 3, 50129 Florence, Italy. *Telephone:* (055) 239-88-13.

PIPE, Martin Charles, CBE; British race horse trainer (retd); b. 29 May 1945; s. of D. A. C. Pipe and M. E. R. Pipe; m. to Mary Caroline; one s.; ed Queen's Coll., Taunton; first trainer's licence 1977; major wins include: Grand National (with Miinnehoma) 1994, Champion hurdle (twice), Welsh National (six times), Irish National, Scottish National, Midlands National, Hennessy Gold Cup (three times), Mackeson Gold Cup; only British trainer to train 200 winners in a season 1989; 15 times National Hunt champion trainer (1989/90, 1990/91, 1991/92, 1992/93, 1995/96, 1996/97, 1997/98, 1998/99, 1999/2000, 2000/01, 2001/02, 2002/03, 2003/04); four winners at Royal Ascot; 28 winners at Cheltenham Festival including record four winners in consecutive years. *Publications:* Martin Pipe: The Champion Trainer's Story (with Richard Pitman) 1992. *Address:* Pond House, Nicholashayne, nr Wellington, Somerset, TA21 9QY, England (office). *Telephone:* (1884) 840715 (office). *Fax:* (1884) 841343 (office). *E-mail:* martin@martinpipe.co.uk (office); www.martinpipe.co.uk (office).

PIPER, Martha Cook, BSc, MA, PhD, OC, OBC; Canadian/American epidemiologist, academic and university administrator; *Chairman, Board of Trustees, National Institute for Nanotechnology;* b. Lorain, OH; ed Univ. of Michigan, Univ. of Connecticut, McGill Univ., Montréal; physical therapist, Sr then Chief Physical Therapist at various US hosps 1967–1973; Dir School of Physical and Occupational Therapy, McGill Univ., Montréal 1979–85, Asst Prof. then Assoc. Prof. 1979–84; Dean, Assoc. Prof., then Prof. of Rehabilitation Medicine and Vice Pres. (Research, later Research and External Affairs), Univ. of Alberta, Edmonton 1985–96; Pres. and Vice-Chancellor, Univ. of British Columbia 1997–2006; Chair. Bd of Trustees Nat. Inst. of Nanotechnology 2008–; fmr Dir Canadian Genetic Diseases Network; mem. Bd of Dirs Bank of Montreal 2006–, Transalta Corpn 2006–, Shoppers Drug Mart Corpn 2007–, Grosvenor Americas Ltd, CARE Canada, Inst. for Research on Public Policy, BC Children's Hosp. Foundation; fmr mem. Bd of Dirs Center for Frontier Engineering Research 1993–97, Telecommunications Research Labs 1993–97, Alberta Research Council 1993–97, Canada Israel Industrial Research Foundation 1994–97, The Conf. Bd of Canada, Pierre Elliot Trudeau Foundation, PrioNet Canada; fmr mem. Advisory Council on Science and Tech. 1996–2004, Protein Eng Network Centre of Excellence (PENCE), Canada Foundation for Innovation, Advisory Bd Vancouver Econ. Devt Comm., Distinguished Profs Selection Cttee, Univ. of Manitoba, Canadian-American Business Council, Nat. Univ. of Singapore Council, Steering Cttee, Asscn of Pacific Rim Univs; fmr Chair. Standing Advisory Cttee on Univ. Research, Asscn of Univs and Colls of Canada; fmr Public Gov., Bd of Canadian Acads of Science; Specially Elected Fellow, Royal Soc. of Canada 2009–; Trustee Dalia Lama Center for Peace and Educ., Vancouver; mem. Trilateral Comm., Canadian Insts of Advanced Research; Hon. Fellow, Merton Coll., Oxford 2007; Hon. DSc (McGill) 1998, (Western Ontario) 2002; Hon. LLD (Dalhousie) 1999, (Toronto) 2001, (Melbourne, Australia) 2003, (Saskatchewan) 2005, (St Francis Xavier) 2006, (Calgary) 2006, (Alberta) 2006, (Victoria) 2006, (Simon Fraser) 2008; Educator of the Year, Learning Partnership 2004 and was recently appointed a. *Address:* c/o Board of Trustees, National Institute for Nanotechnology, 11421 Saskatchewan Drive, Edmonton, AB T6G 2M9, Canada. *E-mail:* nintinfo@nrc.gc.ca. *Website:* nint-innt.nrc-cnrc.gc.ca.

PIQUÉ I CAMPS, Josep, LLB, PhD; Spanish politician, business executive and economist; b. 21 Feb. 1955, Barcelona; ed Univ. of Barcelona; Lecturer in Econ. Theory, Univ. of Barcelona 1977–86, 1990–; Economist, Studies Dept, La Caixa 1984–85; Gen. Dir of Industry, Catalan Autonomous Govt 1986–88; Gen. Man. of Corp. Strategy, Ercros. SA (pvt. chemicals group) 1989–91, Man. Dir 1992, Chair. and CEO 1992–96, various posts in group including Chair. EMESA 1989–91, ERKIMIA SA 1990–96, FERTIBERIA 1993–96, FYSE 1992–93, LISAC 1992, META 1990–94, Sole Admin. FESA 1992–93, mem. Bd Prisma 1991–96, Río Tinto Minera 1991–93, Erkol 1991–96, Rhodiamul 1991–92; Minister of Industry and Energy 1996–2000; Govt Spokesman 1998–2000; Minister of Foreign Affairs 2000–02, of Science and Tech. 2002–04. *Address:* c/o Ministerio de Ciencia y Tecnología, Paseo de la Castellana 160, 28071 Madrid, Spain (office). *Telephone:* (91) 3494000 (office). *Fax:* (91) 4578066 (office). *E-mail:* info@mcyt.es (office). *Website:* www.mcyt.es (office).

PIQUET (SOUTO MAIOR), Nélson; Brazilian fmr racing driver; b. 17 Aug. 1952, Rio de Janeiro; s. of Estácio Souto Maior and Clotilde Maior; m. 1st Maria Clara; m. 2nd Vivianne Leao, one s. racing driver Nelson Angelo "Nelsinho" Piquet Jr; first Grand Prix, Germany 1978; mem. Ensign Grand Prix team 1978, BS McLaren team 1978, Brabham team 1978–85, Williams team 1986–87, Lotus team 1988–89, Benetton team 1990; winner of 23 Grand Prix races; Formula One World Champion 1981, 1983, 1987; lives in Monaco; International Motorsports Hall of Fame 2000. *Leisure interest:* sports.

PIRES, Maria João; Portuguese pianist; b. 23 July 1944, Lisbon; m.; four c.; ed Lisbon Acad. of Music; debut recital aged four; early concert tours of Portugal, Spain and Germany; int. career from 1970, with performances in Europe, Africa and Japan; British debut 1986; debut tour of N America 1988; appearances with numerous famous orchestras and conductors world-wide; repertoire includes Mozart, Schubert, Schumann, Beethoven and Chopin; f. Belgais Foundation for the Study of Arts 1999; moved to San Salvador, Brazil 2006; First Prize, Beethoven Int. Competition, Brussels 1970. *Recordings include:* Complete Mozart Piano Sonatas (Edison Prize, Prix de l'Acad. du Disque Français, Prix de l'Acad. Charles Cros), Debussy Etudes (Grammy Award) 1990, Concertos by Mozart (Grammy Award) 1991. *Leisure interest:* rural life.

PIRES, Maria Madalena Emília; Timor-Leste government official; *Minister of Planning and Finance;* ed La Trobe Univ., Australia; came to Australia as refugee with family at age 14 in 1975; fmr Admin. Nat. Council of Timorese Resistance (CNRT) office, Darwin; fmr Pres. Timorese Asscn of Vic.; mem. World Bank jt assessment mission in Timor-Leste 1999; est. East Timor Devt Office, Melbourne; Head, Nat. Planning and Devt Agency, Timor-Leste 2000–01; joined Ministry of Planning and Finances, held several positions including Sec., East Timor Planning Comm. 2002, Advisor on Planning and External Assistance Man. 2003–04; Sr Coordination Adviser to the UN Deputy Special Representative of the Secretary-General (DSRSG) for Int. Compact on Timor-Leste –2007; Minister of Planning and Finance 2007–. *Address:* Ministry of Planning and Finance, Palácio do Governo, Edif. 5, Av. Presidente Nicolau Lobato, Dili, Timor-Leste (office). *Telephone:* 3339546 (office). *E-mail:* itds@mopf.gov.tl (office).

PIRES, Mario; Guinea-Bissau politician; b. 1949; m.; five c.; trained as economist; fmr Chief of Staff to Pres. Kumba Yalá; Founding mem. Social Renovation Party; Prime Minister (in caretaker govt) of Guinea-Bissau Nov. 2002–Sept. 2003. *Address:* c/o Gabinete do Primeiro Ministro, Avda Unidade Africana, CP 137, Bissau, Guinea-Bissau (office).

PIRES, Gen. Pedro Verona Rodrigues; Cape Verde head of state; *President;* b. 29 April 1934, Sant' Ana, Fogo; s. of Luís Rodrigues Pires and Maria Fidalga Lopes Pires; m. Adélcia Maria da Luz Lima Barreto Pires 1975; two d.; ed Liceu Gil Eanes de São Vicente, Faculty of Science, Lisbon Univ., Portugal; left Portugal to join Partido Africano da Independência da Guiné e Cabo Verde (PAIGC) 1961; mem. PAIGC dels 1961–63; involved in preparation for liberation of Cape Verde 1963–65; mem. Cen. Cttee of PAIGC 1965, of Council of War, PAIGC 1967; re-elected mem. of Commissão Permanente do Comité Executivo da Luta (CEL) and of Council of War 1970; involved in admin. of liberated areas of southern Guinea-Bissau 1971–73; Pres. Nat. Comm. of PAIGC for Cape Verde 1973 (reaffirmed as mem. of Council of War and CEL), appointed an Asst State Commr in first Govt of Repub. of Guinea-Bissau 1973–74; negotiated independence agreements of Cape Verde and Guinea-Bissau 1974; Dir PAIGC policies during transitional govt before independence of Cape Verde 1975; elected Deputy in Nat. Popular Ass. of Cape Verde June 1975–, re-elected 1980; Prime Minister of Cape Verde 1975–91, with responsibility for Finance, Planning and Co-operation; elected Deputy Gen. Sec. Partido Africano da Independência de Cabo Verde (PAICV) 1981, Sec. Gen. 1990–93, fmr Chair. Gen. 1993; Pres. of Cape Verde 2001–; mem. Perm. Comm. of CEL 1977; Amílcar Cabral Medal 1976. *Leisure interests:* philosophy, sociology, politics. *Address:* Presidência da República, CP 100, Plateau, Praia, Santiago (office); c/o PAICV, CP 22, Praia, Santiago, Republic of Cape Verde. *Telephone:* 2616555 (office). *Fax:* 2614356 (office). www.presidenciarepublica.cv

PIRES DE SOUZA, Waldir; Brazilian politician and government official; b. 21 Oct. 1926, Acajutiba, Bahia; s. of José Pires de Souza and Lucída Figueiredo Pires; ed Univ. of Brasília; Sec., State Govt of Bahia 1951–53; State Deputy, PTB party 1955–59, State Deputy, PSD party 1959–64; Gen. Consultant to the Repub. 1963–64; in exile in Uruguay and France, returned to Brazil 1970; Assoc. Prof., Univ. of Dijon, France 1966; Prof., Inst. of Higher Latin American Studies, Univ. of Paris 1968; Minister of Social Security 1985–86; Gov. State of Bahia 1987–89; State Deputy 1991–95, 1999–2003; Comptroller-Gen.

2003–06; Minister of Defence 2006–07. *Address:* c/o Ministry of Defence, Esplanada dos Ministérios, Bloco Q, 70049-900 Brasília, DF, Brazil (office).

PIRIE, Madsen Duncan, MA, PhD, MPhil; British research institute director; *President, Adam Smith Institute;* b. 24 Aug. 1940; s. of Douglas G. Pirie and Eva Madsen; ed Univs of Edinburgh, St Andrews and Cambridge; Republican Study Cttee 1974; Distinguished Visiting Prof. of Philosophy, Hillsdale Coll., Mich. 1975–78; Pres. Adam Smith Inst. 1978–; mem. Citizens' Charter Advisory Panel 1991–95; RC Hoiles Fellow 1975. *Publications:* Freeports 1983, Test Your IQ 1983, Book of the Fallacy 1985, Privatization 1988, Micropolitics 1988, Boost Your IQ 1990, The Sherlock Holmes I.Q. Book 1995. *Leisure interest:* calligraphy. *Address:* 23 Great Smith Street, London, SW1P 3BL, England. *Telephone:* (20) 7222-4995 (office). *Fax:* (20) 7222-4503 (office). *E-mail:* m.pirie@adamsmith.org (office). *Website:* www.adamsmith.org (office).

PIRINSKI, Georgi Georgiev; Bulgarian politician; *Chairman of Narodno Sobraniye (National Assembly);* b. 10 Sept. 1948, New York, USA; m.; two c.; ed English Language Secondary School No. 114, Sofia, Karl Marx Higher Inst. of Econs, Sofia; moved to Bulgaria 1952; Research Assoc., Int. Relations and Socialist Integration Inst. 1972–74; economist, Int. Orgs Div., Ministry of Foreign Trade 1974–76; Advisor, Council of Ministers 1976–80; fmr Deputy Minister and First Deputy Minister of Foreign Trade 1980–89; Deputy Minister and First Deputy Minister of Foreign Trade 1980–90; Deputy Prime Minister Nov. 1989–Feb. 1990, Aug.–Dec. 1990; mem. Parl. for Blagoevgrad in 7th Grand Nat. Ass. (Parl. Group of Bulgarian Socialist Party—BSP), for Plovdiv in 36th Nat. Ass. (Parl. Union for Social Democracy), for Sofia in 37th, 38th, 39th and 40th Nat. Ass. (Parl. Group of Democratic Left) 1995–2005, Pres. (Speaker) 40th Nat. Ass. 2005–; Minister of Foreign Affairs 1995–96 (resgnd); mem. Dels of Nat. Ass. to Parl. Ass of OSCE, Council of Europe and WEU; nominated from BSP for Pres. in Oct. 1996 presidential elections but rejected by Constitutional Court on basis of not being a Bulgarian citizen by birth; mem. BSP 1969–2005 (mem. Presidency and Deputy Chair. Supreme Council 1990–2005), Cen. Cttee Bulgarian CP 1989–90, Coalition for Bulgaria (led by BSP) 2005–. *Address:* Office of the Chairman, Narodno Sobraniye, 1169 Sofia, pl. Narodno Sobraniye 2, Bulgaria (office). *Telephone:* (2) 939-39 (office). *Fax:* (2) 981-31-31 (office). *E-mail:* infocenter@parliament.bg (office). *Website:* www.parliament.bg (office).

PIRK, Jan, MD, DSc; Czech heart surgeon; *Head, IKEM Clinic for Heart Surgery;* b. 20 April 1948, Prague; s. of Otto Pirk and Jitka Pirk; m. Blanka Pirk; two s.; ed Charles Univ., Prague; occupied numerous medical and surgical positions; researcher 1978–90; consultant, Odense Univ. Hosp., Denmark 1990–91, Ochsner Hosp., New Orleans, USA 1983–84; Head, Institutu Klinické a Experimentální Medicíny (IKEM) Clinic for Heart Surgery 1991–; Hon. Mem. Czech Medical Soc. *Publications:* The Effect of Antiaggregation Drugs on the Patency of Grafts in the Arterial System 1980, Improved Patency of the Aortocoronary Bypass by Anti-Trombic Drugs (co-author) 1986, Surgery for Ischaemic Heart Disease in Patients Under Forty (co-author) 1989, An Alternative to Cardioplegia (with M. D. Kellovsky) 1995. *Leisure interests:* skiing, biking, long-distance running, theatre, yachting. *Address:* IKEM Clinic for Heart Surgery, Vídeňská 1958, 140 21, 140 00 Prague 4 (office); V. Domově 28, 130 00 Prague 3, Czech Republic (home). *Telephone:* (23) 605-5015 (office); (2) 72741912 (home). *Fax:* (23) 605-2776 (office). *E-mail:* japx@medicon.cz (office). *Website:* www.ikem.cz (office).

PIRUMOV, Vladimir Semenovich, DrMilSc; naval officer, politician and scientist; b. 1 Feb. 1926, Kirovakan, Armenia; m.; 2 d.; ed Caspian Higher Mil. Marine School, Mil. Marine Acad.; artillery officer, Asst to Commdr of cruiser, Commdr of destroyer Baltic Navy 1948–60; Head of Dept Gen. Staff of Mil. Marine forces 1974–85; teacher, Sr teacher, Head of Chair Mil. Marine Acad. 1963–74; Prof. Mil. Acad. of Gen. Staff 1985–; mem. Russian Acad. of Nat. Sciences; Vice-Pres., Head Section of Geopolitics and Security, Russian Acad. of Sciences 1993; Pres. Cen. of Studies of Problems of Geopolitics and Security at Security Council of Russian Fed. 1993–; First Vice-Pres. Acad. of Geopolitics and Security 2000–; mem. Ed. Bd journals Geopolitica i Besopasnost, Vooruzheniye, Politika, Konversia; P. Kapitsa Silver Medal, Piotr the Great Gold Medal, State Prize of Russian Fed. 1977, Merited Worker of Science of Russian Fed., various scientific awards. *Publications:* over 170 publications including Actual Problems of Security, Regions of Russia and the World, Strategy of Socio-Survival. *Address:* Russian Academy of Natural Sciences, Varshawskoye shosse 8, 113105 Moscow, Russia (office). *Telephone:* (495) 252-55-74 (office). *E-mail:* mediterra@yandex.ru (home).

PIRZADA, Syed Sharifuddin, SPk; Pakistani politician and lawyer; b. 12 June 1923, Burhanpur; s. of S. Vilayat Ali Pirzada and Butul Begum; m. 1st Rafia Sultana (died 1960); m. 2nd Safiya Pirzada; m. 3rd Rashda Pirzada; two s. three d.; ed Univ. of Bombay; Sec. Muslim Students Fed. 1943–45; Hon. Sec. to Quaid-i-Azam, Jinnah 1941–44; Sec. Bombay City Muslim League 1945–47; Prof., Sind Muslim Law Coll. 1947–54; Adviser to Constitution Comm. of Pakistan 1960–61; Chair. Co. Law Comm. 1962; Pres. Karachi High Court Bar Asscn, Pakistan Br. 1964–67; Attorney-Gen. of Pakistan 1965–66, 1968–72, 1977–89; Minister of Foreign Affairs 1966–68, April–Oct. 1993; Minister of Justice 1979–84; mem. or Pres. several asscns and socs; led Pakistan Del. to Session of UN Gen. Ass. 1966–67; Chair. UN Human Rights Sub-Cttee on Minorities 1977; mem. Panel of Perm. Court of Arbitration; mem. Int. Law Comm. 1981–86; Sec.-Gen. Org. of Islamic Conf. 1984–88; Chair. Heritage Council and Amb.-at-large with rank of Fed. Minister 1989–93; mem. Nat. Security Council of Pakistan 1999–; Hon. Sr Adviser to Chief Exec. on Foreign Affairs, Law, Justice and Human Rights 1999–; Judge (ad-hoc), Int. Court of Justice 2000; Chair. Nat. Cttee on Quaid-i-Azam Year 2001; Sr Adviser (Sr Fed. Minister) to Prime Minister on Foreign Affairs, Law, Justice and Human Rights 2002–08; Sr Advocate, Supreme Court. *Publications include:* Evolution of Pakistan 1962, Fundamental Rights and Constitutional Remedies in Pakistan 1966, Some Aspects of Quaid-i-Azam's Life 1978, Collected Works of Quaid-i-Azam Mohammad Ali Jinnah (Vol. I) 1985, (Vol. II) 1986, (Vol. III) 1987; Dissolution of Constituent Assembly of Pakistan 1996. *Leisure interest:* bridge. *Address:* House No. 25/1–4, Phase-V, Zamzama Street, Clifton, Karachi, Pakistan (home). *Telephone:* (21) 5874183 (home).

PISANI-FERRY, Jean; French economist; *Director, Bruegel;* b. 1951; ed Ecole Supérieure d'Electricité, Université Paris V, Centre d'études des programmes économiques; served as Head, Macroeconomic Dept, Centre d'études prospectives et d'informations internationales (CEPII, Paris) 1983–92, Dir CEPII 1992–97; Econ. Adviser to Directorate-Gen. for Econ. and Financial Affairs, EC 1989–92; Sr Econ. Adviser to Minister of Finance 1997–2001; Exec. Pres. Prime Minister's Council of Econ. Analysis 2001–02; Sr Adviser to Dir of Treasury 2002–04; currently Dir Bruegel (econ. think-tank), Brussels; Prof., Université Paris-Dauphine; mem. EC Group of Econ. Policy Analysis. *Address:* Bruegel, 33 Rue de la Charité, Brussels 1210, Belgium (office). *Telephone:* (2) 227-4210 (office). *Fax:* (2) 227-4219 (office). *E-mail:* jean.pisani-ferry@bruegel.org (office). *Website:* www.bruegel.org (office); www.pisani-ferry.net (office).

PISANU, Giuseppe; Italian politician; b. 2 Jan. 1937, Ittiri, Sassari; m.; three s.; Deputy Man. Dir Soc. of Finance and Industry for the Rebirth of Sardinia (SFIRS); Prov. Sec., Regional Sec. (Sardinia), Exec. Sec. to Pres. Democrazia Cristiana (Christian Democrats) 1975–80; elected Deputy 1972–92; Under-Sec. of State for Treasury 1980–83; Under-Sec. of State for Defence 1986–90; Minister of the Interior 2002–06; elected mem. Forza Italia (Sardinia) 1994–; mem. Pres.'s cttee 1994–96, Deputy-Chair. Parl. Group, then Chair. 1996–2001; mem. Defence Cttee; Del. of Italy to CSCE 1998, to WEU 1999. *Address:* c/o Forza Italia, Via dell'Umiltà 36, 00187 Rome, Italy (office). *Telephone:* (06) 67311 (office). *Fax:* (06) 6788255 (office). *E-mail:* lettere@forza-italia.it (office). *Website:* www.forza-italia.it (office).

PISCHETSRIEDER, Bernd; German automotive industry executive; b. 15 Feb. 1948, Munich; ed Technical Univ. Munich; joined BMW AG, Munich as production planning eng 1973; Production Dir BMW South Africa (Pty) Ltd 1982–85; Dir for Quality Control, BMW AG 1985–87, for Tech. Planning 1987–90; deputy mem. Admin. Bd in charge of Production 1990, mem. Admin. Bd 1991, Chair. Admin. Bd 1993–99; fmr Chair. Rover; Chair. Bd of Man. Volkswagen AG 2002–06 (resgnd); mem. Advisory Bd Allianz-Versicherung, Munich; Dr hc (Birmingham) 1996. *Address:* c/o Volkswagen AG, Brieffach 1848-2, 38436 Wolfsburg, Germany.

PISCHINGER, Franz Felix, Prof. Dr Techn., Dr Techn. e.h.; Austrian academic, scientist and business executive; *Chairman of the Board, FEV Motorentechnik GmbH;* b. 18 July 1930, Waidhofen; s. of Franz Pischinger and Karoline Pischinger; m. Elfriede Pischinger 1957 (died 2001); m. Elisabeth Pischinger 2003; four s. one d.; ed Technical Univ. Graz; technical asst Technical Univ. Graz 1953–58; Head of Research Dept, Inst. of Internal Combustion Engines, Prof. List (AVL) 1958–62; leading positions in research and devt with Kloeckner-Humboldt-Deutz AG, Cologne 1962–70; Dir Inst. for Applied Thermodynamics, Aachen Tech. Univ. 1970–97; Pres. and CEO, FEV Motorentechnik GmbH, Aachen 1978–2003, Chair. of the Bd 2003–; Vice-Pres. DFG (German Research Soc.) 1984–90; Fellow Soc. of Automotive Engineers (SAE) 1996–; Dr. hc (Tech. Univ. Graz) 1994; Hon. Prof., Dalian Univ. (People's Repub. of China) 2005; Österreichischer Ehrenring 1954, Deutsches Bundesverdienstkreuz 1978, Cross of Honour for Science and Art, First Class (Austria) 1998; Herbert Akroyd Stuart Award 1962, Carl-Engler-Medaille, Deutsche Wissenschaftliche Gesellschaft für Erdöl, Erdgas und Kohle (DGMK) 1990, Medal of Honour, Verein Deutscher Ingenieure 1993, Soichiro Honda Medal, American Soc. of Mechanical Engineers (ASME) 2000. *Publications:* articles in professional journals. *Address:* FEV Motorentechnik GmbH, Neuenhofstrasse 181, 52078 Aachen, Germany (office). *Telephone:* (241) 5689100 (office). *Website:* www.fev.com (office).

PISTOLETTO, Michelangelo; Italian artist; b. 1933, Biella; worked with his father as painting restorer 1947–58; first solo exhibition at Galleria Galatea, Turin 1960; first solo exhibition in USA at Walker Art Center, Minneapolis 1966; f. Zoo Group of performance artists 1968; associated with 'Arte Povera' movt; works include paintings, sculptures with steel, mirrors and everyday objects, films and video work, and performance art; launched his Progetto Arte manifesto 1994, f. Cittadellarte–Fondazione Pistoletto for the study and promotion of creative projects 1998; Grand Prize, Bienale of São Paulo 1967, Belgian Art Critics' Award 1967, Wolf Foundation Prize 2007. *Works include:* Autoritratto oro 1960, Il Presente–Uomo di schiena 1960–61, Quadri Specchianti (Mirror Paintings), Oggetti in meno (Minus Objects) 1965–66, Venere degli stracci (Venus of the Rags) 1967, Pietra miliare 1967, Opera Ah (performance work) 1979, Anno uno (performance work) 1981. *Publications:* L'uomo nero, il lato insopportabile 1970. *Address:* Cittadellarte–Fondazione Pistoletto, via Serralunga 27, Biella 13900, Italy (office). *Telephone:* (015) 28400 (office). *Fax:* (015) 2522540 (office). *E-mail:* fondazionepistoletto@cittadellarte.it (office). *Website:* www.cittadellarte.it (office).

PISTORIO, Pasquale, M.Electronics; Italian business executive; *Chairman, Telecom Italia SpA;* b. 1936, Sicily; ed Polytechnic of Turin; began career as salesman for Motorola Italy 1967, becoming Dir of Int. Marketing, Phoenix, Ariz. 1977, also Vice-Pres. Motorola Corpn 1977, Gen. Man. Int. Semiconductor Div. 1978–80; Pres. and CEO SGS Group 1980–98 (renamed STMicroelectronics 1998), Pres. and CEO STMicroelectronics 1998–2005, Hon. Chair. 2005–; Chair. Telecom Italia SpA 2007–; f. Pistorio Foundation (charity) 2005; Vice Pres. for Innovation and Research, Confindustria (Confed. of Italian Industrialists); mem. numerous bds including FIAT SpA, Banque de

France, World Econ. Forum Int. Business Council, Govt of Singapore's Internal Advisory Council, French Agency for Innovation, UN ICT Task Force; Hon. Citizen of Singapore 2003; Commendatore al Merito 1974, Chevalier de l'Ordre National du Mérite 1990, Cavaliere del Lavoro 1997, Ouissam Alaouite (Kingdom of Morocco) 1999, Public Service Star (Govt of Singapore) 1999, Chevalier de la Légion d'Honneur 1999, Officier de la Légion d'Honneur 2005; hon. degrees from several univs including Genoa, Malta, Pavia, Catania, Palermo, Sannio, Benevento and Bristol; Akira Inoue Award for Outstanding Achievement in Environmental Health and Safety in the Semiconductor Industry 2000. *Address:* Telecom Italia SpA, Corso d'Italia 41, 00198 Rome, Italy (office). *Telephone:* (6) 3688-2840 (office). *Fax:* (6) 3688-2803 (office). *Website:* www.telecomitalia.com (office).

PITAKAKA, Sir Moses Puibangara, GCMG; Solomon Islands politician; b. 24 Jan. 1945, Zaru Village, Solomon Islands; m. Lois Qilariava 1967; three s. four d.; ed Univ. of Birmingham, Oxford Univ., Univ. of S Pacific, Fiji; Dist Officer, Lands Officer and Magistrate 1972–75; Head of Foreign Affairs, Prime Minister's office 1977–79; Human Resources Devt Man. Unilever Group, Solomon Islands 1983–85; Chair. Citizenship Comm. 1978–88, Nat. Educ. Bd 1980–86, Leadership Code Comm. 1989–94; Commr Judicial and Legal Services Comm. 1982–83; Gov.-Gen. of the Solomon Islands 1994–99; Deacon World Wide Church of God 1993–. *Leisure interests:* walking, reading, canoeing, swimming. *Address:* c/o Government House, PO Box 252, Honiara, Solomon Islands.

PITCHER, Sir Desmond Henry, Kt; British company executive; b. 23 March 1935, Liverpool; s. of George Charles Pitcher and Alice Marion (née Osborne) Pitcher; m. 1st Patricia Ainsworth 1961 (divorced 1973); two d.; m. 2nd Carol Ann Rose 1978 (divorced); two s.; m. 3rd Norma Barbara Niven 1991; ed Liverpool Coll. of Tech. and Commerce; Man. Dir then Vice-Pres. Int. Div. The Sperry Corpn 1961–76; Man. Dir British Leyland Truck and Bus Div. 1976–78, Plessey Telecommunications and Office Systems Ltd 1978–83; Group Chief Exec. The Littlewoods Org. PLC 1983–93, Vice-Chair. 1993–95; Chair. The Mersey Barrage Co. Ltd 1986–96, The Merseyside Devt Corpn 1991–98, The North West Water Group PLC (now United Utilities) 1993–98 (Dir 1990–98); Dir Everton Football Club Co. Ltd 1987–90, Deputy Chair. 1990–98; Dir Northern Advisory Bd of Nat. Westminster Bank PLC 1989–92, Dir (non-exec.) Nat. Westminster Bank 1994–98; Dir Liverpool School of Tropical Medicine 1996–; Chair. Royal Liverpool Philharmonic Social Devt Trust 1992–. *Leisure interests:* football, golf, 19th century history, opera, sailing. *Address:* Folly Farm, Sulhamstead, Berks., RG7 4DF, England. *Telephone:* (118) 930-2326.

PITCHER, Frederick W.; Nauruan/Australian diplomatist and politician; *Minister of Finance and Economic Planning;* ed educated in Australia; early position as Exec. Dir's Adviser, Asian Devt Bank, Manila; Deputy Perm. Rep., UN, New York 2000; mem. Parl. 2004–, mem. Constitutional Review Cttee 2005; served in second Admin of fmr Pres. Ludwig Scotty; Minister for Island Devt and Industry 2004–07, of Finance and Econ. Planning 2007–; Acting Foreign Minister 2007; Pres. Nauru Island Basketball Asscn. *Address:* Ministry of Finance, Government Treasury Building, Aiwo, Nauru (office). *Telephone:* 444-3140 (office). *Fax:* 555-4477 (office). *E-mail:* minister.finance@naurugov.nr (office). *Website:* www.naurugov.nr (office).

PITHART, Petr, JUDr; Czech politician and academic; *First Vice-President of the Senate;* b. 2 Jan. 1941, Kladno; s. of Vilém Pithart and Blažena Pithart (née Krystýnková); m. Drahomíra Hromádková 1964; one s. one d.; ed Charles Univ., Prague (Faculty of Law); Dept of Theory of State and Law, Charles Univ. 1964–70; scholarship Univ. of Oxford, UK 1969–70; labourer 1970–72; co. lawyer 1972–77; signed Charter 77; labourer 1977–79; clerk with Central Warehouses, Prague 1979–89; Spokesman Co-ordination Centre, Civic Forum 1989–90; Prime Minister of Czech Repub. 1990–92; Deputy to Czech Nat. Council 1990–92; mem. and Chair. Senate 1996–98, Vice-Chair. 1998–2000, Chair. 2000, currently First Vice-Pres.; mem. Christian and Democratic Union, Czech Populist Party (KDÚ-ČSL) 1999–, cand. presidential election 2003; Sr Research Fellow, Cen. European Univ., Prague 1992–94; teacher, Faculty of Law, Charles Univ., Prague 1994–; Chief Ed. The New Presence (periodical). *Publications:* numerous articles and essays; Defence of Politics 1974, "1968" 1978, History and Politics 1992, Czechs in the History of Modern Times (co-author) 1992, Who We Are 1999. *Leisure interests:* politics, history, hiking, fishing. *Address:* Senate of the Czech Republic, Valdštejnské nám. 4, 118 11 Prague 1, Czech Republic (office); Podebradova 909, 537 01 Chrudim; Dolni 227, 580 01 Havlickuv Brod, Czech Republic. *Telephone:* (2) 57071111 (office); (4) 69623671. *Fax:* (2) 5753-4484 (office). *E-mail:* pithartp@senat.cz (office); obvod@pithart.cz; petr@pithart.cz (office). *Website:* www.pithart.cz (office).

PITMAN, Sir Brian Ivor, Kt, FIB; British banker; *Senior Adviser, Morgan Stanley;* b. 13 Dec. 1931, Cheltenham; s. of Ronald Ivor Pitman and Doris Ivy Pitman (née Short); m. Barbara Mildred Ann Darby 1954; two s. one d.; ed Cheltenham Grammar School; Asst Gen. Man. Lloyds Bank PLC 1973–75, Jt Gen. Man. 1975–76; Exec. Dir (UK and Asia-Pacific Div.), Lloyds Bank Int. Ltd 1976–78; Deputy Chief Exec. Lloyds Bank Int. Ltd 1978–82; Deputy Group Chief Exec., Lloyds Bank PLC 1982–83, Group Chief Exec. and Dir 1983–97, Chair. 1997–99; Deputy Chief Exec. and Dir TSB Bank PLC 1995–97, Deputy Chair. 1997–2000; Group Chief Exec. and Dir Lloyds TSB Group PLC 1995–97, Chair. 1997–2001; Pres. Chartered Inst. of Bankers 1997–98; fmr Pres. British Bankers Asscn; Dir (non-exec.) Carlton Communications PLC 1998–2004; Chair. Next PLC 1998–2004; mem. Bd of Dirs (non-exec.) Carphone Warehouse Group PLC 2001–, Singapore Airlines 2003–, ITV PLC 2004–, Virgin Atlantic Airways Ltd; Sr Adviser to Morgan Stanley 2001–; mem. Guild of Int. Bankers 2001–, Master 2002–03; Hon. DSc (City Univ.) 1996, (UMIST) 2000. *Leisure interests:* golf, cricket, music. *Address:* Morgan Stanley, 25 Cabot Square, Canary Wharf, London, E14 4QA, England (office). *Telephone:* (20) 7425-8234 (office). *Fax:* (20) 7425-7255 (office). *Website:* www.morganstanley.com (office).

PITMAN, Jennifer (Jenny) Susan, OBE; British consultant, fmr race horse trainer and writer; b. (Jennifer Susan Harvey), 11 June 1946, Leicester; d. of George Harvey and Mary Harvey; m. 1st Richard Pitman 1965 (annulled); two s.; m. 2nd David Stait 1997; ed Sarson Secondary Girls' School; Nat. Hunt trainer 1975–99; Dir Jenny Pitman Racing Ltd 1975–99; Racing and Media Consultant, DJS Racing 1999–; winners include: Watafella (Midlands Nat. 1977), Bueche Giorod (Ferguson Gold Cup 1980), Corbiere (Welsh Nat. 1982, Grand Nat. 1983), Burrough Hill Lad (Anthony Mildmay Peter Cazalet Gold Cup 1983, Welsh Nat. 1983, Cheltenham Gold Cup 1984, King George VI Gold Cup 1984, Hennessey Gold Cup 1984), Smith's Man (Whitbread Trophy 1985), Stears By (Anthony Mildmay Peter Cazalet Gold Cup 1986, Welsh Nat. 1986), Gainsay (Ritz Club Chase 1987, Sporting Life Weekend Chase 1987), Willsford (Midlands Nat. 1990), Crumpet Delite (Philip Cornes Saddle of Gold Final 1988), Garrison Savannah (Sun Alliance Chase 1990, Cheltenham Gold Cup 1991), Wonder Man (Welsh Champion Hurdle 1991), Don Valentino (Welsh Champion Hurdle 1992), Superior Finish (Anthony Mildmay Peter Cazalet Gold Cup 1993), Royal Athlete (Grand Nat. 1995), Willsford (County Hurdle 1989, Scottish Nat. 1995), Mudahim (Irish Nat. 1995), Nathen Lad (Sun Alliance Chase 1996), Indefence (Supreme Novice Hurdler 1996), Master Tribe (Ladbroke Hurdler Leopardstown 1997), Princeful (Stayers Hurdle Cheltenham 1998), Smiths Cracker (Philip Cornes Saddle of Gold Final 1998); first woman to train Grand Nat. winner 1983; numerous awards including Racing Personality of the Year, Golden Spurs 1983, Commonwealth Sports Award 1983, 1984, Piper Heidsieck Trainer of the Year 1983–84, 1989–90, Variety Club of GB Sportswoman of the Year 1984, BBC East Midlands Lifetime Achievement Award 2005. *Publications:* Glorious Uncertainty (autobiog.) 1984, Jenny Pitman: The Autobiography 1999; novels: On the Edge 2002, Double Deal 2002, The Dilemma 2003, The Vendetta 2004, The Inheritance 2005. *Leisure interest:* greyhounds. *Address:* Owls Barn, Kintbury, Hungerford, Berks., RG17 9SX, England (office). *Telephone:* (1488) 668774 (office); (1488) 669191 (home). *Fax:* (1488) 668999 (office). *E-mail:* jpr@owlsbarn.fsbusiness.co.uk (office).

PITSUWAN, Surin, PhD; Thai politician, diplomatist and international organization official; *Secretary-General, Association of South East Asian Nations (ASEAN);* b. 28 Oct. 1949, Nakhon Si Thammarat; s. of Ismael Pitsuwan and Sapiya Pitsuwan; m. Alisa Ariya 1983; three s.; ed Claremont McKenna Coll., Harvard Univ., USA; taught at Thammasat Univ. 1975–86, Academic Asst to Dean of Faculty of Political Science and to Vice-Rector for Academic Affairs 1985–86; columnist, The Nation Review and Bangkok Post newspapers 1980–92; fmr corresp. and analyst, ASEAN Forecast; Congressional Fellow, Office of US Rep. Geraldine Ferraro (q.v.) and Senate Republican Conf. 1983–84; mem. Parl. from Nakhon Si Thammarat Prov. 1986–; Sec. to Speaker of House of Reps 1986; Asst Sec. to Minister of Interior 1988; Deputy Minister of Foreign Affairs 1992–95; Minister of Foreign Affairs 1997–2001; adviser to Int. Comm. on Intervention and State Sovereignty 1999–2001; mem. UN Comm. on Human Security 2001–03; served on ILO's World Comm. on the Social Dimension of Globalization 2002–04; Sec.-Gen. ASEAN 2008–; mem. Democratic Party (fmr Deputy Leader); mem. Advisory Bd Council on Foreign Relations, New York, Int. Advisory Bd Int. Crisis Group, Advisory Bd UN Human Security Trust Fund, 'Wise Men Group' under auspices of the Henri Dunant Centre for Humanitarian Dialogue, Geneva (advising peace negotiations between Acehnese Independence Movt (GAM) and Govt of Indonesia) 2002–04, Islamic Devt Bank's 1440 AH (2020) Vision Comm. –2005; fmr mem. Nat. Reconciliation Comm.; Int. Academic Advisor, Centre for Islamic Studies, Univ. of Oxford, UK; adviser to the Leaders Project (conf. arm of the Cohen Group of fmr US Sec. of Defense William S. Cohen), Washington, DC. *Leisure interest:* reading. *Address:* The ASEAN Secretariat, 70A Jalan Sisingamangaraja, PO Box 2072, Jakarta 12110, Indonesia (office). *Telephone:* (21) 7262991 (office). *Fax:* (21) 7398234 (office). *E-mail:* termsak@aseansec.org (office). *Website:* www.aseansec.org (office).

PITT, Brad; American film actor; b. 18 Dec. 1963, Shawnee, Okla; s. of Bill Pitt and Jane Pitt; m. Jennifer Aniston (q.v.) 2000 (divorced 2005); one d. (with Angelina Jolie); ed Univ. of Missouri; Special Amb. for Nelson Mandela's 46664 campaign against HIV/AIDS 2004. *Films include:* Cutting Glass, Happy Together 1989, Across the Tracks 1990, Contact, Thelma and Louise 1991, The Favor 1992, Johnny Suede 1992, Cool World 1992, A River Runs Through It 1992, Kalifornia 1993, Legend of the Fall 1994, Interview With The Vampire 1994, 12 Monkeys 1995, Seven 1996, Sleepers 1996, Tomorrow Never Dies 1996, Seven Years in Tibet 1997, The Devil's Own 1997, Meet Joe Black 1998, Fight Club 1999, Snatch 2000, The Mexican 2001, Spy Game 2001, Ocean's Eleven 2001, Full Frontal 2002, Confessions of a Dangerous Mind 2002, Sinbad: Legend of the Seven Seas (voice) 2003, Troy 2004, Ocean's Twelve 2004, Mr and Mrs Smith 2005, Babel 2006, Ocean's Thirteen 2007, The Assassination of Jesse James by the Coward Robert Ford (Best Actor, Venice Film Festival 2007) 2007, Burn After Reading 2008, The Curious Case of Benjamin Button 2008. *Television appearances include:* Dallas (series), Glory Days (series), Too Young to Die? (film), The Image (film). *Address:* Creative Artists Agency, 9830 Wilshire Boulevard, Beverly Hills, CA 90212-1825, USA (office). *Telephone:* (310) 288-4545 (office). *Fax:* (310) 288-4800 (office). *Website:* www.caa.com (office).

PITT, Harvey Lloyd, BA, JD; American lawyer and fmr government official; *CEO, Kalorama Partners LLC;* b. 28 Feb. 1945, Brooklyn, NY; s. of Morris Jacob Pitt and Sara (née Sapir) Pitt; m. Saree Ruffin 1984; one s. one d. (and one d. one s. from previous marriage); ed City Univ. of NY (Brooklyn Coll.) and St John's Univ., NY; with Securities and Exchange Comm. (SEC), Washington

1968–78, Legal Asst to Commr 1969, Ed. Institutional Investor Study 1970–71, Special Counsel, Office of Gen. Counsel 1971–72, Chief Counsel Market Regulation Div. 1972–73, Exec. Asst to Chair. 1973–75, Gen. Counsel 1975–78, Chair. 2001–02; f. Kalorama Partners LLC, CEO 2002–; called to Bar, NY 1969, US Supreme Court 1972, DC 1979; Man. Pnr Fried, Frank, Harris, Shriver & Jacobson, Washington 1978–89, Co-Chair. 1997–; Adjunct Prof. of Law George Washington Univ. Nat. Law Centre 1974–82, Univ. of Pa Law School 1983–84; Vice-Pres. Glen Haven Civic Asscn, Silver Spring, Md 1972–73, Pres. 1974; mem. ABA, Fed. Bar Asscn, Admin. Conference of US, American Law Inst.; Hon. LLD (St. John's Univ. School of Law) 2002; Outstanding Young Lawyer Award, Fed. Bar Asscn 1975, Learned Hand Award, Inst. for Human Relations 1988, Brooklyn Coll. Pres. Medal of Distinction 2003. *Address:* Kalorama Partners LLC, 1130 Connecticut Avenue, NW, Suite 800, Washington, DC 20036 (office); 2404 Wyoming Ave, NW, Washington, DC 20008-1643, USA (home). *Telephone:* (202) 721-0000 (office). *Fax:* (202) 721-0007 (office). *E-mail:* info@kaloramapartners.com (office). *Website:* www.kaloramapartners.com (office).

PITTMAN, James A., Jr, MD; American medical scientist and academic; *Distinguished Professor of Physiology and Biophysics, and Professor of Medicine, University of Alabama;* b. 12 April 1927, Orlando, Fla; s. of James A. Pittman and Jean C. Garretson; m. Constance Ming Chung Shen 1955; two s.; ed Davidson Coll. NC and Harvard Medical School; Clinical Assoc., NIH, Bethesda, Md 1954–56; Instructor in Medicine, Univ. of Alabama 1956–59, Asst Prof. 1959–62, Assoc. Prof. 1962–64, Prof. of Medicine 1964–92, Prof. of Physiology and Biophysics 1967–92, Dean, School of Medicine 1973–92, Distinguished Prof. 1992–; Consultant, Children's Hosp. Birmingham, Ala 1962–71; Prof. of Medicine, Georgetown Univ. School of Medicine, Washington, DC 1971–73; Sr Adviser Int. Council on Control of Iodine Deficiency Diseases 1994–96; Master, American Coll. of Physicians, Asscn of American Physicians, American Chemical Soc. etc.; Hon. DSc (Davidson Coll.) 1980, (Alabama) 1984, (Chung Shan Univ., Taiwan) 2005. *Publications:* Diagnosis and Treatment of Thyroid Disease 1963; articles in professional journals. *Leisure interests:* flying, scuba diving, hunting, sailing. *Address:* University of Alabama School of Medicine, SDB 75, 1924 Seventh Avenue South, Birmingham, AL 35294 (office); 5 Ridge Drive, Birmingham, AL 35213, USA (home). *Telephone:* (205) 934-3414 (office), (205) 871-9261 (home). *Fax:* (205) 975-4976 (office). *E-mail:* jap@uab.edu (office); japdoc@msm.com (home). *Website:* main.uab.edu/uasom/show.asp?durki=2023 (office).

PITTMAN, Robert Warren; American media executive; b. 28 Dec. 1953, Jackson, Miss.; s. of Warren E. Pittman and Lanita (née Hurdle) Pittman; m. 1st Sandra Hill 1979 (divorced); one s.; m. 2nd Veronique Choa 1997; one c.; ed Millsaps Coll., Oakland, Pittsburg and Harvard Univs; disc jockey WJDX-FM (Miss.) 1970–72; disc jockey WRIT (Milwaukee) 1972; Research Dir WDRQ (Detroit) 1972–73; Programme Dir WPEZ (Pittsburg) 1973–74; with WMAQ-WKQZ (NY) and NBC Radio 1974–77; with WNBC (NY) 1977–79; exec. producer Album Tracks NBC TV 1977–78; Dir, Vice-Pres., Sr Vice-Pres. Warner Amex Satellite Entertainment Co. (now MTV Networks Inc.) 1979–82, Pres., CEO 1985–86; Exec. Vice-Pres., COO MTV Networks Inc. 1983–85; Pres., CEO Quantum Media Inc. 1987–89; Exec. Adviser Warner Communications Inc. 1989–90; Pres., CEO Time Warner Enterprises 1990–95; CEO Six Flags Entertainment 1991–95; Man. Partner, CEO Century 21 Real Estate 1995–96; Pres., CEO America On-Line Networks 1996–97, Pres., COO America On-Line Inc. 1997–2001, Co-COO 2001–02; Chair. NY Shakespeare Festival 1987–94; dir numerous cos; Golden Plate Award, American Acad. of Achievement 1990, Lifetime Achievement Int. Monitor Award, Int. Teleproduction Soc. 1993 and many others. *Address:* c/o America On-Line, 2200 AOL Way, Sterling, VA 20166, USA.

PIVETTI, Irene; Italian politician; d. of Grazia Gabrielli; m. Paolo Taranta 1988 (separated 1992); ed Catholic Univ. of the Sacred Heart, Milan; journalist; mem. Parl. 1992–, Speaker 1995–96; fmr mem. Lega Nord (Northern League); currently Pres. Unione Democratici per l'Europa (UDEUR, f. 1999). *Address:* Unione Democratici per l'Europa, Largo Arenula 34, 00186 Rome; Camera dei Deputati, Rome, Italy; (06) 684241. *Fax:* (06) 6872593. *E-mail:* udeur@udeur.org. *Website:* www.udeur.org.

PIVOT, Bernard; French journalist; b. 5 May 1935, Lyons; s. of Charles Pivot and Marie-Louise Pivot (née Dumas); m. Monique Dupuis 1959; two d.; ed Centre de formation des Journalistes; on staff of Figaro littéraire, then Literary Ed.; Figaro 1958–74; Chronique pour sourire, on Europe 1 1970–73; Columnist, Le Point 1974–77; producer and presenter of Ouvrez les guillemets 1973–74, Apostrophes, France 2 1975–90, Bouillon de culture 1991–2001, Double Je 2002–05; Ed. Lire 1975–93; Dir Sofica Créations 1986–; mem. Conseil supérieur de la langue française 1989–; Pres. Grévin Acad. 2001–; mem. Académie Goncourt 2004–; Chevalier du Mérite agricole; Grand Prix de la Critique l'Acad. française 1983, Prix Louise Weiss, Bibliothèque Nat. 1989, Prix de la langue française décerne à la Foire 2000. *Publications:* L'Amour en vogue (novel) 1959, La vie oh là là! 1966, Les critiques littéraires 1968, Beaujolaises 1978, Le Football en vert 1980, Le Métier de lire. Réponses à Pierre Nora 1990, Remontrances à la ménagère de moins de cinquante ans (essay) 1998. *Leisure interests:* tennis, football, gastronomy. *Address:* c/o France 2, 7 esplanade Henri de France, 75907 Paris Cedex 15; Les Jonnerys, 69430 Quincié-en-Beaujolais, France (home).

PIVOVAROV, Yuri Sergeyevich, Dr rer. pol; Russian political scientist; *Director, Institute of Scientific Information on Social Sciences (INION), Russian Academy of Sciences;* b. 25 April 1950, Moscow; m.; one s. one d.; ed Moscow Inst. of Int. Relations; Jr then Sr Researcher, Prof., Head of Div., Deputy Dir Inst. of Scientific Information on Social Sciences (INION), USSR (now Russian) Acad. of Sciences 1976–98, Dir 1998–; mem. Exec. Bd Russian Asscn of Political Sciences; mem. Council on Politology, Presidium, Russian Acad. of Sciences; Ed.-in-Chief Gosudarstvo i Pravo (journal), Politicheskaya Nauka (periodical); Corresp. mem. Russian Acad. of Sciences 1997–. *Publications:* Political Culture of Russia after Reforms, Essays on the History of Russian Socio-political Ideas of the 19th and Early 20th Century and over 200 articles. *Address:* INION, Nakhimovsky prosp. 51/21, 117418 Moscow, Russia (office). *Telephone:* (495) 123-88-81 (office). *Website:* www.inion.ru (office).

PIWOWSKI, Marek; Polish/American film director, writer, actor and journalist; b. 24 Oct. 1935, Warsaw; s. of Władysław Piwowski and Jadwiga Piwowska; ed State Acad. of Film, Łodź, Univ. of Warsaw; Visiting Prof., City Univ. of New York; Dir and writer of 17 films which have won 24 int. film festival awards; mem. American Film Inst.; Order of Polonia Restituta. *Films include:* Kirk Douglas 1967, Flybeater 1967, A Cruise 1970, Psychodrama 1972, Corkscrew 1971, Blue Hair 1972, How to Recognize the Vampire 1974, Foul Play 1977, Trouble is My Business 1988, Catch 22 1990, Kidnapping Agata 1993, The Parade Step 1998, The Barracuda's Kiss 1998, The Knife in the Head of Dino Baggio 1999, Olympiad in Zakopane 1999, Executioners 2001, Martin's Law 2001, Body Language 2002, Oskar (dir, scriptwriter) 2005. *Leisure interests:* sailing, skiing, gliders, windsurfing. *Address:* ul. Promenada 21, 00-778 Warsaw, Poland (home). *Telephone:* (22) 841-80-80 (home); 606-600-000 (mobile) (home). *Fax:* (22) 841-80-80 (home). *E-mail:* piwek@eranet.pl (home).

PIZA, Arthur Luiz; Brazilian painter and printmaker; b. 1928, São Paulo; painter and exhibitor 1943–; moved to Paris 1952; works in many important museums and pvt. collections; Purchase Prize 1953 and Nat. Prize for Prints São Paulo Biennale 1959, Prizes at biennales at Ljubljana 1961, Santiago 1966, Venice 1966, Grenchen Triennale 1961, biennales of Norway and Mexico 1980, Puerto Rico 1991, Nat. Asscn of Critics Grand Prize, Brazil 1994. *Publications:* Abstract Painting 1962, Larousse of Paintings (Small Larousse of Paintings, Vol. II) 1979, Bénézit Dictionary of Painters, Sculptors and Engravers 1999, Arthur Luiz Piza 2003. *Address:* 16 rue Dauphine, 75006 Paris, France.

PIZARRO, Artur; Portuguese pianist; b. 1968, Lisbon; regular int. performanes with leading conductors including Esa-Pekka Salonen, Sir Andrew Davis, Charles Dutoit, Franz Welser-Most, Ilan Volkov, Tugan Sokhiev, Yakov Kreizberg, Yannick Nezet-Seguin, Libor Pesek, Vladimir Jurowski, Sir Simon Rattle, Sir Charles Mackerras; as recitalist has performed at many of the world's most prestigious venues and festivals including Kennedy Centre, Washington, Wigmore Hall, London, Aldeburgh Festival, Neues Gewandhaus, Leipzig, Frankfurt Alte Oper, Théâtre du Chatelet and Musee D'Orsay, Paris, Zürich Tonhalle, BBC Proms, London, NHK and Orchard Halls, Japan; chamber music appearances have partnered him with Raphael Oleg, Christian Altenburger, Truls Mork, Toby Hoffmann, the St Lawrence, Muir and Petersen quartets; taught at GSMD 1998–2002; performed complete cycle of Beethoven Piano Sonatas, St John Smith's Square, London 2004–05; f. the Pizarro Trio with violinist Raphael Oleg and cellist Josephine Knight 2005; Medal of Cultural Merit, Portugal 2007; winner, Vianna da Motta Int. Piano Competition 1987, Greater Palm Beach Symphony Invitational Piano Competition 1989, Leeds Int. Piano Competition 1990, Bordalo Prize 1998. *Radio:* Performance On 3, BBC Radio 3. *Recordings include:* Milhaud, Music for Two Pianos (with Stephen Coombs) 1997, Vianna da Motta, The Romantic Piano Concerto 1999, Beethoven Piano Sonatas 2003, Beethoven, Last Three Piano Sonatas 2003, Chopin, Reminiscences 2005, Rodrigo, Complete Piano Works (Ed.'s Choice, Gramophone Magazine) 2005, Chopin, Second and Third Sonatas 2006, Lizst, Hungarian Rhapsodies 2006, Ravel, Complete Solo Works 2007, Piano Duo Music, with Vita Panomariovaite 2007, Ravel, Complete Piano Works, Vol. 2 2008. *Address:* c/o Tom Croxon Management, 22 Hurst Road, Buckhurst Hill, Essex IG9 6AB, England (office). *Telephone:* (20) 8279-2516 (office). *Fax:* (20) 8504-2200 (office). *E-mail:* tom@tomcroxonmanagement.co.uk (office). *Website:* www.tomcroxonmanagement.co.uk (office).

PIZARRO MORENO, Manuel, LicenDer; Spanish lawyer, business executive and politician; ed Univ. Complutense de Madrid; Attorney-Gen. (Advocate of the State); apptd mem. Bd of Dirs Endesa SA 1996, mem. Exec. Cttee 1997–98, Vice-Chair. 1998–2002, Chair. 2002–07; mem. Bd of Dirs Telefónica 2007–08; Chair. Ibercaja, Spanish Savings Banks Confed.; Vice-Chair. Madrid Stock Exchange; fmr Vice-Chair. Bolsa de Madrid, Bolsas y Mercados Espaqoles, Sociedad Holding de Mercados y Sistemas Financieros SA; mem. Spanish Royal Acad. of Legislation and Jurisprudence; Chair. Bd of Trustees, Nat. Park of Ordesa and Monte Perdido; Vice-Chair. Bd of Trustees, Nat. Museum of Archeology; mem. Bd of Trustees, Univ. Pontificia de Salamanca; joined Partido Popular 2008, Partido Popular spokesman, Constitutional Comm., Congress of Deputies 2008–. *Address:* Constitutional Commission, Congress of Deputies, Carrera de San Jerónimo s/n, 28071 Madrid, Spain (office). *Telephone:* (91) 3906000 (office). *Fax:* (91) 4298707 (office). *E-mail:* servicio.informacion@sgral.congreso.es (office). *Website:* www.congreso.es (office).

PIZZO, Philip A., BA, MD; American physician and academic; *Dean, School of Medicine, Stanford University;* b. 6 Dec. 1944, New York City; s. of Vito Pizzo; m. Peggy Pizzo; ed Fordham Univ., Univ. of Rochester School of Medicine; intern, Children's Hosp. Medical Center, Boston 1970–71, Jr Asst Resident 1971–72, Sr Asst Resident 1972–73; Clinical Assoc., Nat. Cancer Inst. 1973–75, Investigator 1975–76, Sr Investigator 1976–80, Head of Infectious Disease Section, Pediatric Br., Nat. Cancer Inst. 1980–96, Chief of Pediatrics 1982–96; Thomas Morgan Rotch Prof. and Chair., Dept of Pediatrics, Harvard Univ. Medical School, Children's Hosp., Boston 1996–2001, also Faculty Dean for Academic Programs 1996–99; Dean, Stanford Univ. School of Medicine 2001–, also Carl and Elizabeth Naumann Prof. of Pediatrics 2001–; Attending Physician, NIH, Bethesda, Md 1976–96; Prof. of Pediatrics, F. Edward Hebert School of Medicine, Bethesda 1987–96; mem. Bd of Dirs Lucile Packard

Children's Hosp. 2001–, Stanford Hosp. and Clinics 2001–; mem. numerous professional socs including American Pediatric Soc. 1995, NAS Inst. of Medicine 1997, American Assn of Physicians 1998; mem. editorial bd numerous journals; Hon. ScD (Fordham) 1996, Hon. MA (Harvard) 1996; numerous awards including US Public Health Service Meritorious Service Award 1985, Outstanding Service Medal 1995. *Publications include:* over 500 papers in professional journals. *Address:* Office of the Dean, Stanford University School of Medicine, 300 Pasteur Drive, Stanford, CA 94305, USA (office). *Telephone:* (650) 723-4000 (office). *E-mail:* philip.pizzo@stanford.edu (office). *Website:* med.stanford.edu (office).

PLACIDO, Michele; Italian actor and director; b. 19 May 1946, Ascoli Satriano, Foggia; m. Simonetta Stefanelli (divorced); three c.; two c. with other pnrs; ed Centro Sperimentale di Cinematografia, Acad. of Dramatic Arts, Rome; made acting debut 1969, has appeared in more than 70 films and numerous tv series; has worked with dirs including Luigi Comencini, Mario Monicelli, Salvatore Samperi, Damiano Damiani, Francesco Rosi, Walerian Borowczyk, Marco Bellocchio, Carlo Lizzani; made directorial debut 1989; jury mem. Venice Film Festival 2006; Bambi Award 1989, Actor's Mission Award, Art Film Festival 1999. *Television:* actor: Il Picciotto 1973, Moses the Lawgiver 1975, Il Passo falso 1983, La Piovra 1983, La Piovra 2 1985, La Piovra 3 1987, La Piovra 4 1989, Scoop 1991, Drug Wars: The Cocaine Cartel 1992, Racket (also story) 1997, La Missione (also writer) 1998, Padre Pio - Tra cielo e terra 2000, Il Sequestro Soffiantini 2002, Un Papà quasi perfetto 2003, Soraya 2003, Il Grande Torino 2004, Karol, un Papa rimasto uomo 2006, Assunta Spina 2006, L'Ultimo padrino 2007. *Films:* actor: Teresa la ladra 1972, Il Caso Pisciotta 1972, La Mano nera - prima della mafia, più della mafia 1973, Mia moglie, un corpo per l'amore 1973, Mio Dio come sono caduta in basso! 1974, Processo per direttissima 1974, Romanzo popolare 1974, Peccati in famiglia 1975, Orlando Furioso movie, 1975, L'Agnese va a morire 1976, La Orca 1976, Divina creatura 1976, Marcia trionfale (Acting Award, David di Donatello Awards, Best Actor, Silver Ribbon Awards) 1976, Corleone 1977, Fontamara 1977, Kleinhoff Hotel 1977, La Ragazza dal pigiama giallo 1977, Casotto 1977, Un Uomo in ginocchio 1978, Io sono mia 1978, Letti selvaggi 1979, Il Prato 1979, Sabato, domenica e venerdì 1979, Ernesto (Best Actor, Berlin Int. Film Festival) 1979, Lulu 1980, Salto nel vuoto 1980, Cargo film, 1981, Les Ailes de la colombe 1981, Tre fratelli 1981, Sciopèn 1982, Ars amandi 1983, Les Amants terribles 1984, Pizza Connection (Best Actor, Silver Ribbon Awards) 1985, Grandi magazzini 1986, Notte d'estate con profilo greco, occhi a mandorla e odore di basilico 1986, Ti presento un'amica 1987, Via Paradiso 1988, Big Business 1988, Come sono buoni i bianchi 1988, Mery per sempre 1989, Afganskiy izlom 1990, Le Amiche del cuore 1992, Uomo di rispetto 1992, Quattro bravi ragazzi 1993, Padre e figlio 1994, Poliziotti 1994, Lamerica 1994, Un Eroe borghese 1995, La Lupa 1996, Le Plaisir 1998, Del perduto amore (FEDIC Award, Venice Film Festival) 1998, Terra bruciata 1999, Un Uomo perbene 1999, La Balia 1999, Panni sporchi 1999, Liberate i pesci! 2000, Tra due mondi 2001, Searching for Paradise 2002, Il Posto dell'anima 2003, L'Odore del sangue 2004, L'Amore ritorna 2004, Romanzo criminale 2005, Arrivederci amore, ciao 2006, Commediasexi 2006, Le Rose del deserto 2006, La Sconosciuta 2006, Smutek paní Snajdrové 2006, Il Caimano 2006, 2061: Un anno eccezionale 2007, Piano, solo 2007, SoloMetro 2007, Estrenando sueños 2007, Liolà 2007; director: Pummarò (writer/dir) 1989, Le Amiche del cuore (writer/dir) 1992, Un Eroe borghese (Special Award, David di Donatello Awards) 1995, Del perduto amore (writer/dir) 1998, Un Altro mondo è possibile 2001, Un Viaggio chiamato amore (writer/dir) 2002, Ovunque sei (writer/dir) 2004, Romanzo criminale (co-writer/dir) (Best Screenplay, David di Donatello Awards (jtly) 2006, Best Director, Silver Ribbon Awards 2006) 2005; other: L'Uomo giusto (producer and writer) 2007. *Address:* c/o Cattleya S.p.A., Via della Frezza, 59, 00186 Rome, Italy (office). *E-mail:* info@cattleya.it (office).

PLANCHON, Roger; French theatrical director and playwright; b. 12 Sept. 1931, Saint-Chamond; s. of Emile Planchon and Augusta Planchon (née Nogier); m. Colette Dompietrini 1958; two s.; bank clerk 1947–49; Founder Théâtre de la Comédie, Lyon 1951; Co-Dir Théâtre de la Cité, Villeurbanne 1957–72; Dir Théâtre Nat. Populaire 1972–2005; Pres. Fondation Molière 1987–; aims to popularize the theatre by extending its units and recreating the classics within a modern social context; Pres. Rhône-Alpes Cinéma; Chevalier de la Légion d'honneur, des Arts et Lettres; Croix de guerre; Prix Georges Lherminier du Syndicat de la critique dramatique 1986, 1998. *Film roles include:* Le grand frère 1982, Danton 1983, Un amour interdit, La septième Cible 1984, Camile Claudel 1988, Radio Corbeau 1989, Jean Galmot, aventurier 1990, L'année de l'éveil 1991, Louis, enfant roi 1992. *Films written and directed:* Dandin 1987, Louis, enfant roi 1992, Lautrec 1998. *Plays:* has directed and acted in over 60 plays by Shakespeare, Molière, Racine, Marivaux, Brecht, Adamov, Vinaver, Dubillard and himself, most recently: Ionesco 1983, L'avare 1986, George Dandin 1987, Andromaque (dir) 1989, Le vieil hiver 1990, Fragile forêt 1990, Les libertins 1994, No Man's Land 1994, Occupe-toi d'Amélie! 1995, Le radeau de la Méduse 1995, La tour de Nesle 1996, Le triomphe de l'amour 1996, Les démons et la Dame de Chez Maxim 1998. *Publications:* plays: La remise 1961, Patte blanche 1965, Bleus, blancs, rouges ou les Libertins 1967, Dans le vent 1968, L'infâme 1969, La langue au chat 1972, Le cochon noir (Prix Ibsen 1974) 1973, Gilles de Rais 1976, Fragile Forêt 1991, Le radeau de la Méduse 1995, L'avare 2001. *Address:* Studio 24, 24 bis rue Emile Decorps, 69100 Villeurbanne, France.

PLANT OF HIGHFIELD, Baron (Life Peer), cr. 1991, of Weelsby in the County of Humberside; **Raymond Plant,** PhD, DLitt; British academic and politician; *Professor of Jurisprudence, King's College London;* b. 19 March 1945, Grimsby; s. of Stanley Plant and Marjorie Plant; m. Katherine Dixon 1967; three s.; ed Havelock School, Grimsby, King's Coll. London and Univ. of Hull; Lecturer, then Sr Lecturer in Philosophy, Univ. of Manchester 1967–79; Prof. of Politics, Univ. of Southampton 1979–94, Pro-Chancellor 1996–2002, Prof. of European Political Thought 2000–02; Prof. of Jurisprudence, King's Coll. London 2001–; Master, St Catherine's Coll. Oxford 1994–2000; Pres. Nat. Council of Voluntary Orgs, Acad. of Learned Socs in the Social Sciences; Hon. Fellow, Harris Manchester Coll., Oxford, St Catherine's Coll., Oxford, Univ. of Cardiff; Hon. DLitt (Hull, London Guildhall); Stanton Lecturer, Univ. of Cambridge 1989–91, Sarum Lecturer, Univ. of Oxford 1991, Boutwood Lecturer, Univ. of Cambridge 2006. *Publications:* Hegel 1973, Community and Ideology 1974, Political Philosophy and Social Welfare 1981, Philosophy, Politics and Citizenship 1984, Conservative Capitalism 1989, Modern Political Thought 1991, Democracy, Representation and Elections 1992, Hegel on Religion 1997, Politics, Theology and History 2000. *Leisure interests:* music, opera, politics. *Address:* 6 Woodview Close, Bassett, Southampton, SO16 3PZ, England (home). *Telephone:* (23) 8059-2448 (office); (23) 8076-9529 (home).

PLANTEY, Alain Gilles; French government official; b. 19 July 1924, Mulhouse; m. Christiane Wioland 1955 (died 1999); four d.; ed Univs of Bordeaux and Paris Sorbonne; Staff of Council of State 1949; French Del. to UN 1951–52; Master of Requests Council of State 1956–74; legal adviser OEEC 1956–57; Prof., Ecole Royale d'Admin, Cambodia, Faculté de Droit and Ecole Nat. d'Admin, Paris 1957–62; Gen. Sec., Agence France-Presse 1958–67; Asst Sec.-Gen. for the Community and African and Malagasy Affairs at the Presidency 1961–66; Amb. to Madagascar 1966–72; Asst Sec.-Gen., WEU 1972–82, Chair. Standing Armaments Cttee 1972–82; Conseiller d'Etat 1974–93; Chair. Int. Court of Arbitration, ICC 1989–96; Pres. Inst. de France 1996; mem. Conseil Int. de l'Arbitrage en matière de Sport 1994; mem. Acad. of Moral and Political Sciences (Inst. of France), American Acad. of Social and Political Science, Int. Council on Commercial Arbitration; Chair. Int. Inst. of Law; Pres., Conf. of Acads, France; Vice-Pres. Inst. Charles de Gaulle; Grand Officier, Légion d'honneur 2000 and numerous other decorations. *Publications:* La réforme de la justice marocaine 1949, La justice répressive et le droit pénal chérifien 1950, Au coeur du problème berbère 1952, Traité pratique de la fonction publique 1956, La formation et le perfectionnement des fonctionnaires 1957, La Communauté 1962, Indépendance et coopération 1964–77, Prospective de l'État 1975, Droit et pratique de la fonction publique internationale 1977, Réformes dans la fonction publique 1978, La négociation internationale 1980, 1994, International Civil Service: Law and Management 1981, Derecho y Práctica de la Función Pública Internacional y Europea 1982, De la politique entre les Etats: Principes de diplomatie 1987, La Fonction publique, traité général 1992, 2002, Tratado de Derecho Diplomático 1992, Diplomatie 2000, La négociation internationale au XXIe siècle 2002, La preuve devant le juge administratif 2003, La fonction publique internationale 2005, Internationel négociation 2007. *Address:* 6 avenue Sully-Prudhomme, Paris 75007, France (home). *Telephone:* 1-44-41-43-26 (office); 1-45-55-26-49 (home). *Fax:* 1-44-41-43-27 (office); 1-45-55-26-49 (home).

PLANTIN, Marcus; British broadcasting executive; *Creative Director, September Films Ltd.;* b. 23 Oct. 1945; s. of Charles P. Plantin and Vera H. Plantin; m. 1980; two s.; ed Surbiton Co. Grammar School, Guildford School of Acting; Producer, BBC TV 1978–84; joined London Weekend TV (LWT), Head Light Entertainment 1985–87, Controller of Entertainment 1987–90, Dir of Programmes 1990–92, 1997; Dir London Weekend Productions and LWT Holdings 1990–92; Network Dir ITV 1992–97, Man. ITV Network Centre 1995–97; Dir of Programmes LWT Productions 1998–2000, LWT/United Productions 2000–01; Dir of Int. Entertainment Formats and Production, Granada TV 2000–01, Dir of Entertainment Content 2001–02; Creative Dir September Films Ltd 2003–. *Leisure interests:* gardening, swimming, travel. *Address:* September Films Ltd., Glen House, 22 Glenthorne Road, London, W6 0NG, England (office). *Telephone:* (20) 8563-9393 (office); (20) 8563-2041 (home). *Fax:* (20) 8741-7214 (office). *E-mail:* september@septemberfilms.com (office); purdenhoe@msn.com (home). *Website:* www.septemberfilms.com (home).

PLANTUREUX, Jean-Henri, (PLANTU); French artist, cartoonist, journalist and editor; *Cartoonist, Le Monde;* b. (Jean-Henri Plantureux), 23 March 1951, Paris; s. of Henri Plantureux and Renée Seignardie; m. Chantal Meyer 1971; four c.; ed Baccalaureate, Lycée Henri IV, Paris; political cartoonist, Le Monde 1972–, L'Express 1991–; caricaturist, Droit de réponse (TV show) 1981–87; Grand Prix de l'Humour noir Granville 1989, Prix du Festival du Scoop (film on Yasser Arafat) 1991, Spanish Gat Perich 1996, UN Political Cartoon Award 2006. *Publications:* Pauvres chéris 1978, La Démocratie? Parlons-en 1979, Les Cours de caoutchouc sont trop élastiques 1982, C'est le goulag 1983, Pas nette, la planète! 1984, Politic-look 1984, Bonne année pour tous 1985, Ça manque de femmes 1986, A la Soupe 1987, Wolfgang, tu feras informatique 1988, Ouverture en bémol 1988, Des fourmis dans les jambes 1989, C'est la lutte finale 1990, Un Vagne Souvenir 1990, Reproche-Orient 1991, Le Président Hip-Hop! 1991, Le Douanier se fait la malle 1992, Ici Maastricht, les Européens parlent aux Européens 1992, Cohabitation à l'Eau de Rose 1993, Le Pire est derrière nous! 1994, Le Petit Mitterrand Illustré 1995, Le Petit Chirac et le Petit Balladur Illustrés 1995, Le Petit Raciste Illustré 1995, Le Petit Communiste Illustré 1995, Le Petit Socialiste Illustré 95, Magic Chirac 1995, Les Années vaches folles 1996, Pas de photos 1997, La France dopée 1998, Le Petit Juge Illustré 1999, L'Année PLANTU 1999, Cassettes, mensonges et vidéo 2001, Ils pourraient dire merci! 2004, À quoi ça rime 2005, Je ne dois pas dessiner 2006, La Présidentielle 2007, Racaille Le Rouge 2007. *Address:* Le Monde, 80 blvd Auguste Blanqui, 75707 Paris Cedex 13, France (office). *Telephone:* 1-57-28-25-30 (office). *Fax:* 1-57-28-21-69 (office). *E-mail:* plantu@lemonde.fr (office). *Website:* www.plantu.net (home).

PLASSNIK, Ursula, DrIur; Austrian politician; b. 23 May 1956, Klagenfurt; m. (divorced); ed Vienna Univ., Coll. d'Europe, Bruges, Belgium; with Ministry of Foreign Affairs, in int. law office and directorates for security policy and CSCE 1981–84; CSCE Del. to Madrid Follow-up Meeting 1981–83, Vienna 1986–87; at Embassy, Berne 1984–86; Rep. Council of Europe 1987–90; at Directorate Gen. for Econ. Policy and EU Coordination, later head of Directorate for Gen. Affairs Council and the European Council 1994–97; at Fed. Chancellery, Cabinet Chief of Dr Wolfgang Schüssel when Fed. Vice Chancellor 1997–2000, when Chancellor 2000–04; Amb. to Switzerland Jan.–Oct. 2004; Minister for Foreign Affairs 2004–08; mem. Austrian People's Party. *Address:* Austrian People's Party, Lichtenfelsgasse 7, 1010 Vienna, Austria (office). *Telephone:* (1) 401-26-0 (office). *Fax:* (1) 401-26-10-9 (office). *E-mail:* email@oevp.at (office). *Website:* www.oevp.at (office).

PLASTERK, Ronald Hans Anton, PhD; Dutch academic and politician; *Minister of Education, Culture and Science;* b. 12 April 1957, The Hague; ed Univ. of Leiden, California Inst. of Tech.; Head of Research Group, Netherlands Cancer Inst., Antoni van Leeuwenhoek Hospital, Amsterdam 1987–2000; Chair in Molecular Biology, VU Univ. Amsterdam 1993–97; Prof. of Molecular Genetics, Univ. of Amsterdam 1997–2000; Prof. of Developmental Genetics, Univ. of Utrecht 2000–07; Dir Hubrecht Lab., Netherlands Inst. for Developmental Biology 2000–07; Minister of Educ., Culture and Science 2007–; mem. European Molecular Biology Org., Bd of Govs Wellcome Trust, Standing Cttee on Genetics, Dutch Health Council; mem. Royal Netherlands Acad. of Arts and Sciences, Royal Dutch Soc. of Sciences and Humanities; mem. Labour Party (PvdA). *Address:* Ministry of Education, Culture and Science, Rijnstraat 50, POB 16375, 2500 BJ The Hague, The Netherlands (office). *Telephone:* (70) 4123456 (office). *Fax:* (70) 4123450 (office). *E-mail:* ocwinfo@postbus51.nl (office). *Website:* www.minocw.nl (office).

PLASTOW, Sir David Arnold Stuart, Kt, CIMgt, FBIM, FRSA; British business executive; b. 9 May 1932, Grimsby, Lincs.; s. of the late James Stuart Plastow and of Marie Plastow; m. Barbara Ann May 1954; one s. one d.; ed Culford School, Bury St Edmunds; apprenticed Vauxhall Motors Ltd 1950; joined Rolls-Royce Ltd, Motor Car Div. Crewe 1958, Marketing Dir Motor Car Div. 1967–71, Man. Dir 1971–72; Man. Dir Rolls-Royce Motors Ltd 1972–74, Group Man. Dir 1974–80; Regional Dir Lloyds Bank 1974–76; Dir Vickers Ltd 1975–92, Man. Dir 1980–86, Chief Exec. 1980–92, Chair. 1987–92; Chair. Inchape PLC 1992–95; Dir GKN Ltd 1978–84; Dir Legal & General 1985–87, Guinness PLC 1986–94, Deputy Chair. 1987–89, Jt Deputy Chair. 1989–94; Deputy Chair. (non-exec.) TSB Group PLC 1991–95; Dir (non-exec.) Cable and Wireless PLC 1991–93, Lloyds TSB 1996–99; Trustee Royal Opera House Trust 1992–93 (Chair. 1992–93); Gov. (non-exec.) BUPA 1990–95 (Deputy Chair. 1992–95); Pres. Soc. of Motor Mfrs and Traders Ltd 1976–78, Deputy Pres. 1978–80; Pres. Motor Industry Research Asscn 1978–81; Vice-Pres. Inst. of Motor Industry 1974–82; Chair. Grand Council, Motor and Cycle Trades Benevolent Fund 1976–78; mem. Eng Council 1981–83, Council CBI, Council, Manchester Business School, Court of Manchester Univ., Council, Regular Forces Employment Asscn, Council, Industrial Soc., Chair. 1983–87, British Overseas Trade Bd 1980–83, British North American Cttee; Dir Tenneco Automotive Inc. 1985–92, 1996–; Chair. MRC 1994–98; Chancellor, Univ. of Luton 1993–; Patron, Coll. of Aeronautical and Automobile Eng 1972–79; Chair. of Govs, Culford School, Bury St Edmunds 1979–; Liveryman, Worshipful Co. of Coachmakers and Coach Harness Makers; Hon. DSc (Cranfield Inst. of Tech.) 1978; Young Businessman of the Year Award (The Guardian) 1976. *Leisure interests:* golf, music. *Address:* c/o Office of the Chancellor, University of Luton, Park Square, Luton, Bedfordshire, LU1 3JU, England.

PLATÉ, Nikolai Alfredovich; Russian chemist; *Vice-President, Russian Academy of Sciences; Director, A. V. Topchiev Institute of Petrochemical Synthesis;* b. 4 Nov. 1934, Moscow; m.; one s. one d.; ed Moscow State Univ.; Jr, later Sr researcher, Head of Lab. Moscow State Univ. 1956, now Prof. Emer.; Dir A. V. Topchiev Inst. of Petrochemical Synthesis; Corresp. mem. USSR (now Russian) Acad. of Sciences 1974, full mem. 1987; Deputy Acad.-Sec. Dept of Gen. and Tech. Chem., Sec. Gen. for Science 1996–02, Vice-Pres. 2002–; Ed.-in-Chief Vysokomolekulyarnye Soyedinenya (Polymer Science); mem. European Acad. of Sciences, Nat. Acad. of Sciences of Ukraine, ACS, Nat. Acad. of Science of Kazakhstan, Nat. Acad. of Tadjikistan, Polish Chemical Soc.; Order for Merits (IV, III, II Degrees), Chevalier de la Légion d'honneur, Order of Orange-Nassau (Netherlands), Cross of Merit (Poland); Dr hc (St Petersburg, Kazan, Tver); USSR State Prize 1985, V. Kargin Prize; S. Lebedev Prize, H. Mark Medal, Austrian Inst. of Chemical Tech. 1999, Russian State Prize 2002, Russian Govt Prize for Science 2004. *Publications:* several books and more than 500 papers in scientific periodicals on polymers of medical application, chemical modifications of polymers, liquid crystal polymers, synthetic polymeric membranes. *Leisure interests:* tennis, driving. *Address:* Institute of Petrochemical Synthesis, Leninsky prospekt 29, 117912 Moscow, Russia (office); Presidium of Russian Academy of Sciences, Leninsky prospekt 14, 117901 Moscow. *Telephone:* (495) 952-59-27 (office); (495) 954-44-85. *Fax:* (495) 954-25-49. *E-mail:* plate@pran.ru (office).

PLATER, Alan Frederick, CBE, FRSL, FRSA; British writer; b. 15 April 1935, Jarrow-on-Tyne; s. of Herbert Richard Plater and Isabella Scott Plater; m. 1st Shirley Johnson 1958 (divorced 1985); two s. one d.; m. 2nd Shirley Rubinstein 1986; three step-s.; ed Kingston High School and King's Coll. Newcastle-upon-Tyne; trained as architect; full-time writer 1960–; has written extensively for radio, TV, films and theatre, also for The Guardian, Listener, New Statesman, etc.; Co.-Chair. Writers' Guild of GB 1986–87, Pres. 1991–95; Visiting Prof., Univ. of Bournemouth 2001–; Hon. Fellow, Humberside Coll. of Educ. 1983; Hon. DLitt (Hull) 1985; Hon. DCL (Northumbria) 1997; Royal TV Soc. Writers' Award 1988, BAFTA Writers' Award 1988, BAFTA Dennis Potter Award 2005, and many other awards. *Plays include:* A Smashing Day, Close the Coalhouse Door, And a Little Love Besides, Swallows on the Water, Trinity Tales, The Fosdyke Saga, Fosdyke Two, On Your Way, Riley!, Skyhooks, A Foot on the Earth, Prez, Rent Party (musical), Sweet Sorrow, Going Home, I Thought I Heard a Rustling, Shooting the Legend, All Credit to the Lads, Peggy for You, Tales From the Backyard, Only a Matter of Time, Barriers. *Films include:* The Virgin and the Gypsy, It Shouldn't Happen to a Vet, Priest of Love, Keep the Aspidistra Flying. *Radio includes:* Only a Matter of Time, Time Added on for Injuries, The Devil's Music. *Television includes:* series: Z Cars, Softly Softly, The Beiderbecke Trilogy; adaptations: The Barchester Chronicles, Fortunes of War, A Very British Coup, Campion, A Day in Summer, A Few Selected Exits, Oliver's Travels, Dalziel and Pascoe; recent plays: Doggin' Around, The Last of the Blonde Bombshells. *Publications:* The Beiderbecke Affair 1985, The Beiderbecke Tapes 1986, Misterioso 1987, The Beiderbecke Connection 1992, Oliver's Travels 1994, Doggin' Around 2006; plays and shorter pieces in various anthologies. *Leisure interests:* reading, theatre, snooker, jazz, grandchildren, talking and listening. *Address:* Alexandra Cann Representation, 12 Abingdon Road, London, W8 6AF, England (office). *Telephone:* (20) 7938-4002 (office).

PLATINI, Michel; French football coach, broadcaster, sports administrator and fmr football player; *President, Union of European Football Associations (UEFA);* b. 21 June 1955, Joeuf; s. of Aldo Platini and Anna Pillenelli; m. Christele Bigoni 1977; one s. one d.; professional footballer AS Nancy-Lorraine 1973–79 (winners Coupe de France 1978), AS St-Etienne 1979–82 (French nat. champions 1981), Juventus (Turin) 1982–85 where he scored 68 goals in 147 games (Italian nat. champions, winners European Cup Winners' Cup 1984, European Championship Cup 1985); player with French nat. team 1982, 1984 (winners European Cup), 1985 (winners Artemio Franqui Intercontinental Cup), 1986; French Nat. Team Coach 1987–92; co-presenter, ed. and consultant French TV 1985–88, consultant 1993–; f. and Pres. Michel Platini Foundation 1987–; Jt Pres. French 1998 World Cup Organising Cttee; Vice-Pres. French Football Fed.; Adviser to Pres. FIFA; mem. Exec. Cttee Union of European Football Associations (UEFA) 2002–, Pres. 2007–; mem. Exec. Cttee FIFA, Vice-Pres. 2007–; Chevalier, Légion d'honneur, Officier, Ordre nat. du Mérite; mem. Laureus World Sports Acad.; Ballon d'or (European footballer of the year) 1983, 1984, 1985, Soulier d'or européen, Top scorer in Italian league 1983, 1984, 1985, World Footballer of the Year 1984, 1985, French Player of the Century. *Publication:* Ma vie comme un match 1987. *Address:* UEFA, Route de Genève 46, Case Postale, 1260, Nyon 2, Switzerland (office). *Telephone:* 848042727 (office). *Fax:* 848012727 (office). *E-mail:* info@uefa.com (office). *Website:* www.uefa.com (office).

PLATONOV, Vladimir Mikhailovich, CandJurSc; Russian politician; b. 24 Dec. 1954, Moscow; m.; one s. one d.; ed Lumumba Univ. of Peoples' Friendship; worked in machine-construction factory 1972–75; investigator Prosecutor's Office, Deputy Prosecutor Moskvoretsky Dist of Moscow 1983–91; pvt. law practice, Exec. Dir Avtum Co. 1991–94; mem. Moscow City Duma 1993, Chair. (Speaker) 1994–; mem. Party Block Choice of Russia; mem. Russian Council of Fed. 1996–; Chair. Cttee on Constitutional Law Feb. 1996–. *Address:* Moscow City Duma, Petrovka str. 22, 103051 Moscow, Russia (office). *Telephone:* (4095) 923-50-80 (office). *Fax:* (495) 753-71-31 (office). *E-mail:* d29@duma.munic.ru (office).

PLATONOV, Vladimir Petrovich, DSc; Belarusian mathematician and academic; b. 1 Dec. 1939, Staiki, Byelorussian SSR; s. of Petr Platonov and Anna Platonova; m. Valentina Platonova 1974; two d.; ed Byelorussian State University; Asst Prof. Byelorussian State Univ. 1963, Prof. 1968, Head of Algebra Dept 1967–71; corresp. mem. Acad. of Sciences of Byelorussian SSR (now Belarus) 1969, mem. 1972 (Pres. 1987–92); Head Algebra Dept, Inst. of Math. 1971–93, Dir 1977–92, Lecturer; mem. Inst. for Advanced Studies, Princeton, NJ 1991–92; Prof., Univ. of Mich., USA 1993, Univ. of Bielefeld 1994, Univ. of Waterloo, Canada 1995–2001; mem. USSR (now Russian) Acad. of Sciences 1987, Belarus Acad. for Educ. 1995, New York Acad. of Sciences 1995; Foreign mem. Indian Nat. Science Acad.; Hon. mem. Chinese-Henan Acad. of Sciences; People's Deputy of the USSR 1989–91; Lenin Prize 1978, Humboldt Prize 1993. *Publications include:* Algebraic groups and number theory 1991, Finite-dimensional division algebras 1992. *Leisure interest:* literature. *Address:* c/o National Academy of Sciences of Belarus, 66 Franziska Skaryny Praspekt, Minsk 220072, Belarus.

PLATT, Nicholas, MA; American diplomatist and educational administrator; *President Emeritus, The Asia Society;* b. 10 March 1936, New York; m. Sheila Maynard; three s.; ed Harvard Coll. and Johns Hopkins Univ. School of Advanced Int. Studies; Chinese language student, Taiwan 1963; Political Officer, Hong Kong 1964–68, Beijing 1973–74, Tokyo 1974–77; staff mem. President Nixon's Del. to China 1972, later mem. US Liaison Office, Beijing; Dir for Japanese Affairs, Dept of State 1977–78; Nat. Security Council staff mem. specializing in Asian Affairs 1978–79; Deputy Asst Sec. for Defense 1980–81; Acting Asst Sec. of State for UN Affairs 1981–82; Amb. to Zambia 1982–84, to the Philippines 1987–91, to Pakistan 1991–92; Pres. Asia Soc. 1992–2004 (retd), Pres. Emer. 2004–; Special Asst to Sec. of State and Exec. Sec., Dept of State 1985–87; mem. Bd of Dirs Fiduciary Trust Int. *Address:* 131 East 69th Street, New York, NY 10021, USA (home). *Telephone:* (212) 772-0724. *Fax:* (212) 772-0732. *E-mail:* nplatt@attglobal.net.

PLATT, Stephen (Steve), BSc (Econ); British journalist; b. 29 Sept. 1954, Stoke-on-Trent; s. of Kenneth Platt and Joyce Pritchard; one d. by Diane Louise Paice; ed Longton High School, Stoke On Trent, Wade Deacon School, Widnes and London School of Econs; teacher, Moss Brook Special School, Widnes 1972–73; Dir Self Help Housing Resource Library, Polytechnic of N London 1977–80; co-ordinator, Islington Community Housing 1980–83; freelance writer and journalist 1983–; News Ed., subsequently Acting Ed. New Society 1986–88; Ed. Midweek 1988–89, Enjoying the Countryside 1988–; Ed. New Statesman and Society 1991–96; Contributing Ed. Channel 4

TV 1996–; Website and Contributing Ed. Time Team 1999– (BAFTA Award for Interactive Entertainment 2002); Dispatches Website Ed. 1999–; UKGLO Award for Outstanding Achievement 1999. *Leisure interests:* football, walking, countryside, gardening, breeding frogs, Paddington Bear, archaeology, ancient history, mountains and music. *Address:* 46 Tufnell Park Road, London, N7 0DT, England (home). *Telephone:* (20) 7263-4185 (home). *Fax:* (870) 124-5850 (home). *E-mail:* mail@steveplatt.net (home). *Website:* www .steveplatt.net.

PLATT, Trevor, PhD, FRS, FRSC; British/Canadian oceanographer; *Head of Biological Oceanography, Bedford Institute of Oceanography;* b. 12 Aug. 1942, Salford, England; s. of John Platt and Lily Platt; m. Shubha Sathyendranath 1988; ed Nottingham, Toronto and Dalhousie Univs; research scientist, Bedford Inst. of Oceanography, Canada 1965–72, Head of Biological Oceanography 1972–; Chair. Int. Ocean-Colow Co-ordinating Group 1996–, Jt Global Ocean Flux Study 1991–93; Huntsman Medal 1992 Hutchinson Medal, Rosenstiel Medal, Plymouth Marine Medal 1999. *Publications:* numerous papers in learned journals. *Leisure interests:* cycling, fly-fishing, languages. *Address:* 33 Crichton Park Road, Dartmouth, NS, B3A 2N9, Canada (home); Bedford Institute of Oceanography, Dartmouth, NS, B2Y 4A2. *Telephone:* (902) 426-3793. *Fax:* (902) 426-9388. *Website:* www.sap.com (office).

PLATTER, Günther; Austrian politician; *Governor of Tyrol;* b. 7 June 2008; m.; two c.; Minister of Defence 2003–07, of the Interior 2007–08; Gov. of Tyrol 2008–; mem. ÖVP (Austrian People's Party). *Address:* Governor of Tyrol, Eduard-Wallnöfer-Platz 3, A 6020 Innsbruck, Tyrol Austria (office). *Telephone:* (5) 125-08-20-02 (office). *Fax:* (5) 125-08-20-05 (office). *E-mail:* buero.lh .platter@tirol.gv.at (office). *Website:* www.tirol.gv.at (office).

PLATTNER, Hasso; German computer executive; *Chairman of the Supervisory Board, SAP AG;* b. 21 Jan. 1944, Berlin; ed Karlsruhe Univ.; consultant IBM 1968–72; co.-f. SAP AG 1972, Chair. SAP America, CEO SAP Markets, Co-Chair., CEO –2003, Chair. Supervisory Bd 2003–; Hon. Prof. Saarbrücken Univ. *Leisure interests:* golf, sailing. *Address:* SAP AG, Neurottstrasse 16, 69190 Walldorf, Germany (office). *Telephone:* (6227) 747474 (office). *Fax:* (6227) 757575 (office). *Website:* www.sap.com (office).

PLAVINSKY, Dmitri; Russian artist; b. 28 April 1937, Moscow; m. Maria Plavinskaya; three d.; ed Moscow Regional Art Coll.; painter and printmaker. *Publication:* Dmitri Plavinsky 2000. *Address:* 370 Fort Washington Avenue #507, New York, NY 10033, USA (office); Arbat str. 51, korp. 2, Apt 97, 121002 Moscow, Russia. *Telephone:* (212) 928-3260; (495) 241-32-29 (Moscow). *E-mail:* plavinsky@aol.com (home).

PLAVŠIĆ, Biljana, PhD; Bosnia and Herzegovina politician and biologist; b. 7 July 1930, Tuzla; m. (divorced); ed Zagreb Univ., Croatia; fmr Prof. of Botany, Sarajevo Univ.; Founding mem. Serbian Democratic Party (SDS); first female mem. of collective Presidency of Bosnia and Herzegovina 1990–92, one of two acting Pres. of Republika Srpska of Bosnia and Herzegovina Feb.–May 1992, then mem. of three-mem. Presidency of Republika Srpska, mem. Supreme Command of the Armed Forces 1992; mem. 'Crisis Cttee' (military and civilian govt which ordered mass expulsion of Muslims and Croats from E and Cen. Bosnia) 1991–92; Vice-Pres., Acting Pres., then Pres. Republika Srpska (Bosnia and Herzegovina) 1992–98; Chair. Serb Nat. Alliance; surrendered herself to trial at War Crimes Tribunal, The Hague Jan. 2001, charged with genocide and crimes against humanity; pleaded guilty on 2 Oct. 2002 to crimes against humanity, charge of genocide dropped by tribunal, sentenced to 11 years' imprisonment Feb. 2003.

PLAYER, Gary Jim; South African professional golfer; b. 1 Nov. 1935, Johannesburg; s. of Francis Harry Audley Player and of the late Muriel Marie Ferguson; m. Vivienne Verwey 1957; two s. four d.; turned professional 1953; first overseas player for 45 years to win US Open Championship 1965; Winner, British Open Championship 1959, 1968, 1974; Piccadilly World Match Play Champion 1965, 1966, 1968, 1971, 1973; US Open Champion 1965; US Masters Champion 1961, 1974, 1978; US Professional Golf Asscn Champion 1962, 1972; Winner, South African Open 13 times; South African PGA Champion 1959, 1960, 1969, 1979, 1982; Winner, Australian Open 7 times; Quadel Sr Classic Champion 1985; third player ever to win all four major world professional titles; holds world record for lowest 18-hole score in any Open Championship (59 in the Brazilian Open 1974); Sr Tour victories include: Sr British Open 1988, 1990, 1997, Sr PGA Champion 1986, 1988, 1990, Long Island Sr Classic, Sr Skins Game 2000; Capt. Rest of the World Team, Pres.'s Cup 2003, 2005; f. Gary Player Group, Gary Player Foundation (rural educ.); golf course designer (over 200 projects world-wide); breeds thoroughbred racehorses; Hon. LLD (St Andrews) 1995, (Ulster) 1997, (Dundee) 1999; South African Sportsman of the Century 1989, Hilton Hotel Lifetime Achievement Award 1995. *Publications:* Gary Player: The Autobiography 1991, The Golfer's Guide to the Meaning of Life 2001, In the Presence of Gary Player. *Leisure interests:* breeding thoroughbred racehorses, farming, educ., family, health, fitness. *Address:* Blair Atholl Farm, Lanseria, Johannesburg (office); Gary Player Stud, POB 189, Colesberg 9795, South Africa (office); POB 785629, Sandton 2146. *Telephone:* (11) 8833333 (office); (11) 6592800 (home). *Fax:* (11) 8834444 (office). *E-mail:* info@garyplayer.co.za (office). *Website:* www.garyplayer.co.za (office).

PŁAŻYŃSKI, Maciej; Polish politician; *Deputy Speaker, Sejm;* b. 10 Feb. 1958, Młynary, Elbląg Prov.; m. Elzbieta Płażyński; two s. one d.; ed Gdańsk Univ.; Co-founder Ind. Students Union (NZS) 1980, Leader NZS Univ. Board, Gdańsk 1980; participant Young Poland Movt; organizer of strikes and activist for underground Solidarity during martial law; Founder and Chair. Gdańsk Height Services Work Cooperative 1983 (employing many unemployed Solidarity activists); Chair. Lech Bądkowski Political Thought Club, Gdańsk 1988; co.-f. Liberal Congress in Gdańsk; mem. Republican

Coalition 1990 (later Conservative Party); Gdańsk Voivoda 1990–96; Vice-Chair. Gdańsk Region Solidarity Election Action (AWS) 1997; Co-founder and mem. Solidarity Election Action Social Movt 1997–; Deputy in Sejm (Parl.) 1997–, Marshal of the Sejm 1997–2001, Deputy Speaker 2005–; mem. Solidarity Election Action Parl. Caucus 1997–2000; Chair. Civic Platform Caucus 2001–; Co-founder and Chair. Civic Platform 2001, later left Party as ind.; Hon. Citizen of Młynary, Puck and Pionki. *Address:* Biuro Poselskie Macieja Płażyńskiego, ul. Szeroka 80/81, 80-835 Gdańsk, Poland (office). *Telephone:* (58) 305-34-15 (office). *Fax:* (58) 305-24-30 (office). *E-mail:* plazynski@nw.senat.gov.pl (office). *Website:* www.plazynski.pl (office).

PLÉAH, Natié; Malian politician; *Minister of Defence and Veterans;* b. 1953, Moutigué, Ké-Macina Circle; m.; seven c.; ed secondary school in Sévaré, Markala Coll., school in Badalabougou, Ecole Nationale d'Admin, Paris, France; began serving Gov.-Gen. Sikasso 1976, held several posts as an admin., including Second Deputy Commdr Ansongo Circle, Deputy Commdr Koulikoro then Yanfolila Circles, Commdr Circle then Koulikoro Timbuktu, Admin. Affairs Advisor to Gov. of Timbuktu, Advisor for Admin. Affairs in Ségou, Chief of Staff to Gov. of Mopti and High Commr of Kayes; Acting High Commr First Econ. Region 2002–04, Gov. of Kayes 2004–05; Gov. Dist of Bamako 2005; Minister of Youth and Sports 2005–07, of the Environment and Sanitation May 2007, of Defence and Veterans 2007–. *Leisure interests:* reading and agricultural activities. *Address:* Ministry of Defence and Veterans, route de Koulouba, BP 2083, Bamako, Mali (office). *Telephone:* 222-50-21 (office). *Fax:* 223-23-18 (office).

PLEISTER, Christopher, Dr rer. pol; German banker; *Chairman, BVR (Federal Association of German Co-operative Banks);* b. 15 May 1948, Hamburg; m.; three s.; ed Ludwig-Maximilians Univ., Munich; with Landesgenossenschaftsbank AG, Hanover 1977–81, Hallbaum, Maier & Co. Landkreditbank AG, Hanover 1981–84; Exec. Man. Norddeutsche Genossenschaftsbank AG 1984, mem. Bd of Man. 1985–90; mem. Bd of Man. DG Bank, Frankfurt-am-Main 1990–99; Chair. Bundesverband der Deutschen Volksbanken und Raiffeisenbanken (BVR — Fed. Asscn of German Cooperative Banks) 2000–; Chair. Supervisory Bd DZ Bank 2001–; Pres. European Asscn of Cooperative Banks (EACB) 2006–. *Address:* BVR, Schellingstrasse 4, 10785 Berlin (office); DZ Band AG, Deutsche Zentral-Genossenschaftsbank, Frankfurt am Main, Platz der Republik, 60265 Frankfurt, Germanyam Main. *Telephone:* (30) 20211000 (BVR) (office). *Fax:* (30) 20211901 (BVR) (office). *E-mail:* pleister@bvr.de (office). *Website:* www .bvr.de (office); www.dzbank.de (office).

PLENDERLEITH, Ian, CBE, MA, MBA, MSI, FCT; British central banker and economist; *Deputy Governor, South African Reserve Bank;* b. 27 Sept. 1943, York; s. of Raymond William Plenderleith and Louise Helen Plenderleith (née Martin); m. Kristina Mary Bentley; one s. two d.; ed King Edward's School, Birmingham, Christ Church, Oxford, Columbia Business School, New York; joined Bank of England 1965, seconded to IMF, Washington, DC 1972–74, Pvt. Sec. to Gov. Bank of England 1976–79; Alt. Dir EIB 1980–86, Head Gilt-Edged Div. 1982–90, Asst Dir 1986–90, Sr Broker to Commrs for Reduction of Nat. Debt 1989–2002, Assoc. Dir 1990–94; Dir Bank of England Nominees Ltd 1994–2002, Exec. Dir Bank of England and mem. Monetary Policy Cttee 1994–2002; Alt. Dir BIS 1994–2002; Dir London Stock Exchange (fmrly mem. Stock Exchange Council) 1989–2001 (Deputy Chair. 1996), Chair. Stock Borrowing and Lending Cttee 1990–95; Chair. G-10 Gold and Foreign Exchange Cttee 1995–2001; Co-Chair. Govt Borrowers' Forum 1991–94; Chair. Sterling Money Markets Liaison Group 1999–2002; Chair. Corpn for Public Deposits 2003–; Deputy Gov. and mem. Monetary Policy Cttee, South African Reserve Bank 2003–; mem. Editorial Cttee OECD Study on Debt Man. 1990–93, Legal Risk Review Cttee 1991–92, Financial Law Panel 1992–94, G-10 Cttee on Global Financial System 1994–2002; mem. Advisory Bd Inst. of Archaeology Devt Trust, Univ. Coll. London 1987–96, Bd of Overseers Columbia Business School 1991–, Fund-raising Planning Group, St Bartholomew's Hosp. 1992–94, Council, British Museum Friends 1993–99, 2000–03, Fund-raising Planning Cttee St Bartholomew's and The London Hosps 1998–2003, Advisory Bd The Actors Centre 2002–, Devt Council Shakespeare's Globe 2002–, Advisory Bd London Capital Club 2002–; Dir City Arts Trust 1997–2003; Fellow, Asscn of Corp. Treasurers; mem. Securities Inst.; Liveryman Innholders' Co. 1977–; Sec. Tillington Cricket Club 1983–2003; Beta Gamma Sigma Medal 1971. *Leisure interests:* archaeology, theatre, cricket, long-distance walking. *Address:* South African Reserve Bank, POB 427, Pretoria 0001 (office); Suite #686, Private Bag X4, Menlo Park, Pretoria 0102, South Africa (home); Goldneys, River, Petworth, W Sussex, GU28 9AU, England. *Telephone:* (12) 313-3139 (office); (12) 346-8179 (home). *Fax:* (12) 313-4767 (office); (12) 346-8179 (home). *E-mail:* ian.plenderleith@resbank.co .za (office); ianplenderleith@yahoo.co.uk (home). *Website:* www.reservebank .co.za (office).

PLENEL, Edwy; French journalist; b. 31 Aug. 1952, Nantes; s. of Alain Plenel and Michèle Bertreux; m. Nicole Lapierre; one d.; ed Institut d'études politiques, Paris; journalist Rouge 1976–78, Matin de Paris 1980; joined Le Monde 1980, Educ. Ed. 1980–82, Legal columnist 1982–90, Reporter 1991, Head Legal Dept 1992–94, Chief Ed. 1994–95, Asst Editorial Dir 1995–96, Ed. 1996–2000, Ed.-in-Chief 2000–04 (resgnd). *Publications:* L'Effet Le Pen 1984, La République inachevée: l'État et l'école en France 1985, Mourir à Ouvéa: le tournant calédonien 1988, Voyage avec Colomb 1991, La République menacée: dix ans d'effet Le Pen 1992, La Part d'ombre 1992, Un temps de chien 1994, Les Mots volés 1997, L'Epreuve 1999, Secrets de jeunesse 2001, La Découverte du monde 2002, Procès 2006. *Address:* c/o Le Monde, 21 bis rue Claude Bernard, 75242 Paris Cedex, France (office).

PLEŞCA, Valeriu; Moldovan politician, business executive and economist; b. 8 Nov. 1958, Dumitreni, Floresti Dist; m.; one s. one d.; ed State Univ. of

Moldova, Acad. of Econ. Studies; Advisor, Ministry of Social Assistance 1983–86, Office of the Chief Prosecutor 1986–91; Head of Gloria V&A Co. 1990–; mem. Parl. 1998– (ind. 2003–), fmr Deputy Chair. Comm. for Rules and Immunities; Minister of Defence 2004–05, 2005–07; Serghei Radonejskii Award 2006. *Publications include:* numerous articles on defence and security policy. *Leisure interests include:* tennis, skiing, hunting. *Address:* c/o Ministry of Defence, 2021 Chişinău şos. Hînceşti 84, Moldova (office).

PLESSNER, Yakir, BS, MS, PhD; Israeli economist and academic; *Associate Professor Emeritus, Department of Agricultural Economics and Management, Hebrew University of Jerusalem;* b. 18 Jan. 1935, Haifa; s. of Martin Plessner and Eva Plessner; m. Ora Ester Frenkel 1959; one s. one d.; ed Iowa State Univ., USA and Hebrew Univ. of Jerusalem; Visiting Lecturer, Univ. of Pennsylvania 1971–73; Sr Lecturer, Hebrew Univ. of Jerusalem 1973–96, now Assoc. Prof. Emer., Dept of Agricultural Econs and Man.; Research Consultant, The World Bank 1977–78; Econ. Adviser to Israel's Minister of Finance 1981–83; Deputy Gov. Bank of Israel 1982–85; mem. Israel's Securities Authority 1982–85; Joseph and Esther Foster Visiting Prof., Brandeis Univ. 1985–86; Visiting Prof., Dartmouth Coll. 1987–88; Visiting Assoc. Prof., Dept of Econs, American Univ., Washington, DC 1992–93, 1999–2000; Consultant, Ministry of Defence 1991–2003; Fellow, Jerusalem Center for Public Affairs 1991–; The Oded Levine Prize of the Operations Research Soc. of Israel 1974, Koret Foundation First Prize for best paper on Israel's economy 1998. *Publications:* The Marketing of Israel's Citrus Fruit in Major European Markets 1976; regular columnist for Globes and Hadashot (daily newspapers); several articles in learned society journals. *Leisure interests:* music, photography, tennis. *Address:* Department of Agricultural Economics and Management, Faculty of Agriculture, Hebrew University, PO Box 12, Rehovot 76100, Israel (office). *Telephone:* (8) 9489373 (office); (8) 9468745 (home). *Fax:* (8) 9466267 (office). *E-mail:* plessner@agri.huji.ac.il (office). *Website:* www.departments.agri.huji.ac.il (office).

PLEŞU, Andrei Gabriel, PhD; Romanian philosopher; b. 23 Aug. 1948, Bucharest; s. of Radu Pleşu and Zoe Pleşu; m. Catrinel Maria Lăcrămioara, 1972; two s.; ed Acad. of Fine Arts and Univ. of Bucharest; Lecturer, Acad. of Fine Arts, Bucharest 1980–82, Prof. 1991–92; Prof., Univ. of Bucharest 1992–, Prof. of Philosophy of Religion 1999–97; Dir of Dilema (weekly); Founder and Rector New Europe Coll., Bucharest 1994–2001; Minister of Culture 1989–91; Minister of Foreign Affairs 1997–99; mem. Romanian Artists' Union 1975, Romanian Writers' Union 1980, World Acad. of Art and Science, Acad. Internationale de Philosophie de l'Art, Geneva, Scientific Advisory Bd Europe Inst., Budapest, Advisory Group for Social Sciences and Humanities in the European Research Area (Research Directorate Gen. of the EU Comm.), Bd Trustees Collegium Budapest, Bd Trustees Maison des Sciences de l'Homme, Paris, Bd Trustees and Advisory Bd Centre for Advanced Study, Sofia; Corresp. mem. Consejo Argentino para las Relaciones Internacionales; Perm. Research Fellow, Wissenschaftskollege, Berlin 1992; Commdr des Arts et des Lettres 1990, Gran Cruz, Orden El Sol del Perú (Peru) 1998, Grand Officier, Légion d'honneur 1999; Hon. PhD (Albert-Ludwig Univ., Freiburg) 2000, (Humboldt Univ., Berlin) 2001; Humboldt Research Fellowship, Univ. of Bonn 1975–77, Univ. of Heidelberg 1983–84, Prize for Art Criticism, Romanian Artists' Union 1980, Prize for Essay, Writers' Asscn, Bucharest 1980, Prize, Ateneu review 1991, Prize, Flacara weekly 1993, New Europe Prize 1993, Prize of Brandenburg Acad. of Sciences, Berlin 1996, Humboldt Medal (Germany) 1998, Hannah Arendt Prize 1998, Goethe Medal, Goethe Inst., Weimar 1999, Konstantin Jireček Medal, South-Eastern European Soc., Berlin 2000 and numerous other prizes. *Publications:* Calatorie in lumea forrnelor (Travel to the World of Forms) 1974, Pitoresc si rnelancolie (Picturesque and Melancholy) 1980, Francesco Guardi 1981, Ochiul si lucrurile (The Eye and the Things) 1986, Minima Moralia (Elements for an Ethics of the Interval) 1988, Jurnalul de la Tescani (The Diary of Tescany) 1992, Limba pasarilor (The Language of Birds) 1993, Faces and Masks of Transition 1996; numerous papers and articles. *Address:* Department of Philosophy, University of Bucharest, Blvd M. Kogalniceanu 64, 70629 Bucharest (office); Str. Paris 14, 71241 Bucharest 1, Romania (home). *Telephone:* (21) 6157187 (office); (21) 2121488 (home).

PLETNEV, Mikhail Vasilievich; Russian pianist, conductor and composer; *Founder, Russian National Orchestra;* b. 14 April 1957, Arkhangelsk; ed Moscow State Conservatory with Yakov Flier and Lev Vlasenko (piano), Albert Leman (composition); gave recitals and played with orchestras in major cities of Russia, Europe, Japan and America; gained reputation as Russian music interpreter; Founder and Chief Conductor Russian Nat. Orchestra 1990–99, Hon. Conductor 1999–, and head of the Conductor Collegium 2006–; tours with orchestra and as piano soloist in various countries; has performed with Haitink, Maazel, Chailly, Tennstedt, Sanderling, Blomstedt, Järvi, Thielemann; also conducted Philharmonia Orchestra, Deutsche Kammerphilharmonie, Norddeutsche Rundfunk Symphony Orchestra, London Symphony Orchestra, Berlin Philharmonic, Bayerische Rundfunk Symphony, Orchestre Nat. de France, Israel Philharmonic, San Francisco Symphony and Pittsburgh Symphony; teacher in Moscow Conservatory 1981–1992; First Prize Int. Tchaikovsky competition, Moscow 1978, People's Artist of Russia 1990, State Prize of Russia 1982, 1993. *Address:* Opus 3 Artists, 470 Park Avenue South, 9th Floor North, New York, NY 10016, USA (office); Russian National Orchestra, Moscow 117335, Orchestrion, Garibaldi 19, Russia (office). *Telephone:* (212) 584-7500 (office); (495) 504-07-81-83 (office). *Fax:* (646) 300-8200 (office); (495) 504-07-88 (office). *E-mail:* info@opus3artists.com (office); info@rno.ru (office). *Website:* www.opus3artists.com (office); www.russianarts.org/rno (office).

PLISETSKAYA, Maya Mikhailovna; Russian ballerina; b. 20 Nov. 1925, Moscow; m. Rodion Shchedrin; ed Moscow Bolshoi Theatre Ballet School; soloist Bolshoi Ballet 1943–90; Artistic Dir Ballet Roma Opera 1984–85, Nat. Ballet of Spain 1987–89; f. Maya Plisetskaya Int. Ballet Competition, St Petersburg 1994; Pres. Imperial Russian Ballet 1996–2005; Hon. mem. Portuguese Dance Centre; Hon. Prof. Moscow Univ. 1993; First Prize, Budapest Int. Competition 1949; People's Artist of the RSFSR 1951; People's Artist of the USSR 1959, Anna Pavlova Prize 1962, Lenin Prize 1964, Hero of Socialist Labour 1985, Légion d'honneur 1986, Triumph Prize 2000, Asturias Prize 2005, Imperial Prize Tokyo, and other decorations. *Main ballet roles:* Odette-Odile (Swan Lake, Tchaikovsky), Raimonda (Raimonda, Glazunov), Zaryema (The Fountain of Bakhchisarai, Asafiev), Kitri (Don Quixote, Minkus), Juliet (Romeo and Juliet, Prokofiev), Girl-Bird, Syunmbike (Shuralye, Yarullin), Laurencia (Laurencia, Krein), Aegina (Spartak, Khachaturian); ballets by R. Shchedrin: Carmen (Carmen Suite), Anna (Anna Karenina) 1972, Nina (The Seagull) 1980, Lady with a Lap-dog 1983, La folle de Chaillot 1992; ballets by M. Béjart: Bolero 1976, Isadora 1977, Leda 1979, Kurazuka 1995, Ave, Maya 2000. *Publication:* I, Maya Plisetskaya. *Address:* Theresien Str. 23, 80333 Munich, Germany (home); 103050 Moscow, Tverskaya 25/9, Apt 31, Russia (home). *Telephone:* (89) 285834 (Munich); (495) 299-72-39 (Moscow). *Fax:* (89) 282057 (Munich) (home); (495) 299-72-39 (Moscow). *Website:* www.plisetskaya.de (office).

PLOIX, Hélène Marie Joseph, MA, MBA; French business executive; *Chairman, Pechel Industies;* b. 25 Sept. 1944, Anould; d. of René Ploix and Antoinette Jobert; m. Alexandre Lumbroso 1988; ed Univ. of Paris, Univ. of California, Berkeley; Man. Consultant, McKinsey and Co., Paris 1968–78; Special Asst to Cabinet of Sec. of State for Consumer Affairs 1977–78; Dir Cie Européenne de Publication 1978–82; Chair. Banque Industrielle et Mobilière Privée 1982–84; mem. of Bd Comm. des Opérations de Bourse 1983–84; Adviser to Prime Minister for Econ. and Financial Affairs 1984–86; Exec. Dir IMF and World Bank, representing France 1986–89; Deputy CEO Caisse des dépôts et consignations 1989–95; Chair. Caisse autonome de refinancement 1990–95, CDC Participations 1992–95; Chair. Pechel Industries 1997–; currently mem. Jt Staff Pension Fund Investments Cttee, UN; mem. Bd of Dirs (non-exec.) BNP Paribas 2003–, Ferring, Publicis 1998–, Lafarge 1999–, The Boots Co. PLC 2000–; Chevalier Ordre Nat. du Mérite, Chevalier Légion d'honneur. *Publications:* Le dirigeant et le gouvernement d'entreprise 2003, Gouvernement d'enterprise 2006. *Leisure interest:* golf. *Address:* Pechel Industries, 162 rue du Faubourg Saint-Honoré, 75008 Paris (office); 42 quai des Ofrèvres, 75001 Paris, France. *Telephone:* 1-56-59-79-59 (office). *Fax:* 1-56-59-79-56 (office). *E-mail:* contact@pechel.com (office). *Website:* www.pechel.com (office).

PLOWDEN, David, BA; American photographer, writer and teacher; b. 9 Oct. 1932, Boston; s. of Roger Stanley Plowden and Mary Plowden (née Butler); m. 1st Pleasance Coggeshall (divorced 1976); m. 2nd Sandra Schoellkopf 1977; three s. one d.; ed Yale Univ.; Asst to Trainmaster, Great Northern Railway 1955–56; self-employed photographer/writer 1962–; Assoc. Prof. Ill. Inst. of Tech. Inst. of Design 1978–85; lecturer Univ. of Iowa School of Journalism 1985–88; Visiting Prof. Grand Valley State Univ. 1988–; numerous photographic exhbns; John Simon Guggenheim Memorial Fellowship 1968; Smithsonian Inst. Award 1970–71, 1975–76; Iowa Humanities Award and Nat. Endowment for the Humanities Award 1987–88. *Publications:* Lincoln and His America 1970, The Hand of Man on America 1971, Floor of the Sky, The Great Plains 1972, Commonplace 1974, Bridges: The Spans of North America 1974, revised edn 2002, Tugboat 1976, Steel 1981, An American Chronology 1982, Industrial Landscape 1985, A Time of Trains 1987, A Sense of Place 1988, End of an Era 1992, Small Town America 1994, Imprints 1997, David Plowden: The American Barn 2003, A Handful of Dust 2006; co-author of numerous books. *Address:* 609 Cherry Street, Winnetka, IL 60093, USA. *Telephone:* (847) 446-2793. *Fax:* (847) 446-2795. *E-mail:* david@davidplowden.com (office). *Website:* www.davidplowden.com (office).

PLOWRIGHT, Dame Joan Ann, DBE; British actress; b. 28 Oct. 1929, Brigg, Lancashire; d. of William Plowright and Daisy Plowright (née Burton); m. 1st Roger Gage 1953 (divorced); m. 2nd Sir Laurence (later Lord) Olivier 1961 (died 1989); one s. two d.; ed Scunthorpe Grammar School and Old Vic Theatre School; mem. Old Vic Company, toured South Africa 1952–53; first leading rôle in The Country Wife, London 1956; mem. English Stage Company 1956; at Nat. Theatre 1963–74; Vice-Pres. Nat. Youth Theatre; Vice-Pres. and mem. Council English Stage Co.; mem. Council, Royal Acad. of Dramatic Art (RADA); Best Actress Soc. of West End Theatre (Filumena) 1978, 18th Crystal Award for Women in Film, USA 1994. *Plays include:* The Chairs 1957, The Entertainer 1958, Major Barbara and Roots 1959, A Taste of Honey (Best Actress (Tony) Award 1960) 1960, Uncle Vanya 1962, 1963, 1964, St Joan (Best Actress (Evening Standard) Award 1964) 1963, Hobson's Choice 1964, The Master Builder 1965, Much Ado About Nothing 1967, Tartuffe 1967, Three Sisters 1967, 1969 (film 1969), The Advertisement 1968, 1969, Love's Labour's Lost 1968, 1969, The Merchant of Venice, 1970, 1971–72, Rules of the Game, Woman Killed with Kindness 1971–72, Taming of the Shrew, Doctor's Dilemma 1972, Rosmersholm 1973, Saturday Sunday Monday 1973, Eden's End 1974, The Sea Gull 1975, The Bed Before Yesterday (Variety Club Award 1976) 1975, Filumena 1977, Enjoy 1980, Who's Afraid of Virginia Woolf? 1981, Cavell 1982, The Cherry Orchard 1983, The Way of the World 1984, Mrs Warren's Profession 1985, Revolution 1985, The House of Bernarda Alba 1986, And a Nightingale Sang 1989, Time and the Conways 1991, Absolutely Perhaps 2003. *Films include:* Equus 1976, Richard Wagner 1982, Britannia Hospital 1981, Brimstone and Treacle 1982, Drowning by Numbers (Variety Club Film Actress of the Year Award 1987) 1987, The Dressmaker 1988, Conquest of the South Pole 1989, I Love You to Death 1989, Avalon 1990, Enchanted April (Golden Globe Award 1993) 1991, Stalin (Golden Globe Award 1993) 1991, Denis the Menace, A Place for Annie 1992, A Pin for the Butterfly 1993, Last Action Hero 1993, Widow's Peak 1994, On Promised Land

1994, Return of the Natives 1994, Hotel Sorrento 1994, A Pyromaniac's Love Story 1994, The Scarlet Letter 1994, Jane Eyre 1994, If We Are Women 1995, Surviving Picasso 1995, Mr. Wrong 1995, 101 Dalmatians 1996, The Assistant 1996, Shut Up and Dance 1997, Tom's Midnight Garden 1997, America Betrayed 1998, Tea with Mussolini 1999, Return to the Secret Garden 2001, Callas Forever 2002, Global Heresy 2002, Bringing Down the House 2003, I Am David 2003, The Great Goose Caper 2003, George and the Dragon 2004, Goose! 2004, Mrs Palfry at the Claremont (AARP Best Actress Award 2006) 2005, Curious George (voice) 2006, The Spiderwick Chronicles 2007. *Television includes:* Merchant of Venice 1973, Daphne Laureola 1977, Saturday Sunday Monday 1977, The Importance of Being Earnest 1988, It May Be the Last Time 1997, Frankie and Hazel 2000, Bailey's Mistake 2001. *Publication:* And That's Not All (autobiog.) 2001. *Leisure interests:* entertaining, music, reading. *Address:* c/o ICM, 76 Oxford Street, London, W1N 0AX, England (office).

PLOWRIGHT, Jonathan Daniel; British pianist; b. 24 Sept. 1959, Doncaster, S Yorks.; s. of Cyril James Plowright and Molly Plowright; m. Diane Rosemary Shaw 1990; ed Stonyhurst Coll., Univ. of Birmingham, Royal Acad. of Music, London, Peabody Conservatory of Music, Baltimore, USA; debut at Carnegie Recital Hall, New York 1984, Purcell Room, London 1985; has performed with all major UK orchestras and numerous int. orchestras; solo recitals throughout UK and many int. tours; regular BBC broadcasts; performed world premiere Constant Lambert's piano concerto, St John's Smith Square 1988; Prof. of Keyboard, Univ. of Chichester, Royal Scottish Acad. of Music and Drama; twelve commercial recordings; Hon. ARAM; McFarren Gold Medal (RAM) 1983, Fulbright Scholarship 1983, Countess of Munster Scholarship, Commonwealth Musician of the Year 1983, winner European Piano Competition 1989. *Leisure interests:* wine, rugby, cricket, fishing. *Website:* www.jonathanplowright.com.

PLOWRIGHT, Rosalind Anne, OBE, LRAM; British singer (mezzo-soprano); b. 21 May 1949; d. of Robert Arthur Plowright and Celia Adelaide Plowright; m. James Anthony Kaye 1984; one s. one d.; ed Notre Dame High School, Wigan, Royal Northern Coll. of Music, Manchester; began career at London Opera Centre 1973–75; Glyndebourne Chorus and Touring Co. 1974–77; debut with ENO as Page in Salome 1975, Miss Jessel in Turn of the Screw 1979 (Soc. of West End Theatre Award), at Covent Garden as Ortlinde in Die Walküre 1980; has sung also in Switzerland, Germany, France, Spain, Portugal, Italy, Netherlands, Denmark, Austria, Greece, USA, Argentina, Chile, Israel; has sung mezzo repertoire 1999–; Metropolitan Opera debut 2003; principal roles include Ariadne, Alceste, Médée, Norma, Tosca; title role and Elizabeth I in Mary Stuart, Maddalena in Andrea Chénier, Antonia in The Tales of Hoffman, Donna Anna in Don Giovanni, Vitellia in La Clemenza di Tito, Madame Butterfly, Manon Lescaut, Suor Angelica, Giorgetta in Il Tabarro, Aida, Abigaille in Nabucco, Desdemona in Otello, Elena in I Vespri Siciliani, Leonora in Il Trovatore, Amelia in Un Ballo in Maschera, Leonora in La Forza del Destino, Violetta in La Traviata, Kundry in Parsifal, Kostelnička in Katya Kabanova, Amneris in Aida, Cassandra in Les Troyens, Eboli in Don Carlos, Fricka in Rheingold and Walküre; First Prize, 7th Int. Competition for Opera Singers, Sofia 1979, Prix Fondation Fanny Heldy, Acad. Nat. du Disque Lyrique 1985. *Television:* House of Elliot 1992, The Man Who Made Husbands Jealous 1997. *Address:* c/o Zemsky/Green Artists Management, 104 West 73rd Street, Suite 1, New York, NY 10023, USA (office); 83 St Mark's Avenue, Salisbury, Wilts., SP1 3DW, England (home). *Website:* www .rosalindplowright.com.

PLUGCHIEVA, Meglena Ivanova, PhD; Bulgarian diplomatist and politician; *Deputy Prime Minister, responsible for European Union Funds;* b. 12 Feb. 1956, Balchik; m.; two c.; ed German Language High School, Varna, Forestry Univ., Sofia; worked as an insp. at Regional Environmental Protection Directorate, Varna 1981–84; a Deputy Dir Varna Regional Forestry Directorate 1984–90; Head of Foreign Relations Dept, Nat. Forestry Directorate 1990–95; mem. Parl. (Bulgarian Socialist Party—BSP) 1995–2001; Deputy Minister of Agric. and Forests 2001–04 (resgnd as mem. Supreme Council of BSP to take this position); Rep. of Bulgaria at Rheinland-Pfalz, Germany 1997–2008, Amb. to Germany 2004–08; Deputy Prime Minister, responsible for EU Funds 2008–; mem. Governing Bd Bulgarian-German Forum 1996–; Bundesverdienstkreuz. *Address:* Council of Ministers, 1194 Sofia, bul. Dondukov 1, Bulgaria (office). *Telephone:* (2) 940-29-99 (office). *Fax:* (2) 980-20-56 (office). *E-mail:* iprd@government.bg (office). *Website:* www .government.bg (office).

PLUMB, Baron (Life Peer), cr. 1987, of Coleshill in the County of Warwickshire; **(Charles) Henry Plumb,** Kt, DL; British politician; b. 27 March 1925; s. of Charles Plumb and Louise Plumb; m. Marjorie Dorothy Dunn 1947; one s. two d.; ed King Edward VI School, Nuneaton; mem. Council Nat. Farmers Union 1959, Vice-Pres. 1964, 1965, Deputy-Pres. 1966–69, Pres. 1970–79; mem. Duke of Northumberland's Cttee of Inquiry on Foot and Mouth Disease 1967–68; Chair. British Agricultural Council 1975–79; Pres. Nat. Fed. of Young Farmers' Clubs 1976–86; Pres. Royal Agricultural Soc. of England 1977, Deputy Pres. 1978; Pres. Int. Fed. of Agricultural Producers 1979–82, Royal Agricultural Benevolent Inst.; MEP (Conservative) 1979–99, Chair. Agricultural Cttee 1979–82, Leader, European Democratic Group (Conservative) 1982–87, 1994–97, Pres. European Parl. 1987–90, Leader British Conservatives in European Parl. 1994–97, Co-Pres. EU/ACP Jt Ass. for Africa/Caribbean/Pacific Countries 1994–99, Hon. Pres. 1999–; Vice-Pres. EPP Group in European Parl. 1994–97; Chancellor Coventry Univ. 1995–; Chair. Agricultural Mortgage Corpn 1994–95; mem. Temporary Cttee of Enquiry into BSE 1996–97; Fellow Royal Agric. Socs, Duchy; Order of Merit, FRG and decorations from Portugal, Luxembourg, Spain, France, Greece, Italy and others; Hon. DSc (Cranfield) 1983; Hon. DLitt (Warwick Coll.); Royal Agricultural Soc. of England Gold Medal 1983. *Leisure interests:* fishing, shooting, country pursuits. *Address:* House of Lords, Westminster, London, SW1A 0PW; The Dairy Farm, Maxstoke, Coleshill, Warwicks., B46 2QJ, England (home). *Telephone:* (20) 7219-1233 (office); (1675) 463133 (Coleshill) (home). *Fax:* (20) 7219-1649 (office); (1675) 464156 (Coleshill). *E-mail:* plumbh@parliament.uk (office).

PLUMBLY, Sir Derek John, KCMG, BA; British diplomatist; *Chairman, Analysis and Evaluation Commission, Sudan;* b. 15 May 1948, Lyndhurst, Hants.; s. of the late John Plumbly and of Jean Plumbly (née Baker); m. Nadia Youssef Gohar 1979; one d. two s.; ed Brockenhurst Grammar School, Magdalen Coll., Oxford; with VSO, Pakistan 1970–71; joined FCO 1972; Arabic language training, MECAS, Lebanon 1973–74; Second Sec. in Jeddah 1975–77; First Sec. in Cairo 1977–80; FCO 1980–84; assigned to Washington, DC 1984–88; Counsellor in Riyadh 1988–92; with UK Mission to UN, New York 1992–96; Dir Drugs and Crime Dept, FCO 1996–97, Dir Middle East and North Africa Dept 1997–2000; Amb. to Saudi Arabia 2000–03, to Egypt 2003–07; Chair. Analysis and Evaluation Comm., established under Sudan Comprehensive Peace Agreement, Khartoum 2008–; Dr hc (Loughborough) 2007. *Leisure interests:* family, reading, travel. *Address:* Analysis and Evaluation Commission, Amarat Street, Khartoum, Sudan (office). *E-mail:* aec.sud@gmail.com (office).

PLUMBRIDGE, Robin Allan, MA; South African business executive (retd) and company director; b. 6 April 1935, Cape Town; s. of the late C. O. Plumbridge and of the late M. A. Plumbridge; m. Celia Anne Millar 1959; two s. two d.; ed St Andrew's Coll., Grahamstown, Univs of Cape Town and Oxford; joined Gold Fields of South Africa Ltd 1957, Asst Man. 1962–65, Man. 1965–69, Exec. Dir 1969–80, CEO 1980–95, Chair. 1980–97; Chair. World Gold Council 1993–95; Dir Standard Bank Group 1980–2005, Newmont Mining Corpn 1983–; Hon. LLD. *Address:* Postnet Suite #107, Private Bag X15, Somerset West 7129; Navarre Farm, Stellenbosch, South Africa (home). *Telephone:* (21) 8551568 (office). *Fax:* (21) 8552170 (office). *E-mail:* rplum@ mweb.co.za (home).

PLUMMER, (Arthur) Christopher (Orme), CC; Canadian actor; b. 13 Dec. 1929, Toronto; m. 1st Tammy Lee Grimes 1956; one d.; m. 2nd Patricia Audrey Lewis 1962 (divorced 1966); m. 3rd Elaine Regina Taylor 1970; public and pvt. schools in Montréal, PQ; professional debut as Faulkland in The Rivals, Ottawa Repertory Theatre; Broadway debut in Starcross Story 1951–52; Maple Leaf Award 1982; numerous appearances in theatres in USA; played many leading Shakespearean roles in productions by the Stratford Canadian Festival Co.; British debut in title role of Richard III, Stratford on Avon 1961 and then in London as Henry II in Anouilh's Becket; a leading actor in the Nat. Theatre Co. of Great Britain 1971–72; has appeared in Nat. Theatre productions of Amphytrion 38, Danton's Death 1971; many TV roles including Hamlet in BBC TV/Danish TV production, Hamlet in Elsinore, Jesus of Nazareth 1977; Hon. DFA (Juilliard School of Performing Arts) 1993; Dr hc (Ryerson Univ., Toronto) 2002, (Univ. of Toronto) 2003, (Univ. of Western Ontario) 2004, (McGill Univ.) 2006; Theatre World Award 1955, Evening Standard Award 1961, Delia Australian Medal 1973, Antoinette Perry (Tony) Award 1974, 1998, Emmy Award 1977, Genie Award 1980, Australian Golden Badge of Honour 1982, Maple Leaf Award, LAFCA 1999, The Sir John Gielgud Award for Excellence in the Dramatic Arts (aka The Golden Quill) 2006, Gov. Gen.'s Performing Arts Award 2001. *Plays:* Earl of Warwick in Anouilh's The Lark, The Dark is Light Enough 1955, Mark Antony in Julius Caesar 1955, Ferdinand in The Tempest 1955, Henry V 1956 1981, The Narrator in Stravinsky's L'Histoire du Soldat 1956, Hamlet 1957, Twelfth Night 1957, The Winter's Tale 1958, Much Ado About Nothing 1958, Henry IV Part 1 1958, The Devil in J.B. 1958, Romeo and Juliet 1960, King John 1960, Much Ado About Nothing 1961, Becket 1961, Richard III 1961, Macbeth 1962, 1988, The Resistible Rise of Arturo Ui 1965–66, The Royal Hunt of the Sun 1965–66, Anthony and Cleopatra 1967, Danton's Death 1971, Cyrano 1973, The Good Doctor 1973, Iago in Othello 1982, Peccadillo 1985, A Christmas Carol 1990, No Man's Land 1994, Barrymore (Tony Award for Best Leading Actor in a Play 1997) 1996, King Lear 2004, A World or Two, Before you Go 2005, Inherit the Wind 2007. *Films include:* The Fall of the Roman Empire, The Sound of Music, Inside Daisy Clover, Triple Cross, Oedipus the King, Nobody Runs Forever, Lock Up Your Daughters, The Royal Hunt of the Sun, Battle of Britain, Waterloo, The Pyx, The Spiral Staircase, Conduct Unbecoming, The Return of the Pink Panther, The Man Who Would be King, Aces High 1976, The Disappearance 1977, International Velvet 1978, The Silent Partner 1978, Hanover Street 1979, Murder by Decree 1980, The Shadow Box 1980, The Disappearance 1981, The Janitor 1981, The Amateur 1982, Dreamscape 1984, Playing for Keeps 1985, Lily in Love 1985, Dragnet 1987, Souvenir 1988, Shadow Dancing, Mindfield 1989, Where the Heart Is 1989, Star Trek VI: The Undiscovered Country 1991, Malcolm X 1992, Wolf 1994, Dolores Claiborne 1994, Twelve Monkeys 1995, Skeletons 1996, The Arrow 1997, The Insider 1999, All the Fine 1999, The Dinosaur Hunter 2000, Dracula 2000, Lucky Break 2001, Blackheart 2001, A Beautiful Mind 2001, Full Disclosure 2001, Ararat 2002, Nicholas Nickleby 2002, Blizzard 2003, Cold Creek Manor 2003, National Treasure 2004, Alexander 2004, Tma 2005, Our Fathers 2005, The New World 2005, Syriana 2005, Inside Man 2006, The Lake House 2006, Man in the Chair 2007, Closing the Ring 2007, Emotional Arithmetic 2007, Already Dead 2007. *Publication:* In Spite of Myself: A Memoir 2008. *Leisure interests:* piano, skiing, tennis, old cars. *Address:* c/o Lou Pitt, The Pitt Group, 9465 Wilshire Boulevard, Suite 480, Beverly Hills, CA 90212, USA (office). *Telephone:* (310) 246-4800 (office). *Fax:* (310) 275-9258 (office).

PLUMMER, James W.; American engineer; fmr Corona Program Man., Div. of Missiles and Space Co., Lockheed Corpn, served as overall systems engineer for Corona, later Vice-Pres. Lockheed Corpn; fmr Under-Sec. USAF; fmr Dir

Nat. Reconnaissance Office; fmr Chair. The Aerospace Corpn; mem. Nat. Acad. of Eng; Hon. Fellow, AIAA; designated as a Space and Missile Pioneer by USAF 1989, honoured by Dir of CIA as a Corona Pioneer 1995, Charles Stark Draper Prize, Nat. Acad. of Eng (co-recipient) 2005. *Address:* c/o National Academy of Engineering, 500 Fifth Street, NW, Washington, DC 20001, USA. *E-mail:* NAEMembershipOffice@nae.edu.

PLUSHENKO, Evgeni Viktorovich; Russian figure skater; b. 3 Nov. 1982, Solnechni, Khabarovsk region in Siberia; s. of Viktor Plushenko and Tatiana Vasilievna; m. Maria Erma 2005; one s.; family moved to Volgograd aged three; began skating aged four; sent to St Petersburg to train under Alexei Mishin aged 11; Nat. Champion 1997–2002, 2004–06; gold medal, Grand Prix Final 2000, 2001, 2004, silver medal, 2002, 2003; gold medal, World Jr Championships 1998; silver medal, European Championships 1999, 2004, gold medal, 2000, 2001, 2003, 2005, 2006; bronze medal, World Championships 1998, silver medal, 1999, gold medal, 2001, 2003, 2004; silver medal, Winter Olympics, Salt Lake City 2002, gold medal, Winter Olympics, Turin 2006; first skater in the world to perform a 4-3-2 (quadruple toe loop-triple toe loop-double loop) jump combination and later a 4-3-3 (quadruple toe loop-triple toe loop-triple loop) jump combination at Cup of Russia 2002; youngest male skater to receive perfect score of 6.0 aged 16; received total of 70 6.0s before new Code of Points judging system was introduced; mem. Ybileiny Sport Club, St Petersburg. *Address:* Ybileiny Sport Club, Yubileiny Sports Palace, 18 Pr. Dobrolyubova. M: Sportivnaya, St Petersburg, Russian Federation. *E-mail:* jimfair@charter.net; info@yubi.ru. *Website:* www .evgeniplushenko.net; www.yubi.ru.

PLYUSHCH, Ivan Stepanovich; Ukrainian politician; b. 11 Sept. 1941, Borzna, Chernigov Dist; m.; one d.; ed Ukrainian Agricultural Acad., Acad. of Social Sciences of Communist Party Cen. Cttee; mem. CPSU 1962–91; worked as agronomist, Dir of collective farms, Dir Sovkhoz 1959–74, party work in Kiev Dist Cttee 1975–84; Deputy Chair. Kiev Dist Soviet 1984–90, Chair. 1990; Deputy to Ukrainian Supreme Soviet 1990; Chair. (Speaker) Verkhovna Rada (parl.) 1991–94, 2000–02; mem. Higher Econ. Bd 1997; mem. People's Democratic Party 1998–; mem. All-Ukrainian Union of Democratic Forces 1998–, Chair. 1999–; rep. of presidential cand. Viktor Yushchenko during elections 2004, now adviser to Pres.; Yaroslav Mudzy Order 1996. *Address:* c/o Office of the President, vul. Bankova 11, 01220 Kiev, Ukraine. *Telephone:* (44) 291-53-33. *Fax:* (44) 293-61-61. *E-mail:* president@adm.gov.ua. *Website:* www .president.gov.ua.

POATY-SOUCHALATY, Alphonse Mouissou; Republic of the Congo politician; fmr Minister of Trade and Small and Medium-sized Enterprises; Prime Minister of the Congo 1989–90; mem. Parti congolais du travail. *Address:* c/o Office of the Prime Minister, Brazzaville, Republic of the Congo.

POCAR, Fausto, LLD; Italian judge, international organization executive and academic; b. 21 Feb. 1939, Milan; ed Univ. of Milan; Prof. of Int. Law, Univ. of Milan, fmr Dean, Faculty of Political Sciences, fmr Vice-Rector Univ. of Milan; Judge, Int. Criminal Tribunal for the Fmr Yugoslavia (ICTY), The Hague 2000–09, also Judge of the Appeals Chamber and mem. Int. Criminal Tribunal for Rwanda (ICTR), Vice-Pres. ICTY 2003–05, Pres. 2005–08; mem. Human Rights Cttee under Int. Covenant on Civil and Political Rights 1984–2000, Rapporteur 1989–90, Chair. 1991–92; Special Rep. of UN High Commr for Human Rights for visits to Chechnya and Russian Fed. 1995–96; has chaired informal working group that drafted declaration on the rights of people belonging to nat. or ethnic, religious or linguistic minorities, Comm. on Human Rights 1992; Italian del. to Cttee on the Peaceful Uses of Outer Space and its Legal Sub-cttee; has lectured at The Hague Acad. of Int. Law; mem. and Treas. Institut de Droit Int.; mem. several other int. law asscn; Grand Ufficiale 2003; Dr hc (Antwerp) 2007, (Buenos Aires) 2008. *Publications:* author of numerous publs on int. law, including human rights and humanitarian law, pvt. int. law and European law. *Address:* International Criminal Tribunal for the Former Yugoslavia, PO Box 13888, EW, 2501 EW, The Hague, Netherlands (office). *Telephone:* (70) 512-5139 (office). *Fax:* (70) 512-5307 (office). *Website:* www.un.org/icty (office).

POCHINOK, Aleksander Petrovich, CandEcon; Russian politician; b. 12 Jan. 1958, Chelyabinsk; m.; one d.; ed Chelyabinsk Polytech. Inst., Inst. of Econs Urals br. USSR Acad. of Sciences; with Chelyabinsk Inst. of Econs 1985–89; People's Deputy Russian Fed.; mem. Supreme Soviet, Chair. Comm. on Budget Planning, Taxation and Prices 1990–93; mem. State Duma (Parl.), Deputy Chair., Chair. Subcttee. on Budget, Taxation, Banks and Finance 1993–97; mem. Political Council Democratic Union of Russia 1994; Head State Taxation Service Russian Fed. 1997–98; Head of Financial Dept of Govt Admin. 1998; Minister of Taxation 1999–2000, of Labour and Social Devt 2000–04; Dir Fed. Labour and Social Protection Agency 2004; Presidential Aide 2004; Deputy Presidential Envoy to Southern Fed. Dist 2004–. *Publications:* I Pay Taxes (with S. Shatalov), Principles of Tax Systems (jtly). *Leisure interest:* sea cruises. *Address:* Sadovo-Kudrinskaya Str. 19, Apt 23, Moscow, Russia. *Telephone:* (495) 201-35-05 (home).

POČIATEK, Ján; Slovak economist and government official; *Minister of Finance;* b. 19 Sept. 1970; m. Ivana Počiatek; one d.; ed Slovak Tech. Univ., Univ. of Econs, Bratislava, Stockholm School of Econs, Sweden, Telenor Corp. Univ., Oslo, Norway; Project Dir, Satellite Communications Div., Telenor Slovakia 1997–2000, Commercial Dir and Vice-Exec. Dir 2000–01, Exec. Dir 2001–06; mem. Bd Dirs Int. Satellite Communication 2001–06; Minister of Finance 2006–. *Address:* Ministry of Finance, PO Box 82, Štefanovičova 5, 817 82 Bratislava, Slovakia (office). *Telephone:* (2) 5958-1111 (office). *Fax:* (2) 5249-8042 (office). *E-mail:* tlacove@mfsr.sk (office). *Website:* www.finance.gov .sk (office).

PODBEREZKIN, Aleksei Ivanovich, DHist; Russian historian and politician; *President, International Non-Government Research and Education Organization;* b. 7 Feb. 1953, Moscow; m.; three d.; ed Moscow State Inst. of Int. Relations; started career as metal worker in Moscow 1968; served in the army; referent Group of Scientific Consultants, USSR Cttee of Youth Orgs 1981–85; Sr Researcher Inst. of World Econs and Int. Relations, Diplomatic Acad., Ministry of Foreign Affairs 1985–90; f. Russian-American Univ. 1990, Pres. 1991–; Pres. Int. Non-Govt Research and Educ. Org. 1992–; adviser to Vice-Pres. of Russia 1991–93; Founder, Chair. and Sec.-Gen. All-Russian Political Movt Spiritual Heritage (Dukhovnoye Naslediye) 1994–; mem. State Duma (Parl.), mem. Communist Party faction 1995–99; Asst to Pres. Dmitry Medvedev 2005–08; Deputy Chair. Cttee on Int. Issues; Founder People's Patriotic Union of Russia 1996–; ed. Observer (analytical monthly); Ed.-in-Chief Russia: Contemporary Political History (annual) 1998–; several state decorations; Adviser of the Year 1998. *Publications:* over 1,200 publs on problems of int. relations, foreign and defence policy, state construction, ideology of state patriotism, economics and financial control. *Leisure interests:* tennis, swimming. *Address:* Dukhovnoye Naslediye, Bakhrushina str. 32, Building 2, 113054 Moscow (office); B. Serpukovsky str. 62/44, Moscow, Russia (home). *Telephone:* (495) 959-20-45 (office); (495) 635-48-94 (home). *E-mail:* podberezkin_a@nasled.ru (office). *Website:* www.viperson.ru (office).

PODESTA, John David, BS, JD; American lawyer and government official; *President and CEO, Center for American Progress;* b. 1 Aug. 1949, Chicago, Ill.; s. of John David Podesta and Mary Kokoris; m. Mary Spieczny 1978; one s. two d.; ed Knox Coll., Illinois, Georgetown Univ. Law Center; attorney, Dept of Justice 1976–77; Special Asst to Dir, ACTION 1978–79; Counsel, Senate Judiciary Cttee 1979–81; Chief Minority Counsel, Senate Judiciary Sub-Cttee 1981–86; Chief Counsel, Senate Agric. Cttee 1987–88; Pres., Gen. Counsel, Podesta Assocs Inc. 1988–93; Asst to the Pres. (Staff Sec.) 1993–95; Asst to Pres. (Deputy Chief of Staff) 1997–98; Chief of Staff to the Pres. 1998–2001; Pres. and CEO Center for American Progress 2001–; Visiting Prof. of Law, Georgetown Univ. Law Center 1995–98, Adjunct Prof. 1998–. *Publication:* Protecting Electronic Messaging 1990. *Address:* Center for American Progress, 805 15th Street, NW, Suite 400, Washington, DC 20005 (office); 3743 Brandywine Street, Washington, DC 20016, USA (home). *Telephone:* (202) 682-1611 (office). *E-mail:* progress@americanprogress.org (office). *Website:* www.americanprogress.org (office).

PODESTÁ SILVA, Carlos Marcial; Paraguayan politician; b. 5 June 1942, Asunción; s. of Julio Podestá Bóveda and Amalia Silva Ojeda; m.; ed Colegio "Sagrado Corazón de Jesús", Nat. Univ. of Asunción, Univ. of Guadalajara; Dir of Communications, of Planning and Public Admin, then Man. Dir Instituto de Bienestar Rural 1972–83; business consultant 1983–92; councillor Entidad Binacional Itaipú 1992–93; Pres. Nat. Emergency Cttee May 1993–; Minister of the Interior 1993–95; titular mem. Governing Bd Asociación Nacional Republicana (Partido Colorado).

PODHORETZ, John, AB; American writer and editor; *Editorial Director, Commentary;* b. 18 April 1961, NY; s. of Norman Podhoretz (q.v.) and Midge (née Rosenthal) Podhoretz; m. 1st Elisabeth Hickey 1996 (divorced); m. 2nd Ayala Cohen; two d.; ed Univ. of Chicago; Exec. News Ed. Insight Magazine 1985–87; contrib. US News and World Report 1987–88; speechwriter to Pres. of USA 1988–89; Asst Man. Ed. Washington Times 1989–91; Sr Fellow Hudson Inst. 1991–94; TV critic NY Post 1994–95, then political columnist; Deputy Ed. The Weekly Standard 1995–97, then movie critic; Editorial Dir Commentary (magazine) 2007–(09), Ed. (2009–); J.C. Penney/Mo. Award for Excellence in Feature Sections 1990. *Publication:* Hell of a Ride: Backstage at the White House Follies 1989–93 1993. *Address:* Commentary, 165 E. 56th Street, New York, NY 10022, USA (office). *E-mail:* letters@ commentarymagazine.com. *Website:* www.commentarymagazine.com (office).

PODHORETZ, Norman, BA, MA, BHL; American writer and editor; b. 16 Jan. 1930, Brooklyn, NY; s. of Julius Podhoretz and Helen Podhoretz (née Woliner); m. Midge R. Decter 1956; one s. (John Podhoretz) three d.; ed Columbia Univ., Jewish Theological Seminary and Univ. of Cambridge; Assoc. Ed. Commentary 1956–58, Ed.-in-Chief 1960–95, Ed.-at-Large 1995–2008; Ed.-in-Chief, Looking Glass Library 1959–60; Chair. New Directions Advisory Comm. US Information Agency 1981–87; Sr Fellow, Hudson Inst. 1995–2003; Fulbright Fellow 1950–51; Kellett Fellow 1950–53; Hon. LLD (Jewish Theological Seminary); Hon. LHD (Hamilton Coll.), (Boston) 1995, (Adelphi) 1996; Hon. DHumLitt (Yeshiva) 1991; Presidential Medal of Freedom 2004. *Publications:* Doings and Undoings: The Fifties and After in American Writing 1964, Making It 1968, Breaking Ranks: A Political Memoir 1979, The Present Danger 1980, Why We Were in Vietnam 1982, The Bloody Crossroads: Where Literature and Politics Meet 1986, Ex-Friends 1999, My Love Affair with America 2000, The Prophets: Who They Were, What They Are 2002, The Norman Podhoretz Reader 2004, World War IV 2007, Why Are Jews Liberal? 2009. *Leisure interest:* listening to music. *Address:* c/o Commentary, 165 East 56th Street, New York, NY 10022, USA (office). *Telephone:* (212) 891-6735 (office). *Fax:* (212) 891-6700 (office). *E-mail:* nhp30@hotmail.com (office).

PODOLSKY, Daniel K., BA, MD; American physician and university administrator; *President, University of Texas Southwestern Medical Centre;* b. 1953; m. Dr. Carol P. Podolsky; three c.; ed Harvard Coll., Harvard Medical School; Clinical Fellow in Medicine, Harvard Medical School 1978–80, Research Fellow 1980–81, Asst Prof. of Medicine 1982–86, Assoc. Prof. 1986–96, Prof. 1996–2008, Mallinckrodt Prof. of Medicine 1998–2008; Asst Resident, Mass Gen. Hosp. 1978–80, Clinical Research Fellow 1980–81, Asst in Medicine 1982–86, Assoc. Physician 1988–93, Physician 1993–2008, Chief of Gastroenterology 1989–2008; Pres. Univ. of Texas SW Medical Center 2008–; Chair. and Scientific Co-Founder GI Co., Framingham, Mass; Chief Academic Officer, Partners HealthCare System, Boston 2005–08; mem. Bd of

Dirs GlaxoSmithKline plc, Antibe Therapeutics, Inc.; Pres. American Gastroenterological Asscn 2003–04; fmr Ed.-in-Chief Gastroenterology (journal); Distinguished Achievement Award, American Gastroenterological Asscn 2007. *Publications:* more than 300 original research and review articles. *Address:* Office of the President, University of Texas Southwestern Medical Center, 5323 Harry Hines Boulevard, Dallas, TX 75235-9002, USA (office). *Telephone:* (214) 648-2508 (office). *Fax:* (214) 648-8690 (office). *E-mail:* daniel.podolsky@utsouthwestern.edu (office). *Website:* www.utsystem.edu/hea/Presidents.htm (office).

PODSIADŁO, Andrzej, BEcons, PhD; Polish banking executive; *President of the Management Board, PKO Bank;* b. 1951; ed Main School of Econs and Planning, Warsaw (now Warsaw School of Econs); fmr teacher, Main School of Planning and Statistics, Warsaw; Dir, Econ. Analysis Team, Planning Comm. of Council of Ministers 1978–88, Under-Sec. and later Sec. of State, Ministry of Finance 1989–92; Pres., Man. Bd, Powszechny Bank Handlowy Gecobank SA 1994; Vice-Pres., Man. Bd, PKO BP 1994–95; Pres., Man. Bd, Powszechny Bank Kredytowy SA 1995–2002; Pres., Man. Bd, PKO Bank 2002–; Vice-Pres. Supervisory Bd, Bank Pocztowy SA 2004–; fmr Chair., Gornoslaski Bank Gospodarczy SA, Powszechne Towarzystwo Emerytalne PBK SA, PTE Ergo Hestia SA, Bank Pekao SA, TUiR Warta; mem. Supervisory Bd, Poskie Koleje Panstwowe, Huta Katowice SA, Fabryka Samochodow Malolitrazowych w Bielsku-Bialej, Bank Wschodni SA, Polska Fundacja Promocji Kadr; fmr Pres., Man. Bd Polish Red Cross; mem. Curriculum Bd, Warsaw Banking School; mem. Council of Banks; Polish Rep., Int. Bank of Econ. Co-operation, Moscow, Int. Investment Bank, Moscow; Vice-Pres., Union of Polish Banks; mem. Bd, Nat. Museum, Warsaw. *Address:* PKO Bank, 15 Puławska Street, 00–975 Warsaw, Poland (office). *Telephone:* (22) 5216000 (office). *Website:* www.pkobp.pl (office).

POFALLA, Ronald; German lawyer and politician; *General Secretary, Christian Democratic Union;* b. 15 May 1959; ed Fachhochschule, Kleve, Univ. of Cologne; mem. Christlich-Demokratische Union (Christian Democratic Union— CDU) 1975–, initially engaged in Junge Union (JU), Chair. JU, North Rhine-Westphalia 1986–92, Gen. Sec. CDU 2005–; mem. Bundestag (Parl.) 1990–, Deputy Chair. CDU/CSU (Christlich-Soziale Union) Parl. Group in Bundestag 2004–05; passed Staatsexamen (Bar examination) 1991, has worked as a lawyer 1991–. *Address:* Christlich-Demokratische Union, Konrad-Adenauer-Haus, Klingelhöferstr. 8, 10785 Berlin, Germany (office). *Telephone:* (30) 220700 (office). *Fax:* (30) 22070111 (office). *E-mail:* info@cdu.de (office). *Website:* www.cdu.de (office); www.ronald-pofalla.de.

POGEA, Gheorghe, PhD; Romanian business executive and politician; *Minister of Economy and Finance;* b. 1 Dec. 1955; m.; two c.; ed Bucharest Polytechnic Inst., École Superieure de Commerce Marseille, France; Dir-Gen. S.C ' Siderurgica SA 1996–2000, S.C Marmosin SA 2001–04, SC Titan Mar SA 2006–08; mem. Democratic Liberal Party (PDL), Pres. PD Org. for Hunedoara Co. 2000–06, Coordinator PDL Strategy Comm. 2005–06; Minister of State 2005–06; Minister of Economy and Finance 2008–. *Address:* Ministry of the Economy and Finance, 050741 Bucharest 5, Str. Apolodor 17, Romania (office). *Telephone:* (21) 3199759 (office). *Fax:* (21) 3122509 (office). *E-mail:* presamfp@mfinante.gv.ro (office). *Website:* www.mfinante.ro (office).

PÖGGELER, Otto, DPhil; German academic; *Professor Emeritus of Philosophy and Director, Hegel-Archiv der Ruhr-Universität;* b. 12 Dec. 1928, Attendorn; m. 1959, two c.; ed Bonn Univ.; Prof. of Philosophy, Ruhr-Universität, Bochum Univ. 1968–94, Prof. Emer. 1994–, Dir Hegel Archives; mem. Rheinland-Westphalia Acad. of Sciences 1977–. *Publications:* Etudes hégéliennes 1985, Martin Heidegger's Path of Thinking 1987, Schritte zu einer Hermeneutischen Philosophie 1994, Heidegger in seiner Zeit 1999, Der Stein hinter Aug. Studien zu Célans Gedichten 2000, Bild und Technik-Heidegger, Klee und die Moderne Kunst 2002. *Address:* Hegel-Archiv der Ruhr-Universität, 44780 Bochum (office); Paracelsusweg 22, 44801 Bochum, Germany (home). *Telephone:* (234) 701160 (home).

POGGIO, Albert Andrew, OBE; British diplomatist; *Representative of Government of Gibraltar in UK;* b. 18 Aug. 1946, Ballymena, N Ireland; one d.; ed Christian Brothers Coll., Gibraltar and City of London Coll.; Rep. of Govt of Gibraltar in UK 1988–; Chair. British Overseas Territories Asscn, Vital Health Group of Cop, Westex Group of Cos; Vice-Chair. Calpe House Trust; Dir Friends of Gibraltar Heritage Soc., SVP Medcruise (Asscn of Mediterranean Ports); Freeman City of London. *Leisure interests:* reading, walking, military memorabilia, sports. *Address:* 150 Strand, London, WC2R IJA (office); The Old House, Manor Place, Chislehurst, Kent, BR7 5QJ, England (home). *Telephone:* (20) 7836-0777 (office). *Fax:* (20) 7240-6612 (office). *E-mail:* a.poggio@gibraltar.gov.uk (office). *Website:* www.gibraltar.gov.uk (office).

POGORELICH, Ivo; Croatian concert pianist; b. 20 Oct. 1958, Belgrade; s. of I. Pogorelich and D. Pogorelich; m. Aliza Kezeradze 1980 (died 1996); ed Tchaikovsky Conservatoire of Moscow, then studied with Aliza Kezeradze; debut recital in Carnegie Hall, New York, USA 1981; has appeared in major concert halls throughout the world; f. Bad Wörishofen Festival (Germany) 1988; inaugurated Ivo Pogorelich Int. Solo Piano Competition, Pasadena, CA 1993; UNESCO Goodwill Amb. 1988; f. Sarajevo Charitable Foundation (to raise funds for people of Bosnia in fields of medicine and health) 1994; Fellow-Commoner, Balliol Coll. Oxford 1993; First Prize, Casagrande Competition, Terni, Italy 1978, First Prize, Montréal Int. Music Competition, Canada 1980, Special Prize, Int. Chopin Competition, Warsaw 1980. *Recordings:* numerous recordings for Deutsche Grammophon, starting with a Chopin recital in 1981 and including works by Bach, Beethoven, Brahms, Chopin, Haydn, Liszt, Mozart, Mussorgsky, Prokofiev, Ravel, Scarlatti, Schumann and the Tchaikovsky Piano Concerto No. 1. *Address:* c/o Kajimoto Concert Management Co. Ltd, Kahoku Building, 8–6–25 Hinza, Chui-ku, Tokyo 104-0061, Japan (office). *Telephone:* (3) 3574-0969 (office). *Fax:* (3) 3574-0980 (office). *Website:* www.kajimotomusic.com (office).

POHAMBA, Hifikepunye; Namibian politician and head of state; *President;* b. 18 Aug. 1935; Sec. of Finance SWAPO 1977–89, Sec.-Gen. SWAPO 1997–2002, Vice Pres. 2002–; Minister of Home Affairs 1990–95, of Fisheries and Marine Resources 1995–98, without Portfolio 1998–2000, of Lands, Resettlement and Rehabilitation 2001–04; Pres. of Namibia 2004–; Swapo Ongulumbashe Medal 1987. *Address:* Office of the President, State House, Robert Mugabe Avenue, PMB 13339, Windhoek, Namibia (office). *Telephone:* (61) 2707111 (office). *Fax:* (61) 221780 (office). *E-mail:* angolo@op.gov.na (office). *Website:* www.op.gov.na (office).

PÖHL, Karl Otto; German economist; b. 1 Dec. 1929, Hanover; m. Dr Ulrike Pesch; two s. two d.; ed Univ. of Göttingen; Head of Dept Ifo-Research Inst., Munich 1955–60; econ. journalist 1961–67; mem. Man. Bd of the Fed. Asscn of German Banks, Cologne 1968–69; Head of Dept Fed. Ministry of Econ. Affairs 1970–71; Head of Econ. and Fiscal Policy Dept, Fed Chancellor's Office 1971–72; State Sec. Fed. Ministry of Finance 1972–77; Vice-Chair. Deutsche Bundesbank 1977–79, Pres. 1980–91; Pnr, Bankhaus Sal Oppenheimer Jr et Cie 1992–98; Dr hc (Georgetown, Ruhr Univ.) 1983, (Tel Aviv Univ.) 1986, (Maryland) 1987, (Buckingham, London) 1992, (Johann-Wolfgang-Goethe Univ.) 2000. *Address:* c/o Frau Janine Helfenstein, Sal. Oppenheim j. & Cie (Schweiz) AG, Uraniastr. 28, 8022 Zürich, Switzerland. *Telephone:* (44) 2142332. *Fax:* (44) 2142241.

POITIER, Sidney; American actor and film director; b. 20 Feb. 1927, Miami; s. of Reginald and Evelyn Poitier; m. 1st Juanita Hardy; four d.; m. 2nd Joanna Shimkus 1975; two d.; ed Western Senior High School, Nassau, Governors High School, Nassau; army service 1941–45; acted with American Negro Theatre 1946; appeared in Anna Lucasta 1948, A Raisin in the Sun 1959; mem. Bd of Dirs Walt Disney Co. 1994–2003, Pres. 1994–2003; Amb. to Japan from the Commonwealth of the Bahamas; Hon. KBE 1974; Silver Bear Award, Berlin Film Festival 1958; New York Film Critics' Award 1958; Acad. Award Best Actor of 1963 (for Lilies of the Field); Cecil B. De Mille Award 1982, Life Achievement Award American Film Inst. 1992, Kennedy Center Honors 1995, Hon. Acad. Award for Lifetime Achievement 2002. *Films include:* No Way Out 1950, Cry, the Beloved Country 1951, Red Ball Express 1952, Go, Man, Go! 1954, Blackboard Jungle 1955, Good-bye, My Lady 1956, Edge of the City 1957, Something of Value 1957, Band of Angels 1957, The Mark of the Hawk 1957, Virgin Island 1958, The Defiant Ones 1958, Porgy and Bess 1959, All the Young Men 1960, A Raisin in the Sun 1961, Paris Blues 1961, Pressure Point 1962, The Long Ships 1963, Lilies of the Field 1963, The Bedford Incident 1965, The Greatest Story Ever Told 1965, A Patch of Blue 1965, The Slender Thread 1965, Duel at Diablo 1966), To Sir, with Love 1967, In the Heat of the Night 1967, Guess Who's Coming to Dinner 1967, For Love of Ivy (also writer) 1968, The Lost Man 1969, They Call Me Mister Tibbs! 1970, Brother John 1971, The Organization 1971, Buck and the Preacher (also dir) 1972, A Warm December (also dir) 1973, Uptown Saturday Night (also dir) 1974, The Wilby Conspiracy 1975, Let's Do It Again (also dir) 1975, A Piece of the Action (also dir) 1977, Stir Crazy dir) 1980, Hanky Panky (dir) 1982, Fast Forward (dir) 1985, Shoot to Kill 1988, Little Nikita 1988, Ghost Dad (dir) 1990, Sneakers 1992, The Jackal 1997, Bicentennial Nigger 2006. *Television includes:* Separate But Equal 1991, Children of the Dust 1995, To Sir, with Love II 1996, Mandela and de Klerk 1997, David and Lisa 1998, Free of Eden (also exec. producer) 1999, The Simple Life of Noah Dearborn 1999, The Last Brickmaker in America 2001. *Publication:* This Life 1981. *Leisure interests:* football, tennis, gardening. *Address:* c/o CAA, 9830 Wilshire Boulevard, Beverly Hills, CA 90210, USA.

POIVRE D'ARVOR, Patrick, LenD; French journalist and radio and television presenter; b. 20 Sept. 1947, Reims (Marne); s. of Jacques Poivre and Madeleine France Jeuge; m. Véronique Courcoux 1971; six c. (two deceased); ed Lycée Georges-Clemenceau, Reims, Instituts d'études politiques, Strasbourg and Paris, Faculties of Law, Strasbourg, Paris and Reims, Ecole des langues orientales vivantes; Special Corresp., France-Inter 1971, journalist 1971–74, Head Political Dept 1975–76, Deputy Chief Ed., Antenne 2 1976–83, Presenter, evening news programme 1976–83, 1987–2008, Deputy Dir News 1989–; Leader-writer Paris-Match, Journal du Dimanche 1983–91; Producer and Compère, A nous deux, Antenne 2 1983–86, A la folie, TF1 1986–88; Compère, Tous en Scène, Canal Plus 1984–85; Compère and Producer Ex libris 1988–99; Compère Vol de nuit 1999–; Presenter and Producer magazine programme Le Droit de savoir, TF1 1990–94; Commdr de l'Ordre des Arts et des Lettres, Chevalier de l'Ordre National du Mérite, Chevalier de la Légion d'Honneur; Prix Interallié 2000, Prix des Lettres du Livre de Poche 2003, Prix Cyrano 2004. *Publications:* Mai 68-Mai 78 1978, Les Enfants de l'aube 1982, Deux amants 1984, Le Roman de Virginie 1985, Les Derniers trains de rêve 1986, La Traversée du miroir 1986, Rencontres 1987, Les Femmes de ma vie 1988, L'Homme d'images 1992, Lettres à l'absente 1993, Les Loups et la bergerie 1994, Elle n'était pas d'ici 1995, Anthologie des plus beaux poèmes d'amour 1995, Un héros de passage 1996, Lettre ouverte aux violeurs de vie privée 1997, Une trahison amoureuse 1997, La fin du monde (collection) 1998, Petit homme 1999, Les rats de garde (collection) 2000, L'Irrésolu 2000 (Prix Interallié), Un enfant 2001, Courriers de nuit (collection) 2002, J'ai aimé une reine 2003, Coureurs des morts (collection) 2003, La Mort de don Juan (Prix Maurice-Genevoix 2205) 2004, Les Plus Beaux Poèmes d'amour 2004, Chasseurs de trésors et autres flibustiers 2005, Pirates et corsaires 2005, Coureurs des mers 2005, Le Monde selon Jules Verne 2005, Confessions 2005, Disparaître 2006, Rêveurs des Mers 2007, J'ai tant rêvé de toi 2007. *Address:* TF1, 1 quai du Point du Jour, 92656 Boulogne-

Billancourt Cedex, France (office). *Telephone:* 1-41-41-23-28 (office). *Fax:* 1-41-41-19-63 (office). *Website:* tf1.lci.fr (office).

POKHAREL, Bhoj Raj; Nepalese civil servant; currently Chief Election Commr. *Address:* Election Commission, Kantipath, Kathmandu, Nepal (office). *Telephone:* (1) 4228663 (office). *Fax:* (1) 4229227 (office). *E-mail:* election@mos.com.np (office). *Website:* www.election-commission.org.np (office).

POKHMELKIN, Victor Valeryevich, CAND.JUR.; Russian politician and jurist; b. 3 Feb. 1960, Perm; m.; one s.; ed Perm State Univ., Moscow State Univ.; docent, lecturer Higher Courses of USSR Ministry of Internal Affairs, Perm; f. and Scientific Head Research Inst. of Legal Policy; mem. State Duma (Parl.) 1993–, mem. Vybor Rosii 1993–99, Union of Rightist Forces 2000–01, Co-Chair. Liberal Russia 2001–04; Deputy Chair. Comm. on Law and Legal Reform; mem. Political Council Demokratichesky Vybor Rossii 1994–; Founder and Chair. Motorists of Russia 2002–. *Publications:* several monographs and scientific publs. *Address:* State Duma, Okhotny Ryad 1, 103265 Moscow, Russia (office). *Telephone:* (495) 692-77-66 (office). *Fax:* (495) 692-32-87 (office). *E-mail:* pokhmelkin@duma.gov.ru (office). *Website:* www.pokhmelkin.ru (office).

POKORNI, Zoltán, AB; Hungarian politician and academic; *Vice President, FIDESZ Party;* b. 10 Jan. 1962, Budapest; s. of János Pokorni and Klara Vincz; m. Andrea Beck 1992; four s.; ed Loránd Eötvös Univ., Budapest; Lecturer, Toldy Ferenc High School, Budapest 1987–94; Founding mem. 1988, spokesman 1988–93, Ed. Democratic Trades Union of Teachers' paper –1993; joined Fed. of Young Democrats–Hungarian Civic Party (Magyar Polgári Párt–FIDESZ) 1993, Vice-Pres. 1994–2001, 2003–, Leader 2001–02; mem. Parl. 1994–; Deputy Head Parl. Group 1994–97, Head 1997–98, personal rep. of Budapest XIIth Dist 1998–; fmr Head FIDESZ Dept for Educational Politics; (FIDESZ) Minister of Educ. 1998–2001; Vice-Pres. Parl. Cttee for Educ. and Science. *Address:* FIDESZ, Szentkirályi u.18, 1088 Budapest, Hungary. *Telephone:* (1) 327-6100 (office). *Fax:* (1) 441-5414 (office). *E-mail:* sajtoosztaly@fidesz.hu (office). *Website:* www.fidesz.hu (office).

POKROVSKY, Boris Aleksandrovich; Russian opera stage director; b. 23 Jan. 1912, Moscow; s. of Aleksandr Pokrovsky and Elisaveta Stulova; m. 1st Anna Nekrasova 1936; m. 2nd Irina Maslennikova 1961; one s. one d; ed Lunacharsky Inst. of Theatre; stage Dir, artistic Dir Gorky Opera Theatre 1937–43; stage Dir Moscow Bolshoi Theatre 1937–82, Dir-Gen. 1952–63, 1967–82; founder and Artistic Dir Moscow Chamber Music Theatre 1972–; Prof. Lunacharsky Inst. of Theatre 1954–; Hon. Pres. Int. Inst. of Theatre 1986; USSR People's Artist 1961, Lenin Prize 1980, State Prizes of USSR and Russia; Golden Mask Theatre Prize 1996. *Productions:* first opera productions in Bolshoi Theatre of many operas by Russian composers, including Francesca da Rimini by Rachmaninov, Semen Kotko and The Gambler by Prokofiev, Dead Souls by Shchedrin; worked with Rostropovich on new productions of Eugene Onegin 1969, Khovanshchina 1995, Bolshoi Theatre; many productions in Moscow Chamber Music Theatre, including The Rake's Progress by Stravinsky, Don Giovanni by Mozart; many productions in European countries, including Life with an Idiot by A. Schnittke, Amsterdam 1993. *Publications:* 10 books and many articles. *Leisure interests:* music, reading. *Address:* c/o Moscow Chamber Music Theatre, Nikolskaya str. 17, 103012 Moscow, Russia. *Telephone:* (495) 929-13-24. *Fax:* (495) 921-06-72.

POKROVSKY, Valentin Ivanovich, DrMed; Russian physician; *Director, Central Scientific Research Institute of Epidemiology; President, Russian Academy of Medical Sciences;* b. 1 April 1929; m. Nina Yakovlevna Pokrovskaya; one s.; ed First Moscow Medical Inst.; mem. CPSU 1959–91; Dir Central Scientific Research Inst. of Epidemiology 1971–; USSR People's Deputy 1989–91; has studied problems of AIDS treatment, meningitis and intestinal diseases; Chair. Scientific Soc. of Microbiologists, Epidemiologists and Parasitologists; mem. Physicians for the Prevention of Nuclear War; mem. WHO Expert Cttee, WHO Global Cttee on AIDS and Diarrhoeal Diseases, Bd Int. Fed. of Infectionists; mem. USSR (now Russian) Acad. of Medical Sciences 1982– (Pres. 1987–), Presidium of USSR (now Russian) Fed. of Space Flight; Hon. mem. Soc. of Microbiologists of Czech Repub.; V. Timakov Prize, D. Ivanovsky Prize. *Publications:* Symptoms, Treatment and Diagnostics of Salmonellesis in Adults 1981, Immuno-ferment Analysis 1985, Symptoms, Pathogenesis and Treatment of Cholera 1988, Small Medical Encylopaedia (ed.) 1991, Encyclopaedia of Health 1992, Epidemiology of Viral Diseases 2000, Cholera in the USSR – Period of the VIIth Pandemia 2000, Social Hygiene Monitoring and Epidemiology Surveillance in Moscow 2000, Cholera – Acute Problems 2000, Manual of Infectious Diseases and Epidemiology 2004, Prion Diseases 2004. *Address:* Russian Academy of Medical Sciences, Solyanka str. 14, 109544 GSP Moscow, Russia (office). *Telephone:* (495) 298-21-37 (home). *Fax:* (495) 921-56-15 (office). *E-mail:* ramn@ramn.ru (office). *Website:* www.ramn.ru (office).

POL, Marek; Polish politician and economist; b. 8 Dec. 1953, Słupsk; m.; one s. one d.; ed Poznań Univ. of Technology and Acad. of Economy, Poznań; mem. staff advancing to Deputy Dir for Financial and Commercial Affairs, Agric. Vehicle Factory, Antoninek, Poznań 1977–93; mem. Polish United Workers' Party (PZPR) 1976–90; Co-Founder Union of Labour (UP) 1992–, Chair. 1998–; Minister of Industry and Trade 1993–95; Govt Plenipotentiary responsible for reforming the cen. econ. admins 1995–97; Deputy Prime Minister and Minister of Infrastructure 2001–04; Deputy to Sjem (Parl.), mem. Social, Health and Family Affairs Cttee, Alternate mem. Cttee on Culture, Science and Educ.; mem. Supervisory Bd Daewoo-FSO 2000–01. *Leisure interests:* walks with family, reading books and journals. *Address:* Sejm, Chancellerie de la Diète, ul. Wiejska 4/6/8, 00-902, Warsaw, Poland (office); Biuro Poselskie Marka Pola, ul. Torowa 2B 62-510 Konin. *Telephone:* (22) 630-1000 (office); (63) 245-3745.

POLAK, Dame Julia Margaret, DBE, MD, DSc, FRCP, FRCPath, FMedSci; British professor and consultant in histopathology; *Emeritus Professor, Department of Chemical Engineering, Imperial College School of Medicine;* b. 29 June 1939, Buenos Aires, Argentina; m. Daniel Catovsky; two s. one d.; ed Univ. of Buenos Aires; various hosp. posts, Buenos Aires 1961–67; Asst Lecturer, Dept of Histochemistry, Royal Postgraduate Medical School, London 1968–69, Lecturer 1970–73, Sr Lecturer 1973–79, Reader 1982–84, Prof. 1984–, Chair. Dept 1992–; Hon. Consultant in Histopathology, Hammersmith Hosp. 1979–, Deputy Dir Dept of Histopathology 1988–; Chair. British Endocrine Pathologists Group 1988–; Chair. Cognate Research Group, Imperial Coll. School of Medicine 1997–, mem. Scientific Advisory Bd Imperial Coll. Inst. of Biomedical Eng, Dir Tissue Eng Centre 1998–2008, currently Prof. Emer., Dept of Chemical Eng; Visiting Prof., Univ. of Texas Health Science Center, Houston 2004; Pres. Tissue and Cell Eng Soc. 1998–; mem. Council Tissue Eng Soc. Int. 2002–05, Acad. of Medical Sciences 2002–05, Stem Cell Advisory Bd Panel Jt MRC/UK Stem Cell Foundation Science Advisory Bd 2005, Panel of Eng and Physical Sciences Research Council Peer Review Coll. 2006–, Panel of MRC Coll. of Experts 2006–; Co-founder and Dir Novathera Ltd (Imperial spin-out co.); European Ed. Tissue Engineering –2004; mem. editorial bd 34 journals; mem. 34 scientific and medical socs; Hon. Fellow, Asscn of Clinical Pathologists 2003; Hon. PhD (Univ. Complutense, Madrid); Dr hc (Sheffield) 2005; Benito de Udaondo Cardiology Prize 1967, Medal of Soc. of Endocrinology 1984, The Cable and Wireless Sir Eric Sharpe Prize for Oncology 1987, Medal, Swedish Soc. of Pathology 1998, Ellison-Cliffe Medal, Royal Soc. of Medicine 2004, Pathology Soc. Award for long services to Pathology 2004, Life Time Achievement Award for contribs to Endocrine Pathology 2006, and others. *Publications:* ed. or author of 25 books, more than 120 review articles and about 1,000 research papers. *Address:* 144 Roderic Hill Building, Department of Chemical Engineering, Imperial College London, South Kensington Campus, Exhibition Road, London, SW7 2AZ (office); 11 Thames Quay, Chelsea Harbour, London, SW10 0UY, England (home). *Telephone:* (20) 7594-5623 (office). *E-mail:* julia.polak@imperial.ac.uk (office). *Website:* www1.imperial.ac.uk/medicine/about/institutes/tissue (office).

POLANČEC, Damir; Croatian business executive and politician; *Deputy Prime Minister and Minister of Economy, Labour and Entrepreneurship:;* b. 1967, Koprivnica; ed Univ. of Zagreb, Leeds Metropolitan Univ.; Import-Export Dept, Podravka dd (food co.) 1992–94, Commercial Assoc. 1994–97, Sr Assoc. 1997, Dir of Cen. Buying 1997–2000, Mem. Bd 2000–; Deputy Prime Minister 2005–08, Deputy Prime Minister and Minister of Economy, Labour and Entrepreneurship 2008–; mem. Man. Cttee, Croatian Handball Asscn; Pres. HC Podravka, Koprivnica 2000–; mem. Croatian Democratic Union. *Address:* Ministry of the Economy, Labour and Entrepreneurship, 10000 Zagreb, ul. grada Vukovara 78, Croatia (office). *Telephone:* (1) 6106111 (office). *Fax:* (1) 6109110 (office). *E-mail:* info@mingorp.hr (office). *Website:* www.mingorp.hr (office).

POLANCO MORENO, Ignacio, BA (Econ), MBA; Spanish media executive; *Chairman, Grupo Prisa;* s. of the late Jesús de Polanco; ed Univ. of Madrid (Complutense), Instituto de Empresa; professional positions at Timón SA and Promotora de Informaciones SA; mem. Bd of Dirs Grupo Prisa 1993–, Corp. Asst to Chair. Prisa –2006, Deputy Chair. Prisa 2006–07, Chair. 2007–; Chair. Timón SA, Promotora de Publicaciones, SL; Pres. El País newspaper. *Address:* Grupo Prisa, Gran Vía 32 28013 Madrid; El País, Miguel Yuste 40, 28037 Madrid, Spain (office). *Telephone:* (91) 337-8200 (El País) (office); (91) 330-1000 (Prisa) (office). *Fax:* (91) 337-7758 (El País) (office); (91) 330-1038 (Prisa) (office). *E-mail:* redaccion@elpais.com (office); sugerencias@prisa.es (office). *Website:* www.elpais.com (office); www.prisa.es (office).

POLAŃSKI, Roman; French film director, writer and actor; b. 18 Aug. 1933, Paris; s. of Ryszard Polański and Bule Katz-Przedborska; m. 1st Barbara Kwiatkowska-Lass (divorced); m. 2nd Sharon Tate 1968 (died 1969); m. 3rd Emmanuelle Seigner; ed Polish Film School, Łódź; Acad. française Pris René Clair for Lifetime Achievement 1999, European Film Acad. Lifetime Achievement Award 2006, Federico Fellini Prize for lifetime achievement 2006. *Film roles include:* A Generation, The End of the Night, See You Tomorrow, The Innocent Sorcerers, Two Men and a Wardrobe, The Vampire Killers, What? 1972, Blood for Dracula (uncredited) 1974, Chinatown 1974, The Tenant 1976, Chassé-croisé 1982, Back in the U.S.S.R. 1992, A Pure Formality 1994, Dead Tired 1994, Tribute to Alfred Lepetit 2000, The Revenge 2002. *Films directed include:* Two Men and a Wardrobe 1958, When Angels Fall, Le Gros et Le Maigre, Knife in the Water (prize at Venice Film Festival 1962), The Mammals (prize at Tours Film Festival 1963), Repulsion (prize at Berlin Film Festival 1965), Cul de Sac (prize at Berlin Film Festival 1966), The Vampire Killers 1967, Rosemary's Baby 1968, Macbeth 1971, What? 1972, Lulu (opera), Spoleto Festival 1974, Chinatown (Soc. of Film and TV Arts Best Dir Award) 1974, Le Prix Raoul-Levy 1975) 1974, The Tenant 1976, Rigoletto (opera) 1976, Tess (Golden Globe Award) 1980, Vampires Ball 1980, Amadeus (play) 1981, Pirates 1986, Frantic 1988, Tales of Hoffmann (opera) 1992, Bitter Moon (Dir, produced, written) 1992, Death and the Maiden 1994, Dance of the Vampire (play) 1997, The Ninth Gate 1999, Icons, A Pure Formality, In Stuttgart 2000, The Pianist (Best Film, Cannes Film Festival 2002, Acad. Award for Best Dir 2003, BAFTA Award for Best Film and Best Dir 2003) 2002, Oliver Twist 2005. *Publication:* Roman (authobiography) 1984. *Address:* c/o ICM, 8942 Wilshire Boulevard, Beverly Hills, CA 90211-1934, USA (office). *Telephone:* (310) 550-4000 (office). *Website:* www.icmtalent.com (office).

POLANYI, John Charles, CC, PhD, FRS, FRSC, FRSE; Canadian academic; *University Professor of Physical Chemistry, University of Toronto;* b. 23 Jan.

1929, Berlin, Germany; s. of Michael Polanyi and Magda Polanyi (née Kemeny); m. Anne Ferrar Davidson 1958; one s. one d.; ed Manchester Grammar School and Manchester Univ., England; Postdoctoral Fellow, Nat. Research Council of Canada 1952–54; Research Assoc., Princeton Univ., USA 1954–56; Lecturer, Univ. of Toronto, Canada 1956–57, Asst Prof. 1957–60, Assoc. Prof. 1960–62, Prof. of Chem. 1962–; many visiting lectureships; mem. numerous prof. asscns; Hon. Foreign mem. AAAS; Foreign Assoc., NAS, USA; Hon. degrees from over 30 univs; shared Nobel Prize for Chemistry 1986; Marlow Medal, Faraday Soc. 1962; British Chemical Soc. Award 1971; Chemical Inst. of Canada Medal 1976; Henry Marshall Tory Medal, Royal Soc. of Canada 1977; Wolf Prize in Chem. (shared with G. Pimentel) 1982; Izaak Walton Killam Memorial Prize 1988; Royal Medal, Royal Soc. 1989. *Publications:* The Dangers of Nuclear War (co-ed.) 1979; author of over 200 scientific papers. *Address:* Lash Miller Chemical Laboratories, Room 262, 80 St. George Street, University of Toronto, Toronto, Ont., M5S 3H6 (office); 142 Collier Street, Toronto, Ont., M4W 1M3, Canada (home). *Telephone:* (416) 978-3580 (office); (416) 961-6545 (home). *Fax:* (416)-978-7580 (office). *E-mail:* jpolanyi@chem.utoronto.ca (office). *Website:* www.utoronto.ca/jpolanyi (office); www.chem.toronto.edu (office).

POLE, Jack Richon, PhD, FBA, FRHistS; British historian, writer, academic and artist; *Profesor Emeritus of American History, University of Oxford; Fellow Emeritus, St Catherine's College, Oxford;* b. 14 March 1922, London; s. of Joseph Pole and Phoebe Rickards; m. Marilyn Mitchell 1952 (divorced 1988); one s. two d.; ed King Alfred School, London, King's Coll. London, Queen's Coll. Oxford and Princeton Univ., USA; served in army, rank of Capt. 1941–46; Instructor in History, Princeton Univ. 1952–53; Asst Lecturer, then Lecturer in American History, Univ. Coll. London 1953–63; Reader in American History and Govt, Cambridge Univ. and Fellow of Churchill Coll. 1963–79, Vice-Master of Churchill Coll. 1975–78; Rhodes Prof. of American History and Insts, Univ. of Oxford and Fellow, St Catherine's Coll., Oxford 1979–89, Fellow Emer. 1989–, Prof. Emer.; Visiting Prof., Univ. of Calif., Berkeley 1960–61, Ghana Univ. 1966, Univ. Chicago 1969, Univ. Beijing 1984, William and Mary Law School 1991; Goleib Fellow, New York Univ. Law School 1990; mem. Selden Soc., MCC; Hon. Fellow, King Alfred School Soc.; Hon. Vice-Pres. British Nineteenth Century Historians 2000–, Int. Comm. for the History of Rep. and Parl. Insts 1991–2001; New Jersey Prize Princeton Univ. 1953, Ramsdell Award, Southern Historical Asscn 1959. *Publications:* Abraham Lincoln and the Working Classes of Britain 1959, Abraham Lincoln 1964, Political Representation in England and the Origins of the American Republic 1966, The Advance of Democracy (ed.) 1967, The Seventeenth Century: The Origins of Legislative Power 1969, The Revolution in America (ed.) 1971, The Meanings of American History (co-ed.) 1971, Foundations of American Independence 1972, The Decision for American Independence 1975, The Idea of Union 1977, The Pursuit of Equality in American History 1978, (revised and enlarged edn) 1993, Paths to the American Past 1979, The Gift of Government: Political Responsibility from the English Restoration to American Independence 1983, Colonial British America (co-ed.) 1984, The American Constitution: For and Against (ed.) 1987, The Blackwell Encyclopedia of the American Revolution (co-ed.) 1991, Freedom of Speech: Right or Privilege? 1998, Blackwell Companion to the American Revolution 2000, The Federalist (ed.) 2005; series co-ed. Early America: History, Context, Culture; contrib. to reference works and professional journals. *Leisure interests:* cricket, painting, writing. *Address:* St Catherine's College, Oxford, OX1 3UJ (office); 20 Divinity Road, Oxford, OX4 1LJ, England (home). *Telephone:* (1865) 271757 (office); (1865) 246950 (home). *Fax:* (1865) 271768 (office). *E-mail:* jack.pole@ntlworld.com (home).

POLEGATO, Mario Moretti; Italian business executive; *President, Board of Directors, Geox SpA;* b. 1952, Crocetta del Montello; m.; one c.; worked in family wine and agricultural business; f. Geox SpA 1995, created and developed a range of 'breathable' footwear, currently Pres., Bd of Dirs and leading shareholder; mem. Bd of Dirs Siparex Italia (pvt. equity fund); mem. arbitration panel Confindustria; Founder ONLUS 'Il Ponte del Sorriso' charitable org. 2004; mem. Aspen Inst. Italia; Hon. Consul-Gen. for North-eastern Italy to Romania 2000, Hon. Affiliate Prof. of Entrepreneurship, ESCP-EAP Business School; Cavaliere al Merito dell'Ordine Nazionale di Romania 2002, Cavaliere del Lavoro 2005; Dr hc (Banatului-Timisoara Univ., Romania) 2003, (Ca' Foscari Univ., Venice); Confindustria Award 1994, Ernst & Young/Il Sole 24 Ore/Borse Italiana Entrepreneur of the Year 2002, Ernst & Young Global Best Italian Entrepreneur in the World 2003, Italian Marketing Asscn Award 2004. *Address:* Geox SpA, Via Feltrina Centro 16, Montebelluna, Treviso, Italy (office). *Telephone:* 04232822 (office). *Website:* www.geox.biz (office).

POLESE, Kim, BS; American computer industry executive; *CEO, SpikeSource Inc.;* ed Univs of California, Berkeley and Washington, Seattle; started career at IntelliCorp, Inc.; Product Man. Sun Microsystems 1988–95 played a role in definition, direction and launch of Java; Co-founder Marimba Inc. 1996, Pres., CEO 1996–2000, Chair. Bd of Dirs 1996–2004; Founder and CEO SpikeSource Inc. 2004–; mem. Exec. Council TechNet; mem. Bd of Dirs Global Security Inst., Univ of Calif. Pres.'s Bd on Science and Innovation, Silicon Valley Leadership Group; Fellow, Center for Engineered Innovation, Carnegie Mellon Univ; named one of Top 25 Most Influential People in America 1997. *Address:* SpikeSource, Inc., 2000 Seaport Blvd, South Building, 2nd Floor, Redwood City, CA 94063, USA (office). *Telephone:* (650) 249-4140 (office). *Fax:* (650) 367-7484 (office). *Website:* www.spikesource.com (office).

POLET, Robert, MBA; Dutch business executive; *CEO, Gucci Group NV;* b. 1955, Kuala Lumpur; m.; two d.; ed Nijenrode and Univ. of Oregon, USA; joined Marketing and Sales Dept, Unilever in 1978, worked in Paris for two years, spent one year in Milan, then moved to Hamburg, Chair. Unilever Malaysia 1990–92, Chair. Van den Bergh's (Dutch subsidiary) 1993–96, Vice-Pres. Home and Personal Care, Unilever HPC Europe, Brussels 1996, Exec. Vice-Pres., later Business Group Pres. and mem. Unilever Exec. Council, Ice Cream and Frozen Foods Europe Business Group, Rotterdam 1997–2001, Pres. Global Business, Ice Cream and Frozen Foods (following merger with Bestfoods and re-org. of Unilever's foods business) 2001–04; CEO Gucci Group NV 2004–; mem. Supervisory Bd Reed Elsevier NV 2007–. *Leisure interests:* spending time with family, sailing, travelling, playing golf. *Address:* Gucci Group NV, Rembrandt Tower, 1 Amstelplein, 1096 HA, Amsterdam, Netherlands (office). *Telephone:* (20) 462-1700 (office). *Fax:* (20) 465-3569 (office). *Website:* www.gucci.com (office).

POLETTI, Alan Ronald, DPhil, FRSNZ; New Zealand physicist; *Professor Emeritus of Physics, University of Auckland;* b. 19 Oct. 1937, New Plymouth; s. of John Poletti and Pearl Poletti; m. 1st Dorothy M. Martin 1961 (died 1994); three s. one d.; m. 2nd Marcia M. Stenson 1996; ed Univ. of Oxford; Prof. of Physics, Univ. of Auckland 1969–98, Head of Dept of Physics 1986–92, now Prof. Emer. *Publications:* over 100 scientific papers. *Leisure interests:* sailing, public history. *Address:* 11 Tole Street, Ponsonby, Auckland, New Zealand (home). *Telephone:* (9) 373-7599 (home).

POLETTO, HE Cardinal Severino; Italian ecclesiastic; *Archbishop of Turin;* b. 18 March 1933, Salgareda, Treviso; ordained priest 1957; parish priest St Mary of the Assumption, Casale 1965; f. Diocesan Centre for Family Ministry 1973; Coadjutant Bishop of Fossano 1980; Bishop of Fossano 1980–89, of Asti 1989–99; Archbishop of Turin 1999–; cr. Cardinal-Priest of S. Giuseppe in via Trionfale 2001. *Address:* Archdiocese of Torino, Via Arcivescovado 12, 10121 Turin, Italy (office). *Telephone:* (011) 5156211 (office). *Fax:* (011) 5156209 (office). *Website:* www.diocesi.torino.it (office).

POLEZHAYEV, Leonid Konstantinovich; Russian politician; *Governor of Omsk Region;* b. 30 Jan. 1940, Omsk; m.; two s.; ed Omsk Inst. of Agric.; different posts in agric. orgs Pavlodar Region, Kazakhstan; 1965–76; Head of Construction Irtysh-Karaganda Canal 1976–82; First Deputy Chair. Karaganda Regional Exec. Cttee 1982–87; Head of Omsk Regional Dept of Melioration and Water Resources 1987–89; Deputy Chair., Chair. Omsk Regional Exec. Cttee 1989–90; Head of Admin. of Omsk Region 1991; Gov. Omsk Region 1995–; mem. Russian Council of Fed. 1993–2001; corresp. mem. Russian and Int. Acads of Eng; Chair. Council of Interregional Asscn Sibirskoe Soglasheniye; Co-Chair. Consulting Council of Admin. Heads of Boundary Territories of Russia and Kazakhstan; Hon. Prof. Omsk State Univ.; Order of Red Banner, Order of St Prince Vladimir and St Prince Daniel, Medal of Valour, Medal of Virgin Lands (300th Anniversary of Russian Fleet); Peace Prize of Kazakhstan. *Publications:* The Path Toward Oneself, Proceed with Caution, The Reform Years. *Leisure interests:* books, history, museums, sport. *Address:* Office of the Governor, 644002 Omsk, Krasny Put 1, Russia (office). *Telephone:* (3812) 24-47-45 (office); (3812) 24-14-15. *Fax:* (3812) 24-23-72 (office). *E-mail:* guptr@omskportal.ru (office). *Website:* www.omskportal.ru (office).

POLFER, Lydie; Luxembourg lawyer and politician; b. 22 Nov. 1952; m. Hubert Wurth (q.v.); one d.; ed Lycée Robert Schuman, Univ. of Grenoble, France, Univ. Centre for Int. and European Research, Grenoble; admitted to Luxembourg Bar 1977; mem. Parl. 1979–; Mayor City of Luxembourg 1982–99; mem. European Parl. 1985–89, 1990–94, 2003–, mem. Group of the Alliance of Liberals and Democrats for Europe, Chair. Del. to ACP-EU Jt Parl. Ass., mem. Cttee on Foreign Affairs; Chair. Democratic Party 1994; Deputy Prime Minister, Minister of Foreign Affairs and External Trade, Minister of Civil Service and Admin. Reform 1999–2005. *Address:* Bât. Altiero Spinelli, 08G258, 60, rue Wiertz 60, 1047 Brussels, Belgium (office). *Telephone:* (2) 284-56-21 (office). *Fax:* (2) 284-96-21 (office).

POLGÁR, László; Hungarian singer (bass); b. 1 Jan. 1947, Somogyszentpál; s. of Lajos Polgár and Anna Kántor; m. Ágnes Gergely; three d.; ed Liszt Ferenc Music Acad., Budapest; scholarship holder 1972–73; soloist, Hungarian State Opera, Budapest 1972–; postgraduate study under Hans Hotter, Hochschule für Musik und Darstellende Kunst, Vienna 1979–81; Lieder recitalist; also sings Oratorio (Verdi's Requiem, etc.); operatic roles include Osmin, Sarastro, Leporello, Figaro, Publius in La Clemenza di Tito, Oroveso in Norma, Rodolfo in La Sonnambula, Basilio in Il Barbiere di Sevilla, Don Geronio in Il Turco in Italia, Philippo II in Don Carlo, Il Guardiano in La Forza del Destino, Conte Walter in Luisa Miller, Fiesco in Simon Boccanegra, Ramphis in Aida, Gurnemanz in Parsifal, Marke in Tristan, Collin in La Bohème, Timur in Turandot, Bluebeard in Duke Bluebeard's Castle, Rocco in Fidelio, Gremin in Eugene Onegin, Boris Godunov; has sung at Staatsoper Wien, Royal Opera House, Covent Garden, Salzburg Festival, Zürich, Munich, Hamburg, Hannover, Paris, Madrid, Venice, Bologna, Florence, Rome, Moscow, Prague, Dresden, Berlin, Stockholm, Buenos Aires, Metropolitan Opera, New York, Philadelphia, Los Angeles, Pittsburgh, Pa; first prizes at competitions: Dvořák, Karlovy Vary 1971, Schumann, Zwickau 1974, Erkel, Budapest 1975, Ostende 1977, Budapest (Hungarian Radio) 1977, Vienna (Hugo Wolf) 1980, Philadelphia (Luciano Pavarotti) 1981, Liszt Prize 1985, Merited Artist 1986. *Recordings include:* Balassa: The Door Outside, Lendvay: La p... respectueuse, Mozart Mass No. 6, Vesperae K. 339, Don Giovanni, La Clemenza di Tito, Petrovic: Crime and Punishment, Handel: Atalanta, Beethoven Fidelio, Die Gezeichneten, Poliuto, Fierrabras, Duke Bluebeard's Castle (Grammy Award 1999), Il Rè (Aida).

POLI, Roberto; Italian energy industry executive; *Chairman, Eni SpA;* b. 1938; Prof. of Corp. Finance, Cattolica di Milano 1966–98; fmr Chair. Rizzoli-Corriere della Sera SpA, Publitania SpA; currently Pres. Poli e Associati SpA (fmrly Poli Morelli & Partners SpA); Chair. Ente Nazionale Idrocarburi (Eni) Group SpA (oil and gas co.) 2002–; mem. Bd of Dirs Fininvest SpA, Mondadori

SpA, Merloni Termosanitari SpA, Coesia SpA, Maire Tecnimont SpA, Perennius Capital Partners SGR SpA. *Address:* Eni SpA, Piazzale Enrico Mattei 1, 00144 Rome, Italy (office). *Telephone:* (06) 59821 (office). *Fax:* (06) 59822141 (office). *E-mail:* segreteriasocietaria.azionisti@eni.it (office). *Website:* www.eni.it (office).

POLIAKOFF, Stephen, CBE; British playwright and film director; b. 1 Dec. 1952, London; s. of the late Alexander Poliakoff and Ina Montagu; m. Sandy Welch 1983; one d. one s.; ed Westminster School and Univ. of Cambridge. *Theatre:* Clever Soldiers 1974, The Carnation Gang 1974, Hitting Town 1975, City Sugar 1976, Strawberry Fields (Nat. Theatre) 1978, Shout Across the River (RSC) 1978, The Summer Party 1980, Favourite Nights 1981, Breaking the Silence (RSC) 1984, Coming in to Land (Nat. Theatre) 1987, Playing with Trains (RSC) 1989, Siena Red 1992, Sweet Panic (Hampstead) 1996, Blinded by the Sun (Nat. Theatre) 1996 (Critics' Circle Best Play Award), Talk of the City (RSC) 1998, Remember This (Nat. Theatre) 1999. *Films:* Runners (original story and screenplay) 1983, Hidden City 1988, Close My Eyes (Best British Film Award, Evening Standard) 1991, Century 1993. *Television:* Stronger Than the Sun 1977, Bloody Kids (aka One Joke Too Many, USA) 1979, Caught on a Train (BAFTA Award) 1980, A Természet lágy ölén 1981, Soft Targets 1982, Die doppelte Welt 1985, She's Been Away (Venice Film Festival Prize) 1989, Frontiers 1996, Food of Love 1998, The Tribe 1998, Shooting the Past (Prix Italia) 1999, Perfect Strangers 2001, The Lost Prince 2003, Friends and Crocodiles 2006, Gideon's Daughter 2006. *Publications:* Plays One 1989, Plays Two 1994, Plays Three 1998, Sweet Panic and Blinded by the Sun, Talk of the City, Shooting the Past, Remember This. *Leisure interests:* watching cricket, going to the cinema. *Address:* 33 Devonia Road, London, N1 8JQ, England. *Telephone:* (20) 7354-2695.

POLING, Harold (Red) Arthur, MBA; American business executive; *Chairman, Eclipse Aviation Corporation;* b. 14 Oct. 1925, Troy, Mich.; s. of Plesant Arthur Poling and Laura Elizabeth Poling (née Thompson); m. Marian Sarita Lee 1957; one s. two d.; ed Monmouth Coll. and Ind. Univ.; with Ford Motor Co., Dearborn, Mich. 1951–59, 1960–, Asst Controller Transmissions and Chassis Div. 1964–66, Controller 1966–67, Engine and Foundry Div. 1967–69, Product Devt Group 1969–72, Vice-Pres. Finance Ford of Europe, 1972–75, Pres. Ford of Europe, Inc., Brentwood, UK 1975–77, Chair. 1977–79, Exec. Vice-Pres. Ford Motor Co., Dearborn, Mich. 1979, Pres. and COO 1985–87, Vice-Chair. and COO 1987–90, Chair. and CEO 1990–93, Chair. 1993–94; currently Chair. Eclipse Aviation Corpn; Sec. Motor Vehicle Mfg Asscn; mem. Pres.'s Export Council, Pres.'s Comm. on Environment; mem. Bd of Dirs Shell Oil Co., Thermadyne Holdings Corpn, Eclipse Aviation Corpn; Co-Chair. Steering Cttee Barbara Bush Foundation for Family Literacy; mem. Nat. 4-H Council and numerous other orgs; Hon. Kt Commdr of the Civil Div. of the Most Excellent Order of the British Empire 1993; hon. degrees (Monmouth Coll.) 1981, (Hofstra Univ.) 1986, (Indiana) 1990, (Detroit) 1990, (Mich. State) 1992; Leadership Award, Eng Soc., Detroit 1987, Man of the Year, Automotive Industries Magazine 1988, Horatio Alger Award 1991, Univ. of Mich. Business Leadership Award 1993, Industry Leader of the Year by Automotive Hall of Fame 1993, Albert Schweitzer Leadership Award 1993. *Address:* Eclipse Aviation Corporation, 2503 Clark Carr Loop SE, Albuquerque, NM 87106, USA (office). *Telephone:* (505) 245-7555 (office). *Fax:* (505) 241-8800 (office). *Website:* www.eclipseaviation.com (office).

POLITI, Mauro; Italian judge and professor of law; *Judge, International Criminal Court;* b. 13 Sept. 1944, Fabrica di Roma; ed Univ. of Florence; Asst Prof. of Pvt Int. Law, Univ. of Cagliari, Sardinia 1976–79; Asst Prof. of Public Int. Law, Univ. of Urbino 1979–83, Assoc. Prof. of Int. Law 1983–86; Assoc. Prof. of Int. Law, Univ. of Trento 1986–90, Prof. 1990–; began judicial career at Tribunal of Florence 1969; Judge Tribunal of Oristano 1972, of Milan 1975–83; Deputy Prosecutor Juvenile Court, Milan 1972–75; Legal Adviser Perm. Mission to UN, NY 1992–2001; ad litem judge Int. Criminal Tribunal for fmr Yugoslavia (ICTY) 2001; Judge, Int. Criminal Court (ICC), The Hague 2003–; mem. Del. to UN Security Council 1995–96; mem. Del. to Preparatory Cttee for ICC 1995–97, 1999–2002; Chair. Sixth Legal Cttee of UN Gen. Ass. 2000–01. *Publications:* books, chapters in books and articles in professional law journals. *Address:* International Criminal Court, Maanweg 174, 2516 AB The Hague, The Netherlands. *Telephone:* (70) 5158515. *Fax:* (70) 5158555. *E-mail:* pio@icc-cpi.int. *Website:* www.icc-cpi.int.

POLITZER, H. David, BS, PhD; American physicist and academic; *Professor of Physics, California Institute of Technology;* b. 31 Aug. 1949, NY; ed Bronx High School of Science, NY, Harvard Univ.; Visiting Assoc., Calif. Inst. of Tech., Pasadena 1975–76, faculty mem. 1976–, Full Prof. 1979–, Head of Physics Dept 1986–88; Nobel Prize in Physics (jt recipient) 2004. *Films:* appeared in minor role in film Fat Man and Little Boy 1989. *Address:* California Institute of Technology, High Energy Physics, 1201 East California Boulevard, Mail Code 452-48, Pasadena, CA 91106-3368, USA (office). *Telephone:* (626) 395-4252 (office). *E-mail:* politzer@theory.caltech.edu. *Website:* www.pma.caltech.edu.

POLKINGHORNE, Rev. Canon John Charlton, Kt, KBE, MA, PhD, ScD, FRS; British ecclesiastic and physicist; b. 16 Oct. 1930, Weston-super-Mare; s. of George B. Polkinghorne and Dorothy E. Charlton; m. Ruth I. Martin 1955; two s. one d.; ed Perse School, Cambridge, Trinity Coll. Cambridge and Westcott House, Cambridge; Commonwealth Fund Fellow Calif. Inst. of Tech. 1955–56; Lecturer, Univ. of Edin. 1956–58; Lecturer, Univ. of Cambridge 1958–65, Reader 1965–68, Prof. of Math. Physics 1968–79; Fellow, Trinity Coll. Cambridge 1954–86; ordained deacon 1981, priest 1982; Curate, St Andrew's, Chesterton 1981–82, St Michael & All Angels, Bedminster 1982–84; Vicar of St Cosmus and St Damian in the Blean 1984–86; Fellow and Dean, Trinity Hall, Cambridge 1986–89, Hon. Fellow 1989–; Pres. Queens' Coll. Cambridge 1989–96, Fellow 1996–, Hon. Fellow 1996–; Canon Theologian,

Liverpool Cathedral 1994–2005; Six Preacher, Canterbury Cathedral 1996–; mem. Church of England Doctrine Comm. 1989–95, General Synod 1990–2000, Human Genetics Advisory Comm. 1996–99, Human Genetics Comm. 2000–02; Hon. Fellow, St Edmund's Coll., Cambridge 2002;; Hon. Prof. of Theoretical Physics, Univ. of Kent 1984–89; Hon. DD (Kent) 1994, (Durham) 1999; Hon. DSc (Exeter) 1994, (Leicester) 1995, (Marquette) 2003; Hon. DHum (Hong Kong Baptist) 2006; Templeton Prize 2002. *Publications:* The Analytic S-Matrix (jointly) 1966, The Particle Play 1979, Models of High Energy Processes 1980, The Way the World Is 1983, The Quantum World 1984, One World 1986, Science and Creation 1988, Science and Providence 1989, Rochester Roundabout 1989, Reason and Reality 1991, Science and Christian Belief 1994, Quarks, Chaos and Christianity 1994, Serious Talk 1995, Scientists as Theologians 1996, Beyond Science 1996, Searching for Truth 1996, Belief in God in an Age of Science 1998, Science and Theology 1998, Faith, Science and Understanding 2000, The End of the World and the Ends of God (ed with M. Welker) 2000, Faith in the Living God (with M. Welker) 2001, The Work of Love (ed.) 2001, The God of Hope and the End of the World 2002, Quantum Theory: A Very Short Introduction 2002, Living with Hope 2003, Science and the Trinity 2004, Exploring Reality 2005, Quantum Physics and Theology 2007, From Physicist to Priest 2007. *Leisure interest:* gardening. *Address:* Queens' College, Cambridge, CB3 9ET, England.

POLLACK, Ilana, BA; Israeli librarian; *Chief Librarian, Weizmann Institute of Science;* b. 13 Aug. 1946, Tel-Aviv; d. of Leon Pinsky and Mala First Pinsky (née Ferszt); m. Joseph Pollack 1977 (died 1994); two s.; ed Re'alit High School, Rishon Le Zion, Tel-Aviv Univ. and Hebrew Univ. Jerusalem; served in Israeli Army 1964–66; joined Weizmann Inst. of Science, Rehovot, Asst Librarian 1966, Librarian in charge of Physics Faculty Library 1975, Chief Librarian, Weizmann Inst. of Science 1983–. *Address:* Wix Library, Weizmann Institute of Science, Rehovot 76100 (office); 22 Shenkin Street, Rishon Le-Zion 75282, Israel (home). *Telephone:* 8-9343583 (office); 3-9692186 (home). *Fax:* 8-9344176 (home). *E-mail:* ilana.pollack@weizmann.ac.il (office). *Website:* www.weizmann.ac.il/WIS-library.home.htm (office).

POLLINI, Maurizio; Italian pianist; b. 5 Jan. 1942, Milan; s. of Gino Pollini and Renata Melotti; m. Maria Elisabetta Marzotto 1968; one s.; has played with Berlin and Vienna Philharmonic Orchestras, Bayerischer Rundfunk Orchestra, London Symphony Orchestra, Boston, New York, Philadelphia, LA and San Francisco Orchestras; has played at Salzburg, Vienna, Berlin, Prague Festivals; recordings for Polydor Int; First Prize Int. Chopin Competition, Warsaw 1960, Ernst von Siemens Music Prize, Munich 1996, Edison Classical Music Award for Best Instrumental Solo Recital 2007, Grammy Award for Best Instrumental Soloist Performance 2007, Disco d'Oro 2007. *Recordings include:* Chopin's Nocturnes (Prix Victoire for Best Classical Recording) 2007. *Address:* Harrison Parrott, 5–6 Albion Court, London, W6 0QT, England (office). *Telephone:* (20) 7229-9166 (office). *Fax:* (20) 7221-5042 (office). *E-mail:* info@harrisonparrott.co.uk (office). *Website:* www.harrisonparrott.com (office).

POLLO, Genc; Albanian politician; *Deputy Prime Minister;* b. 7 April 1963, Tirana; m.; two c.; ed Univ. of Tirana, Univ. of Vienna, Austria; Researcher, Acad. of Sciences 1986–88; adviser to Pres. of Albania 1992–96; Chair. New Democrat Party 2001–; Minister of Educ. and Science 2005–07, Deputy Prime Minister 2007–. *Address:* Office of the Council of Ministers, Bulevardi Dëshmorët e Kombit 1, Tirana, Albania (office). *Telephone:* (4) 250474 (office). *Fax:* (4) 237501 (office). *E-mail:* info@km.gov.al (office). *Website:* www.km.gov.al (office).

POLLOCK, Shaun MacLean; South African professional cricketer; b. 16 July 1973, Port Elizabeth; s. of Peter Pollock and Inez Pollock; m. Tricia Lauderdale; ed Northwood High School, Univ. of Natal, Durban; right-hand batsman, right-arm fast-medium bowler; test debut: South Africa v. England at Centurion, 1st Test 1995; One Day Int. (ODI) debut: South Africa v. England at Cape Town, 1st ODI 1996; First-class debut: Natal B v. Western Province B at Pietermaritzburg 1991; major teams: SA nat. team (fmr Capt.), Natal, SA and Warwicks., UK; in Tests played in 91 matches for a total of 3,120 runs (average 31.51), bowling figures: 371 wickets at an average of 21.98 runs; ODIs: played in 221 matches for 2,270 runs and 305 wickets; First-class: played in 166 matches for 6,262 runs (average 32.95); bowling figures: 610 wickets at an average of 22.58 runs; Wisden Cricketer of the Year 2003. *Leisure interests:* music, golf, reading. *Address:* c/o KwaZulu-Natal Cricket Union, PO Box 47266, Greyville, 4023, South Africa (office).

POLMAN, Paul, BA, MA, MBA, DCL; Dutch business executive; *Group Chief Executive, Unilever PLC;* b. 1956, Enschede; m.; three c.; ed Univ. of Groningen, Univ. of Cincinnati, USA, Univ. of Northumbria, UK; Category Man. and Marketing Dir Baby, FemPro, Cleanser and Beverages, Procter and Gamble France 1986–89, Vice-Pres. and Gen. Man. Procter and Gamble Iberia 1989–95, Vice-Pres. and Gen. Man. Procter and Gamble UK 1995–98, Pres. Global Fabric Care 1998–2001, Group Pres. Procter and Gamble Europe 2001–06; Chief Financial Officer Nestlé SA 2006–08, Exec. Vice-Pres. and Zone Dir for US, Canada, Latin America and The Caribbean 2008; Group Chief Exec. Unilever PLC 2009–; mem. Bd of Dirs Swiss-American Chamber of Commerce, Swiss-Latin American Chamber of Commerce, Alcon Inc.; mem. Supervisory Bd Cereal Partners Worldwide. *Leisure interests:* reading, traveling, sailing, marathons. *Address:* Unilever PLC, Unilever House, 100 Victoria Embankment, London, EC4Y 0DY, England (office). *Telephone:* (20) 7822-5252 (office). *Fax:* (20) 7822-5511 (office). *E-mail:* press-office.london@unilever.com (office). *Website:* www.unilever.com (office).

POLOZKOVA, Lidia Pavlovna; Russian sports official and fmr speed skater; b. 8 March 1939, Zlatoust; d. of Pavel I. Skoblikov and Klavdia N. Skoblikova; m. Alexander G. Polozkov; one s.; six gold medals in Winter

Olympic Games 1960 and 1964; all-round world champion 1963–64; won 40 gold medals, 25 at world championships and 15 in USSR; mem. CPSU 1964–91; Head Dept of Physical Educ., Moscow Higher School of the All-Union Trade Union Movt 1974–88; Sr Vice-Pres. of All-Union Trade Unions Soc. for Physical Culture and Sports 1988–92; Vice-Pres. Russian Speed-Skating Fed. 1992–95; Head, Fund for Support of Sports Veterans 1997–; Hon. mem. Russian Speed-Skating Fed. 1995–; Honoured Master of Sports 1960. *Publications:* numerous publs on sport and physical culture. *Leisure interests:* reading, theatre, forest walking, sports, knitting. *Address:* c/o Russian Speed-Skating Federation, Luzhnetskaya nab. 8, Moscow, Russia. *Telephone:* (495) 201-10-40.

POLTAVCHENKO, Lt-Gen. Georgy Sergeyevich; Russian politician and engineer; b. 23 Feb. 1953, Baku, Azerbaijan; m.; one s.; ed Leningrad Inst. of Aviation Machinery, Higher KGB Courses; constructor, involved in bldg Kama truck plant 1972, worked in unit Leninets, worked in local Comsomol Cttee St Petersburg; on staff in KGB orgs 1979–; with KGB, Leningrad Region 1980–92; People's Deputy of Leningrad Regional Council 1990–93; Head Dept Fed. Service of Tax Police, St Petersburg 1992–99; Rep. of Russian Pres. to Leningrad Region 1999–2000, to Cen. Fed. Dist 2000–; Pres. St Petersburg Basketball Fed. *Address:* Office of the Presidential Representative, Nikolsky per. 6, 130132 Moscow, Russia (office). *Telephone:* (495) 206-12-76 (office); (495) 206-19-37 (office).

POLTORANIN, Mikhail Nikiforovich; Russian politician and journalist; b. 22 Nov. 1939, Leninogorsk, E Kazakhstan Region; m.; two s.; ed Kazakh State Univ., Higher CP School; corresp., Ed.-in-Chief local newspapers in Altai 1966–68, Exec. Sec. Kazakhstanskaya Pravda 1970–75, Corresp. Pravda in Kazakhstan 1975–86, Ed.-in-Chief Moskovskaya Pravda 1986–88, Political Corresp. Press Agency Novosti 1988–90; USSR People's Deputy 1989–91; Minister of Press and Mass Media of Russia 1990–92, Deputy-Chair. of Govt (Deputy Prime Minister) of Russia Feb.–Nov. 1992, Dir Fed. Information Agency 1992–93; mem. State Duma (Parl.) 1993–95; Chair. Cttee on Information Policy and Communications 1994–95; Chair. Bd Moment of Truth Corpn 1994–; mem. Bd of Dirs TV-3 Russia 1998–, Exec. Dir 1999–. *Address:* TV-3, Bersenevskaya nab. 20/2, 109017 Moscow, Russia. *Telephone:* (495) 959-06-37.

POLUNIN, Vyacheslav Ivanovich; Russian mime artist and clown; *Artistic Director, Litsedei;* b. 12 June 1950, Novosil, Orlov Region; s. of Pavlovich Polunin and Nikolayevna Polunina; m. Elena Ushakova; two s.; ed Leningrad Inst. of Culture; f. Theatre of Comic Pantomime Actors Litsedei 1968; f. Leningrad Mime Parade 1982; f. All-Union Festival of Street Theatres 1987, All-Union Congress of Fools 1988, Russian Acad. of Fools; took part in European Caravan of Peace 1989; tours around Europe; lives in UK; Golden Angel Prize of Edin. Festival, Golden Nose Prize, Spain, Lawrence Olivier Prize, England, Triumph Prize, Russia 1999. *Leisure interests:* painting, sculpture, architecture, design. *Address:* Litsedei, Tchaikovskogo ul., 59, St Petersburg, Russia. *Telephone:* (812) 272-8879. *Fax:* (812) 272-2356. *E-mail:* licedei@cityline.spb.ru.

POLVINEN, Tuomo Ilmari, PhD; Finnish historian; *Professor Emeritus, Academy of Finland;* b. 2 Dec. 1931, Helsinki; s. of Eino Ilmari Polvinen and Ilona Vihersalo; m. Eeva-Liisa Rommi 1965; two d.; ed Univ. of Helsinki; Docent, Univ. of Helsinki 1965; Prof. of Modern History, Tampere Univ. 1968–70; Dir-Gen. Nat. Archives of Finland 1970–74; Prof. of Modern History, Univ. of Helsinki 1974–92; Research Prof., Acad. of Finland 1979–95, now Prof. Emer.; Urho Kekkonen Prize 1981. *Publications:* Venäjän vallankumous ja Suomi 1917–1920, I-II 1967, 1971, Suomi kansainvälisessä politiikassa 1941–47, I-III 1979, 1980, 1981, Between East and West: Finland in International Politics 1944–47 1986, J. K. Paasikivi, Valtiomiehen elämäntyö Vol. 1, 1870–1918 1989, Vol. 2, 1918–39 1992, Vol. 3, 1939–44 1995, Vol. 4, 1944–48 1999, Vol. 5, 1948–56 2003, Imperial Borderland: Bobrikov and the Attempted Russification of Finland, 1898–1904 1995. *Address:* Purotie 3 A 10, 00380 Helsinki, Finland (home). *Telephone:* 408554 (home). *E-mail:* tuomo .polvinen@kolumbus.fi (home).

POLZE, Werner, Dr rer. pol; German banker; b. 26 March 1931, Altenburg; m. Margitta Polze 1956; one d.; ed School of Economics, Berlin, Akad. für Staats- und Rechtswissenschaften, Babelsberg (Inst. of Int. Relations); worked for Deutsche Notenbank, Berlin, GDR 1956–66; joined Deutsche Aussenhandelsbank AG 1966, Exec. Vice-Pres. 1969–78, Pres. 1978–91, Spokesman for the Bd 1991–; Deputy Chair. Supervisory Bd, DIHB Deutsche Industrie- und Handelsbank AG, Berlin 1990–. *Address:* Deutsche Aussenhandelsbank AG, Unter den Linden 26/30, 10117 Berlin, Germany.

POMERANTS, Grigory Solomonovich; Russian philosopher and writer; b. 13 March 1918, Vilnius, Lithuania; m. Mirkina Zinaida Aleksandrovna; ed Moscow Inst. of History, Philosophy and Literature; teacher Tula Pedagogical Inst. 1940–41; served in World War II, worked as corresp. of div. newspaper, expelled from CPSU for anti-party activities 1941–45; mem. staff Soyuzenerotrest, newspapers vendor 1946–49; postdoctoral thesis burnt by KGB 1950; was sent to Gulag for dissident activities 1950–53; secondary school teacher; bibliographer Library of Foreign Lit., Moscow, then Library of Public Sciences 1960s and 1970s; freelance contrib. to samizdat 1970s; mem. Acad. of Natural Sciences, Writers Union, PEN Club;Head, Culturological Section, Humanities Research Acad. *Publications:* numerous publs banned in USSR published abroad in the 1970s including Moral Image of the Historic Personality, Unpublished 1972, Dreams of the Earth 1984, Openness to Abyss: Etudes about Dostoyevsky 1989; first three articles published in Russia 1988, Lectures on History of Philosophy 1993, Russian Richness 1994, Exit from Trance 1995, Images of the Eternal 1995. *Address:* c/o Russian PEN Centre, Neglinnaya Street 18/1, bldg 2, Moscow 103031, Russia.

POMEROL, Jean-Charles; French computer scientist, academic and university administrator; *President, Université Pierre et Marie Curie;* b. 1945; ed Univ. Pierre et Marie Curie, Paris; began career as teacher, Lycée Saint-Quentin; Lecturer, Univ. Versailles Saint-Quentin-en-Yvelines; Sr Lecturer, Univ. Pierre et Marie Curie, Paris (UPMC) later Prof. of Computer Science and Dir Teaching and Research Dept, Project Leader CNRS 1995–2000, Dir CNRS-UPMC Lab. for Artificial Intelligence, Vice-Pres. of Science 2002–06, Pres. UPMC 2006–; Pres. Fondation Voir et Entendre; Ed. Revue Française d'Intelligence Artificielle. *Address:* Office of the President, Université Pierre et Marie Curie, 4th Floor, Tour 44, 4 place Jussieu, POB 600, 75252 Paris cedex 05, France (office). *Telephone:* 1-44-27-33-49 (office). *Fax:* 1-44-27-38-29 (office). *Website:* www.upmc.fr/fr/universite/organisation/presidence/jean_charles_pomerol.html (office).

POMMIER, Jean-Bernard; French pianist and conductor; b. 17 Aug. 1944, Beziers; two d. by Irena Podleska; ed Conservatoire de Paris; as pianist has appeared with conductors including: Herbert von Karajan, Bernard Haitink, Pierre Boulez, Riccardo Muti, Gennadi Rozhdestvensky, Leonard Slatkin, Zubin Mehta and Daniel Barenboim; has conducted numerous orchestras including Chamber Orchestra of Europe, Orchestre de Paris; debut with Royal Liverpool Philharmonic Orchestra 1991; Artistic Dir Northern Sinfonia, Newcastle-upon-Tyne 1996–99; Prin. conductor Orchestra Filarmonica di Torino 1997; f. and Artistic Dir Musikè International Acad.; performances world-wide; masterclasses in Chicago, London, Lausanne and Melbourne; Officier, Ordre nat. du mérite; awards include Int. Competition of Young Musicians, Berlin, Prix de la Guilde des artistes solistes Français, Diapason d'Or, Tchaikovsky Prize, Moscow. *Recordings include:* Mozart Piano Concerti (with Sinfonia Varsovia), Poulenc Piano Concerti (with City of London Sinfonia), Brahms Cello Sonatas and Violin Sonatas, Complete Beethoven Piano Sonatas, complete Mozart Sonatas. *Address:* Musiké Académies Productions, Chemin de Praz-Simon 3, 1000 Lausanne, Switzerland. *Website:* www.musike.co.uk.

POMODORO, Arnaldo; Italian sculptor and theatrical designer; b. 23 June 1926, Morciano di Romagna; s. of Antonio Pomodoro and Beatrice Luzzi; has worked as jeweller and goldsmith 1950–; artist-in-residence, Stanford Univ. 1966–67, Univ. of Calif., Berkeley 1968; lecture course, Mills Coll., Oakland, Calif. 1979–82; Grande Ufficiale, Ordine al Merito (Italy) 1986, Cavaliere di Gran Croce dell' Ordine al merito 1996; Hon. DLitt (Dublin) 1992, Hon. DArch (Ancona) 2001; Int. Sculpture Prize, São Paulo Biennale, Brazil 1963, Premio Nazionale di scultura, Venice Biennale 1964, Int. Sculpture Prize (Carnegie Inst., Pittsburgh) 1967, Henry Moore Grand Prize (Hakone Open-Air Museum, Japan) 1981, Praemium Imperiale for Sculpture (Japan Art Asscn) 1990, VII Premio Michelangelo per la Scultura 1998, Ministry of Culture Gold Medal 2005, Premio Lex Spolentina 2006, Guglielmo Marconi Award 2006, ISC Lifetime Achievement in Contemporary Sculpture Award 2008. *Theatrical designs include:* Semiramide, Rome 1982, Orestea, Gibellina, Sicily 1983–85, Alceste, Genoa 1987, Oedipus Rex, Siena 1988, Cleopatra, Gibellina, Sicily 1989, I Paraventi at Bologna 1990, Nella solitudine dei campi di cotone by Koltès, Rome 1991, Benevento 1998, More Stately Mansions by O'Neill, Rome 1992, Oreste by Alfieri, Rome 1993, Stabat Mater by Tarantino, Rome 1994–95, Moonlight by Pinter, Brescia, Rome 1995, Antigone by Anouilh, Taormina 1996, Il Caso Fedra by di Martino 1997, The Tempest, Palermo 1998, Capriccio by Strauss, Naples 2002, Madama Butterfly by Puccini, Torre del Lago 2004, Un Ballo in Maschera by Verdi, Lipsia 2005. *Publications:* L'arte lunga 1992, Arnaldo Pomodoro 1995, Scritti critici per Arnaldo Pomodoro e opere dell'artista 1955–2000 2000, Arnaldo Pomodoro nei giardini del Palais-Royal di Parigi 2003, Arnaldo Pomodoro e il Museo Poldi Pezzoli, La Sala d'Armi 2004, Corona nella Cattedrale di Milwaukee (with Giuseppe Maraniello) 2004, Catalogo della scultura 2007. *Leisure interests:* photography, theatre, literature. *Address:* Via Vigevano 5, 20144 Milan, Italy. *Telephone:* (02) 58104131. *Fax:* (02) 89401303 (office). *E-mail:* info@arnaldopomodoro.it (office). *Website:* www.fondazionearnaldopomodoro.it (office).

PONCE CEVALLOS, Javier; Ecuadorean journalist and government official; *Minister of National Defence;* b. 28 April 1948, Quito; ed Escuela de Sociología y Ciencias Políticas, Univ. Central del Ecuador; columnist El Tiempo newspaper 1966–70; with Ministry of Agriculture 1973–77; Dir Artes cultural review 1977–78; Sec. Gen. Ecumenical Cttee of Projects 1986–97, Coordinator 1997–; Ed. HOY 1992–99, Ed. de investigaciones 1999–2001, columnist 1989–2001; editorial writer and columnist El Universo 2001–; Ed. Enciclopedia Planeta 2002–03; Personal Sec. to Pres. Rafael Correa 2006–08; Minister of Nat. Defence 2008–. *Address:* Ministry of National Defence, Exposición 208, Quito . Ecuador (office). *Telephone:* (2) 221-6150 (office). *Fax:* (2) 256-9386 (office). *Website:* www.midena.gov.ec (office).

PONCE ENRILE, Juan, LLM; Philippine public official and lawyer; b. 14 Feb. 1924, Gonzaga, Cagayan; s. of Alfonso Ponce Enrile and Petra Furagganan; m. Cristina Castañer 1957; one s. one d.; ed Ateneo de Manila, Univ. of the Philippines and Harvard Law School; practising Corpn lawyer and Prof. of Law 1956–64; Under-Sec. of Finance 1966–68; Acting Sec. of Finance; Acting Insurance Commr; Acting Commr of Customs; Sec. of Justice 1968–70; Sec. of Nat. Defence 1970–71 (resgnd), 1972–78, Minister 1978–86 (reappointed under Aquino Govt 1986); Chair. Cttee on Nat. Security, Defense, Peace and Order; mem. Senate and Opposition Leader (Nacionalista Party) 1987–92, 1995–2001, 2004–; arrested Feb. 1990, released March 1990; mem. House of Reps 1992–95, mem. Finance, Appropriations and Steering Cttees; Chair., Bd of Dirs Philippine Nat. Bank until 1978, Nat. Investment and Devt Co., United Coconut Planters Bank, Nat. Disaster Control Center; Dir Philippine Communications Satellite Corpn; Trustee and Sec., Bd of Trustees, Cultural Centre of the Philippines; Chair. Exec. Cttee, Nat. Security

Council; mem. Bd, Nat. Econ. and Devt Authority, Energy Devt, Philippine Nat. Oil Co., Nat. Environmental Protection Council, Philippine Overseas Telecommunications Corpn, Philippine Crop Insurance Corpn; mem. numerous law and commercial asscns; two hon. degrees; Mahaputra Adipranada Medal, Indonesia 1975; Commander, Philippine Legion of Honor 1986. *Publications:* A Proposal on Capital Gains Tax 1960, Income Tax Treatment of Corporate Merger and Consolidation Revisited 1962, Tax Treatment of Real Estate Transactions 1964; also various articles on law, the mil. and govt. *Leisure interests:* reading, golf, tennis, swimming, water-skiing, fishing. *Address:* Senate Office, 5th floor, Room 503, GSIS Bldg., Financial Center, Roxas Blvd., Pasay City; 3/F Vernida IV Building, Leviste Street, Salcedo Village, Makati City (office); 2305 Morado Street, Dasmariñas Village, Makati, Metro Manila, Philippines (home). *Telephone:* (632) 552-6691 (Senate); 813-7934 (office); 844-3915 (home). *Fax:* 818-7392 (office). *E-mail:* senator_enrile@senate.gov.ph; jpenrile@pecabar.ph (office). *Website:* www.senate.gov.ph.

PONCELET, Christian; French politician; *President of the Senate;* b. 24 March 1928, Blaise (Ardennes); s. of Raoul Poncelet and Raymonde Poncelet (née Chamillard); m. Yvette Miclot 1949; two d.; ed Coll. Saint-Sulpice, Paris and Nat. Ecole Professionelle des Postes, Télégraphes et Télécommunications; Deputy to Nat. Assembly for the Vosges 1962–77; Sec. of State, Ministry of Social Affairs 1972–73, Ministry of Employment, Labour and Population 1973–74; Sec. of State for the Civil Service attached to Prime Minister March–May 1974; Sec. of State for the Budget, Ministry of Econ. Affairs and Finance 1974–77, for Relations with Parl. 1977; Conseiller Général, Remiremont 1963–73; Pres. Conseil Général des Vosges 1976–; Sénateur des Vosges 1977–, Pres. Comm. for Finance, Budgetary Control and Econ. Accounts of the Nation to the Senate 1986–98, Pres. of Senate 1998–; mem. European Parl. 1979–80; Mayor of Remiremont 1983–2001; mem. Institut de France. *Leisure interest:* hunting. *Address:* Palais du Luxembourg, 75291 Paris Cedex 06 (office); 17 rue du Etats-Unis, 88200 Remiremont, France (home). *Telephone:* 1-42-34-36-77 (office). *Fax:* 1-42-34-20-94 (office). *E-mail:* c.poncelet@senat.fr (office); presidence@senat.fr (office). *Website:* www.senat.fr (office).

PONDER, Sir Bruce, Kt, MB, BChir, PhD, FRS, FRCP, FRCPath; British medical scientist and academic; *Li Ka-shing Professor of Oncology, University of Cambridge;* b. 1944, Haywards Heath; m.; four c.; ed Univ. of Cambridge; begin career as clinician, St Thomas' Hosp., London; fmr Sr Registrar Oncology Dept, St Bartholomew's Hosp., London; Researcher, Imperial Cancer Research Unit, Mill Hill 1977; Hamilton Fairley Fellowship, Harvard Medical School, USA 1977–78; Researcher, Inst. of Cancer Research, Sutton 1978, also clinical appointment, Royal Marsden Hosp.; Prof. of Oncology, Univ. of Cambridge 1996–, also becoming Head Dept of Oncology, Li Ka-shing Prof. of Oncology 2007–, also Dir Li Ka-shing Centre 2007–; Co-Dir Hutchison/MRC Research Centre; Co-Dir Strangeways Research Labs; Dir Cancer Research UK Cambridge Research Inst.; Founder Fellow, Acad. of Medical Sciences; Ed.-in-Chief Breast Cancer Research; MD Anderson Cancer Center Bertner Award 2007. *Leisure interests:* photography, gardening, golf, travel, wine. *Address:* Cancer Research UK, Cambridge Research Institute, Li Ka Shing Centre, Robinson Way, Cambridge, CB2 0RE, England (office). *E-mail:* bruce.ponder@cancer.org.uk (office). *Website:* www.lksf.org/eng/project/medical/cambridge/main01.shtml (office).

PONOMAREV, Aleksander Sergeyevich; Russian journalist and manager; b. 13 Oct. 1956; m. Nadezhda Ponomareva; one s. one d.; ed Saratov State Univ.; Komsomol work 1979–87; Deputy Ed.-in-Chief Cen. Youth Programme Section, USSR Cen. TV 1987–88, Ed.-in-Chief 1988–91; Dir Creative Union of Experimental TV, Ostankino 1992–93, First Deputy Dir-Gen. Oskankino 1992–93; co-founder and Vice-Pres. Moscow Ind. Broadcasting Corpn (MNVK), Dir-Gen. 1993–, First Vice-Pres. 1997–2001; Deputy Chair. All-Russian State TV Co.; Dir Cultura Camel 2001–. *Address:* Kultura TV Channel, Leningradsky prosp. 22/2, Moscow, Russia. *Telephone:* (495) 234-89-75 (office).

PONS, Bernard Claude, DenM; French physician and politician; b. 18 July 1926, Béziers, Hérault; s. of Claude Pons and Véronique Vogel; m. Josette Cros 1952; one s. three d.; ed Lycées, Marseilles and Toulouse and Faculté de Médecine, Montpellier; gen. practitioner, Cahors 1954; mem. Union pour la nouvelle République 1967–68, Union des Démocrats pour la République 1968–78, Rassemblement pour la République (RPR) 1978–2002, Union pour un Mouvement Populaire (UMP) 2002–; Deputy to Nat. Ass. 1967–69, 1973–86, 1988–95, 1997–2002, Pres. RPR Group 1988–95; Conseiller-Gen. Cajarc canton 1967–78; Sec. of State, Ministry of Agric. 1969–73; mem. Conseil-Gen. Ile-de-France 1978; Sec.-Gen. RPR 1979–84; Paris City Councillor 1983–; Pres. Admin. Council, Paris Câble 1984–; Rep. to Ass. of EC 1984–85; Minister for Overseas Departments and Territories 1986–88; Minister of Town and Country Planning, Equipment and Transport May–Nov. 1995, for Capital Works, Housing, Transport and Tourism 1995–97. *Address:* Union pour un Mouvement Populaire, 55 rue de La Boétie, 75384 Paris Cedex 08 (office); Paris TV câble, 4 villa Thoréton, 75015 Paris, France. *Telephone:* 1-40-76-60-00 (office). *E-mail:* webmaster@u-m-p.org (home). *Website:* www.u-m-p.org (office).

PONSOLLE, Patrick; French business executive; *Chairman, Morgan Stanley France;* b. 20 July 1944, Toulouse; s. of Jean Ponsolle and Marie-Rose Courthaliac; m. Nathalie Elie Lefebvre 1983; two d.; ed Lycées Janson-de-Sailly and Henry IV, Paris, Ecole normale supérieure de la rue d'Ulm, Ecole Nat. d'Admin; civil servant Ministry of Econs and Finance 1973–77; Financial Attaché Embassy, Washington 1977–79; Head of Mission for Dir of Forecasting, Ministry of Econs and Finance 1980; Sec.-Gen. Nat. Accounts and Budgets Comm. 1980–81; Deputy Chief of Staff to Budget Minister 1981–83; Deputy Dir, Asst Man. Dir Compagnie de Suez 1983–87, Man. Dir 1988, Chief Exec. 1991–93; Vice-Chair., Man. Dir then Chair., Man. Dir Suez Int. 1985; Chair. Soc. financière pour la France et les pays d'outre mer (Soffo) 1990–96; Co-Chair. Eurotunnel Group, Chair. Eurotunnel SA 1994–96, Exec. Co-Chair. 1996–2001; Dir Unichem PLC 1998–2006, mem. Bd of Dirs (non-exec.) Alliance Boots PLC 2006–; Adviser Morgan Stanley Dean Witter (now Morgan Stanley) 1999–, Chair. Morgan Stanley France, Vice-Chair. and Man. Dir 2001–; Dir numerous cos including France Télécom, Banque Indosuez; chair. numerous bodies. *Address:* Morgan Stanley France, 61 rue de Monceau, 75008 Paris (office); 3 rue Danton, 75006 Paris, France (home). *Telephone:* 1-42-90-70-00. *Fax:* 1-42-90-70-99 (office). *Website:* www.morganstanley.com.

PONTAL, Jean-François; French business executive; *Adviser, ING Direct France;* b. 17 April 1943, Chaton; m. Martine Lorain-Broca 1968; two c.; ed Centres d'Etudes Supérieures des Techniques Industrielles; human resources consultant Inst. Bossard; Vice-Pres. of Operations, then of Resources and Markets Carrefour, CEO Pryca (Spanish subsidiary), mem. bd with responsibility for S Europe 1993–96; Head Consumer Services Div. France Télécom 1996–2001, apptd Pres. Wanadoo 2000, Exec. Vice-Pres. France Télécom, –2001, CEO Orange (after merger with France Télécom) 2001–03 (retd); Adviser Retail Banking Segment ING Direct France 2003–; mem. Bd of Dirs Sonaecom 2003–, Southwing S.L. 2004–, Investcom LLC 2005–, OTL 2006–; Chevalier, Ordre nat. du Mérite. *Leisure interests:* sailing, tennis. *Address:* c/o ING Direct, Service Clientèle, Libre Réponse 70678, 75568 Paris cedex 12, France (office).

PONTI, Michael; German-American concert pianist; b. 29 Oct. 1937, Freiburg, Germany; s. of Joseph Ponti and Zita Wüchner; m. 1st Carmen Wiechmann 1962 (divorced 1971); one s. two d.; m. 2nd Beatrice van Stappen 1984; one s.; studied under Prof. Gilmour McDonald and Prof. Erich Flinsch; debut in Vienna 1964, in New York 1972; has toured extensively world-wide; over 80 recordings; suffered a stroke 2000, now performs concerts for left hand only; Busoni Award, Italy 1964. *Address:* Heubergstrasse 32, 82438 Eschenlohe, Germany. *Telephone:* (8824) 913754.

PONTING, Richard (Ricky) Thomas; Australian professional cricketer; b. 19 Dec. 1974, Lanceston, Tasmania; s. of Graeme Ponting and Lorraine Ponting (née Campbell); ed Mowbray Primary School, Brooks Senior High School, Launceston; right-handed middle-order batsman, right-arm medium-pace bowler; teams: Tasmania 1992–, Australia 1995– (test debut v. Sri Lanka at Perth, one-day international debut v. South Africa at Wellington, New Zealand); 85 tests for Australia, scored 6,657 runs (average 55.47, highest score 257 v. India 2004) with 14 hundreds and took four wickets; scored 14,790 runs (average 58.22) with 53 hundreds and took 13 wickets in first-class cricket; 212 one-day internationals, scored 7,621 runs (average 42.10) with 16 hundreds; Vice-Capt. Australia 2000– (tests); Capt. Australia (one-day internationals) 2002–; apptd Australia's test Capt. for 2004; Capt. of Australia's World Cup winning side 2003, scored 140 in final v. India; second batsmen ever to score more than 1,500 runs in a calendar year 2003; Allan Border Medal as Australian Cricketer of the Year 2003. *Leisure interests:* football, golf. *Address:* c/o Tasmanian Cricket Asscn, Derwent Street, Bellerive, Tasmania 7018, Australia (office). *Telephone:* (3) 6211-4000 (office). *Fax:* (3) 6244-3924 (office). *E-mail:* info@tascricket.com.au (office). *Website:* www.tastigers.com.au (office).

PONTZIOUS, Richard; American conductor and artistic director; *Artistic Director and Conductor, Asian Youth Orchestra;* has conducted orchestras, bands and choirs in Europe and Asia; Founder, Artistic and Exec. Dir and Conductor, Asian Youth Orchestra 1990–; Bronze Bauhina Star, Hong Kong Govt 2000. *Address:* Suite 15A, One Capital Place, 18 Luard Road, Wanchai, Hong Kong Special Administrative Region, People's Republic of China (office). *Telephone:* (852) 28661623 (office). *Fax:* (852) 28613340 (office). *E-mail:* ayo@asianyouthorchestra.com (office). *Website:* www.asianyouthorchestra.com (office).

POOLE, David James, PPRP, ARCA; British artist; b. 5 June 1931, London; s. of Thomas Herbert Poole and Catherine Lord; m. Iris Mary Toomer 1958; three s.; ed Stoneleigh Secondary Modern School, Wimbledon School of Art, Royal Coll. of Art; Sr Lecturer in Painting and Drawing, Wimbledon School of Art 1961–77; Pres. Royal Soc. of Portrait Painters 1983–91; work in HM The Queen's collection, London and in pvt. collections in Bermuda, Canada, France, Germany, Italy, S Africa, Saudi Arabia, Switzerland and USA. *Portraits include:* HM Queen Elizabeth II, HRH Prince Philip, HM Queen Elizabeth the Queen Mother, HRH Prince Charles, HRH Prince Andrew, HRH Prince Edward, HRH The Princess Royal, Lord Mountbatten, mems of govt, armed forces, industry, commerce, medicine and acad. and legal professions. *Leisure interests:* travel and food, particularly in France. *Address:* Trinity Flint Barn, Weston Lane, Weston, Petersfield, Hants., GU32 3NN, England (home). *Telephone:* (1730) 265075 (home).

POON, Christine A., MS, MBA; American business executive; *Worldwide Chairman, Medicines and Nutritionals and Vice-Chairman, Johnson & Johnson;* b. Cincinnati, OH; d. of James Poon and Virginia Poon; m. Mike Tweedle; ed Northwestern, St Louis and Boston Univs; joined Bristol-Myers Squibb in 1985, various man. positions including Pres. and Gen. Man. Squibb Diagnostics' Canadian operation 1994, Sr Vice-Pres. for Canada and Latin America, Pharmaceutical Operations –1997, Pres. Medical Devices 1997–98, Pres. Int. Medicines 1998–2000; Co. Group Chair. Pharmaceuticals Group, Johnson & Johnson 2000–01, mem. Exec. Cttee and Worldwide Chair. Pharmaceuticals Group 2001–03, Worldwide Chair. Medicines and Nutritionals 2003–, Vice-Chair., mem. Office of the Chair. and mem. Bd Dirs Johnson & Johnson 2005–; mem. Advisory Bd Healthcare Businesswomen's Asscn; mem. Bd Dirs Fox Chase Cancer Center, Phila; ranked by Fortune magazine amongst 50 Most Powerful Women in Business in the US (27th)

2003, (15th) 2004, (12th) 2005, (11th) 2006, (14th) 2007, ranked by Forbes magazine amongst 100 Most Powerful Women (17th) 2004, (43rd) 2005, (26th) 2006, (46th) 2007, (46th) 2008, Healthcare Businesswomen's Assen Woman of the Year 2004. *Address:* Johnson & Johnson, 1 Johnson & Johnson Plaza, Room WH 2133, New Brunswick, NJ 08933, USA (office). *Telephone:* (732) 524-0400 (office). *Fax:* (732) 524-3300 (office). *Website:* www.jnj.com (office).

POON, Chung-Kwong, OBE, BSc, PhD, DSc, CChem, FRSC, JP; Hong Kong chemist, university president and academic; *President Emeritus, The Hong Kong Polytechnic University;* b. 1940, Hong Kong; m.; three c.; ed St Paul's Co-educational Coll., Univ. of Hong Kong, Univ. of London, UK; Post-doctoral Research Fellow, Univ. Coll. London 1967, Calif. Inst. of Tech., USA 1967–68 (Visiting Research Assoc. 1976, 1979); Visiting Research Assoc., Univ. of Southern California 1972; Lecturer in Chem., Univ. of Hong Kong 1968–75, Prof. of Chem. 1982–90, Dean of Faculty of Science 1983–90; Dir Hong Kong Polytechnic 1991–94; Pres. The Hong Kong Polytechnic Univ. 1991–2008, Pres. Emer. 2009–; has chaired or been a mem. of numerous cttees of Hong Kong Govt and of industrial, business and educational sectors, including mem. Legis. Council 1985–91, Preparatory Cttee for Hong Kong Special Admin. Region 1994–97; Founding Chair. Govt's Cttee on Science and Tech. 1988–91; mem. CPPCC Nat. Cttee 1998–; Chair. Radiological Protection Advisory Group 1989–2007; Consultant of Science and Tech. Consulting Cttee, Shenzhen Municipal People's Govt 2000–; mem. Policy Consultative Cttee, Shaanxi Prov. 2000–; mem. Nuclear Safety Consultative Cttee, Guangdong Daya Bay Nuclear Power Station 1986–, Huaqiao Univ. Council 1992–, Shantou Univ. Council 2000–07; Fellow, Univ. Coll. London 1996; Foreign mem. Russian Acad. of Eng 2004; apptd a non-official JP 1989; Hon. Prof. at several univs on Chinese mainland; Gold Bauhinia Star 2002; recipient of UK Commonwealth Scholarship 1964–67, Fulbright Scholarship 1967–68, honoured as one of "Ten Outstanding Young Persons in Hong Kong" 1979. *Address:* Office of the President Emeritus, The Hong Kong Polytechnic University, Yuk Choi Road, Hung Hom, Kowloon, Hong Kong Special Administrative Region, People's Republic of China (office). *Telephone:* 27665381 (office). *Fax:* 27731447 (office). *E-mail:* pckpoon@polyu.edu.hk (office). *Website:* www.polyu.edu.hk (office).

POON, Dickson; Hong Kong business executive; *Group Executive Chairman, Dickson Concepts (International) Ltd.;* s. of Poon Kam Kai; m. 1st Marjorie Yang (divorced); one d.; m. 2nd Michelle Yeoh (q.v.) 1988 (divorced 1991); m. 3rd Pearl Yu 1992; ed St Joseph's Coll., Hong Kong, Uppingham School, UK and Occidental Coll., Los Angeles, USA; apprenticeship in watch-making at Chopard's, Geneva, Switzerland; returned to Hong Kong and opened first Dickson watch and jewellery shop 1980; Co-Founder (with Sammo Hung) DMV film co. 1983; Head Dickson Concepts, Hong Kong, operating more than 240 boutiques and outlets throughout SE Asia and in China; acquired French co. S.T. Dupont label 1987, sold 1997; acquired stake in Harvey Nichols, London 1991, floated co. 1996, pvt. takeover 2002, opened brs in Leeds 1997, Edin. 2002 and Manchester 2003; bought 85% stake in Hong Kong and Shenzhen brs of Japanese dept store Seibu 1996; sole benefactor of Hong Kong Univ.'s Man. Inst. *Address:* Dickson Concepts (International) Ltd., 4th Floor, East Ocean Centre, 98 Granville Road, Tsimshatsui East, Kowloon, Hong Kong (office). *Telephone:* 23113888. *Fax:* 23113323. *Website:* www.dicksonconcepts.com.hk.

POOS, Jacques F.; Luxembourg politician; b. 3 June 1935; m.; three c.; ed Athénée Grand-Ducal, Univ. of Lausanne and Luxembourg Int. Univ.; Ministry of Nat. Economy 1959–62; Service d'Etudes et de Statistiques Economiques (STATEC) 1962–64; Dir Imprimerie Coopérative 1964–76; Pres. SYTRAGAZ 1970–76; MP 1974–76; Minister of Finance, Gov. IBRD, IMF, EIB 1976–79; Dir Banque Continentale du Luxembourg SA 1980–82, Banque Paribas (Luxembourg) SA 1982–84; Vice-Pres. Parti Socialiste 1982; Deputy Prime Minister and Minister of Foreign Affairs, Foreign Trade and Co-operation 1984–99, also of Foreign Trade and Co-operation; Pres. EU Council of Ministers 1985, 1991, 1997; mem. European Parl. 1999–2004, mem. Comm. for Foreign Affairs, Human Rights, Public Security and Defence Policy; fmr Pres. Council of European Union; Hon. DIur (Athens) 2002. *Publications:* Le Luxembourg dans le Marché Commun 1961, Le Modèle Luxembourgeois 1981, La Crise Economique et Financière: est-elle encore maitrisable? 1984; numerous newspaper and periodical articles. *Address:* 45 Square Mayrisch, L-4240 Esch-Alzette, Luxembourg (home). *Telephone:* (352) 556425 (home). *Fax:* (352) 570419 (home). *E-mail:* jacquespoos@hotmail.com (home).

POP, Iggy; American singer, musician (guitar) and actor; b. (James Jewel Osterberg), 21 April 1947, Ann Arbor, Mich.; ed Univ. of Michigan; formed high-school band Iguanas 1962, Prime Movers 1966; concerts in Michigan, Detroit and Chicago; formed The Stooges (originally the Pyschedelic Stooges) 1967, re-formed 2007–; solo artist 1976–; collaborations with David Bowie 1972–; numerous tours and TV appearances. *Film appearances:* Rock & Rule (voice) 1983, Sid and Nancy 1986, The Color of Money 1986, Hardware 1990, Cry-Baby 1990, Atolladero 1995, Tank Girl 1995, Dead Man 1995, The Crow – City of Angels (also known as The Crow II) 1996, The Brave 1997, The Rugrats Movie (voice) 1998, Snow Day 2000, Coffee and Cigarettes 2003, Persepolis (voice) 2007. *Television appearances:* Miami Vice (series), The Adventures of Pete & Pete (series). *Other appearances include:* Driv3r (video game, voice) 2004. *Compositions include:* China Girl (with David Bowie). *Film songs include:* Repo Man (theme song 'Repo Man') 1984, Sid and Nancy (song 'I Wanna Be Your Dog') 1986, Dogs in Space (songs 'Dog Food' and 'Endless Sea') 1987, Slaves of New York (song 'Fall in Love with Me') 1989, Tales from the Crypt (TV series, songs 'Kill City' and 'Five Foot One' for episode 'For Cryin' Out Loud') 1989, Va mourire (1995), Trainspotting (song 'Nightclubbing') 1996, Space Goofs (series theme song) 1997, Full Blast (song 'Loose') 1997, The Brave 1997, Home to Rent (TV series theme song) 1997, Great Expectations (song) 1998, The Wedding Singer (song 'China Girl') 1998, Velvet Goldmine (song 'T.V. Eye') 1998, Whatever (song 'Gimme Danger') 1998, Lock, Stock and Two Smoking Barrels (song 'I Wanna Be Your Dog', as James Oaterberg, Jr) 1998, Radiofreccia (song 'The Passenger') 1998, Born to Lose (song 'Tight Pants') 1999, The Filth and the Fury (song 'No Fun') 2000, Almost Famous (song 'Search and Destroy') 2000, Dogtown and Z-Boys (song 'I Wanna Be Your Dog') 2001, Intimacy (songs 'Consolation Prizes' and 'Penetration', as J. Osterberg alias I. Pop) 2001, Gran Turismo 3: A-Spec (video game) 2001, Killer Barbys vs. Dracula (song 'Candy') 2002, Pro BMX 2 (video game) (song 'The Passenger') 2002, Rugrats Go Wild! (song 'Lust for Life') 2003, Wonderland (song 'Search and Destroy') 2003, The School of Rock (song 'T.V. Eye', as James Osterberg) 2003, The Life Aquatic with Steve Zissou (song 'Search and Destroy') 2004. *Recordings:* albums: with The Stooges: The Stooges 1969, Fun House 1970, Jesus Loves The Stooges 1977, I'm Sick of You 1977, Raw Stooges 1988, Raw Stooges 2 1988, The Weirdness 2007; solo: Raw Power 1973, Metallic KO 1976, The Idiot 1977, Lust For Life 1977, TV Eye Live 1978, Kill City 1978, New Values 1979, Soldier 1980, Party 1981, I'm Sick of You 1981, Zombie Birdhouse 1982, I Got The Right 1983, Blah Blah Blah 1986, Rubber Legs 1987, Live At The Whiskey A Go Go 1988, Death Trip 1988, Instinct 1988, Brick By Brick 1990, American Caesar 1994, Naughty Little Doggie 1996, Heroin Hates You 1997, King Biscuit Flower Hour 1997, Your Pretty Face is Going to Hell 1998, Sister Midnight 1999, Avenue B 1999, Iggy Pop 1999, Hippodrome Paris '77 (live) 1999, Beat 'Em Up 2001, Skull Ring 2003, Preliminaires 2009. *Publications:* I Need More (autobiog.), Iggy Pop's A–Z (autobiog.) 2005. *Website:* www.iggypop.com.

POP, Mihai; Moldovan economist and government official; b. 31 Oct. 1955, Apşa de Mijloc, Transcarpathian Oblast, Ukraine; m.; two c.; ed Chişinău Polytechnic Inst.; Head, Dept for Econ. Planning, Făleşti tobacco factory 1977–86; Industry Coordinator, Făleşti Dist Agricultural and Industrial Agency 1986–89; instructor, organisational agency of Făleşti Dist CP Cttee 1989–90, Head of Finance Dept, then Deputy Head of Finance and Econs Dept 1990–94; Head, State Fiscal Inspectorate of Bălţi Dist 1994–99; Head, Ministry of Finance Fiscal Inspectorate 1999–2005, Deputy Minister of Finance, May–Oct. 2005, Minister of Finance Oct. 2005–08. *Address:* c/o Ministry of Finance, str. Cosmonauţilor 7, 2005 Chişinău, Moldova (office).

POPE, Martin, BS, PhD; American physical chemist and academic; *Professor Emeritus of Physical Chemistry, New York University;* b. 22 Aug. 1918, Lower East Side of New York City; ed City Coll. of New York, Brooklyn Polytechnic Inst.; parents immigrated to USA from Poland; Scientist, Radiation Lab., Brooklyn Navy Yard 1942; First Lt, US Armed Forces, Pacific theatre, World War II 1945; Research Scientist, Balco Research Lab. 1947–51, Tech. Dir 1951–56; Sr Research Scientist, Radiation and Solid State Physics Lab., New York Univ. 1956–60, Research Assoc. Prof. 1960–65, Assoc. Prof. of Chem. 1965–68, Prof. of Chem. 1968–88, Co-Dir Radiation and Solid State Physics Lab. 1968–83, Dir 1983–88, Prof. Emer. of Physical Chem. 1988–; Visiting Prof. in Puerto Rico 1969–70; Scientific Guest of State and Visiting Prof., China 1978, USSR 1987; Visiting Prof., Univ. of Alexandria, Egypt 1981; Guest Lecturer in Leningrad, Moscow, Kiev, Riga, Israel, Gdansk, Kraków, Puerto Rico, Japan, Czechoslovakia and Germany 1980s; Founder Gordon Conf. on Electronic Processes in Organic Materials 1990; mem. Editorial Bd, Mol. Cryst. Liq. Cryst. 1965–94; Fellow, American Physics Soc., New York Acad. of Sciences, AAAS; Fulbright Scholar 1981, Citation of Honor, US Dept of Energy 1988, Citation of Honor, Gordon Research Confs 1990, Townsend Harris Medal, CUNY 1996, Royal Society Davy Medal for "his pioneering work in the field of molecular semiconductors" 2006, Distinguished Lecturer, CUNY Center for Advanced Tech. 2006. *Publications:* Electronic Processes in Organic Crystals (co-author) 1982, Electronic Processes in Organic Crystals and Polymers (co-author) 1992; more than 100 scientific papers in professional journals. *Address:* Department of Chemistry, New York University, 100 Washington Square East, Room 1001, New York, NY 10003-6688, USA (office). *Telephone:* (212) 998-8414 (office). *Fax:* (212) 252-6605 (office). *E-mail:* martin.pope@nyu.edu (office); martin_pope@nyu.edu (office). *Website:* chemxserver.chem.nyu.edu/MPope/index.htm (office).

POPESCU, Dan Mircea, DJur; Romanian politician; *Vice-President, Senate;* b. 6 Oct. 1950, Bucharest; m.; one c.; ed Faculty of Law, Bucharest Univ.; legal adviser, then researcher at Inst. of Political Sciences, Bucharest and Lecturer in Int. Relations, Acad. of Socio-Political Studies, Bucharest 1975–89; mem. Council Nat. Salvation Front, then mem. of Provisional Council of Nat. Union; Presidential Adviser for matters of domestic policy Dec. 1990; Minister of State for Living Standards and Social Security 1991; Minister of Labour and Social Protection 1991–92, Minister of State, Minister of Labour and Social Protection 1992–96; Deputy Prime Minister 1992–96; Dir Romanian Inst. of Social-Democratic Studies 1999–2001; Vice-Pres. Party of Social Democracy in Romania, mem. Exec. Bureau 2001–; Senator 1992–, Pres. Nat. Council 2005–; Pres. Labour Comm. of Senate 1996–2000, Econ. Comm. of Senate 2000–, Vice-Pres. Senate 2003–; Minister of Labour, Social Solidarity and Family 2004; mem. Ass. Council of Europe (Socialist Group) 2003–; Nat. Order of Faithful Service 2003; Grosser Verdienstkreuz mit Stern (Germany) 2005. *Publications:* books and studies in the field of political sciences. *Address:* Senatul României, Calea 13 Septembre 1–3, Bucharest (office); 42–46 Aurel Vlaicu Street, Bucharest, Romania (home). *Telephone:* (21) 3124198 (office). *Fax:* (21) 3158928 (office). *E-mail:* dmpopescu@senat.ro (office).

POPESCU, Dumitru Radu; Romanian writer and editor; *Director General, Editura Academiei Române;* b. 19 Aug. 1935, Păusa Village, Bihor Co.; ed Colls of Medicine and Philology, Cluj; reporter, literary magazine Steaua 1956–69; Ed.-in-Chief literary magazine Tribuna 1969–82, Contemporanul 1982; Dir Gen., Editurii Academiei Române 2006–; Alt. mem. Cen. Cttee Romanian CP 1968–89, mem. 1979–90; Chair. Romanian Writers' Union

1980–90; Corresp. mem. Romanian Acad. 1997–; in custody Jan. 1990; Prize of the Writers' Union 1964, 1969, 1974, 1977, 1980, Prize of the Romanian Acad. 1970, Grand Prize for Balkan Writers 1998, Writers' Union Prize 1994, Writers' Asscn of Bucharest Prize 1997, Grand Prize Camil Petrescu 1995. *Publications:* collections of short stories: Fuga (Flight) 1958, Fata de la miazăzi (A Girl from the South) 1964, Somnul pămîntului (The Earth's Sleep) 1965, Dor (Longing) 1966, Umbrela de soare (The Parasol) 1967, Prea mic pentru un război aşa de mare (Too Little for Such a Big War) 1969, Duios Anastasia trecea (Tenderly Anastasia Passed) 1967, Leul albastru (The Blue Lion) 1981, The Ice Bridge 1980, the Lame Hare 1981, God in the Kitchen 1994, Truman Capote and Nicolae 1995; novels: Zilele săptămînii (Weekdays) 1959, Vara oltenilor (The Oltenians' Summer) 1964, F 1964, Vînătoarea regală (Royal Hunt) 1973, O bere pentru calul meu (A Beer for My Horse) 1974, Ploile de dincolo de vreme (Rains beyond Time) 1976, Impăratul norilor (Emperor of the Clouds) 1976; plays: Vara imposibilei iubiri (The Summer of Impossible Love) 1966, Vis (Dream) 1968, Aceşti îngeri trişti (Those Sad Angels) 1969, Pisica în noaptea Anului nou (Cat on the New Year's Eve) 1970, Pasărea Shakespeare (The Shakespeare Bird) 1973, Rezervaţia de pelicani (The Pelican Reservation) 1983, Iepurele şchiop (The Lame Rabbit) 1980, Orasul îngerilor (The Angel's City) 1985, Powder Mill 1989, The Bride with False Eyelashes 1994, Love is like a Scab 1995; poems: Cîinele de fosfor (The Phosphorus Dog) 1981; essays: Virgule (Commas) 1978, Galaxy 1994, Ophelia's Complex 1998. *Address:* Editura Academiei Române, 050711 Bucharest 5, Calea 13 Septembrie nr. 13, Romania (office). *Telephone:* (21) 3188146 (office). *Fax:* (21) 3182444 (office). *Website:* www.ear.ro (office).

POPESCU, Ioan-Iovitz (Iovitzu), PhD; Romanian professor of optics and plasma physics; *Director, Romanian Centre for Induced Gamma Emission;* b. 1 Oct. 1932, Burila-Mare; s. of Dumitru Popescu and Elvira Popescu; m. Georgeta-Denisa Chiru 1963; ed Univ. of Bucharest; Asst Prof. of Optics and Gaseous Electronics, Univ. of Bucharest 1955–60, Prof., Faculty of Physics 1972–, Dean 1972–77, Rector of Univ. of Bucharest 1981–89; Head of Plasma Physics Lab., Inst. of Physics, Bucharest 1960–67, Scientific Deputy Dir 1970–72; Dir Inst. of Physics and Radiation Tech. 1977–81, Romanian Centre for Induced Gamma Emission 1995–; Alexander von Humboldt Dozenten Stipendium, Kiel Univ. 1967–69; Corresp. mem. Romanian Acad. 1974, Full mem. 1990 (Pres. Physics Section 1990–92); Hon. Citizen of Mehedintzi Co. 1997; Labour Order of Romania 1964, Scientific Merit Order 1981, Commdr Loyal Service Nat. Order 2000; Dr hc (Univ. of Craiova) 1998; Prize for Physics, Romanian Acad. 1966. *Publications:* Ionized Gases 1965, General Physics 1971–75, Plasma Physics and Applications 1981, Plasma Spectroscopy 1987, Optics 1988, The Nobel Prizes for Physics 1901–1998 1998; 165 scientific papers cited in about 1,500 foreign works; numerous articles on gas discharges and pioneering works in optogalvanic and multiphoton spectroscopy. *Leisure interest:* scientometrics, linguistics. *Address:* IGE Foundation, PO Box 34–81, 70350 Bucharest (office); Str. Fizicienilor 6, Bloc M4, Apt 6, 077125 Magurele, Bucharest, Romania (home). *Telephone:* (1) 4574180 (home). *E-mail:* iovitzu@gmail.com (home). *Website:* www.geocities.com/iipopescu (home).

POPESCU, Gen. Mihail Eugeniu, PhD; Romanian army officer; b. 1 April 1948, Carlogani, Olt County; m.; one d.; ed Artillery Officers Mil. School, Mil. Acad., Nat. Defence Coll.; command position, platoon artillery battalion 1969–82; Deputy Commdr and Artillery Chief of Mechanized Div. 1982–92; Artillery Chief 4th Transylvania Army 1984–92; Insp.-Gen. of Artillery, Artillery Gen. Inspectorate 1992–93; Artillery Insp., Gen. Staff Inspectorate 1993–97; Chief of Instruction and Doctrine Directorate, Chief of Army Staff 1997–2000; Chief of Gen. Staff 2000–06; apptd Gen. 2000. *Address:* c/o Ministry of National Defence, 77303 Bucharest, Str. Izvor 13–15, Sector 5, Romania (office).

POPESCU-TĂRICEANU, Călin Constantin Anton, MSc; Romanian politician; *Leader, National Liberal Party parliamentary group;* b. 14 Jan. 1952; m. Ioana Popescu-Tăriceanu; two c.; ed Univ. of Bucharest, Inst. of Civil Eng; started as engineer, Nat. Water Admin, Argeş Co. 1976–77, Industrial Building Co., Bucharest 1977–79; Prof., Faculty of Hydro-technology, Inst. of Civil Eng, Bucharest 1980–91; f. Radio Contact, Romania's first pvt. radio network 1990, Gen. Man. 1992–96; f. Partidul Naţional Liberal (PNL— Nat. Liberal Party) 1990, Exec. Sec. 1990–92, Deputy Chair. 1993–2004, Pres. 2004–05; mem. Constituent Ass. (Parl.) 1990–92, 1996–, Leader of PNL parl. group 2008–; Deputy Prime Minister 1996–97; Minister of Industry and Trade 1996–97; Prime Minister of Romania 2005–08; mem. Economy, Reform and Privatization Comm. 1996–2000; Vice-Pres. Fiscal and Budgetary Policies Comm. 2000–; Assoc. Partner, Automotive Trading Services 1993–; Founding mem. and Chair. Automobile and Importers Asscn 1994–97, 2001–03, Hon. Pres. 2003–. *Publications:* 37 scientific papers and articles on water treatment and distribution. *Address:* Partidul Naţional Liberal, 011866 Bucharest, Blvd Aviatorilor 86, Romania (office). *Telephone:* (21) 2310795 (office). *Fax:* (21) 2310796 (office). *E-mail:* dre@pnl.ro (office). *Website:* www.pnl.ro (office).

POPOFF, Frank Peter, MBA; American business executive and academic; *Harold A. 'Red' Poling Chair of Business and Government, Kelley School of Business, Indiana University;* b. 27 Oct. 1935, Sofia, Bulgaria; s. of Eftim Popoff and Stoyanka Kossoroff; m. Jean Urse; three s.; ed Indiana Univ.; with Dow Chemical Co. 1959–2000, Exec. Vice-Pres. 1985–87, Pres. 1987–92, CEO 1987–96, Chair. 1992–2000, Dir Emer. 2000–; Exec. Vice-Pres., then Pres. Dow Chemical European subsidiary, Switzerland 1976–85; Dir Dow Corning Corpn, Chemical Bank & Trust Co., Midland, The Salk Inst., American Express Co., Shin-Etsu Chemical Co. Ltd, Chemical Financial Corpn, United Technologies Corpn, Qwest Communications International Inc.; mem. Société de Chimie Industrielle (American Section), Chemical Mfrs Asscn (Bd of Dirs); Harold A. "Red" Poling Chair. of Business and Govt, Kelley School of Business, Indiana Univ. 2001–. *Address:* Kelley School of Business, Indiana University, 1309 East Street, Bloomington, IN 47405, USA. *Telephone:* (812) 855-8100 (office). *Website:* www.bus.indiana.edu (office).

POPOV, Anatolii Aleksandrovich, DEconSci; Russian/Chechen politician; b. 10 July 1960, Sovetskoye village, Volgograd Oblast; m.; one s.; ed Volgograd Agricultural Inst.; fmr researcher, agricultural scientific research inst. and irrigation farming scientific research inst.; Sec. of Gorodishchenskii Raion (dist) Cttee of V.I. Lenin Young Communist League (Komsomol), Volgograd Oblast; Adviser to the Council of Ministers of the USSR; fmr Deputy to Head of Man. MENATEP Bank; Financial Dir Rosoboroneksport (Russian Defence Export) State Corpn April–Sept. 1998; fmr Deputy Leader Dept of Food Resources, Govt of Moscow City; Head Centre for Econ. Strategy, Volgograd Oblast; Dir Centre of School of Investment Man. VAPK, Acad. of Nat. Economy, Govt of Russian Fed.; apptd Gen. Dir Direction for the Works of Construction-Restoration in Chechnya (state firm responsible for rebuilding Chechnya) 2001; Deputy Chair. Comm. for the Reconstruction of Chechnya 2002; Prime Minister of the Govt of Chechnya Feb.–Aug. 2003; Acting Pres. Aug.–Oct. 2003; Presidential Asst in Charge of Domestic Politics Dept 2004–. *Address:* c/o Office of the Government, Krasnopresnenskaya nab. 2, 103274 Moscow, Russia (office).

POPOV, Dmitar; Bulgarian politician and judge; fmr judge and Chair. Sofia Municipal Court; Prime Minister of Bulgaria 1990–91.

POPOV, Gavriil Kharitonovich, DEcon; Russian politician and economist; b. 31 Oct. 1936, Moscow; s. of Khariton Popov and Theodora Popov; m. Irina Popov 1968; two s.; ed Moscow State Univ.; mem. CPSU 1959–90; teacher at Moscow Univ. 1960–89, Dean of Econ. Faculty 1977–80; introduced man. and business studies to Moscow Univ., Prof. 1971–; Ed.-in-Chief of journal Voprosy ekonomiki (Questions of Economics) 1988–90; People's Deputy of USSR 1989–91; Co-Chair. Inter-regional Group of Deputies, pressing for radical change; Chair. Moscow City Soviet 1990–91; Mayor of Moscow 1991–92 (resgnd); mem. Consultative Council 1991–2000 (Chair, Foreign Policy Cttee 1996–2000); Pres. Int. Univ. 1991–, Int. Union of Economists 1991–, Free Econ. Soc. of Russia 1991–; Chair. Russian Democratic Reform Movt (RDDR) 1992–; mem. Political Council, Social Democracy Party of Russia 2001–; M. Lomonosov Prize. *Publications include:* more than a dozen books on theory of man. and current political and econ. problems. *Leisure interest:* bees. *Address:* Nikitsky Pereulok 5, 103009 Moscow, Russia. *Telephone:* (495) 956-69-90. *Fax:* (495) 956-80-77.

POPOV, Mihai, DHisSc; Moldovan diplomatist and philologist; b. 1949, Chebruchi, Sloboza Region; ed Kishinev State Univ., Diplomatic Acad. in Moscow; worked as Komsomol and CSPU functionary in Kishinev 1973–83; diplomatic service since 1983; First Counsellor, USSR Embassy, Romania 1986–92; Minister-Counsellor, Moldovan Embassy, Russia 1992–93; Amb. to Belgium 1993–94; Minister of Foreign Affairs 1994–96; Amb. to France 1996–2002; Amb. to Belgium and Rep. to NATO and EU 2002–04; currently Special Advisor for Moldova and European Neighbourhood, East West Inst. (EWI), Brussels. *Address:* EWI Brussels Centre, 83-85 Rue de la Loi, 1040, 1040 Brussels, Belgium (office). *Telephone:* (2) 743-46-10 (office). *Fax:* (2) 743-46-39 (office). *E-mail:* brussels@ewi.info (office). *Website:* www.ewi.info (office).

POPOV, Vadim Aleksandrovich; Belarusian politician; *Chairman, Palata Predstaviteley (House of Representatives);* b. 1940, Demidov, Smolensk Oblast, Russia; m.; two c.; ed Minsk Higher CPSU School, Belarus State Inst. of Agric. Mechanisation; army service 1961–64; Komsomol functionary 1964–71; Dir Sovkhoz Mogilev region 1972–76; party functionary, instructor, Head of Div. Mogilev Regional CP Cttee, First Sec. 1976–92; instructor, Cen. Cttee CP of Belarus 1976–92; worked in agric. roles in complex of Mogilev region 1992–99; First Deputy Minister of Agric. and Food March–July 1999, Minister July–Nov. 2000; mem. Palata Predstaviteley (House of Reps), Nat. Ass. (Parl.) 2000–, Chair. 2000–04, 2007–; Deputy Prime Minister March–June 2001, Prime Minister June–Nov. 2001; Order, Labour Red Banner, three medals; Hon. Diploma Supreme Soviet Belarus SSR. *Address:* House of Representatives, 220010 Minsk, vul. Savetskaya 11, Belarus (office). *Telephone:* (17) 227-25-14 (office). *Fax:* (17) 222-31-78 (office). *E-mail:* admin@gov.house.by (office). *Website:* house.gov.by (office).

POPOV, Viktor Ivanovich, DS; Russian diplomatist (retd); b. 19 May 1918, Moscow; m. Natalia Aleksandrovna Popova; two s.; ed Moscow Inst. of History and Philosophy, Higher Diplomatic School of USSR Ministry of Foreign Affairs; joined Ministry of Foreign Affairs 1954, Counsellor, Democratic Repub. of Viet Nam 1960–61, Embassy in Australia 1967–68, Minister-Counsellor, Embassy in UK 1968; Rector of Acad. of Diplomacy of USSR and Amb. on special assignments, including Iran and Afghanistan, UN Gen. Assembly and UNESCO 1968; Amb. to UK 1980–86; Counsellor, Foreign Ministry 1986–91; Prof. Moscow State Univ., Diplomatic Acad. 1991–; mem. Cen. Auditing Comm. of CPSU 1981–87; USSR State Prize in History, Merited Scientific Worker of the RSFSR, many other Soviet and foreign awards. *Publications:* Anglo-Soviet Relations 1927–29, Anglo-Soviet Relations 1929–37, History of Diplomacy series (co-author), The Country of Traditions Changes 1991, Margaret Thatcher 1991, Life in Buckingham Palace 1993, Queen's Counsellor–Superagent of the Kremlin 1995, Queen Elizabeth II and the Royal Family 1996 and other publications on international relations and USSR foreign policy. *Leisure interests:* tennis, angling, reading. *Address:* Leontyevski per. 14, Apt. 2, 103009 Moscow, Russia. *Telephone:* (495) 229-89-36.

POPOV, Yevgeny Anatolyevich; Russian writer; b. 5 Jan. 1946, Krasnoyarsk; m. Svetlana Anatoliyevna Vasilyeva; one s.; ed Moscow Inst. of Geological Survey; worked as geologist in various regions 1968–73; mem.

USSR Union of Writers 1978, expelled 1979, readmitted 1988; Assoc. mem. Swedish PEN 1980–; founder and mem. bd Russian PEN 1989–; Venets Prize (Corona), Moscow 2000. *Publications:* The Merriment of Old Russia (short stories) 1981, Awaiting Untreacherous Love (short stories) 1989, Wonderfulness of Life (novel) 1990, A Plane to Cologne (short stories) 1991, On the Eve, On the Eve (novel) 1993, The Soul of a Patriot (novel) 1994, Green Musicians (novel) 1998, Thirteen (essays) 1999, Badly Tempered Piano (play), The Bold Boy (play) 2000, A Quiet Barque Named 'Hope' (short stories) 2001, Master Chaos (novel) 2002, Communists (novel) 2003, The Bold Boy (prose, co-author) 2004, Beggars' Opera (prose) 2006. *Address:* Leningradsky prospect 26, korp. 2, Apt 52, 125040 Moscow, Russia. *Telephone:* (495) 612-33-97. *Fax:* (495) 612-33-97. *E-mail:* popov1984@yandex.ru (home).

POPOVIČ, Štěpán, CSc; Czech engineer; *Director-General, Glav Union;* b. 28 Dec. 1945, Ústí nad Labem; m. Iva Popovič; one s. one d.; ed Mechanical Eng and Textile Coll., Liberec, Econs Univ., Prague; with Sklo Union Teplice 1968–89, Dir-Gen. 1989; Dir-Gen. Glav Union 1991–; currently Country Man. for Czech Operations and Gen. Man. Russian Operations, Glaverbel; Pres. Union of Industry and Transport 1992–2000; Chair. of Bd FC Teplice 2000–01; Man. of the Year 1993, 1998. *Leisure interests:* sport, music, playing the piano. *Address:* Glaverbel Czech, Sklářská 450, Teplice, Czech Republic (office). *Telephone:* (417) 502100 (office). *Fax:* (417) 502104 (office). *E-mail:* stepan .popovic@glaverbel.com.cz (office). *Website:* www.glaverbel.com (office).

POPOVSKI, Nikola, MA; Macedonian government minister; b. 24 May 1962, Skopje; ed Univ. of Skopje; mem. Skopje Ass. including service in Ministry of Devt and Cabinet Office of Pres. 1986–90; elected mem. of Parl. 1992–, Chair. Foreign Policy Cttee 1992–94, Environment, Youth and Sport Cttee 1995–98, Financing and Budget Cttee 1998–2002; mem. Parl. Ass., Council of Europe 1993–2002; Pres. of Macedonian Parl. 2002–03; Minister of Finance 2003–06; mem. Social Democratic Alliance of Macedonia (Socijaldemokratski Sojuz na Makedonija). *Address:* Social Democratic Alliance of Macedonia (Socijaldemokratski Sojuz na Makedonija), Bihačka 8, 1000 Skopje, Republic of Macedonia (office). *Telephone:* (2) 3293101 (office). *Fax:* (2) 3293111 (office). *E-mail:* nikopop@yahoo.com (home). *Website:* www.sdsm.org.mk (office).

POPPER, Frank Geoffrey, DèsL; British/French art historian; b. (Franz Gottfried Popper), 17 April 1918, Prague, Czech Repub.; s. of Otto Popper and Paula Goldmann; m. 1st Hella Guth 1946; m. 2nd Aline Dallier 1973; ed Univ. of Paris IV (Paris-Sorbonne); voluntary service in RAF 1941–46; Dir of shipping and travel agencies 1947–53; mem. research group Inst. of Aesthetics, Paris 1961–68; Asst Prof. of Aesthetics and the Science of Art, Univ. of Paris VIII (Vincennes à St-Denis) 1969–71, Dir of Art Dept 1970–83, Temp. Reader 1971–73, Reader 1973–75, Prof. 1975–, Full Prof. 1976–, Prof. Emer. 1985–; also organizes art exhbns; Chevalier, Ordre nat. du Mérite 1998, Commdr, Ordre des Arts et des Lettres 2004. *Publications include:* Kunst-Licht-Kunst (exhbn catalogue) 1966, Lumière et Mouvement (exhbn catalogue) 1967, Naissance de l'Art Cinétique 1967, Origins and Development of Kinetic Art 1968, Art, Action and Participation 1975, Agam 1976, Electra, Electricity and Electronics in the Art of the Twentieth Century (exhbn catalogue) 1983, Art of the Electronic Age 1993, Réflexions sur l'Exil, l'Art et l'Europe 1998, From Technological to Virtual Art 2005. *Leisure interests:* chess, music, literature. *Address:* 6 rue du Marché Saint-Honoré, 75001 Paris, France (home). *Telephone:* 1-42-61-21-38 (home). *Fax:* 1-42-61-21-38 (home). *E-mail:* fpopper@club-internet.fr (home). *Website:* www.arpla.univ-paris8.fr (office).

PORNCHAI, Rujiprapa, BSc, MSc, PhD; Thai business executive and fmr government official; *Chairman, PTT Public Company Ltd;* b. 19 April 1952; ed Kasetsart Univ. of Econs, Thammasart Univ., Univ. of Pennsylvania, USA; fmr Deputy Sec.-Gen. Nat. Econ. and Social Devt Bd; fmr Dir Regional Econ. Devt Cooperation Cttee Office (REDCCO); fmr Exec. Dir Office of the E Seaboard Devt Cttee (OESB); fmr Exec. Dir Office of the S Seaboard Devt Cttee (OSSB); Deputy Perm. Sec. of Energy, Ministry of Energy 2003–06, Perm. Sec. of Energy 2006–; Chair. and Dir Electricity Generating Public Co. (EGCO) –2007 (resgnd); currently Chair. PTT Public Co. Ltd; Chair. Electricity Generating Authority of Thailand. *Address:* PTT Public Co. Ltd, 555 Vibhavadi Rangsit Road, Chatuchak, Bangkok 10900, Thailand (office). *Telephone:* (2) 537-2000 (office). *Fax:* (2) 537-3499 (office). *Website:* www.pttplc .como (office).

POROKHOVSHCHIKOV, Aleksander Shalvovich; Russian actor, film director and scriptwriter; b. 31 Jan. 1939, Moscow; s. of Mikhail Nikolaevich Dudin and Galina Aleksandrovna Porokhovshchikova; m. Irina Valeryevna Zhukova 1995; ed Chelyabinsk Inst. of Medicine, Shchukin High School of Theatre Art; worked in Satire Theatre 1966–71, Taganka Theatre 1971–81, A. Pushkin Theatre 1981–; f. first Russian pvt. film studio Rodina 1987–, Dir Studio; Pres. Cultural Centre "House of A. A. Porokhovshchikov 1871"; Prof. Russian Acad. of Theatre Art; Main Prize Scochi Film Market (Russia) 1993, Spectators Prize, Tver Film Festival, Golden Sail Prize, St Raphaël Russian Film Festival (France) 1994 (all for Film Memory); People's Artist of Russia. *Roles in drama productions include:* Profitable Position, Inspector, Lighting but not Warming, Optimistic Tragedy. *Roles in films include:* Ring 1973, The Star of Captivating Happiness 1975, Diamonds for the Proletariat Dictatorship 1976, Seek the Wind 1979, Family Circle 1980, Living Target 1989, Heir 1992. *Films directed:* The Ninth of May 1988, dir, scriptwriter and actor: Uncensored Memory 1991. *Leisure interests:* music, piano playing, jazz band, nature, diving. *Address:* Prospekt Mira 180, Apt 169, 129366 Moscow, Russia. *Telephone:* (495) 245-26-47. *Fax:* (495) 245-26-47. *E-mail:* vyatkin@npi.ru (home).

POROSHENKO, Petro Oleksiyovych; Ukrainian business executive and politician; *Chairman, Council, Natsionalny Bank Ukrainy (National Bank of Ukraine);* b. 26 Sept. 1965, Bolhrad, Odesa Oblast; ed Taras Shevchenko Univ., Kyiv; Deputy Dir-Gen. Respublika Asscn of Small Businesses and Businessmen 1990–91; Pres. Birzhovy Dim Ukraine 1991–93; Pres. and prin. shareholder PJSC Ukrprominvest 1993–98 (holding co. with control of Roshen confectionary, Mriya bank, Radomysh brewery, Leninsak Kuznia Works, Lutsk automobile plant, Cherkasy bus plant, Channel 5 (5 Kanal) TV station, now Hon. Pres.; mem. Verkhovna Rada (Parl.) 1998–, Chair. Sub-cttee for Securities, Stock and Investment Markets 2000, Budget Cttee 2002–04, currently Chair. Finance and Banking Cttee; mem. United Social Democratic Party of Ukraine –2000; f. Solidarnist party 2000, then joined Party of Regions, then joined Our Ukraine party 2001; apptd mem. Pres.'s Coordinating Council for the Securities Market 1998; Deputy Man. Viktor Yushchenko's presidential campaign 2004; Sec. Nat. Security and Defence Council 2005; Chair. Council of Nat. Bank of Ukraine 2007–; State Prize of Ukraine, Merited Economist of Ukraine, Pylyp Orlyk Int. Prize. *Address:* Natsionalny Bank Ukrainy, 01601 Kyiv, vul. Institutska 9, Ukraine (office). *Telephone:* (44) 253-38-22 (office). *Fax:* (44) 230-20-33 (office). *E-mail:* postmaster@bank.gov.ua (office); press@poroshenko.com.ua; postmaster@ bank.gov.ua (office). *Website:* www.bank.gov.ua (office); www.poroshenko.com .ua (office).

PORPHYRIOS, Demetri; Greek architect; ed Princeton Univ., USA; teacher, Architectural Asscn, London; architect, designed an extension to Magdalen Coll., Oxford, UK; fmr mem. Council Inst. of Architecture. *Publications include:* Classical Architecture.

PORRITT, Sir Jonathon Espie, 2nd Bt, cr. 1963, CBE, BA; British environmentalist and writer; *Founding Director, Forum for the Future;* b. 6 July 1950, London; s. of the late Lord Porritt, 11th Gov.-Gen. of NZ; m. Sarah Staniforth 1986; two d.; ed Eton Coll. and Magdalen Coll. Oxford; trained as a barrister; English teacher, St Clement Danes Grammar School (later Burlington Danes School), Shepherd's Bush, West London 1975–84; Head of English, Burlington Danes School, London 1980–84; Chair. Ecology Party 1979–80, 1982–84; parl. cand. at gen. elections in 1979, 1983; Dir Friends of the Earth 1984–90; Founder Dir Forum for the Future 1996–; Chair. UK Sustainable Devt Comm. 2000–; Co-Dir Prince of Wales Business and Environment Programme; mem. Bd South West Regional Devt Agency 2000, Wessex Water; adviser to many bodies on environmental matters, as well as to individuals, including Prince Charles and Chief Exec. of Marks & Spencer; mem. Advisory Bd BBC Wildlife magazine; Patron Optimum Population Trust. *Publications:* Seeing Green: The Politics of Ecology Explained 1984, Friends of the Earth Handbook 1987, The Coming of the Greens 1988, Save the Earth (ed.) 1990, Where on Earth are We Going? 1991, Captain Eco (for children) 1991, The 'Reader's Digest' Good Beach Guide 1994, Liberty and Sustainability: Where One Person's Freedom is Another's Nuisance 1995, Playing Safe: Science and the Environment (Prospects for Tomorrow) 2000, Making the Net Work: Sustainable Development in a Digital Society 2004, Capitalism: As if the World Matters 2005 (revised edn 2007). *Leisure interests:* walking, cooking. *Address:* 9 Imperial Square, Cheltenham, Glos., GL50 1QB; 9 Lypiatt Terrace, Cheltenham, Glos., GL50 2SX, England (home). *Telephone:* (1242) 262737 (office). *Fax:* (1242) 262757 (office). *E-mail:* a.paintin@forumforthefuture.org.uk (office). *Website:* www.jonathonporritt .com.

PORTAS, Paulo Sacadura Cabral, LLD; Portuguese politician and journalist; b. 12 Sept. 1962, Lisbon; s. of Nuno Portas and Helena de Sacadura Cabral; ed Univ. Católica de Lisboa; began career as journalist with O Tempo (newspaper); mem. political comm. for presidential candidature of Freitas do Amaral 1986; mem. Grupo de Ofir (reform group) 1986; f. O Independente (weekly newspaper) 1988, Dir –1995; jt founder Instituto de Estudos Políticos 1995; Deputy, Assembleia da República (parl.), (CDS/Partido Popular) 1995– (Parl. Leader 1999–2001); Lecturer, Dept of Politics, Univ. Moderna 1995–97; Municipal Deputy, Oliveira de Azeméis 1997; fmr Pres. CDS/Partido Popular (now Partido Popular); fmr MEP; Speaker, Câmara Municipal de Lisboa 2001; Minister of State and of Nat. Defence 2002–05; Distinguished Public Service Award, US Defense Dept 2005. *Address:* c/o Assembleia da República, Palácio de S. Bento, 1249-068 Lisbon, Portugal (office).

PORTER, Andrew Brian, MA; British music critic; *Music Critic, Times Literary Supplement;* b. 26 Aug. 1928, Cape Town, South Africa; s. of Andrew Ferdinand and Vera Sybil Porter (née Bloxham); ed Diocesan Coll., Rondebosch, Cape Town, Univ. Coll., Oxford; music critic, The Financial Times 1950–74; Ed. The Musical Times 1960–67; music critic, The New Yorker 1972–92, The Observer 1992–97, Times Literary Supplement 1997–; Visiting Fellow, All Souls Coll., Oxford 1973–74; Bloch Prof., Univ. of Calif., Berkeley 1981; Corresp. mem. American Musicological Soc. 1993; ASCAP–Deems Taylor Award 1975, 1978, 1982, Nat. Music Theater Award 1988, Words on Music: Essays in Honour of Andrew Porter on the Occasion of His 75th Birthday (co-ed. by David Rosen and Claire Brook) 2003. *Opera:* librettos for The Tempest 1985, The Song of Majnun 1991 and numerous trans. *Publications:* A Musical Season 1974, Wagner's Ring 1976, Music of Three Seasons 1974–77 1978, Music of Three More Seasons 1977–80 1981, Musical Events: A Chronicle 1980–1983 1987, Musical Events: A Chronicle 1983–1986 1989, Verdi's Macbeth: A Sourcebook (ed. with David Rosen) 1984, A Music Critic Remembers 2000; contrib. to Music and Letters, Musical Quarterly, Musical Times, Proceedings of the Royal Musical Association, Atti del Congresso Internazionale di Studi Verdiani. *Leisure interest:* architecture. *Address:* 9 Pembroke Walk, London, W8 6PQ, England (home).

PORTER, Michael E., BSE, MBA, PhD; American economist, academic and consultant; *Bishop William Lawrence University Professor and Director, Institute for Strategy and Competitiveness, Harvard Business School;* b. Ann Arbor, Mich.; two d.; ed Princeton Univ., Harvard Business School, Harvard

Univ.; currently Bishop William Lawrence Univ. Prof., Harvard Business School, also Dir Inst. for Strategy and Competitiveness 2001–; adviser to local and nat. govts; mem. Exec. Cttee Council on Competitiveness; co-Chair. Global Competitiveness Report; has led studies for Govts of India, NZ Canada and Portugal; advises on competitive strategy for US and int. cos including DuPont, Procter & Gamble, Royal Dutch Shell, Taiwan Semiconductor Manufacturing Co.; mem. Bd of Dirs Parametric Technology Corpn, Thermo Electron Corpn; Co-founder an Sr Advisor, Center for Effective Philanthropy; Fellow, Acad. of Man., Royal Swedish Acad. of Eng Sciences, Int. Acad. of Man.; Creu de St Jordi (Spain), Jose Dolores Estrada Order of Merit (Nicaragua), Hon. FRSE 2005; Dr hc (HHL, Leipzig, Univ. of Iceland, Univ. of Los Andres, Colombia, Stockholm School of Econs, Sweden, Erasmus Univ., Netherlands, Hautes Ecoles Commerciales, France, Univ. Tech. de Lisboa, Portugal, Adolfo Ibanez Univ., Chile, INCAE, Central America, Johnson and Wales Univ., Mount Ida Coll.); six McKinsey Awards (for best Harvard Business Review article of the year), Charles Coolidge Parlin Award, American Marketing Asscn 1991, Richard D. Irwin Outstanding Educator in Business Policy and Strategy, Acad. of Man. 1993, Adam Smith Award, Nat. Asscn of Business Economists 1997, Distinguished Award for Contribs in the field of Man. 1998, Acad. of Man. 2003, John Kenneth Galbraith Medal, American Agricultural Econs Asscn 2005, Lifetime Achievement Award, US Econ. Devt Agency 2008. *Publications:* author of 18 books including Competitive Strategy: Techniques for Analyzing Industries and Competitors 1980, Competitive Advantage: Creating and Sustaining Superior Performance (George R. Terry Book Award Acad. of Man.) 1985, The Competitive Advantage of Nations 1990, On Competition 1998, 2008, Can Japan Compete? 2000, Redefining Health Care 2006; contrib. over 125 essays and articles to magazines, journals and newspapers. *Address:* Institute for Strategy and Competitiveness, Ludcke House, Harvard Business School, Soldiers Field Road, Boston, MA 02163, USA (office). *Telephone:* (617) 495-6309 (office). *Fax:* (6170 547-8543 (office). *E-mail:* mporter@hbs.edu (office). *Website:* www.isc.hbs.edu (office).

PORTER, Neil Anthony, PhD, DSc, FInstP, MRIA, FRAS; British physicist and academic; *Professor Emeritus of Electron Physics, University College, Dublin;* b. 4 Sept. 1930, Manchester; s. of Francis Porter and Nora Porter; m. Sheila B. Dunn 1959; one d.; ed St Bede's Coll. Manchester, Univ. of Manchester and Dublin Inst. for Advanced Studies; Asst Univ. Coll. Dublin 1953–54; Jr and Sr Research Fellowship, AERE Harwell 1954–58; Coll. Lecturer, Univ. Coll. Dublin 1958–64, Prof. of Electron Physics 1964–88, Prof. Emer. 1989–; Visiting Prof. Univ. of Tokyo 1981, Weizmann Inst., Israel 1986–87; Hon. Consultant AERE, Harwell 1963–73, Harvard-Smithsonian Center for Astrophysics 1972–90; Dublin Symposium Award 2000. *Publications:* approximately 100 publs on high-energy astrophysics and 10 publs on the history of science; one book. *Leisure interests:* music, history of science, theology. *Address:* Department of Experimental Physics, University College, Belfield, Dublin 4 (office); 5 Westerton Rise, Dublin 16, Ireland (home). *Telephone:* (1) 7062213 (office); (1) 2987870 (home). *E-mail:* naporter@ferdia.ucd.ie (office). *Website:* www.ucd.ie/physics/experimentalphysics.html (office).

PORTER, Peter Neville Frederick, FRSL; Australian poet, writer and broadcaster; b. 16 Feb. 1929, Brisbane, Qld; s. of William R. Porter and Marion Main; m. 1st Jannice Henry 1961 (died 1974); two d.; m. 2nd Christine Berg 1991; ed Church of England Grammar School Brisbane and Toowoomba Grammar School; fmr journalist in Brisbane; came to UK 1951; worked as clerk, bookseller and advertising writer; full-time writer and broadcaster 1968–; Hon. DLitt (Melbourne) 1985, (Loughborough) 1987, (Sydney) 1999, (Queensland) 2001, Queen's Gold Medal for Poetry 2002. *Publications:* Once Bitten, Twice Bitten 1961, Penguin Modern Poets, No. 2 1962, Poems, Ancient and Modern 1964, A Porter Folio 1969, The Last of England 1970, Preaching to the Converted 1972, After Martial (trans.) 1972, Jonah (with A. Boyd) 1973, The Lady and the Unicorn (with A. Boyd) 1975, Living in a Calm Country 1975, New Poetry I (co-ed.) 1975, The Cost of Seriousness 1978, English Subtitles 1981, Collected Poems (Duff Cooper Prize) 1983, Fast Forward 1984, Narcissus (with A. Boyd) 1985, The Automatic Oracle (Whitbread Poetry Award) 1987, Mars (with A. Boyd) 1988, A Porter Selected 1989, Possible Worlds 1989, The Chair of Babel 1992, Millennial Fables 1995, New Writing (ed. with A. S. Byatt) 1997, The Oxford Book of Modern Verse (ed.) 1997, The Shared Heritage: Australian and English Literature 1997, The Oxford Book of Modern Australian Verse (ed.) 1997, Dragons in Their Pleasant Places 1997, Collected Poems 1961–1999 (two vols) 1999, Max is Missing (Forward Poetry Prize 2002) 2001, Saving from the Wreck: Essays on Poetry 2001, Rivers 2002, Afterburner 2004, Eighteen Poems 2007, Better than God 2009; contrib. to various publications. *Leisure interests:* buying records and listening to music, travelling in Italy. *Address:* 42 Cleveland Square, London, W2 6DA, England (home). *Telephone:* (20) 7262-4289 (home). *Fax:* (20) 7262-4289 (home). *E-mail:* peter.porter3@btopenworld.com (home).

PORTER, Robert, AC, MA, DM, DSc, FRACP, FAA; Australian professor of medical research; *Honorary Associate, School of Medecine and Dentistry, James Cook University;* b. 10 Sept. 1932, Port Augusta, S Australia; s. of the late William J. Porter and Amy Porter (née Tottman); m. Anne D. Steell 1961; two s. two d.; ed Univ. of Adelaide and Univ. of Oxford, UK; House Physician and House Surgeon, Radcliffe Infirmary, Oxford 1959–60; Univ. Lecturer in Physiology, Oxford 1961–67; Medical Tutor and Fellow, St Catherine's Coll. Oxford 1963–67; Prof. of Physiology, Monash Univ. 1967–80, Dean 1989–98, Deputy Vice-Chancellor 1992–93; Dir John Curtin School of Medical Research and Howard Florey Prof. of Medical Research, ANU 1980–89; Planning Dean (Medicine), James Cook Univ. of N Queensland, Townsville 1998–99, Dir Research Devt 1999–2008, currently Hon. Assoc., School of Medicine and Dentistry; Rhodes Scholar 1954; Radcliffe Travelling Fellow in Medical Science 1963–64; Sr Fulbright Fellow, Washington Univ. School of Medicine, St Louis 1973; Fogarty Scholar-in-Residence, NIH, Bethesda, Md, USA 1986–87; Chair. Nat. Expert Advisory Group on Safety and Quality in Australian Health Care 1998–2000; Fellow, Royal Australian Coll. of Medical Admins; Hon. DSc (Univ. of Sydney); Centenary Medal 2003. *Publications:* Corticospinal Neurones: Their Role in Movement (with C. G. Phillips) 1977, Corticospinal Function and Voluntary Movement (with R. N. Lemon) 1993; articles on neurophysiology. *Leisure interests:* sport, reading, photography. *Address:* 2 Denison Court, Toomulla, Queensland 4816, Australia (home). *Telephone:* (7) 4781-5330 (office); (7) 4770-7121 (home). *Fax:* (7) 4781-4655 (office). *E-mail:* robport5@bigpond.com (office). *Website:* www.jcu.edu.au/fmhms (office).

PORTES, Richard David, CBE, DPhil, FBA; American economist and academic; *Professor of Economics, London Business School;* b. 10 Dec. 1941, Chicago, Ill.; s. of Herbert Portes and Abra Halperin Portes; m. Barbara Diana Frank 1963 (divorced); one s. one d.; ed Yale Univ., Balliol and Nuffield Colls Oxford; Official Fellow and Tutor in Econs, Balliol Coll. Oxford 1965–69; Asst Prof. of Econs and Int. Affairs, Princeton Univ. 1969–72; Prof. of Econs, Birkbeck Coll., London Univ. 1972–94, Head Dept 1975–77, 1980–83, 1994; Prof. of Econs, London Business School 1995–; Pres. Centre for Econ. Policy Research, London 1983–; Directeur d'Etudes, Ecole des Hautes Etudes en Sciences Sociales, Paris 1978–; fmr Rhodes Scholar, Woodrow Wilson Fellow, Danforth Fellow; Guggenheim Fellow 1977–78; British Acad. Overseas Visiting Fellow 1977–78; Research Assoc., Nat. Bureau of Econ. Research, Cambridge, Mass 1980–; Visiting Prof., Harvard Univ. 1977–78, Univ. of California 1999–2000, Columbia Univ. Business School 2003–04; Vice-Chair. Econs Cttee Social Science Research Council 1981–84; Sec.-Gen. Royal Econ. Soc. 1992–; mem. Bd of Dirs Soc. for Econ. Analysis 1967–69, 1972–80 (Sec. 1974–77); mem. Royal Inst. of Int. Affairs 1973– (Research Cttee 1982–94), Council on Foreign Relations 1978–, Hon. Degrees Cttee, Univ. of London 1984–89; Fellow Econometric Soc. 1983–; mem. Council, Royal Econ. Soc. 1986–92 (mem. Exec. Cttee 1987–); mem. Council, European Econ. Asscn 1992–96; Co-Chair. Bd of Govs and Sr Ed., Economic Policy 1985–; mem. and fmr mem. several editorial bds; mem. Franco-British Council 1996–2002, Comm. on the Social Sciences 2000–03; Hon. DSc (Univ. Libre de Bruxelles) 2000; Hon. PhD (London Guildhall) 2000. *Publications:* The Polish Crisis 1981, Deficits and Detente 1983; Threats to International Financial Stability (co-ed.) 1987; ed.: Global Macroeconomics: Policy Conflict and Cooperation 1987, Blueprints for Exchange Rate Management 1989, Macroeconomic Policies in an Interdependent World 1989, The EMS in Transition: a CEPR Report 1989, External Constraints on Macroeconomic Policy: The European Experience 1991, The Path of Reform in Central and Eastern Europe 1991, Economic Transformation of Central Europe 1993, European Union Trade with Eastern Europe 1995, Crisis? What Crisis? Orderly Workouts for Sovereign Debtors 1995, Making Sense of Globalization 2002, Crises de la Dette 2003; numerous papers and contribs to learned journals. *Address:* London Business School, Regent's Park, London, NW1 4SA, England (office). *Telephone:* (20) 7706-6886 (office). *Fax:* (20) 7724-1598 (office). *E-mail:* rportes@london.edu (office). *Website:* faculty.london.edu/rportes (office).

PORTILLO, Rt Hon. Michael Denzil Xavier, PC, MA; British politician, writer and broadcaster; b. 26 May 1953, London; s. of Luis G. Portillo and Cora W. Blyth; m. Carolyn C. Eadie 1982; ed Harrow Co. Boys' School and Peterhouse, Cambridge; Ocean Transport & Trading Co. 1975–76; Conservative Research Dept 1976–79; Special Adviser to Sec. of State for Energy 1979–81; Kerr McGee Oil (UK) Ltd 1981–83; Special Adviser to Sec. of State for Trade and Industry 1983, to Chancellor of Exchequer 1983–84; MP for Enfield, Southgate 1984–97, for Kensington and Chelsea 1999–2005; Asst Govt Whip 1986–87; Parl. Under-Sec. of State, Dept of Health and Social Security 1987–88; Minister of State, Dept of Transport 1988–90; Minister of State for Local Govt and Inner Cities 1990–92; Chief Sec. to the Treasury 1992–94; Sec. of State for Employment 1994–95, for Defence 1995–97; Shadow Chancellor of the Exchequer 2000–01; freelance writer and broadcaster 1997–2001; Theatre Critic, The New Statesman 2004–06; adviser Kerr McGee Corpn 1997–, mem. Bd of Dirs 2006–; Chair. of jury, Man Booker Prize for Fiction 2008; columnist, The Sunday Times 2004–; Dir (non-exec.) BAE Systems PLC 2002–06; mem. Int. Comm. for Missing Persons in Fmr Yugoslavia; Pres. DebRA (charity working on behalf of people with Epidermolysis Bullosa—EB); British Chair. British-Spanish Tertulias; fmr weekly columnist, The Scotsman. *Television includes:* Portillo's Progress (three-part series for Channel 4), programme in BBC 2's Great Railway Journeys series, Art That Shook the World: Richard Wagner's Ring (BBC 2), Portillo in Euroland, Elizabeth I in the series Great Britons (BBC 2), When Michael Portillo Became a Single Mum (BBC 2) 2003. *Publications:* Clear Blue Water 1994, Democratic Values and the Currency 1998. *Address:* Office of The Rt Hon Michael Portillo, Suite 99, 34 Buckingham Palace Road, London, SW1W 0RH, England (office). *Telephone:* (20) 7931-9422 (office). *Fax:* (20) 7931-6549 (office). *E-mail:* michael@michaelportillo.co.uk (office). *Website:* www.michaelportillo.co.uk (office).

PORTILLO CABRERA, Alfonso Antonio; Guatemalan politician and fmr head of state; ed Universidad Autónoma de Guerrero, Mexico, Universidad Autónoma de México; fmr columnist, daily newspaper Siglo Veintiuno; mem. Editorial Bd Suplemento Económico Pulso; Prof. of Law, Econs and Politics in univs in Latin America; fmr Leader of Democracia Cristiana (DC) Deputies in Congress, Chair. Comm. of Econ., Foreign Trade and Integration; Asst Gen. Sec. DC, Dir DC's Centro de Estudios Socio-Políticos (IGESP); Pres. of Guatemala 2000–04; presently in Mexico, govt seeking to extradite him to face charges of corruption. *Address:* c/o Office of the President, Guatemala City, Guatemala (office).

PORTISCH, Lajos; Hungarian chess player and singer; b. 4 April 1937, Zalaegerszeg; s. of Lajos Portisch, Sr and Anna Simon; mem. MTK-Sport Club; to-ranking player of Hungary's selected team 1962–; nine times Hungarian champion; holder of Int. Grandmaster title 1961–; European team bronze medallist 1961, 1965, 1973, team silver medallist 1970, 1977, 1980; Olympic team bronze medallist 1956, 1966, silver 1970, 1972, 1980, gold 1978; qualified eight times as cand. for the individual chess world title; holder of Master Coach qualification; bass-baritone singer, gives regular concerts; positional style earned him the nickname of the "Hungarian Botvinnik"; Labour Order of Merit (Golden Degree). *Publication:* Six Hundred Endings (co-author with B. Sárközi) 1973. *Leisure interest:* music. *Address:* Néphadsereg utca 10, Hungarian Chess Federation, 1055 Budapest, Hungary. *Telephone:* (1) 111-6616.

PORTMAN, Natalie; American/Israeli actress; b. 9 June 1981, Jerusalem; ed Harvard Univ.; left Israel with her family aged three and moved to USA; discovered by modelling scout at New York pizza parlour aged 11. *Films include:* The Professional (also known as Léon) 1994, Developing 1995, Heat 1995, Beautiful Girls 1996, Everyone Says I Love You 1996, Mars Attacks! 1996, The Diary of Anne Frank 1997, Star Wars: Episode I – The Phantom Menace (as Queen Amidala) 1999, Anywhere But Here, Where the Heart Is 2000, The Seagull 2001, Zoolander 2001, Star Wars: Episode II – Attack of the Clones 2002, Cold Mountain 2003, Garden State 2004, True 2004, Closer (Best Supporting Actress, Golden Globe Awards 2005) 2004, Star Wars: Episode III – Revenge of the Sith 2005, V for Vendetta 2006, Paris, je t'aime 2006, Goya's Ghosts 2006, My Blueberry Nights 2007, Hotel Chevalier 2007, The Darjeeling Limited 2007, Mr Magorium's Wonder Emporium 2007, The Other Boleyn Girl 2008. *Theatre includes:* A Midsummer Night's Dream, Cabaret, Anne of Green Gables (title role), Tapestry. *Address:* c/o ICM, 8942 Wilshire Boulevard, Beverly Hills, CA 90211, USA (office).

PORTMAN, Rachel Mary Berkeley; British composer; b. 11 Dec. 1960, Haslemere; m. Uberto Pasolini; three d.; ed Worcester Coll., Oxford; composer of film and TV scores, for US productions 1992–; British Film Inst. Young Composer of the Year Award 1988. *Compositions for film and television:* Experience Preferred... But Not Essential 1982, The Storyteller (TV series) 1986–88, 1990, Life is Sweet 1990, Oranges Are Not the Only Fruit (TV drama) 1990, Antonia and Jane 1991, Where Angels Fear to Tread 1991, Used People 1992, The Joy Luck Club 1993, Benny and Joon 1993, Friends 1993, Sirens 1994, Only You 1994, War of the Buttons 1994, To Wong Foo – Thanks for Everything! 1995, A Pyromaniac's Love Story 1995, Smoke 1995, The Adventures of Pinocchio 1996, Marvin's Room 1996, Emma (Acad. Award 1997) 1996, Addicted to Love 1997, The Cider House Rules 1999, Chocolat 2000, The Emperor's New Clothes 2001, Hart's War 2002, The Truth About Charlie 2002, Nicholas Nickleby 2002, The Human Stain 2003, Mona Lisa Smile 2003, Lard 2004, The Manchurian Candidate 2004, Because of Winn-Dixie 2005, Oliver Twist 2006, The Lake House 2006, Infamous 2006, The Duchess 2008. *Compositions for stage:* The Little Prince 2003, H2hOpe: The Water Diviner's Tale 2007. *Recordings include:* Rachel Portman Soundtracks (compilation album), numerous soundtrack recordings. *Address:* c/o Chester-Novello, 14-15 Berners Street, London, W1T 3LJ, England (office). *Telephone:* (20) 7612-7549 (office). *Website:* www.chesternovello.com (office).

PORTMAN, Robert (Rob) Jones, BA, JD; American politician, lawyer and government official; b. 19 Dec. 1955, Cincinnati; m. Jane Dudley 1986; two s., one d.; ed Dartmouth Coll., Univ. of Mich. Law School; Assoc., Patton Boggs law firm, Washington, DC 1984–86; Pnr, Graydon, Head and Ritchey, Cincinnati 1986–89, 1991–93; Assoc. Counsel to the Pres. 1989–91, then Dir White House Office of Legis. Affairs; mem. US House of Reps, Second Dist of Ohio 1993–2005, Vice-Chair. Budget Cttee, mem. Ways and Means Cttee, Chair. House Republican Leadership; US Trade Rep. 2005–06; Dir Office of Man. and Budget (OMB) 2006–07; Founding Chair. Coalition for a Drug Free Greater Cincinnati. *Address:* c/o Office of Management and Budget, 725 17th Street and Pennsylvania Avenue, NW, Washington, DC 20503, USA (office).

PORTZAMPARC, Christian de; French architect; b. 9 May 1944, Casablanca, Morocco; s. of Maurice Urvay de Portzamparc and Annick de Boutray; m. Elizabeth Jardim Neves 1982; two s.; ed Ecole Supérieure des Beaux Arts; work includes Hautes Formes housing complex, south-east Paris; City of Music, Parc de la Villette, Paris; office bldg for Crédit Lyonnais, Lille; two housing projects in Japan and Germany, Zac Massena-Seine-Rive-gauche; retrospective exhbn, Pompidou Centre 1996; extension of Palais des Congrés de Paris 1999; French Embassy, Berlin 2000; LVMH Tower, New York (Business Week Architectural Record Prize) 2002; Artistic Creation Chair, Collége de France (first occupant) 2006–; Commdr des Arts et des Lettres; Pritzker Prize for Architecture 1994, Equerre d'argent Award 1995. *Publications:* La Cité de la musique 1986, Scènes d'atelier, Généalogie des formes 1996, Christian de Portzamparc, Le Dantec 1995, Christian de Portzamparc 1996. *Address:* 1 rue de l'Aude, 75014 Paris, France. *E-mail:* studio@chdeportzamparc.com (office). *Website:* www.chdeportzamparc.com (office).

POSNETT, Sir Richard Neil, KBE, CMG, MA; British colonial administrator, barrister and diplomatist (retd); b. 19 July 1919, Kotagiri, India; s. of Rev. Charles Walker Posnett and Phyllis Posnett (née Barker); m. 3rd Eva Inkson 2008; four s. two d. from previous marriages; ed Kingswood School, St John's Coll. Cambridge; RAF 1940; Colonial Admin. Service, Uganda 1941–62; barrister-at-law, Gray's Inn 1950; Chair. Uganda Olympic Cttee 1954–58; Judicial Adviser 1960; Perm. Sec. for External Affairs, Trade and Industry 1961–63; Foreign Office, UK 1964–66; UK Mission to UN 1966–70; briefly HM Commr, Anguilla 1969; Head of West Indian Dept, FCO 1970–72; Gov. and C-in-C, Belize 1972–76; mission to Ocean Island (Banaba) 1977; FCO Adviser on Dependent Territories 1977–79; UK Commr, Bd of British Phosphate Commrs 1978–81; High Commr in Uganda April–Nov. 1979; Gov. and C-in-C Bermuda 1981–83; Lord Chancellor's Panel of Ind. Inspectors 1983–89; Gov. Kingswood School 1985–93; Pres. Godalming-Joigny Friendship Asscn; Pres. Eddystone Housing Asscn; mem. Royal Inst. of Int. Affairs, Royal African Soc., Royal Forestry Soc.; Fellow, Royal Commonwealth Soc.; KStJ 1972. *Achievements include:* first ascent South Portal Peak, Ruwenzori, Uganda 1942. *Publications:* Looking Back at the Uganda Protectorate (contrib.) 1996, The Scent of Eucalyptus – A Journal of Colonial and Foreign Service 2001, Language and Sport in Nation Building (in Empire After); articles in World Today and Uganda Journal. *Leisure interests:* skiing, golf, growing trees. *Address:* Bahati, Old Kiln Close, Churt, Surrey, GU10 2JH, England (home). *Telephone:* (1428) 714147 (home). *E-mail:* bahati@onetel.com (office).

POSOKHIN, Mikhail Mikhailovich; Russian architect; b. 10 July 1948, Moscow; s. of Mikhail Vasilyevich Posokhin and Galina Arkadyevna Posokhina; m. 1st (divorced); one s.; m. 2nd Vitalina Kudzyavtseva; two d.; ed Moscow Inst. of Architecture; Chief Architect Dept of Civil and Residential Construction Mosproyekt-1 1976–80; head of workshop, Dept for Designs of Exemplary Perspective residential area Chertanovo 1980–82; head of workshop, Dept for Designs of Public Bldgs and Edifices Mosproyekt-2 1982–, Gen. Dir 1983; fmr Vice-Chair. Cttee on Architecture and Town-planning of Moscow 1994; mem. Presidium Russian Acad. of Arts, Int. Acad. of Architecture, Acad. Architectural Heritage; The Honour Order, Sergey Radonezhsky Order (2nd and 3rd Degrees), Moscow Daneel Godly Prince Order (2nd Degree), Golden Order of Labour (Bulgary), Golden Order, Russian Acad. of Arts; Merited Architect of Russia, State Prize of Russia, Public Acknowledgement Prize. *Works include:* numerous residential complexes and public edifices including restoration of Cathedral of Christ the Saviour, the Business Centre on Kudrinskaya Square, trade complex on Manege Square, the Gosinny Dvor, reconstruction of the Kremlin and others; 101 projects. *Address:* Mosproyekt-2, 2 Brestskaya str. 5, 123056 Moscow, Russia (office). *Telephone:* (495) 200-56-47 (office).

POSPÍŠIL, Jiří, JUDr; Czech lawyer and politician; *Minister of Justice;* b. 24 Nov. 1975, Chomutov; ed Univ. of Western Bohemia, Plzeň; early career as articled clerk in pvt law firm; mem. Civic Democratic Alliance (Občanská demokratická aliance) 1994–98; mem. Civic Democratic Party (Občanská demokratická strana) 1998–, Chair. Regional Asscn for Plzeň 2003–, mem. Exec. Council 2005–; mem. Parl. 2000–, Shadow Minister of Justice 2003–06, Minister of Justice 2006–, Vice-Chair. Constitutional-Legal Cttee 2002–06, mem. Sub-Cttee for Penal System 2002–06; Expert Asst, Admin. Law Dept, Univ. of Western Bohemia 2002–. *Address:* Ministry of Justice, Vyšehradská 16, 128 10 Prague 2, Czech Republic (office). *Telephone:* 2219977111 (office). *Fax:* 224919927 (office). *E-mail:* info@msp.justice.cz (office). *Website:* www .justice.cz (office).

POSSER DA COSTA, Guilherme; São Tomé and Príncipe politician; *Vice-President, Movimento de Libertação de São Tomé e Príncipe–Partido Social Democrata;* b. 1953; Minister of Foreign Affairs and Co-operation 1987–88, 1990–91; Prime Minister 1999–2001; Vice-Pres. Movimento de Libertação de São Tomé e Príncipe–Partido Social Democrata (MLSTP-PSD). *Address:* Movimento de Libertação de São Tomé e Príncipe–Partido Social Democrata, Riboque Cidade Capital, São Tomé e Príncipe (office). *Telephone:* (12) 22253 (office).

POST, Herschel, MA, LLB; American investment banker; *International Managing Director of Business Development, Christie's International;* b. 9 Oct. 1939; s. of the late Herschel E. Post and of Marie C. Post; m. Peggy Mayne 1963; one s. three d.; ed Yale and Harvard Univs and New Coll. Oxford; Assoc. Davis, Polk & Wordwell (attorneys) 1966–69; Exec. Dir Parks Council of New York City 1969–72; Deputy Admin., Parks, Recreation and Cultural Affairs Admin New York 1973; Vice-Pres. and Man. Euro-clear Operations, JP Morgan & Co. Brussels 1974–78; Vice-Pres. and Deputy Head, Int. Investment Dept JP Morgan, London 1978–83; Pres. Posthorn Global Asset Man. London 1984–90, Shearson Lehman Global Asset Man., London 1984–90; Deputy Chair. London Stock Exchange 1988–95, Chair. Trading Markets Managing Bd 1990–95; Trustee, Earthwatch Europe 1988– (Chair. 1997–); COO Lehman Brothers Int. Ltd 1990–94, Coutts & Co. 1994–95 (CEO, Deputy Chair. 1995–2000); Int. Man. Dir of Business Devt, Christie's Int. PLC 2000–; Chair. Woodcock Foundation 2000–; Deputy Chair. EFG Private Bank Ltd 2002–; Dir Investors Capital Trust 2000–, CRESTCO Ltd 2002–, Ahli United Bank BSC 2002–, Notting Hill Housing Group 2002–. *Address:* Christie's International PLC, 8 King Street, St James's, London, WC1Y 6QT, England (office). *Telephone:* (20) 7839-9060 (office). *Fax:* (20) 7839-1611 (office). *Website:* www.christies.com (office).

POSTE, George, CBE, PhD, FRS, FRCVS, FRCPath, BVSC; British research scientist, business executive and academic; *Del E. Webb Distinguished Professor of Biology, Regents Professor and Director, Biodesign Institute, Arizona State University;* b. 30 April 1944, Polegate, Sussex; s. of the late John H. Poste and of Kathleen B. Poste; m. Linda Suhler 1992; one s. two d.; ed Bristol Univ.; lecturer Royal Post grad. Medical School, Univ. of London 1969–72, Sr. Lecturer 1974; Assoc. Prof. of Experimental Pathology, State Univ. of New York (SUNY) Buffalo 1972–74, Principal Cancer Research Scientist and Prof. of Cell and Molecular Biology 1975–80; Vice-Pres. and Dir of Research Smith Kline & French Labs, Philadelphia, Pa 1980–83, Vice-Pres. Research and Devt Technologies 1983–86, Vice-Pres. Worldwide Research and Preclinical Devt 1987–88, Pres. Research and Devt 1988–89, Exec. Vice-Pres. Research and Devt SmithKline Beecham Pharmaceuticals 1989–91, Pres. Research and Devt 1991–97, Chief Science and Tech. Officer 1997–99; CEO Health Tech. Networks 2000–; partner Care Capital, Princeton 2000–; Research Prof. Univ. of Pa 1981–, Univ. of Tex. Medical Center 1986–; Fleming Fellow Lincoln Coll. Oxford 1995; William Pitt Fellow Pembroke Coll. Cambridge 1996–; Distinguished Visiting, Fellow, Hoover Inst., Stanford

Univ. 2000–; Del E. Webb Distinguished Prof. of Biology and Dir Biodesign Inst., Arizona State Univ. 2003–, Regents Prof. 2006–; Chair. (non-exec.) Orchid Biosciences, Princeton NJ; mem. Bd of Dirs Exelixis, Monsanto; mem. Defense Science Bd of US Dept of Defense, Chair. Task Force on Bioterrorism; mem. NAS Working Group on Defense Against Bioweapons; mem. Human Genetics Advisory Cttee 1996–; mem. Bd Govs Center for Molecular Medicine and Genetics, Stanford Univ. 1992–; mem. Alliance for Ageing 1992–97; Jt Ed. Cell Surface Reviews 1976–83, New Horizons in Therapeutics 1984–; mem. Council on Foreign Relations 2004–; Hon. FRCP 1993; Hon. Fellow Univ. Coll. London 1993; Hon. DSc 1987, (Sussex) 1999; Hon. LLD (Bristol) 1995, (Dundee) 1998; Albert Einstein Award, Global Business Leadership Council 2006. *Publications:* numerous reviews and papers in learned journals. *Leisure interests:* automobile racing, mil. history, photography, desert exploration. *Address:* The Biodesign Institute, Arizona State University, PO Box 875001, Tempe, AZ 85287-5001, USA (office). *Telephone:* (480) 727-8662 (office). *Fax:* (480) 965-2765 (office). *E-mail:* george.poste@asu.edu (office). *Website:* www.biodesign.org (office).

POSTGATE, John Raymond, DPhil, DSc, FRS, FIBiol; British microbiologist and academic; *Professor Emeritus of Microbiology, University of Sussex;* b. 24 June 1922, London; s. of Raymond William Postgate and Daisy Postgate (née Lansbury); m. Mary Stewart 1948; three d.; ed Woodstock School, Kingsbury Co. School, Balliol Coll., Oxford; Sr Research Investigator, Nat. Chemical Lab. 1949–50, Sr Prin. 1950–59; Prin., Sr Prin. Scientific Officer, Microbiology Research Establishment 1959–63; Asst Dir Agricultural and Food Research Council (AFRC) Unit of Nitrogen Fixation, Royal Veterinary Coll. 1963–65; Prof. of Microbiology, Univ. of Sussex 1965–87, Prof. Emer. 1987–, Asst Dir AFRC Unit of Nitrogen Fixation 1965–80, Dir 1980–87; Visiting Prof., Univ. of Illinois 1962–63, Oregon State Univ. 1977–78; Pres. Inst. of Biology 1982–84, Soc. for Gen. Microbiology 1984–87; Hon. DSc (Bath), Hon. LLD (Dundee). *Music:* reviewer of jazz recordings c. 1960–2005. *Publications:* Microbes and Man 1969, (fourth edn) 2000, Biological Nitrogen Fixation 1972, A Plain Man's Guide to Jazz 1973, Nitrogen Fixation 1978, (third edn) 1998, The Sulphate-Reducing Bacteria 1979, (second edn) 1984, The Fundamentals of Nitrogen Fixation 1982, The Outer Reaches of Life 1994, A Stomach for Dissent: The Life of Raymond Postgate (with Mary Postgate) 1994, Lethal Lozenges and Tainted Tea: A Biography of John Postgate (1820–1881) 2001, Looking For Frankie: A Biodiscography of the Jazz Trumpeter Frankie Newton (with Bob Weir) 2003. *Leisure interest:* listening to jazz and attempting to play it. *Address:* 1 Houndean Rise, Lewes, Sussex, BN7 1EG, England (home). *Telephone:* (1273) 472675 (home). *E-mail:* johnp@sussex.ac.uk (home).

POSTLETHWAITE, Peter (Pete), OBE; British actor; b. 16 Feb. 1945, Lancashire; pnr Jacqueline Morrish; one s. one d.; ed Bristol Old Vic. Theatre School; Hon. Fellow Liverpool John Moores Univ. 2005. *Theatre includes:* Macbeth (Bristol), Cyrano de Bergerac, King Lear, Midsummer Night's Dream. *Films include:* The Racer 1975, The Duellists 1977, Fords on Water 1983, A Private Function 1984, Number 27 1988, The Dressmaker 1988, To Kill a Priest 1988, Distant Voices, Still Lives 1988, They Never Slept 1990, Hamlet 1990, The Grass Arena 1991, Split Second 1992, Alien 3 1992, The Last of the Mohicans 1992, Waterland 1992, Anchoress 1993, In the Name of the Father 1993, Sin Bin 1994, Suite 16 1994, The Usual Suspects 1995, When Saturday Comes 1996, James and the Giant Peach 1996, Dragonheart 1996, Crimetime 1996, Romeo + Juliet 1996, Brassed Off 1996, The Serpent's Kiss 1997, The Lost World: Jurassic Park 1997, Bandyta 1997, Amistad 1997, Among Giants 1998, The Divine Ryans 1999, Wayward Son 1999, When the Sky Falls 2000, Rat 2000, Cowboy Up 2001, The Shipping News 2001, Triggermen 2002, Between Strangers 2002, The Limit 2003, Strange Bedfellows 2004, Dark Water 2005, The Constant Gardener 2005, Aeonflux 2005, Ghost Son 2006, Valley of the Heart's Delight 2006, The Omen 2006. *Television includes:* Horse in the House (film) 1978, Doris and Doreen (film) 1978, Afternoon Off (film) 1979, Cyrano de Bergerac (film) 1985, Tales from Sherwood Forest (series) 1987, Coast to Coast (film) 1987, Tumbledown (film) 1989, Treasure Island (film) 1990, Needle (series) 1990, A Child From the South (film) 1991, Martin Chuzzlewit (series) 1994, Sharpe's Enemy (film) 1994, Sharpe's Company (film) 1994, Animal Farm (voice, film) 1999, Butterfly Collectors (film) 1999, Alice in Wonderland (film) 1999, Lost for Words (film) 1999, The Sins (series) 2000, Shattered City: The Halifax Explosion (series) 2003. *Address:* c/o Markham and Froggatt Ltd, 4 Windmill Street, London, W1P 1HF, England.

POTANIN, Vladimir Olegovich; Russian politician and banker; b. 3 Jan. 1961, Moscow; m.; one s., one d.; ed Moscow Inst. of Int. Relations; staff-mem. USSR Ministry of Foreign Trade 1983–90; Head Econ. Co. Interros 1991–92; Vice-Pres., Pres. Joint-Stock Commercial Bank Int. Financial Co. 1992–93; Pres. UNEXIM Bank 1993–, InterRos Financial and Industrial Group (now Interros Holding Co. 1994–; with pnrs acquired several govt oil and mineral assets including Norilsk Nickel (world's largest producer of nickel); First Deputy Chair. Govt of Russian Fed. 1996–97; concurrently Head Interdept Comm. on Co-operation with Int. Financial-Econ. Orgs. and Group of Seven; host reality show The Candidate 2006. *Address:* Interros Company, 9, Bolshaya Yakimanka st., 119180 Moscow, Russia (office). *Telephone:* (495) 785-63-63 (office). *Fax:* (495) 785-63-64 (office). *E-mail:* kirp@pr.interros.ru (office). *Website:* www.interros.ru/eng (office).

POTAPOV, Alexander Serafimovich, CandPhil; Russian journalist; *Editor-in-Chief, Trud newspaper;* b. 6 Feb. 1936, Oktyabry, Kharkov Region, Ukraine; m.; one s.; ed Vilnius State Univ., Lithuania; contrib. Leninskaya Smena (newspaper) 1958–66; Head of Dept, Deputy Ed.-in-Chief Belgorodskaya Pravda (newspaper) 1966–73; Head of Dept Belgorod Regional Exec. CPSU Cttee 1973–75; Ed. Belgorodskaya Pravda 1975–76; instructor CPSU Cen. Cttee 1976–78, 1981–85; Ed.-in-Chief Trud (Labour) newspaper 1985–;

People's Deputy of Russian Fed., mem. Cttee of Supreme Soviet of Russian Fed. on Problems of Glasnost and Human Rights –1993. *Address:* Trud, Nastas'yinsky per. 4, 103792 Moscow, Russia (office). *Telephone:* (495) 299-39-06 (office). *Fax:* (495) 299-47-40 (office). *E-mail:* letter@trud.ru (office). *Website:* www.trud.ru (office).

POTAPOV, Anatoly Victorovich; Russian politician and diplomatist; *Ambassador to Bulgaria;* b. 24 July 1942, Bishkek; m. Tatyana Nikolayevna Potapova; two c.; ed Moscow Inst. of Radio Electronics and Mine Electro Mechanics; Higher Party School at Cen. CPSU Cttee; with Ministry of Foreign Affairs, numerous posts at home and abroad 1986–, Presidium and Ministry of CIS Countries; First Deputy Man. Ministry of Foreign Affairs 1986–92; Pro-Rector Moscow State Inst. of Int. Relations 1992; Counsellor, Russian Fed. Embassy, China 1992–96; Asst to Head of Russian Presidium 1996–98; Deputy Minister, Ministry of CIS Affairs 1998–2001; Deputy Minister of Foreign Affairs 2002–04; Amb. to Bulgaria 2004–. *Address:* Embassy of the Russian Federation, 1087 Sofia, ul. D. Tsankov 28, Bulgaria (office). *Telephone:* (2) 963-16-63 (office). *Fax:* (2) 963-41-03 (office). *E-mail:* info@russia.bg (office). *Website:* www.russia.bg (office).

POTAPOV, Leonid Vasilyevich; Russian politician; b. 4 July 1935, Uakit, Buryatia; m.; two c.; ed Khabarovsk Inst. of Railway Eng, Irkutsk Inst. of Nat. Econs; various positions from engineer to Chief Engineer, Ulan-Ude train factory 1959–76; Head Div. of Industry, then Sec. Buryat Regional CP Cttee 1976–87; Chair. Mary Regional Exec. Cttee Turkmenia 1987–89; Chair. Supreme Soviet Turkmen SSR 1989–90; First Sec. Buryat CPSU Cttee 1990–91; Chair. Supreme Soviet Buryat Autonomous SSR (now Buryatskaya Repub.) 1991–94; Pres. of Buryatskaya Repub. 1994–2007; mem. Council of Fed., Russian Fed. 1993–2001; Hon. Engineer, Buryat Repub.; Order of the Oct. Revolution, Red Banner of Labour, Honour Award, Order of Friendship, Order for Excellent Service to the Native Land (IV degree), Polar Star Order (Mongolia). *Leisure interest:* reading literature on history, philosophy and economics. *Address:* c/o Government House, Sukhe Bator str. 9, 670001 Ulan-Ude, Republic of Buryatia, Russia (office).

POTERBA, James Michael, AB, MPhil, DPhil; American economist and academic; *President and CEO, National Bureau of Economic Research;* b. 13 July 1958, New York, NY; m. Nancy Lin Rose 1984; two s. one d.; ed Harvard Coll., Univ. of Oxford, UK; Jr Research Fellow, Nuffield Coll. Oxford 1982–83; Asst Prof. of Econs, MIT 1983–86, Assoc. Prof. of Econs 1986–88, Prof. of Econs 1988–96, Assoc. Head, Dept of Econs 1994–2000, 2001–06, Mitsui Prof. of Econs 1996–, Head, Dept of Econs 2006–, mem. Program Bd MIT Center for Energy and Environmental Policy Research 1993–, MIT Advisory Cttee on Shareholder Responsibility 2006–; CRSP Visiting Prof. of Finance, Univ. of Chicago GSB 1988; Faculty Research Fellow, Nat. Bureau of Econ. Research (NBER) 1982–85, Research Assoc. 1985–, Assoc. Dir Taxation Research Program, NBER 1989–91, Dir NBER Public Econs Research Program 1991–, Pres. and CEO NBER 2008–; Dir American Finance Asscn 1993–5; Fellow, Center for Advanced Study in Behavioral Sciences 1993–94; George and Karen McCown Distinguished Visiting Fellow, Hoover Inst. 2000–01; Distinguished Scholar, American Council on Capital Formation 2002; CES Distinguished Fellow, Univ. of Munich 2003; TIAA-CREF Inst. Fellow 2004–06; Int. Research Fellow, Inst. for Fiscal Studies, London, UK 2006; Int. Research Fellow, Centre for Business Taxation, Univ. of Oxford 2007–; mem. Research Advisory Bd American Council on Capital Formation 1993–, Advisory Bd Stanford Inst. for Econ. Policy Research 2005–, Econs Advisory Panel Congressional Budget Office 2006–, Retirement Security Task Force, Investment Co. Inst. 2007; First Vice-Pres. Nat. Tax Asscn 2008 (Second Vice-Pres. 2007); mem. Exec. Cttee American Econs Asscn 2001–03, Chair. Honors and Awards Cttee 2006–; Sr Fellow, Inst. for Policy Reform 1992–93; Assoc. Ed. Journal of Finance 1988–2000, Review of Economics & Statistics 1993–2002, Regional Science & Urban Economics 1997–2004; Co-Ed. RAND Journal of Economics 1986–95, Journal of Public Economics 1995–97 (Ed. 1998–2006, Advisory Ed. 2007–); mem. Advisory Bd Journal of Investment Consulting 1998–2005, Journal of Wealth Management 1998–, Retirement Income Review 2002–; mem. Editorial Advisory Bd National Tax Journal 2007–; Fellow, Econometric Soc. 1988, Nat. Acad. of Social Insurance 1992, American Acad. of Arts and Sciences 1996; Trustee, Coll. Retirement Equity Fund (TIAA-CREF) 2006–; John Williams Prize 1980, Marshall Scholarship 1980–83, George Webb Medley MPhil Thesis Prize 1982, Batterymarch Financial Fellowship 1986, James L. Barr Award 1986, Alfred P. Sloan Fellowship 1988, MIT Econs Dept Teacher of the Year 1990, 1993, 1995, Certificate of Excellence, Paul Samuelson Prize, TIAA-CREF 1996, 2004, Woytinsky Lecturer, Univ. of Michigan 1996, Nat. Acad. of Sciences Award for Scientific Reviewing 1999, Duncan Black Prize, Public Choice Soc. 2000, Review of Economics and Statistics Lecturer, Harvard Univ. 2000, Inst. for Fiscal Studies Lecturer, London 2000, David Kinley Lecturer, Univ. of Illinois 2001, MIT Grad. Econs Asscn Teacher of the Year 2002, Watson-Wyatt Lecture, City Univ., London 2002, Hon. Mention, Culp-Wright Book Award, American Risk and Insurance Asscn 2003, Munich Lectures, Centre for Econ. Studies 2003, Marsh & McLennan Lecturer, Furman Univ. 2003, Hahn Lecturer, Royal Econ. Soc. 2003, EFACT Hon. Award, Univ. of Tilburg 2005, Elder Law Journal Lecturer, Univ. of Illinois 2005, American Econs Asscn/American Finance Asscn Jt Luncheon Lecturer 2006, Plenary Lecture, North American Summer Econometric Soc. Meetings 2007. *Publications:* Economic Policy Responses to Global Warming (co-ed. with R. Dornbusch), Tax Policy and the Economy: Vols 6–22 (ed.) 1992–2008, Public Policies and Household Saving (ed.) 1994, Housing Markets in the United States and Japan (co-ed. with Y. Noguchi) 1994, International Comparisons of Household Saving (ed.) 1994), Empirical Foundations of Household Taxation (co-ed. with M. Feldstein) 1996, Borderline Case: International Tax Policy, Corporate Research and Development, and Investment (ed.) 1998, Fiscal Institutions and Fiscal Performance (co-ed. with J. von Hagen) 1999, Fiscal Rules and State Borrowing Costs: Evidence from California and Other States (with K. Rueben) 1999, The Role of Annuity Markets in Financing Retirement (with J. Brown, O. Mitchell and M. Warshawsky) 2001, Fiscal Reform in Colombia: Problems and Prospects (co-ed. with R. Bird and J. Slemrod) 2005; more than 200 book chapters, reviews, articles and papers in professional journals. *Address:* Department of Economics, Massachusetts Inst. of Tech., E52-350, 50 Memorial Drive, Cambridge, MA 02142-1347 (office); National Bureau of Economic Research, Inc., 1050 Massachusetts Avenue, Cambridge, MA 02138-5398; 17 Stults Road, Belmont, MA 02478-3428, USA (home). *Telephone:* (617) 253-6673 (MIT) (office); (617) 868-3900 (NBER) (office). *Fax:* (617) 253-1330 (MIT) (office); (617) 868-2742 (NBER) (office). *E-mail:* poterba@mit.edu (office). *Website:* econ-www.mit.edu/faculty/poterba (office); www.nber.org (office).

POTIER, Benoît; French business executive; *Chairman of the Management Board, Air Liquide;* b. 3 Sept. 1957, Mulhouse; m. Claude Menard; ed Ecole Centrale Paris; joined Research Devt Dept, Air Liquide 1981, positions in Eng and Construction Div. 1993–97, CEO 1997–, mem. Bd 2000–, Chair. Man. Bd 2001–, Chair. and CEO Air Liquide Int., American Air Liquide Inc.; Dir Air Liquide America Holdings, Air Liquide America LP, SOAEO, Air Liquide Italia, AL Air Liquide España, Air Liquide Japan Ltd, Air Liquide Asia Pte Ltd, Air Liquide Canada Inc., Danone Group; mem. Supervisory Bd Michelin; Admin. École Centrale des Arts et Manufactures; mem. Conseil de France, INSEAD; Chevalier, Légion d'Honneur. *Address:* Air Liquide, 75 quai d'Orsay, 75321 Paris Cedex 07, France (office). *Telephone:* 1-40-68-55-55 (office). *Fax:* 1-40-68-58-40 (office). *Website:* www.airliquide.com (office).

POTRČ, Miran; Slovenian politician and lawyer; b. 27 March 1938, Maribor, Slovenia; s. of Ivan Potrč and Olga Potrč; m. Zdenka Potrč 1992; one d.; ed Univ. of Ljubljana; with Secr. of Justice and Public Admin Maribor 1962–63; Head, Legal Dept Mariborska Livarna (Maribor Foundry) 1963–68; Sec. Communal Cttee of League of Communists of Maribor 1968–73; mem. Presidency of Cen. Cttee League of Communists of Slovenia and Pres. Comm. for Socio-Economic Matters and Social Policy 1973; mem. Exec. Cttee Presidency of Cen. Cttee of League of Communists of Slovenia 1974–78; Vice-Pres. Repub. Council of Trade Unions of Slovenia 1978–80; mem. Presidency, Trade Unions of Yugoslavia 1980–82, Pres. 1980–81; Head, Del. of Skupshtina (Parl.) of SR of Slovenia in Fed. Chamber of Repubs and Provs 1982–86; Pres. Skupshtina of SR of Slovenia 1986–90; mem. Parl. of Repub. of Slovenia, Head Parl. Group and mem. Presidium, Party of Democratic Reforms of Slovenia 1990–; Head Parl. Group United List of Social Democrats; fmr Pres. Council, Univ. of Maribor. *Address:* Assembly of the Republic of Slovenia, Tomšičeva 5, 61000 Ljubljana, Slovenia (office). *Telephone:* (1) 215895 (home); (1) 4789637 (office). *Fax:* (1) 4789866 (office). *E-mail:* miran.potrc@dz-ns.si (office).

POTTAKIS, Yannis A.; Greek politician; b. 1939, Corinth; m. Constantina Alexopoulou; two s. one d.; ed Univs of Athens and Munich, Germany; founding mem. of Pasok; mem. Parl. 1977–; Alt. Minister of Nat. Economy 1982–83, Minister of Finance 1983–84, of Agric. 1985–89, of Justice 1995–96; Alt. Minister of Foreign Affairs; Chair. Council of Budget Ministers of EEC 1983. *Address:* 15 Chimaras Street, 14671 Nea Erythrea, Greece. *Telephone:* 8001-631.

POTTER, David Edwin, CBE, PhD, MA, FREng; British business executive; *Chairman, Psion Plc;* b. 4 July 1943, East London, South Africa; s. of Paul James Potter and Mary Agnes Snape; m. Elaine Goldberg 1969; three s.; ed Trinity Coll. Cambridge, Imperial Coll. London; Lecturer, Blackett Lab., Imperial Coll. London 1970–80; Asst Prof., UCLA 1974; Founder, Chair., CEO Psion PLC 1980–; Dir Press Assoc. Ltd 1994–97 (Vice-Chair. 1995–97), London First Centre 1994–, Finsbury Tech. Trust 1995–; Chair. Symbian Ltd 1998–2004; mem. Nat. Cttee of Inquiry into Higher Educ. (Dearing Cttee) 1996–97, Higher Educ. Funding Council for England 1997–2003, Council for Science and Tech., Cabinet Office 1998–2003; Visiting Fellow, Nuffield Coll. Oxford 1998–; Gov. London Business School 2000; Dir Bank of England 2003; Hon. Fellow, Imperial Coll. 1998, London Business School 1998; Hon. DTech (Kingston) 1998, (Brunel) 1998, Hon. DSc (Sheffield) 2000, (Warwick) 2001, (York) 2002, (Edinburgh) 2002; Mountbatten Medal for Outstanding Services to Electronics Industry, Nat. Electronics Council 1994. *Publications:* Computational Physics 1972, contribs to numerous physics journals. *Leisure interests:* flute, gardening, reading, tennis. *Address:* Psion PLC, 10 Park Crescent, London, W1B 1PQ (office); 8 Hamilton Terrace, St John's Wood, London, NW8 9UG, England (home). *Telephone:* (20) 7291-3999 (office). *Fax:* (20) 7291-3991 (office). *E-mail:* david@depotter.net (office). *Website:* www.psion.com (office).

POTTER, John (Jack) E., MA; American postal service executive; *Postmaster General and CEO, United States Postal Service;* m. Maureen Potter; two c.; ed Fordham Univ., Bronx, NY, Massachusetts Inst. of Tech. (Sloan Fellow); began career as distribution clerk, US Postal Service, Westchester, NY 1977, various exec. and man. positions including Sr Vice-Pres. Labour Relations 1998–99, Sr Vice-Pres. Operations 1999–2000, COO and Exec. Vice-Pres. 2000–01, Postmaster Gen. and CEO 2001–; mem. Postal Service Bd of Govs; Vice-Chair. Int. Post Corpn; Chair. Kahala Posts Group; mem. Pres.'s Nat. Hire Veterans Cttee; American Postal Services Bd of Govs Award 1999, Elmo Zumwalt Legacy Award, Marrow Foundation 2003, J. Edward Day Award, Asscn of Postal Commerce 2003, Tom Tully Award, AM Business Media 2006, Roger W. Jones Award for Executive Leadership, American Univ. 2007. *Address:* United States Postal Service, 475 L'Enfant Plaza SW, Washington, DC 20260-0010, USA (office). *Telephone:* (202) 268-2500 (office). *Fax:* (202) 268-4860 (office). *E-mail:* pmgceo@usps.gov (office). *Website:* www.usps.com (office).

POTTER, Myrtle S., BA; American business executive; *CEO, Chapman Properties, Inc.;* b. Las Cruces, NM; one s. one d.; ed Univ. of Chicago; joined Merck & Co. Inc. in 1982, held a variety of sales, marketing and business planning roles, Vice-Pres. Northeast Region Business Group 1993–96; Vice-Pres. Strategy and Econs, US Pharmaceutical Group, Bristol-Myers Squibb 1996–97, Group Vice President of Worldwide Medicines Group 1997–98, Sr Vice-Pres. Sales, US Cardiovascular/Metabolics March–Oct. 1998, Pres. US Cardiovascular/Metabolics 1998–2000; Exec. Vice-Pres., COO and mem. Exec. Cttee Genentech Inc. 2000–04, Co-Chair. Product Portfolio Cttee, Pres. Commercial Operations 2004–05 and mem. Exec. Cttee 2004–05; f. Myrtle Potter and Co. LLC (consulting firm) 2005; CEO Chapman Properties, Inc. (real estate co.) 2006–; mem. Bd of Dirs EV3 Inc., Medco Health Solutions, Inc., Amazon.com 2004–09; Healthcare Business Women's Asscn Woman of the Year Award 2000, Bristol-Myers Squibb Leadership Devt Award 2002, Merck Chairman's Award 2002, ranked 18th Most Powerful Black Exec. in America by Fortune magazine 2002, listed in Time magazine's 15 Young Global Business Influentials 2002, ranked by Fortune magazine amongst 50 Most Powerful Women in Business in the US (29th) 2003, (23rd) 2004, Girl Scouts of the USA Nat. Woman of Distinction Award 2004. *Address:* Myrtle Potter and Company LLC, 2995 Woodside Road, Suite 400, Woodside, CA 94062, USA (office). *Telephone:* (650) 529-0256 (office). *Fax:* (650) 529-0236 (office). *E-mail:* myrtle@myrtlepotter.com (office). *Website:* www.myrtlepotter.com (office).

POTTER, William C., BA, MA, PhD; American research institute director; *Director, Center for Nonproliferation Studies;* b. 8 July 1947, New Brunswick, NJ; ed Southern Ill Univ., Univ. of Mich; started career as research assoc. Univ. of Mich; lecturer Dept of Political Science, Univ. of Calif 1973–76; Post-Doctoral Fellow Stanford Univ. 1976–77; arms control consultant 1976–77; Asst Prof. Tulane Univ.; Asst Dir Center for Int. and Strategic Affairs, UCLA 1979–82, Assoc. Dir 1982–84, Exec. Dir 1984–89; Exec. Officer S Calif Consortium on Int. Studies 1982–83; Visiting Assoc. Prof. UCLA 1979–88; consultant to Lawrence Livermore Nat. Lab. 1982–89, 1992–, Jet Propulsion Lab. 1984–85, RAND Corp. 1984–86; Program Coordinator RAND/UCLA Center for the Study of Soviet Int. Behaviour 1983–85; Prof. Int. Policy Studies, Monterey Inst. of Int. Studies 1989–, Dir Center for Russian and Eurasian Studies 1989–, Dir Center for Nonproliferation Studies 1992–, Inst. Prof. 1998–; mem. several cttees Nat. Acad. of Sciences; mem. Council on Foreign Relations, Pacific Council on Int. Policy, IISS; mem. Advisory Bds UN Disarmament Matters, Center for Policy Studies in Russia; mem. Bd of Trustees UN Inst. for Disarmament Research. *Publications:* SALT and Beyond: A Handbook on Strategic Weapons and Means for Their Control (jtly) 1977, Nuclear Power and Nonproliferation: An Interdisciplinary Perspective 1982, Verification and Arms Control (ed.) 1985, International Nuclear Trade and Nonproliferation: The Challenge of the Emerging Suppliers (ed.) 1990, Nuclear Profiles of the Soviet Successor States (jtly) 1993, The International Missile Bazaar (co-ed.) 1994, Dismantling the Cold War: US and NIS Perspectives on the Nunn-Lugar Cooperative Threat Reduction Program (co-ed.) 1997, Dangerous Weapons, Desperate States (co-ed.) 1999, The Different Faces of Nuclear Terrorism (jtly) 2004; numerous chapters and articles in over eighty scholarly books and journals. *Address:* Center for Nonproliferation Studies, 460 Pierce Street, Monterey, CA 93940 (office); 52 Cuesta Drive, Monterey, CA 93940, USA (home). *Telephone:* (831) 647-3511 (office); (831) 375-3472 (home). *Fax:* (831) 647-3519 (office). *E-mail:* wpotter@miis.edu (office). *Website:* cns.miis.edu (office).

PÖTTERING, Hans-Gert, PhD; German politician; *President, European Parliament;* b. 15 Sept. 1945, Bersenbrueck; two s.; ed Univs of Bonn and Geneva, Institut des Hautes Études Internationales, Geneva; Reserve Officer, Nat. Service 1966–68; European Policy Spokesman, Young Union of Lower Saxony 1974-80; Research Assistant Univ. of Osnabrueck, 1976–79, Lecturer 1989–95, Hon. Prof. 1995–; MEP 1979–, Chair. European Parl. Subcommittee on Security and Defence 1984–94, Vice-Chair. European People's Party–European Democrats Group (EPP–ED) Group 1994–99, Chair. 1999–2007; Leader EPP EU Enlargement Working Group 1996–99, Pres. 2007–; Chair. Europa-Union Deutschland 1997–99; Chair. Osnabrueck Dist CDU 1990–, mem. Exec. Cttee and Fed. Exec. CDU 1999–2007; European Hon. Senator; Grand Order of Merit of the FRG, Grand Decoration of the Repub. of Austria, Grand Cross, Order of St Gregory the Great, Grand Order of Queen Jelena with Sash and Star (Croatia), Dr hc (Babeş-Bolyai-Univ., Cluj-Napoca, Romania); Konsul-Penseler P, Artland-Gymnasium, Quakenbrück, Robert Schuman Medal, EPP-Group, Gold Medal of Mérite Européen, Luxembourg, MEP of the Year 2004 (European Voice), Walter Hallstein Prize (Frankfurt am Main) 2007. *Publications:* Adenauers Sicherheitspolitik 1955–1963. Ein Beitrag zum deutsch-amerikanischen Verhältnis (Adenauer's Security Policy 1955–1963. A Contribution to the German-American relationship) 1975, Die vergessenen Regionen: Plädoyer für eine solidarische Regionalpolitik in der Europäischen Gemeinschaft (The Forgotten Regions: for a European Community Regional Policy Based on Solidarity) (with Frank Wiehler) 1983, Europas vereinigte Staaten – Annäherungen an Werte und Ziele (Europe's United States – Approaches to Values and Objectives) (with Ludger Kühnhardt) 1993, Kontinent Europa: Kern, Übergänge, Grenzen (The Continent of Europe: Nucleus, Transitions, Borders) (with Ludger Kühn-hardt) 1998, Weltpartner Europäische Union (The European Union as a World Partner) (with Ludger Kühnhardt) 2001, Von der Vision zur Wirklichkeit. Auf dem Weg zur Einigung Europas (From Vision to Reality – Towards a United Europe) 2004. *Address:* Office of the President, European Parliament, Bâtiment Paul-Henri Spaak, 11B011, 60 rue Wiertz, 1047 Brussels, Belgium (office). *Telephone:* (2) 284-57-69 (office). *Fax:* (2) 284-97-69 (office). *E-mail:* hans-gert.poettering@europarl.europa.eu (office). *Website:* www.europarl.europa.eu/president/defaulten.htm?biography (office).

POUDEL, Ram Chandra; Nepalese politician; mem. Parl. for Tanahu Dist 1994–99; fmr Deputy Prime Minister; Gen. Sec. Nepali Congress; Minister of Peace and Reconstruction 2007–08; mem. Nepali Nat. Congress party. *Address:* Nepali Congress Party, Bhansar Tole, Teku, Kathmandu, Nepal (office). *Website:* www.nepalicongress.org (office).

POUGATCHEV, Sergueï; Russian politician and banker; *Senator, Council of the Russian Federation;* f. Mejprombank 1992, Dir and later Pres. –2001; co-f. Almazi Yakoutil co.; mem. (Senator) Council of the Fed. for Tver Oblast 2001–. *Address:* Representation of Tver Oblast in the Russian Federation, ul. B. Dmitrovka 26, 103426 Moscow, Russia (office). *Telephone:* (495) 926-65-19 (office). *Fax:* (495) 292-14-85 (office).

POULSEN, Ole Lønsmann, LLM; Danish diplomatist; *Ambassador to India;* b. 14 May 1945, Copenhagen; s. of Aage Lønsmann Poulsen and Tove Alice Poulsen; m. Zareen Mehta 1973; two s.; ed Univs of Pune, India and Copenhagen; with Danchurchaid 1969–73; Head of Section, Ministry of Foreign Affairs 1973–76; Asian Devt Bank, Manila 1976–77; First Sec., New Delhi 1977–80; Alt. Exec. Dir World Bank, Washington, DC 1980–83; Deputy Head of Dept, Ministry of Foreign Affairs 1983–85, Head of Dept 1985–88, Under-Sec. and Amb. 1988–92; Amb. in Vienna, Ljubljana and Sarajevo; Amb. to UN orgs in Vienna 1992–93; State Sec., Amb. 1993–96; Amb. to UK 1996–2001, to People's Repub. of China 2001–04, to Sweden 2004–06, to India 2006–; Kt Commdr of the First Class (Denmark), Grand Cross (Austria), Grand Cross (Sweden), Hon. GCVO (UK). *Leisure interests:* art, music, literature, sports. *Address:* Embassy of Denmark, 11 Aurangzeb Road, 110011 New Delhi, India (office). *Telephone:* (11) 4209-0700 (office). *Fax:* (11) 2379-2891 (office). *E-mail:* delamb@um.dk (office). *Website:* www.ambnewdelhi.um.dk (office).

POUND, Richard (Dick) W., OC, OQ, QC, BCom, BA, BCL, LLD; Canadian fmr Olympic swimmer, lawyer, chartered accountant and university administrator; *Partner, Stikeman Elliott LLP;* b. 22 March 1942, St Catharines, Ont.; ed McGill Univ. and Sir George Williams Univ. (now Concordia Univ.), Montreal; competitor in Olympics Games, Rome 1960, double finalist in 100m freestyle (6th) and 4×100m medley relay (4th); Gold Medal in 110-yard freestyle event, two Silver Medals in 440- and 880-yard freestyle relay, and Bronze Medal in 440-yard medley relay, Commonwealth Games 1962; Canadian Champion in freestyle 1958, 1960–62, butterfly 1961; Sec. Canadian Olympic Asscn 1968–76, Pres. 1977–82; Deputy Chef de Mission, Canadian Olympic Del., Munich 1972; joined IOC in 1978, served on Exec. Bd 1983–91, 1992–2000, Vice-Pres. IOC 1987–91, 1996–2000, Chair. Coordination Comm. for Olympic Games in Atlanta 1996; his investigation of Salt Lake City Winter Olympics scandal led to creation of new ethics watchdog to monitor future interaction between bidding cities and IOC mems; Chair. World Anti-Doping Agency, Lausanne, Switzerland 1999–2007; currently Pnr, Stikeman Elliott LLP, Montréal; mem.Int. Council Arbitration for Sport 2007–; lectured in taxation matters at Faculty of Law, McGill Univ., Montréal and at McGill Centre for Continuing Educ. in Chartered Accountancy program, Past Pres. Grads' Soc. (now McGill Alumni Asscn), fmr Chair. Alma Mater Fund and McGill's Fund Council, mem. Bd Govs 1986 (Chair. 1994–99), Chancellor McGill Univ. 1999–; mem. Quebec and Ontario Bars; has been apptd to Fed. Court Bench and Bar Liaison Cttee; Ed. Legal Notes, CGA Magazine; mem. Canadian Tax Foundation, Asscn de planification fiscale et financière, Canadian Bar Asscn, Int. Fiscal Asscn, Int. Asscn of Practising Lawyers, Int. Olympic Cttee; Hon. Consul Gen. of Norway in Montréal; Hon. PhD (United Sports Acad.) 1989; Hon. LLD (Univ. of Windsor) 1997, (Univ. of Western Ontario) 2004; Dr hc (Laurentian Univ.) 2005, (Beijing Sport Univ.) 2006; Carswell Company Prize, McGill Univ. 1967, Laureus Spirit of Sport Prize 2008. *Publications:* Five Rings Over Korea 1994, Chief Justice W. R. Jackett: By the Law of the Land; Ed.-in-Chief: Annotated Stikeman Income Tax Act (Carswell), Canada Tax Cases (Carswell), Doing Business in Canada; ed. and author of Pound's Tax Case Notes (Carswell). *Address:* ; Stikeman Elliott LLP, 1155 René-Lévesque Blvd. West, 40th Floor, Montréal, PQ H3B 3V2 (office); Chancellor's Office, James Administration Building, McGill University, 845 Sherbrooke Street West, Montréal, PQ H3A 2T5, Canada. *Telephone:* (514) 397-3037 (office). *Fax:* (514) 397-3222 (office). *E-mail:* rpound@stikeman.com (office). *Website:* www.stikeman.com (office); www.mcgill.ca.

POUND, Robert Vivian, MA; American physicist and academic; *Mallinckrodt Professor of Physics, Emeritus, Harvard University;* b. 16 May 1919, Ridgeway, Ont., Canada; s. of V. E. Pound and Gertrude C. Prout; m. Betty Yde Andersen 1941; one s.; ed Univ. of Buffalo and Harvard Univ.; Research Physicist, Submarine Signal Co., Boston, Mass. 1941–42; Staff mem. Radiation Laboratory, MIT 1942–46; Jr Fellow, Soc. of Fellows, Harvard Univ. 1945–48, Asst Prof. 1948–50, Assoc. Prof. 1950–56, Prof. 1956–68, Mallinckrodt Prof. of Physics 1968–89, Prof. Emer. 1989–; Chair. Dept of Physics 1968–72, Dir Physics Labs 1975–83; Zernike Prof. Groningen Univ. 1982; Visiting Prof. Coll. de France 1973, Univ. of Florida 1987; Visiting Fellow, Joint Inst. for Lab. Astrophysics, Univ. of Colorado 1979–80; Visiting Scientist Brookhaven Nat. Lab. 1986–87; Research Fellow, Merton Coll. Oxford 1980; mem. NAS; Foreign Assoc. Académie des Sciences; Fellow, American Acad. of Arts and Sciences, American Physical Soc., AAAS; Fulbright Research Scholar, Oxford Univ. 1951; Fulbright Lecturer, Ecole Normale, Paris 1958; Guggenheim Fellow 1957–58, 1972–73; B. J. Thompson Memorial Award, Inst. of Radio Engineers 1948, Eddington Medal, Royal Astronomical Soc. 1965, Nat. Medal of Science (Pres. of USA) 1990. *Publications:* Microwave Mixers 1948; papers on nuclear magnetism, electric quadrupole interactions, directional correlations of gamma rays, effect of gravity on gamma rays. *Address:* Lyman Laboratory of Physics, Harvard University, Cambridge, MA 02138 (office); 87 Pinehurst Road, Belmont, MA 02478-1502, U.S.A (home). *Telephone:* (617) 495-2873 (office); (617) 484-0254 (home). *E-mail:* pound@physics.harvard.edu (office). *Website:* www.physics.harvard.edu (office).

POUNDS, Kenneth Alwyne, CBE, PhD, FRS; British physicist and academic; *Professor of Space Physics, University of Leicester;* b. 17 Nov. 1934, Leeds, Yorks.; s. of Harry Pounds and Dorothy Pounds (née Hunt); m. 1st Margaret Connell 1961; two s. one d.; m. 2nd Joan Mary Millit 1982; one s. one d.; ed Salt High School, Shipley, Yorks. and Univ. Coll., London; Prof. of Space Physics Univ. of Leicester 1973–, Dir X-ray Astronomy Group 1973–94, Head of Dept of Physics and Astronomy 1986–2002 (on leave of absence 1994–98); Chief Exec. Particle Physics and Astronomy Research Council 1994–98; Pres. Royal Astronomical Soc. 1990–92; mem. Academia Europaea, Int. Acad. of Astronautics; Fellow, Univ. Coll. London 1993, now Hon. Fellow; Leverhulme Research Fellow 2003–05; Hon. DUniv (York), Hon. DSc (Loughborough, Sheffield Hallam, Warwick, Leicester); Gold Medal, Royal Astronomical Soc. 1990. *Publications:* more than 275 scientific publs. *Leisure interests:* sport, music. *Address:* Department of Physics and Astronomy, University of Leicester, University Road, Leicester, LE1 7RH (office); 12 Swale Close, Oadby, Leics., LE2 4GF, England (home). *Telephone:* (116) 252-3509 (office); (116) 271-9370 (home). *Fax:* (116) 252-3311 (office). *E-mail:* kap@le.ac.uk (office). *Website:* www.star.le.ac.uk (office).

POUNGUI, Ange-Edouard; Republic of the Congo politician, economist and banker; *Vice-President, Union panafricaine pour la démocratie sociale;* b. 1942; began career in school, student unions; apptd mem. Nat. Council for Revolution 1968, then mem. Political Bureau, Minister for Finance 1971–73, Vice-Pres. Council of State and Minister for Planning 1973–76; Prime Minister of The Congo 1984–89; fmr Pres. Union pour le Renouveau Démocratique (URD); worked for IMF and African Devt Bank, then Dir-Gen. Cen. African Bank 1976–79, then CEO Congolese Commercial Bank; Dir Cen. Bank of the Congo 1994–2001; currently Vice-Pres. Union panafricaine pour la démocratie sociale. *Address:* c/o Union panafricaine pour la démocratie sociale, BP 1370, Brazzaville, Republic of the Congo (office). *E-mail:* courrier@upads.org (office). *Website:* www.upads.org (office).

POUNTNEY, David Willoughby, CBE, MA; British opera director; *Intendant and Artistic Director, Bregenzer Festspiele;* b. 10 Sept. 1947, Oxford; s. of E. W. Pountney and D. L. Byrt; m. 1st Jane R. Henderson 1980; one s. one d.; m. 2nd Nicola Raab 2007; ed St John's Coll. Choir School, Cambridge, Radley Coll. and St John's Coll. Cambridge; first opera production, Scarlatti's Trionfo dell'Onore, Cambridge 1967; Katya Kabanova at Wexford Festival 1972; Dir of Productions, Scottish Opera 1975–80, notably with Die Meistersinger, Eugene Onegin, Jenůfa, The Cunning Little Vixen, Die Entführung and Don Giovanni; Australian debut in Die Meistersinger 1978; world premiere of Philip Glass' Satyagraha, Netherlands Opera 1980; Prin. Prod. and Dir of Productions, ENO 1982–93, notably with The Flying Dutchman, The Queen of Spades, Rusalka, The Valkyrie and Lady Macbeth of Mtsensk; American debut with Houston Opera, Verdi's Macbeth, returning for the world premiere of Bilby's Doll by Carlisle Floyd, Katya Kabanova and Jenůfa; produced Weill's Street Scene for Scottish Opera 1989; other productions include From the House of the Dead in Vancouver, Dr Faust in Berlin and Paris, The Fiery Angel at the State Opera of S Australia, Adelaide, The Flying Dutchman, Nabucco and Fidelio for the Bregenz Festival, The Excursions of Mr Brouček for the Munich State Opera, the world premiere of Philip Glass' The Voyage at the Met, The Fairy Queen for ENO, Der Kaukasianische Kreidekreis in Zürich, A Midsummer Night's Dream in Venice, Jenůfa, Rienzi and La Forza del Destino for the Vienna Staatsoper 2002, Turandot at Salzburg 2002; engagements include Tristan in Cologne, Aggrippina in Zurich and Les Troyens Deutsche Oper Berlin; Intendant and Artistic Dir Bregenzer Festspiele 2003–; Janáček Medal, SWET Award, Martinu Medal, Olivier Award; Chevalier, Ordre des Arts et des Lettres. *Publications:* Powerhouse; The Doctor of Mydffai (libretto for Peter Maxwell Davies), Mr Emmett Takes a Walk (libretto for Peter Maxwell Davies); several trans. from German, Italian, Russian and Czech. *Leisure interests:* gardening, cooking, croquet. *Address:* IMG Artists, The Light Box, 111 Power Road, London, W4 5PY, England (office); c/o Bregenzer Festspiele, Postfach 311, 6901 Bregenz, Austria (office). *Telephone:* (20) 7957-5800 (office). *Fax:* (20) 7957-5801 (office). *E-mail:* bsegal@imgartists.com (office); info@bregenzerfestspiele.com (office). *Website:* www.imgartists.com (office); www.bregenzerfestspiele.com (office).

POUPARD, HE Cardinal Paul; French ecclesiastic; b. 30 Aug. 1930, Bouzillé; s. of Joseph Poupard and Celestine Guéry; ed Catholic Univ., Angers, Ecole Pratique des Hautes Etudes Sorbonne Univ.; ordained priest 1954; Parochial Minister, Paris and attaché to CNRS 1958; attaché to Sec. of State 1959–71; Rector Institut Catholique de Paris 1971–81; Titular Bishop of Usula 1979, Archbishop 1980; cr. Cardinal 1985; Priest of S. Prassede; Pres. Pontifical Council for Culture 1982–2007, for Inter-Religious Dialogue 2006–07; Commdr, Légion d'honneur, Grand Cross Order of Merit (Germany); Grand Prix Cardinal Crente, Acad. Française, Prix Robert Schuman, Prix Empedocle. *Publications include:* Les Religions 1987, L'Eglise au Défi des Cultures 1989, The Church and Culture 1989, Dieu et la Liberté 1992, Nouvelle Europe 1993, Après Galilée, Science et Foi, Nouveau Dialogue 1994, What Will Give Us Happiness 1992, Dictionnaire des Religions 1993, Le Christianisme à l'aube du troisième millénaire 1999, Where is Your God? Responding to the Challenge of Unbelief and Religious Intolerance Today 2004, Le mariage et la transmission par la famille: Les parents de Thérèse de Lisieux dans la cité d'aujourd'hui 2004, Que sais-je: Les Religions 2004, Foi et cultures au tournant du nouveau millénaire 2005, Chant Grégorien: Art et Prière de l'Eglise 2005, Foi Catholique 2005, L'affaire Galilée 2005, Le christianisme, ferment de nouveauté en Europe 2005, Lumières de Terre Sainte 2005, Le catholicisme au défi des cultures 2006, Des femmes prêtres? 2006, Paul de Tarse : Navigateur de l'espérance 2006, La Voie de la Beauté :

Assemblée plénière de 2006, Voyage apostolique de Benoît XVI à Munich, Altötting et Ratisbonne 2006, Le concile Vatican II 2007. *Address:* Piazza San Calisto, 00120 Vatican City. *Telephone:* (6) 69-88-73-93 (office); (6) 69-89-38-11 (office). *Fax:* (06) 69-88-73-68. *E-mail:* cultura@cultr.va (office). *Website:* www .vatican.va (office).

POURIER, Miguel Arcangel; Netherlands Antilles politician; b. 29 Sept. 1938, Bonaire; m.; three c.; ed Radulphus Coll., Curaçao, Univ. of Tilburg; tax inspector 1962–73, fmr Head Dept Excise and Import Duties, fmr Dir Dept of Taxes; Minister of Devt Co-operation 1973–79, also fmr Minister of Finance, of Econ. Affairs; ABN Bank 1980–91, Dir ABN Trust, Gen. Dir ABN Bank Netherlands Antilles and Aruba; Govt Adviser; fmr Pres. Asscn of Bankers; financial consultant 1991–; Prime Minister of Netherlands Antilles, Minister of Gen. Affairs and Devt Co-operation 1994–98, 1999–2002; Commdr Order of Oranje Nassau. *Leisure interests:* reading, chess, tennis, guitar. *Address:* c/o Ministry of General Affairs and Development Co-operation, Plasa Horacio Hoyer 9, Willemstad, Curaçao, Netherlands Antilles (office).

POUSSOT, Bernard; French business executive; *Chairman, President and CEO, Wyeth;* ed Ecole Supérieure de Commerce de Paris; Chair. Students' Council, Ecole Supérieure de Commerce de Paris 1975; mil. service as civil servant in Casablanca, Morocco 1976–77; began career with Merck and Searle in marketing positions in Europe and USA; joined Wyeth Gen. Man. France 1986–91, Head of Europe 1991–93, Exec. Vice-Pres. 1993–96, Pres. Wyeth International 1996–97, Pres. Wyeth Pharmaceuticals (global pharmaceutical div. of Wyeth) 1997–2006, Pres. and Vice-Chair. Wyeth 2006–, mem. Bd of Dirs, Vice-Chair., Pres. and COO 2007–08, Vice-Chair., Pres. and CEO Jan.– June 2008, Chair., Pres. and CEO June 2008–; mem. Bd Univ. of Pennsylvania School of Dental Medicine, Eisenhower Fellowships, French American Chamber of Commerce, Opera Co. of Philadelphia; Sabin Lifetime Award 2003, Union League Founders Award for Business Leadership 2006. *Address:* Wyeth, 5 Giralda Farms, Madison, NJ 07940-0874, USA (office). *Telephone:* (973) 660-5000 (office). *Fax:* (973) 660-7026 (office). *E-mail:* info@ wyeth.com (office). *Website:* www.wyeth.com (office).

POUZIN, Louis; French computer scientist; *Chairman, Native Language Internet Consortium;* b. 1931, Chantenay-Saint-Imbert (Nièvre); ed Ecole Polytechnique, Paris; on staff, MIT Computer Center 1960s; Dir Cyclades project at Institut de Recherche d'Informatique et d'Automatique, France 1970s; Lecturer, Asscn for Computing Machinery (ACM); Dean of Information Tech., THESEUS (France Telecom inst.) early 1990s; Project Dir, Eurolinc France; Chair. Native Language Internet Consortium 2006–; Chevalier de la Légion d'honneur 2003; Silver Core Award, Int. Fed. for Information Processing, IEEE Internet Award, ACM SIGCOMM Award 1999. *Achievements include:* best known as inventor and advocate of datagram, designed the first packet communications network, Cyclades; also created first forms of command-line interface; his work was broadly used by Vinton Cerf in his development of Internet and TCP/IP. *Publications:* one book and 82 articles on computer networks. *Address:* Native Language Internet Consortium, 17 rue Mesnil, 75116 Paris, France (office). *Telephone:* 1-47-55-14-51 (office). *Fax:* 1-47-55-14-51 (office). *E-mail:* Pouzin@nliconsortium.org (office). *Website:* www .nliconsortium.org (office).

POWATHIL, Most Rev. Joseph, MA, DD; Indian ecclesiastic; *Archbishop Emeritus of Changanacherry;* b. 14 Aug. 1930, Kurumpanadam; s. of Ulahannan Joseph Powathil and Mariyam Joseph Powathil; ed St Berchmans' Coll., Changanacherry, Loyola Coll., Madras, St Thomas Minor Seminary, Parel and Papal Seminary, Pune; ordained RC priest 1962; Lecturer in Econs, St Berchmans's Coll., Changanacherry 1963–72; Auxiliary Bishop of Changanacherry 1972–77, Titular Bishop of Caesarea Philipi, 1972, consecrated Bishop 1972; 1st Bishop of Kanjirappally Diocese, Kerala 1977–85; Archbishop of Changanacherry 1985–2007, Archbishop Emer. 2007–; Chair. Kerala Catholic Bishops' Conf. (KCBC) and Chair. Educational Comm. 1993–96; Pres. Catholic Bishops' Conf. of India (CBCI) 1993–98; Perm. mem. Syro Malabar Bishops' Synod 1993; Chair. CBCI Comm. for Educ. and Clergy, KCBC Comm. for Vigilance 1998–; mem. Comm. for Devt, Justice and Peace; Chair. SMBC Comm. for Ecumenism 1993–; Chair. Inter-Church Council for Educ. 1990–; mem. Asian Synod of Bishops, Post Synodal Council (for Asia) 1998–; mem. Pontifical Comm. for Dialogue with the Orthodox Syrian Church; Chair. Religious Fellowship Foundation 1994; Hon. mem. Pro-Oriente, Vienna 1994. *Address:* Archbishop's House, PO Box 20, Changanacherry 686 101, Kerala, India. *Telephone:* (481) 420040. *Fax:* (481) 422540. *E-mail:* abpchry@md2.vsnl.net.in. *Website:* www.archbishopjosephpowathil .org.

POWELL, Gen. Colin Luther, MBA; American business executive, academic, fmr government official and fmr army officer; *Strategic Limited Partner, Kleiner Perkins Caufield and Byers;* b. 5 April 1937, New York; s. of Luther Powell and Maud A. McKoy; m. Alma V. Johnson 1962; one s. (Michael K. Powell) two d.; ed City Coll. of New York and George Washington Univ.; commissioned US Army 1958, Lt-Gen. 1986; Commdr 2nd Brigade, 101st Airborne Div. 1976–77; Exec. Asst to Sec. Dept of Energy 1979; Sr Mil. Asst to Sec. Dept of Defense 1979–81; Asst Div. Commdr 4th Infantry Div. Fort Carson, Colo 1981–83; Mil. Asst to Sec. of Defense 1983–86; assigned to US V Corps, Europe 1986–87; Nat. Security Adviser, White House, Washington 1987–88; C-in-C US Forces, Fort McPherson, Ga April–Sept. 1989; Chair. Jt Chiefs of Staff 1989–93; Sec. of State 2001–05 (resgnd); public speaker 1993–2000; Strategic Ltd Pnr, Kleiner Perkins Caufield & Byers (venture capital firm) 2005–; investor and mem. Bd Revolution Health Group LLC 2005–; Founder, Advisory Council Chair, Distinguished Scholar, Colin Powell Center for Policy Studies, City Coll. of New York 1997–; Chair. Pres.'s Summit For America's Future 1997–; Founding Chair. America's Promise: The Alliance for Youth 1997–2001; Hon. LLD (Univ. of West Indies) 1994; Legion

of Merit, Bronze Star, Air Medal, Purple Heart, Pres. Medal of Freedom, Pres. Citizen's Medal, Hon. KCB 1993, Order of Jamaica. *Publication:* My American Journey (autobiog. with Joseph E. Persico) 1995. *Address:* Kleiner Perkins Caufield and Byers, 2750 Sand Hill Road, Menlo Park, CA 94025, USA (office). *Telephone:* (650) 233-2750 (office). *Fax:* (650) 233-0300 (office). *Website:* www .kpcb.com (office).

POWELL III, Earl Alexander, AB, AM, PhD; American art museum director; *Director, National Gallery of Art;* b. 24 Oct. 1943, Spartanburg, SC; s. of Earl Alexander Powell and Elizabeth Duckworth; m. Nancy Landry 1971; three d.; ed Williams Coll. and Harvard Univ.; Teaching Fellow, Harvard Univ. 1970–74; Curator, Michener Collection, Univ. of Texas, Austin 1974–76, also Asst Prof. of Art History; Museum Curator, Sr Staff Asst to Asst Dir and Chief Curator, Nat. Gallery of Art, Washington, DC 1976–78, Exec. Curator 1979–80, Dir 1992–; Dir LA Co. Museum of Art 1980–92; other professional appointments; Trustee American Fed. of Arts, Morris and Gwendolyn Cafritz Foundation, Nat. Trust for Historic Preservation, White House Historical Asscn, John F. Kennedy Center for Performing Arts; Chair. Comm. of Fine Arts; mem. Asscn of Art Museum Dirs, Cttee for the Preservation of the White House, Pres.'s Cttee on the Arts and Humanities, American Philosophical Soc., American Acad. of Arts and Sciences; Grand Official, Order of the Infante D. Henrique 1995, Commendatore, Ordine al Merito (Italy) 1998, Chevalier Légion d'honneur 2000, Officier Ordre des Arts et des Lettres 2004, Order of the Aztec Eagle (Mexico) 2007; King Olav Medal 1978, Williams Bicentennial Medal 1995, Mexican Cultural Inst. Award 1996. *Publications:* American Art at Harvard 1973, Selections from the James Michener Collection 1975, Abstract Expressionists and Imagists: A Retrospective View 1976, Milton Avery 1976, The James A. Michener Collection (catalogue) 1978, Thomas Cole monograph 1990. *Address:* 2000B South Club Drive, Landover, MD 20785, USA; National Gallery of Art, Sixth Street and Constitution Avenue, NW, Washington, DC, USA. *Website:* www.nga.gov (office).

POWELL, Jonathan Leslie; British television producer; b. 25 April 1947, Faversham, Kent; s. of James Dawson Powell and Phyllis N. Sylvester (née Doubleday); m. Sally Brampton 1990; one d.; ed Sherborne School and Univ. of East Anglia; script and producer of drama, Granada TV 1970–77; producer, drama serials, BBC TV 1977–83, Head of Drama Series and Serials 1983–87; Controller BBC 1 1987–92; Dir Drama and Co-Production, Carlton TV 1993–2004; Royal TV Soc. Silver Award 1979–80. *Television includes:* Testament of Youth 1979 (BAFTA award), Tinker, Tailor, Soldier, Spy 1979, Pride and Prejudice 1980, The Bell 1982, Smiley's People 1982 (Peabody Medal, USA), The Old Men at the Zoo 1983, Bleak House 1985, Tender is the Night 1985, A Perfect Spy 1987. *Leisure interest:* fly-fishing. *Address:* Flat 1, 158 Lancaster Road, London, W11 1QU, England (office). *Telephone:* (20) 7221-2325 (office).

POWELL, Jonathan Nicholas, MA; British political adviser; *Managing Director of Investment Banking, Morgan Stanley and Co.;* b. 14 Aug. 1956, Fulbeck; s. of Air Vice-Marshal John Frederick Powell and Geraldine Ysolda Powell; m. Karen Drayne (divorced 1997); two s.; pnr Sarah Helm; two d.; ed Univ. Coll. Oxford, Univ. of Pennsylvania, USA; with BBC 1978, Granada TV 1978–79; joined FCO 1979, served in Lisbon 1980–83, FCO, London 1983–85, CSCE, Vienna 1985–89, FCO, London 1989–91, Washington 1991–95; Chief of Staff to Leader of the Opposition 1995–97, to Prime Minister 1997–2007; Man. Dir of European Investment Banking, Morgan Stanley and Co. 2008–. *Publication:* Great Hatred, Little Room: Making Peace in Northern Ireland 2008. *Leisure interests:* walking, skiing. *Address:* Morgan Stanley and Co., 25 Cabot Square, Canary Wharf, London E14 4QA, England (office). *Telephone:* (20) 7425-8000 (office). *Fax:* (20) 7425-8990 (office). *Website:* www .morganstanley.com (office).

POWELL, Michael James David, ScD, FRS; British mathematician and academic; *John Harvey Plummer Professor Emeritus of Applied Numerical Analysis, University of Cambridge;* b. 29 July 1936; s. of William James David Powell and Beatrice Margaret Powell (née Page); m. Caroline Mary Henderson 1959; one s. (deceased) two d.; ed Eastbourne Coll. and Peterhouse, Cambridge; mathematician at AERE, Harwell 1959–76; John Humphrey Plummer Prof. of Applied Numerical Analysis, Univ. of Cambridge 1976–2001, Prof. Emer. 2001–, Professorial Fellow, Pembroke Coll. 1978–; Foreign Assoc. NAS 2001–; Hon. DSc (Univ. of E Anglia) 2001; George B. Dantzig Prize in Math. Programming 1982, Naylor Prize, London Math. Soc. 1983, Gold Medal Inst. of Math. Applications 1996, Sr Whitehead Prize, London Math. Soc. 1999. *Publications:* Approximation Theory and Methods 1981; papers on numerical mathematics, especially approximation and optimization calculations. *Leisure interests:* golf, walking. *Address:* Centre for Mathematical Sciences, University of Cambridge, Wilberforce Road, Cambridge, CB3 0WA (office); 134 Milton Road, Cambridge, CB4 1LE, England (home). *E-mail:* M.J.D.Powell@damtp.cam.ac.uk (office). *Website:* www.damtp.cam.ac.uk (office).

POWELL, Michael K.; American lawyer and fmr government official; *Advisor, Providence Equity Partners Inc.;* s. of Gen. Colin L. Powell (q.v.) and Alma V. Powell; m. Jane Knott Powell; two s.; ed Coll. of William and Mary and Georgetown Univ. Law Center; mil. service as Cavalry Platoon Leader and Troop Exec. Officer, 3/2 Armored Cavalry Reg., Amberg, Germany; fmr Policy Adviser to Sec. of Defense; fmr Judicial Clerk to Chief Judge of US Court of Appeals for DC Circuit; fmr Assoc. O'Melveny & Myers LLP, Washington; fmr Chief of Staff Antitrust Div., Dept of Justice; Chair. Fed. Communications Comm. Jan. 2001–05 (mem. 1997–), also Defense Chair.; Advisor, Providence Equity Pnrs Inc. 2005–; mem. Bd of Visitors, Georgetown Univ. Law Center; Henry Crown Fellow, Aspen Inst. 1999, Sr Fellow Communications and Society Program 2005–; Henry Crown Leadership Award, Aspen Inst. 2004. *Address:* Providence Equity Partners Inc., 50

Kennedy Plaza, 18th Floor Providence RI 02903 (office); Communcations and Society Program, The Aspen Institute, One Dupont Circle, NW, Suite 700, Washington, DC 20036-1133, USA. *Telephone:* (401) 751-1700 (office); (202) 736-5800. *Fax:* (401) 751-1790 (office); (202) 467-0790. *Website:* www.provequity.com (office); www.aspeninstitute.org (office).

POWELL, Robert; British actor; b. 1 June 1944, Salford, Lancs.; s. of John W. Powell and Kathleen C. Powell; m. Barbara Lord 1975; one s. one d.; ed Manchester Grammar School, Manchester Univ.; first job, Victoria Theatre, Stoke On Trent 1964; Hon. MA (Salford) 1990, Hon. DLitt (Salford) 2000; Best Actor, Paris Film Festival 1980, Venice Film Festival 1982. *Television roles include:* Doomwatch 1970, Jude the Obscure 1971, Jesus of Nazareth 1977, Pygmalion 1981, Frankenstein 1984, Hannay (series) 1988, The Sign of Command 1989, The First Circle 1990, The Golden Years 1992, The Detectives 1992–97, Pride of Africa 1997, Kind Hearts and Coronets 1998, Escape (series, voice) 1998, Marple: The Murder at the Vicarage 2004, Holby City (series) 2005–07. *Theatre roles include:* Hamlet 1971, Travesties (RSC) 1975, Terra Nova 1982, Private Dick 1982, Tovarich 1991, Sherlock Holmes 1992. *Films include:* Walk a Crooked Path 1969, The Italian Job 1969, Secrets 1971, Running Scared 1972, Shelley 1972, Asylum 1972, The Asphyx 1973, Mahler 1974, Tommy 1975, Al di là del bene e del male 1977, The Thirty-Nine Steps 1978, Harlequin 1980, Jane Austen in Manhattan 1980, The Survivor 1981, Imperativ 1982, The Jigsaw Man 1983, What Waits Below 1984, D'Annunzio 1985 Laggiù nella giungla 1986, Shaka Zulu 1987, Romeo-Juliet (voice) 1990, Chunuk Bair 1992, The Mystery of Edwin Drood 1993, Hey Mr DJ 2005, Colour Me Kubrick 2005. *Leisure interests:* golf, tennis, cricket, computers. *Address:* c/o Jonathan Altaras Associates, 11 Garrick Street, London, WC2E 9AR, England. *Telephone:* (20) 7836-8722 (office).

POWELL, Sandy; British costume and set designer; b. 7 April 1960; ed St Martin's Coll. of Art and Design, Cen. School of Art, London; Evening Standard Award for film of Edward II, Best Tech. Achievement Award, Evening Standard Award for Orlando 1994, Acad. Award for Shakespeare in Love 1998, BAFTA Award for Velvet Goldmine 1998. *Designs:* costume designer for most shows by The Cholmondoleys and The Featherstonehaughs; stage sets include: Edward II (RSC), Rigoletto (Netherlands Opera) and Dr. Ox's Experiment (ENO); costumes for films include: The Last of England, Stormy Monday, The Pope Must Die, Edward II, Caravaggio, Venus Peter, The Miracle, The Crying Game, Orlando, Being Human, Interview with a Vampire, Rob Roy, Michael Collins, The Butcher Boy, The Wings of the Dove, Felicia's Journey, Shakespeare in Love, Velvet Goldmine, Hilary and Jackie, The End of the Affair, Miss Julie, Gangs of New York, Far From Heaven, Sylvia, The Aviator.

POWELL OF BAYSWATER, Baron (Life Peer), cr. 2000, of Bayswater; **Charles David Powell,** Kt, KCMG, BA; British fmr diplomatist, business executive and policy adviser; *Chairman, Atlantic Partnership;* b. 6 July 1941; s. of Air Vice-Marshal John Frederick Powell OBE; m. Carla Bonardi 1964; two s.; ed King's School, Canterbury, New Coll., Oxford; Diplomatic Service 1963–83; Pvt. Sec. and Foreign Affairs Adviser to Prime Minister 1983–91; Chair. Sagitta Asset Man. Ltd 2001–05, Safinvest 2005–, Magna Holdings 2006–; Chair. Atlantic Partnership; Sr Dir Jardine Matheson and assoc. cos 1991–2000; mem. Bd of Dirs National Westminster Bank (Chair. Int. Advisory Bd) 1991–2000, Mandarin Oriental Hotel Group 1992–, J. Rothschild Name Co. 1993–2003, LVMH Louis-Vuitton-Moët-Hennessy 1995– (Chair. LVMH (UK)), British Mediterranean Airways 1997–2007, Caterpillar Inc. 2001–, Textron Corpn 2001– (mem. Int. Advisory Council), Schindler Corpn 2003–, Yell Group 2003–, Northern Trust Global Services 2005–; Chair. Singapore-British Business Council 1994–2001, Said Business School Foundation, Univ. of Oxford 1997–; Pres. China-Britain Business Council 1993–2007; Chair. Int. Advisory Bd Rolls-Royce, Barrick Gold, Diligence, ACE; Chair. All-Party Parl. Group on Entrepreneurship; Trustee Aspen Inst. 1994–, British Museum 2002–. *Address:* 24 Queen Anne's Gate, London, SW1H 9AA, England (office). *Telephone:* (20) 7799-8811 (office). *Fax:* (20) 7799-8815 (office). *E-mail:* lordpowell@charlespowell.com (office). *Website:* www.atlanticpartnership.com (office).

POWER, Samantha; American academic and journalist; *Anna Lindh Professor of Practice of Global Leadership and Public Policy, Carr Center for Human Rights Policy, John F. Kennedy School of Government, Harvard University;* b. Ireland; ed Yale Univ. and Harvard Law School; moved to USA aged nine; early career as staff mem. CBS Sports and Atlanta affiliate; covered wars in fmr Yugoslavia as reporter for U.S. News and World Report, Boston Globe, and the Economist 1993–96; joined Int. Crisis Group (ICG) as political analyst and helped launch ICG in Bosnia 1996; also worked for Carnegie Endowment for Peace, Washington, DC; adviser to fmr Democratic presidential cand. Wesley Clark 2004; Founding Exec. Dir Carr Center for Human Rights Policy, John F. Kennedy School of Govt, Harvard Univ. 1998–2002, Lecturer in Public Policy 2002–05, Anna Lindh Prof. of Practice of Global Leadership and Public Policy 2005–, took leave of absence 2005–06 to advise US Senator Barack Obama (Democrat from Ill.) on issues of foreign policy; currently a columnist for Time Magazine. *Publications:* A Problem from Hell: America and the Age of Genocide (Pulitzer Prize for Gen. Nonfiction 2003, Nat. Book Critics' Circle Award for Gen. Nonfiction 2003, Council on Foreign Relations' Arthur Ross Prize for the best book on U.S. foreign policy) 2002; Realizing Human Rights: Moving from Inspiration to Impact (co-ed.); Chasing the Flame: Sergio Vieira de Mello and the Fight to Save the World 2008; new introduction to Hannah Arendt's Origins of Totalitarianism; numerous articles on human rights and public policy. *Address:* Carr Center for Human Rights Policy, John F. Kennedy School of Goverment, Harvard University, Rubenstein-217, Mailbox 14, 79 John F. Kennedy Street, Cambridge, MA 02138-5801, USA (office). *Telephone:* (617) 495-3140 (office). *Fax:* (617) 495-4297 (office). *E-mail:* samantha_power@ksg.harvard.edu (office). *Website:* ksgfaculty.harvard.edu/Samantha_Power (office).

POWER, Simon, BA, LLB; New Zealand lawyer and politician; *Minister of Justice, of State Owned Enterprises, of Commerce, Minister Responsible for the Law Commission, Associate Minister of Finance and Deputy Leader of the House;* b. 5 Dec. 1969; m.; ed St Peter's Coll., Victoria Univ.; Assoc. Pnr and Solicitor, Fitzherbert Rowe 1993–97; Solicitor, Kensington Swan 1997; MP for Rangitikei 1999–, mem. Select Cttees on Transport and Industrial Relations 1999–2002, Justice 2002, Educ. and Science 2002–03, Foreign affairs, Defence and Trade 2003–04, Business 2004, Standing Orders 2004–05, Law and Order 2005–08, Chair. Privileges Cttee 2006–08, Senior Whip 2004–05; mem. New Zealand Nat. Party 2003–, Party Spokesman for Labour and Industrial Relations 1999–2002, for Youth Affairs 1999–2004, for Justice 2002–03, for Tertiary Educ. 2002–03, for Defence 2003–04, Veterans' Affairs 2003–04, for Conservation 2004–05, for Law and Order 2005–06, Assoc. Spokesman for Foreign Affairs 2003–04, for Educ. 2004–05; Minister of Justice, of State Owned Enterprises, of Commerce, Minister Responsible for the Law Comm., Assoc. Minister of Finance and Deputy Leader of the House 2008–. *Address:* Ministry of Justice, POB 180, Wellington, New Zealand (office). *Telephone:* (4) 918-8800 (office). *Fax:* (4) 918-8820 (office). *E-mail:* reception@justice.govt.nz (office). *Website:* www.justice.govt.nz (office).

POWERS, Richard; American writer; b. 1957; m. Jane Powers; teacher of creative writing, Univ. of Illinois; John D. and Catherine T. MacArthur Foundation grant 1989. *Publications:* Three Farmers on Their Way to a Dance (Richard and Hinda Rosenthal Foundation Award, American Acad. and Inst. of Arts and Letters, PEN/Hemingway Foundation special citation) 1985, Prisoner's Dilemma 1988, The Gold Bug Variations 1991, Operation Wandering Soul 1993, Galatea 2.2 1995, Gain (American Soc. of Historians James Fenimore Cooper Prize 1999) 1998, Plowing the Dark (American Acad. and Inst. of Arts and Letters Vursell Prize) 2000, The Time of Our Singing (WHSmith Literary Award 2004) 2003, The Echo Maker (Nat. Book Award for Fiction) 2006; contrib. to journals and magazines. *Address:* Gunther Stuhlmann, Box 276, Beckett, MA 01223, USA (office).

POWERS, William C., Jr, BA, JD; American lawyer, university administrator and academic; *President, University of Texas at Austin;* b. 30 May 1946, Los Angeles, Calif.; m. Kim Heilbrun; five c.; ed Univ. of California, Berkeley, Harvard Law School; stationed with LTJG USNR, Bahrain Island in the Persian Gulf 1967–70; Ed. Harvard Law Review 1971–72, Man. Ed. 1972–73; law clerk to Judge Eugene Wright, US Court of Appeals (Ninth Circuit) 1973–74; Teaching Fellow, Harvard Coll. 1973; mem. Washington Bar 1974–80 (resgnd), Texas Bar 1980–; Asst Prof., Univ. of Washington School of Law 1974–77, Assoc. Prof. 1977–78; Visiting Prof., Univ. of Texas School of Law Austin 1977–78, Prof. 1978–, James R. Dougherty Chair for Faculty Excellence 1984–85, Assoc. Dean for Academic Affairs 1984–87, Joseph C. Hutcheson Prof. 1985–86, Judge Benjamin Harrison Powell Prof. 1986–89, Bernard J. Ward Centennial Prof. of Law 1986–89, Fondren Foundation Centennial Chair for Faculty Excellence 1987–88, James R. Dougherty Chair for Faculty Excellence 1991–92, Assoc. Dean for Academic Affairs 1994–95, Hines H. Baker and Thelma Kelley Baker Chair in Law 1990–, Univ. Distinguished Teaching Prof. 1997–, John Jeffers Research Chair in Law 2000–05, Dean School of Law 2000–05, Regents' Chair in Higher Educ. Leadership 2006–, Pres. Univ. of Texas at Austin 2006–, Chair. ExploreUT 2005 (mem. Univ of Texas Corp. Governance Inst.) 2005; Visiting Prof., Univ. of Michigan School of Law 1981, Southern Methodist School of Law, Dallas, Texas 1982–83; Of Counsel, Hogan Dubose & Townsend, Houston, Texas (civil appellate practice) 1998–2003, Hogan & Hogan, Houston 2003–04, Beck, Redden & Secrest, Houston 2004–; worked as legal consultant with US Congress, Brazilian legislature and Tex. legislature; mem. Bd of Dirs Enron Corpn 2001–02, Chair. Special Investigation Cttee 2001–02, mem. Special Litigation Cttee 2001–02, subsequent report known as 'Powers Report' 2002; mem. Advisory Bd Southwestern Legal Foundation 1997–, Organizing Cttee Southwestern Legal Foundation Inst. of Litigation 2000–; mem. Bd Trustees Austin Presbyterian Theological Seminary 2005–; mem. American Law Inst. 1992–, Philosophical Soc. of Tex. 2003–; Fellow, Tex. Bar Foundation 1992–, American Bar Foundation 1993– (Life Fellow 2002–); ABA McKay Award 2003. *Publications:* several books, including Cases and Materials in Products Liability (co-author), Cases and Materials in Torts (co-author), Texas Products Liability Law; articles on tort law and legal philosophy; Co-reporter for "Restatement (Third) of Torts: Apportionment of Liability" 1993–2000, "Restatement (Third) of Torts: Liability for Physical Harm 2001–. *Address:* Office of the President, University of Texas at Austin, PO Box T, MAI 400, G3400, Austin, TX 78713, USA (office). *Telephone:* (512) 471-1232 (office). *Fax:* (512) 471-8102 (office). *E-mail:* president@po.utexas.edu (office). *Website:* www.utexas.edu (office).

POYNTER, John Riddoch, AO, OBE, PhD, FAHA, FASSA; Australian historian, academic and university administrator; *Professor Emeritus and Professorial Fellow, University of Melbourne;* b. 13 Nov. 1929, Coleraine, Victoria; s. of Robert Poynter and Valetta Riddoch; m. 1st Rosslyn M. Rowell 1954 (divorced 1983); two d.; m. 2nd Marion Davidson 1984; ed Trinity Grammar School, Kew, Victoria, Trinity Coll. Univ. of Melbourne and Magdalen Coll. Oxford; Dean, Trinity Coll., Univ. of Melbourne 1953–64, Ernest Scott Prof. of History 1966–75, Dean, Faculty of Arts 1971–73, Pro-Vice-Chancellor 1972–75, Deputy Vice-Chancellor (Research) 1975–82, Deputy Vice-Chancellor 1982–89, Deputy Vice-Chancellor (Academic) 1989–90, Dean, Faculty of Music, Visual and Performing Arts 1991–93, Asst Vice-Chancellor (Cultural Affairs) 1991–94, Prof. Emer. and Prof. Fellow 1995–; Nuffield Dominion Travelling Fellow, London and Oxford 1959; Visiting Fellow, ANU 1968, Carnegie Fellow, Fulbright Grant, USA 1968; Section Ed. Australian

Dictionary of Biography 1972–90; Australian Sec. Rhodes Trust 1974–97; Chair. Melbourne Univ. Press 1976–88; mem. Bd Australian-American Educ. Foundation 1977–84; Rhodes Scholar 1951; Chevalier, Ordre des Palmes Académiques 1981; Australian Dictionary of Biography Medal 2004. *Publications:* Russell Grimwade 1967, Society and Pauperism 1969, A Place Apart 1996, Doubts and Certainties 1997, Mr Felton's Bequests 2003. *Leisure interest:* music. *Address:* The Australian Centre, University of Melbourne, Parkville, Vic. 3052 (office); 38 Brougham Street, North Melbourne, Vic. 3051, Australia (home). *Telephone:* (3) 8344-2104 (office); (3) 9329-8163 (home). *Fax:* (3) 9329-8276 (home). *E-mail:* j.poynter@unimelb.edu.au (office); johnpoynter@fastmail.com (home).

POYNTZ, Rt Rev. Samuel Greenfield, BD, MA, PhD; Irish ecclesiastic (retd); b. 4 March 1926, Manitoba, Canada; s. of Rev. James Poyntz and Catherine Greenfield; m. Noreen H. Armstrong 1952; one s. two d.; ed Portora Royal School, Enniskillen and Trinity Coll. Dublin; curate, St George, Dublin 1950–52, Bray 1952–55, St Michan and St Paul, Dublin 1955–59; Incumbent, St Stephen, Dublin 1959–67, St Ann, Dublin 1967–70, St Ann with St Stephen, Dublin 1970–78; Archdeacon of Dublin 1974–78; mem. Governing Body, Univ. Coll. Cork 1978–87, Court of the Univ. of Ulster 1987–2006; Examining Chaplain to the Archbishop of Dublin 1974–78; Bishop of Cork, Cloyne and Ross 1978–87; Bishop of Connor 1987–95; Chair. Irish Council of Churches 1986–88; Co-Chair. Irish Inter-Church Meeting 1986–88; Vice-Pres. British Council of Churches 1987–90; DLitt hc (Univ. of Ulster) 1995. *Publications:* The Exaltation of the Blessed Virgin Mary 1953, Journey Towards Union 1975, Our Church – Praying with Our Church Family 1983; contrib. A Tapestry of Beliefs 1998, Mary for Earth and Heaven 2002. *Leisure interests:* stamp collecting, rugby football, travel, walking. *Address:* 3 The Gables, Ballinteer Road, Dundrum, Dublin 16, Ireland (home). *Telephone:* (1) 2966748 (home).

POŽELA, Juras, DPhys; Lithuanian physicist; *Senior Researcher, Semiconductor Physics Institute;* b. 5 Dec. 1925, Moscow; s. of Karolis Požela and Eugenija Tautkaitė; m. Rima Poželienė 1953; one s. one d.; ed Vilnius State Univ. and Moscow M. Lomonosov Univ.; Researcher, Sr Researcher, Sector Man., Dir Inst. of Physics and Math., Lithuanian Acad. of Sciences 1952–67; Dir Semiconductor Physics Inst. 1967–85, Sr Researcher 1996–; mem. Seimas (Parl.) 1992–96; Academician Lithuanian Acad. of Sciences 1968, Pres. 1984–92; mem. USSR (now Russian) Acad. of Sciences 1984, European Acad. of Sciences and Arts 1991, Academia Europaea 1993; 3rd Order of Grand Duke Gediminas (Lithuania) 1996; Lenin Prize 1978, Hero of Socialist Labour 1985, USSR State Prize 1988, Lithuanian State Prizes 1965, 1982, Lithuanian Merited Scientist 1965. *Publications include:* Plasma and Current Instabilities in Semiconductors 1981, Physics of High Speed Transistors 1993; more than 200 articles, 9 monographs; about 100 inventions. *Leisure interests:* hunting, chess. *Address:* Lithuanian Academy of Sciences, Gedimino Prospect 3, 2600 Vilnius; Semiconductor Physics Institute, A. Goštauto 11, 2600 Vilnius (office); M. Paco 7/2, apt 7, 2055 Vilnius, Lithuania (home). *Telephone:* (2) 62-71-22 (office); (2) 72-70-22 (home). *Fax:* (2) 62-71-23 (office). *E-mail:* pozela@uj.pfi.lt (office).

POZNER, Vladimir Gerald Dmitri Vladimirovich; Russian broadcaster; *President, Russian Television Academy;* b. 1 April 1934, Paris; s. of Vladimir Aleksandrovich Pozner; m. 1st (divorced); one d.; m. 2nd Yekaterina Orlova; ed Moscow Univ.; worked as trans. of medical biological literature, literary sec. of poet Samuel Marshak 1959–61; Sr Ed., Exec. Sec. Soviet Life 1961–67, Sputnik 1967–70; commentator USA and Britain Broadcasting Service of USSR TV and Radio Cttee 1970–86; political observer Cen. TV 1986–91; author of film scripts; Pres. Russian TV Acad. 1996–; mem. Fed. Tenders Comm. 2004–; mem. Bd of Dirs Transatlantic Partners Against AIDS (TPAA); Communicator of the Year Prize of Soviet Journalists' Union 1986; Communicator of the Year Medal of the Better World Soc. (with Phil Donahue). *Television shows:* regular appearances in Pozner-Donahue show, Multimedia Entertainment Inc. (USA) 1991–95; Meetings with Vladimir Pozner (Moscow Channel, Russia) 1991–94, If 1995, We 1995–2000, Man in a Mask 1996–99, Time and US 1998–2000, Times 2000–. *Publications:* Parting with Illusions 1990, Remembering War (with E. Keyssar 1990), Eyewitness 1992, numerous articles in Russian and American newspapers and magazines. *Address:* c/o Board of Directors, Transatlantic Partners Against AIDS (TPAA), Gazetny Pereulok 5, 3rd Floor, 125993 Moscow, Russia. *Telephone:* (495) 202-71-61 (Moscow); (212) 355-3454 (New York). *Fax:* (495) 230-29-41 (Moscow); (212) 644-1193 (New York).

POZO CRESPO, Mauricio, MEconSci; Ecuadorean banker, government official, banker and economist; ed Pontificia Univ. Católica del Ecuador, Univ. of Colorado, Univ. of Notre Dame, USA; Dir Stock Exchange, Quito; Dir Chamber of Commerce, Quito; Dir Seguros Equinoccial; Tech. Co-ordinator, Ecuadorean Sub-cttee, Pacific Econ. Co-operation Council (PECC); Pres. Investments Tech. Cttee, Inst. Ecuatoriano de Seguridad Social (IESS); Dir Tech. Div., Cen. Bank of Ecuador; Pres. Monetary Council 1981–91; Prof. of Econs, Pontificia Univ. Católica del Ecuador 1987–, Monterrey Tech. Inst. 1987–; Pres. Magna Credit Card 1991–93; Vice-Pres. Produbanco 1993–2000; Pres. Multienlace 2001–02; Minister of Economy and Finance 2003–04 (resgnd). *Address:* c/o Ministry of Economy and Finance, Avda 10 de Agosto 1661 y Jorge Washington, Quito, Ecuador (office).

PRABHAKARAN, Velupillai; Sri Lankan resistance leader; *Leader, Liberation Tigers of Tamil Eelam;* b. 26 Nov. 1954, Velvettithurai, Jaffna Penninsula; m. Mathy Parabhakaran 1984; two s. one d.; participated in Tamil protest movt 1970s, Founder and Leader Liberation Tigers of Tamil Eelam (LTTE); accused of involvement in murder of Mayor of Jaffna 1975, Indian Prime Minister Rajiv Gandhi 1991, convicted in absentia 1998; waged civil war against Sri Lankan Govt for 20 years with objective of securing ind. state for Tamil people.

PRABHJOT KAUR; Indian poet and politician; b. (Matia), 6 July 1924, Langaryal; d. of Nidhan Singh and Rajinder Kaur; m. Col Narenderpal Singh 1948; two d.; ed Khalsa Coll. for Women, Lahore and Punjab Univ.; first collected poems published 1943 (aged sixteen); represented India at numerous int. literary confs; mem. Legis. Council, Punjab 1966; Ed. Vikendrit; mem. Sahitya Akademi (Nat. Acad. of Letters), Exec. Bd 1978; mem. Cen. Comm. for UNESCO, Nat. Writers Cttee of India; Fellow Emer., Govt of India; received honours of Sahitya Shiromani 1964 and Padma Shri 1967; title of Rajya Kavi (Poet Laureate) conferred by Punjab Govt 1964, Sahitya Akademi Award 1964, Golden Laurel Leaves, United Poets Int., Philippines 1967, Grand Prix de la Rose de la France 1968, Most Distinguished Order of Poetry, World Poetry Soc. Intercontinental, USA 1974; Woman of the Year, UPLI, Philippines 1975, Sewa Sifti Award 1980, NIF Cultural Award 1982, Josh Kenya Award 1982, Delhi State Award 1983, Safdar Hashmi Award. *Television:* Ishak Shara Kee Nata (musical play). *Publications:* 50 books, including: Poems: Supne Sadhran 1949, Do Rang 1951, Pankheru 1956, Lala (in Persian) 1958, Bankapasi 1958, Pabbi 1962, Khari 1967, Plateau (French) 1968, Wad-darshi Sheesha 1972, Madhiantar 1974, Chandra Yug 1978, Dreams Die Young 1979, Shadows and Light (Bulgarian) 1980, Him Hans 1982, Samrup 1982, Ishq Shara Ki Nata 1983, Shadows (English and Danish) 1985, Charam Serma, Men Tapu Mukhatab Han–Manas Man the Gagan Mokla (collected poems in four vols); Short Stories: Kinke 1952, Aman de Na 1956, Zindgi de Kujh Pal 1982, Main Amanat Naheen (Hindi), Kuntith, Casket (English); autobiog.: Jeena vi 9k Ada Hai (two vols). *Leisure interests:* reading, travel. *Address:* D-203, Defence Colony, New Delhi 110024, India. *Telephone:* 4622756; 4626045.

PRADA, Michel André Jean Edmond; French civil servant; *Chairman, French Financial Markets Authority;* b. 2 April 1940, Bordeaux; s. of Robert Prada and Suzanne Prada (née Bouffard); m. Annick Saudubray 1963; two s. three d.; ed Lycée Montesquieu Bordeaux, Faculté de Droit et Inst. d'Etudes Politiques de Bordeaux, Ecole Nat. d'Admin; Inspecteur des Finances with Ministry of Econ. and Finance 1966–; Chargé de Mission, Inspection Générale des Finances 1969; Chargé de Mission, Direction de la Comptabilité Publique 1970, Asst Dir 1974, Head of Service 1977, Dir de la Comptabilité Publique 1978–85; Dir of Budget, Ministry of the Economy, Finance and the Budget 1986–88; Chair. Bd Dirs Credit d'équipement des petites et moyennes entreprises (CEPME) 1988–; Chair. Comm. des Opérations de Bourse 1995–2002; Chair. French Financial Markets Authority 2003–, Orchestre de Paris 1989–2000, Inst. d'Etudes Politiques de Bordeaux 1989–, Exec. Cttee Int. Org. of Securities Comms (IOSCO) 1996–98, Tech. Cttee of IOSCO 1998–2001, 2005–; fmr mem. Econ. and Social Council, Nat. Credit Council; Chevalier des Arts et Lettres 1995, Commdr, Légion d'honneur 2002, Grand Officier, Ordre nat. du Mérite 2005. *Address:* Teledoc 335, 139 rue de Bercy, 75572 Paris Cedex 12 (office); 2 rue Cart, 94160 Saint-Mandé, France (home). *Telephone:* 1-53-45-63-04 (office). *Fax:* 1-53-45-63-00 (office). *E-mail:* michel.prada@amf-france-org (office). *Website:* www.amf-france.org (office).

PRADA, Miuccia, PhD; Italian fashion designer; b. 1949; d. of Luisa Prada; youngest granddaughter of Prada founder Mario Prada; m. Patrizio Bertelli; c.; ed Teatro Piccolo, Milan; inherited Prada SpA business from her mother, designer for Prada since 1979, with her husband led co.'s expansion into haute couture, launched collection of women's clothing 1988, Miu Miu collection 1992, men's collection 1994; Council of Fashion Designers of America Int. Award 1993, ranked 22nd by the Financial Times amongst Top 25 Businesswomen in Europe 2005. *Address:* Prada SpA, via Andrea Maffei 2, 20135 Milan, Italy (office). *Telephone:* (02) 76001426 (office). *Website:* www.prada.com (office).

PRADHAN, Lyonpo Om, BA; Bhutanese diplomatist, politician and business executive; *Chairperson, Druk Holding and Investments Ltd;* b. 6 Oct. 1946; m.; three c.; ed Delhi Univ., India; various posts in Ministry of Trade, Industry and Forests 1969–80; Perm. Rep. to the UN 1980–84, 1998–2004; Amb. to India (also accred to Nepal and Maldives) 1984–85, Head of Bhutanese Del. to first and second rounds of boundary talks with China; Deputy Minister, Ministry of Trade and Industry 1985–89, Head of Del. to fifth round of boundary talks with China; Minister for Trade and Industry 1989–98; fmr Chief, Policy Devt and Coordination Monitoring and Reporting Unit, UN Office of High Rep. for the Least Developed Countries, Landlocked Countries and Small Island Developing Sites (UN-OHRLLS); Chair. Druk Holding and Investments Ltd 2007–; mem. Nat. Ass., Council of Ministers; Chair. State Trading Corpn, Chhukha Hydroelectric Project Corpn and Tala Hydroelectric Project Authority; mem. Planning Comm., Nat. Environment Comm. *Address:* Druk Holding and Investments Ltd, PO Box 1127, Motithang, Thimphu, Bhutan (office). *Telephone:* (2) 336257 (office). *Fax:* (2) 336259 (office). *E-mail:* info@dhi.bt (office). *Website:* www.dhi.bt (office).

PRADHAN, Sahana Devi, MEconSc; Nepalese lawyer, women's rights activist and politician; b. 15 July 1932; m. Pushpa Lal Pradhan (died 1978); ed Patna Univ., Tribhuvan Univ., Kathmandu, Delhi Univ., India; began teaching during the ban on political parties 1960; Chair. United Left Front 1990; Minister of Industry 1990–91, of Women, Children and Social Welfare 1997–98, of Foreign Affairs April 2007–08; Sr Partner, Development Law Assocs 1992–; co-f. Forum for Women, Law and Development, Exec. Dir and Pres. 1995–; fmrly consultant to UN Div. for Advancement of Women to Analyze Impact of Strategies on Violence Against Women; mem. Communist Party of Nepal (Unified Marxist-Leninist— UML). *Address:* Communist Party of Nepal, Kathmandu, Nepal (office).

PRADHAN, Trilochan, MSc, PhD; Indian physicist and academic; *Professor Emeritus, Institute of Physics, Bhubaneshwar;* b. 3 Jan. 1929, Ghanashalia, Orissa; s. of Ramachandra and Ahalya Dakshinaray; m. Sanjukta Pradhan 1959; one s. one d.; ed Utkal Univ., Benares Hindu Univ. and Univ. of Chicago; Research Assoc., Univ. of Chicago 1956–57, Niels Bohr Inst., Copenhagen 1957–58; Lecturer in Physics, Ravenshaw Coll., Cuttack 1951–62; Assoc. Prof., Saha Inst. of Nuclear Physics, Calcutta 1962–67, Prof. and Head, Div. of Theoretical Nuclear Physics 1967–74; Founder Dir, Inst. of Physics, Bhubaneshwar 1974–89, Prof. Emer. 1989–; Visiting Prof., Univ. of Virginia 1985; Vice-Chancellor, Utkal Univ. 1989–91; Visiting Scientist, Int. Centre for Theoretical Physics, Trieste 1966–97, Univ. of Syracuse 1967, Univ. of Texas, Austin 1970, Inst. of Theoretical Physics, Gothenberg 1973, KEK, Japan 1985; Meghnad Saha Award, Univ. Grants Comm. of India 1980, Pres. of India's Padma Bhusan Award 1990. *Publications:* The Photon 2001, Quantum Mechanics 2008; about 60 papers on theoretical physics in the areas of elementary particles, atomic physics, plasma physics. *Leisure interests:* gardening, indoor games. *Address:* Institute of Physics, Bhubaneswar 751005 (office); 71 Gajapatinagar, Bhubaneswar 751005, India (home). *Telephone:* (674) 2300637 (office); (674) 2300962. *E-mail:* pradhan@iopb.res .in (office).

PRADIER, Henri Joseph Marie; French engineer; b. 5 Nov. 1931, Sainte-Colombe-lès-Vienne, Rhône; s. of Camille Pradier and Anne-Marie Côte; m. 1st Marie-France Michot (deceased); two s.; m. 2nd Brigitte Dapvril 1973; one s. one d.; ed Institution Robin, Vienne, Lycée du Parc, Lyons and Ecole Polytechnique; consulting engineer 1955–58; Shell Française 1958–67 and 1970; Man. Dir Shell du Maroc 1967–79, Vice-Pres. Distribution 1975–84; Man. Dir Shell Française 1984–92, now Hon. Pres.; Dir Soc. pour l'Utilisation Rationnelle des Gaz (Butagaz) 1975, Shell Chimie 1984, Hosp. Works Française de L'Ordre de Malte (OHFOM) 1992–95, St Joseph and St Luke Hospital, Lyon 1994–97, Publicis 1998–; Chevalier Légion d'honneur, Officer, Order of Orange-Nassau (Netherlands). *Leisure interests:* gardening, sailing, swimming. *Address:* 52 rue du Ranelagh, 75016 Paris, France.

PRAKKE, Lucas, LLD; Dutch academic; *Professor Emeritus of Law, University of Amsterdam;* b. 20 Feb. 1938, Groningen; m. Margaretha M. O. de Bruijn Kops 1965; two s.; ed Gemeentelijk Lyceum, Doetinchem, Univ. of Amsterdam and Columbia Univ. Law School, New York; Asst Prof. of Law, Univ. of Amsterdam 1963–72, Prof. of Dutch and Comparative Constitutional Law 1972–2003, Dean, Faculty of Law 1981–83, Prof. Emer. 2003–; Judge, Civil Service Appeal Tribunal 1977–89; mem. Royal Comm. on Constitution 1982–85; mem. Royal Netherlands Acad. *Publications:* Principles of Constitutional Interpretation in the Netherlands 1970, Toetsing in het publiekrecht 1972, Pluralisme en staatsrecht 1974, Het bestuursrecht van de landen der Europese Gemeenschappen 1986, Bedenkingen tegen het toetsingsrecht (Report of Netherlands Lawyers' Asscn) 1992, Swamping the Lords, Packing the Court, Sacking the King: Address on 'dies natalis' of University of Amsterdam 1994, Handboek van het Nederlandse staatsrecht 1995, Het staatsrecht van de landen van de Europese Unie (5th edn) 1998, Pluralisme van Staatsrecht 2003. *Leisure interests:* history, music, walking. *Address:* Faculteit der Rechtsgeleerdheid, universiteit van Amsterdam, Postbus 1030, 1000 BA Amsterdam (office); Koedijklaan 15, 1406 KW Bussum, Netherlands (home). *Telephone:* (20) 5253966 (office); (35) 6989520 (home). *Fax:* (35) 6989501 (home).

PRANCE, Sir Ghillean Tolmie, Kt, DPhil, FRS; British botanist; *Director of Research, The Eden Project;* b. 13 July 1937, Brandeston, Suffolk; s. of Basil Camden Prance and Margaret Hope Prance (née Tolmie); m. Anne Elizabeth Hay 1961; two d.; ed Malvern Coll., Keble Coll. Oxford; Research Asst, The New York Botanical Garden 1963–66, Assoc. Curator 1966–68, Krukoff Curator of Amazonian Botany 1968–75, Dir of Botanical Research 1975–81, Vice-Pres. 1977–81, Sr Vice-Pres. 1981–88; Dir Inst. of Economic Botany 1981–88; Dir Royal Botanic Gardens, Kew 1988–99; Dir of Research, The Eden Project 1999–; McBryde Prof. Nat. Tropical Botanical Garden 2000–02; Adjunct Prof., City Univ. of New York 1968–99; Dir of Graduate Studies, Instituto Nacional de Pesquisas da Amazônia, Brazil 1973–75; Exec. Dir Org. for Flora Neotropica 1975–88; Visiting Prof. in Tropical Studies, Yale Univ. 1983–88; Visiting Prof., Reading Univ. 1988–; Chair. Bentham-Moxon Trust 1988–99, Brazilian Atlantic Rainforest Trust 1999–, Global Diversity Foundation 1999–; Pres. Linnean Soc. of London 1997–2000; Trustee Au Sable Inst. of Environmental Studies 1984–, Margaret Mee Amazon Trust 1988–96, Worldwide Fund for Nature Int. 1989–93, Horniman Museum 1990–99; Pres. Asscn of Tropical Biology 1979–80, American Asscn of Plant Taxonomists 1984–85, Systematics Asscn 1988–91, Inst. of Biology 2000–02; mem. Bd of Govs Lovaine Trust Co. Ltd 1989–99; Council mem. Royal Horticultural Soc. 1990–2000; Corresp. mem. Botanical Soc. of America 1994; Hon. mem. British Ecological Soc. 1996–; Commendador da Ordem Nacional do Cruzeiro do Sul (Brazil) 2000; Hon. FilDr (Göteborg) 1983; Hon. DSc (Univ. of Kent at Canterbury) 1994, (Portsmouth) 1994, (Kingston) 1994, (St Andrews) 1995, (City Univ., New York) 1998, Dr hc (Bergen) 1996, (Sheffield) 1997, (Florida) 1997, (Liverpool) 1998, (Glasgow) 1999, (Plymouth) 1999, (Keele) 2000, (Exeter) 2000; Henry Shaw Medal, Missouri Botanical Garden 1988, Linnean Medal 1990, Int. Cosmos Prize 1993, Patron's Medal (Royal Geographical Soc.) 1994, Asa Gray Award (American Soc. of Plant Taxonomists) 1998, Int. Award of Excellence (Botanical Research Inst. of Tex.) 1998, Lifetime Discovery Award 1999, Victoria Medal of Honour, Royal Horticultural Soc. 1999, Fairchild Medal for Botanical Exploration 2000, Soc. for Econ. Botany Award 2002, Graziela Barroso Prize Brazilian Botanic Garden Network 2004, Allerton Award, Nat. Tropical Botanical Garden 2005. *Television:* Superteacher (NHK, Japan) 2002. *Publications:* Arvores de Manaus 1975, Extinction is Forever 1977, Biological Diversification in the Tropics 1981, Amazonia–Key Environments 1985, Tropical Forests and World Climate 1986, Leaves 1986, White Gold 1989, Wildflowers for All Seasons 1989, Out of the Amazon 1992, Bark 1993, Rainforests of the World 1998; Ed. 14 books; numerous scientific and gen. articles. *Leisure interests:* bird watching, stamp collecting. *Address:* The Eden Project, Bodelva, Cornwall, PL24 2SG (office); The Old Vicarage, Silver Street, Lyme Regis, Dorset, DT7 3HS, England. *Telephone:* (1726) 811900 (office); (1297) 444991 (home). *Fax:* (1297) 444955 (home). *E-mail:* gprance@edenproject.com (office); gtolmiep@aol.com (home). *Website:* www.edenproject.com (office).

PRAPAS CHARUSATHIRA, General (see Charusathira, General Prapas).

PRASAD, Alok, BA, MA; Indian diplomatist; *High Commissioner to Sri Lanka;* m. Nandini Prasad; two c.; ed Delhi Univ.; joined Indian Foreign Service 1974, has represented India in various capacities in Germany, UN (New York), the Netherlands, Nepal, Burma and Botswana; also worked in Prime Minister's Office; Jt Sec. for Americas Div., Ministry of External Affairs, New Delhi 1995–2000; Deputy Chief of Mission, Washington, DC 2000–04; High Commr to Singapore 2004–06, to Sri Lanka 2006–; Fellow, Center for Int. Affairs, Harvard Univ., USA. *Address:* High Commission of India, 36–38 Galle Road, Colombo 03, Sri Lanka (office). *Telephone:* (11) 2447285 (office); (11) 2580970 (home). *Fax:* (11) 2446403 (office). *E-mail:* hc .colombo@mea.gov.in (office). *Website:* www.hcicolombo.org (office).

PRASAD, Ashoka, MD, FRHistS; Indian psychiatrist and university professor; b. 10 May 1955, Patna; s. of the late Judge Jahnavi Prasad and Usha Prasad; ed Colvin Taluqdar's Coll., Lucknow, GSVM Medical Coll. Kanpur; Resident in Paediatrics and Psychiatry, Castlebar Gen. Hosp., Eire, Resident in Psychiatry, Royal Edin. Hosp., Edin. 1980–83; Research Fellow, Depts of Biochem. and Psychiatry, Univ. of Leeds 1983–85; Kate Stillman Lecturer in Psychiatry, Univ. Coll. Hosp. and Queen Charlotte's Hosp., London 1984–86; Consultant Psychiatrist, Whipps Cross Hosp., Claybury Hosp. and Thorpe Coombe Hosp., London 1986–87; in charge of Psychopharmacology and Hon. Sr Lecturer, Mental Health Research Inst. and Monash Univ., Melbourne, Australia, Assoc. Dept of Psychiatry, Univ. of Melbourne 1987; Visiting Specialist, Kingseat Hosp., NZ 1988; Consultant Psychiatrist, Claybury Hosp., London and St Margaret's Hosp., Essex 1988–89; at Dept of Psychiatry, Dalhousie Univ., Canada, Dept of Psychology, St Mary's Univ., Canada 1989; J. Ernest Runions Fellow, Dept of Psychiatry, Univ. of BC, Vancouver 1989–90; Prof. of Psychiatry, Hahnemann Univ., Phila, USA 1990–91; Adjunct Prof. of Medical Anthropology, Columbia Univ., USA 1990–91, of Anthropology, Univ. of Pa 1991; Medical Dir Phila Consultation Center 1990–92; currently hon. consultant to several bodies, including Jain TV, India, for medical programmes, Hon. Adviser 1993–; several visiting professorships including Harvard Univ. 1986, 1991; Foreign Academician Royal Swedish Acad. of Sciences; Hon. Foreign mem. American Acad. of Arts and Sciences; Dr Med hc (Natal), (Karolinska Inst. Stockholm); Murphy Award 1987, Blueler Award 1987. *Publications:* five books including Biological Basis and Therapy of Neuroses; over 125 publs in various journals. *Leisure interests:* birdwatching, unravelling Greek myths, cricket, history of science and medicine, naturopathy. *Address:* 1 Avas Vikas, Betia Hata, Gorakhpur 273001, India (home). *Telephone:* (551) 334020 (home). *Fax:* (551) 332845 (home). *E-mail:* praashok@gmail.com (home).

PRASAD, Mahabir, LLB, MA; Indian politician; b. 11 Nov. 1939, Ujjarpur Village, Uttar Pradesh; s. of Amar Prasad; m. Udasi Devi; two d.; Gen. Sec., Gorakhpur Uttar Pradesh Congress Cttee 1975–78 (fmr Vice-Pres. and three-times Pres.); fmr Gen. Sec. All-India Congress Cttee; mem. Uttar Pradesh Ass. 1974–77, Lok Sabha 1980, 1984, 1989, Estimates Cttee 1985–86; Deputy Minister for Railways 1986–89; Minister of State for Steel and Mines July–Nov. 1989; Gov. of Haryana 1995–2000. *Address:* Raj Bhavan, Haryana, Chandigarh, India (office).

PRASAD, Mata; Indian politician; b. 11 Oct. 1925, Machi Shahar; s. of Rajji Devi and Jagarup Ram; m. Lekhraji Mata Prasad; three s. two d.; ed Sahitya Ratna; mem. UP Ass. 1957–77, Legis. Council 1980–92; Gen. Sec. UP Congress Cttee 1971–73, 1980–82; mem. UP Congress Legislature Party 1982–86, Treas. 1986–92; Cabinet mem. 1988–89; Chair. UP Congress Cttee SC/ST 1982–88; Gov. of Arunachal Pradesh 1993–99; Chair. Poorvottar Parishad 1993–99; Vice-Pres. Al Dalit Sahitya Acad.; Sec. UP Dalit Varg Sangh; mem. Housing and Devt Bd and Minority Comm., UP; Hon. DLit (Purvanchal Univ.) 1998 numerous awards including Dr Ambedkar Nat. Award 1988, Keerti Bharti 1994, Sahitya Bhusan 1995, Lok Mitra 1997, Bharat Jyoti Award 2001. *Publications:* more than 20 books including works of poetry and drama; Jhopdi Se Raj Bhawan (autobiog). *Address:* 20/25 Indira Nagar, Lucknow 226016, UP, India (office); PO Box Kacheheri, PS Line Bazar, Shekhpura, Jaunpur District, UP (home). *Telephone:* (9415) 207155 (office); (5452) 261835 (home).

PRASAD, Siddheshwar, DLitt; Indian politician; b. 19 June 1929, Bind; s. of Bhikari Mahton; m. Rajkumari Prasad; six c.; Lecturer, Nalanda Coll., Biharsharif 1953–61; mem. Lok Sabha 1962–77; Deputy Minister for Irrigation and Power 1967–71, for Industrial Devt 1971–73, for Heavy Industry Feb.–Nov. 1973, for Irrigation 1973–74, for Energy 1974–77; Minister, Govt of Bihar 1985–88; Gov. of Tripura 1995–99; Chair. Gandhi-Marx Research Inst.; Exec. Chair. Rashtra Bhasha Prachar Samiti; Sec.-Gen. Third World Hindi Conf. *Publications:* Chhayavadottar Kavya, Satyagraha Aur Vigyan, Sahitya Ka Muyankan, Upanishad Chintan Aur Adhunik Jiwan, Ekalavyon Aur Abimanyuon Se, Multi-Dimensional Transformation, Vichar Pravah, New Economic Policy, The Vedic Vision. *Address:* Sector 7, Block 1, 23 Bahadurpur HIG Cology, Kankarbagh, Patna 800020, India (office).

PRASAD, Sunand, MA, PhD; Indian architect; *Partner, Penoyre & Prasad LLP;* b. 22 May 1950, Dehra Dun, India; m. Susan Francis; three c.; ed Cambridge School of Architecture, Architectural Asscn, Royal Coll. of Art;

partner in Edward Cullinan Architects 1976–85; Leverhulme Research Fellow RCA 1985–88; founding partner Penoyre & Prasad LLP 1988–; Vice-Pres. Architectural Asscn 1999–2001; Commr Comm. for Architecture and the Built Environment 1999–; mem. Council and Bd RIBA 2004–; Eternit Award for Architecture 1989, RIBA Regional Award 1991, 1992, RIBA Award 1997, 1999, 2000, 2001, 2003, American Inst. of Architects/UK Excellence in Design Award 1998, Design Sense 1999, numerous other architectural awards. *Publications:* Accommodating Diversity: Housing Design in a Multi-Cultural Society 1998, Paradigms of Indian Architecture 1998, Contemporary Hospital Design (ed) 2005; chapters in Le Corbusier: Architect of the Century 1987, Designing Better Buildings 2003. *Leisure interests:* music, sail boarding. *Address:* Penoyre & Prasad LLP, 28–42 Banner Street, London, EC1Y 8QE, England (office). *Telephone:* (20) 7250-3477 (office). *Fax:* (20) 7250-0844 (office). *E-mail:* s.prasad@penoyre-prasad.net (office). *Website:* www.penoyre-prasad.net (office).

PRASAD SINGH, Balmiki, MA; Indian politician; *Governor of Sikkim;* b. 1 Jan. 1942; m. Karuna Singh; three c.; ed Patna Univ., Oxford Univ.; fmr Lecturer in Political Sciences, Patna Univ.; Deputy Sec., Ministry of Defence 1975–79; Sec. for All Depts under the Chief Sec. and Home Sec., Govt of Assam 1980–82, mem. Assam Planning Bd 1982–84, Agricultural Production Commr, Special Commr and Special Sec., Sec. 1990–92; Jt Sec. Ministry of Steel and Mines 1984–89; Jt Sec., then Additional Sec., Ministry of Home Affairs 1992–93; Additional Sec., Ministry of Environment and Forests 1993–95, Chair. Nat. Cttee on Bio-diversity Conservation, Asia Rep. on Ramar Convention on Wetlands, Gland, Switzerland; Union Culture Sec., Govt of India 1995–97, Union Home Sec. 1997–99; Exec. Dir World Bank, representing India, Bangladesh, Bhutan and Sri Lanka 1999–2002; Gov. of Sikkim 2008–; Jawaharlal Nehru Fellow 1982–84; Queen Elizabeth Fellow, Univ. of Oxford 1989–90; mem. Indian Nat. Trust for Arts and Cultural Heritage 1995–; Gov. of Assam Gold Medal 1991, Gulzarilal Nanda Award 1998, Man of Letters Award, Subabh Int. 2003. *Publications:* Threads Woven: Ideals, Principles & Administration 1975, The Indian National Congress and Cultural Renaissance 1987, The Problem of Change: A Study of North-East India 1987, Culture: the State, the Arts and Beyond 1998, Bahudha and the post-9/11 World 2008; numerous articles and monographs on culture, poverty, ecology and public admin in India and abroad. *Address:* Raj Bhavan, Gangtok, Sikkim, India (office). *Telephone:* (3592) 202400 (office); (3592) 202410 (office). *Fax:* (3592) 202742 (office). *E-mail:* governor-skm@nic.in (office). *Website:* sikkim.gov.in (office).

PRASHAR, Baroness (Life Peer), cr. 1999, of Runnymede in the County of Surrey; **Usha Kumari Prashar,** CBE, BA, FRSA; British civil servant; *First Civil Service Commissioner;* b. 29 June 1948, Nairobi, Kenya; d. of Nauhria Lal Prashar and Durga Devi Prashar; m. Vijay Kumar Sharma 1973; ed Duchess of Gloucester School, Nairobi, Wakefield Girl's High School, Univ. of Leeds, Univs of Leeds and Glasgow; Conciliation Officer, Race Relations Bd 1971–75; Asst Dir Runnymede Trust 1975–77, Dir 1977–84; Residential Fellow, Policy Studies Inst. 1984–86 (mem. Council 1992–97); Dir Nat. Council for Voluntary Orgs 1986–91; Civil Service Commr (part-time) 1990–96, First Civil Service Commr 2000–; Chair. Parole Bd of England and Wales 1997–2000; Deputy Chair. Nat. Literacy Trust 1992–2000, Chair. 2001–; mem. Bd of Dirs (non-exec.) Channel 4 1992–99, Unite PLC 2001–, ITV 2005–, Salzburg Seminar; Vice-Chair. British Refugee Council 1987–89; mem. Arts Council of GB 1979–81, Arts Council of England 1994–97, Study Comm. on the Family 1980–83, Social Security Advisory Cttee 1980–83, Exec. Cttee, Child Poverty Action Group 1984–85, Greater London Arts Asscn 1984–86, London Food Comm. 1984–90, BBC Educational Broadcasting Council 1987–89, Advisory Council, Open Coll. 1987–89, Solicitors' Complaints Bureau 1989–90, Royal Comm. on Criminal Justice 1991–93, Lord Chancellor's Advisory Cttee on Legal Educ. and Conduct 1991–97, Bd Energy Saving Trust 1992–98, King's Fund 2000–, Jt Cttee on Human Rights; Trustee Thames Help Trust 1984–86, Charities Aid Foundation 1986–91, Ind. Broadcasting Telethon Trust 1987–92, Acad. of Indian Dance 1987–91, Camelot Foundation 1996–, Ethnic Minority Foundation 2000–; Chair. English Advisory Cttee, Nat. AIDS Trust 1988–89; Patron Sickle Cell Soc. 1986–, Elfrida Rathbone Soc. 1988–; Chancellor De Montfort Univ. 2000– (Gov. 1996–); Hon. Vice-Pres. Council for Overseas Student Affairs 1986–; Hon. Fellow Goldsmiths' Coll., Univ. of London 1992; Hon. LLD (De Montfort) 1994, (South Bank) 1994, (Greenwich) 1999, (Leeds Metropolitan) 1999, (Ulster) 2000, (Oxford Brookes) 2000; Asian Women of Achievement Award 2002. *Publications include:* contribs to Britain's Black Population 1980, The System: A Study of Lambeth Borough Council's Race Relations Unit 1981, Scarman and After 1984, Sickle Cell Anaemia, Who Cares? A Survey of Screen, Counselling, Training and Educational Facilities in England 1985, Routes or Road Blocks, A Study of Consultation Arrangements Between Local Authorities and Local Communities 1985, Acheson and After: Primary Health Care in the Inner City 1986. *Leisure interests:* reading, music, golf, current affairs. *Address:* House of Lords, Westminster, London, SW1A 0PW (office); First Civil Service Commissioner, 35 Great Smith Street, London, SW 1P 3BQ, England (office). *Telephone:* (20) 7219-6792 (office). *Fax:* (20) 7276-2102 (office). *E-mail:* prasharu@parliament.uk (office). baroness.prashar@cabinet_office.x.grix.gov.uk (office). *Website:* www.civilservicecommissioners.gov.uk (office).

PRAT-GAY, Alfonso; Argentine central bank governor; *Governor, Central Bank of Argentina;* ed Pennsylvania Univ., USA; trained as economist; worked for macro-econ. consultancy, Buenos Aires –1991; country economist (Argentina), JP Morgan, New York 1994, Head of Emerging Market Proprietary Trading Desk, London –1999, Chief of Currency Strategy (cr. Liquidity and Credit Premia Index—LCPI), London 1999–2001; Prof., Univ. of Buenos Aires 2001–02; Gov. Cen. Bank of Argentina 2002–. *Address:* Banco Central de la Republica Argentina, Reconquista 266, 1003 Buenos Aires, Argentina (office). *Telephone:* (11) 4348-3500 (office). *Website:* www.bcra.gov.ar (office).

PRATCHETT, Sir Terence (Terry) David John, Kt, OBE; British writer; b. 28 April 1948, Beaconsfield, Bucks.; m. Lyn Marian Purves 1968; one d.; journalist 1965–80; Press Officer Cen. Electricity Generating Bd 1980–87; Chair. Soc. of Authors 1994–95; Hon. DLitt (Warwick) 1999. *Publications:* Discworld series: The Dark Side of the Sun 1976, Strata 1981, The Colour of Magic 1983, The Light Fantastic 1986, Equal Rites 1987, Mort 1987, Sourcery 1989, Wyrd Sisters 1988, Pyramids (BSFA Award for best novel) 1989, Eric 1989, Guards! Guards! 1989, Moving Pictures 1990, Reaper Man 1991, Witches Abroad 1991, Small Gods 1992, Lords and Ladies 1993, Men at Arms 1993, The Streets of Ankh-Morpork (with Stephen Briggs) 1993, Soul Music 1994, Interesting Times 1994, The Discworld Companion (with Stephen Briggs) 1994, Maskerade 1995, Discworld Map (with Stephen Briggs) 1995, Feet of Clay 1996, Hogfather 1996, The Pratchett Portfolio (with Paul Kidby) 1996, Jingo 1997, The Last Continent 1998, Carpe Jugulum 1998, A Tourist Guide to Lancre (with Stephen Briggs and Paul Kidby) 1998, The Fifth Elephant 1999, Death's Domain (with Paul Kidby) 1999, The Truth 2000, Nanny Ogg's Cookbook (with Stephen Briggs, Tina Hannan and Paul Kidby) 2000, The Last Hero 2001, Thief of Time 2001, Night Watch 2002, The Science of the Discworld I, II, III (with others) 2002, Monstrous Regiment 2003, The Wee Free Men 2003, A Hat Full of Sky 2004, Going Postal 2004, Thud! 2005, Where's My Cow 2005, Wintersmith 2006, Making Money 2007; other fiction: The Carpet People 1971, The Unadulterated Cat (with Gray Jolliffe) 1989, Truckers 1989, Diggers 1990, Wings 1990, Good Omens: The Nice and Accurate Predictions of Agnes Nutter, Witch (with Neil Gaiman) 1990, Only You Can Save Mankind 1992, Johnny and the Dead 1993, Johnny and the Bomb 1996, The Amazing Maurice and his Educated Rodents (Carnegie Medal) 2001, Nation 2008; screenplay: Terry Pratchett's Hogfather (BAFTA Award 2007) 2006; other: short stories. *Leisure interests:* astronomy, gardening, folklore. *Address:* c/o Colin Smythe, PO Box 6, Gerrards Cross, Bucks., SL9 8XA, England (office). *Telephone:* (1753) 886000 (office). *Website:* www.terrypratchettbooks.com (office).

PRATS, Francisco Guerrero; Dominican Republic politician; Gov. Cen. Bank –2003; Sec. of State for External Relations 2003–04; fmr Chair. Council of Ministers of Asscn of Caribbean States. *Address:* c/o Secretariat of State for External Relations, Avenida Independencia 752, Santo Domingo DN, Dominican Republic (office).

PRATT, Cynthia Alexandria, BSc; Bahamian politician; b. 5 Nov. 1945; d. of the late Herman Mackay and Rose Mackay; m. Joseph Benjamin Pratt; six c.; ed Western Sr School, Princess Margaret Hosp. School of Nursing, Aquinas Coll., Nassau, St Augustine's Coll., Raleigh, NC, USA; surgical nurse, Princess Margaret Hosp., Nassau 1971–79; Head Dept of Physical Educ., C. C. Sweeting High School 1978–91; part-time Lecturer and Asst Dir of Student Activities, Coll. of the Bahamas 1991–96; MP (PLP) for St Cecilia, New Providence; fmrly Chief Opposition Whip, House of Ass.; Deputy Prime Minister and Minister of Nat. Security 2002–07; f. St Cecilia's Church Youth and Ladies Club, Dr Keva Bethel Basketball Classic, Cocunut Grove Youth Club; recruiter for St Augustine's Coll., Raleigh, NC; Coach and Rep. of Bahamas overseas in softball, volleyball and basketball; mem. Kappa Delta Pi Soc., Alpha Kappa Mu Honour Soc.; Hon. DHumLitt (Raleigh, NC). *Leisure interests:* arranging sporting events, coaching and meeting people, serving the under-privileged. *Address:* Poincianna Avenue and Six Street, Nassau, NP, The Bahamas (home). *Telephone:* 422-5542 (home).

PRATT, (John) Christopher, OC, CC, RCA, BFA; Canadian painter and printmaker; b. 9 Dec. 1935, St John's, Newfoundland; s. of John Kerr Pratt and Christine Emily (née Dawe) Pratt; m. 1st Mary Frances West 1957 (divorced 2004); two s. two d.; m. 2nd Jeanette Meehan 2007; ed Prince of Wales Coll., St John's, Newfoundland, Memorial Univ. of Newfoundland, Mount Allison Univ., Sackville, NB and the Glasgow School of Art, Scotland; taught as specialist in art, Memorial Univ. 1961–63; freelance artist 1963–; mem. Mount Carmel Town Council 1969–73, Postage Stamp Design Cttee, Ottawa 1970–73, The Canada Council 1976–82, Memorial Univ. Bd of Regents 1972–75; Hon. Chair. Bay Roberts Heritage Soc. 1999–; Hon. DLitt (Memorial) 1972; Hon. LLD (Mount Allison) 1973, (Dalhousie) 1986. *Publications:* Christopher Pratt 1982, The Prints of Christopher Pratt (with Mira Godard) 1991, Christopher Pratt: Personal Reflections on a Life in Art 1995, Christopher Pratt: All My Own Work 2005, A Painter's Poems 2005. *Leisure interests:* offshore sailing, walking/hiking and fly-fishing. *Address:* PO Box 87, Mount Carmel, St Mary's Bay, Newfoundland, A0B 2M0, Canada. *Telephone:* (709) 521-2048 (office); (709) 521-2048 (home). *Fax:* (709) 521-2707 (office).

PRAWER, Siegbert Salomon, MA, DLitt, PhD, LittD, FBA; British university teacher and author (retd); b. 15 Feb. 1925, Cologne, Germany; s. of Marcus Prawer and Eleonora Prawer; brother of Ruth Prawer Jhabvala (q.v.); m. Helga Alice Schaefer 1949; one s. two d. (and one s. deceased); ed King Henry VIII School, Coventry, Jesus Coll., Christ's Coll. Cambridge; Adelaide Stoll Research Student, Christ's Coll. Cambridge 1947–48; Asst Lecturer, then Lecturer, then Sr Lecturer, Univ. of Birmingham 1948–63; Prof. of German, Westfield Coll., London Univ. 1964–69; Taylor Prof. of German Language and Literature, Oxford 1969–86, Prof. Emer. 1986–; Co-editor, Oxford Germanic Studies 1971–75, Anglica Germanica 1973–79; Fulbright Exchange Scholar, Columbia Univ. 1956; Visiting Prof. City Coll., New York 1956–57, Univ. of Chicago 1963–64, Harvard Univ. 1968, Hamburg Univ. 1969, Univ. of Calif. at Irvine 1975, Otago Univ., NZ 1976, Univ. of Pittsburgh 1977, Australian Nat. Univ., Canberra 1980, Brandeis Univ. 1981–82; Resident Fellow, Knox Coll., Dunedin, NZ 1976, Russell Sage Foundation, New York 1988; Fellow Queen's Coll. Oxford 1969–86, Supernumerary Fellow 1986–90, Hon. Fellow 1990, Dean of Degrees 1976–93; Pres. British Comparative Literature Asscn

1984–87, Hon. Fellow 1989; Corresp. Fellow German Acad. of Literature 1989; Pres. English Goethe Soc. 1992–95, Vice-Pres. 1995–; Hon. Dir London Univ. Inst. of Germanic Studies 1967–69, Hon. Fellow 1986; Hon. mem. Modern Languages Asscn of America 1986; Hon. Fellow Jesus Coll. Cambridge 1996–; Hon. DPhil (Cologne) 1985; Hon. DLitt (Birmingham) 1988; Goethe Medal 1973, Gold Medal, German Goethe Soc. 1995; Isaac Deutscher Memorial Prize 1977, Gundolf-Prize of the German Acad. 1986. *Publications:* German Lyric Poetry 1952, Mörike und seine Leser 1960, Heine's Buch der Lieder: A Critical Study 1960, Heine: The Tragic Satirist 1962, The Penguin Book of Lieder 1964, The Uncanny in Literature (inaugural lecture) 1965, Heine's Shake-speare, a Study in Contexts (inaugural lecture) 1970, Comparative Literary Studies: An Introduction 1973, Karl Marx and World Literature 1976, Caligari's Children: The Film as Tale of Terror 1980, Heine's Jewish Comedy: A Study of His Portraits of Jews and Judaism 1983, Coalsmoke and Englishmen 1984, A. N. Stencl–Poet of Whitechapel 1984, Frankenstein's Island–England and the English in the Writings of Heinrich Heine 1986, Israel at Vanity Fair: Jews and Judaism in the Writings of W. M. Thackeray 1992, Breeches and Metaphysics, Thackeray's German Discourse 1997, W. M. Thackeray's European Sketch Books: A Study of Literary and Graphic Portraiture 2000, The Blue Angel 2002, Werner Herzog's Nosferatu 2004, Between Two Worlds: The Jewish Presence in German and Austrian Film 1910–1933 2005; edited: The Penguin Book of Lieder 1964, Essays in German Language, Culture and Society (with R. H. Thomas and L. W. Forster) 1969, The Romantic Period in Germany 1970, Seventeen Modern German Poets 1971; screenplay: Das Kabinett des Dr Caligari (ed and introduction); numerous articles on German, English and comparative literature. *Leisure interest:* portrait drawing. *Address:* The Queen's College, Oxford, OX1 4AW, England (office). *Telephone:* (1865) 279121 (office); (1865) 557614 (home).

PRAWIRO, Radius, MA; Indonesian politician, economist and banker; b. 29 June 1928, Yogjakarta; ed Senior High School, Yogjakarta, Nederlandsche Economische Hoogeschool, Rotterdam, Econ. Univ. of Indonesia; Sec. Defence Cttee, Yogjakarta during revolution 1945; with Army High Command, Yogjakarta 1946–47; Angauta Tentara Pelajar (Army) 1948–51; Officer in Govt Audit Office, Ministry of Finance 1953–65; Vice-Minister, Deputy Supreme Auditor, mem. Supreme Audit Office 1965–66; Gov. Bank Indonesia 1966–73; Chair. Indonesian Asscn of Accountants 1965–; Gov. IMF for Indonesia 1967–72, Alt. Gov. Asian Devt Bank 1967–72; Minister of Trade 1973–78, of Trade and Co-operatives 1978–83, of Finance 1983–88, Co-ordinating Minister of Econs, Finance, Industry and Devt Supervision 1988–93; Chair. Bd of Govs IBRD, IDA, IFC 1971–72; mem. Econ. Council of the Pres. 1968, Nat. Econ. Stabilization Council 1968, Gov. Bd Christian Univ. of Indonesia, Supervisory Bd Trisakti Univ.; Order of Sacred Treasure. *Address:* Jalan Imam Bonjol 4, Jakarta, Indonesia (home).

PRAWIT, Gen. Wongsuwan; Thai army officer and politician; *Minister of Defence;* b. 11 Aug. 1945; ed Chulachomklao Mil. Coll., Army Chief of Staff School, Nat. Defence Coll.; platoon leader, rifle, 2nd Battalion, 3rd combat team 1969, platoon leader heavy mortar, 21st Regt 1971, Commdr rifle co., 2nd Battalion 1974, Officer, Operations and Training, 2nd Infantry Battalion 1976; Staff Officer, Chief of Staff School 1977; Officer, Operations Unit 1979, Deputy Commdr 1st Infantry Battalion, 21st Regt 1980, Commdr 2nd Infantry Battalion, 2nd Regt 1981, Commdr 3rd Infantry Battalion, 12th Regt 1984, Deputy Commdr 12th Infantry Regt 1986, Commdr 1989, Deputy Commanding Gen., 2nd Infantry Div. 1993, Commanding Gen. 1996–97, Deputy Commanding Gen., 1st Army Region 1997–98, Commanding Gen. 2002–03, Commanding Gen. 1st Corps 1998–2000; Army Special Sr Academic 2000–01; Asst Chief of Staff, Operations 2001–02, Asst C-in-C 2003–04, Commdr Chief Royal Thai Army 2004–06; Minister of Defence 2008–. *Address:* Ministry of Defence, Thanon Sanamchai, Bangkok 10200, Thailand (office). *Telephone:* (2) 222-1121 (office). *Fax:* (2) 226-3117 (office). *Website:* www.mod.go.th (office).

PREBBLE, Mark, PhD; New Zealand civil servant; b. 12 May 1951, Auckland; s. of Archdeacon K. R. Prebble and Mary Prebble; brother of Richard William Prebble (q.v.); m. 1st Fenella Druce 1974 (died 1977); m. 2nd Lesley Bagnall 1978; two s. two d.; ed Auckland Grammar School, Auckland Univ. and Victoria Univ. of Wellington; with Treasury, Govt of NZ 1977–82, Dept of Labour 1982–85; Seconded to Prime Minister and Cabinet as Man. Change Team on Targeting Social Assistance 1991–92; Minister (Econ.) NZ High Comm., London 1992–93; Deputy Sec. of Treasury 1993–98; Chief Exec. Dept of Prime Minister and Cabinet 1998–2004; State Services Commr 2004–08 (retd). *Publications:* Smart Cards: Is it Smart to Use a Smart Card? 1990, Information, Privacy and the Welfare State 1990, Incentives and Labour Supply: Modelling Taxes and Benefits (ed. with P. Rebstock) 1992, New Zealand: The Turnaround Economy 1993 and articles in econ., public policy and educational journals. *Leisure interests:* walking, family and gardening. *Address:* c/o Office of the State Services Commissioner, PO Box 329, Wellington 6140, New Zealand.

PREBBLE, Hon. Richard William, CBE, BA, LLB; New Zealand politician and lawyer; b. 7 Feb. 1948, UK; s. of Archdeacon K. R. Prebble; brother of Mark Prebble (q.v.); m. 1st Nancy Prebble 1970; m. 2nd Doreen Prebble 1991; ed Auckland Boys' Grammar School, Auckland Technical Inst. and Auckland Univ.; admitted as barrister and solicitor, NZ Supreme Court 1971; admitted to Bar, Fiji Supreme Court 1973; MP for Auckland Cen. 1975–; Jr Opposition Whip 1978–79; Minister of Transport, of Railways, of Civil Aviation and Meteorological Services, of Pacific Island Affairs, Assoc. Minister of Finance 1984–87; Minister of State-Owned Enterprises, Postmaster-Gen., Minister of Works and Devt and Minister of Pacific Island Affairs 1987–88, of Railways, Police, State-Owned Enterprises and Pacific Island Affairs Jan.–Oct. 1990; Leader ACT New Zealand 1996–2004. *Publications:* I've Been Thinking 1996,

What Happens Next 1997, I've Been Writing. *Leisure interests:* Polynesian and Melanesian culture, opera, drama. *Address:* Parliament Buildings, Wellington, New Zealand (office). *Telephone:* (4) 470-6638 (office). *Fax:* (4) 473-3532 (office). *E-mail:* richard.prebble@parliament.govt.nz (office). *Website:* www.act.org.nz (office).

PREBBLE, Stuart; British media executive; *Managing Director, Liberty Bell Productions;* b. April 1951, London; s. of the late Dennis Stanley Prebble and Jean McIntosh; m.; one d.; ed Beckenham and Penge Grammar School for Boys, Newcastle Univ.; joined BBC as grad. trainee, worked as regional reporter for BBC TV in Newcastle; presenter for Granada TV; Deputy Ed. of World in Action (ITV) 1987, Ed. 1988 (fmr presenter and producer); Head of Granada's Regional Programmes 1990, Head of Factual Programmes 1992; Controller of Network Factual Programmes, ITV Network Centre 1993; CEO Granada Sky Broadcasting and Man. Dir of Channels and Interactive Media, Granada Media Group; CEO ONdigital PLC 1999–2002, ITV 2001–02; Co-founder and Man. Dir Liberty Bell Productions 2002–; RTS Award for Best Factual Series 1995. *Television productions include:* as Exec. Producer: Stars Reunited (BBC 1) 2003–04, Grumpy Old Men (BBC 2) 2003–04, Grumpy Old Women (BBC 2) 2005–, He Says, She Says (BBC 2) 2005–, Three Men in a Boat (BBC 2) 2006, Why We Went To War 2006, The Alastair Campbell Diaries, the Widow's Tale. *Publications:* A Power in the Land 1988, The Lazarus File 1989, Grumpy Old Men – The Official Handbook 2004, Grumpy Old Men – The Secret Diary 2005, Grumpy Old Christmas 2007, Grumpy Old Workers 2007, Grumpy Old Drivers 2008. *Leisure interests:* politics, cinema. *Address:* Liberty Bell Productions, Adamson House, 65 Westgate Road, Newcastle upon Tyne, NE1 1SG, England (office). *Telephone:* (191) 222-1200 (office). *Fax:* (191) 222-1210 (office). *E-mail:* info@libertybell.tv (office). *Website:* www.libertybell.tv (office).

PREDOIU, Cătălin Marian, PhD; Romanian lawyer and government official; *Minister of Justice and Citizens' Freedoms;* b. 27 Aug. 1968; ed Univ. of Bucharest; commercial and corp. governance lawyer; completed a training programme in commercial law at Caen Bar, France 1994; Lecturer in Commercial Law, Univ. of Bucharest 1994–2007; Assoc. Lawyer, ZRP law partnership 2005–; mem. Council of Bucharest Bar Asscn 2003–; Minister of Justice (ind.) 2008–09, of Justice and Citizens' Freedoms 2009–; Prize of Romanian Acad. as a co-author of a law treatise. *Publications:* has published several articles and studies about commercial law. *Address:* Ministry of Justice, 050741 Bucharest 5, Str. Apolodor 17, Romania (office). *Telephone:* (21) 3144400 (office). *Fax:* (21) 3101664 (office). *E-mail:* relatiipublice@just.ro (office). *Website:* www.just.ro (office).

PREM, Gen. Tinsulanonda; Thai politician and army officer; b. 26 Aug. 1920; ed Suan Kularb School and Chulachomklao Royal Mil. Acad., Bangkok; started mil. career as Sub-Lt 1941; Commdr Cavalry HQ 1968; Commdr-Gen. 2nd Army Area 1974; Asst C-in-C Royal Thai Army 1977; Deputy Minister of Interior, Govt of Gen. Kriangsak Chomanan 1977; Minister of Defence 1979–87, later C-in-C; Prime Minister of Thailand 1980–88; Chair. Petroleum Authority of Thailand 1981; Ramathipbodi Order, King of Thailand, Seri Maharajah Mangku Negara (Malaysia) 1984. *Address:* c/o HM Privy Council, Grand Palace, Thanon Na Phra Lan, Bangkok 10200 (office); 279 Sri Ayutthaya Road, Sisao Theves, Bangkok 10300, Thailand.

PRENDERGAST, Sir (Walter) Kieran, KCVO, CMG; British diplomatist; b. 2 July 1942, Campbeltown, Argyll; s. of the late Lt-Commdr J. H. Prendergast and Mai Hennessy; m. Joan Reynolds 1967; two s. two d.; ed Salesian Coll. Chertsey and St Edmund Hall, Oxford; Asst Pvt. Sec. to successive Secs of State, FCO 1976–78; has served at Istanbul, Ankara, Nicosia, The Hague, UK Mission to UN, New York and Tel-Aviv; seconded to staff of last gov. of Rhodesia (Lord Soames) during transition to independence in Zimbabwe; High Commr in Zimbabwe 1989–92, in Kenya 1992–95; Amb. to Turkey 1995–97; UN Under-Sec.-Gen. for Political Affairs 1997–2005 (retd); Goodman UN Fellow, Int. Security Program, Belfer Center for Science and Int. Affairs, Kennedy School of Govt, Harvard Univ. 2005–06. *Leisure interests:* family, reading, walking, wine. *Address:* c/o Foreign and Commonwealth Office, King Charles Street, London, SW1A 2AH, England (office).

PRENTICE, Rt Hon. James (Jim), PC; Canadian lawyer and politician; *Minister of Environment;* b. 20 July 1956, South Porcupine, Ont.; s. of Eric Prentice; m. Karen Prentice; three d.; ed Univ. of Alberta and Dalhousie Univ.; worked in Crowsnest Pass coal mines; as lawyer, specialized in property rights and has handled several relocations, environmental protection suits and cases arising from restricted devt areas; also served as a Commr Indian Claims Comm. of Canada for 10 years; active in Conservative party politics 1976–, cand. for leadership of Progressive Conservative Party of Canada 2003; MP (Conservative Party of Canada) for Calgary Centre-North, Alberta 2004–; Minister of Indian Affairs and Northern Devt and Fed. Interlocutor for Métis and Non-Status Indians 2006–07, of Industry 2007–08, of Environment 2008–; served for seven years on Bd of Dirs Calgary Winter Club, including as Pres. and Chair.; fmr volunteer advocate for learning-disabled children; fmr ice hockey coach. *Address:* Environment Canada, Les Terrasses de la Chaudière, 10 Wellington Street, 28th Floor, Gatineau, PQ K1A 0H3, Canada (office). *Telephone:* (819) 997-1441 (office). *Fax:* (819) 953-0279 (office). *E-mail:* minister@ec.gc.ca (office); prentice.j@parl.gc.ca (office). *Website:* www.ec.gc.ca (office); www.jimprentice.ca; www2.parl.gc.ca/Parlinfo.

PRESCOTT, Edward C., MS, PhD; American economist and academic; *W. P. Carey Chaired Professor, Arizona State University;* ed Swarthmore Coll., Pa, Case-Western Reserve Univ., Cleveland, Carnegie-Mellon Univ., Pittsburgh; Lecturer, Econs Dept, Univ. of Pennsylvania 1966–67, Asst Prof. 1967–71; Asst Prof. of Econs, Grad. School of Industrial Admin, Carnegie-Mellon Univ. 1971–72, Assoc. Prof. 1972–75, Prof. 1975–80; Prof., Dept of Econs, Univ. of

Minnesota 1980–98, 1999–2003, McKnight Presidential Chair in Econs 2003; Prof. of Econs, Univ. of Chicago 1998–99; Prof., Dept of Econs, Ariz. State Univ. 2003–, W. P. Carey Chaired Prof. 2003; Sr Advisor, Research Dept, Fed. Reserve Bank of Minneapolis 1980–2003, Sr Monetary Advisor 2003–; Visiting Prof. of Econs, Norwegian School of Business and Econs 1974–75; Ford Visiting Research Prof., Univ. of Chicago 1978–79; Visiting Prof. of Econs, Northwestern Univ. 1979–80, Visiting Prof. of Finance, Kellogg Grad. School of Man. 1980–82; Regents' Prof., Univ. of Minn. 1996; Leader Nat. Bureau of Econ. Research/NSF Workshop in Industrial Org. 1977–84; Research Assoc., Nat. Bureau of Econ. Research 1988–; Pres. Soc. for the Advancement of Econ. Theory 1992–94, Soc. of Econ. Dynamics and Control 1992–95; Assoc. Ed. Journal of Econometrics 1976–82, Int. Econ. Review 1980–90, Journal of Econ. Theory 1990–92; Co-ed. Econ. Theory 1991; Brookings Econ. Policy Fellow 1969–70; Guggenheim Fellow 1974–75; Fellow, Econometric Soc. 1980, American Acad. of Arts and Sciences 1992; Laurea hc in Economica (Univ. of Rome 'Tor Vergata') 2002; First Lionel McKenzie Lecturer 1990, Walras-Pareto Lecturer 1994, First Lawrence R. Klein Lecturer 1997, Sidrauski Lecturer, Latin America Econometric Soc. 1999, Plenary Lecturer, Soc. for Econ. Dynamics 2001, Richard T. Ely Lecturer, American Econ. Asscn Meetings 2002, Erwin Plein Nemmers Prize in Econs, Northwestern Univ. 2002, Bank of Sweden Prize in Econ. Sciences in Memory of Alfred Nobel (Nobel Prize) (jtly) 2004. *Publications:* Contractual Arrangements for Intertemporal Trade (co-ed.) 1987, Recursive Methods in Economic Dynamics (collaborator) 1989, Applied General Equilibrium Symposium (co-ed.) 1995, Great Depressions of the 20th Century (co-ed.) 2002, Barriers to Riches (co-author) 2000; numerous articles in econs journals. *Address:* Department of Economics, W. P. Carey School of Business, Arizona State University, Tempe, AZ 85287-3806 (office); Research Department, Federal Reserve Bank of Minneapolis, 90 Hennepin Avenue, Minneapolis, MN 55401-1804, USA (office). *Telephone:* 480-965-3531 (Tempe) (office); 612-204-5520 (Minneapolis) (office). *Fax:* 480-965-0748 (Tempe) (office); 612-204-5515 (Minneapolis) (office). *Website:* wpcarey.asu.edu (office); www .minneapolisfed.org (office).

PRESCOTT, John Barry, AC, BComm, FAICD, FAIM, FTSE; Australian business executive; *Chairman, ASC Pty Ltd, QR Ltd;* b. 22 Oct. 1940, Sydney; s. of John Norman Prescott and Margaret Ellen Brownie; m. Jennifer Mary Louise Cahill; one s. three d. (one deceased); ed North Sydney Boys' High School, Univ. of New South Wales, Northwestern Univ. USA; Gen. Man. Transport, Broken Hill Proprietary Co. Ltd (BHP) 1982–87, Exec. Gen. Man. and CEO BHP Steel 1987–91, Dir BHP 1988–98, Man. Dir and CEO BHP 1991–98; Chair. Horizon Pvt. Equity 1998–2005, ASC Pty Ltd 2000–, QR Ltd 2006–; Dir Tubemakers 1988–92, Normandy Mining 1999–2001, Newmont Mining Corpn 2002–; mem. Advisory Bd Booz Allen 1991–2003; mem. Defence Industry Cttee 1988–93, Bd, Business Council of Australia 1995–97; Chair. Mfg Council 1990–95; Patron Australian Quality Council 1990–2000; mem. Int. Council of JP Morgan 1994–2003, Asia Pacific Advisory Cttee of New York Stock Exchange 1995–2005, Council of World Econ. Forum 1996–98, Bd of The Walter and Eliza Hall Inst. of Medical Research 1994–98, Bd of Trustees, The Conf. Bd 1995–2001; Chair., Sunshine Coast Business Council, Queensland 2004–07, Patron 2007–; Hon. LLD (Monash) 1994, Hon. DSc (UNSW) 1995; Centenary Medal 2003. *Leisure interests:* tennis, golf. *Address:* Level 39, 140 William Street, Melbourne, Vic. 3000, Australia (office). *Telephone:* (3) 9642-2518 (office). *Fax:* (3) 9642-2517 (office). *E-mail:* jbp@jbprescott.com (home).

PRESCOTT, John Leslie, PC, DipEconPol; British politician and trade union officialt; b. 31 May 1938, Prestatyn, Denbighshire; s. of John Herbert Prescott and Phyllis Prescott; m. Pauline Tilston 1961; two s.; ed WEA correspondence courses, Ruskin Coll. Oxford, Hull Univ.; trainee chef 1953–55; steward in Merchant Navy 1955–63; Recruitment Officer, Gen. & Municipal Workers Union 1965; contested Southport for Labour 1966; full-time official Nat. Union of Seamen 1968–70; MP for Kingston upon Hull (East) 1970–83, Hull (East) 1983–97, Kingston upon Hull East 1997–; mem. Select Cttee Nationalized Industries 1973–79, Council of Europe 1972–75, European Parl. 1975–79; Parl. Pvt. Sec. to Sec. of State for Trade 1974–76; Opposition Spokesman on Transport 1979–81, Regional Affairs and Devolution 1981–83, on Transport 1983–84, on Employment 1984–87, on Energy 1987–89, on Transport 1988–93, on Employment 1993–94; Deputy Prime Minister and Sec. of State for the Environment, Transport and the Regions 1997–2001, Deputy Prime Minister and First Sec. of State, Head of Office of the Deputy Prime Minister 1997–2006, Deputy Prime Minister 2006–07; British rep. to Parl. Ass., Council of Europe, Strasbourg, France 2007–, also sits on Ass. of Western European Union; mem. Labour Party Nat. Exec. Cttee 1989–, Deputy Leader 1994–2007; mem. Shadow Cabinet 1983–97; North of England Zoological Soc. Gold Medal 1999, Priyadarshni Award 2002. *Publications:* Not Wanted on Voyage: A Report of the 1966 Seamen's Strike 1966, Alternative Regional Strategy: A Framework for Discussion 1982, Planning for Full Employment 1985, Real Needs–Local Jobs 1987, Moving Britain into the 1990s 1989, Moving Britain into Europe 1991, Full Steam Ahead 1993, Financing Infrastructure Investment 1994, Jobs and Social Justice 1994, Prezza: My Story - Pulling No Punches 2008. *Address:* House of Commons, London, SW1A 0AA, England (office). *Telephone:* (20) 7219-6578 (office).

PRESS, Frank, PhD; American geophysicist and academic; *Professor Emeritus of Geophysics, Massachusetts Institute of Technology;* b. 4 Dec. 1924, Brooklyn, New York; s. of Solomon Press and Dora Press (née Steinholz); m. Billie Kallick 1946; one s. one d.; ed Coll. of City of New York and Columbia Univ.; Research Associate, Columbia Univ. 1946–49, Instructor, Geology 1949–51, Asst Prof. of Geology 1951–52, Assoc. Prof. 1952–55; Prof. of Geophysics, Calif. Inst. of Tech. 1955–65, Dir Seismological Lab. 1957–65; Co-Ed. Physics and Chemistry of the Earth 1957–; Chair. Dept of Earth and Planetary Sciences, MIT 1965–77, Prof. Emer. 1981–; Dir Office of Science and

Tech. Policy, Exec. Office of Pres. and Science and Tech. Adviser to Pres. 1977–81; Consultant to USN 1956–57, US Dept of Defense 1958–62, NASA 1960–62, 1965–70; mem. US del. to Nuclear Test Ban Conf. Geneva 1959–61, Moscow 1963; Pres. Science Advisory Comm. 1961–64; Chair. Bd of Advisors Nat. Center for Earthquake Research of the US Geological Survey 1966–76; Planetology Subcomm. NASA 1966–70; Chair. Earthquake Prediction Panel Office of Science and Tech. 1965–66; Fellow, American Acad. of Arts and Sciences 1966, Royal Astronomical Soc.; mem. Nat. Science Bd 1970–77, NAS 1958, Pres. 1981–93; Cecil & Ida Green Sr Fellow, Carnegie Inst. of Washington 1993–97; Dir Washington Advisory Group 1996–; fmr Pres. American Geophysical Union; Chair. Cttee on Scholarly Communication with People's Repub. of China 1975–77; mem. French Acad. of Science, Japan Acad. of Eng, Royal Soc., London; Hon. LLD (City Univ. of NY) 1972, Hon. DSc (Notre Dame Univ.) 1973, (Univ. of Rhode Island, of Arizona, Rutgers Univ., City Univ. of New York) 1979; Townsend Harris Medal Coll. of the City of New York, Royal Astronomical Soc. Gold Medal (UK) 1971, Day Medal Geological Soc. of America, Interior 1972, NASA Award 1973, Killian Faculty Achievement Award, MIT 1975, Japan Prize 1993, Nat. Medal of Science 1994, Philip Hauge Abelson Prize, AAAS 1995, Lomonosov Gold Medal, Russian Acad. of Sciences 1998. *Publications:* Earth (with R. Siever) 1986, Understanding Earth 2000. *Leisure interests:* skiing, sailing. *Address:* Suite 616 S, 2500 Virginia Avenue, Washington, DC 20037, USA. *E-mail:* fpress@ theadvisorygroup.com (office). *Website:* www.theadvisorygroup.com (office).

PRESS, James (Jim) E., BS; American automotive industry executive; *Vice-Chairman and Co-President, Chrysler LLC;* b. 4 Oct. 1946, Los Angeles, Calif.; ed Kansas State Coll. (now Pittsburgh State Univ.); with Ford Motor Co. until 1970; with Toyota Motor Sales, USA Inc., in various positions, since 1970, Sr Vice-Pres. and Gen. Man. Lexus 1995–98, Sr Vice-Pres. Toyota Motor USA Inc. 1998–99, Exec. Vice-Pres. 1999–2001, COO 2001–03, Man. Officer Toyota Motor Corpn 2003–06, Pres. and COO (first non-Japanese) Toyota Motor North America Inc. 2006–07, Bd of Dirs Toyota Motor Corpn (first non-Japanese mem.) 2006–07, mem. Bd of Dirs Toyota Motor Credit Corpn 1999–2007; mem. Bd of Dirs, Vice-Chair. and Pres. Chrysler LLC, Detroit, in charge of N American Sales, Int. Sales, Global Marketing, Product Strategy, and Service and Parts 2007–, mem. Bd Mans and Vice-Chair. Cerberus Operations and Advisory Co. (COAC) LLC; mem. Bd of Dirs and mem. Nominating, Corp. Governance and Public Policy Cttee, Best Buy Co. Inc. 2006–07; Chair. Asscn of Automotive Mfrs; mem. Pittsburgh State Univ., Pittsburgh, Kan., Advisory Bd and Switzer Center School, Torrance, Calif.; mem. Bd Automotive Youth Educational Systems, Asscn of Int. Automobile Mfrs, Detroit Area Council of the Boy Scouts of America, Toyota Technological Inst. at Chicago, Southern Calif. Cttee for Olympic Games; mem. Bd Trustees Coll. of Creative Studies, Detroit, Chadwick School, Rolling Hills, Calif.; Gold Medallion, Int. Swimming Hall of Fame, Distinguished Service Citation Award, Automotive Hall of Fame, named an industry All-Star by both Automotive News and Automobile Magazine. *Address:* Chrysler LLC, 1000 Chrysler Drive, Auburn Hills, MI 48326-2766, USA (office). *Telephone:* (248) 576-5741 (office). *Fax:* (248) 512-9368 (office). *E-mail:* info@chryslerllc.com (office). *Website:* www.chryslerllc.com (office).

PRESSLER, Larry, MA, JD; American politician and lawyer; *President and CEO, Pressler Group LLC;* b. 29 March 1942, Humboldt, SDak; s. of Antone Pressler and Loretta Claussen; m. Harriet Dent 1982; one d.; ed Univ. of South Dakota, Univ. of Oxford, UK (Rhodes Scholar), Harvard Kennedy School of Govt and Harvard Law School; Lt in US Army, Viet Nam 1966–68; mem. House of Reps 1975–79; Senator from South Dakota 1979–97, mem. several Senate cttees, Chair. Commerce, Science and Transport Cttees 1995–96; Congressional Del. to 47th UN Gen. Ass. 1992; mem. US Comm. on Improving the Effectiveness of the UN 1993; Sec. US Del. to Inter-Parl. Union 1981; Dir USAF Bd of Visitory 1987–; Founder, Pres., CEO Pressler and Assocs (now Pressler Group LLC), Washington 1997–; fmr Visiting Prof. of Govt, Univ. of S Dakota; mem. Adjunct Faculty, Native American Oglala Lakota Coll., S Dakota; Sr Fellow UCLA 2001; taught American Govt at Fudan Univ., Shanghai, People's Repub. of China 2005; mem. seven Corp. Bds, including Infosys Technologies, Bangalore, India; mem. Council on Foreign Relations, Vietnam Veterans Memorial Educ. Center Advisory Council; decorations for service as Lt in US Army in Viet Nam. *Publications:* U.S. Senators from the Prairie 1982, Star Wars: The SDI Debates in Congress 1986. *Leisure interests:* running, tennis. *Address:* 800 25th Street, NW, The Plaza, Suite 504, Washington, DC 20037, USA (office). *Telephone:* (202) 210-5330 (office); (202) 546-5959 (home). *Fax:* (202) 333-5854 (office); (202) 333-5854 (home). *E-mail:* lpressler@larrypressler.com (home). *Website:* www.larrypressler.com (office); www.senatorlarrypressler.com.

PRESSLER, Paul S.; American retail executive; b. 1956; ed State Univ. of NY at Oneonta; various positions in branding and marketing, Remco Toys, Mego Toys and Kenner-Parker –1987; Sr Vice-Pres. Product Licensing, The Walt Disney Co. 1987–90, Sr Vice-Pres. Consumer Products 1990–93, Pres. The Disney Stores 1993–96, Pres. Disneyland Resort, Anaheim, Calif. 1996–99, Chair. Global Theme Park and Resorts Div. 1999–2002; Pres. and CEO Gap Inc. 2002–07. *Address:* c/o Gap Inc., 2 Folsom Street, San Francisco, CA 94105, USA (office).

PRESTON, Paul, CBE, MA, DPhil, FRHistS, FBA; British academic; *Prince of Asturias Professor of Contemporary Spanish History, London School of Economics;* b. 21 July 1946, Liverpool; s. of Charles R. Preston and Alice Hoskisson; m. Gabrielle P. Ashford-Hodges 1983; two s.; ed St Edward's Coll. Liverpool, Oriel Coll. Oxford and Univ. of Reading; Research Fellow, Centre for Mediterranean Studies, Rome 1973–74; Lecturer in History, Univ. of Reading 1974–75; Lecturer in Modern History, Queen Mary Coll. London 1975–79, Reader 1979–85, Prof. of History 1985–91; Prof. of Int. History, LSE

1991–94, Prince of Asturias Prof. of Contemporary Spanish History 1994–; regular contrib. to Times Literary Supplement; columnist in ABC, Diario 16 and El País, Madrid; Comendador, Orden del Mérito Civil (Spain) 1987, Caballero Gran Cruz de la Orden de Isabel la Católica 2006; Yorkshire Post Book of the Year 1994, Así fue – La Historia rescatada Prize 1998, Premi Internacional Ramon Llull, Catalan Govt 2005, Trias Fargas Non-Fiction Prize 2006, Marcel Proust Chair of European Acad. 2006. *Publications:* The Coming of the Spanish Civil War 1978, The Triumph of Democracy in Spain 1986, The Spanish Civil War 1986, The Politics of Revenge 1990, Franco: A Biography 1993, Comrades: Portraits from the Spanish Civil War 1999, Doves of War: Four Women of Spain 2003, Juan Carlos: A People's King 2004, We Saw Spain Die 2008. *Leisure interests:* classical music, especially opera, modern fiction. *Address:* Department of International History, London School of Economics, Houghton Street, London, WC2A 2AE (office). *Telephone:* (20) 7955-7107 (office). *Fax:* (20) 8482-9865 (home). *E-mail:* p.preston@lse.ac.uk (office). *Website:* www.lse.ac.uk (office).

PRESTON, Peter John, MA; British journalist; b. 23 May 1938, Barrow-upon-Soar, Leicestershire; s. of John Whittle Preston and Kathlyn Preston (née Chell); m. Jean Mary Burrell 1962; two s. two d.; ed Loughborough Grammar School and St John's Coll. Oxford; editorial trainee, Liverpool Daily Post 1960–63; Political Reporter, The Guardian 1963–64, Educ. Corresp. 1965–66, Diary Ed. 1966–68, Features Ed. 1968–72, Production Ed. 1972–75, Ed. The Guardian 1975–95, Ed.-in-Chief 1995, Ed.-in-Chief The Observer 1995–96, Editorial Dir Guardian Media Group 1996–98; Co-Dir Guardian Foundation 1997–; mem. Scott Trust 1976–; Chair. Int. Press Inst. 1995–97, Asscn of British Eds 1996–99; mem. UNESCO Advisory Group on Press Freedom 2000–04; Gov. British Asscn for Cen. and Eastern Europe 2000–; Hon. Fellow, St John's Coll. Oxford 2003; Hon. DLitt (Loughborough) 1982, (E Anglia), (City Univ.) 1997, (Leicester) 2003; What the Papers Say Award for Lifetime Achievement 2006. *Publications:* Dunblane: Reflecting Tragedy 1996, The 51st State 1998, Bess 1999. *Leisure interests:* football, films, four children. *Address:* The Guardian, 119 Farringdon Road, London, EC1R 3ER, England. *Telephone:* (20) 7278-2332. *Website:* www.guardian.co.uk (office).

PRESTON, Simon John, OBE, MusB, MA, FRAM, FRCM, FRCO, FRCCO, FRSA; British organist and conductor; b. 4 Aug. 1938, Bournemouth; ed Canford School, King's Coll., Cambridge; Sub-Organist, Westminster Abbey 1962–67; Acting Organist, St Albans Abbey 1967–68; Organist and Lecturer in Music, Christ Church, Oxford 1970–81; Organist and Master of the Choristers, Westminster Abbey 1981–87; Conductor, Oxford Bach Choir 1971–74; Artistic Dir, Calgary Int. Organ Festival; Patron, Univ. of Buckingham; mem. Royal Soc. of Musicians, Council of Friends of St John's Smith Square; over 30 recordings; Edison Award 1971; Grand Prix du Disque 1979, Performer of the Year Award, American Guild of Organists 1987. *Leisure interests:* croquet, theatre, opera. *Address:* Little Hardwick, Langton Green, Tunbridge Wells, Kent TN3 0EY, England. *Telephone:* (1892) 862042.

PRESTON, Steven C., BA, MBA; American business executive and fmr government official; b. 4 Aug. 1960; m. Molly Preston; five c.; ed Northwestern Univ., Univ. of Chicago, Ludwig-Maximilians Univ., Munich; Sr Vice-Pres. and Treas., First Data Corpn 1993–97; Chief Financial Officer, then Exec. Vice-Pres. Service Master 1997–2006; Admin. US Small Business Admin, Washington, DC 2006–08; US Sec. of Housing and Urban Devt 2008–09; Chair. Bd of Visitors, Weinberg Coll. of Arts and Sciences, Northwestern Univ. *Address:* c/o Department of Housing and Urban Development, 451 Seventh Street, SW, Washington, DC 20410, USA.

PRÊTRE, Georges; French conductor; b. 14 Aug. 1924, Waziers; s. of Emile Prêtre and Jeanne Prêtre (née Dérin); m. Gina Marny 1950; one s. one d.; ed Lycée and Conservatoire de Douai, Conservatoire national supérieur de musique de Paris and Ecole des chefs d'orchestre; Dir of Music, Opera Houses of Marseilles, Lille and Toulouse 1946–55; Dir of Music Opéra-comique, Paris 1955–59; Dir of Music, l'Opéra de Paris 1959, Artistic Dir 1966, Dir-Gen. of Music 1970–71; conductor of the symphonic asscns of Paris and of principal festivals throughout the world; also conducted at La Scala, Milan and major American orchestras; Conductor Metropolitan Opera House, New York 1964–65, La Scala, Milan 1965–66, Salzburg 1966; First Visiting Conductor, Vienna Symphony Orchestra 1986–91, Opéra Bastille (Turandot) 1997, Opéra-Comique (Pelleas et Melisande) 1998; Turandot at La Scala 2001; concert to celebrate 80th birthday, l'Opéra-Bastille 2004, New Year concert, Vienna 2008; Hon. mem. Gesellschaft der Musikfreunde, Vienna; Officier, Légion d'honneur 1971, Commdr 2003, Chevalier des Palmes Academiques, Haute Distinction République Italienne 1975, Commdr République Italienne 1980; Europa Prize 1982, Victoire de la musique Award for Best Conductor 1997. *Leisure interests:* riding, swimming, aviation, judo. *Address:* Künstleragentur Dr. Raab & Dr. Böhm Gesellschaft m.b.H., Plankengasse 7, 1010 Vienna, Austria (office). *Telephone:* (1) 5120501 (office). *Fax:* (1) 5127743 (office). *E-mail:* office@rbartists.at (office). *Website:* www.rbartists.at (office).

PRETTEJOHN, Nicholas Edward Tucker, BA; British business executive; *CEO and Chairman, Lloyd's Market Board;* b. 22 July 1960; s. of Edward Joseph Tucker Prettejohn and Diana Sally Prettejohn; m. 1st Elizabeth Esch 1986 (divorced 1997); m. 2nd Claire Helen McKenna 1997; two d.; ed Taunton School, Somerset and Balliol Coll., Oxford; Research Assoc., Bain & Co. 1982–91, Partner 1988–91; Dir Apax Partners 1991–94; Dir Corp. Strategy, Nat. Freight Corpn PLC 1994–95; Head of Strategy, Lloyd's of London 1995–97, Man. Dir Business Devt Unit 1997–99, N America Business Unit 1998–99, Chair. and CEO Lloyd's Market Bd 1999–; Dir (non-exec.) Anglo & Overseas Trust PLC 1998–2004; Chair. English Pocket Opera 2001–. *Leisure interests:* opera, music, theatre, horse racing, golf, cricket, rugby. *Address:* Chief Executive's Office, Lloyd's Market Board, One Lime Street, London, EC3M 7HA, England (office). *Telephone:* (20) 7327-1000 (office). *Fax:* (20)

7327-5599 (office). *E-mail:* nicholas.e.prettejohn@lloyds.com (office). *Website:* www.lloyds.com (office).

PRETTY, Katharine Bridget (Kate), PhD, FSA; British archaeologist and college principal; *Principal, Homerton College, Cambridge;* b. 18 Oct. 1945, Cheshire; d. of Maurice Walter Hughes and Bridget Elizabeth Whibley Hughes (née Marples); m. 1st Graeme Lloyd Pretty (divorced 1975); m. 2nd Tjeerd Hendrik van Andel 1988; ed King Edward VI High School for Girls, Birmingham and New Hall, Cambridge; Fellow and Lecturer, New Hall, Cambridge Univ. 1972–91, Emer. Fellow 1995–, Chair, Faculty of Archaeology and Anthropology 1991–, Council of the School of Humanities and Social Sciences 1997–2003, Prin., Homerton Coll., Cambridge Univ. 1991–, Pro-Vice-Chancellor Univ. of Cambridge 2004–; Chair. RESCUE, British Archaeological Trust 1978–83; Vice-Pres. RSA 1999; Medal, British Archaeological Awards 1998. *Publications:* The Excavations of Wroxeter Baths-Basilica 1997. *Leisure interests:* archaeology, botany and gardening. *Address:* Homerton College, Hills Road, Cambridge, CB2 2PH, England (office). *Telephone:* (1223) 507131 (office). *Fax:* (1223) 507130 (office). *E-mail:* kp10002@cam.ac.uk (office). *Website:* www.homerton.cam.ac.uk (office).

PREUSS, Daphne, BS, PhD; American geneticist, business executive and academic; *CEO, Chromatin, Inc;* m.; ed Univ. of Denver, Massachusetts Inst. of Tech.; performed postdoctoral research at Stanford Univ. –1995; joined Dept of Molecular Genetics, Univ. of Chicago 1995, Asst Prof. then Prof., Albert D. Lasker Prof. in Molecular Genetics and Cell Biology 2006–, also Investigator, Howard Hughes Medical Inst.; Co-founder Chromatin, Inc., Chicago 2002, Sr Vice-Pres. then Pres. and Chief Scientific Officer 2007–08, CEO 2008–; mem. Bd of Govs Argonne Nat. Lab. 2003–; David and Lucile Packard Fellow; Searle Scholar; Lifetime Nat. Assoc. NAS. *Address:* Chromatin, Inc., 3440 South Dearborn St, Suite 280, Chicago, IL 60616, USA (office). *Telephone:* (312) 235-3610 (office). *Fax:* (312) 325-3611 (office). *E-mail:* info@chromatininc.com (office); dpreuss@midway.uchicago.edu (office). *Website:* www.chromatininc.com (office); preuss.bsd.uchicago.edu (office).

PRÉVAL, René; Haitian agronomist, politician and head of state; *President;* b. 17 Jan. 1943, Port-au-Prince; m.; two c.; ed Coll. of Jembloux, Belgium; forced to leave Haiti with his family after dispute with Duvalier dictatorship 1963; returned 1975 after five years in USA; worked at Nat. Inst. for Mineral Resources 1975–77; Founding mem. Group for Defence of Constitution; Chair. Cttee Pa Blié investigating disappearance of persons under Duvalier regime 1987–91; Prime Minister Feb.–Sept. 1991; Pres. of Haiti 1996–2001, 2006–; mem. Lespwa Party. *Address:* Office of the President, Palais National, rue de la République, Port-au-Prince (office); c/o La Fanmi Lavalas, blvd 15 Octobre, Tabarre, Port-au-Prince, Haiti. *Telephone:* 222-3024 (office). *E-mail:* webmestre@palaisnational.info (office).

PREVIN, André George; American conductor, pianist and composer; b. (Andreas Ludwig Priwin), 6 April 1929, Berlin, Germany; s. of Jack Previn and Charlotte (née Epstein) Previn; m. 1st Betty Bennett (divorced); two d.; m. 2nd Dory Langan 1959 (divorced 1970); m. 3rd Mia Farrow 1970 (divorced 1979); three s. three d.; m. 4th Heather Hales 1982 (divorced); one s.; m. 5th Anne-Sophie Mutter 2002 (divorced 2006); ed Berlin and Paris Conservatories; began career as film score composer, MGM studios, Los Angeles; Music Dir Houston Symphony, US 1967–69; Music Dir and Principal Conductor, London Symphony Orchestra 1968–79, Conductor Laureate 1979–; composed and conducted approx. 50 film scores 1950–65; guest conductor of most major world orchestras, also Royal Opera House, Covent Garden, Salzburg, Edin., Osaka, Flanders Festivals; Music Dir, London South Bank Summer Music Festival 1972–74; Pittsburgh Symphony Orchestra 1976–84, LA Philharmonic Orchestra 1984–89; Music Dir Royal Philharmonic Orchestra 1985–86, Prin. Conductor 1987–92; Chief Conductor and Music Dir Oslo Philharmonic Orchestra 2004–06, Conductor Laureate 2006–; Hon. KBE 1996; Television Critics' Award 1972, Acad. Award for Best Film Score 1959, 1960, 1964, 1965, Kennedy Center Honor 1998, Glenn Gould Prize 2005, London Symphony Orchestra Lifetime Achievement Award 2008, Gramophone Award for Lifetime Achievement 2008, 10 Grammy Awards. *Television:* series of television specials for BBC and for American Public Broadcasting Service. *Major works:* Symphony for Strings 1965, Overture to a Comedy 1966, Suite for Piano 1967, Cello Concerto 1968, Four Songs (for soprano and orchestra) 1968, Two Serenades for Violin 1969, Guitar Concerto 1970, Piano Preludes 1972, Good Companions (musical) 1974, Song Cycle on Poems by Philip Larkin 1977, Every Good Boy Deserves Favour (music, drama, text by Tom Stoppard) 1977, Pages from the Calendar for solo piano 1977, Peaches for flute and strings 1978, Principals 1980, Outings for brass quintet 1980, Reflections 1981, Piano Concerto 1984, Triolet for Brass 1987, Variations for Solo Piano 1991, Six Songs for Soprano and Orchestra on texts by Toni Morrison 1991, Sonata for Cello and Piano 1992, The Magic Number for soprano and orchestra 1995, Trio for Bassoon, Oboe and Piano 1995, Sonata for Violin 1996, Sonata for Bassoon and Piano 1997, Streetcar Named Desire (opera) 1998, The Giraffes Go to Hamburg for soprano, alto, flute and piano, Three Dickinson Songs for soprano and piano, Diversions for orchestra, Violin Concerto Anne-Sophie 2001, Double Concerto for Violin, Double Bass and Orchestra 2004, Double Concerto for Violin, Viola and Orchestra 2009, Brief Encounter (opera) 2009. *Publications:* Music Face to Face 1971, Orchestra (ed.) 1977, Guide to Music 1983, No Minor Chords: My Days in Hollywood 1992. *Leisure interests:* collecting contemporary art, fencing, American folk art. *Address:* c/o Tanja Dorn, IMG Artists, Carnegie Hall Tower, 152 West 57th Street, 5th Floor, New York, NY 10019, USA (office). *Telephone:* (212) 994-3540 (office). *Fax:* (212) 994-3550 (office). *E-mail:* tdorn@imgartists.com (office). *Website:* www.imgartists.com (office); www.andre-previn.com.

PRICE, Antony, MA; British fashion designer; b. 5 March 1945, Yorks.; s. of Peter Price and Joan Price; ed Bradford Coll. of Art and Royal Coll. of Art; designer for Sterling Cooper 1968–72, for Plaza 1972–79; Chair. of own fashion co. 1979–; British Glamour Award 1989. *Leisure interests:* tropical plants, tropical ornithology, modern and classical music. *Address:* 17 Langton Street, London, SW10 0JL, England. *Telephone:* (20) 7376-7250. *Fax:* (20) 7376-4599.

PRICE, Charles H., II; American business executive and diplomatist (retd); b. 1 April 1931, Kansas City, Mo.; s. of Charles Harry Price and Virginia (née Ogden) Price; m. Carol Ann Swanson 1969; two s. three d.; ed Univ. of Mo.; Pres. and Dir Linwood Securities Co., Kansas City 1960–81; Chair. and CEO, Price Candy Co., Kansas City 1969–81, American Bancorpn., Kansas City 1960–81; Chair. and CEO American Bank and Trust Co., Kansas City 1973–81; Amb. to Belgium 1981–83, to UK 1983–89; Chair. Ameribanc Inc. 1989–92, Pres., COO 1990–92; Chair. Bd of Dirs Mercantile Bank Kansas City, Mo. 1992–96, St Luke's Hosp. Kansas City 1970–81 (Hon. Dir 1989–); Hon. Fellow Regent's Coll., London 1986; several hon. degrees; William Booth Award, Salvation Army 1985, World Citizen of the Year Award, Mayor of Kansas City 1985, Trustee Citation Award Midwest Research Inst. 1987, Distinguished Service Award Int. Relations Council 1989, Mankind Award, Cystic Fibrosis Foundation 1990, Chancellor's Medal, Univ. of Mo. 1992, William F. Yates Medallion, William Jewell Coll. 1996. *Leisure interests:* shooting, golf, tennis. *Address:* One West Armour Boulevard, Suite 300, Kansas City, MO 64111-2089, USA. *Telephone:* (816) 360-6175.

PRICE, Curtis Alexander, AM, PhD, FRCM, FRNCM; American musicologist; *Principal, Royal Academy of Music;* b. 7 Sept. 1945, Springfield, Mo.; ed Southern Illinois Univ., Harvard Univ. with John Ward and Nino Pirotta; teacher, Washington Univ., St Louis 1974–81; teacher, King's Coll. London 1981, Reader 1985, Prof. 1988; Prin. RAM, London 1995–2008; Prof., Univ. of London 2000–; mem. Royal Musical Assen (Pres. 1999–2002); Trustee Musica Britannica and the Handel House Museum; Fellow, King's Coll. London; Hon. RAM; Hon. KBE 2005. *Publications include:* The Critical Decade for English Music Drama 1700–1710 1978, Music in the Restoration Theater: with a Catalogue of Instrumental Music in the Plays 1665–1713 1979, Henry Purcell and the London Stage 1984, H. Purcell: Dido and Aeneas (ed.) 1986, Italian Opera and Arson in Late Eighteenth-Century London 1989, The Impresario's Ten Commandments: Continental Recruitment for Italian Opera in London 1763–4 (with J. Milhous and R. D. Hume) 1992, Man and Music: The Early Baroque Era (ed.) 1993, Purcell Studies (ed.) 1995. *Address:* Royal Academy of Music, Marylebone Road, London, NW1 5HT, England (office). *Telephone:* (20) 7873-7373 (office). *Fax:* (20) 7873-7374 (office). *E-mail:* go@ram.ac.uk (office). *Website:* www.ram.ac.uk (office).

PRICE, Frank; American television and cinema producer and executive; b. 17 May 1930, Decatur, Ill.; s. of William Price and Winifred Price (née Moran); m. Katherine Huggins 1965; four s.; ed Michigan State Univ.; served with USN 1948–49; Writer and Story Ed., CBS-TV, New York 1951–53; with Columbia Pictures, Hollywood 1953–57, NBC-TV 1957–58; Producer, Writer, Universal Television, Calif. 1959–64, Vice-Pres. 1964–71, Sr Vice-Pres. 1971–73, Exec. Vice-Pres. 1973–74, Pres. 1974–78; Pres. Columbia Pictures 1978–79, Chair. and CEO 1979–83; Chair. and CEO MCA Motion Picture Group 1983–86, Price Entertainment 1991–; Chair. Columbia Pictures 1990–91; Dir Sony Pictures Entertainment, Savoy Pictures; Exec. Producer The Virginian 1961–64, Ironside 1965, Kojak, Six Million Dollar Man, Bionic Woman, Rockford Files, Quincy, Rich Man, Poor Man, The Tuskegee Airmen 1996; mem. Writers Guild of America; Peabody Award 1996, NAACP Image Award 1996. *Films include:* Circle of Friends 1995, The Walking Dead 1995, Mariette in Ecstasy 1996, Getting Away with Murder 1996, Texas Rangers 2001, Zeus and Roxanne 1997. *Address:* Price Entertainment Inc., 527 Spoleto Drive, Pacific Palisades, CA 90272, USA (office).

PRICE, Rt Hon. George Cadle, PC; Belizean politician; b. 15 Jan. 1919; s. of William Cadle Price and Irene Price; ed St John's Coll., Belize City and St Augustin Seminary, Mississippi; City Councillor 1947–62; founder-mem. People's United Party (PUP) 1950, Sec. PUP 1950–56, fmr Leader; Pres. Gen. Workers' Union 1947–52; mem. Legislative Council, British Honduras (now Belize) 1954–65; mem. Exec. Council 1954–57, 1961–65; Mayor, Belize City 1956–62; mem. House of Reps 1965–84, Cabinet 1965–84; fmr mem. for Nat. Resources; First Minister 1961–63, leader of del. to London for self-govt constitutional talks; Premier 1964–81, Prime Minister of Belize 1981–84, 1989–93, Minister of Finance and Econ. Planning 1965–84, of Foreign Affairs 1981–84, 1989–90; Chair. Reconstruction and Devt Corpn; Outstanding Alumnus Award (St John's Coll.) 1971. *Address:* c/o House of Representatives, Belmopan, Belize.

PRICE, James Gordon, BA, MD; American physician and academic; *Professor Emeritus of Medicine, University of Kansas;* b. 20 June 1926, Brush, Colo, USA; s. of John Hoover Price and Laurette (née Dodds) Price; m. Janet Alice McSween 1949; two s. two d.; ed Univ. of Colorado; intern, Denver Gen. Hosp.; pvt. practice, family medicine, Brush, Colo 1952–78; Prof. Dept of Family Practice, Univ. of Kan. 1978–93 (Chair. 1978–90), Dean, School of Medicine 1990–93, Prof. Emer. 1993–; nationally syndicated newspaper column, Your Family Physician 1973–86; Medical Ed., Curriculum Innovations 1973–93; mem. Inst. of Medicine, NAS; Pres. American Acad. of Family Physicians 1973–, American Bd of Family Practice 1980–. *Leisure interest:* computer programming. *Address:* 12205 Mohawk Road, Shawnee Mission, Leawood, KS 66209, USA (home). *Telephone:* (913) 491-3072 (home). *E-mail:* jimtad@sbcglobal.net (home).

PRICE, Leontyne; American singer (soprano); b. 10 Feb. 1927, Laurel, Miss.; d. of James A. Price and Kate (née Baker) Price; m. William Warfield 1952 (divorced 1973); ed Central State Coll., Wilberforce, Ohio and Juilliard School of Music; appeared as Bess (Porgy and Bess), Vienna, Berlin, Paris, London, New York 1952–54; recitalist, soloist 1954–; soloist Hollywood Bowl 1955–59, 1966; opera singer NBC-TV 1955–58, San Francisco Opera Co. 1957–59, 1960–61, Vienna Staatsoper 1958, 1959–60, 1961; recording artist RCA-Victor 1958–; appeared Covent Garden 1958–59, 1970, Chicago 1959, 1960, 1965, Milan 1960–61, 1963, 1967, Metropolitan Opera, New York 1961–62, 1963–70, 1972, Paris Opéra as Aida 1968, Metropolitan Opera as Aida 1985 (retd); numerous recordings; Hon. Vice-Chair. US Cttee UNESCO; Fellow American Acad. of Arts and Sciences; Trustee Int. House; Hon. DMus (Howard Univ., Cen. State Coll., Ohio); Hon. DHL (Dartmouth); Hon. Dr of Humanities (Rust Coll., Miss.); Hon. DHumLitt (Fordham); Presidential Medal of Freedom, Order of Merit (Italy), Nat. Medal of Arts 1985, Essence Award 1991, 20 Grammy Awards for classical recordings, Nat. Endowment for the Arts Opera Award 2008.

PRICE, Dame Margaret Berenice, DBE; British singer (soprano); b. 13 April 1941, Tredegar, Wales; d. of the late Thomas Glyn Price and of Lilian Myfanwy Richards; ed Pontllanfraith Grammar School and Trinity Coll. of Music, London; operatic debut with Welsh Nat. Opera in Marriage of Figaro; renowned for Mozart operatic roles; has sung in world's leading opera houses and festivals; has made many recordings of opera, oratorio, concert works and recitals and many radio broadcasts and TV appearances; fmr performer with Bavarian State Opera, Munich; Fellow Coll. of Wales 1991; Hon. Fellow, Trinity Coll. of Music; Hon. DMus (Wales) 1983; Elisabeth Schumann Prize for Lieder, Ricordi Prize for Opera, Silver Medal of the Worshipful Co. of Musicians, Bayerische Kammersängerin. *Major roles include:* Countess in Marriage of Figaro, Pamina in The Magic Flute, Fiordiligi in Così fan tutte, Donna Anna in Don Giovanni, Konstanze in Die Entführung, Amelia in Simon Boccanegra, Agathe in Freischütz, Desdemona in Otello, Elisabetta in Don Carlo, Aida and Norma, Amelia in Ballo in Maschera. *Leisure interests:* cookery, reading, walking, swimming, driving, breeding dogs. *Address:* c/o Stefan Hahn, Agentur Augstein, Im Tal 28, D-80331 Munich, Germany.

PRICE, Michael F.; American financial executive; *Managing Partner, MFP Investors LLC;* b. 1952; m. (divorced); three s.; ed Univ. of Okla; joined Heine Securities Corpn as Research Asst 1975, sole owner, CEO 1988–96; sold co. to Franklin Resources 1996 and f. advisory co. Franklin Mutual Advisers Inc., Pres., CEO 1996–2001; f. and Man. Pnr MFP Investors LLC (investment fund) 2001–; founder and Pres. Michael F. Price Foundation; mem. Bd of Dirs Liquidnet Holdings; Sr Advisor, Michael F. Price School of Business, Univ. of Okla; Fund Action Lifetime Achievement Award 2005. *Address:* MFP Investors LLC, 51 JFK Parkway, Short Hills, NJ 07078, USA. *Telephone:* (973) 921-2201. *Fax:* (973) 921-2236. *E-mail:* mprice@mfpllc.com.

PRICE, Nicholas Raymond Leige (Nick); South African professional golfer; b. 28 Jan. 1957, Durban; m. Sue Price; one s. two d.; turned professional 1977; won Asseng Invitational 1979, Canon European Masters 1980, Italian Open, S African Masters 1981, Vaals Reef Open 1982, World Series of Golf 1983, Trophée Lancôme, ICI Int. 1985, West End S Australian Open 1989, GTE Byron Nelson Classic, Canadian Open 1991, Air New Zealand/Shell Open, PGA Championships, H-E-B Texas Open 1992, The Players' Championship, Canon Greater Hartford Open, Sprint Western Open, Federal Express St Jude Classic, ICL Int., Sun City Million Dollar Challenge 1993, British Open, ICL Int. Honda Classic, Southwestern Bell Colonial, Motorola Western Open, PGA Championship, Bell Canadian Open 1994, Alfred Dunhill Challenge, Hassan II Golf Trophy, Morocco, Zimbabwe Open 1995, MCI Classic 1997, Suntory Open 1999, CVS Charity Classic 2001, Mastercard Colonial 2002; f. golf course designers' Nick Price design 2001; recipient Vardon Trophy 1993, PGA Tour Player of the Year 1986, 1993. *Publication:* The Swing 1997. *Leisure interests:* water skiing, tennis, fishing, flying. *Address:* c/o PGA Tour, 100 Avenue of the Champions, Palm Beach Gardens, FL 33410, USA.

PRICE, Paul Buford, Jr, BS, PhD; American physicist and academic; *Professor, Graduate School, University of California, Berkeley;* b. 8 Nov. 1932, Memphis, Tenn.; s. of the late Paul Buford and Eva (née Dupuy) Price; m. Jo Ann Baum 1958; one s. three d.; ed Davidson Coll., Univ. of Virginia, Univ. of Bristol, Univ. of Cambridge; Physicist Gen. Electric Research Lab., New York 1960–69; Visiting Prof. Tata Inst. of Fundamental Research, Bombay, India 1965–66; Adjunct Prof. of Physics, Rensselaer Polytechnic Inst. 1967–68; Prof. of Physics Univ. of Calif. at Berkeley 1969–2001, Chair. Dept of Physics 1987–91, William H. McAdams Prof. of Physics 1990–92, Dean, Physical Sciences, Coll. of Letters and Science 1992–2001, Prof. in the Grad. School 2001–; Dir Space Science Lab. 1979–85; NASA Consultant on Lunar Sample Analysis Planning Team; mem. Bd Dirs Terradex Corpn 1978–86; mem. Visiting Cttee, Bartol Research Inst. 1991–94, Advisory Cttee, Indian Inst. of Astrophysics 1993–95; Fellow and Chair. Cosmic Physics Div. American Physical Soc.; mem. NAS 1975–, mem. Space Science Bd, Sec. Physical and Math. Sciences Class of NAS 1985–88, Chair. 1988–91, mem. Steering Group on Future of Space Science (NAS) 1994–95, Polar Research Bd (NAS) 1999–2002; Regional Dir Calif. Alliance for Minority Participation 1994–2004; US Ice Core Working Group 2001–03; Fellow, American Geophysical Union, American Astronomical Soc.; Hon. Fellow, Indian Inst. of Astrophysics 2000; Hon. ScD (Davidson Coll.) 1973; Distinguished Service Award, (American Nuclear Soc.) 1964, Ernest O. Lawrence Memorial Award of Atomic Energy Comm. 1971, NASA Medal for Exceptional Scientific Achievement 1973, Scientific Symposium in Honor of P.B. Price's 65th Birthday 1997, Berkeley Citation 2002. *Publications:* (jointly) Nuclear Tracks in Solids, over 530 research papers in specialized journals. *Leisure interests:* skiing, travel, walking, reading. *Address:* Physics Department, University of California, Berkeley, 366 LeConte Hall, Berkeley, CA 94720 (office); 1056

Overlook Road, Berkeley, CA 94708, USA (home). *Telephone:* (510) 642-4982 (office); (510) 548-5206 (home). *Fax:* (510) 643-8497 (office). *E-mail:* bprice@berkeley.edu (office). *Website:* www.physics.berkeley.edu (office).

PRIDEAUX, Sir Humphrey Povah Treverbian, Kt, OBE, MA; British business executive; b. 13 Dec. 1915, London; s. of Walter Treverbian Prideaux and Marion Fenn Prideaux (née Arbuthnot); m. Cynthia V. Birch Reynardson 1939; four s.; ed St Aubyns, Eton Coll. and Trinity Coll., Oxford; Regular army officer 1936–53; Dir Navy, Army & Air Force Insts 1956–63, Chair. 1963–73; Chair. Lord Wandsworth Foundation 1966–92, Trustee 1963–92; Deputy Chair. Liebig's Extract of Meat Co. Ltd 1968–69, Dir 1966–69; Chair. Oxo Ltd 1968–72; Dir WH Smith & Son (Holdings) Ltd 1969, Vice-Chair. 1977–81; Dir Brooke Bond Oxo Ltd 1969–70; Chair. Brooke Bond Liebig 1972–81; Pres. London Life Asscn Ltd 1973–83, Dir 1964–88; Vice-Chair. Morland & Co. 1981–82, Chair. 1983–93; Dir Grindlays (Holdings) PLC 1982–85, Grindlays Bank PLC 1984–85; Hon. DL (Hants.). *Leisure interests:* country pursuits. *Address:* Kings Cottage, Buryfields, Odiham, Hook, Hants., RG29 1NE, England (home). *Telephone:* (1256) 703658 (home). *E-mail:* hptprideaux@aol.com (home).

PRIDIYATHORN, Devakula, BEcons, MBA; Thai government official; b. 15 July 1947, Bangkok; s. of Prince Prididebyabongs Devakula and Mom Taengthai Devakula; m. Prapapan Devakula Na Ayudhya; two s. one d.; ed Wharton School, Univ. of Pennsylvania, USA, Thammasat Univ.; joined Thai Farmers Bank 1971, Dir and Sr Exec. Vice-Pres. –1990; Govt Spokesperson for Prime Minister Gen. Chatichai Choonhavan 1990–91; Deputy Minister of Commerce 1991–92; Pres. Export-Import Bank of Thailand 1993–2001; Gov. Bank of Thailand 2001–06; Minister of Finance 2006–07 (resgnd); mem. Wharton School Exec. Bd for Asia; Kt Order of The Crown Of Thailand, Kt Grand Cross Order of The White Elephant, Grand Companion Order of Chula Chom Klao; Hon. DBA (Chulalongkorn Univ.) 2002, (Mahasarakam Univ.) 2003, Hon. DEcon (Sripatum Univ.) 2003, Hon. DEcon (Univ. Thai Chamber of Commerce) 2006. *Leisure interest:* golf. *Address:* 33 Soi 6, Serivilla 7, Srinakarin Road, Nhongborn, Praves, Bangkok 10250, Thailand (home). *Telephone:* (2) 399-1599 (home). *Fax:* (2) 399-1745 (home).

PRIEDKALNS, Janis, BVSc, PhD, MRCVS; Latvian diplomatist and scientist; *Professor of Anatomy and Histology, Latvian Academy of Medicine;* b. 28 March 1934, Barbele; s. of Karlis Priedkalns and Erna Priedkalns (née Krigers); m. 1964 (died 2000); three s. three d.; ed Univs of Sydney, Australia, Minnesota, USA, Cambridge, UK; veterinary surgeon 1959–60; post grad. studies in microanatomy, embryology, neuroendocrinology 1961–70; appointments at Univ. of Minn., Harvard Medical School, Univs of Munich and Giessen, Collège de France, Univ. of Cambridge; Elder Prof. of Anatomy and Histology, Faculty of Medicine and Dean of Science, Univ. of Adelaide 1966–96, Prof. Emer. 1997–; currently Prof. of Anatomy and Histology, Latvian Acad. of Medicine; mem. Parl. and Rep. to Council of Europe Parl. Ass. 1997; Perm. Rep. to UN, New York 1997–2001; Fellow, Royal Soc. of S Australia 1978–, Latvian Acad. of Sciences 1998–; mem. New York Acad. of Sciences 1989–; Pres. Asscn of Latvian Profs and Scientists 2002–; Dr hc (Agricultural Univ., Latvia) 1997. *Address:* Latvian Academy of Medicine, Dzirciema iela 16, 1007 Rīga (office); Terbatas iela 1, Valmiera 4200, Latvia. *Telephone:* 6745-9752 (office). *Fax:* 6782-8155 (office). *E-mail:* priedkalns@aol.com (home).

PRIESTMAN, Jane, OBE, FCSD; British design management consultant; b. 7 April 1930; d. of the late Reuben Stanley Herbert and Mary Elizabeth Herbert (née Ramply); m. Arthur Martin Priestman 1954 (divorced 1986); two s.; ed Northwood Coll., Liverpool Coll. of Art; design practice 1954–75; Design Man., Gen. Man. Architecture and Design British Airports Authority 1975–86; Dir Architecture and Design British Railways Bd 1986–91; Visiting Prof., De Montfort Univ. 1997–2001; mem. London Regional Transport Design Panel 1985–88, Jaguar Styling Panel 1988–91, Percentage for Art Steering Group, Arts Council 1989–91; mem. Council of Design Council 1996–2000; Gov. Commonwealth Inst. 1987–98, Kingston Univ. 1988–96; Enabler Comm. for Architecture and the Built Environment; Hon. FRIBA; Hon. FRSA; Hon. DrDes (De Montfort) 1994, (Sheffield Hallam) 1998. *Leisure interests:* textiles, city architecture, opera, travel. *Address:* 30 Duncan Terrace, London, N1 8BS, England (home). *Telephone:* (20) 7837-4525 (home). *Fax:* (20) 7837-4525 (home). *E-mail:* jane.priestman@virgin.net (home).

PRIETO JIMÉNEZ, Abel Enrique; Cuban writer, academic and politician; *Minister of Culture;* b. 11 Nov. 1950, Pinar del Rio; joined Communist Party of Cuba 1978, mem. Cen. Cttee 1991–; Deputy, Nat. Ass. of People's Power 1993–; Minister of Culture 1997–; fmr Prof. of Literature, Univ. of Havana, Ed.-in-Chief and Dir Letras Cubanas, Dir Arte y Literatura, Dir Juan Marinello Cultural Centre; fmr Pres. Unión de Escritores y Artistas de Cuba; Premio Nacional de Literatura. *Publications include:* Los bitongos y los guapos 1980, Noche de sábado 1989, El vuelo del gato 1999. *Address:* Ministry of Culture, Calle 2, No 258, entre 11 y 13, Plaza de la Revolución, Vedado, 10400 Havana, Cuba (office). *Telephone:* (7) 55-2260 (office). *Fax:* (7) 66-2053 (office). *E-mail:* atencion@min.cult.cu (office). *Website:* www.min.cult.cu (office).

PRIKHODKO, Sergey Eduardovich; Russian government official; *Adviser to the President;* b. 12 Jan. 1957, Moscow; m.; two d.; ed Moscow State Inst. of Int. Relations; mem. of staff Ministry of Foreign Affairs 1980–93; Head Div. of Baltic Countries, Deputy Dir Second European Dept 1993–97; Asst to Russian Pres. on Int. Problems 1997–98, Deputy Head of Admin, Russian Presidency 1998–99, concurrently Head Dept of Admin on Int. Policy 1998; Adviser to the Pres. 2004–; Public Recognition Award 1999. *Leisure interests:* theatre, literature, fishing, hunting. *Address:* Office of the President, Staraya pl. 4, 103132 Moscow, Russia (office). *Telephone:* (495) 925-35-81 (office). *Fax:* (495) 206-07-66 (office). *E-mail:* president@gov.ru (office). *Website:* www.kremlin.ru (office).

PRIMAKOV, Yevgeniy Maksimovich, DEcon; Russian politician and economist; *President, Russian Federation Chamber of Commerce and Industry;* b. 29 Oct. 1929, Kiev; m.; one d.; ed Moscow Inst. of Oriental Studies; worked for State Comm. on Broadcasting and Television 1953–62; mem. CPSU 1959–91; Columnist and Deputy Ed. (Asia and Africa Desk), Pravda 1962–70; Deputy Dir Inst. of World Econ. and Int. Relations, USSR (now Russian) Acad. of Sciences 1970–77, Dir 1985–, Dir Inst. of Oriental Studies 1977–85; elected to Congress of People's Deputies of the USSR 1989; mem. CPSU Cen. Cttee 1989–91; cand. mem. Politburo 1989–90; Chair. Soviet of the Union June 1989–March 1990; mem. Presidential Council 1989–90; Pres. Gorbachev's Special Envoy to the Gulf 1990–91; Dir Central Intelligence Service of USSR 1991, Foreign Intelligence Service of Russian Fed. 1991–96; Minister of Foreign Affairs 1996–98; Chair of Govt (Prime Minister) 1998–99; Chair. Exec. Council of Russia and Belarus Union 1998–99; mem. Security Council 1996–98; mem. State Duma (Parl.) 1999–, Head Otechestvo faction 2000–; Pres. Russian Fed. Chamber of Commerce and Industry 2001–; Corresp. mem. USSR (now Russian) Acad. of Sciences 1974, mem. 1979, Acad.-Sec., mem. of Presidium 1988–91; specialist on Egypt and other Arab countries; Chief Ed. of and contributor to a number of collective works, including: International Conflicts 1972, The Energy Crisis in the Capitalist World 1975, Years in Large-Scale Policy 1999; Nasser Prize 1975, USSR State Prize 1980, Avicenna Prize 1983. *Publications include:* Egypt under Nasser (with I. P. Belyayev) 1975, The War Which Could Be Avoided 1991, Years at the Top Level of Politics 2000, Eight Months Plus 2001. *Address:* Russian Federation Chamber of Commerce & Industry, Ilyinka str. 6, 103684 Moscow, Russia. *Telephone:* (495) 929-00-01 (office). *Fax:* (495) 929-03-75 (office).

PRIMAROLO, Rt Hon. Dawn, PC; British politician; *Minister of State for Public Health;* b. 2 May 1954; m. 1st 1972 (divorced); one s.; m. 2nd Thomas Ian Ducat 1990; ed Thomas Bennett Comprehensive School, Crawley, Bristol Polytechnic, Univ. of Bristol; mem. Avon Co. Council 1985–87; MP for Bristol S 1987–; Opposition Front Bench Spokesperson on Health 1992–94, on Treasury Affairs 1994–97; Financial Sec. HM Treasury 1997–99, Paymaster Gen. 1999–2007; Minister of State for Public Health 2007–; mem. Labour Party; Patron Royal Chelsea Hosp., Terrence Higgins Trust, Knowle West Against Drugs, Life Skills Project. *Leisure interests:* gardening, opera. *Address:* House of Commons, Westminster, London, SW1A 0AA (office); PO Box 1002, Bristol, BS99 1WH, England (office). *Telephone:* (20) 7219-3608 (London) (office); (117) 909-0063 (Bristol) (office). *Fax:* (117) 909-0064 (Bristol) (office). *E-mail:* primarolod@parliament.uk (office). *Website:* www.dawnprimarolo.labour.co.uk.

PRINCE; American musician, singer, producer and actor; b. (Prince Rogers Nelson), 7 June 1958, Minneapolis, MN; s. of John L. Nelson and Mattie Nelson (née Shaw); m. 1st Mayté Garcia 1996 (divorced 1998); one s. (deceased); m. 2nd Manuela Testolini Nelson; alternatively known as The Artist Formerly Known as Prince (AFKAP) and Symbol; fmr lead singer, Prince and The Revolution; singer with own backing group the New Power Generation 1991–; numerous tours, concerts; own recording studio and record label, Paisley Park; three Grammy awards 1985, Nat. Asscn for the Advancement of Colored People Special Achievement Award 1997, Q Award for Best Songwriter 1990, BRIT Awards for Best International Male Artist 1992, 1993, 1995, 1996, BET Award for Best Male R&B Artist 2006, Grammy Award for Best Male R&B Vocal Performance (for Future Baby Mama) 2008. *Recordings include:* albums: For You 1978, Prince 1979, Dirty Mind 1980, Controversy 1981, 1999 1982, Purple Rain (Acad. Award for Best Original Score, BRIT Award for Best Soundtrack 1985) 1984, Around the World in a Day (Best Soul/Rhythm and Blues Album of the Year, Down Beat Readers' Poll) 1985, Parade 1986, Sign O' The Times 1987, Lovesexy 1988, Batman (film soundtrack) (BRIT Award for Best Soundtrack 1990) 1989, Graffiti Bridge (film soundtrack) 1990, Diamonds and Pearls 1991, (symbol as title) 1992, Come 1994, The Black Album (recorded 1987) 1994, The Gold Experience 1995, Emancipation 1996, Chaos and Disorder 1996, New Power Soul 1998, Rave Un2 The Joy Fantastic 1999, The Rainbow Children 2002, One Nite Alone – Live! 2002, Musicology 2004, 3121 2006, Planet Earth 2007, LotusFlow3r 2009. *Films include:* Purple Rain 1984, Under the Cherry Moon 1986, Sign O' The Times 1987, Graffiti Bridge 1990. *Address:* Paisley Park Enterprises, 7801 Audoban Road, Chanhassen, MN 55317, USA (office). *Website:* www.npgmusicclub.com (office).

PRINCE, Charles (Chuck) O., III, MA, LLM; American banker; ed Univ. of Southern California, Georgetown Univ.; began career as attorney US Steel Corpn 1975–79; joined Commercial Credit Co. (later renamed Citigroup Inc.) 1979, Sr Vice-Pres. and Gen. Counsel 1983–86, Exec. Vice-Pres. 1996–2000, Chief Admin. Officer 2000–01, COO 2001–02, CEO and Dir Citigroup Inc. 2003–07, Chair. and CEO 2006–07; Chair. and CEO Global Corp. and Investment Bank 2002–03; mem. Council on Foreign Relations; mem. Bd of Dirs United Negro Coll. Fund, Teachers' Coll., Columbia Univ., New York; fmr mem. Bd of Dirs New York Urban League; mem. various bar asscns and professional asscns. *Address:* c/o Citigroup Inc., 399 Park Avenue, New York, NY 10043, USA (office).

PRINCE, Harold (Hal) Smith, LittD; American theatre director; b. 30 Jan. 1928, New York; s. of Milton A. Prince and Blanche (née Stern) Prince; m. Judith Chaplin 1962; one s. one d.; ed Emerson Coll.; co-produced Pajama Game 1954–56 (Antoinette Perry Award), Damn Yankees 1955–57 (Antoinette Perry Award), New Girl in Town 1957–58, West Side Story 1957–59, Fiorello! 1959–61 (Antoinette Perry Award, Pulitzer Prize), Tenderloin 1960–61, A Call on Kuprin 1961, They Might Be Giants 1961, Side by Side by Sondheim 1976; produced Take Her, She's Mine 1961–62, A Funny thing

Happened on the Way to the Forum 1962–64 (Antoinette Perry Award), Fiddler on the Roof 1964–72 (Antoinette Perry Award), Poor Bitos 1964, Flora the Red Menace 1965; dir, producer She Loves Me! 1963–64, London 1964, Superman 1966, Cabaret 1966–69 (Antoinette Perry Award), London 1968, Zorba 1968–69, Company 1970–72 (Antoinette Perry Award), London 1972, A Little Night Music 1973–74 (Antoinette Perry Award) (London 1975), Pacific Overtures 1976; co-dir, producer Follies 1971–72; co-producer, dir Candide 1974–75, Merrily We Roll Along 1981; dir A Family Affair 1962, Baker Street 1965, Great God Brown 1972–73, The Visit 1973–74, Love for Love 1974–75, On the Twentieth Century 1978, Evita, London 1978, Broadway 1979, Los Angeles 1980, Chicago 1980, Australia 1980, Vienna 1981, Mexico City 1981, Sweeney Todd, the Demon Barber of Fleet Street 1979–80, London 1980, A Doll's Life 1982, Diamonds 1984, Grind 1985, The Phantom of the Opera (Antoinette Perry Award for Best Dir 1988) 1986, Play Memory, End of the World, Rosa 1987, Grandchild of Kings (The O'Casey Project) (author and dir) 1992, Kiss of the Spider Woman (Toronto, London) 1992, (New York, Vienna) 1993, Show Boat (Toronto) 1993, (New York) 1994, (nat. tour) 1996, Candide 1997, Parade 1998; mem. Council, Nat. Endowment of the Arts, League of New York Theatres; Critics Circle awards, Best Music Award, Evening Standard; Commonwealth Award 1982; John F. Kennedy Center Awards 1994. *Films include:* (co-producer) The Pajama Game 1957, Damn Yankees 1958; (dir) Something for Everyone 1970, A Little Night Music 1978. *Operas:* Ashmedai 1976, Silverlake 1980, Don Giovanni 1989 (New York City Opera); Madame Butterfly 1982; Candide 1982; Willie Stark 1982 (Houston Opera Co.); Turandot 1983 (Vienna Staatsoper); Faust 1990, 1991 (Metropolitan Opera), La Fanciulla del West 1991 (Chicago Lyric Opera, San Francisco Opera). *Publication:* Contradictions (autobiography) 1974. *Address:* Suite 1009, 10 Rockefeller Plaza, New York, NY 10020, USA.

PRINCE, Richard; American painter and photographer; b. 6 Aug. 1949, Panama Canal Zone; began career at Time-Life magazine; trained as a figure painter, began creating collages containing photographs 1975. *Works include:* Untitled (Cigarettes) 1978–79, Untitled (Cowboy) 1980–84, Entertainers 1982–83, Spiritual America 1983, Jokes 1986, My Usual Procedure 1988, The Wrong Joke 1989, Untitled (Hoods) 1989, Girlfriends 1992, Second House, Debutante Nurse 2004. *Publications:* numerous articles and reviews in art magazines. *Address:* c/o Gladstone Gallery, 515 West 24th Street, New York, NY 10011, USA (office). *Telephone:* (212) 206-9300 (office). *Fax:* (212) 206-9301 (office). *E-mail:* richardprin@aol.com (office). *Website:* www.richardprinceart .com (office).

PRINCIPI, Anthony J.; American business executive, fmr government official and fmr naval officer; *Executive Chairman, QTC Management Inc.;* b. 16 April 1944, New York City; m. Elizabeth Ann Ahlering 1971; three s.; ed US Naval Acad., Seton Hall Univ.; service with USN in Vietnam; Chief Defense Counsel, Judge Advocate Gen. Corps, San Diego; Staff Counsel, Commdr US Pacific Fleet; Legis. Counsel, Dept of the Navy 1980; Chair. Bd, Fed. Quality Inst. 1991; Chief Counsel and Staff Dir, US Senate Cttee on Armed Services 1993; Chair. Comm. on Service Mems and Veterans Transition Assistance; COO Lockheed Martin Integrated Solutions 1995–2001; Co-Founder, Pres. and Chair. of Bd, Fed. Network; Pres. QTC Medical Services (now QTC Management Inc.) –1989, currently Exec. Chair.; Deputy Sec. of Veterans' Affairs, 1989, Acting Sec. 1992, Sec. of Veterans' Affairs 2001–04; Chair. 2005 Defense Base Closure and Realignment Comm. 2005; Bronze Star, Vietnamese Cross of Gallantry, Navy Combat Action Medal and other decorations. *Address:* QTC Management Inc., PO Box 5679, Diamond Bar, CA 91765, USA (office). *Telephone:* (909) 859-2101 (office). *Website:* www.qtcm.com (office).

PRINGLE, James Robert Henry, MA; British economist and journalist; *Editor-in-Chief, Central Banking Publications Ltd;* b. 27 Aug. 1939, Surrey; s. of John Pringle and Jacqueline (née Berry) Pringle; m. 1st Rita Schuchard 1966 (divorced 1998); m. 2nd Ikuko Hiroe 2003; ed King's School, Canterbury, King's Coll., Cambridge and London School of Econs; Asst to Ed., then Asst Ed. The Banker, London 1963–67, Ed. 1972–79; mem. editorial staff The Economist, London 1968; Asst Dir, later Deputy Dir Cttee on Invisible Exports 1969–72; Exec. Dir Group of Thirty, Consultative Group on Int. Econ. and Monetary Affairs, New York 1979–86; Sr Fellow, World Inst. for Devt Econs Research of the UN Univ. 1986–89; Sr Research Fellow, David Hume Inst., Edinburgh 1989–91; Dir Graham Bannock and Pnrs 1989–97; Ed.-in-Chief Central Banking Publications Ltd 1990–; fmr Man. Dir Public Policy, The World Gold Council. *Publications:* Banking in Britain 1973, The Growth Merchants 1977, The Central Banks (co-author) 1994, International Financial Institutions 1998. *Leisure interests:* classical music, the theatre. *Address:* 9 Northwood Lodge, Oakhill Park, London, NW3 7LL (home); Central Banking Publications, Tavistock House, Tavistock Square, London, WC1H 9JZ, England (office). *Telephone:* (20) 7388-0006 (office); (20) 7786-4721 (home). *Fax:* (20) 7388-9040 (office). *E-mail:* info@centralbanking.co.uk (office). *Website:* www.centralbanking.co.uk (office).

PRINZ, Birgit; German professional footballer; b. 25 Oct. 1977, Frankfurt; centre forward; teams played for include FSV Frankfurt 1992–98, 1. FFC Frankfurt 1998–2002, Carolina Courage (Women's United Soccer Asscn) 2002, 1. FFC Frankfurt 2002–; represented Germany at World Cup 1995, European Championship 1995, 1997, 1999, 2001, Olympic Games 2000, 2004, 2008; 104 int. caps (2nd highest total), 54 goals (world record) to 19 Sept. 2003; mem. Deutschen Olympischen Sportbund (DOSB) 2006–; won European Championship with Germany 1995, 1997, 2001; bronze medal with Germany at Olympic Games 2000, 2004; won Bundesliga with FSV Frankfurt 1995, 1998, with 1. FFC Frankfurt 1999, 2001, 2002, 2003, 2005; won German Cup with FFC Frankfurt 2000, 2001, 2002; won UEFA Cup with FFC Frankfurt 2002 (Player of the Match); won Founders Cup with Carolina Courage 2003 (Most Valuable Player in the final); won WUSA Championship with Carolina

Courage 2003; won World Cup with Germany 2003 (runner-up 1995); German Female Player of the Year 2001, 2002, 2003, 2004, 2005, 2006, 2007, 2008; FIFA Female Player of the Year 2003, 2004, 2005. *Leisure interests:* badminton, squash, walking her dog. *Address:* c/o 1. FFC Frankfurt, Stadion am Brentanobad, Rödelheimer Parkweg 39, 60489 Frankfurt am Main, Germany. *Website:* www.ffc-frankfurt.de; www.birgitprinz.de.

PRIOR, Baron (Life Peer), cr. 1987, of Brampton in the County of Suffolk; **James Michael Leathes Prior,** PC; British politician and farmer; b. 11 Oct. 1927, Norwich; s. of the late C. B. L. Prior and A. S. M. Prior; m. Jane P. G. Lywood 1954; three s. one d.; ed Charterhouse and Pembroke Coll., Cambridge; MP for Lowestoft 1959–83, for Waveney 1983–87; Parl. Pvt. Sec. to Pres. of Bd of Trade 1963, to Minister of Power 1963–64, to Rt Hon. Edward Heath 1965–70; Vice-Chair. Conservative Party 1965, 1972–74; Minister of Agric., Fisheries and Food 1970–72, Lord Pres. of Council 1972–74; Shadow Spokesman on Home Affairs March–June 1974, on Employment June 1974–79; Sec. of State for Employment 1979–81, for Northern Ireland 1981–84; Chair. GEC 1984–98; Dir Barclays PLC 1984–89, J. Sainsbury PLC 1984–92, United Biscuits 1974–79, 1984–94; mem. Tenneco European Advisory Council 1986–97, AIG Advisory Council; Dir Arab-British Chamber of Commerce; Chair. Royal Veterinary Coll. –1998; Chancellor Anglia Polytechnic Univ. 1992–99; Deputy Chair. MSI Cellular Investments BV 1999–2005, Ascot Underwriting Ltd 2001–06. *Publication:* A Balance of Power 1986. *Leisure interests:* cricket, tennis, golf, gardening. *Address:* House of Lords, Westminster, London, SW1A 0PW (office); Old Hall, Brampton, Beccles, Suffolk MR34 8EE, England (home). *Telephone:* (1502) 575-278 (home). *Fax:* (1502) 575-566 (home).

PRIORY, Richard B., MSc; American energy executive; b. 1946, Lakehurst, NJ; m. Joan Priory; one s., one d.; ed WV Univ. Inst. of Tech., Princeton Univ., Univ. of Mich.; registered professional engineer NC and SC; design and product engineer Union Carbide Corpn 1969–72; Asst Prof. of Structural Eng, Univ. of NC at Charlotte 1973–76; joined Duke Power Corpn as design engineer 1976, various positions including Vice-Pres. Design Eng 1984–91, Exec. Vice-Pres. Power Generation Group 1991–94, Pres. and COO 1994–97, Chair. and CEO 1997–2003 (retd); fmr Dir Dana Corpn; mem. Bd Edison Electric Inst., Asscn of Edison Illuminating Cos; mem. NC Govs Business Council of Man. and Devt, The Conf. Bd, The Business Roundtable, Pres's Advisory Group, US Chamber of Commerce, Business Council; fmr Chair. Inst. of Nuclear Power Operations (INPO); Chair. Charlotte Research Inst. and Foundation Dir Univ. of NC at Charlotte; mem. Nat. Acad. of Eng 1993–; Hon. DSc (WV Univ. Inst. of Tech.); Distinguished Service Award, Charlotte Engineers Club 1998, Alumnus of the Year Award, WV Univ. Inst. of Tech. 1998, Ellis Island Medal of Honor 1999. *Address:* c/o Charlotte Research Institute, 9201 University City Blvd, Charlotte, NC 28223-0001, USA (office).

PRITCHARD, David E., PhD; American physicist, academic and education consultant; *Cecil and Ida Green Professor of Physics, Massachusetts Institute of Technology;* b. 15 Oct. 1941, New York; s. of Edward M. Pritchard and Blanche M. Allen Pritchard; Postdoctoral Fellow, MIT, Cambridge, Mass. 1968, instructor 1968–70, Asst Prof. 1970–75, Assoc. Prof. 1975–80, Cecil and Ida Green Prof. of Physics 1980–; Div. Assoc. Ed. Physics Review Letters 1983–88; Distinguished Traveling Lecturer, LSTG/American Physical Soc. 1991–93; f. Effective Educational Technologies (online educ. co.); mem. NAS; Fellow, AAAS, American Physical Soc., Optical Soc. of America, American Acad. of Arts and Sciences; Broida Prize, American Physical Soc. 1991, Arthur L. Schawlow Prize, American Physical Soc. 2003, Max Born Award Optical Soc. of America 2004, and numerous other awards and honours. *Achievements:* mentored four Nobel Prize winners and four Nat. Thesis Award winners. *Publications:* numerous scientific papers, articles and contribs to books. *Leisure interests:* piano playing, sailing. *Address:* Department of Physics, Massachusetts Institute of Technology, 77 Massachusetts Avenue, Room 26–241, Cambridge, MA 02139 (office); 88 Washington Avenue, Cambridge, MA 02140, USA (home). *Telephone:* (617) 253-6812 (office). *Fax:* (617) 253-4876 (office). *E-mail:* dpritch@mit.edu (office). *Website:* web.mit.edu/ physics/facultyandstaff/faculty/david_pritchard.html (office); www.relate.mit .edu.

PRITZKER, Penny S., BA, MBA, JD; American lawyer and business executive; *Chairman, Classic Residence by Hyatt and TransUnion LLC;* b. 2 May 1959, Chicago; d. of Donald N. Pritzker and Sue Ann Pritzker (neé Sandel); m. Bryan Traubert 1988; one s. one d.; ed Harvard and Stanford Univs; fmr Chair. Superior Bank (now defunct); Chair. Classic Residence by Hyatt 1987–, TransUnion LLC (credit reporting firm) 2005–; Pres. Pritzker Realty Group 1990–; Pnr, Pritzker & Pritzker 1987–; mem. Bd of Dirs William Wrigley Jr Co.; fmr Chair. Chicago Museum of Contemporary Art; mem. Women's Issues Network 1991–, The Chicago Network 1992–, Int. Women's Forum, Council on Foreign Relations, Econ. Recovery Advisory Bd 2009–; mem. Harvard Bd of Overseerers 2002–; served as Nat. Finance Chair for Barack Obama's presidential campaign 2008; ranked 89th by Forbes magazine amongst 100 Most Powerful Women 2005. *Leisure interests:* competing in marathons and recreational ski races. *Address:* 71 South Wacker Drive, Suite 4700, Chicago, IL 60606-4637; Trans Union LLC, 555 West Adams Street, 6th Floor, Chicago, IL 60661-3614, USA (office). *Telephone:* (312) 258-1717 (office). *Website:* www .transunion.com (office); www.hyatt.com (office).

PRITZKER, Robert A., BSIE; American business executive; *President and CEO, Colson Associates;* m. Mayari Pritzker; five c.; ed Ill. Inst. of Tech. (IIL), Calif. Inst. of Tech., Univ. of Ill., Case Inst. of Tech.; co-founder, Pres. and CEO The Marmon Group (pvt. conglomerate of more than 150 cos) 1953–2005 (retd); currently Pres. and CEO Colson Assocs (co-f. 2002); family also owns Global Hyatt Corpn, Pritzker Realty, and other cos; lectured on business man. Univ. of Chicago Grad. School of Business; fmr Assoc. Fellow, Templeton Coll.,

Oxford Univ.; fmr Chair. Nat. Asscn of Manufacturers; Chair. Bd of Trustees Inst. of Tech.; mem. Nat. Acad. of Engineering; Chair. Bd Pritzker Foundation, Chicago; Life Trustee Chicago Symphony Orchestra; mem. Bd of Dirs Field Museum of Natural History, Lincoln Park Zoological Soc., Teachers' Acad. for Math. and Science; Hon. DHumLitt (IIL). *Address:* c/o Pritzker Foundation, 200 West Madison Street, 38th Floor, Chicago, IL 60606, USA (office). *Telephone:* (312) 750-8400. *Website:* www.marmon.com.

PRITZKER, Thomas J., MBA, JD; American business executive; *Chairman and CEO, Global Hyatt Corporation;* s. of Robert A. Pritzker (q.v.) and Mayari Pritzker; m.; four c.; ed Claremont McKenna Coll., Univ. of Chicago; Chair. and CEO Global Hyatt Corpn, The Pritzker Org.; Chair. Marmon Group; Chair., Man. Dir and Co-founder Bay City Capital; Co-founder First Health Group Corpn, Chair. 1990–2001, mem. Bd of Dirs 1985–86, 1990–2002; Founder Triton Container; Founding Gen. Pnr, GKH; Dir Pritzker Philanthropic Fund, Royal Caribbean Cruise Lines; mem. Bd of Trustees, Univ. of Chicago; mem. Interdisciplinary Biosciences Advisory Cttee (Bio-X program), Stanford Univ. *Address:* Global Hyatt Corporation, 71 South Wacker Drive, Chicago, IL 60606, USA (office). *Telephone:* (312) 750-1234 (office). *Fax:* (312) 750-8550 (office). *Website:* www.hyatt.com (office).

PRIX, Wolf D.; Austrian architect and academic; *Design Principal, Coop Himmelb(l)au;* b. 13 Dec. 1942, Vienna; ed Tech. Univ., Vienna, Architectural Asscn, London, UK, Southern Calif. Inst. of Architecture, LA, USA; Cofounder (with Helmut Swiczinsky and Michael Holzer) Coop Himmelb(l)au 1968, now Design Prin.; Prof. of Architecture, Univ. of Applied Arts, Vienna 1993–, Head, Inst. for Architecture, Head, Studio Prix and Vice-Rector, Univ. of Applied Arts 2003–; Visiting Prof., Architectural Asscn, London 1984, Harvard Univ., USA 1990; Adjunct Prof., Southern Calif. Inst. of Architecture, LA 1985–95; Faculty mem. Columbia Univ., New York 1998–; Harvey Perloff Prof., UCLA 1999, Adjunct Prof. 2001; mem. Architectural Council, Fed. Ministry of Science, Research and the Arts 1995–97; mem. Austrian Art Senate, European Acad. of Sciences and Arts, Advisory Cttee for Building Culture, Architectural Asscn of Austria, Architectural Union Santa Clara, Cuba, Architectural Asscn of Italy, Union of German Architects (BDA); Int. FRIBA 2006, American Inst. of Architects (AIA); Dr hc (Universidad de Palermo, Buenos Aires) 2001; Hon. mem. League of German Architects 1989, Hon. FAIA 2006; Officier des Arts et des Lettres 2002; numerous awards including Berlin Prize for Building Art 1982, Austrian Architectural Asscn (AAA) Award 1985, PA Award 1991, European Industrial Architecture Award 1992, Erich-Schelling-Architecture Prize 1992, Tau Sigma Delta Award 1993, Grosser Österreichischer Staatspreis 1999, Gold Medal for Merits to the Fed. State of Vienna 2002, Annie Spink Award for Excellence in Architectural Education 2004, Jencks Award: Visions Built 2008. *Architectural works include:* Rooftop Remodelling Falkestrasse (City of Vienna Award for Architecture 1989) 1983–88, Funder Factory 3 (State of Carinthia Award for Superior Architecture 1989, AAA Award 1990) 1988–89, Los Angeles Art Park (PA Award 1989), Open House (PA Award 1990), Groninger Museum (Dutch Nat. Steel Prize 1992) 1993–94, Seibersdorf Office and Research Centre (AAA Prize 1996) 1993–95, UFA Cinema Centre, Dresden (Neuer Sächsicher Kunstverein Prize 1996, German Architecture Prize 1999, Concrete Architectural Prize 1999, European Steel Design Award 2001) 1993–98, SEG Apt Tower (AAA Award 1999) 1994–98, SEG Remise (Austrian Cement Industry Award 2001) 1994–2000, Wassertum Hainburg (Anerkennungspreis für Architektur des Landes Niederösterreich 2002) 1999, Akron Art Museum (American Architecture Award 2005) 2001–07, Busan Cinema Complex, S Korea 2005–(11), Acad. of Fine Arts, Munich 1992, 2002–05, Space of Contemporary Artistic Creation, Cordoba, Spain 2005, The Great Egyptian Museum, Cairo, Egypt (Int. Architecture Award 2007) 2002, BMW Welt (RIBA European Award 2008, Preis des Deutschen Stahlbaues 2008, World Architecture Festival Award: Production, Wallpaper Design Award 2009: Best New Public Building, Detail Prize 2009 - Innovation Steel) 2001–07; works in progress: Musée des Confluences, Lyon, France 2001–(13); European Central Bank, Frankfurt, Germany 2014; Busan Cinema Center 2011; Cloud Roof, Riva del Garda, Italy 2010; House of Music, Aalborg, Denmark; Museum of Contemporary Art & Planning Exhbn, Shenzhen, China 2007–(10); Dalian Int. Conf. Center, China 2008–(10); Cultural Center Zarautz, Spain. *Publications include:* Coop Himmelb(l)au – Sie leben in Wien 1975, Coop Himmelb(l)au: Architecture is Now 1983; The Vienna Trilogy and One Cinema 1999, Blue Universe: Architectural Manifestos by Coop Himmelb(l)au 2002, Get Off of My Cloud 2005, Dynamic Forces 2007, Coop Himmelb(l)au: Beyond the Blue 2007. *Address:* Coop Himmelb(l)au, Wolf D. Prix / Wolfdieter Dreibholz & Partner ZT, GmbH, Spengergasse 37, 1050 Vienna, Austria (office). *Telephone:* (1) 546-60-0 (office). *Fax:* (1) 546-60-600 (office). *E-mail:* office@coop-himmelblau.at (office). *Website:* www.coop-himmelblau.at (office).

PRLIĆ, Jadranko, DSc; Bosnia and Herzegovina politician and university professor; b. 10 June 1959, Djakovo; m. Ankica Prlić; two d.; ed Univs of Mostar and Sarajevo; worked as a journalist; joined teaching staff, Univ. of Mostar 1987, Prof. Emer. 1999–; Mayor of Mostar 1987–88; fmr Gen. Man. Apro-Mostar agricultural enterprise; Vice-Pres. Govt of Bosnia and Herzegovina 1989–91; during war 1992–95 mem. and official of highest bodies of Croatian people; following signing of Washington (1994) and Dayton (1995) Agreements: Deputy Prime Minister and Minister of Defence; mem. Parl. of Bosnia and Herzegovina and Minister of Foreign Affairs 1996–2001; mem. Council of Ministers 2001–03; Deputy Minister of Foreign Trade and Econ. Relations 2001–03; Founder and Pres. European Movement in Bosnia and Herzegovina; Gov. in IMF for Bosnia and Herzegovina; Pres. Pro-European People's Party; indicted by Int. Criminal Tribunal for the Fmr Yugoslavia for crimes against humanity and war crimes against the non-Croat population March 2005, surrendered voluntarily to Tribunal. *Publications:* Policy of Fluctuating Foreign Exchange Rates 1990, Imperfect Peace 1998, Fuga Della

Storia 2000, Return to Europe 2002, Unfinished Game 2002; numerous articles in field of int. economy, particularly finance and political issues. *Leisure interests:* tennis, soccer, econ. and political literature, etc. *Address:* Srosmeyorova 6, 71000 Sarajevo (office); Grbavička 21C, 71000 Sarajevo, Bosnia and Herzegovina. *Telephone:* (33) 213001 (home). *Fax:* (33) 679275 (office). *E-mail:* jprlic@bih.net.ba (office). *Website:* www.jprlic.ba (home).

PROCTER, Jane Hilary Elizabeth; British journalist; b. London; d. of Gordon H. Procter and Florence Bibby Procter; m. Thomas C. Goldstaub 1985; one s. one d.; ed Queen's Coll. Harley St London; Fashion Asst Vogue 1974–75; Asst Fashion Ed. Good Housekeeping 1975–77; Acting Fashion Ed. Woman's Journal 1977–78; Fashion Writer Country Life 1978–80; Freelance Fashion Ed. The Times, Daily Express 1980–87; Ed. Tatler 1990–99, Ed. Dir PeopleNews Network 1999–2002. *Publication:* Dress Your Best 1983. *Leisure interests:* skiing, sailing.

PRODI, Romano, LLB; Italian academic and politician; b. 9 Aug. 1939, Scandiano; s. of Mario Prodi and Enrica Prodi; m. Flavia Franzoni; two s.; ed Catholic Univ. of Milan, London School of Econs; Prof. of Econs and Industrial Policy, Univ. of Bologna 1971–99, Prof. of Industrial Org. and Policy, 1990–93; Minister of Industry 1978–79; Chair. Scientific Cttee Econ. Research Inst. Nomisma, Bologna 1981–95; Chair. Istituto per le Ricostruzione Industriale (IRI) 1982–89, 1993–94; Founder l'Ulivo (The Olive Tree coalition of centre-left parties) 1995–2007 (evolved into Partito Democratico 2007), Pres. Partito Democratico 2007–08; Pres. Council of Ministers (Prime Minister) 1996–98; Pres. European Comm. 1999–2004; Prime Minister of Italy 2006–08; Chair. Jt UN–AU Peacekeeping Panel 2008–; mem. Asscn di cultura e politica, Il Mulino, Bologna, Asscn Italiana degli Economisti, Rome; Hon. mem. Real Academia de Ciencias Morales y Políticas, Madrid; Hon. Fellow, LSE; numerous hon. degrees. *Publications:* author of numerous scientific publs with particular reference to questions of European industrial policies, public enterprises in Italy and comparative analysis of econ. systems. *Address:* c/o Partito Democratico, Piazza Sant'Anastasia 7, 00186 Rome, Italy (office). *Website:* www.romanoprodi.it.

PROENÇA, Hélder; Guinea-Bissau politician; Minister of Nat. Defence 2005–07. *Address:* c/o Ministry of National Defence, Amura, Bissau, Guinea Bissau (office).

PROFUMO, Alessandro; Italian banking executive; *Managing Director and CEO, UniCredit Group;* b. 17 Feb. 1957, Genoa; ed Luigi Bocconi Univ., Milan; commercial and exec. positions Banco Lariano 1977–87; financial consultant McKinsey & Co. 1987; marketing consultant Bain, Cuneao & Associati 1988–91; Gen. Man. Banking and Parabanking, Riunione Adriatica di Sicurtà (RAS) 1991–94; Deputy Gen. Man. Planning and Group Control, Credito Italiano SpA 1994–95, Chief Gen. Man. 1995–96, CEO 1997–99, Man. Dir and CEO UniCredit Group 1997–, mem. Perm. Strategic Cttee, Corp. Governance, HR and Nominations Cttee; Chair. Supervisory Bd HVB, Bank Austria; Deputy Chair. UniCredit Banca Mobiliare (UBM); mem. Bd of Dirs and Exec. Cttee Asscn Bancaria Italiana (ABI); mem. Bd of Dirs Teatro alla Scala Foundation, Luigi Bocconi Univ., Arnaldo Pomodoro Foundation; mem. Asscn for Devt and Study of Banks and the Stock Exchange, Inst. Int. d'Etudes Bancaires; Cavaliere al Merito del Lavoro 2004. *Publications:* Plus valori (with Giovanni Moro) 2003; numerous articles and studies. *Address:* UniCredit SpA, Piazza Cordusia, 20123 Milan, Italy (office). *Telephone:* (02) 88621 (office). *Fax:* (02) 88628503 (office). *E-mail:* info@unicreditgroup.eu (office). *Website:* www.unicreditgroup.eu (office).

PROGLIO, Henri; French business executive; *Chairman and CEO, Veolia Environnement;* b. 1949, Antibes; ed Haute Ecole de Commerce, Paris; began career with Compagnie Générale des Eaux 1972, Chair. and CEO waste man. and transportation subsidiary 1990–91, Sr Exec. 1991–90, CEO Vivendi Water, Chair. Générale des Eaux and Sr Exec. Vice-Pres. Vivendi 1999–2001, Chair. and CEO Veolia Environnement (fmrly Vivendi Environnement) 2001–; mem. Exec. Cttee Vinci, Elior, Fomento de Construcciones y Contratas, Madrid. *Address:* Veolia Environnement, 36–38 Avenue Kléber, 75116 Paris, Cedex 8, France (office). *Telephone:* 1-71-75-00-00 (office). *Fax:* 1-71-71-15-45 (office). *E-mail:* info@veoliaenvironnement.com (office). *Website:* www .veoliaenvironnement.com (office).

PROKEŠ, Jozef, DSc; Slovak politician; b. 12 June 1950, Nitra; s. of Jozef Prokeš and Elena Manicová; m. 1979; one s. one d.; ed Komenský Univ., Bratislava; research student with Inst. of Physics, Slovak Acad. of Sciences, Bratislava 1973–82; worked for Heavy Current Electrotechnical Works, Čab 1982–85; research worker Inst. of Measurements, Slovak Acad. of Sciences, Bratislava 1985–89; co-f. Forum of Coordinating Cttees of Workers in Slovakia 1989; Chair. Independent Trade Unions 1990; Chair. Trade Union of Research Workers of Slovak Acad. of Sciences 1990; Deputy to Slovak Nat. Council 1990–92; Chair. Slovak Nat. Party (SNP) 1991–92, Hon. Chair. 1992–; Vice-Pres. Slovak Nat. Council 1992–93; Deputy Premier of Slovak Govt 1993–94; Deputy to Nat. Council 1994–; Vice-Chair. Foreign Cttee of Nat. Council 1994–98; Head, Slovak Del. to CSCE 1993–94; mem. Slovak del. to WEU 1995. *Address:* National Council of the Slovak Republic, Mudroňova 1, 812 80 Bratislava, Slovakia (office). *Telephone:* (7) 5934-1111 (office). *E-mail:* k.badulin@nbrb.by.

PROKOPOVICH, Petr Petrovich; Belarusian engineer, politician and central banker; *Chairman, National Bank of the Republic of Belarus;* b. 3 Nov. 1942, Rovno, Brest Region; s. of Petr Prokopovich and Evgeniya Prokopovich; m. Ludmila Prokopovich; one s. one d.; ed Dnepropetrovsk Eng and Construction Inst.; Dir-Gen. Brest Regional Planning and Construction Asscn 1976–96; mem. Supreme Soviet 1990–95; Deputy Head of Admin. of Pres. of Belarus 1996; First Deputy Prime Minister of Belarus 1996–98; Chair. Nat. Bank of the Repub. of Belarus 1998–; Order of Labour Red Banner, Order of

Honour; Honoured Constructor of the USSR Award, Diploma of the Supreme Soviet of Belarus. *Publications:* various articles in Belorusian and foreign edns. *Leisure interests:* billiards, tennis. *Address:* National Bank of the Republic of Belarus, 20 Nezavizimosty Avenue, 220008 Minsk, Belarus (office). *Telephone:* (17) 219-23-03 (office). *Fax:* (17) 227-48-79 (office). *E-mail:* email@nbrb.by (office). *Website:* www.nbrb.by (office).

PRÖLL, Josef; Austrian politician; *Vice-Chancellor and Federal Minister for Finance;* b. 14 Sept. 1968, Stockerau; m.; three c.; ed Univ. of Natural Resources and Applied Life Sciences, Vienna; Official at Chamber of Agric., Fed. Prov. of Lower Austria 1993–98; Official in charge of econ. policy, Austrian Farmers' Fed. 1998–2000, Dir 2001–03; Dir Vienna Farmers' Fed. 1999–2000; Head of Cabinet, Fed. Ministry of Agric., Forestry, Environment and Water Man. 2000–01, Fed. Minister of Agric., Forestry, Environment and Water Man. 2003–08, Vice-Chancellor and Fed. Minister for Finance 2008–; mem. Austrian People's Party, Chair. 2008–. *Address:* Federal Ministry of Finance, Hintere Zollamtstrasse 2b, 1030 Vienna, Austria. *Telephone:* (1) 514-33-0 (office). *Fax:* (1) 512-78-69 (office). *E-mail:* buergerservice@bmf.gv.at (office). *Website:* www.bmf.gv.at (office).

PRONK, Johannes (Jan) Pieter; Dutch international organization official, academic and fmr politician; *Professor of Theory and Practice of International Development, Institute of Social Studies;* b. 16 March 1940, The Hague; m.; one s. one d.; ed Erasmus Univ., Rotterdam; Lecturer, Devt Programming Centre, School of Econs and Netherlands Econ. Inst. 1965–71; mem. Second Chamber (Parl.) 1971–73, 1978–80, 1986–89; Minister for Devt Co-operation 1973–77, 1989–98; Prof. of Int. Devt Policy, Inst. of Social Studies, The Hague 1979–80; Deputy Sec.-Gen. UNCTAD 1980–85, Asst Sec.-Gen. UN 1985–86; First Deputy Chair. Dutch Labour Party 1986–89; Den Uyl Chair, Univ. of Amsterdam 1989; Minister of Housing, Spatial Planning and the Environment 1998–2002; Pres. UN Conf. of Parties of the Convention on Climate Change, The Hague 2000, Bonn 2001, Special Envoy of the Sec.-Gen. for the World Summit on Sustainable Devt, Johannesburg 2002; Chair. Water Supply and Sanitation Collaborative Council 2002–04, Bd Int. Inst. for Environment and Devt, London 2002–04; Prof. of Theory and Practice of Int. Devt, Inst. of Social Studies, The Hague 2003–; Special Rep. of the Sec.-Gen. for Sudan 2004–06; Pres. Soc. for Int. Devt 2008–, Netherlands Interpeace Council 2008–; fmr Treas. Brandt Comm.; Grootlint Orde Palm (Suriname) 1977, Ridder Orde Nederlandse Leeuw (Netherlands) 1978, Gran Cruz Orden Bernardo O'Higgins (Chile) 1993, 26th September Medal (Yemen) 1996, Officier, Légion d'honneur 2001, Officier, Orde Oranje Nassau (Netherlands) 2002; Dr hc (San Marcos Univ., Lima) 1974, (Inst. of Social Studies) 2002; US Business Council for Sustainable Energy Climate e-Award 2001. *Publications:* De Kritische Grens 1994, Catalysing Development? 2004, Willens en Wetens 2005. *Leisure interests:* jogging, skiing. *Address:* Institute of Social Studies, PO Box 29776, 2502 LT The Hague, The Netherlands (office). *Telephone:* (70) 426460 (office). *Fax:* (70) 4260799 (office). *E-mail:* pronk333@planet.nl (office). *Website:* www.iss.nl (office); www.janpronk.nl (home).

PROPPER, Carol, PhD; British economist and academic; *Professor of Economics and Head of Healthcare Management Group, Business School, Imperial College London;* ed Univs of Bristol, Oxford and York, Univ. of Toronto, Canada; Community Worker, Islington, London 1977–79; Research Officer, Nuffield Coll. Oxford 1981–82; Research Economist New Zealand Inst. of Econ. Research 1983–84; Research Fellow Centre for Health Econs, Univ. of York 1986–87, Visiting Fellow 1987–96; Lecturer in Econs, Brunel Univ. 1987–88; Lecturer, Univ. of Bristol 1988–93, Reader 1993–94, Prof. of Econs of Public Policy 1995–2007, Deputy Dir Centre for Market and Public Organisation 1998– (part-time 2007–); Prof. of Econs and Head of Healthcare Man. Group, Imperial Coll. Business School, London 2007–; Visiting Prof., La Follette Inst. for Public Affairs, Univ. of Wisconsin, USA 1993; Research Assoc., Welfare State Programme, LSE 1987–94; Sr Econ. Adviser to NHS Exec. on Regulation of NHS Internal Market 1993–94, Incentives Sanction Group, Dept of Health 1999–, Adding It Up Implementation Group, HM Treasury 2000–; Research Fellow CEPR 1998–; Co-Dir Centre for Social Exclusion, LSE 1997–2007; EC Expert on Social Protection in Europe (DGV) 1991–93; Research Team mem. ECuity Project on Health Care Reform 1992–, COMAC–HSR Project on Equity in Healthcare Finance and Delivery 1992–94; adviser to econ. consultancies; Chair. Cttee on Women in Econs, Royal Econ. Soc. 1998–2001, mem. Council 2000–, Chair. Conf. Programme 2001; Ed. Economic Journal Conference Supplement 2002; mem. Editorial Bd Journal of Health Economics, Health Economics, Fiscal Studies. *Publications include:* The Economics of Social Policy (co-author) 1992, Quasi-Markets: The Emerging Findings (co-ed.) 1994, Who Pays For, Who Gets Health Care: Equity in the Finance and Delivery of Health Care in the UK 1998, Private Welfare and Public Policy (co-ed.) 1999; numerous chapters in books, articles in professional journals and reports. *Address:* Imperial College London, South Kensington Campus, London, SW7 2AZ, England (office). *Telephone:* (20) 7594-9291 (office). *Website:* www3.imperial.ac.uk/business-school (office).

PROSPER, Pierre-Richard, BA, JD; American lawyer and fmr government official; *Counsel, Arent Fox LLP;* b. 1963, Denver, Colo.; ed Boston Coll., Pepperdine Univ.; Deputy Dist Attorney, LA County 1989–94; Asst US Attorney for Cen. Dist. of Calif. 1994–96; war crimes prosecutor UN Int. Criminal Tribunal for Rwanda 1996–98; Special Asst to Asst Attorney Gen. for Criminal Div., US Justice Dept, seconded to US State Dept as Special Counsel and Policy Advisor on War Crimes Issues 1999–2001, Amb.-at-Large, War Crimes Issues, US State Dept 2001–05; Counsel, Arent Fox LLP (law firm), Los Angeles 2005–; mem. UN Cttee on the Elimination of Racial Discrimination, Geneva 2007–; Trustee, Boston Coll. Bd of Trustees. *Address:* Arent Fox LLP, Gas Company Tower, 555 West Fifth Street, 48th Floor, Los Angeles, CA 90013, USA (office). *Telephone:* (213) 629-7400 (office). *Fax:* (213) 629-7401 (office). *E-mail:* prosper.pierre@arentfox.com (office). *Website:* www.arentfox.com (office).

PROSSER, Sir David J., Kt, BSc, FIA; British fmr insurance executive; b. 1944; s. of Ronald and Dorothy Prosser; m. Rosemary Snuggs 1971; two d.; ed Ogmore Grammar School, Univ. of Wales, Aberystwyth; with Sun Alliance and London Assurance Co. 1965–69; Hoare Govett & Co. 1969–73; joined Superannuation Investments Dept, Nat. Coal Bd 1973, Head of Stock Market Activities –1981; Man. Dir Venture Capital CIN Industrial Investments 1981–85, CEO 1985–88; Group Dir Investments, Legal & Gen. PLC 1988–91, Deputy CEO Jan.–Sept. 1991, Group CEO Sept. 1991–2006 (retd); Dir (non-exec.) InterContinental Hotels Group 2003–08, Epsom Downs Racecourse 2003–, Investec 2006–; Chair. Royal Automobile Club 2007–. *Address:* c/o Royal Automobile Club, Pall Mall Clubhouse, 89 Pall Mall, London, SW1Y 5HS, England (office). *Telephone:* (1306) 731113 (office). *E-mail:* sirdavid.prosser@btconnect.com (office).

PROSSER, Sir Ian Maurice Gray, Kt, BComm, FCA, DUniv; British business executive; *Non-Executive Deputy Chairman, BP PLC;* b. 5 July 1943, Bath; s. of Maurice Prosser and Freda Prosser; m. 1st Elizabeth Herman 1964 (divorced 2003); two d.; m. 2nd Hilary Prewer 2003; ed King Edward's School, Bath, Watford Grammar School and Birmingham Univ.; with Cooper Bros (chartered accts) 1964–69; with Bass Charrington Ltd 1969–82, Financial Dir 1978; Vice-Chair. and Financial Dir Bass PLC 1982–84, Vice-Chair. and Group Man. Dir 1984–87, Chair. and CEO 1987–2000, Exec. Chair. 2000, co. then de-merged into Intercontinental Hotels Group PLC, Chair. 2000–2003 (retd); Chair. The Brewers' Soc. 1992–94; Dir (non-exec.) The Boots Co. 1984–96, Lloyds TSB Group PLC 1988–99, BP (later BP Amoco now BP PLC) 1997– (Deputy Chair. 1999–), Glaxo SmithKline PLC 1999–, Sara Lee Inc. 2004–; Chair. Exec., World Travel and Tourism Council 2001–04. *Leisure interests:* bridge, gardening. *Address:* BP PLC, 1 St James Square, London, SW1Y 4PD, England (office). *Telephone:* (20) 7496-4000 (office). *Fax:* (20) 7496-4630 (office). *E-mail:* ian.prosser@imgp.co.uk (office). *Website:* www.bp.com (office).

PROST, Alain Marie Pascal; French motor racing team owner and fmr racing driver; b. 24 Feb. 1955, Saint-Chamond; s. of André Prost and Marie-Rose Karatchian; m. Anne-Marie Prost; two s.; ed Coll. Sainte-Marie, Saint-Chamond; joined Marlboro MacLaren Group 1980, Renault team 1981–83, McLaren TAG team 1984–87, McLaren Honda 1988–89, Ferrari 1990–91, Williams Renault 1993; winner Formula 1 Grand Prix races in France 1981, 1983, 1988, 1989, 1990, 1993, Netherlands 1981, 1984, Italy 1981, 1985, 1989, Brazil 1982, 1984, 1985, 1987, 1988, 1990, South Africa 1982, 1993, Austria 1983, 1985, 1986, Britain 1983, 1985, 1989, 1990, 1993, Belgium 1983, 1987, Europe 1984, Monte Carlo 1984, 1985, 1986, 1988, San Marino 1984, 1986, 1993, Portugal 1984, 1987, 1988, Germany 1984, 1993, Australia 1986, 1988, Mexico 1988, 1990, Spain 1988, 1990, 1993, USA 1989, Canada 1993; Formula 1 World Champion 1985, 1986, 1989, 1993; total 51 Grand Prix wins, 106 podium finishes; technical consultant to McLaren Mercedes 1995; founder and Pres. Prost Grand Prix Team 1997–2002; Hon. OBE 1994; Trophée du champion automobile du siécle en Autriche 1999; Officier, Légion d'honneur;. *Publications:* Vive ma vie 1993.

PROT, Baudouin Daniel Claude; French banker; *CEO, BNP Paribas;* b. 24 May 1951, Paris; s. of André Prot and Marguerite Le Febvre; m. Viviane Abel 1981; one s. one d.; ed Inst. de Sainte-Croix, Neuilly, Ecole Saint-Louis des hautes études commerciales, Ecole nat. d'admin.; Inspecteur, Inspection générale des finances, Paris 1976; Deputy Dir Gen. Energy and Raw Materials, Ministry of Industry 1982–83; joined Banque Nat. de Paris (BNP) 1983, managerial positions depts for Europe 1985–87, metropolitan networks 1987–92, France 1992–96, Deputy Dir-Gen. BNP 1992–96, apptd Dir-Gen. 1996, CEO BNP Paribas 2005–; Chair. Carte bleue group 1991–97; Dir Accor, Veolie Environnement BNP Paribas; mem. Supervisory Cttee PPR SA (fmrly Pinault-Printemps-Redoute); Inspecteur générale des finances 1993; Chevalier, Légion d'honneur, Ordre nat. du Mérite. *Publications:* Armée-Nation, le Rendez-vous manqué 1975, Nationalisations 1977, Réduire l'impôt 1985, Dénationalisation 1986, La Jeunesse inégale 1987, Le Retour de capital 1990. *Leisure interests:* tennis, skiing, sailing. *Address:* BNP Paribas, 16 boulevard des Italiens, 75009 Paris (office); 21 rue Monsieur, 75007 Paris, France (home). *Telephone:* 1-40-14-45-46 (office). *Fax:* 1-40-14-69-73 (office). *E-mail:* baudouin.prot@bnpparibas.com (office). *Website:* www.bnpparibas.com (office).

PROTHEROE, Alan Hackford, CBE, TD, DL; British journalist and broadcasting executive; b. 10 Jan. 1934, St David's, Wales; s. of Rev. B. P. Protheroe and R. C. M. Protheroe; m. 1st Anne Miller 1956 (died 1999); two s.; m. 2nd Rosemary Margaret Louise Tucker 2004; ed Maesteg Grammar School, Glamorgan; reporter, Glamorgan Gazette 1951–53; 2nd Lt, The Welch Regt 1954–56; reporter, BBC Wales 1957–59, Industrial Corresp. 1959–64, Ed. News and Current Affairs 1964–70; Asst Ed. BBC TV News 1970–72, Deputy Ed. 1972–77, Ed. 1977–80; Asst Dir BBC News and Current Affairs 1980–82; Asst Dir-Gen. BBC 1982–87; Man. Dir The Services Sound and Vision Corpn 1987–94; founder-mem. Asscn of British Eds, Chair. 1987; Dir Visnews Ltd 1982–87; Dir Defence Public Affairs Consultants Ltd 1987–; Dir Europac Group Ltd 1990– (Chair. 1990–2000), Chair. E Wessex Reserve Forces Asscn; mem. Inst. of Public Relations; DL for Bucks.; Col TA 1991–96. *Publications:* contribs to journals on media and defence affairs. *Leisure interests:* travel, photography. *Address:* Amberleigh House, 60 Chapman Lane, Flackwell Heath, Bucks., HP10 9BD, England. *Telephone:* (1628) 528492. *Fax:* (1628) 528492 (office).

PROULX, (Edna) Annie, MA; American writer; b. 22 Aug. 1935, Norwich, Conn.; d. of George Napoleon Proulx and Lois Nellie Gill; m. 1st H. Ridgeley

Bullock 1955 (divorced); one d.; m. 2nd James Hamilton Lang 1969 (divorced 1990); three s.; ed Univ. of Vermont and Sir George Williams (now Concordia) Univ., Montréal; freelance journalist, Vt 1975–87; f. Vershire Behind the Times newspaper, Vershire, Vt; short stories appeared in Blair & Ketchums Country Journal, Esquire, etc.; Vt Council Arts Fellowship 1989, Ucross Foundation Residency, Wyo. 1990, 1992; mem. PEN; Guggenheim Fellow 1993; active anti-illiteracy campaigner; Hon. DHumLitt (Maine) 1994; Alumni Achievement Award, Univ. of Vt 1994, New York Public Library Literary Lion 1994, Dos Passos Prize for Literature 1996, American Acad. of Achievement Award 1998. *Publications:* Heart Songs and Other Stories 1988, Postcards (novel) (PEN/Faulkner Award for Fiction 1993) 1992, The Shipping News (Chicago Tribune Heartland Prize for Fiction, Irish Times Int. Fiction Prize, Nat. Book Award for Fiction, Pulitzer Prize for Fiction 1994) 1993, Accordion Crimes 1996, Best American Short Stories (ed.) 1997, Brokeback Mountain (short story, Nat.Magazine Award 1998, O. Henry Awards Prize 1998) 1998, Close Range: Wyoming Stories (New Yorker Book Award Best Fiction 1999, English-Speaking Union's Amb. Book Award 2000, Borders Original Voices Award in Fiction 2000) 1998, That Old Ace in the Hole (Best Foreign Language Novels of 2002/Best American Novel Award, Chinese Publishing Asscn and Peoples' Literature Publishing House 2002) 2002, Bad Dirt: Wyoming Stories 2 2004, Fine Just the Way It Is: Wyoming Stories 3 2008. *Leisure interests:* fly-fishing, canoeing, playing the fiddle. *Address:* PO Box 230, Centennial, WY 82055,; c/o Simon Schuster Inc., 1230 Avenue of the Americas, New York, NY 10020, USA (office). *Fax:* (307) 742-6159.

PROUST, Jean-Paul; French civil servant; *Minister of State of Monaco;* b. 1940; m.; two c.; ed Ecole Nat. d'Admin; various high-level positions within French govt, including Admin., Guadeloupe 1989–91; Prefet of Police, Paris 2001–04; Minister of State of Monaco 2005–; Commdr, Légion d'honneur. *Address:* Boite Postale 522, MC 98015, Monaco (office). *Telephone:* 93-15-80-00 (office). *Fax:* 93-15-82-17 (office). *E-mail:* centre-info@gouv.mc (office). *Website:* www.gouv.mc (office).

PRUAITCH, Patrick; Papua New Guinea politician; *Minister of Finance and the Treasury;* mem. Parl. for Aitape-Lumi; fmr Minister for Forestry, Minister of Finance and the Treasury 2007–; mem. Nat. Alliance Party. *Address:* Department of Finance and Treasury, Vulupindi Haus, Waigani Drive, POB 710, Waigani, Vulupindi Haus, National Capital District, Papua New Guinea (office). *Telephone:* 3128817 (office). *Fax:* 3128844 (office). *E-mail:* enquiries@treasury.gov.pg (office). *Website:* www.treasury.gov.pg (office).

PRUDNIKOV, Gen. Victor Alexeyevich; Russian army officer (retd); b. 4 Feb. 1939, Rostov-on-Don; m.; two s.; ed Armavir Higher Mil. Aviation School of Pilots, Gagarin Mil. Aviation Acad., Mil. Acad. of Gen. Staff; pilot, instructor aviation regt 1959–65; Commdr of squadron, Regt Commdr, Deputy Div. Commdr 1968–75; Commdr Anti-Aircraft Defence Div. 1975–78; Deputy C-in-C 1978–81, First Deputy C-in-C 1981–83; Commdr Anti-Aircraft Defence Army 1983–89; C-in-C Moscow Mil. Command 1989–91; C-in-C Anti-Aircraft Defence Forces of Russia 1991–97; Head of Staff on Co-ordination of Mil. Co-operation CIS Cos 1998–2001. *Leisure interests:* tennis, swimming. *Address:* Ministry of Defence, Myasnitskaya str. 37, 103175 Moscow, Russia (office). *Telephone:* (495) 296-18-00 (office).

PRUEHER, Adm. Joseph W., MS; American diplomatist and naval officer; b. 25 Nov. 1942, Nashville, Tenn.; m. Suzanne Prueher; one s. one d.; ed Montgomery Bell Acad., US Naval Acad., Annapolis, Md, Naval War Coll., Newport, RI and George Washington Univ.; started naval career as Command Ensign, USN, advanced through grades to Adm., C-in-C US Pacific Command, Camp HM Smith, Hawaii 1996–99; Amb. to People's Repub. of China 1999–2001; mem. Bd of Dirs Merrill Lynch 2001–; decorations from govts of Singapore, Thailand, Japan, Korea, Philippines, Indonesia and Australia; multiple awards for combat flying as well as naval and jt service. *Publications:* numerous articles on leadership, mil. readiness and Pacific region security issues. *Address:* c/o Department of State, 2201 C Street, NW, Washington, DC 20520, USA (office). *Website:* www.ml.com (office).

PRUNARIU, Maj.-Gen. (retd) Dumitru-Dorin, PhD; Romanian airspace engineer, cosmonaut and diplomatist; *President of Scientific Board, Romanian Space Agency;* b. 27 Sept. 1952, Brasov; m. Crina Prunariu; two s.; ed Airspace Eng Faculty at Polytechnic Univ., Bucharest, Cosmonaut Training Course, Star City, Russia, Int. Aviation Man. Training Inst. (IAMTI/IIFGA), Montreal, Canada, Nat. Defence Coll., Bucharest, course on applied diplomacy within Ministry of Foreign Affairs; engineer at IAR-BRASOV (aircraft co.) 1976–77; Romanian Air Force 1977–2007; crew member, Soyuz 40 space mission 1981, Chief Inspector for Airspace Activities 1981–89; Deputy Minister to Ministry of Transportation and Chief of Romanian Civil Aviation Dept 1990–91; Sec. Romanian Space Agency 1992–95, mem. Admin. Council 1995–98, Pres. 1998–2004, Pres. Bd 2005–, Pres., Scientific Bd 2008–; Amb. to Russian Fed. 2004–05; Dir Romanian Office for Science and Tech. to the EU, Nat. Authority for Scientific Research 2006–08; Co-leader World Bank Project on reorganization of the higher educ. and research system in Romania 1992–93; Vice-Pres. European Inst. for Risk Man., Security and Communication (EURISC) Foundation 1995–; Chair. S&T Sub-cttee, UN COPUOS 2004–05; Assoc. Prof. of Geopolitics, Faculty of Int. Business and Econs, Acad. of Econ. Studies, Bucharest 1995–; mem. Astronautic Comm., Romanian Acad. 1981–, Int. Aeronautic Fed. 1982–; Founder-mem. Asscn of Space Explorers, Paris 1985, mem. Exec. Cttee 1995–2001; Corresp. mem. Int. Astronautic Acad. 1992, full mem. 2007–; mem. Romanian Nat. COSPAR Cttee 1994–; mem. first Rotary Club of Bucharest 1997–; hon. citizen of several cities; Hon. mem. American Romanian Acad. of Arts and Sciences, registered in Calif., USA 2002; Hero of Romania 1981, Golden Star and Hero of the Soviet Union 1981, Grand Officer of the Order Steaua României (Star of Romania) 2000; Yuri Gagarin Medal, Int. Astronautic Fed. 1982, Hermann Oberth Gold Medal, German Rocket Soc. Hermann Oberth-Wernher von Braun, Germany 1984, and others. *Publications:* author or co-author of several books and numerous scientific papers on space tech. and space flight; studies on security, risk and communication man., geopolitics accomplished within the EURISC Foundation; articles on scientific topics published in Romanian and foreign publs. *Leisure interest:* photography. *Address:* Romanian Space Agency, Mendeleev Str. 21–25, 010632 Bucharest, Romania (office). *Telephone:* (21) 3168722 (office); (21) 2114914 (home). *Fax:* (21) 3128804 (office); (21) 2114914 (home). *E-mail:* dorin52@gmail.com (home); eurisc@eurisc.org (office); dumitru.prunariu@rosa.ro (office). *Website:* www .rosa.ro (office); www.eurisc.org (office); www.prunariu.org (home).

PRUNSKIENĖ, Kazimiera Danutė, DEconSci; Lithuanian politician; *Minister of Agriculture;* b. 26 Feb. 1943, Švenčionėliai Region; d. of Ona Stankevičienė and Pranas Stankevičius; m. 1st Povilas Prunskus 1961; m. 2nd Algimantas Tarvydas 1990 (divorced); one s. two d.; ed Vilnius State Univ.; teacher, then Dean of Faculty, Vilnius State Univ. 1965–85; Deputy Dir Inst. of Econ. Agric. 1986–88; People's Deputy of the USSR 1989–90, mem. USSR Supreme Soviet 1989–90; Deputy Chair. Council of Ministers of Lithuania 1989–90, Chair. 1990–91; mem. Lithuanian Parl. 1990–92, 1996–; Minister of Agric. 2005–; Pres. Lithuanian-European Inst. 1991–; Pres. pvt. consulting firm K. Prunskienė-Consulting 1993–96; Prof. of Econs, Vilnius Gediminas Tech. Univ. 1996–2000; Founder and Pres. Lithuanian Women's Party (later New Democracy Party) 1995–; Chair. Peasants' and New Democracy Union 2001–; mem. CEPS Int. Advisory Council 1992–, Int. Cttee for Econ. Reform and Co-operation 1994–; Pres. Baltic Women's Basketball League 1994–; mem. Council of Women World Leaders 1997–; Order of Grand Duke of Lithuania Gediminas (2nd Degree) and Medal of the Order of Gediminas 2000, Medal of the Independence of Lithuania 2000, Medal of the FRG, Order of Merit 2000, Grand Cross of Merit with Star 2001; Alexander von Humboldt Foundation Scholarship, Minerva Prize (Italy). *Publications:* Amber Lady's Confession 1991, Leben für Litauen 1992, Behind the Scenes 1992, Challenge to Dragon 1992, Price of Liberation 1993, Markt Balticum 1994, Transformation, Co-operation and Conversion 1996, Science and Technology Policy of the Baltic States and International Co-operation 1997, Intellectual Property Rights in Central and Eastern Europe: the Creation of Favourable Legal and Market Preconditions 1998. *Leisure interests:* sports, music, literature, knitting, cooking, walking in the forest. *Address:* Ministry of Agriculture, Gedimino pr. 19, Vilnius 01103 (office); Krivių g. 53a-13, Vilnius 02007, Lithuania (home). *Telephone:* (5) 239-1111 (office). *Fax:* (5) 239-1212 (office). *E-mail:* ministras@zum.lt (office). *Website:* www.zum.lt (office).

PRUSAK, Mikhail Mikhailovich, DEcon; Russian politician and economist; b. 23 Feb. 1960, Ivano-Frankovskaya region, Ukraine; m.; one s. one d.; ed Higher Komsomol School, Acad. of National Econs; Sec. Novgorod regional Komsomol Cttee –1988; Dir Sovkhoz Trudovik Novgorod region 1988–91; People's Deputy, mem. USSR Supreme Soviet, mem. Interregional Deputies' Group 1989–91; Gov. of Novgorod Region 1991–2007 (resgnd); mem. Council of Federal Ass. of Russian Fed. 1996–2001; Chair. Democratic Party of Russia; Vice-Pres. Parl. Ass. Council of Europe 1999–2001; author of numerous works; Corresp. mem. St Petersburg Acad. of Eng; recipient of awards. *Leisure interest:* hunting. *Address:* c/o Office of the Governor, Sophiiyskaya pl. 1, 173005 Veliky Novgorod, Russia (office).

PRUSINER, Stanley B., AB, MD; American physician, biochemist and academic; *Professor of Neurology and Professor of Biochemistry, University of California, San Francisco;* b. 28 May 1942, Des Moines, Ia; s. of Lawrence Prusiner and Miriam Prusiner; m. Sandy Turk; ed Walnut Hills High School, Cincinnati, Ohio, Univ. of Pennsylvania, Univ. of California, San Francisco; US Public Health Service, NIH 1968–71; Internship in Medicine, Univ. of California, San Francisco 1968–69, Residency in Neurology 1972–74, Asst Prof. of Neurology in Residence 1974–80, Lecturer, Dept of Biochemistry and Biophysics 1976–78, Assoc. Prof. of Neurology in Residence 1980–81, Assoc. Prof. of Neurology 1981–84, Prof. of Neurology 1984–, Prof. of Biochemistry 1988–; Asst Prof. of Virology in Residence, Univ. of California, Berkeley 1979–83, Prof. of Virology in Residence 1984–; Potamkin Prize for Alzheimer's Disease Research, American Acad. of Neurology 1991, NIH Christopher Columbus Quincentennial Discovery Award in Biomedical Research 1992, Metropolitan Life Foundation Award for Medical Research 1992, Dickson Prize for Distinguished Scientific Accomplishments, Univ. of Pittsburgh 1992, Charles A. Dana Award for Pioneering Achievements in Health 1992, NAS Richard Lounsbery Award for Extraordinary Scientific Research 1993, Gairdner Foundation Award for Outstanding Achievement in Medical Science 1993, Bristol-Myers Squibb Award for Distinguished Achievement in Neuroscience Research 1994, Albert Lasker Award for Basic Medical Research 1994, Paul Ehrlich Prize, Paul Ehrlich Foundation and FRG 1995, Wolf Prize in Medicine, Wolf Foundation and State of Israel 1996, Keio Int. Award for Medical Science, Keio Univ., Tokyo 1996, Nobel Laureate in Physiology or Medicine (for his discovery of prions) 1997. *Publications:* The Molecular and Genetic Basis of Neurological Disease, Prions Prions Prions (Current Topics in Microbiology and Immunology, Vol. 207), Prions – Novel Infectious Pathogens Causing Scrapie and Creutzfeldt-Jakob Disease, Prion Diseases of Humans and Animals, Slow Transmissible Diseases of the Nervous System, Clinical Companion to the Molecular and Genetic Basis of Neurological Disease 1998, Prion Biology and Diseases 2003, The Molecular and Genetic Basis of Neurologic and Psychiatric Disease 2003. *Address:* Department of Neurology, 513 Parnassus, Box 0518, University of California School of Medicine, San Francisco, San Francisco, CA 94143-0518, USA (office). *Telephone:* (415) 476-4482 (office). *E-mail:* neuroscience@phy.ucsf.edu (office). *Website:* www.ucsf.edu/neurosc/neuro_faculty.html (office).

PRUTKOV, Kozma (see Snodgrass, W. D.).

PRYCE, Jonathan; British actor; b. 1 June 1947, Holywell, North Wales; s. of Isaac Price and Margaret Ellen Price (née Williams); partner Kate Fahy; two s. one d.; ed Royal Acad. of Dramatic Art; Patron Friends United Network, Saving Faces; Dr hc (Liverpool); Tony and Drama Desk Awards, Best Actor, Cannes Film Festival 1995. *Stage appearances include:* Comedians (Tony Award 1976), Nottingham Old Vic 1975, New York 1976, Hamlet (Olivier Award 1980), Royal Court Theatre, London 1980, The Caretaker, Nat. Theatre 1981, Accidental Death of an Anarchist, Broadway 1984, The Seagull, Queen's Theatre 1985, Macbeth, RSC 1986, Uncle Vanya 1988, Miss Saigon (Olivier and Variety Club Awards 1991), Drury Lane 1989, New York 1991, Oliver!, London Palladium 1994, My Fair Lady, Nat. Theatre and Drury Lane, London 2001, A Reckoning, Soho Theatre 2003, The Goat, Almeida Theatre 2004, Dirty Rotten Scoundrels, New York 2005. *Films include:* Something Wicked This Way Comes 1982, The Ploughman's Lunch 1983, Brazil 1985, The Doctor and the Devils 1986, Haunted Honeymoon 1986, Jumpin' Jack Flash 1987, Consuming Passions 1988, The Adventures of Baron Munchausen 1988, The Rachel Papers 1989, Glengarry Glen Ross 1992, Barbarians at the Gate 1992, Great Moments in Aviation 1993, The Age of Innocence 1993, A Business Affair 1993, Deadly Advice 1994, Carrington (Best Actor, Evening Standard Film Awards 1996) 1995, Evita 1996, Tomorrow Never Dies 1997, Regeneration 1997, Ronin 1998, Stigmata 1999, Taliesin Jones 2000, The Suicide Club 2000, Very Annie Mary 2001, Unconditional Love 2001, The Affair of the Necklace 2001, Bride of the Wind 2001, Unconditional Love 2002, Mad Dogs 2002, What a Girl Wants 2003, Pirates of the Caribbean: The Curse of the Black Pearl 2003, De-Lovely 2004, The Brothers Grimm 2005, The New World 2005, Pirates of the Caribbean 2: Dead Man's Chest 2006, Brothers of the Head 2006, The Moon and the Stars 2007, Pirates of the Caribbean: At the World's End 2007, Leatherheads 2007. *Television appearances in:* Roger Doesn't Live Here Anymore (series) 1981, Timon of Athens 1981, Martin Luther 1983, Praying Mantis 1983, Whose Line Is It Anyway? 1988, The Man from the Pru 1990, Selling Hitler 1991, Mr Wroe's Virgins 1993, Barbarians at the Gate 1993, Thicker than Water 1993, Great Moments in Aviation 1993, David 1997, Hey, Mr Producer! The Musical World of Cameron Mackintosh 1998, The Union Game: A Rugby History (series) (voice) 1999, Victoria & Albert 2001, Confessions of an Ugly Stepsister 2002, The Baker Street Irregulars 2007. *Recordings:* Miss Saigon 1989, Nine – The Concert 1992, Under Milk Wood 1992, Cabaret 1994, Oliver! 1995, Hey! Mr Producer 1998, My Fair Lady 2001. *Leisure interests:* painting, drawing. *Address:* c/o Julian Belfrage Assocs, 46 Albemarle Street, London, W1X 4PP, England (office); c/o UTA, 9560 Wilshire Boulevard, Beverly Hills, CA 90212, USA (office). *Telephone:* (20) 7491-4400 (London) (office); (310) 273-6700 (Beverly Hills) (office). *Fax:* (20) 7493-5460 (London) (office); (310) 247-1111 (Beverly Hills) (office).

PRYOR, David Hampton, LLB; American politician and academic; *Dean, Clinton School of Public Service, University of Arkansas;* b. 29 Aug. 1934, Camden, Ark.; s. of Edgar Pryor and Susan Pryor (née Newton); m. Barbara Lunsford 1957; three s. including Mark Pryor (q.v.); ed Univ. of Ark.; admitted to Ark. Bar 1964; mem. Ark. House of Reps 1961–66; served in Congress, House of Reps 1966–72; Gov. of Ark. 1974–79; Senator from Ark. 1979–96; mem. American Bar Asscn, Ark. Bar Asscn; Fellow Inst. of Politics, School of Govt, Harvard Univ. 1999; currently Dean, Clinton School of Public Service, Univ. of Ark.; Democrat. *Address:* University of Arkansas Clinton School of Public Service, Sturgis Hall, 1200 President Clinton Avenue, Little Rock, AR 72201 (office); 2701 Kavanaugh Boulevard, Suite 300, Little Rock, AR 72205, USA (office). *Telephone:* (501) 683-5200 (office). *Fax:* (501) 683-5210 (office). *Website:* clintonschool.uasys.edu (office).

PRYOR, Mark, BA, LLB; American politician and lawyer; *Senator from Arkansas;* b. 1963, Fayetteville; s. of David Hampton Pryor (q.v.); ed Univ. of Ark.; practised law with Wright, Lindsey & Jennings, Little Rock 1982–90; elected to Ark. State House of Reps (Democrat) for two terms 1990; Attorney-Gen. for Ark. 1999–2003, Senator from Ark. 2003–; served as campaign chair. in Ark. for Vice-Pres. Al Gore 2000. *Address:* 257 Dirksen Senate Office Building, Washington, DC 20150, USA (office). *Telephone:* (202) 224-2353 (office). *Fax:* (202) 228-0908 (office). *Website:* pryor.senate.gov (office).

PSAROUDA-BENAKI, Anna; Greek politician, lawyer and academic; b. 12 Dec. 1934, Athens; m. Linos Benakis 1957; ed Pierce Coll. of Athens, Univ. of Athens, Univ. of Bonn, Germany; attorney-at-law 1962–; Researcher, Max Planck Institute for Int. Criminal Law, Freiburg 1962–78; Asst, then Asst Prof., now Prof. of Criminal Law Univ. of Athens 1978–; mem. Vouli (Parl.) 1981–, Alt. Minister of Education 1989, of Culture 1991, of Justice 1992–93; Vice-Pres. Vouli 2002–04, Pres. 2004–07; mem. Asscn of Criminal Attorneys (Vice-Pres.). *Publications:* four books and several articles on criminal matters; political articles. *Leisure interests include:* water skiing, swimming, classical music, literature. *Address:* Skoufa 75, 106 80 Athens; Sina 58, 106 72 Athens, Greece (home). *Telephone:* (210) 3636818 (home). *Fax:* (210) 3645179 (home). *E-mail:* benakis@hol.gr (home).

PSZONIAK, Wojciech Zygmunt; Polish actor; b. 2 May 1942, Lvov, Poland (now Lviv, Ukraine); m.; ed State High Theatre School, Kraków; Asst State High Theatre School, Kraków 1967–72, lecturer 1972–; prin. theatrical roles at Stary Theatre, Kraków 1968–72, Narodowy Theatre, Warsaw 1972–74, Powszechny Theatre, Warsaw 1974–80; presenter TV show Wojtek Pszoniak – pytania do siebie (Pszoniak – Questions to Himself) 1995–96; Gold Cross of Merit 1975, Kt's Cross, Order of Polonia Restituta 1997; Prize of Ministry of Culture (2nd Class) 1975, Masters Award, Montréal Film Festival 1982. *Films:* Wesele (The Wedding) 1973, Ziemia obiecana (The Promised Land) 1975, Austeria 1981, Danton 1982, Je hais les acteurs 1986, Les années-sandwiches 1987, Czerwona Wenecja (Red Venice) 1988, Korczak 1990, Gawin 1991, Le Bal des Casse-Pieds 1992, Coupable d'innocence 1992, Le Vent d'Est 1993, La Chica 1995, Wielki Tydzien 1996, Our God's Brother 1997, L'Atelier (TV) 1999, Deuxième vie 2000, Bajland 2000, Chaos 2001, Le Pacte du silence 2003, Là-haut, un roi au-dessus des nuages (Above the Clouds) 2003, Vipère au poing 2004, Hope 2007. *Plays:* Poskromienie złośnicy (The Taming of the Shrew) 1969, Sen nocy letniej (A Midsummer Night's Dream) 1970, Wszystko dobre, co się dobrze kończy (All's Well That Ends Well) 1971, Biesy 1971, Makbet (Macbeth) 1973, Les gens déraisonnables sont en voie de disparition, Théâtre des Amandiers, Nanterre 1978, Zemsta (Revenge) 1980, Czekając na Godota (Waiting for Godot) 1989, Król Ubu (King Ubu) 1992, The Deep Blue Sea, Apollo Theatre, London 1993, Atelier, Théâtre Hébertot, Paris 1999, Pracownia krawiecka (Tailor's Shop – actor and dir) 2000, Kolacja dla głupca (Supper for Fools) 2001, La boutique au coin de la rue, Théâtre Montparnasse, Paris 2001. *Publication:* Pszoniak & Co. czyli Towarzystwo Dobrego Stołu 1993. *Leisure interests:* classical music, jazz, cooking.

PTASHNE, Mark Stephen, PhD; American biochemist and academic; *Member, Molecular Biology Program, Memorial Sloan-Kettering Cancer Center;* b. 5 June 1940, Chicago, Ill.; s. of Fred Ptashne and Mildred Ptashne; ed Reed Coll. and Harvard Univ.; Jr Fellow, Harvard Soc. of Fellows 1965–68; Lecturer, Dept of Biochem. and Molecular Biology, Harvard Univ. 1968–71, Prof. 1971, Chair. Dept of Biochem. and Molecular Biology 1980–83, Herchel Smith Prof. of Molecular Biology 1993; currently mem. Faculty, Molecular Biology Program, Memorial Sloan-Kettering Cancer Center; Guggenheim Fellow 1973–74; Fellow American Acad. of Arts and Sciences; mem. NAS; Feodor Lynen Lecturer 1988; Prix Charles-Léopold Mayer, Acad. des Sciences, Inst. de France (with W. Gilbert and E. Witkin) 1977; Eli Lilly Award 1975; shared Louisa Gross Horwitz Prize 1985; Gairdner Foundation Int. Award (with Charles Yanofsky) 1985; Cancer Research Foundation Award 1990, Lasker Award 1997. *Publications:* A Genetic Switch 1986, A Genetic Switch: Phage (Lambda) and Higher Organisms 1992, Genes and Signals 2002, Genetic Switch: Phage Lambda Revisited 2004; 122 papers in scientific journals 1950–89. *Leisure interests:* classical music, opera. *Address:* Molecular Biology Program, Memorial Sloan-Kettering Cancer Center, 1275 York Avenue, New York, NY 10021, USA. *Telephone:* (212) 639-2297 (office); (212) 639-5183 (office). *Fax:* (212) 717-3627 (office). *E-mail:* m-ptashne@ski .mskcc.org (office). *Website:* www.mskcc.org/mskcc/html/5781.cfm (office).

PU, Haiqing; Chinese politician; *Director, Three Gorges Project Construction Committee, Office of the State Council;* b. 1941, Nanbu, Sichuan Prov.; ed Chongqing Univ.; joined CCP 1973; Man. Chongqing Iron and Steel Co.; Vice-Gov. Sichuan Prov.; Acting Mayor of Chongqing Municipality 1996–97, Mayor 1997–99, Deputy Sec. CCP Chongqing Municipal Cttee 1997–99; Dir Nat. Metallurgical Industry Bureau 1999–2001 (Sec. CCP Leading Party Group); Deputy Dir Three Gorges Project Construction Cttee, Office of the State Council 2001–03 (Deputy Sec. CCP Leading Party Group), Dir 2003– (Sec. CCP Leading Party Group); Del., 14th CCP Cen. Cttee 1992–97, mem. 15th CCP Cen. Cttee 1997–2002, 16th CCP Cen. Cttee 2002–07. *Address:* Three Gorges Project Construction Committee, Office of the State Council, Beijing, People's Republic of China.

PU, Nai-fu; Taiwanese writer; b. Nanjing; m.; ed Beijing Russian-Language Jr Coll.; imprisoned for various periods in labour-reform camps during anti-intellectual campaigns in China; moved to Hong Kong, subsequently to Taiwan 1983. *Publications include:* Romance in the Arctic, The Woman in the Pagoda, Books Without Names (six vols), The Scourge of the Sea, Red in Tooth and Claw.

PU, Shan, LLD; Chinese academic; b. 27 Nov. 1923, Beijing; m. Chen Xiuying 1951; ed Univ. of Shanghai, Univ. of Michigan, Harvard Univ., USA; Vice-Pres. Chinese Soc. of World Economy 1980–85, Pres. 1985–97, Dir Inst. of World Econs and Politics 1982–88; mem. Nat. Cttee, CPPCC 1988–98, mem. Standing Cttee 1993–98; Pres. Grad. School, Chinese Acad. of Social Sciences 1991–94; Hon. Pres. Chinese Soc. of World Economy 1997–. *Address:* Graduate School, Chinese Academy of Social Sciences, Beijing 100015 (office); 24 Zhan Lan Road, Beijing 100037, People's Republic of China (home). *Fax:* (10) 64362343 (office).

PU, Ta-Hai; Taiwanese government official; b. 3 April 1922, Meihsien, Kwangtung; m.; one s. two d.; ed Chinese Mil. Acad., Chinese Army Command and Gen. Staff Coll. and Chinese Armed Forces Staff Coll.; Section Chief (Col), Taiwan Peace Preservation HQ 1956–57; Dept Head (Col), Gen. HQ, Chinese Army 1957–60; Dept Head (Maj.-Gen.), Personnel Div., Ministry of Nat. Defence 1963–68; Dept Head (Maj.-Gen.), Taiwan Garrison Gen. HQ 1968–72; Dept Head, Cen. Personnel Admin, Exec. Yuan 1972–78; Dir Dept of Personnel, Taipei City Govt 1978–81, Taiwan Provincial Govt 1981–84; Deputy Dir-Gen. Central Personnel Admin, Exec. Yuan 1984, Dir-Gen. 1984–93; Nat. Policy Adviser to the Pres. 1993–. *Leisure interests:* tennis, badminton. *Address:* Office of the Director-General, Central Personnel Administration, Executive Yuan, 109 Huai Ning Street, Taipei, Taiwan. *Telephone:* (2) 361-7072.

PUAPUA, Rt Hon. Sir Tomasi, Kt, PC, KBE; Tuvaluan politician; b. 10 Sept. 1938; s. of Fitilau Puapua and Olive Puapua; m. Riana Tabokai 1971; two s. two d.; ed Fiji School of Medicine and Univ. of Otago, NZ; medical practitioner; Prime Minister of Tuvalu 1981–90, also Minister for Civil Service Admin., Local Govt and Minister for Foreign Affairs; Speaker of Parl. 1993–98; Gov. Gen. of Tuvalu 1998–2005. *Leisure interests:* athletics, rugby, tennis, volleyball, cricket, soccer, fishing, pig and poultry farming, gardening. *Address:* c/o Government House, Vaiaku, Funafuti, Tuvalu (office).

PÚCIK, Brig.-Gen. Vladimír; Slovak air force officer; b. 20 June 1952, Lazisko; m. Viera Púciková; two c.; ed Mil. Acad., Liptovský Mikuláš, Air Defence Mil. Acad., Tver, Royal Coll. Defence Studies, London; promoted to Lt 1976; Deputy Commdr, 52nd Air Surveillance Unit, Stod 1976–77, Commdr

1977–79; promoted to First Lt 1979; Chief of Staff, 54th Air Surveillance Battalion, Nepolisy 1979–81, Commdr 1981–83; promoted to Capt. 1982, to Maj. 1985; Sr Officer, Air Surveillance Branch 3rd AD Div., Žatec 1986–87; Sr Officer, Air Surveillance Dept, HQ of AF and Air Defences, Stará Boleslav 1987–91; promoted to Lt Col 1989; Chief Air Surveillance Branch 1st AD Div., Zvolen 1991–93; Deputy Chief of AD Dept, HQ AF and Air Defence of SR, Trencín 1993–94; promoted to Col 1994; Deputy Commdr in Chief, 3rd AF and Air Defence Corps, Zvolen 1994–98; promoted to Col of Gen. Staff 2000; Deputy Commdr in Chief, Slovak AFs, Zvolen 2000-02; promoted to Brig.-Gen. 2002; Mil. Rep. of Slovakia to NATO and EU 2002–06; Medal for Homeland Service, Medal for Merit of Homeland Defence, Medal for Merit of Czechoslovak Armed Forces, Memorial Medal of Ministry of Defence of Slovak Repub., Mil. Badge of Honour, Slovak Armed Forces. *Leisure interests:* downhill skiing, hiking. *Address:* Ministry of Defence, Kutuzovova 7, 832 47 Bratislava, Slovakia. *Telephone:* (2) 4425-0320. *Fax:* (2) 4425-3242. *E-mail:* iveta.viragova@mod.gov.sk. *Website:* www.mosr.sk.

PUDDEPHATT, Andrew Charles, OBE, BA; British company director; b. 2 April 1950, Luton; s. of Andrew Ross Puddephatt and Margaret Deboo; two c.; ed Kingsbury School, Dunstable and Sidney Sussex Coll. Cambridge; Deputy Leader Hackney Council 1984–85, Leader 1986–89; Dir Nat. Council for Civil Liberties 1989–95; Dir Charter 88 1995–99; Exec. Dir Article 19. *Leisure interests:* music, cinema, walking. *Address:* c/o Article 19, Global Campaign for Freedom of Expression, Lancaster House, 33 Islington High Street, London, N1 9LH, England (office). *Telephone:* (20) 7278-9292. *Fax:* (20) 7713-1356. *E-mail:* andrew@article19.org (office). *Website:* www.article19.org (office).

PUDDEPHATT, Richard John, PhD, FRS, FRSC; British/Canadian chemist and academic; *Professor of Chemistry, University of Western Ontario;* b. 10 Oct. 1943; s. of Harry Puddephatt and Ena Puddephatt; m. Alice Poulton 1969; one s. one d.; ed Univ. Coll. London; Teaching Postdoctoral Fellow Univ. of Western Ontario 1968–70, Prof. of Chem. 1978–; Lecturer, Univ. of Liverpool 1970–77, Sr Lecturer 1977–78; currently Chair. Chemical Inst. of Canada; Nyholm Award 1997, CIC Medal 1998. *Publications include:* The Chemistry of Gold 1978, The Periodic Table of the Elements 1986. *Leisure interest:* gardening. *Address:* Department of Chemistry, Chemistry Building, University of Western Ontario, London, Ont., N6A 5B7, Canada (office). *Telephone:* (519) 679-2111 (office). *Fax:* (519) 661-3022 (office). *E-mail:* pudd@uwo.ca (office). *Website:* www.uwo.ca/chem/Tpuddr (office).

PUENZO, Luis; Argentine film director; b. 24 Feb. 1949, Buenos Aires; worked as storyboard designer in advertising, becoming advertising dir; f. Historias Cinematograficas Cinemania (film production co.) 1974. *Films include:* Luces de mis zapatos (Lights of my Shoes) 1973, Cinco años de vida (Five Years of Life) 1975, The Official Story 1985 (Palme d'Or, Cannes, Acad. Award for Best Foreign Film 1986 and 47 other int. awards), Gringo viejo (Old Gringo) 1989. *Address:* c/o Instituto Nacional de Cinematografía, Lima 319, 1073 Buenos Aires, Argentina.

PUGACHEV, Sergey Victorovich; Russian politician and business executive; b. 4 Feb. 1963, Kostoma; m.; two c.; ed Leningrad State Univ.; credit inspector, Head of Div., mem. Bd of Dirs USSR Promstroibank 1985–90; mem. Bd of Dirs N Trade Bank 1990–92; Chair. Bd of Dirs Int. Industrial Bank (Mezhprombank) 1992–2002; mem. Bureau Russian Union of Businessmen and Entrepreneurs 2002–; mem. Council of Feds, Rep. of Govt, Tuva Repub. 2001–; mem. Cttee on Problems of Fed. and Regional Policy Council of Feds; mem. Russian Acad. of Eng. *Publications include:* Commercial Bank in Conditions of Free Market Relations Formation: Economic and Financial Analysis 1998. *Address:* House of Government, Chuldum str. 18, 667000 Kyzyl (office); Council of Federation, Bolshaya Dmitrovka 26, 103426 Moscow, Russia (office). *Telephone:* (839422) 11284 (Kyzyl) (office); (495) 925-65-19 (Moscow) (office). *Fax:* (839422) 11354 (Kyzyl) (office); (495) 292-14-85 (Moscow) (office). *E-mail:* council@gov.ru (office).

PUGACHEVA, Alla Borisovna; Russian singer; b. 15 April 1949, Moscow; m. 2nd Filipp Kirkorov; one d.; ed M. Ippolitov-Ivanov Music High School, A. Lunacharsky State Inst. of Theatre Art; debut as soloist of Lipetsk vocal-instrumental group 1970; with O Lundstrem Jazz orchestra 1971; soloist, Veselye Rebyata Ensemble 1973–78; f. Song Theatre 1988; numerous prizes and awards including 3rd prize All-Union Contest Moscow, 1974; Grand Prix Int. Competition Golden Orpheus Bulgaria 1975, Int. Festival Sopot 1978; acted in films; tours in USA, Germany, Switzerland, India, France, Italy and other countries; f. Theatre of Songs 1988, Alla Co. 1993, Alla Magazine 1993; toured Russia and other countries in honour of her 60th birthday 2009; USSR People's Artist 1991, Ovation Prize 1994, State Prize of Russia 1995. *Repertoire includes:* numerous songs by popular Soviet composers such as R. Pauls, A. Muromtsev, A. Zatsepin and others, also songs of her own. *Address:* Tverskaya-Yamskaya str., Apt 57, Moscow, Russia (home). *Telephone:* (495) 250-95-78 (home).

PUGIN, Nikolai Andreyevich; Russian industrialist; b. 30 June 1940; ed Gorky Polytechnic Inst.; worker, foreman at car factory 1958–75; chief engineer at gearbox factory 1975–81; Tech. Dir 1981–83, Gen. Dir of Gorky Automobile Works 1983–86; Minister of Automobile Industry 1986–88, of Automobile and Agricultural Machines Industry 1988–91; mem. Russian Eng Acad. 1991–; mem. Russian Acad. of Natural Science 1992–; Pres. ASM Holding Inc. (mfrs of motor vehicles and farm machinery in CIS) 1992–; Chair. Bd GAZ Co. (Nizhny Novgorod); Pres. Ind. Financial Group Nizhegorodskiye Automobili 1994–; Chair. Bd of Dirs Autobank 1996–2002; mem. Nizhny Novgorod Regional Ass. 2002–. *Address:* ASM Holding, 21/5 Kuznetsky Most, 103895 Moscow; GAZ, Lenina prosp. 9, 603046, Nizhny Novgorod; Oblastnaya Duma, Kremlin, korp. 2, 603082 Nizhny Novgorod, Russia. *Telephone:* (495) 921-68-21; (495) 924-53-85; (8312) 56-10-70 (Nizhny Novgorod). *Fax:* (495) 924-39-00. *Website:* www.asm-holding.ru.

PUIG, Lluis de Maria; Spanish politician and historian; *President, Alexander Cirici Institute for European Co-operation;* b. 20 July 1945, Bascara, Gerona; m.; two c.; ed Autonomous Univ. of Barcelona, Ecole des Hautes Etudes de la Sorbonne, Paris; worked in anti-Franco opposition as active mem. of underground Catalan and socialist orgs; Prof. of Contemporary History, Autonomous Univ. of Barcelona; Socialist mem. Cortes for Gerona 1979–; mem. Catalonian Socialist Party Bureau 1986–; Pres. Gerona Fed. of Socialist Party 1993–; mem. Council of Europe Ass. 1983–, Chair. Sub-Cttee on European Social Charter 1984–89, Vice-Pres. Ass. 1993–96; mem. Spanish del. to WEU Ass. 1990–, Vice-Chair. Socialist Group 1992–96, Defence Cttee 1992–94, Chair. Political Cttee 1994–96, mem. Presidential Cttee 1994–, Pres. WEU Ass. 1997–2000; Sec. Alexander Cirici Inst. for European Co-operation 1986–96, Pres. 1996–; Dr hc (Ovidius Univ. of Constanta, Romania) 1998. *Publications:* several books on history of 19th and 20th century Catalonia, books and essays on Europe, articles on domestic and int. politics. *Address:* c/o Assembly of Western European Union, 43 avenue du Président Wilson, 75775 Paris Cedex 16, France.

PUISSOCHET, Jean-Pierre, LLD, PhD; French international judge and lawyer; *Judge, Court of Justice of the European Communities;* b. 3 May 1936, Clermont-Ferrand; s. of René Puissochet and Hélène Puissochet (née Brengues); m. Eliane Millet 1973; one d.; ed Lycée du Parc, Lyon, Inst. for Political Studies, Lyon, School of Law, Lyon, Ecole Nat. d'Admin., Paris; Auditeur, Conseil d'Etat 1962, Maître des Requêtes 1968, Conseiller 1985; Dir Legal Service, Council of EC 1968–70, Dir-Gen. 1970–73; Dir-Gen. Agence Nat. pour l'Emploi 1973–75; Dir Ministry of Industry and Research 1977–79; Dir of Legal Affairs, OECD 1979–85; Dir Int. Inst. of Public Admin. 1985–87; Legal Adviser, Dir of Legal Affairs, Ministry of Foreign Affairs 1987–94; Judge, Court of Justice of the European Communities 1994–; mem. Perm. Court of Arbitration, The Hague 1990–; Officier, Légion d'honneur, Grand Officier Ordre nat. du Mérite, Officier du Mérite agricole, Grand'Uffiziale dell Ordine al Merito (Italy). *Publications:* The Enlargement of the EC 1974; numerous articles on Community and int. law. *Address:* Court of Justice of the European Communities, Plateau du Kirchberg, 2925 Luxembourg (office); 15 rue Jean-Pierre Brasseur, 1258, Luxembourg (home). *Telephone:* 43-03-22-46 (office). *Fax:* 43-03-20-00. *E-mail:* jean-pierre.puissochet@curia.eu.int (office).

PUJATS, HE Cardinal Jānis; Latvian ecclesiastic; *Archbishop of Rīga;* b. 14 Nov. 1930, Nautrani, Rezekne Dist; ed Catholic Seminary, Riga; ordained priest 1951; taught art history and liturgy at Catholic Theological Seminary, Rīga; Vicar General, Metropolitan Curia in Rīga 1979–84; KGB declared him persona non grata 1984; consecrated Bishop 1991; Archbishop of Rīga 1991; cr. Cardinal (in pectore—secretly) 1998, (openly) 2001; Pres. Latvian Bishops' Conf.; mem. Congregation for the Causes of Saints. *Address:* Metropolijas Kurija, Mazā Pils iela 2/a, 1050 Rīga, Latvia (office). *Telephone:* 6222-7266 (office); 6222-0775 (home). *Fax:* 722-0060 (office); 782-0274 (home). *E-mail:* sacerdos@inbox.lv (home).

PUJOL I SOLEY, Jordi, MD; Spanish politician, pharmacologist and business executive; *President, Centre Estudis Jordi Pujol (CEJP);* b. 9 June 1930, Barcelona; s. of Florenci Pujol i Soley and Maria Soley i Mas; m. Marta Ferrusola 1956; seven s.; ed Faculty of Medicine, Univ. of Barcelona; worked in pharmaceutical industry 1953–60; f. Banca Catalana group 1959, Man. Dir 1959–76; f. Convergència Democratica de Catalunya 1974; Councillor, provisional Generalitat 1977–80; mem. Congress, Madrid 1977, 1979; Head Convergència i Unió Parl. Group in Congress 1977–80; mem. Catalan Parl. 1980–; Pres. Generalitat de Catalunya 1980–2003; Vice-Pres. Ass. of European Regions 1988–92, Pres. 1992–96; Pres. Centre Estudis Jordi Pujol (CEJP) 2005–; Dr hc (Brussels, Toulouse, Lyon, Rosario, Argentina, Barcelona). *Publications include:* Una política per Catalunya 1976, Construir Catalunya 1980, Als joves de Catalunya 1988, La Força serena i constructiva de Catalunya 1991, Pensar Europa 1993, Passió per Catalunya 1999, El Libre Roig de Jordi Pujol 2003, Sobre Europa (i altres coses) 2004, Una reflexió necessària 2006, Memòries (1930-1980) 2007. *Leisure interests:* reading, walking, cycling. *Address:* Passeig de Gràcia, 39, 08007 Barcelona, Spain (office). *Telephone:* (93) 5529110 (office). *Fax:* (93) 5529114 (office). *E-mail:* jordipujol@gencat.cat (office). *Website:* www.jordipujol.cat (home).

PUJOLS ALCÁNTARA, José Alberto (Albert); American (b. Dominican Repub.) professional baseball player; b. 16 Jan. 1980, Santo Domingo; s. of Bienvenido Pujols; m. Deidre Pujols 2000; three c.; ed Fort Osage High School, Independence, Mo., Maple Woods Community Coll., Kansas City; emigrated to USA 1996; played in Jayhawk League, Kan. 1999; signed with St Louis Cardinals professional baseball team 1999, assigned to minor leagues 1999–2000; played for Peroia Chiefs 2000, then Potomac Cannons, Memphis Redbirds, first baseman St Louis Cardinals 2001–; Nat. League Batting Champion (average .359) 2003; Co-f. Pujols Family Foundation 2005; Nat. League Rookie of the Year 2001, Sporting News Player of the Year 2003, 2008, Gold Glove Award 2006, Roberto Clemente Award 2008; seven times All-star selection 2001, 2003–08. *Address:* c/o St. Louis Cardinals, 700 Clark Street, St. Louis, MO 63102, USA (office). *Telephone:* (314) 345-9600 (office). *Website:* stlouis.cardinals.mlb.com (office).

PULAT, Abdurakhim; Uzbekistan politician; Chair. Unity People's Movt Party ('Birlik' Xalq Harakati Partiyasi—Birlik) founded in 1988; leading opposition group, banned in 1992; registered as social movt; refused registration as political party 2004), living in self-imposed exile in USA *c.* 2003. *Address:* Unity People's Movement Party ('Birlik' Xalq Harakati Partiyasi—Birlik), c/o Union of Writers of Uzbekistan, Neru ko'ch. 1, 100000 Tashkent,

Uzbekistan (office). *Telephone:* (71) 233-63-74 (office). *E-mail:* webmaster@birlik.net (office). *Website:* www.birlik.net (office).

PULATOV, Timur Iskhakovich; Uzbekistan writer; b. 1939, Bukhara; ed Bukhara Pedagogical Inst., High School of Scriptwriters and Film Directors; freelance writer 1974–; First Sec., Co-ordinator Exec. Bd Int. Soc. of Writers' Unions 1992–; Ed. Literary Eurasia; Order, Friendship of Peoples for devt of lit. and art and strengthening of int. relations 1994. *Publications:* Life Story of a Naughty Boy from Bukhara 1984, Other Populated Points, Properties, Passions of the Bukhara House, Tortoise Tarasi, Swimming Eurasia. *Address:* Moscow City Organization of Russian Writers' Union, B. Nikitskaya str. 50a/5, 121069 Moscow, Russia (office). *Telephone:* (095) 202-87-83 (office).

PULIKOVSKY, Lt-Gen. Konstantin Borisovich; Russian army officer and politician; *Representative of Russian President to Far Eastern Federation District;* b. 9 Feb. 1948, Ussuriysk, Primorsk Territory; ed M. Frunze Mil. Acad., Mil. Acad. of Gen. Staff; mil. posts to rank of Army Commdr 1972; took part in conflict in Chechnya 1994–96; Commdr group of Fed. forces in Chechen Repub. 1996, Deputy Commdr., N Caucasus Mil. District 1997–; leader Krasnodar Org. All-Russian Movt of veterans of local wars and mil. conflicts Boyevoye Bratstvo; Rep. of Russian Pres. to Far Eastern Fed. Dist 2000–. *Publications include:* The Eastern Express: Through Russia With Kim Jong Il 2002. *Address:* Office of the Presidential Representative, Sheronova str. 22, 680030 Khabarovsk, Russia (office). *Telephone:* (4212) 31-30-44 (Khabarovsk) (office); (495) 206-73-52 (Moscow) (office).

PULJIĆ, HE Cardinal Vinko; Bosnia and Herzegovina ecclesiastic; *Archbishop of Vrhbosna;* b. 8 Sept. 1945, Priječani, Banja Luka; s. of Ivan Puljić and Kaja Puljić (née Pletikosa); ed seminary of Šalata, Zagreb and at Đakovo; ordained priest Đakovo 1970; parish vicar Banja Luka, parish priest Sasina, then Ravska; pedagogue, Zmajević seminary, Zadar 1978–87; Parish Priest, Bosanska Gradiška 1987–90; Vice-Rector Catholic Theological Seminary of Vrhbosna, Sarajevo 1990; Archbishop of Vrhbosna 1990–; cr. Cardinal (Cardinal Priest of S. Chiara a Vigna Clara) 1994; travelled to many countries in Europe and N America to publicise the suffering caused by the war in Bosnia and Herzegovina and discuss possible solutions; Hon. Dr Humanitarian Science (Grand Valley State Univ., Mich., USA) 1995; Hon. Dr Pastoral Theology (Catholic Univ. Santa Maria in Apartade, Peru) 2001; Humanist of the Decade and Golden Diploma of Humanism, Int. League of Humanists, Sarajevo 1995. *Publications:* Suffering With Hope: Appeals, Addresses, Interviews 1995, Non cancellato l'uomo – Un grido di speranza da Sarajevo 1997, Per amore dell'uomo–Testimone di pace a Sarajevo 1999. *Address:* Nadbiskupski Ordinarijat, Kaptol 7, BiH 71000 Sarajevo, Bosnia and Herzegovina (office). *Telephone:* (33) 663512 (office); (33) 472430 (office). *Fax:* (33) 472429 (office).

PULLMAN, Bill; American actor; b. 17 Dec. 1953, Hornell, NY; m. Tamara Pullman; three c.; ed Univ. of Massachusetts; fmr drama teacher, bldg contractor, dir of a theatre group; started acting in fringe theatres, New York; f. Big Town Productions (film production co.). *Films include:* Ruthless People, A League of Their Own, Sommersby, Sleepless in Seattle, While You Were Sleeping, Caspar, Independence Day, Lost Highway 1997, The End of Violence 1997, The Thin Red Line 1998, Zero Effect 1998, A Man is Mostly Water 1999, History is Made at Night 1999, The Guilt 1999, Brokedown Place 1999, Lake Placid 1999, Coming To Light: Edward S. Curtis and the North American Indians (voice) 2000, Titan A.E. 2000, Lucky Numbers 2000, Ignition 2001, A Man Is Mostly Water 2001, Igby Goes Down 2002, 29 Palms 2002, Rick 2003, The Grudge 2004, The Orphan King 2005, Dear Wendy 2005, Scary Movie 4 2006, You Kill Me 2007, Nobel Son 2007, Surveillance 2007. *Address:* Big Town Productions, 6201 Sunset Blvd, Suite 80, Los Angeles, CA 90028; c/o J. J. Harris, 9560 Wilshire Boulevard, Suite 500, Beverly Hills, CA 90212, USA. *Telephone:* (323) 962-8099 (Big Town).

PULLMAN, Philip, CBE, BA, FRSL; British writer; b. 19 Oct. 1946, Norwich, Norfolk; m. Jude Speller 1970; two s.; ed Exeter Coll., Oxford; teacher in Oxford 1972–86; part-time Lecturer, Westminster Coll., Oxford 1986–96; Hon. Fellow Univ. of Wales, Bangor; Hon. DLitt (Univ. of East Anglia), (Oxford Brookes Univ.), Hon. DUniv (Univ. of Surrey Roehampton); Booksellers' Asscn/Book Data Author of the Year Award 2001, Booksellers' Asscn Author of the Year 2001, 2002, British Book Awards Author of the Year Award 2002, Whitbread Book of the Year Award 2002. *Publications:* One More River 1973, Count Karlstein 1982, The Ruby in the Smoke (Sally Lockhart series) 1985, The Shadow in the Plate 1986, The Shadow in the North (Sally Lockhart series) 1987, Spring-Heeled Jack 1989, The Tiger in the Well (Sally Lockhart series) 1990, The Broken Bridge 1990, The White Mercedes 1992, The Tin Princess (Sally Lockhart series) 1994, The New Cut Gang: Thunderbolt's Waxwork 1994, The New Cut Gang: The Gas-fitter's Ball 1995, The Wonderful Story of Aladdin and the Enchanted Lamp 1995, The Firework-Maker's Daughter 1995, Northern Lights (aka The Golden Compass, Vol. I, His Dark Materials trilogy) (Carnegie Medal 1996, Guardian Children's Fiction Prize 1996, British Book Awards Children's Book of the Year 1996, CILIP Carnegie Medal 2007) 1995, Clockwork 1996, The Subtle Knife (Vol. II, His Dark Materials trilogy) 1997, The Butterfly Tattoo 1998, Mossycoat 1998, Detective Stories (ed.) 1998, I Was a Rat! 1999, The Amber Spyglass (Vol. III, His Dark Materials trilogy) (British Book Awards WH Smith Children's Book of the Year, Whitbread Children's Book of the Year Prize 2001, Whitbread Book of the Year Award 2001) 2000, Puss-in-Boots 2000, Sherlock Holmes and the Limehouse Horror 2001, Lyra's Oxford 2003, The Scarecrow and his Servant 2004; contrib. reviews to Times Educational Supplement, The Guardian. *Address:* c/o Caradoc King, A. P. Watt Ltd, 20 John Street, London, WC1N 2DR, England (office). *Telephone:* (20) 7405-6774 (office). *Fax:* (20) 7831-2154 (office). *Website:* www.philip-pullman.com.

PULTE, William J.; American construction industry executive; *Founder and Chairman, Pulte Homes Inc.;* m.; 14 c.; started house-building co. William J. Pulte Inc. (now Pulte Home Corpn) 1956, Pres. and Chair. Exec. Cttee 1972–90, Chair. of the Bd 1990–98, 2002–. *Address:* Pulte Homes Inc., 100 Bloomfield Hills Parkway, Suite 300, Bloomfield Hills, MI 48304, USA (office). *Telephone:* (248) 647-2750 (office). *Fax:* (248) 433-4598 (office). *Website:* www.pulte.com (office).

PUNGOR, Ernő, PhD, DrChemSc; Hungarian scientist and academic; *Professor Emeritus of Chemistry, Institute for General and Analytical Chemistry, Budapest University of Technology and Economics;* b. 30 Oct. 1923, Vasszécsény; s. of József Pungor and Franciska Faller; m. 1st Erzsébet Lang 1950; m. 2nd Dr Tünde Horváth 1984; two s. one d.; ed Pázmány Univ., Budapest; Corresp. mem. Hung. Acad. of Sciences 1967, mem. 1976–; Asst Prof. Eötvös Univ., Budapest 1948–53, Assoc. Prof. 1953–62; Prof. Chemical Univ., Veszprém 1962–70; Dir Inst. for Gen. and Analytical Chemistry, Tech. Univ., Budapest 1970–90, now Prof. Emer.; Head Research Group for Tech. Analytical Chem. of Hungarian Acad. of Sciences 1970–93, Pres. Nat. Comm. for Tech. Devt 1990–94; Minister for Tech. Devt 1990–94; Gen. Dir Bay Zoltán Foundation for Applied Research 1994–2001; Pres. Asscn of Eds of European Chemical Journals 1977; mem. Int. Fed. of Scientific Eds Asscn 1981–87; Chair. Working Party of Analytical Chemists of Fed. of European Chemical Socs 1981–87; Chair. Analysis Div. of Hungarian Chemical. Soc.; Head Analysis Group, Hungarian Acad. of Sciences –2001; mem. IUPAC 1973, Chair. Hungarian Nat. Cttee for IUPAC 1985–; Vice-Pres. Electroanalytical Cttee 1985–87; mem. Scientific Advisory Bd of Org. for the Prohibition of Chemical Weapons, Scientific Advisory Bd of Hungarian Govt 1999; Pres. World Fed. of Hungarian Engineers and Architects 1991–95, mem. in perpetuity 1995–, mem. Hungarian Acad. of Sciences; Ed.-in-Chief Hungarian Journal of Chem. 1977–2002; developed new theory of absorption indicators; pioneering work in the field of ion-selective electrodes and in flow-through analytical techniques; Hon. mem. Czechoslovak Acad. Science Chemical Section 1966, Egyptian Pharmaceutical Soc. 1973, Austrian Analytical and Micro-analytical Soc. 1977, Chemical Soc. of Finland 1979, Analytical Chemical Soc. of Japan 1981, Finnish Tech. Soc. 1990, Royal Soc. 1992, Indian Acad. of Sciences 1993, Royal Soc. of Chemistry 1993; Hon. Prof., Agricultural Univ. of Lima 1973; Redwood Lecturer for English Soc. for Analytical Chemistry 1979, Hon. Prof. Árpád Acad., USA 1990, elected mem. Cen. European Hall of Fame for Eng Sciences and Tech. (ITI, USA) 1991; Österreich-Ungarisch Corvinus Kreis Ehrenmitgliedschaft 1994, Grosse Deutsche Verdienstkreuz 1995, Officier, Ordre nat. du Mérite 1996, Decoration of Hungarian Repub. with Star 1998; Dr hc (Tech. Univ. of Vienna) 1983, (Tech. Univ. of Bratislava) 1988, (Bucharest) 1993, (Tech. Univ. of Budapest) 1993 (Lomonosov Univ. Moscow) 1999, (Veszprém Univ. Hungary) 1999, (Babeş-Bolyai Univ.) 2000, Eur. Ing. 1992; Robert Boyle Gold Medal (Royal Soc.) 1986, Talanta Gold Medal 1987, Excellent Inventor Gold Medal 1987, Gold Medal of Hungarian Acad. of Science 1988, Gold Medal, Inst. of Analytical Chemists of Tech. Univ. of Vienna 1988, Fraunhofer Medal (Germany) 1993, Boyle Gold Medal, Royal Soc. of Analytical Chem., UK 1996, Hon. Medal, Fed. of European Chemical Socs 1997, Gold Medal, Arpád Acad., USA 1998, Prize of Hungarian Spiritual Heritage 1999, Pro Scientia Transsylvanica Medal 2000, Medal Appointment of the Univ. of Kassa 2003. *Publications:* Oscillometry and Conductometry 1965, Flame Photometry Theory 1962, Indikátor Elektród (co-author) 1973, Dynamic Characters of Ion Selective Electrodes (co-author) 1988, A Practical Guide to Instrumental Analysis 1994, Magyarország fejlődéséért (For the Development of Hungary) 1996, Éveim, kutatásaim (My Years and My Researches) 1998, Az ionszelektív elektródok elmélete (The Theory of Ion Selective Electrodes) 1998; ed: Ion Selective Electrodes I–V 1973–1989, Coulometric Analysis 1979, Modern Trends in Analytical Chemistry 1984, Bioelectroanalysis I 1987. *Leisure interest:* history. *Address:* Institute for General and Analytical Chemistry, Budapest Univ. of Technology and Economics, St Gellért tér 4, 1111 Budapest (office); Bay Zoltán Foundation for Applied Research, Kondorfa u. 1, 1116 Budapest (office); Meredek u. 4, 1112 Budapest, Hungary (home). *Telephone:* 1-463-4054 (Univ. Inst.); 1-463-0502 (Bay Foundation). *Fax:* 1-463-3408 (Univ. Inst.); 1-463-0503 (Bay Foundation). *E-mail:* pungor@tki.aak.bme.hu (office); pungor@bzaka.hu; pungor@axelero.hu (home).

PURCELL, James Nelson, MPA; American international official and international consultant; b. 16 July 1938, Nashville, Tenn.; s. of James N. Purcell Sr; m. Walda Primm 1961; two d.; ed Furman Univ., Syracuse Univ., New York; Budget Analyst, US Atomic Energy Comm. 1962–66; Man. Analyst, Agency for Int. Devt 1966–68; Deputy Dir Budget Preparation Staff, Office of Man. and Budget (OMB) 1968–72; Sr Examiner Int. Affairs Div. OMB 1972–74; Chief Justice, Treasury Br. OMB 1974–76; Chief Resources Programming and Man. Div., Bureau for Educ. and Cultural Affairs, Dept of State 1976–77; Deputy Budget Dir, Dept of State 1977–78; Exec. Dir Bureau of Admin., Dept of State 1978–79; Deputy Asst Sec., Programmes and Budget, Bureau for Refugee Programs, Dept of State 1979–82, Dir, Asst Sec. Bureau for Refugee Programmes 1982–87; Dir-Gen. Int. Org. for Migration 1988–98; Int. Consultant 1998–; mem. American Soc. of Public Admin.; Distinguished Honor Award, State Dept. *Address:* c/o International Organization for Migration, CP 71, 17 Route des Morillons, 1211 Geneva 19, Switzerland (office); 5113 West Running Brook Road, Columbia, MD 21044, USA (home). *E-mail:* ynpatcol@aol.com.

PURCELL, Philip James, MSc, MBA; American business executive; b. 5 Sept. 1943, Salt Lake City; m. Anne Marie McNamara 1964; seven s.; ed Univ. of Notre Dame, London School of Econs, Univ. of Chicago; Man. Dir consultants McKinsey & Co. Inc., Chicago 1967–78; Vice-Pres. Planning and Admin., Sears, Roebuck and Co., Chicago 1978–82; Pres., CEO then Chair., CEO, Dean Witter Discover & Co., New York 1982–97, Chair., CEO Morgan Stanley,

Dean Witter & Co. (after merger with Morgan Stanley), New York 1997–2005 (co. name changed to Morgan Stanley 2001); Dir New York Stock Exchange 1991–96, AMR Corpn; Trustee Univ. of Notre Dame. *Address:* c/o Morgan Stanley, 1585 Broadway, 39th Floor, New York, NY 10036, USA (office).

PURDUM, Robert L., BS; American business executive; *Operating Partner, American Industrial Partners;* b. 1935, Wilmington, Ohio; m. Arlene Peterson; three s.; ed Purdue Univ.; served USN and Indiana Toll Road Comm. 1956–62; joined Armco Inc. 1962, Dist Eng, Metal Products Div. 1962–66, sales staff 1966–72, Dist Man. 1972–76, Gen. Man. 1976–78; Pres. Midwestern Steel Div. 1978–80, Area Vice-Pres. 1980–82, Group Vice-Pres., CEO Mfg Services Group 1982–86, Exec. Vice-Pres. and COO 1986, Pres. and COO 1986–90, Pres., CEO 1990–93, Chair. 2004; currently Operating Pnr, American Industrial Pnrs (private equity firm), NY; Chair. (non-exec.) Bucyrus International, Inc. 1997–2004, Dir 1997–; mem. Bd of Dirs Berlitz Int. Inc. *Leisure interests:* tennis, hunting, fishing, travel. *Address:* American Industrial Partners, 551 Fifth Avenue, Suite 3800, New York, NY 10176-3801 (office); 26 Horizon Drive, Mendham, NJ 07945, USA (home). *Telephone:* (212) 983-1399 (office). *Fax:* (212) 986-5099 (office). *Website:* www.aipartners.com (office).

PURI, Balraj, MA; Indian human rights campaigner, writer and academic; *Director, Institute of Jammu and Kashmir Affairs;* b. 1928; ed Punjab Univ.; columnist and activist; founding mem. People's Union for Civil Liberties, Convenor Jammu and Kashmir State br.; Dir Inst. of Jammu and Kashmir Affairs, Jammu; several hon. appointments in academic and govt orgs and NGOs; Padma Bhushan 2005; numerous awards including M.A. Thomas Human Rights Award 1995, Mother Teresa Communal Honorary Award 1995. *Publications:* author and co-author of 40 books including Jammu: A Clue of Kashmir Tangle 1966, Abdullah Era 1983, Jammu and Kashmir: Triumph and Tragedy of Indian Federalism 1991, Kashmir towards Insurgency 1995, 5000 years of Kashmir (ed.) 1997, JP on Kashmir 2005, Kashmir Insurgency and After 2008, Muslims of India Since Partition 2008. *Address:* Karan Nagar, Jammu 180005, India (office). *Telephone:* (191) 254-2687 (home). *Fax:* (191) 254-3556 (home). *E-mail:* balraj_puri1@rediffmail.com (office). *Website:* www .humanrightsjournal.com (office).

PURI, Om; Indian actor; b. 18 Oct. 1950, Ambala; Hon. OBE 2004. *Films include:* Jaane Bhi Do Yaaro 1983, Aaghat 1986, Mirch Masala 1986, Genesis 1986, Spices 1986, Dharavi 1992, In Custody 1993, Target 1995, Ghatak 1996, Brothers in Trouble 1996, Ghost and the Darkness 1996, Maachis 1997, My Son the Fanatic 1997, East is East (BAFTA Award 2000) 1999, Hera Pheri 2000, The Zookeeper 2001, Bollywood Calling 2001, Happy Now 2001, Indian 2001, The Mystic Masseur 2001, The Parole Officer 2001, Pitaah 2002, Maa Tujhhe Salaam (voice) 2002, Ansh: The Dangerous Part 2002, Pyaar Diwana Hota Hai 2002, Murder (TV) 2002, Awara Paagal Deewana 2002, Shararat 2002, Chor Machaye Shor 2002, White Teeth 2002 (TV mini-series), Ghaav: The Wound 2002, Ghaav: The Wound 2002, Aapko Pehle Bhi Kahin Dekha Hai 2003, Kash... Aap Hamare Hote 2003, Ek Aur Ek Gyarah 2003, Code 46 2003, Maqbool 2003, The Canterbury Tales, Chupke Se 2003, Second Generation (TV) 2003, Dhoop 2003, Kagaar 2003, Dev 2004, Lakshya 2004, Charlie Wilson's War 2007. *Address:* 703, Trishul-2, Seven Bungalows, Andheri-W, Mumbai 61, India (home). *Telephone:* 6342902 (home).

PURNELL, James Mark Dakin, BA; British politician; *Secretary of State for Work and Pensions;* b. 2 March 1970; s. of John Purnell and Janet Purnell; ed Royal Grammar School, Guildford, Balliol Coll., Oxford; researcher for Shadow Employment Sec. Tony Blair 1989–92; researcher Hydra Assocs (media consultants), London 1992–94; Research Fellow, Inst. for Public Policy Research 1994–95; Head of Corp. Planning BBC 1995–97; Special Adviser to Prime Minister Tony Blair 1997–2001; Labour MP for Stalybridge and Hyde 2001–, Parl. Private Sec. to Ruth Kelly 2003–04, Asst Govt Whip 2004–05, Parl. Under-Sec. of State Dept for Culture, Media and Sport 2005–06, Minister of State for Pensions Dept for Work and Pensions 2006–07, Sec. of State for Culture, Media and Sport 2007–08, Sec. of State for Work and Pensions 2008–. *Leisure interests:* film, music, theatre and football. *Address:* Department for Work and Pensions, Caxton House, Tothill Street, London SW1H 9DA, England (office). *Telephone:* (20) 7712-2171 (office). *Fax:* (20) 7712-2386 (office). *Website:* www.dwp.gov.uk (office).

PURPURA, Dominick Paul, MD; American professor of neuroscience; *Marilyn and Stanley M. Katz Dean, Albert Einstein College of Medicine;* b. 2 April 1927, New York; s. of John R. Purpura and Rose Ruffino; m. Florence Williams 1948; three s. one d.; ed Columbia Univ. and Harvard Medical School; Chair. and Prof., Dept of Anatomy, Albert Einstein Coll. of Medicine 1967–74, Dept of Neuroscience 1974–82, Prof. and Chair. of Neuroscience 1974–82, Dean, Albert Einstein Coll. of Medicine 1984–; Dir Rose F. Kennedy Center for Research in Mental Retardation and Human Devt 1972–82; Dean, Stanford Univ. School of Medicine 1982–84; Pres. Soc. for Neuroscience 1982–83, Int. Brain Research Org. 1987–98, Vice-Pres. for Medical Affairs UNESCO 1961–; Fellow NY Acad. of Sciences; mem. Inst. of Medicine (NAS). *Publications:* numerous scientific papers. *Address:* Albert Einstein College of Medicine, Yeshiva University, Belfer Building, Room 312, 1300 Morris Park Avenue, Bronx, NY 10461, USA (office). *Telephone:* (718) 430-2801 (office). *Fax:* (718) 430-8822 (office). *E-mail:* purpura@aecom.yu.edu (office). *Website:* www.aecom.yu.edu (office).

PURVES, Sir William, Kt, CBE, DSO; British banker (retd); b. 27 Dec. 1931, Kelso; s. of Andrew Purves and Ida Purves; m. 1st Diana T. Richardson 1958 (divorced 1988); two s. two d.; m. 2nd Rebecca Jane Lewellen 1989; ed Kelso High School; with Nat. Bank of Scotland, Kelso 1948–54; joined the Hongkong and Shanghai Banking Corpn 1954, Chief Accountant 1970–74, Man., Tokyo 1974–76, Sr Man. Overseas Operations 1976–78, Asst Gen. Man. Overseas

Operations 1978–79, Gen. Man. Int. 1979–82, Exec. Dir 1982–84, Deputy Chair. 1984–86, Chair. and CEO 1986–92, Exec. Chair. HSBC Holdings PLC 1992–98; Pres. Int. Monetary Conf. 1992, mem. Exec. Council Hong Kong 1987–93; Chair. British Bank of the Middle East 1979–98, Midland Bank PLC 1994–97 (Dir 1987–98); Dir HBSC Americas Inc. 1984–88; Deputy Chair. (non-exec.) Alstom SA 1998–2003; Dir (non-exec.) Shell Transport and Trading Co. PLC 1993–2002, Trident Safeguards Ltd 1999–2003, World Shipping and Investment Ltd 1998–2004, Reuters Founders Share Co. Ltd 1998–, Scottish Medicine Ltd 1999–2003, Interpacific Holding Ltd 2000–, Aquarius Platinum 2004–; Chair. Hakluyt & Co. 2000–; Chair. Royal Hong Kong Jockey Club 1992–93; Fellow Chartered Inst. of Bankers; Trustee Gurkha Welfare Trust; Gov. Queenswood School; Pres. Penguin RFC; Hon. DUniv (Stirling) 1987; Hon. DLaws (Sheffield) 1993; Hon. LLD (Nottingham) 1997; Hon. Dr Business Admin. (Hong Kong Polytechnic) 1993, (Strathclyde) 1996; Dr hc (Hong Kong) 1997, (Napier) 1998, (Hong Kong Open) 1998, (Manchester Science and Tech.) 2000; Grand Bauhinia Medal (HK). *Leisure interests:* golf, rugby. *Address:* 100 Ebury Mews, London, SW1W 9NX, England (home). *Telephone:* (20) 7823-6775 (home). *Fax:* (20) 7824-8351 (home).

PURVIS, Stewart Peter, CBE, BA; British media executive and journalist; *Chair of Television Journalism, City University;* b. 28 Oct. 1947, Isleworth; s. of the late Peter Purvis and the late Lydia Purvis; m. Mary Presnail 1972 (divorced 1993); one d.; two s. with Jacqui Marson; ed Dulwich Coll., Exeter Univ.; fmr presenter Harlech TV; news trainee BBC 1969; Ind. TV News producer 1972, Programme Ed. News at Ten 1980, Ed. Channel 4 News 1983; Deputy Ed. Ind. TV News 1986, Ed. 1989, Ed.-in-Chief 1991, CEO 1995–2003; Pres. EuroNews 1997; Dir Travel News Ltd 1995, London News Radio 1996; Chair of TV Journalism, City Univ. London 2003–; Deputy Chair . King's Cross Partnership (Dir 1996–); Dir (non-exec) Royal Marsden Nat. Health Service Trust; mem. council European Journalism Centre 1996–; Fellow Royal TV Soc.; recipient of two Royal TV Soc. Awards, BAFTA Award for Best News or Outside Broadcast 1987, 1988, Broadcasting Press Guild Award for Best News or Current Affairs Programme 1988. *Leisure interests:* being at home, keeping fit, yoga. *Address:* Department of Journalism, City University, Northhampton Square, London, EC1V 0HB, England (office). *Telephone:* (20) 7040-8783 (office). *Fax:* (20) 7040-8562 (office). *Website:* www.city.ac.uk (office).

PURWAR, A. K.; Indian banker; ed Allahabad Univ.; joined State Bank of India 1968, held numerous positions including CEO Tokyo Br. 1995–98, Chair. State Bank of India 2002–06 (retd); fmr Man. Dir State Bank of Patiala; fmr Lecturer in Commerce, Business Admin Dept, Allahabad Univ.; fmr Chair. FICCI Banking and Financial Insts. *Address:* c/o State Bank of India, Corporate Centre, Madame Cama Road, POB 10121, Mumbai, 400 021, India.

PUSKA, Pekka, MD, PhD, MScS; Finnish epidemiologist and academic; *Director General, National Public Health Institute;* b. 18 Dec. 1945, Vaasa; m. Arja Puska; one s. one d.; ed Univ. of Turku, Univ. of Kuopio; Prin. Investigator, N Karelia Project, Univ. of Kuopio 1972–78; Visiting Prof., Stanford Univ., USA 1983; Research Prof. and Dir Dept of Epidemiology and Health Promotion, Nat. Public Health Inst. 1978–, Dir Div. of Health and Chronic Diseases 1992–2000, Deputy to Dir-Gen. 1995–2000, Acting Dir-Gen. 2000–01, Dir Dept of Noncommunicable Disease Prevention and Health Promotion WHO, Geneva, Switzerland 2001–03, Dir Gen.-Nat. Public Health Inst. 2004–; mem. Parl. 1987–91; Pres. Centre for Health Educ. 1989–95; mem. City Council, Joensuu 1993–97; mem. WHO panel of experts on cardiovascular diseases 1978; Chair. WHO/EURO CINDI working group on smoking 1992–; Dir Int. Quit and Win 1994–2006; Chair. several organizing cttees of int. confs on tobacco and health 1996–; mem. Bd Finnish Cancer Soc. 2004–09; Pres. Finnish Heart Asscn 2004–09; Chair. Nat. Nutrition Council, UKK Inst. (Pres.-Elect 2007–08, Pres. 2009–(10)), World Heart Fed. (Vice-Pres. 2006–), Int. Asscn of Nat. Public Health Insts; mem. Russian Acad. of Natural Sciences; Hon. mem. Hungarian Soc. of Hygiene 2000; Hon. DSc (St St Andrews, Scotland) 1999; WHO Annual Health Educ. Award 1990, Int. Union for Health Educ. AMIE Award 1991, WHO Tobacco Free World Award 1999, Nordic Public Health Award 2005, Rank Prize 2008. *Publications:* 10 books on public health; contrib. of numerous articles to journals. *Address:* National Public Health Institute, Mannerheimintie 166, 00300 Helsinki, Finland (office). *Telephone:* (9) 4744-8200 (office). *Fax:* (9) 4744-8552 (office). *E-mail:* pekka.puska@ktl.fi (office). *Website:* www.ktl.fi (office).

PUSTOVOITENKO, Valery Pavlovich, CandTechSc; Ukrainian politician; *Leader, People's Democratic Party of Ukraine;* b. 23 Feb. 1947, Adamivka, Nikolayev Region; m.; two c.; ed Dnipropetrovsk Inst. of Construction Eng; worked as mechanical eng.; head of trusts in Odessa and Dnipropetrovsk 1965–87; People's Deputy of Ukraine; Chair. Dnipropetrovsk City Soviet 1987–93; mem. Higher Econ. Council, Security Council 1997–; Head election campaign of Pres. Kuchma 1994; mem. Ukrainian Cabinet of Ministers 1994–97; Head of Ukrainian Football Fed. 1996–; mem. People's Democratic Party of Ukraine, currently Leader; mem. Parl.; mem. Political Exec. Council 1996–; Prime Minister of Ukraine 1997–99; Minister of Transport 2000–02. *Address:* c/o Government Offices, M. Hrushevskoga 12/2, 252008 Kiev, Ukraine. *Telephone:* (44) 226 2204.

PUTILIN, Nikolai Georgiyevich; Russian singer (baritone); b. 1954; ed Krasnoyarsk Inst. of Arts; lessons with Nikola Nikolov in Bulgaria; started as singer of Variety Theatre; soloist of Syktyvkar Musical Theatre, Komi Repub. 1983–85; Kazan Opera Theatre 1985–92; Kirov (Mariinsky) Theatre in St Petersburg 1992–; Prizewinner Int. Chaliapin Competition 1989. *Repertoire includes:* over 40 leading roles toured Metropolitan Opera, La Scala, Teatro Comunale di Firenze, Covent Garden, Bolshoi Theatre and others. *Address:* Askonas Holt Ltd, Lincoln House, 300 High Holborn, London, WC1V 7JH,

England (office). *Telephone:* (20) 7400-1700 (office). *Fax:* (20) 7400-1799 (office). *E-mail:* info@askonasholt.co.uk (office). *Website:* www.askonasholt.co.uk (office).

PUTIN, Col Vladimir Vladimirovich, PhD; Russian politician and fmr head of state; *Chairman of the Government (Prime Minister);* b. 7 Oct. 1952, Leningrad (now St Petersburg); s. of Vladimir Spiridonovich Putin and Mariya Ivanovna Putin; m. Lyudmila Putina 1983; two d.; ed Law Dept, Leningrad State Univ.; assigned to work on staff of KGB, USSR 1975–91, with First Chief Dept of KGB and in E Germany 1985–90; asst to Pro-Rector, Leningrad State Univ. 1990; adviser to Chair. of Leningrad City Exec. Cttee 1990–91; Chair. Cttee on Foreign Relations, St Petersburg City Council 1991–96, then also First Deputy Chair. St Petersburg City Govt (First Deputy Mayor) 1994–96; Deputy Head, Admin. of Russian Presidency, Property Man. Directorate 1996–98, then also Deputy Head, Exec. Office of Pres. (Presidential Admin) and Head, Cen. Supervision and Inspections Directorate 1997–98; First Deputy Head, Presidential Admin May–July 1998; Dir Fed. Security Service of Russian Fed. 1998–99; Sec. Security Council of Russia March–Aug. 1999; apptd Chair. of Govt (Prime Minister) Aug. 1999–May 2000, 2008–; Acting Pres. of Russian Fed. Dec. 1999–March 2000, won presidential election 26 March 2000, inaugurated as Pres. of Russian Fed. 7 May 2000–7 May 2008; Chair. United Russia (UR) (Yedinaya Rossiya) party 2008–; Grand Cross Bundesverdienstkreuz (Germany) 2001, Grand Croix, Légion d'honneur 2006, King Abdul Aziz Award, Saudi Arabia 2007, Order of Zayed (UAE) 2007; named Person of the Year by Time magazine 2007. *Leisure interest:* judo. *Address:* Office of the Chairman of the Government, 103274 Moscow, Krasnopresnenskaya nab. 2, Russia (office). *Telephone:* (495) 205-57-35 (office). *Fax:* (495) 205-42-19 (office). *Website:* www.government.ru (office).

PUTINA, Lyudmila; Russian teacher; *First Lady;* b. 6 Jan. 1958, Kaliningrad; m. Vladimir Vladimirvich Putin (Pres. of Russia) 1983; two d.; ed Leningrad State Univ.; early career as airline hostess, Kaliningrad; accompanied husband living in E Germany 1986–90; taught German language advanced courses for teachers at Leningrad State Univ. 1990–94; initiated creation of Center for the Devt of Russian Language. *Leisure interests:* theatre, music, tennis, downhill skiing. *Address:* c/o Office of the President, 103132 Moscow, Staraya pl. 4, Russian Federation. *Telephone:* (495) 925-35-81. *Fax:* (495) 206-07-66. *E-mail:* president@gov.ru. *Website:* www.kremlin.ru.

PUTMAN, Andrée; French designer; b. (Andrée Christine Aynard), 23 Dec. 1925, Paris; d. of Joseph Aynard and Louise Aynard (née Saint-René Taillandier); divorced; two c.; ed Collège d'Hulst, Paris, Conservatoire nat. supérieur de musique, Paris; design columnist for Elle 1952–58, L'Oeil magazines 1960–64; stylist for Prisunic Dept Store 1958–67; Head of Interiors Dept, Mafia Agency 1968–71; Creative Dir Créateurs et Industriels 1971–76; founder and CEO interior design co. Ecart 1978–96; f. Andrée Putman sarl 1997, designing furniture, silver, crystal, tableware, textiles, and fragrance; designed shop interiors for Yves St Laurent, Karl Lagerfeld, Thierry Mugler, Cartier, interiors for Morgańs Hotel, Air France's Concorde, Palladium Disco, New York, Bordeaux Museum of Contemporary Art, Azzedine Alaïa boutique, Paris 1985, Musuem of Fine Arts, Rouen, Ebel boutiques 1988, Wasserturm Hotel, Cologne, Balenciaga rooms, Paris 1989, Le Lac Hotel, Tokyo 1990, Sheraton Hotel, Roissy 1994, Lô Sushi Restaurant, Paris 1999, Ritz Carlton Hotel, Wolfsburgand, Connoly Store, London 2000, French Fed. Haute Couture offices 2000, Pershing Hall Hotel, Paris 2001, Bastide Restaurant, Los Angeles 2002, Lô Sushi II 2003, Bayerischer Hof Hotel Spa, Munich 2005, Inst. Guerlain, Paris 2005, Anne Fontaine boutiques, Paris and Tokyo 2006, Novartis offices, Bâle 2006; cr. film set for Peter Greenaway's film The Pillow Book, silverware and jewellery collection for Christofle 2004; Chevalier, Légion dhonneur, Officier des Arts et des Lettres; Dr hc; European Prize for Interior Architecture 1991, European Grand Prix for Interior Architecture 1991, Crystal Star Award for Design Excellence 1992, Oscar du Design 1993, Grand Prix Nat. de la Création Industrielle 1995, Blenheim Jewelry Display Award 1995, Good Design Award 1995, Business Traveller Award 1995, Starts of Design Award for Lifetime Achievement in Interior Design 1997, Modernism Design Award for Lifetime Achievement, JIDA Star Award, Star award Int. Interior Design Asscn, Chicago 2001, School of Art Inst. of Chicago, German Gala Spa Award 2005, Icon Award for Women in Design, New York 2006. *Address:* Andrée Putman sarl, 83 avenue Denfert-Rochereau, 75014 Paris, France (office). *Telephone:* (1) 55-42-88-55 (office). *E-mail:* archi@andreeputman.com (office). *Website:* www.andreeputman.com (office).

PUTNAM, Gerald D. (Jerry), BS; American business executive; *Vice Chairman, NYSE Euronext Inc.;* b. 21 May 1958; ed Univ. of Pennsylvania and Wharton School; with Walsh Greenwood 1983–87, then with Jefferies and Co., PaineWebber, Prudential, Geldermann Securities, Inc.; f. Terra Nova Trading, LLC 1994, Pres. 1994–99, mem. Bd of Dirs 1994–; Co-Founder, Chair. and CEO Archipelago Holdings Inc., Chicago 1999–2006 (merged with New York Stock Exchange), Pres. and Co-COO NYSE Group Inc., New York 2006-07, Vice Chair. NYSE Euronext Inc. 2007–; elected to Entrepreneurship Hall of Fame, Univ. of Illinois at Chicago 2000, named one of Time Magazine's Outstanding Innovators 2000. *Address:* NYSE Euronext, Inc., 11 Wall Street, New York, NY 10005, USA (office). *Telephone:* (212) 656-3000 (office). *Fax:* (212) 656-2126 (office). *Website:* www.nyse.com (office).

PUTNAM, Hilary, PhD; American academic; *Cogan University Professor Emeritus, Department of Philosophy, Harvard University;* b. 31 July 1926, Chicago, Ill.; s. of Samuel Putnam and Riva Sampson; m. 1st Erna Diesendruck 1948 (divorced 1962); one d.; m. 2nd Ruth A. Hall 1962; two s. one d.; ed Cen. High School of Philadelphia, Univ. of Pa, Harvard Univ. and Univ. of Calif. at Los Angeles; Asst Prof. of Philosophy, Princeton Univ. 1953–60, Assoc. Prof. 1960–61; Prof. of Philosophy of Science, MIT 1961–65; Prof. of Philosophy, Harvard Univ. 1965, Walter Beverly Pearson Prof. of Mathematical Logic and Modern Math. 1976–, then Cogan Univ. Prof., Emer. 2000–; Guggenheim Fellow 1960–61; Corresp. mem. British Acad.; many other fellowships; two hon. degrees. *Publications:* Meaning and the Moral Sciences 1978, Reason, Truth and History 1981, Philosophical Papers (3 vols) 1975–83, The Many Faces of Realism 1987, Representation and Reality 1989, Realism with a Human Face 1990, Renewing Philosophy 1992, Words and Life 1994, Pragmatism: an Open Question 1995, The Threefold Cord 1999, Enlightenment and Pragmatism 2001, The Collapse of the Fact 2002, Ethics without Ontology 2004. *Leisure interests:* hiking, cooking, languages. *Address:* Department of Philosophy, Emerson 207, Harvard University, Cambridge, MA 02138 (office); 116 Winchester Road, Arlington, MA 02174, USA (home). *Telephone:* (617) 495-3921 (office). *E-mail:* hputnam@fas.harvard.edu (office). *Website:* www.fas.harvard.edu/~phildept/putnam.html (office).

PUTTNAM, Baron (Life Peer), cr. 1997, of Queensgate in the Royal Borough of Kensington and Chelsea; **David Terence Puttnam,** Kt, CBE, FRGS, FRSA; British film producer and educationalist; b. 25 Feb. 1941, London; s. of Leonard Arthur Puttnam and Marie Beatrix Puttnam; m. Patricia Mary Jones 1961; one s. one d.; ed Minchenden Grammar School, London; advertising 1958–66, photography 1966–68, film production 1968–2000; Chair. Enigma Productions Ltd 1978–, Spectrum Strategy Consultants 1999–; Dir Nat. Film Finance Corpn 1980–85, Anglia TV Group 1982–99, Village Roadshow Corpn 1989–99, Survival Anglia 1989–99, Chrysalis Group 1993–96; Chair., CEO Columbia Pictures, USA 1986–88; Pres. Council for Protection of Rural England 1985–92; Visiting Lecturer, Univ. of Bristol, Visiting Industrial Prof. 1986–96; Gov. and Lecturer, LSE 1997–; Gov. Nat. Film and TV School 1974–87, (Chair. 1988–96); Chair. Teaching Council 2000–02; mem. Governing Council Royal Photographic Soc., Bd Landscape Foundation; Trustee Tate Gallery 1985–92, Science Museum 1994–2003, IPPR, Royal Acad. of Arts; Chancellor Univ. of Sunderland; Chair. Nat. Endowment for Science, Tech. and the Arts 1998–2003, Nat. Museum of Photography 1994–2003, Film and Television, Teaching Awards Trust; mem. Bd BECTA; Vice-Pres. BAFTA 1995–2002; mem. Educ. Standards Task Force 1997–2001, Arts Council Lottery Panel 1993–97; Pres. UNICEF 2002–; Trustee and Fellow, World Econ. Forum; mem. Gov. Council for Nat. Coll. for School Leadership; Chair. Media and Culture Advisory Group, QCA 2000–03; Lay Canon Durham Cathedral; Chancellor Open Univ. 2006–; BAFTA Acad. Fellowship 2006; Hon. FCSD, Officier, Ordre des Arts et des Lettres 1986; ; Hon. degrees (Bristol, Keele, Leicester, Manchester, Leeds, Birmingham, Southampton, Bradford, Heriot-Watt Edin., Westminster, Humberside, Sunderland, Cheltenham and Glos., Kent, Queens Belfast, London Guildhall Univs, North London, London (City), Royal Scottish Acad., Imperial Coll. London, Sheffield Hallam, American Int. Univ., Richmond, Nottingham, Winchester, Surrey, Navarra, Abertay, Leicester, Middlesex, Brunel, Greenwich); Special Jury Prize for The Duellists, Cannes 1977, two Acad. Awards and four BAFTA Awards for Midnight Express 1978, four Acad. Awards (including Best Film), three BAFTA Awards (including Best Film) for Chariots of Fire 1981, three Acad. Awards and nine BAFTA Awards for The Killing Fields 1985; Michael Balcon Award for outstanding contrib. to the British Film Industry, BAFTA 1982; Palme d'Or (Cannes), one Acad. Award and three BAFTA Awards for The Mission 1987. *Films:* 30 feature film including Bugsy Malone, The Duellists, Midnight Express, Chariots of Fire, Local Hero, The Killing Fields, Cal, The Mission, Memphis Belle, Meeting Venus. *Television:* 15 films including A Dangerous Man, Josephine Baker (Emmy Awards), Without Warning (Golden Globe Award). *Publications:* Rural England: Our Countryside at the Crossroads 1988, Undeclared War: The Struggle to Control the World's Film Industry 1997. *Leisure interests:* If only!. *Address:* Enigma Productions, PO Box 54828, London, SW1A 0WZ, England (office). *Telephone:* (20) 7219-6822 (office). *E-mail:* puttnam@enigma.co.uk (office).

PUYANA, Rafael; Colombian harpsichordist; b. 14 Oct. 1931, Bogotá; s. of Ernesto Puyana and Alicia de Puyana; studied under Wanda Landowska; lives in Spain and Paris; Colombia's Amb. to UNESCO, Paris; Teacher of harpsichord Cursos Manuel de Falla, Granada and Summer Acad. Musica en Compostela, Santiago de Compostela 1976–; gives performances throughout the world; works written for and dedicated to him by several composers including Federico Mompou, Xavier Montsalvatge, Julian Orbón, Alain Louvier and Stephen Dodgson; appeared in two films about life of Domenico Scarlatti (BBC TV and Televisión Española); Grand Prix du Disque (twice), Deutsche Schallplatten Preis for recording of works by François Couperin; Orden de Isabel la Católica (for his contrib. to study and performances of Spanish baroque and contemporary harpsichord music) 1996. *Leisure interest:* collecting 17th and 18th century keyboard instruments and Spanish and S American colonial art. *Address:* 88, rue de Grenelle, 75007 Paris, France (home); Hacienda La Chucua, Carrera 4 No 87-21, Santa Fe de Bogotá, Colombia (home).

PUYOL ANTOLIN, Rafael; Spanish university rector; b. 26 Feb. 1945, Telde, Las Palmas; m. Dolores Martínez-Ferrando; four c.; ed Universidad Complutense; Asst Prof. of Human Geography; Faculty of Geography and History, Universidad Complutense 1975–78, Assoc. Prof. 1978–82, Prof. 1982–, Rector of Univ. 1995–97; mem. editorial bds various journals; Pres. Population Group, Asociación de Geógrafos Españoles 1986–; Vice-Pres. Exec. Cttee Real Sociedad Geográfica. *Publications:* Emigración y desigualdades regionales en España 1979, Población y Espacio 1982, Población y recursos 1984, Población española 1988, Los grandes problemas demográficos 1993, La Unión Europea 1995. *Leisure interests:* music, reading. *Address:* C/Marbella, 50, 28034 Madrid, Spain (home). *Telephone:* (91) 3720480 (home). *Fax:* (91) 3943472.

PUZANOV, Col-Gen. Igor Yevgenyevich; Russian army officer; *Deputy Minister of Defence;* b. 31 Jan. 1947, Tyumen; ed Omsk Gen. Army Command School, M. V. Frunze Mil. Acad., Mil. Acad. of Gen. Staff; Commdr platoon Siberian Mil. Command –1976, Deputy Div. Commdr, then Commdr 1981–88; Deputy Regt Commdr, then Commdr Karpaty Mil. Command 1976–79; served in Afghanistan 1979–81; Head of Gen. Staff Baltic Mil. Command 1988–90; Army Commdr N Caucasian Mil. Command 1990–92; First Deputy Commdr Moscow Mil. Command 1992–2001, Statistics-Sec.; Deputy Minister of Defence 2001–; Merited Mil. Specialist. *Address:* Ministry of Defence, 105175 Moscow, ul. Myasnitskaya 37, Russia (office). *Telephone:* (495) 293-38-54 (office). *Fax:* (495) 296-84-36 (office). *Website:* www.mil.ru (office).

PYAVKO, Vladislav Ivanovich; Russian singer (tenor); b. 4 Feb. 1941, Krasnoyarsk; s. of Nina Piavko and step-s. of Nikolai Bakhin; m. Irina Arkhipova; two s. two d.; ed State Inst. of Theatrical Art, Moscow; studied under S. Rebrikov, Moscow, R. Pastorino, La Scala, Milan; mem. CPSU 1978–89; soloist with Bolshoi Opera 1965–89, Berliner Staatsoper 1989–92; teacher of singing and dramatic art, State Inst. of Theatrical Art 1980–89, Dean of School 1983–89; producer at Mosfilm 1980–83; Vice-Pres. Int. Union of Musicians 1998–; has also sung at Teatro Colón, Buenos Aires, Teatro Comunale, Florence, Opéra la Bastille, Paris, Nat. and Smetana Operas, Prague, Metropolitan, New York, Kirov, St Petersburg and in many other houses; also at many int. festivals; Gold Medal in tenor section, Vervier Int. Competition 1969, Silver Medal, Tchaikovsky Int. Competition 1970, Gold Medal and Pietro Mascagni Silver Medal, Livorno 1984, Gold Plank of Cisternino, Italy 1993; People's Artist of USSR 1983, of Kyrgyzstan 1993 and other awards. *Major roles include:* Hermann in Queen of Spades, Andrei in Mazeppa, Dmitry and Shuisky in Boris Godunov, Andrei and Golitsin in Khovanshchina, Radames, Otello, Manrico in Trovatore, Cavaradossi in Tosca, Pinkerton in Madam Butterfly, Don José in Carmen, Turiddu in Cavalleria Rusticana, Guglielmo Ratcliff. *Recordings:* numerous recordings for leading int. labels including EMI, HMV, Philips, Chant du Monde, Columbia. *Leisure interests:* poetry, photography, cars. *Address:* Bryusov, per. 2/14, Apt 27, 103009 Moscow, Russia. *Telephone:* (495) 229-43-07.

PYE, William Burns, ARCA, FRBS; British sculptor; *President, Hampshire Sculpture Trust;* b. 16 July 1938, London; s. of Sir David Pye and Virginia Pye; m. Susan Marsh 1963; one s. two d.; ed Charterhouse School, Wimbledon School of Art, Royal Coll. of Art; Visiting Prof., California State Univ. 1975–76; kinetic sculpture Revolving Tower 1970; made film Reflections 1971; sculpture 'Zemran' 1971; introduction of tensioned cables with less emphasis on volume 1972; combined working on commissions with smaller work and installations 1972–75; water an integral element of sculptures since mid-70s; first visit to Far East for one-man show (retrospective) 1987; Slipstream and Jetstream (water sculptures) commissioned by British Airports Authority, Gatwick Airport 1988; Balla Frois (100 ft long water sculpture) comm. for Glasgow Garden Festival 1988; Chalice water sculpture for 123 Buckingham Palace Rd, London 1990; cr. Water Wall and Portico for British Pavilion, Expo '92, Seville, Spain; Cristos at St Christopher's Place, London; Downpour at British Embassy, Oman; Cascade at Market Square, Derby 1994; Water Cone at Antony House, Cornwall for Nat. Trust 1996; bronze of Lord Hurd for Nat. Portrait Gallery 1996; Cader Idris at Cen. Square, Cardiff 1998; Prism for Cathay Pacific at Hong Kong Airport 1999; Aquarena Millennium Square, Bristol 2000; Cornucopia at Millfield School; St John's Innovation Park, Cambridge; Millennium Fountain for Wilton House and Sunderland Winter Garden 2001, Jubilee Fountain, Lincoln's Inn, London 2003, Eight Water Sculptures for Serpent Garden, Alnwick Castle 2004, three sculptures at Mariinsky Concert Hall, St Petersburg, eight-metre high water piece near Athens 2006, stone and bronze font for Salisbury Cathedral 2008; Hon. FRIBA 1993, FRBS; Prix de Sculpture, Budapest 1981, Vauxhall Mural Prize 1983, Peace Sculpture Prize 1984, ABSA award for best commission of new art in any medium 1988, Art at Work award for best site-specific comm. 1988, Royal Ueno Museum Award (Japan) 1989. *Leisure interest:* playing the flute. *Address:* The Studio, 22 Langroyd Road, London, SW17 7PL (office); 43 Hambalt Road, London, SW4 9EQ, England (home). *Telephone:* (20) 8682-2727 (Studio) (home). *Fax:* (20) 8682-3218 (home). *E-mail:* william.pye@btconnect.com (office). *Website:* www.williampye.com (office).

PYETSUKH, Vyacheslav Alekseyevich; Russian writer; b. 18 Nov. 1946, Moscow; ed Moscow State Pedagogical Inst.; history teacher Moscow Pedagogical Inst.; work first published in Selskaya Molodezh magazine; freelance writer 1970s–; Emily Clark Balach Prize 1999. *Publications:* Alphabet 1983, New Times 1988, History of the Town of Glupov in New and Newest Times, New Moscow Philosophy 1989, Rommat, I and Others 1990, Cycles 1991, State Child 1997. *Address:* c/o Vagrius Publishers, Troitskaya str. 7/1, building 2, 129090 Moscow, Russia (office). *Telephone:* (495) 785-09-03 (office).

PYNCHON, Thomas Ruggles, Jr, BA; American novelist; b. 8 May 1937, Glen Cove, NY; s. of Thomas R. Pynchon; ed Cornell Univ.; fmr editorial writer, Boeing Aircraft Co.; John D. and Catherine T. MacArthur Foundation Fellowship 1988; American Acad. of Arts and Letters Howells Medal 1975. *Publications:* V (Faulkner Prize for Best First Novel) 1963, The Crying of Lot 49 (Rosenthal Foundation Award 1967) 1965, Gravity's Rainbow (Nat. Book Award) 1973, Mortality and Mercy in Vienna 1976, Low-Lands 1978, Slow Learner (short stories) 1984, In the Rocket's Red Glare 1986, Vineland 1989, Deadly Sins 1994, Mason & Dixon 1996, Against the Day 2006; contrib. short stories to various publs, including Saturday Evening Post. *Address:* Melanie Jackson Agency, 915 Broadway, Suite 1009, New York, NY 10010, USA (office); c/o Penguin Books, 250 Madison Avenue, New York, NY 10016, USA.

PYNE, Natasha; British actress; b. 9 July 1946, Crawley, Sussex; d. of John Pyne and Iris Pyne; m. Paul Copley 1972; ed Hurlingham Comprehensive School, London; entered film industry 1961; mem. Young Vic Theatre Co., Exchange Co. and RSC, Manchester 1980–81; mem. BBC Radio Drama Co. 1985–87, 1994–95. *Stage plays include:* A Party for Bonzo (Soho Poly) 1985–87, Twelfth Night (Middle East and Africa Tour) 1989–90, Rafts and Dreams 1990, Alfie (UK Tour) 1992–93. *Films include:* The Devil-Ship Pirates 1964, The Idol 1966, Taming of the Shrew 1967, The Breaking of Bumbo 1970, Madhouse 1974, One of Our Dinosaurs is Missing 1975. *TV plays include:* Carmilla 1966, Father Dear Father (series) 1968–72, Hamlet, Silas Marner, BBC Play for Today: A Brush with Mr Porter on the Road to Eldorado 1981, Somewhere to Run 1989, Van der Valk (Thames TV) 1990–91, The Bill (Thames TV series) 1991, 1993, 2001, 2003, Virtual Murder (BBC TV) 1992, McLibel! (Channel 4 drama-documentary) 1997, Cadfael III (TV film series) 1997, The Bill 2003. *Radio work includes:* On May-Day (BBC Radio 4 and BBC World Service) 1986, The Snow Queen 1994, Galileo 1995, Ben Hur (serial) 1995, Westway (BBC World Service serial) 1997–98, Young PC (BBC Radio 4 series) 1997, Westway (BBC World Service serial) 1998–2002, Westway (BBC World Service) 1999–2004, Mary Barton (BBC Radio 4) 2001. *Leisure interests:* cycling, reading, cooking, travel, photography, cats, SE Asia. *Address:* c/o Sadie Feast Management, 10 Primrose Hill Studios, Fitzroy Road, London, NW1 8TR, England (office). *Telephone:* (20) 7586-5502 (office). *Fax:* (20) 7586-9817 (office).

PYNZENYK, Viktor Mikhailovich, DEcon; Ukrainian politician and economist; *Leader, Partiya 'Reformy i poryadok' (Reforms and Order Party);* b. 15 April 1954, Smologovitsa; s. of Mikailo Vasilyevich Pynzenyk and Maria Ivanovna Pynzenyk; m. 1st; two d.; m. 2nd Mariya Romanivna Pynzenyk; two s.; ed Lviv State Univ., Asst, then Docent, Sr Researcher, Prof., Chair. Lviv State Univ. 1975–92; mem. Vakhovna Rada (Parl.) 1991–2001; Deputy Chair. Bd on Problems of Econ. Policy 1992; Minister of Economy 1992–93, Deputy Prime Minister 1992–97; Pres. Foundation of Support to Reforms 1993; Chair. Council on Econ. Reforms 1994; Chair. Nat. Council on Statistics 1995; Head, State Comm. on Admin. Reform 1997–99; Head, Partiya 'Reformy i poryadok' (Reforms and Order Party) 1998–; Minister of Finance 2005–06, 2007–09 (resgnd); Dir Inst. of Reforms; Hon. Prof., Mohyla Acad. – Nat. Univ. of Kyiv 1996–, Econs Inst. of Ternopil; named an Honoured Economist of Ukraine 2004. *Publications:* more than 400 papers in professional journals. *Leisure interests:* tourism, music, playing the preferans card game. *Address:* Partiya 'Reformy i poryadok', 01021 Kyiv, vul. Instytutska 28, Ukraine (office). *Telephone:* (44) 585-41-16 (office). *Fax:* (44) 585-41-17 (office). *E-mail:* ref_ord@i.com.ua (office). *Website:* www.prp.org.ua (office).

Q

QABOOS BIN SAID AS-SAID, Sultan of Oman; *Prime Minister and Minister of Foreign Affairs, Defence and Finance;* b. 18 Nov. 1940, Salalah; s. of the late HH Said bin Taimur; m. 1976; ed privately in UK, RMA, Sandhurst; 14th descendant of the ruling dynasty of Albusaid Family; Sultan of Oman (following deposition of his father) July 1970–, also Prime Minister, Minister of Foreign Affairs, Defence and Finance; Hon. KCMG. *Leisure interests:* reading, horse-riding, music. *Address:* Diwan of the Royal Court, PO Box 632, Muscat 113, Sultanate of Oman. *Telephone:* 738711. *Fax:* 739427.

QADDAFI, Col Mu'ammar al- (see Gaddafi, Col Mu'ammar al-).

QADHAFI, Col Mu'ammar al- (see Gaddafi, Col Mu'ammar al-).

QAMAR, Syed Naveed, BSc, MS, MBA; Pakistani politician; *Minister of Privatization and Investment, with additional charge of Finance, Revenue, Economic Affairs and Statistics;* b. 22 Sept. 1955, Karachi; m.; one s. three d.; ed Univ. of Manchester, UK, Northrop Univ. and California State Univ., USA; mem. Computer Science faculty, FAST-NU (then called FAST-ICS) 1988–89; sr mem. Pakistan People's Party, currently mem. Cen. Exec. Cttee; elected mem. Prov. Ass., Sindh 1988–90, mem. Nat. Ass. 1990–93, 1993–96, 1997–99, elected from NA-222 (Tando Muhammad Khan-cum-Hyderabad-cum-Badin) constituency in gen. elections 2008; Prov. Minister (Sindh) for Information 1990; Chair. Privatization Comm. 1993; Fed. Minister for Finance and Privatization 1996; Minister of Privatization and Investment, with additional charge of Finance, Revenue, Econ. Affairs and Statistics 2008–. *Address:* Ministry of Finance, Block Q, Pakistan Secretariat, Islamabad Karachi, Pakistan (office). *Telephone:* (51) 9201941 (office). *Fax:* (51) 9202640 (office). *E-mail:* webmaster@finance.gov.pk (office); naveedqamar@yahoo.com. *Website:* www.finance.gov.pk (office).

QAMBAR, İsa Yunis oğlu; Azerbaijani politician and historian; *Chairman, Müsavat (Equality Party);* b. 24 Feb. 1957, Baku; s. of Yunis Qambarov and Tahira Qambarov; m. Dr Aide Bagirova 1986; two s.; ed Baku State Univ.; researcher, Azerbaijan Acad. of Sciences 1979–82, Inst. of Oriental Studies 1982–90; active participant in democratic movt in late 1980s, head of organizational div. of Popular Front 1990–, Deputy Chair. 1990–91; mem. Supreme Soviet of Azerbaijan 1990–95, Chair. Milli Majlis (Parl.) and Acting Pres. of Azerbaijan 1992–93 (resgnd); Chair. Comm. on Foreign Affairs 1991–92; Chair. Müsavat (Equality Party) 1992–; Co-founder and Chair. Democratic Congress 1999, 2001–03; joined United Opposition Alliance 2002; presidential cand. 2003. *Address:* Müsavat (Equality) Party (Müsavat Partiyası), 1025 Baku, Darnagül qasabasi 30/97, Azerbaijan (office). *Telephone:* (12) 448-23-82 (office); (12) 461-15-00 (home). *Fax:* (12) 448-23-84 (office); (12) 498-31-66 (home). *E-mail:* info@musavat.org (office); isa.gambar@gmail.com (home). *Website:* www.musavat.org (office); www.isagambar.az (home).

QANOONI, Younis; Afghan politician; *Speaker, Wolasi Jirga;* b. 1957, Panjshir Valley; ed Kabul Univ., also studied in India and USA; joined mujahidin troops fighting against Soviet occupation forces 1979–89; Jt Minister of Defence 1993; co-f. Defence of the Motherland and United Nat. Islamic Front for the Salvation of Afghanistan (Unifsa–Northern Alliance) 1996; political head of NA's main Jamiat-i Islami party 2001; Leader NA Del. to Future of Afghanistan Govt Talks, Bonn Nov. 2001; Minister of the Interior, Afghan Interim Authority Dec. 2001–June 2002; Minister of Educ. 2002–04 (resgnd); Head of Nizzat-i-Milli Party 2002; presidential cand. 2004; Founder and Leader Hizb-i Afghanistan-i Nawin (New Afghanistan Party) 2005–; Chair. Nat. Understanding Front (opposition coalition) 2005, currently Speaker of Wolasi Jirga (lower house of parl.). *Address:* c/o Hizb-i Afghanistan-i Nawin (New Afghanistan Party), Kabul, Afghanistan (office).

QARASE, Laisenia, BCom; Fijian politician; *Leader, Soqosoqo Duavata ni Lewenivanua (SDL) (Fiji United Party);* b. 4 Feb. 1941; m.; four s. one d.; ed Ratu Kadavulevu School, Queen Victoria School, Suva Boys' Grammar School, Univ. of Auckland, NZ, British Co-operative Coll., UK, Auckland Tech. Inst.; exec. cadet, Fijian Affairs Bd 1959–66, financial adviser 1979–99; joined Civil Service 1967, Co-operative Officer 1, Co-operatives Dept 1967–68, Asst Registrar of Co-operatives 1969–70, Sr Asst Registrar 1971–72, Chief Asst Registrar 1973–75, Registrar 1976–78; Deputy Sec. of Finance 1978–79; Perm. Sec. for Commerce and Industry 1979–80; Sec. of the Public Service Comm. 1980–83; Prime Minister and Minister for Nat. Reconciliation and Unity July 2000–06 (resigned following Court of Appeal ruling that his Govt was illegal March 7th 2001, reappointed March 15th 2001, dismissed by Acting Pres. Commodore Voreqe Bainimarama in mil. takeover of Govt Dec. 2006), also fmrly Minister for Fijian Affairs, Culture and Heritage, Multi-Ethnic Affairs and Reform of the Sugar Industry; Founder and Leader, Soqosoqo Duavata ni Lewenivanua (SDL) (Fiji United Party) 2001–; Man. Dir Fiji Devt Bank 1983–97, Merchant Bank of Fiji 1997–2000; Chair. South Pacific Fertilizers Ltd 1985–86, Fiji Post & Telecommunications Ltd 1990–91, Fiji TV Ltd 1994–98; Dir Fiji Int. Telecommunication Ltd (FINTEL) 1978–79, Foods Pacific Ltd 1985–86, Fiji Forest Industries Ltd 1988–97, Carlton Brewery (Fiji) Ltd 1989–99, Unit Trust of Fiji 1990–99, Voko Industries Ltd 1993–97, Air Pacific Ltd 1996–98, Colonial Advisory Council 1996–99; Chair. Mavanu Investments Ltd, Qalitu Enterprises Ltd; Dir Mualevu Tikina Holdings Ltd, Yatu Lau Co. Ltd. *Address:* Soqosoqo Duavata ni Lewenivanua (SDL) (Fiji United Party), c/o House of Representatives, Suva, Fiji (office).

QASEM, Subhi, PhD; Jordanian agriculturalist, politician and academic; *Professor Emeritus, University of Jordan;* b. 1934, Palestine; ed Kansas State Univ., Univ. of Minnesota, USA; worked in Ministry of Agric.; Prof. of Agric.,

---

Univ. of Jordan, Dean Faculty of Grad. Studies 1986, Founding Dean Faculties of Sciences, Agric. and Grad. Studies; Minister of Agric. 1991, now Prof. Emer.; consultant in scientific and tech. educ., research and devt, agric. policy and the environment; Fellow Islamic Acad. of Sciences; Medal of the Kawkab (Star) Award, Istiqlal (Independence) Medal. *Address:* PO Box 13300, Amman 11942 (office); Villa No. 7, University District, Abdul Rahim Omar Street, Amman, Jordan (home). *Telephone:* (6) 5346746 (office); (6) 5155200 (home). *Fax:* (6) 5346740 (office). *E-mail:* ubcc@go.com.jo (office).

QASIMI, Sheikha Lubna bint Khalid al-, BSc, MBA; United Arab Emirates information technology manager, business executive and government official; *Minister of Foreign Trade;* ed Al Zahra Secondary School, Sharjah, Calif. State Univ., Chico, USA, American Univ. of Sharjah; computer programmer with Datamation 1981; fmr Dubai br. man. for Gen. Information Authority; Sr Man. Information Systems Dept, Dubai Ports Authority 1993–2000; CEO Tejari.com (online business–to–business marketplace) 2000–; headed Dubai e-Govt Exec. team responsible for instituting e-govt initiatives throughout public sector 2001; Minister of Economy and Planning (first woman minister) 2004, currrently Minister of Foreign Trade; mem. Bd of Dirs Dubai Chamber of Commerce and Industry, Dubai Autism Centre; mem. Bd of Trustees Dubai Univ. Coll., Electronic-Total Quality Man. Coll., Thunderbird, The American Grad. School of Int. Man., Phoenix, Ariz., Zayed Univ., UAE; volunteer for Friends of Cancer Patients' Soc.; Hon. Kentucky Col, Commonwealth of Kentucky 2003; Distinguished Govt Employee Award 1999, Dubai Quality Group Award For Support to Leadership, Quality, and Change 2000, ITP Best Personal Achievement Award 2000, Datamatix IT Woman of the Year 2001, Business.com Personal Contribution Award 2001, Datamatix Outstanding Contribution 2002, UK House of Lords Special Entrepreneurship Award 2004, ranked by Forbes magazine amongst 100 Most Powerful Women (99th) 2007. *Address:* Ministry of Foreign Trade, Abu Dhabi, United Arab Emirates. *Website:* www.tejari.com (office).

QASIMI, HH Sheikh Saqr bin Muhammad al-, (Ruler of Ras al-Khaimah); United Arab Emirates; b. 1920; Ruler of Ras al-Khaimah 1948–; Chair. Rulers' Council of Trucial States –1971; mem. Supreme Council of UAE 1972–. *Address:* The Ruler's Palace, Ras Al-Khaimah, United Arab Emirates.

QASIMI, HH Sheikh Sultan bin Muhammad al-, (Ruler of Sharjah), PhD; United Arab Emirates; b. 1 July 1939; ed Cairo Univ. and Univs of Exeter and Durham, UK; Minister of Educ., UAE 1972; Ruler of Sharjah 1972–; Chair. Sharjah Human Soc., Arab/African Symposium; mem. Arab Historians' Union; Fellow Durham Univ.; Hon. Fellow Centre for Middle Eastern and Islamic Studies 1992; Hon. LLD (Khartoum); Hon. DSc (Univ. of Agric., Faisalabad) 1983; Distinguished Personality Prize, Univ. of Exeter 1993. *Publications:* The Myth of Arab Piracy in the Gulf, The Division of the Omani Empire, The Occupation of Aden, French-Omani Relations, The Arabian Documents in the French Archives, The White Shaikh, The Rebellious Prince, The Return of Holako, Power Struggles and Trade in the Gulf, The Gulf in Historic Maps. *Leisure interest:* reading. *Address:* Ruler's Palace, Sharjah, United Arab Emirates.

QASSEM, Sheikh Naim; Lebanese politician; *Deputy Secretary-General, Hezbollah;* b. 1953; fmr Prof. of Chem.; Founding mem. Hezbullah (Party of God) 1982, Deputy Sec.-Gen. 1991–. *Publication:* Hizbullah: The Story from Within 2005. *Address:* Hezbollah, Beirut, Lebanon. *E-mail:* info@moqawama .net. *Website:* www.moqawama.org.

QAWASMI, Hani-al; Palestinian academic and fmr government official; m.; four c.; fmr admin. Islamic University of Gaza; fmr judge; Sr Admin., Ministry of the Interior and Civil Affairs –2007, Minister of Interior and Civil Affairs 2007 (resgnd). *Address:* c/o Ministry of the Interior and Civil Affairs, Gaza, Palestinian Autonomous Areas (office).

QAYYUM, Malik Muhammad; Pakistani lawyer, judge and government official; *Attorney-General;* b. 18 Dec. 1944; s. of the late Justice Muhammad Akram; Sr Advocate, Supreme Court; began career as legal practitioner 1964; elected Sec., Bar Asscn, Lahore 1970, Pres. Dist Bar Asscn, Lahore 1980; mem. Punjab Bar Council 1984–88; Deputy Attorney-Gen. of Pakistan 1984–88; Judge, Lahore High Court 1988–2001 (resgnd); Attorney-Gen. of Pakistan 2007–; mem. Pakistan Law Comm.; Chief Ed. Pakistan Supreme Court Cases. *Address:* Office of the Attorney General, Supreme Court of Pakistan, Constitution Avenue, Islamabad, Pakistan (office). *Telephone:* (51) 9220581 (office). *Fax:* (51) 9213452 (office). *E-mail:* info@supremecourt.gov.pk (office). *Website:* www.supremecourt.gov.pk (office).

QAZI, Ashraf Jehangir, MA; Pakistani diplomatist; *Special Representative of the Secretary-General for Sudan, United Nations;* b. 1942; s. of the late Qazi Musa (died 1956) and Jennifer Musa; m.; two c.; with Foreign Service of Pakistan 1965–; Amb. to Germany 1990–91, to Russia 1991–94, to People's Repub. of China 1994–97; High Commr to India 1997–2001; Amb. to USA 2002–04; Special Rep. of the UN Sec.-Gen. for Iraq 2004–07, for Sudan 2007–. *Address:* United Nations Assistance Mission for Sudan (UNMIS), Ebeid Khatim Street, PO Box 69, Khartoum, 11111, Sudan (office). *Telephone:* (187) 086000 (office). *Fax:* (917) 3673523 (office). *Website:* www.unmis.org (office).

QI, Huaiyuan; Chinese diplomatist and state official; *President, Chinese People's Association for Friendship with Foreign Countries;* b. 1930, Ezhou City, Hubei Prov.; ed North China People's Univ., Harbin Foreign Languages Coll.; joined CCP 1948; Counsellor, Chinese Embassy, Bonn, FRG 1974–77; Asst to Minister of Foreign Affairs 1984–86, Vice-Minister of Foreign Affairs

1986–91, Dir Foreign Affairs Office of State Council 1991–94; Alt. mem. 13th CCP Cen. Cttee 1987–92, mem. 14th CCP Cen. Cttee 1992–97; Del., 15th CCP Nat. Congress 1997–2002; Pres. Chinese People's Asscn for Friendship with Foreign Countries (CPAFFC) 1994–; mem. Standing Cttee, 9th Nat. Cttee of CPPCC 1998–2003, Vice-Chair. Foreign Affairs Sub-cttee 1998–2003. *Address:* Chinese People's Association for Friendship with Foreign Countries, 1 Taijichang Dajie, Beijing 100740, People's Republic of China (office). *Telephone:* (10) 65125505 (office).

QIAN, Guanlin; Chinese politician; *Deputy Director, State Administration of Taxation;* b. Oct. 1946, Funing, Jiangsu Prov.; ed Shanghai Foreign Trade Inst.; joined CCP 1973; Deputy Head, Customs Dept, Guangzhou City, Guangdong Prov. 1984–86; Deputy Dir, later Dir Prov. Br., Gen. Admin of Customs, Guangdong Prov. 1987–90; Deputy Dir Gen. Admin of Customs 1990–93, Dir 1993–2001; Deputy Dir Nat. Narcotics Control Comm. 1993–2001; Deputy Dir State Admin of Taxation 2001– (Deputy Sec. CCP Leading Party Group); mem. CCP 14th Cen. Cttee for Discipline Inspection 1992–97, Alt. mem. CCP 15th Cen. Cttee 1997–2002. *Address:* State Administration of Taxation, Beijing 100038, People's Republic of China (office). *Website:* www.chinatax.gov.cn (office).

QIAN, Gen. Guoliang; Chinese army officer; *Commander-in-Chief, Shenyang Military Region, People's Liberation Army;* b. 1940, Wujiang, Jiangsu Prov.; ed Mil. Acad. of the Chinese PLA; joined PLA 1958, CCP 1960; Squad Leader, Combat Training Section, Army (or Ground Force), PLA Services and Arms, Staff Officer and Deputy Section Chief 1966, Div. Commdr, PLA 1979–83, Chief of Staff, Army (or Ground Force) 1983–85, Commdr Group Army 1985; rank of Maj.-Gen. 1988–95, Lt.-Gen. 1995–2002, Gen. 2002–; Chief of Staff, PLA Jinan Mil. Region 1993–96; Deputy Mil. Region C-in-C 1996, C-in-C 1996–99 (Deputy Sec. CCP Party Cttee); C-in-C PLA Shenyang Mil. Region 1999–; Alt. mem. 13th CCP Cen. Cttee 1987–92, 14th CCP Cen. Cttee 1992–97, mem. 15th CCP Cen. Cttee 1997–2002, 16th CCP Cen. Cttee 2002–07. *Address:* c/o People's Liberation Army, Ministry of National Defence, Jingshanqian Jie, Beijing, People's Republic of China (office).

QIAN, Lingxi; Chinese university professor and civil engineer; b. 16 July 1916, Wuxi, Jiangsu Prov.; ed Shanghai State-Run Sino-French High School; Prof., Yunnan Univ., Yunnan Prov. 1950, Zhejiang Univ., Zhejiang Prov.; Prof. and Faculty Dir, Dalian Univ. of Tech., Liaoning Prov. 1952, Pres. 1981; Dir-Gen. China Acad. of Mechanics; Pres. Chinese Soc. of Theoretical and Applied Mechanics 1982–; mem. Chinese Acad. of Sciences 1955–, Congress Cttee and Gen. Ass. of Int. Union of Theoretical and Applied Mechanics 1984–, Founding Council of Int. Asscn for Computational Mechanics 1985–; Dept of Tech. Science, Acad. Sinica 1985–; Dr hc (Univ. of Liège) 1987. *Address:* c/o Dalian University of Technology, Research Institute of Engineering Mechanics, Dalian 116024, Liaoning Province, People's Republic of China (office).

QIAN, Liren; Chinese party official; *Adviser, Chinese Association for International Understanding;* b. 20 Aug. 1924, Jiaxing Co., Zhejiang Prov.; s. of Qian Xunyi and Hu Suxian; m. Zheng Yun 1952; one s. one d.; joined CCP 1940; Deputy Sec.-Gen. All-China Fed. of Democratic Youth 1953; Sec.-Gen. All-China Students' Fed. 1956; Dir Int. Liaison Dept Communist Youth League 1959–64; Vice-Chair. All-China Fed. of Youth 1962; Dept Dir Foreign Affairs Office, State Council of People's Repub. of China 1964–65; mem. Standing Council Chinese People's Asscn for Friendship with Foreign Countries 1974–78; Amb. and Perm. Rep. UNESCO 1978–81; Deputy Dir Int. Liaison Dept, Cen. Cttee CCP 1982–83, Dir 1983–85; Pres. Renmin Ribao (People's Daily) 1985–89; mem. CCP Cen. Cttee 1985–92, mem. Propaganda and Ideological Work Leading Group 1988–89; mem. Standing Cttee 8th Nat. Cttee 1993–98; Chair. CPPCC Foreign Affairs Cttee 1995–98; Vice-Pres. Chinese Asscn for Int. Understanding 1995–2003, Adviser 2003–; Hon. Pres. Newspaper Operation and Man. Asscn 1988. *Leisure interests:* reading, swimming. *Address:* c/o Chinese Association for International Understanding, 4 Fuxing Road, Beijing 100860, People's Republic of China. *Telephone:* (10) 83907341. *Fax:* (10) 83907342.

QIAN, Qichen; Chinese diplomatist and state official; *Vice Premier, State Council;* b. Jan. 1928, Tiading Co., Shanghai; m. Zhou Hanqiong; one s. one d.; ed Shanghai Datung Middle School and Communist Youth League School, USSR; joined CCP 1942; mem. CCP Communist Youth League, Shanghai Municipality 1949, Researcher, Gen. Office 1953; Second Sec. Embassy, Moscow, USSR 1955–63, Deputy Section Chief 1955–64, Counsellor 1972–74; Section Chief, Ministry of Higher Educ. 1963, Deputy Dir External Relations Dept 1963; Amb. to Guinea and Guinea-Bissau 1974–76; Dir Information Dept, Ministry of Foreign Affairs 1977–82, later Spokesman, Vice-Minister of Foreign Affairs and Special Envoy to 2nd–11th Round Sino-Soviet Consultations 1982–88, Minister of Foreign Affairs 1988–98; Head of Chinese Del., First Round Sino-Soviet Border Talks 1987; Deputy Dir Comm. for Commemorating 40th Anniversary of UN 1985; Vice-Chair. Organizing Cttee for Int. Year of Peace 1985; State Councillor 1991–93, Vice-Premier of State Council 1993–; Leader Special Admin. Region Preparatory Cttee (to establish post-1997 govt in Hong Kong) 1993–97; Chair. Macao Special Admin. Region Preparatory Cttee 1998, mem. Govt Del., Macao Hand-Over Ceremony 1999; Alt. mem. 12th CCP Cen. Cttee 1982–87, mem. 1985, mem. 13th Cen. Cttee 1987–92, 14th Cen. Cttee 1992–97, 15th CCP Cen. Cttee 1997–2002, Deputy Head Cen. Foreign Affairs Leading Group; mem. Politburo CCP 1992–2002. *Address:* c/o State Council, Beijing, People's Republic of China (office).

QIAN, Renyuan, FAIC; Chinese chemist and academic; *Professor of Chemistry, Institute of Chemistry, Academia Sinica;* b. 19 Sept. 1917, Changshu, Jiangsu; s. of Qian Nantie and Miao Lingfen; m. 1st Hu Miaozhen 1951 (divorced 1956); m. 2nd Ying Qicong 1961 (divorced 1994); one d.; m. 3rd Yu Yansheng 1996; ed Zhejiang Univ., Univ. of Wisconsin, USA; Assoc. Prof.,

Xiamen Univ. 1948–49, Zhejiang Univ. 1949–51; Prof., Inst. of Physical Chem. Acad. Sinica 1951–53, Inst. of Chem. 1956–; Deputy Dir, Inst. of Chem., Acad. Sinica 1977–81, Dir 1981–85; Pres. Chinese Chemical Soc. 1982–86, Exec. Pres. 1984–85; Chair. Polymer Div., Chinese Chemical Soc. 1986–94; mem. Chem. Div., Acad. Sinica 1980, Asia-Pacific Acad. of Materials 1999; Assoc. mem. IUPAC Comm. on Polymer Characterization & Properties 1985–97; Science Premium (3rd class), Acad. Sinica 1956, Advanced Individual Award, Acad. Sinica 1977, Science Award Nat. Science Congress 1978, State Invention Award, (3rd class), State Comm. of Science and Tech. 1980, SINOPEC Science and Tech. Progress Award, (1st class) 1987, Acad. Sinica Natural Science Award (1st class) 1989, 1993, 1998, (2nd class) 1992, State Natural Science Award (2nd class) 1988, 1995, 1999, State Science & Tech. Progress Award (1st class) 1989, Qiushi Prize for Distinguished Scientists 1994, Int. Award, The Soc. of Polymer Science, Japan 1995. *Publications:* over 270 papers in Chinese and int. journals, over 50 reviews and book chapters, four books and four patents. *Leisure interest:* classical music. *Address:* Institute of Chemistry, Academia Sinica, PO Box 2709, Beijing 100080 (office); Flat 304, Apt Building #808, Zhong Guan Cun, Beijing 100080, People's Republic of China (home). *Telephone:* (10) 82612514 (office); (10) 62555505 (home). *Fax:* (10) 62559373 (office). *E-mail:* qianyu@infoc3.icas.ac.cn (office).

QIAN, Gen. Shugen; Chinese army officer; b. Feb. 1939, Wuxi City, Jiangsu Prov.; ed Chongqing Artillery School, PLA Mil. Acad. and Univ. of Nat. Defence; mem. CCP 1956–; entered army 1954; Deputy Div. Commdr 47th Army 1981; Div. Commdr 139th Div. 1983; Deputy Army Commdr 47th Army 1984; Army Commdr 47th Group Army 1985; Chief of Staff, Lanzhou Mil. Region 1992; Deputy Political Commissar, Lanzhou Mil. Region 1993; rank of Lt.-Gen. 1993; Asst to Chief of Gen. Staff 1994; Deputy Chief, PLA Gen. Staff 1995; rank of Gen. 2000; Alt. mem. 13th CCP Cen. Cttee 1987–92, 14th CCP Cen. Cttee 1992–97, mem. 15th CCP Cen. Cttee 1997–2002, 16th CCP Cen. Cttee 2002–07. *Address:* c/o Ministry of National Defence, Jingshanqian Jie, Beijing, People's Republic of China (office). *Telephone:* (10) 6370000 (office).

QIAN, Weichang, (Chien Wei-zang), MA, PhD; Chinese physicist and mathematician; b. 9 Oct. 1912, Wuxi, Jiangsu; s. of Prof. Chien Shen-Yi and Chien Wang Shui Ying; m. Kong Xiang-Ying 1939 (died 2001); one s. two d.; ed Tsinghua Univ., Beijing and Univ. of Toronto, Canada; Research Engineer, Jet Propulsion Lab., Calif. Inst. of Tech., USA 1942–46; returned to China 1946; Prof. of Physics and Applied Math., Tsinghua Univ., Beijing 1946–83, Dean of Studies 1949–58, Vice-Pres. 1956–58; Prof., Beijing Univ., Yanjing Univ.; mem. Standing Cttee All China Fed. of Scientific Socs 1950–58; mem. Standing Cttee, All China Democratic Youth League 1949–58; Head Mechanics Section, Inst. of Math., Acad. Sinica 1951–55; Vice-Dir Inst. of Mechanics; Dir Inst. of Automation 1955–58; mem. Acad. Sinica 1954–58, 1980–, Polish Acad. of Sciences 1956–; mem. State Council Comm. for Scientific Planning 1956–58; Jiangsu Prov. Deputy to NCP 1954–58, 1975–78; Pres. Shanghai Univ. of Tech. 1982, Shanghai Univ. 1994; Dir Shanghai Inst. of Applied Math. and Mechanics 1984; Vice-Chair. CPPCC 6th Nat. Cttee 1983–88, 7th Nat. Cttee 1988–93, 8th Nat. Cttee 1993–98, 9th Nat. Cttee 1998–2003; Chair. Science, Educ., Culture, Public Health and Sports Cttee; Vice-Chair. Cen. Cttee Chinese Democratic League 1983–97, Hon. Chair. 1997–; mem. Draft Cttee Hong Kong Basic Law 1986–91; Vice-Chair. Draft Cttee Macao Basic Law 1988–93; Pres. Soc. of Chinese Language Information Processing 1980–, Chinese Overseas Exchanges Asscn 1990–; Exec. Pres. China Council for the Promotion of Peaceful Reunification 1999–; Ed.-in-Chief, Applied Maths. and Mechanics (Chinese and English edns) 1980–; mem. Editorial Bd, Int. Journal of Eng Science (USA) 1982–, Advances in Applied Maths. (USA) 1984–, Journal of Thin-Walled Structure (USA) 1986–, Finite Elements in Analysis and Design (USA), Chinese Encyclopaedia 1983–; mem. Jt Chinese-US Editorial Bd, Chinese Ed., Concise Encyclopaedia Britannica 1983–; Nat. Science Award 1955, 1982; Beijing Municipal Award for Discoveries 1974, Shanghai Municipal Award for Technological Discoveries 1985. *Publications:* Scientific Discoveries in Chinese History 1953, Theory of Elasticity 1956, Theory of Torsion for Elastic Columns 1956, Large Deflection of Circular Plates 1957, Variational Principles and Finite Elements Methods 1980, Generalized Variational Principles 1984, Mechanics of Penetration 1985 (Nat. Prize for Best Publ 1988), Green's Function and Variational Principles in the Problems of Electromagnetic Fields and Waves 1989, Selected Works of Qian Wei-chang 1989, Applied Mathematics 1991, Foundation of Strength Computation in Electrical Machinery 1993; numerous articles for scientific papers on physics, applied math. and mechanics. *Address:* Shanghai University, 149 Yanchang Road, Shanghai 200072 (office). *Telephone:* (21) 56331245 (office). *Fax:* (21) 56333011 (office).

QIAN, Xuesen, PhD; Chinese scientist; b. 11 Dec. 1910, Shanghai; m. Jiang Ying 1947; one s. one d.; ed Jiaotong Univ. Shanghai, Calif. Inst. of Tech., USA; with MIT, USA 1935; Dir Rocket Section, US Nat. Defence Science Advisory Bd 1945–49; Prof., MIT 1946–49, Calif. Inst. of Tech. 1949–55; Dir China Inst. of Mechanics 1956; Pres. Dynamics Soc. 1956–63; Vice-Chair. Science and Tech. Comm. for Nat. Defence 1978–; mem. Dept for Math., Physics and Chem., Acad. of Sciences 1957–; Vice-Minister Comm. for Science, Tech. and Industry for Nat. Defence 1982–87; Sr Adviser 1987–; Pres. Dynamics Soc. 1957–82; Chair. China Asscn for Science and Tech. 1986–91, Hon. Chair. 1991–; mem. 9th CCP Cen. Cttee 1969–73, 10th CCP Cen. Cttee 1973–77, 11th CCP Cen. Cttee 1977–82, 12th CCP Cen. Cttee 1982–85; Vice-Chair. Nat. Cttee 6th CPPCC 1986–88, 7th 1988–93, 8th 1993–98; Sr Fellow Chinese Acad. of Sciences and Chinese Acad. of Eng 1998–; Hon. Pres. Astronautics Soc. 1980–, Soc. of Systems Eng 1980–; Meritorious Service Medal (for devt of China's first atomic bomb, hydrogen bomb and satellite), CCP Cen. Cttee, State Council and Cen. Mil. Command 1999. *Address:* Chinese Academy of Sciences, 52 San Li He Road, Beijing 100864, People's Republic of China (office).

QIAN, Yi, BS, MS; Chinese environmental scientist and academic; *Professor, Department of Environmental Science and Engineering, Tsinghua University;* b. 1936, Suzhou, Jiangsu Prov.; d. of Qian Mu; ed Tongji Univ., Shanghai, Tsinghua Univ., Beijing; Teaching Asst, Lecturer, Assoc. Prof., then Prof., Dept of Environmental Science and Eng, Tsinghua Univ. 1959–; Dir State Key Jt Lab. of Environmental Simulation and Pollution Control; science consultant, Environmental Protection Comm. of State Council; Vice-Chair., Gen. Cttee of ICSU; Vice-Chair. Eng and Environment Cttee of the World Fed. of Eng Orgs; Deputy, 7th NPC 1988–93, mem. Standing Cttee 8th NPC 1993–98, 9th NPC 1998–2003, Vice-Chair. Cttee of Environment and Resource Protection; mem. Exec. Cttee All-China Women's Fed. 1993; mem. Chinese Acad. of Eng 1994–; Nat. Science and Tech. Advancement Award (2nd Class), State Educ. Comm. Science and Tech. Advancement Award (1st Class) 1987, 2nd Award of Nat. Science and Tech. Progress 2003. *Publications:* Modern Wastewater Treatment Technology; The Prevention and Control of Industrial Environmental Pollution; Water Pollution Volume of Environmental Engineering Handbook; more than 100 research papers. *Address:* Department of Environmental Engineering, Tsinghua University, Beijing 100084, People's Republic of China (office). *Telephone:* (10) 62785684 (office). *Fax:* (10) 62595687 (office). *E-mail:* qiany@tsinghua.edu.cn (office). *Website:* www.tsinghua.edu.cn (office).

QIAN, Yongchang; Chinese politician; *President, China Communication & Transportation Association;* b. 1933, Shanghai City; joined CCP 1953; Vice-Minister of Communications 1982–84, Minister 1984–91; Chair. Bd of Dirs, Hong Kong China Merchants Group 1985–; Pres. China Communications and Transportation Asscn; Alt. mem. 12th Cen. Cttee CCP 1982–87, mem. 13th Cen. Cttee 1987–92. *Address:* c/o Ministry of Communications, Beijing, People's Republic of China (office).

QIAN, Yunlu; Chinese politician; *Secretary-General, 11th CPPCC National Committee;* b. Oct. 1944, Dawu Co., Hubei Prov.; ed Hubei Univ.; joined CCP 1965; sent to do manual labour, Sanli Commune 1968–70; Sec. Publicity Dept, CCP Dawu Co. Cttee, Hubei Prov. 1970–73, later Deputy Sec. Co. Cttee; Sec. Org. Dept CCP Xiaogan Prefectural Cttee, Hubei Prov. 1970–73; fmr Sec. CCP Party Cttee, Xinhe People's Commune, Hanchuan Co., Hubei Prov., later Deputy Sec. CCP Co. Cttee; fmr Magistrate, Dawu Co. (Dist) People's Court; Sec. CCP Communist Youth League Hubei Prov. Cttee 1973–83; Deputy Sec. CCP Hubei Prov. Cttee and mem. Standing Cttee 1983–91; Sec. CCP Wuhan City Cttee 1991–95; Chair. Hubei Prov. Cttee CPPCC 1995–98; Vice-Gov. Guizhou Prov. 1998–99, Gov. 1999–2001; Deputy Sec. CCP Guizhou Prov. Cttee 1998–2000, Sec. 2000–05; Chair. Standing Cttee Guizhou Prov. People's Congress 2003–; Sec., CCP Heilongjiang Prov. Cttee 2005–08; Alt. mem. 14th CCP Cen. Cttee 1992–97, 15th CCP Cen. Cttee 1992–97, mem. 16th CCP Cen. Cttee 2002–07, 17th CCP Cen. Cttee 2007–; Sec.-Gen. 11th CPPCC Nat. Cttee 2008–. *Address:* c/o Guizhou Provincial People's Congress, Guiyang, Guizhou Province, People's Republic of China.

QIAN, Zhengying; Chinese engineer and government official; b. 1923, Jiaxing Co., Zhejiang Prov.; m. Huang Xinbai; ed Dadong Univ., Shanghai; joined CCP 1941; Section Chief, Water Conservancy Bureau (Jiangsu-Anhui Border Regional Govt) 1945–48; Dir Front Eng Div., Dept of Army Service Station, E China Mil. Command) 1945–48; Sec. and Deputy Dir Yellow River Man. Bureau, Shandong Prov. 1948–50; Deputy Head, E China Mil. Admin. Cttee, Dept of Water Conservancy 1949; Deputy Head, Cttee for Harnessing Huaihe River 1950–52; Vice-Minister of Water Conservancy 1952–67, Minister of Water Conservancy and Electrical Power 1970–88; Adviser to State Council 1981–82, mem. 1982–; Vice-Chair. CCP Nat. Comm., Chair. Women, Youth and Legal Affairs Cttee; Adviser to State Flood Control HQ 1988–; mem. 10th Cen. Cttee of CCP 1972–77, 11th Cen. Cttee of CCP 1977–82, 12th Cen. Cttee 1982–87, 13th Cen. Cttee 1987–92, 14th Cen. Cttee 1992–97; Vice-Chair. 7th CPPCC Nat. Cttee 1988–93, 8th CPPCC Nat. Cttee 1993–98, 9th CPPCC Nat. Cttee 1998–2003; Pres. Red Cross Soc. of China 1994–, China-India Friendship Asscn, China Award Foundation for Teachers of Middle and Primary Schools and Kindergartens; Gold Medal (Somalia), China Eng Science and Tech. Prize 2000. *Address:* National Committee of Chinese People's Political Consultative Conference, 23 Taipingqiao Street, Beijing, People's Republic of China (office).

QIAO, Shi; Chinese party official (retd); b. Dec. 1924, Dinghai Co., Zhejiang Prov.; m. Yu Wen; joined CCP 1940; Sec. CP br., Shanghai Middle School 1942; Deputy Sec. Shanghai Dist CP; Sec. Youth Cttee, Hangzhou CP 1950–; Dir Designing Inst. of Jiuquan Iron and Steel Co. 1960–63; Sec. Afro-Asian Solidarity Cttee 1965–Cultural Revolution; Deputy Dir Int. Liaison Dept, CCP Cen. Cttee 1978–82, Dir 1982–83; mem. 12th Cen. Cttee, CCP 1982–87, 13th Cen. Cttee 1987–92, 14th Cen. Cttee 1992–97; mem. Politburo 1985 and Standing Cttee of Politburo 1987–; Vice-Premier, State Council 1986–88; Alt. mem. Secr., Cen. Cttee 1982–85, mem. 1985; Dir Org. Dept, CCP Cen. Cttee 1984–85; Sec. Cen. Cttee of Political Science and Law 1985–87; Head Leading Group for Rectification of Party Style within Cen. Depts 1986–; Sec. Cen. Comm. for Discipline Inspection 1987–93; mem. Politburo, Standing Cttee of Politburo, Secr. CPC Cen. Cttee 1989–92; Perm. mem. Politburo 14th Cen. Cttee 1992–97; Chair. Standing Cttee 8th NPC 1993–98. *Address:* c/o International Liaison Department, Central Committee, Communist Party, Beijing, People's Republic of China.

QIAO, Shiguang; Chinese artist; b. 5 Feb. 1937, Guantao Co., Hebei Prov.; s. of Qiao Lu De and Wang Hao Ling; m. Luo Zhen Ru 1961; two d.; Prof., Cen. Acad. of Arts and Design; Founder-Chair. Chinese Soc. of Lacquer Painting 1990 (group exhbn, Beijing 1990); Dir Chinese Artists Asscn; Dir Int. Culture of Lacquer 1992–; Founder Korea-China Lacquer Art Exchange Exhbn, Seoul 1994. *Publications:* Selected Lacquer Paintings of Qiao Shiguang 1993, The Skill and Artistic Expression of Lacquer Painting 1995, Collection of Qiao Shiguang's Lacquer Paintings 1996. *Leisure interests:* calligraphy, writing poetry. *Address:* The Central Academy of Arts and Design, 34 Dong Huan Bei Lu, Beijing 100020 (office); 3 602 Building, 6 Hong Miao Bei Li, Chao Yang District, Beijing 100025, People's Republic of China (home).

QIN, Huasun; Chinese diplomatist (retd); b. Sept. 1935, Jiangsu Prov.; Counsellor and Deputy Perm. Rep. to Office of UN and other int. orgs Geneva 1984–87; Perm. Rep. Vienna 1987–90; Dir-Gen. Dept of Int. Orgs and Confs Ministry of Foreign Affairs 1990–93; Asst Minister of Foreign Affairs 1993–95; Perm. Rep. to UN 1995–97; mem. CPPCC Nat. Cttee 1998; retd 2004. *Address:* c/o Ministry of Foreign Affairs, 2 Chaoyangmennei Dajie Dongsi, Beijing 100701, People's Republic of China (office).

QIN, Jiaming; Chinese railway executive; *President, China Railway Engineering Corporation;* b. 1945, Guilin, Guangxi Prov.; ed Changsha Railway Univ.; fmr Dir-Gen. China Railway Construction Soc.; fmr Deputy Pres. China Construction Enterprise Man. Asscn; Pres. China Railway Engineering Corpn 1996–; Ministry of Railways Educ. Medal 1989, Henan Provincial Award for Excellent Constructors 1990, Ministry of Railways Excellent Zhigong-Zhi-You 1997, Ministry of Railways Huo-Che-Tou (Locomotive) Medal 1998, State Award for Excellent Constructors 1999. *Address:* China Railway Engineering Corporation, CREC Mansion, Southern Square, Beijing West Railway Station, Beijing 100055, People's Republic of China (office). *Telephone:* (10) 51845159 (office). *Fax:* (10) 51844877 (office). *Website:* www.crecg.com (office).

QIN, Wencai; Chinese energy industry executive; b. Feb. 1925, Shanxi; s. of Qin Wanrong and Qin Wangshi; m. Zhang Huang 1950; one s. three d.; Vice-Minister, Minister of Petroleum Industry, Vice-Pres. Petroleum Corpn of People's Repub. of China 1979–82, China Enterprises Man. Asscn 1991–; Pres. China Nat. Offshore Oil Corpn 1982–87; Chair. China Offshore Oil Service Co., Hong Kong 1985–; Chair. Consultative Cttee 1987–; Chair. Capital Entrepreneurs Club, now Consultant; Vice-Chair. China Corp. Union, China Entrepreneurs Asscn 1991–2003. *Publications:* Facts About China National Offshore Oil Corporation, Oil People in the Chinese Petroleum Industry. *Leisure interests:* reading, sport. *Address:* PO Box 4705, No. 6, Dongzhimznwai Xiaojie, Chaoyang District, Beijing 100027 (office); Apt Sol, Bldg 7, Block 1, Liu Pu Kang, Xicheng District, Beijing, People's Republic of China (home). *Telephone:* (10) 84521002 (office); (10) 62025425 (home). *Fax:* (10) 64602600 (office). *E-mail:* quinwc@cnooc.com.cn (office).

QIN, Xiao, PhD; Chinese business executive; *Chairman, China Merchants Group;* b. 1947; ed Univ. of Cambridge, UK; joined China Int. Trust and Investment Corpn (CITIC) 1986, becoming Vice-Pres. 1994–95, Pres. 1995, Vice-Chair., fmr Deputy Party Sec. and Chair. CITIC Industrial Bank; Chair. China Merchants Group 2001–, China Merchants Bank Co. Ltd 2001–; Chair. Hong Kong Chinese Enterprises Asscn; mem. Toyota Int. Advisory Bd, Asia Business Council; Adviser and Sr Research Fellow, Hong Kong and Macao Research Inst. of State Council Devt and Research Centre; Guest Prof., School of Econs and Man., Tsinghua Univ. and Grad. School of the People's Bank of China; mem. 10th CPPCC; Deputy, 16th Nat. Congress of CCP 2002–07; Rep. 9th NPC 1998–2003. *Publications:* several papers and books in the fields of economics and management. *Address:* China Merchants Group, 40th Floor, China Merchants Building, 168–200 Conaught Road, Central, Hong Kong Special Administrative Region (office); China Merchants Bank Co. Ltd, 7088 Shen Nan Road, Futian District, Shenzhen 518040, Guangdong, People's Republic of China (office). *Telephone:* 25428288 (Hong Kong) (office); (755) 83198888 (Shenzhen) (office). *Fax:* 25448851 (Hong Kong) (office); (755) 83195109 (Shenzhen) (office). *E-mail:* cmhk@cmhk.com (office). *Website:* www.cmhk.com (office); www.cmbchina.com (office).

QIRBI, Abu Bakr Abdallah al-, BSc, MB, ChB, FRCP, FRCPath, FRCP (C); Yemeni diplomatist and medical consultant; *Minister of Foreign Affairs;* b. 6 June 1941, Aden; s. of Abdulla al-Qirbi and Fatoom al-Qirbi; m.; two s.; ed Aden Coll.; Edinburgh Univ. and Univ. of London, UK; Prof. of Clinical Pathology, San'a Univ., Dean Faculty of Science 1979–83, Faculty of Medicine 1982–87, Univ. Vice-Rector 1982–83; Minister of Educ. 1993–94; mem. Consultative Council 1997–2001; Minister of Foreign Affairs 2001–, of Immigrants' Affairs 2006–07; Chair. People's Charitable Soc. 1995–; has made several radio and TV programmes on educ., scientific research, non-governmental work, charity and medical topics; Yemen Unification Medal; WHO Scholarship for Postgraduate Study. *Publications:* author of book on political and development issues in Yemen; more than 40 papers on the biological effects of clinical chemistry, renal disease, gastro-intestinal diseases and numerous papers on politics and social affairs. *Leisure interests include:* tennis, billiards, swimming. *Address:* PO Box 11351, San'a, Yemen (office). *Telephone:* (1) 276555 (office). *Fax:* (1) 276618 (office). *E-mail:* aqirbi@hotmail.com (office). *Website:* www.mofa.gov.ye (office).

QIU, Bojun; Chinese business executive; *Chairman, Zhuhai Jinshan Computer Co. Ltd;* b. 1964, Hebei Prov.; ed Univ. of Science and Tech. for Nat. Defence; developed the Chinese word-processing system WPS; f. Kingsoft Corpn 1988, Dir 1988–, est. Zhuhai Kingsoft Computer Co. Ltd 1993; designed and developed Pangu Office System 1994, WPS97 Chinese processing system 1997; received funds from Legend and reconstructed Kingsoft 1998, establishing two e-commerce websites www.joyo.com and www.xoyow.myrice.com 2000; currently Chair. Zhuhai Jinshan Computer Co. Ltd. *Publications:* A WPS Course, WPS User Guide. *Address:* Zhuhai Jinshan Computer Co., Ltd.,No.8, Lianshan Lane, Lianhuashan, Jida Town, Xiangzhou, Zhuhai 519015, Guangdong, People's Republic of China (office). *Telephone:* (756) 3335688 (office).

QIU, Chunpu; Chinese business executive; b. 1930; joined CCP 1958; Chair. of Bd of Dirs, China Nat. Nonferrous Metals Industry Corpn 1993–; fmr Chair. China Packing Technique Asscn. *Address:* China National Nonferrous Metals

Industry Corporation, 9 Xizhang Hutong, Xicheng District, Beijing 100814, People's Republic of China (office).

QUADEN, Guy, PhD; Belgian economist and banker; *Governor, National Bank of Belgium;* b. 5 Aug. 1945, Liège; ed Univ. of Liège, Univ. of the Sorbonne, Paris, France; Prof. of Econs, Univ. of Liège 1978–; Pres. High Council for Econ. Affairs 1984–88; Exec. Dir Nat. Bank of Belgium 1988–99, Gov. 1999–; Belgian Govt Gen. Commr for the Euro 1996–99; Officier, Légion d'honneur 2001. *Publications include:* Le budget de l'état belge 1980, La crise des finances publiques 1984, L'économie belge dans la crise 1987, Politique économique 1991. *Leisure interests:* soccer, modern art. *Address:* Banque Nationale de Belgique/Nationale Bank van België, 14 boulevard de Berlaimont, 1000 Brussels, Belgium (office). *Telephone:* (2) 221-20-96 (office). *Fax:* (2) 221-32-10 (office). *E-mail:* pressoffice@nbb.be (office). *Website:* www.nbb.be (office).

QUADRIO CURZIO, Alberto, Libera docenza; Italian economist and academic; *Professor of Economics, Università Cattolica del Sacro Cuore;* b. 25 Dec. 1937, Tirano-Valtellina; ed Faculty of Political Sciences, Catholic Univ., Milan, St John's Coll., Cambridge, UK; Assoc. Prof. of Econs, Univ. of Cagliari 1965–68; Assoc. Prof. of Econs, Univ. of Bologna 1968–72, Prof. 1972–75, Chair., Faculty of Political Sciences 1974–75; Prof. of Econs, Università Cattolica del Sacro Cuore, Milan 1976–, Dir Centre of Econ. Analysis 1977–, Chair. Faculty of Political Sciences 1989–; Dir Economia Politica — Journal of Analytical and Institutional Economics (quarterly review) 1984–; mem. Italian Nat. Research Council 1977–88, 2006–; Pres. Italian Econs Asscn 1995–98; mem. Reflection Group on Spiritual and Cultural Dimension of Europe est. by Pres. of EC 2002–04; Pres. Bd for Donato Menichella scholarships, Bank of Italy 2004–07, Scientific Bd for Paolo Baffi Lectures, Bank of Italy 2003–07; mem. Bd for European Investment Bank Prize 1995–2000; has delivered lectures at many Italian and foreign univs; speaker at many confs and seminars in Italy and abroad; mem. Istituto Lombardo-Accad. di Scienze e Lettere, Consulta Stato Città Vaticano, Accad. Naz. dei Lincei; St Vincent Award 1984, W. Tobagi Award 1996, Cortina Ulisse Int. Award 1997, Italian Gold Medal for Contribs to Science and Culture 2000, Capri-San Michele for Econs 2003, Targa alla coerenza Zoli Foundation 2004, Cardano-Beccaria Int. Prize Rotary Pavia 2004, Assoc. Nuova Spoleto Award for Economy 2005. *Publications:* about 350, including Rent, Income Distribution, Order of Efficiency and Rentability 1980, The Gold Problem: Economic Perspectives 1982, Planning Manpower Education and Economic Growth 1983, Sui Momenti costitutivi della Economia Politica (co-author) 1983–84, The Exchange-Production Duality and the Dynamics of Economic Knowledge (co-author) 1986, Industrial Raw Materials: A Multi-Country, Multi-Commodity Analysis (co-author) 1986, The Agro-Technological System towards 2000: A European perspective (co-ed.) 1988, Rent, Distribution and Economic Structure 1990, Structural Rigidities and Dynamic Choice of Technologies (co-author) 1991, Issues on International Development and Solidarity 1992, On Economic Science: Its Tools and Economic Reality 1993, Innovation, Resources and Economic Growth (co-ed.) 1994, Risorse, Tecnologie, Rendita (co-author) 1996, Noi, l'Economia e l'Europa 1996, Rent Resources, Technology (co-author) 1999, Il Made in Italy oltre il 2000 2000, La Società Italiana degli Economisti 2000, Profili della Costituzione Europea 2001, Complexity and industrial clusters (co-ed.) 2002, Il Gruppo Edison: 1993–2003 (co-ed) 2003, La globalizzazione e i rapporti Nord-Est-Sud 2004, Research and Technological innovation (co-ed.) 2005, Research and Technological Innovation: The Challenge for a New Europe (co-ed.) 2006, Industria e Distretti. Un Paradigma di perdurante competitività italiana (co-ed.) 2006, Economisti ed Economia. Per un'Italia europea: paradigmi tra il XVIII e il XX secolo 2007, Intrapresa, sussidiarietà, sviluppo (co-ed.) 2007, Valorizzare un'economia forte. L'Italia e il ruolo della sussidiarietà (co-ed.) 2007, The EU and the Economies of the Eastern European Enlargement (co-ed.) 2008, Democracy, Institutions and Social Justice (co-ed.) 2008,. *Leisure interest:* skiing. *Address:* Facoltà di Scienze Politiche, Università Cattolica del Sacro Cuore, Largo Gemelli, 20123 Milan (office); Via A. Saffi 31, 20123 Milan, Italy (home). *Telephone:* (02) 72342474 (office). *Fax:* (02) 72342475 (office). *E-mail:* alberto.quadriocurzio@unicatt.it (office). *Website:* www.unicatt.it (office).

QUAH, Danny, AB, PhD; British (b. Malaysian) economist and academic; *Professor of Economics and Head, Department of Economics, London School of Economics;* b. 26 July 1958, Penang; m. Kathleen Tyson; two s.; ed Princeton Univ., Harvard Univ.; Asst Prof. of Econs, MIT 1985–91; Prof. of Econs, LSE 1996–, Head of Dept of Econs 2006–; fmr consultant to World Bank, Bank of England, Monetary Authority of Singapore; Gov. Nat. Inst. of Econ. and Social Research 2002–; mem. Editorial Bd Journal of Global Policy 2009–; Fellow, European Econ. Asscn 2004. *Leisure interest:* Taekwon-do. *Address:* Department of Economics, London School of Economics, Houghton Street, London, WC2A 2AE, England (office). *Telephone:* (20) 7955-7535 (office). *E-mail:* dq@econ.lse.ac.uk (office). *Website:* econ.lse.ac.uk/~dquah (office).

QUAID, Dennis; American actor; b. 9 April 1954, Houston, Tex.; s. of William Rudy Quaid and Juanita B. Quaid; m. 2nd Meg Ryan (q.v.) 1991 (divorced); one s.; m. 3rd Kimberly Buffington 2004; one s. one d.; ed Univ. of Houston; appeared on stage in Houston before moving to Hollywood; appeared on stage in New York with brother, Randy Quaid, in True West; performs with rock band The Electrics; wrote songs for films The Night the Lights Went Out in Georgia, Tough Enough, The Big Easy. *Films:* September 30 1955, 1978, Crazy Mama, Our Winning Season, Seniors, Breaking Away, I Never Promised You a Rose Garden, Gorp, The Long Riders, All Night Long, Caveman, The Night the Lights Went Out in Georgia, Tough Enough, Jaws 3-D, The Right Stuff, Dreamscape, Enemy Mine, The Big Easy, Innerspace, Suspect, D.O.A., Everyone's All-American, Great Balls of Fire, Lie Down With Lions, Postcards From the Edge, Come See the Paradise, A 22 Cent Romance,

Wilder Napalu, Flesh and Bone, Wyatt Earp, Something To Talk About 1995, Dragonheart 1996, Criminal Element 1997, Going West 1997, Gang Related 1997, Savior 1997, Switchback 1997, The Parent Trap 1998, Any Given Sunday 1999, Frequency 2000, Traffic 2000, The Rookie 2002, Far From Heaven 2002, Cold Creek Manor 2003, The Alamo 2004, The Day After Tomorrow 2004, Flight of the Phoenix 2004, Synergy 2004, In Good Company 2004, Yours, Mine and Ours 2005, American Dreamz 2006, Smart People 2007, Vantage Point 2008, The Express 2008. *Television includes:* Amateur Night at the Dixie Bar and Grill 1979, Johnny Belinda 1982, Bill: On His Own 1983, Everything That Rises 1998, Dinner with Friends 2001. *Address:* William Morris Agency, 1 William Morris Place, Beverly Hills, CA 90212; c/o Hansen Jacobson Teller Hoberman Newman, Warren, Sloane & Richman, LLP, 450 North Roxbury Drive, 8th Floor, Beverly Hills, CA 90210-4222, USA.

QUAM, Lois E., BA, MA, MHCA; American business executive; *Managing Director, Alternative Investments, Piper Jaffray and Company;* b. 21 June 1961; m. Matt Entenza; two s.; ed Macalaster Coll., Univ. of Oxford, UK; Pres. and CEO Penrose-St Francis Health System, Colo –1989; Dir Research and Evaluation, UnitedHealth Group 1989–93, Vice-Pres. Public Sector Services and Dir Research and Evaluation 1993, Corp. Vice-Pres. Man. Process 1996, CEO American Asscn of Retired Persons (AARP) Health Care Options Div. 1996–98, CEO Ovations, UnitedHealth Group 2002–06, Exec. Vice-Pres. Public and Sr Markets Group 2006–07; mem. Bd of Dirs General Mills Inc. 2007–; Man. Dir of Alternative Investments, Piper Jaffray and Co. 2007–; Sr Advisor to White House Task Force on Nat. Health Care Reform 1993–96; Chair. Minn. Health Care Access Comm. 1989–91; mem. Council on Foreign Relations; Trustee Macalaster Coll.; Rhodes Scholar; ranked by Fortune magazine amongst 50 Most Powerful Women in Business in the US (43rd) 2003, (42nd) 2004, (36th) 2005, (24th) 2006. *Publication:* Wills, Trusts & Estate Planning (co-author) 2001. *Address:* Piper Jaffray & Company, Suite 800 800 Nicollet Mall, Minneapolis, MN 55402, USA (office). *Telephone:* (612) 303-6000 (office). *Website:* www.piperjaffray.com (office).

QUAN, Shuren; Chinese party and government official; b. 1930, Ximing Co., Liaoning Prov.; joined CCP 1949; mem. Standing Cttee CCP Cen. Cttee, Fushun City, Liaoning Prov. 1969–79; Mayor of Fushun 1980–82; Sec. CCP Fushun City Cttee 1980–82; Gov. of Liaoning Prov. 1983–86; Sec. 7th CCP Liaoning Prov. Cttee 1983–85, Deputy Sec. 1985–86, Sec. 1986–93; Chair. Standing Cttee 8th Liaoning Prov. People's Congress 1993–; Alt. mem. 12th CCP Cen. Cttee 1982–87, mem. 13th Cen. Cttee 1987–92, mem. 14th Cen. Cttee 1992–97; Del., 15th CCP Nat. Congress 1997–2002; mem. Standing Cttee 9th CPPCC Nat. Cttee 1998–2003. *Address:* Liaoning Provincial Committee, Shenyang, Liaoning Province, People's Republic of China (office).

QUAN, Zhenghuan; Chinese muralist, painter and university professor; b. 16 June 1932, Beijing; d. of Quan Liang-Su and Qin Xiao-Qing; m. Li Hua-Ji 1959; two d.; ed Cen. Acad. of Fine Arts, Beijing; Asst Lecturer, Cen. Acad. of Fine Arts 1955–56, Cen. Acad. of Applied Arts 1956–59, Lecturer 1959–78, Asst Prof. 1978–87, Prof. and mem. Academic Cttee 1987–; mem. Standing Cttee Artists' Asscn of China. *Murals include:* The Story of the White Snake (Beijing Int. Airport) 1979, Jin Wei filled the Ocean (Beijing Yian Jing Hotel), Dances of China (Beijing Opera House) 1984. *Leisure interests:* Beijing Opera, old movies of 1930–1940s, football. *Address:* Central Academy of Applied Arts, Beijing (office); 3-601, 6/F Hongmiao Beili, 100025, Beijing, People's Republic of China. *Telephone:* (1) 5963912 (office); (1) 5015522.

QUANT, Mary, OBE, FSIA; British fashion, cosmetic and textile designer; *Joint Chairperson, Mary Quant Ltd.;* b. 11 Feb. 1934, London; d. of Jack Quant and Mildred Quant (née Jones); m. Alexander Plunket Greene 1957 (died 1990); one s.; ed Goldsmiths Coll. of Art, London; started career in Chelsea, London 1954; Dir Mary Quant Group of cos 1955–, Jt Chair. Mary Quant Ltd; Dir (non-exec.) House of Fraser 1997–; mem. Design Council 1971–74, UK-USA Bicentennial Liaison Cttee 1973, Advisory Council Victoria and Albert Museum 1976–78; retrospective exhbn of 1960s fashion, London Museum 1974; Sr Fellow, Royal Coll. of Art 1991; Hon. Fellow, Goldsmiths Coll., Univ. of London 1993; Hon. FRSA 1995; Dr hc (Winchester Coll. of Art) 2000; Sunday Times Int. Fashion Award, Rex Award (USA), Annual Design Medal, Soc. of Industrial Artists and Designers, Piavolo d'Oro (Italy), Royal Designer for Industry, Hall of Fame Award, British Fashion Council (for outstanding contrib. to British fashion) 1990. *Publications:* Quant by Quant 1966, Colour by Quant 1984, Quant on Make-up 1986, Mary Quant Classic Make-up and Beauty Book 1996. *Address:* Mary Quant Ltd, 1st Floor, Lynton House, 7-12 Tavistock Square, London, London, WC1H 9LT, England (office). *Telephone:* (20) 7383-2518 (office). *Fax:* (20) 7383-0814 (office). *E-mail:* mqltdldn@ma.kew.net. *Website:* www.maryquant.co.uk (office).

QUARRIE, Donald (Don); Jamaican fmr athlete; b. 25 Feb. 1951, Kingston; ed Univ. of Southern Calif., USA; competed Olympic Games, Munich 1972, reaching semi-final of 200m; Montréal 1976, won gold medal at 200 m and silver medal at 100 m; Moscow 1980, won bronze medal at 200 m; Los Angeles 1984, won silver medal 4×100 m relay; competed Commonwealth Games, Edin. 1970, won gold medals at 100 m, 200 m and 4×100 m relay; Christchurch 1974 won gold medals at 100 m and 200 m; Edmonton 1978 won gold medal at 100 m; coach in Calif., runs sprint clinics in Calif. and around the world. *Address:* c/o PO Box 272, Kingston 5, Jamaica.

QUAYES, Mohamed Mijarul, MPA; Bangladeshi diplomatist; m. Naeema Chaudhury Quayes; ed Univ. of Dhaka, Kennedy School of Govt, Harvard Univ., USA; joined Foreign Service 1982; served in Missions in Tokyo, Geneva and Singapore; Dir Gen., Ministry of Foreign Affairs 2001–05; High Commr to the Maldives 2005–08; Edward S. Mason Fellow in Public Policy and Man., Harvard Inst. for Int. Devt. *Address:* c/o Ministry of Foreign Affairs, Segunbagicha, Dhaka 1000, Bangladesh.

QUAYLE, James Danforth (Dan), BS, JD; American international business consultant and fmr politician; *Chairman, Cerberus Global Investments LLC;* b. 4 Feb. 1947, Indianapolis; s. of the late James C. Quayle and of Corinne (née Pulliam) Quayle; m. Marilyn Tucker 1972; two s. one d.; ed DePauw Univ., Greencastle, Ind., Ind. Univ.; served in Ind. Nat. Guard; court reporter, Huntington Herald Press, Ind. 1965–69, Assoc. Publr and Gen. Man. 1974–76; mem. Consumer Protection Div., Office of Ind. Attorney-Gen. 1970–71; Admin. Asst to Gov. of Ind. 1971–73; Dir Ind. Inheritance Tax Div. 1973–74; admitted to Indiana bar 1974; teacher of business law Huntington Coll. 1975; mem. US House of Reps 1977–79; Senator from Ind. 1981–88; Vice-Pres. of USA 1989–93; Chair. Nat. Space Council 1989; with Circle Investors 1993; currently Chair. Cerberus Global Investments, LLC; Distinguished Visiting Prof., American Grad. School of Int. Man. 1997–99; f. J. D. Quayle & Co. 2000; mem. Huntington Bar Asscn; mem. Hoosier State Press Asscn; Chair. Council on Competitiveness; Republican. *Publications:* Standing Firm 1994, The American Family 1995, Worth Fighting For 1999. *Address:* Cerberus Global Investments LLC, c/o Cerberus Capital Management, L.P., 450 Park Avenue, 28th Floor, New York, NY 10022; Suite 1080, 2425 East Camelback Road, Phoenix, AZ 85016, USA (office). *Telephone:* (602) 840-6750 (office). *Fax:* (602) 840-6936 (office). *E-mail:* lminter@quayleassoc.com (office).

QUDAH, Adel, BA, MA; Jordanian government official; b. Al-Salt; m.; four c.; ed Cairo Univ., Egypt, Univ. of Southern Calif., USA; Gen. Dir Customs Dept, Ministry of Finance 1982–91, Income Tax Dept 1990–91; Pres. Audit Bureau 1991–94; Minister of Supply 1996–2005; Chair. Exec. Privatization Comm. 1996–2005; Minister of Finance July–Nov. 2005; Order of the Jordan Star of the First Order, Order of the Repub. of Egypt of the First Order. *Address:* c/o Ministry of Finance, POB 85, Amman 11118, Jordan (office).

QUEEN LATIFAH; American rap artist and actress; b. (Dana Owens), 18 March 1970, East Orange, NJ; d. of Lance Owens and Rita Bray; worked with female rap act, Ladies Fresh; recorded with producers Dady-O, KRS-1, DJ Mark the 45 King and mems of De La Soul; moved to Motown Records; began acting career with sitcom Living Single; established management company, Flavor Unit Entertainment and label, Flavor Unit Records 1993–; guest appearance on Shabba Ranks' single, Watcha Gonna Do; other recording collaborations with De La Soul and Monie Love; Grammy Award for Best Rap Solo Performance 1994. *Films:* Living Single, Jungle Fever 1991, House Party 2 1991, Juice 1992, My Life 1993, Set It Off 1996, Hoodlum 1997, Sphere 1998, Living Out Loud 1998, The Bone Collector 1999, Bringing Out the Dead 1999, The Country Bears 2002, Brown Sugar 2002, Chicago 2002, Bringing Down the House (also exec. producer) 2003, Scary Movie 3 2003, Barbershop 2: Back in Business 2004, The Cookout (also writer and producer) 2004, Beauty Shop (also producer) 2005, Last Holiday 2006, Ice Age: The Meltdown (voice) 2006, Stranger Than Fiction 2006, Hairspray 2007, The Perfect Holiday 2007, Mad Money 2008, What Happens in Vegas 2008, The Secret Life of Bees 2008. *Television includes:* Living Single (series) 1993, Mama Flora's Family 1998, Queen Latifah Show 1999, Living with the Dead (mini series) 2002, The Muppets' Wizard of Oz 2005, Life Support (Golden Globe Award for Outstanding Performance by a Female Actor in a Television Movie or Miniseries 2008) 2007. *Recordings include:* albums: All Hail The Queen 1989, Latifah's Had It Up 2 Here 1989, Nature Of A Sista 1991, Black Reign 1993, Queen Latifah and Original Flava Unit 1996, Order In The Court 1998, The Dana Owens Album 2004, Trav'lin' Light 2008. *Website:* www.queenlatifah .com.

QUEFFÉLEC, Anne; French concert pianist; b. 17 Jan. 1948, Paris; d. of Henri Queffélec and Yvonne Pénau; m. Luc Dehaene 1983; two s.; ed Conservatoire Nat., Paris (First Prize for Piano 1965, for Chamber Music 1966); since 1968 has played all over Europe, Japan (seven tours), Israel, Africa, Canada and USA; has played with BBC Symphony, London Symphony, Royal Philharmonic, Bournemouth Symphony, Hallé, Scottish Chamber, City of Birmingham Symphony, Miami Symphony, NHK Tokyo, Tokyo Symphony orchestras, Nouvel orchestre philharmonique de Radio-France, Orchestre nat. de Radio-France, Orchestre de Strasbourg, Ensemble Intercontemporain, etc., under conductors including Zinman, Groves, Leppard, Marriner, Boulez, Semkow, Skrowaczewski, Eschenbach, Gardiner, Pritchard, Atherton, etc.; has played at numerous festivals including Strasbourg, Dijon, Besançon, La Roque-d'Anthéron, La Grange de Meslay, Bordeaux, Paris, King's Lynn, Bath, Cheltenham, London Proms; judge in several int. piano competitions; Masterclasses in France (including Ecole normale de musique, Paris), England and Japan; Pres. Asscn des amis d'Henri Queffélec, Asscn musicale 'Ballades'; Chevalier, Légion d'honneur 1998, Officier, Ordre nat. du mérite 2001; first prize, Munich Int. Piano Competition 1968, Prizewinner, Leeds Int. Piano Competition 1969, Best Interpreter of the Year, Victoires de la Musique 1990. *Recordings:* has made about 30 records of music by Scarlatti, Chopin, Schubert, Fauré, Ravel (all his piano works), Debussy, Liszt, Hummel, Beethoven, Mendelssohn, Bach, Satie, complete piano works of Henri Dutilleux 1996 and Mozart and Haydn recitals. *Radio:* many appearances on BBC Radio 3, France Musique and Japanese radio. *Television:* many appearances on musical programmes but has also appeared on literary and religious programmes. *Leisure interests:* children, literature, cycling, theatre, friends, humour, art. *Address:* Christine Talbot-Cooper – International Artists, Stoneville Cottage, Gretton Fields, Cheltenham, Glos. GL54 5HH, England (office); 15 avenue Corneille, 78600 Maisons-Laffitte, France (home). *Telephone:* (1242) 620736 (also fax) (office); 39-62-25-64 (home). *E-mail:* talbotcooper@onetel.com (office). *Website:* www .ctcinternationalartists.com (office). *Fax:* 39-62-25-64 (home).

QUEK, Tan Sri Leng Chan; Malaysian barrister and business executive; *Executive Chairman and CEO, Hong Leong Group Malaysia;* b. 1941; m.; three c.; called to Bar, Middle Temple, UK; has extensive business experience in financial services, manufacturing and real estate; Co-founder, Exec. Chair. and CEO Hong Leong Group Malaysia (includes semiconductor cos, automotive assembly, materials, newsprint, furniture); Exec. Chair. Guoco Group Ltd 1990–; Chair. HL Holdings Sdn Bhd. *Address:* Hong Leong Group Malaysia, Wisma Hong Leong, 18 Jalan Perak, 50450 Kuala Lumpur, Malaysia (office). *Telephone:* (3) 2164-1818 (office). *Fax:* (3) 2164-2477 (office). *E-mail:* info@ hongleong.com (office). *Website:* www.hongleong.com (office).

QUELCH, John Anthony, MA, MBA, MS, DBA, CIMgt; British academic; *Senior Associate Dean and Lincoln Filene Professor, Harvard Business School;* b. 8 Aug. 1951, London; s. of Norman Quelch and Laura Sally Quelch (née Jones); m. Joyce Ann Huntley 1978; ed Exeter Coll. Oxford, Wharton School, Univ. of Pennsylvania, Harvard Univ., USA; Asst Prof., Univ. of Western Ont., Canada 1977–79; Sebastian S. Kresge Prof. of Marketing, Harvard Univ. 1979–98; Dean London Business School 1998–2001; Sr Assoc. Dean and Lincoln Filene Prof. of Business Admin., Harvard Business School 2001–; Chair. Massachusetts Port Authority; Dir (non-exec.) WPP Group PLC, Inverness Medical Innovations, Vistor, Accion Int., Loyalty Management UK, Harvard Business School Publishing; Fellow Int. Acad. of Man. 2000, Hon. Fellow Exeter Coll. Oxford 2002, Hon. Consul Gen., Kingdom of Morocco. *Publications:* How to Market to Consumers 1989, Sales Promotion Management 1989, Cases in Advertising and Promotion Management 1995, Marketing Management 2004, Global Marketing Management 2004, The Global Market 2004, The New Global Brands 2005. *Leisure interests:* squash, tennis. *Address:* Morgan Hall 185, Harvard Business School, Soldiers Field, Boston, MA 02163 (office); 57 Baker Bridge Road, Lincoln, MA 01773, USA (home). *Telephone:* (617) 495-6325 (office); (781) 259-0594 (home). *Fax:* (617) 496-5637 (office). *E-mail:* jquelch@hbs.edu (office); jaquelch@yahoo.com (home).

QUELER, Eve; American conductor; *Music Director, Opera Orchestra of New York;* b. 1 Jan. 1936, New York; ed Mannes Coll. of Music, New York, City Coll. of New York, piano with Isabella Vengerov, conducting with Carl Bamberger, Joseph Rosenstock, Walter Susskind and Igor Markevich; began as pianist, asst conductor New York City Opera 1958 and 1965–70; later became a conductor; guest-conducted Philadelphia, Cleveland, Montréal Symphony, New Philharmonia, Australian Opera, Opéra de Nice, Opera de Barcelona, San Diego Opera, Edmonton Symphony, Nat. Opera of Czechoslovakia, Hungarian State, Hungarian Operahaz, Hamburg Opera, Pretoria, Hamilton, Ont., Opei Bonn and various other orchestras; Music Dir, Opera Orchestra of New York 1968–; Chevalier, Ordre des Arts et des Lettres; Dr hc (Russell Sage Coll., Colby Coll.); Musician of the Month, Musical American Magazine, Martha Baird Rockefeller Fund for Music Award, Sanford Medal, Yale Univ. *Recordings:* Puccini's Edgar, Verdi's Aroldo, Massenet's Le Cid, Boito's Nerone, Strauss' Guntram, Wagner's Tristan und Isolde, Janacek's Jenufa. *Publications:* articles in Musical America and Orpheus magazines. *Leisure interests:* organic gardening, family, women's health issues. *Address:* Robert Lombardo and Assoicates, 61 West 62nd Street, Suite 6F, New York, NY 10023, USA (office); Opera Orchestra of New York, 239 West 72nd Street, Suite 2R, New York, NY 10023, USA (office). *Telephone:* (212) 586-4453 (office); (212) 799-1982 (office). *Fax:* (212) 581-5771 (office). *E-mail:* robert@ robertlombardo.com (office); oony@tiac.net (office). *Website:* www .robertlombardo.com (office); www.operaorchestrany.org (office); www .evequeler.com.

QUESTROM, Allen I., BA; American retail executive; *Chairman and CEO, J. C. Penney Company;* m. Kelli Questrom; ed Boston Univ.; began career with Federated Dept Stores Inc. 1964, Chair. and CEO Rich Div. 1980–, Chair. and CEO fmr Bullock Div. 1984–88, Exec. Vice-Pres. 1988, Chair. and CEO 1990–97; Pres. and CEO Neiman Marcus 1988–90; joined Barneys NY Inc. 1997, Chair., Pres. and CEO 1999–2000; Chair. and CEO J. C. Penney Co. Inc. 2000–; Prin. AEA Investors Inc.; Pnr Mellon Ventures; mem. Bd Dirs Barneys NY Inc.; Dir Nat. Retail Fed.; mem. Nat. Cttee Whitney Museum of American Art, New York; mem. Business Council; Trustee Boston Univ. *Address:* J. C. Penney Company Inc., 6501 Legacy Drive, Plano, TX 75024-3698, USA (office). *Telephone:* (972) 431-1000 (office). *Fax:* (972) 431-1362 (office). *Website:* www.jcpenney.com (office).

QUEYRANNE, Jean-Jack; French politician; b. 2 Nov. 1945, Lyon; s. of Maurice Queyranne and Jeanne Bonavent; First Deputy Mayor of Villeurbanne (Rhône) 1977–88; Parti Socialiste (PS) mem. Rhône Gen. Council 1979–90, Regional Council Rhône-Alps 1986–2002, Pres. 2004–; Nat. Ass. Deputy (alt.) for Rhone 1981–93; mem. PS Steering Cttee, Deputy Nat. Sec. responsible for cultural policy 1983, for press and culture 1985, Party Spokesman 1985, Nat. Del. and Spokesman 1987, Nat. Sec. responsible for audiovisual policy 1988, mem. Nat. Council 1993–94; Mayor of Bron (Rhône) 1989–97, Deputy Mayor 1997–2004; Nat. Ass. Deputy for Rhône 1997–; Minister of State attached to Minister of the Interior, with responsibility for Overseas Depts and Territories 1997–2000; Minister of Relations with Parliament 2000–02. *Leisure interests:* theatre, music, cinema. *Address:* 1 rue Roger Salengro, 69500 Bron (office); Assemblée nationale, 126 rue de l'Université, 75355 Paris 07 SP, France (office). *Telephone:* 4-72-37-50-99 (office). *Fax:* 4-72-37-58-87 (office). *E-mail:* jjqueyranne@assemblee-nationale .fr (office). *Website:* www.assemblee-nationale.fr (office).

QUEZADA TORUÑO, HE Cardinal Rodolfo; Guatemalan ecclesiastic; *Archbishop of Guatemala City;* b. 8 March 1932, Guatemala City; ed in El Salvador, Germany and Rome, Italy; ordained priest 1956; held various pastoral and teaching positions, including Rector Shrine of Our Lady of Guadalupe; Auxiliary Bishop of Zacapa and Titular Bishop of Gadiaufala 1972, Coadjutor Bishop of Zacapa 1975, Bishop of Zacapa 1980, Bishop of Zacapa y Santo Cristo de Esquipulas 1986; Pres. Guatemalan Bishops' Conf. 1988–92; played key role in ending civil war in Guatemala that had lasted for 36 years; Archbishop of Guatemala City 2001–; cr. Cardinal (Cardinal Priest of San Saturnino) 2003. *Address:* Archdiocese of Guatemala, Apartado 723, 7A Avenida 6-21, Zona 1, 01001 Ciudad de Guatemala, Guatemala (office). *Telephone:* (2) 23-21-071 (office). *Fax:* (2) 23-80-004 (office). *Website:* www.riial.org/guatemala/destgua.htm (office).

QUIGLEY, Mike, BSc, BEE; British/Australian business executive; b. 1953; m.; three d.; ed Univ. of New South Wales; joined ITT Australia (now Alcatel Australia) 1971, positions including research and devt, manufacturing, sales and marketing, Gen. Man. for Australia and NZ 1996–99, COO Alcatel USA 1999, later CEO Alcatel USA, Pres. Alcatel N America, mem. Exec. Cttee, Pres. Fixed Communications Activities 2003, Pres. and COO Alcatel 2005–06, COO joint Alcatel-Lucent techs co. after Alcatel acquisition of Lucent 2006–07 (resgnd), also fmr mem. Exec. Bd; mem. Bd Alliance for Telecommunications Industry Solutions. *Address:* c/o Alcatel, 54 rue La Boétie, 75008 Paris, France (office).

QUIGLEY, Sir (William) George (Henry), Kt, CB, PhD, CBIM, FIB, MRIA; British business executive; *Chairman, Short Brothers PLC;* b. 26 Nov. 1929; s. of William G. C. Quigley and Sarah H. Martin; m. Moyra A. Munn 1971; ed Ballymena Acad. and Queen's Univ., Belfast; Asst Prin., NI Civil Service 1955; Perm. Sec. Dept of Manpower Services, NI 1974–76, Dept of Commerce 1976–79, Dept of Finance 1979–82, Dept of Finance and Personnel 1982–88; Deputy Chair. Ulster Bank Ltd 1988–89, Chair. 1989–2001; Dir Irish-American Partnership 1989–; Chair. Short Brothers PLC 1999–, (Dir 1989–), Scottish Fee Support Review 1998–2000, NatWest Pension Fund 1998–2002, Inst. of Dirs (NI) 1990–94, Parades Comm. Review 2001–02, Lothbury Property Trust 2001–, Bd of Inst. of British-Irish Studies, Univ. Coll., Dublin 2006–; Pres. Econ. and Social Research Inst. (Ireland) 1999–2002; Dir Nat. Westminster Bank 1990–99, Ind. News & Media (UK) 2001–; mem. Dearing Cttee on Higher Educ. 1996–97, Qualifications and Curriculum Authority 1997–99; Professorial Fellow, Queen's Univ. Belfast 1988–92; Hon. Fellow, Inst. of Man. of Ireland; Hon. LLD (Queen's) 1996; Hon. DUniv (Ulster) 1998, (Open Univ.) 2005; Compaq Lifetime Achievement Award 1997. *Publication:* Registrum Johannis Mey (co-ed. with E.F.D. Roberts) 1973. *Leisure interests:* historical research, reading, music, gardening. *Address:* Short Brothers PLC, Airport Road, Belfast, BT3 9DZ, Northern Ireland (office). *Telephone:* (28) 9073-3553 (office). *Fax:* (28) 9073-3143 (office).

QUIGNARD, Pascal Charles Edmond, LicenFil; French writer; b. 23 April 1948, Verneuil-sur-Avre, Eure; s. of Jacques Quignard and Anne Quignard (née Bruneau); one s.; ed Lycée de Havre, Lycée de Sèvres and Faculté des Lettres de Nanterre; lecturer 1969–77; mem. Cttee of Lecturing 1977–94; Sec.-Gen. for Editorial Devt, Editions Gallimard; Pres. Int. Festival of Opera and Baroque Theatre, Château de Versailles 1990–94; Pres. Concert des Nations 1990–93; Chevalier, Légion d'honneur; Prix de la Soc. des gens de lettres for his collected works 1998, Grand prix du roman de la Ville de Paris 1998, Prix de la fondation Prince Pierre de Monaco for his collected works 2000. *Publications include:* L'être du balbutiement 1969, Alexandra de Lycophron 1971, La parole de la Délie 1974, Michel Deguy 1975, Echo 1975, Sang 1976, Le lecteur 1976, Hiems 1977, Sarx 1977, Inter aerias fagos 1977, Sur le défaut de terre 1979, Carus 1979, Le secret du domaine 1980, Petits traités (tome I à VIII) 1990, Les tablettes de buis d'Apronenia Avitia 1984, Le vœu de silence (essay) 1985, Une gêne technique à l'égard des fragments 1986, Ethelrude et Wolframm 1986, Le salon de Wurtemberg 1986, La leçon de musique 1987, Les escaliers de Chambord 1989, La raison 1990, Albucius 1990, Tous les matins du monde 1991, Georges de La Tour 1991, La Frontière 1992, Le nom sur le bout de la langue 1993, Le sexe et l'effroi 1994, L'occupation américaine 1994, Rhétorique spéculative 1995, L'amour conjugal 1995, Les septante 1995, La haine de la musique 1996, Vie secrète 1998, Terrasse à Rome (Grand Prix du roman de l'Acad. française 2000) 2000, Albucius 2001, Les ombres errantes (Prix Goncourt 2002) 2002, Sur le jadis 2002, Abîmes 2002, Les Paradisiaques 2005, Sordidissimes 2005, Écrits de l'éphémère 2005, Pour trouver les Enfers 2005, Villa Amalia 2006, L'Enfant au visage couleur de la mort 2006, Triomphe du temps 2006, Ethelrude et Wolframm 2006, Le Petit Cupidon 2006, Requiem 2006, La Nuit sexuelle 2007. *Address:* c/o Éditions Galilée, 9 Rue Linné, 75005 Paris, France (office).

QUIJANO CAPURRO, José Manuel; Uruguayan economist and international organization official; *Director, Mercosur;* Dir Consultora Alianza Cooperativa Internacional, ACI, Uruguay; Advisor, Perm. Secr., Sistema Economico Latinoamericana (SELA) *c.* 2001; fmr consultant with Integración AFAP, Montevideo; mem. Mercosur Sectoral Comm., Dir Mercosur Secr. 2008–. *Address:* Secretaría del Mercosur, Código Postal 11.200, Dr Luis Piera 1992, 1° Piso – Edificio MERCOSUR, Montevideo, Uruguay (office). *Telephone:* (2) 412-9024 (office). *Fax:* (2) 418-0557 (office). *E-mail:* secretaria@mercosur.org.uy (office). *Website:* www.mercosur.int (office).

QUILÈS, Paul; French politician; *Mayor, Cordes-sur-Ciel (Tarn);* b. 27 Jan. 1942, St Denis du Sig, Algeria; s. of René Quilès and Odette Tyrode; m. Josephe-Marie Bureau 1964; three d.; ed Ecole Polytechnique, Paris; engineer, Shell Française 1964–78; Socialist Deputy to Nat. Ass. 1978–83, 1986–88, 1993–; Minister of Town Planning and Housing 1983–85, of Transport 1984–85, of Defence 1985–86, of Posts, Telecommunications and Space 1988–91, of Public Works, Housing, Transportation and Space Research 1991–92, of the Interior and Public Security 1992–93; Chair. Nat. Defence and Armed Forces Comm. 1997–2002; Mayor of Cordes-sur-Ciel (Tarn) 1995–; mem. Econ. and Social Council 1974–75; mem. Foreign Affairs Comm. 2002–. *Publications:* La Politique n'est pas ce que vous croyez 1985, Nous vivons une époque intéressante 1992, Les 577, Un parlement pour quoi faire 2001, Face aux désordres du monde 2005. *Address:* Assemblée nationale, 75355 Paris, France. *Telephone:* (1) 40-63-68-99 (office). *Fax:* (1) 40-63-52-52 (office).

QUILLEN, Daniel G., MA, PhD; American mathematician and academic; *Professorial Fellow and Waynflete Professor of Pure Mathematics, Magdalen College, University of Oxford;* b. 27 June 1940, Orange, NJ; ed Newark Acad. and Harvard Univ.; fmr faculty mem. MIT; Sloan Fellow, Paris, France 1968–69; Visiting mem. Inst. for Advanced Study, Princeton, NJ 1969–70; Guggenheim Fellow, Paris 1973–74; currently Professorial Fellow and Waynflete Prof. of Pure Math., Magdalen Coll., Oxford, mem. Math. Inst.; Cole Prize, American Math. Society 1975, Fields Medal, Int. Congress of Mathematicians, Helsinki 1978. *Publications:* numerous articles in math. journals on definition of higher groups in algebraic K-theory. *Address:* Mathematical Institute, University of Oxford, 24–29 St Giles', Oxford, OX1 3LB, England (office). *Telephone:* (1865) 273560 (office). *Fax:* (1865) 273583 (office). *E-mail:* quillen@maths.ox.ac.uk (office). *Website:* www.maths.ox.ac.uk (office).

QUINLAN, Michael (Mike) R., BS, MBA; American business executive; *Chairman Emeritus, McDonald's Corporation;* b. 9 Dec. 1944, Chicago; s. of Robert Joseph Quinlan and Kathryn (née Koerner) Quinlan; m. Marilyn DeLashmutt 1966; two s.; ed Loyola Univ.; part-time mailroom worker McDonald's Corpn 1963, Asst Buyer 1966, Pres. (USA) 1980–82, CEO 1987–98, Chair. 1989–97, Dir 1979–2002 (retd), now Chair. Emer.; mem. Bd of Dirs Dun & Bradstreet Corpn 1989–, May Dept Stores Co., Warren Resources, Inc. *Leisure interest:* racquetball. *Address:* c/o Board of Directors, Dun & Bradstreet Corporation, 103 JFK Pkwy, Short Hills, NJ 07078, USA.

QUINN, Aidan; American actor; b. 8 March 1959, Chicago; worked with various theatre groups in Chicago before moving to New York; off-Broadway appearances in Sam Shepard's plays Fool for Love and A Lie of the Mind; appeared in Hamlet, Wisdom Bridge Theater, Chicago, numerous other plays. *Films:* Reckless 1984, Desperately Seeking Susan 1985, The Mission 1986, Stakeout 1987, Crusoe 1989, The Handmaid's Tale 1990, The Lemon Sisters 1990, Avalon 1990, At Play in the Fields of the Lord 1991, The Playboys 1992, Benny & Joon 1993, Blink 1994, Legends of the Fall 1994, Mary Shelley's Frankenstein 1994, The Stars Fell on Henrietta 1995, Haunted 1995, Michael Collins 1996, Looking For Richard 1996, Commandments 1997, The Assignment 1997, This is My Father 1998, Practical Magic 1998, In Dreams 1999, Music of the Heart 1999, Songcatcher 2000, Stolen Summer 2002, Evelyn 2002, Song for a Raggy Boy 2003, Cavedweller 2004, Shadow of Fear 2004, Bobby Jones, Stroke of Genius 2004, Plainsong 2004, Return to Sender 2004, Proud 2004, Nine Lives 2005, Dark Matter 2007. *Stage appearances include:* Fool for Love 1983, A Streetcar Named Desire (Theatre World Award) 1988. *Television includes:* An Early Frost 1985, Perfect Witness 1989, Lies of the Twins 1991, A Private Matter 1992, Forbidden Territory: Stanley's Search for Livingstone 1997, The Prince and the Pauper 2000, See You in My Dreams 2000, Two of Us 2000, Benedict Arnold: A Question of Honor 2003, Plainsong 2004, Cavedweller 2004, Miracle Run 2004, Third Watch (series) 2004–05, The Exonerated 2005, Empire Falls 2005, Mayday 2005, The Book of Daniel (series) 2006. *Address:* Framework Entertainment, 9057 Nemo Street, Suite C, West Hollywood, CA 90069; c/o ICM, 8942 Wilshire Boulevard, Beverly Hills, CA 90211, USA.

QUINN, Aidy; Irish singer; b. Co. Tyrone; s. of Tom Quinn and Philomena Quinn; ed St Patrick's Coll., Dungannon; country music singer; Irish World Award for Most Promising New Act 2006, Irish Entertainment Award for Best New Artist 2007. *Recordings:* albums: Born and Bred on Country Music (Irish Country Music Award for Best New Album) 2006. *Address:* Purple Heather Promotions, 8 Forthill Road, Enniskillen, Co. Fermanagh BT74 6AW, Northern Ireland (office); Millbrook House, Galbally, Co. Tyrone, BT70 2NR, Northern Ireland (home). *Telephone:* (28) 6632-3238 (office); (28) 8775-8526 (home). *Fax:* (28) 6632-3225 (office). *E-mail:* erneproms@btinternet.com (office). *Website:* www.aidyquinn.com.

QUINN, Andrea, BA, ARAM; British conductor and music director; *Music Director, Norrlands Opera and Symphony Orchestra;* b. 22 Dec. 1964; m. Roderick Champ 1991; one s. two d.; ed Royal Acad. of Music, London, Nottingham Univ.; Bartók Int. Seminar, Hungary; Music Dir London Philharmonic Youth Orchestra 1994–97, Royal Ballet 1998–2001; Music Dir New York City Ballet 2001–06; Music Dir Norrlands Opera and Symphony Orchestra, Umea, Sweden 2006–; has conducted London Symphony Orchestra, London Philharmonic, Philharmonia, Royal Philharmonic, Hallé, Scottish Chamber, Northern Sinfonia, London Mozart Players and other leading orchestras in UK, Australia, Hong Kong, Sweden, Norway, Italy, Singapore; operas and music theatre pieces conducted include Misper (Glyndebourne), Four Saints in Three Acts (ENO), Harrison Birtwistle's Pulse Shadows (UK tour), Royal Opera House debut conducting Royal Ballet's Anastasia and on tour Cinderella in Turin and Frankfurt and Swan Lake in Japan, China and N America; Fellow, Trinity Coll. of Music 2000. *Dance:* conducted world premiere of Saint-Saens's Carnival of the Animals (choreography Christopher Wheeldon) 2003, Double Feature (Susan Stroman) 2004. *Leisure interests:* art galleries, literature, horse riding, Italian. *Address:* c/o Nicholas Curry, Clarion/Seven Muses, 47 Whitehall Park, London N19 3TW, England (office); Urishay Barn, Michaelschurch Escley, Herefordshire HR2 0LU, England (home). *Telephone:* (20) 7272-4413 (office). *Fax:* (20) 7281-9687 (office). *E-mail:* admin@c7m.co.uk (office); quinnchamp@gmail.com (office). *Website:* www.norrlandsoperan.se.

QUINN, Brian, CBE, MA (Econ), PhD; British banker, economist and consultant; *Chairman, Celtic Football Club;* b. 18 Nov. 1936, Glasgow; s. of Thomas Quinn and Margaret Cairns; m. Mary Bradley 1961; two s. one d.; ed Glasgow, Manchester and Cornell Univs; economist, African Dept IMF 1964–70; Rep. IMF, Sierra Leone 1966–68; joined Bank of England 1970, Econ. Div. 1970–74, Chief Cashier's Dept 1974–77, Head Information Div. 1977–82, Asst Dir 1982–88, Head of Banking Supervision 1986–88, Exec. Dir 1988–96, Acting

Deputy Gov. 1995; Chair. Nomura Bank Int. PLC 1996–99; Vice-Chair. Celtic PLC 1996–2000, Chair. 2000–; Dir (non-exec.) Bankgesellschaft Berlin UK PLC 1996–2001, Britannic Asset Man. 1998–, Nomura Holdings Europe 1998–99; Man. Dir Brian Quinn Consultancy 1997–; Chair. Financial Markets Group, LSE 1996–2001; Consultant World Bank 1997–; Fellow, Inst. of Bankers in Scotland; Hon. MA. *Publications:* ontribs to books and journals. *Leisure interests:* fishing, golf, cycling, soccer. *Address:* Celtic Park, Kerrydale Street, Parkhead, Glasgow, G40 3RE, Scotland (office); 14 Homewood Road, St Albans, Herts., AL1 4BH, England (home). *Telephone:* (1727) 853900. *Fax:* (1727) 866646. *E-mail:* bqconns@aol.com. *Website:* www.celticfc.co.uk.

QUINN, Patrick Joseph, BS, JD; American state official; *Governor of Illinois;* b. 16 Dec. 1948, Hinsdale, Ill.; two s.; ed Georgetown Univ., Northwestern Univ. School of Law; Commr Cook Co. Bd of (Property) Tax Appeals 1982–86; Revenue Dir City of Chicago 1986; Treas. State of Illinois 1991–95; Lt Gov. of Illinois 2003–09, Gov. 2009–; Chair. Blackout Solutions Task Force, Mississippi River Coordinating Council, Illinois Green Govts Coordinating Council, Illinois Biofuels Investment and Infrastructure Working Group, Broadband Deployment Council; Democrat. *Publication:* How to Appeal Your Property Taxes . . . Without a Lawyer. *Address:* Office of the Governor, 207 State House, Springfield, IL 62706, USA (office). *Telephone:* (217) 782-0244 (office). *Fax:* (312) 814-2121 (office). *Website:* www.illinois.gov/gov (office).

QUINN, Ruairi, BArch, RIBA; Irish politician, architect and town planner; *Labour Party Spokesperson on Enterprise, Trade and Employment;* b. 2 April 1946, Dublin; s. of Malachi Quinn and Julia Quinn; m. 1st Nicola Underwood 1969 (divorced), one s. one d.; m. 2nd Liz Allman 1990, one s.; ed Blackrock Coll. and Univ. Coll., Dublin, Athens Center of Ekistics, Greece; Athens Center of Ekistics, Greece 1970–71; Architects' Dept, Dublin Corpn 1971–73; Pnr, Burke-Kennedy Doyle and Pnr 1973–82; mem. Dublin Corpn 1974–77, 1981–82; mem. Seanad Éireann 1976–77, 1981–82; mem. Dáil Éireann 1977–81, 1982–; Minister of State, Dept of the Environment 1982–83; Minister for Labour and Minister for the Public Service 1983–87; Deputy Leader Irish Labour Party 1989, Leader 1997–2002; Treas. Party of European Socialists 2000–, also Vice-Pres.; Dir of Elections for Pres. Mary Robinson (q.v.); Labour Spokesperson on Finance and Econ. Affairs 1990, on European Affairs, on Enterprise, Trade and Employment 2006–; Minister for Enterprise and Employment 1993–94, for Finance 1994–97; mem. Royal Inst. of the Architects of Ireland. *Publication:* Straight Left: A Journey in Politics 2005. *Leisure interests:* athletics, reading, hill walking. *Address:* Dáil Éireann, Kildare Street, Dublin 2 (office); 23 Strand Road, Sandymount, Dublin 4, Ireland (home). *Telephone:* (1) 6183434 (office). *Fax:* (1) 6184153 (office). *E-mail:* ruairi.quinn@oireachtas.ie (office). *Website:* www.ruairiquinn.ie (office).

QUIÑONES AMEZQUITA, Mario Rafael; Guatemalan lawyer and diplomatist; b. 4 June 1933, Quezaltenango; s. of the late Hector Quiñones and of Elisa de Quiñones; m. Yolanda de Quiñones 1963; two s. two d.; ed Univ. of San Carlos and Univ. of Rio Grande do Sul, Brazil; lawyer and notary with law firm of Viteri, Falla, Quiñones, Umaña, Orellana y Cáceres 1959–; Prof. of Law, Rafael Landívar Univ. 1962–, Dean Dept of Legal and Social Sciences 1974–82; Vice-Pres. of Landívar Univ. 1978–82, Pres. March–Oct. 1982; Perm. Rep. to UN 1982–84; Minister of Foreign Affairs 1986–87; Vice-Pres. N and Cen. American Region, Union of Latin Notaries 1978; Pres. Asscn of Lawyers and Notaries of Guatemala 1977; mem. Guatemalan Del. UN Comm. on Int. Trade Law 1974; Dr hc (Univ. Rafael Landivar) 1998; Orden de Malta (Guatemala) and decorations from govts of Spain, Peru, Germany, Argentina and Mexico. *Leisure interests:* reading, music. *Address:* 6A Calle 5-47, Zona 9 – 3er. Nivel, Guatemala City 01009 (office); 3A Ave. 13-81, Zona 14, Guatemala City, 01014 Guatemala. *Telephone:* (2) 331-1721 (office); (2) 368-1449 (home). *Fax:* (2) 337-0186 (home).

QUIÑÓNEZ, Alfonso, MA; Guatemalan lawyer, diplomatist and international organization executive; *Executive Secretary for Integral Development and Director General, Inter-American Agency for Co-operation and Development;* ed Francisco Marroquín Univ. of Guatemala, Georgetown Univ., Washington, DC, Univ. of Maryland, Inter-American Defense Coll., Washington, DC; Professor, Schools of Law and International Relations, Francisco Marroquín Univ. 2001–02; mem. Guatemalan Foreign Service for ten years, held positions of Counsellor in Spain, Minister Counsellor in USA, Amb. and Perm. Rep. to OAS 1998–2000; Exec. Dir Alvaro Arzú Foundation for Peace, Guatemala and Advisor to Mayor of Guatemala City –2001; Dir Dept of Co-operation Policies, OAS 2001, later Dir Office of Policies and Programs for Devt, OAS Exec. Secr. for Integral Devt, later Chief of Staff to Asst Sec.-Gen., Acting Exec. Sec. for Integral Devt and Acting Dir-Gen. Inter-American Agency for Integral Devt 2004–05, Exec. Sec. for Integral Devt and Dir-Gen. Inter-American Agency for Co-operation and Devt 2005–. *Address:* Inter-American Agency for Co-operation and Development, 17th Street and Constitution Avenue, NW, Washington, DC 20006, USA (office). *Telephone:* (202) 458-3000 (office). *Fax:* (202) 458-6319 (office). *E-mail:* diad@oas.org (office). *Website:* www.oas.org (office).

QUIÑÓNEZ ABARCA, Anibal Enrique; Honduran diplomatist and international organization official; b. 7 Jan. 1950, Tegucigalpa; m.; four c.; ed Univ. Nacional Autónoma de Honduras, Univ. de El Salvador; entered Honduran Foreign Service 1973; First Sec. in charge of Consular Affairs, Embassy in Argentina 1973–77, Embassy in Uruguay (concurrent with Paraguay) 1977–78; Amb. to Uruguay and Paraguay 1981–83, to Japan (concurrently to Singapore, Thailand, Brunei, Korea and the Philippines) 1983–85, to Japan 1985–94; Dir-Gen. Foreign Politics, Secr. of External Relations 1996–98; Consul to Greece 1999–2002; Under-Sec. of State, Office of External Relations 2002–04; Sec.-Gen. System of Cen. American Integration (SICA) 2005–08; Great Cross of Diplomatic Merit (Repub. of Korea), Order of the Rising Sun

(Japan), Gran Cruz Placa de Oro de la Orden de Mayo al Mérito (Argentina), Order of the Shining Star (Taiwan), Order of Civil Merit (Spain), Order of Merit (Chile), Order of Morazán (Honduras); Hon. Diploma, Honduran Coll. of Advocates. *Address:* c/o Sistema de la Integración Centroamericana y su Secretaría General, Blv. Orden de Malta No. 470, Urb. Santa Elena, Antigua Cuscatlán, El Salvador, CA, Argentina (office).

QUINTANILLA SCHMIDT, Carlos, BSc; Salvadorean lawyer and politician; b. 5 Aug. 1953, San Miguel; m. Alexandra Rodríguez; two s.; ed José Matías Delgado Univ., San Salvador, American Univ., Washington, DC, USA; Pnr, Guandique-Segovia-Quintanilla, San Salvador (law firm) 1981–; Prof. of Commercial Law, José Matías Delgado Univ. 1985–, Dean, School of Law 1986–92, Deputy Dean of Univ. 1992–; Legal Counsel to Alianza Republicana Nacionalista (ARENA) party 1988–97, mem. Exec. Body 1997–; Vice-Pres. of El Salvador 1999–2004; Vice-Pres. Canadian Chamber of Commerce of El Salvador; mem. Bd of Dirs Fundación Salvadoreña para el Desarrollo Económico y Social (think tank) 2005–. *Address:* Guandique-Segovia-Quintanilla, Pasaje Senda Florida Norte #124, Colonia Escalón, San Salvador, El Salvador (office). *Telephone:* 2245-3444 (office). *Fax:* 2298-6613 (office). *E-mail:* cquintanilla@gsqlaw.com (office). *Website:* www.gsqlaw.com (office).

QUINTON, Baron (Life Peer), cr. 1982, of Holywell in the City of Oxford and County of Oxfordshire; **Anthony Meredith Quinton,** FBA; British academic (retd); b. 25 March 1925, Gillingham, Kent; s. of the late Richard Frith Quinton and Gwenllyan Letitia Quinton; m. Marcelle Wegier 1952; one s. one d.; ed Stowe School, Christ Church, Oxford; served in RAF, Flying Officer and Navigator 1943–46; Fellow, All Souls Coll., Oxford 1949–55, New Coll., Oxford 1955–78 (Hon. Fellow 1998); Pres., Trinity Coll. Oxford 1978–87, Hon. Fellow 1989; Visiting Prof., Swarthmore Coll., Pa 1960, Stanford Univ., Calif. 1964, New School for Social Research, New York 1976–77, Brown Univ., RI 1994; Dawes Hicks Lecturer, British Acad. 1971; Gregynog Lecturer, Univ. of Wales Aberystwyth 1973; T. S. Eliot Lecturer, Univ. of Kent, Canterbury 1976; Robbins Lecturer, Univ. of Stirling 1988; R. M. Jones Lecturer, Queen's Univ., Belfast 1988; Tanner Lecturer, Univ. of Warsaw 1988; Pres., Aristotelian Soc. 1975–76, Soc. for Applied Philosophy 1988–91, Royal Inst. of Philosophy 1990–2004, Asscn of Ind. Libraries 1991–98, Friends of Wellcome Inst. 1992–98; Gov., Stowe School 1963–84, Chair. of Govs 1969–75; Fellow, Winchester Coll. 1970–85; Del., Oxford Univ. Press 1970–76; mem. Arts Council 1979–81; mem. Bd Eds Encyclopaedia Britannica 1985–97; mem. Peacock Cttee; Chair., British Library 1985–90, Kennedy Memorial Trust 1990–97. *Publications:* Political Philosophy (ed.) 1967, The Nature of Things 1973, Utilitarian Ethics 1973, trans. of K. Ajdukiewicz's Problems and Theories of Philosophy (with H. Skolimowski) 1973, The Politics of Imperfection 1978, Francis Bacon 1980, Thoughts and Thinkers 1982, Hume 1998, From Wodehouse to Wittgenstein 1998. *Leisure interests:* sedentary pursuits. *Address:* A-11 Albany, Piccadilly, London, W1J 0AL, England (home); 825 Fifth Avenue, New York, NY 10065, USA (home). *Telephone:* (20) 7287-8686 (home); (212) 838-0800. *Fax:* (20) 7287-9525 (home).

QUINTON, Sir John Grand, Kt, MA, FCIB; British banker; b. 21 Dec. 1929; s. of William Grand Quinton and Norah May Quinton (née Nunn); m. Jean Margaret Chastney 1954; one s. one d.; ed Norwich School, St John's Coll. Cambridge; Asst Gen. Man. Barclays Bank Ltd 1968, Local Dir Nottingham Dist Barclays Bank Ltd 1969–71, Regional Gen. Man. 1971–75, Gen. Man. Barclays Bank Ltd and Dir Barclays Bank UK Ltd 1975–84, Dir Barclays Bank PLC and Sr Gen. Man. 1982–84, Deputy Chair. Barclays Bank PLC 1985–87, Chair. 1987–92; Chair. (non-exec.) Wimpey 1993–95; Chair. Motability Finance Ltd 1978–84, Gov. Motability 1985–. (Hon. Treas. 1998–2003); Chair. Cttee of CEOs, Cttee of London Clearing Bankers 1982–83; Chair. Office of the Banking Ombudsman 1987–92, Cttee of London and Scottish Bankers 1989–91; Dir (non-exec.) Norwich and Peterborough Bldg Soc. 1993–99 (Deputy Chair. 1996–99); Treas. Inst. of Bankers 1980–86; mem. City Capital Markets Cttee 1981–86; mem. NE Thames Regional Health Authority 1974–87; mem. Accounting Standards Cttee 1982–85; Gov. Royal Shakespeare Theatre 1986–2000; Pres. Chartered Inst. of Bankers 1989–90; Chair. Botanic Gardens Conservation Int. 1988–99; Chair. Football Asscn Premier League 1992–99, Metropolitan Police Cttee 1995–2000; mem. Metropolitan Police Authority 2000–04; Trustee Royal Acad. 1987–93, Thrombosis Research Inst. 1993–2001. *Leisure interests:* gardening, music, golf. *Address:* Chenies Place, Chenies, Bucks., WD3 6EU, England (home). *Telephone:* (1923) 284002 (home). *Fax:* (1923) 285579 (home). *E-mail:* sirjquinton@tiscali.co.uk (home).

QUIRK, James Patrick, AO, PhD, DSc, FAA; Australian agricultural scientist and academic; *Professor Emeritus, Faculty of Natural and Agricultural Sciences, University of Western Australia;* b. 17 Dec. 1924, Sydney; s. of J. P. Quirk; m. Helen M. Sykes 1950; one s. one d.; ed Christian Brothers High School, Lewisham, St John's Coll., Univ. of Sydney and Univ. of London; Research Scientist, CSIRO Div. of Soils, Soil Physics Section 1947; CSIRO Sr Postgraduate Studentship, Physics Dept, Rothamsted Experimental Station, England 1950; Research Scientist, Sr Research Scientist, CSIRO 1952–56; Reader in Soil Science, Dept of Agricultural Chem., Waite Agricultural Research Inst., Univ. of Adelaide 1956–62; Carnegie Travelling Fellow, USA 1960; Foundation Prof. and Head, Dept of Soil Science and Plant Nutrition, Univ. of WA 1963–74, Emer. Prof. 1974–, Dir Inst. of Agric. 1971–74, Dir, Waite Agricultural Research Inst. and Prof. 1974–89, Emer. Prof. and Hon. Research Fellow, Univ. of WA 1990–; Prof. Fellow, Dept Applied Math., ANU 1990–96, Hon. Prof. Fellow 1996–; Commonwealth Visiting Prof., Oxford Univ. 1967; Fellow, Australian Acad. of Science (Sec. Biological Sciences 1990–94), Australian Inst. of Agricultural Science, Australian Acad. of Technological Sciences and Eng (mem. Council 1996–), American Soc. of Agronomy, Australian and NZ Asscn for the Advancement of Science; Hon.

mem. Int. Union of Soil Science 1998; Hon. DSc Agric. (Louvain, Belgium) 1978, (Melbourne) 1990, (Western Australia) 1991, (Sydney) 1997; Prescott Medal for Soil Science 1975, Medal of the Australian Inst. of Agricultural Science 1980, Farrer Memorial Medal 1982, Mueller Medal 1988, Brindley Lecturer (USA) 1992, Distinguished Service Award (Soil Science Soc. of America) 1996. *Publications:* about 200 scientific publs. *Leisure interests:* reading, tennis. *Address:* School of Earth and Geographical Sciences (South), University of Western Australia, 35 Stirling Highway-M087, Crawley 6009, Western Australia (office); 70 Archdeacon Street, Nedlands 6009, Western Australia, Australia (home). *Telephone:* (8) 6488-2503 (office); (8) 9386-5948 (home). *Fax:* (8) 9380-2504. *E-mail:* jquirk@agric.uwa.edu.au (office). *Website:* www.are.uwa.edu.au (office).

QUIRK, Baron (Life Peer), cr. 1994, of Bloomsbury in the London Borough of Camden; **(Charles) Randolph Quirk,** Kt, CBE, PhD, DLitt, LLD, FBA; British academic; b. 12 July 1920, Isle of Man; s. of the late Thomas and Amy Randolph Quirk; m. 1st Jean Williams 1946; two s.; m. 2nd Gabriele Stein 1984; ed Cronk y Voddy School, Douglas High School, Isle of Man, Univ. Coll., London; served in RAF 1940–45; Lecturer in English, Univ. Coll. London 1947–54; Commonwealth Fund Fellow, Yale Univ. and Univ. of Mich., USA 1951–52; Reader in English Language and Literature, Univ. of Durham 1954–58, Prof. of English Language 1958–60; Quain Prof. of English, Univ. Coll. London 1960–81; Dir, Univ. of London Summer School of English 1962–67; Survey of English Usage 1959–83; mem. Senate, Univ. of London 1970–85 (Chair. Academic Council 1972–75), Court 1972–85; Vice-Chancellor, Univ. of London 1981–85; Pres., Inst. of Linguists 1983–86, British Acad. 1985–89, Coll. of Speech Therapists 1987–91; Gov., British Inst. of Recorded Sound, English-Speaking Union; Chair., Cttee of Enquiry into Speech Therapy Services, British Council English Cttee 1976–80, Hornby Educational Trust 1979–93; mem. BBC Archives Cttee 1975–79, British Council 1983–91; Trustee, Wolfson Foundation 1987–; Lee Kwan Yew Fellow, Singapore 1985–86; Vice-Pres., Foundation of Science and Tech. 1986–90; mem. House of Lords Select Cttee on Science and Tech. 1999–2002; Fellow, King's Coll. London, Queen Mary Coll. London, Univ. Coll. London, Imperial Coll. London, Academia Europaea; Foreign Fellow, Royal Belgian Acad. Sciences 1975, Royal Swedish Acad. 1986, Finnish Acad. of Sciences 1992, American Acad. of Arts and Sciences 1995; Hon. Fellow, Coll. of Speech Therapists, Inst. of Linguists, Hon. Master, Gray's Inn Bench 1983; hon. degrees (Lund, Uppsala, Poznań, Nijmegen, Paris, Liège, Helsinki, Prague, Reading, Leicester, Salford, London, Newcastle, Bath, Durham, Essex, Open Univ., Glasgow, Bar-Ilan, Brunel, Bucharest, Sheffield, Richmond Coll., Aston, Copenhagen, Queen Margaret); Jubilee Medal, Inst. of Linguists 1973. *Publications:* The Concessive Relation in Old English Poetry 1954, Studies in Communication (with A. J. Ayer and others) 1955, An Old English Grammar (with C. L. Wrenn) 1955, Charles Dickens and Appropriate Language 1959, The Teaching of English (with A. H. Smith) 1959, The Study of the Mother-Tongue 1961, The Use of English (with supplements by A. C. Gimson and J. Warburg) 1962, Prosodic and Paralinguistic Features in English (with D. Crystal) 1964, A Common Language (with A. H. Marckwardt) 1964, Investigating Linguistic Acceptability (with J. Svartvik) 1966, Essays on the English Language–Medieval and Modern 1968, Elicitation Experiments in English (with S. Greenbaum) 1970, A Grammar of Contemporary English 1972 (with S. Greenbaum, G. Leech, J. Svartvik) 1972, The English Language and Images of Matter 1972, A University Grammar of English (with S. Greenbaum) 1973, The Linguist and the English Language 1974, Old English Literature: A Practical Introduction (with V. Adams, D. Davy) 1975, A Corpus of English Conversation 1980; contrib. to many others including Charles Dickens (ed. S. Wall) 1970, A New Companion to Shakespeare Studies 1971, The State of the Language (with J. Svartvik) 1980, Style and Communication in the English Language 1982, A Comprehensive Grammar of the English Language (with S. Greenbaum, G. Leech and J. Svartvik) 1985, Words at Work: Lectures on Textual Structure 1986, English in Use (with Gabriele Stein) 1990, A Student's Grammar of the English Language (with S. Greenbaum) 1990, Grammatical and Lexical Variance in English 1995; papers in linguistic and literary journals. *Leisure interest:* music. *Address:* University College London, Gower Street, London, WC1E 6BT, England (office). *Telephone:* (20) 7219-2226 (office). *Fax:* (20) 7219-5979 (office).

QUIROGA RAMÍREZ, Jorge Fernando, BEng, MBA; Bolivian engineer and politician; *Leader, Acción Democrática Nacionalista (ADN);* b. 5 May 1960, Cochabamba; m. Virginia Gillum 1989; four c.; ed La Salle Coll., Santa Cruz de la Sierra, Texas A&M Univ. and St Edward's Univ., Austin, Tex.; with IBM, Austin, Tex. 1981–88; returned to Bolivia 1988; Econometrician, Mintec 1988; Vice-Pres. Banco Mercantil de Bolivia 1988; mem. Acción Democrática Nacionalista (ADN) 1988–, apptd Deputy Leader 1995, currently Leader; Under-Sec. for Public Investment and Int. Co-operation, Ministry of Planning 1989–90; Minister of Finance 1990–93; Gov. Cooperación Financiera de Inversiones –1993; Dir Andean Devt Corpn –1993; Nat. Sec. Política Social –1993; led electoral campaign of ADN 1993 then worked in pvt. sector; Vice-Pres. of Bolivia 1997–2001, Acting Pres. July–Aug. 2001, Pres. of Bolivia 2001–02; fmr Gov. IBRD and IMF. *Leisure interests:* football, basketball, mountain-climbing. *Address:* Acción Democrática Nacionalista (ADN), La Paz, Bolivia (office). *Website:* www.bolivian.com/adn.

QURAISHI, Abdul Aziz Bin Said Al, MBA, FIBA; Saudi Arabian government official; b. 1930, Hail; s. of Zaid al-Quraishi and Sheikhah Abdul Aziz; m. Amal Abdul Aziz al-Turki 1965; one s. two d.; ed Univ. of Southern California, USA; Gen. Man. State Railways 1961–68; Pres. Gen. Personnel Bureau 1968–74; Minister of State 1971–74; Gov. Saudi Arabian Monetary Agency 1974–83; fmr Gov. for Saudi Arabia, IMF, Arab Monetary Fund; fmr Alt. Gov. for Saudi Arabia, Islamic Devt Bank; fmr mem. Bd of Dirs Supreme Council for Petroleum and Mineral Affairs, Gen. Petroleum and Mineral Org., Public Investment Fund, Pension Fund, Man. Dir Ali Zaid Al-Quraishi & Bros, Riyadh 1983–; fmr Chair. Nat. Saudi Shipping Co., Riyadh 1983; Vice-Chair. Saudi Int. Bank, London 1983–; mem. Int. Advisory Bd, Security Pacific Nat. Bank of LA 1983–; King Abdul Aziz Medal (Second Class), Order of Brilliant Star with Grand Cordon (Taiwan), Order of Diplomatic Merit, Gwan Ghwa Medal (Repub. of Korea), King Leopold Medal (Commdr Class), Belgium, Emperor of Japan Award, Order of Sacred Treasure (First Class) 1980. *Address:* Malaz, Riyadh (office); PO Box 1848, Riyadh 11441, Saudi Arabia (home).

QURASHI, Mazhar Mahmood, PhD, DSc; Pakistani science administrator and researcher; b. 8 Oct. 1925, Gujranwala; s. of Feroz-ud-din Qurashi; m.; four s. five d.; ed Punjab Univ., Manchester Univ.; fmr Sec.-Gen. Pakistan Acad. of Sciences; fmr Dir-Gen. PCSIR Labs, Karachi; fmr Dir Nat. Science Council of Pakistan; fmr Prof. of Physics, Quaid-i-Azam Univ., Islamabad; Sec. Pakistan Asscn for History and Philosophy of Science 1986–; fmr mem. Pakistan Council of Scientific and Industrial Research; Fellow Islamic Acad. of Sciences, Pakistan Acad. of Sciences, Inst. of Physics, London; Open Gold Medal, Pakistan Acad. of sciences 1972, Pakistani Pres. Sitara-i-Imtiaz Award 1991. *Publications:* 10 monographs; numerous research papers in scientific journals. *Leisure interest:* theoretical and experimental study of relation between science and Islam. *Address:* c/o Pakistan Academy of Sciences, Constitution Avenue, G-5, Islamabad (office); House 34, Street 32, F-7/1, Islamabad, Pakistan (home). *Telephone:* (51) 9207789 (office); (51) 2877644 (home). *Fax:* (51) 9206770 (office). *E-mail:* pasisb@yahoo.com (office).

QURAY, Ahmad, (Abu Ala); Palestinian diplomatist and politician; b. 1937, Abu Dis; joined Fatah (largest political group within PLO) 1968, currently mem. Revolutionary Council Cen. Cttee; fmr Minister of Economy and Trade and Minister of Industry, Palestinian Authority; Chief Palestinian Negotiator, Oslo Agreement 1993 and all subsequent Israeli–Palestinian talks including Taba, Cairo, Wye River, and talks in 2007; Deputy and Speaker Palestinian Legis. Council 1996–2003; Prime Minister, Palestinian Authority (PA) 2003–05 (resgnd), Head Nat. Security Council 2004–05; mem. Palestinian Nat. Council; mem. Bd Palestinian Econ. Policy Research Inst., Peres Center for Peace; mem. Bd of Advisers Gleitsman Foundation; Norwegian Royal Order of Merit 1994, Seeds of Peace Foundation Award 1996, Gleitsman Foundation Int. Activist Award 1999. *Publications include:* Hanging Peace; numerous economic essays. *Address:* c/o Palestinian Authority, Jericho Area, West Bank, Palestinian Autonomous Areas. *E-mail:* info@gov.ps. *Website:* www.pna.net.

QURESHI, Moeen, MA, PhD; Pakistani economist, international official and business executive; *Chairman and Managing Partner, EMP Global LLC;* b. 26 June 1930, Lahore; s. of Mohyeddin Ahmad Qureshi and Khursheed Jabin; m. Lilo Elizabeth Richter 1958; two s. two d.; ed Islamia Coll. and Govt Coll., Univ. of Punjab and Indiana Univ., USA; social science consultant, Ford Foundation, Pakistan 1953; Hon. Lecturer, Univ. of Karachi 1953–54; Asst Chief, Planning Comm., Govt of Pakistan 1954–56, Deputy Chief 1956–58; Economist, IMF 1958–61, Div. Chief 1961–65, Adviser Africa Dept 1965–66, Resident Rep. Ghana 1966–68, Sr Adviser 1968–70; Econ. Adviser IFC 1970–74, Vice-Pres. 1974–77, Exec. Vice-Pres. 1977–81; Vice-Pres. Finance, World Bank 1979–80, Sr Vice-Pres. Finance 1980–87, Sr Vice-Pres. Operations 1987–91; Prime Minister of Pakistan July–Oct. 1993; currently Chair. and Man. Pnr EMP Global LLC, Washington DC; mem. Bd Global Trade and Political Risk Insurance Co., American Int. Group; mem. Advisory Bd, American International Group (AIG); mem. Bd Educ. for Employment Foundation; Hilal-i-Imtiaz 1992. *Publications:* various articles in econ. journals. *Leisure interests:* tennis, collecting antiques. *Address:* EMP Global LLC, 2020 K Street NW, Suite 400, Washington, DC 20006, USA (office). *Telephone:* (202) 331-9051 (office). *Fax:* (202) 331-9250 (office). *E-mail:* qureshim@empglobal.net (office). *Website:* www.empglobal.net (office).

QURESHI, Makhdoom Shah Mehmu, BA, MA; Pakistani politician; *Minister of Foreign Affairs, with additional charge of Petroleum and Natural Resources;* b. 22 June 1966, Murree; ed Aitchison Coll., Lahore, Forman Christian Coll., Lahore, Corpus Christi Coll., Cambridge, UK; grew up in Multan; returned to Pakistan following law studies in UK 1983; elected to Prov. Ass. 1985; contested and won local, prov. and nat. elections from his home constituency in Multan; has served as Minister for Planning and Devt Punjab, Minister of Finance, Punjab, and Fed. Minister for Parl. Affairs in Govt of Benazir Bhutto; also served as Chair. Dist Council for Multan and first Dist Nazim under Musharraf admin; represented Pakistan People's Party (PPP) Punjab as their prime ministerial cand. 2002; sr mem. PPP and Pres. PPP Punjab; Minister of Foreign Affairs, with additional charge of Petroleum and Natural Resources 2008–. *Address:* Ministry of Foreign Affairs, Constitution Avenue, Islamabad, Pakistan (office). *Telephone:* (51) 9210335 (office). *Fax:* (51) 9207600 (office). *E-mail:* sadiq@mofa.gov.pk (office). *Website:* www .mofa.gov.pk (office).

R

RA, Eung Chan; South Korean banking executive; *Chairman, Shinhan Financial Group Co. Ltd;* b. 25 Nov. 1938; ed Seonrin Commercial High School; mem. Bd Dirs Cheil Investment Finance 1977–82; Exec. Vice-Pres. Shinhan Bank, Vice-Chair., Pres. and CEO –2001, Chair. Shinhan Financial Group Co. Ltd 2001–; Vice-Chair. Korea-Japan Economy Asscn; Chair. Cttee in Economy and Science Div. of Advisory Council on Democratic and Peaceful Unification. *Address:* Shinhan Financial Group Co. Ltd, 120 Taepyung-ro 2-ga, Jung-gu, Seoul 100-102, South Korea (office). *Telephone:* (822) 6360-3072 (office). *E-mail:* info@shinhangroup.com (office). *Website:* www.shinhangroup.com (office).

RA, Jong-yil, BA, MA, PhD; South Korean academic, university administrator and fmr diplomatist; *President, Woosuk University;* b. 5 Dec. 1940, Seoul; m. Hong Jae-ja; one s. three d.; ed Seoul Nat. Univ., Trinity Coll., Univ. of Cambridge, UK; held teaching posts at several univs including Kyunghee, Southern California, Mich. and Stanford, USA, Cambridge and Sussex, UK; Dir Nat. Intelligence Service 1998–99; fmr mem. Exec. Cttee and fmr Dir-Gen., Millennium Democratic Party (MDP); fmr Special Asst to Pres. for Foreign and Security Affairs; Amb. to UK 2001–03; Sr Adviser to Pres. for Nat. Security 2003; Amb. to Japan 2004–07; Pres. Woosuk Univ. 2007–. *Publications include:* Politics of Western Europe 1982, Cooperation and Conflict 1986, The New Right 1990, Perestroika and its Impacts 1991, Points of Departure 1992, Unfinished War 1994, Man and Politics 1995, In Preparation for the New Millennium 1999, Advantage of Hindsight 2001, Conflict and Resolution in the Korean Church 2002. *Leisure interests:* playing tennis. *Address:* Office of the President, Woosuk University, 490 Hujeong-ri, Samrye-eup, Wanju-kun, Jeollabuk-do, 565-701, Republic of Korea (office). *Telephone:* (63) 290-1003 (office). *Fax:* (63) 290-1004 (office). *Website:* www.woosuk.ac.kr (office).

RÄÄTS, Jaan; Estonian composer and teacher; *Professor Emeritus of Composition, Estonian Academy of Music;* b. 15 Oct. 1932, Tartu; s. of Peeter Rääts and Linda Rääts; m. 1st Marianne Rääts 1958; m. 2nd Ebba Rääts 1983; three c.; ed Tartu Music School with Aleksandra Sarv, Tallinn Conservatory with Mart Saar, Heino Eller; mem. CPSU 1964–90; recording engineer, Estonian Radio 1955–66, Chief Dir Music Programmes, Estonian TV 1966–74; Teacher of composition, Tallinn Conservatory (later Estonian Acad. of Music) 1968–70, 1974–, Prof. 1990–2003, Prof. Emer. 2003–; initiated Estonian Music Days 1979; Vice-Chair. Estonian Composers' Union 1964–74, Chair. 1974–93; People's Artist of the Estonian SSR 1977, 3rd Class Order of the White Star 2002. *Compositions include:* Symphony No. 1 1957, Symphony No. 2 1958, Symphony No. 3 1959, Symphony No. 4 Cosmic 1959, Concerto for chamber orchestra No. 1 1961, Violin Concerto No. 1 1963, Symphony No. 5 1966, Symphony No. 6 1967, Piano Concerto No. 1 1968, 24 Preludes 1968, Toccata 1970, Symphony No. 7 1973, 24 Estonian Preludes 1977, Violin Concerto No. 2 1979, 24 Marginalia 1979, 24 Marginalia for two pianos 1982, Piano Concerto No. 2 1983, Symphony No. 8 1985, Concerto for two pianos and symphony orchestra 1986, Concerto for chamber orchestra No. 2 1987, Piano Concerto No. 3 1990, Concerto for guitar and orchestra 1992, Concerto for trumpet and piano 1994, Concerto for violin and chamber orchestra 1995, Violin Concerto No. 3 1995, Five Sketches for Requiem for symphony orchestra 1999, Concerto for flute, guitar and symphony orchestra 2001, Symphony No. 9, Symphony No. 10, 10 piano sonatas, seven piano trios –2004, six string quartets. *Film scores:* Roosa kübar 1963, Null kolm 1965, Tütarlaps mustas 1966, Supernova 1966, Viini postmark 1967, Gladiaator 1969, Tuulevaikus 1971, Väike reekviem suupillile 1972, Ohtlikud mängud 1974, Aeg elada, aeg armastada 1976, Pihlakaväravad 1982. *Leisure interests:* technology, science. *Address:* c/o Estonian Composers' Union, A. Lauteri Street 7c, 10145 Tallinn, Estonia. *Telephone:* 646-6536 (office); 645-4395 (office); 520-3339 (home); 648-5744 (home). *E-mail:* heliloojatelut@mail.ee (office); emie@emie.ee; ebba@hot.ee (home). *Website:* www.zzz.ee/edition49 (office).

RABAN, Jonathan, BA, FRSL; British author and critic; b. 14 June 1942, Fakenham, Norfolk; s. of Rev. Peter J. C. P. Raban and Monica Sandison; m. 1st Bridget Johnson (divorced 1970s); m. 2nd Caroline Cuthbert 1985 (divorced 1992); m. 3rd Jean Cara Lenihan 1992 (divorced 1997); one d.; ed King's School, Worcester, Peter Symonds School, Winchester, Brockenhurst Grammar and Univ. of Hull; Asst Lecturer, Univ. Coll. of Wales, Aberystwyth 1965–67; Lecturer in English and American Literature, Univ. of E Anglia 1967–69; professional writer 1969–; emigrated to USA 1990; Hon. DLitt (Univ. of Hull); Pacific Northwest Booksellers Asscn Award, Murray Morgan Prize, Governor's Award of the State of Washington. *Publications:* The Technique of Modern Fiction 1969, Mark Twain: Huckleberry Finn 1969, The Society of the Poem 1971, Soft City 1973, Robert Lowell's Poems (ed.) 1974, Arabia Through the Looking Glass 1979, Old Glory (RSL Heinemann Award and Thomas Cook Award 1982) 1981, Foreign Land (novel) 1985, Coasting 1986, For Love and Money 1987, God, Man & Mrs Thatcher 1989, Hunting Mister Heartbreak (Thomas Cook Award 1991) 1990, The Oxford Book of the Sea (ed.) 1992, Bad Land: An American Romance (Nat. Book Critics Circle Award and PEN/West Creative Nonfiction Award 1997) 1996, Passage to Juneau 1999, Waxwings (novel) 2003, My Holy War: Dispatches from the Home Front 2005, Surveillance (novel) 2006; contribs to Harper's, Esquire, New Republic, Atlantic Monthly, New York Review of Books, London Review of Books, Outside, Granta, New York Times Book Review, Vogue, The Guardian, Independent, Financial Times, Wall Street Journal. *Leisure interest:* sailing. *Address:* Aitken Alexander Associates Ltd, 18–21 Cavaye Place, London, SW10 9PT, England (office). *Telephone:* (20) 7373-8672 (office). *Fax:* (20) 7373-6002 (office). *E-mail:* reception@aitkenalexander.co.uk (office). *Website:* www.aitkenalexander.co.uk (office).

RABASSA, Gregory, PhD; American academic and translator; *Distinguished Professor of Romance Languages and Comparative Literature, Queens College/CUNY;* b. 9 March 1922, Yonkers, NY; s. of Miguel Rabassa and Clara Macfarland; m. 1st Roney Edelstein 1957 (divorced 1966); one d.; m. 2nd Clementine Christos 1966; one d.; ed Dartmouth Coll. and Columbia Univ.; mil. service 1942–45; Instructor in Spanish, Columbia Univ. 1947–52, Assoc. Instructor 1952–58, Asst Prof. 1958–63, Assoc. Prof. of Spanish and Portuguese 1963–68; Prof. of Romance Languages, Queens Coll., Flushing, NY 1968–86, Distinguished Prof. 1986–; Assoc. Ed. Odyssey Review 1961–64; mem. Renaissance Soc. of America, PEN Club and other professional asscns; Fulbright-Hays Fellow, Brazil 1965–66; Guggenheim Fellow 1988–89; Croce al Merito di Guerra (Italy), Order of San Carlos (Colombia), Gabriela Mistral Medal (Chile) 1996; Dr hc (Dartmouth Coll.) 1982; Nat. Book Award for trans. 1967, New York Gov.'s Arts Award 1985, Wheatland Translation Prize 1988, Literature Award, American Acad. and Inst. of Arts and Letters 1989, Sandrof Award (Nat. Book Critics Circle) 1993, New York Public Library Literary Lion Award 1993, Gregory Kolovakos Award, PEN 2001, John Steinbeck Award, Southhampton Coll. 2002. *Publications:* O Negro na Ficção Brasileira 1965; A Cloudy Day in Gray Minor (poetry) 1995, If This Be Treason: Translation and its Dyscontents 2005. *Leisure interests:* hiking, birding, jazz. *Address:* Department of Hispanic Languages and Literature, Kiely 243, Queens College/CUNY, Flushing, NY 11367 (office); 140 East 72nd Street, New York, NY 10021, USA (home). *Telephone:* (718) 997-5660 (office); (212) 439-6636 (home). *Fax:* (718) 997-5669 (office). *E-mail:* gregory_rabassa@qc.edu (office). *Website:* qcpages.qc.edu/HLL (office).

RABBANI, Burhanuddin; Afghan politician and academic; *Leader, Jamiat-i-Islami;* b. 1940, Faizabad, Badakhshan Prov.; ed Kabul Univ., Al Azhar Univ., Cairo; fmr Lecturer in Islamic Law, Kabul Univ.; Pres. United Nat. Islamic Front for the Salvation of Afghanistan (UNIFSA) (also known as Northern Alliance); leader Jamiat-i Islami (Islamic Soc.) 1971–; left Afghanistan 1974; made armed raids against govt of Mohammed Daoud from base in Pakistan; returned to Afghanistan 1992; elected Pres. of Afghanistan by Mujahidin Exec. Council 1992; forced to step down when Taliban occupied Kabul 1996; continued to be recognized as Pres. of Islamic State of Afghanistan by UN –2001; currently Leader Jamiat-i Islami party. *Address:* Jamiat-i-Islami, Karte Parwan, Phase 2, Badaam Bagh, Afghanistan (office). *Telephone:* (70) 278950.

RABEE, Hayder K. Gafar, BA; Iraqi teacher of calligraphy; b. 22 Feb. 1962, Najaf; m. Ahalam A. al-Zahawi 1986; two s. one d.; ed Inst. of Fine Arts; calligrapher, Baghdad TV 1982–88; worked as designer, newspapers and magazines 1989–91; teacher, Inst. of Fine Arts, Baghdad 1992–, Head, Calligraphy Dept (evening classes) 1995–; teacher of Arabic Calligraphy, Jordanian Calligraphers' Soc. 1998; Gen. Sec. Iraqi Calligraphers' Soc. 1998–99; mem. Iraqi Plastic Arts Soc. 1996–2002, Iraqi Union of Artists, Iraqi Soc. for Calligraphy Jordanian Calligraphers' Soc., Egyptian Calligraphers' Soc.; State Trophy for Plastic Arts and Calligraphy 1989, 1999, Gold Medal, 2nd World Festival 1992, Third World Festival 1993, Gold Medal for Creativity, Dar Es-Salaam 1st Nat. Festival 1993, Appreciation Prize, 4th Baghdad Nat. Festival 1998, Appreciation Prize in 5th Int. Competition for Calligraphy, Turkey 2001, a main prizewinner, Int. Meeting for Calligraphy of the Islam World, Tehran 2002. *Publication:* Proposed Alphabetic Study for Arabic Calligraphy in Printing 1989. *Leisure interest:* chess. *Address:* al-Waziria, Sec. 301, St. 13 Ho. 50, Baghdad (home); Department of Calligraphy, Institute of Fine Arts, al-Mansur, Baghdad, Iraq (office).

RABEMANANJARA, Gen. Charles; Malagasy politician; *Prime Minister;* b. June 1947, Antananarivo; fmr top policemen, then Head of Gen. Armoured Corps; Dir Presidential Security Cabinet 2004–05; Minister of the Interior and Admin. Reform 2005–09, Prime Minister 2007–. *Address:* Office of the Prime Minister, BP 248, Mahazoarivo, 101 Antananarivo, Madagascar (office). *Telephone:* (20) 2264498 (office). *Fax:* (20) 2233116 (office). *E-mail:* dircom@primature.gov.mg (office). *Website:* www.primature.gov.mg (office).

RABIN, Oskar Yakovlevich; Russian painter; b. 1928, Moscow; m. Valentina Kropovnitskaya; one s.; student of artist and teacher Yevgeny Kropovnitsky; worked in Riga 1946–48; thereafter student of Surikov Art Inst., Moscow; later expelled for unorthodox views; worked until 1958 as loader on railways and on construction sites, painting clandestinely; employed in arts and design centre 1958–67; f. Leonozovo group in Moscow; exhibited in 'Festival of Youth' Exhbn, Moscow 1957; forced to emigrate 1977; now lives in Paris. *Publication:* Memoirs: Three Lives 1986.

RABINOVICH, Itamar, PhD; Israeli university administrator, historian, academic and fmr diplomatist; *Senior Research Fellow, Moshe Dayan Center for Middle Eastern and African Studies, Tel-Aviv University;* b. 1942, Jerusalem; ed UCLA; joined faculty Tel-Aviv Univ. 1971, Dir Moshe Dayan Center for Middle Eastern and African Studies 1980–88, now Sr Research Fellow and Ettinger Prof. of Contemporary Middle Eastern History, Dean of Humanities, Tel-Aviv Univ. 1989–90, Rector 1990–92, Pres. 1999–2007; Israel's Chief Negotiator with Syria and Amb. to USA 1992–96; A.D. White Prof. at Large, Cornell Univ. 1997–2002; fmr Visiting Prof. Univ. of Pa, Univ. of Toronto, Woodrow Wilson Int. Center for Scholars, Inst. of Advanced Studies, Princeton; mem. Trilateral Comm.; Chair. Advisory Council, Wexner Israel Program; Chair. Heseg Project. *Publications:* Syria Under the Ba'th, The War for Lebanon, The Road Not Taken, Early Arab–Israeli Negotiations, The Brink of Peace: Israel and Syria, Waging Peace: Israel and the Arabs at the End of the Century; numerous articles, essays and chapters in books and journals. *Address:* Moshe Dayan Center for Middle Eastern and African Studies, Tel-Aviv University, Ramat Aviv, Tel-Aviv 69978, Israel (office). *Telephone:* (3) 6409646 (office). *Fax:* (3) 6415802 (office). *E-mail:* efratal@post .tau.ac.il (office). *Website:* www.dayan.org (office).

RABINOVITCH, B(enton) Seymour, PhD, FRS; Canadian chemist and academic; *Professor Emeritus of Chemistry, University of Washington, Seattle;* b. 19 Feb. 1919, Montreal, PQ; s. of Samuel Rabinovitch and Rachel Shachter; m. 1st Marilyn Werby 1949 (deceased); m. 2nd Flora Reitman 1980; two s. two d. from 1st m.; ed McGill Univ.; Royal Soc. of Canada Research Fellow 1946–47; Milton Research Fellow, Harvard Univ. 1947–48; Asst Prof., Univ. of Washington, Seattle 1948–53, Assoc. Prof. 1953–57, Prof., Dept of Chem. 1957–85, Prof. Emer. 1985–; Fellow, American Acad. of Arts and Sciences, American Physics Soc.; mem. Silver Soc.; Guggenheim Fellowship 1961; Hon. Liveryman, Worshipful Co. of Goldsmiths, London 2000; Hon. DSc (Technion Univ., Haifa) 1991; Peter Debye Award, Michael Polyani Medal, Sigma Xi Award for Outstanding Research. *Publications:* Textbook of Physical Chemistry 1964, Antique Silver Servers 1991, Contemporary Silver 2000, Contemporary Silver, Part II 2005; Ed. Annual Reviews of Physical Chemistry 1975–85; 220 research papers. *Leisure interest:* silversmithing, decorative silver. *Address:* Department of Chemistry, Box 351700, University of Washington, Seattle, WA 98195 (office); 12530 42nd Avenue, NE, Seattle, WA 98125, USA (home).

RABINOVITCH, Robert, BComm MA, PhD; Canadian broadcasting executive; *Chairman, Board of Governors, McGill University;* b. 1943, Montréal; m.; one s. one d.; ed McGill Univ., Univ. of Pennsylvania; held various positions with Fed. Govt, including Deputy Minister of Communications 1982–85, Under-Sec. of State 1985–86, also held several positions within Privy Council Office, including Deputy Sec. to the Cabinet and Sr Asst Sec. to the Cabinet for Priorities and Planning; Exec. Vice-Pres. and COO Claridge Inc. 1987–99; Pres. and CEO CBC/Radio Canada 1999–2007, Acting Chair. March–Sept. 2005, Sept. 2006; fmr mem. Bd of Dirs Cineplex Odeon, NetStar Communications; Special Advisor, MaxLink Communications, Loews Cineplex; fmr mem. Govt of Canada Direct-to-Home Satellite Broadcasting Policy Review Panel; fmr mem. Canadian Exec. Service Org., CRB Foundation, Samuel and Saidye Bronfman Family Foundation, Canadian Film Centre; Chair. Exec. Cttee Canadian Jewish Congress (Québec) –1999; mem. Bd of Govs McGill Univ. 1997–, Chair. 1999–; mem. Advisory Bd Sauvé Scholars Foundation, McGill Univ., Nunavut Trust Investment Advisory Cttee; Hon. LLD (York Univ.) 2003. *Address:* c/o Board of Governors, McGill University, Room 313, James Administration Building, 845 Sherbrooke Street West, Montréal, PQ H3A 2T5, Canada. *Telephone:* (514) 398-3215. *Fax:* (514) 398-4758. *E-mail:* jennifer.oneil@mcgill.ca. *Website:* www.mcgill.ca/boardofgovernors.

RABINOWITZ, Cay Sophie, MA, PhD; American curator, editor and arts executive; *Artistic Director, Art Basel;* b. 1965, Norfolk, Va; d. of Jeanne and Ralph Rabinowitz; m. Christian Rattemeyer; ed Tufts Univ., Reed Coll., Univ. of Calif., Berkeley, Emory Univ.; DAAD Fellow, Hochschule der Künste, Berlin 1995–96; curator or co-curator for numerous exhbns including Lauretta Rix's Paint and Graphic, Atlanta 1996, Splendid Isolation, Berlin 1997, Patterns of Intention, OSMOS, Berlin 1998, Thinking Loud/Cutting Through, Space 1181, Atlanta 1999, Tonal Bliss, Marietta/Cobb Museum of Art, Atlanta 2001, Scarlett Hooft-Graafland and Jeff Feld, Mary Goldman Gallery, Los Angeles 2003, Erik Schmidt, Henry Urbach Gallery, New York 2004, APEX Summer show, New York 2004; curatorial asst, Venice Biennial 1999; Sr Ed., USA, Parkett Publishers 1999–2008; faculty mem. Parson School of Fine Art, New York 1999–; fmr faculty mem. Emory Univ., Calif. Inst. of the Arts; Artistic Dir, Art Basel and Art Basel Miami Beach 2008–; Contributing Ed. Art Papers Magazine 1998. *Publications:* Escape 1994, Thomas Schutte (jtly) 2001, Julie Mehretu: Black City (jtly) 2007, Fiona Banner's work as work-in-progress 2007; contribs: Financial Times, Artforum, Grand Street, Afterall, Boiler, Self Service; other: numerous exhbn catalogues. *Address:* Art Basel, c/o MCH Swiss Exhibition (Basel) Ltd, 4005 Basel, Switzerland (office). *Telephone:* 582062703 (office). *Fax:* 582063130 (office). *E-mail:* info@artbasel.com (office). *Website:* www.artbasel.com (office).

RABINOWITZ, Harry, (Henry Oliver, Andy Thurlow), MBE; British composer and conductor; b. 26 March 1916, Johannesburg, S Africa; s. of Israel Rabinowitz and Eva Rabinowitz (née Kirkel); m. 1st Lorna T. Anderson 1944 (divorced); one s. two d.; m. 2nd Mitzi Scott 2001; ed Athlone High School, Johannesburg, Univ. of the Witwatersrand and Guildhall School of Music, London; Conductor, BBC Radio 1953–60; Musical Dir BBC TV Light Entertainment 1960–68; Head of Music, London Weekend TV 1968–77; freelance composer and conductor 1977–; Music Dir (TV) Julia and Friends 1986, Paul Nicholas and Friends 1987, series New Faces 1987; has appeared with London Symphony and Royal Philharmonic Orchestras in UK and with the Los Angeles Philharmonic and Boston Pops Orchestras and Orchestra of St Luke's in USA; Musical Dir for world premieres of Cats and Song & Dance; Musical Dir (films) Funeral in Berlin 1966, Puppet on a Chain 1970, Inside Out 1975, All This and World War II 1976, The Greek Tycoon 1978, Roberte 1979, Hanover Street 1979, Goldengirl 1979, La mort en direct 1980, Mon oncle d'Amérique 1980, Chariots of Fire 1981, Time Bandits 1981, Heat and Dust 1983, The Bostonians 1984, Electric Dreams (also actor) 1984, Nemo 1984, Revolution 1985, Return to Oz 1985, Lady Jane 1986, F/X 1986, The Manhattan Project 1986, RoboCop 1987, Masters of the Universe 1987, Maurice 1987, Mangeclous 1988, Camille Claudel 1988, Queen of Hearts 1989, Shirley Valentine 1989, L'Argent, Lord of the Flies 1990, La Voix, Les Carnassiers, Le Petit Garçon, La Baule-les Pins, La Fille des Collines, Eve of Destruction, Jesuit Joe, Jeanne, Putain du Roi, The Ballad of the Sad Café 1991, J'embrasse pas 1991, Howards End 1992, The Remains of the Day 1993, A Business Affair 1994, Gross fatigue 1994, La Fille de d'Artagnan, Death and

the Maiden 1994, Jefferson in Paris 1995, Secret Agent 1996, The Proprietor 1996, The Stupids, The English Patient 1996, Tonka, Surviving Picasso 1996, Wings of the Dove, Amour Sorcier, My Story So Far, City of Angels 1998, A Soldier's Daughter Never Cries 1998, Message in a Bottle 1999, My Life So Far 1999, Cotton Mary 1999, The Talented Mr. Ripley 1999, Place Vendome, The Golden Bowl 2000, Possession 2002, Bon Voyage 2003, Le Divorce 2003, Cold Mountain 2003; has composed and conducted several TV scores including The Charlies Drake Show (series) 1960, I, Claudius (mini-series theme) 1976, Love for Lydia (mini-series theme) 1977, The Marquise 1980, The Sign of Four 1983, Reilly: The Ace of Spies (mini-series) 1983, The Ewok Adventure 1984, The Insurance Man 1986, In a Glass Darkly (aka Agatha Christie's In a Glass Darkly) 1987, L'Amérique en otage 1991, Memento Mori 1992, Alien Empire (BBC); mem. Composers' Guild, BAC&S; Freeman City of London 1995; awarded BASCA Gold Badge for Services to British Music 1985, Radio and TV Industries Award for Best TV Theme 1984, All-Music Gold Award 1991. *Leisure interests:* listening to others making music, edible fungi hunting, wine-tasting. *Address:* 7 East View Cottages, Pursers Lane, Peaslake, Surrey, GU5 PRG, England (home). *Telephone:* (1306) 730674 (home); (503) 224-2541 (USA) (home); 4-90-75-89-47 (France) (home). *E-mail:* mitziscott@aol.com (office).

RABKIN, Mitchell T., MD; American physician, academic and hospital administrator; *Professor of Medicine, Harvard Medical School;* b. 27 Nov. 1930, Boston, Mass.; s. of Morris A. Rabkin and Esther Quint Rabkin; m. Adrienne M. Najarian 1956; one s. one d.; ed Harvard Coll. and Harvard Medical School; trained in medicine, Mass. Gen. Hosp., Boston; U.S. Public Health Service, Nat. Inst. of Health, Bethesda, Md 1957–59; Chief Resident in Medicine, Mass. Gen. Hosp. 1962, medical staff 1963–66, Bd Consultation 1972–80, Hon. Physician 1981–; Gen. Dir Beth Israel Hosp., Boston 1966–80, Pres. 1980–96, now CEO Emer.; Prof. of Medicine, Harvard Medical School 1983–, Pres. Harvard Medical Alumni Council 2000–01; CEO CareGroup, Boston 1996–98; Distinguished Inst. Scholar, Inst. for Educ. and Research, Beth Israel Deaconess Medical Center, Boston 1998–; mem. NAS Inst. of Medicine; mem. Bd Dirs Duke Univ. Health System 1998–2003; Vice-Chair. Bd of Trustees New York Univ. School of Medicine Foundation; Dir Washington Advisory Group, LECG; Fellow AAAS, ACP; Hon. DSc (Brandeis), (Curry Coll., Milton, Mass.), (Mass. Coll. of Pharmacy) 1983, (Northeastern Univ.) 1994; Distinguished Service Award, American Hosp. Asscn 1999, Distinguished Service Medal, Asscn of American Medical Colls 1999. *Publications:* numerous articles in academic journals. *Leisure interests:* sailing, gardening, travel. *Address:* Carl J. Shapiro Institute for Education and Research at Harvard Medical School and Beth Israel Deaconess Medical Center, 330 Brookline Avenue, Boston, MA 02186, USA (office); 124 Canton Avenue, Milton, MA 02186, USA (home). *Telephone:* (617) 667-9400 (office); (617) 696-6614 (home). *Fax:* (617) 667-9122 (office); (617) 696-1008 (home). *E-mail:* mtrabkin@caregroup.harvard.edu (office); mtrabkin@mindspring .com (home). *Website:* www.bidmc.harvard.edu (office).

RABUKA, Maj.-Gen. Sitiveni Ligamamada, OBE, MSc; Fijian politician and army officer; b. 13 Sept. 1948, Nakobo; s. of Kolinio E. V. Rabuka and Salote Lomaloma; m. Suluweti Camamaivuna Tuiloma 1975; two s. two d.; ed Prov. School Northern, Queen Victoria School, NZ Army schools, Indian Defence Services Staff Coll. and Australian Jt Services Staff Coll.; Sr Operational Plans Officer, UN Interim Force in Lebanon (UNIFIL) 1980; Commdr Fiji Bn UNIFL Lebanon 1980–81; Chief of Staff, Fiji July–Dec. 1981; SO 1 Operations and Training, Fiji Army 1982–83, 1985–87; Chief of Mil. Personnel MFO, Sinai, Egypt 1983–84; Commdr Fiji Bn MFO, Sinai, Egypt 1984–85; staged coup 14 May 1987; Adviser on Home Affairs and Head of Security May–Sept. 1987; staged second coup 25 Sept. 1987; declared Fiji a Repub. 7 Oct. 1987; Commdr and Head of Interim Mil. Govt of Fiji Sept.–Dec. 1987; Commdr Fiji Security Forces 1987–91; Minister for Home Affairs, Nat. Youth Service and Army Auxiliary Services 1987–90; Commdr Republic of Fiji Military Forces 1991; Deputy Prime Minister 1991, Minister for Home Affairs 1991; elected Founding Pres. Fijian Political Party 1991; Prime Minister of Fiji 1992–99, fmrly Minister for Home Affairs, Immigration, Fijian Affairs and Rural Devt and Foreign Affairs, fmrly with special responsibility for the Constitutional Review and the Agricultural, Landlords and Tenants Act; Commonwealth Rep. to Solomon Islands 1999–2000; Chair. Cakaudrove Prov. Council 2001–08; Pres. Fijian Political Party (SVT); Commdr, Légion d'honneur 1980, Grand Officier 1997, MSD 1987, OStJ 1987, CF 1998, Order of Tahiti Nui 1998; Dr hc (Cen. Queensland Univ.) 1997. *Publication:* No Other Way 1988. *Leisure interests:* golf, rugby, weightlifting. *Address:* Box 2437, Government Buildings, Savusavu, Fiji (office). *Telephone:* (9) 3323753 (home); (9) 9937023 (mobile) (home). *Fax:* (9) 3323753 (office). *E-mail:* leo@ connect.com.fj (home). *Website:* blighwatershipping.com.fj (office).

RACHDI, Allal; Moroccan civil servant and international organization executive; *Director-General, Islamic Centre for the Development of Trade;* b. 17 June 1951; ed Grande Ecole of Public Admin, Faculty of Law (Political Sciences), Certificate of Trade Policy, GATT, Geneva; sr civil servant at Ministry of Foreign Trade since 1978, participated in devt and implementation of Structural Adjustment programmes, also took part in bilateral and multilateral trade negotiations, particularly in negotiations for accession of Morocco to GATT, co-operation and asscn agreements of Morocco with EU, Uruguay Round negotiations as well as negotiations of several free trade agreements, Dir Foreign Trade Policy, Ministry of Foreign Trade 1994–2000, Co-ordinator at Gen. Secr.; Chair. Nat. Comm. of Foreign Trade Facilitation 1986–2000, Nat. Imports Consultative Comm. 1992–2000; Admin., Common Fund for Commodities, Amsterdam 1998–2000, Moroccan Exports Asscn; mem. Jt Cttee of Pvt./Public Sector; Dir-Gen. Islamic Centre for the Devt of Trade, OIC 2000–. *Address:* Islamic Centre for the Development of Trade, Tours des Habous, Avenue des FAR, BP 13545, Casablanca – Principal 20000,

Morocco (office). *Telephone:* (2) 314974 (office). *Fax:* (2) 310110 (office). *E-mail:* icdt@icdt-oic.org (office). *Website:* www.icdt-oic.org (office).

RACHID-COWLES, Leila Teresa, PhD; Paraguayan diplomatist, politician and academic; m. Frank Cowles Jr; three c.; ed Catholic Univ., Asunción; Prof. of Political Science at acad. insts in Paraguay; various positions in public office including Vice-Minister of Foreign Affairs 1996–98; Amb. to Argentina 1999–2000, to USA 2000–03; Minister of Foreign Affairs 2003–06. *Publications include:* Collection of International Treaties and Acts of the Republic of Paraguay (six vols, with Enrique Bordenave). *Address:* c/o Ministry of Foreign Affairs, Juan E. O'Leary y Presidente Franco, Asunción, Paraguay (office).

RACICOT, Marc F., BA, JD; American lawyer, association executive and fmr politician; *President, American Insurance Association;* b. 24 July 1948, Thompson Falls, Mont.; s. of William E. Racicot and Patricia E. Racicot (née Bentley); m. Theresa J. Barber 1970; two s. three d.; ed Carroll Coll., Helena, Mont., Univ. of Montana; called to Bar, Mont. 1973; served US Army 1973–76, Chief Trial Counsel US Army, Kaiserslautern, Fed. Repub. of Germany 1975–76, resgnd 1976; Deputy Co. Attorney, Missoula (Mont.) Co. 1976–77; Asst Attorney-Gen. State of Mont. 1977–88, Attorney-Gen. 1988–93; Gov. of Montana 1993–2001; Pnr Bracewell & Patterson LLP (now Bracewell & Giuliani, LLP), Washington DC 2001–03; Chair. Republican Nat. Cttee 2002–04; Chair. Bush-Cheney re-election campaign 2004; Pres. American Insurance Asscn 2005–. *Address:* American Insurance Association, 1130 Connecticut Avenue, NW, Suite 1000, Washington, DC 20036, USA (office). *Telephone:* (202) 828-7100 (office). *Fax:* (202) 293-1219 (office). *E-mail:* mracicot@aiadc.org (office). *Website:* www.aiadc.org (office).

RACIONERO GRAU, Luis; Spanish librarian, academic and writer; b. 1940, Seu d'Urgell, Lleida; ed Univ. of Calif., Berkeley, USA, Churchill Coll., Cambridge, UK; industrial engineer, Barcelona 1965; Prof. of Micro Econs, Faculty of Econ. Sciences and Urban Studies, School of Architecture, Barcelona; fmr Dir Spanish Coll., Paris; Dir-Gen. Biblioteca Nacional, Madrid 2001–04. *Publications include:* Taoista textos de estética 1991, Atenas de Pericles 1993, El arte de escribir 1995, La sonrisa de la Gioconda: Memorias de Leonardo 1999, Filosofias del Underground 2000, El pecado original 2001, Oriente y Occidente 2001, El progreso decadente (Espasa de Ensayo Prize) 2001, El alquimista trouador 2003. *Address:* c/o Editorial Planeta, Córcega 273-277, 08008 Barcelona, Spain.

RACZKO, Andrzej, DEcons; Polish economist; *Alternate Executive Director (Poland), International Monetary Fund;* b. 27 Feb. 1953, Kutno; m.; two c.; ed Univ. of Łódź; early career as Asst, then Asst Prof., Inst. of Econs, Univ. of Łódź 1977–86; Chief Specialist on Foreign Cooperation, Łódźkie Towarzystwo Kredytowe Bank SA 1992–93; Econ. Dir Petrobank SA 1993–97, mem. Man. Bd LG Petro Bank SA 1995–97, Dir 1997–99; Man. Mortgage Team, PKO Bank Polski SA 1999–2001; Under-Sec. of State, Ministry of Finance 2001–02, Minister of Finance 2003–04; mem. Bd of Dirs Bank Gospodarki Żywnościowej SA 2002–03; fmr mem. EU negotiating team; fmr Vice-Gov. IMF, Alt. Exec. Dir (Poland) 2004–; fmr Co-Chair. Public Debt Cttee. *Address:* Office of the Alternate Executive Director (Poland), International Monetary Fund, 700 19th Street, NW, Washington, DC 20431, USA (office). *Telephone:* (202) 623-7300 (office). *Fax:* (202) 623-6278 (office). *E-mail:* publicaffairs@imf.org (office). *Website:* www.imf.org (office).

RADAVIDSON, Benjamin Andriamparany; Malagasy politician; *Minister of National Education and Scientific Research;* Minister of the Economy, Finance and the Budget 2002–07, of Nat. Educ. and Scientific Research 2007–; mem. Bd of Govs IMF. *Address:* Ministry of National Education and Scientific Research, BP 247, Anosy, 101 Antananarivo, Madagascar (office). *Telephone:* (20) 2224308 (office). *Fax:* (20) 2223897 (office). *E-mail:* mlraharimalala@yahoo.fr (office).

RADCLIFFE, Paula Jane, MBE, BA; British athlete; b. 17 Dec. 1973, Northwich; d. of Peter Radcliffe and Pat Radcliffe; m. Gary Lough; one d.; ed Univ. of Loughborough; distance runner; World Jr Cross Country Champion 1992; started sr career 1993; fifth place, 5,000m, Olympic Games 1996; won Fifth Avenue Mile, New York 1996, 1997; third place, Int. Asscn of Athletics Feds (IAAF) World Cross Challenge series 1997; fourth place, 5,000m, World Championships 1997; European Cross Country Champion 1998; second place, 10,000m, European Challenge 1998; silver medal, 10,000m World Championships, 1999; fourth place, 10,000m Olympic Games 2000; World Half Marathon Champion 2000, 2001; World Cross Country Champion 2002; gold medallist, 5,000m, Commonwealth Games 2002; gold medallist, 10,000m, European Championships 2002; won London Marathon 2002, 2003, 2005, Chicago Marathon 2002, New York City Marathon 2004, 2007, 2008; set world best time for 5,000m in Flora Light 5km 2003; won Great North Run Half Marathon in world best time 2003; won World Championship's marathon 2005; world record holder for 10,000m, 20,000m and marathon; Capt. GB's Women's Athletic Team 1998–; Hon. DLitt (De Montfort, Loughborough); British Female Athlete of the Year 1999, 2001 and 2002, IAAF World Female Athlete of the Year 2002, BBC Sports Personality of the Year 2002, Sunday Times Sportswoman of the Year 2002. *Publication:* Paula: My Story So Far 2004. *Leisure interests:* dining out, languages, reading, music, cinema, travel, spending time with family and friends. *Address:* c/o Bedford and County Athletics Club, 3 Regent Close, Bedford, MK41 7XG, England (office). *Website:* www.paularadcliffe.com.

RADCLIFFE, Father Timothy Peter Joseph, OP, MA; British ecclesiastic; b. 22 Aug. 1945, London; s. of Hugh Radcliffe and Marie-Therese Pereira; ed Downside School, Le Saulchoir, Paris and St John's Coll., Oxford; entered Dominican Order 1965; Chaplain to Imperial Coll.; Prior of Blackfriars, Oxford 1982–88; Chair. New Blackfriars 1983–88; Provincial of Prov. of England 1988–92; Pres. Conf. of Major Religious Superiors of England and Wales 1991–; Grand Chancellor, Pontifical Univ. of St Thomas (The Angelicum), Rome 1992–2001, Univ. of Santo Tomas, Manila 1992–2001, Ecole Biblique, Jerusalem 1992–2001, Faculty of Theology, Fribourg 1992–2001; Master, Order of Preachers 1992–2001; Hon. Citizen of Augusta (Italy) and Sepahua (Peru); Hon. Fellow, St John's Coll. Oxford, Sarum Canon of Salisbury Cathedral; Hon. DD (Oxford), (Pontifical Univ. of St Thomas), Hon. STD (Providence Coll. RI), Hon. LLD (Barry Univ., Fla) 1996, Hon. DHumLitt (Ohio Dominican Coll.) 1996 (Dominican Univ., Chicago) 2007, (Aquinas Inst., St Louis), Dr hc (Université Catholique de l'Ouest, Angers) 2007; Prix de Littérature Religieuse 2001, Prix Spiritualités d'aujourd'hui 2001, Premio Ecumenico San Nicola 2004, Prix des lecteurs du Procure 2005, Michael Ramsey Award for Theological Writing 2007. *Publications:* El Manantial de la Esperanza 1998, Sing a New Song: The Christian Vocation 1999, I Call You Friends 2001, Seven Last Words of Christ 2004, What is the Point of Being a Christian? 2005, Why go to Church? The Drama of the Eucharist 2008. *Leisure interests:* walking, reading long novels. *Address:* Blackfriars, St Giles, Oxford, OX1 3LY, England (home). *Telephone:* (1865) 278422 (home). *Fax:* (1865) 278403 (home). *E-mail:* timothy.radcliffe@english.op.org (office).

RADDA, Sir George Karoly, Kt, CBE, MA, DPhil, FRS; British medical research director and academic; *Professor and Head of Department of Physiology, Anatomy and Genetics, University of Oxford;* b. 9 June 1936, Gyor, Hungary; s. of Gyula Radda and Anna Bernolak; m. 1st Mary O'Brien 1961 (divorced 1995), two s. one d.; m. 2nd Sue Bailey 1995; ed Pannonhalma and Eötvös Univ., Budapest and Merton Coll. Oxford; Research Assoc., Univ. of Calif., USA 1962–63; Lecturer in Organic Chem., St John's Coll., Oxford Univ. 1963–64, Fellow and Tutor in Organic Chem., Merton Coll. 1964–84, Lecturer in Biochem, Oxford Univ. 1966–84, British Heart Foundation Prof. of Molecular Cardiology 1984–2003, Prof. Emer. 2003, Prof. and Head, Dept of Physiology, Anatomy and Genetics 2006–; Professorial Fellow, Merton Coll. 1984–, Head Dept of Biochem. 1991–96; Chair. MRC Cell. Bd 1988–92; mem. MRC Council 1988–92, Chief Exec. MRC (on leave from Oxford Univ.) 1996–2003; Chair. Nat. Cancer Research Inst. 2001–; mem. Council, Royal Soc. 1990–92, ICRF 1991–96; Ed. Biochemical and Biophysical Research Communications 1977–84; Man. Ed. Biochimica et Biophysica Acta 1977–, Chair. 1989–95; Founder mem. Oxford Enzyme Group 1970–87, Acad. of Medical Sciences 1998; Pres. Soc. for Magnetic Resonance in Medicine 1985–86, Fellow 1994–; Fellow, Int. Soc. of Magnetic Resonance in Medicine 1995–; mem. European Molecular Biology Org. 1997–, Academia Europaea 1999–; Hon. Dir MRC Biochemical and Clinical Magnetic Resonance Unit 1988–96; Hon. FRCR 1985; Hon. Fellow, American Heart Asscn and Citation for Int. Achievement 1987; Hon. FRCP 1997; Hon. DrMed (Berne) 1985, (London) 1991; Hon. DSc (Stirling) 1997, (Sheffield) 1999, (Debrecen, Hungary) 2001, (Birmingham) 2003, (Univ. de la Mediterranée) 2003; Colworth Medal, Biochemical Soc. 1969, CIBA Medal and Prize 1983, Feldberg Prize 1982, British Heart Foundation Prize and Gold Medal for cardiovascular research 1982, Gold Medal, Soc. for Magnetic Resonance in Medicine 1984, Buchanan Medal, Royal Soc. 1987, Rank Prize in Nutrition 1990. *Publications:* articles in books and scientific journals. *Leisure interests:* opera, jazz, swimming. *Address:* Department of Physiology, Anatomy and Genetics, University of Oxford, Sherrington Building, Parks Road, Oxford, OX1 3PT, England (office). *Telephone:* (1865) 282251 (office). *Fax:* (1865) 282252 (office). *E-mail:* george.radda@dpag.ox.ac.uk (office). *Website:* www.dpag.ox.ac.uk/academic_staff/george_radda (office).

RADEBE, Jeffrey (Jeff) Thamsanqa, LLB; South African politician; *Minister of Transport;* b. 18 Feb. 1953, Cato Manor; m. Bridget Radebe; three c.; ed Isibonelo High School, Univ. of Zululand, Leipzig Univ., Germany, Lenin Int. School, Moscow; joined Black Consciousness Movt 1970; Co-Founder Kwamashu Youth Org. 1972; articled clerk with A. J. Gumede & Phyllis Naidoo, E. S. Mchunu & Co. 1976–77; with Radio Freedom 1977–78; Deputy Chief African Nat. Congress (ANC) Rep., Tanzania 1981; headed clandestine political movt of ANC and South African Communist Party (SACP) 1986, Head Political Dept and Co-ordinator of 12 day hunger strike on Robben Island; arrested and sentenced to ten years on Robben Island 1986, sentence reduced to six years, released 1990; Sec. interim leadership group of SACP 1990–91; Deputy Chair. ANC Southern Natal Region 1990–91, Chair. 1991–94; Minister of Public Works, Govt of Nat. Unity 1994–99, of Public Enterprises 1999–2004, currently Minister of Transport, also currently mem. ANC Nat. Exec. Cttee (NEC) and Nat. Working Cttee, Head ANC Policy Unit and NEC Convener in North West Prov.; Hon. LLM (Leipzig); Dr hc (Chicago State Univ.) 1996. *Address:* Ministry of Transport, 159 Forum Bldg, 159 Struben Street, Pretoria 0002 Private Bag X193, Pretoria 0001, South Africa (office). *Telephone:* (12) 3093860 (office). *Fax:* (12) 3283194 (office). *E-mail:* miniprivatesec@dot.gov.za (office). *Website:* www.transport.gov.za (office).

RADER, Gen. Paul A., BA, BD, MTh, DMiss; American fmr university administrator and religious leader; b. 14 March 1934, New York; s. of Lyell M. Rader and Gladys Mina Damon; m. Kay Fuller 1956; one s. two d.; ed Asbury Theological Seminary, Southern Baptist Theological Seminary, Salvation Army's School for Officers' Training, New York, Fuller Theological Seminary; mem. staff Salvation Army Training School, Seoul, Korea 1962–67, Vice-Prin. 1967–71, Training Prin., then Educ. Officer, then Asst Chief Sec. Salvation Army in Korea 1973–77, Chief Sec. with rank of Lt-Col 1977–84; Prin. School for Officers' Training, Suffern, New York 1984–87, Div. Leader 1987–89; Chief Sec. USA Eastern Territory 1989; rank of Commr 1989; Commdr USA Western Territory 1989–94; Pres. The Salvation Army Calif. Corps 1989–94; rank of Gen. of The Salvation Army 1994–99; Pres. Asbury Coll. 2000–06 (retd). *Address:* c/o Office of the President, Asbury College, One Macklem Drive, Wilmore, Ky 40390, USA (office).

RADICE, Vittorio; Italian retail executive; *CEO, La Rinascente;* b. 1957, Como; m. Gemma Radice; two s.; ed Univ. of Milan; home furnishings buyer, Associated Merchandising Corpn; Buying Dir Habitat Int., then Man. Dir Habitat UK 1990–96; Man. Dir Selfridges PLC 1996–98, CEO 1998–2003; Exec. Dir and Head of Home Furnishings, Marks and Spencer PLC 2003–04; CEO La Rinascente, Milan 2005–; Dir (non-exec.) Shoppers Stop India 2000–06, McArthurGlen 2005–, Ishaan plc 2006–. *Leisure interests:* travel, India, art, music. *Address:* la Rinascente s.r.l., Via Washington 70, 20146 Milan (office); Strada 8, Palazzo N, 20089 Rozzano-Milano, Italy (office). *Telephone:* (2) 57583922 (office). *Fax:* (2) 57982015 (office). *E-mail:* vittorio .radice@rinascente.it (office). *Website:* www.rinascente.it (office).

RADIŠIĆ, Živko; Bosnia and Herzegovina politician; *Chairman, Socialist Party;* b. 15 Aug. 1937, Prijedor; m.; two c.; ed Univ. of Sarajevo; Mayor of Banja Luka 1977–82; Minister of Defence of the Fmr Socialist Repub. of Bosnia and Herzegovina 1982–85; Man. Cajavec Holding Co., Banja Luka 1985–92; Chair. Ass., Banja Luka; Pres. and Chair. of the Presidency of Bosnia and Herzegovina 1998–99, 2000–01, Co-Pres. 1999–2001, Mem. of the Presidency 2002; Founding mem. Socialist Party (fmrly Socialist Party of Republika Srpska) 1996–, currently Chair. *Address:* Socialist Party (Socija-listička Partija) (SP), 78000 Banja Luka, Bana Lazarevića 7, Bosnia and Herzegovina (office). *Telephone:* (51) 328750 (office). *Fax:* (51) 328753 (office). *E-mail:* sprs@inecco.net (office).

RADMANOVIĆ, Nebojša; Bosnia and Herzegovina politician; *Member of the Tripartite State Presidency;* b. 1 Oct. 1949, Gračanica; m.; two c.; ed Faculty of Philosophy, Univ. of Belgrade; has held numerous positions in culture and state admin including Dir Bosanska Krajina Archives and Archives of Republika Srpska, Dir Nat. Theatre of Republika Srpska, Banja Luka, Dir and Ed.-in-Chief GLAS, Pres. Exec. Bd Town of Banja Luka, Rep. Nat. Ass., Republika Srpska and Minister of Admin and Local Self-Man.; Serb mem. Tripartite State Presidency 2006–, Chair. 2006–07, 2008–; mem. Alliance of Ind. Social Democrats. *Publications include:* several books and scientific papers. *Address:* Office of the State Presidency, 71000 Sarajevo, Musala 5, Bosnia and Herzegovina (office). *Telephone:* (33) 664941 (office). *Fax:* (33) 472491 (office). *Website:* www.predsjednistvobih.ba (office).

RADNER, Roy, PhD; American economist, applied mathematician and academic; *Professor of Business, Leonard N. Stern School of Business, New York University;* b. 29 June 1927, Chicago; s. of Ella Radner and Samuel Radner; m. 1st Virginia Honoski (died 1976); one s. three d. (one d. deceased); m. 2nd Charlotte V. Kuh 1978; ed Hyde Park High School, Chicago and Univ. of Chicago; served US army 1945–48; Research Assoc., Cowles Comm., Univ. of Chicago 1951–54, Asst Prof. 1954–55; Asst Prof. of Econs Yale Univ. 1955–57; Assoc. Prof. of Econs and Statistics, Univ. of Calif., Berkeley 1957–61, Prof. 1961–79, Chair. Dept of Econs 1965–69; Distinguished mem. tech. staff, AT&T Bell Labs 1979–95; Research Prof. of Econs New York Univ. 1983–95, Prof. of Econs and Information Systems 1995–96, Stern School Prof. of Business 1995–; Guggenheim Fellow 1961–62 and 1965–66; Overseas Fellow, Churchill Coll. Cambridge, UK 1969–70, 1989; Assoc. Ed. Journal of Econ. Theory 1968–, Games and Economic Behavior 1989–, Review of Economic Design 1994–, Information Systems Frontiers, 1999–; mem. NAS; Fellow, American Acad. of Arts and Sciences, Econometric Soc. (Pres. 1973); Distinguished Fellow, American Econ. Asscn, AAAS; Woytinsky Award, Univ. of Mich. 1998. *Publications:* Notes on the Theory of Economic Planning 1963, Optimal Replacement Policy (with others) 1967, Decision and Organization (co-ed.) 1972, Economic Theory of Teams (with J. Marschak) 1972, Demand and Supply in U.S. Higher Education (with L. S. Miller) 1975, Education as an Industry (co-ed.) 1976, Mathematicians in Academia (with C. V. Kuh) 1980, Information, Incentives and Economic Mechanisms (co-ed.) 1987, Perspectives on Deterrence 1989 (co-ed.), Bargaining with Incomplete Information (co-ed.) 1992; and many articles. *Leisure interests:* music, hiking, cross-country skiing. *Address:* Stern School of Business, Kaufmann Management Center, Room 8–87, New York University, 44 W Fourth Street, New York, NY 10012 (office); 3203 Davenport Street, NW, Washington, DC 20008, USA (home). *Telephone:* (212) 998-0813 (office). *Fax:* (212) 995-4228 (office). *Website:* www.stern.nyu.edu/~rradner (office).

RADOJIČIĆ, Igor, MEng; Bosnia and Herzegovina (Republika Srpska) engineer, politician and academic; *President of the National Assembly;* b. 13 Sept. 1966, Banja Luka; m.; two c.; ed Faculty of Electrical Eng, Banja Luka; on staff, Faculty of Electrical Eng, Banja Luka 1991–; mem. Savez nezavisnih socijaldemokrata (Alliance of Ind. Social Democrats), Sec.-Gen. 2003–; Deputy in Nat. Ass., Pres. Nat. Ass. 2006–; Acting Pres. of Republika Srpska Oct.–Dec. 2007. *Publications:* 14 scientific works on signal processing. *Address:* National Assembly, Vuka Karadzica 2, Banja Luka (office); c/o Savez nezavisnih socijaldemokrata, Petra Kočića 5, 78000 Banja Luka, Republika Srpska. *Telephone:* (51) 338117 (office); (51) 318492. *Fax:* (51) 338141 (office); (51) 318495. *E-mail:* predsjednik@snsd.org. *Website:* www .narodnaskupstinars.net (office); www.snsd.org.

RADOŠ, Jozo; Croatian academic, engineer and politician; b. 3 Nov. 1956, Seonica, Tomislavgrad, Bosnia-Herzegovina; m.; three c.; ed Zagreb Univ.; Prof. of History and Electrical Eng, Osijek and Dakovo 1983–1986; Devt Planner, Rade Kondar Co., Zagreb 1986–90; engineer, Zagreb Electric Bulb factory 1990–92; mem. House of Reps 1992–2000; mem. Zagreb City Ass. 1995–97; mem. Croatian Parl. Del. to Parl. Ass. of Council of Europe 1998–2000; Minister of Defence 2000–02; Acting Chair. Croatian Social Liberal Party (HSLS) 2001–02; Chair. Party of Liberal Democrats (Libra) 2002–05, merged with Croatian People's Party to form Croatian People's Party—Liberal Democrats 2005; Homeland War Memorial Certificate. *Address:* c/o Croatian People's Party—Liberal Democrats (CPP) (Hrvatska narodna stranka—Liberalni demokrati) (HNS), 10000 Zagreb, Kneza Mislava

8 Croatia (office). *Telephone:* (1) 4629111 (office). *Fax:* (1) 4629110 (office). *E-mail:* hns@hns.hr (office). *Website:* www.hns.hr (office).

RADOVANOVIĆ, Nikola; Bosnia and Herzegovina government official; ed Ground Forces Acad., GHQ School, King's Coll. London and Univ. of Oxford, UK; Head of Office for Peace and Stability, Ministry of Foreign Affairs –2004; Minister of Defence 2004–07. *Address:* c/o Ministry of Defence, Hamdije Kresevljakovica 98, 71000 Sarajevo, Bosnia and Herzegovina (office).

RADZIKHOVSKY, Leonid; Russian journalist and political analyst; fmr sr columnist for liberal daily newspaper, Segodnya (now defunct); mem. RIA Novosti Expert Council. *Publications:* numerous articles in newspapers and journals. *Address:* c/o Rossiiskaya Gazeta, PO Box 40, ul. Pravdy 24, 125993 Moscow, Russia. *Telephone:* (495) 257-52-52. *Fax:* (495) 973-22-56. *E-mail:* sekretar@rg.ru. *Website:* www.rg.ru.

RADZINSKY, Edvard Stanislavovich; Russian dramatist; b. 23 Sept. 1936, Moscow; s. of Stanislav Radzinsky and Sofia Radzinsky; m. 2nd Yelena Timofeyevna Denisova; ed Inst. of History and Archival Science, Moscow. *Plays include:* My Dream is India 1960, You're All of Twenty-Two, you Old Men! 1962, One Hundred and Four Pages on Love 1964, Kolobashkin the Seducer 1967, Socrates 1977, Lunin 1980, I Stand at the Restaurant 1982, Theatre of the Time of Nero and Seneca 1984, Elderly Actress in the Role of Dostoevsky's Wife 1986, Sporting Scenes 1987, Our Decameron 1989. *Television:* author and narrator of TV series Mysteries of History 1997–. *Publications:* novels: The Last of the Romanovs 1989, Our Decameron 1990; non-fiction: The Last Tsar: The Life and Death of Nicholas II 1992, God Save and Restrain Russia 1993, Stalin 1996, Mysteries of History 1997, Mysteries of Love 1998, Fall of Gallant Century 1998, Collected Works (7 Vols) 1998–99, Rasputin 1999, The Theatrical Novel (memoirs) 1999, Alexander II, The Last Great Tsar 2005. *Address:* Usiyevicha Street 8, Apt 96, 125319 Moscow, Russia (home). *E-mail:* edvard@radzinski.ru (office). *Website:* www.radzinski .ru (office).

RAE, Alexander Lindsay, CNZM, OBE, MAgr.SC, PhD, FRSNZ; New Zealand scientist and academic; *Professor Emeritus of Animal Science, Massey University;* b. 3 Aug. 1923, Eltham; s. of Thomas Rae and Annie Rae; m. Fiona D. Thomas 1957 (died 1998); ed Massey Agricultural Coll. and Iowa State Univ.; Jr Lecturer in Sheep Husbandry, Massey Agricultural Coll. 1944–50; Prof. of Sheep Husbandry, Massey Univ. 1951–80, Prof. in Animal Science 1980–89, Prof. Emer. 1989–; Fellow NZ Inst. of Agricultural Science, Australian Asscn of Animal Breeding and Genetics; Trustee NZ Animal Breeding Trust 1991–2007; NZ Soc. of Animal Production McMeekan Memorial Award 1977, Sir Ernest Marsden Medal for Outstanding Service to Science 1982, Massey Univ. Award for Distinguished Service 1990, New Zealand Medal 1990. *Publications:* research papers on animal genetics and breeding in scientific journals. *Leisure interest:* fishing. *Address:* 16 Wallace Place, Palmerston North 4410, New Zealand (home). *Telephone:* (6) 357-8611 (home).

RAE, Barbara, CBE, RA, RSA; British artist and lecturer; b. 10 Dec. 1943, Falkirk, Scotland; d. of James Rae and Mary Young; one s.; ed Edinburgh Coll. of Art, Moray House Coll. of Educ.; Lecturer, Glasgow School of Art 1975–96; Trustee British School, Rome 1997–2000, Hospitalfield House, Arbroath 1997–99; mem. Bd Royal Fine Art Comm. 1995–; Invited Artist, Royal Hibernian Acad., Dublin 1995, 1996, 2003; numerous group exhbns UK, USA, Germany, Netherlands, Spain; works in public and pvt. collections including Scottish Nat. Gallery of Modern Art, Scottish Arts Council, Univs of Edin., Glasgow and York, Royal Bank of Scotland, Bank of England, TSB Group PLC, HRH the Duke of Edin.; Pres. Soc. of Scottish Artists 1983; mem. Royal Scottish Soc. of Painters and Watercolour (RSW), Royal Glasgow Inst. of the Fine Arts; Hon. Fellow, RCA, London 2003–; Dr hc (Napier Univ., Edin.) 2000; Hon. DLitt (Aberdeen) 2003, (St Andrews) 2008; several awards including Guthrie Award, RSA 1977, May Marshall Brown Award, RSW Centenary Exhibition 1979, Sir William Gillies Travel Award 1983, Calouste Gulbenkian Printmaking Award 1983, Alexander Graham Munro Award, RSW 1989. *Leisure interest:* travel. *Address:* c/o The Adam Gallery, 24 Cork Street, London, England (office). *Telephone:* (20) 7439-6633 (office). *E-mail:* barbararaera@aol.com (office). *Website:* www.barbararae.com.

RAE, Hon. Robert (Bob) Keith, PC, OC, O.Ont., QC, BA, BPhil, LLB; Canadian lawyer, arbitrator and fmr politician; *Partner, Goodmans LLP;* b. 2 Aug. 1948, Ottawa; s. of Saul Rae and Lois George; m. Arlene Perly 1980; three d.; ed public school in Washington, DC, Int. School of Geneva, Univ. of Toronto and Balliol Coll., Oxford; fmr volunteer, legal aid clinics in Toronto and Asst counsel for United Steelworkers of America and Union of Injured Workers; mem. Canadian Fed. Parl. 1978–82; Prov. Leader, New Democratic Party (NDP), Ont. 1982–96; mem. Ont. Prov. Legis. 1982–95; Premier of Ontario 1990–95; Pnr Goodman Phillips & Vineberg (now Goodmans LLP) 1996–; mem. Security Intelligence Review Cttee; mem. Bd of Dirs Hydro One Inc., Niigon Technologies Ltd, Iter Canada Inc., Tembec Ltd., Trojan Technologies; Chair. Forum of Federations, Toronto Symphony Orchestra, Ivesprint, Inc., Inst. for Research on Public Policy; Chancellor Wilfrid Laurier Univ.; Adjunct Prof., Univ. of Toronto; Sr Fellow, Massey Coll.; Dr hc (Law Soc. of Upper Canada), (Univ. of Toronto), (Assumption Univ.). *Publications:* From Protest to Power 1996, The Three Questions: Prosperity and the Public Good 1998, Ontario, A Leader in Learning 2005, Air India, Lessons to be Learned 2005. *Leisure interests:* tennis, golf, fishing, reading, music. *Address:* Goodmans LLP, 250 Yonge Street, Suite 2400, Toronto, ON M5B 2M6, Canada. *Telephone:* (416) 979-2211, ext. 6255. *Fax:* (416) 979-1234 (office); (416) 604-2355 (home). *E-mail:* brae@goodmans.ca (office). *Website:* www.bobrae.ca.

RAFAJLOVSKA, Vera, BEcons; Macedonian economist and government official; *Minister of the Economy;* b. 25 Feb. 1947, Bitola; ed Univs of Bitola and

Skopje; Asst Dir and Pnr, V&F Centre for Econ. and Legal Consulting, Skopje 1991–98; Dir Rafajlovski Consulting DOO 1998–2000, Rafajlovski Revizija DOO 2000–; Minister of the Economy 2006–; fmr Ed.-in-Chief, Economic and Legal Adviser magazine; mem. NSDP party. *Publications:* author and co-author of several books in accounting, taxation, int. financial reporting. *Address:* Ministry of the Economy, Bote Bocevski 9, 1000 Skopje (office); Jurij Gargarin 15, Skopje, Macedonia (office). *Telephone:* (2) 384470 (office). *Fax:* (2) 384472 (office). *E-mail:* minister@economy.gov.mk (office); ms@mt.net.mk (office). *Website:* www.ms.gov.mk (office); www.rafajlovski.com.mk (office).

RAFELSON, Bob; American film director; b. 21 Feb. 1933, New York. *Films directed include:* Head 1968, Five Easy Pieces 1970 (New York Film Critics Award), The King of Marvin Gardens 1972, Stay Hungry 1976, The Postman Always Rings Twice 1981, Black Widow 1987, Mountains of the Moon 1990, Man Trouble 1992, Wet 1993, Armed Response 1994, Blood and Wine 1997, Poodle Springs 1998, Erotic Tales–Porn.com 2002, House on Turk Street 2002. *Address:* c/o William Morris Agency, One William Morris Place, Beverly Hills, CA 90212, USA.

RAFFARIN, Jean-Pierre; French politician; b. 3 Aug. 1948, Poitiers; s. of Jean Raffarin and Renée Michaud; m. Anne-Marie Perrier 1980; one d.; ed Lycée Henri IV, Poitiers, Faculté de Droit, Paris-Assas, Ecole Supérieure de Commerce, Paris; Marketing Dept Cafés Jacques Vabre 1973–76; Adviser, Office of Minister of Labour 1976–81; Pres. Crédit Immobilier Rural de la Vienne 1978–95; Lecturer, Inst. d'Etudes Politiques, Paris 1979–88; Dir-Gen. Bernard Krief Communication 1981–88; Gen. Del. Inst. Euro-92 1988–89; Nat. Del., Deputy Sec.-Gen. and mem. Political Bureau, Parti Républicain 1977–2002; City Councillor, Poitiers 1977–95; Conseiller Régional 1986–88; Pres. Conseil Régional, Poitou-Charentes 1988–2002; mem. European Parl. 1989–95; Deputy Sec.-Gen. and Spokesman for Union pour la Démocratie Française 1993, Sec.-Gen. 1995–2002, mem. Union Pour Un Mouvement Populaire 2002–; Pres. Comm. Arc Atlantique 1994–1998; Minister of Small and Medium-Sized Businesses, of Commerce and Craft Industry 1995–97; mem. Senate (for Vienne) 1995, 1997–2002, 2005–; Vice Mayor of Chasseneuil-du-Poitou 1995–2001; Vice-Pres. Démocratie Libérale 1997–; Pres. Asscn des régions de France 1998–2002; Prime Minister of France 2002–05; Chevalier, Légion d'honneur, Grand Croix, Ordre national du Mérite, Officier, Ordre national du Québec (Canada). *Publications:* La vie en jaune 1977, La publicité nerf de la communication 1983, L'avenir a ses racines 1986, Nous sommes tous les régionaux 1988, Pour une morale de l'action 1992, Le livre de l'Atlantique 1994, Notre Contrat pour l'Alternance 2001, La Nouvelle Gouvernance 2002, La France de Mai 2003, La dernière marche 2007. *Leisure interests:* contemporary painting, regional literature. *Address:* Senat, 15 rue de Vaugirard, 75291 Paris Cedex 06; Union pour un Mouvement Populaire, 55 rue La Boétie 75384 Paris Cedex 08 (office); 7 route de Saint-Georges, 86360 Chasseneuil-du-Poitou, France (home). *Telephone:* 1-42-34-20-00 (Senat) (office); 1-40-76-60-00 (UMP) (office). *Fax:* 1-42-34-26-77 (office). *E-mail:* jpr@carnetjpr.com (office). *Website:* www.senat.fr (office); www.carnetjpr.com.

RAFFENNE, Gen. Jean-Paul; French army officer (retd); *Professor and Director, Senior Executive Seminar, College of International and Security Studies, George C. Marshall Center European Center for Security Studies;* b. 1944; Liaison Officer, Fort Leavenworth, USA 1990–92; Deputy Defence Attaché, Embassy in Washington, DC 1994–96; Head, French Del. to EU Mil. Cttee 2001; Chief French Liaison Officer in unit directing Operation Enduring Freedom (mil. campaign in Afghanistan), Tampa, Fla., USA 2001; Head, Direction du renseignement militaire (mil. intelligence agency) 2002; currently Prof. and Dir, Sr Exec. Seminar, George C. Marshall Center European Center for Security Studies, Germany. *Address:* George C. Marshall Center, Gernackerstrasse 2, 82467 Garmisch-Partenkirchen, Germany (office). *Telephone:* (8821) 750-2680 (office). *E-mail:* cisscontact@marshallcenter.org (office). *Website:* www.marshallcenter.org (office).

RAFIQUE, Muhammad; Pakistani trade union official; *President, National Trade Union Federation of Pakistan;* b. 3 Oct. 1942, Delhi, India; s. of Muhammad Umer; m.; three s. two d.; technician Karachi Water and Sewerage Bd 1971; currently man. of tech. affairs, water treatment plant; joined local union 1972; Treas. Nat. Trade Union Fed. (NTUF), Pres. 1999–; Pres. KMC United Workers Housing Soc.; Best Trade Unionist Award, NTUF-SINDH. *Leisure interest:* singing. *Address:* National Trade Union Federation Pakistan, Bharocha Bldg. 2-B/6, Commercial Area, Nazimabad No. 2, Karachi 74600, Pakistan (office). *Telephone:* (21) 6622361 (office). *Fax:* (21) 6622529 (office). *E-mail:* ntuf@super.netpak (office).

RAFSANJANI, Hojatoleslam Ali Akhbar Hashemi; Iranian ecclesiastic and politician; *Chairman, Assembly of Experts;* b. 25 Aug. 1934, Rafsanjan, Kerman prov.; ed Qom; Speaker, Islamic Consultative Ass. 1980–89; MP –2000; Founding mem. Islamic Repub. Party; Acting C-in-C of the Armed Forces 1988–89; Vice-Chair. Cttee to revise the Constitution 1989; Pres. of the Islamic Repub. of Iran 1989–97; Chair. Expediency Council of Iran 2002–; mem. Ass. of Experts (Majlis-E-Khobregan) representing Tehran, Vice Chair. and First Deputy Speaker 2006–07, Chair. 2007–. *Address:* Expediency Council, POB 13165-311, Pastor Street, Tehran, Iran. *E-mail:* info@maslahat.ir. *Website:* www.maslehat.ir; www.hashemirafsanjani.ir.

RAFTER, Patrick Michael; Australian fmr professional tennis player; b. 28 Dec. 1972, Mount Isa, Queensland; s. of Jim Rafter and Jocelyn Rafter; pnr Lara Feltham; one s.; turned professional 1991; Grand Slam highlights: semi-finalist French Open 1997; winner US Open 1997, 1998; semi-finalist Wimbledon 1999, finalist 2000, 2001; semi-finalist Australian Open 2001; winner Australia Open Doubles title (with Jonas Bjorkman) 1999; sustained serious shoulder injury and took extended break from tennis following Australia's Davis Cup defeat in Dec. 2001; winner of 11 singles titles, 10 doubles titles; announced retirement Jan. 2003; brief comeback (doubles only) 2004; f. Patrick Rafter Cherish the Children Foundation 1999; ATP Newcomer of the Year 1993, Awarded Diploma of Honor International Committee for Fair Play by International Olympic Committee 1997, ATP Tour Stefan Edberg Sportsmanship Award 1997, Australian Sports Personality of the Year Award 1997, Media Sports Personality of the Year Award 1997, ATP Arthur Ash Humanitarian Award 1998, Australian People's Choice Award - Male Sports Star 1998, Awarded Honorary Ambassador for Queensland (presented with the keys to city of Brisbane) 1998, Queensland Young Achiever Award 1998, ATP Tour Stefan Edberg Sportsmanship Award 1998, ATP Tour's Web site Star of the Year Award 1999, Australian People's Choice Award - Male Sports Star 1999, ATP Tour Stefan Edberg Sportsmanship Award 2000, ANSVAR The Bill Brown Community Award 2000, ATP Tour Stefan Edberg Sportsmanship Award 2001, Australian Of The Year 2002. *Leisure interests:* golf, fishing. *Address:* c/o Patrick Rafter Cherish the Children Foundation, POB 1855, Noosa Heads, Queensland 4567, Australia (office). *Fax:* (7) 5455 4433 (office). *Website:* www.cherishthechildren.com.au (office).

RAGHEB, Ali Abu; Jordanian politician; Head Financial and Econ. Affairs Cttee; mem. Nat. Ass.; Prime Minister of Jordan and Minister of Defence 2000–03 resgnd). *Address:* c/o Office of the Prime Minister, PO Box 80, 35216 Amman, Jordan (office).

RAGNEMALM, Hans, LLD; Swedish judge; *Juris Ombudsman;* b. 30 March 1940, Laholm; m. Vivi Ragnemalm 1961; Assoc. Prof. of Public Law, Univ. of Lund 1970–75; Prof. of Public Law, Univ. of Stockholm 1975–87, Dean, Faculty of Law 1984–87; Parl. Ombudsman 1987–92; Judge, Supreme Admin. Court 1992–94, Justice 1999, Pres. 2000–05; currently Juris Ombudsmen; Judge, European Court of Justice 1995–99; Alt. Mem. Court of Conciliation and Arbitration, OSCE. *Publications:* Appealability of Administrative Decisions 1970, Extraordinary Remedies in Administrative Procedure Law 1973, Elements of Administrative Procedure Law 1977, The Constitution of Sweden 1980, Administrative Justice in Sweden 1991; numerous other books and articles. *Address:* c/o Regeringsrätten, PO Box 2293, 103 17 Stockholm, Sweden. *Telephone:* (8) 6176212 (office). *Fax:* (8) 6176234 (office).

RAGON, Michel, Dr d'Etat-ès-Lettres; French writer and lecturer; b. 24 June 1924, Marseille; s. of Aristide Ragon and Camille Sourisseau; m. Françoise Antoine 1968; worked in manual jobs from the age of 14; lived in Paris 1945–, bookseller on the Seine embankments 1954–64; art critic, architectural historian, novelist; Lecturer, l'Ecole Nat. Supérieure des Arts Décoratifs, Paris 1972–85; Chevalier, Ordre du Mérite, Légion d'honneur, Commdr des Arts et des Lettres; Prix de l'Acad. Française et de l'Acad. d'Architecture. *Publications:* Histoire mondiale de l'architecture et de l'urbanisme modernes 1971–78, L'homme et les villes 1975, L'espace de la mort 1981, L'art abstrait 1973–74, L'art pour quoi faire? 1971, 25 ans d'art vivant 1969, Histoire de la littérature prolétarienne en France 1974, L'accent de ma mère 1980, Ma soeur aux yeux d'Asie 1982, Les mouchoirs rouges de Cholet 1984, La louve de Mervent 1985, Le marin des sables 1988, La mémoire des vaincus 1990, Le Cocher du Boiroux 1992, Journal de l'Art Abstrait 1992, Le roman de Rabelais 1994, Les Coquelicots sont revenus 1996, Un si bel espoir 1999, Georges et Louise 2000, Un rossignol chantait 2001, Cinquante ans d'art vivant 2001, Un amour de Jeanne 2003, La ferme d'en haut 2005, Le prisonnier 2007. *Address:* 4 rue du Faubourg Poissonnière, 75010 Paris, France.

RAHEEN, Sayed Makhdoom, MA, PhD; Afghan diplomatist; *Ambassador to India;* b. 1946, Kabul; ed Tehran Univ., Iran; apptd Lecturer, Kabul Univ. 1973; fmr Head of Bureau of Afghan Culture and Art, Ministry of Information, Culture and Tourism; fmr mem. Drafting Cttee of Constitution of Afghanistan; mem. Grand Nat. Ass. (Loya Jirga) 1976; put under house arrest following Communist coup d'etat April 1978; moved to Pakistan after Soviet invasion; apptd mem. High Council and Chair. Cttee of Culture and Publicity, Islamic Unity of Afghanistan Mujahedeen 1982; selected as Head of Radio Free Kabul by Mujahidin parties; served as adviser with rank of Minister to Pres. of Afghan Interim Govt; co-f. Nat. Islamic Movt of Afghanistan in Peshawar, Pakistan 1988; abandoned Afghan resistance and left for USA following disagreements with Jihad leaders 1991; Co-founder and first Chair. Asscn for Peace and Democracy for Afghanistan 1996; mem. Exec. Cttee Loya Jirga, Rome 1998; selected as Minister of Information, Culture and Tourism of Interim Admin, Bonn Conf. 2002; Chair. Kabul City Council 2003; Amb. to India 2007–; Medal for serving the freedom of speech and promoting cultural activities, presented by HM Zahir Shah 2004. *Publications:* Tears of Khorasan, The Mourners, reply to Khalili (poetry), Today's Muslims (in Pashto); several books and articles on culture, literature, history and Islamic Sufism, the works of Sayed Jamaludeen Afghani, Daqiqi Nama, research on Amir Khosrow, and the Relations of Afghanistan and the subcontinent; f. and published resistance magazines and papers, in Dari, Pashto, Urdu, Arabic and English. *Address:* Embassy of Afghanistan, Plot No. 5, Block 50-F, Shanti Path, Chanakyapuri, New Delhi 110 021, India (office). *Telephone:* (11) 26883601 (office). *Fax:* (11) 26875439 (office). *E-mail:* embassyafghanistan@yahoo.co.in (office).

RAHIL, Shafi; Afghan government official; Dir-Gen. Bakhtar News Agency 2005–08. *Address:* c/o Bakhtar News Agency, Ministry of Information and Culture, Mohammad Jan Khan Wat, beside Spinzar Hotel, Kabul, Afghanistan. *Telephone:* (20) 2101304. *Fax:* (20) 2101304.

RAHIM, Arbab Ghulam, MB BS; Pakistani physician and politician; b. 15 Sept. 1956, Mirpurkhas Dist, Sindh Prov.; s. of Arbab Taj Muhammad; m.; ed Cadet Coll. Petaro, Sind Medical Coll., Karachi; Chair. Dist Council, Mirpurkhas 1984–87; Public Health Eng and Rural Devt Adviser to Chief Minister of Sindh 1988; elected to Nat. Ass. 1993, 1996, 1999, Chair. Steering Cttee for Ind. Mems, Standing Cttee on Commerce, Parl. Sec. for Water and

Power; Prov. Minister of Sindh for Local Govt, Katchi Abadis and Public Health Eng 2000, for Works and Services 2003–04; Chief Minister of Sindh and Leader of the House 2004–07; Founding Pres. Sindh Democratic Alliance 1999–2000; beaten with shoes by mob of political activists and fmr servants 7 April 2008. *Address:* Khetlari, Tehsil Diplo, District Tharparkar, Sindh, Pakistan (home). *Telephone:* (21) 5383114 (home).

RAHIM, Q. A. M. A.; Bangladeshi diplomatist and organization official; b. 24 Dec. 1942, Naogaon; m.; two s.; ed Univ. of Dhaka; fmr Del. Bangladesh Missions to Tokyo, London, Doha, Islamabad, Washington, DC and UN, New York; Dir of Secr. SAARC 1990–92, Sec.-Gen. 2002–05; High Commr to Pakistan 1993–98, to Australia (concurrently accred to NZ and Fiji) 1998–99; Prin. Foreign Service Training Acad. 1999–2000; Sec. to the Govt 1999–2000; retd from govt service 2000; Officer on Special Duty (Sec.), Ministry of Foreign Affairs 2000–01; Sec.-Gen. SAARC 2002–05. *Address:* c/o Ministry of Foreign Affairs, Segunbagicha, Dhaka 1000, Bangladesh (office).

RAHIMOV, Saidahmad Borievich; Uzbekistan politician and banker; *Chairman, National Bank for Foreign Economic Activity;* b. 1960; fmr Presidential Adviser for Socioeconomic Affairs; fmr Chair., Auditing Comm.; fmr Man. Asaka Bank; Minister of Finance 2004–05; currently Chair. Nat. Bank for Foreign Economic Activity. *Address:* National Bank for Foreign Economic Activity, 100047 Tashkent, Uzbekistan (office). *Telephone:* (71) 133-62-87 (office). *Fax:* (71) 132-01-72 (office). *E-mail:* webmaster@central.nbu.com (office). *Website:* www.eng.nbu.com (office).

RAHMAN, A. S. F.; Bangladeshi business executive; *Chairman, Beximco Group;* Chair. Beximco Group, including Beximco Pharmaceutical Ltd, Beximco Holdings Ltd, Beximco Agro-Chemicals Ltd, Beximco Foods Ltd, Beximco Synthetics Ltd, Comtrade Beximco Apparels Ltd, Sonali Ansh., Beximco Infusions Ltd; Dir IPDC; mem. Bd of Govs Bangladesh Enterprise Inst. *Address:* Beximco Pharmaceuticals Ltd, 17 Dhanmondi R/A, Road No. 2, Dhaka 1205, Bangladesh (office). *Telephone:* (2) 9127721 (office). *Fax:* (2) 8613470 (office). *Website:* www.beximco.net (office).

RAHMAN, Allah Rakha (A. R.); Indian musician (keyboards), singer and composer; b. (A. S. Dileep Kumar), 6 Jan. 1966, Chennai; s. of the late R. K. Sekhar and of Kareema Begum; ed Padma Seshadri Bal Bhavan, Madras Christian Coll. and Trinity Coll. of Music, London; studied piano aged four; began musical career aged 11 as keyboard player, performing with Illaiyaraja's troupe, later with the orchestras of M. S. Vishwanathan and Ramesh Naidu; mem. local rock bands, including Roots, Magic and Nemesis Avenue; began composing 1987–; f. Panchathan Record Inn studio 1989; performances and recordings with many artists, including Nusrat Fateh Ali Khan, Apache Indian, Zakir Hussein, Dr L. Shankar, Talvin Singh, Dominic Miller, David Byrne and Michael Jackson (Friends of the World, Munich 2002); has created music for many TV and radio advertisements as well as scores for corp. videos and documentaries; fuses music of different traditions (Western classical, reggae, rock and Karnatic music); Padma Shree 2000; SuMu Music Award 1993, R. D. Burman Awards 1993, 1995, Telega Purashkar Award 1992, 1993, 1994, Filmfare Awards 1992–2002, MTV-VMA Award (for song Dil Se Re, from Dil Se..) 1999, Bommai Nagi Reddy Award, Rajiv Gandhi Award. *Film soundtracks include:* Roja (Nat. Film Award 1993, Cinema Express Award 1993) 1992, Vaishnavar 1992, Uzhavan 1993, Thiruda 1993, Pudhiya Mugam 1993, Kizhaku Seemaiyilae 1993, Nippu Ravva 1993, Mawaali Raj 1993, Gentleman (Cinema Express Award 1994) 1993, Ashokan 1993, Duet 1994, Kadhalan (Cinema Express Award 1995) 1994, Karuthamma 1994, May Madham 1994, Pavithra 1994, Super Police 1994, Vandicholai Chinraasu 1994, Bombay 1995, Gang Master 1995, Indira 1995, Muthu 1995, Rangeela 1995, Anthimandaari 1996, Fire 1996, Indian 1996, Love Birds 1996, Mr Romeo 1996, Kadhal Desam (Screen-Videocon Awards 1997, Cinema Express Award 1997) 1996, Daud 1997, Iddaru 1997, Iruvar 1997, Kabhi Na Kabhi 1997, Minsaara Kanavu (Nat. Film Award for Best Music Direction 1998, Screen-Videocon Award 1998) 1997, Ratchakan 1997, 1947/Earth 1998, Dil Se… (Zee Sangeet Award 1999) 1998, Doli Saja Ke Rakhna 1998, Jeans (Cinema Express Award 1999) 1998, En Swasa Kaatre 1999, Kadhalar Dhinam 1999, Muthalvan 1999, Padaiyappa 1999, Pukar 1999, Sangamam 1999, Taal (Screen-Videocon Award 2000, Zee Cine Award 2000, Zee Gold Bollywood Award 2000, Int. India Film Award 2000) 1999, Thakshak 1999, Alai Payuthey 2000, Kandukondain Kandukondain 2000, Rhythm 2000, Thenaali 2000, Zubeidaa 2000, Alli Arjuna 2001, Lagaan 2001, One 2 Ka 4 2001, Parthale Paravasam 2001, Star 2001, Legend of Bhagat Singh 2002, Baba 2002, Saathiya 2002, Nee Manasu Naaku Telusu 2003, Udhaya 2003, Parasuram 2003, Boys 2003, Tian di ying xiong 2003, Tehzeeb 2003, New 2004, Ennaku 20 Unakku 18 2004, Lakeer – Forbidden Lines 2004, Kangalal Kaidhu Sei 2004, Meenaxi: Tale of 3 Cities 2004, Naani 2004, Yuva 2004, Ayitha Ezhuthu 2004, Dil Ne Jise Apna Kaha 2004, Swades 2004, Kisna: The Warrior Poet 2005, Netaji Subhas Chandra Bose: The Forgotten Hero 2005, The Rising: Ballad of Mangal Pandey 2005, Ah Aah: Anbe Aaruyire 2005, Rang De Basanti 2006, Godfather 2006, Provoked 2006, Paani 2006, Mazhab: The Religion 2006, Khazan 2006, Jodhaa Akbar 2008, Jaane Tu Ya Jaane Na 2008, Slumdog Millionaire (Golden Globe Award for Best Musical Score 2009, BAFTA Award for Best Film Music 2009, Academy Award for Best Original Score 2009, Academy Award for Best Original Song (music) 2009) 2008, Yuvraaj 2008, Ghajini 2008. *TV soundtracks include:* Vande Mataram (Screen-Videocon Award 1998) 1997. *Musicals include:* Bombay Dreams (with Don Black) 2001, The Lord of the Rings (with Varttina) (Princess of Wales Theatre, Toronto) 2006. *Recordings include:* Deen Isai Malai (Muslim devotional songs) 1988, Set Me Free (launch album of Malgudi Subha) 1992, Vande Mataram 1997, Jana Gana Mana 2000. *Leisure interest:* singing. *Address:* c/o The Really Useful Group, 22 Tower Street, London, WC2H 9TW, England (office). *E-mail:* contact@arrahman.com (office). *Website:* www.arrahman.com.

RAHMAN, Atta-Ur, BSc, MSc, PhD, FRS, FRSC; Pakistani politician, chemist and academic; *Federal Minister and Chairman, Higher Education Commission and Adviser to the Prime Minister on Science and Technology;* b. 20 Sept. 1942, Delhi, India; s. of Jameel-Ur-Rahman and Amtul Subhan; m. Nargis Begum; ed Coventry Univ. and Univ. of Cambridge, UK, Karachi Univ.; Lecturer in Chem., Karachi Univ. 1964–69, Asst Prof. 1969–74, Assoc. Prof. 1974–81, Prof. 1981–; Fellow, King's Coll. Cambridge 1969–73, Hon. Life Fellow; Co-Dir HEJ Research Inst. of Chem. 1977–81, Dir 1990–; Co-ordinator-Gen., Org. of Islamic Conf. (OIC) Standing Cttee on Scientific and Technological Co-operation (COMSTECH) 1996–; Fed. Minister for Science and Tech. 1999–2002, for Educ. 2002; Chair. Higher Educ. Comm. (rank of Fed. Minister) 2002–; Adviser to Prime Minister and Minister, Ministry of Science and Tech. 2003–04, Adviser to Prime Minister on Science and Tech. 2005–; Pres. Chem. Soc. of Pakistan 1992, Network of Acads of Science in the Countries of the Org. of Islamic Conf. (NASIC) 2004–; Vice-Pres. Pakistan Acad. of Sciences 1997–2001, Pres. 2003–06; Chair. Working Group on Science and Tech. (Pakistan) 1998–2003; Scientific Adviser to CIBA Foundation, London 1995; mem. Nat. Comm. for Science and Tech. 1985–, Steering Cttee for Establishment of Chem. Centre in Trieste, Italy; mem. editorial bds of several int. journals, Advisory Bd Journal of Pharmacy of Istanbul Univ., Turkey 1998; mem. ACS, American Soc. of Pharmacognosy, Swiss Chemical Soc., New York Acad. of Sciences, Russian Acad. of Sciences, Repub. of Uzbekistan Acad. of Natural Sciences; Fellow, Third World Acad. of Sciences 1985 (Vice-Pres. (Cen. and S Asia) Council), Islamic Acad. of Sciences 1988; Foreign Fellow, Korean Acad. of Science and Tech. 2004; Commonwealth Scholar 1985–86; Tamgha-I-Imtiaz (Pakistan) 1983, Sitara-I-Imtiaz (Pakistan) 1991, Hilal-I-Imtiaz 1998, Nishan-I-Imtiaz 2002; Hon. ScD (Cambridge) 1987, Hon. DEduc (Coventry) 2007; several awards, including Pakistan Acad. of Sciences Gold Medal 1977, 1984, 1996, Gold Medal, Govt of Kuwait 1980, Best Scientist of the Year Award, Govt of Pakistan 1986, FPCCI Prize for Technological Innovation (Pakistan) 1985, Scientist of the Year (Pakistan) 1987, Islamic Org. Prize for Science (Kuwait) 1988, First Prize at Sixth Khwrazmi Festival, Pres. of Iran 1993, Baba-I-Urdu Award (Pakistan) 1994, Salimuzzaman Siddiqui Gold Medal, Pakistan Intellectuals Forum 1995, Prime Minister's Gold Medal 1995, Pakistan Acad. of Sciences-INFAQ Foundation Prize in Science 1995, Fed. of Asian Chemical Socs Award (Japan) 1997, Third World Acad. of Sciences Award 1999, UNESCO Science Prize (first Muslim scientist) 1999, ECO Prize 2000, ISESCO Chem. Award 2001, Gold Medal of the Scientific Partnership Charitable Foundation, Inter Bio Screen Ltd, Russia 2004. *Publications:* has written or edited 93 books, mostly published in Europe, USA and Japan, has written 59 book chapters, 611 research papers in leading int. scientific journals and 15 patents. *Leisure interests:* reading, cricket, table tennis. *Address:* Higher Education Commission, Sector H-9, Islamabad (office); House No. 35, Ministers' Enclave, Islamabad, Pakistan (home). *Telephone:* (51) 9259201 (office); (51) 9259202 (office); (21) 9202603 (home). *Fax:* (51) 9259203 (office); (51) 2823850 (home). *E-mail:* chairman@hec.gov.pk (office); attast@comsats.net.pk (home). *Website:* www.hec.gov.pk (office).

RAHMAN, Latifur, LLB, MA; Bangladeshi judge (retd); b. 1 March 1936, Jessore Town; s. of the late Khan Bahadur Lutfor Rahman; ed Jessore Zilla School, Dhaka Coll. and Dhaka Univ.; Lecturer in English, Jagannath Coll. and Suhrawardy Coll., Dhaka; Advocate of the Dhaka High Court 1960; Advocate of the then Supreme Court of Pakistan 1965; Additional Judge, Supreme Court of Bangladesh, High Court Div. 1979, Permanent Judge 1981, Judge of the Appellate Div. 1990; Chief Justice of Bangladesh 2000–01; Chief Adviser of the Caretaker Govt of Bangladesh July–Oct. 2001; Head Interim Govt which conducted elections –2002; mem. Enquiry Comm. into train accident at Majukhan 1989; Chair. Enquiry Comm. into damage to aircraft and naval vessels in cyclone at Chittagong 1991. *Address:* Dhanmondi, Dhaka, Bangladesh (office).

RAHMAN, M. Nefaur; Bangladeshi business executive; fmr Chair. Bangladesh Sugar and Food Industries Corpn. *Address:* c/o Bangladesh Sugar and Food Industries Corporation, Motijheel C/A, Dhaka, 1000, Bangladesh. *Telephone:* (2) 9565869. *E-mail:* chinikal@bttb.net.bd.

RAHMAN, M. Saifur; Bangladeshi chartered accountant and politician; b. March 1932, Maulvibazar, Sylhet Div.; m.; three s. one d.; ed Dhaka Univ.; f. chartered accountancy firm, Rahman Rahman Huq; Minister of Finance, Planning, Commerce and Foreign Trade 1976–1982, of Finance and Planning 2001–06; Chair. of various cabinet cttees 1976–1982, 1991–94; mem. Jatiya Sangsad (Nat. Ass.) 1979–82, 1996–99, 2001; Acting Chair. Bangladesh Jatiyatabadi Dal (Bangladesh Nationalist Party); fmr Chair. Bd Govs IMF, World Bank. *Address:* Bangladesh Jatiyatabadi Dal, Banani Office, House 23, Road 13, Dhaka (office); c/o Rahman Rahman Huq, 9 Mohakhali C/A, 11th floor, Dhaka, 1212 Bangladesh (office). *Telephone:* (2) 8819525 (office). *Fax:* (2) 8813063 (office). *E-mail:* bnpbd@e-fsbd.net (office). *Website:* www.bnpbd.com (office).

RAHMANI, Chérif, PhD; Algerian politician; *Minister of Urban and Rural Planning and the Environment and of Tourism;* b. 16 Jan. 1945, Aïn Oussera; m.; four c.; ed Ecole Nat. d'Admin; fmr Prof., Univ. of Poitiers; fmr Prof., Ecole Nat. d'Admin; fmr Sub-Man. Local Communities, Ministry of the Interior, also Dir Admin and Local Finances and Gen. Man. Local Communities; fmr Inspector Gen., Presidency of the Repub.; fmr Wali de Tébessa; fmr Wali of Algiers; fmr Sec. Gen. to the Ministry of the Interior; Minister of Youth and Sport 1988–89, of Equipment 1989–90, for Equipment and Regional Planning, Minister Gov. of Greater Algiers, on Mission Extraordinary in Charge of Admin of Wilaya of Algiers; currently Minister of Urban and Rural Planning and the Environment and of Tourism; UNEP Champion of the Earth Laureate 2007. *Address:* Ministry of Urban and Rural Planning, the Environment and Tourism, rue des Quatre Canons, Bab-el-Oued, Algiers, Algeria (office). *Telephone:* (21) 43-28-77 (office); (21) 65-23-82 (office); (21) 65-10-68 (office); (21) 66-63-21 (office). *Fax:* (21) 43-28-55 (office). *E-mail:* deeai@ifrance.com (office). *Website:* www.mate-dz.org (office).

RAHMOUNI, Hassan, LLM, PhD; Moroccan lawyer, academic and politician; b. 10 Dec. 1949; m.; four c.; ed Fairfax High School, Va, USA, Univ. Mohamed V, Rabat, Sorbonne Univ., Paris, France; Chief of Legal Service, Office for Industrial Devt, Ministry of Industry 1975–77; Asst Prof., Lecturer and Chair Prof., School of Law and Econs, Mohamed V Univ., Rabat 1977–98; Prof. of Admin. Law, Moroccan Royal Mil. Acad. 1977–80, Prof. of English Terminology in Law 1983–85; Prof. and Staff Coordinator, US Peace Corps, Michigan State Univ. 1981; Prof. of Law, Inst. Nat. d'Aménagement et d'Urbanisme, Ministry of Urban Devt 1981–82; Counsellor to Cabinet of Minister of Admin. Affairs 1987–88; Dir of Gen. Matters, Ministry of Communication 1989–92; Gov. of Mohammedia, apptd by King Hassan II 1992–93; Gov. of Mohammedia (Casablanca) 1994–98; Prof. of Constitutional Law, Political Science and Local Admin., Hassan II Univ. 1998–2005, Vice-Pres. of Hassan II Univ. 2002–03; currently attorney and legal consultant, Casablanca; Visiting Prof., Indiana State Univ. 2000–04, Wayne State Univ. 2000, Purdue Univ. 2001; Program Dir Indiana State Univ., funded by USAID 2003; consultant to Govt of Equatorial Guinea 1992, Govt of Congo 1992; Vice-Pres. Moroccan Nat. Asscn for Governance; mem. Casablanca Order of Lawyers, Moroccan Fulbright Asscn, Nat. Union of Univ. Profs, Nat. Asscn of Civil Service; Trustee Mohammedia School of Law and Social Sciences; Chevalier, Order of the Throne (Morocco) 1994; Green March Medal 1975, Fulbright Scholar, George Wash. Univ. 1985, Fulbright Visiting Specialist Harvard Univ. 2004. *Publications:* English for Economists (co-author) 1985, Droit Administratif et Sciences Administratives (co-author) 1990; numerous book chapters, scholarly articles and conf. papers. *Address:* Quartier Alsace Lorraine, Mers Sultan, Casablanca, Morocco. *Telephone:* 22-541515. *Fax:* 22-541717. *E-mail:* hr@hassanrahmouni.com. *Website:* www.hassanrahmouni.com.

RAI, Aishwarya, (Aishu); Indian actress and model; b. 1 Nov. 1973, Mangalore, Karnataka; d. of Krishnaraj Rai and Vrinda Rai; m. Abhishek Bachchan 2007; studied architecture in Bombay (now Mumbai); worked as model for advertising campaigns and major fashion shows; won Miss Catwalk, Miss Photogenic and Miss Perfect 10 competitions; runner-up in Miss India Contest 1994; winner Miss World Contest 1994; Discovery of the Year (Screen) 1998. *Films include:* Mamagaru 1991, Iruvar (also known as Duo, Iddaru) 1997, Aur Pyar Ho Gaya 1997, Jeans 1998, Aa Ab Laut Chalen 1999, Hum Dil De Chuke Sanam 1999, Taal 1999, Mela – The Great Entertainer 2000, Kandukondain Kandukondain 2000, Josh 2000, Mohabbatein 2000, Dhai Akshar Prem Ke 2000, Hamare Dil Aapke Paas Hai 2000, Sanam Tere Hain Hum 2000, Albela 2001, Devdas (Filmfare Awards, Best Actress 2003) 2002, Hum Tumhare Hain Sanam 2002, Hum Kisi Se Kum Nahin 2002, 23rd March 1931: Shaheed (song) 2002, Shakthi: The Power 2002, Dil Ka Rishta 2003, Kyon Ho Gaya Na 2003, Khakee 2003, Chokher Bali 2003, Kuch Naa Kaho 2003, Khakee 2004, Bride and Prejudice 2004, The Mistress of Spices 2005, Provoked 2006, Umrao Jaan 2006, Guru 2007, The Last Legion 2007, Jodhaa Akbar 2007. *Address:* Aishwarya Rai Fanmail, 12 La Mer, Chandiwala Compound, Bandra (West), Mumbai 400050; 402 Ramlaxmi Niwas, 16th Road, Khar (West), Mumbai 400054, India.

RAIDI; Chinese politician; *Vice-Chairman, 10th Standing Committee, National People's Congress;* b. 1938, Biru Co., northern Tibet; ed Cen. Nationalities Inst., Cen. Political Science and Law Cadre School, Beijing, CCP Cen. Cttee Cen. Party School; Sec. Public Security Div., Nagqu Prefectural Admin. Office, Tibet Autonomous Region 1962–66; worker, Mil. Control Comm., Nagqu Prefecture, PLA Tibet Mil. Region 1966–68, CCP Revolutionary Cttee 1968–72; Sec. CCP Nagqu Autonomous Prefectural Cttee 1972–75; Sec. CCP Tibet Autonomous Regional Cttee 1977–85, Deputy Sec. 1985–2002, Sec. Comm. for Discipline Inspection 1979–85; Chair. Peasants' Fed. of Tibet 1975; Vice-Chair. Revolutionary Cttee, Tibet Autonomous Region 1977–79; Vice-Chair. Standing Cttee Tibet Autonomous Regional People's Congress 1979–83, Chair. 1986–93; Chair. Standing Cttee Tibet Autonomous Regional 6th People's Congress 1993–; Deputy, 8th NPC, Tibet Autonomous Region; Alt. mem. 11th CCP Cen. Cttee 1977–82, mem. 12th CCP Cen. Cttee 1982–87, 13th CCP Cen. Cttee 1987–92, 14th CCP Cen. Cttee 1992–97, 15th CCP Cen. Cttee 1997–2002, 16th CCP Cen. Cttee 2002–07; Vice-Chair. 10th Standing Cttee of NPC 2003–. *Address:* Chinese Communist Party, Tibet Autonomous Region, Lhasa, Tibet, People's Republic of China (office).

RAIGETAL, Larry; Micronesian civil servant; *Director, Department of Youth and Civic Affairs, Yap State Government;* b. 4 July 1968, Lamotrek Atoll; two d.; ed Oxford Univ., UK, Univ. of San Francisco, Calif., USA; Dean of Students, Xavier High School, Chuuk 1992–93; diplomatic functions 1993–2001; Chair. FSM Banking Bd 1998–; Chief of Manpower, Yap State Govt 2001–04; Dir, Dept of Youth and Civic Affairs, Yap State Govt 2007–. *Leisure interest:* fishing. *Address:* Office of the Director, Department for Youth and Civic Affairs, PO Box 430, Yap, FM 96943 (office); Box 254, Colonia Yap, 96943, Micronesia (home). *Telephone:* 320-2168 (office). *Fax:* 320-3898 (office). *E-mail:* lraigetal@mail.fm (home); dyca@mail.fm (office).

RAIKIN, Konstantin Arkadyevich; Russian actor and theatre director; *Artistic Director, Theatre Satirikon;* b. 8 July 1950, Leningrad; s. of Arkady Raikin and Roma M. Joffe; m. Elena Butenko; one d.; ed M. Shchukin Theatre High School, Moscow; theatre Sovremennik 1971–81, debut in Valentin and Valentina; 38 roles including 15 leading, acted in plays of Shakespeare and Russian classics; actor State Theatre of Miniatures (renamed Theatre Satirikon 1987) under Arkady Raikin 1981–87, actor and Artistic Dir 1988–;

Prize for Best Acting, Belgrade Festival 1990, People's Artist of Russia 1992, State Prize 1996, Gold Mask Prize 1996, Stanislavsky Prize 1998, Order of the Fatherland 2000. *Films:* Sensation is Anything 1971, Friends Among Strangers, Strangers Among Friends 1972. *TV Films:* Truffaldino from Bergamo 1976, The Island of Dead Ships 1988, Shadow 1990, Failure Puaro 2002. *Stage appearances include:* Cyrano de Bergerac (Cyrano) 1992, The Magnanimous Cuckold (Bruno) 1994, Metamorphosis (Gregor Zamza) 1995, The Threepenny Opera (Mack the Knife) 1996, Jacques and His Master (Jacques) 1998, Hamlet (Hamlet) 1998, Double Bass 2000. *Plays directed include:* Mowgli 1990, Butterflies Are Free 1993, Romeo and Juliet 1995, The Chioggian Squabbles 1997, Quartet 1999, Chanticleer 2001. *Address:* Theatre Satirikon, Sheremetyevskaya str. 8, 129594 Moscow, Russia. *Telephone:* (495) 289-87-07 (office). *Fax:* (495) 284-49-37 (office). *E-mail:* theatre@satirikon.msk .ru (office). *Website:* www.satirikon.ru (office).

RAIKOV, Gennady Ivanovich; Russian engineer and politician; b. 8 Aug. 1939, Khabarovsk; m.; one s.; ed Omsk State Machine Construction Inst.; mechanical engineer, docent, Omsk State Machine-Construction Inst. 1956–63; lawyer Russian Acad. of Civil Service; engineer, Head of workshop, Deputy Chief Engineer, Branch Dir Omsk Machine Construction production corpn 1961–77; Chief Engineer, Dir-Gen. Tumen Motor Mfg plant 1977–90; Head of City Admin., Tumen City Soviet 1990–93; Deputy Chief Tumennefte-gazstroy Co. 1993, Deputy Dir-Gen. 1995–; Deputy Dir-Gen. Siberian Wood Co., Sweden 1993–95; mem. State Duma of Russian Fed. representing Tyumen dist 1995–, Leader People's Deputy faction 2000, mem. Duma Security Cttee, Mandate Comm., currently Head, Credentials and Ethics Comm.; mem. Perm. Del. of Fed. Ass. of Russian Fed. to Ass. of WEU; Rep. of State Duma to Perm. Comm. of Parl. Ass. Union of Belarus and Russian Fed.; mem. Governmental Comm. of Russian Fed. for participation in APEC forum; Chair. People's Party of the Russian Fed. 2001–04, now mem. United Russia party; Order Sign of Honour, Order of Red Banner of Labour, Order of October Revolution, Order for Service to Motherland (Fourth Degree), Order of Saint Sergei of Radonezh (Second Degree); several medals. *Leisure interest:* ice hockey. *Address:* State Duma, Okhotny Ryad 1, 103265 Moscow, Russia (office). *Telephone:* (495) 292-87-01 (office). *Fax:* (495) 292-87-15 (office).

RAIMI, Samuel (Sam) Marshall; American film director, producer and screenwriter; b. 23 Oct. 1959, Franklin, Mich.; ed Mich. State Univ. *Films include:* as director: The Evil Dead (also producer/writer) 1981, Evil Dead II (also producer/writer) 1987, Darkman 1990, Army of Darkness (also producer/writer) 1993, The Quick and the Dead 1995, A Simple Plan 1998, For Love of the Game 1999, The Gift 2000, Spider-Man 2002, Spider-Man 2 2004, Spider-Man 3 (also writer) 2007; as producer: Hard Target 1993, Timecop 1994, The Grudge 2004, Boogeyman 2005, Rise 2007, 30 Days of Night 2007; as writer: The Hudsucker Proxy 1994. *Television series:* as producer: M.A.N.T.I.S. 1994, Hercules: The Legendary Journeys 1994, American Gothic 1995, Xena: Warrior Princess 1995, Spy Game 1997, Young Hercules 1998, Jack of All Trades 2000, Cleopatra 2525 2000. *Address:* c/o Creative Artists Agency, 9830 Wilshire Boulevard, Beverly Hills, CA 90212–1825, USA. *Telephone:* (310) 288-4545. *Fax:* (310) 288-4800. *Website:* www.caa.com.

RAIMOND, Jean-Bernard; French diplomatist and politician; b. 6 Feb. 1926, Paris; s. of Henri Raimond and Alice Auberty; m. Monique Chabanel 1975; two d.; ed Ecole Normale Supérieure and Ecole Nat. d'Admin.; CNRS 1951–53; Dept of Political Affairs and Cen. Admin. of Ministry of Foreign Affairs 1956–66; Deputy Dir Europe 1967; Asst Dir Office of Minister of Foreign Affairs 1967; Tech. Counsellor, Office of Prime Minister 1968–69; Sec.-Gen. Presidency of the Repub. 1969–73; Amb. to Morocco 1973–77; Dir for N Africa and the Levant 1977–78; Dir Office of Minister of Foreign Affairs 1978; Dir-Gen. for Cultural Relations, Ministry of Foreign Affairs 1979–81; Amb. to Poland 1982–84, to USSR 1984–86; Minister of Foreign Affairs 1986–88; Amb. to Holy See, Rome 1988–91; Deputy to Nat. Ass. from Bouches-du-Rhône (RPR) 1993–2002; Amb. de France 1991; Adviser to the Pres. of the Servier Laboratory 1992–99; Hon. Pres. French-Russian Friendship Soc. (Sofarus), France–Italy Asscn; Officier, Légion d'honneur; Commdr, Ordre nat. du Mérite; Chevalier des Palmes Académiques; Order of Ouissan Alaouite (Morocco), Grand Cross, Order of Pius IX (Holy See). *Publications:* Le Quai d'Orsay à l'épreuve de la cohabitation 1989, Le choix de Gorbatchev 1992, Jean-Paul II, un pape au cœur de l'histoire 1999. *Address:* Société Française des Amis de la Russie, 12 rue Claude Décaen, 75012 Paris (office); 12 rue des Poissonniers, 92200 Neuilly-sur-Seine, France (home). *E-mail:* courrier -sofarus@caramail.com (office). *Website:* www.cybel.fr/html/Communaute/russie/index_comm_russie.htm (office).

RAIMONDI, Ruggero; Monegasque singer (bass) and director; b. 3 Oct. 1941, Bologna, Italy; m. Isabel Maier 1987; operatic debut in La Bohème, Spoleto Festival 1964; debut at Metropolitan Opera, New York in Ernani 1970; engagements include Don Giovanni, Le Nozze di Figaro, Faust, Attila, Nabucco, Don Carlos, Boris Godunov, Don Quichotte, Don Pasquale, Otello, Contes d'Hoffmann, Carmen, Il Viaggio a Rheims, Falstaff, I Vespri Siciliani, I Lombardi, L'Italiana in Algieri, Il Turco in Italia, Tosca, Assassinio nella Cattedrale, Cosi fan' Tutte and others; Commdr des Arts et des Lettres, Officier de la Légion d'honneur, Kt, Order of Malta, Grand Ufficiale della Repubblica Italiana, Citizen of Honour, Athens, Commdr du Mérite Culturel (Monaco). *Opera productions include:* Don Giovanni, The Barber of Seville, Don Carlos. *Films:* Don Giovanni 1979, Six Characters in Search of a Singer 1981, La Truite 1982, Life is a Bed of Roses 1983, Carmen 1984, Boris Godounov 1989, Les couleurs du Diable 1997, Tosca 2001. *Television:* Boris Godunov staged by Joseph Losey at Opéra Nat. de Paris 1980, Six personnages en quête d'un chanteur by Maurice Bejart 1981, Verdi's Requiem 1982, Ernani directed by Kirk Browning (with Milnes and Pavarotti) 1983, José Carreras and Friends: Opera Recital 1991, Le nozze di Figaro directed by

Brian Large 1992, Tosca: In the Settings and at the Times of Tosca, directed by Brian Large (with Malfitano and Domingo) 1992, Il Turco in Italia with Cecilia Bartoli at Zurich Opera House 2001, Così fan tutte staged by Patrice Chéreau 2005. *Recordings include:* Verdi: Aida 1983, 2005, Rossini: L'Italiana in Algeri 1989, Puccini: Turandot 1990, Rossini: Il Viaggio a Reims 1990, Verdi: Don Carlos 1990, Rossini: Il barbiere di Siviglia 1993, Verdi: Un Ballo in Maschera 1998, Mozart: Le Nozze di Figaro 2003, Rossini: La Cenerentola 2003, Rossini: Il Barbiere di Siviglia (DVD) 2005, Verdi: Attila 2005. *Address:* 140 bis rue Lecourbe, 75015 Paris, France (home).

RAINE, Craig Anthony, BA, BPhil; British writer; b. 3 Dec. 1944, Shildon, Co. Durham; s. of Norman Edward and Olive Marie Raine; m. Ann Pasternak Slater 1972; three s. one d.; ed Exeter Coll., Oxford; Lecturer, Exeter Coll., Oxford 1971–72, 1975–76, Lincoln Coll. 1974–75, Christ Church 1976–79; Books Ed. New Review 1977–78; Ed. Quarto 1979–80; Poetry Ed. New Statesman 1981; Poetry Ed. Faber and Faber Ltd 1981–91; Fellow in English, New Coll. Oxford 1991–; Ed. Areté 1999–; Kelus Prize 1979, Southern Arts Literature Award 1979, Cholmondeley Poetry Award 1983, Sunday Times Award for Literary Excellence 1998. *Publications:* The Onion, Memory 1978, A Martian Sends a Postcard Home 1979, A Free Translation 1981, Rich 1984, The Electrification of the Soviet Union (opera) 1986, A Choice of Kipling's Prose (ed.) 1987, The Prophetic Book 1988, '1953' (play) 1990, Haydn and the Valve Trumpet: Literary Essays 1990, Rudyard Kipling: Selected Poetry (ed.) 1992, History: The Home Movie 1994, Clay. Whereabouts Unknown 1996, New Writing 7 1998, A la recherche du temps perdu 1999, In Defence of T.S. Eliot: Literary Essays (Vol. 2) 2000, Collected Poems 1978–1999 2000, Rudyard Kipling: The Wish House and Other Stories (ed.) 2002, T.S. Eliot 2006. *Leisure interests:* music, skiing. *Address:* New College, Oxford, OX1 3BN, England (office).

RAINES, Howell, MA; American journalist and editor; ed Birmingham-Southern Coll. and Univ. of Alabama; journalist, Birmingham Post-Herald 1964, Birmingham (Ala) News 1970; Political Ed. Atlanta Constitution 1971–76, St Petersburg (Fla) Times 1976–78; Nat. Corresp. in Atlanta, NY Times 1978, Atlanta Bureau Chief 1979–81, White House Corresp. 1981–84, Nat. Political Corresp. 1984, Deputy Washington Ed. 1985–87, London Bureau Chief 1987–88, Washington Bureau Chief 1988–93, Editorial Page Ed. 1993–2001, Exec. Ed. 2001–03 (resgnd); currently columnist The Guardian (UK); Pulitzer Prize for feature writing 1992. *Publications:* My Soul Is Rested 1977, Whiskey Man 1977, Fly Fishing Through the Midlife Crisis 1993, The One That Got Away 2006. *Address:* c/o The New York Times, 229 West 43rd Street, New York, NY 10036, USA (office).

RAIS, Amien; Indonesian politician; *General Chairman, Partai Amanat Nasional (PAN) (National Mandate Party);* b. 26 April 1944, Solo, Java; m. Kusnariyati Sri Rahayu; three s. two d.; ed Gadjah Mada Univ., Al Azhar Univ., Cairo, Egypt, Univ. of Notre Dame and Univ. of Chicago, USA; joined Muhammadiyah (Muslim group) 1985, Vice-Chair 1990–95, 1995–98; Chair. People's Consultative Ass. (MPR) 1999–2004; co-f. Partai Amanat Nasional (PAN) (National Mandate Party), Gen. Chair. 1998–; helped found Asscn of Indonesian Muslim Intellectuals (ICMI); Prof., Gadjah Mada Univ., Jogjakarta. *Address:* Partai Amanat Nasional, Jalan H. Nawi 15, Jakarta Selatan 12420, Indonesia (office). *Telephone:* (21) 72794535 (office). *Fax:* (21) 7268695 (office). *Website:* www.geocities.com/CapitolHill/Congress/6678 (office).

RÄISÄNEN, Heikki Martti, MA, DTheol; Finnish professor of New Testament exegesis; *Professor Emeritus, University of Helsinki;* b. 10 Dec. 1941, Helsinki; s. of Martti Olavi Räisänen and Saara Ilona Itkonen; m. Leena Marjatta Wright 1974; three s. one d.; ed Univ. of Helsinki; Lecturer in New Testament Exegesis, Univ. of Helsinki 1969–74, Acting Assoc. Prof. in Biblical Languages 1971–74, Prof. of New Testament Exegesis 1975–2006; Research Prof., Acad. of Finland 1984–94, Acad. Prof. 2001–06, Prof. Emer. 2006–; Dir Exegetical Inst., Univ. of Helsinki 1975–84, 1995–96, Vice-Dean of the Theological Faculty 1978–80, Dir Centre of Excellence 1994–2005; Chief Ed. Vartija 1989–2000; mem. Cttee Finnish Exegetical Soc. 1969–85, Chair. 1980–85; mem. Finnish Acad. of Sciences 1978–, Cttee Soc. for New Testament Studies 1986–89, Academia Europaea 2004; Fulbright Visiting Scholar, Harvard 1970–71; Visiting Scholar, Univ. of Cambridge 1978; Humboldt Visiting Scholar, Tübingen 1980–82; Hon. DD (Edin.) 1990, (Uppsala) 2002; Edward Cadbury Lectures, Univ. of Birmingham 1996, Prize of the Finnish Cultural Foundation 2005, Gad Rausing Prize, Acad. of Letters, Vitterhetsakademi, Stockholm 2006. *Publications:* Die Mutter Jesu im Neuen Testament 1969, Das koranische Jesusbild 1971, The Idea of Divine Hardening 1972, Das 'Messiasgeheimnis' im Markusevangelium 1976, Paul and the Law 1983, The Torah and Christ 1986, The 'Messianic Secret' in Mark's Gospel 1990, Beyond New Testament Theology 1990, Jesus, Paul and Torah 1992, Marcion, Muhammad and the Mahatma 1997, Neutestamentliche Theologie? 2000, Challenges to Biblical Interpretation 2001; numerous books in Finnish; numerous articles on early Christianity. *Leisure interest:* soccer. *Address:* Vantaanjänne 1 B 11, 01730 Vantaa, Finland (home). *Telephone:* (9) 898422 (home). *E-mail:* heikki.raisanen@helsinki.fi (office). *Website:* www.helsinki.fi/teol/hyel (office).

RAISANI, Nawab Muhammad Aslam Khan, MA; Pakistani politician and farmer; *Chief Minister of Balochistan;* b. 5 July 1955, Sarawan, Balochistan; s. of Nawab Ghaus Bakhsh Khan Raisani, fmr Gov. of Balochistan and fed. minister; ed Univ. of Balochistan; Tumandar of Raisani Tribe; became Chief of Sarawan and Raisani tribe following his father's assassination; fmr Deputy Man., BDA; fmr Purchase Officer, PASCO, Jacobabad; apptd as DSP in Balochistan police force following graduation; Minister for Agric., Cooperative, Labour and Manpower in caretaker Prov. Govt Cabinet 1988; Minister for Food and Fisheries in caretaker Prov. Cabinet; elected mem. Prov. Ass. from PB-27 Mastung; mem. Prov. Ass. of Balochistan 1988, 1990,

1993, 2002; joined Pakistan Nat. Party (PNP) 1989, elected Parl. Leader of PNP in Prov. Ass.; apptd Pres. PNP of Balochistan 1990; Minister for Finance in Prov.; joined Pakistan People's Party 1999, mem. Cen. Exec. Cttee; Chief Minister of Balochistan 2008–; Pres. Chamber of Agric., Balochistan; Founder and fmr Pres. Fed. of Chambers of Agric. Pakistan. *Leisure interests:* farming, angling, hiking. *Address:* Office of the Chief Minister, Quetta, Balochistan, Pakistan (office). *E-mail:* info@balochistan.gov.pk (office). *Website:* www.balochistan.gov.pk (office).

RAISER, Konrad; German theologian, academic and fmr organization official; *Visiting Professor, Ecumenical Institute, Château de Bossey;* b. 25 Jan. 1938, Magdeburg; m. Bertha Elisabeth von Weizsaecker 1967; Study Sec., Comm. on Faith and Order, WCC 1969–73, Deputy Gen. Sec. WCC, Gen. Sec. 1992–2004 (retd); Prof. of Systematic Theology and Ecumenics, Univ. of the Ruhr, Bochum 1983–93; currently Visiting Prof., Ecumenical Inst., Château de Bossey, Switzerland; mem. Evangelical Church in Germany (EKD); investor in Oikocredit (microfinance and microcredit org.). *Publications:* Identität und Sozialität 1971, Ökumene im Übergang (Ecumenism in Transition) 1989, Wir stehen noch am Anfang 1994, To Be the Church 1997, For a Culture of Life 2002; more than 200 articles and essays on theological and ecumenical subjects. *Address:* Ecumenical Institute, Château de Bossey, PO Box 1000, 1299 Crans-près-Céligny, Switzerland (office). *Telephone:* (22) 960-7300 (office). *Fax:* (22) 960-7367 (office). *Website:* www.oikoumene.org (office).

RAISMAN, John Michael, CBE, CBIM, MA; British business executive; *Chairman, British Empire and Commonwealth Museum Trust;* b. 12 Feb. 1929, Lahore, India; s. of Sir Jeremy and Renee Mary Raisman (née Kelly); m. Evelyn Anne Muirhead 1953; one s. three d. (one deceased); ed Rugby School, Queen's Coll., Oxford; joined Shell Int. Petroleum Co. Ltd 1953, served in Brazil 1953–60; Gen. Man., Shell Panama 1960–62; Asst to Exploration and Production Co-ordinator, Shell Int. Petroleum, Maatschappij 1963–65; Gen. Man., Shell Co. of Turkey Ltd 1965–69; Pres. Shell Sekiyu KK 1970–73; Head of European Supply and Marketing, Shell Int. Petroleum 1974–77; Man. Dir, Shell UK Oil 1977–78; Deputy Chair. and CEO Shell UK Ltd 1978–79, Chair. and CEO 1979–85; Chair. Shell Chemicals UK Ltd 1979–85; Dir Vickers 1981–90, Glaxo Holdings PLC 1982–90, Lloyds Bank 1985–95, Lloyds TSB 1996–98, Lloyds Merchant Bank Holdings 1985–87, Candover 1990–98, Tandem Computers 1991–97, British Biotech. 1993–98 (Chair. 1995–98); Deputy Chair. British Telecom 1987–91; mem. Pres.'s Cttee of Confed. of British Industry (CBI), Chair. Europe Cttee of CBI 1980–88, Council of Industry for Man. Educ. 1981–85, Oil Industry Emergency Cttee (OIEC) 1981–85, Advisory Council, London Enterprise Agency 1979–85, Investment Bd Electra Candover Pnrs 1985–95, Electronics Industry EDC 1986–88, Business Forum of European Movt, Council for Industry and Higher Educ. 1991–98; Deputy Chair. Nat. Comm. on Educ. 1991–95; Gov. Nat. Inst. of Econ. and Social Research 1981–; mem. Governing Council of Business in the Community 1982–85; mem. Council, Inst. for Fiscal Studies 1982–92; mem. Royal Comm. on Environmental Pollution 1986–87; Chair. Bd of Trustees RA 1986–96; Pro-Chancellor Univ. of Aston 1987–93; Chair. British Empire and Commonwealth Museum Trust 2002–; Hon. DUniv (Stirling) 1983, Hon. LLD (Aberdeen) 1985, (Manchester) 1986, (UWE) 1994; Hon. DSc (Aston) 1992. *Leisure interests:* golf, travel, opera, theatre. *Address:* Netheravon House, Netheravon Road South, London, W4 2PY, England. *Telephone:* (20) 8994-3731. *Fax:* (20) 8742-1000.

RAISS, Sid Ahmed Ould; Mauritanian politician; Minister of Trade and Industry 2007–08, of Finance 2008–. *Address:* Ministry of Finance, BP 181, Nouakchott, Mauritania (office). *Telephone:* 525-20-20 (office).

RAITT, Bonnie Lynn; American blues singer and musician (guitar, piano); b. 8 Nov. 1949, Burbank, Calif.; d. of the late John Raitt; ed Radcliffe Coll.; performer in blues clubs on American E Coast; numerous concert tours and live appearances. *Recordings include:* albums: Bonnie Raitt 1971, Give It Up 1972, Takin' My Time 1973, Streetlights 1974, Home Plate 1975, Sweet Forgiveness 1977, The Glow 1979, Green Light 1982, Nine Lives 1986, Nick of Time (Grammy Awards for Best Female Rock Vocal Performance, Best Female Pop Vocal Performance, Album of the Year 1990) 1989, I'm in the Mood (with John Lee Hooker) (Grammy Award for Best Blues Traditional Record 1990), The Bonnie Raitt Collection 1990, Luck of the Draw (Grammy Award for Best Female Rock Vocal Performance, Best Duet 1992) 1991, Longing in Their Hearts (Grammy Award for Best Pop Album) 1994, Road Tested 1995, Fundamental 1998, Silver Lining 2002, Souls Alike 2005. *Address:* PO Box 626, Los Angeles, CA 90078, USA. *Website:* www.bonnieraitt.com.

RAITT, Lisa, BSc, MSc, LLB; Canadian politician; *Minister of Natural Resources;* m.; two s.; ed St. Francis Xavier Univ., Univ. of Guelph, Osgoode Hall Law School; fmr Corp. Sec., Toronto Port Authority, then Gen. Counsel, Harbourmaster, Pres. and CEO; MP for Halton 2008–; Minister of Natural Resources 2008–; mem. Conservative Party of Canada. *Address:* Natural Resources Canada, 580 Booth Street, Ottawa ON K1A 0E4, Canada (office). *Telephone:* (613) 995-0947 (office). *Fax:* (613) 996-9094 (office). *E-mail:* questions@nrcan.gc.ca (office). *Website:* www.nrcan-rncan.gc.ca (office).

RAJABOV, Safarali; Tajikistani lawyer and politician; b. 2 Sept. 1955, Fayzabad Dist; m. 1976; two s. six d.; ed Dushanbe State Pedagogical Inst.; Dir Special Training Centre, Fayzabad Dist 1980–86; Tech. Coll. N2U, Fayzabad Dist 1986–90; Deputy of Tajikistan Supreme Soviet 1990–95; Sec., Deputy Chair., Chair. Cttee on Legislation and Human Rights 1990–95; Chair. Majlisi Oli (Parl.) of Tajikistan 1995–2000; Minister of Educ. 2000–05; Dr hc (Tajik State Agrarian Univ.) 1998. *Publications:* Independence is Sacred 1997,

Majlisi Oli 1998. *Address:* c/o Ministry of Education, Nisor Mukhammad 13A, 734024 Dushanbe, Tajikistan.

RAJAN, Raghuram G., BTech, MBA, PhD; Indian academic and fmr international organization official; *Eric J. Gleacher Distinguished Service Professor of Finance, Graduate School of Business, University of Chicago;* ed Indian Inst. of Tech., Delhi, Indian Inst. of Man., Ahmedabad, MIT, USA; Officer, Tata Admin. Service 1987; fmr consultant Fed. Reserve Bd, World Bank, IMF; Asst Prof. of Finance, Grad. School of Business, Univ. of Chicago 1991–95, Prof. of Finance 1995–96, Joseph L. Gidwitz Prof. of Finance 1997–2003, Eric J. Gleacher Distinguished Service Prof. of Finance 2006–; Visiting Prof. of Finance, Kellogg School, Northwestern Univ. 1996–97; Bertil Daniellson Visiting Prof. of Banking, Stockholm School of Econs 1996–97; Fischer Black Visiting Prof., MIT 2000–01; Econ. Counselor and Dir of Research, IMF 2003–06; Program Dir for Corp. Finance, Nat. Bureau of Econ. Research; Dir Int. School of Business, Hyderabad; Dir American Finance Asscn 2001–04; Program Dir (Corp Finance) Nat. Bureau of Econ. Research 1998–; mem. Advisory Bd US Comptroller Gen.; mem. Int. Advisory Bd Indian Inst. of Man., Ahmedabad; Adviser Securities and Exchange Bd of India; founding mem. Academic Council, Indian School of Business; mem. Academic Advisory Council, Moodys Investor Services; Assoc. Ed. American Econ. Review, Journal of Financial Intermediation, Review of Financial Studies, Journal of Finance, Quarterly Journal of Economics, Financial Management (various times); Western Finance Asscn Treffstz Prize for Outstanding Academic Achievement 1991, Smith Breeden Prize 1992, 1994, Fifth Annual Small Firm Research Symposium Best Paper Award 1993, Michael Brennan Award 1997, Brattle Prize 2000, 2001, 2002, American Finance Asscn Fischer Black Prize 2003. *Publications:* Saving Capitalism from the Capitalists (co-author) 2003. *Leisure interests:* tennis, squash, history, Indian politics. *Address:* Graduate School of Business, University of Chicago, 5807 South Woodlawn Avenue, Chicago, IL 60637, USA (office). *Telephone:* (773) 702-4437 (office). *E-mail:* raghuram.rajan@chicagogsb.edu (office). *Website:* gsbwww.uchicago.edu/fac/raghuram.rajan/research/ (office).

RAJAPAKSE, Mahinda; Sri Lankan politician, lawyer and head of state; *President, Minister of Defence, Public Security, Law and Order, Religious Affairs, Nation Building and Finance and Planning;* b. 18 Nov. 1945, Hambantota; s. of D. A. Rajapaksa; ed Richmond Coll., Galle, Nalanda and Thurstan Colls, Colombo; fmr lawyer, Tangalle; mem. Parl. for Beliatta 1970; fmr Minister of Labour, of Fisheries, of Ports and Shipping; Leader of the Opposition 2002–04; Prime Minister of Sri Lanka 2004–05; Pres. of Sri Lanka Nov. 2005–, Minister of Defence and of Finance and Planning 2005–07, of Defence, Public Security, Law and Order, Religious Affairs, Nation Building and Finance and Planning 2007–; mem. United People's Freedom Alliance; Pres. Sri Lankan Cttee for Solidarity with Palestine; Chair. Sri Lanka Freedom Party 2006–; Sri Rohana Janaranjana 2000. *Address:* President's Secretariat, Republic Square, Colombo 1, Sri Lanka (office). *Telephone:* (11) 2324801 (office). *Fax:* (11) 2331246 (office). *E-mail:* gosl@presidentsl.org (office). *Website:* www.presidentsl.org (office); www.mahindarajapaksa.com.

RAJAVI, Maryam, BSc; Iranian politician; *President-Elect, National Council of Resistance of Iran;* b. (Maryam Qajar-Azedanllo), 3 Dec. 1953, Tehran; m. Massoud Rajavi 1985; one s. one d.; ed Sharif Univ. of Tech., Tehran; leader anti-Shah student movt; joined Mojahedin-e Khalq Org. (People's Mojahedin of Iran, leading Iranian opposition group) 1970s, parl. cand. for Tehran in 1st post-revolutionary parl. elections 1979; official in social dept 1980–81, organized demonstrations against Khomeini Govt 1980–1981; left Iran for Paris 1982; elected jt-leader of Mojahedin 1985, Sec.-Gen. 1989–93; Deputy C-in-C Nat. Liberation Army of Iran (NLA) 1987–93, launched programme for introduction of women in front-line combat and combat pilots 1987, transformed NLA from infantry to armoured force 1989–93; Pres.-Elect, Nat. Council of Resistance of Iran (540-mem. Parl. in exile) 1993–; proposed platform for women's int. alliance against fundamentalism 1993; prominent int. campaigner for women's rights 1993–; expounded doctrine of democratic Islam as solution to Islamic fundamentalism 1995; Guest Speaker, European Parl. 2004, Int. Human Rights Conf., Paris 2004, Int. Conf. of Jurists, Paris 2004, Parls of Norway and UK 1995–96; numerous lectures, TV appearances, interviews in int. media; awards include Medal of Honour for contrib. to emancipation of women, Nat. Comm. for Gender Equality, Italy 1993, one of The Times 100 Most Powerful Women, UK 1996. *Publications:* Charter of Fundamental Freedoms in Post-dictatorship Iran 1995, Message to Fourth Int. Women's Conf., Beijing 1995, A Message of Tolerance 1995, Women, Islam and Fundamentalism 1996, Women, Voice of the Oppressed 1996, United Against Fundamentalism 1996, Message to Women in Frontline (conf.) 1997, Misogyny, Pillar of Religious Fascism 2003, Message to Int. Federation of Women against Fundamentalism and for Equality (conf.) 2004, Women and Islamic Fundamentalism 2004, Women Empowerment 2005, Women in Leadership 2006, Ten-Point Platform for Future Iran 2006; contrib.: Le Monde, De Welt, Le Figaro, International Herald Tribune. *Leisure interest:* reading. *Address:* National Council of Resistance of Iran, PO Box 2516, London, NW4 2DD, England (office); National Council of Resistance of Iran, 15 rue des Gords, 95430 Auvers-sur-Oise, France (office). *Telephone:* 1-34-48-07-28 (France) (office). *Fax:* 1-34-48-04-33 (France) (office). *Website:* www.ncr-iran.org (office); www.maryam-rajavi.org.

RAJBHANDARI, Pushkar Man Singh; Nepalese diplomatist; Jt Sec., Ministry of Foreign Affairs –2002; Amb. to Pakistan 1983–86, 2002–06 (also accred to Iraq 2003–06, to Iran 2005–06, to Russia, Syria and Afghanistan); Dean of the Asia Group. *Address:* c/o Ministry of Foreign Affairs, Shital Niwas, Maharajgan, Kathmandu, Nepal. *Telephone:* (1) 4416011. *E-mail:* adm@mofa.gov.np. *Website:* www.mofa.gov.np.

RAJESWAR, Thanjavelu, BA (Hons), MA; Indian police officer and government official; *Governor of Uttar Pradesh;* b. 28 Aug. 1926, Salem, Tamil Nadu; m. Mahalaxmi Rajeswar; one s. one d.; ed Presidency Coll., Univ. of Madras; joined Indian Police Service in 1949, posted to erstwhile Hyderabad State, later to Andhra Pradesh, served as Supt of Police in Dist of Nizamabad, Raichur and Guntur and as Deputy Commr of Police in the twin cities of Hyderabad and Secunderabad; joined Intelligence Bureau (IB) in 1962 as Asst Dir, served in Sikkim and Bhutan as OSD and Advisor, respectively 1963–67, Deputy Dir and Jt Dir IB HQ 1967–80, Dir 1980–83; Lt Gov. Arunachal Pradesh (first ever IP/IPS Officer to be apptd to a constitutional post) 1983–85; Gov. of Sikkim 1985–89, of West Bengal 1989–90 (resgnd), of Uttar Pradesh 2004–. *Address:* Raj Bhawan, Lucknow, Uttar Pradesh (office); 9 Anand Lok Colony, New Delhi, India. *Telephone:* (522) 2220494 (office). *Fax:* (522) 2223892 (office). *E-mail:* hgovup@up.nic.in (office). *Website:* www.upgov.nic.in (office).

RAJNA, Thomas, DMus, ARCM; British composer and pianist (retd); b. 21 Dec. 1928, Budapest; s. of the late Dr Nandor Rajna and Hella Eisen; m. Anthea Valentine Campion 1967; one s. two d.; ed Nat. Musical School, Budapest, Franz Liszt Acad. of Music, Budapest and Royal Coll. of Music, London; freelance composer, pianist and teacher, London 1951–63; Prof. of Piano, Guildhall School of Music 1963–70; Lecturer, Univ. of Surrey 1967–70; Sr Lecturer in Piano, Faculty of Music, Univ. of Cape Town 1970–89, Assoc. Prof. 1989–93; launched own record label Amarantha Records 2001; Fellow, Univ. of Cape Town 1981; DMus (Cape Town) 1985; Liszt Prize, Budapest 1947, Artes Award (SABC) 1981, UCT Book Award 1996, Cape Tercentenary Foundation Merit Award 1997. *Compositions include:* film and ballet music, orchestral and chamber music, two piano concertos, Harp Concerto 1990, Amarantha (opera in 11 scenes) 1991–94, Video Games (for orchestra) 1994, Rhapsody for clarinet and orchestra 1995, Fantasy for violin and orchestra 1996, Suite for violin and harp 1997, Stop All the Clocks (four songs on poems by W. H. Auden) 1998, The Creation – A Negro Sermon for unaccompanied choir 2000, Valley Song (opera) 2002–04, Tarantulla for violin and piano 2001, Violin Concerto 2007. *Recordings include:* works by Stravinsky, Messiaen, Scriabin, Granados, Liszt, Schumann, Dohnanyi and own compositions: Amarantha, Suite for violin and harp, Rhapsody for clarinet and orchestra. *Publications:* Dialogues for clarinet and piano 1970, Concerto for harp and orchestra 1990, Suite for violin and piano 1998, Tarantulla for violin and piano 2001, Violin Concerto 2008. *Leisure interests:* chess, swimming. *Address:* 10 Wyndover Road, Claremont, Cape Town, West Cape 7708, South Africa (home). *Telephone:* (21) 6713937 (home). *Fax:* (21) 6713937 (home). *E-mail:* trajna@telkomsa.net (home). *Website:* www.cama.org.za.

RAJOUB, Jibril; Palestinian government official; b. 1953, Dura; m.; three c.; spent 17 years in Israeli prison 1968–85; exiled to Lebanon 1988, returned to West Bank 1994; Chief West Bank Preventive Security Service 1994–2002; Nat. Security Adviser to Yasser Arafat and Head of Nat. Palestinian Security Council 2003–04; mem. Fatah-Revolutionary Council. *E-mail:* fateh@fateh.org. *Website:* www.fateh.net.

RAJOY BREY, Mariano; Spanish politician; *President, Partido Popular;* b. 1955, Santiago de Compostela; m.; two s.; ed Universidad de Santiago de Compostela; fmr Prof. of Law, Univ. of Santiago de Compostela; various positions in Partido Popular (Popular Party) (PP), including Chair. Regional Council, Sec.-Gen., later Deputy Chair. (Pontevedra), Chair. Local Council, mem. Perm. Cttee 1987, Nat. Exec. 1989, Deputy Sec.-Gen. 1991, Pres. 2003–; Vice-Pres. Council of Galicia 1986–87; Nat. Deputy of Pontevedra; Minister of Public Admin 1996–99, of Educ. and Culture 1999–2000; First Deputy Prime Minister and Head of Prime Minister's Office 2000–01; First Deputy Prime Minister and Minister of the Interior 2001–02; First Deputy Prime Minister, Head of Prime Minister's Office and Govt Spokesperson 2002–04; led PP in general elections 2004, 2008; Vice-Pres., Int. Democrat Union (IDU). *Address:* Partido Popular, Génova 13, 28004 Madrid, Spain (office). *Telephone:* (91) 5577300 (office). *Fax:* (91) 3085642 (office). *E-mail:* partidopopular@pp.es (office). *Website:* www.pp.es (office).

RAJU, B. Ramalinga, BCom, MBA; Indian business executive; m. Nandini Raju; two s.; ed Loyola Coll., Vijayawada, Ohio Univ., USA; Co-founder and Chair. Satyam Computer Services Ltd, Satyam Infoway Ltd and Vision-Compass, Inc. 1987–2009 (resgnd), jt ventures include Satyam–GE Software Services Ltd, Satyam Venture Eng Services Pvt. Ltd, Satyam Manufacturing Technologies Ltd, Satyam ideaEdge Technologies Pvt. Ltd, CA Satyam ASP Pvt. Ltd; f. several trusts and charities including Alambana, Naandi and the Byyrajyu Foundation; Chair. Nat. Asscn of Software and Service Cos 2006–07; Dr hc (Andhra Univ.) 2007; Ernst & Young Entrepreneur of the Year Award 2000, 2007, Dataquest IT Man. of the Year Award 2001, Asia Business Leader Award for Corp. Citizen of the Year, Hong Kong 2002. *Leisure interests:* reading, snooker. *Address:* c/o Satyam Computer Services Ltd., Bahadurpally Village, Qutubullapur Mandal, RR District, 500 855, India (office).

RAKE, Sir Michael Derek Vaughan, Kt, FCA; British accountant and business executive; *Chairman, BT Group plc;* b. 17 Jan. 1948; s. of Derek Shannon Vaughan Rake and Rosamund Rake (née Barrett); m. 1st Julia Rake (née Cook) 1970; three s.; m. 2nd Caroline Rake (née Thomas) 1986; one s.; ed Wellington Coll.; with Turquands Barton Mayhew, London and Brussels 1968–74; accountant KPMG (Peat Marwick Mitchell Continental Europe), Brussels 1974, Pnr 1979–, Pnr in charge of Audit, Belgium and Luxembourg 1983–86, Sr Resident Pnr, ME 1986–89, Pnr, London office 1989–, mem. UK Bd 1991–, Regional Man. Pnr, SE Region 1992–94, Chief Exec. London and SE Region 1994–96, COO, UK 1996–98, Sr Pnr, UK and Chair. UK Bd 1998–, Chair. KPMG Europe 1999–2002, Chair. KPMG Int. 2002–07; Chair. BT Group plc 2007–; Deputy Chair. EasyJet 2009–; Chair. Business in the Community 2004–07, Guidelines Monitoring Cttee (pvt. equity oversight group), UK Comm. for Employment and Skills; mem. Bd Dirs Barclays PLC, McGraw Hill Inc., Financial Reporting Council; mem. Bd Prince of Wales Int. Business Leaders' Forum 1998–2007, Britain in Europe Business Leaders' Group 2000–, CBI Pres.'s Cttee 2001–, TransAtlantic Business Dialogue, CBI Int. Advisory Bd, Chartered Man. Inst., DTI's US/UK Regulatory Taskforce, Advisory Council for Business for New Europe, Ethnic Minority Employment Taskforce, SOAS Advisory Bd, Advisory Bd of Judge Inst. at Univ. of Cambridge 2004; Vice-Pres. Royal Nat. Inst. of Blind People (RNIB) 2003–, Reviseur d'Entreprise (Luxembourg); Leader, Advisory Bd HBS Global Leadership Forum 2003–; Assoc. mem. BUPA; Sr Adviser, Chatham House, Global Advisory Bd of Univ. of Oxford Centre for Corp. Reputation; Gov. Wellington Coll.; mem. Bd Guards Polo Club. *Leisure interests:* polo, skiing. *Address:* BT Group plc, BT Centre, 81 Newgate Street, London, EC1A 7AJ, England (office). *Telephone:* (20) 7356-5000 (office). *Fax:* (20) 7356-5520 (office). *E-mail:* btgroup@bt.com (office). *Website:* www.btplc.com (office).

RAKHIMOV, Murtaza Gubaidullovich; Russian politician and head of state; *President, Republic of Bashkortostan;* b. 7 Feb. 1934, Tavakanovo, Bashkiria; s. of Gubaidulla Zufarovich Rakhimov and Galima Abdullovna Rakhimova; m. Luiza Galimovna Rakhimova; one s.; ed Ufa Oil Inst.; operator, then Chief of Oil Rig, Chief Chemist, Chief Engineer, Dir Ufa Oil Processing Plant 1956–90; USSR People's Deputy 1990–92; Chair. Supreme Soviet Repub. of Bashkortostan 1990–93, Pres. 1993–; mem. Russian Council of Fed. (Parl.) 1996–2001; Public Services to Repub. of Bashkortostan, Order of Peter the Great, Labour Red Banner, People's Friendship Order, Honour Symbol, Order of Salavat Yulayev. *Leisure interests:* sports, music, literature. *Address:* The Republic House, 46 Tukayev Street, 450101, Ufa, Bashkortostan, Russia. *Telephone:* (3472) 50-24-06 (office). *Fax:* (3472) 50-01-75 (office). *E-mail:* aprb@admbashkortostan.ru (office). *Website:* www.bashkortostan.ru (office).

RAKHMANIN, Vladimir Olegovich; Russian diplomatist; *Special Envoy, Ministry of Foreign Affairs;* b. 1958, Moscow; ed Moscow Inst. of Int. Relations; on staff USSR (later Russian) Ministry of Foreign Affairs 1980–; Attaché, First Far East Dept, Ministry of Foreign Affairs 1980–82; Third Sec., Embassy in People's Republic of China 1982–83, Third Secretary, Embassy in USA 1983–86, Counsellor 1992–96; Head of Secr., Deputy Foreign Minister 1986–92; Deputy Dir First Asian Dept 1996–98; Dir Dept of Information and Press 1998–2000; Chief of Protocol of the Pres. of the Russian Fed. 2000–01; Amb. to Ireland 2002–06; Special Envoy, Ministry of Foreign Affairs 2006–. *Address:* Ministry of Foreign Affairs, 119200 Moscow, Smolenskaya-Sennaya pl. 32/34, Russia (office). *Telephone:* (495) 244-16-06 (office). *Fax:* (495) 230-21-30 (home). *E-mail:* ministry@mid.ru (home). *Website:* www.mid .ru (office).

RAKHMON, Emomali, BEcons; Tajikistani politician and head of state; *President;* b. (Imamali Sharipovich Rakhmonov), 5 Oct. 1952, Dangar, Kulob Oblast; m.; nine c.; ed Lenin Tajikistan State Univ.; served in USSR army; early jobs as electrician, salesman, as trade union sec. and on various CP cttees; Dir Dangarin Sovkhoz (Soviet farm), Kulob Oblast 1982–92, Chair. Union Cttee 1976–88; Chair. Kulob Oblast Exec. Cttee 1992; Chair. Majlisi Oli (Supreme Ass.) 1992–94; Pres. of Tajikistan 1994–; Leader, People's Democratic Party of Tajikistan; World Peace Corps Acad. Gold Medal 2000. *Address:* Office of the President, 734023 Dushanbe, Xiyoboni Rudaki 80, Tajikistan (office). *Telephone:* (372) 21-04-18 (office). *Fax:* (372) 21-18-37 (office). *E-mail:* mail@president.tj (office). *Website:* www.president.tj (office).

RAKHMONOV, Imamali Sharipovich (see Rakhmon, Imamali Sharipovich).

RAKOTOMAVO, Pascal Joseph; Malagasy politician and business executive; b. 1 April 1934, Antananarivo; ed Coll. of St Michael, Antananarivo, Higher School of Commerce, Lille, France; Minister of Finance and Economy 1982–89; apptd Special Adviser to Pres. of Malagasy Repub. 1989–93; Chair. Bd FIARO 1989–94; Prime Minister of Madagascar 1997–98; Gov. of Antananarivo 2001–02; mem. Association pour la renaissance de Madagascar (Andry sy riana enti-manavotra an'i Madigasikara) (AREMA); Grand-Croix (Second Class), Nat. Order. *Leisure interests:* riding, travelling.

RAKOTONIAINA, Justin; Malagasy politician, academic and diplomatist; b. 1933, Betsileo; fmr Prof. of Law, Univ. of Madagascar; Amb. to Algeria, also accred to Tunisia and Guinea 1973–75; Minister of Nat. Educ. 1975–76; Prime Minister of Madagascar 1976–77; mem. Supreme Revolutionary Council; currently Prof., Faculty of Law, Univ. of Fianarantsoa and Head, Department DEA Peace, Democracy and Devt. *Address:* Department DEA Peace, Democracy and Development, Law Faculty of Law, University of Fianarantsoa, BP 1264–301, Fianarantsoa, Madagascar (office). *Telephone:* (20) 7550849 (office). *Fax:* (20) 7550619 (office). *E-mail:* ufianara@syfed.refer.mg (office). *Website:* www.refer.mg/edu (office).

RAKOTOVAHINY, Emmanuel; Malagasy politician; fmr Chair. Union nat. pour la démocratie et le développement (UNDD); fmr Minister of State for Rural Devt and Land Reform; Prime Minister of Madagascar 1995–96; currently Vice-Pres. Comité pour la Réconciliation Nationale (CRN). *Address:* Comité pour la Réconciliation Nationale (CRN), Antananarivo, Madagascar.

RALPH, Richard Peter, CMG, CVO, MSc; British diplomatist and business executive; *Executive Chairman, Monterrico Metals plc;* b. 27 April 1946, London; s. of the late Peter Ralph and Evelyn Marion Ralph; m. 1st Margaret Elisabeth Coulthurst 1970 (divorced 2001); one s. one d.; m. 2nd Jemma Victoria Elizabeth Marlor 2002; ed The King's School, Canterbury, Univ. of Edin.; served at Embassy in Vientiane, Laos 1970–73, Lisbon, Portugal 1974–77; at FCO 1977–81, 1984–89; High Comm. to Zimbabwe 1981–84, served at Embassy in Washington, DC 1989–93, Amb. to Latvia 1993–95, Gov.

Falkland Islands 1996–99, concurrently Commr S Georgia and S Sandwich Islands, Amb. to Romania (also accred to Moldova) 1999–2002, to Peru 2003–06; Exec. Chair. Monterrico Metals plc 2006–; Pres. Anglo-Peruvian Soc.; Chair. South Georgia Asscn. *Leisure interests:* reading, music, art, motorcycling. *Address:* Monterrico Metals plc, 10 Foster Lane, London, EC2V 6HR (office); 29 Surrey Lane, Battersea, London, SW11 4PA, England (home). *Telephone:* (20) 7776-2900 (office); (20) 7924-4188 (home). *Fax:* (20) 7776-2909 (office). *E-mail:* ralph@monterrico.com (office); richardralph87@hotmail.com (home).

RALSTON, Gen. Joseph W.; American air force officer (retd); *Vice Chairman, Cohen Group;* b. 4 Nov. 1943, Hopkinsville, Ky; m. Diane Dougherty; two s. two d.; ed Miami Univ., Ohio, Cen. Michigan Univ., Army Command and Gen. Staff Coll., Nat. War Coll., Harvard Univ.; mem. reserve officer training program USAF 1965; Vice-Chair. of Jt Chiefs of Staff 1996–2000; concurrently Chair. Jt Requirements Oversight Council, Planning, Programming and Budgeting Systems; Vice-Chair. Defense Acquisition Bd; mem. Nat. Security Council Deputies Comm., Nuclear Weapons Council; Supreme Allied Commdr, Europe 2000–03; C-in-C, US European Command 2000–03; Vice Chair. The Cohen Group 2003–; numerous mil. decorations including Defense Distinguished Service Medal (two awards), Distinguished Service Medal. *Address:* The Cohen Group, 1200 19th Street, NW, Suite 400, Washington, DC 20036, USA (office). *Telephone:* (202) 689-7900 (office). *Fax:* (202) 689-7910 (office). *E-mail:* jralston@cohengroup.net (office). *Website:* www.cohengroup .net/team-jwr.html (office).

RAMA, Carlos M., PhD; Uruguayan writer, lawyer, academic and editor; b. 26 Oct. 1921, Montevideo; s. of Manuel Rama and Carolina Facal; m. Judith Dellepiane 1943; one s. one d.; ed Univ. de la República and Univ. de Paris; journalist 1940–48, 1972–; Exec. Sec. of Uruguayan Bar Asscn 1940–49; Prof. of Universal History in secondary schools 1944–48; Ed. Nuestro Tiempo 1954–56, Gacetilla Austral 1961–73; Prof. of Sociology and Social Research, Prof. of Contemporary History, Prof. of Theory and Methodology of History, Univ. de la República 1950–72; Prof. of Latin American History, Univ. Autónoma de Barcelona 1973–; Pres. PEN Club Latinoamericano en España; Sec. Gen. Grupo de Estudios Latinoamericanos de Barcelona; Commdr, Order of Liberation (Spain), Officier des Palmes académiques (France). *Publications:* La Historia y la Novela 1947, 1963, 1970, 1974, Las ideas socialistas en el siglo XIX 1947, 1949, 1963, 1967, 1976, Ensayo de Sociología Uruguaya 1956, Teoría de la Historia 1959, 1968, 1974, 1980, Las clases sociales en el Uruguay 1960, La Crisis española del siglo XX 1960, 1962, 1976, Itinerario español 1961, 1977, Revolución social y fascismo en el siglo XX 1962, Sociología del Uruguay 1965, 1973, Historia del movimiento obrero y social latinoamericano contemporáneo 1967, 1969, 1976, Los afrouruguayos 1967, 1968, 1969, 1970, Garibaldi y el Uruguay 1968, Uruguay en Crisis 1969, Sociología de América Latina 1970, 1977, Chile, mil días entre la revolución y el fascismo 1974, España, crónica entrañable 1973–77, 1978, Historia de América Latina 1978, Fascismo y anarquismo en la España contemporánea 1979. *Leisure interest:* gardening. *Address:* c/o Monte de Orsá 7, Vallvidrera, Barcelona 17, Spain.

RAMA, Edi; Albanian politician and artist; *Chairman, Socialist Party of Albania;* b. (Edvin Rama), 4 July 1964; ed Albanian Acad. of Arts, Tirana; Prof., Albanian Acad. of Arts; active in democracy movt early 1990s; Founding mem. Movt for Democracy 1996; emigrated to Paris 1997 and returned to Albania 1998; Minister of Culture, Youth and Sports 1998–2000; Mayor of Tirana 2000–; mem. Socialist Party of Albania 2003–, Chair. 2005–; Robert C. Wood Visiting Prof. of Public and Urban Affairs, Univ. of Massachusetts, USA 2003; mem. Regional Advisory Bd of UNDP; Pres. Albanian Municipalities Asscn; fmr Bd mem. Open Society Foundation; UN Poverty Eradication Award 2002, World Mayor 2004, included in Time Magazine's European Heroes list 2005. *Publications:* numerous articles in Albanian and international magazines and newspapers. *Address:* Office of the Mayor, Tirana City Administration, Tirana, Albania (office). *Telephone:* (4) 226100 (office). *E-mail:* info@tirana.gov.al (office). *Website:* www.tirana.gov.al (home); www .ps.al (office).

RAMACHANDRAN, Dato Cherubala Pathayapurayil, MSc, DrMedSc, DAP&E, FIBiol; Malaysian medical scientist and academic; *Chairman, Technical Advisory Group, Global Programme to Eliminate Lymphatic Filariasis, World Health Organisation;* b. 3 June 1936, Kuala Lumpur; s. of KK Madhavan Nair and Kamalam M. Nair; m. Githa Priya Darshini 1966; one s. one d.; ed St John's Inst., Kuala Lumpur, Christian Coll., Madras, India, Univ. of London, UK, Univ. of Liverpool, UK, Tulane Univ., USA, Univ. of Tokyo, Japan; Wellcome Trust Research Scholar and Demonstrator in Medical Parasitology, Liverpool School of Tropical Medicine 1959–62, Research Fellow in Tropical Medicine, Inst. for Medical Research, Kuala Lumpur 1962–63, Head Filariasis Research Div. 1967–70; Asst Prof. in Medical Parasitology Faculty of Medicine, Univ. of Malaysia, Kuala Lumpur 1963–67, Assoc. Prof. in Medical Parasitology and Head School of Biological Sciences Univ. Sains Malaysia, Penang 1970–72, Prof. and Dean 1972–79; Sr Scientist Human Resource Devt Tropical Disease Research WHO, Geneva, Switzerland 1979–87, Man. Research and Devt Filariasis Research Programme, Tropical Disease Research, WHO, Switzerland 1987–92; Chief Filariasis Research and Control, WHO, Geneva 1992–96, Chair., Technical Advisory Group, Global Programme to Eliminate Lymphatic Filariasis; Prof. of Clinical Parasitology, Universiti Putra, Malaysia 1996–2005; Adjunct Prof., Faculty of Medicine, Universiti Technologi MARA, Malaysia; Visiting Prof., Faculty of Tropical Medicine, Mahidol Univ., Bangkok, Thailand; fmr Pres. Malaysian Soc. of Parasitology and Tropical Medicine, mem. Council World Fed. of Parasitologists; Fellow, Liverpool School of Tropical Medicine, UK, Malaysian Scientific Asscn, Acad. of Medicine, Malaysia, Australian Coll. of Tropical Medicine, Acad. of Sciences, Malaysia; Hon. Fellow, Royal Soc. of Tropical Medicine,

London; Sandosham Medal (Malaysia) 1974, Mary Kingsley Medal for Tropical Medicine (UK) 1998, Darjah Setia Pangkuan Negeri (Malaysia) 1999. *Publications:* numerous scientific papers in learned journals. *Leisure interests:* squash, photography, music. *Address:* Apt-8A-4-4, Belvedere Bukit Tunku, 50480 Kuala Lumpur, Malaysia (home). *Telephone:* 26987275 (home). *Fax:* 26986152 (home). *E-mail:* ramacp@hotmail.com (home).

RAMACHANDRAN, Vilayanur S., MD, PhD; Indian neuroscientist, psychologist, physician and academic; *Director, Center for Brain and Cognition and Professor Psychology Department and Neurosciences Program, University of California, San Diego;* b. 1951, Madras; ed Stanley Medical Coll., Trinity Coll., Cambridge; currently Dir Center for Brain and Cognition, Prof. of Psychology, Dept and Neurosciences Program, Univ. of Calif., San Diego; Adjunct Prof. of Biology, Salk Inst.; Ed.-in-Chief Encyclopedia of Human Behavior; Fellow, Neurosciences Inst., La Jolla, Inst. for Advanced Studies in Behavioral Sciences, Stanford; lectures worldwide including BBC Reith Lectures 2003; Trustee San Diego Museum of Art; mem. Nat. Acad. of Sciences (India); Dr hc (Conn. Coll.); Fellowship, All Souls Coll., Oxford, Gold Medal, ANU, Ariens Kappers Medal, Royal Netherlands Acad. of Sciences, Presidential Lecture Award, American Acad. of Neurology, Chancellor's Award for excellence in research, Univ. of Calif. *Publications:* Phantoms in the Brain (co-author) 1998; over 120 papers in scientific journals. *Address:* Center for Brain and Cognition, University of California, 9500 Gilman Drive, #0109, La Jolla, CA 92093-0109, USA (office). *Telephone:* (858) 534-6240 (office). *Fax:* (858) 534-7190 (office). *E-mail:* vramachandran@ucsd.edu (office). *Website:* www.ucsd.edu (office).

RAMADAN, Tariq, MA, PhD; Swiss academic; *Professor of Islamic Studies, Faculty of Theology, University of Oxford;* b. 26 Aug. 1962, Geneva; m.; two s. two d.; ed Univ. of Geneva; fmr Prof. of Islamic Studies and Philosophy, Freiburg Univ.; Prof. of Islamic Studies and Luce Prof. of Religion Conflict and Peacebuilding, Kroc Inst., Univ. of Notre Dame, USA Aug.–Dec. 2004 (visa revoked); Sr Research Fellow, Lokahi Foundation 2004–, Doshisha Univ., Kyoto 2007–; Visiting Prof., St Antony's Coll., Oxford, UK 2004–, holding the Chair Citizenship and Identity, Erasmus Univ., Rotterdam, Netherlands 2007–; Chair. European Muslim Network, Brussels; One of the Seven Innovators of the 21st Century, Time magazine 2000, One of the 100 People of the Year 2004, European of the Year, European Voice 2006, The Muslim News Special Award for Excellence (Faith and Action) for academic and intellectual contrib. to Islamic thought 2007. *Publications:* Islam, le face à face des civilisations, Quel projet pour quelle modernité? 1995, Les Musulmans dans la Laïcité, responsabilités et droits des musulmans dans les sociétés occidentales 1994, To be a European Muslim 1999, Muslims in France: The Way Towards Coexistence 1999, Islam, the West, and the Challenges of Modernity 2001, Jihad, Violence, War and Peace in Islam (in French) 2002, Western Muslims and the Future of Islam 2004, Globalisation: Muslim Resistances 2004, Radical Reform, In the Footsteps of the Prophet 2007, Radical Ijtihad 2008; contrib. of more than 850 articles, reviews and chapters in books and magazines. *Leisure interest:* literature. *Address:* St Antony's College, 62 Woodstock Road, Oxford, OX2 6JF, England (office); 39 rue de la boulangerie, 93200 Saint Denis, France. *Telephone:* (1865) 284700 (office); 1-49-22-01-12. *Fax:* (20) 8810-5142 (office); 1-49-22-00-39. *E-mail:* office@tariqramadan.com (office). *Website:* www.tariqramadan.com (office).

RAMADHANI, Rt Rev. John Acland, BA; Tanzanian ecclesiastic (retd); b. 1 Aug. 1932, Zanzibar; s. of Augustine Ramadhani and Mary Majaliwa; ed Dar es Salaam Univ., Queen's Coll. Birmingham and Univ. of Birmingham; Prin. St Andrew's Teacher Training Coll., Korogwe 1967–69; Warden, St Mark's Theological Coll., Dar es Salaam 1977–79; Bishop of Zanzibar and Tanga 1980–2000; Archbishop of the Prov. of Tanzania 1984–97; Bishop of Zanzibar 2001–02; Chair. Christian Council of Tanzania –2002; Patron Misufini Leprosy Centre. *Leisure interest:* reading. *Address:* c/o Anglican Church of Tanzania, Diocese of Zanzibar, P.O. Box 5, Mkunazini, Zanzibar, Tanzania (office).

RAMADORAI, Subramaniam, BSc, BEng, MSc; Indian business executive; *CEO and Managing Director, Tata Consultancy Services;* b. 6 Oct. 1944, Nagpur; ed Delhi Univ., Indian Inst. of Science, Bangalore, Univ. of Calif. and Massachusetts Inst. of Tech., USA; jr engineer, Tata Consultancy Services (TCS) 1972, later set up TCS's operations in New York 1979, CEO and Man. Dir TCS 1996–, Chair. Tata Technologies Ltd; Chair. CMC Ltd; Ind. Dir (non-exec.) Hindustan Lever Ltd 2002–; mem. Bd of Dirs Nicholas Piramal; IT Adviser to Qingdao City and Hangzhou City, People's Repub. of China; Fellow, Inst. of Electrical and Electronics Engineers, Indian Nat. Acad. of Engineers; Vice-Chair. Nat. Asscn of Software Companies (NASSCOM); Dr hc (Anna Univ., Tamil Nadu) 2004; Hon. DrSc (Sastra Univ.) 2006; Asia Business Leader of the Year Award, Hong Kong 2002, Business India Businessman of the Year 2004, UK Trade and Investment Special Recognition Award 2005, Padma Bhushan 2006, Int. CEO of the Year, LT Bravo Business Awards 2008, Nayudamma Award 2008. *Address:* Tata Consultancy Services, TCS House, Raveline Street, Mumbai 400001, India (office). *Telephone:* (22) 22080522 (office). *Fax:* (22) 67781188 (office). *E-mail:* ceo.office@tcs.com (office). *Website:* www.tcs.com (office).

RAMAHATRA, Maj.-Gen. Victor; Malagasy international business strategy consultant, fmr politician and army officer (retd); b. 6 Sept. 1945, Antananarivo; s. of Pierre Longin Ramahatra and Marie Lucile Ratsimandresy; m. Nivonirina Rajoelson 1971; two s. one d.; ed Saint-Cyr Mil. Acad., France; officer in Corps of Engineers 1967; mil. engineer 1972; Minister of Public Work 1982–87; Prime Minister of Malagasy Repub. 1987–91; Man. locust plague control campaign 1998–2000; fmr Special Adviser to Pres. of Malagasy Repub. in econs and int. affairs; mem. Asscn des Ingénieurs Diplômés de l'Ecole Supérieure du Génie Militaire d'Angers, Asscn des Anciens Elèves de Saint-Cyr (Madagascar), Asscn des Anciens de Saint-Cyr dans la Vie Civile (France); Grand-Croix Ordre du Mérite (France) 1990, Officier Légion d'honneur (France) 2000, Grand Officier de l'Ordre nat. 2000. *Leisure interests:* reading, march/walking, swimming. *Address:* VR. 104P, Fenomanana, 101 Antananarivo (home); PO Box 6004, 101 Antananarivo, Madagascar. *Telephone:* (32) 0208532 (mobile) (home). *Fax:* (202) 223767 (office). *E-mail:* ramfan@moov.mg (home).

RAMAKRISHNAN, T. V., BSc, MSc, PhD; Indian physicist and academic; *DAE Homi Bhabha Professor of Physics, Banaras Hindu University;* ed Banaras Hindu Univ., Columbia Univ., USA; CSIR Junior Research Fellow, Banaras Hindu Univ., Varanasi 1961–62; Lecturer in Physics, Indian Inst. of Tech. (IIT), Kanpur 1966–67, Asst Prof. 1967, 1970–77, Prof. 1977–80; Asst Research Physicist, Univ. of Calif., San Diego, USA 1968–70; Consultant Bell Laboratories, Murray Hill, NJ 1980–81, 1990–91; Coordinator, Research Programme on Disorder, Inst. for Theoretical Physics, Univ. of Calif., Santa Barbara 1983; Prof. of Physics, Banaras Hindu Univ., Varanasi 1984–86, DAE Homi Bhabha Prof. 2003–; Visiting Prof., Dept of Physics, Indian Inst. of Science, Bangalore 1981–84, Prof. of Physics 1986–2003, Distinguished Assoc., Centre for Condensed Matter Theory 2003–; INSA Srinivasa Ramanujan Research Prof. 1997–2002; Visiting Fellow, Princeton Univ. 1978–81, Visiting Prof. and Visiting Research Physicist 1990–91; Rothschild Visiting Prof., Isaac Newton Inst. for Mathematical Sciences, Univ. of Cambridge 2000, Visiting Fellow Commoner, Trinity Coll. and Visiting Prof. 2004; Pres. Indian Acad. of Sciences 2004–06; Vice-Pres. Indian Nat. Science Acad. 2000–03; Fellow, Indian Acad. of Sciences (Bangalore) 1980, Indian Nat. Science Acad. (New Delhi) 1984, American Physical Soc. 1984, Third World Acad. of Sciences (Trieste, Italy) 1991, Nat. Acad. of Sciences (Allahabad) 1993, Royal Soc. (London) 2000, Inst. of Physics (UK) 2000; Foreign Assoc., Acad. of Sciences (Paris) 2005; mem. Scientific Council Centre for Liquid Crystals Research, Bangalore 1996–, Indian Asscn for Cultivation of Science, Kolkata 2004–, Science Advisory Council to the Prime Minister 2005–; mem. Union of Concerned Scientists, USA 1994–; Hon. Prof., Jawaharlal Nehru Centre for Advanced Scientific Research, Bangalore 1993–, Hon. Fellow, TIFR, Mumbai 2004–, Hon. Distinguished Prof., IIT Kanpur 2004–; Padma Sri 2001; Dr hc (Banaras Hindu Univ.) 2004; Devasthale Prize in Physics 1959, Shanti Swarup Bhatnagar Award for Physical Sciences, CSIR 1982, Third World Acad. of Sciences Award in Physics 1990, Mahendralal Sircar Award for Physical Sciences 1994, Alumni Award for Excellence in Research, Indian Inst. of Science 1997, Jawaharlal Nehru Award for Science, MP Council for Science and Technology 1999, C V Raman Centenary Medal, Indian Science Congress 2001, Meghnad Saha Medal, Asiatic Soc. 2002, Distinguished Materials Scientist of the Year, Materials Research Soc. of India 2004, Goyal Prize in Physics, Kurukshetra 2004, Trieste Science Prize 2005. *Address:* Department of Physics, Faculty of Science, Banaras Hindu University, Varanasi 221005, India (office). *Telephone:* (542) 2368390 (Varanasi) (office); (80) 23600228 (Bangalore) (office). *Fax:* (542) 2368468 (Varanasi) (office); (80) 23602602 (Bangalore) (office). *E-mail:* tvrama@physics.iisc.ernet.in (office). *Website:* www.physics.iisc.ernet.in (Bangalore) (office).

RAMANATHAN, V. (Ram), BE, MSc, PhD; Indian scientist and academic; *Victor Alderson Professor of Applied Ocean Sciences and Distinguished Professor of Climate and Atmospheric Sciences, University of California, San Diego;* ed Annamalai Univ., Indian Inst. of Science, State Univ. of New York (SUNY) at Stony Brook (Planetary Atmospheres); Prin. Investigator, NASA Earth Radiation Budget Experiment 1979–; Sr Scientist, Nat. Center for Atmospheric Research (NCAR), Boulder, Colo 1982–86; Affiliate Prof., Colorado State Univ., Fort Collins 1985–88; Visiting Prof., Université Catholique de Louvain, Belgium 1985–88; Prof., Dept of Geophysical Sciences, Univ. of Chicago, Ill. 1986–90; Victor C. Alderson Prof. of Applied Ocean Sciences, and Prof. of Climate and Atmospheric Sciences, Scripps Inst. of Oceanography, Univ. of California, San Diego 1990–, Dir Center for Clouds, Chem. and Climate 1991–, Dir Center for Atmospheric Sciences 1996–, Distinguished Prof. of Atmospheric and Climate Sciences 2004–; First K.R. Ramanathan Visiting Prof., Physical Research Lab., India 1998; Co-Chief Scientist, Indian Ocean Experiment (INDOEX); mem. Bd Dirs Tata Energy Research Inst., Arlington, Va 1992–; Chief Scientist, Cen. Equatorial Pacific Experiment (CEPEX) 1993; Co-Chief Scientist, Indian Ocean Experiment (INDOEX) 1996–2002, Chair. Int. Steering Cttee 1996–2002; Chair. Atmospheric Brown Cloud Project 2005–, Cttee on Strategic Advice, US Climate Change Science Program 2006–; mem. Science Editorial Bd NASA Earth Observatory 1999–, Geophysical Inst. Review Panel for Atmospheric Sciences 2002–, Advisory Bd World Clean Air Congress 2005–, NCAR Earth Observing Lab. External Advisory Cttee 2005–; mem. NAS 2002, Pontifical Acad. of Sciences, 2004, American Philosophical Soc. 2006; Foreign mem. Academia Europaea 1996; Fellow, American Geophysical Union (AGU), American Meteorological Soc., AAAS, American Acad. of Arts and Sciences 1995, Indian Meteorological Soc. 2003; NASA Special Achievement Award 1975, NCAR Outstanding Publication Award 1981, Distinguished Alumnus Award, SUNY 1984, NASA Medal for Exceptional Scientific Achievement 1989, Buys Ballot Medal, Royal Netherlands Acad. of Sciences 1995, Volvo Environment Prize (co-recipient) 1997, elected to Stonybrook 40, SUNY 1998, W.S. Jardetzky Lecturer, Lamont Doherty Observatory, Columbia Univ. 2000, Rossby Medal, American Meteorological Soc. 2002, Alexander M. Cruickshank Lecturer 2003, NSF Pioneer Award 2003, Johannes Gutenberg Lecturer 2004, recognized by AGU Atmospheric Sciences Section for Bjerknes Lecture, Global Dimming and Its Masking Effect on Global Warming 2006, Proceedings of the National Academy of Sciences (PNAS) article, Integrated Model Shows that Atmospheric Brown Clouds and Greenhouse gases have reduced rice harvest in India, recognized as an exceptional paper published in 2006 by Editorial Bd of PNAS, Cozzarelli Prize 2007, Zayed Int. Prize for the Environment,

Category II: Scientific/Technological Achievements in Environment, H.H. Sheikh Mohammad Bin Rashid Al Maktoum (co-recipient) 2007, Henry W. Kendall Memorial Lecturer, MIT 2008. *Publications:* numerous scientific papers in professional journals on mitigation of climate change, climate dynamics, the greenhouse effect, air pollution, clouds, aerosols, satellite radiation measurements and global climate models. *Address:* Center for Clouds, Chemistry and Climate, Scripps Institution of Oceanography, University of California, San Diego, 9500 Gilman Drive, MC 0221, La Jolla, CA 92093-0221, USA (office). *Telephone:* (858) 534-8815 (office). *Fax:* (858) 822-5607 (office). *E-mail:* vram@ucsd.edu (office). *Website:* www-ramanathan.ucsd.edu (office).

RAMANDIMBIARISON, Zaza Manitranja; Malagasy politician and engineer; b. 12 Dec. 1953, Ambatosoratra; s. of André Ramandimbiarison and Delphine Razanamanarivo; m.; one s. two d.; ed France and USA; Deputy Prime Minister in charge of Econ. Programmes, Minister of Transport, Public Works and Regional Planning 2002–07. *Leisure interests:* tennis, football, reading. *Address:* Villa Manarivo, Lot MC, 1209 Mandrosoa, Ivato, 105 Antananarivo, Madagascar (home). *Telephone:* (20) 22-455-77 (home).

RAMAPHOSA, Matamela Cyril, BProc; South African business executive and fmr politician; *Executive Chairman, Shanduka Group;* b. 17 Nov. 1952, Johannesburg; s. of Samuel Ramaphosa and Erdmuth Ramaphosa; m. Tshepo Motsepe; two s. two d.; ed Sekano-Ntoane High School, Soweto, Univ. of Turfloop and Univ. of S Africa; Chair. Univ. br. S African Students' Org. 1974; imprisoned under Section Six of Terrorism Act for 11 months, then for 6 months in 1976; returned to law studies and qualified 1981; apptd legal adviser, Council of Unions of S Africa; Gen. Sec. Nat. Union of Mineworkers 1982–91; Sec.-Gen. African National Congress (ANC) 1991–96, nominated for ANC Pres. 2007; Visiting Prof. of Law, Stanford Univ. 1991; mem. Parl. 1994–96; Chair. of Constitutional Ass. 1994–96; Weapons Inspector N Ireland 2000; Deputy Exec. Chair. New Africa Investments Ltd 1996–99; with Nat. Empowerment Consortium 1996–; Chair. and CEO Molope Group 1999–2000; Chair. Rebserve Ltd 2000–03; Chair. Millennium Consolidated Investments (MCI) 2003; currently Exec. Chair. Shanduka Group; Dr hc (Univs of Natal, Port Elizabeth, Mass., Cape Town, Lesotho, Galway, Ireland); Olaf Palme Prize (Sweden) 1987. *Address:* Shanduka Group, Suite 167, Private Bag X9924, Sandton 2146, South Africa (office). *Telephone:* (11) 3058900 (office). *Fax:* (11) 3058999 (office). *E-mail:* cramaphosa@shanduka.co.za (office). *Website:* www.shanduka.co.za (office).

RAMATHLODI, Ngoako, LLB, MSc; South African politician; b. 21 Aug. 1955, Potgietersrus (Tauatswala); m. Mathuding Ouma Ramatlhodi; one s. one d.; fmr Chair. African Nat. Congress (ANC), Northern Prov.; Deputy Registrar (student affairs), Exec. Asst to Vice-Chancellor Univ. of the N; in exile 1979, Commdr Unkhonto weSizwe; Head Political and Mil. ANC Council, Zimbabwe 1986; Political Sec., Asst to Oliver Tambo and Nelson Mandela (q.v.) 1988–91; Premier of Northern Prov. 1994–2002, of Limpopo Prov. 2002–04; mem. ANC Nat. Exec. Cttee 2007–; Hon. LLD (Univ. of the North, Limpopo). *Publications:* History of the ANC, Charade of Social Emanicipation and National Liberation, Ethnicity: How The ANC Must Govern. *Leisure interests:* music, reading, writing. *Address:* c/o National Executive Committee, African National Congress, PO Box 61884, Marshalltown 2107,, South Africa (office). *Website:* www.anc.org.za (office).

RAMAZANI BAYA, Raymond; Democratic Republic of the Congo politician and diplomatist; b. 17 June 1943; fmr Minister of Information; Amb. to France 1990–96 (resgnd following road accident in France in which two children were killed); joined Congolese Liberation Movt (rebel group based in Gbadolite) following fall of Pres. Mobutu 1997, group entered into transitional govt with other rebel groups and govt of Pres. Joseph Kabila 2003; Minister of Foreign Affairs and Int. Co-operation 2004–07. *Address:* c/o Ministry of Foreign Affairs and International Co-operation, place de l'Indépendence, BP 1700, Kinshasa-Gombe, Democratic Republic of the Congo (office).

RAMBAUD, Patrick; French writer; b. 21 April 1946, Paris; s. of François Rambaud and Madeleine de Magondeau; m. Pham-thi Tieu Hong 1988; mil. service with French AF 1968–69; co-f. Actual magazine 1970–84; Prix Alexandre Dumas 1976, Prix Lamartine 1981, Prix de l'Insolent 1988, Grand Prix du romance, l'Academie Française 1997, Prix Goncourt 1997, Napoleonic Soc. of America Literary Award 2000, Prix Cine-Roman 2001, Prix rabelais 2005. *Plays:* Fregoli (with Bernard Haller) (Théâtre nat. de Chaillot 1991. *Publications:* La Saignée 1970, Les Aventures communautaires de Wao-le-Laid (with Michel-Antoine Burnier) 1973, Les Complots de la liberté: 1832 (with Michel-Antoine Burnier) (Prix Alexandre Dumas) 1976, Parodies (with Michel-Antoine Burnier) 1977, 1848 (with Michel-Antoine Burnier) 1977, Le Roland Barthes sans peine (with Michel-Antoine Burnier) 1978, Comme des rats 1980, La Farce des choses et autres parodies (with Michel-Antoine Burnier) 1982, Fric-Frac 1984, La Mort d'un ministre 1985, Frontière suisse (with Jean-Marie Stoerkel) 1986, Comment se tuer sans en avoir l'air 1987, Virginie Q (Prix de l'Insolent) 1988, Le Visage parle (with Bernard Haller) 1988, Bernard Pivot reçoit... 1989, Le Dernier voyage de San Marco 1990, Ubu Président ou L'Imposteur 1990, Les Carnets secrets d'Elena Ceaucescu (with Francis Szpiner) 1990, Les Mirobolantes aventures de Frégoli 1991, Mururoa mon amour 1996, Le Gros secret 1996, Oraisons funèbres des dignitaires politiques qui ont fait leur temps et feignent de l'ignorer (with André Balland) 1996, La Bataille (Grand Prix du Roman de l'Acad. française 1997, Prix Goncourt 1997, Napoleonic Soc. of America Literary Award 2000) 1997, Le Journalisme sans peine (with Michel-Antoine Burnier) 1997, Les Aventures de Mai 1998, Il neigeait (Prix Ciné-Roman 2001) 2000, L'Absent 2003, L'Idiot du village (Prix de la dédicace sonore 2005) 2004, Le Chat botté 2006, La Grammaire en s'amusant 2007, Chronique du règne de Nicolas I 2008. *Leisure interests:* writing, cooking, walking. *Address:* c/o Editions Grasset, 61 rue des Saints-Pères, 75006 Paris, France.

RAMBERT, Charles Jean Julien, FRSA; French architect; b. 23 March 1924, Arrigny, Marne; s. of Jean Rambert; m. Françoise Coleda 1949; three s.; ed Lycée Pierre-Corneille, Rouen, Inst. Saint-Aspais, Melun and Ecole Nat. Supérieure des Beaux-Arts; architect 1952–, govt-registered architect 1953; Prof. of Construction and History of Art, Ecole de secrétariat technique du bâtiment 1957–82; Arbitrator-expert, Tribunal de Commerce 1960 and de Grande Instance, Versailles 1963, Cour d'Appel de Paris 1971–, Tribunal Administratif de Paris 1979–; Sec. Soc. of Registered Architects 1954–57, Sec.-Gen. 1957, 1st Vice-Pres. 1968; Ed.-in-Chief L'Architecture française 1964–75; Counsellor, Ordre des Architectes de Paris 1964, Treas. 1969, Pres. 1976–78; Pres. Cie des Experts-Architectes, Paris 1978; Asst Dir of Studies, Ecole Nat. Supérieure des Beaux Arts 1965, Prof. of History of Architecture 1969–89; mem. Union Franco-Britannique des Architectes 1969; mem. Acad. d'Architecture 1978, Vice-Pres. 1981; Chevalier, Légion d'honneur, Officier des Arts et Lettres 1967 and other awards. *Publications:* Constructions scolaires et universitaires 1955, L'habitat collectif, Problème urbain 1957, Maisons familiales de plaisance 1959, Magasins 1961, Histoire de l'architecture civile en France 1963, French adapatation of World Architecture 1964, Architecture des origines à nos jours 1968, (English trans. 1969), L'architecture française 1969, L'architecture occidentale 1974 (Audio-visual series), Architecture hispano-mauresque 1980, L'architecture américaine des XIXe et XXe siècles: Chicago, New York. *Leisure interests:* history of art, literature, painting.

RAMDIN, Albert R.; Suriname diplomatist and international organization executive; *Assistant Secretary-General, Organization of American States (OAS);* b. 27 Feb. 1958; m. Charmaine Baksh; one s. one d.; ed schools in Paramaribo and the Netherlands, Univ. of Amsterdam and Free Univ.; career diplomat in public service at nat. and int. level, served as Sr Adviser to Minister of Trade and Industry; worked for two years in pvt. sector before returning to public service; apptd Adviser to Minister of Foreign Affairs and Minister of Finance; Amb. and Perm. Rep. to OAS 1997, Chair. Perm. Council Jan.–March 1998, Inter-American Council for Integral Devt 1999, coordinated Caribbean Community (CARICOM) Ambs' Caucus during Suriname's chairmanship of sub-regional group; apptd to serve concurrently as non-resident Amb. to Costa Rica 1999; Asst Sec.-Gen. for Foreign and Community Relations, CARICOM Secr. 1999; served as Amb. at Large and Special Adviser to Govt of Suriname on Western Hemispheric Affairs –2005; Adviser to OAS Sec.-Gen. with special attention to the Caribbean 2001–05, Asst Sec.-Gen. OAS 2005–. *Address:* Organization of American States, 17th Street & Constitution Avenue, NW, Washington, DC 20006, USA (office). *Telephone:* (202) 458-3000 (office). *Fax:* (202) 458-6319 (office). *E-mail:* OASWeb@oas.org (office). *Website:* www.oas.org (office).

RAMDOSS, Anbumani, MD; Indian physician and politician; *Minister of Health and Family Welfare;* b. 9 Oct. 1968, Puducherry; s. of Dr. S. Ramadoss and Shrimati R. Saraswathi; m.Shrimati Sowmiya Anbumani 1991; three d.; ed Madras Medical Coll., London School of Economics, UK; fmr medical practitioner, Tamil Nadu; mem. Parl. (Pattali Makkal Katchi) from Rajya Sabha 2004–, Minister of Health and Family Welfare 2004–; co-founded Nat. Rural Health Mission 2005; Leader Pattali Makkal Katchi; Pres. Pasumai Thayagam (Green Mother Land). *Address:* Ministry of Health and Family Welfare, Chamber No. 348, Nirman Bhavan, Maulana Azad Road, New Delhi 110 011 (office); 30/34, 4th Cross Street, Kasturibai Nagar, Raja Anamalai Puram, Chennai 600 028, Tamil Nadu, India (home). *Telephone:* (11) 23018863 (office). *Fax:* (11) 23014252 (office). *E-mail:* resp-health@hub.nic.in (office). *Website:* www.mohfw.nic.in (office).

RAMEL, Baron Stig, BA, MA; Swedish diplomatist, writer and fmr administrator; b. 24 Feb. 1927, Lund; s. of Malte Ramel and Elsa née Nyström; m. Ann Marie Wachtmeister 1953; two s. two d.; ed Univ. of Lund; attaché, Ministry of Foreign Affairs 1953; at Embassy in Paris 1954–56; del. to OECD, Paris 1956–58; at Embassy in Washington, DC 1958–60; Ministry of Foreign Affairs 1960–66; Vice-Pres. and Pres. Gen. Swedish Export Asscn 1966–72; Exec. Dir Nobel Foundation, Stockholm 1972–92, Chair. Fund 1992–94; mem. Royal Swedish Acad. of Sciences; Chevalier de la Légion d'honneur; Commdr, Order of Vasa Isabella Catholica and St Olav; White Rose of Finland; Dr hc (Univ. of Lund, Karolinska Inst., Gustavus Adolphus Coll., Loretto Heights Coll.); King Charles XVI Gustaf Medal. *Publications:* Tyckt och Tryckt 1987, Pojken i dörren 1994 (autobiog.), Gustaf Mauritz Armfelt 1997, Smedpojkens dröm 1999, Till En Konstnärssjäl: En Vänbok Till Stig Ramel 2002, Göran Magnus Sprengtporten 200. *Leisure interests:* literature, painting, skiing, orienteering. *Address:* Resedavägen 8, 170 78 Solna, Sweden (home). *Telephone:* (8) 855157 (home). *Fax:* (8) 855716 (home).

RAMGOOLAM, Hon. Navinchandra, LLB, LRCP; Mauritian physician, barrister and politician; *Prime Minister;* b. 14 July 1947, Mauritius; s. of the late Sir Seewoosagur Ramgoolam (first Prime Minister of Mauritius) and Lady Sushill Ramgoolam; m. Veena Ramgoolam 1979; ed Royal Coll. of Surgeons, Dublin, Ireland, London School of Econs and Inns of Court School of Law, London, UK; called to the Bar, Inner Temple 1993; Leader, Mauritius Labour Party (MLP) 1991–, Pres. 1991–92; Leader of Opposition and mem. Nat. Ass. 1991–95; Prime Minister 1995–2000, also Minister of Defence and Home Affairs, External Communications; leader of opposition 2000–2005; Prime Minister 2005–, also Minister of Defence and Home Affairs; acting Minister of Foreign Affairs 2008; mem. Int. Advisory Bd Center for Int. Devt, Harvard Univ. 1999–; Licentiate, Royal College of Surgeons in Ireland; Hon. Fellow London School of Econs 1998; Dr hc (Mauritius) 1998, (Aligarh Muslim Univ.) 1998, (Jawaharlal Nehru Univ.) 2005. *Leisure interests:* reading, music, water skiing, chess. *Address:* Prime Minister's Office, New Treasury Building, Intendance Street, Port Louis, Mauritius (office). *Telephone:* 207-9595 (office).

Fax: 208-8619 (office). *E-mail:* primeminister@mail.gov.mu (office). *Website:* pmo.gov.mu (office).

RAMIREZ, Manuel Aristides (Manny); American (b. Dominican Republic) professional baseball player; b. 30 May 1972, Santo Domingo; s. of Aristides Ramirez and Onelcida Ramirez; m.; ed George Washington High School, NY; left fielder; moved to USA 1985; drafted in first round of amateur draft (13th overall) by Cleveland Indians 1991, debuted 2 Sept. 1993 versus Minnesota; runner-up Rookie of the Year 1994; signed as free agent with Boston Red Sox 2002; led American League in runs-batted-in with 165 in 1999; American League batting champion 2002 with .349 average; led American League in home runs with 43 in 2004; 1,000th career run versus Texas Rangers 23 Aug. 2002; hit 500th home run in 2008; traded to Los Angeles Dodgers 2008; American League All-Star Team 1995, 1998–2007; inducted into New York City Public Schools Athletic Hall of Fame 1999; voted Most Valuable Player, World Series 2004. *Address:* Los Angeles Dodgers, 1000 Elysian Park Ave., Los Angeles, CA 90012-1199, USA. *Telephone:* (323) 224-1500. *Fax:* (323) 224-1269. *Website:* losangeles.dodgers.mlb.com.

RAMÍREZ ACUÑA, Francisco Javier; Mexican politician; b. 22 April 1952, Jamay, Jalisco; m. María de la Paz Verduzco; two s. two d.; ed Universidad de Guadalajara; joined Partido Accíon Nacional (PAN) 1969; Congressional Deputy for Jalisco State 1974–77, 1980–83; Local Rep. to Municipal Pres. of Zapopan 1983–85; Dir Gen. Sistecozome (public transport system of Jalisco) 1995–97; Mayor of Guadalajara 1998–2000; Gov. of Jalisco 2001–2006; Sec. of the Interior 2006–08 (resgnd). *Address:* Partido Accíon Nacional, Avda Coyoacán 1546, Col. del Valle, Juárez 03100, Mexico (office). *Telephone:* (55) 5200-4000 (office). *E-mail:* correo@cen.pan.org.mx (office). *Website:* www.pan.org.mx (office).

RAMIREZ CARRENO, Rafael; Venezuelan politician; *Minister of Energy and Mines and President and CEO, Petróleos de Venezuela SA (PDVSA);* ed Univ. of the Andes and Central Univ. of Venezuela; worked for eng firms Inelectra and Intevep; fmr Head, Enegas (nat. gas regulatory body) –2002; Minister of Energy and Mines 2002–; Pres. and CEO Petróleos de Venezuela SA (PDVSA) 2004–. *Address:* Ministry of Energy and Mines, Edif. Petróleos de Venezuela, Torre Oeste, Avenida Libertador, La Campiña, Apdo 169, Caracas 1010-A (office); Petróleos de Venezuela SA, Edif. Petróleos de Venezuela, Torre Oeste, Avenida Libertador, La Campiña, Apdo 169, Caracas 1010-A, Venezuela (office). *Telephone:* (212) 708-1299 (Ministry) (office); (212) 708-4743 (PDVSA) (office). *Fax:* (212) 708-7014 (Ministry) (office); (212) 708-4661 (PDVSA) (office). *E-mail:* dazaroy@hotmail.com (office). *Website:* www.mem.gov.ve (office).

RAMÍREZ CODINA, Pedro Jeta; Spanish journalist and newspaper executive; *Director, El Mundo (del Siglo Veintiuno);* b. 26 March 1952, Logroño; m. 1st Rocío Fernández Iglesias; m. 2nd Agatha Ruíz de la Prada; one s. one d.; ed Univ. of Navarre; Prof. of Contemporary Spanish Literature, Lebanon Valley Coll., Pa, USA 1973–74; with La Actualidad Económica 1974–76; wrote a weekly column for ABC newspaper; corresp. for El Noticiero Universal, Madrid; Dir of Diario 16 1980; Co-founder, with Alfonso de Salas, Balbino Fraga and Juan González, El Mundo (del Siglo Veinte, now Veintiuno) 1989, Publr and Ed. 1989–. *Address:* El Mundo, Pradillo 42, 28002 Madrid, Spain (office). *Telephone:* (91) 5864800 (office). *Fax:* (91) 5864848 (office). *E-mail:* editor@elmundo.es (office). *Website:* www.elmundo.es (office).

RAMÍREZ CORZO, Luis, MSc; Mexican petroleum industry executive; *Director General, Petróleos Mexicanos (PEMEX);* ed Nat. Univ. of Mexico, Univ. of Louisiana, USA Instituto Tecnológico Autónomo de México; fmr teacher Eng Dept, Nat. Univ. of Mexico; Dir Gen. PEMEX Exploration and Production 2001–04, Dir Gen. PEMEX 2004–; mem. Academia de Ingeniería, Asociación de Ingenieros Petroleros de México, Soc. of Petroleum Engineers of American Inst. of Mechanical Engineers; Nat. Petroleum Eng Prize 2000. *Address:* PEMEX, Avenida Marina Nacional 329, Colonia Huasteca, 11311 México DF, Mexico (office). *Telephone:* (55) 5722-2500 (office). *Fax:* (55) 5531-6321 (office). *Website:* www.pemex.com (office).

RAMÍREZ DE RINCÓN, Marta Lucía, PhD; Colombian politician and lawyer; b. Bogotá; m.; ed Javeriana Pontifical Univ., Univ. of the Andes and Harvard Univ., USA; fmr Prof., Univ. of the Andes; fmr Prof. of Foreign Trade, Faculty of Law, Javeriana Pontifical Univ.; Exec. Pres. Inversiones de Gases de Colombia SA, Federación Colombiana de Compañías Leasing, Nat. Asscn of Finance Insts, Financiera Mazda Crédito SA; fmr Vice-Minster of External Trade, Minister of External Trade 1998–2002; Amb. to France Feb.–Oct. 2002; Minister of Nat. Defence 2002–03; Gen. Man. and Pnr Ramirez and Orozco Int. Strategy Consultants 2004–06; Senator (Partido Social de Unidad Nacional) 2006–; Dir-Gen. Instituto de Comercio Exterior (INCOMEX); Fellow, Center for Int. Affairs, Harvard Univ. *Publications include:* El Contrato de Descuento y la Apertura de Crédito Antecedentes y Perspectivas del Negocio Fiduciario en Colombia, Régimen Legal de las Compañías de Financiamiento Comercial, Los Avances del Proceso de Interación Andina entre 1990 y 1991, El Programa Especial de Cooperación de la CEE para los Países Andines. *Address:* Senado, Bogotá DC, Colombia (office). *E-mail:* martha.ramirez.derincon@senado.gov.co (office); martaluciaramirezderincon@senado.gov.co (office). *Website:* martaluciaramirez.com.

RAMÍREZ LEZCANO, Rubén, MA, MBA; Paraguayan economist, diplomatist and government official; b. 11 Jan. 1966; m. Adriana Cabelluzzi; two s.; ed Univ. of Buenos Aires, Univ. of Paris, Sorbonne, Univ. of California, Los Angeles, USA; with Int. Econ. Affairs Counselling Dept, Pres.'s Office 1989; Sec. Embassy in Buenos Aires, in charge of Commercial Dept 1989–92; Dir Dept of Foreign Trade, Ministry of Foreign Affairs 1994–96; Exec. Sec. Nat. Council for Foreign Trade 1994–96; Counsellor Embassy in Paris and Standing Rep. at UNESCO 1996–98; Consul Gen. Los Angeles, Calif. 1998–99; Gen. Dir Export and Promotion Dept, Ministry of Foreign Affairs 1999–2000; Embassy Minister and Standing Rep. Latin American Integration Asscn, Montevideo, Uruguay 2000; Standing Rep. UN Special Orgs, Geneva, Switzerland 2001–04; Vice Minister for Econ. Relations and Integration 2004–06; Minister of Foreign Affairs 2006–08; mem. Asoc. Nacional Republicana–Partido Colorado (Nat. Republican Asscn–Colorado Party). *Address:* Asociación Nacional Republicana–Partido Colorado, Casa de los Colorados, 25 de Mayo 842, Asunción, Paraguay (office). *Telephone:* (21) 44-4137 (office). *Fax:* (21) 49-7857 (office). *Website:* www.anr.org.py (office).

RAMÍREZ MERCADO, Sergio; Nicaraguan politician and author; b. 5 Aug. 1942, Masatepe, Masaya; s. of late Pedro Ramírez Gutiérrez and Luisa Mercado Gutiérrez; m. Gertrudis Guerrero Mayorga 1964; one s. two d.; ed Univ. Autónoma de Nicaragua; was active in revolutionary student movt and founding mem. of Frente Estudiantil Revolucionario 1962; mem. Cen. American Univ. Supreme Council (CSUCA), Costa Rica 1964, Pres. 1968; mem. Int. Comm. of FSLN (Sandinista Liberation Front) 1975; undertook tasks on diplomatic front, propaganda and int. work on behalf of FSLN leading to overthrow of regime 1979; mem. Junta of Nat. Reconstruction Govt 1979; Vice-Pres. of Nicaragua 1984–90; minority leader, Speaker, Nat. Ass. 1990–94; Pres. Movimiento de Renovación Sandinista (MRS) 1994, MRS pre-cand. for presidency 1996; co-founder literary journal Ventana; mem. Nicaraguan Acad. of Language; Corresp. mem. Royal Spanish Acad.; columnist for numerous newspapers and journals including El Pais, Madrid, La Jornada, Mexico, El Tiempo, Bogota, El Nacional of Caracas, Listín Diario of Santo Domingo, La Opinion, Los Angeles, La Nacion, San Jose, El Tiempo, Tegucigalpa, La Prensa Gráfica, San Salvador, El Periodico in Guatemala, and La Prensa, Managua;; Hon. Prof., Faculty of Humanities, Universidad Pedagógica Francisco Morazán, Honduras 2007; Chevalier des Arts et des Lettres 1993, Order of Merit, First Class, Germany; Dr hc (Universidad Central del Ecuador) 1984, (Universidad Blaise Pascal de Clermont-Ferrand, France) 2000, (Universidad der Catamarca, Argentina) 2007; Bruno Kreisky Prize 1988, Alfaguara Prize (Madrid) 1998. *Publications include:* Cuentos 1963, El cuento centroamericano 1974, Charles Atlas también muere 1976, El cuento nicaragüense 1976, Castigo divino 1988, Confesión de amor 1991, Clave de sol 1992, Cuentos 1994, Oficios compartidos 1994, Un baile de máscaras 1995, Margarita, Está Linda la Mar 1998, Adiós muchachos 1999, Mentiras Verdaderas (2001, Mil y una muertes 2005, El reino animal 2006. *Leisure interests:* classical music, reading. *Address:* c/o MRS, Tienda Katty lc. Abajo, Apdo. 24, Managua, Nicaragua. *Website:* www.sergioramirez.org.ni (office).

RAMÍREZ VALDIVIA, Avil; Nicaraguan fmr lawyer and government official; b. 1964, El Jicaral, León; m.; three c.; ed Universidad Nacional Autónoma de Nicaragua; joined Juventud Democrática Nicaragüense, Movimiento Democrático Nicaragüense 1979; moved to USA 1982, with AmeriFirst Bank, Miami 1983–89; returned to Nicaragua 1989; with USAID 1989; Sub-Dir for Europe, Ministry of Foreign Affairs 1994; Sec. to the Presidency 2001; Deputy Minister of the Interior, Dir of Immigration and Foreign Services 2004; Minister of Nat. Defence 2005–06. *Address:* c/o Ministry of National Defence, Casa de la Presidencia, Managua, Nicaragua (office).

RAMÍREZ VÁZQUEZ, Pedro; Mexican architect; b. 16 April 1919, Mexico; s. of Dolores Vázquez and Max Ramírez; m. Olga Campuzano 1947 (died 1999); two s. two d.; ed Univ. Nacional Autónoma de México; Prof. of Design and City Planning, Nat. School of Architecture, Univ. Nacional Autónoma de México; Sec. of Human Settlements and Public Works of Mexican Govt 1976–82; Chair. Organizing Cttee, Games of XIX Olympiad; lecturer Autonomous Univ. of Mexico 1984; Dir Inst. of Urban Devt and Ecology 1988; Dir of display design Nubia Museum, Egypt 1985; Pres. Soc. of Mexican Architects and Nat. Coll. of Architects of Mexico 1953–58; founding mem. Int. Acad. of Architecture, Sofia 1985; Hon. mem. Council of Socs. of Architects of Spain; Dr hc (Pratt Inst. New York) 1982; Gold Medal of the French Acad. of Architecture 1978, Grand Prix of Twelfth Milan Triennial for prefabricated rural school project, Gold Medal, Eighth São Paulo Biennial for Nat. Museum of Anthropology, Mexico City, Nat. Prize of the Arts 1972, European Museum of the Year Award for Olympic Museum Switzerland 1995, Aga Khan Award for Architecture, Museum Nubia, Syria 2001. *Major works include:* co-author of design for Nat. School of Medicine, Univ. City; plans for several cities in Mexico; numerous prefabricated schools in Mexico (also used in S. America, Europe and Asia); buildings in Mexico City; Secr. of Foreign Affairs, Aztec Stadium, Cía. Mexicana de Aviación, Omega Co. and Congress Bldg, Nat. Museum of Anthropology, Japanese Embassy; Guadeloupe Shrine for 10,000 persons; Cathedral of Villahermosa, Tabasco; Cultural Centre, Tijuana; Monument to Fray Antón de Montesinos, Dominican Repub.; Mexican pavilions at Brussels, Seattle and New York World Fairs; museums of Ciudad Juárez and Mexico City; Nat. Gallery of History and Nat. Gallery of Modern Art, Mexico City; Offices of Int. Olympic Cttee, Lausanne, Switzerland 1981; Olympic Museum Switzerland 1985; Cen. Library and Museum of Anthropology, Toluca, Mexico 1985; Museum of the Major Temple, Mexico City 1985; Chapel of the Virgin of Guadalupe, Vatican 1991; Amparo Museum, Puebla 1991; pavilions of Mexico and Int. Olympic Cttee, Seville 1992; Teotihuacán Museum 1994; Information Centres, Monclova and Saltillo 1994–96; Convention Centre, Mérida 1997. *Leisure interests:* industrial design and design of lead glass objects. *Address:* Avenida de las Fuentes 170, México 01900, DF, Mexico. *Telephone:* (55) 5595-4388. *E-mail:* pramirez@data.net.mx (office). *Website:* www.ramirezvazquezpedro.com.

RAMKALAWAN, Rev. Wavel John Charles, BTheol; Seychelles theologian and politician; *Leader, Seychelles National Party;* b. 15 March 1961, Mahé; m.;

three s.; ed Seychelles Coll., St Paul's Theological Coll., Univ. of Birmingham; Founder and Leader of Parti Seselwa 1991–94; mem. Nat. Ass. 1993–97; Leader of Seychelles Nat. Party; Leader of the Opposition 1998–. *Address:* Seychelles National Party, Arpent Vert, Mant Fleuri, PO Box 81, Victoria (office); St Louis, Mahé, Seychelles (home). *Telephone:* (248) 224124 (office); (248) 516465 (home). *Fax:* (248) 225151 (office). *E-mail:* wavel24@hotmail.com (office).

RAMLI, Rizal, MA, PhD; Indonesian economist, business executive and fmr government official; *President, Board of Commissioners, PT Semen Gresik (Persero) Tbk;* b. 10 May 1953, Padang, West Sumatra; ed Bandung Inst. of Tech., Sophia Univ., Tokyo, Boston Univ., USA; econ. analyst; imprisoned for one year for writing white paper exposing failings of 'trickle-down' econs 1980s; ran ind. consultancy, Jakarta 1990s; Chair. Nat. Logistics Agency (Bulog) 2000; Chief Econs Minister –2001; Coordinating Minister for the Economy, Finance and Industry 2000; Minister of Finance June–July 2001; fmr Sr Consultant Van Zorge, Heffernan and Assocs, Jakarta; Pres. Bd of Comms PT Semen Gresik (Persero) Tbk 2006–. *Address:* PT Semen Gresik (Persero) Tbk, Gedung Utama Semen Gresik, Jl. Veteran, Gresik, 61122, Indonesia (office). *Telephone:* (31) 3981732 (office). *Fax:* (31) 3983209 (office). *Website:* www.semengresik.com (office).

RAMO, Simon, BS, PhD; American engineering executive (retd); b. 7 May 1913, Salt Lake City, Utah; s. of Benjamin Ramo and Clara Ramo (née Trestman); m. Virginia Smith 1937; two s.; ed Univ. of Utah and California Inst. of Tech.; with General Electric Co. 1936–46; Vice-Pres. Operations, Hughes Aircraft Co. 1946–53; with Ramo-Woolridge Corpn 1953–58; Dir US Intercontinental Ballistic Missile Program 1954–58; Dir TRW Inc. 1954–85, Exec. Vice-Pres. 1958–61, Vice-Chair. 1961–78, Chair. 1969–78, consultant 1978–; Pres. The Bunker-Ramo Corpn 1964–66; Chair. TRW-Fujitsu Co. 1980–83; mem. Bd of Dirs Arco Power Technologies; Visiting Prof. of Man. Science, California Inst. of Tech. 1978–; Regents Lecturer, UCLA 1981–82, Univ. of California, Santa Cruz 1978–79; Chair. Center for Study of American Experience, Univ. of Southern California 1978–80; Faculty Fellow, John F. Kennedy School of Govt, Harvard Univ. 1980–84; mem. White House Energy Research and Devt Advisory Council 1973–75; Chair. Pres.'s Comm. on Science and Tech. 1976–77; mem. Bd Advisors for Science and Tech., Repub. of China 1981–84; Chair. Aetna, Jacobs & Ramo Venture Capital 1987–90, Allenwood Ventures, Inc. 1987–; adviser, Axiom Venture Pnrs 1997–; Life Trustee, California Inst. of Tech., Nat. Symphony Orchestra Asscn 1973–83; Trustee Emer., California State Univ.; Pres. Bd Govs Performing Arts Council Music Center, LA 1976–77; Co-Chair. Bd Overseers Keck School of Medicine, Univ. of Southern California (USC) 1999–; mem. Bd of Dirs W.M. Keck Foundation 1983–, LA World Affairs Council 1973–85, Music Center Foundation, LA, LA Philharmonic Asscn 1981–84; Fellow, American Acad. of Political Science, American Acad. of Arts and Sciences, IEEE; mem. Nat. Acad. of Eng (Founder, Council mem. Bueche Award), Int. Acad. of Astronautics, Pacific Council on Int. Policy, Council on Foreign Relations, Inst. for the Advancement of Eng, American Philosophical Soc., American Physical Soc., New York Acad. of Sciences; Hon. DSc (Utah) 1961, (Union Coll.) 1963, (Worcester Polytechnic Inst.) 1968, (Akron) 1969, (Cleveland State) 1976; Hon. DEng (Case Western Reserve) 1960, (Michigan) 1961, (Polytechnic Inst., New York) 1971; Hon. LLD (Carnegie-Mellon) 1970, (USC) 1972, (Gonzaga) 1983, (Occidental Coll.) 1984, (Claremont) 1985; IEEE Electronic Achievement Award 1953, IAS Award 1956, American Inst. of Electronic Engineers Award 1959, American Iron and Steel Inst. Award 1968, Medal of Achievement, American Electronics Asscn 1970, Distinguished Service Medal, Armed Forces Comm. and Electronics Asscn 1970, Medal of Achievement, Western Electronics Mfrs Asscn 1970, USC Award 1971, 1979, Kayan Medal, Columbia Univ. 1972, American Construction Engineers Council Award 1974, IEEE Golden Omega Award 1975, IEEE Founders' Medal 1980, IEEE Centennial Medal 1984, named to Business Hall of Fame 1984, Nat. Medal of Science 1976, 1979, Franklin Inst. Medal 1978, Pres.'s Medal of Science 1981, UCLA Medal 1982, Presidential Medal of Freedom 1983, Aesculapian Award, UCLA 1984, Durand Medal, American Asscn of ind. Architects 1984, John Fritz Medal 1986, Henry Townley Heald Award, IIlinois Inst. of Tech. 1988, Nat. Eng Award, American Asscn of Eng Socs 1988, Franklin-Jefferson Medal 1988, Howard Hughes Memorial Award 1989, Air Force Space and Missile Pioneers Award 1989, Pioneer Award, Int. Council on Systems Eng 1997, NASA Distinguished Public Service Medal 1999, Lifetime Achievement Trophy, Smithsonian Inst. 1999, John F. Kennedy Astronautics Award, American Astronautical Soc. 2000, John R. Alison Award for Industrial Leadership, Air Force Asscn 2000, USC Presidential Medallion 2002, Founders' Award, USC Thornton School of Music 2003, Space Foundation Lifetime Space Achievement Award 2007. *Publications:* Fields and Waves in Modern Radio (with J. R. Whinnery) 1944, 1953, Introduction to Microwaves 1945, Fields and Waves in Communication Electronics (with J. R. Whinnery and Theodore Van Duzer) 1965, Cure for Chaos 1969, Century of Mismatch 1970, Extraordinary Tennis for the Ordinary Player 1970, The Islands of E, Cono and My 1973, The Business of Science 1988, Meetings, Meetings and More Meetings (non-fiction) 2005. *Address:* 9200 Wesst Sunset Boulevard, Suite 801, Los Angeles, CA 90069-3603, USA (office). *Telephone:* (310) 550-8360 (office).

RAMON, Haim, BA; Israeli politician and lawyer; *Vice-Premier and Minister in the Prime Minister's Office;* b. 10 April 1950, Jaffa; s. of Asher Vishnia and Bina Vishnia; m. Prina Tenenbaum (divorced); one s. one d.; ed Tel-Aviv Univ.; fmr Capt. in Israeli Air Force; Chair. Public Council for Youth Exchanges; Nat. Sec. Labour Party's Young Guard 1978–84; co-ordinator Finance Cttee, Labour Party 1984–88, Chair. Labour Party 1988–92; Minister of Health 1992–94, of the Interior 1995–96, 2000–01; apptd mem. Foreign Affairs and Defence Cttee 2001; Minister responsible for Jerusalem Affairs, Prime Minister's Office –2001; Minister without Portfolio 2005–06, of Justice 2006 (resgnd); Vice-Premier of Israel and Minister in Prime Minister's Office 2007–; mem. Knesset 1983–; served on numerous cttees 1983–92 (Labour); fmr Sec.-Gen. Histadrut (Gen. Fed. of Labour in Israel); joined Kadima Party 2005; Chair. Int. Inst. —Histadrut. *Address:* The Knesset, Kiryat Ben-Gurion, Jerusalem, 91950, Israel (office). *Telephone:* 2-6408413 (office). *Fax:* 2-6408412 (office). *E-mail:* ChaimR@knesset.gov.il (office). *Website:* www.knesset.gov.il (office).

RAMOS, Gen. Fidel Valdez; Philippine fmr head of state and army officer; *Chairman, Ramos Peace and Development Foundation;* b. 18 March 1928, Lingayen, Pangasinan; s. of Narciso Ramos and Angela Valdez; m. Amelita Martinez; five d.; ed Nat. Univ. Manila, US Mil. Acad., West Point and Univ. of Illinois; active service in Korea and Viet Nam; Deputy Chief of Staff 1981–84; Acting Chief of Staff, Philippines Armed Forces 1984–86, Chief of Staff 1986–88; Sec. of Nat. Defence 1988–91, cand. for Pres. May 1992; Pres. of the Philippines 1992–98; Chair. Emer. Lakas-Christian Muslim Democrats Party (CMD); Chair. Bd of Dirs Boao Forum for Asia; mem. ASEAN Eminent Persons Group 2005–; f. and Chair. Ramos Peace and Devt Foundation; Légion d'honneur 1987; numerous hon. degrees; Peace Prize Award, UNESCO 1997 and numerous other awards. *Address:* c/o Ramos Peace and Development Foundation, 26th Floor, Export Bank Plaza, Corner Senator Gil Puyat and Chino Roces Avenues, 1200 Makati City (office); 120 Maria Cristina Street, Ayala Alabang Village, Muntinlupa City, Philippines (home). *Telephone:* (2) 8878964 (office). *Fax:* (2) 8878966 (office). *E-mail:* fvr@rpdev.org (office); rpdev@skyinet.net (home). *Website:* www.rpdev.org; www.boaoforum.org.

RAMOS, Maria, BCom, MSc; South African business executive; *Group Chief Executive, Transnet Ltd;* b. Lisbon, Portugal; ed Univ. of the Witwatersrand, Univ. of London, UK, Inst. of Bankers Diploma (CAIB); emigrated as child to South Africa; joined Econ. Planning Dept of African Nat. Congress (ANC) 1990; joined Nat. Treasury, Pretoria as jr 1992, Dir-Gen. 1996–2003; Group Chief Exec. Transnet Ltd (state-owned transport group) 2004–; mem. Bd of Dirs South African Airways (Pty) Ltd, Sanlam Ltd; South Africa's Businesswoman of the Year 2001, ranked by Fortune magazine amongst 50 Most Powerful Women in Business outside the US (29th) 2004, (28th) 2005, (16th) 2006, (14th) 2007. *Address:* Transnet Ltd, Carlton Centre, Room 4936, 49th Floor, 150 Commissioner Street, Johannesburg, South Africa (office). *Telephone:* (11) 308-2309 (office). *Fax:* (11) 308-2312 (office). *Website:* www.transnet.co.za (office).

RAMOS-HORTA, José, MA; Timor-Leste politician and head of state; *President;* b. 26 Dec. 1949, Dili; s. of late Francisco Horta and of Natalina Ramos Filipe Horta; m. Ana Pessoa 1978 (divorced); one s.; ed Hague Acad. of Int. Law, The Netherlands, Int. Inst. of Human Rights, Strasbourg, France, Columbia Univ., Antioch Univ., USA; journalist and broadcaster 1969–74; Minister for External Affairs and Information, Timor-Leste 1975; Perm. Rep. of Fretilin to UN, NY 1976–89; Public Affairs and Media Dir Mozambican Embassy, Washington 1987–88; f., Dir, Lecturer Diplomacy Training Programme, Univ. of NSW 1990–, Visiting Prof. 1996–; Special Rep. Nat. Council of Maubere Resistance 1991–; returned to Timor-Leste Dec. 1999; Vice-Pres. Nat. Council of Resistance 1999–; Sr Minister for Foreign Affairs and Cooperation 2000–06 (resgnd), also Acting Defence Minister June 2006; Prime Minister of Timor-Leste 2006–07, also Minister of Defence; Pres. of Timor-Leste 2007–; served in Timor-Leste Transitional Admin. 2000–02; mem. Bd Timor-Leste Human Rights Centre, Melbourne; Sr Assoc. Mem. St Antony's Coll., Oxford 1987–; Order of Freedom (Portugal) 1996; received Unrepresented Nations and People's Org. Award 1996; shared Nobel Peace Prize 1996 (with Mgr Carlos Ximenes Belo q.v.). *Publications:* Funu: The Unfinished Saga of East Timor 1987; articles in numerous publs worldwide. *Leisure interest:* tennis. *Address:* Office of the President, Palácio das Cinzas, Kaikoli, Dili, Timor-Leste (office). *Telephone:* 3339011 (office). *E-mail:* presidente-tl@easttimor.minihub.org (office).

RAMOS ROSA, António; Portuguese poet and literary critic; b. 17 Oct. 1924, Faro; m. Agripina Costa Marques 1962; one d.; Dir literary reviews, Árvore 1951–53, Cassiopeia 1955, Cadernos do Meio-Dia 1958–60; Grand Oficial, Order of Santiago da Espada; Great Cross, Order of Infante Dom Henrique; Prize of Portuguese Centre of Int. Asscn of Literary Critics 1980, PEN Club's Poetry Prize 1980, 2006, Portuguese Asscn of Writers' Grand Prize 1989, Pessoa Prize 1988, International Poetry Prize of Liège Poetry Biennial 1991, European Poet of the Decade (Collège de l'Europe) 1991, Jean Malrieux Prize (Marseille) 1992; Luís Miguel Nava Poetry Prize 2006. *Publications include:* poetry: Delta seguido de Pela Primeira Vez 1996, Nomes de Ninguém 1997, À Mesa do Vento seguido de As Espirais de Dioniso 1997, A Imobilidade Fulminante 1998; essays: Poesia, Liberdade Livre 1962, A Poesia Moderna e a Interrogação do Real 1979, Incisões Oblíquas 1987, A Parede Azul 1991, As Palavras 2001, Génese 2005. *Address:* c/o Roma Editora, Avenida Roma, 129 r/c Esq., 1700-346 Lisbon, Portugal.

RAMPHAL, Sir Shridath Surendranath, GCMG, OE, OM, ONZ, AC, QC, SC, LLM, FRSA; Guyanese international organization official, barrister and politician; b. 3 Oct. 1928, New Amsterdam; s. of James I. Ramphal and Grace Ramphal (née Abdool); m. Lois Winifred King 1951; two s. two d.; ed Queen's Coll., Georgetown, King's Coll., London, Harvard Law School; Crown Counsel, British Guiana 1953–54; Asst to Attorney-Gen. 1954–56; Legal Draftsman 1956–58; Solicitor-Gen. 1959–61; Legal Draftsman, West Indies 1958–59; Asst Attorney-Gen., West Indies 1961–62; Attorney-Gen., Guyana 1965–73; mem. Nat. Assembly 1965–75; Minister of State for External Affairs 1967–72, Minister of Foreign Affairs 1972–75, of Justice 1973–75; Commonwealth Sec.-Gen. 1975–90; Chancellor Univ. of Guyana 1988–92, Univ. of Warwick 1989–2001, Univ. of West Indies 1989–; Queen's Counsel 1965 and Sr Counsel,

Guyana 1966; mem. Int. Comm. of Jurists, Ind. Comm. on Int. Devt Issues, Ind. Comm. on Disarmament and Security Issues, Ind. Comm. on Int. Humanitarian Issues, World Comm. on Environment and Devt, South Comm., Carnegie Comm. on Deadly Conflict, Bd of Govs Int. Devt Research Center, Canada, Exec. Cttee of Int. Inst. for Environment and Devt, Council of Int. Negotiation Network Carter Center, Georgia, USA 1991–97; Patron One World Broadcasting Trust; Chair. UN Cttee for Devt Planning 1984–87, West Indian Comm. 1990–92, Bd Int. Inst. for Democracy and Electoral Assistance (IDEA) 1995–2001, Advisory Cttee Future Generations Alliance Foundation 1995–97; Pres. World Conservation Union—IUCN 1990–93; Int. Steering Cttee Leadership for Environment and Devt Program Rockefeller Foundation 1991–98; Co-Chair. Comm. on Global Governance 1992–2000; Adviser to Sec.-Gen. of UNCED 1992; Chief Negotiator on Int. Econ. Issues for the Caribbean Region 1997–2001; Facilitator Belize–Guatemala Dispute 2000–02; John Simon Guggenheim Fellowship 1962; Hon. Bencher of Gray's Inn 1981; Fellow, King's Coll., London 1975, LSE 1979, RSA 1981, Magdalen Coll., Oxford 1982; Order of the Repub. (Egypt) 1973; Grand Cross, Order of the Sun (Peru) 1974; Grand Cross, Order of Merit (Ecuador) 1974, Order of Nishaan Izzuddeen (Maldives) 1989, Grand Commdr, Order of Niger 1990, Grand Commdr, Order of the Companion of Freedom (Zambia) 1990, Nishan-e-Quaid-i-Azam (Pakistan) 1990, Order of the Caribbean Community 1991, Commdr Order of the Golden Ark 1994; Hon. LLD (Panjab Univ.) 1975, (Southampton) 1976, (Univ. of The West Indies) 1978, (St Francis Xavier Univ., Halifax, Canada) 1978, (Aberdeen) 1979, (Cape Coast, Ghana) 1980, (London) 1981, (Benin, Nigeria) 1982, (Hull) 1983, (Yale) 1985, (Cambridge) 1985, (Warwick) 1988, (York Univ., Ont., Canada) 1988, (Malta) 1989, (Otago, NZ) 1990; Hon. DHL (Simmons Coll., Boston) 1982; Hon. DCL (Oxon.) 1982, (East Anglia) 1983, (Durham) 1985; Dr hc (Surrey) 1979, (Essex) 1980; Hon. DHumLitt (Duke Univ., USA) 1985; Hon. DLitt (Bradford) 1985, (Indira Gandhi Nat. Open Univ.) 1989; Hon. DSc (Cranfield Inst. of Tech.) 1987; Arden and Atkin Prize, Gray's Inn 1952, Int. Educ. Award (Richmond Coll., London) 1988, RSA Albert Medal 1988, Medal of Friendship, Cuba 2001, Pravasi Bharata Samman Award 2003. *Publications:* One World to Share: Selected Speeches of the Commonwealth Secretary-General 1975–79, Nkrumah and the Eighties (1980 Kwame Nkrumah Memorial Lectures), Sovereignty and Solidarity (1981 Callander Memorial Lectures), Some in Light and Some in Darkness: The Long Shadow of Slavery (Wilberforce Lecture) 1983, The Message not the Messenger (STC Communication Lecture) 1985, The Trampling of the Grass (Econ. Comm. for Africa Silver Jubilee Lecture) 1985, For the South, a Time to Think 1986, Making Human Society a Civilized State (Corbishley Memorial Lecture) 1987, Inseparable Humanity: An Anthology of Reflections of Shridath Ramphal 1988, An End to Otherness (six speeches) 1990, Our Country, The Planet 1992, No Island is an Island and contribs to journals of legal, political and int. affairs, including International and Comparative Law Quarterly, Caribbean Quarterly, Public Law, Guyana Journal, The Round Table, Royal Society of Arts Journal, Foreign Policy, Third World Quarterly, International Affairs. *Leisure interests:* photography, cooking. *Address:* 31 St Mathew's Lodge, 50 Oakley Square, London, NW1 1NB (home); 1 The Sutherlands, 188 Sutherland Avenue, London, W9 1HR, England. *Telephone:* (20) 7266-3409. *Fax:* (20) 7286-2302. *E-mail:* ssramphal@msn.com (office).

RAMPHELE, Mamphela Aletta, MB, ChB, BCom, DPH, PhD; South African physician, anthropologist, business executive and fmr international organization official; *Chairperson, Circle Capital Ventures;* b. 28 Dec. 1947, Pietersburg; d. of Pitsi Eliphaz Ramphele and Rangoato Rahab Ramphele (née Mahlaela); two s.; ed Setotolwane High School, Pietersburg, Univ. of Natal, Univ. of Capetown; community health worker Black Community Programmes, Ktown 1975–77, Ithuseng Community Health Programme, Tzaneen 1978–84; Sr Researcher Dept Social Anthropology, Univ. of Cape Town 1986, Deputy Vice-Chancellor 1991–95, Vice-Chancellor 1996–2000; Researcher and Consultant to Western Cape Hostel Dwellers' Asscn 1986–92; Man. Dir World Bank 2000–05;; Chair. Ind. Devt Trust, Circle Capital Ventures; Co-Chair. Global Comm. on Int. Migration 2004–05; mem. Bd of Dirs (non-exec.) Anglo-American Corpn of SA 1992–95, Old Mutual 1993–, Anglo American 2006–; played key role in formation of Black Consciousness Movt 1969; Patron, Cape Town Opera 2006–; mem. NAMDA 1985–; Hon. DHumLitt (Hunter Coll., New York), 1984, New York Univ.) 2007; Hon. MD (Natal) 1989, (Sheffield) 1998; Dr hc for Distinguished Career (Tufts Univ., Mass.) 1991; Hon. DSc (Univ. Coll., London) 1997; Hon. LLD (Princeton) 1997, (Brown Univ.) 1998, (Mich.) 1998; Dr hc (Inst. of Social Studies, Netherlands) 1997; Hon. DPhil (Univ. of Orange Free State); Barnard Medal of Distinction, Barnard Coll., New York 1991. *Publications:* Children on Frontline (UNICEF report) 1987, Uprooting Poverty: The South African Challenge (with David Philip) 1989 (Noma Award for publishing in Africa 1991), A Bed Called Home: Life in Migrant Labour Hostels of Cape Town (with David Philip) 1993, Mamphela Ramphele: A Life (with David Philip) 1995, Across Boundaries: The Journey of a South African Woman Leader 1996. *Leisure interests:* reading, walking. *Address:* Circle Capital Ventures, 28th Floor, #1 Thibault Square, Cape Town 8001, South Africa (office). *Telephone:* (21) 4252231 (office). *Fax:* (21) 4215541 (office). *Website:* www.circlecapitalventures.co.za (office).

RAMPL, Dieter; German banking executive; *Chairman, UniCredit Group;* b. 5 Sept. 1947, Munich; ed studies in econs in Munich; traineeship with Bayerischen Vereinsbank AG, Munich –1966, positions in Düsseldorf, Frankfurt and NY, 1968–83, mem. Exec. Cttee 1968–87, 1994–98, 1998–2006, Head of Regional Office, Munich 1995–97, Man. Dir Bayerische HypoVereinsbank Aktiengesellschaft (HVB group, cr. through merger between Vereinsbank and Bayerischen Hypotheken und Wechselbank 1998) 1998, Spokesman Group Bd of Man. Dirs 2003–06; Chair. UniCredit SpA 2006–07, Unicredit Group (following merger of Unicredit and Capitalia) 2007–, Chair. Perm. Strategic Cttee, Corp. Governance, HR and Nominations Cttee, Remuneration Cttee, mem. Internal Control and Risks Cttee; with Société de Banque Suisse, Geneva 1966–68; with N American Div., BHF-Bank AG 1983–94; Chair. Supervisory Bd Koenig & Bauer AG, Bayerische Börse AG; Chair. Man. Bd Hypo-Kulturstiftung; Vice-Chair. Supervisory Bd Mediobanca SpA; mem. Supervisory Bd FC Bayern München AG; mem. Bd Dirs Bode Hewitt Beteiligungs AG, ABI (Italian Banking Asscn); Dir (non-exec.) Babcock and Brown; Vice-Chair. Inst. for Int. Political Studies; mem. Bd Dirs AIRC (Italian Asscn for Cancer Research), Bd of Aspen Inst. Italia, Int. Chamber of Commerce; Trustee, European School of Man. and Tech. *Address:* UniCredit Group, Piazza Cordusia, 20123 Milan, Italy (office). *Telephone:* (02) 88621 (office). *Fax:* (02) 88628503 (office). *E-mail:* info@unicreditgroup.eu (office). *Website:* www.unicreditgroup.eu (office).

RAMPLING, Charlotte, OBE; British actress; b. 5 Feb. 1945, Sturmer, England; m. 2nd Jean-Michel Jarre 1978; two s. (one s. from previous marriage); one step-d.; film debut 1963; Chevalier, Ordre des Arts et Lettres 1986; César d'honneur 2001; Chevalier, Légion d'honneur 2002. *Films include:* The Knack 1963, Rotten to the Core, Georgy Girl, The Long Duel, Kidnapping, Three, The Damned 1969, Skibum, Corky 1970, 'Tis Pity She's a Whore, Henry VIII and His Six Wives 1971, Asylum 1972, The Night Porter, Giordano Bruno, Zardoz, Caravan to Vaccares 1973, The Flesh of the Orchid, Yuppi Du 1974–75, Farewell My Lovely, Foxtrot 1975, Sherlock Holmes in New York, Orca The Killer Whale, The Purple Taxi 1976, Stardust Memories 1980, The Verdict 1983, Viva la vie 1983, Beauty and Sadness 1984, He Died with His Eyes Open 1985, Max mon Amour, Max My Love 1985, Angel Heart 1987, Paris by Night 1988, Dead on Arrival 1989, Helmut Newton, Frames from the Edge, Hammers Over the Anvil 1991, Time is Money 1992, La marche de Radetzky (TV film) 1994, Asphalt Tango 1995, The Wings of the Dove 1997, The Cherry Orchard 1999, Signs and Wonders 2000, Hommage à Alfred Lepetit 2000, Aberdeen 2000, The Fourth Angel 2001, Under the Sand 2001, Superstition 2001, Spy Game 2001, See How They Run 2002, Summer Things 2003, I'll Sleep When I'm Dead 2003, Swimming Pool 2003, The Statement 2003, Jerusalem 2003, Vers le sud 2004, Lemming 2005, Basic Instinct 2 2006, Angel 2006, Deception 2007, The Duchess 2008, Babylon A.D. 2008. *Television includes:* numerous appearances including La Femme abandonnée 1992, Murder In Mind 1994, Radetzkymarsch (mini-series) 1995, Samson le magnifique 1995, La Dernière fête 1996, Great Expectations 1999, My Uncle Silas (series) 2000, Imperium: Augustus 2003. *Address:* c/o Artmédia, 20 avenue Rapp, 75007 Paris, France. *Telephone:* 1-43-17-33-00.

RAMQVIST, Lars Henry, PhD; Swedish business executive; *Honorary Chairman, Telefonaktiebolaget L. M. Ericsson;* b. 2 Nov. 1938, Grängesberg; s. of Henry Ramqvist and Alice Ramqvist; m. Barbro Pettersson 1962; one s. one d.; ed Univ. of Uppsala; Section Head, Stora Kopparberg AB 1962–65; with Axel Johnson Inst. 1965–80, Pres. 1975–80; joined L. M. Ericsson Telephone Co. as Vice-Pres. and Head of Information Systems Div. 1980, Pres. and CEO 1990–98, Chair. 1998–2002, Hon. Chair. 2002–, Pres. subsidiary RIFA AB 1984–86, Ericsson Radio AB 1988–90; Vice-Chair. AB Volvo 1998, Chair. 1999–2004 (resgnd); Chair. Skandia Insurance Co. Ltd 1999–2003; mem. Bd of Dirs Svenska Cellulosa Aktiebolaget SCA (publ) 1994–2004, Astra Zeneca; mem. Bd Swedish Eng Employers' Asscn, Asscn of Swedish Eng Industries and Fed. of Swedish Industries (Chair. 1999), European Round Table of Industrialists 1994–2002; mem. Prime Minister's Special Industry Advisory Cttee 1994–; mem. Royal Swedish Acad. of Science, Royal Swedish Acad. of Eng Sciences; Hon. mem. IEEE; Dr hc (Technical Univ. Beijing), (Technical Univ. Moscow). *Address:* c/o Telefonaktiebolaget L. M. Ericsson, Torshamnsgatan 23, Kista, 164-83 Stockholm, Sweden.

RAMSAMY, Pakereesamy (Prega), BA, MBA, PhD; Mauritian economist and international organization official; *Director General, Economic Development Board of Madagascar;* b. 1950, Rose Hill; m. Novia Ramsamy; two d.; with Preferential Trade Area for Eastern and Southern Africa, then Common Market for Eastern and Southern Africa for 14 years; Chief Economist, Southern African Devt Community 1997–98, Deputy Exec. Sec. 1998–2000, Acting Exec. Sec. 2000, Exec. Sec. 2001–05; Dir Gen. Econ. Devt Bd of Madagascar 2006–. *Leisure interests:* reading, indoor games, swimming, fishing. *Address:* Projet Pôles Intégrés de Croissance, Immeuble Ex-Maison de La Réunion, 2ème étage ISORAKA, Antananarivo 101, Madagascar (office). *Telephone:* (20) 2236777 (office). *Fax:* (20) 2230172 (office). *E-mail:* pic@wanadoo.mg (home).

RAMSBOTHAM, Hon. Sir Peter (Edward), Kt, GCMG, GCVO, DL; British diplomatist and administrator; b. 8 Oct. 1919, London; s. of 1st Viscount Soulbury; m. 1st Frances Blomfield 1941 (died 1982); two s. one d.; m. 2nd Zaida Hall 1985; ed Eton Coll. and Magdalen Coll., Oxford; entered diplomatic service 1948; served in Political Div., Allied Control Comm., Berlin 1948–50; First Sec., Foreign Office 1950–53; Head of Chancery, UK del. to UN, New York 1953–57; Foreign Office 1957–62; Head of Chancery, British Embassy, Paris 1962–67; Foreign Office 1967–69; High Commr to Cyprus 1969–71; Amb. to Iran 1971–74, to USA 1974–77; Gov. and C-in-C of Bermuda 1977–80; Dir Commercial Union Assurance Co. 1980–90, Lloyds Bank Ltd 1980–90, Chair. Lloyds Bank Southern Region 1984–90; Chair. Ryder-Cheshire Foundation for the Relief of Suffering 1982–2000; World Memorial Fund for Disaster Relief 1992–96; DL Hants. 1992; Hon. Fellow, Magdalen Coll. Oxford 1991; Croix de Guerre 1945; KStJ 1976; Hon. LLD (Akron Univ.) 1975, (William and Mary Coll.) 1975, (Maryland Univ.) 1976, (Yale Univ.) 1977. *Leisure interests:* gardening, fishing. *Address:* East Lane, Ovington, Alresford, Hants., SO24 0RA, England (home). *Telephone:* (1962) 732515 (home).

RAMSEY, Norman Foster, MA, PhD, DSc; American physicist and academic; *Higgins Professor Emeritus of Physics, Harvard University;* b. 27 Aug. 1915,

Washington, DC; s. of Brigadier-Gen. and Mrs Norman F. Ramsey; m. 1st Elinor Stedman Jameson 1940 (died 1983); four d.; m. 2nd Ellie Welch 1985; ed Columbia, Harvard and Cambridge Univs; Assoc. Univ. of Illinois 1940–42; Asst Prof. Columbia Univ. 1942–46; Research Assoc. MIT Radiation Lab. 1940–43; Expert Consultant to Sec. of War 1942–45; Group Leader and Asscn Division Head, Los Alamos Lab. of Atomic Energy Project 1943–45; Chief Scientist of Atomic Energy Lab., Tinian 1945; Assoc. Prof. Columbia Univ. 1945–47; Head Physics Dept, Brookhaven Nat. Lab. 1946–47; Assoc. Prof. Harvard Univ. 1947–50, Prof. 1950–66, Higgins Prof. of Physics 1966–86, Prof. Emer. 1986–, Sr Fellow, Harvard Soc. Fellows 1970–, Dir Harvard Nuclear Lab. 1948–50 and 1952–53; Air Force Scientific Advisory Cttee 1947–55; Dept Defence Panel on Atomic Energy 1953–58; Scientific Adviser NATO 1958–59; Gen. Advisory Cttee, Atomic Energy Comm. 1960–72; Dir Varian Assocs 1963–66; Pres. Univs Research Asscn 1966–81; Eastman Prof., Oxford Univ. 1973–74; Luce Prof. of Cosmology, Mount Holyoke Coll. 1982–83, Prof. of Physics, Univ. of Va 1983–84; Research Fellow, Jt Inst. Lab. Astrophysics, Univ. of Colo 1986–87; Distinguished Prof., Univ. of Chicago 1987–88; Prof., Williams Coll. 1989; Visiting Prof., Univ. of Mich. 1989–92; Vice-Pres. American Physical Soc. 1977 (Pres. 1978); Chair. Physics Div. American Asscn for Advancement of Science 1977; mem. NAS, American Acad. of Arts and Sciences, American Philosophical Soc., French Acad. of Sciences; Visiting Cttee Nat. Bureau of Standards 1982–; Trustee, Carnegie Endowment for Int. Peace 1962–85 and the Rockefeller Univ. 1976–90; Chair. Bd of Govs, American Inst. of Physics 1980–86; Hon. DSc (Case Western Reserve Univ.) 1968, (Middlebury Coll.) 1969, (Oxford) 1973, (Rockefeller) 1986, (Sussex) 1989, (Chicago, Houston) 1990, (Mich. 1993), (Philadelphia Coll. of Pharmacy and Science) 1995; Hon. DCL (Oxford) 1990; Presidential Order of Merit, Lawrence Award 1960, Davisson-Germer prize 1974, Award for Excellence in Science (Colombia Univ.) 1980, Medal of Honor of IEE 1984, Monie Ferst Prize 1985, Rabi Prize 1985, Karl Compton Award 1986, Rumford Premium 1985, Oersted Medal 1988, Nat. Medal of Science 1988, Nobel Prize in Physics (Jt) 1989, Pupin Medal 1992, Erice Science for Peace Prize 1992, Einstein Medal 1993, Vannevar Bush Award 1995, Alexander Hamilton Award 1995. *Publications:* Nuclear Moments 1953, Nuclear Two-Body Problems 1953, Molecular Beans 1955, 1985, Quick Calculus 1965, 1985, Spectroscopy with Coherent Radiation 1998; and numerous articles in the Physical Review. *Leisure interests:* skiing, walking, sailing, swimming, tennis, reading, conversation, music. *Address:* Lyman Physics Laboratory, Harvard University, Cambridge, MA 02138; 24 Monmouth Court, Brookline, MA 02146, USA (office). *Telephone:* (617) 495-2864 (office). *Fax:* (617) 496-5144 (office). *E-mail:* ramsey@physics.harvard.edu (office). *Website:* www.physics .harvard.edu (office).

RAMSEY, Paul Glenn, AB, MD; American physician and academic; *CEO of UW Medicine and Dean of the School of Medicine, University of Washington;* b. 1949, Pittsburgh; m. Bonnie Ramsey; ed Harvard Coll., Harvard Medical School; Residency in Internal Medicine, Mass Gen. Hosp., Boston 1975–78; Acting Instructor, Dept of Medicine, Univ. of Washington 1980–81, Acting Asst Prof. 1981–82, Asst Prof. 1982–86, Assoc. Prof. 1986–91, Prof. 1991–, Assoc. Chair. Dept of Medicine 1988–90, Chair. 1992–97, Robert G. Petersdorf Endowed Chair. in Medicine 1995, Vice Pres. for Medical Affairs and Dean, School of Medicine 1997–, also CEO UW Medicine and Exec. Vice Pres. of Medical Affairs 2006–; mem. Asscn of American Physicians, NAS Inst. of Medicine; Univ. of Washington School of Medicine Distinguished Teacher Award 1984,1986, 1987, Margaret Anderson Award 1989, Nat. Bd of Medical Examiners John P. Hubbard Award 1999. *Address:* Office of the Dean, UW School of Medicine, University of Washington, 325 Ninth Avenue, Seattle, WA 98104-2499, USA (office). *Telephone:* (206) 744-3000 (office). *Website:* uwmedicine.washington.edu (office).

RAMZI, Rashid; Bahraini (b. Moroccan) athlete; b. 17 July 1980, Morocco; middle-distance runner; competes internationally for Bahrain in 800m, 1,500m and 5,000m; only Bahraini Olympic medallist; raised in Safi, Morocco; competed internationally for Morocco until he joined Bahraini armed forces and gained citizenship in 2002; Silver Medal, 800m, World Indoor Championships 2004; became first athlete in history to win gold medals in 800m and 1,500m at same World Championships and first man to perform this feat in a global championship (World Championships or Olympic Games) since Peter Snell in 1964, World Championships, Helsinki 2005; Silver Medal, 1,500m, World Championships, Osaka 2007; Gold Medal, 1,500m, Olympic Games, Beijing 2008. *Address:* c/o Bahrain Amateur Athletics Federation, PO Box 29269, 12344 Manama, Bahrain. *Telephone:* 684905. *Fax:* 687506. *E-mail:* athletic@batelco.com.bh.

RANA, Madhukar Shumshere J. B., BA, MA; Nepalese economist, academic and fmr government official; *Adjunct Professor, South Asian Institute of Management;* b. 1941, Jawalakhel, Lalitpur; ed McMaster Univ., Canada, Manchester Univ., UK, Geneva Univ., Switzerland, Delhi Univ., India; Manpower Economist, Govt of Canada 1967; fmr Lecturer in Econs, Nippising Univ.; fmr Assoc. Teaching Master, Cambrian Coll. of Applied Arts and Tech; Assoc. Prof., Centre for Econ. Devt and Admin, Tribhuvan Univ., Nepal 1971, then became Exec. Dir; Assoc. Prof., Centre for Econ. Devt and Admin 1971; Chief Econ. Adviser to Ministry of Finance 1983–84; Sr Regional Programme Man. for South Asia, UNDP 1994–95; Special Adviser to Ministry of Foreign Affairs 1996–98; Minister of Finance Jan.–Dec. 2005; currently Adjunct Prof., South Asian Inst. of Man., Kathmandu; Commr SAARC Ind. Comm.; Pres. Shaligram Apartment–Hotel; fmr Pres. Rotary Jawalakhel, Man. Asscn of Nepal; mem. South Asian Ind. Comm. on Poverty Allevation 1991–2001. *Address:* South Asian Institute of Management, Lagankhel, Lalitpur, Kathmandu, Nepal (office). *Telephone:* (1) 5522044 (office). *Fax:* (1) 5522044 (office). *E-mail:* info@saim.edu.np (office). *Website:* www.saim.edu.np (office).

RANA, Pashupati S. J. B. R., BA; Nepalese politician; *Chairman, Rashtriya Prajatantra Party;* b. 7 May 1941, Laxmi Niwas, Kathmandu; s. of the late Gen. Bijaya Shumsher Jung Bahadur Rana and Rani Sarla Devi Rana; m. Rani Usha Rajya Laxmi Devi Rana (Princess of Gwailor); two d.; ed Haileybury, ISC and New Coll., Oxford, UK; mem. Parl. 1973–; Minister of Educ., Transport, Civil Aviation and Tourism 1979, Minister of Water Resources 1983–86, 1995–98, Minister of Panchayat and Local Devt 1986–88, Minister of Foreign Affairs, Finance, Water Resources and Communications 1990, Gen. Sec. Rashtriya Prajatantra Party (Nat. Democratic Party) 1991–97, Chair. 2003–; mem. India-Int. Centre, Int. Council Asia Soc.; Pres. Alliance Française. *Leisure Interests:* reading, European classical music, writing, shooting, trekking. *Address:* Central Secretariat, Rashtriya Prajatantra Party, Charumati Bahal, Chabahil, Kathmandu (office); Bijaya Bas, POB 271, Maharaj Gunj, Kathmandu, Nepal (home). *Telephone:* (1) 4471071 (office); (1) 4437902 (home). *Fax:* (1) 4435173 (office); (1) 4423384 (home). *E-mail:* info@rppnepal.com (office); p-rana@ntc.net.np (home). *Website:* www .rppnepal.org (office).

RANCHOD, Bhadra, BA, LLB, LLM, LLD; South African diplomatist and lawyer; *Member of Faculty, Department of Private and Roman Law, University of Stellenbosch;* b. 11 May 1944, Port Elizabeth; s. of Ghalloo Ranchod and Parvaty Ranchod; m. Vibha M. Desai 1980; two d.; ed Univs of Cape Town, Oslo, Norway and Leiden, The Netherlands; Sr Lecturer, Dept of Pvt. Law, Univ. of Durban-Westville 1972, Prof. of Pvt. Law 1974, Dean, Faculty of Law 1976–79; Advocate of Supreme Court 1973–; mem. Bd of Govs S African Broadcasting Corpn; mem. S African Law Comm.; mem. Human Sciences Research Council, numerous cttees and public bodies etc.; Visiting Scholar, Columbia Univ., New York 1980–81; Amb. and Head of S African Mission to European Communities 1986–92; Minister of Tourism 1993–94; Chair. Minister's Council in House of Dels 1993–94; MP 1994–96; Deputy Speaker, Nat. Ass. 1994–96; High Commr in Australia (also Accred to New Zealand and Fiji Islands) 1996–2001; Faculty of Dept of Pvt. and Roman Law 2001–; Vice-Chair. Bd Christel House Cape Town; Dir Maritime Mutual Insurance Co. (NZ); mem. Advisory Cttee Children's Rights Int. *Publications:* Foundations of the South African Law of Defamation (thesis) 1972, Law and Justice in South Africa 1986; about 100 papers on human rights issues. *Leisure interests:* jogging, reading, travel. *Address:* Department of Private and Roman Law, University of Stellenbosch, Private Bag X1, Matieland, 7602 Stellenbosch (office); 3 Eldorado Street, 7600 Stellenbosch, South Africa (home). *Telephone:* (21) 808-9111 (office); (21) 8833260 (home). *E-mail:* branchod@sun.ac.za. *Website:* law.sun.ac.za/DepartmentofPrivateLaw.htm (office).

RANDALL, Jeff William, BA; British journalist; *Editor-at-Large, The Daily Telegraph;* b. 3 Oct. 1954, London; s. of Jeffrey Charles Randall and Grace Annie Randall (née Hawkridge); m. Susan Diane Fidler 1986; one d.; ed Royal Liberty Grammar School, Romford, Univ. of Nottingham, Univ. of Florida, USA; with Hawkins Publrs 1982–85; Asst Ed. Financial Weekly 1985–86; City Corresp. Sunday Telegraph 1986–88; Deputy City Ed. The Sunday Times 1988–89, City Ed. 1989–94, City and Business Ed. 1994–95, Asst Ed. and Sports Ed. 1996–97; Ed. Sunday Business 1997–2001; Business Ed. BBC 2001–05; Ed.-at-Large The Daily Telegraph 2005–; host Jeff Randall Live (Sky News) 2007–; freelance contrib. Daily Telegraph, Euromoney; Dir Times Newspapers 1994–95; Deputy Chair. Financial Dynamics Ltd 1995–96; Dr hc (Anglia Ruskin Univ.) 2001, (Univ. of Nottingham) 2006; Financial Journalist of the Year, FT-Analysis 1991, Business Journalist of the Year, London Press Club 2000, Sony Gold Award 2003, Communicator of the Year 2004, Business Broadcaster of the Year, Wincott Awards 2004. *Publications:* The Day That Shook the World (co-author). *Leisure interests:* golf, horse racing, football. *Address:* The Daily Telegraph, 111 Buckingham Palace Road, London, SW1W 0DT, England (office). *Website:* www.telegraph.co.uk (office).

RANDEL, Don Michael, MFA, PhD; American musicologist, foundation executive and fmr university administrator; *President, The Andrew W. Mellon Foundation;* b. Panama; m. Carol Randel; four d.; ed Princeton Univ.; Asst Prof., Dept of Fine Arts, Syracuse Univ. 1966–68; Asst Prof. of Music, Cornell Univ. 1968–71, Assoc. Prof. 1971–75, Chair. Dept of Music 1971–76, Prof. of Music 1975–2000, Vice-Provost 1978–79, Assoc. Dean, Coll. of Arts and Sciences 1989–91, Harold Tanner Dean 1991–95, Provost 1995–2000; Pres. Univ. of Chicago 2000–06; Pres. Andrew W. Mellon Foundation 2006–; Vice-Pres. American Musicological Soc. 1977–78 (Ed.-in-Chief Journal of the American Musicological Soc. 1972–74); Fellow, American Acad. of Arts and Sciences 2001–; mem., AAAS, Modern Language Asscn, American Philosophical Soc. 2002–; mem., Bd of Trustees Chicago Symphony Orchestra Asscn 2001–, Music and Dance Theater Chicago 2001; mem., Bd of Govs Partnership for Public Service 2001–; mem., Bd of Dirs Chicago Council on Foreign Relations 2001–, CNA Financial Corpn 2002–. *Publications:* New Harvard Dictionary of Music (Ed.) 1986, Harvard Biographical Dictionary of Music (Ed.) 1996, Harvard Concise Dictionary of Music and Musicians (Ed.) 1999; author of numerous articles in musical journals. *Address:* The Andrew W. Mellon Foundation, 140 East 62nd Street, New York, NY 10065, USA (office). *Telephone:* (212) 838-8400 (office). *Fax:* (212) 500-2302 (office). *E-mail:* inquiries@mellon.org (office). *Website:* www.mellon.org (office).

RANDT, Clark Thorp, Jr, BA, JD; American lawyer and diplomatist; *Ambassador to People's Republic of China;* m. Sarah A. Talcott; two s. one d.; ed Hotchkiss School, Yale Univ., Univ. of Mich. Law School; served with USAF Security Service 1968–72; China rep. Nat. Council for US-China Trade 1974; First Sec. and Commercial Attaché, US Embassy, Beijing 1982–84; pvt. law practice as Pnr, Shearman and Sterling, Hong Kong; Amb. to People's Repub. of China 2001–; mem. NY and Hong Kong Bars; fmr Gov. and First Vice-Pres. American Chamber of Commerce, Hong Kong; mem. Council on Foreign Relations. *Address:* Embassy of the USA, 3 Xiu Shui Bei Jie,

Chaoyang District, Beijing 100600, People's Republic of China (office). *Telephone:* (10) 65323831 (office). *Fax:* (10) 65323178 (office). *Website:* beijing.usembassy-china.org.cn (office).

RANE, Pratapsing Raoji, BSc.; Indian politician; *Speaker, Goa Legislative Assembly;* b. 28 Jan. 1939; s. of Raoji Rane; m.; Chief Minister of Goa 1980–85, 1985–89, 1990, 1994–99, Feb.–March 2005, June 2005–07; Speaker, Goa Legis. Ass. 2007–; mem. various parl. cttees; mem. Indian Nat. Congress; fmr Leader of the Opposition. *Address:* Office of the Speaker, Goa Legislature Secretariat, Alto-Porvorim, Goa 403 521 (office); Golden Acres, Kulan, Sanquelim, Goa, India (home). *Telephone:* (832) 2411040 (office); (832) 2362229 (home). *Fax:* (832) -411054 (office). *E-mail:* assembly@sancharnet .in (office). *Website:* www.goavidhansabha.gov.in (office).

RANGARAJAN, Chakravarthi, PhD; Indian economist, academic and politician; *Chairman, Prime Minister's Economic Advisory Council;* b. 5 Jan. 1932, Ariyalur; s. of B. R. Chakravarty and Rangam Chakravarty; m. Haripriya Chakravarty; one s. one d.; ed Madras Univ., Univ. of Pa, USA; Lecturer, Loyola Coll. Chennai 1954–58, Wharton School of Finance and Commerce, Univ. of Pa 1963–64; Reader, Raj Univ. 1964–65; Prof., Indian Statistical Inst., New Delhi 1965–66; Visiting Assoc. Prof., New York Univ. 1966–68, Visiting Prof. 1972–73; Prof., IIM, Ahmedabad 1968–81; Deputy Gov. Reserve Bank of India 1982–91, Gov. 1992–97; Gov. of Andhra Pradesh 1997–2003; mem. Planning Comm., Indian Govt 1991–92; Chair. Tenth Finance Comm., Ministry of Finance 2003, Twelfth Finance Comm. 2005, Prime Minister's Econ. Advisory Council 2005–; Chair. Task Force on Jammu and Kashmir; Pres. Indian Econ. Asscn 1982, 1994; Hon. Fellow, Indian Inst. of Man., Ahmedabad 1997; Padma Vibhushan 2002; Businessman of the Year, Madras Man. Asscn 1997, Bank of India Award of Excellence 1998, Finance Man of the Decade, Bombay Man. Asscn 1998, Financial Express Award for Economics 1998, Wharton India Econ. Forum Alumni Award 2002. *Publications:* author or co-author: Short-Term Investment Forecasting 1974, Principles of Macro-Economics 1979, Strategy for Industrial Development in the 80s 1982, Innovations in Banking 1982, Agricultural Growth and Industrial Performance in India 1982, Structural Reforms in Industry Banking and Finance 2000; contrib.: Indian Economy: Essays on Money and Finance 1998, Perspectives on Indian Economy 2000, Select Essays on Indian Economy; and more than 40 papers. *Address:* Twelfth Finance Commission, Jawahar Vyapar Bhawan, 1 Tolstoy Marg, New Delhi 110 001, India (office). *Telephone:* (11) 23701110 (office). *Fax:* (11) 23703607 (office). *E-mail:* chrtfc@nic.in (office). *Website:* fincomindia.nic.in (office).

RANGASAMY, Thiru N.; Indian politician; b. 4 Aug. 1950; Chief Minister of Union Territory of Puducherry (fmrly Pondicherry) 2001–08. *Address:* 9 Vinayakar Koil Street, Thilarshpet, Puducherry 605 009, India (home).

RANGEL BRICEÑO, Gen.-in-Chief Gustavo; Venezuelan military officer and government official; b. 16 Aug. 1955, Maracaibo; served as Commdr of Army Infantry Div. 2004–05, Reserve and Nat. Mobilization –2007; Minister of Nat. Defence 2007–09. *Address:* c/o Ministry of National Defence, Edif. 17 de Diciembre, planta baja, Base Aérea Francisco de Miranda, La Carlota, Caracas, Venezuela (office).

RANGEL VALE, José Vicente; Venezuelan politician; b. 10 July 1929, Caracas; s. of José Vicente Rangel Cárdenas and Leonor Vale de Rangel; m. Ana Avalos; one s.; ed Colegio La Salle, Barquismeto, Universidad de los Andes, Cen. Univ. of Venezuela, Univ. of Chile, Univs of Salamanca and Santiago de Compostela, Spain; joined Unión Republicana Democrática aged 16; fmr TV Presenter, Televen, Canal 10; fmr columnist, El Universal, El Informadro, La Tarde, El Regional and Bohemia; cand. in presidential elections 1973, 1978, 1983; elected Deputy to Congress for Estado Miranda; fmr Co-ordinator Movimento Independientes (with Hugo Chávez); Minister of Foreign Affairs 1999–2001, of Defence 2001–02; Vice-Pres. of Venezuela 2002–07. *Publications include:* Tiempo de Verdades, Socialismo y Democracia, Expediente Negro, La Administración de La Justica en Venezuela. *Address:* c/o Central Information Office of the Presidency, Torre Oeste, 18, Parque Central, Caracas 1010, Venezuela (office).

RANIA AL-ABDULLAH, HM Queen of Jordan, BBA; b. (Rania al-Yassin), 31 Aug. 1970, Kuwait; m. Prince Abdullah ibn al-Hussein (King Abdullah II of Jordan) 1993; two s. two d.; ed American Univ., Cairo; est. support network for battered and abused children; Founder Jordan River Foundation 1995; Head Jordan Blood Disease Soc., Int. Advisory Cttee of UNU's Int. Network on Water, Environment and Health (UNU/INWEH), Arab Women Labor Affairs Cttee of Arab Labor Org., Exec. Bd Arab Network for Open and Distance Educ.; Head Queen Rania Soc. for the Support of the Mil. and their Families 2004–; Eminent Advocate for Children, UNICEF 2007–; Pres. Jordanian Soc. for Organ Donation, Nat. Council for Family Affairs, Arab Women's Summit; mem. World Econ. Forum Foundation Bd (Chair. Advisory Council for STARS), UNICEF's Global Leadership Initiative, Bd of Dirs Foundation for Int. Community Assistance, Bd of Dirs The Vaccine Fund, Bd of Dirs Int. Youth Foundation; Int. Pres. Int. Osteoporosis Foundation; Patron Jordanian Psychiatric Rehabilitation Soc.; Friend of Int. Criminal Court; Hon. Pres. Bd of Trustees, Arab Acad. for Banking and Finance, Hon. Chair. Bd of Govs Pacem In Terris Inst., La Rochelle Coll., USA, Hon. Col 2004; Dr hc (Exeter) 2001; Gold Medal of Pres. of Italian Repub. 2002, German Media Prize 2003, ranked by Forbes magazine amongst 100 Most Powerful Women (13th) 2004, (80th) 2005, (81st) 2006, (82nd) 2007, (96th) 2008. *Leisure interests:* reading, water skiing, running, cycling, cooking. *Address:* Royal Palace, Amman, Jordan. *Website:* www.queenrania.jo.

RANIS, Gustav, PhD; American economist and academic; *Frank Altschul Professor Emeritus of International Economics, Yale University;* b. 24 Oct. 1929, Darmstadt, Germany; s. of Max Ranis and Bettina Goldschmidt; m. Ray Lee Finkelstein; two s. one d.; ed Brandeis Univ., Yale Univ.; Social Science Research Council Fellow (Japan) 1955–56; Jt Dir, Pakistan Inst. of Devt Econs, Karachi, Pakistan 1959–61; Assoc. Dir Econ. Growth Center, Yale Univ. 1961–65, Dir 1967–75; Assoc. Prof. of Econs, Yale Univ. 1961–64, Prof. of Econs 1964–82, Frank Altschul Prof. of Int. Econs 1982–2005, Prof. Emer. 2005–; Dir Yale Center for Int. and Area Studies 1996–; Dir Yale-Pakistan Project 1970–71; Asst Admin. for Program and Policy, Agency for Int. Devt, Dept of State 1965–67, Consultant 1962–65, 1967–71, 1984–; Ford Foundation Faculty Fellow, Colegio de Mexico, Mexico City 1971–72; Visiting Prof., Univ. de los Andes, Colombia 1976–77; Consultant UN FAO 1979–; Chief of Mission, ILO Comprehensive Employment Strategy Mission to the Philippines 1973, World Bank/CARICOM Project on Production and Investment Incentives in the Caribbean 1980–82; mem. Oversight Cttee Int. Conf. on Intellectual Property Rights, Nat. Research Council 1991–; mem. Council on Foreign Relations; mem. Editorial Advisory Bd Journal of Int. Devt 1995–, Oxford Devt Studies 1996–; mem. Bd of Trustees and Brandeis Chair. Acad. Affairs Cttee Brandeis Univ.; Sterling Fellow, Yale Univ. 1953; Fellow, Inst. for Advanced Study, Berlin 1993–94; Junior Phi Beta Kappa (Brandeis Univ.) 1951; Dr hc (Brandeis Univ.) 1982. *Publications:* Development of Labor Surplus Economy: Theory and Policy (jtly) 1964, Growth with Equity: The Taiwan Case (jtly) 1979, Comparative Technology Choice in Development (jtly) 1988, Linkages in Developing Economics: A Philippine Study (jtly) 1990, The State of Development Economics, Science and Technology: Lessons for Development Policy (jtly) 1990, Taiwan: From Developing to Mature Economy (ed.) 1992, The Political Economy of Development Policy Change (jtly) 1992, Japan and the U.S. in the Developing World (ed.) 1997, Growth and Development from an Evolutionary Perspective (with John C. H. Fei) 1997, The Economics and Political Economy of Development in Taiwan into the 21st Century 1999, The Economics and Political Economy of Comparative Development into the 21st Century 1999. *Leisure interests:* tennis, squash, hiking. *Address:* Economic Growth Center, P.O. Box 208269, New Haven, CT 06520-8269 (office); 7 Mulberry Road, Woodbridge, CT 06525, USA (home). *Telephone:* (203) 432-3632 (office); (203) 397-2560 (home). *Fax:* (203) 432-3635 (office). *E-mail:* gustav.ranis@yale.edu (office). *Website:* www.yale.edu/~egcenter (office).

RANJEVA, Gen. Marcel; Malagasy politician and army officer (retd); *Minister of Foreign Affairs;* b. 15 Jan. 1944, Antananarivo; s. of the late Rene Ranjeva Raolosoa and Eugenie Raolosoa; m. Michele Rajaonera; two c.; ed Paris I (Sorbonne), France; mem. Christian Students Youth 1960–64; assigned to Army Staff Tech. Bd 1975, then to Dept of Econ. Affairs of Ministry of Defense 1976; apptd Dir of Mil. Operations, Office of Mil. Agricultural Production 1982; Commdr Mil. Acad. 1986; Sec. Gen. Office Malagasy des Tabacs 1992; Chief of Staff, Office of the President 1995–96; Minister of Defence 1996–2002 (resgnd); Minister of Foreign Affairs 2002–; mem. Association des Anciens Elèves de Coëtquidan; Grand Croix de 2ème Classe de La République Malgache, Grand Officier de la Légion d'Honneur, Commandeur de la Légion d'honneur, Officier de l'Ordre National de Mérite. *Address:* Ministry of Foreign Affairs, BP 836, Anosy, 101 Antananarivo, Madagascar (office). *Telephone:* (20) 2221198 (office). *Fax:* (20) 2234484 (office). *E-mail:* contact@madagascar-diplomatie.net (office). *Website:* www .madagascar-diplomatie.net (office).

RANJEVA, Raymond, LLD; Malagasy lawyer and international official; *Judge, International Court of Justice;* b. 31 Aug. 1942, Antananarivo; m. Yvette Madeleine R. Rabetafika 1967; five c.; ed Univ. of Madagascar, Madagascar Nat. School of Admin., Univ. of Paris, France; trainee, Judicial Div., Conseil d'Etat, Paris; Civil Admin., Univ. of Madagascar 1966, Asst Lecturer 1966–72, Lecturer 1972, Dir Dept of Legal and Political Science 1973–82, Prof. 1981–91, Dean of Faculty of Law, Econs, Man. and Social Sciences 1982–88; Prof., Madagascar Mil. Acad., Madagascar School of Admin.; Dir Public Law and Political Science Study Centre; First Rector, Univ. of Antananarivo 1988–90; Man. Dir Jureco (econ., financial and legal databank for advisory and research bodies) 1986–90, Ed. Lettre mensuelle de Jureco 1986–88; Conciliator, IBRD Int. Centre for Settlement of Investment Disputes 1970–; Attorney to Mali, Border Dispute (Burkina Faso/Mali); Consultant on transfer to the State of activities of Eau-Electricité de Madagascar and Electricité de France 1973; Judge, Int. Court of Justice 1991–, Vice-Pres. 2003–06; Founder-mem. Malagasy Human Rights Cttee 1971; mem. and Vice-Pres. Malagasy Acad. 1974, Pres. Ethics and Political Science section 1975–91; mem. Nat. Constitutional Cttee 1975; mem. Court of Arbitration for Sport 1995–; legal adviser to Catholic Bishops' Conf., Madagascar; mem. Governing Body of African Soc. of Int. and Comparative Law, French Soc. of Int. Law, Québec Soc. (Canada); Sec.-Gen. Malagasy Legal Studies Soc.; mem. Pontifical Comm. 'Justice et Paix' 2002–, Curatorium de l'Acad. de Droit Int. 2002–; Commdr, Ordre Nat. Malgache of Madagascar, Chevalier, Ordre de Mérite of Madagascar, Officier, Ordre Nat. of Mali, Grand-Croix nat. malgache 2003. *Address:* International Court of Justice, Peace Palace, Carnegieplein 2, 2517 KJ The Hague, Netherlands (office). *Telephone:* (70) 3022323 (office). *Fax:* (70) 3022409 (office). *E-mail:* information@icj-cij.org (office). *Website:* www.icj-cij.org (office).

RÁNKI, Dezsö; Hungarian pianist; b. 8 Sept. 1951, Budapest; s. of József Ránki and Edith Jecsmen; m. Edit Klukon 1979; two c.; ed Ferenc Liszt Music Acad., Budapest (under Pál Kadosa); has given recitals and appeared with several leading orchestras throughout Europe, including Berlin Philharmonic, Concertgebouw and London Philharmonic; regular concert tours N America and Japan; four-hands piano recitals with Edit Klukon in many European cities 1982–; has taught piano at Budapest Music Acad. since 1973; First Prize, Int. Schumann Competition, Zwickau, GDR 1969, Grand Prix Int. du Disque (Paris) 1972, Liszt Prize 2nd Degree 1973, Kossuth Prize 1978. *Recordings include:* works by Bartók, Brahms, Haydn, Kadosa, Mozart, Ravel and Schumann. *Leisure interests:* gramophone records, sound tapes, books, gardening. *Address:* Béla Simon Artist Management, 29 Goldhurst Terrace, London NW6 3HB, England (office); Ördögorom Lejtő 11/B, 1112 Budapest, Hungary (home). *Telephone:* (20) 7624-7291 (office); (1) 246-4403 (home). *E-mail:* bs@zene91.freeserve.co.uk (office).

RANNEBERGER, Michael E., BA, MA; American diplomatist; *Ambassador to Kenya;* ed Towson State Univ., Baltimore, Md, Univ. of Virginia; Angola Desk Officer 1981–84, worked as mem. of Asst Sec. Crocker's team negotiating independence for Namibia and withdrawal of Cuban troops from Angola; Special Asst to Under-Sec. Armacost 1984–85; Deputy Chief of Mission in Maputo 1986–89, included eight months as Chargé d'affaires during civil war; Deputy Chief of Mission in Asunción 1989–92; Deputy Dir for Cen. American Affairs 1992–94; Deputy Chief of Mission in Mogadishu 1994; set up and ran inter-agency Task Force on Justice and Security-Related Issues in Haiti Jan.–June 1995; Co-ordinator for Cuban Affairs 1995–99; Amb. to Mali 1999–2002; Special Advisor on Sudan 2002–04; Prin. Deputy Asst Sec., Africa Bureau 2004–05; Sr Rep. on Sudan, Bureau of African Affairs Jan.–Aug. 2006; Amb. to Kenya with responsibility for US relations with Somalia 2006–; mem. Sr Foreign Service with rank of Minister-Counsellor; Int. Affairs Fellowship, Council on Foreign Relations, seven Superior Honor Awards, State Dept, Presidential Meritorious Service Award. *Address:* US Embassy, United Nations Avenue, PO Box 606, Village Market, 00621 Nairobi, Kenya (office). *Telephone:* (20) 3636000 (office). *Fax:* (20) 3633410 (office). *E-mail:* ircnairobi@state.gov (office). *Website:* nairobi.usembassy.gov (office).

RANNEY, Helen M., MD, ScD; American physician (retd); b. 12 April 1920, Summer Hill, New York; d. of Arthur C. Ranney and Alesia Ranney (née Toolan); ed Barnard Coll. and Coll. of Physicians and Surgeons, Columbia Univ.; Asst Prof. of Clinical Medicine, Columbia Univ. 1958–60; Assoc. Prof. of Medicine, Albert Einstein Coll. of Medicine 1960–65, Prof. 1965–70; Prof. of Medicine, State Univ. of New York, Buffalo 1970–73; Prof. of Medicine, Dept of Medicine, Univ. of Calif., San Diego 1973–90, Prof. Emer. 1990–, Chair. 1973–86; Distinguished Physician, Department of Veterans' Affairs Medical Center, San Diego, Calif. 1986–91; consultant, Alliance Pharmaceutical Corpn, San Diego 1991–; mem. NAS, Asscn of American Physicians, American Acad. of Arts and Sciences, American Soc. for Clinical Investigation, Inst. of Medicine; Kober Medal, Asscn of American Physicians 1996. *Publications:* papers in medical journals concerned with haemoglobin. *Address:* 6229 La Jolla Mesa Drive, La Jolla, CA 92037, USA (home). *Telephone:* (858) 459-6768 (home). *Fax:* (858) 459-6780 (home). *E-mail:* hranney@ucsd.edu (home).

RANQUE, Denis; French business executive; *Chairman and CEO, Thales;* b. Marseille; ed École Polytechnique, École des Mines; fmrly with Ministry for Industry; joined Thomson group as Dir of Planning 1983, CEO Thomson Tubes Electroniques 1989–92, Chair. and CEO Thomson Sintra ASM 1992–96, CEO Thomson Marconi Sonar 1996–98; Chair. and CEO Thales 1998–; Chair. Ecole Nationale Supérieure des Mines de Paris 2001–, Circle de l'Industrie (French Industrial Asscn) 2002–; Chevalier, Légion d'honneur 1999; Officier, Ordre nat. du Mérite 2003; Hon. CBE 2004. *Leisure interest:* music, sailing. *Address:* Thales, 45 rue de Villiers, 92526 Neuilly-sur-Seine Cedex (office). *Telephone:* 1-57-77-80-00 (office). *Fax:* 1-57-77-86-59 (office). *E-mail:* denis.ranque@thalesgroup.com (office). *Website:* www.thalesgroup.com (office).

RANTANEN, Juha Ilari, MSc, MBA; Finnish business executive; *CEO, Outokumpu Oyj;* b. 25 Jan. 1952, Helsinki; m. Eija Jaaskelainen 1975; three s. one d.; ed Helsinki School of Econs, Int. Man. Inst., Geneva; Man., Internal Accounting, Neste Oy 1977–78, Planning Man. 1979–81, Exec. Vice-Pres., Gas 1986–89, Chemicals 1989–92, Chief Financial Officer 1992–94; Product Line Man., Covering Materials, Partek Oy 1981–84, Vice-Pres., Insulations 1984–86; CEO Borealis A/S 1994–97; Exec. Vice-Pres. Ahlstrom Corpn 1997–98, Pres., CEO 1998–2004; CEO Outokumpu Oyj 2004–; Chair. Moventas Group Jan.–Dec. 2007, Vice Chair. Dec. 2007–; Chair. Finpro; Vice Pres. European Confed. of Iron and Steel Industries (Eurofer); fmr Chair. Bd Forest Industries Fed.; Vice-Chair. Confed. of Finnish Industry and Employers; Pres. Asscn of Plastics Manufacturers in Europe 1994–96; mem. Supervisory Bd Varma-Sampo Mutual Pension Insurance Co. *Address:* Outokumpu Oyj, Riihitontuntie 7, 02201 Espoo, Finland (office). *Telephone:* (9) 4211 (office). *Fax:* (9) 3888 (office). *Website:* www.outokumpu.com (office).

RANTANEN, Paavo Ilmari, MScPol; Finnish diplomatist and business executive; b. 28 Feb. 1934, Jyvaškylä; s. of Vilho Rantanen and Jenny Auer; m. Ritva Lehtinen 1956; two s. one d.; ed Univ. of Helsinki and Acad. for Int. Law, The Hague; entered Ministry of Foreign Affairs 1958; served in embassies in Vienna, Belgrade and Paris 1958–71; Counsellor, Embassy in Brussels and Mission to EC 1971–73; Counsellor, Deputy Chief of Special Mission to CSCE, Geneva 1973–74; Amb.-at-Large 1974–76; Ministry of Foreign Affairs 1976–81; Perm. Rep. to UN Orgs, Geneva 1981–86; Amb. to USA 1986–88; mem. Exec. Bd Int. Relations and Trade Policy, Nokia Group 1988–95, April–Dec. 1995; Minister of Foreign Affairs Feb.–April 1995; Chair. Finnish Inst. for Int. Trade 1996–, Atlantic Council of Finland –2004. *Address:* Laivurinkatu 39 A 4, 00150 Helsinki, Finland (home). *Telephone:* (9) 6221285 (home).

RANTZEN, Esther, CBE, OBE, MA; British television presenter, producer and writer; b. 22 June 1940; d. of Harry Rantzen and Katherine Rantzen; m. Desmond Wilcox 1977 (died 2000); one s. two d.; ed North London Collegiate School and Somerville Coll., Oxford; studio man. making dramatic sound effects, BBC Radio 1963; presenter and producer, That's Life, BBC TV 1973–94, scriptwriter 1976–94; producer, The Big Time (documentary series) 1976–80; presenter, Esther Interviews ... 1988, Hearts of Gold 1988–96, Drugwatch, Childwatch, The Lost Babies (also producer), Esther (talk show) 1994–, The Rantzen Report 1996–, That's Esther 1999–; presenter How to Have a Good Death (BBC) 2006; mem. Nat. Consumer Council 1981–90, Health Educ. Authority 1989–95; Chair. ChildLine (charity); Pres. Asscn of Youth with ME 1996–; numerous charitable activities; Hon. DLitt (South Bank Univ.) 2000; BBC TV Personality of 1975, Variety Club of GB; Richard Dimbleby Award, BAFTA 1988, Snowdon Award for Services to Disabled People 1996, Royal TV Soc. Hall of Fame Award 1997, Champion Community Legal Service 2000. *Publications:* Kill the Chocolate Biscuit (with D. Wilcox) 1981, Baby Love 1985, The Story of Ben Hardwick (with S. Woodward) 1985, Once Upon a Christmas 1996, Esther: The Autobiography 2001, A Secret Life 2003. *Leisure interests:* work and fantasy. *Address:* c/o Billy Marsh Associates, 174–178 North Gower Street, London, NW1 2NB, England (office). *Telephone:* (20) 7388-6858 (office).

RAO, Calyampudi Radhakrishna, MA, ScD, FNA, FRS; American/Indian statistician; *Professor Emeritus of Statistics, Pennsylvania State University;* b. 10 Sept. 1920, Hadagali, Karnataka State; s. of C. D. Naidu and A. Laxmikanthamma; m. Bhargavi Rao 1948; one s. one d.; ed Andhra and Calcutta Univs; Research at Indian Statistical Inst. 1943–46, Cambridge Univ. 1946–48; Prof. and Head of Div. of Theoretical Research and Training 1949–64; Dir Research and Training School, Indian Statistical Inst. 1964–71, Sec. and Dir 1972–76, Jawaharlal Nehru Prof. 1976–84; Univ. Prof., Univ. of Pittsburgh 1979–88; Nat. Prof., India 1987–92; Eberly Prof. of Statistics, Pennsylvania State Univ. 1988–91, Dir Center for Multivariate Analysis 1988–2001, Prof. Emer. 2001–; Ed. Sankhya 1964–80, Journal of Multivariate Analysis 1988–92; Fellow, Inst. of Mathematical Statistics, USA, Pres. 1976–77; Treas. Int. Statistical Inst. 1961–65, Pres. 1977–79; Pres. Int. Biometric Soc. 1973–75; Pres. Forum for Interdisciplinary Math.; mem. NAS, USA; Hon. Fellow, Royal Statistical Soc.; Fellow, American Statistical Asscn, Econometric Soc., Third World Acad. of Sciences; Hon. Prof. Univ. of San Marcos, Lima; Foreign mem. Lithuanian Acad. of Sciences; Hon. mem. Int. Statistical Inst., Inst. of Combinatorics and Applications, Finnish Statistical Soc., Portuguese Statistical Soc.; Hon. Foreign mem. American Acad. Arts and Sciences; Hon. Life Fellow, King's Coll., Cambridge Univ.; Hon. Life mem. Biometric Soc.; Hon. DSc (31 univs); Hon. DLitt (Delhi); Emanuel and Carol Parzen Prize for Statistical Innovation; Bhatnagar Memorial Award for Scientific Research; Padma Vibhushan; Guy Silver Medal Royal Statistical Soc., Meghnad Saha Medal, Nat. Science Acad., J. C. Bose Gold Medal, Wilks Memorial Medal, Calcutta Univ. Gold Medal, Mahalanobis Birth Centenary Gold Medal, Army Wilks Medal, Nat. Science Acad. Ramanujan Medal, Int. Statistics Inst. Mahalanobis Prize, Sankhyiki Bhushan, Pres.'s Nat. Medal for Science, USA 2002. *Publications include:* Advanced Statistical Methods in Biometric Research, Linear Statistical Inference and its Application, Generalized Inverse of Matrices and its Applications, Characterization Problems of Mathematical Statistics (with A. Kagan and V. Linmik) 1973, Estimation of Variance Components and its Applications (with J. Kleffe) 1988, Statistics and Truth 1989, Choquet Deny Type Functional Equations with Applications to Stochastic Models (with D. N Shanbhaq) 1994, Linear Models: Least Squares and Alternatives (with H. Toutenburg) 1995, Matrix Algebra and Its Applications to Statistics and Econometrics (with M. B. Rao) 1998; over 350 research papers in mathematical statistics. *Leisure interest:* writing humorous essays. *Address:* Department of Statistics, Pennsylvania State University, 326 Thomas Bldg, University Park, PA 16802 (office); 826 West Aaron Drive, State College, PA 16803, USA (home). *Telephone:* (814) 865-3194 (office); (814) 234-6209 (home). *Fax:* (814) 863-7114 (office). *E-mail:* crr1@psu.edu (office). *Website:* www.stat.psu.edu/~crrao.

RAO, Chintamani Nagesa Ramachandra, PhD, DSc, FRS, FNA; Indian chemist and academic; *National Research Professor, Linus Pauling Research Professor and Honorary President, Jawaharlal Nehru Centre for Advanced Scientific Research;* b. 30 June 1934, Bangalore; s. of H. Nagesa Rao; m. Indumati Rao 1960; one s. one d.; ed Banaras Univ., Purdue Univ., USA, Mysore Univ.; Lecturer, Indian Inst. of Science, Bangalore 1959–63, Chair. Solid State and Structural Chem. Unit and Materials Research Lab. 1977–84, Dir Indian Inst. of Science 1984–94; Prof., later Sr Prof., Indian Inst. of Tech., Kanpur 1963–77, Dean of Research and Devt 1969–72; Albert Einstein Research Prof. and Pres. Jawaharlal Nehru Centre for Advanced Scientific Research 1995–99, Linus Pauling Research Prof. and Hon. Pres. 1999–; Visiting Prof., Purdue Univ. 1967–68, Univ. of Oxford, UK 1974–75; Prof. IISc, Bangalore; Fellow, King's Coll., Cambridge, UK 1983–84; Chair. Science Advisory Council to Prime Minister of India 1985–89 (and currently), Indo-Japan Science Council, Scientific Advisory Cttee to Union Cabinet 1997–98; fmr Chair. Advisory Bd of Council of Scientific and Industrial Research (India); mem. Atomic Energy Comm. of India; mem. editorial bds of 15 leading scientific journals; Pres. St Catherine's Coll., Oxford 1974–75, Indian Nat. Science Acad. 1985–86, IUPAC 1985–87, Indian Science Congress Asscn 1987–88, Indian Acad. of Sciences 1988–91, Materials Research Soc. of India 1989–91; Nehru Visiting Prof., Univ. of Cambridge, Linnett Visiting Prof. 1998; Gauss Professorship, Acad. of Sciences, Göttingen, Germany 2003; mem. Editorial Bd of 15 leading scientific journals; Founding mem. and Pres. Third World Acad. of Sciences; mem. Pontifical Acad. of Sciences; Titular mem. European Acad. of Arts, Sciences and Humanities; Corresp. mem. Brazilian Acad. of Sciences; Foreign mem. Academia Europaea, Serbian and Slovenian Acads of Science, Yugoslavia, Russian, Czech and Polish Acads of Sciences, American Acad. of Arts and Sciences, Royal Spanish Acad. of Sciences, French Acad. of Sciences, American Philosophical Soc., African Acad., Materials Socs of Japan and Korea, Int. Acad. of Ceramics; Foreign Assoc. NAS; Foreign Fellow, Royal Soc. of Canada; Hon. Foreign mem. Korean Acad. of Science and Tech.; Hon. mem. Japan Acad.; Hon. FRSC 1989; Hon. Fellow, Inst. of Physics, London 2006; Padma Shri 1974, Padma Vibhushan 1985, Commdr Nat. Order of Lion (Senegal) 1999, Karnataka Ratna 2001, Officer de l'Ordre des Palmes Academiques (France) 2002, Order of Scientific

Merit, Grand-Cross (Brazil) 2002, Commdr Order of Rio Branco (Brazil) 2002, Chevalier Légion d'honneur 2005; Dr hc from 41 univs, including Purdue, Bordeaux, Banaras, Mysore, IIT Bombay, IIT Kharagpur, Notre Dame, Novosibirsk, Uppsala, Wales, Wrocław, Caen, Khartoum, Calcutta and Sri Venkateswara Univ.; Marlow Medal, Faraday Soc. 1967, Bhatnagar Award 1968, Jawaharlal Nehru Fellowship, Indian Inst. of Tech. 1973, ACS Centennial Foreign Fellowship 1976, Fed. of Indian Chamber of Commerce and Industry Award for Physical Sciences 1977, Sir C.V. Raman Award 1975, S.N. Bose Medal, Indian Nat. Science Acad. 1980, Royal Soc. of Chem. (London) Medal 1981, Jawaharlal Nehru Award 1988, Hevrovsky Gold Medal, Czechoslovak Acad. 1989, Saha Medal, Indian Nat. Science Acad. 1990, Blackett Lecturer, Royal Soc. 1991, CSIR Golden Jubilee Prize 1991, NAS Int. Science Lecture, USA 1993, Sahabdeen Int. Award of Science, Sri Lanka 1994, Third World Acad. of Sciences Medal in Chem. 1995, Albert Einstein Gold Medal, UNESCO 1996, Asutosh Mookerjee Medal 1996, Shatabdi Puraskar, Indian Scientific Congress 1999, Hallim Distinguished Lecturer, Korean Acad. of Science and Tech. 1999, Centenary Lectureship and Medal, Royal Soc. of Chem. 2000, Hughes Medal, Royal Soc. 2000, Millennium Plaque of Honour, Indian Science Congress 2001, Somiya Award, Int. Union of Materials Research Socs 2004, Dan David Prize 2005, Chemical Pioneer, American Inst. of Chemists 2005, India Science Award, Govt of India 2005, Nat. Research Professorship, Govt of India 2006. *Publications:* 41 books, including Ultraviolet Visible Spectroscopy 1960, Chemical Applications of Infra-red Spectroscopy 1963, Spectroscopy in Inorganic Chemistry 1970, Modern Aspects of Solid State Chemistry 1970, Solid State Chemistry 1974, Educational Technology in Teaching of Chemistry 1975, Phase Transitions in Solids 1978, Preparation and Characterization of Materials 1981, The Metallic and Non-Metallic States of Matter 1985, New Directions in Solid State Chemistry 1986, Chemistry of Oxide Superconductors 1988, Chemical and Structural Aspects of High Temperature Oxide Superconductors 1988, Bismuth and Thallium Superconductors 1989, Chemistry of Advanced Materials 1992, Chemical Approaches to the Synthesis of Inorganic Materials 1994, Transition Metal Oxides 1995, Colossal Magnetoresistance 1998, Understanding Chemistry 1999; more than 1,400 original research papers. *Leisure interests:* gourmet cooking, general reading, music. *Address:* Jawaharlal Nehru Centre for Advanced Scientific Research, Jakkur PO, Bangalore 560064 (office); JNC President's House, Indian Institute of Science Campus, Bangalore 560012, India (home). *Telephone:* (80) 23653075 (office); (80) 23601410 (home). *Fax:* (80) 22082760 (office); (80) 23602468 (office). *E-mail:* cnrrao@jncasr.ac.in (office). *Website:* www.jncasr.ac.in/cnrrao (office).

RAO, G. M. (Grandhi Mallikarjuna); Indian business executive; *Group Chairman, GMR Group;* b. 14 July 1950, Rajam, Andhra Pradesh; m. Varalakshmi Rao; three c.; ed Vizag Eng Coll.; began career with single jute mill, Rajam 1978; Founder GMR Group, Chair. and Man. Dir 1978–2007, Group Chair. 2007–; infrastructure interests in India and abroad including power plants, airports (Hyderabad, Delhi and Istanbul); f. GMR Varalakshmi Foundation; Economic Times Awards for Corp. Excellence Entrepreneur of the Year 2006/07. *Address:* GMR Group, Skip House, 25/, Museum Road, Bangalore 560 025, Karnataka, India (office). *Telephone:* (80) 22070100 (office). *Fax:* (80) 22213091 (office). *E-mail:* info@gmrgroup.in (office). *Website:* www.gmrgroup.co.in (office).

RAO, K. Chandrasekhar, MA,; Indian politician; *President, Telangana Rashtra Samithi;* b. 17 Feb. 1954, Chintamadaka; m. Smt. Kalvakuntla Shobha 1969; one s. one d.; ed Osmania Univ., Hyderabad; mem. Andhra Pradesh Legis. Ass. 1985–2004, Chair. Cttee on Public Undertakings 1992–93, Deputy Speaker 1999–2001; Minister of State, Govt of Andhra Pradesh 1987–88, Cabinet Minister 1997–99; mem. Lok Sabha from Karimnagar, Andhra Pradesh constituency 2004–06 (resgnd), 2006– (re-elected in bye election); Minister without Portfolio May–Nov. 2004, Minister of Labour and Employment 2004–06; Founder and Pres. Telangana Rashtra Samithi. *Address:* 8-2-220/110/1/3, Road No. 14, Banjara Hills, Hyderabad, Andhra Pradesh; Telangana Rashtra Samithi, Karimnagar, India. *Telephone:* (40) 23555798.

RAO, Zihe, MSc, PhD; Chinese biophysicist and biologist; *President, Nankai University;* b. 1950, Nanjing, Jiangsu Prov.; ed Univ. of Science and Tech. of China, Melbourne Univ.; researcher Lab. of Molecular Biophysics, Univ. of Oxford 1989–96; specializes in research concerning proteins related to human health and disease; fmr Prof. of Structural Biology, Tsinghua Univ.; Prof. and Pres. Nankai Univ. 2006–; mem. Chinese Acad. of Sciences 2003–, Dir-Gen. Inst. of Biophysics 2003–07; Pres. Chinese Crystallography Soc.; Vice-Pres. Int. Org. for Biological Crystallography; exec. mem. Chinese Biophysics Asscn (Chair. Macromolecular Cttee); mem. Third World Acad. of Sciences 2004–; Qiushi Outstanding Scientist Prize in Life Sciences, Hong Kong 1999, Yangtze River Distinguished Scholar, Ministry of Educ. 2000, He Liang Heli Foundation Science and Tech. Prize 2003. *Publications:* more than 130 papers in int. scientific journals including Cell, Nature, PNAS, Journal of Molecular Biology, Journal of the American Chemistry Society. *Address:* Office of the President, Nankai University, 94 Wenjin Road, Nankai District, Tianjin 300071, People's Republic of China (office). *Telephone:* (22) 23501631 (office). *Fax:* (22) 23501631 (office). *E-mail:* raozh@nankai.edu.cn (office). *Website:* www.nankai.edu.cn (office).

RAOULT, Eric, LèsScEcon; French politician; *Mayor of Raincy;* b. 19 June 1955, Paris; m. Béatrice Abollivier 1990; ed Inst. d'Etudes Politiques, Paris and Inst. Français de Presse; Parl. Asst to Claude Labbé; Town Councillor, Raincy 1977; Deputy Mayor of Raincy 1983–95, Mayor 1995–; mem. Cen. Cttee of RPR 1982–; Deputy to Nat. Ass. 1986–1995, 2002–, Vice-Pres. 1993–95, 2002–07; mem. Comm. on Foreign Affairs; Regional Councillor, Ile de France 1992; Minister of Integration and the Fight against Exclusion May–Nov. 1995, Deputy Minister with responsibility for Urban Affairs and Integration 1995–97; Nat. Sec. with responsibility for elections 1998–99, with responsibility for Feds and Dom-Tom 1999–2002 (RPR). *Address:* Casier de la Poste, Palais Bourbon, 75355 Paris 07 (office); Mairie, 121 avenue de la Résistance, 93340 Le Raincy, France (office). *Telephone:* 1-43-02-52-94 (office); 1-43-02-77-15 (office). *E-mail:* eraoult@assemblee-nationale.fr (office); ericraoult2007@yahoo.fr (home). *Website:* ericraoult.over-blog.com.

RAPACZYNSKI, Wanda, MPPM, PhD; Polish business executive; *President of the Management Board, Head of Finance and Radio Divisions, Agora SA;* b. 1947; m.; one d.; ed City Univ. of New York and Yale Univ. School of Org. and Man.; began her career as a prof. of psychology, lectured at several univs in New York and Conn.; Post-doctoral Fellow, Educational Testing Service, Princeton, NJ –1980; Researcher and Project Dir, Yale Univ. Family TV Research and Consultation Center 1980–82; fmr Exec., Vice-Pres. and Head of Project Devt Citibank (NY) –1992; apptd Pres. and CEO Agora SA (media corpn) 1992, currently Pres. Man. Bd, Head of Finance and Radio Divs, Pres. Supervisory Bd AMS SA (subsidiary) 2002–; Pres. Supervisory Bd of Polish Union of Pvt. Employers in Media and Advertising 2003–; mem. Advisory Bd of Centre for European Reform, Polish Group in Trilateral Comm. 2002; represents Agora in Polish Confed. of Pvt. Employers; ranked by Fortune magazine amongst 50 Most Powerful Women in Business outside the US (26th) 2001, (47th) 2002, (50th) 2003, (48th) 2004, (45th) 2005, named by Wall Street Journal Europe as one of 30 Most Influential Women in Europe 2001, included by BusinessWeek in list of 50 Stars of Europe 2001, ranked 22nd on list of Europe's 25 Most Successful Businesswomen 2002, placed by BusinessWeek on list of 30 Most Influential People in the Polish Economy 2002, Media Trend Person of the Year statuette 2002, Person of the Year 2002 in the Advertising Industry, Impactor Awards 2003, ranked first by IR Magazine in the Best IR by a CEO/CFO in CEE region category 2003, ranked by the Financial Times amongst Top 25 Businesswomen in Europe (eighth) 2004, (seventh) 2005, (fifth) 2006. *Address:* Agora SA, Czerska 8/10, 00-732 Warsaw, Poland (office). *Telephone:* (22) 5554002 (office). *Fax:* (22) 5554850 (office). *Website:* www.agora.pl (office).

RÂPEANU, Valeriu; Romanian literary critic, historian and editor; b. 28 Sept. 1931, Ploiestiori, Prahova Co.; s. of Gheorghe Râpeanu and Anastasia Râpeanu; m. Sanda Marinescu 1956; one s.; ed Univ. of Bucharest; journalist 1954–69; Vice-Chair. of the Romanian Cttee of Radio and TV 1970–72; Dir Mihai Eminescu Publishing House, Bucharest 1972–90; Prof., Faculty of Journalism and Philosophy, Spiru Haret Univ., Bucharest; mem. Romanian Writers' Union; fmr mem. Cen. Cttee Romanian CP; mem. Int. Assoc. of Literary Critics. *Publications:* the monographs George Mihail-Zamfirescu 1958, Al. Vlahuţă 1964, Noi şi cei dinaintea noastră (Ourselves and Our Predecessors) 1966, Interferenţe spirituale (Spiritual Correspondences) 1970, Călător pe două continente (Traveller on Two Continents) 1970, Pe drumurile tradiţiei (Following Traditions) 1973, Interpretări si înţelesuri (Interpretations and Significances) 1975, Cultură si istorie (Culture and History) (two vols) 1979, 1981; Tărâmul unde nu ajungi niciodată (The Land You Could Never Reach) 1982, Scriitori dintre cele două războaie (Writers between the two World Wars) 1986, La vie de l'histoire et l'histoire d'une vie 1989, N. Iorga: Opera, Omul, Prietenii 1992, N. Iorga, Mincea Eliade, Nae Ionescu 1993, N. Iorga 1994; vols by Nicolae Iorga, Gh. Brătianu, Al. Kiriţescu, Cella Delavrancea, Marcel Mihalovici, I. G. Duca, Gh.I. Brătianu, George Enescu, C. Rădulescu-Motru, C. Brâncuşi; anthology of Romanian drama; essays on François Mauriac, Jean d'Ormesson, Marcel Proust, Aaron Copland, André Malraux, Jean Cocteau. *Leisure interests:* music, art. *Address:* Universitatea Spiru Haret, Strada Ion Ghica nr. 13, Sector 3, Bucharest (office); Str. Mecet 21, Bucharest, Romania. *Telephone:* (21) 3149931 (office). *Fax:* (21) 3149932 (office). *E-mail:* info@spiruharet.ro (office). *Website:* www.spiruharet.ro (office).

RAPHAEL; Spanish singer; b. (Rafael Martos), 5 May 1942, Linares, Jaén; m. Natalia Figueroa 1972; two s. one d.; first prize winner at Salzburg Festival children's singing competition aged nine; subsequently won numerous other competitions; began professional career in Madrid nightclub 1960; rep. of Spain, Eurovision Song Contest 1966, 1967; US debut 1967; toured USSR 1968, Japan 1970, Australia 1971; Broadway debut 1974; celebrated 25th anniversary as professional singer with open-air concert at Bernabé Stadium, Madrid 1985. *Films:* Las gemelas 1963, Cuando tú no estás 1966, Al ponerse el sol 1967, Digan lo que digan 1968, El Ángel 1969, El golfo 1969, Sin un adiós 1970, Volveré a nacer 1973, Ritmo, amor y primavera 1981. *Television:* Donde termina el camino (series) 1978, Horas doradas (series) 1980. *Recordings:* Los hombres lloran también 1964, Sigo siendo aquel 1985, Toda una vida 1985, Las apariencias engañan 1988, Maravilloso corazón 1989, El monstruo de la canción 1990, Andaluz 1990, Fantasia 1994, Brillantes 1994, Monstruo 1995, Desde el fondo de mi alma 1995, Raphael 1998, Dama Dama 1999, Sentado a la vera del camino 1999, Hotel de l'universe 2001, Yo soy aquel 2001, Maldito Raphael 2001, Realite 2003, De vuelta 2003. *Address:* Arie Kaduri Agency, Inc., 16125 NE 18th Avenue, North Miami Beach, FL 33162, USA (office).

RAPHAEL, Farid; Lebanese banker and politician; *Chairman and General Manager, Executive Committee, Banque Libano-Française SAL;* b. 28 Oct. 1933, Dlebta, Kesrouan; s. of Elie Raphael and Evelyne Khalife; m. Ilham Abdel Ahad 1970; one s. three d.; ed Univ. of St Joseph, Beirut, Univ. of Lyons, France; with Cie Algérienne de Crédit et de Banque, Beirut 1956–67; Founder and Gen. Man. Banque Libano-Française SAL 1967–79, Chair. and Gen. Man. Exec. Cttee 1979–; Founder and Vice-Pres. Banque Libano-Française (France) SA (now Banque Française de l'Orient SA), Paris 1976–85, Chair. and Gen. Man. 1985–89, Adviser to BFO-France 1989–; Minister of Justice, Finance, Posts, Telephones and Telecommunications 1976–79. *Address:* Banque Libano-Française, BP 11-808, Tour Liberty, rue de Rome, Beirut 1107-2804 (office); Rue St Charles, Imm. Colette Eddé, Brazilia, Hazmieh, Beirut, Lebanon (home). *Telephone:* (1) 753460 (office). *Fax:* (1) 753461 (office). *E-mail:* farid.raphael@eblf.com (office). *Website:* www.eblf.com (office).

RAPHAEL, Frederic Michael, MA, FRSL; American writer; b. 14 Aug. 1931, Chicago, Ill.; s. of Cedric Michael Raphael and Irene Rose Mauser; m. Sylvia Betty Glatt 1955; two s. one d.; ed Charterhouse, St John's Coll., Cambridge; Lippincott Prize 1961, Prix Simone Genevois 2000. *Publications:* novels: Obbligato 1956, The Earlsdon Way 1958, The Limits of Love 1960, A Wild Sunrise 1961, The Graduate's Wife 1962, The Trouble with England 1962, Lindmann 1963, Orchestra and Beginners 1967, Like Men Betrayed 1970, April, June and November 1972, California Time 1975, The Glittering Prizes 1976, Heaven and Earth 1985, After the War 1988, A Wild Surmise 1991, A Double Life 1993, Old Scores 1995, Coast to Coast 1998, All His Sons 1999, Fame and Fortune 2007; short stories: Sleeps Six 1979, Oxbridge Blues 1980, Think of England 1986, The Hidden I (illustrated by Sarah Raphael) 1990, The Latin Lover and Other Stories 1994; biography: Somerset Maugham and his World 1977, Byron 1982; essays: Cracks in the Ice 1979, Of Gods and Men (illustrated by Sarah Raphael) 1992, France, the Four Seasons 1994, The Necessity of Anti-Semitism 1997, Historicism and its Poverty 1998, Karl Popper 1998, Eyes Wide Open 1999, Personal Terms 2001, The Benefits of Doubt 2002, Rough Copy (Personal Terms II) 2004, Cuts and Bruises (Personal Terms III) 2006, Ticks and Crosses (Personal Terms IV) 2008; translations: Catullus (with K. McLeish) 1976, The Oresteia of Aeschylus 1978, Aeschylus (complete plays, with K. McLeish) 1991, Euripides' Medea (with K. McLeish) 1994, Euripides: Hippolytus, Bacchae (with K. McLeish) 1997, Sophocles Aias (with K. McLeish) 1998, Bacchae 1999, The Satyrica of Petronius 2009; screenplays: Nothing But the Best 1964 (Writers' Guild Best Comedy), Darling (US Acad. Award for Best Original Screenplay, Writer's Guild Best Screenplay, British Film Academy Award) 1965, Far from the Madding Crowd 1967, Two for the Road 1968, Daisy Miller 1974, Rogue Male 1976, Richard's Things 1980, The Man in the Brooks Brothers Shirt (ACE award 1991), Armed Response 1995, Eyes Wide Shut 1998; numerous plays for TV and radio including: The Glittering Prizes (Royal TV Soc. Writer of the Year Award) 1976, From the Greek 1979, The Daedalus Dimension (radio) 1982, Oxbridge Blues 1984, The Thought of Lydia (radio) 1988, After the War 1989, The Empty Jew (radio) 1993, Eyes Wide Open. *Leisure interests:* tennis, bridge. *Address:* c/o Ed Victor Ltd, 6, Bayley Street, Bedford Square, London, WC1B 3HE, England.

RAPLEY, Christopher G., CBE, PhD; British museum director, earth system scientist and academic; *Director, Science Museum, London;* b. 8 April 1947, West Bromwich; s. of Ronald Rapley and Barbara Helen Rapley (née Stubbs); m. Norma Rapley; two d. (twins); ed King Edward's School, Bath, Jesus Coll. Oxford, Victoria Univ. of Manchester, Univ. Coll. London; Head of Remote Sensing, Mullard Space Science Lab., Univ. Coll. London 1982–94, Prof. of Remote Sensing 1991–97, Hon. Prof. 1998–; Exec. Dir Int. Geosphere-Biosphere Programme, Stockholm 1994–97; Dir British Antarctic Survey 1998–2007 (retd); Dir Science Museum, London 2007–; Fellow, St Edmund's Coll. Cambridge 1999–; mem. American Geophysical Union; Chair., Int. Polar Year 2007–08 Planning Group 2003–04; Hon. Prof., Univ. of East Anglia 1999–, Univ. Coll. London 1999–; Edinburgh Medal 2008. *Publications:* more than 120 articles and papers in professional scientific literature. *Leisure interests:* digital photography, jogging. *Address:* Science Museum, Exhibition Road, South Kensington, London, SW7 2DD (office); Flat 3, 51 Bateman Street, Cambridge, CB2 1LR, England (home). *Telephone:* (20) 7942-4000 (office). *E-mail:* christopher.rapley@ntlworld.com (home); feedback@nmsi.ac.uk (office). *Website:* www.sciencemuseum.org.uk (office).

RAPOSO, Mario; Portuguese lawyer and politician; b. Jan. 1929, Coimbra; s. of Mário da Silva Raposo and Adélia Ferreira Bastos; m. Catarina Pera; two s.; ed Univ. of Coimbra; Sub-Insp. for Social Assistance and Sec. to Minister of Finance, resgnd to practise law 1955; mem. Gen. Council, Ordem dos Advogados (Law Soc.) 1972–74, Chair. 1975–77; mem. Exec. Cttee First Nat. Congress of Lawyers 1972, Cttee for Judicial Reform, High Court of Justice 1974; Minister of Justice 1978, 1980–81, 1985–87; mem. Ass. of the Repub. 1978–79, for Social Democratic Party (PSD) Dec. 1979–90; Nat. Ombudsman 1990–91; mem. Council of State 1990–91; First Pres. Ibero-American Inst. of Maritime Law. *Address:* Rua Rodrigo da Fonseco, 149-1, Dt, 1070–242 Lisbon (office); Rua de São Gabriel 7, Alto do Lagoal, 2760–107 Caxias, Portugal (home). *Telephone:* (21) 3826200 (office). *Fax:* (21) 3826209 (office). *E-mail:* marioraposoadvogado@sapo.pt (office); marioraposo.advogado@gmail.com (home).

RAPOTA, Lt-Gen. Grigory Alekseyevich; Russian government official and fmr intelligence officer; b. 5 Feb. 1944, Moscow; m.; three c.; ed Moscow Bauman Higher School of Tech., Inst. of Intelligence Service; mem. First Chief Dept of KGB; worked in USA and Finland; Deputy Dir Intelligence Service Russian Fed. 1994–98; Deputy Sec., Security Council April–Nov. 1998; Dir Gen. Rosvooruzheniye state co. 1998–99; First Deputy Minister of Econ. Devt and Trade 1999–2000; First Deputy Minister of Industry, Science and Tech. 2000–01; Sec.-Gen. Eurasian Econ. Community—EurAsEC 2002–07; Presidential Rep. in the Southern Fed. Okrug 2007–08. *Address:* c/o Office of the Presidential Representative, 344006 Rostov-on-Don, ul. B. Sadovaya 73, Russia (office).

RAPPENEAU, Jean-Paul; French film director and screenwriter; b. 8 April 1932, Auxerre, Yonne; s. of Jean Rappeneau and Anne-Marie Rappeneau (née Bornhauser); m. Claude-Lise Cornély 1971; two s.; ed Lycée Jacques-Amyot, Auxerre, Faculté de droit, Paris; asst dir 1953–57; dir and screenwriter 1958–; Officier, Légion d'honneur, Officier, Ordre Nat. du Mérite, Commdr des Arts et Lettres; 10 César Awards 1990 (including Best Dir, Best Picture), Golden Globe Award for best foreign film 1990, US Nat. Review Bd Best Foreign Film 1990, Grand Prix Nat. du Cinéma 1994. *Films include:* as director: La Maison sur la place, Chronique provinciale 1958; wrote and directed La Vie de château 1966 (Prix Louis-Delluc), Les Mariés de l'An Deux 1970, Le Sauvage 1975, Tout feu, tout flamme 1982; as dir and jt adaptor Cyrano de Bergerac 1990, Le Hussard sur le toit 1995, Bon Voyage (Best Dir Cabourg Romantic Film Festival) 2002; as screenwriter: Signé Arsène Lupin 1959, Le Mariage (in La Française et l'Amour) 1959, Zazie dans le métro 1960, Vie privée 1961, Le Combat dans l'île 1961, L'Homme de Rio 1962, La Fabuleuse aventure de Marco Polo 1965, Les Survivants (TV) 1965, Le Magnifique 1973, Le Sauvage 1975. *Address:* c/o Artmédia, 20 avenue Rapp, 75007 Paris (office); 24 rue Henri Barbusse, 75005 Paris, France (home). *E-mail:* info@artmedia.fr (office).

RASHED, Mahmoud Aboul Leil; Egyptian politician; b. 24 Sept. 1935, Minia; m.; one s. two d.; ed Cairo Univ.; Pres. State High Security Court 1988–90, Giza Primary Court 1990–96; Gov. Kafr El Sheikh 1996–2000, Giza Governorate 2000–04; Minister of Justice 2004–06 (resgnd). *Address:* c/o Ministry of Justice, Justice and Finance Building, Sharia Majlis ash-Sha'ab, Lazoughli Square, Cairo, Egypt (office).

RASHEED, Natheer ar-; Jordanian business executive and civil servant; b. 19 June 1929, Salt; s. of Ahmad al-Rasheed and Sahah al-Hiary; m. Rabia al-Rasheed 1961; four s. one d.; ed mil. courses with British Army and Staff Coll.; Dir-Gen. Intelligence in Jordan 1969–73; fmr Minister of Interior; Chief, Bd of Dirs Jordan Mines Phosphate Co. 1976; Senator 1989–; recipient of three medals. *Leisure interests:* horse-riding (polo), shooting. *Address:* PO Box 6583, Amman, Jordan. *Telephone:* (6) 893102/3 (office); (6) 5523366 (home). *Fax:* (6) 893117.

RASHID, Shaikh Ahmed, MA, LLB; Pakistani politician; b. 6 Nov. 1950, Balra Bazar, Rawalpindi; ed Polytech. Coll., Rawalpindi, Gordon Coll., Punjab Univ.; mem. (Ind.) Nat. Ass. 1985–2008; fmr Minister of Labour and Manpower, of Industries and Production, of Culture and Sports, of Tourism and Investment; Fed. Minister of Information and Broadcasting 2002, for Railways 2006–08; imprisoned in fight for democracy; participated in Geneva Accords, Moscow Conf.; Head of Gulf War Monitoring Programme; Rep. of Pakistan to UN and numerous int. confs. *Publications include:* Farzand-I - Pakistan, Suboatta Hai. *Address:* c/o Ministry of Railways, Block D, Pakistan Secretariat, Islamabad, Pakistan.

RASHID, Ahmed; Pakistani journalist and author; b. 1948, Rawalpindi; m.; two c.; ed Malvern Coll., UK, Government Coll., Lahore, Fitzwilliam Coll., Univ. of Cambridge, UK; fmr Pakistan, Afghanistan and Cen. Asia Corresp. Far Eastern Economic Review; now writes regularly for Daily Telegraph, London, International Herald Tribune, New York Review of Books, BBC Online, The Nation, Lahore and other academic and foreign affairs journals as well as several Pakistani newspapers and magazines; appears on TV and radio including BBC World Service, ABC Australia, Radio France Int. and German Radio; mem. Advisory Bd Eurasia Net of the Soros Foundation; Scholar, Davos World Econ. Forum; consultant for Human Rights Watch; mem. Bd of Advisers Int. Cttee of the Red Cross, Geneva 2004–08; f. Open Media Fund for Afghanistan (charity) 2002; Nisar Osmani Award for Courage in Journalism, Human Rights Soc. of Pakistan. *Publications include:* The Resurgence of Central Asia: Islam or Nationalism, Fundamentalism Reborn: Afghanistan and the Taliban, Jihad: The Rise of Militant Islam in Central Asia, Taliban: Islam, Oil and the New Great Game in Central Asia 2000, Descent into Chaos 2008. *Address:* c/o The Daily Telegraph, 1 Canada Square, Canary Wharf, London, E14 5DT, England (office). *Telephone:* (20) 7538-5000 (office). *Fax:* (20) 7513-2506 (office). *E-mail:* dtnews@telegraph.co.uk (office). *Website:* www.telegraph.co.uk (office); www.ahmedrashid.com.

RASHID, Tan Sri Hussain; Malaysian business executive and banker; fmrly with London Stock Exchange; est. brokerage house 1983; est. Rashid Hussain Berhard group of financial services companies 1996, ceded control 1998; Chair. Exec. Cttee Khazanah Govt holding co. *Address:* c/o D.C.B. Bank Bhd., Menara T.R., 18th Floor, 161B Jalan Ampang, PO Box 10145, 50907 Kuala Lumpur, Malaysia. *Telephone:* (3) 2612444. *Fax:* (3) 2619541. *E-mail:* webmaster@moe.gov.sa (office). *Website:* www.moe.gov.sa (office).

RASHID, Muhammad ibn Ahmad ar-, PhD; Saudi Arabian politician and academic; b. 1944, Al-Majma'a; m.; five s. two d.; ed Imam Mohammed Bin Saud Islamic Univ., Riyadh, Univ. of Indiana, Univ. of Oklahoma; teacher Inst. of Religious Studies, Riyadh 1964–65; Grad. Asst Coll. of Shari'a and Islamic Studies, Makkah 1965–66; sent on mission to USA by King Abdulaziz Univ. 1966–72; Asst Prof. King Saud Univ. 1972–79, Assoc. Prof. 1979–89, Vice-Dean Coll. of Educ. 1974–76, Dean 1976–79; Dir-Gen. Arab Bureau of Educ. for Gulf States 1979–88; Founder of Arab Gulf States Univ. and Vice-Pres. of Founding Cttee 1979–88; Prof. of Educ. King Saud Univ. 1989–94; mem. Saudi Nat. Council 1994–95; Minister of Educ. 1995–2004; Distinguished Fulbright Fellow 1988–89, Distinguished Fellow, World Council for Teacher Training 1989; Gold Medal of Merit (Arab League Educ. Cultural and Scientific Org.). *Publications:* numerous articles and research papers in professional journals. *Leisure interests:* walking, swimming, reading. *Address:* c/o Ministry of Education, PO Box 3734, Airport Road, Riyadh 11481, Saudi Arabia.

RASHID, Rashid Muhammad, BSc; Egyptian business executive and politician; *Minister of Trade and Industry;* b. 1956, Alexandria; ed Alexandria Univ.; f. Fine Foods (Egypt's leading food brand) jt venture with Unilever Mashreq, later Pres. Unilever Middle East, N Africa and Turkey, London; Minister of Trade and Industry 2004–; fmr mem. Bd of Dirs Unilever. *Leisure interests:* horse riding, painting. *Address:* Ministry of Trade and Industry, 2 Latin America Str., Cairo, Egypt (office). *Telephone:* (2) 7921167 (office). *Fax:*

(2) 7955025 (office). *E-mail:* mfti@mfti.gov.eg (office). *Website:* www.mfti.gov.eg (office).

RASI, Satu Marjatta, LLB; Finnish diplomatist; *Under-Secretary of State, Ministry of Foreign Affairs;* b. 29 Nov. 1945, Punkalaidun; m.; ed Helsinki Univ.; attaché, Finnish diplomatic service 1970, Second Sec., London 1972–73, Paris 1974–76, Sec. of Section, Ministry of Foreign Affairs 1977; Counsellor Perm. Mission to the UN 1979; Counsellor, Ministry of Foreign Affairs 1983–86, Dir UN Section, Political Dept 1986; Deputy Perm. Rep. to the UN 1987–91, Perm. Rep. 1997–2005; Chair. Security Council Cttee responsible for monitoring sanctions regime against Iraq 1990; Amb. to India (also accred to Bangladesh, Sri Lanka, Nepal and Bhutan) 1991–95; Dir-Gen. Dept for Int. Devt Co-operation, Ministry of Foreign Affairs 1995–97, Under-Sec. of State 2005–; Vice-Pres. ECOSOC 2002–03, Pres. 2004; Gov., Asian Devt Bank, African Devt Bank, IDB 2005–; Chair. Advisory Bd, UN Peace Building Fund 2007–. *Address:* Ministry of Foreign Affairs, Merikasarmi, Laivastokatu 22, POB 176, 00161 Helsinki (office); Katajanolanlattvei 3, 00160 Helsinki, Finland (office). *Telephone:* (9) 16056400 (office). *Fax:* (9) 16056404 (office). *E-mail:* avs-keo@formin.fi (office). *Website:* formin.finland.fi (office).

RASIZADE, Artur Tahir oğlu; Azerbaijani politician and engineer; *Prime Minister;* b. 26 Feb. 1935, Ganca; m.; one d.; ed Azerbaijan Inst. of Industry; engineer, Deputy Dir Azerbaijan Inst. of Oil Machine Construction 1957–73, Dir 1977–78; Chief Engineer, Trust Soyuzneftemash 1973–77; Deputy Head Azerbaijan State Planning Cttee 1978–81; Head of Section Cen. Cttee of Azerbaijan CP 1981–86; First Deputy Prime Minister 1986–92; adviser, Foundation of Econ. Reforms 1992–96; Asst to Pres. Heydar Aliyev Feb.–May 1996; First Deputy Prime Minister May–Nov. 1996; Prime Minister 1996–, demoted and apptd Deputy Prime Minister Aug. 2003 but resumed role as Prime Minister days later. *Address:* Office of the Prime Minister, 1066 Baku, Lermontov küç. 68, Azerbaijan (office). *Telephone:* (12) 492-66-23 (office). *Fax:* (12) 492-91-79 (office). *E-mail:* nk@cabmin.gov.az (office). *Website:* www.cabmin.gov.az (office).

RASMEY, Keo Puth, MEconSc; Cambodian diplomatist and politician; *Deputy Prime Minister;* b. 1 Oct. 1952, Kompong Cham Prov.; m. Arun Rasmey; one s. one d.; ed Univ. Paris-Sorbonne (Paris IV), France, Univ. of Montreal, Canada; Head of Policy, Admin. and Foreign Affairs, Office of Prince Norodom Ranriddh and Rep. of King Norodom Sihanouk to Asia 1985–91; Head of Del. of Supreme Nat. Council of Cambodia to Tokyo 1992; Amb. to Malaysia, Germany, Slovenia, Malta and Cyprus 1999–2006; Deputy Prime Minister 2006–; mem. United Nat. Front for an Ind., Neutral, Peaceful and Co-operative Cambodia Party (FUNCINPEC) 1991–, Pres. 2006–; Commdr, Légion d'Honneur; Mahasena Medal. *Address:* FUNCINPEC Party, 11 boulevard Monivong (93), Sangkat Sras Chak, Khan Daun Penh, BP 1444, Phnom-Penh, Cambodia (office). *Telephone:* (23) 428864 (office). *Fax:* (23) 218547 (office). *E-mail:* funcinpec@funcinpec.org (office). *Website:* www.funcinpec.org (office).

RASMUSSEN, Anders Fogh, MSc; Danish politician; *Secretary General, NATO;* b. 26 Jan. 1953; m. Anne-Mette Rasmussen; three c.; ed Econ. Univ. of Århus; Consultant to Danish Fed. of Crafts and Small Industries 1978–87; mem. Folketing (Parl.) 1978–, mem. Econ. and Political Affairs Cttee 1982–87, Vice-Chair. 1993–98; Vice-Chair. Housing Cttee 1981–86; Minister for Taxation 1987–92, also for Econ. Affairs 1990–92; Vice-Chair. Econ. and Political Affairs Cttee 1993–98; Prime Minister of Denmark 2001–09; Sec.-Gen. NATO 2009–; mem. Venstre (Liberal Party), Vice-Chair. Nat. Org. Venstre 1985–98, mem. Man. Cttee Parl. Party 1984–87, 1992–2001, Spokesman for Venstre 1992–98, Vice-Chair. Foreign Policy Bd 1998–2001, Chair. Venstre 1998–; Grand Cross of the Portuguese Order of Merit 1992, Commdr (First Degree) of the Order of the Dannebrog 2002, Danish Gold Medal of Merit 2002, Grand Cross of the German Order of Merit 2002, Grand Cross of the Order of Merit of Poland 2003, Grand Cross of the Order of the Oak Crown of Luxembourg 2003, Grand Cross of the Order of Nicaragua 2003, Great Cross of the Pedro Joaquín Chamorro Order 2003, Ordinul Steaua României Mare Cruce 2004, Grand Cross of the Order of the Lithuanian Grand Duke Gediminas 2004, Three Star Order of Latvia 2005, Order of Stara Planina, First Class (Bulgaria) 2006, Grand Cross of the Nordstjärneorden (Sweden) 2007, Grand Cross of the Order of the South Cross (Brazil) 2007; Dr hc (George Washington Univ.) 2002, Hon. DIur (Hampden-Sydney Coll., VA) 2003; Adam Smith Award 1993, Politician of the Year (Dansk Markedsfuringsforbund) 1998, Netherlands Youth Org. for Freedom and Democracy Liberal of the Year 2002, European Leader Award, Polish Leaders Forum 2003, Danish European Movement European of the Year 2003, Robert Schumann Medal 2003, Pedro Joaquin Chamorro Medal, Nicaragua 2003, Best Leader in Denmark 2005, Politician of the Year 2005, Chevalier du St-Chinian 2007. *Publications:* Oprør med skattesystemet 1979, Den truede velstand (co-author) 1980, Kampen om boligen 1982, Fra Socialstat til Minimalstat 1993, I Godvejr og storm (interviews) 2001. *Address:* North Atlantic Treaty Organization Headquarters, Boulevard Leopold III, 1110 Brussels, Belgium (office). *Website:* www.nato.int (office).

RASMUSSEN, Lars Løkke; Danish politician; *Prime Minister;* b. 15 May 1964; ed Copenhagen Univ.; mem. Venstre (Liberal Party); mem. Folketinget (Parl.) 1994–; Minister of the Interior and Health 2001–07, of Finance 2007–09; Prime Minister of Denmark 2009–; Co. Mayor of Frederiksborg Co. 1998–2001. *Address:* Prime Minister's Office, Christiansborg, Prins Jørgens Gård 11, 1218 Copenhagen K, Denmark (office). *Telephone:* 33-92-33-00 (office). *Fax:* 33-11-16-65 (office). *E-mail:* stm@stm.dk (office). *Website:* www.stm.dk (office).

RASMUSSEN, Michael Pram, LLB; Danish business executive; *Chairman, A.P. Møller-Mærsk A/S;* b. 14 Jan. 1955; m. Anne Pram Kjølbye; ed Univ. of Copenhagen; began career with Nye Danske Lloyd 1979; Asst Man.-Dir Baltica Forsikring A/S 1982–84, Man.-Dir 1984–86, Vice-Pres. 1986–88, Pres. 1988–95; Pres. Tryg Forsikring A/S (later renamed Tryg-Baltica Forskring A/S) 1995–96; CEO TopDanmark Forsikring A/S (insurance co.) 1996–; Chair. Mærsk Olie & Gas A/S; Vice-Chair. Forsikring & Pension 2000–03; Vice-Chair. A.P. Møller-Mærsk A/S June–Dec. 2002–03, Chair. 2003–; mem. Bd Dirs Baltica Forsikring A/S 1982–85, William Demant Holdings A/S 1999–, Oticon A/S 1999–, Danmark-Amerika Fondet 2002–, Coloplast A/S 2005–; Dir (non-exec.) Øresundsbro Konsortiet 2001–03. *Address:* A.P. Møller-Mærsk A/S, Esplanaden 50, 1098 Copenhagen K (office); TopDanmark Forsikring A/S, Borupvang 4, 2750 Ballerup, Denmark (office). *Telephone:* 33-63-33-63 (office). *Fax:* 33-63-36-05 (office). *E-mail:* info@maersk.com (office). *Website:* www.maersk.com (office); www.topdanmark.dk (office).

RASMUSSEN, Wilkie, BA, LLB, MA; Cook Islands politician; *Minister of Foreign Affairs and Immigration, Tourism, Cultural Development, Marine Resources and Natural Environment Resources;* b. 21 March 1958, Omoka, Penrhyn; m. Tungane (née Woonton); one s. one d.; ed Univ. of Auckland, NZ; practised as barrister 1996–99; ran pvt. co., Northern Traders Ltd; Cabinet Sec. 1999–2000; High Commr to NZ 2000–02; mem. Parl. for Penrhyn 2002–, Chair. Media Select Cttee 2007, mem. Property Law Select Cttee 2007, Parl. Privileges Select Cttee 2007, CPA Cook Islands Cttee; Minister of Foreign Affairs and Immigration, Tourism, Cultural Devt, Marine Resources and Natural Environment Resources 2005–; Panelist, Pacific Ministers for Post-Forum Dialogue 2006–; Deputy Leader Democratic Party 2007–; Co-Pres. ACP-EU Jt Parl. Ass. 2007–; Chair. Pacific Forum Trade Ministers Meeting 2008; Pres. Tongareva (Penrhyn) Island Cttee; Deacon of Avarua CICC (Cook Islands Christian Church). *Address:* Ministry of Foreign Affairs and Immigration, PO Box 105, Rarotonga, Cook Islands (office). *Telephone:* 29347 (office). *Fax:* 21247 (office). *E-mail:* secfa@mfai.gov.ck (office); wilkie@omoka.co.ck (home).

RASPUTIN, Valentin Grigoriyevich; Russian writer; b. 15 March 1937, Ust-Uda (Irkutsk); ed Irkutsk Univ.; first works published 1961; elected People's Deputy 1989; mem. Presidential Council 1990–91; USSR State Prize 1977, 1987; Hero of Socialist Labour 1987. *Publications:* I Forgot to Ask Lyosha 1961, A Man of This World 1965, Bearskin for Sale 1966, Vasilii and Vasilisa 1967, Deadline 1970, Live and Remember, Stories, 1974, Parting with Matera 1976, Live and Love 1982, Fire 1985, Collected Works (2 vols) 1990, Siberia, Siberia 1991. *Address:* 5th Army Street 67, Apt 68, 664000 Irkutsk, Russia. *Telephone:* (3952) 4-71-00.

RASSADIN, Stanislav Borisovich; Russian literary critic; b. 4 March 1935, Moscow; s. of Boris Matveyevich Rassadin and Varvara Georgievna Rassadin; m. Alina Yegorovna Petukhova-Yakunina 1962; ed Moscow Univ.; mem. Russian PEN Centre. *Publications include:* Poetry of Recent Years 1961, Nikolai Nosov: A Bio-Critical Account 1961, Talk with the Reader: Essay on Literature 1962, The Role of the Reader 1965, Linden Alley 1966, Pushkin the Dramatist 1977, Fonvizin 1980, The Test with a Show: Poetry and Television 1984, Suppositions about Poetry 1988, The Genius and the Villainy or the Case of Sukhovo-Kobylin 1989, After the Flood 1990, I am Choosing Freedom 1990, Very Simple Mandelstam 1994, Russians (Russkiye, ili iz dvoryan v intelligenty) 1995, (enlarged edn) 2005, Bulat Okudzhava 1999, Russkaia Literatura: Ot Fonvizina do Brodskogo 2001, Samoubiitsy: Povest' o Tom Kak My Zhili i Chto Chitali (Suicides) 2002, Kniga Proshchanii (Farewell Book) 2004. *Leisure interest:* work. *Address:* Kosygina Street 5, Apt 335, 117334 Moscow, Russia. *Telephone:* (495) 137-81-84.

RATCLIFFE, David M., BS, LLB; American business executive; *Chairman, President and CEO, Southern Company;* b. Tifton, Ga; m. Cecelia E. Ratcliffe (née Chandler); one s. one d.; ed Valdosta State Univ., Woodrow Wilson Coll. of Law; joined Southern Co. as biologist 1971, served as coordinator for environmental monitoring and compliance programs in power plants, Vice-Pres. Fuel Services, Southern Co. Services 1986–89, Exec. Vice-Pres. 1989–91, Pres. and CEO Miss. Power 1991–95, Group Sr Vice-Pres. of External Affairs 1995–98, Exec. Vice-Pres., Treasurer and Chief Financial Officer, Ga Power 1998–99, CEO Ga Power 1999–2004, Chair., Pres. and CEO Southern Co. 2004–; Chair. Ga Partnership for Excellence in Educ. 2001–04; Dir Fed. Reserve Bank of Ga 2002–07, Chair. 2004–06; Dir Ga Chamber of Commerce (Chair 2005), Ga Research Alliance (Chair. 2005–06), Metro Atlanta Chamber of Commerce; mem. Bd of Dirs CSX Transportation, Nuclear Energy Inst., Edison Electric Inst. (Chair. 2009); mem. Ga Bar Assn; Trustee Woodruff Arts Center; Diversity CEO of the Year Award, Ga Minority Business Awards 2004, Distinguished Alumnus Award, Valdosta State Univ. 2004. *Address:* Southern Company, 30 Ivan Allen Jr Blvd NW, Atlanta, GA 30308-3003, USA (office). *Telephone:* (404) 506-5000 (office). *Fax:* (404) 506-0956 (office). *Website:* www.southernco.com (office).

RATHER, Dan, BA; American broadcast journalist; b. Oct. 1931, Wharton, Tex.; m. Jean Goebel; one s. one d.; ed Sam Houston State Coll., Univ. of Houston, Tex., S Tex. School of Law; writer and sports commentator with KSAM-TV; taught journalism for one year at Houston Chronicle; with CBS 1962; with radio station KTRH, Houston for about four years; News and Current Affairs Dir CBS Houston TV affiliate KHOU-TV late 1950s; joined CBS News 1962; Chief London Bureau 1965–66; worked in Viet Nam; White House 1966; anchorman CBS Reports 1974–75; co-anchorman 60 Minutes CBS-TV 1975–81; anchorman Dan Rather Reporting CBS Radio Network 1977–2006; co-ed. show Who's Who CBS-TV 1977; anchorman Midwest desk CBS Nat. election night 1972–80; CBS Nat. Political Consultant 1964–2006; anchorman Man. Ed. CBS Evening News with Dan Rather 1981–2005, co-anchorman 1993–2005; host Dan Rather Reports, HDNet 2006–; anchored numerous CBS News Special Programmes, including coverage of presidential campaigns in 1982 and 1984; as White House corresp. accompanied Pres. on numerous travels, including visits to Middle East, USSR, People's Repub. of China; numerous acad. honours; ten Emmy awards; Distinguished Achievement for Broadcasting Award, Univ. of Southern Calif. Journalism Alumni Assn, Bob Considine Award 1983. *Publications:* The Palace Guard 1974 (with Gary Gates), The Camera Never Blinks Twice (with Mickey Herskowitz) 1977, I Remember (with Peter Wyden) 1991, The Camera Never Blinks Twice: The Further Adventures of a Television Journalist 1994. *Address:* c/o HDNet, 2909 Taylor Street, Dallas, TX 75226, USA (office). *Telephone:* (214) 651-1446 (office). *Website:* www.hd.net/danrather.html (office).

RATHKE, Most Rev. Heinrich Karl Martin Hans, DTheol; German ecclesiastic; *Bishop and Pastor Emeritus, Evangelical-Lutheran Church of Mecklenburg;* b. 12 Dec. 1928, Mölln, Kreis Malchin; s. of Paul and Hedwig (née Steding) Rathke; m. Marianne Rusam 1955; six s. one d.; ed Univs of Kiel, Erlangen, Tübingen and Rostock; parish priest, Althof bei Bad Doberan 1954–55, Warnkenhagen, Mecklenburg 1955–62, Rostock Südstadt 1962–70; Priest in charge of community service and people's mission, Mecklenburg 1970–71; Bishop of the Evangelical-Lutheran Church of Mecklenburg 1971–84; Presiding Bishop of the United Evangelical Lutheran Church of the GDR 1977–81; Pastor in Crivitz/Mecklenburg 1984–91; Bishop and Pastor Emer. 1991–; Asst Bishop, Evangelical-Lutheran Church of Kazakhstan 1991–93; Hon. DTheol (Rostock) 1999. *Publications:* Ignatius von Antiochien und die Paulusbriefe 1967, Gemeinde heute und morgen 1979, Einstehen für Gemeinschaft in Christus 1980, Kirche unterwegs 1995, Predigthilfen (three vols) 1998–2000, Märtyrer, Vorbilder für das Widerstehen 2002, Mitmenschlichkeit, Zivilcourage, Gottvertrauen – Opfer des Stalinismus 2003. *Address:* Schleifmühlenweg 11, 19061 Schwerin, Germany. *Telephone:* (385) 562887.

RATNAM, Mani; Indian film director and screenwriter; b. 1956, Madras; s. of 'Venus' Gopalrathnam; m. Suhasini Hassan; one s.; ed Madras Univ., Jamnalal Bajaj Inst., Mumbai; fmr man. consultant; worked for TVS Sudaram; f. Madras Talkies film production co. *Films include:* Pallavi Anu Palavi 1983, Mauna Ragam 1986, Nayakan 1987, Agni Nakshatram 1988, Gitanjali 1989, Anjali 1990, Roja 1992, Thiruda Thiruda 1993, Bombay 1994, Dalpati 1995, Chor Chor 1996, Iruvar 1996, Dil Se 1998, Alay Payuthe 2000, Kannathil Muthamittal (A Peck on the Cheek) 2002, Saathiya 2002, Yuva (The Youth) 2004, Ayitha Ezhuthu 2004, Guru 2007. *Address:* 1 Murrey Gate Road, Alwarpet, Chennai 600018, India (office).

RATNER, Gerald Irving; British business executive; *Chief Executive, GeraldOnLine;* b. 1 Nov. 1949, Richmond; s. of Leslie Ratner and Rachelle Ratner; m. 1st (divorced 1989); two d.; m. 2nd Moira Ratner; one s. one d.; ed Hendon County Grammar School, London; Man. Dir Ratners Group 1984, Chair. 1986–91, CEO 1986–92, Dir –1992; Chief Exec. GeraldOnline (online jewellery retailer) 2003–; Dir (non-exec.) Norweb 1991; consultant Tobacco Dock 1993–; Dir Workshop Health and Fitness Club 1997–. *Leisure interests:* cycling, music. *Address:* EdenHouse, Reynolds Road, Beaconsfield HP9 2FL (office); Hampton Lodge, Church Road, Bray, Berks., SL6 1UP, England (home). *Telephone:* (1494) 680173 (office); (1628) 770270 (home). *Fax:* (1494) 680176 (office); (1628) 770270 (home). *E-mail:* gerald@geraldonline.com (office); gerald.ratner@btinternet.com (home). *Website:* www.geraldonline.com.

RATO Y FIGAREDO, Rodrigo, JD, MBA, PhD; Spanish international banker and fmr government official; *Senior Managing Director of Investment Banking, Lazard Ltd;* b. 18 March 1949, Madrid; m.; two d.; ed Complutense Univ. Madrid, Univ. of Calif., Berkeley, USA; mem. Exec. Cttee Partido Popular party 1979–, mem. Parl. 1982–, co-f. party's Econ. Comm., Parl. Sec.-Gen., 1982–84, Econ. Spokesman 1984–86, Sec.-Gen. for Electoral Action 1988, apptd Vice-Sec. 1996; Second Deputy Prime Minister and Minister of Economy and Finance 1996–2000, First Deputy Prime Minister for Econ. Affairs and Minister of Economy 2000–04, including posts as Gov. for Spain on Bds IMF, World Bank, IDB, EIB and EBRD, also in charge of foreign trade relations for Spain; Man. Dir IMF 2004–07 (resgnd); Sr Man. Dir of Investment Banking, Lazard Ltd 2008–. *Address:* Lazard Asesores, Financieros S.A., Serrano 28, 1° Planta, Madrid 28001, Spain (office). *Telephone:* (91) 7818480 (office). *Fax:* (91) 7818492 (office). *Website:* www.lazard.com (office).

RATSIRAHONANA, Norbert; Malagasy lawyer and politician; *Leader, Ny asa vita no ifampitsara (AVI) Party;* b. 18 Nov. 1938, Antsiranana; Pres. Constitutional High Court –1996; Prime Minister of Madagascar 1996–97; Leader Ny asa vita no ifampitsara (AVI—People are judged by the work they do) Party 1997–. *Address:* c/o Office of the Prime Minister, BP 248, Mahazoarivo, 101 Antananarivo, Madagascar.

RATTLE, Sir Simon, Kt, CBE; British conductor; *Artistic Director and Chief Conductor, Berlin Philharmonic Orchestra;* b. 19 Jan. 1955, Liverpool; m. 1st Elise Ross 1980 (divorced 1995); two s.; m. 2nd Candace Allen 1996; pnr Magdalena Kožená; one s.; ed Royal Acad. of Music; won John Player Int. Conducting Competition 1973; has conducted Bournemouth Symphony, Northern Sinfonia, London Philharmonic, London Sinfonietta, Berlin Philharmonic, LA Philharmonic, Stockholm Philharmonic, Vienna Philharmonic, Philadelphia Orchestra, Boston Symphony orchestras, etc.; debut at Queen Elizabeth Hall, London 1974, Royal Festival Hall, London 1976, Royal Albert Hall, London 1976; Asst Conductor, BBC Symphony Orchestra 1977–80; Assoc. Conductor, Royal Liverpool Philharmonic Soc. 1977–80; Glyndebourne debut 1977, Royal Opera, Covent Garden debut 1990; Artistic Dir, London Choral Soc. 1979–84; Prin. Conductor and Artistic Adviser, City of Birmingham Symphony Orchestra (CBSO) 1980–90, Music Dir 1990–98; Artistic Dir South Bank Summer Music 1981–83; Jt Artistic Dir Aldeburgh Festival 1982–93; Prin. Guest Conductor, LA Philharmonic 1981–94, Rotterdam Philharmonic 1981–84; Prin. Guest Conductor Orchestra of the Age of Enlightenment 1992–; Artistic Dir and Chief Conductor Berlin Philharmonic Orchestra 2002–; Hon. Fellow, St Anne's Coll. Oxford 1991; Hon. DMus (Liverpool) 1991, (Leeds) 1993; Edison Award (for recording of Shostakovich's Symphony No. 10) 1987, Grand Prix du Disque (Turangalîla Symphony) 1988, Grand Prix Caecilia (Turangalîla Symphony, Jazz Album) 1988, Gramophone Record of the Year Award (Mahler's Symphony No. 2) 1988, Gramophone Opera Award (Porgy and Bess) 1989, Int. Record Critics' Award (Porgy and Bess) 1990, Grand Prix de l'Acad. Charles Cros 1990, Gramophone Artist of the Year 1993, Montblanc de la Culture Award 1993, Toepfer Foundation Shakespeare Prize (Hamburg) 1996, Gramophone Award for Best Concerto recording (Szymanowski Violin Concertos Nos 1 and 2), Albert Medal (RSA) 1997, Choc de l'Année Award (for recording of Brahms Piano Concerto Op. 15) 1998, Outstanding Achievement Award, South Bank Show 1999, Diapason Recording of the Year Award (complete Beethoven Piano Concertos) 1999, Gramophone Award for Best Opera Recording (Szymanowski's King Roger) 2000, Gramophone Awards for Best Orchestral Recording and Record of the Year (Mahler's Symphony No. 10) 2000, Comenius Prize (Germany) 2004, Classical BRIT Award (for Beethoven Symphonies) 2004, Classical BRIT Award for Classical Recording of the Year (Holst's The Planets) 2007, Gramophone Award for Best Choral Recording (Brahms' Ein deutsches Requiem) 2007; Officier, Ordre des Arts et des Lettres 1995. *Address:* Askonas Holt Ltd, Lincoln House, 300 High Holborn, London, WC1V 7JH, England (office); Berlin Philharmonie Orchestra, Philharmonie, Matthäckirchstrasse 1, 14057 Berlin, Germany (office). *Telephone:* (20) 7400-1706 (office). *Fax:* (20) 7400-1799 (office). *E-mail:* info@askonasholt.co.uk (office). *Website:* www.askonasholt.co.uk (office); www.berliner-philharmoniker.de (office).

RATTNER, Steven (Steve) Lawrence, BA; American journalist, financial industry executive and government official; *Counselor to the Secretary of the Treasury;* b. 5 July 1952, New York; s. of George Seymour Rattner and Selma Ann Silberman; m. P. Maureen White 1986; three s. one d.; ed Brown Univ.; Asst to James Reston, New York Times Corresp., Washington, DC New York and London 1974–82; Assoc. Vice-Pres. Lehman Brothers Kuhn Loeb, New York 1982–84; Assoc. Vice-Pres., Prin., Man. Dir then Head communications group Morgan Stanley and Co., New York 1984–89; Man. Dir then Head communications group Lazard Frères and Co. 1989–97, Deputy CEO and Deputy Chair. 1997–99; Man. Prin. Quadrangle Group LLC 2000–09; Counselor to the Sec. of the Treasury, US Dept of the Treasury, Washington, DC 2009–; Dir Falcon Cable Holding Group 1993–98; mem. Bd of Dirs Cablevision, ProSiebenSat.1 Media AG, InterActiveCorp; mem. Man. Cttee Access Spectrum LLC, Global Energy Decisions, GT Brands; Dir New York Outward Bound Center 1990–2001, mem. Advisory Council 2001–; Harvey Baker Fellow, Brown Univ. 1974; Poynter Fellow, Yale Univ. 1979; mem. Council on Foreign Relations; Assoc. mem. Royal Inst. for Int. Affairs; Trustee Brown Univ. 1987–93, 1994–2000 (Fellow 2000–), Educational Broadcasting Corpn 1990– (Vice-Chair. 1994–98, Chair. 1998–), Metropolitan Museum of Art 1996–, Brookings Inst. 1998–, New America Foundation, 2003–; Chair. Mayor's Fund to Advance NYC 2003–. *Publications:* contrib. to various news publs including New York Times, Wall Street Journal, Los Angeles Times, Newsweek and Financial Times. *Address:* Department of the Treasury, 1500 Pennsylvania Ave, NW, Washington, DC 20220, USA (office). *Telephone:* (202) 622-2000 (office). *Fax:* (202) 622-6415 (office). *Website:* www.ustreas.gov (office).

RATUSHINSKAYA, Irina Borisovna; Russian poet; b. 4 March 1954; m. Igor Gerashchenko 1979; ed Odessa Pedagogical Inst.; teacher Odessa Pedagogical Inst. 1976–83; arrested with husband, Moscow 1981; lost job, arrested again, 17 Sept. 1982, convicted of 'subverting the Soviet regime' and sentenced 5 March 1983 to seven years' hard labour; strict regime prison camp Aug. 1983, released Sept. 1986; settled in UK 1986; f. Democracy and Independence Group April 1989–; poetry appeared in samizdat publs, West European Russian language journals, trans. in American and British press and in USSR 1989–. *Publications include:* Poems (trilingual text) 1984, No, I'm Not Afraid 1986, Off Limits (in Russian) 1986, I Shall Live to See It (in Russian) 1986, Grey Is the Colour of Hope 1989, In the Beginning 1990, The Odessans 1992, Fictions and Lies 1998. *Address:* c/o Vargius Publishing House, Kazakova str. 18, 107005 Moscow, Russia. *Telephone:* (495) 785-09-62.

RATZINGER, Joseph Alois (see BENEDICT XVI, His Holiness Pope).

RAU, Prabha, MSc; Indian politician; *Governor of Himal Pradesh;* b. 4 March 1935, Rohini, Wardha Dist; d. of the late Gulabrao Wasu and Manubai Wasu; Chair. Maharashtra State Comm. for Women 1993–95; Minister of State for Planning, Industry and Educ., Govt of Maharashtra 1972–76, Cabinet Minister for Educ., Sports and Youth Affairs 1976–77, for Co-operation and Tourism 1978, for Revenue and Cultural Affairs 1988–90; Leader of Opposition, Maharashtra State Legis. Ass. 1979, Deputy Leader, Congress Legis. Party, Maharashtra 1985–90; Pres. Maharashtra Pradesh Congress Cttee 1984–89, 2004–08; Gov. Himal Pradesh 2008–; Pradesh Returning Officer (Punjab) for AICC presidential elections 1999, PCC elections 1997, AICC Observer in Andhra Pradesh for Party Organisational Elections 1997; mem. Cen. Election Authority 1999, Congress Working Cttee, Cen. Election Cttee. *Address:* Raj Bhawan, Shimla,, Himachal Pradesh, India (office). *Telephone:* (177) 2624840 (office). *E-mail:* info@himachal.nic.in (office). *Website:* himachal.nic.in (office).

RAUCH, Neo; German artist; b. 1960, Leipzig; ed Hochschule für Grafik und Buchkunst, Leipzig; Asst Lecturer, Hochschule für Grafik und Buchkunst, Leipzig 1993–98; Vincent Award 2002. *Works include:* Das geht alles von ihrer Zeit ab, Stereo, Falle, Schwieriges Gelände 1997, Handel 1999, Weiche 1999, Quiz 2002, Hatz 2002, Haus des Lehrers 2003, Scheune 2003, Gold 2003,

Schmerz 2004. *Address:* Wächterstrasse 11, 04107 Leipzig, Germany (office). *Telephone:* (3) 412135–0 (office). *Website:* www.hgb-leipzig.de (office).

RAUH, Markus, DrScTech; Swiss telecommunications industry executive; b. 1939, St Gallen; ed Swiss Fed. Inst. of Tech. (ETH), Zürich; began career as Sales Man., Sperry Univac 1971–78; Head of Data Systems Dept, Philips AG 1978–83; apptd mem. Corp. Exec. Cttee, Philips Kommunikations Industrie AG 1983, Chair. 1985–88; Pres. Wild Leitz 1988–90; CEO Leica Group 1990–98; apptd Dir Leica Geosystems 1998, Vice-Chair. 2000; Chair. Swisscom AG 1998–2006 (retd); Chair. Synthes Chur AG, Anova Holding AG; Chair. Bd of Dirs AO Foundation; Vice-Chair. Dietiker AG; mem. Bd of Dirs Unaxis Holding AG, The Generics Group AG, Madison Man. AG, Cantonal Bank of St Gallen AG, Sagentia Group 2000–, Madison Pvt Equity Holding Ltd 2002–; mem. Exec. Bd Economiesuisse; Chair. AO ASIF Foundation; Pres. Bd of Trustees, Inst. of Tech. Man., Univ. of St Gallen; Hon. Senator, Univ. of St Gallen 2005. *Address:* c/o AO Foundation, Clavadelerstrasse 8, 7270 Davos Platz, Switzerland. *Telephone:* 814142801. *Fax:* 814142280. *E-mail:* foundation@aofoundation.org. *Website:* www .aofoundation.org.

RAÚL; Spanish professional football player; b. (Raúl González Blanco), 27 June 1977, Madrid; m. Mamen Sanz; two c.; centre forward; teams: Athletico Madrid 1992–95, Real Madrid 1995– (Primera División debut 1994), Spain 1996– (debut v. Czech Republic, Oct. 1996); honours (all with Real Madrid) include: Primera Liga Championship 1994/95, 1996/97, 2000/01, 2002/03; Spanish Super Cup 2001, 2003; Champions League 1998, 2000, 2002; Intercontinental Cup 1998, 2002; Copa del Rey (runner-up) 2002; UEFA Super Cup 2002; 75 caps, 37 goals for Spain. *Address:* c/o Real Madrid club de Fútbol, Conctia Espina, Madrid, 28036, Spain (office). *Telephone:* (91) 3984300 (office). *Fax:* (91) 3440695 (office). *Website:* www.realmadrid.com (office).

RAUSCH, Jean-Marie Victor Alphonse; French politician; b. 24 Sept. 1929, Sarreguemines, Moselle; s. of Victor Rausch and Claire Hessemann; m. 2nd Nadine Haven 1980; two s. by first m.; ed Lycée de Sarreguemines and Ecole française de meunerie, Paris; Dir Moulin Rausch, Woippy 1953–76; Admin. Soc. Anonyme des Moulins Rausch, Woippy 1976–77; Pres. departmental milling syndicate 1967–81; Pres. Millers' Union of Moselle 1974–80; Conseiller-Gen. Metz III 1971, 1976, 1982–88, Pres. of Council 1979–82; Mayor of Metz 1971–2008; mem. Lorraine Regional Council 1974–92, Pres. 1982–92; mem. Nat. Statistical Council 1979, Conseil Nat. du Crédit 1984; numerous other civic, public and professional appointments; Minister of Foreign Trade 1988–91, of Foreign Trade and Tourism 1990–91, of Posts and Telecommunications 1991–92; Deputy Minister attached to Minister of Econ. and Finance in charge of Commerce and Labour April–Oct. 1992; Senator (Moselle) 1974–83, 1983–88, 1992–2001; Pres. Fed. des Asscns de maires de la Moselle 1977–2005, Institut Lorrain de Participation 1984–88, Médiaville 1995–, Metz-interactive 1995–2000, Communauté Numérique Interactive de l'Est 2000–02; Hon. mem. Metz Rotary Club, Acad. de Metz; Chevalier, Légion d'honneur, Commdr, Ordine della Stella della Solidarietà Italiana. *Publication:* Le laminoir et la puce: la troisième génération industrielle 1987 (Grand Prix de la littérature micro-informatique). *Leisure interests:* photography, skiing. *Address:* Médiaville, 42 rue Notre Dame des Champs, 75006 Paris (office); 4 rue Chanoine Collin, 57000 Metz, France (home). *Telephone:* 1-44-39-34-56 (office); 3-87-55-50-00 (home). *E-mail:* hotline@si.mairie-metz.fr (office).

RAUSING, Hans Anders, KBE; Swedish business executive and philanthropist; *Chairman, Ecolean AB;* b. 26 March 1926; s. of Ruben and Elisabeth Rausing; m. Märit Norrby; one s. two c. including Sigrid Rausing; ed Univ. of Lund; Man. Dir Tetra Pak 1954–83, moved to UK 1983, Chair. and CEO Tetra Pak 1983–91, Chair. Bd of Dirs 1985–91, Chair. and CEO Tetra Laval 1991–93, Hon. Chair. 1993–95; Chair. and majority investor Ecolean AB, Helsingborg, Sweden 2001–; f. Märit and Hans Rausing Charitable Foundation 1996, Hans and Märit Rausing Charitable Trust 2002; mem. Russian Council on Business Devt 1995; Hon. KBE 2006; Hon. mem. Royal Swedish Acad. of Eng Sciences, Russian Acad. of Natural Sciences; Hon. Fellow, Isaac Newton Inst., Univ. of Cambridge; Order of People's Friendship 1994; Dr hc (Univ. of Lund) 1979, (Royal Inst. of Tech., Stockholm) 1985, (Stockholm School of Econs) 1987, (American Univ. in London) 1991, (Imperial College London) 2005. *Address:* Wadhurst Park, Wadhurst, East Sussex, TN5 6NT, England (office). *Website:* www.ecolean.com.

RAUSING, Sigrid, BA, MSc, PhD; Swedish anthropologist, philanthropist and publisher; b. 1962, Lund; d. of Hans Anders Rausing and Märit Rausing; m. 1st Dennis Hotz; one s.; m. 2nd Eric Abraham 2003; ed Univ. of York, Univ. Coll. London, UK; wealth derived from family-owned co. Tetra-Pak (manufacturer of drink cartons); f. Ruben and Elisabeth Rausing Trust 1995 (changed name to Sigrid Rausing Trust 2003); co-f. Portobello Books 2005; acquired Granta (magazine and publishing house) 2005; mem. Bd of Dirs Human Rights Watch, Charleston, Sussex; Int. Service Human Rights Award, Global Human Rights Defender Category 2004, Beacon Special Award for Philanthropy 2005, Changing Face of Philanthropy Award, Women's Funding Network 2006. *Publications:* History, Memory, and Identity in Post-Soviet Estonia 2004; articles in academic journals. *Website:* www.sigrid-rausing -trust.org (office).

RAVALOMANANA, Marc; Malagasy business executive, politician and fmr head of state; b. 12 Dec. 1949, Imerikasina; m. Lalao Rakotonirainy; three s. one d.; ed in Imerikasina and in Sweden; f. TIKO (dairy and oil producing co.); owns Malagasy Broadcasting System (TV and radio stations), MAGRO (supermarket chain), FANAMBY (rice-producing co.); elected Mayor of Antananarivo 1999; following disputed victory in presidential elections Dec. 2001, declared himself Pres. of Madagascar Feb. 2002, High Constitutional Court ruled that he had won by an overall majority May 2002, Pres. of Madagascar 2002–09 (resgnd); Vice-Pres. Protestant Church of Madagascar; Dr hc (Univ. of Antananarivo) 2007; Prix Louise Michel 2005. *Address:* c/o Office of the President, Antananarivo, Madagascar (office).

RAVEN, Peter Hamilton, BS, PhD; American botanist, administrator and academic; *President, Missouri Botanical Garden;* b. 13 June 1936, Shanghai, China; s. of Walter Raven and Isabelle Raven (née Breen); m. 1st Tamra Engelhorn 1968; one s. three d.; m. 2nd Patricia Duncan 2001; ed Univ. of California, Berkeley, Univ. of California, Los Angeles; Nat. Science Foundation Postdoctoral Fellow, British Museum, London 1960–61; Taxonomist, Rancho Santa Ana Botanical Garden, Claremont, Calif. 1961–62; Asst Prof., then Assoc. Prof. of Biological Sciences, Stanford Univ. 1962–71; Pres. Mo. Botanical Garden 1971–, Engelmann Prof. of Botany, Washington Univ., St Louis, Mo. 1973–; Adjunct Prof. of Biology, Univ. of Missouri, St Louis 1973–; John D. and Catherine T. MacArthur Foundation Fellow, Univ. of Missouri 1985–90; Chair. Nat. Museum Services Bd 1984–88; mem. Nat. Geographic Soc. Comm. on Research and Exploration 1981, Governing Bd Nat. Research Council 1983–86, 1987–88, Bd World Wildlife Fund (USA) 1983–88, NAS Comm. on Human Rights 1984–87, Smithsonian Council 1985–90; Home Sec. NAS 1987–99; Pres. Org. for Tropical Studies 1985–88; apptd Pres.'s Cttee on the Nat. Medal of Science 2004; mem. Bd of Trustees Nat. Geographic Soc.; Foreign mem. Royal Danish Acad. of Sciences and Letters, Royal Swedish Acad. of Sciences; Fellow, American Acad. of Arts and Sciences, Calif. Acad. of Sciences, AAAS (fmr Pres.), Linnean Soc. of London; Hon. mem. American Soc. of Landscape Architects; several hon. degrees; Distinguished Service Award, American Inst. of Biological Sciences 1981, Int. Environmental Leadership Medal of UNEP 1982, Int. Prize in Biology, Japanese Govt, Pres.'s Conservation Achievement Award 1993, inducted into St Louis Walk of Fame 1995, Field Museum of Natural History Centennial Merit Award 1994, Nat. Medal of Science 2000, Tyler Prize for Environmental Achievement, Int. Cosmos Prize 2003, Gold Veitch Memorial Medal, RHS 2004, Botanical Soc. of America Centennial Award 2006, World Ecology Award 2007, BBVA Foundation Award for Scientific Research in Ecology and Conservation 2008. *Publications:* Papers on Evolution (with Ehrlich and Holm) 1969, Biology of Plants 1970, Principles of Tzeltal Plant Classification 1974, Modern Aspects of Species (with K. Iwatsuki and W. J. Bock) 1986, Understanding Biology (with G. Johnson) 1988; more than 400 professional papers; Ed.: Coevolution of Animals and Plants 1975, Topics in Plant Population Biology 1979, Advances in Legume Systematics 1981, Biology (with G. B. Johnson) 1986, Understanding Biology 1988; contrib. to many other publs. *Leisure interests:* reading, collecting plants. *Address:* Missouri Botanical Garden, PO Box 299, St Louis, MO 63166-0299, USA (office). *Telephone:* (314) 577-5111 (office). *Fax:* (314) 577-9595 (office). *E-mail:* peter.raven@mobot.org (office). *Website:* www .mobot.org (office).

RAVENSDALE, 3rd Baron, cr. 1911, 7th Baronet; **Sir Nicholas Mosley,** Bt, MC; British writer; b. 25 June 1923, London, England; s. of the late Sir Oswald Mosley and of Lady Cynthia Curzon; m. 1st Rosemary Salmond 1947 (divorced 1974, died 1991); three s. one d.; m. 2nd Verity Bailey (née Raymond) 1974; one s.; ed Eton, Balliol Coll., Oxford. *Publications:* novels: Spaces of the Dark 1951, The Rainbearers 1955, Corruption 1957, African Switchback 1958, The Life of Raymond Raynes 1961, Meeting Place 1962, Accident 1964, Assassins 1966, Impossible Object (also screenplay) 1968, Natalie, Natalia 1971, Catastrophe Practice (three plays and a novella) 1979, Imago Bird 1980, Serpent 1981, Judith 1986, Hopeful Monsters (Whitbread Book of the Year) 1990, Children of Darkness and Light 1996, The Hesperides Tree 2001, Inventing God 2003, Look at the Dark 2005; non-fiction: Experience and Religion: A Lay Essay in Theology 1965, The Assassination of Trotsky (also screenplay) 1972, Julian Grenfell: His Life and the Times of his Death 1988–1915 (biog.) 1976, Rules of the Game: Sir Oswald and Lady Cynthia Mosley 1896–1933 (biog.) 1982, Beyond the Pale: Sir Oswald Mosley and Family 1933–1980 (biog.) 1983, Efforts at Truth (autobiog.) 1994, Time at War: A Memoir 2006. *Address:* 2 Gloucester Crescent, London, NW1 7DS, England. *Telephone:* (20) 7485-4514.

RAVIER, Paul-Henri, LenD; French international organization official and civil servant; *Senior Counsellor, French Court of Audit;* b. 9 Sept. 1948, Lyon; s. of the late Philibert André Ravier and of Roselyne Marie Bellon; m. Martine Caffin; one s.; ed Inst. d'Etudes Politiques, Ecole Nat. d'Admin.; joined Trade Dept, Ministry of the Economy and Finance, in charge of bilateral trade relations with SE Asia and Middle East, later Head of Trade Finance Policy Unit, Asst Dir responsible for man. of bilateral trade relations with Eastern Europe, Asia, the Pacific and the Middle East 1985–90, Deputy Sec. 1991–99; adviser on int. econ. issues to Prime Minister Raymond Barre 1980; Jt Deputy Head World Trade Org. 1999–2002; Sr Counsellor, French Court of Audit (Cour des Comptes) 2006–; mem. Bd Agence Française de Développement 1993–99, SNECMA 1994–99, Pechiney 1993–97; Chevalier, Ordre nat. du Mérite 1993, Légion d'honneur 1998. *Leisure interests:* golf, skiing, mountain climbing, cooking, wine tasting. *Address:* Cour des Comptes, 13 rue Cambon, 75001 Paris (office); 2 avenue Frédéric le Play, 75007 Paris, France (home). *Telephone:* 1-42-98-95-00 (office); 1-45-55-42-46 (home). *Fax:* 1-45-56-10-15 (home). *E-mail:* phravier@ccomptes.fr (office); phravier@noos.fr (home). *Website:* www.ccomptes.fr (office).

RAVINET DE LA FUENTE, Jaime; Chilean politician; b. 17 Oct. 1946, Abogado; ed Univ. of Chile; Pres. Fed. of Students of Univ. of Chile 1968–69, Univ. Council 1967–72; Exec. Sec. Presidential Command of Pres. Patricio Azócar 1989; Mayor of Santiago 1990–2000; Pres. Union of Municipalities and Local Govts 1995–97, Union of Latin American Capital Cities 1995–96, World Asscn of Cities and Local Authorities Coordination 1996–97, Latin American Centre of Urban Strategic Devt 1995–97; Vice-Pres. Latin American Org. of Inter-municipal Co-operation; Minister of Housing and Urban Planning

2000–04; Minister of Nat. Defence 2004–06; mem. Exec. Bureau Worldwide Fed. of United Cities 1992–95; mem. Bd of Dirs Universidad Mayor 2006–. *Address:* c/o Board of Directors, Universidad Mayor, Manuel Montt 367, Providencia, Santiago, Chile (office).

RAVITCH, Diane Silvers, PhD; American education scholar and academic; *Research Professor of Education, New York University;* b. 1 July 1938, Houston, Tex.; d. of Walter Cracker and Ann Celia Silvers (née Katz); m. Richard Ravitch 1960 (divorced 1986); three s. (one deceased); ed Wellesley Coll. and Columbia Univ.; Adjunct Asst Prof. of History and Educ., Teachers' Coll., Columbia Univ. 1975–78, Assoc. Prof. 1978–83, Adjunct Prof. 1983–91; Dir Woodrow Wilson Nat. Fellowship Foundation 1987–91; Chair. Educational Excellence Network 1988–91; Asst Sec. Office of Research and Improvement, US Dept of Educ., Washington, DC 1991–93, Counsellor to Sec. of Educ. 1991–93; Visiting Fellow, Brookings Inst. 1993–94, Brown Chair in Educ. Policy 1997–; Sr Research Scholar, New York Univ. 1994–98, Research Prof. in Educ. 1998–; Sr Fellow, Progressive Policy Inst. 1998–2002, Hoover Inst.; Adjunct Fellow, Manhattan Inst. 1996–99; Trustee New York Historical Soc. 1995–98, New York Council on the Humanities 1996–2004; Hon. DHumLitt (Williams Coll.) 1984, (Reed Coll.) 1985, (Amherst Coll.) 1986, (State Univ. of New York) 1988, (Ramopo Coll.) 1990, (St Joseph's Coll., NY) 1991; Hon. LHD (Middlebury Coll.) 1997, (Union Coll.) 1998; Leadership Award, Klingenstein Inst., Teachers Coll. 1994, Horace Kidger Award, New England History Teachers Asscn 1998, Leadership Award, New York City Council of Supervisors and Admins 2004, John Dewey Award, United Fed. of Teachers of New York City 2005, Gaudium Award, Breukelein Inst. 2005, Uncommon Book Award, Hoover Inst. 2005, Kenneth J. Bialkin/Citigroup Public Service Award 2006. *Publications:* The Great School Wars: New York City 1805–1973 1974, The Revisionists Revised 1977, Educating and Urban People (co-author) 1981, The Troubled Crusade: American Education 1945–1980 1983, The School and the City (co-author) 1983, Against Mediocrity (co-author) 1984, The Schools We Deserve 1985, Challenges to the Humanities (co-author) 1985, What Do Our 17-Year-Olds Know? (with Chester E. Finn Jr) 1987, The American Reader (co-ed.) 1990, The Democracy Reader (ed. with Abigail Thernstrom) 1992, National Standards in American Education 1995, Debating the Future of American Education (ed.) 1995, Learning from the Past (ed. with Maris Vinovskis) 1995, New Schools for a New Century (ed. with Joseph Viteretti) 1997, Left Back 2000, City Schools (ed.) 2000, The Language Police 2003, Forgotten Heroes of American Education (co-ed.) 2006, The English Reader (co-ed.) 2006; contrib. articles and reviews to scholarly books and professional journals. *Address:* New York University, 82 Washington Square East, New York, NY 10003, USA (office). *Telephone:* (212) 998-5146 (office). *E-mail:* dr19@hyu.edu (office); gardend@aol .com (home). *Website:* www.dianeravitch.com (office).

RAVONY, Francisque; Malagasy politician and barrister; fmr First Deputy Prime Minister, Transitional Govt; Prime Minister of Madagascar 1993–95, also Minister of Finance and Budget; Minister of Defence 2002–07; Leader Cttee for the Support of Democracy and Devt in Madagascar; fmr Chair. Union des Forces Vives Démocratiques. *Address:* Union des Forces Vives Démocratiques, Antananarivo, Madagascar.

RAWABDEH, Abd ar-Raouf ar-, BSc; Jordanian politician; b. 13 Feb. 1939, Es-Sarih, Irbid; m.; ed American Univ. of Beirut; Minister of Communications 1976–77, of Communications and Health 1977–78, of Health 1978–79, of Public Works and Housing 1989–91, of Educ. and of State for Prime Minister's Affairs 1994–95; Vice-Pres. Nat. Consultative Council 1982–83 (mem. 1978–83; Chair. Bd of Dirs, Jordan Phosphate Mining Co. 1982–85; lecturer School of Pharmacy, Univ. of Jordan 1982–89; Mayor of Amman 1983–86, of Greater Amman 1987–89; Chair. Bd of Dirs Amman Devt Corpn 1983–89; mem. of House of Reps 1989–; Sec.-Gen. Awakening Party (Al-Yakza) 1993–96; Deputy Prime Minister and Minister of Educ. 1995–96; Prime Minister and Minister of Defence 1999–2000; Deputy Sec.-Gen. Nat. Constitutional Party 1996–97; Vice-Chair. Bd of Trustees, Jordan Univ. of Science and Tech.; mem. Jordan Pharmaceutical Asscn 1962–, Royal Soc. for the Conservation of Nature 1994–; Jordan Al-Kawkab Medal (First Degree) 1976, Italian Medal of Honour (Sr Officer) 1983, German Medal of Merit 1984, Al-Nahda Medal (First Degree) 1999. *Publications:* An Outline of Pharmacology, Pharmacy, Democracy, Theory and Application, Education and the Future. *Address:* c/o Office of the Prime Minister, PO Box 80, Amman, Jordan (office).

RAWAL, Tilak, MA, MS, PhD; Nepalese economist, banker and academic; b. 6 Dec. 1950; ed Trihhuvan Univ., Univ. of the Philippines, Dhaka Univ.; Deputy Exec. Dir Agric. Projects Services Centre (APROSC) 1990–91; CEO Agricultural Devt Bank of Nepal 1991–94; Exec. Chair. Rastriya Banijya Bank 1995–99; Gov. Nepal Rastra Bank 2000–05; consultant for several int. orgs, including World Bank, ADB, OECD, FAO, UN, ESCAP; mem. Faculty of Econs, Global Coll. of Man., Kathmandu; mem. Nepal Econ. Asscn. *Publications include:* Corporate Governance and Financial Sector Reform in Nepal 2006; numerous articles. *Address:* c/o Global College of Management, Basuki Marga, Mid-Baneshwor, PO Box No. 24855, Kathmandu, Nepal. *Telephone:* (1) 4488312. *E-mail:* info@proed.edu.np.

RAWI, Najih Mohamed Khalil ar-, MSc, PhD; Iraqi civil engineer, educationalist and fmr government official; b. 4 April 1935, Rawa; m.; one s. two d.; ed Univ. of Wales, Purdue Univ., Oklahoma State Univ.; instructor, Univ. of Baghdad 1967, Asst Prof. of Civil Eng 1971, Prof. 1980; Prof. Emer. 1990–; Dean Higher Inst. of Industrial Eng, Univ. of Baghdad 1968–69; Dean Coll. of Industry (now Tech. Univ.) 1969–70; mem. Bureau of Educ. Affairs, Revolutionary Command Council 1973–74, Council of Higher Educ. 1970–74, 1980–85; Deputy Minister of Municipalities 1974, of Public Works and Housing 1974–77; Minister of Industry and Minerals 1977–78; Vice-Pres. Iraqi Engineers Syndicate 1969–71; Pres. Iraqi Teachers Syndicate 1970–74, Iraqi–Soviet Friendship Soc. 1979–88, Nat. Cttee Tech. and Transfer 1984–89, Man and the Biosphere 1980–89, Int. Geological Correlation Programme 1980–89, Geophysics and Geodesy 1982–89, Council of Scientific Research 1980–89, Iraqi Acad. of Sciences 1996–2001 (mem. 1996–); Head Union of Arab Educators 1983–86; mem. Bd of Trustees, Al-Mustansiryah Univ. 1970–74, Arabian Gulf Univ. 1986–89, Teachers' Union Univ. Coll. 1990–96; mem. Iraq Eng Soc. 1959, American Soc. of Civil Engineers 1967, Council of the World Fed. of Educators 1973–74, 1979–82; Founding Fellow, Islamic Acad. of Sciences 1986; Corresp. mem. Syrian Acad. of Language, Damascus 2001. *Publications:* On Science and Technology (in Arabic) 2003; 65 papers in scientific journals 1960–2003. *Address:* Iraqi Academy of Sciences, Waziriya, A'Adamiah, Baghdad (office); 2/40/635 Hai Al-Jamea, Baghdad, Iraq (home). *Telephone:* (1) 4224202 (office); (1) 5559635 (home). *E-mail:* aos@uruklink.net (office); ahmedelrawi@yahoo.com (home).

RAWLINGS, Hunter R., III, PhD; American academic and fmr university administrator; *Professor, Classics Department, Cornell University;* b. Norfolk, Va; m. Elizabeth Trapnell Rawlings; four c.; ed Haverford Coll., Princeton Univ.; Asst Prof. Univ. of Colo 1970–80, Dept Chair. 1978–88, Prof. 1980–88, Assoc. Vice Chancellor for Instruction 1980–84, Vice-Pres. for Academic Affairs and Research Dean of the System Graduate School 1984–88; Pres. and Prof. of Classics Univ. of Iowa 1988–95; Pres. and Prof. of Classics, Cornell Univ. 1995–, Pres. Emer. 2003–, Interim Pres. 2005–06; fmr Chair. Ivy Council of Presidents; mem. Bd of Dirs American Council on Educ., Exec. Cttee Asscn of American Univs, Nat. Cttee for Selection of Mellon Fellows in Humanities; mem. American Acad. of Arts and Sciences; Woodrow Wilson Fellow, Nat. Defense Educ. Act Fellow, Univ. of Colo Teaching Excellence Award 1979. *Publications:* The Structure of Thucydides' History 1981, The Classical Journal (Ed.); numerous monographs and articles. *Address:* Department of Classics, Cornell University, 120 Goldwin Smith Hall, Ithaca, NY 14853-3201, USA (office). *Telephone:* (607) 255-3354 (office). *Fax:* (607) 254-8899 (office). *E-mail:* sp18@cornell.edu (office). *Website:* www.arts.cornell.edu/classics (office).

RAWLINGS, Flight-Lt Jerry John; Ghanaian fmr head of state and fmr air force officer; b. 22 June 1947, Accra; s. of John Rawlings and Madam Victoria Agbotui; m. Nana Konadu Agyeman; one s. three d.; ed Achimota School and Ghana Military Acad., Teshie; commissioned as Pilot Officer 1969, Flight-Lt 1978; arrested for leading mutiny of jr officers May 1979; leader mil. coup which overthrew Govt of Supreme Mil. Council June 1979; Chair. Armed Forces Revolutionary Council (Head of State) June–Sept. 1979; retd from armed forces Nov. 1979, from air force Sept. 1992; leader mil. coup which overthrew Govt of Dr Hilla Limann Dec. 1981; Head of State 1982–2001; Chief of the Defence Staff 1982–2001; Chair. Provisional Nat. Defence Council 1981–93; Pres. of Ghana 1993–2001. *Leisure interests:* boxing, deep-sea diving, swimming, horse riding, carpentry. *Address:* c/o PO Box 1627, Osu, Accra, Ghana.

RAWLINS, Surgeon-Vice-Adm. Sir John Stuart Pepys, KBE, FRCP, FFCM, FRAeS; British consultant; b. 12 May 1922, Amesbury, Wilts.; s. of Col Commdt Stuart W. H. Rawlins and Dorothy P. Rawlins; m. Diana M. Freshney Colbeck 1944; one s. three d.; ed Wellington Coll., Univ. Coll., Oxford and St Bartholomew's Hosp., London; Surgeon-Lt RNVR 1947; Surgeon-Lt RN, RAF Inst. of Aviation Medicine 1951, RN Physiological Lab. 1957; Surgeon-Commdr RAF Inst. of Aviation Medicine 1961, HMS Ark Royal 1964, US Naval Medical Research Inst. 1967–70; Surgeon-Capt. 1969; Surgeon-Cdre, Dir of Health and Research (Naval) 1973; Surgeon-Rear-Adm. 1975; Dean of Naval Medicine and Medical Officer in charge of Inst. of Naval Medicine 1975–77; Acting Surgeon Vice-Adm. 1977; Medical Dir-Gen. (Navy) 1977–80; Hon. Physician to HM The Queen 1975–80; Dir Diving Unlimited Int. Ltd; Pres. Soc. for Underwater Tech. 1980–84; Chair. Deep Ocean Tech. Inc., Deep Ocean Eng Inc. 1982–90, Trident Underwater Systems Inc. 1986–, Gen. Offshore Corpn (UK) Ltd 1988–90, Europa Hosps Ltd; fmr consultant to Chemical Defence Establishment, Porton Down and British Airways PLC; designed first anti-G suit accepted in RN and RAF, first protective helmet for RN and RAF aircrew, designed and developed an aircraft underwater escape system; Hon. Research Fellow, Univ. of Lancaster, Univ. Coll. Oxford; CStJ; Hon. DTech, (Robert Gordon Univ.); numerous awards and medals, including Royal Navy's Man of the Year 1964, Gilbert Blane Medal, Royal Coll. of Surgeons 1971, Chadwick Naval Prize 1975, Nobel Award of Inst. of Explosive Engineers 1987, Acad. of Underwater Arts and Sciences NOGI Award 1996, Lowell Thomas Award, Explorers Club 2000. *Publications:* numerous papers in fields of aviation and diving medicine and underwater tech. *Leisure interests:* fishing, stalking, riding, judo. *Address:* Little Cross, Holne, Newton Abbot, South Devon, TQ13 7RS, England (home). *Telephone:* (1364) 631249 (home). *Fax:* (1364) 631400 (home). *E-mail:* johnsprawlins@btinternet.com (home).

RAWLINS, Peter Jonathan, MA, FCA, FRSA; British business executive and management consultant; b. 30 April 1951, London; s. of Kenneth Raymond Ivan Rawlins and Constance Amande Malzy; m. 1st Louise Langton 1973 (divorced 1999); one s. one d.; m. 2nd Christina Conway 2000; two s. one d.; ed St Edward's School and Keble Coll. Oxford; with Arthur Andersen & Co., Chartered Accountants, London 1972–85, partner 1983–85; seconded as Personal Asst to CEO and Deputy Chair. Lloyd's of London 1983–84; Dir Sturge Holdings PLC 1985–89, Man. Dir R. W. Sturge & Co. 1985–89, Dir Sturge Lloyd's Agencies Ltd 1986–89; Dir Wise Speke Holdings Ltd 1987–89; CEO The London Stock Exchange 1989–93 (resgnd); consultant, Rawlins Strategy Consulting 1994–; Man. Dir (Europe, Middle East and Africa) Siegel & Gale Ltd 1996–97; Dir Scala Business Solutions NV 1998–2000, Oyster Pnrs Ltd 2001–02; Chair. (non-exec.) Higham Group 2004–05; fmr Chair. Asscn for Research into Stammering in Childhood 1995; Chair. Spitalfields Festival

1998–2003. *Leisure interests:* the performing arts, tennis, shooting, travelling, national heritage. *Address:* Ramley House, Ramley Road, Lymington, Hants., SO41 8LH, England (home). *Telephone:* (1590) 689661 (home). *Fax:* (1590) 689662 (home). *E-mail:* peter@rawlinsp.fsnet.co.uk (home).

RAWNSLEY, Andrew Nicholas James, MA, FRSA; British journalist, broadcaster and author; *Associate Editor and Chief Political Columnist, The Observer;* b. 5 Jan. 1962, Leeds; s. of Eric Rawnsley and Barbara Rawnsley (née Butler); m. Jane Leslie Hall 1990; three d.; ed Lawrence Sheriff Grammar School, Rugby, Rugby School, Sidney Sussex Coll., Cambridge; with BBC 1983–85, The Guardian 1985–93 (political columnist 1987–93); Assoc. Ed. and Chief Political Columnist The Observer 1993–; Presenter Channel 4 TV series A Week in Politics 1989–97, ITV series The Agenda 1996–, Bye Bye Blues 1997, Blair's Year 1998, The Westminster Hour (radio) 1998–, The Unauthorized Biography of the United Kingdom (radio) 1999; Student Journalist of the Year 1983, Young Journalist of the Year 1987, Columnist of the Year, What the Papers Say Award 2000, Book of the Year Award, Channel 4/House Magazine Political Awards 2001, Political Journalist of the Year, Channel 4 Political Awards, 2003. *Publication:* Servants of the People: The Inside Story of New Labour (Channel 4/Politico Book of the year 2001) 2000. *Leisure interests:* skiing, scuba diving, mah jong, books, cinema, food and wine. *Address:* The Observer, 119 Farringdon Road, London, EC1R 3ER, England. *Telephone:* (20) 7278-2332. *E-mail:* a.rawnsley@observer.co.uk (office). *Website:* www.observer.co.uk (office).

RAWSON, Dame Jessica Mary, DBE, MA, DLitt, FBA; British archaeologist, college warden and writer; *Warden, Merton College, University of Oxford;* b. 20 Jan. 1943; d. of Roger Quirk and Paula Quirk; m. John Rawson 1968; one d.; ed New Hall, Cambridge and Univ. of London; Asst Prin. Ministry of Health 1965–67; Asst Keeper II, Dept of Oriental Antiquities, British Museum 1967–71, Asst Keeper I 1971–76, Deputy Keeper 1976–87, Keeper 1987–94; Warden, Merton Coll. Oxford 1994–; Visiting Prof., Kunsthistorisches Inst. Heidelberg 1989, Univ. of Chicago 1994; Chair. Oriental Ceramic Soc. 1993–96; Vice-Chair. Bd Govs, SOAS, Univ. of London 1999–2003; mem. British Library Bd 1999–2003; Hon. DSc (St Andrews) 1997; Hon. DLitt (Sussex) 1998, (Royal Holloway, London) 1998, (Newcastle) 1999. *Publications:* Chinese Jade Throughout the Ages (with J. Ayers) 1975, Animals in Art 1977, Ancient China, Art and Archaeology 1980, Chinese Ornament: The Lotus and the Dragon 1984, Chinese Bronzes: Art and Ritual 1987, The Bella and P.P. Chiu Collection of Ancient Chinese Bronzes 1988, Western Zhou Ritual Bronzes from the Arthur M. Sackler Collections 1990, Ancient Chinese and Ordos Bronzes (with E. Bunker) 1990, The British Museum Book of Chinese Art (ed.) 1992, Chinese Jade from the Neolithic to the Qing 1995, The Mysteries of Ancient China (ed.) 1996, Cosmological Systems and Sources of Art, Ornament and Design 2002, China: The Three Emperors, 1662–1795 (co-ed. with Evelyn Rawski) 2005. *Address:* Merton College, Oxford, OX1 4JD, England (office). *Telephone:* (1865) 276352 (office). *Fax:* (1865) 276282 (office).

RAY, Ajit Nath, MA; Indian judge; b. 29 Jan. 1912, Calcutta; s. of Sati Nath Ray and Kali Kumari Debi; m. Himani Mukherjee 1944; one s.; ed Presidency Coll., Calcutta, Oriel Coll., Oxford and Gray's Inn, London; fmrly practised as a barrister, Calcutta High Court; Judge, Calcutta High Court 1957–69; Judge, Supreme Court of India 1969–73, Chief Justice of India 1973–77; Pres. Int. Law Assn 1974–76, Vice-Pres. 1977–, Vice-Pres. Ramakrishna Inst. of Culture 1981–; mem. Int. Permanent Court of Arbitration 1976–; Pres. Governing Body Presidency Coll., Calcutta 1957–69; Founder-Pres. Soc. for the Welfare of the Blind 1958–80; Treas. Asiatic Soc. 1961–63, Vice-Pres. 1963–65; mem. Karma Samiti Visva Bharati Santiniketan 1963–65, 1967–69, Life mem. 1969–; Hon. Fellow, Oriel Coll., Oxford. *Address:* 15 Panditia Place, Kolkata 700 029, India. *Telephone:* (33) 24541452.

RAY, Robert Francis, BA; Australian politician; *Senator for Victoria;* b. 8 April 1947, Melbourne; m. Jane Ray; ed Rusden State Coll., Monash Univ.; fmr tech. school teacher; Senator for Victoria 1980–, Minister for Home Affairs and Deputy Man. of Govt Business in the Senate 1987–88, for Transport and Communications Jan.–Sept. 1988, for Immigration, Local Govt and Ethnic Affairs and Minister assisting Prime Minister for Multicultural Affairs 1988–90, for Defence 1990–96, currently mem. Finance and Admin Estimates Cttee, Deputy Leader of Govt in Senate 1993–96; mem. Australian Labor Party (ALP) Nat. Exec. 1983–98. *Leisure interests:* films, billiards, tennis, watching Australian Rules football, golf and cricket. *Address:* Office of Senator Robert Ray, Suite 3, Level 2, Illoura Plaza, 424 St Kilda Road, Melbourne, VIC 3004, Australia (home). *Telephone:* (2) 6277-3775 (office). *Fax:* (2) 6277-3086 (office). *E-mail:* senator.ray@aph.gov.au (office). *Website:* www.alp.org.au/people/vic/ray_robert.php (office).

RAY, Siddhartha Shankar, BA, LLB; Indian lawyer and politician; b. 20 Oct. 1920, Calcutta; s. of the late Sudhir Chandra Ray and Shrimati Aparna Devi (Das); m. Maya Bhattacharya 1947; ed Presidency Coll., Univ. Law Coll., Calcutta; called to the Bar, Inner Temple, London; Sr Advocate, Supreme Court 1969; corporate, commercial and constitutional lawyer; appeared in all Courts in India including the Supreme Court, the East Pakistan High Court, the Pakistan Supreme Court (Dhaka Circuit Bench) and Tribunal of Arbitration, Int. Chamber of Commerce, Paris; mem. W Bengal Legis. Ass. 1957–71, 1972–77, 1991–92; mem. Lok Sabha 1971–72, Jr Cen. Govt Counsel 1954–57; Minister of Law and Tribal Welfare, Govt of W Bengal 1957–58; Leader of the Opposition, W Bengal Ass. 1969–71, 1991–92; Cabinet Minister for Educ., Culture, Social Welfare and W Bengal Affairs, Govt of India 1971–72; Chief Minister of W Bengal 1972–77; Gov. of Punjab and Admin. of Chandigarh 1986–89; Amb. to USA 1992–96; High Commr in the Commonwealth of the Bahamas 1994; Gen. Sec. Calcutta Univ. Law Coll. Union 1941–43; Under-Sec. Calcutta Univ. Inst. 1941–44; Univ. Blue in cricket, football and tennis; Individual Champion Athletics, Calcutta Univ. Law Coll. 1941, 1942; mem. Working Cttee Indian Nat. Congress, All India Congress Cttee, Congress Parl. Bd; Pres. Cricket Assn of Bengal 1982–84; mem. Indian Nat. Trust for Art and Cultural Heritage; Trustee Jawaharlal Nehru Memorial Fund (mem. Exec. Cttee); Trustee Nehru Scholarship Trust for Cambridge Univ.; Hon. LLD (Drury Coll., Missouri) 1993. *Leisure interests:* reading, music and sports. *Address:* 2 Beltala Road, Kolkata 700026, India (home). *Telephone:* (33) 4753465.

RAYES, Ghazi al-; Kuwaiti diplomatist; b. 23 Aug. 1935; ed Univ. of Cairo, Egypt; Third Sec., Ministry of Foreign Affairs 1962; at embassies in Washington, DC and Beirut 1965–67; Chair. Int. Affairs Section, Ministry of Foreign Affairs 1967–70; Counsellor, Kuwaiti Embassy, Beirut 1970–73; Amb. to Bahrain 1974–80, to UK 1980–93, to People's Repub. of China 1993–97; Head, Follow-up and Co-ordination Office and Head, Protocol Dept, Ministry of Foreign Affairs 1997. *Address:* c/o Ministry of Foreign Affairs, PO Box 3, 13001 Safat Gulf Street, Kuwait City, Kuwait.

RAYKHELHAUS, Iosif Leonidovich; Russian theatre director; b. 2 June 1947, Odessa, Ukraine; m. Maria Khazina; two d.; ed Moscow Inst. of Theatre Arts; stage Dir Moscow Stanislavsky Theatre 1973; founder and Artistic Dir School of Contemporary Play theatre 1989–; teacher All-Union Inst. of Cinematography 1997–; Prize of Moscow Festival of Chamber Productions Martenitsa 1991; Merited Worker of Arts 1993. *Productions include:* Salute, Don Juan!, A Man Came to a Woman, The Seagull. *Address:* Moscow Theatre School of Contemporary Play, Neglinnaya str. 29/14, 103031 Moscow, Russia (office). *Telephone:* (495) 200-09-00 (office). *Fax:* (495) 200-30-87 (office).

RAYMOND, Lee R., PhD; American oil industry executive (retd); b. 13 Aug. 1938, Watertown, South Dakota; m. Charlene Raymond 1960; ed Univ. of Wisconsin, Univ. of Minnesota; various eng positions Exxon Corpn (now Exxon Mobil Corpn), Tulsa, Houston, New York and Caracas, Venezuela 1963–72, Man. Planning, Int. Co. Div., New York 1972–75, Pres. Exxon Nuclear Co. Div. 1979–81, Exec. Vice-Pres. Exxon Enterprises Inc. Div. 1981–83, Sr Vice-Pres. and Dir Exxon Corpn 1984–86, Pres. and Dir 1987–93, Chair. and CEO 1993–99, Chair. and CEO Exxon Mobil Corpn 1999–2005 (retd), Pres. 1999–2003; Vice-Pres. Lago Oil, Netherlands Antilles 1975–76, Pres. and Dir 1976–79; Pres. and Dir Esso Inter-American Inc., Coral Gables, Fla 1983–84, Sr Vice-Pres. and Dir 1984–; mem. Bd Dirs J. P. Morgan & Co. Inc., New York, Morgan Guaranty Trust Co. of New York, American Petroleum Inst.; mem. Bd Dirs Nat. Action Council for Minorities in Eng Inc., New York 1985–, New American Schools Devt Corpn 1991–, Project Shelter PRO-AM 1991–; mem. American Petroleum Inst. (mem. Bd of Dirs 1987–), The Business Roundtable, American Council on Germany 1986–, British-N American Cttee 1985–, Singapore-US Business Council, Visitors' Cttee Univ. of Wis. Dept of Chem. Eng 1987–, Dallas Cttee on Foreign Relations 1988–, The Conf. Bd 1991–, Bd of Govs, Dallas Symphony Assn; Trustee American Enterprise Inst.; Public Service Star (Distinguished Friends of Singapore Award) 2004, Hon. Citizen of Singapore 2006. *Address:* c/o Board of Trustees, American Enterprise Institute, 1150 Seventeenth Street, NW, Washington, DC 20036, USA (office).

RAYMOND, Réal, MBA; Canadian banker; *Special Advisor, National Bank of Canada;* ed Univ. of Quebec, Montreal; joined National Bank 1970, Sr Vice-Pres. Treasury and Financial Markets 1992–99, Sr Exec. Vice-Pres. Corporate Financing Lévesque Beaubien Geoffrion (now National Bank Financial) 1997–99, Pres. Personal and Commercial Bank 1999–2001, Pres. and COO National Bank of Canada 2001–02, Pres. and CEO 2002–07 (retd), Special Advisor 2007–; Pres. Montreal Museum of Fine Arts Foundation; mem. Bd of Dirs Fondation de l'Univ. du Québec à Montréal, St Mary's Hosp. Foundation, Montreal Symphony Orchestra. *Address:* National Bank of Canada, National Bank Tower, 600 de la Gauchetière West, Montreal, PQ H3B 4L2, Canada (office). *Telephone:* (514) 394-5000 (office). *Fax:* (514) 394-8434 (office). *E-mail:* real.raymond@bnc.ca. *Website:* www.nbc.ca (office).

RAYMUND, Steven A., BS, MA; American computer industry executive; *Chairman, Tech Data Corporation;* b. 16 Nov. 1955, Van Nuys, Calif.; s. of Edward C. Raymund and Annette Leah Raymund; ed Univ. of Oregon, Georgetown Univ. School of Foreign Service, Washington, DC; early position with Manufacturers Hanover Corpn, New York 1980–81; Operations Man. Tech Data Corpn (distributor of computer products f. by Edward Raymund 1974) 1981–84, COO 1984–86, CEO 1986–2006, Chair. 1991–2006, Chair. (non-exec.) 2006–; mem. Bd of Dirs Jabil Circuit Inc. 1996–, WESCO Distribution, Inc. 2006–; Chair. St Petersburg Area Chamber of Commerce 2009; named to Industry Hall of Fame, Computer Reseller News (CRN) 1999. *Address:* Tech Data Corpn, 5350 Tech Data Drive, Clearwater, FL 33760-3122, USA (office). *Telephone:* (727) 539-7429 (office). *Fax:* (727) 538-7803 (office). *E-mail:* info@techdata.com (office). *Website:* www.techdata.com (office).

RAYNAUD, Jean-Pierre; French sculptor; b. 20 April 1939, Courbevoie; s. of André Raynaud and Madeleine Dumay; ed Ecole d'Horticulture du Chesnay; first one-man exhbn Galerie Larcade, Paris 1965; numerous other one-man shows in France, Europe, USA, Japan, Israel; retrospective exhbns. The Menil Collection, Houston, Museum of Contemporary Art, Chicago and Int. Centre of Contemporary Art, Montreal 1991, CAPC, Bordeaux 1993, Paume 1998, Jérôme de Noirmont Gallery, Paris 2001; Grand Prix Nat. de Sculpture 1983; Prix Robert Giron, Palais des Beaux Arts, Brussels 1985; Grand Prix de Sculpture de la Ville de Paris 1986, Prix d'honneur de la Biennale de Venise 1993; Officier des Arts et des Lettres, Chevalier du Mérite, Légion d'honneur. *Work includes:* windows at Cistercian Abbey at Noirlac, Cher 1976–77, large sculpture in gardens of Fondation Cartier pour l'Art Contemporain, Jouy-en-Josas 1985, Autoportrait for City of Québec 1987, Container Zero, Pompidou

Centre, Paris 1988, Carte du Ciel, Grande Arche, Paris La Défense 1989. *Address:* 12 avenue Rhin et Danube, 92250 La Garenne-Colombes, France.

RAYNES, Edward Peter, MA, PhD, FRS; British physicist and academic; *Professor of Optoelectronic Engineering, University of Oxford;* b. 4 July 1945, York; s. of Edward Gordon Raynes and Ethel Mary Raynes; m. Madeline Ord 1970; two s.; ed St Peter's School, York, Gonville and Caius Coll. and the Cavendish Lab., Cambridge; with Royal Signals and Radar Establishment, Malvern 1971–92, Deputy Chief Scientific Officer 1988–92; Chief Scientist Sharp Laboratories of Europe Ltd 1992–98, Dir of Research 1995–98; Visiting Prof., Dept of Eng Science, Univ. of Oxford 1996–98, Prof. of Optoelectronic Eng 1998–; Rank Opto-Electronic Prize 1980, Paterson Medal, Inst. of Physics 1986, Special Recognition Award, Soc. of Information Display 1987. *Publications:* numerous scientific publs and patents; The Physics, Chemistry and Applications of Liquid Crystals (Jt Ed.). *Leisure interests:* choral and solo singing. *Address:* Department of Engineering Science, University of Oxford, Parks Road, Oxford, OX1 3PJ, England (office). *Telephone:* (1865) 273024 (office). *Fax:* (1865) 273905 (office). *E-mail:* peter.raynes@eng.ox.ac.uk (office). *Website:* www.eng.ox.ac.uk/lcoms (office); www.eng.ox.ac.uk (office).

RAYNSFORD, Rt Hon. Wyvill Richard Nicolls (Nick), PC, MA; British politician; b. 28 Jan. 1945, Northampton, Northants.; s. of the late Wyvill Raynsford and Patricia Raynsford (née Dunn); m. Anne Jelley 1968; three d.; ed Repton School, Sidney Sussex Coll. Cambridge, Chelsea School of Art and Design; mem. staff, Soc. of Co-operative Dwellings, AC Nielen, Market Research; Dir SHAC, The London Housing Aid Centre 1976–86, Raynsford & Morris, Housing Consultants 1987–92; Councillor, London Borough of Hammersmith and Fulham 1971–75; MP for Fulham 1986–87, for Greenwich 1992–97, for Greenwich and Woolwich 1997–; mem. House of Commons Environment Select Cttee 1992–93; Front Bench Spokesperson for London 1993–94; Shadow Minister for Housing and Construction, Spokesperson for London 1994–97; Parl. Under-Sec. of State, Minister for London and Construction 1997–99; Minister of State for Housing, Planning and London July–Sept. 1999, for Housing and Planning 1999–2001, for Local Govt and the Regions 2001–04; mem. Nat. Energy Foundation 1989–93. *Publications:* A Guide to Housing Benefits 1982, Making Sense of Localism 2004, Choice Cuts 2004. *Leisure interests:* walking, photography. *Address:* House of Commons, Westminster, London, SW1A 0AA, England (office). *Telephone:* (20) 7219-2773 (office). *Fax:* (20) 7219-2619 (office). *E-mail:* raynsfordn@parliament.uk (office).

RAYTCHEV, Rayko Strahilov, MA; Bulgarian diplomatist; *Permanent Representative, United Nations;* b. 29 March 1955; m.; one d.; ed Higher Inst. of Econs, Sofia, John F. Kennedy School of Govt, Harvard Univ.; joined diplomatic corps as Attaché 1982, becoming Head UN Dept, Co-ordination and Planning Directorate 2000–01, Head UN and Gen. Issues Dept Jan.–Nov. 2001, Deputy Perm. Rep. to UN, New York 2001–05, with Foreign Ministry's NATO and Int. Security Directorate 2005, becoming Head Global Security and Disarmament Dept March–July 2005, Head Arms Control and Int. Security Dept July–Aug. 2005, Chief of Cabinet of Minister of Foreign Affairs 2005–07, Perm. Rep. to UN, New York 2007–; Certificate in Peacekeeping Negotiations and Mediation, Pearson Peacekeeping Centre, Canada 2001. *Address:* Permanent Mission of the Republic of Bulgaria to the United Nations, 11 East 84th Street, New York, NY 10028, USA (office). *Telephone:* (212) 737-4790 (office). *Fax:* (212) 472-9865 (office). *E-mail:* bulgaria@un.int (office). *Website:* www.un.int/bulgaria (office).

RAZ, Joseph, MA, MJr, DPhil, FBA; British (b. Israeli) philosopher and academic; b. 21 March 1939; ed Hebrew Univ., Jerusalem and Univ. of Oxford; Lecturer, Faculty of Law and Dept of Philosophy, Hebrew Univ. 1967–71, Sr Lecturer 1971–72; Fellow and Tutor in Law, Balliol Coll., Oxford 1972–85, also mem. sub-faculty of philosophy 1977–; Ed. (with Prof. A. M. Honoré), The Clarendon Law Series 1984–92; Prof. of Philosophy of Law, Univ. of Oxford and Fellow, Balliol Coll. 1985–2006, Research Prof. and Fellow Emer. 2006–09; Visiting Prof., School of Law, Columbia Univ., New York 1995–2002, Prof., Columbia Univ. Law School 2002–; Foreign Hon. Mem. American Acad. of Arts and Sciences; Dr hc (Katholieke Univ. Brussels) 1994; Hon. DJur (King's Coll., London); first Hector Fix-Zamudio Int. Prize for Legal Research (Univ. Nacional Autonoma de Mexico) 2005. *Publications:* The Concept of a Legal System 1970, Practical Reason and Norms 1975, The Authority of Law 1979, The Morality of Freedom (W.J.M. Mackenzie Book Prize, Political Studies Asscn of the UK, Elaine and David Spitz Book Prize, Conf. for the Study of Political Thought, NewYork) 1986, Ethics in the Public Domain 1994, Engaging Reason 2000, Value, Respect and Attachment 2001, The Practice of Value 2003. *Address:* Balliol College, Oxford, OX1 3BJ, England (office). *Telephone:* (1865) 277721 (office). *Fax:* (1865) 277803 (office). *E-mail:* joseph.raz@law.ox.ac.uk (office). *Website:* josephnraz.googlepages .com.

RAZAFINDRATANDRA, HE Cardinal Armand Gaétan; Malagasy ecclesiastic; *Archbishop Emeritus of Antananarivo;* b. 7 Aug. 1925; ed Inst. Catholique de Paris; ordained priest 1954; parochial and teaching assignments; consecrated Bishop of Majunga 1978; Archbishop of Antananarivo 1994–2005, Archbishop Emer. 2005–; Pres. Bishops' Conf. of Madagascar; mem. Sec.-Gen.'s Special Council for Africa; Congregation for Evangelization of Peoples, Pontifical Council for the Laity; cr. Cardinal 1994; Cardinal-Priest, Basilica of St Sylvester and St Martin of the Hills, Rome 1994. *Address:* Archevêché, BP 3030, Andohalo, 101 Antananarivo, Madagascar. *Telephone:* (20) 2220726. *Fax:* (20) 22664181. *E-mail:* ecar.andohaolo@simicro.mg (office).

RAZAFINJATOVO, Haja Nirina, MA, PhD; Malagasy politician; *Minister of Finance and the Budget;* ed Univ. of Connecticut, USA; fmr teacher Florida International Univ., James Madison Univ., Univ. of Connecticut; served as Computer Specialist at US Embassy, Antananarivo; Minister of Telecommunications, Posts and Communication 2002–04; Minister of Nat. Educ. and Scientific Research 2004–07, of Finance and the Budget 2007–. *Address:* Ministry of Finance and the Budget, BP 61, Antaninarenina, 101 Antananarivo, Madagascar (office). *Telephone:* (20) 2230173 (office). *Fax:* (20) 2264680 (office). *E-mail:* info@mefb.gov.mg (office). *Website:* www.mefb.gov.mg (office).

RAZAK, Dato' Seri Mohamad Najib bin tun Haj Abdul, BA; Malaysian politician; *Prime Minister and Minister of Finance;* b. 23 July 1953, Kuala Lipis, Pahang; m. Toh Puan Indera Datin Sri Rosmah Mansor; five c.; ed Univ. of Nottingham; Exec. Patronas 1974–76; Pengerusi Majuternak 1977–78; mem. Parl. 1976–; Deputy Minister of Energy, Telecommunications and Posts 1978–80, of Educ. 1980–81, of Finance 1981–82; mem. State Ass. for Pakan constituency 1982–86; Menteri Besar Pahang 1982–86; Minister of Culture, Youth and Sports 1986–87, of Youth and Sports 1987–90, of Defence 1990–95, 1999–2008, of Educ. 1995–99, of Finance 2008–; Deputy Prime Minister 2004–09, Prime Minister 2009–; mem. UMNO Supreme Council 1981–; Vice-Pres. UMNO Youth 1982–; Chair. Pahang Foundation 1982–86; Grand Order of Youth (Korea) 1988, Kt Grand Cross, First Class (Thailand), Bintang Yudha Dharma Utama (Indonesia) 1994, Distinguished Service Order (Singapore) 1994, DUBC (Thailand) 1995; Hon. PhD (US Acad. of Sports) 1992, (Nottingham) 2004; Orang Kaya Indera Shahbandar 1976, Darjah Sultan Ahmad Shah 1978, Seri Indera Mahkota Pahang 1983, Darjah Kebesaran Seri Sultan Ahmad Shah 1985, Man of the Year Award, New Straits Times 1990, Panglima Bintang Sarawak 1990, Dato Paduka Mahkota Selangor 1992, Seri Panglima Darjah Kinabalu (SPDK) 2002. *Address:* Prime Minister's Office, Federal Government Administration Center, Bangunan Perdana Putra, 62502 Putrajaya, Malaysia (office). *Telephone:* (3) 88888000 (office). *Fax:* (3) 88883444 (office). *E-mail:* ppm@pmo.gov.my (office). *Website:* www.pmo.gov .my (office).

RAZALEIGH, Tan Sri Tengku Hamzah, PSM, SPMK; Malaysian politician and fmr company executive; b. c. 1936; s. of late Tengku Mohamed Hamzah bin Zainal Abidin (fmr Chief Minister of Kelantan); ed Queen's Univ., Belfast and Lincoln's Inn, London; Chair. of Kelantan Div. of United Malays' Nat. Org. (UMNO) in early 1960s; mem. Kelantan State Assembly for some years; Exec. Dir Bank Bumiputra 1963, Chair., Man. Dir 1970; mem. Parl. for Gua Musang 1969–; Exec. Dir PERNAS 1971–74; Chair. Malaysian Nat. Insurance; led trade mission to Beijing 1971; a Vice-Pres. UMNO 1975; Pres. Assoc. Malay Chambers of Commerce until Oct. 1976; Chair. PETRONAS (Nat. Oil Co.) 1974–76; Minister of Finance 1976–84, of Trade and Industry 1984–87; Chair. IMF Meetings 1978, Asram Devt Bank 1977–, Islamic Devt Bank 1977; mem. United Malays National Organization (Pertubuhan Kebangsaan Melayu Bersatu) (UMNO Baru) (New UMNO). *Address:* United Malays National Organization (Pertubuhan Kebangsaan Melayu Bersatu) (UMNO Baru) (New UMNO), Menara Dato' Onn, 38th Floor, Jalan Tun Ismail, 50480 Kuala Lumpur, Malaysia. *Telephone:* (3) 40429511. *Fax:* (3) 40412358. *E-mail:* email@umno.net.my. *Website:* www.umno-online.com.

RAZBOROV, Alexander A., DPhysMathSci; Russian mathematician, computational theorist and academic; *Leading Researcher, Department of Mathematical Logic, Steklov Mathematical Institute, Russian Academy of Sciences;* b. 16 Feb. 1963; Leading Researcher, Dept of Math. Logic, Steklov Math. Inst., Russian Acad. of Sciences, Moscow; Corresp. mem. Russian Acad. of Sciences; Nevanlinna Prize, Univ. of Helsinki 1990, Tarski Lecturer, Univ. of Calif., Berkeley 2000, Gödel Prize, Asscn for Computing Machinery (with Steven Rudich) 2007. *Publications:* numerous articles in math. journals. *Address:* Steklov Mathematical Institute, Gubkina str.8, 119991 Moscow, Russian Federation (office). *Telephone:* (495) 938-37-44 (office). *Fax:* (495) 135-05-55 (office). *E-mail:* razborov@mi.ras.ru (office); razborov@genesis.mi.ras.ru (office). *Website:* www.mi.ras.ru/~razborov (office).

RAZI, Syed Sibtey, BCom, LLB; Indian politician; *Governor of Jharkhand;* b. 7 March 1939, Jais, Rai Bareli Dist, Uttar Pradesh (UP); s. of the late Syed Wirasat Husain and Razia Begum; m. Chand Farhana 1973; two s. two d.; ed Husainabad Higher Secondary School, Shia Coll., Lucknow Univ.; began political career as student leader, elected Pres. Commerce Asscn, Lucknow Univ.; Pres. Shia Coll. Student Union 1958–59; joined Congress Party in 1969, Gen. Sec. UP Youth Congress 1971–73; Vice-Pres. Youth Welfare Bd, UP Govt 1975–77; mem. Parl. (Rajya Sabha) 1980–85, 1988–98, Chair. Jt Select Cttee on Copyright Amendment Bill 1993, Jt Standing Cttee attached to Ministry of Science and Tech., Environment and Forest 1993–95, Vice-Chair. Rajya Sabha (Panel of Presiding Officers) 1993–95; Gen. Sec. UP Congress Cttee 1980–84, Vice-Pres. 2000–02; mem. UP Legis. Council 1985–88; Minister of Educ. and Muslim Waqf, UP Govt 1985–88; mem. All India Congress Cttee 1985–2004, Jt Sec. 1984–85, Spokesperson 2002–04; mem. Indian Del. led by Prime Minister Indira Gandhi to 9th Non-Aligned Movt Summit, New Delhi 1983, Indian Del. to 42nd UN Gen. Ass. 1986; Vice-Chair. UP Institutional Finance Corpn, UP Govt July–Dec. 1988; Deputy Leader Parl. Congress Party 1993–95; Union Minister of State for Home Affairs 1995–96; Gov. of Jharkhand 2004–; mem. Bd of Dirs Associated Journals Ltd 1988–95; mem. Exec. Cttee CPP 1992–94; Chair. Sarvodaya Degree Coll., Salon, Rai Bareli 1999–2004; mem., NGO del. to Human Rights Comm., Geneva 2000–01, Aligarh Muslim Univ. Court 2002–04, Exec. Council Maulana Azad Urdu Univ., Hyderabad 2002–04; Repertoire of Social Justice Cttee, All India Congress Cttee, Simla Camp 2003; widely travelled abroad. *Address:* Raj Bhavan, Ranchi 834001, Jharkhand (office); D2/3, River Bank Colony, Lucknow, Uttar Pradesh, India. *Telephone:* (651) 2283465 (office). *Fax:* (651) 2201101 (office). *E-mail:* info@rajbhavanjharkhand.nic.in (office). *Website:* rajbhavanjharkhand.nic.in (office).

RAZOV, Sergey Sergeyevich, PhD; Russian diplomatist and economist; *Ambassador to People's Republic of China;* b. 28 Jan. 1953, Sochi, Krasnodar

Territory; m.; two c.; ed Moscow Inst. of Int. Relations; economist, sr economist USSR Trade Mission to Repub. of China 1975–79; head of div., head of group Cen. CPSU Cttee 1979–90; Head Dept of Far East Countries and Indochina, USSR Ministry of Foreign Affairs 1990–92; Amb. to Mongolia 1992–96; Dir Third Dept of CIS Countries, Russian Ministry of Foreign Affairs 1996–99; Amb. to Poland 1999–2002, to People's Repub. of China 2005–; Deputy Minister of Foreign Affairs 2002–05. *Publications:* The People's Republic of China 1991, Foreign Policy of Open Doors of People's Republic of China 1985; articles and other publs. *Address:* Embassy of the Russian Federation, 4 Dong Zhi Men Nei, Bei Zhong Jie, Beijing 100600, People's Republic of China (office). *Telephone:* (10) 65322051 (office). *Fax:* (10) 65324851 (office). *E-mail:* embassy@russia.org.cn (office). *Website:* www.russia.org.cn (office).

RE, HE Cardinal Giovanni Battista; Italian ecclesiastic; *Prefect of the Congregation for Bishops;* b. 30 Jan. 1934, Borno, Brescia; ordained priest 1957; consecrated Bishop 1987; Titular Archbishop of Vescovio; Asst Sec. of State, General Affairs; Prefect of Congregation for Bishops and Pres. Pontifical Comm. for Latin America 2000–; cr. Cardinal 2001, Cardinal Priest of Ss. XII Apostoli Feb. 2001, Cardinal Bishop of Sabina-Poggio Mirteto Oct. 2001. *Address:* Congregation for the Bishops, Palazzo delle Congregazioni, Piazza Pio XII 10, 00193 Rome, Italy (office); Palazzina dell'Arciprete, 00120 Vatican City. *Telephone:* (06) 69884217 (office); (06) 69883942. *Fax:* (06) 69885303 (office). *E-mail:* vati07@cbishops.va (office). *Website:* www.vatican.va/roman_curia/congregations/cbishops/index.htm (office).

REA, Stephen James; Irish actor; b. 1949, Belfast, Northern Ireland; s. of James Rea and Jane Rea (née Logue); m. Dolours Price 1983; two s.; ed Queen's Univ., Belfast; formed (with Brian Friel q.v.) Field Day Theatre Co. 1980; Hon. DLitt (Univ. of Staffs.) 1999, (Univ. of Ulster) 2004, Hon. DUniv (Queen's Univ., Belfast) 2004. *Stage appearances include:* The Shadow of a Gunman, The Cherry Orchard, Miss Julie, High Society, Endgame, The Freedom of the City, Translations, Communication Card, St Oscar, Boesman and Lena, Hightime and Riot Act, Double Cross, Pentecost, Making History, Someone Who'll Watch Over Me 1992 (Broadway, New York), Uncle Vanya 1995; at Nat. Theatre: Ashes to Ashes 1997, Playboy of the Western World, Comedians, The Shaughraun, Cyrano de Bergerac (Nat. Theatre) 2004. *Directed:* Three Sisters, The Cure at Troy, Northern Star 1998. *Films include:* Angel 1982, Company of Wolves 1985, The Doctor and the Devils 1985, Loose Connections 1988, Life is Sweet 1991, The Crying Game 1992, Bad Behaviour 1993, Princess Caraboo 1993, Angie 1994, Interview with the Vampire 1994, Prêt-à-Porter 1994, All Men are Mortal 1994, Citizen X 1994, The Devil and the Deep Blue Sea 1994, Michael Collins 1995, Trojan Eddie 1995, A Further Gesture 1995, The Butcher Boy 1998, Guinevere 1999, The End of the Affair 2000, I Could Read the Sky 2000, Fear Dot Com 2002, Proud 2003, Bloom 2003, The Halo Effect 2004, Romeo and Me 2004, The Good Shepherd 2004, Fluent Dysphasia 2004, Proud 2004, Breakfast on Pluto 2005, River Queen 2005, V for Vendetta 2006, Sixty Six 2006, Until Death 2007, The Reaping 2007. *TV appearances include:* Four Days in July, Lost Belongings, Scout, St Oscar, Not with a Bang, Hedda Gabler, Crime of the Century, Copenhagen 2002, I Didn't Know You Cared. *Address:* c/o ICM, 76 Oxford Street, London, W1N 0AX, England (office). *Telephone:* (20) 7636-6565 (office).

READ, Sir John Emms, Kt, FCA, FIB; British business executive (retd); b. 29 March 1918, Brighton; s. of William E. Read and Daysie E. Read (née Cooper); m. Dorothy M. Berry 1942 (died 2004); two s.; ed Brighton, Hove and Sussex Grammar School and Admin. Staff Coll., Henley-on-Thames; Commdr RN 1939–46; Adm.'s Sec. to Asst Chief of Naval Staff, Admiralty 1942–45, Naval Sec., British Admiralty Tech. Mission, Ottawa 1945–46; Ford Motor Co. 1946–64, Dir of Sales 1961–64; Exec. Dir EMI Ltd 1965, Man. Dir 1966–69, CEO 1969–79, Deputy Chair. 1973–74, Chair. 1974–79; Deputy Chair. Thorn EMI Ltd 1979–80, Dir 1981–87; Chair. Trustee Savings Bank Cen. Bd 1980–88, Trustee Savings Banks (Holdings) Ltd 1980–86, TSB England and Wales 1983–86, TSB Group PLC 1986–88, (Dir TSB England and Wales PLC 1986–88), United Dominions Trust Ltd 1981–85; Dir Dunlop Holdings Ltd 1971–84, Thames Television Ltd 1973–88 (Deputy Chair. 1981–88), Capitol Industries-EMI Inc., USA 1970–83, Wonderworld PLC 1986–97, FI Group PLC 1989–94, Nat. Youth Film Foundation 1987–90, Cadmus Investment Man. Ltd 1993–98, Cafman Ltd (now Cafcash) 1994–2000, Cafinvest Ltd 1994–96; mem. P.O. Bd 1975–77, Royal Naval Film Corpn 1975–83, British Overseas Trade Bd 1976–79; Chair. Electronics Econ. Devt Comm. 1976–80, Armed Forces Pay Review Body 1976–83, Nat. Electronics Council 1977–80, Gov. Admin. Staff Coll., Henley 1974–92; mem. Council of CBI 1977–89, Pres.'s Cttee 1977–84, Chair. Finance Cttee 1978–84; Trustee, Westminster Abbey Trust 1978–87, Charity Aid Foundation 1985–98 (Pres. 1994–98), Crimestoppers Trust 1987–2001; Chair. Cttee of Man. Inst. of Neurology 1980–97, Brain Research Trust 1982–2001 (Pres. 2002–); Pres. Sussex Asscn of Boys' Clubs 1982–97, Cheshire Homes, Seven Rivers, Essex 1979–85, Essex Blind 2004–; Vice-Pres. Inst. of Bankers 1982–89; mem. Cttee of London and Scottish Bankers 1986–88, Governing Body, British Postgraduate Medical Fed. 1982–96; Fellow, RSA 1975–90; Hon. Fellow, Henley Man. Coll. 1993, Univ. Coll. London 1999; Companion, Inst. of Radio Engineers, Chartered Man. Inst.; Hon. DUniv (Surrey) 1987; Hon. DBA (Buckingham) 1988. *Leisure interests:* music, the arts, sport, various charities. *Address:* Flat 68, 15 Portman Square, London, W1H 6LL, England. *Telephone:* (20) 7935-7888.

READ, Piers Paul, MA, FRSL; British writer; b. 7 March 1941, Beaconsfield, Bucks.; s. of Herbert Edward Read and Margaret Ludwig; m. Emily Albertine Boothby 1967; two s. two d.; ed Ampleforth Coll., York and St John's Coll., Cambridge; Artist-in-Residence, Ford Foundation, W Berlin 1964; Sub-Ed. Times Literary Supplement, London 1965; Harkness Fellow Commonwealth Fund, New York 1967–68; Council mem. Inst. of Contemporary Arts (ICA), London 1971–75; Cttee of Man. Soc. of Authors, London 1973–76; mem. Literature Panel Arts Council, London 1975–77; Adjunct Prof. of Writing, Columbia Univ., New York 1980; Chair. Catholic Writers' Guild 1992–97; mem. Bd Aid to the Church in Need 1991–; Trustee Catholic Library 1997–; mem. Council RSL 2001–; Sir Geoffrey Faber Memorial Prize 1968, Somerset Maugham Award 1969, Hawthornden Prize 1969, Thomas More Award (USA) 1976, James Tait Black Memorial Prize 1988. *Publications:* Game in Heaven with Tussy Marx 1966, The Junkers 1968, Monk Dawson 1969, The Professor's Daughter 1971, The Upstart 1973, Alive: The Story of the Andes Survivors 1974, Polonaise 1976, The Train Robbers 1978, A Married Man 1979, The Villa Golitsyn 1981, The Free Frenchman 1986, A Season in the West 1988, On the Third Day 1990, Quo Vadis? The Subversion of the Catholic Church 1991, Ablaze: The Story of Chernobyl 1993, A Patriot in Berlin 1995, Knights of The Cross 1997, The Templars 1999, Alice in Exile 2001, Alec Guinness: The Authorised Biography 2003, Hell and Other Essays 2006. *Leisure interest:* family life. *Address:* 50 Portland Road, London, W11 4LG, England (home). *Telephone:* (20) 7460-2499 (office); (20) 7727-5719 (home). *E-mail:* piersread@dial.pipex.com (office).

READE, Hamish (see GRAY, Simon James Holliday).

REAGAN, Nancy Davis, BA; American actress and fmr First Lady; b. (Anne Francis Robbins), 6 July 1921, New York; d. of Kenneth Robbins and Edith Robbins (née Luckett), step-d. of Loyal Davis; m. Ronald Reagan 1952 (died 2004); one s. one d., one step-s. one step-d.; ed Smith Coll., Mass.; contract actress Metro-Goldwyn-Mayer 1949–56; fmr author syndicated column on prisoners-of-war and soldiers missing in action; civic worker active on behalf of Viet Nam war veterans, sr citizens, disabled children and drug victims; First Lady 1981–89; mem. Bd of Dirs Revlon Group Inc. 1989–; Hon. Nat. Chair. Aid to Adoption of Special Kids 1977; one of Ten Most Admired American Women, Good Housekeeping Magazine 1977, Woman of Year, LA Times 1977, perm. mem. Hall of Fame of Ten Best Dressed Women in US, Lifetime Achievement Award, Council of Fashion Designers of USA 1988, numerous awards for role in fight against drug abuse. *Films include:* The Doctor and the Girl 1949, East Side, West Side 1949, Shadow on the Wall 1950, The Next Voice You Hear 1950, Night Into Morning 1951, It's a Big Country 1951, Talk About a Stranger 1952, Donovan's Brain 1953, Hellcats of the Navy 1957, Crash Landing 1958. *Publications:* Nancy 1980, To Love A Child (with Jane Wilkie), My Turn (memoirs) 1989. *Address:* 2121 Avenue of the Stars, 34th Floor, Los Angeles, CA 90067, USA.

REARDON, Raymond (Ray), MBE; British snooker player; b. 8 Oct. 1932, Tredegar, Wales; s. of Benjamin Reardon and Cynthia Jenkins; m. 1st Susan Carter (divorced); one s. one d.; m. 2nd Carol Lovington 1987; ed Georgeton Secondary Modern School, Tredegar; Welsh Amateur Champion 1950–55; English Amateur Champion 1964; turned professional 1967; six times World Snooker Champion 1970–78; Benson & Hedges Masters Champion 1976; Welsh Champion 1977, 1981, 1983; Professional Players Champion 1982; retd 1992; active in running World Professional Billiards and Snooker Asscn; occasional appearances on BBC TV's Big Break show. *Publications:* Classic Snooker 1974, Ray Reardon (autobiog.) 1982. *Leisure interest:* golf.

REBE, Bernd Werner, DrIur; German academic and fmr university president; b. 5 Sept. 1939, Braunlage; s. of Werner Rebe and Liselotte Rebe; m. 1st Bärbel Bonewitz 1964 (died 1993); two s.; m. 2nd Katharina Ribe (née Becker) 1999; ed Univ. of Kiel, Freie Univ. Berlin and Univ. of Bielefeld; Prof. of Civil Law, Commercial Law, Competition Law and Corpn Law, Univ. of Hannover 1975, Vice-Pres. Univ. of Hannover 1979–81; Pres. Tech. Univ. of Braunschweig 1983–99, Prof. of Constitutional and Media Law 1999–2005; mem. Senate W German Rectors' Conf. 1988; Pres. Rectors' Conf. of Lower Saxony 1989; Hon. Citizen Otto-von-Guericke-Universität Magdeburg. *Publications:* Die Träger der Pressefreiheit nach dem Grundgesetz 1970, Privatrecht und Wirtschaftsordnung 1978, Arbeitslosigkeit—unser Schicksal? 1983, Neue Technologien und die Entwicklung von Wirtschaft und Gesellschaft 1984, Verfassung und Verwaltung des Landes Niedersachsen 1986, Nutzen und Wahrheit: Triebkräfte der Wissenschaftsentwicklung 1991, Die Universität heute—Leitinstitution ohne Leitbild? 1991, Umweltverträgliches Wirtschaften—Wettbewerbsvorteile, Marktchancen, Wohlstandssicherung 1993, Denkerkundungen. Reden wider die Vordergründigkeit 1995, Die unvollendete Einheit. Bestandsaufnahme und Perspektiven für die Wirtschaft 1996, Vision und Verantwortung 1999, Humanität—Wandel—Utopie 2000; Medienrecht als Paradigma "modernen" Rechts? in: FS für Rehbinder, 2002. *Leisure interests:* swimming, skiing, tennis, history, politics. *Address:* Weisser Kuhl 13, 38162 Cremlingen, Germany (home). *Telephone:* (531) 8669292 (home).

REBEK, Julius, Jr., BA, PhD; American chemist and academic; *Director, Skaggs Institute for Chemical Biology, Scripps Research Institute;* b. 11 April 1944, Beregszasz, Hungary; s. of Julius Rebek Sr and Eva Racz; m. (divorced); two d.; ed Univ. of Kansas and Mass. Inst. of Tech. (MIT); lived in Austria 1945–49; Asst Prof., UCLA 1970–76; Assoc. Prof., Univ. of Pittsburgh 1976–80, Prof. 1980–89; Prof., Dept of Chem., MIT 1989–96, Camille Dreyfus Prof. of Chem. 1991–96; Dir Skaggs Inst. for Chemical Biology, Scripps Research Inst. 1996–; Nat. Science Foundation Fellow 1967–70; Sloan Fellow 1977; von Humboldt Fellow 1981; Guggenheim Fellow 1986; mem. ACS, NAS; Fellow, American Acad. of Arts and Sciences; Cope Scholar Award 1991, James Flack Norris Award in Physical Chem. 1997, Chemical Pioneer Award, American Inst. of Chemists 2002, Ronald Breslow Award for Achievement in Biomimetic Chem., ACS 2004, Medal of the Acad. of Sciences, Czech Repub. 2005, Medal of the Nat. Acad. of Sciences, Letters and Arts, Italy 2005, Distinguished Scientist Award, ACS 2006, Evans Award, Ohio State Univ. 2006, Univ. of Oregon Creativity Award in Chemistry, Dance and Music 2007, Humboldt Sr Scientist Award, Germany 2008, Tau-Shue Chou Award, Academica Sinica 2008. *Publications:* 427 publs in scientific journals. *Leisure* *interest:* tennis. *Address:* Rebek Laboratory, Skaggs Institute for Chemical Biology, Scripps Research Institute, 10550 North Torrey Pines Road, La Jolla, CA 92037 (office); 2330 Calle del Oro, La Jolla, CA 92037, USA (home). *Telephone:* (858) 784-2250 (office). *Fax:* (858) 784-2876 (office). *E-mail:* jrebek@scripps.edu (office). *Website:* www.scripps.edu/skaggs/rebek (office).

REBUCK, Gail Ruth, CBE, BA, FRSA; British publishing executive; *Chairman and CEO, Random House Group Ltd;* b. 10 Feb. 1952, London; d. of Gordon Rebuck and Mavis Rebuck; m. Philip Gould (q.v.) 1985; two d.; ed Lycée Français de Londres, Univ. of Sussex; Production Asst, Grisewood & Dempsey (children's book packager) 1975–76; Ed., later Publr Robert Nicholson Publs London Guidebooks 1976–79; Publr Hamlyn Paperbacks 1979–82; Founder Partner Century Publishing Co. Ltd, Publishing Dir Non-Fiction 1982–85, Publr Century Hutchinson 1985–89, Chair. Random House Div., Random Century 1989–91, Chair. and Chief Exec. Random House UK Ltd (now Random House Group) 1991–; mem. COPUS 1995–97, Creative Industries Task Force 1997–2000; mem. Bd of Dirs (non-exec.) Work Foundation 2001–, BSkyB 2002–; mem. Court Univ. of Sussex 1997–, Council RCA 1999–; Trustee Inst. for Public Policy Research 1993–2003; mem. Court of Univ. of Sussex; mem. Advisory Bd Cambridge Judge Inst.; ranked 25th by the Financial Times amongst Top 25 Businesswomen in Europe 2005, Veuve Clicquot Businesswoman of the Year 2009. *Leisure interests:* reading, travel. *Address:* The Random House Group Ltd, 20 Vauxhall Bridge Road, London, SW1V 2SA, England (office). *Telephone:* (20) 7840-8886 (office). *Fax:* (20) 7233-6120 (office). *E-mail:* grebuck@randomhouse.co.uk (office). *Website:* www.randomhouse.co.uk.

REDDY, K. Anji, PhD; Indian pharmaceuticals industry executive; *Chairman, Dr Reddy's Laboratories Ltd;* ed Andhra Christian Coll., Guntur, Univ. of Bombay (now Mumbai), Nat. Chemical Lab., Pune; worked for Indian Drugs and Pharmaceuticals Ltd 1969–75; Founder and Man. Dir Uniloids Ltd 1976–80; Man. Dir Standard Organics Ltd 1980–84; Founder and Chair. Dr Reddy's Laboratories Ltd 1984–; Founder Dr Reddy's Research Foundation, Dr Reddy's Foundation for Human and Social Devt; Chair. Bd of Dirs GAIN Foundation, Geneva; mem. Bd of Dirs Diana Hotels Ltd, Biotech India Consortium Ltd, Biomed Ltd, WaterHealth International, Inc. 2005–; mem. Bd of Trade; Sir P.C. Ray Award, Indian Chemical Manufacturers Asscn 1984, 1992, Achiever of the Year Award, Chemtech Foundation 2000, Padmashri Award 2001. *Address:* Dr Reddy's Laboratories Ltd, Corporate Office, 7-1-27 Ameerpet, Hyderabad 500 016, India (office). *Telephone:* (40) 66511532 (office). *Fax:* (40) 23739666 (office). *Website:* www.drreddys.com (office).

REDDY, K. Srinath, MSc, MD; Indian cardiologist, epidemiologist and academic; *Professor of Cardiology, All India Institute of Medical Sciences;* ed All India Inst. of Medical Sciences, New Delhi, McMaster Univ., Canada; Prof. of Cardiology, All India Inst. of Medical Sciences, New Delhi; coordinator Cardiovascular Health Research Initiative in Developing Countries; Chair. World Heart Fed.'s Scientific Council on Epidemiology and Prevention; mem. WHO Scientific Advisory Cttee on Tobacco Product Regulation; Ed. Nat. Medical Journal of India; Fellow Nat. Acad. of Medical Sciences; Padma Bhushan 2005; WHO Dir-Gen.'s Award for Outstanding Contrib. to Global Tobacco Control 2003, Queen Elizabeth Medal Royal Soc. for Promotion of Health 2005. *Publications:* contrib. over 200 papers and articles in scientific journals. *Address:* All India Institute of Medical Sciences, Sri Aurobindo Marg, Ansari Nagar, New Delhi 110 029, India (office). *Website:* www.aiims.edu.

REDDY, Y. S. Rajasekhara, MBBS; Indian surgeon and politician; *Chief Minister of Andhra Pradesh;* b. 8 July 1949, Pulivendula, Cuddapah Dist; s. of the late Raja Reddy; m. Smt. Vijayalakshmi 1971; one s. one d.; ed M. R. Coll. of Gulbarga, S. V. Medical Coll., Tirupathy; fmr Medical Officer, CSI Campbell Hosp., Jammalamadugu; est. Y.S. Raja Reddy Hosp., Pulivendula 1973; elected to Andhra Pradesh Legis. Ass. (Indian Nat. Congress) 1978, Minister of Rural Devt, Health and Educ. 1980–83, Leader of Opposition 1999–2004; Pres. Andhra Pradesh Congress Cttee 1983–85, 1998–2000; served four terms in Lok Sabha; Chief Minister of Andhra Pradesh 2004–. *Address:* Office of the Chief Minister, Government of Andhra Pradesh, C-Block, 4th Floor, AP Secretariat, Hyderabad (office); Greenlands Circle, Begumpet, Hyderabad, India (home). *Telephone:* (40) 23456698 (office); (40) 23410333 (home). *Fax:* (40) 23452498 (office). *E-mail:* cmap@ap.nic.in (office). *Website:* www.aponline.gov.in (office); www.ysr.in.

REDDY, Y. Venugopal; Indian central banker and academic; *Governor, Reserve Bank of India;* joined Indian Admin. Service in 1964, has held several key positions including Sec. (Banking), Ministry of Finance, Additional Sec., Ministry of Commerce, Jt Sec., Ministry of Finance, Prin. Sec., Govt of Andhra Pradesh; Deputy Gov. Reserve Bank of India 1996–2002, Gov. 2003–; Exec. Dir for India, Sri Lanka, Bangladesh and Bhutan, IMF 2002–; Visiting Prof., Osmania Univ.; Visiting Faculty in Admin. Staff, Coll. of India; fmr Visiting Fellow, LSE. *Publications include:* numerous publications on finance, planning and public enterprises. *Address:* Reserve Bank of India, Central Office Building, Shahid Bhagat Singh Road, POB 10007, Mumbai, 400 001, India (office). *Telephone:* (22) 22661602 (office). *Fax:* (22) 22658269 (office). *E-mail:* helpprd@rbi.org.in (office). *Website:* www.rbi.org.in (office).

REDFORD, (Charles) Robert, Jr; American actor and director; *President, Sundance Group;* b. 18 Aug. 1936, Santa Monica, Calif.; s. of Charles Robert Redford, Sr and Martha W. Redford (née Hart); m. Lola Van Wegenen 1958 (divorced 1985); two s. (one s. died 1959) two d.; ed Van Nuys High School, Univ. of Colorado, Boulder, Pratt Inst. of Design, American Acad. of Dramatic Arts, New York; Founder and Pres. The Sundance Group 1981–, includes Sundance Channel, Sundance Ski Resort, Utah, Sundance Catalog, Sundance Cinemas, North Fork Preservation Alliance, and Sundance Inst., sponsor of

Sundance Film Festival; currently narrator for the Cosmic Collision movie at the Denver Nature and Science Planetarium; Hon. DHumLitt (Bard Coll.) 1995; hon. degrees from Univ. of Colorado, Boulder 1983, Brown Univ. 2008; Audubon Medal 1989, Dartmouth Film Soc. Award 1990, Screen Actors' Guild Award for Lifetime Achievement 1996, Hon. Acad. Award 2002, Kennedy Center Honor 2005. *Films include:* Tall Story 1960, War Hunt 1961, Situation Hopeless But Not Serious 1965, Inside Daisy Clover 1965, The Chase 1965, This Property is Condemned 1966, Barefoot in the Park 1967, Tell Them Willie Boy is Here 1969, Butch Cassidy and the Sundance Kid 1969, Downhill Racer 1969, Little Fauss and Big Halsy 1970, Jeremiah Johnson 1972, The Candidate 1972, How to Steal a Diamond in Four Uneasy Lessons 1972, The Way We Were 1973, The Sting 1973, The Great Gatsby 1974, The Great Waldo Pepper 1974, Three Days of the Condor 1975, All the President's Men 1976, A Bridge Too Far 1977, Ordinary People (dir; Acad. Award and Golden Globe Award for Best Dir 1981) 1980, The Electric Horseman 1980, Brubaker 1980, The Natural 1984, Out of Africa 1985, Legal Eagles 1986, Milagro Beanfield War 1988 (also producer), Promised Land (exec. producer) 1988, Havana 1991, Sneakers 1992, A River Runs Through It (also dir) 1992, Quiz Show (dir) 1994, The River Wild 1995, Up Close and Personal 1996, The Horse Whisperer (also dir and producer) 1997, The Legend of Bagger Vance (also dir and producer) 2000, How to Kill Your Neighbour's Dog (exec. producer) 2000, The Last Castle 2001, Spy Game 2001, The Motorcycle Diaries (exec. producer) 2004, The Clearing 2004, Sacred Planet (narrator) 2004, An Unfinished Life 2005, Charlotte's Web (voice) 2006, The Unforeseen (exec. producer) 2006, Lions for Lambs (also dir) 2007. *Television includes:* Skinwalkers (exec. producer) 2002, Coyote Waits (exec. producer) 2003, A Thief of Time (exec. producer) 2004, Iconoclasts (documentary series) 2005–07. *Address:* c/o Sundance Institute, PO Box 684429, Park City, UT 84068 (office); c/o Sundance Institute, 8530 Wilshire Blvd, 3rd Floor, Beverly Hills, CA 90211-3114 (office); c/o David O'Conner, Creative Artists Agency, 9830 Wilshire Boulevard, Beverly Hills, CA 90212, USA (office). *Telephone:* (801) 328-3456 (Sundance) (office). *Fax:* (801) 575-5175 (Sundance) (office). *E-mail:* institute@sundance.org (office); la@sundance.org (office). *Website:* institute.sundance.org (office).

REDGRAVE, Lynn; British actress; b. 8 March 1943, London; d. of the late Sir Michael Redgrave and Rachel Kempson; sister of Vanessa Redgrave (q.v.); m. John Clark 1967; one s. two d.; ed Cen. School of Speech and Drama; Broadway debut in Black Comedy; other stage appearances include: My Fat Friend 1974, Mrs Warren's Profession, Knock Knock, Misalliance, St Joan, Twelfth Night (American Shakespeare Festival), Sister Mary Ignatius Explains It All for You, Aren't We All?, Sweet Sue, Les Liaisons Dangereuses; one-woman show Shakespeare for My Father (US and Canada tours, also in Melbourne and London 1996) 1993, Moon over Buffalo 1996, The Mandrake Root 2001, Noises Off 2001; numerous TV appearances. *Films:* Tom Jones, Girl With Green Eyes, Georgy Girl, The Deadly Affair, Smashing Time, The Virgin Soldiers, The Last of the Mobile Hot-Shots, Viva La Muerta Tua, Every Little Crook and Nanny, Everything You Always Wanted to Know About Sex, Don't Turn the Other Cheek, The National Health, The Happy Hooker, The Big Bus, Sunday Lovers, Morgan Stewart's Coming Home, Midnight, Getting It Right, Shine 1996, Gods and Monsters 1998, The Annihilation of Fish 1999, Touched 1999, Strike 2000, The Simian Line 2000, Deeply 2000, How to Kill Your Neighbour's Dog 2000, The Next Best Thing 2000, Lion of Oz (voice) 2000, Venus and Mars 2001, Varian's War (TV) 2001, My Kingdom 2001, My Kingdom 2001, My Sister's Keeper (TV) 2002, Spider 2002, Unconditional Love 2002, The Wild Thornberrys Movie 2002, Hansel and Gretel 2002, Anita and Me 2002, Charlie's War 2003, Peter Pan 2003, The White Countess 2005, The Jane Austen Book Club 2007. *Leisure interests:* cooking, gardening, horse riding. *Address:* c/o John Clark, PO Box 1207, Topanga, CA 90290, USA. *Telephone:* (310) 455-1334. *Fax:* (310) 455-1032. *Website:* www.redgrave.com.

REDGRAVE, Sir Steven Geoffrey (Steve), Kt, CBE; British fmr oarsman; b. 23 March 1962, Marlow, Bucks.; m. Elizabeth Ann Redgrave; one s. two d.; ed Marlow Comprehensive School; rep. UK at Jr World Championships 1979, 1980, silver medal (with Clift) rep. Marlow Rowing Club 1976–2000, Leander 1987–2000; stroke, British coxed four, gold medal winners, Los Angeles Olympic Games 1984; gold medals, single scull, coxless pair (with Andy Holmes) and coxed four, Commonwealth Games 1986, coxed pair (with Holmes), World Championships 1986; coxless pair gold medal and coxed pair silver medal (with Holmes), World Championships 1987; gold medal (with Holmes), coxless pair and bronze medal, coxed pair, Olympic Games, Seoul 1988; silver medal (with Simon Berrisford), coxless pairs, World Championships 1989; bronze medal, coxless pair (with Matthew Pinsent q.v.) World Championships, Tasmania 1990; gold medal, coxless pair (with Pinsent), World Championships, Vienna 1991; gold medal, Olympic Games, Barcelona 1992; gold medal, World Championships, Czech Repub. 1993; gold medal, Indianapolis, 1994; gold medal, Finland 1995; gold medal, Olympic Games, Atlanta 1996; gold medal, coxless four (with Pinsent, Foster, Cracknell), Aiguebelette 1997; gold medal, coxless four, Cologne 1998; gold medal, coxless four (with Pinsent, Coode, Cracknell), St Catherines 1999; gold medal, Olympic Games, Sydney 2000; holds record for most consecutive Olympic gold medals won in an endurance event (five); f. Sir Steve Redgrave Charitable Trust, Steve Redgrave Fund (with Comic Relief); Vice-Pres. SPARKS, Steward Henley Royal Regatta; active in raising money for children's charities; Hon. Pres. Amateur Rowing Asscn; Hon. Vice-Pres. British Olympic Asscn, Diabetes UK; Hon. DCL (Durham) 1996, Hon. DSc 2001, (Buckingham) 2001, (Hull), Hon. DLitt (Reading, Nottingham), Hon. DUniv (Buckingham Chiltern, Heriot-Watt, Oxford Brookes, Open Univ.); Hon. DTech (Loughborough), Hon. LLD (Aberdeen) 2007; BBC Sports Personality of the Year 2000, British Sports Writers' Asscn Sportsman of the Year 2000, Laureus Lifetime Achievement Award 2001, BBC Golden Sports Personality 2003. *Publications:* Steven Redgrave's Complete Book of Rowing 1992, A Golden Age (autobiog.)

2000, You Can Win at Life 2005. *Leisure interest:* golf, skiing. *Address:* c/o IMG, McCormack House, Burlington Lane, London, W4 2TH, England (office). *Telephone:* (20) 8233-5300 (office). *Fax:* (20) 8233-5268 (office). *E-mail:* victoria.bryant@imgworld.com (office). *Website:* www.imgworld.com (office); www.steveredgrave.com.

REDGRAVE, Vanessa, CBE; British actress; b. 30 Jan. 1937; d. of the late Sir Michael Redgrave and Rachel Kempson; sister of Lynn Redgrave (q.v.); m. the late Tony Richardson 1962 (divorced 1967, died 1991); two d.; one s. by Franco Reio; ed Queensgate School, London and Cen. School of Speech and Drama; actress 1957–; co-f. Moving Theatre 1974; mem. Workers' Revolutionary Party (Cand. for Moss Side 1979); Fellow, BFI 1988; Chevalier, Légion d'Honneur; Dr hc (Mass.) 1990; Evening Standard Award, Best Actress 1961, Variety Club Award 1961, Cannes Film Festival Award, Best Actress 1966, US Nat. Soc. of Film Critics Award, Leading Actress, Film Critics' Guild (UK) Best Actress Award 1969, Acad. Award, Best Supporting Actress 1978, Award for Best Actress (TV) 1981, Laurence Olivier Award 1984, Tony Award, Best Actress in a Play 2003. *Stage appearances include:* A Midsummer Night's Dream 1959, The Tiger and the Horse 1960, The Taming of the Shrew 1961, As You Like It 1961, Cymbeline 1962, The Seagull 1964, 1985, The Prime of Miss Jean Brodie 1966, Daniel Deronda 1969, Cato Street 1971, Threepenny Opera 1972, Twelfth Night 1972, Antony and Cleopatra 1973, 1986, Design for Living 1973, Macbeth 1975, Lady from the Sea 1976 and 1979 (Manchester), The Aspern Papers 1984, Ghosts 1986, A Touch of the Poet 1988, Orpheus Descending 1988, A Madhouse in Goa 1989, The Three Sisters 1990, Lettice and Lovage 1991, When She Danced 1991, Isadora 1991, Heartbreak House 1992, The Master Builder 1992, Maybe 1993, The Liberation of Skopje 1995, John Gabriel Borkman 1996, The Cherry Orchard 2000, The Tempest 2000, Long Day's Journey into Night 2003; Dir and acted in Antony and Cleopatra, Houston, Tex. 1996, John Gabriel Borkman 1996, Song at Twilight 1999, Lady Windermere's Fan 2002. *Television includes:* Second Serve 1986, A Man for All Seasons 1988, Orpheus Descending 1990, Young Catherine 1991, What Ever Happened to Baby Jane? 1991, Great Moments in Aviation 1993, They 1993, Down Came a Blackbird 1995, The Wind in the Willows 1995, Two Mothers for Zachary 1996, The Willows in Winter 1996, Bella Mafia 1997, If These Walls Could Talk 2 2000, Jack and the Beanstalk: The Real Story 2001, The Gathering Storm 2002, The Locket 2002, Byron 2003, Nip/Tuck (series) 2004–05, The Shell Seekers 2006. *Films include:* Morgan—A Suitable Case for Treatment 1965, Sailor from Gibraltar 1965, Camelot 1967, Blow Up 1967, Charge of the Light Brigade 1968, Isadora Duncan 1968, The Seagull 1968, A Quiet Place in the Country 1968, Dropout, The Trojan Women 1970, The Devils 1970, The Holiday 1971, Mary Queen of Scots 1971, Katherine Mansfield (BBC TV) 1973, Murder on the Orient Express 1974, Winter Rates 1974, 7% Solution 1975, Julia 1977, Agatha 1978, Yanks 1978, Bear Island 1979, Playing for Time (CBS TV) 1979, Playing for Time 1980, My Body My Child (ABC TV) 1981, Wagner 1982, The Bostonians 1983, Wetherby 1984, Prick Up Your Ears 1987, Comrades 1987, Consuming Passions 1988, King of the Wind 1989, Diceria dell'intore 1989, The Ballad of the Sad Cafe 1990, Howards End 1992, Breath of Life, The Wall, Sparrow, They, The House of the Spirits, Crime and Punishment, Mother's Boys, Little Odessa, A Month by the Lake 1996, Mission Impossible 1996, Looking for Richard 1997, Wilde 1997, Mrs Dalloway 1997, Bella Mafia (TV) 1997, Deep Impact 1998, Cradle Will Rock 2000, The Pledge 2001, The Gathering Storm (TV) 2002, Crime and Punishment 2002, The Fever 2004, The Keeper 2005, Short Order 2005, The White Countess 2005, Thief Lord 2006, Venus 2006, How About You 2007, The Riddle 2007, Atonement 2007, Evening 2007, Gud, lukt och henne 2008; produced and narrated documentary film The Palestinians 1977. *Publications:* Pussies and Tigers 1963, An Autobiography 1991. *Leisure interest:* changing the status quo. *Address:* c/o Gavin Barker Associates, 2d Wimpole Street, London, W1M 7AA, England (office).

REDHEAD, Michael Logan Gonne, PhD, FBA; British professor of philosophy; *Co-director, Centre for Philosophy of Natural and Social Science, London School of Economics;* b. 30 Dec. 1929, London; s. of Robert Arthur Redhead and Christabel Lucy Gonne Browning; m. Jennifer Anne Hill 1964; three s.; ed Westminster School, Univ. Coll. London; Prof. of Philosophy of Physics, Chelsea Coll., London 1984–85, King's Coll. London 1985–87; Prof. of History and Philosophy of Science, Cambridge Univ. 1987–97; Fellow, Wolfson Coll. Cambridge 1988–, Vice-Pres. 1992–96; Co-Dir Centre for Philosophy of Natural and Social Science, LSE 1998–, Centennial Prof. 1999–2002; Fellow, King's Coll. London 2000; Tarner Lecturer, Trinity Coll. Cambridge 1991–94; Visiting Fellow, All Souls Coll. Oxford 1995; Pres. British Soc. for Philosophy of Science 1989–91; Fellow, British Acad.; Lakatos Award for Philosophy of Science 1988. *Publications:* Incompleteness, Nonlocality and Realism 1987, From Physics to Metaphysics 1995. *Leisure interests:* poetry, music, tennis. *Address:* Centre for Philosophy of Natural and Social Science, Lakatos Building, Room T111, London School of Economics, Houghton Street, London, WC2A 2AE (office); 119 Rivermead Court, London, SW6 3SD, England (home). *Telephone:* (20) 7955-6552 (office); (20) 7736-6767 (home). *Fax:* (20) 7955-6869 (office); (20) 7731-7627 (home). *E-mail:* mlr1000@cam.ac.uk (office). *Website:* www.lse.ac.uk/collections/CPNSS (office).

REDING, Viviane, PhD; Luxembourg journalist and politician; *Commissioner for Information Society and Media, European Commission;* b. 27 April 1951, Esch-sur Alzette; m.; three c.; ed Sorbonne, Paris; journalist, Luxemburger Wort 1978–99; mem. Parl. 1979–89; communal councillor, City of Esch 1981–99; Pres. Luxembourg Union of Journalists 1986–98; Nat. Pres. Christian-Social Women 1988–93; MEP 1989–99; Pres. Cultural Affairs Cttee 1992–99; Vice-Pres. Parti Chrétien-Social 1995–99; Vice-Pres. Civil Liberties and Internal Affairs Cttee 1997–99; EU Commr for Educ. and Culture 1999–2004, for Information Soc. and Media 2004–; mem. Benelux Parl., N Atlantic Ass. (Leader Christian Democrat/Conservative Group); Officier, Légion d'honneur; Dr hc (Hu Chen Univ. of Taiwan) 2004, (Univ. of Genoa) 2004, (Univ. of Torino) 2004; St George's Cross, Generalitat of Catalunya 1992, Gold Medal of European Merit 2001, Robert Schuman Medal 2004, Prince of Asturias Int. Cooperation Prize 2004, Gloria Artins Medal of Honour (Poland) 2005. *Address:* Commission of the European Communities, 200 rue de la Loi, 1049 Brussels, Belgium (office). *Telephone:* (2) 298-16-00 (office). *Fax:* (2) 299-92-01 (office). *E-mail:* viviane.reding@ec.europa.eu (office). *Website:* ec.europa.eu/commission_barroso/reding/index_en.htm (office).

REDRADO, Martín; Argentine economist and central banker; *Governor, Banco Central de la República Argentina;* ed Harvard Univ., USA; fmrly with Salomon Brothers, USA; fmr Man. Dir Security Pacific Bank; Pres. Nat. Securities Comm. 1991; fmr Chair. Emerging Markets Cttee, Int. Org. of Securities Comms (IOSCO); est. Fundación Capital 1994, Chief Economist –2001; Sec. of State, Technological Educ. Section, Ministry of Educ. 1996; Sec. for Trade and Int. Econ. Relations 2002–04; currently Gov. Banco Central de la República Argentina. *Publications include:* Cómo sobrevivir a la Globalización (How to Survive Globalization) 2002, Exportar para crecer (Exports for Growth) 2003. *Address:* Banco Central de la República Argentina, Reconquista 266, C1003ABF Buenos Aires, Argentina (office). *Telephone:* (11) 4348-3500 (office). *Fax:* (11) 4348-3955 (office). *E-mail:* sistema@bcra.gov.ar (office). *Website:* www.bcra.gov.ar (office).

REDSTONE, Sumner Murray, BA, LLB; American lawyer and business executive; *Executive Chairman, Viacom Inc.;* b. (Sumner Murray Rothstein), 27 May 1923, Boston; s. of Michael Redstone and Belle Redstone (neé Ostrovsky); m. Phyllis Redstone (divorced 2002); one s. one d.; ed Harvard Univ.; served as 1st Lt, US Army 1943–45; called to Bar of Mass. 1947; Special Asst to US Attorney-Gen., Washington, DC 1948–51; Pnr, Ford, Bergson, Adams, Borkland & Redstone (law firm), Washington, DC 1951–54; Pres. and CEO Nat. Amusements Inc., Dedham, Mass. 1967–, Chair. Bd 1986–87, Chair. Viacom Inc., New York 1987–2006, CEO 1996–2006, Exec. Chair. Viacom 2006–, Exec. Chair. CBS Corpn 2006–; Prof., Boston Univ. Law School 1982, 1985–86; Chair. Corp. Comm. on Education Tech. 1996–; mem. Corpn, New England Medical Center 1967–, Mass. Gen. Hosp.; Sponsor, Boston Museum of Science; mem. Bd of Dirs Boston Arts Festival, John F. Kennedy Library Foundation; mem. Nat. Asscn of Theatre Owners, Theatre Owners of America, Motion Picture Pioneers (mem. Bd of Dirs), Boston Bar Asscn, Mass. Bar Asscn; mem. Exec. Cttee Will Rogers Fund; mem. Bd of Overseers Boston Museum of Fine Arts; mem. Exec. Bd Combined Jewish Philanthropies; Hon. LLD (Boston Univ.) 1994; Hon. LHD (New York Inst. of Tech) 1996; Army Commendation Medal, Legends in Leadership Award, Emory Univ. 1995, Lifetime Achievement Award American Cancer Society 1995, Trustees Award Nat. Acad. of TV Arts and Sciences 1997, Robert F. Kennedy Memorial Ripple of Hope Award 1998, Int. Radio and TV Gold Medal Award 1998, Nat. Conf. of Christians and Jews Humanitarian Award 1998, numerous other awards. *Publications:* A Passion to Win (autobiog.) 2001. *Address:* Viacom Inc., 1515 Broadway, New York, NY 10036 (office); National Amusements Inc., 200 Elm Street, Dedham, MA 02026 (office); 98 Baldpate Hill Road, Newton, MA 02159, USA (home); CBS Corporation, 51 West 52nd Street, New York, NY 10019-6188 (office). *Telephone:* (212) 258-6000 (Viacom) (office); (212) 975-4321 (CBS) (office). *Fax:* (212) 258-6464 (Viacom) (office); (212) 975-4516 (CBS) (office). *Website:* www.viacom.com (office); www.national-amusements.com (office); www.cbscorporation.com (office).

REDWOOD, Rt Hon. John Alan, PC, MA, DPhil; British politician; *Shadow Secretary of State for Deregulation;* b. 15 June 1951, Dover, Kent; s. of William Charles Redwood and Amy Emma Champion; m. Gail Felicity Chippington 1974 (divorced 2004); one s. one d.; ed Kent Coll., Canterbury and Magdalen and St Antony's Colls, Oxford; Fellow, All Souls Coll. Oxford 1972–85, 2003–05; Investment Adviser, Robert Fleming & Co. 1973–77; Dir (fmrly Man.) N. M. Rothschild & Sons 1977–87; Dir Norcros PLC 1985–89, Jt Deputy Chair. 1986–87, Chair. (non-exec.) 1987–89; Head, Prime Minister's Policy Unit 1983–85; MP for Wokingham 1987–; Parl. Under-Sec. of State, Dept of Trade and Industry 1989–90, Minister of State 1990–92, Minister of State, Dept of Environment 1992–93; Sec. of State for Wales 1993–95; unsuccessful cand. for leadership of Conservative Party 1995; Opposition Front Bench Spokesman on Trade and Industry 1997–99, on the Environment 1999–2000; Shadow Sec. of State for Deregulation 2004–05; Chair. Econ. Policy Review, Conservative Party 2005–; Chair. Mabey Securities, Concentric PLC; Dir (non-exec.) BNB Resources PLC; Visting Prof., Univ. of Middx Business School; Parliamentarian of the Year Awards 1987, 1995, 1997. *Publications:* Reason, Ridicule and Religion 1976, Public Enterprise in Crisis 1980, Value for Money Audits (with J. Hatch) 1981, Controlling Public Industries (with J. Hatch) 1982, Going for Broke 1984, Equity for Everyman 1986, Popular Capitalism 1989, The Global Marketplace 1994, The Single European Currency (with others) 1996, Our Currency, Our Country 1997, The Death of Britain? 1999, Stars and Strife 2001, Just Say No 2001, Third Way – Which Way? 2002, Singing the Blues 2004, I Want to Make a Difference – But I Don't Like Politics 2006. *Leisure interests:* water sports, village cricket. *Address:* House of Commons, Westminster, London, SW1A 0AA, England (office). *Telephone:* (20) 7219-4205 (office). *Fax:* (20) 7219-0377 (office). *E-mail:* redwoodj@parliament.uk (office). *Website:* wwww.johnredwoodsdiary.com (office); www.wokinghamconservatives.com (office).

REED, Bruce; American fmr government official; *President, Democratic Leadership Council;* b. Coeur d'Alene, Idaho; ed Princeton Univ., Univ. of Oxford, UK; served as chief speechwriter for Senator Al Gore 1985–89; policy dir Democratic Leadership Council 1990–91; deputy campaign man. for policy Clinton-Gore presidential campaign 1992, then Asst to Pres., Head Domestic Policy Council 1997–2001; Pres. Democratic Leadership Council, Washington,

DC 2001–, also Ed.-in-Chief Blueprint (journal). *Publication:* The Plan: Big Ideas for Change in America (with Rahm Emanuel) 2009. *Address:* Democratic Leadership Council, 600 Pennsylvania Avenue, SE, Suite 400, Washington, DC 20003, USA (office). *Telephone:* (202) 546-0007 (office). *Fax:* (202) 544-5002 (office). *Website:* www.ndol.org (office).

REED, Charles Bass, BS, MS, EdD; American academic and university administrator; *Chancellor, California State University System;* b. 29 Sept. 1941, Harrisburg, Pa; s. of the late Samuel Ross Reed and Elizabeth Johnson Reed; m. Catherine A. Sayers 1964; one s. one d.; ed George Washington Univ.; Asst Prof., then Assoc. Prof., George Washington Univ. 1963–70; Asst Dir Nat. Performance-based Teacher Educ. Project 1970–71; Co-ordinator, Research and Devt in Teacher Educ., Fla Dept of Educ. 1971–72, Assoc. for Planning and Co-ordination 1972–74, Dir Office of Educational Planning, Budgeting and Evaluation 1974–79; Educ. Policy Co-ordinator, Exec. Office of Fla Gov. Bob Graham 1979–80, Dir of Legis. Affairs 1980–81, Deputy Chief of Staff 1981–84, Chief of Staff 1984–85; Chancellor, State Univ. System of Fla 1985–98, Calif. State Univ. System 1998–; mem. Pres.'s Roundtable, Nat. Bd for Professional Teaching Standards 2005–, mem. Bd of Dirs Policy Consensus Initiative 2005–, ACT, Inc 2002–, Council for Higher Educ. Accreditation 2004–, Nat. Center for Educational Accountability 2002–,; Chair. Bd of Dirs Regional Tech. Strategies Inc.; Fulbright 50th Anniversary Distinguished Fellow, Peru 1996; mem. Council on Foreign Relations, Hispanic Asscn of Colls and Univs 1998–, Nat. Business-Higher Educ. Forum 1992–, American Council on Educ. (Joint Editorial Board 2003–), Asscn of Governing Bds of Univs and Colls (Council of Pres 2001–),; mem. Advisory Cttee New Voters Project 2003–; mem. Exec. Advisory Council, Systems & Computer Tech. Corpn 1998–; Trustee Long Beach Memorial Medical Center 1998–; mem. Mayor's Blue Ribbon Task Force on Infrastructure, City of Los Angeles 2003, Nat. Alliance of Business 2001–03, Nat. Advisory Council, Hope for Kids 1995–98; Dr hc (Stetson Univ.) 1987, (George Washington Univ.) 1987, (St. Thomas Univ.) 1988, (Waynesburg Coll.) 1990, (Fla State Univ.) 1997, (British Open Univ.) 2000; George Washington Univ. Football Hall of Fame 1990, Floridian of the Year, Orlando Sentinel 1990, Southern Regional Education Bd's Lamar R. Plunkett Award 2001. *Address:* Office of the Chancellor, California State University System, 401 Golden Shore, Suite 641, Long Beach, CA 90802-4210, USA (office). *Telephone:* (562) 951-4700 (office). *Fax:* (562) 951-4986 (office). *E-mail:* creed@calstate.edu (office). *Website:* www.calstate.edu (office).

REED, David Patrick, BS, MS, PhD; American computer scientist and academic; *Adjunct Professor of Media Arts and Sciences, Massachusetts Institute of Technology Media Laboratory;* b. 30 Jan. 1952, Portsmouth, Va; ed Massachusetts Inst. of Tech.; Asst Prof. of Computer Science and Eng, MIT Lab. for Computer Science –1983; apptd Vice-Pres. Research and Devt and Chief Scientist, Software Arts (creator of VisiCalc, the first electronic spreadsheet) 1983; spent seven years as Vice-Pres. and Chief Scientist for Lotus Development Corpn; spent four years at Interval Research Corpn; working at Viewpoints Research Inst. 2001–; Visiting Scientist, MIT Media Lab., Adjunct Prof. of Media Arts and Sciences 2002–; HP Fellow, Hewlett-Packard Labs 2003–; has acted as strategic adviser to small and large tech.-based businesses and consultant on advanced computing and communications tech.; has played key role on Advisory Bd of Vanguard research and advisory programme (now part of Technology Transfer Inst.); Fellow, Diamond Technology Pnrs Diamond Exchange Program; World Tech. Award in Communication Tech., The World Tech. Network 2004. *Achievements include:* pioneer in design and construction of internet protocols, distributed data storage and PC software systems and applications; co-inventor of the end-to-end argument, often called the fundamental architectural principle of the internet; discovered Reed's Law, a scaling law for group-forming network architectures; along with Metcalfe's Law, Reed's Law has significant implications for large-scale network business models. *Publications:* numerous scientific papers in professional journals on densely scalable, mobile and robust RF network architectures and highly decentralized systems architectures. *Address:* The Media Laboratory, Building E15-492, 77 Massachusetts Avenue, Cambridge, MA 02139-4307, USA (office). *Telephone:* (617) 253-6469 (office). *Fax:* (617) 258-6264 (office). *E-mail:* dpreed@mit.edu (office). *Website:* www.media.mit.edu (office); www.reed.com (office).

REED, Ishmael Scott; American writer and poet; b. 22 Feb. 1938, Chattanooga, Tenn.; s. of Bennie S. Reed and Thelma Coleman; m. 1st Priscilla Rose 1960 (divorced 1970); two s.; m. 2nd Carla Blank; one d.; ed Univ. of Buffalo; Co-founder and Dir Reed, Cannon & Johnson Co. 1973–; Assoc. Fellow, Calhoun House, Yale Univ. 1982–; Founder (with Al Young) and ed., Quilt magazine 1981–; Guest Lecturer, Univ. of Calif., Berkeley 1968, then Sr Lecturer, now Lectuer Emer.; mem. usage panel, American Heritage Dictionary; Assoc. Ed. American Book Review; Exec. Producer Personal Problems (video soap opera); collaborator in multimedia Bicentennial mystery, The Lost State of Franklin (winner Poetry in Public Places contest 1975); Chair. Berkeley Arts Comm.; Advisory Chair. Co-ordinating Council of Literary Magazines; Pres. Before Columbus Foundation 1976–; Nat. Endowment for Arts Writing Fellow 1974; Guggenheim Fellow 1975; mem. Authors' Guild of America, PEN; Publr Konch magazine; Nat. Inst. of Arts and Letters Award 1975, Rosenthal Foundation Award 1975, Michaux Award 1978, ACLU Award 1978. *Publications:* fiction: The Free-Lance Pallbearers 1967, Yellow Back Radio Broke Down 1969, Mumbo Jumbo 1972, The Last Days of Louisiana Red 1974, Flight to Canada 1976, The Terrible Twos 1982, Reckless Eyeballing 1986, Cab Calloway Stands in for the Moon 1986, The Terrible Threes 1989, Japanese By Spring 1993; poetry: Catechism of a Neoamerican Hoodoo Church 1970, Conjure: Selected Poems 1963–1970 1972, Chattanooga 1973, A Secretary to the Spirits 1978, Calafia: The California Poetry (ed.) 1979, New and Collected Poems 1988, New and Collected Poems 1964–2006

2006; non-fiction: The Rise, Fall and. . .? of Adam Clayton Powell (with others) 1967, 19 Necromancers from Now (ed.) 1970, Yardbird Reader (five vols, ed.) 1971–77, Yardbird Lives! (ed., with Al Young) 1978, Shrovetide in Old New Orleans 1978, Quilt 2–3 (ed., with Al Young, two vols) 1981–82, God Made Alaska for the Indians 1982, Writin' is Fightin': Thirty-Seven Years of Boxing on Paper (ed.) 1988, Ishmael Reed: An Interview 1990, The Before Columbus Foundation Fiction Anthology: Selections from the American Book Awards 1980–1990 (ed., with Kathryn Trueblood and Shawn Wong) 1992, Airin' Dirty Laundry 1993, Multi-America 1996, The Reed Reader (ed.) 2000. *Address:* c/o Penguin Putnam Inc., 375 Hudson Street, New York, NY 10014, USA. *E-mail:* uncleish@aol.com. *Website:* www.ishmaelreedpub.com.

REED, John C., MD, PhD; American clinical scientist; *President and CEO, Professor and Donald Bren Presidential Chair, The Burnham Institute for Medical Research;* b. 11 Oct. 1958, New York; ed Univ. of Virginia, Charlottesville, Univ. of Pennsylvania School of Medicine; Postdoctoral Fellow in Molecular Biology, Wistar Inst. of Anatomy and Biology, Philadelphia 1986–88; Resident in Clinical Pathology, Dept of Pathology and Lab. Medicine, Univ. of Pennsylvania Hosp. 1986–89, Research Assoc., Dept of Pathology and Laboratory Medicine, Univ. of Pennsylvania 1988–89, Asst Prof. 1989–92, Asst Dir Lab. of Molecular Diagnosis, Univ. of Pennsylvania Hosp. 1989–92; Dir Oncogene and Tumor Suppressor Gene Program, The Burnham Inst. for Medical Research, La Jolla, Calif. 1992–95, then Assoc. Prof. and Leader Apoptosis and Cell Death Research Program, Scientific Dir Burnham Inst. 1995–2003, Deputy Dir NCI Cancer Center 1994–2003, Pres. and CEO The Burnham Inst. 2003–, also Prof. and Donald Bren Presidential Chair; Assoc. mem. Univ. of California, San Diego Cancer Center 1993–; Adjunct Prof., Dept of Biology, San Diego State Univ. 1996–; Adjunct Prof., Dept of Molecular Pathology, Univ. of California, San Diego School of Medicine 1997–; Chair. Translational Apoptosis Research Cttee for Prostate Cancer, CaP-CURE 1999–; mem. Advisory Cttee, Specialized Center of Research on Leukemia and Lymphoma, Univ. of California, San Diego 2001–; mem. Editorial Bd Antisense Research and Development 1993–96, Oncology Reports 1993–99, Cell Death and Differentiation 1994–99, Clinical Cancer Research 1994–99, Molecular Carcinogenesis 1994–, Cancer Gene Therapy 1994–, Advances in Leukemia and Lymphoma 1995–, Cancer Research 1995–, Journal of Inflammation 1996–97, Receptors and Signal Transduction 1996–98, Molecular and Cellular Differentiation 1996–98, Journal of Immunology 1996–98, Journal of Clinical Investigation 1996–, Antisense and Nucleic Acid Drug Development 1996–, Frontiers in Bioscience 1996–, Journal of Biological Chemistry 1996–, BLOOD 1997–, Current Opinion in Oncologic and Endocrine and Metabolic Drugs 1998–2000, Neoplasia 1998–, International Journal of Oncology 1998–, Tumor Targeting 1999–, Nature Reviews 2000–, Current Opinion in Investigational Drugs 2000–, Expert Opinion on Therapeutic Targets 2001–, Cell Cycle 2001–; William R. Drell Chair in Molecular Biology 1995; mem. AAAS 1981, American Soc. for Microbiology 1986, American Asscn for Cancer Research 1990, American Asscn of Univ. Pathologists 1991, Acad. of Clinical Lab. Physicians and Scientists 1991–93, Eastern Cooperative Oncology Group 1991, Clinical Cancer Research 1992, American Hematology Soc. 1992, CALGB 1994, American Soc. for Investigative Pathology 1995, Fed. of American Socs for Experimental Biology 1996, Int. Forum for Corp. Dir 1998; Presidential Award, Reticuloendothelial Soc. 1985, Sheard Stanford Award, American Soc. of Clinical Pathologists 1985, Upjohn Achievement Award 1986, Stohlman Memorial Scholar Award, Leukemic Soc. of America 1994, Local Hero in the Fight Against Breast Cancer Award, Susan G. Komen Foundation 1998, 1st Inaugural D. Wayne Calloway Memorial Lecturer, Memorial Sloan-Kettering Cancer Center 1999, 35th Annual Harold G. Pritzker Memorial Lecture Presenter, Mount Sinai Hosp., Univ. of Toronto 1999, ranked No. 1 Hottest Researcher in Life Sciences WorldWide Inst. for Scientific Information 1999, 2000, 2000 Decade of the Brain Award, American Acad. of Neurology 2000, Warner-Lambert/Parke Davis Award, American Soc. for Investigative Pathology 2000, Harry B. Van Dyke Award, Columbia Univ. 2001. *Publications:* more than 750 articles in scientific journals. *Address:* The Burnham Institute for Medical Research, 10901 N Torrey Pines Road, La Jolla, CA 92037, USA (office). *Telephone:* (858) 795-5301 (office). *Fax:* (858) 646-3199 (office). *E-mail:* president@burnham.org (office). *Website:* www.burnham.org (office).

REED, John Francis (Jack), BS, JD; American politician; *Senator from Rhode Island;* b. 12 Nov. 1949, Providence, RI; s. of Joseph Reed and Mary Monahan; ed US Mil. Acad. and Harvard Univ.; commissioned, 2nd Lt US Army 1971, served with 82nd Airborne Div. 1973–77; Asst Prof. US Mil. Acad., West Point, NY 1977–79; resgnd from Army 1979; called to Bar, DC 1982, Rhode Island 1983; Assoc. Sutherland, Asbill & Brennan, Washington, DC 1982–83, Edwards & Angelli, Providence 1983–89; mem. Rhode Island State Senate 1984–90; mem. 102–104th US Congresses 1990–96; Senator from Rhode Island 1996–; Vice-Chair. NE-Midwest Congressional Coalition; Democrat. *Leisure interests:* reading, hiking. *Address:* 728 Hart Senate Office Building, Washington, DC 20510, USA (office). *Telephone:* (202) 224-4642 (office). *Fax:* (202) 224-4680 (office). *Website:* reed.senate.gov (office).

REED, John Shepard, MS; American business executive; b. 7 Feb. 1939, Chicago; m. 1st (divorced), four c.; m. 2nd Cindy McCarthy 1994; ed Washington and Jefferson Coll., Mass Inst. of Tech., Alfred P. Sloan School of Man. (MIT); served with US Army Eng Corps, Korea; fmr Trainee Goodyear Tire & Rubber; joined Citicorp/Citibank 1965, fmrly responsible for operating group, consumer business, fmr Sr Vice-Pres., Chair. and Chief Exec. 1984–98; Jt Chair. and CEO Citigroup (merger between Citicorp and Travelers Group) 1998–2000; Interim Chair. NY Stock Exchange (NYSE) 2003 then Chair. 2004–05; Chair. Coalition of Service Industries, Services Policy Advisory Cttee to the US Trade Rep.; mem. Bd of Dirs Altria Group Inc. (fmly Philip

Morris Inc.) 1979–2003, 2004–, Manpower Demonstration Research Corpn; fmr mem. Bd of Dirs Monsanto Co.; mem. Business Council, Business Roundtable Policy Cttee; mem. Corpn of MIT; fmr mem. Bd Memorial Sloan-Kettering Cancer Center, Rand Corpn, Spencer Foundation, American Museum of Natural History; Trustee Center for Advanced Studies in Social and Behavioral Sciences. *Address:* c/o Board of Directors, Altria Group Inc., 120 Park Avenue, New York, NY 10017, USA (office).

REED, Lou, BA; American musician (guitar), singer, poet and film actor; b. (Louis Firbank), 2 March 1942, Brooklyn, New York; s. of Sidney Joseph Reed and Toby Reed (née Futterman); m. Sylvia Morales 1980; ed Syracuse Univ.; songwriter and recording artist 1965–; founder mem., lead singer The Velvet Underground 1964–70, 1993–; toured with Andy Warhol's The Exploding Plastic Inevitable; solo artist 1971–93; mem. AFofM, Screen Actors' Guild; Heroes Award 1997, American Master, PBS Documentary Series 1998; Commdr, Ordre des Arts et des Lettres. *Film appearance:* Berlin 2007. *Recordings:* albums: with The Velvet Underground: The Velvet Underground & Nico 1967, White Light/White Heat 1967, The Velvet Underground 1969, Loaded 1970, Live at Max's Kansas City 1972, Squeeze 1973, 1969: Velvet Underground Live 1974, Live With Lou Reed 1974, Live MCMXCIII 1993; solo: Lou Reed 1972, Transformer 1972, Rock 'n' Roll Animal 1972, Berlin 1973, Sally Can't Dance 1974, Lou Reed Live 1975, Metal Machine Music 1975, Coney Island Baby 1976, Rock and Roll Heart 1976, Walk on the Wild Side 1977, Live: Take No Prisoners 1978, Street Hassle 1978, Vicious 1979, The Bells 1979, Growing Up in Public 1980, Rock 'n' Roll Today 1980, The Blue Mask 1982, Legendary Hearts 1983, Live in Italy 1984, New Sensations 1984, Mistrial 1986, New York 1989, Songs for Drella (with John Cale) 1990, Magic and Loss 1992, Set the Twilight Reeling 1996, Live in Concert 1997, Perfect Night: Live in London 1998, Ecstasy 2000, American Poet 2001, Extended Versions 2003, The Raven 2003, Animal Serenade 2004, Le Bataclan '72 2004. *Publications:* Between Thought and Expression (selected lyrics) 1991, Pass Thru Fire 2000. *Address:* Primary Talent International, Fifth Floor, 2–12 Pentonville Road, London, N1 9PL, England (office); Sister Ray Enterprises, 584 Broadway, Room 609, New York, NY 10012, USA (office). *Telephone:* (20) 7833-8998 (office). *Fax:* (20) 7833-5992 (office). *E-mail:* mail@primary.uk.com (office). *Website:* www.loureed.org.

REEDER, Franklin S., BA; American consultant and fmr government official; *President, The Reeder Group;* b. 25 Oct. 1940, Philadelphia, Pa; s. of the late Simon Reeder and Hertha Strauss; m. Anna Marie Seroski 1962; one s. two d.; ed Univ. of Pennsylvania and George Washington Univ.; with US Treasury Dept 1961–64; Defense Dept 1964–70; Office of Man. and Budget, Exec. Office of Pres. of USA 1970–71, 1980–97, Dir 1995–97; currently Pres. The Reeder Group; Deputy Dir House Information System, US House of Reps 1971–80; fmr Chair. Computer Systems Security and Privacy Advisory Bd (now Information Security and Privacy Advisory Bd), Nat. Inst. of Standards and Tech. (NIST); Chair. Center for Internet Security; columnist and Contributing Ed. Government Executive magazine; Fellow, Nat. Acad. of Public Admin; Hon. Certified Information Security Man. (CISM) 2003; numerous awards including Presidential Rank Award as Meritorious Sr Exec.; mem. Govt Computer News Information Resources Man. Hall of Fame. *Leisure interests:* running, swimming, bicycling, watching baseball. *Address:* The Reeder Group, 3200 N Nottingham Street, Arlington, VA 22207 (office); c/o The Center for Internet Security, POB 433, Hershey, PA 17033, USA. *Telephone:* (703) 536-6635 (office). *Fax:* (703) 536-1774 (office). *E-mail:* reeder@bellatlantic.net. *Website:* csrc.nist.gov/ispab; www.cisecurity.org.

REES, Sir Dai (David Allan), Kt, PhD, DSc, FIBiol, FRSC, FRS; British scientist and academic; b. 28 April 1936, Silloth; s. of James A. Rees and Elsie Bolam; m. Myfanwy Owen 1959; two s. one d.; ed Hawarden Grammar School, Clwyd and Univ. Coll. of N Wales, Bangor; Univ. of Edin. 1960, Asst Lecturer in Chem. 1961, Lecturer 1962–70, Section Man. 1970–72; Prin. Scientist Unilever Research, Colworth Lab. 1972–82; Assoc. Dir (part-time) MRC Unit for Cell Biophysics Kings Coll., London 1980–82; Dir Nat. Inst. for Medical Research 1982–87; Sec., then Chief Exec. MRC 1987–96, MRC scientist 1996–; Chair. European Medical Research Councils 1989, Pres. European Science Foundation 1994–2001; Visiting Professorial Fellow, Univ. Coll., Cardiff 1972–77; mem. Royal Soc. Council 1985–87; Hon. FRCP 1986; Hon. FRCPE 1998; Hon. Fellow, King's Coll., London 1989, Univ. Coll. of N Wales 1988; Hon. DSc (Edin.) 1989, (Wales) 1991, (Stirling) 1995, (Leicester) 1997, (York) 2007; Colworth Medal, Biochemical Soc. 1970, Carbohydrate Award, Chemical Soc. 1970, Philips Lecturer, Royal Soc. 1984. *Publications:* articles on carbohydrate biochemistry and cell biology. *Leisure interests:* river cruising, reading, listening to music. *Address:* Ford Cottage, 1 High Street, Denford, Kettering, Northants., NN14 4EQ, England (home). *E-mail:* drees@nimr.mrc.ac.uk (home).

REES, Baron (Life Peer), cr. 2005, of Ludlow in the County of Shropshire; **Martin John Rees,** MA, PhD, FRS, OM; British astronomer and academic; *President, The Royal Society;* b. 23 June 1942; s. of Reginald J. Rees and Joan Rees; m. Caroline Humphrey 1986; ed Shrewsbury School and Trinity Coll., Cambridge; Fellow, Jesus Coll., Cambridge 1967–69; Research Assoc. Calif. Inst. of Tech. 1967–68, 1971; mem. Inst. for Advanced Study, Princeton 1969–70, Prof. 1982–96; Visiting Prof., Harvard Univ. 1972, 1986–87; Prof., Univ. of Sussex 1972–73; Plumian Prof. of Astronomy and Experimental Philosophy, Univ. of Cambridge 1973–91, Royal Soc. Research Prof. 1992–2002, Prof. of Cosmology and Astrophysics 2004–; Astronomer Royal 1995–; Master Trinity Coll., Cambridge 2004–; Fellow, King's Coll., Cambridge 1969–72, 1973–2003; Visiting Prof., Imperial Coll., London 2001–, Leicester Univ. 2001–; Dir Inst. of Astronomy 1977–82, 1987–91; Regents Fellow, Smithsonian Inst. 1984–88; mem. council Royal Soc. 1983–85, 1993–95, Pres. 2005–; Pres. Royal Astronomical Soc. 1992–94, British Asscn for the Advancement of Science 1994–95; Trustee British Museum 1996–2002, Inst. for Advanced Study, Princeton, USA 1998–, Nat. Endowment for Sciences, Tech. and Arts 1998–2001, Kennedy Memorial Trust 1999–2004, Inst. for Public Policy Research 2001: Foreign Assoc. NAS; mem. Academia Europaea 1989, Pontifical Acad. of Sciences 1990; Foreign mem. American Philosophical Soc., Royal Swedish Acad. of Science, Russian Acad. of Sciences, Norwegian Acad. of Arts and Science, Accad. Lincei (Rome), Royal Netherlands Acad., Finnish Acad. of Arts and Sciences; Hon. Fellow, Trinity Coll., Darwin Coll. and Jesus Coll., Cambridge, Indian Acad. of Sciences, Univ. of Wales, Cardiff 1998, Inst. of Physics 2001; Foreign Hon. mem. American Acad. of Arts and Sciences; Officier, Ordre des Arts et des Lettres; Hon. DSc (Sussex) 1990, (Leicester) 1993, (Copenhagen, Keele, Uppsala, Newcastle) 1995, (Toronto) 1997, (Durham) 1999, (Oxford) 2000; Heinemann Prize, American Inst. of Physics 1984, Gold Medal (Royal Astronomical Soc.) 1987, Guthrie Medal, Inst. of Physics 1989, Balzan Prize 1989, Robinson Prize for Cosmology 1990, Bruce Medal, Astronomical Soc. of Pacific 1993, Science Writing Award, American Inst. of Physics 1996, Bower Award (Franklin Inst.) 1998, Rossi Prize, American Astronomical Soc. 2000, Cosmology Prize of Peter Gruber Foundation 2001, Einstein Award, World Cultural Congress 2003, Crafoord Prize, Royal Swedish Acad. 2005, Niels Bohr Medal, UNESCO 2005. *Television:* What We Still Don't Know (documentary series, Channel 4) 2004. *Publications:* Perspectives in Astrophysical Cosmology 1995, Gravity's Fatal Attraction (with M. Begelman) 1995, Before the Beginning 1997, Just Six Numbers 1999, Our Cosmic Habitat 2001, Our Final Century? 2003; edited books; articles and reviews in scientific journals and numerous gen. articles. *Address:* Trinity College, Cambridge, CB2 1TQ (office); Institute of Astronomy, Madingley Road, Cambridge CB3 0HA, England (office). *Telephone:* (1223) 338412 (office). *E-mail:* mjr@ast.cam.ac.uk (office). *Website:* www.ast.cam.ac.uk/IoA/staff/mjr (office); www.trin.cam.ac.uk/index.php?pageid=172 (office).

REES, Roger; British actor; b. 5 May 1944, Aberystwyth, Wales; ed Camberwell and Slade Schools of Art; with RSC 1967–; Assoc. Dir Bristol Old Vic Theatre Co. 1986–. *Stage appearances include:* Hindle Wakes 1964, The Taming of the Shrew, Othello, Major Barbara, Macbeth, Twelfth Night, The Suicide, The Adventures of Nicholas Nickleby, Hapgood, Hamlet, Love's Labours Lost, The Real Thing, Double Double (also writer), Indiscretions, The End of the Day. *Film appearances include:* Star 80 1983, God's Outlaw 1986, Mountains of the Moon 1990, If Looks Could Kill 1991, Stop! Or My Mom Will Shoot 1992, Robin Hood: Men in Tights 1993, The Substance of Fire 1996, Sudden Manhattan 1997, Trouble on the Corner 1997, Next Stop Wonderland 1998, A Midsummer Night's Dream 1999, The Bumblebee Flies Away 1999, BlackMale 2000, 3 A.M. 2001, Return to Never Land (voice) 2002, The Scorpion King 2002, Frida 2002, The Emperor's Club 2002, Crazy Like a Fox 2003, Garfield 2 (voice) 2006, The Prestige 2006, The Treatment 2006, East Broadway 2007, The Invasion 2007. *Television appearances include:* Under Western Eyes 1975, Bouquet of Barbed Wire (mini-series) 1976, The Comedy of Errors 1978, Macbeth 1979, The Voysey Inheritance 1979, The Adventures of Nicholas Nickleby (mini-series) 1982, Saigon: The Year of the Cat 1983, A Christmas Carol 1984, The Ebony Tower 1984, The Return of Sam McCloud 1989, Imaginary Friends (mini-series) 1987, The Modern World: Ten Great Writers (mini-series) 1988, Singles (series) 1988–89, The Finding 1990, Charles and Diana: Unhappily Ever After 1992, The Tower 1993, M.A.N.T.I.S (series) 1994, The Possession of Michael D. 1995, Cheers 1989–91, Boston Common (series) 1996, Titanic 1996, LIBERTY! The American Revolution (mini-series) 1997, Damian Cromwell's Postcards from America (series) 1997, The Crossing 2000, Double Platinum 1999, The West Wing 2000–05, Grey's Anatomy 2007.

REES-MOGG, Baron (Life Peer), cr. 1988, of Hinton Blewett in the County of Avon; **William Rees-Mogg;** British journalist and publisher; *Chairman, Pickering and Chatto Publishers Ltd;* b. 14 July 1928, Bristol; s. of the late Edmund Fletcher and Beatrice Rees-Mogg (née Warren); m. Gillian Shakespeare Morris 1962; two s. three d.; ed Charterhouse and Balliol Coll., Oxford; Pres. Oxford Union 1951; Financial Times 1952–60, Chief Leader Writer 1955–60, Asst Ed. 1957–60; City Ed. Sunday Times 1960–61, Political and Econ. Ed. 1961–63, Deputy Ed. 1964–67; Ed. of The Times 1967–81, Dir The Times Ltd 1968–81; Vice-Chair. BBC 1981–86; Chair. Arts Council 1982–89; Chair. Broadcasting Standards Council 1988–93; mem. Exec. Bd Times Newspapers Ltd 1968–81, Dir 1978–81; Dir Gen. Electric Co. 1981–97; Chair. and Propr Pickering and Chatto Publishers Ltd 1983–; Chair. Sidgwick and Jackson 1985–89, Int. Business Communications PLC 1994–98, Fleet Street Publications 1995–; Dir M & G Group 1987, EFG Pvt. Bank and Trust Co. 1993–2005, Value Realization Trust PLC 1996–98, Newsmax Media, Inc., USA 2000–06; columnist, The Times 1992–, The Mail on Sunday 2004–; mem. Int. Cttee Pontifical Council for Culture 1983–87; Hon. LLD (Bath) 1977, (Leeds) 1992. *Publications:* The Reigning Error: the Crisis of World Inflation 1974, An Humbler Heaven 1977, How to Buy Rare Books 1985, Blood in the Streets (with James Dale Davidson) 1987, The Great Reckoning (with James Dale Davidson) 1992, Picnics on Vesuvius 1992, The Sovereign Individual (with James Dale Davidson) 1997. *Leisure interest:* collecting. *Address:* Pickering & Chatto Publishers Ltd, 21 Bloomsbury Way, London, WC1A 2TH, England (office). *Telephone:* (20) 7242-2241 (office). *Fax:* (20) 7405-6216 (office). *E-mail:* amtraco@btconnect.com (office). *Website:* www.pickeringchatto.com (office).

REESE, Colin Bernard, MA, PhD, ScD, FRS; British chemist and academic; *Professor Emeritus of Chemistry, King's College London;* b. 29 July 1930, Plymouth; s. of the late Joseph Reese and Emily Reese; m. Susanne L. Bird 1968; one s. one d.; ed Dartington Hall School and Clare Coll., Cambridge; Research Fellow, Clare Coll. 1956–59, Harvard Univ., USA 1957–58; Official Fellow and Dir of Studies in Chem., Clare Coll. 1959–73; Univ. Demonstrator in Chem., Univ. of Cambridge 1959–63, Asst Dir of Research 1963–64, Univ. Lecturer in Chem. 1964–73; Daniell Prof. of Chem., King's Coll. London 1973–98, Fellow 1989–, Prof. of Organic Chem. 1999–2003, Prof. Emer. 2003–. *Publications:* scientific papers mainly in chemistry journals. *Address:* 21 Rozel Road, London, SW4 0EY, England (home); Department of Chemistry, King's College London, Strand, London, WC2R 2LS, England (office). *Telephone:* (20) 7848-2260 (office); (20) 7498-0230 (home). *Fax:* (20) 7848-1771 (office). *E-mail:* colin.reese@kcl.ac.uk (office).

REESE, Stuart Harry, BA, MBA; American business executive; *Chairman, President and CEO, Massachusetts Mutual Life Insurance Company (Mass-Mutual);* b. 3 May 1955, Richmond, Va; s. of Allison Reese and Virginia Saul; m. Elizabeth Garr 1976; three d. one s.; ed Gettysburg Coll., Dartmouth Coll.; Securities Analyst Aetna 1979–81, Sr Securities Analyst 1981–82, Dir Treas. Investment Planning 1982–83, Sr Investment Officer 1983–84, Asst Vice-Pres. 1984–85, Man. Dir 1985–89, Vice-Pres., Man. Dir Capital Markets 1989–93; Chair. and CEO Babson Capital Man., Massachusetts Mutual Life Insurance Co. (MassMutual) 1993–99, Exec. Vice-Pres. and Chief Investment Officer Massachusetts Mutual Life Insurance Co. (MassMutual) 1999–2005, Pres. and CEO 2005–, Chair. 2007–, Chair. Exec. Cttee, mem. Corp. Governance Cttee, Investment and Operations Cttee. *Address:* Massachusetts Mutual Life Insurance Company (MassMutual), 1295 State Street, Springfield, MA 01111-0001, USA (office). *Telephone:* (413) 788-8411 (office). *Fax:* (413) 744-6005 (office). *E-mail:* info@massmutual.com (office). *Website:* www .massmutual.com (office).

REETZ, Manfred T., BA, MS, PhD; German chemist and academic; *Director, Max-Planck-Institut für Kohlenforschung;* b. 13 Aug. 1943, Hirschberg; ed Washington Univ., St Louis, MO, Univ. of Mich., Ann Arbor, USA, Göttingen Univ.; Postdoctoral Fellow, Univ. Marburg 1971–72, Asst Prof. 1973–78, Prof. 1980–91; Guest Prof., Univ. of Wis., Madison, USA 1978; Assoc. Prof., Bonn Univ. 1978–80; Guest Prof., Fla State Univ. 1991–; Dir, Max-Planck-Institut für Kohlenforschung 1991–, Dir Dept of Synthetic Organic Chem. 1993–, Chair. Studiengesellschaft Kohle mbH 1993–; mem. Advisory Bd, Inst. für Organische Katalyseforschung, Rostock 1993–, Catalysis Nat. Research School Combination (NRSC), Leeuwenhorst, Netherlands 1999–2000; mem. Int. Advisory Bd Chem. Dept, Nagoya Univ. 2006–07; Senator, Chemistry Section, Deutsche Akademie der Naturforscher Leopoldina 2007–; mem. Editorial Advisory Bd Nachrichten aus Chemie, Technik und Laboratorium 1994–99, Topics in Organometallic Chemistry 1997–, Advanced Synthesis and Catalysis 2000–, Russian Journal of Organic Chemistry 2000–; mem. German Chemical Soc. (Dir 1990–95, Vice-Pres. 1995); mem. Deutsche Akademie der Naturforscher Leopoldina 1997–, Nordrheinwestfälischen Akademie der Wissenschaften 2001–; Hon. Prof., Ruhr-Univ. Bochum 1992, Shanghai Inst. of Organic Chem. 2007; Chemical Industries Prize 1976, Jacobus van't Hoff Prize 1977, Göttingen Acad. of Sciences Chem. Prize 1978, Otto-Bayer Prize 1986, Deutsche Forschungsgemeinschaft Leibniz Prize 1989, Nagoya Gold Medal of Organic Chem. 2000, Hans Herloff Inhoffen Medal 2003, Cliff S. Hamilton Award in Organic Chem. 2005, Karl-Ziegler-Prize 2005, Ernst Hellmut Vits-Prize 2006, Prelog Medal. *Address:* Department of Synthetic Organic Chemistry, Max-Planck-Institut für Kohlenforschung, Kaiser-Wilhelm-Platz 1, 45470 Mülheim an der Ruhr, Germany. *Telephone:* (208) 306-2000 (office). *Fax:* (208) 306-2985 (office). *E-mail:* reetz@mpi-muelheim .mpg.de (office). *Website:* www.mpi-muelheim.mpg.de/kofo/institut/ arbeitsbereiche/reetz/reetz_e.html (office).

REEVE, Sir Anthony, KCMG, KCVO, MA; British business executive and diplomatist (retd); *Chairman, The Curzon Corporation;* b. 20 Oct. 1938, Wakefield; s. of Sidney Reeve and Dorothy Reeve (née Mitchell); m. 1st Pamela Margaret Angus 1964 (divorced 1988); one s. two d.; m. 2nd Susan Doull (née Collins) 1997; ed Queen Elizabeth Grammar School, Wakefield, Marling School, Stroud and Merton Coll., Oxford; joined Lever Bros and Assocs 1962–65; entered Diplomatic Service 1965; Middle East Centre for Arab Studies 1966–68; Asst Political Agent, Abu Dhabi 1968–70; First Sec. FCO 1970–73; First Sec., later Counsellor, Washington 1973–78; Head of Arms Control and Disarmament Dept FCO 1979–81; Counsellor, Cairo 1981–84; Head Southern Africa Dept, FCO 1984–86; Asst UnderSec. of State 1986–88; Amb. to Jordan 1988–91; Amb. to, later High Commr in SA 1991–96; Chair. Foundation, SA 1998–2001; Dir (non-exec.) Barclays Pvt. Bank 1997–2001; Chair. Curzon Corpn 1998–. *Leisure interests:* music, golf. *Address:* Box Tree Cottage, Horsley, Stroud, Glos., GL6 0QB, England (home). *Telephone:* (1453) 832891. *E-mail:* anthony.reeve@btinternet.com.

REEVE, Michael David, MA, FBA; British academic; *Emeritus Fellow, Pembroke College, University of Cambridge;* b. 11 Jan. 1943, Bolton, Lancs.; s. of Arthur Reeve and Edith Mary Barrett; m. Elizabeth Klingaman 1970 (divorced 1999); two s. one d.; one s. with Emma Gee; ed King Edward's School, Birmingham, Balliol Coll., Oxford; Harmsworth Sr Scholar, Merton Coll., Oxford 1964–65; Woodhouse Research Fellow, St John's Coll., Oxford 1965–66; Tutorial Fellow, Exeter Coll., Oxford 1966–84, Emer. Fellow 1984–; Kennedy Prof. of Latin, Univ. of Cambridge 1984–2006, Dir of Research, Faculty of Classics 2006–07, Fellow, Pembroke Coll. 1984–2007, Emer. Fellow 2008–; Visiting Prof., Univ. of Hamburg 1976, McMaster Univ. 1979, Univ. of Toronto 1982–83; Ed., Classical Quarterly 1981–86; Ed.-in-Chief Cambridge Classical Studies –2007; Corresp. mem. Akad. der Wissenschaften, Göttingen 1990–; Chair., Advisory Council, Warburg Inst. 2008–; Foreign mem. Istituto Lombardo, Milan 1993–. *Publications:* Longus, Daphnis and Chloe 1982, contributions to Texts and Transmission 1983, Cicero, Pro Quinctio 1992, Vegetius 2004, Geoffrey of Monmouth 2007; articles in European and American journals. *Leisure interests:* chess, music, gardening, mountain walking. *Address:* Pembroke College, Cambridge, CB2

1RF, England (office). *Fax:* (1223) 335409 (office). *E-mail:* mdr1000@cam.ac .uk (office).

REEVES, Keanu; Canadian actor; b. 2 Sept. 1964, Beirut, Lebanon; s. of Samuel Nowin Reeves and Patricia Reeves; ed Toronto High School for Performing Arts; training at Second City Workshop, Toronto; Toronto stage debut in Wolf Boy; other stage appearances in For Adults Only, Romeo and Juliet; bass guitarist, rock band Dogstar 1996–2002. *Television films:* Letting Go 1985, Act of Vengeance 1986, Babes in Toyland 1986, Under the Influence 1986, Brotherhood of Justice 1986, Save the Planet (TV special) 1990. *Films:* Prodigal, Flying 1986, Youngblood 1986, River's Edge 1987, Permanent Record 1988, The Night Before 1988, The Prince of Pennsylvania 1988, Dangerous Liaisons 1988, 18 Again 1988, Bill and Ted's Excellent Adventure 1988, Parenthood 1989, I Love You to Death 1990, Tune In Tomorrow 1990, Bill and Ted's Bogus Journey 1991, Point Break 1991, My Own Private Idaho 1991, Bram Stoker's Dracula 1992, Much Ado About Nothing 1993, Even Cowgirls Get the Blues, Little Buddha 1993, Speed 1994, Johnny Mnemonic 1995, A Walk in the Clouds 1995, Chain Reaction, Feeling Minnesota, The Devil's Advocate 1996, The Last Time I Committed Suicide 1997, The Matrix 1999, The Replacements 2000, The Watcher 2000, The Gift 2000, Sweet November 2001, The Matrix Reloaded 2003, The Matrix Revolutions 2003, Something's Gotta Give 2003, Thumbsucker 2005, Constantine 2005, A Scanner Darkly 2006, The Lake House 2006, Street Kings 2008. *Address:* c/o Kevin Houvane, CAA, 9830 Wilshire Boulevard, Beverly Hills, CA 90212-1825; 581 North Crescent Heights Boulevard, Los Angeles, CA 90048, USA.

REEVES, Most Rev. Sir Paul Alfred, KStJ, ONZ, GCMG, GCVO, QSO, MA, LTh; New Zealand ecclesiastic, administrator and academic; *Chancellor, Auckland University of Technology;* b. (Paul Alfred Reeves), 6 Dec. 1932, Wellington; s. of D'Arcy Lionel Reeves and Hilda Mary Reeves; m. Beverley Watkins 1959; three d.; ed Wellington Coll., Vic. Univ. of Wellington, St John's Theological Coll., Auckland and St Peter's Coll., Oxford; Deacon 1958; Priest 1960; Curate, Tokoroa, NZ 1958–59, St Mary the Virgin, Oxford 1959–61, Kirkley St Peter, Lowestoft 1961–63; Vicar, St Paul, Okato, NZ 1964–66; Lecturer in Church History, St John's Coll., Auckland 1966–69; Dir of Christian Educ. Diocese of Auckland 1969–71; Bishop of Waiapu 1971–79, of Auckland 1979; Primate and Archbishop of New Zealand 1980–85; Gov.-Gen. of New Zealand (first Maori) 1985–90; Rep. of Anglican Church to UN 1991–93; Dean Te Rau Kahikatea Theological Coll., Auckland 1994–95; Prof. Auckland Univ. of Tech. 2000–05, Chancellor 2005–; Chair. Environmental Council 1974–76, Bioethics Council 2002–; Deputy Leader Comm. of Observers S. African elections 1994; Leader Comm. of Observers Ghanaian elections 1996; Chair. Fijian Constitutional Review Comm. 1995–96; Visiting Prof., Univ. of Auckland 1997–2000; Special Envoy of Commonwealth Secr. to Guyana 2000–; Hon. Fellow and Trustee St Peter's Coll., Oxford 1980; Hon. DCL (Oxon.) 1985; Hon. LLD (Vic., NZ); Hon. DD (General, New York); Dr hc (Edin.) 1994; Companion of Order of Fiji 1999. *Leisure interests:* swimming, sailing, jogging. *Address:* Auckland University of Technology, Private Bag 92006, Auckland (office); 16E Cathedral Place, Parnell, Auckland, New Zealand (home). *Telephone:* (9) 917-9672 (office); (9) 302-2913 (home). *Fax:* (9) 917-9983 (office); (9) 309-9912 (home). *E-mail:* paul.reeves@aut.ac.nz (office); sirpaulreeves@xtra.co.nz (home). *Website:* www.aut.ac.nz (office).

REEVES, Saskia; British actress; b. 1962, London; d. of Peter Reeves; ed Guildhall School of Music and Drama, London; toured S America, India and Europe with Cheek By Jowl theatre co. appearing in A Midsummer Night's Dream and The Man of Mode; subsequent stage appearances include Metamorphosis (Mermaid), Who's Afraid of Virginia Woolf? (Young Vic), Measure for Measure (Young Vic), Separation (Hampstead Theatre), Smelling A Rat (Hampstead Theatre), Ice Cream (Royal Court), The Darker Face of the Earth; appeared in BBC TV In My Defence series. *Films:* December Bride 1990, Antonia and Jane 1991, Close My Eyes 1991, In the Border Country 1991, The Bridge 1992, Traps 1994, I.D. 1995, The Butterfly Kiss 1995, Different for Girls 1996, Much Ado About Nothing 1998, L.A. Without a Map 1998, Heart 1999, Ticks 1999, Bubbles 2001, The Tesseract 2003, The Knickerman 2004, Fast Learners 2006. *Television includes:* A Woman of Substance 1983, Children Crossing 1990, Cruel Train 1995, Plotlands 1997, A Christmas Carol 1999, Dune (mini-series) 2000, Suspicion 2003, Island at War (mini-series) 2004, A Line in the Sand 2004, The Commander: Virus 2005, The Strange Case of Sherlock Holmes and Arthur Conan Doyle 2005, The Last Days of the Raj 2007. *Address:* c/o Markham & Froggatt Ltd, 4 Windmill Street, London, W1P 1HF, England.

REFALO, Michael A., BA, LLD, FRSA; Maltese politician, lawyer and diplomatist; *High Commissioner to UK;* b. 25 Feb. 1936; s. of Edward Refalo; m. Blanche Smith; one s. three d.; ed St Aloysius Coll., Univ. of Malta; lawyer 1961; fmr Pres. of Students' Council; MP 1971–; Parl. Sec. for Tourism 1987–94; Minister for Youth and the Arts 1994–95, for Justice and the Arts 1995–96; Shadow Minister and Opposition Spokesman on Tourism 1996–98; Minister for Tourism 1998–2005; High Commr to UK 2005–; Ed. for nine years of Sunday Nationalist Party newspaper; mem. Nationalist Party; Companion of Honour, Nat. Order of Merit (Malta) 2007. *Publications:* editorials and articles in other newspapers. *Address:* High Commission of Malta, Malta House, 36–38 Piccadilly, London, W1J 0LE, England (office). *Telephone:* (20) 7292-4800 (office). *Fax:* (20) 7734-1831 (office). *E-mail:* maltahighcommission .london@gov.mt (office).

REGÀS, Rosa, BPhil; Spanish writer and journalist; b. 1933, Barcelona; m.; five c.; ed Barcelona Univ.; editorial staff with Seix Barral 1964–70, with Edhasa; f. and Publisher, La Gaya Ciencia 1970–, journals Arquitectura Vis, Cuadernos de la Gaya Ciencia 1976–; trans. for UN 1983–94; Head of Culture Dept of Casa de América, part of Foreign Affairs Ministry 1994–98; Gen. Dir Biblioteca Nacional de España 2004–07 (resgnd); Chevalier de la Legion d'Honneur 2005, Creu de Sant Jordi, Generalitat de Catalunya 2005; Premio Grandes Viajeros 2005. *Publications include:* fiction: Memoria de Almator (novel) 1991, Azul (novel) (Premio Nadal) 1994, Pobre corazón (short stories) 1996, Barcelona, un día (short stories) 1998, Luna Lunera (novel) (Premio Ciudad de Barcelona) 1999, La canción de Dorotea (novel) (Premio Planeta) 2001, contrib. short stories to anthologies, including Relatos para un fin de milenio 1998, Cuentos solidarios 1999, Mujeres al alba 1999, La paz y la palabra 2003; non-fiction: La cuina de l'ampurdanet (leaflet) 1985, Ginebra (leaflet) 1988, Canciones de amor y de batalla: 1993–1995 (articles) 1995, Viaje a la luz del Cham 1995, Una revolución personal 1997, Desde el mar 1997, España: una nueva mirada (leaflet) 1997, Más canciones 1995–1998 (articles) 1998, La creación, la fantasía y la vida (essay) 1998, Sangre de mi sangre (essay) 1999, Diario de una abuela de verano (biog.) 2004, El valor de la protesta (articles) 2004; contrib. essays to collections, including Retratos literarios 1997, Ser mujer 2000, and to numerous journals and periodicals. *Address:* c/o Biblioteca Nacional, Paseo de Recoletos 20, 28071 Madrid, Spain. *E-mail:* arcano@rosaregas.net. *Website:* www.rosaregas.net.

REGESTER, Michael; British crisis management consultant; *Director, Regester Larkin Ltd;* b. 8 April 1947, Godalming; s. of Hugh Regester and Monique Levrey; m. 1st Christine Regester 1969 (divorced 1993); two d.; m. 2nd Leanne Moscardi 1994 (divorced 2003); one s. one d.; ed St Peter's School, Guildford; Man. Public Affairs, Gulf Oil Corpn, Europe, W Africa and Middle East 1975–80; Co-Founder and Jt Man. Dir Traverse-Healy and Regester Ltd 1980–87; Man. Dir Charles Barker Traverse-Healy Ltd 1987–89; Man. Dir Regester PLC 1990–94; Dir Regester Larkin Ltd 1994–. *Publications:* Crisis Management 1987, Investor Relations (with N. Ryder) 1990, Issues and Crisis Management (with J. Larkin) 2008. *Leisure interests:* sailing, golf, tennis, opera, cooking. *Address:* Regester Larkin Ltd, 16 Doughty Street, London, WC1N 2PL, England (office). *Telephone:* (20) 7831-3839 (office). *Fax:* (20) 7831-3632 (office). *E-mail:* mregester@regesterlarkin.com (office). *Website:* www.regesterlarkin.com (office).

REGIS, John, MBE; British fmr athlete; b. 13 Oct. 1966, Lewisham; s. of Antony Regis and Agnes Regis; winner, UK 200m 1985 (tie), 100m 1988, Amateur Athletics Asscn 200m 1986–87; UK record for 200m, World Championships 1987; World Championships bronze medallist 200m, silver medal, Olympic Games Seoul 1988, 300m indoor record holder Commonwealth Games 1990; silver medal 200m 1991, gold medal 4×100m relay 1991; gold medal 200m, 4×100m relay, 4×400m relay 1993; gold medal World Cup 1994, mem. British team Olympic Games, Atlanta 1996; retd 2000; mem. GB bobsleigh training team 2000; Head Athletics Div., Stellar Group Ltd (athletics man. team) 2000–; coach UK Athletics sprint-relay team 2001–. *Leisure interests:* golf, tennis, martial arts. *Address:* The Stellar Group Limited, 16 Stanhope Place, London, W2 2HH, England. *Telephone:* (20) 7298-0080. *Fax:* (20) 7298-0099. *E-mail:* JRegis1@aol.com. *Website:* www.stellargroup.co.uk.

REGO, Paula; British artist; b. 26 Jan. 1935, Lisbon, Portugal; d. of José Figueiroa Rego and Maria de San José Paiva Figueiroa Rego; m. Victor Willing (died 1988); one s. two d.; ed St Julian's School, Carcavelos, Portugal, Slade School of Fine Art, Univ. Coll., London; Assoc. Artist to Nat. Gallery 1990; Sr Fellow, RCA 1989; Dr hc (St Andrews, Univ. of E Anglia), (Rhode Island School of Design, USA) 2000, (London Inst.) 2002, (Univ. Coll. London) 2004, (Oxford) 2005, (Univ. of Roehampton) 2005. *Television:* The South Bank Show 1992, Artsworld 'The Passion of Paula Rego' 2001, Paula Rego (BBC Four) 2002. *Publications:* Monograph Phaidon 1992, 1997, Peter Pan (etchings) 1992, Nursery Rhymes (etchings) 1994, Pendle Witches (etchings) 1996, Children's Crusade (etchings) 1999, Monograph 2002, Complete Graphic Work 2003, Jane Eyre 2003. *Address:* c/o Marlborough Fine Art, 6 Albemarle Street, London, W1X 4BY, England. *Telephone:* (20) 7629-5161.

REGY, Claude, LLB; French theatre director; *Artistic Director, Les Ateliers Contemporains;* b. 1 May 1923, Nîmes; s. of Marcel Régy and Suzanne Picheral; ed Univs of Algiers, Lyons and Paris; dir plays by Marguerite Duras, Harold Pinter, James Saunders, Tom Stoppard, Edward Bond, David Storey 1960–70, by Nathalie Sarraute, Peter Handke, Botho Strauss 1970–80, by Maeterlinck, Wallace Stevens, Leslie Kaplan, Victor Slavkine 1980–90, by Gregory Motton, Henri Meschonnic, Charles Reznifoff, Jon Fosse, David Harrower 1990–2000; dir Ivanov (Chekhov) 1985, Huis-Clos (J. P. Sartre) 1990 (both at Comédie Française), Melancholia Théâtre (J. Fosse) 2001, 4.48 Psychose (S. Kane) 2002, Variations sur la mort (J. Fosse) 2003; dir operas Die Meistersinger (Wagner), Théâtre du Chatelet 1990, Jeanne d'Arc au Bûcher (Honegger), Opéra Bastille 1992, Carnet d'un Disparu (Janacek), Kunsten Festival des Arts, Festival d'Aix-en-Provence 2001; Artistic Dir Les Ateliers Contemporains 1976–; Officier des Arts et des Lettres; Grand Prix Nat. du Théâtre 1992, Grand Prix des Arts de la Scène de la Ville de Paris 1994. *Film:* Conversation avec Nathalie Sarraute 1989. *Publications:* Espaces Perdus 1991, L'Ordre des Morts 1999, L'Etat d'Incertitude 2002. *Leisure interest:* country house. *Address:* Les Ateliers Contemporains, 68 rue J. J. Rousseau, 75001 Paris, France. *Telephone:* 1-48-87-95-10 (office); 1-42-33-34-11 (home).

REHMAN, Maulana Fazlur; Pakistani politician; b. 21 Aug. 1953, Abdulkhel Banyala area in Dera Ismail Khan dist, North-West Frontier Prov.; s. of Mufti Mehmood; ed Dar-al-Ulum Haqania, Akura, Khatak; Sec.-Gen. Jamiat-e-Ulema-e-Islam 1974–2007, now heads own faction of JUI, Jamiat-e-Ulema-e-Islam—Fazl 2007–, also Sec.-Gen. Muttahida Majlis-e-Amal political coalition; mem. Nat. Ass., fmr Leader of the Opposition. *Address:* c/o Jamiat-e-Ulema-e-Islam (JUI), Jamia al-Maarf, al-Sharia, Dera Ismail Khan, Pakistan.

REHME, Robert; American film producer; b. 5 May 1935, Cincinnati, Ohio; m.; two d.; ed Univ. of Cincinnati; Pres. and CEO Avco Embassy Pictures 1978–81; Pres. Worldwide Distribution and Marketing, Universal Pictures, then Pres. Theatrical Motion Picture Group 1981–83; Co-Chair. and CEO New World Entertainment Inc. 1983–89; Co-Founder and Pnr Neufeld/Rehme Productions 1989; currently Head Rehme Productions, Los Angeles; Pres. Acad. of Motion Picture Arts and Sciences 1992–93, 1997–2001; mem. Bd of Trustees American Film Inst., Chair Center for Advanced Film and TV Studies (CAFTS–AFI Conservatory) 2000–; mem. BAFTA. *Films:* Vice Squad 1982, Flight of the Intruder 1991, Necessary Roughness 1991, Patriot Games 1992, Beverly Hills Cop 3 1994, Clear and Present Danger 1994, Blind Faith 1998, Lost in Space 1998, Black Dog 1998, Bless the Child 2000, Gods and Generals 2003. *Television:* Lightning Force (series) 1991, Woman Undone 1996, Gridlock 1996, For the Future: The Irvine Fertility Scandal 1996, Escape: Human Cargo 1998, Love and Treason 2001, Conviction 2002, Deacons for Defense 2003. *Address:* Rehme Productions, 1145 Gayley Avenue, Suite 301, Los Angeles, CA 90024, USA (office). *Telephone:* (310) 824-3371 (office). *Fax:* (310) 824-5459 (office).

REHN, Elisabeth, BSc, DSc; Finnish politician and international organization official; b. 6 April 1935, Helsinki; m. Ove Rehn 1955 (deceased); one s. three d.; ed Univ. of Helsinki; mem. Parl. 1979–95, fmr leader Swedish People's Party; Minister of Defence 1990–95, Minister for Women's Equality 1991–95; cand. in Finnish Presidential election 1994, 2000; MEP 1995–96; fmr UN Under-Sec.-Gen.; UN Special Rapporteur for Human Rights in Fmr Yugoslavia 1995–98; UN Under-Sec.-Gen., Special Rep. of UN Sec.-Gen. in Bosnia and Herzegovina 1998–99; UNIFEM Ind. Expert on impact of war on women 2001–02; Chair. Working Table I, (Human Rights and Democratisation), Stability Pact for SE Europe, Brussels 2003–04; Chair. Finnish Asscn for Educ. and Training of Women in Crisis Prevention 1997; mem. Advisory Council Intellibridge, Washington, DC, UN Dept of Peacekeeping Review Bd, Court of Conciliation and Arbitration, OSCE 1994, Int. Steering Cttee of Engendering The Peace Process; mem. UNICEF Finnish Cttee 1982–94, Chair. 1988–93; Vice Chair. Finnish Red Cross 1984–88; Chair. Bd of Trustees, WWF Finland 2000–06; Vice Chair. Suomen Unifem ry 2003–05, Chair. of Del. 2006–; mem. Advisory Bd Femmes Africa Solidarité 2005–; Patron United World Coll. project in Bosnia and Herzegovina 2005–, Chair. Bd of Educ. from Conflict to Internationalism 2006–; hon. mem. UNICEF Finland 1994, Zonta Int. 1996; Commdr of the Order of the White Rose of Finland 1992, Cross of Liberty, First Class with Grand Star (Finland) 2002, First Class Order of the Cross of Terra Mariana (Estonia) 2003; Hon. DSc (Swedish School of Econs and Business Admin) 1994. *Leisure interests:* fine arts, sports, nature. *Address:* Saarentie 22, 02400 Kirkkonummi, Finland (home). *Telephone:* (9) 2952842 (home). *E-mail:* elisabeth.rehn@kolumbus.fi (home). *Website:* www.elisabethrehn.com.

REHN, Olli, DPhil; Finnish politician; *Commissioner for Enlargement, European Commission;* b. 31 March 1962, Mikkeli; m. Merja Rehn; one c.; ed Macalester Coll., USA, Univ. of Helsinki, Univ. of Oxford, UK; Chair. Centre Youth of Finland 1987–89; Deputy Chair. Centre Party of Finland 1988–94; mem. Helsinki City Council 1988–94; mem. Parl. 1991–95; Special Adviser to Prime Minister 1992–93, Econ. Policy Adviser 2003–04; mem. European Parl. 1995–96; Head of Cabinet, EC 1998–2002, EU Commr for Enterprise and the Information Soc. . July–Nov. 2004, for Enlargement 2004–; Prof. and Dir of Research, Dept of Political Science and Centre for European Studies, Univ. of Helsinki 2002–03; columnist in several newspapers and magazines. *Publications:* Europe's Next Frontiers 2006, Suomen eurooppaiainen valinta ei ole suhdannepolitiikkaa 2006. *Leisure interests:* football, reading, rock and jazz. *Address:* European Commission, 200 rue de la Loi, 1049 Brussels, Belgium (office). *Telephone:* (2) 295-79-57 (office). *Fax:* (2) 295-85-61 (office). *E-mail:* cab-rehn-web-feedback@ec.europa.eu (office). *Website:* ec.europa.eu/commission_barroso/rehn/index_en.htm (office).

REICH, Otto Juan; Cuban-American consultant and fmr government official; *President, Otto Reich Associates LLC;* b. 1945, Cuba; ed Univ. of N Carolina, Georgetown Univ.; Lt, 3rd Civil Affairs Detachment, Panama Canal Zone, US Army 1967–69; Asst Admin. Econ. Assistance to Latin America and the Caribbean, USAID 1981–83; Special Adviser to Sec. of State 1983–86; Founder and Man. Office of Public Diplomacy for Latin America, the Caribbean and US Dept of State 1983–86; Amb. to Venezuela 1986–89; Alt. Rep. to UN Human Rights Comm., Geneva 1991–92; Asst Sec. of State for Western Hemisphere Affairs 2001–02, Special Envoy Nov. 2002–Jan. 2003; Presidential Special Envoy for Latin America, Nat. Security Council 2003–04; Pnr, later Pres. Brock Group (consulting firm) 1989–2001; currently Pres. Otto Reich Assocs LLC (consulting firm), Washington, DC; co-host CNN Int.'s Choque de Opiniones public affairs programme 1998–2001; Dir Center for a Free Cuba, Washington, DC; lobbyist for numerous cos including Bacardi and Lockheed Martin; fmr Washington Dir Council of the Americas; fmr Community Devt Co-ordinator for City of Miami, FL; fmr Int. Rep. of FL Dept of Commerce; fmr staff asst, US House of Reps; Meritorious Honour Award, Dept of State. *Address:* Otto Reich Associates LLC, 1101 30th Street, NW, Suite 200, Washington, DC 20007, USA (office). *Telephone:* (202) 333-1360 (office). *E-mail:* ora@ottoreichassociates.com (office). *Website:* www.ottoreichassociates.net (office).

REICH, Robert Bernard, BA, MA, JD; American political economist, academic and fmr government official; *Professor of Public Policy, Goldman School of Public Policy, University of California, Berkeley;* b. 24 June 1946, Scranton, Pa; s. of Edwin Saul and Mildred Dorf Reich (née Freshman); m. Clare Dalton 1973; two s.; ed Dartmouth Coll., Univ. of Oxford, UK, Yale Univ.; Asst Solicitor-Gen., US Dept of Justice, Washington, DC 1974–76; Dir of Policy Planning Fed. Trade Comm., Washington 1976–81; mem. Faculty, John F. Kennedy School of Govt, Harvard Univ. 1981–92; fmr Econ. Adviser to Pres. Bill Clinton (q.v.); Sec. of Labor 1993–97; Univ. Prof., Maurice B. Hexter

Prof. of Social and Econ. Policy, Brandeis Univ. Grad. School for Advanced Studies in Social Welfare 1997–2006; Prof. of Public Policy, Goldman School of Public Policy, Univ. of Calif., Berkeley 2006–; Chair. Biotechnology Section US Office Tech. Assessment, Washington 1990–91; Co-founder and Chair. Editorial Bd The American Prospect 202-03; mem. Nat. Governing Bd, Common Cause 1982–88; mem. Mass Comm. on Mature Industries 1985–87; mem. Bd of Dirs Business Enterprise Trust 1986–93, Econ. Policy Inst. 1988–93, 2002–03; Trustee Dartmouth Coll. 1988–93; Contributing Ed. The New Republic, Washington 1982–93; Rhodes Scholar 1968; Dr hc (Dartmouth Coll.) 1994, (Univ. of New Hampshire) 1997, (Wheaton Coll.) 1998, (Emory Univ.) 1999, (Bates Coll.) 2001, (Grinnell Coll.) 2002; Mass Teachers Asscn Award for Excellence 1997, Lifetime Achievement Award, Nat. Ass. of Voluntary Health and Social Welfare Orgs 1997, Eleanor Roosevelt Award for Public Service, Americans for Democratic Action 2001, Vaclev Havel Humanitarian Prize 2003. *Publications:* The Next American Frontier 1983, Tales of a New America 1987, The Power of Public Ideas (co-author) 1987, The Work of Nations 1991, Putting People First 1997, Locked in the Cabinet 1997, The Future of Success 2001, Reason: Why Liberals Will Win the Battle for America 2004, Supercapitalism: The Transformation of Business, Democracy and Everyday Life 2007. *Address:* Richard & Rhoda Goldman School of Public Policy, 301 GSPP Main, 2607 Hearst Avenue, University of California, Berkeley, CA 94720-7320, USA (office). *Telephone:* (510) 642-0551 (office). *E-mail:* rreich@berkeley.edu (office); bob@RobertReich.org. *Website:* gspp.berkeley.edu/people/faculty/reich.htm (office); www.robertreich.org.

REICH, Steve, MA; American composer; b. 3 Oct. 1936, New York; s. of Leonard Reich and June Carroll; m. Beryl Korot 1976; two s.; ed Cornell Univ., Juilliard School of Music, Mills Coll.; studied composition with Berio and Milhaud; also studied at the American Soc. for Eastern Arts and in Accra and Jerusalem; f. own ensemble 1966; Steve Reich and Musicians have completed numerous tours world-wide 1971–; his music performed by maj. orchestras and ensembles in United States and Europe; recipient of three Rockefeller Foundation Grants 1975–81 and a Guggenheim Fellowship; mem. American Acad. of Arts and Letters 1994–, Bavarian Acad. of Fine Arts 1995; Regent Lectureship, Univ. of Calif., Berkeley 2000; Montgomery Fellowship, Dartmouth Coll.; Commdr des Arts et Lettres 1999; Dr hc (Calif. Inst. of the Arts) 2000; Koussevitzky Foundation Award 1981, Schumann Prize, Columbia Univ. 2000, Praemium Imperiale Music Laureate, Japan 2006. *Major works include:* It's Gonna Rain (tape) 1965, Come Out (tape) 1966, Melodica (tape) 1966, Piano Phase for two pianos or two marimbas 1967, Violin Phase for violin and tape or four violins 1967, My Name Is for three tapes recorders and performers (manuscript only) 1967, Pendulum Music for 3 or 4 microphones, amplifiers and loudspeakers 1968, Four Organs for four electric organs and maracas 1970, Phase Patterns for four electric organs 1970, Drumming for 4 pairs of tuned bongo drums, 3 marimbas, 3 glockenspiels, 2 female voices, whistling and piccolo 1970–71, Clapping Music for two musicians clapping 1972, Music for Pieces of Wood for five pair of tuned claves 1973, Music for Mallet Instruments, Voices, and Organ 1973, Six Pianos 1973, Music for 18 Musicians (Grammy Award for Best Contemporary Composition 1995) 1974–76, Music for a Large Ensemble 1978, Variations for Winds, Strings, and Keyboards 1979, Octet 1979, Tehillim for voices and ensemble 1981, Vermont Counterpoint for amplified flute and tape 1982, The Desert Music for 10 singers (amplified) and reduced orchestra 1984, Eight Lines for ensemble 1983, Sextet for percussion and keyboards 1984, New York Counterpoint for amplified clarinet and tape, or 11 clarinets 1985, Six Marimbas (transcription of Six Pianos 1973) for 6 marimbas 1986, Three Movements for orchestra 1986, Electric Counterpoint for electric guitar or amplified acoustic guitar and tape, amplified guitar soloist and tape, or guitar ensemble 1987, The Four Sections for orchestra 1987, Different Trains for string quartet and tape (orchestrated 2000) (Grammy Award for Best Contemporary Composition 1990) 1988, The Cave (with Beryl Korot) for amplified voices and ensemble 1993/2003, Duet for two solo violins and string ensemble 1993, Typing Music 1993, Nagoya Marimbas for two marimbas 1994, City Life for amplified ensemble 1995, Proverb for voices and ensemble 1995, Triple Quartet for amplified string quartet (with pre-recorded tape), or three string quartets, or string orchestra 1998, Know What Is Above You for four women's voices and 2 percussion 1999, Electric Guitar Phase for electric guitar and pre-recorded tape (arrangement of Violin Phase 1967) 2000, Tokyo/Vermont Counterpoint for KAT MIDI mallet and pre-recorded tape (arrangement of Vermont Counterpoint 1981) 2000, Three Tales (video opera, video by Beryl Korot) 2002, Dance Patterns for 2 xylophones, 2 vibraphones, 2 pianofortes 2002, Cello Counterpoint for amplified cello and multi-channel tape 2003, You Are (Variations) (text by Rabbi Nachman of Breslov (English), Psalms (Hebrew), Wittgenstein (English) and Pirke Avot (Hebrew) for amplified ensemble and voices, no brass, 2 marimbas, 2 vibraphones, 4 pianofortes, strings, and voices 2004, The Daniel Variations 2006, Double Sextet (Pulitzer Prize in Music 2009) 2008. *Recordings include:* Come Out, Violin Phase, It's Gonna Rain, Four Organs, Drumming, Six Pianos, Music for Mallet Instruments, Voices and Organ, Music for a Large Ensemble, Octet and Variations for Winds, Strings and Keyboards, Music for 18 Musicians, The Desert Music, Electric Counterpoint, Different Trains, The Four Sections, Nagoya Marimbas, City Life, Proverb, Hindenburg (in collaboration with Beryl Korot). *Address:* c/o Elizabeth Sobol, IMG Artists, Carnegie Hall Tower, 152 West 57th Street, 5th Floor, New York, NY 10019, USA (office); c/o Andrew Rosner, Allied Artists 42, Montpelier Square, London, SW7 1JZ, England (office). *Telephone:* (212) 994-3500 (New York) (office); (20) 7589-6243 (London) (office). *Fax:* (212) 994-3550 (New York) (office); (20) 7581-5269 (London) (office). *E-mail:* esobol@imgartists.com (office). *Website:* www.imgartists.com (office); www.alliedartists.co.uk (office); www.stevereich.com.

REICH-RANICKI, Marcel; German author and literary critic; b. 2 June 1920, Wloclawek; s. of David Reich and Helene Auerbach; m. Teofila Langnas 1942; one s.; in Berlin 1929–38; deported to Poland 1938; publr, reader and literary critic, Warsaw until 1958; returned to Germany 1958; regular literary critic Die Zeit 1960–73; guest lecturer in US univs 1968–69; regular guest Prof. of Modern German Literature in Univs of Stockholm and Uppsala 1971–75; Man. Ed. Frankfurter Allgemeine Zeitung 1973–88 (retd); Hon. Prof., Univ. of Tübingen 1974–; DPhil hc (Univ. of Augsburg) 1992, (Univ. of Brandenberg) 1997, (Univ. of Düsseldorf) 2001, (Univ. of Utrecht) 2001; Dr hc (Humboldt-Universität zu Berlin) 2006; Heine-Plakette 1976, Ricarda Huch Prize 1981, Goethe-Plakette 1984, Thomas-Mann-Preis 1987, Ludwig-Börne-Preis 1995, Hess Kulturpreis 1999, Goldenes Kamera 2000, Friedrich-Hölderin-Preis 2001, Ehrendoktorwürde der Universität Utrecht 2001, und der Universität München 2002, Goethe Preis 2002, sowie das Große Verdienstkreuz mit Stern 2002. *Publications:* Deutsche Literatur in West und Ost 1963, Literarisches Leben in Deutschland 1965, Literatur der kleinen Schritte 1967, Lauter Verrisse 1970, Uber Ruhestörer-Juden in der deutschen Literatur 1973, Zur Literatur der DDR 1974, Nachprüfung, Aufsätze über deutsche Schriftsteller von gestern 1977, Entgegnung, Zur deutschen Literatur der siebziger Jahre 1979, Betrifft Goethe 1982, Lauter Lobreden 1985, Nichts als Literatur, Aufsätze und Anmerkungen 1985, Mehr als ein Dichter, Über Heinrich Böll 1986, Thomas Mann und die Seinen 1987, Herz, Ärzt und Literatur 1987, Thomas Bernhard, Aufsätze und Reden 1990, Max Frisch, Aufsätze 1991, Reden auf Hilde Spiel 1991, Ohne Rabatt—Über Literatur aus der DDR, Der doppelte Boden 1992, Günter Grass, Aufsätze 1992, Die Anwälte der Literatur 1994, Martin Walser 1994, Vladimir Nabokov 1995, Ungeheuer oben. Über Bertolt Brecht 1996, Der Fall Heine 1997, 'Mein Leben' 1999, Vom Tag gefordert 2001, Erst leben, dann spielen. Über polnische Literatur 2002, Sieben Wegberiter, Schriftsteller des 20. Jarhunderts 2002, Goethe noch einmal 2002, Kritik als Beruf 2002 und Meine Bilder. Portraits und Aufsätze 2003; Der Kanon. Die deutsche Literatur. (Ed.). *Leisure interests:* literature, theatre, music. *Address:* Gustav-Freytag-Strasse 36, 60320 Frankfurt am Main, Germany.

REICHARDT, Robert Heinrich, DPhil; Austrian/Swiss sociologist and academic; b. 2 May 1927, Basel; s. of Heinrich Reichardt and Magdalena Reichardt (née Bachlehner); m. Dr Isolde Dünhofen; ed Univ. of Basel; Research Assoc., Princeton Univ. 1960–61; Asst Inst. for Social Sciences, Univ. of Basel 1962–64; Dir Dept for Sociology, Inst. for Higher Studies, Vienna 1964–66; Prof., Univ. of Vienna 1966–; Exec. Dir Inst. for Research on Socio-Econ. Devt, Austrian Acad. of Sciences 1977–84, Head Comm. for Sociology of Arts and Music 1990–; mem. Austrian Acad. of Sciences 1978–; Fellow, Collegium Ramazzini Carpi, Italy 1990, Academia Artium et Scientiarum Europaea 1991; Co-operative Prize, Univ. of Basel 1960, Gold Medal of Honour, City of Vienna 1993. *Publications:* Die Schallplatte als kulturelles und ökon. Phänomen, Bedürfnisforschung im Dienste der Stadtplanung, Überleben wir den technischen Fortschritt (with others), Einführung in die Soziologie für Juristen. *Leisure interests:* composition, playing the piano.

REICHMANN, Paul; Canadian real estate industry executive; b. 23 Sept. 1930, Vienna, Austria; s. of Samuel Reichmann and Renée Reichmann; moved to France as child then to Tangier and around N Africa; moved to Toronto 1954; with brothers Ralph and Albert Reichmann formed Olympia & York Developments Ltd (business engaged mainly in real estate but with investments in Gulf Canada, The Consumers Gas Co., Abitibi-Price real estate) 1975; completed First Canadian Place, Toronto (five million sq. ft of offices) 1975; purchased eight office bldgs in Manhattan, New York 1976; completed building of World Financial Center (ten million sq. ft ft of offices) in New York 1987; responsible for concept and realization of Canary Wharf project in London's Docklands 1987, fmr Exec. Chair. Canary Wharf Group PLC, sold to investors 2005; Chief Exec. of Reichmann Group of Cos, including Int. Property Corpn (with interests in real estate devt projects in Mexico); Trustee and Unitholder Retirement Residence Real Estate Investment Trust, CPL Long Term Care Real Estate Investment Trust —2004 (retd); Trustee IPC US Income Commercial Real Estate Investment Trust –2006; f. PR Capital Corpn 2006. *Address:* c/o Canary Wharf Group PLC, 1 Canada Square, Canary Wharf, London, E14 5AB, England (office).

REICHS, Kathleen (Kathy) J., BA,MA, PhD; American writer and forensic anthropologist; b. Chicago; m. Paul Reichs; two d. one s.; ed American Univ., Northwestern Univ.; Asst Prof., Northern Illinois Univ. 1974–78; Instructor, Stateville Correctional Facility, Joliet, Ill. 1975–78; Asst Prof., Davidson Coll. 1981–83; Lecturer, Univ. of North Carolina at Charlotte 1978–81, 1983–87, Asst Prof. 1987–88, Assoc. Prof. 1988–96, Prof. 1996– (currently on leave); works as forensic anthropologist at Office of the Chief Medical Examiner, State of North Carolina and Laboratoires des Sciences Judiciaires et de Médecine Légale, Canada; Visiting Prof., Univ. of Pittsburgh 1987, Visiting Assoc. Prof., Concordia Univ. 1988–89, McGill Univ. 1988–97 (summers); mem. American Acad. of Forensic Sciences, Sec. Physical Anthropology Section 1994–95, Chair, Physical Anthropology Section 1995–96, mem. Bd of Dirs 1996–2002, mem. Exec. Cttee 2000–; mem. Bd of Dirs American Bd of Forensic Anthropology 1986–93, Vice Pres. 1989–93; mem. Canadian Nat. Police Services Advisory Council; producer for TV series "Bones"; named one of Canada's 100 Most Powerful Women 2004, Premio Piemonte Grinzane Noir, Vincitore Sezione Giallo Internazionale Award, Italy 2007. *Publications:* Déjà Dead (Ellis Award for Best First Novel) 1997, Death du Jour 1999, Deadly Decisions 2000, Fatal Voyage 2001, Grave Secrets 2002, Bare Bones 2003, Monday Mourning 2004, Cross Bones 2005, Bones to Ashes 2007, Devil Bones 2008, 206 Bones 2009. *Address:* c/o Simon & Schuster, Inc., 1230 Avenue of the Americas, New York, NY 10020, USA. *E-mail:* kjreichs@aol.com. *Website:* www.kathyreichs.com (office).

REICHSTUL, Henri Philippe; Brazilian business executive; *CEO, Brenco (Brazilian Renewable Energy Company);* b. 12 April 1949; Vice-Pres. Banco Interamerican Express –1999; Pres. Petrobras 1999–2002; CEO Globopar SA 2002–03; Founding Pnr, G&R Gestao Empresarial (consulting firm); currently CEO Brenco (Brazilian Renewable Energy Co.); mem. Bd of Dirs Ashmore Energy Int., REPSOL-YPF, PSA-Peugeot Citroen; mem. Consulting Bd Lhoist Brazil; mem. Admin. Council, Grupo Pão de Açúcar 2003–; mem. Admin. Council, Vivo Participações 2006–. *Address:* Brenco, Avenida Brigadeira Faria Lima, 1309 4° andar, São Paulo CEP 01452-002, Brazil (office). *Telephone:* (11) 3095-2250 (office). *E-mail:* brenco@brenco.com.br (office). *Website:* www.brenco.com.br (office).

REID, Allen (Alan) Forrest, AM, PhD, DSc, FAA, FTSE; Australian scientist; b. 26 March 1931, New Zealand; s. of V. C. Reid and L. E. Reid; m. Prudence M. Little; two s. one d. two step-d.; ed Univ. of NZ, Christchurch, ANU, Canberra, Cornell Univ., New York; joined CSIRO 1959, research scientist 1972–82, Chief Research Scientist 1972–82, Chief Div. of Mineral Engineering 1982–84, Dir Inst. of Energy and Earth Resources 1984–87, Inst. of Minerals, Energy and Construction 1988–97; Chair. Australia Environmental Resources NL 1996–97, Dir 1997–; Chair. Australian Petroleum Co-operative Research Centre 1991–2003; Dir Australian Minerals and Energy Environmental Foundation 1991–; high pressure mineral, Reidite, named after him 2001; CSIRO Rivett Medal 1970, Ian Wark Medal, Australian Acad. of Science 2008. *Publications:* Urban Air Pollution in Australia (ed) 1997, more than 80 scientific papers and six patents. *Leisure interests:* art collecting, oil painting. *Address:* 178 Ward Street, North Adelaide, South Australia 5006, Australia (home). *E-mail:* alan.reid@kern.com.au (home).

REID, David E., CA; British business executive; *Non-Executive Chairman, Tesco plc;* b. 1947, Zambia; two d.; ed Fettes Coll.; qualified as chartered accountant; worked for Peat Marwick, Philips Industries and BAT Industries –1985; joined Tesco plc 1985, mem. Bd of Dirs 1985–, Dir of Finance 1985–97, Deputy Chair. 1997–2004, Chair. (non-exec.) 2004–; Dir (non-exec.) Reed Elsevier Group PLC; Chair. Kwik-Fit Group; Founder and Trustee The Fettes Foundation; mem. Inst. of Chartered Accountants, Scotland. *Address:* Tesco plc, New Tesco House, Delamare Road, Cheshunt, Herts., EN8 9SL, England (office). *Telephone:* (1992) 632222 (office). *Fax:* (1992) 630794 (office). *E-mail:* info@tesco.com (office). *Website:* www.tesco.com (office).

REID, Harry, JD; American politician; *Senator from Nevada and Senate Majority Leader;* b. 2 Dec. 1939, Searchlight, Nevada; s. of Harry Reid and Inez Reid; m. Landra Joy Gould; four s. one d.; ed Utah State Univ., George Washington Univ.; City Attorney, Henderson, Nev. 1964–66; Trustee, Southern Nev. Memorial Hosp. Bd 1967–69, Chair. Bd of Trustees 1968–69; mem. Nev. Ass. 1969–70; Lt-Gov. of Nev. 1970–74; Chair. Nev. Gaming Comm. 1977–81; Congressman, US House of Reps, Washington, DC 1983–87; Senator from Nevada 1987–, Minority Leader 2004–07, Majority Leader 2007–; mem. numerous Senate cttees; mem. Bd of Dirs of American Cancer Soc., of Legal Aid Soc., of YMCA; Democrat; Hon. LLD (Southern Utah State Coll.) 1984; Nat. Jewish Hosp., Humanitarian Award 1984. *Address:* 528 Hart Senate Office Building, Washington, DC 20510, USA (office). *Telephone:* (202) 224-3542 (office). *Fax:* (202) 224-7327. *Website:* reid.senate.gov (office).

REID, Rt Hon. John, PC, PhD; British politician and sports administrator; b. 8 May 1947, Bellshill, Lanarkshire; s. of the late Thomas Reid and Mary Reid; m. 1st Catherine McGowan (died 1998); two s.; m. 2nd Carine Adler 2002; ed St Patrick's Sr Secondary School, Coatbridge and Stirling Univ.; Research Officer, Labour Party 1979–83; Political Adviser to Neil Kinnock (q.v) 1983–85; Organizer, Scottish Trade Unionists for Labour 1985–87; MP for Motherwell N 1987–97, for Hamilton N and Bellshill 1997–2005, for Airdrie and Shotts 2005–; Opposition Spokesman on Children 1989–90, on Defence 1990–97; Minister of State for Defence 1997–98; Minister for Transport 1998–99; Sec. of State for Scotland 1999–2000; Sec. of State for NI 2000–02; Chair. of the Labour Party and Minister without Portfolio 2002–03; Leader of the House of Commons and Pres. of the Privy Council April–June 2003; Sec. of State for Health 2003–05, for Defence 2005–06, for the Home Department 2006–07 (resgnd); Chair. Celtic Football Club, Glasgow 2007–; mem. Armed Forces Cttee and Reserved Forces Cttee 1996–97. *Leisure interests:* football, reading history, crossword puzzles. *Address:* House of Commons, London, SW1A 0AA, England; Celtic FC Ltd, Celtic Park, Glasgow, G40 3RE, Scotland. *Telephone:* (20) 7219-4118; (871) 226-1888 (Celtic). *Fax:* (20) 7219-2771. *E-mail:* reidj@parliament.uk. *Website:* www.johnreidmp.com; www.celticfc.net.

REID, Sir Robert Paul (Bob), Kt, MA; British business executive; *Chairman, ICE Futures;* b. 1 May 1934, Cupar, Fife; m. Joan Mary Reid 1958; three s.; ed St Andrews Univ.; joined Shell 1956, Sarawak Oilfields 1956–59, Head of Personnel Nigeria 1959–67; Africa and S. Asia Regional Org. 1967–68, Personal Asst and Planning Adviser to Chair. Shell & BP Services, Kenya 1968–70, Man. Dir Nigeria 1970–74, Man. Dir Thailand 1974–78; Vice-Pres. Int. Aviation and Products Training 1978–80, Exec. Dir Downstream Oil, Shell Co. of Australia Int. Petroleum Co. 1984–90, Chair. and Chief Exec. Shell UK 1985–90; Chair. Foundation for Man. Educ. 1986–2003; Chair. British Railways Bd 1990–95, London Electricity PLC 1994–97, Sears PLC 1995–99, Rosyth 2000 1995–, ICE Futures (fmly Int. Petroleum Exchange of London) 1999–, Milton Keynes Partnership Cttee 2004–; Deputy Gov. Bank of Scotland 1997–2004; mem. Bd of Dirs The Merchants Trust 1995–, Siemens plc 1998–2006, CHC Helicopter Corpn 2004–, Benella Ltd 2004–, Diligenta Ltd 2005–, Avis 1997–2004, Sun Life Assurance Co. of Canada 1997–2004, HBOS 2001–04; Chancellor Robert Gordon Univ. 1993–2004; Hon. LLD (St Andrews) 1987, (Aberdeen) 1988, (Sheffield Hallam) 1995, (South Bank) 1995, (Kent) 2003. *Leisure interest:* golf, opera. *Address:* ICE Futures, 1 Saint Katherine's Way, London, E1 9UN (office); 24 Ashley Gardens, London, SW1P 1QD, England (home). *Telephone:* (20) 7481-0643 (office). *Fax:* (20) 7860-1786 (office). *E-mail:* kathleen.murray@theice.com (office). *Website:* www.theice.com (office).

REID, Timothy Escott, BA, MA, MLitt; Canadian investor, business executive and public servant; b. 21 Feb. 1936, Toronto, Ont.; s. of Escott Meredith Reid and Ruth Reid (née Herriot); m. Julyan Fancott 1962; one s. one d.; ed Univ. of Toronto, Yale Univ., Univ. of Oxford (Rhodes Scholar), Harvard Grad. School of Business; Exec. Sec. Canadian Inst. of Public Affairs 1962–63; Asst to Pres., Asst Prof. of Econs, Research Assoc. for Public Policy, York Univ. 1963–72; mem. Ont. Legis. Ass. 1967–71; Prin. Admin., Manpower and Social Affairs, OECD, Paris 1972–74; joined Public Service of Canada 1974, subsequently Deputy Sec. Treasury Bd, Office of Comptroller-Gen. of Canada, Asst Deputy Minister, Dept of Regional Econ. Expansion, Exec. Dir Regional and Industrial Program Affairs, Dept of Regional Industrial Expansion, Asst Deputy Minister responsible for Tourism Canada 1984–85; Dir and mem. exec. Cttee Canada Mortgage and Housing Corpn 1980–82, Canadian Labour Market and Productivity Centre 1989 (Co-Chair. Bd of Dirs 1993–97); headed 18-nation OECD study visit to Japan 1984; Prof. of Business Man. and Dean, Faculty of Business, Ryerson Polytechnical Inst. 1985–89; Commr Ont. Securities Comm. 1987–89; Prime Minister's Business Rep., Pacific Business Forum APEC 1994–95; Pres. Canadian Chamber of Commerce 1989–98, ReMan Canada Inc. 1998–2001; Founding mem. and Venture Investor XPV Capital Corpn 2001–; Chair. Bd of Dirs Ontario Lottery and Gaming Corpn 2004–06; mem. Bd of Dirs Inst. of Public Admin of Canada 1985–87, Canadian Exec. Service Org. 1991–95, Inst. of Corporate Dirs 1999–2003, VIA Rail Canada Corpn 2000–07; mem. Int. Trade Advisory Cttee (ITAC), Govt of Canada 1991–97; Gov. Univ. of Toronto Governing Council 2002– (Exec. Cttee 2006–); Patron, Canadian Inst. of Int. Affairs 1999–2003; 125 Anniversary Commemorative Medal, Canada 1992, Queen's Golden Jubilee Medal 2002. *Publications:* Contemporary Canada: Reading in Economics 1969, Student Power and the Canadian Campus (with Julyan Reid) 1969. *Leisure interests:* tennis, swimming, pilates. *Address:* 25 Scrivener Square, Suite 904, Toronto, ON M4W 3Y6, Canada (home).

REIDY, Carolyn Kroll, AB, MA, PhD; American publishing executive; *President and CEO, Simon and Schuster, Inc.;* b. (Carolyn Judith Kroll), 2 May 1949, Washington, DC; d. of Henry Kroll and Mildred Kroll; m. Stephen Kroll Reidy 1974; ed Middlebury Coll. Vt and Indiana Univ.; various positions, Random House, New York 1975–83; Dir of Subsidiary Rights, William Morrow & Co., New York 1983–85; Vice-Pres. Assoc. Publr, Vintage Books, Random House, New York 1985–87; Assoc. Publr, Random House (concurrent with Assoc. Publr and Publr of Vintage Books) 1987–88; Publr, Vintage Books 1987–88, Anchor Books, Doubleday, New York 1988; Pres. and Publr, Avon Books, New York 1988–92; Pres. and Publr, Simon and Schuster Trade Div. 1992–2001, Pres. Adult Publishing Div., Simon and Schuster 2001–08, Pres. and CEO 2008–; Dir NAMES Project 1994–98, New York Univ. Center for Publishing 1997–2008, Literacy Partners, Inc. 1999–, Nat. Book Foundation 2000–; Matrix Award 2002. *Address:* Simon and Schuster, 1230 Avenue of the Americas, New York, NY 10020, USA (office). *Telephone:* (212) 698-7323 (office). *Fax:* (212) 698-7035 (office). *E-mail:* carolyn.reidy@simonandschuster.com (office). *Website:* simonandschuster.com (office).

REIJNDERS, Lucas, PhD; Dutch scientist and academic; *Professor of Environmental Science, University of Amsterdam;* b. 4 Feb. 1946, Amsterdam; s. of C. Reijnders and C. M. Reijnders-Spillekom; one c.; ed Univ. of Amsterdam; Dir Environmental Inst. Univ. of Groningen 1974–80, mem. staff Nat. Environmental Office 1980–, Prof. of Environmental Science Univ. of Amsterdam 1988–; Prof. of Environmental Science, Open Univ., Heerlen 1999–; Winner, Gouden Ganzeveer 1990, Erewimpel ONRI 1992. *Publications:* Food in the Netherlands 1974, A Consumer Guide to Dutch Medicines 1980, Plea for a Sustainable Relation with the Environment 1984, Help the Environment 1991, Environmentally Improved Production and Products 1995, Agriculture in the Low Countries 1997, Travel Through the Ages 2000, Eating Patterns 2005, Energy 2006, Principles of Environmental Science 2008. *Leisure interest:* 19th-century literature. *Address:* Anna van den Vondelstraat 10, 1054 GZ Amsterdam, Netherlands. *Telephone:* (20) 525-62-69. *Fax:* (20) 525-74-31. *E-mail:* l.reijnders@science.uva.nl (office). *Website:* www.science.uva.nl (office).

REILLY, (David) Nicholas (Nick), CBE, MA, FIMI; British automotive executive; *President, GM Asia Pacific;* b. 17 Dec. 1949, Anglesey, N Wales; s. of the late John Reilly and of Mona (née Glynne Jones) Reilly; m. Susan Haig 1976; one s. two d.; ed Harrow School, St Catharine's Coll. Cambridge; investment analyst 1971–74; joined Gen. Motors 1975, Finance Dir Moto Diesel Mexicana 1980–83, Supply Dir Vauxhall Motors 1984–87, Mfg Dir Vauxhall Ellesmere Port 1990–94, Vice-Pres. Quality Gen. Motors Europe 1994–96, Chair., Man. Dir Vauxhall Motors 1996–2001, Chair. (non-exec.) 2001, Vice-Pres. European Sales and Marketing, Gen. Motors Europe 2001, Pres. and CEO GM Daewoo Auto and Technology Co. 2002–06, Pres. GM Asia Pacific and GM Group Vice Pres. 2006–, also Chair. GM Daewoo Auto and Technology Co. Bd of Dirs; Vice-Pres. IBC 1987–90, Chair. IBC Vehicles 1996–; mem. Bd Saab GB 1996; Chair. Chester, Ellesmere, Wirral Training and Enterprise Council 1990–94, Training Standards Council 1997–2001, Adult Learning Inspectorate 2001; Pres. Soc. of Motor Mfrs and Traders 2001–02. *Leisure interests:* skiing, swimming, sailing, golf, watching sports, music, opera, theatre. *Address:* GM Asia Pacific, 10th Floor, Jinmao Tower, 88 Century Avenue, Pudong City, Shanghai 200121, Peoples Republic of China (office). *Telephone:* (9) 1288055 (office). *Website:* www.gm.com (office).

REILLY, Kevin P., BA, MA, PhD; American university administrator; *President, University of Wisconsin System;* m. Kate Reilly; three c.; ed Univ. of Notre Dame, Indiana Univ. of Minn.; teaching assoc. Dept of English, Univ.

of Minn. 1974–79; various posts NY State Bd of Regents 1979–92; Assoc. Provost for Acad. Programs State Univ. of NY System 1992–95, Sec. 1995–96; Provost and Vice Chancellor Univ. of Wis. (UW)-Extension 1996–2000, Chancellor 2000–04, Pres. UW System 2004–; Chair. American Council of Educ.'s Comm. on Adult Learning and Educational Credentials; mem. Steering Cttee of four statewide Wis. econ. summits. *Publications:* has written and edited books and articles on higher education policy, accreditation, biography and Irish studies. *Address:* University of Wisconsin System, Office of the President, 1720 Van Hise Hall, 1220 Linden Drive, Madison, WI 53706, USA (office). *Telephone:* (608) 262-2321. *Fax:* (608) 262-3985. *E-mail:* kreillly@uwsa.edu. *Website:* www.uwsa.edu.

REIMAN, Leonid Dododjonovich; Russian engineer and government official; *Minister of Information and Communications Technologies;* b. 12 July 1957, Leningrad (now St Petersburg); m.; one s. one d.; ed Leningrad Inst. of Electro-Tech. Communications; engineer, head of workshop Leningrad Telephone Exchange 1979–85; posts at Leningrad City Telephone Network 1985–88, later Deputy Head, Chief Eng, Dir of Int. Relations, Dir of Investments, First Deputy Dir-Gen. Jt Stock Co. Peterburgskaya Telefonnaya Set 1988–99; First Deputy Chair. State Cttee on Telecommunications Russian Fed. July–Aug. 1999; Chair. 1999–2000; Minister of Communications and Information Tech. 1999–2004; Deputy Minister for Transport and Communications April 2004; Minister of Information and Communications Techs April 2004–. *Address:* Ministry of Information and Communications Technologies, 103375 Moscow, Tverskaya str. 7, Russia (office). *Telephone:* (495) 771-81-00 (office). *Fax:* (495) 771-87-18 (office). *Website:* www.minsvyaz.ru (office).

REIN, Jeffrey A., BS; American retail executive; *Chairman and CEO, Walgreen Company;* b. 28 Feb. 1952, New Orleans, La; ed Univ. of Arizona; joined Walgreens as Asst Man., Tucson 1982–84, Store Man., Tex. 1984–90, Dist Man., New Mexico 1990–96, Divisional Vice-Pres. and Treas. 1996–2000, Vice-Pres., Marketing Systems and Services 2000–01, Exec. Vice-Pres., Marketing 2001–03, Pres. and COO 2003–06, Pres. 2003–07, CEO 2006–, Chair. 2007–; mem. Bd of Dirs Nat. Asscn of Chain Drugstores, Midwest Young Artists, Midtown Educational Foundation, Retail Industry Leaders Asscn; Chair. American Cancer Soc., Illinois Div. of CEOs Against Cancer. *Address:* Walgreen Co., 200 Wilmot Road, Deerfield, IL 60015, USA (office). *Telephone:* (847) 914-2500 (office). *Fax:* (847) 914-2804 (office). *E-mail:* info@walgreens.com (office). *Website:* www.walgreens.com (office).

REINÅS, Jan; Norwegian business executive; *Adviser, Management Assessment Partners AG;* b. 1945; Pres. Scandinavian Airlines System (S.A.S.) Norway –1993, CEO S.A.S. 1993–94; CEO Norske Skog 1994–2003; Chair. Norsk Hydro ASA 2004–07 (resgnd); Adviser, Management Assessment Pnrs AG 2007–; mem. Bd of Dirs Schibsted ASA, Swiss Int. Air Lines. *Address:* MAP AG, Basteiplatz 7, 8001 Zurich, Switzerland (office). *Telephone:* (44) 289-8887 (home). *Fax:* (44) 289-8889 (office). *E-mail:* info@mgmtassessment.com (office). *Website:* www.mgmtassessment.com (office).

REINEMUND, Steven S., MBA; American business executive; b. 1949; ed US Naval Acad., Univ. of Va; served as officer US Marine Corps 1970–75, achieved rank of Capt. 1975; joined PepsiCo 1984, Pres. and CEO Pizza Hut Div. 1986–91, Pres. and CEO Pizza Hut Worldwide 1991–92, Pres. and CEO Frito-Lay N America 1992–96, Chair. and CEO Frito-Lay Inc. 1996–1999, Pres. and COO PepsiCo Inc. 1999–2001, Chair. and CEO PepsiCo Inc. 2001–06 (retd); mem. Bd of Dirs Johnson & Johnson 2003–, Exxon Mobil Corpn 2007–, Marriott International Inc. 2007–, American Express Co., Business Council of New York State Inc.; fmr Chair. Nat. Minority Supplier Devt Council; mem. Nat. Advisory Bd The Salvation Army 1990–99, Chair. 1996–99; fmr mem. Nat. Council of La Raza; Trustee US Naval Acad. Foundation; Exec. Fellow, The Exec. Program, Darden School of Business, Univ. of Virginia 2007; Pres.'s Award, Nat. Council of La Raza 1997, Excellence in Bd Leadership Award, Nat. Ass. of Nat. Voluntary Health and Social Welfare Orgs 1998, Order of Auxiliary Service Medal, Salvation Army 1998, William Booth Award 1999. *Address:* c/o PepsiCo Inc., 700 Anderson Hill Road, Purchase, NY 10577-1444, USA (office).

REINER, Rob; American actor, writer, director and producer; b. 6 March 1947, New York, NY; s. of Carl Reiner and Estelle Reiner (née Lebost); m. 1st Penny Marshall 1971 (divorced); m. 2nd Michele Singer 1989; three c.; ed UCLA; co-f. Castle Rock Entertainment (now subsidiary of Warner Bros. Entertainment); has appeared with comic improvisation groups The Session and The Committee; Chair. First 5 Calif. Children and Families Comm. 1995–2006 (resgnd). *Films:* Enter Laughing 1967, Halls of Anger 1970, Where's Poppa 1970, Summertree 1971, How Come Nobody's on Our Side? 1975, Fire Sale 1977, This is Spinal Tap (also dir and writer) 1984, The Sure Thing (dir) 1985, Stand By Me (dir) 1986, Throw Momma from the Train 1987, The Princess Bride (dir and prod.) 1987, When Harry Met Sally (dir and prod.) 1989, Postcards from the Edge 1990, The Spirit of '76 1990, Misery (also dir and prod.) 1990, A Few Good Men (dir and prod.) 1992, Sleepless in Seattle 1993, Bullets Over Broadway 1994, Mixed Nuts 1994, North (dir and prod.) 1994, Bye Bye Love 1995, The American President (dir and prod.) 1995, For Better or Worse 1996, The First Wives Club 1996, Mad Dog Time 1996, Ghosts of Mississippi (dir and prod.) 1996, Primary Colors 1998, Spinal Tap: The Final Tour (dir, writer and prod.) 1998, EdTV 1999, The Story of Us (also dir and prod.) 1999, The Majestic 2001, Alex & Emma (also dir and prod.) 2003, Rumor Has It... (dir) 2005, Everyone's Hero (voice) 2006, The Bucket List (dir and prod.) 2007. *Television includes:* The Glen Campbell Goodtime Hour (writer, series) 1969, All in the Family (series) 1971–78, The Super (prod.) 1972, Thursday's Game 1974, Free Country (series, also prod.) 1978, More Than Friends (also writer and prod.) 1978, The T.V. Show (also writer and prod.) 1979, Million Dollar Infield (also writer and prod.) 1982, Morton & Hayes (series, writer and prod.) 1991, But Seriously (exec. prod.) 1994, I Am Your Child (dir, writer) 1997, Everyday Life 2004. *Address:* c/o Castle Rock Entertainment, 335 North Maple Drive, Suite 135, Beverly Hills, CA 90210, USA.

REINFELDT, Fredrik, BS; Swedish politician; *Prime Minister;* b. 4 Aug. 1965, Stockholm; m. Filippa Reinfeldt (neé Holmberg) 1992; three c.; ed Stockholm Univ.; Chair. Swedish Conscripts Council, Swedish Defence Staff 1986; with Skandinaviska Enskilda Banken, Täby 1986–87; Deputy Chair. Regional Section, Young Moderates, Stockholm 1988–90, Chair. 1990–92, Chair. Exec. Cttee 1992–95; mem. Regional Section, Moderate Party, Stockholm 1992–2003, mem. Bd 1995–2002, mem. Exec. Cttee Moderate Party Group in Riksdag (Parl.) 1999–2003, Group Leader and First Deputy Chair. 2002–03, Chair. 2003–, mem. Bd Moderate Party 2002–, Party Chair. 2003–; Deputy Sec. Stockholm City Commr 1990–91, Sec. 1991; mem. Riksdag (Parl.) 1991–, Alt. Riksdag Cttee on Taxation 1991–94, mem. Cttee on Finance 1994–2001, Alt. Cttee on EU Affairs 2001–02, Chair. Cttee on Justice 2001–02, Alt. Advisory Council on Foreign Affairs 2002–03; Deputy Chair. Cttee on Finance 2002–03, mem. Advisory Council on Foreign Affairs 2003–06, Prime Minister 2006–; Deputy Chair. Swedish Central Conscripts Council 1985–86; Chair. Democratic Youth Community of Europe 1995–97; mem. Bd Swedish Nat. Union of Students 1989–90; Pres. Youth of European People's Party 1997–99. *Address:* Prime Minister's Office, Rosenbad 4, 103 33 Stockholm (office); Moderata Samlingspartiet (MS) (Moderate Party), Stord Nygatan 30, POB 2080, 113 12 Stockholm, Sweden. *Telephone:* (8) 405-10-00 (office); (8) 676-80-00 (MS). *Fax:* (8) 723-11-71 (office); (8) 21-61-23 (MS). *E-mail:* registrator@primeminister.ministry.se (office); registrator@primeminister.ministry.se. *Website:* www.sweden.gov.se/sb/d/577 (office); www.moderat.se.

REINHARD, Keith Leon; American advertising executive; *Chairman Emeritus, DDB Worldwide Communications Group Inc.;* b. 20 Jan. 1935, Berne, Ind.; s. of Herman Reinhard and Agnes Reinhard; m. Rose-Lee Simons 1976; two d.; four s. one d. by previous m.; ed public schools in Berne; commercial artist, Kling Studios, Chicago 1954–56; man. tech. communications Dept Magnavox Co., Fort Wayne, Ind. 1957–60; creative/account exec., Biddle Co., Bloomington, Ill. 1961–63; Exec. Vice-Pres., Dir Creative Services and Pres. Needham, Harper & Steers Inc., Chicago 1964; then Chair. and CEO Needham, Harper & Steers/USA, Chicago; also Dir Needham, Harper & Steers Inc.; Chair. and CEO DDB Needham Worldwide Inc. (later DDB Worldwide Communications Group Inc.) New York 1986–2001, Chair. 2001-06, Chair. Emer. 2006–. *Address:* c/o DDB Worldwide Communications Group Inc., 437 Madison Avenue, New York, NY 10022, USA.

REINHARDT, Klaus, DrPhil; German army officer (retd); b. 15 Jan. 1941, Berlin; m. Heide-Ursula Reinhardt (née Bando) 1966; two s.; ed Univ. of Freiburg; joined army as officer cadet, Mountain Infantry; Commdr Mountain Infantry 1986–88; Commdr Army Führungsakademie 1990–93; Commdg Gen. III Corps 1993–94; Gen.-Lt, Commdr German Army, Koblenz 1994–96; Commdg Gen. of NATO Peace-keeping Unit in Kosovo (Kfor) 1999–2000; Commdr NATO Forces, Heidelberg 2000; retd 2001; currently Lecturer, Univ. of Augsburg and Univ. of Munich; fmr Vice Pres. Clausewitz Soc., now Pres.; mem. Int. Advisory Bd World Security Network Foundation. *Publication:* Wende vor Moskau 1998. *Leisure interests:* classical music, skiing, mountaineering, travel. *Address:* Karthäuserhofweg 10, 56075 Koblenz, Germany. *Telephone:* (261) 55690.

REINHOUDT, David N.; Dutch chemist and academic; *Scientific Director, MESA+ Research Institute, University of Twente;* b. 1942; ed Delft Univ. of Tech.; Researcher, Shell NV 1970–75; part-time Prof. (extraordinarius), Univ. Twente 1975–78, Full Prof. 1978–, Scientific Dir, MESA+ Research Inst., Enschede 1999–; Chair. NanoNed (Dutch network for nanotechnology) 2002–; Chair. Nat. Foundation for Supramolecular Chemistry, European Supramolecular Science and Tech. Foundation; Vice-Chair. Nat. Org. for Applied Science (STW) 1996–; mem. Editorial Bd several journals including European Journal of Organic Chemistry, Journal of Supramolecular Chemistry, New Journal of Chemistry; mem. Royal Dutch Acad. of Sciences (KNAW), ACS, Royal Dutch Chemical Soc.; Fellow, AAAS 1997–, Inst. of Physics; Kt of the Order of the Dutch Lion 2002; Izatt-Christensen Award 1995, Simon Stevin Meesterschap 1998. *Publications:* more than 750 scientific publications, patents, review articles, and books. *Address:* Faculty of Science and Technology/SMCT, Universiteit Twente, Postbus 217, Enschede, 7500 AE, Netherlands (office). *Telephone:* (53) 4892980 (office). *Fax:* (53) 4894645 (office). *E-mail:* d.n.reinhoudt@utwente.nl (office). *Website:* smct.tnw.utwente.nl/people/staff_members/prof_dr_ir_david_n_reinhoudt (office).

REINICHE, Dominique; French business executive; *President and Chief Operating Officer, European Union Group, The Coca-Cola Company;* b. 13 July 1955; ed ESSEC Business School, Cergy-Pontoise; began career as Brand Man. at Procter & Gamble France, promoted to Assoc. Advertising Man.; worked for Kraft Jacobs Suchard; joined Coca-Cola Enterprises in 1992, Group Vice-Pres. and Gen. Man. (France) Coca-Cola Enterprises 1998–2003, Sr Vice-Pres. and Pres. Coca-Cola Enterprises Europe 2003–05, Pres. and COO European Union Group, The Coca-Cola Co. 2005–; mem. Bd Dirs The AXA Group 2005–; Pres. Union des annonceurs (French advertiser asscn), UNESDA (European Soft Drink Asscn); mem. Bd ECR (Efficient Consumer Response) Europe; mem. Advisory Bd ING Direct; mem. Exec. Bd Medef (French employers' org.); Chevalier, Legion d'honneur 2002; ranked by Fortune magazine amongst 50 Most Powerful Women in Business outside the US (22nd) 2003, (39th) 2004, (25th) 2005, (40th) 2006, (44th) 2007, ranked by the Financial Times amongst Top 25 Businesswomen in Europe (20th) 2007. *Address:* The Coca-Cola Co., PO Box 1734, Atlanta, GA 30301, USA (office). *Telephone:* (404) 676-2121 (office). *Fax:* (404) 676-6792 (office). *Website:* www.coca-cola.com (office).

REINIG, Gen. Gaston; Luxembourg military officer; *Chief of Staff;* b. 17 Nov. 1956, Diekirch; ed Royal Mil. Acad., Brussels, French Infantry School, Montpellier; Commdr Luxembourg contingent, NATO Allied Command Europe Mobile Force Land (AMF (L)) 1984–87, Rep. to NATO Maintenance and Supply Org. Cttee 1992–95; Deputy Head of Command, Control and Communications Div., EC Monitoring Mission HQ, Sarajevo 1997; Perm. Mil. Rep. to NATO, Brussels 1998–2002, to WEU 2000–02, to EU 2000–02; Head of Mil. Centre of Diekirch (Armed Forces Operational Centre) 2002–08; Chief of Staff 2008–; Commdr, Ordre du Mérite, Officier, Ordre de la Couronne de Chêne, Croix d'Honneur et de Mérite militaire en bronze, Officier avec Couronne dans l'Ordre de Mérite civil et militaire Adolphe de Nassau, Commdr, Ordre de Mérite civil et militaire de la Couronne de Chêne; ECMM Medal for Service with the EC Monitor Mission, Army Commendation Medal. *Address:* Etat-Major de l'Armée, 34–38 rue Goethe, BP 1873, 1018 Luxembourg, Luxembourg (office). *Telephone:* 26-84-82-1 (office). *Fax:* 26-84-56-06 (office). *E-mail:* secretariat.cema@ema.etat.lu (office). *Website:* www.armee.lu (office).

REINO, Fernando, LicenDer; Portuguese diplomatist (retd); b. Aug. 1929, Felgar, Moncorvo; s. of Abel Reino and Julia Janeiro Reino; m. Maria Gabriela Vaz Reino 1962; two d.; ed Univ. of Coimbra, Univ. of Strasbourg, NATO Defence Coll.; entered the Foreign Service 1958, Political and NATO Depts, Lisbon 1958–60, Portuguese del. to NATO, Paris 1960–61, Portuguese Embassy, Tokyo 1961–62, Chargé d'affaires titular, Antananarivo 1962–63, Consul-Gen. Cape Town 1963–66, Chargé d'affaires, Tunis 1966–71, Deputy Head of Mission to the EEC 1971–73; Dir Int. Econ. Org. Dept, Lisbon 1973–74; Head of Co-operation and Tech. Assistance Dept and Co-ordinator Nat. Decolonization Comm. 1974–75; Amb. to Norway and Iceland 1977–80, Head of Civilian Staff of the Pres. 1980–81; Perm. Rep. to the UN and other Int. Orgs, Geneva 1981–85; Amb. to Spain 1985–88; Perm. Rep. to UN 1989–92; fmr Prof., Universidade Nova and Univs of Coimbra and Lusiada; decorations from Portugal, Spain, Brazil, Italy, the Vatican, Germany, Norway, Iceland, Greece, Venezuela. *Leisure interests:* writing, reading, music, gardening, trekking. *Address:* Quinta do Rio Touro, Azoia, 2705-001 Cabo da Roca, Sintra, Portugal (home). *Telephone:* (219) 292862 (home). *Fax:* (219) 292360 (home). *E-mail:* f.reino@mail.telepac.pt (home). *Website:* www.quinta-riotouro.com/english.

REINSHAGEN, Gerlind; German writer; b. 4 May 1926, Königsberg; d. of Ekkehard Technau and Frieda Technau; m. 1949; ed studies in pharmacy and art, Berlin; freelance author of novels, theatre and radio plays, screenplays, poetry, essays and criticism; mem. German PEN; mem. Deutsche Akad. der darstellenden Künste; Fördergabe Schillerpreis, Baden Württemberg 1974, Mühlheimer Dramatikerpreis 1977, Roswitha von Gandersheim Medaille 1984, Ludwig Mülheimes Preis 1993, Niedersächsischer Kunstpreis 1997, Niedersächsischer Staatspreis 1999. *Plays:* Doppelkopf 1968, Leben und Tod der Marilyn Monroe 1971, Himmel und Erde 1974, Sonntagskinder 1976, Frühlingsfest 1980, Eisenherz 1982, Die Clownin 1988, Feuerblume 1987, Tanz, Marie! 1989, Die fremde Tochter 1993, Die grüne Tür 1999. *Television:* Doppelkopf 1972, Himmel und Erde 1976, Sonntagskinder 1981. *Radio:* 12 radio plays. *Publications:* novels: Rovinato 1981, Die flüchtige Braut 1984, Zwölf Nächte 1989, Jäger am Rand der Nacht 1993, Am grossen Stern 1996, Göttergeschichte 2000; Gesammelte Stücke (collected pieces) 1986, Joint Venture 2003, Vom Feuer 2006, Die Frau und die Stadt 2007; contribs to theatrical journals and yearbooks etc. *Address:* Rheingaustrasse 2, 12161 Berlin, Germany. *Telephone:* (30) 8217171.

REISMAN, Heather; Canadian publishing executive; *CEO, Indigo Books & Music Inc.;* b. Montreal; m. Gerald Schwartz; four c.; ed McGill Univ.; Co-founder and Man. Dir Paradigm Consulting 1979–92; Pres. Cott Corpn 1992–96; Founder, Pres. and CEO Indigo Books, Music and Café, Inc. 1996–2001, Pres. and CEO Indigo Books & Music Inc. (following merger with Chapters Inc. 2001) 2001–; mem. Bd of Dirs Onex Corpn, Right to Play; fmr mem. Bd of Dirs Magna Int., Suncor, Rogers Communications, Inc., Williams-Sonoma Inc.; Dir and Officer Mt Sinai Hosp.; fmr Gov. McGill Univ., Toronto Stock Exchange; mem. Bilderberg Steering Cttee; Dr hc (Ryerson Univ.) 2006; Int. Distinguished Entrepreneur Award, Univ. of Manitoba, John Molson School of Business Award of Distinction, Concordia Univ.; inducted into Waterloo Entrepreneur Hall of Fame, Univ. of Waterloo. *Publications include:* numerous articles on media, communications, manufacturing and retailing. *Address:* Indigo Books & Music Inc., 468 King Street West, Suite 500, Toronto, ON M5V 1L8, Canada (office). *Telephone:* (416) 364-4499 (office). *Fax:* (416) 364-0355 (office). *Website:* www.chapters.indigo.ca (office).

REISS, Timothy James, BA, MA, PhD, FRSC; British/Canadian/American academic; *Professor Emeritus of Comparative Literature and Distinguished Scholar in Residence, New York University;* b. 14 May 1942, Stanmore, Middx; s. of James Martin Reiss and Joan Margaret Ping; m. 2nd Patricia J. Hilden 1988; two s. one d. from previous m.; ed Hardye's School, Dorchester, Manchester Univ., Sorbonne, Paris and Univ. of Illinois, USA; Instructor to Asst Prof., Yale Univ. 1968–73; Assoc. Prof., Univ. de Montréal 1973–79, Prof. and Chair. of Comparative Literature 1979–84; Prof. of Comparative Literature, Modern Languages and Philosophy, Emory Univ. 1983–86, Samuel C. Dobbs Prof. of Comparative Literature and French 1986–87; Prof. and Chair. of Comparative Literature New York Univ. 1987–94, 2005–06, Prof. 1994–2005, Prof. Emer. and Distinguished Scholar in Residence 2007–; Visiting Prof., Univ. of Toronto 1976–77, Univ. of British Columbia 1979, New York Univ. 1982, Univ. of Montreal 1984–87, Grad. Center, CUNY 1985, State Univ. of NY, Binghamton 1990, Univ. of California, Berkeley 1996–97, Univ. of Oregon 1999–2000, Stanford Univ. 2001, 2002–03, 2004; mem. Acad. of Literary Studies 1986; Morse Fellowship, Paris 1971–72, Canada Council Sr Fellowship, Oxford 1977–78, Social Sciences Research Council of Canada Sr Fellowship, Oxford 1983–84, ACLS Sr Fellowship 1986–87, Guggenheim Fellowship, Cambridge 1990–91, Outstanding Academic Book 1983, 1993, Forkosch Prize in Intellectual History 1992, various other fellowships and awards. *Publications:* Toward Dramatic Illusion 1971, Science, Language and the Perspective Mind (ed.) 1973, Tragedy and Truth 1980, De l'ouverture des disciplines (ed.) 1981, The Discourse of Modernism (Choice Best Academic Book Award) 1982, Tragique et tragédie dans la tradition occidentale (ed.) 1983, The Uncertainty of Analysis 1988, The Meaning of Literature (Forkosch Prize, Choice Best Academic Book Award) 1992, Knowledge, Discovery and Imagination in Early Modern Europe 1997, For the Geography of a Soul (ed.) 2001, Against Autonomy: Global Dialectics of Cultural Exchange 2002, Sisyphus and Eldorado (ed.) (2nd revised edn) 2002, Mirages of the Selfe 2003, Music, Writing and Cultural Unity in the Caribbean (ed.) 2005, Topographies of Race and Gender: Mapping Cultural Representations, two vols (co-ed.) 2007; more than 150 essays and book chapters. *Address:* Department of Comparative Literature, New York University, 19 University Place, 3rd Floor, New York, NY 10003-4556 (office); 2233 East 6th Street, Tucson, AZ 85719, USA (home). *Telephone:* (520) 795-0706 (home). *Fax:* (212) 995-4377 (office). *E-mail:* timothy.reiss@nyu.edu (office). *Website:* www.nyu.edu/fas/dept/complit (office).

REITEN, Eivind Kristofer; Norwegian energy and light metal industry executive and fmr politician; *President and CEO, Norsk Hydro ASA;* b. 2 April 1953, Midsund; m.; two c.; ed Univ. of Oslo; jr exec. officer, Ministry of Fisheries 1979–82; Sec. to Centre Party's Parl. Group 1982–83; State Sec. Ministry of Finance 1983–; Minister of Fisheries 1985–86, of Petroleum and Energy 1989–90; Man. Hydro Agri Div., Norsk Hydro 1986–88, Asst Gen. Man. Hydro Agri 1988, Pres. Energy Div. 1988, Dir Special Projects 1991–92, Pres. Refining and Marketing Div. 1992–96, Pres. Hydro Aluminium Metal Products 1996–98, Exec. Vice-Pres. and mem. Corp. Man. Bd, Norsk Hydro ASA 1999–2001, Pres. and CEO 2001–, Chair. StatoilHydro (after acquisition of Norsk Hydro by Statoil) 1–4 Oct. 2007 (resgnd); Chair. Bd Norwegian Postal Service 1995–99, Int. Primary Aluminium Inst. 1998–2000, Telenor 2000–01; mem. Bd Cen. Bank of Norway 1988–94, Norske Skog 1995–2000; mem. Green Tax Comm. 1994–95. *Address:* Norsk Hydro ASA, Drammensveien 264, 0283, Oslo, Norway (office). *Telephone:* 22-53-81-00 (office). *Fax:* 22-53-27-25 (office). *E-mail:* info@hydro.com (office). *Website:* www.hydro.com (office).

REITER, Janusz; Polish diplomatist and international affairs scholar; b. 6 Aug. 1952, Kościerzyna; s. of Stanisław Reiter and Hilda Reiter; m. Hanna Reiter 1975; two d.; ed Warsaw Univ.; foreign affairs commentator, Życie Warszawy (daily) 1977–81 (dismissed during martial law); Co-founder Foundation for Int. Ventures and Centre for Int. Studies in Warsaw; mem. Dziekania Club of Political Thought; staff writer, Przegląd Katolicki (weekly) 1984–89, Gazeta Wyborcza (daily) and Polish TV 1989–90, Rzeczpospolita (daily); Amb. to FRG 1990–95; Chair. Bd and Pres. Center for Int. Relations, Warsaw 1998; Amb. to USA 2005–07; Co-founder Council for Foreign Policy; mem. Council on European Integration; Great Cross of Merit with the Star and Ribbon (Germany). *Publication:* Roads to Europe. *Leisure interests:* music, travelling, literature. *Address:* c/o Center for International Relations, Emilii Plater 25, 00-688 Warsaw, Poland (office). *E-mail:* info@reiter.org.pl (office).

REITH, Gen. Sir John, Kt, KCB, CBE; British army officer; commissioned into Parachute Regiment 1969; fmr Chief of Staff, 20 Armoured Brigade, Detmold, W Germany; fmr co. commdr, 3rd Battalion, Parachute Regiment, fmr Commdr, 1st Battalion; Chief of Staff, 1 (UK) Armoured Div., Verden, W Germany 1988; deployed to Gulf for Operation Granby 1990–91; Commdr 4th Armoured Brigade, Munster and Osnabruck 1992; fmr Commdr, British Forces, fmr Commdr, UN Sector SW; Supervisor, Washington Agreement –1994; Dir Int. Orgs, Ministry of Defence, London 1994–95, Dir of Mil. Operations 1995–97; Commdr, Allied Command Europe Mobile Force (Land) 1997–2000; Asst Chief of Defence Staff (Policy), Cen. Staff, Ministry of Defence 2000–01; Chief of Jt Operations, Perm. Jt HQ, Northwood 2001–04; Deputy Supreme Allied Command Europe (DSACEUR), NATO 2004– 07 (retd). *Address:* c/o Ministry of Defence, Main Bldg, Whitehall, London, SW1A 2HB, England.

REITH, Peter, BEcons, LLB; Australian company director, consultant, international organization official and fmr politician; b. 15 July 1950, Melbourne; s. of A. C. Reith and E. V. Reith (née Sambell); m. Julie Treganowan 1971; four s.; ed Monash Univ.; Supreme Court 1975; worked as solicitor 1976–82; mem. Westernport Waterworks Trust and Cowes Sewerage Authority 1977–82; Councillor Shire of Phillip Island 1976–81, Pres. 1980–81; mem. various cttees and authorities; MP for Flinders 1982–83, 1984–2001; Deputy Leader of the Opposition 1990–93; Shadow Special Minister of State 1993, responsible for Mabo 1994; Shadow Minister for Defence Jan.–Sept. 1994, Shadow Minister with responsibility for Mabo Jan.–May 1994; Shadow Minister for Defence May–Sept. 1994; Shadow Minister for Foreign Affairs 1994–95, for Industrial Relations and Man. of Opposition Business in the House 1995–96; Minister for Industrial Relations and Leader of the House of Reps and Minister Assisting the Prime Minister for the Public Service 1996–97; Minister for Workplace Relations and Small Business and Leader of the House of Reps 1997–98, Minister for Employment, Workplace Relations and Small Business and Leader of the House of Reps 1998–2001; Minister for Defence 2001; Dir representing Australia, Repub. of Korea, New Zealand and Egypt, EBRD 2003–06, Alt. Dir 2006–; mem. Asscn of Christian Community Colls.; co-ordinator Free Legal Aid Services; Founding Sec. and mem. Newhaven Coll. *Publication:* The Reith Papers. *Leisure interests:* golf, reading. *Address:* European Bank for Reconstruction and Development (EBRD), One Exchange Square, 175 Bishopsgate, London, EC2A 2JN, England (office); 1A Camperdown Street, Brighton East, Vic. 3187, Australia (home). *Telephone:* (20) 7338-

6000 (office). *Fax:* (20) 7338-6100 (office). *E-mail:* australiaoffice@ebrd.com (office); peterreith@bigpond.com.au. *Website:* www.ebrd.com (office).

REITHOFER, Norbert, Dr-Ing; German automotive industry executive; *Chairman of the Board of Management, BMW AG;* b. 1956, Penzberg; ed Technische Universität München; joined BMW 1987, has served in numerous sr man. positions including Dir Body-in-White Production Div. 1991–94, Tech. Dir BMW South Africa 1994–97, Pres. BMW Mfg Corpn, USA, SC 1997–2000, mem. Bd of Man. with responsibility for production 2000–06, Chair. Bd of Man. BMW AG 2006–. *Address:* BMW AG, 130 Petuelring, Munich 80788, Germany (office). *Telephone:* (89) 382-0 (office). *Fax:* (89) 382-258-58 (office). *E-mail:* info@bmwgroup.com (office). *Website:* www.bmw.com (office); www .bmwgroup.com (office).

REITMAN, Ivan, MusB; Canadian film director and producer; b. 27 Oct. 1946, Komarmo, Czechoslovakia; s. of Leslie Reitman and Clara R. Reitman; m. Genevieve Robert 1976; one s. two d.; ed McMaster Univ.; moved to Canada 1951; Hon. LLD (Toronto); Dir of the Year, Nat. Asscn of Theater Owners 1984, Canadian Genie Special Achievement Award 1985, Star on Hollywood Walk of Fame 1997. *Stage shows produced:* The Magic Show 1974, The National Lampoon Show 1975, Merlin 1983 (also Dir). *Films:* (dir and exec. producer) Cannibal Girls 1973; (producer) They Came From Within 1975, Death Weekend 1977, Blackout 1978, National Lampoon's Animal House 1978 (People's Choice Award 1979), Heavy Metal 1981, Stop! Or My Mom Will Shoot 1992, Space Jam 1996, Private Parts 1996; (producer and dir) Foxy Lady 1971, Meatballs 1979, Stripes 1981, Ghostbusters 1984, Legal Eagles 1986, Twins 1988 (People's Choice Award 1989), Ghostbusters II 1989, Kindergarten Cop 1990, Dave 1993, Junior 1994, Father's Day 1996, Six Days/Seven Nights 1998, Doomsday Man 1999; (exec. producer) Rabid 1976, Spacehunter: Adventures in the Forbidden Zone 1983, Big Shots 1987, Casual Sex? 1988, Feds 1988, Beethoven 1992, Beethoven's 2nd 1993, Commandments 1996, Road Trip (exec. producer) 2000, Evolution (exec. producer and dir) 2001, Killing Me Softly (exec. producer) 2002, Old School (exec. producer) 2003, Eurotrip (exec. producer) 2004, Trailer Park Boys: The Movie (exec. producer) 2006, Disturbia (exec. producer) 2007. *TV series:* (producer and dir) Delta House 1978, Alienators: Evolution Continues (exec. producer) 2001. *TV films:* (exec. producer) The Late Shift 1996; mem. Dirs Guild of America. *Address:* Building 489, 100 University City Plaza, Universal City, CA 91608, USA (office).

REITZ, Edgar; German film director; b. 1 Nov. 1932, Morbach; m. Salome Kammer 1995; one s.; co-f. Institut für Filmgestaltung 1963; co-f. (with son Christian Reitz) Reitz Reitz & Media, Munich; f. Edgar Reitz Filmproduktion GmbH. *Films include:* Mahlzeiten (appeared in UK as Lust for Love) 1966–67, Die Reise nach Wien 1973, Picnic 1975, Stunde Null 1976, Deutschland im Herbst (with others) 1977–78, Der Schneider von Ulm 1978, Heimat 1980–84, Die zweite Heimat 1991, Die Nacht der Regisseure 1995, Heimat 3: Chronik einer Zeitenwende (TV) 2004, Heimat-Fragmente: Die Frauen 2006. *Address:* Reitz Reitz & Media, Rottmannstraße 11, 80333 Munich; Edgar Reitz Filmproduktion GmbH, Imhofstraße 5, 80805 Munich, Germany. *Telephone:* (89) 2724524 (Reitz Reitz & Media); (89) 2723276. *Fax:* (89) 2719760 (Reitz Reitz & Media); (89) 2719760. *Website:* www.edgar-reitz.de.

REITZLE, Wolfgang, DEng; German business executive; *CEO, Linde AG;* b. 7 March 1949, Ulm; m. Nina Ruge 2001; two c.; ed Munich Tech. Univ.; with BMW AG 1976–99, becoming mem. Exec. Bd 1987–93, Chair. Exec. Bd 1993–99; Group Vice-Pres. Ford Motor Co. 1999–2002, also Chair. and CEO Premier Automotive Group 1999–2002; mem. Exec. Bd Linde AG 2002–, CEO 2003–; mem. Supervisory Bd Deutsche Telekom AG, KION Group GmbH, KION Holding 1 GmbH; Hon. Prof., Munich Technical Univ. 2005–; Man. Magazine Man. of the Year 2006. *Address:* Linde AG, Leopoldstrasse 252, 80807 Munich, Germany (office). *Telephone:* (89) 35757-01 (office); (89) 35757-1321 (office). *Fax:* (89) 35757-1075 (office); (89) 35757-1398 (office). *E-mail:* info@linde.com (office). *Website:* www.linde.com (office).

RELL, M. Jodi; American politician and state official; *Governor of Connecticut;* b. 16 June 1946, Norfolk, Va; m. Lou Rell; one s. one d.; ed Old Dominion Univ. and Western Conn. State Univ.; served in Conn. House of Reps for ten years, fmr Asst Minority Leader and Deputy Minority Leader; Lt-Gov. of Conn. 1994–2004, presided over Senate, mem. Prison and Jail Overcrowding Comm., Gov.'s Law Enforcement Council, State Finance Advisory Cttee; est. Lt-Gov.'s Comm. on State Mandate Reform 1995; Gov. of Conn. 2004–; fmr Pres. Nat. Order of Women Legislators; fmr mem. Nat. Conf. of Lt-Govs; mem. Bd Trustees Regional YMCA of Western Conn., Candlewood Lions Club; Lions Club Int. Foundation Melvin Jones Fellow 2003; Republican; Hon. LLD (Hartford) 2001, (New Haven) 2004; honoured by Uniformed Professional Fire Fighters, AmeriCares, Arthritis Foundation, CT Race for the Cure, Conn. Library Asscn, Conn. Chapter of American Coll. of Health Care Admins, Conn. Preservation Council, Conn. Fed. of Business and Professional Women, among others. *Address:* Executive Office of the Governor, State Capitol, 210 Capitol Avenue, Hartford CT 06106, USA (office). *Telephone:* (860) 566-4840 (office). *E-mail:* Governor.Rell@po.state.ct.us (office). *Website:* www.ct.gov/ governorrell (office).

REMEDIOS, Alberto Telisforo, CBE; British singer (tenor); b. 27 Feb. 1935, Liverpool; s. of Albert Remedios and Ida Remedios; m. 1st Shirley Swindells 1958; one s.; m. 2nd Judith Hosken 1965; one s. one d.; studied with Edwin Francis, Liverpool; joined Sadler's Wells Opera Co. 1955; now sings regularly with ENO and Royal Opera House, Covent Garden; has made numerous appearances in USA, Canada, Argentina, Germany, France and Spain and appeared in concert with major British orchestras; Queen's Prize, Royal Coll. of Music; First Prize, Int. Singing Competition, Sofia, Bulgaria; Sir Reginald Goodall Award Wagner Soc. 1995. *Recordings include:* Wagner's Der Ring des Nibelungen and Tippett's A Midsummer Marriage. *Leisure interests:* football, motoring, record collecting. *Address:* c/o Stuart Trotter, 21 Lanhill Road, London, W9 2BS, England. *Telephone:* (20) 7289-6315.

REMENGESAU, Tommy Esang, Jr, BS; Palauan politician and fmr head of state; b. 28 Feb. 1956, Koror; s. of Thomas O. Remengesau, Sr and Ferista Esang Remengesau; m. Debbie Mineich; two s. two d.; ed Grand Valley State Univ., Mich. and Michigan State Univ., USA; Admin./Planner, Palau Bureau of Health Services 1980–81; Public Information Officer, Palau Legislature 1981–84; Senator, Nat. Congress 1984–92; Vice-Pres. and Minister of Admin. 1993–2001, Pres. of Palau 2001–09 (re-elected 2004); rep. to IMF 1997–; led several official dels to Taiwan (Repub. of China); hosted first Taiwan-Pacific Allies Summit 2006; named by Time magazine a Hero of the Environment 2007. *Leisure interest:* fishing (twice Grand Champion All-Micronesia Fishing Derby). *Address:* c/o Office of the President, PO Box 6051, Koror, PW 96940, Palau.

REMINGTON, Deborah Williams, BFA; American artist; b. 25 June 1935, Haddonfield, NJ; d. of Malcolm van Dyke Remington and Hazel Irwin Stewart; ed San Francisco Art Inst.; work in many public collections including Whitney Museum, New York, Pompidou Centre, Paris and Bibliothèque Nat., Paris, Smithsonian American Art Museum, Washington DC; mem. Nat. Acad., New York 1999–; Hassam & Speicher Purchase Prize, Nat. Endowment Fellowship 1979, Guggenheim Fellowship 1984, American Acad. and Inst. of Arts and Letters 1988, Pollock-Krasner Foundation Grant 1999, Benjamin Altman Prize for Painting, Nat. Acad. 2003. *Achievements:* interviewed for Archives of American Art, Smithsonian Inst. 1972, 2004. *Leisure interests:* gardening/horticulture. *Address:* 309 West Broadway, New York, NY 10013, USA (home). *Telephone:* (212) 925-3037 (home). *Fax:* (212) 925-3037 (office). *E-mail:* deborahremington@aol.com (home). *Website:* www.deborahremington .com (office).

REMNICK, David J., AB; American journalist, editor and writer; *Editor-in-Chief, The New Yorker;* b. 29 Oct. 1958, Hackensack, NJ; s. of Edward C. Remnick and Barbara Remnick (née Seigel); m. Esther B. Fein; two s. one d.; ed Princeton Univ.; reporter, The Washington Post 1982–91; staff writer, The New Yorker 1992–, Ed.-in-Chief 1998–; Livingston Award 1991, George Polk Award 1994, Helen Bernstein Award 1994. *Publications:* Lenin's Tomb: The Last Days of the Soviet Empire (Pulitzer Prize for General Non-fiction 1994) 1993, The Devil Problem (and other true stories) 1996, Resurrection: The Struggle for a New Russia 1997, King of the World: Muhammad Ali and the Rise of an American Hero 1998, Life Stories: Profiles from The New Yorker (ed.) 1999, Wonderful Town: Stories from The New Yorker (ed.) 1999, Reporting: Writings from The New Yorker 2006; contrib. to newspapers and periodicals. *Address:* The New Yorker, 4 Times Square, New York, NY 10036, USA (office). *E-mail:* themail@newyorker.com (office). *Website:* www .newyorker.com (office).

RÉMY, Pierre-Jean (see Angrémy, Jean-Pierre).

REN, Jianxin; Chinese judge; b. Aug. 1925, Fencheng (now Xiangfen) Co., Shanxi Prov.; ed Eng Coll., Beijing Univ.; joined CCP 1948; Sec., Secr. N China People's Govt 1948–49; Sec. Gen. Office, Cen. Comm. for Political Science and Law, Sec. Cen. Comm. for Legis. Affairs 1949–54; Sec. Legis. Affairs Bureau, State Council 1954–59; Section Leader, Div. Chief, China Council for the Promotion of Int. Trade (CCPIT) 1959–71, Dir Legal Dept, CCPIT, lawyer 1971–81, Vice-Chair. CCPIT 1981–83; Vice-Pres. Supreme People's Court 1983–88, Pres. 1988–98; Sec.-Gen. Leading Group of Cen. Cttee for Political Science and Law 1989, Deputy Sec. and Sec.-Gen. Cen. Cttee 1990; Chair. Soc. of Chinese Judges 1994–; Hon. Chair China Law Soc. (fmr Vice-Pres.), China Foreign Econ. Trade and Arbitration Cttee, China Maritime Arbitration Cttee (fmr Chair.); Hon. Pres. China Int. Law Soc. (fmr Vice-Pres.); Dir China Training Centre for Sr Judges; Prof. (part-time) Beijing Univ.; mem. 13th CCP Cen. Cttee 1987–92, 14th CCP Cen. Cttee 1992–97, Sec. Secr. 14th CCP Cen. Cttee 1992–97; Del., 15th CCP Nat. Congress 1997–2002; Sec. CCP Cen. Comm. for Political Science and Law 1992–98; Vice-Chair. 9th Nat. Cttee CPPCC 1998–2003. *Address:* National Committee of Chinese People's Political Consultative Conference, 23 Taipingqiao Street, Beijing, People's Republic of China (office).

REN, Meie, BSc, PhD; Chinese geographer and academic; b. 8 Sept. 1913, Ningbo City, Zhejiang Prov.; ed Nat. Cen. Univ., Beijing, Univ. of Glasgow, UK; Prof., Geography Dept, Nanjing Univ. 1986–; Chair. of Asscn for Devt and Man. of Coastal Zones 1986–; mem. Chinese Acad. of Sciences 1980–, Dept of Earth Sciences, Academia Sinica 1985–; Hon. Chair. Chinese Geographical Soc., China Soc. for Oceanography; Victoria Medal (Royal Soc. of Geography) 1986; Ho Leung Ho Lee Foundation Earch Sciences Prize 2006. *Address:* Geography Department, Nanjing University, Nanjing City, Jiangsu Province, People's Republic of China (office).

REN, Zhengfei; Chinese business executive; *CEO, Huawei Technologies Company Ltd;* b. 1944, Jiangsu; ed Chongqing Univ.; joined People's Liberation Army 1970, engineer and officer; transferred to civilian work 1978; joined CCP 1978; co-f. Huawei Techs 1987, currently CEO. *Address:* Huawei Technologies Co. Ltd, Bantian, Longgang District, Shenzen, 518129, China (office). *Telephone:* (755) 28780808 (office). *Website:* www.huawei.com (office).

RENARD, Ian Andrew, BA, LLM; Australian lawyer and university administrator; *Chancellor; , University of Melbourne;* m. Diana Renard; four d.; ed Univ. of Melbourne; fmr Resident Tutor in Law, Ormond Coll. and Newman Coll., Univ. of Melbourne, Grad. Rep. Univ. of Melbourne 1994, Deputy Chancellor 2001–05, Chancellor 2005–; Pnr, Allens Arthur Robinson 1979–2001, Man. Pnr 1989–91; Trustee R E Ross Trust, The Queen's Trust;

fmr Pres. Library Bd of Vic.; fmr Treas. Free Kindergarten Asscn; fmr Dir Royal Children's Hosp.; Supreme Court Prize 1969, Australian Library and Information Asscn Redmond Barry Award. *Publications:* Takeovers and Reconstructions in Australia (co-author). *Address:* Office of the Chancellor, 8th Floor, Raymond Priestley Building, University of Melbourne, Melbourne, Vic. 3010, Australia (office). *Telephone:* (3) 8344-6167 (office). *Fax:* (3) 9347-5904 (office). *E-mail:* chancellor@ unimelb.edu.au (office). *Website:* www .unimelb.edu.au/about/governance/chancellor.html (office).

RENDELL, Edward Gene, BA, JD; American state official; *Governor of Pennsylvania;* b. 5 Jan. 1944, New York City; s. of Jesse T. Rendell and Emma Rendell (née Sloat); m. Marjorie Osterlund 1971; one s.; ed Univ. of Pennsylvania, Villanova Univ. Law School; served in US Army; Asst Dist Attorney, Chief Homicide Unit, Phila 1968–74, Deputy Special Prosecutor, Phila 1976, Dist Attorney 1978–85; partner Ballard Spahr Andrews & Ingersoll, LLP; Mayor of Phila 1992–99; Gen. Chair. Democratic Nat. Cttee 1999–2001; Gov. of Pennsylvania 2003–; Lecturer in Law, Univ. of Pennsylvania; mem. ABA, Pennsylvania Dist Attorneys' Asscn, Phila Bar Asscn, B'nai B'rith, United Jewish Org., Jewish War Vets; Democrat; Man of the Year Award, VFW 1980, American Cancer League 1981, Distinguished Public Service Award, Pa Co. Detectives' Asscn. *Address:* Office of the Governor, 225 Main Capitol Building, Harrisburg, PA 17120, USA (office). *Telephone:* (717) 787-2500 (office). *Website:* www.governor.state.pa.us (office).

RENDELL OF BABERGH, Baroness (Life Peer), cr. 1997, of Aldeburgh in the County of Suffolk; **Ruth Barbara Rendell,** (Barbara Vine), CBE, FRSL; British crime novelist; b. 17 Feb. 1930; d. of Arthur Grasemann and Ebba Kruse; m. Donald Rendell 1950 (divorced 1975), remarried 1977 (died 1999); one s.; ed Loughton County High School; Dr hc (Essex) 1990; Arts Council Nat. Book Award for Genre Fiction 1981, Sunday Times Award for Literary Excellence 1990 and other awards. *Publications include:* From Doon with Death 1964, To Fear a Painted Devil 1965, Vanity Dies Hard 1965, A New Lease of Death (aka Sins of the Father) 1967, Wolf to the Slaughter 1967, The Secret House of Death 1968, The Best Man to Die 1969, A Guilty Thing Surprised 1970, No More Dying Then 1971, One Across, Two Down 1971, Murder Being Once Done 1972, Some Lie and Some Die 1973, The Face of Trespass 1974, Shake Hands Forever 1975, A Demon in My View 1976, A Judgement in Stone 1976, A Sleeping Life 1978, Make Death Love Me 1979, The Lake of Darkness 1980, Put on by Cunning (aka Death Notes) 1981, Master of the Moor 1982, The Speaker of Mandarin 1983, The Killing Doll 1984, The Tree of Hands 1984, An Unkindness of Ravens 1985, Live Flesh 1986, Heartstones 1987, Talking to Strange Men 1987, The Veiled One 1988, The Bridesmaid 1989, Mysterious 1990, Going Wrong 1990, The Strawberry Tree 1990, Walking on Water 1991, Kissing the Gunner's Daughter 1992, The Crocodile Bird 1993, Simisola 1994, Blood Lines 1996, The Keys to the Street 1997, Road Rage 1997, A Sight for Sore Eyes 1998, Harm Done 1999, Babes in the Wood 2002, The Rottweiler 2003, Thirteen Steps Down 2004, End in Tears 2005, The Water's Lovely 2006, Not in the Flesh 2007, Portobello 2008; as Barbara Vine: A Dark-Adapted Eye 1986, A Fatal Inversion 1987, The House of Stairs 1988, Gallowglass 1990, King Solomon's Carpet 1991, Asta's Book 1993, The Children of Men 1994, No Night is Too Long 1994, The Keys to the Street 1996, The Brimstone Wedding 1996, The Chimney Sweeper's Boy 1998, Grasshopper 2000, The Blood Doctor 2002, The Minotaur 2005, The Water's Lovely 2007, The Birthday Present 2008; short story collections: The Fallen Curtain 1976, Means of Evil 1979, The Fever Tree 1982, The New Girlfriend 1985, Collected Short Stories 1987, Undermining the Central Line (with Colin Ward) 1989, The Copper Peacock 1991, Blood Lines 1995, Piranha to Scurfy and Other Stories 2001; other: A Warning to the Curious: The Ghost Stories of M. R. James (ed.) 1987, Ruth Rendell's Suffolk 1989, The Reason Why: An Anthology of the Murderous Mind (ed.) 1995, Harm Done (ed.) 2000. *Leisure interests:* reading, walking, opera. *Address:* House of Lords, London, SW1A 0PW (office); 26 Cornwall Terrace Mews, London, NW1 5LL, England. *Telephone:* (20) 7219-2185 (office).

RENDLE, Michael Russel, MA; British business executive; b. 20 Feb. 1931, Kuala Lumpur, Malaya; s. of the late H. C. R. Rendle; m. Heather Rinkel 1957; two s. two d.; ed Marlborough Coll. and New Coll., Oxford; joined Anglo-Iranian Oil Co. (now British Petroleum) 1954; served in UK, Trinidad, Aden; Man. Dir BP Trinidad 1967–70, BP Australia 1974–78; Dir BP Trading (London) 1978–81; Man. Dir BP Co. 1981–86; Chair. TBI PLC (fmrly Markheath PLC) 1991–94; Deputy Chair. Imperial Continental Gas Asscn 1986–87, British-Borneo Petroleum Syndicate 1986–2000, Tace PLC 1991; Dir Willis Faber PLC (now renamed Willis Group PLC) 1985–98, Petrofina SA 1986–87, FIM Ltd 1989– (Chair. 1992–), Campbell and Armstong PLC 1992–98 (Chair. 1996–98), OIS Int. Inspection PLC 1993–96 (Chair. 1995–96), M.D.U. Ltd 1998–2001; Willis Ltd 2005–; mem. Willis Pension Trustees 1985– (Chair. 1999–); mem. London Bd Westpac Banking Corpn 1978–89; mem. British Overseas Trade Bd 1982–86, INSEAD Int. Council and UK Advisory Bd 1984–86; Chair. UNICE Social Affairs Cttee 1984–87; mem. Marlborough Coll. Council 1987–95. *Leisure interests:* golf, music, various outdoor sports. *Address:* 10 Trinity Square, London, EC3P 3AX, England. *Telephone:* (20) 7481-7152. *Fax:* (20) 7481-7154.

RENÉ, (France) Albert; Seychelles politician; *Leader, Seychelles People's Progressive Front;* b. 16 Nov. 1935, Mahé; s. of Price René and Louisa Morgan; m. 1st Karen Handley 1956; one d.; m. 2nd Geva Adam 1975; one s.; m. 3rd Sarah Zarquani 1993; one d.; ed St Louis Coll., Victoria, Seychelles Coll., St Maurice, Switzerland, St Mary's Coll., Southampton, UK, King's Coll., London; called to Bar 1957; Founder and Leader Seychelles People's United Party (later Seychelles People's Progressive Front) 1964–; mem. Parl. 1965; Minister of Works and Land Devt 1975–77; Prime Minister 1976–77; Pres. of Seychelles 1977–2004, also C-in-C, Minister of Econ. Devt and Housing

1977–78, of Internal Affairs and Finance 1977–79, of Finance 1977–78, of Youth and Community Devt 1978–80, of Finance and Industries 1981–89, of Planning and External Relations 1984–89, of Industry 1986–93, of Community Devt 1993, of Defence 1986–93, of Tourism 1988–89, of Internal Affairs, Defence and Legal Affairs; Order of the Golden Ark 1982. *Leisure interests:* gardening, fishing. *Address:* Seychelles People's Progressive Front (SPPF), PO Box 1242, Victoria, Seychelles (office). *Telephone:* 324622 (office). *Fax:* 225070 (office). *E-mail:* people@sppf.sc (office). *Website:* www.sppf.sc (office).

RENFREW OF KAIMSTHORN, Baron (Life Peer), cr. 1991, of Hurlet in the District of Renfrew; **Andrew Colin Renfrew,** PhD, ScD, FBA, FSA; British archaeologist; *Research Fellow, McDonald Institute for Archaeological Research, University of Cambridge;* b. 25 July 1937, Stockton-on-Tees; s. of the late Archibald Renfrew and Helena D. Renfrew; m. Jane M. Ewbank 1965; two s. one d.; ed St Albans School, St John's Coll., Cambridge and British School of Archaeology, Athens; Lecturer in Prehistory and Archaeology, Univ. of Sheffield 1965–70, Sr Lecturer 1970–72, Reader in Prehistory and Archaeology 1972; Prof. of Archaeology and Head of Dept, Univ. of Southampton 1972–81; Disney Prof. of Archaeology, Univ. of Cambridge 1981–2004, Dir McDonald Inst. for Archaeological Research 1990–2004, Fellow 2004–; Fellow, St John's Coll., Cambridge 1981–86; Master Jesus Coll., Cambridge 1986–97, Professorial Fellow 1997–2004, Fellow Emer. 2004–; Foreign Assoc. Nat. Acad. of Sciences, USA; Visiting Lecturer, UCLA 1967; mem. Ancient Monuments Bd for England 1974–84, Royal Comm. on Historical Monuments 1977–87, Historic Buildings and Monuments Comm. for England 1984–86, Ancient Monuments Advisory Cttee 1984–2002, British Nat. Comm. for UNESCO 1984–86; Foreign mem. American Philosophical Asscn 2006; Trustee, British Museum 1991–2001; Hon. FSA (Scotland); Hon. FRSE 2001; Hon. LittD (Sheffield) 1990, (Southampton) 1995, (Edinburgh) 2004, (Liverpool) 2004, (St Andrews) 2006; Dr hc (Faculty of Letters, Univ. of Athens) 1991; Rivers Memorial Medal, British Anthropological Inst. 1979, Sir Joseph Larmor Award 1961, Huxley Memorial Medal, Royal Anthropological Inst. 1991, Prix Int. Fyssen, Fondation Fyssen, Paris 1997, Language and Culture Prize, Univ. of Umeå, Sweden 1998, Rivers Memorial Medal, European Science Foundation Latsis Prize 2003, Bolzan Prize 2004. *Publications:* The Emergence of Civilization 1972, Before Civilization 1973, The Explanation of Culture Change (ed.) 1973, British Prehistory (ed.) 1974, Transformations: Mathematical Approaches to Culture Change 1979, Problems in European Prehistory 1979, An Island Polity 1982, Theory and Explanation in Archaeology (ed.) 1982, Approaches to Social Archaeology 1984, The Archaeology of Cult 1985, Peer, Polity Interaction and Socio-Political Change (ed.) 1986, Archaeology and Language: The Puzzle of Indo-European Origins 1987, The Idea of Prehistory (co-author) 1988, Archaeology: Theories, Methods and Practice (co-author) 1991, The Cycladic Spirit 1991, The Archaeology of Mind (co-ed. with E. Zubrow) 1994, Loot, Legitimacy and Ownership 2000, Archaeogenetics (ed.) 2000, Figuring It Out 2003, Archaeology, The Key Concepts (co-ed.) 2005; contribs to Archaeology, Scientific American, Phylogenetic Methods and the Prehistory of Languges (co-ed.) 2006. *Leisure interests:* contemporary arts, coins, travel. *Address:* c/o Curtis Brown Ltd, Haymarket House, 28–29 Haymarket, London, SW1Y 4SP, England (office); Room 3.2, West Building, McDonald Institute for Archaeological Research, Downing Street, Cambridge, CB2 3ER, England (office). *Telephone:* (20) 7393-4400 (office); (1223) 333521 (office). *Fax:* (20) 7393-4401 (office); (1223) 333536 (office). *E-mail:* des25@cam.ac.uk (office). *Website:* www .mcdonald.cam.ac.uk (office).

RENGIFO RUIZ, Marciano; Peruvian government minister and fmr army general; b. 25 Sept. 1934, Bellavista, San Martin; ed Escuela Militar de Chorrillos, Lima, Ecole Militaire St Cyr, France, Univ. de Piura, Centro de Altos Estudios Nacionales; numerous sr positions in Peruvian Army 1973–91; Mil. Rep. at OAS 1991; co-founder and mem. Perú Posible political party, mem. Manifesto Cttee 1999–2001; mem. Congress for San Martin 2000–, Pres. Defence Cttee 2000–02; First Vice-Pres. of Congress 2003–04; Minister of Defence 2005–06. *Address:* c/o Ministry of Defence, Avenida Arequipa 291, Lima 01, Peru (office).

RENNERT, Wolfgang; German conductor and music and opera director; *Principal Guest Conductor, Semperoper, Dresden;* b. 1 April 1922, Cologne; s. of Dr Alfred Rennert and Adelheid (née Nettesheim) Rennert; m. 1st Anny Schlemm 1957 (divorced 1968); one s.; m. 2nd Ulla Berkéwicz 1971 (divorced 1975); m. 3rd Simone Kaempf 2004; ed Mozarteum Salzburg; Chief Conductor and Deputy Dir of Music, Frankfurt 1953–67; Head of Opera, Staatstheater am Gärtnerplatz 1967–71; Dir of Music and Dir of Opera, Nat. Theatre, Mannheim 1980–85; Perm. Guest Conductor, State Opera, Berlin 1970–2000; Guest Conductor, Royal Opera, Copenhagen 1975–79; Prin. Guest Conductor, Semperoper, Dresden 1991–; Prin. Guest Conductor, Portuguese Symphony Orchestra, Lisbon 1998–2002; guest appearances with Vienna State Opera, Munich and Hamburg Operas, Royal Opera House Covent Garden, San Francisco Opera, Dallas Opera, Salzburg Festival, Munich Festival and Venice, Rome and Palermo opera houses, Japanese Festival, Osaka. *Address:* Holbeinstrasse 58, 12203 Berlin, Germany. *Telephone:* (30) 8333094.

RENNIE, Heughan Bassett (Hugh), CBE, BA, LLB, QC; New Zealand barrister, company director and fmr broadcasting executive; b. 7 April 1945, Wanganui; s. of the late W. S. N. Rennie and of Reta Rennie; m. 1st Caroline Jane Harding 1967 (died 1992); three s.; m. 2nd Penelope Jane Ryder-Lewis 1998; ed Wanganui Collegiate School, Victoria Univ., Wellington; part-time law clerk, Wanganui 1960–67, legal officer, NZ Electricity, Wellington 1967–70; barrister and solicitor, Macalister Mazengarb Parkin and Rose (later Macalister Mazengarb Perry Castle), Wellington 1970–91, Partner 1972–, Sr Litigation Partner 1982–, Chair. 1989–91; sole barrister, Wellington 1991–95; QC 1995–; Chair., Fourth Estate Group 1970–88, Broadcasting

Corpn of NZ (BCNZ) 1984–88, Govt Cttee on Restructuring BCNZ 1988, Chatham Is. Enterprise Trust 1990–2001, Policy Cttee, Dictionary of NZ Biography 1991–2001, Ministerial Inquiry into Auckland Power Supply Failure 1998, Royal NZ Ballet 1999–2003, The Marketplace Co. Ltd 1999–; Dir United Broadcasters Ltd 1981–84, Roydhouse Publishing Ltd 1981–88, Fletcher Challenge Ltd 1992–99, BNZ Finance Ltd 1993–97, Bank of NZ 1997–; Ed. Wellington Dist Law Soc. newspaper 1973–84; mem. NZ Law Soc. Cttees on Professional Advertising and Public Affairs 1981–84, NZ Council for Law Reporting 1983–87, Govt Advisory Cttee to statutory mans of Equiticorp 1989–; mem. Sir David Beattie Chair of Communications Trust Bd (VUW) 1986–90, Scientific Cttee, Nat. Heart Foundation 1988–94; Trustee Broadcasting History Project Trust Bd 1988–2004; NZ Medal 1990. *Leisure interests:* history, travel, writing, cycling, reading. *Address:* Harbour Chambers, 10th Floor, Equinox House, 111 The Terrace, PO Box 10-242, Wellington 6143, New Zealand (office). *Telephone:* 499-2684 (office); 472-9503 (home). *Fax:* 499-2705 (office). *E-mail:* hughrennie@legalchambers.co.nz (office). *Website:* www.harbourchambers.co.nz (office).

RENO, Janet, BA, LLB; American lawyer, politician and fmr government official; b. 21 July 1938, Miami, Fla; d. of Henry Reno and Jane Wood; ed Cornell and Harvard Univs; admitted to Florida Bar 1963; Assoc. Brigham & Brigham 1963–67; Pnr, Lewis & Reno 1967–71; Staff Dir Judiciary Comm. Fla House of Reps, Tallahassee 1971–72; Admin. Asst State Attorney, 11th Judicial Circuit Fla, Miami 1973–76; State Attorney 1978–93; Pnr, Steel, Hector & Davis, Miami 1976–78; US Attorney-Gen. (first woman) 1993–2001; unsuccessful Democratic cand. for Gov. of Fla 2002; mem. Bd of Dirs Innocence Project; mem. ABA, American Law Inst., American Judicature Soc.; Democrat; Women First Award, YWCA 1993, National Women's Hall of Fame 2000, Lindy Boggs Award (Stennis Center) 2003. *Music includes:* exec. producer Song of America (compilation) 2007. *Address:* c/o Board of Directors, Innocence Project, 100 Fifth Avenue, 3rd Floor, New York, NY 10011, USA. *Telephone:* (212) 364-5340. *E-mail:* info@innocenceproject.org. *Website:* www.innocenceproject.org.

RENO, Jean; French actor; b. (Juan Moreno Jederique y Jimenez), 30 July 1948, Casablanca, Morocco; four c.; m. 3rd Zofia Borucka 2006; Nat. Order of Merit (France) 2003. *Films include:* L'Hypothèse du tableau volé 1979, Claire de femme 1979, Voulez-vous un bébé Nobel? 1980, L'Avant dernier 1981, Les bidasses aux grandes manoeuvres 1981, La passante du Sans-Souci 1982, Ballade sanglante 1983, Le dernier combat 1983, Subway 1985, Signes Extérieurs de Richesse 1983, Ne quittez pas 1984, Alea 1984, Notre Histoire 1984, Le téléphone sonne toujours deux fois 1985, Subway 1985, Strictement personnel 1985, Zone rouge 1986, I Love You 1986, The Big Blue 1988, La Femme Nikita 1990, L'homme au Masque d'Or 1990, L'Opération Corned Beef 1991, Loulou Graffiti (also wrote screenplay) 1991, Kurenai no buta (aka Porco rosso) 1992, La vis (The Screw) 1993, Paranoïa 1993, Les Visiteurs (The Visitors) 1993, The Professional (Léon) 1994, Les truffes 1995, French Kiss 1995, Beyond the Clouds 1995, Mission: Impossible 1996, Le jaguar 1996, For Roseanna 1997, Un amour de sorcière (Witch Way Love) 1997, Le soeurs soleil 1997, Couloirs du temps: Les visiteurs 2 1998, Godzilla 1998, Ronin 1998, Tripwire 1999, The Crimson Rivers (Les Rivières pourpres) 2000, Just Visiting 2001, Wasabi 2001, Rollerball 2002, The Quiet American 2002, Jet Lag (Décalage horaire) 2002, Ruby & Quentin (Tais-toi!) 2003, Crimson Rivers 2: Angels of the Apocalypse 2004, L'Enquête corse 2004, Hotel Rwanda 2004, L'Empire des loups 2005, La tigre e la neve (The Tiger and the Snow) 2005, The Pink Panther 2006, The Da Vinci Code 2006, Flyboys 2006, Flushed Away (voice) 2006. *Television includes:* L'Aéropostale, courrier du ciel (mini-series) 1980, Quelques hommes de bonne volonté (mini-series) 1983, Et demain viendra le jour 1984, Un homme comblé 1985, Tender Is the Night (miniseries) 1985, Pour venger Pépère 1986, Monsieur Benjamin 1987, Flight from Justice 1993. *Address:* Chez les Films du Dauphin, 25 rue Yves-Toudic, 75010 Paris, France.

RENSCHLER, Andreas; German automotive industry executive; *Member, Board of Management, Daimler AG;* b. 1958, Stuttgart; joined Daimler-Benz 1988, fmrly Asst to Chair., led projects in Latin America and developing four-wheel drive vehicles, later Pres. Mercedes-Benz US Int., Inc., Pres. Smart Car Unit, DaimlerChrysler AG (now Daimler AG) 2004, now Head, Daimler Trucks Div., mem. Bd of Man., Daimler AG 2005–; Pres. Commercial Vehicle (CV) Bd of Dirs, European Automobile Mfrs Asscn 2008–; mem. Bd of Dirs Unaxis Holding AG 2005. *Address:* Daimler AG, Epplestrasse 225, 70546 Stuttgart, Germany. *Telephone:* (711) 17-0 (office). *Fax:* (711) 17-22244 (office). *Website:* www.daimler.com (office).

RENTCHNICK, Pierre, MD; Swiss physician and editor; b. 17 July 1923, Geneva; s. of Jacques Rentchnick and Blanche (Spiegel) Rentchnick; m. Paule Adam 1948; one s.; ed Univs of Geneva and Paris; Ed.-in-Chief, Médecine et Hygiène, Geneva 1956–93; Recent Results in Cancer Research; Ed. Springer, Heidelberg and New York 1962–83, Bulletin de l'Union int. contre le cancer, Geneva 1962–80; f. Kiwanis-Club, Geneva 1966, Pres. 1976–77; f. Int. Soc. for Chemotherapy 1959; Fellow, New York Acad. of Sciences, Medical Soc. of Prague, French Soc. of Infectious Pathology; Prix Littré (France) 1977. *Publications:* Esculape chez les Soviets 1954, Klinik und Therapie der Nebenwirkungen 1963, Esculape chez Mao 1973, Ces malades qui nous gouvernent 1976, Les orphelins mènent-ils le monde? 1978, Ces malades qui font l'Histoire 1983, Ces nouveaux malades qui nous gouvernent 1988–96; numerous publs on antibiotics in infectious diseases, on ethical problems, euthanasia etc. *Leisure interests:* skiing, golf, swimming, art (Netzuke). *Address:* Résidence La Gracieuse, Chemin des Vignes 14, 1027 Lonay, Switzerland (home). *Telephone:* (21) 8019257 (home). *Fax:* (22) 7765047 (home).

RENTON OF MOUNT HARRY, Baron (Life Peer), cr. 1997, of Offham in the County of East Sussex; **(Ronald) Tim(othy) Renton,** PC, MA, DL; British politician, business executive and author; b. 28 May 1932, London; s. of R. K. D. Renton CBE and Mrs Renton MBE; m. Alice Fergusson 1960; two s. three d.; ed Eton Coll., Magdalen Coll., Oxford; joined C. Tennant Sons & Co. Ltd 1954, with Tennants subsidiaries in Canada 1957–62, Dir 1964–73, Man. Dir Tennant Trading Ltd 1964–73; Dir Silvermines Ltd 1967–84, Australia and New Zealand Banking Group 1967–76, J. H. Vavasseur & Co. Ltd 1971–74; mem. BBC Gen. Advisory Council 1982–84; contested (Conservative) Sheffield Park 1970; MP for Mid-Sussex 1974–97; Parl. Pvt. Sec. to Rt Hon. John Biffen, MP 1979–81, to Rt Hon Geoffrey Howe, MP 1983–84; Parl. UnderSec. of State FCO 1984–85, Minister of State FCO 1985–87; Parl. Sec. to HM Treasury and Govt Chief Whip 1989–90, Minister for the Arts and for the Civil Service 1990–92; mem. Select Cttee on Nationalized Industries 1974–79, Vice-Chair. Conservative Parl. Trade Cttee 1974–79, Chair. Conservative Foreign and Commonwealth Council 1982–84; mem. Select Cttee on Nat. Heritage 1995–97; mem. House of Lords European Communities Cttee 1997–; Chair. House of Lords European Cttee on Agric. and Environment 2004–; Vice-Pres. Conservative Trade Unionists 1978–80, Pres. 1980–84; Chair. Outsider Art Archive 1995–2000, Sussex Downs Conservation Bd 1997–2005, South Downs Jt Cttee 2005–; Vice-Chair. British Council 1992–98; Dir (non-exec.) Fleming Continental European Investment Trust PLC, Chair. 1999–2002; Parl. Consultant Robert Fleming Holdings 1992–97; mem. Council Sussex Univ. 2000–; Fellow Industry and Parl. Trust 1977–79; mem. Advisory Bd, Know-How Fund for Cen. and Eastern Europe 1992–99; mem. APEX, Council Roedean School 1982–2005 (Pres. 1998–2005), Devt Council, Parnham Trust, Criterion Theatre Trust; Trustee Mental Health Foundation 1985–89; Founding Pres. (with Mick Jagger) of Nat. Music Day 1992–97; Green Ribbon Political Award for Environmental Campaigning 2000, Bowland Award, Asscn of Areas of Outstanding Natural Beauty 2000. *Publications:* The Dangerous Edge 1994, Hostage to Fortune 1997, Chief Whip 2004. *Leisure interests:* writing, mucking about in boats, listening to opera, growing vines. *Address:* House of Lords, London, SW1A 0PW; Mount Harry House, Offham, Lewes, East Sussex, BN7 3QW, England. *Telephone:* (1273) 471450 (office); (20) 7219-3308. *Fax:* (1273) 471450 (office). *E-mail:* rentont@parliament.uk (office).

RENTZEPIS, Peter M., PhD; American chemist, electrical engineer and academic; *Presidential Chair and Professor of Chemistry and Electrical and Computer Engineering, University of California, Irvine;* b. 11 Dec. 1934, Kalamata, Greece; s. of Michael Rentzepis and Leuci Rentzepis; m. Alma Elizabeth Keenan; two s.; ed Denison, Syracuse and Cambridge Univ.; mem. Tech. Staff Research Labs Gen. Electric Co., New York, then mem. Tech. Staff, Bell Labs, NJ, Head, Physical and Inorganic Chem. Research Dept; Presidential Chair. and Prof. of Chem. and Electrical and Computer Eng, Univ. of Calif., Irvine 1986–, Dir CX (IT) 2; Adjunct Prof. of Chem., Univ. of Pa, of Chem. and Biophysics, Yale Univ. 1980–; Visiting Prof., Rockefeller Univ., 1971, MIT –1975, of Chem. Univ. of Tel Aviv; mem. numerous academic cttees and editorial bds including US Army Cttee on Energetic Materials Research and Tech. 1982–83; Dir NATO Advanced Study Inst. 1984–; Co-founder and Chair. Bd Call/Recall Inc. 1996–; mem. Bd of Dirs KRIKOS—Science and Tech. for Greece, Bd of Dirs The Quanex Corpn 1984; mem. Advisory Bd Uniloc Corpn, Physical Chem. Div. Nat. Inst. of Science and Tech.; mem. US AmCCOM Advisory Cttee, US Army ARRACOM Exec. Science Advisory Cttee, NATO Advanced Study Insts (Dir), Int. Science Foundation; mem. NAS 1978, American Physical Soc., AAAS, etc.; mem. Nat. Acad. of Greece 1980; Hon. ScD (Denison) 1981, (Carnegie-Mellon) 1983; Hon. DPhil (Syracuse) 1980; American Chem. Soc. Peter Debye Prize in Physical Chemistry, American Physical Soc. Irving Lungmuize Prize in Chemical Physics, Scientist of the Year 1978, NY Acad. of Sciences Cressy Morison Award in Natural Sciences and other awards. *Publications:* more than 400 on lasers, photochemistry, picosecond spectroscopy; 68 patents. *Address:* Department of Chemistry, University of California, 579, 580A Rowland Hall, Mail Code 2025, Irvine, CA 92697 (office); Call/Recall, Inc. Sytems Division, 6160 Lusk Blvd., Suite C-206, San Diego, CA 92121, USA. *Telephone:* (949) 824-5934 (office); (858) 550-0596 (Call/Recall). *Fax:* (949) 824-2761 (office); (858) 550-0917 (Call/Recall). *E-mail:* pmrentze@uci.edu (office); info@call-recall.com. *Website:* www.chem.uci.edu/people/faculty/pmrentze (office); www.call-recall.com.

RENWICK, Glenn M., BS, MEng; American insurance industry executive; *President and CEO, The Progressive Corporation;* b. 22 May 1955; ed Univ. of Canterbury, Christchurch, NZ, Univ. of Florida at Gainesville; joined The Progressive Corpn (automobile insurance co.) 1986, Auto Product Man. for Fla 1986–88, Pres. of Mid-Atlantic, then Calif. Divs, sr positions in Consumer Marketing Dept –1998, Business Tech. Process Leader 1998–2000, Dir 1999–, CEO Insurance Operations 2000–01, Pres. and CEO 2001–. *Address:* The Progressive Corporation, 6300 Wilson Mills Road, Mayfield Village, OH 44143, USA (office). *Telephone:* (440) 461-5000 (office). *Fax:* (440) 603-4420 (office). *Website:* www.progressive.com (office).

RENWICK OF CLIFTON, Baron (Life Peer), cr. 1997, of Chelsea in the Royal Borough of Kensington and Chelsea; **Robin William Renwick,** KCMG, MA; British diplomatist and business executive; *Vice-Chairman, Investment Banking, JP Morgan; Vice-Chairman, JPMorgan Cazenove;* b. 13 Dec. 1937; s. of Richard Renwick and Clarice Renwick; m. Annie Colette Giudicelli 1965; one s. one d.; ed St Paul's School, Jesus Coll., Cambridge and Univ. of Paris (Sorbonne); army 1956–58; entered Foreign Service 1963; Dakar 1963–64; Foreign Office 1964–66; New Delhi 1966–69; Pvt. Sec. to Minister of State, FCO 1970–72; First Sec., Paris 1972–76; Counsellor, Cabinet Office 1976–78; Head, Rhodesia Dept, FCO 1978–80; Political Adviser to Gov. of Rhodesia 1980; Visiting Fellow, Center for Int. Affairs, Harvard Univ. 1980–81; Head of Chancery, Washington 1981–84; Asst Under-Sec. of State, FCO 1984–87;

Amb. to S Africa 1987–91, to USA 1991–95; Chair. Save and Prosper 1996–98, Fluor Ltd 1996–; Dir Robert Fleming (Deputy Chair. Robert Fleming Holdings Ltd 1999–2001), BHP Billiton plc 1997–2005, Fluor Corpn 1997–, SAB Miller 1999–, Compagnie Financière Richemont AG 1995–, Kazakhmys plc 2005–; Vice-Chair. (Investment Banking) JPMorgan, Vice-Chair. JPMorgan Cazenove 2004–; Deputy Chair. Fleming Family and Partners 2000–; Dir British Airways 1996–2006; Trustee The Economist; Hon. LLD (Witwatersrand) 1991, (American Univ. in London) 1993; Hon. DLitt (Coll. of William and Mary) 1993. *Publication:* Economic Sanctions 1981, Fighting with Allies 1996, Unconventional Diplomacy in Southern Africa 1997. *Leisure interests:* tennis, fishing, islands. *Address:* House of Lords, London, SW1A 0PW; JPMorgan Cazenove, 10 Aldermanbury, London, EC2V 7RF, England (office). *Telephone:* (20) 7219-5353 (House of Lords); (20) 7325-6375 (office). *Website:* www.jpmorgancazenove.com (office).

RENYI, Thomas A., BA, MBA; American banking executive; *Executive Chairman, Bank of New York Mellon Corporation;* b. 1946; m. Elizabeth Renyi; two s. one d.; ed Rutgers Univ.; joined The Bank of New York Co. Inc. 1971, Pres. 1992–98, Vice Chair. 1992–98, CEO 1997–2007, Chair. 1998–2007, Exec. Chair. Bank of New York Mellon Corpn (after merger with Mellon Financial Corpn) 2007–; fmr Chair. New York Bankers Asscn; mem. Bd of Dirs Public Service Enterprise Group Inc., The Clearing House, World Trade Center Memorial Foundation; Chair-elect The Financial Services Roundtable; mem. Bd of Mans New York Botanical Garden; mem Bd of Trustees Bates Coll., Rutgers Univ., Catholic Charities of the Archdiocese of New York. *Address:* Bank of New York Mellon Corporation, 1 Wall Street, 10th Floor, New York, NY 10286, USA (office). *Telephone:* (212) 495-1784 (office). *Fax:* (212) 809-9528 (office). *Website:* www.bnymellon.com (office).

REPIN, Vadim Viktorovich; Russian violinist; b. 31 Aug. 1971, Novosibirsk, Siberia; s. of Viktor Antonovich Repin and Galina Georgievna Repina; m. Nato Gabunia (divorced); ed Novosibirsk Music School with Zakhar Bron; toured Europe since 1985; debut in London (Barbican) 1988, in USA 1990; performances with the Royal Concertgebouw, Suddeutscher Rundfunk, Royal, Israel and St Petersburg Philharmonic Orchestras, NHK, Tokyo Metropolitan, Hallé, and Kirov Orchestras, Berlin and Sydney Symphony Orchestras; USA appearances with the Cleveland, Chicago, Minnesota Symphonies and Los Angeles Philharmonic; season 1996–97 with New York Philharmonic; worked with conductors including Menuhin, Bychkov, Gergiev, Prêtre, Rozhdestvensky, Jansons and Boulez; chamber music partners include Boris Berezovsky, Bella Davidovich and Alexander Melnikov; lives in Switzerland; Wienawski competition winner, Poznań 1982, Tibor Varga competition winner, Sion 1985, Queen Elizabeth competition winner, Brussels 1990. *Recordings include:* Shostakovich No. 1 and Prokofiev No. 2 with the Hallé Orchestra under Nagano 1995, Prokofiev Violin Sonatas and Five Melodies with Berezovsky 1995, Tchaikovsky and Sibelius Concertos with the London Symphony under Krivine 1996, Tchikovsky and Shostakovich piano trios with Berezovsky and Yablonsky 1997, Lalo Symphonie Espagnole with the London Symphony Orchestra under Nagano 1998, Tutta Bravura (with Markovich) 1999, Vadim Repin au Louvre (with Berezovsky, Barachovsky, Lakatos, Gothoni) 1999, Tchaikovsky and Myaskovsky violin concertos with the Kirov Orchestra under Gergiev 2002, A Night of Encores (recorded live with the Berlin Philharmonic under Jansons) 2004, Taneyev Piano Quintet and Trio (Gramophone Award for Best Chamber Recording 2006), Brahms Violin Concerto 2009. *Address:* Interclassica Music Management, Schönburgstrasse 4, 1040 Vienna, Austria (office). *Telephone:* (1) 5853980 (office). *E-mail:* eleanorhope@interclassica.com (office). *Website:* www.vadimrepin.com.

REPŠE, Einars, BS; Latvian politician and banker; *Minister of Finance;* b. 9 Dec. 1961, Jelgava; s. of Aivars-Rihards Repše and Aldona Repše (née Krasauska); m. Diana Vagale 1988 (divorced); two s. one d.; ed Latvia State Univ.; engineer, Latvian Acad. of Sciences 1986–90; entered politics as Co-founder of Latvian Nat. Independence Movt (LNNK) 1988; mem. Parl. 1990–91, 2003–; Gov. Bank of Latvia 1991–2001; Founder and Chair. New Era (Jaunais laiks) 2002; Prime Minister of Latvia 2002–04; Minister of Defence 2004–05, of Finance 2009–; Commdr Order of the Three Stars 1997. *Leisure interest:* aviation. *Address:* Ministry of Finance, Smilšu iela 1, Rīga 1050, Latvia (office). *Telephone:* 6609-5405 (office). *Fax:* 6609-5503 (office). *E-mail:* info@fm.gov.lv (office). *Website:* www.fm.gov.lv (office).

RESCHER, Nicholas, PhD; American philosopher and author; *Professor of Philosophy, University of Pittsburgh;* b. 15 July 1928, Hagen, Germany; s. of Erwin Hans Rescher and Meta Anna Rescher; m. 1st Frances Short 1951 (divorced 1965); one d.; m. 2nd Dorothy Henle 1968; two s. one d.; ed Queens Coll., New York, Princeton Univ.; Assoc. Prof. of Philosophy, Lehigh Univ. 1957–61; Prof. Univ. of Pittsburgh 1961–, Dir Center for Philosophy of Science 1982–89; Consultant RAND Corpn 1954–66, Encyclopaedia Britannica 1963–64, North American Philosophical Publs 1980–; Ed. American Philosophical Quarterly 1964–94; Sec.-Gen. Int. Union of History and Philosophy of Science 1969–75; Pres. American Philosophical Asscn (Eastern Div.) 1989–90, American Catholic Philosophical Asscn 2003–04, American Metaphysical Soc. 2004–05; mem. Academia Europea, Institut Int. de Philosophie, Acad. Int. de Philosophie des Sciences; Guggenheim Fellow 1970–71; visiting lectureships at Univs of Oxford, Munich, Konstanz, Western Ontario and others; Hon. mem. Corpus Christi Coll. Oxford; six hon. degrees; Alexander von Humboldt Prize 1983, Aquinas Medal. *Publications:* more than 90 books including The Coherence Theory of Truth 1973, Methodological Pragmatism 1977, Scientific Progress 1978, The Limits of Science 1984, Ethical Idealism 1987, Rationality 1988, A System of Pragmatic Idealism (three vols) 1992–94, Pluralism 1993, Predicting the Future 1997, Paradoxes 2001, Philosophical Reasoning 2001, Metaphysics 2005, Epistemetrics 2006; numerous articles in many areas of philosophy. *Leisure interests:* reading

history and biography. *Address:* 1012 Cathedral of Learning, University of Pittsburgh, Pittsburgh, PA 15260 (office); 1033 Milton Avenue, Pittsburgh, PA 15218, USA (home). *Telephone:* (412) 624-5950 (office); (412) 243-1290 (home). *Fax:* (412) 383-7506 (office). *E-mail:* rescher@pitt.edu (office). *Website:* www.pitt.edu/~rescher (office).

RESHETNIKOV, Fedor Grigorevich, DTechSci; Russian physical chemist; *Adviser, A.A. Bochvar All Union Scientific and Research Institute of Inorganic Materials;* b. 25 Nov. 1919, Sumy, Ukraine; s. of Grigory Pavlovich Reshetnikov and Elisaveta Ivanovna Reshetnikova; m. Tatyana Frolovna Reshetnikova 1948; one d.; ed Moscow Inst. of Non-Ferrous Metals, Dzerzhinsky Artillery Acad.; engineer, metallurgy works, Kazakhstan 1942, Perm 1944–45; mem. CPSU 1947–91; scientific research work 1946–; Head Lab., First Deputy Dir, A. A. Bochvar All Union Scientific and Research Inst. of Inorganic Materials 1966–92, adviser 1992–; Corresp. mem. USSR (now Russian) Acad. of Sciences 1974–92, mem. 1992–; six Orders; USSR State Prize 1951, 1975, 1985, Khlopin Prize, Russian Acad. of Sciences. *Publication:* Development, Production and Operation of Nuclear Power Reactor Fuels and numerous articles on physical chem. and tech. of radioactive and rare metals, nuclear fuels and structural materials for nuclear reactor cases. *Leisure interests:* touring, fishing, music. *Address:* A.A. Bochvar All Union Scientific and Research Institute of Inorganic Materials, Rogov Street 5, 123060 Moscow; Peschany Ln. 4, Apt. 310, 125252 Moscow, Russia (home). *Telephone:* (495) 196-66-61 (office); 198-26-80 (home). *Fax:* (495) 196-65-91 (office).

RESIN, Vladimir Iosifovich, PhD; Russian politician and civil engineer; *Head of Department, City-Planning Policy, Development and Reconstruction of the City of Moscow;* b. 21 Feb. 1936, Minsk; s. of Josif Resin and Rosa Ressina; m. Marta Yakovlevna Chadayeva 1958; one d.; ed Moscow Mining Inst.; worked in orgs of USSR Ministry of Coal Industry and Ministry of Ass. and Special Construction; Deputy, First Deputy, then Head, Moscow Dept of Eng and Construction 1974–; Head, Moscow Industrial Construction Dept 1985–; Chair. Moscow Construction Cttee 1989–91; Deputy Chair. Exec. Cttee, Moscow City Council 1989–91; Deputy Premier, Moscow City Govt 1991–92, First Vice-Premier 1992–; Head, Dept of Moscow Architecture, Construction, Prospective Devt Complex and Reconstruction 1992–2000, Head of Complex of Architecture, Construction, Devt and Reconstruction of City (CACDR) 2000–02, Head of Dept, City-Planning Policy, Devt and Reconstruction of City 2002–; First Deputy Mayor of Moscow 2000–02; Prof. Russian G. V. Plekhanov Econ. Acad. 1996, Moscow Int. Univ.; Corresp. mem. Russian Acad. of Architecture and Construction Sciences, Russian Eng Acad.; Sr Fellow, Inst. of Civil Engineers 2000; author of 30 inventions; Hon. Prof. (Moscow State Lomonosov Univ.), (Moscow Int. Univ.) 2000, (Russian Acad. of Sciences) 2005; awarded 21 State Prizes; other awards and distinctions include Distinguished Constructor of Russian Fed., Honoured Constructor of Moscow, Order of Russian Orthodox Church (four). *Publications:* Managing the Development of a Large City: A Systems Approach; and numerous other publs. *Leisure interest:* work. *Address:* Moscow City Government, Department of Moscow Architecture, Construction, Development and Reconstruction, Nikitsky per. 5, 103009 Moscow, Russia. *Telephone:* (495) 925-46-26; (495) 291-09-47. *Fax:* (495) 200-53-22; (495) 956-81-40.

RESNAIS, Alain; French film director; b. 3 June 1922, Vannes; s. of Pierre Resnais and Jeanne Resnais (née Gachet); m. 1st Florence Malraux 1969; m. 2nd Sabine Azéma 1998; ed Institut des Hautes Etudes Cinématographiques, Paris; Special Prize (Cannes) for Mon Oncle d'Amerique 1980; Grand Prix du Cinéma 1986, Prix Louis-Delluc 1993, Prix Méliès 1994, Silver Bear for Lifetime Achievement, Berlin 1998; Légion d'honneur. *Short films directed (1948–59) include:* Van Gogh 1948, Guernica (with Robert Hessens) 1950, Les statues meurent aussi (with Chris Marker) 1952, Nuit et brouillard 1955. *Feature films include:* Hiroshima mon amour 1959, L'année dernière à Marienbad 1961, Muriel 1963, La guerre est finie 1966, Je t'aime, je t'aime 1968, Stavisky 1974, Providence 1977, Mon oncle d'Amérique 1980, La vie est un roman 1983, L'amour à mort 1984, Mélo 1986, I want to go home 1989, Smoking/No Smoking 1993 (César awards for best dir, best film), On connait la chanson 1998 (César Award for Best French Film), Pas sur la bouche (Not on the Lips) 2003, Private Fears in Public Places (Best Dir Venice Film Festival) 2006. *Address:* c/o Intertalent, 5 rue Clément Marot, 75008 Paris (office); 70 rue des Plantes, 75014 Paris, France (home).

RESNIK, Regina; American singer (mezzo-soprano); b. 30 Aug. 1924; d. of Samuel Resnik and Ruth Resnik; m. 1st Harry W. Davis 1947; one s.; m. 2nd Arbit Blatas 1975; ed Hunter Coll., New York; opera début as Lady Macbeth, New Opera Co. 1942; Mexico City 1943; New York City Opera 1943–44; Metropolitan Opera 1944–1983; sang 80 roles, soprano and mezzo-soprano, became regular mem. Royal Opera, London, Vienna State Opera, Bayreuth, Salzburg, San Francisco, Chicago, La Scala, Milan, Paris, Buenos Aires, Berlin, Brussels, etc.; Stage Dir for maj. productions Hamburg, Venice, Sydney, Vancouver, Strasbourg, Warsaw, Lisbon, Madrid, Wiesbaden; appeared on Broadway in Cabaret 1987, in A Little Night Music 1990, New York City Opera, 50th anniversary celebrations Danny Kaye Playhouse; Trustee Hunter Foundation, Metropolitan Opera Guild Bd; Commdr, Ordre des Arts et des Lettres; Dr hc (Hunter) 1991; Lincoln Center and Vienna State Opera awards; Pres.'s Medal;. *Address:* American Guild of Musical Artists, 1727 Broadway, New York, NY 10019, USA.

RESTAD, Gudmund; Norwegian politician; b. 19 Dec. 1937, Smøla; s. of Ola Restad and Olga Marie Dalen; m. Britt Jorun Wollum 1959; three c.; ed officers' training school (anti-aircraft artillery), business school, Nat. Police Acad.; sergeant at Ørland airport 1959–61, country police Ørland and Orkdal 1961–67; detective constable/inspector Crime Police Centre 1967–73; training in police investigation in Denmark and Germany 1967; Lecturer, Nat. Police Training School 1973–75; sergeant in Smøla 1975–85; mem. Parl. 1985–2001;

Chair. Local Council, Smøla 1980–85, mem., Chair., Deputy Chair. Nordmøre Interkommunale Kraftlag (Nordmøre Electricity Bd) 1982–91; mem. Bd Central Police Org. 1969–73, Møre og Romsdal Centre Party 1982–83, The Centre Party 1983–89; mem. Judiciary Cttee Storting (Parl.) 1985–89; mem., Deputy Chair. Finance Cttee 1989–97; Minister of Finance and Customs 1997–2000; Deputy Chair. Defence Cttee 2000–01. *Address:* c/o Stortinget, 0026 Oslo, Norway.

RÉTORÉ, Guy; French theatre director; b. 7 April 1924; s. of Hervé Rétoré and Aline Henry; ed Univ. of Paris; Public Relations Dept, SNCF until 1955; Actor and Producer, Théâtre de Boulevard until 1955; f. La Guilde (theatrical company), Menilmontant, East Paris 1954; opened Théâtre de Menilmontant 1958; Dir Maison de la Culture, Menilmontant 1962; Dir Théâtre de l'Est Parisien (TEP) 1963– (also gives concerts, ballets, films and confs); Chevalier Légion d'honneur, Officier Ordre nat. du Mérite, Officier des Arts et des Lettres. *Plays produced include:* La fille du roi (Cosmos) 1955, Life and Death of King John 1956, Grenadiers de la reine (Farquhar, adapted by Cosmos) 1957, L'avare (Molière), Les caprices de Marianne (Musset), La fleur à la bouche (Pirandello), Le médecin malgré lui (Molière), Le manteau (Gogol, adapted by Cosmos) 1963, La Locandiera (Goldoni), Arden of Faversham 1964, Monsieur Alexandre (Cosmos) 1964, Macbeth (Shakespeare) 1964, Turcaret (Lesage) 1965, Measure for Measure (Shakespeare) 1965, Le voyage de Monsieur Perrichon (Labiche) 1965, Live Like Pigs (Arden), The Silver Tassie (O'Casey) 1966–67, Les 13 soleils de la rue St Blaise (A. Gatti), La machine (Jean Cosmos) 1968–69, Lorenzaccio (Musset), The Threepenny Opera (Brecht), Major Barbara (Shaw) 1969–70, Les ennemis (Gorki), L'âne de l'hospice (Arden) 1970–71, Sainte Jeanne des abattoirs (Brecht) 1971–72, Macbeth (Shakespeare) 1972–73, Androclès et le lion 1974–75, Coquin de coq (O'Casey) 1975–76, L'ôtage (Claudel) 1976–77, Le camp du drap d'or 1980, Fin de partie, tueur sans gage 1981, Le Chantier 1982, Clair d'usine 1983, 325000 francs 1984, Entre passions et prairie (Denise Bonal) 1987, Arturo Ui 1988, Clair de Terre 1989, Chacun pleure son Garabed 1991. *Address:* TEP, 159 avenue Gambetta, 75020 Paris, France. *Telephone:* 1-43-63-20-96. *Fax:* 1-43-64-07-50. *Website:* www.theatre-estparisien.net.

REUBER, Grant Louis, OC, PhD, LLD, FRSC; Canadian economist; *Senior Advisor, Sussex Circle;* b. 23 Nov. 1927, Mildmay, Ont.; s. of Jacob Daniel Reuber and Gertrude Catherine Reuber; m. Margaret Louise Julia Summerhayes 1951 (deceased); three d.; ed Walkerton High School, Univ. of W Ontario, Harvard Univ., Sidney Sussex Coll., Cambridge; with Econ. Research Dept Bank of Canada 1950–52; Econ. and Int. Relations Div. Dept of Finance 1955–57, Deputy Minister of Finance Govt of Canada 1979–80; at Univ. of W Ontario 1957–78, Asst Prof. 1957–59, Assoc. Prof. 1959–62, Prof. Econ. Dept 1962–78, Dean of Social Science 1969–74, Acad. Vice-Pres. and Provost, mem. Bd of Govs 1974–78; Chair. Ont. Econ. Council 1973–78; Sr Vice-Pres. and Chief Economist Bank of Montreal 1978–79, Exec. Vice-Pres. 1980–81, Dir, Deputy Chair. and Deputy Chief Exec. 1981–83, Pres. 1983–87, Deputy Chair. 1987–90; Chancellor Univ. of Western Ont. 1988–93; Lecturer, Grad. School of Business, Univ. of Chicago 1992–93; Chair. Canada Deposit Insurance Corpn 1993–99 (Dir 1999–), Canada Merit Scholarship Foundation 1994–; Dir Hermitage Museum Foundation of Canada Inc. 2000–; Sr Adviser and Dir Sussex Circle (consulting firm); Gov. Royal Ont. Museum 2000–03; Pres. and Dir Ditchley Foundation of Canada 1989–; Sr Fellow, C. D. Howe Inst. 2000–; Hon. LLD (Wilfred Laurier Univ.) 1983, (Simon Fraser Univ., Univ. of W Ont.) 1985, (McMaster Univ.) 1994. *Publications:* The Cost of Capital in Canada (with R. J. Wonnacott) 1961, (with R. E Caves): Canadian Economic Policy and the Impact of International Capital Flows 1970, Private Foreign Investment in Development 1973, Canada's Political Economy 1980. *Leisure interests:* tennis, reading. *Address:* Sussex Circle, 50 O'Connor Street, Suite 1424, Ottawa, ON K1P 6L2 (office); 90 Glen Edyth Drive, Toronto, ON M4V 2V9, Canada (home). *Telephone:* (613) 567-3200 (office); (416) 924-4971. *Fax:* (613) 567-4627 (office); (416) 924-4784 (home). *Website:* www.sussexcircle.com (office).

REUTERSWÄRD, Carl Fredrik; Swedish artist, writer and sculptor; b. 4 June 1934, Stockholm; s. of Wilhelm Reuterswärd and Thérèse Ingeström; m. 1st Anna Tesch 1958 (divorced 1968); two s. two d.; m. 2nd Mona Moller-Nielsen 1974; one s.; m. 3rd Tonie Lewenhaupt 1997; ed Ecole de Fernand Léger, Paris and Royal Coll. of Art, Stockholm; first artist to use lasers 1965; Prof., Royal Coll. of Art, Stockholm 1965–70; since 1952 active in drawing, painting, sculpture, holography, scenography, graphics, design and architectural comms; prin. themes: Nonsens 1952–58; Cigars and Games 1958–63; Exercise 1958–64; Lazy Lasers and Holy Holos 1965–74; a trilogy: Kilroy (anybody) 1962–72, CAVIART (a somebody) 1972–82; works in public collections in Sweden, USA, Germany, France, England, Switzerland, Netherlands, Norway and Denmark, including Nat. Museum, Stockholm, Museum of Modern Art and Metropolitan Museum of Art, New York, MIT Museum, Cambridge, Mass, Städtische Kunsthalle, Düsseldorf, Musée Nat. d'Art Moderne, Paris, Tate Modern, London and Stedelijk Museum, Amsterdam; Prins Eugen Medal bestowed by King Carl Gustaf XVI 1984, Lifetime Achievements Award 1997. *Works include:* Non-Violence, bronze sculpture on perm. display in front of UN Bldg, New York since 1988 (UN Award of Honour 1999, Daily Points of Right Award 2000), Non-Violence, bronze sculpture on perm. display in Chaoyang Park, Beijing 2008. *Publications:* Kafka, Wahlstrom and Widstrand 1981, Caviart 1982, Making Faces 1984, Mes Autres Moi 1989, Style is Fraud 2004, Non-Violence och andra offentliga verk 2005, Skuggor och Glas 2006, From One Side to the Other 2006. *Address:* 6 rue Montolieu, 1030 Bussigny/Lausanne, Switzerland (home). *Telephone:* (21) 7010514 (home). *Fax:* (21) 7012675 (home). *E-mail:* cf.reutersward@gmail.com (office).

REVIGLIO, Franco; Italian economist and academic; b. 3 Feb. 1935, Turin; ed Univ. of Turin; asst in Faculty of Law, Univ. of Turin 1959–64, currently Prof. of Financial Science; economist, IMF, Washington, DC 1964–66; Prof., Univ. of Urbino 1966–68; mem. Cen. Tax Comm. and Tech. Cttee for Tax Reform, Ministry of Finance 1976–79, Minister of Finance 1979–81; mem. Municipal Council of Turin 1981–83; Chair. Tech. Comm. on Public Expenditure Ministry of Treasury 1981–83; mem. Tech. Cttee for Econ. Programming Ministry of the Budget 1981–89, Minister of the Budget 1992–93; Chair. Ente Nazionale Idrocarburi 1983–89; Sr Advisor, Wasserstein Perella 1990–92; Senator 1992–94; Chair. and Man. Dir Azienda Energetica Metropolitana Torino 2000–06; Sr Advisor, Lehman Brothers 2002–07; St Vincent Prize for Econs 1998, Walter Tobagi Prize 1998. *Publications:* La finanza della sicurezza sociale (co-author) 1969, Spesa pubblica e stagnazione dell'economia italiana 1975, Le chiavi del 2000 1990, Meno Stato più mercato: Come ridurre lo Stato per risanare il Paese 1994, Lo Stato imperfetto 1996, Come siama entrati in Europa 1998, Sanità senza vincoli di spesa? 1999; contrib. of numerous essays and articles to journals and newspapers. *Address:* Departimento di Scienze Economiche e Finanziarie G. Prato, Facoltà di Economia – Università di Torino, Corso Unione Sovietica 218bis, 10134 Turin, Italy (office). *Telephone:* (011) 6706080 (office); (02) 645750 (home). *Fax:* (011) 6706062 (office). *E-mail:* franco.reviglio@unito.it (home). *Website:* www.econ .unito.it (office).

REXHEPI, Bajram; Serbian (Kosovan) politician; b. 3 June 1954, Kosovska Mitrovica (Mitrovice); m. Shpresa Rexhepi; one d.; ed Faculty of Medicine, Priština Univ. and Univ. of Zagreb; postgraduate studies in Zagreb 1985; worked as gen. surgeon and endoscopic specialist at regional hosp., Kosovska Mitrovica 1985–90; mem. 'Kosovo Assembly'; joined separatist ethnic Albanian Kosovo Liberation Army March–June 1999, spent three months serving as field doctor in operating zone of Shala; Pres. Kosovska Mitrovica Municipal Council and Mayor of divided town's southern section 1990; mem. Democratic Party of Kosovo; first Prime Minister of Kosovo 2002–04; twice awarded title of 'Hairstyle of the Year' by Priština weekly magazine. *Address:* c/o Democratic Party of Kosovo (DPK) (Partia Demokratike e Kosovës—PDK), 10000 Priština, Rruga Nënë Terezë 20, Kosovo and Metohija, Serbia, Serbia (office). *Telephone:* (44) 156774 (office). *E-mail:* pdk@pdk-ks.org (office). *Website:* www.pdk-ks.org (office).

REYES-HEROLES GONZÁLEZ GARZA, Jesús, BEcons, PhD; Mexican civil servant and petroleum industry executive; *Director General, Petróleos Mexicanos (PEMEX);* b. 1950, Mexico City; ed Instituto Autónomo de México (ITAM), Massachusetts Inst. of Tech., USA; began career as Research Asst, Banco de México; served in various civil service roles including Dir-Gen. Treas. Planning 1983–88, Gen. Coordinator of Foreign Affairs Secr. Advisers 1989–90; Dir-Gen. GEA Grupo de Economistas y Asociados (consultancy firm) 1991–94; Mexican mem. Asia-Pacific Econ. Cooperation (APEC) Group of Eminent Persons 1993–94; Dir-Gen. Banco Nacional de Obras y Servicios Públicos (Banobras) 1994–95; Mexican Sec. of Energy 1995–97; Amb. to USA 1997–2000; Exec. Pres. GEA StructurA (consultancy) 2001–06; Dir-Gen. Petróleos Mexicanos (PEMEX) 2006–; mem. PRI (Institutional Revolutionary Party) 1972–, Pres. PRI Nat. Comm. on Ideology 1994; fmr mem. Bd of Dirs Banamex, Citigroup, Wal-Mart Mexico; fmr Trustee Gonzalo Río Arronte Foundation, Universidad Iberoamericana (FICSAC). *Publications:* several articles in academic journals. *Address:* Petróleos Mexicanos (PEMEX), Marina Nacional 329, Colonia Huasteca, CP 11311, México, DF, Mexico (office). *Telephone:* (55) 1944-2500 (office). *Fax:* (55) 1944-9378 (office). *E-mail:* info@pemex.com (office). *Website:* www.pemex.com (office).

REYES LÓPEZ, Juan Francisco; Guatemalan politician and business executive; b. 10 July 1938; m.; three c.; ed John Carroll High School, Birmingham, Ala, USA, Escuela Militar del General de Armas Bernardo O'Higgins, Santiago de Chile, Universidad Rafael Landivar, Guatemala City; primary school teacher; army officer 1960–61; in pvt. business 1961–89; Pres. Comité Coordinador de Asociaciones Agrícolas, Comerciales, Industriales y Financieras (CACIF) 1979–80, Pres. 1980; Man. Instituto Guatemalteco de Seguridad Social 1982; mem. Frente Republicano Guatemalteco (FRG) party, mem. Nat. Exec. Cttee 1991–99; Deputy to Congreso (Parl.) 1990–94, Chair. Comm. on Foreign Relations 1990, mem. Comm. on Finance 1990–94, First Vice-Pres. Exec. Bd 1994; Vice-Pres. of Guatemala 2000–04; Orden del General O'Higgins 1989, Orden de la Estrella Brillante 1995. *Address:* c/o Office of the President, Guatemala City, Guatemala (office).

REYN, Evgeny Borisovich; Russian poet and writer; b. 29 Dec. 1935, Leningrad; m. Nadejda Reyn 1989; one s.; ed Leningrad Tech. Inst.; freelance poet published in samizdat magazine Sintaksis and émigré press abroad in magazines Grani, Kovcheg; participated in publication of almanac Metropol; literary debut in Russia 1984; Prof., Moscow M. Gorky Inst. of Literature; mem. Writers' Union, Union of Moscow Writers, Russian PEN Centre; Peterburg Prize of Arts 'Tsarskoye Selo' 1995, State Prize of Russia in Literature and Art 1996, Ind. Alexander Block Literature Award 1999, Alfred Tepfer Foundation Pushkin Prize (Gamburg, Germany) 2003, State Pushkin Prize in Literature and Art 2004, Grinzane Cavour Prize (Turin, Italy) 2004, Petropol Prize in Literature and Arts, St Peterburg 2005. *Television:* Kuprin 1967, The Thcukokkala 1969, The Tenth Chapter 1970, Journeys with Josef Brodsky 1993, Josef Brodsky: The Hatchings to Portrait 1996. *Publications:* The Names of Bridges 1984, Shore Line 1989, The Darkness of Mirrors 1989, Breda 1995, Irretrievable Day 1991, Counter-Clockwise 1992, Nezhnosmo 1993, Selected Poems 1993, The Prognostication 1994, The Top-booty 1995, The Others 1996, The News Stages of the Life of The Moscow Beau Monde 1997, Balkony 1998, Arch over Water 2000, The Remarks of Marathon Man: Inconclusive Memoirs 2003, The Overground Transition 2004, After Our Age 2005, My Best Addressman... 2005, The Poems, Prose, Essays 2006. *Address:*

Leningradsky Prospect, 75, Apt 167, 125057 Moscow (home). *Telephone:* (499) 157-20-14 (home). *Fax:* (495) 203-46-78 (office). *E-mail:* Reyne@cnt.ru (home).

REYNDERS, Didier, LLB; Belgian politician; *Deputy Prime Minister and Minister of Finance and of Institutional Reform;* b. 6 Aug. 1958, Liège; ed Inst. St Jean Berchmans, Liège, Univ. of Liège; lawyer 1981–85; Gen. Man. Ministry of Wallonia Region 1985–88; Chair. Belgian Nat. Railway Co. (SNCB) 1986–91; Chef de Cabinet of Deputy Prime Minister, Minister of Justice and Inst. Reform 1987–88; Chair. Nat. Airways Co. 1991–93; Vice-Chair. Parti Réformateur Libéral (PRL) 1992; Deputy, House of Reps 1992; Head PRL Group in Liège Council 1995, Chair. PRL-FDF (Front Démocratique des Francophones) Group 1995; Chair. Fed. Provinciale et d'Arrondissement de Liège of PRL 1995–; Lecturer, Hautes Ecoles Commerciales, Liège; Minister of Finance 1999–2007 (resgnd) reappointed Deputy Prime Minister and Minister of Finance and of Institutional Reform Dec. 2008–; Pres. Mouvement Réformateur (MR) (Reformist Movt); Chevalier, Ordre de Léopold 2000. *Address:* Federal Public Service of Finance, 33 boulevard du Roi Albert II, BP 70, 1030 Brussels (office); Mouvement Réformateur (MR) (Reformist Movement), 84–86 ave de la Toison d'Or, 1060 Brussels (office); En Jonruelle 27, 4000 Liège, Belgium (home). *Telephone:* (2) 233-81-11 (office); (2) 500-35-11 (office). *Fax:* (2) 233-80-03; (2) 500-35-00 (home). *E-mail:* info@minfin.be (office); mr@mr.be (office). *Website:* www.minfin.fgov.be (office); www.mr.be (office).

REYNOLDS, Albert; Irish politician and business executive; b. 3 Nov. 1935, Rooskey, Co. Roscommon; m. Kathleen Coén; two s. five d.; ed Summerhill Coll., Sligo; fmr Chair. C & D Petfoods; mem. Longford Co. Council 1974–79; elected mem. Dáil 1977; Minister for Posts and Telegraphs and Transport 1979–81, for Industry and Energy March–Dec. 1982, for Industry and Commerce 1987–88, for Finance and the Public Service 1988–89, of Finance 1989–91; Taoiseach (Prime Minister) 1992–94; Vice-Pres. Fianna Fáil 1983–92, Pres. 1992–94; mem. Bd of Govs European Investment Bank; Gov. for Ireland, Bd of Govs World Bank, IMF; apptd Dir Jefferson Smurfit 1996; Hon. LLD (Univ. Coll., Dublin) 1995; Dr hc from one Irish, three British, four US and one Australian univs. *Leisure interests:* racing, swimming. *Address:* Apt 4, Four Seasons Hotel, Ballsbridge, Dublin 4, Ireland (home). *Fax:* (1) 6601998 (home).

REYNOLDS, Anna, FRAM; British singer (mezzo-soprano); b. 5 June 1930, Canterbury; d. of Paul Grey Reynolds and Vera Cicely Turner; m. Jean Cox 1994; ed Benenden School, Royal Acad. of Music; studied with Prof. Debora Fambri, Rome; has appeared at many int. festivals including Spoleto, Edin., Aix-en-Provence, Salzburg Easter Festival, Vienna, Bayreuth, Tanglewood; has sung with leading orchestras all over the world including Chicago Symphony, New York Philharmonic, Berlin Philharmonic, London Symphony, etc.; has appeared in opera performances in New York Metropolitan, La Scala, Milan, Covent Garden, Bayreuth, Rome, Chicago Lyric Opera, Teatro Colón, Buenos Aires, Teatro Fenice, Venice and many others. *Leisure interests:* reading, piano, travel, world-wide correspondence. *Address:* Peesten 9, 95359 Kasendorf, Germany. *Telephone:* (9228) 1661. *Fax:* (9228) 8468 (home). *E-mail:* jjaspercox@t-online.de (home).

REYNOLDS, Burt; American actor; b. 11 Feb. 1936, Waycross, Ga; s. of Burt Reynolds, Sr; m. 1st Judy Carne (divorced 1965); m. 2nd Loni Anderson 1988 (divorced 1994); one adopted s.; ed Florida State Univ.; mem. Dirs Guild of America. *Stage appearances include:* Mister Roberts, Look, We've Come Through, The Rainmaker. *Films include:* Angel Baby 1961, Operation CIA 1965, Navajo Joe 1967, Impasse 1969, Skullduggery 1970, Deliverance 1972, Everything You've Always Wanted to Know about Sex But Were Afraid to Ask 1972, The Man Who Loved Cat Dancing 1973, Hustle 1975, Silent Movie 1976, Gator (also dir) 1976, Nickelodeon 1976, Smokey and the Bandit 1977, Hooper (also producer) 1978, Starting Over 1979, The Cannonball Run 1981, Sharky's Machine (also dir) 1981, City Heat 1984, Stick (also dir) 1984, Rent A Cop 1987, Switching Channels 1988, Physical Evidence 1989, Breaking In 1989, B. L. Stryker 1989, Modern Love 1990, Alby's House of Bondage 1990, Cop and a Half 1993, Striptease 1996, Mad Dog Time 1996, Boogie Nights (Golden Globe for Best Supporting Actor) 1997, Raven 1997, Waterproof 1998, Mystery Alaska 1998, The Hunter's Moon 1998, Pups 1999, Big City Blues (also producer) 1999, Mystery Alaska 2000, The Crew 2000, The Last Producer 2000, The Hermit of Amsterdam 2001, Driven 2001, Tempted 2001, Hotel 2001, The Hollywood Sign 2001, Auf Herz und Nieren 2001, Snapshots 2002, Time of the Wolf 2002, The Librarians 2003, Gumball 3000: The Movie 2003, The Librarians 2003, Without a Paddle 2004, Grilled 2005, The Longest Yard 2005, Delgo 2005, The Dukes of Hazzard 200, Forget About It 2005, Legend of Frosty the Snowman (video, voice) 2005, Cloud 9 2006, End Game 2006, Broken Bridges 2006, In the Name of the King: A Dungeon Siege Tale 2007, Deal 2007, Randy and the Mob 2007. *Television appearances include:* Riverboat 1959–60, Pony Express, Gunsmoke 1962–65, Hawk 1966, Dan August 1970, B. L. Stryker: The Dancer's Touch 1989, Evening Shade 1990–94, The Cherokee Kid 1996, Johnson County War (mini-series) 2002, Miss Lettie and Me 2002, Hard Ground 2003, Ed (episode) 2003, The King of Queens (episode) 2005, Duck Dodgers (episode) 2005, Freddie (episode) 2006. *Other work includes:* Grand Theft Auto: Vice City (video game, voice) 2002. *Publication:* My Life (autobiog.) 1994. *Address:* William Morris Agency, 1 William Morris Place, Beverly Hills, CA 90212; Jeffrey Lane & Associates, 8380 Melrose Avenue, Suite 206, Los Angeles, CA 90069, USA. *Website:* www .burtreynolds.com (office).

REYNOLDS, Debbie Mary Frances; American actress and singer; b. 1 April 1932, El Paso, TX; m. 1st Eddie Fisher 1955 (divorced 1959); one d. (Carrie Fisher (q.v.)) one s.; m. 2nd Harry Karl 1960 (divorced 1973); m. 3rd Richard Hamlett 1985 (divorced 1994); film debut in June Bride 1948; stage debut at Blis-Hayden Theater 1952; nightclub act mid-1960s–; founder Debbie Reynolds Professional Rehearsal Studios, North Hollywood late 1970s; Prin. Debbie Reynolds Hotel/Casino and Hollywood Motion Picture Museum, Las Vegas 1993–; Nat. Hon. presented by Girl Scouts USA 1966–69, Nat. Film Soc. Humanitarian Award. *Theatre includes:* Irene 1973, Annie Get Your Gun, Woman of the Year 1983, The Unsinkable Molly Brown (nat. tour) 1989. *Films:* June Bride 1948, The Daughter of Rosie O'Grady 1950, Three Little Words 1950, Two Weeks with Love 1950, Mr Imperium 1951, Singin' in the Rain 1952, I Love Melvin 1953, The Affairs of Dobie Gillis 1953, Give a Girl a Break 1953, Susan Slept Here 1954, Athena 1954, Hit the Deck 1955, The Tender Trap 1955, The Catered Affair 1956, Bundle of Joy 1956, Tammy and the Bachelor 1957, This Happy Feeling 1958, The Mating Game 1959, Say One for Me 1959, It Started with a Kiss 1959, The Gazebo 1959, The Rat Race 1960, The Pleasure of his Company 1961, The Second Time Around 1961, How the West Was Won 1962, Mary, Mary 1963, My Six Loves 1963, The Unsinkable Molly Brown 1964, Goodbye Charlie 1964, The Singing Nun 1966, Divorce American Style 1967, How Sweet It Is! 1968, What's the Matter with Helen? 1971, Charlotte's Web (voice) 1973, Kiki's Delivery Service (voice) 1989, Heaven & Earth 1993, Mother 1996, In & Out 1997, Zack and Reba 1998, Rudolph the Red-Nosed Reindeer: The Movie (voice) 1998, Rugrats in Paris: The Movie – Rugrats II (voice) 2000. *Television:* The Debbie Reynolds Show 1969, Aloha Paradise (series) 1981, Sadie and Son 1987, Perry Mason: The Case of the Musical Murder 1989, Battling for Baby 1992, Halloweentown 1998, The Christmas Wish 1998, A Gift of Love: The Daniel Huffman Story 1999, Virtual Mom 2000, Rugrats (series, voice) 2000–04, These Old Broads 2001, Halloweentown II: Kalabar's Revenge 2001, Halloweentown III: Halloweentown High 2004, Lolo's Cafe (voice) 2006, Will & Grace (series) 1999–2006, Return to Halloweentown 2006,. *Publication:* Debbie: My Life (with David Patrick Colombia) 1987. *Address:* William Morris Agency, 1 William Morris Place, Beverly Hills, CA 90212; Debbie Reynolds Studios, 6514 Lankershim Blvd, North Hollywood, CA 91606-2409, USA.

REYNOLDS, Francis Martin Baillie, QC, DCL, FBA; British barrister, legal scholar and academic; *Emeritus Professor of Law, University of Oxford;* b. 11 Nov. 1932, St Albans; s. of Eustace Baillie Reynolds and Emma Holmes; m. Susan Shillito 1965; two s. one d.; ed Winchester Coll. and Worcester Coll. Oxford; Bigelow Teaching Fellow, Univ. of Chicago 1957–58; lecturer, Worcester Coll. Oxford 1958–60, Fellow 1960–2000, Emer. Fellow 2000–; barrister, Inner Temple 1960, Hon. Bencher 1979; Reader in Law, Univ. of Oxford 1977, Prof. of Law 1992–2000, Emer. Prof. 2000–; Ed. The Law Quarterly Review 1987–; Visiting lecturer, Univ. of Auckland 1971, 1977; Visiting Prof. Nat. Univ. of Singapore 1984, 1986, 1988, 1990–92, 1994, 1996, 1997, 2000, 2003, 2005, Univ. Coll. London 1987–89, Univ. of Melbourne 1989, Monash Univ. 1989, Univ. of Otago 1993, Univ. of Sydney 1993, Univ. of Auckland 1995, Univ. of Hong Kong 2002; Titular mem. Comité Maritime Int; Hon. QC; Hon. Prof. Int. Maritime Law Inst., Malta. *Publications:* Bowstead and Reynolds on Agency, 13th–18th edns. 1965–2006, Benjamin's Sale of Goods, 1st–7th edns (jtly) 1974–2006, English Private Law (jtly) 2000, Carver on Bills of Lading (jtly with Sir G. Treitel) 2001, 2005. *Leisure interests:* music, walking. *Address:* 61 Charlbury Road, Oxford, OX2 6UX, England (home). *Telephone:* (1865) 559323 (home). *Fax:* (1865) 511894 (home). *E-mail:* francis .reynolds@law.ox.ac.uk (home).

REYNOLDS, Paula Rosput, BA; American business executive; *Chairman, President and CEO, Safeco Corporation;* b. Newport, RI; m. Stephen P. Reynolds; ed Wellesley Coll., Mass; Chair., Pres. and CEO AGL Resources, Atlanta, Ga 2000–05; Pres., CEO and mem. Bd of Dirs Safeco Corpn 2006–, Chair. 2008–; mem. Bd of Dirs Coca-Cola Enterprises (Chair. Audit Cttee), Delta Air Lines, United Way of Metropolitan Atlanta; ranked 40th by Fortune magazine amongst 50 Most Powerful Women in Business in the US 2006, ranked by Forbes magazine amongst 100 Most Powerful Women (58th) 2006, (48th) 2007, (100th) 2008. *Address:* Safeco Corporation, Safeco Plaza, Seattle, WA 98185-0001, USA (office). *Telephone:* (206) 545-5000 (office). *Website:* www .safeco.com (office).

REYNOLDS, Sir Peter William John, Kt, CBE; British business executive; b. 10 Sept. 1929, Singapore; s. of Harry Reynolds and Gladys Reynolds; m. Barbara Anne Johnson 1955; two s.; ed Haileybury Coll.; with Unilever Ltd 1950–70, Trainee, Man. Dir, then Chair., Walls Ltd; Asst Group Man. Dir Ranks Hovis McDougall 1971, Group Man. Dir 1972–81, Chair. 1981–89, Deputy Chair. 1989–93; mem. Consultative Bd for Resources Devt in Agric. 1982–84; Deputy Chair. AvisEurope PLC 1988–; Dir of Industrial Devt Bd for Northern Ireland 1982–89, Guardian Royal Exchange Assurance PLC 1986–99; Chair. of Resources Cttee of Food and Drink Fed. 1983–86; mem. Bd of Dirs Boots Co. PLC 1986–2000, Guardian Royal Exchange PLC 1986–99, Avis Europe PLC 1988–2001, Cilva Holdings PLC 1989, Nationwide Anglia Bldg Soc. 1990–92; Chair., Pioneer Concrete (Holdings) 1990–99; mem. Peacock Cttee 1985–86; High Sheriff of Buckingham 1990–91. *Leisure interests:* beagling, riding (occasionally), watching rugby football, reading, gardening. *Address:* Rignall Farm, Rignall Road, Great Missenden, Bucks., HP16 9PE, England. *Telephone:* (1240) 64714.

REZA, (Evelyne Agnès) Yasmina; French novelist, dramatist, screenwriter and actress; b. 1 May 1959, Paris; d. of the late Jean Reza and of Nora (née Heltaï) Reza; one s. one d.; ed Lycée de St-Cloud, Paris Univ. X, Nanterre, Ecole Jacques Lecoq; Chevalier, Ordre des Arts et des Lettres; Prix du jeune théâtre Beatrix Dussane-André Roussin de l'Acad. française 1991. *Stage appearances include:* Le Malade imaginaire 1977, Antigone 1977, Un Sang fort 1977, La Mort de Gaspard Hauser 1978, L'An mil 1980, Le Piège de Méduse 1983, Le Veilleur de nuit 1986, Enorme changement de dernière minute 1989, La Fausse suivante 1990. *Plays directed include:* Birds in the Night 1979, Marie la louve 1981. *Plays written include:* Conversations après un enterrement (Molière Award for Best Author, Prix des Talents nouveaux de la Soc. des auteurs et compositeurs dramatiques, Johnson Foundation prize) 1987, La Traversée de l'hiver 1989, La Métamorphose (adaptation) 1988, 'Art' 1994, L'Homme du hasard 1995, Trois versions de la vie 2000, Une pièce espagnole 2004, Le Dieu du carnage 2007. *Screenplays written include:* Jusqu'à la nuit (also dir) 1984, Le Goûter chez Niels 1986, A demain 1992, Le Pique-nique de Lulu Kreutz 2000. *Publications:* novels: Hammerklavier 1997, Une Désolation (trans. as Desolation) 1999, Adam Haberberg 2003, Nulle part 2005, Dans la luge d'Arthur Schopenhauer 2005; non-fiction: L'aube le soir ou la nuit (trans. as Dawn, Dusk or Night) 2007. *Address:* c/o Marta Andras (Marton Play), 14 rue des Sablons, 75116 Paris, France.

REZAZADEH, Hossein; Iranian weightlifter; b. 12 May 1978, Ardabil; m.; competes in 105 kilogrammes and over (heaviest category); won snatch (world record of 212.5 kilogrammes) and clean and jerk (world record of 260.5 kilogrammes, combined world record of 472.5 kilogrammes) for gold medal Olympic Games, Sydney 2000; gold medals in snatch, clean and jerk, combined (world record of 472.5 kilogrammes) World Weightlifting Championships, 2002; gold medals in snatch and combined, bronze medal in clean and jerk World Weight Lifting Championships, Canada 2003; won snatch and clean and jerk (world record of 262.5 kilogrammes) for gold medal Olympic Games, Athens, 2004; mem. Saipa club; Iranian Badge of Courage in 2000 Int. Weightlifting Fed. World's Best Weightlifter 2000, 2002, voted Champion of Champions of Iran 2002. *Leisure interests:* cooking. *Address:* c/o Weightlifting Federation of Iran, POB 15745-175, Varzandeh Street, Shiroudi Stadium, Tehran, Iran. *Website:* www.iriwf.com.

REZEK, Francisco, LLD, JSD; Brazilian lawyer, judge and fmr politician; b. 18 Jan. 1944, Cristina, Minas Gerais; s. of Elias Rezek and Baget Baracat Rezek; ed Fed. Univ. of Minas Gerais, Sorbonne, France, Univ. of Oxford, UK, Harvard Univ., USA, The Hague Acad. of Int. Law, The Netherlands; Attorney of the Repub., Supreme Court 1972–79; Prof. of Int. and Constitutional Law Univ. of Brasília 1971–, Chair. Law Dept 1974–76, Dean, Faculty of Social Studies 1978–79; Prof. of Int., Law Rio Branco Inst. 1976–; Justice of Supreme Court 1983–90, 1992–97; Foreign Minister 1990–92; mem. Perm. Court of Arbitration 1987–2004; Judge, Int. Court of Justice, The Hague 1997–2006; currently legal adviser Advocacia Gandra Martins (law firm), São Paulo. *Publications:* Droit des traités: particularités des actes constitutifs d'organisations internationales 1968, La conduite des relations internationales dans le droit constitutionnel latino-américain 1970, Reciprocity as a Basis of Extradition 1980, Direito dos Tratados 1984, Public International Law 1989. *Address:* Sociedade de Advogados, Rua Dr. Renato Paes de Barros, 717 - 8 andar, Itaim Bibi, São Paulo SP, 04530-001, Brazil (office). *E-mail:* contato@franciscorezek.adv.br (office).

REZNIK, Genry Markovich, Cand.Jur.; Russian barrister; b. 11 May 1938, Leningrad; m. Larissa Yulianovna Reznik; one s.; ed Kazakhstan Univ., Moscow Inst. of Law; various positions at Acad. of Ministry of Internal Affairs 1975–82, including Internal Investigator, Investigation Dept, Kazakh Repub.; Lecturer in Law, All-Union Legal Acad. 1982–98; f. Reznik, Gagarin, Abushakhmin and Pnrs, Moscow (law firm); Dir Inst. of Bar Int. Union of Advocates; mem. Moscow Helsinki Group 1989–; Chair. Moscow Bar Asscn; mem. of Council, Fed. Chamber of Lawyers 2004. *Achievements include:* mem. USSR volleyball youth team. *Publications:* over 100 articles on criminal law. *Address:* Reznik, Gagarin, Abushakhmin and Partners, Schmidtovskiy pr. 3, 123100 Moscow, Russia (office). *Telephone:* (495) 205-27-09 (office). *Fax:* (495) 256-72-52 (office).

RHEINGOLD, Arnold L., BS, MS, PhD, FAAS; American chemist and academic; *Professor, Department of Chemistry and Biochemistry, University of California, San Diego;* b. 6 Oct. 1940, Chicago, Ill.; ed Case Western Reserve Univ., Cleveland and Univ. of Maryland; Project Man., Glidden Co., Cleveland 1963–65; Research Assoc., Virginia Polytechnic Inst. and State Univ., Blacksburg, Va 1969–70; Prof. of Chem., State Univ. of New York (SUNY), Plattsburgh 1970–82, Visiting Scholar, SUNY, Buffalo 1980–81; Visiting Prof. and Sr Scientist, Univ. of Delaware, Newark 1981–84, Assoc. Prof. 1984–87, Prof. 1987–2003; Prof., Univ. of California, San Diego 2003–; Councillor, ACS 1998–2001, Chair.-elect Inorganic Div. 2001, Chair. 2002; mem. Editorial Bd ACS Journal – Organometallics 1990–, Journal of Cluster Science 1993–95, ACS Journal – Inorganic Chemistry 1994–96, 2001–, Organometallic Synthesis 1995–, Inorganica Chimica Acta 2003–; mem. Jt Board-Council, Chemical Abstracts 1998–2001; mem. American Crystallographic Asscn, Int. Council on Main Group Chem. *Publications:* more than 1430 articles in scientific journals. *Address:* Department of Chemistry and Biochemistry, University of California, San Diego, 9500 Gilman Drive, La Jolla, CA 92093-0358, USA (office). *Telephone:* (858) 822-3870 (office). *Fax:* (858) 822-3872 (office). *E-mail:* arheingold@ucsd.edu (office). *Website:* www-chem.ucsd.edu (office).

RHINES, Peter Broomell, PhD; American academic and scientist; *Professor of Oceanography and Atmospheric Sciences, University of Washington, Seattle;* b. 23 July 1942, Hartford, Conn.; s. of Thomas B. Rhines and Olive S. Rhines; m. 1st Marie Lenos 1968 (divorced 1983); m. 2nd Linda Mattson Semtner 1984; one s.; ed Loomis School, MIT, Trinity Coll., Cambridge, England; Sloan Scholar, MIT 1960–63, NSF Fellow 1963–64; Marshall Scholar, Cambridge 1964–67; Asst Prof. of Oceanography MIT 1967–71; Research Scientist, Cambridge Univ. 1971–72; mem. Scientific Staff, Woods Hole Oceanographic Inst. 1972–84, Dir Center for Analysis of Marine Systems 1979–82, oceanographic research cruises 1968–2009; Prof. of Oceanography and Atmospheric Sciences, Univ. of Washington, Seattle 1984–; Guggenheim Fellow, Christ's Coll. Cambridge, England 1979–80; Natural Environment Research Council Visiting Fellow, UK 1983; mem. Science Advisory Bd Bjerknesj Climate Center, Bergen, Norway 2005–, Bipolar Atlantic Circulation project, Univ. of Bergen 2007–; Fellow, American Geophysical Union, American Meteorological Soc., American Acad. of Arts and Sciences, Queen's Fellow in Marine Sciences, Australia; mem. NAS; de Florez Award, MIT 1963, Creativity Award, NSF 1996, Stommel Research Award, American Meteorological Soc. 1998, Haurwitz Lecturer, American Meteorological Soc. 2005, Gledden Fellow, Univ. of Western Australia 2005. *Publications:* research papers on general circulation of the oceans, waves and climate; contrib. to films on oceanography for BBC and Public Broadcasting System, USA. *Leisure interests:* classical guitar, conversation and the out-of-doors. *Address:* School of Oceanography, University of Washington, Box 357940, Seattle, WA 98195 (office); 5753 61st Avenue NE, Seattle, WA 98105, USA (home). *Telephone:* (206) 543-0593 (office); (206) 522-5753 (home). *E-mail:* rhines@ocean.washington.edu (office). *Website:* www.ocean.washington.edu/people/faculty/rhines/rhines.html (office).

RHOADS, James Berton, PhD; American archivist; *Professor Emeritus of History, Western Washington University;* b. 17 Sept. 1928, Sioux City, Ia; s. of James H. Rhoads and Mary K. Rhoads; m. S. Angela Handy 1947; one s. two d.; ed Univ. of California, Berkeley and The American Univ., Washington, DC; held various positions at Nat. Archives 1952–65; Asst Archivist, Civil Archives 1965–66; Deputy Archivist of USA 1966–68, Archivist of USA 1968–79; Pres. Rhoads Assocs Int. 1980–84; Dir Grad. Program in Archives and Records Man., Western Washington Univ. 1984–94, Prof. of History 1987–94, Prof. Emer. 1994–, Dir Center for Pacific Northwest Studies 1994–97; mem. Cttee on Soviet-American Archival Co-operation 1986–91, Bd of Trustees Washington State Historical Soc. 1986–95, Washington State Historical Records Advisory Bd 1990–97, Acad. of Certified Archivists 1989– (Pres. 1992–94); Pres. Int. Council on Archives 1976–79; Vice-Pres. Intergovernmental Council on Gen. Information Program, UNESCO 1977–79, and mem. numerous other related orgs; Fellow, Soc. of American Archivists, Pres. 1974–75. *Publications:* numerous articles in professional journals. *Leisure interests:* reading, philately. *Address:* 3613 Illinois Lane, Bellingham, WA 98226, USA. *Telephone:* (360) 676-1235.

RHODES, Frank Harold Trevor, DSc, PhD; American geologist, academic and fmr university president; *President Emeritus, Cornell University;* b. 29 Oct. 1926, Warwickshire, England; s. of Harold C. Rhodes and Gladys (Ford) Rhodes; m. Rosa Carlson 1952; four d.; ed Univ. of Birmingham; Post-doctoral Fellow, Fulbright Scholar, Univ. of Ill. 1950–51, Visiting Lecturer in Geology summers of 1951–52, Asst Prof., Univ. of Ill. 1954–55, Assoc. Prof. 1955–56, Dir Univ. of Ill. Field Station, Wyoming 1956; Lecturer in Geology, Univ. of Durham 1951–54; Prof. of Geology and Head Dept of Geology, Univ. of Wales, Swansea 1956–68, Dean Faculty of Science 1967–68; Prof. of Geology and Mineralogy, Coll. of Literature, Science and Arts, Univ. of Michigan 1968–77, Dean 1971–74, Vice-Pres. for Academic Affairs 1974–77; Pres. Cornell Univ. 1977–94, Prof. of Geology 1977–95, Pres. Emer. 1995–; Dir John Heinz III Center for Science, Econs and the Environment 1996–98; Vice-Pres. Dyson Charitable Trust 1996–98; Prin. Washington Advisory Group 1997–; mem. Atlantic Philanthropics 1995 (Chair. 2000–05); mem. Nat. Science Bd 1987–98 (Chair. 1994–96), American Philosophical Soc. 1991– (Pres. 1999–), Johnson Foundation Bd 2000–, Goldman Sachs Foundation Bd 2000–; mem. Int. Advisory Panel King Abdullah Univ. of Science and Tech.; Trustee Andrew W. Mellon 1984–99; Jefferson Lecturer, Univ. of Calif., Berkeley 1999; 36 hon. degrees; Bigsby Medal, Geological Soc. 1967, Higher Educ. Leadership Award, Comm. on Ind. Colls and Univs 1987, Justin Smith Morrill Award 1987, Clark Kerr Medal, Univ. of Calif., Berkeley 1995. *Publications:* The Evolution of Life 1962, Fossils 1963, Geology 1972, Evolution 1974, Language of the Earth 1981, (Ed.) Successful Fund Raising for Higher Education: The Advancement of Learning 1997, The Creation of the Future: The Role of the American University 2001; over 70 maj. scientific articles and monographs and some 60 articles on educ. *Address:* 603 Cayuga Heights Road, Ithaca, NY, 14850 (home); Cornell University, 3104 Snee Hall, Ithaca, NY 14853, USA. *E-mail:* mjw11@cornell.edu.

RHODES, Richard Lee, BA; American writer; b. 4 July 1937, Kansas City, Kan.; s. of Arthur Rhodes and Georgia Collier Rhodes; m. Ginger Untrif 1993; two c. by previous m.; ed East High School, Kansas City, Yale Univ.; Trustee Andrew Drumm Inst., Independence, Mo. 1990–, Atomic Heritage Foundation 2004–, Cypress Fund 2005–; Fellowships: John Simon Guggenheim Memorial Foundation 1974–75, Nat. Endowment for the Arts 1978, Ford Foundation 1981–83, Alfred P. Sloan Foundation 1985, 1993, 1995, 2001, MacArthur Foundation Program on Peace and Int. Co-operation 1990–91, 2008–09; Hon. DHumLitt (Westminster Coll., Fulton, Mo.) 1988; Hon. Mem. American Nuclear Soc. 2001. *Publications:* non-fiction: The Inland Ground: An Evocation of the American Middle West 1970, The Ozarks 1974, Looking for America: A Writer's Odyssey 1979, The Making of the Atomic Bomb (Nat. Book Critics' Circle Award for Gen. Non-fiction, Nat. Book Award for Non-fiction 1987, Pulitzer Prize for Non-fiction 1988) 1987, Farm: A Year in the Life of an American Farmer 1989, A Hole in the World: An American Boyhood 1990, Making Love: An Erotic Odyssey 1992, Nuclear Renewal: Common Sense about Energy 1993, Dark Sun: The Making of the Hydrogen Bomb 1995, How To Write 1995, Trying To Get Some Dignity: Stories of Triumph Over Childhood Abuse (with Ginger Rhodes) 1996, Deadly Feasts: Tracking the Secrets of a Terrifying New Plague 1997, Visions of Technology (ed) 1999, Why They Kill 1999, Masters of Death 2001, John James Audubon: The Making of an American (biog.) 2004, The Audubon Reader (ed) 2006, Arsenals of Folly: Nuclear Weapons in the Cold War 2007; fiction: The Ungodly 1973, Holy Secrets 1978, The Last Safari 1980, Sons of Earth 1981. *Address:* c/o Janklow & Nesbit Assocs, 455 Park Avenue, New York, NY 10021, USA (office). *Telephone:* (212) 421-1700 (office). *E-mail:* Rhodes.Today@comcast.net (office). *Website:* www.RichardRhodes.com.

RHODES, William Reginald, BA; American banking executive; *Chairman, President and CEO, Citibank NA;* b. 15 Aug. 1935, New York; s. of Edward R. and Elsie Rhodes; ed Brown Univ.; joined Citibank 1957, served in various sr positions, Latin America and Caribbean 1957–77, Head, Latin American corp. business and Sr Exec., Int. Citibank NA, New York 1977–91, Vice-Chair. 1991–2001, mem. Bd of Dirs 1991–, Sr Vice-Chair. 2001–03, Chair. 2003–, Pres. and CEO 2005–, Sr Vice-Chair. Citigroup, Inc. 1999–, Chair. and CEO Citicorp Holdings, Inc. 2003–, Pres. 2005–; fmr chair. several advisory cttees which negotiated debt-restructuring agreements for Argentina, Brazil, Jamaica, Mexico, Peru and Uruguay during 1980s, and S Korea 1998; mem. Bd of Dirs Conoco-Phillips, Private Export Funding Corpn; Chair. Americas Soc., Council of the Americas, USA–Korea Business Council; First Vice-Chair. Inst. of Int. Finance; mem. Bd of Dirs USA–Russia Business Council, USA–Hong Kong Business Council, Foreign Policy Asscn; mem. Int. Advisory Bd, Pres. of SA, Pres. of Colombia; mem. Pvt. Sector Advisory Bd, Inter-American Devt Bank, Int. Policy Cttee, US Chamber of Commerce, Lincoln Center Consolidated Corporate Fund Leadership Cttee, Art Business and Chair.'s cttees, Metropolitan Museum of Art, Bd of Overseers, Watson Inst. for Int. Studies; Chair. Emer. Bd of Trustees, Northfield Mount Hermon School; mem. Council on Foreign Relations, The Group of Thirty, The Economic Club of New York; Chevalier Légion d'Honneur, France; DHumLitt hc (Brown Univ.). *Address:* Citigroup Inc., 399 Park Avenue, New York, NY 10022, USA (office). *Telephone:* (212) 559-1000 (office). *Website:* www.citibank.com.

RHODES, Zandra Lindsey, CBE, FCSD, FSIAD; British textile and fashion designer; b. 19 Sept. 1940, Chatham, Kent; d. of Albert James Rhodes and Beatrice Ellen (née Twigg); ed Medway Coll. of Art and Royal Coll. of Art; set up print factory and studio 1965; began producing dresses using own prints 1966; Founder-Pnr and designer, Fulham Clothes Shop, London 1967–68; freelance designer, producing own collections for British and US markets 1968–75; Founder and Man. Dir (with Anne Knight and Ronnie Stirling) Zandra Rhodes (UK) Ltd and Zandra Rhodes (Shops) Ltd 1975–86; opened first shop in London 1975; Man. Dir all Zandra Rhodes cos 1975–; other shops in Bloomingdale's, New York, Marshall Field's, Chicago, Seibu, Tokyo and Harrods, London; licences include: Wamsutta sheets and pillowcases (USA) 1976, Eve Stillman Lingerie (USA) 1977, CVP Designs, interior fabrics and settings (UK) 1977, Philip Hockley decorative furs (UK) 1986, Zandra Rhodes saris (India) 1987, Littlewoods catalogues (UK) for printed T-shirts and intasia sweaters 1988, Hilmet silk scarves and men's ties (UK) 1989, Bonnay perfume (UK) 1993, Coats Patons needlepoint (UK) 1993, Pologeorgis Furs (USA) 1996, Zandra Rhodes II handpainted ready-to-wear collection (Hong Kong) 1995, Grattons Catalogue sheets and duvets (UK) 1996; costume designs The Magic Flute, The Pearl Fishers, San Diego Opera 2001, Aida, ENO 2007; f. Zandra Rhodes Museum of Fashion and Textiles, UK 1996; Hon. Fellow, Kent Inst. of Art and Design 1992; Hon. DFA (Int. Fine Arts Coll., Miami) 1986; Dr hc (RCA) 1986; Hon. DD (CNAA) 1987, Hon. DLitt (Westminster) 2000; Designer of the Year, English Fashion Trade 1972, Royal Designer for Industry 1974, Emmy Award for Best Costume Designs in Romeo and Juliet on Ice, CBS TV 1984, Alpha Award, New Orleans 1985, 1991, Woman of Distinction Award, Northwood Inst., Dallas 1986, Observer Award as top UK Textile Designer 1990, Hall of Fame Award, British Fashion Council 1995. *Publications:* The Art of Zandra Rhodes 1984, The Zandra Rhodes Collection by Brother 1988. *Leisure interests:* travelling, drawing, gardening, cooking. *Address:* Zandra Rhodes Head Office, 79–85 Bermondsey Street, London, SE1 3XF, England (office). *Telephone:* (20) 7403-5333 (office). *Fax:* (20) 7403-0555 (office). *E-mail:* zrhodesent@aol.com (home). *Website:* www.zandrarhodes.com.

RHYS-JAMES, Shani, BA, MBE; Australian artist and painter; b. 2 May 1953, Australia; d. of Harold Marcus Rhys-James and Jeannie James-Money; m. Stephen West 1977; two s.; ed Parliament Hill Girls School, Loughborough Coll. of Art and Cen. St Martin's Coll. of Art and Design; came to London aged nine; regular exhbns with Martin Tinney, Cardiff 1991–2006, Stephen Lacey, London; work in art collections of Nat. Museum of Wales, Newport Museum and Art Gallery Cyfartha Castle, Merthyr Tydfil, Usher Gallery, Arts Council of England, Gallery of Modern Art, Glasgow, Wolverhampton Art Gallery, Birmingham City Museum and Art Gallery, Nat. Library of Wales, London Borough of Tower Hamlets, BBC Wales, Glyn Vivian Museum and Art Gallery, New Hall, Cambridge, Serwood Foundation; featured artist, Carlow Festival 2000, Royal Cambrian Acad. three-person show 2001; invited artist, Discerning Eye 2004; mem. Royal Cambrian Acad. 1994; frequent radio and TV appearances; hon. fellow Hereford and UWIC Art Colls First Prize, Mostyn Open, Llandudno 1991, Gold Medal for Fine Art, Royal Nat. Eisteddfod, Ceredigion 1992, First Prize, Hunting/Observer Art Prizes 1993, BBC Wales Visual Artist Award 1994, BP Nat. Portrait Award, Gold Medal for Fine Art Royal Nat. Eisteddfod, First Prize Hunting/Observer Prize, Jerwood Prize 2003, Welsh Woman of the Year in Culture 2003, Creative Wales Award 2006. *Television includes:* Blood Ties 1993, Painting the Dragon 2000, The Little Picture 2000, Paintings from Paradise 2000, Shani Rhys-James: A Conversation 2004,. *Radio:* Relative Values, BBC Wales 2008. *Publications:* The Black Cot 2004, Essay Edward Lucie-Smith (illustrations) 2005, Imaging the Imagination 2005; DVD: Shani Rhys-James. *Leisure interests:* music, films, plays, books, writing, restoring our Welsh farm and French house and studio.

RI, Kwang-gun; North Korean government official; Chief Econ. Councilor to Germany mid-1990s; Minister of Foreign Trade 2001-04; fmr Chair., North Korean Football Asscn. *Address:* c/o Ministry of Foreign Trade, Pyongyang, Democratic People's Republic of Korea (office).

RIBAR, Monika; Swiss business executive; *President and CEO, Panalpina Group;* b. 1959; ed Univ. of St Gallen, Stanford Univ., USA; Financial Controller, BASF Vienna, Austria 1984–86; Head of Strategic Planning, Fides Group (KPMG), Zürich 1986–90; Controlling and IT Dept, Panalpina Group 1991–92, SAP Global Project Man. 1992–95, Corp. Controller 1995–2000, Chief Information Officer 2000–05, mem. Exec. Bd 2005–, Chief Financial Officer 2005–06, Pres. and CEO 2006–; mem. Bd of Dirs Bank Julius Bär Ltd, Zürich 2001–, Logitech Int. SA 2004–. *Address:* Panalpina World Transport (Holding) Ltd, Viaduktstrasse 42, 4002 Basel, Switzerland (office). *Telephone:* (61) 2261111 (office). *Fax:* (61) 2261101 (office). *E-mail:* info@panalpina.com (office). *Website:* www.panalpina.com (office).

RIBEIRO, Inacio; Brazilian fashion designer; m. Suzanne Clements 1992; one s.; ed Cen. St Martin's Coll. of Art and Design, London; fmrly designer, Brazil; design consultant in Brazil (with wife) 1991–93; f. Clements Ribeiro (with wife), London 1993; first collection launched Oct. 1993, numerous collections since; first solo show London Fashion Week March 1995; Creative Dir (with wife) Cacharel, Paris 2000–07; fashion shows since in London, Paris, Brazil, Japan; consultant to cos in UK and Italy; winners, Designer of the Year New Generation Category 1996. *Address:* BCPR, Unit 18, Archer Street Studios, 10–11 Archer Street, London, W1D 7AZ (office); Clements Ribeiro Trading Ltd, 17 Alexander Street, London, W2 5NT, England. *Telephone:* (20) 7229-9680 (office). *E-mail:* inacioribeiro@hotmail.com (office).

RIBEIRO, João Ubaldo Osório Pimentel, LLB, MS; Brazilian writer and journalist; b. 23 Jan. 1941, Itaparica, Bahia; s. of Manoel Ribeiro and Maria Felipa Osório Pimentel Ribeiro; m. 1st Maria Beatriz Moreira Caldas 1962; m. 2nd Mônica Maria Roters 1971; m. 3rd Berenice de Carvalho Batella Ribeiro 1982; one s. three d.; ed Fed. Univ. of Bahia Law School and School of Admin. and Univ. of Southern California, USA; Reporter, Jornal da Bahia, Salvador 1958–59, City Ed. and Columnist 1960–63; Chief Ed. Tribuna da Bahia 1968–73; Columnist O Globo, Rio de Janeiro, O Estado de São Paulo, São Paulo; Editorial-writer Folha de São Paulo 1969–73; Prof. of Political Science, Fed. Univ. of Bahia 1965–71, Catholic Univ of Bahia 1967–71; mem. Brazilian Acad. of Letters; Jabuti Prize (Brazilian Book Chamber) 1971, 1984; Golfinho de Ouro (Govt of Rio), Premio Camões 2008, and many other awards. *Publications:* novels: Setembro Não Tem Sentido 1968, Sargento Getúlio 1971, Vila Real 1980, Viva o Povo Brasileiro 1984, O Sorriso do Lagarto 1989, O Feitiço da Ilha do Pavão 1997, Miséria e Grandeza do Amor de Benedita 2000, Diário do Farol 2002; short stories: Vencecavalo e o Outro Povo 1973, Livro de Histórias 1983, Ein Brasilianer in Berlin (autobiog.) 1994, Você me mata, Mãe gentil 2004, A gente se acostuma a tudo 2006, O rei da noite 2008. *Leisure interests:* microscopy (protozoa), music (Bach), sports (soccer, fishing). *Address:* c/o Academia Brasileira de Letras, Av. Presidente Wilson 203, Castelo, CEP 20030-021, Rio de Janeiro RJ; c/o Editora Nova Fronteira SA, Rua Bambina 25, 22251-050 Rio de Janeiro, R.J.; Rua General Urquiza, 147/401, 22431-040 Rio de Janeiro, R.J., Brazil (home). *Telephone:* (21) 537-8770 (office); (21) 239-8528 (home). *Fax:* (21) 286-6755. *Website:* www.academia.org.br.

RIBEIRO PEREIRA, Lt-Gen. Augusto Heleno; Brazilian military officer; served in Brazilian mil. mission, Paraguay 1981–83; Mil. Attaché to France 1996–98; Head, Centro de Comunicação do Exército 2002–04; C-in-C UN Stabilization Mission in Haiti (MINUSTAH) 2004–05; Head of Cabinet for Mil. Command 2006. *Address:* Quartel General do Exército, Bloco B Térreo, Setor Militário Urbano, 70630-901 Brasília, DF, Brazil (office). *Website:* www.gabcmt.eb.mil.br.

RIBERHOLDT, Gunnar; Danish diplomatist; *President, Danish-French Chamber of Commerce;* b. 7 Nov. 1933, Naestved; s. of Poul G. Riberholdt and Erna M. Andersen; one s. one d.; ed US univs and Univ. of Copenhagen; Ministry of Foreign Affairs 1958–62; Sec. of Embassy, Danish Perm. Mission to European Communities 1962–64, Deputy Head of Mission 1964–65; Head of Section, Ministry of Foreign Affairs 1965–69; Econ. Counsellor, Paris 1969–72; Dir Ministry of Foreign Affairs 1973–75; Dir-Gen. European Econ. Affairs 1975–77; Amb., Perm. Rep. of Denmark to European Communities (now EU) 1977–84, 1992–94; Amb. to France 1984–91; Amb., Personal Rep. of Minister for Foreign Affairs to Intergovernmental Confs on Political Union and on Econ. and Monetary Union 1991–92; Amb., Head Danish Del. to OECD 1991–92; Perm. Rep. to NATO 1995–99; Amb. to Italy (also accred to Cyprus, Malta and San Marino) 1999–2003; Pres. Danish-French Chamber of Commerce 2004–. *Address:* Oestbanegade 5, 2100 Copenhagen, Denmark (home). *Telephone:* 35-43-03-05 (home). *E-mail:* clarinet@mail.dk.

RIBOUD, Franck; Swiss food industry executive; *Chairman and CEO, Groupe Danone;* b. 7 Nov. 1955; ed Ecole Polytechnique, Lausanne; joined BSN Group (renamed Groupe Danone 1994) 1981, various positions in man. control div., sales and marketing div. and business div. including Brand Man., Sales Rep., Regional Sales Force Trainer, Regional Man., Sales Man., Key Account Sales Man., Dept Man., involved in acquisition of Nabisco's European activities 1989, Gen. Man. Evian Water 1990–92, Gen. Man. Devt BSN 1992–94, Vice-Pres. and Gen. Man. Groupe Danone 1994–96, Chair. and CEO 1996–; mem. Bd of Dirs Fiat SpA –2000, Scottish & Newcastle PLC 2000–03, Accor 2001–, Lacoste France (Chair. 2006–), L'Oréal SA 2002–, Renault SAS 2000–. *Address:* Groupe Danone, 17 boulevard Haussmann, 75009 Paris, France (office). *Telephone:* 1-44-35-20-20 (office). *Fax:* 1-42-25-67-16 (office). *E-mail:* info@danone.com (office). *Website:* www.danone.com (office).

RICCI, Christina; American actress; b. 12 Feb. 1980, Santa Monica, Calif.; d. of Ralph Ricci and Sarah Ricci; began acting career in commercials. *Films:* Mermaids 1990, The Hard Way 1991, The Addams Family 1991, The Cemetery Club 1993, Addams Family Values 1993, Casper 1995, Now and Then 1995, Gold Diggers: The Secret of Bear Mountain 1995, That Darn Cat 1996, Last of the High Kings 1996, Bastard Out of Carolina 1996, Ice Storm 1997, Little Red Riding Hood 1997, Fear and Loathing in Las Vegas 1998, Desert Blue 1998, Buffalo 66 1998, The Opposite of Sex 1998, Small Soldiers

1998, Pecker 1999, 200 Cigarettes 1999, Sleepy Hollow 1999, The Man Who Cried 2001, All Over the Guy 2001, Prozac Nation 2001, Pumpkin 2002, Miranda 2002, The Laramie Project 2002, Anything Else 2003, Monster 2003, I Love Your Work 2003, Cursed 2005, Penelope 2006, Home of the Brave 2006, Black Snake Moan 2006, Speed Racer 2008. *Address:* c/o Toni Howard, ICM, 8942 Wilshire Boulevard, Beverly Hills, CA 90211, USA.

RICCI, Nino, BA, MA; Canadian writer; b. 23 Aug. 1959, Leamington; s. of Virginio Ricci and Amelia Ricci (née Ingratta); m. Erika de Vasconcelos 1997; ed York Univ., Toronto, Concordia Univ., Montreal; taught Creative Writing and Canadian Literature at Concordia Univ.; Pres. Canadian Centre, Int. PEN 1995–96; Writer in Residence, Univ. of Windsor 2005–06; Alistair MacLeod Award for Literary Achievement. *Publications:* Lives of the Saints (Books in Canada First Novel Award, Gov. Gen's Award for Fiction, Betty Trask Award, Winifred Holtby Prize for Best Regional Novel, F.G. Bressani Prize) 1990, In a Glass House 1993, Where She Has Gone 1997, Testament 2003 (Trillium Book Award), The Origin of Species (Gov. Gen's Award for Fiction) 2008. *Address:* c/o Anne McDermid & Associates, 83 Willcocks Street, Toronto, ON M5S 1C9, Canada (office). *Telephone:* (416) 324-8845 (office). *Fax:* (416) 324-8870 (office). *E-mail:* info@mcdermidagency.com (office); author@ ninoricci.com (office). *Website:* www.mcdermidagency.com (office); www .ninoricci.com.

RICCI, Ruggiero; American violinist; b. 24 July 1918, San Francisco; s. of Pietro Ricci and Emma Bacigalupi; m. 1st Ruth Rink 1942; m. 2nd Valma Rodriguez 1957; m. 3rd Julia Whitehurst Clemenceau 1978; two s. three d.; ed under Louis Persinger, Mischel Piastro, Paul Stassévitch and Georg Kulenkampff; debut with Manhattan Symphony Orchestra, New York 1929; first tour of Europe 1932; served USAF 1942–45; Prof. of Violin, Indiana Univ. 1970–73, The Juilliard School 1975–78, Univ. of Mich. 1982–87, Hochschule für Musik, Mozarteum, Salzburg, Austria 1989–2002; played first performances of the violin concertos of Ginastera, Von Einem and Veerhoff; specializes in violin solo literature; Cavaliere Order of Merit (Italy); Officier, Ordre des Arts et des Lettres 2004. *Recordings:* over 500 recordings, including the first complete recording of Paganini Caprices. *Publication:* Left Hand Violin Technique 1987, Ricci on Glissando 2007. *Address:* 1099 West Chino Canyon Road, Palm Springs, CA 92262, USA (home). *Telephone:* (760) 320-9785 (home). *Fax:* (760) 320-4768 (home). *E-mail:* jricci1@dc.rr.com (home). *Website:* www.ruggieroricci.com.

RICCIARDONE, Francis Joseph; American diplomatist; b. Boston, Mass; m. Dr Marie Ricciardone; two d.; ed Dartmouth Coll., NH; taught in int. schools Italy 1973–76, Iran 1976–78; entered Foreign Service 1978; served in Turkey 1979–81; research analyst for Turkey, Greece and Cyprus US Dept of State, Washington, DC 1981–82; country officer for Iraq 1982–85; political officer, Cairo 1986–89; led Civilian Observer Unit, Multi nat. Force and Observers, Sinai Desert 1989–91; Deputy Chief of Mission (desig.), Baghdad Embassy 1991–93; Political Adviser to Multinational relief operation, Northern Iraq 1993; Office of Dir.-Gen., US Dept of State, Washington, DC 1993–95; Deputy Chief of Mission and Chargé d'affaires, Ankara 1995; Sec. of State's Special Rep. for Transition in Iraq 1999–2001; Dir Task Force on the Coalition Against Terrorism 2001; Amb. to the Philippines and Palau 2002–05, to Egypt 2005–08; Meritorious Honor Award 1984, Dir-Gen.'s Award for Political Reporting 1988. *Address:* Department of State, 2201 C Street NW, Washington, DC 20520, USA (office). *Telephone:* (202) 647-4000 (office). *Fax:* (202) 647-6738 (office). *Website:* www.state.gov (office).

RICCIOTTI, Rudy; French architect; b. 1952, Algiers, Algeria; ed School of Engineers, Geneva, UPAM, Marseille; freelance architect in Bandol 1980; Prof., Inst. of Art, Marseille-Luminy 1995–; Visiting Prof., Ecole Spécial d'Architecture Paris 1997–98; Scientific Adviser, Ecole d'architecture de Grenoble 2000–; has participated in numerous publs, confs and exhbns; Chevalier de la Légion d'honneur, des Arts et des Lettres; competition entries for remodelling for arte TV station in Strasbourg and Quai de Brainly Museum of Early History in Paris were both awarded prizes, won competitions, including Salle de Musique Actuelle et Contemporaine, Boulogne-Billancourt 2007, Siège d'ITER, Cadarache 2007, Stade Jean Bouin, Paris 2007, École Internationale ITER, Manosque 2007. *Works include:* Bibliothèque de prêt de Draguignan 1986, Centre des loisirs de jeunes, Bandol 1986, Ecole Jean de Florette, St Cyr 1991, city centre pedestrian redevelopment, Bandol 1991, highway information and control centre, Marseille 1992, Salle de spectacles et de cinéma, Pierrelatte (prize winner) 1993, Salle des Fêtes, Port Saint Louis du Rhône 1994, Stadium, Vitrolles 1994, Villa Chaix, Ramatuelle 1995, Base nautique, Bandol 1995, Aire ludique, Lyon-Gerland 1996, Centre d'entretien autoroutier A20, Uzerche 'Collège 900' Auriol 1996, Villa Gros, Gémenos 1997, Collège 600, Saint Ouen 1997, beach redevelopment, Lecques, St Cyr-sur-Mer 1998, Great Hall, Faculty of Science, Marseille 1998, Foyer restaurant of CREPS, Boulouris 1998, Villa Lyprendi, Toulon 1998, Salle de spectacles, Manosque (prize winner) 1999, Maisons individuelles EDF (competition) 1999, Musée des Arts Premiers, Quai Branly, Paris (competition) 1999, Cinéma-casino, St Cyr-sur-Mer 1999, urban redevelopment of Celle Ligure, Italy 1999, Villa and Marmonier swimming pool, La Garde 1999, Villa and Le Goff swimming pool, Marseille 1999, Salle de musique actuelle, Nîmes (prize winner) 2000, project for seaside railway station, Marseille (competition) 2000, renovation of Abbaye de Montmajour, Arles (with E. Cresever, Y. Van Lieshout, F. Deslaugiers) 2000, Concert Room, Potsdam, Germany 2000, Collection Yvon Lambert, Avignon (with A. Putman) 2000, Nat. Photographic Centre, Paris 2001, Pôle santé Hosp., Carpentras (with J.-P. Cassulo) 2001, concert and event halls of Les Tanzmatten, Selesteatt (with G. Heintz) 2001, Musée des Civilisations, Marseille 2004, Nat. Choreographic Centre, Aix-en-Provence 2004, Social Centre Consolat-Mirabeau, Marseille 2004, underground parking, Brussles 2004, reuse and redevelopment of

Grands moulins, Université Paris VII 2005, Rive Gauche, Paris 13ème 2005, Navy Testing and Survey Centre at Le Mourillon, Toulon 2005, Museum of European and Mediterranean Civilisations, Educational Complex, La Bouilladisse. *Leisure interest:* collecting contemporary art. *Address:* Rudy Ricciotti Architecte, 17 blvd Victor Hugo, 83150 Bandol, France (office). *Telephone:* (4) 94-29-52-61 (office). *Fax:* (4) 94-32-45-25 (office). *E-mail:* rudy.ricciotti@ wanadoo.fr (office). *Website:* www.rudyricciotti.com (office).

RICE, Anne, (Anne Rampling, A. N. Roquelaure), BA, MA; American writer; b. 4 Oct. 1941, New Orleans, La; m. Stan Rice 1961; one s. one d. (deceased); ed Texas Women's Univ., San Francisco State Coll., Univ. of Calif., Berkeley; mem. Authors' Guild. *Publications:* Interview with the Vampire 1976, The Feast of All Saints 1979, Cry to Heaven 1982, The Claiming of Sleeping Beauty (as A. N. Roquelaure) 1983, Beauty's Punishment (as A. N. Roquelaure) 1984, The Vampire Lestat 1985, Exit to Eden (as Anne Rampling) 1985, Beauty's Release (as A. N. Roquelaure) 1985, Belinda (as Anne Rampling) 1986, The Queen of the Damned 1988, The Mummy, or Ramses the Damned 1989, The Witching Hour 1990, The Tale of the Body Thief 1992, Lasher 1993, Taltos 1994, Memnoch the Devil 1995, Servant of the Bones 1996, Violin 1997, Pandora 1998, Armand 1998, Vittorio the Vampire 1999, Merrick 2000, Blood and Gold 2001, The Master of Rampling Gate (short story) 2002, Blackwood Farm 2002, Blood Canticle 2003, Christ the Lord: Out of Egypt 2005, Christ the Lord: The Road to Cana 2008, Called out of Darkness: A Spiritual Confession (auto-biog.) 2008. *Address:* c/o Alfred A. Knopf Inc., 1745 Broadway, Suite B1, New York, NY 10019-4305, USA. *Website:* www.annerice.com.

RICE, Condoleezza, PhD; American academic and fmr government official; *Thomas and Barbara Stephenson Senior Fellow on Public Policy, Hoover Institution, Stanford University;* b. 14 Nov. 1954, Birmingham, Ala; ed Univ. of Denver, Univ. of Notre Dame; teacher at Stanford Univ., Calif. 1981–2001, Provost 1993–99, Thomas and Barbara Stephenson Sr Fellow on Public Policy, Hoover Inst. and Prof. of Political Science 2009–; Special Asst to Dir of Jt Chiefs of Staff 1986; Dir, then Sr Dir of Soviet and East European Affairs, Nat. Security Council 1989–91; Special Asst to Pres. for Nat. Security Affairs 1989–91; primary foreign policy adviser to presidential cand. George W. Bush 1999–2000; Asst to Pres. for Nat. Security Affairs and Nat. Security Advisor 2001–04; Sec. of State 2005–09; fmr mem. Bd of Dirs Chevron Corpn, Charles Schwab Corpn, William and Flora Hewlett Foundation and numerous other bds; Sr Fellow, Inst. for Int. Studies, Stanford; Fellow, American Acad. of Arts and Sciences; Trustee John F. Kennedy Center for the Performing Arts, Washington, DC; Dr hc (Morehouse Coll.) 1991, (Univ. of Alabama) 1994, (Univ. of Notre Dame) 1995, (Mississippi Coll. School of Law) 2003, (Univ. of Louisville) 2004; ranked by Forbes magazine amongst 100 Most Powerful Women (first) 2004, (first) 2005, (second) 2006, (fourth) 2007, (seventh) 2008. *Publications:* Uncertain Allegiance: The Soviet Union and the Czechoslovak Army 1984, The Gorbachev Era (co-author) 1986, Germany Unified and Europe Transformed (co-author) 1995; numerous articles on Soviet and East European foreign and defence policy. *Address:* Hoover Institution, 434 Galvez Mall, Stanford University, Stanford, CA 94305-6010, USA (office). *Telephone:* (650) 723-1754 (office). *Fax:* (650) 723-1687 (office). *Website:* www.hoover.org (office).

RICE, Dorothy P., BA; American academic and fmr government official; *Professor Emerita, Institute for Health and Aging, University of California, San Francisco;* b. 11 June 1922, Brooklyn, New York; d. of Gershon Pechman and Lena Schiff; m. John D. Rice 1943; three s.; ed Brooklyn Coll., New York, Univ. of Wisconsin; Dept of Labor 1941–42; War Production Bd 1942–44; Nat. War Labor Bd 1944–45; Nat. Wage Stabilization Bd 1945–47; Health Economist, Public Health Service 1947–49, Public Health Analyst 1960–62, 1964–65; Social Science Analyst, Social Security Admin. 1962–64, Chief, Health Insurance Research Branch 1965–72, Deputy Asst Commr Office of Research and Statistics 1972–76; Dir Nat. Center for Health Stats. Hyattsville, Md 1976–82; Prof.-in-Residence, Dept of Social and Behavioral Sciences, Inst. for Health and Aging, Univ. of Calif., San Francisco 1982, Inst. for Health Policy Studies, Univ. of Calif., San Francisco 1982–94, Prof. Emer. 1994–; numerous honours and awards. *Publications:* more than 250 articles in professional journals. *Address:* Institute for Health and Aging, Department of Social and Behavioral Sciences, School of Nursing, University of California, 3333 California Street, Suite 340, San Francisco, CA 94118 (office); 13895 Campus Drive, Oakland, CA 94605, USA (home). *Telephone:* (415) 476-2771 (office); (510) 638-7150 (home). *Fax:* (415) 502-5208 (office); (510) 638-1429 (home). *E-mail:* dorothy.rice@ucsf.edu (office); drice39223@aol.com (home). *Website:* nurseweb.ucsf.edu/iha (office).

RICE, Jerry; American professional football player (retd); b. 13 Oct. 1962, Starkville, Miss.; s. of Joe Nathan; m. Jacqui Rice; three c.; ed Miss. Valley State Coll.; wide receiver; drafted in first round by San Francisco 49ers, Nat. Football League (NFL) 1985, played with 49ers 1985–2000, Oakland Raiders 2001–03, Seattle Seahawks 2004, Denver Broncos 2005 (retd in preseason); holds 38 NFL records including most touchdowns receiving (197), most passes received (1,549) and most yards receiving (22,895); only player in NFL history to catch three touchdown passes in two Super Bowl games; currently broadcast commentator and radio talk show host; Sporting News NFL Player of the Year 1987, 1990, Sports Illustrated NFL Player of the Year 1986, 1987, 1990, 1993. *Publications:* Rice 1996, Go Long!: My Journey beyond the Game and the Fame (autobiog.) 2007. *Leisure interest:* golf. *Address:* c/o Sports Sunday, NBC11, 2450 North First Street, San Jose, CA 95131, USA. *Telephone:* (408) 432-6221. *Website:* www.nbc11.com/sportssunday; www .jerryricefootball.com.

RICE, Stuart Alan, BS, AM, PhD; American chemist and academic; *Professor Emeritus of Chemistry, James Franck Institute, University of Chicago;* b. 6

Jan. 1932, New York City; s. of Laurence Harlan Rice and Helen Rayfield; m. 1st Marian Coopersmith 1952 (died 1994); two d.; m. 2nd Ruth O'Brien 1997; one s.; ed Brooklyn Coll. and Harvard Univ.; Asst Prof. Dept of Chem. and Inst. for the Study of Metals, Univ. of Chicago 1957–59, Assoc. Prof. Inst. for the Study of Metals (later James Franck Inst.) 1959–60, 1960–69, Louis Block Prof. of Chem. 1969, Louis Block Prof. of Physical Sciences 1969–71, Chair. Dept of Chemistry 1971–77, Frank P. Hixon Distinguished Service Prof. 1977–81, now Prof. Emer., Dean, Div. of Physical Sciences, Univ. of Chicago 1981–95; mem. NAS, Nat. Science Bd 1980–; Foreign mem. Royal Danish Acad. of Science and Letters 1976; Alfred P. Sloan Fellow 1958–62, Guggenheim Fellow 1960–61, NSF Sr Postdoctoral Fellow and Visiting Prof., Univ. Libre de Bruxelles 1965–66; Nat. Insts of Health Special Research Fellow and Visiting Prof., H. C. Orsted Inst., Univ. of Copenhagen 1970–71; Fairchild Distinguished Scholar, Calif. Inst. of Tech. 1979; Fellow, American Acad. of Arts and Sciences; Newton-Abraham Prof., Oxford Univ. 1999–2000; Bourke Lecturer, Faraday Soc. 1964; Baker Lecturer, Cornell Univ. 1985–86; Centenary Lecturer, Royal Soc. of Chemistry 1986–87; John Howard Appleton Lecturer, Brown Univ. 1995; lecturer, numerous univs in USA and abroad; Hon. DSc (Brooklyn Coll., Notre Dame Coll.) 1982; A. Cressy Morrison Prize in Natural Sciences, New York Acad. of Sciences 1955, ACS Award in Pure Chem. 1962, Marlow Medal, Faraday Soc. 1963, Llewellyn John and Harriet Manchester Quantrell Award 1970, Leo Hendrik Baekeland Award 1971, Peter Debye ACS Prize 1985, Joel Henry Hildebrand Award, ACS, Centennial Medal, Harvard Univ. 1997, Nat. Medal of Science 1999, Hirschfelder Prize in Theoretical Chem. 2002–03. *Publications:* Poly-electrolyte Solutions (with Mitsuru Nagasawa) 1961, Statistical Mechanics of Simple Liquids (with Peter Gray) 1965, Physical Chemistry (with R. S. Berry and John Ross) 1980, Optical Control of Molecular Dynamics (with Meishan Zhao) 2000; and 650 papers on chemical physics in scientific journals. *Leisure interests:* reading, carpentry, collecting antique scientific instruments. *Address:* The James Franck Institute, The University of Chicago, 5640 Ellis Avenue, Chicago, IL 60637 (office); 5517 S. Kimbark Avenue, Chicago, IL 60637, USA (home). *Telephone:* (773) 702-7199 (office); (773) 667-2679 (home). *Fax:* (773) 702-5863 (office); (773) 667-0454 (home). *E-mail:* s-rice@uchicago.edu (office).

RICE, Susan Elizabeth, BA, MPhil, PhD; American government official and diplomatist; *Permanent Representative, United Nations;* b. 17 Nov. 1964, Washington, DC; ed Stanford Univ. and Univ. of Oxford, UK; Man. Consultant, McKinsey and Co., Toronto, Canada 1991–93; Dir for Int. Orgs and Peacekeeping, Nat. Security Council, Washington, DC 1993–95, Special Asst to the Pres. and Sr Dir for African Affairs 1995–97,; Asst Sec. of State for African Affairs, US State Dept 1997–2001; Sr Fellow, Foreign Policy and Global Economy and Devt Program, Brookings Inst., Washington, DC 2002–08; Sr Adviser for Nat. Security Affairs on the Kerry-Edwards presidential campaign 2004; Sr Foreign Policy Advisor on Obama presidential campaign 2008; Perm. Rep. to UN, New York 2009–. *Address:* Permanent Mission of the United States to the UN, 799 United Nations Plaza, New York, NY 10017, USA (office). *Telephone:* (212) 415-4000 (office). *Fax:* (212) 415-4443 (office). *E-mail:* usa@un.int (office). *Website:* www.un.int/usa (office).

RICE, Thomas Maurice, PhD, FRS; American/Irish scientist and academic; b. 26 Jan. 1939, Dundalk, Ireland; s. of James Rice and Maureen Rice; m. Helen D. Spreiter 1966; one s. two d.; ed Univ. Coll. Dublin and Univ. of Cambridge; asst lecturer, Dept of Mathematical Physics, Univ. of Birmingham 1963–64; Research Assoc. Dept of Physics, Univ. of Calif. at San Diego, La Jolla 1964–66; Bell Laboratories, Murray Hill, NJ 1966–81; Prof. of Theoretical Physics, ETH, Zürich 1981–2004; mem. NAS; Hon. MRIA; Hewlett-Packard Europhysics Prize 1998, John Bardeen Prize 2000. *Address:* Theoretische Physik, ETH-Hönggerberg, 8093 Zürich, Switzerland. *Telephone:* (1) 6332581. *Fax:* (1) 6331115 (office). *E-mail:* rice@itp.phys.ethz.ch (office). *Website:* www.itp.phys.ethz.ch/staff/rice (office).

RICE, Sir Timothy (Tim) Miles Bindon, Kt; British songwriter; b. 10 Nov. 1944, Amersham; s. of Hugh Gordon Rice and Joan Odette Rice; m. Jane Artereta McIntosh 1974, one s. one d.; pnr Nell Sully, one d.; ed Lancing Coll.; with EMI Records 1966–68, Norrie Paramor Org. 1968–69; founder and fmr Dir GRRR Books Ltd 1978, Pavilion Books Ltd 1981; Chair. Foundation for Sport and the Arts 1991–; mem. Main Cttee MCC 1992–94, 1995– (Pres. 2002–03); Dr hc (Univ. of Sunderland) 2006; 12 Ivor Novello Awards, three Tony Awards, six Grammy Awards. *Lyrics for musicals:* (music by Andrew Lloyd Webber q.v. unless otherwise specified): Joseph and the Amazing Technicolor Dreamcoat 1968, Jesus Christ Superstar 1970, Evita 1976, Blondel (music by Stephen Oliver) 1983, Chess (music by Benny Andersson and Bjorn Ulvaeus) 1984, Cricket 1986, Starmania/Tycoon (with music by Michael Berger) 1989–90, Aladdin (film musical, music by Alan Menken) 1992, The Lion King (film musical, music by Elton John) 1993 (theatre version 1997), Beauty and the Beast (music by Alan Menken) 1994 (some lyrics for stage version), Heathcliff (music by John Farrar) 1995, King David (music by Alan Menken) 1997, Aida (music by Elton John) 1998, The Road to El Dorado (music by Elton John) 1999; songs include: Don't Cry For Me Argentina, I Know Him So Well, Can You Feel The Love Tonight? (Acad. Award, Golden Globe, with Elton John 1994), I Don't Know How To Love Him, A Winter's Tale, Circle Of Life, Any Dream Will Do, A Whole New World (Acad. Award, Golden Globe, with Alan Menken 1992), All Time High (from film Octopussy), You Must Love Me (Acad. Award, Golden Globe, with Andrew Lloyd Webber 1996), One Night In Bangkok; lyrics for songs with composers, including Paul McCartney, Mike Batt, Freddie Mercury, Graham Gouldman, Marvin Hamlisch, Rick Wakeman, John Barry. *Publications:* Evita (with Andrew Lloyd Webber) 1978, Joseph and the Amazing Technicolor Dreamcoat 1982, Treasures of Lords 1989, Oh, What a Circus (autobiog.) 1995, The Complete Eurovision Song Contest Companion (jtly) 1998, founder and original author, with Paul Gambaccini, Jonathan Rice and Mike Read, of the Guinness Book of Hit Singles and related titles. *Leisure interests:* cricket, history of popular music, chickens. *Address:* Lewis & Golden, 40 Queen Anne Street, London, W1M 0EL, England (office). *Website:* www.timrice.co.uk (office).

RICH, Adrienne, AB; American writer; b. 16 May 1929, Baltimore; d. of Arnold Rich and Helen Elizabeth Jones; m. Alfred Conrad (died 1970); three s.; ed Radcliffe Coll.; Teacher, New York Poetry Center 1966–67; Visiting Lecturer, Swarthmore Coll. 1967–69; Adjunct Prof., Columbia Univ. 1967–69; Lecturer, City Coll. of New York 1968–70, Instructor 1970–71, Asst Prof. of English 1971–72, 1974–75; Visiting Prof. of Creative Literature, Brandeis Univ. 1972–73; Prof. of English, Rutgers Univ. 1976–79; Prof.-at-Large, Cornell Univ. 1981–87; Lecturer and Visiting Prof, Scripps Coll. 1983, 1984; Prof. of English and Feminist Studies, Stanford Univ. 1986–93; Marjorie Kovler Visiting Lecturer, Univ. of Chicago 1989; Clark Lecturer, Trinity Coll., Cambridge 2002; Guggenheim Fellow 1952, 1961; MacArthur Fellowship 1994–99; Hon. LittD (Wheaton Coll.) 1967, (Smith Coll.) 1979, (Brandeis Univ.) 1987, (Wooster Coll.) 1989, (Harvard) 1990, (City Coll. of New York) 1990; Yale Series of Younger Poets Award 1951, Ridgely Torrence Memorial Award, Poetry Soc. of America 1955, Shelley Memorial Award 1971, Nat. Book Award 1974, Ruth Lilly Prize 1987, Brandeis Medal in Poetry 1987, Nat. Poetry Assen Award 1989, LA Times Book Award 1992, Frost Silver Medal (Poetry Soc. of America) 1992, The Poets' Prize 1993, Acad. of American Poets, Fellowship 1993, Dorothea Tanning Award 1996, Lannan Foundation Literary Award for Lifetime Achievement 1999, Bollingen Prize for Poetry 2003, Medal for Distinguished Contribution to American Letters, Nat. Book Foundation 2006. *Publications:* A Change of World 1951, The Diamond Cutters and Other Poems 1955, Snapshots of a Daughter-in-Law 1963, Necessities of Life 1962–65, 1965–68 1969, Leaflets, Poems 1965–68, The Will to Change 1971, Diving into the Wreck 1973, Of Woman Born: Motherhood as Experience and Institution 1976, On Lies, Secrets and Silence: Selected Prose 1966–78 1979, A Wild Patience Has Taken Me This Far: Poems 1978–81 1981, Blood, Bread and Poetry: Selected Prose 1979–85 1986, Your Native Land, Your Life 1986, Time's Power: Poems 1985–88 1989, An Atlas of the Difficult World: Poems 1988–91 1991, Collected Early Poems, 1950–1970 1993, What Is Found There: Notebooks on Poetry and Politics 1993, Dark Fields of the Republic: Poems 1991–95 1995, Midnight Salvage: Poems 1995–1998 1999, Arts of the Possible: Essays and Conversations 2001, Fox: Poems 1998–2000 2001, The Fact of a Doorframe: Poems 1950–2000 2002, The School Among the Ruins: Poems 2000–2004 2004. *Address:* c/o Steven Barclay Agency, 12 Western Avenue, Petaluma, CA 94952, USA (office). *Telephone:* (707) 773-0454 (office). *E-mail:* steven@barclayagency.com (office). *Website:* www.barclayagency.com (office).

RICH, Alexander, MD; American molecular biologist and academic; *William Thompson Sedgwick Professor of Biophysics, Massachusetts Institute of Technology;* b. 15 Nov. 1924, Hartford, Conn.; s. of Max Rich and Bella Shub; m. Jane Erving King 1952; two s. two d.; ed Harvard Coll. and Harvard Medical School; served in USN 1943–46; Research Fellow, Gates and Crellin Labs, Calif. Inst. of Tech. 1949–54; Chief of Section on Physical Chem., Nat. Inst. of Mental Health, Bethesda, Md 1954–58; Visiting Scientist, Cavendish Lab., Cambridge, UK 1955–56; Assoc. Prof. of Biophysics, MIT 1958–61, Prof. 1961–, William Thompson Sedgwick Prof. of Biophysics 1974–; Fairchild Distinguished Scholar, Calif. Inst. of Tech., Pasadena 1976; Visiting Prof., Coll. de France, Paris 1987; Sr Consultant, Office of Science and Tech. Policy, Exec. Office of the Pres. 1977–81; Chair. Perm. Science Cttee, American Acad. of Arts and Sciences 1967–71, Basic Research Cttee of Nat. Science Bd 1978–82, Biotech. Programme of NAS Cttee on Scholarly Communication with the People's Republic of China 1986–93; Co-Chair. Scientific and Academic Advisory Cttee of Weizmann Inst. of Science, Israel 1987–93; mem. or fmr mem. numerous cttees etc., including Marine Biological Lab., Woods Hole, Mass., 1965–77, 1987–96, Advisory Bd NAS Acad. Forum 1975–82, Scientific Advisory Bd Stanford Synchrotron Radiation Project 1976–80, US–USSR Jt Comm. on Science and Tech. 1977–82, Council Pugwash Conferences on Science and World Affairs 1977–82, Bd of Dirs Medical Foundation, Boston, Mass. 1981–90, Governing Bd Nat. Research Council 1985–88, Cttee on USSR and E Europe of Nat. Research Council 1986–92, Exec. Cttee, Council of NAS 1985–88, External Advisory Cttee of Center for Human Genome Studies, Los Alamos, NM 1989–97, Nat. Critical Technologies Panel of Office of Science and Tech. Policy, Washington, DC 1990–91; mem. Visiting Cttee, Calif. Inst. of Tech., Pasadena 1999–2005; on editorial bds of numerous publs, including Journal of Molecular Evolution 1983–94, Proteins, Structure, Function and Genetics 1986–91, Genomics 1987–, Journal of Biotechnology 1987–92, EMBO Journal 1988–90; mem. ACS and other socs, NAS 1970– (mem. Exec. Cttee 1985–88), Pontifical Acad. of Sciences, The Vatican 1978, American Philosophical Soc. 1980; Sr mem. Inst. of Medicine, Washington, DC 1990; Fellow, Nat. Research Council 1949–51, American Acad. of Arts and Sciences 1959, Guggenheim Foundation 1963, AAAS 1965; Foreign mem. French Acad. of Sciences 1984; Assoc. mem. European Molecular Biology Org. 1984;; Hon. mem. Japanese Biochemical Soc. 1986; Dr hc (Rio de Janeiro) 1981; Hon. PhD (Weizmann Inst.) 1992; Hons DSc (Eidgenössische Technische Hochschule, Zurich) 1993, (Freie Universität Berlin) 1996; Skylab Achievement Award, NASA 1974; Theodore von Karmen Award 1976, Presidential Award, New York Acad. of Sciences 1977, James R. Killian Faculty Achievement Award, (MIT) 1980, Jabotinsky Medal, New York 1980, Nat. Medal of Science, Washington, DC 1995, Linus Pauling Medal, ACS 1995, Merck Award, American Soc. for Biochem. and Molecular Biology, Washington 1998, Bower Award for Achievement in Science, Franklin Inst. Pa 2000, Sigma Xi Proctor Prize for Achievement in Science, Raleigh, NC 2001, Passano Award, Passano Foundation 2002, Lomonosov Large Gold Medal, Russian Acad. of Sciences 2002, Lifetime Achievement Award, Inst. of Human Virology, Baltimore 2002, Biotechnology Achievement Award, New York Univ. School of Medicine 2003.

Publications: Structural Chemistry and Molecular Biology (co-ed.) 1968; Primary and Tertiary Structure of Nucleic Acids and Cancer Research (co-ed.) 1982; more than 500 publications in the fields of molecular structure of nucleic acid components, nucleic acids and polynucleotides, physical chem. of nucleotides and polynucleotides, molecular structure of proteins, mechanism of protein synthesis, molecular biology of the nucleic acids, X-ray crystallography, origin of life. *Leisure interests:* ocean sailing in small boats, growing tomato plants, collecting fossils. *Address:* Department of Biology, Room 68-233, Massachusetts Institute of Technology, 77 Massachusetts Avenue, Cambridge, MA 02139 (office); 2 Walnut Avenue, Cambridge, MA 02140, USA (home). *Telephone:* (617) 253-4715 (office); (617) 547-1637 (home). *Fax:* (617) 253-8699 (office). *E-mail:* mitbio@mit.edu (office). *Website:* mit.edu/biology/www/index.html (office).

RICH, Frank Hart, Jr, BA; American journalist and critic; b. 2 June 1949, Washington, DC; s. of Frank Hart Rich and Helene Aaronson; m. 1st Gail Winston 1976; two s.; m. 2nd Alexandra Rachelle Witchel 1991; ed Harvard Univ.; Film Critic and Sr Ed. New Times Magazine 1973–75; Film Critic, New York Post 1975–77; Film and TV Critic, Time Magazine 1977–80; Chief Drama Critic, New York Times 1980–93, Op-Ed. Columnist 1994–, also Sr Adviser to Culture Ed.; Assoc. Fellow, Jonathan Edwards Coll., Yale Univ. 1998–. *Publications:* Hot Seat: Theater Criticism for the New York Times 1980–93 1998, Ghost Light 2000, The Greatest Story Every Sold 2006. *Address:* The New York Times, 229 West 43rd Street, New York, NY 10036, USA (office). *Website:* topics.nytimes.com/top/opinion/editorialsandoped/oped/columnists/frankrich/index.html (office).

RICH, Patrick Jean Jacques; French/Swiss/Canadian business executive (retd); b. 28 March 1931, Strasbourg; s. of the late Henri Rich and Marguerite Rich; m. Louise Dionne 1961; two s. one d.; ed Univ. of Strasbourg and Harvard Univ., USA; worked for Alcan Aluminium Ltd in Guinea, France, UK, Argentina, Spain and Italy 1959–70, Area Gen. Man. for Latin America 1971–75, Exec. Vice-Pres. Europe, Latin America and Africa 1976–77, mem. Bd 1978–86; Exec. Vice-Pres. Alcan Aluminium Ltd and CEO Aluminium Co. of Canada 1978–81; Exec. Vice-Pres. Europe, Africa, Middle East and Chair. Alcan Aluminium SA 1978–86; CEO Société Générale de Surveillance Holding SA, Geneva 1987–89; Deputy Chair. BOC Group PLC 1990–91, Chief Exec. 1991–92, Chair. 1992–94 (non-exec. 1994) and Chief Exec. 1992–94; Chair. Royal Packaging Industries Van Leer, Netherlands 1988–95, IMEC Research Project 1995–; Trustee Bernard van Leer Foundation 1982–99; Gov. Van Leer Group Foundation 1982–99, Van Leer Jerusalem Inst. 1995–99; mem. (non-exec.) Bd, La Farge Cement (Canada) 1977–81, Bekaert 1978–87, IMI Geneva 1977–81; Croix de la Valeur Militaire, Army Corps citation, Médaille Commémorative Combattants d'Algérie. *Leisure interests:* opera, walking, skiing, piano playing, reading, sailing. *Address:* 6, route des Mandarins, 3963 Crans Montana, Switzerland (office). *Telephone:* (22) 310-76-14 (office); (27) 481-45-89 (home). *Fax:* (22) 310-76-14 (office); (27) 481-07-89 (home). *E-mail:* pjj.rich@gmail.com (home).

RICHARD, Alain; French government official; *Mayor of Saint Ouen L'Aumône;* b. 29 Aug. 1945, Paris; m. Elisabeth Couffignal 1988; one s. one d. and one s. by previous m.; ed Lycée Henri IV, Paris, Institut d'Etudes Politiques, Ecole Nat. d'Admin; Auditor, Conseil d'Etat 1971, Maître des requêtes 1978, Conseiller d'Etat 1993–95; Mayor, St Ouen l'Aumône 1977–97, 2001–; Deputy, Val d'Oise 1978–93, Senator 1995–97; Vice-Pres. Commission des lois 1981–86, Nat. Ass. 1987–88; Minister of Defence 1997–2001; Founder and Vice-Pres. Forum for Man. of Towns 1985–97; mem. Nat. Office, Parti Socialiste Unifié 1972–74; mem. Cttee Parti Socialiste 1979, Exec. Bd 1988; mem. Bd Inst. for Int. Relations 1991–97. *Address:* Hôtel de Ville, 2 place Pierre Mendès-France, Saint-Ouen l'Aumône, 95318 Cergy-Pontoise Cedex (office); 28 rue René Clair, 95310 St Ouen l'Aumône, France. *Telephone:* 1-34-21-25-00 (office). *Fax:* 1-34-64-35-65 (office). *E-mail:* courrier@ville-saintouenlaumone.fr (office). *Website:* www.ville-saintouenlaumone.fr (office).

RICHARD, Alison Fettes, MA, PhD; British university administrator and professor of anthropology and environmental studies; *Vice-Chancellor, University of Cambridge;* b. 1 March 1948, Kent, England; d. of Gavin Sharp Richard and Joyce Napier Matthews; m. Robert E. Dewar; one s. (deceased) two d.; ed Newnham Coll., Cambridge and King's Coll., London; joined faculty of Yale Univ., USA 1972, Dir of Grad. Studies 1980–86, Prof. of Anthropology 1986–2003, Chair. Dept of Anthropology 1986–90, Prof. of Environmental Studies, Yale School of Forestry and Environmental Studies 1990–2003, Dir Peabody Museum of Natural History 1991–94, Provost Yale Univ. 1994–2002, Franklin Muzzy Crosby Prof. of the Human Environment 1998, Prof. Emer. 2003–; Vice-Chancellor Univ. of Cambridge 2003–; mem. Bd of Dirs World Wildlife Fund US 1995–2004, Liz Claiborne/Art Ortenberg Foundation, Tany Meva Foundation, Madagascar; Officier, Ordre Nat. (Madagascar) 2005; Dr hc (Peking Univ.) 2004, (Univ. of Antananarivo, Madagascar) 2005, (York Univ., Toronto) 2006, (Univ. of Edinburgh) 2006, (Queen's Univ., Belfast) 2008, (Anglia Ruskin Univ.) 2008. *Publications include:* Primates in Nature 1985, Behavioral Variation: Case Study of a Malagasy Lemur 1978; numerous articles in scientific journals. *Address:* Office of the Vice-Chancellor, University of Cambridge, The Old Schools, Trinity Lane, Cambridge, CB2 1TN, England (office). *Telephone:* (1223) 332290 (office). *Fax:* (1223) 339669 (office). *E-mail:* v-c@admin.cam.ac.uk (office). *Website:* www.admin.cam.ac.uk/offices/v-c/richard.html (office).

RICHARD, Sir Cliff, Kt, OBE; British singer, musician (guitar) and actor; b. (Harry Rodger Webb), 14 Oct. 1940, India; s. of Rodger Webb and the late Dorothy Webb; ed Riversmead School, Cheshunt; leader Cliff Richard and The Shadows; later, solo artist; regular int. concert tours, various repertory and variety seasons; own television series on BBC and ITV; mem. Equity; Hon. DUniv (Middx) 2003; numerous awards. *Films:* Serious Charge 1959, Expresso Bongo 1960, The Young Ones 1961, Summer Holiday 1962, Wonderful Life 1964, Finders Keepers 1966, Two a Penny 1968, His Land, Take Me High 1973. *Stage appearances:* musicals Time, Dominion Theatre, London 1986–87, Heathcliff, UK tour and Hammersmith Apollo, London 1996–97. *Recordings include:* albums: Cliff 1959, Cliff Sings 1959, Me And My Shadows 1960, Listen To Cliff 1961, 21 Today 1961, The Young Ones 1961, 32 Minutes And 17 Seconds With Cliff Richard 1962, Summer Holiday 1963, Cliff's Hit Album 1963, When In Spain 1963, Wonderful Life 1964, Aladdin And His Wonderful Lamp 1964, Cliff Richard 1965, More Hits By Cliff 1965, When In Rome 1965, Love Is Forever 1965, Kinda Latin 1966, Finders Keepers 1966, Cinderella 1967, Don't Stop Me Now 1967, Good News 1967, Cliff In Japan 1968, Two A Penny 1968, Established 1968, The Best Of Cliff 1969, Sincerely 1969, It'll Be Me 1969, Cliff Live At The Talk Of The Town 1970, About That Man 1970, His Land 1970, Tracks 'n' Grooves 1970, The Best Of Cliff Vol. Two 1972, Take Me High 1973, Help It Along 1974, The 31st February Street 1974, I'm Nearly Famous 1976, Every Face Tells A Story 1977, 40 Golden Greats 1977, Small Corners 1978, Green Light 1978, Thank You Very Much (Cliff & The Shadows) 1979, Rock 'n' Roll Juvenile 1979, I'm No Hero 1980, Love Songs 1981, Wired For Sound 1981, Now You See Me... Now You Don't 1982, Dressed For The Occasion 1983, Silver 1983, Rock 'n' Roll Silver 1983, Cliff & The Shadows 1984, Always Guaranteed 1987, Private Collection 1988, Stronger 1989, From A Distance – The Event 1990, Together 1991, Cliff Richard: The Album 1993, The Hit List 1994, Songs From Heathcliff 1995, Heathcliff Live 1996, Cliff Richard At The Movies 1996, The Rock 'n' Roll Years 1997, Real As I Wanna Be 1998, The Whole Story 2001, Wanted 2001, The Singles Collection 2002, Cliff At Christmas 2003, Something's Goin' On 2004, Two's Company: The Duets 2006, Love: The Album 2007. *Publications:* Questions 1970, The Way I See It 1972, The Way I See It Now 1975, Which One's Cliff? 1977, Happy Christmas from Cliff 1980, You, Me and Jesus 1983, Mine to Share 1984, Jesus, Me and You 1985, Single-Minded 1988, Mine Forever 1989, My Story: A Celebration of 40 Years in Showbusiness 1998. *Leisure interests:* tennis. *Address:* c/o Cliff Richard Organisation, PO Box 46C, Esher, Surrey KT10 0RB, England (office). *Telephone:* (1372) 467752 (office). *Fax:* (1372) 462352 (office). *E-mail:* general@cliffrichard.org (office). *Website:* www.cliffrichard.org.

RICHARD, Baron (Life Peer), cr. 1990, of Ammanford in the County of Dyfed; **Ivor Seward Richard,** PC, MA, QC; British politician, lawyer and diplomatist; b. 30 May 1932, Cardiff; s. of Seward Thomas and Isabella Irene Richard; m. 1st Geraldine Moore 1956 (divorced 1961); one s.; m. 2nd Alison Mary Imrie 1962 (divorced 1984); one s. one d.; m. 3rd Janet Armstrong Jones 1989; one s.; ed Cheltenham Coll., Pembroke Coll., Oxford; called to the Bar 1955; MP for Barons Court 1964–74; Parl. Pvt. Sec. to Sec. of State for Defence 1966–69; Under-Sec. of State for Defence for Army 1969–70; QC 1971; Perm. Rep. to UN 1974–79; EC Commr for Social Affairs, Employment, Educ. and Vocational Training Policy 1981–84; Leader of Opposition in the House of Lords 1992–97; Lord Privy Seal and Leader of the House of Lords, 1997–98; Chair. World Trade Centre Wales Ltd (Cardiff) 1985–97; Chair. Richard Comm. on the Welsh Ass. 2002–04; Chair. Rhodesia Conf., Geneva 1976; Counsel to Chadbourne, Parke, Whiteside and Wolff, New York 1979–81; Labour; Hon. Fellow, Pembroke Coll. 1981–. *Publications:* Europe or the Open Sea 1971, We, the British 1983, Unfinished Business: Reforming the House of Lords 1998; and articles in various political journals. *Leisure interests:* playing piano, watching football, talking. *Address:* House of Lords, Westminster, London, SW1A 0PW, England. *Telephone:* (20) 7219-1495. *E-mail:* richardi@parliament.uk.

RICHARD, Jean Barthélemy, DèsSc; French historian; b. 7 Feb. 1921, Kremlin-Bicêtre; s. of Pierre Richard and Amélie Grandchamp; m. Monique Rivoire 1944; three s. two d.; ed Ecole des Chartes, Ecole Française de Rome and Sorbonne, Paris; Asst Archivist, Dijon 1943–55; Prof., Univ. of Dijon 1955–88, Dean, Faculté des Lettres 1968–71; mem. Acad. des Inscriptions, Inst. de France and other learned socs; Officier, Légion d'honneur, Grand Officier, Ordre du Mérite, Commdr des Palmes académiques; Dr hc (Cyprus Univ.) 2006; Gold Medal for Altaic Studies, Indiana Univ. *Publications:* The Latin Kingdom of Jerusalem 1953, Les ducs de Bourgogne 1954, L'Esprit de la Croisade 1969, La papauté et les missions d'Orient 1977, Histoire de la Bourgogne 1978, St Louis 1983, Le livre des remembrances de la secrète du royaume de Chypre 1983, Histoire des Croisades 1996, Au-delà de la Perse et de l'Arménie 2005; five vols in Variorum Reprints on Crusades and Oriental History 1976–2003. *Leisure interests:* garden and forest activities. *Address:* 12 rue Pelletier de Chambure, 21000 Dijon; Les Billaudots, 71540 Igornay, France. *Telephone:* (3) 80-66-10-28; (3) 85-82-82-98.

RICHARD, Pierre, BEng; French business executive; b. 9 March 1941, Dijon; s. of Henri Richard and Marguerite Richard (née Genty); m. Aleth Sachot 1966; three c.; ed Univ. of Dijon and Univ. of Pennsylvania, USA; teacher, Inst. of Urbanism, Paris 1967–68; Asst Dir-Gen. Public Devt Corpn, new town of Cergy-Pontoise 1967–72; Tech. Adviser to Sec. of State for Housing 1972–74, to Gen. Secr. for the Pres. of the Rep. 1974–78; Dir Gen. for Local Communities, Ministry of the Interior 1978–82; Asst Dir-Gen. of Treasury, Dept of Local Devt 1983–93; Man. Dir Crédit Local de France (CLF) 1993–, Co-Chair. Dexia Group (after merger between CLF and Crédit Communal de Belgique) 1996–99, Deputy Dir 1999, Pres. Supervisory Bd Dexia Crédit Local de France 2000, Group CEO and Chair. Exec. Bd Dexia Group 2000–05, Chair. Bd of Dirs 2006–08; Pres. Group of Specialized Financial Insts 1991–93; Pres. Inst. of Decentralization 1993–95; Pres. Admin. Bd, Ecole Nat. des Ponts et Chaussées 1994–; Dir Municipal Bond Investors Assurance 1990–, Air France 1995–, Banque européenne d'investissement 1994–, Le Monde 1995–; Chevalier, Légion d'honneur; Officier, Ordre nat. du Mérite. *Publications:* Les Communes françaises d'aujourd'hui, Le Temps des citoyens pour une démocratie décentralisée 1995. *Leisure interest:* horseriding. *Address:* c/o Dexia Group, Square de Meeûs 1, 1000 Brussels, Belgium (office).

RICHARDS, Gen. Sir David, Kt, KCB, CBE, DSO, ADC; British army officer; *Chief of General Staff;* b. 1952; ed Eastbourne Coll., Royal Artillery, Univ. Coll. Cardiff; regimental duty (29 Commando Regt RA, C Anti-Tank Battery Royal Horse Artillery, 11th Armoured Brigade) in the Far East, Germany and UK, including three tours of NI 1974–83; Commdr field battery in 47th Field Regt, 11th Armoured Brigade 1984–86, Chief of Staff, Berlin Infantry Brigade 1984–86; instructor, Staff Coll., Camberley 1986–89; Commdr 3rd Regt Royal Horse Artillery 1989–94; Col Army Plans, Ministry of Defence 1994–96; promoted to Brig. 1996; Commdr 4th Armoured Brigade 1996–98; Chief Jt Force Operations, Perm. Jt HQ 1998–2001; promoted to Maj. Gen. 2001; Chief of Staff Allied Rapid Reaction Corps 2001–02; Asst Chief of Gen. Staff 2002–05; Commdr Allied Rapid Reaction Corps 2005–08, Commdr Int. Stabilisation and Assistance Force in Afghanistan 2006–07; Chief of Gen. Staff 2008–. *Address:* Ministry of Defence, Main Building, Whitehall, London, SW1A 2HB, England (office). *Telephone:* (20) 7218-9000 (office). *E-mail:* public@ministers.mod.uk (office). *Website:* www.mod.uk (office).

RICHARDS, Ed; British government official; *CEO, Office of Communications (Ofcom);* began career as researcher with Diverse Production Ltd; worked with London Economics Ltd (consultancy firm); fmr adviser to Gordon Brown MP; served as Controller of Corporate Strategy at BBC; fmr Sr Policy Adviser to Prime Minister Tony Blair for media, telecoms, internet and e-govt; Sr Pnr, Strategy and Market Devts, Ofcom 2003–05, COO 2005–06, CEO 2006–; mem. Bd of Dirs Donmar Warehouse Ltd. *Address:* Ofcom, Riverside House, 2a Southwark Bridge Road, London, SE1 9HA, England (office). *Telephone:* (20) 7981-3000 (office). *Fax:* (20) 7981-3333 (office). *Website:* www.ofcom.org.uk (office).

RICHARDS, Emma, MBE; British yachtswoman; winner Mobil North Sea Race, Banff–Stavanger, Sigma 400 1998, Fastnet Open 60 Team Group Four, Class One; Round Isle of Wight Race, 60 ft Trimaran Fujicolor 1999, Transat Jacques Vabre, double-handed Transatlantic, Open 50 Pindar, Class 2 Monohull 1999, Europe One New Man Star, single-handed Transatlantic race, Open 50 Pindar, Class Two Monohull 2000, RORC 75th Anniversary Round Britain and Ireland Race, Open 50 Pindar, double-handed 2000, OOPS! Cup eight-race series, Scandinavia, 60 ft Trimaran Toshiba 2001; joined Nautor Challenge Amer Sports Too for start of leg four of Volvo Ocean Race 2002; became first woman to sail single-handed across the Atlantic from west to east in a monohull boat 2002; first British woman and youngest competitor to complete Around Alone race May 2003. *Publication:* Around Alone 2004. *Address:* c/o Camilla Green/Victoria Fuller, Pitch PR, First Floor, 39–43 Brewer Street, London, W1F 9UD, England (office). *Telephone:* (20) 7494-1616 (office); (7775) 585437 (Mobile). *Fax:* (20) 7287–0773. *E-mail:* victoria@pitchpr.co.uk; camilla@pitchpr.co.uk. *Website:* www.pindar.com; www.emmarichards.com.

RICHARDS, Sir Francis Neville, Kt, KCMG, CVO, DL, MA; British diplomatist and academic; *Honorary Professor, School of Social Sciences and Director, Centre for Studies in Security and Diplomacy, University of Birmingham;* b. 18 Nov. 1945; s. of Sir Francis Brooks Richards; m. Gillian Bruce Nevill 1971; one s. one d.; ed Eton Coll. and King's Coll., Cambridge; with Royal Green Jackets 1967, served with UN Force in Cyprus (invalided 1969); joined FCO 1969, served in Moscow 1971; UK Del. to Mutual and Balanced Force Reducations negotiations, Vienna 1973; FCO 1976–85 (Asst Pvt. Sec. to Sec. of State 1981–82); Econ. and Commercial Counsellor, New Delhi 1985–88; FCO 1988–90 (Head S Asian Dept); High Commr to Namibia 1990–92; Minister, Moscow 1992–95; Dir (Europe) FCO 1995–97, Deputy Under-Sec. of State 1997–98; Dir Govt Communications HQ (GCHQ) 1998–2003; Gov. and C-in-C of Gibraltar 2003–06; Hon. Prof., School of Social Sciences and Dir Centre for Studies in Security and Diplomacy, Univ. of Birmingham 2007–; Trustee, Imperial War Museum, London 2007–. *Leisure interests:* walking, travelling, riding. *Address:* Centre for Studies in Security and Diplomacy, European Research Institute, University of Birmingham, Edgbaston, Birmingham, B15 2TT, England (office). *Telephone:* (121) 414-6950 (office). *Fax:* (121) 414-2693 (office). *E-mail:* cssd-bham@bham.ac.uk (office). *Website:* www.cssd.bham.ac.uk (office).

RICHARDS, George Maxwell, MSc, PhD; Trinidad and Tobago professor of chemical engineering, politician and head of state; *President;* b. 1931, San Fernando; m.; two c.; ed Queen's Royal Coll., Port of Spain, Univs of Manchester and Cambridge, UK; staff trainee, United British Oilfields of Trinidad, Ltd 1950–51; held several managerial posts at Shell Trinidad Ltd 1957–65; Sr Lecturer in Chemical Eng, Univ. of the West Indies (UWI), St Augustine 1965–70, Prof. 1970, later Dean Faculty of Chemical Eng, Deputy Prin. and Pro-Vice-Chancellor UWI 1980–85, Acting Prin. 1984–85, Prin. and Pro-Vice-Chancellor 1985–86, now Prof. Emer.; Chair. Salaries Review Comm. 1977–2003; Pres. Trinidad and Tobago 2003–; fmr Chair. Nat. Training Bd, Inst. of Marine Affairs; fmr mem. Bd Trinidad Publishing Co., TRINTOC, National Gas Co., etc.; fmr mem. Bd Nat. Advisory Council; mem. Asscn of Professional Engineers of Trinidad and Tobago, Inst. of Chemical Engineers, London, UK, Inst. of Petroleum, London, Royal Soc. of Chem., UK; Chaconia Medal of the Order of the Trinity (CMT), Class 1 (Gold) for public service. *Address:* Office of the President, President's House, Circular Road, St Ann's, Port of Spain, Trinidad (office). *Telephone:* 624-1261 (office). *Fax:* 625-7950 (office). *E-mail:* presoftt@carib-link.net (office). *Website:* www.gov.tt (office).

RICHARDS, Sir Isaac Vivian Alexander (Viv), KGN, OBE; Antiguan fmr cricketer; b. 7 March 1952, St John's, Antigua; s. of Malcolm Richards; m. Miriam Lewis; one s. one d.; ed Antigua Grammar School; right-hand batsman, off-break bowler, cover-point fielder; played for Leeward Islands 1971–91 (Capt. 1981–91), Somerset 1974–86, Queensland 1976–77, Glamorgan 1990–93; 121 Tests for W Indies 1974–91, 50 as Capt., scoring 8,540 runs (average 50.2) including 24 hundreds and holding 122 catches; scored record 1,710 runs in a calendar year (11 Tests in 1976); scored 36,212 first-class runs (114 hundreds, only W Indian to score 100 hundreds); toured England 1976, 1979 (World Cup), 1980, 1983 (World Cup), 1984, 1988 (as Capt.), 1991 (as Capt.); 187 limited-overs ints scoring 6,721 runs (11 hundreds including then record 189 not out v. England at Old Trafford 1984); Chair. Selectors, W Indies Cricket Bd 2002–04; Dr hc (Exeter) 1986; Wisden Cricketer of the Year 1977; one of Wisden's Five Cricketers of the Century 2000; Cricket Hall of Fame 2001. *Publications:* (with David Foot) Viv Richards (autobiog.) 1982, Cricket Masterclass 1988, Hitting Across The Line (autobiog.) 1991, (with Bob Harris) Sir Vivian (autobiog.) 2000. *Leisure interests:* music, football, golf, tennis. *Address:* c/o West Indies Cricket Board, PO Box 616, St John's, Antigua.

RICHARDS, Sir John (Charles Chisholm), KCB, KCVO; British military officer (retd); b. 21 Feb. 1927, Wallasey; s. of Charles Richards and Alice Milner; m. Audrey Hidson 1953; two s. one d.; ed Worksop Coll. Notts.; joined Royal Marines 1945; served in commando units and HM ships worldwide; Canadian Army Staff Coll. 1959–61; Naval Staff in Ministry of Defence 1963–64; Instructor, Army Staff Coll., Camberley 1965–67; CO 42nd and 45th RM Commandos; Chief of Staff, British Defence Staff, Washington, DC and del. to UN 1972–74; Brig. Commdg 3rd Commando Brigade 1975–77; Maj.-Gen. 1977; Commdt-Gen. Royal Marines (with rank of Lt-Gen.) 1977–81; Rep. Col Commdt Royal Marines 1989–90; HM Marshal of the Diplomatic Corps 1982–92; Dir (non-exec.) DSC Communications (Europe) Ltd 1986–93, Andrew Ltd 1987–94; Extra Equerry to HM The Queen 1992; Freeman, City of London 1982; numerous foreign awards including decorations from FRG, France, Netherlands, Spain, Mexico, Italy, Norway, Senegal, UAE, Malawi, Bahrain, Qatar and Oman. *Leisure interests:* golf, gardening, swimming, military history. *Address:* c/o NatWest Bank, 5 Market Place, Kingston-upon-Thames, KT1 1JX, England.

RICHARDS, Keith; British musician (guitar), singer and songwriter; b. (Keith Richard), 18 Dec. 1943, Dartford, Kent; s. of Bert Richards and Doris Richards; m. 1st Anita Pallenberg; two s. (one deceased) one d.; m. 2nd Patti Hansen 1983; two d.; ed Sidcup Art School; founder mem., The Rolling Stones 1962–; composer (with Mick Jagger) of numerous songs 1964–; Nordoff-Robbins Silver Clef 1982, Grammy Lifetime Achievement Award 1986, Ivor Novello Award for Outstanding Contribution to British Music 1991. *Films:* Sympathy for the Devil 1970, Gimme Shelter 1970, Ladies and Gentlemen, the Rolling Stones 1974, Let's Spend the Night Together 1983, Hail Hail Rock 'n' Roll 1987 (with Chuck Berry, Eric Clapton and Friends), Flashpoint 1991, Voodoo Lounge 1994, Pirates of the Caribbean: At World's End (actor) 2007, Shine a Light 2007. *Recordings include:* albums: with The Rolling Stones: The Rolling Stones 1964, The Rolling Stones No. 2 1965, Out Of Our Heads 1965, Aftermath 1966, Between The Buttons 1967, Their Satanic Majesties Request 1967, Beggar's Banquet 1968, Let It Bleed 1969, Get Yer Ya-Ya's Out 1969, Sticky Fingers 1971, Exile On Main Street 1972, Goat's Head Soup 1973, It's Only Rock And Roll 1974, Black And Blue 1976, Some Girls 1978, Emotional Rescue 1980, Tattoo You 1981, Still Life 1982, Undercover 1983, Dirty Work 1986, Steel Wheels 1989, Flashpoint 1991, Voodoo Lounge 1994, Stripped 1995, Bridges to Babylon 1997, Forty Licks 2002, Live Licks 2004, A Bigger Bang 2005; solo: Hail Hail Rock 'n' Roll (with Chuck Berry) 1987, Talk Is Cheap 1988, Live At The Hollywood Palladium 1991, Main Offender 1992. *Publication:* According to the Rolling Stones (autobiog., jtly) 2003. *Address:* Munro Sounds, 5 Wandsworth Plain, London, SW18 1ES, England (office). *Telephone:* (20) 8877-3111 (office). *Fax:* (20) 8877-3033 (office). *Website:* www.rollingstones.com; www.keithrichards.com.

RICHARDS, Peter, MA, MD, PhD, FRCP, FMedSci; British professor of medicine (retd); *Honourary Fellow, Hughes Hall, University of Cambridge;* b. 25 May 1936, London; s. of Dr William Richards and Barbara Taylor; m. 1st Anne Marie Larsen 1959 (divorced); one s. three d.; m. 2nd Carol Anne Seymour 1987; ed Monkton Combe School, Emmanuel Coll., Cambridge, St George's Hosp. Medical School and Royal Postgrad. Medical School; MRC Clinical Research Fellow and Tutor in Medicine, Royal Postgrad. Medical School 1964–67; Lecturer, St Mary's Hosp. Medical School 1967–70; Consultant Physician, NW Surrey Hosps 1970–73; Sr Lecturer and Consultant Physician, St George's Hosp. and Medical School 1973–79; Dean, St Mary's Hosp. Medical School 1979–95; Prof. and Hon. Consultant Physician, St Mary's Hosp. 1979–95; Pro-Rector (Medicine), Imperial Coll. of Science, Tech. and Medicine, London 1988–95; Medical Dir and Consultant Physician, Northwick Park and St Mark's NHS Trust 1995–99; Pres. Hughes Hall, Cambridge 1998–2006, now Hon. Fellow; Medical Adviser to Parl. Health Service Commr 1999–2001; mem. Gen. Medical Council (GMC) 1994, Deputy Chair. GMC Professional Conduct Cttee 1999–2001; Chair. Fulbright Award, Univ. of Calif., San Francisco 1990; Hon. Fellow, Emmanuel Coll., Cambridge 2002; Kt, Order of the White Rose of Finland 2001. *Achievements:* responsible (with Prof. Sir Eric Ash) for the introduction of medicine to Imperial Coll. *Publications:* The Medieval Leper 1977, Understanding Water, Electrolytes and Acid/Base Metabolism 1983, Learning Medicine 1983, Living Medicine 1990, Student's Guide to Entry to Medicine 1996, New Learning Medicine 1997; scientific papers on renal disease, metabolism, student selection and educ. *Leisure interests:* social history, music, cycling, mountain walking, Finland. *Address:* Hughes Hall, Cambridge, CB1 2EW, England (office). *Telephone:* (1223) 334890 (office). *Fax:* (1223) 311179 (office). *E-mail:* pr229@cam.ac.uk (office). *Website:* www.hughes.cam.ac.uk (office).

RICHARDS, Sir Rex Edward, Kt, DSc, FRS, FRSC; British chemist and university administrator (retd); b. 28 Oct. 1922, Colyton, Devon; s. of H. W.

Richards and E. N. Richards; m. Eva Edith Vago 1948; two d.; ed Colyton Grammar School, Devon, St John's Coll., Oxford; Fellow, Lincoln Coll., Oxford 1947–64; Dr Lee's Prof. of Chem., Oxford 1964–70; Fellow, Exeter Coll., Oxford 1964–69; Warden Merton Coll., Oxford 1969–84; Vice-Chancellor Univ. of Oxford 1977–81; Chancellor Univ. of Exeter 1982–98; Tilden Lecturer 1962; Research Fellow, Harvard Univ., USA 1955; Assoc. Fellow, Morse Coll., Yale, USA 1974–79; Chair. Oxford Enzyme Group 1969–83; Dir Oxford Instruments Group 1982–91; Dir Leverhulme Trust 1985–93; Pres. Royal Soc. of Chem. 1990–92; mem. Chem. Soc. Council 1957, 1988, Faraday Soc. Council 1963, Royal Soc. Council 1973–75, Advisory Bd for Research Councils 1980–82, Advisory Council for Applied Research and Devt 1984–87; Dir IBM United Kingdom Holdings, IBM (UK) 1978–82; Chair. British Postgraduate Medical Fed. 1986–93, Nat. Gallery Trust 1995–99; Trustee of CiBA Foundation 1978–97, Nat. Heritage Memorial Fund 1979–84, Tate Gallery 1982–88, 1991–93, Nat. Gallery 1982–93, Henry Moore Foundation 1989–2002 (Vice-Chair. 1993–94, Chair. 1994–2001); Commr Royal Comm. for Exhbn of 1851 1984–97; Foreign Assoc. Acad. des Sciences, Inst. de France 1995–; Hon. Fellow, St John's Coll., Lincoln Coll., Oxford 1968, Merton Coll., Oxford 1984, Thames Polytechnic 1991; Hon. FRCP 1987; Hon. FBA 1990; Hon. FRAM 1991; Hon. DSc (East Anglia) 1971, (Exeter) 1975, (Leicester) 1978, (Salford) 1979, (Edin.) 1981, (Leeds) 1984, (Birmingham) 1993, (London) 1994, (Oxford Brookes) 1998, (Warwick) 1999; Hon. DLitt (Dundee) 1977, (Kent) 1987; Hon. ScD (Cambridge) 1987; Corday-Morgan Medal, Chemical Soc. 1954, Davy Medal, Royal Soc. 1976, Award in Theoretical Chem. and Spectroscopy, Chemical Soc. 1977, Epic Award 1982, Medal of Honour, Bonn Univ. 1983, Royal Medal, Royal Soc. 1986, Pres.'s Medal, Soc. of Chemical Industry 1991. *Publications:* numerous contribs to scientific journals. *Leisure interests:* painting and sculpture. *Address:* Suite 4, West Heanton, Buckland Filleigh, Beaworthy, Devon, EX21 5PJ, England (home). *Telephone:* (1409) 821985 (home). *E-mail:* rex.richards@merton.ox.ac.uk (home).

RICHARDS, Simon Paul, BA, LLB, MEcon,; Dominican diplomatist and lawyer; b. 19 April 1937, Wesley; ed London Univ., Univ. of the West Indies and City Univ. of New York; Asst Master Dominica Grammar School 1958–60, Sr Master 1963–66; caseworker City of New York Dept of Social Services 1967–74; admitted to Bar of England and Wales 1975, of the State of NY 1977, of US Dist Courts for Southern and Eastern Dists of NY 1978, of Dominica 1980; practised law in New York 1977–, currently a sr trial attorney in pvt. practice; Counsellor, Deputy Perm. Rep. and Chargé d'Affaires Perm. Mission of Dominica to the UN at various times 1982–95, Perm. Rep. 1995–2002. *Address:* c/o Ministry of Foreign Affairs, Government Headquarters, Kennedy Avenue, Roseau, Dominica (office).

RICHARDSON, George Barclay, CBE, MA; British economist and publisher (retd); b. 19 Sept. 1924, London; s. of George Richardson and Christina Richardson; m. Isabel A. Chalk 1957 (divorced 1999); two s.; ed Aberdeen Cen. Secondary School and other schools in Scotland, Univ. of Aberdeen and Corpus Christi Coll., Oxford; Admiralty Scientific Research Dept 1944; Lt RNVR 1945; Intelligence Officer, HQ Intelligence Div., British Army of the Rhine 1946–47; Third Sec. HM Foreign Service 1949; student, Nuffield Coll., Oxford 1950; Fellow, St John's Coll. Oxford 1951–88; Univ. Reader in Econs, Univ. of Oxford 1969–73; Warden, Keble Coll. Oxford 1989–94; Pro-Vice-Chancellor, Univ. of Oxford 1988–94; Del. Oxford Univ. Pres. 1971–74, Chief Exec. 1974–88; mem. Econ. Devt Cttee for Electrical Eng Industry 1964–73, Monopolies Comm. 1969–74, Royal Comm. on Environmental Pollution 1973–74; Econ. Adviser, UKAEA 1968–74; mem. Council, Publishers' Asscn 1981–87; Hon. DCL (Oxford); Hon. LLD (Aberdeen). *Publications:* Information and Investment 1960, 1991, Economic Theory 1964, The Economics of Imperfect Knowledge 1998; articles in academic journals. *Leisure interests:* reading, music, swimming. *Address:* 33 Belsyre Court, Observatory Street, Oxford, OX2 6HU, England (home). *Telephone:* (1865) 510113 (home). *Fax:* (1865) 510113 (home). *E-mail:* george.richardson@keble.oxford.ac.uk.

RICHARDSON, George Taylor, CM, OM, BComm, LLD; Canadian business executive (retd); b. 22 Sept. 1924, Winnipeg, Manitoba; s. of the late James A. Richardson and Muriel Richardson (née Sprague); m. Tannis Maree Thorlakson 1948; two s. one d.; ed Grosvenor and Ravenscourt Schools, Winnipeg and Univ. of Manitoba; joined family firm of James Richardson & Sons, Ltd (grain trader), Winnipeg 1946, Vice-Pres. 1954, Pres. 1966–93, Chair. 1993–2000 (retd), Hon. Chair. and Dir Emer. 2000–; fmr mem. Bd of Dirs Dupont Canada Inc., Canada Packers Inc., Inco Ltd., Tundra Oil & Gas Ltd; fmr Vice-Pres. Canadian Imperial Bank of Commerce; fmr Chair. Great-West Life Assurance Co.; fmr Gov (first Canadian-born) Hudson's Bay Co.; fmr mem. Bd of Govs Univ. of Manitoba (Chair. 1960–64); Patron, Western Canada Aviation Museum; Hon. Dir Canada Aviation Hall of Fame; Hon. LLD (Manitoba, Winnipeg). *Leisure interests:* hunting, helicopter flying. *Address:* James Richardson & Sons Ltd, Richardson Building, 1 Lombard Place, Winnipeg, Manitoba, R3B 0Y1 (office); Briarmeade, 850 PR 200, St Germain South, MB R5A IE8, Canada (home). *Telephone:* (204) 953-7944 (office); (204) 253-4221 (home). *Fax:* (204) 942-6339 (office); (204) 255-4208 (home). *E-mail:* george.richardson@jrsl.ca (office).

RICHARDSON, Graham; Australian politician, broadcaster and journalist; b. 27 Sept. 1949, Kogarah, Sydney; s. of Frederick James Richardson and Catherine Maud Richardson; m. Cheryl Gardener 1973; one s. one d.; ed Marist Brothers Coll., Kogarah; state organizer Australian Labor Party, NSW 1971–76, Gen. Sec. 1976–94, State Campaign Dir 1976; Vice-Pres. Nat. Labor Party 1976, Del. to Nat. Conf. 1977–94, convenor Nat. Industrial Platform Cttee; Senator for NSW 1983–94; Minister for the Environment and the Arts 1987–90, for Sports, Tourism and Territories 1988–90, for Social Security 1990, of Transport and Communications 1991–92, of Health 1993–94; political commentator on election coverage and journalist, The Nine Network 1994–; journalist, The Bulletin 1994–; fmr Chair. Senate Estimates Cttee 1986, Senate Select Cttee on TV Equalization; mem. several senate cttees and three ministerial cttees; fmr mem. Bd Sydney Organizing Cttee for the Olympic Games. *Leisure interests:* golf, reading, skiing, tennis. *Address:* Macquarie Radio Network, Level 8, 368 Sussex Street, Sydney, NSW 2000 (office); 24 Artarmon Road, Willoughby, NSW 2028, Australia.

RICHARDSON, Joely; British actress; b. 9 Jan. 1965, London; d. of the late Tony Richardson and of Vanessa Redgrave (q.v.); m. Tim Bevan 1992 (divorced); one d.; ed Lycée Français de Londres, St Paul's Girls' School, London, Pinellas Park High School, Fla, The Thacher School, Ojai, Calif. and Royal Acad. of Dramatic Art. *Plays include:* Steel Magnolias 1989, Lady Windermere's Fan 2002. *Films include:* The Charge of the Light Brigade (uncredited) 1968, The Hotel New Hampshire 1984, Wetherby 1985, Drowning by Numbers 1988, A proposito di quella strana ragazza (About That Foreign Girl) 1989, King Ralph 1991, Shining Through 1992, Rebecca's Daughters 1992, I'll Do Anything 1994, Sister, My Sister 1995, Believe Me 1995, Loch Ness 1996, Hollow Reed 1996, 101 Dalmatians 1996, Event Horizon 1997, Wrestling with Alligators 1998, Under Heaven 1998, Toy Boys 1999, Return to Me 2000, Maybe Baby 2000, The Patriot 2000, The Affair of the Necklace 2001, Shoreditch 2003, The Fever 2004, The Last Mimzy 2007. *Television appearances include:* Body Contact 1987, Behaving Badly 1989, Heading Home 1991, Lady Chatterley's Lover 1993, The Tribe 1998, The Echo 1998, Nip/Tuck (series) 2003–06, Fallen Angel 2003, Lies My Mother Told Me 2005, Wallis & Edward 2005, Fatal Contact: Bird Flu in America 2006. *Address:* c/o Finch and Partners, First Floor, 6 Heddon Street, London, W1B 4B (office); c/o ICM London, 4-6 Soho Square, London, W1D 3PZ, England (office). *Telephone:* (20) 7851-7140 (office); (20) 7432-0800 (ICM) (office). *Fax:* (20) 7287-6420 (office). *Website:* www.finchandpartners.com (office); www.icmtalent.com (office).

RICHARDSON, Keith, MA; British writer, administrator and fmr journalist; *Trustee, Friends of Europe;* b. 14 June 1936, Wakefield, Yorks.; s. of Gilbert Richardson and Ellen Richardson; m. Sheila Carter 1958; three d.; ed Wakefield Grammar School, Univ. Coll., Oxford; feature writer, The Financial Times 1960–63; Industrial Ed. and European Corresp. The Sunday Times 1964–68, 1970–83; Production Man. GKN 1969–70; Head of Group Public Affairs, BAT Industries 1983–88; Sec.-Gen. The European Round Table of Industrialists 1988–98; Trustee, Friends of Europe. *Publications:* Monopolies and Mergers 1963, Do it the Hard Way 1971, Daggers in the Forum 1978, Reshaping Europe 1991, Beating the Crisis 1993, Europe Made Simple 1998. *Leisure interest:* mountaineering. *Address:* c/o Friends of Europe, La Maison de l'Europe at the Bibliotheque Solvay, Leipoldpark, 137 Rue Belliard, 1040 Brussels, Belgium (office). *Telephone:* (2) 737-91-45 (office). *Fax:* (2) 738-75-97 (office). *E-mail:* info@friendsofeurope.org (office). *Website:* www.friendsofeurope.org (office).

RICHARDSON, Miranda; British actress; b. 3 March 1958, Southport, Lancs.; d. of William Alan Richardson and Marian Georgina Richardson (née Townsend); ed Old Vic Theatre School, Bristol. *Theatre appearances include:* Moving 1980–81, All My Sons, Who's Afraid of Virginia Woolf?, The Life of Einstein, A Lie of the Mind 1987, The Changeling, Mountain Language 1988, Etta Jenks, The Designated Mourner 1996, Aunt Dan and Lemon 1999. *Film appearances:* Dance with a Stranger (debut 1985; Best Actress Award, Evening Standard), The Innocent, Empire of the Sun, The Mad Monkey, Eat the Rich, Twisted Obsession, The Bachelor 1992, Enchanted April 1992 (Golden Globe Award for Best Comedy Actress 1993), The Crying Game 1992, Damage (BAFTA Award for Best Supporting Actress 1993), Tom and Viv 1994, La Nuit et Le Moment 1994, Kansas City, Swann 1995, Evening Star 1996, The Designated Mourner 1996, The Apostle 1996, All For Love, Jacob Two Two and the Hooded Fang 1998, The Big Brass Ring 1998, Sleepy Hollow 1999, Blackadder Back and Forth 1999, Chicken Run (voice) 2000, Get Carter 2000, The Hours 2001, Spider 2002, The Hours 2002, The Actors 2003, The Rage in Placid Lake 2003, Falling Angels 2003, The Prince and Me 2004, Churchill: The Hollywood Years 2004, The Phantom of the Opera 2004, Wah-Wah 2005, Harry Potter and the Goblet of Fire 2005, Merlin's Apprentice 2005, Starry Night 2005, Wah-Wah 2005, Provoked 2006, Paris, je t'aime 2006, Southland Tales 2006, Spinning into Butter 2007, Puffball 2007, Fred Claus 2007. *Television appearances include:* The Hard Word, Sorrel and Son, A Woman of Substance, After Pilkington 1987, Underworld, Death of the Heart, Blackadder II 1985, Blackadder the Third 1987, Blackadder Goes Forth 1989, Die Kinder (mini-series) 1990, Sweet as You Are (Royal TV Soc.'s Best Actress Award), Fatherland (Golden Globe Award), Saint X 1995, Magic Animals, Dance to the Music of Time 1997, The Scold's Bridle, Merlin 1997, Alice 1998, Ted and Ralph 1998, The Miracle Maker (voice) 2000, Snow White 2001, The Lost Prince 2003, Gideon's Daughter 2006, Final Chance to Save 2006, The Life and Times of Vivienne Vyle 2007. *Leisure interests:* gardening, junkshops, music, occasional art, reading, softball, walking. *Address:* c/o ICM, Oxford House, 76 Oxford Street, London, W1D 1BS, England (office). *Telephone:* (20) 7636-6565 (office). *Fax:* (20) 7323-0101 (office). *Website:* www.icmtalent.com (office).

RICHARDSON, Peter Damian, BSc, DSc, PhD, FRS, FCGI, DIC; British mechanical engineer, physiologist and academic; *Professor of Engineering and Physiology, Brown University;* b. 22 Aug. 1935, West Wickham; s. of the late Reginald W. Richardson and Marie S. Richardson; one d.; ed Imperial Coll. London, Brown Univ., USA; demonstrator Dept of Mechanical Eng, Imperial Coll. 1955–58; went to USA 1958; Visiting Lecturer Brown Univ. 1958–59, Research Assoc. 1959–60, Asst Prof. of Eng 1960–65, Assoc. Prof. 1965–68, Prof. 1968–84, Prof. of Eng and Physiology 1984–, Chair. Univ. Faculty 1987–; Chair. Exec. Cttee Center Biomedical Eng 1972–; Consultant to Industry US Govt Agencies; Fellow, ASME, Life Fellow 2001; mem. American Soc. of

Artificial Internal Organs; Founding Fellow, American Inst. of Medical and Biological Eng 1991; Fellow of the City and Guilds of London Inst. 2003; Inaugural Fellow, Biomedical Eng Soc. 2005;; Sr Scientist Award, Alexander Von Humboldt Foundation 1976, Laureate in Medicine, Ernst Jung Foundation 1987. *Publications:* Principles of Cell Adhesion (with M. Steiner) 1995; contribs to many professional journals. *Leisure interests:* country life. *Address:* Division of Engineering and Department of Molecular Pharmacology, Physiology and Biotechnology, Box D, Brown University, Providence, RI 02912-9104, USA. *Telephone:* (401) 863-2687.

RICHARDSON, Robert Coleman II, BS, MS, PhD; American academic and physicist; *F.R. Newman Professor of Physics, Cornell University;* b. 26 June 1937, Washington, DC; s. of Robert Franklin Richardson and Lois (Price) Richardson; m. Betty Marilyn McCarthy 1962; two d.; ed Virginia Polytechnic Inst. and State Univ., Duke Univ.; served in US Army 1959–60; Research Assoc., Cornell Univ., Ithaca, NY 1966–67, Asst Prof. 1968–71, Assoc. Prof. 1972–74, Prof. 1975–87, F.R. Newman Prof. of Physics 1987–, Sr Vice Provost for Research 1998–, Dir of Lab. of Atomic and Solid State Physics 1990–97; Chair. Int. Union Pure and Applied Physics Comm. (C-5) 1981–84; mem. Nat. Science Bd 1998–2004, mem. Exec. Cttee 2000–04; mem. Bd of Dirs AAAS 2000–04; mem. Bd of Dirs Brookhaven Science Assocs 1998–, Associated Univs Inc. 2005–; mem. NAS 1986–, Bd Assessment Nat. Bureau of Standards 1983–; mem. Editorial Bd Journal of Low Temperature Physics 1984–; Foreign mem. Finnish Acad. of Science and Letters 1993; Fellow, AAAS 1981, American Physical Soc. 1983, American Acad. of Arts and Sciences 1995; mem. NAS; mem. Bd of Trustees Duke Univ., mem. Exec. Cttee 2001–; Guggenheim Fellow 1975, 1983; Dr hc (Ohio State Univ.) 2000; Simon Memorial Prize (jtly), British Physical Soc. 1976, Oliver E. Buckley Prize (jtly) 1981, Nobel Prize for Physics (jtly) 1996, Distinguished Grad. School Alumnis Award, Virginia Polytechnic Inst. and State Univ. 2003. *Publications include:* more than 95 articles in scientific journals. *Leisure interests:* photography, gardening. *Address:* Senior Vice Provost for Research, 222 Day Hall, Cornell University, Ithaca, NY 14853, USA (office). *Telephone:* (607) 255-7200 (office). *Fax:* (607) 255-9030 (office). *E-mail:* rcr2@cornell.edu (office). *Website:* www.lassp.cornell.edu/lassp_data/rcr.html (office).

RICHARDSON, Hon. Ruth, LLB; New Zealand politician, economic consultant and company director; b. 13 Dec. 1950, Wanganui; d. of Ross Pearce Richardson and Rita Joan Richardson; m. Andrew Evan Wright 1975; one s. one d.; ed Canterbury Univ., NZ; fmr Legal Adviser, Federated Farmers; Nat. Party MP for Selwyn 1981–94; Shadow Minister for Finance 1987; Minister of Finance 1990–93; consultant Ruth Richardson (NZ) Ltd 1994–; Dir Reserve Bank of NZ 1999–2004; Chair. Kula Fund 1997–, Jade Corpn 2000–; mem. Bd of Dirs Centre for Ind. Studies 1999–, LECG Corporation 2003–. *Publications:* Making a Difference 1995. *Leisure interests:* gardening, running, swimming. *Address:* Newtons Road, RD5, Christchurch, New Zealand (office). *Telephone:* (3) 347-9146 (office). *Fax:* (3) 347-9136 (office). *E-mail:* ruth@rrnz.co.nz (office). *Website:* www.rrnz.com.

RICHARDSON, Sir Tom, KCMG, MA; British diplomatist; b. 6 Feb. 1941, Manchester; s. of Arthur Legh Turnour Richardson and Penelope Margaret Richardson (née Waithman); m. Alexandra Frazier Wasiqullah (née Ratcliff) 1979; ed Westminster School, Christ Church, Oxford; postings in Ghana, Tanzania, FCO, Milan, New York; Cen. Policy Review Staff 1980–81; Counsellor, Embassy, Rome 1982–86; Head Econ. Relations Dept, FCO 1986–89; Deputy Perm. Rep. to UN 1989–94; Deputy Political Dir FCO 1994–96; Amb. to Italy 1996–2000; Chair. Governing Body, British Inst. of Florence 2003–08; Pres. British–Italian Soc. 2007–; mem. Council, British School of Rome 2002–06; Trustee Monte San Martino Trust 2003–. *Leisure interests:* reading, music, walking, Italy.

RICHARDSON, William (Bill) Blaine, MA; American politician, diplomatist and state official; *Governor of New Mexico;* b. 15 Nov. 1947, Pasadena, Calif.; m. Barbara Flavin 1972; ed Tufts Univ., Fletcher School of Law and Diplomacy; staff mem., US House of Reps. 1971–72, Dept of State 1973–75, US Senate Foreign Relations Cttee 1975–78; Exec. Dir NM State Democratic Cttee 1978, Bernalillo Co. Democratic Cttee 1978; business exec. in Santa Fe 1978–82; mem. US House of Reps from 3rd Dist NM 1982–97; Perm. Rep. to UN, New York 1997–98; US Sec. of Energy 1998–2001; Sr Man. Dir Kissinger McLarty Assocs 2001; Adjunct Prof. of Public Policy, Harvard Univ. 2001; Gov. of NM 2003–; unsuccessful cand. for Democratic party nomination for US Pres. 2007; nominated as US Sec. of Commerce 2008, requested that nomination be withdrawn Jan. 2009; fmr mem. NATO 2000 Bd. *Address:* Office of the Governor, 490 Old Santa Fe Trail, Room 400, Santa Fe, NM 87501, USA (office). *Telephone:* (505) 476-2200 (office). *Website:* www.governor.state.nm.us (office).

RICHARDSON, William Chase, MBA, PhD; American university administrator and foundation executive; b. 11 May 1940, Passaic, NJ; s. of Henry B. Richardson and Frances Richardson (née Chase); m. Nancy Freeland 1966; two d.; ed Trinity Coll., Hartford, Conn. and Univ. of Chicago; Research Assoc. and Instructor, Univ. of Chicago 1967–70; Asst Prof., Univ. of Washington, School of Public Health and Community Medicine 1971–73, Assoc. Prof. 1973–76, Prof. of Health Services 1976–84, Chair. Dept of Health Services 1973–76, Graduate Dean, Vice-Provost for Research, 1981–84; Exec. Vice-Pres., Provost and Prof. Dept of Family and Community Medicine, Pennsylvania State Univ. 1984–90; Pres. Johns Hopkins Univ. 1990–95, Pres. Emer. 1995–, Prof., Dept of Health Policy Man. 1990–95, Prof. Emer. 1995–; Pres. and CEO W.K. Kellogg Foundation, Battle Creek, Mich. 1995–2005; mem. Inst. of Medicine, NAS, American Acad. of Arts and Sciences; Fellow, American Public Health Asscn; Kellogg Fellow; mem. Bd of Dirs Exelon Corpn 2005–, CSX Corpn, Bank of NY (now Bank of New York Mellon Corpn); Dr hc (Univ. of Michigan) 2006; Trinity Whitlock Award, Mary H. Bachmeyer Award, Univ. of Chicago. *Publications:* numerous articles in professional journals. *Address:* c/o W.K. Kellogg Foundation, One Michigan Avenue East, Battle Creek, MI 49017-4058, USA (office).

RICHARDSON OF DUNTISBOURNE, Baron (Life Peer), cr. 1983, of Duntisbourne in the County of Gloucestershire; **Gordon William Humphreys Richardson,** KG, PC, MBE, TD; British banker; b. 25 Nov. 1915, London; s. of John Robert and Nellie Richardson (née Humphreys); m. Margaret Alison Sheppard 1941; one s. one d.; ed Nottingham High School and Gonville and Caius Coll., Cambridge; S. Notts. Hussars Yeomanry 1939, Staff Coll., Camberley 1941; called to the Bar, Gray's Inn 1947; mem. Bar Council 1951–55; Industrial and Commercial Finance Corpn Ltd 1955–57; Dir J. Henry Schroder and Co. 1957–62; Chair. J. Henry Schroder Wagg and Co. Ltd 1962–72; Chair. Schroders Ltd 1965–73, J. Henry Schroder Banking Corpn (USA) 1967–69, Schroders AG (Switzerland) 1967, Schroders Inc. (USA) 1969–73; Dir Bank of England 1967–73, Gov. 1973–83; Dir BIS 1973–93, Vice-Chair. 1985–88, 1991–93; Chair. Cttee on Turnover Taxation 1963–64; Vice-Chair. Legal and Gen. Assurance Soc. Ltd 1959–70, Lloyds Bank Ltd 1962–66; Vice-Chair. Chase Manhattan Int. Advisory Council 1996–2000; Dir Rolls-Royce (1971) Ltd 1971–73, ICI 1972–73; mem. Int. Advisory Bd Chemical Bank 1986–96, Chair. 1986–96; Chair. Morgan Stanley Int. Inc. 1986–96; mem. Co. Law Amendment Cttee 1959–62; mem. Court, London Univ. 1962–65; mem. Nat. Econ. Devt Council 1971–73, 1980–83; Chair. Industrial Devt Advisory Bd 1972–73, 'Group of Ten' 1982–83, 'Group of Thirty' 1985–91, Hon. Chair. 'Group of Thirty' 1991–; Dir Glyndebourne Arts Trust 1982–88, Royal Opera House 1983–88; Chair. Pilgrim Trust 1984–89; Hon. Master of Bench of Gray's Inn 1973; one of HM Lts for City of London 1974; High Steward of Westminster Cathedral 1985–89; Deputy High Steward, Univ. of Cambridge 1982–; Deputy Lt for Glos. 1983–; Hon. Fellow, Wolfson Coll. and Gonville and Caius Coll., Cambridge Univ.; Hon. DSc (The City Univ.) 1975, (Univ. of Aston in Birmingham) 1979, Hon. LLD (Cambridge) 1979, Hon. DCL (East Anglia) 1984; Benjamin Franklin Medal, RSA 1984. *Address:* House of Lords, London, SW1A 0PW; 25 St Anselm's Place, London, W1K 5AF, England. *Telephone:* (20) 7219-5353 (House of Lords); (20) 7629-4448.

RICHIE, Lionel, BS (Econs); American singer, songwriter and musician; b. 20 June 1949, Tuskegee, AL; m. Diane Alexander 1996; ed Tuskegee Univ.; mem. The Commodores 1968–82; various tours, concerts; solo artist 1982–; ASCAP Songwriter Awards 1979, 1984–96, numerous American Music Awards 1979–, Grammy Awards include: Best Pop Vocal Performance 1982, Album of the Year 1985, Producer of the Year (shared) 1986; Lionel Richie Day, Los Angeles 1983, two Nat. Asscn. for the Advancement of Colored People (NAACP) Image Awards 1983, NAACP Entertainer of the Year 1987, Acad. Award for Best Song 1986, Golden Globe Award for Best Song 1986. *Compositions include:* with The Commodores: Sweet Love 1975, Just To Be Close To You 1976, Easy 1977, Three Times A Lady 1979, Sail On 1980, Still 1980, Oh No 1981; for Kenny Rogers: Lady 1981; for Diana Ross: Missing You 1984; solo hits: Endless Love, film theme duet with Diana Ross 1981, Truly 1982, All Night Long 1983, Running With The Night 1984, Hello 1984, Stuck On You 1984, Penny Lover (with Brenda Harvey) 1984, Say You Say Me 1986, Dancing On The Ceiling 1987, Love Will Conquer All 1987, Ballerina Girl 1987, My Destiny 1992, Don't Wanna Lose You 1996; contrib. We are the World (with Michael Jackson), USA for Africa 1985. *Recordings include:* albums: with The Commodores: Machine Gun 1974, Caught In The Act 1975, Movin' On 1975, Hot On The Tracks 1976, Commodores 1977, Commodores Live! 1977, Natural High 1978, Greatest Hits 1978, Midnight Magic 1979, Heroes 1980, In The Pocket 1981; solo: Lionel Richie 1982, Can't Slow Down 1983, Dancing On The Ceiling 1986, Back To Front 1992, Louder Than Words 1996, Time 1998, Encore 2002, Coming Home 2006, Just Go 2009. *Address:* John Reid Management, 505 South Beverly Drive, Suite 1192, Beverly Hills, CA 90212 (office); c/o Island Records, 825 Eighth Avenue, New York, NY 10019, USA (office). *Website:* www6.islandrecords.com/site/artist_home.php?artist_id=342 (office).

RICHMOND, Sir Mark Henry, Kt, ScD, FRS; British academic and scientist; *Member of Staff, School of Public Policy, University College London;* b. 1 Feb. 1931, Sydney, Australia; s. of Harold Sylvester Richmond and Dorothy Plaistowe Tegg; m. 1st Shirley Jean Townrow 1958 (divorced); one s. one d. (and one d. deceased); m. 2nd Sheila Travers 2000; ed Epsom Coll., Clare Coll., Univ. of Cambridge; mem. scientific staff, Medical Research Council 1958–65; Reader in Molecular Biology, Univ. of Edin. 1965–68; Prof. of Bacteriology, Univ. of Bristol 1968–81; Vice-Chancellor and Prof. of Molecular Bacteriology, Victoria Univ. of Manchester 1981–90; mem. Public Health Laboratory Service Bd 1976–85; Chair. Cttee of Vice-Chancellors and Prins of the UK 1987–89, Microbiological Food Safety Cttee 1989–90, Science and Eng Research Council 1990–94; Group Head of Research, Glaxo 1993–95, Science Adviser 1995–96; mem. staff School of Public Policy, Univ. Coll. London 1996–; mem. Int. Science Advisory Cttee, UNESCO 1996–2001; mem. and fmr mem. numerous bds; Robert Koch Award 1977. *Publications:* numerous scientific articles. *Leisure interests:* gardening, hill walking, opera. *Address:* School of Public Policy, The Rubin Building, University College London, 29 Tavistock Square, London, WC1H 9QU, England (office). *Telephone:* (20) 7679-4968 (office). *Fax:* (20) 7679-4969 (office). *E-mail:* m.richmond@ucl.ac.uk (office). *Website:* www.ucl.ac.uk/spp (office).

RICHTER, Burton, PhD; American physicist and academic; *Senior Fellow, Freeman Spogli Institute for International Studies, Stanford University;* b. 22 March 1931, Brooklyn, New York; s. of Abraham Richter and Fannie (Pollack) Richter; m. Laurose Becker 1960; one s. one d.; ed Massachusetts Inst. of Tech.; joined Stanford Univ. 1956, Research Assoc. in Physics, High Energy Physics Lab., Stanford Univ. 1956–59; mem. group building first electron storage ring and conducting a colliding beam experiment extending validity of quantum electrodynamics; Asst Prof., Stanford Univ. 1959–63, Assoc. Prof. 1963–67, Prof. 1967–2006, Paul Pigott Prof. in Physical Sciences 1980–2006, Sr Fellow, Freeman Spogli Inst. for Int. Studies 2005–; worked at Stanford Linear Accelerator Center (SLAC) 1963–99, Tech. Dir 1982–84, Dir 1984–99, Dir Emer. 1999–2006; est. group that built a high-energy electron positron machine (SPEAR) and has continued to develop new accelerator and detector techniques including most recently the SLAC linear collider; fmr Pres. IUPAP; fmr mem. Bd of Dirs Varian Assocs, AREVA; mem. Bd of Dirs Litel Instruments; mem. Visiting Cttee Commissairat à l'Energie Atomique; sabbatical year at CERN, Geneva 1975–76; Loeb Lecturer, Harvard Univ. 1974, DeShalit Lecturer, Weizmann Inst. 1975; mem. NAS 1977; Fellow, American Acad. of Arts and Sciences 1989, American Physical Soc. (Pres. 1994), AAAS; E. O. Lawrence Medal 1976, Nobel Prize for Physics (jtly with Samuel Ting q.v.) for discovery of the heavy, long-lived 'psi' particle 1976. *Publications:* more than 300 articles in various scientific journals 1963–89. *Address:* Stanford Linear Accelerator Center, 2575 Sand Hill Road, Menlo Park, CA 94025, USA (office). *Telephone:* (650) 926-2601 (office). *E-mail:* brichter@slac.stanford.edu (office). *Website:* www-group.slac.stanford.edu/do/people/richter.html (office).

RICHTER, Gerhard; German artist; b. 9 Feb. 1932, Dresden; s. of Horst Richter and Hildegard Richter; m. 1st Marianne Richter (née Eufinger); m. 2nd Isa Richter (née Genzken) 1982; m. 3rd Sabine Richter (née Moritz) 1995; one s. two d.; ed Staatliche Kunstakademien Dresden and Düsseldorf; emigrated to West Germany 1961; Visiting Prof. Kunstakademie Hamburg 1967, Coll. of Art, Halifax, Canada 1978; Prof. Staatliche Kunstakademie Düsseldorf 1971–; mem. Akad. der Künste, Berlin; one-man shows in galleries and museums all over world 1964–; paintings in public collections in Berlin, Cologne, Basle, Paris, New York, Chicago, Toronto, London, etc.; mem. Acad. of Arts, Berlin; Dr hc (Université catholique de Louvain-la-Neuve, Belgium) 2001; Kunstpreis Junger Westen 1966, Arnold Bode Preis 1981, Oskar Kokoschka Prize (Austria) 1985, Wolf Prize 1994–95, Venice Biennial Art Festival Jury Prize 1997, Praemium Imperiale, Japan 1997, Wexner Prize 1998, Nordrhein-Westfalen State Prize 2000. *Address:* Osterrietweg 22, 50996 Cologne, Germany; c/o Marian Goodman, 24 West 57th Street, New York, NY 10019, USA. *Website:* www.gerhard-richter.com.

RICHTER, Horst-Eberhard, MD, DPhil; German psychiatrist and academic; *Honorary Director, Centre for Psychosomatics, University of Giessen;* b. 28 April 1923, Berlin; s. of Otto Richter and Charlotte Richter; m. Bergrun Luckow 1947; one s. two d.; ed Berlin Univ.; Dir Advisory and Research Centre for Childhood Emotional Disturbances, Wedding Children's Hosp., Berlin 1952–62; Physician, Psychiatric Clinic, W Berlin Free Univ. 1955–62; Dir Berlin Psychoanalytic Inst. 1959–62; Chief of Dept of Psychosomatic Medicine, Univ. of Giessen 1962–, Dir Centre for Psychosomatics 1973, now Hon. Dir; Dir Sigmund-Freud Inst, Frankfurt am Main 1992–2002; mem. PEN, Germany; Hon. citizen, city of Giessen 2007; Research Prize, Swiss Soc. of Psychosomatic Medicine 1970, Theodor-Heuss Prize 1980, Goethe-Plakette der Stadt Frankfurt 2002, Morehouse Coll., Atlanta Gandhi King Ikeda Award 2003, Hon. Medal for Medicine, Univ. Giessen 400th anniversary 2007, German Medical Profession Paracelsus Medal 2008. *Publications:* Eltern, Kind und Neurose 1963, Herzneurose (with D. Beckmann) 1969, Patient Familie 1970, Giessen-Test (with D. Beckmann) 1972, Die Gruppe 1972, Lernziel Solidarität 1974, The Family as Patient 1974, Flüchten oder Standhalten 1976, Der Gotteskomplex 1979, Alle redeten vom Frieden 1981, Sich der Krise stellen 1981, Zur Psychologie des Friedens 1982, Die Chance des Gewissens 1986, Leben statt Machen 1987, Die hohe Kunst der Korruption 1989, Russen und Deutsche 1990, Umgang mit Angst 1992, Wer nicht leiden will, muss hassen 1993, Psychoanalyse und Politik 1995, Als Einstein nicht mehr weiterwusste 1997, Wanderer zwischen den Fronten 2000, Das Ende der Egomanie 2002, Ist eine andere Welt möglich? Für eine solidarische Globalisierung 2003, Die Krise der Männlichkeit in der unerwachsenen Gesellschaft 2006, Die seelische Krankheit Friedlosigkeit ist heilbar 2008. *Address:* Friedrichstrasse 28, 35392 Giessen, Germany (office). *Telephone:* (641) 9945625 (office). *Fax:* (641) 74350 (office). *E-mail:* h.e.richter@t-online.de (office).

RICHTHOFEN, Hermann, Freiherr von, DJur; German diplomatist; b. 20 Nov. 1933, Breslau; s. of Herbert Freiherr von Richthofen and Gisela Freifrau von Richthofen (née Schoeller); m. Christa Gräfin von Schwerin 1966; one s. two d.; joined diplomatic service 1963; served Saigon and Djakarta; Head of Dept Perm. Rep. Office of FRG for GDR 1975–78; Dir German and Berlin Dept Ministry of Foreign Affairs 1978–80; Dir Working Party on German Policy, Fed. Chancellery 1980–86; Dir Gen. Legal Dept Ministry of Foreign Affairs 1986, Political Dept 1986–88; Amb. to UK 1988–93; Perm. Rep. to NATO 1993–98; Trustee 21st Century Trust, London; Gov. Ditchley Foundation; Hon. Prof., Cen. Connecticut State Univ., hon. mem. Deutsch-Britische Gesellschaft, Berlin; Officer's Cross Order of Kts of Malta, Commdr's Cross Order of Merit (Italy), Commdr, Légion d'honneur, Grand Officer's Cross Order of Infante D. Henrique (Portugal), Grand Cross Order of Merit (Luxemburg), Kt Commdr's Cross 2nd Class (Austria), Hon. GCVO, Grand Cross Order of Merit (Germany), Commdr's Cross Order of Merit (Poland) 2003; Hon. LLD (Birmingham). *Leisure interests:* literature, history, arts, music. *Address:* Beckerstrasse 6A, 12157 Berlin, Germany (home).

RICKE, Kai-Uwe; German telecommunications executive; *Member, Supervisory Board, Kabel Baden-Württemberg GmbH & Co. KG;* b. Oct. 1961, Krefeld; ed European Business School, Schloss Reichartshausen, Germany; began career as asst to Bd of Bertelsmann, Guetersloh, later Head of Sales and Marketing, Scandinavian Club (subsidiary); CEO Talkline and Talkline PS Phone Service, Elmshorn 1990–95, Chair. and CEO 1995–98; Chair. Bd Man. DeTeMobil Deutsche Telekom Mobilnet (now T-Mobile Deutschland) 1998–2000, Chair. T-Mobile Int. 2000–01, COO and mem. Bd of Man. Deutsche Telekom AG 2001, Chair. Bd of Man. and CEO 2002–06 (resgnd); mem. Supervisory Bd Kabel Baden-Württemberg GmbH & Co. KG, Heidelberg 2007–. *Address:* Supervisory Board, Kabel Baden-Württemberg GmbH & Co. KG, m Breitspiel 2-4, 69126 Heidelberg, Germany (office). *Telephone:* (6221) 3330 (office). *Website:* www.kabelbw.de (office).

RICKETTS, Sir Peter, KCMG, BA; British diplomatist; *Permanent Under-Secretary and Head of Diplomatic Service;* b. 30 Sept. 1952; m.; two c.; ed Univ. of Oxford; entered FCO 1974; with Mission in New York, USA 1974–75; Desk Officer, Cen. and Southern Africa Dept 1975–76; Third then Second Sec., Embassy in Singapore 1976–78; Second then First Sec., Del. to NATO, Brussels 1978–81; Desk Officer, Near East and N Africa Dept 1982–83; Asst Pvt. Sec., Office of Sec. of State 1983–86; First Sec., Chancery, Embassy in Washington, DC 1986–89; Deputy Head of Security Policy Dept 1989–91; Head, Hong Kong Dept 1991–94; Counsellor, EC and Finance, Embassy in Paris 1994–97; Deputy Political Dir 1997–99; Dir for Int. Security 1999–2000; Chair. Jt Intelligence Cttee and Intelligence Coordinator, Cabinet Office 2000–01; Dir-Gen. (Political) FCO 2001–03, Perm. Rep. to NATO, Brussels 2003–06, Perm. Under-Sec. and Head of Diplomatic Service 2006–. *Address:* Foreign and Commonwealth Office, King Charles Street, London, SW1A 2AH, England (office). *Telephone:* (20) 7008-2150 (office). *E-mail:* PUS.Action@fco.gov.uk (office). *Website:* www.fco.gov.uk (office).

RICKMAN, Alan; British actor; b. 21 Feb. 1946, London; ed Chelsea Coll. of Art, Royal Coll. of Art and Royal Acad. of Dramatic Art (RADA); repertory theatre in Manchester, Leicester, Sheffield and Glasgow; spent two seasons with RSC at Stratford; later appeared at Bush Theatre, Hampstead and Royal Court Theatre; Time Out Award 1991, Evening Standard Film Actor of the Year 1991, BAFTA Award 1991, Golden Globe Award 1996, Emmy Award 1996, Variety Club Award 2002. *Stage appearances include:* Les Liaisons Dangereuses (RSC Stratford, London and Broadway), The Lucky Chance, The Seagull (Royal Court), Tango at the End of Winter (Edin. Festival and West End London) 1991, Hamlet (Riverside Studios) 1992, Antony and Cleopatra (Nat. Theatre) 1998, Private Lives (West End and Broadway) 2001–02. *Plays directed:* The Winter Guest (W Yorkshire Playhouse and Almeida, London) 1995, My Name is Rachel Corrie (Royal Court, London) 2005, (Playhouse, London) 2006, New York 2006. *Radio includes:* The Seagull, A Good Man in Africa, A Trick to Catch the Old One. *Television appearances include:* The Barchester Chronicles 1982, Pity in History 1984, Revolutionary Witness, Spirit of Man 1989, Rasputin (USA) 1995. *Films include:* Die Hard 1988, The January Man 1989, Close My Eyes 1991, Truly, Madly, Deeply 1991, Closetland 1991, Robin Hood: Prince of Thieves 1991, Bob Roberts 1992, Mesmer 1993, An Awfully Big Adventure 1994, Sense and Sensibility 1995, Michael Collins 1996, Rasputin 1996, Dark Harbour 1997, The Judas Kiss 1997, Dogma 1998, Galaxy Quest 1999, Blow Dry 1999, Play 2000, The Search for John Gissing 2000, Harry Potter and the Philosopher's Stone 2001, Harry Potter and the Chamber of Secrets 2002, Love Actually 2003, Harry Potter and the Prisoner of Azkaban 2003, Something the Lord Made 2004, Harry Potter and the Goblet of Fire 2005, Snowcake 2006, Perfume: The Story of a Murderer 2006, Nobel Son 2007, Harry Potter and the Order of the Phoenix 2007, Sweeney Todd 2007. *Film directed:* The Winter Guest 1997 (Best Film, Chicago Film Festival 1997). *Address:* c/o ICM, Oxford House, 76 Oxford Street, London, W1D 1BS, England.

RICKS, Christopher Bruce, BA, BLitt, MA, FBA; British academic and writer; *Professor of Poetry, University of Oxford;* b. 18 Sept. 1933, London; s. of James Bruce Ricks and Gabrielle Roszak; m. 1st Kirsten Jensen 1956 (divorced 1975); two s. two d.; m. 2nd Judith Aronson 1977; one s. two d.; ed King Alfred's School, Wantage, Oxon., Balliol Coll., Oxford; 2nd Lt Green Howards 1952; Andrew Bradley Jr Research Fellow, Balliol Coll. Univ. of Oxford 1957, Fellow, Worcester Coll. 1958–68; Prof. of English, Bristol Univ. 1968–75; Fellow, Christ's Coll., Prof. of English, Univ. of Cambridge 1975–86, King Edward VII Prof. of English Literature 1982–86; Prof. of English, Boston Univ. 1986–98, Warren Prof. of the Humanities 1998–, Co-Dir Editorial Inst. 1999–; elected Prof. of Poetry, Univ. of Oxford 2004–(09); Visiting Prof., Univ. of California, Berkeley and Stanford Univ. 1965, Smith Coll. 1967, Harvard Univ. 1971, Wesleyan 1974, Brandeis 1977, 1981, 1984, USA; Distinguished Visiting Fellow in Residence, Columbia Univ. 2006; Vice-Pres. Tennyson Soc.; Fellow, American Acad. of Arts and Sciences 1991; Hon. Fellow, Balliol Coll. 1989, Worcester Coll. 1990, Christ's Coll. Cambridge 1993; Hon. DLitt (Oxford) 1998, (Bristol) 2003; George Orwell Memorial Prize 1979; Beefeater Club Prize for Literature 1980, Distinguished Achievement Award Andrew W. Mellon Foundation 2004. *Publications:* Milton's Grand Style 1963, Tennyson 1972, Keats and Embarrassment 1974, The Force of Poetry 1984, T. S. Eliot and Prejudice 1988, Beckett's Dying Words 1993, Essays in Appreciation 1996, Reviewery 2002, Allusion to the Poets 2002, Decisions and Revisions in T. S. Eliot 2003, Dylan's Visions of Sin 2003; editor: Poems and Critics: An Anthology of Poetry and Criticism from Shakespeare to Hardy 1966, A. E. Housman: A Collection of Critical Essays 1968, Alfred Tennyson: Poems 1842 1968, John Milton: Paradise Lost and Paradise Regained 1968, The Poems of Tennyson 1969, The Brownings: Letters and Poetry 1970, English Poetry and Prose 1540–1674 1970, English Drama to 1710 1971, Selected Criticism of Matthew Arnold 1972, The State of the Language (with Leonard Michaels) 1980, The New Oxford Book of Victorian Verse 1987, Collected Poems and Selected Prose of A. E. Housman 1988, The Faber Book of America (with William Vance) 1992, Inventions of the March Hare: Poems 1909–1917 by T. S. Eliot 1996, The Oxford Book of English Verse 1999, Selected Poems of James Henry 2002, Samuel Menashe: New and Selected Poems (Ed.) 2006; contrib. to professional journals. *Address:* 39 Martin Street, Cambridge, MA 02138, USA; Lasborough Cottage, Lasborough Park, Tetbury, Glos., GL8 8UF, England. *Telephone:* (617) 354-7887 (USA); (1666) 890252 (England).

RICKSON, Ian, BA; British theatre director; ed Essex Univ., Goldsmiths' Coll., London Univ.; freelance Dir King's Head, The Gate, Chichester Festival Theatre; Special Projects Dir Young People's Theatre 1991–92; Assoc. Dir Royal Court Theatre 1993–98, Artistic Dir 1998–2006. *Plays:* Royal Court Theatre productions: Killers 1992, SAB 1992, Wildfire 1992, Ashes and Sand 1994, Some Voices 1994, Pale Horse 1995, Mojo 1995, The Lights 1996, The Weir 1997, Dublin Carol 2000, Mouth to Mouth 2001, Boy Gets Girl 2001, The Night Heron 2002, Fallout 2003, The Sweetest Swing in Baseball 2004, The Seagull 2006; other productions: Rinty (Group Theatre, Belfast) 1990, Who's Breaking (Battersea Arts Centre) 1990, First Strike (Soho Poly) 1990, Queer Fish (Battersea Arts Centre) 1991, Me and My Friend (Chichester Festival Theatre) 1992, The House of Yes (Gate Theatre) 1993, La Serva Padrona (Broomhill) 1993, Mojo (Chicago) 1996, The Day I Stood Still (Cottesloe Theatre) 1997, The Hothouse (Lyttelton) 2007, The Seagull (New York) 2008. *Address:* c/o Judy Daish Associates Ltd, 2 St Charles Place, London, W10 6EG, England (office).

RICO, Francisco, PhD; Spanish academic; *Professor of Medieval Hispanic Literature, Universidad Autónoma de Barcelona;* b. 28 April 1942, Barcelona; s. of the late Cipriano Rico and María Manrique; m. Victoria Camps 1966; three s.; ed Univ. of Barcelona; Prof. of Medieval Hispanic Literature, Universidad Autónoma de Barcelona 1971–; Visiting Prof., The Johns Hopkins Univ. 1966–67, Princeton Univ. 1981, Scuola Normale Superiore di Pisa 1987; Gen. Dir Centre of Spanish Letters, Ministry of Culture 1985–86; Ed. Book Series: Letras e ideas, Filología, Biblioteca clásica; mem. Royal Spanish Acad. 1986–; Foreign mem. British Acad. 1992, Accad. dei Lincei 2000, Accad. della Crusca 2003; Premio Internacional Menéndez Pelayo 1998, Premio Nacional de Investigacioń 2004, Premio Natalino Sapegno 2005; Commdr Ordre des Palmes Académiques (France) 1994. *Publications:* El pequeño mundo del hombre 1970, The Spanish Picaresque Novel and the Point of View 1970, Vida u obra de Petrarca (Vol. 1) 1974, Historia y crítica de la literatura española (eight vols) 1980–84, Breve biblioteca de autores españoles 1990, El sueño del humanismo (De Petrarca a Erasmo) 1993, Critical Edition of Cervantes' Don Quixote 1998, el texto del Quijote 2005. *Leisure interest:* contemporary literature. *Address:* Santa Teresa 38, 08172 St Cugat del Vallès, Barcelona; Apartado 1, Universidad Autónoma de Barcelona, Barcelona 08193 Bellaterra-Barcelona, Spain. *Telephone:* (93) 674-07-08; (93) 581-15-26. *E-mail:* iefhf@telefonica.net (office). *Website:* www.uab.es (office).

RICÚPERO, Rubens, LLB; Brazilian international organization official, fmr diplomatist and politician; b. 1 March 1937, São Paulo; m. Marisa Parolari; four c.; ed Univ. of São Paulo and Rio Branco Inst.; Prof. of Theory of Int. Relations, Univ. of Brasília 1979–95; Prof. of History of Brazilian Diplomatic Relations, Rio Branco Inst. 1980–95; with Ministry of Foreign Relations 1981–93, Minister of the Environment and Amazonian Affairs 1993–94, of Finance March–Sept. 1994; Perm. Rep. to UN, Geneva 1987–91; Chair. GATT Council of Reps 1989–91, Contracting Parties 1989–91, GATT Cttee on Trade and Devt 1989–91, GATT Informal Group of Developing Countries 1989–91 (also Spokesman); Amb. to USA 1991–93, to Italy 1995; led Brazilian dels to UN Comm. on Human Rights and Conf. on Disarmament, Geneva; Chair. Finance Cttee, UN Conf. on Environment and Devt, Rio de Janeiro 1992; Sec.-Gen. UNCTAD 1995–2004; Dir Fundação Armando Alvares Penteado 2005–; Pres. Consultative Comm. Conversando com as Nações Unidas (CNU)-Brasil 2006–; Lifetime Achievement Award, World Summit of Young Entrepreneurs of the World Trade Univ. 2004. *Publications:* several books on int. relations, econ. devt problems, int. trade and diplomatic history. *Address:* c/o CNU-Brasil, Rua Plínio Barreto, 285, São Paulo Brazil (office). *Telephone:* (11) 3254-1677. *Fax:* (11) 3254-1675. *Website:* www.cnu-brasil.org.br.

RIDDELL, Clayton (Clay) H., BSc; Canadian geologist and business executive; *Chairman and CEO, Paramount Resources Limited;* b. Winnipeg; ed Univ. of Manitoba; Founder Paramount Resources Ltd, currently Chair. and CEO; fmr Pres. Canadian Soc. of Petroleum Geologists; fmr Chair. Canadian Asscn of Petroleum Producers; co-owner Calgary Flames ice hockey team; Dr hc (Univ. of Man.). *Address:* Paramount Resources Limited, 4700 Bankers Hall, West 888 3rd Street SW, Calgary, AB T2P 5C5, Canada (office). *Telephone:* (403) 290-3600 (office). *Fax:* (403) 262-7994 (office). *Website:* www.paramountres.com (office).

RIDDICK, Frank Adams, Jr., MD; American physician; *CEO Emeritus and Director, Ochsner Clinic Foundation;* b. 14 June 1929, Memphis; s. of Frank Adams Riddick Sr and Falba Crawford Riddick; m. Mary Belle Alston 1952; two s. one d.; ed Vanderbilt and Washington Univs; Staff Physician, Ochsner Clinic, New Orleans 1961–, Asst Medical Dir 1969–73, Assoc. Medical Dir 1973–75, Medical Dir 1975–92, Trustee, Alton Ochsner Medical Foundation 1973–, CEO 1991–2001, now CEO Emer.; Clinical Prof. of Medicine, Tulane Univ., New Orleans 1977–; Chair. Council on Medical Educ., American Medical Asscn 1982–84, Council of Ethical and Judicial Affairs 1995–; mem. NAS Inst. of Medicine; mem. Bd of Govs American Bd of Internal Medicine; Master, American Coll. of Physicians; Distinguished Physician Award, American Soc. of Internal Medicine 1980; Physician Exec. Award, American Coll. of Medical Group Admins 1984; Distinguished Alumnus Award, Vanderbilt Univ. School of Medicine 1988. *Publications:* 56 scientific papers. *Leisure interest:* travel. *Address:* Ochsner Clinic, 1516 Jefferson Highway, New Orleans, LA 70121; 1923 Octavia Street, New Orleans, LA 70115, USA (home). *Telephone:* (504) 838-4001 (office); (504) 897-1737 (home). *Website:* www.ochsner.org (office).

RIDE, Sally, PhD; American scientist, academic and fmr astronaut; *Hibben Professor of Space Science, University of California, San Diego;* b. 26 May 1951, Los Angeles; d. of Dale Ride and Joyce Ride; m. Steven Hawley (divorced); ed Westlake High School, Los Angeles and Stanford Univ.; astronaut trainee, NASA 1978–79, astronaut 1979–87; on-orbit capsule communicator STS-2 mission, Johnson Space Center, NASA, Houston; on-orbit capsule communicator STS-3 mission NASA, mission specialist STS-7 1983; Scientific Fellow, Stanford Univ. 1987–89; Dir Calif. Space Inst., Univ. of Calif. at San Diego 1989–96, Prof. of Physics 1989–; Pres. Space.com 1999–2000; co-founder Imaginary Lines Inc., Pres. 2000–; mem. Presidential Comm. on Space Shuttle 1986, Presidential Comm. of Advisers on Science and Tech. 1994–; mem. Bd of Dirs Apple Computer Inc. 1988–90; Jefferson Award for Public Service, von Braun Award, Lindbergh Eagle, two Nat. Space Flight Medal. *Publications:* To Space and Back (with Susan Okie) 1986, Voyager: An Adventure to the Edge of the Solar System (with Tam O'Shaughnessy) 1992, The Third Planet: Exploring the Earth from Space (with Tam O'Shaughnessy) 1994, The Mystery of Mars 1999, Exploring Our Solar System (with Tam O'Shaughnessy) 2003, Space (with Mike Goldsmith) 2005. *Address:* California Space Institute, 9500 Gilman Drive, Dept 0524, University of California at San Diego, La Jolla, CA 92093-0524, USA (office). *Telephone:* (619) 534-5827 (office). *Fax:* (619) 822-1277 (office). *Website:* www.calspace.ucsd.edu (office).

RIDGE, Thomas (Tom) Joseph, BA, JD; American consultant and fmr politician; b. 26 Aug. 1945, Munhall, Pa; m. Michele Moore 1979; one s. one d.; ed Harvard Univ. and Dickinson School of Law, Carlisle, Pa; admitted to Pa Bar 1972; practising lawyer, Erie, Pa 1972–82; Asst Dist Attorney, Erie, Pa 1979–82; mem. US House of Reps 1983–95; Gov. of Pa 1995–2001; Dir US Office of Homeland Security 2001–03, Sec. Dept of Homeland Security 2003–05 (resgnd); Founder, Pres. and CEO Ridge Global LLC (consulting firm), Washington, DC 2006–; mem. Bd of Dirs Home Depot Inc. 2005–; Nat. Co-Chair. Flight 93 Memorial Fundraising Campaign; numerous awards including Bronze Star for Valor, Woodrow Wilson Award, Veterans of Foreign Wars Dwight D. Eisenhower Award, John F. Kennedy Nat. Award, Ellis Island Medal of Honor, ABA John Marshall Award, US Nat. Guard Harry S. Truman Award, Pa Wildlife Fed. Conservationist of the Year Award, US-Mexico Chamber of Commerce Good Neighbor Award, American Cancer Soc. Nat. Medal of Honor, Mister Rogers Award, Champion of Public TV Award, Intrepid Freedom Award, Esperanza Leadership Award. *Address:* Ridge Global LLC, 1101 16th Street, NW, Suite 308, Washington, DC 20036, USA (office). *Telephone:* (202) 833-2008 (office). *Fax:* (202) 833-2009 (office). *E-mail:* press@ridgeglobal.com (office). *Website:* www.ridgeglobal.com (office).

RIDLEY, Brian Kidd, PhD, FRS, FInstP, CPhys; British physicist and academic; *Professor Emeritus of Physics, University of Essex;* b. 2 March 1931, Newcastle upon Tyne; s. of Oliver Archbold Ridley and Lillian Beatrice Ridley; m. Sylvia Jean Ridley; one s. one d.; ed Yorebridge (Askrigg) and Gateshead Grammar Schools, Univ. of Durham; Research Physicist, Mullard Research Labs 1956–64; Lecturer to Reader, Dept of Physics, Univ. of Essex 1964–86, Prof. of Physics 1986–91, Research Prof. 1991–2007, Prof. Emer. 2007–; several visiting professorial appointments including Cornell, Stanford and Princeton Univs; Paul Dirac Medal and Prize, Inst. of Physics 2001. *Publications:* Time, Space and Things 1976, The Physical Environment 1979, Quantum Process in Semiconductors 1982, Electrons and Phonons in Semiconductor Multilayers 1997, On Science 2001. *Leisure interests:* piano, tennis. *Address:* School of Computing Science and Electronic Engineering, University of Essex, Colchester, CO4 3SQ, England (office). *Telephone:* (1206) 872873 (office). *Fax:* (1206) 872900 (office). *E-mail:* bkr@essex.ac.uk (office). *Website:* www.essex.ac.uk/dces/people/profile.aspx?id=63 (office).

RIEBER-MOHN, Georg Fredrik; Norwegian lawyer; *Justice, Supreme Court;* b. 13 Aug. 1945, Lillehammer; m. Kari Nergaard 1967; two s. one d.; ed Univ. of Oslo; Deputy Gov. Western Prison Dist 1971–74; Asst Judge, Magistrates' Court of Stavanger 1975–76; Dist Attorney (Regional Head of Prosecutions) 1976–80; Gen. Dir Prison and Probation Service 1980–85; Judge, Appeal Court 1985–86; Gen. Dir of Public Prosecutions 1986–97 (resgnd); Justice, Supreme Court of Norway 1997–; Commdr, Order of St Olav. *Publications:* numerous articles on law issues and wild salmon conservation efforts. *Leisure interests:* fly fishing, hunting, literature. *Address:* Høyesterettsplass 1, Oslo 1 (office); Somdalen, 3525 Hallingby, Norway (home). *Telephone:* 22-03-59-15 (office); 32-13-00-08 (home). *Fax:* 22-33-23-55 (office). *E-mail:* georg.fr.rieber.mohn@hoyesterett.no (office).

RIEDLBAUCH, Václav; Czech composer; *Professor, Academy of Performing Arts;* b. 1 April 1947, Dýšina; m.; two s.; ed Prague Conservatoire; Lecturer, Prague Acad. of Performing Arts, Sr Lecturer, Sec. Dept of Composition 1984–; Chief Composer Nat. Theatre Opera 1987–89; Dir Gen. Czech Philharmonic Orchestra 2000–; Prof., Acad. of Performing Arts, Prague 2000–; Chair. Young Composers Section, Czech Composers' and Performing Artists' Union 1982–; Artist of Merit 1987. *Compositions include:* musical dramatic works: Macbeth (ballet for soloist and group dancers and large orchestra) 1979–82; symphonic works: The Rozmberk Sonata for Winds and Percussion Instruments 1971, Symphony 1972, Symphony with Refrain 1973, Concerto-Battle for Organ and Orchestra 1973, Deadly Rondo for Orchestra 1975, The Story – Symhonic narration 1983; chamber instrumental music: Sonatina for James for Violin and Piano 1971, Cathedrals – Organ toccata 1972, The Picture (Still Life with a Dead Nightingale) for flute and piano 1974, Tale for Flute, Violin, Violoncello and Piano 1974, Lamento for Clarinet and Piano 1975, Ballads for Violin and Piano 1975, Stories for Bass-clarinet and Piano 1975, Allegri e Pastorali for wind quintet 1976, Luring for Flute and Piano 1977, Canons for Piano 1977, Parade for Organ 1978, Pastorali e Concerti for brass quintet 1978, Concertie Trenodi for wind octet 1979, The Curtain – Movement for organ 1982, Conjunction – Game for two organs or other keyboard instruments 1983; vocal works: Touzenec pisni – Songs for Tenor and Piano After Verses by R. Tagore 1975, Songs from Rejdova for Soprano, Contralto, Violin and Piano 1976, Tesknice (nostalgic songs) – Three folk songs for two flutes-a-bec and three-part children's choir 1976, Wedding

Singing for girls, female or male choirs after Sappho 1978, Rather-Or Cycle for Children – Seven children's choirs to words by R. Steindl 1978, Songs and Games to Excerpts from Shakespeare for six singers, two violins, oboe and violoncello 1979, Teachers Song (celebration of Bohemian baroque) for organ and children's choir to words by V. Fischer 1980, The Primer – Excerpts from beginnings at school – Four polyphonic pieces for children's choir 1980, Daidalos the Creator, for male choir with barytone solo after Ovid 1982; instructive works: Special Book of Prague – A book of polyphonic compositions for accordion 1972, Pastorale for Three Flutes-a-bec 1973, The Wizard – Accordion school for children 1973–76, SU South Bohemian Nocturnes, for two violins, violoncello, accordion and trumpet 1979, Reversals for children's accordion 1980, SU 2' Povidacky (talks) – Eight polyphonic pieces for two violins 1982. *Address:* Academy of Performing Arts, Malostranské nám. 12, 110 00 Prague 1 (office); Revoluční 6, 110 00 Prague 1, Czech Republic (home). *Telephone:* (2) 57533956 (office); (2) 22310710 (home). *Fax:* (2) 57530405 (office).

RIEKSTIŅŠ, Māris; Latvian lawyer, diplomatist and politician; *Minister of Foreign Affairs;* b. 8 April 1963, Riga; m.; two c.; ed Univ. of Latvia; teacher, Faculty of Pedagogy, Latvian Sports Inst. 1982–85; Deputy Chair. and Desk Officer, Cttee of Latvian Youth Orgs 1987–91; lawyer, Faculty of Law, Univ. of Latvia 1989–93; Chair. Control Cttee of Strategic Goods of Repub. of Latvia 1995–2004, Diplomatic Service Agency's Shareholders' Council 1996–2004, Advisory Council for Membership of Latvia in WTO 1999–2004, Supervisory Cttee on Org. of NATO Aspirant Countries Summit in Riga Jan.–July 2002; Head of Latvian del. for negotiations on sea border delimitations with Estonia 1995–96, Lithuania 1996–99, Latvian del. to US-Baltic Partnership Charter 1997–98, Latvian-Italian Econ. Working Group 1998–2004; several positions within Ministry of Foreign Affairs, including Desk Officer, Political Dept of Europe Div. and Dir Western Europe and Europe Divs Jan.–Nov. 1992, Under-Sec. of State 1992–93, Sec. of State 1993–2004, Head of Latvian del. for accession negotiations with NATO 2002–04, Amb. to USA 2004–07 (also accred to Mexico 2006–07); Chief of Staff to Prime Minister Jan.–Nov. 2007; Minister of Foreign Affairs Nov. 2007–; Commdr, Royal Norwegian Order of Merit 1998, Grand Officer, Royal Norwegian Order of Merit 2000, Grand Officier, Ordre nat. du Mérite 2001, Order of the Lithuanian Grand Duke Gediminas (Fourth Class) 2001, Order of the Cross of Terra Mariana (Third Class, Estonia) 2003, Ordem do Infante D. Henrique Grande Oficial (Portugal) 2003, Commdr, Three Star Order of Latvia 2003, 'Grand Official', Order of Merit of the Italian Repub. 2004. *Address:* Ministry of Foreign Affairs, 3 Valdemara str., Rīga 1395, Latvia (office). *Telephone:* 6701-6201 (office). *Fax:* 6782-8121 (office). *E-mail:* mfa.cha@mfa.gov.lv (office). *Website:* www.mfa.gov.lv (office).

RIES, Col Nico; Luxembourg army officer; b. 30 July 1953; m.; two c.; ed Royal Mil. Acad., Brussels, Belgium, Staff Coll., Compiegne and Ecole Supérieure de Guerre Interarmées, Paris, France; joined Luxembourg Army 1973; apptd to Mil. Instruction Centre 1978–94, held positions successively as Infantry Platoon Leader, Co. Commdr, Personnel Officer, Deputy Commdr; Logistics Officer, Army Staff 1994–98; Asst Chief of Staff 1998–2002, Chief of Staff 2002–08; participated in EC Monitor Mission (ECMM) in fmr Yugoslavia 1991, 1997; Chevalier Ordre de Mérite civil et militaire d'Adolphe de Nassau 1994, Officier Ordre grand-ducal de la Couronne de Chêne 1994, Grand Officier, Ordre du Mérite of Grand Duchy of Luxembourg 2004, Commdr, Ordre Nat. de la Légion d'Honneur 2005, Grande Oficial da Ordem Militar de Avis (Portugal) 2005, Grand Officier Ordre de Viesturs (Latvia) 2006; Verdienstkreuz 1st Class (Germany) 1988, Croix d'Honneur et de Mérite militaire en bronze 1998, Croix de 25 ans de service 1999, Meritorious Service Medal (USA) 1998, Medal of EC Monitor Mission in fmr Yugoslavia 1998. *Address:* c/o Etat-Major de l'Armée, 34–38 rue Goethe, BP 1873, 1018 Luxembourg, Luxembourg (office).

RIESENHUBER, Heinz Friedrich, Dr rer. nat; German politician; b. 1 Dec. 1935, Frankfurt; s. of Karl Riesenhuber and Elisabeth Riesenhuber (née Birkner); m. Beatrix Walter 1968; two s. two d.; ed Gymnasium in Frankfurt and Univs of Frankfurt and Munich; with Erzgesellschaft mbH, c/o Metallgesellschaft, Frankfurt 1966–71; Tech. Man. Synthomer-Chemie GmbH, Frankfurt 1971–82; joined CDU 1961, mem. CDU Hesse Presidium 1968–, Chair. Frankfurt Br. 1973–78, Untermain Br. 1978–; mem. Bundestag 1976–, mem. Cttee on Econ and Tech. 1993– (Chair. 2001–02); Fed. Minister for Research and Technology 1982–93; Chair. and mem. of numerous supervisory bds and advisory panels; Hon. Prof., Univ of Frankfurt; Distinguished Service Cross, Commdr, Légion d'honneur and numerous other decorations; Dr hc (Weizmann Inst., Israel, Berg Acad., Poland, Surrey, Göttingen); Cicero Speaker's Award 1995. *Publications:* Japan ist offen; articles in specialist journals. *Leisure interests:* reading, golf. *Address:* Bundestag, Platz der Republik 1, 11011 Berlin, Germany (office). *Telephone:* (30) 22777381 (office). *Fax:* (30) 22776381 (office). *E-mail:* heinz.riesenhuber@bundestag.de (office).

RIESS, Adam G., BS, AM, PhD; American astrophysicist and academic; *Professor of Astronomy and Physics, Johns Hopkins University;* b. 1969; ed Massachusetts Inst. of Tech., Harvard Univ.; Miller Fellow, Univ. of California, Berkeley 1996–99; mem. Sr Science Science Staff, Space Telescope Science Inst., Baltimore, Md 1999–2005; Prof. of Physics and Astronomy, Johns Hopkins Univ., Baltimore 2006–; led study for High-z Team which provided first direct and published evidence that expansion of Universe was accelerating and filled with Dark Energy 1998; Prin. Investigator of Higher-z SN Team that found and measured 20 most distant type Ia supernovae known through competitive awarding of more than 800 orbits of Hubble Space Telescope Time in five cycles and $2million in grants 2002–; mem. Jt Dark Energy Mission Science Definition Team 2004, Jt Dark Energy Mission Science Working Group 2008; Founding mem. science team for four active dark energy programmes: ESSENCE, ADEPT, SDSS II SN Survey and Pan-STARRS; Fellow, American Acad. of Arts and Sciences 2008; Margaret Weyerhaeuser Jewett Memorial Fellowship 1993, Distinction in Teaching Award, Harvard Univ. 1994, GSAS Merit Fellow, Harvard Univ. 1995, Science Magazine's Research 'Breakthrough of the Year' 1998, Trumpler Award, Astronomical Soc. of the Pacific 1999, Time Magazine Innovator Award 2000, AURA Science Award 2000, STScI Science Merit Award 2000, 2001, Bok Prize, Harvard Univ. 2001 Time Magazine 'Six Who Probed Cosmos', Esquire Magazine 'Best and Brightest' Award 2003, Helen B. Warner Prize, American Astronomical Soc. 2003, Raymond and Beverly Sackler Prize, Tel-Aviv Univ. 2004, Laurels for Achievement Award, Int. Acad. of Astronautics 2004, Townes Prize in Cosmology, Univ. of California, Berkeley 2005, ISI Most Highly Cited 2006, Shaw Prize in Astronomy (co-recipient) 2006, Kavli Frontier of Science Fellow 2007, Gruber Prize in Cosmology (co-recipient) 2007, MacArthur Fellow 2008, Discover Magazine Twenty Under 40 2008. *Publications:* more than 80 scientific papers in professional journals on measurements of the cosmological framework with supernovae (exploding stars) and Cepheids (pulsating stars); more than 20 tech. reports. *Address:* Department of Physics and Astronomy, 207 Bloomberg Center, The Johns Hopkins University, 3400 North Charles Street, Baltimore, Baltimore, MD 21218-2686, USA (office). *Telephone:* (410) 516-4474 (office). *Fax:* (410) 516-7239 (office). *E-mail:* ariess@pha.jhu.edu (office). *Website:* physics-astronomy.jhu.edu (office); www.stsci.edu/~ariess (office).

RIESS-PASSER, Susanne; Austrian lawyer, business executive and fmr politician; *Director General, Bausparkasse Wüstenrot AG;* b. 3 Jan. 1961, Braunau; ed Univ. of Innsbruck; joined Freedom Party as Press Officer 1987, succeeded Jörg Haider as leader 2000–02; Vice-Chancellor and Minister for Public Affairs and Sports 2000–02; Gen. Dir Bausparkasse Wüstenrot AG 2004–; Deputy Chair. Bundestheater Holding. *Address:* Bausparkasse Wüstenrot AG, Alpenstraße 70, 5033 Salzburg, Austria (office). *Telephone:* 57070 110 (office). *Fax:* 057070 109 (office). *Website:* www.wuestenrot.at (office).

RIESTER, Walter; German politician and trade union official; b. 27 Sept. 1943, Kaufbeuren; ed Labour Acad. Frankfurt; apprentice tiler 1957–60; tiler 1960–68; youth training officer German TU Fed. Baden-Württemberg Region 1970, Departmental Gen. Sec. for Youth Questions Stuttgart Region 1970–77; Admin. Sec. IG Metall Geislingen 1977–78, Second Deputy 1978–79, Sec. Dist HQ IG Metall Stuttgart 1980–88, Dist Man. 1988–93, Second Chair. IG Metall Germany 1993–98; Fed. Minister of Labour and Social Affairs 1998–2002; mem. (SPD) Bundestag (Parl.) 2002–. *Address:* Willi-Bleicher-Straße 3, Schillerbau II, 73033 Göppingen; Deutscher Bundestag, Platz der Republik 1, 11011 Berlin, Germany (office). *Telephone:* (30) 22772041 (office). *Fax:* (30) 22776042 (office). *E-mail:* walter.riester@bundestag.de (office). *Website:* walterriester.de (office).

RIFBJERG, Klaus; Danish author; *Adjunct Professor of Languages, Copenhagen Business School;* b. 15 Dec. 1931, Copenhagen; s. of Thorvald Rifbjerg and Lilly Nielsen; m. Inge Merete Gerner 1955; one s. two d.; ed Princeton Univ., USA and Univ. of Copenhagen; Literary Critic, Information 1955–57, Politiken 1959–65 (Copenhagen daily newspapers); Literary Dir Gyldendal Publrs 1984–92, mem. Bd of Dirs 1992–98; Prof. of Aesthetics, Laererhøjskole, Copenhagen 1986; Adjunct Prof. of Languages, Copenhagen Business School 2003–; Grant of Honour from the Danish Dramatists 1966, Grant of Honour from the Danish Writers' Guild 1973; Dr hc (Lund) 1991, (Odense) 1996; Aarestrup Medal 1964, Danish Critics' Award 1965, Danish Acad. Award 1966, Golden Laurels 1967, Soren Gyldendal Award 1969, Nordic Council Award 1970, PH Prize 1979, Holberg Medal 1979, H. C. Andersen Prize 1988, Johannes V. Jensen Prize 1998, Prize for Nordic Writers, Swedish Acad. 1999, Danish Publicists' Award 2001, Danish Language Soc. Award 2001. *Publications include:* novels: Den Kroniske Uskyld 1958, Operaelsken 1966, Arkivet 1967, Lonni Og Karl 1968, Anna (Jeg) Anna 1970, Marts 1970 1970, Leif den Lykkelige JR. 1971, Til Spanien 1971, Lena Jorgensen, Klintevej 4, 2650 Hvidovre 1971, Brevet til Gerda 1972, R.R. 1972, Spinatfuglene 1973, Dilettanterne 1973, Du skal ikke vaere ked af det Amalia 1974, En hugorm i solen 1974, Vejen ad hvilken 1975, Tak for turen 1975, Kiks 1976, Twist 1976, Et Bortvendt Ansigt 1977, Tango 1978, Dobbeltgœnger 1978, Drengene 1978, Joker 1979, Voksdugshjertet 1979, Det sorte hul 1980, De hellige aber 1981, Maend og Kvinder 1982, Jus 1982, En omvej til Klostret 1983, Falsk Forår 1984, Borte tit 1986, Engel 1987, Rapsodi i blåt 1991; short stories: Og Andre Historier 1964, Rejsende 1969, Den Syende Jomfru 1972, Sommer 1974, Det. Svage Køn 1989; non-fiction: I Medgang Og Modgang 1970, Deres Majestæt! 1977; plays: Gris Pa Gaflen 1962, Hva Skal Vi Lave 1963, Udviklinger 1965, Hvad en Mand Har Brug For 1966, Voks 1968, Ar 1970, Narrene 1971, Svaret Blaeser i Vinden 1971, Det Korte af det lange 1976; poems: Livsfrisen 1979 and several other vols of poetry; 20 radio plays, essays, several film and TV scripts. *Address:* c/o Copenhagen Business School, Solbjerg Plads 3, 2000 Frederiksberg; c/o Gyldendal Publishers, 3 Klareboderne, 1001 Copenhagen, Denmark.

RIFKIN, Joshua, BS, MFA; American conductor, musicologist and composer; b. 22 April 1944, New York; s. of Harry H. Rifkin and Dorothy Helsh; m. Helen Palmer 1995; one d.; ed Juilliard School and New York, Göttingen and Princeton Univs; Musical Adviser, Assoc. Dir Nonesuch Records 1963–75; Asst, Assoc. Prof. of Music, Brandeis Univ. 1970–82; Dir The Bach Ensemble 1978–; Visiting Prof. New York Univ. 1978, 1983, 2000, Yale Univ. 1982–83, Princeton Univ. 1988, Stanford Univ. 1989, King's Coll. London 1991, Univ. of Basel 1993, 1997, Ohio State Univ. 1994, Univ. of Dortmund 1996, Schola Cantorum Basiliensis 1997, 2001, Univ. of Munich 2000; Fellow, Inst. for Advanced Study, Berlin 1984–86; guest conductor English Chamber Orchestra, Los Angeles Chamber Orchestra, St Louis Symphony Orchestra, St Paul Chamber Orchestra, Scottish Chamber Orchestra, BBC Symphony Orchestra, Bayerische Staatsoper, San Francisco Symphony Orchestra, City of Glasgow Symphony Orchestra, Jerusalem Symphony Orchestra, Prague Chamber Orchestra; contributed to the revival of interest in the ragtime music of Scott Joplin; as a musicologist has researched Renaissance and Baroque music; recreated J. S. Bach's Wedding Cantata BWV 216 (fragment, originally 1728) 2005; Dr hc (Dortmund) 1999; Gramophone Award 1983. *Recordings:* Bach Mass in B minor 1982, Bach Magnificat 1983, numerous Bach cantatas 1986–2001, Rags and Tangos 1990, Haydn Symphonies 1994, Silvestre Revueltas 1999, rags by Scott Joplin, Mozart Posthorn Serenade, fanfares and sonatas by Pezel and Hammerschmidt, sonatas by Biber, vocal music by Busnois, Josquin. *Publications:* articles on Haydn, Schütz, Bach and Josquin in The Musical Times, Musical Quarterly and other journals, and in the New Grove Dictionary of Music and Musicians. *Leisure interests:* food and wine, cinema, his daughter. *Address:* 100 Montgomery Street, Cambridge, MA 02138, USA. *Telephone:* (617) 876-4017 (office). *Fax:* (617) 441-5572 (office). *E-mail:* jrifkin@compuserve.com.

RIFKIND, Rt Hon. Sir Malcolm Leslie, KCMG, PC, QC, LLB, MSc; British politician and business executive; b. 21 June 1946; s. of the late E. Rifkind; m. Edith Steinberg 1970; one s. one d.; ed George Watson's Coll. and Univ. of Edinburgh; Lecturer, Univ. of Rhodesia 1967–68; called to Scottish Bar 1970; MP for Edin., Pentlands 1974–97; Parl. Under-Sec. of State, Scottish Office 1979–82, FCO 1982–83; Minister of State, FCO 1983–86; Sec. of State for Scotland 1986–90, for Transport 1990–92, for Defence 1992–95, for Foreign and Commonwealth Affairs 1995–97; Pres. Scottish Conservative and Unionist Party 1998–; MP for Kensington and Chelsea 2005–, Shadow Work and Pensions Sec. 2005, mem. Jt Cttee on Conventions 2006–; Chair. (non-exec.) ArmorGroup 2004–; Dir (non-exec.) Aberdeen Asset; consultant to BHP Billiton, PwC; fmr mem. Bd of Dirs Ramco Energy; mem. Queen's Bodyguard for Scotland, Royal Co. of Archers; Patron Tory Reform Club; Hon. Col 162 Movt Control Regt, Royal Logistic Corps (V); Commdr Order of Merit (Poland); Hon. LLD (Napier) 1998. *Leisure interests:* walking, field sports, reading. *Address:* House of Commons, Westminster, London, SW1A 0AA (office). *Telephone:* (20) 7219-5683 (office). *Fax:* (20) 7219-4213 (office). *E-mail:* shaylorc@parliament.uk (office). *Website:* www.malcolmrifkind.co.uk (office).

RIGBY, Jean Prescott, ARAM, ARCM, ABSM; British singer (mezzo-soprano); b. Fleetwood, Lancs.; d. of Thomas Boulton Rigby and Margaret Annie Rigby; m. James Hayes 1987; three s.; ed Elmslie Girls' School, Blackpool, Birmingham School of Music, RAM and Opera Studio; studied piano and viola at Birmingham then singing at RAM with Patricia Clark, with whom she continues to study; Prin. Mezzo-Soprano, ENO 1982–90, roles include Mercedes, Marina, Lucretia, Dorabella, Octavian, Penelope, Jocasta, Helen (King Priam), Rosina; debut Covent Garden 1983, roles have included Tebaldo, Mercedes, Hippolyta, second Lady, Magic Flute and Olga, Eugene Onegin, Nicklausse (Hoffman), Irene in Theodora, Emelia in Otello, Genevieve in Pelleas and Melisande, Edwige in Rodelinda; Glyndebourne debut 1984, sang Nancy in Albert Herring and Mercedes in Carmen 1985; American debut 1993; TV appearances in Così fan tutte and film on Handel; videos of Xerxes, Rigoletto, Lucretia, Carmen, Albert Herring; also sings concert repertoire and has made recordings with Giuseppe Sinopoli; Hon. FRAM 1989; Hon. Assoc., Birmingham Conservatoire 1996, Hon. Fellow 2007; numerous prizes and scholarships at RAM including Countess of Munster, Leverhulme, Peter Stuyvesant, RSA scholarships and the Prin.'s Prize; Royal Overseas League and Young Artists' Competition 1981. *Recordings:* more than 50 recordings, ranging from Bach, Handel, Vivaldi and Debussy to Birtwistle and McMillan. *Leisure interests:* theatre, sport, British heritage. *Address:* c/o Askonas Holt Ltd, Lincoln House, 300 High Holborn, London, WC1V 7JH, England (office). *Telephone:* (20) 7400-1700 (office). *Fax:* (20) 7400-1799 (office). *E-mail:* info@askonasholt.co.uk (office). *Website:* www.askonasholt.co.uk (office).

RIGBY, Peter William Jack, MA, PhD; British medical research scientist and academic; *Professor of Developmental Biology and Chief Executive, Institute of Cancer Research, University of London;* b. 7 July 1947, Savernake; s. of Jack Rigby and Lorna Rigby; m. 1st Paula Webb 1971 (divorced 1983); m. 2nd Julia Maidment 1985; one s.; ed Lower School of John Lyon, Harrow and Jesus Coll. Cambridge; mem. scientific staff, MRC Lab. of Molecular Biology, Cambridge 1971–73; Helen Hay Whitney Foundation Research Fellow, Stanford Univ. Medical School 1973–76; Lecturer, Sr Lecturer in Biochemistry, Imperial Coll. London 1976–83; Reader in Tumour Virology, Univ. of London 1983–86; Head, Genes and Cellular Controls Group and Div. of Eukaryotic Molecular Genetics, MRC Nat. Inst. for Medical Research 1986–2000; Chief Exec. Inst. of Cancer Research, Univ. of London 1999–, also Dir of Research, Prof. of Developmental Biology 2001–; mem. Science Council, Celltech Therapeutics 1982–2003; European Ed. Cell 1984–97; mem. Scientific Advisory Bd Somatix Therapy Corpn 1989–97, KuDos Pharmaceuticals 1999–; Scientific Cttee Cancer Research Campaign 1983–88, 1996–99; non-exec. Dir, Royal Marsden NHS Foundation Trust 2001–; mem. of Council, Acad. of Medical Sciences 2002–04, St George's Hospital Medical School 2003–; mem. Bd of Govs, Beatson Inst. for Cancer Research, Glasgow 2003–; mem. Nat. Council and Chair. of Medical Research Cttee, Muscular Dystrophy Campaign 2003–; Chair. Principal Research Fellowship Interviewing Cttee, Wellcome Trust 2004–; mem. Strategy Bd, Biotechnology and Biological Sciences Research Council 2005–; Chair. Hexagen Tech. Ltd 1996–99; Chair. Scientific Advisory Bd Proflix 1996–2004; Fellow, Acad. of Medical Sciences 1999; Carter Medal, Clinical Genetics Soc. 1994. *Publications:* papers on molecular biology in scientific journals. *Leisure interests:* narrow boats, listening to music, sport. *Address:* Chester Beatty Laboratories, Institute of Cancer Research, 237 Fulham Road, London, SW3 6JB, England (office). *Telephone:* (20) 7153-5125 (office). *Fax:* (20) 7352-0272 (office). *E-mail:* peter.rigby@icr.ac.uk (office). *Website:* www.icr.ac.uk (office).

RIGG, Dame (Enid) Diana Elizabeth, DBE; British actress; b. 20 July 1938, Doncaster, Yorks.; d. of Louis Rigg and Beryl (Helliwell) Rigg; m. 1st Menahem Gueffen 1973 (divorced 1976); m. 2nd Archibald Hugh Stirling 1982 (divorced 1993); one d.; ed Fulneck Girls' School, Pudsey, Yorks, RADA; professional début as Natella Abashwilli (The Caucasian Chalk Circle), York Festival 1957; repertory Chesterfield and Scarborough 1958; Chair. MacRobert Arts Centre, Univ. of Stirling, Chancellor Univ. of Stirling 1997–; Prof. of Theatre Studies, Oxford Univ. 1998–; Dir United British Artists 1982–; a Vice-Pres. Baby Life Support Systems (BLISS) 1984–; Visiting Prof. of Contemporary Theatre Oxford Univ. 1999; mem. Arts Council Cttee 1986; mem. British Museum Devt Fund, Asscn for Business Sponsorship of the Arts; Assoc. Artist of RSC, Stratford and Aldwych 1962–79; mem. Nat. Theatre 1972; Dr hc (Stirling Univ.) 1988; Hon. DLitt (Leeds) 1992, (South Bank) 1996; Plays and Players Award for Best Actress (Phaedra Britannica 1975, Night and Day 1978), BAFTA Award for Best Actress in Mother Love 1990, Evening Standard Award for Best Actress (Medea 1993, Mother Courage and Her Children 1996, Who's Afraid of Virginia Woolf? 1996), Tony Award for Best Actress in Medea 1994, Special Award for The Avengers, BAFTA 2000. *Roles with RSC include:* Andromache (Troilus and Cressida), 2nd Ondine, Violanta and Princess Bertha (Ondine), Philippe Trincant (The Devils), Gwendolen (Becket), Bianca (The Taming of the Shrew), Madame de Tourvel (The Art of Seduction), Helena (A Midsummer Night's Dream), Adriana (Comedy of Errors), Cordelia (King Lear), Nurse Monika Stettler (The Physicists), Lady Macduff (Macbeth); toured Eastern Europe, USSR, USA in King Lear, Comedy of Errors 1964; Viola (Twelfth Night), Stratford 1966. *Roles there included:* Dottie Moore (Jumpers) 1972, Hippolita ('Tis Pity She's A Whore) 1972, Lady Macbeth (Macbeth) 1972, Célimène (The Misanthrope), Washington and New York 1973, 1975, The Governor's Wife (Phaedra Britannica) 1975; rejoined Nat. Theatre at the Lyttelton to play Ilona in The Guardsman 1978. *Other stage appearances include:* Heloise (Abelard and Heloise) London 1970, LA, New York 1971, Eliza Doolittle (Pygmalion) London 1974, Ruth Carson (Night and Day) London 1978, Colette, Seattle and Denver 1982, Hesione Hushabye (Heartbreak House) London 1983, Rita in Little Eyolf, London 1985, Cleopatra in Antony and Cleopatra, Chichester 1985, Wildfire, London 1986, Phyllis in Follies 1987, Love Letters, San Francisco 1990, Cleopatra in All for Love, London 1991, Berlin Bertie 1992, Medea 1993 (London and Broadway), Mother Courage and Her Children, London, 1995, Who's Afraid of Virginia Woolf?, London 1996–97, Phèdre 1998, Britannicus 1998, Humble Boy 2001, Suddenly Last Summer (Theatregoers' Award for Best Actress 2005) 2004, All About my Mother London 2007. *Films include:* A Midsummer Night's Dream 1969, The Assassination Bureau 1969, On Her Majesty's Secret Service 1969, Julius Caesar 1970, The Hospital 1971, Theatre of Blood 1973, A Little Night Music 1977, The Great Muppet Caper 1981, Evil under the Sun 1982, Snow White 1988, Cannon Movie Tales: Cinderella 1988, A Good Man in Africa 1994, Parting Shots 1999, Heidi 2005, The Painted Veil 2006. *Television appearances include:* Sentimental Agent 1963, A Comedy of Errors 1964, The Hothouse 1964, The Avengers (series) 1965–67, Women Beware Women 1965, Married Alive 1970, Diana (series) 1973, In This House of Brede 1975, Three Piece Suite 1977, Clytemnestra in The Serpent Son 1979, The Marquise 1980, Hedda Gabler 1981, Rita Allmers in Little Eyolf 1982, Regan in King Lear 1983, Witness for the Prosecution 1983, Bleak House 1984, Host, Held in Trust, A Hazard of Hearts 1987, Worst Witch 1987, Unexplained Laughter 1989, Mother Love 1989, Host, Mystery! 1989 (USA), Running Delilah 1994, Zoya 1995, The Haunting of Helen Walker 1995, The Fortunes and Misfortunes of Moll Flanders 1996, Samson and Delilah 1996, Rebecca 1997 (Emmy Award for Best Supporting Actress 1997), The Mrs Bradley Mysteries: Speedy Death 1998, The Mrs. Bradley Mysteries (series) 1999, In the Beginning (mini-series) 2000, The American 2001, The 100 Greatest TV Characters (Mrs Peel) 2001, Victoria & Albert 2001, Charles II: The Power and the Passion (mini-series) 2003. *Publications:* No Turn Unstoned 1982, So To The Land 1994. *Leisure interests:* reading, writing, cooking, travel. *Address:* c/o ARG, 4 Great Portland Street, London, W1W 8PA, England.

RIGGIO, Leonard S.; American business executive; *Chairman, Barnes & Noble, Inc.;* b. 1941, New York; m. (divorced); two d.; ed Brooklyn Tech. High School, New York Univ.; fmrly with New York Univ. campus bookstore; opened Waverly Student Book Exchange 1965; f. Barnes & Noble Bookstores 1971, Chair., CEO Barnes & Noble Inc. 1986–, now Chair., also Chair. barnesandnoble.com inc.; Chair. of Bd, Prin. Beneficial Owner Software Etc. Stores, Mpls, MBS Textbook Exchange, Inc.; Chair. Bd Dia Art Foundation; mem. Bd of Dirs Children's Defense Fund, Black Children's Community Crusade, Brooklyn Tech Foundation, Italian American Foundation; Ellis Island Medal of Honor, Frederick Douglas Medallion, Anti-Defamation League Americanism Award Dr. hc (Baruch College, Bentley College). *Address:* Barnes & Noble, Inc., 122 5th Avenue, New York, NY 10011, USA (office). *Telephone:* (212) 633-3300 (office). *Fax:* (212) 675-0413 (office). *Website:* www.barnesandnobleinc.com (office).

RIGGS, Lorrin Andrews, AB, MA, PhD; American psychologist and academic; *Professor Emeritus of Psychology, Brown University;* b. 11 June 1912, Harput, Turkey; s. of Ernest Wilson Riggs and Alice Riggs (née Shepard); m. 1st Doris Robinson 1937 (died 1993); two s.; m. 2nd Caroline Cressman 1994; ed Dartmouth Coll. and Clark Univ.; NRC Fellow, Biological Sciences, Univ. of Pa 1936–37; Instructor Univ. of Vermont 1937–38, 1939–41; with Brown Univ. 1938–39, 1941–, Research Assoc., Research Psychologist Nat. Defense Research Cttee, Asst Prof., Assoc. Prof. 1938–51, Prof. of Psychology 1951–, L. Herbert Ballou Foundation Prof. of Psychology 1960–68, Edgar J. Marston Univ. Prof. of Psychology 1968–77, Prof. Emer. 1977–; Guggenheim Fellow,

Univ. of Cambridge 1971–72; mem. American Psychological Asscn (Div. Pres. 1962–63), Eastern Psychological Asscn (Pres. 1975–76), AAAS (Chair. and Vice-Pres. Section 1 1964), Optical Soc. of America, NAS, American Physiological Soc., Int. Brain Research Org., Soc. for Neuroscience, Soc. of Experimental Psychologists, American Acad. of Arts and Sciences, Asscn for Research in Vision and Ophthalmology (Pres. 1977); William James Fellow, American Psychological Soc. 1989; Hon. DSc (Brown Univ.) 2001; Howard Crosby Warren Medal, Soc. of Experimental Psychologists 1957, Jonas S. Friedenwald Award, Asscn for Research in Ophthalmology 1966, Edgar D. Tillyer Award, Optical Soc. of America 1969, Charles F. Prentice Award, American Acad. of Optometry 1973, Distinguished Scientific Contribution Award, American Psychological Asscn 1974, Kenneth Craik Award, Cambridge Univ. 1979, Frederick Ives Medal, Optical Soc. of America 1982. *Publications:* numerous scientific articles on vision and physiological psychology. *Address:* 80 Lyme Road, Hanover, NH 03755, USA. *Telephone:* (603) 643-2342. *E-mail:* clriggs@bigplanet.com (home).

RIIS, Povl, MD, DM, FRCP; Danish physician, academic and editor; *Chairman, AgeForum;* b. 28 Dec. 1925, Copenhagen; s. of Lars Otto Riis and Eva Elisabeth Riis (née Erdmann); m. Else Harne 1954 (died 1997); one s. three d.; ed Univ. of Copenhagen; specialist in internal medicine 1960, gastroenterology 1963; Head of Medical Dept B, Gentofte Univ. Hosp. 1963–76; Prof. of Internal Medicine, Univ. of Copenhagen 1974–96 (title and functions preserved externally), Vice-Dean Faculty of Medicine 1979–82; Head of Gastroenterological Dept C, Herlev Co. Hosp. 1976–96; Asst Ed. Journal of the Danish Medical Asscn 1957–67, Chief Ed. 1967–90; Ed. Bibliothek for Laeger 1965–90, Danish Medical Bulletin 1968–90, Nordic Medicine 1984–91; mem. Bd, Danish Soc. for Internal Medicine 1962–67, Danish Anti-Cancer League 1970–75, Danish Soc. for Theoretical and Applied Therapy 1972–77, Int. Union against Cancer 1978–86; mem. Danish Medical Research Council 1968–74, Chair. 1972–74; mem. Danish Science Advisory Bd 1972–74, Co-Chair. 1974; mem. Nordic Scientific Co-ordination Cttee for Medicine 1968–72, Chair. 1970–72; Chair. Nordic Medical Publs Cttee 1970–72; Vice-Pres. European Science Foundation (ESF) 1974–77, mem. Exec. Council 1977–83; Chair. ESF Cttee on Genetic Manipulation 1975–77, Chair. ESF Liaison Cttee on Genetic Manipulation 1977–83; mem. Council for Int. Org. of Medical Sciences Advisory Cttee 1977; mem. Trustees Foundation of 1870 1976, Trier-Hansen Foundation 1977–, Hartmann Prize Cttee 1986–2002, Buhl Olesen Foundation 1982–, Madsen Foundation 1978–, Jakobsen Foundation 1989–, Brinch Foundation 1990–96; Chair. Danish Central Scientific-Ethical Cttee 1979–98, Nat. Medical Bd Danish Red Cross 1985–94, Int. Org. of Inflammatory Bowel Diseases 1986–89; mem. Nat. Cttee on Scientific Misconduct 1992–99; Danish Foreign Office del. Helsinki negotiations, Hamburg 1980; mem. Bd Danish Helsinki Cttee; mem. Nuffield Foundation Working Party on Ethics 1999–2002, Ethical Collegial Council, Danish Dental Asscn 2000–, Ethical Collegial Council, Danish Medical Asscn 2000–03; mem. Medical Advisory Bd NetDoktor 1999–; Evaluator EU 1999–; Adviser Augustinus Foundation 1999–; mem. Int. Cttee of Medical Journal Eds 1980–90, Editorial Bd, Acta Medica Scandinavica, Journal Int. Medicine 1980, Ethics Bd, Danish Medical Asscn 1980–82, WHO European Advisory Cttee for Medical Research 1980–85, Scientific Bd, Danish Nat. Encyclopaedia 1991–2001, Editorial Bd JAMA 1994–; Chair. Nat. Medical Bd of Danish Red Cross; Chair. Nat. Center for First Aid and Health Promotion 1991, AgeForum 1996–, Bd Epidemiological Research, Univ. of Århus 2004–; mem. Preid. Cttee Foundation of Psychiatry 1996–; Hon. Mem. Icelandic Medical Asscn 1978, Swedish Medical Soc., Finnish Medical Soc., Danish Soc. of Gastroenterology 1995 and 2004; Hon. MRCP (UK) 1991; Hon. DMed (Univ. of Odense) 1996, (Gothenburg); Alfred Benzon Prize, August Krogh Prize 1974, Christensen-Ceson Prize 1976, Klein-Prize 1980, Barfred-Pedersen Prize 1980, Hagedorn Prize 1983, Nordic Gastro Prize 1983, Nordic Language Prize in Medicine 1993, Danish Prize of Honour in Research Ethics 2003, National Prize of Honour, JL-Foundation 2005, Medal of Honour, Icelandic Medical History Soc. 2005. *Television:* several contribs to Danish Broadcasting System for radio and TV. *Publications:* contrib.: Handbook of Scientific Methodology (in Danish) 1971–, World Medical Association Helsinki Declaration 1975, We Shall All Die – But How? (in Danish) 1977; author: Handbook of Internal Medicine (in Danish) 1968, Grenzen der Forschung 1980; Community and Ethics (in Danish) 1984, Medical Ethics (in Danish) 1985, Ethical Issues in Preventive Medicine 1985, Medical Science and the Advancement of World Health 1985, Bearing and Perspective 1988, The Appleton Consensus 1988, Face Death 1989, Ethics in Health Education 1990, The Future of Medical Journals 1991, Research on Man: Ethics and Law 1991, Scientific Misconduct – Good Scientific Practice 1992, Health Care in Europe after 1992 1992, A Better Health Service – But How? (in Danish), The Culture of General Education 1996, Drugs and Pharmacotherapy 1997, The Time That Followed (in Danish) 1998, Ethics and Clinical Medicine (in Danish) 1998, Can Our Nat Heritage Survive? (in Danish) 1999, Frailty in Aging (in Danish) 1999, Ethics and Evidence-based Pharmacotherapy 2000, Can We Not Do It A Little Better? 2000, In That We Believe 2001, Fraud and Misconduct in Biomedical Research 2001, The Ethics of Research Related to Health Care in Developing Countries 2002; 48 AgeForum publs 1996–2007; Council of Europe, Ethical Eye: Biomedical Research 2004; many articles in medical journals; lyrics to contemporary Danish compositions, trans of lyrics. *Leisure interests:* tennis, music, mountain walking, botany, linguistics. *Address:* AgeForum, Skibshusvej 52 B^3, 5000, Odense C (office); Nerievej 7, 2900 Hellerup, Denmark (home). *Telephone:* 65484050 (office); 39629688 (home). *Fax:* 65484051 (office); 39629588 (home). *E-mail:* aef@aeldreforum.dk (office). *Website:* www.aeldreforum.dk (office).

RIIS-JØRGENSEN, Birger; Danish diplomatist; *Ambassador to UK;* m. Karin Riis-Jørgensen; fmr Dir for West and East Africa, Ministry of Foreign Affairs, State Sec., Ministry for Foreign Affairs –2006; Amb. to UK 2006–. *Address:* Royal Danish Embassy, 55 Sloane Street, London, SW1X 9SR, England (office). *Telephone:* (20) 7333-0200 (office). *Fax:* (20) 7333-0270 (office). *E-mail:* lonamb@um.dk (office). *Website:* www.amblondon.um.dk (office).

RILEY, Bridget Louise, CH, CBE, ARCA; British artist; b. 24 April 1931, London; d. of John Fisher and the late Bessie Louise Riley (née Gladstone); ed Cheltenham Ladies' Coll., Goldsmiths Coll. of Art and Royal Coll. of Art, London; first one-woman exhbn in London at Gallery One 1962, followed by others in England, USA, Italy, Germany, Ireland, Switzerland, Australia and Japan; has exhibited in group shows in Australia, Italy, France, Netherlands, Germany, Israel, USA, Japan and Argentina; represented GB at Biennale des Jeunes, Paris 1965, at Venice Biennale 1968; retrospective exhbn Europe and UK 1970–72; second retrospective exhbn touring America, Australia and Japan 1978–80; Arts Council Touring Exhbn 1984–85; retrospective exhbn Tate Britain 2003; solo exhbn Museum of Contemporary Art, Sydney 2004–05; paintings, drawings and prints in public collections in England, Ireland, Switzerland, Netherlands, Austria, Germany, Japan, Israel, USA, Australia and NZ; Founder-mem. and fmr Dir SPACE Ltd; mem. RSA; Trustee, Nat. Gallery 1981–88; Dr hc (Manchester) 1976, (Exeter) 1997, (Ulster) 1986, (Oxford) 1993, (Cambridge) 1995, (De Montfort) 1996; Hon. DLitt (Cambridge) 1995; AICA Critics Prize 1963, Prize in Open Section, John Moores Liverpool Exhbn 1963, Peter Stuyvesant Foundation Travel Bursary to USA 1964, Maj. Painting Prize, Venice Biennale 1968, Prize at Tokyo Print Biennale 1971, Gold Medal at Grafikk-bienniale, Fredrikstad, Norway 1980, Praemium Imperiale 2003. *Address:* c/o Karsten Schubert, 47 Lexington Street, London, W1R 3LG, England (office). *Telephone:* (20) 7734-9002 (office). *Fax:* (20) 7734-9008 (office). *E-mail:* mail@karstenschubert.com (office). *Website:* www.karstenschubert.com (office).

RILEY, Richard Wilson, LLB; American lawyer and fmr politician; *Partner, Nelson Mullins Riley & Scarborough LLP;* b. 2 Jan. 1933, Greenville, South Carolina; s. of E. P. Riley and Martha Dixon Riley; m. Ann Yarborough 1957; three s. one d.; ed Greenville Sr High School, Furman Univ. and SC School of Law; Lt in USN Legal Counsel to US Senate Cttee of Olin D. Johnston 1960; with family law firm 1961–62; mem. SC House of Reps 1962–66, S Carolina Senate 1966–76; S Carolina State Chair. for Jimmy Carter's Presidential Election Campaign 1976; Gov. of S Carolina 1979–87; Personnel Dir for Pres. Bill Clinton's Transition Team 1991–92; US Sec. of Educ. 1993–2001; Pnr, Nelson, Mullins, Riley & Scarborough LLP (law firm) 1987–93, 2001–; mem. Bd of Trustees, Carnegie Corpn of NY; mem. Bd ACT Inc., Knowledge Works Foundation, Furman Univ.; Distinguished Visiting Prof., Univ. of S Carolina 2001–, Distinguished Prof. of Govt, Politics, and Public Leadership, Richard W. Riley Inst., Furman Univ. *Address:* Nelson, Mullins, Riley & Scarborough, Suite 900, Poinsett Plaza, 104 South Main Street, Greenville, SC 29601-2122, USA (office). *Telephone:* (864) 250-2290 (office). *Fax:* (864) 232-2925 (office). *Website:* www.nelsonmullins.com (office).

RILEY, Robert (Bob), BA; American politician and state official; *Governor of Alabama;* b. 3 Oct. 1944, Ashland, Ala; m. Patsy Adams; one s. three d.; ed Clay Co. High School, Univ. of Ala; fmr propr of poultry and egg business, automobile dealership, trucking co. grocery story and pharmacy; mem. Ashland City Council 1972–76; mem. US House of Reps from Ala 1996–2002, Asst Whip; Gov. of Ala 2003–; Republican. *Address:* Office of the Governor, State Capitol, 600 Dexter Avenue, Suite N104, Montgomery, AL 36130–2751, USA (office). *Telephone:* (334) 242-7100 (office). *Fax:* (334) 353-0004 (office). *Website:* www.governor.state.al.us (office).

RILEY, Terence; American museum curator; *Director, Miami Art Museum;* ed Univ. of Notre Dame and Columbia Univ., New York; f. architectural practice with John Keenen; curator of 'Paul Nelson Filter of Reason' inaugural exhbn at Arthur Ross Architectural Galleries, Columbia Univ. 1989, Dir –1991; directed exhbns. on work of Iacov Chernikhov and restaging of Museum of Modern Art's (MoMA) first exhbn on architecture: 'Exhibition 15: The International Style and The Museum of Modern Art', New York; adjunct faculty mem. 1987–; joined MoMA 1991, Chief Curator of Architecture and Design 1992–2006, organized exhbns on the works of, amongst others, Frank Lloyd Wright, Rem Koolhaas 1994, Bernard Tschumi, Mies van der Rohe 2001; Instructor, Harvard Design School 2001–; Dir Miami Art Museum 2006–. *Publications include:* The Un-Private House (jtly with Glenn D. Lowry) 2002, MoMA QNS Box Set 2002; The Changing of the Avant-garde (Ed.) 2002. *Address:* Miami Art Museum, 101 West Flagler Street, Miami, FL 33130, USA (office). *Telephone:* (305) 375-3000 (office). *Website:* www.miamiartmuseum.org (office).

RILEY, Terry Mitchell, MA; American composer, pianist and raga singer; b. 24 June 1935, Colfax, CA; s. of Wilma Ridlofi and Charles Riley; m. Ann Yvonne Smith 1958; three c.; ed San Francisco State Univ., Univ. of California, studied with Duane Hampton, Adolf Baller and Pandit Pran Nath; Creative Assoc., Center for Creative and Performing Arts, Buffalo 1967; taught music composition and N Indian raga at Mills Coll. 1971–83; freelance composer and performer 1961–; launched Minimal Music Movt with composition and first performance of In C 1964; Guggenheim Fellowship 1980. *Compositions include:* The Harp of New Albion for solo piano in just intonation, Sunrise of the Planetary Dream Collector, Sri Camel, The Ten Voices of the Two Prophets, Chorale of the Blessed Day, Eastern Man, Embroidery, Song from the Old Country, G-Song, Remember This Oh Mind, The Ethereal Time Shadow, Offering to Chief Crazy Horse, Rites of the Imitators, The Medicine Wheel, Song of the Emerald Runner, Cycle of five string quartets, Trio for violin, clarinet and cello 1957, Concert for two pianos and tape 1960, String Trio 1961, Keyboard Studies 1963, Dorian Reeds for ensemble 1964, In C 1964, A Rainbow in the Curved Air 1968, Persian Surgery

Dervishes for electronic keyboard 1971, Descending Moonshine Dervishes 1975, Do You Know How it Sounds? for low voice, piano and tabla 1983, Cadenza on the Night Plain for string quartet 1984, Salome Dances for Peace string quartet 1988, Jade Palace for orchestra and synthesiser 1989, Cactus Rosary for synthesiser and ensemble 1990, June Buddhas for chorus and orchestra 1991, The Sands for string quartet and orchestra 1991, Four Woelfi Portraits for ensemble 1992, The Saint Adolf Ring chamber opera 1993, Ritmos and Melos 1993, El Hombre string quartet 1993, Ascension for solo guitar 1993, The Heaven Ladder for piano four hands 1996, Three Requiem Quartets 1997, Autodreamographical Tales for narrator and instruments 1997. *Leisure interests:* music, gardens and orchards. *Address:* c/o Robert Friedman Presents, 1353 4th Avenue, San Francisco, CA 94122, USA. *Telephone:* (415) 759-1992. *Fax:* (415) 759-6663. *E-mail:* robert@rfpresents .com. *Website:* terryriley.com.

RIMAWI, Fahid Nimer ar-, BA; Jordanian journalist; *Publisher and Editor-in-Chief, Al Majd;* b. 1942, Palestine; m.; two s. five d.; ed Cairo Univ., Egypt; Ed. Difa (newspaper) 1965–67; Ed.-in-Chief, Jordan News Agency 1968–70; Sec. Editorial Bd of Afkar (magazine) 1970–73; Dir Investigating Dept of Al-Raiue (newspaper) 1975–76; writer Al-Destour (newspaper) 1978–81; Political Writer, Al-Raiue (newspaper) 1981–85; Corresp. al Talie'ah (magazine) Paris 1982–85; political writer 1985–94; Publr and Ed.-in-Chief Al Majd (weekly). *Publications:* Mawaweel Fi al Layl Al Taweel, short stories in Arabic 1982. *Address:* PO Box 926856, Amman 11190 (office); Dahiyat al-Rashid, Amman, Jordan. *Telephone:* (6) 5530553 (office); (6) 5160615 (home). *Fax:* (6) 553 0352. *E-mail:* almajd@almajd.net (office). *Website:* www.almajd.net (office).

RIMINGTON, Dame Stella, DCB, MA; British fmr civil servant; b. 1935; m. John Rimington 1963; two d.; ed Nottingham High School for Girls, Edinburgh Univ.; Dir-Gen. Security Service 1992–96; Dir (non-exec.) Marks and Spencer 1997–2004, BG PLC 1997–2000, BG Group 2000–, GKR. Group (now Whitehead Mann) 1997–2001; Chair. Inst. of Cancer Research 1997–2001; Trustee Royal Marsden Hosp., Refuge (charity); Gov. Town Close House Preparatory School, Norwich; Hon. Air Commodore 7006 (VR) Squadron Royal Auxiliary Air Force 1997–2001; Hon. LLB (Nottingham) 1995, (Exeter) 1996, (London Metropolitan Univ.) 2004; Spirit of Everywoman Award 2007. *Publications:* Intelligence, Security and the Law (non-fiction) 1994, Open Secret (autobiog.) 2001, At Risk (novel) 2004, Secret Asset (novel) 2006, Illegal Action (novel) 2007, Dead Line (novel) 2008. *Address:* PO Box 1604, London, SW1P 1XB, England.

RIMŠĒVIČS, Ilmārs, BA, MBA; Latvian economist and central banker; *Governor, Bank of Latvia;* b. 30 April 1965, Rīga; ed Rīga High School No. 6, Rīga Tech. Univ., St Lawrence Univ. and Clarkson Univ., USA; Deputy Chair. Econs Cttee, Popular Front of Latvia 1989–90; Man. Foreign Operations Dept and Head of Securities Dept, Latvijas Zemes banka 1990–92; Deputy Gov. Bank of Latvia 1992–2001, Chair. Bd 1992–2001, Gov. 2001–. *Address:* Bank of Latvia (Latvijas Banka), K. Valdemāra iela 2A, 1050 Rīga, Latvia (office). *Telephone:* (2) 6702-2300 (office). *Fax:* (2) 6702-2420 (office). *E-mail:* info@ bank.lv (office). *Website:* www.bank.lv (office).

RINDLER, Wolfgang, PhD; British physicist and academic; *Professor of Physics, University of Texas at Dallas;* b. 18 May 1924, Vienna; s. of Dr Ernst Rindler; m. 1st Phyllis Berla 1959 (died 1966); m. 2nd Linda Veret 1977; two s. one d.; ed Ruthin Grammar School, Liverpool Univ., Imperial Coll., London; asst lecturer Univ. of Liverpool 1947–49; lecturer Sir John Cass Coll., London 1949–56; Asst Prof. Cornell Univ., USA 1956–63; Assoc. and Full Prof. Southwest Center for Advanced Studies, Dallas, Texas 1963–69, Prof. of Physics, Univ. of Texas at Dallas 1969–; Visiting Prof. Univ. of Vienna, Univ. of Rome, Max-Planck Inst. at Munich and Potsdam, King's Coll. London; Visiting Fellow Churchill Coll., Cambridge 1990; mem. Foreign Editorial Bd Rendiconti di Matematica 1984–; Assoc. Ed. American Journal of Physics 1988–91; Foreign mem. Acad. of Sciences of Turin, Italy 2000; Hon. mem. Austrian Acad. of Sciences 1998; Gold Medal of Honour, City of Vienna 1996. *Publications:* Special Relativity 1960, Essential Relativity 1969, Introduction to Special Relativity 1982, Spinors and Space-Time (with R. Penrose) Vol. I 1984, Vol. II 1986, Relativity: Special, General, and Cosmological 2001, numerous research and encyclopedia articles on special and gen. relativity and cosmology. *Address:* Physics Department, University of Texas at Dallas, Richardson, TX 75080-3021 (office); 7110 Spring Valley Road, Dallas, TX 75254, USA (home). *Telephone:* (972) 883-2880 (office); (972) 387-9768 (home). *E-mail:* rindler@utdallas.edu (office). *Website:* www.utdallas.edu/dept/physics (office).

RINEHART, Georgina (Gina) Hope; Australian business executive; *Chairman, Hancock Prospecting Pty Ltd;* b. 9 Feb. 1954, Perth, WA; d. of Lang Hancock; m. Francis Rinehart (deceased); four c.; ed Univ. of Sydney; joined Hancock Group as personal asst to her father 1973, Exec. Chair. Hancock Prospecting Pty Ltd and Hancock Prospecting Pty Ltd Group 1992–; ranked by Forbes magazine amongst 100 Most Powerful Women in the World (84th) 2007, (98th) 2008. *Address:* Hancock Prospecting Pty Ltd, 28–42 Ventnor Avenue, West Perth 6005, WA, Australia (office). *Telephone:* (8) 9429-8222 (office). *Fax:* (8) 9429-8268 (office). *E-mail:* Mail@hancockprospecting .com.au (office). *Website:* www.hancockprospecting.com.au (office).

RINGEL, Johannes; German banking executive; b. 1941, Breslau; ed Volkswirtschafts-Studium; joined WestLB (Westdeutsche Landesbank Girozentrale) 1969, Dir Dept of Planning 1974–84, Dir Cen. Control Bureau 1984–87, mem. Exec. Cttee 1987–03, CEO WestLB 2002–04; mem. Exec. Bd Steag AG 2001–. *Address:* c/o WestLB, Herzogstrasse 15, 40217 Düsseldorf, Germany (office).

RINGHOLM, Bosse; Swedish politician; *Chairman, Stockholm Branch, Social Democratic Party;* b. 18 Aug. 1942, Falköping; m. Kerstin Pehrsson; three c.; Chair. Social Democratic Youth 1967–72; Political Adviser, Ministries of Interior and Labour 1973–76; mem. Stockholm Co. Council 1973–97; Alt. mem./mem. Riksdag 1976, 1982; Dir Ministry of Educ. and Science 1976–82; Lead Co. Councillor for Transport 1983–85, for Finance 1989–91, 1994–97, Opposition Lead Co. Councillor 1986–88, 1991–94; Dir Gen. Nat. Labour Market Bd 1997–99; Minister for Finance 1999–2004; Deputy Prime Minister 2004–06, temp. Minister of Foreign Affairs March 2006; mem. Exec. Cttee Social Democratic Party (Sveriges Socialdemokratiska Arbetareparti—SAP), Chair. Stockholm Br., Social Democratic Party 2001–. *Address:* Sveriges Socialdemokratiska Arbetareparti, Sveavägen 68, 105 60 Stockholm (office); Källu. 33, 122 62, Enskede, Sweden (home). *Telephone:* (8) 786-40-00 (office); (8) 649026 (home). *Fax:* (8) 204257 (office). *E-mail:* info@sap.se (office). *Website:* www.socialdemokraterna.se (office).

RINGIER, Michael; Swiss publishing and media executive; *Chairman, Ringier AG;* b. 30 March 1949, Zofingen; s. of Hans Ringier and Eva Ringier (née Landolt); ed Hochschule St Gallen; est. himself professionally outside of family-owned firm Ringier working as a journalist, travelled to Germany to work for Grüner + Jahr and H. Bauer; joined Ringier 1985 working with brother, Christoph, becoming CEO 1985, two brothers were Co-Chair. –1991, Pres. Bd of Dirs 1991–97, took over operational man. of Ringier AG as mem. Bd of Dirs 1997–2000, COO Ringier AG 2000–03, Chair. Ringier Holding AG (largest media corpn in Switzerland) 2003–, Chair. Publishing Cttee. *Address:* Ringier AG, Dufourstrasse 23, 8008 Zürich, Switzerland (office). *Telephone:* (44) 259-61-11 (office). *Fax:* (44) 259-86-35 (office). *E-mail:* info@ringier.ch (office). *Website:* www.ringier.com (office).

RINI, Snyder; Solomon Islands politician; *Minister of Finance and Treasury;* b. 27 July 1948; ed Univ. of Papua New Guinea, Univ. of Technology, Lae, Papua New Guinea; Financial Controller, Brewer Solomons Agriculture Ltd. 1975–80; Perm. Sec. for Ministry of Natural Resources 1989, for Ministry of Nat. Planning and Devt 1994–95, for Ministry of Agric. and Fisheries 1997; mem. Parl. for Marovo, Western Prov. 1997–; Minister for Finance and Treasury 2000–01, Deputy Prime Minister for Nat. Planning and Devt 2001–02, Deputy Prime Minister and Minister for Finance and Treasury 2002–03, Deputy Prime Minister and Minister for Educ. and Human Resources Devt 2003–06, Prime Minister April–May 2006 (resgnd); Minister of Finance and Treasury 2007–; mem. Bd of Dirs Devt Bank of Solomon Islands 1976–84, Central Bank of Solomon Islands 1982–84, 1990–96, Solomon Islands Port Authority 1982–84, Nat. Provident Fund 1976–86 (Chair. 1990–96), Solomon Islands Electricity Authority 1988–89. *Address:* Ministry of Finance and Treasury, POB 26, Honiara, Solomon Islands (office). *Telephone:* 22535 (office). *Fax:* 20392 (office). *E-mail:* finance@welkam .solomon.com.sb (office).

RINNE, Risto, MEng; Finnish petroleum industry executive; *President and CEO, Neste Oil Oyj;* b. 1949; with Fortum Corpn (later Neste Oil Oyj) 1975, Pres. Neste Oyj Finland 1999–2004, Pres. Oil Sector Finland 2004, Pres., CEO and Chair. Exec. Team Neste Oil Oyj 2004–; Chair. Bd of Dirs Chemicals Industry Fed. Finland, Finnish Oil and Gas Fed.; mem. Bd of Dirs European Petroleum Industry Asscn (EUROPIA). *Address:* Neste Oil Oyj, Keilaranta 8, PO Box 95, 00095 Espoo, Finland (office). *Telephone:* (10) 45811 (office). *Fax:* (10) 4584442 (office). *Website:* www.nesteoil.com (office).

RINPOCHE, Samdhong; Tibetan academic and politician; *Chief Minister of Tibetan Government in Exile;* b. (Lobsang Tenzin), 5 Nov. 1939, Nagdug, Tibet; ed monastic studies, Univ. of Drepung, Tibet (rehoused in India after Chinese occupation), Monastery of Gyuto, Dalhousie, India; various positions in Tibetan colls in Simla, Darjeeling and Dalhousie, India; Vice-Pres. Congress of Tibetan Youth 1970–73; Prof. Cen. Inst. of Higher Tibetan Studies, Benares (now Varanasi), India 1971–2001, apptd Dir 1988; mem. Standing Cttee Asscn of Indian Univs 1994–, Pres. 1998–; fmr Pres. Tibetan Parl. in Exile; elected Kalon Tripa (Chief Minister) of Tibetan Govt in Exile 2001; Vice-Pres. Library of Tibetan Works and Files, Dharamsala, India; Adviser World Peace Univ., USA; mem. Cttee for Charter of Tibetans in Exile and Future Constitution of Tibet; mem. Bd of Dirs Tibetan Schools, New Delhi, India; mem. Bd of Dirs Asiatic Soc., Calcutta; mem. Bd of Dirs Foundation for Universal Responsibility, New Delhi; mem. Directorate of Indian Council for Philosophical Research; mem. Directorate Krishnamurti Foundation, India; advisory mem. Inst. of Asian Democracy, NY, USA. *Publications include:* numerous academic essays and newspaper articles. *Address:* Kashag Secretariat, Central Tibetan Administration, Dharamsala 176215, Dist Kangra, H.P., India (office). *Telephone:* (18) 92222218 (office). *Fax:* (18) 92224914 (office). *E-mail:* kadrung@gov.tibet.net (home). *Website:* www.tibet.net (office).

RINTZLER, Marius Adrian; German singer; b. 14 March 1932, Bucharest, Romania; m. Sanda Dragomir 1964; ed Acad. of Music, Bucharest; soloist with Bucharest Philharmonic 1959; debut in opera in Bucharest as Don Basilio in Il Barbiere di Siviglia 1964; went to Germany 1966; leading bass at Düsseldorf's Deutsche Oper am Rhein 1968–; guest singer with major opera cos, including Metropolitan, San Francisco, Glyndebourne, Paris, Brussels, Munich; repertoire includes various roles in Richard Strauss' Rosenkavalier (Ochs), Capriccio (La Roche), Schweigsame Frau (Morosus), in Rossini's La Cenerentola (Don Magnifico), Il Barbiere (Bartolo), in Richard Wagner's Ring (Alberich), in Mozart's Don Giovanni (Leporello), Die Entführung (Osmin); appears with major symphony orchestras in Europe and USA, including Philharmonia (London), Berlin Philharmonic, Cleveland Symphony; also gives recitals, TV appearances in England, Germany and France; Kammersänger. *Address:* Friedingstrasse 18, 40625 Düsseldorf, Germany (home). *Telephone:* (211) 297083 (home).

RIO, Neiphiu; Indian politician; *Chief Minister of Nagaland;* b. 11 Nov. 1950, Tuophema village, Kohima Dist; s. of the late Guolhoulie Rio; m.; one s. five d.; ed St Joseph's Coll., Darjeeling and Kohima Arts Coll.; mem. Nagaland Legis. Ass. 1989–2002, 2004–; State Minister of Sports and School Educ. 1989–91, of Higher and Tech. Educ., Arts and Culture 1991–93, of Works and Housing 1993–98, of Home Affairs 1998–2002; Chair. Nagaland Industrial Devt Corpn (NIDC), Nat. Khadi and Village Industries Bd (NKVIB), Devt Authority of Nagaland; Chief Minister of Nagaland 2003–; Leader Democratic Alliance of Nagaland 2004–; Hon. Vice-Pres. Indian Red Cross Soc.; Lifetime Deputy Gov. (Hon.), Bd Govs American Biographical Inst. Research Asscn 1999–. *Leisure interests* games, sports, reading, music. *Address:* Office of the Chief Minister, Government of Nagaland, Civil Secretariat, Kohima 797 001, India (office).

RIORDAN, Richard, BA, JD; American business executive, lawyer and fmr politician; *Of Counsel, Bingham McCutchen LLP;* b. 1930, Flushing, NY; m. 1st Eugenia Riordan; six c. (two deceased); m. 2nd Jill Riordan; ed Univ. of Calif., Santa Clara, Princeton Univ., Univ. of Mich. Law School; served in US Army in Korean War; after law school f. Riordan and McKinzie (law firm); Mayor of LA 1993–2001; Co-founder LEARN 1991; f. Riordan Foundation; Sec. for Educ. for Calif. 2003–05; Of Counsel, Bingham, McCutchen LLP 2005–; mem. Republican Party; Business Person of the Year, Los Angeles Business Journal 2005. *Address:* Bingham McCutchen LLP, 355 South Grand Avenue, Los Angeles, CA 90071-3106, USA (office). *Telephone:* (213) 680-6400 (office). *Fax:* (213) 680-6499 (office). *E-mail:* richard.riordan@bingham.com (office). *Website:* www.bingham.com (office).

RÍOS MONTT, Gen. Efraín; Guatemalan politician and army officer (retd); *Secretary-General, Frente Republicano Guatemalteco (FRG);* b. 1927; joined army 1943; defence posting, Washington, DC 1973; contested presidential election for Christian Democratic coalition 1974; Mil. Attaché, Madrid; fmr Commdr Honour Guard Brigade; Dir Mil. Acad.; installed as leader of mil. junta after coup March 1982; Minister of Nat. Defence March–Sept. 1982; Pres. of Guatemala, also C-in-C of the Army 1982–83; overthrown Aug. 1983; Sec.-Gen. Frente Republicano Guatemalteco (FRG) 1988–; Pres. of Guatemalan Congress 1995–96, 2001–03; unsuccessful presidential cand. for FRG 2003 elections; mem. Parl. (FRG) 2007–. *Address:* Frente Republicano Guatemalteco, 3A Calle 5-50, Zona 1, Guatemala City, Guatemala (office). *Telephone:* 2238-0826 (office). *Website:* www.frg.org.gt (office).

RIPA DI MEANA, Carlo; Italian politician and journalist; b. 15 Aug. 1929, Marina di Pietrasanta, Lucca; m. 1st Gae Aulenti (q.v.) (divorced); m. 2nd Marina Punturieri; journalist on Il Lavoro (weekly journal of the Confederazione Generale Italiana del Lavoro) and on L'Unità (Italian daily) 1950–53; co-f. and ran weekly Nuova Generazione 1953–56; co-f. and Ed. magazine Passato e Presente 1957; publisher's ed. for Feltrinelli and Rizzoli 1958–66; resgnd from Italian CP 1957, joined Italian Socialist Party (PSI) 1958; Sec.-Gen. Club Turati, Milan 1967–76; Regional Councillor, Lombardy, Leader, Socialist Party group in the Council 1970–82; mem. Bd La Scala Theatre, Milan 1970–74; Chair. Venice Biennale 1974–79; head of int. relations, Italian Socialist Party 1979–80; MEP 1979–84, –1999; Comm. of the European Communities (responsible for Citizen's Europe, information, culture and tourism) 1985–89, (responsible for communication) 1986–89, (responsible for environment, nuclear safety and civil protection) 1989–93; Minister for the Environment 1992–93, leader Green Party 1993–98 (left PSI); Pres. Italia Nostra (environmental org.) 2005–07; apptd Chair. Istituto per la Cooperazione economica internazionale e i problemi dello sviluppo 1983. *Publications:* Un viaggio in Viet Nam 1956, Dedicato a Raymond Roussel e alle sue impressioni d'Africa 1965, Il governo audiovisivo 1973. *Address:* c/o Italia Nostra, Via Sicilia 66, 00187 Rome, Italy.

RIPKEN, Calvin Edward (Cal), Jr; American business executive and fmr professional baseball player; b. 24 Aug. 1960, Havre de Grace, Md; s. of the late Cal Ripken Sr; m. Kelly Ripken; one s. one d.; ed Aberdeen High School, Md; player minor league teams in Bluefield, Miami, Charlotte, Rochester 1978–81; shortstop Baltimore Orioles 1978–2001; highest single season fielding percentage 1990; maj. league record for consecutive games played (breaking Lou Gehrig's record of 2,130 in 1995), 2,632 ending in 1998; 4,000 home runs, 3,000 hits (2000); retd 2001; purchased Utica Blue Sox Class A minor league team 2002, renamed to Aberdeen IronBirds (affiliate of Baltimore Orioles); f. The Kelly and Cal Ripken, Jr Foundation (now Cal Ripkin Sr Foundation) 1992; currently Head, Ripken Baseball Group; Rookie of the Year, Int. League 1981, Rookie of the Year, Baseball Writers Asscn, American League 1982, Silver Slugger Award 1983–86, 1989, 1991, 1993–94, Golden Glove Award 1991–92, Sportsman of the Year, Sports Illustrated 1995; elected to Baseball Hall of Fame 2007. *Publications:* Play Baseball The Ripken Way (with Bill Ripken) 2004, Parenting Young Athletes the Ripken Way 2006. *Address:* Ripken Baseball, 1427 Clarkview Road, Suite 100, Baltimore, MD 21209, USA (office). *Telephone:* (410) 823-0808 (office). *Fax:* (410) 823-0850 (office). *Website:* www.ripkenbaseball.com (office).

RIPPON, Angela, OBE; British broadcaster and journalist; b. 12 Oct. 1944, Plymouth, Devon; d. of John Rippon and Edna Rippon; m. Christopher Dare 1967 (divorced); ed Plymouth Selective School for Girls; Presenter and Reporter, BBC TV Plymouth 1966–69; Ed., Producer, Dir and Presenter, Westward TV (ITV) 1969–73; Reporter, BBC TV Nat. News 1973–75, Newsreader 1975–81; Founder and Presenter TV-am Feb.–April 1983; Arts Corresp. for WNETV (CBS), Boston, 1983; Reporter and Presenter BBC and ITV 1984–; Vice-Pres. Int. Club for Women in TV 1979–, British Red Cross, NCH Action for Children, Riding for the Disabled Asscn; Dir Nirex 1986–89; Chair. English Nat. Ballet 2000–04; Dr hc (American Int. Univ.) 1994; New York Film Festival Silver Medal 1973, Newsreader of the Year (TV and Radio Industries Club) 1975, 1976, 1977, TV Personality of the Year 1977, Emmy Award 1984 (Channel 7 Boston), Sony Radio Award 1990, New York Radio

Silver Medal 1992, Royal TV Soc. Hall of Fame 1996, European Woman of Achievement 2002 and other awards. *TV appearances include:* Angela Rippon Meets (documentary), Antiques Roadshow, In the Country, Compere, Eurovision Song Contest 1976, The Morecambe and Wise Christmas Show 1976, 1977, Royal Wedding 1981, Masterteam (BBC) 1985, 1986, 1987, Come Dancing 1988–, What's My Line? 1988–, Healthcheck, Holiday Programme, Simply Money (Family Finance Channel) 2001–, Channel 5 News 2003–, Live with Angela Rippon (ITV) 2004–06, Top Gear 2006, Sun, Sea & Bargain Spotting, Cash in the Attic. *Radio series include:* Angela Rippon's Morning Report for LBC 1992, Angela Rippon's Drive Time Show, LBC 1993, The Health Show (BBC Radio 4), Friday Night with Angela Rippon (BBC Radio 2), LBC Arts Programme 2003–. *Publications:* Riding 1980, In the Country 1980, Mark Phillips – The Man and his Horses 1982, Victoria Plum (eight children's books) 1983, Angela Rippon's West Country 1982, Badminton: A Celebration 1987, Fabulous at 50 – And Beyond 2005. *Leisure interests:* cooking, tennis, reading, theatre. *Address:* c/o Knight Ayton Management, 114 St Martin's Lane, London, WC2N 4BE, England (office). *Telephone:* (20) 7836-5333 (office). *Fax:* (20) 7836-8333 (office). *E-mail:* info@knightayton.co.uk (office). *Website:* www.knightayton.co.uk (office).

RISDAHL JENSEN, Tom; Danish diplomatist; *Ambassador to Sweden;* b. 28 Sept. 1947, Hjørring; m. Helle Bundgaard; Amb. to UK 2001–06, to Sweden 2006–; Commdr, Order of the Dannebrog 2005. *Address:* Embassy of Denmark, Jakobs Torg 1, 10323 Stockholm, Sweden (office). *Telephone:* (8) 406-75-00 (office). *E-mail:* stoamb@um.dk (office). *Website:* www .ambstockholm.um.dk (office).

RISHTON, John; British business executive; *President and CEO, Royal Ahold NV;* b. 21 Feb. 1958; worked for Ford Europe in various exec. positions; fmr Chief Financial Officer British Airways Plc; Exec. Vice-Pres. and Chief Financial Officer Royal Ahold NV 2006–07, mem. Corp. Exec. Bd 2006–, Acting Pres. and CEO July–Nov. 2007–, Pres. and CEO Nov. 2007–; mem. Bd of Dirs (non-exec.) Rolls Royce Group Plc. *Address:* Royal Ahold NV, Albert Hijnweg 1, 1507 EH Zaandam, The Netherlands (office). *Telephone:* (75) 659-9111 (office). *Fax:* (75) 659-8350 (office). *E-mail:* info@ahold.com (office). *Website:* www.ahold.com (office).

RISSEEUW, A. H. J. (Ton), MSc; Dutch business executive; *Chairman of the Supervisory Board, Koninklijke KPN NV;* b. 9 Nov. 1936; Founder and Chair. Exec. Bd Getronics NV 1976–99; Chair. Supervisory Bd Koninklijke KPN NV 2001–, Groeneveld Groep BV, Intergamma BV; mem. Supervisory Bd Heineken Nederlands Beheer BV –2000, Heineken NV 2000–07, Samas-Groep NV 1999–2006, TNO 1997–2007, Blokker Holding BV; mem. Bd of Dirs Stichting ING Aandelen (ING Trust Office) 2002–06, Chair. 2005–06; mem. Advisory Council Deloitte Netherlands. *Address:* Koninklijke KPN NV, Maanplein 5, 2516 CK The Hague, Netherlands (office). *Website:* www.kpn .com (office).

RISTE, Olav, DPhil; Norwegian historian and academic; b. 11 April 1933, Volda; s. of Olav Riste and Bergliot Meidell; m. Ruth Pittman 1964; ed Univs of Oslo and Oxford; Lecturer, Volda Gymnas 1963–64; Historian, Office of Mil. History (with leaves of absence) 1964–79, Dir 1979–80; Research Fellow, Charles Warren Center, Harvard Univ. 1967–68; Visiting Scholar, LSE 1971, 1986; Visiting Prof. Freie Univ. Berlin 1972–73; Dir Research Centre for Defence History (with leaves of absence) 1980–87; Adjunct Prof. of History, Univ. of Bergen 1980–2003, Univ. of Oslo 1998–2003; Guest Scholar, Woodrow Wilson Center, Washington, DC 1982; Dir Norwegian Inst. for Defence Studies 1988–95, Research Dir 1996–2003; Fellow, Norwegian Acad. of Science and Letters 1984; Kt (First Class), Royal Order of St Olav 2003. *Publications:* The Neutral Ally 1965, Norway and the Second World War (ed.) 1966, Norway 1940–45: The Resistance Movement 1970, London-regjeringa: Norge i krigsalliansen 1940–45 I-II 1973–79, Western Security: The Formative Years (ed.) 1985, Norge i Krig: Utefront 1987, Otto Ruge: Felttoget (ed.) 1989, Fredsgeneralen (ed.) 1995, 'Strengt hemmelig.' Norsk etterretningsteneste 1945–70 (with A. Moland) 1997, The Norwegian Intelligence Service 1945–1970 1999, Norway's Foreign Relations: A History 2001. *Leisure interests:* classical music, skiing. *Address:* Husarveien 18, 1396 Billingstad, Norway (home). *Telephone:* 66-84-63-05 (home). *Fax:* 66-98-11-08 (home). *E-mail:* oriste@c2i.net (home).

RITA, Mateus Meira; São Tomé and Príncipe politician; Minister of Foreign Affairs and Co-operation 2002–04. *Address:* c/o Ministry of Foreign Affairs and Co-operation, Avenida 12 de Julho, CP 111, São Tomé, São Tomé e Príncipe (office).

RITBLAT, Sir John Henry, Kt, FSVA, FRICS, FRSA; British business executive; *Chairman, European Real Estate Private Equity Advisory Council;* b. 3 Oct. 1935; m. 1st Isabel Paja 1960 (died 1979); two s. one d.; m. 2nd Jill Rosemary Zilkha (née Slotover) 1986; ed Dulwich Coll., Coll. of Estate Management, Univ. of London; Chair. The British Land Co. PLC 1970 (Man. Dir 1971–2004), Chair. and Chief Exec. The British Land Corpn 1991–2006, Hon. Pres. 2006–; Chair. European Real Estate Pvt. Equity Advisory Council, Lehman Brothers 2006–; Founder and Chair. Conrad Ritblat & Co., Consultant Surveyors and Valuers 1958, Man. Dir 1970, Chair. Conrad Ritblat Group PLC 1993–; Chair. Colliers Conrad Ritblat Erdman 2000–; Man. Dir Union Property Holdings (London) Ltd 1969, Crown Estates Paving Commn. 1969–; mem. Bd of Govs Weizmann Inst. 1991–, London Business School 1991– (Hon. Fellow 2000, Deputy Chair. 2005); Dir and Gov. RAM 1998– (Deputy Chair. 1999–, Hon. Fellow 2000); mem. Council, Business in the Community 1987–, Prince of Wales' Royal Parks Tree Appeal Cttee 1987–, Patrons of British Art (Tate Gallery), Nat. Art. Collections Fund, British Library Bd 1995–; Pres. British Ski Fed. 1994–; Trustee, The Wallace Collection 2003– (Chair. 2005); Life mem. Royal Inst. of GB; Hon. FRIBA 2006; Hon. DLitt (London

Metropolitan Univ.) 2005. *Leisure interests:* golf, skiing, real tennis, books, architecture. *Address:* 10 Cornwall Terrace, Regent's Park, London, NW1 4QP; Lehman Brothers, European Headquarters, 25 Bank Street, London, E14 5LE, England. *Telephone:* (20) 7486-4466. *Fax:* (20) 7935-5552.

RITCHIE, Guy; British film director; b. 10 Sept. 1968, Hatfield, Herts.; s. of John Ritchie and Amber Mary Ritchie; m. Madonna Ciccone (q.v.) 2000; one s. one step-d.; ed Standbridge Earls; directed numerous pop videos 1980s; British Ind. Film Award 1998, London Film Critics' Circle Award 1999. *Films:* The Hard Case 1995, Lock, Stock and Two Smoking Barrels 1998, Snatch 2000, What it Feels Like For a Girl (video) 2001, The Hire: Star 2001, Swept Away 2002, Mean Machine (supervising producer) 2002, Revolver 2005, RocknRolla 2008. *Television:* The Hard Case 1995, Lock, Stock and Two Smoking Barrels (series exec. producer) 2000, Suspect 2007. *Leisure interests:* karate, judo. *Address:* c/o Creative Arts Agency, 2 Queen Caroline Street, Hammersmith, London, W6 9DX, England.

RITCHIE, Ian Charles, CBE, RA, RIBA, FRSA, MRIAI, DipArch; British architect; *Principal, Ian Ritchie Architects Ltd;* b. 24 June 1947, Hove; s. of Christopher Ritchie and Mabel Long; pnr Jocelyne van den Bossche; one s.; ed Polytechnic of Central London (now Univ. of Westminster); project architect Foster Assocs 1972–79; in pvt. practice, France 1976–78; ind. consultant 1979–81; Founder Partner Chrysalis Architects 1979–81; Co-Founder Rice Francis Ritchie 1981, Dir 1981–87, Consultant 1987–89; Prin. Ian Ritchie Architects Ltd 1981–; comms include: Eagle Rock House, Sussex, several projects for the Louvre, Paris, including work on the Louvre Pyramids and Sculpture Courts, Nat. Museum of Science, Tech. and Industry, La Villette, pharmacy at Boves, France, cultural centre, Albert, France, Ecology Gallery, Natural History Museum, London, Stockley Business Park offices, Oxford Science Park offices, Glass Towers, Reina Sofia Museum of Modern Art, Madrid, Glass Hall, Leipzig Int. Exhbn Centre, Bermondsey and Wood Lane Stations for London Underground, EdF HV electricity pylons, France, Royal Opera House Theatre, Tower Bridge, London, Crystal Palace Concert Platform, White City re devt, Theatre Royal Production Centre, Plymouth, Scotland's Home of Tomorrow, Glasgow, Spire of Dublin Nat. Monument, 3rd Millennium Light Monument, Milan, Hayward Gallery Exhbns, London, Potters Field Devt, London, British Museum masterplan, Crossrail station, London, RSC Courtyard Theatre, Stratford upon Avon; numerous exhbns; Chair. Royal Acad. Collections and Library Cttee 2000–, RA Magazine Editorial Bd 2003–; RA Prof. of Architecture 2004–; mem. RA Council 1999, 2005–06; Visiting Prof. Tech. Univ. Vienna 1994–95; Special Prof., Leeds Univ. School of Civil Eng 2001–04; Pres. Europan UK 1997–2003; Gov. and Adviser RSC 2001–; mem. RSC Int. Council 2007–; Royal Fine Art Commr 1995–99; Adviser to Lord Chancellor's Dept 1999–2004, to The Ove Arup Foundation 2002–, to Columbia Univ. Pres.'s Ad Hoc Cttee 2007–; mem. Design Bd London Docklands Devt Corpn 1990–96, Council Steel Construction Inst. 1994–97, Advisory Bd City Journal 1994–99, Research Cttee Nat. Maritime Museum 1995–97, Royal Fine Art Comm. 1995–99; CABE Commr 1999–2001 (Emer. Commr 2002–); mem. IABSE, Scientists for Global Responsibility, UK Construction Foresight Panel 1996–98; Adviser, Natural History Museum 1991–95; mem. European Construction Tech. Platform, Brussels 2005–08, mem. UK Construction Tech. Platform 2006–; regular int. lecturer and architectural judge; Hon. DLitt (Westminster), Hon. Prof. of Architecture (Liverpool Univ.); numerous awards including Architectural Design Silver Medal 1983, Iritecna Prize for Europe (Italy) 1991, Eric Lyons Memorial Award for Housing in Europe 1992, Commonwealth Asscn of Architects Robert Matthews Award 1994, AIA Awards 1997, 2003, 2008, Civic Trust Award 1997, RIBA Awards 1998 (two), 2000, 2003, 2004, 2007, RIBA Stephen Lawrence Award 1998, RFAC Arts Building of the Year 1998, RFAC Sports Building of the Year 2000, RFAC Building of the Year 2003, two Design Council Millennium Product Awards 1999, IABSE Int. Outstanding Structure Award 2000, Regeneration of Scotland Supreme Award 2000, British Construction Industry Special Award 2000, Copper Building of the Year 2000, CDA Innovation in Copper Award 2000, 2003, Abercrombie Awards: Best New Building and Overall Abercrombie Architectural Design Award 2004. *Films:* La cité en lumière (co-scripted/dir) 1986, The Spire of Dublin 2003. *Television:* (scripted, directed or produced): Sandcastles (BBC) 1990, Architect and Engineer 1995, Skyscrapers 1999, Surveillance (Channel 4) 2001. *Publications:* (Well) Connected Architecture 1994, The Biggest Glass Palace in the World 1997, Ian Ritchie: Technoecology 1999, Plymouth Theatre Royal Production Centre 2003, The Spire 2004, RSC Courtyard Theatre 2006, Leipzig Glass Hall (construction drawings) 2007. *Leisure interests:* art, swimming, reading, writing, poetry, etching. *Address:* Ian Ritchie Architects Ltd, 110 Three Colt Street, London, E14 8AZ, England (office). *Telephone:* (20) 7338-1100 (office). *Fax:* (20) 7338-1199 (office). *E-mail:* mail@ianritchiearchitects.co.uk (office). *Website:* www.ianritchiearchitects.co.uk (office).

RITCHIE, Ian Russell, MA; British barrister, business executive and sports administrator; *CEO, All England Lawn Tennis Club;* b. 27 Nov. 1953, Leeds; s. of Hugh Ritchie and Sheelah Ritchie; m. Jill Middleton-Walker 1982; two s.; ed Leeds Grammar School, Trinity Coll. Oxford; Barrister (Middle Temple) 1976–77; Industrial Relations Adviser, Eng Employers' Fed. 1978–79; joined Granada TV 1980, Head Production Services 1987–88; Dir of Resources, Tyne-Tees TV 1988–91, Man. Dir 1991–93, Group Deputy Chief Exec. Yorkshire Tyne-Tees TV PLC 1993; Man. Dir Nottingham Studios, Cen. TV 1993–94; Man. Dir London News Network 1994–96; CEO, subsequently COO Channel 5 Broadcasting 1996–97; Man. Dir Russell Reynolds Assocs 1997–98; Chief Exec. Middle East Broadcasting Centre 1998–2000; CEO Assoc. Press (AP) TV News 2000–04, Vice-Pres. Global Business and Man. Dir AP Int. 2003; CEO All England Lawn Tennis Club 2005–; mem. Bd of Dirs Football League, Wembley National Stadium Ltd. *Leisure interests:* golf, tennis, theatre. *Address:* The All England Lawn Tennis and Croquet Club, Church Road, Wimbledon, London, SW19 5AE, England (office). *Telephone:* (20) 8944-1066 (office). *Fax:* (20) 8947-8752 (office). *Website:* www.wimbledon.org/en_GB/about/guide/club.html (office).

RITHAUDDEEN AL-HAJ BIN TENGKU ISMAIL, Y.M. Tengku Ahmad, PMN, SPMP, SSAP, PMK, LLB; Malaysian politician and barrister; *Pro-Chancellor, National University of Malaysia;* b. 24 Jan. 1932, Kota Bharu; s. of Y. M. Tengku Ismail and Y. M. Besar Zabidah Tengku abd Kadir; m. Y. M. Tengku Puan Sri Datin Noor Aini 1957; three s. two d.; ed Nottingham Univ. and Lincoln's Inn, UK; mem. of royal family of Kelantan; Circuit Magistrate in Ipoh 1956–58, Pres. of Sessions Court 1958–60; Deputy Public Prosecutor and Fed. Counsel 1960–62; mem. Council of Advisers to Ruler of State of Kelantan (MPR), resgnd to enter pvt. practice; Chair. East Coast Bar Cttee of Malaya; Chair. Sri Nilam Co-operative Soc., Malaysia; mem. Malayan Council 1967, 1968, 1969, 1970; Sponsor, Adabi Foundation, Kelantan Youth; Adviser, Kesatria; Chair. Farmers' Org. Authority; Minister with Special Functions Assisting Prime Minister on Foreign Affairs 1973–75; mem. Supreme Council, United Malays' Nat. Org. 1975–; Minister for Foreign Affairs 1975–81, 1984–86, for Trade and Industry 1981–83, for Information 1986, of Defence 1986–90; Jt Chair. Malaysia-Thailand Devt Authority (Gas and Oil); Chair. Kinta Kellas Investments PLC 1990–, Idris Hydraulic (Malaysia) Berhad 1991–, Concrete Eng Products Berhad, Road Builder (Malaysia) Holdings Berhad; Pres. UN Asscn of Malaysia (UNAM); Adviser, KPMG Peat Marwick Malaysia; Pro-Chancellor Nat. Univ. of Malaysia; Chair. Univ. of Nottingham Malaysia Campus; Deputy Pres. Football Asscn of Malaysia. *Leisure interest:* golf. *Address:* c/o Office of Public Relations, Universiti Kebangsaan Malaysia, 43600 UKM, Bangi, Selangor Darul Ehsan, Malaysia. *Telephone:* (3) 89250651. *Fax:* (3) 89254890. *E-mail:* puspa@pkrisc.cc.ukm.my. *Website:* www.ukm.my.

RITOÓK, Zsigmond; Hungarian professor of Latin; *Professor Emeritus, University of Budapest;* b. 28 Sept. 1929, Budapest; s. of Zsigmond Ritoók and Ilona Ritoók (née Gaylhoffer); m. Ágnes Ritoók (née Szalay); one s. two d.; ed Univ. of Budapest; teacher 1958–1970; Research Fellow, Centre of Classical Studies of Hungarian Acad. of Sciences 1970–86; Prof. of Latin, Univ. of Budapest 1986–99, Prof. Emer. 2000–; Corresp. mem. Acad. of Sciences 1990–93, mem. 1993–, Vice-Pres. Section of Linguistics and Literary Scholarship 1990–96, Pres. 1996–99; mem. Academia Latinitati Fovendae, Rome 1984–, Academia Europaea; Corresp. mem. Österreichische Akad. der Wissenschaften 1998–; Gen. Sec. Hungarian Soc. of Classical Studies 1980–1985, Co-Pres. 1985–1991, Pres. 1991–1997; Széchenyi Prize 2001. *Publications:* Everyday Life in Ancient Greece 1960, The Golden Age of Greek Culture (co-author) 1968, (revised and enlarged) 1984, 2006, Theatre and Stadium 1968, Greek Singer of Tales 1973, Sources for the History of Greek Musical Aesthetics 1982 (all in Hungarian); Griechische Musikästhetik (in German) 2004; more than 130 papers in Hungarian and foreign periodicals. *Address:* Mátyás u. 20, 1093 Budapest, Hungary (home). *Telephone:* (1) 217-4033 (home).

RITTENMEYER, Ronald Allen, BSc, MBA; American business executive; *President and CEO, Electronic Data Systems Corpn (EDS);* b. 22 May 1947, Wilkes-Barre, Pa; m. Hedy Rittenmeyer; two c.; ed Wilkes Univ., Pa, Rockhurst Univ., Mo.; Vice-Pres. of Operations, Frito-Lay Inc. 1974–76; fmr Vice-Pres. Middle East and Worldwide Operations, PepsiCo Food Int.; fmr Pres. and COO Merisel; COO Burlington Northern Railroad 1994; Pres. and COO Ryder TRS Inc. 1997–98; Chair., CEO and Pres. RailTex Inc. 1998–2000; CEO and Pres. AmeriServe 2000; Chair., CEO and Pres. Safety-Kleen Inc. 2001–04; Man. Dir The Cypress Group, NY 2004–05; Co-COO and Exec. Vice-Pres. Global Service Delivery Div., Electronic Data Systems Corpn (EDS) 2005, Pres. and COO 2006–07, Pres. and CEO 2007–, Chair. 2007–08 (following acquisition of EDS by Hewlett-Packard Aug. 2008); fmr mem. Bd of Dirs AmeriServe, RailTex, Ryder TRS, Groceryworks.com, Sterling Chemicals, Merisel, Safety-Kleen, US Chamber of Commerce, American Heart Asscn; fmr Chair. ExcellerateHRO; mem. Bd of Dirs Nat. Kidney Foundation of N Texas; mem. Exec. Bd Southern Methodist Univ. Cox School of Business; mem. Business Council, Gov.'s Business Council; mem. Bd of Visitors US Army War Coll. *Address:* Electronic Data Systems Corpn, 5400 Legacy Drive, Plano, TX 75024-3199, USA (office). *Telephone:* (972) 604-6000 (office). *Fax:* (972) 605-6033 (office). *E-mail:* info@eds.com (office). *Website:* www.eds.com (office).

RITTER, August William (Bill), Jr; American lawyer, politician and state official; *Governor of Colorado;* b. 6 Sept. 1956, Denver, Colo; s. of William Ritter and Ethel Ritter; m. Jeannie Ritter 1984; four c.; ed Colorado State Univ., Univ. of Colorado School of Law; Deputy Dist Attorney for City and Co. of Denver 1981–87, 1992–93, Dist Attorney 1993–2006; moved with his wife Jeannie to Zambia as missionaries for Roman Catholic Church 1987–89, opened food distribution and educ. centre; held post in US Attorney's office 1990–92; advised US Attorney Gen. John Ashcroft following attack on World Trade Center 11 Sept., 2001; Gov. of Colo 2007–; Vice-Pres. Nat. Asscn of Dist Attorneys; fmr Chair. American Prosecutors Research Inst., Bd Promoting Anti-Violence through Educ.; fmr mem. Bd Nat. Asscn of Drug Court Professionals, Denver Foundation's Human Services Cttee, Mile High United Way Bd, Denver Public Schools' Comm. on Secondary School Reform; Democrat. *Address:* Office of the Governor, 136 State Capitol, Denver, CO 80203-1792, USA (office). *Telephone:* (303) 866-2471 (office). *Fax:* (303) 866-2003 (office). *E-mail:* governor@state.co.us (office). *Website:* www.colorado.gov/governor (office).

RITTER, Gerhard A., DPhil; German historian and academic; *Professor Emeritus of Modern History, University of Munich;* b. 29 March 1929, Berlin; s. of Wilhelm Ritter and Martha Ritter (née Wietasch); m. Gisela Kleinschmidt

1955; two s.; ed Arndt.-Oberschule, Berlin, Univ. of Tübingen, Free Univ., Berlin; research, Univ. of Oxford, UK 1952–54; Asst, Free Univ., Berlin 1954–61, Prof. of Political Science 1962–65; Prof. of Modern History, Univ. of Münster 1965–74; Prof. of Modern History, Univ. of Munich 1974–94, Prof. Emer. 1994–; fmr Guest Prof., Washington Univ., St Louis, Mo., USA, Univ. of Oxford, Univ. of California, Berkeley, USA, Tel-Aviv Univ., Israel; mem. Senate and Main Cttee, Deutsche Forschungsgemeinschaft (German Research Soc.), Bonn 1973–76; Chair. Asscn of Historians of Germany 1976–80; mem. Bavarian Acad. of Sciences, Munich, Comm. for History of Parliamentarism and Political Parties, Historische Kommission, Berlin; Hon. Fellow, St Antony's Coll. Oxford; Dr hc (Univ. Bielefeld) 1994, (Humboldt Univ., Berlin) 1999. *Publications:* Die Arbeiterbewegung im Wilhelminischen Reich 1959, Parlament und Demokratie in Grossbritannien 1972, Deutsche Sozialgeschichte 1870–1914 (with Jürgen Kocka) 1982, Arbeiterbewegung, Parteien und Parlamentarismus 1976, Die II. Internationale 1918/19. Protokolle, Memoranden, Berichte und Korrespondenzen 1980, Staat, Arbeiterschaft und Arbeiterbewegung in Deutschland 1980, Die deutschen Parteien 1830–1914 1985, Social Welfare in Germany and Britain 1986, Der Sozialstaat 1991, Wahlen in Deutschland 1946–91 (with M. Niehuss) 1991, Das Deutsche Kaiserreich 1871–1914 1992, Arbeiter im Deutschen Kaiserreich 1871–1914 (with Klaus Tenfelde) 1992, Grossforschung und Staat in Deutschland 1992, Der Umbruch von 1989/91 und die Geschichtswissenschaft 1995, Arbeiter, Arbeiterbewegung und soziale Ideen in Deutschland 1996, Soziale Frage und Sozialpolitik in Deutschland seit Beginn des 19. Jahrhunderts 1998, Über Deutschland, Die Bundesrepublik in der deutschen Geschichte 2000, Continuity and Change. Political and Social Developments in Germany after 1945 and 1989/90 2000. *Leisure interests:* sailing, tennis. *Address:* Windscheidstrasse 41, 10627 Berlin, Germany (home). *Telephone:* (30) 31015794 (home). *Fax:* (30) 31019614 (home). *E-mail:* GARitter@web.de (home).

RITTER, Jorge Eduardo, PhD; Panamanian lawyer, politician and diplomatist; b. 1950, Panama City; s. of the late Eduardo Ritter Aislán; m.; two c.; ed Pontificia Univ. Javeriana, Colombia; Clerk to Legis. Comm. 1973–77; Lecturer in Constitutional and Civil Law, Univ. of Panama; fmr mem. Governing Council, Inst. for Human Resources Training and Devt; Vice-Minister of Labour and Social Welfare 1977–78; Pvt. Sec. and Adviser to Pres. of Panama 1978–81; Minister of Foreign Affairs (desig.) 1981; teacher, Nat. Political Training Coll. of the Guardia Nacional 1981; Minister of Interior and Justice 1981–82; Amb. to Colombia 1982–86; Perm. Rep. to UN 1986–88; Minister of Foreign Affairs 1988–89, 1998–99; Minister for Canal Affairs 1998–99; Vice-Chair. Bd Panama Canal Comm. 1998–99; Chair. Exec. Council Nat. Telecommunications Inst. 1981; Chair. Bd Civil Aviation Authority 1981–82, Panama Canal Authority 1998–99; mem. Bd Banco Ganadero 1980–90; Pnr Ritter, Díaz y Ahumada 1982–; mem. Academia Panameña de la Lengua 2007–. *Publication:* Los Secretos de la Nunciatura 1990. *Address:* Calle José Gabriel Duque, La Cresta, Las Torres (C-6), PO Box 0819-08253, Panamá, Panama (office). *Telephone:* (507) 264-0521 (office). *Fax:* (507) 264-0524 (office). *E-mail:* jritter@cwpanama.net (home).

RITTERMAN, Dame Janet Elizabeth, DBE, MMus, PhD, FRNCM; music college director (retd); b. (Janet Elizabeth Palmer), 1 Dec. 1941, Sydney, Australia; d. of Charles Eric Palmer and Laurie Helen Palmer; m. Gerrard Peter Ritterman 1970; ed North Sydney Girls' High School and New South Wales State Conservatorium of Music, Australia, Univ. of Durham and King's Coll. London, UK; pianist, accompanist, chamber music player, music educator; Sr Lecturer in Music, Middx Polytechnic 1975–79, Goldsmiths Coll. Univ. of London 1980–87; Head of Music, Dartington Coll. of Arts 1987–90, Dean Academic Affairs 1988–90, Acting Prin. 1990–91, Prin. 1991–93; Visiting Prof. of Music Educ., Univ. of Plymouth 1993–2005; Dir Royal Coll. of Music 1993–2005; Chair. Assoc. Bd Royal Schools of Music (Publishing) Ltd 1993–2005, The Mendelssohn and Boise Foundations 1996–98, 2002–04, Advisory Council, Arts Research Ltd 1997–2005, Fed. of British Conservatoires 1998–2003; Vice-Pres. Nat. Asscn of Youth Orchestras 1993–, Royal Coll. of Music 2005–; mem. Music Panel, Arts Council of England 1992–98, Council Royal Musical Asscn 1994–2004 (Vice-Pres. 1998–2004), Bd ENO 1996–2004, Exec. Cttee Inc. Soc. of Musicians 1996–99, Arts and Humanities Research Bd 1998–2004 (Post grad. Panel 1998–2002, Chair. Post grad. Cttee 2002–04), Nominating Cttee Arts and Humanities Research Council 2005–07, Bd Nat. Youth Orchestra 1999–2007, Steering Cttee, London Higher Educ. Consortium 1999–2005, Arts Council of England 2000–02, Dept for Educ. and Skills Advisory Group, Music and Dance Scheme 2000–05, Council of Goldsmiths Coll., Univ. of London 2002–07, Bd Anglo-Austrian Soc. 2005–, Bd The Voices Foundation 2005–, Advisory Bd Inst. for Advanced Studies in the Humanities, Univ. of Edinburgh 2005–, Advisory Council Inst. of Germanic and Romance Studies 2005– and Inst. of Musical Research Univ. of London 2006–, Educ. Advisory Group Nuffield Foundation 2007–; Trustee, Countess of Munster Musical Trust 1993–, Prince Consort Foundation 1993–2005, Plymouth Chamber Music Trust 2006–; Gov. Associated Bd Royal Schools of Music 1993–2005, Purcell School 1996–2000, Heythrop Coll. Univ. of London 1996–2006, Dartington Coll. of Arts 2005–08, Middlesex Univ. 2005–, Univ. Coll. Falmouth 2008–; mem. Österreichischer Wissenschaftsrat 2002–; mem. Court, Worshipful Co. of Musicians 2005–; Fellow, Royal Northern Coll. of Music 1996, Dartington Coll. of Arts 1997, Higher Educ. Acad. 2007; Sr Fellow RCA 2004; Hon. RAM 1995, Hon. GSMD (Guildhall School of Music and Drama) 2000; Hon. DUniv (Univ. of Cen. England) 1996, (Middx Univ.) 2005; Hon. DLitt (Univ. of Ulster) 2004. *Publications:* articles in learned journals, France, Germany, Australia and UK. *Leisure interests:* reading, theatre-going, country walking.

RITTNER, Luke Philip Hardwick; British arts administrator; *Chief Executive, Royal Academy of Dance;* b. 24 May 1947, Bath; s. of Stephen

Rittner and Joane Rittner; m. Corinna Frances Edholm 1974; one d.; ed Blackfriars School, Laxton, City of Bath Tech. Coll., Dartington Coll. of Arts and London Acad. of Music and Dramatic Art; Asst Admin. Bath Festival 1968–71, Jt Admin. 1971–74, Admin. Dir 1974–76; Founder and Dir Asscn for Business Sponsorship of the Arts 1976–83; Sec.-Gen. Arts Council of Great Britain 1983–90; UK Cultural Dir Expo '92 1990–92; Chair. English Shakespeare Co. 1990–94; Dir Marketing and Communications, Sotheby's Europe 1992–99; Chief Exec. Royal Acad. of Dance 1999–; Chair. London Chorus (fmrly The London Choral Soc.) 1994–, Exec. Bd London Acad. of Music and Dramatic Art 1994–; Artistic Adviser to Spanish Arts Festival, London 1991–94; Gov. Urchfont Manor, Wiltshire Adult Educ. Centre 1982–83; mem. Music Panel, British Council 1979–83, Council Victoria and Albert Museum 1980–83, J. Sainsbury Arts Sponsorship Panel 1990–96, Olivier Awards Theatre Panel 1992, Council Almeida Theatre 1997–2001; non-exec. mem. Bd Carlton Television 1991–93; Trustee Bath Preservation Trust 1968–73, Theatre Royal, Bath 1979–82; Foundation Trustee Holburne Museum, Bath 1981–83; mem. Dance Panel, Olivier Awards 2003; Hon. Doctorate (Bath) 2004. *Leisure interest:* the arts. *Address:* Royal Academy of Dance, 36 Battersea Square, London, SW11 3RA, England (office). *Telephone:* (20) 7326-8000 (office). *Fax:* (20) 7924-3129 (office). *E-mail:* info@rad.org.uk (office). *Website:* www.rad.org.uk (office).

RITZ, Hon. Gerry, PC; Canadian politician; *Minister of Agriculture and Agri-Food, Minister for the Canadian Wheat Board;* b. 19 Aug. 1951, Delisle, Sask.; m. Judy Ritz; two s.; mem. Reform Party of Canada 1997–2000, Canadian Alliance 2000–03, Conservative Party of Canada 2003–; MP for Battlefords-Lloydminster 1997–; Sec. of State for Small Business and Tourism 2007; Minister of Agric. and Agri-Food 2007–, also Minister for the Canadian Wheat Bd. *Address:* Agriculture and Agri-Food Canada, Sir John Carling Building, 930 Carling Avenue, Ottawa, ON K1A 0C5, Canada (office). *Telephone:* (613) 759-1059 (office). *Fax:* (613) 759-1081 (office). *E-mail:* info@agr.gc.ca (office). *Website:* www.agr.gc.ca (office); www.gerryritzmp.com (home).

RITZEN, Jozef (Jo), MSc, PhD; Dutch politician, economist and university administrator; *President, Maastricht University;* b. 3 Oct. 1945, Heerlen, Limburg Prov.; m Hanneke Smulders; four c; ed Univ. of Tech., Delft, Erasmus Univ., Rotterdam; Prof. of Educ. Econs, Nijmegen Univ. 1981–83; Prof. of Public Sector Econs, Erasmus Univ., Rotterdam 1983–89; sometime adviser to Minister of Social Affairs; Minister of Educ., Culture and Science 1989–99; Special Adviser to the Human Devt Network, IBRD (World Bank) 1998, Vice-Pres. for Devt Policy 1999–2003; Pres. Maastricht Univ. 2003–. *Address:* Universiteit Maastricht, PO Box 616, 6200 MD Maastricht, Netherlands (office). *Telephone:* (43) 3883155 (office). *Fax:* (43) 3834883 (office). *Website:* www.unimaas.nl (office).

RIVALDO; Brazilian professional football player; b. (Vito Barbosa Ferreira), 19 April 1972, Recife; s. of the late Romildo Borreira; one s. one d.; played with Paulista, Santa Cruz 1989–91, Magi-Mirin 1992, Corinthians 1993, Palmeiras 1994–96, Deportivo La Coruña (Spain) (21 goals in 41 matches) 1996–97, FC Barcelona (Spain) 1997–2002, AC Milan (Italy) 2002–03, signed for Cruzeiro Jan. 2004 but left team 90 days later, with Olympiakos 2004–07, AEK Athens 2007–; scored eight goals for Brazil nat. team in 14 World Cup finals games; FIFA World Player of the Year 1999, Ballon D'Or, Best Player in Europe (France) 1999. *Address:* AEK FC, Grammou str. 69-71, 151 24 Marousi, Greece. *Telephone:* (210) 6121371. *Fax:* (210) 6121618. *E-mail:* info@aekfc.gr. *Website:* www.aekfc.gr; www.rivaldo-10.gr (office).

RIVAS-MIJARES, Gustavo, MSc, DrIng; Venezuelan environmental engineer and academic; b. 7 Nov. 1922, Valencia; s. of J. A. Rivas-Montenegro and Amparo Mijares de Rivas; m. Ligia Cardenas 1946; four c.; ed Liceo Pedro Gual, Valencia, Univ. Cen. de Venezuela, Caracas and Univs of Michigan and California, USA; Prof. of Sanitary Eng, Faculty of Eng, Univ. Cen. de Venezuela 1945–85, Dean, Grad. School 1973–76, Prof. Emer. 1985–; Pres. Nat. Acad. of Physics, Math. and Natural Science 1981–85; Dir Nat. Council of Scientific and Tech. Research 1968–72; fmr Dir Venezuela Inst. of Scientific Research; Pres. Superior Council, Universidad Simón Bolívar, Caracas, Venezuela 1988–91; Chair. Pan-American Eng Acad. 1998; mem. Nat. Acad. of Sciences, Venezuela, Nat. Acad. of Eng (USA), Nat. Acad. of Eng (Mexico), Nat. Acad. of Guatemala, Royal Acad. of Sciences (Spain), Academia Panamericana de Ingenieri, TWAS (fmrly Third World Acad. of Sciences); Fellow, Third World Acad. of Sciences 1988; Foreign Assoc., Nat. Acad. of Eng (USA, Mexico, Spain); Nat. Science Prize (Venezuela) 1986; several awards including Libertador Bolívar 1989. *Publications:* several books, including Supply Water and Sewerage 1957, Treatment of Purification of Water 1963, Wastewater 1967; 136 research papers. *Address:* Department of Sanitary Engineering, Faculty of Engineering, Universidad Central de Venezuela, Ciudad Universitaria, Los Changuaramos, Zona Postal 104, Caracas 1051 (office); Urb. Santa Rosa de Lima, Calle C, Res. Jarama, Apt. 7–A, Caracas, Venezuela (home). *Telephone:* (2) 991-7156 (home). *Fax:* (2) 484-6611 (office). *E-mail:* acfmn@ccs.internet.ve (office).

RIVERA, Chita; American actress, singer and dancer; b. (Dolores Conchita Figueroa del Rivero), 23 Jan. 1933, Washington, DC; d. of Pedro Julio Figuerva del Rivero; m. Anthony Mordente (divorced); one c.; ed American School of Ballet, New York; performs in nightclubs and cabarets around the world; Kennedy Center Honor 2002. *Stage appearances include:* Call Me Madam, Guys and Dolls, Can-Can, Seventh Heaven, Mister Wonderful, West Side Story, Father's Day, Bye Bye Birdie, Threepenny Opera, Flower Drum Song, Zorba, Sweet Charity, Born Yesterday, Jacques is Alive and Well and Living in Paris, Sondheim–A Musical Tribute, Kiss Me Kate, Ivanhoe, Chicago, Bring Back Birdie, Merlin, The Rink 1984 (Tony Award 1984), Jerry's Girls 1985, Kiss of the Spider Woman 1993 (Tony Award for Best Actress in a Musical), Chita Rivera: The Dancer's Life. *Films:* Chicago 2002,

Kalamazoo? 2005. *Television includes:* Kojak and the Marcus Nelson Murders 1973, The New Dick Van Dyke Show 1973–74, Kennedy Center Tonight–Broadway to Washington!, Pippin 1982, The Mayflower Madam 1987. *Address:* c/o Gayle Nachlis, William Morris Agency, 1325 Avenue of the Americas, New York, NY 10019, USA.

RIVERA, Geraldo, BS, JD; American broadcaster and journalist; b. 4 July 1943, New York; s. of Cruz Allen Rivera and Lillian Friedman; m. 3rd Sheri Rivera (divorced 1984); m. 4th C. C. Dyer 1987; two s. two d.; ed Univ. of Arizona, Brooklyn Law School, Univ. of Pennsylvania; with Eyewitness News WABC-TV, New York 1970–75; reporter, Good Morning America programme ABC-TV 1973–76; corresp. and host, Good Night America programme 1975–77; corresp. and Sr Producer, 20/20 Newsmagazine 1978–85; host, syndicated talk show The Geraldo Rivera Show, New York 1987–98; host, CNBC Rivera Life Show 1994, investigative show on cable CNBC Upfront Tonight 1998–2000, Travel Channel documentaries: Voyager – Sail to the Century, NBC 1994–2001, Geraldo Rivera Specials; war reporter in Afghanistan, Somalia, Lebanon, Israel and Sudan, Fox News Channel 2001–02, currently host Geraldo at Large; ten Emmy Awards, three Peabody Awards, Kennedy Journalism Award 1973, 1975, Columbia DuPont Award and numerous other awards. *Publications:* Willowbrook 1972, Miguel 1972, Island of Contrasts 1974, A Special Kind of Courage 1976, Exposing Myself 1991. *Address:* Geraldo at Large, FOX News Network, LLC, 1211 Avenue of the Americas, New York, NY 10036, USA (office). *Telephone:* (212) 852-7002 (office). *Fax:* (212) 301-8588 (office). *E-mail:* Atlarge@foxnews.com (office). *Website:* www.foxnews.com (office).

RIVERA CARRERA, HE Cardinal Norberto, DD; Mexican ecclesiastic; *Archbishop of Mexico City and Archbishop Primate of Mexico;* b. 6 June 1942, La Purísima, Durango; s. of Ramón Rivera Cháidez and Soledad Carrera de Rivera; ed Conciliary Seminary, Durango, Gregorian Univ., Rome; ordained priest 1966; Prof. of Dogmatic Theology Seminario Mayor, Durango 1967–85; Prof. of Ecclesiology, Pontificia Universidad de México 1982–85, mem. sr council 1993–95, vice-grand councillor 1995–; Bishop of Tehuacán 1985; Archbishop of Mexico City 1995–; Archbishop Primate of Mexico 1995–; cr. Cardinal 1998, Cardinal-Priest of St Francesco d'Assisi a Ripa Grande; mem. numerous cttees and councils, including the permanent Sinod of Bishops; Pres., Episcopal Commission for Culture, Inter-religion Council of Mexico, Ecumenical Council of Mexico, Exec. Council of Mexico City Historic Centre. *Address:* Curia Arzobispal, Aptdo Postal 24-433, Durango 90, 5°, Col Roma, CP 06700 México, DF, Mexico (office). *Telephone:* (5) 208-3200 (office). *Fax:* (5) 208-5350 (office). *E-mail:* arzobisp@arquidiocesismexico.org.mx (office). *Website:* www.arzobispadomexico.org.mx (office).

RIVERO CASTAÑEDA, Raúl Ramón; Cuban journalist and poet; b. 1945, Morón, Camagüey; m. Blanca Reyes Castañón; ed Havana Univ. School of Journalism; Co-founder satirical magazine Caimán Barbudo 1966; Moscow correspondent Prensa Latina (govt press agency) 1973–76, then worked for science and culture service, Cuba; independent journalist 1988–; Co-founder and Dir Cuba Press news agency 1995–2003, contributing to newspapers and journals abroad, including El Nuevo Herald, The Miami Herald, Encounter magazine; correspondent for French press agency, Reporters sans frontières; fmr regional vice-chair. for Cuba, Inter-American Press Asscn Cttee on Freedom of the Press and Information; accused of collaborating with the USA and sentenced to 20 years' imprisonment by govt April 2003, released Nov. 2004; mem. Manuel Márquez Sterling Journalists' Asscn; Reporters sans frontières Fondation de France prize 1997, Inter-American Press Asscn Grand Prize for Press Freedom, Columbia Univ. Graduate School of Journalism Maria Moors Cabot Prize 1999, World Press Freedom Prize 2004. *Publications:* poems include: Suite de la muerte, Patria 1994, Orden de registro, Oración de septiembre, Foto en La Habana, Ensayo sobre la tiranía. *Address:* c/o Reporters sans frontières, 5 rue Geoffroy-Marie, 75009 Paris, France. *Telephone:* 1 44 83 84 84. *Fax:* 1 45 23 11 51. *E-mail:* rsf@rsf.org. *Website:* www.rsf.org.

RIVETTE, Jacques; French film director; b. 1 March 1928, Rouen; s. of André Rivette and Andrée Rivette (née Amiard); ed Lycée Corneille, Rouen; began career as journalist and film critic for Cahiers du Cinéma, Gazette du Cinema et Arts 1953–82; worked as cameraman on short films by Eric Rohmer and François Truffaut; asst to Jacques Becker on Ali Baba and the Forty Thieves, Jean Renoir on French Cancan; began directing short films 1949, made first feature film 1960; known as one of the originators of the Nouvelle Vague (New Wave) style of French cinema; Chevalier, Ordre nat. du Mérite; Grand Prix nat. 1981, Leopard of Honour, Locarno Int. Film Festival 1991, Prix Friedrich Wilhelm Murnau for Outstanding Lifetime Achievement 1998. *Films:* Aux quatre coins (short) 1949, Le Quadrille (short) 1950, Le Divertissement (short) 1952, Le Coup du berger (short) 1956, Paris nous appartient (Sutherland Trophy, London Film Festival) 1960, La Religieuse 1966, L'Amour fou (Sutherland Trophy, London Film Festival) 1969, Out 1: noli me tangere 1971, Out 1: Spectre 1972, Essai sur l'agression 1974, Naissance et mont de Prométhée 1974, Céline et Julie vont en bateau (Special Prize of the Jury, Locarno) 1974, Noroît 1976, Duelle (une quarantaine) 1976, Paris s'en va (short) 1981, Le Pont du Nord 1981, Merry-Go-Round 1981, L'Amour par terre 1984, Hurlevent 1985, La Bande des quatre (FIPRESCI Prize 1989) 1988, La Divertimento 1991, La Belle noiseuse (Grand Jury Prize, Cannes, Best Film, César Awards, French Syndicate of Cinema Critics Award, Kinema Junpo Best Foreign Language Film) 1991, Jeanne la Pucelle I: Les batailles 1994, Jeanne la Pucelle II: Les prisons 1994, Haut bas fragile 1995, Secret défense 1998, Va savoir (Jury Special Prize, Valladolid) 2001, Histoire de Marie et Julien 2003, Ne touchez pas la hache 2007. *Address:* VMA, 20 avenue Rapp, Paris 75007, France (office). *E-mail:* d.leprestre@vma.fr (office). *Website:* www.vma.fr (office).

RIVIERE, Francis Osborne, BSc, MSc; Dominican politician and economist; ed Univ. of the West Indies, Trinity Coll., Dublin; Minister of Foreign Affairs and of Trade and Marketing, Dominica 2001–05; Acting Prime Minister Nov. 2003–Jan. 2004; currently consultant, Save the Children (charity). *Leisure interests* volunteer work, sport, light classical music, jazz. *Address:* c/o Save the Children, Bath Estate, PO Box 169, Roseau (office); 6 Francis Lane, Roseau, Dominica (home). *Telephone:* 4482090 (office); 4484872 (home). *Fax:* 4482090 (office).

RIVLIN, Alice Mitchell, MA, PhD; American economist and fmr government official; *Director, Greater Washington Research Program, Brookings Institution;* b. 4 March 1931, Philadelphia; d. of Allan Mitchell and Georgianna Fales; m. 1st Lewis A. Rivlin 1955 (divorced 1977); two s. one d.; m. 2nd Sidney G. Winter 1989; ed Bryn Mawr Coll. and Radcliffe Coll.; mem. staff, Brookings Inst. Washington, DC 1957–66, 1969–75, 1983–93, Dir of Econ. Studies 1983–87, apptd Sr Fellow, Johnson Chair. 1999, currently Dir Greater Washington Research Program; Dir Congressional Budget Office 1975–83; Prof. of Public Policy, George Mason Univ. 1992; Deputy Dir US Office of Man. and Budget 1993–94, Dir 1994–96; Vice-Chair Fed. Reserve Bd 1996–99; Chair. Dist of Columbia Financial Control Bd 1998–2001; Visiting Prof. Public Policy Inst., Georgetown Univ.; mem. Bd of Dirs BearingPoint, Washington Post Co.; mem. American Econ. Asscn (Nat. Pres. 1986); MacArthur Fellow 1983–88. *Publications:* The Role of the Federal Government in Financing Higher Education 1961, Microanalysis of Socioeconomic Systems (jtly) 1961, Systematic Thinking for Social Action 1971, Economic Choices (jtly) 1986, The Swedish Economy (jtly) 1987, Caring for the Disabled Elderly: Who Will Pay? 1988, Reviving the American Dream 1992, The Economic Payoff from the Internet Revolutioin 2001, Beyond the Dot.coms 2001, Restoring Fiscal Sanity 2004. *Address:* Brookings Institution, Center on Urban and Metropolitan Policy, 1755 Massachusetts Avenue, NW, Washington, DC 20036-2188, USA (office). *Telephone:* (202) 797-6026 (office). *Fax:* (202) 797-2965 (office). *E-mail:* ARivlin@brookings.edu (office). *Website:* www.brookings.edu (office).

RIX, Timothy John, CBE, BA, CIMgt, FRSA, FInstD; British publisher; b. 4 Jan. 1934, Maidenhead, Berks.; s. of the late Howard T. Rix and of Marguerite Selman Rix; m. 1st Wendy E. Wright 1960 (divorced 1967); m. 2nd Gillian Greenwood 1968; one s. two d.; ed Radley Coll., Clare Coll., Cambridge and Yale Univ., USA; joined Longmans Green & Co. Ltd 1958, Overseas Educ. Publr 1958–61, Publishing Man. Far East and SE Asia 1961–63, Head, English Language Teaching Publishing 1964–68, Div. Man. Dir 1968–72, Jt Man. Dir 1972–76, Chief Exec. Longman Group Ltd 1976–90, Chair. 1984–90; Chair. Addison-Wesley-Longman Group Ltd 1988–89; Chair. Pitman Examinations Inst. 1987–90; mem. Bd of Dirs Pearson Longman Ltd (now Pearson PLC) 1979–83, Goldcrest Television 1981–83, Yale Univ. Press Ltd, London 1984–, ECIC (Man.) Ltd 1990–92, Blackie & Son Ltd 1990–93, B.H. Blackwell Ltd 1991–95, Geddes and Grosset Ltd 1996–98, Jessica Kingsley Publrs Ltd 1997–2007, Frances Lincoln Ltd 1997–2008, Meditech Media Ltd 1997–2003, Scottish Book Source 1999–2007, Central European Univ. Press 1999–2005; Pres. Publrs' Asscn 1981–83; mem. British Library Bd 1986–96, British Council Bd 1988–97, Health Educ. Authority Bd 1995–99; Chair. Book Trust 1986–88, British Library Centre for the Book 1989–95, Book Marketing Ltd 1990–2003, Soc. of Bookmen 1990–92, British Library Publishing 1992–2003, Book Aid Int. 1994–2006, Bell Educational Trust 1994–2001, Nat. Book Cttee 1997–2003, Edinburgh Univ. Press 2001–07, Advisory Bd of Centre for Publishing Studies, Univ. of Stirling 2000–; mem. Oxford Brookes Univ. Devt Cttee 1991–96, Finance Cttee, Oxford Univ. Press 1992–2002, Council, Ranfurly Library Service 1992–94, Advisory Council, Inst. of English Studies, London Univ. 2000–08; Gov. English-Speaking Union 1998–2005; Hon. Pres. Independent Publrs' Guild 1993–2008; Dr hc (Univ. of Stirling) 2006. *Publications:* articles on publishing in trade journals. *Leisure interests:* reading, landscape, wine. *Address:* Flat 1, 29 Barrington Road, London, N8 8QT, England (home). *Telephone:* (20) 8348-4143 (home). *Fax:* (20) 8348-4143 (home). *E-mail:* tim@rixpublishing.co.uk (home).

RIZA, Iqbal, MA; Pakistani UN official; *Special Advisor to the Secretary-General on the Alliance of Civilizations, United Nations;* b. 20 May 1934, Lonavla, India; s. of Sharif Alijan; m. 1959; two s.; ed Univ. of Punjab, Lahore, Fletcher School of Int. Law, Boston; Pakistan Foreign Service 1958–77; served in Madrid 1959–61, Bonn 1962–64, Khartoum 1964–66, London 1966–68; Dir Foreign Service Acad., Lahore 1968–71; Deputy Chief of Mission, Paris and Deputy Perm. Rep. to UNESCO 1972–76; joined UN 1978, Sec. Cttee on the Exercise of the Inalienable Rights of the Palestinian People 1978–80, Prin. Officer, UN Dept of Public Information 1980–82; assigned to negotiations in Iran–Iraq war 1981–87; Dir Office for Special Political Affairs 1983–88, Div. for Political and Gen. Ass. Affairs 1988–89; Chief, UN Observer Mission for verification of the electoral process in Nicaragua (ONUVEN) 1989–90; Chief of Mission of UN Transition Team in El Salvador March–Aug. 1990; Special Rep. of UN Sec.-Gen. and Chief of UN Observer Mission in El Salvador (ONUSAL) 1991–93; Asst Sec.-Gen. for Peace-keeping Operations 1993–96, Coordinator of UN operations in Bosnia-Herzegovina Feb.–Dec. 1996, Under-Sec.-Gen., Chef de Cabinet in Exec. Office of Sec.-Gen. 1997–2005 (retd); currently Special Advisor to UN Sec-Gen. on the Alliance of Civilizations; mem. UN Advisory Bd on Human Security. *Leisure interests:* reading, music, riding. *Address:* c/o Executive Office of the UN Secretary-General, United Nations Plaza, New York, NY 10017, USA (office).

RIZAYEV, Ramiz Gasangulu oglu, DrChemSc; Azerbaijani chemist and diplomatist; b. 2 Nov. 1939, Nakhichevan; m.; one s. one d.; ed Azerbaijan State Univ.; corresp. mem. Azerbaijan Acad. of Sciences 1983; Dir Inst. of Inorganic and Physical Chem. Azerbaijan Acad. of Sciences 1985–93; Plenipotentiary Rep., then Amb. of Azerbaijan to Russian Fed. 1993–2006; numerous inventions in the field of oil extraction and oil processing, 36 patents in various cos; mem. Scientific Council on Catalysis, Russian Acad. of Sciences; mem. Int. Acad. of Eng Sciences 2000–; mem. Ed. Bd Neftekhimiya (journal); Honoured Engineer of Russian Fed. 2000. *Publications:* 250 scientific articles on problems of oil chem. and chemical catalysis. *Address:* c/o Ministry of Foreign Affairs, 1009 Baku, S. Qurbanov küç. 4, Azerbaijan.

RIZO CASTELLÓN, José; Nicaraguan lawyer and politician; ed Catholic Univ. of Chile; Vice-Pres. of Nicaragua 2002–05 (resgnd); mem. Partido Liberal Constitucionalista (PLC), unsuccessful cand. for Pres. of Nicaragua 2006. *Address:* c/o Partido Liberal Constitucionalista (PLC), Semáforos Country Club 100 m al este, Apdo 4569, Managua, Nicaragua. *Telephone:* 278-8705. *Fax:* 278-1800.

RIZZOLI, Angelo, Jr; Italian film producer and publisher; b. 12 Nov. 1943, Como; s. of Andrea Rizzoli and Lucia Rizzoli (née Solmi); m. Eleonora Giorgi 1979; one c.; fmr Pres. and Man. Ed. Rizzoli Editore, Pres. Cineriz Distributori Associati; Pres. Rizzoli Film 1978–. *Films produced include:* Per grazia ricevuta 1971, Paura e amore 1988, Acque di primavera 1989, Stanno tutti bene 1990, Pore aperte 1990, La Settimana della sfinge 1990, In nome del popolo sovrano 1990, The Comfort of Strangers 1990, To Meteoro vima tou pelargou 1991, Paris s'eveille 1991, Il Ladro di bambini 1992, Un Altra vita 1992, Padre e figlio 1994, Anche i commercialisti hanno un'anima 1994,. *Television productions include:* Le Ragazze di Piazza di Spagna (TV series) 1998, Le Ali della vita 2000, Padre Pio 2000, Gioco di specchi 2000, Piccolo mondo antico 2001, Le Ali della vita 2 2001, Cuccioli 2002, Tutti i sogni del mondo 2003, Ferrari 2003, I Ragazzi della via Pal 2003, Al di la delle frontiere (miniseries) 2004, Il Bell'Antonio (miniseries) 2005, 48 ore (series) 2006, La Provinciale 2006, La Freccia nera (miniseries) 2006, Capri (series) 2006, Mafalda di Savoia (miniseries) 2006, Le Ragazze di San Frediano 2007, Il Giudice Mastrangelo (series) 2005–07. *Address:* Via Angelo Rizzoli 2, 20132 Milan, Italy (office). *Telephone:* (02) 25841.

RO, Tu-chol; North Korean politician; *Vice Premier;* Deputy, Supreme People's Ass.; Vice-Chair State Planning Comm. –2003; Vice Premier 2003–;. *Address:* Office of the Vice Premier of the Cabinet, Pyongyang, Democratic People's Republic of Korea.

ROA-KOURI, Raúl, BSc; Cuban diplomatist; *Ambassador to the Holy See;* b. 9 July 1936, Havana; s. of Raúl Roa and Ada Kouri; m. 1st 1960 (divorced); one d.; m. 2nd 1972 (divorced); one d.; m. 3rd 1975 (divorced); one d.; m. 4th Lillian Martino de Roa-Kouri 1996; ed Univ. of Havana, Columbia Univ., New York, USA; Counsellor, Embassy of Cuba in Chile 1959; Deputy Perm. Rep. to UN 1959–60; Amb. to Czechoslovakia 1961–63, to Brazil 1963–64; Dir of Trade Policy, Ministry of Foreign Trade 1964–66; Dir-Gen. of Int. Dept Ministry for Food Industries 1967–70; Dir-Gen. of Nat. Cttee for Econ., Scientific and Tech. Co-operation 1971–72; Perm. Sec. CMEA Nat. Cttee for Econ. Scientific and Tech. Co-operation 1972–76; Sr Political Adviser to Vice-Pres. of Council of State in charge of Foreign Affairs 1976–78; Perm. Rep. to UN 1978–84; Vice-Minister of Foreign Affairs 1984–92; Amb. to UNESCO 1993–94; Amb. to France 1994–98; mem. Scientific Council, Higher Inst. for Int. Relations, Havana 2001–; Chair. Nat. Comm. for UNESCO 2000–04; Amb. to the Holy See 2004–, to Sovereign Order of Malta 2005–; Hon. Mem. Cuban Soc. of Int. Law; Orden de Mayo al Mérito, Gran Cruz (Argentina), Grand Officier, Ordre nat. du Mérite (France), Order of Merit, First Degree (UAR), Magna Cruce Equitem Ordinis Piani 2007; Enrique Hart Medal (Cuba), First Mención Género Testimonio Premio Casa de las Américas 2000. *Publications:* Bolero y otras Prosas 2000, En el Torrente 2003, Roa x Roa 2003. *Leisure interests:* music, literature, writing. *Address:* Via Aurelia 137/5a, 00165 Rome, Italy (office); Calle 38 No. 508, Miramar, Playa, Havana, Cuba (home). *Telephone:* (6) 39366680 (office); (6) 6371289 (Rome) (home). *Fax:* (6) 636685 (office). *E-mail:* embajador@cubassede.com (office); rauljroa@yahoo.it (home).

ROBB, Charles Spittal, BBA, JD; American lawyer, academic and fmr politician; *Distinguished Professor of Law and Public Policy, George Mason University;* b. 26 June 1939, Phoenix, Ariz.; s. of James Spittal Robb and Frances Howard Robb (née Woolley); m. Lynda Johnson (d. of late Pres. Lyndon B. Johnson) 1967; three d.; ed Cornell Univ., Univ. of Wisconsin and Univ. of Virginia; admitted to Va Bar 1973; law clerk to John D. Butzner, Jr, US Court of Appeals 1973–74; admitted to US Supreme Court Bar 1976; Attorney, Williams, Connolly and Califano 1974–77; Lt-Gov. of Va 1978–82, Gov. 1982–86; Pnr, Hunton and Williams 1986–89; Senator from Virginia 1989–2001; Chair. Democratic Govs' Asscn 1984–85, Democratic Leadership Council 1986–88; Chair Educ. Comm. of the States, Educ. Sub-Cttee of the Nat. Govs Asscns' Standing Cttee on Human Resources; Chair. Southern Govs' Asscn 1984–85; Pres. Council of State Govts 1985–86; Distinguished Prof. of Law and Public Policy, George Mason Univ. 2001–; mem. Pres.'s Foreign Intelligence Advisory Bd, Sec. of State's Arms Control and Non-proliferation Advisory Bd, FBI Dir's Advisory Bd; mem. Bd of Dirs Space Foundation, Thomas Jefferson Program in Public Policy, Concord Coalition, Center for the Study of the Presidency; MITRE Corpn (Vice Chair. 2006–); mem. American, Va Bar Asscns, Va Trial Lawyers' Asscn; Co-Chair. Pres.'s Comm. on Intelligence Capabilities 2004; mem. Iraq Study Group, Inst. of Peace 2006; Bronze Star, Viet Nam Service Medal with four stars, Vietnamese Cross of Gallantry with Silver Star; Raven Award 1973; Seven Socs. Org. Award, Univ. of Va. *Address:* School of Law, George Mason University, Room 415, 3301 North Fairfax Drive, Arlington, VA 22201, USA (office). *Telephone:* (703) 993-8000 (office). *Fax:* (703) 993-8088 (office). *Website:* www.law.gmu.edu (office).

ROBB, Graham Macdonald, PhD, FRSL; British writer; b. 2 June 1958, Manchester; m. Margaret Hambrick 1986; ed Univ. of Oxford, Goldsmiths Coll., London and Vanderbilt Univ., Nashville, Tenn., USA; British Acad. Fellowship 1987–90; New York Times Book of the Year 1994, 1999 and 2001,

Whitbread Biography of the Year Award 1997, R.S.L. Heinemann Award 1998. *Publications include:* Le Corsaire – Satan en Silhouette 1985, Baudelaire Lecteur de Balzac 1988, Scènes de la Vie de Bohème (ed.) 1988, Baudelaire (trans.) 1989, La Poésie de Baudelaire et la Poésie Française 1993, Balzac 1994, Unlocking Mallarmé 1996, Victor Hugo: A Biography 1998, Rimbaud 2000, Strangers: Homosexual Love in the 19th Century, The Discovery of France (Duff Cooper Prize, Ondaatje Prize 2008) 2007; contribs to Times Literary Supplement, Daily Telegraph, London Review of Books, New York Times. *Leisure interest:* cycling. *Address:* Rogers, Coleridge & White Ltd, 20 Powis Mews, London, W11 1JN, England (office). *Telephone:* (20) 7221-3717 (office). *Fax:* (20) 7229-9084 (office). *E-mail:* info@rcwlitagency.com (office). *Website:* www.rcwlitagency.com (office).

RÖBBELEN, Gerhard Paul Karl, Dr rer. nat; German professor of plant breeding; *Professor Emeritus, University of Göttingen;* b. 10 May 1929, Bremen; s. of Ernst Röbbelen and Henny Röbbelen; m. Christa Scherz 1957; two s. one d.; ed Univs of Göttingen and Freiburg; Asst Prof. Inst. of Agronomy and Plant Breeding, Univ. of Göttingen 1957–67, Prof. and Head Div. of Cytogenetics 1967–70, Dir of Inst. 1970–94, Dean Faculty of Agric. 1971–72, Prof. Emer. 1994–; Visiting Prof. Univ. of Mo., USA 1966–67; Ed. Plant Breeding 1976–2000; mem. German Soc. for Genetics (Pres. 1969–70, 1977–79), European Asscn for Research in Plant Breeding–EUCARPIA (Chair. Section for Oil and Protein Crops 1978–86, Pres. 1986–89), German Botanical Soc., Asscn for Applied Botany, Genetics Soc. of Canada, German Soc. Fat Research (Pres. 1989–92), German Soc. of Plant Breeding (Pres. 1991–96), Acad. of Sciences, Göttingen 1981, Acad. Leopoldina 1990; Order of Merit 1st Class (Germany) 2001; Hon. DAgric. (Kiel) 1976, (Halle/Saale) 1997, (Brno Czech Repub.) 2001; Norman Medal, German Soc. of Fat Science 1984, Chevreul Medal, Asscn Française pour l'Etude des Corps Gras 1989, Eminent Scientist Award, Paris 1999. *Publications:* more than 300 articles on research into plant genetics and breeding. *Leisure interests:* music, mountain climbing, gardening. *Address:* 8 Von Sieboldstrasse, 37075 Göttingen (office); 9 Tuckermannweg, 37085 Göttingen, Germany. *Website:* www.uni-goettingen .de (office).

ROBBINS, John B., MD; American immunologist and academic; *Head, Laboratory of Developmental and Molecular Immunity, National Institute of Child Health and Human Development;* Chief, Lab. of Developmental and Molecular Immunity, Nat. Inst. of Child Health and Human Devt, NIH 1983–; fmr Chair. WHO Ad Hoc Cttee; Albert Lasker Award for Clinical Research (jtly) 1996, Albert B. Sabin Gold Medal Award 2001. *Publications:* Bacterial Vaccines (ed.) 1987, The Awakened Heart 1997, Diet for a New America – How Your Food Choices Affect Your Health, Happiness, and the Future of Life on Earth 1998, Internal Medicine on Call (co-author) 2002, Reclaiming Our Health – Exploding the Medical Myth and Embracing the Sources of True Healing 2004. *Address:* Office of the Chief, Laboratory of Developmental and Molecular Immunity, National Institute of Child Health and Human Development, 6A/2A06, 31 Center Drive, Bethesda, MD 20892, USA (office). *Telephone:* (301) 496-0850 (office). *E-mail:* robbinsj@nichd.nih.gov (office). *Website:* www.nichd.nih.gov (office).

ROBBINS, Keith Gilbert, DPhil, DLitt, FRSE; British historian, academic and fmr university vice-chancellor; b. 9 April 1940, Bristol; s. of Gilbert Henry John Robbins and Edith Mary Robbins; m. Janet Carey Thomson 1963; three s. one d.; ed Bristol Grammar School, Magdalen Coll. Oxford, St Antony's Coll. Oxford; Lecturer, Univ. of York 1963–71; Prof. of History, Univ. Coll. of N Wales, Bangor 1971–79; Prof. of Modern History, Univ. of Glasgow 1980–91; Vice-Chancellor Univ. of Wales, Lampeter 1992–2003, now Hon. Professorial Fellow in Depts of History and Theology/Religious Studies and Pres. Centre for Comparative Study of Modern British and European Religious History; Sr Vice-Chancellor Univ. of Wales 1995–2001; Pres. Historical Asscn 1988–91; Winston Churchill Travelling Fellow 1990. *Publications:* Munich 1938, 1968, Sir Edward Grey 1971, The Abolition of War 1976, John Bright 1979, The Eclipse of a Great Power: Modern Britain 1870–1975 1983, 1870–1992 (2nd edn) 1994, The First World War 1984, Nineteenth-Century Britain: Integration and Diversity 1988, Appeasement 1988, Blackwell Dictionary of Twentieth-Century British Political Life (ed.) 1990, Churchill 1992, History, Religion and Identity in Modern Britain 1993, Politicians, Diplomacy and War in Modern British History 1994, Bibliography of British History 1914–1989 1996, Great Britain: Identities, Institutions and the Idea of Britishness 1997, The World Since 1945: a Concise History 1998, The British Isles 1901–1951 2002, Britain and Europe 1789–2005 2005, England, Ireland, Scotland, Wales: The Christian Church 1900-2000 2008. *Leisure interests:* walking, music. *Address:* Rhyd y Fran, Cribyn, Lampeter, Ceredigion, SA48 7NH, Wales (home). *Telephone:* (1570) 470349 (home). *E-mail:* profkgr@clara .co.uk (home).

ROBBINS, Tim, BA; American actor, director and screenwriter; b. 16 Oct. 1958, West Covina, Calif.; s. of folk singer Gil Robbins; pnr Susan Sarandon (q.v.); three c.; ed UCLA; began career as mem. Theater for the New City; Founder and Artistic Dir The Actors' Gang 1981–; Founder Havoc Inc. (production co.). *Theatre:* as actor: Ubu Roi 1981; as dir: A Midsummer Night's Dream 1984, The Good Woman of Setzuan 1990; as writer, with Adam Simon: Alagazam, After the Dog Wars, Violence: The Misadventures of Spike Spangle, Farmer, Carnage – A Comedy (rep. USA at Edin. Int. Festival, Scotland); as writer: Embedded 2004. *Films as actor:* No Small Affair 1984, Toy Soldiers 1984, The Sure Thing 1985, Fraternity Vacation 1985, Top Gun 1986, Howard the Duck 1986, Five Corners 1987, Bull Durham 1988, Tapeheads 1988, Miss Firecracker 1989, Eric the Viking 1989, Cadillac Man 1990, Twister 1990, Jacob's Ladder 1990, Jungle Fever 1991, The Player 1992, Bob Roberts (also writer and dir) 1992, Amazing Stories: Book Four 1992, Short Cuts 1993, The Hudsucker Proxy 1994, The Shawshank Redemption

1994, Prêt-à-Porter 1994, I.Q. 1994, Dead Man Walking (writer and dir) 1995, Nothing to Lose 1997, Arlington Road 1999, Cradle Will Rock (also writer and dir) 1999, Austin Powers: The Spy Who Shagged Me 1999, Mission to Mars 2000, High Fidelity 2000, Antitrust 2001, Human Nature 2001, The Truth About Charlie 2002, The Day My God Died 2003, Mystic River (Golden Globe for Best Supporting Actor 2004, Critics' Choice Award for Best Supporting Actor 2004, Screen Actors Guild Best Supporting Actor Award 2004, Acad. Award for Best Supporting Actor 2004) 2003, Code 46 2003, The Secret Life of Words 2005, War of the Worlds 2005, La Vida secreta de las palabras 2005, Zathura: A Space Adventure 2005, Catch a Fire 2006, Tenacious D: The Pick of Destiny 2006, Noise 2007. *Television:* Queens Supreme (pilot episode and series dir) 2003. *Address:* Havoc Inc., 16 West 19th Street, 12th Floor, New York, NY 10011 (office); c/o Elaine Goldsmith Thomas, ICM, 40 West 57th Street, New York, NY 10019 (office); The Actors' Gang at The Ivy Substation, 9070 Venice Blvd., Culver City, CA 90232, USA (office). *Website:* www.theactorsgang.com (office).

ROBBINS, Tom, BA; American writer; b. 22 July 1936, Blowing Rock, NC; s. of George T. Robbins and Katherine Robinson Robbins; m. 1st Terrie Lunden 1967 (divorced 1972); one s.; m. 2nd Alexa d'Avalon 1987; ed Virginia Commonwealth Univ. and Univ. of Washington; operated black market ring in S Korea 1956–57; int. news Times-Dispatch, Richmond, Va 1959–62; Art Critic, The Seattle Times and contrib. to Artforum and Art in America etc. 1962–65; Art Critic, Seattle Magazine 1965–67; Bumbershoot Golden Umbrella for Lifetime Achievement 1998, Writers' Digest 100 Best Writers of the 20th Century 2000. *Films:* Even Cowgirls Get the Blues 1994. *Publications:* novels: Another Roadside Attraction 1971, Even Cowgirls Get the Blues 1976, Still Life With Woodpecker 1980, Jitterbug Perfume 1984, Skinny Legs and All 1990, Half Asleep in Frog Pajamas 1994, Fierce Invalids Home from Hot Climates 2000, Villa Incognito 2003, Wild Ducks Flying Backward 2005, B is for Beer 2009. *Leisure interests:* volleyball, white magick, psychedelic plants, art, pop culture and religions. *Address:* PO Box 338, La Conner, WA 98257, USA (home).

RÖBEL, Udo; German editor; b. 20 Jan. 1950, Neustadt, Weinstrasse; Restaurant Ed. for Rheinpfalz and Mil. Service Corresp. for DPA and AP 1969–71; mem. editorial staff BILD newspaper, Frankfurt, Kettwig, and Aachen-zum-Schluss 1972–82; Deputy Ed.-in-Chief Express newspaper, Cologne 1983–89; journalistic adviser Heinrich-Bauer-Verlag 1989–92; mem. Chief Editorial Staff Bild 1993–97, Ed.-in-Chief Bild 1998–2000, Ed.-in-Chief Bild.de 2001–05; Ed. Fairpress.biz 2005–; Wächter-Preis, Deutschen Tagespresse 1985. *Website:* www.fairpress.biz (office).

ROBERT, Jacques Frédéric, DenD; French professor of law; *President, Centre français de Droit comparé;* b. 29 Sept. 1928, Algiers, Algeria; s. of Frédéric Robert and Fanny Robert; m. Marie-Caroline de Bary 1958; two s. two d.; ed Lycée E. F. Gautier, Algiers, Univs. of Algiers and Paris, CNRS; Prof. of Law, Univs of Algiers 1956–60, Rabat, Morocco 1960–62, Grenoble 1962–65; Dir Maison franco-japonaise, Tokyo 1965–68; Prof. of Law, Univ. of Nanterre 1968–69, Univ. of Paris II 1969–; Contributor, Le Monde and La Croix 1970–; Dir Revue de droit public 1977–; Pres. Univ. of Paris II (Panthéon) 1979–85; Pres. of Centre français de Droit comparé 1985–; mem. Conseil Constitutionnel 1989–98; mem. Japan Acad. 1997; Commdr Légion d'honneur, Ordre nat. du Mérite, Order of Honour Austria; Order of the Sacred Treasure (Japan), Officier, Ordre des Palmes académiques; Prix Paul Deschanel 1954. *Publications:* Les violations de la liberté individuelle 1954, La monarchie marocaine 1963, Le Japon 1970, Introduction à l'Esprit des Lois 1973, Libertés publiques 1988, L'Esprit de défense 1988, Libertés et droits fondamentaux (5th edn) 2002, Droits de l'homme et Libertés fondamentales (7th edn) 1999, Le juge constitutionnel, juge des libertés 1999, La Garde de la République 2000, Enjeux du siècle: nos libertés 2002, La fin de la Laicité 2004, Les richesses du droit 2005. *Leisure interests:* music, photography, swimming. *Address:* Centre français de Droit comparé, 28 rue Saint-Guillaume, 75007 Paris (office); 105 Boulevard Murat, 75016 Paris, France (home). *Telephone:* 1-44-39-86-24 (office); 1-40-71-87-05 (home). *Fax:* 1-44-39-86-28 (office); 1-46-51-37-29 (home). *E-mail:* cfdc@legiscompare.com (office).

ROBERT, Lorin S.; Micronesian diplomatist; *Secretary of Foreign Affairs;* ed American Univ. School of Int. Service, Washington, DC, Univ. of Oxford, UK; joined Dept of Foreign Affairs 1984, posts have included Deputy Chief of Mission for Embassy in Tokyo, Deputy Asst Sec. for Asian Affairs, Asst Sec. Asia Pacific and Multilateral Affairs Div., Deputy Sec. for the Dept 2001–07, Sec. of Foreign Affairs 2007–; Chair. Bd of Trustees Micronesian Fisheries Authority; fmr Alternate Gov. IBRD and Asian Devt Bank; has represented Micronesia on various UN panels. *Address:* Department of Foreign Affairs, PS123, Palikir, Pohnpei State, 96941, Federated States of Micronesia (office). *Telephone:* 320-2641 (office). *Fax:* 320-2933 (office). *E-mail:* foreignaffairs@mail.fm (office).

ROBERTO CARLOS; Brazilian professional footballer; b. (Roberto Carlos da Silva), 10 April 1973, Garca, São Paulo; s. of Oscar and Vera Lúcia; m. to Alexandra; three d.; ed Colonel José Levy School, São Paulo; left-back; teams: Uniao 1989–92 (professional debut 1992), Palmeiras 1992–95 (45 matches, four goals), Internazionale 1995–96 (30 matches, five goals), Real Madrid, Spain 1996–2007, Fenerbahçe, Turkey 2007–, Brazil 1992– (debut v. USA); 95 international caps, eight goals; club titles include: São Paulo Championship with Palmeiras 1993, 1994, Brazilian Championship with Palmeiras 1993, Primera Liga with Real Madrid 1996/97, 2000/01, 2002/03, 2006/07, Champions' League with Real Madrid 1998, 2000, 2002, Intercontinental Cup with Real Madrid 1998, 2002, Spanish Super Cup with Real Madrid 2001, 2003, Copa del Rey (runner-up) with Real Madrid 2002, UEFA Super Cup with Real Madrid 2002; international honours include: Olympic Games (bronze medallist) 1996, Copa America 1997, 1999, World Cup 2002 (runner-up 1998). *Address:* c/o Fenerbahçe Sports Club, Fenerbahçe Sükrü Saracoglu Stadium, Kiziltoprak, Kadıköy, Istanbul, Turkey (office). *Telephone:* (216) 5421907 (office). *Fax:* (216) 5421960 (office). *E-mail:* editor@fenerbahce.org (office). *Website:* www.fenerbahce.org (office); robertocarlos03.terra.com.br.

ROBERTS, Bernard, FRCM; British concert pianist; b. 23 July 1933, Manchester; s. of William Wright Roberts and Elsie Alberta Ingham; m. 1st Patricia May Russell 1955 (divorced 1987); two s.; m. 2nd Caroline Ireland 1992; ed William Hulme's Grammar School, Manchester, Royal Coll. of Music, London; won Scholarship to RCM 1949; début as concert pianist, Wigmore Hall, London 1957; Piano Prof., RCM 1962–99; tutor, Chetham's School of Music, Manchester 1999–; numerous solo recitals and concerto performances, chamber music player; Fellow, Royal Welsh Coll. of Music and Drama 2004; Hon. DUniv (Brunel). *Recordings include:* Beethoven's 32 piano sonatas and Bach's 48 preludes and fugues. *Leisure interests:* philosophy, religion, model railways. *Address:* Uwchlaw'r Coed, Llanbedr, Gwynedd, LL45 2NA, Wales. *Telephone:* (1341) 241532. *E-mail:* caroline.ireland@virgin.net. *Website:* http://freespace.virgin.net/caroline.ireland/intro.html.

ROBERTS, Brian Leon, BS; American communications industry executive; *Chairman and CEO, Comcast Corporation;* b. 28 June 1959, Philadelphia, Pa; s. of Ralph J. Roberts and Suzanne F. Roberts; m. Aileen Kennedy 1985; one s. two d.; ed Wharton School of Finance Univ. of Pennsylvania; Vice-Pres. Operations, Comcast Cable Communications Inc. 1985–86, Exec. Vice-Pres. Comcast Corpn 1986–90, Pres. 1990, CEO 2001–, Chair. 2004–, also mem. Bd of Dirs, Pres. 1992– (acquired AT&T Broadband 2002); mem. Bd of Dirs Nat. Cable & Telecommunications Asscn, Chair. 1995–96, 2005–07; Chair. CableLabs 1999–2001, 2003–05, 2007–; Vice-Chair. Walter Katz Foundation; mem. Bd of Dirs Turner Broadcasting System, QVC Network, Bank of NY, Simon Wiesenthal Center, Viewer's Choice, CableLabs (Chair. 1999–2001, 2003–05), Cable TV Asscn; Co-Chair. Resource Devt Campaign for United Way of Southeastern Pennsylvania 2003; Founding Co-Chair. Philadelphia 2000 (nonpartisan host cttee for Republican Nat. Convention) 2000; honoured by The Police Athletic League of Philadelphia 2002, Steven J. Ross Humanitarian Award, UJA Fed. of New York 2003, Humanitarian Award, Simon Wiesenthal Center 2004, named by Institutional Investor magazine as one of America's top CEOs 2004–08, honoured by Nat. Asscn for Multi-ethnicity in Communications 2005, honoured by Partnership for a Drug-Free America 2005, inducted into Cable Television Hall of Fame 2006, Distinguished Vanguard Award for Leadership 2007, recognized by Big Brothers and Big Sisters for outstanding leadership in the community and for serving as a role model to youth 2008. *Achievement:* earned Silver Medals with US squash team at Maccabiah Games, Israel 1981, 1985, 1997, Gold Medal 2005. *Address:* Comcast Corpn, Floor 33, East Tower, 1500 Market Street, Philadelphia, PA 19102-2148, USA (office). *Telephone:* (215) 665-1700 (office). *Fax:* (215) 981-7790 (office). *E-mail:* lisa_orio@comcast.com (office). *Website:* www.comcast.com (office).

ROBERTS, (Charles) Patrick; American politician; *Senator from Kansas;* b. 20 April 1936, Topeka, Kan.; s. of Wes Roberts and Ruth Roberts (née Patrick); m. Franki Fann 1970; one s. two d.; ed Kan. State Univ.; served with US Marine Corps 1958–62; Publr Litchfield Park, Ariz. 1962–67; Admin. Asst to US Senator F. Carlson 1967–68, to US Congressman Keith Sebelius 1968–70; mem. 97th to 104th US Congresses 1980–97; Senator from Kan. 1997–, Chair. Senate Select Cttee on Intelligence; Republican. *Address:* 302 Hart Senate Office Building, Washington, DC 20510, USA (office). *Telephone:* (202) 224-4774 (office). *Website:* roberts.senate.gov (office).

ROBERTS, Dato Seri Paduka Sir Denys Tudor Emil, KBE, BCL, QC, SPMB, MA; British judge and administrator; b. 19 Jan. 1923, London; s. of William David Roberts and Dorothy Eliza Morrison; m. 1st B. Marsh 1949; one s. one d.; m. 2nd Fiona Alexander 1985; one s.; ed Aldenham School, Wadham Coll., Oxford and Lincoln's Inn; Capt., Royal Artillery 1943–46; English Bar 1950–53; Crown Counsel, Nyasaland (now Malawi) 1953–59; Attorney-Gen., Gibraltar 1960–62; Solicitor-Gen., Hong Kong 1962–66, Attorney-Gen. 1966–73, Colonial Sec. 1973–76, Chief Sec. 1976–78, Chief Justice Hong Kong 1978–88, of and Brunei 1979–88, of Brunei Darussalam 1979–2001; Pres. Court of Appeal for Bermuda 1988–94, Court of Final Appeal Hong Kong 1997; Pres. MCC 1989–90; Hon. Bencher Lincoln's Inn and Court of Final Appeal, Hong Kong Special Admin. Region; Pres. St Albans Cricket Club; Hon. Fellow,Wadham Coll.; Seri Paduka Makhuta Brunei. *Publications:* eight books (including four novels) 1955–. *Leisure interests:* writing, cricket, tennis, walking. *Address:* c/o St Albans Cricket Club, Clarence Park, Clarence Road, St Albans, Herts., AL1 4NF, England; Leithen Lodge, Innerleithen, Peeblesshire, EH44 6NW, Scotland. *Telephone:* (1727)850388; (1896) 830297 (Scotland). *Fax:* (1896) 830726.

ROBERTS, Sir Derek Harry, Kt, CBE, BSc, FRS, FEng; British physicist, business executive, fmr university provost and fmr university president; b. 28 March 1932, Manchester; s. of Harry Roberts and Alice Roberts (née Storey); m. Winifred Short 1958; one s. one d.; ed Manchester Cen. High School and Manchester Univ.; Research Scientist, Plessey Co. 1953–67; Gen. Man. Plessey Semiconductors 1967–69; Dir Plessey Allen Clark Research Centre 1969–73; Man. Dir Plessey Microsystems Div. 1973–79; Dir of Research, The General Electric Co. PLC 1979–83, Tech. Dir 1983–85, Jt Deputy Man. Dir (Tech.) 1985–88, Dir 1988–; Visiting Prof., Univ. Coll., London 1979, Provost and Pres. 1989–99, 2002–03; Pres. BAAS 1996–97, Sr Research Fellow, School of Public Policy 1999–; mem. Bd of Dirs Ludwig Inst. for Cancer Research; Hon. Fellow, Univ. Coll. London, British Asscn for the Advancement of Science; Hon. DSc (Bath) 1982, (Loughborough) 1984, (City) 1985, (Lancaster) 1986, (Manchester) 1987, (Queens Univ., Belfast) 1990; Hon. DUniv (Open) 1984, (Salford), (Essex), (London) 1988. *Publications:* about 30 tech. papers in learned soc. journals. *Leisure interests:* gardening, reading. *Address:* The Old

Rectory, Maids Moreton, Buckingham, England (home). *Telephone:* (1280) 813470 (home).

ROBERTS, Dorothy Elizabeth, AMusA, LMus; pianist and abstract painter; b. 1930, Brisbane, Qld, Australia; m. (divorced); one s.; ed Sydney Conservatorium of Music, studied with Adelina de Lara in London, also with Clara Schumann; concerts at Balliol Coll., Oxford, Purcell Room, South Bank, London; performed Liszt's Piano Concerto in E Flat with London Symphony Orchestra at Royal Albert Hall, London; other concerto performances with the Hallé Orchestra, Northern Sinfonia Orchestra and London Bach Players; recitals in the UK, Germany, Australia, France, The Netherlands, Canada; television appearance with the Hallé Orchestra; other television appearances with Richard Bonynge, including playing with the BBC Orchestra; Hon. DLit (Univ. of Bradford) 1995. *Address:* Alveley House, 17 Lindum Road, Lincoln, LN2 1NS, England (home).

ROBERTS, Sir Ivor Anthony, KCMG, MA; British diplomatist (retd); b. 24 Sept. 1946, Liverpool; s. of the late Leonard Moore Roberts and Rosa Maria Roberts (née Fusco); m. Elizabeth Bray Bernard Smith 1974; two s. one d.; ed St Mary's Coll., Crosby, Keble Coll., Oxford; entered diplomatic service 1968, with Middle East Centre for Arab Studies 1969, Third, then Second Sec. Paris 1970–73, Second, then First Sec. FCO 1973–78, First Sec. Canberra 1978–82, Deputy Head of News Dept FCO 1982–86, Head Security Co-ordination Dept FCO 1986–88, Minister and Deputy Head of Mission, Madrid 1989–93, Chargé d'affaires Belgrade 1994–96; Amb. to Yugoslavia 1996–97, to Ireland 1999–2003, to Italy 2003–06 (retd); Fellow, Inst. of Linguists 1991; Sr Assoc. Mem. St Antony's Coll., Oxford 1998–99; Hon. Fellow, Keble Coll., Oxford 2001. *Leisure interests:* opera, skiing, golf, photography. *Address:* c/o Foreign and Commonwealth Office, King Charles Street, London, SW1A 2AH England.

ROBERTS, John D., PhD; American chemist and academic; *Institute Professor Emeritus of Chemistry, California Institute of Technology;* b. 8 June 1918, Los Angeles, Calif.; s. of Allen Andrew Roberts and Flora Dombrowski; m. Edith M. Johnson 1942; three s. one d.; ed Univ. of California at Los Angeles; Instructor, UCLA; Nat. Research Fellow in Chem., Harvard Univ. 1945–46, Instructor 1946; Instructor, MIT 1946–47, Asst Prof. 1947–50, Assoc. Prof. 1950–53; Guggenheim Fellow, Calif. Inst. of Technology 1952–53, Prof. of Organic Chem. 1953–72, Inst. Prof. of Chem. 1972–88, Prof. Emer. 1988–, Lecturer 1988–, Chair. Div. of Chem. and Chemical Eng 1963–68, Acting Chair. 1972–73, Dean of the Faculty 1980–83, Vice-Pres. and Provost 1980–83; Visiting Prof., Ohio State Univ. 1952, Harvard Univ. 1959–60, Univ. of Munich 1962; Distinguished Visiting Prof., Univ. of Iowa 1967; Visiting Prof., Stanford Univ. 1973; Noyce Visiting Prof. of Science, Grinnell Coll. 2001; Distinguished Grad. Lecturer, Scripps Research Inst. 1996; mem. NAS, Chair. Section of Chem. 1968–71, of Math. and Physical Sciences 1976–78, Class I 1977–79, Counsellor 1980–83; mem. American Philosophical Society 1974, Counsellor, Class I 1983–86; Dr hc (Munich); Hon. DSc (Temple Univ., Wales, Scripps Research Inst.); numerous awards, including Nat. Medal of Science 1990, Welch Award 1990, Arthur C. Cope Award 1994, NAS Award in Chemical Sciences 1999, Nakanishi Prize 2001. *Publications:* Nuclear Magnetic Resonance 1958, Spin-Spin Splitting in High Resolution Nuclear Magnetic Resonance Spectra 1961, Molecular Orbital Calculations 1961, Basic Principles of Organic Chemistry 1965, Modern Organic Chemistry 1967, Organic Chemistry, Methane to Macromolecules 1971, At the Right Place at the Right Time 1990, ABC's of FT NMR 2000; and numerous articles 1940–. *Leisure interests:* tennis, skiing, sailing, classical music, colour photography. *Address:* California Institute of Technology, 358 Crellin Laboratory, Pasadena, CA 91125, USA (office). *Telephone:* (626) 395-6036 (office). *E-mail:* robertsj@caltech.edu (office). *Website:* www.cce.caltech.edu/faculty/roberts_j/index.html (office).

ROBERTS, John G., Jr, AB, JD; American lawyer and judge; *Chief Justice, Supreme Court;* b. 27 Jan. 1955, Buffalo, NY; m. Jane Sullivan Roberts; one s. one d.; ed Harvard Coll., Harvard Law School; fmr Man. Ed. Harvard Law Review; Law Clerk to Hon. Henry Friendly, US Court of Appeals for the Second Circuit 1979–80, to Assoc. Justice William Rehnquist, Supreme Court 1980–81; Special Asst to the Attorney-Gen., Dept of Justice 1981–82; Assoc. Counsel to the Pres., Office of the White House Counsel 1982–86; Assoc. Hogan & Hartson 1986, Pnr 1987–89, 1993–2003; Prin. Deputy Solicitor-Gen., US Dept of Justice 1989–93; Judge US Court of Appeals for DC Circuit 2003–05; Chief Justice Supreme Court 2005–; mem. American Law Inst., American Acad. of Appellate Lawyers; Dept of Justice Edmund J. Randolph Award. *Address:* United States Supreme Court, Supreme Court Bldg, 1 First Street, NE, Washington, DC 20543, USA (office). *Telephone:* (202) 479-3000 (office). *Fax:* (202) 479-2971 (office). *Website:* www.supremecourtus.gov (office).

ROBERTS, Julia; American actress; b. (Julie Fiona Roberts), 28 Oct. 1967, Smyrna, Ga; m. 1st Lyle Lovett 1993 (divorced 1995); m. 2nd Daniel Moder 2002; two s. one d.; ed Campbell High School; UNICEF Goodwill Amb. 1995; f. film production co. Red Om Films Inc. (fmrly Shoelace Productions); American Cinematheque Award 2007. *Films include:* Firehouse 1987, Satisfaction 1988, Mystic Pizza 1988, Blood Red 1989, Steel Magnolias (Golden Globe Award 1990) 1989, Flatliners 1990, Pretty Woman 1990, Sleeping with the Enemy 1991, Dying Young 1991, Hook 1991, The Player 1992, The Pelican Brief 1993, I Love Trouble 1994, Prêt à Porter 1994, Mary Reilly 1994, Something to Talk About 1996, Michael Collins 1996, Everyone Says I Love You 1996, My Best Friend's Wedding 1997, Conspiracy Theory 1997, Stepmom 1998, Notting Hill 1999, Runaway Bride 1999, Erin Brockovich (Acad. Award for Best Actress 2001) 2000, The Mexican 2001, America's Sweethearts 2001, Ocean's Eleven 2001, Grand Champion 2002, Full Frontal 2002, Confessions of a Dangerous Mind 2002, Mona Lisa Smile 2003, Closer 2004, Ocean's Twelve 2004, The Ant Bully (voice) 2006, Charlotte's Web (voice) 2006, Charlie Wilson's War 2007. *Address:* Red Om Films Inc., 145 West 57th Street, 19th Floor, New York, NY 10019 (office); Creative Artists Agency, 9830 Wilshire Boulevard, Beverly Hills, CA 90212-1825, USA (office). *Telephone:* (212) 243-2900 (Red Om) (office); (310) 288-4545 (office). *Fax:* (212) 243-2973 (Red Om) (office); (310) 288-4800 (office). *Website:* www.caa.com (office).

ROBERTS, Julian, BA, FCA, MCT; British accountant and business executive; *CEO, Old Mutual Group plc;* m. Marion Roberts; three s. one d.; ed Univ. of Stirling; qualified as accountant at PricewaterhouseCoopers 1983; with C E Heath 1987–93; mem. Bd of Dirs and Chief Financial Officer Aon UK Holdings Ltd 1993–98; Group Finance Dir Sun Life & Provincial Holdings plc 1998–2006; Group Finance Dir Old Mutual Group plc 2000–06, CEO Skandia 2006–08, CEO Old Mutual Group plc 2008–. *Leisure interests:* watching sports, playing golf, supporting his children at their rugby, football and hockey fixtures. *Address:* Old Mutual Place plc, 5th Floor, Old Mutual Place, 2 Lambeth Hill, London, EC4V 4GG, England (office). *Telephone:* (20) 7002-7000 (office). *Fax:* (20) 7002-7200 (office). *E-mail:* matthew.gregorowski@omg.co.uk (office). *Website:* www.oldmutual.com (office).

ROBERTS, Kevin John; British advertising executive; *CEO, Saatchi & Saatchi Worldwide Inc.;* b. 20 Oct. 1949, Lancaster; s. of John Roberts and Jean Roberts (née Lambert); m. 1st Barbara Beckett; one d.; m. 2nd Rowena Joan Honeywill 1974; two s. one d.; Brand Man. Gillette Co., London 1972–74; Group Marketing Man., Procter & Gamble, Geneva 1975–82; Vice-Pres. Pepsico, Nicosia 1982–86; Pres. and CEO Pepsi Cola Canada, Toronto 1987–89; COO Lion Nathan, Auckland 1990–96; CEO Saatchi & Saatchi Worldwide Inc., New York City 1997–, Publicis Groupe SA, Superscape Group PLC; Prof. of Sustainable Enterprise and Sr Fellow, Waikato Man. School, Univ. of Waikato, New Zealand; inaugural CEO in Residence, Judge Inst. of Man., Cambridge Univ. UK; Chair.USA Rugby Bd 2006–; Hon. Prof., Peruvian Univ. of Applied Sciences 2007; Dr hc (Univ. of Waikato) 1998; New Yorker for New York Award 2004. *Publication:* Peak Performing Organisations (co-author) 2000, Lovemarks: The Future Beyond Brands 2004, sisomo: The Future on Screen 2005, Lovemarks Effect: Winning in the Consumer Revolution 2006. *Leisure interests:* rugby, tennis, art, travel, music. *Address:* Saatchi & Saatchi Worldwide Inc., 375 Hudson Street, New York, NY 10014-3620, USA (office); Waikato Management School, The University of Waikato, Private Bag 3105, Hamilton, New Zealand. *Telephone:* (212) 463-2000 (office); (7) 858-5013 (NZ). *Fax:* (212) 463-2367 (office). *E-mail:* kevin_roberts@mngt.waikato.ac.nz. *Website:* www.saatchi.com/worldwide (office); www.saatchikevin.com; www.mngt.waikato.ac.nz.

ROBERTS, Matthew Vernon, MA, MPhil, DipMassComm; Saint Lucia journalist, educator and fmr politician; *Resident Tutor and Head, School of Continuing Studies, University of the West Indies;* b. 29 July 1954, Castries; m. Catherine (Kate) Regis 1980; one s. three d.; ed Univ. of West Indies, Jamaica, City Univ., London, UK; primary school teacher 1969–72; Asst Ed. The Voice newspaper 1972–80; fmr Public Relations Officer, Saint Lucia Tourist Bd; fmr Regional Communications Consultant, Caribbean Family Planning Affiliation; fmr Chief Information Officer Govt Information Service; currently Resident Tutor and Head, School of Continuing Studies, Univ. of West Indies; Speaker of House of Ass. –2003. *Leisure interests:* reading, swimming, gardening. *Address:* University of the West Indies, School of Continuing Studies, The Morne, Castries (office); Clavier Ridgeway, Entrepot Summit, PO Box 927, Castries, Saint Lucia (home). *Telephone:* 453-6486 (office); 452-7282 (home). *Fax:* 452-4080 (office). *E-mail:* uwislu@candw.lc (office).

ROBERTS, Michèle Brigitte, MA (Oxon.), ALA, FRSL; British novelist and poet; *Professor of Creative Writing Emerita, University of East Anglia;* b. 20 May 1949, Herts.; d. of Reginald Roberts and Monique Caulle; m. 1st Howard Burns 1984 (divorced 1987); m. 2nd Jim Latter 1991 (divorced 2004); two step-s.; ed Convent Grammar School, Somerville Coll., Oxford and University Coll. London; British Council Librarian, Bangkok 1973–74; Poetry Ed. Spare Rib 1974, City Limits 1981–83; Visiting Fellow Univ. of E Anglia 1992, Univ. of Nottingham Trent 1994; Visiting Prof. Univ. of Nottingham Trent 1996–2001; Prof. of Creative Writing, Univ. of E Anglia 2002–07, Emer. 2008–; Chair. Literary Cttee British Council 1998–2002; judge, Booker Prize 2001; mem. Soc. of Authors; Chevalier, Ordre des Arts et des Lettres 2001; Hon. MA (Nene) 1999; WHSmith Literary Award 1993. *Plays:* The Journeywoman 1988, Child-Lover 1995. *Television film:* The Heavenly Twins (Channel 4) 1993. *Publications include:* novels: A Piece of the Night 1978, The Visitation 1983, The Wild Girl 1984, The Book of Mrs Noah 1987, In the Red Kitchen 1990, Daughters of the House 1992, Flesh and Blood 1994, Impossible Saints 1997, Fair Exchange 1999, The Looking-Glass 2000, The Mistressclass 2003, Reader, I Married Him 2005, Paper Houses (autobiog.) 2007; Mind Readings (co-ed.) 1996; short stories: During Mother's Absence 1993, Playing Sardines 2001; essays: Food, Sex and God 1998; poetry: The Mirror of the Mother 1986; plays: Psyche and the Hurricane 1991, Child Lover 1993, All the Selves I Was 1995. *Leisure interests:* reading, talking with friends, cooking, gardening, looking at art. *Address:* Aitken Alexander Associates Ltd, 18–21 Cavaye Place, London, SW10 9PT, England (office). *Telephone:* (20) 7373-8672 (office). *Fax:* (20) 7373-6002 (office). *E-mail:* reception@aitkenalexander.co.uk (office). *Website:* www.aitkenalexander.co.uk (office); www.micheleroberts.com (home).

ROBERTS, Nora, (J. D. Robb); American writer; b. 10 Oct. 1950, Silver Spring, Md; mem. Romance Writers of America, Novelists Inc.; various Romance Writers of America Awards, named as one of 100 People Who Shape Our World, Time magazine 2007. *Publications:* Irish Thoroughbred 1981, Blithe Images 1982, Song of the West 1982, Search for Love 1982, Island of Flowers 1982, The Heart's Victory 1982, From This Day 1983, Her Mother's Keeper 1983, Reflections 1983, Once More with Feeling 1983, Untamed 1983,

Dance of Dreams 1983, Tonight and Always 1983, This Magic Moment 1983, Endings and Beginnings 1984, Storm Warning 1984, Sullivan's Woman 1984, Rules of the Game 1984, Less of a Stranger 1984, A Matter of Choice 1984, The Law is a Lady 1984, First Impressions 1984, Opposites Attract 1984, Promise Me Tomorrow 1984, Partners 1985, The Right Path 1985, Boundary Lines 1985, Summer Desserts 1985, Dual Images 1985, Night Moves 1985, Playing the Odds 1985, Tempting Fate 1985, All the Possibilities 1985, One Man's Art 1985, The Art of Deception 1986, One Summer 1986, Treasures Lost, Treasures Found 1986, Risky Business 1986, Lessons Learned 1986, Second Nature 1986, A Will and a Way 1986, Home for Christmas 1986, Affaire Royale 1986, Mind Over Matter 1987, Temptation 1987, Hot Ice 1987, Sacred Sins 1987, For Now, Forever 1987, Command Performance 1987, The Playboy Prince 1987, Brazen Virtue 1988, Local Hero 1988, Irish Rose 1988, The Name of the Game 1988, Rebellion 1988, The Last Honest Woman 1988, Dance to the Piper 1988, Skin Deep 1988, Sweet Revenge 1989, Loving Jack 1989, Best Laid Plans 1989, Gabriel's Angel 1989, Lawless 1989, Public Secrets 1990, Taming Natasha 1990, Night Shadow 1991, Genuine Lies 1991, With This Ring 1991, Night Shift 1991, Without a Trace 1991, Luring a Lady 1991, Courting Catherine 1991, A Man for Amanda 1991, For the Love of Lilah 1991, Suzannah's Surrender 1991, Carnal Innocence 1992, Unfinished Business 1992, The Welcoming 1992, Honest Illusions 1992, Divine Evil 1992, Captivated 1992, Entranced 1992, Charmed 1992, Second Nature 1993, Private Scandals 1993, Falling for Rachel 1993, Time Was 1993, Times Change 1993, Boundary Lines 1994, Hidden Riches 1994, Nightshade 1994, The Best Mistake 1994, Night Smoke 1994, Born in Fire 1994, Born in Ice 1995, True Betrayals 1995, Born in Shame 1996, Montana Sky 1996, From the Heart 1997, Sanctuary 1997, Holding the Dream 1997, Daring to Dream 1997, Finding the Dream 1997, The Reef 1998, The Winning Hand 1998, Sea Swept 1998, Homeport 1999, The Perfect Neighbor 1999, Megan's Mate 1999, Enchanted 1999, Rising Tides 1999, Inner Harbor 1999, Carolina Moon 2000, The Villa 2001, Heaven and Earth 2001, Three Fates 2002, Chesapeake Blue 2002, Key of Knowledge 2003, Key of Light 2003, Once Upon a Midnight 2003, Birthright 2003, Remember When 2003, Blue Dahlia 2004, Key of Valor 2004, Northern Lights 2005, Blue Smoke (Quill Award for Romance) 2006, Angels Fall (Quill Award for Book of the Year and for Romance 2007) 2006, Heart of the Sea 2007, Divine Evil 2007, The Hollow 2008, High Noon 2008, Tribute 2008, The Pagan Stone 2008, Black Hills 2009, Vision in White 2009; as J. D. Robb: Only Survivors Tell Tales 1990, Naked in Death 1995, Glory in Death 1995, Rapture in Death 1996, Ceremony in Death 1997, Vengeance in Death 1997, Holiday in Death 1998, Immortal in Death 1998, Silent Night 1998, Loyalty in Death 1999, Conspiracy in Death 1999, Witness in Death 2000, Judgment in Death 2000, Seduction in Death 2001, Out of this World 2001, Betrayal in Death 2001, Reunion in Death 2002, Purity in Death 2002, Imitation in Death 2003, Remember When 2003, Portrait in Death 2003, Once Upon a Midnight 2003, Divided in Death 2004, Visions in Death 2004, Memory in Death 2006, Born in Death 2006, Innocent in Death 2007, Strangers in Death 2008, Creation in Death 2008, Salvation in Death 2008. *Address:* Writers' House Inc., 21 W 26th Street, New York, NY 10010, USA (office). *Telephone:* (212) 685-2400 (office). *Fax:* (212) 685-1781 (office). *E-mail:* write2nora@msn.com. *Website:* www.noraroberts.com.

ROBERTS, Sir Richard John, Kt, BSc, PhD, FRS; British scientist; *Chief Scientific Officer, New England Biolabs;* b. 6 Sept. 1943, Derby; s. of John Walter Roberts and Edna Wilhelmina Roberts; m. 1st Elizabeth Dyson 1965 (deceased); one s. one d.; m. 2nd Jean Tagliabue 1986; one s. one d.; ed Univ. of Sheffield; Research Fellow, Harvard Univ. 1969–70, Research Assoc. in Biochemistry 1971–72; Sr Staff Investigator, Cold Spring Harbor Lab. Research Inst., Long Island 1972–86, Asst Dir for Research 1986–92; Research Dir New England Biolabs 1992–2005, Chief Scientific Officer 2005–; Chair. NCI Bd of Scientific Counselors 1996–2000; Chair. Scientific Advisory Bd Celera 1998–2002, MultiGene Biotech 1998–; Chair. Steering Cttee on Genetics and Biotech. ICSU 1998–; mem. Editorial Bd Bioinformatics 1985–2002, Current Opinions in Chemical Biology 1997–2001; mem. Scientific Advisory Bd Genex Corpn 1977–85, Molecular Tool 1994–2000, Oxford Molecular Group 1996–99, Conservation Law Foundation 1998–, PubMed Central 2000–03, Orchid Biosciences 2000–03, Center for Functional Genomics SUNY Albany 2002–, Diversa Corpn 2003–, PubChem 2004–, Rain Dance Techs 2004–, ICGEB 2005–; mem. Bd Albert Schweitzer Acad. of Medicine 1998–2003, Vice-Pres. 2003–; Exec. Ed. Nucleic Acids Research 1987–; Patron Oxford Int. Biomedical Centre 1994–; Adviser to Dir NASA Astrobiology Program 2000–; Vice-Chair. Int. Science Advisory Bd, JDW Inst. of Genome Sciences, Hangzhou, China 2003–; Distinguished Scientist, Research Scholar, Boston Univ. 2003–; Hon. MD (Uppsala) 1992, (Bath) 1994; Hon. DSc (Sheffield) 1994, (Derby) 1995, (Chinese Univ. of Hong Kong) 2005; Nobel Prize in Physiology or Medicine (for the discovery of 'split genes') 1993, American Acad. of Achievement Golden Plate Award 1994, Univ. of Sheffield Convocation Award 1994, Gabor Medal of the Royal Soc. 2007. *Publications:* Nucleases (co-ed.) 1982, The Applications of Computers to Research on Nucleic Acids (co-ed.) 1982. *Leisure interest:* croquet. *Address:* New England Biolabs, 240 County Road, Ipswich, MA 01938-2723, USA (office). *Telephone:* (978) 380-7405 (office). *Fax:* (978) 380-7406 (office). *E-mail:* roberts@neb.com (office). *Website:* www.neb.com (office).

ROBERTSON, Dawn, BA; American retail executive; *President, Old Navy;* b. Birmingham, Ala; m. Tom Robertson; two c.; ed Auburn Univ.; held several sr positions at May Company 1983–96; Pres and CEO McRae's (div. of Saks Inc.) Jackson, Miss. 1997–98; Exec. Vice Pres. Federated Merchandising Group 1998–2000, Pres. and Chief Merchandising Officer Federated Direct (online and catalog business div. for Macy's and Bloomingdale's) 2000-02; Man. Dir Myer (fmrly Myer Grace Bros), Melbourne, Australia 2002–06; Pres. Old Navy Div., Gap Inc., San Francisco 2006–; ranked by Fortune magazine amongst 50 Most Powerful Women in Business outside the US (30th) 2004, (37th) 2005. *Address:* Old Navy, 2 Folsom Street, San Francisco, CA 94105, USA (office). *Telephone:* (650) 952-4400 (office). *Fax:* (415) 427-2553 (office). *Website:* www .oldnavy.com (office).

ROBERTSON, Geoffrey Ronald, QC, BA, LLB, BCL; Australian/British judge and lawyer; *Head, Doughty Street Chambers;* b. 30 Sept. 1946, Sydney; s. of Francis Robertson and Bernice Beattie; m. Kathy Lette (q.v.) 1990; one s. one d.; ed Epping Boys' High School and Univs of Sydney and Oxford; Rhodes scholar; solicitor, Allen, Allen & Hemsley 1970; called to bar, Middle Temple, London 1973; QC 1988; Visiting Prof., Univ. of NSW 1979, Univ. of Warwick 1981; leader, Amnesty missions to S Africa 1983–90; consultant on Human Rights to Govt of Australia 1984; founding mem. and Head, Doughty Street Chambers 1990–; Counsel to Royal Comm. on gun-running to Colombian drug cartels 1991; Asst Recorder 1993–99, a Recorder 1999–; Master of Bench, Middle Temple 1997–; Chief Counsel Comm. on Admin. of Justice in Trinidad and Tobago 2000; Appeal Judge, UN Special Court for War Crimes in Sierra Leone 2002–07; Chair. Staff Panel on Reform of UN Justice 2006; mem. Exec. Council Justice; Hon. LLD (Sydney) 2006; Freedom of Information Award 1992. *Radio:* Chair. You the Jury (BBC Radio 4). *Plays:* The Trials of Oz (BBC) 1992. *TV series:* Hypotheticals, Granada TV, ABC and Channel 7 (Australia). *Publications:* Reluctant Judas 1976, Obscenity 1979, People Against the Press 1983, Geoffrey Robertson's Hypotheticals 1986, Does Dracula Have AIDS ? 1987, Freedom, The Individual and The Law 1989, The Justice Game 1998, Crimes Against Humanity 1999, Media Law (with A. Nicol) 2002, The Tyrannicide Brief 2006, The Levellers - The Putney Debates 2007. *Leisure interests:* tennis, opera, fishing. *Address:* Doughty Street Chambers, 11 Doughty Street, London, WC1N 2PL, England (office). *Telephone:* (20) 7404-1313 (office); (20) 7624-3268 (home). *Fax:* (20) 7404-2283 (office); (20) 7624-7146 (home). *E-mail:* g.robertson@doughtystreet.co.uk (office). *Website:* www .doughtystreet.co.uk (office).

ROBERTSON, Lloyd, OC; Canadian broadcaster; *Chief Anchor and Senior Editor, CTV News;* b. 19 Jan. 1934, Stratford, Ont.; m. Nancy; four d.; with CJCS radio, Stratford 1952, CJOY, Guelph 1953; with CBC 1954, positions in Winnipeg, Ottawa, Anchor Nat. News 1970–76; joined CTV 1976, Chief Anchor and Sr Ed. CTV News 1983–, Presenter, CTV News with Lloyd Robertson; Hon. Chair. Terry Fox Run 1992; Hon. LLD (Royal Roads Univ.) 2006; Gemini Award 1992, 1994, 1997, Cen. Canadian Broadcasters Asscn Broadcaster of the Year 1992, Radio TV News Dirs' Asscn Pres.'s Award 1993, Toronto Sun Reader's Voice Award for Favourite TV Anchor 1994, Canadian Asscn of Broadcasters (CAB) Gold Ribbon Award for Broadcast Excellence 1995–96, CAB Hall of Fame 1998, Canada's Favourite News Anchor, TV Times Readers' Choice Awards 1998, 1999. *Address:* CTV News, CTV Television Network, PO Box 9, Station O, Scarborough, ON M4A 2M9, Canada (office). *Telephone:* (416) 332-5000 (office). *Website:* www.ctv.ca (office).

ROBERTSON, Marion Gordon (Pat), BA, MDiv; American minister and broadcasting executive; *Chairman and CEO, Christian Broadcasting Network;* b. 22 March 1930, Lexington, Va; s. of A. Willis Robertson and Gladys Churchill; m. Adelia Elmer; two s. two d.; ed Washington and Lee Univ., Yale Univ., New York Theology Seminary; founder and CEO Christian Broadcasting Network, Va Beach, Va 1960–; ordained Minister Southern Baptist Convention 1961–87; founder and Chancellor Regent Univ. (fmrly CBN Univ.) 1977–; founder and Chair. Operation Blessing Int. Relief and Devt Inc. 1978–, Int. Family Entertainment Inc. 1990–97, Asia Pacific Media Corpn 1993–; Chair. Starguide Digital Networks Inc. 1995–, Porchlight Entertainment Inc. 1995–; founder and Pres. Christian Coalition 1989–, American Center for Law and Justice 1990–; cand. for Republican nomination for Pres. 1988; Dir United Va Bank, Norfolk; mem. Nat. Broadcasters (Dir 1973–); Knesset Medallion, Israel Pilgrimage Cttee, Faith and Freedom Award, Religious Heritage America, Bronze Halo Award, Southern Calif. Motion Picture Council, George Washington Honor Medal, Freedom Foundation at Valley Forge 1983. *Publications:* Shout it from the Housetops: The Story of the Founder of the Christian Broadcasting Network (jtly) 1972, My Prayer for You 1977, The Secret Kingdom 1982, Answers to 200 of Life's Most Probing Questions 1984, Beyond Reason 1984, America's Dates with Destiny 1986, The Plan 1989, The New Millennium 1990, The New World Order 1991, The End of the Age 1995. *Address:* The Christian Broadcasting Network, 977 Centreville Turnpike, Virginia Beach, VA 23463, USA (office). *Telephone:* (757) 226-7000 (office). *Website:* www.patrobertson.com; www.cbn.com (office).

ROBERTSON, Paul Douglas, BSc (Econ.), MA, PhD; Jamaican politician; b. 7 July 1946, St Andrew; m.; two d.; ed Univ. of the West Indies (UWI), Univ. of Michigan, USA; teacher, Oberlin High School 1965–68; teaching asst, Dept of Govt, UWI 1968–69, Lecturer 1976; Research Fellow, Inst. of Social and Econ. Research 1973–74; Research Assoc., Inst. of Urban Affairs, Asst Prof., Dept of Political Science, Howard Univ. 1974–76; Chair. JAMAL Foundation 1977–78; Special Adviser, Ministry of Justice 1977; Special Asst to Prime Minister 1978, 1980; Deputy Gen. Sec. for Admin, People's Nat. Party 1978–80, Gen. Sec. 1983–91, nat. campaign dir 2007; Deputy Leader of Govt Business in Senate 1989–93; MP for SE St Catherine 1993–2007; Minister without Portfolio 1989, of Information and Culture 1989, of Public Services and Information 1991, of Foreign Affairs 1992–93, of Foreign Affairs and Foreign Trade 1993–95, of Industry, Investment and Commerce 1995–97, of Industry and Investment 1997–2000, of Foreign Affairs 2000–01, apptd Minister of Devt 2001–. *Address:* c/o People's National Party, 89 Old Hope Rd, Kingston 6, Jamaica. *Telephone:* 978-1337. *Fax:* 927-4389. *E-mail:* information@pnpjamaica.com. *Website:* www.pnpjamaica.com.

ROBERTSON, Shirley, OBE; British sailor; b. 15 July 1968, Dundee, Scotland; m. Jamie Boag 2001; ed Heriot-Watt Univ.; sailed in Yngling class

2001–, previously sailed in Europe class; position: helm; Olympic results include ninth Barcelona 1992, fourth Atlanta 1996, gold medal Sydney 2000, gold medal Athens 2004; results in other competitions include silver medal Europe World Championships 1998, bronze medal Europe World Championships 1999, silver medal Europe European Championships 1999, bronze medal Pre-Olympic Regatta 1999, silver medal Europe World Championships 2000, 14th Yngling World Championships 2001, 16th Yngling World Championships, bronze medal Olympic Test Event 2002, gold medal Olympic Class Week 2003, gold medal Princess Sophia Trophy 2003, fourth Olympic Class Week 2003, bronze medal SPA Olympic Class Regatta 2003, gold medal Pre-Olympic regatta 2003; took one year break from sailing 2005; host Mainsail (monthly CNN TV show); mem. London Organising Cttee of the Olympic Games (LOCOG) Sport Advisory Group; BBC South Sports Personality of the Year 2000, Int. Sailing Fed. World Sailor of the Year 2000, Sailor of the Year 2002, Yachtsman of the Year 2004, Spirit of Scotland Top Scot award 2004. *Leisure interests:* cycling, films, dancing, socializing with friends. *Telephone:* (1983) 299202. *E-mail:* jogrindley@wight365.net. *Website:* www .shirleyrobertson.com; edition.cnn.com/CNNI/Programs/main.sail.

ROBERTSON, Thomas S., PhD; British academic; *Reliance Professor of Management and Private Enterprise and Dean, Wharton School, University of Pennsylvania;* b. 16 Nov. 1942, Gourock, Scotland; m. Diana Robertson; three c.; ed Wayne State Univ., Northwestern Univ.; Asst Prof., Anderson School, UCLA 1966–68; Asst Prof., Harvard Business School 1968–70; Assoc. Prof., Wharton School, Univ. of Pennsylvania 1971–76, Prof. 1976–94, Chair. of Marketing Dept 1978–84, 1988–94, Assoc. Dean for Exec. Educ. 1984–88, Pomerantz Prof. of Marketing 1987–94, Reliance Prof. of Man. and Pvt. Enterprise 2007–, Dean, Wharton School 2007–; Deputy Dean, London Business School 1994–98; Dean, Goizueta Business School, Emory Univ. 1998–2004, Exec. Faculty Dir Inst. for Developing Nations 2006–07; Planning Forum Award 1993, Best Paper Award, European Marketing Acad. 1995, Best Paper Award, Winter Conf., American Marketing Asscn 1996. *Publications include:* Handbook of Consumer Behavior (co-ed.) 1991, Perspectives on Consumer Behavior (co-ed.) 1991. *Address:* Wharton School, University of Pennsylvania, 1000 SH-DH, Philadelphia, PA 19104, USA (office). *Telephone:* (215) 898-4715 (office). *Fax:* (215) 573-5001 (office). *E-mail:* Robertson@ wharton.upenn.edu (office). *Website:* wharton.upenn.edu (office).

ROBERTSON OF PORT ELLEN, Baron (Life Peer), cr. 1999, of Islay in Argyll and Bute; **George Islay MacNeill Robertson;** PC, FRSA, GCMG; British business executive; *Deputy Chairman and Chairman, Audit Committee, TNK-BP;* b. 12 April 1946, Port Ellen, Isle of Islay, Argyll; s. of George P. Robertson and Marion Robertson; m. Sandra Wallace 1970; two s. one d.; ed Dunoon Grammar School and Univ. of Dundee; Scottish Organizer, Gen. & Municipal Workers' Union 1968–78; MP for Hamilton 1978–97, for Hamilton South 1997–99; Parl. Pvt. Sec. to Sec. of State for Social Services 1979; Opposition Spokesman on Scottish Affairs 1979–80, on Defence 1980–81, on Foreign and Commonwealth Affairs 1981–93; Prin. Spokesman on European Affairs 1984–94; Shadow Spokesman for Scotland 1994–97; Sec. of State for Defence 1997–99; Sec.-Gen. of NATO 1999–2003; Chair. Scottish Labour Party 1977–78; Vice-Chair. Bd British Council 1985–94; Exec. Deputy Chair. Cable & Wireless (C&W) 2003–06, Chair. Cable & Wireless International 2006–07, Sr Int. Adviser Cable and Wireless PLC 2007–; mem. Bd of Dirs Smiths Group 2004–06, Weir 2004–, Western Ferries (Clyde) Ltd, Scottish Devt Agency 1975–78, Scottish Tourist Bd 1974–76; Sr Counsellor, The Cohen Group, Washington, DC 2004–; Chair. Comm. on Global Road Safety 2004–; mem. Steering Cttee Königswinter Conf. 1983–92; mem. Council, Royal Inst. of Int. Affairs 1984–91, Jt Pres. 2001–; Deputy Chair. Ditchley Foundation 1989–; Deputy Chair. TNK-BP 2006–, Chair. Audit Cttee 2006–; Elder Brother, Trinity House 2001–; Pres. Hamilton Burns Club 2002–; Hon. Regimental Col London Scottish (Volunteers), Hon. FRSE; Kt of the Thistle (UK), Kt Grand Cross, Order of St Michael and St George (UK), Presidential Medal of Freedom (US), Grand Cross, Order of Merit (Germany, Italy, Poland, Hungary, Luxembourg), Grand Cross, Order of Star of Romania, Order of Jesus (Portugal), Order of Isabel the Catholic (Spain), Order of Leopold (Belgium), Order of Oranje-Nassau (Netherlands); Hon. LLD (Dundee, Bradford, St Andrews, Baku State Univ., Azerbaijan, Glasgow Caledonian, Stirling, West of Scotland), Hon. DSc (Cranfield – Royal Mil. Coll. of Science), Dr hc (European Univ., Armenia, Acad. of Sciences, Kyrgystan, School of Political and Administrative Studies, Bucharest, Romania; Winston Churchill Medal of Honour (English Speaking Union) 2003, Transatlantic Leadership Award (European Inst., Washington DC) 2003, Award for Distinguished Int. Leadership (Atlantic Council of USA) 2003, Presidential Medal of Freedom 2003, Distinguished Service Medal, US Dept of Defense. *Publication:* Islay and Jura: photographs by George Robertson 2006. *Leisure interests:* photography, golf, walking, family, reading. *Address:* House of Lords, London, SW1A 0PW (office); c/o BP plc, 1 St James's Square, London SW1Y, England (office). *Telephone:* (20) 7219-3000 (office). *Website:* www.tnk-bp.com (office).

ROBINS, Lee Nelken, MA, PhD; American social scientist and academic; *Professor Emerita of Social Science in Psychiatry, School of Medicine, Washington University;* b. 29 Aug. 1922, New Orleans, LA; m. 1st Eli Robins 1946 (died 1994); four s.; m. 2nd Hugh Chaplin, MD 1998; ed Radcliffe Coll. and Harvard Univ.; Research Assoc. Prof. Dept of Psychiatry, Washington Univ., St Louis, Mo. 1962–66, Research Prof. of Sociology in Psychiatry 1966–68, Prof. of Sociology in Psychiatry 1968–91, Prof. Dept of Sociology 1969–91, Univ. Prof. of Social Science, Prof. of Social Science in Psychiatry 1991–2001, Prof. Emer. 2001–; NIMH Special Research Fellowship, Washington Univ. 1968–70; mem. Inst. of Medicine (NAS); Research Scientist Award 1970, 1990, Lifetime Achievement Award, American Public Health Asscn 1994, Special Presidential Commendation, American Psychiatric Asscn 1999, 2nd Century Award, Wash. Univ. 2000, Distinguished Scientific Contrib. Award, Soc. for

Research into Child Devt 2003, Peter H. Raven Lifetime Award, Acad. of Science, St Louis 2006, Distinguished Clinical Research Scientist in the Addictions, American Journal on Addictions 2007 and many other awards. *Publications include:* Deviant Children Grown Up: A Sociological and Psychiatric Study of Sociopathic Personality 1966, The Vietnam Drug User Returns 1974, Validity of Psychiatric Diagnosis 1989, Psychiatric Disorders in America 1991, Straight and Devious Pathways from Childhood to Adulthood 1990; also written 267 journal articles and 26 psychiatric interviews. *Address:* Washington University School of Medicine, Department of Psychiatry, St Louis, MO 63110, USA (office). *Telephone:* (314) 362-2471 (office); (314) 361-0204 (home). *Fax:* (314) 362-2470 (office); (314) 361-6010 (home). *E-mail:* robinsl@psychiatry.wustl.edu (office); leerobins@sbcglobal.net (home). *Website:* www.psychiatry.wustl.edu (office).

ROBINS, Sir Ralph Harry, Kt, DL, BSc, FREng; British business executive; *Deputy Lieutenant, Derbyshire;* b. 16 June 1932, Heanor; s. of Leonard Haddon and Maud Lillian Robins; m. Patricia Maureen Grimes 1962; two d.; ed Imperial Coll., Univ. of London; Devt Engineer, Rolls-Royce 1955–66, Exec. Vice-Pres. Rolls-Royce Inc. 1971, Man. Dir Rolls-Royce Industrial and Marine Div. 1973, Commercial Dir Rolls-Royce Ltd 1978, Man. Dir Rolls-Royce PLC 1984–89, Deputy Chair. 1989–92 and Chief Exec. 1990–92, Chair. Rolls Royce 1992–2003; Chair. Defence Industries Council 1986–, Alter Technology Group; Deputy Lt Derbyshire 2002–; Pres. Soc. of British Aerospace Cos. 1986–87, Deputy Pres. 1987–88; Dir (non-exec.) Standard Chartered 1988–2004, Schroders 1990–2002, Marks & Spencer 1992–2001, Cable & Wireless 1994– (Chair. (non-exec.) 1998–2003), Marshall Holdings; mem. Council for Science and Tech. 1993–98; Fellow of Imperial Coll.; Hon. FRAeS; Hon. FIMechE 1996; Commdr Order of Merit (Germany) 1996; Hon. DSc (Cranfield) 1994, Hon. DBA (Strathclyde) 1996; Hon. DEng (Sheffield) 2001, (Nottingham) 2003. *Leisure interests:* tennis, golf, music, classic cars. *Address:* c/o Rolls-Royce PLC, 65 Buckingham Gate, London, SW1E 6AT, England. *Telephone:* (20) 7222-9020. *Fax:* (20) 7227-9185.

ROBINSON, Anne Josephine; British journalist and broadcaster; b. 26 Sept. 1944; m. 1st Charles Wilson; one d.; m. 2nd John Penrose; ed Farnborough Hill Convent and Les Ambassadrices, Paris, France; reporter Daily Mail 1967–68, Sunday Times 1968–77; Women's Ed. Daily Mirror 1979–80, Asst Ed. 1980–93, columnist 1983–93; columnist Today 1993–95, The Times 1993–95, 1998–2001, The Sun 1995–97, Daily Express 1997–98, The Daily Telegraph 2003–; Hon. Fellow, John Moores Univ. 1996. *Radio work includes:* Anne Robinson Show (BBC Radio 2) 1988–93. *Television:* presenter and writer (BBC) Points of View 1988–98, Watchdog 1993–2001, Going for a Song 1999–2000, The Weakest Link 2000– (also US version 2001–02), Great Britons 2002, Test the Nation 2002–, Guess Who's Coming to Dinner? 2003, Outtake TV 2003–, Travels with My Unfit Mother 2004, What's the Problem? 2005. *Publication:* Memoirs of an Unfit Mother (autobiog.) 2001. *Leisure interests:* walking her dogs. *Address:* CSS Presenters, Drury House, 34–43 Russell Street, London WC2B 5HA, England (office). *Telephone:* (20) 7078-1457 (office). *Fax:* (20) 7078-1401 (office). *E-mail:* tracey.chapman@css -stellar.com (office). *Website:* www.bbc.co.uk/weakestlink (office).

ROBINSON, (Arthur Napoleon) Raymond, LLB, MA, SC; Trinidad and Tobago politician, barrister, economist and fmr head of state; b. 16 Dec. 1926, Calder Hall; s. of James Andrew Robinson and Emily Isabella Robinson; m. Patricia Jean Rawlins 1961; one s. one d.; ed Bishop's High School, Tobago, London Univ., St John's Coll., Oxford and Inner Temple, London; MP, West Indies 1958–61; Rep. of Trinidad and Tobago Council of Univ. of West Indies 1960–62; Minister of Finance and Gov. for Trinidad Bd of Govs of IMF and IBRD 1961–67; Deputy Leader People's Nat. Movt 1967–70; Minister of External Affairs 1967–68; Dir of the Foundation for the Establishment of an Int. Criminal Court 1971; Chair. Democratic Action Congress 1971–86; Rep. for Tobago East, House of Reps 1976–80; Chair. Tobago House of Ass. 1980–86; Leader Nat. Alliance for Reconstruction 1986–91; Prime Minister of Trinidad and Tobago 1986–91, also Minister of the Economy; Minister Extraordinaire and Minister for Tobago Affairs; Adviser to the Prime Minister 1995–97; Pres. of Trinidad and Tobago 1997–2003; mem. UN Expert Group on Crime and the Abuse of Power 1979; Vice-Chair. Parliamentarians for Global Action 1993, Pres. 1995–96, Hon. Patron 1997–; Visiting Scholar, Harvard Univ. 1971; Hon. Fellow, St John's Coll., Oxford 1989; Chief of Ile Ife 1991; KStJ 1992; Hon. LLD (West Indies); Studentship Prize, Inner Temple; Distinguished Int. Criminal Law Award 1977, Defender of Democracy Award, Parliamentarians for Global Action 1997 and numerous other honours and awards. *Publications:* The New Frontier and the New Africa 1961, Fiscal Reform in Trinidad and Tobago 1966, The Path of Progress 1967, The Teacher and Nationalism 1967, The Mechanics of Independence 1971, Caribbean Man 1986; contributions to Encyclopaedia Britannica. *Leisure interests:* walking, swimming, travel, reading, modern music. *Address:* 21 Ellerslie Park, Maraval, Trinidad, Trinidad and Tobago (home).

ROBINSON, (Francis) Alastair Lavie; British banker; b. 19 Sept. 1937, London; s. of the late Stephen Robinson; m. Lavinia Napier 1961; two d.; ed Eton Coll.; Gen. Man. Mercantile Credit Co. 1971–78; Chair. Exec. Cttee then CEO and Pres. Barclays America Corpn, USA 1981–83; Regional Gen. Man. Barclays Bank Int. 1983–87; Dir Personnel, Barclays Bank PLC 1987–90, Exec. Dir 1990–96, Group Vice-Chair. 1992–96; Dir RMC PLC 1996–; Dir Marshall of Cambridge (Holdings) Ltd 1996–, Portman Bldg Soc. 1998–. *Leisure interests:* music, country pursuits, golf. *Address:* 24 Clarendon Street, London, SW1V 4RF, England.

ROBINSON, Geoffrey; British politician; b. 25 May 1938; s. of Robert Norman Robinson and Dorothy Jane Robinson (née Skelly); m. Marie Elena Giorgio 1967; one s. one d.; ed Emanuel School, Univ. of Cambridge, Yale Univ.; Research Asst Labour Party 1965–68; Sr Exec. Industrial Reorganization Corpn 1968–70; Financial Controller British Leyland 1971–72; Man. Dir Leyland Innocenti, Milan 1972–73; Chief Exec. Jaguar Cars 1973–75, Meriden Motor Cycle Workers' Co-operative 1978–80 (Dir 1980–82); MP for Coventry NW 1976–; HM Paymaster General 1997–98; Opposition Spokesman on Science 1982–83, on Regional Affairs and Industry 1983–86. Chair. TransTec PLC 1986–97; Dir W Midlands Enterprise Bd 1980–84; mem. Bd or Dirs Coventry City Football Club 1996, 2002-, Acting Chair. 2005–07; Labour. *Publications:* The Unconventional Minister (autobiog.) 2000. *Leisure interests:* reading, architecture, gardens. *Address:* c/o House of Commons, London, SW1A 0AA, England (office). *Telephone:* (20) 7219-4083 (office). *Fax:* (20) 7219-0984 (office). *E-mail:* robinsong@parliament.uk (office). *Website:* www .epolitix.com/EN/MPWebsites/Geoffrey+Robinson (office).

ROBINSON, Sir Gerrard Jude, Kt, FCMA; British business executive; *Chairman, Moto Hospitality Ltd;* b. 23 Oct. 1948; s. of Antony Robinson and Elizabeth Ann Robinson; m. 1st Maria Ann Borg 1970 (divorced 1990); one s. one d.; m. 2nd Heather Peta Leaman 1990; one s. one d.; ed St Mary's Coll., Castlehead; started work aged 16 as a cost clerk in a Matchbox toy factory; Works Accountant, Lesney Products 1970–74; Financial Controller Lex Industrial Distribution and Hire 1974–80; Finance Dir Coca-Cola 1980–81, Sales and Marketing Dir 1981–83, Man. Dir 1983–84; Man. Dir Grand Metropolitan (GrandMet) Contract Services 1984–87; led a man. buy-out of GrandMet catering div. 1987; Chief Exec. Compass GP PLC 1987–91, Granada Group PLC 1991–95, Chair. 1995–2001; Chair. London Weekend Television 1994–96, ITN 1995–97, BSkyB 1995–98, Arts Council 1998–2004, Allied Domecq 2002–05, Moto Hospitality Ltd 2006–; Hon. DLitt (Ulster); Hon. DSc (Econs) (Queen's) 1999. *Television:* I'll Show Them Who's Boss (series), Can Gerry Robinson Fix the NHS. *Publication:* I'll Show Them Who's Boss 2004. *Leisure interests:* golf, opera, chess, skiing, reading, music.

ROBINSON, Sir Ian, Kt, BSc, FREng, FIChemE, FRSE; British business executive; *Chairman, Ladbrokes PLC;* b. 3 May 1942, East Boldon, Durham; s. of Thomas Robinson and Eva Robinson; m. Kathleen Crawford Robinson (née Leay) 1967; one s. one d.; ed Leeds Univ., Harvard Business School, MA, USA; chartered engineer; fmr Chair. and Man.-Dir of Eng Div., Trafalgar House PLC; Chair. Amey PLC 2001–03; CEO Scottish Power 1995–2001; Chair. Hilton Group PLC 2001–06, Chair. Ladbrokes PLC (after restructuring of Hilton Group) 2006–; Chair. Scottish Advisory Task Force for Welfare to Work 1997–2000; Chair. Scottish Enterprise 2001–03; Dir (non-exec.) Scottish & Newcastle PLC 2004–, Compass Group PLC 2006–; mem. Advisory Bd Siemens UK; mem. Dept of Trade and Industry Overseas Project Bd 1993–97, Offshore Industry Advisory Bd 1993–95, CBI Scottish Business Council 1995–98, Take Over Panel 2004–; Scottish Businessman of the Year, Business Insider's Corp. Elite Awards 1996, George E. Davis Medal for Outstanding Contribution to Chemical Eng 1998. *Leisure interests:* golf, gardening. *Address:* Ladbrokes PLC, Imperial House, Imperial Drive, Rayners Lane, Harrow, Middx, HA2 7JW, England (office). *Telephone:* (20) 8868-8899 (office). *Fax:* (20) 8868-8767 (office). *Website:* www.ladbrokesplc.com (office).

ROBINSON, James D., III, BS, MBA; American business executive; *Co-Founder and General Partner, RRE Ventures LLC;* b. 19 Nov. 1935, Atlanta, Ga; s. of James D. Robinson Jr and Josephine Crawford; m. 1st Bettye Bradley (divorced); one s. one d.; m. 2nd Linda Gosden 1984; two s. two d.; ed Georgia Inst. of Tech., Harvard Graduate School of Business Admin.; Officer, US Naval Supply Corps 1957–59; various depts of Morgan Guaranty Trust Co. 1961–66, Asst Vice-Pres. and Staff Asst to Chair. and Pres. 1967–68; Gen. Partner, White, Weld & Co. 1968–70; Pres., CEO American Express Int. Banking Corpn 1970–73; Exec. Vice-Pres. American Express Co. 1970–75, Pres. 1975–77, Dir 1975–93, Chair. Bd 1977–93; Chair. American Express Credit Corpn 1973–75; Pres. J. D. Robinson Inc. 1993–; Chair. and CEO RRE Investors 1994, Gen. Pnr RRE Ventures LLC 1999–; Dir Bristol-Meyers Squibb Co., Chair. 2005–08; Dir The Coca-Cola Co., Novell Inc.; Dir and Chair. Emer. New York City Partnership, Chamber of Commerce Inc.; Hon. Chair. Memorial Sloan-Kettering Cancer Center; mem. Council on Foreign Relations, US Japan Business Council, Comm. for Econ. Devt; Hon. mem. Bd of Trustees, The Brookings Inst. *Address:* RRE Ventures, 126 East 56th Street, 22nd Floor, New York, NY 10022, USA (office). *Telephone:* (212) 418-5100 (office). *Fax:* (212) 688-0289 (office). *Website:* www.rre.com (office).

ROBINSON, Janet L., BA; American newspaper executive; *President and CEO, The New York Times Company;* ed Salve Regina Coll., Newport, RI, Exec. Educ. Program at Amos Tuck School, Dartmouth, Hanover, NH; public school teacher 1972–83; joined The New York Times in 1983, served in a variety of sr advertising positions for the newspaper as well as for The New York Times Co. Women's Magazine Group and Sports Magazine Group, Sr Vice-Pres. Advertising of The Times 1995–96, Pres. and Gen. Man. The New York Times newspaper 1996–2004, Sr Vice-Pres. Newspaper Operations 2001–04, Exec. Vice-Pres. and COO The New York Times Co. 2004, Pres. and CEO 2004–; mem. Bd The Advertising Council 1997–, Vice-Chair. 2001–04, 2004–; Hon. DBA (Salve Regina Univ.) 1998; ranked by Fortune magazine amongst 50 Most Powerful Women in Business in the US (48th) 2003, (34th) 2004, ranked by Forbes magazine amongst 100 Most Powerful Women (77th) 2005, (74th) 2006, (45th) 2007, (83rd) 2008. *Address:* The New York Times Co., 620 Eighth Avenue, New York, NY 10018-1405, USA (office). *Telephone:* (212) 556-1234 (office). *Fax:* (212) 556-7389 (office). *Website:* www.nytco.com (office).

ROBINSON, John Harris, BSc, CEng, FREng, FIChemE, FRSA; British business executive; b. 22 Dec. 1940; s. of Thomas Robinson and Florence Robinson; m. Doreen Alice Gardner 1963; one s. one d.; ed Woodhouse Grove School, Univ. of Birmingham; with ICI PLC 1962–65, Fisons PLC 1965–70, PA Consulting Group 1970–75, Woodhouse and Rixson 1975–79; Man. Dir Healthcare Div., Smith & Nephew PLC 1979–82, Dir 1982–89, Deputy CEO 1989–90, CEO 1990–97, Chair. 1997–99; Chair. Bonar PLC 1997–2001, UK Coal (fmrly RJB Mining) 1997–2003, George Wimpey PLC 1999–2007 (Dir (non-exec.) 1999–2007), Railtrack June–Nov. 2001, Paragon Healthcare Group 2002–06; Dir (non-exec.) Delta PLC 1993–2001, Esporta Group Ltd 2006–07; Chair. Healthcare Sector Group, Dept of Trade and Industry 1996–2001, mem. Industrial Devt Advisory Bd 1998–2001; mem. Council CBI 1991– (Chair. Tech. and Innovation Cttee 1998–2001), mem. Pres.'s Cttee 2001–; Chair. Council and Pro-Chancellor Univ. of Hull 1998–2006; mem. Cttee of Univ. Chairmen 1998–2006; Pres. Inst. Chemical Engineers 1999, Inst. of Man. 2002; Liveryman, Engineers Co. Ltd (Jr Warden) 2005; Hon. DEng (Birmingham) 2000; Hon. DUniv (Bradford) 2000; Hon. DBA (Lincoln) 2002, Hon. DrSc (Hull) 2006. *Leisure interests:* theatre, cricket, golf. *Address:* 10 Greycoat Place, London, SW1P 1SB, England (office). *Telephone:* (20) 8290-0911 (office). *Fax:* (560) 053-2780 (office). *E-mail:* terri@jrconsultants.org (office).

ROBINSON, Mary, LLM, DCL, SC, MRIA; Irish academic, international civil servant and fmr head of state; *Professor of Practice, School of International and Public Affairs, Columbia University;* b. 21 May 1944, Ballina, Co. Mayo; d. of Dr Aubrey Bourke and Dr Tessa O'Donnell; m. Nicholas Robinson 1970; two s. one d.; ed Mount Anville, Trinity Coll. Dublin, King's Inns, Dublin and Harvard Univ., USA; Barrister 1967, Sr Counsel 1980; called to English Bar (Middle Temple) 1973; Reid Prof. of Constitutional and Criminal Law, Trinity Coll. Dublin 1969–75, lecturer in European Community Law 1975–90; Founder and Dir Irish Centre for European Law 1988–90; Senator 1969–89; Pres. of Ireland 1990–97; UN High Commr for Human Rights and UnderSec.-Gen. 1997–2002; Chancellor Dublin Univ. 1998–; mem. Dublin City Council 1979–83; mem. New Ireland Forum 1983–84; mem. Irish Parl. Jt Cttee on EC Secondary Legislation 1973–89; mem. Vedel Cttee on Enlargement of European Parl., EC 1971–72, Saint-Geours Cttee on Energy Efficiency, EC 1978–79, Advisory Bd of Common Market Law Review 1976–90, Irish Parl. Jt Cttee on Marital Breakdown 1983–85, Editorial Bd of Irish Current Law Statutes Annotated 1984–90, Advisory Cttee of Interights, London 1984–90, Int. Comm. of Jurists, Geneva 1987–90, Cttee of Man., European Air Law Assen 1989–90, Scientific Council of European Review of Public Law 1989–90, Euro Avocats, Brussels 1989–90; Gen. Rapporteur, Human Rights at the Dawn of the 21st Century, Council of Europe, Strasbourg 1993; Prof. of Practice Columbia Univ. School of Int. and Public Affairs (NY) 2004–; Pres. Cherish (Irish Assen of Single Parents) 1973–90; Founder and Pres. Realizing Rights: The Ethical Globalization Initiative 2002–; founding mem. and Chair. Council of Women World Leaders 2002–; Vice Pres. Club of Madrid; mem. American Philosophical Soc.; mem. Bd of Dirs Vaccine Fund; mem. Leadership Council UN Global Coalition on Women and AIDS; mem. Advisory Bd Earth Inst.; Extraordinary Prof., Univ. of Pretoria; Hon. mem. NY Bar Assen, American Soc. of Int. Lawyers, Bar of Tanzania; Hon. Fellow, Trinity Coll. Dublin, Inst. of Engineers of Ireland, Royal Coll. of Physicians in Ireland, Hertford Coll. Oxford, LSE, Royal Coll. of Psychiatrists, London, Royal Coll. of Surgeons, Ireland, Royal Coll. of Obstetricians and Gynaecologists, London; Hon. Bencher King's Inns, Dublin, Middle Temple, London; Dr hc (Nat. Univ. of Ireland, Cambridge, Brown, Liverpool, Dublin, Montpellier, St Andrews, Melbourne, Columbia, Nat. Univ. of Wales, Poznań, Toronto, Fordham, Queens Univ. Belfast, Northeastern Univ., Rennes, Coventry, Dublin City, Essex, Harvard, Leuven, London, Seoul, Univ. of Peace, Costa Rica, Uppsala, Yale, Basle, Nat. Univ. of Mongolia, A. Schweitzer Univ. Berne); Berkeley Medal, Univ. of Calif., Medal of Honour, Univ. of Coimbra, Medal of Honour, Ordem dos Advogados (Portugal), Gold Medal of Honour, Univ. of Salamanca, Andrés Bello Medal, Univ. of Chile, New Zealand Suffrage Centennial Medal, Freedom Prize, Max Schmidheiny Foundation (Switzerland), UNIFEM Award, Noel Foundation (USA), Marisa Bellisario Prize (Italy) 1991, European Media Prize (Netherlands) 1991, CARE Humanitarian Award (USA) 1993, Int. Human Rights Award, Int. League of Human Rights 1993, Liberal Int. Prize for Freedom 1993, Stephen P. Duggan Award (USA) 1994, Council of Europe North South Prize (Portugal) 1997, Collar of Hussein Bin Ali (Jordan) 1997, F. D. Roosevelt Four Freedoms Medal 1998, Erasmus Prize (Netherlands) 1999, Fulbright Prize (USA) 1999, Garrigues Walker Prize (Spain) 2000, William Butler Prize (USA) 2000, Indira Gandhi Peace Prize (India) 2000, Sydney Peace Prize, Amnesty Int. Amb. of Conscience Award 2004. *Address:* Columbia University School of International and Public Affairs, 420 West 118th Street, New York, NY 10027 (office); Realizing Rights: The Ethical Globalization Initiative, 271 Madison Avenue, Suite 1007, New York, NY 10016, USA. *Telephone:* (212) 854-5406 (office). *Fax:* (212) 864-4847 (office). *Website:* www.sipa.columbia.edu (office); www.realizingrights.org.

ROBINSON, Nick; British journalist; *Political Editor, BBC;* b. 5 Oct. 1963, Macclesfield, Cheshire; ed Cheadle Hulme School, Univ. Coll., Oxford; trainee producer on programmes, including Brass Tacks, Newsround, Crimewatch 1986, then Deputy Ed. On the Record, Panorama; fmr presenter Late Night Live and Weekend Breakfast (both on BBC Radio Five Live), Westminster Live (BBC 2); fmr Chief Political Corresp., BBC News 24, presenting Straight Talk and One to One –2002; Political Ed. ITV News 2002–05; columnist of political 'Notebook' in The Times 2003–; Political Ed. BBC 2005–. *Leisure interest:* sailing. *Address:* BBC Westminster, 4 Millbank, London, SW1P 3JA, England (office). *Website:* www.bbc.co.uk/nickrobinson (office).

ROBINSON, Rt Hon. Peter David, MLA; British politician; *First Minister, Northern Ireland Assembly;* b. 29 Dec. 1948, Belfast; s. of the late David McCrea Robinson and Sheila Robinson; m. Iris Collins, MP 1970; two s. one d.; ed Annadale Grammar School, Castlereagh Coll. of Further Educ.; fmr estate agent; Founding mem. Ulster Democratic Unionist Party (DUP) and mem. Cen. Exec. Cttee 1973– (Sec. 1974–79), Gen. Sec. DUP 1975–79, Deputy Leader 1980–, Spokesman on Constitutional Affairs; MP for Belfast E, House of Commons 1979– (resgnd seat Dec. 1985 in protest against Anglo-Irish Agreement; re-elected Jan. 1986); mem. for Belfast E, NI Ass. 1982–86 (Chair.

Environment Cttee 1982–86), mem. NI Select Cttee 1994, Shipbuilding Group 1997, mem. for Belfast E, NI Ass. 1998–2000 (Ass. suspended 11 Feb. 2000, restored 30 May 2000), Minister for Regional Devt 1999–2000, 2001–02, for Finance and Personnel 2007–08, First Minister NI Ass. 2008–; Leader DUP 2008–; mem. Castlereagh Borough Council 1977–2008, Alderman 1978, Deputy Mayor 1978, Mayor 1986; mem. NI Forum 1996–98, NI Sports Council; Democratic Unionist; Hon. Dir Voice Newspaper Ltd, Crown Publications; Freedom of Borough of Castlereagh. *Publications:* Ulster – The Facts 1982 (jtly); booklets: Give Me Liberty, Hands Off the UDR, IRA/ Sinn Fein, The North Answers Back 1970, Capital Punishment for Capital Crime 1978, Ulster the Prey, Carson Man of Action, A War to Be Won, It's Londonderry, Self-inflicted 1981, Ulster in Peril 1981, Savagery and Suffering 1981, Their Cry Was "No Surrender" 1989, The Union Under Fire 1995, Victims. *Leisure interests:* breeding Japanese Koi, bowling, golf. *Address:* House of Commons, Westminster, London, SW1A 0AA, England (office); Strandtown Hall, 96 Belmont Avenue, Belfast, BT4 3DE (office); 51 Gransha Road, Dundonald, BT16 0HB, Northern Ireland (home). *Telephone:* (20) 7219-3506 (Westminster) (office); (28) 9047-3111 (Belfast) (office). *Fax:* (20) 7219-5854 (Westminster) (office); (28) 9047-1797 (Belfast) (office). *E-mail:* peter.robinson.mp@btconnect.com (office). *Website:* www.peterrobinson.org (office).

ROBINSON, William (Smokey), Jr; American R&B and soul singer, songwriter and producer; b. 19 Feb. 1940, Detroit; m. 1st Claudette Robinson 1959; two c.; m. 2nd Frances Robinson; fmr singer with The Matadors; singer with The Miracles 1954–72, also billed as Smokey Robinson and The Miracles 1967–72; solo artist 1973–; Vice Pres. Motown 1961–88; Exec. Producer and composer on film, Big Time 1977; numerous TV appearances; f. SFGL Foods, Inc.; Dr hc (Howard Univ.) 2006; Grammy Award for Best R&B Vocal Performance 1988, Grammy Living Legend Award 1989, Soul Train Heritage Award 1991, Motor City Music Award for Lifetime Achievement 1992, Kennedy Center Honor 2006, Q Award for Outstanding Contribution to Music 2006; elected to Rock And Roll Hall Of Fame 1988. *Compositions include:* most recordings with The Miracles –1968; also The Way You Do The Things You Do (recorded by The Temptations) 1964, My Guy (co-writer, recorded by Mary Wells) 1964, My Girl (recorded by The Temptations) 1965. *Recordings include:* albums: with The Miracles: The Fabulous Miracles 1963, The Miracles On Stage 1963, Doin' Mickey's Monkey 1964, Going To A Go-Go 1966, Make It Happen 1967, Special Occasion 1968, Time Out For... 1969, What Love Has Joined Together 1970, A Pocketful Of Miracles 1970, One Dozen Roses 1971, Flying High Together 1972; solo: Smokey 1973, Pure Smokey 1974, A Quiet Storm 1975, Smokey's Family Robinson 1976, Deep In My Soul 1977, Big Time (OST) 1977, Love Breeze 1978, Smokin' Motown 1979, Where There's Smoke 1979, Warm Thoughts 1980, Being With You 1981, Yes It's You Lady 1982, Touch The Sky 1983, Essar 1984, Smoke Signals 1986, One Heartbeat 1987, Love Songs 1988, Love, Smokey 1990, Double Good Everything 1991, Ballads 1995, Our Very Best Christmas 1999, Intimate 1999, Food For The Spirit 2004, Timeless Love 2006. *Address:* Richard de la Font Agency Inc., 4845 S Sheridan Road, Suite 505, Tulsa, OK 74145-5719, USA (office); SFGL Foods, Inc., 100 North Brand Avenue, #200, Glendale, CA 91203, USA. *Telephone:* (818) 500-0420. *Fax:* (818) 501-6959. *Website:* www.smokeyrobinsonfoods.com.

ROBLES, Dayron; Cuban athlete; b. 19 Nov. 1986, Guantánamo; sprinter and hurdler; world record holder in 110m hurdles of 12.87 seconds, set at Golden Spike Ostrava meet 12 June 2008; finished sixth in 110m hurdles at World Youth Championships, Sherbrooke, Canada 2003; Silver Medal, World Jr Championships, Grosseto, Italy 2004, Cen. American and Caribbean Championships, Nassau, Bahamas, 60m hurdles, World Indoor Championships, Moscow 2006 (personal best time of 7.46 seconds); Gold Medal, 110m hurdles, Cen. American and Caribbean Games, Cartagena, Colombia 2006, Panamerican Games, Rio de Janeiro 2007, Int. Asscn of Athletics Feds (IAAF) World Athletics Final, Stuttgart 2007, Olympic Games, Beijing 2008 (12.93 seconds); finished fourth in 110m hurdles, World Championships, Osaka 2007. *Address:* c/o Federacion Cubana de Atletismo, 13 y 3 Vedado 601, C/o Comite Olimpico Cubano, 14000 Havana, Cuba. *Telephone:* (7) 952103. *Fax:* (7) 335310. *E-mail:* estadio@inder.co.cu.

ROBLES, Marisa, HRCM, FRCM; British concert harpist; b. 4 May 1937, Madrid, Spain; d. of Cristóbal Robles and María Bonilla; m. 3rd David Bean 1985; two s. one d. from previous marriages; ed Madrid Royal Conservatoire of Music; Prof. of Harp, Madrid Royal Conservatoire of Music 1958–63; Harp Tutor, Nat. Youth Orchestra of GB 1964–85; Prof. of Harp, Royal Coll. of Music, London 1969–94; Artistic Dir World Harp Festival, Cardiff, Wales 1991, World Harp Festival II 1994; appearances as soloist with all maj. orchestras in GB and throughout the world, including New York Philharmonic; chamber music performances with Marisa Robles and Friends, Marisa Robles Harp Ensemble, Marisa Robles Trio and other chamber groups; solo recitals in Australia, Canada, Europe, Japan, NZ, S America and the USA; many TV appearances and radio performances; masterclasses in GB and abroad; four recordings of Mozart's Flute and Harp Concerto with James Galway (q.v.) and more than 20 other recordings. *Publications:* several harp pieces and arrangements. *Leisure interests:* theatre, indoor plants, nature in general, cooking, spending private time with family. *Address:* 38 Luttrell Avenue, London, SW15 6PE, England (home). *Telephone:* (20) 8785-2204 (home).

ROBLES ORTEGA, HE Cardinal Francisco; Mexican ecclesiastic; *Archbishop of Monterrey;* b. 2 March 1949, Mascota, Jalisco; ed studies in Mexico and at Pontifical Gregorian Univ., Rome; ordained priest of Autlán, Jalisco 1976; Parish Priest in Menor de Autlan 1979–91; Auxiliary Bishop of Toluca and Titular Bishop of Bossa 1991–96; Bishop of Toluca 1996–2003; Archbishop of Monterrey, Nuevo León 2003–; cr. Cardinal 2007; represented Mexico at Special Ass. of the Synod of Bishops for America 1997. *Address:* Archdiocese of Monterrey, Apartado 7, Zuazua 1100, 64000 Monterrey, Nuevo León, Mexico (office). *Telephone:* (8) 345-24-66 (office). *Fax:* (8) 345-35-57 (office). *E-mail:* info@arquidiocesismty.org.mx (office). *Website:* www.arquidiocesismty.org.mx (office).

ROBOZ, Zsuzsi, PS, FRSA; British artist; b. 15 Aug. 1939, Budapest, Hungary; d. of Imre Roboz and Edith Grosz; m. A. T. (Teddy) Smith 1964; ed Royal Acad. Schools, London and with Pietro Annigoni in Florence; various comms 1956–, including scenes back-stage at Windmill Theatre, London 1964, theatre card of ballet movements for Theatre Museum 1979, portrait of HRH Alice, Duchess of Gloucester 1981, portraits painted include Dame Ninette de Valois, Lord Olivier and Lucian Freud; rep. in perm. public collections at Tate Gallery, London, Nat. Portrait Gallery, London, Theatre Museum, London, Museum of Fine Arts, Budapest, Graves Art Gallery, Sheffield, Bradford Museum and City Art Galleries, St Andrew's Convent, London, Barnwell Church, Northants, New Scotland Yard, London, Durham Univ., St John's Coll., Cambridge, Royal Festival Hall, London, Pablo Casals Museum, Jamaica; also rep. in various pvt. collections; Guest of Honour, Spring Festival, Budapest 1984. *Publications include:* Women and Men's Daughters (with William Wordsworth) 1970, Chichester 10, Portrait of a Decade (with Stan Gebler Davis) 1975, British Ballet Today (with James Monahan) 1980, British Art Now (with Edward Lucie-Smith q.v.) 1993, Twentieth Century Illusions 1998, Roboz – A Painter's Paradox (with John Russell Taylor) 2006. *Leisure interests:* classical music, reading, swimming. *Address:* 6 Bryanston Court, George Street, London, W1H 7HA, England (home). *Telephone:* (20) 7723-6540 (home). *Fax:* (20) 7724-6844 (home).

ROBREDO, Rafael Miranda; Spanish business executive; *CEO, Endesa Internacional;* ed Instituto Católico de Artes e Industrias (ICAI), EOI; trained as industrial engineer; Chair. Endesa Internacional 2002, CEO 2002–, also mem. Bd Endesa SA, CEO 1997–; Vice-Pres. AUNA, Enersis; fmr mem. Bd of Dirs Tudor SA, Campofrío SA, Elcogas SA, Sevilland de Electricidad SA; mem. American Man. Asscn, Social Council of Autonomous Univ. of Madrid, Circolo de Empresarios, Econ. Advisory Bd RWE Energie; fmr Pres. FECSA; Vice-Pres. Comité Español Consejo Mundial de la Energía; Gran Cruz Orden del Mérito Civil 1999. *Address:* Endesa SA, Ribera de Loira 60, 28042 Madrid, Spain (office). *Telephone:* (91) 2131000 (office). *Fax:* (91) 5645496 (office). *E-mail:* info@endesa.es (office). *Website:* www.endesa.es (office).

ROBSON, Alan David, AM, BAgrSc, PhD, FTSE, FACE, FACEL, FAIAS; Australian professor of agriculture and university administrator; *Vice-Chancellor, University of Western Australia;* ed Univ. of Melbourne, Univ. of WA; several positions at Univ. of Western Australia, including Dean of Faculty of Agric., Head of School of Agric., Prof. of Agric. (Soil Science), Deputy Vice-Chancellor and Provost 1993–2004, Vice-Chancellor 2004–, also currently Hackett Prof. of Agric.; mem. Premier's Science Council; mem. Bd CSIRO; Fellow, Acad. of Tech. Sciences and Eng (Australia) 1987; Australian Medal of Agric. Science 1987. *Address:* Office of the Vice Chancellor, University of Western Australia, 35 Stirling Highway, Crawley, WA 6009, Australia (office). *Telephone:* (8) 6488-2808 (office). *Fax:* (8) 6488-1013 (office). *E-mail:* alan.robson@uwa.edu (office). *Website:* www.uwa.edu.au (office).

ROBSON, Bryan, OBE; British professional football manager and fmr professional football player; b. 11 Jan. 1957, Chester-le-Street; s. of Brian Robson and Maureen Lowther; m. Denise Robson 1979; one s. two d.; ed Birtley Lord Lawson Comprehensive; teams: West Bromwich Albion 1974–81; 1981–94 with Manchester United, FA Cup winners 1983, 1985, 1990; Euro Cup Winners' Cup 1991; winner of League Championship 1992–93, 1993–94; the only British capt. to lead a side to three FA Cup wins; 90 caps (65 as capt.), scoring 26 int. goals; player, Man. Middlesbrough Football Club 1994–2001, Bradford City 2003–04, West Bromwich Albion 2004–06, Sheffield United FC 2007–08; Asst Coach English nat. team 1994; Hon. BA (Salford) 1992, (Manchester) 1992. *Publication:* United I Stand 1983. *Leisure interests:* golf, horse racing. *Address:* c/o Sheffield United Football Club, Bramall Lane, Sheffield, S2 4SU, England.

ROBSON, Sir Robert (Bobby) William, Kt, CBE; British professional football manager and fmr football player; b. 18 Feb. 1933, Sacriston, Co. Durham; s. of Philip Robson and Lilian Robson; m. Elsie Mary Gray 1955; three s.; ed Waterhouses Secondary Modern, Co. Durham; player Fulham 1950–56, 1962–67, West Bromwich Albion 1956–62; 20 caps for England; Man. Vancouver FC 1967–68, Fulham 1968–69, Ipswich Town 1969–82 (won FA Cup 1978, UEFA Cup 1981), England nat. team 1982–90, PSV Eindhoven 1990–92, 1998 (won Dutch title twice), Sporting Lisbon 1993, Porto 1994–96 (won Portuguese title twice), Barcelona 1997–98 (won Spanish Cup, European Cup Winner's Cup), Newcastle United 1999–2004; Vice Pres. League Mans Asscn; consultant Irish nat. football team; Hon. MA (Univ. of E Anglia) 1997; Hon. DCL (Newcastle Univ.) 2003; inducted into English Football Hall of Fame 2003. *Publications:* Time on the Grass (autobiog.) 1982, So Near and Yet So Far: Bobby Robson's World Cup Diary 1986, Against the Odds 1990, My Autobiography: An Englishman Abroad 1998, Farewell But Not Goodbye 2005. *Leisure interests:* golf, gardening, reading, squash. *Address:* c/o League Managers Association, The Camkin Suite, 1 Pegasus House, Pegasus Court, Tachbrook Park, Warwick, CV34 6LW, England (office).

ROBUCHON, Joël; French chef and restaurateur; b. 7 April 1945, Poitiers; s. of Henri Robuchon and Julienne Douteau; m. Janine Pallix 1966; one s. one d.; ed Petit séminaire de Mauléon sur Sèvre; Apprenti 1960–63, Commis 1963–64, Chef de Partie 1965–69, Chef 1969–73, Chef de Cuisine 1974–78, Dir Hotel Nikko de Paris 1978–81, Propr and Chef, Restaurant Jamin, Paris 1981–93, Restaurant Laurent, Paris 1992–2001, Restaurant Joël Robuchon 1994–96, Man. Restaurant l'Astor, Paris 1996–, L'Atelier de Joël Robuchon, Paris 2003–, L'Atelier de Joel Robuchon and Joel Robuchon at The Mansion,

Las Vegas 2005–; Man. Relais du Parc 1992; numerous demonstrations overseas; Compagnon du Tour de France des Devoirs Unis; Titular mem. Acad. Culinaire de France; Pres. du Salon SIREST 1998–2002, (Cuisine Section) Meilleurs Ouvriers de France Competition 1991, Chaîne Thématique Gastronomique GOURMET TV 2002–; Conseiller de la marque 'Reflets de France' (Groupe Carrefour) 1996; mem. Council, Ordre du Mérite Agricole 1998–; Head Editorial Cttee Larousse Gastronomique; Commdr dans l'Ordre du Mérite Agricole; Officier des Arts et des Lettres; Chevalier, Ordre Nat. du Mérite; Chevalier, Légion d'honneur; professional awards include: Prix Prosper Montagné 1969, Prix Pierre Taittinger 1970, Trophée National de l'Académie Culinaire de France 1972, Meilleur Ouvrier de France 1976, Lauréat du Prix Hachette 1985, Chef de l'Année 1987, Chef of the Century, Gault Millau Guidebook 1990, Int. Herald Tribune Best Restaurant in the World 1994, 3 Stars Michelin Guide; also some 15 gold, silver and bronze medals. *Television:* Cuisinez Comme un Grand Chef (TF1) 1996–99, Bon Appétit Bien Sûr (FRANCE 3) 2000–. *Publications:* Ma cuisine pour vous, Simply French, Le meilleur et le plus simple de Robouchon, Les dimanches de Joël Robuchon, Le meilleur et le plus simple de la pomme de terre, Recettes du terroir d'hier et d'aujourd'hui, Le carnet de route d'un compagnon cuisinier, L'atelier de Joël Robuchon, Le meilleur et le plus simple de la France, Cuisinez comme un grand chef (Grand Prix du Meilleur Ouvrage, Acad. Nat. de Cuisine 1999), Le meilleur et le plus simple pour maigrir, Bon appétit bien sûr (Best Book of Cuisine Award, 7th Salon Int. du Livre Gourmand de Périgueux 2002), The Complete Robuchon 2008. *Leisure interest:* tennis. *Address:* c/o La Table de Joel Robuchon, 16, Avenue Bugeaud, 75016 Paris, France. *Website:* www.joel-robuchon.com; www.robuchon.com.

ROCARD, Michel Louis Léon, LèsL; French politician; b. 23 Aug. 1930, Courbevoie (Hauts-de-Seine); s. of Yves Rocard and Renée Favre; m. 2nd Michèle Legendre 1972 (divorced); two s.; one s. one d. from 1st m.; m. 3rd Sylvie Geoffroy-Emmanuelli; ed Lycée Louis-le-Grand, Paris, Univ. of Paris, Ecole Nat. d'Admin; Nat. Sec. Asscn des Etudiants socialistes, French Section of Workers' Int. (Socialist Party) 1955–56; Insp. des Finances 1958, Econ. and Financial Studies Service 1962, Head of Budget Div., Forecasting Office 1965, Insp. Gen. des Finances 1985; Sec.-Gen. Nat. Accounts and Budget Comm. 1965; Nat. Sec. Parti Socialiste Unifié (PSU) 1967–73; Cand. in first round of elections for presidency of French Repub. 1969; Deputy (Yvelines) to Nat. Ass. 1969–73, 1978–81; left PSU to join Parti Socialiste (PS) 1974, mem. Exec. Bureau 1975–81, 1986–, Nat. Sec. in charge of public sector 1975–79, First Sec. 1993–94; Mayor of Conflans-Sainte-Honorine 1977–94; Minister of State, Minister of Planning and Regional Devt 1981–83, of Agric. 1983–85; Prime Minister of France 1988–91; mem. Parl. for Yvelines 1986–88; mem. European Parl. 1994–2009; mem. Senate 1995–97; Chair. Cttee on Devt and Co-operation 1997–99, Employment and Social Affairs 1999–2001, Culture, Educ. and Youth Matters 2001–03; Grand-Croix, Ordre nat. du Mérite, Commdr du Mérite agricole, Grand Cross, Order of Christ (Portugal), Grand Officer, Order of the Tunisian Repub. and numerous other decorations. *Publications:* Le PSU et l'avenir socialiste de la France 1969, Des militants du PSU présentés par Michel Rocard 1971, Questions à l'Etat socialiste 1972, Un député, pourquoi faire? 1973, Le marché commun contre Europe (with B. Jaumont and D. Lenègre) 1973, L'inflation au cœur (with Jacques Gallus) 1975, Parler vrai 1979, A l'épreuve des faits: textes politiques (1979–85) 1986, Le cœur à l'ouvrage 1987, Un pays comme le nôtre, textes politiques 1986–89 1989, Les Moyens d'en sortir 1996, L'art de la paix (essay) 1998, Mes idées pour demain 2000, Pour une autre Afrique 2001, Entretiens 2001, Si la gauche savait 2005. *Leisure interests:* skiing, sailing, gliding. *Address:* 266 blvd Saint-Germain, 75007 Paris (office); 10 rue Philippe Paget, 78380 Bougival, France (home). *Telephone:* 1-47-05-25-00 (office). *Fax:* 1-45-51-42-04 (office). *E-mail:* mrocard .paris@noos.fr (office).

ROCCA, Costantino; Italian professional golfer; b. 4 Dec. 1956, Bergamo; m. Antonella Rocca 1981; one s. one d.; fmr factory worker and caddie; turned professional 1981; qualified for PGA European Tour through 1989 Challenge Tour; won Open V33 Da Grand Lyon and Peugeot Open de France; first Italian golfer to be mem. European Ryder Cup team 1993; mem. European Ryder Cup team 1995, 1997; plays on European Seniors Tour 2007–. *Leisure interests:* fishing, football. *Address:* c/o Golf Club Bergamo, L'Albenza, Via Longoni 12, 24030 Almenno S.Bartolomeo BG, Italy. *Telephone:* (035) 640707. *Fax:* (035) 640028. *Website:* www.europeantour.com.

ROĆEN, Milan; Montenegrin diplomatist and politician; *Minister of Foreign Affairs;* b. 23 Nov. 1950, Žabljak; m. Stana Roćen; one s.; ed Belgrade Univ.; journalist, Ekonomska Politika magazine 1976–79; worked in Information and Propaganda Dept of Pres. of Cen. Cttee of League of Communists of Montenegro 1979–82, Political Chief of Staff 1982–88; Deputy Minister of Foreign Affairs 1988-92; Minister-Counsellor for Political Affairs, Fed. Repub. of Yugoslavia Embassy, Moscow 1992–97; Foreign Policy Advisor to Prime Minister of Repub. of Montenegro 1997–98, to Pres. 1998–2003; Chief Political Advisor to Prime Minister of Montenegro 2003, Feb.–Sept. 2006; Amb. of Serbia and Montenegro to Russian Fed. (also accred to Kazakhstan, Uzbekistan, Turkmenistan, Tajikistan, Kyrgyzstan and Georgia) 2003–06; Co-ordinator Pro-independence Bloc and Gen. Man. of campaign for referendum on independence Feb.–May 2006; Minister of Foreign Affairs 2006–; mem. Democratic Socialist Party of Montenegro. *Address:* Ministry of Foreign Affairs, 81000 Podgorica, Stanka Dragojevića 2, Montenegro (office). *Telephone:* (81) 224609 (office). *Fax:* (81) 224670 (office). *E-mail:* mip@mn.yu (office). *Website:* mip.vlada.cg.yu (office).

ROCHA, John, CBE; British fashion designer; b. 1953, Hong Kong; m. Odette Rocha; ed Croydon Coll. of Design and Technology, London Coll. of Fashion; moved to London 1970; opened a design business in Kilkenny, Ireland 1977, later moved to Dublin; worked briefly in Milan 1987–89 then returned to Ireland; menswear line 1993, jeans line 1997; regular collections at all major int. fashion shows; has also designed interiors for hotels and office blocks including The Morrison Hotel, Dublin; launched John Rocha at Waterford Crystal collection 1997; f. Three Moon Design Studio, Dublin; British Designer of the Year 1994. *Address:* Three Moon Design Studio, 10 Ely Place, Dublin 2, Ireland (office). *Telephone:* (1) 662-9225 (office). *Fax:* (1) 662-9226 (office). *E-mail:* info@johnrocha.ie (office). *Website:* www.johnrocha.ie (office).

ROCHA, José Luis; Cape Verde diplomatist and international organization official; b. 1956, São Vicente; ed Univ. of Louvain, Belgium; joined Ministry of Planning and Co-operation 1981, Chief of Div. and Dir of Int. Co-operation Dept 1982–95; Amb. to Belgium and Luxembourg 1995–99; Perm. Rep. of Org. Int. de la Francophonie to EU 2000; currently Dir-Gen. of Political Affairs, Ministry of Foreign Affairs, Co-operation and Communities. *Address:* Ministry of Foreign Affairs, Co-operation and Communities, Palácio das Comunidades, Achada de Santo António, Praia, Santiago, Cape Verde (office). *Telephone:* 2615727 (office). *Fax:* 2616262 (office). *E-mail:* mne@gov.cv (office).

ROCHA VIEIRA, Lt-Gen. Vasco Joaquim, MA; Portuguese administrator and army officer; *Chancellor, Portuguese Chancery for Honours;* b. 16 Aug. 1939, Lagoa; s. of João da Silva Vieira and Maria Vieira Rocha e Vieira; m. Maria Leonor de Andrada Soares de Albergaria 1976; three s.; ed Tech. Univ. of Lisbon; Prof. Mil. Acad. Lisbon 1968–69; Army Staff course 1969–72; engineer Urbanization Dept Urban Council, Lisbon 1969–73; Sec. for Public Works and Communications, Govt of Macao 1974–75; Dir Engineers Branch, Portuguese Army 1975–76; Army Chief-of-Staff 1976–78; Mil. Rep. of Portugal, SHAPE, Mons, Belgium 1978–82; Army War Coll. course 1982–83; Nat. Defence course 1983–84; Prof. Army War Coll. Lisbon 1983–84; Deputy Dir Nat. Defence Inst. Lisbon 1984–86; Minister for Portuguese Autonomous Region of the Azores 1986–91; Gov. of Macao 1991–99; Chancellor Portuguese Chancery for Honours 2006; Grand Cross of the Military Order of Christ 1996; Grand Cross, Order of Prince Henry; Knight Commdr Mil. Order of Aviz; service medals; Order of Infante D. Henrique 2001; decorations from Brazil, France, Belgium, USA and Japan. *Leisure interests:* tennis, golf. *Address:* c/o Chancelaria das Ordens Honoríficas Portuguesas, Presidência da República, Palácio Nacional de Belém, Calçada da Ajuda, 1340-022 Lisbon (office); Quinta Patino Lote 52, Alcoitão, 2645-143 Alcabideche, Portugal (home). *Telephone:* (213) 614695 (office); (214) 693232 (home). *Fax:* (214) 607258 (home). *E-mail:* vascojrv@yahoo.com (home). *Website:* www.ordens.presidencia.pt (office).

ROCHE, (Eamonn) Kevin; American (b. Irish) architect; *Principal, Kevin Roche John Dinkeloo and Associates LLC;* b. 14 June 1922, Dublin, Ireland; s. of Eamon Roche and Alice Roche (née Harding); m. Jane Tuohy 1963; two s. three d.; ed Univ. Coll. Dublin and Illinois Inst. of Tech.; with Eero Saarinen & Assocs 1950–66, Chief Designer 1954–66; Pnr, later Prin. Kevin Roche John Dinkeloo and Assocs LLC 1966–; Pres. American Acad. of Arts and Letters 1994–97; Academician, Nat. Inst. of Arts and Letters, American Acad. in Rome 1968–71; mem. Fine Arts Comm., Washington, DC, Acad. d'Architecture; Academician Nat. Acad. of Design; mem. Bd of Trustees, Woodrow Wilson Int. Center for Scholars, Smithsonian Inst. Accad. Nazionale di San Luca 1984; Hon. LLD (Ireland Nat. Council for Educational Awards); Brunner Award, Nat. Acad. of Arts and Letters 1965, Brandeis Univ. Creative Arts Award 1967, ASID 1976 Total Design Award, Acad. d'Architecture 1977 Grand Gold Medal, Pritzker Architecture Prize 1982, Gold Medal Award for Architecture, American Acad. of Arts and Letters 1990, Gold Medal AIA 1993, AIA 25 Year Award 1995, and other awards. *Major works include:* IBM World Fair Pavilion, New York, Oakland Museum, Rochester Inst. of Tech., Ford Foundation HQ, New York, Fine Arts Center, Univ. of Massachusetts, Power Center for the Performing Arts, Univ. of Michigan, Creative Arts Center, Wesleyan Univ., Middletown, Conn., Coll. Life Insurance Co. of America HQ, Indianapolis. Master Plan, Galleries and Wings, Metropolitan Museum of Art, New York, Office Complex, UN Devt Corpn, New York, Denver Center for the Performing Arts, Denver, Colo, John Deere & Co., West Office Bldg, Moline, Ill., Union Carbide Corpn World HQ, Conn., General Foods Corpn HQ, Rye, NY, John Deere Insurance Co. HQ, Moline, Ill., Bell Telephone Labs, Holmdel, NJ, Morgan Bank HQ, New York, Northern Telecom HQ, Atlanta, Ga, E.F. Hutton HQ, New York, Bouygues HQ, Paris, IBM Hudson Hills Computer Research Lab., New York, UNICEF HQ, New York, Leo Burnett Company HQ, Chicago, Corning Glass Works HQ, Corning, NY, Merck and Co. HQ, Readington, NJ, Dai Ichi-Seimei Norinchukin Bank HQ, Tokyo, The Jewish Museum, New York, Museum of Jewish Heritage Holocaust Memorial, New York, Nations Bank Plaza, Atlanta, Ga, Tata Cummins, India, Menara Maxis, Kuala Lumpur, Malaysia, Pontiac Marina Hotel and Office Bldg, Singapore, Total System Services Corpn HQ, Columbus, Ga, MIT Cen. Athletic Facility, Cambridge, Mass, Shiodome Block B Devt, Tokyo, Research and Devt Facilities, Lucent Technologies, Lisle, Naperville, Ill., Denver, Co., Allentown, Pa, Nuremberg, Germany, New York Univ. Palladium Student Dormitory, New York Univ. Kimmel Center, Santander Cen. Hispano HQ, Madrid, Bouygues SA Holding Co. HQ, Paris, S.E.C. HQ, Washington, DC, Nat. Conf. Centre, Dublin, Ireland. *Address:* Kevin Roche John Dinkeloo and Associates, 20 Davis Street, PO Box 6127, Hamden, CT 06517, USA (office). *Telephone:* (203) 777-7251 (office). *Fax:* (203) 777-2299 (office). *E-mail:* kroche@krjda.com (office). *Website:* www.krjda.com (office).

ROCHEFORT, Jean; French actor; b. 29 April 1930, Dinan (Côtes-du-Nord); s. of Celestin Rochefort and Fernande Guillot; m. 3rd Françoise Vidal 1989; one s. one d.; two s. one d. from previous marriages; ed Conservatoire nat. d'art dramatique; mem. Jury, Cannes Int. Film Festival 2003; Chevalier de la Légion d'honneur; Officier des Arts et Lettres; Trophée Dussane 1970, César 1975 (for Que la fête commence), 1978 (for Best Actor of the Year, in Le Crabe-tambour), best actor awards Montreal 1982, Brussels 1982, Locarno 1984, César d'honneur 1999. *Films include:* 20,000 Leagues Under the Sea 1960, La

Porteuse de pain 1964, Qui êtes-vous Polly Magoo? 1967, Les Dimanches de la vie 1967, Le Temps de mourir 1970, Céleste 1970, L'Œuf 1971, l'Héritier 1972, Le Fantôme de la liberté 1974, Un divorce heureux 1975, Isabelle devant le désir 1975, Que la fête commence 1975, Les Magiciens 1976, Un éléphant ça trompe énormément 1976, Le Crabe-tambour 1977, Chère inconnue 1980, Un étrange voyage 1981, l'Indiscrétion 1982, Le grand frère 1982, Un dimanche de flic 1983, L'Ami de Vincent 1983, Réveillon chez Bob, Frankenstein 90 1984, La Galette du roi 1986, Tandem 1987, Le Moustachu 1987, Je suis le seigneur du château 1989, Le Mari de la coiffeuse 1990, Le Château de ma mère 1990, Le Bal des casse-pieds 1992, La prochaine fois le feu 1993, Tombés du ciel 1994, Tom est tout seul 1995, Les grands ducs 1996, Ridicule 1996, Barracuda 1997, Le Vent en emporte autant 1999, Rembrandt 1999, Le Placard 2001, Honolulu Baby 2001, La Vie sans secret de Walter Nions 2001, L'Homme du train 2002, Blanche 2002, Fanfan la tulipe (voice) 2003, Il était une fois Jean-Sébastien Bach (voice) 2003, Saint-Germain ou La négociation (TV) 2003, Les Clefs de bagnole 2003, RRRrrrr!!! 2004, La Dernière minute 2004, Les Dalton 2004, Akoibon 2005, L'Enfer 2005, Ne le dis à personne 2006, Désaccord parfait 2006, Mr. Bean's Holiday 2007, J'ai toujours rêvé d'être un gangster 2007. *Television:* Le Scénario défendu 1984, L'Enigme blanche 1985, Eleveur de chevaux, Nosferatu (mini-series) (voice) 2002. *Leisure interest:* riding. *Address:* c/o Artmédia, 20 avenue Rapp, 75007 Paris, France.

ROCHER, Guy, CC, OQ, PhD, FRSC; Canadian sociologist and academic; *Professor of Sociology, University of Montréal;* b. 20 April 1924, Berthierville, PQ; s. of the late Barthélemy Rocher and Jeanne Magnan; m. 1st Suzanne Cloutier 1949; m. 2nd Claire-Emmanuèle Depocas 1985; four d.; ed Univ. of Montréal, Univ. Laval and Harvard Univ.; Asst Prof. Univ. Laval 1952–57, Assoc. Prof. 1957–60; Prof. of Sociology, Univ. of Montréal 1960–; Deputy Minister of Cultural Devt Govt of Québec 1977–79, of Social Devt 1981–82; mem. Royal Comm. on Educ. in Québec 1961–66; Vice-Pres. Canada Council of Arts 1969–74, Cttee on Univ. Research, Royal Soc. of Canada 1989–90; Pres. Radio-Québec 1979–81; mem. American Acad. of Arts and Sciences; Hon. LLD (Laval) 1996; Dr hc Sociology (Moncton) 1997, (Univ. of Québec at Montréal) 2002; Prix Marcel-Vincent (ACFAS) 1989, Prix Léon-Gérin (Québec Govt) 1995, Prix Molson 1997, Prix Esdras-Minville 1998; Outstanding Contrib. Award (Canadian Asscn Sociology and Anthropology) 1988, Médaille Pierre Chauveau (Royal Soc. of Canada) 1991, Prix William Dawson, Royal Soc. of Canada 1999. *Films:* subject of film by Anne-Marie Rocher: Guy Rocher, Sociologist as Protagonist. *Publications:* Introduction à la sociologie générale 1969, Talcott Parsons et la sociologie américaine, Le Québec en mutation 1973, Ecole et société au Québec 1975, Entre les rêves et l'histoire 1989, Le Québec en jeu 1992, Entre droit et technique 1994, Etudes de sociologie du droit et de l'éthique 1996, Théories et emergence du droit 1998, May Weber, Rudolf Stammler et le matérialisme historique 2001, Le Droit à l'égalité 2001; and numerous articles on sociology, on sociology of law, of education and of health and on the evolution of Québec society. *Leisure interests:* tai-chi, skiing, swimming, concerts, reading. *Address:* Faculté de Droit, Université de Montréal, C.P. 6128, Succursale Centre-Ville, Montréal, PQ, H3C 3J7 (office); 4911 Chemin de la Côte-des-Neiges, Apt. 409, Montréal, PQ, H3V 1H7, Canada (home). *Telephone:* (514) 343-5993 (office); (514) 344-0882 (home). *Fax:* (514) 343-7508 (home). *E-mail:* guy.rocher@umontreal.ca (office).

ROCK, Allan, BA, LLB, QC; Canadian lawyer, fmr politician and fmr diplomatist; *Attorney, Sutts Strosberg LLP;* b. 30 Aug. 1947, Ottawa; m. Deborah Hanscom; three s. one d.; ed Univ. of Ottawa; pvt. practice –1993; MP for Etobicoke Centre 1993–2004; Minister of Justice and Attorney Gen. 1993–97, Minister of Health 1997–2002, Minister of Industry 2002–03; Perm. Rep. to UN Jan. 2004–06; attorney Sutts Strosberg LLP, Windsor, Ont. 2006–; Special Advisor on Sri Lanka to UN on subject of Children and Armed Conflict; Chair. Trust Fund for War-Affected Children in Northern Uganda; mem. Security Council Report's Int. Advisory Group; Fellow, American Coll. of Trial Lawyers; fmr Treas. (CEO) Law Soc. of Upper Canada. *Address:* Sutts Strosberg LLP, 600 Westcourt Place, 251 Goyeau Street, Windsor, ON N9A 6V4, Canada (office). *Telephone:* (519) 561-6219 (office). *Fax:* (519) 561-6203 (office). *E-mail:* arock@strosbergco.com (office). *Website:* www.strosbergco.com (office).

ROCKBURNE, Dorothea; American artist; b. 18 Oct. 1934, Montréal, PQ, Canada; m. 1951 (divorced); one d.; ed Ecole des Beaux-Arts, Montréal, Black Mountain Coll., NC, Montréal Museum School; work in many public collections including Whitney Museum, Museum of Modern Art, Metropolitan Museum of Art, artist-in-residence, American Acad. in Rome 1991, Bellagio Study Centre, Italy 1997; secco frescoes at Hilton Hotel, San Jose, Calif. 1992, Sony HQ, New York 1993, Edward T. Grignoux U.S. Courthouse, Portland, Maine 1996, Univ. of Mich., Mich. 1997, secco frescoes at American Embassy, Kingston, Jamaica 2009; Guggenheim Fellow 1972; Nat. Endowment for the Arts 1974; Visiting Artist, Skowhegan School of Painting and Sculpture 1984; Avery Distinguished Prof. Bard Coll. Annandale-on-Hudson, NY 1986, mem. Dept of Art, American Acad. of Arts and Letters 2001; Hon. DFA (Coll. for Creative Studies) 2002; Art Inst. of Chicago Witowsky Painting Award 1972, Creative Arts Award, Brandeis Univ. 1985, Lifetime Achievement Award, American Acad. of Arts and Letters 1999, American Acad. of Arts and Letters, Dept of Art 2001, Pollock-Krasner Foundation Grant 2002, Nat. Acad. of Design, Pike Award for Watercolour 2002, Art Omi Int.,. Francis J. Greenberger Award 2003. *Leisure interests:* astronomy, music, mathematics, theatre, poetry, friends. *Address:* 140 Grand Street, 2WF, New York, NY 10013, USA. *Telephone:* (212) 226-4471. *Fax:* (866) 351-4234. *E-mail:* drockburne@gmail.com (office). *Website:* www.dorothearockburne.com (office).

ROCKEFELLER, David, PhD; American banker; b. 12 June 1915, New York; s. of John Davison Rockefeller, Jr and Abby Greene (née Aldrich) Rockefeller; brother of Laurance; m. Margaret McGrath 1940 (died 1996); two s. four d.; ed Harvard Coll., London School of Econs, Univ. of Chicago; Sec. to Mayor Fiorello H. La Guardia, New York 1940–41; Asst Regional Dir US Office of Defense, Health and Welfare Services 1941–42; served in US Army (Capt.) 1942–45; Foreign Dept Chase Nat. Bank 1946–48, Second Vice-Pres. 1948–49, Vice-Pres. 1949–51, Sr Vice-Pres. 1951–55; Exec. Vice-Pres. Chase Manhattan Bank 1955–57, Vice-Chair. Bd 1957–61, Pres and Chair. Exec. Cttee 1961–69, CEO 1969–80, Chair. of Bd 1969–81, Chair. Chase Int. Investment Corpn 1961–81, Chase Int. Advisory Cttee 1980–99; Chair. Bd Rockefeller Group Inc. 1981–95, Rockefeller Center Properties, Inc. 1996–, Rockefeller Center Properties Inc. Trust; Chair. Rockefeller Univ. 1950–75, Chair Exec. Cttee 1975–, Council on Foreign Relations 1970–85, Americas Soc. 1981–92, Rockefeller Brothers Fund Inc. 1981–87 and numerous other chairmanships; Trustee Rockefeller Family Fund, Carnegie Endowment for Int. Peace, Museum of Modern Art, Chicago Univ., etc.; Grand-Croix, Légion d'honneur; Hon. LLD from 13 univs; Hon. DEng (Colorado School of Mines) 1974, (Notre Dame Univ.) 1987; Hadrian Award, World Mathematics Fund 1994, Presidential Medal of Freedom 1998, numerous American and foreign awards. *Publications:* Unused Resources and Economic Waste 1940, Creative Management in Banking 1964, Memoirs 2002. *Leisure interest:* sailing. *Address:* c/o Chase Manhattan Bank, Room 5600, 30 Rockefeller Plaza, New York, NY 10112, USA.

ROCKEFELLER, John Davison, IV, BA; American politician; *Senator from West Virginia;* b. 18 June 1937, New York; s. of John Davison Rockefeller, III and Blanchette F. Rockefeller (née Hooker); m. Sharon Percy 1967; three s. one d.; ed Harvard and Yale Univs and Int. Christian Univ., Tokyo; mem. Nat. Advisory Council, Peace Corps 1961, Special Adviser to Dir 1962, Operations Officer in Charge of work in Philippines until 1963; Bureau of Far Eastern Affairs, US State Dept 1963, later Asst to Asst Sec. of State for Far Eastern Affairs; consultant, President's Comm. on Juvenile Delinquency and Youth Crime 1964, White House Conf. on Balanced Growth and Econ. Devt 1978, Pres.'s Comm. on Coal 1978–80; field worker, Action for Appalachian Youth Program 1964; mem. W Virginia House of Dels 1966–68; Sec. of State W Virginia 1968–72; Pres. W Virginia Wesleyan Coll., Buckhannon 1973–75; Gov. of W Virginia 1977–85, Senator from W Virginia 1984–, Chair. Senate Steel Caucus, Bipartisan Cttee on Comprehensive Health Care, Vice-Chair. Senate Select Cttee on Intelligence; mem. Foreign Relations Cttee; Democrat. *Publications:* articles in magazines. *Address:* US Senate, 531 Hart Senate Building, Washington, DC 20510, USA (office). *Telephone:* (202) 224-6472 (office). *Website:* rockefeller.senate.gov (office).

ROCKLEY, 3rd Baron; **James Hugh Cecil;** British merchant banker; *Chairman, Hall and Woodhouse;* b. 5 April 1934, London; m. Sarah Cadogan 1958; one s. two d.; ed Eton Coll. and New Coll. Oxford; with Wood Gundy & Co., Canada 1957–62; joined Kleinwort Benson Ltd 1962, apptd to Bd 1970, Head, Corp. Finance Div. 1983, Vice-Chair. 1985–93, Chair. 1993, Vice-Chair. Kleinwort Benson Group PLC 1988–93, Chair. 1993–96; Chair. Dartford River Crossing 1988–93, Kleinwort Devt Fund 1991–93, Midland Expressway 1992–93, Hall and Woodhouse 2001–; Dir, Equity and Law 1980–92, Christies Int. 1989–98, Cobham (fmrly FR Group) 1990–2002, Abbey Nat. 1990–99, Foreign and Colonial Investment Trust 1992–2003, Cadogan Group 1996–, Dusco (UK) 1996–2001. *Address:* Lytchett Heath, Poole, Dorset, BH16 6AE, England. *Telephone:* (20) 7730-4567 (office); (1202) 622228 (home).

ROCKWELL, John Sargent, PhD; American journalist and author; b. 16 Sept. 1940, Washington, DC; s. of Alvin John and Anne Hayward; m. Linda Mevorach; one d.; ed Harvard Univ., Univ. of Munich, FRG and Univ. of Calif., Berkeley; music and dance critic, Oakland (Calif.) Tribune 1969; Asst Music and Dance Critic, Los Angeles Times 1970–72; freelance music critic, New York Times 1972–74, staff music critic 1974–91, Ed. Arts and Leisure section 1998–; European Cultural Corresp. and Prin. Classical Recordings Critic, New York Times, Paris 1992–94, Sr Cultural Corresp. and Columnist 2002–04, Dance Critic 2005–06; Dir Lincoln Center Festival, Lincoln Center for the Performing Arts, New York 1994–98; Chevalier de l'ordre des Arts et Lettres. *Publications:* All American Music: Composition in the Late 20th Century 1983, Sinatra: An American Classic 1984, The Idiots 2003, Outsider: John Rockwell on the Arts 1967–2006 2006. *Address:* 543 Broadway, #10, New York, NY 10012, USA (home). *Telephone:* (212) 334-5073 (home). *Fax:* (212) 334-5073 (home). *E-mail:* rockwell.johnse@mac.com (home).

ROCKWELL, Sam; American actor; b. 5 Nov. 1968, Daly City, Calif. *Films include:* Clownhouse 1989, Last Exit to Brooklyn 1989, Teenage Mutant Ninja Turtles 1990, Strictly Business 1991, In the Soup 1992, Light Sleeper 1992, Jack and His Friends 1992, Happy Hell Night 1992, Dead Drunk 1992, Somebody to Love 1994, The Search for One-eye Jimmy 1994, Drunks 1995, Basquiat 1996, Box of Moon Light 1996, Glory Daze 1996, Mercy 1996, Bad Liver and a Broken Heart 1996, Prince Street (TV series) 1997, Subway Stories: Tales from the Underground (TV) 1997, Lawn Dogs 1997, Arresting Gena 1997, Jerry and Tom 1998, Louis & Frank 1998, Safe Men 1998, Celebrity 1998, The Call Back 1998, A Midsummer Night's Dream 1999, The Green Mile 1999, Galaxy Quest 1999, Charlie's Angels 2000, BigLove 2001, Heist 2001, Pretzel 2001, D.C. Smalls 2001, 13 Moons 2002, Running Time 2002, Welcome to Collinwood 2002, Stella Shorts 1998–2002 (video) 2002, Confessions of a Dangerous Mind 2002, Matchstick Men 2003, Piccadilly Jim 2004, The Hitchhiker's Guide to the Galaxy 2005, The F Word 2005, Robin's Big Date 2005, Snow Angels 2007, Joshua 2007, The Assassination of Jesse James by the Coward Robert Ford 2007, Woman in Burka 2008, Choke 2008, Frost/Nixon 2008. *Address:* c/o The Gersh Agency, 130 West 42nd Street, New York, NY 10036, USA (office).

RODAS, Armando, MA, DJur; Ecuadorean lawyer and politician; b. 1966; fmr lawyer; adviser to Pres. of Ecuador; Vice-Minister of Economy and Deputy

Sec. of Public Admin –2006, Minister of Economy and Finance 2006 (resgnd). *Address:* c/o Ministry of the Economy and Finance, Avda 10 de Agosto 1661 y Jorge Washington, Quito, Ecuador (office).

RODAS BACA, Patricia Isabel, PhD; Honduran politician; *Minister of Foreign Affairs;* b. 22 June 1962, Comayagüela; d. of Modesto Rodas Alvarado and Margarita Baca Sarravia de Rodas Alvarado; m. Rodolfo Gutiérrez González; one s.; ed Univ. Nacional Autónoma de Honduras, Univ. Nacional de Andalucía, Spain; Pres. Partido Liberal de Honduras 2005–09; Minister of Foreign Affairs 2009–. *Address:* Ministry of Foreign Affairs, Centro Cívico Gubernamental, Antigua Casa Presidencial, Blvd Kuwait, Contiguo a la Corte Suprema de Justicia, Tegucigalpa, Honduras (office). *Telephone:* 234-1962 (office). *Fax:* 234-1484 (office). *Website:* www.sre.hn (office).

RODAS MELGAR, (Róger) Haroldo; Guatemalan civil servant and international organization executive; *Minister of Foreign Affairs;* fmr Adviser, Ministry of Economy; Sec.-Gen. Secretaría de Integración Económica Centroamericana (SIECA) 1997–2007; Minister of Foreign Affairs 2008–. *Publications:* articles in professional journals. *Address:* Ministry of Foreign Affairs, 2a Avda La Reforma 4-47, Zona 10, Guatemala City, Guatemala (office). *Telephone:* 2331-8410 (office). *Fax:* 2331-8510 (office). *E-mail:* webmaster@minex.gob.gt (office). *Website:* www.minex.gob.gt (office).

RODAT, Robert, MFA; American screenwriter; b. 1953, NH; ed Univ. of Southern Calif. Film School. *Film screenplays include:* Tall Tale 1995, Fly Away Home 1996, Saving Private Ryan 1998, The Patriot 2000. *Television:* TV screenplays include The Comrades of Summer 1992, The Ripper 1997, 36 Hours to Die 1999. *Address:* c/o Hohman Maybank Lieb, 9229 Sunset Blvd., Suite 700, Los Angeles, CA 90069, USA. *Telephone:* (310) 274-4600. *Fax:* (310) 274-4741. *E-mail:* info@hmllit.com.

RODDICK, Andrew (Andy) Stephen; American professional tennis player; b. 30 Aug. 1982, Omaha, NE; s. of Jerry Roddick and Blanche Roddick; number one US jr 1999–2000 and number one world jr 2000, won six world jr singles and seven doubles titles, including US and Australian Open jr singles titles; turned professional 2000; 15 singles titles: Atlanta 2001, Houston 2001, 2002, Washington 2001, Memphis 2002, Canada TMS 2003, Indianapolis 2003, 2004, Queen's 2003, 2004, Cincinnati TMS 2003, St Poelten 2003, US Open 2003, Miami 2004, San Jose 2004; two doubles titles: Delray Beach 2001 (with Jan-Michael Gambill), Houston 2002 (with Mardy Fish); ranked second Champions Race 2004; fmrly coached by Brad Gilbert; f. Andy Roddick Foundation charity for children 2001. *Leisure interests:* music, films, skydiving. *Address:* c/o Andrew S. Roddick Foundation, Inc., Helping Children Today For Tomorrow, 2901 Clint Moore Road, #109, Boca Raton, FL 33496, USA (office). *Telephone:* (561) 392-2652 (office); (954) 340-7471 (office). *Fax:* (561) 392-6883 (office). *Website:* www.andyroddick.com (office); www.arfoundation.org (office).

RODGER OF EARLSFERRY, Baron (Life Peer), cr. 1992, of Earlsferry in the District of North East Fife; **Alan Ferguson Rodger,** PC, QC, MA, LLD, DPhil, DCL, FBA, FRSE; British advocate and chief justice; *Lord of Appeal in Ordinary;* b. 18 Sept. 1944; s. of Prof. Thomas Ferguson Rodger and Jean Margaret Smith Chalmers; ed Glasgow Univ., New Coll., Oxford; mem. Faculty of Advocates 1974, Clerk of Faculty 1976–79; Advocate Depute 1985–88; Home Advocate Depute 1986–88; Solicitor-Gen. for Scotland 1989–92; Lord Advocate 1992–95; Senator, Coll. of Justice in Scotland 1995–96; Lord Justice-Gen. of Scotland and Lord Pres. of the Court of Session 1996–2001; a Lord of Appeal in Ordinary 2001–; Pres. Expert Witness Inst. 2002–, Holdsworth Club 1998–99; mem. Mental Welfare Comm. for Scotland 1981–84, UK Del. to Comm. Consultative des Barreaux de la Communauté Européenne 1984–89, Acad. of European Pvt. Lawyers 1994–; Dyke Jr Research Fellow, Balliol Coll., Oxford 1969–70; Fellow, New Coll., Oxford 1970–72; Maccabaean Lecturer, British Acad. 1991; Visitor St. Hugh's Coll. Oxford 2003–; Hon. Bencher, Lincoln's Inn 1992, Inn of Court of Northern Ireland 1998; Hon. mem. SPTL 1992; Hon. LLD (Aberdeen) 1999, (Edin.) 2001. *Publications:* Owners and Neighbours in Roman Law 1972, Gloag and Henderson's Introduction to the Law of Scotland (Asst Ed.) 1995. *Leisure interest:* walking. *Address:* House of Lords, London, SW1A 0PA; The Expert Witness Institute (EWI), 1st Floor, 7 Warwick Court, London WC1R 5DJ, England. *Telephone:* (20) 7219-3135; (870) 366-6367 (EWI) (office). *Fax:* (870) 411-2470 (EWI). *E-mail:* info@ewi.org.uk. *Website:* www.ewi.org.uk.

RODGERS, Jimmie, MD; Solomon Islands physician and international organization executive; *Director-General, Secretariat of the Pacific Community;* holds degree in health admin; Under-Sec., later Perm. Sec. for Health, Ministry of Health and Medical Services, Solomon Islands 1990–96; joined Secr. of the Pacific Community (SPC) as Dir of Programmes in 1996, later redesignated as Deputy Dir-Gen. based in Noumea, Head of SPC Suva Regional Office 1998, later Sr Deputy Dir-Gen., Dir-Gen. SPC 2005–. *Address:* Secretariat of the Pacific Community Headquarters, BP D5, 98848 Noumea Cedex, New Caledonia (office). *Telephone:* 26-20-00 (office). *Fax:* 26-38-18 (office). *E-mail:* JimmieR@spc.int (office). *Website:* www.spc.int (office).

RODGERS, Joan, CBE, BA, FRNCM; British singer (soprano); b. 4 Nov. 1956, Whitehaven, Cumbria; d. of the late Thomas Rodgers and of Julia Rodgers; m. Paul Daniel (q.v.) 1988 (divorced); two d.; ed Whitehaven Grammar School, Univ. of Liverpool and Royal Northern Coll. of Music, Manchester; first maj. professional engagement as Pamina in The Magic Flute, Aix-en-Provence Festival 1982; début at Metropolitan Opera House, New York, in same role 1995; other appearances include title role of Theodora at Glyndebourne, The Governess in Turn of the Screw for Royal Opera House, Blanche in Dialogues des Carmélites for ENO and in Amsterdam, Marschallin in Der Rosenkavalier for Scottish Opera and title role of Alcina for English Nat. Opera; regular appearances at Royal Opera House, English Nat. Opera, Glyndebourne, Promenade Concerts and with leading British and European cos; concert engagements in London, Europe and USA with conductors including Solti, Barenboim, Mehta, Rattle, Harnoncourt and Salonen; numerous recordings; Kathleen Ferrier Memorial Scholarship 1981; Dr hc (Liverpool); Royal Philharmonic Soc. Award as Singer of the Year 1997, Evening Standard Award for Outstanding Individual Performance in Opera 1997. *Leisure interests:* walking, cooking, horse riding. *Address:* c/o Ingpen and Williams Ltd, 7 St George's Court, 131 Putney Bridge Road, London, SW15 2PA, England (office). *Telephone:* (20) 8874-3222 (office). *Fax:* (20) 8877-3113 (office). *Website:* www.ingpen.co.uk/ (office).

RODGERS, Nile; guitarist and record producer; b. 19 Sept. 1952, New York, USA; mem. New World Rising 1960s; founder-mem. Big Apple Band 1972–76; became Chic 1977–; also solo artiste and record prod.; mem. The Honeydrippers with Robert Plant, Jimmy Page, Jeff Beck; leader own trio, Outloud; co-founder Ear Candy record label 1989; owner Sumthing Distribution (music distribution co.). *Recordings:* Albums: with Chic: C'Est Chic 1978, Risqué 1979, The Best of Chic 1980, Real People 1982, Take It Off 1982, Tongue In Chic 1982, Believer 1983, Freak Out 1987, Chic-Ism 1992; Solo albums: Adventures In The Land of The Good Groove 1983, B-Movie Matinee 1985, Singles include: Dance Dance Dance 1977, Everybody Dance 1978, Le Freak (No. 1, USA) 1978, I Want Your Love 1979, Good Times (No. 1, USA) 1979, My Forbidden Lover 1979, My Feet Keep Dancing 1980, Soup For One 1982, Jack Le Freak 1987, Chic Mystique 1992; As writer, producer with Bernard Edwards: Norma Jean, Norma Jean Wright 1977, He's The Greatest Dancer, Sister Sledge 1979, We Are Family, Sister Sledge 1979, Love Somebody Today, Sister Sledge 1979, Upside Down, Diana Ross 1980, Diana, Diana Ross 1982, Why, Carly Simon 1982; Record producer for artists including David Bowie, Madonna, Duran Duran, Aretha Franklin, Jeff Beck, Mick Jagger, Al Jarreau, Grace Jones, Johnny Mathis, Marta Sanchez. *Address:* Sumthing Distribution, 9 East 45th Street, 3rd Floor, New York, NY 10017, USA. *Website:* www.nilerodgers.com; www.sumthing.com.

RODGERS, Patricia Elaine Joan, MA, DPolSc; Bahamian diplomatist; b. Nassau; ed School of St Helen & St Catherine, Abingdon, Univ. of Aberdeen, Graduate Inst. of Int. Relations, St Augustine, Trinidad, Inst. Universitaire des Hautes Etudes Int., Univ. of Geneva; Counsellor and Consul, Washington, DC 1978–83; Alt. Rep. to OAS 1982–83; Deputy High Commr (Acting High Commr) to Canada 1983–86, High Commr 1986–88; High Commr to UK (also Accred to France, Belgium and Germany) 1988–92; mem. Bahamas Del. to UN Conf. on Law of the Sea 1974, 1975, OAS Gen. Ass. 1982, Caribbean Co-ordinating Meeting (Head of Del.), OAS 1983, Canada/Commonwealth Caribbean Heads of Govt Meeting 1985, Commonwealth Heads of Govt Meeting Nassau 1985, Vancouver 1987; Adviser to Bahamas Del., Annual Gen. Meetings of World Bank and IMF 1978–82; mem. Commonwealth Observer Group, Gen. Elections Lesotho 1993; apptd. Perm. Sec., Ministry of Tourism 1995; currently Perm. Sec. Ministry of Foreign Affairs. *Publications:* Mid-Ocean Archipelagos and International Law: A Study of the Progressive Development of International Law 1981. *Leisure interests:* folk art, theatre, gourmet cooking, gardening. *Address:* Ministry of Foreign Affairs and Public Service, East Hill Street, POB N-3746, Nassau, Bahamas (office). *Telephone:* 302-9300 (office). *Fax:* 328-8212 (office). *E-mail:* mfabahamas@batelnet.bs (office); carridad68@yahoo.com (home).

RODGERS OF QUARRY BANK, Baron (Life Peer), cr. 1992, of Kentish Town in the London Borough of Camden; **William Thomas Rodgers,** PC, MA; British politician and administrator; b. 28 Oct. 1928, Liverpool; s. of William Arthur Rodgers and Gertrude Helen Rodgers; m. Silvia Schulman 1955; three d.; ed Sudley Road Council School, Quarry Bank High School, Liverpool and Magdalen Coll., Oxford; Gen. Sec. Fabian Soc. 1953–60; Labour Cand. for Bristol West 1957; Borough Councillor, St Marylebone 1958–62; MP for Stockton-on-Tees 1962–74, for Stockton Div. of Teesside 1974–83; Parl. Under-Sec. of State, Dept of Econ. Affairs 1964–67, Foreign Office 1967–68; Leader, UK del. to Council of Europe and Ass. of WEU 1967–68; Minister of State, Bd of Trade 1968–69, Treasury 1969–70; Chair. Expenditure Cttee on Trade and Industry 1971–74; Minister of State, Ministry of Defence 1974–76; Sec. of State for Transport 1976–79; Opposition Spokesman for Defence 1979–80; left Labour Party March 1981; Co-founder Social Democratic Party March 1981, mem. Nat. Cttee 1982–87, Vice-Pres. 1982–87; Dir-Gen. RIBA 1987–94; Chair. Advertising Standards Authority 1995–2000; Leader Liberal Democratic Peers 1998–2001; Liberal Democrat. *Publications:* Hugh Gaitskell 1906–1963 (Ed.) 1964, The People Into Parliament (co-author) 1966, The Politics of Change 1982, Ed. and co-author Government and Industry 1986, Fourth Among Equals 2000. *Leisure interests:* reading, walking, cinema. *Address:* House of Lords, London, SW1A 0PW (office); 43 North Road, London, N6 4BE, England. *Telephone:* (20) 7219-3607 (office); (20) 8341-2434 (home). *Fax:* (20) 7219-2377 (office); (20) 8347-7133 (home).

RODIER, Jean-Pierre; French business executive and mining engineer; *Advisor, CVC Capital Partners (France) SA;* b. 4 May 1947, Reims; s. of Pierre Rodier and Gabrielle Sayen; m. Michèle Foz 1969; ed Lycée de Saumur, Lycée de Pamiers, Lycée de Pierre-en-Fermat, Toulouse; Asst Sec.-Gen. Mines Directorate, Ministry of Industry 1975–78, Sec.-Gen. 1978; Head of Econs and Budget mission of Dir-Gen. of Energy and Raw Materials 1979; Head of Raw Material and Subsoil Dept 1981–83; tech. adviser to Prime Minister's Office 1983–84; Dir of Gen. Man. Penarroya mining and metallurgy Co. 1984–85, Asst Dir-Gen. 1985–86, Pres. and Dir Gen. 1986–88; Pres. Bd Dirs Metaleurop 1988–91; Deputy Admin. Mining Union 1991–94; Pres. Assn of Enterprise and Personnel 2001–; Pres. and Dir-Gen. Pechiney 1994–2003; Advisor, CVC Capital Pnrs (France) SA 2004–; mem. Bd of Dirs Vedanta Resources 2004–; Pres. Bd Dirs Ecole nat. supérieure des techniques industrielles et des mines d'Alès 1992–95; Chevalier de la Légion d'Honneur. *Address:* CVC Capital

Partners (France) SA, 40 rue La Pérouse, 75116 Paris, France (office). *Telephone:* 1-45-02-23-00 (office). *Fax:* 1-45-02-23-01 (office). *Website:* www .cvceurope.com (office).

RODIN, Judith, PhD; American physician, fmr university president and foundation executive; *President, The Rockefeller Foundation;* b. 9 Sept. 1944, Philadelphia, Pa; d. of Morris Rodin and Sally (Winson) Seitz; m. 1st 1978; one s.; m. 2nd Paul Verkuil 1994; ed Univ. of Pennsylvania and Columbia Univ.; Nat. Science Foundation Postdoctoral Fellow, Univ. of Calif. 1971; Asst Prof. of Psychology, New York Univ. 1970–72; Asst Prof. Yale Univ. 1972–75, Assoc. Prof. 1975–79, Prof. of Psychology 1979–83, Dir of Grad. Studies 1982–89, Philip R. Allen Prof. of Psychology 1984–94, Prof. of Medicine and Psychiatry 1985–94, Chair. Dept of Psychology 1989–91, Dean Grad. School of Arts and Sciences 1991–92, Provost 1992–94; Prof. of Psychology, Medicine and Psychiatry, Univ. of Pa 1994–2004, Pres. Univ. of Pa 1994–2004; Pres. Rockefeller Foundation 2005–; Chair. John D. & Catherine T. MacArthur Foundation Research Network on Determinants and Consequences of Health-Promoting and Health-Damaging Behavior 1983–93; Chair. Council of Pres.'s, Univs Research Asscn 1995–96; has served on numerous Bds of Dirs, including Int. Life Sciences Inst. 1993–, Aetna Life & Casualty Co. 1995–, AMR Corpn, Comcast Corpn, Citigroup; has served as mem. of numerous professional cttees, including Pres. Clinton's Cttee of Advisors on Science and Tech., Pa Women's Forum 1995–; chief ed. Appetite 1979–92; has served on numerous editorial bds; mem. Bd of Trustees, Brookings Inst. 1995–; Fellow, AAAS, American Acad. of Arts and Sciences; Hon. DHumLitt (New Haven) 1994, (Medical Coll. of Pa and Hahnemann Univ.) 1995; numerous awards and prizes, including 21st Century Award, Int. Alliance, Glass Ceiling Award, American Red Cross. *Publications:* author or co-author of 12 books on the relationship between psychological and biological processes in human health and behaviour; more than 200 chapters and articles in academic journals. *Leisure interests:* tennis, travel, reading. *Address:* The Rockefeller Foundation, 420 Fifth Avenue, New York, NY 10018-2702, USA (office). *Telephone:* (212) 869-8500 (office). *Fax:* (212) 764-3468. *Website:* www.rockfound.org (office).

RODIONOV, Gen. Igor Nikolayevich; Russian politician and army officer (retd); b. 1 Dec. 1936, Kurakino, Penza Region; m.; one s.; ed Orel Tank Higher Mil. School, Mil. Acad. of Armoured Units, Mil. Acad. of Gen. Staff; Asst to Commdr, master sgt's student's co. Orel Tank Higher School 1965–67; in Group of Soviet Troops in Germany 1957–64; Commdr tank co., Deputy Commdr tank bn 1964–67; Deputy Commdr tank regt, Commdr Regt, Deputy Commdr, Commdr div. Carpathian Mil. Command 1970–78; Commdr Army corps Cen. Group of Troops 1980–83; Commdr 5th Army Far E. Mil. Command 1983–85; Commdr Army of Turkestan Mil. Command, participant of war in Afghanistan 1985–86; First Deputy Commdr Moscow Mil. Command 1986–88; Commdr Caucasian Mil. Command, involved in dispersal of demonstration in Tbilisi 1989; Chief Mil. Acad. of Gen. Staff 1989–96; Minister of Defence of Russian Fed., mem. Security Council and Defence Council 1996–97; discharged by Pres. Yeltsin; joined CP of Russian Fed. 1998; mem. State Duma (Parl.), CP faction 1999–2003, Rodina (Homeland) faction 2003–. *Address:* State Duma, Okhotny Ryad 1, 103265 Moscow, Russia. *Telephone:* (495) 292-50-14.

RODIONOV, Piotr Ivanovich; Russian politician; b. 26 Jan. 1951, Przhevalsk, Kyrgyz SSR; m.; three c.; ed Leningrad Inst. of Vessel Construction, Leningrad Inst. of Finance and Econs, Higher School of Commerce, Acad. of Nat. Econs; with USSR Ministry of Gas Industry; Chief Technologist, Head of Div., with Lentransgas 1984–88; Dir-Gen. Lentransgas 1989–96; mem. Bd of Dirs Russian Jt Gazprom 1996–2006, First Deputy Chair. 2001–06; currently investor Severneftegazdobyca (oil and natural gas co.); rep. of Russian Govt to Gazprom 1996, to United Energy System of Russia 1996; Minister of Oil and Gas Industry 1996–97; mem. Govt Comm. for Operational Problems 1996–97; Chair. Bd of Dirs Menatep St Petersburg Bank 1998–; Hon. Worker of Gas Industry. *Address:* c/o Gazprom, Nametkina str. 16, 117884 Moscow, Russia.

RODKIN, Gary M., BEcons, MBA; American food industry executive; *President and CEO, ConAgra Foods Inc.;* b. 6 April 1952; m. Barbara Rodkin; one s. one d.; ed Rutgers Univ., Harvard Business School; held marketing and man. positions General Mills 1979–95 including Pres. Yoplait-Colombo 1992–95; Pres. Tropicana N America 1995–98; Pres. and CEO Pepsi Cola N America 1999–2002, Pres. PepsiCo Beverages and Foods 2002–03, Chair. CEO 2002–05; Pres. and CEO ConAgra Foods Inc., Omaha 2005–; mem. Bd of Dirs United Industries Corpn 2005–. *Address:* ConAgra Foods Inc., 1 ConAgra Drive, Omaha, NE 68102-5001, USA (office). *Telephone:* (402) 595-4000 (office). *Fax:* (402) 595-4707 (office). *Website:* www.conagra.com (office).

RODRIGO, Nihal; Sri Lankan diplomatist and international organization official; *Adviser to the President on Foreign Affairs;* Asst Lecturer, Univ. of Ceylon; with Foreign Service, including diplomatic missions in Australia, Germany, India, Switzerland and USA; Deputy Perm. Rep. to UN, New York, Perm. Rep., Geneva; Dir-Gen. for S Asia, SAARC, Sec.-Gen. 1999–2002; co-ordinated activities of Non-Aligned Movt under Sri Lanka's chairmanship 1976–79, del. to summit confs 1976–, Chair. Political Cttee 1995; mem. Advisory Bd on Disarmament of UN Sec.-Gen.; mem. several presidential cttees, including Acquisition of Art Works for State Collections, Foreign Affairs, Human Rights and Information Strategy; mem. Man. Bd Bandar-anaike Centre for Int. Studies; Amb. to China, Mongolia and People's Repub. of China 2004–07; Adviser to Pres. of Sri Lanka on Foreign Affairs 2007–. *Address:* c/o President's Secretariat, Republic Square, Colombo 1, Sri Lanka. *Telephone:* (11) 2324801. *Fax:* (11) 2331246. *E-mail:* gosl@presidentsl.org. *Website:* www.presidentsl.org.

RODRIGUES, Christopher John, BA, MBA, FRSA; British business executive and government official; *Chairman, VisitBritain;* b. 24 Oct. 1949; s. of Alfred John Rodrigues and Joyce Margaret Rodrigues (née Farron-Smith; m. Priscilla Purcell Young 1976; one s. one d.; ed Univ. of Cambridge, Harvard Univ., USA; fmr man. trainee Spillers; fmrly with McKinsey, American Express; fmr COO, fmr Chief Exec. Thomas Cook; Chief Exec. Bradford & Bingley Bldg Soc. (now Bradford & Bingley PLC) 1996–2004; Pres. and CEO Visa International 2004–06; Chair. VisitBritain 2007–; founder dir Financial Services Authority 1997–2003; mem. Bd of Dirs (non-exec.) Energis PLC 1997–2003, Ladbrokes plc (fmly Hilton Group) 2003–; mem. Exec. Cttee World Travel and Tourism Council; mem. of the Council and Exec. Cttee National Trust. *Leisure interests:* cooking, rowing, opera. *Address:* VisitBritain, Thames Tower, Black's Road, Hammersmith, London, W6 9EL, England (office). *Telephone:* (20) 8846-9000 (office). *Website:* www.visitbritain.com (office).

RODRIGUES, Roque Félix de Jesus; Timor-Leste politician; fmr Vice-Minister for Educ., Culture and Youth 2001; Minister for Defence –2006 (resgnd).

RODRIGUES, Gen. Sunith Francis, MA; Indian army officer (retd) and government official; *Governor of the Punjab and Administrator of Union Territory of Chandigarh;* b. 19 Sept. 1933, Bombay (now Mumbai); m. Jean Rodrigues; two s. one d.; ed St Xavier's High School, Bombay, Defence Services Staff Coll. (DSSC), Royal Coll. of Defence Studies, UK; joined Jt Services Wing, Indian Mil. Acad. 1949, commissioned into Regt of Artillery 1952, commanded mountain artillery regt 1970–71, served as Gen. Staff Officer during Indo-Pak War at a Corps HQ 1971, of a div. 1973–75, commanded mountain brigade at high altitude 1975–77, Chief Instructor (Army) at DSSC 1978–81, commanded div. deployed at high altitude on becoming Maj.-Gen. 1981, Chief of Staff of a corps 1983–85, Dir-Gen. Mil. Training and promoted to rank of Lt-Gen. 1985–86, commanded corps in northern sector 1986–89, apptd Hon. ADC to Pres. 1987, served as Vice-Chief of Army Staff 1987–89, GOC-in-C Cen. Command April–Oct. 1989, GOC-in-C Western Command Nov. 1989–June 1990, Chief of Army Staff 1990–93; Dir Int. Centre, Goa 1993–99; served two terms on Nat. Security Advisory Bd; mem. Exec. Council Goa Univ. for seven years, Man. Cttee Goa Chamber of Commerce and Industry; Gov. of Punjab and Admin. of Union Territory of Chandigarh 2004–; mem. Goa Planning Bd, Bd Govs Goa Inst. of Man.; Vishisht Seva Medal (VSM) for distinguished service 1972, Param Vishisht Seva Medal (PVSM) 1988. *Leisure interests:* social and literary pursuits. *Address:* Office of the Governor, Chandigarh, Punjab (office); Pb. Raj Bhawan, Sector 6, Chandigarh, Punjab, India (home). *Telephone:* (172) 2740740 (office); (172) 2740740 (home). *E-mail:* governor@punjabmail.gov.in (office). *Website:* punjabgovt.nic .in (office).

RODRIGUES-BIRKETT, Carolyn; Guyanese politician; *Minister of Foreign Affairs;* b. 16 Sept. 1973, Santa Rosa, Region One; m.; two c.; ed Saskatchewan Federated Coll., Canada, Univ. of Guyana; began career as teacher, Santa Rosa Primary School; Asst Co-ordinator, later Co-ordinator for Amerindian Projects, Social Impact Amelioration Program 1993–2001; Minister of Amerindian Affairs 2001–08, of Foreign Affairs 2008–. *Address:* Ministry of Foreign Affairs, Takuba Lodge, 254 South Road and New Garden Street, Bourda, Georgetown, Guyana (office). *Telephone:* 226-1607 (office). *Fax:* 225-9192 (office). *E-mail:* minfor@guyana.net.gy (office). *Website:* www .sdnp.org.gy/minfor (office).

RODRIGUEZ, Alexander (Alex) Emmanuel; American professional baseball player; b. 27 July 1975, New York, NY; m. Cynthia Scurtis 2002; one d.; ed Westminster Christian High School, Miami, FL; shortstop and third baseman; Maj. League teams: Seattle Mariners 1994–2000, Texas Rangers 2001–2003, NY Yankees 2004–; first high school player to trial for Team USA 1993; represented US Junior National Squad 1993; Maj. League debut 8 July 1994 (third 18-year-old shortstop to play Maj. Leagues since 1900); est. Seattle record for average, runs, hits, doubles and total bases 1996; traded to NY Yankees 2004; led American League (AL) in home runs 2001, 2002 (with 57 home runs, sixth highest in AL history), 2003, 2005, 2007; youngest player ever to hit 500 home runs; f. Alex Rodriguez Foundation 1998; USA Baseball Junior Player of the Year 1993, National Baseball Student Athlete of the Year 1993, finalist for USA Baseball Golden Spikes Award for top amateur player 1993 (while still at school), Sporting News Maj. League Player of the Year 1996, 2002 2007, Associated Press Maj. League Player of the Year 1996, Silver Slugger 1996, 1998–2002, 2005–07, Baseball America Maj. League Player of the Year 2000, 2002, Rawlings Gold Glove 2002, 2003 for shortstop, American League Most Valuable Player 2003, 2005, 2007. *Leisure interests:* basketball, golf, boating. *Address:* New York Yankees, Yankee Stadium, East 161st Street and River Avenue, New York, NY 10452, USA (office). *Telephone:* (718) 293-4300 (office). *Fax:* (718) 293-8431 (office). *Website:* newyork.yankees.mlb.com (office). arod.mlb.com/players/rodriguez_alex.

RODRÍGUEZ, Francisco González; Spanish banking executive; *Chairman and CEO, Banco Bilbao Vizcaya Argentaria;* b. 19 Oct. 1944, Chantada, Galicia; m.; two d.; ed Univ. of Madrid; began career as computer programmer, Nixdorf, Germany 1970s; est. Stock Broking Co.; led restructuring and privatisation of Argentaria (collection of state banks) 1996, Argentaria merger with Banco Bilbao Vizcaya (BBA) 2000; Co-Chair. Banco Bilbao Vizcaya Argentaria (BBVA) 2000–02, Chair. and CEO 2002–. *Leisure interest:* golf. *Address:* Banco Bilbao Vizcaya Argentaria SA, Gran Vía 1, 48001 Bilbao, Vizcaya, Spain (office). *Telephone:* (94) 4875555 (office). *Fax:* (94) 4876161 (office). *E-mail:* atencion.clientes@grupobbva.com (office). *Website:* www.bbv .es (office).

RODRIGUEZ, Narciso; American fashion designer; b. 27 Jan. 1961, New Jersey; ed Parsons School of Design, New York; Women's Designer Asst, Anne Klein under Donna Karan 1985–91, Women's Ready-to-Wear, Calvin Klein 1991–95; Women's and Men's Design Dir TSE, New York, Women's Creative Dir Cerruti, Paris 1995–97; Women's Design Dir Loewe, Spain 1997; Narciso Rodriguez signature collection presented Milan 1997; Best New Designer, VH1 Fashion Awards 1997, Perry Ellis Award, Council of Fashion Designers of America (CFDA) 1997, Hispanic Designers Moda Award 1997, New York Magazine Award 1997, Womenswear Designer of the Year, CFDA 2002, 2003. *Address:* Narciso Rodriguez LLC, 30 Irving Place, # 9, New York, NY 10003, USA (office); 22-32 ave. Victor Hugo, 75116 Paris, France. *Telephone:* (212) 677-2989 (office). *Fax:* (212) 677-2475 (office). *Website:* www.narcisorodriguez .com.

RODRÍGUEZ ARAQUE, Ali; Venezuelan politician, lawyer and diplomatist; *Minister of Finance;* b. 9 Sept. 1937, Ejido, Venezuela; ed Univ. Cen. de Venezuela, Univ. de los Andes; practised law; mem. Parl. 1983; mem. Nat. Council of Energy; Chair. Chamber of Deputies Comm. of Energy and Mines 1994–97; Vice-Chair., Bicameral Comm. of Energy and Mines; Senator 1999–2004; fmr Minister of Energy and Mines 1999–2000; Pres. of OPEC Conf. 2000, Sec.-Gen. 2001–02; Pres. and CEO Petróleos de Venezuela SA (PDVSA) 2002–04; Minister of Foreign Affairs 2004–06, of Finance 2008–; Amb. to Cuba 2006–08. *Publications:* various articles on public policy in the field of energy, including Privatisation Process of the Oil Industry in Venezuela 1997. *Address:* Ministry of Finance, Edif. Ministerio de Finanzas, esq. Carmelitas, Avda Urdaneta, Caracas, Venezuela (office). *Telephone:* (212) 802-1404 (office). *Fax:* (212) 802-1413 (office). *E-mail:* consultapublica@mf.gov .ve (office). *Website:* www.mf.gov.ve (office).

RODRIGUEZ CUADROS, Manuel, DJur; Peruvian diplomatist and politician; b. 1949, Cusco; m.; four c.; ed Universidad Nacional Mayor de San Marcos; Asst Dir of Integration, Ministry of Foreign Affairs 1984–85, Dir Econ. Affairs 1985–86, Vice-Minister of Foreign Affairs –2003, Minister 2003–05; Perm. Rep. to UN, New York 1988–89, to Int. Orgs, Geneva –2006; Chair. 62nd Session UN Comm. on Human Rights, Geneva 2006; currrently Dir-Gen. Instituto Sudamericano de Relaciones Internacionales y Medio Ambiente. *Publication:* Delimitación Marítima con Equidad: El caso de Perú y Chile. *Address:* c/o Ministry of Foreign Affairs, Jirón Lampa 535, Lima 1, Peru (office).

RODRÍGUEZ ECHEVERÍA, Miguel Angel, PhD; Costa Rican international organization official, fmr head of state, economist and business executive; b. 9 Jan. 1940, San José; m.; ed Univ. de Costa Rica, Univ. of Calif., Berkeley; Lecturer and Economist, Univ. of Costa Rica 1963; Research Asst, Univ. of Calif., Berkeley 1965–66; Dir of Planning Office and Presidential Adviser on Political Econs and Planning 1966–68; Dir Cen. Bank 1967–70; columnist for La Nación 1967–68; with Ministry of Planning 1968–69; Visiting Economist, Univ. of Calif.; with Ministry of the Presidency 1970; exec. with Empacadora de Carne de Cartago and Abonos Superior SA 1970–71; Pres. Agrodinámica Int. SA and subsidiaries 1974–87; Lecturer in Econs, Univ. of Costa Rica and Univ. Autónoma de Centro América 1978; mem. of Counsel (legal and econ. advisers) 1982; mem. nat. political directorate Partido Unidad Social Cristiano 1984, mem. Exec. 1994; Dir Banco Agro Industrial y de Exportaciones SA 1986–87; gen. adviser Grupo Ganadero Int. de Costa Rica SA 1989–90; Deputy Legis. Ass. 1991–92; Vice-Pres. (for Cen. America), Christian Democratic Org. of Latin America 1991, Pres. 1995; Pres. of Costa Rica 1998–2002; Sec.-Gen. OAS Sept.–Oct. 2004 (resgnd). *Publications:* El mito de la Racionalidad del Socialismo 1963, El Orden Jurídico de la Libertad 1967, Contributions to Economic Analysis. Production Economics: A Dual Approach to Theory and Applications 1978, Nuestra Crisis Financiera: Causas y Soluciones 1979, De las Ideas a la Acción 1988, Al Progreso por la Libertad 1989, Libertad y Solidaridad: Una Política Social para el Desarrollo Humano 1992, Una Revolución Moral: Democracia, Mercado y Bien Común 1992, Por una Vida Buena, Justa y Solidaria 1993; numerous articles and contribs on econs. *Address:* c/o Organization of American States, 17th Street & Constitution Avenue, NW, Washington, DC 20006, USA (office).

RODRÍGUEZ GARCÍA, José Luis, PhD; Cuban politician; *Minister of Economy and Planning;* b. 18 March 1946, Havana; mem. Cen. Cttee, CP of Cuba 1997–; Deputy Nat. Ass. of People's Power 1998–; Minister of Economy and Planning 1998–; currently Vice-Pres. Council of Ministers; mem. Scientific Council, Inst. of Int. Relations, Cuban Acad. of Sciences. *Address:* Ministry of Economy and Planning, 20 de Mayo, entre Territorial y Ayestarán, Plaza de la Revolución, Havana, Cuba (office). *Telephone:* (7) 881-8789 (office). *Fax:* (7) 33-3387 (office). *E-mail:* mep@ceniai.inf.cu (office).

RODRÍGUEZ GIAVARINI, Adalberto; Argentine politician and economist; ed Univ. of Buenos Aires; fmr Comptroller Gen. Trust of State Cos.; Pres. and owner macroecons analysis co.; Chair. Microecons, Univ. of Buenos Aires 1972–78; Co-ordinator Postgrad. Studies in Econs, Univ. of Salvador 1980–83; Sec. of State for Budget, Ministry of Economy 1983–85, for Planning, Ministry of Defence 1986–89; elected mem. Chamber of Deputies 1995; Minister of Foreign Affairs, Int. Trade and Religion –2001; mem. Bd of Dirs and Exec. Cttee Fundación Carolina de Argentina, fmr Pres.; Visiting Prof., Univ. of Belgrano 1994; Prof. of Econs, School of Econs and Business Admin. 1995; mem. various academic insts and advisory bds; guest columnist maj. daily newspapers in Argentina and abroad. *Address:* c/o Fundación Carolina de Argentina, Buenos Aires, Argentina. *E-mail:* info@fundacioncarolina.org.ar. *Website:* www.fundacioncarolina.org.ar.

RODRIGUEZ GÓMEZ, Jorge, PhD; Venezuelan psychologist and politician; b. 9 Nov. 1965, Caracas; s. of Jorge Rodríguez; ed Luis Razetti School of Medicine, Central Univ. of Venezuela and Andrés Bello Catholic Univ.; Pres. Student Union, Luis Razetti School of Medicine 1987–88; Pres. Venezuelan Fed. of Univs. 1988–92; Resident Doctor, Venezuelan Inst. of Social Security 1995; joined Movimiento Quinto República (MVR) 2000; in pvt. medical practice 2002–03; Pres. Nat. Electoral Team 2003–05; Pres. Nat. Electoral Council 2005–06; Vice–Pres. of Venezuela 2007. *Address:* Movimiento Quinto República, Calle Lima, cruce con Avda Libertador, Los Cabos, Caracas, Venezuela (office). *Telephone:* (212) 782-3808 (office). *Fax:* (212) 782-9720 (office).

RODRÍGUEZ HERRER, Elvira; Spanish politician; *President, Assembly of Madrid;* b. 15 May 1949; m.; four c.; ed Universidad Complutense de Madrid; lawyer; Inspector and State Auditor 1972–74; Head of Fiscal Section, Seville Property Del. 1974–75; Chief of Finance Unit, Directorate of the Treasury 1975–78; Asst Dir-Gen. Social Security 1978–84; Asst Dir-Gen. Nat. Audit Office 1984–96; Dir-Gen. of Budgets 1996–2000; Sec. of State for Budgets and Expenditure, Ministry of Property 2000; Minister of the Environment 2003–04; Minister of Transport, Community of Madrid 2006–07; Pres. Ass. of Madrid 2007–; mem. Comms preparing first Gen. Plan of Public Accounts 1981, 1983; Nat. Audit Office Rep. on Comm. of Principles and Public Norms 1991–94. *Address:* Assembly of Madrid, Plaza de la Asamblea de Madrid, 1, 28018, Madrid, Spain (office). *Telephone:* (91) 7799500 (office). *E-mail:* asamblea@asambleamadrid.es. *Website:* www.asambleamadrid.es (office).

RODRÍGUEZ IGLESIAS, Gil Carlos, PhD; Spanish judge and professor of law; b. 26 May 1946, Gijón; m. Teresa Diez Gutiérrez 1972; two d.; ed Univ. of Oviedo and Univ. Autónoma de Madrid; Asst Univs of Oviedo, Freiburg, Autónoma of Madrid and Complutense of Madrid 1969–77; lecturer, Univ. Complutense of Madrid 1977–82, Prof. 1982–83, Prof. of Int. Law 2003–; Prof., Univ. of Granada 1983–2003, Dir Dept of Int. Law 1983–86; Judge, Court of Justice of European Communities 1986–2003, Pres. 1994–2003; Jean Monnet Chair of European Community Law, Dir Dept of European Studies, Instituto Universitario Ortega y Gasset 2004–05; Co-dir Revista de Derecho Comunitario Europeo; mem. Bd of Dirs Fundación Real Instituto Elcano; mem. Editorial Bds of several law reviews; mem. Curatorium, Max Planck Inst. for Int. Public Law and Comparative Law, Heidelberg;; Hon. Bencher Gray's Inn 1995, King's Inn, Dublin; Hon. Fellow, Soc. of Advanced Legal Studies, London; Hon. Mem. Academia Asturiana de Jurisprudencia; Orden de Isabel la Católica, Orden de San Raimundo de Peñafort; Dr hc (Turin) 1996, (Babeş-Bolyai Cluj-Napoca, Romania) 1996, (Sarre Univ.), (Univ. of Ohrid, Bulgaria); Walter-Hallstein Prize 2003. *Publications:* El régimen jurídico de los monopolios de Estado en la Comunidad Económica Europea 1976; numerous articles and studies on EC law and int. law. *Address:* c/o Board of Directors, Fundación Real Instituto Elcano, Príncipe de Vergara, 51, 28006 Madrid, Spain. *E-mail:* info@rielcano.org. *Website:* www.realinstitutoelcano.org.

RODRÍGUEZ MARADIAGA, HE Cardinal Oscar Andrés; Honduran ecclesiastic; *Archbishop of Tegucigalpa;* b. 29 Dec. 1942, Tegucigalpa; ordained priest 1970; Bishop 1978; Sec. Gen. Latin American Episcopal Conference 1987–91, Pres. Econ. Cttee 1991–95; Archbishop of Tegucigalpa 1993–; Pres. Conference of Latin American Bishops 1995–99; cr. Cardinal 2001, Cardinal Priest of S Maria della Speranza; served as Vatican spokesperson to IMF and World Bank on Third World debt; Pres. Caritas Internationalis, Caritas Confederation (network of Catholic relief and devt orgs) 2007–. *Address:* Conferencia Episcopal de Honduras, Los Lavreles, Comayagüela, Apdo 3121, Tegucigalpa, Honduras (office). *Telephone:* 2370353 (office); 2372366 (home). *Fax:* 2222337 (office). *Website:* www .cardinalrodriguez.info; www.caritas.org.

RODRÍGUEZ MENDOZA, Miguel; Venezuelan international organization official, lawyer and diplomatist; *Senior Fellow, International Centre for Trade and Sustainable Development;* ed Cen. Univ. of Venezuela, Univ. of Manchester, UK, Ecole des Hautes Etudes en Sciences Sociales, France; First Sec. Perm. Mission of Venezuela to UN 1978–81; Dir for Consultation and Co-ordination, Latin American Econ. System 1982–88; Special Adviser to Pres. on int. econ. affairs 1989–91; Minister of State, Pres. Inst. of Foreign Trade 1991–94; Pres. Comm. of Cartagena Agreement 1993; Chief Trade Adviser, OAS –1998; Visiting Scholar, Georgetown Univ., Washington, DC 1998–; Jt Deputy Dir-Gen. WTO 1999–2002; Of Counsel Van Bael & Bellis, Geneva 2002–04; Transatlantic Fellow, German Marshall Fund of the US 2005–; Sr Fellow, Int. Centre for Trade and Sustainable Devt, Geneva; apptd Chair. WTO panel to decide US challenge on EU system of protecting products with geographical names 2004. *Publications:* numerous articles in books and journals; has edited numerous books. *Address:* International Centre for Trade and Sustainable Development, International Environment House 2, Chemin de Balexert 7, 1219 Châtelaine, Geneva, Switzerland (office). *Telephone:* (22) 917-8492 (office). *Fax:* (22) 917-8093 (office). *Website:* www.ictsd.org (office).

RODRÍGUEZ PARRILLA, Bruno, LLB; Cuban diplomatist and government official; *Minister of Foreign Relations;* b. 22 Jan. 1958, Mexico City, Mexico; m.; one s.; mem. Cen. Cttee, CP of Cuba 1990–, Head of Cultural Policy Matters 1992–; Deputy Perm. Rep. to UN, New York 1993–95, Perm. Rep. 1995–2003; Deputy Minister for Foreign Relations in charge of Latin America and the Caribbean and for information and communication 2003–04, First Deputy Minister for Foreign Relations 2004–09, Minister of Foreign Relations 2009–. *Address:* Ministry of Foreign Relations, Calzada 360, esq. G, Vedado, Havana, Cuba (office). *Telephone:* (7) 55-3537 (office). *Fax:* (7) 33-3460 (office). *E-mail:* cubaminrex@minrex.gov.cu (office). *Website:* www.cubaminrex.cu (office).

RODRÍGUEZ VELTZÉ, Eduardo, MPA; Bolivian lawyer, judge and fmr head of state; b. 2 March 1956, Cochabamba; m. Fanny Elena Arguedas Calle; four c.; ed Universidad Mayor de San Simón, Harvard Univ., USA; fmr Resident Co-ordinator, UN Latin American Inst. for the Prevention of Crime and the Treatment of Offenders (ILANUD); fmr Lecturer, Universidad Andina Simón Bolívar, Universidad Mayor de San Andrés; Pres. of the Supreme Court 2004–05; Interim Pres. of Bolivia 2005–06. *Address:* c/o Ministry of the Presidency, Palacio de Gobierno, Plaza Murillo, La Paz, Bolivia (office).

RODRIQUEZ, Julián Isaias, PhD; Venezuelan lawyer, poet and politician; *Attorney General;* ed Univs of Santa Maria and Zulia and Cen. Univ. of Venezuela; legal adviser to Ministry of Agric. 1969; fmr Attorney-Gen.; Chief Attorney of Aragua 1990–91; Senator for Aragua 1998; First Vice-Pres. Nat. Constituency Ass. 1999–2000; Vice-Pres. of Venezuela 2000; Attorney Gen. 2000–; Prof., Univ. of Carabobo; regular columnist for El Siglo; consultant to Veterinary Asscn 1971; mem. Movimiento Quinta República. *Publications:* legal: New Labour Procedures 1987, Legal Stability in Labour Laws 1993; poetry: Pozo de cabrillas, Con las aspas de todos los molinos, Los tiempos de la sed; contrib. numerous articles. *Address:* c/o Ministry of the Interior and Justice, Edif. Ministerio del Interior y Justicia, esq. de Platanal, Avda Urdaneta, Caracas 1010, Venezuela. *Telephone:* (212) 506-1101. *Fax:* (212) 506-1559. *E-mail:* webmaster@mij.gov.ve. *Website:* www.mij.gov.ve.

ROED-LARSEN, Terje, PhD; Norwegian diplomatist, politician and international organization official; *Under-Secretary-General and Special Envoy for the Implementation of Security Council Resolution 1559, United Nations;* b. 22 Nov. 1947; m. Mona Juul; taught sociology and philosophy at Univs of Bergen and Oslo; Founder and Exec. Dir Inst. of Applied Social Sciences (FAFO) 1991, Hon. Chair. Programme for Int. Co-operation and Conflict Resolution; fmr Deputy Foreign Minister; facilitated negotiations between reps of Israel's Labour Govt and Palestinian Liberation Org. (PLO) leading to signing of Declaration of Principles, Washington, DC 13 Sept. 1993; Amb. and Special Adviser to Norwegian Foreign Minister for the Middle East Peace Process 1993, 1998–; UN Deputy Sec.-Gen. and Special Co-ordinator in the Occupied Territories, Gaza 1994–96; Minister of Planning 1996–98; Special Co-ordinator for the Middle East Peace Process and Personal Rep. of the UN Sec.-Gen. to the PLO and Palestinian Authority 1999–2005; Under-Sec.-Gen. and Special Envoy for the Implementation of UN Security Council Resolution 1559 (calling for Syrian withdrawal from Lebanon and disarmament of Hezbollah) 2004–; Pres. Int. Peace Acad., New York 2005–. *Address:* International Peace Academy, 777 United Nations Plaza, New York, NY 10017-3521 (office); Executive Office of the UN Secretary-General, United Nations Plaza, New York, NY 10017, USA. *Telephone:* (212) 687-4300 (office); (212) 906-5791 (UN) (office). *Fax:* (212) 983-8246 (office); (212) 906-5778 (UN) (office). *E-mail:* ipa@ipacademy.org (office). *Website:* www.ipacademy.org (office); www.un.org (office).

ROEDER, Robert Gayle, BA, MS, PhD; American biologist and academic; *Arnold O. and Mabel S. Beckman Professor and Head, Laboratory of Biochemistry and Molecular Biology, The Rockefeller University;* b. 3 June 1942, Boonville, IN; s. of Frederick Roeder and Helene Roeder (née Bredenkamp); m. 1st Suzanne Himsel 1964 (divorced 1980); one s. one d.; m. 2nd Cun Jing Hong 1990; one d.; ed Wabash Coll., Crawfordsville, IN, Univ. of Illinois, Urbana, Univ. of Washington, Seattle; Postdoctoral Fellow, Dept of Embryology, Carnegie Inst. of Washington, Baltimore, Md 1971; Asst Prof. of Biological Chem., Washington Univ. School of Medicine, St Louis, Mo. 1971–75, Assoc. Prof. 1975–76, Prof. 1976–82, James S. McDonnell Prof. of Biochemical Genetics 1979–82; Prof. and Head, Lab. of Biochemistry and Molecular Biology, The Rockefeller Univ., New York 1982–, Arnold O. and Mabel S. Beckman Prof. 1985–; Chair. Gordon Research Conf. on Nucleic Acids 1982; mem. Research Grant Review, NIH Molecular Biology Study Section 1975–79; mem. Scientific Advisory Bd Roche Inst. of Molecular Biology 1992–95, Second Int. Review, Karolinska Inst. Center for Biotechnology 1993, Scientific Review Bd, Howard Hughes Medical Inst. 1994–99, Nat. Inst. of Child Health and Human Devt 1995–2000; mem. Editorial Bd Journal of Biological Chemistry 1979–84, Nucleic Acids Research 1980–82, Molecular and Cellular Biology 1980–85, Cell 1990–93, Biological Chemistry Hoppe-Seyler 1994–99, Molecular Cell 1999–; mem. NAS 1988, ACS, American Soc. for Biochemistry and Molecular Biology, American Soc. for Microbiology, American Soc. for Virology, Soc. for Developmental Biology, The Harvey Soc. of New York (Pres. 1994–95), The New York Acad. of Sciences, The Protein Soc.; Fellow, AAAS 1992, American Acad. of Microbiology 1992, American Acad. of Arts and Sciences 1995; Assoc. mem. European Molecular Biology Org. 2003; Hon. DSc (Wabash Coll.) 1990, (Washington Univ.) 2005; Gilbert Scholar, Wabash Coll., US Public Health Service Predoctoral Fellowship 1965–69, Outstanding Biochemistry Grad. Student Award, Univ. of Washington 1967, American Cancer Soc. Postdoctoral Fellow 1969–71, NIH Research Career Devt Award 1973–78, Dreyfus Foundation Teacher-Scholar Award 1976–81, ACS Eli Lilly Award in Biological Chem. 1977, US Steel Award in Molecular Biology, NAS 1986, Outstanding Investigator Award, Nat. Cancer Inst. 1986–2000, Harvey Soc. Lecturer 1988, Passano Award 1995, Lewis S. Rosenstiel Award for Distinguished Work in Basic Medical Sciences 1995, Louisa Gross Horwitz Prize 1999, Alfred P. Sloan Prize, General Motors Cancer Research Foundation 1999, Gairdner Foundation Int. Award 2000, Dickson Prize in Medicine, Univ. of Pittsburgh 2001, ASBMB-Merck Award 2002, Albert Lasker Award for Basic Medical Research 2003. *Publications:* more than 400 articles in scientific journals. *Address:* Laboratory of Biochemistry and Molecular Biology, Rockefeller University, 1230 York Avenue, New York, NY 10021, USA (office). *Telephone:* (212)327-7600 (office). *Fax:* (212) 327-7949 (office). *E-mail:* roeder@rockefeller.edu (office). *Website:* www.rockefeller.edu/labheads/roeder/roeder.html (office).

ROEG, Nicolas Jack, CBE; British film director; b. 15 Aug. 1928, London; s. of Jack Nicolas Roeg and Mabel Roeg; m. 1st Susan Rennie Stephen 1957 (divorced); four s.; m. 2nd Theresa Russell (divorced); two s.; m. 3rd Harriett

Harper; ed Mercers School; started in film industry as clapper-boy; Fellow, BFI 1994; Hon. DLitt (Hull) 1995; Hon. DFA (Brooklyn Coll., City Univ. of New York) 2004. *Films include:* as cinematographer: The Caretaker 1963, The Masque of the Red Death, Nothing but the Best 1964, Fahrenheit 451 1966, Far from the Madding Crowd 1967, Petulia 1968; as dir: Performance (with Donald Cammell) 1968, Walkabout 1970, Don't Look Now 1972, The Man who Fell to Earth 1975, Bad Timing 1979, Eureka 1983, Insignificance 1984, Castaway 1985, Track 29 1987, Aria (Sequence) 1988, Cold Heaven 1989, The Witches 1989, Sweet Bird of Youth 1989, Without You I'm Nothing (exec. producer) 1990, Young Indy – Paris 1916 1991, Cold Heaven 1991, Heart of Darkness 1993, Two Deaths 1994, Full Body Massage 1995, Hotel Paradise 1995, Samson and Delilah 1996, The Sound of Claudia Schiffer 2001, Puffball 2007; co-writer film script for Night Train 2002. *Address:* c/o Independent, 32 Tavistock Street, London, WC2E 7PB, England (office). *Telephone:* (20) 7257-8734 (office). *Fax:* (20) 7240-9029 (office). *E-mail:* mail@ independentfilmcompany.com (office). *Website:* independentfilmcompany.com (office).

ROEHM, Carolyne Jane, BFA; American fashion designer; b. 7 May 1951, Kirksville, Mo.; d. of Kenneth Smith and Elaine Bresee (née Beaty); m. 1st Axel Roehm 1978 (divorced 1981); m. 2nd Henry R. Kravis 1985 (divorced 1993); ed Washington Univ., St Louis; designed sportswear for Kellwood Co. New York 1974–75; apprentice at Oscar de la Renta, Rome 1975–84; Pres. Carolyne Roehm Inc. (fashion design house) 1984–91; lifestyle contributor to Good Morning America TV show; mem. Council of Fashion Designers of America (Pres. 1989–90). *Publications:* Passion for Flowers 1997, Carolyne Roehm's Summer Notebook 1999, Carolyne Roehm's Fall Notebook 1999, Carolyne Roehm's Winter Notebook 1999, Carolyne Roehm's Spring Notebook 2000, At Home with Carolyne Roehm 2001, Presentations 2005, A Passion for Parties 2006. *Leisure interests:* gardening, skiing, tennis, opera, playing the piano. *Address:* POB 648, Sharon, CT 06069, USA. *Website:* www .carolyneroehm.com.

ROELL, Stephen A., BSc; American business executive; *Chairman and CEO, Johnson Controls Inc.;* ed St Ambrose Univ., Northeastern Univ.; began career as accountant Arthur Young & Co. 1971; Div. Controller, FMC Corpn 1975–82; joined Johnson Controls Inc. 1982, Operations Controller, Systems and Services Div. 1982, becoming Div. Controller, later Treas. and Corp. Controller, Sr Vice-Pres. and Chief Financial Officer 1991–2004, Exec. Vice-Pres. 2004, Vice-Chair. 2005–07, CEO 2007–, Chair. 2008–; mem. Bd Dirs Interstate Battery System of America Inc., Wheaton Franciscan Healthcare-Southeast Wis., Hunger Task Force; Trustee, Boys & Girls Club of Greater Milwaukee; mem. Financial Execs Inst. *Address:* Johnson Controls Inc., 5757 North Green Bay Avenue, Milwaukee, WI 53209, USA (office). *Telephone:* (414) 524-1200 (office). *Fax:* (414) 524-2077 (office). *E-mail:* info@ johnsoncontrols.com (office). *Website:* www.johnsoncontrols.com (office).

ROELS, Harry J. M.; Dutch energy industry executive; b. 26 July 1948; ed Univ. of Leiden; began career as oil engineer, Royal Dutch/Shell 1972, various eng and man. positions including Head Exploration and Production Offices, Chief Engineer in Turkey, Tech. Man. Norske Shell, Norway, Dir Enterprise Devt, Shell Int. Petroleum Inst., The Hague, Dir Offshore Bureau then Gen. Man. Aardolie Maatschappij, The Netherlands, Office Coordinator for Latin America, Shell Int. Petroleum Co., London, UK, Regional Business Dir for Middle E and Africa, sr man. positions in Malaysia and Brunei, apptd Man. Dir Royal Dutch Petroleum Co. 1999; Pres. and CEO RWE AG 2003–07, Chair. RWE Energy, RWE Thames Water –2006. *Address:* c/o RWE AG, Opernplatz 1, 45128 Essen, Germany (office).

ROEMER, John E., AB, PhD; American economist and academic; *Elizabeth S. and A. Varick Stout Professor of Political Science and Economics, Yale University;* b. 1 Feb. 1945, Washington, DC; s. of Milton I. Roemer and Ruth Rosenbaum Roemer; m. Carla Natasha Muldavin 1968; two c.; ed Harvard Univ., Univ. of California, Berkeley; math. teacher, Lowell High School and Pelton Jr High School, San Francisco 1969–74; consultant UNCTAD, Geneva 1978; Asst Prof. of Econs, Univ. of Calif., Davis 1974–78, Assoc. Prof. 1978–81, Prof. of Econs 1981–2000; Elizabeth S. and A. Varick Stout Prof. of Political Science and Econs, Yale Univ. 2000–; Visiting Prof., Harvard Univ. 1994, Univ. de Cergy-Pontoise 1995, New York Univ. 1999, Ecole Polytechnique, Paris 2004, EHESS, Marseilles 2005, Univ. de Paris I 2006; Dir Program on Economy, Justice and Society 1988–2000; Guggenheim Fellow; Fellow, Econometric Soc. 1985, American Acad. of Arts and Sciences 2006; Russell Sage Fellow 1998–99; Corresponding Fellow, British Acad. 2005. *Publications:* A General Theory of Exploitation and Class 1982, Free to Lose 1988, Egalitarian Perspectives 1994, A Future for Socialism 1994, Theories of Distributive Justice 1996, Equality of Opportunity 1998, Political Competition 2001, Democracy, Education and Equality 2006. *Address:* Department of Political Science, 124 Prospect Street, Room 208, Box 208301, Yale University, 124 Prospect Street, New Haven, CT 06520, USA (office). *Telephone:* (203) 432-5249. *Fax:* (203) 432-6196. *E-mail:* john.roemer@yale.edu (office). *Website:* www.yale.edu/polisci (office).

ROESKY, Herbert Walter, DrSc; German chemist and academic; *Professor Emeritus, Institute of Inorganic Chemistry, University of Göttingen;* b. 6 Nov. 1935, Laukischken; s. of Otto Roesky and Lina Roesky; m. Christel Roesky 1964; two s.; ed Univ. of Göttingen; Lecturer 1970, Univ. of Frankfurt, Prof. of Inorganic Chem. 1970–80; Dir Inst. of Inorganic Chem., Univ. of Göttingen 1980, now Prof. Emer., Dean Dept of Chem. 1985–87; Visiting Prof., Auburn Univ., USA 1984, Tokyo Inst. of Tech. 1987; mem. Gesellschaft Deutscher Chemiker (Vice-Pres. 1995), ACS, Chemical Soc., London, Gesellschaft Deutscher Naturforscher und Ärzte, Deutsche Bunsen-Gesellschaft für Physikalische Chemie, Göttinger Akad., Akad. Leopoldina, Austrian Acad. of Sciences, Russian Acad. of Sciences 1999; Foreign Assoc., Acad. des

Sciences, France, Romanian Acad. of Sciences; mem. Selection Bd, Alexander von Humboldt-Stiftung 1973–84, numerous editorial bds; Hon. FRSC 2007; Wöhler Prize 1960, French Alexander von Humboldt Prize 1986, Leibniz Prize 1987, Alfred-Stock-Gedächtnispreis 1990, Georg Ernst Stahl Medal 1990; Manfred and Wolfgang Flad Prize 1994, Grand Prix Fondation de la maison de la chimie, Carus Prize 1998, Wilkinson Award 1999, ACS Inorganic Award 2004, Wittig-Grignard-Preis 2005. *Publications:* six books and more than 1,000 learned papers and articles. *Leisure interest:* antique collecting. *Address:* Institute of Inorganic Chemistry, University of Göttingen, Tammannstrasse 4, 37077 Göttingen, Germany (office). *Telephone:* (551) 393001 (office). *Fax:* (551) 393373 (office). *E-mail:* hroesky@gwdg.de (office). *Website:* www.roesky.chemie.uni-goettingen.de (office).

ROGACHEV, Igor Alekseevich, PhD; Russian diplomatist and politician; b. 1 March 1932, Moscow; s. of Aleksey Petrovich Rogachev; m. Dioulber Rogacheva; one s. one d. (adopted); ed Moscow Inst. of Int. Relations 1955, USSR Ministry of Foreign Affairs; worked as interpreter in China 1956–58; joined diplomatic service 1958; Attaché, Embassy in China 1959–61; mem. Cen. Admin. USSR Ministry of Foreign Affairs 1961–65; First Sec. Embassy, USA 1965–69; Counsellor Embassy, China 1969–72; Deputy Head, Far Eastern Dept, Ministry of Foreign Affairs 1972–75, Head Asian Section, Dept of Planning of int. policies 1975–78, Head of South-East Asia Dept 1978–83, Head First Far East Div. 1983–86, Chief Dept of Socialist Countries of Asia 1986–87, Deputy-Minister of Foreign Affairs 1986–91; Head USSR del. Sino-Soviet talks on frontier issues 1987–91, int. talks on Cambodia 1988–91; Special Envoy to South Korea 1991; Amb.-at-Large to Democratic People's Repub. of Korea 1992; Amb. to People's Repub. of China 1992–2005; mem. Fed. Council for Amur Region 2005–; Vice-Chair. Russian–Chinese Friendship Soc. 1992–; mem. Editorial Bd Far Eastern Affairs journal; Academician Int. Acad. of Information Processes and Tech.; Order of the Badge of Honour 1971, Order of the Friendship of Peoples 1982, Order of Friendship 1996, Order of Honour 1999, Honoured Diplomatic Service Worker of Russian Fed. 2002; several medals. *Publications:* numerous articles and essays on Asian Pacific region. *Leisure interests:* playing the piano, tennis, reading, theatre. *Address:* Sovet Federatsii (Federation Council), 103426 Moscow, ul. B. Dmitrovka 26, Russia (office). *Telephone:* (495) 203-90-74 (office). *Fax:* (495) 203-46-17 (office). *E-mail:* post_sf@gov.ru (office). *Website:* www.council.gov.ru (office).

ROGÉ, Pascal; French pianist; b. 6 April 1951, Paris; two s.; ed Paris Conservatoire, private studies with Lucette Descaves, Pierre Pasquier and Julius Katchen; début Paris 1969, London 1969; specialist in Ravel, Poulenc, Debussy, Satie; soloist with leading orchestras; exclusive recording contract with Decca, London; Premiers Prix for Piano and Chamber Music at the Paris Conservatoire 1966, First Prize Marguerite Long-Jacques Thibaud Int. Competition 1971, Grand Prix du Disque and Edison Award 1984, Gramophone Award for Best Instrumental Recording 1988, Best Chamber Music Recording 1997. *Leisure interests:* reading, tennis, riding, golf. *Address:* Clarion/Seven Muses, 47 Whitehall Park, London, N19 3TW, England (office); Lorentz Concerts, 3 rue de la Boétie, 75008 Paris, France; 17 avenue des Cavaliers, 1224 Geneva, Switzerland. *Telephone:* (20) 7272-4413 (office). *E-mail:* admin@c7m.co.uk (office). *Website:* www.c7m.co.uk (office).

ROGEL, Steven R., BS; American business executive; *Chairman and CEO, Weyerhaeuser Company;* ed Univ. of Washington, Seattle, Dartmouth Coll., Massachusetts Inst. of Tech.; began career with Regis Paper Co. 1966–70; Asst Man. St Anne-Nackawic Pulp and Paper, Nackawic, NB, Canada 1970–72; Tech. Dir Wilamette Industries, Inc., Albany, Ore. 1972, Pres. and COO 1991–95, Pres. and CEO 1995–97; mem. Bd Dirs, Pres. and CEO Weyerhaeuser Co. 1997–2008, Chair. 1999–; mem. Bd Dirs Kroger Co., Union Pacific Corpn; fmr Chair. American Forest & Paper Asscn, Nat. Council for Air and Stream Improvement, Inc.; fmr Co-Chair. Wood Promotion Network; fmr Vice-Pres. Admin Western Region Boy Scouts of America, mem. Nat. Exec. Bd Boy Scouts of America; Trustee, Pacific Univ. *Address:* Weyerhaeuser Co., 33663 Weyerhaeuser Way South, Federal Way, WA 98063-9777, USA (office). *Telephone:* (253) 924-2345 (office). *Fax:* (253) 924-2685 (office). *E-mail:* PubRelations@weyerhaeuser.com (office). *Website:* www.weyerhaeuser.com (office).

ROGERS, Gen. Bernard William, MA; American army officer (retd); b. 16 July 1921, Fairview, Kan.; s. of the late W. H. Rogers and Mrs Rogers; m. Ann Ellen Jones 1944; one s. two d.; ed Kansas State Coll., US Mil. Acad., Univ. of Oxford, US Army Command and Gen. Staff Coll., US Army War Coll.; Commdg Officer, Third Bn, Ninth Infantry Regt, Second Infantry Div., Korea 1952–53; Commdr, First Battle Group, 19th Infantry, 24th Infantry Div., Augsburg, FRG 1960–61; Exec. Officer to the Chair., Jt Chiefs of Staff, the Pentagon 1962–66; Asst Div. Commdr, First Infantry Div., Repub. of Viet Nam 1966–67; Commdt of Cadets, US Mil. Acad. 1967–69; Commdg Gen., Fifth Infantry Div., Fort Carson, Colo 1969–70; Chief of Legis. Liaison, Office of the US Sec. of the Army 1971–72; Deputy Chief of Staff for Personnel 1972–74; Commdg Gen., US Army Forces Command, Fort McPherson, Ga 1974–76; Chief of Staff, US Army 1976–79, Supreme Allied Commdr Europe, NATO 1979–87, C-in-C US Forces Europe 1979–87; Rhodes Scholar 1947–50; Hon. Fellow, Univ. Coll., Oxford; Hon. LLD (Akron, Boston); Hon. DCL (Oxford) 1983; Distinguished Grad. Award, US Mil. Acad. 1995, George C. Marshall Medal, Asscn of US Army 1999, DSC, Defense Distinguished Service Medal, DSM of Army, Navy and Air Force, Silver Star, Legion of Merit, Bronze Star, Air Medal. *Publications:* Cedar Falls-Junction City: a Turning Point 1974, NATO's Strategy: An Undervalued Currency 1985, The Realities of NATO Strategy 1985, NATO's Conventional Defense Improvements Initiative: A New Approach to an Old Challenge, NATO's 16 Nations 1986, Western Security and European Defense RUSI 1986, NATO and US National Security: Misperception Versus Reality 1987, Soldat und Technik 1987, Arms Control and NATO, The Council for Arms Control 1987, Arms Control: for NATO, the Name of the Game is Deterrence, Global Affairs 1987; contribs to Atlantic Community Quarterly 1979, Foreign Affairs 1982, NATO Review 1982, 1984, RUSI 1982, Strategic Review, Nato's 16 Nations 1983, Géopolitique 1983, Europa Archiv 1984, Leaders Magazine 1984. *Leisure interests:* golf, reading. *Address:* 1467 Hampton Ridge Drive, McLean, VA 22101, USA (home). *Telephone:* (703) 448-0188 (home). *Fax:* (703) 827-8335 (home). *E-mail:* rogers1467@aol.com (home).

ROGERS, George Ernest, PhD, DSc, FAA; Australian biochemist and academic; *Professor Emeritus and Honorary Visiting Research Fellow, School of Molecular and Biomedical Science, University of Adelaide;* b. 27 Oct. 1927, Melbourne; s. of Percy Rogers and Bertha Beatrice Rogers (née Baxter); m. 2nd Racheline Aladjem 1972; two d.; ed Caulfield Grammar School, Univ. of Melbourne and Trinity Coll., Cambridge, England; Scientist, Wool Research, CSIRO 1951–53, Research Scientist, Div. of Protein Chem. 1957–62; Research Scientist, Univ. of Cambridge, England 1954–56; Reader in Biochem., Univ. of Adelaide 1963–77, Prof. of Biochem. 1978–92 and Chair. Dept of Biochem. 1988–92, now Prof. Emer., Hon. Visiting Research Fellow 1993–; Visiting Fellow, Clare Hall, Cambridge 1970; Program Man., Premium Quality Wool CRC 1995–2000; Visiting Scientist, Univ. de Grenoble, France 1977; Guest Scientist, NIH, Bethesda, USA 1985; CSIRO studentship 1954–56; Bourse Scientifique de Haut Niveau 1977; mem. Australian Soc. of Biochemistry and Molecular Biology, New York Acad. of Sciences; Eleanor Roosevelt Int. Cancer Research Fellow 1985; Fellow, Australian Acad. of Science 1977; Lemberg Medal, Australian Biochemical Soc. 1976, Centenary Federation Medal 2003. *Publications include:* The Keratins (jtly) 1972, The Biology of Wool and Hair (jtly) 1989; 170 publs in scientific journals on wool and hair growth, hair structure and sheep transgenesis. *Leisure interests:* family activities, swimming, golf, gardening. *Address:* School of Molecular and Biomedical Science, University of Adelaide, Adelaide, SA 5005 (office); 1 Gandys Gully Road, Stonyfell, SA 5066, Australia (home). *Telephone:* (8) 8303-4624 (office); (8) 8332-4143 (home). *Fax:* (8) 8303-7532 (office). *E-mail:* george.rogers@adelaide.edu.au (office). *Website:* www.mbs.adelaide.edu.au/people/biochem/grogers (office).

ROGERS, Grant Simon, BA; British artist, art historian and lecturer; *Educator, Imperial War Museum;* b. 4 March 1964, Singapore; s. of Keith Rogers and Diane Rogers; ed Crofton School, Price's Coll., and Portsmouth Coll. of Art, Hampshire, England; founder mem. Cubit Street Artists 1986–1992; lecturer at Nat. Gallery, Nat. Portrait Gallery, Wallace Collection, Victoria and Albert Museum, British Museum, Imperial War Museum 1990–2002; Family and Informal Educ. Co-ordinator Imperial War Museum 2002–. *Television:* BBC television and radio, Channel 4 TV. *Films:* animated: TVC cartoons; Father Christmas; Grandpa; When the Wind Blows. *Publications:* numerous articles in UK press. *Leisure interests:* hedonism and futile introspection. *Address:* 66–68 Camberwell Road, London, SE5 0EG, England (home). *Telephone:* (20) 7416-5329 (office); (7977) 010477 (office). *E-mail:* grogers@iwm.org. *Website:* www.iwm.org.uk (office).

ROGERS, James E., BBA, JD; American energy industry executive; *Chairman, President and CEO, Duke Energy Corporation;* b. 1947, Birmingham, Ala; m. Mary Anne Rogers; one s. two d.; ed Emory Univ., Univ. of Ky; fmr Asst Attorney-Gen. Commonwealth of Ky; fmr Deputy Gen. Counsel for Litigation and Enforcement and Asst to Chief Trial Counsel FERC (Fed. Energy Regulatory Comm.); fmr Pnr Akin, Gump, Strauss, Hauer & Feld (law firm), Dallas, Tex.; Exec. Vice-Pres. Enron Corpn, Houston, TX –1988; Chair., Pres. and CEO PSI Energy Inc. (renamed Cinergy Corpn) 1988, Pres. and CEO Duke Energy (after merger of Cinergy and Duke Corpns) 2006–, Chair. 2007–; Dir Fifth Third Bancorp and Fifth Third Bank, Duke Realty Corpn; Gen. Chair. Greater Cincinnati-N Ky United Way Campaign 1997; Hon. LLD (Indiana State Univ.) 1991; named to Univ. of Ky Coll. of Business and Econs Hall of Fame; Ellis Island Medal of Honor 2007. *Address:* Duke Energy Corporation, 526 South Church Street, Charlotte, NC 28202-1803, USA (office). *Telephone:* (704) 594-6200 (office). *Fax:* (704) 382-3814 (office). *Website:* www.duke-energy.com (office).

ROGERS, Paul; British actor; b. 22 March 1917, Plympton, Devon; s. of Edwin Rogers and Dulcie Myrtle Rogers; m. 1st Jocelyn Wynne 1939 (divorced 1955); two s.; m. 2nd Rosalind Boxall 1955; two d.; ed Newton Abbot Grammar School, Devon and Michael Chekhov Theatre Studio; first stage appearance at Scala Theatre 1938; Stratford-on-Avon Shakespeare Memorial Theatre 1939; RN 1940–46; with Bristol Old Vic Co. 1947–49, London Old Vic 1949–53, 1955–56; Clarence Derwent Award 1952, Tony Award 1967. *Plays include:* The Merchant of Venice 1952, The Confidential Clerk 1953, Macbeth 1954, The Taming of the Shrew; toured Australia as Hamlet 1957; The Elder Statesman 1958, King Lear 1958, Mr. Fox of Venice 1959, The Merry Wives of Windsor 1959, A Winter's Tale 1959, One More River 1959, JB 61, Photo Finish 1962, The Seagull 1964, Season of Goodwill 1964, The Homecoming 1965, 1968, Timon of Athens (Stratford) 1965, The Government Inspector 1966, Henry IV (Stratford) 1966, Plaza Suite 1969, The Happy Apple 1970, Sleuth (London 1970, New York 1971), Othello (Old Vic) 1974, Heartbreak House (Nat. Theatre) 1975, The Marrying of Ann Leete (Aldwych) 1975, The Return of A. J. Raffles (Aldwych) 1975, The Zykovs (Aldwych) 1976, Volpone, The Madras House (Nat. Theatre) 1977, Half Life (Nat. Theatre), Eclipse (Royal Court Theatre) 1978, Merchant of Venice (Birmingham Repertory Co.) 1979, You Never Can Tell (Lyric, Hammersmith) 1979, The Dresser (New York) 1981–82, The Importance of Being Earnest (Nat. Theatre) 1982, A Kind of Alaska (Nat. Theatre) 1982, The Applecart (Haymarket) 1986, Danger: Memory! (Hampstead Theatre, Old Vic) 1986, King Lear 1989, Other People's Money (Lyric) 1990. *Films include:* Murder in the Cathedral 1952, Beau Brummell 1954, The Beachcomber 1954, Svengali 1954, Our Man in Havana

1959, The Trials of Oscar Wilde 1960, A Circle of Deception 1960, No Love for Johnnie 1961, The Mark 1961, Life for Ruth 1962, The Pot Carriers 1962, The Wild and the Willing 1962, Billy Budd 1962, Stolen Hours 1963, The Third Secret 1964, He Who Rides a Tiger 1965, Decline and Fall… of a Birdwatcher 1968, A Midsummer Night's Dream 1968, The Shoes of the Fisherman 1968, The Looking-Glass War 1969, Three Into Two Won't Go 1969, The Reckoning 1969, I Want What I Want 1972, The Homecoming 1973, The Abdication 1974, Lost in the Stars 1974, The Old Curiosity Shop 1975, Nothing Lasts Forever 1984, Oscar and Lucinda 1997. *Television includes:* Othello 1955, A Midsummer Night's Dream 1958, The Prince and the Pauper 1962, Photo Finish 1966, A Tragedy of Two Ambitions 1973, Little Lord Fauntleroy 1976, Barriers (mini-series) 1980, The Executioner 1980, Struggle (series) 1983, Edwin 1984, Connie (series) 1985, London Embassy (mini-series) 1987, The Lady's Not for Burning 1987, Porterhouse Blue 1987, The Fear (series) 1988, The Tenth Man 1988, The Return of the Native 1994. *Leisure interests:* books, gardening. *Address:* 9 Hillside Gardens, Highgate, London, N6 5SU, England. *Telephone:* (20) 8340-2656.

ROGERS, Thomas (Tom) Sydney, BA, JD; American media executive and lawyer; *Vice-Chairman, Tivo, Inc.;* b. 19 Aug. 1954, New Rochelle, NY; s. of Sydney Michael Rogers Jr and Alice Steinhardt; m. Sylvia Texon 1983; two s. one d.; ed Wesleyan Univ., Columbia Univ.; attorney with Wall Street law firm 1979–81; called to New York Bar 1980; Sr Counsel US House of Reps Sub cttee on Telecommunications, Consumer Protection and Finance 1981–86; Vice-Pres. Policy Planning and Business Devt, NBC 1987–88; Pres. NBC Cable 1988–89, NBC Cable and Business Devt 1989–99; Exec. Vice-Pres. NBC 1992–99; Vice-Chair. NBC Internet 1999; Chair. and CEO Primedia Inc. 1999–2003; Chair. TRget Media LLC 2003–05; Sr Operating Exec. for media and entertainment, Cerberus Capital Man. (private equity firm) 2004–05; mem. Bd of Dirs Tivo, Inc. 2003, Vice-Chair. 2004–05, CEO and Pres. 2005–; mem. Bd of Dirs Teleglobe, Chair. 2004–; Pres. and CEO Int. Council, Nat. Acad. of TV Arts and Sciences 1994–97, Chair. 1998–99; mem. New York State Bar Asscn, Int. Radio and TV Soc. *Address:* Tivo Inc., 2160 Gold Street, POB 2160, Alviso, CA 95002-2160, USA (office). *Telephone:* (408) 519-9100 (office). *Fax:* (408) 519-5330 (office). *Website:* www.tivo.com (office).

ROGERS OF RIVERSIDE, Baron (Life Peer), cr. 1996, of Chelsea in the Royal Borough of Kensington and Chelsea; **Richard George Rogers,** Kt, CH, AADipl, MArch, RA; British architect; b. 23 July 1933, Florence, Italy; s. of Nino Rogers and Dada Geiringer; m. 1st Su Brumwell 1961; three s.; m. 2nd Ruth Elias 1973; two s.; ed Architectural Asscn, London, Yale Univ.; Fulbright, Edward D. Stone and Yale Scholar; Chair. Rogers Stirk Harbour Pnrs (fmrly Richard Rogers Partnership); Pres. Nat. Communities Resource Centre; Chief Advisor to the Mayor on Architecture and Urbanism; Dir River Café Ltd; Saarinen Prof., Yale Univ. 1985; has also taught at Architectural Asscn, London, at Cambridge, Princeton, Columbia, Harvard, Cornell, McGill and Aachen Univs and at UCLA; Vice-Chair. Arts Council of England 1994–97; mem. UN Architects' Cttee, Barcelona Urban Strategy Council; Trustee Tate Gallery 1981–89 (Chair. 1984–88), London First 1993–98, UK Bd Médecins du Monde; Reith Lecturer 1995; Hon. FRIBA, FAIA 1986; Hon. Chair. Architecture and Planning Group, House of Lords 2006–; Chevalier Légion d'honneur 1986; Dr hc (Westminster) 1993, (RCA) 1994, (Bath) 1994, (South Bank) 1996; Hon. DLitt (Univ. Coll., London) 1997; winner of numerous int. competitions, including Centre Pompidou, Paris 1971–77, Lloyd's HQ, London 1978; Constructa Prize 1986, 1992, Eternit Int. Prize 1988; 22 RIBA awards 1969–, Royal Gold Medal RIBA 1985, twelve Civic Trust Awards 1986–2006, Thomas Jefferson Memorial Foundation Medal in Architecture 1999, Praemium Imperiale Award 2000, Pritzker Laureate 2007, Minerva Medal 2007 and many other awards. *Works include:* major int. work: masterplanning: Royal Docks, London 1984–86, Potsdamer Platz, Berlin 1991, Shanghai Pu Dong Financial Dist 1992, Greenwich Peninsula Masterplan 1997–98; airports and HQ bldgs: PA Tech., Cambridge 1975–83, PA Tech., Princeton, NJ, USA 1984, European Court of Human Rights, Strasbourg 1990–95, Marseille Airport 1992, Law Courts, Bordeaux, France 1992–98, VR Techno offices and lab., Gifu, Japan 1993–98, Channel 4 HQ 1991–94; recent projects: masterplanning and design of Heathrow Airport Terminal 5 1989–, Montevetro Housing, Battersea, London 1994–2000, ParcBIT Devt, Majorca 1994–, Lloyd's Register of Shipping HQ, London 1995–99, 88 Wood Street, London 1995–99, New Millennium Experience, Greenwich, London 1996–99, Minami Yamashiro Primary School 1995–2003, Mossbourne Community Acad. 2002–04, masterplanning of Piana di Castello, Florence 1997–, New Area Terminal, Barajas Airport, Madrid (RIBA Stirling Prize 2006) 1997–2005, Nat. Ass. for Wales 1998–2006, Law Courts, Antwerp 1999–2006, 122 Leadenhall Street 2002–. *Publications:* Richard Rogers and Architects 1985, A+U: Richard Rogers 1978–88 1988, Architecture: A Modern View 1990, A New London (with Mark Fisher) 1992, Reith Lecturer 1995, Cities for a Small Planet 1997, Richard Rogers The Complete Works (Vols I–III) 1999, Cities for a Small Country 2000, Richard Rogers: Architecture of the Future 2006, Richard Rogers 2006. *Leisure interests:* friends, food, travel, art, architecture. *Address:* Thames Wharf, Rainville Road, London, W6 9HA; House of Lords, London, SW1A 0PW, England. *Telephone:* (20) 7385-1235; (20) 7219-5353 (House of Lords). *Fax:* (20) 7385-8409. *E-mail:* enquiries@rsh-p.com (office). *Website:* www.rsh-p.com (office).

ROGERSON, Philip Graham; British business executive; *Chairman, Carillion plc;* b. 1 Jan. 1945, Manchester; s. of Henry Rogerson and Florence Rogerson; m. Susan Janet Kershaw 1968; one s. two d.; ed William Hulme's Grammar School, Manchester; with Dearden Harper, Miller & Co. Chartered Accountants 1962–67; with Hill Samuel & Co. Ltd 1967–69; with Thomas Tilling Ltd 1969–71; with Steetly Ltd 1971–72; with J.W. Chafer Ltd 1972–78; joined ICI 1978, Gen. Man. Finance 1989–92; Man. Dir Finance British Gas PLC 1992–94, Exec. Dir 1994–96, Deputy Chair. 1996–98; Deputy Chair. (non-exec.) Aggreko PLC 1997–98; Chair. (non-exec.) Pipeline Integrity Int. 1998–, British Biotech 1999–, Octopus Capital PLC 2000–, Copper Eye Ltd 2001–, Thus Group plc 2004–, Carillion plc 2004–; Deputy Chair. Viridian Group PLC 1998, Chair. 1999–2005; Chair. (non-exec.) Aggreko PLC, Aggreko USA LLC), Bertram Group Ltd 1999–, Project Telecom PLC 2000–, KBC Advanced Technologies PLC; mem. Bd of Dirs (non-exec.) Halifax Bldg Soc. (now Halifax PLC) 1995–98, Shandwick Int. PLC 1997–, LIMIT PLC 1997, Int. Public Relations 1997–98, Wates City of London Properties 1998–; Trustee Changing Faces 1997–, School for Social Entrepreneurs 1997–. *Leisure interests:* golf, theatre, opera, ballet. *Address:* Carillion plc, Birch Street, Wolverhampton, WV1 4HY, England. *Telephone:* (19) 0244-2431 (office). *Fax:* (19) 0231-6165 (office). *Website:* www.carillionplc.com (office).

ROGGE, Jacques; Belgian international organization official and surgeon; *President, International Olympic Committee;* b. 1942, Ghent; m.; two c.; fmr orthopaedic surgeon and sports medicine lecturer; participated as Olympic sailing competitor 1968, 1972, 1976; Pres. Belgian Nat. Olympic Cttee 1989–92; Pres. European Olympic Cttee 1989–2001, Chef de mission, two winter and three summer Olympic Games (Chief Co-ordinator, Olympic Games 2000, 2004); mem. Int. Olympic Cttee (IOC) 1991–, Pres. 2001–; UNEP Champion of the Earth Laureate 2007. *Address:* International Olympic Committee, Château de Vidy, 1007 Lausanne, Switzerland (office). *Telephone:* (21) 6216111 (office). *Fax:* (21) 6216216 (office). *Website:* www.olympic.org (office).

ROGOFF, Ilan; Israeli concert pianist and conductor; b. 26 July 1943; s. of Boris Rogoff and Sofija Rogoff; m. Vesna Zorka Mimiça 1985; two d.; ed Israel Acad. of Music, Royal Conservatoire, Brussels, Mannes Coll., Juilliard School, New York; has performed all over Israel, Europe, N. America, Latin America, S. Africa, Japan and Far East with Israel Philharmonic Orchestra and many other orchestras; plays mostly works by Romantic composers including Beethoven, Schumann, Brahms, Chopin, Liszt, César Franck, Rachmaninov, Tchaikovsky, Piazzolla; has performed twentieth-century and contemporary works including world premiere of concerti by John McCabe and by Ivan Erod; has performed with various chamber music groups including Enesco Quartet, Orpheus Quartet, Amati Trio, Festival Ensemble, Matrix Quintet, Sharon Trio and Quartet, soloists of Vienna Chamber Orchestra and Vienna Philharmonic Orchestra; conducting début 1985, with Israel Philharmonic 1988; radio performances and TV appearances in UK, Spain, Austria, Germany, Israel, Canada, USA, SA, Colombia, Ecuador, Venezuela and Argentina; lectures and recital/lectures, masterclasses; various int. awards. *Recordings include:* Chopin in Mallorca, Chopin Concerti (version for piano and string quintet), Portraits by Schumann, numerous works by Bach–Busoni, César Franck, Schumann, Schubert, Chopin, Beethoven and Liszt, transcriptions for piano solo of works by Astor Piazzolla. *Publications:* Transcriptions for Piano Solo of Works by Astor Piazzolla, Ed Two Chopin Concerti for Piano and String Quartet; articles on music published in Scherzo magazine (Madrid), Piano magazine (London). *Leisure interests:* water sports, reading, visual arts, theatre, cinema and music research. *Address:* Estudio/Taller, Calle Bartomeu Fons 13, 07015 Palma de Mallorca, Spain (home). *Telephone:* (71) 707016 (home). *Fax:* (71) 707703 (home). *E-mail:* ilanrogoff@telefonica.net (home). *Website:* www.ilanrogoff.com.

ROGOFF, Kenneth S., BA, MA, PhD; American economist, international finance official and academic; *Thomas D. Cabot Professor of Public Policy, Harvard University;* b. 22 March 1953, Rochester, NY; s. of Stanley Miron Rogoff and June Beatrice Rogoff; m. Natasha Lanre; one s. one d.; ed Yale Univ., Massachusetts Inst. of Tech., Cambridge, Mass.; Economist, Int. Finance Div., Fed. Reserve Bd of Govs 1980–83; economist, Research Dept, IMF 1982–83; Assoc. Prof. of Econs, Univ. of Wis. 1985–88; Prof. of Econs, Univ. of Calif., Berkeley 1989–92; Prof. of Econs and Int. Affairs, Princeton Univ. 1992–94, Charles and Marie Robertson Prof. of Int. Affairs 1995–99; Prof. of Econs, Harvard Univ. 1999–, Thomas D. Cabot Prof. of Public Policy 2004–, Dir Harvard Center for Int. Devt 2003–04; Economic Counsellor and Dir, Research Dept, IMF 2001–05; Vice Pres. American Econ. Asscn 2007; Research Assoc. Nat. Bureau of Econ. Research 1985–; mem. Econ. Advisory Panel Fed. Reserve Bank of New York 2004–; mem. Academic Advisory Panel, Cen. Bank of Sweden 2005–; mem. Advisory Cttee Inst. for Int. Econs 2001–; Assoc. Ed. Review of Economics and Statistics 1993–, Economics Letters 1993–96, Journal of International Economics 1995–, Quarterly Journal of Economics 1984–95, Journal of Economic Perspectives 1987–90; mem. Council on Foreign Relations 2004–, Trilateral Comm. 2003–; Fellow, Econometric Soc. 1990–, German Marshall Foundation 1991, American Acad. of Arts and Sciences 2001–; World Econ. Forum Fellow 2003–; Guggenheim Fellow 1998; Nat. Fellow, Hoover Inst. 1986; Alfred P. Sloan Research Fellow 1986. *Achievements include:* Int. Grandmaster of Chess (World Chess Fed.) 1978–. *Publications include:* Foundations of International Macroeconomics (with Maurice Obstfeld) 1996, Workbook for Foundations of International Macroeconomics 1998; numerous contribs to learned journals and newspapers. *Leisure interests:* swimming, chess, cinema. *Address:* Harvard University, Department of Economics, Littauer Center 232, Cambridge, MA 02138-3001 (office); 3723 Harrison Street, NW, Washington, DC 20015, USA (home). *Telephone:* (617) 495-4022 (office); (202) 363-4529 (home). *Fax:* (617) 495-7730 (office). *E-mail:* krogoff@harvard.edu (office). *Website:* www.economics.harvard.edu/faculty/rogoff (home).

ROGOV, Sergey Mikhailovich, Dr. Hist.; Russian political scientist; *Director, Institute for USA and Canadian Studies, Russian Academy of Sciences;* b. 22 Oct. 1948, Moscow; m.; one s. one d.; ed Moscow State Inst. of Int. Relations; jr, sr researcher, head of sector Inst. for USA and Canadian Studies, Russian Acad. of Sciences 1976–84, Rep. of Inst. for USA and Canadian Studies to USSR Embassy, Washington, DC 1984–87, Leading

Research Fellow, Moscow 1987–89, Chief Dept of Mil. and Political Studies 1989–91, Deputy Dir 1991–95, Dir 1995–; mem. Scientific Council of Ministry of Foreign Affairs, of Security Council; counsellor Cttee on Foreign Relations of State Duma; mem. Russian Acad. of Nat. Sciences; Corresp. mem. Russian Acad. of Sciences 2002–. *Publications:* 16 books on foreign policy of USSR and Russian Fed., Russian-American relationship, mil. aspects of foreign policy, problems of nat. security and over 300 scientific publs and articles. *Address:* Institute for USA and Canadian Studies, Russian Academy of Sciences, Khlebny Pereulok 2/3, 121814 Moscow, Russia (office). *Telephone:* (495) 290-58-75 (office). *Fax:* (495) 200-12-07 (office). *E-mail:* srogov@rambler.ru (office). *Website:* iskran.iip.net/engl/index-en.html (office).

ROGOWSKI, Michael, Dr rer. pol; German business executive; *Chairman, Supervisory Board, Voith AG;* b. 13 March 1939, Stuttgart; m. Gabriele Rogowski; two c.; ed Univ. of Lausanne, Technical Univ. of Karlsruhe; Man. Dir SISCO GmbH, Frankfurt 1973; joined J.M. Voith GmbH (Voith later AG) as Dir of Personnel and Stock Man., Dir Propulsion Tech. Div. 1982–92, Man. Rep. 1986–92, Chair. Man. Bd 1992–97, Chair. Group Exec. Bd 1997–2000, Chair. Supervisory Bd 2000–; Vice-Chair. Freudenberg & Co. Kommanditgesellschaft; mem. Presidency, Bund Deutscher Industrie (BDI), Vice-Pres. 1997–98, Pres. 2001–04; mem. Supervisory Bd Talanx AG/HDI Versicherung, IKB Deutsche Industrie-Bank AG, Carl Zeiss AG, Kloeckner & Co. AG; fmr mem. Supervisory Bd KSB AG (resgnd 2005), KfW Kreditanstalt für Wiederaufbau (resgnd 2005), Deutsche Messe AG (resgnd 2005); mem. Bd of Dirs Stichting Administratiekantoor EADS; mem. Pay Policy Council Gesamtmetall (Metal Workers' Union); mem. Bd Asscn of German Mechanical and Plant Engineers (VDMA) 1992–, Vice-Pres. 1993, Pres. 1996–98; mem. Advisory Bd Carlyle Europe Pnrs 2002–. *Address:* Voith AG, St Pöltenerstrasse 43, PO Box 2000, 89522 Heidenheim, Germany (office). *Telephone:* (7321) 370000 (office). *Fax:* (7321) 3770000 (office). *Website:* www.voith.de (office).

ROGOZHKIN, Aleksandr Vladimirovich; Russian scriptwriter and film director; b. 3 Oct. 1950, Leningrad; ed Leningrad State Univ., All-Union Inst. of Cinematography; worked in TV cos in Leningrad; cinema debut in 1980s. *Films directed include:* Ryzhaya, ryzhaya 1981, Radi neskolkikh strochek 1985, Miss millionersha 1988, Karaul (FIPRESCI Prize for Best Film Moscow Int. Film Festival, Alfred Bauer Prize, Berlin Festival 1989) 1989, The Guard 1990, Tretya planeta (also writer) 1991, Chekist 1992, Akt (also writer) 1993, Zhizn s idiotom (also writer) 1993, Osobennosti natsionalnoy okhoty (also writer, Nika Award for Best Dir) 1995, Blokpost (story, Silver Dolphin for Best Dir Tróia Int. Film Festival 1998, Best Dir Karlovy Vary Int. Film Festival 1998) 1998, Osobennosti natsionalnoy rybalki (also writer) 1998, Boldino Fall 1999, Osobennosti natsionalnoy okhoty v zimniy period 2000, Kukushka (also writer, Grand Prix Honfleur Festival of Russian Cinema, Dialog Prize 2002, Silver Dolphin for Best Dir Tróia Int. Film Festival 2002, FIPRESCI Prize for Best Film Moscow Int. Film Festival, Nika Award for Best Film and Best Dir) 2002, Sapiens (also writer) 2004, Peregon (also writer) 2006. *Address:* Gertsena str. 21, apt 8, 191065 St Petersburg, Russia (home). *Telephone:* (812) 311-76-81 (home).

ROGOZIN, Dmitry Olegovich, CandPhil; Russian journalist, politician and diplomatist; *Ambassador to NATO;* b. 21 Dec. 1963, Moscow; s. of Oleg Konstantinovich Rogozin and Tamara Rogozina; m. Tatyana Serebryakova; one s.; ed Moscow State Univ.; worked in USSR Cttee of Youth Orgs; one of founders Research and Educ. Co. RAU Corp. 1986–90; one of Party of People's Freedom 1990; Pres. Asscn of Young Political Leaders of Russia Forum-90; f. Congress of Russian Communities 1993; active in nat. movt; took part in resurrection of numerous churches; mem. State Duma (Regions of Russia, now Rodina) 1997–; Co-Founder and Leader Rodina pre-election bloc 2003, Leader Rodina—People's Patriotic Union faction 2004–; Chair. Cttee on Int. Affairs 2000–03, Deputy Chair. 2003–04; Deputy Chair. Cttee on Nationalities, State Duma; Chief Negotiator with EU on problems of Kaliningrad Region –2004; Amb. to NATO 2008–. *Publications:* Russian Answer 1996 and other books and articles on Russian people and Russian Culture. *Leisure interests:* master of sports, handball. *Address:* Mission of the Russian Federation to NATO, NATO Headquarters, Blvd Leopold III, 1110 Brussels, Belgium (office). *Telephone:* (2) 707-41-11 (office). *Fax:* (2) 707-45-79 (office). *E-mail:* natodoc@hq.nato.int (home). *Website:* www.nato.int (office).

ROH, Moo-hyun; South Korean politician and fmr head of state; b. 1946, Kimhae, S. Kyonsang Prov.; m.; one s. one d.; ed Pusan Commercial High School; mil. service, rank of corporal; served as judge in Taejon Dist court 1977; practised as human rights lawyer 1978; elected lawmaker 1988; elected mem. ruling Millennium Democratic Party's (MDP, later renamed Democratic Party) Supreme Council 2000–03; Minister of Maritime Affairs and Fisheries 2000–01; Pres. of the Repub. of Korea 2003–08; stripped of constitutional powers following impeachment vote March 2004, returned to office May 2004 after Constitutional Court overturned impeachment. *Leisure interests:* mountain climbing and bowling. *Address:* Democratic Party, 15, Gisan Bldg, Yeongdeungpo-gu, Seoul, Republic of Korea (office). *Telephone:* (2) 784-7007 (office). *Fax:* (2) 784-6070 (office). *Website:* www.minjoo.or.kr (office).

ROH, Tae-woo; South Korean politician; b. 4 Dec. 1932, Daegu; m. Roh (née Kim) Ok Sook 1959; one s. one d.; ed Taegu Tech. School, Kyongbuk High School, Korean Mil. Acad., US Special Warfare School, Repub. of Korea War Coll.; served in Korean War 1950; Commanding Gen. 9th Special Forces Brigade 1974–79, 9th Infantry Div. Jan.–Dec. 1979, Commdr Capital Security Command 1979–80, Defence Security Command 1980–81, Four-Star Gen. 1981, retd from army July 1981; Minister of State for Nat. Security and Foreign Affairs 1981–82, Minister of Sports 1982, of Home Affairs 1982; Pres. Repub. of Korea 1988–93; mem. Nat. Ass. 1985; Chair. Democratic Justice Party 1985–87, Pres. 1987–90; Jt Pres. Democratic Liberal Party (DLP)

1990–92 (had to quit the ruling party by agreement); Pres. Seoul Olympic Organizing Cttee 1983, Korean Amateur Sports Asscn 1984, Korean Olympic Cttee 1984; arrested Nov. 1995, charged with aiding Dec. 1979 Coup Dec. 1995; also charged with taking bribes; convicted of mutiny and treason, sentenced to 22½ years' imprisonment Aug. 1996; numerous decorations. *Publications:* Widaehan pot'ougsaram ui shidae 1987, Korea: A Nation Transformed 1990. *Leisure interests:* tennis, swimming, golf, music, reading.

ROHANI, Hassan, DJur, PhD; Iranian government official; b. 1948; ed Qom; fmr Deputy Speaker, Majlis (parl.); currently mem. and rep. of Ayatollah Khamenei, Supreme Leader of Iran on Supreme Nat. Security Council (Sec. –2005); Deputy Chair. Expediency Council; Dir Center for Strategic Studies, Iran; mem. Ass. of Experts. *Address:* Center for Strategic Studies, No. 840, Opposite Niavaran Park, Tehran 19547, Iran (office). *Telephone:* (21) 2295051 (office). *Fax:* (21) 2801272 (office). *E-mail:* info@csr.ir (office). *Website:* www.csr.ir (office).

ROHATYN, Felix George; American investment banker and diplomatist; *Senior Advisor, Lehman Brothers Holdings Inc.;* b. 29 May 1928, Vienna, Austria; s. of Alexander Rohatyn and Edith Rohatyn (née Knoll); m. 1st Jeannette Streit 1956; three s.; m. 2nd Elizabeth Fly 1979; ed Middlebury Coll., Vt; moved to USA 1942; joined Lazard Freres & Co. (investment bankers) 1948, Gen. Pnr 1961–97; Amb. to France 1997–2000; Founder and Pres. Rohatyn Assocs LLC 2001–; Sr Advisor Lehman Brothers Holdings Inc. 2006–; mem. Bd of Govs NY Stock Exchange 1968–72; Chair. Municipal Assistance Corpn (MAC) 1975–93; mem. Bd of Dirs LVMH (Moet Hennessy Louis Vuitton), Publicis Groupe SA, Rothschild Continuation Holdings AG, Lagardere; Trustee, Center for Strategic and Int. Studies; mem. Council on Foreign Relations; mem. American Acad. of Arts and Sciences; eight hon. degrees; Commdr, Légion d'honneur. *Publications:* The Twenty-Year Century: Essays on Economics and Public Finance 1983, Money Games: My Journey Through American Capitalism 1950–2000 2003, Bold Endeavors: How our Government Built America, and Why it Must Rebuild Now 2009. *Address:* Rohatyn Associates LLC, 280 Park Avenue, 27th Floor, New York, NY 10017 (office); Lehman Brothers Holdings Inc., 745 7th Avenue, New York, NY 10019, USA (office). *Telephone:* (212) 984-2975 (office); (212) 526-7000 (Lehman Brothers) (office). *Fax:* (212) 984-2976 (office); (212) 526-8766 (Lehman Brothers) (office). *E-mail:* felix.rohatyn@rohatyn.com (office). *Website:* www.lehman.com (office).

ROHDE, Bruce C., BBA, JD; American lawyer and food industry executive; *Chairman and CEO Emeritus, ConAgra Foods Inc.;* b. 17 Dec. 1948, Sidney, Neb.; ed Creighton Univ., Omaha, NE Creighton School of Law; with McGrath, North, Mullin and Kratz (law firm) 1973–96; Pres. and Vice-Chair. ConAgra Foods Inc. 1996–97, CEO 1997–98, Chair. and CEO 1998–2005, now Chair. and CEO Emer.; mem. Bd of Dirs Grocery Mfrs of America, Preventive Medicine Research Inst.; Vice-Chair. Bd of Dirs Creighton Univ., Nat. Campaign Chair. Willing to Lead: The Campaign for Creighton Univ. 2005–; Chair. Bd Dirs Strategic Air and Space Museum; mem. Pvt. and Public, Scientific, Academic and Consumer Food Policy Cttee (PAPSAC), Harvard Univ.; mem. STRATCOM (US Strategic Command) Consultation Cttee; mem. Nat. Infrastructure Advisory Council, US Dept of Homeland Security; Business Information Professional of the Year Award 2000, Frost & Sullivan Food and Beverage CEO of the Year 2004. *Address:* c/o Willing to Lead: The Campaign for Creighton University, Development Office, 2500 California Plaza, Omaha, NE 68178, USA (office).

ROHDE, Helmut; German politician and journalist; b. 9 Nov. 1925, Hanover; m. 1st Hanna Müller 1950; one s.; m. 2nd Ruth Basenaü 1983; ed Acad. for Labour, Political Studies and Econs; journalist, German Press Agency; Press Officer, Ministry for Social Affairs, Lower Saxony; mem. Parl. (Bundestag) 1957–87; mem. European Parl. 1964; Parl. State Sec. Fed. Ministry of Labour and Social Affairs 1969–74; Chair. SPD Working Group for Issues Concerning Employees 1973–84; Fed. Minister for Educ. and Science 1974–78; Deputy Chair. SPD, Bundestag 1979; Prof., Univ. of Hanover 1985–; Hon. Prof. (Univ. Bremen) 1994; Paul Klinger Prize 1974, Gold Medal, Asscn of War-Blinded, Grosses Bundesverdienstkreuz mit Stern und Schulterband 1995, Landesmedaille, Lower Saxony 1995. *Publications:* Sozialplanung – Theorie und Praxis der deutschen Sozialdemokratie, Gesellschaftspolitische Planung und Praxis, Für eine soziale Zukunft; numerous articles on social and education policy. *Leisure interests:* modern art, music, modern jazz. *Address:* c/o Sozialdemokratische Partei Deutschlands (SPD) (Social Democratic Party of Germany) Willy-Brandt-Haus, Wilhelmstr. 141, 10963 Berlin; Sanddornweg 3, 53757 St Augustin, Germany. *Telephone:* (2241) 333593.

ROHMER, Eric, (pseudonym of Maurice Henri Joseph Schérer); French film director; b. 21 March 1920, Tulle, Corrèze; s. of Antoine Schérer and Marie Monzat; m. Thérèse Barbet 1957; two s.; ed in Paris; school teacher and journalist until 1955; film critic of Revue du cinéma, Arts, Temps modernes, La Parisienne 1949–63; Co-founder and fmr Co-editor La Gazette du cinéma (review); fmr co-editor Cahiers du cinéma; Co-dir Soc. des Films du Losange 1964–; made educational films for French TV 1964–70; Officier des Arts et Lettres, Chevalier, Légion d'honneur; Prix Max-Ophuls 1970 (for Ma nuit chez Maud); Prix Louis-Delluc 1971, Prix du Meilleur Film du Festival de Saint-Sébastien 1971, Prix Méliès 1971 (all for Le genou de Claire), Prix Special Soc. des Auteurs et Compositeurs 1982, Best Dir Award, Berlin Film Festival 1983, Lifetime Achievement Golden Lion Award, Venice Film Festival 2001. *Wrote and directed:* Présentation ou Charlotte et son steak 1951, Véronique et son cancre 1958, Le signe du lion (first feature) 1959, La boulangère de Monceau 1962, La carrière de Suzanne 1963, La collectionneuse 1966, Ma nuit chez Maud 1969, Le genou de Claire 1970, L'amour l'après-midi 1972, La Marquise d'O 1976, Percival le Gallois 1978, La Femme de l'Aviateur, Le Beau Mariage 1981, Pauline à la Plage 1982, Les Nuits de la pleine lune 1984, Le Rayon Vert

1985, Four Adventures of Reinette and Mirabelle 1986, My Girlfriend's Boyfriend 1986, A Tale of Springtime 1990, A Winter's Tale 1992, L'Arbre, Le Maire et la Mediathèque 1993, Les Rendez-vous de Paris 1995, Conte d'été 1996, An Autumn Tale 1998, The Lady and the Duke 2001, Triple Agent 2004, Le canapé rouge 2005, Les Amours d'Astrée et de Céladon 2007. *Publications:* Alfred Hitchcock, Charlie Chaplin 1973, Six contes moraux 1974, L'organisation de l'espace dans le "Faust" de Murnau 1977, The Taste for Beauty 1991, Mozart or Beethoven 1995. *Address:* Les Films du Losange, 22 avenue Pierre 1er de Serbie, 75116 Paris, France. *Telephone:* 1-44-43-87-10.

ROHNER, Marcel, PhD; Swiss banker; *Group CEO, UBS AG;* b. 4 Sept. 1964; ed Univ. of Zürich; research and teaching asst, Inst. for Empirical Research in Econs, Univ. of Zürich 1990–92; Asst to the Global Head of Derivatives, Union Bank of Switzerland 1992–93; Int. Finance Div. Controlling, Market Risk Control, SBC Zürich 1993–95; Head, Market Risk Control Europe, Warburg Dillon Read 1995–98; Head, Market Risk Control UBS AG 1998–99, Group Chief Risk Officer 1999–2001, COO and Deputy CEO Pvt. Pvt. Banking unit of UBS Switzerland 2001–02, mem. Group Exec. Bd 2002–, CEO Wealth Man. and Business Banking 2002–04, Chair. and CEO Wealth Man. and Business Banking 2004–05, Deputy Group CEO 2006–07, Group CEO 2007–, Chair. and CEO Investment Bank 2007–08; Vice-Chair. Swiss Bankers Asscn, Bd of Trustees, Swiss Finance Inst. *Address:* UBS AG, Postfach 8098, Zürich, Switzerland (office). *Telephone:* 442341111 (office). *Fax:* 442399111 (office). *E-mail:* info@ubs.com (office). *Website:* www.ubs.com (office).

ROHOVIY, Vasyl Vasylyovich, CandEcons; Ukrainian politician and economist; b. 2 March 1953, Mirivka, Kiev region; s. of Vasyl Loginovich and Zinaida Mikhailivna Rohoviy; m. Svetlana Mikhailivna Rogovaya; one s.; ed Kiev Inst. of National Econs, Ukrainian Acad. of Sciences; engineer and economist Kiev Artem Production co. 1974–75, 1976–77; sr mechanic Odessa Mil. Command 1975–76; jr researcher Inst. of Econs, then Scientific Sec. Dept of Econs, Ukrainian Acad. of Sciences 1980–88; Chief Expert, Head of Sector, then Head of Div. Ukrainian Council of Ministers 1988–94; First Deputy Minister of Econs 1994–98, Minister 1998–99, 2000–01; First Deputy Head of Admin., Office of the Pres. 2000; Deputy Prime Minister for Econ. Policy 2001–02; Presidential Adviser 2002; currently Deputy Sec. of Econ, Social and Environmental Security Council, Nat. Security and Defense Council of Ukraine; apptd mem. Supervisory Council UkrExImBank JSC—State Export-Import Bank of Ukraine 2003. *Address:* c/o Council of National Security and Defense of Ukraine, 11 Bankova str., 01220 Kiev, Ukraine (office). *Telephone:* (44) 254-40-25. *Website:* www.rainbow.gov.ua.

ROHR, Hans Christoph von, PhD; German business executive; *Chairman, FIW German Institute for Competition and Market Economy;* b. 1 July 1938, Stettin; s. of Hansjoachim von Rohr; m.; two c.; ed Univs of Heidelberg, Vienna, Bonn and Kiel and Princeton Univ.; joined Klöckner-Werke AG, Bremen; subsequently held leading position with Klöckner subsidiary in Argentina; worked for Fisser & von Doornum, Einden; mem. Bd Klöckner & Co. Duisburg 1984; Chair. Exec. Bd Klöckner-Werke AG 1991–95; Man. Chair. Industrial Investment Council GmbH 1997; Chair. (non-exec.) ING Barings (Germany) 1996–2001; Chair. FIW German Inst. for Competition and Market Economy, Cologne; Chair. Supervisory Bd Balfour Beatty GmbH, Munich; Partner, TaylorWessing Lawyers, Düsseldorf. *Address:* Semmelweisstrasse 34, 45470 Mülheim, Ruhr, Germany.

ROHRER, Hans Heinrich, PhD; Swiss physicist; b. 3 June 1933, Buchs, St Gallen; m. Rose-Marie Egger 1961; two d.; ed Swiss Fed. Inst. of Tech.; Post-Doctoral Fellow, Rutgers Univ., NJ 1961–63; with IBM Research Lab., Rüschlikon 1963–97; sabbatical, Univ. of Calif., Santa Barbara 1974–75; research appointments at CSIC, Madrid 1997–2001, RIKEN, Waco, Japan 1998, Tohoku Univ., Sendai, Japan 1997–2005; mem. Swiss Acad. of Tech. Sciences 1998–; Foreign Assoc. NAS 1988–; Hon. mem. Swiss Physical Soc. 1990–, Swiss Asscn of Engineers and Architects 1991–; Hon. DSc (Rutgers Univ.) 1986; Dr hc (Marseille, Madrid) 1988, (Tsukuba, Japan) 1994, (Wolfgang Goethe Univ., Frankfurt) 1995, (Tohoku, Japan 2000; King Faisal Int. Prize for Science 1984, Hewlett Packard Europhysics Prize 1984, Nobel Prize for Physics (with Ernst Ruska and Gerd Binnig) for work in pioneering devt of scanning tunnelling microscope 1986; Cresson Medal, Franklin Inst., Phila 1986; named to Nat. Inventors Hall of Fame 1994. *Address:* Rebbergstr. 9D, 8832, Wollerau, Switzerland (home). *Telephone:* (1) 7841572 (home). *Fax:* (1) 7841379 (home). *E-mail:* h.rohrer@gmx.net (home).

ROITHOVÁ, Zuzana, DenM, MBA; Czech physician and politician; b. 30 Jan. 1953, Prague; m.; one s.; ed Charles Univ., Prague, Wharton Univ., USA, Sheffield Hallam Univ., UK; radiologist, Dist Hosp., Beroun 1978–79, Univ. Hosp. Motol, Prague 1979–85, Univ. Hosp., Kralovske Vinohadry, Prague 1985–90 (Dir 1990–98); Vice-Chair. Hosp. Asscn of Czech Repub. 1991–98; Minister of Health Jan.–June 1998; Senator 1998–2004, Chair. Senate Cttee on Health Care and Social Policy 2000–02; Chair. Int. European Movt in Czech Repub. 2000–02; mem. Perm. Del. of Czech Parl. to WEU; mem. European Parl. (Group of European People's Party—Christian Democrats and European Democrats) 2004–, Vice-Chair. Cttee on the Internal Market and Consumer Protection, Substitute mem. Cttee on Women's Rights and Gender Equality, mem. Del. for Relations with the Countries of Cen. America, Del. to ACP-EU Jt Parl. Ass.; Pres. Czech Council of European Movt 2000–01; Deputy Chair. Christian Democratic Union-Czechoslovak People's Party (Křesťanská a demokratická unie-Československá strana lidová—KDU-ČSL) Party 2001–03; Chair. Admin. Bd Hosp. of Merciful Sisters of St Karel Boromejsky 2002–05; Charles Univ. Jubilee Medal 1998. *Publications include:* papers in medical journals. *Leisure interests:* sport, mountaineering. *Address:* European Parliament, Bâtiment Altiero Spinelli, ASP 3F365, 60 rue Wiertz, 1047 Brussels, Belgium (office). *Telephone:* (2) 284-54-85. *Fax:* (2) 284-94-85 (office). *E-mail:* zroithova@europarl.eu.int (office). *Website:* www.europarl.eu.int (office); www.roithova.cz.

ROIZMAN, Bernard, ScD; American scientist and academic; *Joseph Regenstein Distinguished Service Professor of Virology, Departments of Microbiology, Molecular Genetics and Cell Biology and Biochemistry and Molecular Biology, University of Chicago;* b. 17 April 1929, Romania; m. Betty Cohen 1950; two s.; ed Temple Univ., Phila, Pa, Johns Hopkins Univ., Baltimore, Md; Instructor of Microbiology, Johns Hopkins Univ. 1956–57, Research Assoc. 1957–58, Asst Prof. 1958–65; Assoc. Prof. of Microbiology, Univ. of Chicago 1965–69, Prof. 1969–84, Prof. of Biophysics 1970–, Chair. Interdepartmental Cttee on Virology 1969–85, 1988–, Joseph Regenstein Prof. of Virology 1981–83, Joseph Regenstein Distinguished Service Prof. of Virology 1984–; Chair. Dept of Molecular Genetics and Cell Biology 1985–88; fmr Ed. of numerous specialist scientific publs and mem. Editorial Bd Journal of Virology 1970–, Intervirology 1972–85, Virology 1976–78, 1983–; Ed.-in-Chief Infectious Agents and Diseases 1992–96; mem. or fmr mem. numerous grant review panels, int. panels, including Chair. Herpes Virus Study Group, Int. Cttee for Taxonomy of Viruses 1971–94, Chair. Bd of Dirs 1991–; Scientific Advisory Bd, Showa Univs Center 1983–; mem. Int. Microbial Genetics Comm., Int. Asscn of Microbiological Sciences 1979–86; numerous nat. panels on vaccines, cancers; Scholar in Cancer Research at American Cancer Soc., Inst. Pasteur (with Andre Lwoff), Paris 1961–62; Travelling Fellow, Int. Agency for Research Against Cancer (with Dr Klein), Stockholm, Sweden 1970; Fellow, Japanese Soc. for Promotion of Science, American Acad. of Arts and Sciences, American Acad. of Microbiology; mem. NAS, Inst. of Medicine, American Asscn of Immunologists, Soc. for Experimental Biology and Medicine, American Soc. for Microbiology (ASM), for Biological Chemists, Soc. for Gen. Microbiology (UK), American Soc. for Virology, Chinese Acad. of Eng, Hungarian Acad. of Science; Hon. DHumLitt (Govs State Univ., Ill.) 1984; Hon. MD (Ferrara) 1991; Hon. DSc (Paris) 1997, (Valladolid, Spain) 2001; J. Allyn Taylor Int. Prize in Medicine 1997, Bristol-Myers Squibb Award for Distinguished Achievement in Infectious Disease Research 1998, ICN Int. Prize in Virology 1988, NIH Outstanding Investigator Award 1988–2001, NIH-NCI Merit Award 2003, ASM Life-time Achievement Award 2008. *Publications:* author or co-author of approx. 600 papers in scientific journals and books; ed. or co-ed. of 20 books. *Address:* Marjorie B. Kohler Viral Oncology Laboratories, University of Chicago, 910 East 58th Street, Chicago, IL 60637 (office); 5555 South Everett Avenue, Chicago, IL 60637, USA (home). *Telephone:* (773) 702-1898 (office); (773) 493-2986 (home). *Fax:* (773) 702-1631 (office); (773) 493-9042 (home). *E-mail:* bernard.roizman@bsd.uchicago.edu (office). *Website:* microbiology.uchicago.edu/roizman.htm (office).

ROJAS DE MORENO DÍAZ, María Eugenia; Colombian politician; *Leader, Alianza Nacional Popular (ANAPO);* b. 1934; d. of the late Gen. Gustavo Rojas Pinilla (Pres. of Colombia 1953–57); m. Samuel Moreno Díaz; two s.; fmr mem. of the Senate; Majority Leader, Bogotá City Council; Leader Alianza Nacional Popular (ANAPO) 1975–. *Address:* Alianza Nacional Popular (ANAPO), Carrera 18, No 33-95, Santa Fe de Bogotá, DC, Colombia. *Telephone:* (1) 287-7050 (office). *Fax:* (1) 245-3138 (office). *E-mail:* anapo@neutel.net.co (office).

ROJAS PENSO, Juan Francisco; Venezuelan economist and consultant; b. 18 Sept. 1952; ed Andrés Bello Catholic Univ., Caracas and CENDES; Prof., Univ. Cen. de Venezuela and Univ. Simón Bolívar; Official, Council of Acuerdo de Cartagena (Cartagena Agreement, now Andean Community of Nations) 1977–79, 1982–85, Alt. Plenipotentiary Rep. and Dir Corporación Andina de Fomento 1985–87; Councillor (Econ. Affairs) to Colombia 1980–81; Dir-Gen. of Econ. Integration, Venezuelan Inst. of Foreign Trade 1985–87; Dir Commercial Policy Dept, Latin American Integration Asscn 1989–93, Deputy Sec.-Gen. 1993–99, Sec.-Gen. 1999–2005; ind. consultant to various orgs including Andean Community of Nations, OAS, Friedrich Ebert Foundation, numerous cos. and trade unions; columnist for Question (magazine), Venezuela Analítica, Aporrea.org, Tinku.org, IntegraciónyComercio.com, Redvoltairenet.org. *E-mail:* jrojas_penso@yahoo.es. *Website:* www.analitica.com.

ROJAS RAMÍREZ, José Alejandro, PhD; Venezuelan politician and economist; *Executive Director, The World Bank;* b. 3 Sept. 1959, Caracas; s. of José Alejandro Rojas Leon and Carmen Ramírez Tovar; m.; one s.; ed Universidad Central de Venezuela, Inst. of Petroleum and Univ. of Paris II (Sorbonne), France; fmr Sr Economist, Office of Programming and Macroeconomic Analysis, IDB, also Gov. (for Venezuela), IDB; Exec. Dir for Panama and Venezuela, Inter American Devt Bank, Washington, DC; Deputy Minister, then Minister of Finance 1999–2001; fmr Adviser to Pres. and Bd of Dirs, Cen. Bank of Venezuela; fmr Vice-Pres. Petroleos de Venezuela (PDVSA) 2004; Pres. Ass. of Fondo Latinoamericano de Reservas (FLAR), Consultant Council, Andean Community of Nations; Alt. Exec. Dir (representing Mexico, Costa Rica, El Salvador, Guatemala, Honduras, Nicaragua, Venezuela and Spain), World Bank, Washington, DC –2008, Exec. Dir 2008–; mem. Bd of Dirs Compañía de Energía Eléctrica del Estado Venezolano (CADAFE), Electrificación del Caroni (EDELCA) CA; consultant several cos and orgs; Dir Quantitative Methods Dept, Universidad Central de Venezuela, mem. Postgrad. Scientific Cttee; Prof. of Econometrics and Math. Econs, Universidad Católica Andrés Bello, Caracas, of Operational Research, Instituto Politécnico de las Fuerzas Armadas, Caracas; mem. Colegio de Estadístico de Venezuela, Royal Econometric Soc., UK. *Publications:* numerous research papers. *Address:* MC12-1211, World Bank Group, 1818 H Street, NW, Washington, DC 20433, USA (office). *Telephone:* (202) 458-2095 (office). *Fax:* (202) 522-1575 (office). *E-mail:* jrojasramirez@worldbank.org (office). *Website:* www.worldbank.org (office).

ROJO, Luis Angel, PhD; Spanish economist, academic and fmr central banker; *Member, Board of Directors and Adviser, Banco Santander Central Hispano, SA;* b. 6 May 1934, Madrid; s. of Luis Rojo and Luisa Duque de Rojo; m. Concepción de Castro 1958; two s. one d.; ed Univ. of Madrid and London School of Econs; economist, Research Dept Ministry of Commerce 1959–68; Asst Prof. Dept of Econ. Analysis, Faculty of Econs, Complutense Univ. of Madrid, 1959–65, Prof. of Econ. Analysis 1966–84, now Prof. Emer.; Gen. Dir of Research and Studies, Bank of Spain 1971–88, Deputy Gov. 1988, Gov. –2000; Adviser to IMF 2002; mem. Bd of Dirs and Adviser to Banco Santander Central Hispano, SA 2005–, Chair. Audit Cttee 2006–; Chair. Fundación pro Real Academia; mem. Bd of Dirs Corporación Financiera Alba; mem. Group of Wise Men apptd by ECOFIN Council to study integration of European financial markets; mem. Academia de Ciencias Morales y Políticas 1985–, Asociación de Amigos del Museo del Prado, Spanish Royal Acad. of Language.; Premio Rey Juan Carlos I de Economía 1986, Premio Rey Jaime I de Economía 2006. *Publications:* Keynes y el pensamiento macroeconómico actual 1965, El Nuevo Monetarismo 1971, Renta, precios y balanza de pagos 1975, Marx: Economía y sociedad (with V. Pérez Díaz) 1984, Keynes: su tiempo y el nuestro 1984. *Address:* c/o Board of Dirs, Banco Santander Central Hispano, SA, Plaza de Canalejas, 1, 28014 Madrid, Spain (office). *Telephone:* (91) 5881111 (office). *Website:* www.gruposantander.com (office).

ROJO GARCÍA, Francisco Javier; Spanish politician; *President of the Senate;* b. 2 March 1949, Pamplona; m.; two d.; early political work with Gen. Workers Union 1976–79; Prov. Councillor, Álava 1979–83, City Councillor for Vitoria-Gasteiz (Álava) 1983–84; mem. Gen. Ass. of Álava 1983–87; Councillor of the Presidency of Álava 1987–93, Deputy Mayor of Vitoria-Gasteiz 1991–96; Senator for Álava 1993–2004, Pres. of the Senate 2004–; mem. Basque Parl. 2001–02, mem. Human Rights Cttee and Basque Radio and TV Control Cttee; Sec.-Gen. Basque Socialist Party-Basque Left (PSE-EE), Álava 2000–05, Pres. 2005–; Sec. of Institutional Relations, Spanish Socialist Workers' Party (PSOE) Fed. Exec. Comm. 2002–04; Grand Cross, Order of Civil Merit, Grand Cross, Isabel la Católica; Dr hc (Piura Public Univ., Peru) 2006. *Address:* Office of the President of the Senate, Plaza de la Marina Española 8, 28071 Madrid, Spain (office). *Telephone:* (91) 5381000 (office). *Fax:* (91) 5381003 (office). *E-mail:* webmaster@senado.es (office). *Website:* www.senado.es (office).

ROKITA, Jan, LLM; Polish politician and lawyer; b. 18 June 1959, Kraków; s. of Tadeusz Rokita and Adela Rokita; m. Nelli Arnold 1994; one d.; ed Jagiellonian Univ., Pontifical Acad. of Theology, Kraków; fmr active mem. of Independent Students' Union (NZS) 1980–82; interned under Martial Law 1982; banned by the Communist authorities from practising law 1983–89; co-founder and participant Freedom and Peace Movt 1985–88; founder and mem. Intervention and Law-abidingness Comm. of Solidarity Trade Union 1986–89; mem. Civic Cttee attached to Lech Wałęsa (q.v.) 1988–90; organizer and Chair. Int. Conf. on Human Rights, Kraków 1988; participant Round Table negotiations 1989; Chair. Special Parl. Comm. of Inquiry in respect of archives of the former Communist Security Service (Rokita Comm.) 1989–90; Deputy Chair. Civic Parl. Caucus 1989–90, Deputy Chair. Democratic Union Parl. Caucus 1991–96, Deputy Chair. Freedom Union Parl. Caucus 1996–97, mem. Solidarity Election Action Parl. Caucus 1997–2001; Deputy Chair. Civic Platform Parl. Caucus 2001–03, Chair. 2003–05; Chair. Parl. Comm. for Admin. and Internal Affairs 1997–2000; Minister-Chief of Office of Council of Ministers 1992–93; Chair. Conservative People's Party (SKL) 1998–2001; mem. Special Parl. Comm. of Inquiry into the Rywin Affair 2003–04; mem. Civic Platform (PO) (Platforma Obywatelska); POLCUL Foundation Award (Australia) 1988, Stefan Kisielewski Award 2003, Edward J. Wende Award 2003, Man of the Year (Wprost weekly magazine, Poland) 2003, Top Parliamentarian (Polityka weekly magazine, Poland) 2003. *Publications:* political and historical journalism; Alfabet Rokity 2004. *Leisure interests:* classical music, jazz, ancient Greek philosophy, bicycle riding. *Address:* Biuro Posła Jana Rokity, 31-143 Kraków, ul. Basztowa 15/10, Poland. *Telephone:* (12) 4300186. *Fax:* (12) 4263560. *Website:* www.janrokita.pl.

ROLANDIS, Nikos A.; Cypriot politician, business executive and barrister; b. 10 Dec. 1934, Limassol; m. Lelia Aivaliotis; one s. two d.; ed Pancyprian Gymnasium Nicosia, Middle Temple, London; called to the bar, Middle Temple 1956; practised law in Cyprus for short time before entering business; owner of industrial and commercial cos; Founding mem. Democratic Group (now Democratic Party); f. Liberal Party 1986, Pres. 1986–98; Minister of Foreign Affairs 1978–83; mem. House of Reps 1991–96; Vice-Pres. Liberal Int. 1994–99; Minister of Commerce, Industry and Tourism 1998–2003. *Publications include:* numerous articles. *Address:* 13 Ayias Agapis, Strovolos, Nicosia, Cyprus (home). *Telephone:* 22591900 (office); 22353811/2 (home). *Fax:* 22591700 (office); 22353100 (home). *E-mail:* nikos@yolandis.com (home).

ROLDÓS AGUILERA, Leon; Ecuadorean lawyer, university administrator and politician; b. 21 July 1942, Guayaquil; ed Vicente Rocafuerte High School, Univ. of Guayaquil; practised as lawyer in Guayaquil; Lecturer, Prof. Vicente Rocafuerte Lay Univ. Law School 1967, later Dean; Chair. Monetary Bd 1979–81; Vice-Pres. of Ecuador 1981–83; presidential cand. (Partido Socialista Ecuatoriano (PSE) 1992; Rector, Univ. of Guayaquil 1994–2004; presidential cand. (ind.) 2002, (Red Ética y Democratica-Izquierda Democrática coalition) 2006; currently mem. Partido Roldosista Ecuatoriano (PRE). *Address:* c/o Partido Roldosista Ecuatoriano (PRE), Quito, Ecuador. *Telephone:* (2) 246-8227. *Fax:* (2) 246-8229. *E-mail:* info@viviendolademocracia.org.

ROLFE JOHNSON, Anthony, CBE; British singer; b. 5 Nov. 1940, Tackley, Oxon.; m. Elisabeth Jones Evans; one s. two d. and two s. from previous m.; has appeared with all major UK opera cos and with Netherlands Opera, Hamburg State Opera, Zürich Opera, at the Monnaie Theatre, Brussels, La Scala Milan, Metropolitan Opera New York and at Aix-en-Provence and Salzburg Festivals; concerts with all major UK orchestras and with Chicago Symphony, Boston Symphony, New York Philharmonic and Cleveland orchestras in USA. *Recordings include:* Acis and Galatea, Saul, Hercules, Jephtha, Alexander's Feast, Esther, Solomon, Semele, Messiah, J. S. Bach's St Matthew Passion and St John Passion, Peter Grimes, Samson, Oedipus Rex, Orfeo, War Requiem. *Roles include:* Fenton in Falstaff, Albert Herring, Don Ottavio in Don Giovanni, Tamino in The Magic Flute, Essex in Gloriana, Ferrando in Così fan tutte, Male Chorus in Rape of Lucretia, Orfeo in Monteverdi's Orfeo, Jupiter in Semele and Aschenbach Death in Venice.

RÖLLER, Lars-Hendrik, BS, MSc, MA, PhD; German economist and academic; *President, European School of Management and Technology;* m.; three c.; ed Texas A&M Univ. and Univ. of Pennsylvania, Phila, USA; Research Asst, Dept of Econs, Univ. of Pennsylvania 1983–86, Inst. for Law and Econs 1986–87, Lecturer, Dept of Econs 1986; Asst Prof. of Econs, Institut Européen d'Admin des Affaires (INSEAD), Paris, France 1987–91, Assoc. Prof. 1991–95, Prof. 1995–99; Prof. of Econs and Chair. Inst. of Industrial Econs, Humboldt Univ., Berlin 1995–; Dir Centre for Econ. Policy Research, London 1992, Co-Dir Industrial Org. Programme 1995–2003; Dir Inst. for Competitiveness and Industrial Change Wissenschaftszentrum Berlin für Sozialforschung 1994–2007, now Research Prof.; Research Fellow, Forschungsinstitut zur Zukunft der Arbeit (IZA), Bonn 1999–2006; Prof. (part-time), Norwegian School of Econs and Business Admin 2003; Chief Competition Economist, EC 2003–06; Pres. European School of Man. and Tech., Berlin 2006–; Visiting Prof., Dept of Applied Econs, Univ. Autonoma, Barcelona, Spain 1989; Visiting Scholar, Starr Center for Applied Econs, New York Univ., USA 1992, Grad. School of Business, Stanford Univ. 1993; mem. Exec. Bd European Asscn for Research in Industrial Econs 1999–2004 (Pres. 2005–07), Scientific Cttee of INSEAD Foundation 1999–, Advisory Bd, Centre for Competition Policy, Univ. of East Anglia, Norwich 2004–, Conselho Consultativo, Universidade Nova de Lisboa, Portugal 2005–, Alexander von Humboldt Foundation, Scientific Council for Transatlantic Cooperation (TransCoop) 2003–, American Econ. Asscn, Exec. Bd Vereins für Socialpolitik 2001–03, German-French Council of Econ. Advisers, 2003–06; Ed. Managerial and Decision Economics 1993–98, International Journal of Industrial Organization 1999–2004; mem. editorial bds of several int. journals; Fellow, European Econ. Asscn 2004; Best Teacher Award, INSEAD 1998, Gossen Award Verein für Socialpolitik 2002. *Publications:* Situation und Perspektiven der deutschen Raumfahrtindustrie 1998, The Corporate Structure of UK and German Manufacturing Firms 1999, Europas Nätverksindustrier: Telekommunikationer Avregleringen i Europa 1999, The Political Economy of Industrial Policy: Does Europe Have an Industrial Policy? 2000, Die Soziale Marktwirtschaft in der neuen Weltwirtschaft 2001; contrib. of numerous articles to professional journals. *Address:* European School of Management and Technology, Schlossplatz 1, 10178 Berlin, Germany (office). *Telephone:* (30) 21231-0 (office). *Fax:* (30) 21231-9 (office). *E-mail:* roeller@esmt.org (office). *Website:* www.esmt.org (office).

RÖLLER, Wolfgang, Dr rer. pol; German bank executive; *Honorary Chairman, Dresdner Bank AG;* b. 20 Oct. 1929, Uelsen, Lower Saxony; m.; three s.; ed Univs of Berlin and Frankfurt; joined Dresdner Bank AG, Frankfurt am Main, Deputy mem. Bd of Man. Dirs 1971–73, Full mem. 1973–85, Chair. Man. Bd 1985–93, Chair. Supervisory Bd 1993–97, now Hon. Chair.; Chair. Supervisory Bd ABD Securities Corpn, New York, Metallgesellschaft AG, Deutscher Investment-Trust Gesellschaft für Wertpapieranlagen mbH, Frankfurt, Dresdnerbank Investment Man. Kapitalanlage GmbH, Frankfurt, Heidelberger Zementwerke AG; mem. Supervisory Bd Allianz AG Holding, Munich, Daimler-Benz AG, Stuttgart, Degussa AG, Frankfurt, Henkel KGaA –2005, Düsseldorf, Hoechst AG, Frankfurt; Fried. Krupp GmbH, Essen; Rheinisch-Westfälisches Elektrizitätswerk AG (fmr Chair. Supervisory Bd), Essen; fmrly Chair. Deutsche Lufthansa AG, Cologne. *Address:* c/o Dresdner Bank AG, Jürgen-Ponto-Platz 1, 60329 Frankfurt am Main, Germany.

ROLLIER, Michel; French business executive; b. 19 Sept. 1944, Annecy, Haute Savoie; s. of François Rollier; m.; three c.; ed Institut d'Etudes Politiques, Université de Droit, Paris; with Aussedat-Rey (int. paper group) 1971–96, Controller, facilities, divs and group 1973–82, Unit Operational Man. 1982–87, Chief Financial Officer 1987–94, Deputy Man. Dir 1994–96; Chief Legal Officer and Dir for Financial Operations, Compagnie Générale des Établissements Michelin 1976, mem. Michelin Group Exec. Council and Chief Financial and Legal Officer 1999–, Co-Man. Pnr 2005–06, Sole Man. Pnr 2006–07, CEO and Man. Gen. Pnr 2007–; Officier, Légion d'honneur 2009. *Address:* Compagnie Générale des Établissements Michelin, 23 place des Carmes-Déchaux, 63040 Clermont-Ferrand, France (office). *Telephone:* 4-73-32-20-00 (office). *Fax:* 4-45-66-15-53 (office). *E-mail:* info@michelin.com (office). *Website:* www.michelin.com (office).

ROLLINS, Edward (Ed) J., BA, MA; American political campaign consultant; *Chairman, Rollins Strategy Group;* b. 1943, Vallejo, Calif.; ed California State Univ., Chico; intern for Speaker of Calif. Ass.; Dean, Washington Univ. St Louis 1970; fmr Co-chair. and CEO Nat. Republican Congressional Cttee (first non-member of Congress); led numerous presidential election campaigns including Ronald Reagan 1984, Ross Perot 1992; served admins of Pres. Nixon, Pres. Ford and Pres. Reagan, fmr Asst to President and White House Political Dir; currently Chair. Rollins Strategy Group, Washington, DC; Nat. Campaign Chair. and Sr Advisor to Mike Huckabee Republican presidential nomination campaign 2007; Econ. Advisor to Jiangsu Prov., People's Republ of China, also to Nanjing and Jinan; Co-chair. R& International (consulting firm), Beijing; fmr political commentator CBS News. *Publication:* Bare Knuckles and Back Rooms: My Life in American Politics (with Tom DeFrank) 1996. *Address:* c/o Republican National Committee, 310 First Street, SE, Washington, DC 20003, USA.

ROLLINS, Kevin B., BA, MBA; American business executive; *Senior Advisor, TPG Capital LP;* ed Brigham Young Univ.; Vice-Pres. and Pnr, Bain & Co. (man. consultants) –1996; joined Dell Inc. and held positions successively as Pres. Dell Americas, Vice-Chair. Dell Inc., Pres. and COO, Pres., CEO and Dir 2004–07 (resgnd); Sr Advisor TPG Capital LP 2007–; mem. US Pres.'s Advisory Cttee for Trade Policy and Negotiation, US Business Council, Computer Systems Policy Project; mem. Pres.'s Leadership Council, Brigham Young Univ., Marriott School Nat. Advisory Council; inducted into Hall of Fame, Utah Information Tech. Asscn (UITA) 2004. *Address:* TPG Capital LP, 301 Commerce Street, Suite 3300, Fort Worth, TX 76102, USA (office). *Telephone:* (817) 871-4000 (office). *Fax:* (817) 871-4010 (office). *Website:* www .texaspacificgroup.com (office).

ROLLINS, Theodore Walter (Sonny); American jazz musician; b. 7 Sept. 1930, New York; s. of Walter Rollins and Valborg Solomon; m. 1st Dawn Finney 1956 (divorced); m. 2nd Lucille Pearson 1959 (died 2004); ed High School, New York; began rehearsing while in high school, with Thelonious Monk; recorded with Bud Powell 1949; wrote standards 'Airegin' and 'Oleo' recorded with Miles Davis 1953; played and recorded with Clifford Brown/ Max Roach 1955; took sabbatical playing on Williamsburg Bridge, New York 1959–61; scored and played music for film Alfie 1966; has appeared in Jazz Heritage series, Smithsonian Inst. and at Newport Jazz Festival; numerous concert tours in Europe, Far East; annual concert tours of Europe, Japan, USA with Concert Orchestra 1973–; Guggenheim Fellow 1972; Dr hc (Bard Coll.) 1993; Hon. DMus (Long Island Univ.) 1998, (New England Conservatory of Music) 2002; Hon. DArts (Wesleyan Univ.) 1998; Hon. DFA (Duke Univ.) 1999; Tufts Univ. Lifetime Achievement Award 1996, Nat. Asscn of Recording Arts and Science Lifetime Achievement Award 2005, Grammy Award for Best Jazz Instrumental Solo (for Why Was I Born?) 2006. *Recordings include:* albums: Saxophone Colossus 1957, Freedom Suite 1958, This Is What I Do 2000, Live in London Vol. 2 2005, Without A Song: The 9/11 Concert 2005. *Address:* Route 9G, Germantown, NY 12526, USA. *Telephone:* (518) 537-6112 (office). *Fax:* (518) 537-4342 (office). *Website:* www.sonnyrollins.com.

ROMAHI, Seif al-Wady, PhD; Jordanian diplomacy expert and human resources development consultant; b. 28 Dec. 1938, Muzera, Palestine; s. of Ahmed al-Hajj Abdul-Nabi; m. Zaka al-Masri 1971; one s. two d.; ed Lebanese State Univ., Univ. Coll. London, Southern Illinois Univ., USA and Univ. of Birmingham, UK; Admin. Adviser to Cabinet of Prime Minister of Jordan Wasfi al-Tall; Area Educ. Supt, Ministry of Educ., Qatar 1960–64; seconded to Office of the Ruler of Abu Dhabi, Pres. UAE 1968–73; Rep. League of Arab States in USA 1970–72; Assoc. Prof. of Middle East Studies and Political Science, Southern Ill. Univ., USA 1971–72; Minister Plenipotentiary, Foreign Ministry, UAE 1973–91, set up UAE Embassies in Beijing, Tripoli, Tokyo and Seoul; Founder and Prof., Diplomatic Training Centre, UAE 1980–82; Co-founder and Chief Rep. Nat. Bank of Abu Dhabi in Japan 1982–86; Prof. of Int. Law, Diplomacy and Islamic Civilization, Int. Univ. of Japan, Sophia Univ., Tokyo; Founder, Gen. Man. Arab Int. Co. for Investment and Educ. 1988–91, Chair. 1990–94; founder Applied Science Univ., Amman, Jordan, Prof. of Diplomacy and Int. Law 1990–95, American Univ. of the Middle East in Jordan, House of Euro-Arab Experts in Jordan 1992– (also Chair.); Co-Founder Islamic-American Univ. Coll., Chicago; planner Jordan Women's Univ. (now Petra Univ.), Zaitouneh Jordanian Univ., Graduate Studies Univ. in Jordan, Middle East Acad. for Aviation; contrib. (with HE Dr Abdul-Razzaq al-Sanhouri) to writing the Consitution of UAE; co-author Abu Dhabi Public Service Code; Co-Chair. Planning Cttee for British Univ. of Dubai; consultant for establishment of RAK British Univ., UAE 2002–; mem. Acad. of Islamic Research (India), Japanese Acad. of Middle East Studies, Middle East Studies Asscn of USA and Canada, Middle East Inst., Washington, DC, British Soc. for Middle East Studies, Japanese Assoc. for Middle Eastern Studies; Order of Independence (Jordan) 1979; Hon. PhD (World Univ.) 1985. *Publications:* Economics and Political Evolution in Arabian Gulf States 1973, The Palestinian Question and International Law 1979, Studies in International Law and Diplomatic Practice 1980, Arab Customs and Manners 1984; contribs to professional and scientific journals. *Leisure interests:* calligraphy, art, travel, poetry, listening to music, painting and drawing, reading, research. *Address:* PO Box 35087 Hotel Jordan, Amman 11185, Jordan. *Telephone:* (6) 5537028 (home). *Fax:* (6) 5528328 (home). *E-mail:* seif-romahi@yahoo.co.uk.

ROMAN, Martin, LLB; Czech business executive; *Chairman and CEO, ČEZ a.s.;* b. 1969; ed Faculty of Law, Charles Univ., Prague, St Gallen Univ., Switzerland, Karl-Ruprechtsuniversität, Heidelberg, Germany; Sales Dir Wolf Bergstrasse ČR s.r.o. 1992–94; CEO Janka Radotín a.s. 1994–99, Chair. Bd of Dirs 1998–99; Chair. and Gen. Dir ŠKODA a.s., Pilsen 1999–2000, Chair. and CEO ŠKODA Holding 2000–04; Dir, Chair. and CEO, ČEZ a.s. 2004–. *Address:* ČEZ a.s., Hlavni Sprava, Duhova 2/1444, 140 53 Prague 4, Czech Republic (office). *Telephone:* (271) 131111 (office). *Fax:* (271) 132001 (office). *E-mail:* cez@cez.cz (office). *Website:* www.cez.cz (office).

ROMAN, Petre, PhD, DTech; Romanian academic and politician; *Senator and Chairman, Democratic Force of Romania (Forţa Democrâta din România) (FDR);* b. 22 July 1946, Bucharest; s. of Valter Roman and Hortensia Roman; m. Mioara Georgescu; two d.; ed Petru Groza High School, Bucharest, Bucharest Polytechnic Inst. and Nat. Polytechnic Inst. of Toulouse, France; fmrly Prof. and Head of Dept Hydraulics Dept, Faculty of Hydroenergy, Bucharest Polytechnic Inst.; Founding mem. Nat. Salvation Front 1989, Pres. 1992–93, became Democratic Party (PD) 1993–2003, Pres. 1993–2001; Prime Minister 1989–91; mem. Parl. 1992–, Chair. Defence, Public Order and Nat. Security Cttee, Chamber of Deputies 1992–96; Special Rapporteur of North Atlantic Ass. 1993–96; Co-Pres. Union of Social Democrats (USD=PD+PSDR—Party of Social Democracy in Romania) 1995–97; Senator for Bucharest (USD), Chair. of Senate 1996–97, Senator for Bucharest (PD),

Chair. of Senate 1997–99, Senator 2000–; cand. in presidential elections 1996; Acting Pres. Parl. Ass. of the Black Sea Econ. Cooperation 1997–98; Deputy Prime Minister, Minister of Foreign Affairs 1999–2000; Founder and Chair. Democratic Force of Romania (Forţa Democrâta din România) (FDR) 2004–; Grand Cross of Merit (France), Grand Cross of Nat. Order of Repub. of Ecuador, High Award of Repub. of Colombia; Traian Vuia Award, Romanian Acad. 1990. *Publications:* The Nuclear Energy File: Risk and Security (co-author) 1978, Water and Pollution (co-author) 1978, Introduction to the Physics of Fluid Pollution 1981, The Movement of the Compressible Fluids with Heat Transfer 1982, Special Problems in Hydromechanics (co-author) 1985, Hydrology and the Protection of Water Quality 1989, Fluid Mechanics 1989, Dynamic Hydrology (co-author) 1990, Le devoir de liberté 1992, Freedom as Duty 1994, Romania incotro? 1995, Political Notebook: A Political Vision on Romania's Development Strategy at the Threshold of Centuries 1999. *Leisure interests:* sports, hunting, reading, hiking. *Address:* Democratic Force of Romania (Forţa Democrâta din România) (FDR), 030627 Bucharest 3, Calea Călăraşi 76; Senatul României, Piata Revolutiei nr. 1, sector 1, Bucharest, Romania (office). *Telephone:* (21) 3150200 (office). *E-mail:* contact@fortademocratatimis.ro; webmaster@senat.ro (office).

ROMAÑA, Oscar José Ricardo, BA, BL; Peruvian government minister, politician and diplomatist; *Representative in Mexico, Organization of American States;* b. 7 Feb. 1947, Lima; m.; three c.; ed Univ. Católica y San Marcos, Univ. of Oxford, Johns Hopkins Univ.; 2nd, then 1st Sec. Peruvian Embassy, USA; Counsellor in Belgium and at EU; Head Dept of Int. Political Econs/ Econ.; Sec.-Gen. Presidency of the Repub.; Amb. to Canada, Bolivia; Dir-Gen. of Planning, of Judicial Affairs; Amb. to Thailand, concurrently to Viet Nam and Laos; Perm. Rep. ESCAP; Amb. to Ecuador; Dir Acad. of Diplomacy; Sub-Sec. for American Affairs, later Sec. for Foreign Affairs; Minister of Foreign Affairs 2005–06; OAS Rep. in Mexico 2007–; Del. to Confs of PECC, PBEC, APPF, APEC; Prof. of Int. Law Univ. Nacional de San Marcos y de Derecho; mem. Colegio de Abogados de Lima, Soc. Peruana de Derecho Int., Oxford Soc., Center of Int. Understanding; Hon. mem. Soc. Boliviana de Historia, Soc. de la Acad. Boliviana de Estudios Int., Siam Soc., Sociedad Fundadores de la Independencia; Hon. Prof., Univ. Andina Simon Bolivar, Quito; Hon. law doctorates (Winnipeg, Bangkok, Univ. Andina, Univ. Aquino); several decorations from Peruvian and foreign govts; Nat. Award of Culture. *Publications:* Derecho Internacional y Política Exterior 1995, Una Visión Latinoamericana del Asia Pacifico 1999, Las Nuevas Relaciones Bilaterales Perú-Ecuador 2000, Perú y Ecuador: Socios en el siglo XXI. *Address:* CDM Polanco, Delegacion Miguel Hidalgo, Apartado Postal 11560, México, DF, Mexico (office). *Telephone:* (55) 280-1208 (office); (55) 280-1147 (office). *Fax:* (55) 281-7390 (office). *E-mail:* OASMexico@oas.org (office). *Website:* www.oas.org (office).

ROMANI, Roger; French politician; *Senator of Paris (Ile-de-France);* b. 25 Aug. 1934, Tunis, Tunisia; s. of Dominique Romani and Madeleine Santelli; m. Joelle Fortier 1971; began career as an asst dir with ORTF; various positions in pvt. offices of Govt Ministers of Posts and Telecommunications, of Information, of State, of the Prime Minister 1967–71; Conseiller de Paris (Paris-Majorité-2ème secteur, then UDP-3ème, then RPR-5ème secteur) 1971–2001; adviser, Office of Jacques Chirac (Minister of Agric. and of Devt 1973, of Interior 1974, Prime Minister 1974–76); Deputy to Mayor of Paris 1977–2001; mem. Conseil Régional, Ile-de-France 1977; Senator of Paris (Ile-de-France) 1977–93, 2002–, Vice-Pres. RPR Group in Senate 1983–86, Pres. 1986–88, Vice-Pres. Group of RPR, later of Union pour un Mouvement Populaire 2002–, mem. Comm. of Foreign Affaires, of Defence and the Armed Forces, Titular mem. Higher Council of the Mil. Reserve 2004–; Vice-Pres. Conseil général de Paris (Departmental Ass.) 1982–2001; Pres. Group 'Rassemblement pour Paris' 1983–2001; Nat. Sec. RPR 1984–86, mem. Political Cttee 1998–2000; adviser to fmr Prime Minister Chirac 1986–88; Minister-Del. for Relations with the Senate 1993–95; Minister for Relations with Parl. 1995–97; adviser to Pres. Chirac 1997–2002; Hon. Pres. Mouvement nat. des élus locaux. *Address:* Sénat, Palais du Luxembourg, Casier postal, 75291 Paris Cedex 06, France (office). *Telephone:* 1-42-34-20-00 (office). *Fax:* 1-42-34-26-77 (office). *E-mail:* r.romani@senat.fr (office). *Website:* www .senat.fr/senfic/romani_roger59312e.html (office).

ROMANO, Sergio, LLD; Italian diplomatist and historian; b. 7 July 1929, Vicenza; s. of Romano Romano and Egle Bazzolo; m. Mary Anne Heinze 1954; two s. one d.; ed Liceo C. Beccaria, Milan, Univ. of Milan, Univ. of Chicago; foreign corresp. and film critic for Italian radio and newspapers, Paris, London and Vienna 1948–52; entered Italian Foreign Service 1954; Vice-Consul, Innsbruck, Austria 1955; Sec., Italian Embassy, London 1958–64; Pvt. Sec. to Minister of Foreign Affairs 1964; mem. Diplomatic Staff of the Pres. of the Repub. 1965–68; Counsellor (later Minister), Italian Embassy, Paris 1968–77; Dir-Gen. of Cultural Relations, Ministry of Foreign Affairs 1977–83; Guest Prof. Faculty of Political Sciences, Univ. of Florence 1981–83; Italian Perm. Rep. Atlantic Council, Brussels 1983–85, Amb. to USSR 1985–89 (resgnd); currently columnist for Corriere della Sera (newspaper) and Panorama (magazine), also contributes opinion articles to Limes, Affari Esteri, Corriere del Ticino, Les Echos; fmr Visiting Professor, Harvard Univ., Univ. of California, Berkeley; Prof. of History of International Relations, Bocconi Univ. 1992–98; mem. Ateneo Veneto, Venice, Accad. Olimpica, Vicenza; corresp. mem. Royal Acad. of Brussels; Pres. Balzan Foundation Prize Cttee; Grand' Ufficiale of the Italian Order of Merit, Commdr Légion d'honneur, other European and Latin-American honours; Dr hc (Inst. d'Etudes Politiques, Paris) (Univ. of Macerat), (Inst. of World History, Russian Acad. of Sciences. *Publications:* Crispi, Progetto per una Dittatura 1973, 1986, La Quarta Sponda 1977, Histoire de l'Italie du Risorgimento à nos jours 1977, Italie 1979, Giuseppe Volpi, Industria e Finanza tra Giolitti e Mussolini 1979, La Francia dal 1870 ai nostri giorni 1981, Benedetto Croce, La Philosophie comme histoire de la Liberté (Ed.) 1983, La Lingua e il Tempo 1983, Giovanni Gentile,

La Filosofia al Potere 1984, Florence, Toscane 1988, Giolitti, Lo Stile del Potere 1989, Disegni per una Esposizione 1989, L'Italia scappata di mano 1993, Cinquant'anni di storia mondiale: La pace e le guerre da Yalta ai nostri giorni 1995, Lo scambio ineguale: Italia e Stati Uniti da Wilson a Clinton 1995, Le Italie parallele 1996, Lettera ad un amico ebreo 1997, Storia d'Italia dal Risorgimento ai nostri giorni 1998, Confessioni di un revisionista 1998, I luoghi della storia 2000, La pace perduta 2001, Un'amica difficile, conversazioni con Gilles Martinet su due secoli di relazioni italo-francesi 2001, I volti della storia 2001, Memorie di un conservatore 2002, Il rischio americano 2003, Giovanni Gentile. Un filosofo al potere negli anni del Regime 2004, Anatomia del terrore. Colloquio con Guido Olimpio 2004, Europa, storia di un'idea. Dall'impero all'unione 2004, La quarta sponda: La guerra di Libia 1911-1912 2005, ibera Chiesa. Libero Stato? 2005, Saremo moderni? Diario di un anno 2007. *Address:* c/o Corbaccio Inc. via Gherardini 10, 20145 Milan, Italy.

ROMANOV, Piotr Vasilyevich, DTechSc; Russian politician; b. 21 July 1943, Kansk, Krasnoyarsk territory; m.; three c.; ed Siberia Inst. of Tech.; engineer, then chief of workshop, Chief Engineer, Dir-Gen. Krasnoyarsky Production Unit of Mil. Chemical Enterprise Enisey 1967–96; mem. Russian Council of Fed. 1993; Co-Chair. Russian Nat. Sobor 1992–93, mem. Org. Cttee All-Russia Congress of Russian Communists, Co-Chair. Co-ordination Council All-Russia Congress of Russian Communists 1994–; mem. State Duma 1995–, currently First Deputy Chair. of State Cttee on Ecology, mem. Comm. on Problems of North Caucasus; Sec. Cen. Cttee CP of Russian Fed. 1997–; mem. Russian Acad. of Eng Sciences; Hero of Socialist Labour; Distinguished Chemist of Russian Fed.; Order of Lenin; Sergei Radonezhsky Medal. *Publications:* I Am Piotr Romanov: About the Times and Myself 1995, With a Son's Care about Russia 1995, The Sovereign Cross 1997. *Leisure interests:* winter sports, gathering mushrooms and berries, gardening. *Address:* State Duma, Okhotny Ryad 1, 103265 Moscow (office); pr. Mira 108, 660017 Krasnoyarsk, Russia. *Telephone:* (495) 292-18-10 (office). *Fax:* (495) 292-40-58 (office). *Website:* www.duma.gov.ru (office).

ROMASZEWSKI, Zbigniew, PhD; Polish politician; b. 2 Jan. 1940, Warsaw; m.; one d.; ed Warsaw Univ., Inst. of Physics, Polish Acad. of Sciences; researcher, Inst. of Physics, Polish Acad. of Sciences 1964–83 (dismissed); ed. Acta Physica Polonica, Inst. of Physics, Jagiellonian Univ., Kraków 1984–; participant relief action in support of repressed workers in Radom and Ursus 1976; mem. Defence Cttee of Workers (KOR) 1977–81, admin. Intervention Office; admin. Helsinki Watch Group 1979–80, ed. Madrid Report; mem. Solidarity Ind. Self-Governing Trade Union 1980–, Chair. Intervention and Law Observance Cttee 1980–81, mem. Bd Presidium Mazovia Br. and Nat. Cttee 1982; ran Solidarity (underground radio) 1982; imprisoned 1982–84; organizer of first Int. Human Rights Confs in Kraków (illegal) 1988, Leningrad (USSR) 1990, Warsaw 1998; Senator 1989–, Chair. Human Rights and the Rule of Law Cttee; mem. Latin American Constitutional Lawyers Asscn 2001–; Ind.; Aurora Award (jt recipient with his wife for achievement in the fields of human rights and democracy) 1987. *Leisure interest:* mountain trekking. *Address:* ul. Wiejska 6, 00-902 Warsaw, Poland (office). *Telephone:* (22) 6252465 (office). *E-mail:* biuro@romaszewski.pl (office); senator@romaszewski.pl (office). *Website:* www.romaszewski.pl (office).

ROMER, Christina Duckworth, BA, PhD; American economist, academic and govnernment official; *Chair, Council of Economic Advisers;* b. 25 Dec. 1958, Alton, Ill.; m. David Romer; three c.; ed Glen Oak High School, Canton, Ohio, Coll. of William and Mary, Massachusetts Inst. of Tech.; Asst Prof. of Econs, Woodrow Wilson School, Princeton Univ. 1985–88; Acting Assoc. Prof. of Econs, Univ. of California, Berkeley 1988–90, Assoc. Prof. of Econs 1990–93, Class of 1957 Prof. of Econs 1997–; Chair., Council of Econ. Advisers, The White House 2009–; Fellow, American Acad. of Arts and Sciences 2004; Research Assoc., Program in Monetary Econs, Nat. Bureau of Econ. Research 1990–, Co-Dir 2003–; mem. Cttee on Honors and Awards, American Econ. Asscn 2004–, Vice-Pres. 2006; Grad. Fellowship Research Grant, NSF 1981–84, Alfred P. Sloan Doctoral Fellowship 1984–85, Research Grant 1987–90, Nat. Bureau of Econ. Research Olin Fellowship 1987–88, Alfred P. Sloan Research Fellowship 1989–91, Presidential Young Investigator Award 1989–94, John Simon Guggenheim Memorial Foundation Fellowship 1998–99, Faculty Award for Women Scientists and Engineers 1991–96, Research Grant 2000–03, 2006–09, Distinguished Teaching Award, Univ. of California, Berkeley 1994, Social Science Research Council Grant 1985–86. *Publications:* as co-ed.: Reducing Inflation: Motivation and Strategy 1997. *Address:* Council of Economic Advisors, Eisenhower Executive Office Bldg, 17th St and Pennsylvania Ave, NW, Washington, DC 20502, USA (office). *Telephone:* (202) 395-5042 (office). *Fax:* (202) 395-6958 (office). *Website:* www.whitehouse.gov/administration/eop/cea (office).

RÖMER, Michael, PhD; German business executive; b. 1946; lab. head of industrial chemicals, Merck Darmstadt 1978–83; worked in process devt chemistry 1983–88; worked at EM Industries, USA 1988–90, Head, Industrial Chemicals Div. 1990–93; apptd Rep. Mem., Exec. Bd, Merck KGaA 1993, apptd mem. Exec. Bd and Gen. Pnr 1994, Vice-Chair. Exec. Bd 2000–05, Chair. Exec. Bd 2005–07; Chair. Hessian Chapter, German Chemical Industry Asscn; Chair. Tech. and Environment Cttee, German Chemical Industry Asscn; Pres. Darmstadt Chamber of Industry and Commerce; Chair. of Industry and Research Cttee of German Chambers of Commerce; mem. Bd of Fed. of Trade Asscns in Hesse; mem. Supervisory Bd, Frankfurt RhineMain GmbH. *Address:* c/o Merck KGaA, Frankfurter strasse, 64293 Darmstadt, Germany (office).

ROMER, Roy R., BS, LLB; American education administrator and fmr politician; *Chairman, Strong American Schools;* b. 31 Oct. 1928, Garden City, Kan.; s. of Irving Rudolph and Margaret Elizabeth Romer (née Snyder); m. Beatrice Miller 1952; five s. two d.; ed Colo State Univ., Univ. of Colo, Yale Univ.; farmed in Colo 1942–52; admitted to Colo Bar 1952; ind. practice, Denver 1955–66; mem. Colo House of Reps 1958–62, Colo Senate 1962–66; Commr for Agric. for Colo 1975; State Treas. 1977–86; Gov. of Colo 1987–98; Supt of Schools, LA Unified School Dist 2001–06; Chair. Strong American Schools (non-profti) 2007–; owner Arapahoe Aviation Co., Colo Flying Acad., Geneva Basin Ski Area, Chain Farm Implement and Industrial Equipment Stores in Colo, Fla and Va; Gov. Small Business Council; fmr mem. Agric. Advisory Cttee, Colo Bd of Agric., Colo Bar Asscn; Chair. Nat. Educ. Goals Panel, Democratic Govs' Asscn 1991, Democratic Nat. Cttee. *Address:* Strong American Schools, 1150 17th Street, NW, Suite 875, Washington, DC 20036, USA (office). *Telephone:* (202) 552-4560 (office). *Fax:* (202) 552-4570 (office). *E-mail:* info@EDin08.com (office). *Website:* edin08.com (office).

ROMERO, Edward L.; American business executive and fmr diplomatist; b. 2 Jan. 1934, Albuquerque, NM; m. Cayetana García; four c.; ed Los Angeles State Coll., Calif., Citrus Coll.; Founder, Chair. and CEO Advanced Sciences Inc. (merged with Commodore Applied Technologies, Inc.); f. Valor Telecommunications Southwest LLC, RTM International (Spain); Amb. to Spain 1998–2000; mem. Bd of Dirs Bank of America 2003–06; mem. President's Hispanic Advisory Cttee, US Trade Reps Services Policy Advisory Cttee; mem. Albuquerque Hispano Chamber of Commerce; Nat. Finance Chair. Richardson for Pres. campaign 2007; Hon. Brother of Int. Brotherhood of Researchers, Toledo, Spain, Noble Hon. Brother of Illustrious and Most Ancient Brotherhood of Mozarabic Knights, Toledo, Spain, Hon. Academic of World Acad. of Science and Tech., Valencia, Spain; Knight of the Order of the Holy Sepulchre of Jerusalem, Madrid, Spain; Nat. Hispanic Businessman of the Year, Hispanic Chamber of Commerce 1989. *Address:* c/o Albuquerque Hispano Chamber of Commerce, 1309 4th Street, SW, Albuquerque, NM 87102, USA (office).

ROMERO, Pepe; American classical guitarist; b. 3 Aug. 1944, Málaga, Spain; s. of Celedonio Romero and Angelita Romero (née Gallego); m. 1st Kristine Eddy 1965; m. 2nd Carissa Sugg 1987; one s. three d.; ed various music acads in USA, including Music Acad. of the West; began career in Seville, Spain, as part of Romero Quartet 1951, re-formed in USA 1960; averages 200–250 concerts a year world-wide; recordings number more than 50 solos, plus others with the Romero Quartet and various orchestras; Artist-in-Residence, Univ. of Southern Calif. 1972, Univ. of Calif., San Diego 1984. *Publications:* Guitar Method, Guitar Transcriptions for 1, 2 and 4 guitars. *Leisure interests:* photography, chess. *Address:* c/o Tim Fox, Columbia Artists Management, Inc., 1790 Broadway, New York, NY 10019, USA (office). *E-mail:* TFox@cami.com (office). *Website:* www.peperomero.com (office).

ROMERO-BARCELÓ, Carlos Antonio, BA, LLB, JD; American politician, lawyer and real estate executive; b. 4 Sept. 1932, San Juan, Puerto Rico; s. of Antonio Romero-Moreno and Josefina Barceló-Bird; m. 1st; two s.; m. 2nd Kathleen Donnelly 1966; one s. one d.; ed Phillips Exeter Acad., NH, Yale Univ., Univ. of Puerto Rico; admitted to bar, San Juan, Puerto Rico 1956; Pres. Citizens for State 51 1965–67; Mayor of San Juan 1969–77; Pres. New Progressive Party 1974–86, Chair. 1989; Pres. Nat. League of Cities 1974–75; Gov. of Puerto Rico 1977–85; Chair. Southern Govs Conf. 1980–81; Resident Commr in Washington, DC 1993–2001 (serving in US Congress); in pvt. practice 2001–; mem. Council on Foreign Affairs 1985–, Int. Platform Asscn 1985–, League of United Latin American Citizens (LULAC); Hon. LLD (Univ. of Bridgeport, Conn.) 1977; James J. and Jane Hoey Award for Interracial Justice, Catholic Interracial Council of NY 1977; Special Gold Medal Award, Spanish Inst., New York 1979; US Attorney-General's Medal 1981. *Publications:* Statehood is for the Poor 1973, Statehood for Puerto Rico, Vital Speeches of the Day 1979, Puerto Rico, USA: The Case for Statehood, Foreign Affairs 1980, The Soviet Threat to the Americas, Vital Speeches of the Day 1981. *Leisure interests:* reading, horse riding, tennis, swimming, water sports, golf. *Address:* Centro de Seguros, Building 701, Ponce de Leòn Avenue # 412, Miramar, PR 00907 (office); PO Box 364351, San Juan, PR 00936, Puerto Rico. *Telephone:* (787) 724-0526; (787) 724-0511. *Fax:* (787) 724-0959 (office). *E-mail:* rbarcelo@prtc.net (office).

ROMERO KOLBECK, Gustavo, MA; Mexican economist and public official; b. 3 July 1923, Mexico City; s. of Gustavo Kolbeck and Ana María Kolbeck (née de Romero); m. Leonor Martínez 1950; one s. two d.; ed Nat. Univ. of Mexico, George Washington Univ. and Chicago Univ.; Prof., Nat. School of Econs 1949, Nat. Univ. of Mexico 1966; Dir School of Econs Anahuac Univ. 1967–70; Economist Bank of Mexico 1944–45; Research Dept of Banco de Comercio 1946; Head of Dept of Econ. Studies, Banco Nacional de México 1949–54; Deputy Dir and Dir of Public Investments, Ministry of Programming and Budget 1954–62; Founder and Dir Centre for Econ. Study of Pvt. Sector 1963–65; mem. Bd of Govs CONCANACO 1967; Founder and Dir Business Trends and Expansión (journals) 1967–69; Amb. to Japan 1971–73, to USSR 1982–83; Dir-Gen. Financiera Nacional Azucarera SA 1973, Nacional Financiera, SA 1974–76, Bank of Mexico 1976–82; Alt. Gov. World Bank 1974–76, IMF and IADB 1976–82; Dir-Gen. Banco Obrero, SA 1983; decorations from Japan, France, FRG, Brazil and other countries. *Leisure interests:* swimming, reading. *Address:* Rubén Darío 45-2, Cd. Rincón del Bosque 11580, México DF, Mexico (home).

ROMERO MENA, Gen. Carlos Humberto; Salvadorean army officer and fmr head of state; b. Chalatenango; s. of late José María Romero and of Victoria Mena de Romero; m. Gloria Guerrero de Romero; two s. two d.; ed Capitán General Gerardo Barrios Mil. School, Escuela de Armas y Servicios, Escuela de Comando y Estado Mayor Manuel Enrique Araujo; Section Commd., Adjutant and Paymaster, Capt.-Gen. Gerardo Barrios Mil. School and other mil. bodies; Regt Commdr Cavalry; Second Officer 1st Infantry Regt; Sub-Dir Escuela de Armas y Servicios and Head Dept Personnel, Gen. Staff Armed Forces; Mil. Attaché to Embassy, Mexico; Head of Staff of

Presidency of Repub.; Minister of Defence and Public Security; Pres. Cen. American Defense Council 1973–77; Pres. of Repub. of El Salvador 1977–79 (overthrown in coup); del. 7th Conf. of American Armies 1966, 2nd Conf. of Cen. American Defense Council 1960, 6th Conf. of American Intelligence Officials 1967; Partido de Conciliación Nacional.

ROMERO ORELLANA, Gen. Otto Alejandro; Salvadorean politician and army officer; b. 4 April 1955, Chalatenango; ed Escuele Militar Capt. Gen. Gerardo Barrios; fmr Section Commdr, First Bn, Oscar Osorio Artillery Brigade; Exec. Sec., Ministry of Nat. Defence 1994; Commdr, Third Military Zone, Infantry Brigade, Domingo Monterrosa 2002; Gen. Inspector of Armed Forces 2002, Minister of Nat. Defence –2007; several nat. and int. decorations. *Address:* c/o Ministry of National Defence, Alameda Dr Manuel Enrique Araújo, Km 5, Carretera a Santa Tecla, San Salvador, El Salvador (office).

ROMETTY, Virginia (Ginni), BSc; American business executive; *Senior Vice-President, Enterprise Business Services, IBM Global Services, International Business Machines Corporation;* b. 1957; ed Northwestern Univ.; began career with General Motors Corpn; joined Int. Business Machines Corpn (IBM), becoming Gen. Man. Global Insurance and Financial Services Sector, Gen. Man. IBM Global Services, Americas, later becoming Man. Pnr, Business Consulting Services –2005, Sr Vice-Pres. Enterprise Business Services 2005–; named by Time magazine amongst Global Business Influential 2002, ranked by Fortune magazine amongst 50 Most Powerful Women in Business in the US (15th) 2005, (16th) 2006, (17th) 2007, ranked by Forbes magazine amongst 100 Most Powerful Women (97th) 2008. *Leisure interest:* scuba diving. *Address:* International Business Machines Corporation (IBM), Somers, NY 10589, USA (office). *Telephone:* (914) 766-2100 (office). *E-mail:* grometty@us.ibm.com (office). *Website:* www.us.ibm.com (office).

ROMITI, Cesare, BEcons; Italian business executive; b. 24 June 1923, Rome; m. Luigina Gastaldi; two s.; joined Bombrini Parodi Delfino (BPD) Group 1947; Gen. Man. Finance and Co-ordination SNIA Viscosa 1968–70; Man. Dir and Gen. Man. Alitalia Airlines 1970–73, Italstat (IRI group) 1973–74; Head Corp. Finance Planning and Control Dept, Fiat SpA 1974–76, Man. Dir Fiat SpA and Vice-Chair. IHF 1976–96, Chair. 1996–98, Man. Dir Fiat Auto SpA 1989–90; Dir Mediobanca 1991; Chair. Rizzoli Corriere della Sera newspaper and publishing group 1998; Head RSC Editori 1998–; mem. Exec. Cttee Italian Stock Cos. Asscn, Bd Turin Industrial Asscn, Confindustria, Aspen Inst. Italia, Advisory Bd Deutsche Bank, Alcatel Alsthom, Council of Int. Advisers, Swiss Bank, Bd Int. Advisers, Westinghouse Electric SA; received 18-month suspended sentence and banned from holding corp. office April 1997, case on appeal; indicted on charges of corruption and bribery June 1998.

ROMNEY, (Willard) Mitt, BA, JD, MBA; American business executive, politician and fmr state official; b. 12 March 1947, Detroit, Mich.; s. of the late George Romney, fmr Gov. of Mich., and Lenore Romney; m. Ann Romney; five s.; ed Cranbrook School, Bloomfield Hills, Mich., Brigham Young Univ., Harvard Univ. Business School, Harvard Law School; Vice-Pres. Bain & Co. (man. consulting firm) 1978–84, Co-founder Bain Capital (investment firm) 1984–99, CEO (interim) Bain & Co. 1990–92; CEO Salt Lake City Organizing Cttee for 2002 Winter Olympics 1999–2002; Gov. of Mass. 2003–07; unsuccessful cand. for Republican nomination for Pres. of US 2007–08; f. Free and Strong America PAC, Inc. 2008; mem. Bd of Dirs Marriott International 1992–2002, 2009–. *Address:* c/o Free and Strong America PAC, Inc., 80 Hayden Avenue, Lexington, MA 02421, USA. *E-mail:* Info@FreeStrongAmerica.com; info@mittromney.com. *Website:* www.freestrongamerica.com; www.mittromney.com.

ROMULO, Alberto (Bert) G., BSc, BL; Philippine politician; *Secretary of Foreign Affairs;* b. Camiling, Tarlac province; s. of Carlos P. Romulo; m. Rosie Lovely Tecson; five c.; ed De La Salle Univ., Universidad de Madrid, Spain; fmr Sec. of Budget and Man., Chair. Devt Budget Co-ordinating Cttee, mem. Monetary Bd; fmr Senator, Majority Leader; Exec. Sec. –2004; Sec. of Foreign Affairs 2004–; Gintong Ama Award, Philippines Free Press Most Outstanding Senator. *Address:* Department of Foreign Affairs, DFA Building, 2330 Roxas Blvd, Pasay City, 1330 Metro Manila, The Philippines (office). *Telephone:* (2) 8344000 (office). *Fax:* (2) 8321597 (office). *E-mail:* webmaster@dfa.gov.ph (office). *Website:* www.dfa.gov.ph (office).

RONALD, Mark H., BA, BSc, MSc; American aerospace and defence industry executive; *Chairman, BAE Systems Inc.;* ed Bucknell Univ., Polytechnic Inst. of New York; served as Vice-Pres., Program Man. Litton Industries, Amecon Div.; fmr Pres., COO and mem. Bd of Dirs AEL Industries; COO and mem. Bd of Dirs BAE Systems plc, CEO and Pres. BAE Systems Inc., USA –2006, Chair. BAE Systems Inc. 2007–; mem. Bd of Dirs Cobham plc, Alliant Tech Systems (ATK), DynCorp International LLC 2007–; mem. Exec. Cttee and Bd of Govs, Aerospace Industries Asscn; mem. Bd of Govs Electronic Industries Alliance; Hon. CBE 2005; Distinguished Engineering Alumni Awards (Bucknell Univ., Polytechnic Inst. of New York), Marine Corps Scholarship Foundation Semper Fidelis Award 2005, John Curtis Sword Award 2006. *Address:* BAE Systems, Inc., 1601 Research Blvd., Rockville, MD 20850, USA (office). *Telephone:* (301) 838-6000 (office). *Fax:* (301) 838-6925 (office). *Website:* www.baesystems.com/WorldwideLocations/UnitedStates (office).

RONALDINHO GAÚCHO; Brazilian/Spanish football player; b. (Ronaldo de Assis Moreira), 21 March 1980, Pôrto Alegre, Rio Grande do Sul, Brazil; s. of the late João de Assis Moreira and of Miguelina de Assis Moreira; attacking midfielder; won World Youth Cup with Brazil Under-17 team (voted Player of the Tournament), Egypt 1997; teams played for include Gremio de Pôrto Alegre (35 appearances, 14 goals) 1998–2001, Paris St Germain, France (55 appearances, 17 goals) 2001–03, FC Barcelona, Spain (207 appearances, 94 goals) 2003–08, AC Milan, Italy 2008–; more than 83 caps and 33 goals for Brazil (as of July 2008) 1999–, won Copa America 1999 (scoring six goals), won World Cup 2002; won Champions League with FC Barcelona 2005; mem. Bronze Medal-winning team, Men's Football, Olympic Games, Beijing 2008; wears No. 80 shirt; became Spanish citizen Jan. 2007; EFE Trophy (best South American player in Spanish leagues) 2004, FIFA World Footballer of the Year 2004, 2005, UEFA (Union of European Football Asscns) Team of the Year 2004, 2005, 2006, Best Foreign Player in La Liga 2004, 2006, European Footballer of the Year (Ballon d'Or) 2005, FIFPro (int. professional football players' union) World Player of the Year 2005, 2006, UEFA Club Footballer of the Year 2005–06, FIFPro World XI 2005, 2006, 2007, FIFA Club World Cup Bronze Ball Award 2006. *Address:* c/o AC Milan SpA, via Turati 3, 20121 Milan, Italy. *Website:* www.acmilan.com; www.ronaldinhogaucho.com.

RONALDO; Brazilian/Spanish professional football player; b. (Ronaldo Luiz Nazario de Lima), 22 Sept. 1976, Bento Ribeiro, Rio de Janeiro; s. of Nelio Nazario de Lima and Sonia Nazario de Lima; m.; teams: Social Ramos, Rio (at age 15) (12 games, 8 goals), São Cristóvão, Rio Second Div. (54 games, 36 goals), Cruzeiro, Brazil (60 games, 58 goals), PSV Eindhoven, Netherlands (58 games, 54 goals), Barcelona, Spain (49 games, 47 goals), Inter Milan 1997–2002 (90 games, 53 goals); transferred to Real Madrid after the World Cup 2002; Brazilian Nat. Team 1994– (67 int. caps, 47 goals); played for winning team World Cup 1994 (at age 17), 2002 (Winner Golden Boot) and Copa America 1997 (Brazil); Spanish Cup and European Cup Winners' Cup (Barcelona) 1997; World Soccer Magazine World Player of the Year 1996, FIFA World Footballer of the Year 1996, 1997, 2002, European Footballer of the Year 1997, 2002. *Address:* c/o FC Real Madrid, Estadio Santiago Bernabeu, Paseo de la Castellana 104, Madrid, Spain. *Website:* www.realmadrid.com (office); www.r9ronaldo.com (home).

RONALDO DOS SANTOS AVEIRO, Cristiano; Portuguese professional footballer; b. 5 Feb. 1985, Funchal, Madeira; s. of Dinis Aveiro; began career as youth player with CD Nacional, Madeira 1995–97; with Sporting Clube de Portugal 2002–03; signed as winger for Manchester United 2003–; first cap for Portugal against Kazakhstan 2003; represented Portugal at Summer Olympics, Athens 2004; Officer, Order of Infante D. Henrique, Medal of Merit, Order of Immaculate Conception of Vila Viçosa (House of Braganza) numerous awards including Portuguese Footballer of the Year 2006–07, Barclays Golden Boot 2007–08, UEFA Club Footballer of the Year 2007–08, FIFPro World Player of the Year 2008, Ballon d'Or European Footballer of the Year 2008, FIFA World Player of the Year 2008. *Address:* Manchester United Football Club, Sir Matt Busby Way, Old Trafford, Manchester, M16 0RA, England (office). *Telephone:* (161) 868-8000 (office). *Website:* www.manutd.com (office).

RONAY, Egon, LLD; British publisher and journalist; b. Pozsony, Hungary; m. 2nd Barbara Greenslade 1967; one s. (and two d. by previous marriage); ed School of Piarist Order, Budapest, Univ. of Budapest and Acad. of Commerce, Budapest; trained in kitchens of family catering firm and abroad; managed five restaurants in family firm; emigrated from Hungary 1946; Gen. Man. two restaurant complexes in London before opening own restaurant The Marquee 1952–55; gastronomic and good living columnist, Sunday Times 1986–91 and Sunday Express 1991, weekly columnist on eating out, food, wine and tourism, Daily Telegraph and later Sunday Telegraph 1954–60; weekly column, The Evening News 1968–74; Ed. Egon Ronay's Guide to Eating at the Airport 1992–94; mem. Acad. des Gastronomes (France) 1979; Founder Int. Acad. of Gastronomy; Founder and Pres. British Acad. of Gastronomes; Founder and Ed. the Egon Ronay Guides 1957, Publr and Ed. 1957–85; Médaille de la Ville de Paris 1983, Chevalier de l'Ordre du Mérite Agricole 1987. *Publications:* Egon Ronay's Guides 1957–84 annually, The Unforgettable Dishes of My Life 1989. *Telephone:* (20) 7584-1384 (office). *E-mail:* egon@egonronay.com (office).

RONČEVIĆ, Berislav; Croatian politician; b. 23 June 1960, Borovik; m.; Vlatka Cindori; four c.; ed Secondary Law School, Našice, Univ. of Zagreb; joined Croatian Democratic Union (Hrvatska demokratska zajednica—HDZ) 1990, mem. Našice br., HDZ 1992, Chair. 1998, Man. City Council, Našice 1992, HDZ Pres. in local parl., Našice 1998, Vice-Chair. and mem. Osijek and Baranja Co. Subsidiary of HDZ 2000–; Head of Legal and Personnel Service, Hrvatske Šume (Forests of Croatia, forest man. co.), Našice 1990, Asst Dir Regional Dept 1995; Deputy Mayor Našice 1998–2002, Mayor 2003; mem. Sabor (Parl.) 2000–; Minister of Defence 2003–07, of Interior 2008; Chair. Našice Handball Club 2000–; mem. Doris Pejačević folklore orchestra of Našice 2002–. *Leisure interests:* handball, cycling, tennis. *Address:* Croatian Democratic Union, 10000 Zagreb, trg Žrtava fašizma 4, Croatia (office). *Telephone:* (1) 4553000 (office). *Fax:* (1) 4552600 (office). *E-mail:* hdz@hdz.hr (office). *Website:* www.hdz.hr (office).

RONG, Zhijian, (Larry Yung Chi Kin); Chinese business executive; *Chairman, President and Managing Director, CITIC Pacific Ltd;* b. 1942, Shanghai; s. of Rong Yiren; m., three c.; ed Tianjin Univ.; began career as intern in hydraulic power plant near Changbai Mountain, Jilin Prov.; co-founded Elcap Electronics Plant, Hong Kong 1978; co-founded Automation Design Co. Ltd, Calif., USA 1982; joined CITIC Pacific Ltd as Vice-Pres., Hong Kong 1986, Dir 1990–, currently Chair., Pres. and Man. Dir, also Chair. Audit Cttee, Exec. Dir CITIC Group; mem. CPPCC; Steward, Hong Kong Jockey Club; mem. Gov.'s Business Council 1994–97; Dr hc (Hong Kong Univ. of Science and Tech.) 1998. *Address:* CITIC Pacific Limited, 32 Floor, CITIC Tower, 1 Tim Mei Avenue, Central, Hong Kong Special Administrative Region, People's Republic of China (office). *Telephone:* 28202111 (office). *Fax:* 28772771 (office). *Website:* www.citicpacific.com (office).

RONTÓ, Györgyi; Hungarian biophysicist and academic; *Professor Emeritus of Biophysics, Semmelweis University;* b. 13 July 1934, Budapest; d. of György Rontó and Erzsébet Lanczkor; m. Dr Dezső Holnapy 1961; two s.; ed Semmelweis Univ. of Medicine, Budapest; Prof. of Biophysics, Semmelweis Univ. 1980, now Prof. Emer., Dir Semmelweis Univ. Inst. of Biophysics

1982–99; Head of Research Group for Biophysics of the Hungarian Acad. of Sciences 1982–; Gen. Sec. Hungarian Biophysical Soc. 1969–90, Vice-Pres. 1990–98, Hon. Pres. 2002–; Vice-Pres. Asscn Int. de Photobiologie 1988–92; officer, European Soc. for Photobiology; mem. Nat. Cttee of COSPAR (Cttee on Space Research); specialises in effects of environmental physical and chemical agents on nucleo-proteins; special interest in biological dosimetry of environmental and artificial UV radiations and in exo/astrobiology; Medal of the Hungarian Biophysical Soc. 1990, 2004, Apáczai Csere János Award 1994, Environment Award 1996, Gold Ring, Semmelweis Univ. 1999. *Publications:* A biofizika alapjai (An Introduction to Biophysics With Medical Orientation) (co-author) 1981 (also English and German edns), Light in Biology and Medicine (Vol. 2) 1991; more than 140 articles. *Leisure interests:* arts, architecture, gardening. *Address:* 1094 Budapest, Tűzoltó-u. 34–47 (home); PO Box 263, 1444 Budapest, Hungary (home). *Telephone:* (1) 267-6261 (home); (1) 459-1500 (home). *Fax:* (1) 266-6656 (home). *E-mail:* gyorgyi.ronto@eok.sote .hu (office).

ROOCROFT, Amanda, FRNCM; British singer (soprano); b. 9 Feb. 1966, Coppull; d. of Roger Roocroft and Valerie Roocroft (née Metcalfe); m. 2nd David Gowland 1999; two s.; ed Royal Northern Coll. of Music; appearances include Sophie in Der Rosenkavalier, Welsh Nat. Opera 1990, Pamina in The Magic Flute, Covent Garden 1991, 1993, Fiordiligi in Così fan tutte, Glyndebourne 1991, European tour with John Eliot Gardiner 1992, Bavarian State Opera 1993, 1994, Covent Garden 1995, Giulietta in I Capuleti e I Montecchi, Covent Garden 1993, Ginevra in Ariodante, ENO 1993, Donna Elvira in Don Giovanni, Glyndebourne 1994, New York Metropolitan Opera 1997, Amelia in Simon Boccanegra, Bavarian State Opera 1995, Mimi in La Bohème, Covent Garden 1996, Countess in Marriage of Figaro, Bavarian State Opera 1997, New York Metropolitan Opera 1999, Cleopatra in Giulio Cesare, Covent Garden 1997, Desdemona in Otello, Bavarian State Opera 1999, Covent Garden 2001, Jenůfa, Glyndebourne 2000, Berlin 2002, Katya Kabanova, Glyndebourne 1998, Covent Garden 2000, Meistersinger, Royal Opera House 2002; debut at BBC Promenade Concert and Edin. Festival 1993; regular concert engagements and recitals; Fellow, Univ. of Cen. Lancs. 1992; Hon. DMus (Manchester) 2003; Kathleen Ferrier Prize 1988, Silver Medal, Worshipful Co. of Musicians 1988, Royal Philharmonic Soc./Charles Heidsieck Award 1990, Barclay Opera Award 2000, Outstanding Achievement In Opera, Laurence Olivier Awards 2007 (for Jenůfa, ENO 2006). *Recordings include:* Amanda Roocroft (solo album) 1994, Mozart and his Contemporaries 1996, Vaughan Williams Serenade to Music (with Matthew Best) 1990, Così fan tutte (with John Eliot Gardiner) 1993, Schoenberg String Quartet No. 2 (with Britten Quartet) 1994, Vaughan Williams Sea Symphony (with Andrew Davies), Mahler Symphony No. 4 (with Simon Rattle), Vaughan Williams Pastoral Symphony (with Bernard Haitink). *Television documentaries include:* The Girl from Coppull, The Debut (Granada TV), Hard Pressed for Signals (Channel 4), Jenufa (BBC Wales). *Leisure interests:* theatre, cinema, reading, cooking. *Address:* Askonas Holt Ltd, Lincoln House, 300 High Holborn, London, WC1V 7JH, England (office). *Telephone:* (20) 7400-1700 (office). *Fax:* (20) 7400-1799 (office). *E-mail:* info@askonasholt.co.uk (office). *Website:* www.askonasholt.co.uk (office).

ROOD, Johannes (Jon) Joseph Van, PhD, MD; Dutch immunologist and academic; b. 7 April 1926, The Hague; s. of Albert van Rood and Rientje Röell; m. Sacha Bsse. van Tuyll van Serooskerken 1957; one s. two d.; ed Univ. of Leiden; worked in bloodbanking 1952–; in charge of Bloodbank and foundation of Dept of Immunohaematology, Univ. Hosp., Leiden 1957; work in tissue typing 1958–; worked on antibody synthesis in Public Health Research Inst., New York 1962; Lecturer in Immunohaematology, Univ. of Leiden 1965–1991, Prof. in Internal Medicine 1969–1991; Founder Eurotransplant 1967, Stichting Europdonor 1970 (Chair. –2000); fmr Pres. World Marrow Donor Asscn. *Publications:* Leukocyte Antibodies in Sera of Pregnant Women 1958, Platelet Survival 1959, Erythrocyte Survival with DFP 32 1961, Leukocyte Groups, the Normal Lymphocyte Transfer Test and Homograft Sensitivity 1965, Platelet Transfusion 1965, The Relevance of Leukocyte Antigens 1967, A Proposal for International Co-operation: EUROTRANSPLANT 1967, Transplantation of Bone-marrow cells and Fetal Thymus in an Infant with Lymphonenic Immunological Deficiency 1969, The 4a and 4b Antigens: Do They or Don't They? 1970, Anti HL-A 2 Inhibitor in Normal Human Serum 1970, HL-A Identical Phenotypes and Genotypes in Unrelated Individuals 1970, HL-A and the Group Five System in Hodgkin's Disease 1971, The (Relative) Importance of HL-A Matching in Kidney Transplantation 1971, Simultaneous Detection of Two Cell Populations by Two Colour Fluorescence and Application to the Recognition of B Cell Determinants 1976, HLA-linked Control of Susceptibility to Tuberculoid Leprosy and Association with HLA-DR types 1978. *Leisure interest:* sailing. *Address:* c/o Europdonor Foundation, Plesmanlaan 1b, 2333 BZ Leiden, Netherlands.

ROONEY, Mickey; American actor; b. (Joe Yule, Jr), 23 Sept. 1920, Brooklyn, NY; s. of Joe Yule and Nell Carter; m. 1st Ava Gardner 1942 (divorced 1943); m. 2nd Betty J. Rase 1944 (divorced 1949); two s.; m. 3rd Martha Vickers 1949 (divorced); m. 4th Elaine Mahnken (divorced 1958); m. 5th Barbara Thomason 1958; four c.; m. 6th Margie Lang 1966 (divorced 1967); m. 7th Carolyn Hockett (divorced); one s. and one adopted s.; m. 8th Jan Chamberlin 1978; two step s.; ed in Dayton Heights, Vine Street Grammar School and Pacific Mil. Acad.; served AUS, World War II; first appeared in vaudeville with parents; later appeared with Sid Gould; numerous TV programmes including series The Mickey Rooney Show; Special Acad. Award 1940, Tony Award for Best Musical Actor 1980. *Films include:* Judge Hardy's Children, Hold That Kiss, Lord Jeff, Love Finds Andy Hardy, Boystown, Stablemates, Out West With the Hardys, Huckleberry Finn, Andy Hardy Gets Spring Fever, Babes in Arms, Young Tom Edison, Judge Hardy and Son, Andy Hardy Meets Debutante, Strike Up the Band, Andy Hardy's Private Secretary, Men of Boystown, Life Begins for Andy Hardy, Babes on Broadway, A Yank at Eton, The Human Comedy, Andy Hardy's Blonde Trouble, Girl Crazy, Thousands Cheer, National Velvet, Ziegfeld Follies, The Strip, Sound Off, Off Limits, All Ashore, Light Case of Larceny, Drive a Crooked Road, Bridges at Toko-Ri, The Bold and Brave, Eddie, Private Lives of Adam and Eve, Comedian, The Grabbers, St Joseph Plays the Horses, Breakfast at Tiffany's, Somebody's Waiting, Requiem for a Heavyweight, Richard, Pulp, It's a Mad, Mad, Mad, Mad World, Everything's Ducky, The Secret Invasion, The Extraordinary Seaman, The Comic, The Cockeyed Cowboys of Calico County, Skidoo, B.J. Presents, That's Entertainment, The Domino Principle, Pete's Dragon, The Magic of Lassie, Black Stallion, Arabian Adventure, Erik the Viking, My Heroes Have Always Been Cowboys 1991, Little Nimo: Adventures in Slumberland (voice) 1992, Silent Night Deadly Night 5: The Toymaker, The Milky Life, Revenge of the Red Baron, That's Entertainment III, Outlaws: The Legend of O.B. Taggart 1994, Making Waves 1994, Kings of the Court (video) 1997, Killing Midnight 1997, Boys Will Be Boys 1997, Animals 1997, Michael Kael contre la World News Company 1998, Sinbad: The Battle of the Dark Knights 1998, Babe: Pig in the City 1998, The Face on the Barroom Floor 1998, The First of May 1999, Holy Hollywood 1999, Internet Love 2000, Lady and the Tramp II: Scamp's Adventure (video) (voice) 2001, Topa Topa Bluffs 2002, Paradise 2003, Strike the Tent 2004, Night at the Museum 2006. *Television includes:* Brothers' Destiny 1995, Stories from My Childhood (series) (voice) 1998, Phantom of the Megaplex 2000, Life with Judy Garland: Me and My Shadows (uncredited singing voice) 2001. *Stage appearances in:* Sugar Babies 1979, The Will Rogers Follies 1993. *Publications:* I.E. An Autobiography 1965, Life Is Too Short 1991, Search for Sunny Skies 1994, Sinbad: The Battle of the Dark Knights 1998, The First Day of May 1998, The Face on the Barroom Floor 1998, Babe: Pig in the City 1998. *Address:* PO Box 3186, Thousand Oaks, CA 91359, USA. *Website:* www.mickeyrooney.com.

ROOS, Björn O., PhD; Swedish chemist and academic; *Professor of Theoretical Chemistry, University of Lund;* b. 28 June 1937, Malmö; m.; four d.; ed Univ. of Stockholm; Sarskild Forskartjanst (Sr Scientist Fellowship), Swedish Natural Science Research Council 1972–78, Asst Prof. 1978–83; Prof. and Head, Dept of Theoretical Chemistry, Univ. of Lund 1983–; Ed. Theoretica Chimica Acta 1985–96; mem. Editorial Bd ChemPhysChem, International Journal of Quantum Chemistry, Molecular Physics, Chemistry Physics Letter; mem. Nobel Cttee for Chemistry 1986–91, Ordinary mem. 1992–2000; mem. Int. Acad. of Quantum Molecular Sciences 1991– (Treas. 1997–2005); mem. ACS, Swedish Asscn of Chemists, Danish Asscn of Chemists, Finnish Asscn of Chemists; Swedish Asscn of Chemists Nordblad-Ekstrand Gold Medal 1977, Univ. of Bratislava Comenius Gold Medal 1996, Royal Soc. of Sciences Celsius Gold Medal 1996, Swedish Asscn of Chemists Bror Holmberg Medal 1997, World Asscn of Theoretically Oriented Chemists (WATOC) Schrodinger Medal 1999, Tokyo Univ. Morino Prize 2001. *Publications:* more than 300 articles in scientific journals. *Leisure interests:* stamp collecting, fishing. *Address:* Department of Theoretical Chemistry, University of Lund, Chemical Center, PO Box 124, 221 00 Lund (office); Protokollgr. 12, 226 47, Lund, Sweden (home). *Telephone:* (46) 222-82-51 (office); (46) 46-120692 (home). *Fax:* (46) 222-45-43 (office). *E-mail:* Bjorn.Roos@teokem.lu.se (office). *Website:* www.teokem.lu.se/~roos (office).

ROOSEN, Gustavo; Venezuelan politician and business executive; ed Andrés Bello Catholic Univ., Caracas, New York Univ., USA; Vice-Pres. Venezuelan Banking Asscn 1981–83; Pres. Caracas Chamber of Commerce 1986–88; Minister of Educ. 1989–92; Pres. Petróleos de Venezuela 1992–95; Pres. CANTV (CA Nacional Teléfonos de Venezuela) 1995–, CEO 2002–07 (resgnd). *Address:* c/o CANTV, Final Av. Libertador, Centro Nacional de Telecomunicaciones, Nuevo Edf. Administrativo, Planta Baja, Caracas, Venezuela (office).

ROOTS, Ott, PhD; Estonian environmental scientist; *Director and Chief Scientist, Estonian Environmental Research Institute, Estonian Environmental Research Centre;* b. 9 May 1946, Tallinn; s. of Dr Otto Roots and Ida Roots (née Lass); m. Marika Voit; one s.; ed Tallinn Tech. Univ., Inst. of Chem., Estonian Acad. of Sciences; Engineer-Lt, Co. Vice-Commdr, 537 Soviet Army Bldg Bn 1969–71; scientist, Inst. of Zoology and Botany, Estonian Acad. of Sciences 1971–74, Baltic Sea Dept, Inst. of Thermo- and Electrophysics 1974–84; Chief Researcher Baltic Br., Inst. of Applied Geophysics 1984–90; Chief Researcher Water Protection Lab., Tallinn Tech. Univ. 1990–92; Sr Scientist Dept of Environmental Carcinogenesis, Inst. of Experimental and Clinical Medicine 1992–94; Lecturer, Tallinn Tech. Univ. 1993, Helsinki Univ. 1995, Tallinn Pedagogical Univ. 1997; Monitoring Counsellor, Environment Information Centre, Ministry of the Environment 1993–2000, Councillor, Dept of Environmental Man. and Tech., Ministry of the Environment 2000–02; Monitoring Co-ordinator, Estonian Environmental Research Centre (EERC) 2000–05, Monitoring Councillor 2005–, Dir and Chief Scientist, Estonian Environmental Research Inst. 2005–, mem. Scientific Council of EERC; Del. Helsinki Comm. (HELCOM) (expert on persistent organic contaminants) 1974–, UN ECE ICP (expert on monitoring) 1994–; Coordinator Finnish-Estonian Training Project (environmental monitoring) 1996–; mem. Estonian Chem. Soc. 1995–, Nat. Geographic Soc., Washington 1996–, New York Acad. of Sciences 1997–, Estonian Nature Fund 1998–2002, Estonia Chemicals Safety Comm. 2000–, Estonian Toxicological Comm., Ministry of Educ. 2001–, Steering Cttee on the Support Project of Chemicals Control in Estonia 2002–05, Estonian Science Soc. 2004–, American Scientist Soc. 2006–, European Lysimeter Research Group, Estonian Co-ordinator –2007, Advisory Bd Scientific Journal Ecological Chemistry (St. Petersburg Univ. and Thesa); mem. Editorial Bd Open Petroleum Engineering Journal 2008–; Amb. Int. HCH and Pesticides Asscn –2003; Bronze Medal, Environmental Protection Exhbn (Russia) 1982, honoured by Ministry of the Environment, Estonia, for work in environmental protection 1996, by Ministry of Social Affairs for work on Govt Chemical Safety Comm. 2003, by Ministry of the Environment (Honour Certificate) for great and long-term contrib. to Estonian environmental protection 2006. *Publications include:* Polychlorinated Biphenyls and Chlororganic Pesticides in the Ecosystem of the Baltic Sea 1992, Toxic Chlororganic Compounds in the Ecosystem of the Baltic Sea 1996, The Effect of Environmental Pollution on Human Health in the Baltic States 1999, Persistent Bioaccumulative and Toxic Chemicals in Central and Eastern European Countries (co-author) 2000, Regionally Based Assessment of Persistent Toxic Substances (co-author) 2003, Ohtlikud Ained Eesti Keskkonnas; contrib. to publs for Estonian Environment Information Centre; more than 190 scientific articles in learned journals. *Leisure interests:* environmental protection, sport (especially basketball), music. *Address:* Estonian Environmental Research Centre, Marja Str. 4D, Tallinn 10617 (office); Paekaare 46-64, 13613 Tallinn, Estonia (home). *Telephone:* (2) 611-2964 (office). *Fax:* (2) 611-2901 (office). *E-mail:* ott.roots@klab.ee (office); ott.roots@ smail.ee (home). *Website:* www.klab.ee (office).

ROP, Anton, MA; Slovenian economist and politician; b. 27 Dec. 1960, Ljubljana; ed Univ. of Ljubljana; Asst Dir Slovene Inst. for Macroeconomic Analysis and Devt 1985–92; State Sec. Ministry of Econ. Relations and Devt 1993; Minister of Labour, Family and Social Affairs 1996–2000, of Finance 2002; Prime Minister 2002–04; Pres. Liberal Democratic Party (Liberalna Demokracija Slovenije—LDS), Leader, Parl. Group 2004–. *Leisure interests:* reading, sport. *Address:* National Assembly, Subiceva 4, 1000 Ljubljana (office); Liberalna Demokracija Slovenije, Republike trg 3, 1000 Ljubljana, Slovenia (office). *Telephone:* (1) 4789569 (office). *Fax:* (1) 4789870 (office). *E-mail:* anton.rop@dz-rs.si (office); toner@lds.si (office). *Website:* www.lds.si (office).

ROPER, Warren Richard, MSc, PhD, FRS, FRSNZ; New Zealand chemist and academic; b. 27 Nov. 1938, Nelson; s. of Robert J. Roper and Nancy L. Robinson; m. Judith D. C. Miller 1961; two s. one d.; ed Nelson Coll., Univ. of Canterbury and Univ. of N Carolina, USA; Lecturer, Univ. of Auckland 1966, Prof. of Chem. 1984–2007; Visiting Lecturer, Univ. of Bristol, UK 1972; Visiting Prof., Univ. of Leeds, UK 1983, Univ. of Rennes, France 1984, 1985, Stanford Univ., USA 1988; Visiting Prof., Univ. of Sydney 2001; Fellow, New Zealand Inst. of Chem., Japan Soc. for Promotion of Science 1992; Hon. DSc (Canterbury) 1999; Royal Soc. of Chem. Award in Organometallic Chem. 1983, ICI Medal, NZ Inst. of Chem., 1984, Centenary Lecturer, Royal Soc. of Chem. 1988, Hector Medal, Royal Soc. of NZ 1991, Inorganic Chem. Award, Royal Australian Chemical Inst. 1992, G.T. Seaborg Lecturer, Univ. of California, Berkeley 1995, Dwyer Medal, Univ. of NSW 2000, Stone Lecturer, Univ. of Bristol 2003, Arthur D. Little Lecturer, MIT 2005. *Publications:* more than 200 original papers and reviews in scientific journals. *Leisure interests:* listening to music (especially opera), walking. *Address:* Department of Chemistry, The University of Auckland, Private Bag, Auckland (office); 26 Beulah Avenue, Auckland 0630, New Zealand (home). *Telephone:* (9) 373-7999 (office); (9) 478-6940 (home). *E-mail:* w.roper@auckland.ac.nz (office). *Website:* www.che.auckland.ac.nz (office).

RORSTED, Kasper; Danish business executive; *CEO, Henkel AG;* b. 24 Feb. 1962, Århus; m.; four c.; ed Int. Business School, Copenhagen, Exec. Summer Program, Harvard Business School, USA; various man. positions in marketing and distribution with Oracle and Digital Equipment Corpn –1995; various man. positions at Compaq, including Head of Compaq Enterprise Business Group in Europe, Middle East & Africa (EMEA) 1995–2001, Vice-Pres. and Gen. Man. Compaq, EMEA Region 2001–02, Sr Vice-Pres. and Gen. Man. Hewlett Packard, EMEA Region 2002–04; Exec. Vice-Pres., Human Resources, Purchasing, Information Technologies, Infrastructure Services 2005–07, Henkel KGaA, Vice-Chair. Man. Bd Henkel KGaA and Exec. Vice-Pres. Human Resources and Infrastructure Services 2007–08, CEO Henkel Group AG, responsible for Human Resources, Infrastructure Services 2008–; mem. Bd of Dirs Cable & Wireless (UK), Ecolab Inc., Henkel of America Inc., Henkel Cen. Eastern Europe GmbH (Austria), Henkel Belgium NV, Henkel France SA, Henkel Norden AB (Sweden); mem. Man. Bd Henkel Group and Chair. 2005–, Exec. Vice-Pres. Human Resources and Infrastructure Services 2005–, CEO Henkel Group 2008–, Exec. Vice-Pres. Human Resources, Purchasing, Information Technologies and Infrastructure Services, Henkel KGaA (subsidiary of Henkel Group) 2005–, Vice-Chair. Man. Bd Henkel KGaA 2007–08, Chair. Henkel KGaA 2008–. *Address:* Henkel AG & Co. KGaA, Henkelstrasse 67, Düsseldorf 40191, Germany (office). *Telephone:* (211) 797-0 (office). *Fax:* (211) 7982484 (office). *E-mail:* info@henkel.com (office). *Website:* www.henkel.com (office).

ROS, Enrique Jorge, LLD; Argentine lawyer and diplomatist; b. 16 July 1927; ed Univs of Buenos Aires and Paris; practised as lawyer 1949–54; joined diplomatic service 1954; served at Perm. Mission to OAS 1956–58, UN 1959–63; Chargé d'Affaires, The Hague 1965–67; served at Embassy in London 1967–71; Head of Mission, Beijing 1973–75; Amb. to Israel 1976–77; Perm. Rep. to UN, New York 1977–80; Dir-Gen. Foreign Policy Bureau, Ministry of Foreign Affairs 1980, Under-Sec. for Foreign Affairs 1980–82; Amb. to Spain 1982–84, to Japan 1984–89, to Viet Nam (non-resident) 1985–89; mem. Higher Council of Ambs of Ministry of Foreign Affairs 1990–; Chair. Bilateral Admin. Comm. of River Plate 1991; decorations from Bolivia, Brazil, Chile, Colombia, Ecuador, Paraguay, Peru, Venezuela, Japan. *Leisure interests:* reading, gardening. *Address:* c/o Ministry of Foreign Affairs, International Trade and Worship, Esmeralda 1212, C1007ABR Buenos Aires, Argentina.

ROSA BAUTISTA, Leonidas; Honduran lawyer and politician; *Attorney-General;* b. 4 Feb. 1947, Lepaera; s. of Leonidas Rosa and Alejandrina Vda. de Rosa; m. Abogada Irma Violeta Suazo de Rosa; three c.; ed Instituto Ramón Rosa, Gracias, Lempira, Universidad Nacional Autónoma de Honduras; fmr

legal adviser to Main Directorate of Transport; Vice Minister of the Interior and of Justice 1978–1980; Deputy to Constituent Nat. Ass. 1980–82; fmr Prof., Universidad Nacional Autónoma de Honduras; Minister of Foreign Affairs 2003–05; Attorney-Gen. 2005–; Sr Pnr and Dir, Bufete Rosa y Asociados, S.A. de C.V. (law firm), Tegucigalpa; Pres. Honduran Bar Assocn 1990–92; Prof., Universidad Nacional Autónoma de Honduras. *Address:* Bufete Rosa y Asociados, S.A. de C.V., Edificio Rosa y Asociados, Colonia San Rafael Retorno Kobe n. 29, Tegucigalpa (office); Office of the Attorney-General, Fiscal General del Estado, Ministerio Público, Lomas del Guijarro, Tegucigalpa, Honduras (office). *Telephone:* 239-2688 (Bufete Rosa) (office). *Fax:* 239-2718 (Bufete Rosa) (office). *E-mail:* lrosab@bufeterosa.com (office). *Website:* www .bufeterosa.com (office).

ROSALES BOLAÑOS, Antenor; Nicaraguan lawyer, banking executive and central banker; *Governor, Banco Central de Nicaragua;* b. 1955, Leon; s. of Rodolfo Rosales and Angela Bolaños; ed Central American Univ., Managua; joined Sandinista Nat. Liberation Front 1970, Pres.Nat. Asscn of Students of Eng. and Allied Careers and Coordinator Exec. Cttee Revolutionary Student Front, joined Sandinista People's Army and served as commdr during insurrection of Esteli, retd with rank of Col 1999; fmr mem. Bd of Dirs Superintendency of Banks and Other Financial Institutions; Co-founder and fmr Dir ProCredit Bank; fmr Dir Intercontinental Bank; Gov. Banco Central de Nicaragua (Cen. Bank of Nicaragua) 2007–; Alternate Gov., Inter-American Devt Bank. *Address:* Banco Central de Nicaragua, Carretera Sur, Km 7, Apdos 2252/3, Zona 5, Managua, Nicaragua (office). *Telephone:* 255-7171 (office). *Fax:* 265-0561 (office). *E-mail:* bcn@bcn.gob.ni (office). *Website:* www.bcn.gob.ni (office).

ROSALES GUERRERO, Manuel; Venezuelan politician; b. 12 Dec. 1952, Santa Bárbara, Zulia; m. Eveling Trejo de Rosales; eight c.; Auditor, Colón Municipal Council 1973–74; Councillor, Santa Bárbara 1979–82; Deputy Zulia Legis. Ass. 1983–94; Mayor of Maracaibo 1996–2000; Gov. Zulia prov. 2001–08; Mayor of Maracaibo 2008–09; fled country to avoid corruption charges April 2009; unsuccessful cand. in presidential election 2006; fmr mem. Acción Democrática; f. Un Nuevo Tiempo party 2000.

ROSATI, Dariusz Kajetan, DEcon; Polish economist and politician; b. 8 Aug. 1946, Radom; s. of Angelo Rosati and Wanda Pleszczyńska; m. Teresa Nowińska 1971; one s. one d.; ed Main School of Planning and Statistics, Warsaw; scientific researcher, Main School of Planning and Statistics (now Cen. School of Commerce), Warsaw 1969–, Asst Prof. 1978, Prof. 1990–; with Citibank, New York 1978–79; Visiting Prof., Princeton Univ., NJ 1986–87; Founder and first Dir Inst. of World Economy, Warsaw School of Econs 1985; Dir Foreign Trade Research Inst., Warsaw 1988–91; Partner, TKD-Ernst & Young Poland 1989–92; Head UN Section for Cen. and E Europe, Geneva 1991–95; Minister of Foreign Affairs 1995–97; mem. Council of Monetary Policy of Nat. Bank of Poland 1998–2004; mem. Bd Dirs Int. Exchange Program (IREX), Washington, DC 1998–2001; currently Chair. WTO panel on US subsidies on upland cotton; mem. Polish United Workers' Party (PZPR) 1966–90; mem. Cttee on Econ. Reform 1987–90, team of econ. advisors to Prime Minister 1988–89, Econ. Strategy Cttee to the Cabinet 1994–97; Adviser to Pres. of EC 2001–; Rector Richard Łazarski Univ. of Commerce and Law, Warsaw 2003–; mem. European Parl. (Socialist Group) 2004–, mem. Cttee on Econ. and Monetary Affairs, Substitute mem. Cttee on Foreign Affairs, Sub-cttee on Security and Defence, Vice-Chair. Temporary Cttee on Policy Challenges and Budgetary Means of the Enlarged Union 2007–2013, mem Del. to ACP-EU Jt Parl. Ass.; mem. Polish Econ. Soc. 1969–, Econ. Studies Cttee Polish Acad. of Sciences 1999–, European Econ. Asscn, European Asscn of Comparative Econ. Studies; Silver Cross of Merit 1981, Kt's Cross Order of Poland Restituta 1989, Orders of Merit from France, Italy, Greece, Ukraine and Lithuania. *Publications:* Decision-Making 1977, Inflation 1989, Export Policies 1990, Polish Way to Market 1998, An Agenda for a Growing Europe: The Sapir Report 2004, Facing the Challenge: Lisbon Strategy for growth and employment 2004, New Europe: Report from Transformation 2005; more than 250 scientific articles. *Leisure interests:* sports, reading. *Address:* ul. Bagatela 10/4, 00–585 Warsaw, Poland (office); European Parliament, Bâtiment Altiero Spinelli, 07H247, 60 rue Wiertz, 1047 Brussels, Belgium (office). *Telephone:* (22) 6215275 (Warsaw) (office). *Fax:* (2) 2847182 (Warsaw) (office). *E-mail:* piotr.stolarczyk@rosati.pl (office); dariusz@rosati.pl (office); drosati@europarl.eu.int (office). *Website:* www .rosati.pl (office).

ROSATTI, Horacio; Argentine lawyer, academic and fmr government official; b. Santa Fe; elected mem. Constituent Ass. 1994; Mayor of Santa Fe 1995–99; Co-Judge, Supreme Court 2002–03; Attorney-Gen. of the Treasury 2003–04; Minister of Justice, Security and Human Rights 2004–05; fmr Dean of Faculty of Law, Catholic Univ. of Santa Fe; fmr Dean Universidad del Litoral; Corresp. mem. Instituto de Federalismo; mem. Partido Justicialista (PJ). *Address:* c/o Ministry of Justice, Security and Human Rights, Sarmiento 329, 1041 Buenos Aires, Argentina (office).

ROŞCA, Iurie; Moldovan journalist and politician; *Deputy Chairman of Parliament;* b. 31 Oct. 1961, Teleneşti; m.; three c.; ed Moldova State Univ.; active in pro-democracy movement in 1980s; Ed., Teleradio-Moldova Co.; mem. Parl. 1994–, Deputy Chair. of Parl. 1998–2000, 2005–, mem. Standing Bureau of Parl.; Chair. People's Christian Democratic Party 1994–. *Publications:* Escape from the Darkness 1995, Exercises of Lucidity 2000. *Address:* Office of the Deputy Speaker, Chisinau, Stefan cel Mare 105 (office); People's Christian Democratic Party (Partidul Popular Creştin Democrat—PPCD), 2009 Chişinău, str. Nicolae Iorga 5, Moldova (office). *Telephone:* (22) 23-73-09 (Parl.) (office); (22) 23-45-47 (office). *Fax:* (22) 23-20-65 (Parl.) (office); (22) 23-86-66 (office). *E-mail:* rosca@parlament.md (office); magic@ppcd.md (office). *Website:* www.parlament.md; www.ppcd.md (office).

ROSCITT, Richard R. (Rick), BEng, MBA; American business executive; *Chairman, Sapien LLC;* ed Stevens Inst. of Tech., Sloan School of Management, MIT; joined AT&T 1973, fmr Pres. AT&T Business Services, then Pres. and CEO AT&T Solutions, fmr mem. Operations Group, AT&T; Chair. and CEO ADC Telecommunications 2001–03; Pres. and COO MCI Group 2003–04; Chair. Sapien LLC 2005–; Chair. (non-exec.) Orion Telecommunications, SMOBILE Systems; Pnr Core Value Pnrs Investments; mem. Bd of Trustees Stevens Inst. of Tech. *Address:* Sapien Corporate Headquarters, 7 Washington Street, Morristown, NJ 07960, USA (office). *Telephone:* (866) 372-7436 (office). *Fax:* (973) 944-7558 (home). *E-mail:* info@sapiensoftware.com (office). *Website:* www.sapiensoftware.com (office).

ROSE, Sir Clive (Martin), GCMG, MA, FRSA, FICDDS; British diplomatist (retd); b. 15 Sept. 1921, Banstead, Surrey; s. of the late Bishop Alfred Rose; m. Elisabeth MacKenzie Lewis 1946 (deceased 2006); two s. three d.; ed Marlborough Coll. and Christ Church, Oxford; Rifle Brigade (rank of Maj., mentioned in despatches), Europe, India, Iraq 1941–46; Commonwealth Relations Office 1948; High Comm. Madras 1948–49; Foreign Office 1950; served in Bonn, Montevideo, Paris, Washington and London 1950–73; Imperial Defence Coll. 1968; Amb. and Head of UK Del. to Mutual and Balanced Force Reduction talks, Vienna 1973–76; Deputy Sec. to Cabinet Office 1976–79; UK Perm. Rep. on N Atlantic Council 1979–82; Consultant to Control Risks Group Ltd 1983–95; Chair. Control Risks Information Services Ltd 1991–93 (Dir 1986–93); Pres. Emergency Planning Asscn 1987–93; mem. Advisory Bd Royal Coll. for Defence Studies 1985–92; Chair. Council Royal United Services Inst. 1983–86, Vice-Pres. 1986–93, Vice-Patron 1993–2001; Vice-Pres. Suffolk Preservation Soc. 1988–2007 (Chair. 1985–88), Vice-Patron 2007. *Publications:* Campaigns Against Western Defence: NATO's Adversaries and Critics 1985, The Soviet Propaganda Network: a Directory of Organisations Serving Soviet Foreign Policy 1988, The Unending Quest: A Search for Ancestors 1996, Detente, Diplomacy and MBFR (Contrib.) 2002, Alice Owen: The Life and Times and Marriages of a Tudor Lady 2006, Fanfare for Lavenham (epic poem) 2007. *Leisure interests:* gardening, genealogy, writing poetry. *Address:* Chimney House, Lavenham, Suffolk, CO10 9QT, England (home).

ROSE, Gen. Sir (Hugh) Michael, KCB, CBE, DSO, QGM, DL; British army officer (retd); b. 5 Jan. 1940, India; s. of the late Lt-Col Hugh Rose and of the late Barbara Allcard; m. Angela Shaw 1968; two s.; ed Cheltenham Coll., St Edmund Hall, Oxford and Royal Coll. of Defence Studies; commissioned, Gloucestershire Regt Territorial Army Volunteer Reserve 1959; RAF Volunteer Reserve 1962; Coldstream Guards 1964; served Germany, Aden, Malaysia, Gulf States, Dhofar, NI, Falkland Islands; Brigade Maj., 16 Para. Brigade 1973–75; CO 22 SAS Regt 1979–82; Command, 39 Infantry Brigade 1983–85; Commdt School of Infantry 1987–88; Dir Special Forces 1988–89; GOC NE Dist and Commdr 2nd Infantry Div. 1989–91; Commdt Staff Coll. 1991–93; Commdr UK Field Army and Insp.-Gen. of Territorial Army 1993–94; Commdr (UN Forces in) Bosnia-Herzegovina 1994–95; Adjutant Gen. 1995–97; Aide de Camp Gen. to the Queen 1995–97; Col Coldstream Guards 1999–; fmr Dir Control Risks Group; Hon. DLitt (Nottingham) 1999. *Television:* presenter Power House 2000. *Publications:* Fighting for Peace 1998, Washington's War 2007. *Leisure interests:* sailing, skiing. *Address:* c/o Regimental H.Q. Coldstream Guards, Wellington Barracks, Birdcage Walk, London, SW1E 6HQ, England.

ROSE, Irwin (Ernie), BS, PhD; American biologist and academic; *Specialist, Department of Physiology and Biophysics, College of Medicine, University of California, Irvine;* b. 16 July 1926, Brooklyn, NY; m. Zelda Budenstein Rose; ed Washington State Coll., Univ. of Chicago; Radio Technician, USN during Second World War; faculty mem., Yale Univ. Medical School Dept of Biochemistry 1954–63; Sr Mem., Fox Chase Cancer Center, Phila 1963–95 (retd); Specialist, Dept of Physiology and Biophysics, Coll. Medicine, Univ. of Calif., Irvine 1995–; mem. NAS; Nobel Prize in Chemistry (jt recipient) 2004. *Address:* Department of Physiology and Biophysics, College of Medicine, University of California, Irvine, CA 92697, USA (office). *Telephone:* (949) 824-4097 (office). *Fax:* (949) 824-8571 (office). *Website:* www.ucihs.uci.edu/pandb (office).

ROSE, Sir John E.V., MA, FRAeS; British business executive; *Chief Executive, Rolls-Royce plc;* b. 1953, Blantyre, Malawi; m. Felicity Rose; two s. one d.; ed Univ. of St Andrews, Scotland; fmrly with First Nat. Bank of Chicago and Security Pacific; joined Rolls-Royce 1994, Dir of Corp. Devt 1989–1994, mem. Bd 1992–, Pres. and Chief Exec. Rolls-Royce plc 1993–96, Man. Dir Aerospace Group 1995–, Chief Exec. 1996–; Dir (non-exec.) Eli Lilly & Co. 2003–; mem. JP Morgan Int. Council, CBI Int. Advisory Bd, Englefield Advisory Bd; Trustee Eden Project; fmr Pres. European Asscn of Aerospace Industries and Soc. of British Aerospace Cos; Fellow, Royal Aeronautical Soc.; Hon. DSc (St Andrews) 1975. *Leisure interests:* scuba diving, skiing, the arts. *Address:* Rolls-Royce plc, 65 Buckingham Gate, London SW1E 6AT, England (office). *Telephone:* (20) 7222-9020 (office). *Fax:* (20) 7227-9178 (office). *Website:* www.rolls-royce.com (office).

ROSE, Matthew K., BS; American transport industry executive; *Chairman, President and CEO, Burlington Northern Santa Fe Corporation;* b. 1960; ed Univ. of Missouri; began career as Man. Trainee Missouri Pacific Railroad 1981; various positions Schneider National, International Utilities; Vice-Pres. Triple Crown Services –1993; joined Burlington Northern 1993, Vice-Pres. Vehicles and Machinery 1994–95, Vice-Pres. Chemicals 1995–96 (following merger with Santa Fe 1995), Sr Vice-Pres. Merchandise Business Unit 1996–97, Sr Vice-Pres. and COO 1997–99, Pres. and COO 1999–2000, Pres. and CEO 2000–, also Chair. 2002–; Chair. Asscn of American Railroads; mem. Bd of Dirs AMR Corpn, Centex Building Community, Center for Energy & Econ. Devt; mem. Gov. of Tex. Business Council, Business Roundtable; mem. Bd Trustees Texas Christian Univ.; mem. NW Univ. Transportation Center Business Advisory Cttee; American Soc. Transportation and Logistics Distinguished Logistics Professional Award 2007. *Address:* Burlington Northern Santa Fe Corpn, 2650 Lou Menk Drive, Fort Worth, TX 76131-2830, USA (office). *Telephone:* (800) 795-2673 (office). *Fax:* (817) 352-7171 (office). *Website:* www.bnsf.com (office).

ROSE, Richard, BA, DPhil, FBA; American writer, academic and consultant; *Professor of Public Policy, University of Aberdeen;* b. 9 April 1933, St Louis, Mo.; s. of Charles Imse Rose and Mary C. Rose; m. Rosemary J. Kenny 1956; two s. one d.; ed Clayton High School, Mo., Johns Hopkins Univ., LSE, Oxford; worked in political public relations, Miss. Valley 1954–55; reporter, St Louis Post-Dispatch 1955–57; Lecturer in Govt, Univ. of Manchester 1961–66; Prof. of Politics Strathclyde Univ. 1966–82, Prof. of Public Policy and Dir Centre for the Study of Public Policy 1976–2005; Prof. of Public Policy, Univ. of Aberdeen 2005–; Specialist Adviser, House of Commons Public Admin Cttee 2002–03; Consultant Psephologist, The Times, ITV, Daily Telegraph, etc. 1964–; Sec. Cttee on Political Sociology, Int. Sociology Asscn 1970–85; Founding mem. European Consortium for Political Research 1970; mem. US/UK Fulbright Comm. 1971–75; Guggenheim Fellow 1974; Visiting scholar at various insts, Europe, USA, Hong Kong; mem. Home Office Working Party on Electoral Register 1975–77; Co-Founder British Politics Group 1974–; Convenor Work Group on UK Politics, Political Studies Asscn 1976–88; mem. Council Int. Political Science Asscn 1976–82; Tech. Consultant OECD, UNDP, World Bank, Council of Europe, Int. IDEA; Dir SSRC Research Programme, Growth of Govt 1982–86; Ed. Journal of Public Policy 1985–, Chair. 1981–85; Scientific Adviser, New Democracies Barometer, Paul Lazarsfeld Soc., Vienna 1991–; Sr Fellow in Governance, Oxford Internet Inst. 2003–05; Hon. Vice-Pres. UK Political Studies Asscn; Hon. Fellow American Acad. of Arts and Sciences, Finnish Acad. of Science and Letters, Acad. of Learned Socs in the Social Sciences 2000; Hon. PhD, Örebro Univ. (Sweden); AMEX Prize in Int. Econs 1992, Lasswell Prize for Lifetime Achievement, Policy Studies Org. 1999; Lifetime Achievement Award, UK Political Studies Asscn 1990. *Publications:* numerous books on politics and public policy including Politics in England 1964, People in Politics: Observations Across the Atlantic 1970, Governing Without Consensus: An Irish Perspective 1971, International Almanack of Electoral History (co-author) 1974, The Problem of Party Government 1974, Northern Ireland: A Time of Choice 1976, Managing Presidential Objectives 1976, What is Governing? Purpose and Policy in Washington 1978, Can Government Go Bankrupt? (co-author) 1978, Do Parties Make A Difference 1984, Understanding Big Government 1984, Public Employment in Western Nations (co-author) 1985, Taxation by Political Inertia (co-author) 1987, Ministers and Ministries 1987, Presidents and Prime Ministers, The Postmodern President 1988, Ordinary People in Public Policy 1989, Training With Trainers? How Germany Avoids Britain's Supply-side Bottleneck (co-author) 1990, The Loyalties of Voters (co-author) 1990, Lesson-Drawing in Public Policy 1993 Inheritance in Public Policy (co-author) 1994, What is Europe? 1996, How Russia Votes (co-author) 1997, Democracy and Its Alternatives, Understanding Post-Communist Societies (co-author) 1998, A Society Transformed: Hungary in Time-Space Perspective, International Encyclopedia of Elections (co-author) 2000, The Prime Minister in a Shrinking World 2001, Elections without Order: Russia's Challenge to Vladimir Putin (co-author) 2002, Elections and Parties in New European Democracies 2003, Learning from Comparative Public Policy 2005; hundreds of papers in academic journals. *Leisure interests:* architecture, music, writing. *Address:* Centre for the Study of Public Policy, University of Aberdeen, Aberdeen, AB24 3QY (office); 1 East Abercromby Street, Helensburgh, G84 7SP, Scotland (home). *Telephone:* (1436) 672164 (home). *Fax:* (1436) 673125 (home). *E-mail:* richard.rose@abdn.ac.uk (office). *Website:* www.abdn.ac.uk/cspp (office).

ROSE, Sir Stuart Alan Ransom, Kt; British retail industry executive; *Executive Chairman and CEO, Marks and Spencer Group PLC;* b. 17 March 1949; s. of Harry Ransom Rose and Margaret Ransom Rose; m. Jennifer Cook 1973; one s. one d.; ed St Joseph's Convent, Dar-es-Salaam, Tanzania, Bootham School, York; various exec. positions with Marks & Spencer PLC 1971–89, Commercial Exec. (Europe), CEO Marks & Spencer Group PLC 2004–, Exec. Chair. 2008–; CEO Multiples, Burton Group PLC 1989–97, Argos PLC 1998, Booker PLC 1998–2000, Iceland Group PLC (after merger with Booker) 2000, Arcadia PLC 2000–02; Chair. British Fashion Council 2003–; Business Leader of the Year, World Leadership Forum 2007. *Address:* Marks and Spencer Group PLC, Michael House, Baker Street, London, W1U 8EP, England (office). *Telephone:* (20) 7935-4422 (office). *Fax:* (20) 7487-2679 (office). *E-mail:* info@marksandspencer.com (office). *Website:* www.marksandspencer.com (office).

ROSEANNE; American comedienne and actress; b. (Roseanne Cherrie Barr), 3 Nov. 1952, Salt Lake City; d. of Jerry Barr and Helen Barr; m. 1st Bill Pentland 1974 (divorced 1989); m. 2nd Tom Arnold 1990 (divorced 1994); three c. (from previous m.); m. 3rd Ben Thomas 1994; one s.; fmr window dresser, cocktail waitress; worked as comic in bars and church coffeehouse, Denver; produced forum for women performers Take Back the Mike, Univ. of Colo; performer, The Comedy Store, LA; featured on TV special Funny and The Tonight Show; TV special, On Location: The Roseanne Barr Show 1987; star of TV series, Roseanne (ABC) 1988–97; Host Search for America's Funniest Mom 2007–; Emmy Award (Outstanding Leading Actress in a Comedy Series) 1993. *Films:* She Devil 1989, Look Who's Talking Too (voice) 1990, Freddy's Dead: The Final Nightmare 1991, Even Cowgirls Get the Blues 1994, Blue in the Face 1995, Unzipped 1995, Meet Wally Sparks 1997, Home on the Range (voice) 2004, A Dairy Tale (voice) 2004. *Television includes:* Little Rosie (series) (voice) 1990, Backfield in Motion 1991, Rosey and Buddy Show (series) (voice) 1992, The Woman Who Loved Elvis 1993, Even Cowgirls Get the Blues 1993, General Hospital (series) 1993, Saturday Night Special (series) 1996,

The Roseanne Show (host) 1998–, Get Bruce 1999. *Publications:* My Life as a Woman 1989, Roseanne: My Lives 1994. *E-mail:* askroseanne@roseanneworld.com. *Website:* www.roseanneworld.com.

ROSELLE, David, PhD; American mathematician and university administrator; *Director, Winterthur Museum and Country Estate;* b. 30 May 1939, Vandergrift, Pa; s. of William Roselle and Suzanne Clever; m. Louise H. Dowling 1967; one s. one d.; ed West Chester State Coll. and Duke Univ.; Asst Prof. Univ. of Md 1965–68; Assoc. Prof., Prof. La State Univ. 1968–74; Prof. Va Polytechnic Inst. and State Univ. 1974–87, Dean, Grad. School 1979–81, Dean of Research and Grad. Studies 1981–83, Univ. Provost 1983–87; Pres. Univ. of Ky 1987–90, Univ. of Del. 1990–2007, Emer. Pres. 2007–; Dir Winterthur Museum and Country Estate 2008–; numerous grants and honours; several hon. degrees. *Publications:* numerous mathematics articles in graph theory and combinatorics. *Leisure interests:* golf, reading, jogging. *Address:* Office of the Director, Winterthur Museum and Country Estate, Route 52, Wilmington, DE 19735 (office); 14 Laurel Ridge Lane, Wilmington, DE 19807, USA (home). *Telephone:* (302) 888-4770 (office); (302) 421-3603 (home). *E-mail:* roselle@udel.edu (office). *Website:* www.winterthur.org (office).

ROSEMAN, Saul, MS PhD; American biochemist and academic; *Professor of Biology, Johns Hopkins University;* b. 9 March 1921, Brooklyn, NY; s. of Emil Roseman and Rose Roseman (née Markowitz); m. Martha Ozrowitz 1941; one s. two d.; ed City Coll. of New York and Univ. of Wisconsin; Instructor to Asst Prof., Univ. of Chicago 1948–53; Asst Prof. to Prof. of Biological Chem. and chemist, Rackham Arthritis Research Unit, Univ. of Mich. 1953–65; Prof. of Biology, Johns Hopkins Univ. 1965–, Chair. Dept of Biology 1969–73, 1988–90, Dir, McCollum-Pratt Inst. 1969–73, 1988–90; Ralph S. O'Connor Prof. of Biology; Consultant, NIH, Nat. Cystic Fibrosis Research Foundation, NSF, American Cancer Soc., Hosp. for Sick Children, Toronto; Scientific Counsellor to Nat. Cancer Inst.; Counsellor to American Soc. of Biological Chemists; mem. Editorial Bd Journal of Biological Chemistry 1962–75, Journal of Lipid Research 1967–73, Journal of Membrane Biology 1969–80, Biochimica et Biophysica Acta 1971–75, Biochemistry 1976–80; mem. American Soc. of Biological Chemists, American Acad. of Arts and Sciences, ACS, NAS, AAAS, Biophysical Soc., American Asscn of Univ. Profs; Fellow, American Acad. of Microbiology 1992; Hon. mem. Biochemical Soc. of Japan; Hon. MD (Univ. of Lund, Sweden) 1984; Sesquicentennial Award (Univ. of Mich.) 1967, 15th Annual T. Duckett Jones Memorial Award, Helen Hay Whitney Foundation 1973, Rosensteihl Award (Brandeis Univ.) 1974, Gairdner Foundation Int. Award 1981, Townsend Harris Medal, City Coll. of New York 1987, Lynch Lecturer, Univ. of Notre Dame 1989, Special Award, 11th Int. Symposium on Glycoconjugates, Toronto, Canada 1991, Van Niel Lecturer, Stanford Univ. 1992, Karl Meyer Award, Soc. of Complex Carbohydrates 1993. *Publications:* 300 original articles in scientific journals. *Leisure interests:* sailing, music, reading, athletics. *Address:* Department of Biology, Mudd 214A, The Johns Hopkins University, 3400 North Charles Street, Baltimore, MD 21218-2685 (office); 8206 Cranwood Court, Baltimore, MD 21208, USA (home). *Telephone:* (410) 516-7333 (office); (410) 516-6110 (office); (410) 486-7439 (home). *Fax:* (410) 516-5213 (office). *E-mail:* roseman@jhu.edu (office). *Website:* www.bio.jhu.edu/Directory/Faculty/Roseman/Default.html (office).

ROSEN, Charles, PhD; American pianist and writer; *International Chairman of Performing and Musicology, Royal Northern College of Music and Drama;* b. 5 May 1927, New York, NY; s. of Irwin Rosen and Anita Gerber; ed Juilliard School of Music, Princeton Univ., Univ. of Southern California; studied piano with Moriz Rosenthal and Hedwig Kanner-Rosenthal 1938–45; recital début, New York 1951; first complete recording of Debussy Etudes 1951; première of Double Concerto by Elliott Carter, New York 1961; has played recitals and as soloist with orchestras throughout America and Europe; has made over 35 recordings including Stravinsky: Movements with composer conducting 1962, Bach: Art of Fugue, Two Ricercares, Goldberg Variations 1971, Beethoven: Last Six Sonatas 1972, Boulez: Piano Music, Vol. I, Diabelli Variations, Beethoven Concerto No. 4, 1979, Schumann: The Revolutionary Masterpieces, Chopin: 24 Mazurkas 1991; Prof. of Music, State Univ. of NY 1972–90; Guggenheim Fellowship 1974; Messenger Lectures, Cornell Univ. 1975, Bloch Lectures, Univ. of Calif., Berkeley 1977, Gauss Seminars, Princeton Univ. 1978; Norton Prof. of Poetry, Harvard Univ. 1980–81; George Eastman Prof., Balliol Coll., Oxford 1987–88, Prof. of Music and Social Thought, Univ. of Chicago 1988–96; Int. Chair. of Performing and Musicology, Royal Northern Coll. of Music and Drama 2006–09; Hon. DMus (Trinity Coll., Dublin 1976, Leeds Univ. 1976, Durham Univ.); Dr hc (Cambridge) 1992; Nat. Book Award 1972, Edison Prize, Netherlands 1974, Musical America Instrumentalist of the Year 2008. *Publications:* The Classical Style: Haydn, Mozart, Beethoven 1971, Beethoven's Last Six Sonatas 1972, Schoenberg 1975, Sonata Forms 1980, Romanticism and Realism: The Mythology of Nineteenth-Century Art (with Henri Zerner) 1984, The Musical Language of Elliott Carter 1984, Paisir de jouer, plaiser de penser 1993, The Frontiers of Meaning: Three Informal Lectures on Music 1994, The Romantic Generation 1995, Romantic Poets, Critics and Other Madmen 1998, Critical Entertainment: Music Old and New 2000, Beethoven's Piano Sonatas: A Short Companion 2001, Piano Notes 2003; contrib. to books, newspapers and journals. *Address:* c/o Owen/White Management, Flat 6, 22 Brunswick Terrace, Hove, East Sussex BN3 1HJ, England (office). *Telephone:* (1273) 727127 (office). *Fax:* (1273) 527038 (office). *E-mail:* info@owenwhitemanagement.com (office). *Website:* www.owenwhitemanagement.com (office).

ROSÉN, Haiim B., PhD; Israeli professor of linguistics and classics; *Professor Emeritus, Tel-Aviv University;* b. 4 March 1922, Vienna, Austria; s. of the late Georg Rosenrauch and Olga Gerstl; m. Hannah Steinitz 1953; one s.; ed schools in Vienna, Hebrew Univ., Jerusalem, Ecole Pratique des Hautes Etudes and Coll. de France, Paris; went to Palestine 1938; schoolteacher, Tel-Aviv 1944–49; mem. Faculty, Hebrew Univ. Jerusalem 1949–, Prof. of Gen. and Indo-European Linguistics 1968–, Head, Dept of Linguistics 1973–86; Prof. of Classics and Hebrew Linguistics, Tel Aviv Univ. 1961–91, Prof. Emer. 1991–; mem. Israeli Nat. Acad. of Sciences and Humanities; Rep. of Israel, Perm. Int. Cttee of Linguists; visiting professorships at Univ. of Chicago, Univ. of Paris, Coll. de France, Univ. of Tübingen etc.; Israel State Prize in the Humanities 1978, Humboldt Research Award 1993. *Publications:* about 25 books including Ha-Ivrit Shelanu (Our Hebrew Language) 1955, East and West–Selected writings in linguistics, three vols 1982–94, Herodoti Historiae edition in the Bibliotheca Teubneriana, two vols 1987–97; about 200 articles on classical philology, general, Indo-European and Hebrew linguistics. *Address:* 13, Bruria, Jerusalem 93184, Israel. *Telephone:* 2-6784236.

ROSEN, Hilary B.; American music industry executive; *Founding Partner, Berman Rosen Global Strategies LLC;* ed George Washington Univ.; worked for Gov. Brendan Byrne and Senator Bill Bradley; worked on transition team of Senator Dianne Feinstein 1992; government affairs specialist with Liz Robbins Assocs and later with her own firm; joined Recording Industry Asscn of America 1987, Chair. and CEO 1998–2003; involved in establishing Secure Digital Music Initiative, passage of Digital Performance Rights Act, US ratification of World Intellectual Property Org. treaties regarding copyright laws, adoption of Digital Millennium Copyright Act; Founding Pnr Berman Rosen Global Strategies LLC (intellectual property consultant), Washington, DC 2006–; Founding Bd mem. Rock the Vote; Bd mem. Ford's Theater, Human Rights Campaign Foundation, Kaiser Family Foundation, LifeBeat, Meridian Int. Center, Nat. Cancer Foundation, Nat. Music Council, Y.E.S. to Jobs; American Civil Liberties Union Torch of Liberty.

ROSEN, Milton William, BS; American engineer and physicist; b. 25 July 1915, Philadelphia, Pa; s. of Abraham Rosen and Regina Rosen (Weiss); m. Josephine Haar 1948; three d.; ed Univ. of Pennsylvania, Univ. of Pittsburgh and California Inst. of Tech.; engineer, Westinghouse Electric and Mfg Co. 1937–38; engineer-physicist, Naval Research Lab., Washington, DC 1940–58, Scientific Officer, Viking Rocket 1947–55, Head, Rocket Devt Branch 1953–55, Tech. Dir Project Vanguard (earth satellite) 1955–58; engineer, NASA 1958–74; Chief of Rocket Vehicle Devt Programs 1958–59, Asst Dir Launch Vehicle Programs 1960–61, Dir Launch Vehicles and Propulsion 1961–63; Sr Scientist, Office of DOD and Interagency Affairs, NASA 1963–72; Deputy Assoc. Admin. for Space Science (Eng) 1972–74; Exec. Sec. Space Science Bd 1974–78; Exec. Sec. Cttee on Impacts of Stratospheric Change, NAS 1978–80, Cttee on Underground Coal Mine Safety 1980–83; Exec. Dir Space Applications Board 1983–85; Chair. Greater Washington Asscn of Unitarian Churches 1966–68; Study Leader, Inst. for Learning in Retirement, American Univ., Washington, DC 1987–; first James H. Wyld Award for the Application of Rocket Power 1954. *Publication:* The Viking Rocket Story 1955. *Leisure interests:* music, art collecting, rug making. *Address:* 5610 Alta Vista Road, Bethesda, MD 20817, USA (home). *Telephone:* (301) 530-1497 (home). *E-mail:* sallyrosen@earthlink.net (home).

ROSENAU, James N., AM, PhD; American political scientist and academic; *University Professor of International Affairs, George Washington University;* b. 25 Nov. 1924, Philadelphia, Pa; s. of Walter N. Rosenau and Fanny Fox Baum; m. Hongying Wang; one s. two d.; ed Bard Coll., Johns Hopkins, Princeton, Columbia and New York Univs; Instructor in Political Science, Douglass Coll., Rutgers Univ. 1949–54, Asst Prof. 1954–60, Assoc. Prof. 1960–62, Prof. 1962–70, Acting Chair. 1963–64, Faculty Fellow 1965–66, Chair. New Brunswick Dept of Political Science 1968–70; Research Assoc., Center for Int. Studies, Princeton Univ. 1960–70; Prof. of Political Science, Ohio State Univ. 1970–73; Dir Inst. for Transnational Studies, Univ. of Southern Calif. 1973–92, Prof. of Political Science and Int. Relations 1973–92, Dir School of Int. Relations 1976–79; Sr Fellow, Center for Int. and Strategic Affairs, UCLA 1979–92; Univ. Prof. of Int. Affairs, George Washington Univ. 1992–; Visiting Prof. of Political Science, McGill Univ., Montréal 1990; Visiting Prof. of Int. Relations, UN Univ. for Peace, Costa Rica 1991; Co-Prin. Investigator (with Ole R. Holsti), Foreign Policy Leadership Project, NSF 1979–81, 1983–85, 1988–89, 1992–94, 1997–99; Pres. Int. Studies Asscn 1984–85; mem. Transparency Int. Council on Governance Research 1995–; Guggenheim Fellowship 1987–88. *Play:* Kwangju: An Escalatory Spree (two-act play, produced at Odyssey Theater, LA 1991). *Publications include:* Turbulence in World Politics: A Theory of Change and Continuity 1990, Governance without Government 1991, The United Nations in a Turbulent World: Engulfed or Enlarged? 1992, Global Voices 1993, International Relations Theory 1993, Thinking Theory Thoroughly: Coherent Approaches to an Incoherent World (with Mary Durfee) 1995, Along the Domestic-Foreign Frontier: Exploring Governance in a Turbulent World 1997, Strange Power: Shaping the Parameters of International Relations and International Political Economy 2000, Information Technologies and Global Politics: The Changing Scope of Power and Governance 2002, Distant Proximities: Dynamics Beyond Globalization 2003, The Study of World Politics, Vol. 1: Theoretical and Methobiological Challenge 2006, The Study of World Politics, Vol. 2: Globalization and Governance 2006; author or ed. of more than 40 books, 200 articles. *Address:* George Washington University, Gelman 709G, 2130 H Street, NW, Washington, DC 20052, USA (office). *Telephone:* (202) 994-3060 (office). *Fax:* (202) 994-0792 (office); (202) 994-4571 (office). *E-mail:* jnr@gwu.edu (office). *Website:* www.gwu.edu/~elliott/faculty/rosenau.cfm (office).

ROSENBERG, Pamela, BA, MA; American music administrator; *Intendant (General Manager), Berlin Philharmonic Orchestra;* b. Los Angeles, Calif.; m. Wolf Rosenberg (deceased); two c.; ed Univ. of California at Berkeley, Ohio State Univ., Guildhall School of Music, London; previous positions at Netherlands Opera, Amsterdam, Deutschen Schauspielhaus, Hamburg;

Scenic Supervisor, subsequently Artistic Admin. Frankfurt Opera; Co-Dir Stuttgart Opera 1991–2000; Gen. Dir San Francisco Opera 2001–06; Intendant (Gen. Man.) Berlin Philharmonic Orchestra 2006–(10). *Address:* Stiftung Berliner Philharmoniker, Herbert-von-Karajan-Str. 1, Berlin 10785, Germany (office). *Telephone:* (30) 254-88-0 (office). *Fax:* (30) 261-48-87 (office). *E-mail:* presse@berliner-philharmoniker.de (office). *Website:* www.berlin -philharmonic.com (office).

ROSENBERG, Pierre Max; French curator; b. 13 April 1936, Paris; s. of Charles Rosenberg and Gertrude Rosenberg; m. 2nd Béatrice de Rothschild 1981; one d.; ed Lycée Charlemagne, Faculté de droit de Paris and Ecole du Louvre; Chief Curator Dept des Peintures, Musée du Louvre 1983, Inspecteur gén. des musées 1988, Conservateur gén. du Patrimoine 1990–94, Pres. and Dir 1994–2001; Curator Musée Nat. de l'Amitié et des Relations franco-américaines de Blérancourt 1981–93; mem. Acad. Française 1995; Foreign mem. American Acad. Arts and Sciences, American Philosophical Soc., Accad. Naz. dei Lincei, Accad. Naz. di San Luca, Accad. del Disegno, Florence, Accad. Pietro Vanucci, Accad. Clementina, Ateneo Veneto, Istituto Veneto di Scienze, Lettere ed Arti; Hon. Fellow, Royal Academy, London; Chevalier Ordre des Arts et des Lettres, Ordre nat. du Mérite, Officier Légion d'honneur, Grand officier de l'ordre du Mérite (Italy), Commdr de l'ordre du Mérite (Germany). *Publications include:* Il Seicento francese 1970, Georges de La Tour 1973, Chardin. Tout l'œuvre peint 1983, Peyron 1983, Saint-Non. Fragonard. Panopticon italiano. Un diario di viaggio ritrovato. 1759-1761 1986, Fragonard. Tout l'œuvre peint 1989, Les frères Le Nain. Tout l'œuvre peint 1993, Nicolas Poussin. 1594-1665 1994, Antoine Watteau 1996, Georges de La Tour 1998, Julien de Parme, 1736-1799 1998, La pittura in Europa 1999, From Drawing to Painting 2000, Michel-François Dandré-Bardon: 1700-1783 2001, Jacques-Louis David: 1748-1825 2002, De Raphaël à la Révolution. Les relations artistiques entre la France et l'Italie 2005, Gesamverzeichnis Französische Gemälde des 17. und 18. Jahrhunderts in deutschen Sammlungen 2005, En Amérique seulement 2006, Dictionnaire amoureux du Louvre 2007. *Address:* 35 rue de Vaugirard, 75006 Paris (home); Institut de France, 23 quai Conti, 75006 Paris, France (office). *Telephone:* 1-45-48-78-13 (home). *E-mail:* pierre.rosenberg@wanadoo.fr (home).

ROSENBERG, Richard Morris, BA, MBA, LLB; American banker; b. 21 April 1930, Fall River, Mass.; s. of Charles Rosenberg and Betty Peck; m. Barbara K. Cohen 1956; two s.; ed Suffolk and Golden Gate Univs; Publicity Asst, Crocker-Anglo Bank, San Francisco 1959–62; Banking Services Officer, Wells Fargo Bank 1962–65, Asst Vice-Pres. 1965–68, Vice-Pres. Marketing Dept 1968, Vice-Pres. Dir of Marketing 1969, Sr Vice-Pres. Marketing and Advertising Div. 1970–75, Exec. Vice-Pres. 1975, Vice-Chair. 1980–83; Vice-Chair. Crocker Nat. Corpn 1983–85; Pres. and COO Seafirst Corpn 1986–87; Dir, Pres. and COO Seattle-First Nat. Bank 1985–87; Vice-Chair. Bd Bank America Corpn San Francisco 1987–90; Chair. and CEO BankAmerica Corpn/ Bank of America 1990–91, Chair. Bank America Corpn 1990–96 (retd); mem. Bd of Dirs Buck Inst. for Age Research, Health Care Property Investors, Inc., San Francisco Symphony, Naval War Coll. Foundation; mem. Advisory Bd Shorenstein Properties LLC; fmr mem. Bd of Dirs Airborne Express, Northrop Grumman Corpn, Pacific Mutual Life Insurance Co., United Way; Chair. Exec. Council Univ. of Calif. Medical Center; mem. State Bar of Calif.; Trustee, Calif. Inst. of Tech. *Leisure interests:* tennis, avid reader, history. *Address:* c/o Shorenstein Properties LLC, Bank of America Center, 555 California Street, 49th Floor, PO Box 37000 San Francisco, CA 94104, USA. *Telephone:* (415) 772-7000. *Website:* www.shorenstein.com.

ROSENBERG, Steven A., BA, MD, PhD; American physician and immunologist; *Chief of Surgery, National Cancer Institute;* b. 2 Aug. 1940, New York; s. of Abraham Rosenberg and Harriet Wendroff; m. Alice R. O'Connell 1968; three d.; ed Bronx High School of Science and Johns Hopkins Univ., Harvard Univ., Intern, Peter Bent Brigham Hosp. Boston 1963–64, Surgical Resident 1968–69, further surgical training 1972–74; Fellow in Immunology, Harvard Medical School 1969–70, NIH 1970–72; Chief of Surgery, Nat. Cancer Inst. Bethesda, Md 1974–; Prof. of Surgery, Uniformed Services Univ. of Health Sciences and George Washington Univ. School of Medicine and Health Sciences, Washington, DC; mem. American Soc. of Clinical Oncology (fmr mem. Bd of Dirs), Inst. of Medicine, NAS, Soc. of Univ. Surgeons, American Surgical Asscn, American Asscn for Cancer Research, American Asscn of Immunologists; Meritorious Service Medal, US Public Health Service 1981, 1986, Friedrich Sasse Prize, Univ. of West Berlin, Germany 1986, Nils Alwell Prize 1987, Distinguished Alumnus Award, Johns Hopkins Univ. 1987, Simon M. Shubitz Prize, Univ. of Chicago Cancer Research Center 1988, Griffuel Prize for Research, French Asscn for Research on Cancer 1988, Milken Family Foundation Cancer Award 1988, Armand Hammer Cancer Prize 1985, 1988, Karnofsky Prize 1991, Ellis Island Medal of Honor 1998, John Wayne Award for Clinical Research 1996, Heath Memorial Award 2002, Flance-Karl Award 2002, American-Italian Cancer Foundation Prize 2003, Richard V. Smalley, MD, Memorial Award 2002. *Publications:* eight books and more than 800 articles in medical journals. *Address:* Center for Cancer Research, Building 10-CRC, Room 3-3940, 10 Center Drive, MSC 1201, Bethesda, MD 20892 (office); National Cancer Institute, 9000 Rockville Pike, Building 10, Room 3-3940, Bethesda, MD 20892, USA (office). *Telephone:* (301) 496-4164 (office). *Fax:* (301) 402-1738 (office). *E-mail:* SAR@nih.gov (office). *Website:* ccr.cancer .gov (office).

ROSENFELD, Arthur H., PhD; American physicist and academic; *Professor Emeritus of Physics, University of California, Berkeley;* b. 1927; ed Univ. of Chicago; specialist in energy efficiency tech.; joined Dept of Physics, Univ. of Calif., Berkeley 1955, worked with particle physics group of Luis Alvarez, Prof. of Physics 1957–94, Prof. Emer. 1994–; Founder and Dir Energy Efficient Buildings Program (later Center for Building Science), Lawrence Berkeley Nat. Lab. 1975–94, Co-f. Heat Islands Research Project 1985; Sr Adviser to US Dept of Energy's Asst Sec. for Energy Efficiency and Renewable Energy 1994–99; Commr, Calif. Energy Comm. 2000–, Chair. Research, Devt and Demonstration Cttee, second mem. Energy Efficiency Cttee; Co-founder American Council for an Energy Efficient Economy (ACEEE), Univ. of Calif. Inst. for Energy Efficiency, Center for Energy and Climate Solutions; Szilard Award for Physics in the Public Interest 1986, Carnot Award for Energy Efficiency, US Dept of Energy 1993, Enrico Fermi Award 2006. *Publication:* The Art of Energy Efficiency. *Address:* California Energy Commission, 1516 Ninth Street, MS-35, Sacramento, CA 95814, USA (office). *Telephone:* (916) 654-4930 (office). *Fax:* (916) 653-3478 (office). *E-mail:* ahrosenfeld@lbl.gov (office). *Website:* www.energy.ca.gov/commission/commissioners/rosenfeld .html (office).

ROSENFELD, Irene B., PhD; American business executive; *Chairman and CEO, Kraft Foods Inc.;* ed Cornell Univ.; joined Kraft Foods in 1981, worked in market research and product man., later Exec. Vice-Pres. Kraft and Gen. Man. Desserts and Snacks, Exec. Vice-Pres. Beverages and Marketing Dir Beverages 1991–96, Exec. Vice-Pres. Kraft and Pres. Kraft Canada 1996–2000, Group Vice-Pres. Kraft Foods N American Operations, Tech., Procurement and Information Systems for Canada, Puerto Rico and Mexico 2000–02, Group Vice-Pres. Kraft Foods N America 2002–03 (resgnd), CEO Kraft Foods Inc. 2006–, Chair. 2007–; Chair. and CEO Frito-Lay Inc. (div. of PepsiCo Inc.) 2004–06; mem. Bd Dirs AutoNation Inc.; Chair. Grocery Mfrs of America Industry Affairs Council 2001; Co-Chair. Jt GMA/Food Marketers Inst. Trading Pnr Alliance, Food and Health Strategy Group; fmr Chair. Food and Consumer Products Mfrs of Canada; mem. The Economic Club of Chicago; Trustee, Cornell Univ.; elected to YWCA Acad. of Women Achievers, ranked by Fortune magazine amongst 50 Most Powerful Women in Business in the US (31st) 2004, (27th) 2005, (fifth) 2006, (fifth) 2007, Masters of Excellence Award Center for Jewish Living 2005, ranked by Forbes magazine amongst 100 Most Powerful Women (11th) 2006, (ninth) 2007, (sixth) 2008. *Leisure interests:* playing the piano, rollerblading. *Address:* Kraft Foods Inc., 3 Lakes Drive, Northfield, IL 60093, USA (office). *Telephone:* (847) 646-2000 (office). *Fax:* (847) 646-6005 (office). *E-mail:* info@kraft.com (office). *Website:* www .kraft.com (office).

ROSENNE, Shabtai, LLB, PhD; Israeli lawyer and diplomatist (retd); b. 24 Nov. 1917, London, England; s. of Harry Rowson and Vera Rowson; m. Esther Schultz 1940; two s.; ed Univ. of London and Hebrew Univ. of Jerusalem; Advocate (Israel), Political Dept, Jewish Agency for Palestine 1946–48; Legal Adviser, Ministry of Foreign Affairs 1948–66; Deputy Perm. Rep. to UN 1967–71; Perm. Rep. to UN, Geneva 1971–74; Ministry of Foreign Affairs 1974–82; mem. Israeli del. to UN Gen. Asss 1948–83, Vice-Chair. Legal Cttee Gen. Ass. 1960; mem. Israeli del. to Armistice Negotiations with Egypt, Jordan, Lebanon and Syria 1949; mem. Israel del. to UN Conf. on Law of the Sea 1958, 1960, Chair. 1973, 1978–82; Chair. Israel del. to UN Conf. on Law of Treaties 1968, 1969, mem. other UN confs; Govt Rep. before Int. Court of Justice in several cases; mem. Int. Law Comm. 1962–71, UN Comm. on Human Rights 1968–70; Visiting Prof., Bar Ilan Univ. 1976–; Arthur Goodhart Visiting Prof. of Legal Science, Univ. of Cambridge 1985–86; Belle van Zuylen Visiting Prof., State Univ. of Utrecht 1986–87, Univ. of Amsterdam 1987; Visiting Scholar, Univ. of Va 1988–92; Hon. mem. Inst. of Int. Law 1963–, Rapporteur, Termination and Modification of Treaties 1965; Fellow, Jewish Acad. of Arts and Sciences 1981; Hon. mem. Inst. of Int. Law 1963–, American Soc. of Int. Law 1976; Israel Prize 1960, Certificate of Merit, American Soc. of Int. Law 1968, Manley O. Hudson Medal 1999, The Hague Prize for Int. Law 2004. *Publications:* International Court of Justice 1957, The Time Factor in Jurisdiction of the International Court of Justice 1960, The Law of Treaties: Guide to the Vienna Convention 1970, Procedure in the International Court 1983, Practice and Methods of International Law 1984, Developments in the Law of Treaties 1945–86 1989, Documents on the International Court of Justice 1991, An International Law Miscellany 1993, The World Court: What It Is And How It Works 1995, The Law and Practice of the International Court 1920–1996 (four vols) 1997, The United Nations Convention on the Law of the Sea 1982: A Commentary (seven vols) (Gen. Ed.) 1985–2003, The Perplexities of Modern International Law 2004, Provisional Measures in International Law: The International Court of Justice, the International Tribunal for the Law of the Sea 2005; numerous articles, mainly on law. *Leisure interests:* reading, music. *Address:* PO Box 3313, Jerusalem 91033, Israel. *Telephone:* (2) 6524339. *Fax:* (2) 6526401. *E-mail:* rosennes@ netvision.net.il (home).

ROSENSHINE, Allen Gilbert, BA; American advertising executive (retd); *Chairman Emeritus, BBDO Worldwide;* b. 14 March 1939; s. of Aaron Rosenshine and Anna Zuckerman; m. Suzan Weston-Webb 1979; two s.; ed Columbia Coll.; copywriter, J.B. Rundle, New York 1962–65; copywriter, Batten, Barton, Durstine & Osborn, New York 1965, copy supervisor 1967, Vice-Pres. 1968, Assoc. Creative Dir 1970, Sr Vice-Pres. and Creative Dir 1975–77, Exec. Vice-Pres. 1977–80, Pres. 1980–82, CEO 1981–86, Chair. 1983–86; Pres. and CEO BBDO Int. New York 1984–86; Pres. and COO Omnicom Group, New York 1986–88, CEO BBDO Worldwide (subsidiary), New York 1989–2004, Chair. 1989–2006, now Chair. Emer.; Founding mem. Partnership for a Drug-Free America, currently Vice Chair. and Exec. Creative Dir; mem. Creative Review Cttee, Advertising Council; mem. Bd of Dirs Business for Diplomatic Action. *Address:* c/o BBDO Worldwide, 1285 Avenue of the Americas, New York, NY 10019, USA (office). *Website:* www .allenrosenshine.com.

ROSENTHAL, Gert, MA; Guatemalan economist and diplomatist; *Permanent Representative, United Nations;* b. 11 Sept. 1935, Amsterdam, Netherlands; s. of Ludwig Rosenthal and Florence Rosenthal (née Koenigsberger); m.

Margit Uhlmann; four d.; ed American School of Guatemala, Univ. of California, Berkeley, USA, Universidad de San Carlos de Guatemala; worked in pvt. sector 1959–67; economist, Nat. Planning Secr. 1960–64, Head Econ. Devt Div. 1965, Sec.-Gen. (rank of Minister) 1969–70, 1973–74; Officer in charge of external financing, Ministry of Finance 1966–67; Asst to Sec.-Gen., Secr. of Cen. American Common Market (SIECA) 1968, Project Dir UNCTAD project to promote SIECA, Guatemala City 1972–73; Prof. of Econ. Devt and Public Finance, Universidad Rafael Landivar, Guatemala 1969–74; Dir Sub-regional Office UN ECLA, Mexico 1974–85, Deputy Exec. Sec. UN ECLA, Santiago, Chile 1985–87, Exec. Sec. (rank of Under-Sec.-Gen. of UN) 1988–97; mem. Oversight Comm. of Guatemalan Peace Accords 1998; Perm. Rep. to UN, New York 1998, 2008–; Pres. UN Econ. and Social Council (ECOSOC) 2003–04; Minister of Foreign Affairs 2006–08; Dr hc (Universidad del Valle) 1996. *Publications:* numerous publs on devt issues 1960–. *Address:* Permanent Mission of Guatemala to the United Nations, 57 Park Avenue, New York, NY 10016, USA (office); Calle de los Duelos #6, Antigua, Guatemala (home). *Telephone:* (212) 679-4760 (office); 832-3659 (home). *Fax:* (212) 685-8741 (office); 832-3666 (home). *E-mail:* guatemala@un.int (office); grosenthal@guate.net (home). *Website:* www.un.int/guatemala (office).

ROSENTHAL, Sir Norman Leon, Kt, BA; British art curator; b. 8 Nov. 1944; s. of Paul Rosenthal and Kate Zucker; m. Manuela Beatriz Mena Marques 1989; two d.; ed Westminster City Grammar School, Univ. of Leicester; librarian Thomas Agnew & Sons 1966–68; Exhbns Officer, Brighton Museum and Art Gallery 1970–71, Exhbn Organizer Inst. Contemporary Arts 1974–76, Exhbns. Sec. RA 1977–2008; freelance curator 2008–; organizer of many exhbns including: Art into Society, I.C.A. 1974, A New Spirit in Painting, 1981, Zeitgeist, W Berlin 1982, German Art of the Twentieth Century and Staatsgalerie, Stuttgart 1985–86, Italian Art of the Twentieth Century, Royal Acad 1989, Metropolis, Berlin 1991, American Art in the Twentieth Century and Martin-Gropius Bau, Berlin 1993, Sensation 1997, Charlotte Salomon, RA 1998, Apocalypse RA 2000, The Genius of Rome 2001, Botticelli's Dante 2001, The Aztecs 2002/03, Kirchner 2004, Illuminating the Renaissance—The Triumph of Flemish Manuscript Painting in Europe 2004, The Art of Philip Guston 2004, Turks: A Journey of a Thousand Years 600–1600 2005; TV and radio broadcasts on contemporary art; mem. Opera Bd, Royal Opera House 1994–98, Bd Palazzo Grassi, Venice 1995–; Hon. Fellow RCA 1987; Officier, Ordre des Arts et des Lettres 2003, Cavaliere Ufficiale, Order of Merit (Italy) 1992, Cross, Order of Merit (Germany) 1993; Hon. DLitt (Southampton) 2003; German/British Forum Award 2003. *Television and radio:* undertakes many television and radio broadcasts and frequently addresses international conferences. *Publications:* contributes numerous articles and essays to catalogues and journals throughout the world. *Leisure interest:* music, especially opera. *Address:* c/o The Royal Academy of Arts, Burlington House, Piccadilly, London, W1J 0BD, England (office).

ROSENTHAL, Thomas Gabriel, MA, PhD; British publisher, critic and broadcaster; b. 16 July 1935; s. of the late Erwin I. J. Rosenthal and Elisabeth Charlotte Marx; m. Ann Judith Warnford-Davis; two s.; ed Perse School, Cambridge and Pembroke Coll., Cambridge; served in RA 1954–56; joined Thames and Hudson Ltd 1959, Man. Dir Thames and Hudson Int. 1966; joined Martin Secker and Warburg Ltd as Man. Dir 1971, Dir Heinemann Group of Publrs 1972–84, Man. Dir William Heinemann Int. Ltd 1979–84, Chair. World's Work Ltd 1979–84, Heinemann Zsolnay Ltd 1979–84, Kaye and Ward Ltd 1980–84, William Heinemann, Australia and SA 1981–82, Pres. Heinemann Inc. 1981–84; Jt Man. Dir and Jt Chair. André Deutsch Ltd 1984, CEO 1987–96, Sole Man. Dir and Chair. 1987, Chair. 1984–98; Chair. Frew McKenzie (Antiquarian Booksellers) 1985–93, Bridgewater Press 1997–; Art Critic The Listener 1963–66; Chair. Soc. of Young Publrs 1961–62; mem. Cambridge Univ. Appointments Bd 1967–71, Exec. Cttee Nat. Book League 1971–74, Cttee of Man. Amateur Dramatic Club, Cambridge (also Trustee), Council RCA 1982–87, Exec. Council Inst. of Contemporary Arts 1987–99 (Chair. 1996–99); Trustee Phoenix Trust, Fitzwilliam Museum, Cambridge 2002–; mem. Editorial Bd Logos 1989–93. *Publications:* Monograph on Jack B. Yeats 1964, Monograph on Ivon Hitchens (with Alan Bowness) 1973; A Reader's Guide to European Art History 1962, A Reader's Guide to Modern American Fiction 1963, Monograph on Arthur Boyd (with Ursula Hoff) 1986, The Art of Jack B. Yeats 1993, Sidney Nolan 2002, Paula Rego: The Complete Graphic Works 2004, Joseph Albers: Formulation Articulation 2006; articles in journals and newspapers. *Leisure interests:* opera, pictures, bibliomania. *Address:* Flat 7, Huguenot House, 19 Oxendon Street, London, SW1Y 4EH, England (home). *Telephone:* (20) 7839-3589 (home). *Fax:* (20) 7839-0651 (home).

ROSENZWEIG, Mark Richard, PhD; American psychologist, neuroscientist and academic (retd); *Professor of Graduate Studies, University of California, Berkeley;* b. 12 Sept. 1922, Rochester, New York; s. of Jacob Rosenzweig and Pearl Grossman Rosenzweig; m. Janine S. A. Chappat 1947; one s. two d.; ed Univ. of Rochester and Harvard Univ.; served US Navy 1944–46; Asst Prof., Univ. of Calif., Berkeley 1951–56, Assoc. Prof. 1956–60, Prof. 1960–91, Prof. Emer. 1991–, Prof. of Grad. Studies 1994–; Assoc. Research Prof. Inst. of Basic Research in Science, Univ. of Calif. 1958–59, Research Prof. 1965–66; main area of interest: neural mechanisms of learning and memory formation; main findings: plastic anatomical and neurochemical responses of the nervous system of vertebrates to training and differential experience, specific neurochemical processes required for formation of the successive stages of memory, requirement of protein synthesis in brain for formation of long-term memory; Fellow AAAS, American Psychological Soc., American Psychological Asscn; Charter mem. Int. Brain Research Org., Soc. for Neuroscience; mem. NAS, American Physiological Soc., Société Française de Psychologie; mem. Exec. Cttee, Int. Union of Psychological Science, Vice-Pres. 1980–84, Pres.

1988–92, Past Pres. 1992–96, mem. US Nat. Cttee for Int. Union of Psychological Science 1985–96, Chair. 1985–88; mem. Int. Cttee on Social Science Information and Documentation 1972–80 (Pres. 1976–78); mem. Advisory Cttee for Int. Council of Scientific Unions (N.A.S.—N.R.C.) 1985–88; Ed. Annual Review of Psychology 1968–94; Dr hc (Université René Descartes, Sorbonne, Paris) 1980, (Université Louis Pasteur, Strasbourg) 1997; Distinguished Scientific Contrib. Award (American Psychological Asscn) 1982, Award for Distinguished Contributions to Int. Advancement of Psychology (American Psychological Asscn) 1997. *Publications:* Psychology: An introduction (with P. H. Mussen) 1973, Biologie de la Mémoire 1976, Neural mechanisms of learning and memory (Co-Ed. with E. L. Bennett) 1976, Physiological Psychology (with A. L. Leiman) 1982, 1989, Psychophysiology: Memory, motivation and event-related potentials in mental operations (Co-Ed. with R. Sinz) 1983, La recherche en psychologie scientifique (with D. Sinha) 1988, International Psychological Science: Progress, Problems and Prospects 1992, Biological Psychology (with A.L. Leiman and S. M. Breedlove) 1996, 1999, International Handbook of Psychology (Co-Ed.) 2000, History of the International Union of Psychological Science (co-author) 2000, Biological Psychology (with S. M. Breedlove and A. L. Leiman) 2001; Biological Psychology (with S. M. Breedlove and N. V. Watson) 2004; book chapters and articles in scientific journals. *Address:* Department of Psychology, 3133 Tolman Hall, University of California, Berkeley, CA 94720-1650, USA (office). *Telephone:* (510) 642-7132 (office); (510) 642-5292 (office). *Fax:* (510) 642-5293 (office). *E-mail:* memory@socrates.berkley.edu (office). *Website:* psychology.berkeley.edu/faculty/profiles/mrosenzweig.html (office).

ROSHAL, Leonid Mikhailovich, MD, DSc; Russian paediatrician; *Executive Director, Moscow Institute of Emergency Children's Surgery and Traumatology;* b. 27 April 1933, Livnya, Orel Region; s. of Mikhail Filippovich Roshal and Emilia Lazarevna Roshal; m. 1st; one s.; m. 2nd Veda Zuponcic; ed Moscow Medical Inst.; paediatrician and specialist, paediatric surgeon Moscow hosps 1957–61; jr then sr researcher, then sr research paediatric surgeon MONIKI Inst. 1961–81; Dir Emergency Surgery and Children's Trauma Dept, Moscow Pediatric Scientific Research Inst.1981–, Exec. Dir Moscow Inst. of Emergency Children's Surgery and Traumatology 2003–; Chair. Int. Task Force Cttee on Paediatric Disaster Medicine; mem. Exec. Cttee World Asscn for Emergency and Disaster Medicine, Exec. Cttee Russian Union of Paediatrics; Pres. Int. Charitable Fund for Children in Disasters and Wars; mem. Bd of Dirs Russian Asscn of Paediatric Surgery, British Asscn of Paediatric Surgeons, Georgian Acad. of Medical Sciences; organized and carried out rescue operations and rendered medical assistance following earthquakes and wars in many countries in Europe, Asia and America; took part in negotiations with terrorists taking hostages in Moscow theatre Sept. 2002, provided medical assistance to hostages and negotiated release of some children; acted as intermediary during Beslan school siege; elected Children's Doctor of the World by Moscow Journalists Community 1995; Order of Courage 2002; awarded title of National Hero 2002, Person of the Year (chosen by several Russian periodicals) 2002; numerous other awards. *Publications:* 7 books and more than 200 scientific articles on surgery and problems of children in catastrophes and wars. *Leisure interest:* music. *Address:* Children's Hospital, B. Polyanka str. 20, 103118 Moscow, Russia. *Telephone:* (495) 238-30-00 (office); (495) 137-87-08 (home). *Fax:* (495) 230-29-98. *E-mail:* roshal@lamport.ru.

ROSHCHEVSKY, Mikhail Pavlovich; Russian physiologist; *Chairman, Presidium of Komi Scientific Centre;* b. 5 March 1933; m.; two d.; ed Ural State Univ.; jr then sr researcher, scientific sec. Ural Research Inst. of Agric. 1958–60; Sr Researcher, Inst. of Biology Komi ASSR 1960–70; Deputy Chair. Presidium Scientific Cen. Komi ASSR 1970–83, Chair. 1983–; Dir Inst. of Physiology Komi Scientific Cen. Ural br. USSR Acad. of Sciences 1983–; Corresp. mem. USSR (now Russian) Acad. of Sciences 1987, mem. 1990; studies of ecological-physiological aspects of blood circulation, electrophysiology of heart, electrocardiology; mem. Dept of Physiology Russian Acad. of Sciences. *Publications:* books and scientific works. *Address:* Presidium of Komi Scientific Centre, Kommunisticheskaya str. 24, 167982 Syktyvkar, Komi Republic, Russia. *Telephone:* (8212) 24-16-08 (office); (8212) 42-25-11 (home). *Fax:* (8212) 24-22-64 (office). *E-mail:* roshchevsky@presidium.komisc.ru (office). *Website:* www.komisc.ru/en (office).

ROSI, Francesco; Italian film director; b. 1922, Naples; apprenticed as asst to Antonioni and Visconti; Dir first feature, La Sfida (The Challenge) 1958. *Films:* Salvatore Giuliano, Hands Over the City, More than a Miracle, Just Another War, Lucky Luciano, The Mattei Affair, Three Brothers, Chronicle of a Death Foretold, To Forget Palermo, Diario napoletano 1992, The Truce 1997.

ROSNER, Robert, PhD; American physicist, astronomer and astrophysicist; *Director, Argonne National Laboratory;* b. 26 June 1947, Garmisch-Partenkirchen, Germany; s. of Heinz Rosner and Faina Rosner; m. Marsha R. Rosner 1971; two d.; ed Brandeis Univ., Harvard Univ.; Asst Prof., later Assoc. Prof. of Astronomy, Harvard Univ. 1978–86; Chair of Astronomy and Astrophysics, Univ. of Chicago 1991–97, William E. Wrather Distinguished Service Prof. 1998–; Assoc. Lab. Dir and Chief Scientist, Argonne Nat. Lab. 2002–05, Dir 2005–; Rothschild Visiting Prof., Newton Inst. for Math. Sciences, Univ. of Cambridge, UK 2004; Life mem. Clare Hall, Cambridge 2005–; mem. External Advisory Cttee for the Nat. Ignition Facility, Lawrence Livermore Nat. Lab., Steering Cttee of the Interagency Task Force on High Energy Density Physics, Scientific Advisory Cttees Max Planck Inst. for Solar System Research, Lindau, Germany, and Astrophysical Inst. Potsdam, Germany; mem. American Acad. of Arts and Sciences 2001; Foreign mem. Norwegian Acad. of Science and Letters 2004; Fellow, American Physical Soc. 1988; Hon. PhD (Illinois Inst. of Tech.) 2007, (Northern Illinois Univ.) 2008;

Woodrow Wilson Fellow, Gordon Bell Prize (Supercomputing) 2000, Thompson Lecturer, Nat. Center for Atmospheric Research 2001, ISI 'Highly Cited Researcher' 2002, Rosseland Lecturer, Univ. of Oslo 1998, Parker Lecturer, American Astronomical Soc./Solar Physics Div. 1995. *Publications:* more than 190 publs in scientific journals. *Leisure interests:* sailing, skiing, hiking. *Address:* Enrico Fermi Institute, University of Chicago, 5640 South Ellis Avenue, Chicago, IL 60637, USA (office). *Telephone:* (773) 702-0560 (office). *E-mail:* r-rosner@uchicago.edu (office).

ROSOMAN, Leonard Henry, OBE, RA, FSA; British artist and teacher; b. 27 Oct. 1913, London; s. of Henry Edward Rosoman and Lillian Blanche Rosoman (née Spencer); m. 1st Jocelyn Rickards 1963 (divorced 1968); m. 2nd Roxanne Wruble Levy 1994; ed Deacons School, Peterborough, King Edward VII School of Art, Univ. of Durham, RA Schools and Cen. School of Art and Design, London; taught Reimann School, London 1937–39; Official War Artist to Admiralty 1943–45; taught Camberwell School of Art, London 1946–47; taught Edin. Coll. of Art 1947–56, Chelsea School of Art, London 1956–57, RCA, London 1957–78; freelance artist 1978–; designed and painted vaulted ceiling in Lambeth Palace Chapel, London; exhbns at Rowland Browse & Delbanco and Fine Art Soc., London, Lincoln Center and Touchstone Gallery, New York, State Univ. of New York at Albany, Oldham Art Gallery, David Paul Gallery, Chichester and Royal Acad. of Art; Winston Churchill Fellow 1966–67; Hon. ARCA; Hon. mem. Royal Scottish Soc. of Painters in Water Colours, Royal West of England Acad.; Hon. Fellow, Edinburgh Coll. of Art 2005. *Leisure interests:* travel, bicycling. *Address:* 7 Pembroke Studios, Pembroke Gardens, London, W8 6HX, England. *Telephone:* (20) 7603-3638.

ROSS, André Louis Henry, LenD; French diplomatist; b. 13 March 1922, Calais; s. of René Ross and Yvonne Alexander; m. Thérèse Anne Guéroult 1951; ed Univ. of Paris and Ecole nat. d'admin; First Counsellor, Bangkok 1964–66; Amb. to Laos 1968–72, Zaïre 1972–78, India 1979–83, Japan 1983–85; Sec.-Gen. Ministry of Foreign Affairs 1985–87; Amb. of France 1985; Sr Adviser Indosuez Bank 1987–95; mem. Council of French Museums 1988–96; mem. Comm. des archives diplomatiques 1988–; Pres. France-Amérique, Paris 1993–98; Chair. Foundation for Japanese Civilization, Tanaka Foundation 1991–98; Commdr, Légion d'honneur, Ordre nat. du Mérite. *Leisure interests:* the arts, history and mathematics. *Address:* c/o Ministry of Foreign Affairs, 37 quai d'Orsay, 75351 Paris, France (office).

ROSS, Dennis B., PhD; American academic, government official and diplomatist; *Special Envoy to the Middle East, US State Department;* b. 26 Nov. 1948, San Francisco; m. Deborah Ross; one s. two d.; ed Univ. of California, Los Angeles; Deputy Dir Office of Net Assessment, US Defense Dept, Washington, DC 1982–84, 1989–92; Exec. Dir of program on Soviet Int. Behavior sponsored by Univ. of California, Berkeley and Stanford Univ. 1984–86; Dir Near East and S Asian Affairs, Nat. Security Council (during Reagan Admin); Dir Policy Planning Office, US State Dept 1988–92, Special Middle East Co-ordinator 1992–2001, helped achieve the 1995 Interim Agreement and brokered the Hebron Accord 1997; Counsellor and Ziegler Distinguished Fellow, Washington Inst. for Near East Policy 2001–08, part-time counsellor 2008–09; Special US Envoy to Middle East, US State Dept 2009–; Adjunct Lecturer, Kennedy School of Govt, Harvard Univ. 2002–04; Fred and Rita Richman Distinguished Visiting Prof., Brandeis Univ. 2003, 2005; Allis-Chalmers Distinguished Prof. of Int. Affairs, Marquette Univ. 2004–05; Adjunct Prof., Georgetown Univ. School of Foreign Service 2006–07, also Adjunct Prof. of Govt, Georgetown Univ. 2007; Bartels World Affairs Fellow, Cornell Univ. 2005; Chair. Inst. for Jewish People Policy Planning, Jerusalem; has served as Foreign Affairs Analyst for Fox News Channel; Hon. DHumLitt (Amherst Coll.) 2002, Dr hc (Jewish Theological Seminary, Syracuse Univ.); UCLA Alumnus of the Year; Presidential Medal for Distinguished Fed. Civilian Service, Truman Peace Prize from Harry S. Truman Research Inst. for the Advancement of Peace, Hebrew Univ. of Jerusalem 2008. *Publications include:* The Missing Peace: The Inside Story of the Fight for Middle East Peace 2004, Statecraft: And How to Restore America's Standing in the World 2007; numerous articles in learned journals and newspapers. *Address:* Department of State 2201 C St, NW, Washington, DC 20520, USA (office). *Telephone:* (202) 647-4000 (office). *Fax:* (202) 647-6738 (office). *Website:* www.state.gov (office).

ROSS, Diana; American singer and actress; b. 26 March 1944, Detroit; d. of Fred Ross and Ernestine Ross; m. 1st Robert Ellis Silberstein 1971 (divorced 1976); three d.; m. 2nd Arne Naess 1985 (died 2004); one s.; fmr lead singer the Supremes (later Diana Ross and the Supremes), solo singer 1970–; citation from Vice-Pres. Humphrey for efforts on behalf of Pres. Johnson's Youth Opportunity Programme, from Mrs Martin Luther King and Rev. Abernathy for contrib. to Southern Christian Leadership Conf. cause, Billboard, Cash Box and Record World magazine awards as world's outstanding female singer, Grammy Award 1970, Female Entertainer of the Year, Nat. Asscn for the Advancement of Colored People 1970, Cue Award as Entertainer of the Year 1972, Golden Apple Award 1972, Gold Medal Award, Photoplay 1972, Antoinette Perry Award 1977, Golden Globe Award 1972, Kennedy Center Honor 2007, BET Lifetime Achievement Award 2007. *Films include:* Lady Sings the Blues 1972, Mahogany 1975, The Wiz 1978. *Recordings include:* albums: I'm Still Waiting 1971, Touch Me In The Morning 1973, Diana 1980, Why Do Fools Fall in Love? 1981, Eaten Alive 1984, Chain Reaction 1986, Workin' Overtime 1989, Surrender 1989, Ain't No Mountain High Enough 1989, The Forces Behind the Power 1991, The Remixes 1994, Take me Higher 1995, Gift of Love 1996, The Real Thing 1998, Every Day is a New Day 1999, Voice of Love 2000, Gift of Love 2000, Blue 2006, I Love You 2006. *Publication:* Secrets of a Sparrow (autobiog.) 1993. *Address:* c/o Phil Symes, Cowan Symes Associates, 35 Soho Square, London, W1V 5DG, England. *Website:* www.dianaross.com.

ROSS, Rt Hon. Lord Donald MacArthur, PC, MA, LLB, FRSE; British judge (retd); b. 29 March 1927, Dundee; s. of John Ross and Jessie MacArthur Thomson; m. Dorothy M. Annand 1958 (died 2004); two d.; ed High School of Dundee and Univ. of Edinburgh; nat. service with Black Watch 1947–49; TA rank of Capt. 1949–58; Advocate 1952; QC (Scotland) 1964; Vice-Dean, Faculty of Advocates 1967–73, Dean 1973–76; Sheriff Prin. of Ayr and Bute 1972–73; Senator, Coll. of Justice, Scotland and Lord of Session 1977–97; Lord Justice Clerk of Scotland and Pres. of Second Div. of the Court of Session 1985–97; Chair. Judicial Studies Cttee for Scotland 1997–2001; mem. Parole Bd for Scotland 1997–2002; Deputy Chair. Boundary Comm. for Scotland 1977–85; mem. Scottish Cttee of Council on Tribunals 1970–76, Cttee on Privacy 1970; mem. Court of Heriot Watt Univ. 1978–90 (Chair. 1984–90); mem. Council Royal Soc. of Edin. 1997–99, Vice-Pres. 1999–2002; Lord High Commr to Gen. Ass. of Church of Scotland 1990, 1991; Hon. LLD (Edin.) 1987, (Dundee) 1991, (Abertay, Dundee) 1994, (Aberdeen) 1998; Hon. DUniv (Heriot Watt) 1988; Royal Soc. of Edinburgh Bicentenary Medal 2004. *Publication:* contrib. to Stair Memorial Encyclopaedia of Scots Law. *Leisure interests:* gardening, walking, travelling. *Address:* 7/1 Tipperlinn Road, Edinburgh, EH10 5ET, Scotland. *Telephone:* (131) 447-6771. *Fax:* (131) 446-3813. *E-mail:* rosd33@aol.com (home).

ROSS, Ian Gordon, AO, MSc, PhD, FAA; Australian chemist and academic; b. 5 July 1926, Sydney; s. of Gordon R. Ross and Isabella M. Jenkins; m. Viola Bartlett 1975; ed Univs of Sydney and London; Research Assoc., Fla State Univ. 1953; Lecturer, then Reader in Physical Chem., Univ. of Sydney 1954–67, Prof. of Chem. 1968–90; Pro-Vice-Chancellor ANU 1975, 1989–90, Deputy Vice-Chancellor 1977–88; Chair. Australian Research Grants Cttee 1977–79, Inquiry into Govt Labs 1982–83, Australian & New Zealand Asscn for the Advancement of Science 1984–86, Communication Research Inst. of Australia 1994–2004; Sec. for Science Policy, Australian Acad. of Science 1989–93; Dir Anutech Pty Ltd 1979–97; Hon. LLD; H. G. Smith Medal, Royal Australian Chem. Inst. 1972. *Publications:* scientific papers on theoretical chemistry and molecular spectroscopy. *Address:* 16/18 George Street, Queanbeyan, NSW 2620, Australia. *Telephone:* (2) 6297-3510. *Fax:* (2) 6299-6324.

ROSS, James Hood, BA; British business executive; *Chairman, Leadership Foundation for Higher Education;* b. 13 Sept. 1938, London; s. of Capt. T. D. Ross RN and Lettice Ferrier Hood; m. Sara B. V. Purcell 1964; one s. two d.; ed Sherborne School, Jesus Coll., Oxford and Manchester Business School; British Petroleum Co. PLC 1959–92, Gen. Man. BP Zaïre, Burundi and Rwanda, Gen. Man. BP Tanker Co., Gen. Man. Stolt-Nielsen (USA), Gen. Man. Corp. Planning BP, Chief Exec. BP Oil Int., Chair. and Chief Exec. BP America; Chief Exec. Cable & Wireless PLC 1992–95; Chair. Littlewoods Org. 1996–2002, Nat. Grid Group PLC (later) 1999–2002, Co-Chair. Nat. Grid Transco (after Nat. Grid merger with Lattice) 2002–04; mem. Bd of Dirs (non-exec.) McGraw Hill Inc. 1988–, Schneider Electric 1996, Datacard Inc. 1997–, Prudential PLC 2004–; Trustee, The Cleveland Orchestra 1988–; Chair. Leadership Foundation for Higher Education 2003–. *Leisure interests:* music, gardening, sailing. *Address:* Leadership Foundation for Higher Education, 88 Kingsway, London, WC2B 6AA, England (office). *Telephone:* (20) 7841-2800 (office). *Fax:* (20) 7681-6219 (office). *Website:* www.lfhe.ac.uk (office).

ROSSANT, Janet, PhD, FRS, FRSC; British/Canadian geneticist; *Chief of Research, The Hospital for Sick Children;* b. 13 July 1950, Chatham; d. of Leslie Rossant and Doris Rossant; m. Alex Bain 1977; one s.; ed St Hugh's Coll., Oxford Univ., Darwin Coll., Cambridge Univ.; Research Fellow in Zoology, Oxford Univ. 1975–77; Asst Prof. of Biological Sciences, Brock Univ., Ont., Canada 1977–82, Assoc. Prof. 1982–85; Assoc. Prof. of Molecular and Medical Genetics, Univ. of Toronto 1985–88, Prof. 1988–, Univ. Prof. 2001–, Sr Investigator, Programme in Devt and Foetal Health, Samuel Lunenfeld Research Inst. 1985–2005; currently Chief of Research, Hospital for Sick Children; Pres. Soc. for Developmental Biology; mem. American and Canadian Socs for Cell Biology; Gibb's Prize for Zoology, Oxford 1972, Beit Memorial Fellowship 1975, E.W.R. Steacie Memorial Fellowship 1983, Howard Hughes Int. Scholar 1991, MRC Distinguished Scientist 1996, McLaughlin Medal (Royal Soc. of Canada) 1998, NCIC/Eli Lilly Robert L. Noble Prize 2000, Killam Prize for Health Sciences 2004, Michael Smith Prize for Health Research 2005. *Publications:* Experimental Approaches to Mammalian Embryonic Development (with R. A. Pedersen) 1986, Mouse Development (with P. P. L. Tam) 2001; over 200 articles in scientific journals. *Leisure interests:* running, cooking, theatre. *Address:* The Hospital for Sick Children, 555 University Avenue, Room 884, Toronto, ON M5G 1X8, Canada (office). *Telephone:* (416) 813-7929 (office). *E-mail:* janet.rossant@sickkids.ca (office). *Website:* www.sickkids.ca/rossant/default.asp (office).

ROSSEL, Eduard Ergartovich, CandTechSc; Russian politician; *Governor of Sverdlovsk Region;* b. 8 Oct. 1937, Bor, Gorki region; m.; one d.; ed Sverdlovsk Ore Inst.; master construction site, head of construction trust Sreduralstroi; supervised construction of Krasnouralsk superphosphate factory, Nevyansk cement factory, Nizhny Tagil metallurgy plant; head Sverdlovsk regional exec. cttee, then Gov. Sverdlovsk Region 1991–93, tried to proclaim Ural Repub., discharged by Pres. Yeltsin, re-elected Head of Admin. and Gov. Sverdlovsk Region 1995–; mem. Russian Council of Fed. 1993–94, 1995–2001; Chair. Sverdlovsk regional Duma 1994–95; Founder and Chair. Org. Preobrazhenie Otechestva; Pres. Asscn for Econ. Co-operation of Ural Region 1995–; mem. Bd Union of Russian Govs 1996; mem. Int. Acad. of Regional Devt and Co-operation; mem. United Russia (UR) (Yedinaya Rossiya); Order 'Decoration of Honour' 1975, 1980, Order for Achievement to Fatherland Fourth Degree 1996, Third Degree 2000; Lenin Centenary Anniversary Medal

'For Valiant Labour' 1970, Honoured Constructor of Russian Soviet Federal Socialist Repub. 1983. *Address:* Governor's Office, Oktyabrskaya pl. 1, 620031 Ekaterinburg, Russia (office). *Telephone:* (343) 217-87-17 (office). *Fax:* (343) 378-18-30 (office). *E-mail:* so@midural.ru (office). *Website:* www.rossel.ru.

ROSSELLINI, Isabella; American actress and model; b. 18 June 1952, Rome; d. of Roberto Rossellini and Ingrid Bergman; m. 1st Martin Scorsese (q.v.) 1979 (divorced 1982); m. 2nd Jonathan Wiedemann (divorced); one d.; ed Acad. of Fashion and Costume, Rome; and New School for Social Research, New York; worked briefly as costume designer for father's films; went to New York 1972; worked as journalist for Italian TV; cover-girl for Vogue 1980; contract to model Lancôme cosmetics 1982–95; Vice-Pres. Lancaster Cosmetics GPs Marketing Dept 1995–. *Films include:* A Matter of Time 1976, White Nights 1985, Blue Velvet 1986, Tough Guys Don't Dance 1987, Siesta 1987, Zelly and Me, Cousins 1989, Wild at Heart 1990, The Siege of Venice 1991, Death Becomes Her, The Pickle, The Innocent, Fearless 1994, Wyatt Earp 1994, Immortal Beloved 1994, The Innocent 1995, The Funeral 1996, Big Night 1996, Left Luggage 1998, The Imposters, The Real Blonde 1998, Rodger Dodger 2002, Empire 2002, The Tulse Luper Suitcases, Part 1: The Moab Story 2003, The Saddest Music in the World 2003, The Tulse Luper Suitcases, Part 2: Vaux to the Sea 2004, King of the Corner 2004, Heights 2005, La Fiesta del chivo 2005. *Television includes:* Ivory Hunters 1990, Lies of the Twins 1991, The Gift 1994, Crime of the Century 1996, The Odyssey 1997, Don Quixote 2000, Napoleon 2002, Monte Walsh 2003, Legend of Earthsea 2004. *Publications:* In the Name of the Father, the Daughter and the Holy Spirits: Remembering Roberto Rossellini 2006. *Address:* c/o United Talent Agency, 9560 Wilshire Blvd., Suite 500, Beverly Hills, CA 90212, USA.

ROSSELLÓ, Hon. Pedro, BS, MD, MPH; American politician and surgeon; b. 5 April 1944, San Juan, Puerto Rico; m. Irma Margarita Nevares; three s.; ed Notre Dame Univ., Yale Univ., Harvard Univ., Univ. of Puerto Rico; fmr paediatric surgeon, Prof. of Medicine; Dir of Health, City of San Juan 1985–87; cand. elections to Congress 1988; Chair. New Progressive Party 1991–99; Gov. of Puerto Rico 1993–2001, unsuccessful cand. 2004; mem. Senate 2005–; Pres. Council of State Govts 1998; Chair. Democratic Govs' Asscn, Southern Govs' Asscn 1998–2001, Southern Int. Trade Council 1998–99, Southern Tech. Council 1998–99, Southern Growth Policies Bd 1999–2000; mem. Advisory Council Welfare to Work Partnership, USA, Democratic Nat. Cttee, Nat. Advisory Bd of Initiative and Referendum Inst., Bd of Dirs US–Spain Council and other bodies; five times men's singles tennis champion, Puerto Rico; Hon. LLD (Notre Dame) 1995, (Mass.) 1995; Pres.'s Award, US Hispanic Chamber of Commerce 1996, LULAC 1998, Rolex Achievement Award 1999. *Address:* Senado-Capitolio, POB 9023431, San Juan, 00902-3431, Puerto Rico (home). *Telephone:* (787) 724-2030, ext. 2931 (office). *E-mail:* lmuniz@senadopr.us (office). *Website:* www.senadopr.us/senadores/sen_prossello.php (office).

ROSSI, Guido, LLM; Italian business executive and academic; b. 16 March 1931, Milan; ed Univ. of Pavia and Harvard Law School; fmr Prof. of Commercial Law, Univs of Trieste, Venice and Pavia; fmr Prof. of Law, State Univ. of Milan; Chair. CONSOB (Italian cos and stock exchange regulatory body) 1981–82; Senator, Repub. of Italy (tenth legislature); Chair. Montedison SpA, Milan 1993–95, Ferruzzi Finanziaria SpA 1993; Dir Eridiana Beghin-Say 1993; Commr Italian Football Fed. 2006; Chair. Telecom Italia SpA 2006–07 (resgnd). *Publications include:* Trasparenza e Vergogna, La Società e La Borsa 1982, La Scalata del mercato 1986; several other books and numerous studies on subjects of corp. enterprises, the securities market and anti-trust legislation. *Address:* c/o Telecom Italia SpA, Corso d'Italia 41, 00198 Rome, Italy (office).

ROSSI, José Lucien André, DenD; French politician and lawyer; *President, Agence de Développement Economique de la Corse;* b. 18 June 1944, Ajaccio, Corsica; s. of Pierre Rossi and Emilie Leca; m. Denise Ferri 1968; two d.; ed Ecoles Sainte-Lucie and Castelvecchio, Lycée Fesch, Ajaccio, Faculté de Droit and Inst. d'Etudes Politiques, Paris; Asst Faculté de Droit, Paris 1969–73; served in pvt. office of Minister of Labour 1972, Minister of Educ. 1972–74; Press Officer to Minister of Health 1974–75; Parl. Relations Officer to Minister of Labour 1975–78, to Minister of Educ. 1978; pvt. office of Pres. of Senate 1981–82; mem. Conseil Général, Corsica 1973–, Pres. 1985–98; Conseiller Régional, Corsica 1975–85; Deputy Mayor of Ajaccio 1983–90, 1995–; Pres. Corsica Tourism and Leisure Agency 1983–84; Pres. Regional Information Centre 1979–85; Deputy to Nat. Ass. 1988–94; Sec.-Gen. Parti Républicain 1989–91; Mayor of Grosseto-Prugna 1990–95; Vice-Pres. Union pour la Démocratie Française (UDF) group in Nat. Ass. 1993–94; Minister of Industry, Posts and Telecommunications and Foreign Trade 1994–95; Deputy to Nat. Ass. 1995–2002; Deputy Sec.-Gen. UDF 1996–97; Titular Judge Higher Court of Justice 1997–; Pres. Démocratie Liberale Group, Nat. Ass. 1998–2000, Assemblée de Corse 1998–2004, Vice-Pres. Démocratie Libérale 2000–02; currently Pres. Agence de Développement Economique de la Corse. *Publication:* Les Maires de grandes villes en France 1972. *Address:* Agence de Développement Economique de la Corse, Immeuble Le Regent, 1 Avenue Eugène Macchini, 20000 Ajaccio, France (office); 461 boulevard Rive Sud, 20166 Porticcio, France (home). *Telephone:* 4-95-50-91-00 (office). *Fax:* 4-95-50-91-60 (office). *E-mail:* adec@corse-adec.org (office). *Website:* www.corse-adec.org (office).

ROSSI, Valentino; Italian motorcycle racer; b. 16 Feb. 1979, Urbino; s. of Graziano Rossi and Stefania Rossi; began in go-karts, then minimoto before progressing to motorcycles; won first World Championship Grand Prix at Brno, Czech Repub. 1996; by 2004 68 Grand Prix victories; World Champion 125cc class 1997, 250cc class 1999, 500cc class 2001, MotoGP class 2002, 2003, 2004, 2005; currently races for Yamaha team. *Leisure interests:* football, skiing. *E-mail:* info@yamahamotogp.com.

ROSSIER, William; Swiss economist and international organization official; b. 25 Oct. 1942; ed Univ. of Lausanne; joined Foreign Econ. Service 1970; Head Secr., Conf. on Security and Co-operation in Europe, Geneva 1972–73; Deputy Head Div. for Gen. Foreign Econ. Questions, Berne 1973–76; Counsellor, Mission to the EC, Brussels 1976–80; with Fed. Office for External Econ. Affairs 1981–88, apptd Head Div. in charge of Relations with Countries of Eastern Europe and the People's Repub. of China 1981, later Head Div. in Charge of Relations with Western Europe; fmrly involved in negotiations with GATT, OECD, UNCTAD; Plenipotentiary Amb. of Switzerland to Int. Econ. Orgs in Geneva (GATT/WTO, UNCTAD, UN-ECE, EFTA); fmr Chair. EFTA, ECE, UNCTAD Trade and Devt Bd; Chair. World Trade Org. Gen. Council 1996; Perm. Rep. to EFTA, Sec.-Gen. 2000–06. *Address:* c/o Federal Department of Foreign Affairs (FDFA), Bundeshaus West, 3003 Berne 7, Switzerland (office). *Telephone:* 313222111 (office). *Fax:* 313234001 (office). *E-mail:* info@eda.admin.ch (office). *Website:* www.eda.admin.ch (office).

ROSSIN, Lawrence G., BA; American diplomatist and UN official; *Principal Deputy Special Representative of the Secretary General, Interim Admin. in Kosovo, United Nations;* b. 3 Nov. 1952; m. Debra J. McGowan; one s. one d.; ed Claremont Men's Coll., California, NATO Defence Coll., Rome, Massachusetts Inst. of Tech.; fmr Dir, Chief of Mission Authority and Overseas Staffing State Dept; fmr Counsellor for Political Affairs, The Hague and Port-au-Prince; fmr Peru Desk Officer; fmr Staff Asst to Secs of State for Inter-American Affairs; Dir Inter-American Affairs, Nat. Security Council 1993–94; Deputy Chief of Mission, Spain 1995–98; Dir Office S Cen. European Affairs, Dept of State, led dels to Rambouillet and Paris confs on Kosovo 1999, directed govt outreach to Kosovo Liberation Army (KLA); first Chief of Mission, Kosovo, opened and headed American Office, Pristina 1999–2000, responsible for all policy initiatives and collaboration with UN Interim Admin. in Kosovo and NATO Kosovo Force; Amb. to Croatia 2001–2003; Special Asst to Pres. and Sr Dir for Strategic Planning and Southwest Asia, Nat. Security Council 2003–04 (retd from US Sr Foreign Service); Sec.-Gen.'s Prin. Deputy Special Rep. for UN Interim Admin. in Kosovo 2004–06; Sec.-Gen.'s Prin. Deputy Special Rep. for the UN Stabilization Mission in Haiti (MINUSTAH) 2006–07; Sr Int. Coordinator, Save Darfur Coalition 2007–08; Prin. Deputy Special Rep. of the UN Sec. Gen., Interim Admin. in Kosovo 2008–; State Dept Award for Valour, three Superior Hon. Awards, Meritorious Hon. Award. *Address:* Press Office, UNMIK HQ, Shop 1, Luan Haradinaj Street (Police Avenue), Pristina,, Kosovo, Serbia (office). *Telephone:* (38) 504604 (office); (212) 963-8442 (New York) (office). *Website:* www.unmikonline.org (office).

ROSSINI MIÑÁN, Renzo Guillermo, BEcons, MSc (Econ); Peruvian central banker; *General Manager, Banco Central de Reserva del Perú;* ed Univ. of the Pacific, London School of Econs, UK, courses with CAF, FMI, BID, The British Council, JICA and Studienzentrum Gerzensee-Suiza, Univ. of Piura; joined Banco Cen. de Reserva del Perú 1982, worked in Dept of Analysis and Financial Planning, Dept of Global Analysis and Dept of Conjunctural Research 1982–91, Head of Dept of External Sector Analysis 1988–90, Deputy Man. of Research and Global Analysis 1990–91, Chief Economist, Banco Cen. de Reserva del Perú 1991–2003, Gen. Man. 2003–; Prof. of Political Economy, Univ. of the Pacific 1998–; Dir Fondo Consolidado de Reservas Previsionales; mem. American Econ. Asscn, Latin American and Caribbean Econ. Asscn, Comité Editorial de la Revista Economía Chilena; Assoc. Asociación Civil Pro Universidad del Pacífico. *Publications include:* El Sesgo Anti-Exportador de la Política Comercial en el Perú (with Adrian Armas and Luis Palacios) 1990, Liberalización del Comercio Exterior en el Perú 1991, Estabilización y Dolarización en el Perú: Comentarios 1993; numerous book chapters and articles in professional journals. *Address:* Banco Central de Reserva del Perú, Jirón Antonio Miró Quesada 441–445, Lima 1, Peru (office). *Telephone:* (1) 4278307 (office). *Fax:* (1) 4266125 (office). *E-mail:* rrossini@bcrp.gob.pe (office). *Website:* www.bcrp.gob.pe (office).

ROSSINOT, André, DenM; French politician and physician; *Mayor of Nancy;* b. 22 May 1939, Briey, Meurthe-et-Moselle; s. of Lucien Rossinot and Jeanne Fondeur; m. 3rd Françoise Cordelier 1985; one s. one d.; three c. from previous marriages; ed Lycée Poincaré and Faculty of Medicine, Nancy; early career as ear, nose and throat specialist in pvt. practice; Town Councillor, Nancy 1969–71; Mayor of Nancy 1983–; Vice-Pres. Greater Nancy Urban Council 1996–2001, Pres. 2001–; Deputy to Nat. Ass. (UDF) 1978–86, 1988–93, 1995–97, Vice-Pres. 1988–89; Pres. Parti Radical 1983–88, 1994–97, Hon. Pres. 1997–, Co-Pres. 2005–07, Nat. Vice-Pres. UDF 1983–90, 1994–; mem. Political Bureau Union pour la France 1990–, UDF 1991–2000; Minister for Relations with Parl. 1986–88, of Civil Service 1993–95; Pres. Conf. Permanente des caisses de crédit municipal 1987–93; Pres. Nouveau Contrat Social 1992–, TGV 1994–99, Fed. nat. des agences d'urbanisme 1995–, Inst. nat. du génie urbain 1996–98, Asscn Seine-Moselle-Rhône 1999–; Founder and Pres. Agence des villes 1998–; Vice-Pres. Asscn des Eco Maires 1990–; Sec-Gen. l'Association des maires des grandes villes de France (AMGVF) 2001–; Chevalier, Légion d'honneur, Commdr Order of Merit (Germany). *Publication:* Stanislas, Le Roi philosophe 1999. *Leisure interests:* walking, tennis, fishing. *Address:* Hôtel de Ville, place Stanislas, 54000 Nancy, France. *Telephone:* (3) 83-85-30-00 (office). *Fax:* (3) 83-32-90-96 (office). *E-mail:* arossinot@mairie-nancy.fr (office). *Website:* www.mairie-nancy.fr (office).

ROSSITER, Robert E., BBA; American automotive industry executive; *Chairman, President and CEO, Lear Corporation;* b. Detroit; ed Northwood Univ.; joined Lear Corpn (automotive supplier) 1973, various position in sales man. and operations, mem. Bd of Dirs 1988–, Pres. and COO 1988–2000, Pres. and COO Int. Operations, Sulzbach, Germany 1997–2000, Pres. Lear Corpn 2000–03, CEO 2000–, Chair. 2003–, also currently Pres.; Vice-Chair. Michigan Minority Business Devt Council; mem. Bd Trustees Mfg Alliance, Northwood Univ.; mem. Soc. of Automotive Engineers, Int. Supplier Advisory Council,

Automotive Advisory Council. *Address:* Lear Corporation, 21557 Telegraph Road, Southfield, MI 48086-5008, USA (office). *Telephone:* (248) 447-1500 (office). *Fax:* (248) 447-1722 (office). *Website:* www.lear.com (office).

ROSSWALL, (Per) Thomas; Swedish scientist, ecologist and academic; b. 20 Dec. 1941, Stockholm; Science Sec. Swedish Council fo Planning and Coordination of Research 1975–77; Dir SCOPE/UNEP Int. Nitrogen Unit, Royal Swedish Acad. of Sciences 1977–80, Exec. Dir Geosphere-Biosphere Programme: A Study of Global Change 1987–94; Asst Prof. in Microbiology and Assoc. Prof. in Soil Ecology, Univ. of Agric. Sciences, Uppsala 1980–84, Rector 1994–2000, Prof. of Water and Environmental Studies 2000–; Prof., Dept of Water and Environmental Studies, Linköping Univ. 1984–92; Dir Int. START Secr., Washington, DC 1992–93; Prof. of Water and Environmental Studies, Univ. of Stockholm 1992–94; Dir Int. Foundation for Science 2000–01; Exec. Dir Int. Council for Science 2002–08; Ed. in Chief Ecological Bulletins 1975–85; mem. Bd for Polar Research, Ministry of Educ. 1993–96, Scientific Council Foundation for Strategic Environmental Research 1994–97, Cttee on Global Biogeochemical Cycles, Natural Science Research Council 1994–99, Environmental Advisory Council Ministry of the Environment 1995–2001, Bd of Inst. for Ecological Sustainability 1999–2001, Bd of Foundation for Int. Cooperation in Research and Higher Educ. 2000–04, Bd Beijer Inst. of Ecological Econs 2001–; Sec.-Gen. SCOPE 1986–88; Chair. Int. Cttee on Microbial Ecology 1980–83; mem. Council of Int. Cell Research Org. 1987–91, European Environmental Research Org. 1990–2004, Exec. Cttee Int. Soc. for Tropical Ecology 1995–2005, Int. Scientific Advisory Bd UNESCO 1996–2004; mem. Bd Millennium Ecosystem Assessment 2003–05; mem. ed. bds; Ed.-in-Chief Ecological Bulletins 1975–85; mem. Editorial Bd (past or present) Advances in Microbial Ecology, Biogeochemistry, Global Biogeochemical Cycles, Soil Biology and Biochemistry, Biology and Fertility of Soils, FEMS Microbial Ecology Journal, Landscape Ecology, MIRCEN Journal of Applied Microbiology and Biotechnology, European Journal of Soil Biology, Revista Estudos Avançados (USP), Brazil; Fellow, Academia Europaea 1989, Royal Swedish Acad. of Sciences 1989, Royal Swedish Acad. of Agric. and Forestry 1995, Swedish Royal Patriotic Soc. 1996, Royal Acad. of Arts and Sciences, Uppsala 1999, World Acad. of Arts and Science 2006; Assoc. Fellow, Acad. of Sciences for the Developing World 2002; Hon. mem. World Acad. of Young Scientists 2004; Royal Order of Merit 12th Grade with Serafim Ribbon (Sweden) 2000; Second Prof. John Roger Porter Memorial Lecturer, Univ. of Bombay, India 1981, First Industrial Memorial Lecturer, Haarlem, the Netherlands 1989, Fourth Hendrik De Waard Lecturer, Univ. of Groningen, the Netherlands 1990, Award of Excellence in Ecosystem Science, Natural Resources Ecology Lab., Colorado State Univ. 2002, Carl Gustaf Bernhard Lecturer, Royal Swedish Acad. of Sciences 2003, ISI Highly Cited Researcher 2003, Beijer Fellow, The Beijer Inst. of Ecological Econs 2007, Medal of Finnish Acad. of Science and Letters 2008. *Publications:* more than 10 edited books; more than 100 papers in scientific journals. *Address:* 57 chemin du Belvédère, 06530 Le Tignet, France (home). *Telephone:* (4) 93-09-93-47 (home). *E-mail:* thomas.rosswall@gmail.org (office). *Website:* www.icsu.org (office).

ROST, Andrea; Hungarian operatic soprano; b. 1962, Budapest; d. of Ferenc Rost and Erzsébet Privoda; ed Ferenc Liszt Acad. of Music, Budapest; operatic debut as Juliette in Gounod's Romeo et Juliette, Budapest 1989; solo artist at Wiener Staatsoper 1991; La Scala debut as Gilda in Rigoletto 1994; debut, Metropolitan Opera, New York as Adina in L'Elisir d'amore 1996; took part in Superconcert with José Carreras and Plácido Domingo, Budapest 1996; appeared as Elisabeth in Donizetti's opera, London 1997; debut, Tokyo Opera, as Violetta 1998; took part in concert in memory of Lehár with José Carreras and Plácido Domingo, Bad Ischl, Austria 1998; has also appeared at Staatsoper, Vienna, Salzburg Festival, Opéra Bastille, Paris, Royal Opera House, Covent Garden and Chicago Opera; Lammermoori Lucia debut, Munchen, Wigmore Hall recital, London, Valencia recital 2002; Traviata debut, Deutsche Oper, Berlin, Desdemona, Otello, Tokyo, Lammermoori Lucia premier, Covent Garden, London 2003, Gilda, Rigoletto, Metropolitan, New York 2004; First Prize, Helsinki Competition 1989, Bartók Béla – Pásztory Ditta Award, Ferenc Liszt Artistic Merit of Honour 1997, Nat. Artistic Merit of Honour 1999, Medal Obersovszky, Prima Primissima Award 2003, Kossuth Prize 2004. *Recordings include:* Mozart – Le nozze di Figaro (Susanna) 1994, Mahler – Symphony No. 8 1995, Verdi – Rigoletto (Gilda) 1995, Mendelssohn – Elias (die Witwe/ein Engel) 1996, Andrea Rost – Le delizie dell'amor 1997, Gaetano Donizetti – Lucia Di Lammermoori (Lucia) 1998, A Tribute to Operetta 1999, Amore II 2000, Escape Through Opera 2001, Erkel: Bánk bán (Melinda) 2003, ...che cosa è amor... [Mozart Arias] 2004. *DVD videos include:* Johann Strauss Gala 2000, Wolfgang Amadeus Mozart: Don Giovanni (Zerlina) 2000, A Verdi Gala from Berlin 2002, Erkel: Bánk bán (Melinda) (opera film) 2003. *Address:* Theateragentur Dr Hilbert, attn z.Hd.: Christine Sienel, Maximilianstrasse 22, 80539 Munich, Germany (office); c/o Katalin Zsigo, Pf. 190, 1276 Budapest (office); Nefelejes u. 27, 2040 Budaörs, Hungary (home). *Telephone:* (89) 290747-0 (office). *Fax:* (89) 290747-90 (office); (23) 416-583 (home). *E-mail:* agentur@hilbert.de (office); info@andrearost.com (home). *Website:* www.hilbert.de (office); www.andrearost.com (home).

ROST, Yuri Mikhailovich; Russian journalist and photographer; b. 1 Feb. 1939, Kiev, Ukraine; s. of Arkadyevich Rost and Georgiyevna Rost; m. (divorced); columnist Komsomolskaya Pravda (newspaper) 1966–79; reviewer Literaturnaya Gazeta (newspaper) 1979–94; author TV programme Stables of Rost 1994–97; reviewer Obshchaya Gazeta (newspaper) 1993–; mem. Russian PEN Centre; Prizes of Acad. of Free Press 1998, 1999; Tsarskoye Selo Artistic Prize 1999; Gilyarovsky Medal 1990; Triumph Prize. *Publications include:* People 1980, 10 Short Stories about Leningrad 1976, Everest 1983, My View 1988, Armenian Tragedy 1990; Birds (jtly); numerous essays. *Leisure interest:* collecting smoking pipes. *Address:* Makarenko str. 1/19, Apt. 21, 103062 Moscow, Russia (home).

RØSTVIG, Maren-Sofie, PhD; Norwegian fmr professor of English literature; b. 27 March 1920, Melbo; d. of Olaf Røstvig and Sigrid Røstvig; ed Univ. of Oslo and Univ. of Calif. Los Angeles; imprisoned by Nazi regime 1943, subsequently released; joined Resistance Movt and published underground newspaper until end of World War II 1944–45; Reader in English Literature, Univ. of Oslo 1955–67, Prof. 1968–87, Sr Research Fellow 1988, retd 1990; mem. Norwegian Acad. of Science and Letters; Mil. Medal of Participation in World War II. *Publications:* The Happy Man. Studies in the Metamorphoses of a Classical Ideal 1600–1760 (two vols) 1954–58, The Hidden Sense and Other Essays 1963, Fair Forms 1975, Configurations. A Topomorphical Approach to Renaissance Poetry 1994; contribs to learned journals and collections of scholarly essays on English literature. *Address:* 14 Urb. Rosa de Piedras, Carretera de Coín, 29650 Mijas, Málaga, Spain. *Telephone:* (95) 2486938. *Fax:* (95) 2485125 (home).

ROTELLA, Stephen J., BEcons, MBA; American banking executive; *President and COO, Washington Mutual, Inc.;* m.; one d.; ed State Univ. NY, Stony Brook and Albany; held various positions with JP Morgan Chase 1987–2005, including COO Chase Home Finance 1998–2001, mem. Exec. Cttee and CEO 2001–04, fmr Chair. Housing Advisory Bd, mem. Bd of Dirs –2005; mem. Exec. Cttee, Pres. and COO Washington Mutual, Inc. 2005–, Pres., Retail Banking 2008–; mem. Bd of Dirs Mortgage Bankers Asscn, St Barnabas Medical Center, NJ; mem. Exec. Cttee Financial Services Roundtable's Housing Policy Council. *Address:* Washington Mutual Inc., 1301 Second Avenue, Seattle, WA 98101, USA (office). *Telephone:* (206) 461-2000 (office). *E-mail:* info@wamu.com (office). *Website:* www.wamu.com (office).

ROTFELD, Adam Daniel, PhD; Polish politician and academic; *Researcher and Chairman, International Consultative Committee, Polish Institute of Foreign Affairs;* b. 1938; ed Diplomatic-Consular Faculty, Main School of Foreign Service and Faculty of Journalism, Warsaw Univ., Faculty of Law and Admin, Jagiellonian Univ., Kraków; Resident Fellow, Inst. of East-West Security Studies, New York, USA 1984–85; Assoc. Prof. and Prof. in Humanities, Univ. of Warsaw 2001–; Researcher in Int. Law and Int. Relations, Polish Inst. of Int. Affairs 1961–89; Ed. Int. Affairs magazine, Warsaw, and Head of European Security Dept 1978; Leader, Project on Building a Co-operative Security System in and for Europe, Stockholm Int. Peace Research Inst. (SIPRI) 1989, Dir SIPRI 1991–2002, apptd Personal Rep. OSCE Chairman-in-Office to settle conflicts in Trans-Dniester region of Moldova 1992; Ed. SIPRI Yearbook: Armaments, Disarmament and International Security 1991–; mem. Nat. Security Council 2001–; apptd Under-Sec. of State, Ministry of Foreign Affairs 2001, Sec. of State 2003–05; Minister of Foreign Affairs Jan.–Oct. 2005; Researcher and Chair. Int. Consultative Cttee, Polish Institute of Foreign Affairs 2006–; mem. Royal Swedish Acad. of War Studies 1996, Governing Bd of Hamburg Inst. for Peace Research and Security Policy at Univ. of Hamburg 1995, Advisory Bd to UNESCO Studies on Peace and Conflict 1993–, Advisory Bd of Geneva Centre for Democratic Control of Armed Forces 2001, and many other research centres. *Publications:* has published and ed more than 20 books and over 300 articles on legal and political aspects of relations between Germany and Cen. and Eastern Europe after World War II, human rights, cooperative security, CSBMs, multilateral security structures, and political and legal aspects of security system in Europe, including The New Security Dimensions: Europe after NATO and EU Enlargements 2001.

ROTH, Daryl; American theatre producer; m. Steven Roth; five c.; ed New York Univ.; began career as interior designer; f. Daryl Roth Productions, New York and Daryl Roth Theater 1996–; f. DR2 Theater 2002–; mem. Bd of Dirs Lincoln Center Theater 1992–, Sundance Inst., New York State Council on the Arts, Albert Einstein Coll. of Medicine; Louis Marshall Award (Jewish Theological Seminary), Albert Einstein Coll. of Medicine Spirit of Achievement Award, Chairman Award (National Corporate Theatre Fund), Tisch School of Arts Award for Artistic Leadership. *Plays produced include:* Nick and Nora 1991, Twilight: Los Angeles 1992 1993, Three Tall Women (Pulitzer Prize) 1994, How I Learned to Drive (Pulitzer Prize) 1998, Wit (Pulitzer Prize) 1999, Snakebit, Villa Villa, The Bomb-itty of Errors; The Play About the Baby, Harlem Song, The Goat, or Who Is Sylvia? (Tony Award for Best Play) 2002, The Tale of the Allergist's Wife 2002, Medea 2003, Proof (Tony Award for Best Play and Pulitzer Prize) 2003, Anna in the Tropics (Pulitzer Prize) 2004, Caroline, or Change 2004, Who's Afraid of Virginia Woolf 2004, Mambo Kings 2005. *Address:* Daryl Roth Productions, 152 West 57th Street, 21st Floor, New York, NY 10019, USA (office). *Telephone:* (212) 957-1222 (office). *Fax:* (212) 957-1024 (office). *Website:* www.rothproductions.com (office); www.dr2theatre.com; darylroththeatre.com.

ROTH, Joe; American film executive and producer; b. 1948; fmrly production asst various commercials and films; fmrly lighting dir Pitched Players, also producer; co-f. Morgan Creek Productions 1987–89; Chair. Twentieth Century Fox Film Corpn 1989–92; f. Caravan Pictures 1992–94; Chair. Walt Disney Motion Pictures Group 1994–97, Walt Disney Studios, Burbank 1997–2000; f. Revolution Studios 2000–07; Producer Sony Pictures Entertainment, Inc. 2007–; mem. Bd of Dirs Pixar Studios 2000–06; majority owner Seattle Soccer Group (Major League Soccer team in Seattle) 2007–. *Films produced include:* Tunnelvision, Cracking Up, Americathon, Our Winning Season, The Final Terror, The Stone Boy, Where the River Runs Black, Bachelor Party, Off Beat, Streets of Gold (also Dir), Revenge of the Nerds (also Dir), Young Guns, Dead Ringers, Skin Deep, Major League, Renegades, Coupe de Ville (also Dir), Enemies: A Love Story; films for Caravan Pictures include Walt Disney's The Three Musketeers, Angie, Angels in the Outfield, I Love Trouble, A Low Down Dirty Shame, Houseguest, The Jerky Boys, Heavyweights, Tall Tale, While

You Were Sleeping 1995, Before and After 1996, Tears of the Sun 2003, Daddy Day Care 2003, Hollywood Homicide 2003, Mona Lisa Smile 2003, The Forgotten 2004, An Unfinished Life 2005, The Great Debaters 2007, Demons 2007, Hellboy II: The Golden Army 2008. *Film directed:* Freedomland 2005. *Address:* c/o Sony Pictures Entertainment Inc., 10202 West Washington Blvd., Culver City, CA 90232, USA. *Website:* www.sonypictures.com; www.mlsinseattle.com.

ROTH, John Andrew, MEng; Canadian communications executive; b. 6 Oct. 1942, Alberta; s. of Henry Roth and Sophia Brix; m. Margaret Anne Roth 1968; ed McGill Univ., Montreal; with RCA 1964–69; joined Nortel 1969, Head Wireless Div. 1991–93, Pres. Nortel N. America 1993–95, Group COO 1995–97, Chief Exec. 1997–2001. *Leisure interest:* making stained-glass windows. *Address:* R.R. #5, Morningview, Orangeville, ON LGW 2Z2, Canada (office).

ROTH, Klaus Friedrich, PhD, FRS; British mathematician and academic; *Honorary Research Fellow, Department of Mathematics, University College London;* b. 29 Oct. 1925, Breslau, Germany; s. of the late Dr Franz Roth and Mathilde Roth; m. Dr Melek Khairy 1955 (died 2002); ed St Paul's School, London, Peterhouse, Cambridge and Univ. Coll., London; Asst Master Gordonstoun School 1945–46; postgraduate student Univ. Coll., London 1946–48; mem. Math. Dept, Univ. Coll., London 1948–66 (title of Prof. in Univ. of London conferred 1961), Fellow 1979, Hon. Research Fellow, Dept of Math. 1996–; Prof. of Pure Math. (Theory of Numbers), Imperial Coll., London 1966–88, Visiting Prof. 1988–96, Fellow 1999; Visiting Lecturer, MIT 1956–57, Visiting Prof. 1965–66; Foreign Hon. Mem. AAAS 1966; Hon. Fellow, Peterhouse, Cambridge 1989; Hon. FRSE 1993; Fields Medal (Int. Math. Union) 1958, De Morgan Medal (London Math. Soc.) 1983, Sylvester Medal (Royal Soc.) 1991. *Publications:* papers in journals of learned socs. *Leisure interests:* chess, cinema, ballroom dancing. *Address:* Colbost, 16A Drummond Road, Inverness, IV2 4NB, Scotland (home).

ROTH, Philip Milton, MA; American writer; b. 19 March 1933, Newark, NJ; s. of Bess Finkel Roth and the late Herman Roth; m. 1st Margaret Martinson 1959 (died 1968); m. 2nd Claire Bloom (q.v.) 1990 (divorced 1994); ed Bucknell Univ. and Univ. of Chicago; in US Army 1955–56; Lecturer in English, Univ. of Chicago 1956–58; Visiting Lecturer, Univ. of Iowa Writers' Workshop 1960–62; Writer-in-Residence, Princeton Univ. 1962–64, Univ. of Pennsylvania 1967–80; Distinguished Prof. of Literature, Hunter Coll. 1989–92; Visiting Lecturer, State Univ. of NY, Stony Brook 1967, 1968; Houghton Mifflin Literary Fellow 1959; Guggenheim Fellowship Grant 1959–60, Rockefeller Grant 1965, Ford Foundation Grant 1966; mem. American Acad. of Arts and Letters 1970–; Dr hc (Harvard Univ.) 2003; Daroff Award of Jewish Book Council of America 1959, Nat. Inst. of Arts and Letters Award 1959, Nat. Arts Club's Medal of Honor for Literature 1991, Karel Capek Prize 1994, Nat. Medal of Arts 1999, Gold Medal in Fiction, American Acad. of Arts and Letters 2000, Nat. Book Foundation Medal for Distinguished Contribution to American Letters 2002, PEN/Nabokov Award for Lifetime Achievement 2006, PEN/Saul Bellow Award for Achievement in American Fiction 2007. *Publications:* Goodbye Columbus (novella and stories) 1959, Letting Go 1962, When She Was Good 1967, Portnoy's Complaint 1969, Our Gang 1971, The Breast 1972, The Great American Novel 1973, My Life as a Man 1974, Reading Myself and Others (essays) 1975, The Professor of Desire 1977, The Ghost Writer 1979, A Philip Roth Reader 1980, Zuckerman Unbound 1981, The Anatomy Lesson 1983, The Prague Orgy 1985, Zuckerman Bound 1985, The Counterlife (Nat. Book Critics' Circle Award 1987) 1986, The Facts: A Novelist's Autobiography 1988, Deception 1990, Patrimony (Nat. Book Critics' Circle Award 1992) 1991, Operation Shylock (PEN/Faulkner Award) 1993, Sabbath's Theater (Nat. Book Award for Fiction) 1995, American Pastoral (Pulitzer Prize in Fiction 1998) 1997, I Married a Communist (Ambassador Book Award of the English-Speaking Union) 1998, The Human Stain (PEN-Faulkner Award 2001, Prix Médicis Étranger 2002) 2000, The Dying Animal 2001, Shop Talk 2001, The Plot Against America (WHSmith Literary Award 2005, Sidewise Award for Alternate History 2005) 2004, Everyman (PEN/Faulkner Award 2007) 2006, Exit Ghost 2007, Indignation 2008. *Address:* The Wylie Agency, 250 W 57th Street, Suite 2114, New York, NY 10107, USA (office).

ROTH, Tim; British actor; b. 14 May 1961, Dulwich, London; ed Dick Sheppard Comprehensive School, Brixton and Camberwell Coll. of Art; began acting career with fringe groups including Glasgow Citizens Theatre, The Oval House and the Royal Court; appeared on London stage in Metamorphosis; numerous TV appearances including Made in Britain 1982. *Films include:* The Hit 1984, A World Apart 1988, The Cook The Thief His Wife and Her Lover 1989, Vincent & Theo 1990, Rosencrantz and Guildenstern are Dead 1990, Jumpin' at the Boneyard 1992, Reservoir Dogs 1992, Bodies Rest and Motion, Pulp Fiction 1994, Little Odessa 1994, Captives 1994, Rob Roy 1995, Four Rooms 1995, Everyone Says I Love You 1996, Hoodlum 1997, Deceiver 1997, Animals 1997, The Legend of the Pianist on the Ocean 1998, The War Zone (dir) 1999, Vatel 2000, Lucky Numbers 2000, Planet of the Apes 2001, Invincible 2001, The Musketeer 2001, The Beautiful Country 2004, Silver City 2004, Don't Come Knockin' 2005, Dark Water 2005, Jump Shot 2005, Youth Without Youth 2007, Funny Games 2008, The Incredible Hulk 2008. *Address:* Ilene Feldman Agency, 8730 West Sunset Boulevard, Suite 490, Los Angeles, CA 90069, USA (office).

ROTH, Urs Philipp, DrIur; Swiss lawyer; *CEO, Swiss Bankers Association;* b. 1947; joined UBS 1976, worked as Group Gen. Counsel –2001; CEO Swiss Bankers Asscn and Del. of Bd of Dirs 2001–; Chair. Exec. Cttee Int. Financial Centre Switzerland (LAIF); mem. Foundation Bd Swiss Finance Inst. 2005–; teaches at Univ. of Zurich. *Publications:* contrib. numerous papers on banking and stock exchange law. *Address:* Swiss Bankers Association, Aeschenplatz 7,

POB 4182, 4002 Basel, Switzerland (office). *Telephone:* (61) 295-93-93 (office). *Fax:* (61) 272-53-82 (office). *E-mail:* office@sba.ch (office). *Website:* www.swissbanking.org (office).

ROTHBLATT, Martine, PhD, JD, MBA; American laywer and business executive; *Chairman and CEO, United Therapeutics;* b. (Martin Rothblatt), 1954; four c.; ed Univ. of Southern Calif., Queen Mary, Univ. of London; began career with Covington & Burlington, Washington, DC –1983; f. PanAmSat, CD Radio, WorldSpace 1980s; co-f. Sirius Satellite Radio; opened The Law Offices of Martine Rothblatt specializing in satellite communications law; Pres. Geostar 1985–89; opened a second law firm 1989; Pnr Makon & Patusky (law firm), Washington, DC 1990–; endowed the PPH (Primary Pulmonary Hypertension) Cure Foundation to find a treatment for her daughter Jenesis' condition 1994–; f. United Therapeutics (pharmaceutical co.); Founding mem. and Co-Chair. Bioethics Sub cttee, Int. Bar Asscn 1993–; Pres. William Harvey Medical Research Foundation. *Publications include:* The Apartheid of Sex: A Manifesto on the Freedom of Gender 1995, Unzipped Genes: Taking Charge of Baby-Making in the New Millennium 1997. *Address:* United Therapeutics Corporate Headquarters, 1110 Spring Street, Silver Spring, MD, 20910, USA (office). *Telephone:* (301) 608-9292 (office). *Fax:* (301) 608-9291 (office). *Website:* www.unither.com (office).

ROTHENBERG, Alan I., BA, JD; American lawyer and business executive; *Chairman and CEO, 1st Century Bank, N.A.;* b. 10 April 1939, Detroit; m. Georgina Rothenberg; three c.; ed Univ. of Michigan; admitted to Calif. Bar 1964; Assoc. O'Melveny & Myers (law firm), LA 1963–66; Founder and Man. Pnr, Manatt Phelps Rothenberg & Phillips (law firm), LA 1968–90, Pnr, Latham & Watkins, LA 1990–2000 (retd); Instructor in Sports Law, Univ. of Southern Calif. 1969, 1976, 1984, Whittier Coll. of Law 1980, 1984; Pres. and Gen. Counsel LA Lakers (professional basketball team) and LA Kings (professional ice hockey team) 1967–79, LA Clippers (professional basketball team) 1982–89; Pres. US Soccer Fed., Chicago 1990–98, now Hon. Pres. and Life Mem.; Founder and fmr Chair. Major League Soccer 1993, now mem. Bd of Dirs; Chair. Goal Media 1993–; Organizer and Bd Mem. First Los Angeles Bank 1973–84; Founder, Chair. and CEO First Century Bank NA, LA 2004–; Chair. Premier Partnerships (sports and entertainment marketing firm); mem. Bd of Dirs Arden Realty Inc., Zenith National Corpn, California Pizza Kitchen Inc. 2006–; Full Time Neutral, ADR Services (dispute resolution service) 2001–; mem. Soccer Comm. 1984 Olympic Games; mem. Equal Educ. Opportunities Comm. State of Calif. Bd of Educ. 1972–75; mem. Bd of Govs Nat. Basketball Asscn 1971–79; Pres. Constitutional Rights Foundation 1987–90; Chair. Pres. CEO 1994 World Cup Organizing Cttee 1990–94; fmr Vice Pres. Confed. of North, Cen. America and Caribbean Asscn Football (CONCACAF); inducted into US Nat. Soccer Hall of Fame 2007. *Address:* 1st Century Bank, NA, 1875 Century Park East, Suite 1400, Los Angeles, CA 90067, USA (office). *Telephone:* (310) 270-9500 (home). *E-mail:* jdinapoli@1stcenturybank.com (home). *Website:* www.1stcenturybank.com (office).

ROTHENBERG, Susan, BFA; American artist; b. 20 Jan. 1945, Buffalo, New York; d. of Leonard Rothenberg and Adele Cohen; m. George Trakas 1971 (divorced 1976); one d.; ed Cornell Univ., Corcoran Museum School, George Washington Univ.; participated in numerous group exhbns at Museum of Modern Art, Whitney Museum of American Art, Venice Biennale and galleries in Germany, Denmark, Spain, Finland etc.; work exhibited in several public collections in USA and Netherlands; Guggenheim Fellow 1980; moved to New Mexico 1990; Cornell Univ. Alumni Award 1998, Skowhegan Medal for Painting 1998, Rolf Schock Prize for the Visual Arts 2003. *Address:* c/o Sperone Westwater, 415 West 13th Street, New York, NY 10014; c/o Art Foundry, POB 8107, Santa Fe, NM 87504, USA.

ROTHENBERGER, Anneliese; German singer (soprano) and painter; b. 19 June 1926, Mannheim; d. of Josef Rothenberger and Sophie Häffner; m. Gerd W. Dieberitz 1954 (deceased); ed Real- und Musikhochschule, Mannheim; debut, Coblenz Theatre 1947; with State Opera Hamburg, Munich, Vienna 1958–70; guest singer at La Scala, Milan, Metropolitan Opera, New York and Salzburg, Glyndebourne and Munich Festivals, etc.; TV Special 1969–; several exhbns as painter, Germany and Switzerland; recital tours to Russia, Japan, Iceland, Germany and USA; Distinguished Service Cross 1st Class, Great Cross; Echo Award for Lifetime Achievement 2003. *Films:* Oh, Rosalinda 1955, Der Rosenkavalier 1960. *Television:* many appearances on Zweites Deutsches Fernsehen. *Publication:* Melody of My Life 1973. *Leisure interests:* driving, books, painting, modelling, swimming. *Address:* Quellenhof, 8268 Salenstein am Untersee, Switzerland.

ROTHERMERE, 4th Viscount, cr. 1919, of Hemsted; **Jonathan Harold Esmond Vere Harmsworth,** BA; British newspaper publisher; *Chairman, Daily Mail and General Trust PLC;* b. 3 Dec. 1967, London; s. of the late 3rd Viscount Rothermere and Patricia Evelyn Beverley Brooks; m. Claudia Clemence 1993; one s. three d.; ed Gordonstoun School, Scotland, Kent School, Conn., USA, Duke Univ.; joined Mirror Group 1993; joined Northcliffe Newspapers Group Ltd 1995; Deputy Man. Dir, then Man. Dir Evening Standard 1997; Chair. Assoc. Newspapers Ltd 1998–; Chair. Assoc. New Media 1998, Daily Mail and Gen. Trust PLC 1998–; Pres. Newspaper Press Fund 1999–. *Leisure interests:* family, tennis, golf, riding. *Address:* Daily Mail and General Trust PLC, Room 602, Northcliffe House, 2 Derry Street, London, W8 5TT, England (office). *Telephone:* (20) 7938-6613. *Fax:* (20) 7937-0043. *E-mail:* chairman@chairman.dmgt.co.uk (office). *Website:* www.dmgt.co.uk (office).

ROTHMAN, James E., PhD; American biochemist/biophysicist and academic; *Clyde '56 and Helen Wu Professor of Physiology (Chemical Biology), Department of Physiology and Cellular Biophysics, Columbia University;* b. 3 Nov. 1950, Haverhill, Mass; ed Yale Univ. and Harvard Medical School; postdoctoral work at MIT; Asst Prof., Dept of Biochemistry, Stanford Univ. 1978–81, Assoc. Prof. 1981–84, Prof. 1984–88; E. R. Squibb Prof. of Molecular Biology, Princeton Univ. 1988-91; Chairman, Cellular Biochemistry and Biophysics Program, Sloan-Kettering Inst., New York 1991–2003, Paul A. Marks Chair, Memorial Sloan-Kettering Cancer Center, Chair. Cellular Biochemistry and Biophysics Program, Rockefeller Research Lab. 1991–2004, Vice-Chair. Sloan-Kettering Inst. 1994–2003; Prof., Dept Physiology and Cellular Biophysics, Columbia Univ. 2004–05, Clyde '56 and Helen Wu Prof. of Chemical Biology 2005–, Dir Chemical Biology Center 2004–, Dir Columbia Genome Center 2005–, mem. Columbia Cancer Center 2004–; mem. NAS Inst. of Medicine 1995; Fellow, American Acad. of Arts and Sciences 1994; mem. Bd of Sr Eds, Journal of Clinical Investigation 2002–; Assoc. Ed., Annual Review of Biochemistry 2003–; Hon. Mem., Japanese Biochemical Soc. 2005; Dr hc (Univ. of Regensburg) 1995, (Univ. of Geneva) 1997; Eli Lilly Award for Fundamental Research in Biological Chem. 1986, Passano Young Scientist Award 1986, Alexander Von Humboldt Award 1989, Heinrich Wieland Prize 1990, Rosenstiel Award in Biomedical Sciences (with R. Schekman) 1994, V.D. Mattia Award 1994, Fritz Lipmann Award 1995, Gairdner Foundation Int. Award 1996, King Faisal Int. Prize in Science 1996, Felix Hoppe-Seyler Lecturer 1996, Harden Medal 1997, NAS Lounsbery Award 1997, Feodor Lynen Award (with G. Blobel and G. Schatz) 1997, Jacobæus Prize 1999, Dr H.P. Heineken Prize for Biochemistry 2000, Otto-Warburg Medal 2001, Louisa Gross Horwitz Prize (with R. Schekman) 2002, Albert Lasker Award for Basic Medical Research (with R. Schekman) 2002. *Publications:* more than 200 articles in scientific journals. *Address:* Russ Berrie Medical Sciences Pavilion, 1150 St Nicholas Avenue, Room 520, Columbia University, New York, NY 10032, USA (office). *Telephone:* (212) 851-5565 (office). *Fax:* (212) 851-5570 (office). *E-mail:* jr2269@columbia.edu (office). *Website:* www.cumc.columbia.edu/dept/physio/physio2 (office); www.cumc.columbia.edu/dept/physio/Rothman (office).

ROTHSCHILD, Baron David René James de; French banker; *Chairman, N.M. Rothschild & Sons Ltd;* b. 15 Dec. 1942, New York; s. of the late Baron Guy de Rothschild and Baroness Alix Schey de Koromla; m. Olimpia Aldobrandini 1974; ed Lycée Carnot, Paris and Inst. d'Etudes Politiques, Paris; Dir Société Le Nickel 1970–73; Dir-Gen. Cie du Nord 1973–78; Chair. Man. Bd Banque Rothschild 1978–82; Pres.-Dir-Gen. Paris-Orléans Man. 1982–84, Paris-Orléans Banque 1984–86; Chair. Rothschild & Cie Banque 1986–, Rothschild NA Inc. 1986–, Rothschild Canada 1990–; Chair. Man. Bd Saint-Honoré-Matignon (investment co.) 1986–94; Pres.-Dir-Gen. Francarep; Pres. Financière Viticole SA, Rothschild Europe; Dir Cie Financière Martin-Maurel, Imetal, Asscn française des entreprises privées (Afep), Rothschilds Continuation Ltd, etc.; Vice-Pres. Incolder 1990; Deputy Chair. N. M. Rothschild & Sons Ltd, London 1992–2004, Chair. 2004–; Chair. N. M. Rothschild Corporate Finance 1996–; Pres. Fondation Rothschild. *Leisure interests:* golf, skiing, tennis. *Address:* N.M. Rothschild & Sons Limited, New Court, St. Swithin's Lane, London, EC4P 4DU, England (office); 6 rue de Tournon, 75006 Paris, France (home). *Telephone:* (20) 7280-5000 (office). *Fax:* (20) 7929-1643 (office). *Website:* www.rothschild.com (office).

ROTHSCHILD, Sir Evelyn de, Kt; British banker; b. 29 Aug. 1931, London; s. of the late Anthony Gustav de Rothschild; m. 1st Victoria Schott 1972 (divorced 2000); two s. one d.; m. 2nd Lynn Forester 2000; ed Harrow, Trinity Coll., Cambridge; Chair. Economist Newspaper 1972–89, United Racecourses Ltd 1977–94, British Merchant Banking and Securities Houses Asscn (fmrly Accepting Houses Cttee) 1985–89; fmr Chair. N.M. Rothschild & Sons Ltd 1976–2004. *Leisure interests:* art, racing. *Address:* c/o N. M. Rothschild & Sons Ltd, New Court, St Swithin's Lane, London, EC4P 4DU, England. *Telephone:* (20) 7280-5302 (office). *Fax:* (20) 7220-7108 (office). *Website:* www.rothschild.com (office).

ROTHSCHILD, 4th Baron, cr. 1885; **(Nathaniel Charles) Jacob Rothschild,** OM, GBE, BA; British banker and business executive; *Chairman, RIT Capital Partners plc;* b. 29 April 1936; eldest s. of the late Nathaniel Mayer Victor Rothschild, 3rd Baron Rothschild GBE, GM, FRS and Barbara Hutchinson, Baroness Rothschild; succeeded his father 1990; m. Serena Mary Dunn 1961; one s. three d.; ed Eton Coll. and Christ Church, Oxford; Chair. St James's Place Capital PLC (fmrly J. Rothschild Holdings) 1971–96, RIT Capital Partners plc 1980–, Five Arrows Ltd 1980–; Deputy Chair. BSkyB Group plc 2003–; Chair. Bd of Trustees, Nat. Gallery 1985–91, Bd of Trustees Nat. Heritage Memorial Fund 1992–98 (administering Heritage Lottery Fund 1995–98), Yad Hanadiv Foundation; Pres. Inst. of Jewish Affairs 1992–; mem. Council, RCA 1986–92 (Sr Fellow 1992); co-f. Butrint Foundation to record and conserve the archaeological site of Butrint in Albania 1993; Trustee Open Russia Foundation 2001–; Hon. Fellow, City of Jerusalem 1992; Hon. FBA 1998; Hon. FRIBA 1998; Hon. FRAM 2002; Hon. Fellow, King's Coll. London 2002; Commdr, Order of Henry the Navigator (Portugal) 1985; Hon. PhD (Hebrew Univ of Jerusalem) 1992; Hon. DLitt (Newcastle) 1998, (Warwick) 2003; Hon. LLD (Exeter) 1998; Hon. DUniv (Keele) 2000; Hon. DCL (Oxon.) 2002; Hon. DSc (Econs) (London) 2004; Weizmann Award for Humanities and Sciences 1997. *Address:* The Pavilion, Eythrope, Aylesbury, Bucks., HP18 0HS, England. *Telephone:* (1296) 748337.

ROTTERMUND, Andrzej; Polish curator and art historian; *Director, The Royal Castle, Warsaw;* b. 11 May 1941, Warsaw; s. of Julian Lenart and Zofia Lenart; m. Maria Reklewska 1963; one d.; ed Warsaw Univ.; Prof. Inst. of Art, Polish Acad. of Sciences, Warsaw 1990; Dept Dir Nat. Museum, Warsaw 1975–83, The Royal Castle, Warsaw 1987–90 (Dir 1991–); Deputy Minister of Culture and Arts 1991; mem. Polish Acad. of Sciences, Polish Art Historians' Asscn 1987–91, Polish ICOM Cttee 1990–96; organized exhbns in Poland and abroad including Treasures of a Polish King, Dulwich Picture Gallery London 1992, Land of the Winged Horsemen: Art in Poland 1572–1764, USA 1999–2000, Thesauri Poloniae, Austria 2002; Silver Cross of Merit 1977, Meritorious Activist of Culture 1978, Kt's Cross, Order of Polonia Restituta 1988, Officer's Cross 1994, Commdr's Cross 1998, Cross of Merit (Germany) 1999, Ordre de la Couronne (Belgium) 2002, Officier de la Légion d'honneur 2002, and other decorations. *Publications:* 100 books, articles and essays including Katalog rysunków architektonicznych ze zbiorów Muzeum Narodowego w Warszawie (The Catalogue of Architectural Drawings of the Nat. Museum in Warsaw) 1970, Klasycyzm w Polsce (Neoclassicism in Poland) 1984, Zamek Królewski – funkcje i treści rezydencji monarszej wieku Oświecenia (The Royal Castle in the Age of the Enlightenment – the Functions and Symbolic Meaning of the Monarch's Residence) 1988, J. N. L. Durand a polska architektura I połowy XIX wieku (J. N. L. Durand and the Polish Architecture of the First Half of the 19th Century) 1990, Warsaw 2000, The Royal Castle in Warsaw 2003. *Leisure interests:* music, cinema. *Address:* The Royal Castle, pl. Zamkowy 4, 00-277 Warsaw, Poland (office). *Telephone:* (22) 6350808 (office); (22) 6572150 (office). *Fax:* (22) 6357260 (office). *E-mail:* a.rottermund@zamek-krolewski.art.pl (office). *Website:* www.zamek-krolewski.art.pl (office).

ROUCO VARELA, HE Cardinal Antonio María, LicenD, DCL; Spanish ecclesiastic; *Archbishop of Madrid;* b. 20 Aug. 1936, Villalba; s. of Vicente Rouco and María Eugenia Varela; ordained priest 1959; taught at Mondoñedo Seminary, Lugo 1964–66, Univ. of Munich 1966–69, Univ. Pontificia de Salamanca 1969–76 (Vice-Rector 1972–76); Auxiliary Bishop of Santiago de Compostela 1976–84, Archbishop of Santiago de Compostela 1984–94, of Madrid 1994–; cr. Cardinal 1998, Cardinal Priest of S Lorenzo in Damaso; Pres. Spanish Bishops Conf. 1999–2005, 2008–; Gran. Canciller San Dámaso Faculty of Theology. *Publications:* Staat und Kirche im Spanien des XVI Jahrhunderts 1965, Sacramento e diritto: antinomia nella Chiesa (with E. Corecco) 1972. *Leisure interests:* music, reading. *Address:* Arzobispado de Madrid, C/ Bailen 8, 28071 Madrid, Spain (office); Conferencia Episcopal Española, Calle Añastro 1, 28033 Madrid, Spain (office). *Telephone:* (91) 4546100 (office); (91) 3439600 (office). *Fax:* (91) 5427906 (office); (91) 3439602 (office). *E-mail:* infomadrid@planalfa.es (home); conferenciaepiscopal@planalfa.es (office). *Website:* www.archimadrid.es (office); www.conferenciaepiscopal.es (office).

ROUILLY, Jean, LenD; French television executive; *CEO, Lagardère Television International;* b. 21 Dec. 1943, Villennes-sur-Seine; s. of Roger Rouilly and Nicole Antigna; m. Annyck Graton 1987; one s.; ed Lycées Jules Verne and Georges Clémenceau, Nantes, Faculté de Droit, Bordeaux and Inst. d'Etudes Politiques, Bordeaux; Asst to the Dir, Office de Radiodiffusion-Télévision Francaise, 1966–70, Admin. Documentary Programmes 1970–72, Gen. Man. to Del. Gen. of TV Production 1972–74; Sec.-Gen. Production, Antenne 2 1975–81, Asst Dir Finance 1981–85, Production Man. 1985–87, Dir-Gen. Programme Production 1987–90; Asst Dir-Gen. Antenne 2 1987–90; Dir Films A2 1981–87, Dir-Gen. 1987–90; Sec.-Gen. TV5 1983–85; Dir-Gen. Hachette Int. TV (now Europe Images Int.) 1990–2003, CEO 1999–2003; CEO Lagardère Images Int. and Lagardère Networks Int. 2001– (merged in 2007 to form Lagardère TV Int.). *Address:* Lagardère Television International, 149-151 rue Anatole France, 92534 Levallois-Peret Cedex, France (office). *Website:* www.lni.tv (office).

ROULEAU, Joseph-Alfred, OC; Canadian singer (bass); *President, Jeunesses Musicales du Canada;* b. 28 Feb. 1929, Matane, Québec; s. of Joseph-Alfred Rouleau and Florence Bouchard; m. 1st Barbara Whittaker 1952; one d.; m. 2nd Jill Renée Moreau; one s. two d.; ed Coll. Jean de Brebeuf, Montreal, Univ. of Montréal, Conservatoire of Music, Province of Québec; debut at Montréal Opera Guild in Un Ballo in Maschera 1951; Royal Opera House, Covent Garden 1957–87, singing 48 roles; guest artist at prin. opera houses all over the world; tours of Canada 1960, Australia (with Joan Sutherland) 1965, Russia 1966, 1969, Romania, S Africa 1974, 1975, 1976; Paris Opera 1975, Metropolitan Opera, New York 1984, 1985, 1986, San Francisco 1986, 1987; roles include Boris Godunov in Boris Godunov, Philip II and Inquisitore in Don Carlos, Basilio in Barber of Seville, Mephistopheles in Faust, Dosifei in Khovanshchina, Don Quixote in Don Quixote, Ramfis in Aida, Prince Gremin in Onegin, Father Lawrence in Roméo et Juliette, Colline in La Bohème, Raimondo in Lucia di Lammermoor, Titurel in Parsifal, Abimelech in Samson et Dalila, Crespel in Contes d'Hoffman, Arkel in Pelléas et Mélisande, Sarastro, Osmin in Die Entführung, Daland in Der fliegende Holländer, Oroveso in Norma, Don Marco in The Saint of Bleecker Street, Trulove in The Rake's Progress, The Prince in Adriana Lecouvreur, Bartolo; Prof. of Voice, Univ. of Québec 1980–98, mem. Admin. Bd, Prof. Emer. 2004–; mem. Bd Corpn of Montreal Opéra Co. 1980–; Pres., Jeunesses Musicales du Canada 1989– (Prix Joseph Rouleau for Vocal Art named after him 1995); Co-Founder and mem. Bd Concours Musical Int. de Montréal 2002–; Grand Officier, Ordre Nat. du Québec 2004; Dr hc (Université Québec à Rimouski, McGill Univ.); Prix Archambault 1967, La Société St Jean Baptiste Prix Calixa-Lavallée, Montreal 1967, Royal Opera House, Covent Garden Silver Medal 1983, Felix Award for Best Classical Artist of the Year 1989, Prix du Québec pour les Arts d'interprétation 1990, Panthéon de l'art lyrique du Canada 1992, Jeunesses Musicales du Canada Médaille du mérite exceptionnel 1995, Conseil québecois de la musique Prix Opus Hommage 2003, Prix du Gov. Gen. (Performing Arts Award) de Canada 2004, Opéra Canada Prix Ruby 2004, Médaille de la Ville de Marseille 2007. *Recordings include:* scenes from Anna Bolena, Ruddigore, Roméo et Juliette (Gounod), L'Enfance du Christ (Berlioz), Sémiramide, Lucia di Lammermoor, Don Carlos, Aida, Il Trovatore, Renard (Stravinsky), F. Leclerc's Songs, Les abîmes du rêve de Jacques Hêtu (song cycle), French operatic arias (with Royal Opera House Orchestra), Boris Godunov (Prix Félix 2000), Don Carlos/Lucie di Lamermoor, L'Africaine (Meyerbeer, with Domingo & Verrett, San Francisco Opera; Don Carlo, Royal Opera House Covent Garden. *Leisure interests:* tennis, golf, reading. *Address:* c/o Jeunesses

Musicales, 305 avenue du Mont-Royal Est, Montréal, PQ H2T 1P8 (office); 7 Roosevelt, Suite 20, Ville Mont-Royal, PQ H3R 1Z3, Canada (home). *Telephone:* (514) 739-3238 (home); (819) 688-3676 (home); (514) 845-4108 (ext. 232) (office). *Fax:* (514) 739-9135 (home); (514) 845-8241 (office). *E-mail:* Jrouleau@jeunessesmusicales.ca (office); renee_rouleau@hotmail.com (home). *Website:* www.jeunessesmusicales.com (office).

ROUNDS, M. Michael; American state official; *Governor of South Dakota;* b. 24 Oct. 1954, Huron, SDak; m. Jean Rounds; four c.; ed S Dakota State Univ.; fmr pnr Fischer, Rounds & Assocs Inc. (insurance and real estate agency), Pierre; mem. SDak State Senate 1990–2000, Senate Majority Leader 1994–2000; Gov. of SDak 2003–; Republican; Guardian of Small Business, Nat. Fed. of Ind. Business 1992, 1998, Agent of the Year, SDak Ind. Insurance Agents 1999, Special Award, SDak Horsemen 2000. *Leisure interests:* flying, hunting, racquetball, camping, boating, family. *Address:* Office of the Governor, 500 East Capitol Avenue, Pierre, SD 57501, USA (office). *Telephone:* (605) 773-3212 (office). *Website:* www.state.sd.us/governor (office).

ROURKE, Philip Andre (Mickey); American actor; b. 16 Sept. 1956, Schenectady, NY; m. 1st Debra Feuer (divorced); m. 2nd Carre Otis; ed Actors' Studio, New York. *Film appearances include:* Fade to Black, 1941 1979, Heaven's Gate 1980, Body Heat 1981, Diner 1982, Eureka 1983, Rumblefish 1983, Rusty James 1983, The Pope of Greenwich Village 1984, 9½ Weeks 1984, Year of the Dragon 1985, Angel Heart 1986, A Prayer for the Dying 1986, Barfly 1987, Johnny Handsome 1989, Homeboy 1989, Francesco 1989, The Crew 1989, The Desperate Hours 1990, Wild Orchid 1990, On the Sport 1990, Harley Davidson and the Marlboro Man 1991, White Sands 1992, F.T.W., Fall Time, Double Time, Another 9½ Weeks, The Rainmaker 1997, Love in Paris 1997, Double Team 1997, Buffalo '66 1997, Thursday 1998, Shergar 1999, Shades 1999, Out in Fifty 1999, The Animal Factory 2000, Get Carter 2000, The Pledge 2001, The Hire: Follow 2001, Picture Claire 2001, They Crawl 2001, Spun 2002, Once Upon a Time in Mexico 2003, Man on Fire 2004, Domino 2005, Sin City 2005, Stormbreaker 2006, The Wrestler (Golden Globe for Best Actor 2009, BAFTA Award for Leading Actor 2009) 2008, The Informers 2008, Killshot 2008. *Address:* c/o Progressive Artists Agency, 400 South Beverly Drive, Beverly Hills, CA 90212, USA (office).

ROUSE, Cecilia E., PhD; American economist and academic; *Theodore A. Wells '29 Professor of Economics and Public Affairs, Princeton University;* ed Harvard Univ.; currently Theodore A. Wells '29 Prof. of Econs and Public Affairs and Prof. of Econs and Public Affairs, Woodrow Wilson School, Princeton Univ., Founding Dir Princeton Univ. Educ. Research Section, Dir Industrial Relations Section; fmr Sr Ed. The Future of Children, Journal of Labor Economics; fmr mem. MacArthur Foundation's Research Network on the Transition to Adulthood; served in Nat. Econ. Council 1998–99; mem. Council of Econ. Advisers. *Publications:* numerous articles on labour econs and the econs of educ., including Florida's school accountability and voucher programmes, tech.-based programmes in schools in large urban dists, strategies for increasing educational attainment among community college students, and the impact of student loans on post-coll. occupational choices. *Address:* 357 Wallace Hall, Woodrow Wilson School, Princeton University, Princeton, NJ 08544-1013, USA (office). *Telephone:* (609) 258-6478 (office). *Fax:* (609) 258-0549 (office). *E-mail:* rouse@princeton.edu (office). *Website:* wws.princeton.edu (office).

ROUSSEL, Paul Henri Michel; French business executive; b. 3 March 1954, Bayeux; s. of Jacques Roussel and Janine Piton; m. Jacqueline Claire Roussel 1975; one s. one d.; ed Lycée Malherbe, Caen; Head of Group, Havas Conseil 1976–80; Consumer Dir SNIP 4 1981–83; Consumer Dir Robert & Pnrs 1984–86; Commercial and Marketing Dir L'Equipe magazine 1986–89, Deputy Dir-Gen. 1990–92, Dir-Gen. 1993–2003; Deputy Dir-Gen. Groupe Amaury 1995–2003. *Leisure interests:* tennis, football, skiing. *Address:* c/o L'Equipe, 4 rue Rouget de l'Isle, 92793 Issy-les-Moulineaux cedex 09, France.

ROUSSELET, André Claude Lucien, LenD; French business executive; b. 1 Oct. 1922, Nancy; s. of Marcel and Yvonne Rousselet (née Brongniart); m. Catherine Roge (divorced); two s. one d.; ed Lycée Claude Bernard, Paris, Faculté de Droit, Paris and Ecole Libre des Sciences Politiques; Chef de Cabinet, Prefects of Ariège and L'Aube 1944; Sub-Prefect of Condom 1946, Pointe-à-Pitre 1948, Issoudun 1935; Chef de Cabinet, Minister of the Interior 1954; Special Asst Office of Minister of Posts and Telecommunications 1955; Chef de Cabinet, Minister of Justice 1956; Dept of External Relations, Simca 1958; Pres.-Dir-Gen. Socs nouvelles des autoplaces G7 1962–67, 1972–; Deputé for Haute-Garonne 1967–68; Man. Galerie de France and Dir du Cabinet, Pres. of Repub. 1981–82; Pres.-Dir-Gen. Agence Havas 1982–86 (now Dir); mem. Comité stratégique de Havas 1987; Pres.-Dir-Gen. Canal Plus 1984–94; Pres. Soc. éditrice de InfoMatin (Sodepresse) 1994–; Pres. Advisory Council Tonna Electronique 1990, Sodepresse 1995; Dir Information; Pres. Editorial Soc. Sodepresse; Dir Télévision le mensuel (publ.). *Leisure interests:* golf, tennis, painting, skiing. *Address:* 44 avenue Georges V, 75008 Paris; 28 rue Henri Barbusse, 92110 Clichy, France.

ROUSSELY, François; French industrial executive; *Chairman, Crédit Suisse First Boston France;* b. 9 Jan. 1945, Dordogne; ed Paris Inst. of Political Science, French Nat. School of Admin; auditor, State Accounting Office 1978; sr civil servant, Ministry of Interior, Prin. Pvt. Sec. 1981–86; assigned to chair. of a parl. cttee, Assemblée Nat. 1986–88; Dir-Gen. Nat. Police (Ministry of Interior) 1989–91; Gen. Sec. for Admin. of Ministry of Defence 1991–97; Sec.-Gen. and mem. Exec. Cttee Soc. Nat. des Chemins de Fer (SNCF) 1997; Prin. Pvt. Sec. Ministry of Defence 1997–98; Chair. and CEO Electricité de France (EDF) 1998–2004; Chair. Crédit Suisse First Boston, France 2005–, Vice–Chair. Crédit Suisse First Boston, Europe 2005–; mem. Comité de l'Energie Atomique; mem. Bd Usinor, Framatome, Aérospatiale-Matra 1998; mem. Advisory Bd of La Banque de France; Advisor, Int. Business Leaders Advisory Council of Mayor of Beijing, Int. Business Leaders Advisory Council of Gov. of Guangdong 1998; Pres. Bd of Dirs of l'Ecole Nationale de Ponts et Chaussées; mem. Supervisory Bd DALKIA Holding 2000; Chair. EDF Foundation 2001; Admin. AFII (French Agency for Int. Investments) 2002; Officier Légion d'honneur 1998, Ordre nat. du Mérite, des Arts et Lettres 2003; Prix 2004 de l'Association France – Chine 2000. *Leisure interests:* jogging, classical music. *Address:* Crédit Suisse First Boston, 25 Avenue Kléber, 75784 Paris, Cedex 16, France (office). *Telephone:* 1-70-39-00-00 (office). *Fax:* 1-70-39-00-01 (office). *Website:* www.csfb.com (office).

ROUVILLOIS, Philippe André Marie; French government official; *Inspector General of Finance;* b. 29 Jan. 1935, Saumur; s. of Gen. Jean Rouvillois and Suzanne Hulot; m. Madeleine Brigol 1960; four s.; ed Lycée Fustel-de-Coulanges, Strasbourg, Lycée Louis-le-Grand, Faculté de Droit, Paris and Inst. d'Etudes Politiques, Paris; Insp. of Finance 1959; Office of Revenue 1964; Adviser, Pvt. Office of Minister of Econ. and Finance 1966–68; Deputy Dir Office of Revenue, Ministry of Econ. and Finance 1967, Head of Service 1969; Deputy Dir-Gen. of Revenue 1973, Dir-Gen. 1976; Insp.-Gen. of Finance 1982–; Deputy Dir-Gen. SNCF 1983–87, Dir-Gen. 1987–88, Pres. Admin. Bd 1988; Gen. Man. and Pres. Admin. Council, Atomic Energy Comm. (CEA) 1989–95; Pres. CEA-Industrie 1989–92, 1993–99; Pres. Pasteur Inst. 1997–2003, Hon. Pres. 2003–; Commdr Légion d'honneur, Croix de Valeur militaire. *Address:* Inspection générale des finances, 139 rue de Bercy, 75572 Paris, cedex 12 France (office). *E-mail:* igf-contact@igf.finances.gouv.fr (office). *Website:* www.igf.minefi.gouv.fr (office).

ROUVOET, André; Dutch politician; *Deputy Prime Minister and Minister for Youth and Families;* b. 4 Jan. 1962, Hilversum; ed VU Univ. Amsterdam; mem. Reformed Political Fed. 1985–2001; mem. Christian Union 2001–, Leader 2002–; mem. House of Reps 1994–; Deputy Prime Minister and Minister for Youth and Families 2007–; fmr Chair. Dutch Reformed Churches' Youth Welfare Asscn; mem. Bd Protestant Children's Homes Foundation, Foundation for the New South Africa. *Address:* Office of the Prime Minister, Ministry of General Affairs, Binnenhof 20, POB 20001, 2500 EA The Hague, The Netherlands (office). *Telephone:* (70) 3564100 (office). *Fax:* (70) 3564683 (office). *Website:* www.minaz.nl (office).

ROUX, Albert Henri, OBE; French chef and restaurateur; b. 8 Oct. 1935, Semur-en-Brionnais; s. of the late Henri Roux and of Germaine Roux (née Triger); brother of Michel André Roux (q.v.); m. 1st Monique Merle 1959; one s. one d.; m. 2nd Cheryl Deborah 2006; ed Ecole Primaire, St Mandé; mil. service, Algeria; founder (with brother Michel Roux), Le Gavroche Restaurant, London 1967 (now owned jtly with his son Michel Jr), The Waterside Inn, Bray 1972 (now owned solely by Michel Roux); opened 47 Park Street Hotel 1981; opened Le Poulbot, Le Gamin, Gavvers, Les Trois Plats and Rouxl Britannia (all as part of Roux Restaurants Ltd) 1969–87; commenced consultancy practice 1989; f. House of Albert Roux (retail catering co.) 1994; Founder-mem. Acad. Culinaire de Grande Bretagne (now renamed Acad. of Culinary Arts) 1980; Hon. Prof. of Hospitality Man., Bournemouth Univ. 1995–; Maître Cuisinier de France 1968, Officier du Mérite Agricole 1987, Chevalier de la Légion d'Honneur 2005; Hon. DSc (Council for Nat. Academic Awards) 1987, Hon. PhD (Bournemouth Univ.) 1987; Catey Lifetime Achievement Award (with Michel Roux) 1995, Watreford Wegdwood Hospitality Award 1999, AA Lifetime Achievement Award for Hospitality 2007. *Publications:* with Michel Roux: New Classic Cuisine 1983, The Roux Brothers on Pâtisserie 1986, The Roux Brothers on French Country Cooking 1989, Cooking for Two 1991. *Leisure interests:* fishing, racing. *Address:* Albert Roux Consultancy, 539 Wandsworth Road, London, SW8 3JX, England (office). *Telephone:* (20) 7720-6148 (office). *Fax:* (20) 7627-0267 (office). *E-mail:* albertroux@le-gavroche.com. *Website:* www.albertroux.co.uk (home).

ROUX, Bernard Georges Marie; French business executive; *CEO, 3620 Le Numéro des Marques;* b. 15 Aug. 1934, St Raphaël (Var); s. of Edouard Roux and Juliette Boyer; m. 1st Chantel Bergerat; one s. one d.; m. 2nd Laurence Grand; one s. one d.; m. 3rd Roselyne Mainfroy 1983; three s.; ed École de Commerce, Faculté de Droit de Lyon; Commercial Dir Meunier Textiles 1959; Dir-Gen. Centrale voile ameublement (Groupe Rhodiaceta) 1963; joined Axe Publicité 1965, Dir 1967; f. Roux Séguéla agency with Jacques Séguéla 1969; Pres. Roux, Séguéla, Cayzac et Goudard 1991; f. RLC 1992– (changed to Opera-RLC 1993); Pres. and Dir-Gen. Gymnase Club 1997–99; currently CEO, 3620 Le Numéro des Marques. *Leisure interests:* tennis, reading, cinema. *Address:* 8 square Chezy, 92200 Neuilly-sur-Seine, France. *Telephone:* (6) 70-16-69-82 (office). *Fax:* 1-46-41-06-96 (office). *E-mail:* Bernard.Roux@3620.com (office).

ROUX, Jean-Louis, CC; Canadian theatre director, actor and author; b. 18 May 1923, Montreal; s. of Louis Roux and Berthe Leclerc; m. Monique Oligny 1950; one s.; ed Coll. Sainte-Marie and Univ. de Montréal; mem. Les Compagnons de Saint Laurent theatrical co. 1939–42, Ludmilla Pitoëff theatrical co. 1942–46; mil. training 1942–46; founder, Théâtre d'Essai, Montreal 1951; Sec.-Gen., Théâtre du Nouveau Monde 1953–63 (co-founder 1950), Artistic Dir 1966–82; Dir-Gen. Nat. Theatre School of Canada 1982–87; has appeared in more than 200 roles (in both French and English) on stage (Montreal, Stratford, Paris), TV, cinema and radio and directed more than 50 theatrical productions; apptd to Senate 1994–96; Lt Gov. of Québec 1996; Chair. Canada Council for the Arts 1998–2003; mem. Royal Soc. of Canada 1982–; Life Gov. Nat. Theatre School of Canada; Ordre de la Pléiade 1995, KStJ; Chevalier, Ordre Nat. du Québec 1989; Dr hc (Laval Univ.) 1988, (Univ. of Ottawa) 1995; Hon. LLD (Concordia Univ.) 1993; numerous awards and medals including Molson Award 1977, World Theatre Award 1985. *Leisure interests:* reading, chess, swimming, walking. *Address:* 4145 Blueridge

Crescent, Apt. 2, Montreal, PQ H3H 1S7, Canada. *Telephone:* (514) 937-2505. *Fax:* (514) 937-5975.

ROUX, Michel André; French chef and restaurateur; b. 19 April 1941; s. of the late Henri Roux and Germaine Roux (née Triger); brother of Albert Henri Roux (q.v.); m. 1st Françoise Marcelle Becquet (divorced 1979, died 2004); one s. two d.; m. 2nd Robyn Margaret Joyce 1984; ed Ecole Primaire St Mandé, Brevet de Collège; commis pâtissier and cuisinier British Embassy, Paris 1955–57; commis cook to Cécile de Rothschild 1957–59, Chef 1962–67; mil. service 1960–62; Propr Le Gavroche 1967, The Waterside Inn 1972, Le Gavroche (Mayfair) 1981; mem. Acad. Culinaire de France (UK Br.), Asscn Relais et Desserts, Asscn Relais et Châteaux; Chevalier, Ordre nat. du Mérite 1987, Ordre des Arts et des Lettres 1990, Légion d'honneur 2004; Hon. OBE 2002; numerous other decorations; numerous culinary awards including Gold Medal Cuisiniers Français (Paris) 1972, Laureate Restaurateur of the Year 1985. *Publications:* New Classic Cuisine 1983, Roux Brothers on Pâtisserie 1986, At Home with the Roux Brothers 1987, French Country Cooking 1989, Cooking for Two 1991, Desserts, a Lifelong Passion 1994, Sauces 1996, Life is a Menu (autobiog.) 2000, Only the Best 2002, Eggs 2005. *Leisure interests:* shooting, skiing, walking. *Address:* The Waterside Inn, Ferry Road, Bray, Berks., SL6 2AT, England. *Telephone:* (1628) 771966. *Fax:* (1628) 789182. *E-mail:* michelroux@btconnect.com (office). *Website:* www.waterside-inn.co.uk (office).

ROVE, Karl Christian; American political consultant and fmr government official; b. 25 Dec. 1950, Denver; m. 1st Valerie Wainright Rove 1976 (divorced 1980); m. 2nd Darby Tara Rove (née Hickson) 1986; one s.; ed Univ. of Utah, George Mason Univ.; left univ. to become Exec. Dir Coll. Republican Nat. Cttee 1971–73, Chair. 1972; Special Asst to Chair. George Bush Nat. Cttee 1973–75; Finance Dir Va Republican Party, Richmond 1976; Dir Fund for Ltd Govt, Houston 1977–79; Deputy Dir Gov. William P. Clements Jr Cttee 1979–80; Deputy Asst to Gov of Tex. 1980–81; mem. George Bush, Sr's presidential campaign team 1980; Founder and Pres. Karl Rove & Co. (consultancy) 1981–99; political adviser to George W. Bush campaigns for Gov. of Tex. and US Pres. 1993–2001; Sr Advisor and Chief Policy Aide to George W. Bush 2001–07, Deputy Chief of Staff in charge of policy coordination 2005–06; Political Commentator Fox News Channel 2008–; consultant to Gov. Bill Clements 1978, 1986, Tom Phillips, Texas Supreme Court 1988, US Senators Phil. Gramm, Kay Bailey Hutchison and other politicians; teaches grad. students at Univ. of Texas. *Address:* c/o FOX News Channel, 1211 Avenue Of The Americas, New York, NY 10036, USA (office). *Website:* www.foxnews.com.

ROVERATO, Jean-François; French business executive; *Chairman and CEO, Eiffrage SA;* ed Lycée Carnot, Dijon, Ecole Polytechnique, Ecole Nationale des Ponts et Chaussées; engineer, Roads and Bridges, Directorate of Ministry of Construction Equipment 1969–72, Tech. Adviser to Cabinet of Robert Andrew Vivien (Sec. of State for Housing) 1971–72; Dir Public Office of HLM du Val-de-Marne 1972–74; Dir, Guiraudie et Auffève 1975; joined Fougerolle group (became Eiffrage 1993), Dir 1975, CEO Fougerolle Construction 1980, CEO Fougerolle France 1982, CEO Fougerolle International 1984, CEO Eiffrage SA 1985–2007, Chair. and CEO 1987–2007, Pres. 2007–; Chair. and CEO Autoroutes Paris Rhin Rhône 2006–; Pres. AREA 2006–; Chair. Ecole Nationale des Ponts et Chaussées 2006–, Etablissement public de la porte Dorée – Cité nationale de l'histoire de l'immigration 2007–; Officer, Légion d'honneur 2003, Commdr 2009. *Address:* Eiffage SA, 163 Quai du Dr Dervaux, 92601 Asnières-sur-Seine, France (office). *Telephone:* 1-41-32-80-00 (office). *Fax:* 1-41-32-81-13 (office). *E-mail:* info@eiffage.fr (office). *Website:* www.eiffage.fr (office).

ROVERSI, Paolo; Italian photographer; b. 25 Sept. 1947, Ravenna; fashion photographer since 1973, working for numerous int. magazines including British and Italian Vogue, Uomo Vogue and others; advertising for Georgio Armani, Cerruti 1881, Comme des Garçons, Christian Dior, Alberta Ferretti, Romeo Gigli and Yohji Yamamoto; dir commercials. *Publications:* Una Donna 1989, Angeli 1993, Nudi 1999, Libretto 2000, Studio 2006. *Address:* 9 rue Paul Fort, 75014 Paris, France (office). *Telephone:* 1-45-40-40-49 (office). *Fax:* 1-45-40-72-98 (office). *E-mail:* info@paoloroversi.com (office). *Website:* www.paoloroversi.com (office).

ROWE, John W., BS, JD; American lawyer and energy industry executive; *Chairman and CEO, Exelon Corporation;* b. 1946, Wis.; m. Jeanne M. Rowe; one s.; ed Univ. of Wisconsin; joined Isham, Lincoln & Beale (law firm), Chicago 1970, Partner 1978–80, served as Gen. Counsel to Trustees of Chicago, Milwaukee, St Paul & Pacific Railroad Co. 1978–80; Sr Vice-Pres. of Law, Consolidated Rail Corpn (Conrail) 1980–84; Pres. and CEO Cen. Maine Power Co. 1984–89; Pres. and CEO New England Electric System (NEES) 1989–98; Chair., Pres. and CEO Unicom Corpn and Commonwealth Edison 1998–2000; Chair. and CEO Exelon Corpn (following merger of Unicom Corpn and PECO Energy 2000) 2000–; Commr Nat. Comm. on Energy Policy; fmr Chair. Edison Electric Inst., Mass Business Roundtable; mem. Bd of Dirs Sunoco, The Northern Trust Corpn 2002–; fmr mem. Bd of Dirs Unum Provident Corpn, Fleet Boston Financial Corp, Wisconsin Cen. Transportation Co., MidSouth Corpn; mem. Bd of Govs Argonne Nat. Lab., Chicago Urban League, Field Museum, Art Inst. of Chicago, Northwestern Univ., Edison Electric Inst., Chicago Club; mem. The Econ. Club of Chicago, The Commercial Club of Chicago; mem. Bd of Trustees, Bryant Coll. 1994–98, Chicago Council on Foreign Relations, Chicago Historical Soc., Wisconsin Alumni Research Foundation, American Enterprise Inst., The Nature Conservancy (Ill. Chapter); fmr Pres. USS Constitution Museum; Hon. DHumLitt (Bryant Coll.), Hon. DBA (Univ. of Massachusetts at Dartmouth) 2002, Hon. PhD (Illinois Inst. of Tech., Drexel Univ., DePaul Univ., Thomas Coll.); Distinguished Alumni Award, Univ. of Wisconsin, World of Difference Award, Anti-Defamation League 2000, Citizen of the Year Award, City Club of Chicago 2002, Corp. Leadership Award, Spanish Coalition for Jobs 2002, City Club of Chicago's Citizen of the Year Award 2002, Civic Leadership Award, American Jewish Cttee 2004, Founder's Award for Business Leadership, Union League of Philadelphia 2005, Univ. of Arizona Executive of the Year 2007, Illinois Holocaust Museum's Humanitarian Award 2008, named by Institutional Investor magazine as Best Electric Utilities CEO in America 2008. *Address:* Exelon Corpn, PO Box 805398, 48th Floor, 10 South Dearborn Street, Chicago, IL 60680-5398, USA (office). *Telephone:* (312) 394-7398 (office). *Fax:* (312) 394-7945 (office). *E-mail:* info@exeloncorp.com (office). *Website:* www.exeloncorp.com (office).

ROWE, John W., MD; American physician and business executive (retd); b. 1944; ed Univ. of Rochester; began career with residency in internal medicine, Beth Israel Hosp., Boston, later becoming Chief of Gerontology; Clinical and Research Fellow, Mass. Gen. Hosp.; Research Fellow and later Prof. of Medicine, Harvard Medical School (Founding Dir Div. on Aging); Pres. School of Medicine and Chief Exec. Mount Sinai NYU Health 1988–2000 (renamed Mount Sinai/NYU Medical Center and Health System 1999), also Prof. of Medicine and Geriatrics; Chair., Pres. and Chief Exec. Aetna Inc. 2000–06, Exec. Chair. 2006 (retd); Chair. Bd of Trustees Univ. of Conn.; mem. NAS Inst. of Medicine; Fellow, American Acad. of Arts and Sciences; fmr Dir MacArthur Foundation on Successful Aging; mem. Bd of Govs American Bd of Internal Medicine; fmr Pres. Gerontological Soc. of America; Medicare Payment Advisory Comm.; numerous honours and awards. *Publications:* over 200 scientific publs on the aging process; Successful Aging (jt author) 1998. *Address:* 352 Mansfield Road, Storrs, CT 06269-2048, USA. *Telephone:* (860) 486-2333.

ROWE, R. Kerry, BSc, PhD, DEng, FRSC, FCAE; Australian engineer and academic; *Professor of Civil Engineering and Vice-Principal (Research), Queen's University;* ed Univ. of Sydney; worked as geotechnical engineer with Australian Govt Dept of Construction; emigrated to Canada 1978; served 22 years as Prof., Dept of Civil and Environmental Eng, Univ. of Western Ont.; currently Prof. of Civil Eng and Vice-Prin. (Research), Queen's Univ., Kingston; Pres. Int. Geosynthetics Soc. 1990–94, Canadian Geotechnical Soc. 2001–02; Vice-Pres. N American Geosynthetics Soc. 1987–91; Chair. Standards Council of Canada Int. Subcommittee on Geotextiles and Geomembranes 1989–2000, NSERC Civil Eng Grant Selection Cttee 1998–99; Founding Chair. London Dist Section, Canadian Soc. for Civil Eng and Canadian Geotechnical Soc. 1993–96; Tech. Chair. 6th Int. Conf. on Geosynthetics, Atlanta, USA 1998, 6th Canadian Environmental Eng Conf. 2000; mem. Bd of Dirs High Performance Computing Virtual Lab. (Chair. 2000–), Canadian Microelectronics Corpn 2000–, PARTEQ Innovations Inc. (currently Chair.) 2000–, CANARIE Inc. 2003–; mem.; mem. Editorial Bd Canadian Geotechnical Journal (Assoc. Ed. 1983–), Int. Journal for Geotextiles & Geomembranes (Ed. 1997–), Int. Journal on Computers and Geotechnics, Int. Journal for Numerical and Analytical Methods in Geomechanics, Geosynthetics Int., Journal of Japanese Geotechnical Society, Italian Geotechnical Journal, Lowland Technology Int., Geotechnique, Geotechnical Eng, Transport in Porous Media, Int. Journal of Geomechanics (Co-Ed. 2001–), Journal of Environmental Eng and Science, Waste Management; Edward G. Pleva Award, Univ. of Western Ont. 1996, Ont. Confed. of Univ. Faculty Asscns Excellence in Teaching Award 1997, Professional Engineers Ont. Eng Medal 1997, Ont. Ministry of the Environment Award of Excellence 1999, Keefer Medal 2001, Legget Medal 2003, K. Y. Lo Medal 2003, Killam Prize 2004, Int. Geosynthetics Soc. Award 2004. *Publications:* Barrier Systems for Waste Disposal Facilities (jtly), Geotechnical and Geoenvironmental Engineering Handbook (Ed.); more than 400 articles, papers and chapters in journals, conferences and books. *Address:* Department of Civil Engineering, Ellis Hall, Queen's University, Kingston, ON K7L 3N6, Canada (office). *Telephone:* (613) 533-6933 (office). *Fax:* (613) 533-2128 (office). *E-mail:* kerry@civil.queensu.ca (office). *Website:* www.civil.queensu.ca (office).

ROWLAND, Frank Sherwood, PhD; American scientist and academic; *Bren Research Professor, University of California, Irvine;* b. 28 June 1927, Delaware, Ohio; s. of Sidney A. Rowland and Margaret Lois Drake Rowland; m. Joan Lundberg 1952; one s. one d.; ed Chicago and Ohio Wesleyan Univs; Instructor in Chem., Princeton Univ. 1952–56; Asst to Prof., Kansas Univ. 1956–64; Prof., Univ. of Calif. Irvine 1964–, Daniel G. Aldrich Endowed Prof. of Chem. 1985–89, Bren Prof. of Chem. 1989–94, Bren Research Prof. 1994–; Guggenheim Fellow 1962, 1974; mem. American Acad. of Arts and Sciences 1977, NAS 1978– (Foreign Sec. 1994–), American Philosophical Soc. 1995, Inst. of Medicine 1995; Fellow AAAS (Pres. 1992, Chair. Bd Dirs. 1993); numerous lectureships and cttee memberships; 16 hon. degrees; Tyler Prize in Ecology and Energy (now called World Prize for Environmental Achievement) 1983, Japan Prize in Environmental Science and Tech. 1989; Nobel Prize for Chem. 1995, Nevada Medal 1997; numerous other awards. *Publications:* about 380 articles in scientific journals. *Leisure interests:* athletics, opera. *Address:* 571 Rowland Hall, Mail Code 2025, Department of Chemistry, University of California, Irvine, CA 92697 (office); 4807 Dorchester Road, Corona del Mar, CA 92625, USA (home). *Telephone:* (949) 824-6016 (office); (949) 760-1333 (home). *Fax:* (949) 824-2905 (office). *E-mail:* rowland@uci.edu (office). *Website:* www.physsci.uci.edu/~rowlandblake (office); www.chem.uci.edu/people/faculty/rowland (office).

ROWLAND, Sir (John) David, Kt, MA; British business executive (retd); b. 10 Aug. 1933, London; s. of Cyril Arthur Rowland and Eileen Mary Rowland; m. 1st Giulia Powell 1957 (divorced 1991); one s. one d.; m. 2nd Diana L. Matthews 1991; ed Trinity College, Cambridge Univ.; joined Matthews Wrightson and Co. 1956, Dir 1965; Dir Matthews Wrightson Holdings 1972; Dir Project Fullemploy 1973–88; Deputy Chair. Stewart Wrightson Holdings

PLC 1978–81, Chair. 1981–87; Vice-Pres. British Insurance and Investment Brokers Asscn 1980–; Chair. Westminster Insurance Agencies 1981–88; Dir Royal London Mutual Insurance Soc. 1985–86; Deputy Chair. Willis Faber PLC 1987–88; Dir Fullemploy Group Ltd 1989–90; Chair. Sedgwick Group PLC 1989–92; Pres. Templeton Coll., Oxford 1998–2003; mem. Council, Lloyd's 1987–90, Chair. 1993–97; Trustee Somerset House Trust 1997–2003, NatWest Group 1998–2000; Chair. NatWest 1999–2000 (Jt Deputy Chair. 1998–99); mem. Templeton Coll.; Gov. Coll. of Insurance 1983–85, Chair. 1985; Gov. St Paul's Girls School, St Paul's School (also Deputy Chair.) 1991–2007; Hon. Fellow Faculty of Actuaries; Hon. Fellow (Cardiff) 1999, (Templeton Coll., Oxford); Hon. MA (Oxford) 1993; Hon. DPhil (London Guildhall) 1996; Hon. DSc (City) 1997. *Leisure interests:* golf, running slowly, admiring his wife's garden. *Address:* Giffords Hall, Wickhambrook, Newmarket, Suffolk, CB8 8PQ, England (home). *Telephone:* (1440) 820221 (home).

ROWLANDS, Christopher John, MA, FCA, CBIM, FRSA; British business executive; *Deputy Chairman and Chief Operating Officer, Apace Media PLC;* b. 29 Aug. 1951, Leeds; s. of the late Wilfred John Rowlands and of Margaretta Rowlands (née Roberts); m. Alison Mary Kelly 1978; two d.; ed Roundhay School, Leeds, Gonville and Caius Coll., Cambridge; articled clerk Peat Marwick Mitchell 1973–75, Man. 1981, seconded as partner, Zambia 1981–83, Sr Man., London 1983–85; Controller Business Planning Asda Group PLC 1985–86, Div. Dir Group Finance 1986–88, Deputy Man. Dir and Finance Dir Property Devt and Investment 1988–92; Group Finance Dir HTV 1992–93, Chief Exec. 1993–97; Chief Exec. The TV Corpn 1998–2001; Dir (non-exec.), ITouch PLC 2002–05; Deputy Chair. and COO Apace Media PLC 2005–; Deutsche Equity Income Trust PLC 2003–; mem. Council, Ind. TV Asscn Co. 1993–97. *Leisure interests:* family, theatre, church, reading, skiing, tennis, travel, cycling. *Telephone:* (07813) 919458 (office).

ROWLANDS, Gena; American actress; b. (Virginia Cathryn Rowlands), 19 June 1930, Madison, Wis.; m. John Cassavetes 1958 (died 1989); three c.; ed Univ. of Wis., American Acad. of Dramatic Arts; Nat. Bd of Review Career Achievement Award 1996. *Play:* Middle of the Night 1955. *Films include:* The High Cost of Loving 1958, Lonely Are the Brave 1962, The Spiral Road 1962, A Child is Waiting 1963, Tony Rome 1967, Faces 1968, Minnie and Moskowitz 1971, A Woman Under the Influence (Golden Globe Award for Best Actress in a Drama, Nat. Bd of Review Award for Best Actress) 1974, Opening Night (Silver Bear for Best Actress, Berlin Int. Film Festival) 1977, The Brink's Job 1978, Gloria 1980, Tempest 1982, Love Streams 1984, Light of Day 1987, Another Woman 1988, Once Around 1991, Night on Earth 1991, Ted and Venus 1991, Something to Talk About 1995, The Neon Bible 1995, Anything for John 1995, Unhook the Stars 1996, She's So Lovely 1997, Paulie 1998, Hope Floats 1998, The Mighty 1998, Playing by Heart 1998, Taking Lives 2004, The Notebook 2004, The Skeleton Key 2005, Paris, t'aime 2006, Broken English 2007, Persepolis (voice) 2007. *Television includes:* Peyton Place 1967, The Betty Ford Story (Emmy Award) 1987, Face of a Stranger (Emmy Award) 1991, Crazy in Love 1992, Parallel Lives 1994, Grace and Glorie 1998, Hysterical Blindness 2002, Charms for the Easy Life 2002, The Incredible Mrs Ritchie 2003, What If God Were the Sun? 2007. *Address:* c/o ICM, 8942 Wilshire Boulevard, Beverly Hills, CA 90211-1934, USA. *Telephone:* (310) 550-4000.

ROWLATT, Penelope Anne, PhD; British economist (retd); b. 17 May 1936; d. of Theodore Alexander Maurice Ionides and Anne Joyce Ionides (née Cooke); m. Charles Rowlatt 1961; one s. three d.; ed King Alfred School, Somerville Coll. Oxford, Imperial Coll. London, London School of Econs; Chief Economist, Econ. Models Group of Cos 1975–76; Economist, Nat. Inst. of Econ. and Social Research 1976–78; Econ. Adviser, HM Treasury 1978–86; Sr Econ. Adviser, Dept of Energy 1986–88; Dir Nat. Econs Research Assocs 1988–98, Europe Econs 1998–2001; Publr Medicine Today 2001–04; currently ind. econ. consultant; mem. Restrictive Practices Court 1998, Retail Advisory Cttee 1991–94, Royal Comm. on Environmental Pollution 1996–2000, Steering Group, Performance and Innovation Unit, Cabinet Office 1999, Better Regulation Task Force, Cabinet Office 2000; fmr Chair. Gloucester Avenue Man. Ltd; Treas. Royal Econ. Soc. 1999–2008. *Publications include:* Group Theory and Elementary Particles 1966, Inflaction 1992; numerous articles in professional journals on nuclear physics and econs. *Leisure interests:* walking, sailing, eating, drinking, bridge. *Address:* 10 Hampstead Hill Gardens, London, NW3 2PL, England (office).

ROWLEY, Janet Davison, PhB, BS, MD; American physician and academic; *Blum-Riese Distinguished Service Professor, Department of Human Genetics, University of Chicago;* b. (Janet Ballantyne Davison), 5 April 1925, New York; d. of Hurford Henry and Ethel Mary Davison (née Ballantyne); m. Donald A. Rowley 1948; four s.; ed Univ. of Chicago; Research Asst, Univ. of Chicago 1949–50; Prof., Dept of Medicine and Franklin McLean Memorial Research Inst. 1977–84, Blum-Riese Distinguished Service Prof., Dept of Medicine and Dept of Molecular Genetics and Cell Biology 1984–, Blum-Riese Distinguished Service Prof., Dept of Human Genetics 1997–, Interim Deputy Dean for Science, Biological Sciences Div. 2001–02; mem. Nat. Cancer Advisory Bd 1979–84, Nat. Human Genome Research Inst. 1994–97, Chair. 1997–99; mem. Council for Human Genome Research 1999–2004, Advisory Bd G & P Charitable Foundation 1999–, Selection Panel for Clinical Science Award, Doris Duke Charitable Foundation 2000–02; mem. NAS (Chair. Section 41 1995–99), Inst. of Medicine, American Asscn for Cancer Research, American Soc. for Hematology, Genetical Soc. (UK), American Soc. for Human Genetics (Pres. 1993), American Philosophical Soc., American Acad. of Arts and Sciences; visiting lecturer at numerous univs including Second Victor McKusick Lecturer, Johns Hopkins Univ. 2003, Dartmouth 2004, Distinguished Service Lecturer, American Soc. for Human Genetics 2003 and guest speaker for numerous orgs; Co-Founder, Co-Ed. Genes, Chromosomes and Cancer; mem. editorial bd of numerous journals; Fellow AAAS (Nominating Cttee 1998); Hon. DSc (Arizona) 1989, (Pennsylvania) 1989, (Knox Coll.) 1981, (Southern California) 1992, (St Louis) 1997, (St Xavier) 1999, (Oxford, UK) 2000, (Lund, Sweden) 2003, (Lake Forest Coll.) 2008, (Harvard) 2008; numerous awards including First Kuwait Cancer Prize 1984, Prix Antoine Lacassagne, Ligue Nat. Française Contre le Cancer 1987, King Faisal Int. Prize in Medicine (jtly) 1988, Charles Mott Prize, GM Cancer Research Foundation (jtly) 1989, Robert de Villers Award, Leukemia Soc. of America 1993, Gairdner Foundation Award 1996, Nat. Medal of Science 1998, Albert Lasker Award for Clinical Medical Research 1998, Woman Extraordinaire Award, Int. Women's Asscns 1999, Golden Plate Award, American Acad. of Achievement 1999, Philip Levine Award, American Soc. of Clinical Pathology 2001, Mendel Medal, Villanova Univ. 2003, Benjamin Franklin Medal, American Philosophical Soc. 2003, Charlotte Friend Award and Lecture, American Asscn for Cancer Research 2003, Distinguished Alumni Award, Univ. of Chicago 2003, Rosalind Franklin Award, Nat. Cancer Inst. 2004, Kenneth McCredie Lecture, The Leukemia and Lymphoma Soc. 2004, Dorothy P. Landon Prize, American Asscn for Cancer Research 2005. *Publications:* 440 items 1960–. *Leisure interests:* gardening, swimming. *Address:* University of Chicago, 5841 South Maryland Avenue, Room 2115, Chicago, IL 60637-1463 (office); 5310 S University Avenue, Chicago, IL 60615-5106, USA (home). *Telephone:* (773) 702-6117 (office); (773) 493-1845 (home). *Fax:* (773) 702-3002 (office). *E-mail:* jrowley@medicine.bsd.uchicago.edu (office). *Website:* www.uchicago.edu (office).

ROWLING, Joanne Kathleen (J. K.), OBE, BA; British writer; b. 31 July 1965, Chipping Sodbury, England; d. of Peter Rowling and Anne Rowling; m. 1st (divorced); one d.; m. 2nd Neil Murray 2001; one s. one d.; ed Wyedean Comprehensive School, Univ. of Exeter, Moray House Teacher Training Coll.; Chevalier, Ordre des Arts et des Lettres 2009; Hon. DJur (Univ. of Aberdeen) 2006; Premio Príncipe de Asturias 2003, Variety UK Entertainment Personality Award, British Ind. Film Awards 2004, British Book Award for Oustanding Achievement 2008, ranked by Forbes magazine amongst 100 Most Powerful Women (85th) 2004, (40th) 2005. *Publications:* Harry Potter and the Philosopher's Stone (aka Harry Potter and the Sorcerer's Stone) (Smarties Prize, British Book Awards Children's Book of the Year) 1997, Harry Potter and the Chamber of Secrets (Smarties Prize, British Book Awards Children's Book of the Year) 1998, Harry Potter and the Prisoner of Azkaban (Smarties Prize) 1999, Harry Potter and the Goblet of Fire 2000, Quidditch Through the Ages by Kennilworthy Whisp 2001, Fantastic Beasts and Where to Find Them by Newt Scamander 2001, Harry Potter and the Order of the Phoenix (WHSmith People's Choice Fiction Prize 2004) 2003, Harry Potter and the Half-Blood Prince (Quill Book Award for Book of the Year, Best Children's Book, British Book Awards WHSmith Book of the Year 2006, Royal Mail Award for Scottish Children's Books) 2005, Harry Potter and the Deathly Hallows 2007, The Tales of Beedle the Bard 2008. *Address:* c/o Christopher Little Literary Agency, Eel Brook Studios, 125 Moore Park Road, London, SW6 4PS, England (office). *Telephone:* (20) 7736-4455 (office). *Fax:* (20) 7736-4490 (office). *E-mail:* info@christopherlittle.net (office). *Website:* www.christopherlittle.net (office); www.jkrowling.com.

ROWLINSON, Sir John Shipley, FRS, FREng; British scientist and fmr academic; b. 12 May 1926, Handforth, Cheshire; s. of Frank Rowlinson and Winifred Rowlinson (née Jones); m. Nancy Gaskell 1952; one s. one d.; ed Trinity Coll., Oxford; Research Assoc., Univ. of Wis. 1950–51; Research Fellow, then Lecturer, then Sr Lecturer in Chem., Univ. of Manchester 1951–60; Prof. of Chemical Tech., Univ. of London 1961–73; Dr Lee's Prof. of Chem., Univ. of Oxford 1974–93; Fellow, Exeter Coll., Oxford 1974–; A. D. White Prof.-at-Large, Cornell Univ. 1990–96; Royal Soc. of Chem., Mary Upson Prof. of Eng, Cornell Univ. 1988; Physical Sec. and Vice-Pres. Royal Soc. 1994–99; Meldola Medal, Royal Inst. of Chem. 1954; Marlow Medal, Faraday Soc. 1956, Hoffman Lecturer, Gesellschaft Deutscher Chemiker 1980, Faraday Lecturer 1983, Lennard-Jones Lecturer 1985, Leverhulme Medal, Royal Soc. 1993. *Publications:* Liquids and Liquid Mixtures (jtly) 1982 (3rd edn), The Perfect Gas 1963, Thermodynamics for Chemical Engineers (jtly) 1975, Molecular Theory of Capillarity (jtly) 1982, J. D. van der Waals: On the Continuity of the Gaseous and Liquid States (ed.) 1988, Record of the Royal Society 1940–89 (jtly) 1992, Van der Waals and Molecular Science (jtly) 1996, Cohesion: A Scientific History of Intermolecular Forces 2002. *Leisure interest:* mountaineering. *Address:* Physical and Theoretical Chemistry Laboratory, South Parks Road, Oxford, OX1 3QZ (office); 12 Pullens Field, Headington, Oxford, OX3 0BU, England (home). *Telephone:* (1865) 275157 (office); (1865) 767507 (home). *Fax:* (1865) 275410 (office). *E-mail:* john .rowlinson@chem.ox.ac.uk (office). *Website:* www.chem.ox.ac.uk (office).

ROWNY, Lt-Gen. Edward Leon, BCE, MA, MS, PhD; American army officer (retd) and diplomatist; b. 3 April 1917, Baltimore, Md; s. of Gracyan J. Rowny and Mary Ann Rowny (née Rodgers); m. Mary Rita Leyko 1941; four s. one d.; ed Johns Hopkins Univ., Baltimore, US Mil. Acad., Yale Univ.; Second Lt, US Army 1941, served in African campaign 1942, European and Middle Eastern Campaigns 1944–45; Korea 1950–52; Viet Nam 1962–63, with Operations Div of War Dept, Washington, DC 1945–47; Special Asst Tactical Mobility Dept of army 1963–75; Commdg Gen. 24th Infantry Div., Europe 1965–66; Deputy Chief of Staff Logistics, Europe 1968–69; Deputy Chief of Research and Devt 1969–70; Commdg Gen. Intelligence Corps, Korea, 1970–71; Deputy Chair. Mil. Comm. NATO 1971–73; Jt Chiefs of Staff rep. to SALT del., Geneva 1973–79 (retd); Chief Arms Control Negotiator 1981–85; Special Adviser to Pres. 1985–89; Special Counsellor to State Dept 1989–90; Pres. Nat. War Coll. Alumni Asscn 1987–88, Paderewski Living Memorial 1994–; mem. Advisory Bd, Critical Incident Analysis Group, Univ. of Virginia Health System; DSM (twice), Silver Star with two oak leaf clusters (four times), Legion of Merit with four oak clusters (twice), Combat Infantry Badge with star; named Distinguished Mil. Grad. from West Point 1993. *Publication:* It Takes One to Tango 1992. *Address:* c/o Advisory Board, Critical Incident Analysis Group, PO Box 800657, Charlottesville, VA 22908; 1105 S. 23rd Road, Arlington, VA 22202, USA.

ROXAS, Manuel (Mar) II, BEcons; Philippine politician; b. 13 May 1957; grandson of Manuel Roxas, fmr Pres. of Philippines; s. of Senator Gerry Roxas; ed Ateneo de Manila Univ., Wharton Business School, Univ. of Pennsylvania, Kennedy School of Govt, Harvard Univ., USA; fmr Dir Kauswagan Devt Corpn, Myapo Prawn Farm Corpn; fmr Vice-Pres. Progressive Devt Corpn; fmr Dir/Pres. Northstar Capital Inc., Atok Big Wedge Mining Co.; fmr banker, Wall Street, New York, USA; mem. House of Reps, First Dist, Capiz 1992–2001; fmr leader admin.-aligned parties in Lower House of Legislature; Co-Chair. Philippines IT Devt; Sec. Dept Trade and Industry 2001–03; Senator 2004–; Co-founder Books for the Barangay Foundation Inc., Capiz Alliance for Ecological Devt Inc.; mem. Liberal Party, currently Exec. Vice-Pres. *Address:* Room 523, 5/F Senate of the Philippines, GSIS Bldg. Roxas Blvd., Pasay City (office); 157 P. Tuazon Street, Cubao, Quezon City, The Philippines. *Telephone:* (2) 8328280 (office). *E-mail:* mar@marroxas.com (office). *Website:* marroxas.com/new (office).

ROY, Arundhati; Indian writer, artist, actress and activist; b. 1960, Bengal; m. 1st Gerard Da Cunha (divorced); m. 2nd Pradeep Krishen; ed Delhi School of Architecture; fmrly with Nat. Inst. of Urban Affairs; judge, Cannes Film Festival 2000–; faced charges of inciting violence, attacking a court official and contempt of court for opposing Sardar Sarovar dam project in the Narmada valley 2001; Lannan Prize for Cultural Freedom 2002. *Screenplays:* In Which Annie Gives It Those Ones (TV) 1988, Electric Moon 1992, DAM/AGE 2002. *Publications:* The God of Small Things (Booker Prize) 1997, The End of Imagination (essay) 1998, The Cost of Living (essays) 1998, The Great Common Good (essay) 1999, War is Peace 2000, The Algebra of Infinite Justice (essays) 2001, Power Politics 2002, The Ordinary Person's Guide to Empire (essays) 2004; contribs to periodicals. *Address:* c/o South End Press, 7 Brookline Street, Suite 1, Cambridge, MA 02139-4146, USA; c/o India Ink Publishing Co. Pvt. Ltd, C-1, Soami Nagar, New Delhi 110 017, India.

ROY, Donkupar, PhD; Indian politician and government official; *Chief Minister of Meghalaya;* b. 10 Nov. 1954; ed North Eastern Hill Univ., Shillong; worked as prof. before entering politics; first won Shella Ass. seat in Meghalaya as ind. cand. 1987, re-elected 1993, subsequently re-elected three times; joined United Democratic Party (UDP) 1998, currently Head of UDP; held several portfolios under Chief Minister of Meghalaya, including Health, Educ., Finance and Planning Implementation, before becoming Deputy Chief Minister, formed alliance with handful of other parties to form govt under banner of Meghalaya Progressive Alliance, Chief Minister of Meghalaya 2008–. *Address:* Office of the Chief Minister, Shillong 793 001, Meghalaya, India (office). *Telephone:* (364) 2224282 (ext. 2200) (office); (94) 36104815 (mobile) (office); (364) 2227121 (home); (364) 2226599 (home). *Fax:* (364) 2227913 (office). *E-mail:* info@meghalaya.nic.in (office). *Website:* meghalaya.nic.in (office).

ROY, Prannoy, PhD; Indian broadcasting executive, political analyst and economist; *President, New Delhi Television;* b. 15 Oct. 1949; m. Radhika Roy; ed Doon School, Dehradun, Haileybury School, Queen Mary Coll. and Univ. of London, UK, Delhi School of Econs; Chartered Accountant, PriceWaterhouse India 1979–83; Election Analyst 1980–85; Assoc. Prof. Delhi School of Econs 1985–86; Econ. Adviser, Ministry of Finance 1986–87; anchor and Ed.-in-Chief for several TV news, budget and election programmes 1998–; Founder, Pres. New Delhi TV Ltd (NDTV) 1988–; Leverhulme Fellow; Priyadarshini Acad. Bombay Felicitations Award, Dynasty Culture Club Hall of Fame Award for Best Anchor Person 1991, TV and Video Award for Best Anchor Person 1993, B.D. Goenka Award for Excellence in Journalism 1994, 1995, Maharana Mewar Foundation Award for Contrib. to Journalism 1996, Indian Dance Theatre Best Personality of the Year Award 1998, Screen Videocon Award for Lifetime Achievement 1998, Ernst & Young Entrepreneur of the Year Award (Media). *Address:* New Delhi Television Ltd (NDTV), Archana, Greater Kailash Part 1, New Delhi 110 048, India (office). *Telephone:* (11) 26446666 (office). *E-mail:* prannoy@ndtv.com (office). *Website:* www.ndtv.com (office).

ROY SAHARA, Subrata; Indian business executive; *Managing Worker and Chairman, Sahara India Pariwar;* m. Swapna Roy 1974; two s.; f. Sahara Group 1978, currently and Man. Worker and Chair. Sahara India Pariwar, cos include Sahara India Financial Corpn Ltd, Sahara Care House, Sahara Infrastructure and Housing; Noble Citizen Award 1986, Baba-E-Rozgar 1992, Karmaveer Samman 1995, Nat. Citizen Award 2001, Businessman of the Year Award 2002, Global Leadership Award 2004, Lifetime Achievement Award 2004, Mother Teresa Millenium Award for Renowned Industrialist 2005, ITA ICON 2007. *Publications:* Shanti Sukh: Santushti, Maan-Samman: Atmasamman. *Address:* Sahara India Pariwar, Sahara Information and Contact Point, PO Box 2, Gomti Nagar, Lucknow 10, India (office). *Fax:* (522) 2303818 (office). *E-mail:* info@saharaindiapariwar.org (office). *Website:* www.sahara.in (office); www.sahara.in/saharasri.

ROYAL, HRH The Princess; (Princess Anne Elizabeth Alice Louise), LG, GCVO; British; b. 15 Aug. 1950; d. of Queen Elizabeth II (q.v.) and Prince Philip, Duke of Edinburgh (q.v.); m. 1st Capt. Mark Anthony Peter Phillips 1973 (divorced 1992); one s., Peter Mark Andrew, b. 15 Nov. 1977, one d., Zara Anne Elizabeth, b. 15 May 1981; m. 2nd Rear Adm. Timothy Laurence MVO, ADC 1992; ed Benenden School, Kent; Col-in-Chief, 14th/20th King's Hussars, Worcs. and Sherwood Foresters Regt (29th/45th Foot), Royal Regina Rifles, 8th Canadian Hussars (Princess Louise's), Royal Corps of Signals, The Canadian Armed Forces Communications and Electronics Branch, The Royal Australian Corps of Signals, The Royal Scots, Royal New Zealand Corps of Signals, King's Royal Hussars, Royal Logistics Corps; Royal New Zealand Nursing Corps, The Grey and Simcoe Foresters Militia; Chief Commdt, WRNS; Hon. Air Commodore, RAF Lyneham; Pres. WRNS Benevolent Trust, British Acad. of Film and TV Arts, Hunters' Improvement and Light Horse Breeding Soc., Save the Children Fund, Windsor Horse Trials, The Royal School for Daughters of Officers of the Royal Navy and Royal Marines (Haslemere), British Olympic Asscn, Council for Nat. Acad. Awards; Patron, Asscn of Wrens, Riding for the Disabled Asscn, Jersey Wildlife Preservation Fund, The Royal Corps of Signals Asscn, The Royal Corps of Signals Inst., Missions to Seamen, British Knitting and Clothing Export Council, The Army and Royal Artillery Hunter Trials, Gloucs. and North Avon Fed. of Young Farmers' Clubs, Royal Lymington Yacht Club, Royal Port Moresby Soc. for the Prevention of Cruelty to Animals, Horse of the Year Ball, Benenden Ball, British School of Osteopathy, Communications and Electronics Branch Inst., All England Women's Lacrosse Asscn, Home Farm Trust; Vice-Patron, British Show Jumping Asscn; Commdt-in-Chief, St John Ambulance and Nursing Cadets, Women's Transport Service; Freeman of the City of London, of the Fishmongers' Co., Master Warden Farriers' Co., Master and Hon. Liveryman, Carmen's Co., Hon. Liveryman Farriers' Co.; Yeoman, Saddlers' Co.; Life mem. Royal British Legion Women's Section, Royal Naval Saddle Club; mem. Island Sailing Club; Visitor, Felixstowe Coll.; official visits abroad to the 14th/20th King's Hussars in Fed. Repub of Germany 1969, 1975, to see the work of the Save the Children Fund in Kenya 1971, to the 2,500th anniversary celebrations of the Iranian monarchy 1971, to 14th/20th King's Hussars and to see the work of the Save the Children Fund, Hong Kong 1971, to SE Asia 1972, Munich 1972, Yugoslavia 1972, Ethiopia and the Sudan 1973, to visit Worcs. and Sherwood Foresters Regt in Berlin 1973, in Hereford, Fed. Repub. of Germany 1974, to Canada 1974, to Australia 1975, to USA 1977, to Fed. Repub. of Germany and Norway 1978, to Portugal, Fed. Repub. of Germany, Thailand, Gilbert Islands, New Zealand, Australia and the Bahamas, Canada 1979, to Royal Corps of Signals in Cyprus, France, Belgium and Fiji 1980, Royal Corps of Signals in Berlin, Nepal, Worcs. and 14th/20th King's Hussars in Fed. Repub. of Germany; USA, Canada and tour of Africa, North Yemen and Lebanon 1982, to France, Japan, Hong Kong, Singapore, Pakistan, Australia, Netherlands and BAOR 1983, USA, Africa, India, Bangladesh, Fed. Repub. of Germany, UAE 1984; Chancellor, Univ. of London 1981–; has accompanied the Queen and the Duke of Edinburgh on several State Visits; has taken part in numerous equestrian competitions including Montreal Olympics 1976, Horse of the Year Show, Wembley and Badminton Horse Trials; winner of Raleigh Trophy 1971 and Silver Medal in 1975 in Individual European Three Day Event; Hon. Freeman, Farmers' Co., Loriners' Co.; Hon. mem., British Equine Veterinary Asscn, Royal Yacht Squadron, Royal Thames Yacht Club, Minchinhampton Golf Club, Lloyds of London; Hon. Life mem. RNVR Officers' Asscn; Sportswoman of the Year, Sports Writers' Asscn, Daily Express, World of Sport, BBC Sports Personality 1971, Special BAFTA Award 1993. *Publication:* Riding Through My Life 1991. *Address:* Buckingham Palace, London, SW1, England. *Website:* www.royal.gov.uk.

ROYAL, Ségolène; French politician; b. 22 Sept. 1953, Dakar, Senegal; d. of Jacques Royal and Hélène Dehaye; fmr pnr Francois Hollande; two s. two d.; ed Univ. of Nancy, Institut d'Etudes Politiques, Paris, Ecole Nationale d'Admin; Conseillère Gen. La Mothe Saint Héray (Deux-Sèvres); Sec. Comm. for Production and Exchange, Nat. Ass.; mem. Nat. Cttee on Tourism; adviser on environment, town planning and social affairs to Pres. of Repub. 1982–88; Deputy to Nat. Ass. (Parti socialiste) from Deux-Sèvres 1988–; Minister of the Environment 1992–93, Deputy Minister of Educ. 1997–2000, of Family and Childhood 2000–01, of Family Childhood and Disabled Persons 2001–02; Pres. region Poitou-Charenteswon 2004–; Pres. Nat. Council of Socialist Group 1994–95; unsuccessful Parti socialiste cand. in 2007 presidential elections. *Publications:* Le Printemps des Grands Parents 1987, Le Ras-le-bol des Bébés Zappeurs 1989, Pays, Paysans, Paysages 1993, La Vérité d'une femme 1996, Désirs d'avenir 2006, Maintenant 2007, Les Droits de l'Enfant 2007, Ma plus belle histoire, c'est vous 2007. *Address:* Casier de la Poste, Palais Bourbon, 75355 Paris Cedex 07 (office); c/o Parti socialiste (PS), 10 rue de Solférino, 75333 Paris Cedex 07, France. *Telephone:* 1-40-63-93-23 (office); 1-45-56-77-00 (PS). *Fax:* 1-40-63-93-39 (office); 1-47-05-15-78 (PS). *E-mail:* infops@parti-socialiste.fr. *Website:* www.assemblee-nationale.fr (office); www.parti-socialiste.fr; www.desirsdavenir.org.

ROYALL OF BLAISDON, Baroness (Life Peer), cr. 2004, of Blaisdon in the County of Gloucestershire; **Janet Anne Royall,** PC, BA; British politician; *Leader of the House of Lords and Lord President of the Council;* b. 20 Aug. 1955; d. of Basil Royall and Myra Royall; m. Stuart Hercock; two s. one d.; ed Royal Forest of Dean Grammar School, Westfield Coll., Univ. of London; Sec.-Gen. British Labour Group, European Parl. 1979–85; policy adviser to Neil Kinnock, Leader of Opposition 1986–92; Head, European Comm. Office in Wales 2003–04; Govt Spokesperson for Health, for Int. Devt and for FCO 2005–08; Capt., Hon. Corps of Gentlemen at Arms (Chief Whip, House of Lords) 2007–08, mem. Select Cttees on Admin and Works, Privleges and Procedure 2008–, Leader of the House of Lords and Lord Pres. of the Council 2008–; mem. AMICUS (trade union). *Leisure interests:* reading, travel, gardening, swimming. *Address:* House of Lords, Palace of Westminster, London SW1A 0PW, England (office). *Telephone:* (20) 7210-1056 (office). *Fax:* (20) 7210-1017 (office). *E-mail:* royallj@parliament.uk (office). *Website:* www.parliament.uk (office).

ROYO SÁNCHEZ, Arístides, LLB, JD; Panamanian politician, diplomatist and lawyer; *Partner, Morgan & Morgan;* b. 14 Aug. 1940, La Chorrera; s. of Roberto Royas and Gilma Sánchez; m. Adele Ruíz 1963; one s. two d.; ed Nat. Institute, Panama City, Univs of Salamanca and Bologna; Gen. Sec. of the Gen. Solicitorship of the Repub. of Panama 1965–68; Prof. of Consular,

Notarial and Mercantile Law, Univ. of Panama 1968–74; mem. Law Codification Comm. 1969; mem. drafting comms for Penal Code 1970, Constitution 1972; mem. Legis. Comm. of Nat. Council of Legislation 1972–73; Gen. Sec. School of Lawyers of Panama 1973; Pnr, Morgan & Morgan (law firm) 1968–; a negotiator of Torrijos-Carter Canal Treaties between Panama and USA 1977; mem. Org. Comm. of Democratic Revolutionary Party; Minister of Educ. 1973–78; Pres. of Panama 1978–82; Amb. to Spain 1982–84, 1994–96, to France 1996–99, Perm Amb. to OAS 2004–; mem. Nat. Bar Asscn of Panama, Union Iberoamericana de Abogados, Instituto Hispano-Luso-Americano de Derecho Internacional, Instituto de Derecho Comparado de la Universidad Complutense de Madrid, Sociedad Bolivariana de Panamá, Fuji-Baru Asscn; hon. mem. Spanish Law Soc. 1979; Grand Cross, Alfonso X the Wise (Spain) 1977, Extraordinary Grand Cross, Vasco Núñez de Balboa (Panama) 1978; Grand Collar, Order of Manuel Amador Guerrero (Panama) 1978; Grand Collar, Order of Isabel la Católica (Spain) 1979; Grand Cross, Légion d'honneur 1979; Extraordinary Grand Cross, Order of Boyaca (Colombia) 1979; Dr hc (Univ. San Martín de Porres, Lima, Peru) 1979. *Publications:* Philosophy of Law in Cathrein and Del Vecchio 1963, History of Spanish Commercial Code 1964, The Responsibility of the Carrier in Sea Shipping 1965, Extraterritoriality of the Panamanian Criminal Law 1967, Draft Criminal Code of Panama, The Participation of Labourers in the Utilities of Enterprises, Revolution or De Facto Government, Manager in the Enterprise 1970, Commentaries to the Law on Retiring Funds for Journalists 1971, The Technician and the Politician in Public Administration 1973, Popular Consultation of the Law 1972. *Leisure interests:* reading, writing, skiing, jogging. *Address:* Morgan & Morgan, MMG Tower, 16th Floor, 53 E Street, Urbanizacion Marbella, PO Box 0832-00232, World Trade Center, Panama City, Panama (office). *Telephone:* (507) 265-7777 (office). *Fax:* (507) 265-7700 (office). *E-mail:* aroyo@morimor.com (office). *Website:* www.morimor.com (office).

ROZANOV, Yevgeny Grigoryevich, PhD; Russian architect; b. 8 Nov. 1925, Moscow; s. of Grigory Alexandrovich Rozanov and Anastasiya Nikolaevna Rozanova; m. Aida Ilyenkova 1952; one s.; ed Moscow Inst. of Architecture; mem. CPSU 1964–91; Dir of Mezentsev Inst. of Standard and Experimental Design of Culture and Sports Activities 1970–85; major bldgs designed in Essentuki, Vladivostok, Tashkent, Moscow (notably Dinamo Sports Centre); teacher of architecture at Moscow Architectural Inst. 1960–85, Prof. 1953–85; Chair. State Cttee on Architecture and Town Planning 1987–91; Sec. USSR Union of Architects 1981–92; People's Deputy of the USSR 1989–91; mem. USSR (now Russian) Acad. of Arts 1979; Pres. Int. Acad. of Architecture (Moscow br.) 1991–; Vice-Pres. Russian Acad. of Arts 1998–; mem. Russian Acad. of Architecture and Construction Sciences 1997, Acad. of Architecture, Paris 1998; Hon. mem. Acad. of Architecture of Ukraine 1995; Dr hc (Moscow Architectural Inst.) 2001; Khamza Uzbek State Prize 1969, 1970, Navoi Uzbek State Prize 1975, USSR State Prize 1975, 1980, First Prize in Borovitskaya Square Competition, Moscow 1997, People's Architect of USSR 1983. *Publication:* The Works of E. G. Rozanov 1995. *Leisure interests:* painting, drawing, sculpture, music. *Address:* International Academy of Architecture, 6, Secodn Brestskaya Street 6, Rooms 8–9, 125047 Moscow (office); Kosygina Street 9, Apt. 74, Moscow, Russia (home). *Telephone:* (495) 972-47-85 (office); (495) 137-56-09 (home). *Fax:* (495) 972-47-85.

ROZANOVA, Irina Yuryevna; Russian actress; b. 22 July 1961, Ryazan; ed Moscow Inst. of Theatre Arts; actress, Moscow Mayakovsky Theatre 1985–96, Moscow Theatre on Malaya Bronnaya 1996–; Merited Actress of Russian Fed. *Films include:* Intergirl 1989, Serf, Gambrinus 1990, Cynics 1991, Encore, Once More Encore! 1992, End of the Operation Resident, Red Stone, The Black Veil 1995, The Rifleman of the Voroshilov Regiment 1999, Dva tovarishcha 2001, Mechanical Suite 2001, Dikarka 2001, Spartacus and Kalashnikov 2002, Life Is Full of Fun 2003, Diary of a Kamikaze 2003, Fatalisty (TV series) 2003, Break Point 2004, Kolya-Perekati Pole 2005, Tanker Tango 2006, Svyaz 2006, Katerina (TV miniseries) 2007, Glyanets 2007. *Theatre includes:* Illusion, King Lear, Wood-Goblin, Abyss, Idiot, Provincial Girl. *Address:* Moscow Theatre on Malaya Bronnaya, M. Bronnaya str. 4, 103104 Moscow, Russia (office); B. Bronnaya str. 8, Apt 21, 103104 Moscow, Russia (home). *Telephone:* (495) 290-40-83 (office); (495) 202-23-42 (home). *Fax:* (495) 125-74-32 (home).

ROZARIO, Patricia, OBE; singer (soprano); b. 1960, Bombay, India; m. Mark Troop; one d.; ed Guildhall School of Music; concerts with Songmakers' Almanac, including tour to USA; solo recitals, South Bank, London and elsewhere; frequent performances of Bach, Handel, Mozart; Vaughan Williams' Serenade to Music, BBC Proms 1988; Schumann's Paradies und der Peri, Madrid with Gerd Albrecht; appearances at Bath and Edin. Festivals; season 1993–94 included Wexford Festival appearance, tour of Germany with BBC Nat. Orchestra of Wales/Otaka, Hong Kong Philharmonic, world premiere of Taverner's Apocalypse, BBC Proms; season 1994–95 included recital in Lebanon, Purcell Room with Nash Ensemble; sang Les illuminations at St John's Smith Square, London 1997; performed in Handel's Triumph of Time and Truth, BBC Proms 1999; British Song Prize, Barcelona, Maggie Teyte Prize, Sängerforderungspreis, Salzburg Mozarteum, Guildhall School of Music Gold Medal, Asian Women of Achievement Arts and Culture Award 2002. *Operatic roles include:* Giulietta (Jommelli's La schiava liberata) for Netherlands Opera, Gluck's Euridice for Opera North, Mozart's Bastienne and Pamina for Kent Opera, Ilia on Glyndebourne tour, Ismene in Lyon production of Mithridate and Zerlina at Aix, Statue in Rameau's Pygmalion and Purcell's Belinda for Kent Opera; Florinda in Handel's Rodrigo at Innsbruck, Nero in L'incoronazione di Poppea and Massenet's Sophie; concert performance of Il re pastore, Queen Elizabeth Hall, London, world premiere of John Casken's Golem, as Miriam, Almeida Festival, London, Ismene at Wexford Festival 1989, cr. title role in premiere of Taverner's Mary of Egypt,

Aldeburgh Festival 1992, season 1992–93 in Monteverdi's Il combattimento, ENO and Haydn's L'infedeltà delusa, Garsington Opera, Romilda in Serse, Brussels 1996. *Recordings include:* Mahler Symphony No. 4, London Symphony Orchestra, Songs of the Auvergne with John Pritchard (conductor), Haydn Stabat Mater with Trevor Pinnock (conductor), Golem (Gramophone Award 1991), Taverner: We Shall See Him As He Is, Mary of Egypt, To a Child Dancing in the Wind; Spanish Songs, Britten's Rape of Lucretia. *Address:* c/o Rayfield Artists, Southbank House, Black Prince Road, London, SE1 7SJ, England (office). *Telephone:* (20) 7193-1531 (office). *E-mail:* ben@rayfieldartists.com (office). *Website:* www.rayfieldartists.com/patriciarozario .html (office).

ROZENTAL, Andrés, AM, MEconSc; Mexican diplomatist and consultant; *President, Rozental & Asociados;* b. 1945, Mexico City; s. of Vivian Holzer Tamara Rozental and Sandra Rozental; ed Universidad de las Américas, Mexico, Univ. of Pennsylvania, USA, Univ. of Bordeaux, France; Amb. to OAS 1971–74; Perm. Rep. to UN, Geneva 1982–83; Amb. to Sweden 1983–88; Deputy Foreign Minister 1988–94; Amb. to UK 1995–97; Amb.-at-Large and Special Presidential Envoy for Pres. Fox 2000–02; Founder and Pres. Rozental & Asociados (consultancy), Mexico City 1997–; Pres. Mexican Council on Foreign Relations 2002–06; part-time Prof. of Int. Relations, Instituto Tecnológico Autónomo de México (ITAM); Chair. Bd Latinoamericana de Duty Free, Grupo Industrial Omega; mem. Bd of Dirs New India Investment Trust, Aeroplazas de Mexico, Fumisa, Mittal Steel Mexico, Int. Inst. for Democracy and Electoral Assistance (Int. IDEA), Pacific Council on Int. Policy; mem. Bd of Govs Int. Devt Research Centre 2007–; mem. Bd of Advisors Latin America Advisor, Inter-American Dialogue 2005–; fmr mem. Editorial Bd Reforma (newspaper); Sr Nonresident Fellow, The Brookings Inst., Washington, DC 2007–; Grand Cross of the Polar Star (Sweden), Grand Cross, Civil Merit Order (Spain), Officier, Ordre Nat. du Mérite (France), Eminent Amb. of Mexico 1994. *Publications:* three books on Mexican foreign policy and numerous articles on int. affairs. *Address:* Rozental & Asociados, Campos Elíseos no 345, Edif. Omega, piso 6, Mexico City DF, Mexico (office). *Telephone:* (55) 5279-6090 (office). *Fax:* (55) 5279-6089 (office). *E-mail:* andres@mexconsult.com (office).

ROZES, Simone, LenD, DèsSc, DES; French lawyer; *Honorary President, Cour de Cassation;* b. 29 March 1920, Paris; d. of Léon Ludwig and Marcelle Cetre; m. Gabriel Rozes 1942; one s. one d.; ed Lycée de Sèvres, Lycée de St-Germain-en-Laye, Univ. of Paris, Ecole Libre des Sciences Politiques; trainee lawyer, Paris 1947–49; Surrogate Judge, Bourges 1949–50; Judge 1951–; attaché, Justice Dept 1951–58; Admin. Chief, Cabinet of the Minister of Justice 1958–62, Vice-Pres. Tribunal de Grande Instance de Paris 1969–73, Pres. 1975–81; Dir Reformatory Educ. 1973–76; mem. UN Crime Prevention and Control Cttee 1977; Advocate-Gen. European Court of Justice 1981–84; First Advocate Gen. 1982–84; Pres. Cour de Cassation (Chief Justice) 1984–88, Hon. Pres. 1989–; Int. and Nat. Arbitrator 1989–; Pres. Int. Soc. of Social Defence, fmr Pres. Soc. of Comparative Law; Hon. Vice-Pres. Int. Asscn of Penal Law; Inst. Frederik R. Bull; mem. Bd Alliance Française, Vice-Pres. 1994–; Grand Croix, Légion d'honneur; Officier, Ordre nat. du Mérite; Médaille de l'Educ. Surveillée, Médaille de Admin. Pénitentiaire, Commdr Cross, Order of Merit (FRG); Hon. LLD (Edin.). *Publication:* Le Juge et l'avocat (jtly) 1992. *Leisure interest:* travelling. *Address:* c/o Cour de Cassation, 5 quai de l'Horloge, 75055 Paris Cedex 01 (office); 34 rue Bayen, 75017 Paris, France. *Telephone:* 1-43-80-16-67 (office). *Fax:* 1-47-63-42-90 (office). *E-mail:* simone.rozes@neuf.fr (office). *Website:* www.courdecassation .fr (office).

RÓŻEWICZ, Tadeusz; Polish poet and playwright; b. 9 Oct. 1921, Radomsko; ed Jagiellonian Univ., Kraków; fmr factory worker and teacher; mem. Art Acad. of Leipzig; Corresp. mem. Bavarian Acad. of Fine Arts 1982–, Acad. of Arts (GDR); Order of Banner of Labour (2nd class) 1977, Great Cross of Polonia Restituta Order 1996; Dr hc (Wrocław) 1991, (Silesian Univ., Katowice) 1999, (Jagiellonian Univ.) 2000, (Kraków) 2000, (Warsaw) 2001; State Prize for Poetry 1955, 1956, Literary Prize, City of Cracow 1959, Prize of Minister of Culture and Art 1962, State Prize 1st Class 1966, Austrian Nat. Prize for European Literature 1982, Prize of Minister of Foreign Affairs 1974, 1987, Golden Wreath Prize for Poetry (Yugoslavia) 1987, Władysław Reymont Literary Prize 1999; Home Army Cross, London 1956, Alfred Jurzykowski Foundation Award, New York 1966, Medal of 30th Anniversary of People's Poland 1974, Nike Literary Prize 2000, Premio Librex Montale, Literary Prize (Italy) 2002. *Plays include:* Kartoteka (The Card Index), Grupa Laokoona (Laocoön's Group), Świadkowie albo nasza mała stabilizacja (The Witnesses), Akt przerywany (The Interrupted Act), Śmieszny staruszek (The Funny Man), Wyszedł z domu (Gone Out), Spaghetti i miecz (Spaghetti and the Sword), Maja córeczka (My Little Daughter), Stara kobieta wysiaduje (The Old Woman Broods), Na czworakach (On All Fours), Do piachu (Down to Sand), Białe małżeństwo (White Marriage), Odejście Głodomora (Starveling's Departure), Na powierzchni poematu i w środku: nowy wybór wierszy, Pułapka (The Trap), Próba rekonstrukcji, (Spread Card Index), Kartoteka rozrzucona (The Card Index Scattered). *Prose includes:* Tarcza z pajęczyny, Opowiadania wybrane (Selected Stories), Na powierzchni poematu (They Came to See a Poet) 1991, Płaskorzeźba (Bas-Relief) 1991, Nasz starszy brat 1992, Historia pięciu wierszy 1993. *Publications:* 15 vols of poetry including Niepokój (Faces of Anxiety), Czerwona rękawiczka (The Red Glove), Czas, który idzie (The Time Which Goes On), Równina (The Plain), Srebrny kłos (The Silver Ear), Rozmowa z księciem (Conversation with the Prince), Zielona róża (The Green Rose), Nic w płaszczu Prospera (Nothing in Prosper's Overcoat), Twarz (The Face), Duszyczka (A Little Soul), Poezje (Poetry) 1987, Słowo po słowie (Word by Word) 1994, Zawsze fragment (Always the Fragment) 1996, Zawsze fragment: Recycling (Always the Fragment: Recycling) 1999, Matka odchodzi (The Mother Goes) 2000, Nożyk profesora (The

Professor's Knife) 2001, Szara strefa 2002, Wyjście 2004. *Address:* ul. Promien 16, 51-659 Wrocław, Poland (home). *Telephone:* (71) 3452126 (home). *Fax:* (71) 3452126 (home).

ROZHDESTVENSKY, Gennadiy Nikolayevich; Russian conductor; b. 4 May 1931, Moscow; s. of Nikolai Anosov and Natalia Rozhdestvenskaya; m. Viktoria Postnikova; one s.; ed Moscow State Conservatoire; Asst Conductor, Bolshoi Theatre 1951, Conductor 1956–60, Prin. Conductor 1965–70, Artistic Dir 2000–01; Chief Conductor of USSR Radio and TV Symphony Orchestra 1961–74; Chief Conductor Stockholm Philharmonia 1974–77, 1992–95, Moscow Chamber Opera 1974–83; Founder, Artistic Dir, Chief Conductor, State Symphony Orchestra of Ministry of Culture 1983–92; Prin. Conductor BBC Symphony Orchestra 1978–82, Vienna Symphony Orchestra 1980–83; has been guest conductor of numerous orchestras throughout Europe, America and Asia; Chair. of Conducting, Moscow State Conservatoire 1965–; Hon. mem. Swedish Royal Acad. 1975, Royal Acad. (UK); Légion d'honneur, Order of the Rising Sun (Japan); People's Artist of the RSFSR 1966, People's Artist of the USSR 1976, Hero of Socialist Labour 1991, Lenin Prize 1970 and other awards. *Publications:* The Fingering of Conducting 1974, Thoughts about Music 1975; numerous articles. *Leisure interest:* music. *Address:* c/o Robert Slotover, Allied Artists, 42 Montpelier Square, London, SW7 1JZ, England (office). *Telephone:* (20) 7589-6243 (office). *Fax:* (20) 7581-5269 (office). *E-mail:* robert@alliedartists.co.uk (office). *Website:* www.alliedartists.co.uk (office).

ROZHKOV, Pavel Alekseyevich; Russian politician and fmr wrestler; *First Vice-President and Chairman, Executive Committee, Russian Paralympic Committee;* b. 30 June 1957, Ramenskoye, Moscow region; m. Larisa Viktorovna Rozhkova; ed Moscow Inst. of Physical Culture; metal worker Radipribor plant 1974–75; coach Urozhai classical wrestling team Moscow 1977–78; jr researcher All-Union Research Inst. of Physical Culture, Moscow 1979–82; coach State Sports Cttee 1982–87; docent Cen. State Inst. of Physical Culture, Moscow 1992; Sr coach Olympic Greek-Roman wrestling team 1992–96; Dir-Gen. Olymp-Tour co., Moscow 1997–99; Deputy Minister of Physical Culture, Sports and Tourism 1999, First Deputy Minister 1999–2000; Chair. State Cttee on Physical Culture, Sports and Tourism 2000–02, First Deputy Chair. 2002; currently First Vice-Pres. and Chair. Exec. Cttee, Russian Paralympic Cttee. *Address:* Russian Paralympic Committee, 32-40 Office, 42, Leninskiy prospect, 119119 Moscow, Russia (office). *Telephone:* (495) 930-79-21 (office). *Fax:* (495) 938-85-21 (office). *E-mail:* npcrus@paralymp.ru (office). *Website:* www.paralymp.ru (office).

ROZOVSKY, Mark Grigorievich; Russian theatre director and scriptwriter; b. 3 April 1937, Petropavlovsk; ed Moscow Univ. Higher Scriptwriters' School; f. and managed 'Our Home' (amateur studio theatre) with fellow students of Moscow Univ. 1958–70; theatre officially disbanded 1970, revived in 1987 as professional co. U Nikitskikh Vorot; wrote 3 books on theatre, dir versions of Karamzin, Kafka, Dostoevsky and others in Leningrad, Moscow and Riga 1970–87; Chief Dir Moscow State Music Hall 1974–79; Dir Orpheus and Eurydice (rock-opera) 1975 and a musical adaptation of 'Strider' jtly with Georgii Tovstonogov, by L. N. Tolstoy for Gorky Theatre, Leningrad; Theatre of Nations Prize Hamburg and Avignon 1979. *Other productions include:* Amadeus (P. Shaffer) for Moscow Arts Theatre; libretto for opera about Mayakovsky; work for TV including documentary on Meyerhold, Triumphal Square 1984; works for Gorky Theatre, Leningrad and Theatre of Russian Drama, Riga, Latvia and his own Studio Theatre, Moscow; Romances with Oblomov, Alexandrinsky Theatre, St Petersburg 1992. *Address:* Theatre U Nikitskikh Vorot, 103009 Moscow, Bolshaya Nikitskaya Str. 23/9, Russia. *Telephone:* (495) 291-84-19.

RUAN, Chongwu; Chinese politician; b. 1933, Huai'an Co., Hebei Prov.; ed Moscow Auto-Eng Inst.; Deputy Dir Shanghai Materials Research Inst.; joined CCP 1952; Deputy Sec. Shanghai Municipal Scientific Workers' Asscn; Science and Tech. Counsellor, Chinese Embassy in Bonn 1978; Vice-Mayor Shanghai 1983–85; Sec. CCP, Shanghai Municipality 1983–85; Minister of Public Security 1985–87; Vice-Minister Science and Tech. Comm., State Council 1987–89, of Labour 1989–93; Sec. CPC 2nd Hainan Provincial Cttee 1993; Gov. of Hainan Prov. 1993–98; mem. 12th CCP Cen. Cttee 1982–87, 13th Cen. Cttee 1987–92, 14th Cen. Cttee 1992–97; Del., 15th CCP Nat. Congress 1997–2002; mem. 9th Standing Cttee of NPC 1998–2003. *Address:* c/o National People's Congress, Beijing, People's Republic of China (office).

RUBADIRI, (James) David, PhD; Malawi diplomatist, academic, author and poet; b. 19 July 1930, Luila; m.; nine c.; ed King's Coll., Cambridge, Univ. of Bristol, Makerere Univ. Coll., Kampala; Prin. Soche Hill Coll. (now part of Univ. of Malawi) 1962–63; fmr Acting Prov. Educ. Officer, Southern Prov.; Amb. to UN and USA 1963–65; various academic and admin. posts, Univ. of Makerere, Kampala 1965–75; Sr Lecturer Dept of Literature, Univ. of Nairobi 1976–84; Prof. and Head Dept of Languages and Literature and Social Science Educ., Univ. of Botswana 1984–95; Perm. Rep. to the UN 1995–2000; Vice Chancellor Univ. of Malawi 2001–05; Chair. Bd of Trustees Univ. of Livingstonia 2005–; Visiting Prof. of English Literature, Northwestern Univ. 1972, Univ. of Ife 1978–80; Dr hc (Univ. of Strathclyde) 2005; Malawi Independence Medal. *Publications:* literary books, poetry and plays. *Address:* c/o Board of Trustees, University of Livingstonia, PO Box 37, Livingstonia, Malawi.

RUBBIA, Carlo; Italian physicist and academic; *Professor of Physics, Università degli Studi di Pavia;* b. 31 March 1934, Gorizia; s. of Silvio Rubbia and Bice Rubbia; m. Marisa Rubbia; one s., one d.; ed high school, Pisa and Rome Univs and Columbia Univ., USA; joined CERN as Sr Physicist 1961, mem. Cttee CERN 1985–89, Dir-Gen. 1989–93; Higgins Prof. of Physics, Harvard Univ. 1970–88; currently Full Prof. of Physics, Pavia Univ.; Pres. Ente per le Nuove tecnologie, l'Energia e l'Ambiente (ENEA) 1999–2005; Adviser, EC Commr for Research and Educ. Policies 2002; mem. Papal Acad. of Science 1986–; mem. American Acad. of Arts and Sciences, Accad. dei Lincei, European Acad. of Sciences, Accademia dei XL, Pontifical Acad. of Sciences, Polish Acad. of Sciences (Foreign Mem.), Croatian Acad. of Sciences and Arts, Royal Society, UK, (Foreign Mem.), NAS (Foreign Mem.), Russian Acad. of Sciences (Foreign Mem.), Third World Acad. of Sciences, European Acad. of Sciences, Société Européenne de Culture, Ateneo Veneto, Société Française de Physique, Istituto Lombardo, Austrian Acad. of Sciences; Cavaliere di Gran Croce (Knight Grand Cross) 1985, Officier de la Légion d'Honneur 1989, Polish Order of Merit 1993; Dr hc (Geneva) 1983, (Carnegie Mellon) 1985, (Genoa) 1985, (Udine) 1985, (La Plata, Argentina) 1986, (Northwestern) 1986, (Camerino) 1987, (Chicago) 1987, (Loyola) 1987, (Boston) 1988, (Sofia, Bulgaria) 1990, (Moscow)1991, (Chile) 1991, (Polytechnic Univ. of Madrid) 1992, (Padova) 1992, (Tech. Univ. of Rio de Janeiro) 1993, (Trieste) 1994, (Oxford) 1994, (Catholic Univ. of Lima, Peru) 1994, (Nat. Univ. of St Antonio Abad of Cusco, Peru) 1994, (Bordeaux) 1998, (Haute Savoie) 1999, (St John's Univ.) 2003, (Università di Torino) 2004; Nobel Prize for Physics 1984, Leslie Prize for Exceptional Achievements 1985, Jesolo d'Oro 1986. *Address:* Physics Department, Università degli Studi di Pavia, Corso Strada Nuova 65, 27100 Pavia, Italy (office). *Telephone:* 0382-504217 (office). *Fax:* 0382-504529 (office). *Website:* www.unipv.it (office).

RUBENSTEIN, Edward, MD; American physician, scientist and academic; *Professor Emeritus of Medicine (Clinical), School of Medicine, Stanford University;* b. 5 Dec. 1924, Cincinnati; s. of Louis Rubenstein and Nettie Nathan; m. Nancy Ellen Millman 1954; three s.; ed Cincinnati Univ. Coll. of Medicine; Laboratory Asst, Dept of Physiology, Cincinnati Univ. 1947; Intern, then Jr Asst, then Sr Asst Resident in Medicine, Cincinnati Gen. Hosp. 1947–50, Medical Chief, Psychosomatic Service 1953–54; Research Fellow, May Inst., Cincinnati 1950; Chief of Medicine, USAF Hosp., March Airforce Base 1950–52; Sr Asst Resident in Medicine, Barnes Hosp., St Louis 1952–53; Chief, Clinical Physiology Unit, San Mateo Co. Gen. Hosp. 1955–63, Chief of Medicine 1960–70; Prof. of Medicine and Assoc. Dean of Postgraduate Medical Educ., Stanford Univ. School of Medicine 1971, now Prof. Emer.; Founding Ed.-in-Chief Scientific American Medicine 1977–93; mem. Inst. of Medicine of NAS 1981–, Soc. of Photo-Optical Engineers 1981–; Master, American Coll. of Physicians 1987; TV documentary Being Human 1979; research in synchrotron radiation; Fellow, AAAS 1992–, Royal Soc. of Medicine 1992; Henry Kaiser Award 1989, Albion Walter Hewlett Award 1995. *Publications:* Intensive Medical Care 1971, Handbook on Synchrotron Radiation Vol. 4 (ed.), Introduction to Molecular Medicine (ed.), Synchrotron Radiation in the Life Sciences (ed.); numerous scientific papers. *Address:* Stanford University School of Medicine, 300 Pasteur Drive, Stanford, CA 94305, USA (office). *Telephone:* (650) 343-2992 (office). *Fax:* (650) 343-2992 (office). *E-mail:* exr@leland.stanford.edu (office). *Website:* med.stanford.edu (office).

RUBENSTEIN, Howard Joseph, LLB; American lawyer and public relations executive; *President, Rubenstein Associates Inc.;* b. 3 Feb. 1932, New York; s. of Samuel Rubenstein and Ada Sall; m. Amy Forman 1959; three s.; ed Univ. of Pa, Harvard Univ. and St John's Law School; admitted New York State Bar 1960; Pres. Rubenstein Assocs Inc. (public relations consultants), New York 1954–, also Chair. Rubenstein Communications, Inc.; Co-Chair. Holocaust Comm. 1993; mem. Exec. Cttee Real Estate Bd of New York, NYC & Co., Asscn for a Better New York; mem. Bd of Dirs Albert Einstein Coll. of Medicine 1997–; mem. Mayor's Business Advisory Council, New York 1996–, communications adviser Gov.'s Jerusalem 3000 Cttee 1996–; mem. Bd of Govs Jewish County Relations Council 1999–; Trustee Police Athletic League, Inner City Scholarship Fund of the Archdiocese of New York, Foundation for Nat. Archives; mem City Univ. of New York Business Leadership Council; Hon. LLD (St John's Law School) 1990. *Address:* Rubenstein Associates Inc., 1345 Avenue of the Americas, New York, NY 10105 (office); 993 Fifth Avenue, New York, NY 10028, USA (home). *Telephone:* (212) 843-8000 (office). *E-mail:* info@rubenstein.com (office). *Website:* www.rubenstein.com (office).

RUBIANO SÁENZ, HE Cardinal Pedro; Colombian ecclesiastic; *Archbishop of Santafé de Bogotá;* b. 13 Sept. 1932, Cartago; ordained priest 1956; Bishop of Cúcuta 1971–83; Coadjutor Archbishop of Cali 1983–85, Bishop of Cali 1985–94; Archbishop of Santafé de Bogotá 1994–; cr. Cardinal 2001, Cardinal Priest of Trasfigurazione di Nostro Signore Gesù Cristo 2001; mem. Congregation for Catholic Educ., Pontifical Council for the Pastoral Care of Migrants and Itinerant People; Apostolic Admin. of Popayán 1990–91. *Address:* Arzobispado, Carrera 7 N. 10–20, Bogotá, DC1, Colombia (office). *Telephone:* (1) 3505511 (office). *Fax:* (1) 3347867 (office). *Website:* www.arquibogota.org.co (office).

RUBIK, Ernő, BA; Hungarian inventor, architect and designer; b. 13 July 1944, Budapest; s. of Ernő Rubik, Sr and Magdolna Szántó; one s. two d.; ed Univ. of Tech. Educ., Budapest, Hungarian Acad. of Applied Arts and Design, Budapest, Budapest School of Commercial Art; consecutively Asst Prof., then Assoc. Prof., Acad. of Applied Arts, Dir of Postgraduate Studies 1983–86; Hon. Prof. Acad. of Crafts and Design, Budapest 1987; inventor of Rubik's Cube 1974, and other games and puzzles; Pres. Rubik Studio; Pres. Hungarian Acad. of Eng 1990–96; Labour Order of Merit Gold Medal of the Hungarian People's Repub.; Toy of the Year Award 1981–82 of UK, FRG, Italy, Sweden, Finland, France, USA, State Prize 1983. *Publications:* co-author and ed. of A bűvös kocka (The Magic Cube) 1981, Rubik's Magic 1986, Rubik's Cubic Compendium 1987. *Leisure interests:* swimming, skiing, sailing. *Address:* Rubik Studio, Városmajor u. 74, 1122 Budapest, Hungary (office). *Telephone:* (1) 356-9533 (office). *Website:* www.rubiks.com (office).

RUBIKS, Alfrēds; Latvian politician; *Chairman, Latvian Socialist Party;* b. 1935, Daugavpils, Latvia; m.; two s.; ed Rīga Tech. Higher School and

Leningrad Higher Party School; mem. CPSU 1958–91; engineer and foreman, Riga Electrotechnical Plant 1957–61; Komsomol and party work; Sec. Latvian Komsomol Cen. Cttee; First Sec. of Leningradsky Region of Rīga Regional CP Cttee 1976–82; Minister of Local Industry for Latvian SSR 1982–84; Chair. Exec. Cttee Rīga City Council of People's Deputies 1984–90; First Sec. Cen. Cttee Latvian CP 1990–91; USSR People's Deputy 1989–91; mem. CPSU Cen. Cttee 1990–91; mem. CPSU Politburo July 1990–91; arrested by Latvian authorities Aug. 1991, accused of high treason; elected to Saeima (Parl.) 1993; sentenced to eight years' imprisonment 1995; released 1997; mem. Saeima 1998–; Chair. Latvian Socialist Party 1998–. *Address:* Saeima, Jecaba Str. 11, 1811 Rīga; Latvian Socialist Party, Burtnieku iela 23, Rīga, Latvia. *Telephone:* 6755-5535. *Fax:* 6755-5535. *Website:* www.latsocpartija.lv.

RUBIN, Hon. James P., BA, MIA; American fmr government official, academic and broadcast journalist; b. 1960, New York; m. Christiane Amanpour; one s.; ed Columbia Univ.; Research Dir Arms Control Asscn, Washington DC 1985–89, also consultant to US Senate Foreign Relations Cttee on nuclear arms control issues; fmr staff mem., US Senate Foreign Relations Cttee, Sr Foreign Policy Adviser to Joseph R. Biden, Jr (q.v.); Sr Adviser and spokesman for US Rep. to UN Madeleine Albright (q.v.) 1993–96; Dir of Foreign Policy and Spokesman Clinton/Gore presidential campaign Aug.–Nov. 1996; Sr Adviser to Sec. of State 1996–97; Asst Sec. of State for Public Affairs 1997–2000; Pnr, Brunswick 2001–04; Visiting Prof. of Int. Relations, LSE 2001–04; foreign policy adviser John Kerry US presidential campaign 2004; Anchor, World News Tonight, Sky News (UK) 2005–06, World Affairs Commentator 2006–; Vice Chair. Atlantic Partnership; mem. Bd of Dirs Columbia Univ. School of Int. Affairs, Int. Rescue Cttee, UK; mem. Council on Foreign Relations; John Jay Award for Distinguished Professional Achievement (Columbia Univ.) 1998, Distinguished Service Award, Sec. of State 2000. *Address:* Sky News, British Sky Broadcasting, Grant Way, Middlesex, TW7 5QD, England (office). *Telephone:* (20) 7705-3000 (office). *Website:* www.skypressoffice.co.uk/SkyNews (office).

RUBIN, Louis Decimus, Jr, PhD; American writer, academic and publisher; *Professor Emeritus of English, University of North Carolina;* b. 19 Nov. 1923, Charleston, SC; s. of Louis Decimus Rubin, Sr and Janet Weinstein Rubin; m. Eva Maryette Redfield 1951; two s.; ed High School of Charleston, Coll. of Charleston, Univ. of Richmond and Johns Hopkins Univ.; U.S. Army 1943–46; instructor in English Johns Hopkins Univ. 1948–54; Exec. Sec. American Studies Asscn 1954–56 (also fmr Vice-Pres.); Assoc. Ed. News Leader, Richmond, Va 1956–57; Assoc. Prof. of English, Hollins Coll., Prof., Chair. of Dept 1960–67, Prof. of English Univ. of NC 1967–73, Univ. Distinguished Prof. 1973-89, Prof. Emer. 1989–; Visiting Prof. La. State Univ., Univ. of Calif. at Santa Barbara, Harvard Univ.; lecturer, Aix-Marseille at Nice, Kyoto Summer American Studies Seminars; USICA, Austria, Germany; Ed. Southern Literary Studies Series, Louisiana State Univ. Press 1965–90; Co-Ed. Southern Literary Journal 1968–89; Co-founder and Editorial Dir Algonquin Books, Chapel Hill 1982–91; fmr Pres. Soc. for Study of Southern Literature; fmr Chair. American Literature Section, Modern Language Asscn; mem. SC Acad. of Authors, Fellowship of Southern Writers; Hon. DLitt (Richmond, Clemson, Coll. of Charleston, Univ. of the South, Univ. of NC, Ashville, Univ. of NC Chapel Hill); Richard Beale Davis Award for Lifetime Achievement in Southern Letters, Society for Study of Southern Literature 2004. *Publications:* author: Thomas Wolfe: The Weather of His Youth 1955, No Place on Earth 1959, The Faraway Country 1964, The Golden Weather (novel) 1961, The Curious Death of the Novel 1967, The Teller in the Tale 1967, George W. Cable 1969, The Writer in the South 1972, William Elliott Shoots a Bear 1975, The Wary Fugitives 1978, Surfaces of a Diamond (novel) 1981, A Gallery of Southerners 1982, The Even-Tempered Angler 1984, The Edge of the Swamp: a study in the Literature and Society of the Old South 1989, The Mockingbird in the Gum Tree 1991, Small Craft Advisory 1991, The Heat of the Sun (novel) 1995, Babe Ruth's Ghost 1996, Seaports of the South 1998, A Memory of Trains 2000, An Honorable Estate 2001; editor: Southern Renascence 1953, Idea of an American Novel 1961, South 1961, Comic Imagination in American Literature 1973, The Literary South 1979, American South 1980, The History of Southern Literature 1985, An Apple for My Teacher 1986, Algonquin Literary Quiz Book 1990, A Writer's Companion 1995. *Leisure interests:* baseball, classical music, reading. *Address:* 702 Gimghoul Road, Chapel Hill, NC 27514, USA (home).

RUBIN, Robert, BA, LLB; American financial services industry executive, lawyer and fmr government official; b. 29 Aug. 1938, New York; s. of Alexander Rubin and Sylvia Rubin (née Seiderman); m. Judith L. Oxenberg 1963; two s.; ed Harvard Univ., LSE, Yale Univ. Law School; lawyer, Cleary, Gottlieb, Steen & Hamilton New York 1964–66; joined Goldman, Sachs 1966, Vice-Chair. & Co-COO 1987–90, Co-Chair. 1990–92; Chair. New York Host Cttee 1992 Democratic Convention; Asst to Pres. Clinton for Econ. Policy 1993–95; Sec. of Treasury 1995–99; Chair. Exec. Cttee and mem. Office of the Chair. Citigroup Inc. 1999–2007, Chair. Nov.–Dec. 2007, Sr Advisor 2007–09 (resgnd); mem. Bd Trustees Mount Sinai-New York University Health; mem. Advisory Bd Insight Venture Partners, Taconic Capital Advisors LLC, General Atlantic LLC; Special Advisor Tinicum Capital Partners, LP; mem. Harvard Corpn 2002–; Vice-Chair. Council on Foreign Relations 2003–07, Co-Chair. 2007–; fmr mem. Bd of Dirs Ford Motor Co., Harvard Management Co., New York Stock Exchange, New York Futures Exchange, New York City Partnership, Center for Nat. Policy; Chair. Local Initiatives Support Corpn (LISC); launched Hamilton Project 2006; mem. Africa Progress Panel 2007–; Hon. DHumLitt (Yeshiva Univ.) 1996; Hon. LLD (Univ. of Miami) 2008; Nat. Asscn of Christians and Jews Award 1977, Columbia Business School Award 1996, Euromoney Magazine's Finance Minister of the Year Award 1996, Medal for High Civic Service, Citizens' Budget Comm. 1997, Foreign Policy Asscn Medal 1998, Jefferson Award, American Inst. for Public Service 1998, Award of Merit, Yale Univ. 1998, Paul Tsongas Award 1998, Global Leadership Award, UN Asscn 1998. *Publication:* In an Uncertain World: Tough Choices from Wall Street to Washington 2003 (with Jacob Weisberg). *Leisure interest:* fly fishing. *Address:* c/o Citigroup Inc., 399 Park Avenue, New York, NY 10043, USA (office).

RUBIN, Vera Cooper, MA, PhD; American astronomer; *Senior Fellow, Department of Terrestrial Magnetism, Carnegie Institution of Washington;* b. (Vera Florence Cooper), 23 July 1928, Philadelphia; d. of Philip Cooper and Rose Applebaum Cooper; m. Robert J. Rubin 1948 (died 2008); three s. one d.; ed Vassar Coll., Cornell Univ., Georgetown Univ.; Research Assoc. to Asst Prof., Georgetown Univ. 1955–65; mem. Staff Dept of Terrestrial Magnetism, Carnegie Inst. of Wash. 1965–, now Sr Fellow; Distinguished Visiting Astronomer, Cerro Tololo Inter-American Observatory 1978, Chancellor's Distinguished Prof. of Astronomy Univ. of Calif., Berkeley 1981; Pres.'s Distinguished Visitor, Vassar Coll. 1987; B. Tinsley Visiting Prof., Univ. of Texas 1988; Oort Visiting Prof., Univ. of Leiden 1995; has observed at Kitt Peak Nat. Observatory, Lowell, Palomar, McDonald, Las Campanas, Chile Observatories; Chair. Nat. Comm. for Int. Astronomical Union 1998–2000; Assoc. Ed. Astronomical Journal 1972–77, Astrophysical Journal of Letters 1977–82; mem. Council American Astronomical Soc. 1977–80, Nat. Science Bd 1996–2002; mem. Editorial Bd Science Magazine 1979–87, mem. Sr Editorial Bd 1998–; mem. Council Smithsonian Inst. 1979–85, Space Telescope Science Inst. 1990–92; Pres. Galaxy Comm. Int. Astronomical Union 1982–85; mem. Bd Science Service 2003–; Judge, Intel Science Talent Search 2001–; mem. NAS, American Acad. of Arts and Sciences, American Philosophical Soc., Pres.'s Cttee to select recipients of Nat. Medal of Science, Pontifical Acad. of Sciences; Hon. DSc (Creighton Univ.) 1978, (Harvard Univ.) 1988, (Yale Univ.) 1990, (Williams Coll.) 1993, (Univ. of Michigan) 1996, (Ohio State Univ.) 1998, (Smith Coll.) 2001, (Grinnell Coll.) 2002, (Ohio Wesleyan) 2004, (Princeton Univ.) 2005; Hon. DHL (Georgetown) 1997; Nat. Medal of Science 1993, Dickson Prize for Science, Carnegie Mellon Univ. 1994, Jansky Lecturer, Nat. Radio Astronomy Observatory 1994, Russel Lecturer, American Astronomical Soc. 1995, Helen Hogg Prize, Canadian Astronomical Soc. 1997, Weizmann Women and Science Award 1996, Gold Medal Royal Astronomical Soc., London 1996, Canadian Astronomy Soc. Helen Hogg Prize 1997, Peter Gruber Foundation Cosmology Prize 2003, Astronomical Soc. of the Pacific Catherine Wolfe Bruce Medal 2003, NAS Watson Medal 2004. *Publications:* Bright Galaxies, Dark Matters 1999; over 150 scientific papers on the dynamics of galaxies in specialist journals. *Leisure interests:* family, garden, hiking, travel. *Address:* Department of Terrestrial Magnetism, Carnegie Institution of Washington, 5251 Broad Branch Road, NW, Washington, DC 20015, USA (office). *Telephone:* (202) 478-8861 (office). *E-mail:* rubin@dtm.ciw.edu (office). *Website:* www.ciw.edu/rubin (office).

RUBINA, Dina Ilyinichna; Israeli writer; b. 19 Sept. 1953, Tashkent, Uzbekistan; ed Tashkent State Conservatory; music teacher Tashkent Inst. of Culture 1977–90; literary debut in Yunost magazine 1971; emigrated to Israel 1990; book publications, theatrical stagings, film, newspaper editing (Pyatnitza and others); Head Dept of Public and Cultural Relations, The Jewish Agency in Russia 1999–2003; Ministry of Culture Award 1982, Arye Dulchin Award (Israel) 1991, Israel Writers' Union Award 1995, Best Book of literary season, France 1996. *Films:* Zavtra, kak obychno 1984, Na Verhney Maslovke 2004. *Publications:* The Double-Barrelled Name (short stories) 1990, In Thy Gates 1994, An Intellectual Sat Down on the Road 1995, Here Comes the Messiah 1997, The Escort Angel 1998, The Last Wild Boar from Pontevedra Forest 1998, High Water in Venice 1999, Several Hurried Words of Love (short stories) 2003. *Leisure interest:* travelling. *Address:* Et Ha'zmir, 11/8, 98491 Maale-Adumim, Israel (home). *Telephone:* 2-5352435 (home). *Fax:* 2-5352435 (home). *E-mail:* web@dinarubina.com (home). *Website:* www.dinarubina.com (home).

RUBINSTEIN, Amnon, BA, LLM, PhD; Israeli author, academic and fmr politician; *Professor of Law, Radzyner School of Law, Interdisciplinary Center (IDC), Herzliya;* b. 5 Sept. 1931, Tel-Aviv; s. of Aaron Rubinstein and Rachel Rubinstein (née Vilozny); m. Ronny Havatzeleth 1959; one s. one d.; ed Hebrew Univ. of Jerusalem, London School of Econs; mil. service in Israeli Defence Forces; fmr Dean, Faculty of Law and Prof. of Law, Tel-Aviv Univ.; mem. Knesset (Parl.) 1977–2001 (resgnd), mem. Constitution and Justice Cttee (Chair. 1999–2001), State Audit Cttee; Minister of Communications 1984–87, of Energy and Infrastructure and Science and Tech. 1992–93, of Educ. and Culture 1993–96; currently Prof. of Law, Interdisciplinary Center (IDC), Herzliya, fmr Dean Radzyner School of Law; Dr hc (Bradford) 1968, (Hewbrew Union Coll., Jerusalem) 1969. *Publications:* Jurisdiction and Illegality 1965, The Zionist Dream Revisited 1985 (French trans. Le Rêve et l'histoire), The Constitutional Law of Israel (5th edn) 1997, From Herzl to Rabin 1999. *Leisure interests:* music, drama, swimming. *Address:* Radzyner School of Law, Interdisciplinary Center Herzliya, Kanfei Nesharim Street, POBox 167, Herzliya 46150, Israel. *Telephone:* 9-9527325 (office). *Fax:* 9-9513075 (office). *E-mail:* amnon_r@idc.ac.il (office). *Website:* portal.idc.ac.il/en/main/academics/law/Pages/General.aspx (office).

RUBINSTEIN, Ariel, BSc, MA, MSc, PhD; Israeli economist and academic; *Professor of Economics and Salzberg Chair, Tel-Aviv University;* b. 13 April 1951, Jerusalem; s. of Yehuda Rubinstein and Leah Rubinstein; m. Yael Rubinstein; one s. one d.; ed The Hebrew Univ.; Sr Lecturer, Dept of Econs, The Hebrew Univ. 1981–84, Assoc. Prof. 1984–86, Prof. 1986–1990; Prof. of Econs and Salzberg Chair, Tel-Aviv Univ. 1990–, Chair. Dept of Econs 1991–93; Lecturer in rank of Prof. Princeton Univ., USA 1991–2004; Prof. of Econs, New York Univ. 2004–; fmr Visiting Prof., Nuffield Coll. Oxford 1979–80, LSE 1986–89, Univ. of Chicago 1988, Univ. of Pennsylvania 1989, Columbia Univ., New York 1990, Russell-Sage Foundation 1996–97; Assoc.

Ed. Econometrica 1984–92, Journal of Econ. Theory 1986–94, Games and Economic Behavior 1988–2002, Mathematics of Social Sciences 1993–2001; mem. Editorial Bd Review of Economic Studies 1987–88 (Foreign Ed. 1988–92), Review of Economic Design 1993–, Economics and Philosophy 1994–, International Journal of Game Theory 1995–2000, NAJ Economics 2001–; mem. Advisory Cttee Journal of European Economic Association 2003–; mem. Exec. Bd Theoretical Economics 2005–; Fellow, Econometric Soc. 1985– (Pres. 2004), Israeli Acad. of Sciences 1995–, European Econ. Asscn 2004–; mem. European Acad. of Sciences and Arts; Foreign Hon. mem. American Acad. of Arts and Sciences 1994–, American Econ. Asscn 1995–, Hon. Fellow, Nuffield Coll. 2002–; Dr hc (Tilburg) 2002; Michael Bruno Memorial Award 2000, Pras Israel 2002, Nemmers Prize, Northwestern Univ. 2004, EMET Prize 2006. *Publications:* Bargaining and Markets (with M. Osborne) 1990, A Course in Game Theory (with M. Osborne) 1994, Modeling Bounded Rationality 1998, Economics and Language 2000, Lecture Notes in Microeconomic Theory: The Economic Agent 2005, Economic Tales 2009, more than 80 articles in academic journals. *Address:* School of Economics, Tel-Aviv University, Tel-Aviv 69978, Israel (office). *Telephone:* (3) 6409601 (office); (3) 6421111 (home). *Fax:* (3) 6409908 (office). *E-mail:* rariel@post.tau.ac.il (office). *Website:* arielrubinstein.tau.ac.il (office).

RUCKAUF, Carlos Federico; Argentine politician; b. 10 July 1944; m.; three c.; ed Nat. Univ. of Buenos Aires; Asst Sec. Insurance Union 1969–72; Labour Judge 1973–75; Sec. Trabajo de la Nación (Labour of the Nation) 1975–76; Pres. Partido Justicialista de Capital Federal (Fed. Justice Party) 1983, Vice-Pres. 1993, Pres. 1994; Senatorial Cand. 1983; Nat. Deputy 1987–89, 1991–93; Amb. to Italy, Malta and FAO 1989–91; Pres. Foreign Affairs Comm. 1991–93; Minister of the Interior 1993; apptd Vice-Pres. of Argentina 1995; Gov. Buenos Aires Prov. 1999–; Minister of Foreign Affairs 2002–03; mem. Parl. (Partido Justicialista—PJ) 2003–07; Kt of the Grand Cross, Order of Merit (Italy) 1995, Grand Cross, Order Bernardo O'Higgins (Chile) 1996, Medal of the Congress of Deputies (Spain) 1997, Commdr, Légion d'honneur (France) 1997, Alaoui Order (Morocco) 1998, Grand Cross, Ordem Nacional do Cruzeiro do Sul (Brazil) 1998, Special Grand Cross, Nat. Order of Merit (Paraguay) 1999. *Address:* c/o Ministry of Foreign Affairs, International Trade and Worship, Esmeralda 1212, 1007 Buenos Aires, Argentina (office).

RUCKELSHAUS, William Doyle; American business executive and fmr government official; *Strategic Director, Madrona Venture Group LLC;* b. 24 July 1932, Indianapolis, Ind.; s. of John K. Ruckelshaus and Marion Covington Ruckelshaus (née Doyle); m. Jill E. Strickland 1962; one s. four d.; ed Portsmouth Priory School, RI and Princeton and Harvard Univs; served with US Army 1953–55; admitted to Ind. Bar 1960; attorney with Ruckelshaus, Bobbit & O'Connor 1960–68; Partner, Ruckelshaus, Beveridge, Fairbanks & Diamond (fmrly Ruckelshaus, Beveridge & Fairbanks), Sr Partner 1974–76; Deputy Attorney-Gen. Ind. 1960–65; Minority Attorney, Ind. State Senate 1965–67; mem. Ind. House of Reps 1967–69; Asst Attorney-Gen., US Civil Div., Dept of Justice 1969–70; Dir Environmental Protection Agency 1970–73, 1983–84; Acting Dir FBI 1973; Deputy Attorney-Gen. 1973; Sr Vice-Pres. Weyerhaeuser Co. 1976–83; mem. firm Perkins Coie, Seattle 1985–88; Chair. CEO Browning-Ferris Industries Inc., Houston 1988–95; Founder and Prin. Madrona Investment Group (now Madrona Venture Group LLC) 1996–, now Strategic Dir; Chair. World Resources Inst., Washington, DC 1999–2006; mem. Bd of Dirs Cummins Engine Co., Inc., Vykor, Isilon Systems; fmr Dir Peabody Int. Corpn, Church and Dwight Co. Inc.; fmr Chair. Bd Geothermal Kinetics Inc., Trustees of Urban Inst.; mem. Bd American Paper Inst., Council on Foreign Relations, Twentieth Century Fund; mem. Public Interest Advisory Cttee Harvard Univ. Medical Project, Bd of Overseers, Harvard J.F.K. School of Govt, Bd of Regents, Seattle Univ., World Resource Inst. (Chair. 1998–), Comm. on Ocean Policy 2001–, Science Advisory Bd, Nat. Oceanic and Atmospheric Admin 2003–; Chair. Salmon Recovery Funding Bd for State of Washington, Puget Sound Cleanup, Univ. of Washington and Washington State Univ. Policy Consensus Center, Seattle Aquarium Soc.; Co-Chair. Puget Sound Partnership 2005–; Trustee, Pacific Science Center Foundation, Seattle Chamber of Commerce, The Conservation Foundation, Seattle Art Museum; mem. bd numerous other non-profit orgs, several US Bar asscns; numerous awards and distinctions. *Publication:* Reapportionment – A Continuing Problem 1963. *Leisure interests:* tennis, fishing, reading. *Address:* Madrona Investment Group LLC, 1000 2nd Avenue, Suite 3700, Seattle, WA 98104, USA (office). *Telephone:* (206) 674-3009 (office). *Fax:* (206) 674-3013 (office). *E-mail:* bill@madrona.com (office). *Website:* www.madrona.com (office).

RÜCKER, Joachim; German UN official; b. 30 May 1951; one s.; two d.; has served in several positions within Ministry of Foreign Affairs including Head, Budget and Finance Div. 2002–05; Mayor of Sindelfingen, Germany 1993–2001; Deputy High Rep. for Admin and Finance, Office of the UN High Rep., Sarajevo, Bosnia and Herzegovina 2001–02; Deputy Special Rep. of Sec.-Gen. in charge of EU Pillar for Econ. Reconstruction, UN Interim Admin Mission in Kosovo (UNMIK) 2005–06, Special Rep. of Sec.-Gen. and Head of UNMIK 2006–08. *Address:* c/o United Nations Mission in Kosovo, 10000 Prishtina, Kosovo (office). *E-mail:* ruecker@un.org (office). *Website:* www.joachim-ruecker.de.

RÜCKL, Jiří; Czech business executive and fmr politician; *President, Rückl Crystal Ltd;* b. 20 Oct. 1940, Prague; s. of Jiří Rückl and Věra Rückl; m. Jana Hrabánková; two d.; ed Econ. Univ., Prague; specialist positions in glassware 1961–90; Pres. Rückl Crystal 1992–; Dir, Ministry of Industry 1990–92; Councillor for Nibor 1994–; Senator 1996–2004. *Publications include:* specialist papers about glass production. *Address:* Rückl Crystal a.s., 26705 Nižbor 141, Czech Republic (office). *Telephone:* (3) 11696232 (office). *Fax:* (3) 11693510 (office). *E-mail:* ruckl@ruckl.cz (office). *Website:* www.ruckl.eu (office); www.ruckl.cz (office).

RUDD, Sir (Anthony) Nigel (Russell), Kt, DL, FCA; British business executive; *Chairman, Invensys plc;* b. 31 Dec. 1946; m. Lesley Elizabeth Rudd (née Hodgkinson) 1969; two s. one d.; ed Bemrose Grammar School, Derby; chartered accountant 1968; Div. Finance Dir London & Northern Group 1970–77; Chair. C. Price & Son Ltd 1977–82; Chair. Williams Holdings (later Williams PLC) 1982–2000; Deputy Chair. Raine Industries 1992–94 (Chair. (non-exec.) 1986–92); Dir Pilkington PLC 1994, Chair. 1995–2006; Deputy Chair. Boots PLC 2002, Chair. 2003–06, Chair. Alliance Boots PLC (after merger with Alliance Unichem) 2006–07; Chair. (non-exec.) Pendragon PLC 1989–, East Midlands Electricity 1994–97 (Dir 1990–97), Kidde 2000–03, BAA plc 2007–; Deputy Chair. Invensys plc Jan.–July 2009, Chair. July 2009–; Dir (non-exec.) Williams Man. Services 1985–96, Westminster Securities 1987–96, Gartmore Value Investment 1989–93, Gartmore 1993–96, Derby Pride 1993–98, Mithras Investment Trust 1994–98, Barclays Bank 1996–2009 (Deputy Chair. 2004–09), BAE Systems 2006–, Sappi Ltd 2006–; mem. European Round Table of Industrialists –2001, Council CBI 1999–; mem. Chartered Accountants' Co.; DL Derbyshire 1996; Freeman, City of London; Hon. DTech (Loughborough) 1998; Hon. DUniv (Derby) 1998. *Leisure interests;* golf, skiing, theatre, field sports. *Address:* Invensys plc, Portland House, Bressenden Place, London, SW1E 5BF, England (office). *Telephone:* (20) 7834-3848 (office). *Fax:* (20) 7834-3879 (office). *Website:* www.invensys.com (office).

RUDD, Kevin, BA; Australian politician; *Prime Minister;* b. 21 Sept. 1957, Nambour, Queensland; m. Therese Rudd; two s. one d.; ed Australian Nat. Univ.; joined Dept of Foreign Affairs and Trade 1981, worked in Embassies in Stockholm and Beijing; Chief of Staff to Queensland State Opposition Leader 1988–92; Premier, Queensland State Govt 1989–92, Dir-Gen. of Cabinet 1992–95; China Consultant, KPMG 1996–98; Adjunct Prof. of Asian Languages, Univ. of Queensland 1997–; mem. Parl. (Labor Party) for Griffith 1998–, Chair. Fed. Parl. Labor Party's Cttee on Foreign Affairs, Defence and Trade 1998–2001, Shadow Minister for Foreign Affairs 2001–04, Shadow Minister for Foreign Affairs and Int. Security 2004–05, Shadow Minister for Foreign Affairs, Trade and Int. Security 2005–07; Leader, Australian Labor Party 2006–; Prime Minister 2007–; mem. Australian-American Leadership Dialogue; mem. Advisory Council, Australia-Asia Centre, Korea-Australia Centre. *Publications include:* numerous articles on Chinese politics. *Address:* Australian Labor Party (ALP), POB 6222, Kingston, ACT 2604 (office); Griffith Electorate Office, POB 476A, 653 Wynnum Road, Morningside, Brisbane, Qld 4170, Australia (office). *Telephone:* (2) 6120-0800 (office); (7) 3899-4031 (office). *Fax:* (7) 3899-5755 (office). *Website:* www.pm.gov.au (office); www.kevinrudd.com.

RUDDEN, Bernard (Anthony), LLD, DCL, FBA; British professor of law; *Professor Emeritus, University of Oxford;* b. 21 Aug. 1933, Carlisle; s. of John Rudden and Kathleen Rudden; m. Nancy Campbell 1957; three s. one d.; ed City of Norwich School and St John's Coll., Cambridge; Fellow and Tutor, Oriel Coll. Oxford 1965–79; Prof. of Comparative Law, Univ. of Oxford and Fellow, Brasenose Coll. Oxford 1979–99, Prof. Emer. 1999–; Hon. LLD (McGill) 1979. *Publications:* Soviet Insurance Law 1966, The New River 1985, Basic Community Cases 1987, Source-Book on French Law (co-author) 1991, Basic Community Law (co-author) 1996, Law of Property 2002. *Address:* 15 Redinnick Terrace, Penzance, Cornwall, TR18 4HR, England (home). *Telephone:* (1736) 360395 (home). *E-mail:* bernard.rudden@law.ox.ac.uk (office).

RUDDLE, Francis Hugh, PhD, FAAS; American biologist and academic; *Professor Emeritus of Biology and Human Genetics, Yale University;* b. 19 Aug. 1929, West New York, NJ; s. of Thomas Hugh Ruddle and Mary Henley (née Rodda); m. Nancy Marion Hartman 1964; two d.; ed Wayne State Univ., Detroit and Univ. of California, Berkeley; Research Assoc., Child Research Center of Mich., Detroit 1953–56; NIH Postdoctoral Fellow, Dept of Biochem., Univ. of Glasgow, Scotland 1960–61; Asst Prof., Yale Univ. 1961–67, Assoc. Prof. 1967–72, Prof. of Biology and Human Genetics 1972, Chair. Dept of Biology 1977–83, 1988, Ross Granville Harrison Prof. of Biology 1983–88, Sterling Prof. of Biology 1988, now Prof. Emer.; Pres. American Soc. of Human Genetics 1985; Pres. American Soc. of Cell Biology 1986; mem. NAS, American Genetic Asscn, American Soc. of Biological Chemists, American Soc. of Zoologists, Genetics Soc. of America. *Leisure interest:* boating. *Address:* Department of Molecular, Cellular and Developmental Biology, Yale University, Kline Biology Tower, KBT 1010A, New Haven, CT 06511 USA (office). *Telephone:* (203) 432-3520 (office). *Fax:* (203) 432-5690 (office). *E-mail:* frank.ruddle@yale.edu (home). *Website:* www.biology.yale.edu (office).

RUDDOCK, Joan Mary, BSc, ARCS; British politician; b. 28 Dec. 1943; d. of Ken Anthony and Eileen Anthony; m. Dr Keith Ruddock 1963 (died 1996); ed Pontypool Grammar School for Girls and Imperial Coll. London; worked for Shelter (nat. campaign for the homeless) 1968–73; Dir Oxford Housing Aid Centre 1973–77; Special Programmes Officer with unemployed young people, Manpower Services Comm. 1977–79; Man., Reading Citizens Advice Bureau 1979–87; Chair. Campaign for Nuclear Disarmament (CND) 1981–85, Vice-Chair. 1985–86; MP for Lewisham Deptford 1987–; mem. Select Cttee on Televising House of Commons; mem. British Del., Council of Europe 1988–89; Shadow Spokesperson on Transport 1989–92, on Home Affairs 1992–94, on Environmental Protection 1994–97; Parl. UnderSec. of State for Women 1997–98; Co-Founder Women Say No to GMOs 1999; mem. Select Cttee on Modernization 2001–05, Select Cttee on Environment, Food and Rural Affairs 2003–05, Select Cttee of Int. Devt 2005–; Founder and Co-ordinator UK Women's Link with Afghan Women 2001; Labour; Hon. Fellow, Goldsmith's Coll., Univ. of London 1996, Laban Centre, London; Frank Cousins Peace Award 1984. *Publications:* CND Scrapbook 1987, The CND Story (contrib.)

1983, Voices for One World (contrib.) 1988. *Leisure interests:* gardening, music, art. *Address:* House of Commons, Westminster, London, SW1A 0AA, England (office). *Telephone:* (20) 7219-4513 (office). *Fax:* (20) 7219-6045 (office). *E-mail:* adamss@parliament.uk (office). *Website:* www.joanruddock.org.uk (office).

RUDDOCK, Hon. Philip M., BA, LLB; Australian solicitor and politician; b. 12 March 1943, Canberra; s. of the Hon. Max S. Ruddock; m. Heather Ruddock 1971; two d.; ed Barker Coll., Horsby, Sydney Univ.; Shadow Minister for ACT and Shadow Minister Assisting Opposition Leader on Public Service Matters 1983–84, Immigration and Ethnic Affairs 1984–85, 1989–93, Shadow Minister for Social Security and Sr Citizens 1993, mem. Shadow Cabinet 1996; Minister for Immigration and Multicultural Affairs 1996–2001, also Minister Assisting Prime Minister for Reconciliation 1998–2001, 2002–03, Minister for Immigration and Multicultural and Indigenous Affairs 2001–02; Attorney Gen. 2003–07. *Leisure interests:* jogging, bushwalking, gardening, opera, reading. *Address:* PO Box 6022, House of Representatives, Parliament House, Canberra 2600 (office); Level 3, 20 George Street, Hornsby, NSW 2077, Australia. *Telephone:* (2) 6277-7300 (office). *Fax:* (2) 6273-4102 (office). *Website:* www.ruddockmp.com.au.

RUDENSTINE, Neil Leon, PhD; American university administrator and academic; *Chairman, ARTstor Inc.;* b. 21 Jan. 1935, Ossining, NY; s. of Harry Rudenstine and Mae Rudenstine; m. Angelica Zander 1960; one s. two d.; ed Princeton Univ., Oxford Univ., Harvard Univ.; instructor, English Dept, Harvard Univ. 1964–66, Asst Prof. 1966–68, Prof. of English and Pres., Harvard Univ. 1991–2001, now Pres. Emer.; Assoc. Prof. of English, Princeton Univ. 1968–73, Dean of Students 1968–72, Prof. of English 1973–88, Dean of Coll. 1972–77, Provost 1977–88, now Provost Emer.; Exec. Vice-Pres. Andrew W. Mellon Foundation, New York 1988–91; mem. Council on Foreign Relations; Chair. of the Advisory Bd, ARTstor Inc. 2001–, also Chair. Bd of Trustees; mem. Bd of Dirs New York Public Library, Goldman Sachs Foundation; mem. Council on Foreign Relations, American Philosophical Soc., Cttee for Econ. Devt; Trustee Princeton Univ., New York Public Library, Goldman Sachs Foundation, Courtauld Inst. of Art, American Acad. in Berlin, Barnes Foundation, Council on Econ. Devt; Fellow, American Acad. of Arts and Sciences; Hon. Fellow, New Coll., Oxford, Emmanuel Coll., Cambridge; Dr hc (Harvard, Oxford, Princeton, Yale). *Publications:* Sidney's Poetic Development 1967, English Poetic Satire: Wyatt to Byron (with George Rousseau) 1972, In Pursuit of the PhD (with William G. Bowen) 1992, Pointing Our Thoughts 2001. *Address:* 41 Armour Road, Princeton, NJ 08540 USA (home); ARTstor, 151 East 61st Street, New York NY 10021 (office). *Telephone:* (212) 500-2420 (office); (609) 683-7516 (home). *Fax:* (212) 500-2418 (office). *Website:* www.artstor.org (office).

RUDIN, Alexander Izraliyevich; Russian cellist and conductor; *Artistic Director and Chief Conductor, Musica Viva Chamber Orchestra;* b. 25 Nov. 1960, Moscow; m. Rudina Olga Ryurikovna; two s.; ed Gnessin Music Inst., Moscow State Conservatory; has appeared as a soloist with numerous orchestras including Royal Philharmonic, Danish Radio, St Petersburg Philharmonic, Moscow Philharmonic, Austrian Symphony, Bolshoi Theatre; has worked as conductor with orchestras in Finland, Germany, Italy, Norway, Russia; has participated in festivals in Edin., Istanbul, Kuhmo, Vaasa; Artistic Dir and Chief Conductor Musica Viva Chamber Orchestra 1987–; Artistic Dir Int. Festival Music Ensembles; Prof., Moscow State Conservatory; Visiting Prof. Sibelius Acad., Helsinki; winner of Concertino Prague 1973, J. S. Bach Competition, Leipzig 1976, Nat. Competition, Vilnius 1977. *Address:* Vrubel Hall, 10/12 Lavrushinsky Pereulok, Moscow; Malaya Ostroumovskaya str. 1/10, Apt. 46, 107014 Moscow, Russia (home). *Telephone:* (495) 241-6881 (office); (495) 268-15-77 (home). *Fax:* (926) 220-4009 (office). *E-mail:* musica-viva@mail.ru (office). *Website:* musicaviva.ru/eng (office).

RUDIN, Scott; American film and theatre producer; b. 14 July 1958, New York; production asst, asst to theatre producers Kermit Bloomgarden and Robert Whitehead; Casting Dir, Producer with Edgar Scherick; Exec. Vice-Pres. Production 20th Century Fox 1984–86, Pres. Production 1986–87; f. Scott Rudin Productions 1990–. *Films produced:* He Makes Me Feel Like Dancing 1982 (Outstanding Children's Program Emmy Award 1982, Feature Documentary Acad. Award 1982), Mrs Soffel 1984, Flatliners 1990, Pacific Heights 1990, Regarding Henry 1991, Little Man Tate 1991, The Addams Family 1991, Sister Act 1992, Jennifer Eight 1992, Life With Mikey 1993, The Firm 1993, Searching for Bobby Fischer 1993, Sister Act 2 1993, Addams Family Values 1993, I.Q. 1994, Nobody's Fool 1994, Sabrina 1995, Clueless 1995, Up Close and Personal 1996, Ransom 1996, Marvin's Room 1996, The First Wives' Club 1996, In and Out 1997, Twilight 1998, The Truman Show 1998, A Civil Action 1998, Wonder Boys 1999, Rules of Engagement 1999, Brokeback Mountain 1999, Angela's Ashes 1999, Bringing Out the Dead 1999, Sleepy Hollow 1999, Shaft 2000, Rules of Engagement 2000, Zoolander 2001, The Royal Tenenbaums 2001, Iris: A Memoir of Iris Murdoch 2001, Orange County 2002, The Hours 2002, Changing Lanes 2002, Marci X 2003, The School of Rock 2003, The Stepford Wives 2004, The Manchurian Candidate 2004, The Village 2004, I Heart Huckabees 2004, Team America: World Police 2004, The Life Aquatic with Steve Zissou 2004, Closer 2004, Lemony Snicket's A Series of Unfortunate Events 2004, Freedomland 2005, Failure to Launch 2006, The Queen 2006, Venus 2006, Notes on a Scandal 2006, No Country for Old Men 2007, Margot at the Wedding 2007, The Darjeeling Limited 2007, Nothing Is Private 2007, There Will Be Blood 2007, The Other Boleyn Girl 2008, Stop Loss 2008. *Theatre:* Passion 1994 (Tony Award Best Musical 1994), Indiscretions 1995, Hamlet 1995, Seven Guitars 1995, A Funny Thing Happened on the Way to the Forum 1996, Skylight 1997, On the Town (New York Shakespeare Festival) 1997, The Chairs 1998, The Judas Kiss 1998, Closer (London) 1998, Amy's View 1999, Wide Guys 1999, Copenhagen 1999 (Tony Award). *Address:* Scott Rudin Productions, 10th Floor, 120 West 45th Street, New York, NY 10036; c/o Miramax Films Inc., 8439 West Sunset Blvd, West Hollywood, CA 90069, USA.

RUDINI, Gen.; Indonesian army officer; b. 15 Dec. 1929, Malang, E. Java; s. of R. I. Poespohandojo and R. A. Koesbandijah; m. Oddyana Rudini 1959; one s. two d.; ed Breda Mil. Acad., Netherlands, reaching rank of Second Lt; Commdr Kostrad Infantry/Airborne Brigade 1972–73; Commdr Indonesian contingent of UN Peace-keeping Force in Middle East 1973–76; Commdr Kostrad Airborne Combat 1976–81; Commdr N. and Cen. Sulawesi Mil. Region, Manado 1981, later Commdr of Kostrad; Chief of Staff, Indonesian Army 1983–88; Minister of Home Affairs 1988–93, concurrently Chair. of the Election Cttee. *Leisure interests:* sport, music. *Address:* c/o Ministry of Home Affairs, Jalan Merdeka Utara 7, Jakarta Pusat, Indonesia.

RUDMAN, Michael P.; American publishing executive; b. 1950, New York; ed Univ of Michigan and New York Univ; Pres. and CEO Nat. Learning Corpn, also Dir; Pres. and CEO Delaney Books Inc., also Dir; Pres. Frank Merriwell Inc., also CEO, Dir; mem. Asscn of American Publishers. *Address:* National Learning Corporation, 212 Michael Drive, Syosset, NY 11791, USA. *Website:* www.passbooks.com.

RUDMAN, Warren Bruce, LLB; American fmr politician and lawyer; *Co-Chairman, Stonebridge International LLC;* b. 18 May 1930, Boston, Mass.; s. of Edward G. Rudman and Theresa (née Levenson) Rudman; m. Shirley Wahl 1952; one s. two d.; ed Valley Forge Mil. Acad., Syracuse Univ., Boston Coll. Law School; rank of Capt. US Army 1952–54; admitted to NH Bar, mem. law firm Stein, Rudman and Gormley 1960–69; Attorney-Gen. NH, Concord 1970–76; Pnr Sheehan, Phinney, Bass and Green 1976–80; Fiscal Agent Gov. Walter Peterson's campaign 1968, Special Counsel to Gov. Peterson 1969–70; Republican Senator from NH 1980–92; co-founder Concord Coalition 1992–; Deputy Chair. Fed. Reserve Bank of Boston 1993; Pnr Paul, Weiss, Rifkind, Wharton and Garrison LLP 1993–; Co-Chair. Stonebridge International LLC; Founder, Chair. Bd Trustees Daniel Webster Jr Coll., New England Aeronautical Inst. 1965–81; fmr mem. Sr Advisory Cttee, John F. Kennedy School of Govt, Harvard Univ.; fmr Dir Chubb Corpn, Raytheon Corpn, Dreyfus Corpn; mem. American Legion, Sub-Cttee on Defense Co-operation of the North Atlantic Ass., Sec. of State's Advisory Panel on Overseas Security; Bronze Star. *Address:* Stonebridge International LLC, 555 Thirteenth Street, NW Suite 300 West, Columbia Square, Washington, DC 20004-1109, USA (office). *Telephone:* (202) 223-7320 (home). *Fax:* (202) 637-8600 (office). *E-mail:* wrudman@stonebridge-international.com (office). *Website:* www.stonebridge-international.com (office).

RUELLE, David Pierre, PhD; French research mathematician and physicist; *Professor Emeritus, Institut des Hautes Etudes Scientifiques;* b. 20 Aug. 1935, Ghent, Belgium; s. of Pierre Ruelle and Marguerite de Jonge; m. Janine Lardinois 1960; one s. two d.; ed high school at Mons and Free Univ. of Brussels; Research Asst and Privatdozent, ETH, Zürich 1960–62; mem. Inst. for Advanced Study, Princeton, NJ, USA 1962–64; mem. Acad. des Sciences 1985, Academia Europaea 1993; Foreign Assoc. NAS 2002–; Foreign mem. Accad. Nazionale dei Lincei 2003–; Foreign Hon. mem. American Acad. of Arts and Sciences 1992; Hon. Prof., Institut des Hautes Etudes Scientifiques, Bures-sur-Yvette 1964–2000; Chevalier, Légion d'honneur; Dannie Heineman Prize 1985, Boltzmann Medal 1986, Matteuci Medal 2004, Henri Poincaré Prize 2006. *Publications:* Statistical Mechanics: Rigorous Results 1969, Thermodynamic Formalism 1978, Elements of Differentiable Dynamics and Bifurcation Theory 1989, Chance and Chaos 1991. *Address:* I.H.E.S., 91440 Bures-sur-Yvette (office); 1 avenue Charles-Comar, 91440 Bures-sur-Yvette, France (home). *Telephone:* 1-60-92-66-52 (office); 1-69-07-61-52 (home). *Website:* www.ihes.fr/~ruelle (office).

RUFIN, Jean-Christophe, MD; French writer and doctor; *Ambassador to Senegal;* b. 28 June 1952, Bourges; s. of Marcel Rufin and Denise Bonneau; one s. two d.; ed Lycées Janson-de-Sailly and Claude Bernard, Paris, Pitié-Salpêtrière School of Medicine, Paris, Institut d'études politiques, Paris; Hosp. Intern, Paris 1975–81, Dir of Clinic and Asst Hôpitaux de Paris 1981–83, attaché Hôpitaux de Paris 1983–86; Chief of Mission of Sec. of State for Human Rights 1986–88; Cultural Attaché French Embassy in Brazil 1989–90; Vice-Pres. Médecins sans Frontières 1991–93; Adviser to Minister of Defence 1993–95; Dr, Nanterre Hosp. 1994–95; Practitioner, Saint Antoine Hospital, Paris 1995–98; Dir French Red Cross 1994–96, Inst. Pasteur, Groupe France Télévisions, l'Office français de protection des réfugiés et apatrides 2005–; Medical Dir, then Pres. Action contre la faim 2002–07; Amb. to Senegal (also accred to Gabon) 2007–; Lecturer, Inst. d'études politiques 1991–2002, Univ. Paris XIII-Nord 1993–95, Coll. interarmée de défense; Dir of Research, Inst. des relations ints et stratégiques 1996–99; mem. Supervisory Bd Express-Expansion Group 2005; mem. Acad. Française 2008–; Chevalier des Arts et des Lettres, Chevalier de la Légion d'Honneur; Dr hc (Laval Univ., Catholic Univ. of Louvain). *Publications:* Le Piège humanitaire 1986, L'Empire et les nouveaux barbares 1992, La Dictature libérale (Prix Jean-Jacques Rousseau) 1994, L'Aventure humanitaire 1994, L'Abyssin (Prix Goncourt, Prix Méditerranée) 1997, Sauver Ispahan 1998, Les Causes perdues (Prix Bergot, Prix Interallié) 1999, Rouge Brésil (Prix Goncourt) 2001, Globalia 2004, La Salamandre 2005, Le Parfum d'Adam 2006, Un Léopard sur le garrot 2008,. *Leisure interest:* mountain climbing. *Address:* Embassy of France, 1 rue El Hadj Amadou Assane Ndoye, BP 4035, Dakar, Senegal (office). *Telephone:* 33-839-5100 (office). *Fax:* 33-839-5181 (office). *E-mail:* webmestre.dakar-amba@diplomatie.gouv.fr (office); acf12@wanadoo.fr (home). *Website:* www.ambafrance-sn.org (office).

RUGAR, Daniel, PhD; American scientist; *Manager, Nanoscale Studies, IBM Almaden Research Center;* ed Stanford Univ.; Research Assoc. in Applied

Physics, Stanford Univ.; joined IBM in 1984, contributed to early devts of atomic force microscopy, especially for imaging magnetic materials and for applications to data storage; currently Man. Nanoscale Studies, IBM Almaden Research Center, San Jose, Calif.; has received IBM internal awards for contribs to scanning probe microscopy, near field optical data storage and single spin detection 1999–2000, Distinguished Lecturer, IEEE Magnetic Soc., Scientific American 50 Award for research leadership in the field of imaging 2004, World Tech. Award in Materials, The World Tech. Network (co-recipient) 2005. *Achievements include:* co-inventor thermo-mechanical recording technique that is basis of IBM 'Millipede' AFM storage device; pioneered mechanical detection of ultrasmall forces, achieving current record of 800 zeptonewtons in a 1 Hertz bandwidth; made first demonstrations of magnetic resonance force microscopy (MRFM) 1992, work reached key milestone with manipulation and detection of individual electron spin 2004. *Publications:* more than 100 scientific papers in professional journals on scanning microscopy; 20 patents. *Address:* IBM Almaden Research Center, Mailstop K13/D1, 650 Harry Road, San Jose, CA 95120-6099, USA (office). *Telephone:* (408) 927-2027 (office). *Fax:* (408) 927-2100 (office). *E-mail:* rugar@almaden .ibm.com (office). *Website:* almaden.ibm.com (office).

RUGARLI, Giampaolo; Italian writer; b. 5 Dec. 1932, Naples; s. of Mirko Rugarli and Rubina De Marco; m. Maria Pulci 1985; three c.; ed legal studies; bank dir since 1972; a dir of Cariplo 1981–85; contrib. Messaggero and Corriere della Sera and other reviews; Premio Bagutta Opera Prima 1987; Premio Capri 1990, Premio Selezione Campiello. *Publications:* Il Superlativo assoluto, La troga, Il nido di ghiaccio, Diario di un uomo a disagio, Andromeda e la notte, L'orrore che mi hai dato 1987, Una montagna australiana 1992, Per i pesci non è un problema 1992, I camini delle fate 1993, Il manuale del romanziere (The Novelist's Handbook) 1993, L'infinito, forse 1995, Una gardenia ni capilli 1997, Il bruno dei crepuscoli (Leopardi) 1998, La Viaggiatrici del tram numero 4 2001, Il Cavaliere e la vendita della saggezza 2002, La mia Milano 2003, I giardini incantati 2005, La luna di Malcontenta 2006, Il buio di notte 2008. *Leisure interest:* gardening. *Address:* Via Colle di Giano 62, Olevano Romano 00035, Italy. *Telephone:* (06) 9564518.

RUGGIERO, Renato; Italian diplomatist; *Senior Adviser, Citigroup;* b. 9 April 1930, Naples; ed Univ. of Naples; entered diplomatic service 1955; served in São Paulo, Moscow, Washington, DC; Counsellor, Belgrade 1966; Counsellor for Social Affairs, Perm. Mission to European Communities 1969; Chef de Cabinet Pres. of Comm. of European Communities 1970–73, Dir-Gen. of Regional Policy 1973–77, Comm. Spokesperson 1977; Co-ordinator EEC Dept, Ministry of Foreign Affairs 1978; Diplomatic Counsellor of Pres. of Council 1979; Chef de Cabinet of Minister of Foreign Affairs 1979; Perm. Rep. to European Communities 1980–84; Dir-Gen. for Econ. Affairs, Ministry of Foreign Affairs 1984–85; Sec.-Gen. Ministry of Foreign Affairs 1985–87, Minister of Foreign Trade 1987–91; Dir-Gen. WTO 1995–99; Chair. ENI June–Sept. 1999; Vice-Chair. Schroder Salomon Smith Barney Int., Chair. Schroder Salomon Smith Barney Italy 2000; Minister of Foreign Affairs 2001–02; Vice-Chair. Citigroup's European Investment Bank and Chair., Citigroup Switzerland, Zurich 2002, currently Sr Adviser and mem. European Advisory Bd, Citigroup; Chair. Int. Advisory Bd, Unicredit HVB; Personal Rep. of Pres. of Council, Econ. Summits Bonn 1978, Tokyo 1979, Venice 1980, London 1984, Bonn 1985, Tokyo 1986, Venice 1987; Pres. Exec. Cttee OECD; Hon. KCMG; Kt, Grand Cross, Order of Merit. *Address:* Citigroup, Foro Buonaparte 16, 20121 Milan, Italy (office). *Telephone:* (2) 86484212 (office). *Fax:* (2) 86484222 (office). *E-mail:* renato.ruggiero@citi.com (office). *Website:* www.citibank.com (office).

RUGGIERO, Riccardo; Italian telecommunications industry executive; *Managing Director, Executive Director and Member of Strategy Committee, Telecom Italia SpA;* b. 26 Aug. 1960, Naples; s. of Renato Ruggiero; Sales Man. Fininvest SpA 1986–88; Sales and Marketing Man. AT&T Italia 1988–90; Asst to CEO, Olivetti Group 1990, Vice-Pres. Int. Customers and Communications Sales Devt 1992–94, Vice-Pres. Telemedia Sales and Marketing Devt 1994–96, CEO Infostrada (subsidiary co.) 1996–2001, also CEO Italia On Line 1996–99; joined Telecom Italia Group 2001, Head, Telecom France Business Unit 2001, CEO Telecom Italia Domestic Wireline Business Unit 2001–02, CEO Telecom Italia SpA 2002–07, CEO of Operations 2005, currently Man. Dir, Exec. Dir and Mem. of Strategy Cttee; mem. Bd of Dirs Societa Azionaria Fabbrica Italiana Lavorazione Occhiali SpA 2005–. *Address:* Telecom Italia SpA, Corso d'Italia 41, 00198 Rome, Italy (office). *Telephone:* (6) 3688-2840 (office). *Fax:* (6) 3688-2803 (office). *Website:* www.telecomitalia.com (office).

RÜHE, Volker; German politician; *Chairman, Bundestag Foreign Policy Committee;* b. 25 Sept. 1942, Hamburg; m. Anne Rühe 1968; two s. one d.; ed Univ. of Hamburg; fmr teacher; mem. Hamburg City Council 1970–76; mem. Bundestag 1976–, Chair. Foreign Policy Cttee 2002–; Deputy Chair. CDU/CSU Parl. Group 1982–89, 1998–; Sec. Gen. CDU 1989–92, Deputy Party Leader 1998–2002; Minister of Defence 1992–98. *Address:* Deutscher Bundestag, Platz der Republik 1, 11011 Berlin (office). *Telephone:* (30) 22773610 (office). *E-mail:* volker.ruehe@bundestag.de (office). *Website:* www .bundestag.de (home).

RUHUL AMIN, M. M., LLB, MA; Bangladeshi judge; *Chief Justice of Bangladesh;* b. 23 Dec. 1942, Laxmipur; ed Dhaka Univ., Nat. Judicial Coll., USA; began career as asst judge in fmr East Pakistan, promoted to dist judge 1984, served courts in Chittagong, Cox's Bazar, Kishoreganj and Jessore, visited several US courts to learn about alternative dispute resolution and court admin 1990, apptd High Court Judge 1994, visited Sri Lanka, India and Nepal to learn about their judicial services and salary structure of judges; Judge, Sr Appellate Div., Supreme Court of Bangladesh 2003–08; Chair. Judicial Service Comm. 2004–08; Chief Justice of Bangladesh 2008–. *Address:* Supreme Court of Bangladesh, Dhaka 2, Bangladesh (office).

RUIJGH, Cornelis Jord, DPhil; Dutch academic; *Professor Emeritus of Ancient Greek Language, University of Amsterdam;* b. 28 Nov. 1930, Amsterdam; s. of Jord Ruijgh and Trijntje Swart; ed Univ. of Amsterdam and Ecole Pratique des Hautes Etudes, Paris; Asst in Greek Philology, Univ. of Amsterdam 1954–66, Lecturer in Ancient Greek Language 1966–69, Prof. of Ancient Greek Language, Dialectology and Mycenology 1969–95, Prof. Emer. 1995–; mem. Royal Netherlands Acad., Int. Perm. Cttee of Mycenaean Studies 1970–; Prix Zographos 1957, Michael Ventris Memorial Award 1968. *Publications:* L'élément achéen dans la langue épique, 1957, Etudes sur la grammaire et le vocabulaire du grec mycénien 1967, Autour de 'te épique' 1971, Scripta Minora I 1991, Scripta Minora II 1996 etc. *Leisure interest:* music. *Address:* Keizersgracht 800, 1017 ED Amsterdam, Netherlands. *Telephone:* (20) 6247995.

RUINI, HE Cardinal Camillo; Italian ecclesiastic; *Vicar General of Rome;* b. 19 Feb. 1931, Sassuolo; ed Pontifical Gregorian Univ. and Almo Collegio Capranica, Rome, Italy; ordained priest 1954; returned to Reggio Emilia and taught philosophy at diocesan seminary until 1968; taught dogmatic theology at Studio Teologico Interdiocesano di Modena-Reggio-Emilia-Carpi-Guastalla 1968–86, Headmaster 1968–77; taught dogmatic theology at Studio Teologico Accademico Bolognese 1977–83; Chaplain to Catholic Univ. grads 1958–66; Del. for Catholic Action 1966–70; Pres. John XXIII Diocesan Cultural Centre 1968; Auxiliary Bishop of Reggio Emilia and Guastalla and Titular Bishop of Nepte 1983; Vice-Pres. Preparatory Cttee, Ecclesial Convention of Lorreto 1985; elected mem. Bishops' Comm. for Catholic Educ., Culture and School 1985; Sec.-Gen. Italian Episcopal Conf. 1986, Pres. 1991–2007; mem. Cen. Cttee for Marian Year 1987–88; Consultor, Congregation for Bishops 1988–; elected mem. Council of Gen. Secr., 8th Gen. Ass. of Synod of Bishops 1990; Archbishop and Pro-Vicar Gen. of Pope for Diocese of Rome 1991, Vicar Gen. and Archpriest of Patriarchal Lateran Basilica, Grand Chancellor Pontifical Lateran Univ. and Pres. Emer. Peregrinatio ad Petri Sedem 1991–; Relator for Special Ass. for Europe of Synod of Bishops, Vatican City 1991; cr. Cardinal (Cardinal Priest of S. Agnese fuori le mura) 1991; mem. Cttee of the Great Jubilee of the Year 2000. *Publications:* has published many essays and research work since 1971. *Address:* Piazza S Giovanni in Laterano 4, 00184 Roma, Italy (office). *Telephone:* (06) 6988-6436 (office). *Website:* www.vatican .va (office).

RUITENBERG, Elis Joost, DVM, PhD; Dutch professor of immunology; b. 24 May 1937, Amersfoort; s. of E J. Ruitenberg and D. H. van Mechelen; m. Christiane Friederike Ambagtsheer 1963; three d.; ed Univ. of Utrecht; veterinarian, Lab. Zoonoses, Nat. Inst. of Public Health, Bilthoven 1964, Head Pathology Lab. 1970–86, Dir Div. of Immunology 1979, Vaccine Production 1980–86, Dir Div. of Microbiology and Immunology, Nat. Inst. of Public and Environmental Protection, Bilthoven 1984, Deputy Dir-Gen. –1986; Prof. of Veterinary Immunology, Univ. of Utrecht 1984, now Prof. Emer.; Gen. and Scientific Dir Sanquin Blood Supply Foundation (CLB) 1989–2001; Prof. of Int. Healthcare, Vrije Universiteit, Amsterdam 2001–; Chair. Netherlands-Vietnam Medical Cttee 1998–; mem. Non-exec. Bd AGLAIA BioMedical Ventures B.V.; Visiting Prof., Nat. School of Public Health, Madrid, Spain 1987; retd, mem. numerous advisory cttees including Advisory Council for Devt Research, Advisory Bd Royal Numico N.V.; mem. Royal Netherlands Acad. of Arts and Sciences; Schimmel Viruly Award 1976, Annual Award, Nat. Journal of Veterinary Medicine 1977, Award Medical Acad., Poznan, Poland, Kt, Order of Netherlands Lion 1988, Schornagel Award 1996. *Publications include:* Anisakiasis, Pathogenesis, Diagnosis and Prevention 1970, Preventive Screening of Adults (with D.A.T. Griffiths) 1987, Statistical Analysis and Mathematical Modelling of AIDS (with J.C. Jager) 1988, AIDS Impact Assessment Modelling and Scenario Analysis (with J.C. Jager) 1992; numerous articles on immunology, vaccinology, pathology and parasitology. *Leisure interests:* European languages, history, cycling. *Address:* c/o Non-Executive Board, AGLAIA BioMedical Ventures B.V., Professor Bronkhorstlaan 10-XI, 3723 MB Bilthoven, Netherlands. *Telephone:* (30) 2296090. *Fax:* (30) 2296099. *E-mail:* info@aglaia-biomedical.com. *Website:* www.aglaia-biomedical.com.

RUIZ, Hector de Jesus, BEng, MEng, DEng, PhD; Mexican business executive; *Chairman and CEO, Advanced Micro Devices (AMD), Inc.;* b. 25 Dec. 1945, Piedras Negras, Coahuila; m. 1st (deceased); one s.; m. 2nd Judy Ruiz; two step-c.; ed Univ. of Texas, Austin, Rice Univ.; held various positions with Texas Instruments; fmr Pres. Semiconductor Products Sector, Motorola; COO and Pres. Advanced Micro Devices (AMD), Inc. 2000–02, CEO 2002–, Chair. 2004–; Chair. Spansion Inc.; mem. Bd of Dirs Eastman Kodak Co., Semiconductor Industry Asscn; mem. Pres.'s Council of Advisors for Science and Tech., Hispanic Professional Engineers; Fellow, Int. Eng Consortium 2002–; Hispanic Engineer Nat. Awards Conference Hall of Fame 2000. *Address:* Advanced Micro Devices, Inc., 1 AMD Place, Sunnyvale, CA 94088, USA (office). *Telephone:* (408) 749-4000 (office). *Fax:* (408) 749-4291 (office). *Website:* www.amd.com (office).

RUIZ, Raoul; Chilean film director and scriptwriter; b. 25 July 1941, Puerto Montt; m. Valeria Sarmiento; ed Univ. of Chile; began career in avant-garde theatre writing over 100 plays 1956–62; first feature film 1968; fled Chile during fascist coup 1973, settled in Paris, France; mem. jury Cannes Film Festival 2002. *Films include:* Tres tristes tigres (Golden Leopard, Locarno International Film Festival 1969) 1968, Que hacer? 1972, La Expropriacion 1974, Colloque de chiens (César Award) 1977, L'Hypothèse du tableau volé 1978, Les trois couronnes du matelot 1983, Les Destins de Manoel (KNF Award, Rotterdam Int. Film Festival) 1985, L'Ile au trésor 1991, Dark at noon 1992, L'Oeil qui ment 1993, Trois vies et une seule mort (Critics Award, São Paulo International Film Festival 1996) 1996, Généalogies d'un crime (Silver Bear, Berlin Int. Film Festival) 1997, Le Temps Retrouvé 1998, Shattered Image 1998, Comédie de l'innocence 2000, Combat d'amour en songe

(FIPRESCI Prize) 2000, Les Âmes fortes 2001, Cofralandes, rapsodia chilena (FIPRESCI Prize) 2002, Ce jour-là 2003, Días de campo 2004, Klimt 2005, Le Domaine perdu 2005.

RUIZ-GALLARDÓN JÍMENEZ, Alberto; Spanish lawyer and politician; *Mayor of Madrid;* b. 11 Dec. 1958, Madrid; s. of José María Ruiz-Gallardón; m. María del Mar Utrera; four s.; ed Complutense Univ., Madrid, San Pablo CEU Univ.; began career working in prov. courts in Málaga; elected to Madrid City Council 1983; mem. Partido Popular Exec. 1986; elected as mem. Regional Parl. for Autonomous Community of Madrid 1987, spokesperson in the Senate for Partido Popular parl. group 1987–95; Pres. Community of Madrid 1995–2003; Mayor of Madrid 2003–; mem. Partido Popular. *Address:* Alcalde de Madrid, Palacio de Cibeles, Plaza de Cibeles 1, 4ª planta, 28014 Madrid, Spain (office). *Telephone:* (91) 5880022 (office). *Fax:* (91) 5882662 (office). *E-mail:* relinternacionales@munimadrid.es (office). *Website:* www.munimadrid.es (office).

RUIZ GUINAZU, Magdalena; Argentine journalist; b. 13 Feb. 1935, Buenos Aires; four c.; fmr mem. Comision Nacional por la desaparicion de Personas (National Commission on the Disappearance of People); currently host Magdalena Tempranisimo, Radio Continental and La vuelta con Magdalena (Back with Magadalena) 2002–; columnist La Nación and Pagina 12 newspapers; Co-founder and fmr Pres. Asociación para la Defensa del Periodismo Independiente (Asociación Periodistas) (press freedom org.); Officer, Legion d'Honneur, Order of Merit (Italy); Martin Fierro de Oro (Gold Martin Fierro Award) for Lifetime Achievement 1994, Int. Women's Media Foundation Lifetime Achievement Award 2003, Diamond Konex, Communication-Journalism 2007. *Publications include:* Huésped de un verano 1994, Había una vez...la vida 1995, Qué mundo nos ha tocado! (with Father Rafael Braun) 2001, Historias de hombres, mujeres y jazmines 2002. *Address:* c/o Asociación Periodistas, Piedras 1675 Oficina B, Secretaría de Derechos, 1140 Buenos Aires, Argentina. *E-mail:* magdalena@continental.com.ar (office). *Website:* www.continental.com.ar; www.magdalenatempranisimo.blogspot.com.

RUIZ MATEOS, Gerardo; Mexican business executive and politician; *Secretary of the Economy;* ed Instituto Tecnológico de Estudios Superiores de Monterrey; Dir Gen. Automotive Moulding Mexico (now Linde Pullman Mexico) 1989–; Pres. Mexican Foundation for Rural Devt 1995; mem. Nat. Action Party 1995–, Exec. Sec. Nat. Exec. Cttee 1996–98, mem. Cttee 2002–05; Pres. Surveillance Comm., Nat. Council 2001–02; Admin and Finance Coordinator, Felipe Calderón's Presidential Campaign 2005–06; Coordinator of Cabinets and Special Projects of the Pres.'s Office 2006–08; Sec. of the Economy 2008–; mem. Council of the Social Union of Mexican Businessmen 1996–2000, Pres. 2000. *Address:* Secretariat of State for the Economy, Alfonso Reyes 30, Col. Hipódromo Condesa, 06170 Mexico City, Mexico (office). *Telephone:* (55) 5729-9100 (office). *Fax:* (55) 5729-9320 (office). *Website:* www.economia.gob.mx (office).

RUKAVISHNIKOV, Aleksander Yulianovich; Russian sculptor; b. 2 July 1950, Moscow; s. of Yulian Rukavishnikov and of Anagelina Filippova; m. Olga Mikhailovna Rukavishnikova; one s.; ed Surikov Moscow State Inst. of Arts; freelance artist; Prof., Surikov Inst.; mem. Presidium, Russian Acad. of Fine Arts; mem. Union of Artists; People's Artist of the Russian Fed. *Major works include:* portraits: Feofan Grek 1977, Sergey of Radonezh 1981, Dmitry Donskoy 1982, Aleksander Peresvet 1983, John Lennon 1982, Tamara Bykova 1983; Vladimir Vysotsky memorial; installation Intrusion 1988; Tatishchev monument, Togliatti 1997; Dostoyevsky statue 1997, Nikulin monument 2000. *Address:* Bolshaya Molchanovka str. 10, Moscow (office); Granatny per. 11, Apt 30, 103001 Moscow, Russia (home). *Telephone:* (495) 290-67-60 (office); (495) 291-05-52 (home). *Fax:* (495) 291-01-52 (home).

RUKINGAMA, Luc, PhD; Burundian academic and fmr politician; *Senior Programme Specialist and Chief, Higher Education Unit, Regional Office for Education in Africa, United Nations Educational, Scientific and Cultural Organization (UNESCO);* b. 1952, Kiremba; m. Thérèse Niyonzima; two s. two d.; ed Sorbonne, Paris; mem. Parl.; fmr Minister for Higher Educ., for Cooperation, for Foreign Affairs and Cooperation; Minister of Communication and Govt Spokesman 2000–01; fmr Co-Pres. Union pour le Progrès National (UPRONA); unsuccessful presidential cand. 2001; currently Sr Programme Specialist and Chief of Higher Educ. Unit, UNESCO/BREDA; Chevalier, Ordre des Palmes Académiques, Medaille de l'Unité Nationale, UNESCO Medal. *Publications:* Voyage au Congo d'André Gide ou la stéréotype au cœur de l'image 1995; numerous articles. *Leisure interests:* reading, sport, music. *Address:* UNESCO Regional Office for Education in Africa, 12, avenue L. S. Senghor, Dakar, Senegal (office); Avenue de Juillet no 4, Kiriri, PO Box 1810, Bujumbura, Burundi (home). *Telephone:* 849-23-41 (office); 226561 (home). *Fax:* 226561 (home). *E-mail:* l.rukingama@unesco.org (office). *Website:* www.dakar.unesco.org/education_en/index.shtml (office).

RUKMANA, Siti Hardijanti; Indonesian business executive and politician; b. 1949; d. of the late Gen. Suharto (Pres. of Indonesia) and Siti Hartinah; m. Indra Rukmana Kowara; Pres. Citra Lamtoro Gung Persada (construction, pharmaceutical, telecommunications and media corpn); apptd Minister of Social Affairs 1998; presidential cand. 2004 elections; Chair. Indonesian Social Workers' Asscn, United Pvt Radio Broadcasting Service of Indonesia, Indonesian Blood Donor Asscn, Org. for Indonesian Youth; mem. Parti Karya Peduli Bangsa (PKPB). *Address:* Citra Lamtoro Gung Persada, Jakarta, Indonesia.

RULI, Genc, DEcon; Albanian economist, academic and politician; *Minister of Economy, Trade and Energy;* b. 4 Nov. 1958; m.; ed Univ. of Tirana; Lecturer in Econs, Univ. of Tirana 1982–90, Prof. of Finance and Accounting 1996–; Minister of Finance June-Dec. 1991, of Finance and the Econony 1992–93, of Economy, Trade and Energy 2007–; Deputy, People's Ass. for Tirana 1991, for Gjirokaster 1992–96, Chair. Perm. Parl. Comm. for Finance and Economy 1994–96; Chair. Bd of Govs Albanian Inst. of Insurance 1992–; Chair. Inst. for Contemporary Science 1996–2005; mem. Democratic Party of Albania. *Address:* Ministry of Economy, Trade and Energy, Bulevardi Dëshmorët e Kombit 2, Tirana, Albania (office). *Telephone:* (4) 227617 (office). *Fax:* (4) 234052 (office). *E-mail:* kabineti@mete.gov.al (office). *Website:* www.mete.gov.al (office).

RUMENS, Carol, PGDip, FRSL; British writer and poet; *Professor of Creative Writing, University of Hull;* b. (Carol-Ann Lumley), 10 Dec. 1944, London, England; m. David Rumens 1965 (divorced); two d.; ed Univ. of London and Arden School of Theatre, Manchester; Writing Fellow Univ. of Kent 1983–85; Northern Arts Writing Fellow 1988–90; Writer-in-Residence, Queen's Univ., Belfast 1991–, Univ. Coll., Cork 1994, Univ. of Stockholm 1999; Creative Writing Tutor, Queen's Univ. Belfast 1995–99, Univ. of Wales, Bangor 2000–; Prof. of Creative Writing, Univ. of Hull 2005–; mem. Int. PEN, Soc. of Authors, The Welsh Academi; Alice Hunt Bartlett Prize (Jt Winner) 1981, Prudence Farmer Award 1983, Cholmondeley Award 1984, First Prize, BT Section, Nat. Poetry Competition 2002, First Prize Peterloo Poetry Competition 2003. *Publications:* A Strange Girl in Bright Colours 1973, Unplayed Music 1981, Scenes from the Gingerbread House 1982, Star Whisper 1983, Direct Dialling 1985, Selected Poems 1987, Plato Park 1987, The Greening of the Snow Beach 1988, From Berlin to Heaven 1989, Thinking of Skins: New and Selected Poems 1993, Best China Sky 1995, The Miracle Diet (with Viv Quillin) 1997, Holding Pattern 1998, Hex 2002, Collected Poems 2004, Poems 1968–2004 2005; contrib. ed. of numerous anthologies; contrib. to periodicals; trans. poems for collections of Russian poetry. *Address:* 100A Tunis Road, London, W12 7EY, England. *Telephone:* (7917) 860326 (home). *E-mail:* c.rumens@hull.ac.uk (office); carol@rumens.fslife.co.uk (office).

RUMHI, Muhammad bin Hamad bin Saif al-; Omani petroleum engineer and government official; *Minister of Oil and Gas;* fmr Prof. of Petroleum Eng., Sultan Qaboos Univ.; Minister of Oil and Gas 1997–; Chair. Petroleum Devt Oman 2003–. *Address:* Ministry of Oil and Gas, POB 551, Muscat 113 (office); Petroleum Development Oman (PDO), Bait Saih Maleh Building, Mina Al Sahel Street, PO Box 81, 113 Muscat, Oman (office). *Telephone:* 24603333 (Ministry) (office); 24678111 (PDO) (office). *Fax:* 2469672 (Ministry) (office); 24677106 (PDO) (office). *E-mail:* external-affairs@pdo.co.om (office). *Website:* www.mog.gov.om (office); www.pdo.co.om (home).

RUML, Jan; Czech journalist and fmr politician; *Chairman, Olympic Watch;* b. 5 March 1953, Prague; m. Marie Ruml; two s.; ed grammar school, Prague, Faculty of Law, Univ. of Plzeň; stoker, woodcutter, hosp. technician, mechanic, bookseller, cattle-minder; signed Charter 77, Feb. 1977; freelance journalist 1977–79; mem. Cttee for Protection of the Unjustly Persecuted 1979–89; in custody, indicted for subversive activities 1981–82; co-founder Lidové noviny (monthly samizdat) 1988–90; spokesman of Charter 77 1990; First Deputy Minister of Interior of CSFR 1990–91; Deputy Minister of Interior 1991–92; mem. Civic Democratic Party (ODS) 1992–97; Deputy to House of Nations, Fed. Ass. June–Dec. 1992; Minister of Interior of Czech Repub. 1992–97; mem. Interdepartmental Anti-drug Comm. 1993–97, Comm. for Prevention of Crime 1994–97; mem. of Parl. 1996–98, Senator 1998–2004, Vice-Pres. of Senate (Parl.) 2000–04; Founder Freedom Union (US), Chair. 1998–99; Chair. Olympic Watch; Hon. Medal of the French Nat. Police 1992. *Films:* Hledání Pevného Bodu (Looking for a Stable Point). *Publication:* (with Jana Klusáková) What Was, Is and Will Be (in Czech). *Address:* Olympic Watch, Sokolska 18, 12000 Prague 2, Czech Republic (office). *E-mail:* info@olympicwatch.org (office). *Website:* www.olympicwatch.org (office); www.janruml.cz.

RUMMEL, Reinhard Franz, DrIng; German scientist and academic; *Professor of Physical Geodesy, Institut für Astronomische und Physikalische Geodäsie, Technische Universität München;* b. 3 Dec. 1945, Landshut; m. Renate Schophaus 1970; one s. one d.; ed Hans Leinberger Gymnasium, Technische Univ. Munich and Technische Hochschule, Darmstadt; Research Assoc. Dept of Geodetic Science, Ohio State Univ., Columbus, Ohio 1974–76; scientist, German Geodetic Research Inst. and Bavarian Acad. of Science, Munich 1976–80; Prof. of Physical Geodesy, Faculty of Geodetic Eng, Delft Univ. of Tech. 1980; currently Prof., Institut für Astronomische und Physikalische Geodäsie,Technische Uiversität München; mem. Netherlands Acad. of Science; Speuerwerkpreis, KIVI, Netherlands 1987. *Publications:* Zur Behandlung von Zufallsfunktionen und -folgen in der physikalischen Geodäsie 1975, Geodesy's Contribution to Geophysics 1984, Satellite Gradiometry 1986, Encyclopedia of Earth System Science, Vol. II (on geodesy) 1992. *Address:* Institut für Astronomische und Physikalische Geodäsie, Room 3610, Technische Universität München, Arcisstrasse 21, 80290 Munich, Germany (office). *Telephone:* (89) 28923190 (office). *Fax:* (89) 28923178 (office). *E-mail:* rummel@bv.tum.de (office). *Website:* tau.fesg.tu-muenchen.de (office).

RUMSFELD, Donald H., BA; American business executive, fmr politician and fmr government official; *Distinguished Visiting Fellow, Hoover Institution, Stanford University;* b. 9 July 1932, Chicago; s. of George Rumsfield and Jeannette Rumsfeld (née Husted); m. Joyce Pierson 1954; one s. two d.; ed New Trier High School, Ill., Princeton Univ.; aviator, USN 1954–57; Admin. Asst, House of Reps 1957–59; investment broker, A. G. Becker & Co., Chicago 1960–62; mem. 88th–91st Congresses; Republican; Asst to Pres. and Dir Office of Econ. Opportunity 1969–70; Dir Econ. Stabilization Program, Counsellor to Pres. 1971–72; Amb. to NATO, Brussels 1973–74; White House Chief of Staff 1974–75; Sec. of Defense 1975–77, 2001–06, currently non-paid consultant to Defense Dept; mem. Cabinet 1969–73, 1974–77; Pres., CEO then Chair. G. D. Searle and Co., Skokie, Ill. 1977–85; Sr Advisor, William Blair and Co. 1985–90; Chair. and CEO General Instrument Corpn 1990–93; Chair. Gilead Sciences, Inc. 1997–2000; Pres. Special Middle East Envoy 1983–84; Chair.

Eisenhower Exchange Fellowships 1986–93, US Ballistic Missile Threat Comm. 1998–99; mem. Presidential Advisory Cttee on Arms Control 1982–86, Nat. Econ. Comm. 1988–89, Trade Deficit Review Cttee, US Comm. to Assess Nat. Security, Space Man. and Org. 2000–01; Distinguished Visiting Fellow, Hoover Inst., Stanford Univ. 2007–; f. Rumsfeld Foundation 2007; 11 hon. degrees; Presidential Medal of Freedom 1977, Woodrow Wilson Award 1985, Outstanding Pharmaceutical CEO 1980, Eisenhower Medal 1993, Statesmanship Award, Claremont Inst. 2007 and many other awards. *Leisure interests:* skiing, squash, ranching, reading. *Address:* c/o Hoover Institution, 434 Galvez Mall, Stanford University, Stanford, CA 94305-6010, USA (office). *Website:* www.hoover.org.

RUMYANTSEV, Aleksandr Yu., Dr Phys., Math., Sciences; Russian physicist and diplomatist; *Ambassador to Finland;* b. 26 July 1945, Kushka, Turkmenistan; m.; one d.; ed Moscow Inst. of Physics and Engineering; trained as engineer; jr, then sr researcher, head of division, Dir of Scientific Devt Russian Scientific Centre, Kurchatov Inst. of Atomic Energy 1969–94, Dir 1994–2001; Minister of Atomic Energy of the Russian Fed. 2001–04; Head Fed. Agency for Atomic Energy 2004–05; Amb. to Finland 2006–; Prof. Moscow Inst. of Physics and Eng; Chair. Bd of Trustees Global Energy Int. Prize 2005–; mem. Bd of Dirs Nuclear Soc. of the Russian Fed.; mem. Russian Acad. of Sciences (corresp. mem. 1997–2000); USSR State Prize 1986; Order of Honour 2001. *Publications include:* over 100 scientific papers on new methods of solid-state physics studies by means of stationary nuclear reactors. *Address:* Embassy of Russia, Tehtaankatu 1b, 00140 Helsinki, Finland (office). *Telephone:* (9) 661876 (office). *Fax:* (9) 661006 (office). *E-mail:* rusembassy@co.inet.fi (office). *Website:* www.rusembassy.fi (office).

RUNDQUIST, Dmitri Vasilyevich; Russian geologist and mineralogist; b. 10 Aug. 1930; m.; two d.; ed Leningrad Inst. of Mines; jr, then sr researcher, Deputy Dir All-Union Research Inst. of Geology 1954–84; Dir Inst. of Geology and Geochronology Russian Acad. of Sciences 1984–90, Head of Lab. 1990–; Corresp. mem. USSR (now Russian) Acad. of Sciences 1984, mem. 1990, Acad.-Sec. Dept of Geology, Geophysics, Geochemistry and Mining Sciences 1996–2002; research in mineralogy, petrography, developed theory on laws of mineral deposit location; USSR State Prize; Merited Geologist of Russian Fed. *Publications include:* Greisen Deposits 1971, Zones of Endogenic Mineral Deposits 1975, Precambrian Geology 1988. *Address:* Vernadsky State Geological Museum, Morkhovaya 11, 103009 Moscow, Russia. *Telephone:* (495) 203-53-87.

RUOSLAHTI, Erkki, MD, PhD; Finnish medical scientist and academic; *Distinguished Professor, The Burnham Institute for Medical Research;* ed Univ. of Helsinki, Calif. Inst. of Tech.; various appts Univ. of Helsinki, Univ. of Turku, City of Hope Nat. Medical Center, Duarte, Calif., USA; joined The Burnham Inst. 1979, Pres. and CEO 1989–2002, Distinguished Prof. 2002–; Adjunct Distinguished Prof., Dept of Molecular, Cellular and Developmental Biology, Univ. of Calif., San Diego 2006– (after establishment of program affiliation with Burnham); mem. NAS, Inst. of Medicine, American Acad. of Arts and Sciences, European Molecular Biology Org., Finnish Acad. of Sciences; Nobel Fellow, Karolinska Inst., Stockholm; Knight of the Order of the White Rose, Finland; Hon. MD (Lund, Sweden); Gairdner Foundation Int. Award, G. H. A. Clowes Award, American Asscn for Cancer Research, Robert J. and Claire Pasarow Foundation Award, Jacobaeus Int. Prize, Jubilee Award British Biochemical Soc., Japan Prize in Cell Biology (jtly), Science and Tech. Foundation of Japan 2005. *Publications:* numerous articles and essays in prof. journals. *Address:* The Burnham Institute, 10901 North Torrey Pines Road, La Jolla, CA 92037, USA (office). *Telephone:* (805) 893-5358 (office). *Fax:* (805) 893-5805 (home). *E-mail:* ruoslahti@burnham.org (office). *Website:* www.burnham.org (office).

RUPEL, Dimitrij, PhD; Slovenian politician, diplomatist and writer; b. 7 April 1946, Ljubljana; m. Marjetica-Ana Rudolf-Rupel; ed Ljubljana Univ., Brandeis Univ. (Mass., USA); worked as journalist in Yugoslav newspapers and magazines; was considered as dissident for criticism of Yugoslav Communist regime; Asst Prof., Ljubljana Univ. 1980–89, Prof. 1989–; Lecturer, Queen's Univ. (Canada) 1977–78, New School for Social Research, NY (USA) 1985, Cleveland State Univ. (USA) 1989; Co-founder Cultural-Political journal Nova Revija 1984–87; Founder and first Pres. Opposition Slovenian Democratic Alliance Party 1989–90; Minister of Foreign Affairs 1990–93, mem. first elected Govt of Slovenia 1990, Chair. Cttee for Culture, Educ. and Sports; mem. State Ass. 1992–95; elected Mayor of Ljubljana 1994–97; Amb. to USA 1997–2000; Minister of Foreign Affairs 2000–08; Prime Minister's Special Foreign Affairs Envoy 2008–; Boris Kidrič Prize 1986, Golden Medal of Honour of the Repub. of Slovenia 1992. *Publications include:* novels: Half Way to the Horizon 1968, White Rooms 1970, Secretary of the Sixth International 1971, Tea and Guns at Four 1972, Fifth Floor of the Three-Floor House 1972, Time in It the Cruel Hangman 1974, Chi Square 1975, The Family Connection 1977, Cold Storms, Mad Homes 1978, Pleasant Life 1979, Max 1983, Follow the Addressee, Job 1984, Forgotten Invited 1985, Why is the World Upside Down? 1987, Lion's Share 1989, Story About Time 1989; non-fiction: Reading 1973, Free Words 1976, Words and Acts 1981, Reality Tests 1982, Sociology of Literature 1982, Sociology of Culture and Art 1986, Words of God and Words Divine 1987, Slovenian Intellectuals 1989, Slovenian Holidays and Everydays 1990, Slovenian Faith 1992, Slovenian Path to Independence and Recognition 1992, Secret of the State (memoirs) 1992, Disenchanted Slovenia 1993, Time of Politics 1994, Unity, Happiness, Reconciliation 1996, Freedom Against State 1998, Meetings and Partings 2001, Taking Over the Success Story 2004; plays: Less Terrible Night 1981, Job 1982, PDFS (Follow the Addressee) 1984; film screenplay: Oxygen 1971. *Address:* c/o Office of the Prime Minister, 1000 Ljubljana, Gregorčičeva 20, Slovenia (office).

RUPÉREZ, Francisco Javier, LLB; Spanish diplomatist and politician; *Consul-General, Chicago;* b. 24 April 1941, Madrid; m. Rakela Cerovic; two d.; ed El Pilar Coll., Univ. of Madrid; joined Diplomatic Service 1965, posts in Addis Ababa 1967–69, Warsaw 1969–72, Helsinki 1972–73; mem. Del. to CSCE, Helsinki 1972–73, to Int. Orgs, Geneva 1973–75; Chief of Staff of Under-Sec. of Foreign Affairs 1976; Chief of Staff of Ministry of Foreign Affairs 1976–77; mem. Exec. Cttee, Union of Democratic Centre (UCD) 1977–82; Mem. Parl. for Cuenca 1979–82, 1986–89, for Madrid 1989–93, for Ciudad Real 1993–2000; Amb. and Head of Del. to Madrid Session of CSCE 1980–82; First Spanish Amb. to NATO 1982–83; Senator and Mem. Regional Parl. of Castilla La Mancha 1983–86; Vice-Pres. Democratic People's Party (PDP) 1983–87; Pres. Christian Democratic Party 1987–89; Vice-Pres. People's Party (PP) 1989–90, Spokesman in Parl. Defence Cttee 1989–91, Spokesman in Parl. Foreign Affairs Cttee 1991–96; Vice-Pres. NATO Parl. Ass. 1994–96, Pres. Parl. Ass. 1998–2000; Pres. Parl. Ass. of OSCE 1996–98; Pres. Spanish Atlantic Asscn (AAE) 1996–2000; Pres. Foreign Affairs Cttee, House of Deputies 1996–2000; Pres. Christian-Democratic Int. (CDI) 1998–2000; Pres. Cttee on Defence, House of Deputies 2000; Amb. to USA 2000–04; Asst Sec.-Gen. and Exec. Dir UN Counter-Terrorism Exec. Directorate 2004–07; Consul-Gen. to Chicago 2007–; Pres. Foundation for Humanism and Democracy 1989–2000; Co-founder Cuadernos para el Diálogo (monthly political magazine) 1963–77; lectures regularly and directs courses at Int. Univ. Menéndez Pelayo, Univ. of Madrid and the Diplomatic School; Gran Cruz de la Orden de Isabel la Católica, Comendador de la Orden de Carlos III, Oficial de Isabel la Católica, Oficial de la Orden del Mérito Civil, Orden Bernardo O'Higgins (Chile), Gran Cruz de Vasco Núñez de Balboa (Panama), Grand Ordre de Léopold II (Belgium), Comendador con Placa de la Orden del Infante Don Enrique (Portugal), Kt Commdr of the Order of Alistical (Jordan), Kt Commdr, Order of the Arab Repub. of Egypt, Officier, Légion d'honneur (France). *Publications include:* Confessional State and Religious Liberty 1970, Europe Between Fear and Hope 1976, Spain in NATO 1986, First Book of Short Stories 1987, Kidnapped by ETA: Memoirs 1990, The Price of a Shadow (novel) 2005, El espejismo multilateral 2009; contribs to co-authored books and numerous articles in the Spanish press and specialized publs. *Address:* Consulate-General of Spain, 180 North Michigan Avenue, Suite 1500, Chicago, IL 60601, USA (office). *Telephone:* (782) 45-89 (office). *Fax:* (312) 782-1635 (office). *E-mail:* conspainchicago@sbcglobal.net (office); javieruperez@hotmail.com (home). *Website:* www.mae.es/Consulados/Chicago (office).

RUPNIK, Jacques, MA PhD; French political scientist and academic; *Director of Research, National Foundation for Political Science, Centre for International Studies and Research (CERI);* b. 21 Nov. 1950, Prague, Czech Republic; s. of Anton Rupnik and Micheline Bauvillain-Rupnik; m.; ed Harvard Univ., Sorbonne, Institut d'Etudes Politiques de Paris; Research Assoc., Russian Research Center, Harvard Univ. 1974–75; Eastern Europe specialist BBC World Service 1977–82; Prof., Institut d'Etudes Politiques de Paris 1982–96; adviser to Czech Pres. Vaclav Havel 1990–92; Exec. Dir Int. Comm. for Balkans, Carnegie Endowment for Int. Peace 1995–96; mem. Ind. Int. Comm. on Kosovo 1999–2000; Visiting Prof., Coll. of Europe 1999–, Harvard Univ. 2006; currently Research Dir Nat. Foundation for Political Science, Centre for Int. Studies and Research (CERI); adviser to EC 2007–; Ordre Nat. du Mérite 1995, Order of T.G. Maseryk, Czech Repub. 2002. *Television:* writer and presenter, The Other Europe (6-part documentary series) (Channel 4 TV, UK) 1988. *Publications:* The Other Europe 1988, Unfinished Peace 1996, Le Europe en face à l'élargissement 2004; numerous books and articles focused on central and Eastern Europe, and the Balkans. *Address:* Centre for International Studies and Research (CERI), 56 rue Jacob, 75006 Paris, France (office). *Telephone:* 1-58-71-70-51 (office); 1-49-57-08-54 (home). *Fax:* 1-58-71-70-90 (office). *E-mail:* rupnik@ceri-sciences-po.org (office); jacquesrupnik@hotmail.com (home). *Website:* www.ceri-sciencespo.com/cherlist/rupnik.htm (office).

RUPP, George, PhD; American international organization official, university president and professor of religion; *President and CEO, International Rescue Committee;* b. 22 Sept. 1942, Summit, NJ; m. Nancy Katherine Farrar 1964; two d.; ed Univ. of Munich, Germany, Princeton Univ., Yale Divinity School, Univ. of Sri Lanka, Harvard Univ.; Faculty Fellow in Religion, Johnston Coll., Univ. of Redlands, Calif., 1971–73, Vice-Chancellor 1973–74; Asst Prof. of Theology, Divinity School, Harvard Univ. 1974–76, Assoc. Prof. of Theology and Chair. Dept of Theology 1976–77, Dean and John Lord O'Brian Prof. of Divinity 1979–85; Dean for Acad. Affairs and Prof. of Humanistic Studies, Univ. of Wisconsin-Green Bay 1977–79; Pres. and Prof. of Religious Studies, Rice Univ. 1985–93; Pres. and Prof. of Religion, Columbia Univ., New York 1993–2002; Pres. and CEO Int. Rescue Cttee 2002–; mem. Bd Inst. of Int. Educ., Council on Foreign Relations, Interaction and other orgs; Hon. DLit (Columbia) 1993; Alexander Hamilton Medal, Columbia Univ. 2002, Centennial Medal for Contrib. to Society, Harvard Univ. Grad. School of Arts and Sciences 2004, Gold Medal, Nat. Inst. of Social Sciences 2005, Woodrow Wilson Award, Princeton Univ. 2006. *Publications:* Christologies and Cultures: Toward a Typology of Religious Worldviews 1974, Culture-Protestantism: German Liberal Theology at the Turn of the Twentieth Century 1977, Beyond Existentialism and Zen: Religion in a Pluralistic World 1979, Commitment and Community 1989, Globalization Challenged 2006; numerous book chapters and articles. *Address:* International Rescue Committee, 122 East 42nd Street, 12th Floor, New York, NY 10168, USA (office). *Telephone:* (212) 551-3002 (office). *Website:* www.theirc.org (office).

RUPPRECHT, Rudolf, DipEng; German business executive; *Member of the Supervisory Board, MAN Aktiengesellschaft;* b. 12 Jan. 1940, Berlin; ed Munich Tech. Univ.; began career as sales engineer, MAN Group 1966, various positions including Tech. Dir MAN subsidiary in Argentina, Exec. Dir Diesel Engines Div. 1981–84, apptd mem. Exec. Bd MAN B&W Diesel AG,

Augsburg 1984, Chair. Exec. Bd 1989–93, Chair. Exec. Bd MAN Nutzfahr-zeuge AG, Munich 1993–96, Chair. Exec. Bd MAN Aktiengesellschaft, Munich 1996–2004, now mem. Supervisory Bd; mem. Supervisory Bd Bayerische Staatsforsten AöR, KME AG, Salzgitter AG, SMS GmbH (Chair.). *Address:* MAN Aktiengesellschaft, Ungererstrasse 69, 80805 Munich, Germany (office). *Telephone:* (89) 360980 (office). *Fax:* (89) 36098250 (office). *E-mail:* public .relations@ag.man.de (office). *Website:* www.man.de (office).

RUPRECHT, William F.; American auctioneer and business executive; *President, CEO and Director, Sotheby's Holdings, Inc.;* b. St Louis; ed Univ. of Colorado, Univ. of Vermont; began career as apprentice to furniture maker, Vermont; joined Sotheby's 1980, Dir of Marketing Sotheby's Inc., New York 1986–92, Dir of Marketing Sotheby's worldwide 1992–94, Man. Dir Sotheby's N and S America 1994–2000, Pres., CEO and Dir Sotheby's Holdings, Inc. 2000–. *Address:* Sotheby's, 1334 York Avenue at 72nd Street, New York, NY 10021, USA (office). *Telephone:* (212) 606-7000 (office). *Fax:* (212) 606-7107 (office). *Website:* www.sothebys.com (office).

RUSBRIDGER, Alan, BA, MA; British journalist; *Editor, The Guardian and Executive Editor, The Observer (UK);* b. 29 Dec. 1953, Lusaka, Zambia; s. of G. H. Rusbridger and B. E. Rusbridger (née Wickham); m. Lindsay Mackie 1982; two d.; ed Cranleigh School, Magdalene Coll., Cambridge; reporter Cambridge Evening News 1976–79; reporter The Guardian 1979–82, diary ed. and feature writer 1982–86, special writer 1987–88, launch ed. Weekend Guardian 1988–89, Features Ed. 1989–93, Deputy Ed. 1993–95, Ed. 1995–; TV critic and feature writer The Observer 1986–, Exec. Ed. 1996–; Washington Corresp. London Daily News 1987; Chair. Photographer's Gallery 2001–; mem. Bd Guardian Newspapers Ltd 1994–, Guardian Media Group 1999–; mem. Scott Trust 1997–; Ed. of the Year, What the Papers Say Awards (Granada TV) 1996, 2001, Nat. Newspaper Ed., Newspaper Industry Awards 1996, Editor's Ed., Press Gazette 1997, Judges' Award, What the Papers Say 2006. *Television:* presenter of What the Papers Say (Granada TV) 1983–94, co-writer (with Ronan Bennett) of Fields of Gold (BBC TV) 2001. *Publications:* New World Order (ed.) 1991, Altered State (ed.) 1992, Guardian Year 1994, The Coldest Day in the Zoo 2004, The Wildest Day at the Zoo 2005, The Smelliest Day at the Zoo 2007. *Leisure interests:* golf, music, painting. *Address:* The Guardian, 119 Farringdon Road, London, EC1R 3ER, England (office). *Telephone:* (20) 7278-2332 (office). *Fax:* (20) 7239-9997 (office). *Website:* www.guardian.co.uk (office).

RUSCHA, Edward (Ed) Joseph; American artist; b. 16 Dec. 1937, Omaha, Neb.; s. of Edward Joseph Ruscha and Dorothy Driscoll; m. Danna Knego 1967; one s.; ed Chouinard Art Inst., LA; first one-man exhbn LA 1963; produced films Premium 1970, Miracle 1975; maj. exhbns, San Francisco Museum of Modern Art 1982, Musée St Pierre, Lyons, France 1985, Museum of Contemporary Art, Chicago 1988, Centre Georges Pompidou, Paris 1989, Serpentine Gallery, London 1990, Museum of Contemporary Art, LA 1990, Robert Miller Gallery, New York 1992, Thaddaeus Ropac, Salzburg, Austria 1992; first public comm., for Miami Dade Cultural Center's Main Library, Miami, Fla 1985; other comms. include Great Hall, Denver Cen. Library 1994–95, Auditorium Getty Center, Los Angeles 1997; represented in numerous perm. collections; Guggenheim Foundation Fellowship 1971; mem. American Acad. of Arts and Letters 2001. *Publications:* 12 books, including Twenty-six Gasoline Stations 1963, The Sunset Strip 1966. *Address:* c/o Leo Castelli Gallery, 59 East 79th Street, New York, NY 10021 (office); Kornelia Tamm Fine Arts, 28 Willa Cather Road, Santa Fe, NM 87540, USA. *Website:* www.edruscha.com.

RUSH, Geoffrey; Australian actor; b. 6 July 1951, Toowoomba, Queensland; s. of Roy Baden Rush and Merle Kiehne; m. Jane Menelaus 1988; one s. one d.; studied at Jacques Lecoq School of Mime, Paris, began professional career with Queensland Theatre Co.; Hans Christian Andersen Amb. 2005–; Hon. DLitt (Univ. of Queensland). *Films include:* The Wedding 1980, Starstruck 1981, Twelfth Night 1985, Midday Crisis 1994, Dad and Dave on our Selection 1995, Shine (Acad. Award, BAFTA Award, Australian Film Inst. Award, Golden Globe Award, numerous other awards) 1995, Children of the Revolution 1996, Les Miserables 1997, Elizabeth 1998, Shakespeare in Love (BAFTA Award for Best Supporting Actor) 1998, The Magic Pudding 1999, Mystery Men 1999, House on Haunted Hill 1999, Quills 1999, Tailor of Panama 2001, Lantana 2001, Frida 2002, The Banger Sisters 2002, Swimming Upstream 2003, Ned Kelly 2003, Finding Nemo (voice) 2003, Pirates of the Caribbean: The Curse of the Black Pearl 2003, Intolerable Cruelty 2003, Harvie Krumpet (voice) 2003, The Life and Death of Peter Sellers (Best Actor in a Miniseries or TV Movie, Golden Globe Awards 2005, Screen Actors Guild Awards 2005, Emmy Award for Best Actor in a Mini-Series or Movie 2005) 2004, Swimming Upstream 2005, Munich 2005, Candy 2006, Pirates of the Caribbean: Dead Man's Chest 2006, Pirates of the Caribbean: At World's End 2007, Elizabeth: The Golden Age 2007. *Theatre includes:* Hamlet 1994, The Alchemist 1996, The Marriage of Figaro 1998, The Small Poppies 1999, Exit the King 2009; also dir of numerous productions. *Television includes:* Menotti 1980–81, The Burning Piano 1992, Mercury 1996, Bonus Mileage 1996, Frontier (mini-series) 1997. *Address:* c/o Shanahan Management, PO Box 478, King's Cross, NSW 2011, Australia.

RUSHAYLO, Col-Gen. Vladimir Borisovich; Russian politician and international organization official; b. 28 July 1953, Tambov; m.; three c.; ed Omsk Higher School of Militia, USSR Ministry of Internal Affairs; militiaman 1972–76; investigator Moscow Dept of Internal Affairs 1976–88, later Head Moscow Dept of Internal Affairs; Head Dept for Struggle against Organized Crime 1988–93, 1998–99, Head Regional Dept for Struggle against Organized Crime 1993–96; Counsellor Council of Fed. 1996–98; Deputy Minister of Internal Affairs 1998–99, Minister of Internal Affairs 1999–2001; Sec. Security Council of Russia 2001–04; Exec. Sec. and Chair. Exec. Cttee CIS

2004–07; Head, CIS mission to observe presidential election in Belarus 2006; mem. Presidium of Russian Govt, Security Council; Order of Sign of Honour; Order for Personal Courage and numerous other decorations. *Address:* c/o Office of the Executive Secretary, Commonwealth of Independent States, 220000 Minsk, Kirava 17, Belarus (office).

RUSHDIE, Sir (Ahmed) Salman, Kt, MA, FRSL; British writer and academic; *Distinguished Writer-in-Residence, Emory University;* b. 19 June 1947, Bombay (now Mumbai), India; s. of Anis Ahmed and Negin (née Butt) Rushdie; m. 1st Clarissa Luard 1976 (divorced 1987, died 1999); one s.; m. 2nd Marianne Wiggins 1988 (divorced 1993); one step-d.; m. 3rd Elizabeth West 1997 (divorced); one s.; m. 4th Padma Lakshmi 2004; ed Cathedral and John Connon Boys' High School, Bombay, Rugby School, England, King's Coll., Cambridge; mem. Footlights revue, Univ. of Cambridge 1965–68; actor, fringe theatre, London 1968–69; advertising copywriter 1969–73; wrote first published novel Grimus 1973–74; part-time advertising copywriter while writing second novel 1976–80; mem. Int. PEN 1981–, Soc. of Authors 1983–, Exec. Cttee Nat. Book League 1983–, Council Inst. of Contemporary Arts 1985–, British Film Inst. Production Bd 1986–, PEN American Center (pres. 2004–06); Distinguished Writer in Residence, Emory Univ., Atlanta 2007–; Exec. mem. Camden Cttee for Community Relations 1977–83; Distinguished Fellow in Literature, Univ. of East Anglia 1995; Hon. Prof. MIT 1993; Hon. Spokesman Charter 88 1989; Hon. DLitt (Bard Coll.) 1995; Booker McConnell Prize for Fiction 1981, Arts Council Literature Bursary 1981, English Speaking Union Literary Award 1981, James Tait Black Memorial Book Prize 1981, Kurt Tucholsky Prize Sweden 1992, Prix Colette Switzerland 1993, Austrian State Prize for European Literature 1994, Whitbread Fiction Award 1996, British Book Awards Author of the Year 1996, London Int. Writers Award 2002, Booker of Bookers Prize 2008, James Joyce Award 2008; Commdr., Ordre des Arts et des Lettres 1999. *Television film screenplays:* The Painter and the Pest 1985, The Riddle of Midnight 1988. *Film appearance:* Then She Found Me 2007. *Publications:* Grimus 1975, Midnight's Children 1981, Shame (Prix du Meilleur Livre Etranger 1984) 1983, The Jaguar Smile: A Nicaraguan Journey 1987, The Satanic Verses 1988, Is Nothing Sacred (lecture) 1990, Haroun and the Sea of Stories (novel) 1990, Imaginary Homelands: Essays and Criticism 1981–91 1991, The Wizard of Oz 1992, East, West (short stories) 1994, The Moor's Last Sigh (novel) 1995, The Vintage Book of Indian Writing 1947–97 (ed. with Elizabeth West) 1997, The Ground Beneath Her Feet 1999, Fury 2001, Step Across the Line: Collected Non-Fiction 1992–2002 2002, Telling Tales (contrib. to charity anthology) 2004, Shalimar the Clown 2005, The Enchantress of Florence 2008; articles for New York Times, Washington Post, The Times and Sunday Times. *Leisure interests:* films, chess, table tennis, involvement in politics, especially race relations. *Address:* English Department, Emory University, N-302 Callaway Center, 537 Kilgo Circle, Atlanta, GA 30322, USA (office). Wylie Agency (UK) Ltd, 4–8 Rodney Street, London, N1 9JH, England (office). *Telephone:* (404) 727-6420 (office). *Fax:* (404) 727-2605 (office). *E-mail:* english@emory.edu (office). *Website:* www.english.emory.edu (office).

RUŠKO, Pavol; Slovak politician; b. 20 Aug. 1963, Liptovský Hrádok; m.; two c.; ed Comenius Univ.; Sports Ed. Slovak TV 1985, Head Dept of Program Research, Head of Transmitting Centre and Deputy of Gen. Dir 1989–94; with Lottop Co. 1994–96; Gen. Dir and Co-Owner TV Markiza 1995–2000, Chair. STS Markiza Bd of Owners 2000–; Dir-Gen. Slovenska Televizna Spolocnost; Chair. New Citizens' Alliance (NCA) (Aliancia nového občana—ANO) 2001–07; Vice-Chair. Nat. Council of Slovak Repub. 2002–03; Deputy Prime Minister and Minister of the Economy, and Admin and Privatization of Nat. Property 2003–05. *Address:* c/o New Citizens' Alliance (NCA) (Aliancia nového občana—ANO), Drobného 27, 841 01 Bratislava, Slovakia. *Telephone:* (2) 6920-2918. *Fax:* (2) 6920-2920. *E-mail:* ano@ano-aliancia.sk. *Website:* www .ano-aliancia.sk.

RUSMAJLI, Ilir; Albanian lawyer and politician; b. 24 April 1965, Elbasan; ed Univ. of Tirana; fmrly Minister of Foreign Affairs; Deputy Prime Minister 2005–07; Minister of Justice 2007 (resgnd).

RUSNOK, Jiří, DipEconEng; Czech politician and economist; *Executive Advisor to the Management Committee and Director of Pensions, ING Bank Czech Republic/Slovak Republic;* b. 16 Oct. 1960, Ostrava-Vítkovice; m.; two c.; ed Univ. of Economics, Prague; various positions in state admin.; Econ. Adviser, Czech-Moravian Confed. of Trade Unions 1992–98; mem. Czech Social Democratic Party (CSDP) 1998–; Deputy Minister for Labour and Social Affairs 1998–2001; Minister of Finance 2001–02, of Industry and Trade 2002–03; Exec. Advisor to the Man. Cttee and Dir of Pensions, ING Bank Czech Repub./Slovak Repub. 2003–; Vice Pres. Czech Pension Funds Asscn 2003–; mem. World Bank Governing Council 2001–02; fmr mem. Bd of Govs EBRD. *Leisure interests:* nature, history, botany. *Address:* ING Bank, Nádražní 25, 150 00 Prague 5, Czech Republic (office). *Telephone:* 257473111 (office). *Fax:* 257473555 (office). *E-mail:* komunikace@ing.cz (office). *Website:* www.ing.cz (office).

RUSSELL, Sir George, Kt, CBE, BA, FRSA, CBIM, FID; British business executive; *Deputy Chairman, ITV PLC;* b. 25 Oct. 1935; s. of William H. Russell and Frances A. Russell; m. Dorothy Brown 1959; three d.; ed Gateshead Grammar School, Univ. of Durham; Vice-Pres. and Gen. Man. Welland Chemical Co. of Canada Ltd 1968, St Clair Chemical Co. Ltd 1968; Man. Dir Alcan UK Ltd 1976; Asst Man. Dir Alcan Aluminium (UK) Ltd 1977–81, Man. Dir 1981–82; Man. Dir and CEO British Alcan Aluminium 1982–86; Dir Alcan Aluminiumwerke GmbH, Frankfurt 1982–86, Alcan Aluminium Ltd 1987–2000; Group Chief Exec. Marley PLC 1986–89, Chair. and CEO 1989–93, Chair. (non-exec.) 1993–97; Deputy Chair. Channel Four TV 1987–88; Chair. Ind. TV News (ITN) 1988; Chair. Ind. Broadcasting Authority (IBA) 1989–90, Ind. Television Comm. (ITC) 1991–96; Chair.

Camelot Group PLC 1995–2002; Chair. Luxfer Holdings Ltd 1976; mem. Bd of Dirs Northern Rock Building Soc. (now Northern Rock PLC) 1985–2006, 3i Group PLC 1992–2001 (Chair. non-exec. 1993–2001), Taylor Woodrow PLC 1992–2004 (Deputy Chair. 2000–03); Chair. Northern Devt Co. 1994–99; Deputy Chair. Granada PLC 2002–04, ITV PLC 2003–; Dir Wildfowl & Wetlands Trust 2002–; Visiting Prof., Univ. of Newcastle-upon-Tyne 1978; mem. Northern Industrial Devt Bd 1977–80, Washington Devt Corpn 1978–80, IBA 1979–86, Civil Service Pay Research Unit 1980–81, Council CBI 1984–85, Widdicombe Cttee of Inquiry into Conduct of Local Authority Business 1985; Fellow, Inst. of Industrial Mans; Trustee Beamish Devt Trust 1985–90, Thomas Bewick Birthplace Trust; Hon. FRIBA 1993; Hon. FRTS 1994; Hon. FRAM 2001; Hon. DEng (Newcastle upon Tyne) 1985; Hon. DBA (Northumbria) 1992; Hon. LLD (Sunderland) 1995, (Durham) 1997. *Leisure interests:* tennis, badminton, bird watching. *Address:* c/o ITV plc, 200 Gray's Inn Road, London, WC1V 8HF, England (office). *Telephone:* (844) 881-5662 (office). *Fax:* (844) 556-3854 (office).

RUSSELL, Ian, CBE, BCom; British chartered accountant and business executive; *Chairman, Advanced Power AG Advisory Board;* b. 16 Jan. 1953, Edinburgh; s. of James Russell and Christine Clark; m. Fiona Russell 1975; one s. one d.; ed Univ. of Edinburgh; Finance Dir HSBC Asset Man., Hong Kong 1987–90; Dir Finance Control, Tomkins, London 1991–94; Finance Dir Scottish Power plc 1994, Deputy CEO 1998–2001, CEO 2001–06; Industrialist in Residence, 3i Group (pvt. equity firm) 2007–, Chair. Advanced Power AG Advisory Bd (after 3i investment in Advanced Power) 2007–; mem. Bd of Dirs Johnston Press plc, JPMorgan Fleming Mercantile Investment Trust plc; Head Govt Comm. on Nat. Youth Volunteering Strategy 2004–05; mem. Edinburgh Int. Festival Council, Scottish Council of the Prince's Trust. *Leisure interests:* golf, rugby. *Address:* Advanced Power AG, Baarer Str. 12, 6300 Zug, Switzerland (office); 3i Group, 16 Palace Street, London SW1E 5JD, England (office). *Telephone:* 417297297 (office); (20) 7928-3131 (3i) (office). *Fax:* 417297299 (office); (20) 7928-0058 (3i) (office). *E-mail:* info@advancedpower.ch (office). *Website:* www.advancedpower.ch (office); www.3i.com (office).

RUSSELL, Ken; British film director and stage producer; b. 3 July 1927, Southampton; s. of Henry Russell and Ethel Smith; m. 1st Shirley Kingdam (divorced 1978); four s. one d.; m. 2nd Vivian Jolly 1984; one s. one d.; m. 3rd Hetty Baines 1992 (divorced 1997); one s.; ed Nautical Coll., Pangbourne; fmr actor and freelance magazine photographer; Hon. DLitt (Univ. Coll., Salford) 1994; Prix Italia 1985. *Films:* French Dressing 1964, Billion Dollar Brain 1967, Women in Love 1969, The Music Lovers 1970, The Devils 1971, The Boyfriend 1971, Savage Messiah 1972, Mahler 1973, Tommy 1974, Lisztomania 1975, Valentino 1977, Altered States 1981, Gothic 1986, Aria (segment) 1987, Salome's Last Dance 1988, The Lair of the White Worm 1988, The Rainbow 1989, Whore 1990, Prisoners of Honour 1991, Lion's Mouth 2000, The Fall of the Louse of Usher 2002, Revenge of the Elephant Man 2004, Trapped Ashes 2006; as actor: The Russia House 1990, Brothers of the Head 2006. *Opera directed:* The Rake's Progress (Maggio Musicale, Florence) 1982, Die Soldaten (Opéra de Lyon) 1983, Madama Butterfly (Spoleto) 1983, L'Italiana in Algeri (Geneva) 1984, La Bohème (Macerata Festival) 1984, Faust (Vienna) 1985, Mefistofele (Genoa) 1987, Princess Ida (London Coliseum) 1992, Salome (Bonn) 1993. *Television directed:* documentaries: Elgar, Bartok, Debussy, Henri Rousseau, Isadora Duncan, Delius, Richard Strauss, Clouds of Glory, The Mystery of Dr Martini, The Secret Life of Arnold Bax, Elgar: Fantasy of a Composer on a Bicycle 2002; series: Lady Chatterley's Lover. *Publications:* A British Picture: an Autobiography 1989, Altered States: The Autobiography of Ken Russell 1991, Fire Over England 1993, Mike and Gaby's Space Gospel 1999, Beethoven Confidential/Brahms Gets Laid (novel biogs) 2007, Elgar: The Erotic Variations/Delius: A Moment with Venus (novel biogs) 2007; four novellas. *Leisure interests:* music, walking. *Address:* 16 Salisbury Place, London, W1H 1FH, England.

RUSSELL, Kurt von Vogel; American actor; b. 17 March 1951, Springfield, Mass; s. of Bing Oliver Russell and Louise Julia Russell (née Crone); m. Season Hubley 1979 (divorced); one s.; pnr Goldie Hawn; one s.; lead role in TV series The Travels of Jamie McPheeters 1963–64; child actor in many Disney shows and films; professional minor league baseball player 1971–73; numerous TV guest appearances; mem. Professional Baseball Players' Asscn, Stuntman's Asscn; Co-founder Cosmic Entertainment (production co.) 2003; recipient five acting awards, ten baseball awards, one golf championship. *Films include:* Follow Me, Boys! 1966, Mosby's Marauders 1967, Guns in the Heather 1968, The One and Only, Genuine, Original Family Band 1968, The Horse in the Gray Flannel Suit 1968, The Computer Wore Tennis Shoes 1969, The Barefoot Executive 1971, Fools' Parade 1971, Now You See Him, Now You Don't 1972, Charley and the Angel 1973, Superdad 1973, The Strongest Man in the World 1975, The Captive: The Longest Drive 2 1976, Used Cars 1980, Escape from New York 1981, The Thing 1982, Silkwood 1983, Swing Shift 1984, Mean Season 1985, Best of Times 1986, Big Trouble in Little China 1986, Overboard 1987, Tequila Sunrise 1988, Winter People 1989, Tango & Cash 1989, Backdraft 1991, Unlawful Entry 1992, Captain Ron 1992, Tombstone 1993, Stargate 1994, Executive Decision 1996, Escape from LA 1996, Breakdown 1997, Soldier 1998, 3000 Miles to Graceland 2001, Vanilla Sky 2001, Interstate 60 2002, Dark Blue 2002, Miracle 2004, Jiminy Glick in La La Wood 2004, Dreamer 2005, Sky High 2005, Poseiden 2006, Grindhouse 2007, Death Proof 2007, Cutlass 2007. *Television series include:* Sugarfoot 1957, Travels with Jamie McPheeters 1963–64, The New Land 1974, The Quest 1976. *Television films include:* Search for the Gods 1975, The Deadly Tower 1975, Christmas Miracle in Caulfield USA 1977, Elvis 1979, Amber Waves 1988. *Address:* Cosmic Entertainment, 9255 Sunset Boulevard, Suite 1010, West Hollywood, CA 90069; Creative Artists' Agency, 9830 Wilshire Boulevard, Beverly Hills, CA 90212-1825, USA. *Telephone:* (310) 275-8080 (Cosmic Entertainment).

RUSSELL, Paul; British lawyer and music industry executive; *Founding Partner, R2M Music LPP & LLC;* b. 3 July 1944, London; m. Elizabeth Russell; three s. two d.; ed Coll. of Law; fmrly band mem. Red Diamond; fmrly with law firm Balin & Co.; joined CBS 1973, fmrly Man. Dir, Pres. Sony Music Europe 1993–; Chair. Sony Music Europe 1997–2000; Sr Vice-Pres. Sony Music Entertainment Inc. 2000–; Chair. Sony ATV Music Publishing 2000–, Chair. Sony ATV Music Publishing 2000–; Founding Pnr R2M Music LPP & LLC; co-f. Brit Awards; f. Platinum Europe Awards. *Leisure interests:* music, films, theatre, golf, swimming, all sports. *Address:* Compton House, Lake Road, Wentworth, Surrey, GU25 4QW, England (office). *Telephone:* (1344) 845661 (office). *Fax:* (1344) 841730 (office). *E-mail:* pr44@btopenworld.com (office).

RUSSELL, Stuart, BA, PhD; British computer scientist and academic; *Professor of Computer Science, University of California, Berkeley;* b. 1962, Portsmouth; ed St Paul's School, London, Wadham Coll., Univ. of Oxford, Stanford Univ.; Programmer, IBM Systems Eng Centre, Warwick 1978–80; Programmer, graphics research project, IBM Scientific Center, Los Angeles 1981; Teaching Asst, Computer Science Dept, Stanford Univ. 1983, Research Asst 1985–86; Asst Prof., Computer Science Div., Univ. of California, Berkeley 1986–91, Assoc. Prof. 1991–96, Prof. 1996–, Michael H. Smith and Lotfi A. Zadeh Chair in Eng 2001, Chair. Computer Science Div. 2006–, also Chair. Dept of Electrical Eng and Computer Sciences 2008–; Fellow, American Asscn for Artificial Intelligence 1997– (mem. Exec. Council 1997–2000); Fellow, Asscn for Computing Machinery 2003–; mem. British Scientists Abroad (Chair. 1993–96); numerous awards including NSF Presidential Young Investigator Award 1990, IJCAI Computers and Thought Award (co-winner) 1995. *Publications:* over 150 papers on artificial intelligence; The Use of Knowledge in Analogy and Induction 1989, Do the Right Thing: Studies in Limited Rationality (with Eric Wefald) 1991, Artificial Intelligence: A Modern Approach (with Peter Norvig) 1995. *Address:* Computer Science Division, 387 Soda Hall, University of California, Berkeley, CA 94720-1776, USA (office). *Telephone:* (510) 642-8736 (office). *E-mail:* russell@cs.berkeley.edu (office). *Website:* www.cs.berkeley.edu/~russell (office).

RUSSELL, William (Willy) Martin; British writer; b. 23 Aug. 1947; s. of William Russell and Margery Russell; m. Ann Seagroatt 1969; one s. two d.; ed St Katharine's Coll. of Educ., Liverpool; ladies hairdresser 1963–69; teacher 1973–74; Fellow in Creative Writing, Manchester Polytechnic 1977–78; Founder-mem. and Dir Quintet Films; Hon. Dir Liverpool, Playhouse; work for theatre includes: Blind Scouse (three short plays) 1971, When the Reds (adaptation) 1972, John, Paul, George, Ringo and Bert (musical) 1974, Breezeblock Park 1975, One for the Road 1976, Stags and Hens 1978, Educating Rita 1979, Blood Brothers (musical) 1983, Our Day Out (musical) 1983, Shirley Valentine 1986; screenplays include: Educating Rita 1981, Shirley Valentine 1988, Dancing Through the Dark 1989; TV and radio plays; Hon. MA (Open Univ.) 1983; Hon. DLit (Liverpool Univ.) 1990. *Publications:* Breezeblock Park 1978, One for the Road 1980, Educating Rita 1981, Our Day Out 1984, Stags and Hens 1985, Blood Brothers 1985, Shirley Valentine 1989, The Wrong Boy (novel) 2000; songs and poetry. *Leisure interests:* playing the guitar, composing songs, gardening, cooking. *Address:* c/o Casarotto Company Ltd, National House, 60–66 Wardour Street, London, W1V 3HP, England. *Telephone:* (20) 7287-4450. *Website:* www.willyrussell.com.

RUSSELL BEALE, Simon, CBE, BA; British actor; b. 12 Jan. 1961, Penang, Malaya; s. of Lt-Gen. Sir Peter Beale and Lady Beale; ed Gonville and Caius Coll., Cambridge; Assoc. Artist of RSC 1986; Patron, English Touring Theatre; Pres. Anthony Powell Soc. *Theatre includes:* (Traverse Theatre, Edin.): Die House, Sandra/Manon, Points of Departure, The Death of Elias Sawney; (Lyceum, Edin.): Hamlet (Royal Court, London): Women Beware Women, The Duchess of Malfi, Volpone, Rosencrantz and Guildenstern are Dead, Candide, Money 1999, Sommerfolk, Hamlet (Royal Nat. Theatre) 2000, Uncle Vanya (Olivier Award for Best Actor 2003; Donmar Warehouse, London) 2002, Macbeth (Almeida, London) 2005, The Philanthropist (Evening Standard Award for Best Actor 2005) (Donmar Warehouse, London) 2005, Monty Python's Spamalot (Palace Theatre, London) 2006. *RSC productions include:* The Winter's Tale, The Art of Success, Everyman in his Humour, The Fair Maid of the West, The Storm, Speculators, The Constant Couple, The Man of Mode, Restoration, Mary and Lizzie, Some Americans Abroad, Playing with Trains, Troilus and Cressida, Edward II (title role), Love's Labours Lost, The Seagull, Richard III (title role), The Tempest, King Lear, Ghosts, Othello. *Films include:* Orlando 1992, Persuasion 1995, Hamlet 1996, The Temptation of Franz Schubert 1997, An Ideal Husband 1999, Blackadder Back & Forth 1999, The Gathering 2002, Deep Water (voice) 2006. *Television includes:* A Very Peculiar Practice, Downtown Lagos (mini-series) 1992, The Mushroom Picker (mini-series) 1993, A Dance to the Music of Time (mini-series) (Royal TV Soc. Award for Best Actor 1997, BAFTA Award for Best Actor 1998) 1997, The Temptation of Franz Schubert 1997, Alice in Wonderland 1999, The Young Visiters 2003, Dunkirk 2004. *Leisure interests:* medieval history, music, history of religion. *Address:* c/o Anthony Powell Society, 7 Ormonde Gate, Chelsea, London, SW3 4EU, England.

RUSSO, Patricia F., BA; American communications industry executive; b. 1953, Trenton, NJ; m.; two step-c.; ed Lawrence High School, Georgetown Univ., Harvard Business School; Sales and Marketing Man. Exec., IBM 1973–81; joined AT&T, Murray Hill, NJ 1981, Pres. business unit, Business Communications Systems 1992–96, Exec. Vice-Pres. Strategy Business Devt and Corp. Operations 1997–99, Exec. Vice-Pres. and CEO Service Provider Networks Group 1999–2000, Pres. and CEO Lucent Technologies Inc. (spin-off of AT&T) 2002–03, Chair. and CEO 2003–06, CEO jt Alcatel-Lucent co.

(following Alcatel acquisition of Lucent) 2006–08; Chair. Avaya, Inc. (fmr Business Communications Systems unit of Lucent Technologies) –2001; Pres. and COO Eastman Kodak 2001–02; mem. Bd of Dirs Xerox Corpn, Schering-Plough Corpn (Chair. Governance Cttee), New Jersey Manufacturers Insurance Co., Georgetown Univ.; Vice-Chair. Nat. Security Telecommunications Advisory Cttee 2003–06; mem. Network Reliability Interoperability Council; Trustee, Georgetown Univ.; Hon. DEng (Stevens Inst. of Tech.); Dr hc (Columbia Coll., SC); ranked by Fortune magazine amongst 50 Most Powerful Women in Business in the US 1998–2000, (26th) 2001, (15th) 2002, (21st) 2003, (14th) 2004, (14th) 2005, and amongst 50 Most Powerful Women in Business outside the US (first) 2006, (fourth) 2007, ranked by Forbes magazine amongst 100 Most Powerful Women (56th) 2004, (13th) 2005, (25th) 2006, (10th) 2007, ranked by the Financial Times amongst Top 25 Businesswomen in Europe (seventh) 2007. *Address:* c/o Alcatel–Lucent, 54, rue de la Boétie, 75008 Paris, France. *Telephone:* 1-40-76-10-10. *E-mail:* execoffice@alcatel-lucent.com.

RUSSO, Rene; American actress; b. 17 Feb. 1954, Burbank, Calif.; d. of Shirley Russo; one d.; fmrly model Eileen Ford Agency. *Film appearances include:* Meanwhile in Santa Monica 1988, Major League 1989, Mr Destiny 1990, One Good Cop 1991, Freejack 1992, Lethal Weapon 3 1992, In the Line of Fire 1993, Major League II 1994, Outbreak 1995, Get Shorty 1995, Tin Cup 1996, Ransom 1996, Buddy 1997, Lethal Weapon 4 1998, The Thomas Crown Affair 1999, The Adventures of Rocky and Bullwinkle 2000, Showtime 2002, Big Trouble 2002, 2 for the Money 2005, Yours, Mine & Ours 2005. *Television appearance:* Sable (series) 1987. *Address:* c/o Progressive Artists Agency, 400 South Beverly Drive, Suite 216, Beverly Hills, CA 90212, USA.

RUSSO JERVOLINO, Rosa; Italian lawyer and politician; *Mayor of Naples;* b. 17 Sept. 1936, Naples; ed Univ. of Rome; worked in Research Dept CNEL 1961–68; joined Legis. Div. Ministry of the Budget 1969; mem. staff, subsequently Nat. Vice-Pres. Centro Italiano femminile 1969–78; mem. Nat. Exec. Women's Movt of Christian Democrat (DC) Party 1968–78, Pres. 1992; Nat. Organizer DC Family Div. 1974; Senator 1979–94; Deputy Camera dei deputati 1994–2001; Minister for Social Affairs 1989–92, of Educ. 1992–94, of the Interior 1998–99; Mayor of Naples 2001–; Chair. Parl. Supervisory Comm. of RAI (nat. TV and radio Corpn) 1985–. *Address:* Comune di Napoli, Piazza Municipio, Palazzo San Giacomo, 80100 Naples, Italy (office). *Telephone:* (081) 7951111 (office). *Fax:* (081) 7954517 (office). *E-mail:* sindaco@comune.napoli.it (office). *Website:* www.comune.napoli.it (office).

RUST, Edward B., Jr, BA, MBA, JD; American insurance industry executive; *Chairman and CEO, State Farm Insurance Companies;* b. Ill.; ed Illinois Wesleyan Univ., Bloomington, Southern Methodist Univ., Dallas, Tex.; joined Tex. Regional Office, State Farm 1975, Pres. and CEO State Farm Insurance Cos 1985–87, Chair. and CEO 1987–, also Chair. and CEO State Farm Mutual Automobile Insurance Co., Pres. and CEO State Farm Fire and Casualty Co.; mem. Bd of Dirs Caterpillar Inc., Peoria, Helmerich and Payne Inc., McGraw-Hill Cos Inc.; Co-Chair. The Business Roundtable for seven years; Chair. Emer. Ill. Business Roundtable, Business Higher Educ. Forum; fmr Chair. American Enterprise Inst., Financial Services Roundtable, Nat. Alliance for Business, Insurance Inst. for Highway Safety; Dir Achieve, Nat. Center for Educational Accountability; mem. Business Advisory Council, Illinois Coll. of Commerce and Business Admin; mem. Bd of Trustees, The Conf. Bd, Illinois Wesleyan Univ.; fmr mem. Advisory Council Stanford Univ. Grad. School of Business, Bd of Overseers Inst. for Civil Justice; fmr Trustee, American Inst. for Property and Liability Underwriters; mem. Tex. and Ill. bar asscns. *Address:* State Farm Insurance Cos, 1 State Farm Plaza, Bloomingon, IL 61710-0001, USA (office). *Telephone:* (309) 766-2311 (office). *Fax:* (309) 766-3621 (office). *E-mail:* info@statefarm.com (office). *Website:* www.statefarm .com (office).

RUSTAMOV, Elman Siraj oglu, CandEconSci, DEconSci; Azerbaijani economist and central banker; *Chairman, National Bank of Azerbaijan;* b. 29 June 1952, Jabrail dist; m.; three c.; ed Azerbaijan Nat. Economy Inst. (named after D. Bunyadzade); economist, Scientific Research Inst. of Economy, USSR State Planning Cttee July–Dec. 1973, Head Economist 1980–90, Doctorantura 1990–92; with Azerbaijan Nat. Economy Inst. 1973–78; mil. service, Smolensk, USSR 1974–75; Chief of Dept of Economy, Baku Fine Broadcloth Union of Azerbaijan SSR, Ministry of Light Industry 1978–80; Chief Adviser, Presidential Apparatus of Azerbaijan Repub. 1991–92; First Deputy Chair. Man. Bd Nat. Bank of Azerbaijan 1992–93, Deputy Chair. Man. Bd Agrarian – Industrial Union Jt Stock Bank 1993–94, First Deputy Chair. Man. Bd Nat. Bank of Azerbaijan 1994–95, Admin. for Azerbaijan at World Bank Group, MIGA and EBRD 1995, Chair. Man. Bd Nat. Bank of Azerbaijan 1995–. *Address:* National Bank of Azerbaijan, 32 Rashid Beybutov Avenue, Baku 370014, Azerbaijan (office). *Telephone:* (12) 931122 (office). *Fax:* (12) 935541 (office). *E-mail:* rustamov@nba.az (office). *Website:* www.nba.az (office).

RUSTIN, Jean; French artist; b. 3 March 1928, Moselle; s. of Georges Rustin and Andrée Carrat; m. Elsa Courand 1949; two s. (one deceased); ed Ecole Nationale Supérieure des Beaux Arts, Paris; works displayed at Musée d'Art Moderne, Paris and numerous other museums and centres in Europe and the USA; subject of books including Rustin by Edward Lucie-Smith 1991. *Publications:* Enfer = Rustin 1996, La quête de la figuration 1999. *Leisure interest:* the violin. *Address:* 110 rue Carnot, 93170 Bagnolet (office); Fondation Rustin, 38, Boulevard Raspail, 75007 Paris, France; Fondation Rustin, 21 Joseph Wautersstraat, 2600 Antwerp, Belgium. *Telephone:* 1-42-84-46-35 (Paris) (office); (3) 232-70-25 (Antwerp). *Fax:* 6–81–59–97–03 (Paris) (office). *E-mail:* charlotte@rustin.eu (office). *Website:* www.rustin.eu (office).

RUTAN, Elbert L. (Burt), BS; American aerospace engineer; *Owner, Scaled Composites, LLC;* b. 17 June 1943, Portland, Ore.; m. 4th Tonya Rutan; ed Calif. Polytechnic Univ.; first solo flight in Aeronca Champ aeroplane aged 16 1959; flight test project engineer, USAF, Edwards Air Force Base 1965–72; Dir Bede Test Center for Bede Aircraft, Newton, Kan. 1972–74; f. Rutan Aircraft Factory to develop light aircraft for homebuilt aircraft market 1974; f. Scaled Composites, LLC 1982, designed several aircraft including Voyager aircraft that his brother Dick and Jeana Yeager flew in first nonstop, un-refuelled flight around the world 1986, SpaceShipOne (first pvt. vehicle to achieve suborbital, 62.5 miles/100 km, spaceflight), Raytheon Beechcraft Starship, Proteus, VariEze, Long-EZ, Quickie, Quickie 2, Defiant, and Boomerang; won $10 million Ansari X Prize for making two flights in SpaceShipOne within two weeks 29 Sept. and 4 Oct. 2004. *Address:* Scaled Composites, LLC, 1624 Flight Line, Mojave, CA 93501, USA (office). *Telephone:* (661) 824-4541 (office). *Fax:* (661) 824-4174 (office). *Website:* www.scaled.com (office).

RUTELLI, Francesco; Italian politician; b. 14 June 1954, Rome; m. Barbara Palombelli; two c.; mem. Camera dei Deputati (Parl.) (Radicals) 1983–93, then mem. Green Party, then Founder mem. Democrats party; Minister for Environment (resgnd after one day) 1993; Mayor of Rome 1993–2001; mem. European Parl. 1999–2004; Pres. Democrazia è Libertà–La Margherita (Democracy is Liberty–The Daisy) 2001–07, mem. Partito Democratico (Democratici di Sinistra and Democrazia è Libertà–La Margherita) 2007–; Deputy Prime Minister and Minister of Cultural Assets and Activities 2006–08; Chair. Parl. Cttee for the Security of the Repub. (COPASIR) 2008–. *Address:* Partito Democratico, Piazza Saint'Anastasia 7, 00186 Rome, Italy (office). *Telephone:* (06) 675471 (office). *Fax:* (06) 67547319 (office). *E-mail:* info@partitodemocratico.it (office). *Website:* www.partitodemocratico .it (office).

RUTHVEN, Kenneth Knowles, PhD; British academic; *Visiting Professor of English, University of Adelaide;* b. 26 May 1936; ed Univ. of Manchester; Asst Lecturer, Lecturer, Sr Lecturer, Univ. of Canterbury, Christchurch, NZ 1961–72, Prof. of English 1972–79; Prof. of English, Univ. of Adelaide, Australia 1980–85, Univ. of Melbourne, Vic., Australia 1985–99, Prof. Emer. 2000–; Visiting Prof. of English, Univ. of Adelaide 2002–. *Publications:* A Guide to Ezra Pound's Personae 1969, The Conceit 1969, Myth 1976, Critical Assumptions 1979, Feminist Literary Studies: An Introduction 1984, Ezra Pound as Literary Critic 1990, Beyond the Disciplines: The New Humanities (ed.) 1992, Nuclear Criticism 1993, Faking Literature 2001; Southern Review (Adelaide) (ed.) 1981–85, Interpretations series (gen.) 1993–96 (19 vols). *Address:* 27 Fairleys Road, Rostrevor 5073, South Australia, Australia (home). *Telephone:* (8) 8336-6348 (home). *E-mail:* kruthven@chariot.net.au (home). *Website:* www.arts.adelaide.edu.au/humanities/english (office).

RUTKIEWICZ, Ignacy Mikołaj; Polish journalist; *President, Foundation Press Centre for Central and Eastern Europe;* b. 15 April 1929, Vilna; s. of Józef Rutkiewicz and Maria Rutkiewicz (née Turkułł); m. Wilma Helena Koller 1961; two s.; ed Poznań Univ.; Ed., Ed.-in-Chief Wrocławski Tygodnik Katolicki (weekly) 1953–55; journalist, Zachodnia Agencja Prasowa (ZAP) 1957–66, Polska Agencja Interpress 1967–70; Ed. Odra (monthly) 1961–81, Ed.-in-Chief 1982–90, mem. Editorial Council 1991–; Co-Founder, mem. Editorial Council Więź (monthly), Warsaw 1958–; Pres.-Ed.-in-Chief Polish Press Agency (PAP), Warsaw 1990–92, 1992–94; Adviser to Prime Minister, Warsaw 1994–95; TV journalist TV Centre of Training, Polish TV (TVP) 1994–96; Sec. TV Comm. for Ethics 1996–; Ed.-in-Chief Antena (weekly) 1998; Adviser to Minister of Culture and Arts 1998–99; Sr Ed. On-line News, TVP 1999–; Co-founder and Vice-Pres. Polish-German Asscn, Warsaw 1990–2001; Vice-Pres. Alliance Européenne des Agences de Presse, Zürich 1991–92; mem. Exec. Bd, Asscn of Polish Journalists (SDP) 1980–82, Pres. 1993–95; mem. Council on Media and Information, Pres.'s Office 1993–95; mem. Euroatlantic Asscn 1995–; mem. Bd Foundation Press Centre for Cen. and Eastern Europe 1996–, (Pres. 2001–), Programme Bd Nat. Club of Friends of Lithuania 1996–, Programme Bd Polish Press Agency 1998–2002; Assoc. mem. Orbicom (int. network of UNESCO Chairs in Communications) 2000–; Kt, Order of Polonia Restituta 1981; City of Wrocław Award 1963, B. Prus Award of SDP 1990, Phil epistémoni Award, Jagiellonian Univ., Kraków 1991. *Publications:* author or co-author of more than 10 books; Transformation of Media and Journalism in Poland 1989–1996 (author and co-ed.), How to be Fair in the Media: Guidelines not only for TV journalists. *Leisure interests:* literature, recent history, foreign languages, mountain trips, skiing. *Address:* Ośrodek Nowe Media TVP, ul. Woronicza 17, 00-999 Warsaw (office); Al. Jerozolimskie 42/55, 00-024 Warsaw, Poland (home). *Telephone:* (22) 5477082 (office); (22) 8275813 (home). *E-mail:* ignacy.rutkiewicz@waw.tvp.pl (office). *Website:* www .wiadomosci.tvp.pl (office).

RUTSKOY, Maj.-Gen. Aleksandr Vladimirovich, CandEconSc; Russian politician and military officer; b. 16 Sept. 1947, Proskurov, Kamenets Podolsk Region (now Khmelnitsky, Ukraine); s. of Vladimir Alexandrovich Rutskoy and Zinaida Iosifovna Rutskaya; m. 3rd Irina Rutskaya; three s. one d.; ed Higher Air Force Coll., Barnaul, Y. Gagarin Higher Air Force Acad., Acad. of Gen. Staff; fmr mem. CPSU (expelled 1991); Regimental Commdr, Afghan War 1985–86; Deputy Commdr Army Air Force 1988; RSFSR People's Deputy, mem. Supreme Soviet, mem. Presidium of Supreme Soviet 1990–91; Leader Communists for Democracy (renamed People's Party of Free Russia 1991, renamed Russian Social Democratic Party 1994); Vice-Pres. RSFSR (now Russian Fed.) 1991–93; Head Centre for the Operational Supervision of the Progress of Reforms 1991–93; Leader Civic Union coalition 1992–93; declared Acting Pres. of Russia by Parl. Sept. 1993; arrested as one of organizers of failed coup d'état Oct. 1993; freed on amnesty Feb. 1994; Chair. Social-Patriotic Movt Derzhava 1994; Gov. of Kursk Region 1996–2000; mem. Council Europe Parl. 1996–2000; Pro-Rector Moscow State Social Univ. 2001; Hero of Soviet Union 1988, Order of Lenin, seven Russian and Afghan orders; 15 medals. *Publications include:* Agrarian Reform in Russia 1992,

Unknown Rutskoy 1994, About Us and Myself 1995, Finding Faith 1995, Lefortovo Protocols 1995, March Records 1995, Bloody Autumn 1996, Liberal Reforms – Strong Power 1996. *Leisure interests:* painting, gardening, designing, fishing. *Telephone:* (495) 292-66-98.

RUTT, Rev. Canon Cecil Richard, CBE, MA, DLitt; British ecclesiastic; b. 27 Aug. 1925, Langford, Beds.; s. of Cecil Rutt and Mary Hare Turner; m. Joan M. Ford 1969; ed Huntingdon Grammar School, Kelham Theological Coll. and Pembroke Coll., Cambridge; RNVR 1943–46; ordained 1951; curate St George's, Cambridge 1951–54; Church of England Mission to Korea 1954–74, consecrated Bishop 1966, Bishop of Taejon, Repub. of Korea 1968–74; Bishop of St Germans, Cornwall 1974–79; Bishop of Leicester 1979–90; Chair. Advisory Council for Relations of Bishops and Religious Communities 1980–90; joined RC Catholic Church as layman 1994, became priest 1995; mem. Anglican/Orthodox Jt Doctrinal Discussions 1983–89; Hon. Canon Diocese of Plymouth 2001; Bard of the Gorseth of Cornwall 1976, Chaplain 1993; Chaplain, Order of St John of Jerusalem 1978; Hon. Fellow, Northumbrian Univs E Asia Centre 1990–; Order of Civil Merit, Peony Class (Korea) 1974; Hon. DLitt (Confucian Univ., Seoul) 1974; Tasan Cultural Award (for writings on Korea) 1964. *Publications:* Korean Anglican Hymnal (ed.) 1961, Korean Works and Days 1964, P'ungnyu Han'guk (in Korean) 1965, An Anthology of Korean Sijo 1970, The Bamboo Grove 1971, James Scarth Gale and His History of the Korean People 1972, Virtuous Women 1974, A History of Hand Knitting 1987, The Book of Changes (Zhouyi): A Bronze Age Document 1996, Korea: A Cultural and Historical Dictionary (with Keith Pratt) 1999, The Martyrs of Korea 2002; contribs to various Korean and liturgical publications. *Address:* 3 Marlborough Court, Falmouth, Cornwall, TR11 2QU, England. *Telephone:* (1326) 312276. *E-mail:* richard@ruttc.fsnet .co.uk (home).

RUTTENSTORFER, Wolfgang, DEcon; Austrian business executive; *Chairman of the Executive Board and CEO, OMV AG;* b. 1950, Vienna; m.; three c.; ed Univ. of Econs and Business Admin, Vienna; joined OMV AG 1976, with Planning and Control Dept 1985, Head of Strategic Devt 1989–90, Head of Marketing 1990, mem. Exec. Bd 1992–97, 2000–, CEO and Chair., Exec. Bd 2002–; Deputy Minister of Finance 1997–2000. *Address:* OMV AG, Otto Wagner Platz 5, 1090 Vienna, Austria (office). *Telephone:* (1) 40440-21401 (office). *Fax:* (1) 40440-29496 (office). *E-mail:* wolfgang.ruttenstorfer@omv .com (office). *Website:* www.omv.com (office).

RUTTER, John Milford, CBE, MA, DMus; British composer and conductor; *Director, The Cambridge Singers;* b. 24 Sept. 1945, London; m. JoAnne Redden 1980; two s. (one deceased) one step-d.; ed Highgate School and Clare Coll., Cambridge; Dir of Music Clare Coll., Cambridge 1975–79; part-time Lecturer in Music, Open Univ. 1975–87; Founder and Dir The Cambridge Singers 1981–; Hon. Fellow, Westminster Choir Coll., Princeton; Hon. DMus (Lambeth) 1996; Ivor Novello Classical Music Award 2007. *Compositions include:* The Falcon 1969, Gloria 1974, Bang! (opera for young people) 1975, The Piper of Hamelin (opera for young people) 1980, Requiem 1985, Magnificat 1990, I my best beloved's am (unaccompanied choral work for BBC Sounding the Millennium series) 1999, Mass of the Children 2003; numerous carols, anthems and songs; orchestral works and music for TV. *Recordings include:* original version of Fauré Requiem 1984. *Publications:* Opera Choruses (ed.) 1995, European Sacred Music (ed.) 1996, Christmas Motets (ed.) 1999. *Address:* Old Laceys, St John's Street, Duxford, Cambridge, CB22 4RA, England (home).

RUTTER, Sir Michael Llewellyn, Kt, CBE, MD, FRS, FRCP, FRCPsych; British academic; *Research Professor, Institute of Psychiatry, King's College London;* b. 15 Aug. 1933; s. of Llewellyn Charles Rutter and Winifred Olive Rutter; m. Marjorie Heys 1958; one s. two d.; ed Univ. of Birmingham Medical School, training in paediatrics, neurology and internal medicine 1955–58; practised at Maudsley Hosp. 1958–61; Nuffield Medical Travelling Fellow, Albert Einstein Coll. of Medicine, New York 1961–62; scientist with MRC Social Psychology Research Unit 1962–65; Sr Lecturer, then Reader, Univ. of London Inst. of Psychiatry 1966–73; Prof. of Child Psychiatry 1973–98, Research Prof. 1998–; Dir MRC Research Centre for Social, Genetic and Developmental Psychiatry 1994–98; Hon. Dir MRC Child Psychiatry Unit 1984–98; Fellow, Center for Advanced Study in Behavioral Sciences, Stanford Univ. 1979–80; guest lecturer at many insts in Britain and America; Pres. Soc. for Research in Child Devt 1999–2001 (Pres. elect 1997–99); Clinical Vice-Pres. Acad. of Medical Sciences 2004–07; Hon. Fellow, British Psychological Soc. 1978, American Acad. of Pediatrics 1981, Royal Soc. of Medicine 1996; Hon. doctorates (Leiden) 1985, (Catholic Univ. of Leuven) 1990, (Birmingham) 1990, (Edin.) 1990, (Chicago) 1991, (Minnesota) 1993, (Jyväskylä) 1996, (Warwick) 1999, (E. Anglia) 2000. *Publications:* Children of Sick Parents 1966: A Neuropsychiatric Study in Childhood (jtly) 1970, Education, Health and Behaviour (ed. jtly) 1970, Infantile Autism (ed.) 1971, Maternal Deprivation Reassessed (ed.) 1981, The Child with Delayed Speech (jtly) 1972, Helping Troubled Children (jtly) 1975, Cycles of Disadvantage (jtly) 1976; Child Psychiatry (ed. jtly) 1976, (2nd edn as Child and Adolescent Psychiatry 1985), Autism (ed. jtly) 1978, Changing Youth in a Changing Society (jtly) 1979, Fifteen Thousand Hours: Secondary Schools and Their Effect on Children 1979, Scientific Foundations of Developmental Psychiatry (ed.)1981, A Measure of Our Values: Goals and Dilemmas in the Upbringing of Children (jtly) 1983, Lead versus Health (jtly) 1983, Juvenile Delinquency 1983, Developmental Neuropsychiatry (ed.) 1983, Stress, Coping and Development (ed. jtly) 1983, Depression and Young People (ed. jtly) 1986, Studies of Psychosocial Risk: The Power of Longitudinal Data (ed.) 1988, Parenting Breakdown: The Making and Breaking of Intergenerational Links (jtly) 1988, Straight and Devious Pathways from Childhood to Adulthood (ed. jtly) 1990, Biological Risk Factors for Psychosocial Disorders (ed. jtly) 1991, Developing Minds (jtly) 1993, Development Through

Life: A Handbook for Clinicians (ed. jtly) 1994, Stress, Risk and Resilience in Children and Adolescents (ed. jtly) 1994, Psychological Disorders in Young People 1995, Antisocial Behaviour by Young People (jtly) 1998, Genes and Behaviour: Nature-Nurture Interplay Explained 2006. *Leisure interests:* fell walking, tennis, wine tasting, theatre. *Address:* Institute of Psychiatry, King's College London, Box P080, De Crespigny Park, London SE5 8AF (office); 190 Court Lane, Dulwich, London, SE21 7ED, England (home). *Telephone:* (20) 7848-0882 (office). *Fax:* j.wickham@iop.kcl.ac.uk (office). *Website:* www.iop.kcl .ac.uk/iopweb/departments/home/?locator=10 (office).

RÜÜTEL, Arnold, PhD, DrAgrSc; Estonian politician, agronomist and fmr head of state; *Honorary Chairman, Estonian People's Union;* b. 10 May 1928, Laimjala, Saaremaa Island; s. of Feodor Rüütel and Juuli Rüütel; m. Ingrid Rüütel (née Ruus) 1935; two d.; ed Jäneda Agric. Coll., Estonian Agricultural Acad.; Sr Agronomist, Saaremaa Dist, Estonian SSR 1949–50; mil. service 1950–55; teacher, Tartu School of Mechanization of Agric. 1955–57; Deputy Dir Estonian Inst. of Livestock-breeding and Veterinary Sciences 1957–63; mem. CPSU 1964–90; Dir Tartu Model State Farm 1963–69; Rector Estonian Agric. Acad. 1969–77; Agricultural Sec. of Cen. Cttee of Estonian CP 1977–79; First Deputy Chair. Council of Ministers of Estonia 1979–83; Chair. Presidium of Supreme Soviet of Estonian SSR 1983–90, of Supreme Council of Repub. of Estonia 1990–92; Deputy Pres. of USSR Presidium of Supreme Soviet 1984–91; mem. Constitutional Ass. 1991–92; Founder, Dir Inst. for Nat. Devt and Cooperation 1993–2001; Founder and Chair. Estonian Rural People's Party (Maarava) 1994–99, Chair. Estonian People's Union 1999–2000, Hon. Chair. 2000–01; mem. Riigikogu (Parl.) 1995–2001, Vice-Chair. 1995–97, Chair. ruling coalition's council 1995–99; Head Del. of Riigikogu to Baltic Ass. 1995–99, mem., alternately Chair. Presidium 1995–99; presidential cand. 1996; Pres. of Estonia 2001–06; Chair. Estonian Soc. for Nature Protection 1981–88, Keep Estonian Sea Clean, Forselius (educational org.); Pres. Estonian Green Cross 1993–2001; mem. Tallinn City Council 1993–2001; Chair. Estonian Soc. for Nature Conservation 1981–88 (Hon. mem. 1989–), B.G. Forselius Soc. 1989–2002, Hon. Chair. 2002–, Movt 'Protect the Estonian Sea' 1993–2002 (Hon. Chair. 2002–); Pres. Estonian Nat. Org. of the Green Cross Int. 1993–2001; Foreign mem. Ukranian Acad. of Agrarian Sciences 2002; Hon. mem. Estonian Academic Agricultural Soc. 2002–, Int. Raoul Wallenberg Foundation 2002–; Collar of Order of Grand Cross of Terra Mariana (Estonia) 2001, Grand Cross Order of the White Rose with Collar (Finland) 2001, Grand Cross Order of the White Eagle (Poland) 2002, Grand Cross Royal Order of St Olaf (Norway) 2002, Grand Cross Order of Merit (Hungary) 2002, Grand Cross Order of Adolph de Nassau (Luxembourg) 2003, Grand Collar Order of Infant D. Henrique (Portugal) 2003, Grand Collar Nat. Order of Merit (Malta) 2003, Grand Collar Nat. Order of Merit (Romania) 2003, Grand Collar Order of Makarios III (Cyprus) 2004, Grand Cross with Collar, Order of Merit (Italy) 2004, Order of Falcon (Iceland) 2004, Order of 1st Class of Vytautas the Great (Lithuania) 2004, Order of 1st Class White Double Cross (Slovak Repub.) 2005; Dr hc (Bentley Coll.) 1991, (Estonian Agricultural Univ.) 1991, (Univ. of Helsinki) 2002, (Nat. Agricultural Univ. of Ukraine) 2002, (Univ. of Naples II) 2002, (Szent Istvan Univ., Hungary) 2004, (L.N. Gumilyov Eurasian Nat. Univ. of Kazakhstan) 2004, (Yerevan, Armenia) 2004; Rotary Foundation Distinguished Service Award 2002, Andres Bello Commemorative Medal 2002. *Publications:* Tuleviku taassünd (The Rebirth of the Future) (memoirs) 2003. *Leisure interests:* nature protection, sports. *Address:* Estonian People's Union (Eestimaa Rahvaliit), Pärnu mnt. 30–6, Tallinn 10141, Estonia (office). *Telephone:* 644-8578 (office). *Fax:* 648-5053 (office). *E-mail:* erl@erl.ee (office). *Website:* www.erl.ee (office).

RUYS, Anthony; Dutch business executive; b. 20 July 1947, Antwerp, Belgium; m. Melanie E. van Haaften; two s.; ed Univ. of Utrecht, Harvard Business School; marketing trainee Van den Bergh & Jurgens 1974–80; Marketing Dir Cogra Lever S.A. 1980–84, Chair. 1984–87; Chair. Van den Bergh Italy; mem. Bd Italian Unilever Cos 1987–89; Chair. Van den Bergh Netherlands; mem. Bd Dutch Unilever Cos 1989–92; Sr Regional Man. Food Exec., North European Region, Unilever NV 1992–93; mem. Exec. Bd Heineken NV 1993–96, Vice-Chair. 1996–2002, Chair. 2002–05; Dir TRN, BAT Europe (Netherlands) BV, Rembrandt Foundation, Gtech Corpn, NH Hotels SA 1994–2003; Pres. Supervisory Bd Rijksmuseum, Amsterdam, Stop Aids Now Foundation, ECR Europe 2004–06; mem. Supervisory Bd Gtech Holdings Corpn (now Lottomatica Italy), USA, ABN Ambro Bank, Sara Lee Int. B.V., Rijksmuseum, Amsterdam, Tourism Recreation Netherlands, Aiesec Netherlands 1996–2004, Veerstichting 1997–2007; mem. Bd of Dirs Netherlands Asscn for Int. Affairs, Int. Chamber of Commerce Netherlands, Nationaal Fonds Kunstbehoud, British American Tobacco PLC 2006–, Luchthaven Schipol NV, Rothmans Europe 1997–2001, Robeco Group NV 2001–04, Trilateral Comm. 2003–06, European Round Table of Industrialists 2004–05; mem. European Advisory Bd Harvard Business School 2003–07; mem. Int. Council INSEAD. *Address:* c/o Heineken NV, Tweede Weteringsplantsoen 21, Postbus 28, 1000 Amsterdam AA, Netherlands (office).

RUZICKA, Karel Zdenek; Czech musician and composer; b. 2 June 1940, Prague; s. of Zdenek Ruzicka and Vlasta Ruzicka; m. Marie-José; one s.; ed Conservatory of Prague; pianist, Semafor Theatre, Prague 1960–66; mem. Prague Radio Big Band 1966–90; teacher Conservatory of Jaroslav Jezek, Prague 1969; imprisoned for political activities 1969; pianist, composer, arranger, conductor 1970–2000; f. Karel Ruzicka Jazz Quartet; has toured and performed in Canada, Poland, Cuba, France and Czech Repub.; has collaborated with Laco Deczi's Jazz Cellula septet, Czech–Polish Big Band, Veleband All-Stars and with numerous musicians including Rudolf Dasek (guitarist), Jarmo Sermila (trumpeter), Jiri Stivin(flutist), Wilson de Oliveira (saxophonist); Celebration Jazz Mass and Te Deum compositions performed during The Prague Spring Music Festival and also in Europe and USA; Monte Carlo Int. Jazz Festival composition awards (Interlude) 1977, (Echoes) 1978,

(Triste) 1979; numerous awards from the Czech Composers Soc. and Musical Acad. of Monaco. *Recordings:* 10 albums, 100 compositions, including Fata Morgana, Going Home, Flight, Celebration Jazz Mass, Te Deum. *Publications:* Jazz Echoes, Best of Arta. *Leisure interest:* literature. *Address:* c/o Conservatory of Jaroslav Jezek, Roskotova 4/1692, 14000 Prague 4 (office); Devonska 1, 15200 Prague 5, Czech Republic (home). *E-mail:* karuz@barr.cz (home); karuzjazz@gmail.com (home).

RUZIMATOV, Farukh Sadilloyevich; Tajikistani ballet dancer and ballet director; *Artistic Director, Mikhailovsky Theater Ballet Company;* b. 26 June 1963, Tashkent; ed Vaganova Acad. of Russian Ballet; soloist State Academic Mariinsky Theatre 1981–86, Prin. Dancer 1986–2007; guest dancer Bolshoi Theatre, Moscow; Prin. Guest Dancer, American Ballet Theater 1990–91; Artistic Dir Mikhailovsky Theater Ballet Company, St Petersburg 2007–; Pres. Farukh Ruzimatov The Renaissance of the Dance Art Foundation 2006–; chevalier, Order For the Spiritual Renaissance of Russia; Silver Medallist, Sixth Varna Int. Competition 1983, awarded special diploma by Paris Acad. of Dance, Honoured Artist of Russia 1995, Golden Sofit Award 1995, Baltika Prize 1998, Peoplés Artist of Russia 2000. *Principal roles include:* Albert in Giselle, Siegfried in Swan Lake, Basil in Don Quixote, The Prince in The Nutcracker, José in Carmen, Golden Slave in Sheherazade, Désiré Prince in Sleeping Beauty, James in La Sylphide, Solor in Bayadere, Ali in Corsair, Abderahman in Raymonda, Ferhad in Fokin's The Legend about love, Tariel in Vinogradov's The Knight in Tiger Skin. *Address:* Mikhailovsky Theatre, Arts Square, 1, St Petersburg, Russia (office). *Telephone:* (812) 595-43-05 (office). *E-mail:* pr@ mikhailovsky.ru (office). *Website:* www.mikhailovsky.ru (office).

RUZOWITZKY, Stefan; Austrian film director and screenwriter; b. 25 Dec. 1961, Vienna; m.; two d.; ed Univ. of Vienna; began career by directing documentaries and commercials and also music videos for N'Sync, Scorpions and Die Prinzen. *Films:* Tempo (Max Ophüls Preis) 1996, Die Siebtelbauern (The Inheritors; aka The One-Seventh Farmers) (Best Picture, Rotterdam Film Festival, Flanders Film Festival, prize at Int. Film Festival, Valladolid) 1998, Anatomie (Anatomy) 2000, All the Queen's Men (Die Männer Ihrer Majestät) 2001, Anatomie 2 2003, Die Fälscher (The Counterfeiters) (Academy Award for Best Foreign Language Film 2008) 2007. *Address:* c/o Miriam Rönn, Corporate Communications, Studio Babelsberg AG, August-Bebelstr. 26–53, 14482 Potsdam, Germany. *Telephone:* (331) 721-21-32. *Fax:* (331) 721-21-35. *E-mail:* mroenn@studiobabelsberg.com. *Website:* www.studiobabelsberg.com.

RYABOV, Nikolai Timofeyevich; Russian politician, lawyer and diplomatist; b. 9 Dec. 1946, Salsk, Rostov Region; ed Rostov Univ.; mem. CPSU 1968–91; worked as tractor driver, engineer Salsk Agricultural Machine Factory 1966–72; taught in higher educ. school of Rostov Region 1973–90; People's Deputy of Russia 1990–93; mem. Supreme Soviet 1990–92, Chair. Sub-Cttee for legis. 1990–91; Chair. Council of Repubs 1991–92, Deputy Chair. Supreme Soviet 1992–93; Deputy Chair. Constitutional Comm. 1991–93, Chair. Cen. Election Comm. of Russian Fed. 1993–96; Amb. to Czech Repub. 1996–2000, to Azerbaijan 2000–04, to Moldova 2004–06. *Address:* c/o Ministry of Foreign Affairs, 119200 Moscow, Smolenskaya-Sennaya pl. 32/34, Russia.

RYABOV, Vladimir Vladimirovich, PhD; Russian composer and pianist; *Composer in Residence, Moscow Symphony Orchestra;* b. 15 Sept. 1950, Chelyabinsk; m. 1st; one d.; m. 4th Ellen Levine; ed Moscow State Conservatory (expelled twice for non-conformist attitudes), Gnessin Pedagogical Inst. of Music (under Aram Khachaturyan), Leningrad State Conservatory; taught composition in Leningrad and Sverdlovsk conservatories 1977–81; Artistic and Repertoire Consultant, Moscow Symphony Orchestra 1993–; toured as pianist in Russia, Finland, USA, Germany, Austria, Hungary, Italy and Spain, performing standard repertoire and own compositions; mem. Int. Informatization Acad.; winner First S. Prokofiev Int. Composers' Competition 1991, Merited Artist of Russia 1995, Pushkin Gold Medal 1999. *Film:* The Life of Frederic Chopin (pianist) 1992. *Compositions include:* over 30, including 4 symphonies (Nine Northern Tunes 1977, Pushkin 1980, Listen! 1981, In Memoriam of J. Brahms 1983), 5 string quartets, works for full and chamber orchestras, sonatas and other compositions for piano, violin, viola, organ, choir, song cycles on Russian poetry and English, American, Spanish and German poetry in Russian trans., transcriptions of classical music and folk songs, 6 cycles of sacred music, European Cathedrals (7 cycles for different chamber ensembles), Norwegian Suite for symphony orchestra. *Leisure interests:* reading Russian poetry on stage, collecting illustrations of owls. *Address:* Novoyasenevsky pr. 14, kor. 2 Apt. 48, Moscow 117574, Russia (home); Orisaarentie 6E, 00840 Helsinki, Finland (home). *Telephone:* (495) 143-97-13 (Moscow) (home); (9) 6984059 (Helsinki) (home). *E-mail:* moscowsymphonyorchestra@mtu-net.ru (office). *Website:* www .moscowsymphony.ru (office).

RYAN, Alan James, BA, MA, DLitt, FBA; British political scientist, academic and writer; *Warden, New College, University of Oxford;* b. 9 May 1940, London; s. of James W. Ryan and Ivy Ryan; m. Kathleen Alyson Lane 1971; one d.; ed Christ's Hospital and Balliol Coll. Oxford; Fellow, New Coll. Oxford 1969–; Reader in Politics, Univ. of Oxford 1978–88; Prof. of Politics, Princeton Univ. 1988–96, Mellon Fellow, Inst. for Advanced Study 1991–92; Warden, New Coll., Oxford 1996–; Visiting Prof., City Univ. of New York 1967–, Univ. of Texas 1972, Univ. of Calif., Santa Cruz 1977, Univ. of Witwatersrand 1973, 1978, ANU 1974–75, Univ. of Cape Town 1982–84; Visiting Fellow, ANU 1979; de Carle Lecturer, Univ. of Otago 1983; Fellow, Center for Advanced Studies in the Behavioral Sciences 2002–03; del. Oxford Univ. Press 1982–87; Almoner Christ's Hosp. 1998–. *Publications:* The Philosophy of John Stuart Mill 1970, The Philosophy of the Social Sciences 1970, J. S. Mill 1974, Property and Political Theory 1984, Property 1987, Russell: A Political Life 1988, John Dewey and the High Tide of American Liberalism 1995, Liberal Anxieties and

Liberal Education 1998. *Leisure interests:* dinghy sailing, long train journeys. *Address:* Warden's Lodgings, New College, Oxford, OX1 3BN, England. *Telephone:* (1865) 279501 (office). *Fax:* (1865) 724047 (office). *E-mail:* alan .ryan@new.ox.ac.uk (office). *Website:* new.ox.ac.uk (office); users.ox.ac.uk/ ajryan.

RYAN, Arthur (Art) Frederick; American insurance industry executive; b. 14 Sept. 1942, Brooklyn, NY; s. of Arthur Ryan and Gertrude Wingert; m. Patricia Kelly; two s. two d.; ed Providence Coll.; Area Man. Data Corpn Washington, DC 1965–72; Project Man. Chase Manhattan Corpn and Bank, New York 1972–73, Second Vice-Pres. 1973–74, Vice-Pres. 1974–75, Operations Exec. 1978, Exec. Vice-Pres. 1982, later Vice-Chair., Pres. 1990–94; CEO Prudential Insurance Co. of America (now Prudential Financial Inc.) 1994–2007, Chair. 1994–2008; mem. American Bankers Asscn. *Address:* c/o Prudential Financial Inc., 751 Broad Street, 24th Floor, Newark, NJ 07102, USA (office).

RYAN, Meg; American actress; b. 19 Nov. 1961, Fairfield, Conn.; m. Dennis Quaid (q.v.) 1991 (divorced); one s.; ed Bethel High School and New York Univ.; fmrly appeared in TV commercials; TV appearances in As the World Turns, One of the Boys, Amy and the Angel, The Wild Side, Charles in Charge; f. Prufrock Pictures (production co., fmrly Fandango Films) 1994. *Films:* Rich and Famous 1981, Amityville III-D, Top Gun, Armed and Dangerous, Innerspace, D.O.A., Promised Land, The Presidio, When Harry Met Sally, Joe Versus the Volcano, The Doors, Prelude to a Kiss, Sleepless in Seattle, Flesh and Bone, Significant Other, When a Man Loves a Woman, I.Q., Paris Match, Restoration, French Kiss 1995, Two for the Road 1996, Courage Under Fire 1996, Addicted to Love 1997, City of Angels 1998, You've Got Mail 1998, Hanging Up 1999, Lost Souls 1999, Proof of Life 2000, Kate & Leopold 2001, In the Cut 2003, Against the Ropes 2004, In the Land of Women 2007, The Deal 2008, My Mom's New Boyfriend 2008, The Women 2008. *Address:* c/o Steve Dontanville, ICM, 8942 Wilshire Boulevard, Beverly Hills, CA 90211, USA.

RYAN, Richard, BA, MA; Irish diplomatist; *Ambassador to Netherlands;* b. 1946, Dublin; m.; three c.; ed Oatlands Coll. and Univ. Coll., Dublin; joined Dept of Foreign Affairs 1973, First Sec., Perm. Mission to EC, Brussels 1980 (seconded to Comm. of EC 1982–83); Counsellor, Embassy in London 1983, Minister-Counsellor (Political) 1988, Amb. to Repub. of Korea 1989, to Spain (also accred to Algeria, Andorra and Tunisia) 1994–98; Perm. Rep. to UN, New York 1998–2005; Amb. to Netherlands 2005–; Hon. DLitt (Univ. of St Thomas) 2003. *Publications:* Ledges 1970, Ravenswood 1973. *Leisure interests:* shooting, archery, swimming. *Address:* Embassy of Ireland, Dr Kuyperstraat 9, 2514 BA The Hague, Netherlands (office). *Telephone:* (70) 3630993 (office). *Fax:* (70) 3617604 (office). *E-mail:* thehagueembassy@dfa.ie (office). *Website:* www.embassyofireland.nl (office).

RYAN, Thomas M. (Tom), BS; American pharmacist and retail executive; *Chairman, President and CEO, CVS Caremark Corporation;* b. 15 Aug. 1952, NJ; m. Cathy Ryan; four c.; ed Univ. of Rhode Island; began career as pharmacist, CVS Pharmacy Inc. 1975, various man. and professional positions including Pres. and CEO CVS Pharmacy Inc. 1994–, Vice-Chair. and COO CVS Corpn 1996–98, Chair. 1999–2007, Pres. and CEO CVS Caremark Corpn 1998–2007 (following merger of Caremark Rx Inc. and CVS Corpn), Chair. 2007–; Dir FleetBoston Financial Corpn, Reebok Int. Ltd, Yum! Brands Inc., Tricon Global Restaurants Inc.; Co-Chair. Blue Ribbon Steering Cttee, Univ. of RI, Chair. Leadership Gifts Cttee, URI Convocation Center; Hon. DHumLitt (Univ. of RI) 1999. *Address:* CVS Caremark Corpn, 1 CVS Drive, Woonsocket, RI 02895, USA (office). *Telephone:* (401) 765-1500 (office). *Fax:* (401) 766-2917 (office). *E-mail:* storecomments@cvs.com (office). *Website:* www .cvs.com (office).

RYAZANOV, Eldar Aleksandrovich; Russian film director, writer and television broadcaster; b. 18 Nov. 1927, Samara; studied at VGIK under Pyriev, Kozintsev and Eisenstein; writes most of his own scripts (often together with playwright Emil Braginsky); Chevalier, Légion d'honneur; State Prize of USSR, State Prize of Russia, People's Artist of the USSR 1984, People's Artist of Russia. *Films include:* Voices of Spring 1955, Carnival Night 1956, The Girl without an Address 1957, How Robinson was Created 1961, The Hussar Ballad 1962, Let Me Make a Complaint 1964, Look out for the Cars 1966, The Zigzag of Success 1968, The Old Rascals 1971, The Amazing Adventures of Italians in Russia 1973, The Irony of Fate 1975, An Official Romance 1978, Garage 1979, Put in a Word for the Poor Hussar 1981, Railway Station for Two 1983, A Cruel Romance 1984, Forgotten Melody for Flute 1988, Dear Elena Sergeevna 1988, The Promised Heaven 1991 (Nika Prize 1992), The Prediction 1993, Hey, Fools! 1996, The Old Horses 2000, The Quiet Streams 2000, The Key of the Bedroom 2003, Andersen. Life Without Love 2006; numerous TV productions, including interviews with Boris Yeltsin and Naina Yeltsin 1993. *Television:* The Paris Secrets (series), The Conversations on Fresh Air (series), The Woman's Summer (series). *Publication:* Not Summarizing (memoirs), Nostalgia (poems), The Prediction (novel), Irony of Fate, The Quiet Streams, Eldar TV or My Portrait's Gallery (memoirs) 2002. *Address:* Bolshoi Tishinski per. 12, Apt 70, 123557 Moscow, Russia. *Telephone:* (495) 721-83-70; (495) 546-94-15. *Fax:* (495) 546-94-15 (office).

RYBKIN, Ivan Petrovich, DrPolitSch, CandTechSc; Russian politician; b. 20 Oct. 1946, Semigorovka, Voronezh Region; m.; two d.; ed Volgograd Inst. of Agric. Acad. of Social Sciences at Cen. Cttee CPSU; Sr Engineer Kolkhoz Zavety Ilyicha Volgograd Region 1968–69; Lecturer, Prof., Head of Chair, Deputy Dean, Volgograd Inst. of Agric. 1970–87; Sec. Party Cttee 1983–87, First Sec. CPSU Dist Cttee in Volgograd, Second Sec. Volgograd Regional Cttee CPSU 1987–91; Head of Div. Cen. Cttee CP of RSFSR 1991; People's Deputy of Russia 1990–93; one of founders and Co-Chair. faction Communists of Russia 1990–91; mem. Agrarian Party, concurrently co-founder Socialist

Party of Workers 1991–93; Deputy in State Duma (Parl.) 1993–96, Chair. 1994–95; mem. Council on Personnel Policy of Pres. Yeltsin 1994–95, mem. Security Council 1994–96, Sec. 1996–98; head of group negotiating with Chechen leaders 1996–98; Deputy Prime Minister 1998; Plenipotentiary Rep. of Russian Pres. to CIS states 1998; Chair. Political Union Regions of Russia, concurrently of Election Bloc 1995–96; Chair. Political Consultative Council of Pres. of Russia 1999–2000; cand. in 2004 presidential elections; Prize for Contribution to Peace with Chechnya (Ichkeria) 1996. *Publications:* State Duma, Fifth Attempt, We are Doomed to Consensus, Russia and the World: The Way to Security; numerous articles. *Address:* c/o Socialist Party, Novo-Basmannaya str. 14, Building 1, 107078 Moscow, Russia (office).

RYCHETSKY, Pavel, JuDr; Czech politician and judge; *Chairman, Constitutional Court;* b. 17 Aug. 1943, Prague; m.; three c.; ed Charles Univ.; Sr Lecturer and Asst Prof., Dept of Civil Law, Charles Univ. Law School, Prague 1966–70, compelled to leave for political reasons; worked as co. lawyer for Fortuna commercial agency, Mladá fronta publrs and for housing devt co-operative; mem. CP 1966–69; Co-founder and signatory Charter 77; Co-founder Civic Forum, Rep. Civic Forum Liberal Club and later of Civic Movt; Public Prosecutor-Gen. of Czech Repub. 1990; Deputy Prime Minister and Chair. Legis. Council of the then Czech and Slovak Fed. Repub. 1990; f. solicitor's practice 1992; Lecturer in Political Sciences, Prague School of Econs Faculty of Int. Relations 1992; joined Czech Social Democrat Party 1995; elected Senator for Strakonice Constituency No. 12, later Chair. Constitutional Law Cttee of the Senate; Deputy Prime Minister of Czech Repub. and Chair. Govt Legis. Council 1998–2003; Chair. Govt Council for Research and Devt 1998–2002, Govt Council for Roma Community Affairs 1998–2002, Govt Council for Ethnic Minorities 1998–2002; Minister of Justice 2000–01, 2002–03; Chair. Constitutional Court, Brno 2003–; Chair. Czech Lawyers' Asscn 1990–92; Pres. Bd Trustees Pro-Bohemia Foundation 1992–98; Founder Práchensko Region Citizens' Endowment Fund; Officier de la Légion d'honneur 2005. *Address:* The Constitutional Court of the Czech Republic, Jostova 8, 660 83 Brno 2, Czech Republic (office). *Telephone:* (54) 2214360 (office). *Fax:* (54) 2218326 (office). *E-mail:* pavel.rychetsky@usoud.cz (office). *Website:* www.usoud.cz (office).

RYCKMANS, Pierre, (Simon Leys), PhD; Belgian academic and writer; b. 28 Sept. 1935, Brussels; m. Chang Han-fang; three s. one d.; ed Univ. of Louvain; taught Chinese Literature, ANU, then Prof. of Chinese Studies, Univ. of Sydney 1987–93; Fellow, Australian Acad of Humanities; mem. Acad. Royale de Littérature Française (Brussels) 1991–; Officer Ordre de Léopold, Commdr Ordre des Arts et Lettres 1999; Prix Stanislas-Julien (Institut de France), Prix Jean Walter (Acad. Française), The Independent (UK) Foreign Fiction Award 1992, Christina Stead Prize for Fiction (NSW) 1992, Prix Bernheim 1999, Prix Renaudot 2001, Prix Henri Gal (Acad. Française) 2001, Prix Guizot 2004, Prix Femina (100th anniversary) 2004, Prix del Duca (Acad. Française) 2005. *Film:* The Emperor's New Clothes (Dir Alan Taylor, Producer U. Pasolini) 2001, adapted from Simon Leys' The Death of Napoleon. *Publications:* (under pen-name Simon Leys) The Chairman's New Clothes: Mao and the Cultural Revolution 1977, Chinese Shadows 1977, The Burning Forest 1985, La Mort de Napoléon 1986 (English trans. 1991), Les Entretiens de Confucius 1989, L'humeur, l'honneur, l'horreur 1991, The Analects of Confucius 1996, Essais sur la Chine 1998, The View from the Bridge 1996, The Angel and the Octopus 1999, Protée et autres essais 2001, Les Naufragés du Batavia 2003, La Mer dans la littérature française 2003, Les idées des autres 2005, The Wreck of the Batavia 2005, Le Bonheur des petits poissons 2008; (under own name Pierre Ryckmans) Les Propos sur la peinture de Shitao 1969, La Vie et l'oeuvre de Su Renshan, rebelle, peintre et fou 1970. *Address:* 6 Bonwick Place, Garran, ACT 2605, Australia. *Fax:* (2) 6281-4887.

RYDBERG-DUMONT, Josephine; Swedish business executive; *CEO, IKEA of Sweden;* served as Man. IKEA Catalogue Production to Gen. Man. IKEA of Sweden, responsible for purchasing and product devt of IKEA Group, currently CEO and mem. Group Man., IKEA of Sweden AB; ranked 30th by Fortune magazine amongst 50 Most Powerful Women in Business outside the US 2006. *Address:* IKEA of Sweden AB, Almhult, Kronoberg, Sweden (office). *Website:* www.ikea-group.ikea.com (office).

RYDER, Guy; British trade union official; *General Secretary, International Trade Union Confederation (ITUC);* b. 3 Jan. 1956, Liverpool; ed Univ. of Cambridge; Asst, Int. Dept, Trade Union Congress (TUC) 1981–85; Sec. Industry Trade Section, Int. Fed. of Commercial, Clerical, Professional and Tech. Employees (FIET), Geneva, Switzerland 1985–88; Sec. Workers' Group, ILO 1993–96, 1996–98, Sec. Worker's Group, Int. Labour Conf. 1994–98, Dir of Bureau for Workers' Activities, ILO 1998–99, Chief of Cabinet 1999–2001, Special Adviser to Dir-Gen. –2001; Asst Dir, then Dir ICFTU, Geneva 1988–98, Gen. Sec. 2002–06, Gen. Sec. Int. Trade Union Confed. (formed after merger of ICFTU with World Confed. of Labour and eight nat. trade union orgs 2006–. *Address:* International Trade Union Confederation (ITUC), 5 blvd Roi Albert II, 1210 Brussels, Belgium (office). *Telephone:* (2) 224-02-10 (office). *Fax:* (2) 201-58-15 (office). *E-mail:* press@ituc-csi.org (office). *Website:* www.ituc-csi.org (office).

RYDER, Winona; American actress; b. (Winona Horowitz), 29 Oct. 1971, Winona, Minn.; d. of Michael Horowitz and Cynthia Istas; ed Petaluma Jr High School, San Francisco and acting classes at American Conservatory Theatre, San Francisco. *Films:* Lucas 1986, Square Dance 1987, Beetlejuice 1988, '1969' 1988, Heathers 1989, Great Balls of Fire! 1989, Welcome Home, Roxy Carmichael 1990, Edward Scissorhands 1990, Mermaids 1990, Night on Earth 1991, Bram Stoker's Dracula 1992, The Age of Innocence 1993, The House of the Spirits 1993, Reality Bites 1994, Little Women 1994, How to Make an American Quilt 1995, Boys 1996, The Crucible 1996, Looking for Richard 1996, Alien Resurrection 1997, Celebrity 1998, Girl, Interrupted 1999, Autumn in New York 2000, Lost Souls 2000, Mr Deeds 2002, S1m0ne 2002, The Day My God Died (voice) 2003, The Heart is Deceitful Above All Things 2004, The Darwin Awards 2006, A Scanner Darkly 2006, The Ten 2007, Sex and Death 101 2007, The Last Word 2008. *Television:* The Simpsons (episode: Lisa's Rival, voice) 1994, Dr Katz, Professional Therapist (episode: Monte Carlo, voice) 1996, From the Earth to the Moon (mini-series) 1998, Strangers with Candy (episode: The Last Temptation of Blank) 2000, Friends (episode: The One with Rachel's Big Kiss) 2001. *Address:* c/o Thruline Entertainment, 9250 Wilshire Blvd, Beverly Hills, CA 90212, USA. *Telephone:* (310) 595-1500. *E-mail:* info@thrulinela.com. *Website:* www.thruline.com.

RYDER OF WENSUM, Baron (Life Peer), cr. 1997, of Wensum in the County of Norfolk; **Richard Andrew Ryder,** OBE, PC, BA; British politician; b. 4 Feb. 1949; s. of Richard Stephen Ryder and Margaret MacKenzie; m. Caroline Mary Stephens 1981; one s. (deceased) one d.; ed Radley Coll., Magdalene Coll., Cambridge; journalist 1972–75; Political Sec. to Margaret Thatcher, Leader of the Opposition and Prime Minister 1975–81; MP for Mid-Norfolk 1983–97; Parl. Pvt. Sec. to Financial Sec. to the Treasury 1984, Parl. Pvt. Sec. to Foreign Sec. 1984–86; Govt Whip 1986–88; Parl. Sec. Ministry of Agric. 1988–89; Econ. Sec. to Treasury 1989–90; Paymaster Gen. 1990; Parl. Sec. to Treasury and Govt Chief Whip 1990–95; Chair. Conservative Foreign and Commonwealth Council 1984–89; Chair. Eastern Counties Radio 1997–2001, Inst. of Cancer Research 2005–; Vice-Chair. BBC Govs 2002–04, Chair. (Acting) 2004; Dir Great Bradley Farms, also dir of other family businesses. *Address:* House of Lords, Westminster, London, SW1A 0PW, England (office). *Telephone:* (20) 7219-3000 (office). *Fax:* (20) 7219-5979 (office). *Website:* www.parliament.uk (office).

RYDIN, Bo, BSc; Swedish business executive; *Chairman Emeritus, Svenska Cellulosa Aktiebolaget SCA;* b. 7 May 1932; s. of Gunnar Rydin and Signe Rydin (née Höög); m. 1st Monika Avréus 1955 (died 1992); m. 2nd Françoise Yon 1997; with Stockholms Enskilda Bank 1956–57; Marma-Långrör AB 1957–60; AB Gullhögens Bruk 1960, Pres. 1965–71; Pres. and CEO Svenska Cellulosa AB SCA 1972–88, Chair. and CEO 1988–90, Chair. 1990, Chair. Emer. 2002–; Chair. AB Industrivärden, Graningeverken, Skanska AB –2002, Hon. Chair. 2002–; Vice-Chair. Svenska Handelsbanken, mem. Bd SAS Ass. of Reps; Vice-Chair. Volvo 1988–93; Chair. Fed. of Swedish Industries 1993–94; mem. Skandia 1983–93; mem. Royal Swedish Acad. of Eng Sciences, Royal Swedish Acad. of Agric. and Forestry; King's Medal 12th Dimension of Order of the Seraphim; Hon. DEcon; Hon. DTech. *Leisure interests:* golf, hunting, opera. *Address:* AB Industrivärden, Storgatan 10, Box 5403, 114 84 Stockholm (office); Karlavägen 3, 114 24 Stockholm, Sweden (home).

RYKIEL, Sonia; French fashion designer; b. 25 May 1930, Paris; d. of Alfred Flis and Fanny Tesler; m.; one s. one d.; began designing rabbit-hair sweaters which est. her reputation 1963; opened own boutique, Paris 1968; opened further boutiques specializing in men's knitwear and household linens 1976, 1981; launched first perfume 7e Sens 1979; supervised renovation of Hotel Crillon, Paris 1982; first boutique opened New York 1983; launched first children's collection 1984; Vice-Pres. Chambre Syndicale du Prêt-à-Porter des Couturiers et des Créateurs de Mode, Paris 1982; launched Sonia Rykiel perfume 1997; Hon. Prof. China Textile Univ., Shanghai 1998; Officier Ordre des Arts et Lettres 1993, Légion d'honneur 1996; Award for Design Excellence (Costume Cttee, Chicago Historical Soc. *Publications:* Et je la voudrais nue 1979, Célébration 1988, La collection 1989, Colette et la mode 1991, Collection terminée, collection interminable 1993, Tatiana Acacia (jtly) 1993, Les lèvres rouges 1996, Sonia Rykiel (memoirs) 1997. *Address:* Sonia Rykiel C.D.M. S.A, 175 boulevard Saint Germain, 75006 Paris, France. *Telephone:* 1-49-54-60-00. *Fax:* 1-49-54-60-96. *E-mail:* info@soniarykiel.fr. *Website:* www.soniarykiel.com.

RYLANCE, Mark; British actor and director; b. 1960, Ashford, Kent; ed Royal Acad. of Dramatic Art and Chrysalis Theatre School, Balham; joined The Citizen's Theatre, Glasgow 1980; has since worked with RSC, Royal Nat. Theatre, Royal Opera House, Scottish Ballet, Shared Experience, Bush Theatre, Tricycle Theatre, London Theatre of Imagination, Contact Theatre, Oxford Playhouse, Project Theatre, Dublin, Mermaid Theatre, Royal Court, American Repertory Theatre, Boston, Theatre for a New Audience, New York, Pittsburgh Playhouse, Thelma Holte; now assoc. actor, RSC; Artistic Dir Shakespeare's Globe 1996–2005; Artistic Dir Phoebus Cart; performances include the title role in Phoebus Cart's production of Macbeth (also Dir) and Proteus in The Two Gentlemen of Verona, Shakespeare's Globe's Prologue Season 1996, title role in Henry V in Shakespeare's Globe's opening season 1997, Bassanio in The Merchant of Venice and Hippolito in The Honest Whore, Shakespeare's Globe 1998, Cleopatra in Antony and Cleopatra, Shakespeare's Globe 1999, Life x3 2000, Twelfth Night, Shakespeare's Globe 2002, Vincentio in Measure for Measure, Shakespeare's Globe 2004; Olivier Award for Best Actor 1994. *Television appearances include:* The Grass Arena, Love Lies Bleeding, In Lambeth, Incident in Judea, The Government Inspector, Leonardo da Vinci. *Films:* Prospero's Books, Angels and Insects, Institute Benjamenta, Hearts of Fire, Intimacy 2001, The Other Boleyn Girl 2008. *Address:* Markham and Froggatt Ltd, 4 Windmill Street, London, W1T 2HZ, England (office). *Telephone:* (20) 7636-4412 (office).

RYLKO, HE Cardinal Stanisław; Polish ecclesiastic; *President of the Pontifical Council for the Laity;* b. 4 July 1945, Andrychów; ordained priest of Kraków 1969; fmr Prof. of Pastoral Theology, Kraków Theological Acad.; apptd Head of Youth Section of Pontifical Council for the Laity 1988, responsible for planning celebrations for World Youth Day; later served as official of Vatican Secr. of State; apptd Titular Archbishop of Novica and Sec. Pontifical Council for the Laity 1995, Pres. Pontifical Council for the Laity 2003–2 April 2005, 21 April 2005–; cr. Cardinal 2007. *Address:* Pontifical Council for the Laity, Piazza S. Calisto 16, 00153 Rome, Italy (office); 00120

Città del Vaticano, Italy. *Telephone:* (06) 6988-7322 (office); (06) 6988-7141 (office). *Fax:* (06) 6988-7214 (office).

RYMAN, Robert; American painter; b. 30 May 1930, Nashville, Tenn.; m. 1st Lucy Lippard (divorced); m. 2nd Merrill Wagner; ed George Peabody Coll. for Teachers, Nashville; in US Army Reserve band during Korean War 1950–52; moved to New York to try and make it as jazz saxophonist; first exhibited in staff show at Museum of Modern Art when working as a guard there 1958; began painting full-time 1961; mem. American Acad. of Arts and Letters. *Address:* c/o Pace Wildenstein, 32 East 57th Street, 2nd floor, New York, NY 10022, USA. *Telephone:* (212) 421-3292. *Fax:* (212) 421-0835. *Website:* www .pacewildenstein.com.

RYMBAI, J. Dringwel, BEd; Indian politician; *Chairman, Meghalaya Economic Development Council;* b. 26 Oct. 1934; m. Peggymon Pathaw; two s. three d.; high school teacher –1988; entered Meghalaya Legis. Ass. representing Jirang constituency in Ri-Bhoi 1988, later Deputy Speaker, re-elected 1993, Speaker 1993; Minister of Food and Civil Supply 1993; held portfolios of Consumer Affairs, Taxation, Information Tech. and Tourism and Fisheries 2003–06; Minister for Parl. Affairs –2006; elected Leader Congress Legislature Party 2006; Chief Minister of Meghalaya with responsibility for Cabinet Affairs, Industries, Personnel, Planning, Political Programme Implementation and Taxation 2006–07; Chair. Meghalaya Econ. Devt Council 2007–. *Address:* Meghalaya Economic Development Council, Planning Department, Government of Meghalaya, Shillong, Meghalaya, India (office). *Telephone:* 2224828 (office); 2224388 (home).

RYNNE, Etienne Andrew, MA, MRIA, FSA; Irish archaeologist and academic; *Professor Emeritus of Archaeology, National University of Ireland, Galway;* b. 11 Sept. 1932, Dublin; s. of Dr Michael Rynne and Nathalie Fournier; m. Aideen Lucas 1967; four s. one d.; ed Terenure Coll., Dublin, Ecole des Roches, Verneuil-sur-Avre, France, Clongowes Wood Coll., Clane, Co. Kildare and Univ. Coll. Dublin; part-time Archaeological Asst, Nat. Museum of Ireland 1954–56, Asst, Irish Antiquities Div. 1957–66, Asst-Keeper 1966–67; Lecturer in Celtic Archaeology, Univ. Coll., Galway (now Nat. Univ. of Ireland, Galway) 1967–78, Prof. of Archaeology 1978, now Prof. Emer.; Hon. Curator Galway City Museum 1972–86; Pres. Royal Soc. of Antiquaries of Ireland 1985–89, Galway Archaeological & Historical Soc. 1989–95; Ed. North Munster Antiquarian Journal 1964; mem. Royal Irish Acad.; Travelling Studentship Prize, Nat. Univ. of Ireland 1956. *Publications:* Ed. North Munster Studies 1967, Figures from the Past 1987; about 200 articles in learned journals. *Leisure interests:* archaeology (visiting ancient sites, museums etc.), art history, sport (boxing, athletics). *Address:* c/o Department of Archaeology, National University of Ireland, Galway, University Road, Galway, Ireland. *Website:* www.nuigalway.ie/archaeology.

RYRIE, Sir William Sinclair, KCB, MA, FRSA; British merchant banker and fmr civil servant; b. 10 Nov. 1928, Calcutta, India; s. of Rev. Dr Frank Ryrie and Mabel M. Ryrie; m. 1st Dorrit Klein 1953 (divorced 1969); two s. one d.; m. 2nd Christine G. Thomson 1969; one s.; ed Heriot's School, Edinburgh, Edinburgh Univ.; army service, Lt Intelligence Corps in Malaya 1951–53 (despatches 1953); joined Colonial Office as Asst Prin. 1953; seconded to Govt of Uganda 1956–58; Prin., UN Affairs, Colonial Office 1959–63; Prin., Balance of Payments Div. of HM Treasury 1963–66, Asst Sec. for Int. Monetary Affairs 1966–69; Prin. Pvt. Sec. to Chancellor of the Exchequer 1969–71; Under-Sec., Public Sector Group in Treasury 1971–75; Econ. Minister, Embassy in USA and Exec. Dir of IMF, IBRD, IDA, IFC 1975–79; Second Perm. Sec., Domestic Economy Sector, HM Treasury 1980–82; Perm. Sec. Overseas Devt Admin. 1982–84; Exec. Vice-Pres. and Chief Exec. Int. Finance Corpn, World Bank Group 1984–93; Exec. Dir Barings PLC 1994–95, Vice-Chair. ING Barings Holding Co. Ltd 1995–98; Chair. Baring Emerging Europe Trust 1994–2002; Deputy Chair. Commonwealth Devt Corpn 1994–98; Dir W S. Atkins Ltd 1994–2001, First NIS Regional Fund 1994–99, Ashanti Goldfields Co. 1995–2000; mem. Group of Thirty 1992–2002; Council mem. Overseas Devt Inst. 1994–2000; Pres. Edin. Univ. Devt Trust 1994–99; Dir CARE UK 1993–2001. *Publication:* First World, Third World 1995. *Leisure interests:* walking, photography. *Address:* Hawkwood, Hawkwood Lane, Chislehurst, Kent, BR7 5PW, England. *Telephone:* (20) 8295-1853 (home). *Fax:* (20) 8468-7495 (office). *E-mail:* billryrie@btinternet.com (home).

RYTTER, Jakob, LLD; Danish diplomatist; b. 17 Dec. 1932, Århus; s. of the late Ejnar I. J. Rytter and Ingeborg J. Rytter; m. Suzanne Engelsen 1963 (died 1986); two d.; ed Marselisborg Gymnasium, Århus, Lycée de Fontainebleau, Univ. of Århus, Institut d'Etudes Politiques, Paris; mil. service 1960; entered Danish Foreign Office 1961, Sec. of Embassy, Bonn 1963–66, del. to UN Gen. Ass., New York 1966, 1968, First Sec., Tel-Aviv 1969–72, Counsellor Danish EC Representation, Brussels 1973–78, Dir EC Affairs, Danish Foreign Ministry 1978–83, Deputy Perm. Rep., Danish EC Representation 1983–86; Amb. to Israel 1986–89, 1992–96, Amb., Perm. Rep. to the EC, Brussels 1989–92; Amb. to the Netherlands 1996–2001, Perm. Rep. to OPCW, The Hague 1998–2001; Chair. Admin. and Financial Council, European Schools 1977–78; Commdr (First Class) Order of Dannebrog 1998. *Address:* Esplanaden 28, 1263 Copenhagen K, Denmark (home). *Telephone:* 33-33-97-98 (home).

RYU, Seung-min; South Korean table tennis player; b. 5 Aug. 1982; began playing table tennis age nine; plays for Sichuan team club; won Gold Medal at Athens Olympics 2004, Men's Singles, ITTF Pro Tour Killerspin US Open 2004; Bronze Medal, Men's Team Event, Beijing Olympics 2008; ranked No. 8 in the world (ITTF) as of 5 Dec. 2007. *Address:* c/o Korea Table Tennis Association, Room 411, 88 Olympic Center, Oryun-Dong, Songpa-ku, Seoul, Republic of Korea. *Telephone:* (2) 4204240. *Fax:* (2) 4205913. *E-mail:* tabletennis@sports.or.kr. *Website:* www.koreatta.or.kr.

RYWIN, Lew; Polish film producer and business executive; b. 10 Nov. 1945, Niżne Alkiejewo; m. Eżbieta Sitek; one s.; ed Warsaw Univ.; Asst Inst. of Applied Linguistics, Warsaw Univ. 1969–70; Head Dept Orgmasz, Warsaw 1970–78; fmr interpreter and Sec. Main Bureau of Co-operation with Foreign Countries, Polish Interpress Agency; Man. Poltel Commerce Bureau of Polish Radio and TV Cttee 1983–88, 1st Deputy Chair. 1988–91; Chair. Heritage Films 1991–97, Canal+ Polska 1997–; Co-Founder and mem. Polish Interpreters' Assch 1981–; convicted of soliciting a bribe, sentenced to two and a half years in prison and a fine of 100,000 Polish Złoty April 2004, released 2006. *Films produced include:* Korczak 1990, Europa, Europa 1991, Pierścionek z orłem w koronie (The Crowned-Eagle Ring) 1992, Schindler's List (Humanitas Prize, jt recipient with co-producer 1994) 1993, Pułkownik Kwiatkowski (Colonel Kwiatkowski) 1994, Les Milles 1995, Tato (Dad) 1995, Erotic Tales II 1995, Der Unhold 1996, Wielki Tydzień (Holy Week) 1996, Matka swojej matki (Mother of Her Own Mother) 1996, Sara 1996, Ostatni rozdział (Last Chapter) 1997, 13 Posterunek (13 Police Station) 1997, Un Air Si Pur (exec. producer) 1997, Jakub kłamca (Jacob the Liar) 1998, Podróże (Travels) 1998, Złoto dezerterów (Deserter's Gold) 1998, Brute 1998, Pan Tadeusz (Last Foray in Lithuania) 1999, Wiedzmin 2002, The Pianist (exec. producer) 2002, Pornografia 2003. *Leisure interests:* tennis, fishing. *Address:* c/o Heritage Films, ul. Marszałkowska 2/65, 00-581 Warsaw, Poland (office). *Telephone:* (22) 6252553 (office). *Fax:* (22) 6252601 (office). *E-mail:* heritage@heritage.com.pl (office).

RYZHKOV, Nikolai Ivanovich; Russian politician; b. 28 Sept. 1929, Donetsk; m. Lyudmila Sergeyevna Ryzhkova; one d.; ed S. M. Kirov Ural Polytechnic Inst.; mem. CPSU 1956–91; Chief Engineer 1965–70, Deputy Dir, later Dir S. Orzhonikidze Ural Factory of Heavy Machine Bldg 1970; Gen. Dir of Production Uralmash Factory 1971–75; First Deputy Minister of Heavy and Transport Machine Bldg 1975–79; mem. Cen. Cttee CPSU in charge of Heavy Industry 1981–90; mem. Politburo 1985–90; Chair. Council of Ministers 1985–90; First Deputy Chair. of Gosplan 1979–82; Head Econ. Affairs 1982–85; Deputy of the USSR Supreme Soviet 1974–89; People's Deputy of the USSR 1989–91; cand. for Pres. of Russia 1991; Chair. Bd Tveruniversalbank; 1993–95, Pres. Int. Public Union; leader pre-election bloc 'Power to People'; mem. State Duma 1995–99, Chair. deputies bloc Narodovlastiye 1996–; mem. Fed. Council 2002–, Chair. Comm. for Natural Monopolies, mem. Cttee of Local Govt; mem. Acad. of Social Sciences, Acad. of Tech. Sciences, Int. Eng Acad., Int. Acad. of Man.; Order of Lenin (twice), Order of Red Banner of Labour (twice) and other decorations; USSR State Prizes 1969, 1979. *Publication:* Perestroika: a series of betrayals. *Address:* Sovet Federatsii (Federation Council), 103426 Moscow, ul. B. Dmitrovka 26, Russia (office). *Telephone:* (495) 203-90-74 (office). *Fax:* (495) 203-46-17 (office). *E-mail:* post_sf@gov.ru (office). *Website:* www.council.gov.ru (office).

RYZHKOV, Vladimir Aleksandrovich, DHist; Russian politician; b. 3 Sept. 1966, Altai Territory; ed Altai State Univ.; Deputy Head, Altai Territory Soc. of Encouraging Perestroika 1988–90; Deputy Chair. Altai Territory Movt Democratic Russia 1990–91; Vice-Gov. Altai Territory; mem. State Duma (Parl.) 1993–2007, mem. Cttee on Fed. and Regional Policy 1994–95, First Deputy Chair. State Duma 1997–99, ind. mem. 2000–05; Deputy Chair. faction Russia Our Home 1996–97, Chair. 1999–2000; founding mem. Democratic Alternative 2004, Co-Chair. Republican Party of Russia 2006, now associated with The Other Russia coalition. *Publications:* Chetvertaya respublika (The Fourth Republic in Russia) 1999; more than 80 articles on contemporary policy. *E-mail:* press-centre@theotherrussia.ru (office). *Website:* www.ryzkov.ru (office).

RYZHOV, Yuri Alexeevich, DTech; Russian politician, scientist, diplomatist and university administrator; *President, International Engineering University;* b. 28 Oct. 1930, Moscow; m.; two d.; ed Moscow Physical Tech. Inst.; mem. CPSU 1961–90; engineer 1954–60; Sr Researcher, Moscow Inst. of Aviation 1960–92, Prof. 1970, Pro-Rector 1972–86, Rector 1986–92; mem. Presidium of the Supreme Soviet of USSR 1989–91; Chair. Scientific Cttee of the Soviet Parl. 1989–91; mem. Presidential Council of the Russian Fed. 1991–2000; mem. USSR (now Russian) Acad. of Sciences 1987; mem. Interregional Group of Deputies 1989; Amb. to France 1992–98; Pres. Int. Eng Univ. 1999–; Chair. Russian Pugwash Group. *Leisure interest:* music. *Address:* International Engineering University, 119991 Moscow, Leninsky prosp. 6, Russia (office). *Telephone:* (495) 236-50-66 (office); (495) 135-12-44 (home). *Fax:* (495) 236-14-69 (office). *E-mail:* info@miu.ru (office). *Website:* www.miu.ru (office).

S

SAÁ, Adolfo Rodríguez; Argentine lawyer and politician; b. 25 July 1947, San Luis; s. of Juan Rodríguez Saá and Lilia Ester Paez Montero; m.; five c.; ed Nat. Univ. of Buenos Aires; lawyer 1971–; Rep. of Partido Justicialista (PJ—Justice Party) 1971–83; Prov. Deputy and Pres. Justicialista Block 1973–76; Prov. Congressman 1976–85; Nat. Congressman (PJ) 1983–91; Nat. Councillor 1987–94; Pres. Partido Justicialista (San Luis Dist) 1985–95, Third Vice-Pres. Nat. Partido Justicialista 1996–2000; Gov. of San Luis Prov. 1983–2001; Interim Pres. of Argentina Dec. 2001–Jan. 2002; unsuccessful cand. for Pres. 2003. *Address:* c/o Partido Justicialista (PJ), Buenos Aires, Argentina (office). *Website:* www.pj.org.ar.

SAADAT, Air Chief Marshal Kaleem; Pakistani air force officer; b. 12 Dec. 1951; joined Pakistan Air Force 1971, fmr Dir of Plans, Air HQ, fmr Deputy Chief of Air Staff (operational), Chief of Air Staff 2003–06; fmr Asst Commdt, Coll. of Flying Training, Risalpur; mem. Nat. Security Council; Pres. Pakistan Squash Fed. 2003–; Hilal-e-Imtiaz, Sitar-e-Imtiaz, Sitar-e-Basalat. *Address:* Pakistan Squash Federation, Mushaf Squash Complex, Jinnah Stadium, Aabpara, Islamabad, Pakistan (office). *Telephone:* (51) 9201517 (office). *Fax:* (51) 9201527 (office). *E-mail:* paksquash@yahoo.com (office). *Website:* www.paksquash.com (office).

SAADAWI, Nawal el-, MA, MD; Egyptian writer and physician; b. 27 Oct. 1931, Kafr Tahla; m. 1st Ahmed Helmi (divorced); m. 2nd (divorced); m. 3rd Sherif Hetata 1964; one s. one d.; ed Cairo Univ., Columbia Univ., New York, USA; novelist and writer, particularly on feminist issues 1956–; worked Rural Health Centre, Tahla 1955–57; Dir-Gen. Ministry of Health 1958–72; writer, High Inst. of Literature and Science 1973–78; psychiatrist 1974–; fmr Ed.-in-Chief, Health magazine; fmr Asst Gen.-Sec. Medical Asscn; fmr researcher, Faculty of Medicine, Ain Shams Univ., Cairo 1973–78; worked for UN as Dir African Training and Research Center for Women in Ethiopia 1978–80, adviser to UN Econ. Comm. for West Africa, Lebanon; arrested and detained in Egypt for three months 1981; Founder, Arab Women's Solidarity Asscn 1982, Pres. 1982–91 (prohibited by Egyptian govt); fled to USA 1991 after name appeared on fundamentalist death list, taught at Duke Univ. and Washington State Univ., Seattle; returned to Egypt 1996; formally charged with apostasy 2007, court dismissed all charges; First Degree Decoration of the Republic of Libya 1989; Hon. DUniv (York) 1994, (Univ. of Illinois at Chicago) 1996, (Univ. of St Andrews, Scotland) 1997, (Univ. of Tromso, Norway) 2003; Dr hc (Université libre de Bruxelles) 2007; High Council of Literature Award 1974, Short Story Award (Cairo) 1974, Franco-Arab Literary Award (Paris) 1982, Literary Award of Gubran 1988, XV Premi Int. Catalunia Award 2003, North South Prize, Council of Europe 2004, Inana Int. Prize 2005. *Publications:* Memoirs of a Woman Doctor 1958, Two Women in One 1968, Women and Sex 1971, She Has No Place in Paradise (short story) 1972, Woman at Point Zero 1975, God Dies by the Nile 1976, The Hidden Face of Eve: Women in the Arab World (non-fiction) 1977, The Circling Song 1977, The Veil (short story) 1978, Death of an Ex-Minister 1979, Memoirs from the Women's Prison 1983, My Travels Around the World 1986, The Fall of the Imam 1987, The Innocence of the Devil 1992, Nawal el-Saadawi in the Dock 1993, The Well of Life and The Thread: Two Short Novels 1993, The Nawal el-Saadawi Reader 1997, A Daughter of Isis: The Autobiography of Nawal el-Saadawi 1999, Walking Through Fire: A Life of Nawal el-Saadawi 2002, The Novel 2005, God Resigns in the Summit Meeting 2007; contrib. to newspapers and magazines. *Leisure interests:* swimming, walking. *Address:* 19 Maahad Nasser, Shoubra, 11241, Cairo, Egypt. *Telephone:* 2022279. *Fax:* 2035001. *E-mail:* shns@tedata.net.eg. *Website:* www.nawalsaadawi.net.

SAAKASHVILI, Mikheil, LLM, SJD; Georgian politician, lawyer and head of state; *President;* b. 21 Dec. 1967, Tblisi; s. of Nikoloz Saakashvili and Giuli Alasania; m. Sandra Roelofs; two s.; ed Faculty of Int. Relations, Kyiv State Univ., Ukraine, Columbia Univ. Law School, New York, USA, George Washington Univ., Washington, DC, USA, Int. Inst. of Human Rights, Strasbourg, France, Norwegian Inst. of Human Rights; worked for Patterson, Belknap, Webb & Tyler (law firm), New York 1994; returned to Ukraine 1995; mem. Parl. (Union of Citizens of Georgia) 1995, Chair. Parl. Cttee responsible for creating new electoral system, ind. judiciary and non-political police force 1995–2000; Vice-Pres. Parl. Ass. of Council of Europe 2000; Minister for Justice 2000–01 (resgnd); resgnd from Union of Citizens of Georgia Party 2001; f. Nat. Movt opposition party 2001; elected Head, City Council of Tblisi 2002–03; Pres. of Georgia 2004–; named Man of the Year by panel of journalists and human rights activists 1997. *Address:* Office of the President, 0105 Tbilisi, P. Ingorovka 7, Georgia (office). *Telephone:* (32) 99-00-70 (office). *Fax:* (32) 99-88-87 (office). *E-mail:* secretariat@admin.gov.ge (office). *Website:* www.president.gov.ge (office).

SAAKIAN, Suren Mushegovich; Armenian politician; b. 1 Jan. 1958; m.; three c.; ed Yerevan State Univ.; Chair. of Nuclear Physics, Yerevan State Univ. 1979–81; Researcher, Inst. of Physical Studies, Armenian SSR Acad. of Sciences 1981–88; Head, Lazernaya Tekhnika Div. 1988–90; Head, Armenian Ministry of Higher Educ. Dept 1990–91; Deputy Minister of Internal Affairs 1991; Minister of Armenian State Tax Service 1991–94; envoy to Russian Fed. 1994–96, Amb. to Russian Fed. 1999–2002; Rep. to Bd of Int. Econs Cttee 1996–99. *Address:* c/o Ministry of Foreign Affairs, 375010 Yerevan, Republic Square, Government House 2, Armenia (office).

SAATCHI, Charles; British advertising executive and art collector; *Partner, M&C Saatchi;* b. 9 June 1943; s. of Nathan Saatchi and Daisy Saatchi; brother of Maurice Saatchi (q.v.); m. 1st Doris Lockhart 1973 (divorced 1990); m. 2nd Kay Saatchi 1990 (divorced 2001); one d.; m. 3rd Nigella Lawson; ed Christ's Coll. Finchley; fmr jr copywriter, Benton & Bowles (US advertising agency), London; Assoc. Dir Collett Dickenson Pearce 1966–68; with Ross Cramer formed freelance consultancy, Cramer Saatchi, Dir 1968–70; Co-Founder (with Maurice Saatchi), of Saatchi and Saatchi (advertising agency) 1970, (Saatchi & Saatchi PLC 1984), Dir 1970–93, Pres. 1993–95; co-founder and partner M&C Saatchi Agency 1995–; f. The Saatchi Gallery 2003. *Address:* M&C Saatchi, 36 Golden Square, London, W1R 4EE (office); The Saatchi Gallery, County Hall, Southbank, London SE1 7PB, England. *Telephone:* (20) 7543-4500. *Website:* www.mcsaatchi.com; www.saatchi-gallery.co.uk.

SAATCHI, Baron (Life Peer), cr. 1996, of Staplefield in the County of West Sussex; **Maurice Saatchi,** BSc; British advertising executive and politician; *Partner, M&C Saatchi;* b. 21 June 1946; s. of Nathan Saatchi and Daisy Saatchi; brother of Charles Saatchi (q.v.); m. Josephine Hart 1984; one s.; one step-s.; ed London School of Econs; Co-Founder Saatchi & Saatchi Co. 1970; Chair. Saatchi & Saatchi Co. PLC 1984–94, Dir –1994; Co-Founder and Partner, M&C Saatchi Agency 1995–; Chair. Megalomedia PLC 1995–; Dir (non-exec.) Loot 1998–; Shadow Treasury Minister in House of Lords 1999–2003, Cabinet Office Minister 2001–03; Co-Chair. Conservative Party 2003–05; mem. Council RCA 1997–2000; Gov. LSE 1996–; Trustee Victoria and Albert Museum 1988–96; MacMillan Prize for Sociology 1967. *Publication:* The War of Independence 1999, Happiness Can't Buy Money 1999, The Bad Samaritan 2000, Poor People! Stop Paying Tax! 2001, The Science of Politics 2001, If This is Conservatism, I Am a Conservative 2005, In Praise of Ideology 2006. *Address:* M&C Saatchi, 36 Golden Square, London, W1F 9EE, England (office). *Telephone:* (20) 7543-4510 (office). *Fax:* (20) 7543-4502 (office). *E-mail:* maurices@mcsaatchi.com (office). *Website:* www.mcsaatchi.com (office).

SAAVEDRA, Gustavo Fernández; Bolivian politician and diplomatist; b. 1941, Cochabamba; m.; three c.; ed San Simón Univ.; Exec. Sec., Secr. of Integration, La Paz 1969–70; Head Legal Dept, Comm. on Cartagena, Lima, Peru 1970–76; Dir of Consultation and Latin American Co-ordination, Caracas, Venezuela 1976–77; Consulting Dir-Gen. Coprinco y Asociados Consultores 1977–78, Pres. 1979–80, 1982–83; Minister of Integration 1978, of Foreign Affairs 1979, 1984–85, 2001–02; Consultant to UNCTAD 1980–83, 1987–89, 1993–98; Rep. of Ministries of Industry and Foreign Affairs, Quito, Ecuador 1980–81, Geneva, Switzerland 1985–87; Amb. to Brazil 1983–84; Exec. Dir Muller y Asociados Consultores 1987–89, Network of Advising and Man. SA 1993; Vice-Presidential cand. 1989; Minister of the Presidency 1989–93; Co-ordinator Nat. Dialogue 1997; Rep. Andean Corpn of Promotion in Peru 1998–99; Gen. Consul of Bolivia in Chile 2000–01; Special Rep. of the OAS Sec-Gen. and Head, Misión Especial de Acompañamiento al Proceso Democrático y Electoral de la República de Nicaragua (Special Mission Accompanying the Democratic Process and Elections of Repub. of Nicaragua) 2006. *Address:* Casilla 7ll, La Paz, Bolivia. *Telephone:* (2) 278-2614. *Fax:* (2) 278-6793. *E-mail:* gustavof@acelerate.com.

SAAVEDRA-ALESSANDRI, Pablo, LLM, JSD; Chilean lawyer and international organization executive; *Secretary, Inter-American Court of Human Rights (Corte Interamericana de Derechos Humanos);* ed Univ. of Notre Dame Law School, USA; Deputy Sec. Inter-American Court of Human Rights (IACHR) (Corte Interamericana de Derechos Humanos) –2003, Sec. 2003–. *Address:* Corte Interamericana de Derechos Humanos, Apdo Postal 6906-1000, San José, Costa Rica (office). *Telephone:* 2234-0581 (office). *Fax:* 2234-0584 (office). *E-mail:* corteidh@corteidh.or.cr (office). *Website:* www.corteidh.or.cr (office).

SABA, Elias, BLitt; Lebanese economist and politician; b. 1932; s. of Shukri Saba and Guilnar Abou Haidar; m. Hind Sabri Shurbagi 1960; five d.; ed American Univ. of Beirut and Univ. of Oxford, UK; Econ. Adviser to Ministry of Finance and Petroleum, Kuwait and Kuwait Fund for Arab Econ. Devt 1961–62; Chair. Dept of Econs, American Univ. of Beirut 1963–67, Assoc. Prof. of Econs 1967–69; Deputy Prime Minister of Lebanon, Minister of Finance and of Defence 1970–72; Econ. and Financial Adviser to the Pres. 1972–73; Chair., Gen. Man. St Charles City Centre SARL 1974–; Vice-Chair. Banque du Crédit Populaire, Chair. Allied Bank, Beirut 1983; Chair., CEO The Associates, SARL 1981–; Minister of Finance 2004–05; mem. Nat. Dialogue Cttee 1975. *Publication:* Postwar Developments in the Foreign Exchange Systems of Lebanon and Syria 1962. *Leisure interests:* hunting, vintage and classic cars. *Address:* c/o Ministry of Finance, 4e étage, Immeuble MOF, place Riad es-Solh, Beirut, Lebanon.

SABA, Shoichi, BEng, FIEEE; Japanese business executive; b. 28 Feb. 1919; s. of Wataru Saba and Sumie Saba; m. Fujiko Saito 1945 (deceased); two s. (one deceased) one d.; ed Tokyo Imperial Univ.; Pres. Toshiba Corpn 1980–86, Chair. 1986–87, Adviser 1987–; Dir ICI (UK) 1985–91 and numerous other bodies; Vice-Chair. Keidanren 1986–92, Vice-Chair. Bd of Councillors 1992–94, Advisor 1994–; Chair. Electronic Industries Asscn of Japan 1986–87, The Japan Inst. of Industrial Eng 1982–88, Japan Int. Devt Org. Ltd (JAIDO) 1989–94, Japan Machinery Fed., Nat. Bd of Govs, Nat. Asscn, Boy Scouts of Nippon 1994–; Chair. Bd of Trustees Int. Christian Univ.; Pres. Japanese Ind. Standards Cttee 1994–; mem. Public Review Bd, Andersen Worldwide SC (USA) 1991–98; Foreign Assoc. Nat. Acad. of Eng, USA; Foreign mem. Royal Swedish Acad. of Eng Science; Commdr's Cross, Order of Merit (FRG) 1988, Hon. CBE (UK) 1989, Order of the Sacred Treasure (1st Class) 1990, Hon. KBE (UK) 1993; Progress Prize (IEE of Japan) 1958, Blue Ribbon Medal (Govt of Japan) 1980. *Leisure interests:* golf, yachting. *Address:* c/o Toshiba Corpn, 1-1 Shibaura 1-chome, Minato-ku, Tokyo 105, Japan.

SABAH, Sheikh Ahmad Fahad al-Ahmad al-, BSc; Kuwaiti politician; *Director, National Security Agency;* b. 1963; ed Univ. of Kuwait, Kuwait Military Acad.; officer Kuwaiti Army 1985–90, reaching rank of Maj.; Deputy Chair. Public Authority for Youth and Sports 1992–2000, Chair. (rank of cabinet minister) 2000; Minister of Information 2000; Minister of Energy 2002; fmr Chair. Kuwait Petroleum Corpn; Sec.-Gen., OPEC Jan.–Dec. 2005; Pres. Kuwait Olympic Cttee 1990–2001; Dir Nat. Security Agency 2006–; fmr Pres. Olympic Council of Asia; mem. IOC 2001–; fmr Chair. Nat. Council for Culture, Arts and Literature; Hon. degrees from Dong-A Univ., Repub. of Korea, Taipei Univ., Taiwan, American Acad. Kingdom of Saudi Arabia Sports Medal. *Leisure interest:* sport. *Address:* National Security Agency, Kuwait City, Kuwait (office).

SABAH, Sheikh Jaber Mubarek al-Hamad as-; Kuwaiti politician; *First Deputy Prime Minister, Minister of the Interior and Minister of Defence;* b. 1948; fmr Head of Admin. Affairs, Ministry of Amiri Diwan; fmr Gov. Hawally prov., Al-Ahmadi prov.; fmr Minister of Social Affairs, of Information; Deputy Prime Minister and Minister of Defence 2001–06; First Deputy Prime Minister and Minister of the Interior and of Defence 2006–. *Address:* Ministry of Defence, POB 1170, 13012 Safat, Kuwait City, Kuwait (office). *Telephone:* 4848300 (office). *Fax:* 4846059 (office). *Website:* www.mod.gov.kw (office).

SABAH, Muhammad Sabah as-Salim as-, PhD; Kuwaiti politician and diplomatist; *Deputy Prime Minister and Minister for Foreign Affairs;* b. 1955; ed Univ. of Calif. and Harvard Univ., USA; Lecturer of Econs, Faculty of Commerce, Economy and Political Sciences, Kuwait Univ. 1979–85, Kuwaiti Institute of Scientific Research 1987–88; Amb. to USA 1993–2001; Minister of State for Foreign Affairs 2001–03; Minister of Foreign Affairs 2003–; Deputy Prime Minister 2006–. *Address:* Ministry of Foreign Affairs, POB 3, Gulf Street, 13001 Safat, Kuwait City, Kuwait (office). *Telephone:* 2425141 (office). *Fax:* 2412169 (office). *E-mail:* emad@mofa.org (office). *Website:* www.mofa.gov.kw (office).

SABAH, Sheikh Nasser al-Muhammad al-Ahmad as-; Kuwaiti government official and diplomat; *Prime Minister;* b. 1940; ed secondary education in Britain; Univ. of Geneva; began career at Ministry of Foreign Affairs 1964; Perm. Rep. to UN, Geneva 1965–68; Consul-Gen., Kuwaiti Embassy, Switzerland 1967–68; Amb. to Iran 1968–79; Under-Sec., Ministry of Information 1979–85; Minister of Information 1985–88, of Social Affairs and Labour 1988–90, of State for Foreign Affairs 1990–98, of Amiri Diwan Affairs 1998–2006; Prime Minister of Kuwait 2006–. *Address:* Office of the Prime Minister, Council of Ministers, General Secretariat, Kuwait City, Kuwait (office). *E-mail:* info@cmgs.gov.kw (office). *Website:* www.cmgs.gov.kw (office).

SABAH, HH Sheikh Nawaf al-Ahmad al-Jaber as-; Kuwaiti government official; b. 1937; Gov. of Hawalli 1962–78; Minister of the Interior 1978–88; Minister of Defence 1988–92; Deputy Prime Minister and Minister of the Interior from 2003, First Deputy Prime Minister 2003–06; proclaimed Crown Prince 20 Feb. 2006–. *Address:* Diwan of HH The Crown Prince, POB 4, 13001 Safat, Kuwait (office).

SABAH, Sheikh Sabah al-Ahmad al-Jaber as-, (Amir of Kuwait); b. 1928; ed Mubarakiyyah Nat. School, Kuwait and privately; mem. Supreme Cttee 1955–62; Minister of Public Information and Guidance and of Social Affairs 1962–63, of Foreign Affairs 1963–91, acting Minister of Finance and Oil 1965, Minister of the Interior 1978; Deputy Prime Minister 1978–91; acting Minister of Information 1981–84; fmrly First Deputy Prime Minister and Minister of Foreign Affairs; Prime Minister 2003–06; Amir of Kuwait 2006–. *Address:* Bayan Palace, Amiry Diwan, Kuwait.

SABAH, Sheikh Salem Abd al-Aziz Sa'ud as-, BA (Econs); Kuwaiti central bank governor; *Governor and Chairman of Board of Directors, Central Bank of Kuwait;* b. 1 Nov. 1951; ed American Univ. of Beirut, Lebanon; Econ. Analyst Studies Section, Foreign Operations Dept, Cen. Bank of Kuwait 1977–78, Head 1978–80, Deputy Man. and Head of Investment and Studies Section 1980–84, Deputy Man. and Head of Inspection Section, Banking Supervision Dept March–Aug. 1984, Man. Banking Supervision Dept 1984–85, Exec. Dir for Banking Supervision and Monetary Policy 1985–86, Deputy Gov. Feb.–Sept. 1986, Gov. and Chair. Bd of Dirs 1986–; Chair. Bd of Dirs Inst. of Banking Studies; Alternate Gov. of the State of Kuwait, IMF and Arab Monetary Fund; mem. Higher Planning Council, Higher Petroleum Council, Bd of Dirs Kuwait Investment Authority, Higher Cttee for Econ. Devt and Reform (Chair. of Sub-Cttee); Gov. of the Year Award, Euromoney magazine 1988, Personality in Banking Management Award, Arab Research Center 1997. *Publications include:* Casting Light on the Monetary Policy and the Kuwaiti Economy 1988, Recent Issues of Central Bank Policy in Kuwait 1989, Prominent Landmarks in the Operation of the Central Bank of Kuwait 1995, Monetary Policy and the Role of the Central Bank of Kuwait: Current Concerns and Future Prospects 1997. *Address:* Central Bank of Kuwait, POB 526, 13006 Safat, Abdullah as-Salem Street, Kuwait City, Kuwait (office). *Telephone:* 2449200 (office). *Fax:* 2402715 (office). *E-mail:* cbk@cbk.gov.kw (office). *Website:* www.cbk.gov.kw (office).

SABAN, Haim; American/Israeli media executive; *CEO, Saban Capital Group, Inc.;* b. Alexandria, Egypt; m. Cheryl Saban; ed agricultural school, Israel; fled to Tel-Aviv with his parents aged 12 after Suez War 1956; served in Israeli Defense Force; est. leading tour business; relocated to France 1975, est. ind. record co. that sold over 18 million records in eight years; moved to Los Angeles, USA 1983, launched chained of recording studios that become leading suppliers of music for TV; f. Saban Entertainment 1988, merged with Fox Kids Network 1995, acquired Fox Family Channel (restructured as Fox Family Worldwide) 1997, sold to Walt Disney Co. 2001; Founder and CEO Saban Capital Group, Inc. (SCQ) 2002–; acquired ProSiebenSat.1 Media AG, Chair. Supervisory Bd –2007 (co. sold); with group of investors acquired Bezeq

The Israel Telecommunication Corp., Ltd. 2005, Univision Communications Inc. 2007; apptd to California Bd of Regents 2002–(13); Founder Saban Inst. for the Study of the American Political System, Univ. of Tel-Aviv; f. Saban Family Foundation 1999; f. Saban Center for Middle East Policy, Brookings Inst. 2002, currently Chair. Int. Advisory Bd; mem. Bd of Trustees Brookings Inst. *Address:* Saban Capital Group, Inc., 10100 Santa Monica Blvd, Los Angeles, CA 90067, USA (office). *Telephone:* (310) 557-5100 (office). *Website:* www.saban.com (office).

SABANCI, Güler; Turkish business executive; *Chairman and Managing Director, Hacı Ömer Sabancı Holding A.Ş.;* b. 1955, Istanbul; d. of İhsan Sabancı and Yüksel Sabancı; ed TED Ankara Coll. and Bosphorus Univ.; worked for LASSA Tyre Manufacturing and Trading Co., Kocaeli Prov. 1978; Gen. Man. and mem. Bd KORDSA Tyre Cord Manufacturing and Trading Co. 1985–99, led teams that set up several jt ventures for Sabancı Group such as Brisa, Beksa and Dusa International LLC, Pres. Tire and Reinforcement Materials Group –2004, Chair. Hacı Ömer Sabancı Holding A.Ş. (also Head of Human Resources Cttee) 2004–; Founder and Chair. Bd of Trustees Sabancı Univ. 2002–; Chair.-Elect Sabancı Foundation, VAKSA; ranked by The Wall Street Journal amongst 30 Most Powerful Women in Europe 2004, ranked by Fortune magazine amongst 50 Most Powerful Women in Business outside the US (20th) 2004, (17th) 2005, (11th) 2006, (eighth) 2007, ranked by Forbes magazine amongst 100 Most Powerful Women (65th) 2006, (65th) 2007, (75th) 2008, ranked by the Financial Times amongst Top 25 Businesswomen in Europe (eighth) 2005, (ninth) 2006, (eighth) 2007. *Leisure interest:* running vineyard producing wine under her own brand name. *Address:* Hacı Ömer Sabancı Holding A.Ş., Sabancı Center 4.Levent, 34330 Istanbul, Turkey (office). *Telephone:* (212) 2816600 (office); (212) 2816611 (office). *Fax:* (212) 2810272 (office). *E-mail:* info@sabanci.com (office). *Website:* www.sabanci.com (office).

SABATIER, Robert; French writer; b. 17 Aug. 1923, Paris; s. of Pierre Sabatier and Marie Exbrayat; m. Christiane Lesparre 1957; fmr manual worker and factory exec.; produced journal La Cassette; mem. Acad. Goncourt; Commdr, Légion d'honneur, Ordre nat. du Mérite, des Arts et Lettres, Officier du Mérite agricole; Lauréat de la Soc. des gens de lettres 1961, Prix de Poésie Louis Montalte 2005. *Publications:* Alain et le nègre 1953, Le marchand de sable 1954, Le goût de la cendre 1955, Les fêtes solaires 1955 (Antonin-Artaud Prize, Prix Apollinaire), Boulevard 1956, Canard au sang 1958, St Vincent de Paul, Dédicace d'un navire 1959, La Sainte-Farce 1960, La mort du figuier 1962, Dessin sur un trottoir 1964, Les poisons délectables (poems) 1965, Le Chinois d'Afrique 1966, Dictionnaire de la mort 1967, Les châteaux de millions d'années (poems) 1969 (Grand Prix de Poésie de l'Acad. française 1969), Les allumettes suédoises 1969, Trois sucettes à la menthe 1972, Noisettes sauvages 1974, Histoire de la poésie française des origines à nos jours (eight vols) 1975, Icare et autres poèmes 1976, Les enfants de l'été 1978, Les fillettes chantantes 1980, L'oiseau de demain 1981, Les années secrètes de la vie d'un homme 1984, David et Olivier 1986, Lecture (poetry) 1987, La souris verte 1990, Le livre de la déraison souriante 1991, Olivier et ses amis 1993, Ecriture (poems) 1993, Le cygne noir 1995, Le lit de la merveille 1997, Les masques et le miroir 1998, Le sourire aux lèvres 2000, Olivier 1940 2003, Les Trompettes guerrières 2007. *Address:* c/o Éditions Albin Michel, 22 rue Huyghens, 75014 Paris (office); 64 boulevard Exelmans, 75016 Paris, France (home).

SÁBATO, Ernesto; Argentine writer; b. 24 June 1911, Rojas; m. Matilde Kusminsky-Richter; two s.; ed Universidad Nacional de la Plata; fmr Dir of Cultural Relations, Argentina; has lectured in numerous univs, including Paris, Columbia, Berkeley, Madrid, Warsaw, Bucharest, Bonn, Milan, Pavia, Florence; Pres. Comisión Nacional sobre Desaparición de Personas (CONADEP) 1984; mem. The Club of Rome; Ribbon of Honour, Argentine Soc. of Letters; Prize of the Inst. of Foreign Relations (Stuttgart) 1973, Grand Prize of Argentine Writers' Soc. 1974, Prix Meilleur Livre Etranger for Abaddon el Exterminador (Paris) 1977; Chevalier, Ordre des Arts et des Lettres (France), Chevalier, Légion d'honneur 1978, Gran Cruz de la República Española, Gabriela Mistral Prize 1984, Cervantes Prize, Madrid 1984, Jerusalem Literary Prize 1989. *Publications:* Uno y el universo 1945, Hombres y engranajes 1951, Heterodoxia 1953, El escritor y sus fantasmas 1963, Tres aproximaciones a la literatura de nuestro tiempo (essays) 1969, El túnel 1947, Sobre héroes y tumbas 1961, Abaddon el exterminador (novel) 1976, La resistencia, Narrativa completa 1995, Apologias y rechazos 1995, Antes del fin 1999, La Resistencia 2000. *Address:* Langeri 3135, Santos Lugares, Argentina. *Telephone:* 757-1373.

SABBAH, Michel, PhD; ecclesiastic; *Emeritus Latin (Roman Catholic) Patriarch of Jerusalem;* b. 19 March 1933, Nazareth; ed Patriarchate Seminary of Beit-Jala and in Beirut and Paris; ordained priest 1955; fmr Dir Gen. of Schools, Patriarchate of Jerusalem; priest, Misdar, nr Amman; Pres. Frères Univ. Bethlehem; Latin (Roman Catholic) Patriarch of Jerusalem 1988–2008, Emer. Patriarch 2008–; Pres. Bishops' Conf. for Arab Countries. *Publication:* Lire et Vivre la Bible au Pays de la Bible 2003; eight pastoral letters. *Address:* Office of the Latin Patriarch, POB 14152, 91141 Jerusalem, Israel (home). *Telephone:* 2-6282323 (office). *Fax:* 2-6271652 (office). *E-mail:* chancellery@latinpat.org (office). *Website:* www.lpj.org (office).

SABBIONI, Enrico; Italian biochemist; *Researcher, Institute for Health and Consumer Protection, European Commission Joint Research Center;* currently Researcher, Inst. for Health and Consumer Protection, EC Jt Research Center, Ispra, Italy; Task Leader, Inst. for Health and Consumer Protection (IHCP); mem. European Centre for Validation of Alternative Methods (ECVAM); mem. Int. Soc. for Trace Element Research in Humans; Fellow, Int. Union of Pure and Applied Chem.; mem. Editorial Bd Science of the Total Environment, Alternatives To Lab. Animals; mem. Bd of Dirs Università Carlo Cattaneo (LIUC); Hevesy Medal 2002. *Address:* Institute for Health and

Consumer Protection, European Commission Joint Research Center, Ispra, 21 020 Italy (office). *Telephone:* (332) 789070 (office). *Fax:* (332) 785994 (office). *E-mail:* enrico.sabbioni@jrc.it (office). *Website:* www.jrc.cec.eu.int (office).

SABHARWAL, Yogesh Kumar; Indian judge; b. 14 Jan. 1942; enrolled as Advocate, Delhi 1964; Advocate Indian Railway 1969–81; Advocate Delhi Admin 1973–76, Additional Standing Counsel 1980–81, later Standing Counsel; Cen. Govt Counsel 1980–86; Additional Judge High Court of Delhi 1986–87, Perm. Judge 1987, Acting Chief Justice –1999; Chief Justice High Court of Bombay 1999–2000; Judge Supreme Court of India 2000–05, Chief Justice 2005–07 (retd); fmr Chair. Bd COFEPOSA; fmr Sec., Pres. Delhi High Court Bar Asscn; rep. of Delhi to Bar Council of India 1969–73; fmr Hon. Sec. Int. Law Asscn. *Address:* c/o Supreme Court, Tilak Marg, New Delhi 110 001, India (office).

SABIA, Michael J., BA, MA, MPh; Canadian telecommunications executive; *President and CEO, BCE Inc.;* b. 1954, St Catharines, Ont.; m. Hilary M. Pearson; one d.; ed Trinity Coll., Univ. of Toronto, Yale Univ.; began career with Canadian Fed. Public Service, various sr positions including Dir-Gen., Tax Policy, Dept of Finance, Deputy Sec. of the Cabinet (Plans), Privy Council Office –1993; Vice-Pres. Corp. Devt, Canadian Nat. Railway Authority (CN) 1993, Exec. Vice-Pres. and Chief Financial Officer 1995–99; Vice-Chair. and CEO Bell Canada Int. Inc. 1999–2000, Exec. Vice-Pres. Bell Canada Enterprises (BCE) Inc. and Vice-Chair. Bell Canada 2000, Pres. and COO BCE Inc. March–April 2002, COO Bell Canada March–May 2002, Pres. and CEO BCE Inc. 2003–(08), also CEO Bell Canada. *Address:* BCE Inc., 1000 rue de la Gauchetière Ouest, Suite 3700, Montréal, PQ H3B 4Y7, Canada (office). *Telephone:* (514) 870-8777 (office). *Fax:* (514) 870-4385 (office). *E-mail:* bcecomms@bce.ca (office). *Website:* www.bce.ca (office).

SABIRIN, Syahril, MBA, PhD; Indonesian banker; b. 14 Oct. 1943, Bukittinggi; m.; one s. one d.; ed Univ. Gazah Mada, Yogyakarta, Williams Coll., Williamstown, Mass., Vanderbilt Univ., Nashville, Tenn., USA; mem. staff, Bank Indonesia 1969–93, mem. Bd 1988–93, Gov. 1998–2003; Sr Financial Economist, World Bank, Washington, DC 1993–96; sentenced to three years' imprisonment for role in misuse of state funds in 2002, conviction subsequently overturned. *Leisure interests:* travel, tennis. *Address:* Jalan Ikan Mas No. 96, Blok K, Cinere, Depok 16514, Indonesia (home). *Telephone:* (21) 7535011 (home). *Fax:* (21) 7549101 (home). *E-mail:* sabirin@hotmail.com (home).

SABIT, Abdul Jabar; Afghan lawyer and government official; *Attorney-General;* legal adviser, Ministry of the Interior –2006; Attorney-Gen. 2006–; mem. official del. that visited Afghan prisoners held by US Govt in Guantánamo Bay detainment camp, Cuba 2006. *Address:* Office of the Attorney-General, Ministry of Justice, Pashtunistan Wat, Kabul, Afghanistan (office). *Telephone:* (20) 2101322 (office).

SABORÍO CHAVERRI, Lineth; Costa Rican politician; b. 1962; m. Roger Carvajal Bonilla; Head of Nat. Investigative Police 1997–2001; First Vice-Pres. and Minister of Justice 2002, First Vice-Pres. 2002–06, also Coordinator of Ministries of Justice, Security, the Interior, External Relations and the Inst. of Devt; Minister of Nat. Planning and Econ. Policies 2002–03; Pres. Council of Security and Citizens' Participation 2002–04. *Address:* c/o Ministry of the Presidency and Planning, Avdas 3 y 5, Calle 4, Apdo 10.127, 1000 San José, Costa Rica (office).

SABOURET, Yves Marie Georges; French civil servant; b. 15 April 1936, Paris; s. of Henri Sabouret and Colette Sabouret (née Anthoine); m. 1st Anne de Caumont la Force 1965 (divorced); one s. two d.; m. 2nd Laurence Vilaine 1991; one d.; ed Ecole Nat. d'Admin; Inspecteur des finances 1964–81; tech. counsellor, Office of Minister of Supply and Housing 1968–69; Dir Office of Minister of Labour, Employment and Population 1969–72; Counsellor for Social and Cultural Affairs to Prime Minister Pierre Messmer 1972–74; Conseiller général, Côtes du Nord (Canton de Matignon) 1973–92; Pres. Soc. de développement régional de la Bretagne 1977–2000; Vice-Pres., Soc. Matra 1979; Dir-Gen. Hachette 1981–90, Vice-Pres. 1981–90; Pres. Atlas Copco France 1984–; Co-Dir-Gen. La Cinq 1990; Dir-Gen. NMPP 1994–2003; Chevalier Légion d'honneur, Officier Ordre nat. du Mérite, Croix de la Valeur militaire. *Address:* c/o NMPP, 52 rue Jacques Hillairet, 75012 Paris; 5 rue Mignard, 75116 Paris, France.

SABOURIN, Louis, LLL, PhD, FRSC; Canadian academic; *Professor of International Economic Organizations and Director, Groupe d'Etude de Recherche et de Formation Internationales, Ecole Nationale d'Administration Publique, University of Québec;* b. 1 Dec. 1935, Québec City; s. of Rolland Sabourin and Valeda Caza; m. Agathe Lacerte 1959; one s. two d.; ed Univ. of Ottawa, Univ. of Paris, France, Institut d'Etudes Politiques de Paris, France, Columbia Univ., USA; Prof., Dir Dept of Political Science, Univ. of Ottawa, Dean of Faculty of Social Science; Founder and Dir Inst. of Int. Co-operation and Devt, Visiting Sr Research Fellow, Jesus Coll., Oxford and Queen Elizabeth House, England 1974–75; Pres. OECD Devt Centre, Paris 1977–82; Prof. of Int. Econ. Orgs, Ecole Nationale d'Admin Publique, Univ. of Québec 1983–, Dir Groupe d'Etude, de Recherche et de Formation Internationales 1983–; Visiting Prof., Univ. of Paris (Sorbonne) 1982, Univ. of Notre Dame and Stanford Univ. 1992, Hanoi, Viet Nam 2000; Founding mem. Asia-Pacific Foundation, Montreal Council of Foreign Relations; mem. Pontifical Comm. on Justice and Peace; Pres. Soc. de Droit Int. Economique 1988; Legal Counselor Hudon, Gendron, Harris, Thomas 1989–; Ford Int. Fellow 1962, Canada Council Scholar 1963; mem. Pontifical Acad. of Social Sciences, Rome 1994; Chevalier Pléiade de la Francophonie 1988; Chevalier Légion d'honneur; Dr hc (Sorbonne, Paris) 1998. *Publications:* Le système politique du Canada 1969, Dualité culturelle dans les activités internationales du Canada 1970, Canadian Federalism and International Organizations 1971, Le Canada

et le développement international 1972, Allier la théorie à la pratique: le développement de la Chine nouvelle 1973, International Economic Development: Theories, Methods and Prospects 1973, The Challenge of the Less Developed Countries 1981, La crise économique: contraintes et effets de l'interdépendance pour le Canada 1984, Passion d'être, désir d'avoir, le dilemme Québec-Canada dans un univers en mutation 1992, Les organisations économiques internationales 1994, The Social Dimensions of Globalization 2000, Globalization and Inequalitites 2002, The Governance of Globalization 2004; numerous articles. *Leisure interests:* music, travel, wine-tasting (Grand officier du Tastevin), skiing, tennis, cycling. *Address:* GERFI-ENAP, 4750 avenue Henri-Julien, Montreal, Québec, H2T 3E5, Canada (office). *Telephone:* (514) 849-3989 (office); (514) 735-4541 (home). *Fax:* (514) 849-3369 (office). *E-mail:* lsabourin@hotmail.com (home). *Website:* www.enap.ca (office).

SABRI, Naji, MA, PhD; Iraqi politician and journalist; b. 1951; Foreign Ed. and Man. Ed. al-Thawra Daily 1968–75; Lecturer in English, Coll. of Arts, Univ. of Baghdad 1969–75; Councillor at Iraqi Embassy, London 1975–80; Founder and Dir Iraqi Cultural Centre, London 1977–80; Founder and Ed.-in-Chief UR (journal of modern Arab arts) 1977–80; Dir-Gen. Dar al-Mamun House (trans. and publishing) 1980–90; Ed.-in-Chief Baghdad Observer 1980–98; Founder and Ed.-in-Chief Gilgamesh (journal of modern Iraqi arts) 1986–95; Vice-Pres. Iraqi Nat. Cttee of Educ., Science and Culture 1986–95; Dir-Gen. of Foreign Information, Ministry of Information and Culture 1990–91, Deputy Minister of Information and Culture 1991–95, Adviser to Minister of Information and Culture 1997–98; lecturer, Coll. of Arts, Univ. of Mustansiriya 1995–99; Adviser, Presidential Office 1995–98; Amb . at Ministry of Foreign Affairs, Baghdad 1998; Amb. to Austria and Perm. Rep. to IAEA, UNIDO and UN Office, Vienna 1999–2001; Amb. (non-resident) to Slovakia 2000–01; Minister of State for Foreign Affairs April–Aug. 2001, Minister of Foreign Affairs 2001–03; currently teaches journalism in Qatar. *Publications include:* trans. into Arabic: The Genius of Show (Michael Holroyd), Aspects of Biography (André Maurois), Lectures on Literature (Vladimir Nabokov); several Iraqi political books into English; Iraq's Year Book (Ed.-in-Chief) 1988, 1990, 1995, 1998, 1999.

SABUROV, Yevgeny Fedorovich, DEconSc; Russian economist and poet; b. 13 Feb. 1946, Crimea; m. Tatiana Petrovna; three d.; ed Moscow State Univ.; researcher econ. inst. in Moscow –1990; Deputy Minister of Educ. of Russian Fed. 1990–91; project leader Programme of Econ. Reform in Russia April–Aug. 1991; Deputy Prime Minister, Minister of Econ. Aug.–Nov. 1991; Dir Cen. for Information and Social Tech. of Russian Govt 1991–94; Deputy Head of Govt of Repub. of Crimea Feb.–Oct. 1994; Prof. Acad. of Econs; Dir Inst. for Investment Studies 1995, now Chair Bd of Trustees; Chief Consultant, Menatep Bank 1995; Chair. Bd of Guardians, Inst. for Urban Econs 1996–; Chair. Bd of Dirs Confidential and Investment Bank 1999–2000, Deputy Chair. 2000–; mem. Acad. of Information, Acad. of Social Sciences; poetry published in Europe since 1970, in Russia since 1990; columnist NZ magazine. *Publications:* Gunpowder Conspiracy (poems) 1996, On the Edge of the Lake (selected poems); over 100 articles on problems of econ. reform in Russia; numerous verses in periodicals. *Address:* c/o Board of Trustees, Institute for Urban Economics, 0/1, Tverskaya Street, Moscow 125009, Russia. *Telephone:* (495) 363-50-47. *Fax:* (495) 787-45-20. *E-mail:* mailbox@urbaneconomics.ru. *Website:* www.urbaneconomics.ru.

SACA GONZÁLEZ, Elías Antonio (Tony); Salvadorean politician, business executive and head of state; *President;* b. 9 March 1965, Usulután; m.; three c.; ed Instituto San Agustín de Usulatán, Colegio Cristóbal Colón; fmr sports commentator and journalist; launched TV channel and several radio programmes 1990s including Radio América (with Alfonso Rivas) 1987, Radio Astral 1993; Pres. Asociación Salvadoreña de Radiodifusores (ASDER) 1997–2001, currently Vice-Pres.; Pres. Asociación Nacional de Empresa Privada (ANEP; National Private Enterprise Association) 2001–04; fmr Pres. Círculo de Informadores Deportivos (CID); currently Pres. FEDEPRICAP (Fed. of Cen. American and Dominican Repub. Business Execs); Pres. of El Salvador 2004–; mem. Alianza Republicana Nacionalista (ARENA); Micrófono de Oro 1991, Distinguished Broadcaster Award 2003. *Address:* Ministry for the Presidency, Avenida Cuba, Calle Darió González 806, Barrio San Jacinto, San Salvador, El Salvador (office). *Telephone:* 2248-9000 (office). *Fax:* 2248-9370 (office). *E-mail:* casapres@casapres.gob.sv (office). *Website:* www.casapres.gob.sv (office).

SACCOMANI, Fabrizio, BEcons; Italian banking executive; *Director-General, Bank of Italy;* b. 22 Nov. 1942, Rome; m.; ed Bocconi Univ., Princeton Univ., USA; joined Bank of Italy 1967, with Supervision Office 1967–70, with Int. Econ. Corpn Dept, then Econ. Research Dept 1975–84, Head of Foreign Dept 1984–97, Cen. Man. for Int. Affairs 1997–2003, Dir-Gen. 2006–; Rep. at Int. Relations Cttee, European Cen. Bank, Cttee on the Global Financial System, BIS, Econ. and Finance Cttee, EU; with Economist, Exchange and Trade Relations Dept, then Asst to Exec. Dir for Italy, IMF 1970–75; Chair. Foreign Exchange Policy Sub-Cttee, European Monetary Inst. 1991–97; Vice-Pres. EBRD 2003–06; mem. Bd of Dirs Einaudi Inst. for Econs and Finance, Istituto Italiano di Tecnologia; mem. Istituto Affari Internazionali, Società Italiana degli Economisti. *Address:* Bank of Italy, Via Nazionale 91, 00184 Rome, Italy (office). *Telephone:* (06) 47921 (office). *E-mail:* email@bancaditalia.it (office). *Website:* www.bancaditalia.it (office).

SACHS, Jeffrey David, BA, MA, PhD; American academic and economist; *Quetelet Professor of Sustainable Development and Director, The Earth Institute, Columbia University;* b. 5 Nov. 1954, Detroit, Mich.; s. of Theodore Sachs and Joan Sachs; m. Sonia Ehrlich; one s. two d.; ed Harvard Univ.; Research Assoc. Nat. Bureau of Econ. Research, Cambridge, Mass. 1980–85; Asst Prof. of Econs Harvard Univ. 1980–82, Assoc. Prof. 1982–83, Galen L.

Stone Prof. of Int. Trade 1984–2001; Dir Harvard Inst. for Int. Devt 1995–2002, Center for Int. Devt –2002; Quetelet Prof. of Sustainable Devt and Prof. of Health Policy and Man. and Dir The Earth Inst., Columbia Univ. 2002–; adviser, Brookings Inst., Washington, DC 1982–; Special Adviser to UN Sec.-Gen. Kofi Annan on Millennium Devt Goals 2002–06, Dir Millennium Project; Founder and Chair. Exec. Cttee Inst. of Econ. Analysis, Moscow 1993–; Chair. Comm. on Macro econs and Health, WHO 2000–01; Co-Chair. Advisory Bd The Global Competitiveness Report; mem. Int. Financial Insts Advisory Comm., US Congress 1999–2000; econ. adviser to various govts in Latin America, Eastern Europe, the fmr Soviet Union, Asia and Africa, Jubilee 2000 movt; fmr consultant to IMF, World Bank, OECD and UNDP; adviser to Pres. of Bolivia 1986–90; Fellow, World Econometric Soc.; Research Assoc. Nat. Bureau of Econ. Research; syndicated newspaper column appears in more than 50 countries; mem. American Acad. of Arts and Sciences, Harvard Soc. of Fellows, Brookings Panel of Economists, Bd of Advisers, Chinese Economists Soc.; Distinguished Visiting Lecturer to LSE, Univ. of Oxford, Tel-Aviv, Jakarta, Yale Univs; BBC Reith Lecturer 2007; Commdr's Cross Order of Merit (Poland) 1999; Hon. PhD (St Gallen) 1990, (Universidad del Pacífico, Peru) 1997, (Lingnan Coll., Hong Kong) 1998, (Varna Econs Univ., Bulgaria) 2000, (Iona Coll., New York) 2000; Frank E. Seidman Award in Political Econ. 1991, Berhard Harms Prize (Germany) 2000, Distinguished Public Service Award, Sec. of State's Open Forum 2002, Sargent Shriver Award for Equal Justice 2005. *Publications:* Economics of Worldwide Stagflation (with Michael Bruno) 1985, Developing Country Debt and the Economic Performance (Ed.) 1989, Global Linkages: Macroeconomic Interdependence and Cooperation in the World Economy (with Warwick McKibbin) 1991, Peru's Path to Recovery (with Carlos Paredes) 1991, Macroeconomics in the Global Economy (with Felipe Larrain) 1993, Poland's Jump to the Market Economy 1993, The Transition in Eastern Europe (with Olivier Blanchard and Kenneth Froot) 1994, Russia and the Market Economy (in Russian) 1995, Economic Reform and the Process of Global Integration (with A. Warner) 1995, The Collapse of the Mexican Peso: What Have We Learned? (jtly) 1995, Natural Resource Abundance and Economic Growth (with A. Warner) 1996, The Rule of Law and Economic Reform in Russia (co-ed.) 1997, Economies in Transition (co-Ed.) 1997, The End of Poverty 2005, Common Wealth: Economics for a Crowded Planet 2008; more than 200 scholarly articles. *Leisure interests:* skiing, biking, watching ballet. *Address:* The Earth Institute at Columbia University, 405 Low Library, 535 West 116th Street, MC 4335, New York, NY 10027, USA (office). *Telephone:* (212) 854-8704 (office). *Fax:* (212) 854-8702 (office). *E-mail:* director@ei.columbia.edu (office). *Website:* www.earth.columbia.edu/about/director (office).

SACHS, Leo, PhD, FRS; British/Israeli biologist and academic; *Otto Meyerhof Professor of Molecular Biology, Department of Molecular Genetics, Weizmann Institute of Science;* b. 14 Oct. 1924, Leipzig, Germany; s. of Elias Sachs and Louise Sachs; m. Pnina Salkind; one s. three d.; ed City of London School, Univ. of Wales, Bangor, Trinity Coll., Cambridge; research scientist in genetics, John Innes Inst. 1951–52; Research Scientist, Weizmann Inst. of Science, Rehovot, Israel 1952–, Assoc. Prof. 1960, est. Dept of Genetics and Virology 1960, Prof. 1962, Head, Dept of Genetics 1962–89, Dean Faculty of Biology 1974–79, now Otto Meyerhof Prof. of Biology; mem. European Molecular Biology Org. 1965, Israel Acad. of Sciences and Humanities 1975; Foreign Assoc. NAS 1995–; Foreign mem. European Acad. 1998; Samuel Rudin Visiting Prof., Coll. of Physicians and Surgeons, Columbia Univ., USA 1980; Charles B. Smith Visiting Research Prof., Memorial Sloan-Kettering Cancer Center, USA 1981; Hon. Fellow, Univ. of Wales 1999, Hon. Life Mem. Int. Cytokine Soc. 2001–; Dr hc (Bordeaux) 1985, Hon. DMed (Lund) 1997; Israel Prize for Natural Sciences 1972, Harvey Lecturer, Rockefeller Univ., USA 1972, Rothschild Prize in Biological Sciences 1977, Wolf Prize in Medicine 1980, Bristol-Myers Award for Distinguished Achievement in Cancer Research 1983, Royal Soc. Wellcome Foundation Prize 1986, R. E. Bob Smith Lecturer, Univ. of Texas Cancer Center, USA 1986, General Motors Cancer Research Foundation Lecturer, Walter and Elisa Hall Inst., Australia 1986, Karl Bayer Lecturer, Univ. of Wisconsin, USA 1987, Jan Waldenstrom Lecturer, Swedish Soc. of Medicine 1987, Sloan Prize, General Motors Cancer Research Foundation 1989, Warren Alpert Foundation Prize, Harvard Medical School, Mass 1997, Donald Van Slyke Distinguished Lecturer, Brookhaven Nat. Lab., USA 1997, Ham-Wasserman Lecturer, American Soc. of Hematology 2000, Emet Prize for Life Sciences 2002. *Publications:* papers in various scientific journals on stem cells, blood cells, devt and cancer research. *Leisure interests:* music, museums. *Address:* Department of Molecular Genetics, Weizmann Institute of Science, Belfer 226, Rehovot 76100, Israel (office). *Telephone:* (8) 9344068 (office). *Fax:* (8) 9344108 (office). *E-mail:* leo.sachs@weizmann.ac.il (office). *Website:* www.weizmann.ac.il/molgen/members/sachs.html (office).

SACIRBEY, Muhamed, BA, JD, MBA; Bosnia and Herzegovina lawyer, diplomatist and politician; b. 20 July 1956, Sarajevo; s. of Nedzib Sacirbey and Aziza Sacirbey; m. Susan Walter; ed Tulane Univ. and Columbia Univ. New York; left Sarajevo with his parents for Turkey and North Africa in 1963; moved to USA in 1967; admitted New York Bar 1981; attorney, Booth & Baron New York 1981–83; Financial Analyst, Vice-Pres. Standard Poor's Corpn New York 1983–85; Financial Investment Banking, Trepp & Co. New York 1985–87; Sr Vice-Pres. and Man. Dept of Investment Security, Pacific Merchant Bank, New York 1987–91; Pnr and Consultant, Princeton Finance, New York 1991–92; served at Perm. Mission of Repub. of Bosnia-Herzegovina to the UN, New York 1992–95, Perm. Rep. 1996–2000; Minister of Foreign Affairs of Bosnia-Herzegovina 1995–96; int. arrest warrant issued for him by Interpol over allegations of misuse of $2.3 million of govt funds during his time as UN Perm. Rep. 2001; arrested in March 2003, held in Metropolitan Correction Center Prison, Manhattan, New York, USA facing extradition charges since 25 March 2003; Man of the Year, Tulane Univ. (USA) 1996, Lifetime Achievement Award, Decapo Tolerance Foundation 1999. *Leisure interests:* athletic activities, reading.

SACKER, Ulrich, PhD; German cultural administrator; b. 16 March 1951, Luenen; s. of Erich and Dorothea Sacker; m. Christina Sacker; one s.; ed Univ. of Münster, Munich, Aix-en-Provence, France; mem. Bureau Int. de Documentation et de Liaison Franco-Allemandes, Paris; Prof. of French and Russian, Univ. of Bonn, Cologne; Commr Promotion of Germany Worldwide, Goethe-Institut HQ Munich, Dir Goethe-Institut San Franciso, USA, Hong Kong, London 2000–, Regional Dir Goethe-Institut Northwestern Europe 2000–. *Address:* Goethe-Institut, 50 Princes Gate, Exhibition Road, London, SW7 2PH, England (office). *Telephone:* (20) 7596-4048 (office). *Fax:* (20) 7594-0211 (office). *E-mail:* sacker@london.goethe.org (office). *Website:* www.goethe.de/london (office).

SACKETT, Penny Diane, PhD; Australian (b. American) physicist, astronomer and academic; *Chief Scientist of Australia;* b. 28 Feb. 1956, Lincoln, Neb.; ed Univ. of Nebraska, Univ. of Pittsburgh; fmr reporter for Science News; fmr J. Seward Johnson Fellow, Inst. of Advanced Study, Princeton; fmr Program Dir Nat. Science Foundation; fmr Prof., Univ. of Groningen, Netherlands; fmr Researcher and Prof. of Astronomy, Kapteyn Astronomical Inst., Netherlands; Dir ANU Research School of Astronomy and Astrophysics 2002–07, also Dir Mount Stromlo and Siding Spring Observatories 2002–07; Chief Scientist of Australia 2008–; Elected Int. Fellow, Royal Astronomical Soc.; mem. Bd of Dirs Asscn of Univs for Research in Astronomy, Giant Magellan Telescope –2008; mem. Australian Astronomical Soc., American Astronomical Soc., Int. Astronomical Union, Asscn for Women in Science. *Address:* Office of the Chief Scientist, Science and Research Division, Department of Innovation, Industry, Science and Research, GPO Box 9839, Canberra, ACT 2601, Australia (office). *Telephone:* (2) 6276-1843 (office). *E-mail:* chief.scientist@innovation.gov.au (office). *Website:* innovation.gov.au/ScienceAndResearch/Pages/Office_of_the_Chief_Scientist.aspx (office).

SACKS, Sir Jonathan Henry, PhD; British rabbi; *Chief Rabbi, United Hebrew Congregations of the Commonwealth;* b. 8 March 1948, London; s. of the late Louis Sacks and of Louisa (née Frumkin) Sacks; m. Elaine Taylor 1970; one s. two d.; ed Christ's Coll. Finchley, Gonville & Caius Coll., Cambridge, New Coll., Oxford, London Univ., Jews' Coll., London and Yeshivat Etz Hayyim, London; Lecturer in Moral Philosophy, Middx Poly. 1971–73; Lecturer in Jewish Philosophy, Jews' Coll., London 1973–76, in Talmud and Jewish Philosophy 1976–82, Chief Rabbi Lord Jakobovits Prof. (first incumbent) in Modern Jewish Thought 1982–, Dir Rabbinic Faculty 1983–90, Prin. 1984–90; Chief Rabbi of the United Hebrew Congregations of the British Commonwealth of Nations 1991–; Assoc. Pres. Conf. of European Rabbis 2000–; Visiting Prof. of Philosophy Univ. of Essex 1989–90; currently Visiting Prof. of Philosophy Hebrew Univ., Jerusalem and of Theology and Religious Studies King's Coll., London; Rabbi Golders Green Synagogue, London 1978–82, Marble Arch Synagogue, London 1983–90; Ed. Le'ela (journal) 1985–90; mem. CRAC; Presentation Fellow King's Coll., London 1993; Sherman Lecturer, Manchester Univ. 1989, Reith Lecturer 1990, Cook Lecturer 1997; Hon. Fellow Gonville and Caius Coll., Cambridge 1993; Hon. DD (Cantab.) 1993, (Archbishop of Canterbury) 2001; Dr hc (Middx Univ.) 1993, (Haifa Univ., Israel) 1996, (Yeshiva Univ., NY) 1997, (St Andrews Univ.) 1998; Hon. LLD (Univ. of Liverpool) 1997; Jerusalem Prize 1995. *Publications:* Torah Studies 1986, Tradition and Transition (essays) 1986, Traditional Alternatives 1989, Tradition in an Untraditional Age 1990, The Persistence of Faith (Reith Lecture) 1991, Orthodoxy Confronts Modernity (Ed.) 1991, Crisis and Covenant 1992, One People?: Tradition, Modernity and Jewish Unity 1993, Will We Have Jewish Grandchildren? 1994, Faith in the Future 1995, Community of Faith 1995, The Politics of Hope 1997, Morals and Markets 1999, Celebrating Life 2000, Radical Then Radical Now 2001, The Dignity of Difference: How To Avoid the Clash of Civilizations 2002, The Chief Rabbi's Hagadah 2003, To Heal a Fractured World 2005. *Leisure interests:* walking, music. *Address:* Adler House, 735 High Road, London, N12 0US, England (office). *Telephone:* (20) 8343-6301 (office). *Fax:* (20) 8343-6310 (office). *E-mail:* info@chiefrabbi.org (office). *Website:* www.chiefrabbi.org (office).

SACKS, Oliver Wolf, MD, FRCP, CBE; British neurologist, writer and academic; *Professor of Neurology and Psychiatry and University Artist, Columbia University;* b. 9 July 1933, London; s. of Dr Samuel Sacks and Dr Muriel Elsie (Landau) Sacks; ed St Paul's School, London and Queen's Coll., Oxford; Research Asst, Parkinsonism Unit, Mt Zion Hospital, San Francicso 1960–61; Resident, UCLA 1962–65; Consultant Neurologist, Headache Unit, Montefiore Hosp., Bronx, New York 1966–68, Beth Abraham Hosp., Bronx 1966–2007, Bronx Psychiatric Center 1966–91, Little Sisters of the Poor, NY 1972–, Bronx Developmental Services 1974–76; Consultant Neurologist and mem. Medical Advisory Bd, Gilles de la Tourette Syndrome Asscn, New York 1974–; Asst Prof. of Neurology, Albert Einstein Coll. of Medicine, Bronx 1975–78, Assoc. Clinical Prof. 1978–85, Clinical Prof. 1985–2007; Adjunct Prof. of Psychiatry, New York Univ. (NYU) School of Medicine 1992–2007, Consulting Neurologist, NYU Comprehensive Epilepsy Center 1999–2007; Prof. of Neurology and Psychiatry, Medical Center, Columbia Univ. 2007–, Columbia Univ. Artist 2007–; mem. American Acad. of Neurology, American Fern Soc., Authors' Guild, British Pteridological Soc., Bronx Co. and NY State Medical Socs, New York Mineralogical Club, New York Stereoscopic Soc., PEN, Soc. for Neuroscience; Hon. Fellow, American Acad. of Arts and Letters 1996, American Acad. of Arts and Sciences, American Neurological Asscn, Asscn of British Neurologists, Jonathan Edwards Coll., Yale Univ., New York Acad. of Sciences, New York Inst. for the Humanities at NYU, Queen's Coll., Oxford, Royal Coll. of Physicians. Univ. of California, Santa Cruz, Cowell Coll.; Hon. DHumLitt (Georgetown Univ.) 1990, (Staten Island Coll., CUNY)

1991; Hon. DSc (Tufts Univ.) 1991, (New York Medical Coll.) 1991, (Bard Coll.) 1992; Hon. DMedSc (Medical Coll. of Pennsylvania), (Karolinska Institutet, Stockholm) 2003; Hon. LLD (Gallaudet Univ.) 2005; Hon. DCL (Oxford Univ.) 2005, (Pontificia Universidad Católica del Perú) 2006; Oskar Pfister Award, American Psychiatric Asscn 1988, Harold D. Vursell Memorial Award, American Academy and Inst. of Arts and Letters 1989, Prix Psyche' 1991, Nat. Headache Foundation Professional Support Award 1991, Presidential Citation, American Acad. of Neurology 1991, Special Presidential Award, American Neurological Asscn 1991, Communicator of the Year Award, Royal Nat. Inst. for the Deaf 1991, Award for Educ. in Neuroscience, Asscn of Neuroscience Depts and Programs 1991, Lewis Thomas Prize for the Scientist as Poet, Rockefeller Univ. 2002, Public Communication Award, Nat. Science Foundation 2004, Mental Health Award, Coalition of Voluntary Mental Health Asscns 2004, E.A. Wood Scientific Writing Award, American Crystallographic Asscn 2004. *Publications:* Migraine 1970, Awakenings (Hawthornden Prize 1974, Book of the Year, The Observer 1973, The Scriptor Award, Univ. of Southern California 1991) 1973A Leg to Stand On 1984, The Man Who Mistook His Wife For A Hat 1985, Seeing Voices: A Journey Into The World of the Deaf (Odd Fellows Social Concern Book Award 1991, Mainichi Publishing Culture Award, Tokyo, Best Natural Science Book 1996) 1989, An Anthropologist on Mars (Esquire/Apple/Waterstone's Book of the Year) 1995, The Island of the Colourblind 1996, Uncle Tungsten (New York Times Editors' Choice, Jewish Quarterly Wingate Prize, Literature Award of the German Chemical Industry Fund 2004) 2001, Oaxaca Journal 2002, Musicophilia: Tales of Music and the Brain 2007. *Address:* 2 Horatio Street, 3G, New York, NY 10014 (home); Neurological Institute, Columbia University, New York, NY 10032 USA (office). *Telephone:* (212) 633-8373 (home); (212) 305-3806 (office). *Fax:* (212) 633-8928 (home); (212) 305-1343 (office). *E-mail:* os2177@columbia.edu (office); mail@oliversacks.com (home). *Website:* www.cumc.columbia.edu/dept/ps (office); www.oliversacks.com.

SADANG, Elbuchel; Palauan politician; *Minister of Finance;* legislator for Ngaraard State 1990–2001; Dir Bureau of Nat. Treasury, Ministry of Finance 1994–2001; Minister of Finance 2001–, also serves as Gov. for Asian Devt Bank and IMF on behalf of Palau.; mem. Asian Pacific Asscn for Fiduciary Studies, Island Govt Finance Officers Asscn; fmr mem. Bd of Trustees Civil Service Pension Plan, charged with pension fraud 2008 along with other bd mems. *Address:* Ministry of Finance, PO Box 6011, Koror, PW 96940, Palau (office). *Telephone:* 488-2561 (office). *Fax:* 488-2168 (office). *E-mail:* esadang@palaugov.net (office). *Website:* www.palaugov.net/minfinance/mofinance.html (office).

SADCHIKOV, Nikolai Ivanovich; Russian diplomatist; *Ambassador to the Holy See;* b. 20 March 1946, Moscow; s. of Ivan Sadchikov and Ludmila Sadchikova; m. Olga Olegovna Sadchikova; one s. one d.; ed Moscow State Inst. of Int. Relations; attaché, Dept of Middle East, USSR Ministry of Foreign Affairs 1970–72; Third Sec., USSR Embassy, North Yemen 1972–76; Counsellor, Dept of Int. Econ. Orgs, USSR Ministry of Foreign Affairs 1976–80; UN Secr. New York, 1980–83; Counsellor, USSR Mission to UN, New York 1983–86; Counsellor, Office of the Minister of Foreign Affairs 1986–90; Counsellor, Russian Embassy, UK 1990–95; Deputy Dir Dept of Consular Affairs, Ministry of Foreign Affairs 1995–97; Consul-Gen., New York 1997–99; Dir Dept of Consular Affairs, Ministry of Foreign Affairs, Russian Fed. 1999–2001; Amb. to Sweden 2001–05, to the Holy See 2005–; Order of Honour 2006. *Leisure interests:* serious music, theatre, classical literature. *Address:* Embassy of the Russian Federation, Via della Conciliazione 10, 00193 Rome, Italy (office). *Telephone:* (06) 6877078 (office). *Fax:* (06) 6877168 (office). *E-mail:* russsede@libero.it (office).

SADIK, Nafis, MD; Pakistani international organization official and physician; *Special Envoy of the Secretary-General for HIV/AIDS in Asia, United Nations;* b. 18 Aug. 1929, Jaunpur, India; d. of Mohammad Shoaib and Iffat Ara; m. Azhar Sadik 1954; one s. two d. and two adopted d.; ed Loretto Coll. Calcutta, Calcutta Medical Coll., Dow Medical Coll. Karachi and Johns Hopkins Univ.; Intern, Gynaecology and Obstetrics, City Hosp., Baltimore, Md 1952–54; civilian medical officer in charge of women's and children's wards in various Pakistani armed forces hosps. 1954–63; Resident, Physiology, Queen's Univ., Kingston, Ont. 1958; Head, Health Section, Planning Comm., on Health and Family Planning, Pakistan 1964; Dir of Planning and Training, Pakistan Cen. Family Planning Council 1966–68, Deputy Dir-Gen. 1968–70, Dir-Gen. 1970–71; Tech. Adviser, UN Population Fund (UNFPA) 1971–72, Chief, Programme Div. 1973–77, Asst Exec. Dir 1977–87, Exec. Dir UNFPA 1987–2000; fmrly UN Under-Sec.-Gen.; Sec.-Gen. Int. Conf. on Population and Devt 1994; UN Special Envoy for HIV/AIDS in Asia 2002–; Pres. Soc. for Int. Devt 1994–97; Fellow ad eundem, Royal Coll. of Obstetricians and Gynaecologists; Order of Merit, First Class (Egypt) 1994, Hilal-I-Imtiaz (Pakistan); Hon. DHumLitt (Johns Hopkins) 1989, (Brown) 1993, (Duke) 1995; Hon. LLD (Wilfrid Laurier) 1995; Hon. DSc (Mich.) 1996, (Claremont) 1996, (Long Island) 1997, (Tulane) 1999, (Univ. of the West Indies) 2000; Hon. DLitt (Nepal Tribhuvan) 1998; Hon. DEcon (Nihon) 1999; Dr hc (Al-Ahfad) 2000; Bruno H. Schubert-Stiftung Prize 1995, Hugh Moore Award 1976, Women's Global Leadership Award 1994, Peace Award (UNA) 1994, Prince Mahidol Award 1995, Population Award, UN 2001, Defender of Democracy, Peoples Global Action 2006. *Publications:* Population: National Family Planning Programme in Pakistan 1968, Population: The UNFPA Experience (ed.) 1984, Population Policies and Programmes: Lessons Learned from Two Decades of Experience 1991, Making a Difference: Twenty-five Years of UNFPA Experience 1994; articles in professional journals. *Leisure interests:* bridge, reading, theatre, travel. *Address:* Special Envoy of the UN Secretary-General for HIV/AIDS in Asia, 300 East 56th Street, 9J New York, NY 10022, USA (office). *Telephone:* (212) 826-5025 (home). *Fax:* (212) 758-1529 (office). *E-mail:* sadik@unfpa.org (office).

SADOVNICHY, Victor Antonovich, D.Phys-MathSC; Russian physicist and university administrator; *Rector, Moscow State University 'M. V. Lomonsov';* b. 3 April 1939, Krasnopavlovka, Kharkov Region; m.; three c.; ed Moscow State Univ. 'M. V. Lomonsov'; Asst, Docent, Deputy Dean Chair of Mechanics and Math., Moscow State Univ. 'M. V. Lomonsov' 1972–78, Prof., Prorector 1982–84, First Pro-Rector 1982–92, Rector 1992–, also Chair. Dept of Math. Analysis; Pres. Russian Union of Rectors, Eurasia Univ. Asscn; Corresp. mem. Russian Acad. of Sciences 1994, mem. 1997, mem. Presidium; Dir Inst. of Math. Problems of Complex Systems 1995–; Prof., Int. Acad. of Marketing; mem. Russian Acad. of Tech. Sciences; Sec.-Gen. Asscn of USSR Univs. 1987–91; Vice-Pres. Int. Acad. of Higher School 1992–; mem. Perm. Cttee, Pres. Conf. of Rectors of Europe; mem. Yedinaya Rossia (United Russia) party; Hon. mem. Russian Acad. of Educ.; Order of Merit for the Country, Class III, two Orders of the Red Banner of Labor, Order St Prince Daniil Moskovsky, Commdr Legion d'Honneur, Order For Merit (Ukraine), order Dostyk; Lomonosov Prize 1973, USSR State Prize laureate 1989, Russian Fed. State Prize for Science and Tech. 2002, Medal for Distinguished Labor, Medal for the 850th Anniversary of Moscow, Francisc Scorina Medal (Belarus), Kazakhstan State Prize. *Address:* Moscow State University 'M. V. Lomonsov', Leninskie Gory, 119992 Moscow, Russia (office). *Telephone:* (495) 939-27-29 (office). *Fax:* (495) 939-01-26 (office). *E-mail:* rector@rector.msu.ru (office). *Website:* www.msu.ru (office).

SADR, Moqtada as-; Iraqi religious leader; b. 12 Aug. 1973; s. of Grand Ayatollah Muhammad al-Sadr (died 1999); f. al-Hawzah weekly newspaper; est. Mahdi Army (Shiite resistance group) and Sadr Bureau in Sadr City, suburb of Baghdad 2003.

SADUR, Nina Nikolayevna; Russian writer and playwright; b. 15 Oct. 1950, Novosibirsk; d. of Nikolai Sadur; one d.; ed Moscow Inst. of Culture, Moscow M. Gorky Inst. of Literature; literary debut in Sibirskiye Ogni magazine; freelance writer; mem. USSR Writers' Union 1989. *Plays include:* Chardym, My Brother Chichikov, Weird Baba, Move Ahead. *Publications:* New Amazons (collected stories) 1991, Irons and Diamonds (short stories), German (novel). *Address:* Vagrius Publishers, Troitskaya str. 7/1, Bldg 2, 129090 Moscow, Russia (office). *Telephone:* (495) 785-09-63 (office).

ŠADŽIUS, Rimantas, LLM; Lithuanian physicist and politician; b. 8 Oct. 1960, Vilnius; m. Dalia Šadžius; one s. one d.; ed Lomonosov Moscow State Univ., Russia and Vilnius Univ.; began career as scientific researcher specialising in quantum chem. and solid-state physics; Deputy Minister of Social Security and Labour 2003–04, of Health 2004–06, of Finance 2006–07; Minister of Finance 2007–08; mem. Lithuanian Social Democratic Party (LSDP); mem. Lithuanian Asscn of Physicists. *Address:* c/o Lithuanian Social Democratic Party (Lietuvos Socialdemokratų Partija), Barboros Radvilaites g. 1, Vilnius 01124, Lithuania. *Telephone:* (5) 261-3907. *Fax:* (5) 261-5420. *E-mail:* info@lsdp.lt. *Website:* www.lsdp.lt.

SÆBØ, Magne, DTheol; Norwegian fmr professor of Old Testament theology; *Professor Emeritus of Old Testament Theology, Free Faculty of Theology (Church of Norway);* b. 23 Jan. 1929, Fjelberg; s. of Samson Sæbø and Malla Ølfaernes; m. Mona Uni Bjørnstad 1953; three s.; ed Free Faculty of Theology, Oslo and Univ. of Oslo; studied Old Testament and Semitic languages in Jerusalem, Kiel and Heidelberg; teacher of Biblical Hebrew, Univ. of Oslo 1961–70; Lecturer in Old Testament, Free Faculty of Theology (Church of Norway) 1969–70, Prof. 1970–99, Dean 1975–77, 1988–90, now Prof. Emer.; Ed.-in-Chief int. project on Hebrew Bible/Old Testament: The History of Its Interpretation I–III; Ed.-in-Chief Tidsskrift for Teologi og Kirke (Univ. Press), Oslo 1977–94; mem. Bd Norwegian Bible Soc. 1965–91, Chair. O.T. Trans. Cttee 1968–78, Gen. Trans. Cttee 1978–91; Chair. Norwegian Israel Mission 1978–87; mem. WCC Consultation on the Church and the Jewish People 1976–81; Chair. Lutheran European Comm. on the Church and the Jewish People, Hanover 1979–82; Pres. Int. Org. for the Study of Old Testament 1995–98; mem. Royal Soc. of Science and Letters, Trondheim, Norwegian Acad. of Science and Letters, Oslo, Nathan Söderblom Soc., Uppsala; received on 65th birthday Festschrift Text and Theology 1994; Kt 1st Class of Royal Norwegian Order of St Olav 1994; Fridtjof Nansen Award for Eminent Research 1995. *Publications:* Sacharja 9-14. Untersuchungen von Text und Form 1969, Gjennom alle tider 1978, Ordene og Ordet. Gammeltestamentlige studier 1979, Salomos ordsprak, Forkynneren, Høysangen, Klagesangene (Commentary) 1986, On the Way to Canon: Creative Tradition History in the Old Testament 1998, The Book of Esther, (Ed.), Megilloth, Edn Biblia Hebraica Quinta 2004; articles in int. journals and theology books. *Leisure interests:* biographies, stamp collecting, mountain walking. *Address:* Lars Muhles vei 34, N-1338 Sandvika, (home); The Free Faculty of Theology, POB 5144, Majorstua, N-0302 Oslo, Norway (office). *Telephone:* 22-59-05-00 (office); 67-54-38-06 (home). *Fax:* 22-69-18-90 (office); 67-54-38-06 (home). *E-mail:* msabo@mf.no (office); m-saebo@online.no (home).

SAEED, Hassan, PhD; Maldivian politician; ed Int. Islamic Univ. Malaysia, Univ. of Queensland, Australia; Attorney-Gen. of Maldives 2003–07 (resgnd); Pres. Maldives Alumni Asscn of Int. Islamic Univ. Malaysia; mem. and Deputy Leader Dhivehi Rayyithunge Party (DRP) (Maldivian People's Party) –2007; mem. New Maldives Movt 2007–, cand. for Pres. 2008. *Address:* c/o New Maldives Movement, Malé, Maldives (office).

SAEMALA, Francis Joseph, BA; Solomon Islands diplomatist and civil servant; b. 23 June 1944; m. Eve Mercy 1974; four s. one d.; ed Victoria Univ., Wellington, NZ; Head of Planning, Cen. Planning Office 1976; Sec. to Independence Timetable Talks Del. and Jt Sec. to Constitutional Conf. in London 1977; Special Sec. to Chief Minister 1976, to Prime Minister 1978–81; Sec. to Leader of the Opposition 1981–82; Perm. Sec. Ministry of Foreign Affairs and Int. Trade 1982–83; Perm. Rep. to UN 1983–90; elected mem. Parl.

1989, Chair. Parl. Foreign Relations Cttee 1992–93, 1995; Chair. Solomon Islands Ports Authority Bd 1991–93; Deputy Prime Minister, Minister of Foreign Affairs 1993–94. *Publications:* Our Independent Solomon Islands, Solomon Islands in Politics in Melanesia. *Address:* Auki, Malaita Province, Solomon Islands.

SÁENZ ABAD, Alfredo; Spanish banker; *Second Vice-Chairman and CEO, Santander Central Hispano SA;* b. Nov. 1942, Getxo, Vizcaya; ed Univ. of Valladolid, Deusto Univ., Bilbao; mem. Bd Dirs and Exec. Vice-Pres. Tubacex (Basque steel pipe producer) 1965–80; Dir of Planning, Banco de Vizcaya 1981; Man. Dir Banca Catalana 1983, Chair. –1993; Man. Dir Banco Bilbao Vizcaya 1988, First Vice-Pres. 1990–93; Pres. Banco Español de Crédito (Banesto) 1994–2002; Second Vice-Chair. and CEO Santander Central Hispano SA (subsequently Banco Santander) 2002–; Vice-Chair. Compañía Española de Petróleos (CEPSA) 2002–; mem. Bd Dirs San Paolo IMI SpA, Auna Operadores de Telecomunicaciones SA; Dir (non-exec.) France Telecom España SA. *Address:* Santander Central Hispano SA, 1 Plaza de Canalejas, 28014 Madrid, Spain (office). *Telephone:* (91) 5581111 (office). *Fax:* (91) 5226670 (office). *E-mail:* info@grouposantander.com (office). *Website:* www.grouposantander.com (office).

SAFAYEV, Sodyk Solihovich; Uzbekistan politician and diplomatist; *Chairman, Senat Foreign Affairs Committee;* b. 1954; ed Harvard Univ.; First Deputy Minister of External Econ. Relations –1993; Minister of Foreign Affairs 1993–94, 2003–05, First Deputy Minister 2001–03; Amb. to Germany 1994–96, to USA 1996–2001; Rep. to Afghanistan 2001–03; currently Chair. Senat (Senate) Foreign Affairs Cttee. *Address:* Office of the Chairman, Senat Foreign Relations Committee, Senat, 100029 Tashkent, Mustaqillik maydoni 6, Uzbekistan (office). *Telephone:* (71) 138-26-66 (office). *Fax:* (71) 138-29-01 (office). *Website:* www.parliament.gov.uz (office).

SAFIN, Marat Mikhailovic; Russian professional tennis player; b. 27 Jan. 1980, Moscow; s. of Misha Safin and Rausa Islanova; started playing aged six; moved to train in Valencia, Spain aged 14; turned professional 1997; winner ATP Tennis Masters Series, Toronto 2000, Paris 2000, 2002, 2004, Madrid 2004, Beijing 2004; winner US Open 2000, Australian Open 2005; ATP Newcomer of the Year 1998, ATP Most Improved Player 2000, Newcomer of the Year Laureus World Sports Awards, Monte Carlo 2000. *Address:* c/o Russian Tennis Federation, Lutzhnetskaya Nab 8, 119871 Moscow, Russia. *Telephone:* (495) 923 21 37. *Fax:* (495) 924 6427. *E-mail:* arta@russport.ru. *Website:* www.maratsafin.com.

SAFIRE, William; American journalist and author; *Chairman, The Dana Foundation;* b. 17 Dec. 1929, New York; s. of Oliver C. Safir and Ida Safir (née Panish); m. Helene Belmar Julius 1962; one s. one d.; ed Syracuse Univ.; reporter, New York Herald Tribune Syndicate 1949–51; Corresp. WNBC-WNBT, Europe and Middle East 1951, Radio and TV Producer, WNBC, New York 1954–55; Vice-Pres. Tex McCrary Inc. 1955–60; Pres. Safire Public Relations Inc. 1960–68; Special Asst to Pres. Nixon, Washington 1968–73; Columnist, New York Times, Washington 1973–; Chair. The Dana Foundation 2000–; mem. American Acad. of Arts and Sciences, Pulitzer Bd; Trustee, Syracuse Univ.; Pulitzer Prize for Distinguished Commentary 1978, Presidential Medal of Freedom 2006. *Publications:* The Relations Explosion 1963, Plunging into Politics 1964, Safire's Political Dictionary 1968, Before the Fall 1975, Full Disclosure 1977, Safire's Washington 1980, On Language 1980, What's the Good Word? 1982, Good Advice (with Leonard Safir) 1982, I Stand Corrected 1984, Take My Word for It 1986, Freedom (novel) 1987, You Could Look It Up 1988, Words of Wisdom 1989, Language Maven Strikes Again 1990, Leadership (with Leonard Safir) 1990, Coming To Terms 1991, The First Dissident 1992, Good Advice on Writing (with Leonard Safir) 1992, Lend Me Your Ears 1992, Safire's New Political Dictionary 1993, Quote the Maven 1993, In Love With Norma Loquendi 1994, Sleeper Spy 1995, Watching My Language 1997, Spreading the Word 1999, Scandalmonger 1999, Let A Smile Be Your Umbrella 2001, No Uncertain Terms 2003, The Right Word 2004. *Address:* The Dana Foundation, 900 15th Street, NW, Washington, DC 20005, USA (office). *Telephone:* (202) 682-4545 (office). *Fax:* (202) 682-2662 (office). *E-mail:* wsafire@dana.org (office). *Website:* www.dana.org (office).

SAFONOV, Col-Gen. Anatoly Yefimovich; Russian politician; *Special Representative to the President of the Russian Federation in International Co-operation for Combating Terrorism and Transitional Organized Crime;* b. 5 Oct. 1945, Krasnoyarsk; m. Galina Nikolayevna Safonova; one s. one d.; ed Krasnoyarsk Polytechnic Inst., Higher KGB School, Minsk; engineer-topographer, expeditions to regions of Chukotka, Magadan, Yakutia, Krasnoyarsk –1969; KGB service –1970, Head Counter-Espionage Dept 1983–87, Head, Territorial KGB 1988–92; Deputy Minister of Security 1992–93; First Deputy Dir Fed. Service of Security, Russian Fed. 1994–97, Chair. Cttee on Security Problems of Union State of Russia and Belarus 1997; People's Deputy of Russian Fed. 1990–93; Deputy Minister of Foreign Affairs 2002–; Special Rep. to the Pres. of the Russian Fed. for int. co-operation in combating terrorism and transitional organized crime 2004–; Corresp. mem. Int. Acad. of Information Tech.; Amb. Extraordinary and Plenipotentiary; Hon. Worker of Counterespionage; Hon. Worker MFA of Russia; governmental and departmental awards. *Address:* Ministry of Foreign Affairs, Smolenskaya-Sennaya pl. 32–34, 121200 Moscow, Russia (office). *Telephone:* (095) 244-95-20 (office). *Fax:* (095) 244-16-57 (office). *E-mail:* safonov@mid.ru (office).

SAFONOVA, Yelena Vsevolodovna; Russian actress; b. 14 June 1956, Leningrad; d. of Vsevolod Safonov; m.; ed All-Union Inst. of Cinematography, Leningrad Inst. of Theatre, Music and Cinema; actress Mosfilm Studio 1986–; David di Donatello Prize (Italy) for Best Role (Black Eyes) 1988. *Films include:* Return of Butterfly, Winter Cherries, Winter Cherries 2, Winter Cherries 3, Sofia Kovalevskaya, Secret of the Earth, Strange Call, Confrontation, Sleuth, Continuation of the Clan, Taxi Blues, Butterflies, Music for December, The President and His Woman, All Red, Alissa 1998, Woman's Own 1999, The Sky Will Fall 2000, Poklonnik 2001, Zayats nad bezdnoy 2006, La Traductrice 2006. *Television:* Next II (series) 2003. *Address:* Taganskaya pl. 31/22, Apt. 167, 109004 Moscow, Russia. *Telephone:* (495) 278-07-36.

SAFRA, Joseph; Brazilian banker; *Chairman, Grupo Safra SA;* b. 1934, Beirut, Lebanon; s. of Jacob Safra and Esther Safra; m. Vicky Safra (neé Sarfatty); two s.; currently Chair. Grupo Safra SA, family business group that includes Banco Safra SA (f. 1967), Banco JS de Investimento (f. 1998), Bank Jacob Safra, Switzerland (f. 2000), Safra Nat. Bank of New York, Safra Asset Man. Corpn, Banque Safra-Luxembourg SA, Banque Safra-France SA, Banco Safra (Cayman Islands) Ltd, Safra Int. Bank and Trust Ltd, Aracruz Celulose SA; Pres. Safra Cultural Inst.; Perm. mem. Advisory Council, Albert Einstein Soc. *Address:* Safra National Bank of New York, 546 5th Avenue, New York, NY 10036, USA (office); Banco Safra SA, venida Paulista 2100, 58160-789 São Paulo, Brazil. *Telephone:* (212) 704-5500 (office). *Fax:* (212) 704-5527 (office). *Website:* www.safra.com.br (office).

SAGALAYEV, Eduard Mikhailovich; Russian journalist; b. 3 Oct. 1946, Samarkand; m.; one s. one d.; ed Samarkand Univ., Acad. of Social Sciences Cen. Cttee CPSU; Dir, Sr Ed. Cttee on TV and Radio Samarkand; on staff, Deputy Exec. Sec. Leninsky Put 1969–72; Exec. Sec. Komsomolets Uzbekistana Tashkent 1972–73; instructor Propaganda Div. Cen. Comsomol Cttee Moscow 1973–75; Deputy Ed.-in-Chief programmes for youth, USSR Cen. TV 1975–80, Ed.-in-Chief 1980–88; Ed.-in-Chief Information section of Cen. TV 1988–90; Dir Gen. Studio Channel IY 1990; First Deputy Chair. All-Union State Radio and TV Corpn 1991–92; Dir Gen. TV Ostankino Jan.–July 1992; Founder and Pres. TV-6, Moscow's first ind. broadcasting co. 1992–96, 1997–; Chair. Russian TV and Broadcasting co. (RTR) 1996–97; now Chair. Bd of Dirs and Pres. Moscow Ind. Broadcasting Corpn, Deputy Chair. Bd of Dirs ORT (Channel 1); Co-Chair. Int. TV and Radio Broadcasting Policies Comm. 1990–97; Dir-Gen. RTR Signal Co.; Chair. Bd of USSR Journalists' Union 1990–91; Chair. Confed. of Journalists' Unions of CIS 1992–97, Pres. Nat. Asscn of TV and Radio Producers of Russia 1995–; mem. Acad. of Russian TV 1995–, Fed. Tenders Comm. 2004–; USSR State Prize 1978; Order of Friendship (twice). *Address:* National Association of TV and Radio Producers, Myasnitskaya str. 13/11, 101000 Moscow, Russia. *Telephone:* (495) 924-24-38. *Fax:* (495) 923-23-18.

SAGARRA, Eda, MA, DPhil, LittD, MRIA; Irish professor of German and university administrator; *Professor Emerita, Trinity College Dublin;* b. 15 Aug. 1933, Dublin; d. of Kevin O'Shiel and Cecil Smiddy; m. Albert Sagarra i Zacarini 1961; one d.; ed Loreto Convent, Foxrock, Farnborough Hill Convent, Hants., England, Univ. Coll. Dublin and Univs of Freiburg, Zürich and Vienna; jr lecturer, lecturer, Univ. of Manchester 1958–68; Special Lecturer in German History 1968–75; Prof. of German, Trinity Coll. Dublin 1975–98, Dean of Visiting Students 1979–86, Prof. Emer. 1998–, Registrar 1981–86, Pro-Chancellor 2000–; Chair. Irish Research Council for the Humanities and Social Sciences 2000–, Salzburg Univ. Arts Faculty 2002–; mem. Council, Royal Irish Acad. (Sec. 1993–2000), Nat. Council for Educational Awards 1991–96; mem. Standing Cttee for Humanities, European Science Foundation 1996–2002; mem. Germanistische Kommission of German Research Council 1982–90; mem. Bd Inst. of Germanic Studies of Univ. of London 1983–87; mem. Academia Europaea 1991–, Quality Review Group 1998–, Max Planck Inst., Quality Review Group, Swiss Research Council 2001–, Bd Giessen Univ., Germany; Bundesverdienstkreuz (Austria); Bundesverdienstkreuz (FRG); Goethe Medal 1990, Jacob and Wilhelm Grimm Prize 1995. *Publications:* Tradition and Revolution 1971, A Social History of Germany 1648–1914 1977, Theodor Fontane: Der Stechlin 1986, Literatur und Anthropologie um 1800 (Ed. with Jürgen Barkhoff) 1992, Companion to German Literature 1494 to the Present (with Peter Skrine) 1997, Germany in the 19th Century: History and Literature 2001; scientific bibliographies/review essays on German women writers; articles on legal, social and literary history of servants in Germany. *Leisure interests:* golf (county golfer 1969–75), ornithology, cooking, European politics. *Address:* 5066 Arts Building, Trinity College, Dublin 2 (office); 30 Garville Avenue, Rathgar, Dublin 6, Ireland (home). *Telephone:* (1) 6081373 (office); (1) 4975967 (home). *Fax:* (1) 6772694 (office). *E-mail:* esagarra@irchss.ie (office); esagarra@tcd.ie (home).

SAGDEEV, Roald Zinnurovich, DSc; Russian physicist and academic; *Distinguished University Professor and Director, East-West Space Science Center, University of Maryland;* b. 26 Dec. 1932, Moscow; m. Susan Eisenhower (grand-d. of the late US Pres. Dwight Eisenhower) 1990; ed Moscow State Univ.; Research Worker, Inst. of Atomic Energy, USSR Acad. of Sciences 1956–61; Head of Lab., Inst. of Nuclear Physics, Siberian Dept, Acad. of Sciences 1961–70, Inst. of High Temperature Physics of USSR Acad. of Sciences 1970–73; Prof. Novosibirsk State Univ. 1964–73; Dir Inst. of Space Research 1973–88, Sr Researcher 1988–; Distinguished Univ. Prof., Univ. of Md, USA 1990–, Founder and Dir East-West Space Science Center 1992–; Corresp. mem. USSR (now Russian) Acad. of Sciences 1964, mem. 1968–; specialist on global warming, plasma physics, controllable thermonuclear synthesis, cosmic ray physics; mem. Council of Dirs Int. Fund for Survival and Devt of Mankind 1988–; Head Scientific-Methodical Centre for Analytical Research, Inst. of Space Research 1988–; mem. NAS Swedish Royal Acad., Max Planck Soc.; USSR People's Deputy 1989–91; Order of October Revolution, Order of Red Banner and other decorations; Dr hc (Tech. Univ. Graz, Austria) 1984; Hero of Socialist Labour 1986; Lenin Prize 1984. *Address:* 2309A Computer and Space Sciences Building, University of Maryland, College Park, MD 20742, USA (office). *Telephone:* (301) 405-8051 (office). *E-mail:* rs124@umail.umd.edu (office). *Website:* www.physics.umd.edu/people/faculty/sagdeev.html (office).

SAGER, Dirk; German broadcast journalist; b. 13 Aug. 1940, Hamburg; m. Irene Dasbach-Sager; one s. one d.; fmrly with Radio RIAS Berlin; fmr corresp. ZDF TV, East Berlin, Washington DC, Chief of Moscow Office 1990–97, 1998–2004, Chief of Brandenburg Office 1997–98, Ed. Kennzeichen D. (political TV show) 1984–90; Hanns-Joachim-Friedrichs-Preis 2002. *Publications include:* Betrogenes Rubland 1996, Russlands hoher Norden 2005, Berlin-Saigon 2007, Pulverfass Russland 2008. *Leisure interest:* reading. *Address:* Zweites Deutsches Fernsehen (ZDF), 55100 Mainz, Germany (office). *Telephone:* (6131) 702161 (office). *Fax:* (6131) 702170 (office). *E-mail:* ia@zdf .de (office). *Website:* www.zdf.de (home).

SAGET, Louis Joseph Édouard; French government official (retd); b. 27 April 1915, Paris; s. of Pierre Saget and Jeanne Saget (née Barbare); m. Anne Vincens 1940; six c.; ed Lycée Janson-de-Sailly, Paris, Sorbonne; Mayor of Tananarive 1954–56; First Counsellor, French Embassy, Madagascar 1959–60; High Commr in Comoro Islands 1960–62; Commissaire aux Comptes, European Launcher Devt Org. 1963–66; Gov. of French Somaliland 1966–67; High Commr in Djibouti 1967–69; Conseiller maître à la Cour des Comptes 1970–84; Pres. Agence nat. pour l'amélioration de l'habitat 1971–78, Comm. de terminologie du ministère de la Défense 1973–87; Investigator, Comité central d'enquête sur le coût et le rendement des services publics 1974–84; mem. Electoral Comm. for French living abroad 1977–88, Cttee for Fiscal Matters, Customs and Exchange 1987–93; mem. town council of Méréville 1969–95; Officier Légion d'honneur, Commdr Ordre nat. du Mérite, Croix de guerre, Commdr de l'Etoile noire, Commdr de l'Ordre nat. Malgache, Grand Commdr of the Order of the Star of Ethiopia, Commdr de l'Etoile équatoriale de Gabon, Nat. Order of Upper Volta, Order of the Leopard of Zaire, Grand Officier Ordre du Croissant Vert des Comores. *Leisure interest:* nature. *Address:* 1 rue de Laborde, 91660 Méréville, France (home).

SAGLIO, Jean-François; French mining engineer; b. 29 July 1936, Toulon; s. of Georges Saglio; m. Odile Bertrand 1968; two s. one d.; ed Ecole Polytechnique and Ecole Supérieure des Mines, Paris; engineer, govt del., Algiers 1960–61; mining engineer, Mines de Metz 1961–66; Founder/Dir Agence de Bassin Rhin-Meuse, Metz 1966–69; Adviser, Cabinet of Pres. of France 1969–73; Head, Perm. Secr. for Study of Water Problems of Paris 1971–73; Dir in charge of Pollution and Nuisance, Ministry of Environment 1973–78; Pres. Dir-Gen. Agence Foncière et Technique de la Région Parisienne 1979–81; Dir of Innovation and Valorization of Research, Elf Aquitaine, also Dir of New Projects 1981–84; Pres. Dir-Gen. INOVELF 1981–84; Asst Dir-Gen. Soc. Elf-France 1984; Asst Dir-Gen. Refineries and Distribution, Soc. Nat. Elf Aquitaine 1984; Dir-Gen. of Industry, Ministry of Industry, Posts & Telecommunications and Tourism 1987–88; Dir Soc. Roussel-Uclaf 1989–91; Vice-Pres. SCH Consultants; Pres. Admin. Council Rhin-Meuse 1992–97, ERSO 1993; Dir-Gen. CEA Industrie 1992–94; Pres. Dexter SA 1992–99, Inst. français de l'environnement 1995–98; Pres. BNFL SA 1996; mem. Conseil Général des Mines 1991–99; Officier, Légion d'honneur, Ordre nat. du Mérite; Croix de la Valeur militaire. *Address:* 143 rue de la Pompe, 75116 Paris, France (home). *Telephone:* 1-45-53-05-44 (home).

SAGUIER CABALLERO, Bernardino Hugo, PhD; Paraguayan diplomatist and international organization executive; *Secretary-General, Latin American Integration Association (Asociación Latinoamericana de Integración—ALADI);* b. 21 July 1945; m.; three c.; ed Catholic Univ. of Asunción, Nat. War Coll., Asunción, Acad. of Int. Law, The Hague, European Inst. of Business Admin, Fontainebleau, France; joined Foreign Ministry, held various posts as Sec. to Comms, etc. 1962–75, Pvt. Sec. to Minister of Foreign Affairs 1965–68, Chef de Cabinet 1968–70, Dir of Int. Orgs, Treaties and Instruments 1970–75, Dir responsible for binational entity of Itaipu 1975–89, Under-Sec. of State for Foreign Affairs 1989–92; Perm. Rep. to the UN 1992–99; Amb. and Perm. Rep. to Latin American Integration Asscn (Asociación Latinoamericana de Integración—ALADI) and Mercosur c. 2005; Sec.-Gen. ALADI 2008–; fmr Head del. negotiations on Treaty of the Common Market of the Southern Cone (Mercosur), on Mercosur–US trade and investment agreement; fmr mem. del. to sessions of UN Gen. Ass. and meetings of OAS, Rio Group, River Plate Basin and Latin American Free Trade and Integration Asscns; fmr Prof., Diplomatic Acad., Ministry of Foreign Affairs; fmr Lecturer at Catholic Univ., Asunción and Higher Police Coll., Asunción; decorations from China, Brazil, S Africa, Argentina, Spain, Ecuador, Chile and others. *Address:* Secretaría General, Asociación Latinoamericana de Integración, Calle Cebollatí 1461, Barrio Palermo, Casilla de Correo n° 20.005, CP 11200, Montevideo, Uruguay (office). *Telephone:* (2) 419-10-14 (office); (2) 410-33-63 (office). *Fax:* (20) 418-45-66 (office). *E-mail:* sgaladi@aladi.org (office). *Website:* www.aladi.org (office).

SAHABDEEN, Desamanya Abdul Majeed Mohamed, BA, PhD; Sri Lankan foundation president, entrepreneur, fmr civil servant and scholar; *Chairman, Sifani Group of Companies;* b. 19 May 1926, Gampola; s. of Abdul Majeed and Shaharwan Majeed; m. Ruchia Halida 1959; one s. one d.; ed Univ. of Ceylon; joined Ceylon Civil Service 1950, served as Sec., Dir, Commr, Chair. several maj. Govt orgs. until 1973; Visiting Head, Dept of Western Philosophy, Univ. of Sri Lanka, Vidyodaya (now Sri Jayawardanapura) 1957–59; Chair. Majeedsons Group of Cos 1973–, Sifani Group of Cos; Chair. Muslim Law (Amendments) Cttee 1990; Founder and Chair. A.M.M. Sahabdeen Trust Foundation 1991, for Educ. and Social Devt; Mohamed Sahabdeen Int. Awards for Science, Literature and Human Devt est. by Act. of Parl. 1991; f. Mohamed Sahabdeen Inst. for Advanced Studies and Research in Pahamune 1997; Pres. Ceylon Muslim Scholarship Fund 1999; Chair. Pahamune House (Narammala, Sri Lanka) Rehabilitation Centre for Children –2005; mem. Presidential Comms on Delimitation of Electoral Dists 1988, Taxation 1989, Finance and Banking 1990, Industrialization 1990, Public Service Comm.

1989; mem. Press Council 1998; Vice-Patron Sri Lanka-India Friendship Soc. 1998; received Desamanya (highest civilian honour) 1992. *Publications:* several articles and books on philosophy and allied subjects, including Sufi Doctrine in Tamil Literature 1986, God and the Universe 1995, The Circle of Lives. *Leisure interests:* philosophy, classical music. *Address:* A.M.M. Sahabdeen Trust Foundation, 30/12 Bagatalle Road, Colombo 03, Sri Lanka; No. 86, 4th Floor, Galle Road, Colombo 03, Sri Lanka (office). *Telephone:* (11) 2399601 (office); (11) 2399602 (office); (11) 2586327 (home); (11) 2502447 (home); (11) 2399605 (office). *Fax:* (11) 2399603 (office); (11) 2399604 (office); (11) 2399604 (office). *E-mail:* sifanicare@eureka.lk (office); ammstrust@gamil .com (office). *Website:* www.ammstrustfoundation.org (office).

SAHADE, Jorge, PhD; Argentine astrophysicist; b. 23 Feb. 1915, Alta Gracia (Córdoba); s. of Nallib Jorge Sahade and María Kassab; m. 1st Myriam Stella Elkin Font 1948 (died 1974); one s. one d.; m. 2nd Adela Emilia Ringuelet 1975; ed Colegio de Monserrat, Córdoba, Univ. of Córdoba, Univ. of La Plata; Fellow, Univ. of La Plata at Univ. of Chicago (Yerkes Observatory) 1943–46; Prof., Univ. of Córdoba 1948–55, Dir Córdoba Observatory 1953–55; Guggenheim Fellow, Univ. of Calif., Berkeley 1955–57, Research Astronomer 1957–58, 1960; Prof. and Head Div., Univ. of La Plata Observatory 1958–71, in charge of two-m telescope project 1958–69, Dir Observatory 1968–69, Dean Faculty of Exact Sciences 1969; Dir Inst. of Astronomy and Space Physics, Buenos Aires 1971–74; Pres. Argentine Astronomical Asscn 1963–69; Pres. Comm. 29, Int. Astronomical Union (IAU) 1964–67, Vice-Pres. Exec. Cttee IAU 1967–73, Pres. 1985–88, Adviser 1988–91, Vice-Pres. Comm. 38 1988–91, Pres. 1991–94; Pres. Argentine Space Agency (CONAE) 1991–94; Emer. Researcher, CONICET 1995; Scientific Co-ordinator of Argentinian participation, Gemini Project 1996–2001; Chair. COSPAR Advisory Panel on Space Research in Developing Countries 1973–79, Pres. 1979–82; mem. Bd Dir Nat. Research Council 1969–73, 1996, Exec. Bd ICSU 1972–76, Gen. Cttee 1972–80, COSTED 1973–79; mem. Bd Dir Div. V, Int. Astronomical Union 1997–2003; Visiting Prof. at numerous univs: Indiana, Sussex, Mons, Collège de France, Int. School for Advanced Study (Trieste), San Marcos (Peru), Porto Alegre (Brazil); Visiting Astronomer Dominion Astrophysical Observatory, Victoria, BC, later Visiting Research Officer; Visiting Scientist Max-Planck Institut-für-Astrophysik, FRG, Cerro Tololo Interamerican Observatory, Chile, Trieste Observatory; Guest Investigator at numerous observatories; Assoc. Royal Astronomical Soc. 1970, COSPAR 1992; Founder-mem. Argentine Acad. of Aeronautical and Space Sciences 1989; mem. Buenos Aires Nat. Acad. of Sciences 2001–, mem. Argentine Nat. Acad. of sciences, Nat. Acad. of Sciences (Córdoba) 1972–; Foreign, Corresp. mem. numerous acads; Hon. Prof. Univ. of San Marcos, Peru 1987; Hon. mem. Argentine Asscn of Friends of Astronomy 1970, Argentine Astronomical Asscn 1985; Dr hc (Córdoba) 1987, (San Juan) 1996; Golden Planetarium Award 1973, Konex Award 1983, Diploma of Recognition, World Cultural Council 1987; Asteroid (2605)=1974 QA named Sahade at the proposal of the discoverer 1986, Consagración Científica Medal 1988; IAU Symposium No. 151 dedicated to J. Sahade; CASLEO's 2.15m telescope named Jorge Sahade 1996, Gold Medal, Argentine Asscn of Friends of Astronomy 1999; Conf. Room of Cen. American Suyapa Observatory, Nat. Autonomous Univ. of Honduras named after him 2000. *Publications:* books and 190 research papers in int. journals. *Leisure interests:* music, travel, walking. *Address:* Observatorio Astronómico, FCAG, Universidad Nacional de La Plata, B 1900 CGA- La Plata (office); 53-448 (p. 11 #1), B 1900 BAV- La Plata, Argentina (home). *Telephone:* (221) 423-6593/4 (office); (221) 482-4639 (home). *Fax:* (221) 423-6591 (office). *E-mail:* sahade@fcaglp .unlp.edu.ar (office). *Website:* www.fcaglp.unlp.ar (office).

SAHAKIAN, Bako; Azerbaijani government official; *'President of the Republic of Nagornyi-Karabakh';* b. 30 Aug. 1960, Xankandi (Stepanakert); m.; two c.; ed Stepanakert High School, Artsakh State Univ.; served in Soviet Army 1978–80; metalworker and mechanical engineer, Stepanakert Mechanical Works 1981–83; worked on restoration of historical monuments 1983–87; worked for Stepanakert dist council 1987–90; various roles within 'Repub. of Nagornyi-Karabakh' Self Defence Forces including Deputy Commdr of External Relations and Commdr of HQ 1990–97; Asst to Minister for Home Affairs and Nat. Security 1997–99; Minister for Home Affairs 1999–2001; Head, State Dept for Nat. Security 2001–07; 'Pres. of Repub. of Nagornyi-Karabakh' 2007–; Fighting Cross Order, Sparapet Vazgen Sargsian, Order of Peter the Great (Russia). *Address:* 'Office of the President of the Republic of Nagornyi-Karabakh', Xankandi, 20 February Street 3, Nagornyi-Karabakh, Azerbaijan (office). *Telephone:* (1) 45-222 (office). *Fax:* (1) 45-222 (office). *E-mail:* ps@president.nkr.am (office). *Website:* www.president.nkr.am (office).

SAHAYA, Dinesh Nandan, MA; Indian police officer and politician; *Governor of Tripura;* b. 2 Feb. 1936, Madhepur, Madhubani Dist, Bihar; s. of the late Deva Nandan Sahaya and Kishori Devi; m. Manju Sahaya; one s. two d.; ed Patna Coll.; began career as Lecturer, H. D. Jain Coll., Ara (Composite Bihar Univ.); selected for Indian Police Service as R.R. and allotted to Bihar Cadre 1960, held various sr positions in the field and Secr., also with CBI, retd as Dir-Gen. of Police 1994; entered public life and joined Samata Party 1995, Sr Vice-Pres. Bihar Pradesh Samata Party and mem. Nat. Exec. 1995–2000; Gov. of Chhattisgarh (first) 2000–03, of Tripura 2003–; Chair. Bihar State Br. of UN Students Asscn, Deputy Leader of del. on Goodwill Mission to Ceylon 1959; Patna Coll. Blue, Pres.'s Police Medal for Distinguished Services (highest award in Police Service). *Publications:* contrib. of articles to journals and magazines. *Leisure interests:* avid reader of books, particularly on political and social science, NGOs and voluntary orgs. *Address:* Raj Bhavan, Kunjaban, Tripura (office); 'Sai Niwas' 123, Patliputra Colony, Patna, Bihar, India. *Telephone:* (381) 222-4091 (office); (381) 222-5767 (office). *Fax:* (381) 222-4350 (office). *E-mail:* govtrp@trp.nic.in (office). *Website:* tripura.nic.in (office).

SAHE AL KAFAJE, Galib Nahe; Iraqi artist; b. 1932, Emara; m. 1967; three d.; ed Inst. of Fine Arts, Baghdad and Acad. of Fine Arts, Rome; Instructor Inst. of Fine Arts, Baghdad 1966, Acad. of Fine Arts, Baghdad 1969; work includes mural at fmr Saddam Airport 1987, 130 graphics at Rashed Hotel, Baghdad; works in collection at fmr Saddam Art Center and have been widely exhibited in European cities, New Delhi, Cairo etc.; several awards. *Leisure interest:* handicrafts in gold. *Address:* Dawoody, Street 15 No 102, Baghdad, Iraq (home). *Telephone:* 5423690.

SAHEL, El Mostafa, LenD; Moroccan politician and diplomatist; *Permanent Representative, United Nations;* b. 5 May 1946, Ouled Frej, El Jadida; s. of Maati Sahel and Hajja Ghita; m. Farida Benmansour Nejjai 1972; two s.; ed Lycée Mohamed V, Casablanca, Univ. Mohamed V, Rabat and Univ. de Sorbonne, Paris; Insp. des Finances 1968–70; Financial Controller 1970–74; Head of Service of Working Budget 1974–81, Equipment Budget 1981–86; Dir of Budget 1986–91; Sec.-Gen. Ministry of Finance 1992–93; Dir-Gen. of Communal Equipment Funds 1993–; Minister for Maritime Fisheries and Merchant Marine 1993–97, of Admin. Affairs and Relations with Parl. 1997–98; Chair. SOMED Investment Group (devt co.) 1998–2001; Prefect of Rabat region 2001–02; Minister of Interior 2002–06; Perm. Rep. to UN, New York 2006–; Ordre de Mérite, Ordre du Trône. *Leisure interest:* golf. *Address:* Permanent Mission of Morocco, 866 Second Avenue, 6th and 7th Floors, New York, NY 10017, USA (office). *Telephone:* (212) 421-1580 (office). *Fax:* (212) 980-1512 (office). *E-mail:* morocco@un.int (home). *Website:* www.un.int/morocco (home).

SAHGAL, Nayantara; Indian journalist and novelist; b. (Nayantara Pandit), 10 May 1927, Allahabad; d. of Ranjit Sitaram Pandit and Vijaya Lakshmi Pandit; m. 1st Gautam Sahgal 1949 (divorced 1967); one s. two d.; m. 2nd E. N. Mangat Rai 1979; ed Wellesley Coll., USA; Adviser English Language Bd, Sahitya Akademi (Nat. Acad. of Letters), New Delhi 1972–75; Scholar-in-Residence, holding creative writing seminar, Southern Methodist Univ., Dallas, Texas 1973, 1977; mem. Indian Del. to UN Gen. Ass. 1978; Vice-Pres. Nat. Exec., People's Union for Civil Liberties 1980–85; Fellow, Radcliffe Inst. (Harvard Univ.) 1976, Wilson Int. Center for Scholars, Washington, DC 1981–82, Nat. Humanities Center, NC 1983–84; mem. jury Commonwealth Writers' Prize 1990, Chair. Eurasia Region 1991; Annie Besant Memorial Lecture (Banaras Hindu Univ.) 1992; Arthur Ravenscroft Memorial Lecture (Univ. of Leeds) 1993; mem. American Acad. of Arts and Sciences 1990; Foreign Hon. mem. American Acad. Arts and Sciences 1990; Hon. DLitt (Leeds) 1997; Diploma of Honour, Int. Order of Volunteers for Peace, Salsomaggiore, Italy 1982, Sinclair Prize 1985, Doon Ratna Citizens' Council Prize 1992, Wellesley Coll. Alumni Achievement Award 2002, Pride of Doon Award 2002, Woodstock School Alumni Achievement Award 2004. *Publications:* Prison and Chocolate Cake 1954, A Time to Be Happy 1958, From Fear Set Free 1962, This Time of Morning 1965, Storm in Chandigarh 1969, History of the Freedom Movement 1970, The Day in Shadow 1972, A Situation in New Delhi 1977, A Voice for Freedom 1977, Indira Gandhi's Emergence and Style 1978, Indira Gandhi: Her Road to Power 1982, Rich Like Us (Sinclair Prize 1985, Sahitya Akad. Award 1987) 1985, Plans for Departure 1985 (Commonwealth Writers' Prize 1987), Mistaken Identity 1988, Relationship: Extracts from a Correspondence 1994 (co-author), Point of View 1997, Before Freedom: Nehru's Letters to His Sister 1909–47 (ed.) 2000, Lesser Breeds 2003; contrib. to newspapers and magazines including India Today. *Leisure interests:* walking, reading, music. *Address:* 181B Rajpur Road, Dehra Dun, 248009 Uttaranchal, India. *Telephone:* (135) 2734278 (home). *E-mail:* ebd@ebdbooks.com (office).

ŞAHIN, Mehmet Ali; Turkish politician; *Minster of Justice;* b. 1950, Ekincik; m.; four c.; ed Faculty of Law, Istanbul Univ.; early career as lawyer; fmr Mayor Fatih Municipality; Founding mem. AK Party; Deputy Prime Minister and Minister of State responsible for Sport and Youth Affairs 2002–07, Minister of Justice 2007–. *Address:* Ministry of Justice, Adalet Bakanlığı, 06659 Kizilay, Ankara, Turkey (office). *Telephone:* (312) 4177770 (office). *Fax:* (312) 4173954 (office). *Website:* www.adalet.gov.tr (office).

SAHINGUVU, Yves, MD; Burundian ophthalmologist and politician; *First Vice-President;* b. 20 Dec. 1949, ; m.; three c.; ed Univ. of Kinshasa, Catholic Univ. of Leuwen, Belgium; physician in pvt practice in Kinshasa 1984–97; Fmr Asst Prof., Faculty of Medicine, Univ. of Kinshasa; mem. Parl. for Muramvya 1998–, Senator 2002–05, mem. Union for Nat. Progress (UPRONA); First Vice-Pres. of Burundi 2007–. *Address:* Office of the First Vice-President, Bujumbura, Burundi (office). *Website:* presidence.burundi-gov.bi (office).

SAHL, Morton (Mort) Lyon, BS; American comedian; b. 11 May 1927, Montreal, Canada; s. of Harry Sahl; m. 1st Sue Babior 1955 (divorced 1957); m. 2nd China Lee; one c.; ed Compton Jr Coll., Univ. of Southern Calif.; Ed. Poop from the Group; magazine writing; many night club engagements; radio and TV performances, including Comedy News TV show, Steve Allen Show, Jack Paar Show, Eddie Fisher Show, Nightline, Wide Wide World; monologues on long-playing records; in Broadway revue, The Next President 1958; one-man show Broadway 1987; Mort Sahl: The Loyal Opposition (TV) 1989; Visiting Lecturer, Claremont McKenna Coll. 2007–. *Films include:* In Love and War 1958, All the Young Men 1960, Johnny Cool 1963, Doctor, You've Got to Be Kidding 1967, Nothing Lasts Forever 1984, (TV) Inside the Third Reich 1982. *Publication:* Heartland 1976. *Address:* c/o Gould Center for Humanistic Studies, Claremont McKenna College, 850 Colombia Avenue, Claremont, CA 91711-6420; 2325 San Ysidro Drive, Beverly Hills, CA 90210, USA. *Website:* www.mortsahl.com.

SAHLIN, Mona; Swedish politician; *Chairman, Sveriges Socialdemokratiska Arbetareparti (SAP—Swedish Social Democratic Party);* b. 9 March 1957, Sollefteå; m. Bo Sahlin; three c.; ed Correspondence School, Swedish Cooperative Movt 1978–80; Sec. State Employees' Union 1980–82; Mem. Parl. (Riksdag) 1982–90; Minister of Employment 1990–91; Gen. Sec. Sveriges Socialdemokratiska Arbetareparti (SAP—Social Democratic Party of Sweden) 1992–94, Chair. 2007–; Govt Rep. Bd of Swedish Sports Confed. 1983–90; Chair. Cttee on Working Hours 1982–90; mem. Bd Centre for Working Life 1982–90; Deputy Prime Minister and Minister with Special Responsibility for Equality Issues 1994–95; self-employed 1995–98; Minister, Ministry of Industry, Employment and Communications 1998–2002; Minister (Democracy and Integration Issues), Ministry of Justice 2002–04, Minister for Sustainable Devt 2004–06. *Address:* Sveriges Socialdemokratiska Arbetareparti (SAP), Sveavägen 68, 105 60 Stockholm, Sweden (office). *Telephone:* (8) 700-26-00 (office). *Fax:* (8) 21-93-31 (office). *E-mail:* info@sap.se (office). *Website:* www.socialdemokraterna.se (office).

SAHNOUN, Mohamed; Algerian diplomatist, fmr UN official and international organization official; *President, Caux Forum for Human Security;* b. Chlef; Deputy Sec.-Gen. OAU (in charge of Political Affairs) 1964–73, League of Arab States (for Arab-African dialogue) 1973–75; Amb. to FRG, to France, to USA 1984–89, to Morocco 1989–1990; Perm. Rep. to the UN 1982–84; Sec. of the Maghreb Union 1989–90; Counsellor to the Pres. of Algeria for Foreign Affairs 1990–92; UN Special Rep. in Somalia 1992; OAU Special Rep. in the Congo 1993; UN/OAU Special Envoy in Great Lakes Region of Africa 1997–2006 (resgnd); Pres. Initiatives of Change Int. 2006–08; Founder and Pres. Caux Forum for Human Security 2008–; fmr Special Adviser to Sec.-Gen. UN Conf. on Environment and Devt, UNCED; fmr Special Adviser to Culture of Peace Prog. UNESCO, Paris, War-Torn Societies Project UNRISD, Geneva; fmr Exec. Dir Earth Charter Project; fmr mem. World Comm. on Environment and Devt (Brundtland Comm.); mem. Bd Int. Inst. for Sustainable Devt (IISD), Winnipeg, Int. Council for Human Rights; Distinguished Fellow, US Inst. of Peace, Washington 1992–93; Pearson Fellow, Int. Devt Research Centre (IDRC), Ottawa, Canada 1993–94; mem. Univ. for Peace Council, Costa Rica and consulant on Africa Programme. *Publications:* Somalia: The Missed Opportunities 1994, Managing Conflicts in the Post-Cold War Era 1996. *Address:* Initiatives of Change International, PO Box 3, 1211 Geneva 20, Switzerland (office). *Telephone:* 227491620 (office). *Fax:* (office). *E-mail:* iofc-international@iofc.org (office). *Website:* www.iofc.org (office).

SAIBOU, Brig. Ali; Niger politician and army officer; fmr Chief of Staff of Armed Forces; fmr Acting Head of State; Pres. Mouvement nat. pour une Société de développement (MNSD); Chair. of the Higher Council for Nat. Orientation (fmrly Conseil militaire Suprême) 1987–89; Pres. of the Council of Ministers 1989–91, Minister of Nat. Defence 1987–91, of Interior 1987–89 (stripped of exec. power Aug. 1991).

SAID, Sayyid Fahad bin Mahmoud as-; Omani politician; m. Sayyidah Berthe Fahad Al-Said; Deputy Prime Minister for Legal Affairs, then Deputy Prime Minister for the Council of Ministers. *Address:* c/o Ministry of Legal Affairs, POB 578, Ruwi 112, Oman (office).

SAID, Sayyid Faisal bin Ali as-; Omani diplomatist and politician; b. 1927, Muscat; attached to Ministry of Foreign Affairs, Muscat 1953–57; lived abroad 1957–70; Perm. Under-Sec. Ministry of Educ. 1970–72; Minister of Econ. Affairs 1972; Perm. Rep. to UN, Amb. to USA 1972–73; Minister of Educ. 1973–76, of Omani Heritage 1976, of Culture 1979. *Address:* c/o Ministry of National Heritage and Culture, PO Box 668, Muscat 113, Oman.

SAID, Wafic Rida; Saudi Arabian (b. Syrian) financier; *Chairman, Said Holdings Limited;* b. 1939, Damascus; s. of Dr Rida Said; m. Rosemary Thompson; one s. one d. (and one s. deceased); ed in Lebanon and at Inst. of Banking, London; began banking career at UBS Geneva 1962; f. TAG System Construction for design and construction projects in Saudi Arabia 1969; became Saudi Arabian citizen 1981; f. SIFCORP Holdings (int. investment co.) 1981; Chair. of several pvt. cos including Said Holdings Ltd and Sagitta Asset Man. (Bermuda) Ltd; mem. Oxford Univ. Court of Benefactors; Trustee Said Business School Foundation; Gov. RSC, London; Amb. and Perm. Del. to UNESCO of St Vincent and the Grenadines 1996–; mem. Oxford Univ. Court of Benefactors; f. Karim Rida Saïd Foundation 1982; Hon. Fellow, Trinity Coll., Oxford; Grand Commdr Ordre de Mérite du Cèdre (Lebanon), Ordre Chérifien (Morocco); Sheldon Medal, Univ. of Oxford 2003. *Leisure interests:* horse racing, collecting art and antiques. *Address:* Said Holdings Limited, 31 Reid Street, Hamilton HM 12, Bermuda (office); Karim Rida Said Foundation, 4 Bloomsbury Place, London, WC1A 2QA, England. *Telephone:* (20) 7691-2772. *Fax:* (20) 7691-2780. *E-mail:* heather.gray@saidholdings.com (office); admin@krsf.org. *Website:* www.shl.bm (office); www.krsf.org; www.waficsaid.com.

SAIDENOV, Anvar Galimullaevich, MS; Kazakhstani banker and economist; *Governor, National Bank of Kazakhstan;* b. 19 Sept. 1960; ed Moscow State Univ. M.G. Lomonsov, Univ. of London; worked for European Bank for Reconstruction and Development (EBRD), London 1993–96; Deputy Gov. Nat. Bank of Kazakhstan 1996–98, First Deputy Chair. 2002–04, Gov. 2004–; Exec. Dir, State Cttee of Kazakhstan for Investment, Gov. Agency of Kazakhstan for Investment; Vice-Minister of Finance, 1999–2000; Acting Chair. then Chair. Halyk People's Savings Bank of Kazakhstan 2000–02, Gov. Council of Dirs 2002–. *Address:* National Bank of Kazakhstan, Koktem-3 21, 050000 Almaty, Kazakhstan (office). *Telephone:* (727) 259-68-00 (office). *Fax:* (727) 270-47-03 (office). *E-mail:* hq@nationalbank.dz (office). *Website:* www.nationalbank.kz (office).

SAIER, Oskar, DJurCan; German ecclesiastic; *Archbishop Emeritus of Freiburg;* b. 12 Aug. 1932, Wagensteig; s. of Adolf Saier and Berta Saier; ed Univs of Freiburg, Tübingen and Munich; ordained Priest of Freiburg im

Breisgau 1957; Vicar, Study and Research Asst, Kanonist. Inst., Univ. of Munich 1963–70; Dir Mayor Seminar St Peter, Black Forest 1970–77; Auxiliary Bishop of Freiburg and Titular Bishop of Rubicon 1972, Archbishop of Freiburg 1978–2002 (resgnd), Archbishop Emer. 2002–07; Chair. Pastoral Comm. of German Conf. of Bishops 1979–98; mem. Vatican Congregation for the Clergy 1984–99; Second Chair. of German Conf. of Bishops 1987–99; Freeman of Buchenbach 1972, of St Peter, Black Forest 1977 and of Bethlehem 1984; Hon. Senator, Univ. of Freiburg 2003; Order El Sol del Peru 1990, Grosses Bundesverdienstkreuz 1992, Verdienstmedaille des Landes Baden-Württemberg 1997, Grosses Bundesverdienstkreuz mit Stern; Hon. DrTheol (Freiburg) 2002. *Publication:* Communio in der Lehre des Zweiten Vatikanischen Konzils 1973. *Address:* Ludwigstrasse 42, 79104 Freiburg, Germany (home).

SAIF, Abdulla Hassan; Bahraini banker; *Economic Affairs Adviser to the Prime Minister;* b. 10 March 1945, Muharraq; ed Inst. of Cost and Man. Accountants, UK, IMF Inst. and other int. forums; apprentice, Bahrain Petroleum Co. 1957, served in all depts. –1971; Head of Finance and Admin. Civil Aviation Directorate 1971–74; Deputy Dir-Gen. Bahrain Monetary Agency 1974–77, Dir-Gen. 1977, fmr Gov.; Chair. Gulf Int. Bank BSC; Minister of Finance and Nat. Economy 1999–2005; Economic Affairs Adviser to Prime Minister 2005–; Chair. Specific Council for Training of Banking Sector; mem. Bd of Dirs Gulf Air Co., Org. for Social Insurance, Civil Service Pension Bd; Alt. Gov. IMF; Dr hc (DePaul Univ. Chicago) 2002. *Address:* c/o Office of the Prime Minister, POB 1000, Government House, Government Road, Manama, Bahrain (office). *Telephone:* 17253361 (office). *Fax:* 17533033 (office).

SAIF AL-ISLAM, HRH Mohamed al-Badr, fmr Imam of the Yemen; b. 1927; ed Coll. for Higher Education, San'a; Minister for Foreign Affairs 1955–61, Minister of Defence and C-in-C 1955–62; succeeded to Imamate on the death of his father, Imam Ahmed Sept. 1962; led Royalist Forces in civil war 1962–68; replaced by Imamate Council May 1968; in exile in Saudi Arabia 1968.

SAIFUDIN (see SEYPIDIN).

SAIFULLAH KHAN, Javed, BA, MBA; Pakistani business executive; *Chairman, Saif Holdings;* ed Carnegie Mellon Univ., Univ. of Pittsburgh, USA; joined Saif Group of Cos 1973, Chair. Saif Holdings 1990–, holding co. of Saif Group consisting of interests in telecommunications, information tech., cement and textiles, including Pakistan Mobile Communications Pvt. Ltd, Saif Telecom Ltd, Transworld Assocs Pvt. Ltd, Saif Textile Mills; Sr Advisor Galen Capital Group LLC, USA; mem. Bd of Dirs Pakistan Int. Airlines Corpn, Pakistan Mobile Communications Ltd, Lok Virsa; mem. Bd of Investment, Govt of Pakistan; mem. Exec. Cttee Pakistan Petroleum Exploration and Production Cos; fmr Chair. Cen. Man. Cttee, All Pakistan Textile Mills Asscn; fmr mem. Task Force, Information Tech. and Telecommunication Advisory Bd, Ministry of Science and Tech.; Sitara I Imtiaz 2007. *Address:* Saif Group, Kulsum Plaza 42, Blue Area, Islamabad, Pakistan (office). *Telephone:* (51) 2823924 (office). *Fax:* (51) 2277843 (office). *E-mail:* info@saifgroup.com (office). *Website:* www.saifgroup.com (office).

SAIGA, Fumiko; Japanese diplomatist and judge; *Judge, International Criminal Court;* b. 30 Nov. 1943; ed Tokyo Univ. of Foreign Studies; with Int. Convention Div., Treaties Bureau 1980–83; First Sec., Perm. Mission to UN, New York 1983–88, Asst Dir UN Policy Div., UN Affairs Bureau Feb. 1988, Deputy Dir Social Co-operation Div., UN Affairs Bureau 1988–89, Dir Ocean Div., Econ. Affairs Bureau 1989–92, Counsellor, Embassy in Copenhagen 1992–96, Minister, Perm. Mission to UN 1996–98; Vice-Gov. Saitama Pref. 1998–2000; Consul-Gen. of Japan in Seattle 2000–02, Amb. and Perm. Rep. to UN 2002–03, Amb. to Norway (also accred to Iceland) 2003–07, Amb. in charge of Human Rights 2005–08; Judge (Pre-Trial Div.), Int. Criminal Court, The Hague, Netherlands 2008–; mem. Cttee on Elimination of Discrimination Against Women (CEDAW) 2001–. *Address:* International Criminal Court, PO Box 19519, 2500 CM The Hague, The Netherlands (office). *Telephone:* (70) 515-8515 (office). *Fax:* (70) 515-8555 (office). *E-mail:* info@icc-cpi.int (office). *Website:* www.icc-cpi.int (office).

SAIGOL, Mian Naseem; Pakistani business executive; *Chairman, Saigol Group of Companies;* Chair. Saigol Group of Cos, conglomerate with interests in automobiles, eng, power, information tech., including Kohinoor Textile Mills; Chair. Pak Elektron Ltd (PEL); Chair. and CEO Kohinoor Power Co. Ltd; est. Union Bank 1991; mem. Commonwealth Business Council, mem. Bd of Dirs 2006–08;. *Address:* Pak Electron Ltd, 17 Aziz Avenue, Canal Bank, Lahore, Pakistan (office). *Telephone:* (42) 5717364-5 (office). *Fax:* (42) 5715105 (office). *Website:* www.pel.com.pk (office).

SAIJO, Hideki; Japanese singer; b. (Kimoto Tatsuo), 13 May 1955, Hiroshima; popular recording artist 1972–; has released over 80 singles, appeared in six feature films, four plays, seven musicals and 23 TV dramas; producer and performer annual Stop AIDS benefit concert. *Singles Include:* Ai Suru Kisetsu, Jyonetsu no Arashi, Chigereta Ai, Young Man, Itsumo no Hoshi ga Nagare. *Publications:* Bali Sutairu no Ie. *Leisure interests:* scuba diving, golf. *Website:* www.earth-corp.co.jp/HIDEKI.

SAINSBURY, Keith J., BS, PhD; New Zealand marine research scientist; *Director, SainSolutions Pty Ltd;* b. 22 Feb. 1951, Christchurch; ed Univ. of Canterbury; research scientist NZ Ministry of Agric. and Fisheries 1975–76; research scientist Commonwealth Scientific and Industrial Research Org. (CSIRO), Australia 1977–78, project leader Man. Australian Tropical Fisheries Resources 1978–79, Man. Pelagic Fisheries Resources Program and Multi-Div. Program for Design and Evaluation of Marine Management Strategies 1990–97, Man. Multiple Use Management of Exclusive Economic Zone

program 1997–2002, Sr Prin. Research Scientist and Program Leader Div. of Marine Research 2002–; Prof. of Marine Systems Science, Univ. of Tasmania; mem. Bd of Commrs Australian Fisheries Man. Authority; Pres. SainSolutions, Tasmania, Dir SainSolutions Pty Ltd; Vice-Chair. of the Bd. Marine Stewardship Council, mem. Tech. Advisory Bd; mem. Advisory Cttee Pew Fellows Program in Marine Conservation; The Australian Book Publishers' Asscn Award for Outstanding Design and Production of an Australian Book 1985, Japan Prize for contrib. to understanding of shelf ecosystems and their sustainable utilization 2004. *Publications:* Continental Shelf Fishes of Northern and Northwestern Australia (co-author) 1985; contrib. numerous chapters in books and articles in journals including Journal of Marine Science. *Address:* SainSolutions Pty Ltd. 41 Powell Road, Blackmans Bay, Tasmania. *Telephone:* (3) 62291767. *E-mail:* ksainsbury@netspace.net.au. *Website:* www.sainsolutions.net.

SAINSBURY, (Richard) Mark, DPhil, FBA; British academic; *Professor of Philosophy, University of Texas at Austin;* b. 2 July 1943, London; s. of Richard Eric Sainsbury and Freda Margaret Horne; m. 1st Gillian McNeill Rind 1969 (divorced); one s. one d.; m. 2nd Victoria Goodman 2000; ed Sherborne School, Corpus Christi Coll., Oxford; Radcliffe Lecturer in Philosophy, Magdalen Coll., Oxford 1968–70; Lecturer in Philosophy, St Hilda's Coll., Oxford 1970–73, Radcliffe Lecturer in Philosophy, Brasenose Coll., Oxford 1973–75; Lecturer in Philosophy, Univ. of Essex 1975–78, Bedford Coll., Univ. of London 1978–84, King's Coll., London 1984–87, Reader 1987–89, Stebbing Prof. of Philosophy 1991–2003; Prof. of Philosophy, Univ. of Texas at Austin 2002–; Ed. Mind 1990–2000; Radcliffe Fellow 1987–88; Fellow, King's Coll., London 1994, British Acad. 1998; Leverhulme Sr Research Fellow 2000–02. *Publications:* Russell 1979, Paradoxes 1988, Logical Forms 1991, Departing From Frege 2002, Reference Without Referents 2005. *Leisure interest:* baking bread. *Address:* Department of Philosophy, WAG 403A, 1 University Station, University of Texas, Austin, TX 78712, USA (office). *Telephone:* (512) 417-5433 (office). *E-mail:* marksainsbury@mail.utexas.edu (office). *Website:* www.utexas.edu/cola/depts/philosophy (office).

SAINSBURY OF PRESTON CANDOVER, Baron (Life Peer), cr. 1989, of Preston Candover in the County of Hampshire; **John Davan Sainsbury,** KG, MA; British business executive; b. 2 Nov. 1927, London; s. of the late A. J. (later Baron) Sainsbury; m. Anya Linden 1963; two s. one d.; ed Stowe School and Worcester Coll., Oxford; Dir J Sainsbury Ltd 1958–92, Vice-Chair. 1967–69, Chair. & CEO 1969–92, Pres. 1992–; Chair. Anglo-Israel Asscn 2001–; Dir Royal Opera House, Covent Garden 1969–85 (Chair. 1987–91), The Economist 1972–80, Royal Opera House Trust 1974–84, 1987–97; Chair. Friends of Covent Garden 1969–81, Benesh Inst. of Chorology 1986–87, Dulwich Picture Gallery 1994–; Vice-Pres. Contemporary Arts Soc. 1984–; mem. Council, Retail Consortium 1975–79, Pres. 1993–97; mem. Nat. Cttee for Electoral Reform 1976–85; Jt Hon. Treas. European Mov. 1972–75; Fellow, Inst. of Grocery Distribution 1973; Hon. Fellow Worcester Coll., Oxford 1982; Gov. Royal Ballet School 1965–76, 1987–91, Royal Ballet 1987– (Chair. 1995–); Trustee Nat. Gallery 1976–83, Westminster Abbey Trust 1977–83, Tate Gallery 1982–83, Rhodes Trust 1984–98, Prince of Wales Inst. of Architecture 1992–96; Hon. Bencher, Inner Temple 1985; Hon. DSc (London) 1985; Hon. DLitt (South Bank) 1992; Albert Medal (RSA) 1989. *Address:* House of Lords, London, SW1A 0PW, England. *Telephone:* (20) 7219-5353.

SAINSBURY OF TURVILLE, Baron (Life Peer), cr. 1997, in the County of Buckinghamshire; **David John Sainsbury,** MBA; British business executive and fmr government official; b. 24 Oct. 1940; s. of Sir Robert Sainsbury; m. Susan C. Reid 1973; three d.; ed King's Coll., Cambridge and Columbia Univ., NY; joined J Sainsbury 1963, Finance Dir 1973–90, Deputy Chair. J Sainsbury PLC 1988–92, Chair. and CEO 1992–98, Dir J Sainsbury USA Inc.; Parl. Under-Sec. of State for Science and Innovation 1998–2006; mem. Cttee of Review of Post Office (Carter Cttee) 1975–77; fmr Trustee, Social Democratic Party (SDP); mem. Gov. Body, London Business School 1985– (Chair. 1991–98); Visiting Fellow, Nuffield Coll., Oxford 1987–95; mem. IPPR Comm. 1995–97; Chair. Transition Bd, Univ. for Industry 1998–99; f. Gatsby Charitable Foundation 1967 (one of Sainsbury Family Charitable Trusts); Hon. FREng 1994; Hon. LLD (Cambridge) 1997. *Publications:* Government and Industry: A New Partnership 1981, Wealth Creation and Jobs (with C. Smallwood) 1987. *Address:* House of Lords, London, SW1A 0PW, England (office). *Telephone:* (20) 7219-1493 (office).

ST ARNAUD, Bill, BEng, MEng, PEng; Canadian computer engineer; *Chief Research Officer and Director of Network Projects, CANARIE Inc.;* b. 1951; ed Carleton Univ. School of Eng; Consultant and Chief Engineer, Switzer Engineering 1975–79; Project Man., Motorola, Inc. 1979–81; Founder and Pres. TSA Proforma 1981–88; consultant for several high-tech start-ups 1988–92; Project Dir, Vision 2000 1992–93; Sr Dir of Network Projects, CANARIE Inc. 1993–, led devt, coordination and implementation of world's first nat. optical R&D Internet network, CA*net3, Chair. CA*net 3 Tech Applications Cttee 1994–, currently, Chief Architect of CA*net4; mem. various cttees and bds, including Bd of Trustees for The Internet Society (ISOC), NomComm Cttee for Internet Corpn for Assigned Names and Numbers (ICANN), UKlight Steering Cttee, GLORIAD Policy Cttee, Neptune Canada Oversight Cttee, Global Lambda Integrated Facility Policy Cttee, Steering Cttee SPIE Tech. Group on Optical Networks 2000–, amongst others; NSF Reviewer; Ed. CAnet-3-NEWS@canarie.ca; mem. Editorial Bd Optical Networking Magazine; Globecomm Fellow, Center for Global Communications 2000; World Tech. Award in Communication Tech., The World Tech. Network 2005. *Publications:* numerous scientific papers in professional journals. *Address:* CANARIE Inc., 4th Floor, 110 O'Connor Street, Ottawa, ON K1P 5M9, Canada (office). *Telephone:* (613) 785-0426 (office). *Fax:* (613) 943-5443 (office). *E-mail:* bill.st.arnaud@canarie.ca (office); bill.st.arnaud@gmail.com (home). *Website:* www.canarie.ca/~bstarn (office); billstarnaud.blogspot.com.

ST AUBIN de TERÁN, Lisa Gioconda, (Lisa Duff-Scott), FRSL; British author; *Director, Teran Foundation;* b. (Lisa Gioconda Carew), 2 Oct. 1953, London; d. of Jan Rynveld Carew and Joan Mary St Aubin; m. 1st Jaime Terán 1970 (divorced 1981); one d.; m. 2nd George Macbeth 1981 (divorced 1989, deceased); one s.; m. 3rd Robbie Duff-Scott (divorced) 1989; one d.; pnr Mees van Deth; ed James Allen's Girls' School, Dulwich; travelled widely in France and Italy 1969–71; managed sugar plantation in Venezuelan Andes 1971–78; moved to Italy 1983; fmr Vice-Pres. Umbria Film Festival, now Hon. Pres.; CEO Radiant Pictures 2002 (film production co.); f. Teran Foundation and Makua Coll. of Tourism and Agriculture, Mozambique 2004; Somerset Maugham Award 1983, John Llewelyn Rhys Award 1983, Eric Gregory Award for Poetry 1983. *Screenplays:* The Slow Train to Milan (co-writer with Michael Radford), The Hacienda, The Blessing, A Woman Called Solitude, The Orange Sicilian (co-writer with Alex Macbeth, animated feature film). *Television:* wrote and presented documentaries Santos to Santa Cruz in Great Railway Journeys series (BBC) 1994, Great Railway Journeys of the World (BBC and PBS). *Radio:* adapted and read (for BBC) Off the Rails 1995, The Bay of Silence 1996. *Publications:* fiction: Keepers of the House 1982, The Slow Train to Milan 1983, The Tiger 1984, The Bay of Silence 1986, Black Idol 1987, The Marble Mountain (short stories) 1989, Joanna 1990, Nocturne 1993, Distant Landscapes (novella) 1995, The Palace 1998, The Virago Book of Wanderlust and Dreams (ed.) 1998, Southpaw (short stories) 1999, Otto: A Novel 2004, Sapa's Blessing and Other Stories 2005, Swallowing Stones 2006; poetry: The Streak 1980, The High Place 1985; memoirs: Off the Rails 1989, Venice: The Four Seasons 1992, A Valley in Italy 1994, The Hacienda 1997, My Venezuelan Years 1997, Memory Maps 2001, Mozambique Mysteries 2007. *Leisure interests:* travelling, medicinal plants, gardening, architecture, falconry, antiques, reading, Mozambique. *Address:* Caixa Postal 81, Ilha de Moçambique, Provincia de Nampula (home); c/o Teran Foundation, Sunset Boulevard Guest House, Mossuril Sede, Distrito Mossuril, Provincia de Nampula, Mozambique (office). *E-mail:* info@teranfoundation.org (office). *Website:* www.teranfoundation.org (office).

SAINT-GEOURS, Frédéric; French civil servant and business executive; *Chairman, Union des Industries et Métiers de la Métallurgie (UIMM);* b. 20 April 1950, Clamart (Hauts-de-Seine); s. of Jean Saint-Geours, fmr Pres. Comm. des opérations de bourse; m. Eva Bettan; three c.; ed Institut d'Etudes Politiques and Ecole Nationale d'Admin, Paris; joined Ministry of Finance 1975, worked as forecaster for Finance Minister Jacques Delors, held series of govt posts in finance, including adviser to Pres. of Nat. Ass., finally Chief Tech. Advisor to Sec. of State for the Budget, Henri Emmanuelli 1984–86; Deputy Chief Financial Dir PSA Peugeot-Citroën 1986–88, Financial Dir 1988–90, Deputy Dir-Gen. Automobiles Peugeot 1990, oversaw Jean Todt's successful Peugeot 905 sports car campaigns 1991, 1992, 1993, Dir-Gen. Automobiles Peugeot 1998–2007; Chair. Union des Industries et Métiers de la Métallurgie (UIMM) 2007–. *Address:* Union des Industries et Métiers de la Métallurgie, 56 avenue de Wagram, 75017 Paris, France (office). *Telephone:* 1-40-54-20-20 (office). *Fax:* 1-47-66-22-74 (office). *E-mail:* uimm@uimm.fr (office). *Website:* www.uimm.fr (office).

ST JOHN OF FAWSLEY, Baron (Life Peer), cr. 1987, of Preston in the County of Northampton; **Norman Antony Francis St John-Stevas,** PC, MA, BCL, PhD, FRSL; British politician, barrister, writer and journalist; b. 18 May 1929; s. of the late Stephen Stevas and Kitty St John O'Connor; ed Ratcliffe, Fitzwilliam Coll., Cambridge, Christ Church, Oxford and Yale Univ.; Barrister, Middle Temple 1952; Lecturer, King's Coll., London 1953–56; Tutor in Jurisprudence, Christ Church, Oxford 1953–55, Merton Coll., Oxford 1955–57; Founder mem. Inst. of Higher European Studies, Bolzano 1955; Legal Adviser to Sir Alan Herbert's Cttee on Book Censorship 1954–59; Legal and Political Corresp., The Economist 1959–64; Conservative MP for Chelmsford 1964–87; Sec. Conservative Party Home Affairs Cttee 1969–72; mem. Fulbright Comm. 1961; mem. Parl. Select Cttee Race Relations and Immigration 1970–72, on Civil List 1971–83, on Foreign Affairs 1983–87; Parl. Under-Sec. for Educ. and Science 1972–73; Minister of State for the Arts 1973–74; Shadow Cabinet 1974–79, Shadow Leader of the House of Commons 1978–79, Opposition Spokesman on Educ. 1974–78, Science 1974–78 and the Arts 1974–79; Chancellor of the Duchy of Lancaster 1979–81; Leader of the House of Commons 1979–81; Minister for the Arts 1979–81; Vice-Chair. Cons. Parl. NI Cttee 1972–87; Vice-Chair. Cons. Group for Europe 1972–75; Chair. Royal Fine Art Comm. 1985–99; Master Emmanuel Coll., Cambridge 1991–96, Life Fellow 1996; Vice-Pres. Theatres Advisory Council 1983; Founder mem. Christian-Social Inst. of Culture, Rome 1969; mem. Council RADA 1983–88, Nat. Soc. for Dance 1983–, Nat. Youth Theatre 1983– (Patron 1984–), RCA 1985–; Trustee Royal Philharmonic Orch. 1985–88, Decorative Arts Soc. 1984–; Hon. Sec. Fed. of Conservative Students 1971–73; Ed. The Dublin (Wiseman Review) 1961; Romanes Lecturer, Oxford 1987; Hon. FRIBA; Hon. DD (Susquehanna, Pa) 1983; Hon. DLitt (Schiller) 1985, (Bristol) 1988; Hon. LLD (Leicester) 1991; Hon. DArts (De Montfort) 1996; Silver Jubilee Medal 1977; Kt Grand Cross, St Lazarus of Jerusalem 1963; Cavaliere Ordine al Merito della Repubblica (Italy) 1965, Commendatore 1978; Grand Bailiff Mil. and Hospitaller Order of St Lazarus of Jerusalem. *Publications:* Obscenity and the Law 1956, Walter Bagehot 1959, Life, Death and the Law 1961, The Right to Life 1963, Law and Morals 1964, The Literary Essays of Walter Bagehot 1965, The Historical Essays of Walter Bagehot 1968, The Agonising Choice 1971, The Political Essays of Walter Bagehot 1974, The Economic Works of Walter Bagehot 1978, Pope John Paul, His Travels and Mission 1982, The Two Cities 1984. *Leisure interests:* reading, talking, listening to music, travelling, walking, appearing on TV. *Address:* House of Lords, London, SW1A 0PW; 7 Brunswick Place, Regent's Park, London, NW1 4PS; 15 North Court, Great Peter Street, Westminster, London SW1P 3LL, England. *Telephone:* (20) 7219-3199 (House of Lords).

SAINZ MUÑOZ, Most Rev. Faustino, DCL; Spanish ecclesiastic and diplomatist; *Apostolic Nuncio to UK;* b. 5 June 1937, Almadén; ordained priest 1964; entered diplomatic service of the Holy See 1970, served in Pontifical Representations in Senegal and Scandinavia, then in Council of Public Affairs of the Church, Vatican Secr. of State, dispatched as part of Holy See's del. to preparatory talks of CSCE 1975, returning to Vatican 1975, apptd liaison with Poland, Hungary, and later USSR and Yugoslavia, travelled to Latin America 1978, accompanied Cardinal Antonio Samoré in successfully averting war between Chile and Argentina over the Beagle conflict, accompanied Pope John Paul II on his visit to his native Poland June 1979; consecrated Titular Archbishop of Novaliciana 1988; Apostolic Pro-Nuncio to Cuba 1988–92, Apostolic Nuncio to Democratic Repub. of the Congo 1992–99, to EU 1999–2004, to UK 2005–; Hon. LLD (Aberdeen) 2007. *Leisure interests:* Real Madrid fan, walking and tennis enthusiast. *Address:* Apostolic Nunciature, 54 Parkside, Wimbledon, London, SW19 5NE, England (office). *Telephone:* (20) 8944-7189 (office). *Fax:* (20) 8947-2494 (office). *E-mail:* nuntius@globalnet.co.uk (office).

SAITO, Akihiko, PhD; Japanese engineer and business executive; *Chairman, DENSO Corporation;* ed Nagoya Univ.; joined Toyota Motor Corpn 1968, responsible for several tech. assignments, including work in vibration testing, chassis design, product planning and production eng, mem. team that handled product planning work for Toyota's best-selling car, the Corolla 1980, served as Chief Engineer in devt of sixth and seventh generation Corollas, Gen. Man. Product Planning Div. 1987–91, mem. Bd of Dirs 1991–, Man. Dir 1996–98, Sr Man. Dir 1998–2001, Exec. Vice-Pres. 2001–05; Vice-Chair. DENSO Corpn 2005–07, Chair. 2007–. *Address:* DENSO Corpn, 1-1 Showa-cho, Kariya, Aichi 448-8661, Japan (office). *Telephone:* (556) 25-5511 (office). *Fax:* (566) 25-4509 (office). *E-mail:* info@globaldenso.com (office). *Website:* www.globaldenso.com (office).

SAITO, Atsushi; Japanese business executive; *President and CEO, Tokyo Stock Exchange Group;* ed Keio Univ.; joined Nomura Securities Co. Ltd 1963, stationed twice in New York for a total of 10 years, apptd Dir 1986, several exec. positions including Vice Pres. 1995–98 (retd); Pres. Sumitomo Life Investment Co. Ltd 1998–2002, Chair. 2002–03; Pres. and CEO Industrial Revitalization Corpn of Japan 2003–07; Pres. and CEO Tokyo Stock Exchange Group 2007–. *Address:* Tokyo Stock Exchange Group, 2-1 Nihombashi Kabutocho, Chuo-ku, Tokyo 103-0026, Japan (office). *Telephone:* (3) 3666-0141 (office). *Website:* www.tse.or.jp (office).

SAITO, Gunzi, PhD; Japanese scientist and academic; *Professor, Department of Chemistry, Kyoto University;* b. 10 March 1945, Otaru, Hokkaido; s. of Nenosuke Saito and Toyo Saito; m. Atsuko Nishikawa 1971; three s.; ed Otaru Choryo High School, Hokkaido Univ.; Postdoctoral Fellow, Emory Univ., Atlanta, Ga, USA 1973–74, Guelph Univ., Ont., Canada 1975–76; Welch Fellow Univ. of Tex., Dallas, USA 1977–78; Research Assoc., Inst. for Molecular Science, Okazaki 1979–84; Assoc. Prof., Inst. for Solid State Physics, Tokyo Univ. 1984–89; Prof., Dept of Chem., Faculty of Science, Kyoto Univ. 1989–; mem. Science Council, Ministry of Educ., Sport and Culture 1996–2003; Inoue Award 1988, Nishina Award 1988, Japan Surface Science Award 1991, The Chemical Soc. of Japan Award 2003. *Publications:* Organic Superconductors (co-author) 1998; more than 500 scientific articles on organic superconductors, organic metals and other organic functional materials. *Address:* Chemistry Division, Graduate School of Science, Kyoto University, Sakyo-ku, Kitashirakawa, Kyoto 606-8501 (office); 35-1-504 Kakinoki-cho, Nishigamo, Kita-ku, Kyoto 603-8821, Japan (home). *Telephone:* (75) 753-4035 (office); (75) 493 1046 (home). *Fax:* (75) 783 4038 (office); (75) 493 1046 (home). *E-mail:* saito@kuchem.kyoto-u.ac.jp (office). *Website:* bake.kuchem.kyoto-u.ac.jp/ossc (office).

SAITO, Katsutoshi; Japanese insurance industry executive; *President and Representative Director, Dai-ichi Mutual Life Insurance Company;* Sr Man. Dir Dai-ichi Mutual Life Insurance Co. –2004, Pres. and Rep. Dir 2004–; Chair. Life Insurance Asscn of Japan; mem. Bd of Dirs Japan Cancer Soc. *Address:* Dai-ichi Mutual Life, 13-1, Yurakucho 1-chome, Chiyoda-ku, Tokyo 100-8411, Japan (office). *Telephone:* (3) 3216-1211 (office). *E-mail:* info@dai-ichi-life.co.jp (office). *Website:* www.dai-ichi-life.co.jp (office).

SAITO, Nobufusa, DSc; Japanese chemist and academic; b. 28 Sept. 1916, Tokyo; m. Haruko Umeda 1944; one s. two d.; ed Tokyo Imperial Univ.; fmr Asst Prof., Kyushu and Seoul Univs., Prof. Inorganic Chem., Tokyo Univ. 1956–65, Prof. Inorganic and Nuclear Chem., 1965–77, Dir Radioisotope Centre 1970–77; Chief Researcher, Inst. of Physical and Chemical Research 1959–76; fmr Consultant to IAEA, Dir of Isotopes Div. 1963–65; Prof. Inorganic and Analytical Chem. Toho Univ. 1978–87, Dean, Faculty of Science 1979–82; Pres. Japan Chemical Analysis Centre 1990–96; Dir Japan Radioisotopes Asscn 1967–; Tech. Adviser, Japan Atomic Energy Research Inst. 1966–2000; mem. Chemical Soc. of Japan (Vice-Pres. 1976–78, Pres. 1981–82, Hon. mem. 1987–), ACS, Atomic Energy Soc. of Japan, Japan Soc. for Analytical Chem. (Pres. 1979–80, Hon. mem. 1980–), Japan Soc. of Nuclear and Radiochemical Sciences (Hon. mem. 2000–), Balneological Soc. of Japan (Hon. mem. 2006–); Royal Decoration of Second Order of Sacred Treasure 1987; Chem. Soc. of Japan Award 1974; Nat. Purple Ribbon Medal for Chemistry 1979. *Publication:* Analytical Chemistry (jtly) 2001. *Leisure interests:* music, travel. *Address:* 5-12-9, Koshigoe, Kamakura 248-0033, Japan (home). *Telephone:* (467) 31-3178 (home). *Fax:* (467) 31-3639 (home).

SAITO, Tetsuo, BSc, MSc, DEng; Japanese engineer, academic and politician; *Minister of the Environment;* b. 5 Feb. 1952, Ōchi Dist, Shimane Pref.; ed Tokyo Inst. of Tech.; joined Shimizu Corpn 1976; Visiting Fellow, Princeton

Univ., USA 1986–89; mem. House of Reps for Chugoku Dist 1993–; Parl. Sec., Vice-Minister for Science and Tech. 1999–2004; Chair. Cttee on Educ., Culture, Sports, Science and Tech., House of Reps; Chair. Policy Research Council of New Komeito Party 2006–08; Minister of the Environment 2008–. *Leisure interest:* swimming. *Address:* Ministry of the Environment, 1-2-2, Kasumigaseki, Chiyoda-ku, Tokyo 100-8975, Japan (office). *Telephone:* (3) 3581-3351 (office). *Fax:* (3) 3502-0308 (office). *E-mail:* moe@eanet.go.jp (office). *Website:* www.env.go.jp (office).

SAITO, Toshitsugu, BA, MBA; Japanese politician; m.; two c.; ed Sophia Univ. and Univ. of Washington; Pres. Japan Jr Chamber 1984; mem. House of Reps. for Shizuoka Prefecture, 5th Electoral Dist 1986–; Dir Youth Div., Party Org. HQ, Liberal Democratic Party 1991, Dir Communications Div., Policy Research Council 1995, Dir-Gen. Information Research Bureau 1996, Deputy Chair. Diet Affairs Cttee 1996, Acting Chair. Public Relations HQ 1999, Dir-Gen. Int. Bureau 2001; Parl. Vice-Minister, Ministry of Posts and Telecommunications 1992; Chair. Standing Cttee on Commerce and Industry, House of Reps 1997, Standing Cttee on Local Admin 1999; Minister of State and Dir-Gen. of Defense Agency 2000–. *Address:* Liberal Democratic Party (Jiyu-Minshuto), 1-11-23, Nagata-cho, Chiyoda-ku, Tokyo 100-8910, Japan (office). *Telephone:* (3) 3581-6211 (office). *E-mail:* koho@ldp.jimin.or.jp (office). *Website:* www.jimin.jp (office); toshitsugu.com.

SAITOTI, George, PhD; Kenyan mathematician and politician; *Minister of State for Provincial Administration and Internal Security;* ed Univ. of Warwick, UK; fmr Prof. of Math. and Chair. Dept of Math., Univ. of Nairobi; mem. E African Legis. Ass. 1974–77; Dir and Exec. Chair. Kenya Commercial Bank 1977–82; nominated MP 1983; Minister of Finance and Planning 1983–85, of Finance 1986–93, of Planning and Nat. Devt 1993–98; Vice-Pres. of Kenya 1989–97, 1999–2002, also Minister of Home Affairs 2001–02; Minister of Educ., Science and Technology 2003–Feb. 2006, Nov. 2006–Jan. 2008; Minister of State for Prov. Admin. and Internal Security 2008–; Chair. Annual Meetings Bd of Govs, IMF and World Bank Group 1990. *Address:* Office of the Minister of State for Provincial Administration and Internal Security, c/o Office of the President, Harambee House, Harambee Ave, POB 30510, Nairobi, Kenya (office). *Telephone:* (20) 227411 (office). *Website:* www.officeofthepresident.go.ke (office).

SAITOV, Oleg; Russian boxer; b. 26 May 1974, Jigalevsk, Samara Region; won gold medal for welterweights at 1996 Summer Olympics, Atlanta and 2000 Summer Olympics, Sydney, won bronze medal 2004 Summer Olympics, Athens; won gold medal European Amateur Boxing Championships 2004; named Best Boxer of Sydney Olympic Games 2000; Honored Master of Sports of Russia 1995; Fair Play Award, Russian Olympic Cttee 1998. *Address:* c/o Russian Olympic Committee, Luzhnetskaya Nab. 8, 119992 Moscow, Russia (office).

SAJJADPOUR, Seyed Mohammad Kazem, PhD; Iranian diplomatist; ed George Washington Univ., USA; Post-doctoral Fellow, Harvard Univ.; taught at Coll. of Int. Relations, Tehran Univ., Azad Univ., National Defence Univ. of Iran; fmr Dir Inst. for Political and Int. Studies, Ministry of Foreign Affairs; fmr Amb. and Deputy Perm. Rep. to UN and other Int. Orgs, Geneva; mem. Bd of Advisers, Dialogues: Islamic World-US-The West program, New York Univ.; fmr Dir-Gen. Inst. for Political and Int. Studies (IPIS), Tehran, currently Sr Fellow. *Address:* Institute for Political and International Studies, Shaheed Bahonar (Niavaran) Avenue, Shaheed Aghaee St, Tehran, Iran (office).

SAKAGUCHI, Chikara; Japanese politician; b. 1 April 1934; ed Mie Univ.; mem. House of Reps for Tokai dist. 1976–, fmr Dir Finance Cttee; Minister of Labour 1993–94, of Health, Labour and Welfare 2000–04; fmr Chair. Komeito Policy Bd, currently Vice Rep. New Komeito. *Address:* c/o New Komeito, 17, Minami-Motomachi, Shinjuku-ku, Tokyo 160-0012, Japan (office). *Telephone:* (3) 3353-0111 (office). *Website:* www.komei.or.jp (office); www.shugiin.go.jp (office); www.chikara.serio.jp.

SAKAIYA, Taichi, (pseudonym of Kotaro Ikeguchi); Japanese economist, politician, author and fmr civil servant; b. 13 July 1935, Osaka; ed Tokyo Univ.; with Ministry of Int. Trade and Industry 1960–78, directed 1970 World Exposition in Osaka and 1975 Okinawa Int. Ocean Exposition; became full-time writer 1978; Chair.Event and Project Cttee Osaka 21st Century Plan 1982; Pres. Asian Club Foundation 1985; mem. Cttee for Ten Year Support for Regions Stricken by the Hanshin Awaji, Kobe Earthquake 1995; Co-Chai. US–Japan 21st Century Cttee 1996; Minister of State for Econ. Planning responsible for econ. policy and further econ. restructuring in Japan 1998–2000; Special Adviser to the Prime Minister 2000; mem. Advisory Bd for Japan, Lehman Brothers Holdings Inc. 2005–; mem. Bd of Dirs Osaka Securities Exchange Co. Ltd. Chair. Sakaiya Advisory Cttee 2002; fmr Pres. Asia Crime Foundation Asscn. *Publications include:* Yudan 1975, Dankai no sedai (Baby Boom Generation), Chika Kakumei (The Knowledge-Value Revolution), Nihon to wa Nanika (What is Japan?), Soshiki no seisui (The Rise and Fall of Organizations). *Address:* c/o Lehman Brothers Japan Inc., Roppongi Hills, Mori Tower, 6-10-1, Roppongi, Minato-ku, Tokyo 106-6131, Japan (office). *Telephone:* (3) 6440-3000 (office). *Website:* www.lehman.co.jp (office).

SAKAKI, Hiroyuki, BS, MS, PhD; Japanese scientist and academic; *Professor, Institute of Industrial Science, University of Tokyo;* b. 6 Oct. 1944, Aichi; s. of Yone-ichiro Sakaki and Fumiko Sakaki; m. Mutsuko Sakaki 1973; one s. four d.; ed Univ. of Tokyo; Assoc. Prof., Inst. of Industrial Science, Univ. of Tokyo 1973–87, Prof. 1987–, Prof., Research Center for Advanced Science and Tech. 1988–98; Visiting Scientist, IBM T. J. Watson Research Center (group of Dr Leo Esaki) 1976–77;; Dir for Quantum Wave Project (Japan's governmental project for Exploratory Research for Advanced Tech. (ERATO)) 1988–93; Dir for Japan–US Jt Research Project on Quantum Transition 1994–98; IBM Science Prize 1989, Hattori-Hokokai Prize 1990, Japan Applied Physics Soc. Prize 1983, 1990, Shimazu Science Prize, Outstanding Achievement Award, IECEJ 1991, David Sarnoff Award, IEEE 1996, Fujiwara Prize 2000, Medal with Purple Ribbon (Japan) 2001, Esaki Award 2004, Japan Acad. Prize (jtly) 2005. *Leisure interests:* listening to classical music, looking at paintings. *Address:* Sakaki Laboratory, Ee-403, Institute of Industrial Science, University of Tokyo, 4-6-1 Komaba, Meguro-ku, Tokyo 153-8505 (office); 1–41–5 Kagahara, Tsuzukiku, Yokohama 224, Japan (home). *Telephone:* (3) 5452-6235 (office); (45) 943-1539 (home). *E-mail:* sakaki@iis.u-tokyo.ac.jp (office). *Website:* quanta.iis.u-tokyo.ac.jp (office).

SAKAMOTO, Ryûichi, MA; Japanese composer, musician and actor; b. 17 Jan. 1952, Tokyo; m. Akiko Yano 1979; ed Shinjuku High School, Composition Dept, Tokyo Fine Arts Univ.; began composing at age of ten; mem. group Yellow Magic Orchestra 1978–83; worked with David Sylvian 1982–83; solo recording artist, composer 1982–; conductor, arranger, music for Olympic Games opening ceremony, Barcelona, Spain 1992. *Film appearances:* Merry Christmas Mr Lawrence 1982, The Last Emperor 1987, New Rose Hotel 1998. *Film soundtracks:* Daijôbu, mai furendo 1983, Merry Christmas Mr Lawrence 1982, Koneko monogatari 1986, The Last Emperor (with David Byrne and Cong Su, Acad. Award) 1987, Ôritsu uchûgun Oneamisu no tsubasa 1987, The Laser Man (title song) 1988, The Handmaid's Tale 1990, The Sheltering Sky 1990, Tacones lejanos 1991, Topâzu 1992, Wuthering Heights 1992, Wild Palms (TV series) 1993, Little Buddha 1993, Rabbit Ears: Peachboy 1993, Wild Side 1995, Snake Eyes 1998, Love is the Devil 1998, Gohatto 1999, Poppoya (theme) 1999, Alexei to izumi 2002, Derrida 2002, Femme Fatale 2002, Los Rubios 2003, Life Is Journey 2003, Appurushîdo 2004, Original Child Bomb 2004, Tony Takitani 2004, Hoshi ni natta shonen 2005, Zarin 2005, Silk 2007. *Recordings include:* albums: Thousand Knives 1978, B-2 Unit 1980, Hidariudeno (A Dream Of The Left Arm) 1981, Coda 1983, Ongaku Zukan (A Picture Book Of Music) 1984, Illustrated Musical Encyclopedia 1984, Esperanto 1985, Miraiha Yarô (A Futurist Chap) 1986, Media Bahn Live 1986, Oneamisno Tsubasa (The Wings Of Oneamis) 1986, Neo Geo 1987, Playing The Orchestra 1988, Tokyo Joe 1988, Sakamoto Plays Sakamoto 1989, Grupo Musicale 1989, Beauty 1989, Heartbeat 1991, Neo Geo (with Iggy Pop) 1992, Sweet Revenge 1994, Soundbites 1994, Hard To Get 1995, 1996 1996, Music For Yohji Yamamoto 1997, Smoochy 1997, Discord 1998, Love Is The Devil 1998, Raw Life 1999, Intimate 1999, Space 1999, BTTB 1999, Gohatto 1999, Complete Index of Gut 1999, Cinemage 2000, Casa 2002; singles: Bamboo Houses (with David Sylvian) 1982, Forbidden Colours (with David Sylvian) 1983, Field Work (with Thomas Dolby) 1986, Risky 1988, We Love You 1991, Moving On 1994, Prayer/Salvation 1998, Anger 1998. *Address:* David Rubinson Management, PO Box 411197, San Francisco, CA 94141, USA (office).

SAKANE, Masahiro; Japanese business executive; *Chairman, Komatsu Ltd;* b. 7 Jan. 1941, Shimane Pref.; ed Osaka City Univ.; joined Komatsu Ltd 1963, COO Komatsu Dresser Co. 1990–94, Man. Dir 1994–97, Exec. Man. Dir 1997–99, Exec. Vice-Pres. 1999–2001, Pres. 2001–07, CEO 2003–07, Chair. 2007–; Vice-Chair. Japan Construction Equipment Mfrs Asscn 2001–04, Chair. 2004–; mem. Bd of Exec. Dirs Japan Business Fed., Chair. Sub-Saharan Africa Cttee 2003–, Deputy Chair. Japan-Russia (NIS) Business Cooperation Cttee 2003–; Japan Inst. of Invention and Innovation Nat. Commendation for Invention 2003. *Address:* Komatsu Ltd, 2-3-6 Akasaka, Minato-ku, Tokyo 107-8414, Japan (office). *Telephone:* (3) 5561-2687 (office); (3) 5561-2616 (office). *Fax:* (3) 3505-9662 (office). *E-mail:* info@komatsu.com (office). *Website:* www.komatsu.com (office).

SAKINE, Ahmat Awat; Chadian politician; Dir-Gen of the Treasury –2004; Minister of the Economy and Finance 2004–05. *Address:* c/o Ministry of the Economy and Finance, BP 816, N'Djamena, Chad (office).

SAKMANN, Bert, BA, MD; German physician; *Director, Department of Cell Physiology, Max-Planck-Institut für medizinische Forschung;* b. 12 June 1942, Stuttgart; s. of Berthold Sakmann and Annemarie Schaeffer Sakmann; m. Dr Christiane Wulfert 1970; two s. one d.; ed Univ. of Tübingen, Univ. of Munich, Univ. Hosp., Munich, Univ. of Göttingen; Research Asst, Max-Planck-Institut für Psychiatrie, Munich 1969–70; British Council Fellow, Dept of Biophysics, Univ. Coll., London 1971–73; Research Asst, Max-Planck-Institut für biophysikalische Chemie, Univ. of Göttingen 1974–79, Research Assoc., Membrane Biology Group 1979–82, Head, Membrane Physiology Unit 1983–85, Dir 1985–87, Prof. Dept of Cell Physiology 1987–89; Dir Dept of Cell Physiology Max-Planck-Institut für medizinische Forschung, Heidelberg 1989–; Prof. of Physiology, Univ. of Heidelberg 1990–; Foreign mem. NAS 1993, Royal Soc., UK 1994; Hon. DSc (London) 1999; shared Nobel Prize for Medicine or Physiology 1991 for discoveries about single-ion channels in cells; numerous other awards, prizes and guest lectures. *Publications:* The Visual System: Neurophysiology, Biophysics and Their Clinical Applications 1972 (contrib.), Advances in Pharmacology and Therapeutics 1978 (contrib.), Single Channel Recording 1983 (jtly), Membrane Control of Cellular Activity 1986 (contrib.), Calcium and Ion Channel Modulation 1988 (contrib.), Neuromuscular Junction 1989 (contrib.); numerous articles including Nobel Lecture in 'Les Prix Nobel' 1991. *Leisure interests:* music, reading, tennis, skiing. *Address:* Max-Planck-Institut für medizinische Forschung, R.242, Jahnstrasse 29, PO Box 10 38 20, 69120 Heidelberg, Germany (office). *Telephone:* (6221) 486460 (office). *Fax:* (6221) 486459 (office). *E-mail:* sakmann@mpimf-heidelberg.mpg.de (office). *Website:* wzp.mpimf-heidelberg.mpg.de (office).

SAKO, Soumana, PhD, MPA; Malian politician, civil servant and international civil servant; *Executive Secretary, African Capacity Building Foundation;* b. 23 Dec. 1950, Nyamina; s. of Sayan Sako and Djeneba Traore; m. Cisse Toure; two s. two d.; ed Univ. of Pittsburgh, Pa, USA, Ecole Nationale d'Admin du Mali; Staff mem. Gen. Inspectorate, Office of the Pres. of Repub. of Mali 1974; Admin. and Finance Man., Operation Puits Project 1975–76; Staff mem. Ministry of Industrial Devt and Tourism 1981; Adviser Ministry of Foreign Affairs and Int. Co-operation 1981–82; Sr Adviser Ministry of Planning and Econ. Man. 1982–84; Dir of Sr Staff, Ministry of State-Owned Enterprises 1985–87; Minister of Finance and Commerce Feb.–Aug. 1987; Deputy Controller-Gen. Office of the Pres. 1988–89; UNDP official serving in Cen. African Repub. 1989–91, Sr Economist for Madagascar and Comoros Islands 1993–97; Prime Minister of Mali 1991–92; Prof. of Devt Econs and Public Finance, Univ. of Mali 1997–2000; int. consultant 1998–; Exec. Sec. African Capacity Bldg Foundation, Harare Jan. 2000–08; Commdr, Nat. Order of Mali 2000, Grand-Officer 2005; AFGRAD Distinguished Alumnus 1992, Sennen Andriamirado Prize of Excellence 2000. *Publication:* Determinants of Public Policy—A Comparative Analysis of Public Expenditure Patterns in African States Trade Related Capacity Building. *Leisure interests:* soccer, chess, gardening. *Address:* PO Box 1502, Harare (office); The African Capacity Building Foundation, Intermarket Life Towers, 7th Floor, Corner Jason Moyo/Sam Nujoma Street, Harare, Zimbabwe; BP 433, Bamako, Mali; Villa f4 bis 48, Sema Gexco Bamako, Mali (home). *Telephone:* (4) 702931 (Harare) (office); (4) 744512 (Harare); 236196 (Bamako) (home). *Fax:* (4) 702915 (Harare) (office); 229748 (Bamako). *E-mail:* s.sako@acbf-pact.org (office); dbtymz@gmail.com. *Website:* www.acbf-pact.org (office).

SAKS, Gene; American actor and director; b. 8 Nov. 1921, New York; m. Beatrice Arthur (divorced); two s. one d.; ed Cornell Univ.; began acting career off-Broadway at Provincetown Playhouse and the Cherry Lane Theatre; appeared in Dog Beneath the Skin (Auden), Him (e.e. cummings), The Bourgeois Gentilhomme (Molière); Broadway appearances in Mr Roberts, South Pacific, Middle of the Night, The Tenth Man, A Shot in the Dark, Love and Libel, A Thousand Clowns; debut as dir on Broadway with Enter Laughing 1963. *Plays directed:* Nobody Loves an Albatross, Half a Sixpence, Generation, Mame, Same Time, Next Year, California Suite, I Love My Wife (Tony Award), Brighton Beach (Tony Award), Biloxi Blues 1985 (Tony Award), Broadway Bound 1986, A Month of Sundays 1987, Rumours 1988, Jake's Woman 1992, Lost in Yonkers (original Broadway stage production), Barrymore 1997. *Films directed:* Barefoot in the Park 1967, The Odd Couple 1968, Cactus Flower 1969, Last of the Red Hot Lovers 1972, Brighton Beach Memoirs 1986, Cin cin 1991, Bye Bye Birdie (TV) 1995. *Film appearances:* A Thousand Clowns 1965, Prisoner of Second Avenue 1965, The One and Only 1978, Lovesick 1983, The Goodbye People 1984, The Good Policeman 1991, Nobody's Fool 1994, IQ 1994, Deconstructing Harry 1997. *Address:* c/o ICM, 40 West 80th Street, 1, New York, NY 10024, USA.

SAKSKOBURGGOTSKI, Simeon; Bulgarian politician and fmr King of Bulgaria; *Leader, National Movement for Stability and Progress;* b. 16 June 1937, Sofia; s. of the late King Boris III and of Queen Joanna; m. Margarita Gómez y Acebo 1962; four s. one d.; ed in England, Victoria Coll., Alexandria, Egypt, Lycée Français, Spain and Valley Forge Mil. Acad., USA; proclaimed King of Bulgaria 1943; deposed 1946; sought refuge in Egypt in 1947; has since lived mainly in Spain; Constitutional Court ruled in 1998 that confiscation of royal property by communist regime had been illegal; returned to Bulgaria 1996; Founder and Leader, Nat. Movt for King Simeon II (renamed Nat. Movt for Stability and Progress 2007) 2001–; Prime Minister of Bulgaria 2001–05. *Address:* National Movement for Stability and Progress (Natsionalno dvizhenie za stabilnost i vazhod), 1000 Sofia, ul. Vrabcha 23, Bulgaria (office). *Telephone:* (2) 980-38-09 (office). *Fax:* (2) 980-38-07 (office). *E-mail:* ndsv@ndsv.bg (office). *Website:* www.ndsv.bg (office).

SAKURAI, Masamitsu, CBE, BSc; Japanese business executive; *Chairman and Representative Director, Ricoh Company Ltd;* b. 8 Jan. 1942, Tokyo; m. Yokohama Sakurai; ed Faculty of Science and Tech., Waseda Univ.; joined Ricoh Co. Ltd 1966, Gen. Man. of Eng Admin Office 1980–84, Pres. Ricoh UK Products Ltd 1984–92, apptd Dir 1992, Gen. Man. of Purchasing Div. 1992–93, Pres. Ricoh Europe BV 1993–94, Man.-Dir Ricoh Co. Ltd 1994–95, Gen. Man. Research and Devt Group 1995–96, Pres., COO and CEO 1996–2007, Chair. and Rep. Dir 2007–. *Leisure interests:* travel, golf, reading. *Address:* Ricoh Co. Ltd, 8-13-1 Ginza, Chuo-ku, Tokyo 104-8222, Japan (office). *Telephone:* (3) 6278-2111 (office). *Fax:* (3) 3543-9329 (office). *E-mail:* info@ricoh.com (office). *Website:* www.ricoh.com (office).

SAKURAI, Takahide; Japanese insurance executive; *Advisor, Dai-ichi Mutual Life Insurance Company;* Chair. The Dai-ichi Mutual Life Insurance Co. –2004, Advisor 2004–; Vice-Chair. Bd of Councillors, Japan Business Fed. (JBF) 2002, Japan Fed. of Econ. Orgs (Keidanren) 2004; Corp. Auditor, JFE Holdings Inc. 1999, The Tokyo Group 2001, Asahi Breweries Ltd 2004; Acting Chair. Keizai Koho Center; mem. Bd of Dirs Imperial Hotel Ltd 1999–, IY Bank Co. Ltd 2001; Vice-Chair. Keizai Koho Centre, Japan Inst. for Social and Econ. Affairs 2000; mem. Advisory Cttee, Ritsumeikan Asia Pacific Univ., Steering Cttee, The 21st Century Public Policy Inst. 2004. *Address:* Dai-ichi Mutual Life Insurance Company, 13-1 Yurakucho 1-chome, Chiyoda-ku, Tokyo 100-8411, Japan (office). *Telephone:* (3) 3216-1211 (office). *Fax:* (3) 5221-4360 (office). *Website:* www.dai-ichi-life.co.jp (office).

SALA, Marius, PhD; Romanian linguist and academic; *Director, Institutul de Lingvistică 'Iorgu Iordan – Al Rosetti', Bucharest;* b. 8 Sept. 1932, Vaşcău, Bihor Co.; s. of Sabin Sala and Eleonora Tocoianu; m. Marina Sala 2003; one d.; ed Coll. of Philology, Bucharest Univ.; researcher, Inst. of Linguistics 'Iorgu Iordan – Al Rosetti', Bucharest 1955–90, Deputy Dir 1990–94, Dir 1994–; Prof. Faculty of Foreign Languages, Bucharest; Visiting Prof., Heidelberg 1971, Málaga 1968, 1970, 1973, 1979, Madrid 1978, 1981, 1987, Mexico City 1981, Cologne 1984, Frankfurt 1992, Oviedo 1994, Nancy 1999; Corresp. mem. Royal Acad. Spain 1978, Mexican Inst. of Culture 1981, Romanian Acad. 1993, Full mem. 2001, Acad. Nacional de Letras, Montevideo 1994–, Academia Peruana de la Lengua, Lima 2004–, Int. Cttee of Onomastic Studies 1969; mem. Int. Cttee of the Mediterranean Linguistic Atlas 1960; mem. Man. Junta of the Int. Asscn of Hispanists 1974–80; mem. Cttee Soc. of Romance Linguistics 1974–80, 1989–1995, hon. mem. 2003; mem. Perm. Int. Cttee of Linguists 1987–92; Prize of Romanian Acad. 1970, Prize of Mexican Acad. Centennial 1976. *Publications:* Contribuţii la fonetica istorică a limbii române (Contributions to the Historical Phonetics of the Romanian Language) 1970, Estudios sobre el judeo-español de Bucarest 1970, Phonétique et Phonologie du Judéo-Espagnol de Bucarest 1971, Le judéo-espagnol 1976, Contributions à la phonétique historique du roumain 1976, El léxico indígena del español americano, Apreciaciones sobre su vitalidad (co-author) 1977, El español de América, (Vol. 1), Léxico (co-author) 1982, Limbile lumii. Mică enciclopedie (The Languages of the World: A Concise Encyclopaedia) (co-author), 1981, Les langues du monde (Petite Encyclopédie) (co-author) 1984, Etimologia şi Limba Română (Etymology and the Romanian Language) (co-author) 1987, Vocabularul Reprezentativ Al Limbilor Romanice (The Representative Vocabulary of the Romance Languages) (co-author) 1988, El problema de las lenguas en contacto 1988, Enciclopedia Limbilor Romanice (Encyclopaedia of the Romance languages) (co-author) 1989, Unité des langues romanes 1996, Limba română, limbă romanică (Romanian Language, Romance Language) 1997, Limbi în contact (Languages in Contact) 1997, De la latină la română (From Latin to Romanian) 1998, Lenguas en contacto 1998, Introducere în etimologia limbii române (Introduction to the Etymology of Romanian) 1999, May We Introduce the Romanian Language to You? (co-author) 1999, Du latin au roumain 2000, Limbile Europei (The Language of Europe) (jtly) 2001, Ratengo kara rumaniago he – rumania goshi 2001, Made in Spain 1 – Logos, Made in Spain 2 – Packaging 2002, Made in Spain 3 – Editorial 2002, Made in Spain 4 2003, Made in Spain 5 2003, From Latin to Romanian: The Historical Development of Romanian in a Comparative Romance Context 2005. *Leisure interests:* philately, cooking. *Address:* Institutul de Lingvistică, Calea 13 Septembrie 13, 79515 Bucharest, B.O. 42-37 (office); Aleea Bistra 1, E1, 39, Bucharest, Romania (home). *Telephone:* 3182452 (office); 3182416 (office); 7457564 (home). *Fax:* 3182417 (office). *E-mail:* inst@lingv.ro (office).

SALA-I-MARTÍN, Xavier, MA, PhD; Spanish (Catalan) economist and academic; *Professor of Economics, Columbia University;* b. 17 June 1963, Barcelona; ed Univ. Autònoma, Barcelona, Harvard Univ., USA; Assoc. Prof., Yale Univ., USA 1990–95; Visiting Prof., Univ. Pompeu Fabra, Barcelona 1994–2006; Prof. of Econs, Columbia Univ., USA 1996–; Visiting Prof., Harvard Univ. 2003–04; Research Assoc., Nat. Bureau of Econ. Research, Cambridge, Mass 1991–; Sr Econ. Advisor, World Econ. Forum 2002–; consultant, IMF 1993–2001, World Bank 1996–2001; Assoc. Ed. Journal of Economic Growth 1995–; Pres. Barcelona Football Club 2006, CEOs Without Borders 2006–; NSF Award 1998, King Juan Carlos I Prize for Social Sciences 1998, Kenneth Arrow Prize 1999, King Juan Carlos I Prize for Econs 2004. *Publications include:* Apuntes de Crecimiento Económico 1994, Economic Growth 1995, Economia Liberal para No Economistas y No Liberales, Converses amb Xavier Sala-i-Martin 2007; numerous articles in learned journals. *Address:* Columbia University, Department of Economics, International Affairs Building, MC 3308, 420 West 118th Street #1005, New York, NY 10027, USA (office). *Telephone:* (212) 854-7055 (office). *Fax:* (212) 854-8059 (office). *E-mail:* xs23@columbia.edu (office). *Website:* www.columbia.edu/~xs23 (office).

SALADINO ARANDA, Irving Jahir; Panamanian athlete; b. 23 Jan. 1983, Colón; World and Olympic men's long jump Champion; Silver Medal, World Indoor Championships, Moscow 2006 (set South American indoor record of 8.29m); won five (Oslo, Rome, Zurich, Brussel, Berlin) out of six Golden League events in same season 2006; jumped 8.56m May 2006 (South American record); jumped 8.53m (–0.2m/s wind) to win Grande Prêmio Rio Caixa de Atletismo, Rio de Janeiro 13 May 2007; Gold Medal, World Championships, Osaka 2007 (jump of 8.57m); set new personal record of 8.73m (+1.2m/s wind) during FBK-Games, Hengelo May 2008; Gold Medal, Olympic Games, Beijing 2008 (jump of 8.34m; Panama's first Olympic gold medallist). *Address:* c/o Federacion Panamena de Atletismo, Avenida Jose Agustin Arango, Estadio Rommel Fernandez, Planta Baja, Panama City, Panama. *Telephone:* 2335649. *Fax:* 2776852. *E-mail:* sassoagu@cwp.net.pa.

SALAKHITDINOV, Makhmud, DSc; Uzbekistan mathematician; b. 23 Nov. 1933, Namangan, Uzbek SSR; s. of Salahiddin Shamsuddinov and Zuhra Shamsuddinova; m. Muharram Rasulova 1955; three s. one d.; ed Cen. Asian State Univ.; Asst Tashkent State Univ. 1958–59; Scientific Fellow, Chief of Section, Deputy Dir then Dir Inst. of Math. Uzbek SSR Acad. of Sciences 1959–85, Chief, Differential Equation Section 1974–, Vice-Pres. Uzbek SSR Acad. of Sciences 1984–85, Pres. 1988–94, Chair. Dept of Physical and Math. Sciences 1994–; Chief of Chair. (Jt), Tashkent State Univ. 1980–85; Minister of Higher and Secondary Specialized Educ. of Uzbek SSR 1985–88; Uzbekistan People's Deputy 1990–; Ed. papers of Uzbekistan Acad. of Sciences; Fellow, Islamic World Acad. of Sciences (IAS) 1993–; Al-Bairuni Prize1974; Honoured Scientist of Uzbek SSR; Badge of Honour 1974, Uzbek State Prize. *Publications:* more than 150 scientific papers; Mixed-Complex Type Equation 1974, Ordinary Differential Equation 1982; contribs to professional publs. *Leisure interests:* walking, reading fiction. *Address:* Uzbekistan Academy of Sciences, st. Acad. Gulyamova Yaya, 70, 700047 Tashkent, Uzbekistan (office). *Telephone:* (71) 133-14-45 (office). *Fax:* (71) 133-49-01 (office). *E-mail:* academy@uzsci.net (office). *Website:* www.academy.uz (office).

SALAKHOV, Tair Teimur ogly; Azerbaijani/Russian painter; *Vice-President, Russian Academy of Fine Arts;* b. 29 Nov. 1928, Baku, Azerbaijan; m. Varvara Salakhova; three d.; ed Azerbaijan Azim-zade Higher School of

Fine Arts, Moscow State Inst. of Fine Arts; Docent, Prof. Azerbaijan State Inst. of Arts 1963–74, also teacher Baku Aliyev Art School; Chair. Exec. Bd Azerbaijan Union of Artists 1972–74; Head of Studio Moscow State Inst. of Fine Arts 1974–92; First Sec. Exec. Bd USSR Union of Artists 1973–91; mem. Exec. Bd USSR Acad. of Fine Arts, Sec. 1986–; author of numerous portraits, landscapes, theatre decorations; Sec. Academician for painting section Russian Acad. of Arts 1979–, Vice-Pres. Russian Acad. of Arts 1996–; mem. Acad. of Arts of Kyrghyz Repub., Azerbaijan Acad. of Arts; Corresp. mem. French Acad. of Fine Arts 1986–, San Fernando Royal Academy of Fine Arts (Spain), Real Academia San Fernando, Madrid –1998; Hon. Pres. Int. Asscn of Art, Paris; Hon. mem. Austrian Soc. of Fine Arts 1975, Acad. of Fine Arts, Kazakhstan, Acad. of Fine Arts, Kyrgyzstan; Hon. citizen Trenton, NJ, Santa Fe, NM and Billings, Mont.; Order of Istiglal of Azerbaijan 1998, Order of Za Zaslugi pered Otechestvom (3rd class) (Russia) 1998; Prize of Cen. Komsomol Cttee 1959, Akhundov Prize of Azerbaijan SSR 1964, USSR State Prize 1968, State Prize of Azerbaijan 1970 (for picture New Sea), Grekov's Gold Medal 1977, Hero of Socialist Labour 1989, People's Painter of Russia 1996–. *Address:* 3 Mamedyarov lane, h.1 'Icheri Sheher', Baku, Azerbaijan (home); Russian Academy of Arts, Prechistenka str. 21, 119034 Moscow (office); Kutizovskiy pr. 18, ap.29, 121151 Moscow, Russia. *Telephone:* (495) 201-39-71. *Fax:* (495) 201-39-71. *Website:* www.rah.ru.

SALAKHOVA, Aidan; Russian artist; b. 1964, Moscow; ed Surikov Art Inst.; Jt Owner, First Gallery, Moscow; f. Aidan Gallery, Moscow 1992. *Address:* Aidan Gallery, 1st Tverskaya-Yamskaya Str. 22, 3rd Floor, Moscow 125047, Russian Federation (office). *Telephone:* (495) 251-3734 (office). *Fax:* (495) 250-9166 (office). *E-mail:* info@aidan-gallery.ru (office). *Website:* www.aidan-gallery.ru (office).

SALAMA, Hussein Samir Abdul-Rahman, PhD, DSc; Egyptian entomologist and academic; *Research Professor Emeritus, National Research Centre;* b. 26 Jan. 1936, Gharbia; m.; two c.; ed Ain Shams Univ., Cairo Univ.; Research Asst, Entomology Research Unit, Nat. Research Centre (NRC) 1956–62, Researcher 1962–67, Assoc. Research Prof. 1967–73, Research Prof. of Entomology, NRC 1973, Vice-Pres. NRC, Pres. 1988–92, Research Prof. Emer. 1996–; Pres. Research Council for Basic Sciences, Egyptian Acad. of Scientific Research and Tech., Nat. Cttee for Biological Sciences, Egyptian Inst. for Scientific Culture 1991; fmr Pres. Int. Union of Biological Sciences, now mem. Exec. Cttee; Vice-Pres. Entomological Soc. of Egypt; mem. Bd Egyptian Acad. of Sciences, African Acad. of Sciences; Post-Doctoral Fellow, Dept of Entomology, Univ. of Alberta 1963–65, Fellow, Islamic Acad. of Sciences 1987, African Acad. of Sciences 1990, TWAS 1994; State Prize for Biological Sciences 1973, Golden Medal of Nat. Research Centre 1981, Golden Medal of the Entomological Soc. of Egypt 1982, African Acad. of Sciences Prize for Agric. 1991 and numerous other awards. *Publications:* 230 scientific publs and review articles. *Address:* National Research Centre, Plant Protection Department, Tahrir Street, Dokki, 12311 Cairo (office); 76 Mohyee Abonlezz str., Dokki, Cairo, Egypt (home). *Telephone:* (2) 3669908 (office); (2) 3377399 (home). *Fax:* (2) 3370931 (office); (2) 7488167 (office). *E-mail:* info@nrc.sci.eg (office); hsarsalama@hotmail.com. *Website:* www.nrc.sci.eg (office).

SALAMÉ, Ghassan, MPhil, PhD; Lebanese politician, academic and fmr UN official; *Professor of International Relations, Institut d'Etudes Politiques, Paris;* b. 18 May 1951, Kfarzebian (Mount Lebanon); two d.; ed Paris III Univ., Paris I Univ., St-Joseph Univ.; taught Political Science at Saint-Joseph Univ., Beirut, American Univ. of Beirut and Paris I Univ.; Rockefeller Fellow in Int. Relations, Brookings Inst., Washington, DC 1981, Visiting Fellow 1985–86; mem. Social Science Research Council, New York 1985–90, Co-Dir 'State, Nation and Integration in the Arab World' study program 1986–91; Minister of Culture 2000–03; Prof. of Int. Relations, Institut d'Etudes Politiques, Paris, France 1988–; Co-founder and Chair. Euro-Mediterranean Studies, European Univ. Inst., Florence, Italy; Sr Adviser to UN Sec.-Gen. 2003–06; mem. Bd L'Institut du Monde Arabe, Paris 1998–2000, Arab Thought Forum 1995–98, Haut Conseil de la Francophonie 2003–06, Int. Crisis Group 2004–, Arab Anti-Corruption Org. 2005–, The Bibliotheca Alexandrina 2005–, Int. Peace Acad. 2007–; Chevalier, Légion d'honneur 2003. *Publications:* author or ed. 12 books, including Al-mujtama' wa al-dawla fi al-mashriq al-arabi (State and Society in the Arab Levant) 1987, The Foundations of the Arab State 1987, The Politics of Arab Integration 1988, Democracy without Democrats: Politics of Liberalization in the Arab and Muslim World (ed.) 1994, Appels d'empire: ingérences et résistances à l'âge de la mondialisation (Phoenix Award; APELF Award) 1996, Quand L'Amerique refait le monde 2005, and others; articles published in several periodicals, including La Revue Française de Science Politique, Foreign Policy, The Middle East Journal, Security Dialogue. *Address:* Fondation Nationale des Sciences Politiques-Institut d'Etudes Politiques de Paris, 27 rue Saint-Guillaume, 75337 Paris Cedex 07, France (office). *Telephone:* 1-45-49-72-40 (office). *Fax:* 1-42-22-40-26 (office). *E-mail:* ghassan.salame@sciences-po.fr (office). *Website:* www.sciences-po.fr (office).

SALAMEH, Riad T., BA(Econ); Lebanese banker; *Governor, Banque du Liban;* b. 17 July 1950, Beirut; s. of Toufic Salamé and Renée Salamé; ed Coll. Notre Dame de Jamhour, American Univ. of Beirut; with Merrill Lynch, Beirut 1973–76, 1978–85, Paris 1976–78, Sr Vice-Pres. and Financial Counsellor, Paris 1985–93; Gov. Banque du Liban 1993–; Chevalier Légion d'honneur; Best Arab Banker Award, Euromoney 1996, World's Best Cen. Bank Gov., Euromoney 2006. *Address:* Banque du Liban, Hamra, rue Masraf Loubnan, PO Box 11-5544, Beirut, Lebanon (office). *Telephone:* (1) 750000 (office). *Fax:* (1) 747600 (office). *E-mail:* bdlg0@bdl.gov.lb (office). *Website:* www.bdl.gov.lb (office).

SALAMI, Alawi Salih as-, BA; Yemeni politician; b. 21 Dec. 1945, Radaa; ed Univ. of Baghdad, Iraq; Gen. Man. Financial and Admin. Affairs, Ministry of Educ. 1970–73; Gen. Man. Budget Gen. Office 1973–75; Deputy, Budget Div. 1975–86, with rank of Vice-Minister 1986; Minister of Finance 1986–94; Gov. Yemen Cen. Bank 1994–97; Deputy Prime Minister and Minister of Finance –2006. *Address:* c/o Ministry of Finance, San'a, Yemen (office).

ŠALAMUN, Tomaž, MA; Slovenian poet, writer and academic; *Visiting Professor, University of Richmond;* b. 4 July 1941, Zagreb, Yugoslavia; m. 1st Marusa Krese 1969 (divorced 1975); m. 2nd Metka Krašovec (1979); one s. one d.; ed Univ. of Ljubljana, Univ. of Iowa; Asst Curator Modern Gallery, Ljubljana 1968–70; Asst Prof., Acad. of Fine Arts, Ljubljana 1970–73; workshops Univ. of Tennessee at Chattanooga 1987–88, 1996; Visiting Writer, Vermont Coll. 1988, Berlin 2003–04, Bogliasco Foundation 2004; Consul, Slovenian Cultural Attaché, New York 1996–97; currently Distinguished Writer-in-Residence and Visiting Prof. Univ. of Richmond, USA; mem. PEN, Slovenian Writers' Asscn, Slovenian Acad. of Science and Art; Mladost Prize 1969, residencies at Yaddo 1973–74, 1979, 1986, 1989, MacDowell Colony 1986, Karoly Foundation, Vence, France 1987, Maisons des écrivains étrangers, Saint-Nazaire, France 1996, Civitella Ranieri, Umbertide, Italy 1997, Bogliasco Foundation 2002, Fulbright Fellowship 1987, Jenko Prize 1988, Pushcart Prize 1994, Civitella Raneiri Fellowship 1997, Prešeren Prize 1999, Alta Marea Prize 2002, Festival Prize, Constanta 2004, Europäische Preis für Poesie, Münster (Germany) 2007, Jenko Prize 2007. *Publications:* Turbines: Twenty-One Poems 1973, Snow 1973, Pesmi (Poems) 1980, Maske (Masks) 1980, Balada za Metka Krašovec (trans. as A Ballad for Metka Krašovec) 1981, Analogije svetlobe 1982, Glas 1983, Sonet o mleku 1984, Soy realidad 1985, Ljubljanska pomlad 1986, Mera casa 1987, Ziva rana, zivi sok 1988, The Selected Poems of Tomaz Salamun 1988, Otrok in jelen 1990, Painted Desert: Poems 1991, The Shepherd, The Hunter 1992, Ambra 1994, The Four Questions of Melancholy: New and Selected Poems 1997, Crni labod 1997, Knjiga za mojega brata 1997, Homage to Hat and Uncle Guido and Eliot 1998, Morje 1999, Gozd in kelihi 2000, Feast 2000, Ballad for Metka Krašovec 2001, Table 2002, Poker 2003, Od tam 2003, Blackboards 2004, Z Arhilohom po Kikladih 2004, The Book For My Brother 2006; contrib. to anthologies and periodicals. *Address:* Dalmatinova 11, 1000 Ljubljana, Slovenia (home). *Telephone:* (1) 2314522 (home). *Fax:* (1) 4304843 (home). *E-mail:* metka.krasovec@siol.net (home).

SALAS COLLANTES, Javier; Spanish association executive; *President, European Federation of Cleaning Industries (FENI/EFCI);* b. 1949; ed Faculty of Econs Univ. of Madrid; joined Instituto Nacional de Industria 1973, apptd Chair. 1990; Chair. Iberia 1993–95; mem. Bd of Dirs Telvent; fmr Pres. Fundación Entorno; Pres. Asociación Profesional de Empresas de Limpieza (ASPEL) 2005–, European Fed. of Industrial Cleaning (FENI/EFCI) 2007–. *Leisure interest:* hill-trekking. *Address:* ASPEL, General Alvarez de Castro, 41, 1° Madrid 28010 (office); European Federation of Cleaning Companies, Rue de l'Association 27, 1000 Brussels, Belgium (office). *Telephone:* (2) 225-83-30 (Brussels) (office). *Fax:* (2) 225-83-39 (Brussels) (office). *E-mail:* office@feni.be (office). *Website:* www.feni.be (office); asociados.aspel.es (office).

SALAS FALGUERAS, Margarita, PhD; Spanish biologist and academic; *Professor in Research, Severo Ochoa Centre for Molecular Biology, Universidad Autónoma de Madrid;* b. 30 Nov. 1938, Canero, Oviedo (Asturias); m. Dr Eladio Viñuela (died 1999); ed Univ. Complutense of Madrid; Post-doctorate work, Dept of Biochemistry, New York Univ. 1964–67; Prof. of Molecular Genetics, Univ. Complutense of Madrid 1968–92; Prof. in Research, Severo Ochoa Centre for Molecular Biology, Consejo Superior de Investigaciones Científicas-Universidad Autónoma de Madrid (CSIC-UAM), Madrid 1974–; Pres. Spanish Inst. 1995–2003; mem. Bd Cervantes Inst. 1996–; mem. European Molecular Biology Org. (EMBO) 1983, American Soc. for Virology 1983, Royal Acad. of Exact Sciences, Physics and Natural Sciences 1988, Academia Europaea 1988, Inter-American Medical and Health Asscn 1993, American Acad. of Microbiology 1996, European Acad. of Science and Arts 1997, American Soc. for Biochemistry and Molecular Biology 1997, Spanish Royal Acad. 2001, NAS 2007–; Hon. Pres. Royal Acad. of Medicine of Asturias and Leon 1996–; Hon. mem. Spanish Soc. of Biochemistry and Molecular Biology 1998–; Great Cross of the Civil Order of Alfonso X el Sabio 2003; Dr hc (Oviedo) 1996, (Tech. Univ. of Madrid) 2000, (Extremadura) 2002, (Murcia) 2003, (Cádiz) 2004; Leonardo Torres Quevedo Award 1963, Santiago Ramón y Cajal Award 1973, Ferrer Foundation Severo Ochoa Award in Research 1986, UNESCO Carlos J. Finlay Award 1991, King Jaime I Award for Research 1994, Medal of the Principality of Asturias 1997, Medal of Honour for the Promotion of Invention, García Cabrerizo Foundation 1997, Grupo Correo Award for Human Values 1998, Research Award, Community of Madrid 1998, Mexico Award for Science and Tech. 1998, Charter 100 Heroine Award 1998, Spanish Soc. of Biochemistry and Molecular Biology Medal 1999, Santiago Ramón y Cajal National Award in Research 1999, L'Oréal-UNESCO For Women in Science Award 2000, Ind. Foundation Award for Universal Spanish Woman 2000, Gold Medal, Community of Madrid 2002, Medal of Honour, Int. Univ. Menéndez y Pelayo 2003, FCG Int. Science and Research Award 2004, Medalla de Oro al Mérito en el Trabajo 2005. *Publications:* more than 300 articles in scientific journals. *Address:* Severo Ochoa Centre for Molecular Biology, Universidad Autónoma de Madrid, Cantoblanco, 28049 Madrid, Spain (office). *Telephone:* (914) 975070 ext. 8435 (office). *Fax:* (914) 974799 (office). *E-mail:* webmaster@cbm.uam.es (office). *Website:* www.cbm.uam.es (office).

SALAYEV, Eldar Unis ogly, D.Phys-Math.Sc; Azerbaijani scientist and politician; b. 31 Dec. 1933, Nakhichevan City; s. of Yunis Sala oglu Salayev and Telly Tahir kizi Salayeva; m. Dilara Ashraf Guseynova; two s.; ed Azerbaijan Univ.; mem. CPSU 1963–91; Jr Researcher, Deputy Dir Inst. of Physics, Azerbaijan Acad. of Sciences 1956–73, Dir 1973–83; Corresp. mem. Acad. of Sciences of Azerbaijan 1980, mem. 1983, Pres. 1983–97; mem. Council on co-ordination of scientific activities of Acads of Sciences, Presidium of USSR Acad. of Sciences 1985–91; Chair. Repub. Council, Presidium of Acad. of Sciences of Azerbaijan; Ed.-in-Chief Doklady Akademii Nauk Azerbaijana; Deputy to USSR Supreme Soviet 1985–89; USSR People's Deputy 1989–91; Merited Worker of Arts of Azerbaijan. *Publications:* Dynamics and Statistics, Non-linear Effects on Layer Crystals, Type of Selenite Gallium 1993; more than 200 scientific publs in numerous journals. *Leisure interest:* sport. *Address:* c/o Azerbaijan Academy of Sciences, 9, F.Agayev Street, 1141 Baku, Azerbaijan. *Telephone:* (12) 4923529. *Fax:* (12) 4925699. *E-mail:* info@science .az. *Website:* www.science.az.

SALAZAR, Ken Lee, BA, JD; American lawyer, politician and government official; *Secretary of the Interior;* b. 2 March 1955, Alamosa, Colo; s. of Henry Salazar and Emma Salazar; m. Hope Salazar; two d.; ed Centauri High School, Conejos Co., St Francis Seminary, Colorado Coll., Univ. of Michigan Law School; worked as a farmer for more than 30 years, helped establish El Rancho Salazar partnership 1981; Assoc. Sherman & Howard (law firm), Denver Colo 1981–86; Chief Legal Counsel to Gov. of Colo 1986–90, apptd Exec. Dir Colo Dept of Natural Resources 1990–94; returned to pvt. law practice 1994–98; elected Colo Attorney Gen. 1999–2005; Dir Parcel, Mauro, Hultin & Spaanstra 1994–98; Senator from Colo 2005–08; US Sec. of the Interior, Washington, DC 2009–; mem. ABA, American Judicature Soc., Hispanic Bar Asscn, Denver Bar Asscn, Colorado Bar Asscn, American Farmland Trust, Pres.'s Council; mem. Bd of Trustees Colorado Coll.; Democrat; Hon. LLD (Colorado Coll.) 1993, (Univ. of Denver) 1999; Distinguished Alumni Award, Univ. of Michigan Law School. *Address:* Department of the Interior, 1849 C Street, NW, Washington, DC 20240, USA (office). *Telephone:* (202) 208-3100 (office). *Fax:* (202) 208-5048 (office). *E-mail:* webteam@ios.doi.gov (office). *Website:* www .doi.gov (office).

SALBER, Herbert; German diplomatist and international organization executive; *Director, Conflict Prevention Centre, Organization for Security and Co-operation in Europe;* b. 26 April 1954, Aachen; m.; three d.; ed Bonn Univ., Toulouse Univ., France; served in Fed. Armed Forces prior to univ. studies; entered training for diplomatic service, posted to Belgrade and Nicaragua before returning to Bonn 1990, involved with Geneva Conf. on Disarmament, Nuclear Non-Proliferation Treaty and Biological Weapons Convention, Rep. to UN Special Comm. (UNSCOM) 1995, Deputy Head of German Perm. Mission to OSCE 1996–2000, Head of OSCE Centre, Almaty, Kazakhstan 2000–01, Special Adviser to Portuguese OSCE Chairmanship on Cen. Asia 2002–03; Head of Div. for EU relations with CIS, South-Eastern Europe, Turkey, Asia, Africa and Latin America, Fed. Foreign Office, Berlin 2003–04; Head of Dept for Econ. and Scientific Relations, Embassy in Moscow 2004–06; Dir OSCE Conflict Prevention Centre 2006–. *Address:* OSCE Conflict Prevention Centre, Kärntner Ring 5–7, 1010 Vienna, Austria (office). *Telephone:* (1) 514-36-122 (office). *Fax:* (1) 514-36-96 (office). *E-mail:* info@osce.org (office). *Website:* www .osce.org/cpc (office).

SALEH, Field Marshall Ali Abdullah; Yemeni army officer and head of state; *President;* b. 21 March 1942, Beit al-Ahmer, Sanhan Dist.; m.; several c.; entered mil. service 1958; participated in 1974 coup; Mil. Gov., Taiz Prov. until June 1978; mem. Provisional Presidential Council, Deputy C-in-C of Armed Forces June–July 1978; Pres. of Yemen Arab Repub. 1978–90, Pres. Presidential Council of Repub. of Yemen 1990–94, of Repub. of Yemen 1994–; C-in-C of Armed Forces 1978–90; Sec.-Gen. People's Gen. Congress 1982; rank of Marshal 1997; Hon. M.Mil.Sc.; Nat. Republican Award. *Address:* Office of the President, San'a, Republic of Yemen (office). *Fax:* (1) 274147 (office).

SALEH, Ali Bin Saleh al-, BCom; Bahraini politician; *Chairman, Shura Consultative Council;* b. 28 Dec. 1942; s. of Saleh Al Saleh; m. Afaf Radhi Salman Almousawi 1970; one s. two d.; ed Ain Shams Univ., Cairo; dir of several public cos 1975–95; Minister of Commerce 1995–2006; Chair. Bahrain Promotions and Marketing Bd 1995–2000, Bahrain Convention and Exhbn Bureau, Bahrain Stock Exchange; Deputy Chair. Bahrain Chamber of Commerce and Industry 1975–93, Deputy Chair. Shura (Consultative Council) 1993–95, Chair. 2006–; mem. Bd of Trustees Univ. of Bahrain 1985–95, Bahrain Centre for Studies and Research, Econ. Devt Bd. *Leisure interests:* reading, music, travel. *Address:* Shura Council, PO Box 2991, Shaikh Duajj Road, Ghudaibura, Bahrain (office). *Telephone:* 17748888 (office). *E-mail:* info@shura.gov.bh (office). *Website:* www.shura.gov.bh (office).

SALEH, Amrullah; Afghan government official; *Head, National Security Directorate;* b. Panjshir Prov.; ed high school educ., Afghanistan; served as trans. between CIA officers and Northern Alliance leader Ahmad Shah Massoud 2001, helped remove Taliban from power with support of US-led coalition late 2001; fmr Chief Liaison Officer with foreign mil. and diplomatic corps, Kabul; fmr political officer, spokesman and relief co-ordinator; fmr Deputy Chief of Afghanistan Intelligence, focused on foreign relations; Sr mem. Nat. Security Directorate, Head of Directorate 2004–; Hon. DSc (Cleary Univ., Mich.) 2005. *Address:* National Security Directorate, Kabul, Afghanistan (office). *E-mail:* ahmad.afg@gmail.com.

SALEH, Maj.-Gen. Bakri Hassan; Sudanese military officer and government official; *Minister of the Presidency;* Mil. Officer, Revolutionary Command Council for Nat. Salvation (RCC–NS) 1989–; Chief of Security Forces 1997; Minister of Presidential Affairs 2001; fmr Minister of Nat. Defence; currently Minister of the Presidency; mem. Nat. Congress. *Address:* c/o National Congress, Khartoum, Sudan (office).

SALEH, Jaime Mercelino; Dutch government official, chief justice and university professor; *Minister of State, Netherlands Antilles;* b. 20 April 1941, Bonaire; m. Marguerite Marie Halabi; two s. two d.; ed State Univ. of Utrecht; Deputy Public Prosecutor, Netherlands 1967–68; Curaçao 1968–74; attorney-at-law, Curaçao 1971–74; Deputy mem. High Court of the Netherlands Antilles 1974–76; Justice 1976–79; Chief Justice High Court of Justice of the Netherlands Antilles and Aruba 1979–90, Vice-Pres. Dutch Navy Mil. Court for the Netherlands Antilles 1978–79, Pres. Dutch Navy Mil. Court for the Netherlands Antilles and Aruba 1979–90; Gov.-Gen. of Netherlands Antilles 1990–2002; Minister of State 2004–; Prof., Univ. of Utrecht 2005–; Order of Merit of Corps Consulaire 1989; Order of Libertador en el grado de Gran Cordón, Venezuela 1996; Order of Knighthood of the Dutch Lion; Commdr, Order of Orange Nassau 2002; Royal Medal 1980, Almirate Luis Brion Naval Medal 1994, Dutch ICN Dales Award for Integrity 2004, Dutch Lawyers Asscn Award 2008. *Publications:* various works on law and politics, with particular reference to the Netherlands Antilles. *Address:* B7 Villapark Zuurzak, Willemstad, Curaçao, Netherlands Antilles (home). *Telephone:* (9) 7382800 (home). *Fax:* (9) 7382801 (home). *E-mail:* marlex@cura.net (home).

SALEH ABBAS, Youssouf, LLM; Chadian politician; *Prime Minister;* b. 1953, Abéché, Ouaddai Region; Head, Multilateral Co-operation Div. and Dir of Int. Co-operation, Ministry of Foreign Affairs 1979–81; Diplomatic Adviser to Pres. 1981; Dir Cabinet of Head of State 1981–82; Adviser to Dir-Gen., Ministry of Foreign Affairs 1992–96; Vice-Pres. Sovereign Nat. Conf. Jan.–April 1993; Dir-Gen. Ministry of Planning and Co-operation 1996–97; mem. Movt for Democracy and Justice in Chad 1998–2001; Special Rep. to UN and EUFOR (peacekeepng force) 2007–08; Adviser to Pres. on Int. Relations and Co-operation 2006–08; Prime Minister 2008–. *Address:* Office of the Prime Minister, BP 463, N'Djamena, Chad (office). *Telephone:* 52-63-39 (office). *Fax:* 52-69-77 (office). *E-mail:* cpcprimt@intnet.td (office). *Website:* www.primature -tchad.com (office).

SALEK, Lt-Col Mustapha Ould; Mauritanian army officer and politician; ed Saumur Mil. Acad., France; Chief of Staff of Armed Forces 1968–69, March 1978; fmr Dir Soc. Nat. d'Import/Export (SONIMEX); Commdr Third Mil. Region 1977; Head of State and Chair. Mil. Cttee for Nat. Recovery (later for Nat. Salvation) 1978–79; sentenced to 10 years' imprisonment for plotting against Pres. Haidalla March 1982.

SALEM, Elie Adib, PhD; Lebanese politician, academic and university administrator; *President, University of Balamand;* b. 5 March 1930, Bterram Kurah; s. of Adib Salem and Lamia Salem (née Malik); m. Phyllis Sell; two s. two d.; ed American Univ. of Beirut, Univ. of Cincinnati, USA, Johns Hopkins Univ., USA; Instructor in Public Admin, American Univ. of Beirut 1954–56, Assoc. Prof. of Political Studies and Public Admin 1962–68, Asst Dean of Arts and Sciences 1966–68, Chair. Middle East Area Program and Prof. of Political Studies and Public Admin 1969–74, Chair. Dept of Political Studies and Public Admin 1972–74, Dean of Arts and Sciences 1974–82; Asst Prof. of Middle East Politics, School of Advanced Int. Studies, Johns Hopkins Univ. 1956–62; Visiting Prof., Dept of Govt and Research Scholar Int. Devt Research Center, Ind. Univ. 1968–69; Deputy Prime Minister and Minister of Foreign Affairs 1982–84; Adviser to Pres. on Foreign Affairs 1984–88; Founder and Pres. Lebanese Centre of Policy Studies 1988–; Pres. Univ. of Balamand 1993–. *Publications include:* The Arab Public Administrative Conference 1954, Political Theory and Institutions of the Khawarij 1956, Modernization without Revolution: Lebanon's Experience 1973, 'Rusum Dar al-Khilafah al Abbasiyah' manuscript by Hlal al Sab' (trans.) 1977, Violence and Diplomacy in Lebanon 1982–88 1994; articles in professional journals. *Leisure interests:* tennis, swimming, table tennis. *Address:* Université de Balamand, PO Box 100, Tripoli (office); Sibnai, Baabda, Villa Salem, Beirut, Lebanon. *Telephone:* (6) 930250, ext. 103 (office). *Fax:* (6) 930278 (office); (6) 400742 (office). *E-mail:* president@balamand.edu.lb (office). *Website:* www.balamand.edu.lb (office).

SALERNO, F. Robert; American car rental industry executive; *President and Chief Operating Officer, Avis Budget Group, Inc.;* b. Springfield, Mass; m., one d.; ed Marquette Univ.; Vice-Pres., Eastern Region and Zone Devt, Avis Rent-a-Car 1982–87, Vice-Pres. Field Operations 1987–90, Sr Vice-Pres. and Gen. Man. 1990–95, Exec. Vice-Pres. of Operations 1995–96, Pres. and COO 1996–2002, Pres. and COO Cendant Car Rental 2002–03, CEO Cendant Vehicle Rental Services Div. 2003–05, Pres. and COO Avis Budget Group Inc. (cr. after Cendant separated into four units) 2005–. *Address:* Avis Budget Group Inc., 6 Sylvan Way, Parsippany, NJ 07054, USA (office). *Telephone:* (973) 496-3500 (office). *Fax:* (888) 304-2315 (office). *Website:* www .avisbudgetgroup.com (office).

SALGADO, Sebastião Ribeiro, Jr, PhD; Brazilian photographer; b. 8 Feb. 1944, Aimorés, Minas Gerais; m. Lélia Deluiz Wanick 1967; two s.; ed São Paulo Univ., Vanderbilt Univ., USA, Univ. of Paris; with Brazilian Ministry of Finance 1968–69; with Investment Dept, Int. Coffee Org., London 1971–73; photo-reporter, working in Europe, Africa (particularly covering drought in Sahel) and Latin America 1973–, with Sygma News Agency of Paris 1974, with Gamma Agency 1975–79, mem. Magnum Photos 1979–; numerous solo exhbns Europe, Brazil, Israel, China, Canada, Cuba, including L'Afrique des Colères 1977–78, Sahel – L'Homme en Détresse 1986, Other Americas 1986–90, UNICEF Special Rep. 2001; many prizes, including Kodak/City of Paris Award for book Autres Amériques 1984, Oskar Barnack Prize, World Press Photos, the Netherlands, for work in Sahel 1985, Int. Center of Photography Photojournalist of the Year Award, New York 1986, 1988, Photographer of the Year Award, American Soc. of Magazine Photographers 1987, Olivier Rebbot Award, Overseas Press Club, New York 1987, King of Spain Award 1988, Erich Salomon Award, Germany 1988, Erna and Victor Hasselblad Award, Sweden 1989, Grand Prix Nationaux 1995, UNESCO Prize for Culture in Brazil. *Publications:* several books of photographs and exhbn catalogues, including Autres Amériques 1986, Sahel: L'Homme en Détresse 1986, Les Cheminots 1988, Sahel: El Fin del Camino 1988, Workers: An Archaeology of the Industrial Age 1993, Terra: Luta dos Sem-Terra 1997, Exodus 2000, O Fím do Pálio 2003, Um Incerto Estado de Graça 2004, O Berço da Desigualdade

2005, Africa 2007. *Address:* c/o Amazonas Images, 93 Quai de Valmy, 75010 Paris, France (office). *Telephone:* 1-42-09-90-68 (office). *E-mail:* amazonas@amazonasimages.fr (office). *Website:* www.amazonasimages.com (office).

SALGADO MENDÉZ, Elena, MA; Spanish government official and telecommunications executive; *Minister of the Economy and Finance;* b. 1949, Ourense; ed Universidad Politécnica de Madrid, Escuela Organización Industrial, Universidad Complutense de Madrid; industrial engineer Universidad Politécnica de Madrid 1972; with Econs Dept, School of Industrial Org. 1976–82; Dir Dept of Studies, Inst. for Small and Medium-sized Businesses, Ministry of Industry 1982–84; Dir-Gen. for Personnel Expenditure and Public Pensions, Ministry of Economy and Finance 1985–91; Sec.-Gen. for Communications, Supervision of Postal and Telecommunication Policy, Ministry of Public Works 1991–96; Dir of Strategic Consulting Services, Lenci Consulting SL 1997–2002; Exec. Dir Vallehermoso Telecom 2002–03; apptd Pres. Nueva Información Telefónica 2003; Minister of Health and Consumer Affairs 2004–07, of Public Admin.2007–09, of the Economy and Finance 2009–; Pres. Bd of Dirs Hispasat SA, Correos y Telégrafos; mem. Bd of Dirs Abertis Telecom 2004, Telefónica SA, Caja Postal, Hunosa, RENFE, Trasmediterranea, Nat. Mint; mem. Advisory Council, Arthur Andersen 1999–2000, Social Council, Universidad Politécnica de Madrid 1999–2002; Gran Cruz de la Orden del Mérito Civil 1987, Gran Cruz de la Orden de Mérito Militar con distintivo blanco 1996. *Leisure interest:* cinema. *Address:* Ministry of the Economy and Finance, Alcalá 9, 28014 Madrid, Spain (office). *Telephone:* (91) 5958348 (office). *Fax:* (91) 5958486 (office). *E-mail:* informacion.alcala@meh.es (office). *Website:* www.meh.es (office).

SALGADO TAMAYO, Wilma, PhD; Ecuadorean economist and government official; b. 20 Oct. 1952, Pifo; ed Liceo Municipal Fernández Madrid, Univ. Católica del Ecuador, Univ. of Paris, Sorbonne, Univ. Nacional Autónoma, Mexico; Researcher, Univ. Católica del Ecuador 1973–74; Researcher and Dir Econ. Forecasting, Banco Central del Ecuador 1986–91; Econ. Adviser to Pres. 1991; Researcher, Centro Andino de Acción Popular 1993; Prof., Univ. Andina Simón Bolívar 1994–2002; Consultant to WFP 1999–2001; Gen. Man. Agencia de Garantía de Depósitos 2003–04; mem. Andean Parl. 2007–; Minister of Economy and Finance July–Sept. 2008 (resgnd). *Address:* General Secretariat, Andean Parliament, 70-61 Avenida 13, Bogotá, Colombia (office). *Telephone:* (1) 217-3357 (office). *Fax:* (1) 348-2805 (office). *E-mail:* correo@parlamentoandino.org (office). *Website:* www.parlamentoandino.org (office).

SALIBA, George, MA; Maltese business consultant and fmr diplomatist; b. 27 Jan. 1944; m. Yvonne Saliba; three c.; ed Plater Coll. Oxford, UK and Johns Hopkins Univ., USA; clerk in Finance Dept, Univ. of Malta 1964–66, Lecturer in Politics 1971–73; Lecturer in Social Studies, Malta Polytechnic 1971; regular columnist with Maltese language weekly and TV and radio commentator 1971–73; Sec.-Man. of leading agricultural co-operative 1974; Public Relations Officer, Kuwait Embassy, Malta 1974–76; Gen. Man. Animal Feedmill 1976–81; Amb. (non-resident) to countries of Arabian Gulf 1981–85; Amb. to Saudi Arabia 1985–87, to Libya (Chair. of Social Cttee of Diplomatic Corps, Head of European Group and Dean of Diplomatic Corps) 1987–93, to Russia 1993–97; Perm. Rep. to UN, New York 1997–99; Amb. to USA and Amb. (non-resident) to Mexico 1999–2003, High Commr to Canada 2000–03; Amb.-designate to Libya from 2004; currently business consultant to Libya; Founder Maltese Arab Friendship Soc. 1980. *Address:* DBHS, PO Box 8342, Tripoli, Libya (office). *Telephone:* (21) 3331576 (office); (21) 637466 (home). *Fax:* (21) 4442742 (office). *E-mail:* gs@dbms.com.mt (office); gbsaliba@yahoo.com (home).

SALIH, Barham, BE; Iraqi politician; *Deputy Prime Minister for National Security;* b. 1960, Kurdistan; ed Univ. of Cardiff, Univ. of Liverpool, UK; joined Patriotic Union Kurdistan (PUK) 1976, served as spokesman in London, UK; Rep. to US, Patriotic Union Kurdistan and Kurdistan Regional Govt 1991–2001; Regional Admin. Sulaimaniya; Deputy Prime Minister for Nat. Security Affairs 2004–05; Minister of Planning and Devt Co-operation 2005–06, Deputy Prime Minister for Nat. Security 2006–. *Address:* Ministry of National Security Affairs, North Gate, Baghdad, Iraq (office). *Telephone:* (1) 888-9071 (office).

SALIH, Khaled, BA, MA, PhD; Iraqi academic and government official; *Official Spokesperson, Kurdistan Regional Government;* b. 16 Feb. 1957, Sulaimania, Kurdistan; ed Gothenburg Univ., Sweden; fmr Lecturer in Int. and Middle E Politics, Dept of Political Science, Gothenburg Univ. 1989–97; Sr Lecturer, Univ. of Linkøping, Sweden 1997–98; Associate Prof. in Middle E Politics, Centre for Contemporary Middle E Studies, Univ. of Southern Denmark, Odense 1998–; mem. Kurdistan Int. Constitutional Advisory Team 2003, also served as political adviser to Kurdistan Regional Govt and Kurdistan Nat. Ass.; Official Spokesperson for Kurdistan Regional Govt 2006–; fmr Advisory Ed. Democratiya (journal). *Publications:* State-Making, Nation-Building and the Military: Iraq, 1941-1958 1996, The Future of Kurdistan in Iraq (co-ed.) 2005. *Address:* Kurdistan Regional Government, Council of Ministers Building, Arbil, Kurdish Autonomous Region, Iraq; Center for Contemporary Middle East Studies, University of Southern Denmark, Campusvej 55, 5230 Odense, Denmark. *Telephone:* 6550 2183. *Fax:* 6550 2161. *E-mail:* salih@hist.ou.dk. *Website:* www.krg.org; www.humaniora.sdu.dk/middle-east.

SALIH, Muhammad; Uzbekistani writer, poet and politician; *Chairman, Freedom Democratic Party of Uzbekistan (Erk);* b. 20 Dec. 1949, Xorazm; m.; five c.; ed Tashkent State Univ., Moscow High Literary Inst.; mil. service in army 1968–70; worked as screenwriter in 1980s; wrote letter to Politbureau protesting political situation in Uzbekistan 1984; work published in Soviet newspapers 1985–86; elected Chair. Union of Writers of Uzbekistan 1988; co-f. Birlik (Unity People's Movt) 1988; f. Freedom Democratic Party of Uzbekistan (Erk) 1990, currently Chair.; Deputy, Oly Majlis (Supreme Ass. — Parl.) 1990–92 (resgnd); presidential cand. 1990; f. Democratic Forum 1992; refused offer of Deputy Prime Minister role in return for dissolution of Democratic Forum 1992, arrested and jailed for three days, and subsequently put under house arrest, left Uzbekistan to continue political activity abroad 1992; received sentence in absentia of 15 and a half years 1999; f. Nat. Salvation Cttee 2005; living in exile in Norway. *Publications:* The Golden Head of the Avenger (screenplay), more than 20 books, including: Oydinlik sari 1993, Etikodning chorrahasi bolmaydi 1994, Ikror 1995, Devlet sirlari (in Turkish) 1997, Turkistan suuru (in Turkish) 1997, Agaclar sair olsa (in Turkish) 1997, Yolnoma (in Uzbek) 1999, Yolname (in Turkish) 2002, The Articles 2003, Valfajr, Ko'men nashriyoti, Konya 2005, Publisistika, Izdatelstvo Bilgeoguz 2005. *Address:* c/o Freedom Democratic Party of Uzbekistan (O'zbekiston Erk Demokratik Partiyasi), 100055 Tashkent, Ipakchi ko'ch. 38, Uzbekistan (office). *Telephone:* (71) 120-65-30 (home). *E-mail:* erkparty@yahoo.com (office). *Website:* www.muhammadsalih.info (office).

SALIH MUHAMMAD, Osman, BSc; Eritrean politician; *Minister of Foreign Affairs;* b. 1948; ed Haile Selassie I Univ. (Addis Ababa Univ.), Ethiopia; Head, Eritrean People's Liberation Front refugee schools, Sudan 1983–87; Head, Educ. Dept 1987; Commr for Eritrean Refugees' Affairs 1987–92; mem. Nat. Ass. 1993–; Minister of Educ. 1993–2007, of Foreign Affairs 2007–; mem. People's Front for Democracy and Justice (PFDJ), mem. Exec. Bd 1993–, mem. Cen. Ass. 1993–. *Address:* Ministry of Foreign Affairs, PO Box 190, Asmara, Eritrea (office). *Telephone:* (1) 127838 (office). *Fax:* (1) 123788 (office). *E-mail:* tesfai@wg.eol (office).

SALIJ, Rev. Jacek; Polish ecclesiastic and professor of theology; *Professor, Cardinal Stefan Wyszyński University;* b. 19 Aug. 1942, Budy; ed Acad. of Catholic Theology, Warsaw; ordained priest 1966; Asst Acad. of Catholic Theology (now Cardinal Stefan Wyszyński Univ.), Warsaw 1970–71, Asst Prof. 1971–90, Extraordinary Prof. 1990–99, Ordinary Prof. 2000–; Co-Founder Gaudium Vitae Movt 1979–; mem. Council of Educ. attached to the Pres. of Poland 1992–95, Main Council of Higher Educ. 1993–96; consultant to Educ. of Faith Comm. of Episcopate of Poland 1997–; mem. Polish Soc. of Philosophy 1982–, PEN Club 1989–. *Publications:* Modlitwa za świętych w liturgii rzymskiej 1974, Królestwo Boże w was jest 1980, Legendy dominikańskie (composition and translation) 1982, Rozpacz pokonana 1983, Rozmowy ze św. Augustynem 1985, Pytania nieobojętne 1986, Dekalog 1989, Wiara na co dzień 1994, Nadzieja poddawana próbom 1995, Nasze czasy są OK. 1997, Praca nad wiarą 1999, Divinations, Astrology, Reincarnation (in Russian). *Leisure interest:* cycling. *Address:* ul. Freta 10, 00-227 Warsaw, Poland (office).

SALIKHOV, Shavkat Ismailovich; Uzbekistan biochemist; *President, Uzbek Academy of Sciences;* fmr Dir Sadykov Inst. of Bioorganic Chemistry; fmr CHAP/Uzbekistan Program Man.; Pres. Uzbek Acad. of Sciences 2006–. *Address:* Uzbek Academy of Sciences, 70 Acad. Gulyamov street, 100047 Tashkent, Uzbekistan (office). *Telephone:* (71) 136-76-29 (office). *Fax:* (71) 133-49-01 (office). *Website:* www.uzsci.net/academy (office).

SALIM, Salim Ahmed; Tanzanian diplomatist; b. 23 Jan. 1942, Pemba Island, Zanzibar; m. Amne Salim; three c.; ed Lumumba Coll., Zanzibar, Univ. of Delhi, India, and Columbia Univ., USA; Publicity Sec. of UMMA Party and Chief Ed. of its official organ Sauti ya UMMA 1963; Exec. Sec. United Front of Opposition Parties and Chief Ed. of its newspaper; Sec. Gen. All-Zanzibar Journalists Union 1963; Amb. to UAR 1964–65; High Commr to India 1965–68; Dir African and Middle East Affairs Div., Ministry of Foreign Affairs 1968–69; Amb. to People's Repub. of China and Democratic People's Repub. of Korea June–Dec. 1969; Perm. Rep. to UN 1970–80 (Pres. of Gen. Ass. 1979), also High Commr to Jamaica, accred to Guyana, Trinidad and Tobago, Barbados and Amb. to Cuba 1971–80; Chair. UN Special Cttee on Decolonization 1972–80; Minister of Foreign Affairs 1980–84, Prime Minister of Tanzania 1984–85, Deputy Prime Minister, Minister of Defence and Nat. Service 1986–89; Sec.-Gen. OAU 1989–2001; a fmr Vice-Pres. of Tanzania; Chair. UN Security Council Cttee on Sanctions against Rhodesia Jan.–Dec. 1975; fmr del. of Tanzania at int. confs; mem. Bd of Dirs South Centre (inter-governmental body) 2002–05; Pres. Julius K. Nyerere Foundation 2001–; African Union Special Envoy for Darfur Talks and Chief Mediator for the Inter-Sudanese Peace Talks on the Darfur Conflict 2004–08; Hon. LLD (Univ. of Philippines); Hon. DH (Univ. of Maiduguri, Nigeria) 1983; Hon. DCL (Univ. of Mauritius) 1991; Hon. Dr of Arts (Univ. of Khartoum, Sudan) 1995; Hon. PhD (Univ. of Bologna, Italy) 1996. *Address:* c/o Ministry of foreign Affairs and International Co-operation, Kivukoni Road, P.O. Box 9000, Dar es Salaam, Tanzania (office). *Website:* www.nyererefoundation.or.tz (office).

SALINAS DE GORTARI, Carlos, PhD; Mexican fmr head of state; b. 1948, Mexico City; ed Nat. Univ. of Mexico and Harvard Univ.; Asst Prof. of Statistics, Nat. Univ. of Mexico 1970; Research Asst Harvard Univ. 1974; taught Public Finance and Fiscal Policy in Mexico 1976, 1978; Asst Dir of Public Finance, Ministry of Finance 1971–74, Head of Econ. Studies 1974–76, Asst Dir of Financial Planning 1978, Dir-Gen. 1978–79; Dir-Gen. of Econ. and Social Policy, Ministry of Programming and Budget 1979–81; Dir-Gen. Inst. of Political, Social and Econ. Studies 1981–82; Minister of Planning and Fed. Budget 1982–87; named as pres. cand. by Partido Revolucionario Institucional 1987, Pres. of Mexico 1988–94. *Publications:* Mexico: The Policy and the Politics of Modernization 2002; numerous articles and essays. *Address:* c/o Partido Revolucionario Institucional (PRI), Edif. 2, Insurgentes Norte 59, Col. Buenavista, Del. Cuauhtémoc, 06359 México, DF, Mexico.

SALINAS PLIEGO, Ricardo B., BA, MBA; Mexican business executive; *Chairman and President, Grupo Elektra SA de CV;* b. 1956; m. María Laura Medina; three c.; ed Instituto Tecnológico y de Estudios Superiores de Monterrey, Tulane Univ., USA; fmrly with Arthur Andersen, Brinkman Co.;

joined Grupo Elektra Sa de CV1981, Pres. 1989–, Chair. 1993–, business interests in retail, broadcasting, telecommunications and financial services, including TV Azteca, Banco Azteca, Elektra, Iusacell, Unefon; Chair. Exec. Cttee Grupo Salinas; est. Empresario Azteca Program, Empresario Azteca Asscn (ASMAZ); f. Fundación Azteca 1997. *Address:* Grupo Elektra, SA de CV, Avenida Insurgentes Sur 3579, Colonia, Tlalpán La Joya, 14000 México DF, Mexico (office). *Telephone:* (55) 8582-7000 (office). *Fax:* (55) 8582-7822 (office). *Website:* www.grupoelektra.com.mx (office).

SALINGER, Jerome David (J. D.); American writer; b. 1 Jan. 1919, New York, NY; s. of Sol Salinger and Miriam Salinger (née Jillich); m. 2nd Claire Douglas 1953 (divorced 1967); one s. one d.; m. 3rd Colleen O'Neill; ed Manhattan public schools, Valley Forge Mil. Acad., Columbia Univ.; travelled in Europe 1937–38; army service with 4th Infantry Div. (Staff Sergeant) 1942–46;; mem. Légion d'honneur. *Publications:* The Catcher in the Rye (novel) 1951, For Esme with Love and Squalor (short stories, aka Nine Stories) 1953, Franny & Zooey (novel) 1961, Raise High the Roof-Beam, Carpenters and Seymour: An Introduction (novel) 1963, Hapworth 16, 1924 1997; contrib. numerous stories to magazines, mostly in the New Yorker 1948–. *Address:* Harold Ober Associates Inc., 425 Madison Avenue, New York, NY 10017, USA (office).

SALISBURY, David Murray, MA; British financial services industry executive; *Chairman and CEO, Dimensional Fund Advisors Ltd;* b. 18 Feb. 1952; s. of Norman Salisbury and Isobel Sutherland Murray; m. Lynneth Mary Jones 1977; two d.; ed Harrow School, Trinity Coll., Oxford; joined J. Henry Schroder Wagg & Co. Ltd 1974, Chief Exec. Schroder Capital Man. Int. Inc. 1986–2001, Jt Chief Exec. Schroder Investment Man. Ltd 1995–97, Chair. 1997–2001; Dir Dimensional Fund Advisers Inc. 1991–96, Chair. and CEO London Dimensional Fund Advisors Ltd, London 2002–; Gov. Harrow School 1996–99. *Leisure interests:* tennis, skiing. *Address:* Dimensional Fund Advisors Ltd, 7 Down Street, London, W1J 7AJ (office); The Dutch House, West Green, Wintney, Hants. RG27 8JN, England. *Telephone:* (20) 7016-4500 (home). *Fax:* (20) 7495-4141 (office). *Website:* www.dfaus.com (office).

SALISBURY, 7th Marquess of; **Most Hon. Robert Michael James Gascoyne-Cecil,** PC, DL; British politician and university chancellor; *Chancellor, University of Hertfordshire;* b. 30 Sept. 1946; s. of the late 6th Marquess of Salisbury; m. Hannah Ann Stirling 1970; two s. three d.; ed Eton Coll., Univ. of Oxford; MP for Dorset S 1979–87; mem. House of Lords 1992–, sits in House of Lords as Lord Gascoyne-Cecil 1999–, on leave of absence 2002–; Parl. Under-Sec. of State for Defence 1992–94; Lord Privy Seal 1994–97; Shadow Leader of House of Lords 1997–98; Chair. Council of Royal Veterinary Coll. 1999–2007; Chancellor Univ. of Hertfordshire 2005–; fmr Pres. Herts. Agric. Soc.; DL Herts. 2007; mem. Conservative Party. *Address:* Hatfield House, Hatfield, Herts., AL9 5NF, England. *Telephone:* (20) 7351-7458 (office). *Fax:* (20) 7351-7450 (office).

SALJE, Ekhard Karl Hermann, MA, PhD, FRS, FGS, FInstP, FRSA; British/German professor of mineralogy and petrology; *Professor of Mineralogy and Petrology and Head, Department of Earth Sciences, University of Cambridge;* b. 26 Oct. 1946, Hanover; s. of Gerhard Salje and Hildegard Salje (née Drechsler); m. Elisabeth Démaret; one s. four d.; ed Univ. of Hanover, Univ. of Cambridge, UK; Prof. of Crystallography, Univ. of Hanover 1983–86; Lecturer in Mineral Physics, Univ. of Cambridge 1986–92, Prof. 1992–94, Prof. of Mineralogy and Petrology 1994–, Head, Dept of Earth Sciences 1998–; Pres. Clare Hall, Cambridge 2002–08; Visiting Prof. in Paris, Grenoble, Le Mans (France), Nagoya (Japan), Bilbao (Spain), Max Planck Institute for Mathematics, Leipzig 2008–09, Univ. of Paris VII 2009; Pres. Alexander von Humboldt Asscn (UK) 2004–, European Trust UK; Programme Dir Cambridge-MIT Inst. CMI 2001–03; mem. Bd Univ. of Hamburg, Germany 2004–; mem. Working Party, Royal Soc. on Nuclear Waster, British Pugwash Group, Wissenschaftsrat Germany; Bd mem. EIT Poland 2008, Parl. Office for Science and Tech.; Fellow, Akad. Leopoldina (Germany); Hon. Fellow, Darwin Coll., Cambridge 2001, Clare Hall 2008; Chevalier des Palmes académiques; Abraham-Gottlieb-Werner Medal 1997, Schlumberger Medal 1997, Humboldt Research Prize 1999, Ernst Ising Prize 2000, Gold Medal, Univ. of Hamburg 2002, Agricola Medal for Mineralogy 2006. *Publications:* over 400 scientific publs including book on phase transitions in ferroelastic and co-elastic crystals. *Leisure interests:* music, painting. *Address:* Department of Earth Sciences, University of Cambridge, Downing Street, Cambridge, CB2 3EQ, England (office). *Telephone:* (1223) 333478 (office). *E-mail:* es10002@esc.cam .ac.uk (office). *Website:* www.esc.cam.ac.uk/new/v10/index_mineralogy.html (office).

SALKIND, Ilya; film producer; b. 1947, Mexico City; s. of Alexander Salkind; ed Univ. of London; Assoc. Producer, Cervantes, The Light at the Edge of the World, Spain, 1974; f. Illya Salkind Co., Los Angeles (film production co.), currently CEO and Pres.. *Films produced include:* Bluebeard 1972, The Three Musketeers 1973, The Four Musketeers 1974, The Twist 1976, The Prince and the Pauper 1977, Superman 1978, Superman II 1980, Superman III 1983, Supergirl 1984, Santa Claus: The Movie 1985, Christopher Columbus: The Discovery 1992, Heads N TailZ 2005, Young Alexander the Great 2007. *Television includes:* Superboy (series) 1988–92. *Website:* www .ilyasalkindcompany.com.

SALL, Macky; Senegalese politician; b. 11 Dec. 1961, Fatick; m.; two c.; ed Université Cheikh Anta Diop, Institut Français du Pétrole, Paris; Head of Div., Société des Pétroles du Sénégal (PETROSEN) 1993–2002, Dir-Gen. 2000–01; fmr Special Adviser to the Pres. on Energy and Mining; Minister of Energy, Mining and Hydraulics 2001–03, concurrently Minister for Equipment and Transport Oct.–Nov. 2002; Minister of State, Minister of the Interior and Local Communities, Govt Spokesperson 2003–04; Prime Minister of

Senegal 2004–07; Pres. Nat. Ass. June–Nov. 2007; fmr mem. Parti démocratique sénégalais (PDS). *Address:* c/o Parti démocratique sénégalais (PDS), blvd Dial Diop, Immeuble Serigne Mourtada Mbacké, Dakar, Senegal (office).

SALLAH, Halifa; Gambian politician, sociologist and editor; *Leader, People's Democratic Organization for Independence and Socialism;* currently Leader, People's Democratic Org. for Independence and Socialism and Coordinator (Nat. Alliance for Democracy and Devt), represents constituency of Serrekunda Central; expelled from Nat. Ass. for membership of two political parties 2005, re-elected later same year; unsuccessful cand. in presidential election 2006; mem. Pan-African Parl.; Co-Ed. Foroyaa (newspaper). *Address:* People's Democratic Organization for Independence and Socialism (PDOIS), POB 2306, 1 Sambou Street, Churchill, Serrekunda, The Gambia (office). *Telephone:* 4393177 (office). *Fax:* 4393177 (office). *E-mail:* foroyaa@qanet.gm (office). *Website:* www.foroyaa.com.

SALLAH, Ousman Ahmadou, BA; Gambian diplomatist and business executive; *Managing Director, Dandimay Enterprise;* b. 26 July 1938, Kudang; s. of Ahmadou Jabel Sallah and Haddy Sallah; m. Ramou Sallah 1966; two s. two d.; ed Trinity Coll., Hartford, Conn., School of Int. Affairs, Columbia Univ., New York, London School of Econs; Asst Sec., Prime Minister's Office 1967; Asst Sec. Ministry of External Affairs 1967–68, Deputy Perm. Sec. 1973–74; First Sec., Head of Chancery and Acting High Commr, London 1971; Amb. to Saudi Arabia (also accred to Egypt, Iran, Kuwait, Qatar and UAE) 1974–79, to USA 1979–83; Perm. Rep. to UN 1979–83; Perm. Sec. Ministry of External Affairs and Head of Gambian Diplomatic Service 1982–87, Amb. to USA and Perm. Rep. to UN 1987–94; Consultant, World Bank 1996–99; Man. Dir Dandimay Enterprise 1999–; Hon. LLD (Trinity Coll., Hartford); Diploma in Int. Relations and Diplomacy from UNITAR . *Leisure interest:* tennis. *Address:* PO Box 667, Banjul, The Gambia. *Telephone:* 820-39-12 (office); 820-39-13 (home); 653-82-64. *Fax:* 820-39-06 (office). *E-mail:* torodo@sentoo.sn (office); sallahlamtoro@yahoo.com (home).

SALLE, David, MFA; American artist; b. 1952, Okla; s. of Alvin S. Salle and Tillie D. Salle (née Brown); ed California Inst. of Arts; retrospective exhbn Museum of Contemporary Art, Chicago 1987; Guggenheim Fellow 1986. *Address:* c/o Gagosian Gallery, 980 Madison Avenue, New York, NY 10021, USA.

SALLEH, Dato' Seri Mohd Nor, BSc, MSc, PhD; Malaysian scientist and academic; *Secretary General, Malaysian Academy of Sciences;* b. 20 Oct. 1940, Negeri Sembilan; s. of Mohammed Nor and Nyonya Nor; m. Habiba Alias 1966; two s. one d.; ed Univ. of Adelaide, Australia, Australian Forestry School, Canberra, ITC Delft, Netherlands, Michigan State Univ., USA; Deputy Conservator of Forests, Forest Dept Peninsular Malaysia 1965, Dir Forest Inventory 1971; Dir Forestry Research Inst., Kepong 1977–85; Dir Gen. Forest Research Inst. of Malaysia (FRIM) 1985–95 (retd); Adjunct Prof., Univ. Putra Malaysia 1994–96, Univ. Malaysia Sabah 2001–; Vice-Pres. Int. Union of Forest Research Orgs. (IUFRO) 1986–90, Pres. 1991–95; Pres. Malaysian Nature Soc. 1978–; mem. Nat. Environment Quality Council 1995–; fmr Vice Pres. Malaysian Acad. of Sciences, now Sec. Gen.; mem. Advisory Cttee Nat. Science Center, Nat. Planetarium and Nat. Park; mem. Malaysian Human Rights Comm. 2000–02; mem. Bd of Dirs Forest Trends, CIFOR, InterAcad. Council; mem. Panel of Eminent Experts on Ethics in Food and Agricultural of FAO 2000, Scientific and Tech. Advisory Panel of Global Environmental Facility, FAO High-Level Panel of External Experts on Forestry (Chair. 2003), Ind. Panel to Review the Tropical Forestry Action Plan; Chair. IUCN East Asia Group on Sustainable Use Initiative; fmr Chair Asia Pacific Asscn of Forest Research Insts; Trustee Int. Network on Bamboo and Rattan; Dr hc (Nat. Univ. of Malaysia) 1992, (Aberdeen) 1993; KMN 1981, DSNS 1989, Award of Third World Network of Scientific Orgs. for Public Understanding of Science 1991; Langkawi Environmental Award 1991, Nat. Science Award 1993. *Publications:* The Tropical Garden City 1990, The Malaysian Marine Heritage 1991, over 100 articles and contribs. to seminars, books and journals. *Leisure interests:* squash, badminton, reading, nature-oriented activities. *Address:* Malaysian Academy of Sciences (Akademi Sains Malaysia), 902-4 Jalan Tun Ismail, 50480 Kuala Lumpur, Malaysia (office). *Telephone:* (3) 26949898 (office). *Fax:* (3) 26945858 (office). *E-mail:* admin@ akademisains.gov.my (office). *Website:* www.akademisains.gov.my (office).

SALLEO, Baron; Ferdinando; Italian diplomatist and business executive; *Vice-Chairman, MCC SpA;* b. 2 Oct. 1936, Messina; s. of the late Baron Carmelo and Maria Carla Stagno d'Alcontres; m. Anna Maria Riegler; two c.; ed Univ. of Rome; joined diplomatic service 1960, assigned to Directorate-Gen. for Political Affairs, Third Sec. in Paris 1963; Second Sec., Foreign Minister's Cabinet, Rome 1964; Deputy Consul Gen., New York 1966–69; Counsellor in Prague 1969–72; Head of NATO Desk, Ministry of Foreign Affairs 1974–77; Minister in Bonn 1977–81; Deputy Dir-Gen. for Devt Co-operation, Ministry of Foreign Affairs 1982–86, Special Envoy and Minister Plenipotentiary of First Class and Dir-Gen. 1986; Amb. and Perm. Rep. to OECD 1986–88; Dir-Gen. Econ. Affairs, Ministry of Foreign Affairs 1988–1989; Amb. to USSR (later Russian Fed.) 1989–93; Dir-Gen. Political Affairs, Ministry of Foreign Affairs 1993–94, Sec.-Gen., Ministry of Foreign Affairs 1994–95; Amb. to USA 1995–2003; currently Vice-Chair. MCC SpA (merchant bank), Rome; mem. Int. Advisory Council, Textron Inc.; Visiting Prof. of Devt Policy, Faculty of Political Science, Univ. of Florence 1982–84; Prof. of Theory of Int. Relations, Faculty of Political Science, LUISS Univ., Rome 1984–86; Grand Cross OMRI (Italy), Grand Cross Verdienstkreuz (Germany), Légion d'honneur; Hon. Doctor of Laws (St Thomas Univ., Miami, Fla). *Publications:* Diario Fotografico del Marchese di San Giuliano, Palermo, Sellerio, 1984, Albania: Un Regno per Sei Mesi, Palermo, Sellerio 2000 (later translated into Albanian). *Address:* MCC SpA, Via Piemonte, 51, 00187 Rome, Italy (office).

Telephone: (06) 47911 (office). *Fax:* (06) 47913130 (office). *E-mail:* mcc@mcc.it (office). *Website:* www.mcc.it (office).

SALLES, Walter; Brazilian film director and screenwriter; b. 12 April 1956, Rio de Janeiro; mem. jury Cannes Film Festival 1999, 2002. *Films include:* Socorro Nobre (Fipa d'Or 1996) 1995, Foreign Lane (Grand Prix du Public Rencontres de Cinéma de Paris 1995), Central do Brasil (co-directed) (Golden Bear Berlin Int. Film Festival, Best Screenplay Sundance Inst.-NHK, Best Foreign Film British Acad. Awards, Best Foreign Film Golden Globes) 1998, O Primeiro Dia (co-directed) (Best Latin-American Film Mexican Acad. Awards) 1998, Abril Despedaçado (Little Golden Lion Award Venice Film Festival) 2001, Diarios de Motocicleta (The Motorcycle Diaries) 2004, Dark Water 2005, Paris, Je T'aime 2006, Linha de Passe 2008. *Address:* c/o The Endeavour Agency, 9601 Wilshire Boulevard, 10th Floor, Beverly Hills, CA 90212, USA. *Telephone:* (310) 248-2000. *Fax:* (310) 248-2020.

SALLINEN, Aulis Heikki; Finnish composer and academic; b. 9 April 1935, Salmi; s. of Armas Rudolf Sallinen and Anna Malanen; m. 1st Pirkko Holvisola 1955 (died 1997); four s.; m. 2nd Maisa Lokka 1999; ed Sibelius Acad.; primary school teacher 1958–60; Man. Finnish Radio Orchestra 1960–70; Prof. of Arts, Sibelius Acad. 1965–76; mem. Bd of Dirs TEOSTO (Finnish Composers' Copyright Soc.) 1970–84, Chair. 1988–90; mem. Swedish Royal Music Acad. 1979–; mem. Finnish Composers' Soc., Sec. 1958–73, Chair. 1971–73; fmr mem. Bd Finnish Nat. Opera; Hon. DPhil (Turku) 1991, (Helsinki) 1994; Nordic Council Music Prize 1978, Prof. of Arts for Life (by the Finnish Govt) 1981, Wihuri Int. Sibelius Prize 1983. *Compositions include:* eight symphonies, violin concerto, cello concerto, flute concerto and other orchestral music, five string quartets and other chamber music; film score for The Iron Age 1983. *Operas include:* The Horseman 1975, The Red Line 1978, The King Goes Forth to France 1982, Kullervo 1988, The Palace 1993, King Lear 1999. *Address:* c/o TEOSTO, Lauttasaarentie 1, 00 200 Helsinki 20, Finland (office).

SALLING, Augusta; Greenlandic politician; *Deputy, Delegation from Greenland, Nordic Council;* b. 1954; ed Greenland Coll. of Educ.; teacher, deputy head then man. head of school, Qeqertarsuaq 1980–86; Gen. Man. Disko Havfiskeri SpA 1986–93; mem. Qeqertarsuaq Local Council 1993–2001; Mayor of Qeqertarsuaq 1993–97; mem. Landtag (Atassut) 1999–, Chair. 2002–05; Minister of Economy 2001–02; Vice-Premier and Minister of Finance 2003; Vice Chair., Landsting and Deputy, Nordic Council, Del. from Greenland 2005–, also Deputy Centre Group. *Address:* Nordic Council, Delegation from Greenland, Grønlands Landstings Bureau, POB 1060, 3900 Nuuk, Greenland (office). *Telephone:* 345000 (office). *Fax:* 324606 (office). *E-mail:* aus@gh.gl (office). *Website:* www.nanoq.gl (office).

SALLOUKH, Fawzi; Lebanese government official and diplomatist; *Minister of Foreign Affairs and Emigrants;* b. 1931, Qammatieh; m. Hind Basma; three c.; ed American Univ. Beirut; Prof. 1955–57; Dir of Public Relations, Franklin Publishing 1957–60; Amb. to Sierra Leone 1964–71; Cen. Dept, Ministry of Foreign Affairs 1971–78; Amb. to Nigeria 1978–85, to Algeria 1985–87; Dir of Econ. Affairs 1987–90; Amb. to Austria 1990–94, to Belgium 1994–95; Sec.-Gen. Islamic Univ. 1998–; Minister of Foreign Affairs and Emigrants 2005–06 (resgnd, resignation not accepted), 2008–. *Address:* Ministry of Foreign Affairs and Emigrants, rue Sursock, Achratieh, Beirut, Lebanon (office). *Telephone:* (1) 333100 (office). *E-mail:* info@emigrants.gov.lb (office). *Website:* www.emigrants.gov.lb (office).

SALMAN, Sheikh Ali; Bahraini politician; *President, Al-Wefaq (Islamic National Accord Association—INAA);* ed in Qom; Shia cleric; exiled to Dubai 1995, then sought asylum in London, returned to Bahrain 2001; currently Pres. Al-Wefaq (Islamic Nat. Accord Asscn —INAA); mem. Parl. for Jid Hafas 2006–. *E-mail:* webmaster@alwefaq.org. *Website:* www.alwefaq.org; www.toqa.net.

SALMON, Peter Andrew, BA; British broadcasting executive; *Chief Creative Officer, BBC Vision;* b. 15 May 1956, Burnley; m.; four s.; ed Univ. of Warwick; fmr Dir of Programmes, Granada TV and Controller of Factual Programmes, Channel 4; fmr producer and Series Ed. BBC TV, later Head of Features, BBC Bristol, Controller, BBC One 1997–2000, Dir BBC Sport 2000–05; CEO The Television Corpn 2005–06; Chief Creative Officer, BBC Vision 2006–; mem. Bd Liverpool Culture Co. 2005–. *Leisure interests:* cycling, football, tennis. *Address:* BBC Television, Television Centre, Wood Lane, London, W12 7RJ, England (office). *Telephone:* (20) 8743-8000 (office). *Website:* www.bbc.co.uk (office).

SALMON, Robert; French journalist; b. 6 April 1918, Marseille; s. of Pierre Salmon and Madeleine Blum; m. Anne-Marie Jeanprost 1942; five c.; ed Lycée Louis le Grand, Ecole Normale Supérieure and at the Sorbonne; Founder Mouvement de Résistance Défense de la France; mem. Comité Parisien de Libération; Leader Paris Div., Mouvement de Libération Nationale; mem. Provisional Consultative Ass. 1944, First Constituent Ass. 1945; Founder Pres. and Dir Gen. France-Soir 1944; fmr Pres. Soc. France-Editions (Elle, Le Journal de Dimanche, Paris-Presse, etc.), Hon. Pres. 1976–; fmr Pres. Soc. de Publications Economiques (Réalités, Connaissance des Arts, Entreprise, etc.); Sec.-Gen. Féd. Nat. de la Presse 1951–77; Hon. Pres. French Cttee Int. Press Inst. 1973; mem. Admin. Council Fondation Nat. des Sciences Politiques 1973–93; Prof. Inst. d'Etudes Politiques, Univ. of Paris and Ecole Nat. d'Admin 1967–88; mem. Haut Conseil de l'audiovisuel 1973–82; fmr mem. Comm. de la République Française pour l'UNESCO; Commdr, Légion d'honneur, Croix de guerre, Rosette de la Résistance, Médaille des évadés. *Publications:* Le sentiment de l'existence chez Maine de Biran 1943, Notions élémentaires de psychologie 1947, L'organisation actuelle de la presse française 1955, Information et publicité 1956, L'information économique, clé de la prospérité 1963, Chemins Faisant (two vols) 2004, La route de chaque jour me suffit 2006. *Leisure interests:* yachting, skiing, gardening. *Address:* c/o Jaques André Editeur, Edition Cei, 5 Rue Bugeaud, 69006 Lyon (office); 4 rue Berlioz, 75116 Paris, France (home).

SALMOND, Alex Elliot Anderson, MA; British politician; *First Minister of Scotland;* b. 31 Dec. 1954, Linlithgow, Scotland; s. of Robert F. Salmond and Mary S. Milne; m. Moira McGlashan; ed Linlithgow Acad., St Andrews Univ.; Vice-Pres. Fed. of Student Nationalists 1974–77, St Andrews Univ. Students' Rep. Council 1977–78, Founder-mem. Scottish Nat. Party (SNP) 79 Group 1979, mem. SNP Nat. Exec. Cttee 1981–82, 1983–, SNP Exec. Vice Convener for Publicity 1985–87, SNP Nat. Convener (Leader) 1990–2000, 2004–; Asst Economist, Dept of Agric. and Fisheries 1978–80; Economist, Bank of Scotland 1980–87; MP for Banff and Buchan 1987–, SNP Parl. Spokesperson on Constitution and Fishing 1997–99; MSP for Banff and Buchan 1999–2001; First Minister of the Scotland 2007–; Visiting Prof. of Econs, Univ. of Strathclyde. *Leisure interests:* golf, reading. *Address:* Office of the First Minister, The Scottish Parliament, Edinburgh, EH99 1SP (office); 17 Maiden Street, Peterhead, Aberdeenshire, AB42 1EE, Scotland (office). *Telephone:* (1779) 470444 (Constituency Office) (office); (131) 348-5000 (Edinburgh) (office). *Fax:* (1779) 474460 (office); (131) 348-5601 (office). *E-mail:* firstminister@scotland.gsi.gov.uk (office); alex.salmond.msp@scottish.parliament.uk (office). *Website:* www.snp.org (office); www.scottish.parliament.uk (office).

SALOLAINEN, Pertti Edvard, MSc(Econ); Finnish diplomatist and politician; b. 19 Oct. 1940, Helsinki; s. of Edvard Paavali Salolainen and Ella Elisabeth Salolainen; m. Anja Sonninen 1964 (died 2005); one s. one d.; ed Helsinki School of Econs; TV journalist, Finnish Broadcasting Co. 1962–65, producer 1965–66, corresp. in London 1966–69, mem. Working Cttee, Supervisory Bd 1970–87; journalist, BBC, London 1966; Head of Dept, Finnish Employers' Confed. 1969–89; mem. Parl. 1970–96, 2007–, Chair. Foreign Affairs Cttee 2007–; Minister for Foreign Trade 1987–95; Deputy Prime Minister 1991–95; Head, negotiating team for entry of Finland into EU 1993–95, negotiating team of GATT (Uruguay Round); Amb. to UK 1996–2004; Chair. Finance Cttee IPU 1982–87; Hon. Founder Worldwide Fund for Nature Finland 1972; mem. Supervisory Bd's Working Cttee Outokumpu Mining Co. 1979–91; mem. Supervisory Bd Suomi-Salama Insurance Co. 1980–91, Finnair 1995–2002; mem. Legal Cttee Nordic Council 1982–87; Freeman of City of London 1998; holds mil. rank of Maj.; several solo exhbns of art and photographs in Finland, Germany and UK; Nat. Coalition Party (Leader 1991–94); Grand Cross of the Lion of Finland 1994, Grand Cross of the Nordstjerna Order (Sweden) 1996; Grand Cross of the FRG, of Hungary, of Austria, of Estonia (Maaria Maa); Medal of Merit, Finnish Defence Force 1997; Int. Conservation Award, Worldwide Fund for Nature, Gold Medal of Merit, Finnish Asscn for Nature Conservation. *Leisure interests:* nature conservation, photography, sports, tennis, swimming. *Address:* Parliament of Finland, 00100 Helsinki, Finland. *Telephone:* (50) 5122270 (office). *E-mail:* pertti.salolainen@eduskunta.fi (office). *Website:* web.eduskunta.fi (office).

SALOMÃO, Tomaz Augusto, BA MA; Mozambican international organization official; *Executive Secretary, Southern African Development Community;* b. 16 Oct. 1954, Inhambane Prov.; m.; ed Commercial and Industrial School Vasca da Gama-Inhambane, Commercial Inst. of Lurenco Marques, Eduardo Mondlane Univ.; expert for study unit of Montepio Savings Bank of Mozambique 1974–76; expert at Ministry of Industry and Trade 1976–78; head of production unit at CIFEL 1978–81; Sec. of State for Nat. Defence 1983–89; lecturer Eduardo Mondlane Univ. 1990–93; Deputy-Minister of Planning and Finance 1990–94, Minister of Planning and Finance, Gov. for Mozambique at African Devt Bank, IMF, World Bank 1994–99; Chair. SADC Transport and Communications Ministers' Cttee 2000–02, Chair. SADC Ministers' Cttee on ICTs 2002–03; Chair. African Union Ministers' Cttee on ICTs 2003–04; Minister of Transport and Communications of Mozambique 2000–04; Exec. Sec. SADC 2005–; mem. Ass. of the Repub. (Parl.) 2005–. *Leisure interests:* music, swimming, soccer, jogging, tennis, reading, gardening. *Address:* SADC House, Government Enclave, Private Bag 0095, Gaborone, Botswana. *Telephone:* 3951863 (office). *Fax:* 3972848 (office). *E-mail:* registry@sadc.int (office). *Website:* www.sadc.int (office).

SALONEN, Esa-Pekka, FRCM; Finnish conductor and composer; *Principal Conductor and Artistic Advisor, Philharmonia Orchestra;* b. 30 June 1958, Helsinki; ed Sibelius Acad., Helsinki, studied composition with Rautavaara and conducting with Panula, studied composition with Niccolò Castiglioni and Franco Donatoni in Italy; conducting debut with Finnish Radio Symphony Orchestra 1979; London conducting début with the Philharmonia Orchestra 1983, Prin. Guest Conductor, Philharmonia Orchestra 1984–94, Oslo Philharmonic Orchestra 1985–; Music Dir and The Walt and Lilly Disney Chair, Los Angeles Philharmonic Orchestra 1992–2009; Prin. Conductor and Artistic Adviser, Philharmonia Orchestra, London 2008–; Prin. Conductor Swedish Radio Symphony Orchestra 1985–95; Artistic Adviser, New Stockholm Chamber Orchestra 1986; Artistic Dir Helsinki Festival 1995–96; co-founder and Artistic Dir Baltic Sea Festival 2003–; Dr hc (Sibelius Acad.) 2003; Officier Ordre des Arts et des Lettres 1998; Siena Prize, Accad. Chigiana 1993, Royal Philharmonic Soc. Opera Award 1995, Litteris et Artibus Medal (Sweden) 1996, Royal Philharmonic Soc. Conductor Award 1997, Helsinki Medal 2005, Musical America Musician of the Year 2006. *Compositions:* orchestral: Concerto for alto saxophone and orchestra 1980–81, Giro 1982–97; chamber music: YTA I for alto flute 1985, YTA II for piano 1985, YTA III for cello 1986, FLOOF for soprano and chamber ensemble 1990, Mimo II 1992, LA Variations 1996, Gambit 1998, Five Images after Sappho 1999, Mania 2000, Foreign Bodies 2001. *Film appearance:* Sketches of Frank Gehry 2006. *Address:* c/o Van Walsum Management, 4 Addison Bridge Place, London W14 8XP, England (office); Philharmonia Orchestra, 6th Floor, The Tower Building, 11

York Road, London SE1 7NX, England (office). *Telephone:* (20) 7371-4343 (office); (20) 7921-3900 (office). *Fax:* (20) 7371-4344 (office); (20) 7921-3950 (office). *Website:* www.vanwalsum.com (office); www.philharmonia.co.uk (office). *E-mail:* orchestra@philharmonia.co.uk (office).

SALOUM, Nasir ibn Muhammad as-, PhD; Saudi Arabian engineer; b. 4 Nov. 1936, Medina; resident engineer, Ministry of Communications 1965; Head of Study Dept, Ministry of Communications 1965–68; Deputy Minister of Communications 1976–96, Minister 2000; Minister of Transport 1991–2000; mem. Bd of Saudi Arabian Railways Authority. *Leisure interests:* reading, travel. *Address:* c/o Ministry of Communications, Airport Road, Riyadh 11178, Saudi Arabia.

SALTANOV, Aleksander Vladimirovich; Russian diplomatist; *Deputy Minister of Foreign Affairs;* b. 14 Feb. 1946, Moscow; m.; two s.; ed Moscow State Inst. of Int. Relations; attaché, USSR Embassy, Kuwait 1970–74; attaché, Third then Second Sec., Dept of Near East and N Africa, Ministry of Foreign Affairs 1974–79, Counsellor, Head of Sector, then Head of Div. 1986–92, Dir of Dept 1999–2001; Consul then Gen., Consulate in Aleppo (Syria) 1979–83; First Sec. then Counsellor, USSR Embassy, Syria 1983–86; Amb. to Jordan 1992–98; Deputy Minister of Foreign Affairs 2001–. *Address:* Ministry of Foreign Affairs, Smolenskaya-Sennaya pl. 32–34, 119200 Moscow, Russia (office). *Telephone:* (495) 244-47-15 (office). *Fax:* (495) 244-92-39 (office). *E-mail:* saltanov@mid.ru (office). *Website:* www.mid.ru (office).

SALTER, John Rotherham, MA, CEnv, FCMI, FCIWM, FRGS, FRSA, ACIArb; British international business lawyer, solicitor and academic; *Visiting Professor of Law, Cranfield University;* b. 2 May 1932, London; s. of Herbert Salter and Nora Salter; m. Cynthia Brewer 1961; one s. two d.; ed Queen Elizabeth's School, Ashridge Coll., Lincoln Coll., Oxford and King's Coll. London; Lt RA 1951–53; partner, Denton Hall 1961–94, consultant 1994–99; Chair. Environmental Law Group 1994–98, Chair. Maj. Projects Group 1994–98; Vice-Chair. IBA Cttee of Energy and Natural Resources Law 1976–79, IBA Cttee on Int. Environmental Law 1979–82; Chair. North Sea Gas Gathering Consortium 1979–80; Chair. Section on Business Law, Int. Bar Asscn 1986–88; Chair. ABA Cttee on Int. Law 1993–95, Legal Issues Group of ISWA 1994–2000; Treas. Anglo-American Real Property Inst. 1985–86; Trustee, Petroleum Law Educ. Trust 1980–98, IBA Educ. Trust 1983–95; consultant, UNIDO 1983–84; Vice-Chair. ABA Cttee on Comparative Govt Law 1988–91; Chair. IBA Cttee on Oil and Gas Construction Law 1989–93; mem. Bd Int. Capital Markets Group 1987–89; mem. Law Soc.'s Planning Panel 1991–97; Legal Assoc., Royal Town Planning Inst. 1992–98; Chair. The Silver Soc. 1986–87, The Care Foundation 1994–2001, Hospice in the Weald 1994–2001, IBA Standing Cttee on UN and World Orgs (UNWOC) 1995–2000, Murray Soc. 1996–98; Pres. The Wine Label Circle 1986–87; Dir John Ray Initiative 1997–2004; mem. Soc. of Chemical Industry, London Chapter of Lamda Alpha Int., Advisory Cttee on Integrated Environmental Man. by Distance Learning, Bath Univ., Scientific and Tech. Cttee, ISWA 1994–2000; Visiting Fellow Cranfield Univ. 1993–, mem. of Court 1995–, Visiting Prof. of Law 1997–, Chair. Legislation and Policy Unit 2000–08; mem. Sr Common Room, Lincoln Coll., Oxford 1991–; mem. of Court Worshipful Co. of Fan-Makers 1997–, Tercentenary Master Fan Maker 2009; Pnr, John Salter & Assocs 1999–; mem. Advisory Panel, US Inst. of Peace 2001–08; Hon. Mem. Bar of Madrid 1987–, ISWA 2000–, ICC (UK) 2000–, IBA 2001–; Freeman of London and of Glasgow; Hon. Fellow Centre for Petroleum and Mineral Law and Policy, Univ. of Dundee. *Television appearances:* The Law is Yours series. *Publications:* Planning Law for Industry (co-author) 1981, UK Onshore Oil and Gas Law 1986, Corporate Environmental Responsibility – Law and Practice 1992; contrib. to UK Oil and Gas Law 1984, Halsbury's Laws of England (Vol. 58) 1986, Law of the European Communities 1986, Vaughan's Law of the European Communities Service 1990, Environment and Planning Law 1991, Frontiers of Environmental Law 1991, Directors' Guide to Environmental Issues 1992, European Community Energy Law 1994, European Environmental Law 1994, How to Understand an Act of Parliament (with D. J. Gifford) 1996, Understanding the English Legal System (with D. J. Gifford) 1997, Sauce Labels (1750–1950) 2002, Wine Labels (1730–2003) 2004; numerous articles in professional journals. *Leisure interests:* the arts, archaeology, sailing, tennis, bowls. *Address:* John Salter and Associates, 120 Oak Hill Road, Sevenoaks, Kent TN13 1NU (office); Jumpers Hatch, Oak Hill Road, Sevenoaks, Kent, TN13 1NU, England (home). *Telephone:* (1732) 458338 (office); (1732) 458388 (home). *Fax:* (870) 052-2008 (office); (1732) 458388 (home). *E-mail:* john_salter@sky.com (home). *Website:* fanmakers.com (office).

SALTYKOV, Boris Georgievich, C.ECON.SC.; Russian politician and economist; *President, Russian House of International Science and Technology Cooperation;* b. 27 Dec. 1940, Moscow; s. of Georgy Saltykov and Evdokia M. Saltykova (née Pukaleva); m. Lubov N. Klochkova 1972; two d.; ed Moscow Inst. of Physics and Tech.; researcher, Head of lab., Head of Div. Cen. Inst. of Econ. and Math. USSR (now Russian) Acad. of Sciences 1967–86; Head of Div. Inst. of Econ. and Forecasting of Progress in Science and Tech. (now Forecasting of Econ.) USSR Acad. of Sciences 1986–91; Deputy Dir Analytical Centre USSR Acad. of Sciences 1991; Minister of Science, Higher School and Tech. Policy of Russian Fed. 1991–92; Deputy Prime Minister of Russian Fed. 1992–93; Minister of Science and Tech. Policy 1993–96; Pres. Russian House of Int. Science and Tech. Cooperation 1996–; mem. State Duma (Parl.) 1993–95; Chair. Russian Comm. for UNESCO 1992–97; Dir-Gen. Fed. State Unitary Co. Russian Technologies 1998–2000; Hon. Foreign mem. American Acad. of Arts and Letters 1999–. *Leisure interest:* cars. *Address:* Russian House of International Science and Technology Cooperation, Bryusov per. 11, 125009 Moscow (office); Protochny per. 11, ap. 99, 121099 Moscow, Russia

(home). *Telephone:* (495) 229-58-40 (office); (495) 241-44-03 (home). *Fax:* (495) 200-32-77 (office); (495) 229-59-01. *E-mail:* bsaltykov@osi.ru (office).

SALVADOR CRESPO, María Isabel; Ecuadorean politician; b. 1962; Minister of Tourism 2005–07, of External Relations, Trade and Integration 2007–08 (resgnd). *Address:* c/o Ministry of External Relations, Trade and Integration, Avenida 10 de Agosto y Carrión, Quito, Ecuador (office).

SALVATORI, Carlo; Italian banking executive; *CEO, Unipol Gruppo Finanziario SpA;* b. 7 July 1941, Sora, Prov. of Frosinone; ed Univs of Bologna and Siena; began career with Banca Naz. del Lavoro (BNL); Deputy Gen. Man. Cassa di Risparmio di Parma 1980–87; Gen. Man. in charge of Business Devt Div., BNL 1987–90; Gen. Man., then Man.-Dir, Banco Ambrosiano Veneto 1990–96; Gen. Man. and Dir Cariplo 1996–98; Man.-Dir Banca Intesa 1998–2000; Chair. UniCredito Italiano SpA 2002–06; CEO Unipol Gruppo Finanziario 2006–; Chair. CreditRas Vita, CreditRas Assicurazioni; Deputy Chair. Mediobanca SpA –2006, Inst. for Int. Political Studies (IPSI); mem. Bd of Dirs Riunione Adriatica di Sicurtà (RAS), Abi, Ras; mem. Man. Bd and Gen. Council, Assonime. *Address:* Unipol Gruppo Finanziario SpA, Via Stalingrado 45, 40128 Bologna, Italy (office). *Telephone:* (051) 6097111 (office). *Fax:* (051) 375349 (office). *Website:* www.unipolonline.it (office).

SALZ, Anthony Michael Vaughan, LLB, FRSA; British lawyer; *Executive Vice-Chairman, N M Rothschild & Sons Limited;* b. 30 June 1950, Tavistock, Devon; s. of Michael H. Salz and Veronica Edith Dorothea Elizabeth Salz (née Hall); m. Sally Ruth Hagger 1975; one s. two d.; ed Summerfields School, Oxford, Radley Coll. and Univ. of Exeter; Articled Clerk, Kenneth Brown Baker Baker 1972–74, Asst Solicitor 1974–75; Asst Solicitor, Freshfields 1975–77, seconded to Davis Polk & Wardwell, New York 1977–78, Solicitor, Freshfields 1978–80, Partner 1980–96, Sr Partner 1996–2000, Co-Sr Pnr Freshfields Bruckhaus Deringer 2000–06; Vice-Chair. Bd of Govs, BBC 2004–06, Acting Chair. 2006; Exec. Vice-Chair. N M Rothschild & Sons (investment bank) 2006–; mem. Bd of Dirs Media Standards Trust 2007–; mem. Tate Gallery Corp. Advisory Group 1997– (Chair. 1997–2002); mem. Business Action on Homelessness Exec. Forum, Business in the Community (BITC) Nat. Educ. Leadership Team; Trustee Tate Foundation, Eden Project, Paul Hamlyn Foundation, St Brides Appeal, Habitat for Humanity GB. *Publications include:* contribs to various legal books and journals. *Leisure interests:* fishing, soccer, sports, theatre, arts. *Address:* N M Rothschild & Sons Limited, New Court Street, Swithin's Lane, London, EC4P 4DU, England (office). *Telephone:* (20) 7280-5000 (office). *Fax:* (20) 7929-1643 (office). *Website:* www.rothschild.com (office).

SALZA, Enrico; Italian banking executive; *Chairman of the Management Board, Intesa Sanpaolo SpA;* b. 1937, Turin; Deputy Chair. and CEO Il Sole 24 Ore 1971–89; Deputy Chair. Sanpaolo 1984–95; Dir and mem. Exec. Cttee Sanpaolo IMI SpA (now Intesa Sanpaolo SpA) 1998–2001, Deputy Chair. Man. Bd 2001–04, Chair. Sanpaolo IMI Group 2004–07, Chair. Man. Bd Intesa Sanpaolo SpA 2007–; CEO Cerved SpA –2002; Chair. Italconsult SpA; Founder and first Chair. Confindustria Young Entrepreneurs; fmr Chair. Turin Chamber of Commerce, Unioncamere Piemontese; Dir Centro Congressi Torino Incontra, Nomisma; fmr Dir Union Bank of Switzerland, Compagnia di San Paolo; mem. Bd Govs ICC; Hon. Chair. Associazione Sviluppo Scientifico e Tecnologico of Piedmont. *Address:* Intesa Sanpaolo SpA, Piazza San Carlo 156, 10121 Turin, Italy (office). *Telephone:* (011) 5551 (office). *Fax:* (011) 5557007 (office). *E-mail:* info@intesasanpaolo.it (office). *Website:* www.intesasanpaolo.it (office).

SAM-SUMANA, Samuel, BSc; Sierra Leonean business executive and politician; *Vice-President;* b. 17 April 1962, Koidu Town, Kono Dist; s. of the late Chief Sam-Sumana and Haja Sia Hawa Sam-Sumana; m.; three c.; ed Metropolitan State Univ., Minn., USA, America Inst. of Diamond Cutting and Polishing, Deerfield Beach, Fla, USA, Knollwood Computer and Business School, St Louis Park, Minn.; fmr System Officer of network support for Prudential Financial Group, USA; fmr Vice-Pres. Network Support System, Allina Health Services and Seagate Technologies, USA; served as Regional Man. for C-12 International, Tex., USA (co. engaged in diamond buying in Sierra Leone, Guinea and Liberia); fmr Man. Dir United Diamond Mining Co., Kodu Town, Kono Dist; CEO Aries Rehabilitation Construction and Supplies (ARCS) SL Ltd –2007; mem. All People's Congress party, mem. 'Five-Man Committee'; Vice-Pres. of Sierra Leone 2007–; Vice-Chair. Kono-Union Chapter USA, Minn. *Address:* c/o Office of the President, Tower Hill, Freetown, Sierra Leone (office). *Telephone:* (22) 22467 (office). *E-mail:* vicepresident@statehouse.gov.sl (office). *Website:* www.statehouse.gov.sl (office).

SAMA, Koffi, DMV; Togolese lawyer and politician; b. 1944, Amoutchou, Ogou Prefecture; m.; ed Lycée Bonnecarrère, Lomé and Ecole Nat. Vétérinaire de Toulouse, France; qualified as a vet 1972; Minister of Youth, Sport and Culture 1981–84; Dir-Gen. SOTOCO (Société Togolaise de Coton) 1990–96; Minister of Health 1996–99, of Nat. Educ. and Research 1999–2002; Prime Minister of Togo 2002–05; Special Advisor to Pres. 2005; mem. Rassemblement du peuple togolais—RPT (fmr Sec.-Gen.); Officier, Ordre de Mono, Grand Officier, Ordre du Mérite agricole. *Address:* c/o Rassemblement du peuple togolais (RPT), pl. de l'Indépendance, BP 1208, Lomé, Togo (office).

SAMAK, Sundaravej; Thai politician; b. 13 June 1935, Bangkok; m. Khunying Surat Sundaravej; two c.; ed Thammasat Univ.; mem. Democratic Party 1968–76; mem. Parl. 1973–76, 1979–83, 1986–90, 1992–2000, 2007–; Deputy Minister of Agriculture 1975–76, Deputy Minister of Interior 1976, Minister of Interior 1976–77, of Transport 1983–86, 1990–91; Founder and Leader Prachakorn Thai party 1979–2000; Deputy Prime Minister 1992; Gov. of Bangkok 2000–03; presenter of tv talk shows Chao Nee Tee Muang Thai (This Morning in Thailand), Samak Dusit Kid Tam Wan (Daily Views) and radio talk show Kho Tet Ching Wan Ni (The Facts of Today) 2006, also presenter TV cooking show Tasting, Grumbling 2001–; Founder and Leader People Power Party (PPP) (Palang Prachachan) 2007–; Prime Minister Feb.–Sept. 2008, stripped of post after Constitutional Court unanimously ruled that he violated country's constitution by taking part in TV cooking show. *Address:* People Power Party (PPP) (Palang Prachachan), 1770 Thanon Petchaburi Tat Mai, Bang Gapi, Huay Kwang, Bangkok 10310, Thailand (office). *Telephone:* (2) 686–7000 (office). *Website:* www.ppp.or.th (office).

SAMAKUVA, Isaias; Angolan politician; *President, União Nacional para a Independência Total de Angola (UNITA);* b. 8 July 1946, Cunje; fmr Treas., União Nacional para a Independência Total de Angola (UNITA), Chief of Logistics mid-1980s, Rep. in Paris 1998–2002, fmr Interim Leader, Pres. 2003–. *Address:* União Nacional para a Independência Total de Angola (UNITA), Luanda, Angola. *Website:* www.kwacha.net; www.samakuva.com.

SAMAR, Sima, DMed; Afghan politician, physician and human rights activist; *Chairperson, Afghanistan Independent Human Rights Commission;* b. Feb. 1957, Jaghori, Ghazni; ed Kabul Univ.; exiled in Pakistan following Soviet invasion; Founder and Dir Shuhada Org., f. Shuhada hosp. for Afghan women and children, Quetta, Pakistan 1989, founder of three medical clinics, four hosps and girls' schools in rural Afghanistan (also providing medical training, literacy programmes and food aid), f. school for refugee girls in Quetta, f. Shuhada Org.; mem. Women Living Under Muslim Law; political activist and opponent of women's subjugation under Taliban regime; Vice-Chair. and Minister of Women's Affairs, Afghan Interim Admin 2001–02; currently Chair. Afghanistan Ind. Human Rights Comm.; UN Special Rapporteur for Human Rights in Sudan 2005–; Hon. LLD (Univ. of Alberta) 2004; Hon. DHumLitt (Brown Univ.) 2005; Community Leadership Award, Ramon Magsaysay Award Foundation 1994, Global Leader for Tomorrow, World Econ. Forum 1995, 100 Heroines Award 1998, Paul Gruniger Human Rights Award 2001, Voice of Courage Award, Women's Comm. for Refugee Women and Children 2001, John Humphrey Freedom Award 2001, Women of the Month, Canada 2001, Women of the Year (on behalf of the Afghan Women), Ms. Magazine 2001, Best Social Worker, Mailo Trust Foundation, Pakistan 2001, Int. Human Rights Award, Int. Human Rights Law Group 2002, Freedom Award, Women's Asscn for Freedom and Democracy, Spain 2002, Lawyers Cttee for Human Rights Award 2002, Silver Banner Award, Italy 2002, Women for Peace, Together for Peace Foundation, Rome 2002, Silver Rose Award, Brussels 2003, Perdita Huston Human Rights Award 2003, UN Asscn of the Nat. Capital Area 2003, Jonathan Mann Award for Health and Human Rights 2004, Profile in Courage Award 2004, Paul Schiller Stiftung Award 2004, Global Women's Rights Award 2007, Ypres Peace Prize 2008, Asia Democracy and Human Rights Award 2008, ranked by Forbes magazine amongst 100 Most Powerful Women (74th) 2004, (28th) 2006, (92nd) 2007. *Address:* Afghanistan Independent Human Rights Commission, Pul-i-Surkh, Karti 3, Kabul (office); Shura Street, Karte3, Close to Katib University, District 6th, Kabul, Afghanistan (home). *Telephone:* (20) 2500676 (office); (70) 276283. *Fax:* (20) 2500677 (office). *E-mail:* aihrc@aihrc.org.af (office); sima_samar@yahoo.com (home). *Website:* www.aihrc.org.af (office).

SAMARANCH TORELLO, Marqués de Samaranch; **Juan Antonio;** Spanish diplomatist and international sports official; *Honorary President, International Olympic Committee;* b. 17 July 1920, Barcelona; s. of Francisco Samaranch and Juana Torello; m. María Teresa Salisachs Rowe 1955 (died 2000); one s. one d.; ed German Coll., Higher Inst. of Business Studies, Barcelona; mem. Spanish Olympic Cttee 1954–, Pres. 1967–70; mem. IOC 1966, Vice-Pres. 1974–78, Pres. 1980–2001, Hon. Pres. 2001–; Amb. to USSR (also accred to Mongolia) 1977–80; fmr Chair. La Caixa (savings bank), now Hon. Chair., Pres. Int. Boat Show, now Hon. Pres.; numerous decorations from many countries; Dr hc; Seoul Peace Prize 1990. *Leisure interests:* philately, art. *Address:* Avda Diagonal 520, 08006 Barcelona, (office); Avda Pau Casals, 24, 08021 Barcelona, Spain (home). *Telephone:* (93) 2003560 (office). *Fax:* (93) 4145931 (office). *E-mail:* jasamaranch@jas-sl.com (office).

SAMARAS, Antonis C., BA (Econs), MBA; Greek politician; *Minister of Culture;* b. 23 May 1951, Athens; s. of Constantinos Samaras and Eleni Samaras; m. Georgia Kritikou 1990; one s. one d.; ed Amherst Coll., Harvard Business School, USA; mem. Parl. for Messinia 1977–; Minister of Finance 1989, of Foreign Affairs 1989–90, 1990–92; Founder-Pres. Politiki Anixi Party (POLAN) 1993–2002; joined New Democracy party 2002; MEP 2004–07 (resgnd); mem. Parl. for Messinia 2007–; Minister of Culture 2009–. *Leisure interests:* tennis, swimming, music, poetry, reading. *Address:* Ministry of Culture, Odos Bouboulinas 42, 106 82 Athens (office); 10 Mourouzi Street, Athens 10674, Greece. *Telephone:* (210) 8894800 (office). *Fax:* (210) 8894805 (office). *E-mail:* dpse@hch.culture.gr (office). *Website:* www.culture.gr (office).

SAMARASEKERA, Indira V., OC, PhD, FRSC, FCAE; Canadian (b. Sri Lankan) professor of metals and materials engineering and university administrator; *President and Vice-Chancellor, University of Alberta;* b. 1952, Colombo; two c.; ed Univ. of Ceylon, Univ. of Calif., USA, Univ. of BC, Canada; fmr mechanical engineer, Refinery of Ceylon Petroleum Corpn; emigrated to Canada 1977; fmr Hays-Fulbright Scholar; fmr Dir of Student Affairs, Minerals, Metals and Materials Soc. of AIME; apptd Prof. Dept of Metals and Materials Eng and Centre for Metallurgical Process Eng, Univ. of BC 1980, first Dofasco Chair in Advanced Steel Processing 1996, Vice-Pres. Research 2000–05; Pres. and Vice-Chancellor Univ. of Alberta 2005–; mem. Bd of Dirs Discovery Parks Inc., Genome BC, Canadian Microelectronics Corpn, Michael Smith Foundation for Health Research, The Stem Cell Network, Canadian Genetics Diseases Network, Provincial Health Services Authority; mem. Science and Eng Advisory Cttee, Alberta Ingenuity Fund, Presidential Advisory Cttee, MIT, Carnegie Mellon Univ.; Vice-Chair. UNESCO Forum Scientific Cttee for Europe and N America; fmr Pres. Metallurgical Soc. of CIM; fmr mem. Nat. Research Council of Canada, Nat. Advisory Bd on Minerals and Metals, BC Research Inst. for Children and Women's Health, Killam Selection Cttee for Canada Council for the Arts, Int. Review Cttee for Ontario Challenge Fund, Aquanet-NCE; fmr mem. Bd Children and Women's Health Center of BC, TRIUMF; E.W.R. Steacie Fellow 1991; Iron and Steel Soc. of AIME Robert W. Hunt and Charles H. Herty Best Paper Awards (jtly), UK Materials Soc. Williams Prize and Ablett Prize, TMS Extraction and Processing Technology Award, Univ. of BC Killam Prize and McDowell Medal for research excellence, BC Science Council Award for New Frontiers in Research. *Address:* Office of the President, 3-1 University Hall, University of Alberta, Edmonton, Alberta T6G 2J9, Canada (office). *Telephone:* (780) 492-3212 (office). *Fax:* (780) 492-9265 (office). *E-mail:* president@ualberta.ca (office). *Website:* www.president.ualberta.ca (office).

SAMARAWEERA, Mangala; Sri Lankan politician; *Leader, Sri Lanka Freedom Party—Mahajana Wing (SLFP—M);* b. 21 April 1956; s. of Mahanama Samaraweera and Khema Samaraweera; ed St Martin's School of Art, London, UK; fmr Design Consultant Nat. Design Centre of Sri Lanka; Organizer for Matara, Sri Lanka Freedom Party (SLFP) 1983–, Chief Opposition Whip and Treas. SLFP 2002–04, currently Asst Sec.; mem. Parl. 1989–; fmr Minister of Post and Telecommunications, of Urban Devt, Construction and Public Utilities; fmr Deputy Minister of Finance; Minister of Ports, Aviation, Information and Media and Deputy Minister of Educ. –2005; Minister of Foreign Affairs 2005–07, of Ports and Aviation 2005–07; f. Sri Lanka Freedom Party—Mahajana Wing (SLFP—M) 2007, Leader 2007–; exec. mem. UNESCO. *Address:* Sri Lanka Freedom Party—Mahajana Wing (SLFP—M), Colombo 1, Sri Lanka (office).

SAMARDŽIC, Vice Adm. Dragan; Montenegrin naval officer and government official; *Chief of the General Staff of the Army of Montenegro;* b. 14 May 1963, Kotor; m. Branka Samardžic; one s. one d.; ed Naval Acad., Gen. Staff School, War Coll., Belgrade; commissioned as Ensign in Montenegrin Navy, served aboard 401-type missile gun boats as Weapons Officer, XO, CO and Commdr of Squadron 1985–95; various positions in 18th Flotilla HQ including Chief of Staff and Deputy Flotilla Commdr 1995–2001, Flotilla Commdr 2001–03; Deputy of Mil. Cabinet to Pres. of State Union of Serbia and Montenegro, Belgrade 2003; Chief of Staff Naval Corps and promoted to Flag Officer 2003–05; C-in-C Serbia and Montenegro Navy 2005–06; Deputy Chief of Gen. Staff of the Army of Montenegro 2006–07; Asst Minister for Material Resources, Ministry of Defense 2007–08; Chief of the Gen. Staff of the Army of Montenegro 2008–; Cavaliere dell ordine al merito della erpubblica italiana; numerous decorations from Montenegrin govt. *Address:* Ministry of Defense, Jovana Tomasevica 29, 81000 Podgorica, Montenegro (office). *Telephone:* (81) 483561 (home). *Fax:* (81) 224702 (office). *E-mail:* kabinet@mod.cg.yu (office). *Website:* www.vlada.cg.yu/odbrana (office); www.vcg.cg.yu (office).

SAMATER, Gen. Mohammed Ali; Somali politician and army officer; b. 1931, Chisimaio; ed Intermediate School, Mogadishu, Mil. Acad., Rome, Mil. Acad., Moscow; Commdt Somali Police 1956, Maj.-Adjutant 1958–65; Brig.-Gen. Nat. Army 1967, Maj.-Gen. 1973; Sec. of State for Defence 1971–76, C-in-C Armed Forces 1971–78; fmr Vice-Pres. Political Bureau, Somali Socialist Revolutionary Party; Minister of Defence 1976–81, 1982–89; First Vice-Pres. Supreme Revolutionary Council (now Council of Ministers) 1982–90; Prime Minister of Somalia 1987–90; Chair. Defence and Security Cttee, Supreme Council of the Revolution 1980–82, Vice-Pres. of Council 1981–82.

SAMBI, Ahmed Abdallah; Comoran politician, business executive and head of state; *President;* b. 5 June 1958, Mutsamudu, Anjuouan; m. Hadjira Djoudi 1988; two s. five d.; ed in Saudi Arabia, Sudan and Hawzat Al Qaaim Coll., Iran; f. madras for girls 1986, imprisoned for 21 days following riot after closure of school by authorities in 1987; co-f. Ulézi Radio and TV Ulézi 1990; co-f. National Front for Justice Party 1990, soon left politics to concentrate on business activities; owner of factories producing mattresses, bottled water, and perfume; Pres. of Comoros 2006–. *Leisure interests:* basketball, football, tennis. *Address:* Office of the Head of State, BP 521, Moroni, The Comoros (office). *Telephone:* (74) 4808 (office). *Fax:* (74) 4829 (office). *Website:* www.beit-salam.km (office).

SAMBROOK, Richard, BA, MSc; British media executive; *Director, World Service and Global News Division, BBC;* b. 24 April 1956, Canterbury; m.; two c.; ed Oakwood Grammar School, Maidstone, Reading Univ., Birkbeck Coll. London Univ.; trainee journalist Thomson Regional Newspapers 1977; spent three years with Celtic Press in Welsh Valleys and South Wales Echo; joined BBC as sub-ed. in radio newsroom 1980, later producer and programme ed. on nat. TV news, sr producer and deputy ed. Nine O'Clock News, News Ed. BBC Newsgathering 1992–96, Head of Newsgathering 1996–99, Deputy Dir News Div. 1999–2001, Dir BBC News 2001–04, Dir World Service and Global News Div. 2004–. *Address:* BBC World Ltd, Woodlands, 80 Wood Lane, London, W12 0TT, England (office). *Telephone:* (20) 8433-2000 (office). *Fax:* (20) 8743-9256 (office). *Website:* bbcworld.com (office).

SAMBU, Soares; Guinea-Bissau politician; *Minister of Natural Resources;* Pres. Cttee on Agric., Fisheries, Natural Resources, Environment and Tourism 1997–98; mem. Cen. Cttee Partido Africano da Independência da Guiné e Cabo Verde (PAIGC), fmr Dir election campaign; mem. Nat. Ass., Deputy Speaker –2003; Minister of Foreign Affairs, Int. Co-operation and Communities 2004–05, of Natural Resources 2007–. *Address:* Ministry of Natural Resources, CP 311, Bissau, Guinea-Bissau (office). *Telephone:* 215659 (office). *Fax:* 223149 (office).

SAMHAN, Mohammad Jasim, MA, MScS; United Arab Emirates diplomatist; b. 1950, Ras Al Khaimah; m.; four c.; ed Goddard Coll. and Syracuse Univ., USA; worked for Dept of Water and Electricity 1966–68, with Nat. Oil Co. 1972–74; joined diplomatic corps 1974, with Consulate in Karachi 1975, then with del. to UN, rank of Counsellor 1981, with Consulate in Bombay 1981, rank of Minister Plenipotentiary; Dir Dept of Int. Orgs and Confs, Arab League 1982–84, Dept of Arab Homeland 1984–87, UAE Interests section Feb.–Nov. 1987; Perm. Rep. to Arab League 1988–90, also Amb. to Tunisia 1988–92; Perm. Rep. to UN, New York 1992–2001. *Address:* c/o Ministry of Foreign Affairs, POB 1, Abu Dhabi, United Arab Emirates.

SAMIOS, Nicholas Peter, PhD; American physicist and academic; *Director, RIKEN BNL Research Center, Brookhaven National Laboratory;* b. 15 March 1932, New York; s. of Peter Samios and Niki Samios; m. Mary Linakis 1958; two s. one d.; ed Columbia Coll., Columbia Univ., New York; Instructor, Dept of Physics, Columbia Univ. 1956–59, Adjunct Prof. 1970–; Asst Physicist Brookhaven Nat. Lab. Dept of Physics 1959–62, Assoc. Physicist 1962–64, Physicist 1964–68, Group Leader 1965–75, Sr Physicist 1968–, Chair. Div. of Particles and Fields 1975–76, Chair. PEP Experimental Program Cttee (of SLAC & LBL) 1976–78, Chair. Dept of Physics 1975–81, Deputy Dir 1981, Acting Dir 1982, Dir 1982–97, Deputy Dir RIKEN BNL Research Center 1998–, now Dir; Adjunct Prof., Stevens Inst. of Tech. 1969–75; mem. Bd Dirs Stony Brook Foundation 1989, Adelphi 1989–97, Long Island Asscn 1990–97; mem., fmr mem. or fmr chair. numerous specialist cttees and bds; Corresp. mem. Akademia Athenon 1994–; mem. NAS; Fellow, American Physical Soc. 1964 (mem. Exec. Cttee 1976–77), American Acad. of Arts and Sciences; E.O. Lawrence Memorial Award 1980, New York Acad. of Sciences Award in Physical and Math. Sciences 1980, AUI Distinguished Scientist 1992, W.K.H. Panofsky Prize 1993, Bruno Pontecorvo Prize, Jt Inst. for Nuclear Research, Moscow 2001. *Address:* RIKEN BNL Research Center, Building 510A, Room 1-70, Physics Department, Brookhaven National Laboratory, Upton, NY 11973-5000, USA (office). *Telephone:* (631) 344-6281 (office). *Fax:* (631) 344-4906 (office). *E-mail:* samios@bnl.gov (office). *Website:* www.bnl.gov/riken (office).

SAMMONS, Mary F., BA; American retail executive; *Chairman and CEO, Rite Aid Corporation;* b. 1947, Portland, Ore.; ed Maryhurst Coll.; began career with Fred Meyer Inc. 1973, sr positions in all areas of operations and merchandising, Pres. and CEO Fred Meyer Stores (food, drug and gen. merchandise retailer) –1999; Pres. and COO Rite Aid Corpn 1999–2003, mem. Bd of Dirs, Pres. and CEO 2003–08, Chair. 2007–, CEO 2008–, Pres. The Rite Aid Foundation; Chair. Nat. Asscn of Chain Drug Stores 2003–; mem. Bd of Dirs First Horizon Nat. Corpn; mem. Exec. Cttee Nat. Asscn of Chain Drug Stores; ranked by Fortune magazine amongst 50 Most Powerful Women in Business in the US (37th) 2003, (33rd) 2004, (39th) 2005, (34th) 2006, (35th) 2007, ranked by Forbes magazine amongst 100 Most Powerful Women (40th) 2004, (27th) 2005, (16th) 2006, (15th) 2007, (18th) 2008. *Address:* Rite Aid Corpn, PO Box 3165, Harrisburg, PA 17105 (office); Rite Aid Corpn, 30 Hunter Lane, Camp Hill, PA 17011, USA (office). *Telephone:* (717) 761-2633 (office). *Fax:* (717) 975-5871 (office). *E-mail:* contacttheboard@riteaid.com (office). *Website:* www.riteaid.com (office).

SAMMUT, Salv; Maltese trade union official; *President, General Workers' Union;* b. 4 March 1947, Lija; m.; two s. one d.; ed Diploma in Social Studies and Industrial Relations, Univ. of Malta; mem. Nat. Comm. for Health and Safety 1994, Bd Health and Safety Authority 2001; Vice-Pres. General Workers' Union (GWU) 1999–2001, Pres. 2001–, represents GWU at int. congresses and confs relating to EU issues on matters dealing with trade unions; mem. EU Advisory Cttee on Health and Safety; substitute mem. Bilbao Agency on Health and Safety. *Radio:* readings of two novels and several short stories and poems have been broadcast. *Publications include:* book of poetry (second place, Prize of the Year nat. award). *Leisure interests:* reading, writing literature. *Address:* The General Workers' Union, Workers' Memorial Building, South Street, Valletta, VLT 11 (office); The Quest, Maisonette 2, Block R, Mtarfa, RBT 10, Malta (home). *Telephone:* 21244300 (office); 21454903 (home). *Fax:* 21234911 (office). *E-mail:* ssammut@gwu.org.mt (office); sammutsalv@hotmail.com (home). *Website:* www.gwu.org.mt (office).

SAMOILOVA, Tatyana Yevgeniyevna; Russian film actress; b. 4 May 1934, Leningrad; d. of Eugeniy V. Samoilov and Zinaida I. Levina-Samoilova; one s.; ed Shchukin Theatre School; Merited Artist of the RSFSR, Order of the Badge of Honour; Special Prize for personal creative achievements in cinematography 1990. *Films:* The Mexican 1955, Letyat zhuravli (The Cranes are Flying) (Cannes Festival Palm Award) 1957, Neotpravlennoye pismo (The Unsent Letter) 1959, Leon Garros ishchet druga (Leon Garros Looks for a Friend) 1960, Alba Regia 1961, They Went East 1964, Italiani brava gente (Attack and Retreat) 1965, Anna Karenina 1968, A Long Way to a Short Day 1972, Vozvrata net (No Return) 1973, Okean (Ocean) 1974, Brillianty dlya diktatury proletariata (Jewels for the Dictatorship of the Proletariat) 1975, 24 chasa (24 hours) 2000. *Television:* Moskovskaya saga 2004. *Address:* Spiridonyevsky per. 8/11, 103104 Moscow, Russia. *Telephone:* (495) 254-34-68.

SAMPAIO, Jorge Fernando Branco de; Portuguese fmr head of state; b. 18 Sept. 1939; m. Maria José Ritta; one s. one d.; leader of students union and led protests against govt as student in Lisbon 1960–61; following graduation as lawyer defended several political prisoners; fmr mem. Socialist Left Movt then joined Socialist Party (PS), elected deputy Portugeuse Nat. Parl. 1979, Pres. Parl. Bench 1986–87, Sec.-Gen. 1989–91; mem. European Comm. for Human Rights 1979–84; Mayor of Lisbon 1989–95; Pres. of Portugal 1996–2006; UN Special Envoy to Stop Tuberculosis 2006–07; UN High Rep. to the Alliance of Civilizations 2007–. *Leisure interests:* music, golf. *Address:* Alliance of Civilizations, c/o United Nations, New York, NY 10017, USA (office). *Telephone:* (917) 367-5118 (office). *E-mail:* ContactAOC@unops.org (office). *Website:* www.unaoc.org (office).

SAMPEDRO, José Luis; Spanish fmr economist and novelist; b. 1 Feb. 1917, Barcelona; s. of Luis Sampedro and Matilde Saez; m. 1st Isabel Pellicer Iturrioz 1944 (deceased); one d.; m. 2nd Olga Lucas 2003; ed Madrid Univ.; Civil Service, Ministry of Finance 1935–50, 1957–62; Asst Prof. of Econ. Structure, Madrid Univ. 1947–55, Prof. 1955–69; Economist, Ministry of Commerce 1951–57; Adviser to Spanish Del. to UN 1956–58; Special Prof. of Econ. Sociology, Madrid Univ. 1962–65; Asst Gen. Dir Banco Exterior de España 1962–69; Visiting Prof. Univ. of Salford 1969–70, Univ. of Liverpool 1970–71; Econ. Adviser Customs Bureau, Ministry of Finance 1971–79; nominated mem. Senate 1977–79; Econ. Adviser Banco Exterior de España 1979–81; Vice-Pres. Fundación Banco Exterior de España 1981–84; mem. Real Academia Española 1990; Spanish Nat. Award for new playwrights 1950, Nat. Gold Medal for Fine Arts 2005, Gold Medal, Madrid City. *Publications:* Economics: Principles of Industrial Location 1954, Effects of European Economic Integration 1957, Economic Reality and Structural Analysis 1958, The European Future of Spain 1960, Regional Profiles of Spain 1964, Decisive Forces in World Economics 1967, Economic Structure 1969, Conscience of Underdevelopment 1973, Inflation Unabridged 1976, El Mercado y la Globalización 2002; Fiction: Congreso en Estocolmo 1952, El Río que nos lleva 1962, El Caballo Desnudo 1970, Octubre, Octubre 1981, La Sonrisa Etrusca 1985, La Vieja Sirena 1990, Mar al Fondo 1993, Mientras la Tierra Gira 1993, Real Sitio 1993, La Estatua de Adolfo Espejo 1994, La Sombra de los Días 1994, Fronteras 1995, El Amante Lesbiano 2000, Los Mongoles en Bagdad 2003; plays: La Paloma de Cartón 1950, Un sitio para vivir 1956. *Leisure interest:* human communication. *Address:* Cea Bermúdez 51, 28003 Madrid, Spain. *Telephone:* (91) 5442860. *Website:* www.clubcultura.com/clubliteratura/clubescritores/sampedro.

SAMPER GNECCO, Armando; Colombian agricultural economist; b. 9 April 1920, Bogotá; s. of the late Daniel Samper Ortega and of Mayita Gnecco de Samper; m. Jean K. de Samper 1945; two s. two d.; ed Cornell Univ., USA; research and teaching posts in agricultural econs, Colombia 1943–49; Inter-American Inst. of Agricultural Sciences of OAS, Turrialba, Costa Rica 1949–69, Head of Scientific Communications Service 1949–54, Dir of Regional Services 1955–60, Dir of Inst. 1960–69, Dir Emer. 1969–; Visiting Prof., Univ. of Chicago 1954–55; Minister of Agric. 1966–67, 1969–70; Agricultural Adviser, Banco de la República, Bogotá 1970–72; Chancellor Univ. de Bogotá 1971; FAO Asst Dir-Gen. for Latin American Affairs, Santiago, Chile 1972–74; Pres. Nat. Corpn for Forestry Research and Devt (CONIF), Bogotá 1975–77, Consultant Delsa Ltd 1978–92; Dir-Gen. Colombian Sugar Cane Research Centre (Cenicaña) 1978–90, Dir Emer. 1990–; consultant COLCIENCIAS 1990–91; mem. Bd Int. Centre of Tropical Agriculture 1967–76 (Chair. 1973–76, Chair. Emer. 1976–), Foundation for Higher Educ. 1978–95 (Chair. 1984–89), UN Science and Tech. Cttee 1981–83, Nat. Council of Science and Tech. 1982–86, Gimnasio Moderno 1989–, Oil Palm Research Center 1991–, Aquaculture Research Centre 1993–; Chair. Emer., Colombian Program for the Admin of Agric. Research 1990–; Vice-Chair. Bd Colombian Corpn for Agric. Research 1993–94; mem. Nat. Acad. Econ. Sciences 1984–. *Publications:* Importancia del Café en el Comercio Exterior de Colombia 1948, Desarrollo Institucional y Desarrollo Agrícola (3 Vols) 1969, El Cuatrenio de la Transformación Rural 1966–70, Los Estudios Microeconómicos en Colombia 1988, Evolución de la Investigación en Caña de Azúcar en el Valle del Cauca 1930–79 1998. *Address:* Apartado Aéreo 100-286, Santa Fe de Bogotá, Colombia. *Telephone:* (1) 611-0941 (office). *Fax:* (1) 616-4813.

SAMPERMANS, Françoise, LèsL; French business executive; *Publishing Consultant and Director, UPM-Kymmene;* b. 10 July 1947, Paris; d. of Jacques Durand and Jeannine Behot; one s. one d.; joined CIT-TRANSAC 1974; est. public relations service, Chapelle Darblay 1978; Head of Public Relations, Entreprise et Crédit 1981; Dir of Communications, Transmission, Group Thomson 1982; subsequently Deputy Dir, Dir of Communications, Alcatel CIT; Dir of Communications, Alcatel NV 1987, Alcatel Alsthom 1987; Dir-Gen. Générale Occidentale 1991–95; Pres. Dir-Gen. Groupe Express 1992–95; Vice-Pres. Québecor-Europe 1996–; Pres., Dir-Gen. Nouvel Economiste 1999–; Dir-Gen. Marianne and L'Evènement du Jeudi 1999–; Vice-Pres. Nouvelles Messageries de la Presse Parisienne 2000–04; mem. Bd UPM-Kymmene (Finland), currently Publishing Consultant, Dir; mem. Bd DATEM (France); Chevalier, Ordre des Arts et des Lettres. *Address:* 18 rue Charles Silvestri, 94300 Vincennes, France.

SAMPHAN, Khieu (see Khieu Samphan).

SAMPLE, Steven Browning, BS, MS, PhD; American electrical engineer and university administrator; *President, University of Southern California;* b. 29 Nov. 1940, St Louis; m. Kathryn Sample (neé Brunkow); two d.; ed Univ. of Illinois, Urbana-Champaign; Sr Scientist, Melpar Inc., Falls Church, Va 1965–66; Assoc. Prof. of Electrical Eng, Purdue Univ. 1966–73; Deputy Dir Ill. Bd of Higher Educ., Springfield 1971–74; Exec. Vice Pres. of Academic Affairs, Dean Grad. Coll. and Prof. of Electrical Eng, Univ. of Neb. 1974–82; Prof. of Electrical and Computer Eng and Pres. State Univ. of New York, Buffalo 1982–91; Pres. Univ. of Southern Calif. 1991–, holder, Robert C. Packard Pres.'s Chair; Co-founder Asscn of Pacific Rim Univs; fmr Chair. Asscn of American Univs (AAU); Fellow, Nat. Acad. of Eng 1998–, American Acad. of Arts and Sciences 2003–; Dr hc (Canisius Coll., Buffalo) 1989, (Sheffield, UK) 1991, (Hebrew Union Coll.) 1994, (Purdue) 1994, (Neb.) 1995, (Northeastern) 2004, (Notre Dame) 2005, (State Univ. of NY, Buffalo) 2006; Los Angeles Area Chamber of Commerce Distinguished Business Leader Award, Central City Asscn of Los Angeles Heart of the City Award, Chancellor Charles P. Norton Medal, State Univ. of NY, Buffalo, Nat. Conference of Christians and Jews Humanitarian Award, Jewish Fed. Council of Greater Los Angeles Hollzer Memorial Award, Los Angeles Co. Econ. Devt Corpn Eddy Award, Alumni Achievement Award, Univ. of Illinois, Chancellor Charles P. Norton Medal, SUNY Buffalo 2004, IEEE Founders Award 2008. *Achievements include:* has licensed numerous patents in field of digital appliance controls to major manufacturers. *Publications:* The Contrarian's Guide to Leadership 2001;

numerous journal articles and published papers in science, eng and higher educ. *Address:* Office of the President, University of Southern California, Los Angeles, CA 90089, USA (office). *Telephone:* (213) 740-2111 (office). *Fax:* (213) 821-1342 (office). *Website:* www.usc.edu/president (office).

SAMPRAS, Pete; American fmr professional tennis player; b. 12 Aug. 1971, Washington, DC; s. of Sam Sampras and Georgia Sampras; m. Brigette Wilson 2000; one s.; turned professional 1988; holds men's record for most Grand Slam singles titles (14); US Open Champion 1990, 1993, 1995, 1996, 2002; Grand Slam Cup Winner 1990; IBM/ATP Tour World championship–Frankfurt Winner 1991; US Pro-Indoor Winner 1992; Wimbledon Singles Champion 1993, 1994, 1995, 1997, 1998, 1999, 2000; European Community Championships Winner 1993, 1994; ranked No. 1 1993–98 (record); winner Australian Open 1994; RCA Championships 1996, ATP Tour World Championships, 1996, Australian Open 1997; winner San José Open 1997, Philadelphia Open 1997, Cincinnatti Open 1997; Munich Open 1997, Paris Open 1997, Hanover Open 1997, Advanta Championship 1998; mem. US Davis Cup Team 1991, 1995; won 64 WTA Tour singles titles, two doubles titles and US \$ 43,280,489; Chair. ATP Tour Charities Programme 1992; investor, pnr and special consultant Tennis Magazine 2003–; Co-founder Pure Sports Management, LLC 2007; f. Acres for Charity Fund; Jim Thorpe Tennis Player of the Year 1993, ATP Tour Player of the Year 1993–97, US Olympic Cttee Sportsman of the Year 1997, inducted into Int.Tennis Hall of Fame 2007. *Leisure interests:* golf, basketball, Formula 1 racing. *Address:* Pure Sports Management, LLC, 609 Deep Valley Drive, Suite 200, Rolling Hills, CA 90274, USA. *Telephone:* (310) 265-4451. *Fax:* (310) 807-9255. *E-mail:* info@ puresportsmgmt.com. *Website:* www.puresportsmanagement.com; www .petesampras.com (office).

SAMS, Jeremy Charles; British director, writer and composer; b. 12 Jan. 1957; s. of Eric Charles Sydney Sams and Enid Sams (née Tidmarsh); one s.; ed Whitgift School, Magdalene Coll., Cambridge, Guildhall School of Music. *Plays:* Dir The Wind in the Willows (Tokyo) 1993, 1995, (Old Vic) 1995, Neville's Island (Nottingham Playhouse and West End), Forty Years On (West Yorks. Playhouse), Maria Friedman by Special Arrangement (Donmar Warehouse and West End), Enjoy (Nottingham Playhouse), Wild Oats (Royal Nat. Theatre) 1995, Passion (West End) 1996, Marat/Sade (Royal Nat. Theatre) 1997, 2 Pianos 4 Hands (Birmingham Repertory and West End) 1999, Spend Spend Spend (Plymouth and West End) 1999–2000, (tour) 2001, Noises Off (Royal Nat. Theatre) 2000, (West End, Broadway and tour) 2001, What The Butler Saw (Theatre Royal Bath and tour) 2001, Benefactors (West End) 2002, Water Babies (Chichester Festival Theatre) 2003, Little Britain Live (tour) 2005; translated A Fool and His Money: Time And The Room (Nottingham Playhouse), Les Parents Terribles/Indiscretions (Royal Nat. Theatre/Broadway), Mary Stuart, The Miser (Royal Nat. Theatre), The Park (RSC), Becket (West End), The Rehearsal (Almeida and West End), Saturday, Sunday and Monday (Chichester Festival Theatre), Leonce and Lena (Crucible Theatre, Sheffield), The Coffee House (Chichester Festival Theatre), Seven Doors (Chichester Festival Theatre), Scapino (Chichester Festival Theatre); as adaptor: Chitty Chitty Bang Bang (West End and Broadway); as lyricist: Amour (Broadway) 2002; as composer: Arcadia, The Rehearsal, Kean, Talking Heads, The Scarlet Pimpernel, The Wind in the Willows, Ghetto, Merry Wives of Windsor, Some Americans Abroad, Ring Round The Moon, The Country Wife, Jumpers, Don Carlos, Edward II, As You Like It. *Music:* composed for film Enduring Love (Ivor Novello Award), The Mother; for BBC: Have Your Cake, Persuasion (BAFTA Award), Old Times, Uncle Vanya, Welcome Home Comrades, Nativity Blues, Down Town Lagos; translated (opera) The Ring (ENO 2001–(05), The Merry Widow (Royal Opera), Der Kuhhandel (Juilliard School, New York), The Threepenny Opera (lyrics) (Donmar Warehouse & ART, Boston), La Bohème, Marriage of Figaro, Macbeth, The Force of Destiny (ENO), The Magic Flute (ENO, Opera 80, Scottish Opera), Cendrillon (Welsh Nat. Opera), Orpheus in the Underworld (Opera North, D'Oyly Carte), L'Étoile, The Reluctant King (Opera North), Così fan tutte (ENO). *Address:* c/o The Agency, 24 Pottery Lane, London, W11 4LZ, England (office). *Telephone:* (20) 7727-1346 (office).

SAMSONOWICZ, Henryk, PhD; Polish politician, historian and academic; *Professor, Instytut Historyczny, Warsaw University;* b. 23 Jan. 1930, Warsaw; m. Agnieszka Lechowska; one s. one d.; ed Warsaw Univ.; Staff mem. Warsaw Univ. 1950–, Asst, Sr Asst, Lecturer 1950–60, Asst Prof. 1960–69, Prof., History Inst. 1969–, Dean Dept of History 1969–74, Rector 1980–82; mem. Civic Cttee attached to Lech Wałęsa (q.v.), Chair. Science and Educ. Comm., Solidarity Trade Union 1988–89; Head Dept of Social Sciences, Polish Acad. of Sciences 2001–; participant Round Table plenary debates, mem. group for political reforms and team for science, educ. and tech. progress Feb.–April 1989; Minister of Nat. Educ. 1989–90; Deputy Head Scientific Research Cttee 1994–97; mem. Polish Historical Soc., Chair. Gen. Bd 1977–82, Soc. for Advancement and Propagation of Sciences 1980–, Academia Europaea 1992–94, Acad. des Belles Lettres, Polish Acad. of Sciences 1994–; Gold Cross (Hungary); Commdr's Cross, Order of Polonia Restituta; Gold Cross of Merit; Officier, Légion d'honneur; Dr hc (Duquesne Univ., USA, High School of Educ., Kraków, Nicolaus Copernicus Univ., Toruń, Marie Curie-Skłodowska Univ., Lublin); Nat. Educ. Comm. Medal. *Publications:* books include: Bürgerkapital in Danzig des XV Jh 1970, Złota jesień polskiego Średniowiecza (Golden Autumn of the Polish Middle Ages) 1971, Dzieje miast i Polsce (History of the Towns of Poland) 1984, Republic of Nobles 1990, Dziedzictwo Średniowiecza (Heritages of the Middle Ages) 1994, Miejsce Polski w Europie (Poland's Place in Europe) 1996, Europe – North-South 1999; numerous articles. *Address:* Instytut Historyczny Uniwersytetu Warszawskiego, ul. Krakowskie Przedmieście 26/28, 00-325 Warsaw (office); ul. Wilcza 22 m. 5, 00-544 Warsaw, Poland (home). *Telephone:* (22) 8261988 (office); (22) 6214061 (home). *Fax:* (22) 8261988 (office). *E-mail:* wydzial1@pan.pl (office).

SAMUELSON, Paul Anthony, BA, MA, PhD, LLD, DLitt, DSc; American economist and academic; *Institute Professor Emeritus, Professor of Economics Emeritus and Gordon Y. Billard Fellow, Massachusetts Institute of Technology;* b. 15 May 1915, Gary, Ind.; s. of Frank Samuelson and Ella Lipton; m. 1st Marion E. Crawford 1938 (died 1978); four s. (including triplets) two d.; m. 2nd Risha Eckaus 1981; ed Hyde Park High School Chicago, Univ. of Chicago and Harvard Univ., Cambridge, Mass; Prof. of Econs at MIT 1940–65, Inst. Prof. 1966–85, Inst. Prof. Emer. 1986–, Gordon Y. Billard Fellow 1986, mem. Radiation Lab. Staff 1944–45; Visiting Prof. of Political Economy, New York Univ. 1987–; Consultant to Nat. Resources Planning Bd 1941–43, to War Production Bd 1945, to US Treasury 1945–52, 1961–74, to Rand Corpn 1949–75, to Council of Econ. Advisers 1960–68, to Fed. Reserve Bd 1965–, to Finance Cttee, NAS 1977–, to Loomis, Sayles & Co. Boston and to Burden Investors Services Inc.; mem. Research Advisory Bd Cttee for Econ. Devt 1960, Advisory Bd to Pres. Eisenhower's Comm. on Nat. Goals 1960, Nat. Task Force on Econ. Educ. 1960–61, Special Comm. on Social Sciences of Nat. Science Foundation 1967–68, Comm. on Money and Credit; Econ. Adviser to Pres. Kennedy during election campaign; author of report to Pres. Kennedy on State of American Economy 1961; Assoc. Ed. Journal of Public Econs, Journal of Int. Econs, Journal of Nonlinear Analysis; NAS Guggenheim Fellow 1948–49; mem. American Acad. of Arts and Sciences, American Economic Asscn (Pres. 1961), Int. Econ. Asscn (Pres. 1965–68, Lifetime Hon. Pres.); Fellow American Philosophical Soc., Econometric Soc. (Council mem.), Vice-Pres. 1950, Pres. 1951); Corresp. Fellow British Acad.; Corresp. mem. Leibniz-Akad. der Wissenschaften und der Literatur; 34 hon. degrees; numerous awards including David A. Wells Prize 1941, John Bates Clark Medal 1947, Nobel Prize for Economic Science 1970, Albert Einstein Commemorative Award 1971, Alumni Medal, Univ. of Chicago 1983, Britannica Award 1989, Gold Scanno Prize, Naples 1990, Medal of Science 1996, John R. Commons Award 2000; MIT est. Paul A. Samuelson Professorship in Econs 1991. *Publications:* Foundations of Economic Analysis 1947, Economics 11 edns 1948–1980, 12th–18th edns (with William D. Norhaus) 1985–2005 (trans. into 40 languages), Readings in Economics (Ed.), seven edns 1955–73, Linear Programming and Economic Analysis (jtly) 1958, 1987, Collected Scientific Papers of Paul A. Samuelson (Vols I–V) 1966–86; author and jt author of numerous articles on econs. *Leisure interest:* tennis. *Address:* Massachusetts Institute of Technology, Department of Economics, E52-383, Cambridge, MA 02139, USA (office). *Telephone:* (617) 253-3368 (office). *Fax:* (617) 253-0560 (office). *Website:* econ-www.mit.edu (office).

SAMUELSSON, Bengt Ingemar, DMS, MD; Swedish medical chemist, academic and organization executive; *Chairman, Nobel Foundation;* b. 21 May 1934, Halmstad; s. of Anders Samuelsson and Stina Nilsson; m. Inga Bergstein 1958; two c.; ed Karolinska Inst. Stockholm; Asst Prof. Karolinska Inst. 1961–66, Prof. of Medical and Physiological Chem. 1972–, Chair. Dept of Physiological Chem. 1973–83, Dean, Faculty of Medicine 1978–83, Rector 1983–95; Research Fellow, Harvard Univ. 1961–62; Prof. of Medical Chem. Royal Veterinary Coll. Stockholm 1967–72; mem. Nobel Cttee of Physiology or Medicine 1984–89, Chair. 1987–89; Chair. Nobel Foundation 1993–; mem. Bd of Dirs Svenska Handelsbanken AB, Pharmacia & Upjohn, The Liposome Co., NicOx; mem. Advisory Bd Odlander Fredrikson & Co. AB; mem. Research Advisory Bd Swedish Govt 1985–88, Nat. Comm. on Health Policy 1987–90, European Science and Tech. Ass. 1994; Special Advisor to Commr for Research and Educ., EC 1995; mem. Royal Swedish Acad. of Sciences; Foreign Assoc. NAS; Foreign mem. Royal Soc. (London), Mediterranean Acad. of Sciences, Acad. Europaea, French Acad. of Sciences, Spanish Soc. of Allergology and Clinical Immunology, Royal Nat. Acad. of Medicine (Spain), Int. Acad. of Sciences; Hon. Prof. Bethune Univ. of Medical Sciences, Changchun, China 1986; Hon. mem. Asscn of American Physicians, AAAS, Swedish Medical Asscn, American Soc. of Biological Chemists, Italian Pharmacology Soc., Acad. Nat. Medicina de Buenos Aires, Int. Soc. of Haematology; Hon. DSc (Chicago) 1978, (Illinois) 1983, (Louisiana State Univ.) 1993; Dr hc (Rio de Janeiro) 1986, (Complutense Univ., Madrid) 1991, (Milan) 1993; Hon. DUniv (Buenos Aires) 1986; recipient of numerous honours and awards including Louisa Gross Horwitz Award 1975, Lasker Award 1977, Gairdner Foundation Award 1981, Nobel Prize in Physiology or Medicine 1982, Abraham White Science Achievement Award 1991, City of Medicine Award 1992, Maria Theresa Medal 1996. *Publications:* articles in professional journals. *Address:* Nobel Web AB, PO Box 5232, 102 45 Stockholm, Sweden (office). *Fax:* (8) 663-17-55 (office). *E-mail:* comments@nobelprize.org (office). *Website:* nobelprize.org (office).

SAMUELSSON, Håkan, MSc, Dipl-Ing; Swedish business executive; *Chairman of the Executive Board, MAN AG;* b. 19 March 1951, Motala; ed Royal Inst. of Tech., Stockholm; joined Scania AB 1977, Dir Powertrain 1988, Tech. Dir Scania Latin America 1993, mem. Exec. Bd Scania AB 1996; Chair. Exec. Bd MAN Nutzfahrzeuge AG 2000–, mem. Exec. Bd MAN AG 2000–, Chair. 2005–, mem. Supervisory Bd and Chair. Man Roland Druckmaschinen AG 2005–, Man Ferrostaal AG. *Address:* MAN AG, PO Box 201363, 80013 Munich (office); MAN AG, Landsberger Straße 110, 80339 Munich, Germany (office). *Telephone:* (89) 36098-0 (office). *Fax:* (89) 36098-250 (office). *E-mail:* info@man .de (office). *Website:* www.man.de (office).

SAMUKAI, Brownie J.; Liberian government official; *Minister of Defence;* ed American Univ.; fmr Deputy Minister of Defense, Deputy Minister of State for Presidential Affairs; fmr Chief of Police; fled Liberia and worked with UN in East Timor and Tanzania; Minister of Defence 2006–. *Address:* Ministry of Defence, Benson Street, POB 10-9007, 1000 Monrovia, Liberia (office). *Telephone:* 226077 (office).

SAMURA, Sorious; Sierra Leonean filmmaker and journalist; maker of film and TV documentaries and programmes for various media outlets; mem. Bd

Insight News Television, London; debut documentary Cry Freetown about civil war in Sierra Leone, broadcast 2000, within four weeks of film's transmission, plans were made for deployment of UN peace-keeping force in Sierra Leone; arrested along with mems of Channel 4 (UK) TV crew in Liberia on alleged espionage charges 2000, imprisoned for one week; now lives in UK; Dr hc (Univ. of East Anglia) 2003; CNN African Journalist of the Year 1999, Rory Peck Award 1999, Mohamed Amin Award 1999, Amnesty International Media Award for TV Documentary 2000, George Foster Peabody Award 2000, ICRC Dignity in Conflict Award 2000, Columbia-DuPont Award 2001, BAFTA Award for News and Current Affairs Journalism 2001, TV Documentary Award, One World Media Awards 2000, 2001, two Emmy Awards, two further Amnesty International Media Awards, Prix Europa, Japan Prize, Harry Chapin Media Award, three Overseas Press Club of America Awards, Golden Nymph, Monte Carlo Television Festival, Bronze World Medal, New York Festivals. *Films documentaries:* Cry Freetown 1999, Return to Freetown 2000, Exodus from Africa 2001, 21st Century War 2002, Living with Hunger 2003. *Address:* c/o Insight News Television Ltd, The Clockhouse, 28 Old Town, London, SW4 0LB, England (office). *Telephone:* (20) 7738-8344 (office). *Fax:* (20) 7498-2030 (office). *E-mail:* insight@insightnewstv.com (office). *Website:* www.insightnewstv.com (office).

SAMYN, Gilles; French/Belgian banking executive; *CEO, Compagnie Nationale à Portefeuille (CNP);* b. 2 Jan. 1950, Cannes; m. Myriam Goethals; five c.; ed Solvay Business School, Université Libre de Bruxelles; Asst Solvay Business School 1969–75, Lecturer 1975; Adviser Mouvement Co-operatif Belge 1972–74; with Groupe Bruxelles Lambert 1974–82; Ind. Adviser 1982–83; joined Groupe Frère-Bourgeois 1983, becoming Man. Dir Erbe SA 1986–, Dir Cie Nationale à Portefeuille 1988–, currently CEO and mem. Exec. Cttee; mem. Bd of Dirs Groupe Bruxelles Lambert 1987–, Pargesa Holding 1992–, Transcor, Astra Group, Groupe Flo, Entremont Alliance, Gruppo Banca Leonardo, Imetal, CLT-UFA. *Address:* Compagnie Nationale à Portefeuille, Rue de la Blanche Borne 12, 6280 Gerpinnes (Loverval), Belgium (office). *Telephone:* (71) 60-60-60 (office). *Fax:* (71) 60-60-70 (office). *E-mail:* cnp@cnp.be (office). *Website:* www.cnp.be (office).

SAN GIACOMO, Laura; American actress; b. 14 Nov. 1962, West Orange, NJ; m. 1st Cameron Dye (divorced 1998); one s.; 2nd Matt Adler 2000; ed Morris Knolls High School, NJ, Carnegie Mellon Univ., Pa; started career in regional theatre productions. *Theatre includes:* North Shore Fish, Beirut, The Love Talker, Italian American Reconciliation. *Films include:* Sex, Lies and Videotape (New Generation Award, LA Film Critics' Asscn) 1989, Pretty Woman 1990, Vital Signs 1990, Quigley Down Under 1990, Once Around 1991, Under Suspicion 1991, Where the Day Takes You 1992, Nina Takes a Lover 1994, Stuart Saves His Family 1995, Eat Your Heart Out 1997, Suicide Kings 1997, Apocalypse 1997, With Friends Like These . . . 1998, Mom's on the Roof, House on a Hill 2003, Havoc 2005, Checking Out 2005. *Television includes:* The Stand (miniseries) 1994, Just Shoot Me (series) 1997–2003, Sister Mary Explains It All 2001, Jenifer 2001, Saving Grace (series) 2007. *Address:* More Medavoy Management, 7920 West Sunset Boulevard, Suite 401, Los Angeles, CA 90046, USA.

SAN MIGUEL RODRIGUEZ, Walker, BA; Bolivian lawyer and government official; *Minister of National Defence;* b. 6 Aug. 1963, Ciudad de La Paz; m. Tatiana Núñez Ormachea; ed Universidad Mayor de San Andrés, Univ. of Salamanca, Spain, Univ. of Nancy, France; fmr Dir Lloyd Bolivian Airlines; fmr Exec. Chair. Colegio de Abogados de La Paz; Vice-Chair. Colegio Nacional de Abogados de Bolivia; Minister of Nat. Defence 2006–; mem. Nat. Acad. of Judicial Sciences of Bolivia, Inter-American Fed. of Lawyers. *Address:* Ministry of National Defence, Plaza Avaroa, esq. Pedro Salazar y 20 de Octubre 2502, La Paz, Bolivia (office). *Telephone:* (2) 232-0225 (office). *Fax:* (2) 243-3153 (office). *E-mail:* comunicaciones@mindef.gov.bo (office). *Website:* www.mindef.gov.bo (office).

SANADER, Ivo, PhD; Croatian politician; *Prime Minister;* b. 8 June 1953, Split; m.; two d.; ed Univ. of Innsbruck, Austria; Programme Ed., later Ed.-in-Chief Logos publishing house, Split 1983–88; mem. Editorial Bd Mogućnosti (Possibilities) magazine 1987–90; man. own cos, Innsbruck 1988–91; Gen. Man. Croatian Nat. Theatre, Split 1991–92; mem. Parl. (House of Reps of Croatian Parl.) 1992–, Minister of Science and Tech. 1992–93; Deputy Minister of Foreign Affairs 1993–95; Chief of Staff to Pres. of Repub. of Croatia and Sec.-Gen. Defence and Nat. Security Council 1995–96; Deputy Minister of Foreign Affairs 1996–2000; Prime Minister of Croatia 2003–; Pres. Croatian Democratic Union (Hrvatska Demokratska Zajednica—HDZ) 2000–; Deputy Chair. Foreign Affairs Cttee 2000; mem. Croatian Writers' Asscn, Croatian-PEN. *Publications:* author of several books on literary history and contemporary politics. *Leisure interests:* golf, reading, music. *Address:* Office of the Prime Minister, 10000 Zagreb, trg sv. Marka 2, Croatia (office). *Telephone:* (1) 4569220 (office). *Fax:* (1) 6303019 (office). *E-mail:* predsjednik@vlada.hr (office). *Website:* www.vlada.hr (office).

SANAKOYEV, Dimitri I.; Georgian government official; *President of the Provisional Administration of South Ossetia;* b. 31 Jan. 1969, Tskhinvali, S Ossetian Autonomous Oblast, Georgian SSR; fought on Ossetian side during Georgian–Ossetian conflict 1991–92; Minister of Defence in breakaway region of S Ossetia 2000; Prime Minister 2001–03; apptd Pres. of the Provisional Admin of S Ossetia by Georgian Pres. Mikheil Saakashvili 2007; mem. The Salvation Union of S Ossetia (political party). *Address:* Office of the President, Provisional Administration of South Ossetia, 1427 Shida Kartli Mkhare, Gori Region, Kurta, Georgia (office). *Website:* www.soa.ge (office).

SANBAR, Samir H., BBA; Lebanese international civil servant and consultant; b. 9 March 1934, Haifa; s. of Habib Sanbar and Georgette Khoury; ed American Univ. of Beirut; Deputy Ed. Al Howadeth, Al-Sayyad (Arab weeklies) and journalist with various Lebanese, Arab and int. media; Political Ed. Al-Usbu Al Araby (pan-Arab weekly), Beirut 1954–65; Information Officer of Special Rep. of Sec.-Gen. for UNYOM 1964; Special Asst to Personal Rep. of Sec.-Gen. of UNITAR 1965–70; Special Asst to Exec. Dir UNITAR 1970–73; accompanied UN Sec.-Gen. on all visits to Middle East 1973–87; Dir UN Information Centre, Beirut, Chief, Information Services of ECWA and Co-ordinator of UN public information activities in Gulf countries 1975–82; special assignment to assist Office of Sec.-Gen. in liaison and media functions during establishment of UNIFIL 1978–82; Chief UN Centres Services 1982–87; Dir UN Information Centres, Dept of Public Information 1987–93; Special Rep. of UN Sec.-Gen. to head UN mission to verify Referendum in Eritrea 1993; Asst Sec.-Gen. UN Dept of Public Information 1994–98; int. communications consultant. *Publication:* Hold on to Your Dreams; (short stories in Arabic): Characters From Ras Beirut, Aleikum Salam (Greetings).

SANBERK, Özdem; Turkish diplomatist (retd); b. 1 Aug. 1938, Ankara; s. of Halil Turgut Sanberk and Nimet Sanberk; m. Sumru Sanberk; one d.; ed Lycée de Galatasaray, Faculty of Law, Univ. of Istanbul; fmrly at Embassies in Bonn, Paris, Madrid; fmr Foreign Policy Adviser to Prime Minister Turgut Ozal; Amb. to EU 1987–91, to UK 1995–2000; fmr Under-Sec. to Ministry of Foreign Affairs 1990–95; Dir Turkish Econ. and Social Studies Foundation 2000–04, mem. Foreign Affairs Cttee 2004–; mem. Advisory Bd Euro Horizons (consulting firm); mem. Turkish-Armenian Reconciliation Comm., Turkish–Greek Forum; specialist on Turkish–EU relations, the Western Alliance, the Middle East second-track diplomacy and conflict resolution; broadcaster on domestic and foreign policy issues on radio and both Turkish and foreign TV; Comendador de la Orden de Mérito (Spain), Comendador de la Orden de Isabel la Católica (Spain); Verdienstmedaille des Verdienstordens (Germany). *Publications:* numerous articles in Turkish and int. newspapers. *Leisure interests:* reading, walking, music. *Address:* c/o Advisory Board, Euro Horizons, Karanfil Caddesi Mor Karanfil Sokak No:6, 34330 Levent - Istanbul, Turkey. *Website:* www.eurohorizons.com.

SANCAR, M. Sitki, MSc; Turkish petroleum industry executive; b. 10 Aug. 1941, Gemlik, Bursa; m. Ayse Sancar 1968; one s. one d.; ed Univs of Istanbul and Tulsa, Okla; well site geologist, Turkish Petroleum Co. (TPAO) 1967–70, research geologist and Dist Man. 1974–79, Chair. and Gen. Man. 1993–99; Gen. Dir MTA-Mineral Research & Exploration Inst. of Turkey 1979–88; Deputy Under-Sec. Ministry of Energy 1988–93; Adviser to Ministry of Energy 1999–; mem. Asscn of Petroleum Geologists of Turkey; Hon. mem. Chamber of Petroleum Engineers of Turkey. *Publications:* several scientific papers. *Address:* Binses Sitesi, 4 Cad. 21, Ümitköy, 06530 Ankara, Turkey (home). *Telephone:* (312) 2351095 (home). *E-mail:* mssancar@tr.net (home).

SANCHEZ, Felix; American athlete; b. 30 Aug. 1977, New York, NY; ed University City High School, San Diego, Calif., Mesa Community Coll., San Diego, Univ. of Southern Calif.; sprinter and 400m hurdler; represents Dominican Republic (birthplace of his parents); 400m hurdles personal best 47.25 seconds (Paris, France Aug. 2003), 400m 44.90 seconds (Gateshead, UK Aug. 2001), 200m 20.87 seconds (Irvine, CA May 2001); winner: World Championships 400m hurdles 2001 (1st Dominican Republic World Championship medal), 2003, International Amateur Athletics Federation Grand Final 400m hurdles 2002, six Golden League 400m hurdles 2003, Pan-American Games 400m hurdles 2003; 5th place IAAF Grand Prix Final 400m 2002, gold medal 400m hurdles Olympic Games, Athens 2004; ranked 1st in 2004 at 400m hurdles; ranked 6th among top 100 athletes of the year 2003; won 43 consecutive 400m hurdles races; hurdles coach Harvard-Westlake School, Calif. *Address:* c/o Harvard-Westlake School Athletics Department, 3700 Coldwater Canyon, North Hollywood, CA 91604, USA.

SÁNCHEZ DE LOZADA, Gonzalo; Bolivian politician; b. 1 July 1930; m. Ximena Iturralde Monje; one s. one d.; ed Univ. of Chicago; Founder and Man. Telecine Ltda (documentary and commercial film production) 1953–57; Founder and Gen. Man. Andean Geo-Services Ltd 1957–62; Founder and Pres. Compañía Minera del Sur (COMSUR) 1962–79, Pres. 1980–82; mem. Parl. 1979–80, 1982–85; Senator for Cochabamba and Pres. Senate 1985–86; Minister for Planning and Coordination 1986–88; Presidential cand. 1989; Leader, Movimiento Nacionalista Revolucionario (Histórico) (MNR) 1988–; Pres. of Bolivia 1993–97, 2002–03. *Address:* c/o Movimiento Nacionalista Revolucionario (MNR), Calle Estados Unidos y Panamá, Pasaje Puerto Príncipe 1487, Miraflores, La Paz, Bolivia (office).

SÁNCHEZ GALÁN, José Ignacio; Spanish industrial engineer and business executive; *Chairman and CEO, Iberdrola SA;* b. Sept. 1950, Salamanca; ed Eng Tech. School (ICAI), Universidad Pontificia de Comillas, Madrid; Commercial Dir SE Acumulador Tudor SA, Operations Man., Man. Dir Industrial Batteries Div., Pres. and CEO several cos in Grupo Tudor 1972–91; Gen. Man. and CEO ITP 1991–95; CEO Airtel Movil 1995–2001; Vice-Chair. and CEO Iberdrola SA 2001, now Chair. and CEO, also Chair. Iberdrola Renovables SA, Iberdrola Immobiliaria SA, El Desafio Español 2007 SA (co. that manages participation of Spanish boat in America's Cup); Dir Page Ibérica, Bodegas Matarromera; mem. Bd Nutreco Holding BV, Page Iberica, GALP, Red Electrica de España, Bodegas Matarromera, Corporación IBV, Puleva Biotech and other cos; mem. Advisory Bd Accenture Energy; mem. Advisory Cttee Prince of Asturias Endowed Chair in Information Tech., Univ. of New Mexico; mem. Círculo de Empresarios Vascos, Círculo de Empresarios (Madrid), Círculo de Economía, Asociación para el Progreso de la Dirección, American Man. Asscn; Trustee, Fundación Universitaria Pontificia de Salamanca, Fundación Atapuerca, Fundación Consejo España-Estados Unidos, Fundación de Estudios Financieros, Fundación Premysa, Fundación Iberdrola; fmr Prof., School of Industrial Engineers, ICAI; Best CEO in European Utilities sector, Institutional Investor magazine 2007, Top Exec. of the Year, Platts Global Energy Awards 2006, three Best CEO awards,

Investor Relations magazine. *Leisure interests:* hunting, horse riding. *Address:* Iberdrola, Cardenal Gardoqui 8, 48008 Bilbao, Spain (office). *Telephone:* (4) 4794811 (office). *Fax:* (4) 4705069 (office). *E-mail:* informacion@iberdrola.com (office). *Website:* www.iberdrola.es (office).

SÁNCHEZ-VICARIO, Arantxa; Spanish fmr professional tennis player; b. 18 Dec. 1971, Barcelona; d. of Emilio Sánchez and Marisa Vicario; most successful Spanish tennis player ever; turned professional in 1984 and won first professional title at Brussels 1988; winner French Open Women's title 1989, 1994, 1998, Int. Championships of Spain 1989, 1990, Virginia Slims Tournaments Newport 1991, Washington 1991, Canadian Open 1992, Australian Open Women's Doubles 1992, Mixed Doubles 1993, US Open 1994; named Int. Tennis Fed. World Champion 1994; silver medal (doubles), bronze medal (singles) 1992 Olympics; silver medal (singles), bronze medal (doubles) 1996 Olympics; Spanish Fed. Cup team 1986–98, 2000–01; winner of 14 Grand Slam titles, 96 WTA Tour titles and over US $16 million in prize money at retirement Nov. 2002; mem. Spanish Olympic Cttee 2001; Infiniti Commitment to Excellence Award 1992, Tennis Magazine Comeback Player of the Year 1998, Principe de Asturiasi Award (Spain) 1998, Int. Tennis Fed. Award of Excellence 2001. *Publication:* The Young Tennis Player: A Young Enthusiast's Guide to Tennis 1996. *Leisure interests:* soccer, water skiing, reading, horse riding, languages. *Address:* IMG, 1360 East 9th Street, Suite 100, Cleveland, OH 44114, USA (office).

SANCHO-ROF, Juan, DChemEng; Spanish business executive; *Vice-President, Board of Directors, Técnicas Reunidas Internacional SA;* b. 9 Feb. 1940, Madrid; m. Paloma Suils; two s. three d.; ed Universidad Complutense de Madrid and Instituto de Estudios Superiores de la Empresa, Barcelona; Technical–Commercial post Petronor SA (Petróleos del Norte) 1970–76, Deputy Gen. Man. 1976–85; Chair. and CEO Repsol Petróleo SA 1985, Pres. 1995, then Pres. Petronor and Exec. Vice-Pres. of Downstream, Repsol YPF –2003; mem. Bd of Dirs Gas Natural SDG 2003; currently Vice-Pres. Bd of Dirs Técnicas Reunidas Internacional, SA; Pres. Gen. Council of the Colls of Chemists of Spain. *Publications:* several technical works. *Address:* Técnicas Reunidas Internacional SA, Arapiles 13, Madrid, Spain, (office). *Telephone:* (91) 5920300 (office). *Fax:* (91) 5920397 (office). *Website:* www .tecnicasreunidas.es (office).

SANDAGE, Allan Rex, PhD, DSc; American astronomer and academic; *Staff Astronomer Emeritus, The Observatories, Carnegie Institution of Washington;* b. 18 June 1926, Iowa City; s. of Charles H. Sandage and Dorothy M. Briggs; m. Mary L. Connelly 1959; two s.; ed Univ. of Illinois and Calif. Inst. of Tech.; staff mem. Mount Wilson and Palomar Observatories 1952–; Asst Astronomer Hale Observatories, Calif. 1952–56, Astronomer 1956–, now Staff Astronomer Emer.; Sr Research Astronomer, Space Telescope Scientific Inst., NASA 1986–; Homewood Prof. of Physics, Johns Hopkins Univ., Baltimore 1987–88; Visiting Astronomer, Univ. of Hawaii 1986; Visiting Lecturer, Harvard Univ. 1957; Consultant, NSF 1961–63; Assoc. Ed. Annual Review of Astronomy and Astrophysics 1990–; mem. Cttee on Science and Public Policy 1965; Philips Lecturer, Haverford Coll. 1968; Research Assoc. ANU 1968–69; Fulbright-Hayes Scholar 1972; Grubb-Parson Lecturer, Royal Astronomical Soc. 1992; mem. Royal Astronomical Soc., American Astronomical Soc.; numerous hon. degrees; Helen Warner Prize of American Astronomical Soc. 1960, Russell Prize 1973, Eddington Medal, Royal Astronomical Soc. (UK) 1963, Pope Pius XI Gold Medal, Pontifical Acad. of Sciences 1966, Gold Medal, Royal Astronomical Soc. (UK) 1967, Rittenhouse Medal 1968, Nat. Medal of Scientific Merit 1971, Elliott Gresson Medal, Franklin Inst. 1973, Gold Medal of Pacific Astronomical Soc. 1975, Crafoord Prize, Swedish Acad. of Science 1991, Adion Medal, Observatoire de Nice 1991, Tomalla Gravity Prize, Swiss Physical Soc. 1992, Gruber Cosmology Prize 2000. *Publications:* numerous scientific papers and Hubble Atlas of Galaxies. *Leisure interests:* bread-making, gardening. *Address:* Carnegie Observatories, 813 Santa Barbara Street, Pasadena, CA 91101 (office); 8319 Josard Road, San Gabriel, CA 91775, USA (home). *Telephone:* (818) 285-5086 (home). *Website:* www.ociw .edu/research/asandage.

SANDBERG, Baron (Life Peer), cr. 1997, of Passfield in the County of Hampshire; **Michael Graham Ruddock Sandberg,** Kt, CBE, FCIB, FRSA; British banker (retd); b. 31 May 1927, Thames Ditton, Surrey; s. of the late Gerald Arthur Clifford Sandberg and Ethel Marion (née Ruddock) Sandberg; m. Carmel Mary Roseleen Donnelly 1954; two s. two d.; ed St Edward's School, Oxford; mil. service 1945–48, commissioned into 6th Duke of Conaught's Own Lancers, Indian Army, later 1st King's Dragoon Guards; joined Hongkong and Shanghai Banking Corpn 1949, Deputy Chair. 1973–77, Chair. 1977–86; Chair. British Bank of the Middle East 1980–86; Pres. Surrey County Cricket Club 1987–88; Vice-Pres. Chartered Inst. of Bankers 1984–87; JP Hong Kong 1972–86; Dir New World Devt Ltd, Winsor Ind. Corpn; mem. of Exec. Council of Hong Kong 1978–86; Treasurer Univ. of Hong Kong 1977–86; Chair. of Stewards, Royal Hong Kong Jockey Club 1981–86, Hon. Steward 1986; Freeman City of London; Liveryman Worshipful Co. of Clockmakers; Hon. LLD (Hong Kong) 1984, (Pepperdine) 1986. *Publication:* The Sandberg Watch Collection 1998. *Leisure interests:* horse racing, cricket, bridge, horology. *Address:* House of Lords, London, SW1A 0PW (office); 11 St James's Square, London, SW1Y 4LB (office); Waterside, Passfield, Liphook, Hants., GU30 7RT, England (home). *Telephone:* (20) 7219-5353 (House of Lords) (office); (20) 7930-9924 (office); (1428) 751225 (home). *Fax:* (20) 7930-7028 (office); (1428) 751636 (home). *E-mail:* patriciawhetnall@btconnect.com (office).

SANDER, Heidemarie Jiline (Jil); German fashion designer; b. 1944, Wesselburen; ed studied textile eng; stylist on fashion magazine; designs clothes for working women; owns own co. Jil Sander AG, fmr Chair.; first boutique opened, Hamburg 1968; boutiques in Germany, Paris, Chicago and San Francisco 1973–2000; first collection designed 1973; launched first fragrances, Woman Pure and Man. Pure 1977; introduced menswear range Jan. 1997; left Jil Sander AG 2000 after co. sold to Prada, returned as Chief Designer 2003. *Leisure interests:* modern art, gardening. *Address:* Jil Sander AG, Osterfeldstr 32–34, 22529 Hamburg, Germany (office). *Telephone:* (40) 22529 (office). *Fax:* (40) 5533034 (office). *E-mail:* info@JilSander.de (office). *Website:* www.jilsander.com (office).

SANDERLING, Kurt; German conductor; b. 19 Sept. 1912, Arys; m. 1st Nina Bobath 1941; m. 2nd Barbara Wagner 1963; three s.; Conductor Moscow Radio Symphony Orchestra 1936–41, Leningrad Philharmonic 1941–60, Chief Conductor Dresden State Orchestra 1964–67; guest appearances at Prague, Warsaw, Salzburg and Vienna Festivals; with Leipzig Gewandhaus Orchestra, New Philharmonia Orchestra 1972–; conducted LA Philharmonic 1991; Chief Prof. of Conducting, Leningrad Conservatory; retd 2002; numerous awards and prizes (USSR and GDR). *Address:* c/o Norman McCann International Artists Ltd, The Coach House, 56 Lawrie Park Gardens, London, SE26 6YJ (office); The Music Partnership Ltd, 41 Adlebert Terrace, London, SW8 7BH, England (office); Am Iderfenngraben 47, 13156 Berlin, Germany. *Telephone:* 9167558. *Fax:* 9167558.

SANDERS, Bernard (Bernie), BS; American politician; *Senator from Vermont;* b. 8 Sept. 1941, Brooklyn, NY; m. Dr Jane O'Meara Sanders; two s. two d.; ed James Madison High School, Brooklyn, Brooklyn Coll., Univ. of Chicago; moved to Vt 1964; worked as carpenter and journalist; political career began when he joined anti-Vietnam War Liberty Union Party 1971, resgnd 1977; unsuccessful ind. cand. for election to Senate 1972, 1974, and for Gov. of Vt 1972, 1976, 1986; worked as writer and Dir American People's Historical Soc.; Mayor of Burlington 1981–86; cand. in elections for US House of Reps 1988, mem. House of Reps for Vermont-At Large Dist 1991–2006 (first ind. mem. of House since 1950, longest-serving ind. mem. of the House), mem. Cttee on Financial Services, Cttee on Govt Reform; Co-founder House Progressive Caucus, chaired group for its first eight years; Senator from Vermont 2007–; mem. faculty, Harvard Univ. 1989, Hamilton Coll. 1991; Ind. (caucuses with Democrats and is counted as Democrat for purposes of cttee assignments). *Radio:* regular guest appearances on the Thom Hartmann radio programme for Friday segment Brunch with Bernie. *Publication:* Outsider in the House (autobiography) 1997. *Address:* 332 Dirksen Bldg, Washington, DC 20510, USA (office). *Telephone:* (202) 224-5141 (office). *Fax:* (202) 228-0776 (office). *Website:* sanders.senate.gov (office); bernie.org (office).

SANDERS, Donald Neil, AO, CB, BEcons; Australian banker; b. 21 June 1927, Sydney; s. of L. G. Sanders and R. M. Sanders; m. Betty Elaine Constance 1952; four s. one d.; ed Wollongong High School, Univ. of Sydney; Commonwealth Bank of Australia 1943–60; Australian Treasury 1956; Bank of England 1960–61; with Reserve Bank of Australia 1961–87, Supt, Credit Policy Div. of Banking Dept 1964–66, Deputy Man. of Banking Dept 1966–67, of Research Dept 1967–70, Chief Man. of Securities Markets Dept 1970–72, of Banking and Finance Dept 1972–74, Adviser and Chief Man. 1974–75, Deputy Gov. and Deputy Chair. of Bd 1975–87; with Australian Embassy, Washington, DC 1968; Man. Dir Commonwealth Banking Corpn 1987–91; Man. Dir CEO Commonwealth Bank of Australia 1991–92; Chair. H-G Ventures Ltd 1995–2000; Dir Lend Lease Corpn Ltd, MLC Ltd 1992–99, Queensland Investment Corpn 1992–98, Australian Chamber Orchestra Pty Ltd 1992–99. *Leisure interests:* golf, music. *Address:* 'Somerset', Taralga Road, via Goulburn, NSW 2580, Australia. *Telephone:* (2) 4840-2095. *Fax:* (2) 4840-2058 (home).

SANDERS, Jeremy Keith Morris, BSc, PhD, ScD, FRS; British scientist, academic and university administrator; *Professor of Chemistry and Deputy Vice Chancellor, University of Cambridge;* b. 3 May 1948, London; s. of Sidney Sanders and Sylvia Sanders (née Rutman); m. Louise Elliott 1972; one s. one d.; ed Wandsworth School, Imperial Coll., London, Univ. of Cambridge; Research Assoc. in Pharmacology, Stanford Univ., USA 1972–73; Demonstrator in Chem., Univ. of Cambridge 1973–78, Lecturer 1978–92, Reader 1992–96, Prof. of Chem. 1996–, Head, Dept of Chem. 2000–06, Deputy Vice Chancellor, Univ. of Cambridge 2006–; Fellow, Selwyn Coll., Cambridge 1976–; mem. Editorial Bd Magnetic Resonance in Chem. 1984–92, Journal of the Chem. Soc. Perkins Transactions 1988–93; mem. Editorial Advisory Bd, Chemical Soc. Reviews 1996–2002, Chair. 2000–02; Assoc. Ed. New Journal of Chem. 1998–2000; mem. Int. Supervisory Bd, Nat. Research Consortium on Catalysis (Netherlands) 1999–; mem. Scientific Bd, Inst. of Chemical Research of Catalonia 2002–; mem. Scientific Advisory Bd, Cresset BioMolecular Discovery Ltd 2002–; Chair. Chem. sub-panel, 2008 Research Assessment Exercise 2004–; Visiting Fellow, Japan Soc. for Promotion of Science 2002; AstraZeneca Lecturer, Univ. of Alberta, Canada 2003, Merck-Frosst Lecturer, Simon Fraser Univ. 2003, IAP Lecturer, Columbia Univ. 2003, J. Clarence Karcher Lecturer, Univ. of Okla. 2005, Barré Lecturer, Univ. of Montreal 2007; Meldola Medal, Royal Institute of Chemistry 1975, Hickinbottom Award, Royal Society of Chemistry 1981, Pfizer Award 1984, 1988, Josef Loschmidt Prize, Royal Soc. of Chem. 1994, Pedler Lecturer, Royal Soc. of Chem. 1996, Izaat Christensen Award, USA 2003. *Publication:* Modern NMR Spectroscopy (with B. K. Hunter), 2nd edn 1993. *Address:* Chemical Laboratory, Cambridge University, Lensfield Road, Cambridge, CB2 1EW, England (office). *Telephone:* (1223) 336411 (office). *Fax:* (1223) 336017 (office). *E-mail:* jkms@cam.ac.uk (office). *Website:* www.ch.cam.ac.uk (office); www-sanders.ch .cam.ac.uk (office).

SANDERS, Sir Ronald Michael, Kt, KCMG, KCN, MA; Antigua and Barbuda diplomatist, international relations consultant, business executive and writer; b. 26 Jan. 1948, Guyana; m. Susan Ramphal 1975; ed Sacred Heart RC School, Guyana and Boston Univ., USA, Univ. of Sussex, UK; Man. Dir Guyana Broadcasting Service, Public Affairs Adviser to Prime Minister of Guyana 1973–76; Lecturer in Communications, Univ. of Guyana 1975–76; Consultant to Pres. of Caribbean Devt Bank, Barbados 1977–78; Special Adviser to the Minister of Foreign Affairs of Antigua and Barbuda 1978–82; Deputy Perm. Rep. of Antigua and Barbuda to the UN, New York 1982–83; Antigua and Barbuda Amb. Extraordinary and Plenipotentiary accred to UNESCO 1983–87; Antigua and Barbuda High Commr in UK 1984–87, 1995–2004 (also accred to FRG 1986–87, 1996–2004, to France 1996–2004), Chief Foreign Affairs Rep. with Ministerial Rank 1999–2004; Deputy Chair. Caribbean Financial Action Task Force 2002–; Pres. Caribbean Broadcasting Union 1975–76; Chair. Caribbean Sub-Group at UNESCO 1983–85; mem. Bd Dirs of Caribbean News Agency 1976–77; mem. Inter-Governmental Council of the Int. Programme for the Devt of Communications at UNESCO 1983–87; mem. Exec. Bd UNESCO 1985–87; Visiting Fellow, Univ. of Oxford 1987–89; freelance broadcaster with BBC World Service 1987–89; Consultant (Int. Rels.) Atlantic Tele-Network, US Virgin Islands 1989–97; mem. Bd of Dirs Swiss American Nat. Bank of Antigua 1990–97, Guyana Telephone and Telegraph Co. 1991–97, Innovative Communication Corpn, US Virgin Islands 1998 (Exec. Dir for Int. Relations 2004); mem. Advisory Council Commonwealth Broadcasting Asscn 2005–; currently columnist Antigua Sun newspaper. *Publications:* Broadcasting in Guyana 1978, Antigua and Barbuda: Transition, Trial, Triumph 1984, Inseparable Humanity: Anthology of Reflections of the Commonwealth Secretary-General (ed.) 1988, Antigua Vision: Caribbean Reality, Perspectives of Prime Minister Lester Bird (ed.) 2002, Crumbled Small: The Commonwealth Caribbean in World Politics 2005; numerous articles on media ownership and control, communication and development and Antarctica. *Leisure interests:* reading, West Indian history, cinema. *E-mail:* ronaldsanders29@hotmail.com.

SANDERSON, Bryan Kaye, CBE, BSc; British business executive; *Chairman, QGS Synergy;* b. 14 Oct. 1940, Co. Durham; s. of Eric Sanderson and Anne Sanderson; m. Sirkka Kärki 1966; one s. one d.; ed Dame Allan's School, London School of Econs, UK, Int. Man. Inst. (IMEDE) Lausanne, Switzerland; VSO Peru 1962–64; joined British Petroleum (BP) 1964, Sr Rep. for SE Asia and China 1984–87, CEO BP Nutrition 1987–90, CEO BP Chemicals, then BP Amoco Chemicals 1990–97, mem. Bd BP 1992–2000; Dir (non-exec.) Corus (fmrly British Steel) 1994–2000, Six Continents hotel group 2001–03; Chair. (non-exec.) BUPA 2001–06; Dir (non-exec.) Standard Chartered PLC 2002–03, Exec. Chair. 2003–06; Chair. QGS Synergy 2007–; Chair. Northern Rock PLC 2007–08; mem. Advisory Group to the Labour Party on Industrial Competition Policy 1997–98, Dept for Trade and Industry (DTI) Advisory Group on Competitiveness 1998, King's Fund Man. Cttee 1999, DTI Co. Law Steering Group 1998, DTI Industrial Devt Advisory Bd 2000–04; Pres. CEFIC 1998–2000; Gov. LSE 1997, Vice-Chair. Govs 1998–2004; Dir Sunderland Football Club PLC 1998–, Durham Co. Cricket Club 2005–; Chair. Learning and Skills Council 2000–04, Sunderland Urban Regeneration Co. 2001–; mem Commonwealth Business Council; Hon. FIChemE 2002; Hon. DBA (Sunderland) 1998, (York) 1999. *Leisure interests:* reading, golf, walking, gardening. *Address:* QGS Synergy, Endurance House, Colmet Court, Seventh Avenue, Team Valley, NE11 0EF, England (office). *E-mail:* business@qgs-synergy.co.uk (office). *Website:* www.qgs-synergy.co.uk (office).

SANDERSON, Theresa Ione (Tessa), CBE, OBE; British sports administrator and fmr athlete; b. 14 March 1956, St Elizabeth, Jamaica; ed Bilston Coll. of Further Educ.; silver medal for javelin Euro Championships 1978; gold medal Commonwealth Championships 1978, 1986, 1990; gold medal (Olympic record), Olympic Games, LA 1984; gold medal World Cup 1992; competed Olympic Games, Atlanta 1996; retd from sport 1997; sports presenter Sky News 1989–92; Bd mem. English Sports Council 1998–; Vice-Chair. Sport England 1999–; Patron, Disabled Olympics; apptd to work with Newham Council to head Newham 2012 Sports Acad. 2006; Hon. Fellow, Wolverhampton Polytechnic; Hon. BSc (Birmingham); Sunday Times Life Times Achievement Award 2004. *Publication:* My Life in Athletics (autobiog.) 1985. *Leisure interest:* cardiofunk (low impact aerobic exercise workout). *Address:* The Newham Unit for the 2012 Games, The Old Dispensary, Romford Road, London Tel: 0 London, E15 4BZ, England. *Telephone:* (20) 8430-3693. *E-mail:* matthewjfisher@hotmail.co.uk. *Website:* www.tessa.co.uk.

SANDIFORD, Rt Hon. Sir Lloyd Erskine, PC, JP, MA (ECON.); Barbadian politician and educationalist; *President, Sandiford Centre for Public Affairs;* b. 24 March 1937; s. of the late Cyril G. Sandiford and of Eunice Sandiford; m. Angelita P. Ricketts 1963; one s. two d.; ed Coleridge-Parry Secondary School, Harrison Coll., Barbados, Univ. Coll. of the W Indies, Jamaica and Univ. of Manchester, UK; Asst Master, Modern High School, Barbados 1956–57, Kingston Coll., Jamaica 1960–61; part-time Tutor and Lecturer, Univ. of the W Indies, Barbados 1963–65; Sr Grad. Master, Harrison Coll. 1964–66; Asst Tutor, Barbados Community Coll. 1976–86; mem. Barbados Senate 1967–71, MP for St Michael S 1971–99; Personal Asst to Prime Minister 1966–67; Minister of Educ. 1967–71, of Educ., Youth Affairs, Community Devt and Sport 1971–75, of Health and Welfare 1975–76; Deputy Prime Minister and Minister of Educ. and Culture 1986–87; Prime Minister of Barbados and Minister of Finance 1987–93, Prime Minister and Minister of Econ. Affairs and the Civil Service 1987–94, also of Defence; Visiting Scholar, Penn State Univ., Harrisburg, Pa, USA; mem. Democratic Labour Party, Asst Sec., Gen. Sec., Pres. 1974–75; Founder, Acad. of Politics; Pres. Sandiford Centre for Public Affairs; mem. Council of Freely Elected Presidents and Prime Ministers, Carter Center, Atlanta; Life mem. Barbados Cricket Asscn; currently tutor Barbados Community Coll.; Order of the Liberator (Venezuela), Kt of St Andrew 2000; Barbados Scholar 1956, Distinguished Fellow, Sir Arthur Lewis Inst. of Social and Econ. Studies, Univ. of the W Indies 1999, Pres.'s Medal of Excellence, Bowie State Univ., Md. *Poetry:* Ode to the Environment, When She Leaves You. *Publications:* The Essence of Economics 1997, Caribbean Politics and Society 2000, Speeches (six vols). *Leisure interests:* choral singing, reading, gardening, swimming, cricket. *Address:*

Hillvista, Porters, St James, Barbados. *Telephone:* 422-3458 (home). *Fax:* 422-0281 (home). *E-mail:* lesandiford@carbsurf.com (home).

SANDLE, Michael Leonard, FRBS, DFA, RA; British artist; b. 18 May 1936, Weymouth, Dorset; s. of Charles E. Sandle and Dorothy G. Sandle (née Vernon); m. 1st Cynthia D. Koppel 1971 (divorced 1974); m. 2nd Demelza Spargo 1988 (divorced 2004); one s. one d.; ed Douglas High School, Isle of Man, Douglas School of Art and Tech. and Slade School of Fine Art; studied lithography, Atelier Patris, Paris 1960; began sculpture 1962; held various teaching posts in UK 1961–70 including Leicester and Coventry Colls of Art; resident in Canada 1970–73; Visiting Prof., Univ. of Calgary 1970–71; Visiting Assoc. Prof., Univ. of Victoria, BC 1972–73; Lecturer in Sculpture, Fachhochschule für Gestaltung, Pforzheim, FRG 1973–77, Prof. 1977–80; Prof., Akad. der Bildenden Künste, Karlsruhe 1980–99; resgnd from RA 1997, re-elected 2004; Kenneth Armitage Fellow 2004–; various exhbns in UK and internationally since 1957 including V. Biennale, Paris 1966, Documenta IV, Kassel 1968, Documenta VI 1977, Whitechapel Art Gallery, London 1988, Württembergischer Kunstverein, Stuttgart 1989, Ernst Múzeum, Budapest 1990; works in many public collections in UK, Germany, Australia, USA etc.; Nobutaka Shikanai Prize, 1st Rodin Grand Prize Exhbn, Japan 1986; Henry Hering Memorial Medal, Nat. Sculpture Soc. of America 1995. *Achievement:* designed architecture and executed sculpture for the Malta Siege Memorial, Grand Harbour, Valletta 1999–92; designed the Int. Memorial for Seafarers sited at the Int. Maritime Org's HQ, London 2001. *Address:* 26 De-Beavoir Place, London, N1 4EP (home); c/o Royal Society of British Sculptors, 108 Old Brompton Road, London, SW7 3RA, England (office). *E-mail:* michael-sandle@supanet.com (home).

SANDLER, Adam, BFA; American actor and screenwriter; b. 9 Sept. 1966, Brooklyn, New York; s. of Stanley Sandler and Judy Sandler; m. Jackie Sandler; two d.; ed New York Univ.; People's Choice Award 2000. *Albums:* They're All Gonna Laugh at You! 1993, What the Hell Happened to Me? 1996, What's Your Name? 1997, Stan and Judy's Kid 2000, Shhh..Don't Tell 2004. *Films include:* Going Overboard (1989, Shakes the Clown 1992, Coneheads 1993, Airheads (1994), Mixed Nuts 1994, Billy Madison 1995, Happy Gilmore 1996, Bulletproof 1996, The Wedding Singer 1998, The Water Boy 1998, Big Daddy 1999, Little Nicky 2000, Punch-Drunk Love 2002, Mr Deeds 2002, Anger Management 2003, 50 First Dates 2004, Spanglish 2004, The Longest Yard 2005, Click 2006, Reign Over Me 2007, I Now Pronounce You Chuck and Larry 2007, You Don't Mess with the Zohan 2008. *Television appearances include:* actor, writer Saturday Night Live 1991–95, Saturday Night Live Mother's Day Special 1992, MTV Music Video Awards 1994, Saturday Night Live Presents Pres. Bill Clinton's All-Time Favorites 1994, 37th Annual Grammy Awards 1995, ESPY Awards 1996. *Screenplays:* (co-writer) Billy Madison, Happy Gilmore, The Water Boy, You Don't Mess with the Zohan. *Publications:* Little Nicky 2000. *Address:* c/o The Endeavor Agency, 9601 Wilshire Blvd., 10th Floor, Beverly Hills, CA 90212; Agency for Performing Arts, 888 7th Avenue, Suite 602, New York, NY 10106 (office); c/o Brillstein-Grey Entertainment, 9150 Wilshire Boulevard, Suite 350, Beverly Hills, CA 90212, USA. *Website:* www.adamsandler.com.

SANDLER, Joanne; American international organization official; ran consulting business that provided organizational devt support to women's orgs, New York; joined UNIFEM 1997, fmr Chief of Organisational Learning and Resource Devt and Deputy Dir for Programmes, Ad Interim Exec. Dir –2008; has served on bd of dirs of several orgs including Asscn for Women's Rights in Devt, Gender at Work, Women Make Movies. *Address:* c/o UNIFEM Headquarters, 304 East 45th Street, 15th Floor, New York, NY 10017, USA (office).

SANDLER, Ron, CBE, MA, MBA; South African business executive; *Chairman, Northern Rock plc;* b. 5 March 1952, Durban, South Africa; s. of Bernard M. Sandler and Carla Sandler; m. Susan Lee 1977; two s.; ed Queens' Coll. Cambridge, Stanford Univ., USA; ran LA office of Boston Consulting, USA, then London office of Booz Allen; f. own man. consultancy firm 1988; apptd. Chair. Quadrex Holdings 1990; joined Lloyd's of London 1994, Chief Exec. 1995–99, COO Nat. Westminster Bank PLC 1999–2000; Chair. Kyte Group 2000–, Computacenter 2001–08; Head, Inquiry into Long-term Savings 2001; led Govt-sponsored review of UK Long Term Savings Industry 2002; Exec. Chair. Northern Rock plc Feb.–Oct. 2008, Chair. (non-exec.) Oct. 2008–; Trustee Royal Opera House 1999–; fmr Pres. Chartered Inst. of Bankers. *Address:* Northern Rock plc, Northern Rock House, Gosforth, Newcastle-upon-Tyne, NE3 4PL (office); 5 Southside, Wimbledon, London, SW19 4TG, England (home). *Telephone:* (191) 285-7191 (office); (20) 8946-1179 (home). *Fax:* (191) 284-8470 (office). *Website:* www.northernrock.co.uk (office).

SANDMO, Agnar, DR.ECON.; Norwegian economist and academic; *Professor of Economics, Norwegian School of Economics and Business Administration;* b. 9 Jan. 1938, Tønsberg; m. Tone Sverdrup 1959; two s. one d.; ed Tønsberg Gymnasium and Norwegian School of Econs and Business Admin.; Grad. Fellow, Norwegian School of Econs and Business Admin. 1963–66, Asst Prof. of Econs 1966–71, Prof. 1971–, Vice-Rector 1985–87; Visiting Fellow, Catholic Univ. of Louvain 1969–70; Visiting Prof., Univ. of Essex 1975–76; mem. Petroleum Price Bd 1976–80 and several Govt bds and cttees on social science and gen. research policy; Fellow, Econometric Soc.; mem. Norwegian and Swedish Acads of Science; Pres. European Econ. Asscn 1990; Order of St Olav 1997; Dr hc (Univ. of Oslo) 1997; Research Council of Norway Prize for Outstanding Research 2002. *Publications:* articles and books on econs and econ. policy. *Address:* Norwegian School of Economics and Business Administration, Helleveien 30, 5045 Bergen (office); Øyjordsbotten 28A, 5038 Bergen, Norway (home). *Telephone:* 55-95-92-76 (office); 55-25-65-86 (home). *E-mail:* agnar.sandmo@nhh.no (office). *Website:* www.nhh.no (office).

SANDOVAL, Arturo; American musician (trumpet); b. 1949, Artemisa, Cuba; m. Marianela Sandoval; one s.; ed Nat. School of Art; began trumpet playing aged 12 and made first public appearances in Cuba aged 13; played in group with Chucho Váldez until 1981; formed own group, Irakere, in 1981 and now undertakes annual maj. world tour; granted political asylum in USA 1990; currently Prof. of Music, Florida Int. Univ.; opened Arturo Sandoval Jazz Club, Miami Beach 2006; festival appearances at Tokyo, Newport, Montreux, Antibes, Chicago, The Hague and the Hollywood Bowl; several record albums; numerous Grammy and Billboard Awards. *Recordings include:* albums: Havana (with David Amram) 1976, New York (with David Amram) 1977, Irakere 1979, To a Finland Station (with Dizzy Gillespie) 1982, Breaking the Sound Barrier 1983, No Problem 1986, Tumbaito 1987, Straight Ahead 1988, Classics 1989, Arturo Sandoval 1989, Flight to Freedom 1991, I Remember Clifford 1992, Danzón 1993, Dream Come True 1993, Passion 1993, Cubano 1994, Arturo Sandoval y el Tren Latino 1995, Double Talk (with Ed Calle) 1996, Swingin' 1996, Just Music 1997, Hot House 1998, Americana 1999, Sunset Harbour (with Ed Calle) 1999, Los Elefantes (with Wynton Marsalis) 1999, For Love or Country 2000, Piedras y Flores (with Amaury Gutiérrez) 2001, L.A. Meetings 2001, My Passion for the Piano 2002, From Havana With Love 2003, Trumpet Evolution 2003, Rumba Palace (Latin Grammy for Best Latin Jazz Album 2007) 2007. *Address:* Turi's Music Enterprises Inc., 6701 Collins Avenue, Regency No. 1, Miami Beach, FL 33141, USA (office). *Telephone:* (305) 866-6511 (office). *Fax:* (305) 866-6516 (office). *E-mail:* fanmail@arturosandoval.com. *Website:* www.arturosandoval .com.

SANDOVAL CÓRDOVA, Wellington, MD; Ecuadorean physician and government official; ed Universidad Central del Ecuador, Univ. of Michigan, USA and Univ. of Toronto, Canada; dir of mobile hosp. during Paquisha war 1981; cardiovascular and thoracic surgeon, Armed Forces Hosp., Quito 1977–91; Dir Hosp. Metropolitano, Quito 1992–2005; Prof. and Head of Surgery, Faculty of Medical Sciences, Universidad Internacional del Ecuador 2004–; Minister of Public Health April–Dec. 2005; Pres. Inst. for Social Security 2006–07; Minister of Nat. Defence 2007–08 (resgnd). *Address:* Universidad Internacional del Ecuador, Avenida Jorge Fernández y Simón Bolívar, Quito, Ecuador (office). *Telephone:* (2) 298-5600 (office). *Fax:* (2) 298-5666 (office). *E-mail:* informa@internacional.edu.ec (office). *Website:* www .internacional.edu.ec (office).

SANDOVAL IÑÍGUEZ, HE Cardinal Juan; Mexican ecclesiastic; *Archbishop of Guadalajara;* b. 28 March 1933, Yahualica, Jalisco; s. of Esteban Sandoval and María Guadalupe Iñiguez; ed Seminario Diocesano de Guadalajara, Pontifica Universidad Gregoriana; ordained as a Catholic priest 1957; teacher Seminario de Guadalajara 1961, Prof. of Philosophy, Vice-Rector 1971, Rector 1980; Bishop's Coadjutor, Juárez 1988, Bishop of Juárez 1992; Archbishop of Guadalajara 1994–; cr. Cardinal 1994, Cardinal Priest of Nostra Signora di Guadalupe e S Filippo Martire in Via Aurelia; mem. IV Latin American Archbishop's Conf., Santo Domingo 1992. *Address:* Arzobispado, Calle Liceo 17, Apdo. 1-331, 44100 Guadalajara, Mexico. *Telephone:* (3) 614-5504. *Fax:* (3) 658-2300. *Website:* www.arquidiocesisgdl.org.mx.

SANDRE, Didier (Didier de Maffre); French actor; b. 17 Aug. 1946, Paris; s. of Pierre Maffre and Geneviève Gevril; one d.; m. 2nd Nada Strancar 1990; ed Lycée d'Enghien-les-Bains, Collège Estienne, Paris; stage roles include: Dom Juan, La Tempête, Le Conte d'hiver, Phèdre, L'Ecole des Femmes, Le Misanthrope, Tartuffe, Les Paravents, Fausse Suivante, Terre Etrangère, Martyr de Saint-Sébastien, Madame de Sade, Le Mariage de Figaro, Le Soulier de Satin, Ivanov, Le Chemin Solitaire, Partage de Midi, Dinner with Friends, Thomas Becket, Bérénic, Histoire du Soldat; Chevalier des Arts et des Lettres, Chevalier Ordre nat. du Mérite; Prix Syndicat de la Critique; Molière Prize for Best Actor 1996. *Plays include:* Lulu 1973, Penthésilée 1973, Don Juan 1973, The Tempes 1974, L'abîme1974, Le Précepteur 1975, Phèdre1975, 1998, Dommage qu'elle soit une putain 1975, La passion du Général Franco 1976, Les cordonniers 1976, Les paysans 1976, La jeune fille Violaine 1977, Les contes des mille et une nuits1977, Lentz 1977, Les Moliere De Vitez (L'école des femmes,Tartuffe, Don Juan, Le Misanthrope) 1978–80, Sur les ruines de Carthage 1981, A Winter's Tale 1981, Peer Gynt 1981, Les Paravents 1983, Tonio Kröger 1983, Terre étrangère 1984, Ajax 1984, La Fausse suivante 1985, L'Illusion 1985, Madame de Sade 1984, Le Martyre de Saint-Sébastien 1984, Le Mariage de Figaro 1987, Le Soulier de satin 1987, Comment Wang-Fô fut sauvé 1988, Ivanov 1989, Le Chemin solitaire 1989, Partage de Midi 1990-91, Andromaque 1992, Contre-jour 1993, Maison d'arrêt 1993, Célimène et le cardinal 1993, An Ideal Husband 1995, 1996–97, la neuvième symphonie1996, Dîner entre amis 1998, Becket 2000, Bérénice 2001, Les Couleurs De La Vie 2002, Le Laboureur De Bohême 2003, Monsieur Chasse! 2004, L'Auteur De Beltraffio 2005, Ma Vie Avec Mozart 2006, La Femme D'Avant 2006, La Danse De Mort 2007, Alberto Et Moravia2007. *Films include:* La Java des ombres 1983, Train d'enfer 1985, Code Name: Emerald 1985, La Femme de ma vie 1986, Les Mannequins d'osier 1989, Boulevard des hirondelles 1991, Mensonge 1993, 3000 scénarios contre un virus 1994, Petits arrangements avec les morts 1995, Conte d'Automne 1997, Le mystère Paul 2000, Hell 2006. *Television includes:* Médecins de nuit 1978, Le Misanthrope 1980, Peer Gynt 1981, Saint Louis ou La royauté bienfaisante 1982, Capitaine X 1983, Deux amies d'enfance 1983, Richelieu ou La journée des dupes 1983, La Fausse suivante 1985, L'Année terrible 1985, Manon Roland 1989, Jeanne d'Arc: le pouvoir de l'innocence 1989, Les Grandes familles 1989, Le Chemin solitaire 1990, Ivanov 1990, L'Amour assassin 1992, Turbulences 1992, Une famille formidable 1992–2007, Sandra princesse rebelle 1995, l'Allée du roi 1996, La Femme d'un seul homme 1998, Passion interdite 1998, Intime conviction 1998, Deux frères 2000, L'Enfant éternel 2002, Saint-Germain ou La négociation 2003, Les Amants du Flore 2006, Le Sang noir 2007, Moi, Louis, enfant de la mine 2007. *Leisure interests:* music, gardening. *Address:* c/o Agents Associés Guy Bonnet, 201 rue Faubourg St Honoré, 75008 Paris, France (office). *Telephone:* 1-42-56-04-57 (office). *Fax:* 1-53-76-00-96 (office). *E-mail:* bonnetguy@wanadoo.fr (office); didiersandre@ didiersandre.info (office). *Website:* www.didiersandre.info (office).

SANDRI, HE Cardinal Leonardo, BCL; Argentine ecclesiastic; *Prefect of the Congregation for the Oriental Churches;* b. 18 Nov. 1943, Buenos Aires; born to parents of Italian descent; ordained priest in Buenos Aires 1967; entered Vatican diplomatic corps 1974, served at Vatican Embassy in Madagascar, worked at Secr. of State 1977–89, assigned to Nunciature in USA 1989–91, returned to the Vatican 1991–97; apptd Titular Archbishop of Aemona 1997; Apostolic Nuncio to Venezuela 1997–2000, to Mexico 2000; Substitute (Sostituto) Sec. for Gen. Affairs, Secr. of State 2000–07; Prefect of the Congregation for the Oriental Churches 2007–; cr. Cardinal 2007. *Address:* Congregation for the Oriental Churches, Via della Conciliazione 34, Palazzo del Bramante, 00193 Rome, Italy (office). *Telephone:* (06) 6988-4282 (office). *Fax:* (06) 6988-4300 (office). *E-mail:* info@vatican.va (office). *Website:* www .vatican.va/roman_curia/congregations/orientchurch (office).

SANDS, Peter, MPA; British banking executive; *Group Chief Executive, Standard Chartered PLC;* b. 8 Jan. 1962; m.; four c.; ed Univ. of Oxford, Harvard Univ., USA (Harkness Fellow); grew up in Asia; joined McKinsey & Co. 1988, worked extensively in banking and tech. sectors, Pnr 1996–2002, mem. Bd of Dirs 2000–02; Group Finance Dir and Group Exec. Dir Standard Chartered PLC 2002–06, Group Chief Exec. 2006–. *Address:* Standard Chartered Bank PLC, 1 Aldermanbury Square, London, EC2V 7SB, England (office). *Telephone:* (20) 7280-7088 (office). *Fax:* (20) 7600-2546 (office). *E-mail:* info@standardchartered.com (office). *Website:* www.standardchartered.com (office).

SANDS, Sarah; British editor and writer; *Deputy Editor, London Evening Standard;* b. (Sarah Harvey), 3 May 1961, Cambridge; m. 1st Julian Sands; one s.; m. 2nd Kim Fletcher; two c.; ed Goldsmiths Coll., London; worked at Kent and Sussex Courier 1983–86; worked at Evening Standard, London, as diary reporter, Ed. of the Londoner's Diary, later Features Ed., then Assoc. Ed. 1986–95; Deputy Ed. The Daily Telegraph 1996–2005, responsible for The Daily Telegraph Saturday edn, Ed. The Sunday Telegraph 2005–06; Consulting Ed. The Daily Mail 2006–08; Ed.-in-Chief Reader's Digest UK 2008–09; Deputy Ed., London Evening Standard 2009–. *Publications:* novels: Playing the Game 2003, Hothouse 2005, Chiswick Wives 2006. *Address:* London Evening Standard, Northcliffe House, 2 Derry Street, London, W8 5TT, England (office). *Telephone:* (20) 7938-6000 (office). *Fax:* (20) 7937-2648 (office). *E-mail:* editor@standard.co.uk (office). *Website:* www.standard.co.uk (office).

SANDSTRÖM, Sven, BA, MBA, PhD; Swedish banker and international finance official; *Member of the Council and Treasurer, World Conservation Union;* ed Univ. of Stockholm, Stockholm School of Econs, Royal Inst. of Tech.; consultancy work 1966–68; Research Assoc., MIT and Harvard Business School, USA 1969–72; joined IBRD 1972, Project Analyst, Urban Projects Dept 1973, Deputy Div. Chief 1977, Div. Chief 1979, Div. Chief Urban Devt and Water Supply, S Asia Projects 1986, Dir Southern Africa Dept 1987–90, Dir Office of the Pres. 1990–91, Man. Dir 1991–2001, Chair. Operation Cttee, Chair. Information and Knowledge Man. Council; Secretariat Dir. Int. Task Force on Global Public Goods, Stockholm, 2003–06; Vice-Chair. Voluntary Replenishment Mechanism, Global Fund to Fight AIDS, Tuberculosis and Malaria; mem. Governing Council and Treas. World Conservation Union (IUCN); Coordinator and Chair. fo the replenishment of African Devt Fund of African Devt Bank; fmr Special Adviser to EU, Adviser to World Bank; mem. Bd of Dirs AES Corpn. *Address:* IUCN Headquarters, Rue Mauverney 28, Gland 1196, Switzerland (office). *Telephone:* (22) 999-0000 (office). *Fax:* (22) 9990002 (office). *E-mail:* webmaster@iucn.org (office). *Website:* www.iucn.org (office).

SANDURA, Wilson Runyararo, BA, LLB; Zimbabwean judge; *Judge of Appeal, Supreme Court;* b. 29 July 1941, Shamva; s. of the late Fore Sandura and Gilliet Sandura; m. 1st Joyce Alexis Sandura 1972 (divorced 1976); m. 2nd Caroline Elizabeth Sandura 1985; two s. one d.; ed Mavuradonha Mission, Goromonzhi High School, Morehouse Coll., USA, Univ. of London, UK; called to the Bar, Lincoln's Inn, London; pvt. practice as barrister 1973–80; Regional Magistrate 1980–82; Perm. Sec., Ministry of Justice 1982–83; Judge, High Court 1983–84, Judge Pres. 1984–97, 2000, Supreme Court 1998–, currently Judge of Appeal; Chair. delimitation comms 1985, 1989, 1990, 1991, 1995, 2000. *Leisure interest:* gardening. *Address:* Supreme Court, PB 870, Causeway, Harare, Zimbabwe (office). *Telephone:* (4) 736951 (office). *E-mail:* supreme_court@gta.gov.zw (office).

SANDVED, Arthur Olav, DPhil; Norwegian professor of English; b. 2 Feb. 1931, New York; s. of Ole Sandved and Ane Aarsland; m. Ruth Øgaard 1953; three d.; ed Univ. of Oslo; Lecturer in English Language, Univ. of Trondheim 1959–63, Univ. of Oslo 1963–71; Reader in English Philology, Univ. of Oslo 1971–74, Prof. of English Language 1974–96; mem. Norwegian Acad., Royal Norwegian Acad. Trondheim; Hon. Stipend from Norwegian Govt 2004–. *Publications:* Studies in the Language of Caxton's Malory and that of the Winchester Manuscript 1968, An Advanced English Grammar (with P. Christophersen) 1969, Introduction to Chaucerian English 1985, Vers fra Vest (anthology of Old English verse translated into Norwegian) 1987, Peter Plogmann (extracts from Piers Plowman translated into Norwegian) 1990, Paradise Lost (translated into Norwegian) 1993, trans. King Lear into Norwegian 1995, trans. the three parts of King Henry VI into Norwegian 1996, trans. Henry VIII into Norwegian 1997, Fra 'Kremmersprog' til Verdensspråk (history of English studies in Norway 1850–1943) 1998, trans. A History of Reading into Norwegian 1999, trans. Joseph Andrews into

Norwegian 1999, trans. Revelation of Divine Love into Norwegian 2000, Fra 'Kremmersprog' til Verdensspråk, Vol. II (1945–57) 2002, trans. Canterbury Tales (extracts) into Norwegian 2002, Engelsk språkguide (a handbook of English usage), Norwegian adaptation of J. Svartvik and R. Svartvik, Handbok i Engelska, 2003, Paradise Regained (translated into Norwegian) 2005, King Arthur and His Knights: Selected Tales by Sir Thomas Malory (ed. E. Vinaver) (translated into Norwegian) 2007. *Address:* I. F. Gjerdrums vei 74, 1396 Billingstad, Norway. *Telephone:* 66-84-57-77.

SANÉ, Pierre Gabriel Michel, MSc, MBA; Senegalese administrator and UN official; *Assistant Director-General, United Nations Educational, Scientific and Cultural Organization (UNESCO);* b. 7 May 1948, Dakar; s. of Nicolas Sané and Thérèse Carvalho; m. Ndeye Coumba Sow 1981; one s. one d.; ed Lycée Van Vollenhoven, Dakar, Ecole Supérieure de Commerce de Bordeaux, France, Ecole Nouvelle d'Organisation Economique et Sociale, Paris, London School of Econs, UK, Carleton Univ., Ottawa, Canada; Vice-Pres. Fédération des Etudiants d'Afrique Noire en France 1971–72; auditor with audit firms in France 1973–77; Deputy Gen. Man. Société Sénégalaise Pharmaceutique (Senepharma) 1977–78; joined Int. Devt Research Centre (IDRC) 1978, various positions Ottawa, Nairobi and Dakar, to Regional Dir W and Cen. Africa, Dakar 1988–92; mem. Amnesty Int. 1988–, Sec.-Gen. 1992–2001; Asst Dir-Gen. UNESCO, Paris 2001–; Pres. PANAF 92 1991–92, Founding mem. Int. Cttee; winner, Concours Nat. de Commercialisation, France 1972. *Publications:* papers and reports on African devt, science and tech. and human rights research man. for IDRC. *Leisure interests:* reading, travelling, music, museums, arts. *Address:* UNESCO, 1 rue Miollis, 75732 Paris Cedex 15, France (office). *Telephone:* 1-45-68-39-23 (office). *Fax:* 1-45-68-57-20 (office). *E-mail:* p.sane@unesco.org (office). *Website:* www.unesco.org (office).

SANEJOUAND, Jean Michel, DenL; French painter; b. 18 July 1934, Lyon; s. of Henri Felix Sanejouand and Angèle Fardel; m. Michelle Bourgeois 1957; two s.; ed Institut d'études politiques, Faculté de Droit, Lyon; self-taught in art; worked as artist, Lyon 1955–59, Paris 1959–93, Vaulandry 1993–; 'charges-objets' (assemblage works) 1963–67, 'organisations d'espaces' (environmental works) 1967–75, 'calligraphies d'humeurs' (calligraphic works on canvas) 1968–77, 'espaces-peintures' (painted and drawn works) 1978–86, black and white paintings 1987–93, sculptures 1988–, colour paintings 1993–96; 'sculptures-peintures' (paintings of sculptures) 1997–2002; retrospective exhbn Centre Georges Pompidou, Paris, 1995; Espaces critiques (imaginary landscapes organized with earlier works) 2002–. *Address:* Belle-Ville, 49150 Vaulandry, France. *Telephone:* (2) 41-82-88-71. *E-mail:* web-site@sanejouand.com (office). *Website:* www.sanejouand.com (office).

SANFORD, Marshall (Mark), Jr, BA, MBA; American state official; *Governor of South Carolina;* b. 28 May 1960, Fort Lauderdale, Fla; m. Jenny Sullivan; four s.; ed Furman Univ., SC, Univ. of Va Darden Business School; with Goldman Sachs –1988; with CRC Realty 1988–89; Prin. Southeastern Partners 1989; Propr Norton & Sanford 1992, Prin. 1993–95, 2001–03; mem. US House of Reps 1995–2001; Gov. of SC 2003–; Republican; Taxpayers' Best Friend Award, Nat. Taxpayers Union, Deficit Hawk Award, Concord Coalition Citizens Council, Taxpayer Hall of Fame, Taxpayers for Common Sense, Golden Bulldog Award, Watchdogs of the Treasury Inc., Spirit of Enterprise Award, US Chamber of Commerce, Congressional Youth Leadership Council Award. *Address:* Office of the Governor, POB 12267, Columbia, SC 29211, USA (office). *Telephone:* (803) 734-2100 (office). *Fax:* (803) 734-5167 (office). *E-mail:* mark@sc.gov (office). *Website:* www.scgovernor.com (office).

SANGAJAVYN, Bayartsogt, MSc; Mongolian economist and politician; *Minister of Finance;* b. 28 March 1967, Selenge; m.; two c.; ed Lomonosov Moscow State Univ., Baden-Wuerttemberg Acad. for Foreign Trade, Nat. Univ. of Mongolia, Columbia Univ.; Sec. Youth Comm., Nat. Central Hospital 1980–82; Vice-Chair. Mongolian Youth Comm. Cttee 1990–91; mem. State Baga Hural (Parl.) 1990–92; Pres. Mongolian Youth Union 1991–97; mem. Great Hural (Parl.) 1996–2000, 2004–06, 2008–; Cabinet mem. and Minister of Nature and Environment 1998; adviser to Tovhon Khan Ltd 2002–04; Chief, Cabinet Secr. of Govt 2004–06; Minister of Finance 2008–. *Address:* Ministry of Finance, Government Building 2, United Nation's street - 5/1, Chingeltei District, Ulan Bator, Mongolia (office). *Telephone:* (11) 262712 (office). *Fax:* (11) 320247 (office). *E-mail:* bayartsogt_s@mof.gov.mn (office). *Website:* www.mof.gov.mn (office).

SANGALA, Aaron; Malawi politician; *Minister of National Defence;* mem. Parl.; Deputy Minister of Health 2006–07; Deputy Minister of Women and Child Devt 2007–08; Minister of Nat. Defence 2008–. *Address:* Ministry of National Defence, Private Bag 339, Capital Hill, Lilongwe 3, Malawi (office). *Telephone:* 8893906 (office). *Fax:* 1789600 (office). *E-mail:* defence@malawi.gov.mw (office). *Website:* www.malawi.gov.mw/Defence/Home%20Defence.htm (office).

SANGARE, Oumou; Malian singer and songwriter; b. 1968, Bamako; m. Ousmane Haidara; one c.; began singing aged five; first performance at Stade des Omnisports aged six; mem. Nat. Ensemble of Mali; mem. Djioliba percussion 1986–89; solo artiste with own backing group 1989–; regular concert tours in W Africa and Europe; first US concert 1994; campaigner for women's rights; apptd Amb. to FAO 2003; Performance of the Year 1993; numerous African Music Awards. *Recordings include:* Moussolou (Women) (Best Selling Album of the Year 1990) 1990, Ko Sira (Marriage Today) (European World Music Album of the Year 1993) 1993, Worotan 1996, Moussolou 1999, Ko Sira 2000, Oumou (compilation) 2003, Seya 2009; appears on African Blues 1998, Beloved 1998; also recordings with Ali Farka Touré, Trilok Gurtu. *Address:* c/o World Circuit Records, First Floor, Shoreditch Stables, 138 Kingsland Road, London, E2 8DY, England (office). *E-mail:* post@worldcircuit.co.uk (office). *Website:* www.worldcircuit.co.uk (office).

SANGER, David John, FRAM, FRCO, ARCM; British organist; b. 17 April 1947, London; s. of Stanley C. Sanger and Ethel L. F. Sanger; ed Eltham Coll., London and Royal Acad. of Music; studied organ in Paris with Marie-Claire Alain and later with Susi Jeans 1966–68; freelance soloist and teacher of organ 1969–; has performed throughout Europe and in USA and Canada; Prof. of Organ, RAM 1983–89, Visiting Prof. of Organ 1989–97; Pres. Royal Coll. of Organists 2009–(11); has recorded six organ symphonies of Louis Vierne and complete organ works of César Franck; Hon. FASC; First Prize, Int. Organ Competition, St Albans 1969, Kiel 1972. *Publication:* Play the Organ (organ tutor for beginners) 1990, Organ Works of Louis Vierne (co-Ed.) 2009. *Leisure interests:* fell-walking, racquet sports, swimming, gardening. *Address:* Old Wesleyan Chapel, Embleton, Cumbria, CA13 9YA, England (home). *Telephone:* (17687) 76628 (home). *Fax:* (17687) 76628 (home). *E-mail:* david.sanger@virgin.net (home). *Website:* www.davidsanger.co.uk (home).

SANGER, Frederick, OM, CH, CBE, PhD, FRS; British research biochemist; b. 13 Aug. 1918, Rendcomb, Glos.; s. of Frederick Sanger and Cicely Crewdson; m. Joan Howe 1940; two s. one d.; ed Bryanston School and St John's Coll., Cambridge; joined biochemical research staff at Univ. of Cambridge 1940; Beit Memorial Fellowship 1944–51; mem. Scientific Staff, Medical Research Council 1951–83; Fellow, King's Coll., Cambridge 1954, Hon. Fellow 1983; Corresp. mem. Asociación Química de Argentina; mem. Acad. of Science of Argentina and Brazil, World Acad. of Arts and Science, Russell Cttee against Chemical Weapons 1981–; Foreign Assoc. NAS, French Acad. of Sciences; Hon. Foreign mem. American Acad. of Arts and Sciences 1958; Hon. mem. American Soc. of Biological Chemists, Japanese Biochemical Soc.; Hon. DSc (Leicester, Oxford, Strasbourg, Cambridge) 1983; Corday-Morgan Medal and Prize, Chemical Soc. 1951, Nobel Prize for Chem. 1958 and (jtly) 1980, Alfred Benzon Prize 1966, Royal Medal (Royal Soc.) 1969, Hopkins Memorial Medal 1971, Gairdner Foundation Annual Award 1971, 1979, Hanbury Memorial Medal 1976, William Bate Hardy Prize 1976, Copley Medal 1977, G.W. Wheland Award 1978, Louisa Gross Horwitz Prize 1979, Albert Lasker Basic Medical Research Award, Columbia Univ. (with W. Gilbert q.v.) 1979, Gold Medal, Royal Soc. of Medicine 1983. *Publications:* numerous papers on protein and nucleic acid structure and metabolism in scientific journals. *Leisure interests:* boating, gardening. *Address:* Far Leys, Fen Lane, Swaffham Bulbeck, Cambridge, CB5 0NJ, England (home). *Telephone:* (1223) 811610.

SANGHELI, Andrei; Moldovan business executive and fmr politician; *Director-General, Limagrain Moldova SRL;* b. 20 July 1944, Grinautsy; m.; one s.; ed Kishinev Agric. Inst., Kishinev Higher CP School; mem. CPSU 1967–91; agronomist, Deputy Dir, Dir of collective farms, Moldova 1971–75, Sec. Kamenka Regional CP Cttee 1975–79, Vice-Chair. Council of Collective Farms of Moldova 1979–80; Chair. Dondushansk Regional Exec. Cttee; First Sec. Regional CP Cttee 1980–86; First Deputy-Chair. Council of Ministers, Chair. State Agric.-Industrial Cttee 1986–89, First Deputy Prime Minister of Moldova; Minister of Agric. and Food 1990–92; Prime Minister of Moldova 1992–96; currently Dir-Gen. Limagrain Moldova SRL (agricultural co.); Chair. Union of Agrarians 1997–. *Address:* Limagrain Moldova SRL, 2004 Chisinau, bd. Stefan cel Mare, 162, Moldova (office). *Telephone:* (22) 21-00-49 (office). *Fax:* (22) 21-00-67 (office). *E-mail:* limagrain@moldovacc.md (office).

SANGMA, Shri Purno Agitok, MA, LLB; Indian lawyer and politician; b. 1 Sept. 1947, Chapahati Village, West Garo Hills Dist; m. Soradini K. Sangma 1973; two s. two d.; ed Dalu High School, St Anthony's Coll. Shillong and Dibrugarh Univ.; mem. Lok Sabha 1977–79, 1980–84, 1985–89, 1991–, Speaker 1996–98; Deputy Minister, Ministry of Industry 1980–82, Ministry of Commerce 1982–85; Minister of State for Commerce 1985–86, for Home Affairs 1986; Minister of State (Independent Charge) for Labour 1986–88; Chief Minister of Meghalaya State 1988–90; Minister of State (Independent Charge) for Coal 1991–95, also for Labour 1993–95; Minister of Information and Broadcasting 1995–96; del. to various int. confs; Founder mem. Nationalist Congress Party; left party to join All India Trinamool Congress 2004; Tata Workers' Union Michael John Roll of Honour for Distinguished Contrib. to the Cause of Labour and to the Parl. System 1997, Golden Jubilee Award of the Indian Nat. Trade Union Congress 1997, Saraswati Nat. Eminence Award for Public Leadership, South Indian Educ. Soc. 2003. *Leisure interests:* reading, discussion, music, indoor games. *Address:* c/o All India Trinamool Congress, 30B Harish Chatterjee Street, Kolkata 700 026 (office); 34, Aurangzeb Road, New Delhi 110 011 (home); Walbakgre, Tura PO, West Garo Hills, Meghalaya, India (home). *Telephone:* (33) 24540881 (office); (11) 23018396. *Fax:* (33) 24540880 (office). *E-mail:* pasangma@sansad.nic.in (office). *Website:* www.trinamoolcongress.com (office).

SANGUINETI, Edoardo; Italian writer; b. 9 Dec. 1930, Genoa; s. of Giovanni Sanguineti and Giuseppina Cocchi; m. Luciana Garabello 1954; three s. one d.; ed Univ. degli Studi, Turin; Prof. of Italian Literature, Univ. of Salerno 1968–74, Genoa 1974–2000; Town Councillor of Genoa 1976–81; mem. Chamber of Deputies 1979–83; Cavaliere di Gran Croce al merito della Repubblica Italiana 1996, Satrape Transcendant Grand Maître O.G.G. du Coll. de Pataphysique 2001. *Publications:* Laborintus 1956, Opus metricum 1960, Interpretazione di Malebolge 1961, Tre studi danteschi 1961, Tra liberty e crepuscolarismo 1961, Alberto Moravia 1962, K. e altre cose 1962, Passaggio 1963, Capriccio italiano 1963, Triperuno 1964, Ideologia e linguaggio 1965, Il realismo di Dante 1966, Guido Gozzano 1966, Il Giuoco dell' Oca 1967, Le Baccanti di Euripide (trans.) 1968, Fedra di Seneca (trans.) 1969, T.A.T. 1969, Teatro 1969, Poesia Italiana del Novecento 1969, Il Giuoco del Satyricon 1970, Orlando Furioso (with L. Ronconi) 1970, Renga (with O. Paz, J. Roubaud, C. Tomlinson) 1971, Storie Naturali 1971, Wirrwarr 1972, Catamerone 1974, Le Troiane di Euripide (trans.) 1974, Giornalino 1976, Postkarten 1978, Le Coefore di Eschilo (trans.) 1978, Giornalino secondo 1979, Stracciafoglio 1980, Edipo tiranno di Sofocle (trans.) 1980, Scartabello 1981, Segnalibro 1982,

Alfabeto apocalittico 1984, Scribilli 1985, Faust, un travestimento 1985, Novissimum Testamentum 1986, Smorfie 1986, La missione del critico 1987, Bisbidis 1987, Ghirigori 1988, Commedia dell'Inferno 1989, Lettura del Decameron 1989, Senzatitolo 1992, I Sette contro Tebe di Eschilo (trans.) 1992, Dante reazionario 1992, Gazzettini 1993, Per musica 1993, Satyricon di Petronio (trans.) 1993, Opere e introduzione critica 1993, Malebolge (with E. Baj) 1995, Libretto 1995, Per una critica dell'avanguardia poetica (with J. Burgos) 1995, Tracce (with M. Lucchesi) 1995, Minitarjetas 1996, Orlando Furioso, un travestimento ariostesco 1996, Corollario 1997, Il mio amore è come una febbre (with S. Liberovici) 1998, Cose 1999, Don Giovanni di Molière (trans.) 2000, Il chierico organico 2000, Verdi in Technicolor 2001, La Festa delle donne di Aristofane (trans.) 2001, Sei personaggi.com 2001, L'amore delle tre melarance 2001, Atlante del Novecento italiano 2001, L'orologio astronomico 2002, Il gatto lupesco 2002, Carol Rama 2002, Il cerchio di gesso del Caucaso di Brecht (trans.) 2003, Omaggio a Goethe 2003, Omaggio a Shakespeare 2004, Mikrokosmos 2004, Schede gramsciane 2004, Genova per me 2005, L'illusione comica di Corneille (trans.) 2005, Quaderno di traduzioni (trans.) 2006, Mantova, 13.9.6 2006, Come si diventa materialisti storici 2006, Teatro antico (trans.) 2006, Smorfie 2007. *Leisure interests:* to live. *Address:* Via Pergolesi 20, 16159 Genoa, Italy (home). *Telephone:* (10) 7452050 (home). *Fax:* (10) 7452050 (home).

SANGUINETTI CAIROLO, Julio María; Uruguayan lawyer and politician; b. 1936; m. Marta Canessa; one s. one d.; mem. Gen. Ass. 1962–73; Minister of Industry and Labour 1969–72, of Educ. and Culture 1972–73; then Pres. Comisión Nacional de Artes Plásticas and Pres. of UNESCO Comm. for promotion of books in Latin America; Pres. of Uruguay 1985–89, 1995–2000; Leader (Foro Batllista) Colorado Party 1989–94; Pres. Nat. Fine Arts Council. *Address:* c/o Office of the President, Casa de Gobierno, Edif. Libertad, Avda Luis Alberto de Herrera 3350, esq. Avda José Pedro Varela, Montevideo, Uruguay.

SANHÁ, Issufo; Guinea-Bissau politician; Minister of the Economy 1998–2007, of Finance 2007–09; mem. Partido Africano da Independência da Guiné e Cabo Verde (PAIGC). *Address:* Partido Africano da Independência da Guiné e Cabo Verde, CP 106, Bissau, Guinea-Bissau (office). *Website:* www .paigc.org (office).

SANKARANARAYANAN, Kateekal; Indian politician; *Governor of Nagaland and Arunachal Pradesh;* b. 15 Oct. 1932; s. of the late A. Sankaran Nair and K. Lekshmi Amma; active mem. students' org. from 1946; elected to 5th Kerala Legis. Ass. (KLA) from Thrithala, 6th KLA from Sreekrishnapuram, 8th KLA from Ottappalam, 11th KLA from Palghat Constituency, as Indian Nat. Congress mem.; Convenor United Democratic Front 1985–2001; Minister for Agric., Animal Husbandry and Dairy Devt and Community Devt 11–25 April 1977, 27 April–Oct. 1978; Chair. Cttee on Govt Assurances 1980–82, Cttee on Public Accounts 1989–91; Minister for Finance and Excise 2001–04, continued as MLA –2006; served as minister in state govt of Kerala; Gov. of Nagaland Feb. 2007–, of Arunachal Pradesh (Additional Charge) during absence on leave of S. K. Singh Sept. 2007–. *Address:* Raj Bhawan, Kohima, Nagaland (office); Raj Bhawan, Itanagar 791 111, Arunachal Pradesh, India. *Telephone:* (370) 2242881 (Kohima) (office); (370) 2242881 (Kohima) (home); (360) 2212508 (Itanagar) (office); (360) 2212432 (Itanagar) (office); (360) 2212394 (Itanagar) (home); (360) 2212418 (Itanagar) (office). *E-mail:* info@ nagaland.nic.in (office); info@arunachalgovernor.gov.in (office). *Website:* nagaland.nic.in (office); arunachalpradesh.nic.in (office); arunachalgovernor .gov.in (office).

SANKEY, John Anthony, CMG, PhD; British diplomatist (retd); b. 8 June 1930, London; m. Gwendoline Putman 1958; two s. two d.; ed Cardinal Vaughan School, Kensington; Peterhouse, Cambridge, NATO Defence Coll., Rome, Univ. of Leeds; Colonial Office 1953, UK Mission to UN, New York 1961, FCO 1964, Guyana 1968, Singapore 1971, Malta 1973, The Hague 1975, Special Counsellor for African Affairs, FCO 1980–82; High Commr in Tanzania 1982–85; Perm. Rep. to the UN in Geneva 1985–90; Sec.-Gen. Soc. of London Art Dealers 1991–96; Dir Int. Art and Antiques Loss Register 1993–96; Chair. Tanzania Devt Trust 1999–2004. *Leisure interest:* Victorian sculpture. *Address:* 108 Lancaster Gate, London, W2 3NW, England. *Telephone:* (20) 7723-2256.

SANO, Seiichiro; Japanese business executive; *Executive Director and President, SANYO Electric Co. Ltd;* b. 20 Nov. 1952, Osaka; ed Kwansei Gakuin Univ.; joined SANYO Electric Co. Ltd 1977, Human Resources Div., Audio Business 1977–89, Labour Admin Div., Human Resources HQ 1989–92, Man. Labour Admin Div. 1992–97, Man. Human Resouces Dept 1997–2000, Gen. Man., Gen. Affairs/Human Resources 2000–07, Gen. Man. Human Resources Group 2001–03, Gen. Man. Corp. Admin Dept 2003–05, Vice-Pres. 2005–07, Exec. Dir and Pres. 2007–. *Address:* SANYO Electric Co. Ltd, 5-5 Keihan-Hondori, 2-chome, Moriguchi, Osaka 570-8677, Japan (office). *Telephone:* (6) 6991-1181 (office). *Fax:* (6) 6991-5411 (office). *E-mail:* info@sanyo .com (office). *Website:* www.sanyo.com (office).

SANT, Alfred, MSc, MBA, DBA; Maltese politician; *Leader, Malta Labour Party;* b. 28 Feb. 1948; ed Univ. of Malta, Inst. Int. d'Admin Publique, Paris, Boston Univ. and Harvard Business School, USA; Second Sec., First Sec., Malta Mission to European Communities, Brussels 1970–75; adviser on gen. and financial man. Ministry of Parastatal and People's Industries, Valletta 1977–78; Man. Dir Medina Consulting Group 1978–80; Exec. Deputy Chair. Malta Devt Corpn 1980–82; consultant to pvt. and public sectors 1982–; Chair. Metal Fond Ltd, Bottex Clothing 1982–84, First Clothing Cooperative 1983–87; Lecturer, Man. Faculty, Univ. of Malta 1984–87; Adviser to Prime Minister on econ. and diplomatic affairs 1985–87; Chair. Dept of Information, Malta Labour Party 1982–92; Pres. Malta Labour Party 1984–88, Leader 1992–; mem. Parl. 1987–; Prime Minister of Malta 1996–98; Leader of the Opposition 1998–2009. *Plays:* Fio. dell Tal-Katioral 1994, Oabel Tiftau L-Inujesta 1999. *Publications:* Min Hu Evelyn Costa? (plays) 1979, L-Ewwel Weraq tal-Bajtar (novel), Silg fuq Kemmuna (novel) 1985, Malta's European Challenge (essay) 1995, Bejgh u Xiri (novel) 1999, La Bidu, La Tmiem (novel) 2001, Confessions of a Maltese European 2003; contrib. articles in the press and professional publs. *Leisure interests:* travel, reading, writing, listening to music, farming. *Address:* 18a, Victory Street, B'Kara, Malta (home). *Telephone:* 21495742 (office). *E-mail:* alfred.sant@gov.mt (office). *Website:* alfredsant.org.

SANTANA, Carlos; Mexican musician; b. 20 July 1947, Autlán de Navarro; s. of José Santana; played Tijuana night clubs; debut with the Santana Blues Band 1966, played at Woodstock Festival Aug. 1969; guitarist, Santana Man. 1987–; Prin. Guts and Grace Records 1993; performed with Mike Bloomfield, Al Kooper, Buddy Miles, McCoy Turner, Jose Feliciano, Herbie Hancock, Wayne Shorter, Alice Coltrane, Aretha Franklin, Mahavishnu John Mclaughlin; co-founder Milagro Foundation supporting young people in the arts, health and education 1998; Santana Band first to earn CBS Record's Crystal Globe Award, multiple Best Pop-Rock Guitarist in Playboy Magazine's Readers' Poll, Grammy for Best Rock Instrumental Performance 1988, Nosotros Golden Eagle Legend Award 1992, Recording Acad. (NARAS) tribute concert and induction into Hollywood Rock Walk, Billboard Magazine Century Award 1996, ten Bay Area Music Awards, BAMMY Hall of Fame, Chicano Music Awards Latino Music Legend of the Year 1997, Rock 'n' Roll Hall of Fame, Hollywood Walk of Fame 1998, also won nine Grammys Feb. 2000, Latin Recording Acad. Person of the Year 2004; numerous civic and humanitarian commendations. *Films:* Viva Santana 1988, Sacred Fire 1993, A History of Santana: The River Of Color And Sound 1997, A Supernatural Evening With Santana 2000. *Recordings include:* albums: Santana 1969, Abraxas 1970, Santana III 1971, Greatest Hits 1974, Moonflower 1977, Inner Secrets 1978, Zebop! 1981, Shango 1982, Freedom 1987, Freedom 1987, Viva Santana 1988, Milagro 1992, Sacred Fire 1993, Dance Of The Rainbow Serpent 1995, Live At The Fillmore 1997, Best of Santana 1998, Supernatural 1999, All That I Am 2005. *Address:* Santana Management, PO Box 10348, San Rafael, CA 94912, USA (office). *E-mail:* info@jensencom.com. *Website:* www .santana.com (office).

SANTANA CARLOS, António Nunes de Carvalho; Portuguese diplomatist; *Ambassador to UK;* b. 20 March 1945, Lisbon; m. Maria Santana Carlos; one s.; ed Univ. of Lisbon; joined Foreign Service 1971, posts included Second Sec., Embassy in Tokyo 1974–76, Head of Cipher Dept, Foreign Office 1976, First Sec., Dept of Int. Econ. Orgs, Foreign Office 1979, served in Perm. Mission in Geneva, Switzerland 1982–86, Minister Counsellor, Luanda, Angola 1986–90, Dir Multilateral Affairs Dept, Foreign Office 1990–93, Deputy Dir-Gen. of Political and Econ. Affairs, Foreign Office 1993–94, Dir Office of Econ. Affairs 1994, Chargé de Mission to Minister of Foreign Affairs for Lisbon World Exhbn 1995, Sr Rep. to China-Portugal Jt Liaison Group 1996, also served as Pres. Interministerial Comm. on Macau, Chargé de Mission to Minister of Foreign Affairs for East Timor affairs 2000–02, Dir-Gen. of Foreign Policy 2000–02, Amb. to People's Repub. of China (also accred to Mongolia) 2002–06, to UK 2006–; Grand Cross of the Order of Christ 2002, Grand Cross of the Order of Merit, Grand Officer of the Order Infante D. Henrique, Grand Officer of the Order Wissan Alouite (Morocco), Kt of the Order Rio Branco (Brazil). *Leisure interests:* sailing, golf, walking. *Address:* Embassy of Portugal, 11 Belgrave Square, London, SW1X 8PP, UK (office). *Telephone:* (20) 7235-5331 (office). *Fax:* (20) 7235-0739 (office); (20) 7245-1287 (office). *E-mail:* london@portembassy.co.uk (office).

SANTANA LOPES, Pedro; Portuguese lawyer and politician; b. 29 June 1956, Lisbon; five c.; ed Univ. of Lisbon; joined Social Democratic Party 1976, Vice-Pres., Pres. 2004–05; fmr Sec. of State for Culture; fmr Mayor of Figueira da Foz, then Lisbon 2002–July 2004, Feb. 2005–Oct. 2005; Prime Minister of Portugal July 2004–Feb. 2005 (resgnd); currently mem. Parl. *Address:* c/o Partido Social Democrata (PSD) (Social Democratic Party) Rua de São Caetano 9, 1249-087, Lisbon, Portugal (office). *Telephone:* (21) 3952140 (office). *Fax:* (21) 3976967 (office). *E-mail:* psd@psd.pt (office). *Website:* www .psd.pt (office).

SANTER, Jacques, DenD; Luxembourg politician; b. 18 May 1937, Wasserbillig; s. of Josef Santer and Marguerite Santer; m. Danièle Binot; two s.; ed Athénée de Luxembourg, Univs of Paris and Strasbourg and Inst. d'Etudes Politiques, Paris; advocate, Luxembourg Court of Appeal 1961–65; attaché, Office of Minister of Labour and Social Security 1963–65; Govt attaché 1965–66; Parl. Sec. Parti Chrétien-Social 1966–72, Sec.-Gen. 1972–74, Pres. 1974–82; Sec. of State for Cultural and Social Affairs 1972–74; mem. Chamber of Deputies 1974–79; Municipal Magistrate, City of Luxembourg 1976–79; Minister of Finance, of Labour and of Social Security 1979–84; Prime Minister, Minister of State and Minister of Finance 1984–89, Prime Minister, Minister of State, of Cultural Affairs and of the Treasury and Financial Affairs 1989–94, now Hon. Minister of State; MEP 1975–79, 1999–2004, Vice-Pres. 1975–77; Pres. European Comm. 1994–99; Chair. Bd CLT-UFA 2004–; Chair. Bd Unicredit International Bank 2005, mem. Bd RTL Group 2005–; Hon. LLD (Wales) 1998, (Miami Univ.), (Sacred Heart Univ., Ohio), (Univ. of Urbino, Italy), (Kyoto Univ., Japan) and others; Prize Prince d'Asturias (Spain) 1998, Robert Schumann Prize, Jean Monnet Medal (Lausanne, Switzerland) and others. *Leisure interests:* walking, swimming. *Address:* 33 boulevard F. D. Roosevelt, 2450 Luxemburg (office); 69 rue J.-P. Huberty, 1742 Luxemburg (home). *Telephone:* 478-8155 (office); 42-00-40 (home). *Fax:* 26-27-08-37 (office); 26-43-09-99 (home). *E-mail:* jacques.santer@me.etat.lu (office).

SANTER, Rt Rev. Mark, MA, DD; British ecclesiastic; b. 29 Dec. 1936, Bristol; s. of Rev. Canon E. A. R. Santer and Phyllis C. Barlow; m. 1st

Henriette Cornelia Weststrate 1964 (died 1994); m. 2nd Sabine Böhmig Bird 1997; one s. two d.; ed Marlborough Coll., Queens' Coll. and Westcott House, Cambridge; Curate All Saints Cuddesdon 1963–67; Tutor Cuddesdon Coll., Oxford 1963–67; Dean and Fellow Clare Coll., Cambridge 1967–72; Asst Lecturer in Divinity, Univ. of Cambridge 1968–72; Principal Westcott House 1973–81; Area Bishop of Kensington 1981–87; Bishop of Birmingham 1987–2002; Co-Chair. Anglican/RC Int. Comm. 1983–99; Hon. Fellow Clare Coll., Cambridge 1987, Queens' Coll., Cambridge 1991; Hon. DD (Birmingham) 1998, (Lambeth) 1999; Hon. DUniv (Univ. of Cen. England) 2003. *Publications:* Documents in Early Christian Thought (with M. F. Wiles) 1975, Their Lord and Ours (ed.) 1982. *Address:* 81 Clarence Road, Birmingham, B13 9UH, England (home). *Telephone:* (121) 441-2194 (home). *E-mail:* msanter@btinternet.com (home).

SANTO CARVALHO, Evaristo do Spirito; São Tomé and Príncipe politician; Prime Minister of São Tomé e Príncipe July–Oct. 1994; mem. Partido de Convergência Democrática-Grupo de Reflexão (PCD-GR) (expelled from party July 1994). *Address:* c/o Office of the Prime Minister, São Tomé, São Tomé e Príncipe.

SANTORUM, Rick, MBA, JD; American fmr politician; *Senior Fellow, Ethics and Public Policy Center;* b. 10 May 1958, Winchester, Va; s. of Aldo Santorum and Catherine Dughi; m. Karen Garver 1990; two s. two d.; ed Pa State Univ., Pa State Coll., Univ. of Pittsburgh and Dickinson Law School; mem. Bar of Pa 1986; Admin. Asst to State Senator Doyle Corman, Harrisburg, Pa 1981–86; Exec. Dir Local Govt Cttee Pa State Senate 1981–84, Transport Cttee 1984–86; Assoc. Attorney, Kirkpatrick and Lockhart, Pittsburgh 1986–90; mem. Congress from 18th Pa Dist 1991–95; Senator from Pennsylvania 1995–2007; Sr Fellow, Ethics and Public Policy Center, Washington, DC 2007–, est. and directs America's Enemies program; contrib. Fox News 2007–; Republican. *Publication:* It Takes a Family: Conservatism and the Common Good 2005. *Leisure interests:* golf, cross-country skiing, racquet sports. *Address:* c/o Melissa Anderson, Ethics and Public Policy Center, 1015 15th Street, NW, Suite 900, Washington, DC 20005 (office); 127 Seminole Drive, Pittsburgh, PA 15228, USA (home). *Telephone:* (202) 715-3495 (office). *Fax:* (202) 408-0632 (office). *E-mail:* manderson@eppc.org (office). *Website:* www.eppc.org (office).

SANTOS CALDERÓN, Francisco; Colombian journalist and politician; *Vice-President;* b. 14 Oct. 1961, Bogotá; ed Univ. of Kansas, Univ. of Texas at Austin, USA; in late 1980s taught journalism and US–Latin American relations at several Colombian univs including Universidad Central, Universidad Javeriana, Universidad Jorge Tadeo Lozano; fmr Ed. El Tiempo (daily newspaper); kidnapped with other journalists by Pablo Escobar, leader of Medellín drug cartel 1990, held for eight months; Nieman Fellow, Harvard Univ. 1992; moved to Madrid, Spain and worked as journalist for daily newspaper El País 2000–02; Vice-Pres. of Colombia 2002–; co-f. Fundación Pais Libre (Free Country Foundation); Paul Harris Medal, Rotary Int. *Address:* c/o Office of the President, Palacio de Nariño, Carrera 8a, No. 7–26, Bogotá, Colombia (office). *Telephone:* (1) 562-9300 (office). *Fax:* (1) 286-8063 (office).

SANTOS CALDERÓN, Juan Manuel; Colombian politician; *Minister of National Defence;* b. 10 Aug. 1951, Bogotá; m. María Clemencia Rodríguez; two s. one d.; ed Cartagena Naval Acad. of Colombia, Univ. of Kansas, USA, London School of Econs, UK, Harvard Univ., USA; fmr leader Colombian Del. to Int. Coffee Org. negotiations, London; fmr journalist, Deputy Dir and Pres. Editorial Bd El Tiempo (daily); apptd Minister of Foreign Trade 1991; Vice-Pres. 1993; apptd Minister of Finance and Public Credit 2000; managed Pres. Alvaro Uribe's re-election campaign 2006; Minister of Nat. Defence 2006–; Pres. UNCTAD 1992–96, UN ECLA 1997–99; fmr Vice-Pres. Press Freedom Comm. of Inter-American Press Soc.; Founder and Chair. Fundación Buengobierno; Bernardo O'Higgins en el Grado de Comendador 1996, Gran Oficial de la Orden Nacional Francesca del Mérito 2001; Fulbright and Neiman Fellowships, King of Spain Prize for journalism. *Publications:* several books including The Third Way, An Alternative for Colombia. *Address:* Ministry of National Defence, Centro Administrativo Nacional (CAN), Avda El Dorado carrera 52, Bogotá, DC, Colombia (office). *Telephone:* (1) 266-0185 (office). *Fax:* (1) 266-0351 (office). *E-mail:* yoljime@mindefensa.gov.co (office). *Website:* www.mindefensa.gov.co (office).

SANTOS LÓPEZ, Samuel; Nicaraguan politician; *Minister of Foreign Affairs;* b. 13 Dec. 1938, Managua; s. of Samuel Santos Fernández and Lucila López Bermúdez; m. Annelly Molina de Santos; early business career with several managerial roles including roles at Publicidad Noble y Asociados, Honduras, Hotel Best Western Las Mercedes, Inversiones Inmobiliaras Acuario S.A., Inmobiliarios Penta S.A., Inmobiliarios Alpha S.A., Inmobiliarios Beta S.A; Founder and fmr Dir Stock Market of Nicaragua; mem. Nat. Govt for Reconstruction 1979–85; Vice-Pres. Nat. Devt Bank 1979–80; Minister in charge of Reconstruction of Managua 1980–85; Mayor of Managua 1984–85; Finance Sec. Frente Sandinista de Liberación Nacional (FSLN) 1992–, Exec. Sec. –2001, Int. Relations Spokesperson 2001–06; Minister of Foreign Affairs 2007–; mem. Chamber of Commerce, Chamber of Tourism, Union of Latin American Capital Cities, Exec. Cttee of the Bolivian Congress for Town Devt, Works Comm. for the Inter-Oceanic Canal of Nicaragua. *Address:* Ministry of Foreign Affairs, Del Cine González al Sur sobre Avenida Bolivar, Managua, Nicaragua (office). *Telephone:* (2) 244-8000 (office). *Fax:* (2) 228-5102 (office). *E-mail:* samuel.santos@cancilleria.gob.ni (office). *Website:* www.cancilleria.gob.ni (office).

SANTOS-NEVES, Augusto R., BA, MBA; Brazilian diplomatist; *Ambassador to UK;* b. 1944, Rio de Janeiro; m. Mary Joan Hershberger; two s. one d.; ed Instituto Rio Branco, Fundação Getulio Vargas, Columbia Univ., USA; joined diplomatic service 1966, Asst to Foreign Minister 1977–79, Chief of Staff to Sec. Gen. of Foreign Ministry 1985–88; Consul Gen. in New York 1988–92; Amb. to Mexico 1992–96 (also accred. to Belize 1995–96), to Canada 1996–99; Sec. for Policy Planning, Foreign Ministry 1999–2001, Consul Gen. in Houston, Tex. 2001–03, Amb. to Russian Fed. 2003–08 (also accred. to Kazakhstan, Belarus, Georgia, Turkmenistan and Uzbekistan), to UK 2008–; Légion d'honneur, Ordre Nat. du Mérite, Order of Rio Branco. *Address:* Embassy of Brazil, 32 Green Street, London, W1K 7AT, England (office). *Telephone:* (20) 7399-9000 (office). *Fax:* (20) 7399-9100 (office). *E-mail:* info@brazil.org.uk (office). *Website:* www.brazil.org.uk (office).

SANTOS ORDÓÑEZ, Elvin Ernesto, BSc; Honduran engineer, business executive and politician; b. 18 Jan. 1963, Tegucigalpa; s. of Elvin Santos Lozano and Sonia Ordóñez de Santos; m. Becky Manzanares de Santos; four c.; ed Lamar Univ., USA; CEO Santos y Compañia Construction Co.; fmr Consul in Austin, Tex; fmr Chair. Honduras Chamber of Industry and Construction, Dir Honduras Pvt. Enterprise Council, Nat. Asscn of Industrialists; mem. Partido Liberal de Honduras; Vice-Pres. of Honduras 2006–08 (resgnd); Partido Liberal candidate for 2009 presidential election; mem. Colegio de Ingenieros Civiles de Honduras, American Soc. of Civil Engineers. *Address:* Partido Liberal, Col. Miramonte, Tegucigalpa, Honduras (office). *Telephone:* 232-0520 (office). *Fax:* 232-0797 (office). *E-mail:* multimedia@partidoliberal.net (office). *Website:* www.partidoliberal.net (office).

SANTOS RIVERA, Rebeca Patricia; Honduran politician; *Minister of Finance;* fmr consultant, Honduran Social Security Inst.; consultant, World Bank Resident Mission in Honduras –2006; Vice Minister of Finance 2006, Minister of Finance 2006–. *Address:* Ministry of Finance, 5A Avda, 3A Calle, Tegucigalpa, Honduras (office). *Telephone:* 222-1278 (office). *Fax:* 238-2309 (office). *E-mail:* despacho@sefin.gob.hn (office). *Website:* www.sefin.gob.hn (office).

SANTOS SIMÃO, Leonardo, LicMed, MSc; Mozambican politician and medical practitioner; *Executive Director, Joaquim Chissano Foundation;* b. 6 June 1953, Mandlakaze; s. of Antonio Santos Simão Sitoi and Amélia Muchanga; m. Josephine P. Simão; two d.; ed Liceu Salazar, Maputo, Eduardo Mondlane Univ., Univ. of London, UK, Boston Univ., USA; Dir Centre of Dist Formation of Chicumbane, Gaza 1981–1982; Prov. Health Dir Zambezia Prov. 1982–84; Dir Prov. Hosp. of Quelimane, Zambezia Prov. 1984–88; Minister of Health 1988; apptd Prof. of Medicine, Eduardo Mondlane Univ. 1988; Minister of Foreign Affairs and Co-operation 1994–95; currently Exec. Dir Joaquim Chissano Foundation; Chair. Nat. Mine Clearance Comm.; mem. Cen. Cttee Frelimo Party; mem. Medical Asscn of Mozambique, Mozambique Asscn of Public Health; Great Cross, Order of Rio Branco (Brazil) 1996, Order of Good Hope, II Grade (South Africa) 1997, Great Cross, Order of Merit (Portugal) 1998, Order of Eduardo Mondlane (Mozambique) 2005, Diploma of Honour (Mozambique) 2005. *Leisure interests:* music, reading, swimming. *Address:* The Joaquim Chissano Foundation, 954, Av. Zimbabwe, Maputo, Mozambique (office). *Telephone:* (21) 484000 (office). *Fax:* (21) 484001 (office). *E-mail:* l.simao@fjchissano.org.mz (office). *Website:* www.fjchissano.org.mz (office).

SAOUMA, Edouard; Lebanese international organization official and agricultural engineer; b. 6 Nov. 1926, Beirut; m. Inès Forero; one s. two d.; ed St Joseph's Univ. School of Eng, Beirut, Ecole nat. Supérieure d'Agronomie, Montpellier, France; Dir Tel Amara Agricultural School 1952–53, Nat. Centre for Farm Mechanization 1954–55; Sec.-Gen. Nat. Fed. of Lebanese Agronomists 1955; Dir-Gen. Nat. Inst. for Agricultural Research 1957–62; mem. Governing Board, Nat. Grains Office 1960–62; Lebanese del. to FAO 1955–62, Deputy Regional Rep. for Asia and Far East 1962–65, mem. of Secr. 1963–, Dir Land and Water Devt Div. 1965–75, Dir-Gen. of FAO 1976–93; Minister of Agric., Fisheries and Forestry Oct.–Nov. 1970; Hon. Prof. of Agronomy, Agric. Univ. of Beijing; Accademico Corrispondente dell' Accademia Nazionale di Agricoltura (Italy); Order of the Cedar (Lebanon), Said Akl Prize (Lebanon); Chevalier du Mérite agricole (France), Grand Croix, Ordre nat. du Tchad, du Ghana, de la Haute Volta (Burkina Faso), Gran Cruz al Mérito Agrícola (Spain), Kt Commdr Order of Merit (Greece), Orden del Mérito Agrícola (Colombia), Gran Oficial del Orden de Vasco Núñez de Balboa (Panama), Orden al Mérito Agrícola (Peru), Order of Merit (Egypt, Mauritania), Grand Officier, Ordre de la République (Tunisia), Grand Officier, Ordre Nat. (Madagascar); Dr hc from 16 univs. *Publications:* technical publs in agric. *Address:* PO Box H0210, Baabda, Lebanon.

SAPIN, Michel; French politician; b. 9 April 1952, Boulogne-Billancourt; m. Yolande Millan 1982; three c.; ed Ecole Normale Supérieure, Paris and Ecole Nat. d'Admin; joined Parti Socialiste 1975; elected Deputy Nat. Ass. for Indre 1981–86, 2007–, for Hauts-de-Seine 1986–91, Sec. 1983–84, Vice-Pres. 1984, Chair. of the Cttee for Law 1988–91; town councillor, Nanterre 1989–94; Minister Del. for Justice 1991–92; Minister of Economy and Finance 1992–93, of Civil Service, of Admin. Reform 2000–02; Regional Councillor Ile de France 1992–94; mem. Council for Monetary Policy of Banque de France 1994–95; Mayor of Argenton-sur-Creuse 1995–2004; Gen. Councillor of Indre 1998–; Pres. Centre Regional Council 1998–2000, 2004–07, Vice-Pres. 2000–01; First Vice-Pres. Asscn of the Regions of France 1998–2000; Nat. Sec. on Economy, Parti Socialiste 2007–. *Address:* Assemblée Nationale, 126 Rue de l'Université 753555 Paris (office). *Telephone:* 1-40-63-93-16 (office). *E-mail:* msapin@assemblee-nationale.fr (office). *Website:* www.assemblee-nationale.fr (office).

SAPORTA, Marc, LLD; French writer; b. 20 March 1923; s. of Jaime Saporta and Simone Nahmias; m. 1st Denise Kleman 1949 (died 1966); m. 2nd Michèle Truchan 1972; three d.; ed Univ. of Paris and Univ. of Madrid, Spain; worked in Dept of Cultural Activities, UNESCO 1948–53, Asst Ed. Informations et Documents 1954–71, Ed. 1971–78; Ed.-in-Chief Dept of Publs, US Information Agency, Paris 1978–84; Literary Critic, L'Express 1954–71, La Quinzaine

Littéraire 1966–71. *Radio:* 1917 La Relève 1967. *Publications:* Les lois de l'air 1953, La convention universelle du droit d'auteur de UNESCO 1952, Le grand défi: USA-URSS, I 1967, II 1968 (ed. and co-author), Histoire du roman américain 1970, La vie quotidienne contemporaine aux USA 1972, Go West 1976, William Faulkner (ed. and co-author) 1983, Henry James (ed. and co-author) 1983, I. B. Singer (ed. and co-author) 1984, Nathalie Sarraute (ed. and co-author) 1984, Marguerite Duras (ed. and co-author) 1985, Vivre aux Etats-Unis 1986, André Breton ou le Surréalisme Même (ed. and co-author) 1988, Israel 1988, Les Erres du Faucon, une psychobiographie de William Faulkner 1989, Le roman américain 1997; novels: Le furet 1959, La distribution 1961, La quête 1961, Composition numéro un 1962, Les invités 1964. *Leisure interest:* ice-skating. *Address:* 9 rue Saint-Didier, 75116 Paris, France.

SAPUTO, Emanuele (Lino); Canadian business executive; *Chairman, Saputo Inc.;* b. 1937, Italy; s. of Guiseppe Saputo and Maria Saputo; m. Mirella Saputo; two s. one d.; family emigrated to Canada 1952; with parents f. dairy processor Saputo Inc. 1954, Chair. 1969–, Pres. 1969–2004, CEO 1998–2004; mem. Bd of Dirs Tembec Inc. 2006–07; mem. Bd of Trustees TransForce Income Fund 2008–; f. Jolina Capital (investment co.). *Address:* Saputo Inc., 6869 Metropolitain Boulevard East, Saint-Leonard, PQ H1P 1X8, Canada (office). *Telephone:* (514) 328-6662 (office). *Fax:* (514) 328-3364 (office). *Website:* www.saputo.com (office).

SAR, Kheng; Cambodian politician; *Deputy Prime Minister and Minister of the Interior;* b. 15 Jan. 1951, Prey Veng; m. Nhem Sakhan; mem. Cen. Cttee Cambodian People Party 1984–, Pres. Org. Comm. 1990–; Deputy Prime Minister 1992–, Co-minister of the Interior 1998–2006, Minister of the Interior 2006–; fmr Acting Prime Minister; Chair. Nat. Census Cttee; fmr Co-Chair. Nat. Cttee to Support Commune/Sangkat; Membership Award, Natural Sciences Acad. of the Russian Fed. 2002. *Address:* Ministry of the Interior, 275 blvd Norodom, Khan Chamkarmon, Phnom-Penh, Cambodia (office). *Telephone:* (23) 721190 (office). *Fax:* (23) 721190 (office). *E-mail:* info@interior.gov.kh (office). *Website:* www.interior.gov.kh (office).

SARABHAI, Mrinalini; Indian dancer and choreographer; *Founder-Director, Darpana Academy of Performing Arts;* b. 11 May 1918, Madras; d. of Shri Swaminadhan and Smt. Ammu Swaminadhan; m. Dr Vikram A. Sarabhai; ed American Acad. of Dramatic Arts; studied dance with Meenakshi Sundaram Pillai and Thakazhi Kunchu Kurup; studied under Meenakshi Sundaram Pillai; Founder-Dir Darpana Acad. of Performing Arts, Ahmedabad 1949–; Chair. Handicrafts & Handloom Devt Corpn of Gujarat State; Chair. Friends of Trees, Gujarat State; mem. Sangeet Natak Acad., New Delhi; Pres. Alliance Française, Prakriti; Exec. Cttee Int. Dance Council 1990; adviser to many arts and cultural insts in India; Trustee Sarvodaya Int. Trust; Fellow, Sangeet Natak Akademi 1994; Kerala Kalamandalam Fellowship 1995; Hon. Consultant, Nat. Centre for Performing Arts, Bombay; Padma Shri 1965, Padma Bhushan 1992; Hon. DLitt (Univ. of East Anglia) 1997; French Archives Internationales de la Danse Medal (first Indian), Sangeet Natak Akademi Fellowship, New Delhi 1994, Gold Medal, Govt of Mexico for choreography of the Ballet Folklorico of Mexico. *Publications:* Staging a Sanskrit Classic – Bhasa's Vision of Vasavadatta (with John D. Mitchell) 1992, one novel, textbook on Bharata Natyam, a book on various classical dance-dramas, children's books and articles in newspapers and journals. *Leisure interests:* reading, watching TV, writing, dancing, social work. *Address:* Darpana Academy of Performing Arts, Usmanpura, Ahmedabad 380013, Gujarat, India (office). *Telephone:* (79) 2755-1389 (office). *Fax:* (79) 2755-0566 (office). *E-mail:* mrinalini@darpana.com (office). *Website:* www.darpana.com (office).

SARABI, Habiba; Afghan politician, haematologist, pharmacist and women's rights activist; *Governor of Bamiyan Province;* b. 5 Dec. 1957, Mazar-e Sharif; m.; three c.; ed Aisha Durani High School, Kabul Univ.; licensed pharmacist; with Nat. Inst. of Medicine, Kabul 1983–87; teacher, Intermediate Medical Inst., Kabul 1988–96; exile in Pakistan 1996–2001; Prof. and Gen. Man. Afghanistan Inst. of Learning 1997–2001; medical aid to women and children in refugee camps on Afghanistan-Pakistan border 2001; Dir of Humanitarian Assistance for the Women and Children of Afghanistan, Peshawar 2002; Minister of Women's Affairs 2002–04; Gov. of Bamiyan Prov. (first female gov. in Afghanistan) 2005–; est. Band-e Amir Nat. Park; WHO Fellowship Training Programme, All India Inst. of Medical Science 1998; Jason Award, USA 2005, Malalai Maiwand Medal from Pres. Karzai 2005, named by Time magazine a Hero of the Environment 2008. *Address:* Chawney, Governor's Office, Bamyan, Afghanistan (office). *Telephone:* 799300120 (office); 202400008 (home). *E-mail:* bamyangovernor@yahoo.com (office).

SARACENO, Chiara, PhD; Italian sociologist and academic; *Research professor, Wissenschaftszentrum Berlin fuer Sozialforschung;* b. 20 Oct. 1941, Milan; m.; two d.; Assoc. Prof. then Full Prof., Faculty of Sociology, Univ. of Trento –1990, Vice Rector 1989–90; Prof. of Sociology of the Family, Faculty of Political Sciences, Univ. of Turin 1990–2008, Chair.Dept of Social Sciences 1991–97, Chair Univ. Gender and Women Studies Center (CIRSDe) 1997–2006, Chair.PhD Programme in Comparative Social Research 1996-2005; Research Prof., Wissenschaftszentrum Berlin fuer Sozialforschung 2006–; Kt of the Grand Cross. *Publications:* Genere. La costruzione sociale del femminile e del maschile (ed with Simonetta Piccone Stella) 1996, Separarsi in Italia (with Marzio Barbagli) 1998, Sociologia della famiglia (with Manuela Naldini) 2001, Età e corso della vita 2001, Commissione d'indagine sull'esclusione sociale, Rapporto sulle politiche contro la povertà e l'esclusione sociale. 1997–2001 2002, Social Assistance Dynamics in European Welfare States (ed.) 2002, Diversi da chi? Gay, lesbiche, transessuali in un'area metropolitana (ed.) 2003, Mutamenti della famiglia e politiche sociali in Italia 2003, Dinamiche assistenziali in Europa (ed.) 2004, Quality of Life in the Enlarged European Union (ed. with A. Alber and T. Fahey) 2007, Childhood.-Changing Contexts (ed. with A. Leira) 2008, Families, Aging and Social Policy (ed.) 2008; numerous scientific papers in academic journals on comparative family changes, gender patterns, family and social policies, poverty and anti-poverty policies in comparative perspective. *Address:* Wissenschaftzentrum Berlin fuer Socialforschung Reichpietschufer 50, 10785 Berlin, Germany (office). *Telephone:* (30) 25491378 (office). *Fax:* (30) 25491360 (office). *E-mail:* chiara.saraceno@unito.it (office); saraceno@wzb.eu (office). *Website:* www.wzb.eu (office).

SARAIVA GUERREIRO, Ramiro Elysio; Brazilian diplomatist; b. 1918, Salvador; s. of José Affonso Guerreiro and Esther Saraiva Guerreiro; m. Gloria Vallim Guerreiro 1947; one s. one d.; ed Univ. of Brazil and Rio Branco Inst. (Diplomatic Acad.); Foreign Service 1945; Brazilian Mission to UN 1946–69; Embassies, La Paz 1950–51, Washington, DC 1956–58; Minister-Counsellor, Montevideo 1966–67, Deputy Del. to Meeting of Chiefs of American States 1967; Del. Emergency Special Session of UN Gen. Ass. 1967; Asst Sec.-Gen. of Int. Orgs, Ministry of Foreign Affairs 1967–79; mem. del. to numerous UN Gen. Assemblies; Under-Sec.-Gen. of External Policy 1969; Rep. at meetings of Comm. of Sea Bed and Ocean Floor 1969–72; Chief of Del. UN Conf. on Law of the Sea 1968–77, 26th Session of GATT 1970, Geneva 1970–74, Disarmament Cttee 1970–74, Chief of Section of Brazilian-German Cttee on Econ. Co-operation and Science and Tech. 1974, 1975, 1977; Amb. to France 1978–79; Minister of Foreign Affairs 1979–85; Chief of Dels. to 24th–28th UN Gen. Assemblies 1979–83; mem. Geographical Soc. (Rio de Janeiro), American Soc. of Int. Law, Brazilian Soc. of Air Law, Argentine Council for Int. Relations. *Leisure interests:* reading, golf. *Address:* c/o Ministério das Relações Exteriores, Esplanada dos Ministérios 70170, Brasília, DF, Brazil.

SARAIVA MARTINS, HE Cardinal José; Portuguese ecclesiastic; *Prefect of the Congregation for the Causes of Saints;* b. 6 Feb. 1932, Gagos, Guarda; ed Pontifical Gregorian Univ., Pontifical Univ. of St Thomas Aquinas, Rome; ordained priest 1957, Bishop 1988; fmr teacher Claretianum, Rome; fmr teacher Pontifical Urbanian Univ., Rector 1977–80, 1980–83, 1986–88; Titular Archbishop of Thuburnica 1988; Prefect of the Congregation for the Causes of Saints 1998–; cr. Cardinal 2001, Cardinal Deacon of Nostra Signora del Sacro Cuore. *Address:* Congregation for the Causes of Saints, Palazzo delle Congregazioni, Piazza Pio XII 10, 00193 Rome, Italy (office). *Telephone:* (06) 69884247 (office). *Fax:* (06) 69881935 (office). *Website:* www.vatican.va/roman_curia/congregations/csaints (office).

SARAMAGO, José; Portuguese writer and poet; b. 16 Nov. 1922, Azinhaga; m. Pilar del Rio; one c.; ed principally self-educated; Prémio da Críticos Portugueses 1979, Prémio Cidade de Lisboa 1980, Prémios PEN Clube Portugues 1982, 1984, Prémio Literario Municipio de Lisboa 1982, Prémio da Critica, Associação Portuguesa de Criticos, Prémio Don Dinis 1986, Grinzane Cavour Prize 1987, Mondello Prize 1992, Grande Prémio de Romance e Novela da Associação Portuguesa de Escritores 1992, Brancatti Literary Prize 1992, Flaiano Prize 1992, Prémio Vida Literária da Associação Portuguesa de Escritores 1993, Prémio Consagração Soc. Portuguesa de Autores 1995, Luís de Camões Prize 1995, Nobel Prize for Literature 1998. *Publications include:* novels: Terra do pecado 1947, Manual de pintura e caligrafia (trans. as Manual of Painting and Calligraphy) 1976, Levantado do chão 1980, Memorial do convento (trans. as Baltasar and Blimunda) 1982, O ano da morte de Ricardo Reis (trans. as The Year of the Death of Ricardo Reis) 1984, A jangada de pedra (trans. as The Stone Raft) 1986, História do cerco de Lisboa 1989, O Evangelho Segundo Jesus Cristo (trans. as The Gospel According to Jesus Christ) 1991, Ensaio sobre a cegueira (trans. as Blindness) 1995, Todos os nomes (trans. as All the Names) 1999, O Homeru Duplicado (trans. as The Double) 2000, La caverna 2001, Ensaio sobre a Lucidez 2004, As Intermitências da Morte (trans. as Death with Interruptions) 2005, As Pequenas Memórias 2006, A Viagem do Elefante (trans. as The Elephant's Journey) 2008; short stories: Objecto quase trans. as Quasi Object) 1978, Poética dos cinco sentidos – O ouvido 1979, Telling Tales (contrib. to charity anthology) 2004; poetry: Os poemas possíveis 1966, Provavelmente alegria 1970, O ano de 1993 1975; plays: A noite 1979, Que farei com este livro? 1980, A segunda vida de Francisco de Assisi 1987, In Nomine Dei 1993, Don Giovanni ou O dissoluto absolvido 2005; opera librettos: Blimunda 1990, Divara 1993, Il dissoluto assolto 2005; other writing: Deste mundo e do outro 1971, A bagagem do viajante 1973, O embargo 1973, Os opiniões que o DL teve 1974, Os apontamentos 1976, Viagem a Portugal 1981, Cadernos de Lanzarote 1994–96, O poeta perguntador (ed.) 1979. *Address:* Los Topes 3, 35572 Tias, Lanzarote, Canary Islands, Spain; Ray-Güde Mertin, 1 Friedrichstrasse, 61348 Bad Hamburg 1, Germany.

SARANDON, Susan Abigail; American actress; b. 4 Oct. 1946, New York; d. of Philip Tomalin and Lenora Criscione; m. Chris Sarandon 1967 (divorced 1979); one d. with Franco Amurri; two s. with Tim Robbins (q.v.); ed Catholic Univ. of America; numerous TV appearances. *Films include:* Joe 1970, Lady Liberty 1971, The Rocky Horror Picture Show 1974, Lovin' Molly 1974, The Great Waldo Pepper 1975, The Front Page 1976, Dragon Fly 1976, Walk Away Madden, The Other Side of Midnight 1977, The Last of the Cowboys 1977, Pretty Baby 1978, King of the Gypsies 1978, Loving Couples 1980, Atlantic City 1981, Tempest 1982, The Hunger 1983, Buddy System 1984, Compromising Positions 1985, The Witches of Eastwick 1987, Bull Durham 1988, Sweet Hearts Dance 1988, Married to the Mob, A Dry White Season 1989, The January Man 1989, White Palace, Thelma and Louise 1991, Light Sleeper 1991, Lorenzo's Oil, The Client, Little Women 1995, Safe Passage 1995, Dead Man Walking (Acad. Award for Best Actress 1996) 1996, James and the Giant Peach 1996, Illuminata 1998, Twilight 1998, Stepmom 1999, Anywhere But Here 1999, The Cradle Will Rock 1999, Rugrats in Paris 2000, Joe Gould's Secret 2000, Cats and Dogs 2001, Igby Goes Down 2002, The Banger Sisters

2003, The Nazi Officer's Wife 2003, Last Party 2000 2003, Noel 2004, Shall We Dance? 2004, Alfie 2004, Elizabethstown 2005, Romance & Cigarettes 2005, Irresistible 2006, In the Valley of Elah 2007, Mr. Woodcock 2007, Emotional Arithmetic 2007, Bernard and Doris 2007, Enchanted 2007, Speed Racer 2008. *Stage appearances include:* A Coupla White Chicks Sittin' Around Talkin', An Evening with Richard Nixon, A Stroll in the Air, Albert's Bridge, Private Ear, Public Eye, Extremities, Exit the King. *Address:* c/o Samuel Cohen, ICM, 40 West 57th Street, New York, NY 10019, USA (office).

SARASTE, Jukka-Pekka; Finnish conductor; *Artistic Advisor, Lahti Symphony Orchestra;* b. 22 April 1956, Heinola; m. Marja-Lisa Ollila; three s. one d.; ed Sibelius Acad., Helsinki; debut with Helsinki Philharmonic 1980; Prin. Conductor and Music Dir Finnish Radio Symphony Orchestra 1987–2001, now Conductor Laureate; Music Dir Toronto Symphony Orchestra 1994–2001; Prin. Guest Conductor BBC Symphony Orchestra 2002–05; Chief Conductor and Music Dir Oslo Philharmonic Orchestra 2006–; Artistic Advisor Lahti Symphony Orchestra 2008–, Artistic Dir Lahti Sibelius Festival 2008–; has been guest conductor with Boston Symphony Orchestra, Cleveland Orchestra, San Francisco Orchestra, Frankfurt Radio Orchestra, NY Philharmonic Orchestra, London Philharmonic Orchestra, Orchestre Philharmonique de Radio France, BBC Symphony Orchestra, Munich Philharmonic Orchestra; has toured Japan, Hong Kong, Taiwan, Germany, USA, Canary Islands Festival; Artistic Adviser Finnish Chamber Orchestra; Dr hc (Univ. of York, UK). *Recordings include:* complete Sibelius symphonies 1995 (with Finnish Radio Symphony Orchestra) Mussorgsky (with Toronto Symphony Orchestra) Nielsen Symphonies 4, 5 (with Finnish Radio Symphony Orchestra), Romeo and Juliet Suite (Prokofiev). *Address:* c/o Till Janczukowicz, Columbia Artists Management GmbH, 18 Albrechtstrasse, 10117 Berlin, Germany (office); Lahti Symphony Orchestra Office, Sibelius Hall, Ankkurikatu 7, 15140 Lahti Finland. *Telephone:* 172 2518526 (office). *Website:* www.sinfonialahti.fi.

SARAYA, Osama, BA; Egyptian journalist and editor; *Editor-in-Chief, Al Ahram (The Pyramids);* b. 24 March 1952; ed Cairo Univ.; has held various positions at Al-Ahram (state-owned daily newspaper) since 1975, including Econs Ed., Supervisor of the Econ. Page (weekly edn), Dir of Arab Econs Dept, Man. of Al-Ahram Regional Press Inst., Dir of Al-Ahram office in Saudi Arabia, Ed.-in-Chief 2005–, supervised training programmes for Egyptian, Arab and African journalists of Al-Ahram Regional Press Inst., represented Al-Ahram in Arab and int. conventions, est. The Devt and Environment Media Unit in Al-Ahram Regional Press Inst.; mem. Egyptian Journalists Syndicate, fmr Sec.-Gen. and Treas.; helped establish Nat. Democratic Party—NDP (ruling party), mem. sub-cttee of NDP's policy secr.; Gen. Union for Egyptians Abroad Unity Prize 2005. *Address:* Al Ahram, Sharia al-Galaa, Cairo 11511, Egypt (office). *Telephone:* (2) 5801600 (office). *Fax:* (2) 5786023 (office). *E-mail:* ahramdaily@ahram.org.eg (office). *Website:* www.ahram.org.eg (office).

SARBANES, Paul Spyros, BA, LLB; American lawyer and fmr politician (retd); b. 3 Feb. 1933, Salisbury, Md; s. of Spyros P. Sarbanes and Matina (née Tsigounis) Sarbanes; m. Christine Dunbar 1960; two s. one d.; ed Princeton Univ., Balliol Coll., Oxford, UK, Harvard Law School; Rhodes Scholar, Balliol Coll., Oxford 1954–57; admitted to Md Bar 1960; law clerk to circuit judge 1960–61; Assoc., Piper and Marbury, Baltimore 1961–62; Admin. Asst to Chair. Council of Econ. Advisers 1962–63; Exec. Dir Charter Revision Comm., Baltimore 1963–64; Assoc., Venable, Baetjer & Howard, Baltimore 1965–70; mem. Md House of Dels 1967–71, US House of Reps 1971–76, Senator from Md 1977–2007 (retd), Chair. Cttee on Banking, Housing and Urban Affairs 2001–07, fmr ranking mem. Senate Sub-cttee on Int. Econ. Policy, Export and Trade Promotion, co-author Sarbanes-Oxley Act; Democrat; Paul H. Douglas Ethics in Govt Award, Univ. of Illinois 2003, Woodrow Wilson Award, Princeton Univ. 2007. *Address:* Tower 1, Suite 1710, 100 South Charles Street, Baltimore, MD 21201, USA.

SARBAYEV, Kadyrbek Telmanovich; Kyrgyzstani diplomatist and politician; *Minister of Foreign Affairs;* b. 9 Dec. 1966, Frunze; ed Far Eastern State Univ.; joined Ministry of Foreign Affairs 1992; Third, then Second Sec., Embassy in Beijing 1993–96; First Sec., Ministry of Foreign Affairs 1996–97; Deputy Head of Dept, Office of the Prime Minister 1997; Chief of Dept Ministry of Foreign Affairs 1997–99, 2003; Counsellor, Embassy in Berlin 2000, Embassy in Beijing 2001–03; Deputy Minister and Nat. Co-ordinator Shanghai Co-operation Org. 2004–05; Deputy Minister of Foreign Affairs 2005–07; Amb. to China 2007–09; Minister of Foreign Affairs 2009–. *Address:* Ministry of Foreign Affairs, 720040 Bishkek, bul. Erkindik 57, Kyrgyzstan (office). *Telephone:* (312) 62-05-45 (office). *Fax:* (312) 66-05-01 (office). *E-mail:* gendep@mfa.gov.kg (office). *Website:* www.mfa.kg (office).

SARCINELLI, Mario; Italian banker, economist and academic; *Chairman, Dexia Crediop;* b. 9 March 1934, Foggia; m. Giovanna Longardi; two s.; ed Univ. of Pavia, Univ. of Cambridge; joined Bank of Italy 1957, fmr Head Data Processing and Information Systems Dept, Cen. Man. for Banking Supervision 1976, Deputy Dir-Gen. 1976; Econ. Adviser to Italian Del. to UN 1960; Dir-Gen. Treasury 1982–91; Minister of Foreign Trade April–July 1987; Vice-Pres. EBRD 1991–94; Chair. Monetary Cttee 1989–90, Banca Nazionale del Lavoro SpA 1994–98; Chair. Diners Club Sim p.a. 1999–2001; Prof. of Int. Monetary Econs, Università degli Studi di Roma 'la Sapienza'1998–2002; Lecturer in Global Banking, LUISS Guido Carli 2001–04, Pres. Centro di Ricerca per il Diritto d'Impresa (CERADI) 1999–2004; Chair. Dexia Crediop, Rome 2007–; alt. mem. EEC Cttee of Govs of Cen. Banks 1978–81, Bd of Dirs BIS 1978–81; Officier Légion d'honneur, Cavaliere del Lavoro 1996; Dr hc Univ. of Bari. *Address:* Dexia Crediop, Via Venti Settembre 30, 00187 Rome, Italy (office). *Telephone:* (06) 47711 (office). *Fax:* (06) 47715961 (office). *E-mail:* mario.sarcinelli@dexia-crediop.it; (office). *Website:* www.dexiacrediop.it (office).

SARDENBERG, Ronaldo Mota; Brazilian diplomatist; *Chairman, National Telecommunication Agency of Brazil (Anatel);* b. 8 Oct. 1940, Itú; s. of Irto Sardenberg and Ruth S. da Mota Sardenberg; m.; four c.; ed Univ. of Brazil Law School, Rio Branco Inst., Brazilian Foreign Service Acad.; joined External Relations Ministry 1964, Adviser, Econ., Tech. and Commodities Div. 1964–67, mem. staff Embassy in Washington, DC 1967–70, mem. staff Perm. Mission to UN, New York 1970–74, Political Adviser in Multilateral and Afro-Asian Affairs 1974–76, Co-ordinator of Policy Planning 1976–78, Special Sec. for Political and Econ. Affairs, Int. Bilateral Area then Head Policy Planning team 1978–82, apptd Chargé d'Affaires, Embassy in Moscow 1982, rank of Amb. 1983, Amb. to USSR 1985–89, to Spain 1989–90; Perm. Rep. to UN, New York 1990–94 (Pres. Security Council Oct. 1993), 2003–07; Sec. for Strategic Affairs, Presidency of the Repub. 1995–98; Minister for Special Projects 1999; Minister of Science and Tech. 1999–2003; Chair. Inter-Ministerial Cttees on Wood Production 1997, Bi-oceanic Transport Corridors 1996, Lands Owned by Fed. Govt in State of Pará 1996; Chair. Bd Dirs Anatel (Nat. Telecommunications Agency) 2007–. *Address:* Anatel, SAUS Quadra 06, Bloco H, 70070-940, Brasília Brazil (office). *Telephone:* (61) 2312-2063 (office). *Fax:* (61) 2312-2201 (office). *E-mail:* sardenberg@anatel.gov.br (office). *Website:* www.anatel.gov.br (office).

SARDJOE, Ramdien; Suriname politician; *Vice-President;* b. 10 Oct. 1935, Dist Suriname; mem. Parl. 1964–80, 1987–; Chair. Vooruitstrevende Hervormings Partij (VHP); Speaker, Nat. Ass. –2005; Perm. Rep. of Suriname Nat. Ass. to Jt Parl. ACP-EU Meeting, Co-Pres. –2004; Vice-Pres. of Suriname 2005–; Officer, Order of the Netherlands Lion, Officer, Order of the Yellow Star, Grand Officer, Order of the Yellow Star. *Address:* Office of the Vice-President, Paramaribo, Suriname (office).

SARDO, Gabriele, LLB; Italian diplomatist; *Ambassador to Canada;* b. 9 Jan. 1944, Trieste; ed Univ. of Trieste; entered Foreign Service 1968; assigned to Directorate General for Political Affairs 1968–70; Vice Consul, Munich 1970–973; posted to Buenos Aires, Argentina 1973–1975; served in Foreign Ministry Cabinet 1975–77; posted to Mexico City 1977–82; First Counsellor in Washington, DC 1984–91; with Middle East Dept, Ministry of Foreign Affairs 1991–1993, Coordinator for the Schengen Convention Implementation 1995–1996; Deputy Head, Minister's Cabinet 1996–98; Head, Perm. Representation to UNESCO, Paris 1998–2002; Diplomatic Counsellor for Minister for Environment and Protection of Natural Resources, Rome 2002–06; Amb. to Canada 2006–. *Address:* Embassy of Italy, 275 Slater Street, 21st Floor, Ottawa, ON K1P 5H9, Canada (office). *Telephone:* (613) 232-2401 (office). *Fax:* (613) 233-1484 (office). *E-mail:* ambasciata.ottawa@esteri.it (office). *Website:* www.ambottawa.esteri.it (office).

SARFATI, Alain; French architect and town planner; b. 23 March 1937, Meknès, Morocco; s. of Maurice Sarfati and Sarah Levy de Valencia; two d.; ed Lycée Poeymirau, Meknès, Lycée Laknal, Sceaux, Ecole des Beaux Arts, Paris and Inst. d'Urbanisme, Univ. de Paris; town planner, Inst. d'Urbanisme, Paris region 1966; Founder of review A.M.C. and Atelier de Recherche et d'Etudes d'Amènagement (AREA) 1967; Prof. of Architecture, Nancy 1969; Prof. and Head of Dept, Ecole des Beaux Arts, Paris-Conflans 1979–; architectural adviser, Ministère de l'Equipement, de l'Urbanisme, du Logement et des Transports 1985–; Vice-Pres. of Construction Planning, Ministère de l'Equipement, du Logement, des Transports et de la Mer 1988–; mem. Consultative Cttee Centre Scientifique et Technique du Bâtiment 1990–; Vice-Pres. Ordre Nat. des Architectes 1992–96; work includes housing, schools, hosps, leisure centres and Centre des Archives du Monde du Travail, Roubaix 1993; Chevalier, Ordre du Mérite, Officier des Arts et Lettres. *Leisure interests:* opera, cinema, art, golf, skiing. *Address:* Atelier de Recherche et d'Etudes d'Amènagement, 43 rue Maurice Ripoche, 75014 Paris (office); 79 rue du Cherche-Midi, 75006 Paris, France (home). *Telephone:* 1-58-14-24-00 (office). *Fax:* 1-58-14-24-13 (office). *E-mail:* sarea@sarea.fr (office). *Website:* www.sarea.fr (office).

SARGENT, Ronald (Ron) L., BA, MBA; American retail executive; *Chairman and CEO, Staples Inc.;* b. 1956; ed Harvard Univ., Harvard Business School; began retail career with The Kroger Co., man. positions in operations, human resources, strategy, sales and marketing –1989; Regional Vice-Pres. of Operations, Staples Inc. 1989–91, Head of Staples Direct 1991, Vice-Pres. Staples 1991–94, Pres. Staples Contract & Commercial 1997, Pres. N American Div. 1997–98, Pres. and COO Staples Inc. 1998–2002, Pres. and CEO 2002–05, Chair. and CEO 2005–; fmr mem. Bd of Dirs Literacy Volunteers of America; mem. Bd of Dirs Kroger Co., Mattel, Inc., Yankee Candle Co., Bd of Advisers Boston Coll. Carroll School of Man. *Address:* Staples Inc., 500 Staples Drive, Framingham, MA 01702, USA (office). *Telephone:* (508) 253-5000 (office). *Fax:* (508) 253-8989 (office). *E-mail:* info@staples.com (office). *Website:* www.staples.com (office).

SARGENT, Wallace Leslie William, PhD, FRS, ARAS; British astronomer and academic; *Ira S. Bowen Professor of Astronomy, California Institute of Technology;* b. 15 Feb. 1935, Elsham, Lincs.; s. of Leslie Sargent and Eleanor Sargent; m. Anneila I. Cassells 1964; two d.; ed Scunthorpe Tech. High School and Manchester Univ.; Research Fellow in Astronomy, Calif. Inst. of Tech. 1959–62; Sr Research Fellow, Royal Greenwich Observatory 1962–64; Asst Prof. of Physics, Univ. of Calif., San Diego 1964–66; Asst Prof. of Astronomy, Calif. Inst. of Tech. 1966–68, Assoc. Prof. 1968–71, Prof. 1971–81, Exec. Officer for Astronomy 1975–81, Ira S. Bowen Prof. of Astronomy 1981–, Dir Palomar Observatory 1997–2000; Alfred P. Sloan Foundation Fellow 1968–70; Visiting Fellow, Sterrewacht, Leiden Univ. 2005; Vice-Pres. American Astronomical Soc. 2004–07; mem. MIT Center for Space Research Advisory Cttee 2003–(09); mem. NAS 2005–; Fellow, American Acad. of Arts and Sciences; Helen B. Warner Prize, American Astronomical Soc. 1969, George Darwin Lecturer, Royal Astronomical Soc. 1987, Dannie Heineman Prize,

American Astronomical Soc. 1991, Bruce Gold Medal, Astronomical Soc. of the Pacific 1994, Thomas Gold Lecturer, Cornell Univ. 1995, Sackler Lecturer, Harvard Univ. 1995, Sackler Lecturer, Univ. of California, Berkeley 1996, Henry Norris Russell Lecturer, American Astronomical Soc. 2001, Icko Iben Lecturer, Univ. of Illinois 2002. *Publications:* numerous papers in scientific journals. *Leisure interests:* reading, gardening, watching sports, oriental rugs. *Address:* Department of Astronomy 105–24, California Institute of Technology, Pasadena, CA 91125 (office); 400 South Berkeley Avenue, Pasadena, CA 91107, USA (home). *Telephone:* (626) 356-4055 (office); (626) 795-6345 (home). *Fax:* (626) 568-9352. *E-mail:* wws@astro.caltech.edu (office). *Website:* www.astro.caltech.edu/~wws (office).

SARGSYAN, Sos Artashesovich; Armenian actor; b. 24 Oct. 1929, Armenia; m. Nelli Sargsyan (née Martirosian); three d.; ed Yerevan Theatre Inst.; acted with Sundukian Theatre 1954–; acted in films 1960–; USSR People's Deputy 1989–91; Artistic Man. Hamazgain Theatre; People's Artist of Armenian SSR 1972, Armenian State Prize for work in the theatre 1979, People's Artist of USSR 1985, Mesrop Mastots Prize 1998. *Films:* Tchanaparh 1962, Tern u tzaran 1963, Msyo Zhake yev urishner 1966, Yerankyuni 1967, Aprum er mi mard 1968, Menq, yev mer sarere 1970, Heghnar aghbyur 1971, Khatabala 1971, Solyaris 1972, Hndzan 1974, Qaos 1974, Zhayre 1975, Yerkunq 1977, Nahapet 1977, Komissiya po rassledovaniyu 1978, Huso astgh 1978, Kyanqi lavaguyn kese 1979, Yot sarits ayn koghm 1980, Dzori Miro 1981, Gikor 1982, Tchermak anurjner 1985, Khndzori aygin 1985, Pod znakom odnorogoy korovy 1986, Vozneseniye 1988, Quartet 1988, Khachmeruki deghatune 1988, I povtoritsya vsyo 1989, Urakh avtobus 2001, Mayak 2006. *Plays:* King John, The Judge, Pepo, Othello, The Apple Garden; more than 40 plays. *Publications:* At This Side of the Curtain 1991, DIY Branches 1991, The Break Off 2000. *Address:* Yerevan State Institute of Theatre and Cinema, Amirian 26, Yerevan (office); Terian 63 fl. 20, Yerevan, Armenia (home). *Telephone:* (10) 53-62-21 (office); (10) 58-26-60 (home). *Fax:* (10) 53-62-33 (office). *E-mail:* institute@highfest.am (office).

SARID, Yossi, MA; Israeli journalist, fmr politician and journalist; b. 1940, Rehovot; m.; three c.; ed New School for Social Research, New York, USA; served in artillery corps and as a mil. corresp.; mem. Knesset 1974–2006, served on Educ. and Culture Cttee 1974–77, House Cttee 1974–92, Immigration and Absorption Cttee 1996–99 and Foreign Affairs and Security Cttee 1972–92, 1996–99; Minister of Environment 1993–96, of Educ. 1999–2000 Chair. Meretz–Yahad Party and Leader of the Opposition –2006; currently political columnist Ha'aretz (daily newspaper). *Address:* c/o Ha'aretz (The Land), 21 Schocken Street, Tel-Aviv 61001, Israel (office). *Telephone:* 3-5121212 (office). *Fax:* 3-6810012 (office). *E-mail:* contact@haaretz.co.il (office). *Website:* www.haaretz.co.il (office).

SARIN, Arun, MS, MBA; American/Indian telecommunications industry executive; b. 21 Oct. 1954, Pachmarhi, MP; m.; two c.; ed Indian Inst. of Tech., Univ. of Calif.; fmr corp. developer, Pacific Telesis Group, San Francisco, Chief Financial Officer, Chief Strategy Officer, Pacific Bell, Vice-Pres., Gen. Man. San Francisco Bay Area Telephone Co. (div. of Pacific Bell); Sr Vice-Pres. of Corp. Strategy and Devt, AirTouch Communications (on demerger from Pacific Telesis), Pres. and CEO AirTouch Int., Pres. AirTouch Communications, CEO USA and Asia Pacific region 1999–2000, Vodafone Airtouch PLC; CEO Infospace 2000–01, Accel-KKR Telecom, San Francisco 2001–03, Vodafone Group plc 2003–08; Dir (non-exec.) Vodafone 2000–03, Charles Schwab Corpn –2003, Cisco Systems –2003, Gap Inc. –2003. *Address:* c/o Vodafone Group plc, Vodafone House, The Connection, Newbury, Berks., RG14 2FN, England. *Telephone:* (1635) 33251. *Fax:* (1635) 686111. *Website:* www.vodafone.com.

SARKAR, Manik; Indian politician; *Chief Minister of Tripura;* b. 22 Jan. 1949, Radhakishorepur; ed Maharaja Bir Bakram Coll., Calcutta Univ.; mem. Communist Party of India—Marxist 1968–, mem. State Cttee 1972, State Secr. 1978, mem. Central Cttee 1985, State Sec. 1993, State Left Front Convenor, mem. Politburo 1998; mem. Tripura Legis. Ass. 1980–; Chief Minister of Tripura 1998–. *Address:* Chief Minister's Secretariat, Agartala, Tripura, India (office). *Telephone:* (381) 2324000 (office). *Fax:* (381) 2223201 (office). *E-mail:* cmo-trp@hub.nic.in (office). *Website:* tripura.nic.in (office).

ŠARKINAS, Reinoldijus; Lithuanian economist and central banker; *Chairman, Board of Governors, Bank of Lithuania;* b. 16 July 1946, Toliūnų Village, Ukmergės Dist; m.; two d.; ed Vilnius Univ.; Chief Engineer Spindulys factory and Head Div. of Labour and Earnings Lithuanian Chemicals Co. 1968–72; Deputy Head Dept of Planning and Finance, Head Financial Accounting Dept, Ministry of Educ. 1972–80; Finance Adviser, Ministry of Educ., Repub. of Cuba 1980–82; Deputy Head, Head of Culture and Health Care Financing Dept, Dir Budget Dept, Ministry of Finance 1983–90; Deputy Minister and Sec., Ministry of Finance 1991–95, Minister of Finance 1995–96; mem. Bd Bank of Lithuania 1992–95, Chair. Bd of Govs 1996–; Commdr's Cross, Order of Lithuanian Grand Duke Gediminas 2003. *Address:* Bank of Lithuania (Lietuvos bankos), Gedimino pr. 6, Vilnius 01103, Lithuania (office). *Telephone:* (5) 268-0006 (office). *Fax:* (5) 262-8124 (office). *E-mail:* info@lb.lt (office). *Website:* www.lb.lt (office).

SARKISOV, Ashot Arakelovich; Russian nuclear energy specialist; *Adviser, Nuclear Safety Institute, Russian Academy of Sciences;* b. 30 Jan. 1924, Tashkent, USSR; s. of Arakel A. Sarkisov and Evgeniya B. Grigoryan; m. Nelli G. Sarkisov 1951; two s.; ed F. Dzerzhinsky Higher Marine Eng School, Leningrad Univ.; worked as engineer Baltic fleet; Chair. Higher Marine School, Sevastopol; Deputy Dir Naval Acad.; Chair. Scientific-Tech. Council of the Navy; Head of Dept, Inst. for Nuclear Safety; Chair. Expert Council on Navy and Shipbuilding; Chair. Panel of Experts, Int. Scientific and Eng Program on Radioactive Waste; Corresp. mem. USSR (now Russian) Acad. of Sciences 1981, mem. and Adviser, Nuclear Safety Inst. 1990–, 1994; research in theory of dynamic processes and automatic protection of nuclear plants, problems of safety and security in nuclear energy; nine Orders of the USSR and of Russia; many medals. *Publications include:* Dynamics of Nuclear Power Plants of Submarines 1964, Nuclear Propulsion Power Plants 1968, Dynamic Regimes in the Operation of Nuclear Propulsion Power Plants 1971, Physics of Transitional Processes in Nuclear Reactors 1983, Nuclear Propulsion Power Plants and Steam Generators 1985, Thermo-Electric Generators with Nuclear Sources of Heat 1987, Physical Principles of Nuclear Steam-Productive Plants 1989, Nuclear Submarine Decommissioning and Related Problems 1996, Analysis of Risks Associated with Nuclear Submarine Decommissioning, Dismantling and Disposal 1999, Remaining Issues in the Decommissioning of Nuclear Powered Vessels 2003, Overcoming Impediments to US–Russian Cooperation on Nuclear Nonproliferation 2004, Status, Problems and Priorities of NS Complex Decommissioning in the North-West Russia (Basic Provisions of Strategic Master Plan Initial Phase) 2004, Strategic Approaches in Solving Decommissioning Problems of Retired Russian Nuclear Fleet in the Northwest Region: Executive Summary of Strategic Master Plan, Phase 1 2004, Strengthening US–Russian Cooperation on Nuclear Nonproliferation Recommendations for Action 2005, Scientific and Technical Issues in the Management of Spent Nuclear Fuel of Decommissioned Nuclear Submarines 2006, Atomic Legacy of the Cold War at the Artic Seabed. Radioecological Consequences and Technical and Economic Problems of Radiation Remediation at the Arctic Seas 2006, Strategic Master Plan for Decommissioning of the Retired Russian Nuclear Fleet and Environmental Rehabilitation of Its Supporting Infrastructure in Northwest Russia. Priority Project Programme 2006, Strategic Master Plan for Decommissioning of the Retired Russian Nuclear Fleet and Environmental Rehabilitation of Its Supporting Infrastructure in Northwest Russia. Executive Summary 2007. *Leisure interests:* tennis, history of the navy. *Address:* Nuclear Safety Institute, Russian Academy of Sciences, B. Tulskaya str. 52, 115191 Moscow, Russia. *Telephone:* (495) 958-14-59 (office); (495) 955-22-80 (office). *Fax:* (495) 958-00-40 (office). *E-mail:* sarkisov@ibrae.ac.ru (office). *Website:* www.ibrae.ac.ru (office).

SARKISSIAN, Aram; Armenian politician; *Leader, Republic (Hanrapetutiun);* b. 2 Jan. 1961, Ararat; m.; three c.; ed Yerevan School of Arts, Yerevan Polytechnical Inst.; army service 1981–83; various positions with Ararat-stroytrust 1989–93; Asst Dir-Gen., then Deputy Dir-Gen. Araratcement 1993–98, Exec. Dir 1998–99; mem. Republican Party of Armenia, Yerkrapah Union of Volunteers; Prime Minister of Armenia 1999–2000; in pvt. business; Leader Republic (Hanrapetutiun); Chair. Armenian Democratic Party. *Address:* Republic, 0002 Yerevan, Mashtotsi Avenue 37/30, Armenia (office). *Telephone:* (10) 53-86-34 (office). *E-mail:* republic@arminco.com (office). *Website:* www.hanrapetutyun.am (office).

SARKISSIAN, Serge; Armenian politician and head of state; *President;* b. 30 June 1954, Xankandi (Stepanakert, Nagornyi Karabakh Autonomous Oblast, Azerbaijan SSR); m. Rita Sarkissian 1983; two d.; ed Yerevan State Univ.; USSR army 1972–74; metal turner, Electrical Devices Factory, Yerevan 1975–79; Komsomol Sec., Head of Propaganda section City Cttee, Stepanakert 1979–88; Head of Self-Defence Cttee, Nagornyi Karabakh 1989–93; Deputy Supreme Council (Parl.) 1990–93, Minister of Defence 1993–95, 2000–07, of Nat. Security 1995–96, 1999, of Internal Affairs and Nat. Security 1996–99; Chief of Staff to Pres. 1999–2000; Sec. Council of Nat. Security 1999–2007; mem. Republican Party of Armenia (RPA) 2006–, Chair. Party Council 2006–07, Chair. RPA 2007–; Prime Minister 2007–08; Pres. of Armenia 2008–; Chair. Bd of Trustees, Yerevan State Univ.; Chair. Chess Federation of Armenia; Order of Martakan Khach, Kt of the Golden Eagle Order, Hero of Artsakh, Armenian Battle Cross, Tigran Mets. *Address:* Office of the President, 375077 Yerevan, Marshal Baghramian Street, Armenia (office). *Telephone:* (10) 52-02-04 (office). *Fax:* (10) 52-15-51 (office). *E-mail:* frd@gov.am (office). *Website:* www.president.am (office); www.serzhsargsyan.com.

SARKISSIAN, Tigran, PhD; Armenian politician and central banker; *Prime Minister;* b. 29 Jan. 1960, Kirovakan (now Vanadzor); m.; two s. one d.; ed Voznesenskii Financial and Econ. Inst., Leningrad (now St Petersburg), USSR; Chief of Dept for Foreign Econ. Relations, Scientific Research Inst. of Econ. Planning 1987–90; Chair. Republican Council of Young Specialists and Scientists 1988–93; mem. Supreme Council of the Repub. of Armenia and Chair. of Standing Comm. for Financial, Credit and Budget Affairs 1990–95; Dir of Scientific Research Inst. of Social Reforms 1995–98; Chair. Armenian Banks Assen 1995–98; Chair. Cen. Bank of Armenia 1998–2008; Prime Minister 2008–. *Address:* Office of the Prime Minister, 0010 Yerevan, Republic Square 1, Government Building, Armenia (office). *Telephone:* (10) 52-03-60 (office). *Fax:* (10) 15-10-35 (office). *Website:* www.gov.am/enversion/premier_2/primer_home.htm (office).

SARKISYAN, Armen, CandPhys-MathSc; Armenian academic, politician and diplomatist; b. 1953, Yerevan; m.; two s.; ed Yerevan State Univ.; Docent, Yerevan State Univ. 1979–84; researcher Cambridge Univ. UK 1984–85; Lecturer, Yerevan State Univ. 1985–90, Head Dept of Math. Modelling; Prof., London Univ. 1992–; apptd. Chargé d'affaires, then Amb. to UK 1992–2000; Amb., Doyen of Armenian Diplomatic Corps to Europe (also accred to Belgium, Netherlands, Vatican City, Luxembourg) 1993–96; Prime Minister 1996–97; mem. IISS, London; Hon. Mem. Royal Soc. of Int. Relations and Cen. of Strategic Studies, Oxford Univ. *Publications:* author of numerous articles on politology, theoretical physics, astronomy and math. modelling. *Address:* c/o Ministry of Foreign Affairs, Government House 2, Republic Square 1, 375010 Yerevan, Armenia.

SARKISYAN, Fadey Tachatovich, DTechSci; Armenian scientist and politician; b. 18 Sept. 1923, Yerevan; s. of Tachat Sarkisyan and Maria Sarkisyan;

m. Tatiana Roubenovna; one d.; ed Yerevan Polytechnical Inst. and Mil. Acad. of St Petersburg; mem. CPSU 1945–91; responsible for new techniques in devt and Scientific Centres of USSR Ministry of Defence 1945–63; Gen. Dir Yerevan Computer Research Inst. 1963–77; Chair. Council of Ministers of Armenian SSR 1977–89; Deputy to USSR Supreme Soviet 1979–89; Academician-Sec. Nat. Acad. of Sciences of Armenia 1989–93, Pres. 1993–2006; Dir Eurasia Centre, Univ. of Cambridge; mem. Nat. Ass. of Armenia 1974–99; State Prize of the USSR 1971, 1981, State Prize of the Ukraine 1986. *Publications:* more than 200 scientific articles. *Leisure interests:* new technologies, literature, music. *Address:* c/o Armenian Academy of Sciences, 24 Marshal Baghramian Avenue, Yerevan 375019 (office); 10/1 Zarobyan Street, Apt. 11, Yerevan 375019, Armenia (home). *Telephone:* (10) 527419 (home).

SARKÖZY DE NAGY BOCSA, Nicolas Paul Stéphane, LLM; French politician, barrister, civil servant and head of state; *President;* b. 28 Jan. 1955, Paris; s. of Paul Sarközy de Nagy Bocsa and Andrée Mallah; m. 1st Marie-Dominique Culioli 1982 (divorced 1996); two s.; m. 2nd Cecilia Ciganer-Albeniz 1996 (divorced 2007); one s.; m. 3rd Carla Bruni 2008; ed Inst. of Political Studies, Paris, Paris Univ.; barrister, Paris 1981–87; Assoc., Leibovici Claude Sarközy 1987; mem. Neuilly-sur-Seine Municipal Couincil 1977–83, Mayor of Neuilly-sur-Seine 1983–2002; Vice-Chair. Hauts-de-Seine Gen. Council, responsible for Educ. and Culture 1986–88, Chair. 2004; RPR Deputy to Nat. Ass. from Hauts-de-Seine 1988–2002; Govt Spokesman 1993–95; Minister of the Budget 1993–95, of Communications 1994–95, of the Interior, Internal Security and Local Freedoms 2002–04, of the Economy, Finance and Industry 2004, of the Interior and Town and Country Planning 2005–07 (resgnd); Pres. of France 2007–, Co-Prince of Andorra 2007–; Nat. Sec. RPR responsible for Youth and Training 1988, for Activities, Youth and Training 1989, Deputy Gen.-Sec. responsible for local branches 1992–93, mem. Political Bureau 1993, -Gen. Sec. RPR 1998, Interim Pres. April–Oct. 1999, Pres. RPR Regional Cttee of Hauts-de-Seine 2000; Leader RPR-DL List, European Elections 1999; Pres. Union pour un Mouvement Populaire (UMP) 2004–07; Chevalier, Légion d'honneur 2004, Grand Cross of the Légion d'honneur 2007, Grand Cross of the Ordre national du Mérite 2007, Stara Planina (Bulgaria) 2007, Commdr Ordre de Léopold (Belgium). *Publications:* Georges Mandel, moine de la politique 1994, Au bout de la passion, l'équilibre (co-author) 1995, Libre 2001, La République, les Religions, l'Espérance 2004, Témoignage 2006. *Leisure interests:* tennis, cycling. *Address:* Office of the President, Palais de l'Elysée, 55–57 rue du Faubourg Saint Honoré, 75008 Paris, France (office). *Telephone:* 1-42-92-81-00 (office). *Fax:* 1-47-42-24-65 (office). *Website:* www.elysee.fr (office); www.sarkozy.fr.

SARMADI, Morteza, BSc, MA; Iranian politician and diplomatist; *Deputy Foreign Minister for Euro-American Affairs;* b. July 1954, Tehran; m. Fatima Hosseini 1982; four d.; ed Sharif Univ., Tehran; joined Ministry of Foreign Affairs 1981, Dir-Gen. of Press and Information 1982–89, Deputy Foreign Minister for Communication 1989–97, Deputy Foreign Minister for Europe and America 1997–, Amb. to UK 2000–05, Deputy Foreign Minister for Euro-American Affairs 2005–; Sr Del. Iran-Iraq peace talks; Trustee, Islamic Thought Foundation, Islamic Repub. News Agency, Islamic High Council of Propagation Policy, Inst. for Political and Int. Studies. *Publications:* numerous political articles. *Leisure interests:* reading, writing, watching TV, spending time with family. *Address:* Ministry of Foreign Affairs, Shahid Abd al-Hamid Mesri Street, Ferdowsi Avenue, Tehran Iran (office). *Telephone:* (21) 61151 (office). *Fax:* (21) 33212763 (office). *E-mail:* matbuat@mfa.gov.ir (office). *Website:* www.mfa.gov.ir (office).

SARMI, Massimo, BEng; Italian postal service executive; *CEO and Managing Director, Poste Italiane SpA;* b. 4 Aug. 1948, Malcesine; ed Univ. of Rome; Gen. Man. TIM 1995–98, Telecom India 1998–2001; CEO Siemens, Italy 2001–02; CEO and Man. Dir Poste Italiane SpA 2002–; Prof., Univ. 'La Sapienza' and Univ. 'Luiss', Rome; mem. Admin. Bd Univ. Bocconi, Milan 2006–, mem. Int. Post Corpn; American Chamber of Commerce Business and Culture Award 2006, Business and Culture Award 2006, GEI Award 2007. *Address:* Poste Italiane SpA, Viale Europa 190, Rome 00144, Italy (office). *Telephone:* (06) 59587162 (office). *Fax:* (06) 59589100 (office). *E-mail:* sarmim@posteitaliane.it (office). *Website:* www.poste.it (office).

SARNE, Tanya, BA; British fashion designer; *Founder and Creative Director, Ghost Ltd;* b. 15 Jan. 1945, London; d. of Jean-Claude Gordon and Daphne Tucar; m. Michael Sarne 1969 (divorced); one s. one d.; ed Sussex Univ.; worked as a model then as a teacher, then briefly in film production; travelled extensively throughout S America and Europe; returned to England and set up co. importing Alpaca wool knitted garments influenced by traditional Inca designs which launched career in 1970s; introduced Scandinavian labels In Wear and Laize Adzer to UK; est. successful labels Miz 1978–83; Founder and Creative Dir Ghost 1984–; British Apparel Export Award for Womenswear 1993, 1995. *Leisure interests:* cooking, tennis. *Address:* Ghost Ltd, The Chapel, 263 Kensal Road, London, W10 5DB, England (office). *Telephone:* (20) 8960-3121 (office). *Fax:* (20) 8960-8374 (office). *E-mail:* info@ghost.co.uk (office). *Website:* www.ghost.co.uk (office).

SARNEY, José; Brazilian politician and author; *Senator for Amapá;* b. 24 April 1930, Pinheiro, Maranhão; s. of Sarney de Araújo Costa and Kyola Ferreira de Araújo Costa; m. Marli Macieira Sarney; two s. one d.; Asst to Maranhão State Gov. 1950; Maranhão State Rep. 1956, re-elected 1958, 1962; elected Gov. of Maranhão 1965; State Senator (Arena Party, now Partido Democrático Social—PDS) 1970; Nat. Pres. Arena 1970; fmr Chair. PDS; mem. Partido Frente Liberal 1984, PMDD; Acting Pres. of Brazil March–April 1985, Pres. 1985–90; Senator 1971–85, 1991–, Pres. of the Senate 2003–05; fmr Pres. Nat. Congress; mem. Brazilian Acad. of Letters; Brazilian Union of Writers Aluízio de Azevedo Award 2003. *Publications:* A canção inicial 1952, Norte das Águas (Tales of Rain and Sunlight) 1970, Os maribondos de fogo 1978, O Dono do Mar (The Master of the Sea) 1995, Saraminda 2003, Saudades Mortas 2004, Tempo de Pacotilha 2004. *Leisure interests:* literature, painting. *Address:* Senado Federal, Praça dos Três Poderes, Brasília DF, 70165-900, Brazil (office). *Telephone:* (61) 3311-4141 (office). *E-mail:* sarney@senador.gov.br (office). *Website:* www.senado.gov.br/web/senador/jsarney (office).

SARR, HE Cardinal Théodore-Adrien; Senegalese ecclesiastic; *Archbishop of Dakar;* b. 28 Nov. 1936, Fadiouth; ordained priest of Dakar 1964; Bishop of Kaolack 1974–2000; Archbishop of Dakar 2000–; cr. Cardinal 2007; first Vice-Pres. Symposium of Episcopal Confs of Africa and Madagascar; also served as Pres. Bishops' Conf. of Senegal, Mauritania, Cape Verde and Guinea-Bissau. *Address:* Archeveche, BP 1908, Avenue Jean XXIII, Dakar, Senegal (office). *Telephone:* 8890600 (office). *Fax:* 8234875 (office).

SARRAJ, Eyad Rajab el-, PhD; Palestinian human rights activist and psychiatrist; *Medical Director, Gaza Community Mental Health Programme;* b. Beersheva; m.; two c.; ed Inst. of Psychiatry, London Univ., Harvard Univ.; Founder and Medical Dir Gaza Community Mental Health Programme; Co-Founder and Commr-Gen. Palestinian Independent Comm. for Citizens' Rights; arrested three times for criticism of Palestinian Nat. Authorities; mem. Int. Rehabilitation Centre for Torture Victims; mem. Co-ordinating Cttee Campaign Against Torture Victims; Trustee Palestinian Initiative for the Promotion of Global Dialogue and Democracy (MIFTAH); fmr mem. Int. Council on Human Rights Policy; Martin Ennals Award for Human Rights Defenders 1998. *Publications:* numerous articles in journals and newspapers. *Address:* Gaza Community Mental Health Programme, POB 1049, Gaza, Palestinian Autonomous Areas. *Telephone:* (7) 2865949 (office). *Fax:* (7) 2824072 (office). *E-mail:* eyad@gcmhp.net (office). *Website:* www.gcmhp.net (office).

SARRE, Claude-Alain, DèsL, DHist; French business executive and writer; b. 10 April 1928, Douai; s. of Henri Sarre and Claudine Vau; m. Simone Allien 1952; two s. one d.; ed Univ. de Lille, Inst. d'Etudes Politiques, Paris, Univ. d'Aix-Marseille; with Cie Air France; joined Soc. André Citroën 1955, Commercial Dir 1968, Chair., Man. Dir Soc. Automobiles Citroën and Soc. Commerciale Citroën 1968–70; joined Lainière de Roubaix-Prouvost Masurel SA 1970, Pres., Dir-Gen. 1972–77; Chair. Inst. de Devt industriel 1975–77; Dir Soc. Sommer-Allibert 1976; Pres. and Dir Gen. Nobel-Bozel 1978–82; Dir Conseil nat. du patronat français 1983–88; Pres. Council of Improvement, Magni; Chevalier, Légion d'honneur 1975, Palmes Académiques 2007; Prix Mignet Acad. d'Aix-en-Provence 1995, Prix de Beaujour, Acad. de Marseille 1999, Médaille de vermeil, Ville de Paris 2002. *Publications:* Informatisation des entreprises françaises 1981, Vivre sa soumission 1997, Un procès de sorcière 1999, Les Panhard et Levassor 2000, Le dossier-verité du Concorde 2002, Livre de raison de Casimir de Montvalon 2003, Louise de Condé 2005, Souvenirs de la Marquise de Saint-chamais 2006. *Address:* Le grand pin, La Crémade Nord, 13100 Le Tholonet, France (home). *Telephone:* 4-42-66-96-22 (office). *E-mail:* ca.sarre@club-internet.fr (home).

SARRIS, Michalis, DEcon; Cypriot government minister and banker; b. 14 April 1996, Nicosia; ed London School of Econs, UK, Wayne State Univ., USA; joined research dept Central Bank of Cyprus 1972; moved to Bank of Cyprus 1974; Dir World Bank 1975–2004; Minister of Finance 2005–08, of Defence (acting) 2007–08; mem. Bd Laiki Group Dir. *Address:* c/o Ministry of Finance, corner M. Karaolis Street and G. Afxentiou Street, 1439 Nicosia, Cyprus (office).

SARTORIUS, Norman, MD, PhD, FRCPsych; German/Croatian psychiatrist and psychologist; *President, International Association for the Improvement of Mental Health Programmes;* b. 28 Jan. 1935, Münster, Germany; s. of Prof. F. Sartorius Doz and Dr F. Fischer-Sartorius; m. Vera Pecikozić 1963; one d.; ed Univ. of Zagreb, Univ. of London; Consultant, Dept of Psychiatry, Univ. of Zagreb 1959–64; Research Fellow, Inst. of Psychiatry, Univ. of London 1964–65; WHO medical officer in psychiatric epidemiology 1967–68; Medical Officer in charge of Epidemiological and Social Psychiatry and Standardization of Psychiatric Diagnosis, Classification and Statistics, WHO 1969–73, Chief, Office of Mental Health 1974–76, Dir Div. of Mental Health 1976–93; Pres. World Psychiatric Asscn (WPA) 1993–99, currently Scientific Dir WPA Global Programme Against Stigma and Discrimination because of Schizophrenia; also currently Pres. Int. Asscn for Improvement of Mental Health Programmes; Pres. AEP 1999–2001; Prof., Univ. of Zagreb; Visiting Prof., Univ. of Geneva, Univ. of Prague, St Louis Univ., Univ. of Beijing, Univ. of London; corresp. mem. Royal Spanish Acad. of Medicine, Croatian Acad. of Arts and Science; mem. Mexican Acad. of Medicine, Peruvian Acad. of Medicine; Council of WPA, WHO Expert Advisory Panel on Mental Health; Hon. Fellow, Royal Coll. of Psychiatrists, UK, Royal Australian and New Zealand Coll. of Psychiatrists, Amercan Coll. of Psychiatry; Distinguished Fellow, American Psychiatric Asscn; Hon. mem. Medical Acad., Croatia, Hon. mem. of numerous professional and scientific orgs; Hon. DrMed (Umeå), (Prague); Hon. DSc (Bath); Rema Lapouse Medal, Prince Mahidol Prize for Medicine 2005, Harvard Prize in Psychiatric Epidemiology, Burgholzli Prize. *Publications:* more than 350 articles, numerous books (author or ed.) on schizophrenia, transcultural psychiatry, mental health policy, scientific methodology, ethics, human rights and stigma. *Leisure interests:* chess, reading, history. *Address:* 14 Chemin Colladon, 1209, Geneva, Switzerland. *Telephone:* (22) 7882331 (office). *Fax:* (22) 7882334 (office).

SARTZETAKIS, Christos A., LLD; Greek fmr head of state and lawyer; b. 6 April 1929, Salonika; m. Efi Argyriou; one d.; ed Salonika Univ. and Law Faculty, Paris (Sorbonne); called to Bar 1954; apptd JP 1955, Judge of 1st Instance 1956; Investigating Magistrate in Lambrakis affair (which inspired

Vasilis Vasilikos' novel Z, later made into film) 1963–64; postgrad. studies Paris 1965–67; mem. Société de Législation Comparée, Paris 1966–; fmr mem. Admin. Council Hellenic Humanistic Soc.; arrested and detained on unspecified charges 1969; reinstated as an Appeal Judge 1974; Sr Appeal Judge, Nauplion 1981, Justice of Supreme Court 1982–85; Pres. of Greece 1985–90; mem. Société de Législation Comparée, Paris 1966–; fmr mem. Admin. Council Hellenic Humanistic Soc.; hon. mem. High Court of Portugal, Literary Soc. of Thessalonica, Hon. Prof. Dimokrition Univ. of Thrace. *Address:* c/o Office of the President, Odos Vas. Georgiou 2, 100 28 Athens (office); Aghias Sophias str. 6, 152 36 Nea Penteli, Attikis, Greece (home).

SARUNGI, Philemon, MD, MCh; Tanzanian surgeon and politician; ed Bugema Coll., Medical Univ. of Szeged, Hungary, Univ. of Vienna, Austria, Univ. of Shanghai, China; Medical Officer, Muhimbili Hosp. 1971–72; Lecturer in Surgery, Univ. of Dar es Salaam 1972–76; Prof. and Head of Dept of Orthopaedics/Trauma, Muhimbili Medical Center 1977–84, Dir-Gen. 1984–90; Minister for Health 1990–95; Regional Commr, Coast Region 1996–97, Kilimanjaro Region 1998–2000; mem. Parl. for Tarime Constituency 2000–, Minister for Defence and Nat. Service 2000–06. *Address:* c/o Ministry of Defence and National Service, POB 9544, Dar es Salaam, Tanzania (office).

SARY IENG (see Ieng Sary).

SASAKAWA, Yohei; Japanese foundation executive; *Chairman, The Nippon Foundation;* b. 1939, Tokyo; s. of Ryoichi Sasakawa; ed Meiji Univ.; Trustee, Nippon Foundation 1981–88, Acting Pres. 1988–89, Pres. 1989–2005, Chair. 2005–; Founder and Trustee, Sasakawa Memorial Health Foundation 1974, US-Japan Foundation 1980, Scandinavia-Japan Sasakawa Foundation 1984, GB Sasakawa Foundation 1985, Sasakawa Peace Foundation 1986, Sasakawa Africa Asscn 1986, Sasakawa Young Leaders Fellowship Fund 1987, Sasakawa Pacific Island Nations Fund 1989, Sasakawa Cen. Europe Fund 1990, Foundation Franco-Japonaise Sasakawa 1990, Sasakawa Pan Asia Fund 1992; Vice-Chair. Sasakawa Japan-China Friendship Fund 1990; adviser, Tokyo Foundation, AsiaResearch Fund; WHO Global Alliance for Elimination of Leprosy (GAEL) 2001, WHO Goodwill Amb. for Leprosy Elimination 2004; Goodwill Amb. for the Human Rights of People Affected by Leprosy, Ministry of Foreign Affairs 2007; Hon. Prof., Yanbian Univ. 2000, China Medical Univ. 2003, Harbin Medical Univ. 2004, Heilongjiang Univ. 2004, Shanghai Maritime Univ. 2004; Grand Officier, Ordre du Mono (Togo) 1989, La Grande Etoile de Djibouti 1995, Order of Merit for Distinguished Service, Third Grade (Peru) 1996, Order of Friendship (Russian Fed.) 1996, Al Hussein Bin Ali Decoration for Accomplishment, First Degree (Jordan) 1998, Order of Merit in the Rank of Grand Officer (Romania) 2000, Officier, Ordre Nat. (Madagascar) 2003, Commdr, Ordre Royal du Monisaraphon (Cambodia) 2003, Commdr, Ordre Nat. du Mali 2006, Coast Guard Legion of Honour (Degree of Maginoo) 2007; Dr hc (Univ. of Bucharest) 2000, (Univ. of Cape Coast) 2000, (Acad. of Man., Mongolia) 2003, (World Maritime Univ.) 2004; Medal for Merits, Third Degree (Ukraine) 1996, Frantsiska Scarina Medal (Belarus) 1996, China Health Medal 1997, WHO Health-for-All Gold Medal 1998, Decerne la Medaille d'Honneur de Menerbes (France) 2000, Int. Leprosy Union Millennium Gandhi Award 2001, Vaclav Havel Memorial Medal 2001, Nat. Construction Medal (Cambodia) 2003, Yomiuri Int. Cooperation Prize (Japan) 2004, Int. Gandhi Award (India) 2006. *Publications (in English):* Those with Wisdom Fail for Wisdom 1996, Real Faces of the World Unknown to the Ministry of Foreign Affairs 1998, This Country and That Country 2004, The Day Leprosy is Eradicated from the World 2004. *Address:* The Nippon Foundation, 1-2-2 Akasaka, Minato-ku, Tokyo 107-8404, Japan (office). *Telephone:* (3) 6229-5121 (office). *Fax:* (3) 6229-5120 (office). *Website:* (office).

SASAKI, Hajime, MSc; Japanese computer industry executive; *Chairman, NEC Corporation;* b. 6 April 1936; ed Univ. of Tokyo; joined NEC Corpn 1961, designed integrated circuits for communications applications 1961–82, Gen. Man. VLSI Devt Div. 1982–84, Gen. Man. Microcomputer Products Div. 1984–86, Vice-Pres. 1986–88, Assoc. Sr Vice-Pres. 1988–91, Exec. Vice-Pres. 1994–96, Sr Exec. Vice-Pres. 1996–99, Chair. and Rep. Dir 1999–2008, Chair. 2008–; mem. Bd Dirs Komatsu Ltd; Exec. Dir Semiconductor Industry Research Inst. Japan 1994–96; Pres. Semiconductor Leading Edge Technologies Inc. 1996–98; Chair. Communications Industry Asscn of Japan (CIAJ) 1999–2000; Sheffield Fellowship, Yale Univ. 2006; IEEE Fellow 1996; Foreign Assoc. Nat. Acad. of Eng 2000; Inst. of Electronics Information and Communications Engineers (IEICE) Fellow 2000; IEEE Life Fellow 2001; Chevalier, Légion d'honneur 2006; Science and Tech. Agency Award, Govt of Japan 1997, IEEE Third Millennium Medal 2000, IEICE Achievement Award 2001, IEEE Robert N. Noyce Medal 2001, Deming Prize for Individuals 2005. *Address:* NEC Corporation, 7-1 Shiba 5-chome, Minato-ku, Tokyo 108-8001, Japan (office). *Telephone:* (3) 3454-1111 (office). *Fax:* (3) 3798-1510 (office). *E-mail:* a-shikimori@ay.jp.nec.com (office); Lwojtecji@necusa.com (office). *Website:* www.nec.com (office).

SASAKI, Mikio, DEng; Japanese business executive; *Chairman, Mitsubishi Corporation;* b. 8 Oct. 1937; m.; c.; ed Waseda Univ.; joined Mitsubishi Corpn 1960, various sr and man. positions including assignments in Chile 1973, Iran 1979–83, USA 1980s, Germany and UK 1990s, apptd Dir Mitsubishi Corpn 1992, Man. Dir 1994–98, Pres. 1998–2004, Chair. 2004–; Chair. Japan Foreign Trade Council Inc. 2004–. *Address:* Mitsubishi Corporation, 6-3, Marunouchi 2-chome, Chiyoda-ku, Tokyo 100-8086, Japan (office). *Telephone:* (3) 3210-2121 (office). *Fax:* (3) 3210-8583 (office). *E-mail:* info@mitsubishicorp.com (office). *Website:* www.mitsubishicorp.com (office).

SASSEN, Saskia, MA, PhD; American sociologist and academic; *Robert S. Lynd Professor of Sociology, Columbia University;* b. (Saskia Sassen Van Elsloo), 1949, The Hague, Netherlands; m. Richard Sennett; ed Université de Poitiers, Univ. of Notre Dame, Harvard Univ.; fmr Ralph Lewis Prof. of Sociology, Univ. of Chicago; Centennial Visiting Prof., LSE; currently Robert S. Lynd Prof. of Sociology, Univ. of Columbia; Visiting Scholar Russell Sage Foundation, Woodrow Wilson Int. Center for Scholars, Center for Advanced Study in the Behavioral Sciences; Dir project on global cities and cross-border networks, Inst. of Advanced Studies, UNU, Tokyo; Co-Dir Economy Section, Global Chicago Project; mem. Social Science Research Council (SSRC) Working Group on New York City sponsored by Russell Sage Foundation 1985–90, SSRC Cttee on Hispanic Public Policy sponsored by Ford Foundation 1987–91, New York-London Comparative Study sponsored by UK Econ. and Social Research Council, UN Centre on Regional Devt and MIT-sponsored project on Economic Restructuring in the US and Japan 1988–90, Research Working Group on Informal Sector, Stanford Univ. Project on Mexico–US Relations, Immigration and Econ. Sociology Project (Russell Sage Foundation) 1992–95, Comparative Urban Studies Project, Woodrow Wilson Center 1992–, Group of Lisbon sponsored by Science Program of EU and Gulbenkian Foundation 1993–, NAS Panel on Urban Data Sets, Council of Foreign Relations; Chair. Information Tech., Int. Co-operation and Global Security Cttee of the SSRC; mem. Advisory Panel, Queens Borough, Pres. Claire Shulman's Blue Ribbon Panel on Govt, NY State Industrial Corpn Council; mem. French Govt's Ministry of Urban Affairs scientific jury, Belgian Govt's Agency on Science and Tech. in the Office of the Prime Minister; mem. several editorial bds; Fellow American Bar Foundation, Wissenschaftszentrum, Berlin; Dr hc (Delft Univ., Netherlands); recipient of awards from the Ford Foundation, Tinker Foundation, Revson Foundation, Chicago Inst. for Architecture and Urbanism, Twentieth Century Fund; Nat. Prize of the American Inst. of Certified Planners; Distinguished Lecturer, Inst. for Advanced Studies, Vienna, Henry Luce Lecturer, Clark Univ., Georg Simmel Lectures, Humboldt Univ., Eilert Sundt Lecture, Univ. of Oslo. *Publications include:* The Mobility of Labor and Capital 1988, The Global City 1991, Cities in a World Economy 1994, Losing Control? Sovereignty in an Age of Globalization 1996, Migranten, Siedler, Flüchtlinge, Globalization and its Discontents – Selected Essays 1984–98 1998, Guests and Aliens 1999, Global Networks/Linked Cities 2002, Territory, Authority, Rights: From Medieval to Global Assemblages 2006, A Sociology of Globlaization 2006, Deciphering the Global: Its Spaces, scales and subjects 2007; books translated into 19 languages. *Address:* Department of Sociology, Columbia University, 422 Fayerweather Hall, 1180 Amsterdam Avenue, New York, NY 10027, USA (office). *Telephone:* (212) 854-0790 (office). *Fax:* (212) 854-2963 (office). *E-mail:* sjs2@columbia.edu (office). *Website:* www.sociology.columbia.edu (office); www.columbia.edu/~sjs2/ (office).

SASSER, Hon. James (Jim) Ralph, JD; American lawyer, fmr diplomatist and fmr politician; *Senior Counselor, APCO Worldwide;* b. 30 Sept. 1936, Memphis, Tenn.; s. of Joseph Ralph Sasser and Mary Nell Sasser (née Gray); m. Mary Ballantine Gorman 1962; one s. one d.; ed Vanderbilt Univ.; served US Marine Corps Reserve 1958–65; pnr, Goodpasture, Carpenter, Woods & Sasser, Nashville 1961–76; Chair. Tennessee Democratic State Cttee 1973–76; Senator from Tennessee 1977–95; Amb. to People's Repub. of China 1996–99; Foreign Policy Adviser to Vice-Pres. Al Gore 2000; J. B. and Maurice C. Shapiro Prof., Elliott School of Int. Affairs, George Washington Univ. 2000–02; currently Sr Advisor to FedEx Corpn and Sr Counselor to APCO Worldwide, Washington, DC; mem. Bd of Dirs GreenHunter Energy, Inc. 2008–; mem. Council on Foreign Relations, ABA, UN Asscn; Trustee Nat. Geographic Soc. *Address:* c/o APCO Worldwide, 700 12th Street, NW, Suite 800, Washington, DC 20005, USA (office). *Telephone:* (202) 778-1010 (office). *Website:* www.apcoworldwide.com (office).

SASSOON, David; British fashion designer; b. 5 Oct. 1932, London; s. of George Sassoon and Victoria Gurgi; ed Chelsea Coll. of Art and Royal Coll. of Art; designer, Belinda Bellville 1958; first ready-to-wear collection 1963; Dir Belinda Bellville 1964; Licensee Vogue Butterick USA 1966 (became Bellville Sassoon 1970); Dir and sole shareholder Bellville Sassoon 1983–; Trustee Fashion and Textile Museum. *Leisure interests:* theatre, ballet. *Address:* Bellville Sassoon, 18 Culford Gardens, London, SW3 2ST, England. *Telephone:* (20) 7581-3500 (office). *Fax:* (20) 7581-0151 (office). *E-mail:* D.S@bellvillesassoon.com (office). *Website:* www.bellvillesassoon.com (office).

SASSOON, Vidal; British hair stylist; b. 17 Jan. 1928, London; s. of Nathan Sassoon and Betty (née Bellin) Sassoon; m. (divorced 1980); two s. two d.; ed New York Univ.; served with Palmach Israeli Army; cr. a form of hairstyling based on Bahaus and geometric forms; Founder and Chair. Vidal Sassoon Inc.; Pres. Vidal Sassoon Foundation; f. Vidal Sassoon Centre for the Study of Antisemitism and Related Bigotries at Hebrew Univ., Jerusalem; Fellow, Hair Artists Int; French Ministry of Culture Award, Award for Services Rendered, Harvard Business School, Intercoiffure Award, Cartier, London 1978. *Address:* Vidal Sassoon International Center for the Study of Antisemitism, Hebrew University of Jerusalem, Mount Scopus, 91905 Jerusalem, Israel (office). *Telephone:* (2) 5882494 (office). *Fax:* (2) 5881002 (office). *E-mail:* ukvidals.im@pg.com (office).

SASSOU-NGUESSO, Gen. Denis; Republic of the Congo army officer and head of state; *President;* b. 1943, Edou; joined Congolese Armed Forces 1960, mil. training in Cen. Africa, Algeria and France 1961–68; mem. Parti Congolais du Travail (PCT) 1970–, First Vice-Pres., Mil. Cttee Parti Congolais du Travail (PCT), co-ordinator of PCT activities 1977–79, Pres. PCT 1979–, Leader, Forces Démocratiques Unies (alliance of six parties including PCT) 1994–95; Minister of Defence 1975; Pres. of the Republic of the Congo 1979–92, 1997–; Chair. African Union 2006–07. *Address:* Palais du Peuple, Brazzaville, Republic of the Congo (office). *Telephone:* 81-17-11 (office). *E-mail:* contact@presicongo.cg (office). *Website:* www.presidence.cg (office).

SASSU, Alexandru; Romanian politician and television executive; *President and Director-General, Televiziunea Română (TVR);* b. 26 Oct. 1955; ed Faculty of Electronics and Telecommunications, Tech. Inst., Bucharest; fmr Vice-Pres. Partidul Democrat (PD—Democratic Party); fmr mem. Chamber of Deputies 1992–2004, fmr mem., Sec. and Vice-Pres. Comm. of Culture, Art and Mass Media; Interim Dir-Gen. Televiziunea Română (TVR—state broadcaster) May–Sept. 2007, Pres. and Dir-Gen. 2007–. *Address:* Televiziunea Română, PO Box 63-1200, Calea Dorobanţilor 191, 015089 Bucharest, Romania (office). *Telephone:* (21) 2312704 (office). *Fax:* (21) 2307514 (office). *E-mail:* tvr@tvr.ro (office). *Website:* www.tvr.ro (office).

SASTRY, S. Shankar, PhD; Indian electrical engineer, computer scientist and academic; *Dean, College of Engineering, University of California, Berkeley;* ed Indian Inst. of Tech., Univ. of Calif., Berkeley; Asst Prof., MIT 1980–82; Gordon McKay Prof., Harvard Univ. 1994; Dir, Electronics Research Lab., Berkeley 1996–99, Chair., Dept of Electrical Eng, Univ. of California, Berkeley 2001–04, also Prof. of Electrical Eng and of Computer Sciences and Bioengineering and Dir, Center for Information Tech. in the Interest of Soc. (CITRIS) 2005–07, Dir Emer. 2007–, Dean, Coll. of Eng 2007–; fmr Visiting Prof., Australian Nat. Univ., Univ. of Rome, Univ. of Pisa, Inst. Nat. Polytechnique de Grenoble, Center for Intelligent Control Systems, MIT; Chair., Int. Computer Science Inst. (ICSI) 2004–; mem. Nat. Acad. of Eng. 2001–; fmr Assoc. Ed., IEEE Transactions on Automatic Control, IMA Journal of Control and Information, Journal of Biomimetic Systems and Materials, International Journal of Adaptive Control and Signal Processing; Fellow, IEEE 1994–; MA hc (Harvard) 1994; numerous awards including Pres. of India Gold Medal 1977, Eckman Award, American Automatic Control Council 1990. *Publications:* over 250 technical papers; books include Essays in Mathematical Robotics (jt author), Adaptive Control: Stability, Convergence and Robustness (jt author) 1989, A Mathematical Introduction to Robotic Manipulation (jt author) 1994, Nonlinear Systems: Analysis, Stability and Control 1999, An Invitation to 3D Vision: From Images to Models (jt author) 2003. *Address:* Dean's Office, 320 McLaughlin Hall # 1700, UC Berkeley, Berkeley, CA 94720-1700, USA (office). *E-mail:* sastry@eecs.berkeley.edu (office). *Website:* www.eecs.berkeley.edu/Faculty/Homepages/sastry (office).

SATA, Genichiro; Japanese politician; b. 22 Dec. 1952; ed Hokkaido Univ.; served as Sec. to Minister of Finance 1986; mem. House of Reps for Gunma Prefecture constituency 1990–; Deputy Sec.-Gen. LDP 1997–2004, Chief Deputy Sec.-Gen. 2004–, other LDP positions have included Deputy Chair. Diet Affairs Cttee, Vice-Chair. Political Reform HQ, Dir Construction Div., Deputy Dir Communications Div.; Parl. Vice-Minister of Finance 1995, Vice-Minister of Educ., Science, Sports and Culture 1996, Vice-Minister of Posts and Telecommunications 2000, Sr Vice-Minister of Internal Affairs and Communications 2002, Minister of State for Regulatory Reform, for Admin. Reform, for Special Zones, for Structural Reform and for Regional Revitalization 2006 (resgnd). *Address:* c/o Liberal-Democratic Party—LDP (Jiyu-Minshuto), 1-11-23, Nagata-cho, Chiyoda-ku, Tokyo 100-8910, Japan. *E-mail:* koho@ldp.jimin.or.jp. *Website:* www.sata-genichiro.jp.

SATCHELL, Keith, BSc, FIA; British insurance industry executive; *Chairman, Rothesay Life Ltd;* b. 3 June 1951; worked for UK Provident then joined Friends Provident 1986, Divisional Gen. Man. 1987–95, apptd Man. Dir Business Operations 1995, Exec. Dir Friends Provident Life Office 1992–2001, CEO 1997–2001, Group CEO and mem. Bd of Dirs Friends Provident plc 2001–07; mem. Bd of Dirs F & C Asset Man. plc 1995–2007; Chair. Barnett Waddingham LLP 2007–; Chair. Rothesay Life Ltd (insurance co. est. in UK as wholly-owned subsidiary of Goldman Sachs Group, Inc.) 2008–; fmr mem. Supervisory Bd of European Alliance Pnrs B.V., Swiss Mobiliar Cooperative Co.; mem. of Sr Bd Banco Comercial Português SA; Chair. Asscn of British Insurers 2005–07. *Address:* Rothesay Life Ltd, PO Box 545, Redhill, Surrey, RH1 1YX (office); Barnett Waddingham LLP, Cheapside House, 138 Cheapside, London, EC2V 6BW, England (office). *Telephone:* (20) 7776-2200 (Barnett Waddingham) (office). *Fax:* (20) 7776-3800 (office). *Website:* www .rothesaylife.co.uk (office); www.barnett-waddingham.co.uk (office).

SATHIRATHAI, Surakiart, LLM, MALD, SJD; Thai politician and economist; b. 7 June 1958, Bangkok; m. Thanpuying Dr. Suthawan Sathirathai; one s.; ed Chulalongkorn Univ., Tufts Univ., Harvard Univ., USA; policy adviser to Prime Minister 1988–92, to Nat. Ass. 1989–91, to Prime Minister on econ. affairs 1991–92; Co-founder Siam Premier Int. Law Office Ltd 1990, Chair. Exec. Bd 1990–2001; Dean and Assoc. Prof., Chulalongkorn Univ. 1992–95; Chair. Crown Property Bureau, Securities Exchange Comm., House Select Cttee on Budget Review 1995–96, PTTEP Co. Ltd 1998–2000, Laem Thong Bank Co. Ltd 1998–99, Petroleum Authority of Thailand, Thai Oil Co. Ltd 1999–2000; Minister of Finance 1995–96; Vice-Chair. of Prime Minister's Advisory Council on Econ. and Foreign Affairs 1996–97; Councillor of State 1997–2001; Pres. Inst. of Social and Econ. Policy (ISEP) 1997–2001; Chair. Foundation for the Inst. of Social and Econ. Policy 1999–2001; Minister of Foreign Affairs 2001–05; Deputy Prime Minister 2005–06; Kt Grand Cordon (Special Class) of the Most Noble Order of the Crown of Thailand, Kt Grand Cross (First Class) of the Most Exalted Order of the White Elephant. *Address:* c/o Siam Premier International Law Office Limited, 26th Floor, The Offices at Central World, 999/9 Rama 1 Road, Pathumwan, Bangkok 10330, Thailand (office). *Website:* www.siamlaw.co.th.

SATO, Humitaka, PhD; Japanese astrophysicist and academic; *Professor Emeritus of Astrophysics and Relativity, Kyoto University;* b. 23 March 1939, Yamagata; s. of Mokichi Sato and Kane Sato; m. Keiko Okazaki 1965; one s. one d.; ed Kyoto Univ.; Prof. of Astrophysics and Relativity, Kyoto Univ. 1974–2006, Dean Faculty of Sciences 1993, Prof. Emer. 2006–; Dir Yukawa Inst. for Theoretical Physics 1976–80; Pres. Physical Soc. of Japan 1998–2000; Nishina Prize 1973, Purple Medal of Honour 1999. *Publications:* Black Holes 1976, Discovery of Big Bang 1983, Invitation to Cosmology 1988. *Address:* Yukawa Memorial Foundation, Yukawa Institute of Theoretical Physics,

Kyoto University, Kitasirakawa, Sakyo-ku, Kyoto 606-8502, Japan (office). *E-mail:* sato@tap.scphys.kyoto-u.ac.jp (office). *Website:* www.kyoto-u.ac.jp (office).

SATO, Masatoshi, BEcons; Japanese insurance industry executive; *President and CEO, Sompo Japan Insurance Inc;* b. 2 March 1949, Toshima-ku; ed Keio Univ.; joined Yasude Fire & Marine Insurance Co. Ltd 1972, Man. Yamanashi Br. 1994–96, Gen. Man. System Planning Dept 1996, Gen. Man. Information System Dept 1997–99, Gen. Man. Presidential Staff Office 1999–2000, Dir and Gen. Man. Presidential Staff Office 2000–02, Dir and Man. Exec. Officer 2002–05, Pres. and CEO Sompo Japan Insurance Inc. 2006–; Pres. and Rep. Dir Sompo Japan Reseach Inst.; Dir Nippon Keidanren Cttee on Nature Conservation. *Address:* Sompo Japan Insurance Inc., 26-1, Nishi-Shinjuku 1-chome, Shinjuku-ku, Tokyo 160-8338, Japan (office). *Telephone:* (3) 3349-3111 (office). *Fax:* (3) 3349-4697 (office). *Website:* www.sompo-japan.com (office).

SATO, Mikio, BSc, PhD; Japanese mathematician and academic; *Professor Emeritus, Research Institute for Mathematical Sciences, Kyoto University;* b. 1928; ed Tokyo Univ.; Lecturer, Tokyo Univ. 1960–63, Prof. 1968–70;; Prof., Osaka Univ. 1963–68; Prof., Research Inst. for Math. Sciences (RIMS), Kyoto Univ. 1970–92, Prof. Emer. 1992–, Dir RIMS 1987–91; mem. NAS 1993–; Asahi Prize of Science 1969, Japan Acad. Prize 1976, Fujiwara Prize 1987, Rolf Schock Prize in Math., Royal Swedish Acad. of Sciences 1997, Wolf Prize 2003. *Publications:* numerous articles in math. journals on algebraic analysis and theory of hyperfunctions. *Address:* Research Institute for Mathematical Sciences, Kyoto University, Kyoto 606-8502, Japan (office). *Fax:* (75) 7537276 (office). *E-mail:* sato@kurims.kyoto-u.ac.jp (office). *Website:* www.kurims .kyoto-u.ac.jp (office).

SATO, Ryuzo, PhD, DEcon; Japanese economist and academic; b. 5 July 1931, Akita-ken; m. Kishie Hayashi 1959; one s. one d.; ed Hitotsubashi Univ., Tokyo, Johns Hopkins University, Baltimore, Md, USA; Fulbright Scholar, Johns Hopkins Univ. 1957–62; Prof. of Econs Brown Univ. 1967–85; C.V. Starr Prof. of Econs New York Univ. 1985–2006 (retd), Dir Center for Japan–US Business and Econ. Studies, New York Univ. Stern School of Business –2006; Adjunct Prof. of Public Policy, John F. Kennedy School of Govt Harvard Univ. 1983; Guggenheim Fellow; Ford Foundation Fellow; Yomiuri newspaper Rondan Prize, Nihon-Keizai newspaper Economics Award (Nikkei Prize). *Publications:* Theory of Technical Change and Economic Invariance 1981, Research and Productivity (with G. Suzawa) 1983, Growth Theory and Technical Change 1996, Production, Stability and Dynamic Invariance 1999. *Leisure interests:* skiing, music, gardening. *Address:* c/o Center for Japan–US Business and Economic Studies, Stern School of Business, 44 West Fourth Street, KMC 7-91, New York, NY 10012, USA (office).

SATO, Yoshio; Japanese insurance industry executive; *President, CEO and Representative Director, Sumitomo Life Insurance Company;* Man. Dir Sumitomo Life Insurance Co. –2007, Pres., CEO and Rep. Dir 2007–; mem. Bd of Dirs Life Insurance Asscn of Japan; Trustee Japan Inst. of Life Insurance. *Address:* Sumitomo Life Insurance Co., 1-4-35 Shiromi, Chuo-ku, Osaka 540-8512, Japan (office). *Telephone:* (6) 6937-1435 (office). *E-mail:* info@sumitomolife.co.jp (office). *Website:* www.sumitomolife.co.jp (office).

SATOH, Yukio, BA; Japanese diplomatist; *Vice Chairman, Japan Institute of International Affairs;* b. 6 Oct. 1939; m.; two c.; ed Tokyo Univ. and Univ. of Edinburgh, UK; entered Foreign Service 1961, with Ministry of Foreign Affairs, Tokyo, then Embassy, Washington, DC –1976, Dir Div. of Security Affairs, American Affairs Bureau, Ministry of Foreign Affairs 1976–77, Pvt. Sec. to the Foreign Minister 1977–79, Counsellor, London 1981–84, also Consul-Gen., Dir Policy Coordination Div. 1985–87, Asst Vice-Minister for Parl. Affairs, Ministry of Foreign Affairs 1987–88; Chief of Prefectural Police, Miyazaki 1984–85; Consul-Gen., Hong Kong 1988–90; Dir-Gen. North American Affairs Bureau and Dir-Gen. Information Analysis, Research and Planning Bureau, Ministry of Foreign Affairs 1990–94, Amb. to the Netherlands 1994–96, to Australia 1996–98; Perm. Rep. to the UN 1998–2002; Pres. The Japan Inst. of Int. Affairs 2002–09, Vice-Chair. 2009–. *Publications:* numerous articles on Japanese foreign and security policy. *Address:* The Japan Institute of International Affairs, Kasumigaseki Building 11 Floor, 3-2-5 Kasumigaseki, Chiyoda-ku, Tokyo, 100-6011, Japan (office). *Telephone:* (03) 3503-6625 (office). *Fax:* (03) 3503-7411 (office). *E-mail:* satoh@jiia.or.jp (office). *Website:* www.jiia.or.jp/en.

SATRAPI, Marjane, MA; Iranian writer, illustrator and film director; b. (Marjan Ebrahimi-Ripa), 22 Sept. 1969, Rasht; ed Visual Communication School of Fine Arts, Tehran, École des Arts Decoratifs de Strasbourg, France. *Film:* Persepolis (dir and writer with Vincent Paronnaud) (Sutherland Trophy, British Film Inst. Awards 2007, Jury Prize, Cannes Film Festival 2007, Special Jury Prize, Cinemanila Int. Film Festival 2007, César Award for Best First Work 2007, Audience Award, Rotterdam Int. Film Festival 2008, Audience Award, São Paulo Int. Film Festival 2007, Most Popular Film, Vancouver Int. Film Festival 2007) 2007. *Publications:* Persepolis: The Story of a Childhood (four vols) 1999–2002, Persepolis 2: The Story of a Return (adapted as screenplay 2007) 2005, Embroideries 2005, Chicken with Plums 2006; several children's books; contrib. illustrations to French magazines and periodicals. *Address:* 13 rue de Thorigny, 75003 Paris, France (home). *Telephone:* 6-64-99-04-52 (home). *Fax:* 1-42-72-65-15 (home). *E-mail:* marjanesatrapi@yahoo.fr (home).

SATTAR, Abdul, MA; Pakistani diplomatist; b. 1931; m. Yasmine Sattar 1955; one s. two d.; ed Punjab Univ. and Fletcher School, USA; served in Pakistan Missions in Saudi Arabia, Sudan and the USA; Amb. of Pakistan to Austria 1975–78, to India 1978–82, 1990–92, to USSR 1988–90; Dir, then Dir-Gen. and Additional Sec. at Foreign Office, for Asia 1982–86; Foreign Sec.,

Islamabad 1986–88; Sr Del. to Geneva Talks on Afghanistan 1988; Minister of Foreign Affairs 1999–2002; Distinguished Fellow, US Inst. of Peace, Washington, DC 1994; mem. Nat. Security Council. *Publications:* Pakistan in Perspective, 1947–97 (co-author); articles in learned journals on nuclear non-proliferation and regional studies. *Address:* House 7, College Road, F-7/3, Islamabad, Pakistan (home). *Telephone:* (51) 2270476 (home). *Fax:* (51) 2270476 (home). *E-mail:* sattara@comsats.net.pk (home).

SATTERFIELD, David M., BA; American diplomatist; *Senior Advisor to the Secretary of State and Coordinator for Iraq;* b. Baltimore; ed Univ. of Maryland, Georgetown Univ.; joined US State Dept. 1980, served in Saudi Arabia, Tunisia, Lebanon and Syria and staff mem. Bureau of Near Eastern Affairs, Bureau of East Asian and Pacific Affairs and Intelligence and Research; Dir for Exec. Secretarial Staff and for Near East and South Asian Affairs, Nat. Security Council 1993–96; Dir Office of Israel and Arab-Israeli Affairs 1996–98; Amb. to Lebanon 1998–2001, Deputy Asst Sec. for Near Eastern Affairs 2001–04, Prin. Deputy Asst. Sec. of State for Near Eastern Affairs 2004–05; Deputy Chief of Mission, Embassy in Baghdad 2005–06; Sr Advisor to Sec. of State and Coordinator for Iraq 2006–; Presidential Meritorious Exec. Rank Award, Dept of State Distinguished Honor Award, Dept Sr Performance Award, six Dept of State Superior Honor Awards. *Address:* Department of State, 2201 C Street, NW, Washington, DC 20520, USA (office). *Telephone:* (202) 647-5056 (office). *Fax:* (202) 647-6738 (home). *Website:* www.state.gov (office).

SATYANAND, Hon. Anand, PCNZM, QSO, KStJ, LLB; New Zealand lawyer, judge and ombudsman; *Governor-General;* b. 22 July 1944, Auckland; m. Susan Satyanand; three c.; ed Univ. of Auckland Law School; admitted to the Bar 1970; practised law with Crown Solicitors' Office and Pnr, pvt. law practice; Dist Court Judge, Palmerston N and Auckland, with specialist warrant for criminal jury trials 1982–94; Parl. Ombudsman 1995–2005; Gov.-Gen. of NZ 2006–; Chair. Confidential Forum for Fmr In-Patients of Psychiatric Hosps –2006; Registrar of Pecuniary Interests of Mems of Parl. –2006; mem. Bd of Dirs NZ Inst. of Int. Affairs, Transparency Int.; fmr exec. NZ Rugby League; Hon. LLD (Auckland Univ.) 2006. *Address:* Government House, Private Bag 39995, Wellington Mail Centre, Lower Hutt 5045, Wellington, New Zealand (office). *Telephone:* (4) 3898055 (office). *Fax:* (4) 3895536 (office). *E-mail:* info@govthouse.govt.nz (office). *Website:* www.gov-gen.govt.nz (office).

SA'UD, HM The King of Saudi Arabia; Abdullah ibn Abd al-Aziz as-; *Head of State and Prime Minister;* b. 1924, Riyadh; s. of the late King Abdul Aziz ibn Sa'ud and Fahda bint Asi ash-Shuraim; brother of HRH Crown Prince Sultan ibn Abd al-Aziz as-Sa'ud; Commdr Nat. Guard 1962–2005; Second Deputy Prime Minister 1975–82, First Deputy Prime Minister and Commdr Nat. Guard 1982–2005; became Crown Prince June 1982; succeeded to throne upon death of half-brother HM King Fahd 1 Aug. 2005; Patron Nat. Heritage and Cultural Festival, Jenadriyah 1985–. *Leisure interests:* hunting, horse racing. *Address:* Royal Diwan, Riyadh, Saudi Arabia.

SA'UD, Prince Ahmed ibn Abd al-Aziz as-; Saudi Arabian government official; b. 1940; Deputy Minister of the Interior 1978–. *Address:* Ministry of the Interior, POB 2933, Airport Road, Riyadh 11134, Saudi Arabia (office). *Telephone:* (1) 401-1111 (office). *Fax:* (1) 403-1185 (office).

SA'UD, HRH Prince Bandar ibn Sultan ibn Abd al-Aziz as-, MA; Saudi Arabian diplomatist and army officer; *Secretary-General, National Security Council;* b. 2 March 1949, Taif; s. of HRH Crown Prince Sultan ibn Abd al-Aziz as-Sa'ud; m. HRH Princess Haifa bint Faisal ibn Abd al-Aziz as-Sa'ud; four s. four d.; ed RAF Coll., Cranwell, USAF Advanced Program and Johns Hopkins Univ.; fighter pilot, Royal Saudi Air Force 1969–82; in charge of special Saudi Arabian liaison mission to USA for purchase of AWACS and other defence equipment 1981; Defence and Mil. Attaché, Saudi Arabian Mil. Mission to USA 1982–83; Amb. to USA 1983–2005; promoted to rank of Minister 1995; Sec.-Gen. Nat. Security Council 2005–; numerous medals and decorations, including Hawk Flying Medal of Aviation, King Faisal Medal, King Abdul Aziz Sash, as well as honours from other nations. *Leisure interests:* flying, racquetball, reading. *Address:* c/o Ministry of Foreign Affairs, PO Box 55937, Riyadh 11544, Saudi Arabia (office). *Telephone:* (1) 405-5000 (office).

SA'UD, HRH Prince Nayef ibn Abd al-Aziz as-; Saudi Arabian politician; *Minister of the Interior;* b. 1934; brother of King Abdullah ibn Abd al-Aziz as-Sa'ud; Gov. of Riyadh 1953–54; Minister of State for Internal Affairs 1970–75, Minister of the Interior 1975–; Pres., Supreme Council for Information; Chair. Supreme Cttee on the Hajj; Head, Ministerial Oversight Cttee on the WTO; Head, Ministerial Cttee on Morality. *Address:* Ministry of the Interior, POB 2933, Airport Road, Riyadh 11134, Saudi Arabia (office). *Telephone:* (1) 401-1111 (office). *Fax:* (1) 403-1185 (office).

SA'UD, HRH Prince Salman ibn Abd al-Aziz as-; Saudi Arabian politician; *Governor of Riyadh;* b. 13 Dec. 1936; s. of the late King Abd al-Aziz as-Sa'ud and Hussah bint Ahmad as-Sudairi; brother of HRH King Abdullah ibn Abd al-Aziz as-Sa'ud; m.; Gov. of Riyadh 1962–, in this role also arbitrates disputes among mems of the royal family; Chair. Bd Riyadh Water and Sanitary Drainage Authority and numerous other orgs; active in Abdul Aziz Foundation. *Leisure interest:* reading. *Address:* Office of the Governor, Riyadh, Saudi Arabia (office).

SA'UD, HRH Prince Sa'ud al-Faisal as-, BA (Econs); Saudi Arabian politician and diplomatist; *Minister of Foreign Affairs;* b. 1941, Riyadh; s. of the late King Faisal ibn Abd al-Aziz as-Sa'ud; ed Princeton Univ., USA; fmr Deputy Minister of Petroleum and Mineral Resources 1971–74; Minister of State for Foreign Affairs March–Oct. 1975, Minister of Foreign Affairs Oct. 1975–; Leader del. to UN Gen. Ass. 1976; Special Envoy of HM King Khalid

ibn Abd al-Aziz as-Sa'ud in diplomatic efforts to resolve Algerian–Moroccan conflict over Western Sahara and the civil war in Lebanon; mem. Saudi Arabian del. to Arab restricted Summit, Riyadh, Oct. 1976 and to full Summit Conf. of Arab League, Oct. 1976; Founding mem. King Faisal's Int. Charity Soc. *Leisure interest:* reading. *Address:* Ministry of Foreign Affairs, Nasseriya Street, Riyadh 11124, Saudi Arabia (office). *Telephone:* (1) 401-5000 (office). *Fax:* (1) 403-0159 (office). *Website:* www.mofa.gov.sa (office).

SA'UD, HRH Prince Sa'ud bin Abdullah bin Thunayan as-, BEng; Saudi Arabian business executive; *Chairman, SABIC;* ed King Sa'ud Univ.; early career as engineer, Riyadh Municipality, becoming Dir-Gen. for survey and drawings; Under-Sec. for Planning and Programmes, Ministry of Municipality and Rural Affairs 1989; currently Chair. Admin. Bd Saudi Basic Industries Corpn (SABIC); Chair. Royal Comm. for Jubail and Yanbu; mem Bd Utility and Water Co. of Jubail and Yanbu, Royal Family Bd, Prince Salman's Social Centre; mem several cttees formed by Royal Decree to regulate needs of Al-Jouf, Jizan, northern border and Hail areas in Saudi Arabia, in addition to villages and areas in western coast and needs of people of Yanbu Governor-ates; mem jt cttee that supervises co-ordination and follows work between Ministry of Municipality and Rural Affairs, Ministry of Transportation, Ministry of Agric. and Higher Cttee for Childhood. *Address:* Saudi Basic Industries Corporation, PO Box 5101, Riyadh 11422, Saudi Arabia (office). *Telephone:* (1) 225-8000 (office). *Fax:* (1) 225-9000 (office). *E-mail:* info@sabic.ocm (office). *Website:* www.sabic.com (office); www.thunayan-al-saud.com.

SA'UD, HRH Crown Prince Sultan ibn Abd al-Aziz as-; Saudi Arabian politician; *First Deputy Prime Minister, Minister of Defence and Aviation and Inspector General;* b. 5 Jan. 1928, Riyadh; s. of the late King Abd al-Aziz as-Sa'ud and Hussah bint Ahmad as-Sudairi; brother of King Abdullah ibn Abd al-Aziz as-Sa'ud; son, Prince Bandar ibn Sultan ibn Abd al-Aziz as-Sa'ud; ed at court and abroad; Gov. of Riyadh 1947; Minister of Agric. 1954, of Transportation 1955; mem. most Saudi dels to Arab and Islamic Summit confs, State visits and UN Gen. Ass. Sessions 1962–75; Vice-Pres. Supreme Cttee of Educ. Policy; Minister of Defence and Aviation and Insp. Gen. 1962–82; Chair. Ministerial Cttee for Econ. Offset Program 1982–; Chair. Bd Saudia Airlines 1963–; Chair. Council of Manpower 1980; Second Deputy Prime Minister, Minister of Defence and Civil Aviation and Insp. Gen. 1982–; Chair. Bd of Gen. Enterprise of Mil. Industries 1985–, Bd for Nat. Comm. for Wildlife Conservation and Devt 1986–, Supreme Council for Islamic Affairs 1994–; Supreme Pres. and Chair. Trustees Sultan ibn Abd al-Aziz Charity Foundation 1995–; Chair. Ministerial Cttee on Environment 1995–; Vice-Pres. Supreme Econ. Council 2000–; Chair. High Comm. for Tourism 2000–; named Crown Prince 2005; First Deputy Prime Minister, Minister of Defence and Aviation and Insp. Gen. 2005–; Order of Merit (First Class) from many countries. *Address:* Ministry of Defence and Civil Aviation, PO Box 26731, Airport Road, Riyadh 11165, Saudi Arabia (office). *Telephone:* (1) 476-9000 (office). *Fax:* (1) 405-5500 (office).

SA'UD, HRH Prince Talal ibn Abd al-Aziz as-; Saudi Arabian politician and international official; *President, Arab Gulf Programme, United Nations Development Organizations (AGFUND);* b. 1934; s. of the late King Abd al-Aziz as-Sa'ud; brother of King Abdullah ibn Abd al-Aziz as-Sa'ud; son, Prince Walid ibn Talal; ed Prince's School, Royal Palace, Riyadh; positions held in his early 20s include responsibility for the Royal Palaces, Minister of Communications; fmr Minister of Economy and Finance; fmr Amb. to France; f. Riyadh's first girls' school 1957, first pvt. hosp. 1957 and Mecca's first coll. for boys 1957; passport cancelled 1962; exile in Egypt (for activities promoting human rights and democracy); returned to Saudi Arabia 1964; fmr Special Envoy, UNICEF; Pres. Arab Gulf Programme for UN Devt Orgs 'AGFUND'; Pres. Arab Council for Childhood and Devt. *Leisure interests:* history, amateur radio, swimming. *Address:* AGFUND, PO Box 18371, Riyadh 11415, Saudi Arabia (office); 7 rue Beaujon, 75008 Paris, France. *Telephone:* 1-43-80-22-97 (office). *E-mail:* HRH.Office@agfund.org (office). *Website:* www.princetalal.net.

SA'UD, HRH Prince Turki al-Faisal ibn Abd al-Aziz as-, LLB, MA; Saudi Arabian diplomatist; *Chairman, King Faisal Center for Research and Islamic Studies;* b. 15 Feb. 1945; s. of the late King Faisal ibn Abd al-Aziz as-Sa'ud; m. HRH Princess Nouf bint Fahad; three s. three d.; ed Lawrenceville School, NJ, Princeton and Georgetown Univs, USA, Univs of Cambridge and London, UK; adviser to Royal Court 1973–77; Dir-Gen. Saudi Arabian Intelligence Dept 1977–2001; Del. to Afghanistan 1997–98; Amb. to Court of St James (UK), London 2003–05, to USA 2005–06; Co-founder King Faisal Foundation; Chair. Bd of Dirs King Faisal Center for Research and Islamic Studies; Trustee Effat Coll., Jeddah. *Address:* King Faisal Center for Research and Islamic Studies, PO Box 51049, Riyadh 115434, Saudi Arabia (office). *Telephone:* (1) 465-2255 (office). *Fax:* (1) 465-9993 (office). *E-mail:* sjameel@kff.com (office). *Website:* www.kff.com (office).

SAUDARGAS, Algirdas; Lithuanian politician, biophysicist and diplomatist; *Ambassador to the Holy See;* b. 17 April 1948, Kaunas; m. Laima Saudargenė; one s. one d.; ed Kaunas Inst. of Medicine; research Asst Inst. of Math. and Information Tech. Lithuanian Acad. of Sciences 1972–77; Sr Lecturer Lithuanian Acad. of Agric. 1977–82; researcher Kaunas Inst. of Medicine (now Acad.) 1982–90; Founder mem. Sąjūdis Movt, Chair. Sąjūdis Seimas (Parl.) Political Cttee 1988–90; elected to Supreme Soviet Repub. of Lithuania 1990; Minister of Foreign Affairs 1990–92, 1996–99; mem. official del. Repub. of Lithuania to negotiations with Soviet Union; mem. Seimas, Cttee on Foreign Affairs, mem. Seimas del. to European Parl. 1992–2004 Chair. Sub-cttee on European Affairs 1995–2004; Chair. Lithuanian Christian Democratic Party 1995– (mem. 1989–); mem. Seimas Del. to OSCE 2003–04; Amb. to the Holy See, Vatican City 2004–. *Leisure interest:* reading. *Address:* Embassy of Lithuania, Via G. G. Porro 4, 00197 Rome, Italy (office); L. Stuokos-Gucevičiaus Str. B/10, Apt. 3, 2001 Vilnius, Lithuania (home).

Telephone: (06) 8078259 (office). *Fax:* (06) 8078291 (office). *E-mail:* amb.va@urm.lt (office).

SAUDEK, Jan; Czech photographer; b. 13 May 1935, Prague; s. of Gustav Saudek and Pavla Saudková; m. 1st Marie Geislerová 1958 (divorced 1973); m. 2nd Marie Šrámková 1974 (died 1993); two s. three d.; studied reproduction photography at graphic school; factory worker 1953–83; over 400 solo exhbns world-wide, over 300 jt exhbns; works include Man Holding New Born Child 1966, Artist's Father of the Cemetery 1972, Mother and Daughter 1979, Walkman 1984, Desire 1985, The Wedding 1990, The Deep Devotion 1994, Pretty Girl I Loved 1995, Joan of Arc 1998; Chevalier, Ordre des Arts et des Lettres 1990; Award for album cover 'Soul Asylum' 1999. *Films include:* Jerôme du Missolz 1991, Jan Saudek (series) 1993, Jan Saudek – Czech Photographer (Documentary), Telewizia Wroslaw, Poland 1997. *Publications include:* Il Teatro de la Vita 1980, The World of Jan Saudek 1983, Jan Saudek – 200 Photographs 1953–1986 1987, Life, Love, Death and Such Other Trifles 1992, Theatre of the Life 1992, The Letter 1995, Jubilations and Obsessions 1995, Album 1997, Jan Saudek... 1998, Love is a 4 Letter Word 1999, Single, Married, Divorced, Widower 1999, Realities 2002, Saudek 2005, Best of Jan Saudek 2005, Chains of Love 2007. *Leisure interests:* women, running long distances, painting, drinking. *Address:* Blodkova 6, 130 00 Prague 3, Czech Republic. *Telephone:* 737960682 (office). *Fax:* 22711482 (office); 22726845 (home). *E-mail:* jan@saudek.com (office). *Website:* www.saudek.com (office).

SAUER, Fernand Edmond; French international official, pharmacist and lawyer; *Honorary Director for Public Health, European Commission;* b. 14 Dec. 1947, St Avold, Moselle; m. Pamela Sheppard; one s. two d.; ed Univs of Strasbourg and Paris II; fmr hosp. pharmacist and pharmaceutical insp. French Ministry of Health; joined European Comm., Brussels, Head of Pharmaceuticals 1986; Exec. Dir European Agency for Evaluation of Medicinal Products (EMEA), London 1994–2000; Dir for Public Health, EC, Luxembourg 2001–06, Hon. Dir 2006–; Hon. Fellow, School of Pharmacy, Univ. of London; Hon. mem. Royal Pharmaceutical Soc.; Chevalier, Légion d'honneur, Ordre Nat. du Mérite. *Address:* DG Sanco C – Public Health and Risk Assessment, Jean Monnet Building, Office C5/120, European Commission, rue Alcide de Gasperi, 2920 Luxembourg (office). *Telephone:* 43-01-32-71-9 (office). *Fax:* 43-01-34-51-1 (office). *E-mail:* Fernand.Sauer@cec.eu.int (office). *Website:* www.ec.europa.eu.

SAUER, Louis, FAIA; American architect, urban planner and academic; b. 15 June 1928, Forest Park, Ill.; s. of Frank J. Sauer and Jeanne LaFazia; m. 1st Elizabeth Mason 1956; two c.; m. 2nd Perla Serfaty 1990; ed Univ. of Pennsylvania, Int. School of City Planning, Venice, Italy, Illinois Inst. of Tech.; Prin. Louis Sauer Assoc. Architects, Phila, Pa 1961–79; Prof. of Architecture, Univ. of Pa 1974–79, Carnegie-Mellon Univ., Pittsburgh, Pa 1979–85, Univ. of Colo 1985–89; Commr, Ville de Montreal Jacques Viger Comm. 1991–; Pnr, Archiris Inc., Pittsburgh 1981–84; Prin. Louis Sauer Architect, Boulder, Colo 1985–89; Dir of Urban Design, Daniel Arbour and Assocs, Montreal, Canada 1989–2000; currently teacher at Royal Melbourne Inst. of Tech. (RMIT) School of Architecture and Design, Australia; fmr consultant to USAID to advise govts of Lebanon, Egypt and Portugal on low-income housing devt; Nat. Endowment for the Arts Design Fellowships 1978; over 50 design and public service awards. *Work includes:* Water Plaza and high-rise housing, Cincinnati, renewal plan for Fells Point waterfront, public open-space landscape, pvt. housing and housing for the elderly, Baltimore, new town Devt for Golf Course Island, Reston, Va, Oaklands Mills Village Center, Columbia, Md, housing at Society Hill, Phila; work in Canada includes master-plans for Verdun Nuns Island 1991, Bois-Franc St-Laurent New Town 1992, Ville de Laval 1993, Angus C. P. Rail Rosemont Community 1993, Gatineu City Town Centre 1993, Ile Bizard Town Centre 1993. *Leisure interests:* gardening, fishing. *Address:* c/o RMIT University, School of Architecture and Design, 124 La Trobe Street, Melbourne, Vic. 3000, Australia.

SAUERBREY, Ellen Richmond; American politician and diplomatist; *Assistant Secretary of State for Population, Refugees and Migration;* b. 9 Sept. 1937, Baltimore; ed Western Md Coll.; fmr teacher; Rep. of Northern Md District, Md State Legislature 1978–94, Minority Leader 1986–94; Nat. Chair. American Legis. Exchange Council 1990–91; US Rep., UN Comm. on Human Rights 2001; Del. to Econ. and Social Council 2002, 2003; US Rep. to UN Comm. on Status of Women –2006; Asst Sec. of State for Population, Refugees and Migration 2006–; f. Project Freedom. *Address:* Bureau of Population, Refugees and Migration, Office 5824, Department of State, 2201 C Street, NW, Washington, DC 20520, USA (office). *Telephone:* (202) 647-7360 (office). *Website:* www.state.gov (office).

SAUERLÄNDER, Willibald, DPhil; German art historian; *Director Emeritus, Zentralinstitut für Kunstgeschichte;* b. 29 Feb. 1924, Waldsee; s. of Wilhelm Sauerländer and Anita Sauerländer-Busch; m. Brigitte Rückoldt 1957; one s.; ed Univ. of Munich; Visiting mem. Inst. for Advanced Study, Princeton 1961–62, 1973; Prof. of History of Art, Univ. of Freiburg Br. 1962–70; Dir Zentralinstitut für Kunstgeschichte, Munich 1970–89, Dir Emer. 1989–; Visiting Prof., Inst. of Fine Arts, New York Univ. 1964–65, Collège de France, Paris 1981, Univ. of Wisconsin 1982, Harvard Univ. 1984–85, Univ. of California, Berkeley 1989; Mellon Lectures, Washington 1991, New York Univ. 1992; mem. Bayerische Akad. der Wissenschaften, Medieval Acad. of America, British Acad., Soc. Nat. des Antiquaires de France, Royal Soc. of Antiquaries, London, Kon. Acad. Voor Wetenschappen, Letteren en Schone Kunsten van Belgie, Acad. Europaea, Acad. des Inscriptions et Belles-Lettres, American Acad. of Arts and Sciences; Dr hc (Perteziontо Scuola Normale, Pisa, Italy); Grand Prix de la Societé française d'archéologie 2007. *Publications:* Die Kathedrale von Chartres 1954, Jean-Antoine Houdon: Voltaire 1963, Gotische Skulptur in Frankreich 1140-1270 1970, Das Königsportal in Chartres 1984, Das Jahrhundert der grossen Kathedralen 1990, Initiälen 1996, Gegenwart der Kritik 1999, Cathedrals and their Sculptures 2000. *Leisure interests:* reading, travelling. *Address:* c/o Zentralinstitut für Kunstgeschichte, Meiserstrasse 10, 80333 Munich; Victoriastrasse II, 80803 Munich, Germany (home). *Telephone:* (89) 5591546; (89) 390988 (home).

SAUL, Hon. David John, JP, PhD; British/Bermudian politician (retd) and business consultant; b. 27 Nov. 1939, Bermuda; s. of John A. Saul and Sarah Elizabeth Saul; m. Christine Hall 1963; one s. one d.; ed Mt St Agnes Acad., Saltus Grammar School, Loughborough Coll. UK, Queen's and Toronto Univs, Canada; teacher 1962–67; consultant to Ont. Educ. Communications Authority 1970–72, to Bermuda Dept of Educ. 1972–73; Visiting Prof., Univ. of Toronto 1972; Perm. Sec. Ministry of Educ. 1972–76; Financial Sec. Ministry of Finance 1976–81; Chief Admin. Officer, Gibbons Co. 1981–84; Pres. Fidelity Int. Bermuda Ltd 1984–95, Bermuda Audubon Soc. 1998, Bermuda Debating Soc. 1998; Chair. Bermuda Council on Int. Affairs 1983–85; Dir Bermuda Monetary Authority 1986–88, 1997–99, London Bermuda Reins Co. Ltd, Bermuda Track and Field Asscn 1987–99, Fidelity Investments 1984–, Lombard Odier (Bermuda) Ltd 1989–, Odyssey Marine Exploration, Inc. 2001–; Trustee Bermuda Underwater Exploration Inst. 1992–99 (Life Trustee 1999); mem. House of Ass. 1989–97; Minister of Finance 1989–95; Prime Minister of Bermuda 1995–97; mem. Bermuda Defence Bd 1997–2001; Fellow, Explorers' Club. *Leisure interests:* scuba diving, fly-fishing, canoeing, oil painting, ocean cruising, exploration. *Address:* Rocky Ledge, 18 Devonshire Bay Road, DV 07, Bermuda (home). *Telephone:* 236-7338 (home). *Fax:* 236-5087 (home). *E-mail:* davidjsaul@aol.com (home).

SAUL, Ralph Southey, BA, LLB; American lawyer, business executive and fmr stock exchange official; *Chairman, Executive Committee, Knox & Company;* b. 21 May 1922, Brooklyn, NY; s. of Walter Emerson and Helen Douglas; m. Bette Jane Bertschinger 1956; one s. one d.; ed Univ. of Chicago and Yale Law School; war service, USNR 1943–46; attached to American Embassy, Prague 1947–48; admitted to DC Bar 1951, to New York Bar 1952; Assoc., firm of Lyeth and Voorhees, New York City 1951–52; Asst Counsel to Gov. of New York State 1952–54; Staff Attorney, Radio Corpn of America 1954–58; with Securities and Exchange Comm. 1958–65, Dir Div. of Trading and Markets 1963–65; Vice-Pres. for Corporate Devt, Investors Diversified Services, Inc. 1965–66; Pres. American Stock Exchange 1966–71; Vice-Chair. First Boston Corpn 1971–74; Chair. and CEO INA Corpn, Phila, 1975–81; Chair. CIGNA Corpn (fmrly Connecticut Gen. and INA Corpn) 1982–84; Co-founder Peers and Co. 1985; currently Chair. Exec. Cttee Knox & Co.(investment banking and corp. advisory firm); mem. Bd of Dirs American Buildings Corpn, Horace Mann Educators Corpn, PH II, Inc., Commonwealth Ventures, Brookings Inst., Cttee for Econ. Devt, Regulatory Advisory Cttee of New York Stock Exchange; mem. Advisory Bd to Grad. School of Educ., University of Pennsylvania; fmr mem. Bd of Dirs Sun Co. 1976, Certain Teed Corpn 1983, Drexel Burnham (fmr Chair.) 1989; mem. ABA, Council on Foreign Relations. *Leisure interest:* golf. *Address:* Knox & Co., 33 Riverside Avenue, 5th Floor, Westport, CT 06880, USA (office). *Telephone:* (203) 226-6288 (office). *Fax:* (203) 226-8022 (office). *Website:* www.knoxandco.com (office).

SAUMAREZ SMITH, Charles Robert, CBE, PhD, FSA; British gallery administrator; *Secretary and CEO, Royal Academy of Arts;* b. 28 May 1954, Redlynch, Wilts.; s. of the late William Hanbury Saumarez Smith and of Alice Elizabeth Harness Saumarez Smith (née Raven); m. Romilly Le Quesne Savage 1979; two s.; ed King's Coll. Cambridge, Harvard Univ., USA, Univ. of London, Warburg Inst.; Christie's Research Fellow in Applied Arts, Christ's Coll. Cambridge 1979–82; apptd Asst Keeper Victoria & Albert (V&A) Museum 1982, with special responsibility for V&A/RCA MA course in History of Design, Head of Research 1990–94; Dir Nat. Portrait Gallery 1994–2002, Nat. Gallery 2002–07; Sec. and CEO Royal Academy of Arts 2007–; Slade Prof., Univ. of Oxford 2002; Chair. English Art Museum Dir's Conf. 1999–2003; Pres. Museum Asscn 2004–06; mem. Advisory Council, Warburg Inst. 1997–2003, Inst. of Historical Research 1999–2004, Expert Panel for Museums, Libraries and Archives of the Heritage Lottery Fund 1998–2002; Gov. Univ. of the Arts 2005–; Hon. Fellow, RCA 1991; Hon. FRIBA 2000; Hon. DLitt (Univ. of E Anglia) 2001, (Westminster) 2002, (London) 2003, (Sussex) 2003, (Essex) 2005. *Publications:* The Building of Castle Howard (Alice Davis Hitchcock Medallion) 1990, Eighteenth Century Decoration 1993, The National Portrait Gallery 1997. *Address:* Royal Academy of Arts, Burlington House, Piccadilly, London, W1J 0BD, England (office). *Telephone:* (20) 7300-8020 (office). *E-mail:* chiefexecutive@royalacademy.org.uk (office). *Website:* www.royalacademy.org.uk (office).

SAUNDERS, Jennifer; British actress and writer; b. 6 July 1958; m. Adrian Edmondson; three d.; ed Cen. School of Speech and Drama, London; Hon. Rose, Montreux 2002. *Theatre:* An Evening with French and Saunders (nat. tour) 1989, Me and Mamie O'Rourke 1993, French and Saunders Live in 2000 (nat. tour) 2000. *Television series:* The Comic Strip Presents... 1990, Girls on Top, French and Saunders 1992–, Absolutely Fabulous 1993–2005 (Emmy Award 1993), Let Them Eat Cake 1999, Mirrorball 2000, Jam and Jerusalem 2006, The Life and Times of Vivienne Vyle 2007. *Films include:* The Supergrass 1984, Muppet Treasure Island 1996, Spice World the Movie, Maybe Baby 2000, Shrek 2 (voice) 2004, L'Entente cordiale 2006. *Publications:* A Feast of French and Saunders (with Dawn French) 1992, Absolutely Fabulous: The Scripts 1993, Absolutely Fabulous 'Continuity' 2001. *Address:* c/o Maureen Vincent, United Agents, 12–26 Lexington Street, London, W1F 0LE, England (office). *Telephone:* (20) 3214-0800 (office). *Fax:* (20) 3214-0801 (office). *E-mail:* info@unitedagents.co.uk (office). *Website:* unitedagents.co.uk (office).

SAUNDERS, Stuart John, MD, FRCP, FCPSA, FRSSAf; South African physician, academic and university administrator; *Senior Advisor, South Africa*

Program, Andrew W. Mellon Foundation; b. 28 Aug. 1931, Cape Town; s. of the late Albert Frederick Saunders and of Lilian Emily; m. 1st Noreen Merle Harrison 1956 (died 1983); one s. one d.; m. 2nd Anita Louw 1984; ed Christian Brothers Coll. and Univ. of Cape Town; Registrar in Pathology and Medicine, Groote Schuur Hosp. and Univ. of Cape Town 1955–58, Lecturer and Sr Lecturer 1961–70, Prof. and Head of Medicine Dept 1971–80, Deputy Principal for Planning, Univ. of Cape Town 1978–80, Vice-Chancellor and Prin. Univ. of Cape Town 1981–96, Vice-Chancellor Emer. 1996–, Co-founder Liver Clinic and Liver Research Unit; Research Asst Royal Postgraduate Medical School, London 1959–60; Fellow in Medicine, Harvard Medical School and Mass. Gen. Hosp. 1963–64; currently Sr Advisor for South Africa program, Andrew W. Mellon Foundation; Past Pres. SA Inst. of Race Relations; Fellow, Royal Coll. of Physicians, London 1971, Royal Soc. of South Africa 1995, Coll. of Medicine of South Africa 1996; Life Fellow, Univ. of Cape Town; Hon. Fellow, Coll. of Medicine SA; Grand Counsellor, Order of the Baobab; Hon. LLD (Aberdeen), (Sheffield), (Princeton), (Rhodes); Hon. DSc (Toronto), (Cape Town). *Publications:* Access to and Quality in Higher Education: A Comparative Study 1992, Vice-Chancellor on a Tightrope 1999; numerous scientific publications particularly in the field of liver diseases. *Leisure interests:* reading, fishing. *Address:* c/o Office of the Vice-Chancellor, University of Cape Town, Private Bag, Rondebosch 7701, Cape Town; 45 Belvedere Avenue, Oranjezicht, 8001 Cape Town, South Africa. *Telephone:* 453035. *Fax:* 4620047.

SAUR, Klaus Gerhard, DHumLitt; German publisher; *CEO and Partner, Walter de Gruyter Publishing House GmbH;* b. 27 July 1941, Pullach; s. of Karl-Otto Saur and Veronika Saur; m. Lilo Stangel 1977; one s. one d.; ed High School, Icking and Commercial High School, Munich; Marketing Man. Vulkan-Verlag, Essen 1962; Publishing Man. KG Saur, Munich 1963, Publishing Dir 1966; Pres. KG Saur New York and KG Saur, London 1977–2003; Man. Dir KG Saur Munich 1988–2004, Chair. Bd –2004; CEO and Pnr, Walter de Gruyter Publishing House GmbH, Berlin and New York 2005–; Founder, World Guide to Libraries, Publrs Int. Directory; mem. Bd F.A. Brockhaus Bibliographical Inst., Mannheim; Vice-Pres. Goethe-Institut, Germany; Hon. Prof., Univ. of Glasgow, Humboldt-Univ. Berlin; Hon. Fellow, Tech. Univ. of Graz; Hon. mem. Austrian Library Asscn 1998, German Library Asscn, Bavarian Acad. of Belle Arts; Senator hc (Ludwig Maximilians Univ., Munich) 1992, (Leipzig) 2001, (Friedrich Alexander Univ., Erlangen) 2007; Bundesverdienstkreuz der Bundesrepublik Deutschland, Officier Ordre des Arts et Lettres (France), Sächsischer Verdienstordern 2002, Bayerischer Verdienstordern 2002; Hon. DPhil (Marburg) 1985, (Ishevsk, Russia) 1997, (Pisa, Italy) 1998, (Simmons Coll., Mass.) 1992; Hon. Medal City of Munich 1988, Hon. Bene Merenti Medal, Bavarian Acad. of Sciences 1997, Helmut-Sontag Award, Asscn of German Libraries 1999, Großes Österreichisches Verdienstkreuz der Wessenschaftund Künste 2003, Max-Hermann-Award, German State Library. *Publications:* World Biographical Information System, Pressehandbuch für Exportwerbung, World Guide to Libraries. *Leisure interests:* special German exile literature 1933–45, int. politics, history of publishing and book trade. *Address:* Verlag Walter de Gruyter, Genthinerstr. 13, 10785 Berlin (office); Beuerbergerstr. 9, 81479 Munich, Germany (home). *Telephone:* (30) 26005312 (office); (89) 74994651 (home). *Fax:* (30) 26005369 (office); (89) 74994652 (home). *E-mail:* klaus.saur@degruyter.com (office). *Website:* www.degruyter.com (office).

SAURA, Carlos; Spanish film director; b. 4 Jan. 1932, Huesca; m.; two c.; ed film school in Madrid; professional photographer 1949–; teacher, Instituto de Investigaciones y Experiencias Cinematograficos, Madrid 1957–64, dismissed for political reasons. *Films include:* La Prima Angelica, La Caza (Silver Bear, Berlin Film Festival), Blood Wedding, Carmen (flamenco version), El Amor Brujo, El Dorado 1987, The Dark Night 1989, Ay Carmela! 1990, Sevillanas 1992, Dispara! 1993, Flamenco 1995, Taxi 1996, Pajarico 1997, Tango 1998, Esa Luz! 1998, Goya 1999, Salome 2002, El Séptimo día 2004, Iberia 2005, Fados 2007. *Website:* www.carlos-saura.com.

SAUVAGE, Jean-Pierre, BEng, PhD; French chemist and academic; *Director of Research, Organo-Mineral Chemistry Laboratory, Université Louis Pasteur;* b. 21 Oct. 1944, Paris; ed Ecole Nationale Supérieure de Chimie, Strasbourg, Université Louis Pasteur; Post-doctoral Researcher, Univ. of Oxford, UK 1973–74; Research Asst, CNRS, Strasbourg 1971–75, Research Assoc. 1975–79, Master of Research 1979, Sr Researcher 1979–81, Prof. 1981–, Dir of Research, Organo-Mineral Chem. Lab., Univ. Louis Pasteur, Strasbourg 1988–; mem. Editorial Bd Bioorganic Chem. Frontiers, Act Chimica Scandinavia, Bulletin of the Chemical Society of Japan, New Journal of Chem., Compte Rendu de l'Academie des Sciences, Bulletin de la Société Française de Chimie, Inorganic Chem. 1997–99, Structure and Bonding 1997–; Ed.-in-Chief Chemical Society Reviews 1997–2000; mem. French Acad. of Sciences 1997–; mem. Japanese Soc. for the Promotion of Science 1994–; Hon. lecturer at numerous int. univs including Utrecht 1992, Sydney 1994, Kansas State Univ. 1995, Berkeley 1995, Texas A&M Univ. 1996, Notre Dame Univ. 1996, Univ. of Chicago 1998, Univ. of Montreal 1999, Hebrew Univ. of Jerusalem 2001; CNRS Bronze Medal 1978, Silver Medal 1988, French Acad. of Sciences Jean-Baptiste Dumas Award 1980, Société Française de Chimie Award in Organic Chem. 1987, Eidgenössische Technische Hochschule (ETH) Zurich Prelog Gold Medal 1994, Univ. of Geneva World Nessim Habif Award 1995. *Address:* Laboratoire de Chimie Organo-Minérale, UMR 7513, Université Louis Pasteur, Institut Le Bel, 4, rue Blaise Pascal, 67070 Strasbourg, Cedex, France (office). *Telephone:* 3-90-24-13-61 (office). *Fax:* 3-90-24-13-68 (office). *E-mail:* sauvage@chimie.u-strasbg.fr (office). *Website:* www-chimie.u-strasbg.fr/~lcom (office).

SAVAGE, Francis Joseph, CMG, LVO, OBE, KCMG; British administrator, diplomatist and consultant; b. 8 Feb. 1943, Preston; s. of Francis Fitzgerald Savage and Mona May Savage (née Parsons); m. Veronica Mary McAleenan 1966; two s.; ed St Stephen's Catholic School, Welling, N Kent Coll., Dartford; joined Foreign Office 1961, Embassy, Cairo 1967–70, Washington, DC 1971–73, Vice-Consul, Aden 1973–74, Foreign Office 1974–78, Consul, Düsseldorf 1978–82, Consul, Peking (now Beijing) 1982–86, First Sec., Lagos and Consul, Benin 1987–90; First Sec./Counsellor, Foreign Office 1990–93; Gov. of Montserrat 1993–97, The British Virgin Islands 1998–2002; Chair. Friends of British Virgin Islands 2005–; adviser to FCO 2003–; freelance consultant 2003–; mem. Bd Visar Trust 2002–; adviser on overseas territories to FCO; Trustee, Montserrat Foundation 2008–; Kt Commdr, Order of St Gregory the Great 2002; Montserrat Badge of Honour 2000. *Leisure interests:* cricket, travel, volcano watching. *Address:* c/o Foreign and Commonwealth Office, King Charles Street, London, SW1A 2AH (office); 19 Cleeve Park Gardens, Sidcup, Kent, DA14 4JL, England (home). *Telephone:* (20) 8309-5061 (home). *E-mail:* frank.savage@fco.gov.uk (office); fjsavage@savagef.fsnet.co.uk (home).

SAVARIN, Charles Angelo; Dominican politician; *Minister of Public Utilities, Energy, Ports and the Public Service;* b. 2 Oct. 1943, Portsmouth, Dominica; m. Clara Etienne; one s. two d.; ed Dominica Grammar School, Roseau, Ruskin Coll., Oxford Univ., England; Asst Master, Dominica Grammar School 1963–70; Gen. Sec., Dominica Civil Service Asscn 1966–83; Senator, House of Ass. 1979–85; Minister without Portfolio, Prime Minister's Office 1983–85; Minister Councillor, Dominica High Comm., London, 1985–86; Amb. of Dominica to UN, EU and selected European countries, Geneva 1986–93; Gen. Man., Nat. Devt Corpn 1993–95; mem. Parl. for Roseau Cen. Constituency 1995–; mem. Dominica Freedom Party (fmr Leader); Minister of Tourism –2005, Minister of Foreign Affairs, Trade, Labour and Public Service 2005–07, of Public Utilities, Energy, Ports and the Public Service 2007–. *Address:* Ministry of Public Utilities, Energy, Ports and the Public Service, Government Headquarters, Kennedy Avenue, Roseau, Dominica (office). *Telephone:* 4482401 (office).

SAVARY, Jérôme; French theatre director and actor; b. 27 June 1942, Buenos Aires, Argentina; s. of Jacques Savary and Claire Hovelaque; one s. two d.; ed Collège Cévenol, Haute-Loire, les Arts-Déco, Paris; studied music Paris; moved to France 1947; became jazz musician New York 1961; returned to France; f. Compagnie Jérôme Savary 1965, subsequently called Grand Magic Circus, then Grand Magic Circus et ses animaux tristes 1968–; theatre dir 1969–; Dir Centre Dramatique Nat. du Languedoc-Roussillon, Béziers and Montpellier 1982–85; Dir Carrefour Européen, Théâtre-du 8e, Lyon 1986–88; Dir Théâtre Nat. de Chaillot, Paris 1988–2000; Dir Opéra Comique, Paris 2000–07; Dir about 80 plays and shows in Europe, Brazil, Argentina, Canada, USA, Israel; several TV films of plays and operas and three films for cinema; Chevalier, Ordre des Arts et des Lettres, Légion d'honneur, Grand Badge of Hon. (Austria); Prix Dominique for Cyrano de Bergerac, Molière Award for Best Musical 1987, Victoire de la Musique for Best Musical (for Cabaret) 1987, Best Dir for Cabaret Spain 1993. *Publications:* La Vie privée d'un magicien ordinaire 1985, Ma vie commence à 20h30 1991, Magic Circus 1966–96, 30 ans d'aventures et d'amour 1996, Havana Blues 2000, Dictionnaire Amoureux du Spectacle 2004. *Address:* c/o Opéra Comique, 5 rue Favart, 75002 Paris, France.

SAVÉANT, Jean-Michel, DèsSc; French chemist and academic; *Emeritus Research Director, Centre National de la Recherche Scientifique, Université Paris 7 – Denis Diderot;* b. 19 Sept. 1933, Rennes; ed Ecole Normale Supérieure, Paris, Instituto di Chimica Fisica dell'Universita de Padova, Italy; Asst Dir, Chem. Lab., Ecole Normale Supérieure, Paris 1968–70; Prof., Univ. Paris 7 – Denis Diderot 1971–85, CNRS Research Dir 1985–2000, Emer. 2000–; Prof., Calif. Inst. of Tech. (Caltech), Pasadena, CA, USA 1988–89; mem. Editorial Bd Journal of the American Chemical Society, Inorganic Chem., Journal of Physical Organic Chem., ChemPhysChem, Journal of Electroanalytical Chem.; mem. Acad. des Sciences 2000–; Assoc. Foreign mem. NAS 2001–; French Chemical Soc. Prix Louis Ancel 1966, CNRS Silver Medal 1976, Royal Soc. of Chem. Faraday Medal 1983, Medaglia Luigi Riccoboni 1983, Prix Emile Jungfleisch, Acad. des sciences 1989, Electrochemical Soc. Palladium Medal 1993, Societa Chimica Italiana Luigi Galvani Medal 1997, Manuel Baizer Award, Electrochemical Soc. 2002, Bruno Breyer Medal, Royal Australian Chemical Inst. 2005. *Address:* Laboratoire d'Electrochimie Moléculaire, CNRS UMR 7591, Université Paris 7 – Denis Diderot Tour 44, Case 7107, 2, place Jussieu, 75251 Paris, Cedex 05, France (office). *Telephone:* 1-44-27-55-82 (office). *Fax:* 1-44-27-76-25 (office). *E-mail:* saveant@paris7.jussieu.fr (office). *Website:* www.lemp7.cnrs.fr (office).

SAVELYEVA, Lyudmila Mikhailovna; Russian actress; b. 24 Jan. 1942, Leningrad (now St Petersburg); ed Vaganova Ballet School, Leningrad; soloist, Kirorskiy (Mariinskiy) Theatre 1961–65; People's Artist of the RSFSR 1985. *Films include:* War and Peace (Natasha), by Bondarchuk 1966–67, The Sunflowers (de Sica) 1971, Flight 1971, The Headless Horseman 1973, The Seagull 1973, Yulia Vrevskaya 1978, The Hat 1982, The Fourth Year of War 1983, Success 1985, Another's Belaya and Ryaboy 1986, White Rose–Emblem of Grief, Red Rose–Emblem of Love 1989, The Mystery of Nardo 1999, The Tender Age 2000. *Television:* Anna Karenina (miniseries) 20075. *Theatre productions include:* The Price (Miller), M. Rozovsky theatre. *Address:* Tverskaya Str. 19, Apt. 76, 103050 Moscow, Russia. *Telephone:* (495) 299-99-34.

SAVI, Toomas, PhD; Estonian physician and politician; b. 30 Dec. 1942, Tartu; m. Kirsi Savi; two d.; ed Tartu State Univ.; Chief Physician, USSR light athletics team, concurrently Sr Researcher Tartu State Univ. 1970–80; nat. team physician at Olympic Games in Munich 1972, Montreal 1976, Moscow 1980, Lillehammer 1994; Chief Physician, Tartu Medical Centre of Physical Educ. 1979–93; Asst Medical Officer, Kuopio Univ. Hosp. and Kajaani Hosp.,

Finland 1991–92; mem. Tartu Town Council 1989–93, 1996–97, 1999–2000; Deputy Mayor of Tartu 1993–95; mem. Eesti Reformierakond (Estonian Reform Party) 1994–; Speaker of Riigikogu (State Ass.) 1995–2003, Deputy Speaker 2003–04; Observer, European Parl. 2003–04; mem. European Parl. (Group of the Alliance of Liberals and Democrats for Europe) 2004–, Del. for Relations with Canada, mem. Cttee on Devt, Substitute mem. Cttee on Regional Devt, Del. to the ACP-EU Jt Parl. Ass.; Founder-mem. Estonian Olympic Cttee 1989–; Pres. Estonian Skiing Asscn 1999–; mem., Tartu Rotary Club 1993–, Bd Eluterve Eesti exercise asscn 1994–, Bd Estonian Asscn 2001–, Supervisory Bd of Tartu St Mary's Church Foundation 2003–; Grand Cross, Royal Norwegian Order of Merit 1998, Nat. Order of Merit (Malta) 2001, Grand Cross, Ordre nat. du Mérite (France) 2001, Commdr Grand Cross, Order of the Lion (Finland) 2002, Badge of the Order of the Nat. Coat of Arms (Second Class) (Estonia) 2003, Grand Officier of the Order of Infante Dom Henrique (Portugal) 2003. *Address:* European Parliament, Bâtiment Altiero Spinelli, 09G210, 60 rue Wiertz, 1047 Brussels, Belgium (office); Näituse 22-8, 50 407 Tartu, Estonia. *Fax:* (2) 284-9814 (office). *E-mail:* tsavi@europarl.eu.int (office). *Website:* www.europarl.eu.int (office).

SAVILL, Dame Rosalind Joy, DBE, FSA, FRSA; British museum director; *Director, The Wallace Collection;* b. 12 May 1951, Hants.; d. of Dr Guy Savill and Lorna Williams; one d.; ed Wycombe Abbey School, Chatelard School, Montreux and Univ. of Leeds; Museum Asst, Ceramics Dept, Victoria & Albert Museum 1973–74; Museum Asst and Sr Asst, The Wallace Collection 1974–78, Asst to Dir 1978–92, Dir 1992–; Pres. French Porcelain Soc. 1999–; mem. Arts Panel, Nat. Trust 1995–, Art Advisory Cttee, Nat. Museums & Galleries of Wales 1998–2003, Museums and Collections Advisory Cttee English Heritage 1998–2002, Royal Mint Advisory Cttee 1999–; Gov. Camden School for Girls 1996–; Fellow, British Acad. 2006–; Trustee Somerset House 1997–2004, Campaign for Museums 1999–, Holburne Museum of Art, Bath 2004–; Dr hc (Buckinghamshire and Chiltern Univ. Coll.); Leverhulme Scholar 1975, Getty Scholar 1985, Nat. Art Collections Fund Prize 1990, European Women of Achievement Award 2005. *Publications:* The Wallace Collection Catalogue of Sèvres Porcelain (three vols) 1988; articles, reviews, contribs to exhbn catalogues etc. *Leisure interests:* music, birds, wildlife, gardens. *Address:* The Wallace Collection, Hertford House, Manchester Square, London, W1U 3BN, England. *Telephone:* (20) 7563-9512 (office). *Fax:* (20) 7224-2155. *E-mail:* rosalind.savill@wallacecollection.org (office). *Website:* www.the-wallace-collection.org.uk (office).

SAVIN, Anatoliy Ivanovich, DTechSc; Russian specialist in radio analysis and systems analysis; b. 6 April 1920; ed Bauman Tech. Inst., Moscow; mem. CPSU 1944–91; fmrly employed as engineer and constructor; constructor with machine-bldg plant 1944–51; positions of responsibility on eng side of radio-tech. industry 1951–; Gen. Dir Scientific and Production Asscn Kometa 1973–98, Scientific Dir 1999–; Corresp. mem. Acad. of Sciences 1979, mem. 1984–, Prof. 1984; Academician Russian Acad. of Sciences; main research has been on complex radio-tech. automatized informational systems; inventor of cosmic radio-telescope KRT-10; Acad. of Sciences Raspletin Prize 1972, Lenin Prize 1972, Hero of Socialist Labour 1976, State Prizes 1946, 1949, 1951, 1981. *Address:* Kometa Association, Velozavodskaya Str. 5, 109280 Moscow, Russia. *Telephone:* (495) 275-15-33.

SAVISAAR, Edgar; Estonian politician; *Mayor of Tallinn and Chairman, Estonian Centre Party (Eesti Keskerakond);* b. 31 May 1950, Harjumaa, Harju Co.; m. Vilya Savisaar; two s. two d.; ed Tartu Secondary School, Tartu State Univ.; worked in governmental insts dealing with planning of economy 1980–88; Academic Dir Mainor consultancy co. 1988–89; mem. CP –1990; Leader Estonian Popular Front; Vice-Chair. Council of Ministers of Estonian SSR and Head of State Plan Cttee 1989 (resgnd), Chair. Council of Ministers 1990–91, then Prime Minister of Repub. of Estonia following independence 1991–92; Minister of Economy 1990; Deputy Speaker of Riigikogu 1992–95; Chair. Estonian Centre Party (Eesti Keskerakond) –1995 (resgnd), re-appointed Chair. following split in party 1996–; Deputy Prime Minister and Minister of the Interior April–Nov. 1995, dismissed from posts following scandal over taped conversations; Chair. Tallinn City Council 1996–99; Mayor of Tallinn 2001–04, 2007–; briefly Prime Minister of Estonia following legis. election 2003; Minister of Econ. Affairs and Communications 2005–07; Order of State Coat of Arms 2001. *Publications include:* four books. *Address:* Estonian Centre Party (Eesti Keskerakond), Toom-Rüütli 3/5, Tallinn 10130 (office); Office of the Mayor, Tallinn City Government, Vabaduse väljak 7, Tallinn 15199, Estonia (office). *Telephone:* 627-3460 (office); 640-4141 (Mayor's office) (office). *Fax:* 627-3461 (office); 640-4327 (Mayor's office) (office). *E-mail:* keskerakond@keskerakond.ee (office); foreign@tallinnlv.ee (office). *Website:* www.keskerakond.ee (office); www.tallinn.ee (office); savisaar.blogspot.com (home).

SAVOLA, Kai Kari; Finnish theatre director; b. 30 Sept. 1931, Helsinki; s. of Tauno Savola and Hilppa Korpinen; m. Terttu Byckling 1958; two s. one d.; ed Helsinki Univ.; Admin. Dir Helsinki Student Theatre 1959–62; Man. Dir Finnish Drama Agency 1962–65; Literary Man. Helsinki City Theatre 1965–68; Dir-Gen. Tampere Workers' Theatre 1968–73; Dir Finnish Nat. Theatre 1973, Dir-Gen. 1974–92; stage direction of Finnish, English, Russian and Japanese drama; designed the two experimental stages of the Finnish Nat. Theatre (with Prof. Heikki Siren) 1976, 1987; Hon. Prof. 1983; Commdr, Order of White Rose of Finland 1991, Golden Medal of Honour of Tampere 1973, Golden Medal, Helsinki 1992. *Publications:* translations of English and German plays into Finnish. *Address:* Laivurinkatu 39 A 12, 00150 Helsinki, Finland. *Telephone:* (9) 636939. *Fax:* (9) 636939. *E-mail:* f.savola@kolumbus.fi (office).

SAVOSTYANOV, Maj.-Gen. Yevgeny Vadimovich, Cand.Tech.Sc.; Russian politician; b. 28 Feb. 1952, Moscow; m.; two s.; ed Moscow Mining Inst.; Jr researcher Inst. of Physics of the Earth USSR Acad. of Sciences 1975–77; researcher Inst. for Problems of Complex Use of Mineral Wealth USSR Acad. of Sciences 1975–90; Founder and Co-Chair. Club of Voters of Acad. of Sciences for election of Andrey Sakharov and other scientists as people's deputies from Acad. of Sciences; Asst to Chair. Moscow City Soviet, then Dir-Gen. Dept Moscow Mayor's Office 1990–91; mem. Co-ordination Council Movt Democratic Russia; mem. Org. Cttee of Democratic Reforms 1991; Deputy Dir Russian Fed. Service of Counterespionage, Head of Dept Moscow and Moscow Region 1991–94; Adviser to Chair. Russian Fed. of Ind. Trade Unions 1995–96; Deputy Head Admin. of Russian Presidency 1996–98; Vice-Pres. Moscow Oil and Gas Co. (MOGC) 1999–2005; Chair. Supervisory Bd Kemerovo Mining Co. 2000; mem. Bd of Dirs Sibir Energy plc 2004; unsuccessful cand. for Pres. of Russian Fed. 2000.

SAVOVA, Olga B.; Russian actress and singer (mezzo-soprano); b. 14 Nov. 1964, Leningrad; m. Yefimov Dmitri; two s.; ed Leningrad State Inst. of Music Theatre and Cinematography, Leningrad State Conservatory; actress at Leningrad Tovstonogov Drama Theatre –1995; singer at Mariinsky Opera Theatre (Kirov Opera) 1995–; repertoire includes Verdi's Requiem, Emilia in Othello, Eboli in Don Carlos, Flora in La Traviata, Carmen, Amneris and Preziosilla, Olga in Eugene Onegin, Prokofiev's Semyon Kotko, Azucena in Il Trovatore, Marfa in Tsar's Bride, Bobilikha in Rimsky-Korsakov's The Snow Maiden, Blanche in The Gambler by Prokofiev, Lyubov in Mazeppa, Marina Mnishek in Boris Godunov, Hélène in War and Peace, Paulina in The Queen of Spades and Teresa in La Sonnambula; performances in France, Belgium, Holland, Italy, Japan, China and Israel; Voci Verdiani International Competition prizewinner, Italy 1992. *Leisure interests:* diving, skiing. *Address:* St Petersburg State Academic Mariinsky Opera Theatre, Teatralnaya pl.1, St Petersburg 130000, Russia (office).

SAVOY, Guy; French chef and restaurateur; *Proprietor, Restaurant Guy Savoy;* b. 24 July 1953, Nevers; m. Marie Danielle Amann 1975; one s. one d.; for three years Chef at La Barrière de Clichy, Paris; Propr Restaurant Guy Savoy, Paris 1980–, Restaurant Le Bistrot de l'Etoile Troyon 1989–, Restaurant Le Bistrot de l'Etoile-Niel 1989–, Restaurant Le Bistrot l'Etoile-Lauriston 1991, Restaurant La Butte Chaillot 1992, Les Bookinistes 1994, Le Cap Vernet, Paris 1995; Légion d'Honneur. *Publications:* Les Légumes gourmands 1985, La Gourmandise apprivoisée 1987, La Cuisine de mes bistrots 1998, 120 recettes comme à la maison 2000. *Leisure interest:* modern painting. *Address:* Restaurant Guy Savoy, 18 rue Troyon, 75017 Paris (office); 101 boulevard Pereire, 75017 Paris, France (home). *Telephone:* 1-43-80-40-61 (office); 1-42-67-25-95 (Bistrot de l'Étoile). *Fax:* 1-46-22-43-09 (office). *Website:* www.guysavoy.com (office).

SAVVINA, Iya Sergeyevna; Russian actress; b. 2 March 1936, Voronezh; ed Moscow State Univ.; played leading role in adaptation of Chekhov's The Lady with the Lap-dog 1960; acts in cinema and on stage with Mossovet Theatre, Moscow 1960–78, with Moscow Arts Theatre 1978–; USSR State Prize 1983, USSR People's Artist 1990. *Films include:* Lady with a Lapdog 1960, A Gentle Woman 1960, Asya's Happiness (State Prize 1990) 1967, Anna Karenina 1968, A Day in the Life of Dr Kalinnikova 1974, A Lovers' Romance 1975, An Open Book, 1980, Garage 1980, Private Life 1983, Last, Last the Fascination… 1985, Mother and Son 1990, Lev Trotsky 1993, Postelnyye stseny 2005; numerous stage roles in classical and contemporary works. *Address:* Bolshaya Gruzinskaya Str. 12, Apt. 43, 123242 Moscow, Russia. *Telephone:* (495) 254-97-39.

SAWA, Metropolitan Michał Hrycuniak, ThD; Polish ecclesiastic; *Metropolitan of Warsaw and All Poland; Primate of the Polish Autocephalous Orthodox Church;* b. 15 April 1938, Śniatycze; ed Christian Acad. of Theology, Warsaw, Univ. of Belgrade; teacher Orthodox Seminary, Warsaw 1962–, Rector Int. Section 1964–65; Rector Orthodox Theological Seminary, Jabłeczna 1970–79; Assoc. Prof. and Prof. Christian Acad. of Theology, Warsaw 1966–, Prof. of Theological Sciences 1990–; ordained deacon 1964; ordained priest 1966; Dir Chancellery of Metropolitan of Warsaw and All Poland 1966–70; Superior Monastery of St Onufrey at Jabłeczna 1970–79; ordained Bishop 1979, Bishop of Łódź and Poznań 1979–81, of Białystok and Gdańsk 1981–99; Archbishop 1987; Metropolitan of Warsaw and All Poland, Primate of the Polish Autocephalous Orthodox Church 1998–; Orthodox Ordinary of the Polish Armed Forces 1994–98, rank of Brig.-Gen. 1996; f. quarterly publs of Diocese of Białystok and Gdańsk and of Orthodox Ordinate of Polish Armed Forces; Dean and Prof. of Chair of Orthodox Theology, Univ. in Białystok 1999–; Ed.-in-Chief Kalendarz Polskiego Autokefalicznego Kościoła Prawosławnego, Elpis, Rocznik Teologiczny (annual), Cerkiewny Wiestnik (quarterly), Wiadomości Polskiego Autokefalicznego Kościoła Prawosławnego (monthly); Hon. Prof. of Theological Sciences; Dr hc (Thessaloniki Univ., Greece), (Bialystok, Poland), St Vladimir's Orthodox Seminary, NY, USA. *Publication:* Prawosławne pojmowanie małżeństwa (The Orthodox Understanding of Marriage) 1994, Chrystus najwiernigszy pryjacrel (Christ the Only Beloved Friend) 2003, Croba (Speeches) 2004. *Address:* Al. Solidarności 52, 03-402 Warsaw, Poland (office). *Telephone:* (22) 6190886 (office). *Fax:* (22) 6190886 (office).

SAWADOGO, Philippe; Burkinabè diplomatist and politician; *Minister of Culture, Tourism and Communication, Spokesperson for the Government;* b. 26 May 1954; CEO Festival Panafricain du Cinéma et de la Télévision de Ouagadougou 1984–96; Amb. to France 1996–2006, also Perm. Del. UNESCO; Minister of Culture, Tourism and Communication, Spokesperson for the Govt 2007–. *Address:* Ministry of Culture, Tourism and Communication, 03 BP 7007, Ouagadougou 03, Burkina Faso (office). *Telephone:* 50-33-09-63 (office). *Fax:* 50-33-09-64 (office). *E-mail:* mcat@cenatrin.bf (office). *Website:* www.culture.gov.bf (office).

SAWALLISCH, Wolfgang; German conductor; b. 26 Aug. 1923, Munich; m. Mechthild Schmid (died 1998); one s.; ed Wittelsbacher Gymnasium, Munich; studied under Profs. Ruoff, Haas and Sachsse; mil. service 1942–46, POW in Italy; conductor Augsburg 1947–53; Musical Dir Aachen 1953–58, Wiesbaden 1958–60, Cologne Opera 1960–63; Conductor Hamburg Philharmonic Orchestra 1960–73, Hon. mem. 1973–; Prin. Conductor Vienna Symphony Orchestra 1960–70, Hon. mem. and Hon. Conductor 1980; Prof. Staatliche Hochschule für Musik, Cologne 1960–63; Musical Dir Bayerische Staatsoper Munich 1971–92; Prin. Conductor Bayerisches Staatsorchester –92; Perm. Conductor Teatro alla Scala, Milan; conducted at many Festivals; recordings in Germany, USA and Britain; Hon. Conductor NHK Symphony Orchestra, Tokyo 1967; Artistic Dir Suisse Romande Orchestra, Geneva 1973–80; Dir Bayerische Staatsoper, Munich 1982–92; Music Dir Philadelphia Orchestra 1993–2003, Conductor Laureate 2003–; Co-founder Wolfgang Sawallisch Stiftung 2003; mem. Bavarian Acad. of Fine Arts; Pres. Richard Strauss Soc., Munich; Dr hc (Curtis Inst., Philadelphia), (Princeton Univ.); Accademico Onorario Santa Cecilia; Österreichisches Ehrenkreuz für Kunst und Wissenschaft, Bayerischer Verdienstorden, Bruckner-Ring of Vienna Symphony Orchestra 1980, Grosses Bundesverdienstkreuz (mit Stern), Bayerische Maximiliansorden für Wissenschaft und Kunst 1984, Orden der aufgehenden Sonne am Halsband, Japan, Robert-Schumann-Preis 1994, Suntory Special Music Prize, Japan, Golden Baton Toscanini Teatro Scala, Milan; Chevalier Légion d'honneur, Commdr des Arts et des Lettres, Cavaliere di Gran Croce (Italy). *Publications:* Im Interesse der Deutlichkeit – Mein Leben mit der Musik 1988, Kontrapunkte 1993. *Address:* Hinterm Bichl 2, 83224 Grassau/Chiemsee, Germany. *Telephone:* (49) 86412315. *Fax:* (49) 86414501. *E-mail:* graphil@gmx.de. *Website:* www.sawallisch-stiftung.de.

SAWCHUK, Arthur R., BSc; Canadian business executive; m. Mary Sawchuk; one s. one d.; ed Univ. of Manitoba; joined DuPont Eng group, Kingston, Ont. 1958; transferred to Montreal, holding managerial positions in Fibres Marketing 1967; Div. Man. Home Furnishings, Toronto 1974; Man. Corp. Planning and Devt 1981; Div. Man. Packaging 1984; Vice-Pres. and Gen. Man. Fibres and Intermediate Chemicals 1985; Sr Vice-Pres. and mem. Corp. Policy Advisory Council 1988; Pres., CEO and Dir DuPont Canada Inc. 1992–97, Chair. 1995–97; Chair. Manulife Financial Corpn 1998–2008 (retd); mem. Bd of Dirs Manitoba Telecom Services Inc., Bowater Inc. Canadian Inst. for Advanced Research; fmr Dir Canadian Chemical Producers' Asscn, Avenor Inc., Mfrs Life Insurance Co., Ontario Hydro. *Address:* c/o Manulife Financial, 200 Bloor Street East, Toronto, ON, M4W 1E5, Canada (office).

SAWERS, Sir John, KCMG, BSc; British diplomatist; *Permanent Representative, United Nations;* b. 26 July 1955; m.; three c.; ed Univ. of Nottingham; Prin. Pvt. Sec. to Foreign Sec. 1992–95; Int. Fellow, Harvard Univ. 1995; served at Embassy in Washington, DC 1996–98; Foreign Affairs Adviser to Prime Minister 1999–2001; Amb. to Egypt 2001–03; Political Dir Foreign and Commonwealth Office 2003–07; Perm. Rep. to UN, New York 2007–. *Address:* Permanent Mission of the United Kingdom to the United Nations, 1 Dag Hammarskjöld Plaza, 885 Second Avenue, New York, NY 10017, USA (office). *Telephone:* (212) 745-9200 (office). *Fax:* (212) 745-9316 (office). *E-mail:* uk@un.int (office). *Website:* www.ukun.org (office).

SAWIRIS, Naguib, MTA; Egyptian business executive; *Chairman and CEO, Orascom Telecom Holding S.A.E.;* m.; four c.; ed German Evangelical School, Cairo, Swiss Inst. of Tech. (ETH), Switzerland; joined Orascom 1979, Chair. CEO Orascom Telecom Holding S.A.E. (after Orascom split into separate operating cos) 1997–, mem. GSM Asscn (representing Orascom Telecom Holdign 2003–; mem. Int. Advisory Cttee New York Stock Exchange Bd of Dirs; Jt Chair. Italian-Egyptian Business Council 2006–07; Chair. Egyptian Company for Mobile Services (MobiNil); mem. Bd of Dirs Arab Thought Foundation, Egyptian Council for Foreign Affairs, Consumer Rights Protection Asscn, Cancer Soc. of Egypt; Trustee and head of Financial Cttee French Univ. in Cairo. *Address:* Orascom Telecom, 2005A Nile City Towers, South Tower, Cornish El Nile Ramlet Beaulac, Cairo 11221, Egypt (office). *Telephone:* (2) 4615050 (office). *Fax:* (2) 4615054 (office). *Website:* www.orascomtelecom.com (office).

SAWYER, Amos, PhD; Liberian academic and political activist; *Chairman, Governance Reform Commission of Liberia;* ed Univ. of Liberia, Northwestern Univ., USA; Chair. Constitution Drafting Comm. 1980s; fmrly installed as Leader of Interim Govt of Nat. Unity (by national conference of Liberian leaders that included leaders of political parties, civil society organizations and of combined guerrilla forces which overthrew regime of fmr Pres. Samuel Doe 1990) Aug. 1990, inaugurated Nov. 1990; fmr Leader Liberian People's Party; fmr Dir Inst. of Research and Dean Coll. of Social Science and Humanities, Univ. of Liberia; currently Co-Dir and Research Scholar, Workshop in Political Theory and Policy Analysis, Indiana Univ.; Chair Governance Reform Commission of Liberia. *Publications:* The Emergence of Autocracy in Liberia: Tragedy and Challenge 1992, Beyond Plunder: Toward Democratic Governance in Liberia 2005. *Address:* Workshop in Political Theory and Policy Analysis, Indiana University, 513 North Park, Bloomington, IN 47408-3895, USA (office); Governance Reform Commission, Ministry of Information Building, Third Floor, Monrovia, Liberia (office). *Telephone:* (812) 855-0441 (Bloomington) (office); (6) 833924 (Monrovia) (office). *Fax:* (812) 855-3150 (Bloomington) (office). *E-mail:* asawyer@indiana.edu (office); acsawyer45@aol.com (office). *Website:* www.indiana.edu/~workshop (office).

SAWYER, Diane, BA; American broadcast journalist; *Co-Anchor, Good Morning America, ABC News;* b. 22 Dec. 1945, Glasgow, Ky; d. of E. P. Sawyer and Jean W. Sawyer (née Dunagan); m. Mike Nichols 1988; ed Wellesley Coll.; reporter, WLKY-TV, Louisville, Ky 1967–70; Admin. White House Press Office 1970–74; mem. Nixon-Ford transition team 1974–75; Asst to Richard Nixon (fmr US Pres.) 1974, 1975; Gen. Reporter, later State Dept Corresp.,

CBS News 1978–81, apptd Co-Anchor Morning News 1981, Co-Anchor Early Morning News 1982–84, Corresp. and Co-Ed. 60 Minutes 1984–89; Co-Anchor PrimeTime Live (now Primetime Thursday), ABC News 1989–, Good Morning America 1999–; nine Emmy awards, Nat. Headliner Awards, George Foster Peabody Award for Public Service, Robert F. Kennedy Journalism Award, Special Dupont Award, Ohio State Award, IRTS Lifetime Achievement Award, inducted TV Acad. of Fame 1997, ranked by Forbes magazine amongst 100 Most Powerful Women (26th) 2004, (55th) 2005, (60th) 2006, (62nd) 2007, (65th) 2008. *Address:* Good Morning America, 147 Columbus Avenue, New York, NY 10023-5900, USA (office). *Telephone:* (212) 456-2060 (office). *Fax:* (212) 456-1246 (office). *Website:* abcnews.go.com/GMA (office).

SAYARI, Sheikh Hamad Sa'ud al-, MA; Saudi Arabian economist and central banker; *Governor, Saudi Arabian Monetary Agency;* b. 1941; ed Univ. of Md, USA; early career teachings econs at Inst. of Public Admin., Riyadh; Dir-Gen. Saudi Industrial Devt Fund 1979–80; Controller Gen. Saudi Arabian Monetary Agency (SAMA) 1979–80, Vice-Gov. 1980–83, Acting Gov. 1983–85, Gov. 1985–, also Chair. Bd of Dirs; mem. Supreme Econ. Council; mem. Bd of Dirs Public Investment Fund (Sec.-Gen. 1973–74), Gulf Investment Corpn. *Address:* Saudi Arabian Monetary Agency, POB 2992, Riyadh 11169, Saudi Arabia (office). *Telephone:* (1) 463-3000 (office). *Fax:* (1) 466-2966 (office). *E-mail:* info@sama.gov.sa (office). *Website:* www.sama.gov.sa (office).

SAYAVONG, Khammy; Laotian government official; *President, People's Supreme Court;* b. 9 April 1944, Khai Village; m. Boun Ngiem; ed Inst. of Party, Moscow, Russia; Head of Propaganda and Training Div., Vientiane Prov. 1992–95; Vice-Chair. Propaganda and Training Cen. Cttee 1996–98; Vice-Chair. Cen. Control Cttee 1999–2000; Pres. People's Supreme Court 2001–. *Address:* Office of the President, People's Supreme Court, c/o Ministry of Justice, Ban Phonxay, Vientiane (office); Sisavat Village, Chanthabouly District, Vientiane Municipality, Laos (home). *Telephone:* (21) 412170 (office); (21) 212355 (home). *Fax:* (21) 451371 (office). *E-mail:* lao99006@laotel.com (office).

SAYED, Karimat El, PhD; Egyptian academic and physicist; *Emeritus Professor of Solid State Physics, Ain Shams University;* m.; two s. one d.; ed Ain Shams Univ., Cairo, Univ. Coll. London; currently Emer. Prof. of Solid State Physics, Ain Shams Univ., Cairo; UNESCO-L'Oréal Award for Women in Science 2003. *Address:* Physics Department, Faculty of Science, Ain Shams University, Elkhalifa Elmaamoon Street, Abbassia, Cairo, Egypt (office). *Telephone:* (2) 282-2189 (office). *Fax:* (2) 284-2123 (office). *E-mail:* karima@frcu.eun.eg (office). *Website:* sci.shams.edu.eg (office).

SAYED, Mostafa Amr as-, BSc, PhD, FAAS; American scientist and academic; *Julius Brown Chair and Regents Professor and Director, Laser Dynamics Laboratory, School of Chemistry and Biochemistry, Georgia Institute of Technology;* b. 8 May 1933, Zifta, Egypt; s. of Amr El-Sayed and Zakia Ahmed; m. Janice Jones 1957; three s. two d.; ed Ain Shams Univ., Cairo, Egypt, Florida State, Yale and Harvard Univs, Calif. Inst. of Tech.; Prof., Univ. of Calif., LA 1961–64; Ed.-in-Chief Journal of Physical Chem. 1980–; Julius Brown Prof. and Dir Laser Dynamics Lab., Ga Inst. of Tech. 1994–, Regents Prof. 2000–; Visiting Prof., American Univ. of Beirut 1968, Univ. of Paris 1976, 1991; Mem.-at-Large US Nat. Research Council Cttee for IUPAC 1987–91 (Chair. 1990–92); mem., American Acad. of Sciences 1980, Third World Acad. of Arts and Sciences 1984, NSF 2000; mem. NAS; Alexander von Humboldt Sr Fellow, Tech. Univ. of Munich 1982; Fellow, American Acad. of Arts and Sciences 1986, AAAS, American Physical Soc. 2000; mem. Bd of Trustees Assoc. Univs Inc. 1988–91; mem. Advisory Cttee NSF Chem. Div. 1990–93; Dr hc (Hebrew Univ.) 1993; Fresenius Nat. Award in Pure and Applied Chem. 1967, Alexander von Humboldt Sr US Scientist Award, 1982, King Faisal Int. Prize in Sciences (Chem.) 1990, Harris Award, Univ. of Nebraska 1995, Nat. Medal of Science 2007, and many other honours and awards. *Publications:* many articles in scientific journals. *Address:* Department of Chemistry and Biochemistry, Office 104-B (LDL), Georgia Institute of Technology, 901 Atlantic Drive, Atlanta, GA 30332 (office); 579 Westover Drive, Atlanta, GA 30305, USA (home). *Telephone:* (404) 894-0292 (office); (404) 352-0453 (home). *Fax:* (404) 894-7452 (office). *E-mail:* mostafa.el-sayed@chemistry.gatech.edu (office). *Website:* www.chemistry.gatech.edu/faculty/El-Sayed (office).

SAYEED, Hafiz Mohammad; Pakistani military leader; fmr Prof. of Eng., Univ. of Tech. and Eng, Lahore; Co-Founder and Leader, Lashkar-e-Taiba (banned militant group), Founder and Leader Jamaat-ud-Dawa; detained, then placed under house arrest 2002, released Nov. 2002. *Address:* Jamaat-ud-Dawa, Bdehai Road, Peshawar, Pakistan. *Telephone:* (521) 2262189. *Fax:* (521) 2260800. *E-mail:* Jdawa@hotmail.com. *Website:* www.jamaatuddawa.org.

SAYEED, Mufti Mohammed; Indian politician; b. 1936; joined Nat. Conf. party 1950, left to join Congress Party, then left to join Janata Dal, rejoined Congress Party, left and f. People's Democratic Party 1999, fmr Chair. now Patron; fmr Minister of Home Affairs (India's first Muslim Home Minister); daughter kidnapped by Kashmiri militants 1989, released in exchange for militants; Chief Minister of Jammu and Kashmir 2002–05 (resgnd). *Address:* c/o People's Democratic Party, Jammu, Jammu and Kashmir, India (office).

SAYEF, Abdul Rasul; Afghan politician and academic; *Leader, Tanzim-i Dawat-i Islami (Organization for Invitation to Islam);* ed Kabul Univ., Al-Azhar Univ., Cairo, Egypt; fmr Prof. of Islamic Law, Shariat in Kabul –1973, tenure ended when he plotted with Burhanuddin Rabbani, Ahmed Shah Massoud and Gulbuddin Hekmatyar to overthrow Pres. Daoud Khan from Panjshir Valley; fmr mem. Akhwan-ul-Muslimeen (Muslim Brotherhood); fought against Soviet occupying forces Afghanistan during 1980s, chair. first rebel alliance 1980, one of the most important resistance leaders during Soviet invasion that ended in 1992; Leader Islamic Union for the Liberation of

Afghanistan (Ittihad-i Islami Bara-yi Azadi—only anti-Taliban Pashtun leader to be part of Northern Alliance), now called Tanzim-i Dawat-i Islami (Organization for Invitation to Islam) 2005–; mem. constitutional Loya Jirga 2003–04 (chaired one of working groups); elected to Wolasi Jirga (House of People, Nat. Ass.). *Address:* Tanzim-i Dawat-i Islami (Organization for Invitation to Islam), Ansari Square, Road 1, District 4, Kabul; Wolasi Jirga, Darul Aman Road, Kabul, Afghanistan. *Telephone:* (70) 277007. *Website:* www.nationalassembly.af.

SAYEGH, Bishop Selim Wahban, PhD; Jordanian ecclesiastic; *Titular Bishop of Aquae in Proconsulari and Vicar General for Transjordan;* b. 15 Jan. 1935, Jordan; s. of Wahban Sayigh; ed Lateran Univ., Rome; Pres. of the Latin Patriarchal Court, Jerusalem 1967–79; Rector of the Latin Patriarichal Seminary 1976–81; Titular Bishop of Aquae in Proconsulari, Vicar Gen. for Transjordan 1982–; Commdr of the Equestrian Order of the Holy Sepulchre of Jerusalem. *Publications:* Le Statu Quo des Lieux-Saints 1971, The Christian Family's Guidebook. *Leisure interests:* chess, table tennis, volleyball, history, ecclesiastical law. *Address:* Latin Vicariate, PO Box 851379, Amman 11185, Jordan. *Telephone:* (6) 5929546. *Fax:* (6) 5920548. *E-mail:* info@ourladyofpeacecentre.org (office). *Website:* www.ourladyofpeacecentre.org (office).

SAYEH, Antoinette Monsio, PhD; Liberian economist and government official; *Minister of Finance;* b. 12 July 1958, Monrovia; one s.; ed Swarthmore Coll., Fletcher School, Tufts Univ., USA; fmrly with Ministry of Planning, Ministry of Finance; worked for 17 years at World Bank, positions included Country Dir for Benin, Niger and Togo 2000–03 and working on public finance man. and civil service reform in Pakistan; Minister of Finance 2006–; Lucretia Mott Award, Swarthmore Coll., Service to Country Award, Govt of Niger. *Address:* Ministry of Finance, Broad Street, POB 10-9013, 1000 Monrovia 10, Liberia (office). *Telephone:* 47510680 (office). *Website:* www.finance.gov.lr (office).

SAYLES, John Thomas, BS; American writer, film director, actor and scriptwriter; b. 28 Sept. 1950, Schenectady, NY; s. of Donald John Sayles and Mary Sayles (née Rausch); pnr, Maggie Renzi; ed Williams Coll.; John D. MacArthur Award, Eugene V. Debs Award, John Steinbeck Award, John Cassavettes Award, Ian McLellan Hunter Award. *Films include:* Return of the Secaucus Seven (dir, screenwriter, actor, ed.) (Los Angeles Film Critics Award) 1980, Baby It's You (dir, screenwriter) 1983, Lianna (dir, screenwriter, actor, ed.) 1983, The Brother from Another Planet (dir, screenwriter, actor, ed.) 1984, Matewan (dir, screenwriter, actor) 1987, Eight Men Out (dir, screenwriter, actor) 1989, Bruce Springsteen: Video Anthology 1978–1988 (dir videos Born in the USA, Glory Days, I'm on Fire), City of Hope (dir, screenwriter, actor, ed.) 1991, Passion Fish (dir, screenwriter, actor, ed.), The Secret of Roan Inish (dir, screenwriter, ed.) 1994, Lone Star (dir, screenwriter, ed.) 1996, Men With Guns (dir, screenwriter, ed.) 1997, Limbo (dir, screenwriter, ed.) 1999, Sunshine State (dir, screenwriter, ed.) 2002, Casa de los babys (dir, screenwriter, ed.) 2003, Silver City (dir, screenwriter, ed.) 2004, Honeydripper (dir, screenwriter, actor, ed.) (Jury Prize for Best Screenplay, San Sebastian Film Festival 2007, NAACP Image Award for Outstanding Ind. or Foreign Film 2008) 2007; writer: Piranha 1978, The Lady in Red 1979, Battle Beyond the Stars 1980, The Howling 1981, Alligator 1981, The Challenge 1982, Enormous Changes at the Last Minute 1983, The Clan of the Cave Bear 1986, Something Wild 1986, Wild Thing 1987, Breaking In 1989, Men of War 1994, The Spiderwick Chronicles 2008; actor: Malcolm X 1992, Straight Talk 1992, Matinee 1993, My Life's in Turnaround 1993, Gridlock'd 1997, Girlfight (also producer) 2000. *Television:* writer: A Perfect Match 1980, Unnatural Causes 1986, Shannon's Deal (also dir) 1989, Piranha 1995. *Publications:* Pride of the Bimbos 1975, Union Dues 1979, Thinking in Pictures 1987, I-80 Nebraska, M.490-M.205 (O. Henry Award) 1975, Breed, Golden State (O. Henry Award) 1977, Hoop, The Anarchists' Convention 1979, New Hope for the Dead (play) 1981, Turnbuckle (play), Los Gusanos 1991, Dillinger in Hollywood 2004. *Address:* c/o Lucy Stille, Paradigm, 360 N Crescent Drive, North Building, Los Angeles, CA 90210, USA (office). *Website:* www.johnsayles.com.

SBEIH, Nouria (see SUBEEH, Nouriya Subeeh Barrak as-).

SCACCHI, Greta; Italian/British actress; b. 18 Feb. 1960, Milan, Italy; one d. by Vincent D'Onofrio; one s. by Carlo Mantegazza; ed Bristol Old Vic Drama School. *Films:* Das Zweite Gesicht, Heat and Dust, Defence of the Realm, The Coca-Cola Kid, A Man in Love, Good Morning Babylon, White Mischief, Paura e Amore (Three Sisters), La Donna della Luna, Presumed Innocent, Shattered, Fires Within, Turtle Beach, The Player, Salt on Our Skin, The Browning Version, Jefferson in Paris 1994, Country Life 1995, Emma 1996, The Serpent's Kiss 1997, The Red Violin 1998, Ladies Room 1999, The Manor 1999, Tom's Midnight Garden 2000, Looking for Alibrandi 2000, One of the Hollywood Ten 2000, Cotton Mary 2000, Festival in Cannes 2002, Baltic Storm 2003, Sotto falso nome 2004, Beyond the Sea 2004, Flightplan 2005, The Book of Revelation 2006, The Handyman 2006, Icicle Melt 2006, L'Amour caché 2007, Brideshead Revisited 2008. *Television:* The Ebony Tower, Dr. Fischer of Geneva, Waterfront (Australia), Rasputin (Emmy Award 1996), The Odyssey (series) 1996, Macbeth 1998, The Farm (Australia) 2000, Daniel Deronda, Jeffrey Archer – The Truth 2002, Maigret: L'ombra cinese 2004, Marple: By the Pricking of My Thumbs 2006, Broken Trail 2006, Nightmares and Dreamscapes: From the Stories of Stephen King (miniseries) 2006, The Trojan Horse (miniseries) 2008, Miss Austen Regrets 2008. *Theatre:* Cider with Rosie, In Times Like These, Airbase, Uncle Vanya 1988, A Doll's House, Miss Julie, Simpatico, A Midsummer Night's Dream, Easy Virtue, The Guardsman 2000, Old Times 2000, The True-Life Fiction of Mata Hari 2002, The Deep Blue Sea 2008. *Address:* c/o Conway van Gelder, 3rd Floor, 18–12 Jermyn Street, London, SW1Y 6HP, England (office).

SCACE, Arthur R.A., CM, QC, MA, LLB; Canadian lawyer and banking industry executive; *Chairman, Bank of Nova Scotia;* b. Toronto; ed Univ. of Toronto, Univ. of Oxford, Harvard Univ., Osgoode Hall; called to the bar, Ontario 1967; began career at McCarthy Tétrault (law firm) 1967, became Pnr 1972, Man. Pnr, Toronto 1989–96, Nat. Chair. 1997–99, currently Counsel; mem. Bd of Dirs Scotiabank (Nat. Bank of Nova Scotia) 1997–, Chair. 2004–; Dir The Canada Life Assurance Co., Canada Life Financial Corpn 2000–04; fmr Chair. Canadian Opera Co.; fmr Treas. Law Soc. of Upper Canada; mem. Bd of Dirs Garbell Holdings Ltd, Gardiner Group Capital Ltd, Gerdau Ameristeel Corpn, Lallemand Inc., N.M. Davis Corpn Ltd, Sceptre Investment Counsel Ltd, estJet Airlines Inc.; fmr mem. Bd of Dirs The Canada Life Assurance Co., Canada Life Financial Corpn, Brompton Equity Split Corpn, Brompton Split Banc Corpn; Sec., Rhodes Scholarships in Canada; Hon. DIur (Law Soc. of Upper Canada), (York Univ.); Robinette Medal, Osgoode Hall Law School 2003. *Publication:* The Income Tax Law of Canada (co-author). *Address:* The Bank of Nova Scotia, 44 King Street West, Toronto, ON M5H 1H1, Canada (office). *Telephone:* (416) 866-6161 (office). *Fax:* (416) 866-3750 (office). *E-mail:* ascace@mccarthy.ca (office). *Website:* www.scotiabank.ca (office).

SCAGLIA, Silvio; Italian telecommunications industry executive; *Founder and Chairman, Babelgum;* b. 1958, Lucerne, Switzerland; m.; three c.; ed Polytechnic Univ. of Turin; began career as consultant with McKinsey and Bain & Co.; fmr CEO Omnitel (now Vodafone Italy); f. Fastweb (fibre-to-the-home (FTTH) broadband co.) 1999, CEO 1999–2003, Chair. 2003–07, currently mem. Bd of Dirs; Founder and Chair. Babelgum (on-demand TV over the internet service) 2007–. *Address:* Babelgum, Block J, East Point Business Park, Fairview, Dublin 3, Ireland (office). *E-mail:* info@babelgum.com (office). *Website:* www.babelgum.com (office).

SCAIFE, Brendan Kevin Patrick, PhD, DSc (Eng), MRIA, CEng, FIET, CPhys, FInstP; Irish electrical engineer and academic; b. 19 May 1928, London; s. of James Scaife and Mary Kavanagh; m. Mary Manahan 1961; three s. one d.; ed Cardinal Vaughan Memorial School, London, Chelsea Polytechnic and Queen Mary Coll. London; GEC Research Labs, Wembley 1953–54; Scholar, School of Theoretical Physics, Dublin Inst. for Advanced Studies 1954–55; Inst. for Industrial Research and Standards, Dublin 1955–56; Electricity Supply Bd Dublin 1956; Coll. of Tech., Dublin 1956–61; Lecturer in Electronic Eng, Trinity Coll. Dublin 1961–66, Fellow 1964, Reader 1966, Assoc. Prof. 1967–72, Prof. of Eng Science 1972–86, Prof. of Electromagnetics 1986–88, Sr Fellow 1987–88, Fellow Emer. 1988–; Visiting Prof., Univ. of Salford 1969–82; Fellow, Inst. of Engineers of Ireland, Inst. of Eng and Tech.; Boyle Medal, Royal Dublin Soc. 1992. *Publications:* Complex Permittivity (compiler) 1971, Studies in Numerical Analysis (ed.) 1974, Principles of Dielectrics (revised edn) 1998, The Mathematical Papers of Sir William Rowan Hamilton Vol. IV (ed.) 2000. *Address:* Department of Electronic and Electrical Engineering, Trinity College, Dublin 2 (office); 6 Trimleston Avenue, Booterstown, Blackrock, Co. Dublin, Ireland (home). *Telephone:* (1) 6081580 (office); (1) 2693867 (home). *Fax:* (1) 6772442 (office). *E-mail:* bscaife@eircom.net (home).

SCAJOLA, Claudio; Italian lawyer and politician; *Minister of Economic Development;* b. 15 Jan. 1948, Imperia, Liguria; m.; two c.; mem. staff Inpdap; Chair. Unità Sanitaria Locale of Imperia 1980–83; Mayor of Imperia 1990–95; mem. Camera dei Deputati (Forza Italia) for Liguria 1996–; Minister of the Interior 2001–02, for Implementation of Govt Programs 2003–04, of Productive Activities 2005–06, of Econ. Devt 2008–; Pres. Parl. Cttee for the Information and Security Services and for the Secrets of the State 2007–08; Chair. ANCI Liguria, Rivera Trasporti. *Publication:* Ai Confini d'Italia: Storia e Immagini del Ponente Ligure. *Address:* Ministry of Economic Development, Via Veneto 33, 00187 Rome, Italy (office). *Telephone:* (06) 420434000 (office). *Fax:* (06) 47887964 (office). *E-mail:* segreteria.ministro@attivitaproduttive.gov.it (office); scajola_c@camera.it (office). *Website:* www.sviluppoeconomico.gov.it (office); www.claudioscajola.it.

SCALES, Prunella Margaret Rumney, CBE; British actress; b. (P M R Illingworth), Sutton Abinger; d. of John Richardson Illingworth and Catherine Scales; m. Timothy West (q.v.) 1963; two s.; ed Moira House, Eastbourne, Old Vic Theatre School, London, Herbert Berghof Studio, New York; in repertory, Huddersfield, Salisbury, Oxford, Bristol Old Vic etc.; seasons at Stratford and Chichester 1967–68; numerous radio broadcasts, readings, poetry recitals, fringe productions; has directed plays at numerous theatres including Bristol Old Vic, Arts Theatre, Cambridge, Nottingham Playhouse, W Yorkshire Playhouse (Getting On); Pres. Council for the Protection of Rural England 1997–2002; Amb. Howard League for Penal Reform 2007–; Freeman of City of London 1990; Hon. DLitt (Bradford) 1995, (East Anglia) 1996. *Plays include:* The Promise 1967, Hay Fever 1968, The Wolf 1975, Make and Break 1980, An Evening with Queen Victoria 1980, The Merchant of Venice 1981, Quartermaine's Terms 1981, When We Are Married 1986, Single Spies (double bill) 1988, School for Scandal, Long Day's Journey into Night (Nat. Theatre), Happy Days 1993, Staying On 1996, Some Singing Blood (Royal Court), The Mother Tongue, The Editing Process 1994, The Birthday Party 1999, The Cherry Orchard 2000, The External 2001, Too Far to Walk (King's Head) 2002, A Woman of No Importance 2004, Gertrude's Secret, New End Theatre 2007. *Films include:* Laxdale Hall 1953, Waltz of the Toreadors 1962, What Every Woman Wants 1954, Hobson's Choice 1954, The Crowded Day 1954, The Hound of the Baskervilles 1978, The Boys from Brazil 1978, The Wicked Lady 1983, The Lonely Passion of Judith Hearne 1987, Consuming Passions 1988, A Chorus of Disapproval 1988, Howards End 1992, Freddie as F.R.O.7 (voice) 1992, Sherwood's Travels 1994, Second Best 1994, Wolf 1994, An Awfully Big Adventure 1994, Phoenix 1997, An Ideal Husband 1998, Stiff Upper Lips 1998, Mad Cows 1999, The Ghost of Greville Lodge 2000, Brand Spanking 2004, Helix 2006. *Radio includes:* After Henry,

Smelling of Roses 2000, Ladies of Letters 2001, 2004, Rumpole 2007. *Television includes:* Pride and Prejudice (mini-series) 1952, What Every Woman Wants 1954, The Crowded Day 1954, Television Playhouse – French for Love 1955, Room at the Top (uncredited) 1959, Television Playhouse – The New Man 1960, The Secret Garden (series) 1960, The Seven Faces of Jim – The Face of Genius 1961, Coronation Street 1961, Marriage Lines (series) 1961–66, On the Margin (series) 1966, Jackanory 1970, Thirty-Minute Theatre – Blues in the Morning 1971, Country Matters – The Ring of Truth 1973, Seven of One – One Man's Meat 1973, Comedy Playhouse – The Big Job 1974, Decisions, Decisions 1975, Play of the Month – The Apple Cart 1975, Fawlty Towers (series) 1975, 1979, Escape from the Dark 1976, BBC 2 Playhouse – The Achurch Letters 1977, Mr. Big (series) 1977, Pickersgill People (series) 1978, Target 1978, Doris and Doreen 1978, Bergerac 1981, A Wife Like the Moon 1982, Grand Duo 1982, S.W.A.L.K. (series) 1982, Never the Twain 1982, Outside Edge 1982, The Merry Wives of Windsor 1982, Wagner (mini-series) 1983, Mapp and Lucia (series) 1985–86, Absurd Person Singular 1985, Unnatural Causes 1986, The Index Has Gone Fishing 1987, What the Butler Saw 1987, When We Are Married 1987, After Henry (series) 1988–92, Beyond the Pale 1989, A Question of Attribution 1991, My Friend Walter 1992, Woodcock 1994, The Rector's Wife (series) 1994, Fair Game 1994, Look at the State We're In! (mini-series) 1995, Signs and Wonders 1995, Breaking the Code 1995, Searching (series) 1995, Lord of Misrule 1996, Emma 1996, Dalziel & Pascoe 1996, Breaking the Code 1996, The Tale of Mrs. Tiggy-Winkle and Mr. Jeremy Fish (voice) 1998, The Big Knights (series; voice) 1999, Midsomer Murders – Beyond the Grave 2000, Silent Witness – Faith 2001, Station Jim 2001, Dickens 2002, Looking for Victoria 2003, Casualty 2004, Essential Poems for Christmas 2004, Where the Heart Is 2005, The Shell Seekers 2006, The Royal 2008. *Publications:* So You Want To Be An Actor?. *Leisure interests:* gardening, crosswords, canal boat. *Address:* c/o Jeremy Conway, 18–21 Jermyn Street, London, SW1Y 6HP, England (office). *Telephone:* (20) 7287-0077 (office). *Fax:* (20) 7287-1940 (office). *E-mail:* vena@conwayvg.co.uk (office). *Website:* www.conwayvg.co.uk (office).

SCALFARI, Eugenio, DIur; Italian editor and journalist; b. 6 April 1924, Civitavecchia; m. Simonetta de Benedetti 1959; two d.; contrib. Il Mondo, L'Europeo 1950–; Promoter Partito Radicale 1958, L'Espresso 1955–, Ed.-in-Chief 1963–68, Man. Dir 1970–75; Promoter La Repubblica 1976–, Ed.-in-Chief 1976–96, Dir 1988–; Deputy to Parl. 1968–72; currently columnist, La Repubblica and L'Espresso; Siena Award 1985, Journalist of the Year Award 1986, Premio Ischia alla Carriera 1996, Premio St Vincent alla Carriera. *Publications:* Rapporto sul Neocapitalismo Italiano, Il Potere Economico in URSS, L'Autunno della Repubblica, Razza Padrona, Interviste ai Potenti, L'Anno di Craxi, La Sera Andavamo in Via Veneto, Incontro con Io, La Morale Perduta, La Ruga Sulla Fronte. *Address:* c/o La Repubblica, Via Cristoforo Colombo 90, 00147 Rome, Italy. *Telephone:* (06) 49821.

SCALFARO, Oscar Luigi; Italian politician, lawyer and fmr head of state; b. 9 Sept. 1918, Novara; ed Università Cattolica del Sacro Cuore, Milan; elected Christian Democrat (DC) MP for Turin-Novara-Vercelli 1948; Sec. then Vice-Chair. Parl. Group and mem. Nat. Council of DC, mem. of DC Cen. Office during De Gasperi's leadership, Under-Sec. of State at Ministry of Labour and Social Security in Fanfani Govt, Under-Sec. in Ministry of Justice, Under-Sec. in Ministry of Interior 1959–62; Minister of Transport and Civil Aviation in Moro, Leone and Andreotti Govts, Minister of Educ. in second Andreotti Govt; Vice-Chair. House of Deputies; Minister of the Interior 1983–87; mem. House of Deputies Comm. for Foreign and Community Affairs; Pres. of Italy 1992–99; currently mem. Senato della Repubblica (Senator for Life) 1999–, mem. Gruppo Misto 2006–. *Address:* Senato della Repubblica, Piazza Madama, 00186 Rome, Italy. *E-mail:* scalfaro_o@posta.senato.it. *Website:* www.senato.it.

SCALIA, Antonin, AB, LLB; American lawyer and judge; *Associate Justice, Supreme Court;* b. 11 March 1936, Trenton, NJ; s. of S. Eugene Scalia and Catherine L. Scalia (née Panaro); m. Maureen McCarthy 1960; five s. four d.; ed Georgetown Univ., Univ. of Fribourg, Switzerland and Harvard Univ. Law School; called to Bar, Ohio 1962, Virginia 1970; Assoc. Jones, Day, Cockley & Reavis, Cleveland 1961–67; Assoc. Prof., Univ. of Va Law School 1967–70, Prof. 1970–74; Gen. Counsel Office of Telecommunications Policy, Exec. Office of President 1971–72; Chair. Admin. Conf. US, Washington 1972–74; Asst Attorney Gen., US Office of Legal Counsel, Justice Dept 1974–77; Prof., Law School, Univ. of Chicago 1977–82; Visiting Prof., Georgetown Law Center 1977, Stanford Law School 1980–81; Judge, US Court of Appeals (DC Circuit) 1982–86; Assoc. Justice, US Supreme Court 1986–; Hon. Master of the Bench, Inner Temple, London 1986. *Publication:* A Matter of Interpretation 1998. *Address:* United States Supreme Court, One First Street, NE, Washington, DC 20543, USA (office). *Telephone:* (202) 479-3211 (home). *Website:* www.supremecourtus.gov (office).

SCANLAN, John Oliver, MEng, PhD, DSc, MRIA, FIEE, FIEEE; Irish electronic engineer and academic; *Professor Emeritus of Electronic Engineering, University College Dublin;* b. 20 Sept. 1937, Dublin; s. of John Scanlan and Hannah Scanlan; m. Ann Weadock 1961; ed St Mary's Coll., Dundalk, Univ. Coll. Dublin; Research Engineer, Mullard Research Labs., Surrey, UK 1959–63; Lecturer, Univ. of Leeds, UK 1963–68, Prof. of Electronic Eng 1968–73; Prof. of Electronic Eng, Univ. Coll. Dublin 1973–2002, Prof. Emer. 2002–; Sec. Royal Irish Acad. 1981–89, Pres. 1993–96; Dir Bord Telecom Eireann 1984–97; Golden Jubilee Medal, IEEE Circuits and Systems Soc. 1999. *Publications:* Analysis and Synthesis of Tunnel Diode Circuits 1966, Circuit Theory (Vols 1 and 2) 1970. *Leisure interests:* music, golf. *Address:* Department of Electronic and Electrical Engineering, Engineering Building, University College Dublin, Belfield, Dublin 4, Ireland (office). *Telephone:* (1) 7161909 (office). *Fax:* (1) 2830921 (office). *E-mail:* eleceng@ucd.ie (office). *Website:* eleceng.ucd.ie (office).

SCARAMUZZI, Franco; Italian agricultural scientist; *President, Accademia dei Georgofili;* b. 26 Dec. 1926, Ferrara; s. of Donato Scaramuzzi and Alberta Rovida; m. Maria Bianca Cancellieri 1955; one s. one d.; Prof. of Pomology, Univ. of Pisa 1959, Univ. of Florence 1969, now Prof. Emer.; Rector Magnificus, Univ. of Florence 1979–91; Pres. Int. Soc. of Horticultural Science 1986–90; Pres. Accademia dei Georgofili 1986–; mem. Soviet (now Russian) Acad. of Agricultural Sciences 1982–; Pres. Società di San Giovanni Battista 2001–; Hon. Pres. Italian Horticultural Soc. 1976–, Italian Acad. of Vine and Wine; Hon. mem. Rotary; Cavaliere di Gran Croce 1998; Dr hc (Bucharest); Gold Medal of the Minister of Education, 1983, Gold Medal of Univ. of Florence. *Publication:* Fruit Pomology. *Address:* Accademia dei Georgofili, Logge Uffizi Corti, 50122 Florence (office); Viale Amendola 38, 50121 Florence, Italy (home). *Telephone:* (55) 213360 (office); (55) 2342825 (home). *Fax:* (55) 2302754 (office). *E-mail:* accademia@georgofili.it (office). *Website:* www.georgofili.it (office).

SCARDINO, Dame Marjorie Morris, DBE, JD, BA; American/British journalist, lawyer and business executive; *CEO, Pearson PLC;* b. 25 Jan. 1947, Flagstaff, Ariz.; d. of Robert Weldon Morris and Beth Lamb Morris; m. Albert James Scardino 1974; two s. one d.; ed Baylor Univ., Univ. of San Francisco; started career as reporter, Associated Press; Pnr, Brannen, Wessels and Searcy law firm, Savannah, Ga 1975–85; Co-founder (with husband) and Publr The Georgia Gazette Co. (won Pulitzer Prize) 1978–85; Pres. The Economist Newspaper Group Inc., New York 1985–93, Chief Exec. The Economist Group, London 1993–97, CEO Pearson PLC 1997–; mem. Bd of Dirs (non-exec.) Nokia Corpn 2001–; mem. Bd of Trustees The MacArthur Foundation, Carter Center, Victoria & Albert Museum; Hon. Fellow, London Business School, City and Guilds of London Inst., RSA; Hon. LLD (Exeter); Hon. DHumLitt (New School Univ.); Dr hc (Heriot-Watt), (Brunel); Veuve Clicquot Businesswoman of the Year Award 1998, Benjamin Franklin Medal, RSA 2001, ranked by Fortune magazine amongst 50 Most Powerful Women in Business outside the US (first) 2001, (first) 2002, (first) 2003, (third) 2004, (third) 2005, (fifth) 2006, (third) 2007, ranked by Forbes magazine amongst 100 Most Powerful Women (59th) 2004, (18th) 2005, (31st) 2006, (17th) 2007, (20th) 2008. *Leisure interests:* horse riding, playing golf, watching Manchester United football team. *Address:* Pearson PLC, 80 Strand, London, WC2R 0RL, England (office). *Telephone:* (20) 7010-2300 (office). *Fax:* (20) 7010-6601 (office). *E-mail:* marjorie.scardino@pearson.com (office). *Website:* www.pearson.com (office).

SCARF, Herbert Eli, AB, MA, PhD; American economist and academic; *Sterling Professor of Economics, Yale University;* b. 25 July 1930, Philadelphia, Pa; s. of Louis H. Scarf and Lena Elkman; m. Margaret Klein 1953; three d.; ed Temple Univ. and Princeton Univ.; worked at RAND Corpn, Santa Monica, Calif. 1954–57; Asst and Assoc. Prof., Dept of Statistics, Stanford Univ., Calif. 1957–63; Fellow, Center for Advanced Study in the Behavioral Sciences, Stanford, Calif. 1962–63; Prof. of Econs, Yale Univ. 1963–70, Stanley Resor Prof. of Econs 1970–78, Sterling Prof. of Econs 1979–; Dir Cowles Foundation for Research in Econs 1967–71, 1981–84, Dir Div. of Social Sciences 1971–72, 1973–74; Visiting Prof., Stanford Univ., Calif. 1977–78, Mathematical Sciences Research Inst. Spring 1986; Ford Foundation Sr Faculty Fellowship 1969–70; Fellow, Econometric Soc., Pres. 1983; Fellow, American Acad. of Arts and Sciences; mem. NAS 1976–, American Philosophical Soc.; Distinguished Fellow, American Econ. Assn 1991; Hon. LHD (Chicago) 1978; Lanchester Prize, (Operations Research Soc. of America) 1974, Von Neumann Medal 1983. *Publications:* Studies in the Mathematical Theory of Inventory and Production (with K. Arrow and S. Karlin) 1958, The Optimality of (S, s) Policies in the Dynamic Inventory Problem 1960, The Computation of Economic Equilibria (with Terje Hansen) 1973, Applied General Equilibrium Analysis (ed with John Shoven) 1984; articles in learned journals. *Leisure interests:* music, reading, hiking. *Address:* Cowles Foundation, Yale University, PO Box 208281, New Haven, CT 06520-8281; 88 Blake Road, Hamden, CT 06517, USA (home). *Telephone:* (203) 432-3693 (office); (203) 776-9197 (home). *Fax:* (203) 432-6167 (office). *E-mail:* herbert.scarf@yale.edu (office). *Website:* cowles.econ.yale.edu/faculty/scarf.htm (office); cowles.econ.yale.edu/~hes/index.htm (office).

SCARFE, Gerald A., CBE; British cartoonist; b. 1 June 1936, London; m. Jane Asher; two s. one d.; joined Daily Mail as political cartoonist 1966; began working with Sunday Times (London) 1967; has contributed cartoons to Punch 1960–, Private Eye 1961–, Time 1967–; exhibited at Grosvenor Gallery (group exhbns) 1969, 1970, Pavillion d'Humour, Montreal 1969, Expo 1970, Osaka 1970; animation and film directing BBC 1969–; designer and dir of animation for Pink Floyd The Wall concerts and film 1975–78; consultant designer and character design for film Hercules 1997; Hon. Fellow, London Inst. 2001; Hon. LLD (Liverpool) 2001, (Dundee) 2007; Zagreb Prize for BBC film Long Drawn Out Trip 1973, BAFTA Award for Scarfe on Scarfe 1987, Olivier Award for Absolute Turkey 1993, Cartoonist of the Year, British Press Awards 2006. *Television includes:* dir. and presenter Scarfe on Art, Scarfe on Sex, Scarfe on Class, Scarfe in Paradise; subject of Scarfe and His Work with Disney (South Bank Special). *Theatre design:* Ubu Roi (Traverse Theatre) 1957, What the Butler Saw (Oxford Playhouse) 1980, No End of Blame (Royal Court, London) 1981, Orpheus in the Underworld (English ENO, Coliseum) 1985, Who's a Lucky Boy (Royal Exchange, Manchester) 1985, Born Again 1990, The Magic Flute (LA Opera) 1992, An Absolute Turkey 1993, Mind Millie for Me (Haymarket, London) 1996, Fantastic Mr. Fox (LA Opera) 1998, Peter and the Wolf (Holiday on Ice, Paris and world tour) 2000, The Nutcracker 2002,. *Publications:* Gerald Scarfe's People 1966, Indecent Exposure 1973, Expletive Deleted: The Life and Times of Richard Nixon

1974, Gerald Scarfe 1982, Father Kissmass and Mother Claus 1985, Scarfe by Scarfe (autobiog.) 1986, Gerald Scarfe's Seven Deadly Sins 1987, Line of Attack 1988, Scarfeland 1989, Scarfe on Stage 1992, Scarfe Face 1993, Hades: The Truth at Last 1997, Drawing Blood: Forty-five Years of Scarfe Uncensored 2005. *Leisure interests:* drawing, painting, sculpting. *Address:* c/o Simpson Fox Associates, 52 Shaftsbury Avenue, London, W1D 6LP, England (office). *Telephone:* (20) 7434-9167 (office). *Website:* www.geraldscarfe.com (office).

SCARGILL, Arthur; British trade union official; *General-Secretary, Socialist Labour Party;* b. 11 Jan. 1938, Worsborough, Yorks.; s. of the late Harold Scargill and of Alice Scargill; m. Anne Harper 1961; one d.; ed White Cross Secondary School; worked first in a factory, then Woolley Colliery 1955; mem. Barnsley Young Communist League 1955–62; mem. Nat. Union of Mineworkers (NUM) 1955–, NUM Br. Cttee 1960, Br. del. to NUM Yorks. Area Council 1964, mem. NUM Nat. Exec. 1972–, Pres. Yorks. NUM 1973–82, Pres. NUM 1981–2002, Hon. Pres. and Consultant July 2002–; Chair. NUM Int. Cttee; Pres. Int. Miners Org. 1985–; mem. Labour Party 1966–95; mem. TUC Gen. Council 1986–88; f. Socialist Labour Party 1996, Gen.-Sec. 1996–; contested Newport East 1997, Hartlepool 2001. *Address:* Socialist Labour Party, PO Box 112, Leigh, WN7 4WS (office); National Union of Mineworkers, 2 Huddersfield Road, Barnsley, S. Yorks., S70 2LS, England. *Telephone:* (870) 850-3576 (office). *E-mail:* info@socialist-labour-party.org.uk (office). *Website:* www.socialist-labour-party.org.uk (office).

SCARLETT, Sir John McLeod, Kt, KCMG, OBE, MA; crown servant; *Chief, Secret Intelligence Service (MI6);* b. 18 Aug. 1948, London; s. of the late James Henri Stuart Scarlett and of Clara Dunlop Scarlett (née Morton); m. Gwenda Mary Rachel Stilliard 1970; one s. three d. (and one s. deceased); ed Epsom Coll., Magdalen Coll., Oxford; with Secret Intelligence Service 1971–2001, FCO London 1971–73, 1977–84, 1988–91, 1994–2001 (Dir of Security and Public Affairs 1999–2001), Third Sec., Nairobi 1973–74; language student 1974–75; Second, later First Sec., Moscow 1976–77; First Sec., Paris 1984–88, Political Counsellor, Moscow 1991–94; Chair. Jt Intelligence Cttee and Intelligence and Security Dir, Cabinet Office 2001–04; Chief, Secret Intelligence Service (MI6) 2004–. *Leisure interests:* history, family. *Address:* Secret Intelligence Service, PO Box 1300, London, SE1 1BD, England (office). *Website:* www.sis.gov.uk (office); www.mi6.gov.uk (office).

SCARONI, Paolo, MBA; Italian business executive; *CEO, Eni SpA;* b. 28 Nov. 1946, Vicenza; m.; three c.; ed Univ. of Bocconi, Milan, Columbia Univ., New York, USA; staff mem. Chevron 1969–71; consultant, McKinsey & Co. 1972–73; joined Saint Gobain Group 1973, various exec. positions including Financial Man. St German Italia, Gen. Man. Balzaretti & Modigliani SpA, Chair. Borma SpA and Air Industrie SpA –1978; Gen. Del. St Gobain Venezuela, Colombia, Ecuador and Peru, Caracas 1978–81; Gen. Del. St Gobain Italia 1981–84; Chair. St Gobain Flat Glass Div., Paris 1984; Chair. and Man. Dir St Gobain Vitrage SA; CEO St Gobain Group –2002; Chair. Fabbrica Pisana SpA, Vegla GmbH, Cristaleria Espanola SA, Saint Roch SA; Vice-Chair. and Man. Dir Techint 1985; Vice-Chair. Falck SpA 1986–88; Man. Dir SIV SpA 1993–95; Group CEO Pilkington PLC 1996–2002; CEO and COO Enel SpA 2002–05; CEO Eni SpA 2005–; Chair. Alliance Unichem (UK) 2005–06; Vice-Chair. Sadi SpA; mem. Bd Dirs Assicurazioni Generali, LSEG (London Stock Exchange Group) plc, Veolia Environnement (Paris), Fondazione Teatro alla Scala; Pres. Unindustria Venice 2001–; mem. Exec. Cttee Confindustria; mem. Exec. Bd BAE Systems, London, Alstom SA, Paris, Alliance UniChem; mem. Bd of Overseers, Columbia Business School, New York; Officier, Légion d'honneur 2007. *Publication:* Professione manager 1985. *Leisure interests:* reading, skiing, golf, football. *Address:* Eni SpA, Piazzale Enrico Mattei 1, 00144 Rome, Italy (office). *Telephone:* (06) 59821 (office). *Fax:* (06) 59822141 (office). *E-mail:* segreteriasocietaria.azionisti@eni.it (office); ufficio.stampa@eni.it (office). *Website:* www.eni.it (office).

SCAZZIERI, Roberto, MLitt, DPhil, DrScPol; Italian economist and academic; *Professor of Economics, University of Bologna;* b. 1 May 1950, Bologna; s. of Guerrino Scazzieri and Fosca Lambertini; m. Maria Cristina Bacchi 1983; one s.; ed Liceo Minghetti, Bologna, Univ. of Bologna, Univ. of Oxford, UK; Asst Lecturer, Univ. of Bologna 1974–79, Lecturer in Theory and Policy of Econ. Growth 1980–83, in Econ. Principles 1983–86, in Advanced Econ. Analysis 1985–87, Assoc. Prof. of Econs, Faculty of Political Sciences 1986–87, Full Prof. of Econs, Faculty of Econs and Commerce and Dept of Econs 1990–, mem. Teaching Bd, PhD Programme in Science, Tech. and Humanities 2007–; Prof. of Econs, Faculty of Statistics, Univ. of Padua 1987–90; Visiting Scholar, Dept of Applied Econs, Univ. of Cambridge 1987, 1989, Research Assoc. 1992–93; Visiting Fellow, Clare Hall 1992, Life mem. 1992; Visiting Fellow, Gonville and Caius Coll. 1999, mem. 1999–, Centre for Research in the Arts, Social Sciences and Humanities, Univ. of Cambridge 2004; Resident Fellow, Bologna Inst. of Advanced Study 1997, Founding Scientific Dir 2000–03, Deputy Scientific Dir 2003–06; Visiting Prof., Univ. of Lugano, Switzerland 1997; Visiting Research Fellow, Centre for History and Econs, King's Coll., Cambridge 2005, Visiting Scholar, Gonville and Caius College and Clare Hall 2007–08; Man. Ed. and Review Ed. Structural Change and Economic Dynamics; Assoc. Ed. Journal of Economic Methodology; mem. Steering Cttee Bologna-Cambridge-Harvard Sr Seminars Network, Bologna Inst. for Advanced Study, Steering Cttee European Consortium of Humanities Centres and Institutes 2002–; mem. Man. Bd European Summer School in Structural Change and Econ. Dynamics, Selwyn Coll., Cambridge 1995–; mem. Scientific Cttee Int. Centre for the History of Univs and Science 1994–, Scientific Cttee Centre for Research on Complex Automated Systems (CASY), Univ. of Bologna 2002–; mem. Man. Bd 'Federigo Enriques' Centre for Epistemology and History of Sciences, Univ. of Bologna 2001–; Foundation Fellow, Kyoto Univ.; Rector's Del., Bologna-Clare Hall Fellowship 1993–; mem. Bologna Acad. of Sciences 1994–; Bonaldo Stringher Prize Scholarship (Bank of Italy) 1974, St Vincent Prize for Econs 1985, Linceo Prize for Econs, Nat. Lincei Acad. 2004. *Publications:* Efficienza produttiva e livelli di attività 1981, Protagonisti del pensiero economico (co-author) 1977–82, Sui momenti costitutivi dell'economia politica 1983 (co-author), Foundations of Economics: Structures of Inquiry and Economic Theory 1986, The Economic Theory of Structure and Change 1990, A Theory of Production: Tasks, Processes and Technical Practices 1993, Production and Economic Dynamics 1996, Incommensurability and Translation. Kuhnian Perspectives on Scientific Communication and Theory Change 1999, Knowledge, Social Institutions and the Division of Labour 2001, Economics of Structural Change (co-author) 2003, Reasoning, Rationality, and Probability (co-author) 2008, Markets, Money and Capital – Hicksian Economics for the Twenty First Century (co-author) 2008, Migration of Ideas (co-author) 2008, Capital, Time and Transitional Dynamics (co-author) 2009,; numerous articles. *Leisure interests:* reading and conversation, art, walking. *Address:* Università degli Studi di Bologna, Piazza Scaravilli 2, 40126 Bologna (office); Via Garibaldi 5, 40124 Bologna, Italy (home). *Telephone:* (051) 2098146 (office); (051) 2098132 (Secretary) (office). *Fax:* (051) 2098040 (office). *Website:* www.economia.unibo.it (office); www.dse.unibo.it (office); www.crassh.cam.ac.uk (office); www.isa.unibo.it (office).

SCHAAL, Barbara A., BS, MPh, PhD; American/German plant biologist and academic; *Spencer T. Olin Professor in Arts & Sciences, Washington University in St Louis;* b. 1947, Berlin, Germany; ed Univ. of Illinois, Chicago, Yale Univ.; became US citizen in 1956; grew up in Chicago; mem. Faculty, Univ. of Houston, Ohio State Univ. –1980; joined Faculty, Washington Univ. in St Louis 1980, currently Spencer T. Olin Prof. in Arts & Sciences; Assoc. Ed. Molecular Biology and Evolution, The American Journal of Botany, Molecular Ecology, Conservation Genetics; Pres. Botanical Soc. of America 1995–96; fmr Soc. for the Study of Evolution; mem. Bd of Trustees St Louis Acad. of Sciences, Missouri Chapter of the Nature Conservancy; mem. NAS 1999, Vice-Pres. (first woman) NAS 2005–; Fellow, AAAS. *Achievements include:* recognized for her work on the genetics of plant species, particularly for her studies using DNA sequences to understand evolutionary processes such as gene flow, geographical differentiation, and the domestication of crop species. *Publications:* numerous scientific papers in professional journals. *Address:* 304 McDonnell Hall, Department of Biology, Washington University, Campus Box 1129, One Brookings Drive, St Louis MO 63130-4899, USA (office). *Telephone:* (314) 935-6822 (office). *E-mail:* schaal@biology.wustl.edu (office). *Website:* www.biology.wustl.edu/faculty/schaal (office).

SCHABRAM, Hans, DPhil; German academic; *Professor of Medieval English Language and Literature, University of Göttingen;* b. 27 Sept. 1928, Berlin; s. of Paul Schabram and Lucia Schabram; m. Candida Larisch 1956; two s. one d.; ed Univs of Berlin and Cologne; Asst, English Dept, Univ. of Heidelberg 1957–63; Prof. of Medieval English Language and Literature, Univ. of Giessen 1964–67, Univ. of Göttingen 1968–; mem. Akad. der Wissenschaften, Göttingen. *Publications:* 55 publs on English Philology since 1956. *Address:* Seminar für Englische Philologie der Universität, Humboldtallee 13, 37073 Göttingen (office); Heinz-Hilpert-Str. 6, 37085 Göttingen, Germany. *Telephone:* (551) 55444 (home). *Website:* www.uni-goettingen.de (office).

SCHACHMAN, Howard Kapnek, PhD; American biochemist and academic; *Professor of the Graduate School, Division of Biochemistry and Molecular Biology, University of California, Berkeley;* b. 5 Dec. 1918, Philadelphia, Pa; s. of Morris H. Schachman and Rose Kapnek Schachman; m. Ethel H. Lazarus 1945; two s.; ed Mass. Inst. of Technology and Princeton Univ.; Fellow, Rockefeller Inst. for Medical Research, Princeton, NJ, 1947–48; Instructor (Biochemistry), Univ. of California, Berkeley 1948–50, Asst Prof. 1950–54, Assoc. Prof. 1955–59, Prof. of Biochemistry and Molecular Biology 1959–91, Prof. Emer. 1991–94, Faculty Research Lecturer 1994, Prof. of Grad. School 1994–, Chair. Dept of Molecular Biology, Dir Virus Lab. 1969–76; Scholar-in-Residence, Fogarty Int. Center, NIH 1977–78; Carl and Gerty Cori Lecturer, Washington Univ. School of Medicine, St Louis 1993; Pres. American Soc. for Biochemistry and Molecular Biology 1987–88, Chair. Public Affairs Cttee 1989–2000; Pres. Fed. of American Socs for Experimental Biology 1988–89; mem. Scientific Council and Scientific Advisory Bd of Stazione Zoologica Naples, Italy 1988–, Bd of Scientific Consultants of Memorial Sloan-Kettering Cancer Center 1988–97, Bd of Scientific Counselors Nat. Cancer Inst., Div. of Cancer Biology and Diagnosis 1989–92, Cttee on Scientific Freedom and Responsibility 1998–; Special Adviser to Dir of NIH and Ombudsman in the Basic Sciences 1994–; mem. NAS 1968 (Chair. Biochemistry Section 1990–93), AAAS, American Acad. of Arts and Sciences 1966; Foreign mem. Accad. Nazionale dei Lincei, Rome 1996; Hon. DSc (Northwestern Univ.) 1974; Hon. MD (Naples) 1990; ACS (Calif. Section) Award 1958, ACS E. H. Sargent & Co. Award for Chemical Instrumentation 1962, John Scott Award, City of Philadelphia 1964, Warren Triennial Prize, Mass Gen. Hosp. 1965, Merck Award, American Soc. of Biological Chemists 1986, Alexander von Humboldt Award 1990, NAS Panel on Scientific Responsibility and the Conduct of Research 1990–92, Alberta Heritage Foundation for Medical Research Visiting Professorship, Univ. of Alberta 1996, Herbert A. Sober Award, American Soc. for Biochemistry and Molecular Biology 1994, Public Service Award, FASEB 1994, Theodor Sredberg Award 1998, Burroughs Wellcome Fund Lecturer 1999, AAAS Scientific Freedom and Responsibility Award 2001. *Publications:* Ultracentrifugation in Biochemistry 1959; numerous articles in scientific journals. *Leisure interest:* sports. *Address:* Schachman Lab, 176 Stanley Hall #3220, University of California, Berkeley, CA 94720-3220, USA (office). *Telephone:* (510) 642-7046 (office). *Fax:* (510) 642-8699 (office). *E-mail:* howardschachman@berkeley.edu (office). *Website:* mcb.berkeley.edu/faculty/BMB/schachmanh.html (office).

SCHACHT, Henry Brewer, MBA; American business executive; *Managing Director and Senior Advisor, Warburg Pincus LLC;* b. 16 Oct. 1934, Erie, Pa; s.

of Henry Schacht and Virginia Schacht; m. Nancy Godfrey 1960; one s. three d.; ed Yale and Harvard Univs; Investment Man. Irwin Man. Co. 1962–64; Vice-Pres. Finance, Subsidiaries and Int. Areas, Cummins Engine Co., Inc. 1964–69; Pres. Cummins Engine Co., Inc. 1969–77, Chair. 1977–95, CEO 1977–94; Man. Dir Warburg Pincus LLC, New York 1995, Man. Dir and Sr Advisor 2004–; Chair. and CEO Lucent Techs, Murray Hill, NJ 1995–98, 2000–03, now mem. Bd of Dirs; mem. Bd of Dirs Aluminum Company of America (Alcoa); fmr mem. Bd of Dirs CBS, AT&T, Chase Manhattan Corpn, Chase Manhattan Bank NA, Johnson & Johnson, New York Times Co., Avaya; fmr mem. Business Council; Trustee, Metropolitan Museum of Art; fmr Chair. Bd of Trustees Ford Foundation; fmr Trustee Yale Univ., Brookings Inst., Business Enterprise Trust, Calver Educ. Foundation; fmr Sr Mem. The Conf. Bd. *Address:* Warburg Pincus LLC, 466 Lexington Avenue, New York, NY 10017, USA (office). *Telephone:* (212) 878-0600 (home). *Fax:* (212) 878-9351 (office). *Website:* www.warburgpincus.com (office).

SCHADEWALDT, Hans, DrMed; German professor of medical history; *Professor Emeritus, University of Düsseldorf;* b. 7 May 1923, Kottbus; s. of Johannes Schadewaldt and Hedwig Schadewaldt; m. Lotte Schadewaldt 1943; four s.; ed Univs of Tübingen, Würzburg and Königsberg; Lecturer Univ. of Freiburg 1961–63; Prof. History of Medicine, Univ. of Düsseldorf 1963– (now Emer.), Dean, Faculty of Medicine 1976–77; mem. numerous int. medical socs.; mem. North Rhine-Westphalian Acad. of Sciences, Pres. 1990–, Accad. Nazionale Virgiliana Mantova 2001–; Hon. Fellow Royal Soc. of Medicine; Dr hc (Szecein); Officier Ordre du Mérite Culturel, Monaco; Officier Ordre des Palmes Académiques, Paris; Bundesverdienstkreuz, Commdr.'s Cross, Order of Merit; Sarton Medal, Sudhoff Medal, Langerhans Medal, Ernst von Bergmann Medal, Hansen Medal, Hahnemann Medal. *Films include:* History of Diabetes, Dance of Death, Trepanation in Kenya, Folklore Medicine in Kenya. *Television:* Sanfte Medizin (ARD) 1992–2001. *Publications:* Michelangelo und die Medizin seiner Zeit 1965, Die berühmten Ärzte 1966, Kunst und Medizin 1967, Der Medizinmann bei den Naturvölkern 1968, Geschichte der Allergie 1979–83, Die Chirurgie in der Kunst 1983, Das Herz, ein Rätsel für die antike und mittelalterliche Welt 1989, Betrachtungen zur Medizin in der bildenden Kunst 1990, 100 Jahre Pharmakologie bei Bayer 1890–1990 1990, Totentanz und Heilberufe 1993, Chronik der Medizin 1993, Die Seuchen kehren zurück 1994, Paul Ehrlich und die Anfänge der Chemotherapie 2001–02, Sieben Jahre Sanfte Medizin 2002. *Address:* Institute für Geschichte der Medizin, Heinrich-Heine-Univeristät Düsseldorf, Moorenstr. 5, 40225 Düsseldorf (office); Brehmstrasse 82, 40239 Düsseldorf, Germany (home). *Telephone:* (211) 8114053 (office); (211) 623163 (home). *Fax:* (211) 8114053.

SCHAEFER, Henry Frederick, III, BS, PhD; American chemist, researcher and academic; *Graham-Perdue Professor of Chemistry and Director, Center for Computational Chemistry, University of Georgia;* b. 8 June 1944, Grand Rapids, Mich.; s. of Henry Frederick Schaefer, Jr and Janice Christine Trost Schaefer; m. Karen Regine Rasmussen; three s. two d.; ed Massachusetts Inst. of Tech., Stanford Univ.; Prof. of Chem., Univ. of Calif., Berkeley 1969–87; Wilfred T. Doherty Prof. and Dir Inst. for Theoretical Chem., Univ. of Tex. 1979–80; Graham-Perdue Prof. of Chem. and Dir Center for Computational Chem., Univ. of Ga 1987–; Ed. Molecular Physics 1991–, Encyclopedia of Computational Chem. 1995–; Pres. World Asscn of Theoretically Oriented Chemists 1996–; Alfred P. Sloan Research Fellow 1972–74; John Simon Guggenheim Fellow 1976–77; Fellow, American Physical Soc. 1977–, AAAS, American Acad. of Arts and Sciences 2004–; mem. Int. Acad. of Quantum Molecular Sciences; numerous lectureships including Guelph-Waterloo Distinguished Lecturer, Univ. of Guelph and Univ. of Waterloo, Ont., Canada 1991, John M. Templeton Lecturer, Case Western Reserve Univ. 1992, Herbert H. King Lecturer, Kansas State Univ. 1993, Francis A. Schaeffer Lectures, Washington Univ., St Louis 1994, Mary E. Kapp Lecture, Va Commonwealth Univ. 1996, Abbott Lectures, Univ. of ND 1997, C.S. Lewis Lecture, Univ. of Tenn. 1997, Joseph Frank McGregory Lecture, Colgate Univ. 1997, Kenneth S. Pitzer Lecture, Univ. of Calif. at Berkeley 1998, Donald F. Othmer Lectures in Chem., Tokyo 2000, Israel Pollak Lectures, Technion-Israel Inst. of Tech., Haifa 2001, Coochbehar Lectures, Indian Asscn for the Cultivation of Science, Kolkata 2001, Lise Meitner Lecture, Hebrew Univ., Jerusalem 2001, Oakley Vail Lecture, Wake Forest Univ. 2002, Lawrence J. Schaad Lecture, Vanderbilt Univ. 2002, Annual Lecture of the Croatian Chemical Soc., Zagreb 2002, The Pres.'s Lecture, Univ. of Texas at Arlington 2002, Distinguished Theory Lecturer, Max Planck Inst., Mülheim, Germany 2003, John Marks Templeton Lecture, Princeton Univ. 2004, The New Coll. Lectures, Univ. of New South Wales 2004; 14 hon. degrees; ACS Award in Pure Chem. 1979, Leo Hendrik Baekeland Award (ACS) 1983; Schroedinger Medal, World Asscn of Theoretical Organic Chemists 1990, Centenary Medal, RSC, London 1992, ACS Award in Theoretical Chem. 2003, ACS Ira Remson Award 2003, Joseph O. Hirschfelder Prize 2006. *Publications:* The Electronic Structure of Atoms and Molecules 1972, Modern Theoretical Chemistry 1977, Quantum Chemistry 1984, A New Dimension to Quantum Chemistry 1994, Science and Christianity: Conflict or Coherence? 2003; more than 1080 publs in scientific journals. *Leisure interests:* Bible study, running, hiking. *Address:* Center for Computational Chemistry, University of Georgia, 1004 Cedar Street, Athens, GA 30602-2525, USA (office). *Telephone:* (706) 542-0364 (office); (706) 542-2067 (office). *Fax:* (706) 542-0406 (office). *E-mail:* hfs@uga.edu (office). *Website:* ccqc.uga.edu (office).

SCHAEFER, Michael, PhD; German diplomatist; *Ambassador to the People's Republic of China;* b. 1949; m.; three c.; ed Max Planck Inst., Heidelberg, Univ. of Mannheim; joined Foreign Service 1978, overseas postings include Bonn, UN missions in Geneva and New York, Singapore; Head, Western Balkans Task Force, Fed. Foreign Office, Berlin 1999–2001, Special Envoy for S Eastern Europe and Deputy Political Dir 2001–02, Head, Legal Dept 2002, Political Dir 2002–07; Amb. to People's Repub. of China 2007–. *Publications:* Der Sicherheitsmechanismus der Vereinten Nationen 1980, Berufsbild Diplomat: Auswahl und Ausbildung im Auswärtigen Dienst 1995; contrib. to Südosteuropa Mitteilungen, Zeitschrift Vereinte Nationen. *Address:* Embassy of Germany, 17 Dong Zhi Men Wai Dajie, San Li Tun, Beijing 100600, People's Republic of China (office). *Telephone:* (10) 85329000 (office). *Fax:* (10) 65325336 (office). *E-mail:* embassy@peki.diplo.de (office). *Website:* www.beijing.diplo.de (office).

SCHAEFER, William Donald, LLM, JD; American politician (retd); b. 2 Nov. 1921, Baltimore; s. of William Henry Schaefer and Tululu Skipper; ed Baltimore Univ.; law practice, Baltimore 1943–; mem. Baltimore City Council 1955–67, Pres. 1967–71, Mayor of Baltimore 1971–86; Gov. of Md 1986–95, Md State Comptroller 1999–2007; professional lecturer and William Donald Schaefer Chair, School of Public Affairs, Univ. of Md and Inst. for Policy Studies, Johns Hopkins Univ. 1996; fmr Counsel, Gordon, Feinblatt, Rothman, Hoffberger & Hollander; Democrat; numerous hon. degrees; numerous awards including Jefferson Award 1979, Michael A. DiNunzio Award 1981, Distinguished Mayor Award, Nat. Urban Coalition 1982, Best Mayor in America, Esquire Magazine 1984, Commendation, Pres.'s Council on Physical Fitness and Sports 1988, Making Marylanders Safe Award, Marylanders Against Handgun Abuse 1991, Lifetime Achievement Award, American Planning Asscn 1991, Award for Outstanding Leadership, Leadership Md 1992, President's Medal, Johns Hopkins Univ. 1994, Premier Leadership Award, American Cancer Soc. 1995, Schools for Success Lifetime Achievement Award, Md Dept of Educ. 1999, B'nai B'rith Inaugural Lifetime Achievement Award 2000, Md Man of the Century 2000, Speaker's Medallion, Md House of Delegates 2002, Governor's Award for Int. Leadership, World Trade Inst., Woodrow Wilson Award for Public Service 2003. *Address:* c/o Comptroller of Maryland, 80 Calvert Street, Annapolis, MD 21401, USA.

SCHAEFFER, Bogusław, DPhil; Polish/Austrian composer, music critic, playwright and pianist; b. 6 June 1929, Lwów (now Lviv, Ukraine); s. of Władysław Schaeffer and Julia Schaeffer; m. Mieczysława Hanuszewska 1953; one s.; ed State Higher School of Music (student of A. Malawski), Jagiellonian Univ., Kraków (student of Zdzisław Jachimecki); wrote first dodecaphonic music for orchestra, Music for Strings: Nocturne 1953; Assoc. Prof. State Higher School of Music, Kraków 1963–98, Ordinary Prof. of Composition, Higher School of Music, Mozarteum, Salzburg 1986–89, Prof. 1989–; Chief Ed. Forum Musicum 1967–; leads Int. Summer Courses for New Composition in Salzburg and Schwaz (Austria) 1976–; Hon. mem. Int. Soc. for Contemporary Music 1998, Pro Sinfonica 2003; Gold Cross of Merit 1969; Kt's Cross of Polonia Restituta Order 1972; numerous prizes include G. Fitelberg Prize 1959, 1960, 1964, A. Malawski Prize 1962, Minister of Culture and Arts Prize 1971, 1980, Union of Polish Composers Prize 1977, Alfred Jurzykowski Award 1999. *Main compositions:* Extrema, Tertium datur, Scultura, S'alto for alto saxophone, Collage and Form, Electronic Music, Visual Music, Heraclitiana, Missa Electronica, Jangwa, Missa Sinfonica, eight Piano Concertos, Maah, Sinfonia, Hommage à Guillaume for two cellos and piano 1995, Sinfonietta for 16 instruments 1996, Symphony in One Movement 1997, Enigma for Orchestra 1997, Four Psalms for choir and orchestra 1999, Musica Omogènea for 32 violins 1999, Si Quaeris Miracula for soprano and orchestra 2000, Model XXI (Wendepunkt) for piano 2000, De Profundis for soprano and chamber orchestra 2000, Monophonie VIII for 24 violins 2000, Ave Maria for soprano and orchestra 2000, opera Liebesblicke 2000, five violin concertos, three cello concertos, Concerto for vibraphone and orchestra 2001, Concerto for harp, Celtic harp and orchestra 2002, Concerto for saxophone, piano and orchestra 2002, Blues VII for piano and orchestra 2004, Quartet for four cellos 2005, Panorama for orchestra 2005, Fragment III for two actors, clarinet, cello, piano and electronic media 2005, Second Symphony in One Movement 2005, OCSENOT for soprano and ensemble of seven instruments, Impresiónes Liricas for piano and electro-acoustic medias 2005, Model XXXIII for piano 2005, Contemporaneamente o Alternatamente for violin and piano 2005, Model XXXIV for paino 2006, Mini opera, also film and theatre music, Miserere, Organ Concerto, 14 string quartets, Orchestral and Electronic Changes, Concerto for Violin, Piano and Orchestra, Symphony/Concerto for 15 solo instrumentalists and orchestra, Heideggeriana, Winter Musik for horn and piano, Concerto for percussion, electronic media and orchestra. *Plays include:* Three Actors 1970, Darknesses 1980, Screenplay for Sins of Old Age 1985, The Actor 1990, Rehearsals 1990, Séance 1990, Tutam 1991, Rondo 1991, Together 1992, Toast 1991, Harvest 1993, Promotion 1993, Daybreak 1994, Multi 1994, Largo 1996, Stage Demon 1998, Alles 1998, Advertisement 1998, Farniente 1998, Chance 1999, Dwa Te (Two Te) 2000, Skala 2000, Case; plays trans. into 17 languages. *Publications:* Nowa Muzyka. Problemy współczesnej techniki kompozytorskiej (New music. Problems of Contemporary Technique in Composing) 1958, Klasycy dodekafonii (Classics of Dodecaphonic Music) 1964, Leksykon kompozytorów XX wieku (Lexicon of 20th Century Composers) 1965, W kręgu nowej muzyki (In the Sphere of New Music) 1967, Mały informator muzyki XX wieku 1975, Introduction to Composition (in English) 1975, Historia muzyki (Story of Music) 1980, Kompozytorzy XX wieku (20th Century Composers) 1990, Trzy rozmowy (kompozytor, dramaturg, filozof) (Three Conversations: Composer, Playwright and Philosopher) 1992. *Leisure interests:* literature, theatre. *Address:* Osiedle Kolorowe 4, m.6, 31-938 Kraków, Poland; St. Julienstrasse 7A, Apartment 27, 5020 Salzburg, Austria. *Telephone:* (12) 6441960 (Poland) (home). *E-mail:* bsch@ceti.pl (office). *Website:* www.usc.edu/dept/polish_music/composer/schaeffer.html#intro.

SCHAEFFER, Leonard D., BA; American business executive; *Senior Advisor, Texas Pacific Group;* b. 28 July 1945, Chicago; m. Pamela Schaeffer (née Sidford); two c.; ed Princeton Univ.; Man. Consultant Arthur Andersen & Co. 1969–73; Deputy Dir of Man. Illinois Mental Health and Developmental Disabilities, Springfield, Ill. 1973–75; Dir Ill State Bureau of Budget 1975–76;

Vice Pres. Citibank NA, New York 1976–78; Asst Sec., Man and Budget, US Dept of Health and Human Services, Washington, DC 1978, Admin. Health Care Financing Admin (HCFA) 1978–80; Exec. Vice Pres. and COO Student Loan Marketing Asscn 1980–82; Pres. and CEO Group Health Inc., Minneapolis, Minn. 1983–86; Chair. and CEO Blue Cross of Calif. 1986–96, managed transition to WellPoint, Chair. and CEO WellPoint Health Networks Inc. (now WellPoint Inc.) 1993–2004, Chair. 2004–05; Sr Advisor Texas Pacific Group (pvt. investment firm) 2006–; est. Calif. Endowment and Calif. HealthCare Foundation 1996; mem. Bd of Dirs Allergan, Inc., Amgen Inc. 2004–; Chair. Nat. Inst. for Health Care Man.; fmr Chair. Health Insurance Asscn of America, Nat. Health Foundation; Founding Chair. Coalition for Affordable and Quality Healthcare; Chair. WellPoint Foundation; mem. Inst. of Medicine, Nat. Acad. of Science; mem. Bd Trustees, The Brookings Inst.; mem. Bd of Fellows and Co-Chair., Advisory Council, Dept of Healthcare Policy, Harvard Medical School; mem. Advisory Council Dept of Economics, Princeton Univ.; mem. Bd of Councilors, School of Policy, Planning, and Development, Univ. of Southern Calif.; Citation for Outstanding Service, American Acad. of Paediatrics, Distinguished Public Service Award, US Dept of Health, Educ. and Welfare, Exec. Leadership Award, UCLA Anderson School of Man. 2003. *Address:* Texas Pacific Group, 301 Commerce Street, Suite 3300, Fort Worth, TX 76102, USA (office). *Telephone:* (817) 871-4000 (office). *Fax:* (817) 871-4010 (office). *Website:* www.texaspacificgroup.com (office).

SCHAFER, Edward (Ed) Thomas, BA, MBA; American business executive, government official and fmr state governor; b. 8 Aug. 1946, Bismarck, ND; s. of Harold Schafer and Marian Schafer; m. Nancy Jones 1992; four c.; ed Univ. of N Dakota and Univ. of Denver; quality control insp., Gold Seal 1971–73, Vice-Pres. 1974, Chair. Man. Cttee 1975–78, Pres. 1978–85; Owner/Dir H & S Distribution 1976; Pres. Dakota Classics 1986, TRIESCO Properties 1986, Fish 'N Dakota 1990–94; Gov. of N Dakota 1993–2000; Civilian Aide to US Sec. of the Army 2002; Co-founder and CEO Extend America (wireless communications co.) 2000–08; Adviser, Americans for Prosperity 2006–08; US Sec. of Agric., Washington, DC 2008–09; Republican. *Address:* c/o Department of Agriculture, 1400 Independence Avenue, SW, Washington, DC 20250, USA.

SCHÄFERKORDT, Anke; German television executive; *CEO, RTL Television;* b. 1962; began career at Bertelsmann AG in 1988; Exec. Asst for Sales Controlling and Strategic Planning, RTL Television GmbH, Cologne 1991–92, Head, Controlling Dept 1992–93, Dir in charge of Corp. Planning and Controlling Div. 1993–95, Head of Business Affairs, VOX Television 1995–97, Program Dir 1997–99, CEO VOX Television 1999–, COO and Deputy CEO of RTL Television Feb.–Sept. 2005, CEO Sept. 2005–, also in charge of RTL Group's holdings in n-tv and Super RTL networks; ranked by the Financial Times amongst Top 25 Businesswomen in Europe (24th) 2006, (24th) 2007. *Address:* RTL Television GmbH, Aachener Straße 1044, 50858 Cologne, Germany (office). *Telephone:* (221) 456-0 (office). *Fax:* (221) 456-1690 (office). *Website:* www.rtl-television.de (office).

SCHALLER, George Beals, PhD; American zoologist, academic and author; *Vice-President, Science and Exploration Program, Wildlife Conservation Society;* b. 26 May 1933, Berlin, Germany; s. of George Ludwig Schaller and Bettina Iwersen (née Byrd); m. Kay Suzanne Morgan 1957; two s.; ed Univ. of Alaska, Univ. of Wisconsin-Madison; moved to USA in his teens; Fellow, Dept of Behavioral Sciences, Stanford Univ. 1962–63; Research Assoc., Johns Hopkins Univ., Baltimore 1963–66; Adjunct Assoc. Prof., Rockefeller Univ., New York 1966–72; Research Zoologist, Wildlife Conservation Soc. 1966–, Dir Int. Conservation Program, New York Zoological Soc. 1979–88, now Vice-Pres. Science and Exploration Program and Ella Millbank Foshay Chair in Wildlife Conservation; Adjunct Prof., Peking (now Beijing) Univ.; Research Assoc., American Museum of Natural History; Fellow, Guggenheim Foundation 1971; Hon. Dir Explorers' Club 1991; Order of Golden Ark (Netherlands) 1978; Int. Cosmos Prize (Japan) 1996, Tyler Prize for Environmental Achievement 1997, Gold Medal, World Wildlife Fund 1980, Beebe Fellowship, Wildlife Conservation Soc. 2006, Lifetime Achievement Award, Nat. Geographic Soc. 2007, Indianapolis Prize 2008. *Achievement:* recognized as one of the world's leading field biologists, studying wildlife throughout Africa, Asia and S America. *Publications:* The Mountain Gorilla 1963, The Year of the Gorilla 1964, The Deer and the Tiger 1967, The Serengeti Lion (Nat. Book Award 1973) 1972, Mountain Monarchs 1977, Stones of Silence 1980, The Giant Pandas of Wolong (co-author) 1985, The Last Panda 1993, Tibet's Hidden Wilderness 1997, Wildlife of the Tibetan Steppe 1998, Antelopes, Deer and Relatives (co-ed.) 2000. *Leisure interests:* photography, reading. *Address:* Wildlife Conservation Society, 2300 Southern Boulevard, Bronx, New York, NY 10460, USA (office). *Telephone:* (718) 220-6807 (office). *Fax:* (718) 364-4275 (office). *E-mail:* asiaprogram@wcs.org (office). *Website:* www.wcs.org (office).

SCHALLY, Andrew Victor, PhD; American medical researcher and academic; b. 30 Nov. 1926, Wilno, Poland (now Vilnius, Lithuania); s. of Casimir Peter Schally and Maria Schally (née Lacka); m. 1st Margaret Rachel White; one s. one d.; m. 2nd Ana Maria de Medeiros-Comaru 1976 (died 2004); ed Bridge of Allan, Scotland, London Univ., McGill Univ., Montreal, Canada; Asst Prof. of Physiology and Asst Prof. of Biochem., Baylor Univ. Coll. of Medicine, Houston, Tex. 1957–62; Chief, Endocrine and Polypeptide Labs., Veterans Admin. Hosp., New Orleans, La. 1962–2005; Sr Medical Investigator, Veterans' Admin. 1973–99, Distinguished Medical Research Scientist, Veterans' Affairs Dept 1999–; Assoc. Prof. of Medicine, Tulane Univ. School of Medicine, New Orleans, La 1962–67, Prof. of Medicine 1967–2005; Distinguished Leonard Miller Prof. of Pathology, Prof. Div. of Hematology/Oncology and Div. of Endocrinology, Dept of Medicine, Miller School of Medicine, Univ. of Miami; mem. NAS, AAAS and numerous other socs and nat. academies; more than 30 hon. degrees; Chevalier, Légion d'honneur 2004; decorations from USA, Spain, France, Ecuador and Venezuela; Charles Mickle Award 1974, Gairdner Foundation Award 1974, Edward T. Tyler Award 1975, Borden Award in the Medical Sciences (Asscn of American Medical Colls) 1975, Lasker Award 1975, shared Nobel Prize for Physiology or Medicine with Roger Guillemin (q.v.) for discoveries concerning peptide hormones 1977, US Govt Distinguished Service Award 1978. *Publications:* more than 2,000 scientific papers, particularly concerning hormones and cancer. *Leisure interest:* swimming, soccer. *Address:* Veterans Administration Hospital Research Service, 1201 NW 16th Street, Miami, FL 33125 (office); 3801 Collins Avenue, Apt 1506, Miami Beach, FL 33140, USA (home). *Telephone:* (305) 575-3477 (office). *Fax:* (305) 575-3126 (office). *E-mail:* Andrew.Schally@va.gov.

SCHAMA, Simon Michael, CBE, MA; British historian, academic, writer and art critic; *University Professor, Department of History, Columbia University;* b. 13 Feb. 1945, London; s. of the late Arthur Schama and of Gertrude Steinberg; m. Virginia Papaioannou 1983; one s. one d.; ed Christ's Coll., Cambridge; Fellow and Dir of Studies in History, Christ's Coll., Cambridge 1966–76; Fellow and Tutor in Modern History, Brasenose Coll., Oxford 1976–80; Prof. of History (Mellon Prof. of the Social Sciences), Harvard Univ. 1980; Univ. Prof., Columbia Univ. 1997–; art critic, New Yorker 1995–; Contributing Ed., Financial Times 2009–; Vice-Pres. Poetry Soc.; Wolfson Prize 1977, Leo Gershoy Prize, American Historical Asscn 1978, Nat. Cash Register Book Prize for Non-Fiction (for Citizens) 1990. *Television:* Rembrandt: The Public Eye and the Private Gaze (film for BBC) 1992, A History of Britain (series) 2000–01, The Power of Art (series) 2006, The American Future: A History (series) 2008. *Publications:* Patriots and Liberators: Revolution in the Netherlands 1780–1813 1977, Two Rothschilds and the Land of Israel 1979, The Embarrassment of Riches: An Interpretation of Dutch Culture in the Golden Age 1987, Citizens: A Chronicle of the French Revolution 1989, Dead Certainties (Unwarranted Speculations) 1991, Landscape and Memory 1995, Rembrandt's Eyes 1999, A History of Britain Vol. 1: At the Edge of the World? 3000 BC–AD 1603 2000, Vol. 2: The British Wars 1603–1776 2001, Vol. 3: The Fate of Empire 1776–2001 2002, Hang-Ups: Essays on Painting 2004, Rough Crossings: Britain, the Slaves and the American Revolution 2005, Power of Art 2006, The American Future: A History 2008. *Leisure interests:* wine, Dutch bulbs, children's fiction. *Address:* Department of History, 522 Fayerweather Hall, Columbia University, New York, NY 10027, USA (office). *Telephone:* (212) 854-4593 (office). *E-mail:* sms53@columbia.edu (office). *Website:* www.columbia.edu/cu/history (office).

SCHANBERG, Sydney Hillel, BA; American journalist and academic; b. 17 Jan. 1934, Clinton, Mass.; s. of Louis Schanberg and Freda Schanberg (née Feinberg); two d.; ed Harvard Univ.; joined New York Times 1959, reporter 1960, Bureau Chief, Albany, New York 1967–69, New Delhi, India 1969–73, SE Asia Corresp., Singapore 1973–75, City Ed. 1977–80, Columnist 1981–85; Assoc. Ed., Columnist Newsday newspaper, New York 1986–98; chief investigative unit APBnews.com; columnist for Village Voice, NY –2006; currently Adjunct Prof., Dept of Communication and Media, SUNY New Paltz; numerous awards including Page One Award for Reporting 1972, George Polk Memorial Award 1972, Overseas Press Club Award 1972, Bob Considine Memorial Award 1975, Pulitzer Prize 1975, Elijah Parish Lovejoy Award, Colby Coll. 1992. *Publication:* Death and Life of Dith Pran 1985. *Address:* 164 West 79th Street, Apartment 12D, New Paltz, NY 10024, USA (office). *Telephone:* (212) 769-0960 (office). *Fax:* (212) 769-3666 (office). *E-mail:* sydneyschanberg@yahoo.com.

SCHAPIRO, Mary L., BA, JD; American lawyer and stock exchange official; *Chairman, Securities and Exchange Commission;* b. 19 June 1955, New York City; m. Charles A. Caldwell 1980; two c.; ed Franklin and Marshall Coll., George Washington Univ.; called to the Bar, Washington, DC 1980; attorney 1980–81; Gen. Counsel, Futures Industry of America 1984–86, Sr Vice-Pres. 1986–88; Commr SEC 1988–94, Acting Chair. 1993–94; Chair. Commodity Futures Trading Comm. 1994–96; Pres. of Regulation, Nat. Asscn of Securities Dealers (NASD) 1996–2002, Vice-Chair. for regulatory policy oversight, NASD 2002–06, Chair. and CEO 2006–07, CEO Financial Industry Regulatory Authority, Inc. (FINRA) (self-regulatory org. cr. through consolidation of NASD and NYSE Mem. Regulation) 2007–08, also Chair. FINRA Investor Educ. Foundation; Chair. SEC, Washington, DC 2009–; mem. Int. Org. of Securities Comms, Chair. Consultative Cttee 2002–06; fmr mem. Bd of Dirs Duke Energy, Kraft Foods; mem. ABA; mem. Bd of Trustees Franklin and Marshall Coll.; mem. Law and Governance Advisory Bd, RAND Corpn, LRN-RAND Center of Corp. Ethics, Pres.'s Advisory Council on Financial Literacy 2008; Financial Women's Asscn Public Sector Woman of the Year 2000. *Address:* Securities and Exchange Commission, Station Pl., 100 F St, NE, Washington, DC 20549, USA (office). *Telephone:* (202) 942-8088 (office). *Fax:* (202) 942-9646 (office). *E-mail:* help@sec.gov (office). *Website:* www.sec.gov (office).

SCHARP, Anders, MSc; Swedish business executive; *Chairman, AB Nederman & Company;* b. 8 June 1934; ed Royal Inst. of Tech. Stockholm; joined AB Electrohelios 1960 (merged with AB Electrolux 1963), Exec. Vice-Pres. (Production and Research & Devt) 1974; Pres. AB Electrolux 1981, CEO 1986; Chair. Saab-Scania 1990–95; Chair. Saab AB 1995–2006, AB Nederman; Chair., CEO AB SKF 1992–2008; Chair. Incentive AB 1992–98; Chair. White Consolidated Industries 1993–98, fmrly CEO; mem. Bd of Dirs Investor AB 1988–, Vice Chair. 2005–; Chair. AB Nederman & Co.; fmr mem. Bd of Dirs Swedish Asscn of Metalworking Industries, Swedish Metal Trades Employers' Asscn, Swedish Employers' Confed.; mem. Royal Swedish Acad. of Eng. Sciences. *Address:* AB Ph. Nederman & Co., PO Box 602, 251 06 Helsingborg, Sweden (office). *Telephone:* 42-18-87-00 (office). *Fax:* 42-14-79-71 (office). *E-mail:* support@nederman.se (home). *Website:* www.nederman.com (office).

SCHARPING, Rudolf; German politician; b. 2 Dec. 1947, Niederelbert, Westerwald; m. 1st Jutta Scharping (divorced 2000); three c.; m. 2nd Countess Kristina Pilati Borggreve 2000; ed Univ. of Bonn; joined Social Democratic Party (SPD) 1966; State Chair. and Nat. Deputy Chair. Jusos (Young Socialists) 1966; mem. State Parl. of Rhineland-Palatinate 1975; Party Leader of SPD in Rhineland-Palatinate 1985; Leader of Opposition in Rhineland-Palatinate 1987; Minister-Pres. of Rhineland-Palatinate 1991–94; mem. Bundestag (German Parl.) 1994–2005; Leader, SPD 1993–95, Deputy Chair. 1995–2003, Chair. SPD Parl. Group, Leader of the Opposition 1994; Chair. Social Democratic Party of Europe –2003; Minister of Defence 1998–2002; Deputy Chair. Party of European Socialists 1995–2001; Visiting Prof., Fletcher School for Law and Diplomacy, Tufts Univ. 2004; Pres. Bundes Deutscher Radfahrer (Fed. of German Cyclists) 2005–. *Publications:* Was Jetzt Butun Ist 1994, Wir Dürfer Nicht Wegsehen – Der Kosovo-Krieg und Europa 1999; numerous articles on German and European politics. *Address:* c/o Bund Deutscher Radfahrer e.V., Otto-Fleck-Schneise 4, 60528 Frankfurt, Germany (office). *Website:* www.rad-net.de (office).

SCHATZ, Gottfried (Jeff), PhD; Austrian biochemist and academic; *Professor Emeritus of Biochemistry, University of Basel;* b. 18 Aug. 1936, Strem; s. of Andreas Schatz and Anna Schatz; m. Merete Bjorn Petersen 1962; three c.; ed Univ. of Graz; Asst Prof., Univ. of Vienna 1961–64; Postdoctoral Fellow, Public Health Research Inst. City of New York 1964–66; Assoc. Prof., Prof. Cornell Univ. 1968–74; Prof. of Biochemistry, Univ. of Basel 1974–, now Prof. Emer.; Pres. Swiss Science and Tech. Council 2000–03; Chair. Science Council of the Inst. Curie; Scientific Councilor, Inst. Pasteur; mem. Scientific Advisory Bd ORIDIS Biomed GmbH; Fellow, AAAS 2007–; mem. NAS, Royal Swedish Acad., Netherlands Acad. Sciences;; Dr hc (Bratislava) 1996, (Stockholm) 2000; Innitzer Prize 1967, Louis Jeantet Prize 1990, Prix Benoist 1993; Gairdner Award 1998; Hansen Gold Medal 1983; Sir Hans Krebs Medal 1985; Otto Warburg Medal 1988, E. B. Wilson Medal 2000. *Publications:* Jeff's View: on Science and Scientists 2005; about 200 scientific publs in biochemical journals. *Leisure interests:* music, jogging. *Address:* Unterer Rebbergweg 33, 4153 Reinach, Switzerland (home). *Telephone:* (61) 7112795 (office). *Fax:* (61) 7112448 (office). *E-mail:* gottfried.schatz@unibas.ch (office). *Website:* www.chemie.unibas.ch (office).

SCHATZMAN, Evry; French research scientist; b. 16 Sept. 1920, Neuilly; s. of Benjamin Schatzman and Cécile Kahn; four c.; ed Ecole Normale Supérieure; Research Assoc. CNRS 1945, Head of Research 1948; Prof., Univ. of Paris 1954; Dir of Research, CNRS 1976–89; mem. Acad. of Sciences 1985–; Chevalier, Légion d'honneur, Officier, Ordre nat. du Mérite; Prix Holweck 1976, Médaille d'Or, CNRS 1983. *Publications:* Astrophysique générale 1957, Structure de l'Univers 1968, Science et société 1971, Les Enfants d'Uranie 1986, Le Message du photon voyageur 1987, La science menacée 1989, L'expansion de l'Univers 1989, Les étoiles 1990, L'outil théorie 1992, The Stars 1993; more than 200 research papers, mainly on physical processes in astrophysics. *Address:* Institut de France, 23 quai Canti, 75006 Paris; 11 rue de l'Eglise, Dompierre, 60420 Maignelay-Montigny, France (home).

SCHAUB, Alexander, DJ; German lawyer and civil servant; *Of Counsel, Freshfields Bruckhaus Deringer;* b. 14 June 1941, Duisburg; s. of Franz Schaub and Gertrud Stockert; m. Nicole Van der Meulen 1974; one s. two d.; ed Univs of Freiburg, Lausanne, Cologne and Bonn and Coll. of Europe, Bruges; with Fed. Ministry of Econ. Affairs 1971; mem. Secr. of Ralf Dahrendorf 1973; mem. Secr. and Deputy Chef de Cabinet of Guido Brunner 1974–78; Deputy Chef de Cabinet Messrs Davignon and Burke 1980, of Pres. Gaston Thorn 1981; Chef de Cabinet of Willy de Clercq 1985–89; Dir DG External Relations and Trade Policy, EC 1989–90, Deputy Dir-Gen. DG Internal Market and Industrial Affairs 1990–93, Deputy Dir-Gen. DG Industry 1993–95, Dir-Gen. for Competition 1995–2002; Dir-Gen. DG Internal Market and Services 2002–06 (retd); Of Counsel, Freshfields Bruckhaus Deringer, Brussels 2007–; Grosses Silbernes Ehrenzeichen mit Stern (Austria), Verdiensthrent 1 klasse des Verdinstordens der Bundesrepublik Deutschland. *Publications:* Die Anhörung des Europäischen Parlaments in Rechtsetzungsverfahren der EWG 1971, Food Quality in the Internal Market 1993, Gentechnik im Lebensmittelbereich – Die Politik der EG-Kommission 1994 and numerous contribs to legal and professional journals, articles in newspapers etc. *Leisure interests:* tennis, skiing. *Address:* Freshfields Bruckhaus Deringer, Bastion Tower, Place du Champ de Mars/Marsveldplein 5, 1050 Brussels, Belgium (office). *Telephone:* (2) 504-70-00 (office). *Fax:* (2) 504-72-00 (office). *E-mail:* alexander.schaub@freshfields.com (office). *Website:* www.freshfields.com (office).

SCHÄUBLE, Wolfgang, DrIur; German politician and lawyer; *Minister of the Interior;* b. 18 Sept. 1942, Freiburg; s. of Karl Schäuble and Gertrud Schäuble (née Göhring); m. Ingeborg Hensle 1969; one s. three d.; ed Univs of Freiburg and Hamburg; Regional Pres., Junge Union, S Baden 1969–72; worked in admin. of taxes, Baden-Württemberg 1971–72; mem. Bundestag 1972–, Exec. Sec. CDU/CSU Parl. Group 1981–84, Vice-Chair. in charge of Foreign Security and European Policies 2002–; mem. parl., European Council 1975–84; Chair. CDU Cttee on Sport 1976–84; Regional Vice-Pres. S Baden CDU 1982–95, mem. Federal Exec. Cttee CDU, mem. Presidium CDU 2000–; Minister with special responsibility and Head of Chancellery 1984–89, of Interior 1989–91, 2005–; CDU Parl. Leader 1991–2000, Leader 1998–2000; legal practice in Offenburg 1978–84; Chair. Arbeitsgemeinschaft Europäischer Grenzregionen (AGEG) 1979–82; Grosses Bundesverdienstkreuz; Commdr, Ordre nat. du Mérite. *Publications:* Mitten im Leben 2000, Scheitert der Westen? 2003. *Leisure interests:* chess, music. *Address:* Ministry of the Interior, Alt-Moabit 101d, 10559 Berlin, Germany (office). *Telephone:* (30) 186810 (office). *Fax:* (30) 186812926 (office). *E-mail:* poststelle@bmi.bund.de (office). *Website:* www.bmi.bund.de (office).

SCHAVAN, Annette, DPhil; German politician and theologian; *Minister of Education;* b. 1955, Neuss am Rhein; Scientific Adviser, Religious Studies Dept, Cusanuswerk Inst., Bonn 1980–84, Dir 1988–95; Lecturer, Univ. of Düsseldorf 1980–95; Dept Leader for Further Educ., Parish of Aachen 1984–87; Leader, CDU Women's Union 1988–90, mem. Bd, Baden-Württemberg CDU, Chair. Baden-Württemberg 2012 Comm. 2003–; Baden-Württemberg Regional Minister for Culture, Youth and Sport 1995–2005; Pres. Kultusministerkonferenz (KMK) 2001–; Minister of Educ. 2005–; Officier de la Légion d'honneur 2002. *Leisure interests:* rambling. *Address:* Federal Ministry of Education and Research, Hannoversche Straße 28–30, 10115 Berlin, Germany (office). *Telephone:* (30) 18570 (office). *Fax:* (30) 185783601 (office). *E-mail:* bmbf@bmbf.bund.de (office). *Website:* www.bmbf.de (office).

SCHECKTER, Jody David; South African business executive and fmr racing driver; b. 29 Jan. 1950, East London, nr Durban; m. Pam Bailey; two s.; raced karts from age of 11, graduated to motorcycles and racing cars; won SA Formula Ford Sunshine Series in 1970, competed in Britain from 1971; Formula One World Champion 1979, runner-up 1977, third place 1974 and 1976; Grand Prix wins: 1974 Swedish (Tyrrell-Ford), 1974 British (Tyrrell-Ford), 1975 South African (Tyrrell-Ford), 1976 Swedish (Tyrrell-Ford), 1977 Argentine (Wolf-Ford), 1977 Monaco (Wolf-Ford), 1977 Canadian (Wolf-Ford), 1979 Belgian (Ferrari), 1979 Monaco (Ferrari), 1979 Italian (Ferrari); retd from motor racing 1980; est. business in Atlanta, Ga, designing and building simulation equipment for firearms training, later retd; currently owner Laverstoke Park Farm (organic farming), UK. *Leisure interest:* keeping fit. *Address:* Laverstoke Park Offices, Overton, Hampshire, RG25 3DR, England. *Telephone:* (1256) 772800. *Fax:* (1256) 772809. *E-mail:* info@laverstokepark.co.uk. *Website:* www.laverstokepark.co.uk.

SCHEEL, Walter; German politician; b. 8 July 1919, Solingen; m. 1st Eva Kronenberg 1942 (died 1966); one s.; m. 2nd Dr Mildred Wirtz 1969 (died 1985); one s. two d.; m. 3rd Barbara Wiese 1988; ed Reform-Gymnasium, Solingen; served German Air Force, World War II; fmr head of market research org.; mem. Landtag North Rhine-Westphalia 1950–53; mem. Bundestag 1953–74, Vice-Pres. 1967–69; Fed. Minister for Econ. Co-operation 1961–66; Chair. of Free Democrats 1968–74 (Hon. Chair. 1979); Vice-Chancellor, Minister of Foreign Affairs 1969–74; Pres. FRG 1974–79; mem. European Parl. 1958–61; Pres. Bilderberg Conf. –1985; Chair. German Council of European Movt 1980–85; Chair. Bd of Trustees, Friedrich Naumann Foundation 1979–90; Chair. Admin. Council, Germanic Nat. Museum, Nuremberg 1978, Cttee European Music Year 1983–86, Supervisory Bd, DEG-German Investment and Devt Co. 1980–, Directory for Thoroughbreds and Races 1981; Pres. Europa-Union Deutschland 1980–89; mem. Supervisory Bd ROBECO Group 1982–89, Supervisory Bd Thyssen AG 1980–, Supervisory Bd Thyssen Stahl AG 1983–; Hon. Pres. German Fed. of Artists; Hon. Pres. 4th Choir Olympics, Xiamen, People's Repub. of China 2006; Grosses Bundesverdienstkreuz (special class); numerous hon. degrees and awards from Germany and abroad; Theodor Heuss Prize 1971, Peace Prize (Kajima Inst., Tokyo) 1973, Gold Medal, Fondation du Mérite Européen 1984,. *Publications:* Konturen einer neuen Welt 1965, Schwierigkeiten, Ernüchterung und Chancen der Industrieländer 1965, Formeln deutscher Politik 1968, Warum Mitbestimmung und wie 1970, Die Freiburger Thesen der Liberalen (with K.-H. Flach and W. Maihofer) 1972, Bundestagreden 1972, Reden und Interviews 1974–79, Vom Recht des anderen – Gedanken zur Freiheit 1977, Die Zukunft der Freiheit 1979, Nach 30 Jahren; Die Bundesrepublik Deutschland, Vergangenheit, Gegenwart, Zukunft 1979, Die andere deutsche Frage 1981, Wen Schmerzt noch Deutschlands Teilung? 1986. *Leisure interest:* modern art. *Address:* Flemingstrasse 107, 81925 Munich, Germany.

SCHEELE, Sir Nicholas Vernon, Kt, KCMG, BA; British business executive; *Director, British American Tobacco plc;* b. 3 Feb. 1944, Essex; s. of Werner James Scheele and Norah Edith Scheele (née Gough); m. Rosamund Ann Jacobs 1967; two s. one d.; ed Durham Univ.; with Purchasing, Supply, Procurement, Ford of Britain 1966–78; Purchasing, Supply, Procurement Man., Ford of USA 1978–83, Dir Supply Policy and Planning 1983–85, Dir Body and Chassis Parts Purchasing 1985–88; Pres. Ford of Mexico 1988–91; mem. Supervisory Bd Ford Werke AG 1999–2001, Vice-Chair. Jaguar Cars Jan.–April 1992, Chair. and CEO 1992–99, Chair. Ford of Europe –2001, Vice-Pres. for N America, Ford Motor Co. Dearborn, Mich. 2001, COO and Pres. 2001–04, Pres. and Dir responsible for product planning, information tech. and global purchasing 2004; Chair. Prince of Wales Business and Environment Cttee 1999–2006, Mfg Theme Group, Foresight 2020 1999–2002; Chancellor Univ. of Warwick 2002–08; Dir Grupo Proeza, Mexico 2005–, Pegasus Group, USA 2006–; Chair. CMI 2005–08; mem. of Council Midlands Region Inst. of Dirs 1994–99, Exec. Cttee Soc. of Motor Mfrs and Traders, Bd of Dirs British American Tobacco plc 2005–, Advisory Bd British American Chamber of Commerce 1995–99, Fulbright Comm., Univ. of Coventry 1995–, Univ. of Durham 1996–; six hon. doctorates. *Leisure interests:* reading, classical music, tennis, squash. *Address:* c/o Board of Directors, British American Tobacco plc, Globe House, 4 Temple Place, London, WC2R 2PG, England (office).

SCHEEPBOUWER, Adrianus (Ad) Johannes; Dutch telecommunications industry executive; *Chairman of the Board of Management and CEO, Royal KPN;* b. 22 July 1944, Dordrecht; Pres. Air Freight Div. Pakhoed Holding NV (later Pandair Group) 1976–88; Man. Dir PTT Post 1988–98; mem. Bd of Man. Royal KPN NV (fmr holding co. of PTT Post and PTT Telecom) 1992–98, Chair. and CEO TPG 1998–2001, Chair. Bd of Man. and CEO Royal KPN 2001–; Chair. Supervisory Bd Havenbedrijf Rotterdam NV, Supervisory Council of

Maasstad Hosp.; mem. Supervisory Bd Welzorg Group, RFS Holland Holding BV (Wehkamp), Advisory Bd ECP.NL, Rotterdam School of Man.; Chair. Econ. Advisory Council for City of Dordrecht, Audit Cttee 'Sleutelgebieden' of the Innovationplatform; mem. Bd of Foundation for the support of Dutch Bach Asscn, Supervisory Council of Foundation for Nat. Art Collection; Amb. 'Randstad Urgent' (Project International City The Hague). *Address:* Royal KPN, Maanplein 55, 2516 CK The Hague, Netherlands (office). *Telephone:* (70) 451-01-00 (office). *Fax:* (70) 451-01-01 (office). *E-mail:* ad.scheepbouwer@kpn.com (office). *Website:* www.kpn.com (office).

SCHEER, François, DèsSc; French diplomatist (retd); b. 13 March 1934, Strasbourg; s. of Alfred Scheer and Edmée Lechten; m. 2nd Nicole Roubaud 1985; one s. one d.; one s. three d. from 1st m.; ed Faculty of Law, Univ. of Paris, Inst. d'Etudes Politiques de Paris, Ecole Nat. d'Admin; Second Sec. Embassy, Algiers 1962–64; Direction des Affaires Economiques et Financières, Admin Cen. 1964–67; Cultural Attaché Embassy, Tokyo 1967–71; Deputy Dir for Budget 1971, also for Financial Affairs 1972–76; Amb. to Mozambique and Swaziland 1976–77; Deputy Perm. Rep. to European Community 1977–79, Dir of Cabinet to Pres. of European Parl. 1979–81; Dir of Cabinet of Minister of Foreign Affairs 1981–84; Amb. to Algeria 1984–86; Amb. Perm. Rep. for France to EC (now EU) 1986–88, 1992–93; Sec.-Gen. Ministry of Foreign Affairs 1988–92; Amb. to FRG 1993–99; mem. Cttee for Atomic Energy 1988–92; Admin. Cie générale des matières nucléaires (Cogema) 1989–93; mem. Conseil d'Admin. Ecole Nat. d'Admin. 1991–95; adviser, Pres. of Cogema 1999–2001, Pres. Exec. Bd of Areva 2001–; Commdr, Légion d'honneur, Ordre nat. du Mérite. *Address:* 33 rue La Fayette, 75442 Paris Cedex 09 (office); 35 rue Broca, 75005 Paris, France (home). *Telephone:* 1-34-96-12-00 (office); 1-45-81-35-84 (home). *Fax:* 1-34-96-16-12 (office); 1-45-81-35-84 (home). *E-mail:* francois.scheer@areva.com (office); francois.scheer@club-internet.fr (home).

SCHEFFLER, Israel, PhD; American philosopher and academic; *Scholar-in-Residence, Mandel Center, Brandeis University;* b. 25 Nov. 1923, New York; s. of Leon Scheffler and Ethel Grünberg Scheffler; m. Rosalind Zuckerbrod 1949; one s. one d.; ed Brooklyn Coll., Jewish Theological Seminary and Univ. of Pennsylvania; mem. faculty, Harvard Univ. 1952–, Prof. of Educ. 1961–62, Prof. of Educ. and Philosophy 1962–64, Victor S. Thomas Prof. of Educ. and Philosophy 1964–92, Prof. Emer. 1992–, Hon. Research Fellow in Cognitive Studies 1965–66, Co-Dir Philosophy of Educ. Research Center 1983–, Dir 1999–; Scholar-in-Residence, Mandel Center, Brandeis Univ., MA 2003–; Founding mem. Nat. Acad. of Educ. 1965; Fellow, Center for Advanced Study in Behavioral Sciences, Palo Alto, Calif. 1972–73; fmr Pres. Philosophy of Science Asscn, Charles S. Peirce Soc.; Fellow, American Acad. of Arts and Sciences; Hon. AM (Harvard Univ.) 1959; Hon. DHL (Jewish Theological Seminary) 1993; Guggenheim Fellow 1958–59, 1972–73, Mead-Swing Lecturer, Oberlin Coll. 1965, Alumni Award of Merit, Brooklyn Coll. 1967, Distinguished Service Medal, Teacher's Coll., Columbia 1980, Patten Foundation Lecturer, Indiana Univ. 1981. *Publications:* Philosophy and Education 1958, The Language of Education 1960, The Anatomy of Inquiry 1963, Conditions of Knowledge 1965, Science and Subjectivity 1967, Logic and Art (co-ed.) 1972, Reason and Teaching 1973, Four Pragmatists 1974, Beyond the Letter 1979, Of Human Potential 1985, Inquiries 1986, In Praise of the Cognitive Emotions 1991, Work, Education and Leadership (co-author) 1995, Teachers of My Youth 1995, Symbolic Worlds 1997, Visions of Jewish Education (co-ed.) 2003, Gallery of Scholars 2004, Worlds of Truth 2009. *Leisure interests:* reading, crosswords, travel. *Address:* Mandel Center, Brandeis University, Waltham, MA 02454-9110, USA (office). *Telephone:* (781) 736-4998 (office). *E-mail:* israel_scheffler@harvard.edu (office).

SCHEFFLER, Matthias Robert, Dr rer. nat; German physicist and academic; *Director, Theory Department, Fritz Haber Institute;* b. 1951, Berlin; ed Technische Universität Berlin; Scientific Staff mem., Physikalisch-Technische Bundesanstalt, Braunschweig 1978–88; Researcher, IBM T.J. Watson Research Center, Yorktown Heights, NY, USA 1979–80; Researcher, Max-Planck-Inst., Stuttgart 1982; Dir, Theory Dept, Fritz Haber Inst., Berlin 1988–; Visiting Scientist, Instituto de Fisica, Universidade de Sao Paulo, Brazil 1995; Visiting Scientist, Kavli Inst. for Theoretical Physics, Univ. of Calif., Santa Barbara, USA 2002; Hon. Prof., Technische Universität Berlin 1989–, Freie Universitat Berlin 2001–, Visiting Prof., Dalian Inst. of Chem. Physics, Chinese Acad. of Sciences 2004–, Distinguished Visiting Prof., Univ. of California, Santa Barbara 2004–; Dr hc; Max-Planck Research Award for Int. Co-operation 2001, American Vacuum Soc. Medard W. Welch Medal and Prize 2003, Max Born Medal and Prize 2004. *Publications:* 391 articles in scientific journals; Walter Kohn: Personal Stories and Anecdotes Told by Friends and Collaborators (co-ed.) 2003. *Address:* Fritz-Haber-Institut der Max-Planck-Gesellschaft, Faradayweg 4-6, 14195 Berlin-Dahlem, Germany (office). *Telephone:* (30) 8413-4711 (office). *Fax:* (30) 8413-4701 (office). *E-mail:* scheffler@FHI-Berlin.MPG.de (office). *Website:* (office).

SCHEIBE, Erhard A. K., Dr rer. nat; German professor of philosophy (retd); b. 24 Sept. 1927, Berlin; s. of Albert Scheibe and Maria (née Heidenreich) Scheibe; m. Maria Elgert-Eggers 1958; two s. one d.; ed Berlin and Singen High Schools, Univ. of Göttingen; Asst, Max Planck Inst. of Physics, Göttingen 1956–57; Asst and Lecturer, Univ. of Hamburg 1957–64; Prof. of Philosophy, Univ. of Göttingen 1964–83, Univ. of Heidelberg 1983–92; mem. Acad. of Sciences, Göttingen, Acad. of Sciences and Literature, Mainz, Int. Acad. of Philosophy of Science, Brussels; Ehrenmitglied der Allgemeinen Gesellschaft für Analytische Philosophie 2004. *Publications:* Die kontingenten Aussagen in der Physik 1964, The Logical Analysis of Quantum Mechanics 1973, Die Reduktion physikalischer Theorien (Vol. 1) 1997, (Vol. 2) 1999, Between Rationalism and Empiricism – Selected Papers in the Philosophy of Physics (ed. by B. Falkenburg) 2001, Die Philosophie der Physiker 2006. *Leisure interests:* music, art, literature. *Address:* Moorbirkenkamp 2A, 22391 Hamburg, Germany (home). *Telephone:* (40) 5368107 (home).

SCHEID, HE Cardinal Eusébio Oscar, SCI, DTheol; Brazilian ecclesiastic; *Archbishop of Saõ Sebastião do Rio de Janeiro;* b. 8 Dec. 1932, Bom Retiro, Joaçaba; s. of Alberto Reinaldo Scheid and Rosalia Joana Scheid; ed Congregation of Priests of Sacred Heart of Jesus (Dehonian Fathers') Seminary, Seminary of Priests of Heart of Jesus, Corupa, Pontifical Gregorian Univ., Rome, Italy; ordained priest 1960; Prof. of Theology, Christ the King Seminary and Northeast Regional Seminary, Recife 1964–65 Prof. of Dogma and Liturgy, Theological Inst. of Taubate 1965–81; Prof. of Religious Culture, Pontifical Catholic Univ. of São Paulo 1966–68; Coordinator of Catechesis, Taubate 1970–74; Dir Faculty of Theology, Taubate; Bishop of São José dos Campos 1981–91; Archbishop of Florianópolis 1991–2001; attended Fourth Gen. Conf. of Latin American Episcopate, Santo Domingo, Dominican Repub. 1992, Ninth Ordinary Ass. of World Synod of Bishops, Vatican City 1994, Tenth Ordinary Ass. 2001; Archbishop of Saõ Sebastião do Rio de Janeiro and Bishop of Brazil, Faithful of the Oriental Rites 2001–; cr. Cardinal (Cardinal Priest of SS Bonifacio ed Alessio) 2003; Pres. South Region IV of Brazilian Bishops' Conf., currently Counsellor, Pontifical Comm. for Latin America. *Address:* Archdiocese of São Sebastião do Rio de Janeiro, Rua Benjamin Constant 23/502, Gloria, C.P. 1362, 20241-150 Rio de Janeiro, RJ, Brazil (office). *Telephone:* (21) 292-3132 (office). *Fax:* (21) 242-9295 (office). *Website:* www.arquidiocese.org.br (office).

SCHEIFF, Dieter Christian, BA; German business executive; *CEO, Adecco SA;* b. 1952; m.; three c.; ed Univ. of Applied Sciences (Fachhochschule) Aachen; held various sales and marketing roles at 3M 1987–98; joined Johnson and Johnson Cordis 1998, becoming Vice-Pres. for Europe 2001; Head of Sales and Marketing, DIS Deutscher Industrie Service AG 2001–02, CEO 2002–06, CEO Adecco Group SA (following acquisition of DIS by Adecco) 2006–. *Address:* Adecco SA, Sägereistrasse 10, PO Box, 8152 Glattbrugg, Switzerland (office). *Telephone:* (44) 878-8888 (office). *Fax:* (44) 829-8888 (office). *E-mail:* info@adecco.com (office). *Website:* www.adecco.com (office).

SCHEKMAN, Randy W., PhD; American biologist and academic; *Professor of Cell and Developmental Biology, University of California, Berkeley;* b. 30 Dec. 1948, St Paul, Minn.; ed Univ. of California, Los Angeles and Stanford Univ. School of Medicine, Calif.; Cystic Fibrosis Postdoctoral Fellow, Biology Dept, Univ. of California, San Diego, La Jolla 1974–76; Asst Prof., then Assoc. Prof., then Prof., Dept of Biochemistry, Univ. of California, Berkeley 1976–89, Prof. of Cell and Developmental Biology, Dept of Molecular and Cell Biology 1989–, Head, Div. of Biochemistry and Molecular Biology 1990–94, Investigator, Howard Hughes Medical Inst. 1990–, Co-Chair. Dept of Molecular and Cell Biology 1997–2000; Chair. FASEB Conf. on Protein Folding in the Cell 1992, Gordon Conf. on Molecular Membrane Biology 1997; mem. Bd of Scientific Advisors, Jane Coffin Childs Memorial Fund for Medical Research 1992–2000, Scientific Dir 2002–; mem. Eli Lilly Award Cttee 1988–90, Chair. 1990; mem. Advisory Cttee, Pew Scholars Program 1996–2002; Assoc. Ed. Molecular Cell Biology 1988–91, Molecular Biology of the Cell 1992–99 (Ed. 1999–), Annual Reviews of Cell and Developmental Biology 1993–98, Journal of Cell Biology (later Ed.) 1993–; mem. Editorial Bd Journal of Cell Biology 1985–92, Journal of Membrane Biology 1986, Biochemistry 1986–93, Cell 2001–; mem. NAS (Chair. Biochemistry Section 2002–) 1992, Ed.-in-Chief Proceedings of NAS 2007–; mem. NIH Cell Biology (Study Section), American Soc. for Microbiology, American Acad. for Microbiology, American Soc. for Biochemistry and Molecular Biology, American Soc. for Cell Biology (Council mem. 1991–94); Foreign Assoc. European Molecular Biology Org. 2001; Hon. mem. Japanese Biochemical Soc. 1993; Dr hc (Geneva) 1997; Undergraduate Research Award, UCLA Zoology Dept 1970, Woodrow Wilson Fellow 1970, Guggenheim Fellowship 1982–83, Lewis S. Rosenstiel Award in Basic Biomedical Science 1994, Gairdner Foundation International Award 1996, Amgen Award Lecturer Protein Society 1999, Berkeley Faculty Research 1999, Albert Lasker Award for Basic Medical Research 2002, Louisa Gross Horwitz Prize, Columbia Univ. 2002. *Publications:* more than 200 articles in scientific journals on mechanism and control of intracellular protein transport. *Address:* Department of Molecular and Cell Biology, University of California, Berkeley, 401 Barker Hall #3202, Berkeley, CA 94720-3202, USA (office). *Telephone:* (510) 642-5686 (office). *Fax:* (510) 642-7846 (office). *E-mail:* schekman@berkeley.edu (office). *Website:* mcb.berkeley.edu/labs/schekman (office).

SCHELL, Maximilian; Swiss actor; b. 8 Dec. 1930, Vienna; s. of Hermann Ferdinand Schell and Margarete Noe von Nordberg; m. Natalya Andreichenko 1985; one d.; ed Humanistisches Gymnasium, Basel, Freies Gymnasium, Zürich and Univs of Zürich, Basel and Munich; Corporal, Swiss Army 1948–49; various appearances on stage in Switzerland and Germany 1952–55; German début in Children, Mothers and a General 1955; American film début in Young Lions 1958, on Broadway stage in Interlock 1958; Dir Volkstheater, Munich 1981–; Critics' Award (Broadway) 1958; New York Critics' Award 1961, 1978; Golden Globe Award 1961, 1974, 1993; Acad. Award 1961, 1970, 1971, 1978, 1985; Silver Award San Sebastian 1970, 1975; German Fed. Award 1971, 1979, 1980; Film Critics' Award, Chicago 1973; Golden Cup 1974; Bavarian Film Prize 1984. *Films include:* Judgment at Nuremberg 1961, Five Finger Exercise 1961, Reluctant Saint 1962, Condemned of Altona 1962, Topkapi 1964, Return from the Ashes 1965, Beyond the Mountains 1966, The Deadly Affair 1966, Counterpoint 1966, Krakatoa, East of Java 1967, The Castle 1968, First Love 1969, Pope Joan 1971, Paulina 1880 1971, The Pedestrian 1973, The Odessa File 1974, The Man in the Glass Booth 1975, Assassination 1975, Cross of Iron 1977, Julia 1977, Avalanche Express 1978, The Black Hole 1979, The Diary of Anne Frank 1980, The Chosen 1980, Les îles 1983, Phantom of the Opera 1983, Man Under Suspicion 1983, The Assisi

Underground 1984, The Rosegarden 1989, The Freshman 1990, Labyrinth 1990, A Far Off Place 1993, Little Odessa 1995, Through Roses 1996, Left Luggage 1997, Telling Lies in America 1997, Deep Impact 1997, Fisimatenten 1998, Joan of Arc 1998, I Love You, Baby 2000, Festival in Cannes 2001, Das Haus der schlafenden Schönen 2006; Producer, Dir First Love 1969, Tales from the Vienna Woods 1979, Dir and wrote screenplay End of the Game 1975. *Television includes:* Peter the Great (miniseries) 1985, Stalin 1992, Miss Rose White 1992, Liebe, Lügen, Leidenschaft (miniseries) 2002, Der Fürst und das Mädchen (series) 2003–07. *Plays include:* Hamlet, Prince of Homburg, Mannerhouse, Don Carlos, Sappho (Durrell), A Patriot for Me, The Twins of Venice, Old Times, Everyman 1978/79/80; Dir All for the Best, A Patriot for Me, Hamlet, Pygmalion, La Traviata 1975, Tales from the Vienna Woods, Nat. Theatre 1977, The Undiscovered Country, Salzburg Festival 1979/80, Der Seidene Schuh, Salzburg Festival 1985, Der Rosenkavalier (opera) 2005. *Address:* c/o Image Management, Lucile-Grahn-Strasse 48, 81675 Munich; c/o Erna Baumbauer, Keplerstrasse 2, 81679 Munich, Germany. *Telephone:* (89) 478577.

SCHEMAN, L. Ronald, BA, JD; American business executive and fmr international organization executive; *Chairman and CEO, iMalls, Inc.;* m. Lucy Duncan-Scheman; four c. by previous m.; ed Dartmouth Coll., Yale Law School; with Dept of Legal Affairs, OAS 1961–64, Dir Office of Planning 1968–70, Asst Sec. of Man. 1975–83, later Exec. Sec.; Co-founder Pan American Devt Foundation, Exec. Dir 1964–68, Chair. of Bd 1977–82; US Exec. Dir IDB 1993–98; Chair. Int. Finance Div., Greenberg Traurig (law firm) 1998–2000; Dir-Gen. Inter-American Agency for Co-operation and Devt, OAS 2000–07; currently Sr Adviser Kissinger McLarty Assocs, Washington, DC 2997; currently Co-founder, Chair. and CEO iMalls, Inc. Charleston, SC; Founding Exec. Dir Center of Advanced Studies of the Americas 1984–86; fmr Adjunct Prof. in Int. Relations, George Washington Univ. Grad. School; adviser to several govts and corpns as Pres. Porter International Co. 1970–75 and subsequently in as Sr Pnr, Heller, Rosenblatt & Scheman 1989–93; fmr mem. Bd Pan American Devt Foundation, Inter-American Bar Foundation, Inter-American Man. Educ. Foundation (also Pres.), Due Process of Law Foundation, Int. Foundation for Electoral Systems, Americas Fund for Ind. Univs (IESA), Charles E. Smith & Cos, Big Brothers; Pres. Fund for Democracy & Development 1990–93; fmr Pres. Washington Foreign Law Soc.; fmr Vice-Pres. American Foreign Law Asscn. *Publications include:* Foundations of Freedom (co-author) 1965, The Inter-American Dilemma 1988, The Alliance for Progress in Retrospect 1989, Greater America: A New Partnership for the Americas in the Twenty-first Century 2003; numerous articles and editorials in int. publs. *Leisure interests:* farming, amateur vintner. *Address:* iMalls, Inc., 3 Broad Street, Suite 300, Charleston, SC 29401-3011, USA (office). *Telephone:* (843) 723-9480 (office). *Fax:* (843) 414-0799 (office). *E-mail:* info@imallsglobal.com (office). *Website:* www .imallsglobal.com (office).

SCHENKER, Joseph G., MD; Israeli physician; b. 20 Nov. 1933, Kraków, Poland; s. of the late Itzhak Schenker; m. Ekaterina Idels 1959; two s.; ed Herzlia High School, Tel-Aviv and the Hebrew Univ. of Jerusalem; Exec. Chief of Teaching Obstetrics and Gynaecology, Hebrew Univ. Medical School 1977–84; Chair. Dept of Obstetrics and Gynaecology, Hadassah Univ. Hosp., Jerusalem 1978; Prof. Obstetrics and Gynaecology, Hebrew Univ. Jerusalem 1979–; Pres. Israel Soc. of Obstetrics and Gynaecology 1984–92, Deputy Pres. and Sec. 1993–; Pres. Israel Medical Asscn, Jerusalem br. 1984–; Chair. of Directory, Bd Examination in Obstetrics and Gynaecology, State of Israel 1979–83, of Advisory Cttee 1979–86; Acting Chair. of Hadassah Org. of Heads of Depts. 1983–; Chair. Residency Programme, Medical Council 1987, of Cttee Licensing Physicians, Ministry of Health 1987; Pres. of Int. Soc. for Study of Pathophysiology 1983; Chair. European Residency Exchange Programme, Extended European Bd of Gynaecology and Obstetrics 1993– (Pres. of Bd 1994–), Cttee for European Examination for Excellence in Gynaecology and Obstetrics 1993–, FIGO (Int. Fed. of Gynaecology and Obstetrics) Cttee for Study of Ethical Aspects of Human Reproduction 1994– (mem. Exec. Bd FIGO 1991–); Pres. Int. Acad. of Human Reproduction 1996–; Deputy Pres. and Sec. Israel Medical Council 1985–, European Asscn of Gynaecology and Obstetrics; Founder mem. European Soc. of Human Reproduction, Int. Soc. of Gynaecological Endocrinology, Int. Soc. of Study of Pathophysiology of Pregnancy and other orgs; mem. exec. bds and cttees, hon. mem. or mem. numerous int. professional orgs; mem. Editorial Bd Human Reproduction (Oxford), Int. Journal of Gynaecology and Obstetrics (USA), Int. Journal of Foeto-Maternal Medicine (Germany), European Journal of Obstetrics, Gynaecology and Reproductive Biology and several other journals; Hon. Fellow American Coll. of Obstetricians and Gynaecologists, Royal Coll. of Obstetricians and Gynaecologists and other int. orgs; hon. citizen City of Jerusalem; Award for Outstanding Contribution to the Field of Human Reproduction 1999. *Publications:* Recent Advances in Pathophysiological Conditions in Pregnancy (ed.)1984, The Intrauterine Life-Management and Therapy 1986, Female and Male Infertility 1997, Pregnancy and Delivery 1998, Textbook of Gynecology 2000; more than 500 articles in medical journals on obstetrics and gynaecology, new tech. in reproduction, ethical and legal aspects of IVF etc. *Leisure interests:* history, chess. *Address:* Department of Orbital Gynaecology, Hadassah Medical Center, PO Box 12000, Jerusalem 91120 (office); 5 Mendele Street, Jerusalem 91147, Israel (home). *Telephone:* 2-6777779 (office); 2-637775 (home). *Fax:* 2-6432445. *E-mail:* schenker@cc.huji.ac.il (office).

SCHEPISI, Frederic Alan; Australian film writer, director and producer; b. 1939, Melbourne; s. of Frederic Thomas Schepisi and Loretto Ellen Schepisi (née Hare); m. 1st Joan Mary Ford 1960; two s. two d.; m. 2nd Rhonda Elizabeth Finlayson 1973 (divorced 1983); two d.; m. 3rd Mary Rubin 1984; one s.; ed Assumption Coll., Kilmore, Victoria, Marist Brothers' Juniorate, Macedon, Victoria, Marcellin Coll., Melbourne; Carden Advertising, Mel-

bourne, Press TV Production; Paton Advisory Service, Melbourne 1961–64; Victorian Man. Cinesound Productions, Melbourne 1964–66; Man. Dir, The Film House, Melbourne 1966–79, Chair. 1979–92; Chauvel Award 1994, Officer Order of Australia 2004. *Films include:* A Devil's Playground (also screenplay) 1975, The Chant of Jimmie Blacksmith 1978, Barbarosa 1981, Iceman 1983, Plenty 1985, Roxanne 1986, Evil Angels (Australian Film Inst. Award for Best Film 1989) (also known as A Cry in the Dark (Longford Award 1991)) 1990, The Russia House 1990, Mr. Baseball 1991, Six Degrees of Separation 1993, IQ 1994, Fierce Creatures 1997, That Eye the Sky (exec. producer), Last Orders (also screenplay) 2001, It Runs in the Family 2002. *Television includes:* Empire Falls 2005. *Leisure interests:* tennis, swimming. *Address:* PO Box 743, South Yarra, Vic. 3141, Australia.

SCHERAGA, Harold A., PhD; American scientist and academic; *George W. and Grace L. Todd Professor Emeritus, Department of Chemistry and Chemical Biology, Cornell University;* b. 18 Oct. 1921, Brooklyn, New York; s. of Samuel Scheraga and Etta Scheraga; m. Miriam Kurnow 1943; one s. two d.; ed City Coll. of New York and Duke Univ.; ACS Postdoctoral Fellow Harvard Medical School 1946–47; Instructor of Chem. Cornell Univ. 1947–50, Asst Prof. 1950–53, Assoc. Prof. 1953–58, Prof. 1958–92, Todd Prof. 1965–92, Todd Prof. Emer. 1992–; Chair. Chem. Dept 1960–67; Guggenheim Fellow and Fulbright Research Scholar Carlsberg Lab., Copenhagen 1956–57, Weizmann Inst., Rehovoth, Israel 1963; NIH Special Fellow Weizman Inst., Rehovoth, Israel 1970; Visiting Lecturer, Wool Research Labs, CSIRO, Australia 1959; Visiting Prof. Weizmann Inst., Rehovoth, Israel 1972–78, Japan Soc. for the Promotion of Science 1977; Regional Dir. Nat. Foundation for Cancer Research 1982–; mem. NAS, American Acad. of Arts and Sciences; Vice-Chair. Cornell Section ACS 1954–55, Chair. 1955–56, Councillor 1959–62; mem. Advisory Panel in Molecular Biology NSF 1960–62; mem. editorial bd numerous scientific journals; mem. Biochemical Training Cttee, NIH 1963–65, Fogarty Scholar 1984, 1986, 1988, 1989, 1990, 1991; mem. Comm. on Molecular Biophysics Int. Union for Pure and Applied Biophysics 1967–69; mem. Comm. on Macromolecular Biophysics, Int. Union for Pure and Applied Biophysics 1969–75, Pres. 1972–75; mem. Comm. on Subcellular and Macromolecular Biophysics, Int. Union for Pure and Applied Biophysics 1975–81; mem. Exec. Comm. Div. of Biological Chem. ACS 1966–69; Vice-Chair. Div. of Biological Chem. ACS 1970, Chair. 1971; mem. Council Biophysical Soc. 1967–70; mem. Research Career Award Cttee NIH 1967–71; mem. Bd Govs Weizmann Inst., Rehovoth, Israel 1970–97; Fellow, Biophysical Soc. 1999; Hon. life Mem. New York Acad. of Sciences 1985; Hon. Mem. Hungarian Biophysical Soc. 1989; Hon. ScD (Duke Univ.) 1961, (Univ. of Rochester) 1988, (Univ. of San Luis) 1992, (Technion) 1993, (Univ. of Gdansk) 2006; ACS Eli Lilly Award in Bio chem. 1957, Welch Foundation Lecturer 1962, Harvey Lecturer 1968, Gallagher Lecturer 1968–69, Townsend Harris Medal, CCNY 1970, Lemieux Lecturer 1973, Nichols Medal, NY Section, ACS 1974, Hill Lecturer 1976, City Coll. Chem. Alumni Scientific Achievement Award Medal 1977, ACS Kendall Award in Colloid Chem. 1978, Venable Lecturer 1981, Linderstrøm-Lang Medal 1983, Kowalski Medal 1983, Pauling Medal, ACS 1985, Mobil Award, ACS 1990, Repligen Award, ACS 1990, Stein and Moore Award, Protein Soc. 1995, ACS Award for Computers in Chemical and Pharmaceutical Research 1997, Hirschmann Award in Peptide Chem., ACS 1999, Ramachandran Lecturer 2002. *Publications:* Protein Structure 1961, Theory of Helix-Coil Transitions in Biopolymers 1970; more than 1,200 articles in profession journals on the physical chem. of proteins and other macromolecules, structure of water, and the chem. of blood clotting and growth factors. *Leisure interest:* golf. *Address:* 212 Homestead Terrace, Ithaca, NY 14850 (home); Department of Chemistry and Chemical Biology, 660A Baker Laboratory, Ithaca, NY 14853-1301, USA (office). *Telephone:* (607) 272-5155 (home); (607) 255-4034 (office). *Fax:* (607) 254-4700 (office). *E-mail:* has5@cornell.edu (office). *Website:* www.chem.cornell.edu (office).

SCHERBAK, Yuri, MD, PhD, DSc; Ukrainian diplomatist, politician, environmentalist and academic; b. 12 Oct. 1934, Kiev; m. Maria Scherbak; two c.; ed Kiev Medical Inst.; worked as social and political publicist in Ukrainian and Soviet media 1988–91; began active political career 1989, won seat in USSR Supreme Soviet, Chair. Sub-cttee on Energy and Nuclear Safety; f. Ukrainian Green Movt, Leader Zeleny Svit (Green World) 1988, Leader Green Party of Ukraine 1990; apptd Minister of Environmental Protection 1991; Amb. to Israel 1992–94, to USA 1994–98 (also accred to Mexico 1997), to Canada 2000–03; Foreign Policy Adviser to Pres. of Ukraine 1998–2000; Int. Affairs Adviser to Volodymyr Lytvyn, Speaker of the Verkhovna Rada (Parl.) –2006; currently Prof., Vernadsky Inst. for Sustainable Devt; mem. Nat. Security and Defence Council 1991; mem. Acad. of Ecological Sciences of Ukraine, Writers' Union of Ukraine (mem. Bd 1987–89), Cinematographers' Union of Ukraine; Hon. mem. Scientific Studies Inst., Harvard Univ., USA; Yuri Yanovski Literary Prize 1984, Olexander Dovzhenko Prize in Cinematography 1985. *Publications include:* Chornobyl (eye-witness account) 1986, The Strategic Role of Ukraine 1998, Ukarine: Challenge and Choice 2004; 20 books of poetry, prose, plays and essays; over 200 publs on epidemiology, theoretical issues in medicine and ecology. *Address:* c/o Vernadsky Foundation, 119019 Moscow, Gogolevsky blvd 17, office 517, Russia (office). *Telephone:* (495) 697-1662 (office). *Fax:* (495) 690-4792 (office). *E-mail:* info@vernadsky.ru (home). *Website:* www.vernadsky.ru (office).

SCHERER, Frederic M., MA, MBA, PhD; American professor of economics; *Aetna Professor Emeritus of Public Policy and Corporation Management, John F. Kennedy School of Government, Harvard University;* b. 1 Aug. 1932, Ottawa, Ill.; s. of Walter K. Scherer and Margaret Lucey Scherer; m. Barbara Silbermann 1957; one s. two d.; ed Univ. of Michigan, Harvard Univ., Hohenheim Univ.; served in US Army Counter-Intelligence Corps 1954–56; research asst. then assoc. Harvard Business School 1958–63; mem. staff, Princeton Univ. 1963–66, Univ. of Mich. 1966–72, Int. Inst. of Man. 1972–74,

Northwestern Univ. 1976–82, Swarthmore Coll. 1982–89; Chief Economist, US Fed. Trade Comm. 1974–76; Aetna Prof. of Public Policy and Corp. Man., John F. Kennedy School of Govt, Harvard Univ. 1989–2000, Prof. Emer. 2000–; Ludwig Erhard Visiting Prof., Univ. of Bayreuth 2000; Lecturer, Woodrow Wilson School of Public and Int. Affairs, Princeton Univ. 2000–05; Visiting Prof., Haverford Coll., Pa 2004–06; Co-Founder European Asscn for Research in Industrial Econs; pioneering work on theory of research and devt strategy and timing; Lanchester Prize, Operations Research Soc. of America 1964, O'Melveny & Myers Centennial Research Prize 1989, Distinguished Fellow, Industrial Org. Soc. 1999, Lifetime Achievement Award, American Antitrust Inst. 2002. *Publications:* The Weapons Acquisition Process: Economic Incentives 1964, Industrial Market Structure and Economic Performance 1970, Innovation and Growth: Schumpeterian Perspectives 1984, Industry Structure, Strategy and Public Policy 1996, Quarter Notes and Bank Notes: The Economics of Music Composition in the 18th and 19th Centuries 2004. *Leisure interest:* 17th–19th century music. *Address:* 601 Rockbourne Mills Court, Wallingford, PA 19086, USA (home). *Telephone:* (610) 872-2557 (office); (610) 872-2557 (home). *Fax:* (610) 872-2557. *E-mail:* fmscherer@comcast.net (office).

SCHERER, HE Cardinal Odilo Pedro; Brazilian ecclesiastic; *Archbishop of São Paulo;* b. 21 Sept. 1949, São Francisco; born to parents of German descent; ed Pontifical Brazilian Coll., Pontifical Gregorian Univ.; ordained priest in Toledo, Paraná 1976; served as pastor in Diocese of Toledo, taught at and served as rector of several seminaries and religious insts in southern Brazil; worked as official of Vatican's Congregation for Bishops 1994–2001; Auxiliary Bishop of São Paulo and Titular Bishop of Novi 2001–02; Sec.-Gen. Brazilian Bishops' Conf. 2003–; Archbishop of São Paulo 2007–; cr. Cardinal 2007, apptd Cardinal-Priest of S. Andrea al Quirinale; named one of two Secs Fifth Gen. Conf. of Bishops of Latin America and the Caribbean, Brazil 2007. *Address:* Archdiocese of São Paulo, Avenida Higienopolis 890, 01238-908 São Paulo, SP (office); CP 1670, 01064-970 São Paulo, SP, Brazil. *Telephone:* (11) 826-0133 (office). *Fax:* (11) 825-6806 (office). *E-mail:* info@arquidiocesedesaopaulo.org.br (office). *Website:* www.arquidiocesedesaopaulo.org.br (office).

SCHERER, Peter Julian; New Zealand journalist; b. 15 Aug. 1937, Stratford; s. of Arnold F. Scherer and Constance M. White; m. Gaelyn P. Morgan 1964; one s. one d.; ed Browns Bay School and Takapuna Grammar School; joined New Zealand Herald 1955; mem. later Chief, Wellington Bureau 1960–71; Chair. Parl. Press Gallery 1965; leader-writer, Duty Ed., Business News Ed. 1973–76, Editorial Man. 1977–83, Asst Ed. 1977–85; Ed. New Zealand Herald 1985–96; Dir Community Newspapers Ltd 1972–73, Wilson & Horton Group 1989–96, NZ Press Asscn 1991–96; Chair. NZ Associated Press 1985–90, NZ section, Commonwealth Press Union (CPU) 1989–94; Chair. Planning Cttee, North Health Medical Workforce 1996–97; Councillor, CPU, London 1989–94; mem. NZ Press Council 1988–97, Communications and Media Law Asscn 1990–97; mem. Communications Advisory Council NZ Comm. for UNESCO 1989–94; mem. Bd of Control, Newspaper Publishers Asscn of NZ 1991–96; mem. NZ Nat. Cttee for Security Co-operation in Asia-Pacific 1994–96, NZ Div., Inst. of Dirs 1989–96; other professional appointments; CPU Fellowship 1963; Cowan Prize 1959. *Leisure interests:* reading, tennis, gardening, fishing, golf. *Address:* Apartment C, 25 Ring Terrace, St Mary's Bay, Auckland 1001 (home); 267 School Road, Tomarata, RD4 Wellsford 1242, New Zealand (home). *Telephone:* (9) 378-9184 (Auckland) (home); (9) 431-5244 (Wellsford) (home). *Fax:* (9) 431-5244 (Wellsford) (home); (9) 378-9184 (Auckland) (home). *E-mail:* gandpscherer@xtra.co.nz (home).

SCHERPENHUIJSEN ROM, Willem; Dutch business executive; b. 1933, Utrecht; ed Univ. of Amsterdam; Chair. NMB Postbank 1976–92; Chair. Int. Nederlande (formed by merger of NMB Postbank and Internationale Nederlande Groep in 1991) 1992; mem. and Treas. (for Europe) Trilateral Comm.; Founding mem. and Deputy Chair. Institut für Sozialforschung MAITRI e.V; mem. Anthroposophical Soc. 1992–; mem. Advisory Bd Arleen Auger Memorial Fund. *Address:* c/o Institut für Sozialforschung MAITRI e.V., Bruckwiesenweg 5, 73635 Rudersberg, Germany (office).

SCHERRER, Anton, BSc; Swiss business executive; *Chairman, Swisscom AG;* b. 1942; ed Swiss Inst. of Tech. (ETH); headed biological research lab. and experimental brewery at Swiss brewing industry trial facility 1970–73; Plant Man. and Deputy Man. Eglisau (mineral spring) and Deputy Head Tech. Dept Unifontes Group 1973–76; held several man. positions at Brauerei Hürlimann 1977–91, including Deputy Man. and Master Brewer 1977–82, Chief Tech. Officer 1983, Chair. Exec. Bd 1984–89, Del. Bd of Dirs Hürlimann Holding AG 1990–91; fmr Chair. Retail Trade Cttee Migros Cooperative Association, Chair. Admin. Del. 2001–03, Chair. Exec. Bd Migrosbank 2003–05; Vice Chair. Swisscom AG 2005–06, Chair. 2006–; mem. Managerial Cttee Inst. for Marketing and Trade, Univ. of St Gallen. *Address:* Swisscom AG, Alte Tiefenaustrasse 6, 3050 Bern, Switzerland (office). *Telephone:* (31) 3421111 (office). *Fax:* (31) 3426411 (office). *Website:* www.swisscom.ch (office).

SCHETYNA, Grzegorz; Polish politician; *Deputy Prime Minister and Minister of the Interior and Administration;* b. 18 Feb. 1963, Opole; ed Wrocław Univ.; fmr mem. Solidarność Walcząca (Fighting Solidarity); Chair. Ind. Students' Union (Niezależne Zrzeszenie Studentów, NZS), Wrocław Univ. 1986–89, later mem. Presidium NZS Nat. Co-ordinating Cttee; Dir Voivodship Office, Wrocław 1990, Deputy Voivod 1991–92; Chair. Liberal and Democratic Congress (Kongres Liberalno-Demokratyczny), Wrocław 1991, later becoming Sec.-Gen.; mem. Freedom Union (Unia Wolności) 1994–2001; Co-founder Civic Platform (Platforma Obywatelska) 2001; mem. Sejm (Parl.) for Legnica 1997–; Deputy Prime Minister and Minister of the Interior and Admin 2007–; launched Radio Eska, Wrocław 1993. *Leisure interest:* basketball. *Address:*

Ministry of the Interior and Administration, ul. Stefana Batorego 5, 02–591 Warsaw, Poland (office). *Telephone:* (22) 6014427 (office). *Fax:* (22) 6227973 (office). *E-mail:* wp@mswia.gov.pl (office). *Website:* www.mswia.gov.pl (office).

SCHICKEL, Richard, BS; American writer, film critic and film producer; *President, Lorac Productions Inc.;* b. 10 Feb. 1933, Milwaukee; s. of Edward J. Schickel and Helen (née Hendricks) Schickel; two d.; ed Univ. of Wisconsin; Ed. Look Magazine 1957–60, Show Magazine 1960–63; self-employed 1963–; Film Critic, Life Magazine 1965–72, Time Magazine 1973–; Pres. Lorac Productions Inc. 1986–; Consultant, Rockefeller Foundation 1965; Lecturer in History of Art, Yale Univ. 1972, 1976; Guggenheim Fellow 1964; mem. Nat. Soc. of Film Critics, New York Film Critics. *Publications:* The World of Carnegie Hall 1960, The Stars 1962, Movies: The History of an Art and an Institution 1964, The Gentle Knight 1964, The Disney Version 1968, The World of Goya 1968, Second Sight: Notes on Some Movies 1972, His Pictures in the Papers 1974, Harold Lloyd: The Shape of Laughter 1974, The Men Who Made the Movies 1975, The World of Tennis 1975, The Fairbanks Album 1975, Another I, Another You 1978, Singled Out 1981, Cary Grant: A Celebration 1984, D.W. Griffith: An American Life 1984, Intimate Strangers: The Culture of Celebrity 1985, James Cagney, A Celebration 1985, Striking Poses 1987, Schickel on Film 1989, Brando: A Life in Our Times 1991, Double Indemnity 1992, Bogie: A Celebration of Humphrey Bogart (with George Perry) 2006, You Must Remember This: The Warner Bros. Story (with George Perry) 2008; Co-Ed. Film 1967–68; Producer, Dir, Writer: (TV Specials) The Man Who Made the Movies 1973, Funny Business 1978, Into the Morning: Willa Cather's America 1978, The Horror Show 1979, James Cagney: That Yankee Doodle Dandy 1981, From Star Wars to Jedi: The Making of a Saga 1983, Minnelli on Minnelli: Liza Remembers Vincent 1987, Gary Cooper: American Life, American Legend 1989, Myrna Loy: So Nice to Come Home To 1990, Barbara Stanwyck: Fire and Desire 1991, Eastwood & Co: Making Unforgiven 1992, Hollywood on Hollywood 1993, Elia Kazan: A Director's Journey 1995, Clint Eastwood: A Biography 1996, The Moviemakers 1996, Eastwood on Eastwood 1997, The Harryhausen Chronicles 1998, Matinee Idols: Reflections on the Movies 1999; Producer, Writer: TV Life Goes to the Movies 1976, SPFX 1980, Cary Grant, A Celebration 1989. *Address:* Lorac Productions Inc, 1551 South Robertson Blvd, #206, Los Angeles, CA 90035, USA (office). *Telephone:* (310) 286-7234 (office). *Fax:* (310) 286-7236 (office). *E-mail:* rs@lorac.tv (office). *Website:* www.lorac.tv (office).

SCHIEFFER, Robert (Bob), BA; American broadcast journalist; b. Austin, Tex.; m. Patricia Penrose; two d.; ed Texas Christian Univ.; reporter, Fort Worth Star-Telegram; news anchor, WBAP-TV, Dallas; began work at CBS News 1969, Pentagon Corresp. 1970–74, White House Corresp. 1974–79, Chief Washington Corresp. 1982–, anchor, CBS Sunday Nightly News 1973–74, Sunday ed. CBS Evening News, then Sun. Ed. 1976, anchor Saturday ed. CBS Evening News 1976–96, co-anchor, CBS Morning News 1985, anchor and moderator Face the Nation, CBS News 1991–, interim anchor CBS Evening News 2005–06, currently weekly commentator and political analyst; participant numerous CBS special reports including Peace and the Pentagon 1974, Watergate: The White House Transcripts 1974, Mysterious Alert 1974, Ground Zero 1981; six Emmy Awards and two Sigma Delta Chi Awards, Broadcaster of the Year by Nat. Press Foundation 2002, Paul White Award from Radio-TV News Dirs Asscn 2003, Int. Radio and TV Soc. Foundation Award 2004, American News Women's Club Helen Thomas Award for Excellence in Journalism 2004, and numerous other awards. *Publications:* The Acting President (with Gary P. Gates) 1989, This Just In: What I Couldn't Tell You On TV 2003. *Address:* Face the Nation with Bob Schieffer, CBS News, 2020 M Street, NW, Washington, DC 20036, USA (office). *Telephone:* (202) 457-4481 (office). *E-mail:* ftn@cbsnews.com (office). *Website:* www.cbsnews.com (office).

SCHIEFFER, Rudolf; German historian and academic; *President, Monumenta Germaniae Historica;* b. 31 Jan. 1947, Mainz; s. of Theodor Schieffer and Annelise Schreibmayr; Research Assoc. DFG project, Spätantike Reichskonzilien 1971–75; Research Assoc. Monumenta Germaniae Historica, Munich 1975–80; Prof. of Medieval and Modern History, Univ. of Bonn 1980–94; Prof. of Medieval History, Univ. of Munich; Pres. Monumenta Germaniae Historica, Munich 1994–; Corresp. mem. Nordrhein-Westfäl. Acad. of Sciences, Austrian Acad., Goettingen Acad.; Corresp. Fellow, Royal Historical Soc., Medieval Acad. of America, Socio straniero Accad. dei Lincei, Rome. *Publications:* Die Entstehung von Domkapiteln in Deutschland 1976, Hinkmar v. Reims, De ordine palatii (with T. Gross) 1980, Die Entstehung des päpstlichen Investiturverbots für den deutschen König 1981, Die Karolinger 1992, Die Streitschriften Hinkmars v. Reims und Hinkmars v. Laon 2003, Die Zeit des karolingischen Grossreichs 2005. *Address:* Monumenta Germaniae Historica, Postfach 340223, 80099 Munich, Germany (office). *Telephone:* (89) 286382383 (office). *Fax:* (89) 281419 (office). *E-mail:* rudolf.schieffer@mgh.de (office). *Website:* www.mgh.de (office).

SCHIFANI, Renato Giuseppe, LLB; Italian lawyer and politician; *President, Senato della Repubblica;* b. 11 May 1950, Palermo; m. Franca Schifani; two s.; lawyer, Court of Appeal; f. Siculabrokers 1979, becoming Dir; f. GMS (credit agency) 1992; fmr mem. Partito della Democrazia Cristiana; mem. Forza Italia 1995–, Pres. 2001–06; mem. Popolo della Libertà (People of Freedom) 2007–; mem. Senato (Upper House) for Sicily constituency 1996–, Pres. 2008–. *Address:* Senato della Repubblica, Piazza Madama, 00186 Rome, Italy (office). *Telephone:* (6) 67061 (office). *E-mail:* schifani_r@posta.senato.it (office). *Website:* www.senato.it (office).

SCHIFF, András; Hungarian pianist; b. 21 Dec. 1953, Budapest; s. of Odon Schiff and Klara Schiff (née Csengeri); ed Franz Liszt Acad. of Music, Budapest with Pal Kadosa, Gyorgy Kurtag and Ferenc Rados, pvt lessons with George Malcolm, England; recitals in London, New York, Paris, Vienna,

Munich, Florence; concerts with New York Philharmonic, Chicago Symphony, Vienna Philharmonic, Concertgebouw, Orchestre de Paris, London Philharmonic, London Symphony, Philharmonia, Royal Philharmonic, Israel Philharmonic, Berlin Philharmonic, Cleveland, Philadelphia, Washington Nat. Symphony; played at Salzburg, Edinburgh, Aldeburgh, Feldkirch Schubertiade, Lucerne and Tanglewood Festivals; f. Musiktage Mondsee Festival 1989 (Artistic Dir 1989–98); f. own orchestra Cappella Andrea Barca 1999; Prizewinner at 1974 Tchaikovsky Competition in Moscow and Leeds Piano Competition 1975, Liszt Prize 1977, Premio della Accad. Chigiana, Siena 1987, RPS/Charles Heidsieck Award for best concert series of 1988–89, Wiener Flotenuhr 1989, Bartok Prize 1991, Royal Philharmonic Soc.'s Instrumentalist of the Year 1994, Claudio Arrau Memorial Medal 1994, Kossuth Prize 1996, Sonning Prize, Copenhagen 1997, Palladio d'Oro della Città di Vicenza 2003, Musikfest Prize, Bremen 2003, Wigmore Medal 2008. *Recordings include:* Bach Goldberg Variations, Bach Partitas, Bach Piano Concertos, Mendelssohn Concertos 1 and 2, all the Schubert Sonatas, Schubert Trout Quintet, Schumann and Chopin 2, all the Mozart Concertos, Bach Two- and Three-part Inventions, Bach Well-Tempered Klavier, Beethoven Violin and Piano Sonatas with Sandor Vegh, Beethoven Piano Concertos, Bartok Piano Concertos, Tchaikovsky Piano Concerto, Bach English Suites (Grammy Award 1990), Bach French Suites, Lieder with Peter Schreier, Robert Holl and Cecilia Bartoli, etc., Beethoven Piano Sonatas Op. 2 Nos 1–3 and Op. 7 No. 4 2005, Beethoven Piano Sonatas Op. Nos 6–8 2008. *Television:* The Wanderer – A Film About Schubert with Andras Schiff (BBC Omnibus, narrator), Chopin with Andras Schiff (BBC Omnibus, narrator). *Leisure interests:* literature, languages, soccer, theatre, cinema, art. *Address:* Terry Harrison Artists Management, The Orchard, Market Street, Charlbury, Oxon. OX7 3PJ, England (office). *Telephone:* (1608) 810330 (office). *Fax:* (1608) 811331 (office). *E-mail:* artists@terryharrison.force9.co.uk (office). *Website:* www.terryharrison.force9.co.uk (office).

SCHIFF, Heinrich; Austrian cellist and conductor; *Chief Conductor, Vienna Chamber Orchestra;* b. 18 Nov. 1951, Gruunden; ed studied cello in Vienna with Tobias Kühne and André Navarra; London and Vienna debuts 1973; subsequently undertook extensive concert tours in Europe, Japan and USA appearing with maj. orchestras; interpreter of contemporary music including work of Lutosławski, Henze, Krenek and Penderecki and has given first performances of many new works; Artistic Dir Northern Sinfonia 1990–96; prin. guest conductor, Deutsche Kammerphilharmonie 1990–92; Prin. Conductor, Musikkollegium, Winterthur and Copenhagen Philharmonic Orchestra 1995; Chief Conductor, Vienna Chamber Orchestra 2007–. *Address:* Vienna Chamber Orchestra, Schachnerstrasse 27, 1220 Vienna, Austria (office); c/o Intermusica Artists Management Ltd, 16 Duncan Terrace, London, N1 8BZ, England (office). *Telephone:* (1) 203-63-57 (office). *Fax:* (1) 204-37-50 (office). *E-mail:* wiener@kammerorchester.com (office). *Website:* www.kammerorchester.com (office).

SCHIFFER, Claudia; German actress and fmr fashion model; b. 25 Aug. 1970, Düsseldorf; m. Matthew Vaughn 2002; one s. one d.; fashion model for Karl Lagerfeld 1990, model for Revlon 1992–96, Chanel –1997; has appeared on numerous covers for magazines and journals; designs calendars; appears on TV specials; has share in Fashion Café, New York 1995–; announced retirement from modelling 1998; mem. US Cttee UNICEF 1995–98. *Films include:* Richie Rich 1994, Pret-a-Porter 1994, The Blackout 1997, And She Was 1999, Friends and Lovers 1999, Black and White 2000, Chain of Fools 2000, Reckless + Wild 2001, Life Without Dick 2001, Love Actually 2003. *Publication:* Memories 1995. *Address:* c/o Heidi Gross GmbH, Hartungstrasse 5, 20146 Hamburg, Germany. *E-mail:* info@model-management.de.

SCHIFFRIN, André, MA; American editor and publisher; *Director and Editor-at-Large, The New Press;* b. 12 June 1935, Paris, France; s. of Jacques Schiffrin and Simone Heymann; m. Maria Elena de la Iglesia 1961; two d.; ed Yale Univ. and Univ. of Cambridge; with New American Library 1959–63; with Pantheon Books, New York 1962–90, Ed., Ed.-in-Chief, Man. Dir 1969–90; Publr Schocken Books (subsidiary of Pantheon Books Inc.) 1987–90; Pres. Fund for Ind. Publishing 1990–; Founder, Dir and Ed.-in-Chief The New Press, New York 1990–, currrently Ed.-at-Large; Visiting Fellow, Davenport Coll. 1977–79; Visiting Lecturer, Yale Univ. 1977, 1979; mem. Council Smithsonian Inst.; mem. Bd of Dirs New York Council for Humanities; mem. Special Cttee American Centre, Paris 1994–; mem. Visting Cttee of Grad. Faculty The New York School 1995–; other professional appts and affiliations; Hon. Fellow, Trumbull Coll. Yale Univ.; Grinzane Cavour Prize, Italy 2003. *Publications include:* L'Edition sans Editeurs 1999, The Business of Books 2000; contribs to professional journals. *Address:* The New Press, 38 Greene Street, 4th Floor, New York, NY 10013 (office); 250 West 94th Street, New York, NY 10025, USA (home). *Telephone:* (212) 629-8802 (office). *Website:* www.thenewpress.com (home).

SCHIFRES, Michel Maurice René; French journalist; *Vice-President, the Editorial Committee, Le Figaro;* b. 1 May 1946, Orléans; s. of Jacques Schifres and Paulette Mauduit; m. Josiane Gasnier (divorced); two c.; ed Lycée du Mans, Lycée de Caen, Faculté des Lettres de Caen, Centre de Formation des Journalistes; journalist with Combat 1970–72, with Monde 1972–74; Head of Political Affairs Quotidien de Paris 1974–76; Asst Head of Political Affairs France-Soir 1976; Head of Political Affairs Journal du Dimanche 1977, Editorial Dir 1985–89; mem. Comm. on quality of radio and TV broadcasts 1977–79; Editorial Dir France-Soir 1989–92, Asst Dir-Gen. 1992; Asst Editorial Dir Le Figaro (newspaper) 1992–98, Man. Dir 1998–2000, Man. Ed. magazine 2005–07, Vice-Pres. Editorial Cttee 2000–; mem. Editorial Cttee La Revue de l'Intelligent 2003–; Chevalier, ordre nat. du Mérite. *Television:* L'Elysée 1988, Ville de Chiens 1989, Un Siecle d'Ecrivain: Jules Romains 1998. *Publications include:* La CFDT des militants 1972, D'une France à l'autre 1974, L'enaklatura 1987, L'Elysée de Mitterrand 1987, La désertion des énarques 1999. *Leisure interest:* antiques. *Address:* Le Figaro, 37 rue du Louvre, 75002 Paris (office); 150 avenue Emile Zola, 75015 Paris, France (home). *Telephone:* 1-42-21-29-73 (office); 1-40-58-16-64 (home); 6-07-59-40-91. *Fax:* 1-42-21-63-82 (office). *E-mail:* mschifres@lefigaro.fr (office); mschifres@noos.fr (home).

SCHIFTER, Richard, LLB; American lawyer, diplomatist and politician; *Chairman, American Jewish International Relations Institute;* b. 1923, Vienna, Austria; m.; five c.; ed Coll. of the City of New York, Yale Law School; served in US Army 1943–46; practising attorney, Washington, DC until 1981; US Rep. to UN Human Rights Comm. 1983–86; Deputy US Rep. to UN Security Council (with rank of Amb.) 1984–85; Asst Sec. of State for Human Rights and Humanitarian Affairs, Counsellor, Nat. Security Council (organized SE Europe Cooperative Initiative 1996), Dept of State Rep. to CSCE, Special Adviser to Sec. of State 1996–2001; Chair. Center for Democracy and Reconciliation in SE Europe 2001–08; currently Chair. American Jewish Int. Relations Inst.; mem. Bd of Dirs US Inst. of Peace; Grand Decoration of Honour in Gold (Austria) 1998. *Address:* American Jewish International Relations Institute, PO Box 341197, Bethesda, MD 20827, USA.

SCHILLER, Vivian, MA; American media executive; *President and CEO, National Public Radio Inc.;* b. 13 Sept. 1961; ed Cornell Univ., Middlebury Coll.; Russian interpreter and tour guide, Moscow 1984–88; Production Coordinator, Turner Broadcasting System Inc., Moscow 1988, Supervising Producer, Sr Producer, then Vice-Pres. and Gen. Man., Turner Original Productions, Turner Entertainment Networks 1994–2002; fmr Exec. Vice-Pres. CNN Productions, Turner Broadcasting System Inc.; Sr Vice-Pres. and Gen. Man. Discovery Times Channel, The New York Times Co. 2002–05, Sr Vice-Pres. TV and Video 2005–06, Exec. Vice-Pres. and Gen. Man. Discovery Times Channel 2005–06; Sr Vice-Pres. and Gen. Man. NYTimes.com 2006–08; Pres. and CEO, National Public Radio, Washington, DC 2009–; mem. Council on Foreign Relations; five Emmy Awards, two Peabody Awards, two Alfred I. DuPont-Columbia Univ. Award, CableACE Award, Int. Documentary Asscn Award. *Television:* as supervising producer: A Century of Women 1994, Moon Shot 1994; as sr producer: Hank Aaron: Chasing the Dream 1995, Hollywood's Amazing Animal Actors 1996, Biker Women 1996, Survivors of the Holocaust 1996, Animal ER 1996, Pirate Tales 1997, Twin Stories 1997, Warner Bros. 75th Anniversary: No Guts, No Glory 1998, Dying to Tell the Story 1998; as exec. producer: Word Wars 2004, Off to War 2005. *Address:* National Public Radio Inc., 635 Massachusetts Avenue, Washington, DC 20001-3753, USA (office). *Telephone:* (202)513-2000 (office). *Website:* www.npr.org (office).

SCHILTZ, Jean-Louis; Luxembourg lawyer and politician; *Minister for Development Cooperation and Humanitarian Action, Minister for Communications and Minister of Defence;* b. 14 Aug. 1964, Luxembourg; ; m.; three c.; ed Université Paris I Panthéon Sorbonne; worked for Schiltz & Schiltz (law firm), Luxembourg 1989–2004; Academic Asst, Law Faculty Université Paris I Panthéon Sorbonne 1989–90; mem. Cttee Young Bar Asscn 1990, Chair. 1997–98, then mem. Bar Council; MP 2004–, Minister for Devt Cooperation and Humanitarian Action, Minister for Communications and Minister of Defence 2004–; Gov. Asian Development Bank for Luxembourg 2004–; Sec.-Gen. Parti Chrétien Social (Chrëschtlech Sozial Vollekspartei) (PCS/CSV) (Christian Social Party); First Asst, then Chargé de Cours, Centre universitaire de Luxembourg 1991–2004; co-Ed. Assurances et Responsabilité 1994–2004; mem. Editorial Bd European Lawyer, Int. Bar Asscn; fmr mem. Legal Comm., Nat. Olympic Cttee. *Sport achievements:* Luxembourg team fencing champion 1983. *Address:* Parti Chrétien Social (Chrëschtlech Sozial Vollekspartei) (PCS/CSV) (Christian Social Party), 4 rue de l'Eau, BP 826, 2018, Luxembourg. *Telephone:* 22-57-311. *Fax:* 47-27-16. *E-mail:* csv@csv.lu. *Website:* www.csv.lu.

SCHILY, Otto; German politician and lawyer; b. 20 July 1932, Bochum; s. of Franz Schily; m. (divorced); two c.; ed Munich, Hamburg and Berlin Univs; mem. Bundestag 1983–86, 1987–89, 1990–; mem. SPD 1990–, Deputy Chair. 1994–; Minister of the Interior 1998–2005; mem. Presidium Neue Gesellschaft für bildende Kunst; Adviser, Humanist Union. *Address:* Platz der Republik 1, 11011 Berlin (office); Oberanger 38, 80331 Munich, Germany (office). *Telephone:* (30) 22777971 (office). *Fax:* (30) 22776971 (office). *E-mail:* otto.schily@bundestag.de (office). *Website:* www.otto-schily.de (office).

SCHIMMEL, Paul Gordon; American museum curator; *Chief Curator, Museum of Contemporary Art, Los Angeles;* m. Yvonne Schimmel; ed Syracuse Univ., New York Univ.; internship, Contemporary Arts Museum, Houston, Tex., then mem. curatorial staff; fmr Curator, Newport Harbor Art Museum; Chief Curator Museum of Contemporary Art, Los Angeles 1990–, has organized major exhbns including Helter Skelter: Los Angeles Art in the 1990s, Hand-Painted Pop: American Art in Transition 1955–62, Sigmar Polke Photoworks: When Pictures Vanish, Out of Actions: Between Performance and the Object 1949–79; has lectured at Kanazawa Museum of Modern Art, Japan, RCA, London, Centre Georges Pompidou, Paris, Whitney Museum of American Art, J. Paul Getty Museum, Los Angeles Co. Museum of Art, and others; panelist Nat. Endowment for the Arts; Bard Coll. Center for Curatorial Studies Award for Curatorial Excellence. *Publications:* Ecstasy: In and About Altered States (co-ed with Lisa Gabrielle Mark); contrib.: articles in journals and magazines including The Art Book. *Address:* The Museum of Contemporary Art, 250 South Grand Avenue, Los Angeles, CA 90012, USA (office). *Telephone:* (213) 621-2766 (office). *Website:* www.moca.org (office).

SCHINDLER, David W., OC, BSc, DPhil, FRSC; American biologist and academic; *Killam Memorial Professor of Ecology, University of Alberta;* b. 3 Aug. 1940, Fargo, ND; ed N Dakota State Univ., Univ. of Oxford, UK; Asst

Prof. of Biology, Trent Univ., Canada 1966–68; Founder and Dir Experimental Lakes Project, Canadian Dept of Fisheries and Oceans 1968–89; Killam Memorial Prof. of Ecology, Univ. of Alberta 1989–, Chair. Limnology Lab.; Chair. Alberta Br., Safe Drinking Water Foundation; mem. Bd of Dirs Canadian Arctic Resources Cttee (Chair. Cumulative Effects Sub-Cttee); mem. Scientific Advisory Cttee and Aquatic Sciences Cttee, Yukon to Yellowstone; mem. NAS 2002–; Foreign mem. Royal Swedish Acad. of Eng Science 2003–; Assoc. Ed. Canadian Journal of Fisheries and Aquatic Sciences; mem. Editorial Bd Aquatic Sciences; mem. Advisory Bd Ecosytems (journal); Queen's Golden Jubilee Medal 2002, Alberta Order of Excellence 2008; Hon. DSc (N Dakota State Univ., Acadia Univ., Brock Univ., Queen's Univ. and Univs of Victoria, Athabasca, Winnipeg and Lethbridge); Hon. DLaws (Univ. of Windsor, Trent Univ.); Outstanding Achievement Award, American Inst. of Fisheries Research Biologists 1984, Frank Rigler Award, Canadian Soc. of Limnologists 1984, Hutchinson Medal, American Soc. of Limnology and Oceanography 1985, Naumann-Thieneman Medal, Int. Limnology Soc. 1989, First Stockholm Water Prize, Stockholm Water Foundation 1991, Manning Distinguished Achievement Award 1993, First Romanowski Medal, RSC 1994, Walter Bean–Canada Trust Award for Environmental Science 1996, Volvo Environment Prize 1998, J Gordin Kaplan Award for Excellence in Research, Univ. of Alberta 1999, Distinguished mem., Int. Water Acad., Norway 1999, Alberta Science and Tech. Award for Outstanding Leadership in Alberta Science 1999, Natural Sciences and Eng Research Council (NESRC) Award of Excellence 2000, 2001, Douglas H. Pimlott Award for Conservation, Canadian Nature Fed. 2001, NESRC Gerhard Herzberg Canada Gold Medal for Science and Eng 2001, Environment Canada, EcoLogo/Natural Marine Environmental Award 2002, Award of Distinction, City of Edmonton 2002, Killam Prize 2003, Tyler Prize for Environmental Achievement (co-recipient) 2006, David Schindler Endowed Professorship in Aquatic Sciences est. at Trent Univ. 2008. *Publications:* more than 280 articles and reports, more than 20 of them in Science and Nature magazine. *Address:* University of Alberta, Room Z 811, Biological Sciences Building, Edmonton, Alberta T6G 2R3, Canada (office). *Telephone:* (780) 492-1291 (office). *Fax:* (780) 492-9234 (office). *E-mail:* d.schindler@ualberta.ca (office). *Website:* www.biology.ualberta.ca (office).

SCHINZLER, Hans-Jürgen, DJur; German insurance industry executive; *Chairman, Supervisory Board, Munich Re Group;* b. 12 Oct. 1940, Madrid, Spain; m. Monika Somya; three c.; ed Univs of Munich and Würzburg; training at Bayerische Vereinsbank 1968–69; joined Münchener Rückversicherungsgesellschaft (Munich Reinsurance Co.) 1968, mem. Bd of Man. 1981–93, Chair. Bd of Man. 1993–2003, Chair. Supervisory Bd Munich Re Group 2004–, Chair. Bd of Trustees Munich Re Foundation; Deputy Chair. Allgemeine Kreditversicherung AG, Mainz, Allianzversicherung AG, Munich; fmr Chair. Supervisory Bd ERGO Versicherungsgruppe AG, MR Beteiligungen AG; mem. Supervisory Bd Bayerische Hypo- und Vereinsbank AG, Deutsche Telekom AG, METRO AG. *Address:* Munich Re Group, Königinstrasse 107, 80802 Munich, Germany (office). *Telephone:* (89) 38913534 (office). *Fax:* (89) 399056 (office). *Website:* www.munichre.com (office).

SCHIRO, James J., BBA; American business executive; *CEO, Zurich Financial Services;* b. 1946; m. Tomasina Schiro; two. c.; ed St John's Univ., Dartmouth Coll.; joined Price Waterhouse 1967, Chair. Mining Special Services Group 1979–88, Nat. Dir Mergers and Acquisitions Services 1988–91, Vice-Chair. and Man. Partner for New York Metropolitan Region 1991, apptd to Council of Partners 1990, to Gen. Council 1992, Deputy Chair. World Exec. Group and World Bd 1995, Chair. and Sr Partner, Price Waterhouse 1995, CEO 1997, CEO PricewaterhouseCoopers 1998–2001; COO Group Finance, Zurich Financial Services March–May 2002, CEO May 2002–; mem. Bd Dirs PepsiCo 2002–; Vice-Chair. Swiss-American Chamber of Commerce, American Friends of Lucerne Festival (also mem. Bd Trustees); mem. Foundation Bd IMD (business school), Bd Inst. for Advanced Study, Bd Trustees St John's Univ.; Hon. DCS (St John's Univ.) 1994; Ellis Island Medal of Honor 1994, St John's Univ. Alumni Pietas Medal 1992, Avenue of the Americas Asscn's Gold Key Award 1992. *Address:* Zurich Financial Services, Mythenquai 2, 8022 Zurich, Switzerland (office). *Telephone:* (1) 6252525 (office). *Fax:* (1) 6254560 (office). *E-mail:* james.schiro@zurich.com (office). *Website:* www.zurich.com (office).

SCHLAGMAN, Richard Edward, FRSA; British publisher; *Chairman and Publisher, Phaidon Press Ltd;* b. 11 Nov. 1953, London; s. of Jack Schlagman and the late Shirley Schlagman (née Goldston); ed Univ. Coll. School, Hampstead, Brunel Univ.; Co-Founder, Jt Chair., Man. Dir Interstate Electronics Ltd 1973–86; purchased Bush from Rank Org., renamed IEL Bush Radio Ltd 1981, floated on London Stock Exchange 1984, sold as Bush Radio PLC 1986; acquired Phaidon Press Ltd 1990, Chair. and Publr 1990–; mem. Exec. Cttee Patrons of New Art, Tate Gallery 1994–97, Royal Opera House Trust, Glyndebourne Festival Soc., Designers and Arts Dirs Asscn of UK; Patron Bayreuther Festspiele, Salzburger Festspiele, Schubertiades; Pres. Judd Foundation, MARFA, Tex. 1999–2001, mem. Bd 2001–. *Leisure interests:* music, art, architecture. *Address:* Phaidon Press Ltd, Regent's Wharf, All Saints Street, London, N1 9PA, England (office). *Telephone:* (20) 7843-1100 (office). *Fax:* (20) 7843-1212 (office). *E-mail:* richard@phaidon.com (office). *Website:* www.phaidon.com (office).

SCHLECKER, Anton; German retail executive; *CEO, Fa. Anton Schlecker;* b. 1944; m.; two c.; began career as apprentice butcher in father's co. 1965, built first self-service dept store in Ehingen 1967, opened first drugstore in Kirchheim 1975, began expanding into other European countries 1987, currently CEO Fa. Anton Schlecker. *Address:* Fa. Anton Schlecker, Talstrasse 12, 89579 Ehingen, Germany (office). *Telephone:* (73) 91 584-0 (office). *Fax:* (73) 91 584-300 (office). *Website:* www.schlecker.com (office).

SCHLESSINGER, Joseph, PhD; American molecular biologist and academic; *William H. Prusoff Professor and Chairman, Department of Pharmacology, School of Medicine, Yale University;* b. 26 March 1945, Topusko, Croatia; s. of Ehud Schlessinger and Avner Schlessinger; ed The Hebrew Univ., Jerusalem and The Weizmann Inst. of Science, Rehovot, Israel; Postdoctoral Assoc., Dept of Chem., School of Applied and Eng Physics, Cornell Univ., Ithaca, NY 1974–76; Visiting Scientist, Immunology Br., Nat. Cancer Inst., NIH, Bethesda, Md 1977–78; Sr Scientist, Dept of Chemical Immunology, The Weizmann Inst. of Science 1978–80, Assoc. Prof. 1980–85, Prof. 1985–91, The Ruth and Leonard Simon Prof. of Cancer Research, The Weizmann Inst. of Science 1985–91; Research Dir Rorer Biotechology, Inc., Rockville, Md and King of Prussia, Pa 1985–90; The Milton and Helen Kimmelman Prof. and Chair. Dept of Pharmacology, New York Univ. Medical Center 1990–2001; William H. Prusoff Prof. and Chair. Dept of Pharmacology, Yale Univ. School of Medicine, New Haven, Conn. 2001–; Founder SUGEN, Inc. 1991, Plexxikon 2000); mem. Editorial Bd European Molecular Biology Organization (EMBO) Journal, Cell, Molecular Cell, Genes and Development, Molecular Biology of the Cell, Journal of Biological Chemistry, Cancer Research, Journal of Cell Biology, Growth Factors, Protein Engineering, Cell Growth and Differentiation, Structure; mem. EMBO 1982, NAS 2000, American Acad. of Arts and Sciences 2001, Inst. of Medicine 2006, Russian Acad. of Sciences 2006, Croatian Acad. of Sciences 2008; Hon. mem. Japanese Biochemical Soc. 1999; Michael Landau Prize for PhD Thesis 1973, Sara Leedy Prize 1980, Hestrin Prize 1983, Levinson Prize 1984, Keynote Presidential Lecturer, The Endocrine Soc. 1986, Lamport Lecturer, Univ. of Seattle 1993, E. Fisher Lecturer, Univ. of Geneva 1993, E.J. Cohn Lecturer, Harvard Univ. Medical School 1993, Randall Lecturer, Univ. of Pennsylvania 1994, Feigen Lecturer, Stanford Univ. Medical School 1994, Opening Keynote Lecturer, American Soc. for Biochemistry and Molecular Biology 1994, Deans Lecturer, Mount Sinai Medical School 1994, Harvey Lecturer, Rockefeller Univ. 1994, Antoine Lacassagne Prize 1995, Drew-Ciba Prize 1995, Opening Keynote Lecturer, Whitehead Inst. Symposium 1995, Howard Hughes Medical Inst. Symposium on Signal Transduction 1995, Sigma-Tau Lecturer 1995, Lindner Lecturer, The Weizmann Inst. of Science 1996, Burroughs Wellcome Lecturer, Indiana Univ. 1997, Juan March Lecturer 1998, 6th Ray A. and Robert L. Kroc Lecturer, Univ. of Massachusetts Medical School 1999, Bayer Lecturer, Univ. of California, Berkeley 1999, Distinguished Service Award, Miami Nature Biotechnology 1999, 16th Annual Kenneth F. Naidorf Memorial Lecturer, Columbia Univ. 2000, Distinguished Speakers Program, Univ. of Texas Health Science Center 2000, NIH Director's Lecturer 2000, The Taylor Prize 2000, Dan David Prize 2006, Inaugural Pfizer Lecture Michigan 2006, Keith Porter Lecture, ASCB San Diego 2006, NIH-WALS Lecture, Bethesda 2008, Helen Coley-Nauts Lecture, Moscow 2008, 24th Medical Scientist Lecture Series, UC Irvine 2008. *Publications:* more than 450 articles in scientific journals. *Address:* Department of Pharmacology, Yale University School of Medicine, Sterling Hall of Medicine, PO Box 208066, 333 Cedar Street, B-204, New Haven, CT 06520-8066, USA (office). *Telephone:* (203) 785-7395 (office). *Fax:* (203) 785-3879 (office). *E-mail:* joseph.schlessinger@yale.edu (office); Laura.copela@yale.edu (office). *Website:* info.med.yale.edu/pharm (office).

SCHLINK, Bernhard, PhD, JD; German judge, academic and writer; *Professor of Public Law and Legal Philosophy, Humboldt-Universität zu Berlin;* b. 1944, Bethel, nr Bielefeld; s. of the late Prof. Dr Edmund Schlink; ed Heidelberg, West Berlin, Darmstadt, Bielefeld and Freiburg Univs; Prof., Bonn Univ. 1981–91; Judge Constitutional Law Court of North Rhein-Westphalia, Munster 1987–2005; Prof., Frankfurt Univ. 1991–92; Prof., Humboldt Univ., Berlin 1992–; Visiting Prof. of Law, Benjamin Cardozo School of Law, Yeshiva Univ., New York 1994–; qualified as masseur in Calif.; began writing fiction in 1980s. *Publications:* fiction: Selbs Justiz (with Walter Popp, translated as Self's Punishment) 1987, Die Gordische Schleife 1988, Selbs Betrug (translated as Self's Betrayal) 1992, Der Vorleser (translated as The Reader) 1995, Liebesfluchten (short stories; translated as Flights of Love) 2001, Selbst Mord 2005, Die Heimkehr (translated as Homecoming) 2006, Das Wochenende 2008; non-fiction: Weimar: A Jurisprudence of Crisis (with Arthur Jacobson), several books on constitutional law, fundamental separation of powers and admin. law. *Address:* Humboldt-Universität zu Berlin, Lehrstuhl für Öffentliches Recht und Rechtsphilosophie, Juristische Fakultät, Unter den Linden 6, 10099 Berlin, Germany (office). *Telephone:* (30) 20933472 (office). *Fax:* (30) 20933452 (office). *E-mail:* schlink@rewi.hu-berlin.de (office). *Website:* schlink.rewi.hu-berlin.de (office).

SCHLÖGL, Herwig, PhD; German fmr international organization official; b. 17 Aug. 1942; ed Univ. of Marburg; mem. German Perm. Representation to European Econ. Union, Brussels 1969–72; mem. staff Industrial Policy Div., Ministry of Econs 1972–76, Head Foreign Econ. Affairs Div. of Industry Dept 1980–84, Head Div. for Foreign Econ. Policy, Export Promotion 1984–96; Head Econs Dept, German-American Chamber of Commerce, New York 1976–80; Deputy Dir-Gen. for Trade Policy, Bonn 1996–98; Deputy Sec.-Gen. OECD, Paris 1998–2006. *Publications:* books and articles on competition policy and trade issues. *Address:* c/o Organisation for Economic Co-operation and Development, 2 rue André-Pascal, 75775 Paris Cédex 16, France (office).

SCHLÖNDORFF, Volker; German film director; b. 1939, Wiesbaden; m. Margarethe von Trotta (q.v.) 1991; has directed numerous cinema and TV films; mem. German PEN Centre; Officier de l'Ordre Nat. de la Légion d'Honneur 2002 Prize of the Int. Film Critics, Cannes 1966, Konrad-Wolf-Prize 1997, Blue Angel Award for Best European Film 2000. *Films include:* Der junge Törless, Mord und Totschlag, Michael Kohlhaas, Der plötzliche Reichtum der armen Leute von Kombach, Baal, Die Moral der Ruth Halbfass, Strohfeuer, Die Ehegattin, Übernachtung in Tirol, Die verlorene Ehre der Katharina Blum, Die Blechtrommel (The Tin Drum) (Golden Palm of Cannes,

Acad. Award for Best Foreign Film) 1979, Die Fälschung 1981, Circle of Deceit 1982, Eine Liebe von Swann (Swann in Love) 1984, Death of a Salesman 1985, The Handmaid's Tale 1989, Voyager 1991, The Ogre 1996, Palmetto 1997, Die Stille nach dem Schuss 2000, Ten Minutes Older: The Cello (segment) 2002, Der Neunte Tag (The Ninth Day) 2004, Strike 2006, Ulzhan 2007. *Television includes:* Death of a Salesman 1985, Enigma: Eine uneingestandene Liebe 2005, Billy Wilder Speaks 2006.

SCHLOTER, Carsten; German business executive; *CEO, Swisscom AG;* b. 1963, Erlenbach, Main; m.; three c.; ed Univ. of Paris, Dauphine; early career at Mercedes Benz France; held several man. positions at debitel AG –2000, est. and managed debitel France SA 1992–94; Head, Public Com and Mobile Com 2000–01; CEO Swisscom Mobile AG 2001–06, CEO Swisscom AG 2006–; Chair. Bd of Dirs Fastweb SpA. *Leisure interest:* sport. *Address:* Swisscom AG, Alte Tiefenaustrasse 6, 3050 Bern, Switzerland (office). *Telephone:* 313421111 (office). *Fax:* 313426411 (office). *E-mail:* carsten.schloter@swisscom.com (office). *Website:* www.swisscom.ch (office).

SCHLÜTER, Poul Holmskov, LLB; Danish lawyer and fmr politician; b. 3 April 1929, Tønder; s. of Johannes Schlüter; m. 1st Lisbeth Schlüter 1979 (died 1988); two s. one d.; m. 2nd Anne Marie Vessel Schlüter 1989; ed Univs of Århus and Copenhagen; barrister and Supreme Court Attorney; Leader of Conservative Youth Movt (KU) 1944, Nat. Leader 1951; Del. to Int. Congress of World Asscn of Youth 1951, 1954; Chair. Young Conservatives, mem. Exec. Cttee Conservative Party 1952–55, 1971, Nat. Chair. Jr Chamber 1961, Vice-Pres. Jr Chamber Int. 1962; mem. Folketing (Parl.) 1964–94, Prime Minister of Denmark 1982–93; Chair. Jt Danish Consultative Council on UN 1966–68; MP Foreign Affairs Cttee 1968, Chair. 1982; mem. Council of Europe 1971–74; fmr Chair. Conservative People's Party 1974–77, 1981–93; Chair. Danish Del. to Nordic Council and mem. Presiding Cttee 1978–79; Dir Nat. Cleaning Group 1993, Int. Service System (ISS); Co-founder Danish Centre for Political Studies (CEPOS) 2004. *Address:* c/o CEPOS, Vestergade 16, stuen, 1456 Copenhagen, Denmark. *Telephone:* 33-93-24-04. *Fax:* 33-36-07-69. *E-mail:* info@CEPOS.DK. *Website:* www.cepos.dk.

SCHMALENBACH, Werner, DPhil; Swiss art museum director; b. 13 Sept. 1920, Göttingen, Germany; s. of Prof. Dr Herman Schmalenbach and Sala Schmalenbach (née Müntz); m. 1st Esther Grey (died 2001); two d.; m. 2nd Anna Schlüter 2001; ed Basle Grammar School and Univ. of Basle; organiser of exhbns, Gewerbemuseum, Basle 1945–55; Dir Kestner Gesellschaft, Hanover 1955–62; mem. working Cttee, 'Documenta II, III, IV', Kassel 1959, 1964, 1968; German Commr, Venice Biennale 1960, São Paulo Biennale 1961, 1963, 1965; Dir Kunstsammlung Nordrhein-Westfalen, Düsseldorf (Museum of Modern Art) 1962–90; mem. Sotheby's Int. Advisory Bd 1991–2000; Grosses Bundesverdienstkreuz; Officer, Nat. Order of Southern Cross (Brazil). *Publications:* Der Film 1947, Die Kunst Afrikas 1956, Julius Bissier 1963, Kurt Schwitters 1967, Antoni Tàpies 1974, Fernand Léger 1976, Eduardo Chillida 1977, Marc Chagall 1979, Emil Schumacher 1981, Joan Miró 1982, Paul Klee 1986, African Art from the Barbier-Mueller Collection (ed.) 1989, Amedeo Modigliani 1990, Die Lust auf das Bild 1996, Henri Rousseau 1997, Kunst! Reden Schreiben Streiten 2000, Über Die Liebe Zur Kunst Und Die Wahrheit Der Bilder 2004. *Address:* Marktpl. 3, 40213 Düsseldorf (office); Poststrasse 17, 40667 Meerbusch, Germany (home). *Telephone:* (211) 322230 (office); (2132) 77802 (home). *Fax:* (211) 320743 (office).

SCHMID, Hans Heinrich, DTheol; Swiss university rector (retd); b. 22 Oct. 1937, Zürich; s. of Gotthard Schmid and Erika Hug; m. Christa Nievergelt 1962; two s. two d.; ed Zürich and Göttingen Univs; Asst Prof. Univ. of Zürich 1967–69; Prof. for Old Testament, Kirchliche Hochschule Bethel/Bielefeld 1969–76, Univ. of Zürich 1976–88; Rector Univ. of Zürich 1988–2000; Goldenes Ehrenkreuz der Republik Österreich 1996; Hon. DTheol (Leipzig) 1991. *Publications include:* Altorientalische Welt in der alttestamentlichen Theologie (essays) 1974, Der sogenannte Jahwist. Beobachtungen und Fragen zur Pentateuchforschung 1976. *Leisure interest:* conducting a chamber orchestra. *Address:* In der Halden 11, 8603 Schwerzenbach, Switzerland (home). *Telephone:* (1) 8252533 (home). *Fax:* (1) 8252517 (home). *E-mail:* hhschmid@freesurf.ch (home).

SCHMID, Samuel; Swiss lawyer and politician; b. 1947; m.; three s.; ed Univ. of Bern; with Swiss Fed. Finance Admin 1973; joined legal practice, Bern 1973; independent advocate and notary, Lyss 1978–; solicitor with Kellerhals & Pnrs LLC, Bern 1998–; adviser to econ. and trade asscns.; local councillor 1972–74, Pres. Municipality of Rueti 1974–82; mem. Berni Greater Council 1982–93, Chair. Cttee for new Berni State Canton Constitution, mem. Finance Cttee; mem. Nat. Council 1994–98, mem. Standing Cttee for Econ. Affairs and Taxation, Cttee for Econs and Deliveries, Nat. Policy Cttee, Constitutional Affairs Cttee, Comm. for Strategic Questions, Comm. for Reorganization of the Intelligence Service; Pres. Swiss People's Party (Schweizerische Volkspartei) Parl. Group of the Presidential Election Council 1998–99; mem. Comm. for Foreign Policy 1999– (also Vice-Pres.), Comm. for Econs and Deliveries, Comm. for Social Security and Health, Nat. Political Comm.; mem. Upper House of Parl. 2001–; Head of Fed. Dept of Defence, Civil Protection and Sport 2001–08; Vice-Pres. Swiss Confed. 2004, Pres. 2005; Pres. Berni Trade Asscn 1990–; mem. Exec. Cttee Swiss Trade Asscn 1991–; Col, Commdt of infantry regiment 1993–96, Commdt Stv. F Div. 3 1998–99. *Address:* c/o Federal Department of Defence, Civil Protection and Sport, Bundeshaus-Ost, 3003 Bern, Switzerland (office).

SCHMIDBAUR, Hubert, Dr rer. nat; German chemist, academic and consultant; *Professor Emeritus, Technische Universität München;* b. 31 Dec. 1934, Landsberg; s. of Johann B. Schmidbaur and Katharina S. Ehelechner; m. Rose-Marie Fukas; one s. one d.; ed Univ. of Munich; Asst Prof., Univ. of Munich 1960–64; Assoc. Prof., Univ. of Marburg 1964–69; Prof., Univ. of Würzburg 1969–73; Prof. of Chem. and Head of Dept, Tech. Univ. of Munich 1973–2002, Dean Faculty of Science 1983–86, Prof. Emer. 2002–; Assoc. Prof., Univ. of Stellenbosch, SA 2002–06; mem. Göttingen, Leopoldina, Bavarian and Finnish Acads, Senate, German Science Foundation; Dr hc (Westfälische Wilhelms-Universität Münster) 2005 Bundesverdienstkreuz; A. Stock Prize, German Chemical Soc., Wacker Silikon Preis, Bonner Chemie-preis, F. Kipping Award, ACS, Leibniz Award, German Science Foundation, Dwyer Medal, Bailar Medal, Ludwig Mond Medal, Birch Medal, Centenary Medal, Royal Soc. of Chem. *Publications:* about 850, including books, monographs and scientific papers on inorganic, metalorganic and analytical chem. *Address:* Technische Universität München, Lehrstuhl für Anorganische und Analytische Chemie, Lichtenbergstrasse 4, 85747 Garching (office); Konigsbergerstr. 36, 85748 Garching, Germany (home). *Telephone:* (89) 28913130 (office). *Fax:* (89) 28913125 (office). *E-mail:* h.schmidbaur@lrz.tum.de (office). *Website:* aac.anorg.chemie.tu-muenchen.de (office).

SCHMIDT, Andreas; German singer (baritone); b. 30 June 1960, Düsseldorf; m. Jeanne Pascale 2003; two s. three d.; ed studied piano, organ, conducting in Düsseldorf, singing in Düsseldorf and Berlin; youngest mem. Deutsche Oper Berlin 1983; debut Hamburg State Opera 1985, Munich State Opera 1985, Covent Garden London 1986, Vienna State Opera 1988, Geneva Opera 1989, Salzburg Festival 1989, Aix-en-Provence Festival 1991, Metropolitan New York 1991, Edin. Festival 1991, Paris Bastille 1992, Paris Garnier 1993, Glyndebourne Festival 1994, State Opera Berlin 1995, Amsterdam Opera 1995, Bayreuth Festival 1996; has sung with major orchestras, including Berlin, Geneva, Vienna, Munich, London, New York, Israel Philharmonic orchestras, Cincinnati, Cleveland Symphony orchestras, La Scala, Milan; currently Prof., Hochschule für Musik, Dresden; Hon. mem., Richard-Wagner-Verband; first prize Deutscher Musikwettbewerb, several German and int. awards and prizes. *Recordings:* over 130 CDs. *Leisure interests:* fly-fishing, golf, literature, art. *Address:* c/o Hartmut Haase, Artists Management, Aalgrund 8, 31275 Lehrte, Germany (office). *Telephone:* (5175) 953232 (office). *Fax:* (5175) 953233 (office). *E-mail:* artists@t-online.de (office). *Website:* www.artists-haase.de (office).

SCHMIDT, Benno C., Jr; American academic and university administrator; *Chairman, Nations Academy;* b. 20 March 1942, Washington; s. of the late Benno Charles Schmidt, Sr and Martha Chastain; m. 2nd Helen Cutting Whitney 1980; one d. (one s. one d. by previous marriage); ed Yale Coll. and Yale Law School; clerk to Chief Justice Earl Warren 1966–67; Dept of Justice 1967–69; mem. Faculty, Columbia Univ. Law School 1969–86, Dean 1984–86; Pres. and Prof. of Law, Yale Univ. 1986–92; Pres., CEO The Edison Project (now Edison Schools) 1992, now Chair.; Chair. Nations Acad. 2007–; Chair. Bd of Trustees, City Univ. of NY; Dir Nat. Humanities Center, Chapel Hill, NC 1985–; Hon. Master of Bench, Gray's Inn 1988. *Publications:* Freedom of the Press versus Public Access 1976, The Judiciary and Responsible Government 1910–1921 (with A. M. Bickel) 1984; papers on constitutional law, freedom of the press and first amendment issues. *Address:* Edison Schools, 521 Fifth Avenue, 11th Floor, New York, NY 10175, USA (office). *Telephone:* (212) 419-1600 (office). *Fax:* (212) 419-1706 (office). *E-mail:* info@nationsacademy.com. *Website:* www.nationsacademy.com; www.edisonschools.com (office).

SCHMIDT, Brian P., BS, AM, PhD, FAA; American/Australian astronomer and academic; *Australian Research Council Federation Fellow and Scientific Leader, SkyMapper Telescope and Southern Sky Survey, Australian National University;* b. 24 Feb. 1967, Missoula, MT; ed Univ. of Arizona, Harvard Univ.; Post-doctoral Fellow, ANU 1993–94, Post-doctoral Fellow, ANU Mount Stromlo and Siding Spring Observatories 1995–96, Research Fellow 1997–99, Fellow, Research School of Astronomy and Astrophysics 1999–2002, Australian Research Council Professorial Fellow 2003–05, Australian Research Council Fed. Fellow 2005–, Scientific Leader, SkyMapper Telescope and Southern Sky Survey; Chair. LOC and SOC of Astronomical Soc. of Australia's AGM 2002, Australian Time Allocation Cttee (Gemini/AAT/UK-Schmidt) 2002–03, Australia Telesope Nat. Facility Time Allocation Cttee 2002–04, Australian Nat. Acad. LOFAR Working Group 2003, Australian Decade Plan Working Group on Int. Facilities 2004; mem. Major Nat. Research Facility Selection Panel 2001, Council of Astronomical Soc. of Australia 2001–03, Australian Square Kilometre Array Steering Cttee 2001–, Anglo Australian Telescope Bd 2004–; Dir (non-exec.) Astronomy Australia Ltd 2007–; Fellow, Japanese Soc. for the Promotion of Science 1999, NAS 2008; Glenn C. Purviance Scholarship, Univ. of Arizona 1988, Vesto Slipher Scholarship, Univ. of Arizona 1988–89, Most Outstanding Student in Physics, Univ. of Arizona 1989, Danforth Award for Excellence in Teaching, Harvard Univ. 1991, NASA Grad. Student Researchers Program Fellowship Recipient 1992–93, Science Magazine's 'Breakthrough of the Year' 1998, Bok Prize for Outstanding Astronomical Thesis, Harvard Univ. 2000, Inaugural Malcolm McIntosh Prize, Australian Govt 2000, Pawsey Medal, Australian Acad. of Sciences 2001, Harley Wood Lecturer, Astronomical Soc. of Australia 2001, Burbidge Lecturer, Auckland Astronomical Soc. 2001, Inaugural Oliphant Lecturer, Australian Acad. of Science 2001, Vainu Bappu Medal, Astronomical Soc. of India 2002, Dean's Lecturer, Univ. of Western Australia 2004, Australian Academy of Science 50th Anniversary Lecture 2004, Bulletin Magazine's Scientist of the Year 2004, Marc Aaronson Memorial Lecturer 2005, Shaw Prize in Astronomy (co-recipient) 2006, Gurevitch Lecture, Portland State Univ. 2007, Niels Bohr Lecturer, Copenhagen 2007, Gruber Prize for Cosmology (co-recipient) 2007, Sackler Lecturer, Princeton Univ. 2008, ISI Most Cited Australian in Space Sciences 1997–2007 2008. *Publications:* more than 110 scientific papers in professional journals on observational cosmology, studies of supernovae, gamma ray bursts, large surveys, photometry and calibration. *Address:* The Research School of Astronomy and Astrophysics, ANU Mount Stromlo Observatory, via Cotter Road, Weston Creek, ACT 2611, Australia (office). *Telephone:* (2) 6125-8042 (office); (408)

383365 (mobile). *Fax:* (2) 6125-0260 (office). *E-mail:* brian@mso.anu.edu.au (office). *Website:* msowww.anu.edu.au/~brian (office).

SCHMIDT, Chauncey Everett, BS, MBA; American banker and business executive; *Chairman, Cybernet Software Systems Inc.;* b. 7 June 1931, Oxford, Ia; s. of Walter F. Schmidt and Vilda Saxton; m. Anne Garrett McWilliams 1954 (deceased); one s. two d.; ed US Naval Acad., Harvard Graduate School of Business Admin.; with First Nat. Bank of Chicago 1959–75, Vice-Pres. 1965, Gen. Man., London 1966, Gen. Man. for Europe, Middle East and Africa 1968, Sr Vice-Pres. 1969–72, Exec. Vice-Pres. 1972, Vice-Chair. 1973, Pres. 1974–75; Chair. and CEO, Bank of Calif. 1976–84; Chair., Pres., CEO BanCal Tri-State Corpn 1976–84; Chair. Cybernet Software Systems 2004–; Founder and Chair. C.E.Schmidt and Assocs Inc.; Dir Docuton, Barry Financial, UBS Asset Man., Amfac Ltd, Calif. Bankers Clearing House Asscn, Calif. Roundtable, Bay Area Council; Exec. Bd San Francisco Bay Area Council of Boy Scouts of America; Bd of Govs San Francisco Symphony; mem. Fed. Advisory Council of Fed. Res. System, Advisory Council of Japan–US Econ. Relations, SRI Int. Council, Int. Monetary Conf., American Bankers Asscn. *Address:* Cybernet Software Systems Inc., 3031 Tisch Way, Suite 1002, San Jose, CA 95128 (office); 40 Why Worry Farm, Woodside, CA 94062, USA (home). *Telephone:* (408) 615-5700 (office). *Fax:* (408) 615-5707 (office). *E-mail:* css .westcoast@cybernetsoft.com (office). *Website:* www.cybernetsoft.com (office).

SCHMIDT, Christian, PhD, D.SC.ECON.; French economist and academic; *Director, Laboratory of Economics and Sociology of Defence Organizations (LESOD);* b. 20 July 1938, Neuilly-sur-Seine; s. of Paul Schmidt and Jeanne Loriot; m. Marie-Pierre de Cossè Brissac 1988; ed Facultés de Lettres, Droit, Sciences, Inst. d'Etudes Politiques, Paris, Inst. des Hautes Etudes de Défense Nationale, Acad. of Int. Law, The Hague; Research Asst Inst. of Applied Econ. Sciences Laboratoire Coll. de France 1964–67; Asst La Sorbonne 1967–70; Chargé de Mission Forecasting Admin. Ministry of Finances 1970–72; f. Dir Econ. Perspectives 1969–86; Asst Dir French Inst. of War Studies 1980–82; Pres. Charles Gide Asscn for the Study of Econ. Thought 1981–90; Consultant on Econ. Aspects of Disarmament UN 1980; Prof. of Econs Univ. of Paris IX (Paris Dauphine) 1983–; Pres., Founder Asscn française des économistes de défense 1981–, Int. Defence Econ. Asscn 1985–; Dir Lab. of Econs and Sociology of Defence Orgs. (LESOD) 1984–; Co-Dir (Research Group) CNRS 1990–; Chair. Scientific Council of European Soc. of Econ. Thought; mem. Council French Econs Asscn 2000–04, Societé d'Economie Politique 2000–; mem. various editorial bds; Croix de Chevalier, Légion d'honneur; Prix de L'institut (Acad. des Sciences Morales et Politiques) 1986, 1993. *Publications:* Conséquences Economiques et Sociales de la Course aux Armaments 1983, Essai sur l'Economie Ricardienne 1984, La Semantique Economique en Question 1985, Peace, Defence and Economic Analysis 1987, The Economics of Military Expenditures 1989, Penser la Guerre, Penser l'Economie 1991, Game Theory and International Relations 1994, Uncertainty and Economic Thought 1996, Game Theory and International Relations (co-ed.) 1996, The Rational Foundations of Economic Behaviour (co-ed.) 1996, La Theorie des Jeux: Essai d'Interpretation 2001, Game Theory and Economic Analysis 2002; numerous articles in learned journals. *Leisure interests:* theatre, opera. *Address:* Université de Paris-IX Dauphine, Place du Maréchal de Lattre de Tassigny, 75775 Paris cedex 16 (office); 109 rue de Grenelle, 75007 Paris, France (home). *Telephone:* 1-44-05-49-39 (office); 1-45-51-01-78 (home). *Fax:* 1-44-05-46-87 (office); 1-45-51-22-70 (home). *E-mail:* christian.schmidt@dauphine.fr (office); schmidt@magic.fr (home).

SCHMIDT, Eric E., BS, MS, PhD; American computer industry executive; *Chairman of the Executive Committee and CEO, Google Inc.;* b. 27 April 1955, Washington, DC; m. Wendy Schmidt; two c.; ed Princeton Univ., Univ. of California, Berkeley; began career with Bell Labs and Zilog; mem. Research Staff Computer Science Lab., Xerox Palo Alto Research Center (PARC) 1979–83; Software Man. Sun Microsystems 1983–84, Software Dir 1984–85, Vice Pres. Software Products 1985–88, Vice Pres. Gen. Systems Group 1988–91, Chief Tech. Officer 1994–97, Pres. Sun Tech. Enterprises 1991–94; Chair. and CEO Novell Inc. 1997–2001; Chair. of Exec. Cttee and CEO Google Inc. 2001–, Volera Inc.; mem. Bd of Dirs Siebel Systems Inc., Integrated Archive Systems, Tilion, Apple Computer Inc. 2006–; Chair. New America Foundation 2008–; mem. IEEE, American Acad. of Arts and Sciences, Assocn of Computing Machinery. *Address:* Google Inc., 1600 Amphitheatre Pkwy, Mountain View, CA 94043, USA (office). *Telephone:* (650) 330-0100 (office). *Fax:* (650) 618-1499 (office). *Website:* www.google.com (office).

SCHMIDT, Helmut; German politician, economist and publisher; *Co-Publisher, Die Zeit;* b. 23 Dec. 1918, Hamburg; s. of Gustav Schmidt and Ludovica Schmidt; m. Hannelore Glaser 1942; one d.; ed Lichtwarkschule and Univ. Hamburg; Man. Transport Admin. of State of Hamburg 1949–53; mem. Social Democrat Party 1946–; mem. Bundestag 1953–61, 1965–87; Chair. Social Democrat (SPD) Parl. Party in Bundestag 1967–69; Vice-Chair. SPD 1968–84; Senator (Minister) for Domestic Affairs in Hamburg 1961–65; Minister of Defence 1969–72, for Econ. and Finance July–Dec. 1972, of Finance 1972–74; Fed. Chancellor 1974–82; Co-Publr Die Zeit (weekly newspaper), Hamburg 1983–; Co-founder Inter Action Councils 1983; Hon. DCL (Oxford) 1979; Dr hc (Newberry Coll.) 1973, (Johns Hopkins) 1976, (Cambridge) 1976, (Harvard) 1979, (Sorbonne) 1981, (Louvain) 1984, (Georgetown) 1986, (Bergamo) 1989, (Tokyo) 1991, (Haifa) 2000, (Potsdam) 2000 and others; European Prize for Statesmanship (FUS Foundation) 1979, Nahum Goldmann Silver Medal 1980, Athinai Prize 1986. *Publications:* Defence or Retaliation 1962, Beiträge 1967, Strategie des Gleichgewichts (trans. as Balance of Power) 1969, Kontinuität und Konzentration 1976, Als Christ in der politischen Entscheidung 1976, Der Kurs heisst Frieden 1979, Pflicht zur Menschlichkeit 1981, Kunst im Kanzleramt 1982, Freiheit verantworten 1983, Die Weltwirtschaft ist unser Schicksal 1983, Eine Strategie für den Westen (trans. as A Grand Strategy for the West) (Adolphe Bentinck Prize) 1986, Vom deutschen Stolz: Bekenntnisse zur Erfahrung von Kunst 1986, Menschen und Mächte (trans. as Men and Powers) 1987, Die Deutschen und ihre Nachbarn 1990, Mit Augenmass und Weitblick 1990, Einfügen in die Gemeinschaft der Völker 1990, Kindheit und Jugend unter Hitler 1992, Ein Manifest – Weil das Land sich ändern muss (co-author) 1992, Handeln für Deutschland 1993, Jahr der Entscheidung 1994, Was wird aus Deutschland? 1994, Weggefährten 1996, Jahrhundertwende 1998, Allgemeine Erklärung der Menschenpflichten 1998, Globalisierung 1998, Auf der Suche nach einer öffentlichen Moral 1998, Die Selbstbehauptung Europas 2000, Hand aufs Herz 2002, Die Mächte der Zukunft 2005. *Address:* Die Zeit, Speersort 1, Pressehaus, 20095 Hamburg (office); Bundeskanzler a.D., Deutscher Bundestag, Platz der Republik 1, 11011 Berlin, Germany. *Telephone:* (40) 32800 (office); (30) 22771580. *Fax:* (40) 327111 (office); (30) 22770571. *Website:* www .zeit.de (office).

SCHMIDT, Klaus, PhD; German economist and academic; *Professor, Faculty of Economics, Ludwig-Maximilians-Universität München;* b. 16 June 1961, Koblenz; m. Monika Schnitzer; three d.; ed Univs of Marburg, Hamburg and Bonn and London School of Econs; Visiting Asst Prof., MIT, USA 1992; Asst Prof., Univ. of Bonn 1993–95; Full Prof. of Econs, Ludwig-Maximilians-Universität München 1995–; Visiting Prof., Stanford Univ. 2000, Yale Univ. 2004. *Address:* Department of Economics, Ludwig-Maximilians-Universität München, Room 08, Ludwigstr. 28, 80539 Munich, Germany (office). *Telephone:* (89) 21802250 (office). *Fax:* (89) 21803510 (office). *E-mail:* klaus .schmidt@lmu.de (office). *Website:* www.vwl.uni-muenchen.de (office).

SCHMIDT, Maarten, PhD, ScD; Dutch astronomer and academic; *Professor Emeritus of Astronomy, California Institute of Technology;* b. 28 Dec. 1929, Groningen; s. of W. Schmidt and A. W. Haringhuizen; m. Cornelia J. Tom 1955; three d.; ed Univs of Groningen and Leiden; Scientific Officer Univ. of Leiden Observatory 1949–59; Carnegie Fellow, Mt. Wilson Observatory, Pasadena 1956–58; Assoc. Prof. Calif. Inst. of Tech. 1959–64, Prof. of Astronomy 1964–96, Prof. Emer. 1996–; Pres. American Astronomical Soc. 1984–86;; Warner Prize 1964, Rumford Award, American Acad. of Arts and Sciences 1968, Jansky Prize, Nat. Radio Astronomy Observatory 1979, Royal Astronomy Soc. Gold Medal 1980, James Craig Watson Medal, NAS 1991, Bruce Medal 1992,. *Achievements include:* discovered large red shifts in spectra of quasi-stellar radio sources (quasars). *Leisure interest:* classical music. *Address:* California Institute of Technology, 204 Robinson Laboratory, 1201 E California Boulevard, Pasadena, CA 91125, USA (office). *Telephone:* (626) 395-4204 (office). *E-mail:* mxs@astro.caltech.edu (office). *Website:* www .astro.caltech.edu (office).

SCHMIDT, Ole; Danish conductor and composer; b. 14 July 1928, Copenhagen; s. of Hugo Schmidt and Erna S. P. Schmidt; m. Lizzie Rode Schmidt 1960; two d.; ed Royal Danish Acad. of Music, Copenhagen; conducting debut 1955; Conductor, Royal Theatre, Copenhagen 1959–65; Chief Conductor, Hamburg Symphony 1969–70; Conductor Danish Radio Concert Orchestra 1971–73; Chief Conductor and Artistic Dir Århus Symphony 1978–84; Perm. Guest Conductor, Royal Northern Coll. of Music, Manchester 1986–89; Interim Prin. Conductor and Artistic Dir The Toledo Symphony, Ohio 1989–90, now Prin. Guest Conductor; Carl Nielsen Legat 1975; Gramex Award 1975, H.C. Lumbye Award 1988. *Leisure interests:* writing, painting, gardening.

SCHMIDT, Renate; German politician; b. 12 Dec. 1943, Hanau/Main; m.; three c.; worked as programmer, systems analyst and mem. of works cttee of mail-order co.; mem. SPD 1972–; mem. Bundestag (Parl.) 1980–94, 2005–; Deputy Chair. SPD Parl. Party in Bundestag (Chair. of Equal Rights for Woman and Man working group) 1987–90; Vice-Pres. Bundestag 1990–94; Chair. SPD Bavaria 1991–2000; directly elected mem. of Parl. for Nuremberg N in Bavarian Landtag; Chair. SPD Parl. Party in Bavarian Landtag 1994–2002; Deputy Chair. SPD 1997–; Federal Minister for Family Affairs, Senior Citizens, Women and Youth 2002–05; Pres. Bavarian Red Cross 1993–2002, Deutscher Familienverband May–Oct. 2002, Zentralstelle für Recht und Schutz der Kriegsdienstverweigerer aus Gewissensgründen e.V. –Oct. 2002; mem. HBV, AWO, Socialist Youth Germany 'Die Falken', Bund Naturschutz, AIDS-Hilfe, Bd of Trustees of the Deutscher Kinderschutzbund. *Address:* Deutscher Bundestag, Platz der Republik 1, 11011 Berlin (office); Friedrich-List-Str.5, 91054 Erlangen, Germany. *Telephone:* (30) 22772504 (office); (9131) 8126533 (Erlangen). *Fax:* (30) 22776703 (office); (9131) 8126535 (Erlangen). *E-mail:* renate.schmidt@bundestag.de (office); berlin@ renateschmidt.de. *Website:* www.renateschmidt.de.

SCHMIDT, Ulla; German politician; *Minister for Health;* b. 13 June 1949; ed Einhard Municipal Secondary School, Aachen, Tech. Univ. of Aachen, Teachers' Coll., Aachen, Distance Univ. of Hagen; teacher at school for learning disabled, Stolberg 1976–85, at school for remedial educ., Dist of Aachen 1985–90; mem. local and dist personnel councils, of personnel council for teachers at special educ. schools, Office of Minister of Educ. and Cultural Affairs, State of North Rhine-Westphalia 1980–90; mem. SPD 1983–, Chair. Local Party Org., Richterich, mem. Sub-dist Party Exec., Aachen, SPD Party Council, Aachen City Council Housing Policy, Spokeswoman of SPD Group, Aachen, SPD Deputy Chair. for Aachen City Sub-dist 2000–; mem. Bundestag 1990–, mem. Exec. Directorate SPD Parl. Group 1991–2001, Chair. Cross-Sectoral Group for the Equality of Men and Women, SPD Parl. Group, Deputy mem. (later full mem.) Mediation Cttee, Spokeswomen for project group 'Family Policy in the 21st Century', Spokeswomen for ad hoc working group 'Sexual Violence against Children' 1991–98, Deputy Chair. for Labour and Social Affairs, Women, Family Affairs, and Senior Citizens, SPD Rep. on ZDF TV Council 1998–2001; Fed. Minister for Health 2001–02, Minister for Health 2002–; mem. IG BCE, AWO, Child Protection Fed., ASB. *Address:* Ministry for Health, 53109 Bonn (office); Ministry for Health, Am Propsthof 78A, 53121

Bonn, Germany (office). *Telephone:* (30) 18884410 (office). *Fax:* (30) 18884414900 (office). *E-mail:* info@bmg.bund.de (office). *Website:* www.bmg.bund.de (office).

SCHMIDT, Werner; German banking executive; b. 13 July 1943, Sindelfingen; m.; two c.; Man. Landesbank Stuttgart 1971–74, mem. Bd of Man. Dirs 1974–86, Deputy Chair. 1986–89; Chair. Südwestdeutsche Landesbank 1989–99; Chair. Landesbank Baden-Württemberg 1999–2001; Chair. Bd of Man BayernLB (Bayerische Landesbank Girozentrale) 2001–08 (resgnd), Chair. Supervisory Bd Hypo Group Alpe Adria (after acqusition by BayernLB) 2007–08; fmr Deputy Chair. BAWAG (Bank für Arbeit und Wirtschaft AG). *Address:* c/o Bayerische Landesbank Girozentrale, Briennerstrasse 18, 80333 Munich, Germany (office).

SCHMIDT-HOLTZ, Rolf; German lawyer and music company executive; *Chairman of the Management Board and CEO, Sony BMG Music Entertainment;* b. 31 Aug. 1948, Martinsreuth; ed Univs of Erlangen and Kiel, Germany; journalist, television correspondent, Ed.-in-Chief and Publisher, magazines, newspapers; television exec.; Ed.-in-Chief WDR (German public broadcaster) 1986–88; Publr Gruner + Jahr's Stern news magazine 1988, Ed.-in-Chief 1990, mem. Exec. Bd Gruner + Jahr 1989–94; CEO UFA (Bertelsmann TV c.) 1994, CEO CLT-UFA (after merger with CLT) 1997, then merger with Pearson Television to form RTL Group 2000; Chair. and CEO BMG 2001–04, Non-Exec. Chair. Sony BMG (following merger with Sony Music Entertainment) 2004–06, Chair. Man. Bd and CEO 2006–; mem. Bertelsmann Stiftung Bd of Trustees 2005–; Co-Chair. Advisory Bd Art Dirs Club Inst., Berlin 2004–; mem. Supervisory Bd Gruner & Jahr AG, Druck-und Verlagshaus; mem. Bd of Dirs RTL Group SA 2002–. *Address:* Sony BMG Music Entertainment, 550 Madison Avenue, New York, NY 10022-3211, USA (office). *Telephone:* (212) 833-7100 (office). *Fax:* (212) 833-7416 (office). *Website:* www.sonybmg.com (office).

SCHMIDT-JORTZIG, Edzard, DrIur; German lawyer, academic and politician; *Professor of Public Law, Christian-Albrechts Kiel University;* b. 8 Oct. 1941, Berlin; s. of Rear-Adm. Friedrich-Traugott Schmidt and Carla Freiin von Frydag; m. Marion von Arnim 1968; two d. two s.; Academic Counsellor and Prof., Münster 1977; Head Law Dept, Christian-Albrechts Kiel Univ. 1982, Prof. of Public Law 1982–; Higher Admin. and Constitutional Court Judge, Lüneburg 1983–91, 1993–94; mem. Bundestag 1994–2002; Fed. Minister of Justice 1996–98; mem. FDP. *Publications:* Zur Verfassungsmässigkeit von Kreisumlagesätzen 1977, Kommunale Organisationshoheit 1979, Die Einrichtungsgarantien der Verfassung 1979, Kommunalrecht 1982, Gemeindliches Eigentum an Meereshäfen 1985, Reformüberlegungen für die Landessatzung Schleswig-Holstein 1988, Handbuch des Kommunalen Finanz und Haushaltsrechts (with J. Makswit) 1991, Staatsangehörigkeit im Wandel 1997, Wann ist der Mensch tot? 1999. *Address:* Faculty of Law, Christian-Albrechts Kiel University, Olshausenstrasse 40, 24098 Kiel, Germany (office). *Telephone:* (431) 8802125 (office). *Fax:* (431) 8801689 (office). *E-mail:* dekanat@law.uni-kiel.de (office). *Website:* www.uni-kiel.de (office).

SCHMIDT-ROHR, Ulrich, Dr rer. nat; German physicist; *Director, Max Planck Institute for Nuclear Physics;* b. 25 May 1926, Frankfurt an der Oder; s. of Georg Schmidt-Rohr and Ruth Schmidt-Rohr; m. Helma Wernery 1963; four s. one d.; ed Friedrichsgymnasium, Frankfurt an der Oder, Technische Hochschule, Berlin and Brunswick and Univ. of Heidelberg; research Lab., OSRAM 1948–49; Asst, Univ. of Heidelberg 1950–53; FSSP Fellow, MIT 1954; Asst Max Planck Inst. for Medical Research 1955–58; Asst Max Planck Inst. for Nuclear Physics 1958–61, Dir 1966–; Dir Inst. for Nuclear Physics, Kernforschungsanlage, Jülich 1962–65; Hon. Prof. Univ. of Heidelberg 1966. *Publications:* five books; papers on nuclear physics, accelerators and the history of nuclear physics in Germany. *Address:* Max Planck Institut für Kernphysik, Postfach 10 39 80, 69029 Heidelberg, Germany (office). *Telephone:* (6221) 516204 (office). *Website:* www.mpi-hd.mpg.de/english (office).

SCHMIED, Wieland; Austrian art historian and academic; b. 5 Feb. 1929, Frankfurt am Main; m. Erika Schmied 1966; two d.; ed Univ. of Vienna; reader, Insel Verlag, Frankfurt 1960–62; Art Critic, Frankfurter Allgemeinen Zeitung 1960–62; Dir Kestner-Gesellschaft, Hannover 1963–74; Dir Berliner Künstlerprogramm DAAD (Artists-in-Residence Programme) 1978–86; Prof. of Art History, Acad. of Fine Arts, Munich 1986–94, Rector 1988–93; Pres. Int. Summer Acad. of Fine Arts, Salzburg 1981–99; mem. Bayerische Akad. der Schönen Künste 1988–, Dir Abteilung Bildenden Kunst 1992–95, Pres. 1995–2004; Vienna City Prize for Essays 1984, Staatspreis for Essays, Vienna 1992, Friedrich Märker Award for Essays, Munich 1994, Theo Wormland Award, Munich 1997. *Publications:* Schach mit Marcel Duchamp 1980, De Chirico und sein Schatten 1989, Berührungen (essays) 1991, Caspar David Friedrich 1992, 2002, De Chiricos beunruhigende Musen 1993, Ezra Pound. Ein Leben zwischen Kunst und Politik 1994, Edward Hoppers Amerika 1995, Thomas Bernhards Häuser 1995, Francis Bacon 1996, Max Weiler – Ein anderes Bild der Natur. Der Weg zum Spätwerk 1998, Thomas Bernhards Welt. Schauplätze seiner Jugend 1999, Caspar David Friedrich – Zyklus, Zeit and Ewigkeit 1999, Museum der Malerei 1999, Thomas Bernhards Österreich. Schauplätze seiner Romane 2000, Ezra Pound Studien 2000, Giorgio de Chirico – Reise ohne Ende 2001, Der kühle Blick – Kunst der 20er Jahre 2001, H.C. Artmann: Erinnerungen und Essays 2001, Die andere Moderne – De Chirico und Savinio (with Paolo Baldacci) 2001, Geschichte der Bildenden Künste in Österreich Das 20. Jhdt. 2002, Wohin geht die Reise der bildenden Kunst? 2003, Die schwierige Schönheit. Ezra Pound und die bildende Kunst 2003, Hundertwassers Paradiese 2003, Leidenschaft und kühler Blick (essays) 2004, Begegnung mit Samuel Beckett in Berlin 2006; major catalogues on modern art. *Address:* Bayerische Akademie der Schönen Künste, Max Joseph Platz 3, 80539 Munich, Germany (office). *Telephone:* (89) 2900770 (office). *Fax:* (89) 29007723 (office). *E-mail:* bayerische-akademie@gmx.de (office). *Website:* www.badsk.de/home (office).

SCHMITT, Harrison H., BS, PhD; American geologist, business executive, fmr politician and fmr astronaut; *Chairman Emeritus, The Annapolis Center for Science-Based Public Policy;* b. 3 July 1935, Santa Rita, NM; s. of Harrison A. Schmitt and Ethel Hagan Schmitt; m. Teresa Fitzgibbons 1985; ed Calif. Inst. of Tech., Univ. of Oslo, Norway and Harvard Univ.; Fulbright Fellowship 1957–58, Kennecott Fellowship in Geology 1958–59, Harvard Fellowship 1959–60, Harvard Travelling Fellowship 1960, Parker Travelling Fellowship 1961–62, NSF Postdoctoral Fellowship, Dept of Geological Sciences, Harvard 1963–64; has done geological work for Norwegian Geological Survey, Oslo, for US Geological Survey, NM and Montana and in Alaska 1955–56; with US Geological Survey Astrogeology Dept until 1965; Project Chief on photo and telescopic mapping of moon and planets; selected as scientist-astronaut by NASA June 1965; completed flight training 1966; Lunar Module pilot Apollo XVII Dec. 1972; Chief, Astronaut Office, Science and Applications, Johnson Space Center 1974; Asst Admin., Energy Programs, NASA, Washington, DC 1974–76; Senator from New Mexico 1977–83; Consultant 1983–; mem. Pres.'s Foreign Intelligence Advisory Bd 1984–85, Army Sciences Bd 1985–89, Army Research Lab. Tech. Review Bd 1993–; co-leader group to monitor Romanian elections 1990; Chair., Pres. Annapolis Center 1994–98, now Chair. Emer. and mem. Bd of Dirs; Adjunct Prof., Univ. of Wisconsin 1995–; Republican; Lovelace Award, NASA 1989, Gilbert Award, GSA 1989. *Address:* c/o Board of Directors, The Annapolis Center for Science-Based Public Policy, 111 Forbes Street, Suite 200, Annapolis, MD 21401, USA. *E-mail:* Info@AnnCtr.org. *Website:* www.annapoliscenter.org.

SCHMITTER, Philippe, BA, PhD; American academic; *Emeritus Professor, European University Institute;* b. 19 Nov. 1936, Washington, DC; m. (divorced); one d. one s.; ed Dartmouth Coll., Univ. Nacional Autónoma de México, Mexico, Univ. of Geneva, Switzerland, Univ. of Calif. at Berkeley; Research Asst, Univ. of Calif., Berkeley 1961–62, Fellowship Coordinator, Inst. of Int. Studies 1964, Research Political Scientist 1966–67; Lecturer, Sacramento State Coll. 1967; Asst Prof., Dept of Political Sciences, Univ. of Chicago 1967–71, Chair. Cttee on Latin American Studies 1970–73, 1974–76, Assoc. Prof. 1971–75, Founding Chair. Cttee on Western Europe 1974–77, Prof. 1975–84; Dir European Univ. Inst. (EUI) Summer School, Florence, Italy 1983, Prof. Dept of Social and Political Sciences 1982–86, Prof. of Political Science –2004, Emerit. Prof. 2004–; Prof., Stanford Program-in-Paris 1993; Prof., Dept of Political Science, Stanford Univ. 1985–98, Prof. Emer. 1999–; Visiting Prof., Univ. of Brazil 1965–66, INTAL, Buenos Aires 1969, Harvard Univ. 1970, Univs of Geneva 1973–74, Paris I 1976, Mannheim 1977–78, Zurich 1978, Barcelona 1984, Univ. Autónoma de Madrid 1990, Univ. Menendez Pelayo, Valencia 1993, Inst. of Political Studies, Paris 1994, Bilkent Univ., Ankara 1995, Univ. of Siena 1999–2002; Recurrent Visiting Prof. Central European Univ. 2005–; mem. Editorial Bd Comparative Political Studies 1974–77, Armed Forces and Society 1976–82, Historical Social Research 1976–83, Papers: Revista de Sociologia 1979–85, Politics and Soc. 1982–86, Stato e mercato 1983–86, 1997–, Journal of Democracy 1992–, The Encyclopedia of Democracy 1992–, Review Int. de Politique Comparée 1993–, Swiss Political Science Review 1995–, Politique et Sociétés 1995–; mem. numerous academic advisory bds; mem. Société Tocqueville 1977–, Asscn Française de Science Politique 1981–, Schweizerische Vereinigung für Politische Wissenschaft 1981–, Società italiana di scienza politica 1982–, Deutsche Vereinigung für Politische Wissenschaft 1982–; mem. Research Cttee on European Unification, Int. Political Science Asscn 1993–; Int. Fellow, Council on Foreign Relations, New York 1972–73, Fellow, Alexander von Humboldt Stiftung 1977, J.S. Guggenheim Foundation 1978, Center for Advanced Studies in the Behavioural Sciences 1991–92, Collegium Budapest 2005–06; Recurring Visiting Prof., Central European Univ. 2004–; numerous fellowships and research grants; Hon. Prof. Konstanz Univ. 1999–2002; Dissertation Prize, Univ. of Calif., Berkeley 1968, ECPR Lifetime Acheivement Prize 2008, EUSA Contrib. to European Integration Prize 2009, IPSA Mattei Doggan Award 2009, Johan Skytte Prize, Univ. of Uppsala 2009. *Publications:* Corporatism and Public Policy in Authoritarian Portugal 1975, Trends Toward Corporatist Intermediation (co-author) 1984, Patterns of Corporatist Policy-Making (co-author) 1982, La politica degli interessi nei paesi industrializzati (co-author) 1984, Private Interest Government and Public Policy (co-ed.) 1985, Transitions from Authoritarian Rule: Tentative Conclusions about Uncertain Democracies (co-author) 1986, Transitions from Authoritarian Rule: Prospects for Democracy, Vols I-IV (co-author) 1986, Neocorporativismo (co-author) 1992, Sustainable Democracy (co-author) 1995, Governance in the European Union (co-author) 1996, El fin del siglo del corporativismo (co-author) 1998, Portugal: do autoritarismo à democracia 1999, Come democratizzare l'Unione Europea...e perché 2000; numerous articles in professional journals and chapters in books. *Address:* Department of Social and Political Sciences, European University Institute, Badia Fiesolana, Via dei Roccettini, 9, 50016 San Domenico di Fiesole (FI), (office); Via di Monteloro 31/A, 50069 Le Sieci (FI), Italy (home). *Telephone:* 055 4685274 (office); 055 8300613 (home). *Fax:* 055 4685201 (office). *E-mail:* philippe.schmitter@iue.it (office). *Website:* www.iue.it (office).

SCHMÖGNEROVÁ, Brigita, PhD; Slovak international organization official and politician; *Vice-President, European Bank for Reconstruction and Development;* b. 17 Nov. 1947, Bratislava; m.; one s.; ed School of Econs, Bratislava; teacher, Univ. of Athens, Greece and Georgetown Univ., Washington, DC, USA; researcher, Inst. of Econs, Slovak Acad. of Sciences; Lecturer, Univ. of Econs, Bratislava; Econ. Adviser to Pres. of Slovak Repub. 1993; Deputy Prime Minister 1994; mem. Parl. 1995–98; Minister of Finance 1998–2002; Exec. Sec. UN Econ. ECE 2002–05; adviser to IMF, IBRD and EBRD; Vice-Pres. EBRD 2005–; World Finance Minister of the Year Award, Euromoney

Inst. Investor 2000. *Address:* European Bank for Reconstruction and Development, One Exchange Square, London, EC2A 2JN, England (office). *Telephone:* (20) 7338-6000 (office). *Fax:* (20) 7338-6910 (office). *E-mail:* ngr@ebrd.com (office). *Website:* www.ebrd.com (office).

SCHNABEL, Julian, BFA; American painter and film director; b. 26 Oct. 1951, Brooklyn, New York; ed Univ. of Houston, Whitney Museum Ind. Study Program, New York. *Films:* Basquiat 1996, Before Night Falls 2000, Sketches of Frank Gehry 2006, Le Scaphandre et le Papillon (Best Dir, Cannes Film Festival 2007, Best European Film, San Sebastian Film Festival 2007, Best Foreign Film, Nat. Bd of Review 2007, Golden Globe for Best Foreign Language Film, Golden Globe for Best Director 2008) 2007, Berlin 2007. *Publication:* Nicknames of Maître D's and Other Excerpts From Life 1988. *Address:* c/o PaceWildenstein Gallery New York, 32 East 57th Street, New York, NY 10022, USA.

SCHNABEL, Rockwell Anthony; American business executive and fmr diplomatist; *Chairman, Sage LLC;* ed Trinity Coll.; fmr financial analyst; fmr Pres. Bateman, Eichler, Hill, Richards Inc. (now First Union Securities); Co-Founder and Chair. Trident Capital 1993–2001, Advisory Dir 2005; Amb. to Finland 1986–89; Deputy Sec. Dept of Commerce 1989, then Acting Sec. of Commerce; Amb. to EU 2001–05; Founder and Chair. Sage LLC, Los Angeles 2006–; mem. Bd of Dirs Flextronics, Singapore and Lhoist, Brussels; mem. Los Angeles Olympic Cttee 1984; fmr Envoy to The Netherlands; Grand Cross of the Order of the Lion of Finland 1989; Hon. DJur (Pepperdine Univ.); Netherlands Olympic Cttee Medal of Honor 1984, Netherlands Govt Gold Medal 1984, US Dept of Commerce Gold Medal Award. *Publication:* The Next Superpower? The Rise of Europe and Its Challenge to the United States (co-author) 2005. *Address:* Sage LLC, 11111 Santa Monica Boulevard, Suite 2200, Los Angeles, CA 90025, USA (office). *Telephone:* (310) 478-7899 (home). *Fax:* (310) 478-6619 (office). *E-mail:* contact@sagellc.com (office). *Website:* www.sagellc.com (office).

SCHNACKENBERG, Gjertrud, BA; American poet and writer; b. 27 Aug. 1953, Tacoma, Wash.; m. Robert Nozick 1987 (died 2002); ed Mount Holyoke Coll.; Fellow in Poetry, The Radcliffe Inst. 1979–80; Christensen Fellow, Saint Catherine's Coll., Oxford 1997; Visiting Scholar, Getty Research Inst., J. Paul Getty Museum 2000; Fellow, American Acad. of Arts and Sciences 1996; Guggenheim Fellowship 1987–88; Dr hc (Mount Holyoke Coll.) 1985;Daimler Chrysler Berlin Prize Fellow, American Acad., Berlin 2004; Glascock Award for Poetry 1973, 1974, Acad. of American Poets Lavan Younger Poets Award 1983, American Acad. and Inst. of Arts and Letters Rome Prize 1983–84, Amy Lowell Traveling Prize 1984–85, Nat. Endowment for the Arts grant 1986–87, American Acad. of Arts and Letters Award in Literature 1998, Los Angeles Times Book Prize in Poetry 2001. *Publications:* Portraits and Elegies 1982, The Lamplit Answer 1985, A Gilded Lapse of Time 1992, The Throne of Labdacus 2000, Supernatural Love: Poems 1976–1992 2000; contrib. to books and journals. *Address:* c/o Farrar, Straus & Giroux Inc., 19 Union Square West, New York, NY 10003, USA (office).

SCHNAPPER, Dominique, DSc; French sociologist and writer; *Member, Conseil Constitutionnel;* b. 9 Nov. 1934, Paris; d. of Raymond Aron and Suzanne Gauchon; m. Antoine Schnapper 1958; three c; ed Institut d'Etudes Politiques de Paris, Sorbonne, Université Paris V; Prof. Dir of Studies Ecole des Hautes Etudes en Sciences Sociales (Paris) 1980–; mem. Comm. Marceau Long on the reform of the nation 1987, Comm. 2000 1989, Comm. on Drugs Henrion 1994, Comm. on Educ. Fauroux 1995–96; mem. Steering Cttee of French Soc. of Sociology 1991–95, Pres. 1995–99; mem. Conseil Constitutionnel (French Supreme Court) 2001–; Chevalier de la Légion d'honneur, Officier des Arts et des lettres; Prix de l'Assemblée Nat. 1994, Balzan Prize for Sociology 2002. *Publications include:* La Communauté des citoyens 1994, La Rélation a l'autre 1998, Qu'est ce que la citoyénneté? 2000, La Démocratie providentielle 2002, Diasporas et nations 2006, Qu'est ce que l'intégration? 2007. *Address:* Conseil Constitutionnel, 2 rue de Montpension, 75001 Paris (office); Maison des Sciences de l'Homme, 54 blvd Raspail, 75007 Paris, France. *Telephone:* 1-40-15-30-00 (office). *Fax:* 1-40-20-93-27 (office). *E-mail:* relations-exterieures@conseil-constitutionnel.fr (office); schnapp@ehess.fr (office). *Website:* www.conseil-constitutionnel.fr (office).

SCHNEBLI, Dolf, MArch; Swiss architect and planner; *Partner, SAM Architects and Partner Inc.;* b. 27 Dec. 1928, Baden; s. of Robert Schnebli and Margret Heer; m. Jamileh Jahanguiri; one s. two d.; ed Swiss Fed. Inst. of Tech. (ETH), Zürich and Harvard Grad. School of Design, USA; own architectural office 1958; Pnr Ryser, Engeler, Meier 1971; Prof., ETH Zürich 1971, Prof. Emer.; Pnr Schnebli Ammann Ruchat 1990, Schnebli Ammann Menz SAM Architects, now Schnebli Menz SAM Architects, mem. Bd SAM Architects and Pnr Inc. 1997–; Pres. Schnebli Ammann Ruchat & Assocs Architecture, Planning, Urban Design 1994; Hon. mem. BDA, Hon. Prof., South China Univ. 1983; numerous first prizes in architecture competitions and other awards. *Publication:* SAM – Recent Buildings and Projects 1998. *Leisure interests:* visual arts, literature. *Address:* SAM Architects and Partner Inc., Hardturmstrasse 175, PO Box 48, 8037 Zürich (office); Südstrasse 45, 8008 Zürich, Switzerland (home). *Telephone:* (1) 4474343 (office); (1) 3831430 (home). *Fax:* (1) 4474340 (office); (1) 3832737 (home). *E-mail:* dschnebli@samarch.ch (office). *Website:* www.samarch.ch (office).

SCHNEIDER, Cynthia Perrin, PhD; American academic and fmr diplomatist; *Distinguished Professor in Practice of Diplomacy, School of Foreign Service, Georgetown University;* b. 16 Aug. 1953, Pa; ed Harvard Univ., Oxford Univ.; Asst Curator of European Paintings, Museum of Fine Arts, Boston; Asst Prof. of Art History, Georgetown Univ. 1984–90, Assoc. Prof. 1990, Distinguished Prof. in Practice of Diplomacy, School of Foreign Service 2004–, Pfizer Medical Humanities Scholar in Residence, Public Policy Inst. and Dir Life Sciences and Society Initiative 2004–06; Amb. to Netherlands 1998–2001; Nonresident Sr Fellow, Foreign Policy, Saban Center for Middle East Policy, Brookings Inst.; Vice-Chair. Pres.'s Cttee on the Arts and Humanities; fmr mem. Bd of Dirs Nat. Museum of Women in the Arts, Australian-American Leadership Dialogue. *Publications:* Rembrandt's Landscapes 1990, Rembrandt's Landscapes: Drawing and Prints 1990. *Address:* Georgetown University, Box 571444, 3300 Whitehaven Street, NW, Suite 5000, Washington, DC 20057-1485, USA (office). *Telephone:* (202) 687-0703 (office). *Fax:* (301) 924-8715 (office). *E-mail:* schneidc@georgetown.edu (office); cpschneider@restructassoc.com. *Website:* hpi.georgetown.edu/lifesciandsociety (office).

SCHNEIDER, Manfred; German business executive; *Chairman of the Supervisory Board, Bayer AG;* b. 21 Dec. 1938, Bremerhaven; m.; one d.; ed Univs of Freiburg, Hamburg and Cologne; joined Bayer AG, Leverkusen 1966, Head Finance and Accounting Dept of subsidiary co. Duisburger Kupferhütte, later Chair. of Bd; returned to Bayer AG 1981, apptd. Head Regional Co-ordination, Corp. Auditing and Control 1984, mem. Bd of Man. 1987–2002, Chair. 1992–2002, Chair. Supervisory Bd 2002–; Chair. Supervisory Bd, Linde AG, Munich; mem. Supervisory Bd Daimler AG, Stuttgart (mem. Chair.'s Council 2001–), RWE AG, Essen, TUI AG Hanover; Pres. German Chemical Industry Asscn (VCI) 1999–2001. *Address:* Bayer AG, Bayerwerk, Gebäude W11, Kaiser-Wilhelm-Allee, 51368 Leverkusen, Germany (office). *Telephone:* (214) 301 (office). *Fax:* (214) 3066328 (office). *E-mail:* info@bayer.com (office). *Website:* www.bayer.com (office).

SCHNEIDER, Peter; German politician and business executive; *Chairman of the Supervisory Board, Landesbank Baden-Württemberg;* b. 27 July 1958, Riedlingen; m. Rose Marie Schneider 1978; two s.; mem. CDU 1976–; with Co. Dept Sigmaringen 1986–88; Pvt. Sec. to Ministry of Interior Dietmar Schlee 1988–92; worked for Biberach Dist 1992–2006; mem. State Parl. of Baden-Württemberg 2001–; Pres. Sparkassenverband Baden-Württemberg (Savings Bank Asscn of Baden-Württemberg), Stuttgart 2006–; currently Chair. Supervisory Bd Landesbank Baden-Württemberg; Dist Chair. German Red Cross Biberach. *Address:* Sparkassenverband Baden-Württemberg, Am Hauptbahnhof 2, 70173 Stuttgart (office); Landesbank Baden-Württemberg, Am Hauptbahnhof 2, 70173 Stuttgart, Germany (office). *Telephone:* (711) 127-0 (office). *Fax:* (711) 12743544 (office). *E-mail:* Peter.Schneider@sv-bw.de (office); Peter.Schneider@CDU.landtag-bw.de (office). *Website:* www.peter-schneider-bc.de.

SCHNEIDERHAN, Gen. Wolfgang; German army officer; *Inspector General of the Bundeswehr;* b. 26 July 1946, Riedlingen, Donau; m. Elke Schneiderhan (née Speckhardt); two d. three s.; ed Bundeswehr Command and Staff Coll., Hamburg; began career with Bundeswehr (German Armed Forces) 1966; Youth Information Officer, 10th Armoured Div., Sigmaringen 1972–74; Co. Commdr Armoured Battalion 293, Stetten am Kalten Markt 1974–77; Asst Br. Chief, Mil. Intelligence, Armed Forces Staff 1979–81; Asst Chief of Staff, G-3 Operations, Home Defence Brigade 55, Böblingen 1981–83; Sr Officer, G-3, Operations, NATO Cen. Europe HQ, Brunssum, The Netherlands 1983–86; CO Armoured Battalion 553, Stetten am Kalten Markt 1986–88; Chief of Staff, 4th Mechanized Div., Regensburg 1988–90; Sr Officer, Arms Control, NATO HQ, Brussels 1990–92; Dir Faculty of Army Doctrine, Bundeswehr Command and Staff Coll. 1992–94; CO Armoured 39 Brigade Thüringen, Erfurt 1994–97; Asst Chief of Staff, Planning, Fed. Ministry of Defence 1997–99; Chief of Policy and Advisory Staff 2000–02; apptd Chief of Defence 2002; Inspector Gen. of the Bundeswehr 2002–; apptd Brig.-Gen. 1996, Maj.-Gen. 1999, Lt-Gen. 2000, Gen. 2002; Gold Cross of Honour of the Bundeswehr. *Leisure interests:* contemporary history, music. *Address:* Ministry of Defence, Stauffenbergstr. 18, 10785 Berlin, Germany (office). *Telephone:* (30) 200400 (office). *Fax:* (30) 20048333 (office). *E-mail:* poststelle@bmvg.bund400.de (office). *Website:* www.bundeswehr.de (office).

SCHNIEDERS, Richard J., BSc; American food distribution executive; *Chairman, President and CEO, Sysco Corporation;* b. 1949, Remsen, Ia; s. of the late Bob Schnieders and of Helen Schnieders; m. Beth Schnieders; two d.; ed Univ. of Iowa; began career at Randall's Super Valu Stores, Iowa City; with John Morrell & Co., Des Moines, Bettesdorf and Memphis; joined Exec. Devt Program, Hardin's-Sysco, Memphis 1982, Pres. and CEO 1989–90, Chair., Pres. and CEO 1990–92, apptd Sr Vice-Pres. Merchandising Sysco Corpn, Houston, Tex. 1992, mem. Bd Dirs 1997–, Pres. and COO 2000–03, Chair. and CEO 2003–, Pres. 2005–, Chair. Exec. Cttee, Employee Benefits Cttee, mem. Finance Cttee; mem. Bd Dirs Aviall, Inc. *Address:* Sysco Corpn, 1390 Enclave Parkway, Houston, TX 77077-2099, USA (office). *Telephone:* (281) 584-1390 (office). *Fax:* (281) 584-2721 (office). *E-mail:* info@sysco.com (office). *Website:* www.sysco.com (office).

SCHOCKEMÖHLE, Alwin; German show jumper (retd) and horse breeder; b. 29 May 1937, Osterbrock, Kreis Meppen; s. of Aloys Schockemöhle and Josefa Schockemöhle (née Borgerding); m. 2nd Rita Wiltfang; two s. one d.; two d. from previous m.; began riding 1946, in public events 1948; trained in mil. riding 1954–55; reserve for Mil. and Showjumping, Melbourne Olympics 1956; specialized in showjumping 1956–77; first Derby win, riding 'Bachus', Hamburg 1957; continually in int. showjumping events 1960–77; Showjumping Champion FRG (four times); second in European Championship (three times); European Champion riding 'Warwick' 1975, 1976; gold medal (Team Award) Rome Olympics 1960; gold medal (Individual Award) and silver medal (Team Award) riding 'Warwick' Montreal Olympics 1976; currently owner Gestüt und Rennstall Alwin Schockemöhle (stud and racing stables). *Publication:* Sportkamerad Pferd (A Horse for Sports Companions). *Address:* Münsterlandstraße 53, 49453 Mühlen, Germany. *Telephone:* (54) 923823. *Fax:* (54) 923794. *E-mail:* info@alwin-schockemoehle.de. *Website:* www.alwinschockemoehle.de.

SCHOELLER, François; French engineer; b. 25 March 1934, Nancy; s. of Gustave Schoeller and Suzanne Woelflin; m. Colette Canonge 1960; three c.; ed Ecole Polytechnique and Ecole Nat. Supérieure des Télécommunications; engineer, equatorial office of PTT, Brazzaville 1960–63; Chief Eng, Regional Man., Télécommunications de Strasbourg 1963–73; Operational Dir Télécommunications de Marseille 1973–75, Regional Dir Montpellier 1975–80, Regional Dir with grade of Engineer-Gen. 1980; Chair. TéléDiffusion de France 1983–86; Dir Higher Educ. in Telecommunication 1987–94; Pres. France Cables et Radio de México 1994–97; Project Man. France Telecom 1997–98; Man. Consultant, François Schoeller Conseil 1998–; Commdr Ordre nat. du Mérite; Officier, Légion d'honneur. *Publication:* Professional Ethics. *Address:* 6 rue Marietta Martin, 75016 Paris, France (office). *Telephone:* 1-42-15-01-45 (office). *Fax:* 1-42-15-07-16 (office). *E-mail:* schoeller.conseil@wanadoo.fr (office).

SCHOENDOERFFER, Pierre; French writer, scriptwriter and film director; b. 5 May 1928; m. Patricia Chauvel 1957; two s. one d.; served as able seaman on Swedish ship SS Anita Hans 1947–48; combat cameraman in French Expeditionary Corps, Indochina 1952–55, taken prisoner by Viet Minh; mem. Institut de France, Acad. des beaux arts 1988; Pres. Acad. de l'histoire et de l'image 2000; mem. Council, Musée de l'armée 1990, Haut Conseil de la mémoire combattante 1997–; Commdr, Légion d'honneur; Officier, Ordre Nat. du Mérite; Croix de guerre (6 mentions); Chevalier des Palmes académiques; Officier des Arts et Lettres; Médaille militaire; Prix Vauban for literary and cinematographic work 1984, Prix Encre Marine, Prix Erwan Bergot. *Films:* La Passe du Diable (Pellman Award 1958, Award of City of Berlin 1958) 1957, Ramuntcho 1958, Pêcheurs d'Islande 1959, La 317ème Section (Platoon 317) (Award for Best Script, Cannes 1965) 1964, Objectif: 500 Millions 1966, Le Crabe Tambour (Grand Prix du Cinéma Français 1977, Prix Femina Belge 1978, 3 Césars 1978) 1977, L'Honneur d'un Capitaine (Grand Prix du Cinéma de l'Académie Française, Prix Leduc, Grand Prix de l'Académie du Cinéma) 1982, Dien Bien Phu 1992, La Haut 2004. *Documentaries:* Attention Hélicoptère (Gold Sun, Mil. Film Festival, Versailles) 1963, The Anderson Platoon (Oscar, USA 1968, Int. Emmy Award, USA 1968, Prix Italia 1967, Merit Award of Guild of TV Dirs and Producers, UK 1967 and other awards) 1967, La Sentinelle du Matin 1976, Reminiscence (sequel to Anderson Platoon) 1989. *Publications:* La 317ème Section (Prix de l'Académie de Bretagne) 1963, L'Adieu au Roi (Farewell to the King) (Prix Interallié) 1969, Le Crabe Tambour (The Paths of the Sea) (Grand Prix du Roman de l'Académie Française) 1976, Là Haut 1981, Dien Bien Phu, De la Bataille au Film 1992, L'Aile du Papillon (Prix des Sables d'Olonne, Prix Encre Marine, Prix Erwan Bergot, Prix Livre et Mer, Prix Meursault) 2003. *Address:* 15 rue Raynouard, 75016 Paris, France. *Telephone:* 1-40-50-06-41.

SCHOESSLER, Don H.; American engineer; worked as engineer on Corona programme for Lockheed Corpn, collaborated with Eastman Kodak Co. to engineer, supply and process film used in system; later worked at Eastman Kodak Co. and continued to support Corona, U-2 the Nat. Reconnaissance Office reconnaissance projects –1986 (retd); honoured by Dir of CIA as a Corona Pioneer 1995, Charles Stark Draper Prize, Nat. Acad. of Eng (co-recipient) 2005. *Address:* c/o National Academy of Engineering, 500 Fifth Street, NW, Washington, DC 20001, USA. *E-mail:* NAEMembershipOffice@nae.edu.

SCHOLAR, Sir Michael Charles, Kt, KCB, PhD, ARCO; British civil servant and academic; *President, St John's College, Oxford;* b. 3 Jan. 1942, Merthyr Tydfil, Wales; s. of Richard Scholar and Blodwen Scholar (née Jones); m. Angela Sweet 1964; three s. one d. (deceased); ed St Olave's and St Saviour's Grammar School, St John's Coll., Cambridge, Univ. of Calif., Berkeley, Harvard Univ., USA; worked at HM Treasury 1969–93; Sr Int. Man. Barclay's Bank 1979–81; Pvt. Sec. to Prime Minister 1981–83; Perm. Sec., Welsh Office 1993–96; Perm. Sec. Dept of Trade and Industry 1996–2001; Pres. St John's Coll., Oxford 2001–; Dir (non-exec.) Council of Man., Nat. Inst. of Econ. and Social Research 2001–05, Legal and General Investment Man. 2002–07; Chair. Benton Fletcher Advisory Cttee 2004–; Chair. –Desig. Statistics Bd, HM Treasury 2007–; Hon. Fellow, Univ. of Wales (Aberystwyth), St John's Coll., Cambridge, Cardiff Univ.; Dr hc (Glamorgan Univ.). *Leisure interests:* playing the organ and piano, opera, long-distance walking. *Address:* St John's College, Oxford, OX1 3JP, England (office). *Telephone:* (1865) 277419 (office). *Fax:* (1865) 277482 (office). *E-mail:* president@sjc.ox.ac.uk (office). *Website:* www.sjc.ox.ac.uk (office).

SCHOLES, Myron S., BA, MBA, PhD; American/Canadian academic and business executive; *Chairman, Platinum Grove Asset Management, LP;* b. 1 July 1941, Timmons, Ont., Canada; ed McMaster Univ., Canada, Univ. of Chicago; instructor Univ. of Chicago Business School 1967–68; Asst Prof., MIT Man. School 1968–72, Assoc. Prof. 1972–73; Assoc. Prof. Univ. of Chicago 1973–75, Prof. 1975–79, Edward Eagle Brown Prof. of Finance 1979–82; Prof. of Law, Stanford Univ. 1983–, also Peter E. Buck Prof. of Finance; Man. Dir Salomon Bros 1991–93; Dir Center for Research in Security Prices, Univ. of Chicago 1975–81; Sr Research Fellow, Hoover Inst, Stanford Univ. 1988–; Co-founder and Prin. Long-Term Capital Man. (hedge fund) 1994–99; currently Chair. Platinum Grove Asset Man.LP; Dir. Capital Preservation Fund, Capital Preservation Fund II; Research Assoc. NBER; mem. American Econ. Asscn, American Finance Asscn; shared Nobel Prize for Econs 1997 for devising Black-Scholes Model for determining value of derivatives. *Address:* Platinum Grove Asset Management, LP, Reckson Executive Park, Building 4, 1100 King Street, Rye Brook, NY 10573, USA (office). *Telephone:* (914) 690-2100 (office). *Website:* www.ohpp.com (office).

SCHOLEY, Sir David Gerald, Kt, FRSA, CBE; British banker; *Senior Adviser, UBS Investment Bank;* b. 28 June 1935, Chipstead, Surrey; s. of Dudley Scholey and Lois Scholey; m. Alexandra Drew 1960; one s. one d.; ed Wellington Coll., Berks. and Christ Church, Oxford; served in Royal Armoured Corps, 9th Queen's Royal Lancers (Nat. Service) 1953–55, TA Yorkshire Dragoons 1955–57, 3/4 CLY (Sharpshooters) 1957–61, Metropolitan Special Constabulary (Thames Div.) 1961–65; with Thompson Graham & Co. (Lloyd's Brokers) 1956–58; Dale & Co. (Insurance Brokers), Canada 1958–59; Guinness Mahon & Co. Ltd 1959–64; joined S. G. Warburg & Co. Ltd 1964, Dir 1967–, Deputy Chair. 1977–80, Jt Chair. 1980–84; Chair. S.G. Warburg Group PLC (now UBS Investment Bank) 1985–95, SBC Warburg July–Nov. 1995, Sr Adviser 1995–; Dir Mercury Securities PLC 1969, Deputy Chair. 1980–84, Chair. 1984–86; Chair. Swiss Bank Corp. Int. Advisory Council 1995–97; Chair. Close Brothers Group PLC 1999–; mem. Bd of Dirs Orion Insurance Co. Ltd 1963–87, Stewart Wrightson Holdings PLC 1972–81, Union Discount Co. of London Ltd 1976–81, Bank of England 1981–98, British Telecom Ltd 1986–94, Chubb Corpn, USA 1991–, Inst. européen d'admin des affaires (INSEAD) 1991–2004 (Chair. UK Council 1994–97, Int. Council 1995–), Gen. Electric Co. 1992–95, LSE 1993–96, J Sainsbury PLC 1996–2000, Vodafone Group PLC 1998–2005, Anglo American PLC 1999–2005; Sr Adviser Int. Finance Corpn 1996–2005; mem. Export Guarantees Advisory Council 1970–75, Deputy Chair. 1974–75; Chair. Construction Exports Advisory Bd 1975–78; mem. Institut Int. d'Etudes Bancaires 1976–94 (Pres. 1988), Cttee on Finance for Industry, Nat. Econ. Devt Office 1980–87, IISS Studies Council 1984–93, (Hon. Treasurer 1984–90), Business in the Community, Pres.'s Cttee 1988–91, General Motors European Advisory Council 1988–97, Save the Children Fund, Industry and Commerce Group 1989–95 (Lord Mayor's Appeal Cttee 2002–03), London First 1993–96, London Symphony Orchestra Advisory Council 1998–2004, Fitch Int. Advisory Cttee 2001–, Mitsubishi Int. Advisory Cttee 2001–, Sultanate of Oman Int. Advisory Cttee 2002–; Gov. Wellington Coll. 1978–88, 1996–2004 (Vice-Pres. 1998–2004), BBC 1994–2000, Nat. Inst. for Econ. and Social Research; Trustee Glyndebourne Arts Trust 1989–2002, Nat. Portrait Gallery (Chair. of the Trustees) 1992–2005; Hon. DLitt (Guildhall) 1993. *Address:* UBS Investment Bank, 1 Finsbury Avenue, London, EC2M 2PP; Heath End House, Spaniards Road, London, NW3 7JE, England (home). *Telephone:* (20) 7568-2400 (office). *Fax:* (20) 7568-4225 (office). *E-mail:* david.scholey@ubs.com (office). *Website:* www.ubs.com (office).

SCHOLL, Andreas; German singer (countertenor); b. 1967, Eltville; ed Schola Cantorum Basiliensis, Basel, Switzerland; mem. Kiedricher Chorbuben choir as child; soloist, Pueri Cantors Gathering, St Peter's Basilica, Rome 1981; debut int. recital at Théâtre de Grévin, Paris 1993; opera debut in Handel's Rodelinda, Glyndebourne Festival Opera, England 1998; performed at Belgian Royal Wedding Dec. 1999; teacher, Schola Cantorum Basiliensis, Basel 2000–; numerous int. tours and recitals, working with the world's leading Baroque conductors and ensembles, including London Proms 2005; Conseil de l'Europe Award 1992, Fondation Claude Nicolas Ledoux Award 1992, Cannes Classical Award 1998, Artist of the Year, German Kultur Radio 1998, Belgian Musical Press Union Prize 1999. *Recordings include:* Handel's Messiah, Solomon, Italian Cantatas and Opera Arias, Bach's Christmas Oratorio, St Matthew Passion, St John Passion, Solo Cantatas for Alto and B Minor Mass, Vivaldi's Stabat Mater (Gramophone Award) 1996, Nisi Dominus (Edison Award) 2001, Monteverdi's L'Orfeo and 1610 Vespers, works by Pergolesi and Caldara; Heroes (Echo Classic Award) 1999, Wayfaring Stranger 2001, Arcadia 2003, Arias for Senesino (Classical BRIT Award for Singer of the Year 2006) 2005, Crystal Tears (with Julian Behr) 2008. *Address:* Harrison Parrott Ltd, 5–6 Albion Court, London, W6 0QT, England (office). *Telephone:* (20) 7229-9166 (office). *E-mail:* info@harrisonparrott.co.uk (office). *Website:* www.harrisonparrott.com (office).

SCHOLL, Hermann, DrIng; German business executive; *Chairman, Supervisory Council, Robert Bosch GmbH;* b. 21 June 1935, Stuttgart; m.; one d.; ed Univ. of Stuttgart; joined Robert Bosch GmbH, Advanced Eng Dept, Automotive Tech. 1962, Chief Engineer Electronic Fuel Injection 1968–71, Dir of Eng, Electrical and Electronic Engine Equipment 1971–73, Assoc. mem. Bd of Man. 1973–75, Deputy mem. 1975–78, mem. 1978–2003 (Chair. 1993–2003), Man. Pnr Robert Bosch Industrietreuhand KG (holding co.) 1995–, Chair. Supervisory Council Robert Bosch GmbH 2003–; mem. Supervisory Bd BASF AG; Hon. DrIng (Kettering Univ., Mich., USA) 1988, (Tech. Univ. of Munich) 1993. *Address:* Robert Bosch GmbH, Postfach 106050, Stuttgart 70049, Germany (office). *Telephone:* (711) 811-0 (office). *Fax:* (711) 8116630 (office). *Website:* www.bosch.com (office).

SCHOLZ, Olaf; German politician and lawyer; *Minister of Labour and Social Affairs;* b. 14 June 1958, Osnabrück; m. Britta Ernst; joined SPD youth wing 1975; Deputy Chair. Socialist Youth Org. 1982–88; Vice-Pres. Int. Union of Socialist Youth 1987–89; Pnr, Zimmermann, Scholz and Pnrs (law firm), Hamburg 1985–; mem. Bundestag (parl.) 1998–; Minister of the Interior of City of Hamburg May–Oct. 2001; Gen. Sec. SPD 2002–04; Minister of Labour and Social Affairs 2007–; legal adviser to Cen. Asscn of German Consumer Cooperatives 1990–98. *Address:* Büro Olaf Scholz, Deutscher Bundestag, 11011 Berlin (office); Federal Ministry of Labour and Social Affairs, Wilhelmstr. 49, 11017 Berlin, Germany (office). *Telephone:* (30) 22773435 (office); (30) 185270 (Ministry) (office). *Fax:* (30) 22770435 (office); (30) 185272236 (Ministry) (office). *E-mail:* info@bmas.bund.de (office). *Website:* www.olafscholz.de (office); www.bmas.bund.de (office).

SCHOLZ, Rupert, DJur; German lawyer, academic and politician; *Of Counsel, Gleiss Lutz;* b. 23 May 1937, Berlin; m.; ed Free Univ. of Berlin and Univ. of Heidelberg; Prof. of Public Law, Free Univ. of Berlin 1972–78; Chair of Public Law, Univ. of Munich 1978–2005, Prof. Emer. 2005–; Senator for Justice, W Berlin 1981–88, for Fed. Affairs 1983–88; Minister of Defence 1988–90; mem. Bundestag 1990–2002; Of Counsel, Gleiss Lutz (law firm), Berlin 2005–; mem. CDU 1983–. *Address:* Gleiss Lutz, Friedrichstrasse 71,

10117 Berlin, Germany (office). *Telephone:* (30) 800979171 (office). *Fax:* (30) 800979979 (office). *E-mail:* rupert.scholz@gleisslutz.com (office). *Website:* www.gleisslutz.com (office).

SCHÖNBERG, Claude-Michel; French composer; b. 6 July 1944, France; s. of Adolphe Schönberg and Julie Nadás; one s. two d.; m. Charlotte Talbot 2003; started as producer for EMI France and as pop song writer 1967–72; recording his own songs in France 1974–77; recipient of Tony, Grammy, Evening Standard and Laurence Olivier Awards, French 'Molière' and 'Victoires de la musique' for musicals. *Ballet:* Wuthering Heights with the Northern Ballet Theatre 2002. *Compositions:* musicals La Révolution Française 1973, Les Misérables 1980–85, Miss Saigon 1989, Martin Guerre 1996–, Pirate Queen 2006–, Marguerite 2008. *Address:* c/o Cameron Mackintosh Limited, 1 Bedford Square, London, WC1B 3RA, England (office). *Telephone:* (20) 7637-8866 (office).

SCHÖNBORN, HE Cardinal Christoph, OP; Austrian ecclesiastic; *Archbishop of Vienna;* b. 22 Jan. 1945, Skalsko (now in Czech Repub.); ordained priest 1970; student pastor, Univ. of Graz 1973–75; Assoc. Prof. of Dogma, Univ. of Fribourg 1975–76, Prof. of Theology 1976–81, Prof. of Dogmatic Theology 1981–91; apptd Auxiliary Bishop of Vienna 1991, Coadjutor 1995, Archbishop of Vienna 1995–; cr. Cardinal 1998, Cardinal-Priest of Gesù Divin Lavoratore; Pres. Austrian Bishop's Conf. 1998–; curial mem. Congregations for the Doctrine of the Faith, Oriental Churches, and Catholic Educ.; mem. Pontifical Council on Culture, Comm. on the Cultural Heritage of the Church, Special Council for Europe of the Gen. Secretariat of the Synod of Bishops; Ordinary for the faithful of Byzantine Rite in Austria. *Address:* Archdiocese of Vienna, Wollzeile 2, 1010 Vienna, Austria. *Telephone:* (1) 515-52-0. *Fax:* (1) 515-52-3760. *Website:* stephanscom.at.

SCHÖNE, Albrecht, DPhil; German philologist and academic; *Professor Emeritus, University of Göttingen;* b. 17 July 1925, Barby; s. of Friedrich Schöne and Agnes Moeller; m. Dagmar Haver 1952; one s. one d.; ed Univs. of Freiburg, Basle, Göttingen and Münster; Extraordinary Prof. of German Literature, Univ. of Münster 1958; Prof. of German Philology, Univ. of Göttingen 1960–90, Prof. Emer. 1990–; Pres. Int. Asscn for Germanic Studies 1980–85; mem. Akad. der Wissenschaften, Göttingen, Deutsche Akad. für Sprache und Dichtung, Bayerische, Nordrhein-Westfäl. Akad. der Wissenschaften, Austrian and Netherlands Acads; Hon. mem. Modern Language Asscn of America; Foreign Hon. mem. American Acad. of Arts and Sciences; Officier, Ordre nat. du Mérite; Hon. DPhil; Hon. DTheol; several prizes. *Publications:* numerous books and articles on German literature and philology. *Leisure interests:* riding, hunting, painting. *Address:* Grotefendstrasse 26, 37075 Göttingen, Germany (home). *Telephone:* (551) 56449 (home).

SCHÖNFELDER, Wilhelm Heinrich, PhD; German lobbyist and fmr diplomatist; *Head of Government Affairs, Siemens AG;* b. 12 Nov. 1940, Marburg; Dir for European Affairs, Federal Foreign Ministry –1999; Perm. Rep. of Germany to EU, Brussels 1999–2007; Head of Govt Affairs, Siemens AG, Brussels 2007–. *Address:* Siemens, Rue d'Arlon 69-71, 1040 Brussels, Belgium (office). *Telephone:* (2) 286-19-31 (office). *Fax:* (2) 230-97-70 (office). *E-mail:* wilhelm.schoenfelder@siemens.com (office). *Website:* www.siemens.com (office).

SCHRADER, Hans Otto; German business executive; *Chairman of the Executive Board and CEO, Otto Group;* b. 8 Dec. 1956, Bevensen; joined Otto Group 1977, becoming Deputy Head, Hong Kong Office, Vice-Pres. for Import, Vice-Pres. for Merchandising 1993–99, mem. Exec. Bd Otto GmbH & Co. KG 1999–, Otto Group 2005–, Chair. Exec. Bd and CEO 2007–. *Address:* Otto Group, Wandsbeker Strasse 3–7, 22179 Hamburg, Germany (office). *Telephone:* (40) 64610 (office). *Fax:* (40) 64618571 (office). *E-mail:* info@ottogroup.com (office). *Website:* www.ottogroup.com (office).

SCHRADER, Paul Joseph, MA; American screenwriter and director; b. 22 July 1946, Grand Rapids, Mich.; m. 1st Jeannine Oppewall (divorced); m. 2nd Mary Beth Hurt 1983; ed Calvin Coll. and Univ. of Calif. at Los Angeles; film critic for LA Free Press magazine 1970–72; Ed. Cinema magazine 1970–; fmr Prof., Columbia Univ. *Films include:* screenplays/written by: The Yazuka 1974, Taxi Driver 1976, Obsession 1976, Rolling Thunder 1977, Old Boyfriends 1979, Raging Bull 1981, The Mosquito Coast 1986, Light of Day 1987, The Last Temptation of Christ 1988, City Hall 1996, Affliction 1997, Bringing Out the Dead 1999, The Walker (also dir) 2007; directed: Bluecollar (also co-writer) 1978, Hardcore 1978, American Gigolo (also co-writer) 1979, Cat People 1982, Mishima (also co-writer) 1985, Patty Hearst 1989, The Comfort of Strangers 1990, Light Sleeper 1991 (also writer), Witch-hunt 1994, Touch 1997, Forever Mine 1999 (also writer), Auto Focus 2002, Paul Schrader's Exorcist: The Beginning 2005. *Publication:* Transcendental Style in Film: Ozu, Bresson, Dreyer 1972.

SCHRAMECK, Olivier Claude Martin; French politician and civil servant; b. 27 Feb. 1951, Paris; s. of Jean Schrameck and Stéphanie Schrameck (née Epstein); m. Hélene Rioust de Largentaye 1980; one s. one d.; ed Lycées Carnot, Paris and Pasteur, Neuilly-sur-Seine, Univ. of Paris II (Université Panthéon Assas), Ecole Nat. d'Admin., Inst. d'Etudes Politiques, Paris; Auditeur, Conseil d'Etat 1977–83; Governing Commr, Ass. du contentieux et les autres formations de jugement du Conseil d'Etat 1981–82, 1987–88; tech. adviser 1982–84; Chargé de mission, Ministry of the Interior and of Decentralization 1984; Chief of Staff, Sec. of State of Ministry of Nat. Educ., with responsibility for Univs. 1984–85, Dir of Higher Educ. 1985–86; Maître des requêtes, Conseil d'Etat 1983; Chief of Staff, Minister of State, Ministry of Nat. Educ., Youth and Sports 1988–91; Assoc. Prof., Univ. of Paris I (Panthéon- Sorbonne) 1991–97, 2005–; Gen. Reporter to High Council for Integration 1991–93; Sec.-Gen. Constitutional Council 1993–97; mem. Conseil d'Etat 1995, 2005–; Chief of Staff to Prime Minister 1997–2001; mem. Admin. Council, Nat. Caisse of Historic Monuments 1992–97; Amb. to Spain 2002–05; mem. Comité de réflexion et de proposition sur la modernisation et le rééquilibrage des institutions (Cttee for Institutional Reform) 2007–; Chevalier Légion d'honneur, Chevalier Ordre nat. du Mérite. *Publications include:* Les Cabinets ministériels 1995, La Fonction publique territoriale 1995, Matignon, Rive Gauche 1997–2001; numerous articles on decentralization law, immigration and constitutional law. *Address:* Conseil d'Etat, 1 place du Palais Royal, 75001 Paris, France. *Telephone:* 1-40-20-80-51. *Website:* www.conseil-etat.fr.

SCHREIBER, Stuart L., BA, PhD; American chemist and academic; *Scientific Co-Director, Harvard Center for Genomics Research;* ed Univ. of Va, Harvard Univ.; Asst Prof., Yale Univ. 1981–84, Assoc. Prof. 1984–86, Prof. 1986–88; Morris Loeb Prof., Harvard Univ. 1988–, Co-Dir, Harvard Inst. of Chem. and Cell Biology 1997–, Scientific Co-Dir, Harvard Center for Genomics Research 1998–, Assoc. mem., Harvard Univ. Medical School, Molecular and Cell Biology Div. 1988–; Investigator, Howard Hughes Medical Inst., Chevy Chase, MD 1994–, Assoc. mem., Dept of Molecular and Cellular Biology 1994–; Founder and Co-Chair. Scientific Advisory Bd Infinity Pharmaceuticals 2002–06; Founder and Chair. Bd of Scientific and Medical Advisors ARIAD Pharmaceuticals 1991–; Founder ARIAD Gene Therapeutics 1994–; Founder and mem. Scientific Advisory Bd Vertex Pharmaceuticals 1988–90; Advisor, Theravance 2000–04; consultant to Pfizer 1983–91; Founder and Co-Ed. Chemistry and Biology 1993–2004, Founding Ed. 2005–; mem. Bd of Consulting Eds Tetrahedron Publications 1983–; mem. Editorial Bd or Advisory Ed. The Scientist 2005–; Proceedings of NAS 1995–98, Current Biology, Topics in Stereochemistry, Comprehensive Organic Synthesis, Current Opinion in Chemical Biology, Nature Chemical Biology, ACS Chemical Biology, ChemBioChem, Synthesis Letters, Journal of Organic Chemistry, Journal of Medicinal Chemistry, Bioorganic and Medicinal Chemistry Letters, Bioorganic and Medicinal Chemistry; mem. NAS 1995–, American Acad. of Arts and Sciences 1995–; Trustee Rockefeller Univ. 1999–2004; numerous awards including ICI Pharmaceuticals Award for Excellence in Chem. 1986, Arthur C. Cope Scholar Award, ACS 1986, Award in Pure Chem., ACS 1989, Arun Guthikonda Memorial Award, Columbia Univ. 1990, Ciba-Geigy Drew Award for Biomedical Research 1992, Thieme-IUPAC Award in Synthetic Organic Chem. 1992, NIH Merit Award 1992, Rhone-Poulenc Silver Medal, Royal Soc. of Chem. 1992, Eli Lilly Award in Biological Chem., ACS 1993, Leo Hendrik Baekeland Award, ACS 1993, Nat. Cancer Inst. Derek Barton Medal 1999, William H. Nichols Medal 2001, Chiron Corpn Biotechnology Research Award, American Acad. of Microbiology 2001 Soc. for Biomolecular Screening Achievement Award 2004, Asscn of American Cancer Insts Distinguished Scientist Award 2004, Academic Scientist of the Year, Finalist for the 2005 Pharmaceutical Achievement Awards 2005, Thomson Laureate Award in Chem. (with Gerald R. Crabtree) 2006. *Address:* Schreiber Research Laboratory, 7 Cambridge Center, Cambridge, MA 02142 (office); Department of Chemistry and Chemical Biology, Harvard University, 12 Oxford Street, Cambridge, MA 02138-2902, USA (office). *Telephone:* (617) 324-9603 (Lab.) (office); (617) 495-5318 (office). *Fax:* (617) 324-9601 (Lab.) (office); (617) 495-0751 (office). *E-mail:* stuart_schreiber@harvard.edu (office). *Website:* www.schreiber.chem.harvard.edu/index.html (office).

SCHREIER, Ethan J., BSc, PhD; American astronomer; *President, Associated Universities Inc.;* b. New York; ed Bronx High School of Science, City Coll. of NY, MIT; Researcher, American Science and Eng Inc. 1970–73; Sr Scientist, Harvard-Smithsonian Center for Astrophysics 1973; co-founder, Space Telescope Science Inst., Baltimore, Md 1981, becoming Chief Data and Operations Scientist, Assoc. Dir for Next Generation Space Telescope, and Head of Strategic Planning and Devt; Adjunct Prof., Dept of Physics and Astronomy, Johns Hopkins Univ.; Exec. Vice-Pres., Associated Universities Inc. 2001–04, Pres. 2004–; mem. numerous NASA advisory cttees, including Nat. Virtual Observatory Exec. Cttee, Int. Virtual Observatory Alliance Exec. *Address:* Associated Universities Inc., 1400 16th Street, NW, Washington, DC 20036, USA (office). *Telephone:* (202) 462-1676 (office). *Fax:* (202) 232-7161 (office). *E-mail:* ejs@aui.edu (office). *Website:* www.aui.edu (office).

SCHREIER, Peter; German singer (tenor) and conductor; b. 29 July 1935, Meissen; ed Dresden Hochschule für Musik; sang with Dresden State Opera 1959–63; joined Berlin Staatsoper 1963; has appeared at Vienna State Opera, Salzburg Festival, La Scala, Milan, Sadler's Wells, London, Metropolitan Opera, New York and Teatro Colón, Buenos Aires; recital debut London 1978; debut as conductor 1969; has conducted recordings of several choral works by J. S. Bach, Mozart and Schubert; retd as opera singer 1999, continues to conduct. *Address:* Calberlastr. 13, 01326 Dresden, Germany.

SCHREYER, Rt Hon. Edward Richard, PC, CC, C.M.M., CD, MA, LLD; Canadian politician and diplomatist; b. 21 Dec. 1935, Beausejour, Manitoba; s. of John J. Schreyer and Elizabeth Gottfried; m. Lily Schulz 1960; two s. two d.; ed Cromwell Public School, Beausejour Collegiate, United Coll., St John's Coll. and Univ. of Manitoba; mem. for Brokenhead, Manitoba Legislature 1958, re-elected 1959, 1962; Prof. Political Science and Int. Relations, Univ. of Manitoba 1962–65; MP for Springfield Constituency 1965–68, for Selkirk 1968; Leader, Manitoba New Democratic Party 1969–78; Premier of Manitoba, Minister of Dominion-Provincial Relations 1969–77, Minister of Hydro 1971–77, of Finance 1972–74; Leader of the Opposition 1977–78; Gov.-Gen. of Canada 1979–84; High Commr to Australia, also accred to Papua New Guinea and Solomon Islands 1984–88; Amb. to Vanuatu 1984–88; Distinguished Visiting Prof. Univ. of Winnipeg 1989–90, Simon Fraser Univ. 1991; Distinguished Fellow, Inst. of Integrated Energy Systems, Univ. of Victoria 1992–94, Dept of Geography, Univ. of BC 1995–96; Chair. Canadian Shield Foundation 1984–; Dir Perfect Pacific Investments 1989–, China Int. Trust and Investment Corpn (Canada) Ltd 1991–, Swan-E-Set Bay Resort and Country Club 1991–, Habitat for Humanity Canada 1992–, Sask. Energy Conservation and Devt Authority 1993–96, Alt. Fuel Systems Inc. (Calgary) 1994–, Cephalon Oil and Gas Resource Corp. (Calgary) 1994–95; Hon. Dir Sierra Legal Defence Fund 1991–; mem. Int. Assen of Energy Econs, Churchill Econ. Advisory Cttee, Pacific Inst. of Deep Sea Tech.; Counsellor Canada West Foundation 1989–; Sr Adviser Summit Council for World Peace (World Peace Fed.), Washington DC 1991–; Hon. Adviser Canadian Foundation for the Preservation of Chinese Cultural and Historical Treasures 1994–; Hon. Patron John Diefenbaker Soc. 1991–; Chancellor, Brandon Univ. 2002–08; Hon. LLD (Manitoba) 1979, (Mount Allison) 1983, (McGill) 1984, (Simon Fraser) 1984, (Lakehead) 1985; Gov.-Gen. Vanier Award 1975. *Leisure interests:* reading, golf, sculpting, woodworking. *Address:* c/o Office of the Chancellor, Brandon University, 270-18th Street, Brandon, Man. R7A 6A9 (office); 250 Wellington Center, Unit 401, Winnipeg, Man. R3M 0B3, Canada.

SCHREYER, Michaele, PhD; German organization official and fmr politician; *Vice-President, Netzwerks Europäische Bewegung Deutschland;* b. 9 Aug. 1951, Cologne; ed Univ. of Cologne, Free Univ. of Berlin; Research Asst, Inst. for Public Finances and Social Policy, Free Univ. of Berlin 1977–82, Lecturer 1996–99, Lecturer, Otto-Suhr-Institut 2004–; research asst and adviser for Green Caucus, Bundestag 1983–87; Researcher, Inst. for Econ. Research (IFO), Munich 1987–88; Minister for Urban Devt and Environmental Protection in Senate of Berlin 1989–90; mem. State Parl., Berlin 1991–99, mem. Budget and Public Finance Cttee, Chair. Sub-Cttee on Funds for Public Housing 1995–97; Chair. Green Caucus, Berlin Parl. 1998–99; EU Commr for Budget, Financial Control and Fraud Prevention 1999–2004; currently Vice-Pres. Netzwerks Europäische Bewegung Deutschland (non-partisan union of European political orgs); mem. Advisory Bd for Transatlantic Relations and European Affairs, Heinrich Böll Foundation; mem. Advisory Bd Transparency Int. Germany; fmr mem. numerous co. bds; fmr mem. Bd Berlin br. of German Soc. for UN. *Address:* Netzwerk Europäische Bewegung Deutschland, Sophienstr. 28/29, 10178 Berlin, Germany (office). *Telephone:* (30) 3036201 (office). *Fax:* (30) 3036201 (office). *E-mail:* netzwerk@europaeische-bewegung.de (office). *Website:* www.europaeische-bewegung.de (office).

SCHREYER, William Allen, BA; American fmr business executive; *Chairman Emeritus, Merrill Lynch & Co., Inc.;* b. 13 Jan. 1928, Williamsport, Pa; s. of the late William Schreyer and Elizabeth Engel; m. Joan Legg 1953; one d.; ed Pennsylvania State Univ.; with Merrill Lynch & Co., Inc. 1948–93, CEO 1984–92, Chair. 1985–93, Chair. Emer. 1993–; mem. Exec. Cttee Center for Strategic and Int. Studies, Washington, DC, mem. Bd Trustees and Chair. Exec. Cttee Int. Councillor; Hon. DH; Distinguished Alumnus Award (Pa State Univ.). *Leisure interests:* tennis, reading, swimming. *Address:* Merrill Lynch & Co., Inc., 800 Scudders Mill Road, Plainsboro, NJ 08536 (office); 117 Mercer Street, Princeton, NJ 08540, USA (home). *Telephone:* (609) 806-2540. *Fax:* (609) 806-2542. *E-mail:* RARempe@NA2.US.ML.com.

SCHRIEFFER, John Robert, BS, MS, PhD; American physicist and academic; *University Eminent Scholar Professor and Chief Scientist, National High Magnetic Field Laboratory, Florida State University;* b. 31 May 1931, Oak Park, Ill.; s. of John Henry Schrieffer and Louise Anderson; m. Anne Grete Thomson 1960; one s. two d.; ed Mass. Inst. of Technology and Univ. of Illinois; NSF Fellow, Univ. of Birmingham, UK and Univ. Inst. for Theoretical Physics, Copenhagen 1957–58; Asst Prof., Univ. of Chicago 1957–60, Univ. of Ill. 1959–60; Assoc. Prof., Univ. of Ill. 1960–62; Prof., Univ. of Pa 1962, Mary Amanda Wood Prof. of Physics 1962–79, Mary Amada Wood Prof. of Physics 1964–79; Prof. of Physics, Univ. of Calif., Santa Barbara 1980–91, Essan Khashoggi Prof. of Physics 1985, Dir Inst. for Theoretical Physics 1984–89, Chancellor's Prof. 1984–91; Prof. Fla State Univ., Tallahassee 1992–, Chief Scientist Nat. High Magnetic Field Lab. 1992–, Univ. Eminent Scholar, Fla State Univ. System 1996; Vice-Pres. American Physical Soc. 1994–96, Pres. 1996; Andrew D. White Prof. Cornell Univ. 1969–75; mem. NAS, American Acad. Arts and Sciences, American Philosophical Soc. 1974, Royal Danish Acad. of Science and Letters, Nat. Medal of Science Cttee 1996–; Guggenheim Fellow 1967–68; Fellow, American Physical Soc. (Pres. 1997); Dr hc (Geneva, Technische Hochschule, Munich, Univs of Pa, Ill., Cincinatti and Tel-Aviv); Buckley Prize 1968, Comstock Prize (NAS) 1968, Nobel Prize for Physics (with J. Bardeen and L. N. Cooper) 1972, John Ericsson Medal (American Soc. of Swedish Engineers) 1976, Alumni Achievement Award, Univ. of Ill. 1979, Nat. Medal of Science 1985, Superconductivity Award of Excellence (World Congress of Superconductivity) 1996, Robert A. Holton Medal for Distinguished Research Service, Florida State Univ. 2004. *Publication:* Theory of Superconductivity 1964. *Address:* A-307, National High Magnetic Field Laboratory, Florida State University, 1800 E Paul Dirac Drive, Tallahassee, FL 32310-3706, USA. *Telephone:* (850) 644-3203 (office). *Fax:* (850) 645-2486 (office). *E-mail:* schrieff@magnet.fsu.edu (office). *Website:* www.magnet.fsu.edu (office).

SCHROCK, Richard R., AB, PhD; American chemist and academic; *Frederick G. Keyes Professor of Chemistry, Massachusetts Institute of Technology;* b. 4 Jan. 1945, Berne, Indiana; m. Nancy F. Carlson 1971; two s.; ed Univ. of California, Riverside, Harvard Univ., Cambridge Univ., UK; Research Chemist, Cen. Research and Devt Dept, E.I. du Pont de Nemours & Co. 1972–75; Asst Prof. of Chem., MIT 1975–78, Assoc. Prof. 1978–80, Prof. 1980–89, Frederick G. Keyes Prof. of Chem. 1989–; Sherman T. Fairchild Scholar, Calif. Inst. of Tech. 1986, Science and Eng Research Council Visiting Fellow, Univl of Cambridge 1991; ACS Award in Organometallic Chem. 1985 and Harrison Howe Award 1990, Inorganic Chem. Award 1996, Bailar Medal, Univ. of Ill. 1998, ACS Cope Scholar Award 2001, Royal Soc. of Chem. Sir Geoffrey Wilkinson Medal 2002, Nobel Prize in Chemistry (jtly) 2005. *Publications:* numerous papers in scientific journals. *Address:* Department of Chemistry, 6-331, Massachusetts Institute of Technology, 77 Massachusetts Avenue, Cambridge, MA 02139, USA. *Telephone:* (617) 253-1596 (office). *Fax:* (617) 253-7670 (office). *E-mail:* rrs@mit.edu (office). *Website:* web.mit.edu/rrs/www/home.html (office); web.mit.edu/chemistry/www/faculty/schrock (office).

SCHRODER, Baron Bruno Lionel, MBA; British business executive; *Director, Schroders PLC;* b. 17 Jan. 1933; s. of the late Baron Bruno Schroder and Margaret Eleanor Phyllis Schroder (née Darell); m. Patricia Leonie Mary Holt 1969; one d.; ed Eton Coll., Univ. Coll., Oxford, Harvard Business School, USA; Second Lt, Life Guards 1951–53; joined Schroders PLC 1960, Dir 1963–, J. Henry Schroder & Co. Ltd 1966–, Schroders Inc. 1984–; Gov. English Nat. Ballet; mem. Exec. Cttee Air Squadron, Court of Assts Worshipful Co. of Goldsmiths, Liveryman Guild of Air Pilots and Air Navigators; Cross of the Order of Merit (Germany) 2006; Queen Beatrix of Netherlands Wedding Medal. *Leisure interests:* flying, stalking, shooting. *Address:* Schroders PLC, 31 Gresham Street, London, EC2V 7QA, England (office). *Telephone:* (20) 7382-6000 (office). *Fax:* (20) 7288-2006 (office). *Website:* www.schroders.com (office).

SCHRÖDER, Gerhard, LL.B.; German business executive and fmr politician; *Chairman, Nord Stream AG;* b. 7 April 1944, Mossenburg, Lippe; s. of the late Fritz Schröder and of Erika Schröder; m. 1st Eva Schubach; m. 2nd Anna Taschenmacher; m. 3rd Hiltrud Hensen 1984; m. 4th Doris Köpf 1997; one adopted d. one adopted s.; ed Univ. of Göttingen; apprentice as shop asst 1961; joined Sozialdemokratische Partei Deutschlands (SPD) (Social Democratic Party of Germany) 1963, Chair. 1999–2004; lawyer, Hanover 1976; Nat. Chair. of Young Socialists 1978–80; mem. Bundestag 1980–86; Leader of Opposition in State Parl. of Lower Saxony 1986; Minister-Pres. of Lower Saxony 1990–98; Chancellor of Germany 1998–2005; consultant to Ringier Group (publr) Nov. 2005; Chair. Nord Stream AG (consortium owned by OAO Gazprom, BASF AG, E.On AG for construction and operation of planned Nord Stream submarine pipeline) 2006–; mem. Bd of Dirs TNK BP Ltd 2009–; Mittelstandspreis 1997, Quadriga Award 2007. *Address:* Nord Stream AG, Grafenauweg 2, 6304 Zug, Switzerland (office). *Telephone:* (41) 7669191 (office). *Fax:* (41) 7669192 (office). *E-mail:* info@nord-stream.com (office). *Website:* www.nord-stream.com (office).

SCHRÖDER, Ulrich, MCL, DrIur; German banking executive; *CEO, KfW Bankengruppe;* b. 19 March 1952, Melle; m.; three c.; ed Univ. of Münster, Univ. of Illinois, USA; Research Asst, Univ. of Münster 1980–82; with Westdeutsche Landesbank Girozentrale (WestLB), Düsseldorf/Münster 1983–, mem. Bd of Dirs 1983–87, Head of Exec. Secr. 1985–87, Account Man., WestLB Br., London, UK 1987–92, Head of Dept 1991, Head of Münster and Bielefeld Brs 1992–97, Bank Man. 1995, mem. Man. Bd WestLB France 1997–2002, Man. of WestLB Paris Br. and Head of Chemicals/Life Sciences Unit 2001–02, mem. Man. Bd WestLB April–July 2002; mem. Man. Bd NRW.BANK, Düsseldorf/Münster 2002–, Chair. Man. Bd 2006–08; CEO KfW Bankengruppe 2008–; mem. Supervisory Bd Deutsche Post AG, Deutsche Telekom AG, ProHealth AG. *Address:* KfW Bankengruppe, Palmengarten str. 5–9, 60325 Frankfurt am Main, Germany (office). *Telephone:* (69) 7431-0 (office). *Fax:* (69) 7431-2944 (office). *E-mail:* presse@kfw.de (office). *Website:* www.kfw.de/EN_Home/index.jsp (office).

SCHROEDER, Barbet; French film producer, director and actor; b. 26 April 1941, Tehran, Iran; ed Sorbonne, Paris; worked as jazz tour operator Europe, photojournalist India, critic for Cahiers du Cinéma and L'Air de Paris 1958–63; Asst to Jean-Luc Godard on Les Carabiniers 1963; f. own production co. Les Films du Losange 1964; worked as actor and producer. *Films produced:* Méditerranée 1963, La Carrière de Suzanne 1963, La Boulangère de Monceau 1963, Nadja à Paris 1964, Paris vu par... 1965, Fermière à Montfaucon 1967, La Collectionneuse 1967, More 1969, Ma nuit chez Maud 1969, Le Genou de Claire 1970, Sing-Sing 1971, Maquillages 1971, Le Cochon aux patates douces 1971, L'Amour l'après-midi 1972, Céline et Julie vont en bateau 1974, Marquise von O..., Die 1976, Chinesisches Roulette 1976, Perceval le Gallois 1978, Le Pont du Nord 1981, Flügel und Fesseln 1985, Barfly 1987, Single White Female 1992, Kiss of Death 1995, Never Talk to Strangers 1995, Before and After 1996, Desperate Measures 1998, Shattered Image 1998, La Virgen de los sicarios 2000, Murder by Numbers 2002. *Films directed:* More 1969, Sing-Song (documentary) 1971, Le Cochon aux patates douces 1971, La Vallée 1972, General Idi Amin Dada (documentary) 1974, Maîtresse 1976, Koko, the Talking Gorilla (documentary) 1978, Tricheurs 1984, Charles Bukowski (50 four-minute videos) 1985, Barfly 1987, Reversal of Fortune 1990, Single White Female 1992, Kiss of Death 1995, Before and After (also producer) 1996, Desperate Measures 1998, La Virgen de los Sicarios 2000, Murder by Numbers 2002, L'Avocat de la terreur 2007. *Films as actor:* La Boulangère de Monceau 1963, Les Carabiniers 1963, Paris vu par... 1965, Out 1, noli me tangere 1971, Out 1: Spectre 1972, Céline et Julie vont en bateau 1974, Roberte 1979, L'Amour par terre 1984, The Golden Boat 1990, La Reine Margot 1994, Beverly Hills Cop III 1994, Mars Attacks! 1996, La Virgen de los sicarios 2000, Ne fais pas ça 2004, Une aventure 2005, Paris, je t'aime (segment) 2006, Ne touchez pas la hache 2007, The Darjeeling Limited 2007.

SCHROEDER, Manfred Robert, Dr rer. nat; American physicist and academic; *University Professor Emeritus of Physics, University of Göttingen;* b. 12 July 1926, Ahlen, North Rhine-Westphalia, Germany; s. of Karl Schroeder and Hertha Schroeder; m. Anny Menschik 1956; two s. one d.; ed Univ. of Göttingen; joined AT&T Bell Laboratories, Murray Hill 1954, Head of Acoustics Research Dept 1958–63, Dir of Acoustics, Speech and Mechanics Research 1963–69; Dir Drittes Physikalisches Inst., Univ. of Göttingen 1969–91, Univ. Prof. Emer. 1991–; Founder mem. Institut de Recherche et Coordination Acoustique/Musique, Centre Pompidou, Paris; mem. Nat. Acad. of Eng Washington, Göttingen Acad. of Sciences, Max-Planck Soc.; Fellow

American Acad. of Arts and Sciences 1986, New York Acad. of Sciences 1993; holds 45 US Patents in speech and signal processing and other fields; Hon. mem. German Soc. Audiology 2003; Gold Medal, Audio Eng Soc. 1972, Baker Prize Award, Inst. of Electrical and Electronics Engineers, New York 1977, Sr Award, Acoustics, Speech and Signal Processing Soc. 1979, Lord Rayleigh Gold Medal, British Inst. of Acoustics, Gold Medal, Acoustical Soc. of America 1991, Niedersachsenpreis 1992, Helmholtz Medal, German Acoustical Soc. 1995, Rhein Tech. Prize 2003, ISCA Medal, Int. Speech Communication Asscn 2004. *Publications:* Speech and Speaker Recognition 1985, Fractals, Chaos, Power Laws: Minutes From an Infinite Paradise 1991, Number Theory in Science and Communication 1999, Computer Speech: Recognition, Compression, Synthesis 1999 and about 130 articles on acoustics, speech, hearing, microwaves, computer graphics. *Leisure interests:* languages, photography, computer graphics. *Address:* Drittes Physikalisches Institut, Universität Göttingen, Hund-Platz 1, 37073 Göttingen; Rieswartenweg 8, 37077 Göttingen, Germany (home). *Telephone:* (551) 21232 (home); (551) 397713. *Fax:* (551) 397720. *E-mail:* mrs17@aol.com (home). *Website:* www.physik3.gwdg.de/~mrs (office).

SCHROEDER, Patricia Nell Scott, JD; American organization executive and fmr politician; *President and CEO, Association of American Publishers;* b. (Patricia Nell Scott), July 1940, Portland, Ore.; m. James W. Schroeder; one s. one d.; ed Univ. of Minn., Harvard Law School; mem. US House of Reps 1972–96, served on House Armed Services and Judiciary Cttees and several other cttees, Chair. House Select Cttee on Children, Youth and Families 1991–93; Prof., Woodrow Wilson School of Public and Int. Affairs, Princeton Univ. Jan.–June 1997; Pres. and CEO Asscn of American Publrs 1997–; mem. Bd Marguerite Casey Foundation, ABA Center for Human Rights; Chair. Peace PAC, Council for a Livable World; elected to Nat. Women's Hall of Fame, Seneca Falls, New York 1995. *Publications:* Champion of the Great American Family 1989, 24 Years of House Work and the Place is Still a Mess 1998. *Address:* Association of American Publishers Inc., 50 F Street, NW, Suite 400, Washington, DC 20001 (office); 621 Nadina Place, Orlando, FL 34747, USA (home). *Telephone:* (202) 220-4543 (office). *Fax:* (202) 347-3690 (office). *E-mail:* pschroeder@publishers.org (office). *Website:* publishers.org (office).

SCHROEDER, Steven Alfred, MD; American physician and academic; *Distinguished Professor of Health and Health Care, Department of Medicine, University of California, San Francisco;* b. 26 July 1939, New York; s. of Arthur E. Schroeder; m. Sally Ross Schroeder 1967; two s.; ed El Cerrito High School, Stanford Univ., Harvard Univ.; Fellow, Harvard Community Health and Medical Care and Instructor Harvard Medical School 1970–71; Asst Prof. of Medicine and Health Care Sciences, later Assoc. Prof., The George Washington Univ. Medical Center 1971–76; Medical Dir The George Washington Univ. Health Plan 1971–76; Assoc. Prof. of Medicine, Univ. of Calif., San Francisco 1976–80, Prof. 1980–90, Chief, Div. of Gen. Internal Medicine 1980–90, Distinguished Prof. of Health and Health Care, Dept of Medicine 2003–, Dir Smoking Cessation Leadership Center 2003–; Clinical Prof., Univ. of Medicine and Dentistry of NJ, Robert Wood Johnson Medical School 1991–; Pres. Robert Wood Johnson Foundation 1990–99, Pres. and CEO 1999–2003; Founding Chair. Int. Advisory Cttee of The Health Services, Ben-Gurion Univ. of the Negev, Israel 1996–; mem. Bd of Dirs American Legacy Foundation 2000–, Vice-Chair. 2001–; mem. Bd of Overseers, Harvard Coll. 2000–; mem. Editorial Bd New England Journal of Medicine 1994–; mem. Bd of Dirs James Irvine Foundation 2004–, Charles R. Drew Univ. of Medicine and Science 2005–; Visiting Prof. Dept of Community Medicine, St Thomas's Hosp. Medical School, London 1982–83; Pres. Harvard Medical Alumni Asscn 2005–06; numerous hon. degrees. *Publications:* more than 200 articles. *Leisure interests:* climbing, hiking, tennis, gardening, literature, history. *Address:* Smoking Cessation Leadership Center, University of California, 3333 California Street, Suite 430, San Francisco, CA 94143 (office); Box 1211, University of California, San Francisco, San Francisco, CA 94143-1211, USA (office). *Telephone:* (415) 502-1881 (office). *Fax:* (415) 502-5739 (office). *E-mail:* steve.schroeder@ucsf.edu (office). *Website:* smokingcessationleadership.ucsf.edu (office).

SCHUBARTH, Martin, DrIur; Swiss judge and professor of law; *Avocat-Conseil, Rusconi & Associés;* b. 9 June 1942, Basel; m. Musa Retschmedin 1944; one d.; ed Univ. of Basel; began practising as lawyer, Basel 1969; Lecturer, Univ. of Basel 1973; apptd Prof. Univ. of Bonn 1976, Univ. of Hanover 1980; Fed. Judge 1983–2004, Pres. Fed. Supreme Court 1999–2000, Pres. Criminal Court 1999–2002; currently Avocat-Conseil, Rusconi & Associés, Lausanne. *Publication:* Kommentar zum Schweizer Strafrecht 1982 ff. *Address:* Rusconi & Associés, 4 rue de la Paix, CP 7268, 1002 Lausanne (office); Ch. du Levant 44, 1005 Lausanne, Switzerland (home). *Telephone:* (21) 321-50-80 (office); (21) 728-83-82 (home). *Fax:* (21) 320-29-60 (office). *E-mail:* info@rusconi-avocats.ch (office); m.schubarth@bluewin.ch (home). *Website:* www.rusconi-avocats.ch; www.martinschubarth.ch.

SCHUBERT, John M., BChemEng (Hons), PhD; Australian business executive; *Chairman, Commonwealth Bank of Australia;* fmr CEO and Man. Dir Pioneer International Ltd; fmr Chair. and Man. Dir Esso Australia Ltd; mem. Bd of Dirs Commonwealth Bank of Australia 1991–, Chair. 2004–, Chair. Performance and Renewal Cttee, mem. People and Remuneration Cttee; Chair. G2 Therapies Ltd; mem. Bd of Dirs BHP Billiton Ltd 2000–, BHP Billiton PLC 2001–, Qantas Airways Ltd; Chair. Great Barrier Reef Foundation; Fellow, Acad. of Technological Science and Eng, Inst. of Engineers; Hon. mem. and Past Pres. Business Council of Australia. *Address:* Commonwealth Bank of Australia, Level 2, 48 Martin Place, Sydney, NSW 1155, Australia (office). *Telephone:* (2) 9378-2000 (office). *Fax:* (2) 9378-3317 (office). *E-mail:* info@commbank.com.au (office). *Website:* www.commbank.com.au (office).

SCHULBERG, Budd, LLD; American novelist and scriptwriter; b. 27 March 1914, New York, NY; s. of Benjamin P. Schulberg and Adeline Schulberg (née Jaffe); m. 1st Virginia Ray 1936 (divorced 1942); one d.; m. 2nd Victoria Anderson 1943 (divorced 1964); two s.; m. 3rd Geraldine Brooks 1964 (died 1977); m. 4th Betsy Langman 1979; one s. one d.; ed Deerfield Acad. and Dartmouth Coll.; short-story writer and novelist 1936–; screenwriter for Samuel Goldwyn, David O. Selznick and Walter Wanger, Hollywood, Calif. 1936–40; Lt in USN 1943–46, assigned to Office of Strategic Service; taught writing courses and conducted workshops at various insts in US; mem. Authors Guild, Dramatists Guild, American Civil Liberties Union, American Soc. Composers Authors and Publrs, Sphinx, Writers Guild of America East, Bd of Trustees, Humanitas Prize, Advisory Cttee on Black Participation, John F. Kennedy Center for the Performing Arts; Founder and Dir Watts Writers Workshop 1965–, Frederick Douglass Creative Arts Center, New York 1971–; numerous awards for writings, numerous humanitarian awards. *Publications:* novels: What Makes Sammy Run? 1941, The Harder They Fall 1947 (screen adaptation 1955), The Disenchanted 1950, Waterfront 1955, Sanctuary V (Prix littéraire du Festival du cinéma américain de Deauville 2005) 1969, Some Faces in the Crowd (short stories) 1953, From the Ashes: Voices of Watts (ed. and author of introduction) 1967, Loser and Still Champion: Muhammad Ali 1972, The Four Seasons of Success 1972, Swan Watch (with Geraldine Brooks) 1975, Everything That Moves 1980, Moving Pictures: Memories of a Hollywood Prince 1981, Writers in America 1983, Love, Action, Laughter and Other Sad Tales (short stories) 1990, Sparring with Hemingway: And Other Legends of the Fight Game 1995, Ringside 2006; plays, films: Winter Carnival (with F. Scott Fitzgerald) 1939, The Pharmacist's Mate 1951, On the Waterfront (Acad. Award and Screen Writers Guild Award for the screenplay) 1954, A Face in the Crowd (German Film Critics Award) 1957, Wind Across the Everglades 1958, The Disenchanted 1958, What Makes Sammy Run? (TV play 1959, stage 1964), Senor Discretion Himself (musical) 1985, A Table at Ciro's 1987, Joe Louis: For All Time (film documentary) 1988; stories and articles in numerous anthologies; contrib. to Newsday Syndicate, Esquire, Saturday Review, Life, Harper's, Playboy, Intellectual Digest, The New Republic, The New YorkerN New York Times Sunday Book Review. *Leisure interests:* bird watching, boxing, fishing, Mexican archaeology, Black Arts movt. *Address:* c/o Miriam Altshuler Literary Agency, RR #1, Box 5, Old Post Road, Red Hook, NY 12571 (office); c/o Mr Mickey Freiberg, 2221 Pelham, Los Angeles, CA 90046, USA (office); POB 707, Westhampton Beach, NY 11978, USA (home). *Telephone:* (631) 288-0564 (office); (631) 288-1452 (home). *Fax:* (631) 288-1495 (office). *E-mail:* bschulberg@optonline.net (office).

SCHULLER, Gunther Alexander; American composer, conductor, music educator and record producer; b. 22 Nov. 1925, New York, NY; s. of Arthur E. Schuller and Elsie (Bernartz) Schuller; m. Marjorie Black 1948 (died 1992); two s.; ed St Thomas Choir School, New York, Manhattan School of Music; Principal French horn, Cincinnati Symphony Orchestra 1943–45, Metropolitan Opera Orchestra 1945–59; teacher, Manhattan School of Music 1950–63, Yale Univ. 1964–67; Head Composition Dept, Tanglewood 1963–84; Music Dir First Int. Jazz Festival, Washington 1962; active as conductor since mid-1960s with maj. orchestras in Europe and USA; reconstructed and orchestrated Der Gelbe Klang by De Hartmann/Kandinsky; Pres. New England Conservatory of Music 1967–77; Pres. Nat. Music Council 1979–81; Artistic Co-Dir, then Artistic Dir Summer Activities, Boston Symphony Orchestra, Berkshire Music Center, Tanglewood 1969–84, Festival at Sandpoint 1985–98; founder and Pres. Margun Music Inc. 1975–2000, GM Recordings 1981–; mem. American Acad. of Arts and Sciences, American Acad. of Arts and Letters; Hon. DMus (Northeastern Univ.) 1967, (Colby Coll.) 1969, (Ill. Univ.) 1970, (Williams Coll.) 1975, (Rutgers Univ.) 1980, (Oberlin Coll.) 1989, (Fla State Univ.) 1991; Creative Arts Award, Brandeis Univ. 1960, Nat. Inst. Arts and Letters Award 1960, Guggenheim Grant 1962, 1963, ASCAP Deems Taylor Award 1970, Rogers and Hammerstein Award 1971, William Schuman Award, Columbia Univ. 1989, McArthur Foundation Fellowship 1991, McArthur'Genius' Award 1994; Gold Medal American Acad. of Arts and Letters 1996, Order of Merit, Germany 1997, Max Rudolf Award 1998, Pulitzer Prize in Music 1999. *Compositions include:* Horn Concerto No. 1 1945, Vertige d'Eros 1946, Concerto for cello and orchestra 1946, Jumpin' in the Future 1946, Quartet for Four Brasses 1947, Oboe Sonata 1947, Duo Concertante for cello and piano 1947, Symphonic Study (Meditation) 1948, Trio for Oboe, Horn, Viola 1948, Symphony for brass and percussion 1950, Fantasy for Unaccompanied Cello 1951, Recitative and Rondo for violin and piano 1953, Dramatic Overture 1951, Five Pieces for Five Horns 1952, Adagio for flute, string trio 1952, Music for Violin, Piano and Percussion 1957, Symbiosis for violin, piano, percussion 1957, String Quartet No. 1 1957, Contours 1958, Woodwind Quintet 1958, Spectra 1958, Concertino for jazz quartet and orchestra 1959, Seven Studies on Themes of Paul Klee 1959, Conversations 1960, Lines and Contrasts for 16 horns 1960, Abstraction for jazz ensemble 1960, Variants on a Theme of Thelonious Monk 1960, Music for Brass Quintet 1960, Contrasts for woodwind quintet and orchestra 1961, Variants (ballet with choreography by Balanchine) 1961, Double Quintet for woodwind and brass quintets 1961, Meditation for concert band 1961, Concerto for piano and orchestra 1962, Journey into Jazz 1962, Fantasy Quartet for four cellos 1963, Threnos for oboe and orchestra 1963, Composition in Three Parts 1963, Five Bagatelles for Orchestra 1964, Five Etudes for orchestra 1964, The Power Within Us 1964, Five Shakespearean Songs for baritone and orchestra 1964, String Quartet No. 2 1965, Symphony 1965, American Triptych (on paintings of Pollock, Davis and Calder) 1965, Sacred Cantata 1966, Gala Music concerto for orchestra 1966, The Visitation (opera) 1966, Movements for flute and strings, Six Renaissance Lyrics, Triplum I 1967, Study in Textures for concert band 1967, Diptych for brass quintet and orchestra 1967, Shapes and Designs 1968, Concerto for double bass and orchestra 1968, Consequents for orchestra 1969, Fisherman and his Wife (opera) 1970, Concerto da Camera No. 1 1971, Capriccio Stravagante 1972, Tre Invenzioni 1972, Three Nocturnes 1973, Five Moods for tuba quartet 1973, Four Soundscapes 1974, Triplum II 1975, Violin Concerto 1976, Concerto No. 2 for horn and orchestra 1976, Diptych for organ 1976, Concerto No. 2 for orchestra 1977, Concerto for contrabassoon and orchestra 1978, Deaï for three orchestras 1978, Sonata Serenata 1978, Octet 1979, Concerto for trumpet and orchestra 1979, Eine Kleine Posaunenmusik 1980, In Praise of Winds symphony for large wind orchestra 1981, Concerto No. 2 for piano and orchestra 1981, Symphony for organ 1981, Concerto Quaternio 1984, Concerto for alto saxophone 1983, Duologue for violin and piano 1983, On Light Wings piano quartet 1984, Piano Trio 1984, Concerto for viola and orchestra 1985, Concerto for bassoon and orchestra 1985, Farbenspiel Concerto No. 3 for orchestra 1985, String Quartet No. 3 1986, Chimeric Images 1988, Concerto for string quartet and orchestra 1988, Concerto for flute and orchestra 1988, Horn Sonata 1988, On Winged Flight: A Divertimento for Band 1989, Chamber Symphony 1989, Five Impromptus for English horn and string quartet 1989, Impromptus and Cadenzas for chamber sextet 1990, Song and Dance for violin and concert band 1990, Concerto for piano three hands 1990, Violin Concerto No. 2 1991, Brass Quintet No. 2 1993, Reminiscences and Reflections 1993, The Past is the Present for orchestra 1994, Sextet for left-hand piano and woodwind quintet 1994, Concerto for organ and orchestra 1994, Mondrian's Vision 1994, Lament for M 1994, Blue Dawn into White Heat concert band 1995, An Arc Ascending 1996, Ohio River Reflections 1998, A Bouquet for Collage 1988, Fantasia Impromptu for flute and harpsichord 2000, Quod Libet for violin, cello, oboe, horn and harp 2001, String Quartet No. 4 2002, Concerto da Camera No. 2 2002, String Trio 2003, Encounters for jazz orchestra and symphony orchestra 2003, Where the World Ends 2008. *Publications:* Horn Technique 1962, Early Jazz: Its Roots and Musical Development, Vol. I 1968, Musings: The Musical Worlds of Gunther Schuller 1985, The Swing Era: The Development of Jazz 1930–45 1989, The Compleat Conductor 1997. *Address:* GM Recordings, 167 Dudley Road, Newton Center, MA 02459, USA. *Telephone:* (617) 332-6328. *Fax:* (617) 969-1079. *E-mail:* contact@gmrecordings.com. *Website:* www.gmrecordings.com.

SCHULMAN, Joshua G.; American business executive; *CEO, Jimmy Choo;* spent seven years at Gucci Group, first as Worldwide Dir Women's Ready to Wear for Gucci brand and then as Exec. Vice-Pres. Worldwide Merchandising and Wholesale for Yves Saint Laurent brand; Man. Dir of Int. Strategic Alliances for Gap, Inc. and Sr Vice-Pres. Int. Product Devt and Merchandising for Gap Brand –2006; Pres. Kenneth Cole Productions, Inc. New York brand 2006–07; CEO Jimmy Choo (shoe label) 2007–. *Address:* J. Choo Ltd, Ixworth House, 37 Ixworth Place, London, SW3 3QH, England (office). *Telephone:* (20) 7591-7000 (office). *Fax:* (20) 7591-7077 (office). *E-mail:* info@jimmychoo.com (office). *Website:* www.jimmychoo.com (office).

SCHULTE-NOELLE, Henning, MBA; German lawyer and banking executive; *Chairman of the Supervisory Board, Allianz SE;* b. 26 Aug. 1942, Essen; ed Univs of Tübingen, Bonn, Cologne, Edinburgh, UK and Pennsylvania, USA; attorney Eckholt, Westrick and Pnrs, Frankfurt 1974; joined Allianz Group 1975, Head of Chair.'s Office, Munich 1979–83, Head of Regional Office for Northrhine-Westphalia, Cologne 1984–87, mem. Man. Bd Allianz Versicherung 1988–90, Allianz Leben 1988–90 (Chair. 1991), Chair. Allianz AG (called Allianz-Dresdner after acquisition of Dresdner Bank 2001, renamed Allianz SE 2006) 1991–2003, Chair. Supervisory Bd 2003–; mem. Supervisory Bd Thyssen Krupp AG, E.ON AG. *Address:* Allianz SE, Königinstrasse 28, 80802 Munich, Germany (office). *Telephone:* (89) 38000 (office). *Fax:* (89) 38003425 (office). *Website:* www.allianz.com (office).

SCHULTZ, Howard, BS; American business executive; *Chairman, CEO and Chief Global Strategist, Starbucks Corporation;* b. 19 July 1953, Brooklyn, NY; m. Sheri Kersch Schultz; one s. one d.; ed Canarsie High School and Northern Michigan Univ.; began career as sales trainee for Xerox; Vice-Pres. of US Sales, Hammerplast (subsidiary of Swedish-based Perstorp); joined Starbucks Coffee Co. (now Starbucks Corpn) in Sales and Marketing Dept 1982, Chair. 1987– (after buying out original owners), CEO 1987–2000, 2008–, now also Chief Global Strategist; prin. owner Seattle SuperSonics (Nat. Basketball Asscn) professional basketball team and Seattle Storm (Women's Nat. Basketball Asscn) professional basketball team. *Address:* Starbucks Corporation, 2401 Utah Avenue South, Seattle, WA 98134, USA (office). *Telephone:* (206) 447-1575 (office). *Fax:* (206) 447-0828 (office). *Website:* www.starbucks.com (office).

SCHULTZ, Peter G., BS, PhD; American chemist and academic; *Institute Director, Genomics Institute, Novartis Research Foundation;* b. 23 June 1956, Cincinnati, OH; ed Calif. Inst. of Tech. (Caltech), Pasadena, MIT; Asst Prof., Dept of Chem., Calif. Inst. of Tech. (Caltech), Pasadena, Calif. 1985–87, Assoc. Prof. 1987–89, Prof. 1989–99; Prin. Investigator, Lawrence Berkeley Lab. 1985–; Founding Scientist and Chair., Scientific Advisory Bd, Affymax Research Inst., Palo Alto, Calif. 1988–; Investigator, Howard Hughes Medical Inst. 1994–98; Founder and Dir, Symyx Technologies, Palo Alto 1995–; Prof. of Chem., Scripps Research Inst., La Jolla, Calif. 1999–; Inst. Dir Genomics Inst., Novartis Research Foundation, La Jolla 1999–; mem. Bd of Dirs Nanosphere 2005–; Founder and Dir Syrrx Inc. 2000–, Kalypsys 2001–, Phenomix 2002–, Ambrx 2003–, Ilypsa 2004–; mem. American Acad. of Arts and Sciences 1990–, NAS 1993–, Caltech Chem. Advisory Cttee 1998–, Searle Advisory Cttee 1995–, Welch Foundation Scientific Advisory Bd 2002–, Daman Runyon Advisory Bd 1999–2004, Princeton Chem. Advisory Cttee 1994–96; Dr hc (Uppsala Univ., Sweden) 1994; numerous awards including NSF Presidential Young Investigator Award 1985, Alan T. Waterman Award 1988, ACS Award in Pure Chem. 1990, Eli Lilly Award in Biological Chem. 1991, Humboldt Research Award 1992, Wolf Prize in Chem. 1994, Calif. Scientist of the Year 1995, Alfred Bader Award in Bioorganic and Bioinorganic Chem. 2000, Paul

Ehrlich and Ludwig Darmstaedter Prize 2002, Arthur C. Cope Award, ACS 2005. *Address:* Genomics Institute, Novartis Research Foundation, 10675 John Jay Hopkins Drive, La Jolla, CA 92121, USA (office). *Telephone:* (858) 812-1500 (office). *Fax:* (858) 812-1502 (office). *E-mail:* info@gnf.org (office). *Website:* www.gnf.org (office); schultz.scripps.edu.

SCHULTZE, Charles Louis, BA, MA, PhD; American economist and fmr government official; *Senior Fellow Emeritus in Economic Studies, Brookings Institution;* b. 12 Dec. 1924, Alexandria, Va; s. of Richard Lee Schultze and Nora Woolls Schultze (née Baggett); m. Rita Irene Hertzog 1947; one s. five d.; ed Georgetown Univ. and Univ. of Maryland; Economist, Office of Price Stabilization 1951–52, Council of Econ. Advisers 1952–53, 1955–59; Assoc. Prof. of Econs, Indiana Univ. 1959–61; Assoc. Prof., Adjunct Prof. of Econs, Univ. of Md 1961–87; Asst Dir, Bureau of the Budget 1962–65, Dir 1965–68; Sr Fellow, Brookings Inst., Washington, DC 1968–76, 1981–87, 1991–96, Emer. 1997–, Dir Econ. Studies 1987–90, John C. and Nancy D. Whitehead Chair 1997; Chair. Council of Econ. Advisers to Pres. 1977–81; Hon. Pres. American Econ. Asscn 1984. *Publications:* National Income Analysis 1964, The Politics and Economics of Public Spending 1969 (co-author), Setting National Priorities: The 1974 Budget, The Public Use of Private Interest 1977, Other Times, Other Places 1986, American Living Standards (co-ed. and co-author) 1988, Barriers to European Growth (co-ed. and co-author) 1989, An American Trade Strategy: Options for the 1990s (co-ed.) 1990, Memos to the President 1992. *Address:* Brookings Institution, 1775 Massachusetts Avenue, NW, Washington, DC 20036 (office); 5520 33rd Street, NW, Washington, DC 20015, USA (home). *Telephone:* (202) 797-6163 (office). *Fax:* (202) 797-6181 (office). *E-mail:* escomment@brookings.edu (office). *Website:* www.brookings.org/scholars/cschultze.htm (office).

SCHULZ, Ekkehard D., Dr-Ing; German business executive; *Chairman of the Executive Board, ThyssenKrupp AG;* b. 24 July 1941, Bromberg, Westpreussen; m.; two c.; ed Clausthal Mining Acad., Clausthal Univ.; mem. scientific staff and Chief Engineer, Inst. for Gen. Metallurgy and Casting, Clausthal Univ. 1967–72; joined Thyssen Group 1972, Deputy Mem. (Production) Exec. Bd, Thyssen Stahl AG 1985, mem. (Production) 1986, (Tech.) 1988, Chair. 1991; mem. Exec. Bd, Thyssen AG 1991, Chair. 1998, Chair. Exec. Bd, ThyssenKrupp Stahl AG 1997, ThyssenKrupp AG 1999–, Thyssen Krupp Steel AG 1999–2001; Pres. EUROFER, Brussels; mem. supervisory bds/advisory councils, AXA Konzern AG, Commerzbank AG, Hapag Lloyd AG, MAN AG, RAG AG, RWE Plus AG, STRABAG AG; mem. int. advisory Bd, Salomon Smith Barney, New York; mem. Exec. Cttee and Bd, Wirtschaftsvereinigung Stahl und VDEh; mem. Advisory Council of BDI (Vice-Pres.); Hon. Prof. (Clausthal Univ.) 1999. *Address:* ThyssenKrupp AG, August-Thyssen-Strasse 1, 40211 Dusseldorf, Germany (office). *Telephone:* (211) 8240 (office). *Fax:* (211) 82436000 (office). *E-mail:* info@thyssenkrupp.com (office). *Website:* www.thyssenkrupp.com (office).

SCHULZE, Ingo; German writer and journalist; b. 15 Dec. 1962, Dresden; s. of Christa Schulze; m. Natalia Schulze; two d.; ed Univ. of Jena; Dramatic Producer, Theatre of Altenburg 1988–90; founder weekly newspaper in Altenburg 1990–92, weekly newspaper in St Petersburg 1993; writer in Berlin 1993–; Ernst Willner Prize 1995, Aspekte Literature Prize 1995, Berlin Literature Prize 1998, Johannes Bobrowski Medal 1998, Joseph Breitbach Prize 2001, Peter Weiss Prize 2006, Thuringia Literature Prize 2007, Leipzig Book Fair Prize 2007, Premio Grinzane Cavour (Italy) 2008. *Publications:* 33 Augenblicke des Glücks (Aspekte-Literatur-Prize for best debut) 1995, Simple Storys: Ein Roman aus der ostdeutschen Provinz 1998, Von Nasen, Faxen und Ariadnefäden, Fax-Briefe (with Zeichnungen von Helmar Penndorf) 2000, Telling Tales (contrib. to charity anthology) 2004, Neue Leben (novel) 2005, Handy – 13 Geschichten in alter Manier 2007, Adam und Evelyn (novel) 2008, Der Herr Augustin (with Julia Penndorf), Tausend Geschichten sind nicht genug (essays); contrib.: Granta 100 (anthology) 2008. *Address:* Liselotte-Herrmann-Str. 33, 10407 Berlin, Germany (home). *E-mail:* writer@ingoschulze.com (home). *Website:* www.ingoschulze.com.

SCHULZE, Richard (Dick) M.; American retail executive; *Chairman, Best Buy Company, Inc.;* b. St Paul, Minn.; m.; one d.; ed St Paul Cen. High School; tech. electronics training with USAF and Minn. Air Nat. Guard; began career as ind. mfrs rep. for consumer electronics brands 1960s; f. Sound of Music (stereo component retail stores chain) 1966, Chair. and Dir 1966–83; f. Best Buy Co. Inc. (consumer electronics retailer) 1983, mem. Bd Dirs, Chair. and CEO 1983–2002, Chair. 2002–; mem. Minn. Business Partnership; mem. Bd Dirs Pentair Inc., The Nat. Entrepreneur of the Year Inst., Bd Overseers Carlson School of Man., Advisory Bd Science and Tech. Center; Trustee Univ. of St Thomas, Chair. Exec. and Institutional Advancement Cttee; Chair. Bd of Govs Univ. of St Thomas Business School, Best Buy Children's Foundation 1994–; Hon. PhD (Univ. of St Thomas) 1998; Dealer's Pride Award, Dealerscope Merchandising 1997, Corp. Leader of the Year, Juvenile Diabetes Foundation 1999, America's Promise Red Wagon Award for Community Service 1999, Lifetime Achievement Award, Ernst & Young 1999, Outstanding Marketing Exec. of the Year, Minn. DECA 2000. *Address:* Best Buy Company Inc., 7601 Penn Avenue South, Richfield, MN 55423, USA (office). *Telephone:* (612) 291-1000 (office). *Fax:* (612) 292-4001 (office). *E-mail:* info@bestbuy.com (office). *Website:* www.bestbuy.com (office).

SCHUMACHER, Joel, BA; American film director; b. 29 Aug. 1939, New York City; s. of Francis Schumacher and Marian Kantor; ed Parsons School of Design, New York; began to work in fashion industry aged 15; later opened own boutique Paraphenalia; costume designer for Revlon in 1970s; also set and production designer; wrote screenplays Sparkle, Car Wash, The Wiz; also wrote and directed for TV. *Films include:* The Incredible Shrinking Woman 1981, DC Cab (also screenplay) 1983 St Elmo's Fire (also screenplay) 1985, The Lost Boys 1987, Cousins 1989, Flatliners 1990, Dying Young 1991, Falling

Down 1993, The Client 1994, Batman Forever 1995, A Time to Kill 1996, Batman and Robin 1997, Eight Millimeter 1999, Flawless (also screenplay and producer) 1999, Gossip (producer) 2000, Tigerland 2000 Phone Booth 2002, Bad Company 2002, Veronica Guerin 2003, The Phantom of the Opera 2004, The Number 23 2007. *Address:* Joel Schumacher Productions, 400 Warner Boulevard, Burbank, CA 91522, USA (office).

SCHUMACHER, Michael; German motor racing driver; b. 3 Jan. 1969, Hürth-Hermülheim; s. of Rolf Schumacher and the late Elizabeth Schumacher; m. Corinna Betsch 1995; one d. one s.; began professional career 1983; 2nd place, Int. German Formula 3 Championship 1989; driver for Mercedes 1990; Int. German Champion, Formula 3 Championship 1990; European Formula 3 Champion 1990; World Champion, Formula 3, Macau and Fiji 1990; Formula 1 racing driver for the Jordan team 1991, Benetton team 1992–95, Ferrari team 1996–2006 (retd), now Advisor; Grand Prix wins: Argentina 1998, Australia 2000, 2001, 2002, 2004, Austria 2002, 2003, Bahrain 2004, Belgium 1992, 1995, 1996, 1997, 2001, 2002, 2004, Brazil 1994, 1995, 2000, 2002, Britain 1998, 2002, 2004, Canada 1994, 1997, 1998, 2000, 2002, 2003, 2004, China 2006, Europe 1994, 1995, 2000, 2001, 2004, 2006, France 1994, 1995, 1997, 1998, 2001, 2002, 2004, 2006, Germany 1995, 2002, 2004, 2006, Hungary 1994, 1998, 2001, 2004, Italy 1996, 1998, 2000, 2003, 2006, Japan 1995, 1997, 2000, 2001, 2002, 2004, Malaysia 2000, 2001, 2004, Monaco 1994, 1995, 1997, 1999, 2001, Pacific 1994, 1995, Portugal 1993, San Marino 1994, 1999, 2000, 2002, 2003, 2004, 2006, Spain 1995, 1996, 2001, 2002, 2003, 2004, USA 2000, 2003, 2004, 2005, 2006; Formula One World Champion 1994, 1995, 2000, 2001, 2002, 2003, 2004 (record seven times). *Film appearance:* Astérix at the Olympic Games 2008. *Publications:* Formula For Success (with Derick Allsop) 1996, Michael Schumacher (autobiog. with Christopher Hilton) 2000. *Leisure interests:* football, tennis, swimming, skiing. *Address:* c/o Willi Weber, Weber Management GmbH, Tränkestr. 11, 70597 Stuttgart, Germany (office). *Telephone:* (711) 726460 (office). *Fax:* (711) 7264633 (office). *Website:* www.mschumacher.com (office).

SCHUMER, Charles Ellis, BA, JD; American politician; *Senator from New York;* b. 23 Nov. 1950, Brooklyn, NY; s. of Abraham Schumer and Selma Schumer (née Rosen); m. Iris Weinshall 1980; two d.; ed Harvard Univ.; called to Bar NY 1975; mem. staff US Senator Claiborne Pell 1973; Assoc. Paul, Weiss, Rifking, Wharton and Garrison (law firm) 1974; mem. NY State Ass. 1975–80, Chair. Sub cttee on City Man. and Governance 1977, Cttee on Oversight and Investigation 1979; mem. Congress from NY Dist 1981–99, Senator from New York 1999–, mem. Finance, Banking, Judiciary and Rules Cttees; Head, Democratic Senate Campaign Cttee 2006; Democrat. *Publication:* Winning Back the Middle-Class Majority One Family at a Time (with Daniel Squadron) 2007. *Address:* 313 Hart Senate Office Building, Washington, DC 20510, USA (office). *Telephone:* (202) 224-6542 (office). *Fax:* (202) 228-3027 (office). *Website:* schumer.senate.gov (office).

SCHÜSSEL, Wolfgang; Austrian politician; b. 7 June 1945, Vienna; m.; two c.; ed Univ. of Vienna; Sec. Parl. Austrian People's Party (ÖVP) 1968, Chair. 1995–2007, Group Leader in Parl. 2007–; Sec.-Gen. Austrian Econ. Fed. 1975–89; mem. Parl. 1979–, Leader ÖVP Group of Econ. Fed. Parl. Dels 1987; Minister of Econ. Affairs 1989–95; Vice-Chancellor of Austria and Minister of Foreign Affairs 1996–2000, Chancellor of Austria 2000–07; Minister of the Interior Jan. 1, 2007–Jan. 11, 2007; Pres. European Council Jan.– June 2006. *Publications:* several books on issues relating to democracy and economics. *Address:* Austrian People's Party (ÖVP), Lichtenfelsgasse 7, 1010 Vienna, Austria (office). *Telephone:* (1) 401-26-0 (office). *Website:* www.oevp.at (office).

SCHUSTER, Rudolf, PhD; Slovak politician, diplomatist, writer and engineer; b. 4 Jan. 1934, Košice; s. of Alojz Schuster and Mária Benediková; m. Irene Trojáková; two c.; ed Slovak Tech. Univ., Bratislava, Tech. Univ. Košice; designer, Regional Agric. Inst., Bratislava 1960; Asst Hydrology and Hydraulic Inst., Slovak Acad. of Sciences 1960–62; Dir Energy Investment Dept and Tech. Dir E Slovak Steelworks 1963–74; Vice-Mayor of Košice 1975–83, Mayor 1983–86, 1994–99, Chair. E Slovak Region Nat. Cttee 1986–89; Chair. Nat. Council 1989–90; Amb. of Czech Repub. and Slovakia to Canada 1990–92; with Ministry of Foreign Affairs 1993–94; Mayor of Košice 1994–99; Pres. of Slovakia 1999–2004; Order of Labour 1988, Pribina Cross, First Class 1998, Grand Cross of Merit with Collar (Malta) 1999, Grand Gross (Greece) 2000, Grand Star of Romania 2000, Pour le Merite, First Class (Lebanon) 2001, Decoration Jose San Martin (Argentine) 2001, Cross Kenedy (Argentine) 2001, Decoration of Merit with Chain (Chile) 2001, Grand Chain of the Southern Cross (Brasil) 2001, Grand Decoration of the King Tomislav with Ribbon and Star (Croatia) 2001, Grand Cross of Merit (Germany) 2001, Decoration Seraphine (Sweden) 2002, White Eagle, First Class (Poland) 2002, Decoration Isabel La Catolica (Spain) 2002, Knight of the Grand Cross with Grand Gibbon (Italy) 2002, Knight Decoration with Chain (The Holy See) 2002, Golden Lion (Luxembourg) 2002, Golden Lion (Netherlands) 2002, Grand Chain, Prince Don Henrique (Portugal), Golden Honest Insignia of Freedom (Slovenia) 2003, Grand Cross of Merit with Chain (Hungary) 2003, Grand Honest Star Decoration of Merit (Austria) 2004, Decoration Prince Jaroslav the Sage First Class (Ukraine) 2004; Dr hc (Tech. Univ. Košice) 1998, (Wuppertal) 1999, (Moscow) 2001, (Kraków) 2002, (Bratislava) 2002, (St Petersburg) 2002, (Sofia) 2002, (Kiev) 2002, (Ottawa) 2003, (Ostrava) 2003, and four others; Merit Award for Peace and Democratic Achievement 2000 and numerous other decorations. *Achievements:* open-air performance of Bocatius, eight broadcast performances and 21 literary sessions. *Publications:* Ultimatum (memoirs, translated into eight languages) 1997, more than 30 books (travel, crime fiction and detective novels, memoirs); numerous screenplays. *Leisure interests:* documentaries, literature, collecting historical photocameras, film-cameras and cine-projectors. *Address:* c/o Regional Office of the President, Hviezdoslavova 7/A, 040 01 Košice, Slovak Republic (office). *Telephone:* (55) 622-96-17 (office). *Fax:* (55) 622-96-19 (office). *E-mail:* kosice@prezident.gov.sk (office). *Website:* www.prezident.sk/?274 (office).

SCHÜTZ, Klaus; German politician and diplomatist; b. 17 Sept. 1926, Heidelberg; m. Heidi Seeberger 1953; one s. one d.; ed Paulsen-Realgymnasium, Humboldt Univ. zu Berlin, Freie Univ. Berlin and Harvard Univ., USA; war service, seriously wounded 1944–45; Asst, Inst. für Politische Wissenschaften, Freie Univ., Berlin 1951–61; mem. City Ass. 1954–57, 1963–77; mem. Bundestag 1957–61; Liaison Senator between Berlin Senate and Bonn Govt 1961–66; mem. Bundesrat 1961–77, Pres. 1967–68; Under-Sec. Ministry of Foreign Affairs 1966–67; Governing Mayor of West Berlin 1967–77; Chair. Berlin Social Democratic Party 1968–77; Amb. to Israel 1977–81; Dir-Gen. Deutsche Welle 1981–87; Dir Landesanstaltung für Rundfunk NRW, Düsseldorf 1987–93; Pres. Landesverband Berlin des Deutschen Roten Kreuzes 1996–2003. *Leisure interests:* books, baroque music. *Address:* 9 Konstanzerstrasse, 10707 Berlin, Germany (home). *Telephone:* (30) 8813617 (home). *E-mail:* drschuetz@t-online.de (home).

SCHÜTZEICHEL, Rudolf, DPhil; German professor of philology; b. 20 May 1927, Rahms; s. of Matthias Schützeichel and Gertrud Schützeichel; m. Margrit Britten 1955; two d.; ed Univ. of Mainz; Docent Univ. of Cologne 1960–63; Prof. of German Philology, Univ. of Groningen 1963–64, Univ. of Bonn 1964–69, Univ. of Münster 1969–; mem. Akad. Wissenschaften, Göttingen, Kgl. Akad., Göteborg; Hon. DPhil (Leipzig) 1992; Festschrift 1987 (Althochdeutsch 2 Bände Heidelberg); Officer Order of Orange-Nassau. *Publications:* Mundart, Urkundensprache und Schriftsprache 1974, Grundlagen d.w. Mitteldeutsch 1976, Das alem. Memento Mori 1967, Codex. Pal. lat. 52 1982, Mittelrh. Passionsspiel 1978, Gottschald Namenkunde 1982, Addenda und Corrigenda (I) 1982, (II) 1985, (III) 1991, Textgebundenheit 1981, Althochdeutsch. Wörterb. (5th Edn) 1995; Ed. various publs including BNF.NF. 1966–, Sprachwissenschaft 1976–, NOWELE 1983–, Die älteste Überlieferung von Williams Kommentar des Hohen Liedes 2001. *Address:* Potstiege 16, 48161 Münster, Germany. *Telephone:* (251) 861345.

SCHUWIRTH, Lt-Gen. Klaus; German army officer; Commdr of German army's 4th Corps in Potsdam; Dir of Mil. Staff, EU Rapid Reaction Force 2001. *Address:* c/o Ministry of Defence, Stauffenbergstr. 18, 10785 Berlin, Germany (office). *Telephone:* (30) 200400 (office). *Fax:* (30) 200-48333 (office). *Website:* www.bundeswehr.de (office).

SCHUWIRTH, Gen. Rainer; German army officer; b. 12 July 1945, Regensburg, Bavaria; m. Barbara Hackbarth; one s., one d.; enlisted into Fed. Armed Forces 1964; trained as Artillery Officer 1964–66; assignments as Artillery Officer and Honest John Battery Commdr 1966–76; Fed. Armed Forces Command and Staff Coll., Hamburg 1976–78; G2 Staff Officer (Intelligence Estimates), HQ Centag, Heidelberg 1978–81; G3 Staff Officer (Operations) at III Corps, Koblenz 1981–83; Commdr Missile Artillery Bn 150 (Lance), Wesel 1983–85; Asst Br. Chief, Mil. Leadership and Civic Educ., Armed Forces Staff, Fed. Ministry of Defence, Bonn 1985–88, Branch Chief of Mil. Policy 1990–91; Mil. Asst to Fed. Minister of Defence 1988–90; Commdr Armoured Brigade 8, Luneberg 1991–93; Head of Mil. Policy Div., Perm. Mission to NATO 1994–96; Asst Chief of Staff, Armed Forces Staff Politico-Mil. Affairs and Operations, Ministry of Defence 1996–99; Commdg Gen. IV Corps, Potsdam 1999–2001; Dir-Gen., EU Mil. Staff 2001–04; Chief of Staff, SHAPE 2004–07 (retd); contracted by European Defence Agency to produce draft concept for EU to exploit Network Enabled Capabilities (NEC) in support of crisis-man. operations 2007; work with Stiftung Wissenschaft und Politik, Berlin 2008–; Silver Cross of Honour, Fed. Armed Forces, Gold Cross of Honour, Fed. Armed Forces, Cross of Order of Merit, Cross of Order of Merit (First Class), Commdr de l'Ordre nat. de Mérite, Gold Medal, Polish Armed Forces. *Address:* c/o Stiftung Wissenschaft und Politik, Deutsches Institut für Internationale Politik und Sicherheit, Ludwigkirchplatz 3-4, 10719 Berlin, Germany.

SCHWAB, Charles R., BA (Econs), MBA; American business executive; *Chairman and CEO, The Charles Schwab Corporation;* b. 1937, Sacramento; m. Helen O'Neill; five c.; ed Stanford Univ., Stanford Grad. School of Business; f. The Charles Schwab Corpn, San Francisco 1971, Chair. 1986–, CEO 1986–97, 2004–, Co-CEO 1998–2003; mem. Bd The Gap, Inc., Transamerica Corpn, AirTouch Communications, Siebel Systems, Inc.; Chair. Parent's Educational Resource Center, San Mateo; mem. Bd of Trustees, Stanford Univ.; mem. World Business Forum, CEO Org., San Francisco CEO Cttee on Jobs; mem. Bd and Treas. Nat. Park Foundation; co-founder Charles and Helen Schwab Foundation. *Publication:* How To Be Your Own Stockbroker 1984. *Address:* The Charles Schwab Corporation, 101 Montgomery Street, San Francisco, CA 94104 (office); Charles and Helen Schwab Foundation, 1650 South Amphlett Blvd., Suite 300, San Mateo, CA 94402-2516, USA. *Telephone:* (415) 627-7000 (office). *Fax:* (415) 627-5970 (office). *Website:* www.schwab.com (office).

SCHWAB, Klaus, KCMG, DEcon, DrIng, MPA; German foundation director and academic; *Executive Chairman, World Economic Forum;* b. 30 March 1938, Ravensburg, Germany; m. Hilde Schwab; one s. one d.; ed Swiss Federal Inst. of Tech., Univ. of Fribourg, Harvard Univ.; founder and Exec. Chair. World Econ. Forum 1971–; Prof. of Business Policy, Univ. of Geneva 1972–2002; fmr mem. UN High-Level Advisory Bd on Sustainable Devt; fmr Vice-Chair. UN Cttee for Devt Planning; fmr mem. Earth Council; co-f. The Schwab Foundation for Social Entrepreneurship 1998; f. The Forum of Young Global Leaders 2004; Trustee Peres Center for Peace, Israel; Grand Cross of the Nat. Order of Merit, Germany; six hon. doctorates including from Bishops Univ., Quebec, Canada, Univ. Autonoma de Guadalajara, Mexico, LSE, UK); Hon. Prof., Ben Gurion Univ., Israel; The Candlelight Award Foundation for Prevention and Early Resolution of Conflict 2001. *Publications:* several books and The Global Competitiveness Report (annually 1979–). *Leisure interests:* cross-country ski marathons, mountain climbing. *Address:* World Economic Forum, 91–93 route de la Capite, 1223 Cologny/Geneva, Switzerland (office). *Telephone:* (22) 869 1212 (office). *Fax:* (22) 786 2744 (office). *E-mail:* contact@weforum.org (office). *Website:* www.weforum.org (office).

SCHWAB, Susan Carroll, PhD; American academic administrator and fmr government official; ed Williams Coll., Stanford Univ., George Washington Univ.; agricultural trade negotiator, Office of US Trade Rep. 1977–79; Trade Policy Officer, US Foreign Service, American Embassy, Tokyo, Japan 1979–81; Chief Econ. and Legis. Asst, Office of US Senator John C. Danforth 1981–86, Legis. Dir 1986–89; Asst Sec. of Commerce and Dir Gen., US and Foreign Commercial Service, US Dept of Commerce 1989–93; Dir of Corp. Business Devt, Motorola Inc. 1993–95; Dean, School of Public Affairs, Univ. of Md 1995–2003; Pres. and CEO Univ. of Md Foundation 2004–05; Deputy US Trade Rep., Washington, DC 2005–06, US Trade Rep. 2006–09; mem. Council on Foreign Relations; Fellow, Nat. Acad. of Public Admin. *Publications:* Trade-Offs: Negotiating the Omnibus Trade Act 1994; numerous articles in magazines and journals. *Address:* c/o Office of the United States Trade Representative, Winder Bldg, 600 17th Street, NW, Washington, DC 20508, USA.

SCHWAETZER, Irmgard; German politician; *Chairman, Deutsche Komitee Katastrophenvorsorge e.V. (DKKV);* b. 5 April 1942, Münster; ed Univs of Passau, Münster and Bonn; worked in pharmaceutical industry in Germany and abroad 1971–80; joined FDP 1975, Gen. Sec. 1982–84, mem. Presidium 1982, Deputy Chair. 1988–94, Chair. Work-Group on Youth, Family, Employment, Women and Health 1998–; mem. Bundestag 1980–2002; mem. Landesvorstand Nordrhein-Westfalen 1980; Minister of State, Ministry of Foreign Affairs 1987–91; Chair., Nat. Union of Liberal Women 1990–95; Minister for Planning and Construction 1991–94; Regional Pres., Aachen 1997; Chair. Deutsche Komitee Katastrophenvorsorge e.V. (DKKV) 2002–. *Address:* Deutsches Komitee Katastrophenvorsorge e.V., Friedrich-Ebert-Allee 40, 53113 Bonn, Germany (office). *Telephone:* (228) 44601828 (office). *Fax:* (228) 44601836 (office). *E-mail:* info@dkkv.org (office). *Website:* www.dkkv.org (office).

SCHWAN, Gesine Marianne, Dr rer. pol; German political scientist, academic and university administrator; *President, Europa-University Viadrina;* b. 22 May 1943, Berlin; d. of Hildegard Schneider (née Olejak) and Hans R. Schneider; m. Alexander Schwan 1969 (died 1989); one s. one d.; ed Lycée Français de Berlin, Free University of Berlin; Asst Prof. Dept of Political Sciences, Free Univ. of Berlin 1971–77, Prof. 1977–; Fellow Woodrow Wilson Int. Center for Scholars 1980–81; By-Fellow Robinson Coll., Cambridge, UK 1984; Pres. Europa-Univ. Viadrina 1999–; unsuccessful candidate for Pres. of Germany 2004; Fed. Cross of Merits 1993, Verdienstkreuz (1st class) 2002; Urania Medal 1999, Marion Dönhoff Award 2004, Asscn of Berlin Foreign Press Award 2004, Pauline Staegemann Award 2004, Women in Europe Award, Network European Movt Germany 2005, Tolerance Award, Tolerance Ecumenical Foundation 2005. *Publications:* Leszek Kolakowski, Eine Philosophie der Freiheit nach Marx 1971, Die Gesellschaftskritik von Karl Marx 1974, Sozialdemokratie u. Marxismus (with Alexander Schwan) 1974, Sozialismus in der Demokratie; Eine Theorie Konsequent sozialdemokratischen Politik 1982, Der normative Horizont moderner Politik I und II (with Alexander Schwan) 1985, Politik und Schuld: Die zerstörerische Macht des Schweigens 1997; Jahrbuch für Politik (co-ed.) 1991–. *Leisure interests:* music, theatre, travelling. *Address:* Office of the President, Europa-Universität Viadrina, Main building 105, Große Scharrnstraße 59, 15230 Frankfurt an der Oder; Department of Political Science, Free University of Berlin, Ihnestrasse 21, 1000 Berlin 33 (office); Teutonenstrasse 6, 14129 Berlin, Germany (home). *Telephone:* (335) 55344274 (office); (30) 8382340 (Free Univ.) (office); (30) 8038366 (home). *Fax:* (335) 5534600 (office). *E-mail:* president@euv-frankfurt-o.de (office). *Website:* www.euv-frankfurt-o.de (office).

SCHWAN, Severin, Mag.rer.soc.oec., MagIur, DrIur; Austrian pharmaceuticals industry executive; *CEO, Roche Group;* b. 1967; m.; three c.; ed Univ. of Innsbruck, Univs of York and Oxford, UK, Univ. of Louvain, Belgium; trainee, Corp. Finance, Roche, Basel 1993–95, Head of Finance and Admin, Roche, Brussels 1995–98, Head of Finance and Informatics, Roche, Grenzach, Germany and mem. Exec. Bd Roche Deutschland Holding GmbH 1998–2000, Head of Global Finance and Services, Roche Diagnostics, Basel 2000–04, Head of Asia Pacific Region, Roche Diagnostics, Singapore 2004–06, CEO Roche Diagnostics Div. 2006–08, CEO Roche Group 2008–. *Address:* Roche Holding Ltd, Grenzacherstrasse 124, 4070 Basel, Switzerland (office). *Telephone:* (61) 688-11-11 (office). *Fax:* (61) 691-93-91 (office). *E-mail:* info@roche.com (office). *Website:* www.roche.com (office).

SCHWARTZ, Gerald W., OC, BCom, LLB, MBA; Canadian financial services industry executive; *Chairman, President and CEO, Onex Corporation;* b. Toronto, Ont.; ed Univ. of Manitoba, Harvard Univ. Grad. School of Business Admin; fmr specialist in mergers and acquisitions, investment banking firm, New York; Co-founder and Pres. CanWest Capital (renamed CanWest Global Communications) –1983; f. Onex Corpn 1983, Chair., Pres. and CEO 1983–; mem. Bd of Dirs Indigo Books and Music Inc., Canadian Council of Christians and Jews; mem. Cttee of Univ. Resources, Harvard Univ. Bd of Overseers, Business School, Canadian Council of Christians and Jews; Vice-Chair. and mem. Exec. Cttee, Mount Sinai Hosp.; Gov. Jr Achievementof Metro Toronto; Trustee, The Simon Wiesenthal Center; Hon. Dir Bank of Nova Scotia; Hon. LLD (St Francis Xavier Univ.), Hon. DPhil (Tel-Aviv Univ.); inducted into Canadian Business Hall of Fame. *Address:* Onex Corpn, 161 Bay Street, PO Box 700, Toronto, ON M5J 2S1, Canada (office). *Telephone:* (416) 362-7711 (office). *Fax:* (416) 362-5765 (office). *E-mail:* info@onex.com (office). *Website:* www.onex.com (office).

SCHWARTZ, Jonathan Ian; American computer industry executive; *President and CEO, Sun Microsystems Inc.;* b. 20 Oct. 1965; ed Wesleyan Univ.; early career at McKinsey & Co., New York 1987–89; Co-founder and CEO Lighthouse Design –1996, joined Sun Microsystems Inc. 1996 after Sun's acquisition of Lighthouse, held several sr positions including Vice Pres., Venture Fund, Vice Pres., Developer Products, Vice Pres., Enterprise Software, Dir of Product Marketing, Javasoft, Sr Vice Pres. of Corp. Strategy and Planning –2002, Exec. Vice Pres. for Software 2002–04, Pres. and COO 2004–06, Pres. and CEO 2006–. *Address:* Sun Microsystems, Inc., 4150 Network Circle, Santa Clara, CA 95054, USA (office). *Telephone:* (650) 960-1300 (office). *Fax:* (408) 276-3804 (office). *Website:* www.sun.com (office); blogs.sun.com/roller/page/jonathan.

SCHWARTZ, Maxime; French administrator and scientist; b. 1 June 1940, Blois; ed Ecole Polytechnique; entered Inst. Pasteur 1963, Head of Lab. 1973–84, mem. Scientific Council 1973–85, Head of Dept of Molecular Biology 1984–85, Deputy Dir 1985–87, Dir-Gen. 1988–99; Dir Dept Lab. Programming, l'Agence Française de Sécurité Sanitaire des aliments (AFSSA) –2006. *Publications include:* How the Cows Turned Mad 2001. *Address:* c/o Agence Française de Sécurité Sanitaire des aliments, 27–31 avenue du Général Leclerc, 94701 Maisons-Afort Cedex (office); L'Institut Pasteur, 25–28 rue du Dr. Roux, 75015 Paris, France.

SCHWARTZENBERG, Roger-Gérard, DenD; French politician and professor of law; b. 17 April 1943, Pau, Pyrénées-Atlantiques; s. of André Schwartzenberg and Simone Gutelman; ed Inst. d'Etudes Politiques, Paris; Prof. Univ. de Droit, d'Économie et de Sciences Sociales de Paris II 1969–, Inst. d'Etudes Politiques 1972–83; Pres. Mouvement des Radicaux de Gauche 1981–83, Hon. Pres. 1983–; mem. European Parl. 1979–83; Sec. of State, Ministry of Educ. 1983–84; Sec. of State responsible for univs, Ministry of Educ. 1984–86; Deputy for Val de Marne to Nat. Ass. 1986–2000, 2002–07; Sec. to Nat. Ass. 1988–92, 1993–97, Vice-Pres. Foreign Affairs Comm. 1992–2000; Mayor of Villeneuve-Saint-Georges 1989–95, 2001–08; Deputy Judge High Court of Justice and Court of Justice of the Repub. 1993–97; Pres. Groupe parlementaire radical, citoyen et vert 1999–2000; Minister of Research 2000–02; Deputy, Nat. Ass. 2002–07; Chevalier, Légion d"honneur 2009, Grand Officer, Order of Merit (Germany), Grand Decoration of Honour (Austria). *Publications:* books on political and legal topics including La Campagne présidentielle de 1965 1967, ĹAutorité de la chose décidée ou la Force juridique des décisions administratives 1969, La Guerre de succession ou les élections présidentielles de 1969 1969, Traité de sociologie politique 1971, ĺEtat spectacle, Essai sur et contre le star-system en politique 1977, La Droite absolue 1981, La Politique mensonge 1998, 1788: Essai sur la maldémocratie 2006. *Leisure interest:* tennis. *Address:* Université de Droit de Paris, 12 Place du Panthéon, 75005 Paris, France (office).

SCHWARZ, Antoine, LenD; French administrator and business executive; b. 9 Aug. 1943, Paris; s. of Willy Schwarz and Elisabeth du Brusle de Rouvroy; m. Christine Coudreau 1974; two s. one d.; ed Inst. d'Etudes Politiques de Paris, Ecole Nat. d'Admin; Admin. to the Treasury, Ministry of the Economy and Finance 1971–74; Prin. Inst. d'Études Politiques 1972–74; Head Service Juridique et Technique de l'Information 1974; Head of Cabinet André Rossi 1975–76, Raymond Barre 1977; Dir Radio Monte-Carlo 1978–81, Editions Mondiales 1982–83; Counsellor Centre Nat. de la Cinématographie 1984–85; Pres. and Dir-Gen. Soc. Financière de Radiodiffusion (SOFIRAD) 1986–89; Pres. Sofica-valor 1988–89, Consultant 1990; Founder, Pres. Radiofina 1993; Pres. SFP-Productions 1994–99, Sportotal 2000–; CEO Radio France Internationale 2004–08; Chevalier, Ordre nat. du Mérite, Chevalier, Ordre de la Légion d'honneur. *Address:* Sportotal, 51 rue d'Amsterdam, 75008 Paris (office); 20 place de la Motte-Piquet, 75015 Paris, France (home).

SCHWARZ, Gerard; American conductor; *Music Director, Seattle Symphony Orchestra;* b. 19 Aug. 1947, Weehawken, NJ; m. Jody Greitzer 1984; two s. two d.; ed Professional Children's School, Juilliard School; joined American Brass Quintet 1965; Music Dir Erick Hawkins Dance Co. 1966, Eliot Feld Dance Co. 1972; Co-Prin. Trumpet, New York Philharmonic 1973–74; Founding Music Dir Waterloo Festival 1975; Music Dir New York Chamber Symphony 1977–2002, LA Chamber Orchestra 1978–86; est. Music Today series, Merkin Concert Hall, New York 1981 (Music Dir 1988–89); Music Adviser Mostly Mozart Festival, Lincoln Center, New York 1982–84, Music Dir 1984–; Music Adviser Seattle Symphony 1983–84, Prin. Conductor 1984–85, Music Dir 1985–; Artistic Adviser Tokyu Bunkamura's Orchard Hall, Japan 1994–; Music Dir Royal Liverpool Philharmonic Orchestra 2001–06; Guest Conductor, Cosmopolitan Symphony, Aspen Festival Chamber, Tokyo Philharmonic, Residentie, The Hague, St Louis Symphony, Kirov, St Petersburg, Royal Liverpool Philharmonic and Vancouver Symphony Orchestras, City of London Symphonia and London Mozart Players; has conducted many US orchestras and Hong Kong Philharmonic, Jerusalem Symphony, Israeli Chamber and English Chamber Orchestras, London Symphony, Helsinki Philharmonic and Monte Carlo Philharmonic Orchestras, Ensemble Contemporain, Paris and Nat. Orchestra of Spain; operatic conducting debut, Washington Opera 1982; has also conducted Seattle Opera 1986, San Francisco Opera 1991 and New Japan Philharmonic 1998; numerous recordings for Delos, Nonesuch, Angel and RCA labels; numerous TV appearances; Hon. Fellow (John Moores Univ., Liverpool) 2001; Hon. DFA (Fairleigh Dickinson Univ., Seattle Univ.); Hon. DMus (Univ. of Puget Sound); named Conductor of the Year by Musical America Int. Directory of the Performing Arts 1994, Ditson Conductor's Award, Columbia Univ. 1989, two Record of the Year Awards, one Mumms Ovation Award. *Address:* Columbia Artists Management Inc., 1790 Broadway, New York, NY 10019-1412, USA (office);

Seattle Symphony Orchestra, PO Box 21906, Seattle, WA 98111-3669, USA (office). *Telephone:* (212) 841-9500 (office); (206) 215-4700 (office). *Fax:* (212) 841-9744 (office); (206) 215-4701 (office). *E-mail:* info@cami.com (office); info@seattlesymphony.org (office). *Website:* www.cami.com (office); www.seattlesymphony.org (office).

SCHWARZ, Harry Heinz, BA, LLB; South African attorney, politician and diplomatist; b. 13 May 1924, Cologne, Germany; s. of Fritz Schwarz and Alma Schwarz; m. Annette Louise Rudolph 1952; three s.; ed Univ. of Witwatersrand; with SA Air Force (seconded to RAF) during World War II; mem. Middle Temple; practised as attorney and advocate 1949–; Chief Exec. Merchant Bank 1969–74; mem. Johannesburg City Council 1951–57; mem. Transvaal Prov. Council 1958–74, Leader of Opposition 1960–74; MP 1974–91; Amb. to USA 1991–94; Sr Adviser to Hofmeyr Inc., Johannesburg; fmr columnist Sunday Star; Hon. Col 15 Squadron (SA Air Force); Order of Meritorious Service; several hon. doctorates. *Publications:* Poverty Erodes Freedom and articles and book chapters on politics, law and economics. *Leisure interest:* writing. *Address:* Hyde Park Law Chambers, 7 Albury Park, Sandton 2024 (office); 5 Dukes End, 163 Buckingham Avenue, Craighall Park, Johannesburg 2196 (home); PO Box 413063, Craighall 2024, South Africa. *Telephone:* (11) 325-4846 (office); (11) 447-9879 (home). *Fax:* (11) 325-4244 (office). *E-mail:* harry@schwarz.co.za (office).

SCHWARZ-SCHILLING, Christian, DPhil; German politician, consultant and fmr UN official; *President, Dr. Schwarz-Schilling and Partner GmbH;* b. 19 Nov. 1930, Innsbruck, Austria; s. of Prof. Rheinhard Schwarz-Schilling and Duzsa Schwarz-Schilling; m. Marie Luise Jonen 1957; two d.; ed Univs of Berlin and Munich; mem. Landtag, Hesse, FRG 1966–76; Sec.-Gen. Hesse CDU 1966–80, Deputy Chair. 1967–96; Chair. Coordinating Cttee for Media Policy CDU/CSU 1975–83; mem. Bundestag 1976–2002; Minister of Posts and Telecommunications 1982–92; Deputy Chair. CDU/CSU Fed. Medium and Small Business Asscn 1977–97; Pres. Exec. Cttee European Medium and Small Business Union 1979–82; Chair. Inquiries Cttee Bundestag New Information and Communication Technologies 1981–82; Chair. Bundestag Subcttee on Human Rights and Humanitarian Aid 1995–98, Deputy Chair. 1998; Int. Mediator-Arbitrator for Fed. of Bosnia and Herzegovina 1996–98, also for Repub. Srpska 1997; Pres. Dr. Schwarz-Schilling and Pnr GmbH 1993–; Chair. Bd Prima Com AG, Mainz, 1999–, Mox Telecom AG Ratingen 1999–; High Rep. UN Mission in Bosnia and Herzegovina 2006–07; Grosses Bundesverdienstkreuz mit Stern; Hon. DUniv (Bryant Coll., USA) 1997. *Publication:* Unsere Geschichte Schicksal oder Zufall, Lansfristig Sichere Rente. *Leisure interests:* swimming, skiing, piano. *Address:* Dr. Schwarz-Schilling and Partner GmbH, Industriestrasse 35, 63654 Büdingen (office); Am Dohlberg 10, 63654 Büdingen, Germany (home). *Telephone:* (6042) 96440 (office). *Fax:* (6042) 964432 (office). *E-mail:* css@schwarz-schilling.de (office). *Website:* www.schwarz-schilling.de (office).

SCHWARZENBERG, Karel; Czech politician; *Minister of Foreign Affairs;* b. 10 Dec. 1937, Prague; s. of Karel Schwarzenberg and Antonia Schwarzenberg; m.; two s. one d.; ed Univ. of Vienna, Univ. of Graz, Univ. of Munich; family exiled to Austria after Communist takeover of Czech Repub. 1948; Pres. Int. Helsinki Cttee for Human Rights (concerned with human rights issues in fmr USSR, Bulgaria, Kosovo and Czech Repub.) 1984–91; est. Czechoslovak Documentation Centre (archive of prohibited literature) with Dr Vilém Prečan in Bavaria, Germany 1985; returned to Czech Repub. 1990; Chancellor, Office of Pres. 1990–92; Head of first OSCE del. to Nagorno Karabakh, Azerbaijan 1992; mem. Senate (Civic Democratic Alliance, ODA) 2004–, Chair. Foreign Affairs, Defence and Security Cttee 2005–07, Alt. mem. Perm. Del. of Parl. to Parl. Ass. of Council of Europe 2005; mem. Perm. Czech del. to Parl. Ass., NATO 2006–; mem. Caucus of Open Democracy 2006–07; Minister of Foreign Affairs 2007–; mem. Bd of Dirs Forum 2000, 2005–07; Order T.G.M. (Third Class) 2002; Prize for Human Rights, Council of Europe 1989. *Address:* Ministry of Foreign Affairs, Černínský Palác, Loretánské nám. 5, 118 00 Prague 1, Czech Republic (office). *Telephone:* (2) 24181111 (office). *Fax:* (2) 24182048 (office). *E-mail:* info@mzv.cz (office). *Website:* www.mzv.cz (office).

SCHWARZENEGGER, Arnold Alois, BA; American (b. Austrian) state official, actor, business executive and fmr bodybuilder; *Governor of California;* b. 30 July 1947, Graz, Austria; s. of Gustav Schwarzenegger and Aurelia Schwarzenegger; m. Maria Owings Shriver 1985; two s. two d.; ed Univ. of Wisconsin-Superior; went to USA 1968, naturalized 1983; Nat. Weight Training Coach Special Olympics, later Global Amb.; Bodybuilding Champion 1965–80; volunteer, prison rehabilitation programmes; Chair. Pres.'s Council on Physical Fitness and Sport 1990; Nat. Chair. Nat. Inner-City Games Foundation; elected Gov. of Calif. (after recall of Gov. Gray Davis) 2003–; Republican; Jr Mr Europe 1965, Best Built Man of Europe 1966, Mr Europe 1966, Mr International 1968, Mr Universe (amateur) 1969, Mr Olympia 1970–75, 1980, Nat. Theater Owners' Int. Star of the Decade, 1993, Simon Wiesenthal Center Nat. Leadership Award, ShoWest Humanitarian of the Year Award 1997, Boys and Girls Town Father Flanagan Service to Youth Award 2000, American Film Marketing Association (AFMA) World Wide Box Office Champ 2002, Muhammad Ali Humanitarian Award 2002, and numerous other prizes. *Film appearances include:* Stay Hungry 1976 (Golden Globe Award), Pumping Iron 1977, The Jayne Mansfield Story 1980, Conan the Barbarian 1982, Conan The Destroyer 1984, The Terminator 1984, Commando 1985, Raw Deal 1986, Predator 1987, Running Man 1987, Red Heat 1988, Twins 1989, Total Recall 1990, Kindergarten Cop 1990, Terminator II: Judgment Day 1991, Last Action Hero 1993, Dave (cameo) 1993, True Lies 1994, Junior 1994, Eraser 1996, Jingle All the Way 1996, Batman and Robin 1997, End of Days 1999, The Sixth Day 2000, Collateral Damage 2002, Terminator 3: Rise of the Machines 2003, Around the World in 80 Days 2004. *Publications:* Arnold: The Education of a Bodybuilder 1977, Arnold's Bodyshaping for Women 1979, Arnold's Bodybuilding for Men 1981, Arnold's Encyclopedia of Modern Bodybuilding 1985, Arnold's Fitness for Kids (co-author) 1993. *Address:* Office of the Governor, State Capitol Building, Sacramento, CA 95814, USA (office). *Telephone:* (916) 445-2841 (office). *Fax:* (916) 558-3160 (office). *Website:* gov.ca.gov (office).

SCHWARZKOPF, Gen. H. Norman, BS; American army officer (retd); b. 22 Aug. 1934, Trenton, NJ; s. of H. Norman Schwarzkopf and Ruth Bowman; m. Brenda Holsinger 1968; one s. two d.; ed US Mil. Acad. and Univ. of Southern Calif.; 2nd Lt US Army 1956; Deputy Commdr 172nd Infantry Brigade, Fort Richardson, Alaska 1974–76; Commdr 1st Brigade, 9th Infantry Div. Fort Lewis, Wash. 1976–78; Deputy Dir Plans, US Pacific Command, Camp Smith, Hawaii 1978–80; Asst Div. Commdr 8th Infantry Div. (mechanized), US Army Europe, FRG 1980–82; Dir Mil. Personnel Man. Office of Deputy Chief of Staff for Personnel, Washington, DC 1982–83; Commdg Gen. 24th Infantry Div. (mechanized), Fort Stewart, Ga 1983–85; Deputy Commdr US Forces in Grenada Operation 1983; Asst Deputy Chief of Staff Operations, HQ, Dept of Army, Washington, DC 1985–86; Commdg Gen. I Corps, Fort Lewis, Wash. 1986–87; Deputy Chief of Staff for Operations and Plans, HQ, Dept of Army, Washington, DC 1987–88; C-in-C US Cen. Command, MacDill Air Force Base, Fla 1988–91; Commdr Allied Forces in War to liberate Kuwait after invasion and annexation by Iraq (Operation Desert Storm) 1990–91, retd 1992; contrib. and analyst NBC News 1995–; Chair. Starbright Foundation 1995–; Spokesman North American Be Bear Aware and Wildlife Stewardship Campaign, Center for Wildlife Information; Hon. KCB (UK) 1991, Hon. Pvt. French Foreign Legion 1991; DSM, DFC, Silver Star with two oak leaf clusters, Legion of Merit, Bronze Star with three oak leaf clusters, Purple Heart with oak leaf cluster; Grand Officier, Légion d'honneur 1991, Distinguished Order of Kuwait 1991; Distinguished German-American of the Year 2006. *Publication:* It Doesn't Take A Hero (autobiog.) (with Peter Petre) 1992. *Leisure interests:* hunting, fishing, skeet and trap-shooting. *Address:* 400 North Ashley Drive, Suite 3050, Tampa, FL 33602; c/o International Creative Management, 40 West 57th Street, New York, NY 10019, USA.

SCHWARZMAN, Stephen A., BA, MBA; American investment banker; *Chairman and CEO, The Blackstone Group;* b. 14 Feb. 1947, Philadelphia; m. Christine Hearst; three c. from previous marriages; ed Yale Univ., Harvard Business School; began career in Mergers and Acquisitions (M&A) at Lehman Brothers 1977–84, at age 31, elected Man. Dir 1978–84, Chair. M&A Cttee 1981–84; co-founder, Chair. CEO The Blackstone Group 1985–; Chair. Bd The John F. Kennedy Center for the Performing Arts, Washington, DC 2004–; mem. Council on Foreign Relations; mem. Bd NY City Ballet, NY Public Library, Film Soc. of Lincoln Center, Harvard Business School Visiting Cttee, JP Morgan Chase Nat. Advisory Bd, NY City Partnership Bd of Dirs; Trustee Frick Collection. *Address:* The Blackstone Group, 345 Park Avenue, New York, NY 10154, USA (office). *Telephone:* (212) 583-5000 (office). *Fax:* (212) 583-5712 (office). *Website:* www.blackstone.com (office).

SCHWEBEL, Stephen Myron, BA, LLB; American judge, lawyer, arbitrator and mediator; *President of the Administrative Tribunal, International Monetary Fund;* b. 10 March 1929, New York City; s. of Victor Schwebel and Pauline Pfeffer Schwebel; m. Louise I. N. Killander 1972; two d.; ed Harvard Coll., Univ. of Cambridge, UK, Yale Law School; attorney 1954–59; Asst Prof. of Law, Harvard Univ. 1959–61; Asst Legal Adviser, then Special Asst to Asst Sec. of State for Int. Org. Affairs 1961–67; Exec. Vice-Pres. and Exec. Dir American Soc. of Int. Law 1967–73; Consultant, then Counsellor on Int. Law, Dept of State 1967–74, Deputy Legal Adviser 1974–81; Prof. of Int. Law, then Edward B. Burling Prof. of Int. Law and Org., Johns Hopkins Univ., Washington, DC 1967–81; Legal Adviser to US Del. and Alt. Rep. in 6th Cttee, UN Gen. Ass. 1961–65; Visiting Lecturer or Prof., Univ. of Cambridge 1957, 1983, ANU 1969, Hague Acad. of Int. Law 1972, Inst. Univ. de hautes études int., Geneva 1980 and various American univs 1987–; rep. in various cttees UN 1962–74; Assoc. Rep., Rep., Counsel or Deputy Agent in cases before Int. Court of Justice 1962–80; Judge, Int. Court of Justice 1981–2000, Vice-Pres. 1994–97, Pres. 1997–2000; mem. Int. Law Comm. 1977–81, Perm. Court of Arbitration, The Hague 2006–; arbitrator or chair. in int. commercial arbitrations 1982–; mem. Tribunal in Eritrea-Yemen Arbitration 1997–99, Ethiopia-Eritrea Boundary Comm. 2000–; Pres. Barbados-Trinidad and Tobago Arbitration Tribunal 2004–; Pres. Admin. Tribunal, IMF 1994–, Southern Blue Fin Tuna Arbitration 2000; mem. Panels of Arbitrators and of Conciliators of the Int. Centre for the Settlement of Investment Disputes (ICSID) of the World Bank 2000–; mem. Bd of Eds, American Journal of Int. Law 1967–81, 1994–; mem. Council on Foreign Relations, Inst. of Int. Law; mem. Bars of State of New York, Dist of Columbia, Supreme Court of the USA; Hon. Bencher, Gray's Inn 1998–, Hon. Fellow, Lauterpacht Centre for Int. Law, Univ. of Cambridge; Hon. Fellow, Trinity Coll. Cambridge 2005; Hon. LL (Bhopal Univ.) 1983, (Hofstra Univ.) 1997, (Univ. of Miami) 2002; Gherini Prize, Yale Law School 1954, Medal of Merit, Yale Law School 1997, Manley O. Hudson Medal, American Soc. of Int. Law 2000. *Publications:* The Secretary-General of the United Nations 1952, The Effectiveness of International Decisions (ed.) 1971, International Arbitration: Three Salient Problems 1987, Justice in International Law 1994; author of some 175 articles in legal periodicals and the press on problems of international law and relations. *Leisure interests:* music, cycling. *Address:* 1501 K Street, NW, Washington, DC 20005 (office); 1917 23rd Street, NW, Washington, DC 20008, USA (home). *Telephone:* (202) 736-8328 (office); (202) 232-3114 (home). *Fax:* (202) 736-8709 (office); (202) 797-9286 (home). *E-mail:* judgeschwebel@aol.com (office).

SCHWEIGER, Til; German actor, producer and director; b. 19 Dec. 1963, Freiburg, Germany; m. Dana Schweiger; four c.; ed acting acad., Cologne; Best Actor Award, Moscow Film Festival 1997. *Films include:* Manta Manta 1991,

Ebbie's Bluff (Max Ophuls Prize for Best Actor) 1992, Der Bewegte Mann 1994, Maennerpension, Das Superweib, Brute 1996, Knocking on Heaven's Door 1996 (also producer and co-writer), Replacement Killers, Judas Kiss 1997, Der Eisbär (also producer), Der grosse Bagarozy 1998, Magicians 1999, Investigating Sex, Driven 2000, Was tun wenn's brennt 2000, Jetzt oder Nie (producer) 2000, Auf Herz und Nieren (producer) 2000, Joe and Max 2001, Tomb Raider 2 2002, King Arthur 2003, A Surprise Period 2003, The Daltons vs. Lucky Luke 2004, Barfuss 2005, Deuce Bigalow: European Gigolo 2005, Bye Bye Harry! 2006, Wo ist Fred? 2006), Video Kings 2007, Body Armour 2007, Keinohrhasen 2007, Already Dead 2007, The Red Baron 2008. *Address:* c/o Players Agentur Management GmbH, Sophienstr. 21, 10178 Berlin, Germany. *Telephone:* (30) 2851680 (office). *Fax:* (30) 2851686 (office). *E-mail:* mai@players.de (office). *Website:* www.players.de.

SCHWEIKER, Mark, BSc, MAdmin; American fmr politician; *President and CEO, Greater Philadelphia Chamber of Commerce;* b. 31 Jan. 1953, Bucks Co., Pa; s. of John Schweiker and Mary Schweiker; m. Katherine Schweiker; two s. one d.; ed Bloomsberg Univ., Rider Univ.; began career with Merrill Lynch, moving on to McGraw-Hill; first elected to public office as Middletown Township Supervisor 1979; Bucks Co. Commr 1987–94; Lt-Gov. of Pa 1994–2001, Gov. 2001–2003; Pres. and CEO Greater Phila Chamber of Commerce 2003–; numerous awards including Bloomsburg Univ. Alumnus of the Year 1990, Pa Nature Conservancy Award for Outstanding Service to Conservation 1993, Tech. Council of Pa Advocate of the Year 1996, Pa Econ. League Commitment to Excellence in Local Govt Award 1998, Pa League of Cities Outstanding Public Service Award 1999. *Address:* Greater Philadelphia Chamber of Commerce, 200 South Broad Street, Suite 700, Philadelphia, PA 19102, USA (office). *Telephone:* (215) 545-1234 (office). *Fax:* (215) 790-3600 (office). *Website:* www.philachamber.com (office).

SCHWEIKER, Richard Schultz, BA; American business executive and fmr politician; b. 1 June 1926, Norristown, Pa; s. of Malcolm A. Schweiker and Blanche Schultz; m. Claire Joan Coleman 1955; two s. three d.; ed Pennsylvania State Univ.; business exec. 1950–60; mem. US House of Reps. 1960–68; US Senator from Pa 1969–80; Sec. of Health and Human Services 1981–83; Pres. American Council of Life Insurance 1983–94; Chair. Partnership for Prevention 1991–97; mem. Bd of Dirs Tenet Healthcare Corpn 1984, LabOne Inc. 1994–2002; Republican; ten hon. degrees and numerous awards. *Address:* 904 Lynton Place, McLean, VA 22102-2113, USA (office).

SCHWEIKERT, Emile A., PhD; American chemist and academic; *Head, Department of Chemistry and Director, Center for Chemical Characterization, Texas A&M University;* ed Univ. of Paris; currently Head, Dept of Chem. and Dir, Center for Chemical Characterization, Tex. A&M Univ.; mem. Program Advisory Cttee, Nat. Inst. of Standards and Tech. (NIST) Center for Neutron Research (NCNR), Gaithersburg, Md 1997–98; George Hevesy Medal 1986. *Address:* Department of Chemistry, Texas A&M University, College Station, TX 77842, USA (office). *Telephone:* (979) 845-2341 (office). *Fax:* (979) 845-1655 (office). *E-mail:* schweikert@mail.chem.tamu.edu (office). *Website:* www.chem .tamu.edu/faculty/schweikert (office); www.chem.tamu.edu/rgroup/ schweikert (office).

SCHWEITZER, Brian, MS; American politician; *Governor of Montana;* b. 5 Sept. 1955, Havre, Mont.; s. of Adam Schweitzer and Kay Schweiter; m. Nancy Hupp 1981; two s. one d.; ed Colorado and Montana State Univs; began career in irrigation devt working in Africa, Asia, Europe and South America 1981–86; returned to Mont. to raise family and build ranching and irrigation business 1986; apptd by US Sec. of Agric. to serve on Mont. State US Dept of Agric. Farm Service Agency Cttee 1993–99; apptd to Mont. Rural Devt Partnership Bd 1996, Nat. Drought Task Force 1999; cand. US Senate elections 2000; Gov. of Mont. 2005–; Democrat; Sec. of Agric. Award for outreach efforts to Native Americans 1995. *Address:* Office of the Governor, PO Box 200801 State Capitol, Helena, MT 59620-0801, USA (office). *Telephone:* (406) 444-3111 (office). *Fax:* (406) 444-5529 (office). *E-mail:* governor@mt.gov (office). *Website:* governor.mt.gov (office).

SCHWEITZER, Louis, LenD; French business executive; *Chairman, Renault SA;* b. 8 July 1942, Geneva, Switzerland; s. of Pierre-Paul Schweitzer and Catherine Hatt; m. Agnes Schmitz 1972; two d.; ed Inst. d'Etudes Politiques, Paris, Faculté de Droit, Paris and Ecole Nat. d'Admin; Insp. of Finance 1970–; special assignment, later Deputy Dir, Ministry of the Budget 1974–81; Dir du Cabinet to Minister of Budget 1981–83, of Industry and Research 1983, to Prime Minister 1984–86; Prof. Inst. d'Etudes Politiques de Paris 1982–86; Vice-Pres. for Finance and Planning Régie Renault SA 1986–90, Chief Finance Officer 1988–90, Exec. Vice-Pres. 1989–90, Pres. and COO 1990, Chair. and CEO 1992–2005, Chair. 2005–; Chair. (non-xec.) AstraZeneca PLC 2005–; Haute autorité de lutte contre les discriminations et pour l'égalité (HALDE) 2005–; Admin., Société Générale 1989–93, UAP 1988–94, Inst. Pasteur 1988–94, Péchiney 1989–92, IFRI 1989–, Réunion des Musées Nat. 1990–96, Renault Véhicules Industriels 1992–2001, BNP 1993–, Roussel UCLAF 1994–97, Crédit Nat. (now Natexis) 1995–99, Philips 1997–, Volvo AB 2001–; Chair. Ecole des mines de Nancy 1999–, Groupe Le Monde 2008–; Pres. Festival d'Avignon 2005–; Officier, Légion d'honneur, Commdr, Légion d'honneur 2005, Officier, Ordre nat. du Mérite. *Address:* Renault SA, 34 quai du Point du Jour, 92109 Boulogne-Billancourt Cedex (office); 1 rue Dauphine, 75006 Paris, France (home). *Telephone:* 1-41-04-56-94 (office). *Fax:* 1-41-04-62-30 (office). *E-mail:* louis.schweitzer@renault.com (office). *Website:* www.renault.com (office).

SCHWERY, HE Cardinal Henri; Swiss ecclesiastic; *Bishop Emeritus of Sion;* b. 14 June 1932, St Léonard, Valais; s. of the late Camille Schwery and Marguerite Terroux; ed Lycée-Coll. de Sion, Valais, Faculty of Sciences, Univ. de Fribourg, Grand Séminaire de Sion and Pontificia Università Gregoriana,

Rome; ordained priest 1957; teacher of science, math. and religious studies, Lycée-Coll. de Sion 1961–; Rector 1972–77; Dir Pensionnat de la Sitterie (Petit Séminaire) de Sion 1968–72; Diocesan Chaplain, Action Catholique de Jeunesse Etudiante 1958–66; Mil. Chaplain 1958–77; Bishop of Sion 1977–95, Bishop Emer. 1995–; cr. Cardinal 1991; Cardinal-Priest of Ss. Protomartiri a Via Aurelia Antica 1991–; Kt of the Grand Cross, Order of the Holy Sepulchre of Jerusalem. *Publications:* Un Synode extraordinaire 1986, Chemin de Croix, chemin de lumière, L'Année Mariale dans le diocèse de Sion 1987, Sentiers Pastoraux 1988, Sentiers épiscopaux – Regards sur nos familles (two vols) 1992, Magnificat (in collaboration) 1992, Chrétien au quotidien 1996. *Leisure interest:* spirituality. *Address:* c/o Diocèse de Sion, Case postale 2124, rue de la Tour, 1950 Sion 2, Switzerland. *Telephone:* (27) 329-18-18. *Fax:* (27) 329-18-36. *Website:* www.cath-vs.ch.

SCHWIMMER, David, BS; American actor, writer and director; b. 12 Nov. 1966, New York; s. of Arthur Schwimmer and Arlene Schwimmer; ed Beverly Hills High School and Northwestern Univ., Chicago; co-founder Lookingglass Theater Co., Chicago 1988; mem. Bd Dirs Rape Foundation for Rape Treatment Center of Santa Monica. *Theatre includes:* West, The Odyssey, Of One Blood, In the Eye of the Beholder all with Lookingglass Theater Co.), The Master and Margarita (all with Lookingglass Theater Co.), Some Girl(s) (Gielgud Theatre, London) 2005, The Caine Mutiny Court-Martial (Broadway) 2006. *Theatre directed includes:* The Jungle (six Joseph Jefferson Awards), The Serpent, Alice in Wonderland (Edin. Festival, Scotland). *Films include:* Flight of the Intruder 1990, Crossing the Bridge 1992, Twenty Bucks 1993, The Waiter 1993, Wolf 1994, The Pallbearer 1996, Shooting the Moon (exec. producer) 1996, Apt Pupil 1998, Kissing a Fool (exec. producer) 1998, Six Days Seven Nights 1998, The Thin Pink Line 1998, All the Rage 1999, Picking Up the Pieces 2000, Hotel 2001, Dogwater (also Dir), Duane Hopwood 2005, Big Nothing 2006, Run, Fat Boy, Run (dir) 2007. *Television includes:* The Wonder Years 1988, Monty 1993, NYPD Blue 1993, Friends 1994–2004, L.A. Law, The Single Guy (NBC), Happy Birthday Elizabeth: A Celebration of Life 1997, Breast Men 1997, Since You've Been Gone (dir) 1998, Band of Brothers (mini series) 2001, Uprising 2001, Curb Your Enthusiasm (series) 2004; hosted Montreal's 13th Annual Just for Laughs Festival. *Leisure interests:* writing, playing softball and basketball. *Address:* c/o The Gersh Agency, PO Box 5617, Beverly Hills, CA 90210 (office); Lookingglass Theatre Company, 2936 North Southport Avenue, Chicago, IL 60657, USA. *Website:* www.lookingglasstheatre.org.

SCHWIMMER, Walter, LLD; Austrian politician, international organization official and lawyer; *Chairman, International Coordination Committee, World Public Forum – Dialogue of Civilizations;* b. 16 June 1942, Vienna; s. of Walter Schwimmer and Johanna Schwimmer; m. Martina Pucher-Schwimmer; two s.; ed Univ. of Vienna; mem. Nationalrat (Austrian Parl.) 1971–99, Chair. Parl. Cttee on Health 1989–94, on Justice 1995–96; Vice-Chair. Parl. Group, Austrian People's Party (ÖVP) 1986–94; mem. Council of Europe Parl. Ass. 1991–, Vice-Pres. Council of Europe 1996, Jan.–Sept. 1999, Sec.-Gen. 1999–2004; Chair. European People's Party Group–Christian Democrats 1996–99; Dir and Exec. Vice-Pres. Vienna Health Insurance Fund 1979–99; Chair. Int. Coordination, World Public Forum – Dialogue of Civilizations 2005–; mem. Bd Crans Montana Forum 2004–; consultant on int. relations and European affairs 2004–; Hon. Sec.-Gen. Maison de la Méditerranée 2004–; Grosses Goldenes Ehrenzeichen am Bande (Austria) 2004; Grosses Silbernes Ehrenzeichen mit dem Stern (Austria), Grosses Silbernes Ehrenzeichen der Stadt Wien, Grand Cross, Order of the Star of Romania 2001, Commdr's Cross, Order of Grand Duke Gaudemes (Lithuania), Chevalier, Légion d'honneur 2003, Grand Cross of the Equestrian Order of St Agatha (San Marino) 2003, Order of the Aztec Eagle (Mexico), Grande Ufficiale dell'Ordine al Merito (Italy) 2004; Leopold-Kunschak Award 1975, Peter the Great Int. Prize of the Russian Fed., European Pro Humanitate European Foundation for Culture Prize, Germany, Medal of the European Inst. of Moscow, Person of the Year Award (Ukraine) 2002. *Publications:* Christian Trade Unions in Austria 1975, Social Consequences of Inflation 1988, A Union Goes Down in History 1993, Der Traum Europa 2003, The European Dream 2004. *Leisure interests:* books, history, stamps, art. *Address:* World Public Forum – Dialogue of Civilizations, Vienna Headquarters, Stubenring 4, 1010 Vienna, Austria (office); Crans Montana Forum, 41 Avenue Hector Otto, 98000 Monaco (office); Consultancy Office, Dresden 2B, 3400 Klosterneuburg, Austria (office). *Telephone:* (1) 513-01-38-2 (office); 97707000 (office); 224387694 (office). *Fax:* (1) 513-01-38-4 (office); 97707040 (office); 224387649 (office). *E-mail:* schwimmer@wpfdc.at (office); schwimmer.cmf@aon.at (office); schwimmer.consult@aon.at (office). *Website:* www.wpfdc.org (office); www.cmf .ch (office).

SCHWYZER, Robert, DPhil; Swiss molecular biologist and academic (retd); b. 8 Dec. 1920, Zürich; s. of Robert Schwyzer and Rose Schätzle; m. Rose Nägeli 1948; two s. one d.; ed primary school, Nathan Hale, Minneapolis, USA, Canton High School (A), Zürich and Dept of Chem., Univ. of Zürich; Privatdozent, Univ. of Zürich 1951–59, Asst Prof. 1960–63; initiation of Polypeptide Research, Head of Polypeptide Research Group, Ciba Ltd, Basel 1952–63, Asst Man. 1960–63; apptd Prof. and Head of Dept of Molecular Biology, Swiss Fed. Inst. of Tech., Zürich 1963; apptd Prof.-in-Residence, Clinical Research Inst. of Montreal 1991; Werner Award, Swiss Chemical Soc. 1957, Ruzicka Prize, Swiss Fed. Inst. of Tech. 1959, Otto Nägeli Award, Switzerland 1964, Vernon Stouffer Award, American Heart Asscn, Cleveland 1968, Ernesto Scoffone Award 1982, Alan E. Pierce Award, American Peptide Symposia 1985, Rudinger Gold Medal, European Peptide Symposia 1988. *Publications:* scientific papers on syntheses of biologically active polypeptides; structure activity relationships; relationships between structure and biophysical interactions with lipid-bilayer membranes; molecular mechanisms of opioid receptor selection by peptides, new principles governing receptor specificity. *Leisure interests:* mountain climbing, skiing, literature. *Address:* Institut für Molekularbiologie und Biophysik, Eidgenössische Technische Hochschule, Hartriegelstrasse 12, 8180 Bülach, Switzerland (office). *Telephone:* (44) 8607111 (home).

SCHYGULLA, Hanna; German actress; b. 1943, Bundesverdienstkreuz Erster Klasse. *Stage appearances include:* Mother Courage 1979. *Films include:* Die Ehe der Maria Braun (Silberner Bär Berlinale) 1979, Die Dritte Generation 1979, Lili Marleen 1980, Die Fälschung 1981, La Nuit de Varennes 1982, Eine Liebe in Deutschland 1983, The Story of Piera 1983, Miss Arizona 1987, The Summer of Mr. Forbes, Dead Again 1991, Beware of a Holy Whore 1993, The Merchant of Four Seasons 1998, Werckmeister Harmonies 2001, Die Blauwe Grenze 2005, Vendredi ou un autre jour 2005, Winterreise 2006, Auf der anderen Seite 2007. *Television appearances include:* 8 Stunden sind kein Tag (series) 1972, Absolitude 2001. *Leisure interests:* travel, painting.

SCINDIA, Vasundhara Raje, BA; Indian politician; b. 8 March 1953, Bombay (now Mumbai); d. of the late Jivaji Rao Scindia and of Rajmata Vijya Raje Scindia; m. Raja Hemant Singh 1972; one s.; ed Presentation Convent, Kodaikanal, Sophia Coll., Mumbai Univ.; MLA for Dholpur 1984–89; Vice-Pres. Bharatiya Janata Party (BJP) Yuva Morcha 1984–89; Vice-Pres. Rajasthan State BJP 1985–89, Pres. 2002–; mem. Lok Sabha 1989–; Jt Sec. BJP Parl. Cttee 1997; Union Minister for Foreign Affairs 1998–99; Minister for Small Scale Industries and Agric. and Rural Industries (Ind. charge) 1999–2003; State Minister for Personnel and Training, Pensions and Welfare, Personnel, Public Grievance and Pension Ministry, Atomic Energy and Space Dept 1999–2003; Chief Minister of Rajasthan 2003–08; numerous visits abroad for various social causes; UN Women Together Award 2007. *Leisure interests:* reading, music, horse riding, gardening. *Address:* Bharatiya Janata Party, 11 Ashok Road, New Delhi (office); Pratap Chowk, Jhalawar 326 001, India. *Telephone:* (11) 23382234. *Fax:* (11) 23782163 (office). *E-mail:* bjpco@vsnl.com (office); me@vasundhara-raje.com (home). *Website:* www.bjp.org (office); www.vasundhara-raje.com (home).

SCLATER, John G., PhD, FRS; British geophysicist and academic; *Professor, Geosciences Research Division, Scripps Institution of Oceanography, University of California, San Diego;* b. 17 June 1940, Edinburgh, Scotland; s. of John G. Sclater and Margaret Bennett Glen; m. 1st Fredrica R. Sclater 1968 (divorced 1985), two s.; m. 2nd Paula Ann Edwards 1985 (divorced 1991); m. 3rd Naila G. Burchett 1992; ed Stonyhurst Coll., Univs of Edinburgh and Cambridge; Postdoctoral Research Geophysicist, Scripps Inst. of Oceanography 1965–67, Asst Research Geophysicist 1967–72; Assoc. Prof., MIT 1972–77, Prof. 1977–83; MIT Dir, Jt Program in Oceanography with the Woods Hole Oceanographic Inst. 1981–83; Assoc. Dir Inst. for Geophysics, Univ. of Texas at Austin, Prof., Dept of Geological Sciences and Shell Distinguished Chair. in Geophysics 1983–91; Prof. of Marine Geophysics, Scripps Inst. of Oceanography, Univ. of Calif., San Diego 1991–; Fellow, Geological Soc. of America; mem. NAS Geophysical Union; Swiney Lecturer, Edin. Univ. 1976; Shell Distinguished Prof. 1984–89; Guggenheim Fellow 1998–99; Rosenstiel Award 1978; Bucher Medal, American Geophysical Union 1985. *Leisure interests:* running, swimming, golf. *Address:* Scripps Institution of Oceanography, Geosciences Research Division, University of California, San Diego, 9500 Gilman Drive, La Jolla, CA 92093-0220, USA (office). *Telephone:* (619) 534-3051. *E-mail:* jsclater@ucsd.edu (office). *Website:* grd.ucsd.edu (office).

SCLATER, John Richard, CVO, MA, MBA; British business executive and farmer; *Chairman, Graphite Enterprise Trust PLC;* b. 14 July 1940, Camborne; s. of Arthur William Sclater and Alice Sclater (née Collett); m. 1st Nicola Mary Gloria Cropper 1967 (divorced); one s. one d. (deceased); m. 2nd Grizel Elizabeth Catherine Dawson MBE 1985; ed Charterhouse, Gonville and Caius Coll., Cambridge and Yale and Harvard Univs, USA; Commonwealth Fellow 1962–64; Glyn, Mills & Co. 1964–70; Dir Williams, Glyn & Co. 1970–76; Man. Dir Nordic Bank 1976–85, Chair. 1985–87; Dir and Deputy Chair. Guinness Peat Group PLC 1985–87, Jt Deputy Chair. 1987; Dir and Deputy Chair. Guinness Mahon & Co. Ltd 1987, Chair. 1987; Dir Foreign & Colonial Investment Trust PLC 1981–2002, Chair. 1983–2002; Chair. Foreign & Colonial (now Graphite) Enterprise Trust PLC 1986–, Foreign & Colonial Ventures Ltd 1990–98, Berisford PLC 1990–2000 (Dir 1986–2000), Hill Samuel Bank Ltd 1992–96, (Dir 1990–96, Vice-Chair. 1990–92), Foreign & Colonial (now Graphite) Pvt. Equity Trust PLC 1994–2002, Finsbury Life Sciences Investment Trust PLC (renamed Finsbury Emerging Biotechnology Trust PLC 2005, then The Biotech Growth Trust PLC 2007) 1997–, Argent Group Europe Ltd 1998–; Pres. Equitable Life Assurance Soc. 1994–2001 (Dir 1985–2001); Deputy Chair. Yamaichi Int. (Europe) Ltd 1985–97, Union (fmrly Union Discount Co. of London) PLC 1986–96 (Dir 1981–96, Chair. 1996), Grosvenor Group Ltd (fmrly Grosvenor Group Holdings Ltd) 2000–05 (Dir 1999), Grosvenor Estate Holdings 1989–2002; Dir Berner Nicol & Co. Ltd 1968 (Chair. 2002–04, 2005–), James Cropper PLC 1972–2008, Holker Estates Co. Ltd 1974–, Angerstein Underwriting Trust PLC 1985–96, Foreign & Colonial Group (Holdings) Ltd 1989–2001, Fuel Tech (Europe) 1990–98, Millennium & Copthorne Hotels PLC 1996–2007, Wates Group Ltd 1999–2004; Chair. Asscn of Consortium Banks 1980–82; Consultant RP&C Int. 1997–2003; First Church Estates Commr 1999–2001 (mem. Archbishops' Council and Gen. Synod, Church of England 1999–2001); Dir and Gov. Brambletye School 1976–2006; mem. City Taxation Cttee 1973–76, London Bd of Halifax Building Soc. 1983–90, Council of Duchy of Lancaster 1987–2000, CBI City Advisory Group 1988–99; Gov. Int. Students House 1976–99; Trustee The Grosvenor Estate 1973–2005, The Coll. of Arms 1994–; Freeman City of London 1993–; Liveryman Goldsmiths' Co. 1993–. *Leisure interest:* country pursuits. *Address:* Sutton Hall, Barcombe, nr Lewes, E Sussex, BN8 5EB, England. *Telephone:* (1273) 400450. *Fax:* (1273) 401086. *E-mail:* john.sclater@talk21.com.

SCOFIDIO, Ricardo; American artist, architect and academic; *Professor Emeritus of Architecture, Cooper Union for the Advancement of Science and Art;* co-f. (with Elizabeth Diller q.v.), Diller & Scofidio (now Diller Scofidio + Renfro), New York 1979, cr. installations and electronic media projects; Prof. of Architecture, The Cooper Union 1965, now Prof. Emer.; Jt recipient (with Elizabeth Diller) fellowships from Graham Foundation for Advanced Study in the Fine Arts 1986, New York Foundation for the Arts 1986, 1987, 1989, Chicago Inst. for Architecture and Urbanism 1989, Tiffany Foundation Award for Emerging Artists 1990, Progressive Architecture Award (for Slow House) 1991, Chrysler Award for Achievement and Design 1997. *Publications:* (with Elizabeth Diller) Flesh 1995, Back to the Front: Tourisms of War. *Address:* Diller Scofidio + Renfro, 601 West 26th Street, Suite 1815, New York, NY 10001, USA (office). *Telephone:* (212) 260-7971 (office). *E-mail:* disco@dsrny.com (office). *Website:* www.dillerscofidio.com (office).

SCOGNAMIGLIO PASINI, Carlo Luigi, DEcon; Italian politician, economist and business consultant; *President, Aspen Institute Italia;* b. 27 Nov. 1944, Varese; s. of Luigi Scognamiglio and Esther Scognamiglio (née Pasini); m. Cecilia Pirelli; one s. one d.; ed L. Bocconi Univ., Milan, London School of Econs; Asst Lecturer, L. Bocconi Univ., Asst Prof. of Industrial Econs 1968–73, Prof. 1973; Asst Prof. of Finance, Univ. of Padua 1973–79; Prof. of Econs and Industrial Policy, Libera Università Int. degli Studi Sociali, Rome 1979–, Dean and Rector 1984–92; Liberal Party cand. in Milan constituency, elected to Senate 1992, Chair. European Affairs Cttee, mem. Budget Cttee, re-elected to Senate 1994; Pres. of Senate 1994–; Acting Pres. of Italy 1994–96; Pres. Rizzoli-Corriere della Sera 1983–84, Vice-Pres. 1984–; Minister of Defence 1998–99; Co-Founder, Bocconi School of Business Admin 1979; Pres. Aspen Inst. Italia 1995–; Acad. of France Award for Econs 1988. *Publications include:* The Stock Exchange 1973, Industrial Crises 1976, The White Book on PPSS 1981, The White Book on the Italian Financial Market 1982, Theory and Policy of Finance 1987, Industrial Economics 1987, Report to Minister of Treasury of Commission for Privatization of Industry 1990, The Liberal Project 1996. *Leisure interests:* economics, history. *Address:* Aspen Institute Italia, Piazza SS Apostoli 49, 00186 Rome, Italy (office). *Telephone:* (06) 67062835 (office). *Fax:* (06) 67063988 (office). *E-mail:* info@aspeninstitute.it (office); c.scognamigliopasini@senato.it (office). *Website:* www.aspeninstitute.it (office).

SCOLA, HE Cardinal Angelo, PhD, DTheol; Italian ecclesiastic; *Patriarch of Venice;* b. 7 Nov. 1941, Malgrate; s. of Carlo Scola and Regina Colombo; ed Catholic Univ. of Sacred Heart, Milan, Seminary of Saronno, Milan, Seminary of Venegono, Milan, Univ. of Fribourg, Switzerland; ordained priest 1970; successively, until 1991, active collaborator of Comunione e Liberazione, Dir Inst. of Studies for Transition, Milan, collaborator in establishment and mem. Exec. Cttee Italian edn of Rivista Internazionale Communio, pastoral work in Italy and abroad; Research Asst to Chair of Political Philosophy 1979, later Asst to Chair of Fundamental Moral Theology, Univ. of Fribourg; Prof. of Theological Anthropology, Pontifical John Paul II Inst. for Studies on Marriage and Family, Pontifical Lateran Univ., Rome 1982, later Prof. of Contemporary Christology, Faculty of Theology, Rector Magnifico Pontifical Lateran Univ. and Pres. Pontifical John Paul II Inst. for Studies on Marriage and the Family 1995; attended Seventh Ordinary Ass. of World Synod of Bishops as an asst to Special Sec., Vatican City 1987; Bishop of Grosseto 1991–95 (resgnd); Patriarch of Venice 2002–; cr. Cardinal (Cardinal Priest of SS XII Apostoli) 2003; Relator Gen. 11th Gen. Ordinary Ass. of World Synod of Bishops 2005. *Address:* Patriarchat of Venice, S. Marco 320/a, 30124 Venice, Italy (office). *Telephone:* (041) 2702470 (office). *Fax:* (041) 2776493 (office). *Website:* www.venezia.chiesacattolica.it (office).

SCOLA, Ettore; Italian film director and screenwriter; b. 10 May 1931, Trevico (Avellino); m. Gigliola Fantoni 1956; two d.; ed Univ. of Rome; studied law, then worked in journalism and radio; started scriptwriting 1952–. *Films:* Se permettete parliamo di donne 1964, La Congiuntura 1965, Thrilling 1965, L'arcidiavolo 1966, Riusciranno i nostri eroi a ritrovare l'amico misteriosamente scomparso in Africa? 1968, Il commissario Pepe 1969, Dramma della gelosia (tutti i particolari in cronaca) (Jealousy, Italian Style) 1970, Permette? Rocco Papaleo 1971, La più bella serata della mia vita 1972, Trevico—Torino… viaggio nel Fiat-nam 1973, C'eravamo tanto amati 1974, Brutti, sporchi e cattivi 1976 (Best Dir, Cannes Film Festival), Signore e signori buonanotte 1976, Una giornata particolare (A Special Day) 1977 (Special Jury Prizes, Cannes Film Festival), I nuovi mostri 1977, La terrazza 1979, Passione d'amore 1980, Il mondo nuovo 1982, Le bal 1983, Maccheroni 1985, La Famiglia (The Family) 1987, Splendor 1988, Che Orà È? 1989, Il Viaggio di Capitan Fracassa 1990, Mario, Maria e Mario 1992, Romanzo di un giovane povero 1995, I Corti italiani (segment) 1997, La Cena 1998, Concorrenza sleale 2001, Un Altro mondo è possibile (Another World Is Possible) 2001, Lettere dalla Palestina (Letters from Palestine) 2002, Gente di Roma 2003.

SCOLARI, Luiz Felipe; Brazilian professional football manager; b. 9 Nov. 1948, Passo Fundo, Rio Grande do Sul; Man. Club Gremio 1993–96 (three league titles, Brazilian Cup, Libertadores Cup); Man. Palmeiras 1997–2000 (Libertadores Cup); Man. Cruzeiro 2000–01; Man. Brazilian Nat. Team 2001–02, led Brazil to a record fifth world championship in June 2002; resgnd July 2002; Man. Portuguese nat. team Nov. 2002–08; Man. Chelsea FC 2008–09. *Address:* c/o Chelsea FC, Stamford Bridge, Fulham Road, London, SW6 1HS, England.

SCOLES, Giacinto, MSc, FRS; Italian physicist and academic; *Donner Professor of Science, Princeton University;* b. Turin; ed Univ. of Genoa, Univ. of Leiden, Netherlands; began academic career in Physics Dept, Univ. of

Genoa –1961; mem. staff, Univ. of Leiden 1961–64; Prof. of Chem. and Physics, Univ. of Waterloo, Canada –1986, Acting Dir Guelph-Waterloo Centre for Grad. Work in Chem. 1974–75, Dir Centre for Molecular Beams and Laser Chem. 1982–85; Prof. of Solid State Physics, Univ. of Trento 1975–82; Donner Prof. of Science, Princeton Univ. Chem. Dept and Princeton Materials Inst. 1987–; Prof., Depts of Biophysics and Condensed Matter Physics, Int. School for Advanced Studies, Trieste, Italy; long-term collaborator at Elettra Synchrotron Lab., Trieste; Foreign mem. Netherlands Royal Acad. of Arts and Sciences; Lippincott Award, Optical Soc. of America, Coblentz Soc., Soc. for Applied Spectroscopy, E. K. Plyler Prize for Molecular Spectroscopy, Benjamin Franklin Medal in Physics (co-recipient) 2006. *Publications:* numerous scientific papers in professional journals on the devt of helium droplet spectroscopy. *Address:* Department of Chemistry, Princeton University, Princeton, NJ 08544, USA (office). *Telephone:* (609) 258-5570 (office). *E-mail:* gscoles@princeton.edu (office). *Website:* www.princeton.edu/~gscoles (office); prism.princeton.edu (office).

SCOON, Sir Paul, GCMG, GCVO, OBE; Grenadian public administrator; *Chairman, St John's Ambulance Association;* b. 4 July 1935; m. Esmai Monica Lumsden 1970 (deceased); two step-s. one step-d.; ed Inst. of Educ., Leeds, Univ. of Toronto, Canada; teacher, Grenada Boys' Secondary School 1953–67, Chief Ed. Officer 1967–68; with Civil Service 1968, Vice-Pres. Civil Service Asscn 1968, Perm. Sec. 1969, Sec. to Cabinet 1970–72, Deputy Dir, Commonwealth Foundation 1973–78, Gov. Centre for Int. Briefing, Farnham Castle 1973–78, Gov.-Gen. of Grenada 1978–92; Chair. Grenada Tourism Bd 1995–99; currently Chair. St John's Ambulance Asscn; mem. Bd of Dirs Grenada Industrial Devt Corpn; KStJ 2001; Paul Harris Fellow, Rotary Int. 1984. *Publication:* Survival for Service 2003. *Leisure interests:* reading, tennis. *Address:* PO Box 180, St George's, Grenada (home). *Telephone:* 4402180 (home).

SCORSESE, Martin, BA, MA; American film director and writer; b. 17 Nov. 1942, Flushing, NY; s. of Charles Scorsese and Catherine (née Cappa) Scorsese; m. 1st Laraine Marie Brennan 1965; one d.; m. 2nd Julia Cameron (divorced); one d.; m. 3rd Isabella Rossellini (q.v.) 1979 (divorced 1983); m. 4th Barbara DeFina 1985 (divorced); m. 5th Helen Morris 1999; ed New York Univ.; Faculty Asst and Instructor, Film Dept, New York Univ. 1963–66, instructor 1968–70; dir and writer of films: What's a Nice Girl Like You Doing in a Place Like This? 1963, It's Not Just You, Murray 1964, Who's That Knocking At My Door? 1968, The Big Shave 1968; dir play The Act 1977–78; dir and writer of documentaries; Supervising Ed. and Asst Dir Woodstock 1970; Assoc. Producer and Post-Production Supervisor Medicine Ball Caravan 1971; Légion d'Honneur; Edward J. Kingsley Foundation Award 1963, 1964, First Prize, Rosenthal Foundation Awards of Soc. of Cinematologists 1964, named Best Dir, Cannes Film Festival 1986, First Prize, Screen Producer's Guild 1965, Brown Univ. Film Festival 1965, shared Rosellini Prize 1990, Award American Museum of Moving Image 1996, American Film Inst. Lifetime Achievement Award 1997, Int. Fed. of Film Award for Preservation 2001, Kennedy Center Honor 2007. *Films include:* Street Scenes 1970, Boxcar Bertha 1972, Mean Streets 1973, Italianamerican 1974, Alice Doesn't Live Here Any More 1974, Taxi Driver 1976, New York, New York 1977, The Last Waltz 1978, Raging Bull 1980, King of Comedy 1981, After Hours 1985, The Color of Money 1986, The Last Temptation of Christ 1988 (Courage in Filmmaking Award, LA Film Teachers Asscn 1989), Good Fellas 1989, Made in Milan 1990, Cape Fear 1991, The Age of Innocence 1993, Casino 1995, Kundun 1997, Bringing Out the Dead 1999, Gangs of New York (Golden Globe for Best Dir 2003) 2002, The Aviator 2004, The Departed (Nat. Bd of Review Award for Best Dir 2006, Golden Globe for Best Dir 2007, Dirs' Guild of America Award 2007, Acad. Award for Best Picture, Best Dir 2007) 2006, Shine a Light 2007; exec. producer: The Crew 1989, Naked in New York 1994, Grace of My Heart 1996, Kicked in the Head 1996, You Can Count on Me 2000, Deuces Wild 2002, Soul of a Man 2003, Something to Believe In 2004, Brides 2004, The Aviator 2004; producer: The Grifters 1989, Naked in New York 1994, Casino 1996, Kundun 1998, Bringing Out the Dead 1999, Gangs of New York 2002; co-producer Mad Dog and Glory 1993; acted in Cannonball 1976, Triple Play 1981, Dreams 1990, The Muse 1999. *Television includes:* Lady by the Sea: The Statue of Liberty 2004, No Direction Home: Bob Dylan 2005; exec. producer The Blues (mini-series) 2003. *Publications:* Scorsese on Scorsese 1989, The Age of Innocence: The Shooting Script (with Jay Cocks) 1996, Casino (with Nicholas Pileggi) 1996. *Address:* c/o Artists Management Group, 9465 Wilshire Boulevard, Suite 519, Los Angeles, CA 90212; Jeff Doolly Starr & Co., 350 Park Avenue, 9th Floor, New York, NY 10022, USA.

SCOTCHMER, Suzanne, BA, MA, PhD; American economist and academic; *Professor of Economics and Public Policy, University of California, Berkeley;* b. (Suzanne Andersen), 23 Jan. 1950, Seattle; d. of Toivo Andersen and Margaret Andersen; ed Univ. of Washington, Univ. of California, Berkeley; Asst and Assoc. Prof. of Econs, Harvard Univ. 1980–86; Prof. of Econs and Public Policy, Univ. of Calif., Berkeley 1986–, Prof. of Law 2008–; Visiting Prof., Univ. of Southern Calif., NY Univ. School of Law, Univ. of Toronto School of Law, Tel-Aviv Univ. Dept of Econs, Univ. of Auckland Dept of Econs, Univ. of Paris 1, New School of Econs, Moscow, Stockholm School of Econs; Prof. Invité, Univ. of Paris, Cergy-Pontoise; Research Assoc. Nat. Bureau of Econ. Research, US; mem. Bd of Dirs American Law and Econs Asscn; mem. Advisory Bd, Toulouse School of Econs; mem. Bd on Science, Tech. and Econ. Policy, NAS; Sloan Fellowship, Olin Fellowship (Yale), Hoover Nat. Fellowship (Stanford Univ.), Kaufmann Foundation, Nat. Science Foundation Prin. Investigator, France-Berkeley Fund. *Publications:* Innovation and Incentives 2004; many articles on econs in professional journals including Econometrica and Science. *Address:* School of Law and Department of Economics, University of California, Berkeley, Berkeley, CA 94720-7200, USA (office). *Telephone:*

(510) 643-8562 (office). *E-mail:* scotch@berkeley.edu (office). *Website:* socrates .berkeley.edu/~scotch (office).

SCOTLAND OF ASTHAL, Baroness (Life Peer), cr. 1997, of Asthal in the County of Oxfordshire; **Patricia Janet Scotland,** PC, QC, LLB; British barrister and politician; *Attorney General;* b. 1956, Dominica; d. of the late Arthur Leonard Scotland and of Dellie Marie Genevieve; m. Richard Mawhinney 1985; two s.; ed Univ. of London; called to the Bar, Middle Temple 1977, Bencher 1997; mem. the Bar, Antigua, Recorder 2000; mem. Privy Council 2001; Parl. Under-Sec. of State, Foreign and Commonwealth Office 1999–2001; Parl. Sec., Lord Chancellor's Dept 2001–03; Alt. UK Govt Rep. of the European Convention 2002–03; Minister of State, Home Office 2003–07; Attorney Gen. (first woman) 2007–; fmr mem. Comm. for Racial Equality, Gen. Council Bar Race Relations Cttee, Professional Conduct Cttee, Judicial Studies Bd Ethnic Minority Advisory Cttee, House of Commons Working Party on Child Abduction, Legal Advisory Panel on the Nat. Consumer Council, Ind. Cttee for the Supervision of Standards of Telephone Information Services, Nat. Advisory Cttee on Mentally Disordered Offenders; Commr Millennium Comm. 1994–; Chair. HMG Caribbean Advisory Group; Dominican Rep. of Council of The British Commonwealth Ex-Service League; Founder-mem. and fmr Head of Chambers, 1 Gray's Inn Square; fmr Chair. Inner London Educ. Authority Disciplinary Tribunal; fmr mem. BBC World Service Consultative Group; Hon. Pres. Trinity Hall Law Soc.; Hon. Fellow, Cardiff Univ., Soc. for Advanced Legal Studies, Wolfson Coll. Cambridge; Dame, Sacred Mil. Constantinian Order of St George; Dr hc (Westminster, Buckingham, Leicester, East London, Newman Univ. Coll., Birmingham); Black Woman of the Year (Law) 1992, Peer of the Year, House Magazine Awards 2004, Peer of the Year, C4 Political Awards 2004, Parliamentarian of the Year, Political Studies Association Awards 2004, The Spectator Parliamentarian of the Year Awards 2005. *Leisure interests:* church, sport, dancing, theatre. *Address:* Attorney General's Chambers, 20 Victoria Street, London, SW1H 0NS, England (office). *Telephone:* (20) 7271-2400 (office). *E-mail:* CorrespondenceUnit@attorneygeneral.gsi.gov.uk (home). *Website:* www .attorneygeneral.gov.uk (office).

SCOTT, Alastair Ian, PhD, FRS, FRSE; British/American chemist and academic; *Robert A. Welch Chair in Chemistry and D. H. R. Barton Professor of Chemistry, Texas A&M University;* b. 10 April 1928, Glasgow, Scotland; s. of William Scott and Nell Scott (née Newton); m. Elizabeth W. Walters 1950; one s. one d.; ed Univ. of Glasgow; Lecturer in Organic Chem., Univ. of Glasgow 1957–62; Prof., Univ. of British Columbia, Vancouver 1962–65, Univ. of Sussex 1965–68, Yale Univ. 1968–77; Distinguished Prof., Texas A&M Univ. 1977–80, Davidson Prof. of Chem. and Biochemistry 1982–2001, Robert A. Welch Chair in Chem. and D. H. R. Barton Prof. of Chem. 2001–, also Dir Center for Biological NMR; Prof., Dept of Chem., Univ. of Edinburgh 1980–82; mem. ACS, Royal Soc. of Chem. (RSC); Hon. Mem. Pharmaceutical Soc. of Japan 1984; Hon. MA (Yale) 1968; Hon. DSc (Coimbra) 1990, (Univ. Pierre et Marie Curie, Paris) 1992; RSC Corday Morgan Medal 1964, ACS Guenther Award 1975, ACS A.C. Cope Scholar Award 1992, RSC Centenary Lecturer 1994, RSC Tetrahedron Prize 1995, Award in Natural Product Chem. 1995, Robert A. Welch Award in Chem. 2000, Queen's Royal Medal, Royal Soc. of Edin. 2001, Davy Medal, Royal Soc. 2001, Distinguished Tex. Scientist of the Year, Tex. Acad. of Science 2002, ACS Nakanishi Prize 2003, and other awards. *Publications:* Interpretation of Ultraviolet Spectra of Natural Products 1964, Handbook of Naturally Occurring Compounds (co-author) 1972; articles in professional journals. *Leisure interests:* tennis, walking, reading. *Address:* Department of Chemistry, Texas A&M University, College Station, TX 77842, USA (office). *Telephone:* (979) 845-3243 (office). *Fax:* (979) 845-5992 (office). *E-mail:* scott@mail.chem.tamu.edu (office). *Website:* www.chem.tamu .edu (office).

SCOTT, Alexander Brian, DPhil, MRIA; Irish academic; *Professor Emeritus of Late Latin, Queen's University, Belfast;* b. 1 Dec. 1933, Bangor, N Ireland; s. of John Scott and Lil Scott; m. Margaret Byrne 1997; ed Foyle Coll. Londonderry, Queen's Univ. Belfast and Merton Coll. Oxford; temporary lecturer, Magee Univ. Coll. Londonderry 1957–58; Asst Dept of Western Manuscripts, Bodleian Library, Oxford 1958–62; Lecturer, Dept of Humanity, Aberdeen Univ. 1963–64; Lecturer, Dept of Latin, Queen's Univ. Belfast 1964, Reader in Late Latin 1971–92, Prof. of Late Latin 1992–94, Prof. Emer. 1995–. *Publications:* Hildeberti Cenomanensis Carmina Minora 1969, Malachy, a Life 1976, Expugnatio Hibernica, The Conquest of Ireland by Gerald of Wales 1978, Medieval Literary Theory and Criticism c. 1100–1375 1988, Liudprand of Cremona 1992. *Leisure interest:* travelling by train, preferably in France. *Address:* 31 Valentia Road, Drumcondra, Dublin 9, Ireland (home). *Telephone:* (1) 8372924 (home).

SCOTT, Charles Thomas, CA; British business executive; *Chairman, William Hill PLC;* b. 22 Feb. 1949; with Binder Hamlyn 1967–72; Chief Accountant, ITEL Int. Corpn 1972–77; Controller, IMS Int. Inc. 1978–84, Chief Financial Officer 1985–89; Chief Financial Officer, Saatchi & Saatchi Co. (later Cordiant PLC, now Cordiant Communications Group PLC) 1990–91, COO 1991–92, CEO 1993–95, Chair. 1995, Chair. Bates Worldwide 1997; fmr Chair. Robert Walters PLC; Sr Exec. Dir William Hill PLC 2002–04, Chair. 2004–; mem. Bd of Dirs InTechnology PLC, Emcore Corpn, Flybe Group Ltd. *Leisure interests:* golf, tennis. *Address:* William Hill PLC, Greenside House, 50 Station Road, Wood Green, London N22 7TP, England (office). *Telephone:* (20) 8918-3600 (office). *Fax:* (20) 8918-3775 (office). *Website:* www.williamhillplc.co .uk (office).

SCOTT, James, MSc, FRS, FRCP, FMedSci; British physician; b. 13 Sept. 1946, Ashby-de-la-Zouch; s. of Robert B. Scott and Iris O. Scott (née Hill); m. Diane M. Lowe 1976; two s. one d.; ed Univ. of London, London Hosp. Medical Coll.; house surgeon London Hosp. 1971–72; House Physician Hereford Co. Hosp.

July–Dec. 1972; Sr House Officer Queen Elizabeth Hosp., Midland Centre for Neurosurgery and Neurology, Birmingham Jan.–Dec. 1973; Registrar Gen. Hosp., Birmingham Jan.–Dec. 1974, Royal Free Hosp., Academic Dept of Medicine 1975–76; Hon. Sr Registrar, MRC Research Fellow Hammersmith Hosp., Dept of Medicine 1976–80; Postdoctoral Fellow Univ. of Calif., Dept of Biochemistry and Biophysics 1980–83; Clinical Scientist, Head Div. of Molecular Medicine, MRC Research Centre 1983–91; Hon. Consultant Physician Northwick Park Hosp., Harrow 1983–91, Hammersmith Hosp. 1992–97; Prof., Chair. of Medicine Royal Postgraduate Medical School 1992–97; Hon. Dir MRC Molecular Medicine Group 1992–; Dir of Medicine Hammersmith Hosps NHS Trust, Dir Div. of Medical Cardiology 1994–97; Prof. of Medicine, Imperial Coll. School of Medicine 1997–, Deputy Vice-Prin. for Research 1997–, Dir Imperial Coll. Genetics and Genomics Research Inst. 2000–; European Ed. Arteriosclerosis, Thrombosis and Vascular Biology (Journal of American Heart Asscn); several prizes and awards include Graham Bull Prize (Royal Coll. of Physicians) 1989, Squibb Bristol Myers Award for Cardiovascular Research 1993, etc. *Publications:* numerous articles on molecular medicine, molecular genetics, atherosclerosis, RNA modification, RNA editing and gene expression. *Leisure interests:* family and friends, the twentieth-century novel, British impressionist and modern painting, long distance running, swimming. *Address:* Genetics and Genomics Research Institute, The Flowers Building, Imperial College, London, SW7 2AZ, England (office). *Telephone:* (20) 7594-3614 (office). *Fax:* (20) 7594-3653 (office). *E-mail:* j.scott@imperial.ac.uk (office).

SCOTT, (Harold) Lee, Jr, BBA; American retail executive; *Chairman, Executive Committee, Wal-Mart Stores, Inc.;* b. 14 March 1949, Joplin, Mo.; s. of Harold Lee Scott and Avis Viola Scott (née Parsons); m. Linda Gale Aldridge 1969; two s.; ed Pittsburg State Univ., Pittsburg, Kan.; Br. Man. Yellow Freight System, Springdale, Ark. 1972–78; Man. Queen City Warehouse, Springfield, Mo. 1978–79; joined Wal-Mart Stores, Inc., Bentonville, Ark. 1979, Dir of Transportation 1979–83, Vice-Pres. of Distribution, Sr Vice-Pres. of Logistics, Exec. Vice-Pres. of Logistics, mem. Exec. Cttee 1995–, Chair. 2009–; Pres. and CEO Wal-Mart Stores Div. 1996, then COO and Vice-Chair. Pres. 2000–09, CEO 2000–09; Dir Cooper Industries, Inc.; mem. Bd of Dirs Pvt. Truck Council, Washington, DC 1985–86, United Negro Coll. Fund; mem. Republican party. *Leisure interests:* reading, quail hunting. *Address:* Wal-Mart Stores, Inc., 702 SW 8th Street, Bentonville, AR 72716-8611 (office); 611 Prairie Creek Road, Rogers, AR 72756-3019, USA (home). *Telephone:* (479) 273-4000 (office). *Fax:* (479) 277-1830 (office). *Website:* www.walmartstores .com (office).

SCOTT, Mark; Australian editor, media executive and academic; *Managing Director, Australian Broadcasting Corporation (ABC);* s. of Brian Scott; grand-s. of Sir Walter Scott (govt adviser); Editorial Dir John Fairfax Publs –2006, served in a range of sr roles, including Ed.-in-Chief Metropolitan, Regional & Community Newspapers, which included The Sydney Morning Herald, Sun Herald, The Age and Sunday Age; Man. Dir Australian Broadcasting Corpn (ABC) 2006–. *Address:* Australian Broadcasting Corporation (ABC), 700 Harris Street, Ultimo, PO Box 9994, Sydney, NSW 2001, Australia (office). *Telephone:* (2) 8333-1500 (office). *Fax:* (2) 8333-5344 (office). *E-mail:* comments@your.abc.net.au (office). *Website:* www.abc.net.au (office).

SCOTT, Peter Denys John, CBE, MA, QC; British lawyer and arbitrator; b. 19 April 1935; s. of John Ernest Dudley Scott and Joan G. Steinberg; ed Monroe High School, Rochester, New York, USA, Balliol Coll., Oxford; called to Bar 1960, QC 1978; Chair. of Bar 1987 (Vice-Chair. 1985–86); Standing Counsel to Dir-Gen. of Fair Trading 1974–78, to Dept of Employment 1973–78; mem. Interception of Communications Tribunal 1986–, Lord Chancellor's Advisory Cttee on Legal Educ. and Conduct 1991–94; Chair. Inst. of Actuaries Appeal Bd 1995–; Judicial Chair. City Disputes Panel 1997–; Chair. Panel on Takeovers and Mergers 2000–; Harmsworth Scholar of Middle Temple; Bencher of Middle Temple; Chair. Kensington Housing Trust 1999–2002; Chair. Bd of Trustees, Nat. Gallery 2000, Scott Review (NI) 2007–; mem. Investigatory Powers Tribunal 2000–. *Leisure interests:* art, gardening, theatre. *Address:* Fountain Court, Temple, London, EC4Y 9DH (office); 4 Eldon Road, London, W8 5PU, England (home). *Telephone:* (20) 7583-3335 (office); (20) 7937-3301 (home). *Fax:* (20) 7376-1169 (office).

SCOTT, Sir Ridley, Kt; British film director; b. 30 Nov. 1937, South Shields; ed Royal Coll. of Art; Dir of numerous award-winning TV commercials since 1970; Hon. DLitt (Sunderland) 1998. *Films:* Boy and Bicycle (dir, prod.) 1965, The Duellists (dir) 1977, Alien (dir) 1979, Blade Runner (dir, co-prod.) 1982, Legend (dir) 1985, Someone to Watch Over Me (dir, exec. prod.) 1987, Black Rain (dir) 1989, Thelma and Louise (dir, prod.) 1991, 1492: Conquest of Paradise (dir, prod.) 1992, Monkey Trouble (exec. prod.) 1994, The Browning Version (prod.) 1994, White Squall (dir, exec. prod.) 1996, G.I. Jane (dir, prod.) 1997, Clay Pigeons (prod.) 1998, Where the Money Is (prod.) 2000, Gladiator (dir, exec. prod.) (Acad. Award for Best Picture) 2000, Hannibal (dir, prod.) 2001, Black Hawk Down (dir, prod.) 2001, Six Bullets from Now (prod.) 2002, The Hire: Hostage (exec. prod.) 2002, The Hire: Beat the Devil (exec. prod.) 2002, The Hire: Ticker (exec. prod.) 2002, Matchstick Men (dir, prod.) 2003, Kingdom of Heaven (dir, prod.) 2005, In Her Shoes (prod.) 2005, Domino (prod.) 2005, Tristan & Isolde (exec. prod.) 2006, A Good Year (dir, prod.) 2006, American Gangster (dir, producer) 2007, Body of Lies (dir, producer) 2008. *Television:* Z Cars (dir, series) 1962, The Troubleshooters (dir, series) 1965, Adam Adamant Lives! (dir, series) 1966, The Informer (dir, series) 1966, Robert (dir, film) 1967, The Hunger (exec. prod., series) 1997, RKO 281 (exec. prod., series) 1999, The Last Debate (exec. prod., film) 2000, AFP: American Fighter Pilot (exec. prod., series) 2002, The Gathering Storm (exec. prod., film) (Emmy Award for Best Made-for-TV Film) 2002, Numb3rs (exec. prod., series) 2005. *Address:* William Morris Agency, One William Morris Place, Beverly

Hills, CA 90212, USA (office); Scott Free, 42/44 Beak Street, London, W1R 3DA, England. *Telephone:* (310) 859-4000 (office); (20) 7437-3163. *Fax:* (310) 859-4462 (office); (20) 7734-4978. *Website:* www.wma.com (office).

SCOTT, Robert G., BA, MBA; American financial services executive (retd); b. Montclair, NJ; ed Williams Coll., Stanford Graduate School of Business; investment banker, Morgan Stanley 1970–79, Managing Dir 1979–97, Head Capital Market Services, Corp. Finance, Investment Banking Div. –1997, Chief Financial Officer and Exec. Vice-Pres. Morgan Stanley Dean Witter (now Morgan Stanley) 1997–2001, Pres. and COO 2001–03, Dir 2001–04, currently Advisory Dir; mem. Bd of Dirs Archipelago Holdings Inc. 2004–, Genpact Ltd. 2006–; Exec. Vice-Pres. Greater New York Council of Boy Scouts of America; Chair. American Museum of Fly Fishing; mem. Advisory Council Stanford Graduate School of Business; mem. Bd of Trustees New York-Presbyterian Hospital; Excellence in Leadership Award from Stanford Business School 2004. *Address:* c/o Board of Directors, Genpact Ltd, 1251 Avenue of the Americas, Suite 4100, New York, NY 10020, USA (office).

SCOTT, Timothy (Tim), AADipl; British sculptor; b. 18 April 1937, Richmond, Surrey; s. of A. C. Scott and Dorothea Scott; m. Yvonne Jeanne Malkanthi Wirekoon 1958; two s. three d.; ed Lycée Jaccard, Lausanne, Architectural Asscn and St Martin's School of Art, London; worked at Atelier Le Corbusier-Wogenscky and others, Paris 1959–61; Sr Lecturer Canterbury Coll. of Art 1975–76; Head of Fine Art Dept, Birmingham Polytechnic 1976–78; Head Dept of Sculpture, St Martin's School of Art 1980–86; Prof. of Sculpture, Akad. der Bildenden Künste Nürnberg 1993–2002; numerous visiting lectureships in USA, Canada, Australia, Germany, UK, Chile. *Leisure interests:* music, architecture, travel, Sri Lanka, Indian culture, food. *Address:* 'High House', 71 Gangawata Para Anniewatte, Kandy, Sri Lanka (office); Keeper's Cottage, Troutsdale, N Yorks., YO13 9PS (home); 50 Clare Court, Judd Street, London, WC1H 9QW, England (home). *Telephone:* (81) 2226913 (Sri Lanka) (office); (1733) 859087 (UK) (home). *E-mail:* timscottsculptor@ yahoo.com (office).

SCOTT, Tony, MFA; British film director; b. 21 June 1944, Newcastle; m. Donna Wilson; ed Sunderland Coll. of Art, Leeds Coll. of Art, Royal Coll. of Art Film and TV Dept; worked for Derrick Knight & Alan King Assocs; Visual Dir and cameraman on pop promotional films, Now Films Ltd; TV cameraman late 1960s; Film Dir Totem Productions 1972–; Dir Scott Free Enterprises Ltd; Dir of TV and cinema commercials for Ridley Scott and Assocs. *Films:* Loving Memory (writer, editor and dir) 1969, One of the Missing (dir) (Mar Del Plata Festival Grand Prix, Argentina, Prix de la Télévision Suisse, Nyon, Second Prize Esquire Film Festival, USA, Diploma of Merit, Melbourne) 1971, The Hunger (dir) 1983, Top Gun (dir) 1986, Beverley Hills Cop II (dir) 1987, Revenge (dir) 1990, Days of Thunder (dir) 1990, The Last Boy Scout (dir) 1991, True Romance (dir) 1993, Crimson Tide (dir) 1995, The Fan (dir) 1996, Clay Pigeons (exec. prod.) 1998, Enemy of the State (dir) 1998, RKO 281 (exec. prod.) 1999, Where the Money Is (exec. prod.) 2000, The Last Debate (exec. prod.) 2000, Spy Game (dir) 2001, Big Time (exec. prod.) 2001, Six Bullets from Now (exec. prod.) 2002, The Gathering Storm (exec. prod.) 2002, The Hire: Hostage (exec. prod.) 2002, The Hire: Beat the Devil (dir, exec. prod.) 2002, The Hire: Ticker (exec. prod.) 2002, Man on Fire (dir, prod.) 2004, Agent Orange (dir) 2004, In Her Shoes (exec. prod.) 2005, Domino (dir, prod.) 2005, Tristan & Isolde (exec. prod.) 2006, The Assassination of Jesse James by the Coward Robert Ford (prod.) 2006, Déjà Vu (dir) 2006. *Television:* Nouvelles de Henry James (series, dir of part, L'Auteur de Beltraffio) 1976, The Hunger (series, dir of episode, The Swords; also exec. prod.) 1997, AFP: American Fighter Pilot (series exec. prod.) 2002, Numb3rs (series exec. prod.) 2005. *Address:* Creative Artists Agency, 9830 Wilshire Boulevard, Beverly Hills, CA 90212-1825, USA (office); Totem Productions, 8009 Santa Monica Boulevard, Los Angeles, CA 90046, USA (office). *Telephone:* (310) 288-4545 (office). *Fax:* (310) 288-4800 (office). *Website:* www.caa.com (office).

SCOTT, Hon. W. Alexander, JP, BFA; Bermudian politician; b. 1940; m. Olga Scott 1969; one s. one d.; Owner public relations agency; founding mem. and fmr Chair. Big Brothers; mem. Pitt Comm. investigating causes of riots 1977; fmr Senator and Opposition Leader in the Senate; fmr Chair. Progressive Labour Party; MP 1993–2006, Minister of Works and Eng 1998–2003; Premier of Bermuda and Govt Leader 2003–06. *Leisure interest:* photography. *Address:* Progressive Labour Party, Alaska Hall, 16 Court Street, POB 1367, Hamilton, HM 17, Bermuda (office). *Telephone:* 292-2264 (office). *Fax:* 295-7890 (office). *E-mail:* info@plp.bm (office). *Website:* www.plp.bm (office).

SCOTT, Walter, Jr, BS; American business executive; *Chairman, Level 3 Communications Inc.;* b. 21 May 1931; m. Suzanne Scott; three d. one s.; Mrs. Scott has two s.; ed Colorado State Univ.; began career with Peter Kiewit Sons Inc., Omaha 1953, Man. Cleveland Dist 1962–64, Vice-Pres. 1964, Exec. Vice-Pres. 1965–79, Chair. 1979–97 (now Chair. Emer.), Pres., CEO 1979–97, Chair., Dir Level 3 Communications (cr. after spinoff from Peter Kiewit Sons) 1998–, also Chair. Exec. Cttee; mem. Bd of Dirs Berkshire Hathaway, Burlington Resources, Commonwealth Telephone Enterprises, MidAmerican Energy Holdings, RCN Corpn, Valmont Industries, and Peter Kiewit Sons, Inc.; Pres. Joslyn Art Museum, Omaha 1987–97, now Dir; Chair. Bd of Policy Advisors Peter Kiewit Inst. for Information Science, Tech. and Eng, Heritage Services, Omaha Zoological Soc.; Dir Neb. Game and Parks Foundation, Horatio Alger Asscn. *Address:* Level 3 Communications, Inc., 1025 Eldorado Boulevard Broomfield, CO 80021, USA (office). *Telephone:* (720) 888-1000 (office). *Website:* www.level3.com (office).

SCOTT, W(illiam) Richard, PhD; American sociologist and academic; *Professor Emeritus of Sociology and Senior Scholar, Collaboratory for Global Research, Stanford University;* b. 18 Dec. 1932, Parsons, Kan.; s. of Charles H. Scott and Hildegarde Hewit; m. Joy Lee Whitney 1955; three c.; ed Parsons Jr

Coll., Kan., Univ. of Kansas, Univ. of Chicago; Asst Prof., Dept of Sociology, Stanford Univ. 1960–65, Assoc. Prof. 1965–69, Prof. 1969–99, Prof. Emer. 1999–, Chair. Dept of Sociology 1972–75, Dir Orgs. Research Training Program 1972–89; Dir Stanford Center for Orgs. Research 1988–96; Prof. by courtesy, Dept of Health Research and Policy, School of Medicine 1972– and of Educ., School of Educ. and of Organizational Behaviour, Graduate School of Business, Stanford Univ. 1977–, Sr Scholar, John W. Gardner Center for Youth and Their Communities 2002–08, Collaboratory for Global Research; Sr Researcher, Nat. Center for Health Services Research, Dept of Health, Educ. and Welfare, Washington, DC 1975–76; Visiting Prof., Kellogg Grad. School of Man., Northwestern Univ. 1997, Hong Kong Univ. of Science and Tech. 2000; Ed. Annual Review of Sociology 1986–91; mem. Gov. Bd, Comm. on Social and Behavioral Sciences and Educ., NAS 1990–96; Woodrow Wilson Fellow 1954–55; Social Science Research Council Fellow 1958–59, Fellow, Center for Advanced Study in the Behavioral Sciences 1989–90; Resident Fellow, Bellagio Center 2002; mem. Inst. of Medicine; Dr hc (Copenhagen Business School) 2000; Hon. DEcon (Helsinki School of Econs) 2001; Distinguished Scholar Award, Acad. of Man. 1988, Richard D. Irwin Award 1996. *Publications:* Metropolis and Region (with others) 1960, Formal Organizations (with P. M. Blau) 1962, Social Processes and Social Structures 1970, Evaluation and the Exercise of Authority (with S.M. Dornbusch) 1975, Organizations: Rational, Natural and Open Systems 1981, Organizational Environments (with J. W. Meyer) 1983, Hospital Structure and Performance (with A. Flood) 1987, Institutional Environments and Organizations: Structural Complexity and Individualism (with J. W. Meyer) 1994, Institutions and Organizations 1995, Institutional Change and Healthcare Organizations: From Professional Dominance to Managed Care (with others) 2000, Organizations and Organizing (with G.F. Davis) 2007, Between Movement and Establishment (with others) 2009. *Leisure interests:* reading, tennis, cross-country skiing. *Address:* Stanford University Department of Sociology, Building 120, Stanford, CA 94305 (office); 940 Lathrop Place, Stanford, CA 94305, USA (home). *Telephone:* (650) 723-3959 (office); (650) 857-1834 (home). *Fax:* (650) 725-6471 (office). *E-mail:* scottwr@stanford.edu (office). *Website:* www.stanford.edu/dept/soc (office).

SCOTT BROWN, Denise, MArch, MCP, RIBA; American architect, urban designer, writer and academic; *Principal, Venturi, Scott Brown and Associates;* b. 3 Oct. 1931, Nkana, Zambia; d. of Simon Lakofski and Phyllis Hepker; m. 1st Robert Scott Brown 1955 (died 1959); m. 2nd Robert Venturi (q.v.) 1967; one s.; ed Kingsmead Coll. Johannesburg, Univ. of Witwatersrand, Architectural Asscn London and Univ. of Pennsylvania; Asst Prof., Univ. of Pennsylvania School of Fine Arts 1961–65; Assoc. Prof., UCLA 1965–68; mem. Venturi, Scott Brown & Assocs Inc., Philadelphia 1967–, Pnr 1969–89, Prin. 1989–; Visiting Prof., Univ. of Calif., Berkeley 1965, Yale Univ. 1967–71, Univ. of Pennsylvania 1982–83; mem. MIT School of Architecture and Urban Planning Visiting Cttee 1973–1983; Fellow, Butler Coll., Princeton Univ. 1983–, Kassler Lecturer and Whitney J. Oates Fellow, Humanities Council, School of Architecture 2006; Eliot Noyes Visiting Critic, Harvard Univ. 1990; Jury mem. Prince of Wales Prize in Urban Design 1993; mem. Advisory Bd, Carnegie Mellon Univ. Dept of Architecture 1992–, Bd of Overseers for Univ. Libraries, Univ. of Pennsylvania 1995–2004; Adviser to Bd of Visitors, Tyler School of Art and Architecture, Temple Univ. 2008–; Int. FRIBA; numerous other academic and professional appts; Hon. DEng (Tech. Univ. of Nova Scotia) 1991; Hon. DHumLitt (Pratt Inst.) 1992; Hon. DFA (Univ. of Pennsylvania) 1994; Hon. DLit (Univ. of Nev.) 1998; President's Medal, Architectural League of NY 1986; Chicago Architecture Award 1987; Commendatore, Repub. of Italy 1987; Nat. Medal of Arts 1992, Philadelphia Award 1992, Benjamin Franklin Medal Award (RSA) 1993, ACSA–AIA Jt Award for Excellence in Architecture Educ., Topaz Medallion 1996, Giants of Design Award, House Beautiful Magazine 2000, Joseph Pennell Medal, Philadelphia Sketch Club 2000, Edith Wharton Women of Achievement Prize for Urban Planning 2002, Harvard Radcliffe Inst. Medal 2005, Vileck Prize 2007, Athena Award 2007, Nat. Design Mind Award, Cooper Hewitt Nat. Design Museum 2007. *Publications:* Learning from Las Vegas (with R. Venturi and S. Izenour) 1977, A View from the Campidoglio: Selected Essays, 1953–84 (with R. Venturi) 1984, Urban Concepts 1990, Architecture and Decorative Arts: Two Naifs in Japan (with R. Venturi) 1991, Architecture as Signs and Systems for a Mannerist Time (with R. Venturi) 2004; articles in professional journals. *Leisure interests:* travelling, writing, teaching, lecturing. *Address:* Venturi, Scott Brown & Associates Inc., 4236 Main Street, Philadelphia, PA 19127-1696, USA (office). *Telephone:* (215) 487-0400 (office). *Fax:* (215) 487-2520 (office). *E-mail:* info@vsba.com (office). *Website:* www.vsba.com (office).

SCOTT-HERON, Gil; American singer, songwriter, musician (piano) and poet; b. 1 April 1949, Chicago; ed Lincoln Univ., Pa; co-founder, The Midnight Band 1972–; numerous concerts and festival appearances. *Recordings include:* albums: Small Talk At 125th And Lenox 1970, Pieces Of A Man 1971, Free Will 1972, Winter In America (with Brian Jackson) 1974, The First Minute Of A New Day (with the Midnight Band) 1975, From South Africa To South Carolina (with Brian Jackson) 1975, It's Your World (with Brian Jackson) 1976, Bridges (with Brian Jackson) 1977, Secrets (with Brian Jackson) 1978, The Mind Of Gil Scott-Heron 1979, 1980 (with Brian Jackson) 1980, Real Eyes 1980, Reflections 1981, Moving Target 1982, Amnesia Express 1990, Spirits 1994, Minister Of Information 1994, Evolution And Flashback 1999. *Publications:* The Vulture (novel) 1970, Small Talk at 125th and Lenox 1970, The Nigger Factory (novel) 1972, So Far, So Good 1990, Now and Then (poems) 2001, The Last Holiday (poetry) 2008.

SCOTT-JOYNT, Rt Rev. Michael, MA; British ecclesiastic; *Bishop of Winchester;* b. 15 March 1943, Bromley, Kent; m. Louise White 1965; two s. one d.; ed King's Coll. Cambridge and Cuddesdon Theological Coll.; ordained deacon 1967, priest 1968; Curate, Cuddesdon 1967–70; Tutor, Cuddesdon Coll. 1967–71, Chaplain 1971–72; Team Vicar, Newbury 1972–75; Priest-in-Charge, Caversfield 1975–79, Bicester 1975–79, Bucknell 1976–79; Rector, Bicester Area Team Ministry 1979–81; Rural Dean of Bicester and Islip 1976–81; Canon Residentiary of St Albans 1982–87; Dir of Ordinands and In-Service Training, Diocese of St Albans 1982–87; Bishop Suffragan of Stafford 1987–95; Bishop of Winchester 1995–. *Address:* Wolvesey, Winchester, Hants., SO23 9ND, England (office). *Telephone:* (1962) 854050 (office). *Fax:* (1962) 897088 (office). *Website:* www.winchester.anglican.org (office).

SCOTT OF FOSCOTE, Baron (Life Peer), cr. 2000, of Foscote in the County of Buckinghamshire; **Richard Rashleigh Folliot Scott,** BA, LLB; British judge; *Lord of Appeal in Ordinary;* b. 2 Oct. 1934, Dehra Dun, India; s. of the late Lt Col C. W. F. Scott and Katharine Scott (née Rashleigh); m. Rima E. Ripoll 1959; two s. two d.; ed Michaelhouse Coll. Natal, Univ. of Cape Town and Trinity Coll. Cambridge; called to Bar, Inner Temple 1959; practising barrister, Chancery Bar 1960–83; QC 1975; Attorney-Gen. to Duchy of Lancaster 1980–83; Bencher, Inner Temple 1981; Chair. of the Bar 1982–83 (Vice-Chair. 1981–82); High Court Judge, Chancery Div. 1983–91; Vice-Chancellor, County Palatine of Lancaster 1987–91; a Lord Justice of Appeal 1991–94; Vice-Chancellor of the Supreme Court of Justice 1994–2000; Head of Civil Justice 1995–2000; Lord of Appeal in Ordinary 2000–; conducted inquiry into the sale of arms to Iraq 1992–96; Ed.-in-Chief Supreme Court Practice 1996–2001; Hon. mem. American Bar Assoc., Canadian Bar Assoc; Hon. LLD. (Birmingham) 1996, (Buckingham) 1999. *Publications:* Report of the Inquiry into the Export of Defence Equipment and Dual-Use Goods to Iraq and the Related Prosecutions; articles in legal journals. *Leisure interests:* equestrian activities, tennis, bridge. *Address:* House of Lords, London, SW1A 0PW, England. *Telephone:* (20) 7219-3117. *Fax:* (20) 7219-6156.

SCOTT-THOMAS, Kristin, OBE; British actress; b. 24 May 1960, Redruth; m. François Oliviennes; two s. one d.; ed Cen. School of Speech and Drama and Ecole Nat. des Arts et Technique de Théâtre, Paris; stage debut in Schnitzler's La Lune Déclinante Sur 4 ou 5 Personnes Qui Danse while student in Paris; has lived in France since age of 18; Chevalier, Légion d'honneur 2005. *Plays include:* La Terre Etrangère, Naive Hirondelles, Yes Peut-Etre, Bérénice, Three Sisters 2003, The Seagull (Olivier Award for Best Actress 2008) 2007. *Television includes:* L'Ami d'Enfance de Maigret, Blockhaus, Chameleon La Tricheuse, Sentimental Journey, The Tenth Man, Endless Game, Framed, Titmuss Regained, Look At It This Way, Body and Soul. *Films include:* Djamel et Juliette, L'Agent Troublé, La Méridienne, Under the Cherry Moon, A Handful of Dust, Force Majeure, Bille en Tête, The Bachelor, Bitter Moon, Four Weddings and a Funeral (BAFTA Award), Angels and Insects (Evening Standard Film Award), Richard III, The English Patient, Amour et Confusions, The Horse Whisperer 1998, Random Hearts, Up at the Villa, Gosford Park, Life As a House 2001, Petites Coupures 2003, Résistances 2004, The Three Ages of the Crime 2004, Arsène Lupin 2004, Man to Man 2005, Keeping Mum 2005, La Doublure 2006, Ne le dis à personne 2006, The Walker 2007, The Golden Compass (voice) 2007, I've Loved You So Long 2008, The Other Boleyn Girl 2008, Seuls two 2008, Easy Virtue 2008. *Address:* c/o PMK 8500 Wilshire Blvd., #700, Beverly Hills, CA 90211-3105, USA; c/o ARG, 4 Great Portland Street, London, W1W 8PA, England.

SCOTTO, Renata; Italian singer (soprano); b. 24 Feb. 1935, Savona; m. Lorenzo Anselmi; one s. one d.; ed Giuseppe Verdi Conservatory, Milan with Emilio Ghiriardini; debut as Violetta, Teatro Nuovo, Milan 1953; joined La Scala opera co. from 1954; London debut at the Stoll Theatre 1957; US debut in Chicago 1960; Covent Garden debut 1962, as Madama Butterfly; roles at the Metropolitan Opera from 1965, directed Butterfly at the Metropolitan 1986 and sang there for the last time in 1987; numerous festival appearances; sang roles in Adriana Lecouvreur, Andrea Chénier, Anna Bolena, Cavalleria Rusticana, Der Rosenkavalier (Marschallin), Elektra (Klytämnestra), Edgar, Falstaff, Gilda, I Capuleti e i Montecchi, I Lombardi, I Puritani, I Vespri Siciliani (Helena), L'Elisir d'amore, La Bohème, La Sonnambula (Amina), La Straniera, La Traviata, La Voix Humaine, Lucia di Lammermoor, Madama Butterfly, Manon Lescaut, Otello, Pagliacci, Pirata, Robert le Diable, The Medium, Tosca, Trittico, Turandot; as stage dir: Il Pirata, Bellini Festival, Catania, Madama Butterfly, Arena di Verona, Genoa, Thessaloniki, Ancona, Dallas Opera, Lucia di Lammermoor, Thessaloniki, Tosca, Traviata, Sonnambula, Florida Grand Opera, Sonnambula, Detroit; Commendatore della Reppublica (Italy); Dr hc (Saint John's Univ.); Metropolitan Opera Guild Opera News Award 2006. *Publication:* More than a Diva (autobiography) 1984. *Address:* Robert Lombardo Associates, 61 West 62nd Street, Suite 6F, New York, NY 10023, USA (office). *Telephone:* (212) 586-4453 (office). *Fax:* (212) 581-5771 (office). *E-mail:* lewis@rlombardo.com (office). *Website:* www.rlombardo.com (office).

SCOTTY, Ludwig Derangadage; Nauruan politician and fmr head of state; b. 20 June 1948, Anabar; Speaker Parl. –2000; Pres. and Minister of Foreign Affairs 2003 (removed in a no-confidence vote), re-elected Pres. 2004–07 (removed in a no-confidence vote), also Minister of Civil Aviation, of Customs and Immigration and of Public Service. *Address:* c/o Office of the President, Yaren, Nauru (office).

SCOWCROFT, Lt-Gen. Brent, PhD; American consultant, fmr government official and air force officer (retd); *President, Scowcroft Group;* b. 19 March 1925, Odgen, Utah; s. of James Scowcroft and Lucile Balantyne Scowcroft; m. Marian Horner 1951 (died 1995); one d.; ed US Mil. Acad., West Point and Columbia Univ.; Operational and Admin. positions in USAF 1948–53; taught Russian history as Asst Prof., Dept of Social Sciences, US Mil. Acad., W Point 1953–57; Asst Air Attaché, US Embassy, Belgrade 1959–61; Assoc. Prof., Political Science Dept, USAF Acad., Colorado 1962–63, Prof., Head of Dept 1963–64; Plans and Operations Section, Air Force HQ, Washington 1964–66;

various Nat. Security posts with Dept of Defense 1968–72; Mil. Asst to Pres., The White House 1972, Deputy Asst to Pres. for Nat. Security Affairs 1973–75, Asst to Pres. for Nat. Security Affairs 1975–77, 1989–93; Pres. Forum for Int. Policy 1993–; Pres. The Scowcroft Group 1994–; mem. Pres.'s Gen. Advisory Cttee on Arms Control 1977–81; Dir Atlantic Council, US Bd of Visitors USAF Acad. 1977–79, Council on Foreign Relations, Rand Corpn, Mitre Corpn; Vice-Chair. UNA/USA; Chair. Presidential Comm. on Strategic Forces 1983–89; mem. Cttee to Advise Dir of CIA 1995–; Chair. Pres.'s Foreign Intelligence Advisory Bd 2001–04, Eisenhower Inst. 2004–; mem. Cttee of Enquiry into Nat. Security Council 1986–87; Defense DSM, Air Force DSM (with two oak leaf clusters), Legion of Merit (with oak leaf cluster), Air Force Commendation Medal, Nat. Security Medal; Hon. KBE 1993. *Publication:* A World Transformed (with George Bush) 1998. *Address:* The Scowcroft Group, Suite 900, 900 17th Street, NW, Washington, DC 20006, USA (office). *Telephone:* (202) 296-9312 (office). *Fax:* (202) 296-9395 (office). *Website:* www.scowcroft.com (office).

SCRANTON, William Warren, AB, LLB; American lawyer and fmr politician; b. 19 July 1917, Madison, Conn.; s. of Worthington Scranton and Marion Margery Warren Scranton; m. Mary Lowe Chamberlin 1942; three s. one d.; ed Hotchkiss School, Yale Univ. and Yale Univ. Law School; served in USAAF 1941–45; Pa Bar 1946; Assoc. O'Malley, Harris, Harris and Warren 1946–47; Vice-Pres. Int. Textbook Co., Scranton, Pa 1947–52, later Dir and mem. Exec. Cttee; Pres. Scranton-Lackawanna Trust Co. 1954–56; Chair. Bd and Dir Northeastern Pa Broadcasting Co. 1957–61; Special Asst to US Sec. of State 1959–60; mem. US House of Reps 1961–63; Gov. of Pa 1963–67; Special Envoy to Middle East on behalf of Pres.-elect Nixon 1968; Chair. Pres.'s Commission on Campus Unrest 1970; Special Consultant to the Pres. 1974; Perm. Rep. to UN 1976–77; Chair of Bd Northeastern Bank of Pa 1974–76; Chair. UNA; official judge SE Wis. Scientific Fair, Milwaukee 1988–; fmr Dir Cummins Engines Co., IBM Corpn, New York Times Co., Mobil Oil; Republican; numerous hon. degrees. *Leisure interests:* tennis, swimming, hiking.

SCREECH, Rev. Michael Andrew, MA, DLitt, FBA, FRSL; British clergyman and academic; b. 2 May 1926, Plymouth; s. of Richard John Screech MM and Nellie Screech (née Maunder); m. Anne Reeve 1956; three s.; ed Sutton High School, Plymouth and Univ. Coll. London; served Intelligence Corps, mainly Far East; Lecturer then Sr Lecturer, Birmingham Univ. 1951–60; Reader, then Prof. of French, Univ. of London 1960–71, Fielden Prof. of French Language and Literature 1971–84; Sr Research Fellow, All Souls Coll. Oxford 1984–93, Emer. 1993–, Fellow and Chaplain 2001–03; Extraordinary Fellow, Wolfson Coll. Oxford 1993–2001, Hon. Fellow 2001–; ordained deacon 1993, priest 1994; Non-Stipendiary Minister, St Giles' Church, St Margaret's Church, Oxford 1993–; Visiting Prof. London, Ont. 1964, Albany, NY 1969; Johnson Prof. Madison, Wis. 1979; Edmund Campion Lecturer, Regina, Sask. 1985, Dorothy Ford Wiley Prof. of Renaissance Culture, Chapel Hill, NC 1986; Prof. Collège de France 1989; Visiting Prof. Sorbonne 1990; Comité de Publ d'Humanisme et Renaissance 1965–; Corresp. mem. Soc. Historique et Archéologique de Geneva 1988, Institut de France: Acad. des Inscriptions et Belles Lettres, Paris 1999; Fellow, Univ. Coll. London 1980; Ordre National du Mérite 1983, Chevalier, Légion d'honneur 1992; Hon. DLitt (Exeter) 1993; Dr hc (Geneva) 1998; Médaille de la Ville de Tours. *Publications:* The Rabelaisian Marriage 1958, L'Evangélisme de Rabelais 1959, Le Tiers Livre de Pantagruel 1964, Les 52 Semaines de Lefèvre d'Etaples 1965, Les Regrets et Antiquités de Du Bellay 1966, Gargantua 1967, Marot Evangélique 1967, La Pantagrueline Prognostication 1975, Rabelais 1979, Ecstasy and the Praise of Folly 1981, 1988, Montaigne and Melancholy 1983, A New Rabelais Bibliography (with Stephen Rawles) 1987, Montaigne: An Apology for Raymond Sebond 1987, Montaigne: The Complete Essays 1991, Some Renaissance Studies 1992, Rabelais and the Challenge of the Gospel 1992, Clément Marot: A Renaissance Poet Discovers the Gospel 1993, The Doctrina et Politia Ecclesiae Anglicanae of Warden Mocket (ed.) 1995, Monumental Inscriptions in All Souls College, Oxford 1997, Laughter at the Foot of the Cross 1998, Montaigne's Copy of Lucretius 1998, 'Isaiah Berlin' in Armchair Athenians 2001. *Leisure interest:* walking. *Address:* Wolfson College, Oxford, OX2 6UD (office); All Souls College, Oxford, OX1 4AL (office); 5 Swanstonfield, Whitchurch-on-Thames, Reading, RG8 7HP, England (home). *Telephone:* (118) 984-2513 (home). *Fax:* (118) 984-2513 (home). *E-mail:* michael.screech@all-souls.ox.ac.uk (office); michael.screech@btinternet.com (home).

SCRIMSHAW, Nevin Stewart, PhD, MD, MPH; American nutritionist, academic and public health consultant; *President, International Nutrition Foundation Institute and Professor Emeritus, Massachusetts Institute of Technology;* b. Milwaukee, Wis.; s. of Stewart Scrimshaw and Harriet Scrimshaw (née Smith); m. Mary Ware Goodrich 1941; four s. one d.; ed Ohio Wesleyan Univ., Harvard Univ. and Univ. of Rochester; Consultant in Nutrition, Pan American Sanitary Bureau, Regional Office of the Americas, WHO 1948–49, Regional Adviser in Nutrition 1949–53; Dir Inst. of Nutrition of Cen. America and Panama (INCAP), Guatemala 1949–61, Consulting Dir 1961–65, Consultant 1965–; Adjunct Prof., Public Health Nutrition, Columbia Univ. 1959–61, Visiting Lecturer 1961–66; Visiting Lecturer on Tropical Public Health, Harvard Univ. 1968–85; Head, Dept of Nutrition and Food Science, MIT 1961–79, Inst. Prof. 1976–88, Inst. Prof. Emer. 1988–, Dir Clinical Research Center 1962–66, 1979–85, Principal Investigator 1962–86; Visiting Prof., Tufts Univ. 1987; Dir MIT/Harvard Int. Food and Nutrition Program 1979–88; Dir Int. Food and Nutrition Programme, UN Univ. 1976–97, Dir Devt Studies Div. 1986–87, Sr Adviser UN Univ. Food and Nutrition Programme 1998–; Pres. Int. Union of Nutritional Scientists 1978–81; Founding Pres. Int. Nutrition Foundation 1982–; Fellow, American Acad. of Arts and Sciences, AAAS; mem. NAS, Inst. of Medicine and numerous other nat. and foreign scientific socs and asscns; mem. numerous cttees and advisory panels to UN agencies and other orgs; Knight Grand Cross (First

Class) of the Admirable Order of the Direkgunabhorn (Thailand); Int. Award, Inst. of Food Technologists 1969, Goldberger Award in Clinical Nutrition, American Medical Asscn 1969, First James R. Killian Jr Faculty Achievement Award, MIT 1972, McCollum Award, American Soc. for Clinical Nutrition 1975, Conrad A. Elvehjem Award, American Inst. of Nutrition 1976, 1st Bolton L. Corson Medal, Franklin Inst. 1976, Medal of Honor, Fundación F. Cuenca Villoro 1978, Bristol Meyers Award 1988, World Food Prize 1991, McCollum Award, American Soc. of Nutritional Sciences 1999, UN Lifetime Achievement and Service Award 2004; John Boyd Orr Lecturer, British Nutrition Soc., and numerous other awards. *Publications:* 22 books and more than 700 scientific articles on various aspects of human and animal nutrition, nutrition and infection, agricultural and food chemistry and public health. *Leisure interests:* skiing, hiking, gardening. *Address:* PO Box 330, Campton, NH 03223 (office); 115 Sandwich Mount Farm, PO Box 330, Campton, NH 03223, USA (home). *Telephone:* (603) 726-4200. *Fax:* (603) 726-4614. *E-mail:* nscrimshaw@inffoundation.org (office).

SCRIVENER, Christiane; French public official and mediator; *President Ombudsman, Société Générale;* b. 1 Sept. 1925, Mulhouse; d. of Pierre Fries and Louise Fries; m. Pierre Scrivener 1944; one s. (deceased); ed Harvard Business School and Univ. of Paris; businesswoman involved since 1958 in org. of French tech. co-operation with more than 100 countries, devt of int. tech. and industrial exchanges and promotion of French tech. abroad; State Sec. for Consumer Affairs 1976–78; MEP 1979–89; mem. Union pour la Démocratie (UDF); EEC Commr for Taxation and Customs Union and Consumers' Interests 1989–95; Pres. Ombudsman Société Générale 1996–, Plan Int. France 1997–; mem. Bd, Alliance Française 1995–97; Commdr, Légion d'honneur; Grand-croix Ordre de Leopold (Belgium); Grand-croix de Mérite (Luxembourg); Officier de Polonia Restituta (Poland). *Publications:* Le rôle et la responsabilité à l'égard du public 1978, L'Europe, une bataille pour l'avenir 1984, Histoires du petit Troll 1986. *Leisure interests:* skiing, music. *Address:* 21 avenue Robert-Schuman, 92100 Boulogne-Billancourt, France. *Telephone:* 1-48-25-44-11 (home). *E-mail:* ch.scrivener@wanadoo.fr (home).

SCRIVER, Charles Robert, CC, G.O.Q., MD, CM, FRS, FRSC, FAAS; Canadian professor of pediatrics, human genetics and biology; *Alva Professor Emeritus of Human Genetics, McGill University;* b. 7 Nov. 1930, Montreal; s. of Walter DeMoulpied and Jessie Marion Boyd; m. Esther Peirce 1956; two s. two d.; intern Royal Victoria Hosp. Montreal 1955–56, Resident 1956–57, Resident Montreal Children's Hosp. 1956–57, Chief Resident (Pediatrics) 1960–61, physician 1961–; Children's Medical Center, Boston, USA 1957–58; McLaughlin Travelling Fellow Univ. Coll. London, UK 1958–60; Asst Prof. of Pediatrics McGill Univ. 1961, Markle Scholar 1961–66, Assoc. Prof. 1965–69, Prof. of Pediatrics, Genetics and Biology 1969–, Co-Dir MRC Genetics Group 1972–95, Alva Prof. of Human Genetics 1994, Alva Prof. Emer. 2002–; Assoc. Dir Canadian Genetic Diseases Network 1989–98; Pres. Canadian Soc. for Clinical Investigation 1974–75, Soc. for Pediatric Research 1975–76, American Soc. Human Genetics 1986, American Pediatric Soc. 1994–95; mem. Medical Advisory Bd./Scientific Advisory Bd Howard Hughes Medical Inst. 1981–88; Hon. DSc (Manitoba) 1992, (Glasgow, Montreal) 1993, (Utrecht) 1999, (British Columbia) 2002; numerous awards and prizes including Allen Award, American Soc. of Human Genetics 1978, Gairdner Foundation Int. Award 1979, McLaughlin Medal, Royal Soc. of Canada 1981, Canadian Rutherford Lectureship, Royal Soc., London 1983, Ross Award, Canadian Pediatric Soc. 1990, Award of Excellence (Genetic Soc. of Canada) 1992, Prix du Québec 1995, Friesen Award 2001, Querci Prize (Italy) 2001, ASHG Award for Excellence in Human Genetics Educ. 2001. *Publications:* Amino Acid Metabolism and its Disorders (co-author) 1973, Garrod's Inborn Factors in Disease (co-author) 1989, Metabolic Basis of Inherited Disease (6th, 7th, 8th edns, online, Sr Ed.) (co-author) 1989–; author or co-author of more than 500 scientific articles. *Leisure interests:* literature, music, photography. *Address:* 232 Strathearn Avenue, Montreal, PQ H4X 1Y2 (home); Montreal Children's Hospital, 2300 Tupper Street, Montreal, PQ H3H 1P3, Canada (office). *Telephone:* (514) 412-4417 (office). *Fax:* (514) 412-4329 (office). *E-mail:* charles.scriver@mcgill.ca (office).

SCRUTON, Roger, BA, PhD, FRSL; British philosopher and writer; b. 27 Feb. 1944, Buslingthorpe; s. of John Scruton and Beryl C. Haines; m. 1st Danielle Laffitte 1975 (divorced 1983); m. 2nd Sophie Jeffreys 1996; ed High Wycombe Royal Grammar School, Jesus Coll. Cambridge and Inner Temple, London; Fellow, Peterhouse, Cambridge 1969–71; Lecturer in Philosophy, Birkbeck Coll. London 1971–79, Reader 1979–86, Prof. of Aesthetics 1986–92; Prof. of Philosophy, Boston Univ. 1992–95; Founder and Dir The Claridge Press 1987–2004; Ed. The Salisbury Review 1982–2000, now on Editorial Bd; mem. Editorial Bd British Journal of Aesthetics, Arka (Kraków), and openDemocracy.net; unpaid research prof., Buckingham Univ.; Hon. doctorates (Adelphi Univ.) 1995, (Masaryk Univ., Brno, Czech Repub.) 1998; Medal of Merit, First Class (Czech Repub.). *Publications:* Art and Imagination 1974, The Aesthetics of Architecture 1979, The Meaning of Conservatism 1980, The Politics of Culture and Other Essays 1981, Fortnight's Anger (novel) 1981, A Short History of Modern Philosophy 1982, A Dictionary of Political Thought 1982, The Aesthetic Understanding 1983, Kant 1983, Untimely Tracts 1985, Thinkers of the New Left 1986, Sexual Desire 1986, Spinoza 1987, A Land Held Hostage: Lebanon and the West 1987, The Philosopher on Dover Beach (essays) 1989, Francesca (novel) 1991, A Dove Descending (stories) 1991, Conservative Texts: An Anthology 1991, The Xanthippic Dialogues 1993, Modern Philosophy 1993, The Classical Vernacular 1994, Modern Philosophy 1996, Animal Rights and Wrongs 1996, An Intelligent Person's Guide to Philosophy 1997, The Aesthetics of Music 1997, On Hunting 1998, Town and Country (co-ed.) 1998, An Intelligent Person's Guide To Modern Culture 1998, On Hunting 1999, Perictione in Colophon 2000, England: An Elegy 2000, The West and the Rest: Globalization and the Terrorist Threat 2002, Death-

Devoted Heart: Sex and the Sacred in Wagner's Tristan and Isolde 2004, News from Somewhere: On Settling 2004, Gentle Regrets (autobiog.) 2005, A Political Philosophy 2006, Culture Counts: Faith and Feeling in a World Besieged 2007, Beauty 2009. *Leisure interests:* music, literature, hunting. *Address:* Sunday Hill Farm, Brinkworth, Wilts., SN15 5AS, England. *Website:* www.roger-scruton.com.

SCULLY, Sean Paul, BA; American artist; b. 30 June 1945, Dublin; s. of John Anthony Scully and Holly Scully; m. Catherine Lee; ed Croydon Coll. of Art, Newcastle Univ., Harvard Univ.; with Fine Art Dept, Newcastle Univ. 1967–71; Lecturer, Harvard Univ. 1972–73; Lecturer, Chelsea School of Art and Goldsmiths School of Art, London 1973–75; Lecturer, Princeton Univ. 1978–83; Lecturer in Painting, Parsons School of Design, New York 1983–; one-man exhbns in London, LA, New York, Berlin, Washington, etc. 1973–; exhibited at Carnegie Inst., Pittsburgh, Boston Museum of Fine Arts, Chicago Art Inst. 1987, Univ. Art Museum, Berkeley, Calif. 1987, Whitechapel Art Gallery, London 1989, Lenbachhaus, Munich 1989, Palacio Velázquez, Madrid 1989, Mary Boone Gallery, New York 1993, Fort Worth Museum of Modern Art 1993, Galerie Nat. de Jeu de Paume, Paris 1996; works in public collections in UK, USA, Australia, Germany, Ireland; Guggenheim Fellowship 1983; Stuyvesant Foundation Prize 1970, 1972 Prize John Moores Liverpool Exhbn 8, 1974 Prize John Moores Liverpool Exhbn 9. *Address:* Galerie Lelong, 528 West 26th Street, New York, NY 10001, USA; Waddington Galleries, 11 Cork Street, London, W1S 3LT, England. *Telephone:* (212) 315-0470 (NY); (20) 7851-2200 (London). *Fax:* (212) 262-0624 (NY); (20) 7734-4146 (London). *E-mail:* mail@waddington-galleries.com.

SCULTHORPE, Peter Joshua, AO, OBE; Australian composer; b. 29 April 1929, Launceston, Tasmania; s. of Joshua Sculthorpe and Edna Moorhouse; ed Launceston Grammar School, Univ. of Melbourne and Wadham Coll., Oxford; Lecturer, Sr Lecturer in Music, Univ. of Sydney 1963–68; Visiting Fellow, Yale Univ. 1965–67; Reader in Music, Univ. of Sydney 1968–91, Prof. in Musical Composition and Sydney Moss Lecturer in Music 1992–; Visiting Prof. of Music, Univ. of Sussex 1971–72; commissions from bodies including Australian Broadcasting Comm., Birmingham Chamber Music Soc., Australian Elizabethan Theatre Trust, Australian Ballet, Musica Viva Australia, Australian Chamber Orchestra; Hon. DLitt (Tasmania, Sussex); Hon. DMus (Melbourne); Australian Council Composers' Award 1975–77, Australian Film Inst. Award 1980, Ted Albert Award 1993, Sir Bernard Heinze Award 1994, ABC Classic FM Listeners' Choice Award 1998 and numerous other awards. *Compositions published include:* The Loneliness of Bunjil 1954, Sonatina 1954, Irkanda I 1955, II 1959, III 1960, IV 1961, Ulterior Motifs, a musical farce and music for various revues 1957–59, Sonata for Viola and Percussion 1960, Theme and Journey's End (from film They Found a Cave) 1962, The Fifth Continent 1963, String Quartet No. 6 1965, No. 7 1966, No. 8 1969, No. 9 1975, No. 10 1983, No. 11 1990, Sun Music I 1965, Sun Music for Voices and Percussion 1966, Sun Music III 1967, IV 1967, Morning Song for the Christ Child 1966, Red Landscape 1966, Tabuh Tabuhan 1968, Autumn Song 1968, Sea Chant 1968, Sun Music II 1969, Orchestral Suite (from film The Age of Consent) 1968, Sun Music Ballet 1968, Love 200 for pop group and orchestra 1970, The Stars Turn 1970, Music for Japan 1970, Dream 1970, Night Pieces 1971, Landscape 1971, How The Stars Were Made 1971, Ketjak 1972, Koto Music I 1973, II 1976, Rites of Passage 1973, The Song of Tailitnama 1974, Postcard from Nourlangie to Clapham Common 1993, From Saibai 1993, Memento Mori for orchestra 1993, From Ubirr for string quartet and didgeridoo 1994; various works for radio, TV, theatre and film. *Leisure interests:* gardening, collecting Sung ceramics. *Address:* 91 Holdsworth Street, Woollahra, NSW 2025, Australia.

SCUTT, Der, FAIA; American architect and interior designer; b. 17 Oct. 1934, Reading, Pa; s. of George W. Scutt and Hazel Smith; m. Leena Liukkonen 1967; two c.; ed Pennsylvania State Univ., Yale Univ.; Design Pnr, Swanke Hayden Connell & Pnrs 1975–81; Prin. Der Scutt Architect, New York 1981–; mem. American Inst. of Architects, Bd of Govs NY Bldg Congress 1984–92 (Treasurer 1988), Bd of Trustees Chapin Soc. 1984–, Nat. Maritime Historical Soc. 1991–, Ocean Liner Museum, New York 1994; numerous design awards. *Projects include:* One Astor Plaza and Minskoff Theatre, New York 1973, Equitable Life Assurance Data Center, Easton, Pa 1973, Creative Perfumery Center, Teaneck, NJ 1973, Grand Hyatt Hotel, New York 1980, 520 Madison Avenue, NY 1983, Continental Center Office Tower NY 1983, Trump Tower, NY 1983, US HQ Hong Kong Bank, NY 1985, office bldg 625 Madison Avenue, NY 1988, IFF World HQ, NY 1994 and other office bldgs NY. *Address:* Der Scutt, Architect, 114 West 27th Street, 2nd Floor, New York, NY 10001-6211, USA (office). *Telephone:* (212) 725-2300 (home). *Fax:* (212) 481-7094 (office). *E-mail:* info@derscutt.com (office). *Website:* www.derscutt.com (office).

SEABRA, Antônio Luíz; Brazilian business executive; *Chairman, Natura Cosméticos;* b. 1943, São Paulo; began career as trainee in Human Resources Dept, Remington Brazil, Man. 1964–66; f. Natura Cosméticos 1969, mem. Bd of Dirs 1998–, co-Chair. 2001–; Most Valuable Exec. Award, Valor Econômico 2003. *Address:* Natura Cosméticos S.A, Rodavia Régis Bittencourt, s/nº, km 293, Potuverá, 06882-700 Itapecerica da Serra, São Paulo, Brazil (office). *Website:* www.natura.net (office).

SEAGA, The Most Hon. Edward Philip George, BA, PC, ON; Jamaican academic and fmr politician; *Honorary Distinguished Fellow, University of the West Indies at Mona;* b. 28 May 1930, Boston, Mass., USA; s. of Philip Seaga and Erna Seaga (née Maxwell); m. 1st Marie Elizabeth Constantine 1965 (divorced 1995); two s. two d.; m. 2nd Carla Frances Vendryes 1996; ed Wolmers Boys' School, Kingston and Harvard Univ.; Field Researcher with Inst. of Social and Econ. Research (Univ. of West Indies) on devt of child and revival spirit cults; nominated to Upper House, Legis. Council 1959; Asst Sec. to Jamaican Labour Party 1960, Sec. 1962; MP for Western Kingston 1962–2005; Minister of Devt and Social Welfare 1962–67, of Finance and Planning 1967–72; Leader of Jamaican Labour Party Nov. 1974–2005; Leader of Opposition 1974–80 1989; Prime Minister 1980–89; Minister of Finance and Planning, Information and Culture 1980–89, of Defence 1987–89; Chair. Premium Group 1989; Hon. Distinguished Fellow, Univ.of the West Indies at Mona 2005–; Grand Cross, Order of Merit (FRG) 1982; The Order of the Nation 2002 (Jamaica); five Hon. LLD degrees from US univs; Gold Mercury Int. Award (Venezuela) 1981, Dr Martin Luther King Humanitarian Award 1984, Enviromental Leadership Award, UNEP 1987 and other awards. *Publications:* Development of the Child, Revival Spirit Cults, Faith Healing in Jamaica. *Leisure interests:* classical music, reading, hunting, sports, futurology. *Address:* Office of the Board for Graduate Studies and Research, University of the West Indies at Mona, Kingston 7 (office); 24–26 Grenada Crescent, New Kingston, Kingston 5, Jamaica (home). *Telephone:* (876) 977-0655 (office). *E-mail:* edward.seaga@uwimona.edu.jm (office). *Website:* www.mona.uwi.edu (office).

SEAGAL, Steven; American film actor and martial arts expert; b. 10 April 1951, Lansing, Mich.; m. 1st Miyako Fujitoni; one s. one d.; m. 2nd Kelly Le Brock; one s. two d.; moved to Japan aged 17 remaining there for 15 years; established martial arts acads (dojo) in Japan and LA; CEO Steamroller Productions. *Films:* Above the Law 1988, Hard to Kill 1990, Marked for Death 1990, Out for Justice, Under Siege/On Deadly Ground (dir) 1994, Under Siege 2 1995, The Glimmer Man, Executive Decision, Fire Down Below, The Patriot (also producer) 1998, Ticker 2001, Exit Wounds 2001, Half Past Dead 2002, The Foreigner 2003, Out for a Kill 2003, Belly of the Beast 2003, Clementine 2004, Out of Reach 2004, Into the Sun 2005,. *Recording:* Mojo Priest (album) 2007. *Address:* c/o ICM, 8942 Wilshire Blvd, Beverly Hills, CA 90211-1934, USA. *Website:* www.stevenseagal.com.

SEAL, Basil (see BARNES, Julian Patrick).

SEAMAN, Christopher, MA, ARCM; British conductor; *Music Director, Rochester Philharmonic Orchestra;* b. 7 March 1942, Faversham; s. of Albert Edward Seaman and Ethel Margery Seaman (née Chambers); ed Canterbury Cathedral Choir School, The King's School, Canterbury, King's Coll., Cambridge; Prin. Timpanist, London Philharmonic Orchestra 1964–68; Asst Conductor BBC Scottish Symphony Orchestra 1968–70, Chief Conductor 1971–77; Chief Conductor Northern Sinfonia Orchestra 1973–79; Prin. Conductor BBC Robert Mayer Concerts 1978–87; Conductor-in-Residence, Baltimore Symphony Orchestra 1987–98; Chief Guest Conductor Utrecht Symphony Orchestra 1979–83; Music Dir Naples Philharmonic Orchestra, Fla 1993–, Rochester Philharmonic Orchestra, NY 1998–; Artistic Adviser San Antonio Symphony; Dir Symphony Australia Conductor Programme; appears as guest conductor world-wide and has appeared in USA, Germany, France, the Netherlands, Belgium, Italy, Spain, Australia and all parts of the UK; Hon. FGSM 1972. *Leisure interests:* people, reading, shopping, theology. *Address:* Harrison Parrott, 5–6 Albion Court, Albion Place, London, W6 0QT, England (office); Rochester Philharmonic Orchestra, 108 East Avenue, Rochester, NY 14604, USA (office). *Telephone:* (20) 7229-9166 (office); (585) 454-7311 (office). *Fax:* (20) 7221-5042 (office). *E-mail:* info@harrisonparrott.co.uk (office). *Website:* www.harrisonparrott.com (office); www.rpo.org (office).

SEAMAN, Rev. Sir Keith Douglas, KCVO, OBE, MA, LLB, DipHum; Australian ecclesiastic and fmr state governor; b. 11 June 1920, McLaren Vale; s. of the late Eli Semmens Seaman and Ethel Maud Seaman; m. Joan Isabel Birbeck 1946; one s. one d.; ed Unley High School and Univ. of Adelaide; South Australia (SA) Public Service 1937–54; RAAF Overseas HQ, London 1941–45, Flight Lt; entered Methodist ministry 1954; Minister, Renmark 1954–58; Cen. Methodist Mission 1958–77; Dir 5KA, 5AU, 5RM Broadcasting Cos 1960–77 (Chair. 1971–77); Sec. Christian TV Asscn SA 1959–73; mem. Exec. World Asscn of Christian Broadcasting 1963–70; Supt Adelaide Cen. Methodist Mission 1971–77; mem. Australian Govt Social Welfare Comm. 1973–76; Gov. of S Australia 1977–82; KStJ. *Leisure interests:* gardening, reading. *Address:* 93 Rosetta Village, Victor Harbor, SA 5211, Australia. *Telephone:* (8) 85523535. *E-mail:* kdsl@iinet.net.au.

SEARLE, John R., BA, MA, DPhil.; American academic; *Willis S. and Marion Slusser Professor of Philosophy of the Mind and Language, University of California, Berkeley;* b. 1932, Denver, CO; s. of George W. Searle and Hester Beck Searle; m. Dagmar Carboch 1958; two s.; ed Univ. of Wisconsin, Univ. of Oxford, UK; Asst Prof. of Philosophy Univ. of California, Berkeley 1959–64, Assoc. Prof. 1964–67, Prof. 1967–, later Slusser Prof. of Philosophy, Chair. Dept of Philosophy 1973–75, Special Asst to Chancellor for Student Affairs 1965–67; mem. Scholar Council, Library of Congress 2000–; mem. Editorial Bd Journal of Psycholinguistic Research, Linguistics and Philosophy, Philosophy and Artificial Intelligence, Journal of Consciousness Studies, Cognitive Science Series, Harvard Univ.Press; mem. American Acad. of Arts and Sciences 1976–, Cognitive Science Group, Univ. of California, Berkeley 1981–, European Acad. of Science and Art 1993–, Scientific Bd, Vilem Mathesius Centre, Charles Univ., Prague 1994–, Nat. Council of Nat. Endowment of Humanities 1992–96; mem. Bd of Dirs American Council of Learned Socs 1979–87; mem. Bd of Trustees Nat. Humanities Center 1976–90; Fellow and Lecturer, World Econ. Forum, Davos 1991, 1995, 1998, 2001; Educ. TV series in Calif. 1960–74; Advisor to Pres.'s Comm. on Student Unrest (Scranton Comm.) 1970; Hon. Prof., Tsinghua Univ., Beijing 2007, East China Normal Univ., Shanghai 2007; Dr hc (Adelphi) 1993, (Wisconsin) 1994, (Bucharest) 2000, (Torino) 2000, (Lucano) 2003; Rhodes Scholar 1952, Reith Lecturer 1984, Tasan Award, South Korean 2000, Jean Nicod Prize 2000, Jovellanos Prize 2000, Nat. Humanities Medal 2005, Mind and Brain Prize, Torino, Italy 2006, Puffendorf Medal, Sweden 2006. *Publications:* Speech Acts 1969, The Campus War 1972, Expression and Meaning 1979, Intentionality 1983, Minds, Brains and Science 1984, The Foundations of Illocutionary Logic (with

D. Vanderveken) 1985, The Rediscovery of the Mind 1992, (On) Searle on Conversation 1992, The Construction of Social Reality 1995, Mystery of Consciousness 1997, Mind, Language and Society 1998, Conversations with John Searle 2001, La Universidad Desafiada 2002, Consciousness and Language 2002, Liberté et Neurobiologie (trans. as Freedom and Neurology) 2004, Mind, A Brief Introduction 2004. *Leisure interests:* literature, opera, skiing, travel. *Address:* Department of Philosophy, 314 Moses Hall 2390, University of California, Berkeley, CA 94720-2390, USA (office). *Telephone:* (510) 642-3173 (office). *Fax:* (510) 642-5160 (office). *Website:* philosophy .berkeley.edu (office).

SEARLE, Ronald, CBE, RDI, AGI, FRSA; British artist; b. 3 March 1920, Cambridge; s. of the late William James Searle and of Nellie Searle (née Hunt); m. 1st Kaye Webb (divorced 1967, died 1996); one s. one d.; m. 2nd Monica Koenig 1967; ed Central School, Cambridge and Cambridge School of Art; first drawings published 1935–39; served with Royal Engineers 1939–46; POW in Japanese camps 1942–45; contrib. to nat. publs 1946; mem. Punch 'Table' 1956; special features artist, Life magazine 1955, Holiday 1957, The New Yorker 1966–, Le Monde 1995–; Designer of medals for the French Mint 1974–, British Art Medal Soc. 1983–; work represented in Victoria and Albert Museum, Imperial War Museum and British Museum, London, Bibliothèque Nationale, Paris and in several German and US museums; Chevalier de la Légion d'honneur 2006; Venice, Edin., San Francisco and other film festival awards for film Energetically Yours; LA Art Dirs' Club Medal 1959, Philadelphia Art Dirs' Club Medal 1959, Nat. Cartoonists' Soc. Award 1959, 1960, Gold Medal, III Biennale, Tolentino, Italy 1965, Prix de la Critique Belge 1968, Grand Prix de l'Humour noir (France) 1971, Prix d'Humour, Festival d'Avignon 1971, Medal of French Circus 1971, Prix Int. 'Charles Huard' 1972, La Monnaie de Paris Medal 1974, Bundesrechtsanwaltskammer Award (Germany) 1998. *Films designed:* designer of several films including John Gilpin, On the Twelfth Day, Energetically Yours, Germany 1960, Toulouse-Lautrec, Dick Deadeye, or Duty Done 1975; designed animation sequences for films Those Magnificent Men in their Flying Machines 1965, Monte-Carlo or Bust! 1969, Scrooge 1970, Dick Deadeye 1975. *Publications:* Forty Drawings 1946, John Gilpin 1952, Souls in Torment 1953, Rake's Progress 1955, Merry England 1956, Paris Sketchbook 1957, The St Trinian's Story (with Kaye Webb) 1959, USA For Beginners 1959, Russia for Beginners 1960, The Big City 1958 (all with Alex Atkinson), Refugees 1960 1960, Which Way Did He Go? 1961, Escape from the Amazon 1963, From Frozen North to Filthy Lucre 1964, Those Magnificent Men in their Flying Machines 1965, Haven't We Met Before Somewhere? (with Heinz Huber) 1966, Searle's Cats 1967, The Square Egg 1968, Hello—Where Did All the People Go? 1969, Secret Sketchbook 1970, The Second Coming of Toulouse-Lautrec 1970, The Addict 1971, More Cats 1975, Designs for Gilbert and Sullivan 1975, Paris! Paris! (with Irwin Shaw) 1977, Searle's Zodiac 1977, Ronald Searle (monograph) 1978, 1996, The King of Beasts 1980, The Big Fat Cat Book 1982, Illustrated Winespeak 1983, Ronald Searle in Perspective (monograph) 1984, Ronald Searle's Golden Oldies: 1941–1961, 1985, Something in the Cellar 1986, To the Kwai—and Back 1986, Ah Yes, I Remember It Well...: Paris 1961–1975 1987, Non-Sexist Dictionary 1988, Slightly Foxed—But Still Desirable 1989, Carnet de Croquis 1992, The Curse of St Trinian's 1993, Marquis de Sade Meets Goody Two-Shoes 1994, Searle and Searle 2001, Ronald Searle in Le Monde 2002, The Scrapbook Drawings 2005. *Address:* c/o The Sayle Literary Agency, 8B King's Parade, Cambridge, CB2 1SJ, England (office); c/o Eileen McMahon Agency (office). *Telephone:* (1223) 303035 (Cambridge) (office). *Fax:* (1223) 301638 (Cambridge) (office). *E-mail:* rcalder@sayleliteraryagency.com (office); eileenmcmahon@earthlink.net (office). *Website:* www.ronaldsearle.com.

SEARS, Hon. Alfred M., BA, M.Phil., JD; Bahamian politician and lawyer; b. 13 Jan. 1953, Fort Charlotte; s. of Winifred Sears; m. Marion Bethel 1987; three c.; ed Boys' Industrial School, St. Augustine Coll., Columbia Univ., USA, New York Law School, USA, Univ. of the West Indies, Jamaica; f. Interdenominational Christian Youth Assen (ICYA); Lecturer in Caribbean Politics, Hunter Coll., Univ. of New York 1977–87; fmr Attorney, Civil Court of Manhattan, USA, Berthan Macaulay, Jamaica, Gibson & Co., The Bahamas; Founder and Pnr, Sears & Co. (law firm) 1992–; Attorney-Gen. and Minister of Educ. 2002–07; Head of Caribbean Financial Action Task Force (CFTAF) 2002. *Address:* Sears & Co., POB N3645, Nassau N.P., The Bahamas (office). *Telephone:* 326-3481 (office). *Fax:* 326-3483 (office). *E-mail:* info@ searschambers.com (office). *Website:* www.searschambers.com (office); alfredsears.org.

SEBASTIAN, Sir Cuthbert (Montraville), GCMG, OBE, BSc, MD, CM; Saint Christopher and Nevis government official and physician; *Governor-General;* b. 22 Oct. 1921; ed Mount Allison Univ., Dalhousie Univ., Canada; pharmacist and lab. technician, Cunningham Hosp., St Kitts 1942–43; served in RAF 1944–45; Capt. St Kitts Nevis Defence Force 1958–80; Medical Supt, Cunningham Hosp. 1966, Joseph N. France Gen. Hosp. 1967–80; Chief Medical Officer Saint Christopher and Nevis 1980–83; pvt. medical practitioner 1983–95; Gov.-Gen. of Saint Christopher and Nevis 1996–. *Leisure interests:* farming, reading, dancing. *Address:* Government House, Basseterre (office); 6 Cayon Street, Basseterre, St Kitts, Saint Christopher and Nevis, W Indies (home). *Telephone:* 465-2315 (office); 465-2344 (home).

SEBASTIANI, HE Cardinal Sergio; Italian ecclesiastic; *President, Prefecture for Economic Affairs of The Holy See;* b. 11 April 1931, Montemonaco (Ascoli-Piceno); s. of Angelo Sebastiani and Lucia Valeri; ed Pontifical Gregorian Univ., Pontifical Lateran Univ., Pontifical Ecclesiastical Acad.; ordained priest 1956; Sec. of Apostolic Nunciature, Peru 1960; Sec. of Apostolic Nunciature, Brazil 1962; Uditore, Apostolic Nunciature, Chile 1966, Office Chief, Vatican Secr. of State, Counsellor Apostolic Nunciature in Paris, with special assignment to Council of Europe 1974; ordained Titular Archbishop of Cesarea in Mauritania; Apostolic Pro-Nuncio to Madagascar and Apostolic Del. to Réunion and Comoros 1976, Apostolic Nuncio to Turkey 1985; Sec.-Gen. Cen. Cttee of Great Jubilee Year 2000 1994; Pres. Pref. for Econ. Affairs of The Holy See 1997–; cr. Cardinal 2001 (Cardinal-Deacon of S. Eustachio); Commendadore Order of Merit, Italy, Nat. Order of Madagascar, Grand Cross Order O'Higgins, Chile. *Publications:* La Chiesa all'uomo del XX secolo, La Sapienza nell'Antico Testamento. *Address:* Prefecture for the Economic Affairs of the Holy See, Palazzo delle Congregazioni, Largo del Colonnato 3, 00193 Rome (office); Via Rusticucci 13, 00193 Rome, Italy (home). *Telephone:* (06) 69884263 (office). *Fax:* (06) 69885011 (office).

SEBBAN, Guy; French business executive and international organization executive; *Secretary-General, International Chamber of Commerce;* b. Mostaganem; m. Michelle Sebban; ed Ecole de Physique et Chimie de Paris, Univ. of Paris (Sorbonne), Université de Paris Dauphine; fmr Man. at Rhône-Poulenc, later at Aventis, Brussels, in charge of relations with EU insts; Sr Advisor to CEO of Vivendi Universal –2005; Sec.-Gen. ICC 2005–. *Address:* International Chamber of Commerce, 38 cours Albert 1er, 75008 Paris, France (office). *Telephone:* 1-49-53-28-18 (office). *Fax:* 1-49-53-28-35 (office). *E-mail:* sg@ iccwbo.org (office). *Website:* www.iccwbo.org (office).

SEBELIUS, Kathleen, MPA; American politician, government official and fmr state official; *Secretary of Health and Human Services;* b. 15 May 1948, Ohio; d. of fmr Ohio Gov. John Gilligan; m. Gary Sebelius; two s.; ed Univ. of Kansas; first woman employee in Kan. Dept of Corrections 1975–87; mem. Kan. State House of Reps 1987–94, mem. Ethics Comm.; Insurance Commr, Kan. 1994–2002; Gov. of Kan. 2003–09; US Sec. of Health and Human Services, Washington, DC 2009–; Democrat; named amongst Top Ten Public Officials in America, Governing Magazine 2001. *Address:* Department of Health and Human Services, 200 Independence Ave, SW, Washington, DC 20201, USA (office). *Telephone:* (202) 619-0257 (office). *Website:* www.os.dhhs .gov (office).

ŠEBRLE, Roman; Czech decathlete; b. 26 Nov. 1974, Prague; m. Eva Sebrle; one c.; mem. Czech Olympic athletics team, Sydney 2000 (silver medal for decathlon); set world record for decathlon (9,026 points), World Championships, Götzis, Austria May 2001; gold medals in heptathlon, World Indoor Championships, Lisbon March 2001, heptathlon, European Indoor Championships March 2002, decathlon, European Championships Aug. 2002, heptathlon, World Indoor Championships, Budapest 2004, decathlon, Olympic Games, Athens 2004 (set Olympic record with 8,893 points); silver medal in decathlon, World Championships, Paris Aug. 2003; bronze medal, heptathlon, World Championships, Maebashi 1999, heptathlon, World Indoor Championships, Birmingham 2003; Czech Athlete of the Year 2002, 2003. *Leisure interests:* computers, the Internet, football, sci-fi, music, spaghetti. *Address:* c/o Czech Olympic Committee, Benesovská 6, 10100 Prague 10 (office); Ceská Sportovní, a.s., 2A Cisarseým Mlýnem 33, Prague 7, Czech Republic. *Telephone:* (2) 71734734 (office). *Fax:* (2) 71731318 (office). *E-mail:* info@ olympic.cz (office). *Website:* www.ceskasportovni.cz (office).

SECHIN, Igor Ivanovich, PhD; Russian politician and business executive; *Deputy Chairman of the Government (Deputy Prime Minister);* b. 7 Sept. 1960, Leningrad (now St Petersburg); m.; one d.; ed Leningrad State Univ.; army service 1984–86; leading instructor, Exec. Cttee, Dept of Foreign Econ. Relations, Leningrad City Soviet 1988–91; Chief Expert, Asst to Head of Admin to First Vice-Mayor, Chair. Cttee on Foreign Relations, Office of Mayor of Leningrad 1991–96; Expert, Deputy Head of Div., Public Relations Dept, Dept of Foreign Affairs 1996–97; Head, Gen. Admin Dept, Adviser to Deputy Head then Head Chief Control Dept, Admin of the Russian Pres. 1998–99; Head, Secr. of First Deputy Chair., later Chair., Govt of Russian Fed. 1999–2000; Deputy Chief of Staff, Presidential Exec. Office 2002–08, Aide to the Pres. 2004–08; Deputy Chair. of the Govt (Deputy Prime Minister), in charge of industry devt, nuclear power and environment 2008–; mem. Bd of Dirs and Chair. Rosneft Oil Co. 2004–. *Address:* Office of the Government, Krasnopresnenskaya nab. 2, 103274 Moscow, Russia (office). *Telephone:* (495) 205-57-35 (office). *Fax:* (495) 205-42-19 (office). *E-mail:* info@government.ru (office). *Website:* www.government.ru (office).

SECK, Idrissa; Senegalese politician; b. 9 Aug. 1959, Thies; m.; three c.; ed Institut d'Etude Politique, Paris and Princeton Univ., USA; consultant with Price Waterhouse 1986–92; mem. Parti démocratique sénégalais—PDS (Democratic Party), Deputy Sec.-Gen.; fmr Minister Without Portfolio; Sec. of State, Dir Office of the Pres. 2000–02; Prime Minister of Senegal Sept. 2002–April 2004; Mayor of Thies 2002; unsucessful cand. for Pres. 2007. *Address:* c/o Parti démocratique sénégalais (PDS), blvd Dial Diop, Immeuble Serigne Mourtada Mbacké, Dakar, Senegal (office).

SEDAKA, Neil; American singer and composer; b. 13 March 1939; s. of Mac Sedaka and Eleanor Appel; m. Leba M. Strassberg 1962; one s. one d.; ed Juilliard School of Music; recipient of numerous gold records and recording industry awards. *Composed numerous popular songs including:* Breaking Up Is Hard to Do, Stupid Cupid, Calendar Girl, Oh! Carol, Stairway to Heaven, Happy Birthday Sweet Sixteen, Laughter in the Rain, Bad Blood, Love Will Keep Us Together, Lonely Night (Angel Face). *Recordings include:* In the Pocket, Sedaka's Back, The Hungry Years, Steppin' Out, A Song, All You Need Is The Music, Come See About Me, Greatest Hits 1988, Oh! Carol and Other Hits 1990, Timeless 1992, Tales of Love 1997, The Show Goes On 2003. *Address:* c/o Neil Sedaka Music, 641 Lexington Avenue, 14th Floor, New York, NY 10022, USA (office). *Telephone:* (212) 593-0526 (office). *E-mail:* leba@ neilsedaka.com (office). *Website:* www.neilsedaka.com.

SEDGWICK, (Ian) Peter; British business executive; *Member, European Advisory Board, JER Partners;* b. 13 Oct. 1935; m. Verna Mary Sedgwick 1956; one s. one d.; with Nat. Provincial Bank 1952–59, Ottoman Bank Africa and Middle East 1959–69, J. Henry Schroder Wagg & Co. Ltd 1969–90; Dir Schroders Nominees Ltd 1981–95, CEO Schroder Investment Man. Ltd 1985–94, Dir Schroder Unit Trusts Ltd 1987–95, Group Man. Dir Investment Man. Schroders PLC 1987–95, Deputy Chair. (Chair. Desig.) 1995–2000, Chair. 2000–03, CEO (interim) 2001, Dir (non-exec.) Schroder & Co. Inc. 1991–99, Chair. 1996–2002, Pres. and CEO Schroders Inc. New York 1996–2000, Chair. Schroder All-Asia Fund 1991–99, Schroder UK Growth Fund 1994, Pres. CEO Schroder US Holdings Inc. 1996; Dir (non-exec.) Equitable Life Assurance Soc. 1991–2001, INVESCO City & Commercial Investment Trust PLC (fmrly New City & Commercial Trust PLC) 1992; mem. European Advisory Bd JER Pnrs. *Leisure interests:* golf, grandchildren, theatre. *Address:* c/o European Advisory Board, JER Partners, Clarges House, 6–12 Clarges Street, London, W1J 8AD, England. *Telephone:* (20) 7518-4350. *Fax:* (20) 7518-4351. *Website:* www.jer.com.

ŠEDIVÝ, Jaroslav, CSc, DPhil; Czech politician and diplomatist (retd); b. 12 Nov. 1929, Prague; s. of Jaroslav Šedivý and Marie Šedivý; m. Marie Poslušná 1962; one s. one d.; ed Charles Univ., Prague; with Czech Acad. of Sciences 1954–57; scientist, Inst. of Int. Policy and Econ. 1957–70; imprisoned on charges of subversion of the state 1970–71; worker, driver, window cleaner 1972–88; researcher, Prognostic Inst., Prague 1989; adviser to Minister for Foreign Affairs 1989–90; Amb. to France 1990–95, to Belgium, Luxembourg and NATO 1995–97; Perm. Rep. to UNESCO 1993–95; Minister for Foreign Affairs 1997, Jan.–July 1998; Amb. to Switzerland 1998–2002; Adviser, Analysis Section, Ministry of Foreign Affairs 2002–03; Grand Officier, Ordre nat. du Mérite 1994, Chevalier, Ordre de la Légion d'honneur 2005, Ordre of Merit (Czech Repub.) 2005; Dr hc (J.F. Kennedy Univ., Buenos Aires) 1998. *Publications:* Policy and Relations 1969, Humiliated Revolution (published under pseudonym Y. Heřtová) 1978, Metternich contra Napoleon 1998, Palace Černín in the Year Zero 1997, Mystery and Sins of the Templars 1999, Decembrists: Anatomy of an Unsuccessful Coup 2000. *Telephone:* (2) 41431707 (home). *E-mail:* sedivay@seznam.cz (home).

ŠEDIVÝ, Maj.-Gen. Jiří; Czech army officer; b. 3 Jan. 1953, Příbram; m.; two d.; ed Mil. High School, Mil. Univ. for Land Army, Mil. Acad., Brno; mem. CP 1975–89; various commands Czech Army 1975–96, including Commdr, Czech Unit, Implementation Force (IFOR), Bosnia 1996; Commdr Czech Land Army 1997–98, Chief of Gen. Staff 1998–2002; in pvt. sector 2002–; four Mil. Merit Awards, two Memorial Badges. *Leisure interests:* sport, music. *Address:* c/o Ministry of Defence, Tychonova 1, 160 00 Prague 6, Czech Republic.

ŠEDIVÝ, Jiří, MA, PhD; Czech academic, international organization official and fmr government official; *Assistant Secretary General for Defence Policy and Planning, NATO;* b. 1963; s. of Jaroslav Šedivý; m. Lucie Šedivý; one s.; ed King's Coll. London, UK, Charles Univ., Prague; Reader, Int. Relations, Int. Politics and Security Studies, Charles Univ., Prague 1995–2000; Prof. of European Security, Prague Center, New York Univ., USA 2000–03; Dir Inst. of Int. Relations (IIR), Prague 1998–2004; Prof. of Cen. European Security Studies, George C. Marshall European Center for Security Studies, Germany 2004–06; Minister of Defence June–Oct. 2006 (resgnd); Asst Sec. Gen. for Defence Policy and Planning, NATO, Brussels 2007–; Chair. Czech Foundation for the Study of Int. Relations; Chair. Editorial Bd Mezinárodní vztahy (Int. Relations Quarterly), Prague; mem. Editorial Bd Contemporary Security Policy, Birmingham Univ.; mem. Council for Science, Czech Foreign Ministry; aide to fmr Pres. Vaclav Havel 1996–2000. *Publications:* Dilema rozšiřování NATO (The Dilemma of NATO Enlargement) 2001; numerous articles in professional journals on int. security, IR theory, Czech foreign and security policy. *Address:* North Atlantic Treaty Organization (NATO), blvd Léopold III, 1110 Brussels, Belgium (office). *Telephone:* (2) 707-41-11 (office). *Fax:* (2) 707-45-79 (office). *E-mail:* natodoc@hq.nato.int (office). *Website:* www.nato.int (office).

SEDLEY, Rt Hon. Sir Stephen John, Kt, PC, BA; British judge and writer; *Lord Justice of Appeal;* b. 9 Oct. 1939; s. of William Sedley and Rachel Sedley; m. 1st Ann Tate 1968 (divorced 1995); one s. two d.; m. 2nd Teresa Chaddock 1996; ed Mill Hill School, Queens' Coll., Cambridge; writer, musician, trans. 1961–64; called to Bar, Inner Temple 1964, Bencher 1989, QC 1983; mem. Int. Comm. on Mercenaries, Angola 1976; Visiting Professorial Fellow, Univ. of Warwick 1981; Pres. Nat. Reference Tribunals for the Coalmining Industry 1983–88; Visiting Fellow, Osgoode Hall Law School, Canada 1987, Visiting Prof. 1997; Dir Public Law Project 1989–93; Chair. Sex Discrimination Cttee, Bar Council 1992–95; Judge of the High Court of Justice, Queen's Bench Div. 1992–99; Distinguished Visitor, Hong Kong Univ. 1992; Hon. Prof., Univ. of Wales, Cardiff 1993–, Univ. of Warwick 1994–; Visiting Fellow, Victoria Univ. of Wellington, NZ 1998; Judicial Visitor, Univ. Coll. London 1999–; Pres. British Inst. of Human Rights 2000–, British Tinnitus Asscn 2006–; Chair. British Council Advisory Cttee on Governance 2002–05; mem. Admin. Law Bar Asscn (Hon. Vice-Pres. 1992–), Haldane Soc. (Sec. 1964–69); Hon. Fellow, Inst. for Advanced Legal Studies 1997; Dr hc (North London) 1996; Hon. LLD (Nottingham Trent) 1997, (Bristol) 1999, (Warwick) 1999, (Durham) 2001, (Hull) 2002, (Southampton) 2003. *Publications include:* Whose Child? 1987, The Making and Remaking of the British Constitution (with Lord Nolan) 1997, Freedom, Law and Justice 1999, Human Rights: A New World or Business as Usual 2000; editor: Seeds of Love (anthology) 1967, A Spark in the Ashes 1992; translator: From Burgos Jail, by Marcos Ana and Vidal de Nicolas 1964; contrib. essays to numerous books, including Freedom of Expression and Freedom of Information 2000, Judicial Review in International Perspective 2000, Discriminating Lawyers 2000; contrib. to periodicals and journals, including Civil Justic Quarterly, Industrial Law Journal, Journal of Law and Society, Journal of Legal Ethics, Law Quarterly Review, London Review of Books, Modern Law Review, Public Law. *Address:* Royal Courts of Justice, Strand, London, WC2A 2LL, England (office). *Telephone:* (20) 7947-6000 (office). *Website:* www.hmcourts-service.gov.uk (office).

SEDNEY, Jules; Suriname academic and politician; b. 28 Sept. 1922, Paramaribo; s. of Eugene Edwin Leonard Sedney and Marie Julia Linger; m. Ina Francis Waaldyk 1951 (divorced 1985); two s. two d.; one d. by A. Calor; ed Graaf van Zinzendorfschool, Mulo and Univ. of Amsterdam; fmr teacher; held sr post with Cen. Bank of Suriname 1956–58, Pres. 1980; Minister of Finance 1958–63; Dir Industrial Devt Corpn of Suriname and Nat. Devt Bank 1963; left Nationale Partij Suriname (NPS) and joined Progressieve Nationale Partij (PNP) 1967; Prime Minister and Minister of Gen. Affairs 1970–73; Prof. of Econs, Univ. of Suriname 1976–80; Chair. Nat. Planning Council 1980; fmr Dir Suriname Trade and Industry Asscn 1990–92; Chair. Monitoring Group Suriname Structural Adjustment Programme 1992–96, Tripartite Advisory Bd to Govt of Suriname 1994–98, Seniority Bd of Econ. Advisers to Pres. of the Repub. 1998–2000, Center for the Promotion and Protection of Democracy and Civil Soc. 1999; Gran Cordón Simón Bolívar (Venezuela), Groot-Officier Oranje Nassau (Netherlands), Kt, Nederlandse Leeuw (Netherlands). *Publications:* Growth Without Development 1978, To Choose and To Divide 1980, The Future of Our Past 1998. *Leisure interests:* bridge, golf. *Address:* Maystreet 34, Paramaribo, Suriname. *Telephone:* (597) 439114. *Fax:* (597) 421029.

SEEBACH, Dieter, BS, PhD, FRSC; German chemist and academic (retd); *Visiting Professor, Harvard University;* b. 1937, Karlsruhe; m. Ingeborg Reichling (deceased); three c.; ed Univ. of Karlsruhe; Post-doctoral Fellow and Lecturer in Chem., Harvard Univ., USA 1965–66; Prof., Justus Liebig Universität, Giessen 1971–77; Prof., ETH, Zürich 1977–2003, Visiting Prof. 2003–; Visiting Prof. at numerous int. univs including Harvard Univ. 2007; mem. Schweizerischer Chemiker Verband 1981–92, Chemical Soc., Royal Soc. of Chem., Gesellschaft Deutscher Chemiker, Chemical Soc. of Japan, ACS, Neue Schweizerische Chemische Gesellschaft 1992–95 (Hon. mem. 2004–), Deutsche Akad. der Naturforscher Leopoldina 1984–; mem. Advisory Bd Synthesis 1984–, Angewandte Chemie 1985–94, Chimia 1985–, Helvetica Chimische Acta 1986–91; Fellow, Japan Soc. for the Promotion of Science 1985–; Foreign Assoc. NAS (USA) 2007–; Dr hc (Montpellier) 1989; hon. lecturer at numerous int. univs; numerous awards, including Univ. of Karlsruhe Wolf Prize 1964, Stichting Havinga Fonds Havinga Medal 1985, Gesellschaft Deutscher Chemiker Karl Ziegler Prize 1987, Harvard Univ. Tischler Prize 1990, King Faisal Int. Prize in Science (Saudi Arabia) 1999, Marcel Benoist Prize (Switzerland) 2000, Yamada Prize (Japan) 2000, Nagoya Medal (Japan) 2002, A.W. von Hofmann Medal 2003, Tetrahedron Prize 2003, American Peptide Soc. Vincent du Vigneaud Award 2004, Ryoji Noyori Prize 2004, Max Bergmann Medal 2005. *Publications:* more than 800 research papers and numerous lectures world-wide. *Address:* c/o Laboratorium für Organische Chemie, Eidgenössische Technische Hochschule, Hönggerberg HCI H 331, Wolfgang-Pauli-Strasse 10, 8093 Zürich, Switzerland (office). *Telephone:* (1) 632-2990 (office). *Fax:* (1) 632-1144 (office). *E-mail:* seebach@org.chem.ethz.ch (office). *Website:* infosee.ethz.ch/seebach/seebach.html (office).

SEEHOFER, Horst Lorenz; German politician; *Minister President of Bavaria and Chairman Christian Social Union;* b. 4 July 1949, Ingolstadt; m. Karin Seehofer 1985; one s. three d.; ed Verwaltungs und Wirtschaftsakademie, Munich; began career in local govt, Ingolstadt and Eichstätt; joined Christlich-Soziale Union (CSU) 1971, Mem. Parl. for Ingolstadt 1980–, CSU Speaker on Social Affairs 1983–89, Parl. Sec. of State, Ministry of Employment 1989–92, Minister of Health 1992–98, Vice-Chair. CSU 1994–2008, Chair. 2008–, Vice-Chair. CDU/CSU Parl. Group 1998–2004, Regional Chair., Christlich Soziale Arbeitnehmerschaft 2000–, Minister of Food, Agriculture and Consumer Protection 2005–08; Regional Chair. VdK Bayern 2005–06; Minister-Pres. of Bavaria 2008–. *Address:* Franz Josef Strauß-Haus, Nymphenburger Strasse 64, 80335 Munich, Germany (office). *Telephone:* (89) 12430 (office). *Fax:* (89) 1243299 (office). *E-mail:* info@csu-bayern.de (office). *Website:* www.csu.de (office); www.horst-seehofer.de (home).

SEELERT, Robert Louis (Bob); American business executive; *Chairman, Saatchi & Saatchi Worldwide;* Gen. Man. Gen. Foods, 1966–86, Pres. Coffee and Int. Foods Div. 1986–89; Pres. and CEO Kayser-Roth (hosiery group) 1991–94; Pres. and CEO Topco American (grocery co.) 1989–91; Chief Exec. Cordiant Communications Group PLC (frmly. Saatchi & Saatchi, later Cordiant PLC) 1995–97; CEO Saatchi & Saatchi Worldwide 1997–, now Chair. *Address:* Saatchi & Saatchi Worldwide, 375 Hudson Street, New York, NY 10014-3620, USA (office). *Telephone:* (212) 463-2000 (office). *Fax:* (212) 463-9855 (office). *Website:* www.saatchi.com (office).

SEEMAN, Nadrian C., BS, PhD, FRSC; American chemist and academic; *Margaret and Herman Sokol Professor of Chemistry, New York University;* ed Univ. of Chicago, Univ. of Pittsburgh; Postdoctoral researcher, Columbia Univ., New York 1970–72, MIT, Cambridge, Mass 1972–77; Prof., Dept of Chem., New York Univ. 1977–, Margaret and Herman Sokol Chair in Chem. 2001–; Founding Pres. Int. Soc. for Nanoscale Science, Computation and Eng; Fellow, AAAS 1998; Hon. Prof., Universidad Peruana Cayetano Heredia 1998; NATO Advanced Study Fellow 1970, Damon Runyon Fellow 1972–73, NIH Postdoctoral Fellow 1973–76, Sidhu Award 1974, Basil O'Connor Fellow 1978–81, NIH Research Career Devt Award 1982–87, Popular Science Magazine Science and Tech. Award 1993, Feynman Prize in Nanotechnology 1995, Discover Magazine Emerging Tech. Award 1997, Margaret and Herman Sokol Faculty Award in the Sciences 1999, Tulip Award in DNA-Based Computation 2004, MERIT Award, Nat. Inst. of Gen. Medical Sciences 2005, Nano50 Award, Nanotech Briefs 2005, World Tech. Award in Biotechnology, The World Tech. Network 2005, Nichols Medal, New York Section of ACS 2008. *Publications:* Emergence of Function in Molecular Assemblies 2010;

numerous scientific papers in professional journals on DNA nanotechnology, macromolecular design and topology, biophysical chem. of recombinational intermediates, DNA-based computation, and crystallography. *Address:* Room 1066 W, Department of Chemistry, New York University, New York, NY 10003-6688, USA (office). *Telephone:* (212) 998-8395 (office). *Fax:* (212) 260-7905 (office). *E-mail:* ned.seeman@nyu.edu (office). *Website:* seemanlab4.chem.nyu.edu (office).

SEEPAPITSO IV, Chief Kgosi, DipAdmin; Botswana diplomatist; *Paramount Chief, Bangwaketse Tribe;* ed Moeng Coll. and South Devon Tech. Coll., UK; Dist Officer, Botswana 1960; fmr mem. Land Bd; Paramount Chief of Bangwaketse Tribe 1970–; mem. Citizenship Cttee 1982–97, Vision 2016 Task Force 1995; Chair. Sports Comm. 1998; Amb. to USA (also accred to Brazil, Canada, Mexico, Chile and Trinidad and Tobago) 2000–02, to People's Repub. of China (also accred to Repub. of Korea and Singapore) 2002–05. *Address:* Office of the Paramount Chief, Bangwaketse Tribe, Kanye, Botswana.

SEGAL, Anthony (Tony) Walter, MD, PhD, DSc, FRS, FRCP, FMedSci; British medical scientist and consultant physician; *Charles Dent Professor of Medicine and Director, Centre for Molecular Medicine, Department of Medicine, University College London;* b. 24 Feb. 1944, Johannesburg, South Africa; s. of Cyril Segal and Doreen Segal (née Hayden); m. Barbara Miller 1966; three d.; ed Univ. of Cape Town, S Africa and Univ. of London; Sr Clinical Fellow, Wellcome Trust 1979–86; Charles Dent Prof. of Medicine, Univ. Coll., London 1986–, also Dir Centre for Molecular Medicine. *Leisure interests:* golf, sculpture, theatre, art. *Address:* Department of Medicine, University College London, 2nd Floor, Rayne Institute, 5 University Street, London, WC1E 6JJ (office); 48B Regents Park Road, London, NW1 7SX, England (home). *Telephone:* (20) 7679-6175 (office); (20) 7586-8745 (home). *Fax:* (20) 7679-6175 (office). *E-mail:* t.segal@ucl.ac.uk (office). *Website:* www.ucl.ac.uk/CMM (office).

SEGAL, George, BA; American film actor and producer; b. 13 Feb. 1934, New York, NY; s. of George Segal and Fanny Segal (née Bodkin); m. 1st Marion Sobol 1956 (divorced 1983); two d.; m. 2nd Linda Rogoff 1983 (deceased); m. 3rd Sonia Schulz; ed Manhasset Bay School, Great Neck Junior High School, George School, Haverford Coll., Columbia Coll. *Films include:* The Young Doctors 1961, Act One 1962, The Longest Day 1962, Invitation to a Gunfighter 1964, The New Interns 1964, Ship of Fools 1965, King Rat 1965, Who's Afraid of Virginia Woolf? 1966, The Quiller Memorandum 1966, Bye Bye Braverman 1968, No Way to Treat a Lady 1968, The Bridge at Remagen 1969, She Couldn't Say No 1969, The Southern Star 1969, Loving 1970, Where's Poppa? 1970, The Owl and the Pussy Cat 1970, Born to Win 1972, The Hot Rock 1972, A Touch of Class (Golden Globe Award 1972) 1972, Blume in Love 1972, The Terminal Man 1973, California Split 1973, Blackbird 1974, Russian Roulette 1975, The Duchess and the Dirtwater Fox 1976, Fun with Dick and Jane 1976, Rollercoaster 1977, Who is Killing the Great Chefs of Europe? 1978, Lost and Found 1979, The Last Married Couple in America 1980, Stick 1983, The Endless Game (TV) 1989, Look Who's Talking 1990, The Clearing, For The Boys 1991, The Mirror has Two Faces 1996, Flirting with Disaster 1996, The Cable Guy 1996, The November Conspiracy 1997, Heights 2004. *Play:* Art, New York 1999, West End, London 2001. *Television:* Just Shoot Me (NBC sitcom) 1996–2003, Houdini 1998, The Linda McCartney Story 2000. *Leisure interest:* banjo playing. *Address:* c/o Starr & Co., 350 Park Avenue, New York, NY 10022, USA.

SEGAL, Uri; Israeli orchestral conductor; *Principal Guest Conductor, Indiana University;* b. 7 March 1944, Jerusalem; s. of Alexander and Nehama Segal; m. Ilana Finkelstein 1966; one s. three d.; ed Rubin Acad., Jerusalem and Guildhall School of Music, London; debut with Tivoli Orchestra, Copenhagen 1969; Prin. Conductor Bournemouth Symphony Orchestra 1980–82, Philharmonia Hungarica 1981–85; Music Dir Israeli Chamber Orchestra, Chautauqua Festival, NY 1990–2007, Louisville Orchestra, KY 1998–2004; founder/Chief Conductor Century Orchestra, Osaka 1990–98, Laureate Conductor 1998–; currently Prin. Guest Conductor, Ind. Univ.; fmr Prin. Guest Conductor Stuttgart Radio Symphony; orchestras conducted include Berlin Philharmonic, Stockholm Philharmonic, Concertgebouw, Orchestre de Paris, Vienna Symphony, Israel Philharmonic, London Symphony, London Philharmonic, Philharmonia, Orchestra de la Suisse Romande, Warsaw Philharmonic, Spanish Nat. Orchestra, Pittsburgh Symphony, Chicago Symphony, Detroit Symphony, Dallas Symphony, Houston Symphony, Montréal Symphony and Rochester Symphony; tours have included Austria, Switzerland, Spain, Italy, France, UK, Scandinavia and the Far East; operatic debut conducting The Flying Dutchman at Sante Fe Opera 1973, has since conducted opera in Italy, France, Germany, Japan, Israel and USA; recent guest appearances include with Hamburg Symphony, Düsseldorf Symphony, Polish Nat. Orchestra, Orchestre Nat. de Lille, Rochester Philharmonic, Detroit Symphony Orchestra, Jerusalem Symphony, London Philharmonia, Tokyo Chamber Opera Theater; First Prize, Int. Mitropoulos Conducting Competition, New York 1969. *Recordings:* Mahler Symphony No. 4 (with NZ Symphony Orchestra), music by Britten (Bournemouth Symphony), Stravinsky's Firebird Suite and Symphony in C with the Suisse Romande Orchestra), Mozart Piano Concertos with Radu Lupu and the English Chamber Orchestra, Schumann's Piano Concerto with Ashkenazy and the London Symphony, Beethoven Piano Concertos with Rudolf Firkusny and the Philharmonia, Mozart Piano Concertos with Alicia de Larocha and Wiener Symphoniker. *Leisure interests:* reading, photography, cooking. *Address:* Michal Schmidt Artists Management, 59e 54th Street, Suite 83, New York, NY 10022, USA (office). *Telephone:* (212) 421-8500 (office); (54) 801-9086 (Israel) (home). *Fax:* (212) 421-8583 (office). *E-mail:* mws@achmidtart.com (office); usegal@attglobal.net (home). *Website:* www.schmidtart.com (office); www.urisegal.com.

SEGLIŅŠ, Mareks; Latvian lawyer and politician; *Chairman, People's Party;* b. 4 July 1970, Aizpute; ed Aizputes Secondary School, Univ. of Latvia; worked in prosecutor's office and court of Liepāja City; worked in law office Pomerancis un Kreicis 1994–98; elected to 7th Saeima (Parl.) 1998; mem. Parl. (People's Party Parl. Group), Chair. Legal Affairs Cttee, Sub-cttee on Drafting Criminal Procedure Law of the Legal Affairs Cttee, Deputy Chair. Nat. Security Cttee, mem. Baltic Affairs Sub-cttee of Foreign Affairs Cttee, Sports Sub-cttee of Educ., Culture and Science Cttee, Latvian del. to Baltic Ass., Latvia Interparliamentary Co-operation Groups with Australia and NZ, Azerbaijan, Canada, Chile, China, Ecuador, Germany, Italy, Kuwait, Taiwan, Turkey, UK and USA; Minister of Interior 1999–2002, 2007–09; currently Chair. People's Party. *Address:* People's Party, Dzirnavu iela 68, Rīga, Latvia (office). *Telephone:* 6728-6441 (office). *Fax:* 6728-6405 (office). *E-mail:* Mareks.Seglins@saeima.lv (office). *Website:* www.tautaspartija.lv (office).

SEGUELA, Jacques Louis; French advertising executive; b. 23 Feb. 1934, Paris; s. of Louis Seguela and Simone Le Forestier; m. Sophie Vinson 1978; one s. four d.; ed Lycée de Perpignan, Faculté de Pharmacie de Montpellier; reporter, Paris Match 1960; with France Soir group's leisure magazines 1962; produced several TV programmes; joined Delpire 1964, then Axe; f. Roux Seguela Agency; f. Roux Seguela Cayzac & Goudard with Alain Cayzac and Jean Michel Goudard 1978; Vice-Pres. (Euro-RSCG) 1991–96; Chief Creative Officer and Administrator Havas Advertising 1996–2001; est. Bleu comme bleu (restaurant), Paris 1995; Chevalier, Légion d'honneur, Chevalier des Arts et des Lettres; César winner. *Publications:* Terre en rond 1967 (Prix littérature sportive), Ne dites pas à ma mère que je suis dans la publicité, elle me croit pianiste dans un bordel 1979, Hollywood lave plus blanc 1982, Fils de pub 1984, Cache Cache Pub, Demain il sera tros star 1989, C'est gai la pub 1990, Vote au-dessus d'un nid de cocos 1992, Pub Story 1994, La parole de Dieu 1995, le Futur a de l'avenir 1996, 80 ans de publicité Citroën et toujours 20 ans 1999, Le Vertige des urnes 2000, Job Guide des métiers de demain 2001, Tous ego: Havas, moi et les autres 2005, Soeur Courage 2006, La prise de l'Elysée: Les campagnes présidentielles de la Ve République 2007. *Address:* c/o Editions Flammarion, 87 quai Panhard et Levassor, 75647 Paris Cedex 13 (office); Havas Advertising, 84 rue de Villiers, 92300 Levallois-Perret, France.

SÉGUIN, Philippe Daniel Alain, LèsL; French politician; *First President, Cour des Comptes;* b. 21 April 1943, Tunis, Tunisia; s. of Robert Séguin and Denyse Danielle; m. 2nd Béatrice Bernascon; one d.; two s. one d. by first m.; ed Lycée Carnot, Tunis, Lycée de Draguignan, Ecole Normale d'Instituteurs, Var, Faculté des Lettres, Aix-en-Provence and Ecole Nationale d'Admin.; Auditor, Cour des Comptes 1970, Chargé de mission, Office of First Pres., Cour des Comptes 1972–73, Sr Auditor 1977–2003, Audit Dir 2003, First Pres. 2004–; head of scholastic sector, Bd of Educ., Nice 1971; Dir of Studies, Inst. d'Etudes Politiques, Aix-en-Provence 1970–74; Maître de Conferences, Inst. d'Etudes Politiques, Paris 1971–77; Prof. Centre de Formation Professionelle et de Perfectionnement 1971–73; Secr.-Gen. Presidency of the Repub. 1973–74; Asst to Dir of Physical Educ. and Sport 1974–75; Dir Office of Sec. of State responsible for relations with Parl. 1977; Chargé de mission, Office of Prime Minister 1977–78; Deputy for Les Vosges to Nat. Ass. 1978–86, 1988–2002, Vice-Pres. 1981–86; Mayor of Epinal 1983–97; Nat. Sec. RPR 1984–86, Pres. 1997–99, Pres. RPR Conseil de Paris 2001–02; Minister of Social Affairs and Employment 1986–88; Pres. Nat. Ass. 1993–97, Parl. Floor Leader 1997–99; Pres. nat. tripartite comm., French Fed. of Football; Pres. Bd of Govs ILO 2004–; Chevalier des Palmes académiques, du mérite agricole, Officier des Arts et Lettres, de l'Ordre national du Québec, Grand Croix de l'ordre national du Mérite, de l'Ordre de la Pléiade, Grand Cross of the Order of Merit, Germany, Grand Cross of the Order of Merit, Brazil, Grand Cross of the Order of Merit, Chile, Grand Cross of the Royal Order of Merit of Sahamétrei, Cambodia, Grand Cross of Repub. of Tunisia, Grand Cross of the Order of Gorkha-Dakshina-Bahu, Nepal, Grand Cordon de l'Ordre Ouissam Alaouite, Morocco, Commdr Order Stara Planina, Bulgaria, Order of Tahiti-Nui; Hon. DLitt (Loughborough Univ. of Tech.) 1987, (Univ. of Bucharest), (Univ. of Montréal); Bronze Medal, Faculty of Arts,Aix-en-Provence 1967, Médaille de l'Institut d'études politiques d'Aix-en-Provence 1967, Prix de la Fondation Napoléon 1990, Prix des écrivains combattants 1990. *Publications:* Réussir l'alternance 1985, La force de convaincre 1990, Louis Napoléon le Grand 1990, De l'Europe en général et de la France en particulier (jtly) 1992, Discours pour la France 1992, Demain, la France: tome I: La Priorité sociale (jty), Tome II: La Reconquête du Territoire 1993, Ce que j'ai dit 1993, Discours encore et toujours républicains 1994, Deux France (jtly) 1994, 240 dans un fauteuil 1995, C'est quoi la politique? (for children) 1999, Plus français que moi, tu meurs! (essay) 2000, Lettre ouverte à ceux qui veulent encore croire à Paris 2000, Revisiter Montcalm 2002, Itinéraire: Dans la France d'en bas, d'en haut et d'ailleurs 2003. *Address:* Cour des Comptes, 13 rue Cambon, 75001 Paris, France (office). *E-mail:* contact@ccomptes.fr (office). *Website:* www.ccomptes.fr (office).

SEGUY, Georges; French trade union official; *Honorary President, Institut CGT d'Histoire Sociale;* b. 16 March 1927, Toulouse; s. of André Seguy and Gabrielle Monfouga; m. Cécile Sédeillan 1949; two s. one d.; ed Armand-Leygues School, Toulouse; apprentice typographer 1942; mem. French CP 1942–, mem. Cen. Cttee 1954–, Political Bureau 1956–82; arrested by Gestapo and deported to Mauthausen Concentration Camp 1944; electrician, SNCF (French Railways) 1946; mem. Railway Workers' Union, Toulouse 1946–49; Sec. Fédération des cheminots CGT (Confédération Générale du Travail) 1949, Sec.-Gen. 1961–65; Sec. CGT 1965–67, Sec.-Gen. 1967–82; Hon. Pres. Institut CGT d'Histoire Sociale 1982–; mem. Exec. Cttee Fédération syndicale mondiale 1970–83; Officier, Légion d'honneur, Order of the October Revolution 1982. *Publications:* Le mai de la CGT 1972, Lutter (autobiog.) 1975, Le 1er Mai les 100 printemps 1989, la Grève 1993. *Leisure interests:* shooting, fishing. *Address:* Institut CGT d'histoire sociale, 263 rue de Paris, 93516

Montreuil Cedex, France (office). *Telephone:* 1-48-18-84-90 (office). *Fax:* 1-48-18-84-52 (office). *E-mail:* ihs@cgt.fr (office). *Website:* www.ihs.cgt.fr (office).

SEHGAL, Amar Nath, MA; Indian sculptor and painter; b. 5 Feb. 1922, Campbellpur, West Pakistan; s. of Ram Asra Mal and Parmeshwari Devi; m. Shukla Dhawan 1954; two s.; ed Punjab Univ., Govt Coll., Lahore and New York Univ.; one-man exhbn New York 1950–51, Paris 1952, East Africa and India; Hon. Art Consultant to Ministry of Community Devt, Govt of India 1955–66; organized sculpture exhbns in Belgrade 1964, Musée d'Art Moderne, Paris 1965, Pauls-kirche, Frankfurt 1965, Haus am Lutzoplatz West Berlin 1966, Musées Royaux D'Art et Histoire, Brussels 1966, Musée Etat Luxembourg 1966, Wiener Secession, Vienna 1966, Flemish Acad. Arts 1967, Tokyo Int. Fair 1973, etc.; retrospective exhbn Nat. Gallery of Modern Art, New Delhi 1972, City Hall, Ottawa 1975, Aerogolf, Luxembourg 1975, India House, New York 1976, Rathaus, Fransheim, FRG 1977, Frankfurt Airport 1977, Neustadt 1978, Brenners Park, Baden-Baden 1979, Luxembourg 1980; exhbns, Dubai, Abu Dhabi 1980, Jeddah 1981, Chaux de Fond (Switzerland) 1982, Cercle Munster, Luxembourg 1987, Berne 1988, New York 1991, London 1991, New Delhi 1992, Indian Int. Centre 2005; participated in Sculpture Biennale, Musée Rodin, Paris 1966 and UNESCO Conf. on role of art in contemporary soc. 1974; org. Int. Children's Art Workshop UNESCO, Paris 1979; est. The Creative Fund, charitable org.; Fellow, Lalit Kala Akad. 1992; Sculpture Award, Lalit Kala Acad. 1957, President's Award, Lalit Kala Acad. 1958 (donated to Prime Minister Nehru during Chinese invasion), UN Peace Medal 1985, Lalit Kala Acad. Lifetime Acievement Award 2004. *Major works:* Voice of Africa (Ghana) 1959, A Cricketer 1961, Mahatma Gandhi, Amritsar, To Space Unknown (bronze; Moscow) 1963; commissioned to decorate Vidyan Bhawan (India's Int. Conferences Bldg) with bronze sculptural mural depicting rural life of India; bronze work Conquest of the Moon, White House Collection 1969; Anguished Cries (bronze) monument, W Berlin 1971; Gandhi monument, Luxembourg 1971; Monument to Aviation, New Delhi Airport, 1972; Rising Spirit, White House Collection 1978; The Crushing Burden, inaugurated 2nd World Population Conf., Mexico 1984; Victims of Torture, designed for UN; monument to Freedom Fighters of Namibia, Vienna 1986; Bust of Sam Nujoma, Nat. Gallery of Modern Art, New Delhi 1993; Int. Year of Peace sculpture, Head with Horns 1986; Captive, inaugurated at UN Conf. on sanctions against South Africa, Paris 1986; Nari, monument to Women, Int. Women's Day 1986; Flute Player (gift of children of India to UNICEF) 1986; monument to Nehru 1989; exhbn of gold sculptures Luxembourg 1990, The Captive, Palace of Human Rights, Geneva 1999 and Museum of Robben Island, SA 2001; exhbn based on Ramayana and Mahabharata epics 2004; Aiming for Excellence, monumental sculpture, Delhi; works in Jerusalem, Vienna, Paris, West Berlin, Antwerp, Luxembourg, Connecticut, New Delhi. *Film:* film on life and work sponsored by UNESCO Int. Fund for the Promotion of Culture, with music by Yehudi Menuhin and Ravi Shankar. *Television appearance in:* films on life and works 1980, 1990, 2001, 2003. *Publications:* Arts and Aesthetics, Organising Exhibitions in Rural Areas, Der Innere Rhythmus (poems) 1975, Folio of Graphics 1981; folios of graphics with poetry in English, French, Arabic 1981–84, Folio on Ganesha 1991, Lonesome Journey, A Collection of Poems 1996, Awaiting a New Dawn 1997. *Leisure interests:* writing poetry, photography, cooking. *Address:* J-23 Jangpura Extension, New Delhi 110014, India; The Creative Fund, 1 Montée de Clausen, 1343 Luxembourg. *Telephone:* (11) 4319206 (India); (352) 47-02-20 (Luxembourg).

SEIDELMAN, Susan, MFA; American film director; b. 11 Dec. 1952, nr Philadelphia, Pa; ed Drexel Univ. and New York Univ. Film School; directing debut with And You Act Like One Too (Student Acad. Award, Acad. of Motion Picture Arts and Sciences); then Dir Deficit (short film funded by American Film Inst.) and Yours Truly, Andrea G. Stern, The Dutch Master; Hon. PhD (Drexel); Mary Pickford Award for Best Female Dir 2002. *Films:* Smithereens (dir, producer, co-scriptwriter) 1982, Desperately Seeking Susan 1985, Making Mr Right 1987, Cookie 1989, She-Devil 1989, Confessions of a Suburban Girl 1992, Dutch Master 1994, Tales of Erotica 1996, Gaudi Afternoon 2001, The Boynton Beach Club 2005. *Television:* The Barefoot Executive 1995, Sex and The City (pilot episode) 1998, A Cooler Climate 1999, Now and Again (series) 1999, Power and Beauty 2002, The Ranch 2004, The Electric Company 2009. *Leisure interest:* travel. *Address:* c/o Michael Shedler, 350 5th Avenue, New York, NY 10118 (office); c/o Gary Pearl Pictures, 10956 Weyburn Avenue, Suite 200, Los Angeles, CA 90024, USA (office). *E-mail:* stonehedge185@aol.com (office).

SEIDENBERG, Ivan G., BA, MBA; American telecommunications industry executive; *Chairman and CEO, Verizon Communications Inc.;* b. 1946; m. Phyllis Seidenberg; two c.; ed City Univ. of NY, Pace Univ.; began career in communications as cable splicer's asst 1965; sr exec. positions at AT&T; fmr govt affairs dir Bell Atlantic; mem. Bd of Dirs NYNEX Inc. 1991–97, CEO (oversaw merger between NYNEX and Bell Atlantic 1997) –1997; CEO Bell Atlantic (oversaw merger between Bell Atlantic and GTE 1999) 1997–99; co-f. Verizon Wireless (cr. from merger of wireless assets of Bell Atlantic, GTE and Vodafone Airtouch) 1999, Co-CEO 1999–2002, Pres. and CEO Verizon Communications Inc. 2002–03, Chair. and CEO 2004–; mem. Bd of Dirs Honeywell, Museum of TV and Radio, Viacom Inc., Verizon Foundation, Wyeth (pharmaceuticals co.); Dir. Pace Univ. The Hall of Science. *Address:* Verizon Communications Inc., 140 West Street, New York, NY 10007, USA (office). *Telephone:* (212) 395-2121 (office). *Fax:* (212) 571-1897 (office). *E-mail:* info@verizon.com (office). *Website:* www.verizon.com (office).

SEIDMAN, L(ewis) William, AB, LLB, MBA; American fmr government official, publisher, television broadcaster and consultant; b. 29 April 1921, Grand Rapids, Mich.; s. of Frank Seidman and Esther Lubetsky; m. Sarah Berry 1944; one s. five d.; ed Dartmouth Coll., Harvard Univ. and Univ. of Mich.; army service 1942–46; mem. Mich. Bar 1949, DC Bar 1977; Special Asst for Financial Affairs to Gov. of Mich. 1963–66; Nat. Man. Partner, Seidman & Seidman (certified public accountants) New York 1969–74; Asst for Econ. Affairs to Pres. Gerald Ford 1974–77; Dir Phelps Dodge Corpn New York 1977–82, Vice-Chair. 1980–82; Dean, Coll. of Business Admin. Ariz. State Univ. 1982–85; Chair. Fed. Deposit Insurance Corpn (FDIC) 1985–91; mem. Bd of Dirs Fed. Reserve Bank, Chicago, Detroit Br. 1966–70, Chair. 1970; Co-Chair. White House Conf. on Productivity 1983–84; Chair. Resolution Trust Corpn 1989–91; Chief Commentator CNBC-TV 1991–; Publr Bank Director (magazine); mem. Bd of Dirs Pharmaceutical Resources Inc. 2004–, Clark Inc 1998–, Fiserv Inc 1992–, InteliData Techs Corpn, LML Payment Systems Inc; Bronze Star Medal. *Publications:* Full Faith and Credit 1993. *Address:* 825 Audubon Drive, Bradenton, FL 34209 (home); CNBC, 8th Floor, 1025 Connecticut Avenue, NW, Washington, DC 20036, USA (office). *Telephone:* (202) 530-0910 (office). *Fax:* (202) 822-9551 (office). *E-mail:* lws1025@aol.com (office).

SEIERSTAD, Åsne; Norwegian journalist and writer; b. 1970, Oslo; ed Univ. of Oslo; staff, ITAR-TASS news agency, Moscow; covered wars in Chechnya, Kosovo, Afghanistan, Iraq for several Scandinavian newspapers 1994–2004; correspondent, Norwegian television news 1998–2000; award for television reporting from Kosovo, Chechnya and Afghanistan; Journalist of the Year, Norway 2003; EMMA Award, London 2004; Bookseller's Prize, Paris, France 2004. *Publications:* non-fiction: With Their Backs to the World 2000, The Bookseller of Kabul 2002, A Hundred and One Days: A Baghdad Journal 2004, The Angel of Grozny: Inside Chechnya 2008. *Leisure interests:* skiing, nature. *Address:* c/o Virago Press, Brettenham House, Lancaster Place, London, WC2E 7EN, England (office); Tidemands gt. 20, 0260 Oslo, Norway (home). *E-mail:* aaseie@frisurf.no (home). *Website:* www.virago.co.uk (office).

SEIKE, Tomio; Japanese artist and photographer; b. 13 July 1943, Tokyo; m. Junko Seike; ed Sapporo Jr Coll., Japan Photographic Acad.; asst photographer, Japan 1970–74; moved to England 1974; freelance photographer, Tokyo. *Publications include:* Portrait of Zoe, Paris, Waterscape 2003. *Address:* c/o Hamiltons Gallery, 13 Carlos Place, London, W1 2EU, England (office). *Telephone:* (20) 7499-9494 (office). *Fax:* (20) 7629-9919 (office). *E-mail:* info@hamiltonsgallery.com (office). *Website:* www.hamiltonsgallery.com (office).

SEILLIÈRE de LABORDE, Ernest-Antoine; French business executive and fmr civil servant; *President, Business Europe;* b. 20 Dec. 1937, Neuilly-sur-Seine; s. of Jean Seillière de Laborde and Renée de Wendel; m. Antoinette Barbey 1971; two s. three d.; ed Ladycross Coll., Lycée Janson-de-Sailly, Faculty of Law, Paris, Nat. School of Admin.; attaché High Comm. of Algeria 1962; with Ministry of Information 1963, Sec. for Foreign Affairs 1966, mem. French del. at negotiations for EEC, Brussels and Gen. Agreement on Tariffs and Trade, Geneva 1966–69; Adviser on Foreign Affairs 1969, Adviser to the Prime Minister 1969–72, Tech. Adviser to Minister for Foreign Affairs 1972–73; Minister of Armed Forces 1973–74; lecturer Centre for Int. Affairs, Harvard Univ. 1975; Jt Dir-Gen. of Industrial Politics Marine-Wendel 1976, Pres. 1992–2002, Pres. Wendel Investissement 2002– (following merger of CGIP and Marine Wendel); Gen. Dir, Admin. CGIP 1978–87, Pres., Dir-Gen. 1987–2002; Vice-Pres. Carnaud SA (later CMB Packaging) 1984–91; Vice-Chair. Bd Cap Gemini 2000–; Vice-Pres. Fed. of Mechanical Industries 1985; fmrly Vice-Pres. Nat. Council of French Employers (CNPF), Pres. 1997–2005; Pres. MEDEF (French Business Confed.) 1997–2005; Pres. Business Europe (European business lobby group fmrly known as UNICE) 2005–; currently Chair. Bd of Dirs Legrand Holding, Supervisory Bd Oranje-Nassau Groep BV; mem. Supervisory Bd Editis Holding, Peugeot SA, Hermès Int; Officier, Légion d'honneur, Ordre nat. du Mérite. *Address:* Business Europe, avenue de Cortenbergh 168, 1000 Brussels, Belgium (office); Wendel Investissement, 89 rue Taitbout, 75009 Paris, France. *Telephone:* (2) 237-65-11 (Belgium) (office); 1-42-85-30-00 (France) (office). *Fax:* (2) 231-14-45 (Belgium) (office); 1-42-80-68-67 (France) (office). *E-mail:* main@businesseurope.eu (office). *Website:* www.businesseurope.eu (office); www.wendel-investissement.com (office).

SEINFELD, Jerome (Jerry); American comedian; b. 29 April 1955, Brooklyn; s. of Kal Seinfeld and Betty Seinfeld; m. Jessica Sklar 1999; three c.; ed Queens Coll., New York; fmrly salesman; stand-up comedian 1976–; joke-writer Benson (TV series) 1980; cr. (with Larry David) Seinfeld Chronicles (later Seinfeld) 1989, actor Seinfeld (TV series) 1989–97, also co-writer, producer; Emmy Award Outstanding Comedy Series (for Seinfeld) 1993; American Comedy Award 1988, 1992. *Film:* A Uniform Used to Mean Something 2004, Hindsight Is 20/20 2004, Bee Movie (voice, writer and producer) 2007. *Television includes:* The Ratings Game (film) 1984, I'm Telling You for the Last Time 1998. *Publications:* Seinlanguage 1993, Halloween (juvenile) 2002. *Leisure interests:* Zen, yoga. *Address:* c/o Creative Artists Agency, 2000 Avenue of the Stars, Los Angeles, CA 90067, USA.

SEINO, Satoshi; Japanese transport industry executive; *President and CEO, East Japan Railway Company;* b. 1947; joined Japanese Nat. Railways 1970; Vice-Pres. East Japan Railway Co. 2002–06, Pres. and CEO 2006–. *Address:* East Japan Railway Co., 2-2, Yoyogi 2-chome, Shibuya-ku, Tokyo 151-8578, Japan (office). *Telephone:* (3) 5334-1310 (office); (3) 5334-1151 (office). *Fax:* (3) 5334-1297 (office); (3) 5334-1110 (office). *E-mail:* ir@jreast.co.jp (office); bond@jreast.co.jp (office); info@jreast.co.jp (office). *Website:* www.jreast.co.jp (office).

SEIP, Anne-Lise, DPhil; Norwegian historian and academic; *Professor of Modern History, University of Oslo;* b. 6 Nov. 1933, Bergen; d. of Edvin Thomassen and Birgit Thomassen; m. Jens Arup Seip 1960 (died 1992); one s. one d.; ed Univ. of Oslo; Sr Lecturer Inst. of Criminology and Penal Law, Univ. of Oslo 1974–75, Dept of History 1975–85, Prof. of Modern History 1985–; mem. Norwegian Acad. of Science, Det kongelige danske videnskabernes selskab. *Publications include:* Videnskap og virkelighet T.H. Asehehoug 1974,

Eilert Sundt. 1983, Sosialhjelpstaten blir til 1984, Veier til velferdsstaten 1994, Norges historie, Vol.8 1830–70 1997, Demringstid. Johan Sebastian Welhaven og nasjonen 2007; numerous articles. *Leisure interests:* books, music, gardening. *Address:* Gamle Drammensvei 144, 1363 Høvik (home); Department of History, University of Oslo, PO Box 1008, Blindern, 0315 Oslo, Norway (office). *Telephone:* 22-85-68-78 (office); 67-53-40-39 (home). *E-mail:* a.l.seip@hi.uio.no (office). *Website:* www.hf.uio.no/hi/english (office).

SEIPP, Walter, DJur; German banker and business executive; b. 13 Dec. 1925, Langen; m. 1954; two s.; ed Univ. of Frankfurt am Main; Jr Barrister 1950–53; with Deutsche Bank AG 1951–74 (Exec. Vice-Pres. 1970–74); mem. Man. Bd, Westdeutsche Landesbank Girozentrale 1974–77, Vice-Chair. 1978–81; Chair. Man. Bd, Commerzbank AG 1981–91, fmr Chair. Supervisory Bd, now Hon. Chair.; Chair. Supervisory Bd, Berliner Commerzbank AG, Rheinische Hypothekenbank AG, Frankfurt, Essen; Chair. Admin. Bd, Commerzbank Int. SA, Luxembourg, Commerzbank (Schweiz) AG, Zürich; Chair. Supervisory Bd Commerz Int. Capital Man. GmbH, Frankfurt; Chair. Bd of Dirs., Commerzbank Capital Markets Corpn, NY, Commerz-Securities (Japan) Co. Ltd, Commerzbank, SE Asia Ltd, Singapore; mem. Bd of Dirs, Int. Monetary Conf., Wash. (Pres. 1987–88); mem. Supervisory Bd, Bayer AG, Leverkusen, Daimler Benz AG, Stuttgart, Deutsche Shell AG, Hamburg, Vereinigte Industrie-Unternehmungen AG, Bonn, Linde AG Wiesbaden, Allianz Versicherungs AG, Munich, Hochtief AG, Essen, MAN AG, Munich, Thyssen AG, Duisburg; mem. Bd of Man. Dirs. Bundesverband deutscher Banken eV, Cologne; mem. advisory cttee of three cos.

SEITERS, Rudolf; German politician; *President, German Red Cross;* b. 13 Oct. 1937, Osnabrück; s. of Adolf Seiters and Josefine Gördel; m. Brigitte Kolata; three c.; ed Univ. of Münster; qualified as lawyer; joined Junge Union and CDU 1958, Regional Chair. Junge Union, Osnabrück-Emsland 1963–65, Chair. CDU Land Asscn Hanover 1965–68, mem. Junge Union Fed. Exec. Cttee 1967–71, Sr Chair. CDU Land Asscn Lower Saxony 1968–70; Head Econ. and Housing Dept, Office of Regierungspräsident (Regional Gov.), Osnabrück 1967–69; mem. Deutscher Bundestag 1969–; mem. CDU Fed. Exec. Cttee 1971–73; Parl. Party Man. CDU/Christian Social Union (CSU) Parl. Party in Bundestag 1971–76, Sr Parl. Man. 1984–89; Parl. Party Man. 1982–84; Fed. Minister for Special Tasks and Head of Fed. Chancellery 1989–91, of the Interior 1991–93; Deputy Chair. CDU/CSU in Bundestag 1994–; Vice-Pres. Bundestag 1998–2002; Pres. German Red Cross 2003–; Hon. Dr rer. pol; Grosses Bundesverdienstkreuz mit Stern 1995, Grosses Silbernes Ehrenzeichen (Austria) 1995, Officier, Légion d'honneur 1996. *Publications:* Aussenpolitik im 21. Jahrhundert 1996, In der Spur Bleiben 2005. *Address:* Deutschen Roten Kreuzes Generalsekretariat, Carstenstr. 58, 12205 Berlin (office); Spiekerooger Strasse 6, 26871 Papenburg, Germany. *Telephone:* (30) 85404277 (office). *Website:* www.drk.de (office).

SEITZ, John N., BSc; American geologist and petroleum industry executive; *Vice Chairman, Endeavour International Corporation;* ed Univ. of Pittsburgh, Rensselaer Polytechnic Inst. and Univ. of Pennsylvania; Sr Exploration Geologist, Anadarko Petroleum Corpn 1977–82, Chief Geologist 1982–83, Gen. Man. 1983–89, Vice-Pres. of Exploration and Production 1989–95, Sr Vice-Pres. of Exploration 1995–97, Exec. Vice-Pres. of Exploration and Production 1997–99, mem. Bd of Dirs 1997–2003, Pres. and COO 1999–, then CEO –2003; f. North Sea Oil Ventures 2003, Co-CEO Endeavour International (cr. after merger of North Sea Oil Ventures and Continental Southern Resources), Houston Tex 2004, now Vice Chair.; mem. Bd of Dirs Input/Output Inc., Elk Resources, Inc.; mem. American Asscn of Petroleum Geologists, Geological Soc. of America, American Inst. of Professional Geologists, Houston Geological Soc., Soc. of Petroleum Engineers; Trustee American Geological Inst. Foundation; mem. Advisory Bd Spindletop. *Address:* Endeavour International Corporation, 1001 Fannis, Suite 1600, Houston, TX 77002, USA (office). *Telephone:* (713) 307-8700 (office). *Website:* www.endeavourcorp.com (office).

SEITZ, Konrad, MA, DPhil; German diplomatist and writer; b. 18 Jan. 1934, Munich; m. Eva Kautz 1965; Prof. of Classics, Univs of Marburg and Munich 1956–64; entered Foreign Office 1965; served in New Delhi 1968–72, UN Mission, New York 1972–75; main speech writer for Minister of Foreign Affairs 1975; Head, Policy Planning Staff, Foreign Office 1980–87; Amb. to India 1987–90; Co-Chair. Comm. Economy 2000, Baden-Württemberg 1992–93; Amb. to Italy 1992–95, to China 1995–99 (retd); Grosses Bundesverdienstkreuz 1996, Baden-Württemberg Medal of Honour 1998. *Publications:* The Japanese-American Challenge: Germany's Hi-tech Industries Fight for Survival 1990, The Aimless Elites – Are the Germans Losing the Future? (with others), Europa—una Colonia Tecnológica? 1995, Race into the 21st Century – The Future of Europe Between America and Africa 1998, China—a World Power Comes Back 2000; contribs to foreign and econ. journals and newspapers. *Leisure interests:* history of ideas, literature, art, collecting Indian miniature paintings. *Address:* Dahlienweg 4, 53343 Wachtberg-Pech, Germany (home). *Telephone:* (228) 327811 (home). *Fax:* (228) 9325154 (home). *E-mail:* k.seitz@freenet.de.

SEITZ, Hon. Raymond George Hardenbergh; American diplomatist and business executive; *Chairman, Sun-Times Media Group Inc.;* b. 8 Dec. 1940, Honolulu, Hawaii; m. Caroline Gordon Richardson; two s. one d.; ed Yale Univ.; joined Foreign Service 1966, served as Political Officer in Montreal, Political Officer, Embassy in Nairobi, also Vice-Consul, Seychelles 1968–70; Prin. Officer, Bukavu, Zaire 1970–72; served on Secretariat Staff, Washington, DC 1972 then Dir of Staff; Special Asst to Dir-Gen. Foreign Service 1974; Political Officer, London 1975–79; Deputy Exec. Sec., Dept of State 1979–81, Sr Deputy Asst Sec. for Public Affairs 1981–82, Exec. Asst to Sec. Shultz 1982–84; Minister, Embassy in London 1984–89; Asst Sec. of State for European and Canadian Affairs 1989–91; Amb. to UK 1991–94; Vice-Chair.

Lehman Bros. Int. (Europe) (now Lehman Bros Europe Ltd) 1995–2003; currently Chair. Sun-Times Media Group Inc., Chicago; mem. Bd of Dirs The Chubb Corpn, PCCW Ltd; fmr mem. Bd of Dirs Cable and Wireless 1995, BA 1995, Rio Tinto 1996, Pacific Century CyberWorks (PCCW) 1997, Hollinger Int.; Contributing Ed. Conde Nast Traveller magazine (UK) 2004–; Gov. Ditchley Foundation; Hon. DUniv (Herriot-Watt) 1994; Dr hc (Open Univ.) 1997. *Publication:* Over Here 2001. *Address:* Sun-Times Media Group Inc., 350 North Orleans, Chicago, IL 60654, USA (office). *Telephone:* (312) 321-2299 (office). *Fax:* (312) 321-6426 (office). *Website:* www.thesuntimesgroup.com (office).

SEJDIU, Fatmir, PhD; Kosovo politician, academic and head of state; *President;* b. 23 Oct. 1951, Podujeva; m.; three c.; ed Univ. of Priština; Prof. of Law, Univ. of Priština; mem. Ass. of Kosovo –2006, fmr mem. Cttee for Rules and Procedures of Ass., Cttee for Int. Cooperation and EU Integration; Pres. of Kosovo 2006–; mem. and fmr Chair., Democratic League of Kosovo; Dr hc (Tirana). *Publication:* Constitutional Framework of Kosovo (co-author) 2001, The History of State and Law (co-author) 2000, 2005, Agrarian Politics as an Instrument of National Repression (monograph) 2000, Glossary of Parliamentary and Legal Terms (co-author) 2005. *Address:* Office of the President, 10000 Prishtina, Rruga Nëna Terezë, Kosovo (office). *Telephone:* (38) 213222 (office). *Fax:* (38) 211651 (office). *E-mail:* beqiri@president-ksgov.net (office). *Website:* www.president-ksgov.net (office).

SEJIMA, Kazuyo, MArch; Japanese architect; *Principal, SANAA / Kazuyo Sejima & Ryue Nishizawa Associates;* b. 1956, Ibaraki Pref.; ed Japan Women's Univ.; worked for Toyo Ito Architect & Assocs 1981–87; f. Kazuyo Sejima & Assocs 1987; Founder and Prin. (with Ryue Nishizawa) SANAA Ltd/ Kazuyo Sejima & Ryue Nishizawa Assocs 1995–; teacher, Dept of Architecture, Univ. of Ill., USA; Winner Competition for MCH House 1990, Second Prize, Nasunogahara Harmony Hall Design Competition 1991, Second Prize, GID Competition 1992, Second Prize, Commercial Space Design Award 1992, Young Architect of the Year, Japan Inst. of Architects 1992, Grand Prize, Commercial Space Design 1994, Architect of the Year 1994, Vincenzo Scamozzi Architecture Award 2003, Rolf Schock Prize in Visual Arts (with Ryue Nishizawa) 2005. *Architectural works include:* MCH House (Kajima Prize, SD Review) 1990, Platform One Katsuura, Platform Two Yamanashi, Saishunkan Seiyaku Women's Dormitory, Pachinko Parlors I, II & III, Y-House Katsuura, Chino Villa in the Forest, Police Box at Chofu Station, N-House Kumamoto, Yokohama Int. Port Terminal, Apartment Bldg in Gifu, Expo Tokyo 96, Oogaki Multi Media Studio. *Exhibitions include:* Nat. Panasonic Gallery, Tokyo 1989, Artpolis, Kumamoto 1992, Sezon Museum 1993, MA Gallery, Tokyo 1993, Nat. Museum of Modern Art, Seoul, Korea 1994. *Address:* SANAA Ltd/Kazuyo Sejima, Ryue Nishizawa & Associates, 7-A Shinagawa-Soko, 2–2–35 Higashi-Shinagawa, Shinagawa-ku, 140 Tokyo, Japan (office). *Telephone:* (3) 34501757 (office). *E-mail:* sanaa@sanaa.co.jp (office).

SEKERAMAYI, Sydney Tigere, MB, ChB, DTM; Zimbabwean politician; *Minister of State for National Security;* b. 30 March 1944; m.; fmr govt. positions include Minister for Lands and Resettlement, Minister of State Security, Energy Minister; Intelligence Dir; Minister of Defence 2001–; mem. Parl. (Zanu-PF) for Marondera E 2005–08; Senator from Marondera-Hwedza 2008–09; Minister of State for Nat. Security 2009–. *Address:* Ministry of National Security, Chaminuka Building, POB 2278, Harare, Zimbabwe (office). *Telephone:* (4) 700501 (office). *Fax:* (4) 732660 (office).

SEKERINSKA, Radmilla, BSc, MA; Macedonian politician; *Chairperson, National Council for European Integration;* b. 10 June 1972, Skopje; s. of Aleksandar Sekerinski and Jelena Sekerinska; m. Bozidar Jankovski; ed Faculty of Electrical Eng, Skopje Univ., Fletcher School of Law and Diplomacy, Tufts Univ., USA; fmr Public Relations Asst, Open Soc. Inst., Asst at Faculty of Electrical Eng, Skopje Univ.; started political career with Social Democratic Youth of Macedonia 1992, Pres. 1995; mem. Skopje City Council 1996–98; Deputy Coordinator, Spokesperson and mem. Cen. Bd Social Democratic Alliance of Macedonia 1999–, Vice-Chair., Chair. 2006–08; mem. Parl. 1998–2002, 2006–, Ass. Del. to Inter-Parl. Union, Ass. Group for Cooperation with the European Parl. 1998–2002; Deputy Prime Minister, with responsibility for European Integration 2002–06; Pres. Nat. Council for European Integration 2007–; Young Global Leader, World Econ. Forum 2004. *Publications include:* scientific articles. *Address:* Social Democratic Alliance of Macedonia (Socijaldemokratski Sojuz na Makedonija, SDSM), 1000 Skopje, Bihačka 8, Republic of Macedonia (office). *Telephone:* (2) 3293101 (office). *Fax:* (2) 3293111 (office). *E-mail:* president@sdsm.org.mk (office). *Website:* www.sdsm.org.mk (office).

SEKIGUCHI, Ken-Ichi; Japanese insurance industry executive; *Chairman, Meiji Yasuda Life Insurance Company;* Gen. Man. Aomori Br. Meiji Yasuda Life Insurance Co. 1994–96, Gen. Man. Int. Investment Dept, Meiji Yasuda Life Insurance Co. 1996–97, Gen. Man. Global Investment Dept 1997–2000, Gen. Man. Financial Planning Dept 2000–03, later Man. Dir, mem. Bd of Dirs 1999–, Chair. 2005–, mem. Nominating Cttee, Compensation Cttee, Chief Exec. New Market Devt; mem. Bd Dirs UBS Wealth Man., USA (fmrly Paine Webber Group Inc.) 1999–. *Address:* Meiji Yasuda Life Insurance Co., 1-1, Marunouchi 2-chome, Chiyoda-ku, Tokyo 100-0005, Japan (office). *Telephone:* (3) 3283-8293 (office). *Fax:* (3) 3215-8123 (office). *E-mail:* info@meijiyasuda.co .jp (office). *Website:* www.meijiyasuda.co.jp (office).

SEKIYA, Katsutsugu; Japanese politician; ed Chuo Univ., Univ. of British Columbia, Canada; joined Japan Airlines 1963; sec. to a mem. of House of Reps 1966; mem. LDP; mem. for Ehime, House of Reps 1976–2007, Chair. House of Reps Transport Cttee; fmr Minister of Posts and Telecommunications; Minister of Construction 1998–99; Dir-Gen. Nat. Land Agency 1999. *Address:*

c/o Liberal-Democratic Party—LDP (Jiyu-Minshuto) 1-11-23, Nagata-cho, Chiyoda-ku, Tokyo 100-8910, Japan.

SEKIZAWA, Tadashi, BEng; Japanese business executive; *Senior Executive Adviser, Fujitsu Ltd;* b. 6 Nov. 1931, Tokyo; m. Misako Sekizawa; two s.; ed Tokyo Univ.; joined Fujitsu Ltd 1954, Gen. Man. Switching Systems Group 1982–84, Bd Dir 1984, Man. Dir 1986–88, Exec. Dir 1988–90, apptd Pres. and Rep. Dir 1990, later Chair., currently Sr Exec. Adviser; Vice-Chair. Communication Industry Asscn of Japan 1990–98, apptd Chair. 1998, Japan Electronic Industry Devt Asscn 1990. *Leisure interests:* literature, travel, motoring. *Address:* Fujitsu Ltd, Shiodome City Center, 1-5-2, Higashi-Shimbashi, Minato-ku, Tokyo 105-7123, Japan (office). *Telephone:* (3) 6252-2220 (office). *Fax:* (3) 6252-2783 (office). *Website:* www.fujitsu.com (office).

ŠEKS, Vladimir, LLB; Croatian politician; b. 1 Jan. 1943, Osijek; m. Anica Resler-Šeks; one s. one d.; ed Univ. of Zagreb; trainee, Municipal Public Prosecutors Office, Vinkovci 1967–69; Deputy Municipal Public Prosecutor, Vinkovci 1970; Municipal Court Judge, Osijek 1970–71; Deputy Regional Public Prosecutor, Osijek 1971; barrister in prt. law firm 1972–81; sentenced to seven-month prison term for conspiracy against the state 1981; mem. Croatian Democratic Union (Hrvatska demokratska zajednica—HDZ), Vice-Chair. 1989–91, 1995–99, Chair. Rep. Group 1995, Acting Chair. Jan.–April 2000, Chair. Parl. Group 2000, Deputy Chair. Cen. Cttee 2002–03; mem. Sabor (Parl.) 1990–, Deputy Pres. 1992–2000, Pres. 2003–08; Public Prosecutor of Croatia 1992; Chair. State Amnesty Comm. 1996–2000; Chair. Cttee on Constitutional Affairs 1990–92, Deputy Chair. 1995–99; mem. Defence and Nat. Security Council 1995–99, Council for Strategic Decisions of the Pres. 1995–99; Founder and Co-chair. Yugoslav Helsinki Cttee 1987–; mem. Amnesty Int.; Grand Order of King Dmitar Zvonimir, Order of Ante Starčević, Order of Stjepan Radić, Order of the Croatian Trefoil, Vukovar Medal. *Publications:* Expression of Opinion Treated as Offence, Contemplations on the Freedom of Conscience, Dangerous Times, Reminiscences from Prison; over 20 professional papers on law and politics. *Address:* Hrvatska demokratska zajednica, trg Žrtava fašizma 4, 10000 Zagreb, Croatia (office). *Telephone:* (1) 4553000 (office). *Fax:* (1) 4552600 (office). *E-mail:* hdz@hdz.hr (office). *Website:* www.hdz.hr (office).

SELA, Michael, PhD; Israeli immunologist, chemist and academic; *W. Garfield Weston Professor of Immunology, Weizmann Institute of Science;* b. 6 March 1924, Tomaszow, Poland; s. of Jakob Salomonowicz and Roza Salomonowicz; m. 1st Margalit Liebman 1948 (died 1975); two d.; m. 2nd Sara Kika 1976; one d.; ed Hebrew Univ., Jerusalem and Geneva Univ.; joined Weizmann Inst. of Science 1950, Head Dept of Chemical Immunology 1963–75, Vice-Pres. 1970–71, Dean Faculty of Biology 1970–73, mem. Bd of Govs 1970–, Pres. 1975–85, Deputy Chair. 1985–; W. Garfield Weston Prof. of Immunology 1966–; Visiting Scientist, NIH, Bethesda 1956–57, 1960–61; Visiting Prof. Molecular Biology, Univ. of Calif., Berkeley 1967–68; Visiting Prof., Dept of Medicine, Tufts Univ. School of Medicine, Boston 1986–87; Inst. Prof. 1985; Fogarty Scholar-in-Residence, Fogarty Int. Center, Bethesda, Md 1973–74; mem. WHO Expert Advisory Panel of Immunology 1962–; Chair. Council, European Molecular Biology Org. 1975–79; Pres. Int. Union Immunological Socs. 1977–80; Chair. Scientific Advisory Cttee European Molecular Biology Lab. Heidelberg 1978–81; WHO Advisory Cttee on Medical Research 1979–82, WHO Special Programme for Research and Training in Tropical Diseases 1979–81; mem. Council Paul Ehrlich Foundation (Frankfurt) 1980–97; mem. Advisory Bd UCLAF, France 1980–92; Founding mem. Bd Dir Int. Foundation for Survival and Devt of Humanity, Moscow and Washington 1988–92; Nat. mem. Gen. Cttee Int. Council of Scientific Unions 1984–93; mem. Scientific Advisory Group of Experts, Programme for Vaccine Devt, WHO 1987–92; mem. Int. Guidance Panel, Israel Arts and Science Acad. 1987–; Vice-Pres. Asscn Franco-Israélienne pour Recherche Scientifique et Technologique 1992–98; mem. Exec. Bd Int. Council of Human Duties, Trieste 1995–; mem. other int. bodies; serves on many editorial bds., including Exec. Advisory Bd of Dictionary for Science and Tech. 1989–, Ed. Acad. of the Int. Journal of Molecular Medicine 1997, Int. Advisory Bd of Russian Journal of Immunology 2000, Int. Ed. Bd Reviews in Auto-immunity 2001, Cambridge Encyclopedia of the Life Sciences, Handbook of Biochemistry and Molecular Biology, Experimental and Clinical Immunogenetics, Receptor Biology Reviews, Encyclopedia of Human Biology, Encyclopedia of the Life Sciences; mem. Israel Acad. of Sciences and Humanities 1971, Pontifical Acad. of Sciences 1975, Deutsche Akad. der Naturforscher Leopoldina 1989; Foreign mem. Max-Planck Soc., Freiburg 1967, Russian Acad. of Sciences 1994, French Acad. of Sciences 1995; Foreign Assoc. NAS 1976, Italian Acad. of Sciences 1995, American Philosophical Soc. 1995; Fellow Polish Acad. of Arts and Sciences 1998; Hon. mem. American Soc. Biological Chemists 1968, American Asscn of Immunologists 1973, Scandinavian Soc. for Immunology 1971, Harvey Soc. 1972, French Soc. for Immunology 1979, Chilean Soc. for Immunology 1981, Romanian Acad. 1991, Romanian Acad. of Medical Sciences 1991, Romanian Soc. for Immunology; Foreign Hon. mem. American Acad. Arts and Sciences 1971; Commdr's Cross of Order of Merit Award, FRG 1986; Officier, Légion d'honneur, 1987; Caballero, Order of San Carlos (Colombia) 1997; Dr hc (Bordeaux II) 1985, (Nat. Autonomous Univ. of Mexico) 1985, (Tufts Univ.) 1989, Colby Coll. 1989, (Univ. Louis Pasteur) 1990, (Hebrew Univ. of Jerusalem) 1995, (Tel-Aviv) 1999, (Ben Gurion Univ. of the Negev 2001; awarded NIH Lectureship 1973; Israel Prize Natural Sciences 1959, Rothschild Prize for Chem. 1968, Otto Warburg Medal, German Soc. of Biological Chem. 1968, Emil von Behring Prize, Phillipps Univ. 1972, Gairdner Int. Award, Toronto 1980, Prize, Inst. de la Vie Fondation Electricité de France, Lille 1984, Prix Jaubert, Faculty of Science, Univ. of Geneva 1986, Interbrew-Baillet Latour Health Prize 1997, Karl Landsteiner Medal, Toronto 1986, Albert Einstein Gold Medal 1995, Harnak Medal, Max-Planck-Soc. 1996, Wolf Prize in Medicine 1998. *Publications:* over

800 in immunology, biochemistry and molecular biology; Ed. The Antigens (7 Vols published). *Address:* Weizmann Institute of Science, Rehovot, 76100 Israel. *Telephone:* 8-9466969; 8-9471132 (home). *Fax:* 8-9469713. *E-mail:* michael.sela@weizmann.ac.il (office). *Website:* www.weizmann.ac.il/immunology/SelaPub.html (office).

SELANGOR, HRH The Sultan of; Tuanku Sharafuddin Idris Shah Salahuddin Abdul Aziz Shah, DK, SPMS, SSIS, SPMJ; Malaysian; b. 24 Dec. 1945, Klang; s. of the late Sultan Salahuddin Abdul Aziz Shah and Raja Shaidatul Ihsan binti Tengku Badar Shah; m. 1st Raja Zarina binti Raja Zainul 1968 (divorced 1986); m. 2nd Lisa Davis (Puan Nur Lisa Abdullah) 1988 (divorced 1997); two d. one s.; ed Hale School, Perth, Australia and Langhurst Coll., Surrey, England; fmr Regent of Selangor, proclaimed ninth Sultan of Selangor on the death of his father Nov. 2001; held various admin. posts in state and fed. govt services, including Selangor State Secr., Dist Office and Royal Malaysian Police Dept, Kuala Lumpur 1968–; mem. The Conf. of Rulers, Malaysia; Pro-Chancellor Universiti Teknologi MARA 2000; Chancellor Universiti Putra Malaysia 2002; Chair. Semi-Professional Football Asscn; Chair. Bd of Trustees Yayasan Seni Selangor (Selangor Art Foundation), Galeri Shah Alam; Patron Malaysian branch of the Royal Asiatic Soc., Royal Selangor Club; circumnavigated the world on his yacht, S. Y. Jugra 1995–96; participated in Peking to Paris Challenge vintage car race 1997; Hon. Dr of Public Admin (Universiti Teknologi MARA) 2001; Hon. Life Pres. Selangor Football Asscn. *Website:* www.selangor.gov.my.

SELBORNE, 4th Earl, cr. 1882; **John Roundell Palmer,** KBE, FRS; British farmer; b. 24 March 1940; s. of the late Viscount Wolmer; m. Joanna van Antwerp James 1969; three s. one d.; ed Eton Coll., Christ Church, Oxford; Man. Dir Blackmoor Estate Ltd 1962–; Chair. Hops Marketing Bd 1978–82, Agricultural and Food Research Council 1983–89; Pres. Royal Agricultural Soc. of England 1987–88; Chair. Jt Nature Conservation Cttee 1991–97; Chair. House of Lords Select Cttee on Science and Tech. 1993–97; mem. Govt Panel on Sustainable Devt 1994–97; Chair. AMC 1994–2002, UK Chemical Stakeholder Forum 2000–; Dir Lloyds TSB Group 1995–; Chancellor Univ. of Southampton 1996–2006; Pres. Royal Geographical Soc. (with Inst. of British Geographers) 1997–2000; Vice-Pres. Royal Soc. for the Protection of Birds 1996–; elected Hereditary mem. House of Lords 1999–, Chair. Sub-cttee D (Agric. and Environment), House of Lords EU Select Cttee 1999–2003; Chair. Bd of Trustees, Royal Botanic Gardens, Kew 2003–; Hon. LLD (Bristol) 1988; Hon. DSc (Cranfield) 1991, (East Anglia) 1996, (Southampton) 1996, (Birmingham) 2000; Massey-Ferguson Nat. Award for Services to UK Agric. 1990. *Address:* Temple Manor, Selborne, Alton, Hants., GU34 3LR, England. *Telephone:* (1420) 473646.

SELBY, Philip; British composer; b. 6 Feb. 1948; s. of the late George Selby and Sarah Selby (née Knott); m. Rosanna Burrai 1974; one s.; ed Manor Park Grammar School, Nuneaton, Royal Northern Coll. of Music; composition studies with G. Petrassi, C. Camilleri and Karlheinz Stockhausen; appeared as guitar soloist, Birmingham Town Hall 1966, Royal Albert Hall, London 1970, All-India Radio and TV, Pakistani TV, Youth Palace, Tehran, Istanbul Univ.; debut as composer with first performance of From the Fountain of Youth (for guitar and chamber orchestra), Leamington 1975; mem. British Acad. of Composers and Songwriters, Inc. Soc. of Musicians, Performing Right Soc.; Chevalier, Ordre Souverain et Militaire de la Milice du Saint Sépulcre 1988. *Compositions include:* Suite for guitar 1965–67, Two Meditations for Piano 1972–74, Symphonic Dance for orchestra 1973, Ten Little Studies for Guitar Solo 1973–76, Fantasia for guitar 1974, Rhapsody for piano and orchestra 1975, Three Scottish Songs for voice and violin 1975, A Nature Meditation for violin and small orchestra, Guitar Concerto 1976–77, Suite for String Quartet 1977–78, Sonatina for piano 1978, Spirit of the Earth for flute 1978, Branch Touches Branch, pastorale 1979, Isa Upanishad (cantata sacra for double chorus and orchestra) 1979–87, Sonata for timpani 1980, Greek Suite for Oboe Solo 1981, Siddhartha (dance symphony) 1981–84, Logos for trumpet 1982, Ring Out Ye Bells (carol) 1988, Symphony of Sacred Images (for soprano and bass soli, double chorus and orchestra) 1986–92, Anthem for Gibraltar (unison voices and organ) 1994, Beatus Vir (motet) 1995, String Quartet No. 1 (Non Potho Reposare, Amore Coro) 1996–97, Autoritratto Vittorio Alfieri (for soprano, violin and guitar) 1998, Sonata Atma Brahma for Piano 1998–99, Fear No More the Heat of the Sun, madrigal 2001, Agape for solo violin 2001–02, Agape II for solo viola 2002, Eight Poems of J. G. Brown, song cycle 2005, Four American Portraits for speaking choir 2006, Ode to Earth and Sky (for double string orchestra) 2007–08. *Leisure interests:* reading, travel, the arts. *Address:* Hill Cottage, Via 1 Maggio 93, 00068 Rignano Flaminio, Rome, Italy. *Telephone:* (0761) 507945.

SELEBI, Jackie; South African police commissioner and international organization official; fmr Head African Nat. Congress (ANC) Youth Section whilst in exile; mem. ANC Exec. –1991; elected to Parl. 1994; Perm. Rep. to UN, Geneva 1995–98, fmr Chair. UN Human Rights Comm. 54th Session; fmr Chair. Anti-Landmine Conf., Oslo; Nat. Commr South African Police Service 2000–08; fmr Vice-Pres. (African Region) Interpol, Pres. 2004–08 (resgnd); fmr Chair. Justice, Crime Prevention and Security Cluster; appeared in Randburg Magistrates Court where he was charged with corruption 2008; Int. Human Rights Award 1997.

SELEŠ, Monica; American (born Yugoslav) professional tennis player; b. 2 Dec. 1973, Novi Sad, Yugoslavia (now Serbia and Montenegro); d. of the late Karolj Seleš and of Ester Seleš; moved to USA 1986; became US citizen March 1994; semi-finalist, French Open 1989; won French Open 1990, 1991, 1992; Virginia Slims Championships 1990, 1991, 1992; US Open 1991, 1992; Australian Open 1991, 1992, 1993, 1996; Canadian Open 1995, 1996; winner LA Open 1997, Canadian Open 1997, Tokyo Open 1997; quarter-finalist, Wimbledon Championships 1990; youngest number one ranked player in tennis history for women and men, at 17 years three months nine days – Martina Hingis (q.v.) now holds the record; off court for over two years after being stabbed by spectator during Hamburg quarter-final 1993; 59 WTA Tour titles, nine Grand Slam titles and US $14,891,762 in prize money; mem. winning US Fed. Cup team 1996, 1999, 2000; partner, the All-Star Café; played exhibition match Australia 2005; Ted Tinling Diamond Award 1990, Associated Press Athlete of the Year 1990–91, Tennis Magazine Comeback Player of the Year 1995, Flo Hyman Award 2000. *Publication:* Monica: From Fear to Victory 1996. *Leisure interests:* ice skating, horse riding, basketball, guitar, swimming, reading autobiographies. *Address:* c/o International Management Group, 1 Erieview Plaza, Cleveland, OH 44114, USA. *Telephone:* (216) 522-1200.

SELEZNEV, Gennadiy Nikolaevich; Russian politician; *Founder and Chairman, Rossiya;* b. 6 Nov. 1947, Serov, Sverdlovsk Region; m. Irina Borisovna Selezneva 1978; one d.; ed Leningrad Univ. (by correspondence); mem. CPSU 1970–91, CP of Russian Fed. 1992–; work in komsomol 1968–74; Ed.-in-Chief Smena 1974–80, Komsomolskaya Pravda 1980–88, Uchitelskaya Gazeta (newspaper for teachers) 1988–91; First Deputy Ed., Ed.-in-Chief, Pravda 1991–93, dismissed then re-elected 1993; Ed.-in-Chief Pravda Rossii 1995–96; mem. State Duma (Parl.) 1993–, Deputy Chair. 1995–96, Chair. 1996–2003, Deputy, State Duma 2003–07; Co-Chair. Interparl. Ass. of CIS; Chair. Parl. Union of Russia and Belarus 1997–2003; Founder, Chair. Rossiya (political movt) 2000–; expelled from CP 2002; mem. Security Council, Russian Fed. 1998–2003; Deputy Chair. Parl. Ass. of OSCE 1999–; Chair. Respublikanskiy Commercial Bank 2008–; Pres. Russian Equestrian Fed. 2005–; mem. Int. Acad. of Information Russian Acad. of Social Sciences; Hon. Prof. Inst. of Youth, Heilutsiang Univ.; Order of Friendship of Peoples 1984, Order for Service to the Fatherland, Class II, 2000 and other state awards. *Publications:* All Power to Law 1997, Law, Power and Politics: National and Local Levels 1998; numerous articles on the state. *Leisure interests:* reading, swimming, riding. *Address:* 56/4 str. Zemlyanov Val, 109994 Moscow, Russia. *Telephone:* (495) 915-65-53 (office). *Fax:* (495) 915-47-75 (office). *Website:* www.seleznev.org (office).

SELF, Colin Ernest, DFA; British artist; b. 17 July 1941, Rackheath; s. of Ernest Walter Self and Kathleen Augustine Self (née Bellamy); m. 1st Margaret Ann Murrell 1963; m. 2nd Jessica Prendergast 1978; one s. two d.; ed Norwich Art School, Slade School of Fine Art, London Univ.; Drawing Prize Biennale de Paris 1967, Giles Bequest Prize Bradford Biennale 1969, Tolly Cobbold Prize 1979. *Leisure interests:* nature study: in a constant perennial dreamy but acute way, un-academically, all music. *Address:* 31 St Andrew's Avenue, Thorpe, Norwich, Norfolk, NR7 0RG, England.

SELF, William (Will) Woodward, MA; British writer and cartoonist; *Columnist, The Independent;* b. 26 Sept. 1961, London; s. of Peter John Otter Self and Elaine Rosenbloom; m. 1st Katharine Sylvia Anthony Chancellor 1989 (divorced 1996); one s. one d.; m. 2nd Deborah Jane Orr 1997; two s.; ed Christ's Coll., Exeter Coll., Oxford; cartoon illustrations appeared in New Statesman and City Limits 1982–88; Publishing Dir Cathedral Publishing 1988–90; Contributing Ed. London Evening Standard magazine 1993–95; columnist, The Observer 1995–97, The Times 1997–99, Ind. on Sunday 2000–, Evening Standard 2002–, The Independent 2003–; Geoffrey Faber Memorial Prize 1992. *Publications:* short stories: Quantity Theory of Insanity 1991, Grey Area 1994, A Story for Europe 1996, Tough Tough Toys for Tough Tough Boys 1998, Dr Mukti and Other Tales of Woe 2003, Liver 2008; novellas: Cock and Bull 1992, The Sweet Smell of Psychosis 1996; novels: My Idea of Fun 1993, Great Apes 1997, How the Dead Live 2000, Perfidious Man 2000, Feeding Frenzy 2001, Dorian 2002, Dr Mukti 2004, The Book of Dave 2006; non-fiction: Junk Mail (selected journalism) 1995, Sore Sites (collected journalism) 2000, Psychogeography (collected journalism) 2007, The Butt 2008; collected cartoons 1985. *Leisure interest:* walking. *Address:* The Wylie Agency, 17 Bedford Square, London, WC1B 3BA, England (office). *Telephone:* (20) 7908-5900 (office).

SELIGMAN, Joel, AB, JD; American professor of law and university administrator; *President, University of Rochester;* b. 11 Jan. 1950, New York City; m. Friederike Seligman 1982; one s. one d.; ed UCLA, Harvard Law School; attorney, Accountability Research Group, Washington, DC 1974–77; Prof., Northeastern Univ. School of Law 1977–83; Prof., George Washington Univ. Law School 1983–86; Prof., Univ. of Michigan Law School 1987–95; Dean and Samuel M. Fegtly Prof. of Law, Univ. of Arizona Coll. of Law 1995–99; Dean and Ethan A.H. Shepley Univ. Prof., School of Law, Washington Univ., St Louis 1999–2005; Pres. Univ. of Rochester 2005–; mem. Bd of Govs Financial Industry Regulatory Authority; reporter, Nat. Conf. of Commrs on Uniform State Laws, Revision of Uniform Securities Act 1998–2002; Chair. SEC Advisory Cttee on Market Information 2000–01; consultant to US Fed. Trade Comm., Washington, DC 1979–82, US Dept of Transportation 1983, Office of Tech. Assessment 1988–89; Dir Nat. Asscn of Securities Dealers 2004–07; mem. American Law Inst., State Bar of Calif., American Inst. of Certified Public Accountants (fmr mem. Professional Ethics Exec. Cttee. *Publications:* author or co-author of 20 books including (co-author with the late Louis Loss) Securities Regulation (11 vols) and The Transformation of Wall Street: A History of the Securities and Exchange Commission and Modern Corporation Finance; over 40 articles. *Address:* Office of the President, 240 Wallis Hall, University of Rochester, Rochester, NY 14627, USA (office). *Telephone:* (585) 275-8356 (office). *Fax:* (585) 256-2473 (office). *E-mail:* seligman@rochester.edu (office). *Website:* www.rochester.edu/president (office).

SELINGER, Benjamin Klaas, AM, Dr rer. nat, DSc; Australian chemist, environmental consultant and academic; *Professor Emeritus of Chemistry, Australian National University;* b. 23 Jan. 1939, Sydney; s. of Herbert Selinger and Hilde Wittner; m. Veronica Hollander 1967; two s.; ed Sydney Boys High School, Univ. of Sydney, Tech. Univ. Stuttgart and Australian Nat. Univ.; Lecturer in Physical Chem., ANU 1966–71, Sr Lecturer 1971–78, Head, Dept of Chem. 1988–91, Prof. of Chem. 1992–, Prof. Emer. 1999–; Chair. Bd of Nat. Registration Authority for Agric. and Veterinary Chemicals 1993–97; mem. numerous Govt bodies, advisory cttees, etc.; various academic posts overseas; Deputy Chair. ANZAAS 1994–96; Chair. Australian Science Festival Ltd 2001–; Fellow, Royal Australian Chem. Inst., Royal Inst. of GB, Australian Acad. of Tech. Sciences and Eng, Australian Acad. of Forensic Sciences; mem. CHOICE (Council Australian Consumers Asscn) 2000–, Life mem. 2007; consultant, Versel Scientific Consulting; columnist, Canberra Times 1972–, Burke's Backyard magazine 2000–; Alexander von Humboldt Fellow; Archibald Olle Prize 1979, Special Eureka Prize for Science Communication (ABC/Australian Museum) 1991, ANZAAS Medallist 1993, Centenary of Fed. Medal 2003; many other awards and distinctions. *Film:* appeared in An Act of Necessity, Film Australia. *Radio:* Dial-a-Scientist, ABC. *Television:* has appeared in ABC World Series Debates on "Science Is a Health Hazard". *Publications:* Chemistry in the Market Place 1975–98 (5th edn), Thinking with Fourier 1992, Expert Evidence 1992, Why the Watermelon Won't Ripen in Your Armpit 2000. *Leisure interests:* bushwalking, science museums, forensic chem. *Address:* Department of Chemistry, Building 33, Australian National University, Canberra, ACT 0200 (office); 56 Brereton Street, Garran, Canberra, ACT 2605, Australia (home). *Telephone:* (2) 6281-5076 (office); (407) 460339 (mobile). *Fax:* (2) 6285-2832 (home). *Website:* chemistry.anu.edu.au/Staff/BKS/home.html (office).

SELIVON, Mykola Jedosovych, PhD; Ukrainian lawyer, judge and diplomatist; *Ambassador to Kazakhstan;* b. 30 Oct. 1946, Shestovytsya, Chernigiv Region; one s. one d.; ed Faculty of Law, Kyiv Taras Shevchenko State Univ.; Research Fellow, Inst. of State and Law, Acad. of Sciences of Ukraine 1973; apptd Sr Asst Govt Legal Group 1979, later Chief of Legal Dept; fmr Deputy Minister of Cabinet of Ministers, later First Deputy Minister –1996; Judge, Constitutional Court of Ukraine 1996–99, Deputy Chair. 1999–2002, Chair. 2002–06; Amb. to Kazakhstan 2006–; Academician, Ukrainian Acad. of Law Sciences; mem. Perm. Court of Arbitration, The Hague; Order for Service, Third Class; Distinguished Lawyer of Ukraine. *Leisure interests:* classical music, theatre, sport. *Address:* Embassy of Ukraine, 010000 Astana, Auezova 57, Kazakhstan (office). *Telephone:* (7172) 32-60-42 (office). *Fax:* (7172) 32-68-11 (office). *E-mail:* embassy_ua@mbox.kz (office). *Website:* ukrembassy.kepter.kz (office).

SELKOE, Dennis J., BA, MD; American neurologist and academic; *Vincent and Stella Coates Professor of Neurologic Diseases, Harvard Medical School;* b. 25 Sept. 1943, New York; ed Columbia Univ., New York and Univ. of Virginia School of Medicine; US Public Health Service Summer Research Fellow in Pediatrics, Michael Reese Medical Research Inst., Chicago 1966, US Public Health Service Summer Research Fellow in Neurochemistry, McLean Hosp., Belmont, Mass 1968; Intern in Medicine, Hosp. of the Univ. of Pennsylvania, Phidelphia 1969–70; Research Assoc., Nat. Inst. of Neurological Disorders and Stroke, NIH, Bethesda, Md 1970–72; Resident in Neurology, Peter Bent Brigham, Children's and Beth Israel Hosps Boston, Mass 1972–75, Chief Resident in Neurology, Peter Bent Brigham and Children's Hosps 1974–75, United Cerebral Palsy Fellow, Children's Hosp. 1974–75; NIH Postdoctoral Fellow in Neuroscience, Children's Hosp., Harvard Medical School, Boston 1975–78, Research Assoc. in Neuroscience, Children's Hosp. Medical Center 1975–78, Instructor in Neurology, Harvard Medical School 1975–78, Asst Neurologist Children's Hosp. and Brigham and Women's Hosp. 1975–82, Asst Prof. of Neurology, Harvard Medical School 1978–82 (Faculty mem. Div. on Aging 1979–, Program in Neuroscience 1985–), Assoc. Physician (Neurology), Children's Hosp. and Brigham and Women's Hosp. 1982–85, Assoc. Prof. of Neurology 1982–85, Assoc. Prof. of Neurology (Neuroscience) 1985–90, Physician (Neurology), Brigham and Women's Hosp. 1985–92, Dir Center for Neurologic Diseases, Brigham and Women's Hosp. 1985–, Prof. of Neurology (Neuroscience), Harvard Medical School 1990–, Sr Physician (Neurology), Brigham and Women's Hosp. 1992–99, Clinical Assoc. in Neurology, Massachusetts Gen. Hosp. 1997–, Sr Neurologist, Brigham and Women's Hosp. 1999–, Vincent and Stella Coates Prof. of Neurologic Diseases, Harvard Medical School 2001–; Assoc. Neuropathologist, McLean Hosp., Belmont 1978–85; Investigator, Huntington's Disease Research Center Without Walls, Boston 1980–83; Wellcome Visiting Professorship in the Basic Medical Sciences, Louisiana State Univ. Medical School 1995; Rotary Chair for Alzheimer's Disease, Univ. of Leiden (Netherlands) 2000; Co-Chair. Governance Cttee and Chair. Harvard Center for Translational Neurology Research, Harvard Center for Neurodegeneration and Repair, Harvard Medical School 2000–; mem. Medical and Scientific Advisory Bd Alzheimer's Asscn (USA) 1983–90; mem. Exec. Cttee Massachusetts Alzheimer's Disease Research Center 1984–; Founding mem. Dana Alliance for Brain Initiatives 1992–; mem. Scientific Review Bd (Neuroscience) Howard Hughes Medical Inst. 1995–; mem. NIH Nat. Advisory Council on Aging 1998–; Consulting Ed. Journal of Clinical Investigation 1998–; mem. Editorial Bd Neurobiology of Aging 1983–93, Alzheimer's Disease 1986–, Neurodegeneration 1990–93, Neuron 1993–99, Neurobiology of Disease 1993–, Amyloid 1994–, American Journal of Alzheimer's Disease 1997–; mem. Editorial Advisory Bd Synapse 1994–; mem. Editorial Cttee Annual Review of Neuroscience 1996–2001; Editorial Advisor, Neurology, BioMed Central 2000–; American Soc. for Neurology 1973, Soc. for Neuroscience 1980, Massachusetts Neurologic Association 1980, AAAS 1982, American Soc. for Neurochemistry 1983, American Asscn for Neuropathologists 1983, American Neurological Asscn 1983, World Fed. of Neurology 1985, American Soc. for Investigative Pathology 1992, American Soc. for Cell Biology 1998; Fellow, American Acad. of Neurology 1996 (Chair.

Potamkin Prize Cttee 1998–); Hon. MA (Harvard) 1991; Neuropathology Award, Univ. of Virginia School of Medicine 1966, Medical Student Research Award in Experimental Neurology (First Prize), American Acad. of Neurology 1968, Nat. Foundation Merit Award 1968, Univ. Research and Devt Prize, Univ. of Virginia 1969, Teacher Investigator Devt Award, NIH (NINDS) 1978–83, Andrew Floud Memorial Lecturer, The Neurological Inst. 1984, Wood Kalb Foundation Prize for Research on Alzheimer's Disease 1984, Metropolitan Life Foundation Award for Medical Research 1986, McKnight Foundation Award for Neuroscience Research 1988–91, Leadership and Excellence in Alzheimer's Disease (LEAD) Award, NIH Nat. Inst. on Aging 1988–95, Potamkin Prize, American Acad. of Neurology 1989, Arling Lecturer, Univ. of Cincinnati Medical Center 1991, NIH MERIT Award, Nat. Inst. on Aging 1991, Matthew and Marcia Simons Lecturer, Alzheimer's Asscn, Commonwealth of Massachusetts 1992, Lifetime Science Award, Inst. for Advanced Studies in Immunology and Aging, Washington, DC 1992, Distinguished Alumnus/Keynote Speaker, Univ. of Virginia Medical Alumni Symposium 1994, Rita Hayworth Award, Alzheimer's Asscn 1995, Lowell O. Randall Lecturer in Pharmacology, Univ. of Pennsylvania School of Medicine 1996, Royston C. Clowes Annual Memorial Lecturer, Univ. of Texas, Dallas 1996, Arthur Cherkin Memorial Award, UCLA 1996, Leonard Berg Hon. Symposium on Alzheimer's Disease, Washington Univ. School of Medicine 1997, Mathilde Solowey Award in the Neurosciences, NIH Foundation for Advanced Education in the Sciences 1998, Boerhaave Medal, Univ. of Leiden 1998, Frank A. Elliott Lecturer, Penn Neurological Inst., Univ. of Pennsylvania Health System 1999, Robert J. Huebner Memorial Symposium, Kimmel Cancer Center, Jefferson Univ. 1999, Pioneer Award, Alzheimer's Asscn 1999. *Publications:* more than 630 articles in medical journals. *Address:* Brigham and Women's Hospital, Harvard University Center for Neurologic Diseases, HIM 730, 77 Avenue Louis Pasteur, Boston, MA 02115-5817, USA (office). *Telephone:* (617) 525-5200 (office). *Fax:* (617)525-5252 (office). *E-mail:* dselkoe@rics.bwh.harvard.edu (office). *Website:* www.hms.harvard.edu/dms/neuroscience/fac/selkoe.html (office); selkoelab.bwh.harvard.edu (office).

SELLA, George John, Jr, BS, MBA; American business executive; b. 29 Sept. 1928, West New York, NJ; s. of George John Sella and Angelina Dominoni; m. Janet May Auf-der Heide 1955; two s. three d.; ed Princeton and Harvard Univs; joined American Cyanamid Co. 1954, Pres. Europe/Mideast/Africa Div. 1976–77, Corp. Vice-Pres. 1977, Vice-Chair. 1978, Pres. 1979–90, CEO 1983, Chair. 1984, now retd; fmr mem. Bd of Dirs Union Camp Corpn, Bush Boake Allen, Inc., Equitable Cos Inc., Coulter Pharmaceutical Inc.; mem. NAM, Soc. of Chemical Industry, Pharmaceutical Mfrs Asscn; fmr mem. Advisory Cttee InterWest Pnrs. *Address:* c/o InterWest Partners, 2710 Sand Hill Road, Second Floor, Menlo Park, CA 94025, USA.

SELLA, Phillippe; French fmr rugby union player; *Co-Director, Sella Communication;* b. 14 Feb. 1962, Tonneins; centre/wing; 111 appearances with French nat. team 1982–1995, fmr world record number of caps, scored 30 tries including one in every game of the 1986 Five Nations Championship; appeared in three World Cups, retd from nat. team 1995; with English club Saracens 1995–97; still involved in rugby, fmrly co-coach of Barbarians; currently involved in business ventures; co-Dir Sella Communication 2003–. *Address:* Sella Communication, 1 rue du Parc des Princes, 47300 Villeneuve-sur-Lot, France (office). *Telephone:* 5-53-40-15-22 (office). *Fax:* 5-53-36-70-10 (office). *E-mail:* contact@sellacommunication.com (office). *Website:* www.sellacommunication.com (office).

SELLARS, Peter, BA; American theatre and opera director and academic; *Professor, Department of World Arts and Cultures, UCLA;* b. 27 Sept. 1957, Pittsburgh, PA; ed Harvard Univ.; Dir Boston Shakespeare Co. 1983–84; Dir and Man. American Nat. Theater at J.F. Kennedy Center, Washington, DC 1984–86; Artistic Adviser, Boston Opera Theatre 1990; currently Prof., Dept of World Arts and Culture, UCLA; Fellow MacArthur Foundation, Chicago 1983; fmr Visiting Prof. Center for Theatre Arts, Univ. of Calif., Berkeley; Dir New Crowned Hope Festival 2006–. *Productions include:* Ajax, Armida, Così fan tutte, The Death of Klinghoffer, Die Zauberflöte, Don Giovanni, The Electrification of the Soviet Union, Le Grand Macabre, Idomeneo, The Lighthouse, The Marriage of Figaro, Mathis der Maler, Merchant of Venice, The Mikado, El Niño, Nixon in China, Orlando, The Rake's Progress, Saul and Orlando, St Francois d'Assise, Tannhäuser, Theodora, Zangezi. *Address:* Department of World Arts and Cultures, UCLA, Glorya Kaufman Hall 114, 120 Westwood Plaza, Suite 150, Box 951608, Los Angeles, CA 90095-1608, USA (office). *Telephone:* (310) 825-1821 (office). *Website:* www.wac.ucla.edu (office).

SELLECK, Tom; American actor and producer; b. 29 Jan. 1945, Detroit, Mich.; s. of Robert D. Selleck and Martha Selleck; m. 1st Jackie Ray (divorced 1982); one step-s.; m. 2nd Jillie Mack 1987; one d.; ed Univ. of Southern Calif.; mem. Bd Michael Josephson Inst. of Ethics, Advisory Bd Character Counts Coalition (fmr Nat. Spokesperson), Student/Sponsor Partnership Program, New York, Cttee of John F. Kennedy Center for the Performing Arts; fmr Hon. Chair. Skin Cancer Foundation; Spokesman for Nat. Fatherhood Initiative; fmr spokesperson for Los Angeles Mission to Help the Homeless; Hon. LLD (Pepperdine Univ.) 2004; Distinguished American Award, Horatio Alger Asscn 2004. *Films include:* Myra Breckenridge, Midway, Coma, Seven Minutes, High Road to China, Runaway, Lassiter, Three Men and a Baby, Her Alibi 1988, Quigley Down Under, An Innocent Man 1989, Three Men and a Little Lady 1991, Folks 1991, Mr Baseball 1991, Christopher Columbus: The Discovery 1992, In & Out, The Love Letter 1999, Running Mates 2000. *Television includes:* Returning Home, Bracken's World, The Young and the Restless, The Rockford Files, The Sacketts, played Thomas Magnum in Magnum PI 1980–88, Divorce Wars, Countdown at the Super Bowl, Gypsy Warriors, Boston and Kilbride, The Concrete Cowboys, Murder She Wrote, The Silver Fox, The Closer (series) 1998, Last Stand at Saber River, Friends, 1996, 2000, Ruby, Jean and Joe, Broken Trust 1995, Washington Slept Here 2000, Louis l'Amour's Crossfire Trail 2000, Monte Walsh 2003, 12 Mile Road 2003, Reversible Errors 2004, Ike, Countdown to D Day 2004, Stone Cold 2005, Jesse Stone: Night Passage 2006, Jesse Stone: Death in Paradise 2006, Jesse Stone: Sea Change 2007, Las Vegas (series) 2007–08. *Leisure interests:* volleyball (Hon. Capt. US Men's Volleyball Team for 1984 Olympic Games), outrigger canoe specialist, baseball, horseback riding. *Address:* c/o Esme Chandlee, 2967 Hollyridge Drive, Los Angeles, CA 90068, USA. *Telephone:* (323) 962-5704 (office). *Fax:* (323) 962-5705 (office).

SELLERT, Wolfgang, DJur; German legal scholar and academic; *Professor Emeritus and Chairman, Abteilung für Deutsche Rechtsgeschichte, University of Göttingen;* b. 3 Nov. 1935, Berlin; s. of Horst-Günther Sellert and Else Kaiser; m. Dr Urte Wenger 1962; two d.; Asst in Dept for History of German Law, Univ. of Frankfurt 1965–72, Prof. 1972–77; Prof. History of German Law and Civil Law Georg-August Univ., Göttingen 1977–, now Prof. Emer. and Chair. Dept for German Historical Jurisprudence; Dir German-Chinese Inst. of Econ. Law, Univ. of Nanjing 1995–; mem. Akad. der Wissenschaften, Göttingen 1984–. *Publications:* Über die Zuständigkeitsabgrenzung von Reichshofrat und Reichskammergericht 1965, Prozessgrundsätze über Stilus Curiae am Reichshofrat 1973, Die Ordnungen des Reichshofrats 1980, Studien- u. Quellenbuch zur Geschichte der dt. Strafrechtspflege 1989, Recht u. Gerechtigkeit in der Kunst 1991. *Leisure interests:* collecting old manuscripts and baroque literature. *Address:* Konrad-Adenauer-Strasse 25, 37075 Göttingen; Juridicum, Räume 131-133, Platz der Göttinger, Sieben 6, 37073 Göttingen, Germany (office). *Telephone:* (551) 397444 (office); (551) 23771. *Fax:* (551) 394872 (office); (551) 23771. *E-mail:* eszepst@gwdg.de (office). *Website:* www.jura.uni-goettingen.de/privat/w.sellert (office); www.jura.uni-goettingen.de/seminar/lehrstuhl/privatrecht/sellert (office).

SELMER, Knut S., DJur; Norwegian professor of law; b. 7 Nov. 1924, Oslo; m. Elisabeth Schweigaard 1950; one s. one d.; ed Univ. of Oslo; Research Fellow, Univ. of Oslo 1953–58, Prof. of Insurance Law 1959–89; Sec. for revision of Norwegian Marine Insurance Conditions 1957–67; Chair. Public Comm. for revision of Norwegian Insurance Contracts Act 1973–87; Founder and Chair. Norwegian Research Center for Computers and Law 1970–86; Chair. Bd Norwegian Data Inspectorate 1980–96; Chair. Bd Norwegian Legal Information System, Lovdata 1980–89. *Publications:* The Survival of General Average 1958, A Decade of Computers and Law (with J. Bing) 1980, Forsikringsrett 1982; numerous articles on insurance law, tort law and computer law. *Address:* Krusesgate 11, 0263 Oslo 2, Norway.

SELTEN, Reinhard, D.PHIL.NAT.; German economist and academic; *Research Co-ordinator, Experimental Economics Laboratory, University of Bonn;* b. 5 Oct. 1930, Breslau; s. of Adolf Selten and Käthe Luther; m. Elisabeth Langreiner 1959; ed Univ. of Frankfurt am Main; Prof., Freie Univ. Berlin 1969; Prof., Univ. of Bielefeld; Prof. of Econ. Theory, Univ. of Bonn 1984–96, Prof. Emer. 1996–, currently Research Co-ordinator Experimental Econs Lab. (BonnEconLab); mem. Rheinisch-Westfalen Akad. der Wissenschaften; Fellow, Econometric Soc.; Order of Merit, Arts and Sciences 2006;Foreign Hon. mem. American Acad. of Arts and Sciences, Hon. Senator Univ. of Bonn 2007; Dr hc (Bielefeld) 1989, (Frankfurt) 1991, (Graz) 1996, (E Anglia) 1996, (Norwich) 1997, (Cachan) 1998, (Innsbruck) 2000, (Hong Kong) 2003, (Osnabrück) 2006; shared Nobel Prize for Econs 1994, Nordrhein-Westfalen State Prize 2000. *Publications:* Preispolitik der Mehrprodukte-nunternehmung in der stat. Theorie 1970, General Equilibrium with Price Making Firms (with T. Marschak) 1974, Models of Strategic Rationality 1988, A General Theory of Equilibrium Selection in Games (with J. Harsanyi) 1988. *Address:* Laboratorium für Experimentelle Wirtschaftsforschung, Universität Bonn, Adenauerallee 24-42, 53113 Bonn, Germany (office). *Telephone:* (228) 739192 (office). *Fax:* (228) 739193 (office). *E-mail:* rselten@uni-bonn.de (office). *Website:* www.bonneconlab.uni-bonn.de/econlab (office).

SEMAGO, Vladimir Vladimirovich; Russian politician; b. 10 Jan. 1947; m.; one s.; ed Moscow Inst. of Construction Eng, All-Union Acad. of Foreign Trade; with Mosoblstroi 1973–77; Deputy Dir-Gen., Solnechny 1977–81; accountant, tourist co., commerce Dept, State Cttee of Tourism 1981–83; Deputy Chair., Domodedovo Dist Consumers' Union 1983–86; Chief Engineer, State Cttee of Science and Tech. of USSR Council of Ministers 1986–87; Founder Jt Venture Moscow Commercial Club; co-f. Ecology and Energy Resources 1992; mem. CP of Russian Fed. 1993–98; mem. CP faction, later Regions of Russia faction; mem. State Duma 1993–; Founder and leader New Left (political movt) 1999; mem. Cttee on Problems of Women, Family and Youth; Chair. Bd of Dirs Rosebusinesbank; mem. Presidium, Co-ordination Council Round Table of Russian Business; mem. United Russia (UR) (Yedinaya Rossiya). *Leisure interests:* travelling, collecting modern paintings. *Address:* United Russia (UR) (Yedinaya Rossiya), 129110 Moscow, Pereyaslavskii per. 4, Russia. *Telephone:* (495) 786-82-89 (office). *Fax:* (495) 975-30-78. *E-mail:* centrpr@edinros.ru. *Website:* www.er.ru.

SEMAKULA KIWANUKA, Matia Mulumba, PhD; Ugandan government official and diplomatist; *Minister of State of Investment;* m.; several c.; ed Makerere Univ. and Univ. of London, UK; fmr univ. lecturer, researcher and admin.; Sr Presidential Adviser 1979–81; worked with UNEP 1985–87; Counterpart Chief Tech. Adviser and Dir of Planning and Project Coordination for a UNDP project on capacity-building and institutional strengthening 1988–90; Dean, Makerere Univ. School of Post grad. Studies and Research 1991–94; Exec. Dir Man. Training and Advisory Centre, Uganda 1994–96; Amb. and Perm. Rep. to UN, New York 1996–2003, Chair. Gen. Ass.'s Fourth Cttee (Special Political and Decolonization) 2000; Minister of State in Charge of Luwero 2003–05, of Investment 2005–; fmr Minister of Culture, Royal Kingdom of Buganda; mem. Royal Council. *Address:* Office of the Minister of Investment, Ministry of Finance, Appollo Kaggwa Road, Plot 2/4, POB 8147, Kampala, Uganda (office). *Telephone:* (41) 2234700 (office). *Fax:* (41) 2230163 (office). *E-mail:* webmaster@finance.go.ug (office). *Website:* www.finance.go.ug (office).

SEMASHKO, Vladimir Ilich; Belarusian politician; *First Deputy Prime Minister;* Minister of Energy –2003; First Deputy Prime Minister 2003–; Chair. Supervisory Bd Beltransgaz 2007–; Order of Honour 2008. *Address:* Office of the Deputy Prime Ministers, vul. Savetskaya 11, 220010 Minsk, Belarus (office). *Telephone:* (17) 222-68-08 (office). *Fax:* (17) 222-66-65 (office). *Website:* www.btg.by.

SEMEL, Terry, BS; American media executive; *Chairman, Yahoo! Inc.;* b. 24 Feb. 1943, New York; s. of Ben Semel and Mildred (née Wenig) Semel; m. Jane Bovingdon 1977; one s. two d.; ed Long Island Univ., City Coll. of New York; Domestic Sales Man. CBS Cinema Center Films, Studio City, Calif. 1970–72; Vice-Pres., Gen. Man. Walt Disney's Buena Vista, Burbank, Calif. 1972–75; Pres. W.B. Distribution Corpn, Burbank 1975–78; Exec. Vice-Pres., COO Warner Bros. Inc., Burbank 1979–80, Pres., COO 1980–96, Chair., CEO 1994–99; Chair., Co-CEO Warner Music Group Inc. 1995–99; Chair., CEO and Dir Yahoo! Inc. 2001–07, Chair. (non-exec.) 2007–; Vice-Chair. San Diego Host Cttee for Republican Nat. Convention 1996; mem. Bd of Dirs Revlon, Polo Ralph Lauren Corpn, Guggenheim Museum; Vanguard Award from Producers Guild of America 2005. *Address:* Yahoo! Inc., 701 First Avenue, Sunnyvale, CA 94089, USA (office). *Telephone:* (408) 349-3300 (office). *Fax:* (408) 349-3301 (office). *Website:* www.yahoo.com (office).

SEMENOV, Victor Aleksandrovich; Russian politician and business executive; *Chairman of the Supervisory Board, Belaya Dacha Group;* b. 14 Jan. 1958, Novokuryanovo, Moscow Region; m.; one s. one d.; ed Moscow K. Timiryazev Acad. of Agric.; on state farm, later Agric. Co. Belaya Dacha 1980–85; instructor Agric. Dept, Lyubertsy Town CP Cttee 1987–88; Pres. and Dir-Gen. Belaya Dacha 1989–98; Minister of Agric. and Food of Russian Fed. 1998–99; mem. State Duma (Otechestvo faction) 1999–; Chair. Union of Agricultural Scientific Complex Asscns of the Russian Fed. (ASSAGROS); Pres. Russian Interregional Asscn for Assistance of Field Experiments (AAFEI); Founder and Chair. of the Supervisory Bd, Belaya Dacha Group (activities include growing and processing vegetables, planting trees and gardens and landscape design, commercial property); mem. Russian Acad. of Agricultural Sciences. *Leisure interests:* gardening, fishing, hunting. *Address:* Belaya Dacha Group, 2, Yanichkin Proezd, Kotelniki, Lubertsy District, Moscow 140053, Russia (office). *Telephone:* (495) 995-90-00 (office). *E-mail:* info@belaya-dacha.ru (office). *Website:* www.belaya-dacha.ru (office).

SEMENOV, Yuri Pavlovich; Russian mechanical engineer; b. 20 April 1935, Toropets, Kalinin region; m.; two d.; ed Dnepropetrovsk State Univ.; worked in rocket and space industry as engineer, head of group, Leading Designer 1967–72, Chief Designer 1972–78, Deputy Gen. Designer, Chief Designer 1978–81; First Deputy Gen. Designer, Chief Designer of BURAN Orbiter, Manned Spacecrafts and Stations 1981–89, Gen. Designer of ENERGIA Scientific and Production Asscn (NPO ENERGIA) 1989–91, Dir Gen., Gen. Designer 1991–94; Gen. Designer and Pres. S. P. Korolev RSC ENERGIA 1994–2005 (responsible for devt and operation of Buran reusable vehicle, devt, manufacture and operation of Soyuz, Progress-type vehicles, Salyut and Mir in-orbit complexes, rocket segment of the Sea Launch rocket and space complex-RSC, satellite systems based on YAMAL spacecraft of new generation communication satellites and devt of Russian segment of Int. Space Station and its main modules, devt and construction of the AURORA/ONEGA RSC); mem. Int. Acad. of Astronautics 1986; Corresp. mem. USSR (now Russian) Acad. of Sciences 1987, mem. 2000–; Hero of Socialist Labour 1976, Lenin Prize 1978, USSR State Prize 1985, USSR Acad. of Sciences K. Tsyolkovsky Gold Medal 1987, Alan De Emil IAF State Prize 1991, State Prize of Russian Fed. 1999, François-Xavier Bagnoud Aeropace Prize 1999, RAS S. P. Korolev Gold Medal 2001 and others. *Publications:* more than 360 publs including S. P. Korolev Rocket and Space Corporation Energia 1946–96 1996, S. P. Korolev Rocket and Space Corporation ENERGIA at the Turn of Two Centuries 1996–2001 2001. *Leisure interests:* sports. *Address:* c/o S. P. Korolev RSC Energia, Lenina str. 4A, 141070 Korolev, Moscow Region, Russia.

SEMENYAKA, Lyudmila Ivanovna; Russian ballerina; b. 16 Jan. 1952, Leningrad (St Petersburg); m. (divorced); one s.; ed Vaganova Ballet Acad., Leningrad (now St Petersburg); danced with Kirov Ballet 1970–72; Prima Ballerina Bolshoi Theatre Co., Moscow 1972–96; has worked with English Nat. Ballet 1990–91 and Scottish Nat. Ballet; ballet teacher 1994–, with Moscow State Acad. of Choreography 1999–, currently also with Bolshoi Ballet; trained as actress, Studio Theatre of Modern Dramaturgy 2001–03; mem. jury several int. ballet competitions; performed in Europe, USA and Argentina; winner Moscow Int. Ballet competition 1969, 1972, Varna 1972, Tokyo (First Prize and Gold Medal) 1976, Anna Pavlova Prize, Paris 1976, USSR State Prize 1977, USSR People's Artist 1986, Evening Standard Prize 1986. *Films:* Ludmila Semenyaka Danse, The Bolshoi Ballerina, Spartacus, The Stone Flower, Raymonda, The Nutcracker, Fantasy on the Theme of Casanova and others. *Plays:* An Excellent Medicine for Anguish, The Seagull. *Roles include:* all of classical repertoire, debut in Odette/Odile, Swan Lake, Moscow; all of Y. Grigorovitch ballets: Phrygia (Spartak), Anastasia (Ivan the Terrible), Katerina (Stony Flower) etc; roles in ballets by Balanchin, Petit, Lavrovsky, Vassilyev, Boccadoro, Ben Stivenson, May Murdmaa; has partnered Mikhail Baryshnikov, Vladimir Vassilyev, Irek Mukhamedov, Farukh Ruzimatov etc. *Address:* Bolshoi Theatre, Teatralnaya ploshchad 1, Moscow, Russia. *Telephone:* (495) 253-87-42 (home). *Fax:* (495) 253-87-42 (home). *Website:* www.bolshoi.ru (office).

SEMENZA, Giorgio, DrMed; Swiss biochemist and academic; *Emeritus Professor of Biochemistry, Swiss Federal Institute of Technology, Zurich;* b. 23 June 1928, Milan, Italy; s. of Prof. Carlo Semenza and Clementina Gerli; m. Berit Andersson 1958; three c.; ed Univ. of Milan; post-doctoral studies, Univ. of Uppsala 1955–56; Asst Lecturer, Lecturer, Dept of Biochem. Univ. of Zürich 1956–64, Asst Prof. 1964–69; Prof. of Gen. Physiology, Univ. of Milan 1967–69; Prof. of Biochem. Swiss Fed. Inst. of Tech., Zürich 1969–95, Chair. or Co.-Chair., Dean of School of Natural Sciences 1980–82, currently Emer. Prof. of Biochem; Prof. of Biochemistry, Univ. of Milan 1995–2003; Visiting Prof. at numerous foreign univs; Man. Ed. Fed. European Biochemical Soc. (FEBS) Letters 1985–99; mem. editorial advisory bds of a number of scientific journals; mem. Academia Europaea 1989–2006, Istituto Lombardo di Scienze e Lettere, Milan 2000–; Foreign mem. Accad. Nazionale dei Lincei 2006–; Hon. mem. Italian Soc. of Experimental Biology 1978, Spanish Soc. of Biochemistry and Molecular Biology 1997; Hon. PhD (Univ. Autónoma de Madrid) 1985; Hon. MD (Univ. de Nice Sophia Antipolis, France) 1999, (Univ. of Copenhagen, Denmark) 1999; Int. Prize of Modern Nutrition 1975, Iorio-Rustichelli Prize 1985, European Pharmaceutical Industry Research Award 1988, Purkine Gold Medal, Prague 1988. *Publications:* 19 books ed or co-ed; more than 250 publs in peer-reviewed journals. *Leisure interests:* literature, films, theatre. *Address:* c/o Swiss Institute of Technology, ETH-Zentrum, PO Box 35, CH-8092 Zürich, Switzerland; c/o Dipartimento di Chimica, Biochimica e Tecnologie per la Medicina, Università di Milano, Via Saldini 50, 20133 Milan, Italy (office). *E-mail:* semenza@bc.biol.ethz.ch (office).

ŠEMETA, Algirdas Gediminas; Lithuanian economist and government official; *Minister of Finance;* b. 23 April 1962; m.; three c.; ed Univ. of Vilnius; fmr adviser on privatization, Ministry of the Economy, also worked in Econ. Devt Strategy Dept; worked for Chair. Securities Comm. 1996–97; Minister of Finance 1997–99, 2008–; Vice-Pres. AB Nalšia June–Nov. 1999; Sec., Govt Cabinet Office 1999–2001; Dir Gen. Statistics Lithuania 2001–08; mem. Knowledge Economy Forum. *Address:* Ministry of Finance, J. Tumo-Vaižganto 8a/2, Vilnius 01512, Lithuania (office). *Telephone:* (5) 239-0005 (office). *Fax:* (5) 212-6387 (office). *E-mail:* finmin@finmin.lt (office). *Website:* www.finmin.lt (office).

SEMIGIN, Gennady Yuryevich, Dr rer. pol; Russian business executive and politician; *Leader, Patriots of Russia (Patrioty Rossii);* b. 23 March 1964; ed Riga Higher Mil. Political School, Moscow Juridical Inst., Acad. of Finance; army service 1985–90; f. Centre of Econs and Russian AKROS 1990; f. Russian Group of Finance and Industry 1991; mem. Council on Business, Russian Presidency 1992–; mem. Exec. Bd Russian Union of Businessmen, Pres. Russian Group of Finance and Industry 1991–; f. Nat. Public Scientific Fund 1996; Founder and Head, Inst. of Comparative Politology, Russian Acad. of Sciences; Pres. Congress of Russian Business Circles; mem. CP 1998; mem. State Duma (Agrarian faction, then CP faction) 1999–, Deputy Chair. 2000–03; Founder and Leader Patriots of Russia (Patrioty Rossii) 2002–; mem. Comm. on Regulation of Labour and Social Relations, Russian Acad. of Social Sciences, Acad. of Political Sciences; corresp. mem. Acad. of Natural Sciences. *Publications:* Social Partnership in the Contemporary World, Political Stability of Society, ed. New Philosophical Encyclopedia (4 Vols). *Leisure interests:* swimming, tennis, running, classical music, boxing, history, philosophy, art, economics. *Address:* Patriots of Russia (Patrioty Rossii), 119121 Moscow, Smolenskii bulv. 11/2 (office); State Duma, Okhotny Ryad 1, 103205 Moscow, Russia (office). *Telephone:* (495) 692-15-50 (Patrioty Rossii) (office); (495) 292-76-75 (office). *Fax:* (495) 692-15-50 (Patrioty Rossii) (office). *E-mail:* partia-korn@rambler.ru (office). *Website:* www.patriot-rus.ru (office); www.duma.ru (office).

SEMIKHATOV, Mikhail Alexandrovich; Russian geologist; b. 21 Feb. 1932; m.; one s.; ed Moscow State Univ.; jr, sr researcher, head of lab. Inst. of Geology 1954–; Corresp. mem. USSR (now Russian) Acad. of Sciences 1990, mem. 1994; Deputy Ed.-in-Chief Stratigrafiya. Geologicheskaya korrelyatsiya (journal); N. Shatsky Prize. *Publications include:* General Problems of the Proterozoic Stratigraphy in the USSR. *Leisure interest:* expeditions to Siberia. *Address:* Institute of Geology, Russian Academy of Sciences, Pyzhevsky per. 7, 109017 Moscow, Russia. *Telephone:* (495) 230-81-32 (office). *E-mail:* semikhatov@ginran.ru (office).

SEMIZOROVA, Nina Lvovna; Russian ballerina; b. 15 Oct. 1956, Krivoi Rog; d. of Lev Alexandrovich Semizorov and Larisa Dmitrievna Semizorova; m. 1st Maris Liepa 1980; m. 2nd Mark Peretokin 1988; one d.; ed Kiev Choreographic School; danced with Shevchenko Theatre of Opera and Ballet, Kiev 1975–78, with Bolshoi Ballet, Moscow 1978–; many appearances abroad; First Prize, Int. Ballet Competition, Moscow 1977; Artist of Merit of Ukrainian SSR 1977, Honoured Artist of Russia 1987, Laureate of Moscow Komsomol 1987. *Roles include:* Odette/Odile, Lady Macbeth, Giselle, Don Quixote, Sleeping Beauty, La Bayadère, Spartacus, The Golden Age, Paquita, Raymonda, Les Sylphides. *Leisure interest:* reading. *Address:* 2 Zhukovskaya Street, Apt. 8, Moscow, Russia. *Telephone:* (495) 923-40-84 (home). *Fax:* (495) 923-40-84 (home).

SEMKOW, Jerzy, MMus; Polish/ French conductor; b. 12 Oct. 1928, Radomsko; s. of Aleksander Semkow and Waleria Sienczak Semkow; ed Jagiellonian Univ., Kraków, State Higher School of Music (student of A. Malawski), Kraków and Leningrad Music Conservatoire; Asst Conductor, Leningrad Philharmonic Orch. 1954–56; Conductor, Bolshoi Opera and Ballet Theatre, Moscow 1956–58; Artistic Dir and Prin. Conductor, Warsaw Nat. Opera 1960–62; Perm. Conductor, Danish Royal Opera, Copenhagen 1965–68; Prin. Conductor Italian Radio and TV (RAI) Orchestra, Rome 1969–73; Musical Dir and Prin. Conductor Saint Louis Symphony Orchestra 1975–; Artistic Dir and Prin. Conductor, Rochester Philharmonic Orchestra, New York 1986–; Guest Conductor Berlin Philharmonic, London Philharmonic,

Nat. Orchestra of Madrid, Orchestre de la Suisse Romande, Cleveland Symphony Orchestra, Orchestre Nat. de France and the orchestras of Paris, Strasbourg, Lyon, Bordeaux, Monte Carlo, Jerusalem, Stockholm, Frankfurt, St Petersburg, Toronto, New York, Cleveland, Chicago, Boston, Detroit, Washington, Cincinatti, Houston, Dallas, Pittsburgh, Rochester, Utah and Minneapolis; engagements at Covent Garden, La Scala, Milan, Staatsoper, Berlin, Staatsoper, Vienna, Teatro Real, Madrid, Paris Opera, Teatro del Opera, Rome, Maggio Musicale, Florence, La Fenice, Venice, Grand Theatre, Geneva, etc.; master classes at Yale Univ., Manhattan School of Music, New York; Dr hc (Acad. Chopin, Warsaw) 2005; Commdr Cross Order of Polonia Restituta, Gold Cross Gloria Artis, Commdr Ordre des Arts et des Lettres. *Recordings include:* Boris Godunov (Musorgski) with Polish Nat. Radio Symphony Orchestra, Kniaź (Borodin) with Group from Opera of Sofia, Symphony No. 3 and Symphonic Concerto No. 4 (Szymanowski), Symphony Nos 2 and 3 (Scriabin) with Nat. Philharmonic Symphony Orchestra, Warsaw, Beethoven and Schumann works with Saint Louis Orchestra, Brahms' works with Warsaw Philarmonic Orchestra, Mozart Symphonies (Disque d'Or). *Leisure interests:* reading, yachting. *Address:* Opus 3 Artists, 470 Park Avenue South, 9th Floor, New York, NY 10016, USA (office). *Telephone:* (212) 584-7569 (office). *Fax:* (616) 300-8200 (office). *E-mail:* icma_publicity@ icmtalent.com (office). *Website:* www.opus3artists.com (office).

SEMPÉ, Jean-Jacques; French cartoonist; b. 17 Aug. 1932, Bordeaux; s. of Ulysse Sempé and Juliette Marson; one s. one d.; ed Ecole Communale à Bordeaux; work has appeared in various publications including: L'Express magazine, Paris-Match, Punch (now defunct), New Yorker, New York Times; has produced an album annually for 30 years for Editions Denoël; Officier des Arts et des Lettres. *Publications include:* Le Petit Nicolas series from 1960, Rien n'est simple 1962, Tout se complique 1963, Sauve qui peut 1964, Monsieur Lambert 1965, La grande panique 1966, St Tropez 1968, Information-Consommation 1968, Des Hauts et des Bas 1970, Face à Face 1972, Bonjour Bonsoir 1974, L'Ascension Sociale de Mr Lambert 1975, Simple question d'equilibre 1977, Un léger décalage 1977, Les Musiciens 1979, Comme par hasard 1981, De bon matin 1983, Vaguement compétitif 1985, Luxe, calme et volupté 1987, Par Avion 1989, L'Histoire de Monsieur Sommer (with Patrick Süsskind) 1991, Ames Soeurs 1991, Insondables Mystères 1993, Raoul Taburin 1995, Les Musiciens 1996, Grands rêves 1997, Beau Temps 1999, Multiples intentions 2003, Sentiments distingués 2007. *Address:* Editions Denoël, 9 rue du Cherche-Midi, 75006 Paris, France (office).

SEMPLE, Sir John Laughlin, KCB, BSc (Econ), MA (Cantab.); British civil servant (retd); b. 10 Aug. 1940, Belfast; s. of the late J. E. Semple and of Violet E. G. Semple; m. Maureen Anne Kerr 1970; two s. one d.; ed Campbell Coll., Belfast and Corpus Christi Coll., Cambridge; joined Home Civil Service, Ministry of Aviation 1961, transferred to NI Civil Service 1962, succession of posts relating to industrial training, financial planning, community relations, physical planning, Belfast Devt and housing policy, Perm. Sec. NI Dept of Finance and Personnel 1988–97, Head. NI Civil Service 1997–2000, (also Second Perm. Sec. NI Office 1998–99), Sec. to NI Exec. Cttee 1999–2000; mem. Consumer Council for Postal Services 2000, Regional Chair. for NI 2000–01; Dir of Northern Ireland Affairs, Royal Mail Group plc 2001–06; Chair. Bd of Trustees NI Police Fund 2001–05; Head Ind. Affordability Review, Dept for Social Devt 2006–07. *Leisure interests:* golf, tennis, skiing, history. *Address:* c/o Affordability Review Team, James House, 2-4 Cromac Avenue, Gasworks Business Park, Ormeau Road, Belfast, BT7 2JA, Northern Ireland (office). *Telephone:* (28) 9081-9581 (office); (28) 9185-2594 (home). *Fax:* (28) 9081-9588 (office); (28) 9185-3949 (home). *E-mail:* affordabilityreview@dsdni.gov.uk (office); johnsemple@utvinternet.com (home).

SEMPRÚN, Jorge; Spanish politician and writer; b. 10 Dec. 1923, Madrid; in exile in France during Spanish Civil War; fought in the French Resistance in World War II, joined Spanish Communist Party 1942, captured by Nazis and sent to Buchenwald concentration camp 1943; returned to Paris 1945; translator with UNESCO 1945–52; led clandestine effort of CP in Spain 1957–62; Minister of Culture 1988–91; mem. Acad. Goncourt, Paris 1996–; Dr hc (Turin) 1990; Prix Fémina 1969, Prix Fémina Vacaresco 1994, Prix Littéraire des Droits de l'Homme 1995, Jerusalem Prize 1997, Nonino Prize 1999, Goethe Medal 2003. *Publications:* Le Grand Voyage (novel, in French), The Autobiography of Federico Sánchez (under pseudonym), Literature or Life 1998, Le Retour de Carola Neher (play) 1998; screenplays for films: Z, La Guerre est finie, L'aveu. *Address:* c/o Penguin Books, 80 Strand, London, WC2R 0RL, England. *Website:* www.academie-goncourt.fr.

SEN, Amartya Kumar, PhD, FBA; Indian economist and academic; *Lamont University Professor Emeritus and Professor of Economics and Philosophy, Harvard University;* b. 3 Nov. 1933, Santiniketan, Bengal; s. of the late Ashutosh Sen and of Amita Sen; m. 1st Nabaneeta Dev 1960 (divorced 1975); two d.; m. 2nd Eva Colorni 1978 (died 1985); one s. one d.; m. 3rd Emma Rothschild; ed Presidency Coll. Calcutta and Trinity Coll., Cambridge; Prof. of Econs, Jadavpur Univ., Calcutta 1956–58; Fellow, Trinity Coll., Cambridge 1957–63; Prof. of Econs, Univ. of Delhi 1963–71, Chair. Dept of Econs 1966–68; Hon. Dir Agricultural Econs Research Centre, Delhi 1966–68, 1969–71; Prof. of Econs, LSE 1971–77, Univ. of Oxford 1977–80, Drummond Prof. of Political Economy 1980–88; Lamont Univ. Prof., Harvard Univ. 1987–98, 2004–, Prof. Emer. 1998–2004, Prof. of Econs and Philosophy 2004–; Master Trinity Coll., Cambridge 1998–2004; Visiting Prof., Univ. of Calif., Berkeley 1964–65; Harvard Univ. 1968–69; Andrew D. White Prof.-at-Large, Cornell Univ. 1978–84; Pres. Int. Econ. Asscn 1986–89; Fellow, Econometric Soc., Pres. 1984; Hon. Prof., Delhi Univ.; Foreign Hon. mem. American Acad. of Arts and Sciences; Hon. Fellow, Inst. of Social Studies, The Hague, Hon. Fellow LSE, Inst. of Devt Studies; Hon. CH 2000; Grand Cross, Order of Scientific Merit (Brazil) 2000; Hon. DLitt (Univ. of Saskatchewan, Canada)

1979, (Visva-Bharati Univ., India) 1983, (Oxford) 1996; Hon. DUniv (Essex) 1984, (Caen) 1987; Hon. DSc (Bath) 1984, (Bologna) 1988; Dr hc (Univ. Catholique de Louvain) 1989, (Padua) 1998; Senator Giovanni Agnelli Inst. Prize for Ethics 1989, Nobel Prize for Econs 1998, UN Econ. and Social Comm. for Asia and the Pacific (UNESCAP) Lifetime Achievement Award 2007. *Publications:* Choice of Techniques: An Aspect of Planned Economic Development 1960, Growth Economics 1970, Collective Choice and Social Welfare 1970, On Economic Inequality 1973, Employment, Technology and Development 1975, Poverty and Famines 1981, Utilitarianism and Beyond (jtly with Bernard Williams) 1982, Choice, Welfare and Measurement 1982, Resources, Values and Development 1984, Commodities and Capabilities 1985, On Ethics and Economics 1987, The Standard of Living 1988, Hunger and Public Action (with Jean Drèze) 1989, Social Security in Developing Countries (jtly) 1991, Inequality Re-examined 1992, The Quality of Life (jtly) 1993, Development as Freedom 1999, The Argumentative Indian: Writings on Indian History, Culture and Identity 2005, Identity and Violence: The Illusion of Destiny 2006; articles in various journals in econs, philosophy and political science. *Address:* Department of Economics, Littauer 205, Harvard University, Cambridge, MA 02138, USA (office). *Telephone:* (617) 495-1871 (office). *Fax:* (617) 496-5942 (office). *E-mail:* slrich@fas.harvard.edu (office). *Website:* www .economics.harvard.edu/faculty/sen (office).

SEN, Mrinal; Indian film director; b. 14 May 1923, Faridpur (now Bangladesh); s. of the late Dinesh Chandra Sen and Saraju Sen; m. Gita Shome 1953; one s.; started making films 1956, directed 24 feature films; mem. jury numerous int. film festivals; Chair. Gov. Council Film & TV Inst. of India 1983–85; Chair. Indian People's Human Rights Comm. 1987–90; Vice-Chair. Fed. of Film Socs of India 1980–92, Cinéma et Liberté (Paris) 1992; Pres. Int. Fed. of Film Socs 1991–; nominated mem. of Rajya Sabha (Upper House of Parl.); Padma Bhushan 1981; Commdr Ordre des Arts et Lettres 1985; Hon. DLitt (Burdwan Univ.) 1981; numerous awards. *Films include:* The Dawn 1956, Wedding Day 1960, Up in the Clouds 1965, Two Brothers 1966, Bhuvan Shome 1968, Calcutta Trilogy—The Interview, Calcutta 71 and Guerrilla Fighter (Calcutta Trilogy 1971–73), Royal Hunt 1976, The Outsiders 1977, Man With an Axe 1978, And Quiet Rolls the Dawn 1979, In Search of Famine 1980, The Kaleidoscope 1982, The Case is Closed 1983, The Ruins 1984, Genesis 1986, Suddenly One Day 1989, World Within, World Without 1992, Antareen 1994, My Land 2002. *Leisure interests:* reading, travelling, loafing about. *Address:* C-501, Talkatora Road, New Delhi 110 001 (office); 4E, Motilal Nehru Road, Kolkata 700029, India (home). *Telephone:* (11) 3351866 (office); (22) 4754799 (home).

SENANI, Mawlawi Abdol Ghafur; Afghan ecclesiastic; fmr Chair. High Council of Ulema and Clergy of Afghanistan. *Address:* c/o High Council of Ulema and Clergy of Afghanistan, Kabul, Afghanistan.

SENDAK, Maurice Bernard, LHD; American illustrator and writer; b. 10 June 1928, New York; s. of Philip Sendak and Sadie (née Schindler) Sendak; ed Art Students League, New York, Boston Univ.; writer and illustrator of children's books 1951–; Co-founder and Artistic Dir The Night Kitchen 1990–; Hans Christian Andersen Illustrators Award 1970, Nat. Medal of Arts 1997. *Publications (writer and illustrator):* Kenny's Window 1956, Very Far Away 1957, The Sign on Rosie's Door 1960, The Nutshell Library 1963, Where the Wild Things Are (Caldecott Medal 1964) 1963, On Books and Pictures 1986, Caldecott and Co. (collection of reviews and articles) 1989, We Are All in the Dumps with Jack and Guy 1993. *Illustrator:* A Hole is to Dig 1952, A Very Special House 1954, I'll Be You and You Be Me 1954, Charlotte and the White Horse 1955, What Do You Say, Dear? 1959, The Moonjumpers 1960, Little Bear's Visit 1962, Schoolmaster Whackwell's Wonderful Sons 1962, Mr. Rabbit and the Lovely Present 1963, The Griffin and the Minor Canon 1963, Nikolenka's Childhood 1963, The Bat-Poet 1964, Lullabies and Night Songs 1965, Hector Protector and As I Went Over the Water 1965, Zlateh the Goat 1966, Higgelty Pigglety Pop, Or There Must Be More To Life 1967, In the Night Kitchen 1970, The Animal Family 1965, In The Night Kitchen Coloring Book 1971, Pictures by Maurice Sendak 1971, The Juniper Tree and Other Tales from Grimm 1973, Outside Over There 1981, The Love for Three Oranges (with Frank Corsaro) 1984, Nutcracker (with Ralph Manheim) 1984, The Cunning Little Vixen 1985, Dear Mili 1988, I Saw Esau 1992, The Ubiquitous Pig 1992; Writer, Dir and Lyricist for TV animated special Really Rosie 1975. *Stage designs:* The Magic Flute 1980, The Love for Three Oranges 1984, L'Enfant et les sortilèges 1987, The Cunning Little Vixen (for New York Opera) 1989, Idomeneo (opera) 1990. *Address:* c/o HarperCollins, Children's Division, 1350 Avenue of the Americas, New York, NY 10019, USA.

SENDANYOYE RUGWABIZA, Valentine, BSc, MSc; Rwandan diplomatist, business executive and international organization executive; *Deputy Director-General, World Trade Organization;* ed Nat. Univ. of Zaïre (now Democratic Repub. of the Congo); sr man. with major Swiss multinational co., first as head of its commercial devt and marketing operations for Cen. Africa, based in Yaoundé, Cameroon, and then as its regional man. for Cen. and West Africa, based in Abidjan, Côte d'Ivoire 1989–97; managed her own co. 1997–2000; joined govt 2000, served simultaneously as Perm. Rep. to UN in Geneva, Head of Del. to WTO and Amb. to Switzerland 2002–05; Deputy Head of Del. for Rwanda's first Trade Policy Review 2004; adviser, Council of Econ. and Social Affairs, Office of Pres. of Rwanda, Kigali –2005; Deputy Dir-Gen. WTO 2005–, Coordinator of African Group in WTO; Founding mem. Rwandese Pvt. Sector Fed., Rwanda Women Entrepreneurs' Org., Rwandese Women Leaders' Caucus; one of two Ambs representing Least Developed Countries in Integrated Framework Working Group. *Address:* World Trade Organization, Centre William Rappard, rue de Lausanne 154, 1211 Geneva 21, Switzerland (office). *Telephone:* (22) 739-51-11 (office). *Fax:* (22) 731-42-06 (office). *E-mail:* enquiries@wto.org (office). *Website:* www.wto.org (office).

SENDERENS, Alain; French restaurateur; b. 2 Dec. 1939, Hyères; s. of René Senderens and Lucette Senderens (née Azan); m. Eventhia Senderens (née Pappadinas) 1974; one s.; ed Lycée de Vic-en Bigorre; apprentice chef, Hôtel des Ambassadeurs, Lourdes 1957–59, La Tour d'Argent, Paris 1963; Sauce Cook Lucas Carton Restaurant 1964–65, Man. 1985–2005; Chief Sauce Cook and Fish Cook, Berkeley, Paris 1965–66, Chief Sauce Cook, Orly Hilton Hotel, Paris 1966–68; Proprietor and Chef, l'Archestrate, Paris 1968–85; Man. Senderens Restaurant 2005–; Chair. Bd of Dirs, Auberge Franc Comtoise, Lucas Carton; Pres. Chambre Syndicale de la Haute Cuisine Française 1990–92, Conseil Nat. des Arts Culinaires 1990–98; Chevalier, Légion d'honneur 1993; Officier des Arts et des Lettres 1985, Ordre nat. du Mérite 1978; Chevalier du Mérite Agricole 1978, Ordre Nat. du Mérite en titre de l'Industrie 1986, Ordre des Palmes Académiques 1993; Officier dans l'Ordre Nat. de la Légion d'honneur 2004; Médaille Vermeil de la Ville de Paris 1988. *Publications:* La Cuisine Réussie 1981, La Grande Cuisine à Petits Prix 1984, Figues sans barbarie 1991, Proust, la Cuisine retrouvée (jtly) 1991, Manger, c'est la santé (jtly) 1992, L'Atelier d'Alain Senderens 1997, Les Festins de Balthazar (jtly) 1997, Le vin et la table d'Alain Senderens 1999. *Leisure interests:* classical music, contemporary art, reading. *Address:* Restaurant Senderens, 9 place de la Madeleine, 75008 Paris (office); 11 place de la Madeleine, 75008 Paris, France (home). *Telephone:* 1-42-65-22-90 (office). *Fax:* 1-42-65-06-23 (office). *E-mail:* restaurant@senderens.fr (office). *Website:* www .senderens.fr (office).

SENDOV, Blagovest Hristov, PhD, DSc; Bulgarian mathematician, academic, politician and diplomatist; *Ambassador to Japan;* b. 8 Feb. 1932, Assenovgrad; s. of Christo Sendov and Marushka Sendov; m. 1st Lilia Georgieva 1958 (divorced 1982); two d.; m. 2nd Anna Marinova 1982; one s.; ed gymnasium in Assenovgrad, Sofia Univ., Moscow State Univ. and Imperial Coll., London; cleaner in Sofia 1949–52; teacher in Boboshevo and Elin Pelin 1956–58; Asst, Dept of Algebra, Univ. of Sofia 1958–60, Asst in Numerical Analysis and Computer Science 1960-63, Asst Prof. of Computer Sciences 1963–67, Prof. of Computer Science 1967, Dean, Faculty of Math. 1970–73, Rector 1973–79; mem. Parl. 1976–90, 1994–, Pres. of Parl. 1995–97, Vice-Pres. 1997–2003; Amb. to Japan 2003–; Vice-Pres. Bulgarian Acad. of Sciences 1980–82, Vice-Pres. and Scientific Sec.-Gen. 1982–88, Dir Centre for Informatics and Computer Tech. 1985–90, Pres. 1988–91; Pres. Comm. of Science 1986–88; Vice-Pres. Int. Fed. for Information Processing 1985–88, Pres. 1989–91; Vice-Pres. World Peace Council 1983–86, IIP— UNESCO 1986–90; Extraordinary Vice-Pres. ICSU 1990–93; mem. Exec. Cttee and Bd Dirs Int. Foundation for Survival and Devt of Humanity 1988–; Hon. Pres. Int. Asscn of Univs 1985–; two Orders of People's Repub. of Bulgaria and many others; Dr hc 1969, 1977; Dimitrov Prize for Science, Honoured Scientist 1984. *Publications:* Numerical Analysis, Old and New 1973, Hausdorff Approximation 1979, Averaged Moduli of Smoothness (monograph); textbooks and more than 150 articles in learned journals. *Leisure interests:* tennis, travelling. *Address:* Embassy of Bulgaria, 5-36-3, Yoyogi, Shibuya-ku, Tokyo 151-0053, Japan (office); 5 Plachkoviza Str., 1126 Sofia, Bulgaria (home). *Telephone:* (3) 3465-1021 (Tokyo) (office); (2) 862-60-83 (Sofia) (home). *Fax:* (3) 3465-1031 (Tokyo) (office); (2) 980-36-36 (Sofia) (office). *E-mail:* bulemb@gol.com (office); sendov2003@yahoo.com (office); bsendov@argo.bas.bg (home).

SENEQUIER, Dominique, DEA; French investment manager and business executive; *Chairman and CEO, AXA Private Equity;* m.; one s. one d.; ed Ecole Polytechnique, Univ. of the Sorbonne, Paris; worked for French Insurance Comm. 1975–80; Group Acquisitions Man., Groupe GAN (insurance co.) 1980–87, Founder and Dir GAN Participations 1987–95; joined AXA Investment Managers 1996, Founder of subsidiary AXA Private Equity, currently Chair. and CEO; mem. Institut des Actuaries Français; acquired Chateau Kirwan and Chateau Clinet wineries in Bordeaux; ranked by Forbes magazine amongst 100 Most Powerful Women (53rd) 2008. *Leisure interest:* playing the piano. *Address:* AXA Private Equity, 20 place Vendôme, 75001 Paris, France (office). *Telephone:* 1-44-45-92-52 (office). *Fax:* 1-44-45-93-31 (office). *E-mail:* mylan.gaillard@axa-im.com (office). *Website:* www .axaprivateequity.com (office).

ŞENER, Abdüllatif, DEcon; Turkish politician; *Deputy Prime Minister and Minister of State;* ed Ankara Univ.; served in several academic posts; entered Parl. 1991 as RP Deputy; Minister of Finance 1996–97; founding mem., Justice and Progress Party (AKP), becoming Deputy Chair.; Deputy Prime Minister and Minister of State 2002–; Pres., Exec. Cttee, e-Transformation Turkey. *Address:* Office of the Deputy Prime Minister, Başbakan yard. ve Devlet Bakanı, Bakanlıklar, Ankara, Turkey (office). *Telephone:* (312) 4191621 (office). *Fax:* (312) 4191547 (office). *E-mail:* abdullatif.sener@ basbakanlik.gov.tr (office).

SENGHAAS, Dieter, DPhil; German professor of social science; *Professor of Peace, Conflict and Development Research, University of Bremen;* b. 27 Aug. 1940, Geislingen; m. Eva Knobloch 1968; one d.; ed Univs of Tübingen, Michigan and Frankfurt and Amherst Coll.; Research Fellow, Center for Int. Affairs, Harvard Univ. 1968–70; Research Dir, Peace Research Inst., Frankfurt (PRIF) 1971–78; Prof. of Int. Relations, Univ. of Frankfurt 1972–78; Prof. of Peace, Conflict and Devt Research, Univ. of Bremen 1978–; mem. several nat. and int. scientific orgs; Dr hc (Tübingen) 2000; Lentz Int. Peace Research Award 1987, Göttingen Peace Award 1999. *Publications:* Aggressivität und kollektive Gewalt 1972, Aufrüstung durch Rüstungskontrolle 1972, Gewalt-Konflikt-Frieden 1974, Weltwirtschaftsordnung und Entwicklungspolitik (5th edn) 1987, Abschreckung und Frieden (3rd edn) 1981, Rüstung und Militarismus (2nd edn) 1982, Von Europa lernen 1982, The European Experience 1985, Die Zukunft Europas 1986, Europas Entwicklung und die Dritte Welt 1986, Konfliktformationen im internationalen System 1988, Europa 2000: Ein Friedensplan 1990, Friedensprojekt Europa 1992,

Wohin driftet die Welt 1994, Zivilisierung wider Willen 1998, Klaenge des Friedens 2001, The Clash Within Civilizations 2001, Zum ewigen Frieden 2004, On Perpetual Peace 2007; ed. or co-ed. of 33 books related to political science, int. affairs, etc. *Leisure interest:* music. *Address:* University of Bremen, 28334 Bremen (office); Freiligrathstrasse 6, 28211 Bremen, Germany (home). *Telephone:* (421) 2182281 (office); (421) 230436 (home). *Fax:* (421) 2187248 (office); (421) 249169 (home). *E-mail:* tmenge@iniis.uni-bremen .de (office). *Website:* www.iniis.uni-bremen.de/homepages/senghaas/index .php (office).

SENILAGAKALI, Jona, MD; Fijian physician, politician and diplomatist; b. 8 Nov. 1929, Waciwaci, Lakeba, Lau Islands; m.; five c.; ed Lau Provincial School, Queen Victoria School, Viti Levu, Fiji School of Medicine, study orthopaedic surgery in Melbourne, Australia and at Vellore Christian Medical Coll. Hosp., India; employed in health service 1954–63; Consultant Surgeon, Labasa Hosp. 1968–70; Lecturer, Fiji School of Medicine 1970–73; Dir of Medical Services 1974–78; Perm. Sec. for Health 1978–81; fmr medical doctor to Repub. of Fiji Mil. Forces; Counsellor, Embassy in Tokyo 1981–83, Consul Gen. to Los Angeles 1983–85, briefly served as roving amb. to Pacific Islands Forum countries; Perm. Sec. in Prime Minister's Office 1986; Perm. Sec. for Foreign Affairs 1987; Interim Prime Minister 2006–07 (following mil. coup of 5 Dec. 2006); Minister of Health 2007–08; Pres. Fiji Medical Asscn 1970–74, 2005–; public mem. Disciplinary Cttee, Fiji Law Soc. 1998–2006; lay preacher, Methodist Church of Fiji and Rotuma; Chief Steward Yarawa Methodist Church; mem. Standing Cttee Methodist Conf. 1989–2002; IBC Achievement Award, Int. Biographical Centre, Cambridge, UK. *Address:* c/o Ministry of Health, PO Box 2223, Government Buildings, Suva, Fiji (office).

SENKO, Vladimir Leonovich; Belarusian diplomatist; *Ambassador to Belgium and Permanent Representative to the European Union and NATO;* b. 5 Aug. 1946; ed Moscow State Inst. of Int. Relations, Diplomatic Acad.; entered diplomatic service 1973, serving with USSR Embassy, Poland 1973–79, Second Sec. 1981–85, First Sec. 1988–91; Third Sec. Fourth European Div. USSR Ministry of Foreign Affairs 1979–81; First Sec. Dept of Socialist Countries, USSR Ministry of Foreign Affairs 1987–88; Deputy Minister of Foreign Affairs, Belarus, 1991–92, Minister 1994–97; Amb. to UK 1994–97, to France (also accred to Spain, Portugal and Rep. to UNESCO) 1998–2004, to Belgium and Perm. Rep. to EU and NATO 2004–. *Address:* Embassy of Belarus, avenue Molière 192, 1050 Brussels, Belgium (office). *Telephone:* (2) 340-02-70 (office). *Fax:* (2) 340-02-87 (office).

SENTAMU, Rt Rev John Tucker Mugabi, LLB, MA, PhD, FRSA; Ugandan ecclesiastic; *Archbishop of York;* b. 1949; m. Margaret Sentamu; two c.; ed Makerere Univ., Univ. of Cambridge, UK; trained barrister and Advocate of the High Court of Uganda; Asst Chaplain Selwyn Coll. Cambridge; ordained 1979; Chaplain, Latchmere Remand Centre 1979–82; curate, St Andrew's Ham in Southwark 1979–82; curate, St Paul's, Herne Hill 1982–83; Priest-in-Charge, Holy Trinity, Tulse Hill 1983–84; Parish Priest St Matthias, Upper Tulse Hill 1983–84; mem. Gen. Synod 1985–96, mem. Standing, Policy and Appointments Cttees; mem. Archbishop's Comm. for Urban Priority Areas 1988–92; mem. Revision Cttee for the Ordination of Women to the Priesthood; Priest-in-Charge, St Saviour, Brixton Hill 1987–89; mem. Family Welfare Asscn 1989–; mem. Decade of Evangelism Steering Group; mem. Exec. Springboard; Prolocutor Convocation of Canterbury 1990–96; Chair. Cttee for Minority Ethnic Anglican Concerns 1990–99; Vicar of the Jt Benefice of Holy Trinity and St Matthias, Tulse Hill 1994–96; Area Bishop of Stepney 1996–2002; Bishop of Birmingham 2002–05, Archbishop of York 2005–; Adviser to the Stephen Lawrence Judicial Inquiry 1997–99; Gov. Univ. of North London 1998–2002; Pres. and Chair. London Marriage Guidance Council 2000–02; Chair. Review into the murder investigation of Damilola Taylor 2001–02; Pres. Youth for Christ, YMCA England; Chair. NHS Haeomoglobinopathy Screening Programme, EC1 New Deal Devt Programme; mem. Health Advisory Cttee HM Prisons, CTE Forum, Birmingham Hosp. NHS Trust; Custodian Trustee Birmingham Diocesan Fund; Trustee, Tower Hamlets Summer Univ.; Deputy Chair. Comm. on Urban Life and Work 2003–; Fellow, Univ. Coll., Christ Church, Canterbury, Queen Mary, Univ. of London; Hon. Fellow Selwyn Coll. Cambridge Freeman of the City of London 2000; Dr hc (Open Univ., Birmingham City Univ.); Hon. DPhil (Gloucestershire); Hon. DD (Birmingham, Hull); Hon. LLD (Leicester); Hon. DL (Sheffield); Midlander of the Year 2003, Yorkshire Man of the Year 2007, Speaker of the Year 2007. *Leisure interests:* music, cooking, reading, athletics, rugby, football. *Address:* Bishopthorpe Palace, Bishopthorpe, York, YO23 2GE, England (office). *Telephone:* (1904) 707021 (office). *Fax:* (1904) 709204 (office). *E-mail:* office@archbishopoyyork.org (office). *Website:* www .bishopthorpepalace.co.uk (office).

SEPE, HE Cardinal Crescenzio; Italian ecclesiastic; *Archbishop of Naples;* b. 2 June 1943, Carinaro, Aversa; ordained priest 1967; consecrated Bishop 1992; Titular Archbishop of Grado; Sec.-Gen. Cttee of the Grand Jubilee of the Year 2000 and of the Presidential Council; Chair. "Peregrinatio ad Petri Sedem"; cr. Cardinal 2001; Cardinal-Deacon of Dio Padre misericordioso 2001–; Prefect of Evangelization of Peoples, Roman Curia 2001–05, 2005–; Archbishop of Naples 2006–. *Address:* Largo Donnaregina 22, 80138 Naples (office); Palazzo di Propaganda Fide, Piazza di Spagna 48, 00187 Rome (office); Villa Betania, Via Urbans VIII 16, 00165 Rome, Italy (home). *Telephone:* (081) 5574111 (Naples) (office). *Fax:* (081) 440943 (Naples) (office). *E-mail:* ucs.na@ iol.it (office). *Website:* www.webdiocesi.chiesacattolica.it/cci_new/vis_diocesi .jsp?idDiocesi=126 (office).

SEPÚLVEDA-AMOR, Bernardo, LLB; Mexican lawyer and politician; *Judge, International Court of Justice;* b. 14 Dec. 1941, Mexico City; s. of Bernardo Sepúlveda and Margarita Sepúlveda; m. Ana Yturbe 1970; three s.; ed Nat. Univ. of Mexico and Queen's Coll., Cambridge; fmrly taught int. law,

El Colegio de México and Faculty of Political Science, Univ. of Mexico; Asst Dir of Juridical Affairs, Ministry of Presidency 1968–70; Dir-Gen. of Int. Financial Affairs, Ministry of Finance 1976–81; Int. Adviser, Minister of Programming and Budget 1981; Amb. to USA March–Dec. 1982; Sec. of Foreign Affairs 1982–88; Amb. to UK 1989–93; Foreign Affairs Adviser to Pres. of Mexico 1993–; mem. UN Int. Law Comm. 1996–2005; fmr Judge ad hoc, Int. Court of Justice, Judge 2006–; Sec. Int. Affairs Institutional Revolutionary Party (PRI) 1981–82; Pres. to UN Sixth Comm. on Transnat. Corpns. 1977–80; Hon. Fellow Queens' Coll., Cambridge 1991; Hon. GCMG; Dr hc (Univ. of San Diego), (Univ. of Leningrad); Premio Príncipe de Asturias, Premio Simón Bolivar; Knights Grand Cross, Most Distinguished Order of St. Michael and St. George (UK), Grand Cross, Order of Isabel The Catholic (Spain), Grand Cross, Order of Civil Merit (Spain), Grand Cross, Order of Cruzeiro do Sul (Brazil), Grand Cross, Order of Rio Branco (Brazil), Grand Cross, Order of Boyacá (Columbia), Ribbon, Order of Kwang-Wha (South Korea), Grand Cross, Order of General San Martin (Argentina), Gran Cordón, Order of the Libertador (Venezuela), Grand Cross, Orden de la Bandera Yugoslava (Yugoslavia), Grand Cross Orden de Cristo (Portugal), Grand Cross, Order Infante Don Henrique (Portugal), Grand Cross, Ordre de la Couronne (Belgium), Grand Officier, Ordre d la Légion d'Honneur (France), Connander INsignia jof the Order of Merit, with the Star (Poland), Superior Commander, Grand Order of the Saviour (Greece), Grand Cross, Order of Vasco Núñez de Balboa (Panama), Grand Cross, Order of the Quetzal (Guatemala), Grand Cordon, Order of the Rising Sun (Japan), Grand Cross, Order of El Sol de Peru (Peru), Order of the Republic, First Class (Egypt), Commander, Order of Distinction (Jamaica). *Publications:* Foreign Investment in Mexico 1973, Transnational Corporations in Mexico 1974, A View of Contemporary Mexico 1979, Planning for Development 1981. *Address:* International Court of Justice, Peace Palace, 2517 KJ, The Hague, Netherlands (office); Rocas 185, México, DF 01900, Mexico. *Telephone:* (70) 3022323 (office); (5) 652-0641. *Fax:* (70) 3649928 (office); (5) 652-9739. *Website:* www.icj-cij.org (office).

SEQUEIRA, Luis, PhD; American plant biologist and academic; *Professor Emeritus, Department of Plant Pathology, University of Wisconsin;* b. 1 Sept. 1927, San José, Costa Rica; s. of Raul Sequeira and the late Dora Jenkins; m. Elisabeth Steinvorth 1954; one s. three d.; ed Harvard Univ.; Teaching Fellow, Harvard Univ. 1949–52; Parker Fellow, Harvard and Instituto Biológico, São Paulo, Brazil 1952–53; Plant Pathologist, Asst Dir, then Dir Coto Research Station, United Fruit Co., Costa Rica 1953–60; Research Assoc., NC State Univ., Raleigh, NC 1960–61; Assoc. Prof., then Prof., Dept of Plant Pathology, Univ. of Wis., Madison 1961–78, Prof., Depts. of Bacteriology and Plant Pathology 1978–82, J.C. Walker Prof. 1982–, now Prof. Emer.; Consultant Agracetus, Madison 1982–93; Chief Scientist, Competitive Grants Office, USDA, Washington, DC 1987–88; research interests include physiology and biochem. of plant–parasite interactions, identification of genes for virulence in pathogens, particularly bacteria and breeding plants for disease resistance; Fellow American Phytopathological Soc. (Pres. 1985–86, Award of Distinction 1994), American Acad. of Microbiology; mem. NAS, Linnean Soc. of London, Nat. Science Bd 1991–; Hon. Prof. (Univ. of Queensland) 1997; E. M. Stakman Award. *Publications:* approximately 260 publs in journals and covering plant pathology, bacteriology, biochem. and genetics. *Leisure interests:* classical music, cross-country skiing. *Address:* 10 Appomattox Court, Madison, WI 53705, USA (home). *Telephone:* (608) 833-3440 (home).

SERAGELDIN, Ismail, BSc, MRP, PhD; Egyptian international organization official; *Director, Bibliotheca Alexandrina;* b. 1944, Guiza; m.; one s.; ed Cairo Univ., Harvard Univ.; fmr lecturer Cairo and Harvard Univs; fmr consultant in city and regional planning; joined World Bank 1972, held numerous positions including Economist in Educ. and Human Resources 1972–76, Div. Chief for Tech. Assistance and Special Studies 1977–80, for Urban Projects in Europe, the Middle E and N Africa 1980–83, Dir for Programs in W Africa 1984–87, Co-Dir for Cen. and Occidental Africa 1987–89, Tech. Dir for Sub-Saharan Africa 1990–92, Vice-Pres. for Environmentally and Socially Sustainable Devt 1992–98, Co-Chair. Non Governmental Org.-Bank Cttee 1997–99, Vice-Pres. for Special Programs 1998–2000; Chair. Global Water Partnership 1996–2000, World Comm. for Water in the 21st Century 1998–2000; currently Dir Bibliotheca Alexandrina (Library of Alexandria); fmr Distinguished Univ. Prof. Univ. of Wageningen, Netherlands; Chair. and mem. of numerous advisory cttees.; Hon. DSc (Indian Agricultural Research Inst.) 1997, (Punjab Agricultural Univ.) 1998, (Tamil Nadu Veterinary and Animal Sciences Univ.) 1998, (Tamil Nadu Agricultural Univ.) 1999, (Egerton Univ., Kenya) 1999, (SNHU, Manchester, NH) 2002, (McGill Univ., Montreal) 2003, (Azerbaijan State Econ. Univ., Baku) 2007,and numerous other hon. degrees. *Publications:* Nurturing Development 1995, Sustainability and the Wealth of Nations 1996, Architecture of Empowerment 1997, Rural Well-Being: From Vision to Action (jtly) 1997, The Modernity of Shakespeare 1998, Biotechnology and Biosafety (jtly) 1999, Very Special Places 1999, Promethean Science (jtly) 2000 and numerous other books and articles. *Address:* Bibliotheca Alexandrina, POB 138, El Shatby, Alexandria, 21526, Egypt (office). *Telephone:* (203) 4839999 (office). *Website:* www.bibalex.org (office); www.serageldin.com.

ŞERBAN, Andrei; Romanian stage director; b. 21 June 1943, Bucharest; s. of Gheorghe Şerban and Elpis Şerban; m.; two c.; ed Bucharest Theatrical and Cinematographic Art Inst.; int. scholarships: Ford 1970, Guggenheim 1976, Rockefeller 1980; associated with Robert Brustein's American Repertory Theatre Company for more than twenty years since 1970; worked also with LaMama Theatre, Public Theater, Lincoln Center, Circle in the Square, Yale Repertory Theatre, Guthrie Theatre, ACT, New York City, Seattle and Los Angeles Operas; in Europe: at Paris, Geneva, Vienna, and Bologna Opera Houses, Welsh Nat. Opera, Covent Garden, Théâtre de la Ville, Helsinki Lilla Teatern, Comédie Française, among others; worked with Shiki Co. of Tokyo,

Japan; has delivered numerous lectures; Gen. Man. Nat. Theatre of Romania 1990–93; Dir Oscar Hammerstein Center for the Performing Arts, Columbia University, New York 1992–; Prize for the Best Performance, World Students' Theatre Festival, Zagreb 1965, Obie Awards, Tony Award, George Abbott Award, Soc. of Stage Dirs and Choreographers, prizes at Avignon, Belgrade and Shiraz Festivals. *Productions include:* (in Romania) Ubu Roi 1966, Julius Caesar 1968, Jonah 1969, An Ancient Trilogy (Medea, The Trojan Women, Elektra) 1990; (in USA) Medea (Euripides) 1970, The Cherry Orchard 1972, Fragments of a Trilogy (Medea, Elektra, The Trojan Women) 1974, As You Like It 1976, Uncle Vanya 1979, The Umbrellas of Cherbourg 1980, The Seagull 1981, Three Sisters 1983, The Miser 1988, Twelfth Night 1989, Sweet Table at the Richelieu 1989, Hamlet 2000, The King Stag 2001. *Opera productions include:* Eugene Onegin 1980, Turandot 1984, Norma 1985, Fidelio (Covent Garden) 1986; Paris Opera: L'Ange de feu 1991, Lucia Di Lammermoor 1995, The Puritans 1997, L'Italienne a Alger 1998, Les Indes Galanates 1999. *Address:* Teatrul Naţional, Bd N. Bălcescu 2, Bucharest, Romania. *Telephone:* 614-56-92.

SERDENGEÇTİ, Süreyya, BS, MA; Turkish economist, central banker and academic; *Director, Stability Institute, Economic Policy Research Foundation of Turkey (TEPAV);* b. Istanbul; m. Çiğdem Son Deniz; ed Middle East Tech. Univ., Ankara, Vanderbilt Univ., Nashville, USA; with Central Bank of Turkey 1980–2006, positions included Foreign Exchange, Markets, External Relations, Communication Depts, Vice Gov. 1998–2001, Gov. 2001-2006; Sr Lecturer, Dept of Econs, TOBB University of Econs and Tech., Ankara 2006–; Dir Stability Inst., Econ. Policy Research Foundation of Turkey. *Address:* TEPAV Sögütözü Cd 43, Sögütözü, Ankara 06560, Turkey (office). *Telephone:* (312) 2925547 (office). *Fax:* (312) 2871946 (office). *E-mail:* serdengecti@tepav .org.tr (office); serdengecti@etu.edu.tr (office).

SERDYUKOV, Anatolii Eduardovich; Russian business executive and politician; *Minister of Defence;* b. 8 Jan. 1962, Kholmskii village, Abin Dist, Krasnodar Krai; m.; ed Leningrad (now St Petersburg) Inst. of Soviet Trade and St Petersburg State Univ.; mil. service 1984–85; worked in furniture shop 1985–95, then Marketing Dir and Dir-Gen. St Petersburg furniture market 1995–2000; Deputy Head, Dist Inspectorate of Taxes, Ministry of Taxes and Dues 2000–01; Deputy Head then Head, St Petersburg Tax Authority 2001–04; Deputy Minister of Taxes and Dues Feb.–July 2004, Head of Fed. Tax Service 2004–07; Minister of Defence 2007–. *Address:* Ministry of Defence, 105175 Moscow, ul. Myasnitskaya 37, Russia (office). *Telephone:* (495) 293-38-54 (office). *Fax:* (495) 296-84-36 (office). *Website:* www.mil.ru (office).

SEREBREAN, Oleg, PhD; Moldovan politician; *Chairman, Social Liberal Party;* b. 1969; ed Universitatea Pedagogică de Stat Ion Creangă, European Inst. of High Int. Studies, Nice, France; Spokesperson, Ministry of Foreign Affairs 1998–99; Deputy Rector Free Univ. of Moldova 1999–2002; Chair. Social Liberal Party 2001–; currently mem. Parl., Democratic Moldova electoral bloc, mem. Cttee for Foreign Policy and European Integration, two Special Cttees, Standing Bureau of Parl. *Publications:* Geopolitics of the Black Sea Region 1998, Politosphere 2001, Politics and Geopolitics 2004, Dictionary of Geopolitics 2006. *Address:* Social Liberal Party (Partidul Social-Liberal), Chişinău, str. Bulgară 24b, Moldova (office). *Telephone:* (22) 27-66-20 (office). *Fax:* (22) 22-36-66 (office). *E-mail:* psl_moldova@yahoo.com (office). *Website:* www.psl.md (office).

SEREBRIER, José, MA; American conductor and composer; b. 3 Dec. 1938, Montevideo, Uruguay; s. of David Serebrier and Frida Serebrier (née Wasser); m. Carole Farley 1969; one d.; ed Univ. of Minn., Curtis Inst. of Music, Phila; started conducting at age of 12; went to USA 1956; studied composition with Aaron Copland and Vittorio Giannini, Curtis Inst., Phila 1956–58 and conducting with Antal Dorati and Pierre Monteux; guest conductor in USA, S America, Australia and Europe; Assoc. Conductor American Symphony Orchestra, with Leopold Stokowski 1962–68; conducted alongside Leopold Stokowski world première of Charles Ives' Fourth Symphony, Carnegie Hall, New York 1964; conducted first performance in Poland of Charles Ives' Fourth Symphony 1971 and premieres of over 100 works; Rockefeller Foundation Composer-in-Residence with Cleveland Orchestra 1968–70; Music Dir Cleveland Philharmonic Orchestra 1968–71; Artistic Dir Int. Festival of Americas, Miami 1984–, Miami Festival 1985– (also Founder); two Guggenheim Fellowships, Ford Foundation Conducting Award, Nat. Endownment for Arts Comm. Award 1969, Ditson Award for Promotion of New Music, Columbia Univ. 1980, Deutsche Schallplatten Critics' Award 1991, UK Music Retailers' Asscn Award for Best Symphony Recording (Mendelssohn symphonies) 1991, Diapason d'Or Recording Award, France, Best Audiophile Recording (Scheherazade), Soundstage 2000, BMI Award, Koussevitzky Foundation Award, Latin Grammy for Best Classical Album of 2004. *Compositions:* Solo Violin Sonata 1954, Quartet for Saxophones 1955, Pequeña música (wind quintet) 1955, Symphony No. 1 1956, Momento psicológico (string orchestra) 1957, Solo Piano Sonata 1957, Suite canina (wind trio) 1957, Symphony for Percussion 1960, The Star Wagon (chamber orchestra) 1967, Nueve (double bass and orchestra) 1970, Colores mágicos (variations for harp and chamber orchestra) 1971, At Dusk, in Shadows (solo flute), Andante Cantabile (strings), Night Cry (brass), Dorothy and Carmine (flute and strings), George and Muriel (contrabass), Winter (violin concerto) 1995, Winterreise (for orchestra) 1999; composed music for several films; all compositions published and recorded; over 350 recordings to date. *Television includes:* int. TV broadcast of Grammys' Ceremony, LA 2002, conducting suite from Bernstein's West Side Story. *Publications:* orchestration of 14 songs by Edvard Grieg 2000, orchestration of Gershwin's works 2002, Suite from Janacek's Makropulos Case 2004; more than 100 works published by Peer Music, Kalmus, Peters Editions, Universal Edition, Vienna. *Leisure interests:*

reading, swimming, football. *Address:* 20 Queensgate Gardens, London, SW7 5LZ, England (office). *Fax:* (212) 662-8073 (office). *E-mail:* caspi123@aol.com (office). *Website:* www.joseserebrier.com.

SERETSE, Brig. Ramadeluka; Botswana lawyer, politician and army officer (retd); *Minister for Defence, Justice and Security;* served as Brig. in Botswana Defence Force, now retd; mem. Parl. for Serowe North East (Botswana Democratic Party) 2004–, Minister for Lands and Housing –2008, for Defence, Justice and Security 2008–. *Address:* Ministry for the Administration of Justice, Gaborone, Botswana.

SERFATY, Abraham, DipEng; Moroccan adviser, mining engineer and lecturer; *Adviser, National Office of Petroleum Research and Development;* b. 12 Jan. 1926, Casablanca; ed Ecole Nat. Supérieure des Mines, Paris; Dir Mining Research Operations Atlas Mountains 1949–50; arrested and imprisoned 1950; under house arrest in France 1952–56; with Mines du Maroc 1956; Head of Cabinet, Sec. of State for Industrial Production and Mines 1958; Dir of Mines and Geology 1959–60; Dir of Devt Research, Sherifian Office of Phosphates 1960–68; univ. lecturer 1962–63, 1964–65, 1968–72; arrested and tortured 1972; in hiding 1972–74; arrested, tortured and sentenced to life imprisonment 1977; released and exiled to France 1991; Lecturer, Univ. of Paris 1992–94; returned to Morocco as Adviser, Nat. Office of Petroleum Research and Devt 2000–. *Publications:* Lutte anti-sioniste et Révolution Arabe 1977, Ecrits de Prison sur la Palestine 1992. *Address:* c/o Ministry of the Economy and Finance, avenue Muhammad V, Rabat, Morocco (office).

SERGEANT, Carol, CBE, BA, MBA; British financial officer; *Chief Risk Director, Lloyds TSB;* b. 1952, Berlin, Germany; d. of Frank Hawksworth and Norah MaCauley; m. Philip Sergeant; one s. one d.; ed Newnham Coll. Cambridge, City Univ. Business School; joined Bank of England 1970s, various positions in research, negotiations with IMF, EEC issues, foreign exchange –1998; joined Financial Services Authority 1998, various positions including Dir Strategic Change, Man. Dir responsible for Regulatory Processes and Risk Directorate, Deputy Chair. Building Societies Comm., Dir Banks and Building Societies, mem. Bd, 2001–03 (resgnd); Chief Risk Dir and mem. Group Exec. Cttee, Lloyds TSB 2004–; mem. Advisory Bd and Strategy Cttee, Cass Business School; mem. Trustee and Audit Cttee, Court of Int. Guild of Bankers. *Leisure interest:* fencing. *Address:* Lloyds TSB Group plc, 25 Gresham Street, London, EC2V 7HN, England (office). *Telephone:* (20) 7356-1116 (office). *Fax:* (20) 7356-1364 (office). *E-mail:* jeanette.craft@lloydstsb.co.uk (office). *Website:* www.lloydstsbgroup.co.uk (office).

SERGEYEV, Ivan Ivanovich; Russian civil servant and diplomatist; *Director General, GlavUpDK, Ministry of Foreign Affairs;* b. 7 Sept. 1941, Electrostal, Moscow Region; Deputy, First Deputy Chair., Exec. Cttee Moscow Regional Soviet 1976–83; Deputy, First Deputy Head, Dept on Problems of Diplomatic Corps USSR (now Russian) Ministry of Foreign Affairs 1983–97; Deputy Minister of Foreign Affairs 1997–2003; Deputy Chair. Bd Black Sea Bank for Trade and Devt 1998–2003; currently Dir Gen. GlavUpDK (Main Admin. for Service to Diplomatic Corps)., Ministry of Foreign Affairs; State Prize of Russia 2002. *Address:* GlavUpDK, 119034 Moscow, Prechistenka, 20, Russia (office). *Telephone:* (495) 230-2329 (office). *Fax:* (495) 230-2329 (home). *E-mail:* info@updk.ru (office). *Website:* updk.ru (home).

SERGEYEV, Victor Mikhailovich, Cand.Math.Sci., DHist; Russian mathematician, political scientist and academic; *Professor of Comparative Politics and Director, Centre for International Research, Moscow State Institute of International Relations;* b. 22 April 1944, Moscow; m. Marina Alekseyevna Sergeyeva; one s.; ed Moscow Inst. of Energy, Moscow State Univ.; Sr Researcher All-Union Research Inst. of Meteorological Service, USSR State Cttee of Standards 1975–78, Problem Lab. of System Analysis, Moscow State Inst. of Int. Relations 1978–86, Prof. of Comparative Politics and Dir Centre for Int. Research 1998–; Head of Lab. Inst. of USA and Canada, USSR (now Russian) Acad. of Sciences 1986–90; Deputy Dir Analytical Centre on Scientific and Industrial Policy, Ministry of Science and Tech. 1998–; mem. Russian Acad. of Nat. Sciences, Asscn of Political Studies, Kant Soc., Russian Asscn of Artificial Intellect, Exec. Bd Centre of Philosophy, Psychology and Sociology of Religion; Hon. mem. Leeds Univ. (UK). *Publications:* numerous scientific works published in Russia and abroad on political and religious culture, cognitive studies etc., including The Wild East 1998, Limits of Rationality 1998. *Leisure interest:* foreign languages. *Address:* Centre for International Research, Moscow State Institute of International Relations, Vernadskogo prosp. 76, 119454 Moscow, Russia (office). *Telephone:* (495) 434-20-44 (office). *Fax:* (495) 434-20-44 (office). *E-mail:* tsmi@mgimo.ru (office); av205@comtv.ru (home).

SERGIENKO, Valentin I., DrChem; Russian chemist; *Chairman, Far East Branch, Russian Academy of Sciences;* b. 18 Aug. 1944, Novosysoyevka, Primorsky territory; m.; two c.; ed Far East State Univ., Vladivostok; has held numerous positions at Inst. of Chemistry, Far East Br., Russian Acad. of Sciences 1970–92, including Jr Researcher, Sr Researcher, Head of Group, Head of Lab., Head of Div., Deputy Dir, Acting Dir, Deputy Chair. Far East Br. of Russian Acad. of Sciences 1992, now Chair., concurrently Head of Div., Inst. of Chem., Far East Br. of Russian Acad. of Sciences; Scientific Head, Inst. of Eng. and Social Ecology, Far East State Tech. Univ.; Dir Far East Br. of Agency for Man. of Property, Russian Acad. of Sciences; mem. Russian Acad. of Sciences (Corresp. mem. 1997–2000); mem. Bd Russian Foundation for Basic Research; Prize of Russian Fed. Govt in the field of science and technology; Order of Labour Red Banner, various medals. *Achievements include:* owner of six patents. *Publications include:* over 160 scientific papers, monographs on theoretical chem., spectrochem., structure of fluorides, tech. of purification and utilization of waste. *Address:* Presidium of Far Eastern

Branch, Russian Academy of Sciences, Svetlanskaya str. 50, Vladivostok 690950, Russia (office). *Telephone:* 4232-22 25 28 (office). *E-mail:* sergienko@hg.febras.ru (office).

SERJEANT, Graham Roger, CMG, CD, MD, FRCP; British medical research scientist and academic; *Professor Emeritus, Faculty of Medicine, University of the West Indies;* b. 26 Oct. 1938, Bristol; s. of Ewart E. Serjeant and Violet E. Serjeant; m. Beryl E. King 1965; ed Sibford School, Banbury, Bootham School, York, Clare Coll., Cambridge, London Hosp. Medical School and Makerere Coll. Kampala; House Physician, London Hosp. 1963–64, Royal United Hosp. Bath 1965–66, Hammersmith Hosp. London 1966; Registrar, Univ. Hosp. of the West Indies 1966–67; Wellcome Research Fellow, Dept of Medicine, Univ. Hosp. of the West Indies 1967–71; Visiting Prof., Dept of Biochemistry, Univ. of Tenn. 1971; mem. scientific staff, MRC Abnormal Haemoglobin Unit, Cambridge 1971–72, Epidemiology Research Unit, Jamaica 1972–74; Dir MRC Labs, Jamaica 1974–99; Prof. of Epidemiology, Faculty of Medicine, Univ. of the West Indies 1981–99, Prof. Emer. 1999–; Visiting Prof. London School of Hygiene and Tropical Medicine 1999, Guy's, King's and St Thomas' Combined Medical School, London 1999; Chair. Sickle Cell Trust (Jamaica); Hon. FRCPE 1998; Hon. Prof. Dept of Public Health, Guy's Hosp., London 1999; Vice-Chancellor's Award for Excellence 1999, PAHO Jamaican Hero of Health 2002. *Publications:* The Clinical Features of Sickle Cell Disease 1974, Sickle Cell Disease (3rd edn) 2001; more than 400 papers on sickle cell disease in medical journals. *Leisure interests* squash, music. *Address:* 14 Milverton Crescent, Kingston 6, Jamaica. *Telephone:* 970-0077 (office); 927 2300 (home). *Fax:* 970-0074 (office). *E-mail:* grserjeant@cwjamaica.com.

SERKIN, Peter Adolf; American concert pianist; b. 24 July 1947, New York; s. of Rudolf Serkin and Irene Busch; m. Regina Serkin; five c.; ed Curtis Inst. of Music; debut, New York 1959; Dr hc (New England Conservatory) 2001; Premio Accademia Musicale Chigian Siena 1983. *Performances:* concert appearances in recital and with orchestras world-wide including Philadelphia, Cleveland, New York, Chicago, Berlin, London, Zürich, Paris and Japan; has premiered works composed for him by Knussen, Takemitsu, Lieberson, Berio; has given benefit performances to aid hunger and war victims. *Address:* c/o CM Artists, 127 West 96th Street, #13B, New York, NY 10025, USA (office). *Telephone:* (212) 864-1005 (office). *Fax:* (212) 864-1066 (office). *Website:* www.cmartists.com/artists/peter_serkin.htm (office).

SEROTA, Sir Nicholas Andrew, Kt, MA; British art gallery director; *Director, The Tate Gallery;* b. 27 April 1946; s. of Stanley Serota and Baroness Serota; m. 1st Angela M. Beveridge 1973 (divorced 1995); two d.; m. 2nd Teresa Gleadowe 1997; ed Haberdashers' Aske's School, Hampstead and Elstree, Christ's Coll., Cambridge and Courtauld Inst. of Art; Regional Art Officer and Exhbn Organizer, Arts Council of GB 1970–73; Dir Museum of Modern Art, Oxford 1973–76; Dir Whitechapel Art Gallery 1976–88; Dir The Tate Gallery, London 1988–; Chair. British Council Visual Arts Advisory Cttee 1992–98 (mem. 1976–98); Sr Fellow Royal Coll. of Art 1996; Trustee Public Art Devt Trust 1983–87, Architecture Foundation 1991–99, The Little Sparta Trust 1995–2007; Commr Comm. for Architecture and the Built Environment 1999–2006; mem. Olympic Delivery Authority 2006–; Hon. Fellow, Queen Mary and Westfield Coll., Univ. of London 1988, RIBA 1992, Goldsmiths Coll., Univ. of London 1994; Hon. DArts (City of London Polytechnic) 1990; Hon. DLitt (Plymouth) 1993, (Keele) 1994, (South Bank) 1996, (Exeter) 2000; Hon. DUniv (Surrey) 1997. *Publication:* Experience or Interpretation: The Dilemma of Museums of Modern Art 1997. *Address:* Tate Britain, Millbank, London, SW1P 4RG, England (office). *Telephone:* (20) 7887-8000 (office). *Fax:* (20) 7887-8007 (office). *Website:* www.tate.org.uk (office).

SERRA, José; Brazilian politician, economist and academic; *Governor of São Paulo;* b. 19 March 1942, São Paulo; m. Monica Serra; two c.; ed Univ. of São Paulo, CEPAL-ILPES, Santiago, Chile, Univ. of Chile, Cornell Univ., USA; Leader Nat. Students' Union 1963–64; forced to flee to Chile for opposing Brazil's fmr mil. regime in early 1970s, in exile for 14 years; Prof. of Econs, Univ. of Chile 1968–73; Prof., Univ. of Campinas; Sec. for Economy and Planning, São Paulo 1983–86; Co-Founder and mem. Brazilian Social Democratic Party (PSDB) 1988, now Pres.; elected Fed. Rep. for São Paulo 1986–94; elected Senator 1994–95, 2002–; Minister of Planning 1995–96; Minister of Health 1998–2002; unsuccessful Presidential cand. 2002; Mayor of São Paulo 2005–06, Gov. of São Paulo 2007–; mem. Inst. for Advanced Study, Princeton Univ., USA 1976–78. *Address:* Palácio dos Bandeirantes, Avenida Morumbi, 4500, 05650–905 São Paulo, SP Brazil (office). *Telephone:* (11) 2193-8000 (office). *Website:* www.saopaulo.sp.gov.br (office).

SERRA, Richard, MFA; American sculptor; b. 2 Nov. 1939, San Francisco, Calif.; m. Clara Weyergraf-Serra; ed Univ. of Calif., Berkeley, Univ. of Calif. Santa Barbara, Yale Univ.; frequent exhbns at Leo Castelli Gallery, New York since 1970; works in many perm. collections including Whitney Museum of Modern Art, Guggenheim Museum, Museum of Modern Art, New York, Art Gallery of Ontario, Stedelijk Museum, Amsterdam; Hon. DFA (Calif. Coll. of Arts and Crafts, Oakland) 1994; Skohegan School Medal 1975, Japan Art Asscn Praemium Imperiale 1994. *Publications:* Weight and Measure 1992, Writings/Interviews 1994. *Address:* c/o Leo Castelli Gallery, 59 East 79th Street, New York, NY 10021; 173 Duane Street, New York, NY 10013, USA. *Website:* www.gagosian.com/artists/richard-serra.

SERRA RAMONEDA, Antoni, PhD; Spanish economist, academic and fmr university rector; *Full Professor of Managerial Economics, Department d'Economia de l'Empresa, Universitat Autònoma of Barcelona;* b. 20 July 1933, Barcelona; s. of Antoni Serra Riera and Enriqueta Ramoneda Ruis; m. Margarita de la Figuera Buñuel 1958; one s. two d.; ed Lycée Français, Barcelona and Univ. Complutense de Madrid; Sec. Faculty of Econ. Sciences, Univ. of Barcelona 1960–64; Founding Mem.of the Universitat Autònoma de

Barcelona and Dept d'Economia de l'Empresa, Univ. Autónoma de Barcelona, Sec.-Gen. 1960–72, Dir Inst. of Educ. Sciences 1977–78, Rector 1980–85, currently Full Prof. of Managerial Econs and mem. Business Efficiency and Competitiveness Group; Treas. Institut d'Estudis Catalans (IEC) 1992–98, Vice-Pres. 1998–2001; Chair. Caixa Catalunya –2005; Pres. Comisión de Control Caja de Pensiones para la Vejez y de Ahorros 1979–82, Sec.-Gen. 1982–84; Pres. Caja de Ahorros de Cataluña 1984; Officier et Chevalier de l'Ordre du Mérite Nat.; Medalla al Mèrit Científic, Medalla Narcís Monturiol al Mèrit Científic i Tecnològic. *Publications:* Libro Blanco sobre los efectos para Cataluña del ingreso de España en la CEE, La industria textil algodonera y el Mercado Común Europeo, Sistema Económico y Empresa. *Address:* Department d'Economia de l'Empresa, Edifici B, Campus UAB, 08193 Cerdanyola; Pl. Bonanova 5, Barcelona 08022, Spain (home). *Telephone:* (93) 5811209 (office); (93) 2478101 (home). *Fax:* (93) 5812555 (office). *E-mail:* gr.becg@uab.es (office). *Website:* selene.uab.es/dep-economia-empresa (office).

SERRA REXACH, Eduardo, LLB; Spanish business executive and fmr politician; *President, Eduardo Serra y Asociados SL;* b. 19 Dec. 1946, Madrid; m. 1st; one s.; m. 2nd Luz del Carmen Municio; ed Complutense Univ., Madrid; began career as state lawyer; mem. staff Ministry of Educ. and Industry –1982; Under-Sec. of Defence 1982–84, Sec. of State for Defence 1984–87, Minister of Defence 1996–2000; Chair. Telettra 1986; Vice-Chair. Cubiertas y MZOV 1989–91, Chair. 1991; Chair. Peugeot Spain 1992, Airtel 1994–96; Chair. UBS Warburg Spain 2000–06; currently Founder and Pres. Eduardo Serra y Asociados (ESYA) SL; mem. Bd of Dirs Zeltia; mem. Advisory Bd Rolls Royce, ASPIDE Group GmbH, Instituto de Empresa, Montrose, ICX Technologies, Everis, European Advisory Group; Patron, Real Instituto Elcano for Int. and Strategic Studies; Vice-Pres. FAD; Pres. Everis Foundation; Chair. Bd of Trustees, Prado Museum, Madrid 2000–; Chair. Elcano Royal Institute, Madrid 2001–05; Pres. Foundation for Assistance Against Drug Addiction 1996–; fmr Pres. Funación DMR Consulting, Spain. *Address:* Eduardo Serra y Asociados SL, Jorge Juan, 78, 28009 Madrid Spain (office). *Telephone:* (91) 4350402 (office).

SERRA SERRA, Narcís, DEcon; Spanish politician; b. 30 May 1943, Barcelona; ed Barcelona Univ. and London School of Econs; Prof. of Econ. Theory, Autonomous Univ. of Barcelona 1976–77; mem. Convergència Socialista de Catalunya 1974–, Minister of Public Works in Catalan Autonomous Govt 1977–79; Mayor of Barcelona 1979; Minister of Defence in Spanish Govt 1982–91, Deputy Prime Minister 1991–95; Gen. Sec. Catalan Socialist Party 1996–2000; Pres. CIDOB Foundation, IBEI Inst.; Hon. Fellow, LSE 1991. *Publications:* Guerra y paz en el siglo XXI – una perspectiva Europea 2003, Europa en construcción – integración, identidades y seguridad 2004, Visiones sobre el Desarrollo en América Latina 2007, Hacia un nuevo pacto social. Políticas económicas para un desarrollo integral en América Latina 2008, The Washington Consensus Reconsidered: Towards a New Global Governance 2008, La transición militar. Reflexiones en torno a la reforma democrática de las fuerzas armadas 2008. *Address:* Fundació CIDOB, Elisabets 12, 08001 Barcelona, Spain (office). *Telephone:* (93) 3180807 (office). *Fax:* (93) 3427550 (office). *E-mail:* lmoya@cidob.org (office). *Website:* www.cidob.org (office).

SERRANO AGUILAR, Nicanor Alejandro; Ecuadorean politician; b. 14 Jan. 1933; m.; four c.; ed Colegio de los Padres Jesuitas, Universidad de Cuenca; fmr engineer and business executive; fmr Councillor Prov. Council of Azuay; Pres. Instituto de Estudios de Régimen Seccional del Ecuador (IERSE); Vice-Pres. of Ecuador 2005–07; Sport and Promotion of Olympism Trophy, Int. Olympic Cttee 2007. *Address:* c/o Office of the Vice-President, Manuel Larrea y Arenas, Edif. Consejo Provincial de Pichincha, 21°, Quito, Ecuador (office).

SERRANO ELIAS, Jorge, PhD; Guatemalan fmr head of state and business executive; b. 26 April 1945; m. Magda Bianchi de Serrano; three s. two d.; ed Univ. of San Carlos, Stanford Univ., USA; Pres. Advisory Council of State 1982–83; Pres. of Guatemala 1991–93 (resgnd).

SERRE, Jean-Pierre, BSc PhD, DèsSc; French mathematician and academic; *Honorary Professor, Collège de France;* b. 15 Sept. 1926, Bages; s. of Jean Serre and Adèle Serre (née Diet); m. Josiane Heulot 1948; one d.; ed Lycée de Nîmes, Ecole Normale Supérieure, Université de Paris; worked at Centre National de la Recherche Scientifique, Paris 1948–54, Université de Nancy 1954–56; Prof. of Algebra and Geometry, Coll. de France 1956–94, Hon. Prof. 1994–; mem. Académie des Sciences, Paris 1977–; Foreign mem. American Acad. of Arts and Sciences 1960–, Royal Soc., London 1974–, Académie Royale Néerlandaise des Sciences 1978–, NAS 1979–, American Philosophical Soc. 1998–, Académie des Sciences de Russie 2003–; Hon. FRS (UK); Hon. mem. London Math. Soc.; Grand officier, Légion d'honneur, Ordre nat. du Mérite; Dr hc (Cambridge) 1978, (Stockholm) 1980, (Glasgow) 1983, (Athens) 1996, (Harvard) 1998, (Durham) 2000, (London) 2001, (Oslo) 2002, (Oxford) 2003, (Bucharest, Barcelona) 2004, (Madrid) 2006; Fields Medal 1954, Prix Peccot-Vimont, Collège de France 1955, Prix Francoeur, Académie des Sciences 1957, Prix Gaston Julia 1970, Médaille Émile Picard, Académie des Sciences 1971, Balzan Prize 1985, Médaille d'or du CNRS 1987, American Math. Soc. Steele Prize 1995, Wolf Prize 2000, Abel Prize 2003. *Publications:* Homologie singulière des espaces fibrés 1951, Faisceaux algébriques cohérents 1955, Groupes algébriques et corps de classes 1959, Corps Locaux 1962, Cohomologie galoisienne 1964, Abelian *l* -adic representations 1968, Cours d'arithmétique 1970, Représentations linéaires des groupes finis 1971, Arbres, amalgames, SL2 1977, Lectures on the Mordell-Weil Theorem 1989, Topics in Galois Theory 1992, Collected Papers (four vols) 1949–1998, Local Algebra 2000, Correspondence Grothendieck-Serre 2004. *Leisure interest:* sport. *Address:* Collège de France, 3 rue d'Ulm, 75005 Paris, France (office); 6 avenue de Montespan, 75116 Paris (home). *Telephone:* 1-44-27-17-90 (office); 1-45-53-35-63 (home). *Fax:* 1-44-27-17-04 (office). *E-mail:* serre@dma.ens.fr (office).

SERREAU, Coline; French film director; b. 29 Oct. 1947, Paris; d. of Jean-Marie Serreau; has acted in several stage plays including Lapin, lapin in Paris; wrote and acted in Bertuccelli's On s'est trompé d'histoire d'amour 1973; directed Oedipus the King for Italian TV; f. trapeze school in Canada. *Films include:* Mais qu'est-ce qu'elles veulent? (documentary) 1975, Pourquoi pas! 1976, Qu'est-ce qu'on attend pour être heureux! 1982, Trois hommes et un couffin (Three Men and a Cradle – also screenwriter) 1985, Romuald et Juliette 1989, Mama, There's a Man in Your Bed 1990, Chaos (also screenwriter) 2003, 18 ans après (also screenwriter) 2003, Saint-Jacques... La Mecque (also screenwriter) 2005.

SERRIN, James B., PhD, FAAS; American mathematician and academic; *Professor Emeritus of Mathematics, University of Minnesota;* b. 1 Nov. 1926, Chicago, Ill.; s. of Helen Wingate Serrin and James B. Serrin; m. Barbara West 1952; three d.; ed Western Michigan Univ. and Indiana Univ.; MIT 1952–54; Univ. of Minn. 1955–, Chair. 1964–65, Regents Prof. of Math. 1969–, Prof. Emer. of Math. 1995–; Fellow, American Acad. of Arts and Sciences; mem. NAS, Finnish Acad. of Science, Soc. for Natural Philosophy (Pres. 1969–70); Hon. DSc (Sussex, Ferrara, Padua, Tours); G. D. Birkhoff Award, American Math. Soc. *Publications:* Mathematical Principles of Fluid Dynamics 1958, New Perspectives on Thermodynamics 1985, The Problem of Dirichlet for Quasilinear Elliptic Differential Equations 1969. *Address:* Department of Mathematics, University of Minnesota, Minneapolis, MN 55455 (office); 4422 Dupont Avenue South, Minneapolis, MN 55409, USA (home). *Telephone:* (612) 624-9530 (office). *Fax:* (612) 626-2017 (office). *E-mail:* serrin@math.umn.edu (office). *Website:* www.math.umn.edu/~serrin (office).

SERVAN-SCHREIBER, Jean-Claude, LenD; French media executive and journalist; b. 11 April 1918, Paris; s. of the late Robert Servan-Schreiber and Suzanne Crémieux; m. 1st Christiane Laroche 1947 (divorced); m. 2nd Jacqueline Guix de Pinos 1955 (divorced); two s. three d.; m. 3rd Paule Guinet 1983 (divorced); ed Exeter Coll., Oxford and Sorbonne; served World War II in Flanders 1940, in Resistance 1941–42, in N Africa 1943, France 1944, Germany 1945; with Les Echos 1946–65, Gen. Man. 1957, Dir 1963–65; Deputy for Paris, Nat. Ass. 1965–67; Asst Sec.-Gen. UNR-UDT 1965; Pres. Rassemblement français pour Israël 1967; Dir-Gen. Régie française de publicité 1968–78; mem. Haut Conseil de l'audiovisuel 1973–81; Pres. Groupe Européen des Régisseurs de Publicité Télévisée 1975–78; mem. Conseil politique, RPR 1977–81; Conseiller du Groupe de Presse L'Expansion 1980–93; Special Adviser Mitsubishi Electric (Europe) 1992–2000; Pres. Inst. Arthur Vernes (Medical and Surgical Center) 1993–; Commdr, Légion d'honneur; Médaille mil.; Commdr Ordre nat. du Mérite; Croix de guerre; Croix du Combattant volontaire de la Résistance; Legion of Merit (USA), etc. *Address:* 147 bis rue d'Alésia, 75014 Paris, France (home). *Telephone:* 1-45-39-96-11 (home). *E-mail:* jcss@orange.fr (home).

SERVATIUS, Bernhard, DJur; German lawyer and academic; *Partner, Servatius Jenckel Noelle;* b. 14 April 1932, Magdeburg; s. of Rudolf Servatius and Maria Servatius; m. Ingeborg Servatius 1985; ed Univs of Fribourg, Hamburg and other univs; lawyer 1959–; Sr Pnr Dr Servatius & Pnr (legal firm), currently Pnr Servatius Jenckel Noelle; Man. Pnr Treubesitz GmbH, Hamburg (trust co.); legal adviser to Axel Springer and Springer Publishing Group 1970; Chair. Supervisory Bd Rheinische Merkur GmbH; Chief Rep. of Axel Springer and Acting Chair. of Man. Admin. Verlagshaus Axel Springer 1984; Chair. Supervisory Bd Axel Springer Verlag 1985–2002; Prof. Hochschule für Musik und Theater, Hamburg; Deputy Chair. Supervisory Bd AWD; mem. Supervisory Bd equitrust Aktiengesellschaft; mem. Advisory Bd EnBW Energie Baden-Württemberg AG, Hapag-Lloyd AG; Bundesverdienstkreuz Erste Klasse; Hon. DPhil. *Address:* Servatius Rechtsanwälte Partnerschaftsgesellschaft, Gänsemarkt 50, 20354 Hamburg, Germany (office). *Telephone:* (40) 35016145 (office). *Fax:* (40) 35016100 (office). *E-mail:* bernhard.servatius@servatius-law.de (office). *Website:* www.servatius-rechtsanwaelte.de (office).

ŠEŠELJ, Vojislav, DJur; Serbian politician; *President, Serbian Radical Party;* b. 11 Oct. 1954, Sarajevo; s. of Nikola Šešelj and Danica Šešelj (née Misita); m. Jadranka Pavlović; four s.; ed Sarajevo Univ.; Docent, Sarajevo Univ. 1981–84; Prof., Prishtina Univ. 1991–, was persecuted by authorities for nationalistic activities, arrested and sentenced to 8 years' imprisonment 1984, released after 22 months; later arrested twice 1990, 1994–95; Head of Četnik (royalist) Movt 1989; Founder and Pres. Serbian Radical Party 1990–; supported war against Croatia 1991; cand. for presidency of Serbia 1997; Deputy Prime Minister 1998–2001; worked and lectured in European countries, USA, Canada; indicted by Int. Criminal Tribunal for the fmr Yugoslavia (ICTY) for crimes against humanity and war crimes Feb. 2003. *Publications:* more than 100 books including Political Essence of Militarism and Fascism 1979, Dusk of Illusions 1986, Democracy and Dogma 1987, Debrozovisation of Public Mentality 1990, Destruction of Serbian National Being 1992, Actual Political Challenges 1993, Are We Threatened with Slobotomia 1994, Selected Works 1994. *Address:* c/o Serbian Radical Party (Srpska Radikalna Stranka), 11080 Belgrade, Zemun, Magistratski trg 3, Serbia (office). *E-mail:* info@srpskaradikalnastranka.rs (office). *Website:* www.vseselj.com (office).

SESHADRI, C. S., BA, PhD; Indian mathematician and academic; *Professor and Director, Chennai Mathematical Institute;* ed Loyola Coll., Madras Univ., Tata Inst. of Fundamental Research, Bombay Univ.; Research Scholar, Tata Inst. of Fundamental Research, Bombay 1953, Prof. 1965–75, Sr Prof. 1975–84; Sr Prof., Inst. of Math. Sciences, Madras 1984–89; Prof. and

Founding Dir Chennai Math. Inst. 1989–; Visiting Prof., Univ. of Paris 1957–60, Harvard Univ. 1974–75, Inst. for Advanced Study, Princeton 1975–76, UCLA, Brandeis Univ., Univ. of Bonn, Kyoto Univ.; Hon. DSc (Banaras Hindu Univ.); Shanti Swarup Bhatnagar Award, Srinivasa Ramanujan Medal, Indian Acad. of Sciences, Third World Acad. of Sciences Science Award, Trieste Science Prize in Math. (co-recipient) 2006. *Publications:* numerous papers in professional journals on algebraic geometry. *Address:* Chennai Mathematical Institute, Plot H1, SIPCOT IT Park, Padur PO, Siruseri 603103, India (office). *Telephone:* (44) 32983441 (office). *E-mail:* css@cmi.ac.in (office). *Website:* www.cmi.ac.in (office).

SESSIONS, Jefferson Beauregard, III, BA, JD; American politician; *Senator from Alabama;* b. 24 Dec. 1946, Hybart, Ala; s. of Jefferson Beauregard Sessions and Abbie Sessions (née Powe); m. Mary Montgomery Blackshear 1969; one s. two d.; ed Huntingdon Coll., Montgomery and Univ. of Alabama; admitted to Ala Bar 1973; Assoc., Guin, Bouldin & Porch, Russellville, Ala 1973–75; Asst US Attorney, US Dept of Justice, Mobile, Ala 1975–77, US Attorney 1981–93; Assoc. Pnr, Stockman & Bedsole Attorneys, Mobile 1977–81; Pnr, Stockman, Bedsole & Sessions 1993–94; Attorney-Gen. for Ala 1996; Senator from Ala 1997–; mem. US Attorney-Gen.'s Advisory Cttee 1987–89, Vice-Chair. 1989; mem. Environment and Public Works Cttee, Judiciary Cttee; mem. Bd Trustees, Exec. Cttee Mobile Bay Area Partnership for Youth 1981–; Chair. Advisory Bd Ashland Place United Methodist Church, Mobile 1982; First Vice-Pres. Mobile Lions Club 1993–94; Capt. US Army Reserves 1975–85; mem. ABA, Ala Bar Asscn., Mobile Bar Asscn; US Attorney-Gen.'s Award for significant achievements in the war against drug-trafficking 1992. *Address:* 493 Senate Russell Office Building, Washington, DC 20510-0001 (office); 1119 Hillcrest, Xing E, Mobile, AL 36695-4505, USA (home). *Telephone:* (202) 224-4124 (office). *Website:* sessions.senate.gov (office).

SESSIONS, William S., JD; American government official and judge; *Vice-Chairman, Governor's Task Force on Homeland Security for the State of Texas;* b. 27 May 1930, Fort Smith, Ark.; s. of Will A. Sessions and Edith A. Steele; m. Alice June Lewis 1952; three s. one d.; ed Baylor Univ.; called to Texas Bar 1959; Pnr, McGregor & Sessions, Waco, Tex. 1959–61; Assoc. Tirey, McLaughlin, Gorin & Tirey, Waco 1961–63; Pnr, Haley, Fulbright, Winniford, Sessions & Bice, Waco 1963–69; Chief, Govt Operations Section, Criminal Div. Dept of Justice 1969–71; US Attorney, US Dist Court (Western Dist) Texas, San Antonio 1971–74, US Dist Judge 1974–80, Chief US Dist Judge 1980–87; Dir Fed. Bureau of Investigation (FBI) 1987–93; Pnr, Sessions & Sessions, LC 1995–2000, Holland & Knight, LLP 2000–; Vice-Chair. Gov.'s Task Force on Homeland Security for the State of Texas 2002; mem. Gov.'s Anti- Crime Comm. 2002, Judiciary Relations Cttee for the State Bar of Texas; fmr Pres. Waco-McLennan Co. Bar Asscn, Fed. Bar Asscn of San Antonio, Dist Judges' Asscn of the Fifth Circuit; fmr mem. Bd Dirs Fed. Judicial Center, Washington, DC; mem. Steering Cttee of Coastal Texas 2020, Innocence Project of Nat. Capital Region, Innocence Comm. for Virginia, Texas Comm. on Judicial Efficiency 1995–97, Texas Comm. on a Rep. Student Body 1997–98; serves as arbitrator and mediator for American Arbitration Asscn, Int. Center for Dispute Resolution, CPR Inst. of Dispute Resolution (Dist Panelist), Nat. Panel of Distinguished Neutrals, Arbitration Appeal Panel; mem. DC Bar, State Bar of Texas, San Antonio Bar Asscn, Fed. Bar Asscn, ABA (Initial Chair. Cttee on Independence of the Judiciary 1997, Hon. Co-Chair. Comm. on the 21st Century Judiciary 2002, mem. Advisory Comm. to Standing Cttee on the Law Library of Congress), American Bar Foundation, Judicature Soc., William S. Sessions American Inn of Court, Nat. Asscn of Fmr United States Attorneys; mem. Bd of Trustees, Nat. Environmental Educ. and Training Foundation Inc. 2001–; Hon. Dir Martin Luther King Jr Fed. Holiday Comm. 1991–93, 1994–; several hon. degrees; Baylor Univ. Law School Lawyer of the Year 1988, Price Daniel Distinguished Public Service Award 2002, listed in The Best Lawyers In America for Alternative Dispute Resolution 2005–06. *Publications:* articles in professional journals. *Leisure interests:* climbing, hiking, canoeing. *Address:* Holland & Knight LLP, Suite 100, 2099 Pennsylvania Avenue, NW, Washington, DC 20006 (office); 112 East Pecan, 29th Floor, San Antonio, TX 78205, USA. *Telephone:* (202) 419-2410 (office). *Fax:* (202) 955-5564 (office). *E-mail:* william.sessions@hklaw.com (office). *Website:* www.hklaw.com (office).

SETCH, Terry, DFA; British artist; b. 11 March 1936, Lewisham, London; s. of Frank Setch and Florence Skeggs; m. Dianne Shaw 1967; one d.; ed Sutton and Cheam School of Art and Slade School of Fine Art; Lecturer, Foundation Dept, Leicester Coll. of Art 1960–64; Sr Lecturer in Fine Art, Cardiff Coll. of Art 1964–2001, in Art History Hayward Gallery, London 1987, Broken Ground, Tate Gallery, London 2003; works in Tate Gallery, Arts Council of Great Britain, British Council, Victoria & Albert Museum and other collections; comms: mural for restaurant, Nat. Museum of Wales 1993; elected to Royal W of England Acad. 2002; Welsh Arts Council Painting Award 1971, Welsh Arts Council Major Artist Award 1978, John Moores Exhbn (Third Prize) 1985, Athena Awards (shortlist prizewinner) 1988. *Radio:* Art Work: Terry Setch, BBC Radio 3 2000, Terry Setch – How I Spend My Sundays, Radio Wales 2001. *Television includes:* Statements, BBC 2 Wales 1990, A Word in Your Eye, HTV Wales 1997, Catalyst, BBC 1 Wales 1997, Painting the Dragon, BBC Wales 2000, Jamie Owen Welsh Journeys, BBC 1 2006. *Publications:* New Work by Terry Setch 1992, Terry Setch: a Retrospective 2001. *Address:* 111 Plymouth Road, Penarth, Vale of Glamorgan, CF64 5DF, Wales (home). *Telephone:* (29) 2071-2113 (home). *E-mail:* setch@terrysetch.co.uk (home). *Website:* www.terrysetch.co.uk (home).

SETCHELL, David Lloyd, MA, FCA; British chartered accountant; b. 16 April 1937, Anston, Yorks.; s. of Raymond Setchell and Phyllis Jane Lloyd; m. Muriel Mary Davies 1962; one s. one d.; ed Woodhouse Grammar School and Jesus Coll., Cambridge; Peat Marwick 1960–64; Shawinigan Ltd 1964–71; Vice-Pres. Gulf Oil Chemicals (Europe) 1971–82; Man. Dir Gulf Oil (GB) Ltd 1982–98; Pres. Inst. of Petroleum 1996–98, Oil Industries Club 1993–95; Council mem. Univ. of Gloucestershire 1994–, Chair. 2002–; Gov. Cheltenham Coll. 1998–2004; Dir Cheltenham Arts Festivals 1994–2005, RAF Personnel and Training Command Bd 2000–06; Fellow Energy Inst. *Leisure interests:* golf, music, theatre. *Address:* South Hayes, Sandy Lane Road, Cheltenham, Glos., GL53 9DE, England. *Telephone:* (1242) 571390.

SETH, Vikram, CBE, MA, PhD; Indian author and poet; b. 1952, Calcutta (now Kolkata); s. of Premnath Seth and Leila Seth; ed Doon School, India, Tonbridge School, UK, Corpus Christi Coll., Oxford, Stanford Univ., USA, Nanjing Univ., People's Repub. of China; Hon. Fellow, Corpus Christi Coll., Oxford 1994; Chevalier des Arts et des Lettres 2001; Commonwealth Poetry Prize 1986, W. H. Smith Literary Prize 1994, Commonwealth Writers' Prize 1994, Pravasi Bharatiya Samman 2005, Padma Shri 2007. *Publications:* Mappings 1980, From Heaven Lake: Travels Through Sinkiang and Tibet 1983, The Humble Administrator's Garden 1985, All You Who Sleep Tonight (trans.) 1985, The Golden Gate: A Novel in Verse 1986, Three Chinese Poets (trans.) 1992, A Suitable Boy (novel) 1993, Arion and the Dolphin (libretto) 1994, Beastly Tales (animal fables) 1994, An Equal Music (novel) 1999, Two Lives (biog.) 2005; several vols of poetry. *Leisure interests:* Chinese calligraphy, music, swimming. *Address:* c/o Jonny Geller, Curtis Brown, Haymarket House, 28-29 Haymarket, London, SW1Y 4SP, England (office). *Telephone:* (20) 7393-4400 (office). *Fax:* (20) 7393-4401 (office). *E-mail:* cb@curtisbrown.co.uk (office).

SETHNESS, Charles Olin, AB, MBA; American government official, financial executive, university administrator and investment banker; *Resident Country Director, Vanuatu, Millennium Challenge Corporation;* b. 24 Feb. 1941, Evanston, Ill.; s. of C. Olin Sethness and Alison Louise Burge; four c. and step-c.; ed New Trier High School, Princeton Univ. and Harvard Business School; Sr Credit Analyst, American Nat. Bank and Trust Co. of Chicago 1963–64; Research Asst, Harvard Business School 1966–67; with Morgan Stanley & Co. 1967–73, 1975–81, Vice-Pres. 1972–73, Man. Morgan & Cie Int. SA, Paris 1971–73, Man. Dir 1975–81; Exec. Dir World Bank Group and Special Asst to Sec. of Treasury 1973–75; Assoc. Dean for External Relations, Harvard Business School, Boston 1981–85; Asst Sec. of the Treasury for Domestic Finance 1985–88; Dir Capital Markets Dept, Int. Finance Corpn 1988–89; Chief Financial Officer IDB 1990–2004; Vice-Pres., Monitoring and Evaluation, interim CEO, Vice-Pres., Accountability, Sr Investment Counsellor and Resident Country Dir, Millennium Challenge Corpn 2004–; Alexander Hamilton Medal, US Treasury Dept 1988. *Leisure interests:* Washington Inst. of Foreign Affairs, Washington Recorder Soc., Nat. Cathedral Choral Soc. *Address:* Millennium Challenge Corporation, P.O. Box 3231, Port Vila, Vanuatu (office); 14525 SW Millikan #80479, Beaverton, OR 97005-2343, USA (home). *Telephone:* (678) 24824 (office); (678) 7756740 (home). *Fax:* (678) 25016 (office). *E-mail:* sethnessc@mcc.gov (office); charlessethness@aol.com (home). *Website:* www.mcc.gov (office).

ŞEULEANU, Dragoş, BA, MBA; Romanian radio journalist, public relations consultant and organization executive; *President, Romanian Chamber of Commerce and Industry;* ed Acad. of Econ. Studies, Bucharest, Romanian-American Business School, Univ. of Washington at Seattle; apptd Pres. Trade-Tourism Dept, Romanian Chamber of Commerce and Industry 2001, Vice-Pres. Romanian Chamber of Commerce and Industry –2007, Pres. 2007–; fmr Pres. Gen. Man. Romania's Radio Broadcasting Corpn (ROR) where he served as Deputy Dir for Programming, later Human Resources Dir, later Sec.-Gen., later CEO during a 15-year career, active radio journalist at ROR, covered Democratic and Republican conventions 2000, 2004; est. Effective Management Solutions (public relations co.); Pres. Foundation for Democracy, Culture and Liberty; Adjunct Fellow (non-resident), New European Democracies Project, Center for Strategic and Int. Studies, Washington, DC; mem. Int. Press Inst., Vienna; Founding mem. Romanian Chapter of Transparency International, Romanian Asscn of Public Relations Professionals; mem. Bd European Broadcasting Union; fmr Vice-Chair. Forum of the Information Society (Romanian Acad.); expert on ethnic politics, governance, business, information tech. and communications, and regional security; Hon. Adviser, Ministry of the Interior 2000; Hon. mem. Romanian Acad. of Scientists, Foundation of the Romanian Gendarmerie Magazine; Young European for 1994 Prize, Del. of EC in Romania 1994, Medal for 'Faithful Service' in the rank of Cavalier, Pres. of Romania. *Address:* Romanian Chamber of Commerce and Industry, Blvd Octavian Goga nr 2, Sector 3, Bucharest 030982, Romania (office). *Telephone:* (21) 319-01-14 (office). *E-mail:* ccir@ccir.ro (office). *Website:* www.ccir.ro (office).

SEVAN, Benon V., MA; Cypriot fmr UN official; b. 18 Dec. 1937; m.; one d.; ed Melkonian Educational Inst. and Columbia Coll. and School of Int. and Public Affairs, Columbia Univ., New York, USA; joined UN 1965; with Dept of Public Information 1965–66; with Secr. of Special Cttee on Decolonization 1966–68; served UN in W Irian (Irian Jaya), Indonesia 1968–72; with Secr. of UN Econ. and Social Council 1973–88; Dir and Sr Political Adviser to Rep. of Sec.-Gen. on Settlement of Situation relating to Afghanistan 1988–89; Personal Rep. of Sec.-Gen. in Afghanistan and Pakistan 1989–92; Rep. of Sec.-Gen. on Implementation of Geneva Accords on Afghanistan 1990–92; Dir Office for Co-ordination of UN Humanitarian and Econ. Assistance Programmes in Afghanistan 1991–92; Asst Sec.-Gen. Dept of Political Affairs 1992–94; Asst Sec.-Gen. for Conf. and Support Services 1994–97; Asst Sec.-Gen. Office of Security Co-ordination 1994–2002; apptd Exec. Dir Office of Iraq Programme 1997–2004, Head Oil-for-Food Program 1996–2003, resgnd from UN 2005, indicted in 2007 by US Govt on charges of bribery and conspiracy to commit wire fraud, in connection with the United Nations Oil-for-Food Program.

SEVELE, Hon. Feleti (Fred), BSc, BA, MA, PhD; Tongan politician, business executive and academic; *Prime Minister and Minister of Finance and Defence;* ed Univ. of Cambridge, UK; mem. Legis. Ass. 1999–, Minister of Labour, Commerce, Industries 2005–08; Interim Prime Minister Feb.–March 2006, Prime Minister (first non-noble) March 2006–, Minister of Finance and Defence 2009–. *Address:* Office of the Prime Minister, POB 62, Taufa'ahau Road, Kolofo'ou, Nuku'alofa, Tonga (office). *Telephone:* 24644 (office). *Fax:* 23888 (office). *E-mail:* fttuita@pmo.gov.to (office). *Website:* www.pmo.gov.to (office).

SEVERIANO TEIXEIRA, Nuno, PhD; Portuguese academic and politician; *Minister of National Defence;* ed Univ. of Lisbon, European Univ. Inst., Florence, Italy, New Univ. of Lisbon; Researcher, European Univ. Inst., Florence 1989–92; Visiting Prof., Dept of Govt, Georgetown Univ., USA 2000; Visiting Fellow, Center for European Studies, Univ. of Calif., Berkeley, USA 2003; Prof., Dept of Political Sciences and Int. Relations, Faculty of Social and Human Sciences, New Univ. of Lisbon, Dir Portuguese Inst. of Int. Relations; Dir Inst. of Nat. Defence 1996–2000; Minister of Internal Admin 2000–02, of Nat. Defence 2006–. *Publications include:* O Ultimatum Inglês. Política Externa e Política Interna no Portugal de 1890 1990, O Poder e a Guerra. Objectvos nacionais e estratégias políticas na entrada de Portugal na Grande Guerra 1914–1918 1996; numerous articles in professional journals. *Address:* Ministry of National Defence, Av. Ilha de Madeira 1, 1400-204, Lisbon, Portugal (office). *Telephone:* (21) 3038528 (office). *Fax:* (21) 3020284 (office). *E-mail:* gcrp@sg.mdn.gov.pt (office). *Website:* www.mdn.gov.pt (office).

SEVERIN, (Giles) Tim, MA, DLitt; British traveller and writer; b. 25 Sept. 1940; s. of Maurice Watkins and Inge Severin; m. Dorothy Virginia Sherman 1966 (divorced 1979); one d.; ed Tonbridge School, Keble Coll., Oxford; Commonwealth Fellow, USA 1964–66; expeditions: led motorcycle team along Marco Polo's route 1961, canoe and launch down River Mississippi 1965, Brendan Voyage from W Ireland to N America 1977, Sindbad Voyage from Oman to China 1980–81, Jason Voyage from Greece to Soviet Georgia 1984, Ulysses Voyage, Troy to Ithaca 1985, Crusade: on horseback from Belgium to Jerusalem 1987–88, Travels on horseback in Mongolia 1990, China Voyage: bamboo sailing raft Hong Kong-Japan-Pacific 1993, Spice Islands Voyage in Moluccas, E Indonesia 1996, Pacific travels in search of Moby Dick 1998, Latin America travels seeking Robinson Crusoe sources 2000; historical novelist 2005–; Hon. DLitt (Trinity Coll., Dublin) 1996; Royal Geographical Soc. Gold Medal, Royal Scottish Geographical Soc. Livingstone Medal. *Publications:* Tracking Marco Polo 1964, Explorers of the Mississippi 1967, The Golden Antilles 1970, The African Adventure 1973, Vanishing Primitive Man 1973, The Oriental Adventure 1976, The Brendan Voyage 1978, The Sindbad Voyage 1982, The Jason Voyage 1984, The Ulysses Voyage 1987, Crusader 1989, In Search of Genghis Khan 1991, The China Voyage 1994, The Spice Islands Voyage 1997, In Search of Moby Dick 1999, Seeking Robinson Crusoe 2002, Viking: Odinn's Child (novel) 2004, Viking: Sworn Brother 2005, Viking: King's Man 2005, Corsair 2007, Buccaneer 2008. *Address:* Inchy Bridge, Timoleague, Co. Cork, Ireland (home). *Telephone:* (23) 88446127 (home). *E-mail:* timsev@eircom.net (home). *Website:* www.timseverin.com.

SEVERINO, Rodolfo, MA; Philippine diplomatist; *Visiting Senior Research Fellow, Institute of Southeast Asian Studies;* b. 22 April 1936, Manila; m. Rowena V. Romero; two s. one d.; ed Ateneo de Manila Univ., Johns Hopkins Univ. School of Advanced Int. Studies, Washington, DC; Assoc. Ed. Manor Press Inc. 1956–59, Philippine Int. 1957–59, Marketing Horizons 1961–64; with Operation Brotherhood, Laos 1959–61; Special Asst to Senator Raul S. Manglapus, Philippine Senate 1961–64; information asst, UN Information Centre, Manila 1964–65; Third, then Second and First Sec., Embassy in Washington, DC 1967–74; Special Asst to Under-Sec. of Foreign Affairs 1974–76, Under-Sec. 1992–97; Chargé d'Affaires, Embassy in Beijing 1976–78; Consul-Gen., Houston, Texas 1979–86; Asst Sec. for Asian and Pacific Affairs 1986–88; Amb. to Malaysia 1988–92; Under-Sec. of Foreign Affairs 1992–97; Sec.-Gen. ASEAN 1998–2003; adviser to Cambodian Govt Jan.–June 2002; Prof., Asian Inst. of Man., Manila 2003–04; currently Visiting Sr Research Fellow, Inst. of Southeast Asian Studies, Singapore; Order of Sikatuna, rank of Datu (Philippines) 1997, rank of Rajah; Royal Award (Cambodia) 2002. *Publications include:* ASEAN Faces the Future 2001, ASEAN Today and Tomorrow 2002, Framing the ASEAN Charter 2005, Southeast Asia in Search of an ASEAN Community 2006. *Address:* Institute of Southeast Asian Studies, 30 Heng Mui Keng Terrace, Pasir Panjang, 119614 (office); 2D Hong San Walk, Palm Gardens #16-06, 689050, Singapore (home). *Telephone:* 67780955 (office); 63101794 (home). *Fax:* 67781735 (office). *E-mail:* severino@iseas.edu.sg (office); roseverino@hotmail.com (home). *Website:* www.iseas.edu.sg (office).

SEVÓN, Leif, LLM; Finnish judge; b. 31 Oct. 1941, Helsingfors; s. of Enzio Sevón and Ulla Sevón; m. (divorced); one s. one d.; ed Univ. of Helsinki; Asst Univ. of Helsinki 1966–71, Asst Prof. 1971–74; Counsellor of Legislation, Ministry of Justice 1973–78; Sr Judge, Chamber Pres. City Court of Helsinki 1979–80; Dir of Legislation, Ministry of Justice 1980–86, Dir-Gen. Dept of Legislation 1986–91; Judge, Supreme Court of Justice 1991; Counsellor, Dept of Trade, Ministry of Foreign Affairs 1991–92; Pres. EFTA Court 1994; Judge, Court of Justice of European Communities 1995–2002; Pres. Supreme Court of Finland 2002–05; Commdr, Grand Cross Order of White Rose of Finland 2003, Nordstjärncorden (Sweden) 2003; Hon. LLD (Stockholm) 1999, (Helsinki) 2000. *Publications:* books, articles and translations. *Address:* c/o The Supreme Court of Finland, Pohjoisesplanadi 3, 00170 Helsinki, Finland (office).

SEVOSTYANOV, Grigory Nikolayevich; Russian historian; *Chief Researcher, Institute of Comprehensive History, Russian Academy of Sciences;* b. 5 April 1916; m.; one s.; ed Novocherkassk Polytech. Inst.; teacher Novocherkassk Polytech. Inst. 1940–41; Asst Deputy Chair. Govt Belorussian SSR 1944–45; Attaché Ministry of Foreign Affairs 1947; Jr, Sr researcher, head of div. Inst. of History USSR Acad. of Sciences 1950–68; head of div., head of Dept Inst. of Comprehensive History USSR Acad. of Sciences 1968–88; Chief Researcher 1988–; mem. USSR (now Russian) Acad. of Sciences 1987; research in history of America and int. relations, problems of history of World War II, workers' movt in USA; USSR State Prize. *Publications:* Policy of Great States in the Far East on the eve of World War II 1961, USA and France in wartime 1939–45: History of International Relations 1974, History of USA 1983–87; and other books and articles. *Address:* Institute of Comprehensive History, Russian Academy of Sciences, Leninsky pr. 32A, 117334 Moscow, Russia. *Telephone:* (495) 938-19-11 (office); (495) 928-86-07 (home).

SEWARD, George Chester, LLB; American lawyer; *Senior Counsel, Seward & Kissel LLP;* b. 4 Aug. 1910, Omaha, Neb.; s. of George F. Seward and Ada L. Rugh; m. Carroll F. McKay 1936 (died 1991); two s. two d.; ed Male High School, Louisville, Ky and Univ. of Virginia; with Shearman & Sterling, New York 1936–53, Seward & Kissel LLP, New York, Washington DC 1953–now Sr Counsel; Dir Witherbee Sherman Corpn 1952–66 (Pres. 1964–66), Howmet Corpn 1955–75, Chas. P. Young Co. 1965–72, Howmedica, Inc. 1970–72; Trustee Benson Iron Ore Trust 1969–80; Founder and Hon. Pres. Business Law Section of Int. Bar Asscn, now Hon. Life Pres.; Chair. Cttee on Corporate Laws of ABA 1952–58, American Bar Foundation Cttee on Model Business Corpn Acts 1956–65, Banking Cttee of ABA 1960–61; Life mem. Council of Section of Business Law of ABA (Chair. 1958–59); mem. House of Dels, ABA 1959, 1963–74, Jt Cttee on Continuing Legal Educ. of the American Law Inst. and ABA 1965–76, Univ. of Va Arts and Sciences Council 1984–93 (Pres. 1991–93), New York Stock Exchange Legal Advisory Cttee 1984–87; Fellow, American Bar Foundation; mem. American Law Inst., Asscn of Bar of City of New York, NY State, Ky, Va and DC Bar Asscns; Trustee Edwin Gould Foundation for Children 1955–96, The Nature Conservancy Eastern Long Island, NY 1975–88, NY Genealogical and Biographical Soc.; George Seward Lecture series sponsored by Int. Bar Asscn, London; Hon. Life Pres. and Life mem. Council of Int. Bar Asscn. *Publications:* Basic Corporate Practice, Seward and Related Families, co-author Model Business Corporation Act Annotated; ed. We Remember Carroll. *Address:* Seward & Kissel LLP, 1 Battery Park Plaza, New York, NY 10004 (office); 48 Greenacres Avenue, Scarsdale, NY 10583, USA (home). *Telephone:* (212) 574-1216 (office). *Fax:* (212) 480-8421 (office). *E-mail:* seward@sewkis.com (office). *Website:* www.sewkis.com (office).

SEWELL, Brian; British art historian and art critic; *Art Critic, Evening Standard;* art critic for Evening Standard newspaper; British Press Awards Critic of the Year 1988, Arts Journalist of the Year 1994, Hawthornden Prize for Art Criticism 1995, Foreign Press Asscn Arts Writer of the Year 2000, The Orwell Prize 2003, Critic of the Year, British Press Awards 2004. *Television includes:* The Works: Minette Walters and the Missing Masterpiece 1996, The Naked Pilgrim 2003, The Road to Santiago 2003, Grand Tour 2006, Dirty Dalì: A Private View 2007. *Publications:* South from Ephesus 1988, The Reviews that Caused the Rumpus 1994, An Alphabet of Villains 1995. *Leisure interests:* dogs, old motor cars. *Address:* The Evening Standard, Northcliffe House, 2 Derry Street, London, W8 5EE, England (office). *Telephone:* (20) 7938-6000 (office). *Fax:* (20) 7938-3637 (office).

SEWELL, Rufus Frederick; British actor; b. 29 Oct. 1967; s. of the late Bill Sewell; London Critics' Circle Best Newcomer 1992, Broadway Theatre World Award 1995, London Evening Standard Award for Best Actor 2006. *Stage appearances include:* Royal Hunt of the Sun, Comedians, The Lost Domain, Peter and the Captain, Pride and Prejudice, The Government Inspector, The Seagull, As You Like It, Making it Better, Arcadia, Translations, Rat in the Skull, Macbeth, Luther, Rock 'N' Roll (London Critics' Circle Best Actor 2006, Best Actor, Laurence Olivier Awards 2007). *Television appearances include:* The Last Romantics, Gone to Seed, Middlemarch, Dirty Something, Citizen Locke, Cold Comfort Farm, Henry IV, Charles II: The Power and the Passion 2003, Taming of the Shrew 2005. *Film appearances include:* Twenty-One 1991, Dirty Weekend 1993, A Man of No Importance 1994, Victory 1995, Carrington 1995, Hamlet 1996, The Woodlanders 1997, Dangerous Beauty 1998, Dark City 1998, Martha, Meet Frank, Daniel and Laurence 1998, Illuminata 1998, At Sachem Farm 1998, In a Savage Land 1999, Bless the Child 2000, A Knight's Tale 2001, Extreme Ops 2002, Victoria Station 2003, The Legend of Zorro 2005, Tristan + Isolde 2006, The Illusionist 2006, Paris, je t'aime 2006, Amazing Grace 2006, The Holiday 2006. *Address:* c/o Julian Belfrage Associates, 46 Albemarle Street, London, W1X 4PP, England. *Telephone:* (20) 7491-4400. *Fax:* (20) 7493-5460.

SEWERYN, Andrzej; Polish actor and theatre director; b. 25 April 1946, Heilbronn, Germany; m.; two s. one d.; ed State Higher School of Drama, Warsaw; actor Athenaeum Theatre, Warsaw 1968–82, Peter Brook's Group 1984–88, perm. mem. Comédie Française, Paris 1993–; co-operation with film, TV and radio; mem. SPATiF (Asscn of Polish Theatre and Film Actors) 1969–82; Chevalier des Arts et des Lettres 1995, Kt's Cross, Order of Polonia Restituta 1997, Ordre Nat. du Mérite 1999; Prize Berlin Int. Film Festival for Conductor 1979, Best Actor, French Film Awards for Unpleasant Man 1996, Prize of Le Syndicat professionnel de la Critique dramatique et musicale de France 1996, Polish TV Award, Polish Film Festival, Gdansk 2000. *Films:* Zenon in The Border 1977, Rościszewski in Without Anaesthetic 1978, Ksiądz in The Brute 1979, Kung-fu 1979, Conductor 1979, Mahabharata 1988, French Revolution 1989, Schindler's List 1994, Journey to the East 1994, Total Eclipse 1995, Unpleasant Man 1996, With Fire and Sword 1998, Billboard 1998, Pan Tadeusz (The Last Foray in Lithuania) 1999, The Primate 2000, The Revenge 2002, Par amour (TV) 2003, A ton image 2004. *Theatre:* (actor) leading roles in Don Carlos, Peer Gynt, Don Juan; (dir) Le Mariage forcé by Molière, Comédie Française 1999, Le Mal court by Jacques Audiberti, Comédie Française 2000, Tartuffe 2002. *Television series:* Kliefhorn in Polish Roads 1977, Marek in On the Silver Globe 1976–79, Bukacki in Połaniecki's Family 1977, Roman in Roman and Magda 1979; numerous other roles on TV. *Address:* Comédie Française, Place Colette, 75001 Paris, France. *Telephone:* 1-44-58-14-00. *Fax:* 1-44-58-14-50.

SEXTON, John Edward, BA, MA, JD; American academic, university administrator and lawyer; *President, New York University;* b. 1944, Brooklyn; m. Lisa Goldberg; one s. one d.; ed Fordham Coll., Fordham Univ., Harvard Law School; Prof. of Religion, St Francis Coll., Brooklyn, NY 1966–73, Dept Chair 1970–1975; Law Clerk, Judges David Bazelon and Harold Leventhal US Court of Appeals 1979-1980, to Chief Justice Warren Burger, US Supreme Court 1980–81; joined Law Faculty, New York Univ. (NYU) 1981, Dean 1988–, now Emer., Benjamin Butler Prof. of Law and Pres. NYU 2001–; served as Special Master Supervising Pretrial Proceedings in Love Canal Litigation 1983–93; Chair New York Acad. of Sciences, Comm. of Ind. Colls and Univs of NY; mem. Bd of Dirs New York State Comm. on Higher Educ., American Council on Educ., Inst. of Int. Educ., Asscn for a Better New York; fmr Pres. American Asscn of Law Schools; Fellow, American Acad. of Arts and Sciences; mem. Asscn of American Univ. Presidents, Council on Foreign Relations; Chair. Bd Fed. Reserve Bank of NY 2003–06, Chair Fed. Reserve Systems Council of Chairs 2006; Dr hc (Fordham Univ., St Francis Coll., St John's Univ., Syracuse Univ., Katholieke Universiteit Leuven). *Publications:* Redefining the Supreme Court's Role: A Theory of Managing the Federal Court System; Procedure: Cases and Materials (jtly) and numerous chapters and articles. *Address:* Office of the President, New York University, 70 Washington Square South, New York, NY 10012, USA (office). *Telephone:* (212) 998-2345 (office). *Fax:* (212) 995-3679 (office). *Website:* www.nyu.edu (office).

SEXWALE, (Gabriel) Tokyo; South African business executive and politician; *Executive Chairman, Mvelaphanda Group Ltd;* b. 5 March 1953, Orlando West, Soweto; s. of Frank Sexwale; m. Judy Moon; one s. one d.; ed Univ. of Botswana, Lesotho, Swaziland; joined African Nat. Congress (ANC) in 1970s; went into exile and underwent officers' mil. training in Soviet Union 1975; returned to South Africa as underground fighter in ANC's Spear of the Nation armed wing 1976, imprisoned for 13 years on Robben Island for guerrilla activities; returned to Johannesburg, served as Head Public Liaison Dept of ANC HQ, then apptd Head Special Projects under Mil. HQ 1989; elected mem. Exec. Cttee ANC, Pretoria-Witwatersrand-Vereeniging (now Gauteng) Prov. 1990, Chair. 1994–97, Premier 1994–97; mem. ANC Nat. Exec. Cttee 1991–97; left politics for business sector and co-f. Mvelaphanda Mining, expanded into Mvelaphanda Holdings Pty Ltd (now Mvelaphanda Group Ltd), Chair. 2002–07, Chair. (non-exec.) 2007, now Exec. Chair., also Chair. of related cos Trans Hex Group Ltd, Mvelaphanda Resources Ltd, Northam Platinum Ltd; Owner, Jonga Entabeni; CEO Batho Bonke; mem. Bd of Dirs GFI-SA, Altech, Gold Fields Ltd, ASBA Group, Desta Power Matla, Voltex, De Montfort Univ., UK; Hon. Consul General of Finland in South Africa; Pres. South African/Russian Business, Technological and Cultural Association; Vice–Pres. South African/Japanese Business Forum; Trustee, Nelson Mandela Foundation; Légion d'Honneur, Cross-of-Valour (Ruby Class) South Africa; Dr. hc (Univ. of Nottingham, UK); Reach and Teach Leadership Award, USA. *Address:* Mvelaphanda Group Ltd., POB 1639, Rivonia 2128, South Africa (office). *Telephone:* (11) 2904200 (office). *Website:* www .mvelagroup.co.za (office).

SEYDOUX FORNIER de CLAUSONNE, Jérôme; French business executive; *Co-President, Pathé;* b. 21 Sept. 1934, Paris; s. of René Seydoux Fornier de Clausonne and Geneviève Schlumberger; m. 1st (divorced); three s. one d.; m. 2nd Sophie Desserteaux-Bessis 1988; one s.; ed Lycées Montaigne, Louis-le-Grand and Buffon; financial analyst Istel, Lepercq and Co. Inc. NY 1962–63; sleeping pnr Bank of Neuflize, Schlumberger, Mallet 1964, Pnr 1966, mem. Bd of Dirs 1969–70; Admin. Schlumberger Ltd 1969, Exec. Vice Pres. 1970, Dir Gen. 1975–76; Admin. Compagnie Deutsch 1964–; mem. Bd of Dirs Danone (fmrly BSN) 1970–2005, fmr Admin.; Pres. Pricel 1976; Pres. Chargeurs 1980–96, later Vice-Pres., Dir-Gen., currently Vice-Chair., CEO and Dir; Pres. Admin. Council of France 5 1986; Pres., Dir-Gen. Pathé Palace (fmrly Pathé Cinema) 1991–2000, later Pres., Dir-Gen. Pathé, Vice-Pres. Supervisory Cttee 2000, currently Co-Pres.; Vice-Pres. Advisory Bd, Mont-Blanc Co. 2000–; Chair. BSkyB 1998–99; owner Libération newspaper. *Leisure interests:* skiing, golf. *Address:* Pathé, 5 rue François 1er, 75008 Paris, France (office). *Telephone:* 1-71-72-30-00 (office). *Fax:* 1-71-72-31-00 (office). *Website:* www.pathe.com (office).

SEYDOUX FORNIER de CLAUSONNE, Nicolas Pierre, LenD, LenScEcon; French business executive; *President-Director-General, Gaumont;* b. 16 July 1939, Paris; s. of René Seydoux Fornier de Clausonne and Geneviève Schlumberger; m. Anne-Marie Cahen-Salvador 1964; two c.; ed Lycée Buffon, Faculté de Droit, Paris, New York Business School and Inst. d'Etudes Politiques, Paris; Head of Legal Service, Cie Int. pour l'Informatique, Paris 1967–70; financial analyst Morgan, Stanley & Co. Inc. New York 1970–71, Morgan & Cie Int. SA Paris 1971–74; Vice-Pres.-Dir-Gen. Gaumont 1974, Pres.-Dir-Gen. 1975–; mem. Bd of Dirs Schlumberger 1982–; Pres. Fédération Nat. des Distributeurs de Films 1988–2001, Bureau de liaison des industries cinématographiques (BLIC) 2000, Asscn de Lutte contre la Piraterie Audiovisuelle (ALPA), Asscn des Producteurs Indépendants (API); Officier Légion d'honneur. *Leisure interests:* vintage cars, skiing. *Address:* Gaumont, 30 avenue Charles de Gaulle, 92200 Neuilly-sur-Seine (office); 5 place du Palais-Bourbon, 75007 Paris, France (home). *Website:* www.gaumont.com (office).

SEYMOUR, Lynn, CBE; Canadian ballet dancer; b. 8 March 1939, Wainwright, Alberta; d. of E. V. Springett; m. 1st Colin Jones 1963 (divorced 1974); three s.; m. 2nd Philip Pace 1974; m. 3rd Vanya Hackel 1983 (divorced 1988); ed Royal Ballet School; graduated into Royal Ballet 1957; promoted to Soloist rank 1958, to Prin. 1958; joined Deutsche Oper, Berlin 1966; Guest Artist, Royal Ballet 1970–78; Artistic Dir of Ballet Bayerische Staatsoper 1979–80; guest artist with other cos including Alvin Ailey; Artistic Dir Greek Nat. Opera Ballet 2006–07 (resgnd); Evening Standard Drama Award 1977. *Ballets:* The Burrow 1958, Swan Lake 1958, Giselle 1958, The Invitation 1960, The Two Pigeons 1961, Symphony 1963, Romeo and Juliet 1964, Anastasia 1966, Dances at a Gathering, The Concert, The Seven Deadly Sins, Flowers 1972, Shukumei, The Four Seasons 1975, Side Show, Rituals 1975, Manon Lescaut 1976, A Month in the Country 1976, Mayerling 1978, Manon 1978, Choreography for Rashomon 1976, The Court of Love 1977, Intimate Letters 1978, Mae and Polly, Boreas, Tattooed Lady, Wolfy, the Ballet Rambert 1987. *Publication:* Lynn: Leaps and Boundaries (autobiog. with Paul Gardner) 1984.

SEZER, Ahmet Necdet, BA, PhD; Turkish judge and fmr head of state; b. 13 Sept. 1941, Afyon; m.; three c.; ed Univ. of Ankara; served in mil. service at Land Forces Acad.; Judge in Ankara, then Dicle; Supervisory Judge High Court of Appeal, Ankara; mem. High Court of Appeal 1983, Constitutional Court 1988–2000, Chief Justice 1998–2000; Pres. of Turkey 2000–07. *Address:* c/o Office of the President, Cumhurbaşkanlığı, Köşku, Çankaya, Ankara, Turkey.

SGORLON, Carlo Pietro Antonio, PhD; Italian novelist and journalist; b. 26 July 1930, Cassacco, Udine; s. of Antonio Sgorlon and Livia Sgorlon; m. Edda Agarinis 1961; ed Liceo Classico di Udine, Univs of Pisa and Munich; secondary school teacher 1953–79; journalist 1969–; Cavaliere di Gran Croce della Repubblica; Accademico pontificio; Enna Prize 1968, Rapallo Prize 1968, Supercampiello Prizes 1973 and 1983, Vallombrosa Prize 1983, Soroptomist Prize 1983, Strega Prize 1985, Hemingway Prize 1987, Palme D'Oro Prize 1988, Nonino Prize 1989, Campano D'Oro Prize 1989, Fiuggi Prize 1989, Un Libro per L'Avvenire Prize 1989, Tascabile S. Benedetto del Tronto Prize 1989, Napoli Prize 1989, Latina Prize 1989, Isola d'Elba Prize 1997, Ennio Flaiano Prize 1997, Rhegium Prize 1997, S. Vidal (Venice) 1999, Libraio Prize (Padua) Fregene Prize 2001, Frontino Prize 2001, Giorgio La Pira Prize (Messina) 2003, PEN Prize (Parma) 2003, Scanno Prize for Literature 2005. *Radio:* Le parole sulla sabbia, La stanchezza di Mose, Il vento nel vigneto, La luna color ametista, Il viaggiatore di Dio (Odorico da Pordendone). *Publications:* Kafka narratore 1961, La Poltrona 1968, Elsa Morante 1972, Il Trono di Legno 1973, Regina di Saba 1975, Gli dei torneranno 1977, La Luna Color Ametista 1978, La Carrozza di Rame 1979, La Contrada 1981, La Conchiglia di Anataj 1983, L'Armata dei Fiumi Perduti 1985, Sette Veli 1986, L'Ultima Valle 1987, Il Caldèras 1988, I Racconti della Terra di Canaan 1989, La Fontana di Lorena 1990, Il Patriarcato della Luna 1991, La Foiba Grande 1992, Il Guaritore 1993, Il Regno dell'Uomo 1994, Il Costruttore 1995, La Malga di Sîr 1997, Il Processo di Tolosa 1998, Il Filo di Seta 1999, La Tredicesima Notte 2001, L'Uomo di Praga 2003, Il Velo oli Maya 2005. *Leisure interests:* painting, carpentry, walking. *Address:* Via Micesio 15, Udine CAP 33100, Italy (home). *Telephone:* (0432) 294140 (office). *Fax:* (0432) 294140 (office).

SGOUROS, Dimitris; Greek pianist; b. 30 Aug. 1969, Athens; s. of Sotirios Sgouros and Marianthi Sgouros; ed Univ. of Athens, Athens Conservatory of Music, Univ. of Maryland, USA, St Peter's Coll., Oxford and RAM, London, UK; debut aged seven, Piraeus 1977; numerous concerts in Europe from 1980; solo piano recital aged 11, to audience of 4,000 at Hirrodus of Atticus Theatre of Athens 1981; first US appearance aged 12, with Nat. Symphony Orchestra of Washington, Carnegie Hall, New York 1982; appeared at Prague Spring Festival with Sir Charles Mackeras and the Czech Philharmonic Orchestra playing Beethoven's Piano Concerto No. 4 1986; played 12 different piano concertos over six nights with Singapore Symphony Orchestra, Sgouros Festival, Singapore 1990; has played in all the major cities and concert houses and on all the major radio and TV stations worldwide; repertoire of 45 piano concertos and large number of solo piano and chamber music works; took part in cultural events at Los Angeles Olympics 1984, Athens Olympics 2004; Rotary Club of Athens Award 1981, Acad. of Athens Award 1982, LA 1984, Athens Conservatory Gold Medal 1984, Tom Brandley Award, Los Angeles 1984, Leonardo da Vinci Int. Prize, The Lions: Melvin Jones Fellow 2000, and many other awards. *Recordings include:* works by Schumann, Brahms, Rachmaninov, Tchaikovsky, Liszt, Mozart and Chopin with the Berlin Philharmonic, London Philharmonic and Sofia Philharmonic Orchestras and the Radio Orchestra of Slovenia, Capriccio's Elysium Recordings (USA), Grieg Piano Concerto with Borusan Istanbul Philharmonic Orchestra 2000, Rachmaninov Piano Concertos Nos 2 and 3 with Cyprus State Orchestra (for Steinway Club 150th anniversary, recorded live). *Leisure interests:* mathematics, conducting opera, languages. *Address:* Tompazi 28, 18537 Piraeus (home); Sahturi 25, 18535 Piraeus, Greece (office). *Telephone:* (693) 2265110 (mobile); (210) 8959778 (office). *Fax:* (210) 8956477 (home); (210) 4538737 (office). *E-mail:* info@sgouros-pianist.com (office). *Website:* www.sgouros -pianist.com (office).

SHA, Zukang; Chinese diplomatist and UN official; *Under-Secretary-General for Economic and Social Affairs, United Nations;* b. Sept. 1947, Jiangsu prov.; m.; one s.; ed Nanjing Univ.; staff mem., Embassy in London 1971–74, in Sri Lanka 1974–80; Attaché and Third Sec., Embassy in India 1980–85; Deputy Div. Dir and First Sec. Dept of Int. Orgs and Conferences 1985–88, Adviser and Deputy Dir-Gen. 1992–95; First Sec. and Adviser, Perm. Mission to UN, New York 1988–92; Amb. for Disarmament Affairs and Deputy Perm. Rep. to UN Office and Other Int. Orgs, Geneva, Switzerland 1995–97; Dir-Gen. Dept of Arms Control 1997–2001; Perm. Rep. to UN, Geneva 2001–07; UN Under-Sec.-Gen. for Econ. and Social Affairs 2007–. *Address:* Office of the Under-

Secretary-General for Economic and Social Affairs, United Nations, Room DC2-2320, New York, NY 10017 USA (office). *E-mail:* esa@un.org (office). *Website:* www.un.org/esa/desa (office).

SHAABAN, Muhammad, PhD; Egyptian diplomatist and UN official; *Under-Secretary-General, United Nations Department for General Assembly and Conference Management;* b. 13 June 1942; m.; three c.; ed Brussels Univ.; rep. to ECOSOC, UNDP and various other cttees 1984–88; Amb. to Belgium and Luxembourg 1993–97, to Denmark and Lithuania 1998–2000; Head of Perm. Mission to EU, Brussels 1993–97; Deputy Minister of Foreign Affairs responsible for Africa 1997–98; Deputy Minister for Information, Research and Assessment 2000–01; Deputy Minister for Foreign Affairs responsible for Europe 2001–04; Nat. Co-ordinator for Reform Initiatives in Middle East 2004–07; Diplomatic Adviser to Speaker of the House, Egyptian Parl. 2004–07; Under-Sec.-Gen., Dept for Gen. Ass. and Conference Man., UN, New York 2007–; Coordinator of First Session of Euro-Mediterranean Parl. Ass. 2005; Order of Merit (Egypt) 1977, Chevalier, Ordre du Mérite (France) 1978, Grand Croix de l'Ordre de la Couronne (Belgium) 1997. *Publications:* The United Nations Secretary-General: The man and the post 1971, The Analysis of International Relations (in Arabic) 1984. *Leisure interests:* tennis, swimming, reading. *Address:* Department for General Assembly and Conference Management, United Nations, New York, NY, 10017, USA (office). *Telephone:* (212) 963-1234 (office). *Fax:* (212) 963-4879 (office). *E-mail:* shaabans@un.org (office). *Website:* www.un.org/Depts/DGACM (office).

SHA'ALAN, Hazim; Iraqi business executive and fmr government official; b. 1947, Diwaniya; ed Baghdad Univ.; started career as man. various branches Iraqi Real Estate Bank; left Iraq in opposition to regime 1985; man. real estate co. in UK; apptd Gov. Diwaniya territory 2003; Interim Minister of Defence 2004–05. *Address:* c/o Office of the Minister of Defence, Green Zone, Baghdad, Iraq.

SHAATH, Nabeel A., BA, MBA, PhD, DJur; Palestinian politician, diplomatist, consultant and academic; b. 1938, Safad; m.; two s. two d.; ed Univ. of Alexandria, Egypt, Univ. of Pa, Wharton School of Business, USA; fmr Business School Prof., taught Finance and Econs, Univ. of Pa, USA 1961–65, academic positions at Univs of Cairo and Alexandria 1965–69; Dean, School of Business Admin, American Univ. in Beirut 1969–75; consultant to several govts, in Org. of Shuaiab industrial zone, Kuwait, power sector in Saudi Arabia, public transportation in Gulf Area; est. Eng and Man. Inst. and Arab Centre for Admin. Devt in Beirut, Cairo and 14 brs in other Arab countries; mem. Fatah Cen. Cttee, del. to Middle E Peace Conf., Madrid 1991; mem. PLO –Israel peace negotiations, Oslo, Norway and Washington, DC; First Head of PLO Del. to UN, Adviser to Yasser Arafat, wrote his speech to UN Gen. Ass. 1974; Palestinian Authority Minister of Planning and Int. Co-operation 1994–2003, Minister of Foreign Affairs 2003–05; Deputy Prime Minister 2005–06; elected to Palestinian Legis. Council, Rep. of Khan Younis, Gaza Strip 1996–; Rep. of Palestine to world media confs, including World Econ. Forum; acting Prime Minister of Palestinian Authority 2005–06, currently Sr Advisor to Palestinian Nat. Authority Pres. *Address:* c/o Fatah, Ramallah, Palestinian Autonomous Areas. *E-mail:* hanishka2@yahoo.com; fateh@fateh. *Website:* www.fateh.net.

SHABDURASULOV, Igor Vladimirovich; Russian civil servant; *President, Triumph Fund;* b. 3 Oct. 1957, Tashkent; m.; three c.; ed Moscow State Univ.; Head, UNESCO Project Great Silk Way, Russian Acad. of Sciences 1983–86; on staff Div. of Science, Culture and Educ., Russian Govt; mem., Admin. of Russian Presidency, then Head, Dept of Culture, Russian Govt 1993–94; Head, Dept of Culture and Information, Russian Govt 1994–98; Deputy Head, Admin. of Russian Presidency, Head Group of Speech Writers April–Sept. 1998; Dir-Gen. Russian Public TV 1998–99; Deputy Head Admin. of Russian Presidency 1999–2000; Pres. Triumph Fund 2000–; Chair. Bd of Dirs TV-6 Co. March–May 2001; mem. Bd of Trustees Virtual Radio and TV Museum. *Address:* Triumph Fund, Povarskaya str. 8/1, 102069 Moscow, Russia (office). *Telephone:* (495) 916-54-96 (office).

SHABIBI, Sinan Muhammad Rida ash-, MA, PhD; *Governor, Central Bank of Iraq;* ed Univs of Manchester and Bristol, UK; consultant on trade, debt and finance; Head, importation and marketing section, Ministry of Oil 1975–77; served in Iraqi Ministry of Planning 1977–80; taught at Baghdad Univ. and Mustansiryah Univ., Iraq; Sr Economist, UNCTAD –2001, consultant 2001–03; Gov. Cen. Bank of Iraq 2003–; spoke at Senate hearings on Iraq Aug. 2002, on disappearance of Iraqi middle class under sanctions, and reconstruction of Iraq, and at AEI Conf. on post-Saddam Iraq Oct. 2002 (mem. follow-up cttee Dec. 2002). *Publications:* OPEC Aid: Issues and Performance 1987, The Arab Share in OPEC Aid: Some Related Facts 1988, Prospects for the Iraqi Economy: Facing the New Reality 1997, Globalisation of Finance: Implications for Macroeconomic Policies and Debt Management 2001. *Address:* Central Bank of Iraq, PO Box 64, Rashid Street, Baghdad, Iraq (office). *Telephone:* (1) 816-5170 (office). *Fax:* (1) 816-6802 (office). *E-mail:* cbi@ cbiraq.org (office). *Website:* www.cbiraq.org (office).

SHAFAREVICH, Igor Rostislavovich, Dr.Phys.-Math.Sc; Russian mathematician; b. 3 June 1923, Zhitomir; m.; two c.; ed Moscow Univ.; Research Officer Moscow Math. Inst. 1943–44; staff mem. Faculty of Mechanics and Math., Moscow Univ. 1944–52; Prof. Moscow Univ. 1953–75 (dismissed for dissident activities); Lecturer and Head of Dept, V. Steklov Math. Inst. 1960–; Corresp. mem. USSR (now Russian) Acad. of Sciences 1958, mem. 1991; mem. Bd Moscow Math. Soc. 1964, Pres. 1970–74; mem. USSR Human Rights Cttee; mem. Political Council, Nat. Salvation Front 1992; Hon. mem. US Acad. of Sciences, Acad. Leopoldina, American Acad. of Arts and Sciences, Royal Soc., London; Dr hc (Paris); Lenin Prize 1959, Heinemann Prize, Göttingen Acad. of Sciences 1975. *Publications include:* Has Russia a Future? and 'Socialism' in

Solzhenitsyn's From Under the Rubble, Socialism as a Phenomenon in Global History 1977, Russophobia 1990. *Address:* V. Steklov Mathematical Institute, Ul. Gubkina 8, 117966 Moscow, Russia. *Telephone:* (495) 135-25-49 (office); (495) 135-13-47 (home).

SHAFEEU, Ismail; Maldivian politician; fmr Minister of Educ. 2002–03; Minister of Home Affairs and Environment 2003–04, of Defence and Nat. Security 2004–08; Chair. Dhiraagu Ltd. *Address:* c/o Ministry of Defence and National Security, Bandaara Koshi, Ameer Ahmed Magu, Malé 20-05, Maldives (office).

SHAFFER, Sir Peter Levin, Kt, CBE, FRSL; British playwright; b. 15 May 1926, Liverpool; s. of Jack Shaffer and Reka Shaffer (née Fredman); ed St Paul's School, London and Trinity Coll., Cambridge; with Acquisitions Dept New York Library 1951; returned to England 1954; with Symphonic Music Dept Boosey and Hawkes 1954; Literary Critic, Truth 1956–57, Music Critic Time and Tide 1957; playwright 1957–; Cameron Mackintosh Prof. of Contemporary Theatre, St Catherine's Coll. Oxford 1994–95; mem. European Acad., Yuste 1998–; Hon. DLitt (Bath) 1992, (St Andrews) 1999; New York Drama Critics' Circle Award 1959–60 (Five Finger Exercise); Antoinette Perry Award for Best Play and New York Drama Critics' Circle Award 1975 (Equus) and 1981 (Amadeus); Evening Standard Drama Award 1957 (Five Finger Exercise) and 1980 (Amadeus), London Drama Critics' Award; Acad. Award for Best Screenplay (Amadeus) 1984; Hamburg Shakespeare Prize 1987; Best Comedy, Evening Standard Award for Lettice and Lovage 1988. *Plays:* Five Finger Exercise, London 1958, New York 1959 (film 1962), The Private Ear and The Public Eye, London 1962, USA 1963, The Royal Hunt of the Sun, London 1964, New York 1964, Black Comedy, London 1965, New York 1967, White Lies, New York 1967 (revised as The White Liars, London 1968 and as White Liars, London 1976), The Battle of Shrivings 1970, Equus, London 1973, New York 1974, Amadeus, London 1979, New York 1980, Yonadab 1985, Lettice and Lovage, London 1987, New York 1990, The Gift of the Gorgon 1992; also performed on stage, Chichester, Guildford, Malvern 1996. *Television:* several TV plays including The Salt Land 1955, Balance of Terror. *Film screenplays:* The Royal Hunt of the Sun 1965, Equus 1977, Amadeus 1984 (all adaptations of his plays). *Radio play:* Whom Do I Have the Honour of Addressing? 1989. *Leisure interests:* architecture, walking, music. *Address:* c/o Macnaughton Lord 2000 Ltd, 19 Margravine Gardens, London, W6 8RL, England (office). *Telephone:* (20) 8741-0606 (office). *Fax:* (20) 8741-7443 (office). *E-mail:* info@ml2000.org.uk (office). *Website:* www.ml2000.org.uk (office).

SHAFIE, Tan Sri Haji (Mohammed) Ghazali, PMN, SSAP, SIMP, SPDK; Malaysian politician; b. 22 March 1922, Kuala Lipis; m. Puan Sri Khatijah binti Abdul Majid; two s.; ed Raffles Coll., Singapore, Univ. Coll. of Wales, London School of Econs; fmr civil servant; assigned to Office of Commr for Malaya, London; later Commr for Fed. of Malaya, New Delhi; Deputy Sec. for External Affairs 1957, Acting Perm. Sec. 1959; Senator 1970–72; Minister with Special Functions 1970–72, also of Information 1971–72; mem. Parl. 1972–; Minister of Home Affairs 1973–81, of Foreign Affairs 1981–84; Govt Special Envoy 1984; Resident Writer, Inst. of Malay World and Civilization 1993–95; Chair. Paremba; Visiting Prof., Nat. Univ. of Singapore; mem. United Malays Nat. Org. (Pertubuhan Kebangsaan Melayu Bersatu) (UMNO Baru) (New UMNO). *Publications include:* Malay Nationalism and Globalisation 1997, Memoir on the Formation of Malaysia 1998, Ghazali Shafie: Malaysia, Asean and the New World Order 2000. *Address:* c/o United Malays National Organization (Pertubuhan Kebangsaan Melayu Bersatu) (UMNO Baru) (New UMNO), Menara Dato' Onn, 38th Floor, Jalan Tun Ismail, 50480 Kuala Lumpur; 15 Jalan Ampang Hilir, 55000 Kuala Lumpur, Malaysia.

SHAFIK, Nemat (Minouche), BA, MSc, DPhil; Egyptian/American economist and international banking official; *Permanent Secretary, Department for International Development;* b. Egypt; m.; two c. three step-c.; ed Univ. of Mass at Amherst, London School of Econs and St Anthony's Coll. Oxford, UK; Econ. Policy Analyst, USAID, Cairo 1983–84, Evaluation Officer, Cairo 1984–85, Consultant, Dakar, Senegal 1986; Econs Tutor, Univ. of Oxford, UK 1987–89, Researcher, Unit for Study of African Economies, Inst. of Econs and Statistics 1989–91; Consultant, Public Econs Div., World Bank, Washington, DC 1988, Consultant, Vice Pres. for Devt Econs 1989, Economist, Int. Econs Dept 1990, Economist, World Devt Report 1992, Country Economist, Cen. European Dept 1992–94, Sr Economist, Office of the Chief Economist 1994–95, Man. Pvt. Sector Team, Middle East and N Africa (MENA) Region 1996–97, Dir Pvt Sector and Finance, MENA 1997–99, Vice-Pres. Pvt Sector Devt and Infrastructure 1999–2003, Vice-Pres. Infrastructure 2003–04; Dir-Gen. Country Programmes and mem. Man. Bd, Dept for Int. Devt (DfID), UK 2004–08, Perm. Sec. 2008–; Adjunct Prof., Econs Dept, Georgetown Univ. 1989–94; Chair. Consultive Group to Assist the Poorest 1999–2004, InfoDev 1999–2004, Global Water and Sanitation Program 1999–2004, Pvt Participation in Infrastructure Advisory Facility 1999–2004, Energy Sector Man. and Advisory Program 1999–2004; Visiting Assoc. Prof., Wharton School, Univ. of Pennsylvania 1996; mem. Bd of Advisory Eds, The Middle East Journal 1996–2002; mem. Bd of Dirs Schutz American School in Egypt 1997–2000; mem. Bd Operating Council, Global Alliance for Workers and Communities, Int. Youth Fed. 1999–2003;. *Address:* Department for International Development, 1 Palace Street, London, SW1E 5HE (office); 61 New End, London, NW3 1HY, England. *Telephone:* (20) 7023-0000 (office). *E-mail:* n-shafik@dfid.gov .uk (office). *Website:* www.dfid.gov.uk (office).

SHAGARI, Alhaji Shehu Usman Aliu; Nigerian teacher and fmr head of state; b. 25 Feb. 1925, Shagari; m.; eight s. ten d.; ed Middle School, Sokoto, Barewa Coll., Kaduna, Teacher Training Coll., Zaria; Science Teacher Sokoto Middle School 1945–50; Headmaster Argungu Sr Primary School 1951–52; Sr Visiting Teacher Sokoto Prov. 1953–58; mem. Fed. Parl. 1954–58; Parl. Sec. to the Prime Minister 1958–59; Fed. Minister of Econ. Devt 1959–60, of Establishments 1960–62, of Internal Affairs 1962–65, of Works 1965–66; Sec. Sokoto Prov. Educ. Devt Fund 1966–68; State Commr for Educ., Sokoto Prov. 1968–70; Fed. Commr for Econ. Devt and Reconstruction 1970–71, for Finance 1971–75; fmr Chair. Peugeot Automobile Nigeria Ltd; mem. Constituent Ass. 1977–83; Presidential candidate for the Nat. Party of Nigeria (NPN) 1979; Pres. of Nigeria and C-in-C of the Armed Forces 1979–83 (deposed by mil. coup), also Minister of Defence 1982–83; under house arrest 1983–86, banned from holding public office and from political activity Aug. 1986; confined to Shagari Village 1986–88; granted unrestricted freedom 1988; Grand Commdr Order of the Niger 1993; Hon. LLD (Ahmadu Bello Univ.) 1976. *Publications:* Wakar Nigeria (poem), Shehu Usman Dan-Fodio: Ideas and Ideals of his Leadership. *Address:* 6A Okoll'e Eboh Street, Ikoyi, Lagos, Nigeria.

SHAH, Prakash, BA, LLB, MCom; Indian diplomatist; *Chairman, PRS International Consultants;* b. 4 July 1939, Bombay; s. of H. Shah; m. Radhika; two d.; joined Indian Foreign Service 1961; Third Sec. EEC 1962–64; Second Sec. Washington, DC 1964–67; Ministry of External Affairs 1967–69; Ministry of Finance 1969–71; First Sec., Petroleum Counsellor, Embassies, Iran and Gulf States 1971–75; Dir Ministry of Petroleum 1975–77; Dir Indian Petrochemicals Ltd, Petrofils Co-operatives Ltd 1976–77; Dir/Jt Sec. Ministry of External Affairs 1977–78; Jt Sec. to Prime Minister 1978–80; High Commr in Malaysia and Brunei 1980–83; Amb. to Venezuela and Consul-Gen. to Netherlands Antilles 1983–85; Jt Sec. Ministry of External Affairs 1985–88, Additional Sec. 1989–90; Dir Kudremakh Iron Ore Ltd 1986; Amb. and Perm. Rep. to UN, Geneva 1991–92; Amb. to Japan 1992–95; Perm. Rep. to UN, New York 1995–97; Special Rep. of UN Sec.-Gen. to Iraq 1998; Dir Pathfinder Int.; Adviser Dodsal Group, UPS, Washington, USA; mem. Bd Khandwala Securities Bombay, Global Educ. Man., Indo-American Arts Council, Hinduja Group, Falcon Corp. Advisors; mem. Indo-Japan Eminent Persons Group; Chair. PRS Int. Consultants; del. to numerous int. confs. *Publications:* articles in professional journals. *Leisure interests:* cricket, tennis, golf, bridge. *Address:* 3102 Forum, Uday Baug, Pune 411013, India (home). *Telephone:* (22) 23676714 (office); (22) 23676717 (home). *Fax:* (22) 66390088 (office). *E-mail:* prakashun@yahoo.com (office); pshah@falconindia.net (office).

SHAH, Saira; British/Afghan journalist; b. 1964; freelance journalist in Afghanistan, covering guerrilla war against Soviet invasion 1986–89, in Baghdad, Iraq, covering Gulf War 1990–91; journalist with Channel Four News (UK). *TV documentary films:* Beneath the Veil (Int. Documentary Asscn Courage under Fire Award) 2001, Unholy War 2001, Death in Gaza (with James Miller, for Frostbite Films/HBO/Channel 4) (BAFTA Award for Current Affairs 2005) 2004. *Publication:* Storyteller's Daughter 2003. *Address:* c/o Michael Joseph, Penguin UK, 80 Strand, London, WC2R 0RL, England.

SHAH, Syed Qaim Ali, BA, LLB; Pakistani lawyer and politician; *Chief Minister of Sindh;* b. 1935, Khairpur dist; s. of Syed Ramzan Ali Shah; m. 1st (deceased); m. 2nd (deceased); m. 3rd; four s. seven d. from three marriages; ed Univ. of Karachi, SM Law Coll., Karachi; elected Chair. Dist Council, Khairpur in Ayub Khan's era; pioneer mem. Pakistan People's Party (PPP) 1967; elected mem. Nat. Ass. 1970; Fed. Minister for Industries and Kashmir Affairs during Zulfikar Ali Bhutto's premiership; Pres. PPP Sindh 1973–77, 1987–97, 2004–; elected mem. Prov. Ass. 1990, later Leader of Sindh Ass., re-elected five times; elected Senator 1997; Chief Minister of Sindh 1988–90, 2008–. *Address:* Chief Minister House, Dr Ziauddin Ahmed Road, Karachi, Sindh (office); Jilani House, Khairpur, Pakistan. *Telephone:* (21) 9202051–4 (office). *E-mail:* info@sindh.gov.pk (office). *Website:* www.sindh.gov.pk (office).

SHAHABUDDEEN, Mohamed, LLB, LLM, BSc, PhD, LLD; Guyanese inter-national judge; *Appeals Judge, United Nations International Criminal Tribunal for the Former Yugoslavia;* b. 7 Oct. 1931, Vreed-en-Hoop; s. of Sheikh Abdul and Jamillah Hamid; m. Bebe Sairah 1955; two s. one d.; ed Univ. of London and Middle Temple London, UK; called to the Bar, Middle Temple, London 1954; pvt. legal practice 1954–59; magistrate 1959; Crown Counsel 1959–62; Solicitor-Gen. (with rank of Justice of Appeal from 1971) 1962–73; Attorney-Gen. 1973–87; Minister of Justice and sometimes Acting Foreign Minister 1978–87; Vice-Pres. of Guyana 1983–87; Judge Int. Court of Justice 1988–97; Judge, Appeals Chamber, UN Int. Criminal Tribunal for Fmr Yugoslavia and for Rwanda 1997–, Vice-Pres. Int. Tribunal for Fmr Yugoslavia 1997–99, 2001–03; Judge, Int. Criminal Court Jan.–Feb. 2009 (resgnd); Chair. Legal Practitioners' Disciplinary Cttee, Advisory Council on the Prerogative of Mercy; mem. Guyana del. to numerous int. confs; Hon. Bencher of the Middle Temple; HQ mem. Int. Law Asscn; mem. Soc. Française pour le droit int., Advisory Bd European Journal of International Law, Bd of Electors of Whewell Professorship of Int. Law of Cambridge Univ., Inst. de Droit int. (first Vice-Pres. 1999–2001), Int. Acad. of Comparative Law; Hon. mem. American Soc. of Int. Law; Order of Excellence, Order of Roraima, Cacique's Crown of Honour (Guyana). *Publications:* several books and articles. *Address:* International Criminal Tribunal for the Former Yugoslavia, Churchillplein 1, 2517 JW The Hague, The Netherlands (office). *E-mail:* shahabuddeen@un.org (office). *Website:* www.icty.org (office).

SHAHEED, Ahmed, PhD; Maldivian government official and politician; *Minister of Foreign Affairs;* m.; one s. two d.; ed Univ. of Wales, Aberystwyth, UK, Univ. of Queensland, Australia; joined Ministry of Foreign Affairs 1982, Attaché, Perm. Mission to UN, New York 1982–84, est. Research and Analysis section, Ministry of Foreign Affairs 1989–91, Officer, Bilateral Relations Dept 1995–96, Head SAARC Div. 1996–98, Head Multilateral Affairs Dept 1998–99, Perm. Sec. 1999–2004; Speech writer for Pres. 1996–; Chief Govt Spokesman 2004–05; Minister of Foreign Affairs 2005–07 (resgnd), 2008–; mem. Dhivehi Rayyithunge Party (DRP) (Maldivian People's Party), Co-

founder and Leader New Maldives faction; Co-founder and Patron Open Soc. Asscn 2006–. *Address:* Ministry of Foreign Affairs, Boduthakurufaanu Magu, Male', 20-077, Maldives (office). *Telephone:* 3323400 (office). *Fax:* 3323841 (office). *E-mail:* admin@foreign.gov.mv (office). *Website:* www.foreign.gov.mv (office).

SHAHEEN, C. Jeanne, BA, MSc; American academic, politician and fmr state governor; *Senator from New Hampshire;* b. 28 Jan. 1947, St Charles, Mo.; d. of Ivan Bowers and Belle Bowers; m. William H. Shaheen; three d.; ed Shippensburg Univ. and Univ. of Mississippi; taught high school in Miss. and New Hampshire; fmr small business owner; directed several NH statewide political campaigns; mem. NH Senate 1990–96; Gov. of NH (first woman) 1997–2003; mem. Democratic Nat. Cttee Comm. on Presidential Nomination Timing and Scheduling 2004; Nat. Chair Kerry-Edwards Cam-paign for Pres. 2004; Sr Fellow, Inst. of Politics, Kennedy School of Govt, Harvard Univ., Dir 2005–07; Senator from New Hampshire 2009–; mem. Bd of Dirs Nellie Mae Educ. Foundation; fmr Sr Fellow, Coll. of Citizenship and Public Service, Tufts Univ.; Democrat. *Address:* 34 Fir Street, Manchester, NH 03101, USA (office). *Website:* www.jeanneshaheen.org (office).

SHAHID, Abdullah; Maldivian politician; m.; three c.; ed Canberra Coll. of Advanced Educ., Australia, Fletcher School of Law and Diplomacy, Tufts Univ., USA; began civil service career in Foreign Ministry 1983; mem. Constitutional Ass. 1994; mem. Parl. 1995–; Exec. Sec. to the Pres. 1995–2005; Minister of State for Foreign Affairs 2005–07, Minister of Foreign Affairs 2007–08. *Leisure interests:* soccer, badminton. *Address:* c/o Ministry of Foreign Affairs, Boduthakurufaanu Magu, Malé 10-307, The Maldives (office).

SHAHRANI, Nematullah, PhD; Afghan politician; *Minister of Hajj and Religious Affairs;* b. Jorm Dist, Badakhshan; ed Abu Hanifa School, Kabul Univ., Al-Azhar Univ., Egypt; fmr Prof. of Sharia, Kabul Univ.; fmr Ed.-in-Chief, Sharayat magazine; Vice-Pres., Transitional Authority 2002–04; Dir Constitutional Drafting Cttee 2002; Minister of Hajj and Religious Affairs 2004–. *Publications include:* Quran Shenaasy (Knowing the Holy Quran), Feqeh Islami Wa Qanoon e Gharb (Islamic Fiqh and Western Law); numerous articles and books on Sharia law. *Address:* Ministry of Hajj and Religious Affairs, nr District 10, Shir Pur, Shar-i-Nau, Kabul, Afghanistan (office). *Telephone:* (20) 2201338.

SHAHRUDI, Ayatollah Sayed Mahmoud Hashemi; Iranian jurist; *Head of the Judiciary;* b. Aug. 1948, Najaf, Iraq; s. of the late Ayatollah Seyed Ali Housseini Shahrudi; ed Alavi School, Iraq; jailed under Baathist regime of Iraq 1974; returned to Iran 1979; teacher of Islamic jurisprudence and methodology, Qum School of Theology 1979–, mem. Supreme Man. Council, Vice-Chair. Asscn of Instructors; est. Inst. of Encyclopedia of Islamic Jurisprudence; currently Head of the Judiciary, Islamic Repub. of Iran; jurist mem. Council of Guardians; mem. Ass. of Experts. *Publications include:* Islamic Criminal Law (discretionary punishments), The Book of Khoms (religious tax) I, II, Hire, Sale, Dormant Partnership, Co-Partnership, Agricultural and Cultivation Partnership etc, Discourses in Islamic Method-ology. *Address:* c/o Ministry of Justice, Panzdah-e-Khordad Square, Tehran, Iran (office). *Website:* www.iranjudiciary.org (office).

SHAHRYAR, Ishaq, BSc, MA; Afghan diplomatist, scientist and business executive; b. 1936, Kabul; m. Hafizah Shahryar; two c.; ed Univ. of Calif., Santa Barbara; awarded scholarship to study chem. in USA 1956, remained in exile; Founder and Pres. Solec Int. Co. 1975–96; Founder and Pres. Solar Utility Co. Inc. 1996–2001; Amb. to USA 2002–03 (resgnd); Univ. of Calif., Santa Barbara Chem. and Biochemistry Distinguished Alumni Achievement Award 2004. *Achievements include:* co-inventor low-cost terrestrial photo-voltaic systems and developer of screen printing of solar cells. *Address:* c/o Ministry of Foreign Affairs, Malak Azghar Rd, Kabul, Afghanistan (office).

SHAHUMI, Suleiman Sasi ash-; Libyan politician; currrently Sec. for Foreign Affairs. *Address:* General Secretariat of the General People's Congress, Tripoli, Libya (office).

SHAIMIYEV, Mintimer Sharipovich; Russian engineer and politician; *President, Republic of Tatarstan;* b. 20 Jan. 1937, Anyakovo, Aktanyshski Dist, Tatar ASSR; s. of Sharip Shaimiev and Naghima Safioullina; m. Sakina Shaimiyeva; two s.; ed Kazan Inst. of Agric.; Engineer, Chief Engineer Service and Repair Station, Mouslyumovski Dist, Tatar ASSR 1959–62; Man. Selkhoztekhnika Regional Asscn, Tatar ASSR 1962–67; Instructor, Deputy Chief of Agricultural Dept, Tatar Regional Cttee of CPSU, Tatar ASSR 1967–69; Minister of Land Improvement and Water Man., Tatar ASSR 1969–83; First Deputy Chair. Council of Ministers, Tatar ASSR 1983, Chair. 1985–89; Sec. Tatar Regional Cttee of CPSU 1983–85, First Sec. 1989–90; Chair. Supreme Soviet, Tatar ASSR 1990–91; Pres. of Tatarstan 1991–, re-elected 1996, 2001, 2005; f. All Russia political movt 1999, now part of United Russia (Yedinaya Rossiya); mem. Acad. of Tech. Sciences; Co-Chair., Higher Council, United Russia Party; Hon. mem. Presidium, Int. Parl. of World Confed. of Kts (under auspices of UN); Hon. mem. Int. Acad. of Informatiza-tion; Hon. Prof., Moscow State Inst. of Int. Relations; Order of Lenin 1966, Order of Red Banner of Labour 1971, Order of Oct. Revolution 1976, Order of Friendship of Peoples 1987, Order for Services to the Fatherland, Grade II 1997; Silver Avitsenna Medal, UNESCO 2001. *Leisure interests:* chess, gardening, skiing. *Address:* Office of the President, 420014 Tatarstan, Kazan, Kreml, Russia (office). *Telephone:* (843) 292-74-66 (office); (843) 291-79-01. *Fax:* (843) 292-78-66 (office). *E-mail:* secretariat@tatar.ru (office). *Website:* www.tatar.ru (office).

SHAKAR, Karim Ebrahim ash-, BA; Bahraini diplomatist; *Ambassador to People's Republic of China;* b. 23 Dec. 1945, Manama; m. Fatima Al-Mansouri 1979; three d.; ed Univ. of New Delhi; joined Ministry of Foreign Affairs 1970;

mem. Perm. Mission to the UN, rising to rank of Second Sec. 1972–76; apptd Chief Foreign Affairs and Int. Org., Bahrain 1977; Perm. Rep. to the UN Office, Geneva and Consul-Gen., Switzerland 1982–87; apptd Amb. (non-resident) to FRG and Austria 1984; apptd. Perm Rep. to the UN Office, Vienna 1982, Perm. Rep. (non-resident) 1984; Perm Rep. to the UN 1987–90; Amb. to UK 1990–95, Amb. (non-resident) to Ireland, Denmark and the Netherlands 1992–95; Dir Int. Directorate at Ministry of Foreign Affairs, Bahrain 1995–2001; Amb. to People's Repub. of China (also accred to Malaysia, the Philippines and Thailand) 2001–; Shaikh Isa Bin Salman Al-Khalifa Medal of Merit 2001. *Leisure interests:* reading, travelling. *Address:* Embassy of Bahrain, 10-06 Liangmaqiao Diplomatic Residence Compound, 22 Dong Fang Dong Lu, Chao Yang Qu, Beijing, People's Republic of China (office). *Telephone:* (10) 65326483 (office). *Fax:* (10) 65326393 (office). *E-mail:* bahembj@yahoo.com (office).

SHAKED, Shaul, PhD; Israeli professor of Iranian studies and comparative religion; *Schwarzmann University Professor Emeritus, Hebrew University of Jerusalem;* b. 8 Feb. 1933, Debrecen, Hungary; m. Miriam Schächter 1960; one s. two d.; ed Hebrew Univ. Jerusalem and SOAS, Univ. of London; Asst Lecturer SOAS 1964–65, Lecturer 1964–65; Lecturer, Assoc. Prof., Prof. Hebrew Univ. Jerusalem 1965–2001, Chair. Dept of Indian, Iranian and Armenian Studies 1971–72, 1974–75, Chair. Dept of Comparative Religion 1972–74, 1977–79, Chair. Ben Zvi Inst. for Study of Jewish Communities in the East 1975–79, Inst. of Asian and African Studies 1981–85, Chair. Academic Bd, Centre for the Study of Christianity 1999–, currently Schwarzmann Univ. Prof. Emer.; mem. Israel Acad. of Sciences and Humanities 1986–, Chair. Section of Humanities and Social Sciences 1995–2001; Visiting Prof., Univ. of Calif. at Berkeley 1969–70, Columbia and New York Univs 1980–81, Univ. of Heidelberg 1987–88; Visiting Fellow, Wolfson Coll., Cambridge, Netherlands Inst. for Advanced Study; Vice-Pres. Societas Iranologica Europaea 1995–99, Int. Academic Union 1998–2001, Pres. 2001–04, Hon. Pres. 2004–; Hon. Fellow, Univ. Coll. London 1995–; Yoram Ben-Porat Prize for Distinguished Research 1993, Israel Prize in Linguistics 2000. *Publications include:* A tentative bibliography of Geniza documents 1964, Amulets and Magic Bowls (with J. Naveh) 1985, Dualism in Transformation 1994, From Zoroastrian Iran to Islam 1995, Magische Texte aus der Kairoer Geniza (with P. Schäfer) (3 vols) 1994–99; articles and book chapters. *Address:* Institute of Asian and African Studies, The Hebrew University, Mount Scopus, Jerusalem 91905, Israel (office). *Telephone:* (2) 6416005 (home). *Fax:* (2) 6446273 (home). *E-mail:* shaul.shaked@huji.ac.il (office). *Website:* religions.huji.ac.il (office).

SHAKER, Mohamed Ibrahim, LLB, DèsScPol; Egyptian diplomatist; *Vice Chairman, Egyptian Council for Foreign Affairs;* b. 16 Oct. 1933, Cairo; m. Mona El Kony 1960; one s. one d.; ed Cairo Univ., Inst. of Int. Studies, Univ. of Geneva, Switzerland; Rep. of Dir-Gen. of IAEA to UN, New York 1982–83; Deputy Perm. Rep. of Egypt to UN, New York 1984–86; Amb. to Austria, Perm. Rep. to UN in Vienna, Gov. on IAEA Bd of Govs, Perm. Rep. to UNIDO 1986–88; Amb. to UK 1988–97, Dean of Diplomatic Corps; fmr mem. Core Group, Programme for Promoting Nuclear Non-proliferation (PPNN) 1987–97, UN Sec.-Gen.'s Advisory Bd on Disarmament Matters 1993–98 (Chair. 1995); Vice Chair. Egyptian Council for Foreign Affairs 1999–, Sawires Foundation for Social Devt 2001–, Regional Information Tech. Inst. 2002–; Order of the Republic (Second Grade) 1976; Order of Merit (First Grade) 1983. *Publications:* The Nuclear Non-Proliferation Treaty: Origin and Implementation, 1959–1979 1980; several articles and contribs to books on nuclear energy and nuclear non-proliferation. *Leisure interests:* tennis, music. *Address:* Egyptian Council for Foreign Affairs, Tower No.2 Osman Buildings, 12th Floor, Kornish El Nile, Maadi, Cairo 11431 (office); 120 Mohie Eldin Abou Elezz, Mohandeseen, Guizeh, Cairo (office); 9 Aziz Osman Street, Zamalek, Cairo, Egypt (home). *Telephone:* (2) 5281091 (home); (2) 3378242 (office); (2) 7359593 (home). *Fax:* (2) 7603552 (office); (2) 7359593 (home). *E-mail:* moshaker@ecfa-egypt.org (office). *Website:* www.ecfa-egypt.org (office).

SHAKESPEARE, Frank; American diplomatist and fmr radio and television executive; b. 9 April 1925, New York; s. of Frank J. Shakespeare, Sr and Frances Hughes Shakespeare; m. Deborah Ann Spaeth Shakespeare 1954; one s. two d.; ed Holy Cross Coll., Worcester, Mass.; Liberty Mutual Insurance Co., Washington, DC 1947–49; Procter and Gamble Co. 1949–50; Radio Station WOR, New York 1950, CBS 1950; Gen. Man. WXIX-TV, Milwaukee, Wis. 1957–59; Vice-Pres. and Gen. Man. WCBS-TV, New York 1959–63; Vice-Pres and Asst to Pres. CBS-TV Network 1963–65; Exec. Vice-Pres. CBS-TV Stations 1965–67; Pres. CBS Television Service Div. 1967–69; Dir US Information Agency 1969–73; Exec. Vice-Pres. Westinghouse Electric Co. 1973–75; Pres. RKO Gen. 1975–83, Vice-Chair. 1983–85; Chair. Bd Radio Free Europe/Radio Liberty Inc. 1982–85; Amb. to Portugal 1985–86, to the Holy See 1986–89; Trustee Heritage Foundation 1979–, Chair. Bd 1981–85; Kt Grand Cross with Palm, Order of the Holy Sepulchre and other honours; nine hon. degrees. *Address:* 303 Coast Boulevard, La Jolla, CA 92037, USA. *Telephone:* (858) 459-8640.

SHAKHANBEH, Abed Ali, LLM, PhD; Jordanian lawyer and politician; b. 1950, Jdaideh-Madba; ed Damascus Univ., Syria, Jordan Univ., Cairo Univ., Egypt; civil servant, lawyer, then judge 1973–93; Sec.-Gen. Court of Control and Admin. Audit 1993–95, Pres. of Court 1995–2001; Pres. Court of Audit 2003; Minister of State for Judiciary Affairs 2001–03, 2003–05; Minister of Justice 2005–07; currently Pres. Anti-Corruption Comm., Amman. *Address:* c/o Ministry of Justice, POB 6040, Amman, Jordan (office).

SHAKHNAZAROV, Karen Georgyevich; Russian film director; *Director-General, Mosfilm Cinema Concern;* b. 8 July 1952, Krasnodar; s. of Georgy Shakhnazarov and Anna Shakhnazarova; m. Darya Igorevna Mayorova 1972; two s. one d.; ed All-Union Inst. of Cinematography; Asst Film Dir Mosfilm Studio 1973–75; on staff Mosfilm 1976–; Artistic Dir VI Creative Union 1987; Chair. Bd Dirs Courier Studio at Mosfilm 1991–, Pres., Dir-Gen. Mosfilm Cinema Concern 1998–; Boris Polevoy Prize 1982, Special Prize of the Jury (Grenoble) 1984, Silver Medal of Int. Film Festival, Lodz 1984, Prize of Int. Film Festival in Moscow for Courier 1986, Comsomol Prize 1986, Brothers Vassilyev State Prize 1988, Special Prize of Karlovy Vary Film Festival for Day of Full Moon 1998, Merited Worker of Arts of Russia, People's Artist of the Russian Fed. 2002. *Film scripts:* debut as scriptwriter Ladies Invite Partners 1981. *Films include:* God Souls 1980, Jazzmen (Diplomas of Int. Film Festivals in London, Chicago, Belgrade 1984) 1983, Winter Night in Gagra 1985, Courier 1986, Town Zero 1989, Assassin (Grand Prix of Int. Film Festival in Belgrade 1991) 1991, Dreams 1993, American Daughter 1995, Day of Full Moon 1998, Poisons or the World History of Poisoning 2001, Rider Named Death 2004. *Leisure interests:* swimming, driving. *Address:* Mosfilmovskaya str. 1, 119858 Moscow, Russia (office). *Telephone:* (495) 745-95-93 (office). *Fax:* (495) 938-20-83 (office). *E-mail:* mosfilm@com2com.ru (office). *Website:* www.mosfilm.ru (office).

SHAKHRAY, Sergey Mikhailovich, LLD; Russian politician; *Head, Accounts Chamber Administration;* b. 30 April 1956, Simferopol; s. of Mikhail A. Shakray and Zoya A. Shakray; m. Tatyana Shakhray 1985; two s. one d.; ed Rostov State Univ.; Head of Law, Moscow State Univ.; People's Deputy of Russia 1990–92; Chair. of the Legis. Cttee of Russian Supreme Soviet 1990; State Councillor on legal issues of Russian Fed. 1991–92; Vice-Prime Minister of Russia 1991–92, 1993, 1994–95; Chair. State Cttee for nat. problems; Founder and Chair. Party of Russian Unity and Consent (PRES) 1993–; Head interim admin in zone of emergency situation in N Ossetia and Ingushetia 1992–93; mem. State Duma (Parl.) 1993; Minister for Nationalities and Nat. Problems 1994–95; Deputy Head of Pres. Yeltsin's Admin, Pres.'s Rep. at Constitutional Court 1996–98; Deputy Chair. Political Consultative Council of Pres. Yeltsin; adviser to Prime Minister 1998–; Prof., Moscow State Inst. of Int. Relations 1999–; Deputy Head, Accounts Chamber Admin 2001–04, Head 2004–; Honoured Jurist of the Russian Fed. *Publications:* Constitution of the Russian Federation. Encylopaedic Dictionary (co-author) 1995, Constitutional Justice in the System of Russian Federalism 2002, Constitutional Law of the Russian Federation 2003, Globalization in the Contemporary World – Political-Legal Aspects 2003, Globalization State Law 2003. *Leisure interests:* fishing, bicycling, badminton, Russian baths. *Address:* Accounts Chamber of the Russian Federation, Zubovskaya str. 2, 119992 Moscow, Russia (office). *Telephone:* (495) 986-00-14 (office). *Fax:* (495) 986-01-53 (office). *E-mail:* zemochka@mail.ru (office); shahray@ach.gov.ru (office). *Website:* www.ach.gov.ru (office).

SHAKIRA; Colombian singer and songwriter; b. (Shakira Isabel Mebarak Ripoll), 2 Feb. 1977, Barranquilla; wrote first song at age of eight, at age 13 signed recording contract with Sony Music Colombia 1990; f. Fundación Pies Descalzos (Barefoot Foundation) 1997; Founding mem. Fundación América Latina en Acción Solidaria; apptd UNICEF Goodwill Amb. 2003; helped organize Live Aid Latino series of concerts 2008–; Hon. Chair. for Educ. Action Week, Global Campaign for Educ., April 2008; Latin Grammy Awards for Best Female Vocal Performance 2000, for Best Music Video (for Suerte) 2002, five MTV Video Awards 2002, MTV Europe Music Award for Best Female 2005, American Music Award for Favorite Latin Music Artist 2005, 2006, Billboard Music Awards for Latin Song of the Year (for La Tortura), for Latin Pop Album Artist of the Year 2005, MTV Video Award for Best Choreography 2006, MTV Latin America Music Award for Song of the Year (for Hips Don't Lie) 2006, Latin Grammy Award for Best Song (for La Totura), for Record of the Year (for La Totura) 2006, MTV Video Music Award for Best Collaboration (for Beautiful Liar with Beyoncé) 2007. *Recordings include:* albums: Magia 1991, Peligro 1993, Pies Descalzos 1996, ¿Dónde Están Los Ladrones? 1998, Laundry Service 2002, Washed And Dried: Laundry Service Limited Edition 2002, Fijación Oral Vol. 1 (Billboard Music Award for Latin Pop Album of the Year 2005, Grammy Award for Best Latin Rock/Alternative Album 2006, Latin Grammy Awards for Best Album and Best Female Pop Vocal Album 2006) 2005, Fijación Oral Vol. 2 2005. *Television:* El Oasis (Colombian TV drama). *Address:* Sony BMG Entertainment, 550 Madison Avenue, New York, NY 10022-3211, USA (office). *Telephone:* (212) 833-7100 (office). *Fax:* (212) 833-7416 (office). *Website:* www.sonybmg.com (office); www.shakira.com.

SHAKOOR, Aishath Azima; Maldivian lawyer, politician and government official; *Attorney-General;* fmr Deputy Minister of Home Affairs; MP apptd by Pres. Maumoon Abdul Gayoom; Pres. Women's Wing of Dhivehi Rayyithunge Party; Attorney-Gen. 2007–. *Address:* Attorney-General's Office, Huravee Building, 3rd Floor, Ameer Ahmed Magu, Malé 20-05, Maldives (office). *Telephone:* 3323809 (office). *Fax:* 3314109 (office). *E-mail:* ashraf@agoffice.gov.mv (office).

SHAKUROV, Sergey Kayumovich; Russian actor; b. 1 Jan. 1942, Moscow; ed Theatre School of Cen. Children's Theatre; with K. Stanislavsky Drama Theatre 1978–88; acted in several other theatres; USSR State Prize 1980, prizes of All-Union Film Festivals for Best Actor 1988, 1991, People's Actor of Russia 1991. *Stage roles include:* Ivanov (Chekhov), Hamlet and others. *Films include:* Svoy sredi chuzhikh, chuzhoy sredi svoikh (At Home among Strangers) 1974, Sto dney posle detstva (100 Days after Childhood) 1975, The Taste of Bread 1979, Portret zheny khudozhnika (Portrait of the Artist's Wife) 1982, Retsept yeyo molodosti (Recipe of Her Youthfulness) 1984, Dogs' Feast 1991, Szwadron (Squadron) 1992, Hagy-Trager 1993, Declaration of Love 1995, Cranberries in Sugar 1995, Armaviz 1998, Pan Tadeusz 1999, Rozhdestvenskaya mysterya 2000, Dikarka 2001, Antikiller 2002, Dnevnik kamikadze (Diary of a Kamikaze) 2003, Antikiller 2: Antiterror 2003. *Television includes:* Vizit k Minotavru (Visit to Minotaurus) (miniseries) 1987, Brezhnev 2005, Master i Margarita (miniseries) 2005. *Address:*

Bibliotechnaya str. 27, Apt. 94, 109544 Moscow, Russia (home). *Telephone:* (495) 270-15-32 (home).

SHALA, Ahmet, BA, MBA, PhD; Kosovo politician; *Minister of the Economy and Finance;* m.; four c.; ed Univ. of Prishtina, Univ. Autonoma de Barcelona, Vaxjo Univ., Sweden; fmr Policy Advisor for Econ. Devt, EU Mission in Kosovo; Deputy Head Dept for Trade and Industry 2000–02; Deputy Man. Dir Kosovo Trust Agency 2002–08; Minister of the Economy and Finance 2008–; Prof. of Marketing Modeling and Statistics, Univ. of Prishtina; f. Cambridge School (English language teaching inst.). *Address:* Ministry of the Economy and Finance, Rruga Bill Klinton dhe Nënë Terezë, 10000 Prishtina, Kosovo (office). *Telephone:* (38) 213115 (office). *Fax:* (38) 213113 (office). *E-mail:* info@mfe-ks.org (office). *Website:* www.mfe-ks.org (office).

SHALALA, Donna Edna, PhD; American professor of political science, university president and fmr government official; *President, University of Miami;* b. 14 Feb. 1941, Cleveland, Ohio; d. of James A. Shalala and Edna Smith; ed Western Coll. and Syracuse Univ.; volunteer, Peace Corps, Iran 1962–64; Asst to Dir Metropolitan Studies Program, Syracuse Univ. 1965–69; Instructor and Asst to Dean, Maxwell Grad. School, Syracuse Univ. 1969–70; Asst Prof. of Political Science, Bernard Baruch Coll., CUNY 1970–72, Prof. of Political Science and Pres. Hunter Coll. 1980–88; Assoc. Prof. of Politics and Educ., Teachers' Coll., Columbia Univ. 1972–79; Asst Sec. for Policy Devt and Research, US Dept of Housing and Urban Devt Washington, DC 1977–80; Chancellor and Prof. of Political Science, Univ. of Wis., Madison 1988–92; US Sec. of Health and Human Services 1993–2001; Pres. Univ. of Miami 2001–; Dir Inst. of Int. Econs 1981–93, Ditchley Foundation 1981–93; mem. Nat. Acad. of Arts and Sciences, American Soc. for Public Admin.; 24 hon. degrees. *Publications:* Neighborhood Governance 1971, The City and the Constitution 1972, The Property Tax and the Voters 1973, The Decentralization Approach 1974. *Leisure interests:* tennis, mountain-climbing, reading, spectator sports. *Address:* Office of the President, University of Miami, 230 Ashe Building, Coral Gables, FL 33146, USA (office). *Telephone:* (305) 284-5155 (office). *E-mail:* dshalala@miami.edu (office). *Website:* www.miami.edu (office).

SHALGAM, Abd ar-Rahman Muhammad, BA; Libyan government official and diplomatist; *Permanent Representative, United Nations;* b. 21 Nov. 1949, Guraifa; s. of Mohamed Shalgam and Rahma Shalgam; m. Mabrouk el-Araby; three s.; ed Cairo Univ., Egypt; Sec. of the People's Cttee for Foreign Liaison and Int. Co-operation 2000–09; Perm. Rep. to UN, New York 2009–; El-Fatah Medal. *Publications include:* Africa in the Future, Religion and Politics in Islamic History, Intimacy (poetry). *Leisure interests:* music, playing the lute and piano. *Address:* Permanent Mission of Libya to the United Nations, 309–315 East 48th Street, New York, NY 10017, USA (office). *Telephone:* (212) 752-5775 (office). *Fax:* (212) 593-4787 (office). *E-mail:* libya@un.int (office). *Website:* www.libya-un.org (office).

SHALHOUB, Anthony (Tony) Marcus, MA; American actor; b. 9 Oct. 1953, Green Bay, Wis.; m. Brooke Adams 1992; two d.; ed Univ. of Southern Maine, Yale School of Drama; spent four seasons with American Repertory Theatre, Cambridge, Mass 1980–84. *Films include:* Longtime Companion 1990, Big Night (Best Supporting Actor Nat. Soc. of Film Critics) 1996, Men in Black 1997, Primary Colors 1998, A Civil Action 1998, The Siege 1998, Galaxy Quest 1999, Impostor 2001, Spy Kids 2001, Spy Kids 2 2002, Men in Black II 2002, Spy Kids 3-D 2003, Against the Ropes 2004, The Great New Wonderful 2005, Careless 2007, American East 2007. *Television includes:* Wings (series) 1991–97, Stark Raving Mad (series) 1999, Monk (also exec. producer) (Best Actor in a Comedy Acad. of Television Arts and Sciences 2003, 2005, Golden Globe 2003, SAG Award 2004, 2005) 2002–, Men in Black: The Series. *Plays:* The Scene 2007. *Address:* Creative Artists Agency, Inc, 9830 Wilshire Blvd., Beverly Hills, CA 90212-1825, USA. *Telephone:* (310) 288-4545. *Fax:* (310) 288-4800. *Website:* www.caa.com.

SHALIKASHVILI, Gen. John, BS, MA; American army officer (retd); *Visiting Professor, Center for International Security and Cooperation, Stanford University;* b. 27 June 1936, Warsaw, Poland; s. of Dimitri Shalikashvili and Maria (Ruediger) Shalikashvili; m. 1st Gunhild Bartsch 1963 (died 1965); m. 2nd Joan Zimpelman 1966; one s.; ed Bradley Univ., Naval War Coll., US Army War Coll., George Washington Univ.; entered US army active duty 1958; various troop and staff assignments Alaska, USA, FRG, Viet Nam, Repub. of Korea 1959–75; Commdr 1st Bn, 84th Field Artillery, 9th Infantry Div., Fort Lewis, Washington 1975–77; Deputy Chief of Staff for Operations, S European Task Force, Vicenza, Italy 1978–79; Commdr Div. Artillery 1st Armored Div. US Army, Nürnberg, FRG 1979–81; Chief, Politico-Mil. Div., later Deputy Dir, Strategy, Plans and Policy, ODCSOPS, the Army Staff, Washington, DC 1981–84; rank of Brig.-Gen. 1983; Asst Div. Commdr 1st Armored Div. US Army, Nürnberg, FRG 1984–86; Dir of Strategy, Plans, Policy, ODCSOPS, the Army Staff, Washington, DC 1986–87; rank of Maj.-Gen. 1986; Commdg Gen. 9th Infantry Div. Fort Lewis, Washington 1987–89; rank of Lt-Gen. 1989; Deputy C-in-C US Army Europe, Heidelberg, FRG 1989–91; Asst to Chair. Jt Chiefs of Staff, Washington, DC 1991–92; rank of Gen. 1992; Supreme Allied Commdr Europe and C-in-C US European Command 1992–93; Chair. Jt Chiefs of Staff 1993–97; Adviser to Pentagon 2000–; currently Visiting Prof. Center for Int. Security and Cooperation, Stanford Univ.; mem. Bd Govs of American Red Cross, Asscn of US Army, Field Artillery Asscn, Retd Officers Asscn, Council on Foreign Relations, American Acad. of Achievement, Bradley Univ. Bd of Trustees; mem. Bd. Dirs Boeing 2000–, Frank Russell Trust Co., L-3 Communications Holdings Inc., Plug Power Inc., United Defense Industries Inc.; numerous decorations, including Mil. Order of the Carabao; Hon. LLD (Univ. of Md, Bradley Univ.; numerous awards. *Address:* Center for International Security and Cooperation, 616 Serra Street, Stanford University, Stanford, CA 94305-

6055, USA. *Telephone:* (425) 882-1923. *E-mail:* brant.shali@verizon.net. *Website:* cisac.stanford.edu.

SHALOM, Silvan, BA, MA, LLB, CPA; Israeli politician and journalist; b. 1958, Tunisia; m. Judy Shalom Nir-Mozes; five c.; ed Tel-Aviv Univ., Ben Gurion Univ.; attained rank of Sergeant during mil. service; mem. Knesset 1992–; Deputy Minister of Defence 1997, Minister of Science and Tech. 1998; Deputy Prime Minister and Minister of Finance 2001–03; Deputy Prime Minister and Minister of Foreign Affairs 2003–06 (resgnd); Chair. Bd of Dirs Israel Electric Co., Dir-Gen. Ministry of Energy and Infrastructure; Deputy Chair. Public Council for Youth Exchange; mem. Exec. of the Broadcasting Authority; Adviser to Ministers of Finance, Econ., Planning and Justice; Israel Airport Authority, Dir Sun d'Or Int. Airlines. *Publications:* numerous articles on the Israeli press. *Address:* Knesset, HaKiryah, Jerusalem 91950, Israel (office). *Telephone:* 2-6408377 (office). *E-mail:* sshalom@knesset.gov.il (office). *Website:* www.knesset.gov.il (office); www.silvan-shalom.co.il.

SHAMANOV, Lt-Gen. Vladimir Anatolyevich; Russian army officer and politician; b. 15 Feb. 1957, Barnaul, Altai territory; m.; one s. one d.; ed Ryazan Higher Military School of Paratroopers, M. Frunze Military Acad. of General Army, Military Acad. of General Staff; Commdr of artillery platoon, Pskov region 1978–85, Bn Commdr 1985–87; Deputy Regt Commdr Kishinev, Moldova 1990–91; Regt Commdr Kirovabad, Azerbaijan 1991–93, Regt moved to Ulyanovsk 1994; Head of Staff Novorossiysk div. 1994–95, transferred to Chechnya as Commdr operation group; Deputy Commdr army group, Ministry of Defence 1995–96; Head of Staff 20th Gen. Troops Army, Voronezh 1998–99; Commdr 58th Army N Caucasus Mil. Command 1999, W Direction of United Group of Fed. Forces 1999; participated in devt and realization of Operation Hunting for Wolves, Grozny, Chechnya 2000; Commdr 58th Army 2000; Gov. Ulyanovsk Region 2000–04; fmr counselor to Minister of Defence Sergei Ivanov; Co-chair. US - Russia Jt Comm. on POW/MIAs –2007; Head, Armed Forces Combat Training Directorate 2007–; Hon. Citizen of Makhachkala, Dagestan; Hero of Russia 1999. *Address:* Ministry of Defence, 105175 Moscow, ul. Myasnitskaya 37, Russia (office). *Telephone:* (495) 293-38-54 (office). *Fax:* (495) 296-84-36 (office). *Website:* www.mil.ru (office).

SHAMASK, Ronaldus; Dutch fashion designer; b. 24 Nov. 1945, Amsterdam; self-educated in design; window-dresser for dept store in Melbourne, Australia 1959; fashion illustrator, The Times and The Observer newspapers, London 1967–68; set and costume designer, Company of Man (multi-media artists' org.) Buffalo, New York 1968–71; subsequently undertook design and clothing comms. for pvt. clients in New York; Founder-pnr with Murray Moss, Moss Shamask, New York 1978–89; opened Moss boutique, Madison Avenue, New York, presented first collection 1979; costume designer, Lucinda Childs Dance Co. premiere of Available Light, Next Wave Fall Festival, Brooklyn Acad. of Music 1983; work exhibited at Hayden Gallery, MIT 1982 and in perm. collection of Smithsonian Inst.; Coty Fashion Award 1981, Fil d'Or, Conf. Int. du Lin 1982.

SHAMGAR, Meir; Israeli lawyer, fmr government official and fmr judge; b. 13 Aug. 1925, Danzig (now Gdańsk, Poland); s. of Eliezer Sterenberg and Dina Sterenberg; m. Geula Shamgar 1955 (deceased); two s. one d.; ed Balfour Coll. Tel-Aviv, Hebrew Univ. and Govt Law School, Jerusalem and Univ. of London; served in Israeli army attaining rank of Brig.-Gen. 1948–68; Mil. Advocate-Gen. 1961–68; Legal Adviser, Ministry of Defence April–Aug. 1968; Attorney-Gen. of Israel 1968–75; Justice, Supreme Court 1975, Deputy Chief Justice 1982, Pres. of Supreme Court (Chief Justice of Israel) 1983–95, Pres. Emer. 1995–; Chair. Comm. of Inquiry into Judiciary in Mil. Justice 1977, into Hebron Massacre 1994, into Murder of Prime Minister Yitzhak Rabin 1995, into Appointment and Powers and Duties of Attorney-Gen. of Israel 1999, into Pollution on Kishon River 2001; Head, govt cttee drafting code for ministers' ethics 2007; mem. Perm. Court of Arbitration, The Hague); mem. Council Open Univ. of Israel, World Jurist Asscn (Peace Through Law); Hon. Fellow, Open Univ. of Israel, Hon. Chair. Council for Ethiopian Jewry; Dr hc (Weizman Inst.) 1987, (Hebrew Univ. Jerusalem) 1990, (Ben Gurion Univ., Beer-Sheva) 1996, (Tel Aviv Univ.) 1997, (Bar Ilan Univ.) 1998; Israel Prize for Special Service to Society and State 1996, Ben Gurion Prize 1998, Democracy Award, Israel Democracy Inst. 2008. *Publications:* The Military Government of the Territories Administered by Israel 1967–80: The Legal Aspects 1982; numerous articles and essays in legal publs. *Address:* Kiriat Ben Gurion, Rehov Shaare Mishpat 1, Jerusalem 91909 (office); 12 Shahar Street, Jerusalem 96263, Israel (home). *Telephone:* 2-6759730 (office); 2-6526130 (home). *Fax:* 2-6759654 (office); 2-6518957 (home).

SHAMI, Misbah-Ud-Din, BSc, MSc, PhD; Pakistani chemist, academic and university administrator; b. 1 Oct. 1930, Jalandhar, India; m.; four c.; ed Punjab Univ., Washington State Univ., USA; Prof., Punjab Univ. 1970, Dean, Faculty of Natural Sciences, Eng and Pharmacy 1973, Pro-Vice-Chancellor 1974–76; mem. Univs' Grants Comm. 1976–80; Chair. Pakistan Science Foundation 1980–90; Ed. Pakistan Journal of Science 1972–79; Adviser to Chancellor, Hamdard Univ., Karachi 1998–; Postdoctoral Fellowship, Royal Soc. 1969; mem. and fmr Pres. Pakistan Asscn for the Advancement of Science, Pakistan Asscn of Scientists and Scientific Professions, Past-Pres. Scientific Soc. of Pakistan; Founding Fellow, Islamic Acad. of Sciences, mem. Council 1994–99; Fellow, Pakistan Acad. of Sciences, Treas. 2005–; Fellow and Past-Pres. Pakistan Inst. of Chemical Engineers; Allama Iqbal Centenary Commemorative Medal, 1979, Nat. Award of the Pakistan Talent Forum 1987, UNESCO Kalinga Prize 1990, Sitara-Imtiaz 1990, UNESCO Niels Bohr Medal 1990, Pakistan Acad. of Sciences Golden Jubilee Medal 2002. *Address:* c/o Pakistan Academy of Sciences, 3-Constitution Avenue, G-5/2, Islamabad, Pakistan. *Telephone:* (51) 9204657. *Fax:* (51) 9206770. *E-mail:* pasisb@yahoo.com.

SHAMIR, Shimon, PhD; Israeli historian, academic and fmr diplomatist; *Professor Emeritus, Department of Middle Eastern and African History, Tel-Aviv University;* b. 15 Dec. 1933, Romania; m. Daniela (née Levin) Shamir 1958; one s. two d.; ed Hebrew Univ. of Jerusalem and Princeton Univ.; Instructor, Lecturer in Modern History of the Middle East, Hebrew Univ. of Jerusalem 1960–66, Fellow, Inst. for Advanced Studies 1978–79; Sr Lecturer, Modern History of the Middle East, Tel-Aviv Univ. 1966, Head of Dept of Middle Eastern and African History 1966–71, Head of Shiloah Center for Middle Eastern and African Studies 1966–73, Assoc. Prof. of Modern History of the Middle East 1970, Head of Grad. School of History 1973–76, mem. Bd of Govs 1974–77, Head of Dept of Middle Eastern and African History 1978–79, Full Prof. 1979, Kaplan Chair in the History of Egypt and Israel 1980, now Prof. Emer., mem. Steering Cttee 1990–91, Headof Tami Steinmetz Center for Peace Research 1992–95; Dir Israeli Academic Center, Cairo 1982–84, mem. Bd of Dirs 1985–93; Amb. to Egypt 1988–90, to Jordan 1995–97; Fellow, Center for Middle Eastern Studies, Harvard Univ. 1968–69; Visiting Assoc. Prof. of Oriental Studies and Political Science, Univ. of Pennsylvania 1976–77, Dept of Near Eastern Studies, Cornell Univ. 1982; Distinguished Fellow, US Inst. of Peace 1991–92; mem. Council for Higher Educ. 1971–76. *Publications:* A Modern History of the Arabs in the Middle East, 1798–1918 1965, Egypt under Sadat: The Search for a New Orientation 1978, Self-Views in Historial Perspective in Egypt and Israel 1981, The Jews of Egypt: A Mediterranean Society in Modern Times 1987, Egypt from Monarchy to Republic (ed.) 1995. *Address:* Department of Middle Eastern History, Gilman Building, Room 405, Tel-Aviv University, Ramat-Aviv, 69 978 Tel-Aviv, Israel (office). *Telephone:* (3) 6409313 (office). *Fax:* (3) 6415802 (office). *E-mail:* shimons@post.tau.ac.il (office). *Website:* www.mideast.tau.ac.il (office).

SHAMIR, Yitzhak, MA; Israeli politician; b. (Yitzhak Yernitsky), 15 Oct. 1915, Ruzinoy, Poland; m. Shulamit; one s. one d.; ed Hebrew Secondary School, Białystok, Warsaw Univ., Hebrew Univ., Jerusalem; emigrated to Palestine 1935; mem. Irgun Zvai Leumi (Jewish Mil. Org.) 1937, then Co-founder and Leader Lohamei Herut Yisrael 1940–48; arrested by British Mandatory Authority 1941, 1946 (exiled to Eritrea); given political asylum in France, returned to Israel 1948; retd from political activity until 1955; sr posts in Civil Service 1955–65; Man. Dir of several business concerns 1965–; mem. Herut Movt 1970–, Chair. Exec. Cttee 1975–92; mem. Knesset 1973–96, Speaker 1977–80; Minister of Foreign Affairs 1980–83, Prime Minister of Israel 1983–84, 1986–92; Deputy Prime Minister 1984–86, Minister of Foreign Affairs 1984–86; Dr hc (Hebrew Union Coll., LA Jewish Inst. of Religion) 1991, (Yeshiva Univ. of NY). *Publication:* Summing Up (memoirs) 1992. *Address:* Beit Amot Mishpat, 8 Shaul Hamelech Boulevard, Tel-Aviv 64733, Israel. *Telephone:* (3) 695-1166 (office).

SHAMKHANI, Rear-Adm. Ali, BSc, MSc, MA; Iranian military officer; b. 1955, Ahvaz, Khuzestan; ed Univ. of Ahvaz, Univ. of State Man. Org.; held various military posts in Iran-Iraq War including Cmmdr Islamic Revolution's Guards Corps (IRGC); Minister in charge of implementation of UN Resolution 598 on ending Iran-Iraq War; Cmmdr of Naval Forces and IRGC and Minister of Defence and Armed Forces Logistics –2005; currently Head, Centre for Strategic Defense Research, Tehran. *Address:* c/o Ministry of Defence, Shadid Yousuf Kaboli Street, Sayed Khandan Area, Tehran, Iran (office).

SHAMLAN, Ali Abdullah ash-, PhD; Kuwaiti geologist, academic and administrator; b. 8 March 1945, Kuwait; m.; ed Kuwait Univ.; Demonstrator, Kuwait Univ. 1967, Asst Prof. 1973, Assoc. Prof. 1978, Prof. 1985–; Chair. Geology Dept, Kuwait Univ. 1975–78, Asst Dean 1978–82, fmr Dean Faculty of Science; Dir-Gen. Kuwait Foundation for the Advancement of Sciences; Chair. Science Coll. Council of Kuwait; fmr Minister of Higher Educ.; mem. Higher Cttee for the Evaluation of the Educational System; mem. Kuwait Univ. Council 1986–, American Soc. of Petroleum Geologists, Soc. of Econ. Palaeontologists and Mineralogists; Fellow, Islamic Acad. of Sciences. *Address:* University of Kuwait, PO Box 5969, 13060 Safat, Kuwait City, Kuwait (office). *Telephone:* 4811188 (office).

SHAMS, Mohammad Jalil, PhD; Afghan economist, academic and politician; *Minister of Economy;* ed Sultan Ghias-ud-din Ghoori High School, Herat, Cairo Univ., Egypt, Bochum Univ., Germany; Asst Prof., School of Econs, Kabul Univ. 1964–66; Vice-Pres. Banke Milli-e-Afghan, Hamburg, Germany 1969–71; Man. Dir Afghan Nat. Bank, London, UK 1971–74; Lecturer in Econs, Essen Polytechnic Germany 1973–74; Deputy Minister of Foreign Affairs 1992–94 (resgnd in protest against internal conflict in Afghanistan); Deputy Minister of Energy and Water 2005–06; Minister of Economy 2006–. *Address:* Ministry of Economy, 5th Floor, Malik Asghar Square, Kabul, Afghanistan (office).

SHAMSIE, Kamila, BA, MFA; Pakistani writer; b. 1973, Karachi; d. of Muneeza Shamsie; ed Hamilton Coll., New York, and Univ. of Mass., Amherst, USA. *Publications include:* In the City by the Sea (Prime Minister's Award for Literature, Pakistan 1999) 1998, Salt and Saffron (Orange's list of 21 Writers for the 21st century) 2000, Kartography 2002, Broken Verses 2005, Burnt Shadows 2009. *Address:* c/o Victoria Hobbs, AM Heath & Co. Ltd, 6 Warwick Court, London, WC1R 5DJ, England (office).

SHAMUZAFAROV, Anvar Shamukhamedovich; Russian politician and architect; b. 10 Nov. 1952; m.; one s.; ed Tashkent Polytech. Inst.; architect, then sr architect, Tashkent Research Inst. of USSR State Cttee on Construction 1974–85; worked in Armenia after earthquake in town restoration projects 1985–88; Chief Expert, Deputy Head of Dept, then Head of Dept Russian State Cttee on Construction (Gosstroi Rossii), Ministry of Construction 1991–96, Chair. 1999–2002; Statistics-Sec., Deputy Minister 1996–98; First Deputy Minister of Land Construction 1998–; consultant to World Bank on problems of financing and reform 1992–98; Chair. Observation Bd Agency of Ipotech Credits (jt stock co.) 1998–99; Friendship of Peoples Order. *Address:* c/o Gosstroi Rossii, Stroitelei str. 8, korp. 2, 117987 Moscow, Russia (office).

SHAN KUO-HSI, HE Cardinal Paul, SJ; Taiwanese ecclesiastic; *Bishop Emeritus of Kaohsiung;* b. 3 Dec. 1923, Puyang; s. of John Shan Cheng-Yin and Maria Teresa Shan Tsung Auo; ordained priest 1955; Dir Chinese Section, Sacred Heart School, Cebu City, Philippines 1957–59; Minister of the House and Socius of the Master of Novices, Jesuit Novitiate, Thuduc, Viet Nam 1961–63; Master of Novices and Rector Manresa House, Changhua, Taiwan 1963–70; Rector, St Ignatius High School, Taipei 1970–76; Pres. Catholic Schools' Asscn, Taiwan 1972–76, Kuangchi Program Service, Taipei 1976–79; Episcopal Vicar of Taipei 1976; consecrated Bishop 1980; Bishop of Hwalien 1980; Pres. Bishops' Comm. for Evangelization within the Chinese Regional Bishops' Conf. 1981; mem. Fed. of Asian Bishops' Confs (FABC) Office for Social Communications 1981, Pres. FABC Office for Interreligious Dialogue 1983–85, FABC Office of Social Communications 1985–91; Pres. Chinese Regional Bishops' Conf. 1987–, Nat. Council of Churches in Taiwan 1991; Bishop of Kaohsiung 1991–2006 (retd) Bishop Emer. 2006–; cr. Cardinal (Cardinal-Priest of S. Crisogono) 1998. *Address:* Bishop's House, 125 Szu-wei 3rd Road, Kaohsiung 80203, Taiwan.

SHANDAL, Abd al-Husayn; Iraqi lawyer and politician; b. 1945, Baghdad; trained and worked as criminal lawyer; Minister of Justice in Transitional Govt 2005; mem. Iraqi Nat. Congress 2005–. *E-mail:* info@inciraq.com (office). *Website:* inciraq.com.

SHANG, Fulin, PhD; Chinese banker; *Chairman, China Securities Regulatory Commission;* b. Nov. 1951, Jinan, Shandong Prov.; ed Beijing Finance and Trade Coll., Southwestern Univ. of Finance and Econs, Chengdu; soldier, PLA 1969–73; worker, Municipal Br., Agricultural Bank of China, Beijing, Yingtaoyuan 1973–78, Deputy Div. Dir Financial Planning Dept, Agricultural Bank of China 1982, then Div. Dir, then Deputy Dept Dir, then Dept Dir; Asst Gov. People's Bank of China 1994–96, Deputy Gov. 1996–2001, Head of Monetary Policy Cttee 1997, Del. to Bank for Int. Settlements (BIS) 1998; Gov. Agricultural Bank of China 2001–03; Chair. China Securities Regulatory Comm. 2002–; Alt. mem. 16th CCP Cen. Cttee 2002–07; mem. 17th CCP Cen. Cttee 2007–. *Publications:* China's Monetary Policy and Credit System of China 1995, The Operation, Efficiency and Development of Central Banks 1996, China's Success in Controlling Inflation and Its Future Policy Orientation 1997, Encyclopedia of Financial Guarantees 1999, A Study on the Transmission Mechanism of Monetary Policy 2000, The Situational Analysis on State-owned Commercial Banks 2002. *Address:* Office of the Chairman, China Securities Regulatory Commission, Focus Place 19, Jin Rong Street, West District, Beijing 100032, People's Republic of China (office). *Telephone:* (10) 66211283 (office). *E-mail:* enadmin@ml.csrc.gov.cn (office); crscweb@publicf.bta.net.cn (office). *Website:* www.csrc.gov.cn (office).

SHANGE, Ntozake, MA; American playwright and poet; b. (Paulette Williams), 18 Oct. 1948, Trenton, NJ; d. of Paul Williams and Eloise Williams; m. David Murray 1977 (divorced); one c.; ed Barnard Coll. and Univ. of S Calif.; mem. Faculty, Sonoma State Univ. 1973–75, Mills Coll. 1975, City Coll. of New York 1975, Douglass Coll. 1978; fmr Artist-in-Residence, Univ. of Florida; performing mem. Sounds in Motion Dance Co.; author, An Evening with Diana Ross: The Big Event 1977; Guggenheim Fellow 1981; mem. Nat. Acad. of TV Arts and Sciences, Acad. of American Poets, PEN America etc.; recipient of numerous drama and poetry awards. *Publications include:* plays: For Colored Girls Who Have Considered Suicide/When the Rainbow is Enuf 1975, A Photograph: Lovers-in-Motion 1977, Boogie Woogie Landscapes 1979, Spell #7 1979, Black and White Two Dimensional Planes 1979, Mother Courage and Her Children 1980, Three for a Full Moon 1982, Bocas 1982, Educating Rita 1982, From Okra to Greens/A Different Kinda Love Story 1983, Three Views of Mt. Fuji 1987, Daddy Says 1989; novels: Sassafrass, Cypress and Indigo 1976, Betsey Brown 1985, The Love Space Demands 1991, I Live in Music 1994, Liliane: Resurrection of the Daughter 1995; poetry: Melissa and Smith 1976, Natural Disasters and Other Festive Occasions 1977, Nappy Edges 1978, Three Pieces 1981, A Daughter's Geography 1983, From Okra to Greens 1984; essays, short stories, non-fiction, adaptations; contribs to magazines and anthologies. *Address:* c/o St Martin's Press, 175 Fifth Avenue, New York, NY 10010, USA.

SHANGHVI, Dilip, BCom; Indian pharmaceutical industry executive; *Chairman and Managing Director, Sun Pharmaceutical Industries Ltd;* m.; two c.; ed Calcutta Univ.; Founder and Man. Dir Sun Pharmaceutical Industries Ltd 1983–, Chair. 1999–; Chair. Bd of Dirs Caraco Pharmaceutical Labs Ltd 1997–; mem. Advisory Cttee Global Bio Pharma Conf. Group; Ernst and Young Entrepreneur of the Year in Health Care and Life Sciences 2005. *Leisure interests* reading, travelling, listening to music. *Address:* Sun Pharmaceutical Industries Limited, 17-B, Mahal Industrial Estate, Mahakali (office); Sun Pharmaceutical Industries Limited, Caves Road, Qudhen East, Mumbai 93, India (office). *Telephone:* (22) 56455645 (office). *Fax:* (22) 56455685 (office). *E-mail:* piedadedsouya@sunpharma.com (office). *Website:* www.sunpharma.com (office).

SHANKAR, Ramamurti, BTech, PhD; Indian physicist and academic; *John Randolph Huffman Professor of Physics, Yale University;* b. 28 April 1947, New Delhi; ed Indian Inst. of Tech., Madras, Univ. of Calif., Berkeley, USA; Jr Fellow, Harvard Soc. of Fellows 1974–77; J. W. Gibbs Instructor of Physics, Yale Univ. 1977–79, Asst Prof. 1979–83, Assoc. Prof. 1983–88, Prof. 1988–, Chair., Dept of Physics 2001–, John Randolph Huffman Prof. of Physics 2004–; Visiting Assoc. Prof., Ecole Normale Supérieure, Paris, France 1982; A.P. Sloan Fellow 1982–86; Visiting Prof., Inst. for Theoretical Physics, Santa Barbara, Calif. 1989; mem. Editorial Bd Journal of Statistical Physics 1988–90; mem. Aspen Center for Physics 1998–2003, Trustee 2004–; mem.

numerous cttees at Yale and elsewhere including Cttee of Visitors, NSF 1999, Dannie Heineman Prize Cttee 1997–98; Fellow, American Physical Soc. 2001–; Byrnes and Sewel Teaching Prize, Yale Univ. 2005. *Publications:* Principles of Quantum Mechanics 1980, Basic Training in Mathematics 1995; numerous journal articles. *Address:* 554 Sloane Physics Laboratory, Department of Physics, Yale University, POB 208120, New Haven, CT 06520, USA (office). *Telephone:* (203) 432-6917 (office). *Fax:* (203) 432-6175 (office). *E-mail:* r.shankar@yale.edu (office). *Website:* pantheon.yale.edu/~rshankar (office).

SHANKAR, Ravi; Indian sitar player and composer; b. 7 April 1920, Varansi; m. Sukanya Rajan 1989; two d. (Anoushka Shankar and Norah Jones) one s. (deceased); ed studied under Ustad Allauddin Khan of Maihar; fmr Dir of Music All-India Radio and Founder of Nat. Orchestra; Founder and Dir Kinnara Schools of Music, Mumbai 1962, Los Angeles 1967; Visiting Lecturer, Univ. of Calif. 1965; concert tours in Europe, USA and the East, major festivals include Edinburgh, Woodstock, Monterey; f. Ravi Shankar Institute for Music and Performing Arts, New Delhi; f. Ravi Shankar Foundation, Calif.; elected to Rajya Sabha (Upper House) 1986; Fellow, Sangeet Natak Akademi 1977; Hon. KBE 2001; numerous hon. degrees; Award of Indian Nat. Acad. for Music, Dance and Drama 1962, Silver Bear of Berlin 1966, Award of Padma Bhushan 1967, Padma Vibhushan 1981, Deshikottam 1981, Int. Music Council UNESCO Award 1975, Ramon Magsaysay Award 1992, Praemium Imperiale 1997, Polar Music Prize 1998, Bharat Ratna (Jewel of India) Award 1999, Grammy Award 2000, ISPA Distinguished Artists Award 2003. *Compositions include:* Concerto No. 1 for Sitar and Orchestra 1971, No. 2 1981, Ghanashyam (opera-ballet, premiered by City of Birmingham Touring Opera) 1989, Kalyan 2001, Mood Circle 2002. *Soundtracks:* for film: Pather Panchali, The Flute and the Arrow, Nava Rasa Ranga, Charly, Gandhi, Chappaqua; for television: Alice In Wonderland. *Recordings include:* Concertos 1 and 2 for Sitar and Orchestra, Raga Jageshwari 1981, Homage To Mahatma Ghandhi 1981, West Meets East (with Yehudi Menuhin and others), In New York 2000, Full Circle: Carnegie Hall 2000. *Film:* Raga 1974. *Publications:* My Music, My Life (autobiog.) 1968, Rag Anurag (Bengali), Ravi: The Autobiography of Ravi Shankar (with others) 1995, From India 1997, Mantram: Chant of India 1997, Raga Jogeshwari 1998. *Address:* Sulivan Sweetland, 1 Hillgate Place, Balham Hill, London, SW12 9ER, England (office); Ravi Shankar Institute for Music and Performing Arts, 7 Chanakyapuri, New Delhi, 110021, India; Ravi Shankar Foundation, 132 North El Camino Real, Suite 316, Encinitas, CA 92024, USA. *Telephone:* (20) 8772-3470 (office). *Fax:* (20) 8673-8959 (office). *E-mail:* info@sulivansweetland.co.uk (office). *Website:* www.sulivansweetland.co.uk (office); www.ravishankar.org.

SHANKARANAND, B., BA, LLB; Indian politician; b. 19 Oct. 1925, Chikodi, Belgaum Dist, Karnataka; s. of Buburao Talwar; m. Kamaladevi Shankaranand; two s. six d.; ed Govt Law Coll., Bombay and R.L. Law Coll., Belgaum; fmrly associated with Republican Party of India and PSP; mem. Lok Sabha 1967–70, 1971–79, 1980–96; Gen. Sec. Congress Party in Parl. 1969–71, mem. Exec. Cttee; Deputy Minister of Parl. Affairs 1971–77; Minister of Health, Educ. and Family Welfare Jan.–Oct. 1980, of Health and Family Welfare 1980–84, of Irrigation and Power Jan.–Sept. 1985, of Law and Justice and Water Resources 1988–89, of Law and Justice July–Nov. 1989, of Petroleum and Natural Gas 1991–93, of Health and Family Welfare 1993–94; mem. numerous cttees; Del. to UNCTAD 1968, UN Gen. Ass. 1969. *Leisure interests:* cricket, football. *Address:* 8 Tees January Marg, New Delhi 110001, India. *Telephone:* 3011307.

SHANKARDASS, Raghuvansh Kumar Prithvinath, MA, LLM; Indian lawyer; b. 9 June 1930, Nairobi, Kenya; s. of P.N. Shankardass and Pushpavati Shankardass; m. Ramma Handoo 1955; ed Trinity Coll., Cambridge, Lincoln's Inn, London; Gen. Sec. Bar Asscn of India 1975–85, Vice-Pres. 1985–; Asst Sec.-Gen. Int. Bar Asscn 1980–82, Vice-Pres. 1984–86, Pres. 1986–88; Gen. Sec. Indian Law Foundation 1975–1991, Pres. 1991–; Chair. Panel of Commrs UN Compensation Comm. 1996–2005; Fellow, American Bar Foundation 1997; Ed. The Indian Advocate 1990–; Pres. Cambridge Univ. Majlis 1953; Vice-Pres. Indian Soc. of Int. Law 2003–06; Trustee India Foundation for the Arts 1994–2000, Talwar Research Foundation 1996, Nurul Hasan Educational and Research Foundation 1998–, Pratichi (India) Trust 2003–; Hon. OBE 1996. *Leisure interests:* golf, music, reading, travel. *Address:* 87 Lawyer's Chambers, Supreme Court of India, New Delhi 110 001 (office); B-12 Maharani Bagh, New Delhi 110 065, India (home). *Telephone:* (11) 23381041 (office); (11) 26830636 (home). *Fax:* (11) 26848104.

SHANKS, Ian Alexander, PhD, FRS, FIEE, FREng, FRSA, FRSE; British scientist; *Honourary Lecturer, Department of Electrical and Electronic Engineering, University of Glasgow;* b. 22 June 1948, Glasgow; s. of Alexander Shanks and Isabella A. Beaton; m. Janice Coulter 1971; one d.; ed Dumbarton Acad., Univ. of Glasgow and Portsmouth Polytechnic; Projects Man. Scottish Colorfoto Labs. Ltd Alexandria 1970–72; Jr Research Fellow, Royal Signals and Radar Establishment, Malvern, later Sr Scientific Officer, Prin. Scientific Officer 1973–82; Sr Scientist, later Prin. Scientist/Sr Man. Unilever Research Lab., Sharnbrook, Beds. 1982–86, Divisional Science Adviser 1994–2000, Vice-Pres. Eng Sciences 2001, Vice-Pres. Physical and Eng Sciences 2001–; Chief Scientist, Thorn EMI PLC 1986; Visiting Prof. of Electrical and Electronic Eng, Univ. of Glasgow 1985–, now Hon. Lecturer; mem. Optoelectronics Cttee The Rank Prize Fund; fmr mem. Science Consultative Group, BBC; fmr mem. Council and Vice-Pres. Royal Soc.; fmr mem. Advisory Bd for Research Councils, Office of Public Service and Science; Chair. Inter-Agency Cttee for Marine Science and Tech. 1991–93; Hon. DEng (Glasgow); Paterson Medal and Prize, Inst. of Physics 1984. *Publications:* 40 research papers and over 75 patents mainly on liquid crystals, displays and biosensors. *Leisure interests:* music, collecting antique pocket watches, scientific instruments and art deco figures. *Address:* Electronics and Electrical Engineering Department, Rankine Building, University of Glasgow, Glasgow G12 8LT, Scotland; Kings Close, 11 Main Road, Biddenham, Bedford, MK40 4BB, England (home). *Telephone:* (1234) 328773 (home).

SHANMUGARATNAM, Tharman Motek, MPA; Singaporean politician; *Minister of Finance;* b. 1958; of Sri Lankan Tamil ancestry; m. Jane Yumiko Ittogi; three s. one d.; ed London School of Econs and Univ. of Cambridge, UK, Harvard Univ., USA; early professional career at Monetary Authority of Singapore, where he was Man. Dir, currently mem. Bd and Deputy Chair.; mem. Parl. for Jurong GRC (Taman Jurong) 2001–; apptd to Cen. Exec. Cttee of People's Action Party 2002, Asst Treas. 2004–; Sr Minister of State, Ministry of Trade and Industry and Ministry of Educ. 2001–03, Acting Minister of Educ. 2003–04, Minister of Educ. 2004–08, Second Minister of Finance 2006–07, Minister of Finance 2007–; Deputy Chair. Nat. Research Foundation; mem. Bd Govt of Singapore Investment Corpn; Co-Chair. Singapore-Liaoning Econ. and Trade Council 2003–; Chair. Ong Teng Cheong Inst. of Labour Studies; Life Trustee Singapore Indian Devt Asscn; Littauer Fellow Award, Harvard Univ., Singapore Public Admin Gold Medal 1999. *Address:* Ministry of Finance, The Treasury 100 High Street, #10-01, Singapore 179434 (office). *Telephone:* 63322717 (office). *Fax:* 63367001 (office). *E-mail:* tharman_s@mof.gov.sg (office). *Website:* www.mof.gov.sg (office).

SHANNON, M. Frances, PhD; Irish biochemist; *Director, John Curtin School of Medical Research, Australian National University;* fmr Researcher, Hanson Centre for Cancer Research, Inst. of Medical and Veterinary Science, Adelaide; currently Group Leader and Dir John Curtin School of Medical Research, ANU; mem. Editorial Bd FEBS Letts (journal of Fed. of European Biochemical Socs); Australian Soc. for Biochemistry and Molecular Biology Boehringer Medal, Lorne Genome Meeting Julian Wells Medal. *Address:* Division of Molecular Bioscience, John Curtin School of Medical Research, GPO Box 334, Canberra, ACT 2601, Australia (office). *Telephone:* (2) 6125-2550 (office). *Fax:* (2) 6125-0415 (office). *E-mail:* frances.shannon@anu.edu.au (office). *Website:* jcsmr.anu.edu.au/org/dmb/cytogene (office).

SHANNON, Richard Thomas, PhD; New Zealand/British historian and academic; *Professor Emeritus, University of Wales, Swansea;* b. 10 June 1931, Suva, Fiji; s. of Edward Arthur Shannon and Grace Shannon (née McLeod); ed Mount Albert Grammar School, Auckland, NZ, Auckland Univ. Coll., Gonville and Caius Coll., Cambridge; Lecturer and Sr Lecturer in History, Univ. Coll. Auckland 1955–57, 1961–62; Lecturer in English History, Univ. of E Anglia, Norwich, UK 1963–65, Sr Lecturer 1965–71, Reader 1971–79; Prof. of Modern History, Univ. of Wales, Swansea 1979–97, Head, History Dept 1982–88, Dean Faculty of Arts 1985–88, Prof. Emer. 1997–; Visiting Fellow, Peterhouse, Cambridge 1988–89; Leverhulme Sr Research Fellowship 1988–90; Fellow, St Deiniol's (Gladstone Foundation) 2000. *Publications:* Gladstone and the Bulgarian Agitation, 1876 1963, The Crisis of Imperialism, 1865–1915 1974, Gladstone, Vol. I 1809–1865 1982, The Age of Disraeli 1868–1881 1992, The Age of Salisbury, 1881–1902 1996, Gladstone Vol. II 1865–1898 1999, A Press Free and Responsible. Self-regulation and the Press Complaints Commission, 1991–2001 2001. *Leisure interest:* mid-Wales borders. *Address:* Flat A, 86 Portland Place, London, W1B 1NU, England; Old School House, Cascob, Presteigne, Powys, LD8 2NT, Wales. *Telephone:* (20) 7436-0214 (London) (home). *E-mail:* dickshannon86@hotmail.com (home).

SHANNON, Robert William Ernest, CBE, BSc, PhD, DTech, FREng, FIMechE; British engineer (retd); *Chairman, Surrey Governors Association;* b. 10 Oct. 1937, Belfast, Northern Ireland; s. of Robert Albert Ernest Shannon and Letitia Shannon; m. Annabelle McWatters 1959; one s. one d.; ed Belfast Tech. High School, The Queen's Univ. Belfast (QUB); Research Fellow, (QUB) 1966–70, Professional Fellow 1996–; Research and Devt, British Gas 1970–83, Dir On Line Inspection Centre 1983–89, HQ Dir of Eng Research 1989–91, Group Dir of Devt 1991–93, Dir of Special Projects, British Gas Global 1993–95; consultant 1995–2007; Exec. Dir ERA Technology; Chair. (non-exec.) Pegasus Engineering Ltd 1996–2000; Dir UCF (NI) Ltd 1997–; mem. Bd Industrial Research and Tech. Unit, NI 1995–2002; mem. Exec. Bd European Prize Foundation Charitable Trust, Dir 1998–2006; Pres. Inst. of Gas Engineers 1993–94, IMechE 1996–97; Chair. NIGC/IRTU Foresight Steering Cttee 1996–2002, Cen. TC54 Harmonization Cttee 1997–2004, IMechE Research and Tech. Cttee 1998–2004 and Council Awards Cttee 1998–, Royal Acad. of Eng Int. Cttee 1998–2004, Inst. of Gas Engineers Research and Tech. Cttee 1998–2003, NI Science Park Foundation Ltd 1999–; Vice-Pres. Royal Acad. of Eng 1998–2003; Chair. Governing Body, The Warwick School, Redhill 1999–; Vice-Chair. Surrey Govs Asscn 2005–07, Chair. 2007–; Vice-Chair. UK Nat. Comm. for UNESCO 2005–; mem. Royal Aeronautical Soc.; Fellow, Irish Acad. of Eng, Inst. of Gas Engineers, British Inst. of Non-Destructive Testing; Hon. DSc; Hon. DTech; MacRobert Award, Inst. of Gas Engineers Gold Medal, Royal Soc. Mullard Medal. *Publications:* Experience with On-Line Inspection 1981; more than 70 scientific publs. *Leisure interests:* reading, gardening, walking. *Telephone:* (1737) 223559. *Fax:* (1737) 223559. *E-mail:* rwe .shannon@btinternet.com (home).

SHANTSEV, Valery Pavlinovich; Russian politician; *Governor, Nizhny Novgorod Region;* b. 1947, Susanino Kostroma Region; m.; one s. one d.; ed Moscow Aviation School, Moscow Inst. of Radiotech., Electronics and Automation, Acad. of Nat. Econs; asst to master factory Salut 1968–75; instructor Perov Dist CP Cttee, Deputy Head Machine Construction Dept Moscow City CP Cttee 1975–85; Chair. Exec. Cttee Perov Dist Soviet, First Sec. Perov Dist CP Cttee, Chair. Perov Dist Soviet of People's Deputies 1985–90; Sec. Moscow City CP Cttee 1990–91; Deputy of Perovo District Council of People's Deputies 1983–93; Deputy of Moscow Soviet 1987–93; Commercial Dir Hockey Club Dynamo 1991–94; Prefect of S Admin. Dist of Moscow 1994–96; Vice-Mayor of Moscow, First Deputy Prime Minister, Moscow Govt and Head of Social Complex 1996–99; Vice-Mayor of Moscow, First Deputy Prime Minister,

Moscow Govt and Head of Econ. Policy and Devt Complex 1999–2001; Vice-Mayor of Moscow and Head of Econ. Policy and Devt Complex 2001–05; Gov. Nizhny Novgorod Region 2005–. *Address:* Office of the Governor, Kremlin, Corpus 1 and 2, Nizhny Novgorod 603082, Russia (office). *Telephone:* (8314) 33-52-51 (office). *Fax:* (8314) 33-49-03. *E-mail:* official@mvs.kreml.nnov.ru. *Website:* www.government.nnov.ru (office).

SHAO, Lt-Gen. Huaze; Chinese journalist, army officer and government official; b. June 1933, Chun'an Co., Zhejiang Prov.; ed PLA Political Cadres' School No. 2, Chinese People's Univ.; joined PLA 1950, CCP 1957; Ed. Jiefangjun Ribao (PLA Daily) 1964; Vice-Dir Jiefangjun Ribao 1981; Dir Propaganda Dept PLA Gen. Political Dept 1985; rank of Maj.-Gen. 1988, Lt-Gen. 1992; Ed.-in-Chief Renmin Ribao (People's Daily) 1989–92, Dir 1992–2000; Chair. All-China Journalists' Asscn 1996–2006; Dean School of Journalism and Mass Communication, Peking Univ.; mem. 14th CCP Cen. Cttee 1992–97, 15th CCP Cen. Cttee 1997–2002; mem. Standing Cttee 9th CPPCC Nat. Cttee 1998–2003. *Address:* College of Journalism and Mass Communication, Peking University, 5 Yiheyuan Road, Hai Dian, Beijing 100871, People's Republic of China (office). *Telephone:* 62754683 (office). *Fax:* 62754485 (office). *E-mail:* sjc18@pku.edu.cn (office). *Website:* sjc.pku.edu.cn (office).

SHAO, Qihui; Chinese administrator and engineer; b. 1934, Yixing, Jiangsu Prov.; ed Harbin Inst. of Tech.; joined CCP 1953; Vice-Gov. Heilongjiang Prov. 1988–89, Gov. 1989–93; mem. 14th CCP Cen. Cttee 1992–97; a Vice-Minister, Ministry of Machine-Building Industry 1994–98; Dir State Admin of Machine-Building Industry 1998–99; Vice-Chair. Econ. Cttee and Standing mem. CPPCC; Dir (non-exec.) Sinotruk (Hong Kong) Ltd; Adviser, Nat. Cttee for Science and Tech. Award; Hon. Chair. Soc. of Automotive Engineers of China, Fed. of Machinery Industry of China; People's Friendship Medal of Russia 1991. *Leisure interest:* photography. *Address:* c/o State Administration of Machine-Building Industry, 46 Sanlihe Lu, Xichen Qu, Beijing, People's Republic of China. *Telephone:* (10) 68594716 (office). *Fax:* (10) 68533673 (office). *E-mail:* sqhw@public3.bta.net.cn (office).

SHAPAR, Howard Kamber, BA, JD; American lawyer; b. 6 Nov. 1923, Boston, Mass; m. Henriette Albertine Emilie van Gerrevink 1977; two s. one d.; ed Amherst Coll., Yale Univ.; Chief Counsel US Atomic Energy Comm.'s Idaho Operations Office 1956–62; Asst Gen. Counsel for Licensing and Regulation, US Atomic Energy Comm. 1962–76; Exec. Legal Dir US Nuclear Regulatory Comm. 1976–82; Dir-Gen. OECD Nuclear Energy Agency, Paris 1982–88; Counsel to Shaw, Pittman, Potts and Trowbridge 1988–98; Past Pres. Int. Nuclear Law Asscn; mem. Bars of State of New Mexico, Court of Appeals for DC, DC Bar Asscn, US Supreme Court; Distinguished Service Award, US Nuclear Regulatory Comm. 1980; Presidential Award of Meritorious Exec. 1981. *Publications:* articles in legal journals and periodicals; papers on atomic energy law. *Address:* PO Box 30242, Bethesda, MD 20824, USA. *Telephone:* (301) 986-5217. *E-mail:* hshapar@bigfoot.com (office).

SHAPIRO, Bernard, OC; Canadian (b. American) academic administrator and fmr government official; *Principal Emeritus, McGill University;* b. 8 June 1935, Montreal; s. of Maxwell Shapiro and Mary Tafler; twin brother of Harold T. Shapiro (q.v.); m. Phyllis Schwartz 1957 (died 2005); one s. one d.; ed McGill Univ., Harvard Univ., USA; Deputy Minister of Educ., Ont. Prov. 1986–89, of Skills Devt 1988–89; Deputy Sec. of Prov. Cabinet, Ont. 1989–90, Deputy Minister and Sec., Man. Bd 1990–91, of Colls and Univs 1991–93; Prof. of Educ. and Public Policy, Univ. of Toronto 1992–94; Prin. and Vice-Chancellor McGill Univ. 1994–2003, now Prin. Emer.; Ethics Commr of Canada 2004–07 (resgnd); Grand Officier, Ordre national du Québec 2004; Hon. LLD (McGill) 1988, (Toronto) 1994, (Ottawa) 1995, (Yeshiva) 1996, (Montreal) 1998, (Edin.) 2000, (Glasgow) 2001, (Bishop's) 2001. *Address:* c/o McGill University, James Administration Building, Room 506, 845 Sherbrooke Street West, Montreal, PQ H3A 2T5, Canada.

SHAPIRO, Ehud, BA, BSc, PhD; Israeli computer scientist and academic; *Harry Weinrebe Professorial Chair of Computer Science and Biology, Weizmann Institute of Science;* b. 1955, Jerusalem; ed Tel-Aviv Univ., Yale Univ., USA; Postdoctoral Fellow, Dept of Computer Science and Applied Math., Weizmann Inst. 1982–93, co-operated closely with Japanese Fifth Generation Computer Systems project to invent high-level programming language for parallel and distributed computer systems, named Concurrent Prolog, on leave of absence 1993–98, Assoc. Prof., Depts of Computer Science and Applied Math., and Biological Chem., holds Harry Weinrebe Professorial Chair of Computer Science and Biology 1998–; Founder and CEO Ubique Ltd (Israeli internet software co.; sold to AOL 1995, sold again to IBM in 1988 following man. buy-out in 1997); World Tech. Award in Biotechnology, The World Tech. Network 2004, Research Leader in Nanotechnology, Scientific American 50 2004. *Achievements include:* studied molecular biology in attempt to build biomolecular computer to operate inside the living body ('Doctor in a Cell'); has also developed method for tracing 'genealogy' of cells in the human body. *Publications:* Algorithmic Program Debugging 1983, Inductive Inference of Theories from Facts 1986, The Art of Prolog: Advanced Programming Techniques (with L. Sterling) 1986 (translated into Japanese, Dutch, French, German and Russian, second edn 1994), Concurrent Prolog: Collected Papers, Vols 1 and 2 (ed.) 1987, Hebrew Prolog for Beginners (with Z. Scherz and O. Maler; in Hebrew) 1988; several scientific papers in professional journals; five US patents. *Address:* Department of Computer Science and Applied Mathematics, Weizmann Institute of Science, Rehovot 76100, Israel (office). *Telephone:* (8) 934-4506 (office). *Fax:* (8) 947-1746 (office). *E-mail:* ehud.shapiro@weizmann.ac.il (office). *Website:* www.wisdom.weizmann.ac.il/~udi (office).

SHAPIRO, Harold Tafler, PhD; American university president and professor of economics; *Professor of Economics and Public Affairs, Department of Economics and Woodrow Wilson School of Public and International Affairs and President Emeritus, Princeton University;* b. 8 June 1935, Montreal, Canada; s. of Maxwell Shapiro and Mary Tafler; twin brother of Bernard Shapiro (q.v.); m. Vivian Shapiro; four d.; ed McGill Univ. and Princeton Univ. Grad. School; Asst Prof. of Econs Univ. of Mich. 1964, Assoc. Prof. 1967, Prof. 1970, Vice-Pres. for Academic Affairs 1977, Pres. 1980–88; Pres. Princeton Univ. 1988–2001, Pres. Emer. 2001–, Prof. of Econs and Public Affairs 1988–; currently Chair. Cttee on Organizational Structure of NIH; mem. Conf. Bd Inc., Bretton Woods Cttee; mem. Pres.'s Council of Advisors on Science and Tech. 1990–92; Chair. Nat. Bioethics Advisory Comm. 1996–; Dir Dow Chemical Co., Nat. Bureau of Econ. Research; mem. Inst. of Medicine of NAS, American Philosophical Soc.; mem. Bd of Overseers, Robert Wood Johnson Medical Center, Bd of Trustees Educational Testing Service 1994–2000, Univ. Corpn for Advanced Internet Devt 2000–; Fellow American Acad. of Arts and Sciences; Trustee, Alfred P. Sloan Foundation, Univ. of Pa Medical Center, Univs Research Asscn, Educational Testing Service. *Address:* 355 Wallace Hall, Princeton University, Princeton, NJ 08544, USA (office). *Telephone:* (609) 258-6184 (home). *Fax:* (609) 258-7120 (office). *E-mail:* hts@princeton.edu (office). *Website:* www.princeton.edu/~hts (office).

SHAPIRO, Irwin I., PhD, FAAS; American physicist and academic; *Timken University Professor, Department of Astronomy, Harvard University;* b. 29 Oct. 1929, New York; s. of Esther Feinberg and Samuel Shapiro; m. Marian Helen Kaplun 1959; one s. one d.; ed Cornell and Harvard Univs; mem. staff., MIT Lincoln Lab. 1954–70, Prof. of Geophysics and Physics 1967–80; Redman Lecturer, McMaster Univ. 1969; Sherman Fairchild Distinguished Scholar, Calif. Inst. of Tech. 1974; Schlumberger Prof., MIT 1980–85, Prof. Emer. 1985–; Sr Scientist, Smithsonian Astrophysical Observatory 1982–; Paine Prof. of Practical Astronomy and Prof. of Physics, Harvard Univ. 1982–97, Timken Univ. Prof., Dept of Astronomy 1997–, Dir Harvard-Smithsonian Center for Astrophysics 1983–2004 (Chair. Bd 1980–81); John C. Lindsay Lecturer, NASA Goddard Space Flight Center 1986; mem. Editorial Bd Celestial Mechanics 1969–75, Annals of Physics 1977–82; Assoc. Ed. Icarus 1969–75; Fellow American Geophysical Union, American Physical Soc.; mem. Int. Astronomical Union, NAS 1974, American Acad. of Arts and Sciences 1969, American Astronomical Soc., American Philosophical Soc. 1998; mem. Radio Science Teams, Mariner Venus–Mercury, Viking and Pioneer–Venus Missions 1970–79, Space Science Bd (NAS) 1977–80, NSF Astronomy Advisory Cttee 1983–86, Task Group on Astronomy and Astrophysics of Nat. Research Council Space Science Bd Study 'Major Directions for Space Science: 1995–2015' 1984–86, Tech. Oversight Cttee of Nat. Earth Orientation Service 1986–, NASA Advisory Council 1987–90; Chair. NASA Astrophysics Sub cttee 1988–92, mem. 1992–96; Albert A. Michelson Medal of Franklin Inst. 1975, Benjamin Apthorp Gould Prize of NAS 1979, John Simon Guggenheim Fellowship 1982, New York Acad. of Sciences Award in Physical and Math. Sciences 1982, Dannie Heineman Award of American Astronomical Soc. 1983, Whitten Medal (American Geophysical Union) 1991, Bowie Medal (American Geophysical Union) 1993, Einstein Medal 1994, Gerard Kuiper Award 1997, Secretary's Gold Medal for Exceptional Service, Smithsonian Inst. 1999. *Publications:* over 350 including Prediction of Ballistic Missile Trajectories from Radar Observations 1958; Ed. of trans. of Mathematical Foundations of Quantum Statistics (Khinchin) 1960; numerous scientific articles, tech. reports and text books for students. *Address:* Harvard-Smithsonian Center for Astrophysics, 60 Garden Street, MS 51, Cambridge, MA 02138 (office); 17 Lantern Lane, Lexington, MA 02421, USA (home). *Telephone:* (617) 495-7100 (office). *Fax:* (617) 495-7105 (office). *E-mail:* ishapiro@cfa.harvard.edu (office). *Website:* cfa-www.harvard.edu (office); cfa-www.harvard.edu/ast (office).

SHAPIRO, Joel, BA, MA; American sculptor; b. 27 Sept. 1941, New York; s. of Dr Joseph Shapiro and Dr Anna Shapiro; m. Ellen Phelan; one d.; ed New York Univ., Peace Corps in India; teacher, Princeton Univ. 1974–75, 1975–76, School of Visual Arts 1977–82; group exhbns in UK, USA, Australia, Germany, the Netherlands 1969–89; Nat. Endowment for the Arts 1975; mem. Swedish Royal Acad. of Art 1994, American Acad. of Arts and Letters 1998; Chevalier, Ordre des Arts et des Lettres 2005; Visual Arts Fellowship, Visual Arts Program, Nat. Endowment for the Arts 1975, Brandeis Univ. Creative Arts Award 1984, Skowhegan Medal for Sculpture 1986, Award of Merit Medal for Sculpture, American Acad. and Inst. of Arts and Letters, New York 1990, Resident in the Visual Arts, American Acad. in Rome 1998–99, Smithsonian Archives of American Art Award 2008. *Commissions:* Verge 2003–2008, 23 Savile Row, London 2008. *Film:* 20 Elements 2005. *Radio:* Giornale radio (interview with Peter Boswell, Radio RAI, Italy) 1999, New York and Company (interview with Leonard Lopate, WNYC-AM, New York) 2001, Leonard Lopate Remote, Whitney Museum of American Art (WNYC-AM) 2002, Art Talk (interview with Edward Goldman, KCRW-FM, Los Angeles) 2004. *Television:* Julião Sarmento/Joel Shapiro 1997, L'Exposition Impossible, Musée d'Orsay, Paris 2005, Joel Shapiro: Twenty Elements (Michael Blackwood Productions, Inc., New York) (DVD) 2006, Getty Museum Audio Tour Interview on Matisse, Nasher Museum 2006. *Address:* c/o Pace Wildenstein, 32 East 57th Street, Second Floor, New York, NY 10022, USA. *Telephone:* (718) 228-1351. *Fax:* (718) 706-0555. *E-mail:* cb@jeshapiro.com (office). *Website:* www.pacewildenstein.com.

SHAPIRO, Larry J., AB, MD; American geneticist, paediatrician and academic; *Dean, School of Medicine, Washington University in St Louis;* b. 6 July 1946, Chicago; m. Carol-Ann Uetake; one s. two d.; ed Washington Univ. in St Louis; intern, St Louis Children's Hosp. 1971–72, resident 1971–73; Research Assoc., Nat. Inst. of Arthritis, Metabolism and Digestive Diseases, Bethesda, Md 1973–75; Asst Prof. of Pediatrics, UCLA 1975–79, Assoc. Prof.

1979–83, Prof. of Pediatrics and Biological Chemistry 1983–91; Investigator, Howard Hughes Medical Inst. 1987–91, also W.H. and Marie Wattis Distinguished Prof.; Prof. and Chair. Dept of Pediatrics, Univ. of California, San Francisco School of Medicine 1991–2003, also Chief of Pediatric Services, Univ. of California, San Francisco Children's Hosp.; Spencer T. and Ann W. Olin Distinguished Prof., Exec. Vice Chancellor for Medical Affairs and Dean, School of Medicine, Washington Univ. in St Louis 2003–; Fellow, AAAS, American Acad. of Pediatrics; mem. NAS Inst. of Medicine, American Acad. of Arts and Sciences, American Pediatric Soc. (Pres. 2003–04), American Soc. for Clinical Investigation, American Soc. for Human Genetics (Pres. 1997), Asscn of American Physicians, Soc. for Inherited Metabolic Disease (Pres. 1986–87), Western Soc. for Pediatric Research (Pres. 1989–90), Soc. for Pediatric Research (Pres. 1991–92); numerous awards including Ross Award, Western Soc. for Pediatric Research 1981. *Address:* Office of the Dean, School of Medicine, Washington University in St Louis, 660 South Euclid Avenue, St Louis, MO 63110, USA (office). *Telephone:* (314) 362-6827 (office). *Website:* medschool.wustl.edu (office).

SHAPIRO, Robert Leslie, BS, JD; American lawyer; b. 2 Sept. 1942, Plainfield, NJ; m. Linell Shapiro; two s. (one deceased); ed Univ. of Calif. at Los Angeles, Loyola Univ. Law School; called to Bar, Calif. 1969, US Court of Appeals 1972, US Dist Court, Calif. 1982; Deputy Dist Attorney, LA 1969–72; sole practice 1972–87; Counsel, Bushkin, Gaims, Gaines, Jonas 1987–88; with Christensen, White, Miller, Fink & Jacobs 1988–95, Pnr, Christensen, Miller, Fink, Jacobs, Glaser, Weil & Shapiro LLP 1995–, currently Head, White-Collar Criminal Defense Section; f. Trial Lawyers for Public Justice 1982; mem. Nat. Asscn of Criminal Defence Lawyers, Calif. Attorneys for Criminal Justice, Bar Asscn; Founder and Chair. Brent Shapiro Foundation for Drug Awareness; American Jurisprudence Award, Bancroft Whitney 1969; Best Criminal Defence Lawyer, Bar Asscn 1993, Lawyer of the Year 1995, Bruce K. Gould Award, Touro Law Center 1997, Author of One of the Ten Best Legal Articles of the Decade, Calif. State Bar Journal, Pro-Bono Lawyer of the Year, Nevada. *Publications:* Search for Justice 1996, Misconception (novel) 2001. *Address:* Glaser, Weil, Fink, Jacobs and Shapiro, LLP, 10250 Constellation Boulevard, 19th Floor, Los Angeles, CA 90067, USA (office). *Telephone:* (310) 556-7886 (office). *Fax:* (310) 556-2920 (office). *E-mail:* rs@glaserweil.com (office). *Website:* www.robertshapiro.com (office); www.brentshapiro.org.

SHAPLEY, Lloyd Stowell, PhD; American professor of mathematics and economics; *Professor Emeritus, Department of Mathematics, UCLA;* b. 2 June 1923, Cambridge, Mass.; s. of Harlow Shapley and Martha Betz; m. Marian Ludolph 1955 (died 1997); two s.; ed Belmont Hill School, Phillips Exeter Acad., Harvard and Princeton Univs; served in US Army Air Corps in meteorology and cryptanalysis 1943–45; research mathematician, RAND Corpn 1948–49, 1954–81; visiting appointments at Calif. Inst. of Tech. 1955–56, Indian Statistical Inst. 1979, Hebrew Univ. of Jerusalem 1979–80, Catholic Univ. of Louvain, Belgium 1982, Nat. Univ. of Defence Tech., China 1987; intermittent teaching, RAND Grad. Inst. 1970; Prof. of Math. and Econs, UCLA 1981–, now Prof. Emer.; Fellow, Econometric Soc., American Acad. of Arts and Sciences; mem. NAS; Hon. PhD (Hebrew Univ. of Jerusalem) 1986; Bronze Star, US Army 1943; Von Neumann Theory Prize, ORSA/TIMS 1981. *Publications:* Geometry of Moment Spaces (with S. Karlin) 1953, Values of Non-Atomic Games (with R. Aumann) 1974. *Leisure interest:* Kriegsspiel. *Address:* Department of Mathematics and Department of Economics, UCLA, Math Sciences Building 6103, 520 Portola Plaza, Los Angeles, CA 90024, USA (office). *Telephone:* (310) 825-3233 (office). *Fax:* (310) 206-6673 (office). *E-mail:* shapley@math.ucla.edu (office). *Website:* www.math.ucla.edu (office).

SHAPOSHNIKOV, Air Marshal Yevgeny Ivanovich; Russian air force officer and politician; b. 3 Feb. 1942, Bolshoy Log, Rostov region; s. of Ivan Sevastinovich Shaposhnikov and Klavdia Stepanova Shaposhnikova; m. Zemfira Nikolayevna Shaposhnikova 1980; one s. two d.; ed Kharkov Higher Aviation School, Y. Gagarin Aviation Acad., Gen. Staff Acad.; served Soviet Army 1959–; Head, Soviet Air Force in Germany 1987–88; First Deputy Commdr All-Union Soviet Air Force 1988–, Commdr 1990–91; Minister of Defence and Head Soviet Armed Forces Aug.–Dec. 1991; C-in-C of the Armed Forces of the CIS 1991–93; Sec. of Security Council, resgnd 1993; rep. of Pres. Yeltsin in Rosvooruzhenie (state-owned armaments exports co.); Gen. Dir Aeroflot 1995–97; Asst to Pres. Russian Fed. 1997–2004; mem. Bd Democratic Reforms Movt 1993–98. *Leisure interests:* literature, theatre, tennis. *Address:* c/o Office of the President, Staraya pl. 4, 103132, Moscow, Russia.

SHAPOVALYANTS, Andrei Georgiyevich; Russian economist; b. 23 Feb. 1952, Moscow; m.; two d.; ed Moscow Plekhanov Inst. of Nat. Econs; researcher, Inst. Elektronika, Main Computation Centre, USSR State Planning Cttee, Head of Div., USSR State Planning Cttee 1969–90; Head, Div. of Financial-Credit Policy, USSR Ministry of Econs and Prognosis 1991; Deputy, First Deputy Minister of Econs and Finance of Russian Fed. 1991–93; Acting Minister of Econs and Finance, First Deputy Minister 1993–98, Minister of Econs 1998–99; mem. Presidium, Russian Govt 1998; Man. Black Sea Bank of Trade and Devt 1999; apptd Pres. Bd of Dirs KAMAZ co. 1999; Dir-Gen. Centre of Reconstruction and Devt of Enterprises 2001; currently mem. Bd of Dirs Murmansk Sea Trade Port,. *Address:* Murmansk Sea Trade Port, 19 prospekt Portovy, Murmansk 183024, Russia (office). *Telephone:* (8152) 48-06-44 (office). *Fax:* (8152) 42-31-27 (office). *E-mail:* mmtp@portmurmansk.ru (office). *Website:* www.portmurmansk.ru (office).

SHARA, Farouk ash-, BA; Syrian politician; *Vice President;* b. 1938; m.; one s. one d.; ed Damascus Univ.; several sr positions in Syrian Airlines 1963–76; Amb. to Italy 1976–80; Minister of State for External Affairs 1980–84, of Foreign Affairs 1984–2006; Vice-Pres. 2006–; several times Acting Minister of Information; Deputy Prime Minister 2001–03; mem. Regional Leadership of Al-Baath Socialist Party 2000–. *Address:* c/o Ministry of Foreign Affairs, Shora Avenue, Muhajireen, Damascus, Syria (office).

SHARANSKY, Natan; Israeli (b. Soviet) politician and human rights activist; *Institute Chairman and Distinguished Fellow, Adelson Institute for Strategic Studies, Shalem Center;* b. 20 Jan. 1948, Donetsk, USSR (now Ukraine); s. of the late Ida Milgrom; m. Natalya (now Avital) Stiglitz 1974; two d.; a leading spokesman for Jewish emigration movt in USSR; arrested by Soviet authorities for dissident activities 1977; received 13-year prison sentence on charges of treason 1978; following worldwide campaign, Soviet authorities released him in exchange for eastern spies held in West and he took up residence in Israel Feb. 1986; mem. Knesset 1996–2006 (resgnd); Minister of Trade and Industry 1996–99, of the Interior 1999–2000; Minister without Portfolio responsible for Jerusalem, Social and Diaspora Affairs 2003–05; currently Inst. Chair. and Distinguished Fellow, Adelson Inst. for Strategic Studies, Shalem Center 2006–; Pres. Beit Hatefutsot (Jewish diaspora museum); fmr Visiting Prof., Brandeis Univ., Waltham, Mass.; fmr Leader, Israel B'Aliyah Party (merged with Likud 2003); US Congressional Gold Medal 1986. *Publications:* Fear No Evil 1988, The Case for Democracy: the Power of Freedom to Overcome Tyranny and Terror (with Ron Dermer) 2005, Defending Identity: It's Indispensable Role in Protecting Democracy 2008. *Address:* Shalem Center, 13 Yehoshua Bin-Nun Street, Jerusalem 93145, Israel (office). *Telephone:* (2) 560-5500 (office). *E-mail:* inquiries@shalem.org.il (office). *Website:* www.shalemcenter.org.il (office).

SHARAPOVA, Maria; Russian professional tennis player; b. 19 April 1987, Nyagan, Siberia; d. of Youri Sharapov and Yelena Sharapova; turned professional 19 April 2001; Women's Tennis Asscn (WTA) singles titles include Tokyo 2003, 2004, 2005, Québec City 2003, Birmingham 2004, 2005, Seoul 2004, WTA Championship 2004, Doha 2005; Wimbledon 2004 (second-youngest Wimbledon Champion in Open era, fourth-youngest winner of any Grand Slam title), US Open 2006; WTA doubles titles, Luxembourg 2003 (with Tamarine Tanasugarn), Japan Open 2003 (with Tanasugarn), Birmingham 2004 (with Maria Kirilenko); coached by father and by Robert Lansdorp; signed with IMG Models 2003; apptd UNDP Goodwill Amb. 2007. *Leisure interests:* fashion, singing, dancing, movies. *Address:* c/o IMG Models, 304 Park Avenue South, 12th Floor, New York, NY 10010, USA. *Website:* www.mariasharapova.com.

SHARAR, Muhammad Dhaifallah, LLB; Kuwaiti lawyer and politician; b. 1948; ed Kuwait Univ.; pvt. law practice 1985–90; elected to Nat. Ass. 1996, Minister of Justice, Awqaf and Islamic Affairs –1998, State Minister for Nat. Ass. Affairs 1998, State Minister for Cabinet and Nat. Ass. Affairs 2001–06; currently Adviser to Amir Sheikh Sabah al-Ahmad al-Jaber al-Sabah. *Address:* c/o Al Diwan Al Amiri, Sief Palace, Building 100, Safat, 13001, Kuwait (office). *E-mail:* amirsoffice@da.gov.kw (office). *Website:* www.da.gov.kw (office).

SHAREEF, Mohammed Hussain; Maldivian government official; fmr Chair. State Trading Org. plc; fmr Dir-Gen. Post and Telecommunications Section, Ministry of Communication, Science and Tech.; currently Chief Govt Spokesman. *Address:* President's Office, Boduthakurufaanu Magu, Malé 20-05, Maldives (office). *Telephone:* 7773394 (office). *Fax:* 3325500 (office). *E-mail:* info@presidencymaldives.gov.mv (office). *Website:* www.presidencymaldives.gov.mv (office).

SHARER, Kevin W., BEng, MBA; American business executive; *Chairman, President and CEO, Amgen Inc.;* ed US Naval Acad., Annapolis and Univ. of Pittsburgh; fmr Consultant, McKinsey & Co.; fmr Exec. Gen. Electric Corpn; Exec. Vice-Pres. and Pres. of Business Markets Div., MCI Communications Corpn –1992; Pres., COO and mem. Bd of Dirs Amgen 1992–2000, CEO 2000–, Chair. 2001–; Chair. Bd of Trustees, LA Co. Museum of Natural History; mem. Bd of Dirs. UNOCAL Corpn, 3M, Northrop Grumman, US Naval Acad. Foundation; mem. The Business Council. *Address:* Amgen Inc., 1 Amgen Center Drive, Thousand Oaks, CA 91320-799, USA (office). *Telephone:* (805) 447-1000. *Fax:* (805) 447-1010. *Website:* www.amgen.com (office).

SHARIATMADARI, Hossein; Iranian newspaper industry executive; *Managing Director, Kayhan;* imprisoned in Tehran before Islamic Revolution of 1979; served as Revolutionary Guards commdr during war with Iraq; currently Man. Dir Kayhan (daily newspaper), Pres. Kayhan Inst. and Rep. of the Supreme Leader of the Islamic Revolution. *Address:* Kayhan, POB 11365-3631, Ferdowsi Avenue, Tehran 11444, Iran (office). *Telephone:* (21) 33110251 (office). *Fax:* (21) 33111120 (office). *E-mail:* kayhan@kayhannews.ir (office). *Website:* www.kayhannews.ir (office).

SHARIF, Ihah ash-, PhD; Egyptian diplomatist; b. 1 Jan. 1954, Cairo; s. of Salaheldin ash-Sharif; m. Asmaa Hussein; two d.; ed Univ. of Paris (Sorbonne), Univ. of Paris XI, France; Diplomatic Attaché, Cen. African Repub. 1981–85; Asst to Minister of State for Foreign Affairs 1985–88; First Sec., Paris 1988–92; Counsellor, Damascus 1994–98; Plenipotentiary Minister, then Head of Mission and Chargé d'affaires, Embassy in Tel-Aviv 1999; Order of Merit, Germany 1999. *Publications:* photographic travel books about 22 countries, including Europe, Myth and Reality 1997, India, Secret and Keys, Germany Today, France, A Country of Djinns and Angels. *Leisure interests:* sport, reading, driving. *Address:* Ministry of Foreign Affairs, Corniche en-Nil, Cairo (Maspiro), Egypt (office). *Telephone:* (2) 5749820 (office). *Fax:* (2) 5748822 (office). *E-mail:* info@mfa.gov.eg (office). *Website:* www.mfa.gov.eg (office).

SHARIF, Mian Mohammed Nawaz; Pakistani politician and industrialist; *President, Pakistan Muslim League—Nawaz (PML—N);* b. 25 Dec. 1949, Lahore; s. of Mian Muhammad Sharif; m. 1971; two s. two d.; ed Govt Coll. and Punjab Univ. Law Coll., Lahore; started work in Ittefaq faction industrial group 1969; Finance Minister, Govt of the Punjab 1981–85, Chief Minister of Punjab 1985–90; Prime Minister of Pakistan 1990–93 (dismissal ruled unconstitutional), resgnd July 1993, Prime Minister 1997–99, concurrently Minister of Defence and Finance (removed in coup by Gen. Pervez Musharraf); sentenced to life imprisonment for terrorism and hijacking April 2000; released from imprisonment, went into exile in Jeddah, Saudi Arabia Dec. 2000, allowed to return to Pakistan Aug. 2007; Pres. Pakistan Muslim League, Punjab 1985, Islami Jamhoori Ittehad 1988; Pres. Pakistan Muslim League—Nawaz (PML—N) 2002–; best known internationally for ordering Pakistan's nuclear tests in response to those of India May 1998; barred by Supreme Court from contesting elections or holding public office early 2009, defied house arrest to lead anti-govt protests that briefly turned violent 15 March 2009, Govt agreed to reinstate deposed Supreme Court judges. *Leisure interests:* social work, photography, hunting, playing cricket. *Address:* Pakistan Muslim League—Nawaz (PML—N), House No. 20-H, Street 10, Sector F-8/3, Islamabad (office); 180–181-H, Ittefaq Colony, Model Town, Lahore, Pakistan. *Telephone:* (51) 2852661 (office); 856069 (home). *Fax:* (51) 2852662 (office). *E-mail:* pmlisb@hotmail.com (office). *Website:* www.pmln.org.pk (office).

SHARIF, Muhammad Safwat esh-; Egyptian politician; b. 1933, Cairo; ed Mil. Acad., Inst. of Strategic Studies; with Presidency of the Repub. 1957–74; Dir Gen. Local Information, State Information Dept 1975, Dir Foreign Information Service, State Information Dept; mem. Arab Information Cttee 1975; Sec., Ministry of Information 1977; Chair. Information Authority 1978; mem. Media Cttee 1979; mem. Constituent Cttee Nat. Democratic Party; Chief, Council of TV and Radio Trustees 1980; Minister of Information 1982–2004. *Address:* c/o Ministry of Information, Radio and TV Bldg, Corniche en Nil, Cairo, Egypt.

SHARIF, Muhammad Shahbaz; Pakistani politician; *Chief Minister of Punjab and President, Pakistan Muslim League—Nawaz;* b. 1950, Lahore; brother of Nawaz Sharif, fmr Prime Minister of Pakistan; m. 1st Nusrat Shahbaz 1973; two s. three d.; m. 2nd Aaliya Honey 1993 (divorced); one d.; m. 3rd Tehmina Durrani; Chief Minister of Punjab 1997–99 (ousted in mil. coup of Gen. Pervez Musharraf 1999); Pres. Pakistan Muslim League—Nawaz 2002–; lived in exile in Saudi Arabia and London before being allowed to return to Pakistan 2007; Chief Minister of Punjab 2008–. *Address:* Office of the Chief Minister, Government of Punjab, 3rd Floor, 3rd Building, Aiwan-e-Iqbal Egerton Road, Lahore, Punjab (office); Pakistan Muslim League—Nawaz, House No. 20-H, Street 10, F-8/3, Islamabad, Pakistan (office). *Telephone:* (42) 9203151 (office); (51) 2852662 (Islamabad). *Fax:* (42) 9203154 (office). *E-mail:* webmaster@punjab.gov.pk (office); pmlisb@hotmail.com (office). *Website:* www.punjab.gov.pk (office); www.pmln.org.pk (office).

SHARIF, Omar; Egyptian actor; b. (Michael Chalhoub), 10 April 1932, Cairo; s. of Joseph Chalhoub and Claire Saada; m. 1st Faten Hamama 1955 (divorced 1967); one s.; m. 2nd 1973; ed Victoria Coll., Cairo; fmr salesman in lumber-import firm; made first film The Blazing Sun 1953; starred in 24 Egyptian films and two French co-production films during following five years; commenced int. film career with Lawrence of Arabia. *Films include:* Lawrence of Arabia, The Fall of the Roman Empire, Behold a Pale Horse, Genghis Khan, The Yellow Rolls-Royce, Doctor Zhivago, Night of the Generals, Mackenna's Gold, Funny Girl, Cinderella-Italian Style, Mayerling, The Appointment, Che, The Last Valley, The Horsemen, The Burglars, The Island, The Tamarind Seed, Juggernaut, Funny Lady, Ace Up My Sleeve, Crime and Passion, Bloodline, Green Ice, Top Secret, Peter the Great (TV), The Possessed, Mountains of the Moon, Michaelangelo and Me, Drums of Fire, Le Guignol, The Puppet, The Rainbow Thief, 588 rue Paradis, Gulliver's Travels (TV), Heaven Before I Die, The 13th Warrior, Mysteries of Egypt. *Publication:* The Eternal Male (autobiog.) 1978. *Leisure interests:* bridge, horse racing. *Address:* c/o Ames Cushing, William Morris Agency, 1 William Morris Place, Beverly Hills, CA 90212, USA.

SHARIF, Osama ash-, BA; Jordanian/Canadian publisher, journalist and media consultant; *Chairman, Media-Arabia;* b. 14 June 1960, Jerusalem; s. of Mahmoud al-Sherif and Aida al-Sherif; m. Ghada Yasser Amr 1984; one s. one d.; ed Univ. of Missouri, Columbia, USA; Chief Ed. The Jerusalem Star 1985–88; Pres. Info-Media, Jordan 1989–; Publr, Chief Ed. and weekly columnist, The Star, Jordan 1990–; Publr Arabian Communications & Publishing (ACP) 1994–97, BYTE Middle East 1994–97, Al Tiqaniyyah Wal 'Amal 1995–97; Chief Ed. and Dir General Arabia.com 1999–2002; Chief Ed. Addustour Newspaper 2003–06; Chair. Media-Arabia 2006–; mem. Royal Cttee for the Nat. Agenda, Amman, Jordan 2005. *Leisure interests:* novel and short-story writing, travel, photography, horse riding. *Address:* Addustour Newspaper, PO Box 591, University Street, Amman 11118, Jordan (office). *Telephone:* (6) 5608000 (office). *Fax:* (6) 5684478 (office). *E-mail:* osama@mediaarabia.com (office). *Website:* www.mediaarabia.com (office).

SHARIFOV, Samir Rauf oğlu, MA; Azerbaijani economist and government official; *Minister of Finance;* b. 7 Sept. 1961; m.; two c.; foreign econ. relations specialist in USSR 1983–91; Deputy Chief, Dept of Int. Econ. Relations, Ministry of Foreign Affairs 1991–95; Chief of Dept, then Exec. Dir Nat. Bank of Azerbaijan 1995–2001; Exec. Dir State Oil Fund of Repub. of Azerbaijan (SOFAZ) 2001–06, also Azerbaijan Rep. and Dir Black Sea Trade and Devt Bank 2001–06; Chair. Govt Comm. on Extractive Industries Transparency Initiative 2003–06; Minister of Finance 2006–. *Address:* Ministry of Finance, 1022 Baku, Samed Vurghun küç. 83, Azerbaijan (office). *Telephone:* (12) 493-30-12 (office). *Fax:* (12) 493-05-62 (office). *E-mail:* office@maliyye.gov.az (office). *Website:* maliyye.gov.az (office).

SHARMA, Arun Kumar, DSc, FNA, F.A.SC., F.N.A.SC., F.TWAS; Indian botanist and cytogeneticist; b. 31 Dec. 1924, Calcutta (now Kolkata); s. of the late Charu Chandra Sharma and of Shovamoyee Sharma; m. Archana Mookerjea 1955; ed Univ. of Calcutta; Research Scholar, Botanical Survey of India 1946–48; Asst Lecturer, Univ. of Calcutta 1948–52, Lecturer 1952–62, Reader 1962–69, Prof. and Head, Dept of Botany 1969–80, Programme Coordinator, Centre of Advanced Study, Dept of Botany 1980–90; Pres. Indian Nat. Science Acad. 1983–84, Golden Jubilee Prof. 1985–90, Hon. Prof. 1990–; Chair. Steering Cttee Nat. Biosource Devt Bd, Govt of India 2000–; Chair. State Biodiversity Bd 2004–; Gen. Pres. Indian Science Congress Asscn 1981; Founding Pres. Fed. of Asian Scientific Acads and Socs 1986–; Fellow, Third World Acad. of Sciences; S. S. Bhatnagar Award in Biology – CSIR 1967, Padma Bhushan, Om Prakash Bhasin Foundation Award 1993, First J. C. Bose Memorial Prize 1994, G. M. Modi Research Award 1994, Centenary Award in Biology 1999, M. N. Saha Memorial Award (Indian Nat. Science Acad.) 1999, Centenary Award (Sataboli Award), Ind. Sci. Cong. Asscn 1999, Vasvik Award 2001, and numerous other awards. *Publications:* Chromosome Techniques: Theory and Practice (with Archana Sharma) 1980, Chromosome in Evolution of Eukaryotic Groups, Vols I and II (with Archana Sharma) 3rd edn 1983, Chromosome Techniques—A Manual (with Archana Sharma) 1994, Plant Chromosomes: Analysis, Manipulation and Engineering (with Archana Sharma) 1999, Chromosome Painting (with A. Sharma) 2002; book chapters, more than 300 articles in professional journals. *Leisure interests:* photography, bird-watching. *Address:* Centre of Advanced Study (Cell and Chromosome Research), Department of Botany, University of Calcutta, 35 Ballygunge Circular Road, Kolkata 700 019 (office); Flat No. 2F2, 18/3 Gariahat Road, Kolkata 700 019, India (home). *Telephone:* (33) 24754681 (office); (33) 24405802 (home). *Fax:* (33) 24764419; (33) 24741042. *E-mail:* nuclaks@cal2.vsnl.net.in (home).

SHARMA, Kamalesh; Indian diplomatist and international organization official; *Secretary-General, Commonwealth;* m. Babli Sharma; one s. one d.; ed Delhi Univ., King's Coll. Cambridge, UK; joined Foreign Service 1965; Head of Divs of Econ. Relations, Int. Orgs and Policy Planning, Foreign Office; Head of Div. Ministry of Finance; served in Bonn, Hong Kong, Saudi Arabia and Turkey; Amb. to fmr GDR, Kazakhstan, Kyrgyzstan; Amb. to UN, Geneva, also Amb. for Disarmament and Spokesman for developing countries in UNCTAD; Amb. to UN, New York 1997–2002; Special Rep. of UN Sec.-Gen. for East Timor (now Timor-Leste) and Head of UN Mission of Support in East Timor (UNMISET) 2002–04; Dir Int. Peace Acad., New York; High Commr to UK 2004–08; Sec.-Gen. The Commonwealth 2008–; Fellow, Weatherhead Center for Int. Affairs, Harvard Univ.; mem. US Foreign Policy Asscn; fmr mem. Bd Dirs Peace Academy, New York, Education Consultants India Ltd; Gov. Ditchley Foundation; Fellow, Harvard Univ., USA; Hon. LLD (De Montfort Univ., UK);Medal of US Foreign Policy Asscn. *Publications include:* Mille Fleurs: Poetry from Around the World (compilation of poems by diplomats and officials) (ed.), Imaging Tomorrow: Rethinking the Global Challange. *Leisure interests:* literature, cosmology, cricket, Indian and western classical music and jazz. *Address:* Commonwealth Secretariat, Marlborough House, Pall Mall, London, SW1Y 5HX, England (office). *Telephone:* (20) 7747-6500 (office). *Fax:* (20) 7930-0827 (office). *E-mail:* info@commonwealth.int (office). *Website:* www.thecommonwealth.org (office).

SHARMA, Nawal Kishore, BA, LLB; Indian politician and journalist; *Governor of Gujarat;* b. 5 July 1925, Dausa, Rajasthan; s. of the late Pandit Mool Chand Sharma; m. Munni Devi; two s.; ed Maharaja Coll., Jaipur; Agra Univ., Hindi Sahitya Sammelan, Prayag, UP; Chair. Municipal Bd, Dausa 1951–56; Pradhan, Panchayat Samiti 1961–65; elected to Lok Sabha 1968, re-elected 1971, 1980, 1984, 1996; Sec. Congress Parl. Party and mem. House Cttee 1971–72; Chair. Cttee on Public Undertakings 1972–73, Jt Select Cttee on Cos (Amendment) Bill 1972–74; Jt Sec. AICC 1974–77, Gen. Sec. 1985, 2003, mem. Working Cttee 1986–87, 1992–94; Pres. INTUC, Rajasthan 1980–82, Pradesh Congress Cttee, Rajasthan 1982–85; Union Minister of State for Finance Nov.–Dec.; Union Minister of State (Ind. Charge) for Petroleum and Natural Gas 1985–86; Chair. Khadi and Village Industries Comm. 1994–96; elected MLA from Jaipur Rural Constituency 1998; Chair. Rajasthan Ass. 1998–2003; Gov. of Gujarat 2004–; Chair. Rajasthan Golden Jubilee Celebration Cttee 1998; Ed. Socialist India, Socialist Bharat; Sec. Gandhi Smriti (Rajghat) for nearly three years; mem. Bd of Rural Electrification Corpn, Govt of India for Jaipur Dist Rural Electrification; Hon. DLitt (Mahatma Gandhi Kashi Vidyapeeth Univ., Varanasi) 1998. *Leisure interests:* reading, writing. *Address:* Raj Bhawan, Sector-20, Gandhinagar 382 020, Gujarat, India (office); B-50, Janata Colony, Jaipur 302004, Rajasthan, (home). *Telephone:* (79) 3243171 (office); (141) 2601723 (home). *Fax:* (79) 3243171 (office). *E-mail:* info@gujaratindia.com (office). *Website:* www.gujaratindia.com (office).

SHARMA, R. S.; Indian energy industry executive; *Chairman and Managing Director, Oil & Natural Gas Corporation () Ltd;* joined Oil & Natural Gas Corpn (ONGC) Ltd as Dir (Finance) 2002–, Acting Chair. and Man. Dir May–Aug. 2006, Chair. and Man. Dir 2006–, mem. Bd of Dirs ONGC Videsh Ltd, Mangalore Refinery & Petrochemicals Ltd, ONGC Mittal Energy Services Ltd, Indian Oil Corpn Ltd; Fellow and mem. Inst. of Cost and Works Accountants of India; Assoc. mem. Indian Inst. of Bankers; India CFO Award 2005 – Excellence in Finance in a PSU, CNBC—TV18 CFO Award 2006 for Excellence in Finance in Oil and Allied Services. *Address:* Oil & Natural Gas Corpn Ltd, Tel Bhavan, Dehradun 248 003, India (office). *Telephone:* (135) 2759561 (office). *E-mail:* info@ongcindia.com (office). *Website:* www.ongcindia.com (office).

SHARMA, Sheel Kant, MS, PhD; Indian diplomatist and international organization executive; *Secretary-General, South Asian Association for Regional Cooperation (SAARC);* b. 10 Jan. 1950; m. Meenu Sharma; ed Indian Inst. of Tech., Mumbai; joined Foreign Service 1973, served as Third Sec., Embassy in Kuwait and Second Sec., Embassy in Saudi Arabia 1976–77,

Under-Sec., Middle East Desk, Ministry of External Affairs 1978–81, Fellow, Inst. of Defence Studies and Analysis, New Delhi 1981–82, Deputy Sec. (North), Ministry of External Affairs 1982–83, First Sec. (Disarmament), Perm. Mission to UN, Geneva and Alt. Rep. to UN Conf. on Disarmament 1983–86, Counsellor and Deputy Chief of Mission, Embassy in Algiers 1986–89, Dir (UN Div.) and Disarmament Head, Ministry of External Affairs, New Delhi 1989–91, Jt Sec. (South and Disarmament) in charge of India's relations with ASEAN, Indo-China and South Pacific 1991–94; seconded to IAEA, Vienna, served as sr professional in External Relations and Policy Coordination Div. 1994–2000; Jt Sec. (Disarmament and Int. Security Affairs) 2000–03, Additional Sec. (Int. Orgs), Ministry of External Affairs 2003–04, Amb. to Austria and Perm. Rep. to all Int. Orgs, Vienna 2004–08, Sec.-Gen. South Asian Asscn for Regional Cooperation (SAARC) 2008–; Chair. G-77 Vienna Chapter 2005; mem. India Int. Centre, India Habitat Centre. *Publications:* articles in journals and UN reports. *Leisure interests:* literature, readings on science and technology, basketball, tennis, swimming, yoga, chess. *Address:* South Asian Association for Regional Co-operation (SAARC), PO Box 4222, Tridevi Marg, Kathmandu, Nepal (office). *Telephone:* (1) 4221785 (home). *Fax:* (1) 4227033 (office). *E-mail:* saarc@saarc-sec.org (office). *Website:* www.saarc-sec.org (office).

SHARMAN, Baron (Life Peer), cr. 1999, of Redlynch in the County of Wiltshire; **Colin Morven Sharman,** OBE, FCA, CIMgt; British chartered accountant and business executive; *Chairman, Aviva plc;* b. 19 Feb. 1943; s. of Col Terence John Sharman and Audrey Emmiline Newman; m. Angela M. Timmins 1966; one s. one d.; ed Bishops Wordsworth School, Salisbury; qualified as accountant with Woolgar Hennel & Co. 1965; joined Peat Marwick Mitchell 1966 (later KPMG Peat Marwick, now KPMG), Man. Frankfurt Office 1970–72, The Hague Office 1972–81 (Partner 1973, Partner-in-Charge 1975), London Office 1981–, Sr Partner, Nat. Marketing and Industry Groups 1987–90, Sr Man. Consultancy Partner 1989–91, Sr Regional Partner, London and SE 1990–93, Sr Partner 1994–98, Chair. KPMG Int. 1997–99; Deputy Chair. Aegis PLC 1999–2000, Chair. 2000–; Chair. BG Group PLC; Dir Reed Elsevier 2002–; Deputy Chair. (non-exec.) Securicor 2003, Chair. (non-exec.) Nov. 2003–; mem. Bd of Dirs Aviva plc 2005–, Chair. 2006–; mem. Industrial Soc.; completed a study of Cen. Govt Audit and Accountability commissioned by Chief Sec. to The Treasury 2002; Hon. mem. Securities Inst.; Dr hc (Cranfield Univ.). *Publication:* Living Culture 2001. *Leisure interests:* food and wine, sailing, opera. *Address:* House of Lords, Westminster, London, SW1A 0IW (office); Aviva plc, St Helen's, 1 Undershaft, London, EC3P 3DQ, England. *Telephone:* (20) 7283-2000 (Aviva). *Fax:* (20) 7662-2753 (Aviva). *Website:* www.aviva.com.

SHARON, Maj.-Gen. Ariel; Israeli politician and army officer (retd); b. 1928; m.; two s.; active in Hagana since early youth; Instructor, Jewish Police units 1947; Platoon Commdr Alexandroni Brigade; Regimental Intelligence Officer 1948; Co. Commdr 1949; Commdr Brigade Reconnaissance Unit 1949–50; Intelligence Officer, Cen. Command and Northern Command 1951–52; studies at Hebrew Univ. 1952–53; in charge of Unit 101, on numerous reprisal operations –1957, Commdr Paratroopers Brigade, Sinai Campaign 1956; studies at Staff Coll., Camberley, UK 1957–58; Training Commdr, Gen. Staff 1958; Commdr Infantry School 1958–69; Commdr Armoured Brigade 1962; Head of Staff, Northern Command 1964; Head, Training Dept of Defence Forces 1966; Head Brigade Group during Six-Day War 1967; resigned from Army July 1973; recalled as Commdr Cen. Section of Sinai Front during Yom Kippur War Oct. 1973, forged bridgehead across Suez Canal; founding mem. Likud party 1973, Leader 1999–2005 (resgnd from party); f. Kadima (Forward) Party 2005; mem. Knesset (Parl.) 1973–74, 1977–2006; Adviser to Prime Minister 1975–77; Minister of Agric. in charge of Settlements 1977–81, of Defence 1981–83, without Portfolio 1983–84, of Trade and Industry 1984–90, of Construction and Housing 1990–92, of Foreign Affairs and Nat. Infrastructure 1996–99; Prime Minister of Israel March 2001–06, also Minister of Immigrant Absorption (suffered stroke in Jan. 2006 and has remained in a coma since then); mem. Ministerial Defence Cttee 1990–92; Chair. Cabinet Cttee to oversee Jewish immigration from USSR 1991–96. *Publication:* Warrior (autobiog.) 1989. *Address:* c/o Office of the Prime Minister, PO Box 187, 3 Rehov Kaplan, Kiryat Ben-Gurion, Jerusalem 91919, Israel (office).

SHARP, Hon. John Randall; Australian politician (retd) and company director; *Chairman, EADS Australia Pacific;* b. 15 Dec. 1954, Sydney; s. of J. K. Sharp; m. Victoria Sharp 1986; two s. one d.; ed The King's School, NSW, Orange Agricultural Coll.; fmr farmer; mem. House of Reps for Gilmore, NSW 1984–93; MP (Nat. Party of Australia) for Hume, NSW 1993–98, Shadow Minister for Tourism and Sport 1988, for Tourism, Sport and Youth Affairs 1988–89, for Land Transport and Shipping 1989–90, for Shipping and Waterfront Reform 1990–93, for Transport 1993–96; Minister for Transport and Regional Devt 1996–97, Deputy Man. of Opposition Business in the House 1990–94; Exec. Dir Linfox (now ADI–Fox) 1999–2001, Corp. adviser 1999–2001; Chair. Thenford Consulting transport consulting co.) 1998–; Chair. Aviation Safety Foundation Australia 2001–; Chair. Power and Data Corpn 2003–; mem. Bd of Dirs EADS Australia Pacific, Australian Aerospace 2002–, French-Australian Chamber of Commerce and Industry, Sky Traders 2005–; Deputy Chair. Regional Express Airlines 2005–; Chair. Pel Air 2006–; mem. Advisory Council Parsons Brinckerhoff 2007–; mem. Univ. of Wollongong Vice-Chancellor's Advisory Bd; mem. Nat. Party of Australia, Hon. Fed. Treas. 2000–05; Chair. Winifred West Foundation 2001–; Co-Chair. Cancer Council of NSW, Southern Highlands Br.; Fellow, Chartered Inst. of Transport; Trustee John McKeown House; Hon. Sec. Nat. Party of Australia. *Leisure interests:* rugby union, scuba diving, skiing, tennis, aviation. *Address:* EADS Australia Pacific, Level 24, AMP Centre, 50 Bridge Street, Sydney, NSW 2000 (office); Ashby Park, Nowra Road, Moss Vale, NSW 2577,

Australia. *Telephone:* (2) 4868-1334 (office). *Fax:* (2) 4868-1474 (office). *E-mail:* info.syd@aerospatiale.com.au (office); sharp@hinet.net.au (office).

SHARP, Phillip Allen, PhD; American biologist, academic and academic administrator; *Institute Professor, Massachusetts Institute of Technology;* b. 6 June 1944, Falmouth, Ky; s. of Joseph W. Sharp and Katherin A. Sharp; m. Ann H. Holcombe 1964; three d.; ed Union Coll., Ky, Univ. of Illinois, California Inst. of Tech. and Cold Spring Harbor, New York; Research Asst, Dept of Chem., Univ. of Ill. 1966–69; Postdoctoral Fellow, Lab. of Prof. Norman Davidson, Calif. Inst. of Tech. 1969–71, Cold Spring Harbor Lab. 1971–72, Sr Research Investigator 1972–74; Assoc. Prof., Center for Cancer Research and Dept of Biology, MIT 1974–79, Prof. 1979–99, Inst. Prof. 1999–; Assoc. Dir Center for Cancer Research 1982–85, Dir 1985–91, Head of Dept of Biology 1991–99; Founding Dir The McGovern Inst. for Brain Research 2000–04; Co-Founder, Chair. Scientific Bd, mem. Bd of Dirs Biogen Idec, Inc., Almylam Pharmaceuticals, Whitehead Inst., MIT 2005–; mem. Scientific Advisory Bd, Fidelity Biosciences Group 2004–; Chair. Gen. Motors Cancer Research Foundation Awards Ass. 1994–, Scientific Advisory Cttee Dana-Farber Cancer Inst. 1996; mem. Cttee on Science, Eng and Public Policy 1992–95, Gen. Motors Cancer Research Foundation Advisory Council 1993–, Pres.'s Advisory Council on Science and Tech. 1991–97, Nat. Cancer Advisory Bd, NIH (Presidential appointment) 1996, Scientific Bd of Advisors, Van Andel Inst. 1996–, Scientific Cttee Ludwig Inst. for Cancer Research 1998–, Bd of Scientific Govs Scripps Research Inst. 1999–; mem. and Trustee Alfred P. Sloan Foundation 1995–2004; mem. Bd Trustees Massachusetts Gen. Hosp., Bd Advisors Polaris Ventures; mem. NAS, NAS Inst. of Medicine, American Acad. of Arts and Sciences, American Philosophical Soc.; Hon. mem. Nat. Acad. of Sciences, Repub. of Korea; Hon. DSc (Univ. of Kentucky, Univ. of Tel-Aviv, Thomas More Coll., Ky, Univ. of Glasgow, Albright Coll., Pa, Rippon Coll., Wis.); Hon. MD (Uppsala Univ.); Dr hc (Union Coll., Ky, Univ. of Buenos Aires); Howard Ricketts Award, Eli Lilly Award, NAS US Steel Foundation Award, Gen. Motors Research Foundation Alfred P. Sloan, Jr Prize for Cancer Research, Gairdner Foundation Int. Award, New York Acad. of Sciences Award in Biological and Medical Sciences, Louisa Gross Horwitz Prize, Albert Lasker Basic Medical Research Award, Dickson Prize (Univ. of Pittsburgh), shared Nobel Prize for Medicine 1993, Benjamin Franklin Medal, American Philosophical Soc. 1999, Walter Prize, Museum of Science, Boston, Nat. Medal of Science 2004, Inaugural Double Helix Medal for Scientific Research, Cold Spring Harbor Lab., AACR Irving Weinstein Distinguished Lectureship Award 2006, Karl Friedrich Bonhoeffer Lecture, Max Planck Inst., Göttigen, Germany, Winthrop-Sears Award, Chemists' Club of New York 2007. *Publications:* numerous papers in scientific journals. *Leisure interests:* family, reading, sports. *Address:* Center for Cancer Research, Room E17-529B, Massachusetts Institute of Technology, 40 Ames Street, Cambridge, MA 02139, USA (office). *Telephone:* (617) 253-6421 (office). *Fax:* (617) 253-3867 (office). *E-mail:* sharppa@mit.edu (office). *Website:* web.mit.edu/sharplab (office).

SHARP, Richard L.; American business executive; b. 12 April 1947; ed Univ. of Virginia, Coll. of William and Mary; joined Circuit City Stores Inc. 1982, several sr positions including Pres. 1984–97, CEO 1986–2000, Chair. 1994–2002; mem. Bd of Dirs Flextronics Int. Ltd 1993–, Chair. 2003–05; fmr Dir and Chair. Carmax Inc. *Address:* c/o Board of Directors, Flextronics International Ltd, 2090 Fortune Drive, San Jose, CA 95131, USA (office).

SHARPE, Kevin Michael, MA, DPhil, FRHistS; British historian, critic, academic and journalist; *Leverhulme Research Professor, Professor of Renaissance Studies and Director, Centre for Renaissance Studies, Queen Mary, University of London;* b. 26 Jan. 1949, Kent; s. of Thomas H. Sharpe and Nell D. Sharpe; ed Sir Joseph Williamson's Math. School, Rochester and St Catherine's Coll., Oxford; Sr Scholar, St Catherine's Coll., Oxford 1971–74; Fellow, Oriel Coll., Oxford 1974–78; Lecturer, Christ Church, Oxford 1976–78; Lecturer in Early Modern History, Univ. of Southampton 1978–89, Reader 1989–, Prof. of History, School of Research and Grad. Studies and Dir of Research 1994–2001; Prof. of Renaissance Studies, Univ. of Warwick 2001–06, Hon. Prof. 2006–; Leverhulme Research Prof., Prof. of Renaissance Studies and Dir Centre for Renaissance Studies, Queen Mary, Univ. of London 2006–; Visiting Fellow, Inst. for Advanced Study, Princeton, NJ 1981; Huntington Library, San Marino, Calif. 1982 (Fletcher Jones Research Prof. 2001–02); Visiting Prof., Stanford Univ. Humanities Center, Calif. 1985–86; Visiting Fellow, Humanities Centre, ANU, Canberra 1990; Visiting Prof., California Inst. of Tech. 1992–93, Mellon Fellowship and Mellon Prof. 2001–02; Visiting Fellow, St Catherine's Coll., Oxford 1996; Adviser to British Art Galleries Project, Victoria and Albert Museum, Lely Exhbn and Conf., Yale Center for British Art and NPG, USA; Fulbright Fellow 1981; ANU Fellowship 1989; Avery Sr Research Fellowship, Huntington Library 1992, Fletcher Jones Sr Fellowship 2001–02; Alexander Von Humboldt Fellowship 2001; Fellow, English Asscn 2002, Max Planck Inst. for History, Göttingen, Germany 2003–04; Yale Center for British Art 2006; Leverhulme Major Research Fellow 2005–07; Wolfson Award 1980, Humboldt Prize Fellowship 2002, Leverhulme Major Fellowship 2005–07. *Radio:* In Our Time, Nightwaves, The Poetry of History. *Television:* Channel 4, Granada TV. *Publications:* Faction and Parliament 1978, Sir Robert Cotton, 1586–1631: History and Politics in Early Modern England 1979, Faction and Parliament: Essays on Early Stuart England (ed.) 1985, Criticism and Compliment: The Politics of Literature in the England of Charles I (Royal Historical Soc. Whitfield Prize 1988) 1987, Politics of Discourse: The Literature and History of Seventeenth Century England (co-ed.) 1987, Politics and Ideas in Early Stuart England 1989, The Personal Rule of Charles I 1992, Culture and Politics in Early Stuart England (co-ed.) 1994, Refiguring Revolutions: Aesthetics and Politics from the English Revolution to the Romantic Revolution (co-ed.) 1998, Reading Revolutions (Soc. for History of Authorship, Readership and Publishing Prize 2001) 2000,

Remapping Early Modern England 2000, Reading, Society, and Politics in Early Modern England (co-ed.) 2004; articles and reviews in The Sunday Times, The Independent, Times Literary Supplement, Spectator, History Today and other journals. *Leisure interests:* cycling, travel, conversation. *Address:* School of English and Drama, Queen Mary, University of London, Mile End Road, London, E1 4NS (office); English and Comparative Literary Studies, University of Warwick, Coventry, CV4 7AL; 97 Livingstone Road, Portswood, Southampton, SO17 1BY, England; 8 Bertie Terrace, Warwick Place, Leamington Spa, CV32 5DZ. *Telephone:* (20) 7862-5013 (office); (24) 7652-3322; (1926) 435606 (Leamington Spa) (home); (23) 8055-3303 (Southampton) (home). *Fax:* (20) 7882-3357 (office). *E-mail:* k.sharpe@qmul.ac.uk (office). *Website:* www.english.qmul.ac.uk (office).

SHARPE, Thomas (Tom) Ridley, MA; British novelist; b. 30 March 1928, London; s. of Rev. George Coverdale Sharpe and Grace Egerton Sharpe; m. Nancy Anne Looper 1969; three d.; ed Lancing Coll., Pembroke Coll., Univ. of Cambridge; social worker 1952; teacher 1952–56; photographer 1956–61; Lecturer in History, Cambridge Coll. of Arts and Tech. 1963–71; full-time novelist 1971–; Laureat, Le Grand Prix de l'Humour Noir, Paris 1986. *Publications:* Riotous Assembly 1971, Indecent Exposure 1973, Porterhouse Blue 1974, Blott on the Landscape 1975, Wilt 1976, The Great Pursuit 1977, The Throwback 1978, The Wilt Alternative 1979, Ancestral Vices 1980, Vintage Stuff 1982, Wilt on High 1984, Grantchester Grind 1995, The Midden 1996, Wilt in Nowhere 2004. *Leisure interests:* photography, gardening. *Address:* 38 Tunwells Lane, Great Shelford, Cambridge, CB2 5LJ, England.

SHARPE, William Forsyth, PhD; American economist and academic; *STANCO 25 Professor Emeritus of Finance, Graduate School of Business, Stanford University;* b. 16 June 1934, Cambridge, Mass; s. of Russell Thornley Sharpe and Evelyn Forsyth Maloy Sharpe (née Jillson); m. 1st Roberta Ruth Branton 1954 (divorced 1986); one s. one d.; m. 2nd Kathryn Dorothy Peck 1986; one step-s. one step-d.; ed Univ. of Calif., Los Angeles; Economist, RAND Corpn 1957–61; Asst Prof. of Econs, Univ. of Washington 1961–63, Assoc. Prof. 1963–67, Prof. 1967–68; Prof., Univ. of Calif., Irvine 1968–70; Timken Prof. of Finance, Stanford Univ. 1970–89, Prof. Emer. 1989–92, Prof. of Finance 1993–95, STANCO 25 Prof. of Finance 1995–99, Prof. Emer. 1999–; Pres. William F. Sharpe Assocs 1986–92; Founder and Chair. Financial Engines Inc. 1996–2003; Hon. DHumLitt (De Paul Univ.) 1997; Dr hc (Alicante Univ.) 2003, (Univ. of Vienna) 2004; Graham and Dodd Award 1972, 1973, 1986, 1988, Nicholas Molodovsky Award 1989, Nobel Prize for Econ. Sciences 1990, UCLA Medal 1998. *Publications:* Economics of Computers 1969, Portfolio Theory and Capital Markets 1970, Asset Allocation Tools 1987, Investments 1999, Fundamentals of Investments (2nd edn) 2000. *Leisure interests:* sailing, all kinds of music. *Address:* Graduate School of Business, Stanford University, Stanford, CA 94305, USA (office). *E-mail:* wfsharpe@stanford.edu (office). *Website:* www.stanford.edu/~wfsharpe (office); www.financialengines.com (office).

SHARPLESS, K(arl) Barry, BA, PhD; American scientist and academic; *W. M. Keck Professor of Chemistry, Scripps Research Institute;* b. 28 April 1941, Philadelphia; s. of Dr E. Dallett Sharpless and Evelyn Anderson Sharpless; m. Jan Sharpless; two s. one d.; ed Dartmouth Coll., New Hampshire, Stanford Univ., Harvard Univ.; mem. Chem. Faculty, MIT 1970–77, 1980–90, Arthur C. Cope Prof. 1987–90; mem. Chem. Faculty, Stanford Univ. 1977–80; W. M. Keck Prof. of Chem., The Scripps Research Inst. (TSRI), La Jolla, Calif. 1990–, Skaggs Inst. for Chemical Biology, TSRI 1996–; mem AAAS 1984, American Acad. of Arts and Sciences 1984, NAS 1985; numerous fellowships including A. P. Sloan Foundation Fellow 1973, Camille and Henry Dreyfus Foundation Fellow 1973, Simon Guggenheim Foundation Fellow 1987; numerous hon. degrees; Hon. mem. RSC 1998; Dr hc (Dartmouth Coll.) 1995, (Royal Inst. of Tech., Stockholm) 1995, (Tech. Univ., Munich) 1995, (Catholic Univ. of Louvain) 1996, (Wesleyan Univ.) 1999; ten prizes from the ACS including Arthur C. Cope Scholar 1986, and Award 1992, San Diego Scientist of the Year 1992, Roger Adams Award in Organic Chem. 1997; Janssen Prize 1986, Prelog Medal, ETH, Zürich 1988, Sammet Award, Goethe Univ., Frankfurt 1988, Chemical Pioneer Award (American Inst. of Chemists) 1988, Scheele Medal (Swedish Acad. of Pharma Sciences) 1991, Tetrahedron Prize 1993, King Faisal Prize for Science (Saudi Arabia) 1995, Microbial Chem. Award, Kitasato Inst., Tokyo 1997, Harvey Science and Tech. Prize, Israel Inst. of Tech. 1998, Organic Reactions Catalysis Soc. Richard Rylander Award 2000, NAS Chemical Sciences Award 2000, Chirality Medal, Italian Chemical Soc. 2000, Nobel Prize in Chem. 2001 (jt recipient), Benjamin Franklin Medal Medal, Philadelphia 2001, Wolf Prize in Science (jtly) 2001, Rhône-Poulenc Medal (UK) 2001, John Scott Prize and Medal, Philadelphia 2001. *Publications:* more than 300 publs in learned journals and 20 patents. *Address:* Scripps Research Institute, 10550 North Torrey Pines Road, La Jolla, CA 92037, USA (office). *Telephone:* (858) 784-7505 (office). *Fax:* (858) 784-7562 (office). *E-mail:* sharples@scripps.edu (office). *Website:* www.scripps .edu (office).

SHARQI, HH Sheikh Hamad bin Muhammad ash-, (Ruler of Fujairah); United Arab Emirates; b. 25 Sept. 1948; ed Mons Mil. Acad., Hendon Police Coll.; Minister of Agric. and Fisheries, UAE Fed. Cabinet 1971; Ruler of Fujairah 1974–; mem. Supreme Council 1974–. *Address:* Emiri Court, PO Box 1, Fujairah, United Arab Emirates.

SHATIGADUD, Col Hassan Mohamed Nur; Somali politician; *Chairman, Rahanwin Resistance Army;* fmr mem. Nat. Security Service; Chair. Rahanwin Resistance Army 1995–; Pres. of self-proclaimed state of South-western Somalia (SWS) 2002; elected mem. Transitional Fed. Govt 2004; Minister of Finance 2005–07. *Address:* c/o Ministry of Finance, Mogadishu, Somalia.

SHATKIN, Aaron Jeffrey, PhD; American scientist and academic; *Professor and Director, Center for Advanced Biotechnology and Medicine, Rutgers University;* b. 18 July 1934, RI; s. of Morris Shatkin and Doris Shatkin; m. Joan Arlene Lynch 1957; one s.; ed Bowdoin Coll. and Rockefeller Univ.; Research Chemist NIH, Bethesda, Md 1961–68; Visiting Scientist, Salk Inst., La Jolla, Calif. 1968–69; mem. Roche Inst. of Molecular Biology, Nutley, NJ 1968–86, Head, Lab. of Molecular Biology 1977–83, Head, Dept of Cell Biology 1983–86; Univ. Prof. of Molecular Biology, Rutgers Univ. 1986–, Prof. of Molecular Genetics and Microbiology, R. W. Johnson Medical School 1986–, Dir and Prof., Center for Advanced Biotechnology and Medicine 1986–; Adjunct Prof. Rockefeller Univ. 1978–87, Princeton Univ. 1984–87; Visiting Prof. Georgetown Univ. Medical School, Washington, DC 1968; Instructor, Cold Spring Harbor Lab. 1972, 1973, 1974, Univ. of Puerto Rico 1978, 1980; Ed.-in-Chief Molecular and Cellular Biology 1980–90; mem. several editorial bds; mem. NAS 1981–, American Acad. of Arts and Sciences 1997; Fellow, American Acad. of Microbiology 1992; Hon. DSc (Bowdoin Coll.) 1979; US Steel Award in Molecular Biology 1977, NJ Pride Award in Science 1989, Thomas Alva Edison Science Award 1991, Asscn of American Medical Colls. Award for Distinguished Research in the Biomedical Sciences 2003. *Publications:* more than 200 publs in scientific journals including original reports and review articles. *Leisure interests:* travel, birds, running. *Address:* Center for Advanced Biotechnology and Medicine, 679 Hoes Lane, Piscataway, NJ 08854 (office); 1381 Rahway Road, Scotch Plains, NJ 07076, USA (home). *Telephone:* (732) 235-5311 (office). *Fax:* (732) 235-5318 (office). *E-mail:* shatkin@cabm .rutgers.edu (office). *Website:* faculty.umdnj.edu/cabm/faculty_shatkin.asp (office).

SHATNER, William, BA; American (b. Canadian) actor and film director; b. 22 March 1931, Montreal, PQ; s. of Joseph Shatner and Anne Shatner; m. 1st Gloria Rand 1956 (divorced 1969); m. 2nd Marcy Lafferty 1973 (divorced 1996); m. 3rd Nerine Kidd 1997 (died 1999); three d.; m. 4th Elizabeth Martin 2001; ed McGill Univ.; appeared Montreal Playhouse 1952, 1953; juvenile roles, Canadian Repertory Theatre, Ottawa 1952–53, 1953–54; appeared Shakespeare Festival, Stratford, Ont. 1954–56; Broadway appearances include: Tamburlaine the Great 1956, The World of Suzie Wong 1958, A Shot in the Dark 1961; founder, Presenter Hollywood Charity Horse Show, Los Angeles 1991–; CEO C.O.R.E. Digital Pictures, Inc., Toronto 1994–; Emmy Award for Outstanding Guest Actor in a Drama Series 2004. *Films include:* The Brothers Karamazov 1957, The Explosive Generation 1961, Judgment at Nuremberg 1961, The Intruder 1962, The Outrage 1964, Dead of Night 1974, The Devil's Rain 1975, Star Trek 1979, The Kidnapping of the President 1979, Star Trek: The Wrath of Khan 1982, Star Trek III: The Search for Spock 1984, Star Trek IV: The Voyage Home 1986, Star Trek V: The Final Frontier (also dir) 1989, Star Trek VI: The Undiscovered Country 1991, National Lampoon's Loaded Weapon 1993, Star Trek: Generations 1994, Ashes of Eden 1995, Star Trek: Avenger 1997, Tek Net 1997, Free Enterprise 1999, Miss Congeniality 2000, Groom Lake (also dir and co-writer) 2002, Dodgeball 2004, Miss Congeniality 2: Armed & Fabulous 2005, Stalking Santa (voice) 2006, The Wild (voice) 2006, Over the Hedge (voice) 2006,. *Albums:* The Transformed Man 1968, Has Been 2004. *TV appearances include:* Star Trek, TekWar (also exec. producer and dir. of two episodes) T.J. Hooker, Land of the Free, The Fresh Prince of Bel-Air, Cosby, Third Rock from the Sun, Boston Legal (Best Supporting Actor in a Series, Miniseries or TV Movie, Golden Globe Awards 2005, Emmy Award for Best Supporting Actor in a Drama 2005) 2004–, Everest (miniseries) 2007. *Publications include:* TekWar 1989, Star Trek Memories (jtly) 1993, Star Trek Movie Memories 1994, Ashes of Eden (jtly) 1995, Man O' War 1996, Tek Kill 1996, The Return 1996, Avenger 1997, Delta Search: Quest For Tomorrow 1997, Delta Search: In Alien Hands 1998, Step into Chaos 1999, Dark Victory 1999, Step Into Chaos 1999, Get a Life (jtly) 1999, The Preserver 2000, Spectre 2000. *Leisure interests:* tennis, yoga, skiing, riding, horse breeding, scuba diving, parasailing. *Address:* c/o Melis Productions Inc., 760 North La Cienega Boulevard, Los Angeles, CA 90069, USA. *Telephone:* (818) 509-2290. *Fax:* (818) 509-2299. *Website:* www .williamshatner.com.

SHATROV, (Marshak) Mikhail Filippovich; Russian dramatist and scriptwriter; b. 3 April 1932; s. of Filipp Semenovich and Cecilia Alexandrovna Marshak; m. Julia Vladimirovna Chernyshova; two d.; ed Moscow Mining Inst.; Pres. and Chair. of Bd of Dirs Zao Moskva-Krasnye Kholmy Co. 1994–; Head of Drama, Theatre, Cinema and TV, Ministry of Culture of the Russian Fed. 2002–; began writing plays in 1955; USSR State Prize 1983. *Plays include:* In the Name of Revolution 1957, The Peace of Brest Litovsk 1962, The Sixth of July 1963, Przevalsky's Horse 1972, The Dictatorship of Conscience 1986, Further... Further... Further 1988. *Film screenplays include:* Two Lines of Tiny Handwriting 1981, Tehran-43 1981, Maybe (for Vanessa Redgrave) 1993. *Publications:* February (novel) 1988, Maybe 1993. *Address:* Serafimovich str. 2, Apt 349, 109072 Moscow, Russia. *Telephone:* (495) 961-22-30 (office); (495) 959-31-68.

SHATTUCK, Mayo A., III, BA, MBA; American energy industry executive; *Chairman, President and CEO, Constellation Energy Group Inc.;* b. 7 Oct. 1954, Boston, Mass; s. of Mayo Adams Shattuck Jr and Jane Bergwall; m. Molly George Shattuck; five c.; ed Williams Coll., Stanford Univ. (Arjay Miller Scholar); analyst, Morgan Guaranty Trust Co. 1976–78; Man. Bain & Co. 1980–83; Pres., COO and Dir Alex Brown Inc. 1991–97; Vice-Chair. Bankers Trust Corpn 1997–99; Co-Chair. and Co-CEO Deutsche Banc Alex Brown Inc. 1999–2001; Pres. and CEO Constellation Energy Group Inc. 2001–, Chair. 2002–; mem. Bd of Dirs Gap Inc. (Chair. Audit and Finance Cttee), Capital One Financial Corpn (Chair. Compensation Cttee), Edison Electric Inst. (Chair. Finance Cttee), Nuclear Energy Inst., Inst. of Nuclear Power Operations, The Walters Art Museum; Chair. Bd of Visitors Univ. of Maryland, Baltimore Co.; mem. Advisory Council Grad. School of Business,

Stanford Univ.; mem. Bd of Trustees Johns Hopkins Medicine; Hon. Doctor of Public Service (Univ. of Maryland, Baltimore Co.). *Leisure interests:* tennis, golf. *Address:* Constellation Energy Group Inc., 750 East Pratt Street, Baltimore, MD 21202, USA (office). *Telephone:* (410) 783-2800 (office). *Fax:* (410) 234-5220 (office). *E-mail:* info@constellation.com (office). *Website:* www.constellation.com (office); www.mayoshattuck.net.

SHAW, Audley, BA, MA; Jamaican politician; *Minister of Finance and Public Service;* b. 13 June 1952, Christiana, Manchester; ed Northern Ill. Univ., USA; began career as Lab. Technician, Jamaica Milk Products; worked for Jamaica Promotions Ltd; fmr Area Literacy Officer, JAMAL Movt; MP for Manchester N E 1993–, served as Shadow Minister of Information and Culture, of Public Utilities and Transport, of Industry and Commerce, fmr Chair. Public Accounts Cttee, Shadow Minister of Finance and Public Service 1997–2007, Minister of Finance and Public Service 2007–; Deputy Leader, Labour Party 1999– (fmr Gen. Sec.). *Address:* Ministry of Finance and the Public Service, 30 National Heroes Circle, Kingston 4 (office); The Jamaica Labour Party, 20 Belmont Road, Kingston 5, Jamaica (office). *Telephone:* 922-8600 (Ministry) (office); 929-1690 (office). *Fax:* 922-7097 (Ministry) (office). *E-mail:* info@mof.gov.jm (office); fitzalbert_2@yahoo.com (office); manchester-ne@jamaicalabourparty.com (office). *Website:* www.mof.gov.jm (office); www.audleyshawjamaica.com (office).

SHAW, Bernard Leslie, PhD, FRS; British scientist and academic; *Professor Emeritus and Honorary Research Professor, School of Chemistry, University of Leeds;* b. 28 March 1930, Springhead, Yorks.; s. of Tom Shaw and Vera Shaw; m. Mary Elizabeth Neild 1951 (died 2003); two s.; ed Hulme Grammar School, Oldham and Manchester Univ.; Sr DSIR Fellow, Torry Research Station, Aberdeen 1953–55; Research Scientist, Ministry of Defence 1955–56; Research Scientist, ICI Ltd 1956–61; Lecturer, School of Chem., Univ. of Leeds 1962–65, Reader 1965–71, Prof. 1971–94, Research Prof. 1995, now Prof. Emer. and Hon. Research Prof.; Visiting Prof., Univ. of Western Ont., Carnegie Mellon Univ. 1969, ANU 1983, Univ. of Auckland 1986, Univ. of Strasbourg 1993; mem. Science and Eng Research Council Chem. Cttee 1975–78, 1981–84; research consultant, Union Carbide Corpn, USA for 31 years; Chemical Soc. Award in Transition Metal Chem. 1975, Tilden Lecturer, Chemical Soc. 1975, Liversidge Lecturer, Royal Soc. of Chem. (RSC) 1987–88, RSC Ludwig Mond Lecturer and Prizewinner 1992–93, Sir Edward Frankland Lecturer and Prizewinner 1995, Calabria Prize for Science 2001. *Publications:* Inorganic Hydrides, Organo-Transition Metal Compounds and Related Aspects of Homogeneous Catalysis and over 400 research papers; several patents. *Leisure interests:* walking, pottery, gardening, tennis, classical music, opera. *Address:* School of Chemistry, University of Leeds, Leeds, LS2 9JT (office); 14 Monkbridge Road, Leeds, West Yorks., LS6 4DX, England (home). *Telephone:* (113) 343-6454 (office); (113) 275-5895 (home). *Fax:* (113) 343-6565 (office). *E-mail:* B.L.Shaw@Leeds.ac.uk (office). *Website:* www.chem.leeds.ac.uk (office).

SHAW, Colin Don, CBE, MA; British fmr broadcasting executive, writer and lecturer; b. 2 Nov. 1928, Liverpool; s. of Rupert M. Shaw and Enid F. Shaw (née Smith); m. Elizabeth A. Bowker 1955; one s. two d.; ed Liverpool Coll., St Peter's Hall, Oxford, Inner Temple; served with RAF 1947–49; joined BBC as radio drama producer 1953–57, variety of posts 1957–69, Sec. to Bd 1969–71, Chief Sec. 1972–77; Dir of TV IBA 1977–83; Dir Programme Planning Secr. Ind. Cos TV Asscn 1983–87; Dir Broadcasting Standards Council 1988–96; mem. Arts Council of GB 1978–80; Gov. English Speaking Union of GB 1976–83; Trustee, Int. Inst. of Communications 1983–89; Hon. Visiting Prof., Univ. of Manchester 1996–99. *Publications:* Deciding What We Watch 1999, Acccountability and the Public Interest in Broacasting (with Andrea Millwood Hargrave); several radio plays and a stage play for children. *Leisure interests:* travel, reading, theatre. *Address:* Lesters, Little Ickford, Aylesbury, Bucks., HP18 9HS, England (home). *Telephone:* (1844) 339225 (home).

SHAW, Fiona, BA, FRSA; Irish actress; b. 10 July 1958, Cork; d. of Dr Denis Joseph Wilson and Mary Teresa Flynn; ed Univ. Coll. Cork, Royal Acad. of Dramatic Art (RADA); joined RSC 1985; Hon. Prof. of Drama, Trinity Coll. Dublin; Officier des Arts et des Lettres 2001; Hon. CBE 2002; Hon. DUniv (Open Univ.) 1999; Hon. LLD (Nat. Univ. of Ireland) 2000; Hon. DLitt (Trinity Coll. Dublin) 2002, (Ulster) 2004; RADA Tree Prize 1982, RADA Ronson Award 1982, Olivier Award, Evening Standard Award for Machinal 1995, Evening Standard Award for Best Actress 2001, RADA Bancroft Gold Medal, OBIE Award, New York 2002, William Shakepeare Award, Washington, DC 2003. *Plays include:* debut in Love's Labours Lost, Julia in The Rivals, Nat. Theatre, Mary Shelley in Howard Brenton's Bloody Poetry, Hampstead, appeared with RSC as Celia in As You Like It, Tatyana in Gorky's Philistines, Madame des Volonges in Les Liaisons Dangereuses, Beatrice in Much Ado About Nothing, Portia in The Merchant of Venice, Kate in The Taming of the Shrew, Mistress Carol in James Shirley's Hyde Park and as Sophocles's Electra; appeared as Rosalind in As You Like It, Old Vic 1990, as Shen Te/Shui Ta in Brecht's The Good Person of Sichuan, Nat. Theatre 1990 (Olivier Award for Best Actress 1990, London Critics' Award for Best Actress 1990), in Hedda Gabler, Abbey Theatre, Dublin and West End 1991 (London Critics' Award 1992), in Beckett's Footfalls, West End 1994, as Richard II in Richard II and in The Waste Land 1996, The Prime of Miss Jean Brodie, Royal Nat. Theatre 1998, Widower's Houses 1999, Medea, Abbey Theatre, Dublin 2000, West End 2001, The Power Book, Nat. Theatre 2002, The Seagull, Edinburgh Festival 2003, Julius Caesar, Barbican 2005, My Life is a Fairy Tale, Lincoln Centre 2005, Readings, Nat. Theatre of Challot, Paris 2005, Woman and Scarecrow, Royal Court Theatre 2006, Happy Days, Royal Nat. Theatre 2007. *Films include:* The Man Who Shot Christmas 1984, Sacred Hearts 1985, My Left Foot 1989, Mountains of the Moon 1990, 3 Men and a Little Lady 1990, London Kills Me 1991, Super Mario Brothers 1992, Undercover Blues 1993, The Waste Land 1995, Persuasion 1995, Jane Eyre 1996, The Avengers 1997, The Butcher's Boy 1997, Anna Karenina 1997, The Last September 1999, The Triumph of Love 2000, Harry Potter and The Philosopher's Stone 2001, Doctor Sleep 2001, The Triumph of Love 2001, Harry Potter and The Chamber of Secrets 2002, Harry Potter and the Prisoner of Azkaban 2004, El sueño de una noche de San Juan (A Midsummer Night's Dream) (voice; English version) 2005, The Black Dahlia 2006, Catch and Release 2006, Fracture 2007, Harry Potter and the Order of the Phoenix 2007. *Radio includes:* Transfiguration 2000, Aiding and Abetting 2000. *Television includes:* The Adventures of Sherlock Holmes – The Crooked Man 1984, Love Song 1985, Iphigenia at Aulis 1990, For the Greater Good 1991, Maria's Child 1992, Shakespeare: The Animated Tales – Twelfth Night 1992, Hedda Gabler 1993, Seascape 1994, Richard II 1997, RKO 281 1999, Gormenghast (BBC) (mini-series) 1999, Mind Games 2001, The Sweetest Thing 2002, Empire (mini-series) 2005, The British Face 2006, Trial and Retribution XIV: Mirror Image 2007. *Leisure interests:* opera, running, snorkling. *Address:* c/o ICM, Oxford House, 76 Oxford Street, London, W1N 0AX, England (office); Eglantine, Montenotte, Cork, Ireland (home). *E-mail:* shawassist@aol.com (home).

SHAW, Sir Neil McGowan, Kt; Canadian business executive; b. 31 May 1929, Montreal; s. of Harold LeRoy Shaw and Fabiola Shaw (née McGowan); m. 1st Frances Audrey Robinson 1952 (divorced 1980); two s. three d.; m. 2nd Elizabeth Fern Mudge 1985; ed Knowlton High School, Lower Canada Coll.; Trust Officer, Crown Trust Co. 1947–54; with Canada Dominion Sugar (now Redpath Industries) 1954–98, Merchandising Man. 1954–66, Vice-Pres. 1967–72, Pres. 1972–80, Vice-Chair. 1981–98; Group Man. Dir Tate and Lyle PLC, England 1980–86, Chair. 1986–93, CEO 1986–92, Exec. Chair. 1992–98 (retd); Redpath Div. Industries Ltd 1972–98 (Vice-Chair. 1981–98); fmrly Chair. Tate and Lyle Holdings Ltd, England, Tate and Lyle Industries Ltd, England, Tate and Lyle Inc., New York; Dir Tunnel Refineries Ltd, England, United Biscuits (Holdings) PLC 1988–97, G.R. Amylum N.V., Brussels, Americare Corpn Alcantara, Lisbon, Canadian Imperial Bank of Commerce, Toronto 1986–2000, A.E. Staley Manufacturing Co., Ill. 1991–98, M & G Investment Income Trust PLC 1991–95; Dir Inst. of Dirs 1986–; Chair. World Sugar Research Org. 1994–96 (Dir 1982–97), Foundation and Friends of Royal Botanic Gardens, Kew 1994– (Trustee 1990–), Anglo-Canadian Support Group CARE 1989–, Business in the Community 1991–95; Gov. Montreal Gen. Hosp., Reddy Memorial Hosp., World Food and Agro Forum 1988–96; mem. Canadian Memorial Foundation 1989–, Council of Advisers to Premier of Québec 1987–, Advisory Council Prince's Youth Business Trust 1990–, London Enterprise Agency 1986–, Food Asscn 1989–, Listed Cos Advisory Cttee 1991–, British N American Cttee 1991–; Chair. and Dir CAPOCO Ltd (Theatre Royal Windsor) 1991–, Atkins Restaurant Co. Ltd 1993–; Dir United World Coll. of Atlantic 1997–2000; Hon. LLD (E London) 1997. *Leisure interests:* sailing, skiing, golf. *Address:* Titness Park, Mill Lane, Sunninghill, Ascot, Berks., SL5 7RU, England (home).

SHAW, Sir Run Run, Kt, CBE; British business executive; b. 4 Oct. 1907, Shanghai, China; s. of the late Shao Hang-yin and Wang Shun-xiang; m. 1st Lily Wang Mee-chun 1932 (died 1987); two s. two d.; m. 2nd Lee Manglan 1997; ed in China; Founder and Chair. Shaw Group of Cos 1959–; Chair. Shaw Foundation HK Ltd 1973–; Pres. Hong Kong Red Cross Soc. 1972–, Hong Kong Arts Festival 1974–88, Bd of Govs. Hong Kong Arts Centre 1978–88, Television Broadcasts Ltd, TVE (Holdings) Ltd 1980–; mem. Council, The Chinese Univ. of Hong Kong 1977–92; Chair. Bd of Trustees, United Coll., Chinese Univ. of Hong Kong 1983–92; Local Adviser on Hong Kong for People's Repub. of China 1992–; mem. Preparatory Cttee, Hong Kong Special Admin. Region 1995–98; Founder, Shaw Coll. Chinese Univ. of Hong Kong 1986; Dr hc (Univ. of Hong Kong, Chinese Univ. of Hong Kong, Univs. of E Asia (Macau), Sussex, New York at Stony Brook, City Polytechnic of Hong Kong, Hong Kong Baptist Coll., Hong Kong Polytechnic, Pepperdine Univ.); Queen's Badge, Red Cross 1982; Commdr Order of Crown of Belgium; Chevalier Légion d'honneur; est. US $1 million Shaw Prize ("Nobel Prize of the East") for scientific researchers in astronomy, math., and life and medical science 2004. *Leisure interests:* shadow-boxing, golf. *Address:* Shaw House, Lot 220, Clear Water Bay Road, Kowloon, Hong Kong Special Administrative Region, People's Republic of China (office). *Telephone:* 27198371 (office).

SHAW, Vernon Lorden; Dominican fmr head of state and civil servant; b. 13 May 1930; m.; four c.; ed Dominica Grammar School, Trinity Coll., Oxford; various appointments at Treasury and Customs Dept, Post Office, Cen. Housing and Planning Authority, Audit Dept, Cen. Housing and Planning Authority 1948–62; Admin. Asst Ministry of Trade and Production 1962–65, Asst Sec. 1965–67; Perm. Sec., Ministry of Educ. and Health 1967, Ministry of External Affairs 1967–71; Chief Establishment Officer 1971–77; Sec. to Cabinet 1977–78 and Amb.-at-Large and Inspector of Missions 1978–90 (retd from public service); temporary resident tutor, Univ. of W Indies School of Continuing Studies 1991–93; Chair. Dominica Broadcasting Corpn 1993–95, Public Service Bd of Appeal 1993–98; Pres. of Dominica 1998–2003; mem. Inst. of Admin. Accounting; Assoc. mem. BIM; Dominica Award of Honour, Sisserou Award of Honour. *Address:* 8 Churchill Lane, Goodwill, Dominica (home). *Telephone:* 448-2361 (home).

SHAW, Yu-Ming, PhD; Taiwanese public servant and academic; b. 3 Nov. 1938, Harbin; m. Shirley Shiow-jyu Lu; one s. one d.; ed Nat. Chengchi Univ., Tufts Univ. and Univ. of Chicago, USA; Asst Prof. of History, Newberry Coll., SC 1967–68, 1972–73; Assoc. Prof. of History, Univ. of Notre Dame, Ind. 1973–82; held various research posts in Asian studies in USA; Dir Asia and World Inst., Taiwan 1983–84; Dean, Grad. School of Int. Law and Diplomacy, Nat. Chengchi Univ. 1984, Dir Inst. of Int. Relations 1984–87, 1994, Prof. of History 1991; Dir-Gen. Govt Information Office and Govt spokesman 1987–91; currently Prof., Chinese Culture Univ., Pres. Cultural Foundation of the

United Daily News Group 1992–; awards from American Council of Learned Socs, Asia Foundation, Inst. of Chinese Culture, USA and others. *Publications include:* China and Christianity 1979, Problems in Twentieth Century Chinese Christianity 1980, Twentieth Century Sino-American Relations 1980, History and Politics in Modern China 1982, International Politics and China's Future 1987, Beyond the Economic Miracle 1988, An American Missionary in China: John Leighton Stuart and Chinese-American Relations 1993. *Address:* Chinese Culture University, 55, Hwa-Kang Road, Yang-Ming-Shan, Taipei 111, Taiwan.

SHAWAYS, Rowsch Nouri, DEng; Iraqi engineer and politician; b. 1947; Head, Kurdish Student Union, Germany; returned to Iraq 1979 joining Kurdish rebellion; Deputy Prime Minister, jt Kurdistan Regional Govt 1996; Prime Minister, Kurdistan Regional Govt Arbil 1996–99; Pres. Iraqi Kurdistan Nat. Ass. 1999–2004; Interim Vice-Pres. 2004–05; Deputy Prime Minister 2005; mem. Political Bureau, Kurdistan Democratic Party. *Address:* Kurdistan Democratic Party, c/o KDP Europe, PO Box 301 516, 10749 Berlin, Germany (office). *Telephone:* (30) 79743741. *Fax:* (30) 79743746. *E-mail:* KDPEurope@t-online.de; party@kdp.se. *Website:* www.kdp.se.

SHAWCROSS, William; British journalist, writer and broadcaster; b. 28 May 1946, Sussex; s. of Baron Shawcross; m. 1st Marina Warner 1972 (divorced 1980); one s.; m. 2nd Michal Levin 1981 (divorced); one d.; m. Olga Forte 1993; ed Eton, Univ. Coll., Oxford; freelance journalist in Czechoslovakia 1968–69; corresp. for The Sunday Times, London 1969–72; Chair. Article 19, Int. Centre on Censorship 1986–96; mem. Bd Int. Crisis Group 1995–, mem. Exec. Cttee 2000–; mem. Council of Disasters Emergency Cttee 1997–; mem Informal Advisory Bd UNHCR 1995–2000. *Publications:* Dubček 1970, Crime and Compromise: Janos Kadar and the Politics of Hungary Since Revolution 1974, Sideshow: Kissinger, Nixon and the Destruction of Cambodia 1979, Quality of Mercy: Cambodia, the Holocaust and Modern Conscience 1984, The Shah's Last Ride 1989, Kowtow: A Plea on Behalf of Hong Kong 1989, Murdoch 1992, Cambodia's New Deal 1994, Deliver Us from Evil: Warlords & Peacekeepers in a World of Endless Conflict 2000, Queen and Country 2002, Allies: The United States, Britain, Europe and the War in Iraq (aka Allies: The US, Britain and Europe in the Aftermath of the Iraq War) 2003; contrib. to newspapers and journals. *Leisure interests:* sailing, walking. *Address:* c/o Greene and Heaton, 37 Goldhawk Road, London, W12 8QQ, England (office). *Telephone:* (20) 8749-0315 (office). *Fax:* (20) 8749-0318 (office). *Website:* www.williamshawcross.com (office).

SHAWN, Wallace, BA; American actor and playwright; b. 12 Nov. 1943, New York; s. of William Shawn and Cecille Lyon; brother-in-law of Jamaica Kincaid (q.v.); pnr Deborah Eisenberg; ed Harvard Univ., Magdalen Coll., Oxford Univ. *Films include:* My Dinner with André (also writer) 1981, Manhattan 1979, The Princess Bride 1987, The Moderns 1988, Scenes from the Class Struggle in Beverly Hills 1989, We're No Angels 1989, Shadows and Fog 1992, Mom and Dad Save the World 1992, Nickel and Dime 1992, The Cemetery Club 1993, Vanya on 42nd Street 1994, Mrs Parker and the Vicious Circle 1994, Clueless 1995, Canadian Bacon 1995, Toy Story (voice) 1995, The Wife 1995, House Arrest 1996, All Dogs Go To Heaven II (voice), Critical Care 1997, My Favorite Martian 1999, Toy Story 2 (voice) 1999, The Prime Gig 2000, Blonde 2001, The Curse of the Jade Scorpion 2002, Love Thy Neighbor 2002, Personal Velocity: Three Portraits 2002, Duplex 2003, The Haunted Mansion 2003, Teacher's Pet (voice) 2004, Melinda and Melinda 2004, The Incredibles (voice) 2004, Chicken Little (voice) 2005, Southland Tales 2006, Tom and Jerry: Shiver Me Whiskers (voice) 2006, Happily N'Ever After (voice) 2007, New York City Serenade 2007. *Television includes:* Clueless (series) 1996–1997, Blonde 2001, Crossing Jordan 2001–06, Mr. St. Nick 2002, Monte Walsh 2003, Karroll's Christmas 2004, Crossing Jordan (series) 2001–06, Gossip Girl 2008, The L Word 2008–09. *Plays:* as writer: A Thought in Three Parts 1976, Marie and Bruce 1979, Aunt Dan and Lemon 1985, The Fever 1990, The Designated Mourner 1996, Grasses of a Thousand Colours 2009. *Stage appearances include:* My Dinner with André, A Thought in Three Parts, Marie and Bruce 1979, Aunt Dan and Lemon 1985, The Fever 1991. *Address:* c/o William Morris Agency, 1325 Avenue of the Americas, New York, NY 10019, USA (office). *E-mail:* plays@wma.com (office). *Website:* www.wma.com (office).

SHAYE, Robert Kenneth, JD; American lawyer, film producer and film industry executive; *Co-Chairman and Co-CEO, New Line Cinema Corporation;* b. 3 March 1939, Detroit, Mich.; s. of Max Shaye and Dorothy Shaye; m. Eva G. Lindsten 1970; two c.; ed Univ. of Michigan, Columbia Univ. Law School; won First Prize in Soc. of Cinematologists' Rosenthal Competition for Best Film Directed by American Under 25; wrote, produced, directed and edited short films and TV commercials, including award-winning shorts, Image and On Fighting Witches; f. New Line Cinema Corpn 1967, Co-Chair. and Co-CEO; mem. Bd of Trustees Neuroscience Inst., Motion Picture Pioneers, American Film Inst., Legal Aid Soc.; mem. New York State Bar. *Films:* Producer and Exec. Producer: Stunts, XTRO, Alone in the Dark, The First Time, Polyester, Critters, Quiet Cool, My Demon Lover, A Nightmare on Elm Street (Parts 1–6), The Hidden, Stranded, Critters 2, Hairspray, Heart Condition, Book of Love (dir), Wes Craven's New Nightmare (also actor), Frequency, Lord of the Rings trilogy, Freddy Vs. Jason, The Last Mimzy. *Television:* Freddy's Nightmare: The Series (exec. producer). *Leisure interest:* cooking. *Address:* New Line Cinema Corporation, 888 Seventh Avenue, New York, NY 10106, USA (office). *Telephone:* (212) 649-4900 (office). *Fax:* (212) 649-4966 (office). *Website:* www.newline.com (office).

SHCHAPOV, Yaroslav Nikolayevich; Russian historian; *Councillor, Institute of Russian History, Russian Academy of Sciences;* b. 6 May 1928, Moscow; s. of Nikolai Mikhailovich Shchapov and Eugenia Nikolayevna Shchapova (née Dobrobozhenko); m. Yulia Leonidovna Shchapova (née

Sinelnikova) 1954; one s.; ed Moscow State Univ.; Sr, Chief Librarian V. Lenin State Library 1952–57; Jr, Sr, Leading, Chief Researcher Inst. of History of USSR, USSR Acad. of Sciences 1957–90; Head Centre of Church and Religious History, Inst. of Russian History, Russian Acad. of Sciences 1990–99, Councillor 1999–; Corresp. mem. USSR (now Russian) Acad. of Sciences 1987; Pres. Russian Soc. of Historians and Archivists 1990–96; Dir County Estate Schapovo Municipal Museum, Podolsk 1998–; Chair. Scientific Council Role of Religion in History 1998–2001; mem. Russian Ass. of the Nobility, Pres. Imperial Orthodox Palestine Soc. 2003–; research in history of old Russia, law, social relations, religion, culture, old Russian manuscripts, Russian-Byzantine relations, Russian Orthodox Church; Hon. mem. Imperial Orthodox Palestine Soc. 1993; Hon. Citizen of Podolsk Dist 2004; Order of Friendship of the Peoples 1988, Church Order St Sergius of Radonezh (Second Class) 1997, Order of Honour 1998, Church Order St Prince Daniil of Moscow 2003; B. Grekov Prize. *Publications:* Byzantine and South Slavic Legal Heritage in Russia of 11th–13th Centuries 1978, State and Church in Early Russia 10th–13th Centuries 1989 (published in USA 1993), Russian Orthodox Church and the Communist State (Documents from Secret Archives) 1996, Historical Country Estates in South Moscow District 2000, Shchapov's Agricultural School 1903–2003: Call Over the Centuries 2003; more than 300 articles. *Leisure interests:* family history. *Address:* Institute of Russian History, Russian Academy of Sciences, D. Ulyanov str. 19, 117036 Moscow, Russia (office). *Telephone:* (495) 126-26-65 (office); (495) 438-22-89 (home). *Fax:* (495) 126-39-55 (office); (495) 438-22-89 (home). *E-mail:* y_schapov@mail .ru (home). *Website:* www.iri-ap.com/irh.html (office).

SHCHEDRIN, Rodion Konstantinovich; Russian composer; b. 16 Dec. 1932, Moscow; s. of Konstantin Mikhailovich Shchedrin and Konkordia Ivanovna Shchedrin; m. Maya Plisetskaya 1958; ed Moscow Conservatoire; Chair. RSFSR (now Russian) Union of Composers 1973–90; USSR People's Deputy 1989–91; mem. Acad. of Fine Arts, Berlin, Bavarian Acad. of Fine Arts; Hon. mem. American Liszt Soc., Rachmaninov Soc., Int. Music Council, Hon. Prof., Moscow Conservatoire, St Petersburg Conservatoire; Lenin Prize, USSR and Russian State Prizes, Russian Union of Composers Prize, Shostakovich Prize, Beethoven Soc. Prize. *Compositions include:* operas: Not Only Love 1961, Dead Souls (operatic scenes in three acts) 1976, Lolita (after V. Nabokov) 1994; ballets: Humpbacked Horse 1960, Carmen Suite 1967, Anna Karenina 1972, The Seagull 1980, Lady with a Lapdog 1985; for orchestra: three symphonies 1958, 1965, 2000, 5 concertos for orchestra 1963, 1968, 1988, 1989, 1998; Self-Portrait 1984, Stykhira 1988, Old Russian Circus Music 1989; 6 concertos for piano and orchestra 1954, 1966, 1973, 1992, 1999, 2003, Concerto for cello and orchestra 1994, Concerto for trumpet and orchestra 1995, Two Tangos by Albéniz for orchestra 1996, Concerto dolce for viola and string orchestra 1997; other: Poetoria 1974, Musical Offering for organ and nine soloists 1983, The Sealed Angel (Russian Liturgy) 1988, Nina and the Twelve Months (musical) 1988, Piano Terzetto 1996, Concerto Cantabile (for violin and strings) 1997, Preludium for 9th Symphony by Beethoven 1999, Lolita-serenade 2001, Parabola concertante (for cello and strings) 2001, Dialogue with Shostakovich 2001, The Enchanted Wanderer (concert opera) 2002, Tanja-Katya 2002, My Age, My Wild Beast 2003; works for chamber orchestra, piano, violin, organ and cello and song cycles, music for theatre and cinema. *Leisure interests:* jogging, fishing, water-skiing, wind surfing. *Address:* Theresienstrasse 23, 80333 Munich, Germany (home); 25/9, Tverskaya St, apt. 31, 103050 Moscow, Russia (home). *Telephone:* (89) 285834 (Munich); (495) 299-72-39 (Moscow). *Fax:* (89) 282057 (Munich). *E-mail:* rshchedrin@yahoo.com (office). *Website:* www.shchedrin.de (office).

SHCHEGOLEV, Igor Olegovich; Russian politician; *Minister of Communications and the Mass Media;* ed Moscow State Inst. of Foreign Languages, Germanic Studies Faculty, Leipzig Univ., Germany; ITAR-TASS Corresp., Paris, France 1993–97, Ed. of European News, ITAR-TASS, Moscow 1997–98, later Deputy Head of ITAR-TASS; Deputy Head of Dept of State Information, Russian Govt 1998; Press Sec. to the Prime Minister, later Head of Dept of State Information 1998–2002; Head of Presidential Press Service 2000–02; Head of Protocol Office of Pres. of Russian Fed. 2002–08; Minister of Communications and the Mass Media 2008–. *Address:* Ministry of Communications and the Mass Media, 125375 Moscow, Ulitsa Tverskaya 7, Russia (office). *Telephone:* (495) 771-8100 (office); (495) 771-8121 (office). *Fax:* (495) 771-8718 (office). *E-mail:* info@minsvyaz.ru (office). *Website:* www.minsvyaz .ru (office).

SHCHERBAKOV, Vladimir Ivanovich, DEconSc; Russian business executive; *Chairman, Board of Directors, Avtotor Group;* b. 5 Dec. 1949, Novo-Sysoyevka, Primorsky territory; s. of Ivan Shcherbakov and Elena Shcherbakova; m. Natalia Shcherbakova; one s.; ed Togliatti Polytech. Inst., Higher Comsomol School; engineer-mechanic; mem. CPSU 1970–91; party work in Togliatti 1971–74; engineer, controller, Chief Planning and Econ. Dept, Volga Motor Car Plant 1970–82; Deputy Dir-Gen., Dir Econ. and Planning Dept, Kama Big Lorries Plant 1982–85; Chief Machine Bldg and Metal Trade Plant Dept, USSR State Cttee for Labour and Social Affairs 1985–88; First Deputy Chief Nat. Economy Man. Dept, USSR Council of Ministers 1988–89; Minister of Labour and Social Affairs 1989–91; Deputy Prime Minister, later First Deputy Prime Minister, Minister of Economy and Planning of the USSR March–Aug. 1991; Pres. Interprivatization Fund 1991–; Chair. Bd of Dirs Avtotor Group of Cos 1995–; Chair. Russian United Industrial Party 1995–97; Vice-Pres. Russian Union of Mfrs and Entrepreneurs 1996–; mem. Admin. Bureau, Vice-Pres. Russian Union of Mfrs and Entrepreneurs 1996; Vice-Pres. Free Econ. Soc. of Russia 1997–; mem. Russian Acad. of Natural Sciences. *Publications* include: about 50 monographs and articles, concerning Big Economic Complexes: Mechanism of Management, Industrial Labour and its Remuneration, New Mechanisms of Labour Remuneration, etc. *Leisure interests:* hunting, sports. *Address:* Avtotor Holding 3, Bldg 3 Solyanka

Street, 109028 Moscow, Russia (office). *Telephone:* (495) 624-60-61 (office). *Fax:* (495) 623-14-11 (office). *E-mail:* scherbakov@avtotor.ru (office). *Website:* www.avtotor.ru (office).

SHEA, Gail; Canadian politician; *Minister of Fisheries and Oceans;* mem. Legis. Ass., PEI 2000–07; Minister of Community and Cultural Affairs 2000–03, of Transportation and Public Works 2003–07, of Fisheries and Oceans 2008–; MP for Egmont 2008–; mem. Conservative Party of Canada. *Address:* Fisheries and Oceans Canada, Centennial Towers, 13th Floor, 200 Kent Street, Station 13228, Ottawa, ON K1A 0E6, Canada (office). *Telephone:* (613) 993-0999 (office). *Fax:* (613) 990-1866 (office). *E-mail:* info@dfo-mpo.gc.ca (office). *Website:* www.dfo-mpo.gc.ca (office).

SHEA, Gail; Canadian politician; *Minister of Fisheries and Oceans;* mem. Legis. Ass., PEI 2000–07; Minister of Community and Cultural Affairs 2000–03, of Transportation and Public Works 2003–07, of Fisheries and Oceans 2008–; MP for Egmont 2008–; mem. Conservative Party of Canada. *Address:* Fisheries and Oceans Canada, Centennial Towers, 13th Floor, 200 Kent Street, Station 13228, Ottawa, ON K1A 0E6, Canada (office). *Telephone:* (613) 993-0999 (office). *Fax:* (613) 990-1866 (office). *E-mail:* info@dfo-mpo.gc.ca (office). *Website:* www.dfo-mpo.gc.ca (office).

SHEA, Jamie Patrick, BA, PhD; British international organization official; *Director, Policy Planning, Private Office of the Secretary-General, NATO;* b. 11 Sept. 1953, London; m.; two c.; ed Univ. of Sussex, Lincoln Coll., Oxford; joined NATO as minute-taker 1981, later Sr Planning Officer and Speechwriter to Sec.-Gen.; Spokesman and Deputy Dir of Information and Press 1993–2001, Dir 2000–03, Temporary Spokesman 2003–04, Deputy Asst. Sec.-Gen. for External Relations 2003–05, Dir Policy Planning, Pvt. Office of the Sec.-Gen. 2005–; Prof. of Int. Relations, Assoc. Prof. of Int. Relations, American Univ., Washington, DC; Adjunct Assoc. Prof. of Int. Relations, James Madison Coll., Mich. State Univ., also Dir MSU Summer School in Brussels; mem. Advisory Council Int. Relations Studies and Programme of Université Libre de Bruxelles and Jean Monnet Visiting Prof.; mem. Advisory Council European Policy Centre, Brussels; Founder and mem. Security and Defence Agenda, Brussels; mem. Centre for European Policy Studies, European-Atlantic Movt, Int. Studies Asscn; Assoc. mem. Inst. Royal des Relations Internationales, Brussels; European Communicator of the Year 1999. *Address:* NATO, 1110 Brussels, Belgium (office). *Telephone:* (2) 707-44-13 (office). *Fax:* (2) 707-35-86 (office). *E-mail:* shea.jamie@hq.nato.int (office). *Website:* www.nato.int.

SHEARER, Alan, OBE; British fmr professional football player; b. 13 Aug. 1970, Gosforth, Newcastle upon Tyne; s. of Alan Shearer and Anne Shearer; m. Lainya Shearer; one s. two d.; coached as a child at Wallsend Boys' Club; striker; played for Southampton 1987–92, Blackburn Rovers 1992–96, becoming the only player in English football ever to score 30 or more goals in three consecutive seasons; signed by Newcastle United for then world record transfer fee of £15 million 1996, became player-coach 2005, retd 2006; played for England 1992–2000 (63 caps, 30 goals), Capt. 1996–2000; first player to score 200 Premiership goals and first to score 100 League goals for two different clubs; Premiership all-time leading scorer with 260 goals in 441 games; Sporting Amb. Newcastle United 2006-07; football commentator Match of the Day and other BBC broadcasts 2006–; Manager, Newcastle United Football Club 2009; Hon. DCL (Northumbria Univ.) 2006; Football Writers' Asscn Footballer of the Year 1994, (Football Asscn) Hall of Fame 1998. *Leisure interest:* golf. *Address:* Match of the Day, BBC Sport, BBC Television Centre, Wood Lane, London, W12 7RJ, England. *Website:* news.bbc.co.uk/sport1/hi/football/match_of_the_day.

SHEARING, Sir George Albert, Kt; British jazz pianist and composer; b. 13 Aug. 1919, London; s. of James Philip Shearing and Ellen Amelia Shearing (née Brightman); m. 1st Beatrice Bayes 1941 (divorced); one d.; m. 2nd Eleanor Geffert 1984; ed Linden Lodge School for the Blind, London; f. and performed with George Shearing Quintet 1949–67, later trio, duo, solo artist; has also led other jazz ensembles; composed many popular songs, including Lullaby of Birdland 1952; musician with Harry Parry, Stéphane Grapelli; played with Mel Tormé, Marian McPartland, Hank Jones, Peggy Lee, Carmen McRae; mem. Bd of Dirs Guide Dogs for the Blind, Hadley School for the Blind, Nat. Braille Press, Lotos Club, Bohemian Club; Hon. DMus (Westminster Coll.) 1975, (Hamilton Coll.) 1994; Top English Pianist 1941–47, Winner All American Jazz polls, Golden Plate Award, American Acad. of Achievement 1968, Helen Keller Achievement Award 1995, BBC Jazz Lifetime Achievement Award 2003. *Recordings include:* albums: Latin Escapade 1956, Velvet Carpet 1956, Black Satin 1957, Burnished Brass 1957, Americana Hotel (with Peggy Lee) 1959, White Satin 1960, The Shearing Touch 1960, Satin Affair 1961, Jazz Concert 1963, My Ship 1974, The Way We Are 1974, Continental Experience 1975, The Reunion (with Stéphane Grappelli) 1976, 500 Miles High 1977, On Target 1979, Two For The Road (with Carmen McRae) 1980, On A Clear Day 1980, Alone Together (with Marian McPartland) 1981, An Evening With Mel Tormé And George Shearing 1982, Top Drawer (with Mel Tormé) 1983, Bright Dimensions 1984, Grand Piano 1985, More Grand Piano 1986, An Elegant Evening (with Mel Tormé) 1986, George Shearing and Barry Treadwell Play The Music Of Cole Porter 1986, Breakin' Out 1987, The Spirit of 1761 (with Hank Jones) 1989, Piano 1989, Paper Moon: Songs Of Nat King Cole 1995, Christmas With The George Shearing Quintet 1998, Back To Birdland (live) 2001, Duets 2002, Rare Delight Of You (with John Pizarelli) 2002, Hopeless Romantics (with Michael Feinstein) 2005. *Publications:* Lullaby of Birdland (autobiog.) 2003. *Address:* International Ventures Inc., 25864 Tournament Road, Suite L, Valencia, CA 91355, USA (office). *Telephone:* (661) 259-4500 (office). *Fax:* (661) 259-1310 (office). *E-mail:* info@ivimanagement.com (office). *Website:* www.ivimanagement.com (office); www.georgeshearing.net.

SHEBBEARE, Sir Thomas (Tom) Andrew, Kt, KCVO, BA; British charity administrator; *Director of Charities to HRH The Prince of Wales;* b. 25 Jan. 1952; s. of the late Robert Austin Shebbeare and Frances Dare Graham; m. Cynthia Jane Cottrell 1976; one s. one d.; ed Malvern Coll., Univ. of Exeter; with World Univ. Service 1973–75; Gen. Sec. British Youth Council 1975–80; Admin. Council of Europe 1980–85; Exec. Dir European Youth Foundation 1985–88; Exec. Dir Prince's Trust 1988–99, CEO 1999–2003; apptd Dir Royal Jubilee Trusts 1988; Dir of Charities to HRH The Prince of Wales 2004–; Dir Inst. for Citizenship Studies 1991–2000, Gifts in Kind 1996, Skills Festival Co. Ltd 1998–; Trustee Nations Inst. for Citizenship Studies Trust (SA) 1995–, InKind Direct; mem. Council Queen's Coll. 1999–; Hon. LLD (Univ. of Exeter) 2005. *Leisure interests:* family, cooking, food and drink. *Address:* Charities Office, Office of the Prince of Wales, Clarence House, St James's Palace, London, SW1 1BA, England (office). *Telephone:* (20) 7860-5930 (office). *Fax:* (20) 7860-5920 (office). *E-mail:* tom@shebbeare.freeserve.co.uk (home). *Website:* www.princeofwales.gov.uk/trusts/index.html (office).

SHECHTMAN, Dan, BS, MS, PhD; Israeli/American physicist and academic; *Philip Tobias Professor of Materials Science, Technion Israel Institute of Technology;* b. Tel Aviv; m. Zipora Shechtman; four c.; ed Technion Israel Inst. of Tech., Haifa; Nat. Research Council Fellow, Wright Patterson Air Force Base, OH, USA 1973–75; Dept of Materials Eng, Technion Israel Inst. of Tech., Haifa 1975–, becoming Philip Tobias Prof. of Materials Science; Prof., Dept of Materials Science and Eng, Ia State Univ., USA 2004–; Research Fellow, Johns Hopkins Univ., Baltimore, MD 1981–83; Researcher, Nat. Inst. of Standards and Tech. (NIST), Gaithersburg, MD 1992–94; mem. Israel Acad. of Sciences, Nat. Acad. of Eng (USA), European Acad. of Sciences 2004–; Friedenberg Fund for the Advancement of Science and Educ. Physics Award 1986, American Physical Soc. Int. Award for New Materials 1987, Technion England Academic Award for Academic Excellence 1987/88, Rothchild Prize in Eng 1990, Weizmann Prize in Science 1993, Israel Prize in Physics 1998, Wolf Prize for Physics 1999, Swedish Royal Acad. of Sciences Gregori Aminoff Prize 2000, EMET Prize in Chem. 2002. *Address:* Technion Israel Institute of Technology, Room 617, Technion City, Haifa 32000, Israel (office). *Telephone:* (4) 8294299 (office). *Fax:* (4) 8295677 (office). *E-mail:* dannys@tx.technion.ac.il (office). *Website:* www.technion.ac.il/technion/materials/shechtman.html (office).

SHECTMAN, Stephen A., BS, PhD; American astronomer; *Staff Member, Carnegie Observatories;* b. 25 Sept. 1949, New York, NY; s. of Arthur Shectman and Dorothy Shectman; divorced; one s. one d.; ed Yale Univ., Calif. Inst. of Tech. (Caltech); Post-Doctoral Scholar in Astronomy and Lecturer in Physics, Univ. of Michigan 1973–75; Alfred P. Sloan Research Fellow 1984–88; staff mem. Carnegie Observatories, Pasadena, Calif. 1975–, Project Scientist, Magellan Telescope Project 1986–2004; mem. American Acad. of Arts and Sciences 1997–; Weber Award for Astronomical Instrumentation, American Astronomical Soc. 2005, Jackson-Gwilt Medal, Royal Astronomical Soc. 2008. *Publications:* numerous articles in astronomical journals. *Leisure interests:* opera, cycling. *Address:* Carnegie Observatories, 813 Santa Barbara Street, Pasadena, CA 91101, USA (office). *Telephone:* (626) 577-1122 (office). *Fax:* (626) 795-8136 (office). *E-mail:* sshectman@ociw.edu (office). *Website:* www.ociw.edu/research/shectman.html (office).

SHEED, Wilfrid John Joseph, MA; American author; b. 27 Dec. 1930, London, England; s. of Francis Joseph Sheed and Maisie Sheed (née Ward); m. 1st Maria Bullitt Dartington 1957 (divorced); three c.; m. 2nd Miriam Ungerer; one s. two d.; ed Lincoln Coll., Oxford Univ.; film reviewer, Jubilee magazine 1959–61, Assoc. Ed. 1959–66; drama critic and fmr book critic, Commonweal magazine, New York; film critic, Esquire magazine 1967–69; Visiting Prof., Princeton Univ. 1970–71; columnist, NY Times 1971–; judge and mem. editorial Bd Book of the Month Club 1972–88; Guggenheim Fellow 1971–72; mem. PEN Club. *Publications include:* A Middle Class Education 1961, The Hack 1963, Square's Progress 1965, Office Politics 1966, The Blacking Factory 1968, Max Jamison 1970, The Morning After 1971, People Will Always Be Kind 1973, Three Mobs: Labor, Church and Mafia 1974, Transatlantic Blues 1978, The Good Word 1979, Clare Boothe Luce 1982, Frank and Maisie 1985, The Boys of Winter 1987, Baseball and Lesser Sports 1991, My Life as a Fan 1993, In Love with Daylight 1995, The House That George Built 2007; ed. of G.K. Chesterton's Essays and Poems 1957, 16 Short Novels 1986; contributes articles to popular magazines. *Address:* c/o Random House, Inc., 1745 Broadway, New York, NY 10019, USA (office). *Telephone:* (212) 782-9000 (office). *Website:* www.randomhouse.com (office).

SHEEHAN, Neil, AB; American journalist and author; b. (Cornelius Mahoney Sheehan), 27 Oct. 1936, Holyoke, Mass; s. of Cornelius Sheehan and Mary O'Shea; m. Susan Margulies 1965; two d.; ed Harvard Univ.; Viet Nam Bureau Chief, UPI, Saigon 1962–64; reporter, New York Times, New York, Jakarta, Saigon, Washington, DC 1964–72, obtained classified Pentagon Papers from Daniel Ellsberg 1971, subsequently published in New York Times winning newspaper Pulitzer Prize; Guggenheim Fellow 1973–74; Adlai Stevenson Fellow 1973–75; Fellow, Lehrman Inst. 1975–76; Rockefeller Foundation Fellow 1976–77; Fellow, Woodrow Wilson Center for Int. Scholars 1979–80; mem. Soc. of American Historians, Acad. of Achievement; Hon. LittD (Columbia Coll., Chicago) 1972; Hon. LHD (American Int. Coll.) 1990, (Lowell Univ.) 1991; recipient of numerous awards for journalism. *Publications:* The Arnheiter Affair 1972, A Bright Shining Lie: John Paul Vann and America in Viet Nam (Nat. Book Award 1988, Pulitzer Prize for non-fiction 1989, J.F. Kennedy Award 1989, chosen by The Modern Library as one of 100 Best Works of Non-Fiction in 20th Century 1999) 1988, After the War Was Over: Hanoi and Saigon 1992; contrib. to The Pentagon Papers 1971; articles and book reviews for popular magazines. *Address:* 4505 Klingle Street, NW, Washington, DC 20016, USA (home).

SHEEHY, Sir Patrick, Kt; British business executive (retd); b. 2 Sept. 1930; s. of Sir John Francis Sheehy and Jean Sheehy (née Newton); m. Jill Patricia Tindall 1964; one s. one d.; ed Ampleforth Coll., Yorks.; served in Irish Guards 1948–50; joined British-American Tobacco Co. 1950, first appointment, Nigeria, Ghana 1951, Regional Sales Man. Nigeria 1953, Ethiopian Tobacco Monopoly 1954, Marketing Dir Jamaica 1957, Gen. Man. Barbados 1961, Netherlands 1967; Dir British-American Tobacco 1970–82, mem. Chair.'s Policy Cttee and Chair. Tobacco Div. Bd 1975; Deputy Chair. BAT Industries 1976–81, Vice-Chair. 1981–82, Chair. 1982–95; Chair. BAT Financial Services 1985–90, Barder Marsh (now Marlborough) 1995–; Dir Eagle Star Holdings 1984–87, British Petroleum 1984–98, The Spectator (1828) Ltd 1988–, Cluff Resources 1992–96, Celtic Football Club 1996–; Dir (non-exec.) Pvt. Bank and Trust Co. 1996–; Chair. Council of Int. Advisors Swiss Bank Corpn 1985–, UK Home Office Inquiry into Police Responsibilities and Rewards 1992–93; CEO Rainbow 1993–; Dir Asda Property Holdings 1994–, currently Chair. (non-exec.); mem. Pres.'s Cttee, CBI 1986–; mem. Trade Policy Research Centre 1984–89, Action Cttee for Europe 1985–; mem. CBI Task Force on Urban Regeneration; Chevalier, Légion d'honneur. *Leisure interests:* golf, reading. *Address:* 11 Eldon Road, London, W8 5PU, England. *Telephone:* (20) 7937-6250.

SHEEN, Charlie; American actor; b. (Carlos Estevez), 3 Sept. 1965, New York; s. of Martin Sheen (q.v.) and Janet Sheen (née Templeton); brother of Emilio Estevez; m. 1st Donna Peele 1995 (divorced 1996); m. 2nd Denise Richards 2003; two d.; ed Santa Monica High School. *Films include:* Red Dawn 1984, The Boys Next Door 1986, Lucas 1986, Ferris Bueller's Day Off 1986, Platoon 1986, The Wraith 1986, Wisdom 1986, A Life in the Day 1986, No Man's Land 1987, Three for the Road 1987, Grizzly II: The Predator 1987, Young Guns 1988, Wall Street 1987, Eight Men Out 1988, Major League 1989, Comicitis 1989, Catchfire 1989, Cadence 1990, Men at Work 1990, Courage Mountain 1990, Navy SEALS 1990, The Rookie 1990, Stockade (Dir), Secret Society, Hot Shots! 1991, Beyond the Law 1992, Hot Shots! Part Deux 1993, Deadfall 1993, The Three Musketeers 1993, The Chase 1994, Major League II 1994, Terminal Velocity 1994, All Dogs Go To Heaven II (voice) 1996, The Arrival (aka Shockwave) 1996, The Shadow Conspiracy 1997, Money Talks 1997, Bad Day on the Block 1997, Postmortem 1998, No Code of Conduct 1998, Free Money 1998, A Letter From Death Row 1998, Five Aces 1999, Being John Malkovich 1999, Rated X 2000, Good Advice 2001, Scary Movie 3 2003, Deeper Than Deep 2003, The Big Bounce 2004. *Television includes:* The Execution of Private Slovik 1974, Silence of the Heart (film), The Boys Next Door (film), Sugar Hill 1999, Spin City (Golden Globe for Best Actor 2002) 2000–02, Two and a Half Men 2003–. *Leisure interests:* baseball, music, film-making. *Address:* c/o Jeffrey Ballard Public Relations, 4814 Lemara Avenue, Sherman Oaks, CA 91403, USA.

SHEEN, Ching-Jing; Taiwanese business executive and property developer; *Chairman, Core Pacific Group;* b. 1947, Nanjing, China; moved with family to Taiwan 1947; joined Sea Snake Gang (triads) 1962; in prison 1966–69; mil. service 1969–71; worked on cargo ships 1971–73; govt clerk 1974; est. co. to buy and sell textile quotas; f. Core Pacific property co. 1985, Core Pacific Securities 1988, negotiated merger between Core Pacific Securities and Yuanta 2000, currently Chair. Core Pacific Group; Chair.. Sheen Chuen-Chi Cultural and Educational Foundation. *Address:* Sheen Chuen-Chi Cultural and Educational Foundation, 125 Nanking East Road, Section 5, Taipei 105, Taiwan; Core Pacific - Yamaichi International (HK) Limited, 36th Floor, Cosco Tower, Grand Millennium Plaza, 183 Queen's Road Central, Hong Kong Special Administrative Region, People's Republic of China (office). *Telephone:* (852) 2826-0700 (Hong Kong) (office). *Fax:* (852) 2536-9916 (Hong Kong) (office). *Website:* www.cpy.com.hk (office).

SHEEN, Martin; American actor; b. (Ramon Estevez), 3 Aug. 1940, Dayton, Ohio; s. of Francisco Estevez and Mary Ann Phelan; m. Janet Templeton 1961; three s. one d.; worked as shipping clerk, American Express Co., New York; Hon. Mayor of Malibu 1989–; Laetare Medal, Univ. of Notre Dame, Indiana 2008. *Stage appearances:* The Connection (début, New York and European tour), Never Live Over A Pretzel Factory, The Subject Was Roses, The Crucible. *Films:* The Incident, Catch-22, Rage, Badlands, Apocalypse Now, Enigma, Gandhi, The King of Prussia, That Championship Season, Man, Woman and Child, The Dead Zone, Final Countdown, Loophole, Wall Street, Nightbreaker, Da 1988, Personal Choice 1989, Cadence (also Dir) 1990, Judgement in Berlin 1990, Limited Time, The Maid 1990, Cadence (also Dir), Hear No Evil, Hot Shots Part Deux (cameo), Gettysburg 1993, Trigger Fast, Hits!, Fortunes of War, Sacred Cargo, The Break, Dillinger & Capone, Captain Nuke and the Bomber Boys, Ghost Brigade, The Cradle Will Rock, Dead Presidents, Dorothy Day, Gospa, The American President, The War At Home, Spawn, Storm 1999, Monument Avenue, Free Money, Lost & Found 1999, Apocalypse New Redux 2001, Catch Me If You Can 2003, Milost mora 2003, The Commission 2003, Jerusalemski sindrom 2004, The Departed 2006, Bobby 2006, Bordertown 2007, Flatland: The Movie 2007, Talk to Me 2007. *Television appearances include:* The Defenders, East Side/West Side, My Three Sons, Mod Squad, Cannon, That Certain Summer, The Execution of Private Slovik, Missiles of October, The Last Survivors, Blind Ambition, Shattered Spirits, Nightbreaker, The Last P.O.W.?, Roswell, The West Wing (Golden Satellite Award 2000, Golden Globe Award 2000) 1999–2006. *Address:* c/o Jeff Ballard, 4814 Lemara Avenue, Sherman Oaks, CA 91403, USA.

SHEEN, Michael, OBE; British actor; b. 5 Feb. 1959, Newport, Gwent; s. of Meyrick Sheen and Irene Sheen; ed Royal Acad. of Dramatic Art. *Films include:* Othello 1995, Mary Reilly 1996, Wilde 1997, Heartlands 2002, The Four Feathers 2002, Bright Young Things 2003, Underworld 2003, Timeline 2003, Laws of Attraction 2004, The Banker 2004, Dead Long Enough 2005,

Kingdom of Heaven 2005, The League of Gentlemen's Apocalypse 2005, Underworld: Evolution 2006, The Queen 2006, Blood Diamond 2006, Music Within 2007, Frost/Nixon 2008, Underworld: Rise of the Lycans 2009. *Television includes:* Gallowglass 1993, Lost in France 1998, The Deal 2003, Dirty Filthy Love 2004, Kenneth Williams: Fantabulosa! 2006, Ancient Rome: The Rise and Fall of an Empire 2006, HG Wells: War with the World 2006. *Address:* Roxanne Vacca Management, 73 Beak Street, London, W1R 9SR, England (office). *Telephone:* (171) 734-8085 (office). *Fax:* (171) 734-8086 (office).

SHEERAN, Josette, BA; American newspaper editor and diplomatist; *Executive Director, United Nations World Food Programme;* b. Orange, NJ; ed Univ. of Colorado; Deputy Man. Ed., Washington Times newspaper 1985–92, Man. Ed. 1992–97; Man. Dir Starpoint Solutions, NY; fmr Pres. and CEO Empower America; Deputy US Trade Rep., Office of US Trade Rep. –2005; Under-Sec. of State for Econ., Business and Agricultural Affairs, US State Dept 2005–07; Exec. Dir UN WFP 2007–; mem. Council on Foreign Relations; mem. Bd of Dirs Overseas Pvt. Investment Corpn; Press Award for Journalistic Achievement, Nat. Order of Women Legislators, nat. award for developing and promoting African-American journalists. *Address:* World Food Programme, Via Cesare Giulio Viola 68, Parco dei Medici, 00148 Rome, Italy (office). *Telephone:* (06) 65131 (office). *Fax:* (06) 6513-2840 (office). *E-mail:* wfpinfo@wfp.org (office). *Website:* www.wfp.org (office).

SHEIKH HUSSEIN, Hussein Mahmud; Somali politician; Minister of Finance 2002–04, of Higher Education and Culture 2004–07. *Address:* c/o Ministry of Higher Education and Culture, Mogadishu, Somalia (office).

SHEIN, Ali Mohammed; Tanzanian politician; Vice-President of Tanzania 2001–. *Address:* Office of the Vice-President, POB 5380, Dar es Salaam, Tanzania (office). *Telephone:* (22) 2113857 (office). *Fax:* (22) 2113856 (office). *E-mail:* makamu@twiga.com (office). *Website:* www.tanzania.go.tz/vpoffice .htm (office).

SHEINWALD, Sir Nigel Elton, Kt, KCMG; British diplomatist; *Ambassador to USA;* b. 26 June 1953, London; s. of Leonard Sheinwald and Joyce Sheinwald; m. Dr Julia Dunne; three s.; ed Harrow Co. Boys' School, Balliol Coll., Oxford; joined Diplomatic Service 1976–, Japanese Desk 1976–77, Embassy, Moscow 1978–79, mem. Lancaster House Conf. team on Zimbabwe 1979–80, Head of Anglo-Soviet Section, FCO 1981–83, Embassy in Washington, DC 1983–87, Deputy Head of Policy Planning Staff, FCO 1987–89, Deputy Head of EC Dept 1989–92, Perm. Rep. to EU, Brussels 1993–95, Head of News Dept, FCO 1995–98, Dir EU Div. 1998–2000, Amb. and Perm. Rep. to EU, Brussels 2000–03; Foreign Policy and Defence Adviser to the Prime Minister and Head, Cabinet Office Defence and Overseas Secr. 2003–07; Amb. to USA 2007–. *Address:* Embassy of the United Kingdom, 3100 Massachusetts Avenue, NW, Washington, DC 20008, USA (office). *Telephone:* (202) 588-7800 (office). *Fax:* (202) 588-7870 (office). *E-mail:* washi@fco.gov.uk (office). *Website:* www.britainusa.com (office).

SHEKHAR MOOSHAHARY, Ranjit; Indian politician and fmr police officer; *Governor of Meghalaya;* b. Oldaguri, Kokrajhar Dist; ed St Anthony's Coll.; joined Indian Police Service 1967, assigned to Kerala cadre, fmr Chief of Crime Br. CID and Vigilance and Anti-Corruption Bureau; fmr mem. Cabinet Secr.; Dir Gen. Nat. Security Guards 2002–05, Border Security Force 2005–08; Gov. of Meghalaya 2008–; Police Medal for Meritorious Service, Pres.'s Police Medal for Distinguished Services. *Address:* Office of the Governor of Meghalaya, Meghalaya Legislative Assembly, Shillong 793001, Meghalaya, India. *Website:* meghalaya.nic.in (office).

SHEKHAWAT, Bhairon Singh; Indian politician; b. 23 Oct. 1923; s. of Devi Singh and Suraj Kanwar; m. Suraj Kanwar; one d.; mem. Rajasthan Legis. Ass. 1952–72, 1977–2002; mem. Rajya Sabha 1974–77; Chief Minister of Rajasthan 1977–80, 1990–92, 1993–98; Vice-Pres. of India 2002–07 (resgnd); fmr Leader, Janata Dal, Bharatiya Janata Party. *Address:* 31 Aurangazeb Road, New Delhi, India (home).

SHELAH, Saharon, PhD; Israeli mathematician and academic; *A. Robinson Chair for Mathematical Logic, Hebrew University of Jerusalem;* b. 3 July 1945, Jerusalem; ed Tel-Aviv Univ. and Hebrew Univ. of Jerusalem; mil. service, Israel Defence Forces Army 1964–67; Teaching Asst, Inst. of Math., Hebrew Univ. of Jerusalem 1967–69, Instructor 1969, Asst Prof. 1971–72, Assoc. Prof. 1972–74, Prof. 1974–, A. Robinson Chair for Math. Logic 1978–; Head, Model Theory Group, Inst. for Advanced Studies, Princeton NJ 1980–81; Lecturer, Dept of Math., Princeton Univ., 1969–70; Asst Prof., UCLA 1970–71; Visiting Prof., Univ. of Wis. 1977–78, Univ. of California, Berkeley 1978, 1982, Dept of Electrical Eng and Computer Science, Univ. of Mich 1984–85, Simon Fraser Univ., Burnaby, BC, Canada 1985, Rutgers Univ., New Brunswick, NJ 1985–86; Distinguished Visiting Prof., Rutgers Univ. 1986–; Chair. European Research Confs: Infinite Combinatorics and its Impact to Algebra, Hattingen, Germany 1999; Vice-Chair. European Science Foundation Meeting, Barcelona, Spain 1997; Head, Israeli Del., US-Israel Conf. in Classification Theory, Chicago, Ill. 1984; Ed. Proceedings American Math. Soc. Summer Conf. on Set Theory, Boulder, Colo 1983, Fundamenta Mathematicae 1994–, Journal of Applied Analysis 1996–, Asian Journal of Mathematics 1998–; mem. Gen. Editorial Bd Journal D'Analyse Mathématique 1992–, Israel Journal of Mathematics 1992; mem. Asscn of Symbolic Logic, Israel Math. Soc., American Math. Soc., Israeli Acad. of Science and Humanities 1988–; Foreign hon. mem. American Acad. of Arts and Sciences 1991; Hon. Ed. Mathematica Japonica 1994–; Erdös Prize 1977, Rothschild Prize in Math. 1982, C. Karp Prize, Asscn for Symbolic Logic 1983, Conf. in Honour of S. Shelah, Tulane Univ., New Orleans 1987, George Polya Prize in Applications of Combinatorial Math., Soc. for Industrial and Applied Math. 1991, Plenary Lecturer, Canadian Math. Soc. Annual Meeting 1992, Plenary Lecturer, European

Logic Colloquium, Haifa, Israel 1995, Gödel Lecturer, Asscn for Symbolic Logic Annual Meeting, Madison, WI 1996, Israel Prize in Math. 1998, Japanese Asscn of Math. Sciences Prize 1999, Janos Bolyai Prize, Hungarian Acad. of Sciences 2000, Wolf Foundation Prize in Math. 2001. *Publications:* more than 840 articles in math. journals. *Address:* Einstein Institute of Mathematics, Hebrew University of Jerusalem, Edmond Safra Campus, Givat Ram, Kaplun 205, 91904 Jerusalem, Israel (office). *Telephone:* (2) 658-41-22 (office). *Fax:* (2) 563-07-02 (office). *E-mail:* shelah@math.huji.ac.il (office). *Website:* shelah.logic.at (office).

SHELBY, Richard Craig, AB, LLB; American politician; *Senator from Alabama;* b. 6 May 1934, Birmingham, Ala; s. of O. H. Shelby and Alice L. Skinner; m. Annette Nevin 1960; two s.; ed Univ. of Alabama; Law Clerk, Supreme Court of Ala 1961–62; law practice, Tuscaloosa, Ala 1963–79; Prosecutor, City of Tuscaloosa 1964–70; US Magistrate, Northern Dist of Ala 1966–70; Special Asst Attorney-Gen., State of Ala 1969–70; Pres. Tuscaloosa Co. Mental Health Asscn 1969–70; mem. Ala State Senate 1970–78; mem. 96th–99th US Congresses, 7th Ala Dist 1979–87; Senator from Alabama 1987–, Chair. Senate Banking Cttee 2003–; fmr mem. Exec. Cttee Ala State Democratic Party; joined Republican Party 1994; mem. ABA. *Address:* 110 Hart Senate Building, Washington, DC 20510 (office); 1414 High Forest Drive, North Tuscaloosa, AL 35406, USA (home). *Telephone:* (202) 224-5744. *Fax:* (202) 224-3416. *Website:* shelby.senate.gov.

SHELDRICK, George Michael, MA, PhD, FRS; British scientist and academic; *Professor of Structural Chemistry, University of Göttingen;* b. 17 Nov. 1942, Huddersfield; s. of George Sheldrick and Elizabeth Sheldrick; m. Katherine E. Herford 1968; two s. two d.; ed Huddersfield New Coll. and Jesus Coll., Cambridge; Fellow, Jesus Coll., Cambridge and Univ. Demonstrator/Lecturer, Univ. of Cambridge 1966–78; Prof. of Structural Chem., Univ. of Göttingen 1978–; mem. Akad. der Wissenschaften zu Göttingen 1989; Leibniz Prize, Deutsche Forschungsgemeinschaft 1987, Patterson Prize, American Crystallographic Asscn 1993; Meldola Medal, Royal Soc. of Chem. (RSC) 1970, Corday-Morgan Medal, RSC 1978, Award for Structural Chem., RSC 1981, Carl-Hermann Medal, Deutsche Gesellschaft für Kristallographie 1999; mineral Sheldrickite named after him 1996, Dorothy Hodgkin Prize, British Crystallographic Asscn 2004, Max Perutz Prize, European Crystallographic Asscn 2004. *Achievements include:* author of widely used computer programme for crystal structure determination (SHELX). *Publications:* more than 750 scientific papers. *Leisure interests:* chess, tennis. *Address:* Department of Inorganic Chemistry, University of Göttingen, Tammannstr. 4, 37077 Göttingen, Germany. *Telephone:* (551) 393021 (office). *Fax:* (551) 392582 (office). *E-mail:* gsheldr@shelx.uni-ac.gwdg.de (office). *Website:* shelx.uni-ac.gwdg.de (office).

SHELLEY, Howard Gordon, OBE; British concert pianist and conductor; b. 9 March 1950, London; s. of Frederick Gordon Shelley and Anne Taylor; m. Hilary MacNamara 1975; one s. one step-s.; professional debut at Wigmore Hall, London 1971; soloist with all London and prov. British orchestras; regular tours to USA and Canada, Australia, Hong Kong and Europe; three piano concertos written for him (Cowie, Chapple, Dickinson); conducting debut with London Symphony Orchestra 1985; Assoc. Conductor, London Mozart Players 1990–92, Prin. Guest Conductor 1992–98; Music Dir, Prin. Conductor Uppsala Chamber Orchestra, Sweden 2001–03; opera conducting debut 2002; current engagements as conductor or soloist or combined role of conductor/soloist; Hon. FRCM 1993; Dannreuther Concerto Prize 1971. *Repertoire:* from Mozart through Liszt to Gershwin; first pianist to perform in concert complete solo piano works of Rachmaninov 1983. *Recordings include:* over 100 recordings including complete solo piano music of Rachmaninov (nine vols) and complete Rachmaninov song-cycle (three vols), Chopin Preludes, Sonatas, Scherzi, Impromptus, Schumann Carnival, Kinderszenen, Hummel solo piano works, Clementi sonatas, piano concertos of many British composers including Alwyn, Carwithen, Dickinson, Ferguson, Rubbra, Tippett and Vaughan Williams, the symphonies of Alice Mary Smith, Gershwin's piano concerto and rhapsodies, piano concertos of Balakirev, Korngold (Left Hand), Liapounov, Hindemith's Four Temperaments, Szymanowski's Symphony No. 4 and Messiaen's Turangalila; conducting from the keyboard has recorded the Mendelssohn piano concertos and Mozart piano concertos (six vols); Hummel piano concertos (eight vols), Cramer piano concertos with the London Mozart Players; with the Tasmanian Symphony Orchestra has recorded piano concertos by Moscheles, Herz, Hiller, Kalkbrenner; conducting the Royal Philharmonic Orchestra has recorded Mozart symphonies 35 and 38 and Schubert symphonies 3 and 5; with Tasmanian Symphony Orchestra Reinecke symphonies 2 and 3; and with Orchestra Svizzera Italiana in Lugano Haydn's London symphonies. *Television:* documentary on Ravel with Tasmanian Symphony Orchestra (Australian Broadcasting Co.) featured Shelley as presenter, conductor and pianist (Gold Medal for Best Arts Biog., 40th New York Festival Awards); documentary on Rachmaninov by Hessische Rundfunk (Channel 4). *Address:* c/o Caroline Baird Artists, Pinkhill House, Oxford Road, Eynsham, Oxon., OX29 4DA (office); 38 Cholmeley Park, London, N6 5ER, England (home). *Telephone:* (1865) 882771 (office). *Fax:* (1865) 882771 (office). *E-mail:* caroline@cbartists.sol.co.uk (office). *Website:* www.carolinebairdartists.co.uk (office).

SHELOV-KOVEDYAYEV, Fedor Vadimovich; Russian politician; b. 15 June 1956, Moscow; m.; two c.; ed Moscow State Univ.; researcher, Inst. of History of USSR (now Russian) Acad. of Sciences; mem. Club of Moscow Intellectuals Moskovskaya Tribuna 1989–91; RSFSR People's Deputy; mem. Cttee on Human Rights, Supreme Soviet 1990–93; mem. State Duma 1993–95; mem. Constitutional Comm. on Regional Policy and Co-operation; mem. Parl. Block Coalition of Reforms; First Deputy Minister of Foreign Affairs 1991–92; mem. Political Council, Democratic Choice of Russia Party 1993–96; Co-Chair., Int. Russian Club; Vice-Pres. Expert Fund of Social Research (ELF). *Publications:* History of the Bosphorus from 6th to 14th Century BC and over 90 scientific works. *Address:* International Russian Club, Ogareva str. 5, 103009 Moscow, Russia.

SHELTON, Gen. H(enry) Hugh, MSc; American army officer (retd); b. 2 Jan. 1942, Tarboro, NC; s. of the late Hugh Shelton and of Sarah Shelton (née Laughlin); m. Carolyn L. Johnson; three s.; ed North Carolina State Univ., Auburn Univ., Harvard Univ., Air Command and Staff Coll., Nat. War Coll.; commissioned into Infantry 1963; served in mainland USA, Hawaii, 2 tours of Vietnam; fmrly Commdr 3rd Bn 60th Infantry Div., Fort Lewis, Wash., Asst Chief of Staff for Operations 9th Infantry Div., Commdr 1st Brigade 82nd Airborne Div., Fort Bragg, NC, Chief of Staff 10th Mountain Div., Fort Drum, NY; rank of Brig.-Gen. 1987; Deputy Dir for Operations, Nat. Mil. Command CTR, Jt Staff Operations Directorate 1987–89; Asst Div. Cmmdr for Operations 101st Airborne Div. (Air Assault) (including during Operations Desert Shield and Desert Storm 1990–91) 1989–91; rank of Maj.-Gen. 1991; Commdr 82nd Airborne Div., Fort Bragg, NC 1991–93; rank of Lt-Gen. 1993; Commdr XVIIIth and Fort Bragg Airborne Corps. 1993, Commdr Jt Task Force for Operation Restore Democracy, Haiti 1994; attained rank of Gen. 1996; C-in-C US Special Operations Command 1996–97; Chair. Jt Chiefs of Staff 1997–2001 (retd); Pres. International Operations, M.I.C. Corpn 2002–05; mem. Bd of Dirs Red Hat Corpn 2003–, Anheuser-Busch Cos, CACI International Inc., Ceramic Protection Corpn; recipient Defense DSM (with 2 oak leaf clusters) 1989, 1994, 1997, DSM 1994, Legion of Merit (with oak leaf cluster) 1985, 1991, Bronze Star Medal (with V device, 3 oak leaf clusters) 1968, 1969, 1991, Purple Heart 1967 and numerous other decorations. *Leisure interests:* jogging, woodworking, reading and playing guitar. *Address:* c/o Board of Directors, Red Hat Corporation, 1801 Varsity Drive, Raleigh, NC 27606, USA (office).

SHELTON, Robert Neal, BS, MS, PhD; American physicist, academic and university administrator; *President, University of Arizona;* b. 5 Oct. 1948, Phoenix; m. Adrian Shelton (née Millar) 1969; two s. one d.; ed Stanford Univ., Univ. of California, San Diego; Asst Research Physicist, Univ. of California, San Diego 1975–78; Asst Prof. of Physics, Iowa State Univ. 1978–81, Assoc. Prof. 1981–84, Prof. 1984–87; Prof. of Physics, Univ. California, Davis 1987–2001, Chair. Dept of Physics 1987–90, Vice Chancellor for Research 1990–96, Vice Provost for Research, 1996–2001; Prof. of Physics, Univ. of North Carolina, Chapel Hill 2001–06, Exec. Vice Chancellor and Provost 2001–06; Pres. Univ. of Arizona 2006–, also Prof. of Physics; Fellow, American Physical Soc., AAAS; Ed. Journal of Physics and Chemistry of Solids. *Publications:* over 240 publs. *Address:* Office of the President, University of Arizona, Administration Building, Room 712, PO Box 210066, Tucson, AZ 85721-0066, USA (office). *Telephone:* (520) 621-5511 (office). *Fax:* (520) 621-9323 (office). *E-mail:* robert.shelton@arizona.edu (office). *Website:* www.president.arizona.edu (office).

SHELTON-COLBY, Sally, BA, MA; American fmr diplomatist and international organization official; *Chairman, Helen Keller International/Europe;* b. 29 Aug. 1944, San Antonio; m. William Colby (deceased); ed Univ. of Missouri, Johns Hopkins School of Advanced Int. Studies, Institut des Sciences Politiques, Paris; fmr Deputy Asst Sec. of State for Inter-American Affairs; fmr mem. US Perm. Mission to UN, New York; Amb. to Grenada, Barbados and other Caribbean nations 1979–81; Sr Fellow and Adjunct Prof., Georgetown Univ. Center for Latin American Studies; Asst Admin. for Global Problems, US Agency for Int. Devt 1994–99; Deputy Sec.-Gen. OECD 1999–2002; fmr Vice-Pres. Bankers Trust Co., New York; fmr Dir Valero Energy Corpn, Baring Brother & Co. Ltd's Puma Fund; Pres. Helen Keller International/Europe 2002, now Chair.; mem. American Acad. of Diplomacy 2002–; adviser to several multi-nat. corpns on int. trade and investment strategies; fmr Co-Ed. Global Assessment (econ. journal); Fulbright Scholar. *Address:* Helen Keller International Europe, 45-47, rue Vineuse, 75016 Paris, France (office). *Telephone:* 1-47-64-11-30 (office). *E-mail:* europe-info@hki.org (office). *Website:* www.hki.org/network/Europe.html (office).

SHEMYAKIN, Mikhail Mikhailovich; Russian sculptor and painter; b. (Kardanov), 1943, Moscow; ed Inst. of Painting, Sculpture and Architecture, Leningrad (now St Petersburg); one-man exhbn Leningrad 1962; arrested for dissident activities, interned in lunatic asylums; emigrated in 1971; lived in Paris 1971–81; living in USA 1981–; f. Foundation for Helping Soviet Veterans of the War in Afghanistan 1989; visited Russia frequently after citizenship was restored 1990; created Peter the Great Memorial in St Petersburg; Chief Designer on Gofmaniada film project, Soyuzmultfilm 2006–; mem. European Acad. of Arts, Paris, New York Acad. of Sciences and Arts; Dr hc (San Francisco); State Prize 1993, Pres. of Russia Prize 1995. *Address:* c/o Soyuzmultfilm, 127006, Moscow, ul.Dolgorukovskaya, d.25, Russia.

SHEMYAKIN, Yevgeniy Ivanovich, DTech Sc; Russian mining specialist and academic; *Professor, Moscow State University;* b. 9 Dec. 1929, Novosibirsk; s. of I. Shemyakin and Ella Shemyakina; m. L. T. Petrova 1952; one s. one d.; ed Leningrad Univ.; Sr Research Asst at USSR Acad. of Sciences Inst. of Chemico-Physics 1955–60; head of lab. of USSR Acad. of Sciences Inst. of Theoretical and Applied Mechanics 1960–70; Prof. Novosibirsk State Univ. 1963–87, Chair. of Elasticity 1967–87; Acting Dir of USSR Acad. of Sciences Inst. of Mining (Siberian Div.) 1970–72, Dir 1972–87; Chair. Supreme State Cttee of Attestation, Moscow, 1987–92; Prin. Consultant, Russian Acad. of Sciences Inst. of Dynamics of Geospheres 1987–92; Prof. Moscow State Univ. 1987–, Chair. of Wave and Gas Dynamics 1988–; Vice-Pres. of Presidium, Siberian Div., Acad. of Sciences 1980–85; Chair. Russian Acad. of Sciences Scientific Council on Underground Space and Underground Construction 1994–; mem. of USSR (now Russian) Acad. of Sciences 1984, Royal Swedish Soc. of Engineers 1987, Czech Acad. of Science, Slovak Acad. of Science, Int.

Soc. for Rock Mechanics (Vice-Pres. 1988–92), Int. Mining Congress; mem. CPSU 1963–91; mem. several scientific editorial bds; USSR State Prize 1984. *Publications:* author and co-author of more than 200 scientific and technical papers. *Leisure interests:* ancient history, old underground constructions. *Address:* Department of Mechanics and Mathematics, Moscow Lomonosov State University, Vorobyevy Gory, 119899 Moscow, Russia (office). *Telephone:* (495) 939-37-54 (office); (495) 332-62-63 (home). *Fax:* (495) 939-49-95.

SHEN, Beizhang; Chinese business executive; b. Jan. 1929, Cixi Co., Zhejiang Prov.; ed Jiaotong Univ., Shanghai; Chair. Shanghai Overseas Corpn 1990–; Chair. and Gen. Man., Shanghai Int. Group Corpn 1991; fmr Chair. Shanghai Int. Holding Corpn America 1996, now Hon. Chair; Chair. Chinese Chamber of Commerce in USA 1996; fmr Pres. Shanghai International Trust and Investment Corpn; fmr Dir Shanghai Foreign Econ. and Trade Comm.; mem. 8th CPPCC 1993–98.

SHEN, Dali; Chinese historian and translator; b. 4 Sept. 1938, Yanan; s. of the late Shen Xu and Song Ying; m. Dong Chun 1993; one s. one d.; ed Beijing Foreign Languages Univ.; Prof. titulaire and Dir Doctoral Theses, French Dept, Beijing Foreign Languages Univ. 1957–2005; trans. at UNESCO, Paris 1979–81, réviseur 1985–; Chinese del. WIPO 1984; visiting scholar in France 1990–91; Prof., Univ. of Montreal, Canada 1994, 2005; Prof., INALCO, Paris 1995, Univ. of Aix and Marseille 2003, 2007; Président du Jury 'Grands Reportages', FIPA 1996; del. to Cultural Comm. CIO, Lausanne, Switzerland 1997; mem. Chinese Writers' Asscn 1982–, Editorial Cttee Revue des Deux Mondes (France) 1999–2009; Chevalier, Ordre des Arts et des Lettres 1991, Croix de vermeil du Mérite et Dévouement français 1996; awarded title 'Membre d'honneur' by L'Association des Amis de la Commune de Paris 1981. *Translations include:* Le temps des cerises, Montserrat, Selected Poems of Eugene Pottier (additional trans): Les fleurs jumelles (play) 1982, L'epreuve (novel) 1985, Les trésors de la cité interdite 1986, Poésies choisies de la Commune de Paris 1986, l'Internationale, la Marseillaise, Le Chant du départ, N'a qu'un oeil, La paix du ménage, Le Vésuve, Les couteaux, Les yeux de demain, La vraie Dame aux camélias, Byron et les femmes 2002, Bruges la morte 2002, Biographie de Victor Hugo 2003. *Publications:* The Humble Violet (novel) 1980, The Meteor (novel) 1981, The Children of Yenan (novel, also in French and Italian) 1985, Les fleurs du rêve (poetry) 1986, Les lys rouges (novel) 1987, La flûte des Titans (play) 1987, Le rêve dans le pavillon d'azur, Le temps des cigales, Le tableau de Paris (prose) 1989, L'etoile filante (novel) 1993, (augmented edn) 1995, Voyage en Europe et en Amérique du Nord 1996, La rose de Jéricho (film) 1999; painting and poetry (in Italian, French and English): Matisse/Frasnedi 2001, Chagall/Vangeli 2001, Renoir/Zejtlin 2005, Rublev/Ambrosino 2006, Michelangelo/Günter Roth 2006, Les lettres et arts en France (essay) 2003, Les Amoureux du lac (novel) 2004, Biographie de Berlioz 2005, Lega/Vacca 2008, Roberto Panichi 2009, Su Manshu et Paul Verlaine (étude comparée). *Leisure interest:* music. *Address:* Building No 49-1-4, Dongdaqiaolu, Beijing 100020, People's Republic of China (home). *Telephone:* (10) 65007458 (home). *Fax:* (10) 65007458 (home). *E-mail:* chun.shen@ free.fr (home).

SHEN, Guofang; Chinese forestry engineer; b. 15 Nov. 1933, Jiashan, Zhejiang Prov.; ed Leningrad Forestry Inst.; currently Prof., Beijing Forestry Univ. (Pres. 1986–93); fmr Pres. Chinese Soc. of Forestry; Fellow, Chinese Acad. of Eng 1995–, Vice-Pres. 1998–2006. *Publication:* Silviculture. *Address:* Beijing Forestry University, Xiaozhaang, Haidan District, Beijing 100083, People's Republic of China (office). *Telephone:* (10) 62338279 (office). *Fax:* (10) 62335071 (office). *E-mail:* shengf@public.bta.net.cn (office).

SHEN, Heting; Chinese engineer and business executive; *President and CEO, China Metallurgical Group Corporation;* b. 1954; ed Tianjin Commercial Coll., Postgraduate School of Party School of CCP; fmr Asst Man., Deputy Man. and Man. Furnace Construction Co. of 22nd China Metallurgical Construction Corpn, Gen. Man. 1997–2004, Dir, Pres., Deputy Sec. of Party Cttee and Legal Rep., China Metallurgical Group Corpn 2004–; Nat. Labour Day Prize 2004. *Address:* China Metallurgical Group Corpn, 11 Gaoliangqiao Xiejie, Haidian, Beijing 100081, People's Republic of China (office). *Telephone:* (10) 82169999 (office). *Fax:* (10) 82169988 (office). *E-mail:* mcc@mcc.com.cn (office). *Website:* www.mcc.com.cn (office).

SHEN, Jerry, MEng; Taiwanese computer industry executive; *CEO, ASUS-TeK Computer;* ed Nat. Taiwan Univ.; spent 10 years holding several sr R&D positions at computer cos and IT research insts; Pres. AOOP (ASUS Open Optimal Platform) Group for Motherboard (MB), Graphics Card (VGA), Desktop, Chassis, Digital Home, EMS and Server businesses 1994–2007, CEO ASUSTeK Computer 2008–. *Address:* ASUSTeK Computer Inc., 15 Li-Te Road, Peitou, Taipei 112, Taiwan (office). *Telephone:* (2) 2894-3447 (office). *Fax:* (2) 2892-6140 (office). *E-mail:* info@asus.com (office). *Website:* www.asus .com (office).

SHEN, Jianhua, PhD; Chinese automotive industry executive; *President, Shanghai Automotive Industry Corporation (SAIC) Ltd;* ed Tongji Univ.; Vice-Pres. Shanghai Automotive Industry Corporation (SAIC) Motor Corpn Ltd –2007, mem. Bd of Dirs and Pres. 2007–. *Address:* Shanghai Automotive Industry Corporation (SAIC) Ltd, 5/F Building A, 563 Songtao Road, Zhangjiang, High Technology Park, Pu Dong, Shanghai 201203, People's Republic of China (office). *Telephone:* (21) 50803757 (office). *Fax:* (21) 50803780 (office). *E-mail:* info@saicgroup.com (office). *Website:* www .saicgroup.com (office); www.saicmotor.com (office).

SHEN, Peng; Chinese calligrapher, poet and editor; b. Sept. 1931, Jiangyin, Jiangsu Prov.; began to learn poetry, calligraphy and art from an early age; majored in Chinese literature in coll., later studied journalism; Assoc. Ed.-in-Chief People's Fine Arts Press; fmr Vice-Chair. Chinese Calligraphers Asscn, Chair. 2000, now Hon. Pres.; Sr Ed. and Art Counsellor, China Fine Arts

Publishing Group; Adjunct Prof., Peking Univ., China Ren Min Univ.; Vice-Pres. and Deputy Chair. Nat. Book Reward Evaluation Cttee; est. Art Museum of ShenPeng Calligraphy in Jiangyin, Jiansu Prov. and Mengjin, Henan Prov.; attended China Art Museum Contemporary Famous Calligraphers Exhbn 2005; organized draft Chinese Calligraphy Devt Compendium 2001–2002; Chief Ed. numerous nat. art magazines, including Art China, Chinese Art, Friends of Chinese Fine Art, and Art Guide; Ed. The laws of the People's Republic of China, Carvings Review, Calligraphy, and 500 other magazines; visits to USA, France, Japan, Sweden, USSR, Singapore, Italy, Korea, Malaysia, Canada, Peru, Venezuela, Hong Kong, Macao and Taiwan; mem. Nat. Cttee CPPCC; Hon. Commr China Fed. of Literary and Art Circles; among first group of experts honoured by State Council of China for Special Contribs, Modeling Art Creation Study Award, China Fed. of Literary and Art Circles 2006, China Calligraphy Lan Ting Lifelong Accomplishment Award, China Fed. of Literary and Art Circles and China Calligraphy Asscn 2006, World Peace and Art Authority Prize, UN Acad. *Publications:* academic thesis 'Tradition and yihua' (First Prize, Fourth Art Review Reward, China Fed. of Literary and Art Circles), Origins and Branches (Special Award, Fifth Art Review Reward) Criticism on Calligraphy and Art, Shen Peng's Talks on Calligraphy and Art, San Yu Lyrics on Grass, San Yu Lyrics Continues, Collections of San Yu Poems, Anthology of Contemporary Calligraphers – Shen Peng, Selections of Shen Peng's Calligraphy Works, Collections of Shen Peng's Calligraphy (published in Japan), Shen Peng's Calligraphy of BaiJuyi's Works, Shen Peng's Calligraphy of DuFu's Works, Shen Peng's Running Script of 'Front and Back Chibi', Collections of Running Script, Collections of Regular Script, Script of Words about Yue Yang Pavilion, Shen Peng's Script of Nineteen Ancient Poems, Collections of China Art Museum Contemporary Famous Calligraphers Exhibition. *Address:* People's Fine Arts Press, Beijing, People's Republic of China (office). *Telephone:* (10) 65245237 (home). *Fax:* (10) 65245237 (office).

SHEN, Rong; Chinese writer; b. (Shen Derong), Oct. 1936, Hubei Prov.; Perm. mem. Chinese Writers' Asscn 1985–, China PEN 1986–; mem. Chinese Int. Exchange Asscn 1990–. *Publications:* Forever Green (novel), No Way Out, Light and Dark, A Middle-aged Woman 1980, True and False, The Secret of Taizi Village, Wrong, Wrong, Wrong!. *Address:* Chinese Writers' Association, 15 Nongzhanguan Nanli, Chaoyang District, Beijing, People's Republic of China (office).

SHENG, Huaren; Chinese politician; *Vice-Chairman and Secretary-General, 10th Standing Committee, National People's Congress;* b. 1935, Xieyang Co., Jiangsu Prov.; joined CCP 1954; Office Sec. CCP Party Cttee, Nanjing Chemical Industry Corpn, Jiangsu Prov.; mem. Exec. Council China Council for the Promotion of Peaceful Reunification; Deputy Office Dir CCP Party Cttee, Chemical Fertilizer Industry Corpn, Ministry of Chemical Industry 1965; Deputy Head, Long-Term Planning Group, Ministry of Fuel and Chemical Industries 1970; Deputy Dir, later Dir Planning Dept, Ministry of Chemical Industry; Deputy Gen. Man., later Exec. Deputy Gen. Man. Sinopec Corpn 1983 (Deputy Sec. CCP Leading Party Group), Gen. Man. 1990–98; Vice-Pres. China-ROK Non-Governmental Econ. Asscn; Minister of State Econ. and Trade Comm. 1998–2001; Del., 14th CCP Nat. Congress 1992–97, 15th CCP Nat. Congress 1997–2002; mem. State Leading Group for Science and Tech. 1998; mem. 9th Standing Cttee of NPC 1998–2003; Vice-Chair. and Sec.-Gen. 10th Standing Cttee of NPC 2003–. *Address:* Standing Committee, National People's Congress, Tian'anmen, Beijing 100053, People's Republic of China (office).

SHENG, Zhongguo; Chinese violinist; b. 1941, Chongqing, Sichuan Prov.; s. of Sheng Xue and Zhu Bing; m. Seta Hiroko; ed Moscow Acad. of Music, USSR; fmr Instructor, Cen. Acad. of Music; solo performer (First Class), Cen. Philharmonic Soc.; performed Bach's concerto for two violins with Yehudi Menuhin 1979; performed 15 concerts in five Australian cities 1980; mem. 7th, 8th, 9th, 10th sessions CPPCC; Founder Sheng Zhongguo Foundation; prize at Int. Tchaikovsky Violin Competition 1962, 1st Prize for Musical Instruments at Competitive Performance by Troupes and Insts (Ministry of Culture) 1981. *Recordings:* many albums, including Butterfly Lovers Violin Concerto. *Address:* National Symphony Orchestra, Beijing, People's Republic of China (office).

SHENGELAIA, Eldar; Georgian film director and politician; b. 26 Jan. 1933, Georgia; s. of Nikolai Shengelaia and Nato Vachnadze; brother of Georgiy Nikolayevich Shengelaia (q.v.); m. 1st Ariadna Shengelaia (Shprink) 1957 (divorced 1980); two d.; m. 2nd Nelly Davlianidze 1981; one d.; ed Moscow Inst. of Cinematography; Dir at Mosfilm 1958–59, at Kartuli Pilmi film studio, Georgia 1960–; mem. CPSU 1966–90; Chair. Georgian Film-makers' Union 1976–; fmr sec. USSR Film-makers' Union; teacher, Tbilisi Theatre Inst., Tbilisi State Univ., Head of Film and TV Dept; Deputy, Supreme Soviet of Georgian SSR 1980–85, 1986–90, mem. Presidium 1989–90; elected to Supreme Soviet of Georgian Repub. (representing Democratic Centre) 1990–91; People's Deputy of USSR, USSR Supreme Soviet 1989–91; mem. State Council, Georgia, Parl. Repub. of Georgia 1992–; mem. Georgian Parl. 1995–, Deputy Chair.; Chair. Cultural Comm.; People's Artist of Georgia 1979, People's Artist of USSR 1987; USSR Prize 1985, numerous other prizes. *Films include:* The Legend of the Ice Heart 1957, The Snow Fairy Tale 1958, White Caravan 1963, Mikela 1965, An Extraordinary Exhibition 1968, The Screwballs 1974, Stepmother of Samanishvili 1978, Blue Mountains or an Improbable Event 1984, Tbilisi 9 April Chronicles 1989, Express Information 1994, Dog Rose 1996. *Address:* c/o Georgian Film-makers' Union, Kakabadze Street 2, 380008 Tbilisi (office); Ioseliani Street 37, Flat 58, 380091 Tbilisi, Georgia (home). *Telephone:* (32) 99-75-18 (office); (32) 93-14-05 (Parl.) (office); (32) 99-80-80 (home).

SHENGELAIA, Georgiy Nikolayevich; Georgian film director and actor; b. 11 May 1937, Tbilisi; s. of Nicolai Shengelaia and Nato Vachnadze; brother of Eldar Shengelaia (q.v.); m. 1st Sofiko Chiaureli 1957 (divorced); m. 2nd Ketevan Ninya 1985; three s.; ed Moscow Inst. of Cinematography; freelance artist; mem. Parl., Deputy Chair. 2000; Georgian State Prize 1980. *Films include:* Alaverdoba 1960, He Did Not Want to Kill 1966, Pirosmani 1969, Melodies of Veriysky Suburb 1973, Come into the Grape Valley 1977, The Girl with the Sewing-Machine 1980, Journey of the Young Composer 1985, Kchareba An Gogi 1987, Death of Orpheus 1996, Georgian Grapes 1999. *Roles include:* Dato (Our Yard), Georgi (Otar's Widow), Gela (The Tale About a Girl). *Address:* Kekelidze Street 16, Apt. 12, 380009 Tbilisi, Georgia. *Telephone:* (32) 22-64-11. *Fax:* (32) 99-07-54; (32) 93-50-97.

SHENIN, Col Oleg Semyonovich; Russian politician; b. 22 July 1937, Vladimirskaya, Volgograd Dist; s. of Semyon Sidorovich Shenin and Angelina Nikolaevna Shenina; m. Tamara Aleksandrovna Shenina 1955; one s. two d.; ed Krasnoyarsk Tech. College for Mining, Tomsk Eng Inst. and CPSU Cen. Cttee Acad. of Social Sciences; mem. CPSU 1962–91; various positions including works foreman and trust man. at construction sites in Krasnoyarsk Dist 1955–74; conducted party work 1974–91; First Sec., Achinsk City Cttee, Second Sec., Khakassk Dist Cttee (obkom), Sec., Krasnoyarsk Dist Cttee, First Sec., Khakassk Dist Cttee (obkom) 1974–87; First Sec., Krasnoyarsk Dist Cttee 1987–90; elected USSR People's Deputy 1989; Chair. Krasnoyarsk Dist Council of People's Deputies 1990–91; fmr mem. CPSU Cen. Cttee; mem. Political Bureau, Sec. Cen. Cttee 1990–91; arrested Aug. 1991 for alleged participation in attempted coup d'état; charged with conspiracy Jan. 1992, released Oct. 1992; on trial 1993, released on amnesty 1994; Chair. Union of Communist Parties (SCP-CPSU) 1993–, Int. Comm. for Union and Brotherhood of Peoples 1997–; First Sec. Cen. Cttee CPSU 2000–; mem. Russian Fed. of Natural Sciences. *Leisure interests:* sport, reading, family. *Address:* Union of Communist Parties, Novaya sq. 14, 103132 Moscow, Russia (office); Per Plotnikov 13 Kv. 24, Moscow, Russia (home). *Telephone:* (495) 278-96-33. *Fax:* (495) 278-31-39. *E-mail:* shenin@cea.ru (office). *Website:* www.cea.ru/shenin (office).

SHENNAN, Joseph Hugh, PhD, FRHistS, FRSA; British historian and academic; b. 13 March 1933, Liverpool; s. of Hugh Cringle Shennan and Mary Catherine Jones; m. Margaret King Price 1958; three s.; ed St Edward's Coll. Liverpool, Univ. of Liverpool and Corpus Christi Coll. Cambridge; Asst Lecturer, Lecturer in History, Univ. of Liverpool 1960–65; Lecturer, Sr Lecturer, Reader in History, Lancaster Univ. 1965–74, Prof. of European Studies 1974–79, Prof. of European History 1979–, Pro-Vice-Chancellor (Academic) 1985–93, Deputy Vice-Chancellor 1993–98; Sr Research Scholar (Visiting Fellow), Corpus Christi Coll. Cambridge 1984–85; Founding Ed. European Studies Review (now European History Quarterly) 1970–79. *Publications:* The Parlement of Paris 1968, Government and Society in France 1461–1661 1969, The Origins of the Modern European State 1450–1725 1974, Philippe, Duke of Orleans: Regent of France, 1715–1723 1979, France Before the Revolution 1983, Liberty and Order in Early Modern Europe: The Subject and the State, 1650–1800 1986, Louis XIV 1986, International Relations in Europe, 1689–1789 1995, The Bourbons: History of a Dynasty. *Leisure interests:* golf, the 18th century, watching Liverpool Football Club. *Address:* Bull Beck House, Four Acres, Brookhouse, Lancaster, LA2 9JW, England (home). *Telephone:* (1524) 770517. *E-mail:* j.shennan@lancaster.ac.uk (home).

SHENOUDA III, BA, BD; Egyptian ecclesiastic; b. 3 Aug. 1923; ed Cairo Univ. and Coptic Orthodox Theological Coll.; theological teacher and writer; fmr Bishop and Prof. of Theology, Orthodox Clerical Coll., Cairo; 1st Chair. Asscn of Theological Colls in the Near East; 117th Pope of Alexandria and Patriarch of the See of St Mark of Egypt, the Near East and All Africa (Coptic Orthodox Church) 1971–81, 1985; removed from post by Pres. Sadat and banished to desert monastery Wadi Natroun Sept. 1981, released Jan. 1985. *Address:* Coptic Orthodox Patriarchate, St Mark Cathedral, PO Box 9035, Anba Ruess, 222 Ramses Street, Abbasiya, Cairo, Egypt.

SHEPARD, Donald J., MBA; American insurance industry executive; ed Univ. of Chicago; began career with Life Investors Inc., Ia 1970, served in various man. and exec. positions including Exec. Vice-Pres. and COO 1985–89, Pres. and CEO AEGON USA (following acquisition of Life Investors by AEGON USA 1989) 1989–2002, Chair. Exec. Bd AEGON, The Hague 2002–08; mem. Bd of Dirs Mercantile Bankshares Corpn, European Financial Services Roundtable, US Chamber of Commerce, CSX Corpn, Financial Services Roundtable; Trustee Johns Hopkins Medicine, Johns Hopkins Univ.; mem. Bd of Visitors Univ. of Maryland Univ. Coll. *Address:* c/o Board of Visitors, University of Maryland University College, Office of the President, 3501 University Boulevard East, Adelphi, MD 20783, USA.

SHEPARD, Sam; American playwright, actor, director and screenwriter; b. (Samuel Shepard Rogers), 5 Nov. 1943, Fort Sheridan, Ill.; s. of Samuel Shepard Rogers and Jane Schook Rogers; m. O-Lan Johnson Dark 1969 (divorced); one s.; one s. one d. with Jessica Lange (q.v.); ed Duarte High School, Mount San Antonio Jr Coll. *Television appearances include:* Lily Dale 1996, Purgatory 1999, Hamlet 2000. *Plays include:* Cowboys and Rock Garden (double bill), Chicago, Icarus's Mother and Red Cross (triple bill; Obie Award) 1966, Melodrama Play 1966, The 4-H Club, La Turista (Obie Award) 1967, Forensic and the Navigators (Obie Award) 1968, The Unseen Hand (rock opera) 1969, Cowboy Mouth (with Patti Smith) 1971, The Mad Dog Blues 1971, The Tooth of Crime (Obie Award) 1973, Geography of a Horse Dreamer 1974, Black Dog Beast Bait, Operation Sidewinder, Shaved Splits, Rock Garden (included in Oh! Calcutta!), Curse of the Starving Class (Obie Award) 1978, Buried Child (Pulitzer Prize) 1979, True West 1980, Fool for Love 1982, A Lie of the Mind 1985 (New York Drama Critics Circle Award for Best Play

1986), States of Shock 1991, Simpatico 1994, Eyes for Consuela 1998, The Late Henry Moss 2000, The God of Hell 2004, Kicking a Dead Horse 2007. *Film appearances include:* Days of Heaven 1978, Resurrection 1980, Francis 1982, The Right Stuff 1983, Paris, Texas 1984, Country, Crimes of the Heart, Baby Boom, Defenceless 1989, Voyager 1991, Thunderheart 1992, The Pelican Brief 1994, Safe Passage 1995, The Good Old Boys 1995, Curtain Call 1997, The Only Thrill 1997, Snow Falling on Cedars 1999, One Kill 2000, All the Pretty Horses 2001, Shot in the Heart 2001, Swordfish 2001, Black Hawk Down 2001, The Pledge 2001, The Notebook 2004, Don't Come Knockin' 2005, Stealth 2005, Walker Payne 2006, Bandidas 2006, The Return 2006, Charlotte's Web (narrator) 2006, The Assassination of Jesse James by the Coward Robert Ford 2007, The Accidental Husband 2008. *Screenplay:* Zabriskie Point 1970, Paris, Texas (Palme d'Or, Cannes Film Festival 1984), Fool for Love 1985, Far North (also Dir) 1989, Silent Tongue (also Dir) 1994, Don't Come Knockin' 2005. *Publications:* Hawk Moon 1972, Motel Chronicles 1982, A Murder of Crows (novel) 1996, Cruising Paradise (autobiog.) 1996, Great Dream of Heaven (short stories) 2002, The Rolling Thunder Logbook 2005. *Address:* c/o ICM, 10250 Constellation Boulevard, Los Angeles, CA 90067, USA (office).

SHEPARD, Stephen Benjamin; American journalist, editor and academic; *Founding Dean, Graduate School of Journalism, City University of New York;* b. 20 July 1939, New York; s. of William Shepard and Ruth Shepard (née Tanner); m. Lynn Povich 1979; one s. one d.; ed City Coll., NY, Columbia Univ.; reporter and writer, Business Week 1966–75, Exec. Ed. 1982–84, Ed.-in-Chief 1984–2005; Founding Dean, Grad. School of Journalism, CUNY 2005–; Asst Prof. and Dir Walter Bagehot Fellowship Program in Econs and Business Journalism, Columbia Univ. 1975–76, mem. Bd of Visitors, Grad. School of Journalism 1998–2004; Sr Ed. Newsweek 1976–81; Ed. Saturday Review 1981–82; mem. American Soc. of Magazine Eds (Vice-Pres. 1990–92, Pres. 1992–94), Council on Foreign Relations, Overseas Press Club, Century Asscn; Gov. Soc. of American Business Eds and Writers; Gerald Coeb Foudation Lifetime Achievement Award 1999, Henry Johnson Fisher Award for Magazine Publisher of America 2000, Soc. of American Business Eds and Writers Distinguished Achievement Award 2005. *Address:* Graduate School of Journalism, City University of New York, 219 West 40th Street, New York, NY 10018 (office); 322 Central Park West, New York, NY 10025, USA (home). *Telephone:* (646) 758-7800 (office). *Website:* journalism.cuny.edu/about/deans-corner.php (office).

SHEPHARD OF NORTHWOLD, Baroness (Life Peer), cr. 2005, of Northwold in the County of Norfolk; **Gillian Patricia Shepard,** PC, MA, DL; British politician; b. 22 Jan. 1940; d. of Reginald Watts and Bertha Watts; m. Thomas Shephard 1975; two step-s.; ed North Walsham High School for Girls, St Hilda's Coll., Oxford; Educ. Officer and Schools Inspector 1963–75; Lecturer, Univ. of Cambridge Extra-Mural Bd 1965–87; Councillor Norfolk Co. Council 1977–89 (Chair. Social Services Cttee 1978–83, Educ. Cttee 1983–85); Chair. W Norfolk and Wisbech Health Authority 1981–85, Norwich Health Authority 1985–87; MP for SW Norfolk 1987–97, for Norfolk SW 1997–2005; Co-Chair. Women's Nat. Comm. 1990–91; Parl. Pvt. Sec. to Econ. Sec. to the Treasury 1988–89; Parl. Under-Sec. of State Dept of Social Security 1989–90; Minister of State (Treasury) 1990–92; Sec. of State for Employment 1992–93, for Agric., Fisheries and Food 1993–94, for Educ. 1994–95, for Educ. and Employment 1995–97; Shadow Leader of House of Commons and Shadow Chancellor of Duchy of Lancaster 1997–99; Opposition Spokesman on Environment, Transport and the Regions 1998–99; Deputy Chair. Conservative Party 1991–92, 2002–03; Vice-Pres. Hansard Soc. 1997–2003; mem. Council Univ. of Oxford 2000–; Hon. Fellow, St Hilda's Coll. 1991. *Publications:* The Future of Local Government 1991, Shephard's Watch 2000. *Leisure interests:* music, gardening, France. *Address:* House of Lords, London, SW1A 0PW, England (office). *Telephone:* (02) 7219-4457 (office). *E-mail:* westm@parliament.uk (office).

SHEPHERD, Cybill; American actress; b. 18 Feb. 1950, Memphis, Tenn.; d. of William Jennings Shepherd and Patty Shobe Micci; m. 1st David Ford 1978 (divorced); one d.; m. 2nd Bruce Oppenheim 1987; twin s.; fmr magazine cover girl; eight years of commercials for L'Oréal Préférence. *Films include:* The Last Picture Show 1971, The Heartbreak Kid 1973, Daisy Miller 1974, At Long Last Love 1975, Taxi Driver 1976, Special Delivery 1976, Silver Bears 1977, The Lady Vanishes 1978, Earthright 1980, The Return 1986, Chances Are 1988, Texasville 1990, Alice 1990, Once Upon A Crime 1992, Married to It 1993, The Last Word 1995, Open Window 2005. *Plays include:* A Shot in the Dark 1977, Vanities 1981, The Muse 1999, Marine Life 2000. *Television includes:* The Yellow Rose 1983–84, Moonlighting (Emmy Award 1985) 1985–89, Cybill 1994–98, Due East 2002, Martha Inc.: The Story of Martha Stewart (film) 2003, The Detective 2004, Martha Behind Bars (film) 2005. *Albums include:* Cybill Getz Better 1978, Vanilla 1979, Moonlighting 1984, Somewhere Down the Road 1990, Songs from the Cybill Show 2003, At Home with Cybill 2004. *Publication:* Cybill Disobedience 2000. *Website:* www.cybill.com (office).

SHEPPARD OF DIDGEMERE, Baron (Life Peer), cr. 1994, of Roydon in the County of Essex; **Allen John George Sheppard,** KB, KCVO, BSc; British company director; *Chairman, Namibian Resources;* b. 25 Dec. 1932, London; s. of John Baggott Sheppard and Lily Sheppard (née Palmer); m. 1st Peggy Damaris (née Jones) 1959 (divorced 1980); m. 2nd Mary Stewart 1980; ed Ilford Co. School, London School of Econs; with Ford 1958–68, Chrysler 1968–71, British Leyland 1971–75; with Grand Metropolitan 1975–96, CEO 1986–93, Chair. 1987–96; Pres. London First 1992–, Group Trust PLC 1994–2001, McBride PLC 1995, GB Railways PLC 1996–2004, Unipart 1996–, OneClickHR, Unipart Group of Cos; Vice-Pres. Brewers' Soc. 1987–; Chair. Bd of Trustees, Prince's Youth Business Trust 1990–94, Advisory Bd, British American Chamber of Commerce 1991–94, Business in the Community

1994–97, Namibian Resources 2004–; Gov. LSE 1989–; Dir High Point Rendel 1997–2003, One Click HP PLC, Wyne PLC 2000–, Transware PLC 2001–03; Chancellor Middlesex Univ. 2000–; Hon. Fellow and Gov. LSE;; Hon. LLD (South Bank Univ.) 1994; Dr hc (Westminster) 1998, (Middx) 1999, (LSE) 2001; Gold Medal, British Inst. of Man. 1993. *Publications:* Your Business Matters 1958, Maximum Leadership 1995, various articles in professional journals. *Leisure interests:* reading, gardens, red setter dogs. *Address:* House of Lords, Westminster, London, SW1A 0PW (office); Namibian Resources plc, 302 High Street, Croydon, Surrey, CR0 1NG, England. *Telephone:* (20) 7219-5353 (House of Lords) (office). *E-mail:* namibianplc@btconnect.com. *Website:* www.namibianresources.com.

SHER, Sir Antony, Kt, KBE; British actor, artist and author; b. 14 June 1949, Cape Town, South Africa; Civil partnership with Gregory Doran 2005; ed Webber Douglas Acad. of Dramatic Art; numerous appearances at Nat. Theatre, RSC (RSC Assoc. Artist 1982–) and in West End; directorial debut with Fraser Grace's play Breakfast with Mugabe at The Other Place, Stratford-upon-Avon; Hon. DLitt (Liverpool) 1998 (Exeter) 2003, (Warwick) 2007; Best Actor Awards from The Evening Standard Awards, for performance as Richard III (RSC) 1985, Olivier Award for Best Actor, Soc. of West End Theatres, for performances as Richard III, as Arnold in Torch Song Trilogy 1985, for Stanley 1997, Best Actor Award, Martini TMA Awards, for performance as Titus Andronicus 1996, Peter Sellers Evening Standard Film Award for performance as Disraeli in Mrs. Brown 1998. *Plays include:* John, Paul, Ringo and Bert (Lyric Theatre), Teeth 'n' Smiles, Cloud Nine, A Prayer for My Daughter (Royal Court Theatre), Goosepimples (Hampstead and Garrick Theatres), King Lear, Tartuffe, Richard III, Merchant of Venice, The Revenger's Tragedy, Hello and Goodbye, Singer, Tamburlaine the Great, Travesties, Cyrano de Bergerac, The Winter's Tale, Macbeth, The Roman Actor, The Malcontent, Othello (RSC), Torch Song Trilogy (Albery Theatre), True West, Arturo Ui, Uncle Vanya, Titus Andronicus (Royal Nat. Theatre), Stanley (Royal Nat. Theatre, Circle in the Square Theater, New York), Mahler's Conversion (Aldwych Theatre), ID (Almeida Theatre) 2003, Primo (Royal Nat. Theatre, London) 2005, (Music Box Theater, New York—Drama Desk and Outer Critics' Circle Awards for Best Solo Performance 2005–06, S. Africa Fleur du Cap Award for Best Solo Perfomrance 2005) 2005, Kean (Apollo Theatre) 2007. *Films include:* Mark Gertler: Fragments of a Biography 1981, Shadey 1985, The Young Poisoner's Handbook 1995, Alive and Kicking (aka Indian Summer) 1996, Mrs. Brown 1997, Shakespeare in Love 1998, Churchill: The Hollywood Years 2004, Three and Out 2008. *Television includes:* ITV Playhouse – Cold Harbour, Pickersgill People – The Sheik of Pickersgill 1978, Collision Course 1979, The History Man 1981, Tartuffe 1983, Changing Step 1990, The Land of Dreams 1990, The Comic Strip Presents… – The Crying Game 1992, Genghis Cohn 1993, Moonstone 1996, Hornblower: The Frogs and the Lobsters 1999, Macbeth 2001, The Jury (mini-series) 2002, Home 2003, Murphy's Law – Jack's Back 2004, Primo 2007. *Publications:* Year of the King (theatre journal) 1986, Middlepost (novel) 1988, Characters (paintings and drawings) 1989, Changing Step (screenplay) 1989, The Indoor Boy (novel) 1991, Cheap Lives 1995, Woza Shakespeare! (theatre journal, co-written with Gregory Doran) 1996, The Feast (novel) 1998, Beside Myself (autobiography) 2001, I.D. (play) 2003, Primo (play) 2005, Primo Time (theatre journal) 2005, The Giant (play) 2007. *Address:* c/o Mic Cheetham Literary Agency, 50 Albemarle Street, London, W1S 4BD, England (office). *Telephone:* (20) 7495-2002 (office). *E-mail:* info@miccheetham.com (office). *Website:* www.miccheetham.com (office).

SHERCHAN, Amik; Nepalese politician. Chair. People's Front Nepal (Janamorcha Nepal); Deputy Prime Minister and Minister of Health and Population 2006–07. *Address:* c/o Ministry of Health and Population, Singh Durbar Plaza, Ramshah Path, Kathmandu, Nepal (office).

SHERIMKULOV, Megetkan; Kyrgyzstani politician and diplomatist; b. 17 Nov. 1939, Tchapaevo (Kyrgyzia); m.; three d.; ed Kyrgyz Univ., Moscow Univ.; mem. CPSU 1962–91; Lecturer, Kyrgyz Univ., Prof. 1995–; Prof., Centre of Strategic Studies and Political Sciences, Kyrgyz Nat. Univ. 1998–;Instructor, Div. of Science, Cen. Cttee CP of Kyrgyzia 1971–73; Sec., Party Cttee, Kyrgyz Univ. 1973–76; Sec., Issyk-Kul Regional CP Cttee 1976–80; Head, Div. of Propaganda, Cen. Cttee CP, Kyrgyz SSR 1986–90; Chair. Supreme Soviet (now Uluk Kenesh) of Repub. of Kyrgyzstan 1990–94; cand. for presidency of Kyrgyzstan 1995; Amb. to Turkey 1996–2002. *Address:* c/o Ministry of Foreign Affairs, 720050 Bishkek, Razzakova, 59, Kyrgyzstan (office).

SHERMAN, Bernard (Barry), PhD; Canadian pharmaceuticals industry executive; *Chairman and CEO, Apotex Incorporated;* m.; four c.; ed Univ. of Toronto, Massachusetts Inst. of Tech., USA; major shareholder of Barr Laboratories, New York; f. Apotex Inc. 1974, now Chair. and CEO. *Address:* Apotex Inc., 150 Signet Drive, Weston, ON M9L 1T9, Canada (office). *Telephone:* (416) 749-9300 (office). *Fax:* (416) 401-3835 (office). *Website:* www.apotex.com (office).

SHERMAN, Cindy, BA; American artist; b. 1954, Glen Ridge, NJ; ed State Univ. Coll., Buffalo; work in perm. collections including Museum of Fine Arts, Houston, Museum Boymans-van Beuningen, Rotterdam, Museum of Modern Art, New York, Tate Gallery, London, Centre Pompidou, Paris, Stedelijk Museum, Amsterdam, Metropolitan Museum of Art, New York, San Francisco Museum of Modern Art. *Address:* c/o Metro Pictures, 519 West 24th Street, New York, NY 10011, USA.

SHERMAN, Martin; American playwright; b. 1938, New Jersey; ed Boston Univ. *Plays include:* A Solitary Thing 1963, Fat Tuesday 1966, Next Year in Jerusalem 1968, Night Before Paris 1969, Things Went Badly In Westphalia 1971, Passing By 1974, Soaps 1975, Cracks 1975, Rio Grande 1976, Blackout

1978, Bent 1978, Messiah 1982, When She Danced 1985, Madhouse In Goa 1989, Some Sunny Day 1996, Rose 1999, Chain Play 2001, Passage To India 2002, Absolutely! (Perhaps) 2003,. *Films include:* The Clothes in the Wardrobe 1992, Indian Summer 1996, Mrs Henderson Presents 2005. *Address:* c/o Casarotto Ramsay and Associates Ltd, National House, 60-65 Wardour Street, London, W1V 3HP, England.

SHERPAO, Aftab Ahmad Khan; Pakistani politician; b. 20 Aug. 1944; f. Pakistan People's Party—PPP (Sherpao Group), breakaway faction, faction rejoined PPP 2002; fmr Chief Minister of North-West Frontier Prov.; fmr Minister of Water and Power, of Inter-Prov. Co-ordination and of Kashmir Affairs, Northern Areas and State and Frontier Regions; Minister of the Interior 2004–07. *Address:* c/o Pakistan People's Party, 8, Street 19, F-8/2, Islamabad, Pakistan. *Telephone:* (51) 2255264. *Fax:* (51) 2282741. *E-mail:* ppp@comsats.net.pk. *Website:* www.ppp.org.pk.

SHERRINGTON, David, MA, PhD, FRS, FInstP; British physicist and academic; *Wykeham Professor of Physics Emeritus, University of Oxford;* b. 29 Oct. 1941, Blackpool; s. of the late James A. Sherrington and Elfreda Cameron; m. Margaret Gee-Clough 1966; one s. one d.; ed St Mary's Coll. Middlesbrough and Univ. of Manchester; Asst Lecturer in Theoretical Physics, Univ. of Manchester 1964–67, Lecturer (on leave) 1967–69; Asst Research Physicist, Univ. of Calif., San Diego 1967–69; Lecturer in Solid State Physics, Imperial Coll. London 1969–74, Reader 1974–83, Prof. of Physics 1983–89; Cadre Supérieur, Inst. Laue Langevin, Grenoble 1977–79; Wykeham Prof. of Physics, Univ. of Oxford 1989–2008, now Emer. Prof.; Ulam Scholar, Los Alamos Nat. Lab., USA 1995–96; Fellow, New Coll. Oxford 1989–; Visiting Prof., Hong Kong Univ. of Science and Tech. 1994, Ecole Normale Supérieure, Paris 2003; External Prof., Santa Fe Inst. 2004–; Visiting Scientist, IBM 1975, Schlumberger-Doll Research 1984, Inst. for Advanced Study, Princeton 2003, Univ. of California, Santa Barbara 2003, Univ. of California, San Diego 2008, Los Alamos Nat. Lab.; Fellow, American Physical Soc.; mem. European Acad. of Sciences; Bakerian Lecture, Royal Soc. 2001, Dirac Medal and Prize, Inst. of Physics 2007. *Publications:* articles in scientific journals, co-ed. of seven books. *Leisure interests:* travel, wine, theatre, walking, skiing. *Address:* Rudolf Peierls Centre for Theoretical Physics, 1 Keble Road, Oxford, OX1 3NP (office); 53 Cumnor Hill, Oxford, OX2 9EY, England (home). *Telephone:* (1865) 273963/996 (office); (1865) 862057 (home). *Fax:* (1865) 273947 (office). *Website:* www-thphys.physics.ox.ac.uk/people/DavidSherrington/ (office).

SHERSTYUK, Col-Gen. Vladislav Petrovich, CandTechSc; Russian security official and academic; *Director, Institute of Information Security Issues, Lomonosov Moscow State University;* b. 16 Oct. 1940, Novoplastunovskaya, Krasnodar Region; m.; one s.; ed Moscow State Univ., Higher KGB School; with KGB 1966–; Head Dept of Radioelectronic Espionage Telecommunications, Fed. Agency of Govt Telecommunications and Information 1995–98, Deputy Dir-Gen. 1998, Dir-Gen. 1998–99; First Deputy Sec., Security Council 1999; Dir Fed. Agency of Govt Communications and Information (FAPSI) 2001–02; currently Dir Inst. of Information Security Issues, Lomonosov Moscow State Univ.; Order of Labour Red Banner 1975, Order for Service to Motherland 1996 and numerous other decorations; USSR State Prize 1978, State Prize of Russian Fed. 1996, Red Star 1988. *Address:* Institute of Information Security Issues, Lomonosov Moscow State University, 19234 Moscow, Michurinsky pr. 1, Russia (office). *Telephone:* (495) 932-89-58 (office). *Fax:* (495) 939-20-96 (office). *Website:* www.iisi.msu.ru (office).

SHERWIN, Susan, BA, PhD, FRSC; Canadian academic; *University Research Professor Emerita, Department of Philosophy, Dalhousie University;* b. 6 June 1947, Toronto; ed York Univ., Canada, Stanford and Case Western Reserve Univs, USA; Asst Prof., Dept of Philosophy, Dalhousie Univ. 1974–80, Assoc. Prof. 1980–90, Chair. Dept of Philosophy 1982–87, Prof. 1990–, Co-ordinator Women's Studies 1987–88, 1996–2000, also teaches in Gender and Women's Studies Program, Faculty of Health Professions; mem. Canadian Comm. for UNESCO (Ethics Cttee 2001–03, Sectoral Comm. on Natural and Social Sciences 2001–03), Canadian Soc. for Women in Philosophy (Co-ordinator 1985–86, 1994–95), Canadian Philosophical Asscn (Exec. Cttee 1983–85), Canadian Research Inst. for Advancement of Women, Nova Scotia Women's Health Educ. Network, Canadian Soc. of Bioethics, Int. Asscn of Bioethics (Bd mem. 1995–2000), Int. Feminist Approaches to Bioethics (Jt Coordinator 2001–03); mem. Ethics and Equity Cttee, Royal Coll. of Physicians and Surgeons of Canada, Research Council, Canadian Inst. of Advanced Research 2002–05, CIHR Standing Cttee on Ethics 2000–06; CAUT Sarah Shorten Award 2000, American Soc. for Women and Philosophy Distinguished Woman Philosopher 2004, Killam Prize in Humanities 2006, Canadian Bioethics Soc. Lifetime Achievement Award 2007. *Publications:* Moral Problems in Medicine (co-ed.) 1983, No Longer Patient: Feminist Ethics and Health Care 1992, Health Care Ethics in Canada (co-ed.) 1995, The Politics of Women's Health: Exploring Agency and Autonomy (ed.), Women 1992, Medicine, Ethics, and the Law (co-ed.) 2002, Engaged Philosophy (co-ed.) 2007, Agency and Embodiment (co-ed.) 2009; contribs: numerous articles in journals including Journal of Medicine and Philosophy, Humane Medicine, Bioethics, Politeia. *Address:* Department of Philosophy, Dalhousie University, Halifax, NS B3H4P9, Canada (office). *Telephone:* (902) 494-3393 (office). *Fax:* (902) 494-3518 (office). *E-mail:* susan.sherwin@dal.ca (office). *Website:* philosophy.dal.ca (office).

SHERWOOD, James Blair, BEcons; American shipping industry executive; b. 8 Aug. 1933; s. of William Earl Sherwood and Florence Balph Sherwood; m. Shirley Angela Masser Cross 1977; two step s.; ed Yale Univ.; Lt USNR 1955–58; Man. French Ports, later Asst Gen. Freight Traffic. Man., US Lines Co. 1959–62; Gen. Man. Container Transport Int. Inc. 1963–64; Founder and Pres. Sea Containers Ltd 1965–2006 (resgnd); Chair. Orient-Express Hotels

Ltd 1987–2006, GE Senco SRL 1998–2006, Silja Oy 1999–2006; with Mark Birley est. Harry's Bar Club, London 1979; restored and brought into service Venice Simplon-Orient-Express 1982; Trustee Solomon R. Guggenheim Foundation 1989; Hon. Citizen of Venice, Italy 1990; Order of the Southern Cross (Brazil) 2004. *Publication:* James Sherwood's Discriminating Guide to London 1975. *Leisure interests:* skiing, tennis, sailing. *Address:* Hinton Manor, Hinton Waldrist, Oxon., SN7 8SA, England (home). *Telephone:* (1865) 820260 (home).

SHERZAI, Gul Agha; Afghan politician; *Governor of Nangarhar;* Gov. of Kandahar prior to Taliban takeover, in exile in Quetta, Pakistan 1994–2001, reinstated as Gov. of Kandahar 2002–04, Gov. of Nangarhar 2004–; Minister of Urban Affairs 2003; fmr Minister of Urban Devt and Housing; Minister of Public Works –2004; fmr ministerial adviser to Pres. Hamid Karzai. *Address:* Office of the Governor, Jalalabad, Nangarhar Province, Afghanistan (office).

SHESHINSKI, Eytan, PhD; Israeli economist and academic; *Sir Isaac Wolfson Professor of Public Finance, Department of Economics, Hebrew University of Jerusalem;* b. 29 June 1937, Haifa; s. of Alice Sheshinski and Baruch Sheshinski; m. Ruth H. Sheshinski 1960; four d.; ed Hebrew Univ. Jerusalem, Mass Inst. of Tech., USA; Asst Prof., Harvard Univ. 1966–67; Lecturer, then Assoc. Prof. 1971–74, Prof. of Econs 1974–, now Sir Isaac Wolfson Prof. of Public Finance, Hebrew Univ. of Jerusalem; Visiting Prof., Harvard Univ., Stanford Univ., MIT, Columbia Univ.; Chair. Bd Koor Industries 1990–, Khevrat Ha'Ovdim 1989–92; Fellow, Econometric Soc.; mem. Royal Swedish Acad. of Sciences, American Acad. of Arts and Sciences; American Acad. of Arts and Sciences Award; Dr hc (Stockholm School of Econs). *Publications:* The Optimal Linear Income Tax (Review of Econ. Studies 1972), Inflation and Costs of Price Adjustment (Review of Econ. Studies 1977), Optimum Pricing, Inflation and the Costs of Price Adjustments (ed.) 1993. *Leisure interests:* hiking, sailing. *Address:* Hebrew University of Jerusalem, Mount Scopus, 91905 Jerusalem, Israel (office). *Telephone:* (2) 5883144 (office); (2) 5105681. *Fax:* (2) 5883357 (office); (2) 5195353. *E-mail:* mseytan@mscc.huji.ac.il (office). *Website:* economics.huji.ac.il/sheshinski/index.html (office).

SHESTAKOV, Sergey Vasilyevich; Russian biologist; *Chairman, Department of Genetics, Moscow State University;* b. 23 Nov. 1934, Leningrad; s. of Vasily Ivanovich Shestakov and Ludmila Shestakova; m. Galina A. Grigorieva 1964; one s.; ed Moscow State Univ.; on staff, Moscow State Univ. 1957–, Chair. Dept of Genetics 1980–; Dir Int. Biotech. Centre; Dir N. Vavilov Inst. of Genetics, USSR (now Russian) Acad. of Sciences 1988–91; Corresp. mem. Russian Acad. of Sciences 1987, mem. 2000; Chair. Scientific Council on Genetics 1988–2004; mem. Russian Biotech. Acad., Int. Acad. of Science, New York Acad. of Sciences; Visiting Prof., Mich. State Univ., USA 1992; Fulbright-Hays Fellowship 1975; UNESCO Fellowship Award 1985; Hon. Distinguished Scientist of Russian Fed. 1995, Hon. Prof. (Univ. of Wales) 2000; USSR State Prize 1988, Lomonosov Prize 1995, N. Vavilov Gold Medal 1997, P. Ehrlich Medal (Germany) 2006. *Publications:* papers and articles on molecular genetics of DNA repair and recombination, photosynthesis, nitrogen-fixation, resistance to stresses. *Leisure interest:* sports. *Address:* Department of Genetics, Moscow State University, 119899 Moscow, Russia (office). *Telephone:* (495) 939-35-12 (office). *Fax:* (495) 939-35-12 (office). *E-mail:* shestakovgen@mail.ru (office).

SHESTAKOVA, Tatyana Borisovna; Russian actress; b. 23 Oct. 1948, Leningrad; d. of Boris Shestakov and Aleksandra Shestakova; m. Lev Dodin 1972; ed Leningrad Theatre Inst.; Leningrad Theatre for Children 1972–75; Leningrad Comedy Theatre 1975–80; Bolshoi Drama Theatre 1980–83; Maly Drama Theatre 1983–; has also played for Moscow Arts Theatre; toured abroad 1983, 1987–2001; Dir Stars In the Morning Sky 2005; USSR State Prize 1986, RSFSR Merited Artist 1987, Nat. 'Triumph' Prize 1992. *Films include:* Solyonyy pyos (Salty Dog) 1973, Tsarevich Prosha 1974, Idi i smotri (Go and See) 1985, Podsudimyy (The Accused) 1986. *Theatre roles include:* Liza (The House) 1980, Sonya (Uncle Vanya) 1982, She (The Meek One) 1985, Anfisa (Brothers and Sisters) 1986, Anna (Stars of the Morning Sky) 1987, Lebyadkina (The Possessed), Lubov Andreevna (The Cherry Orchard) 1994, Dame Elegant (Roberto Zucco) 1994, Katya and Ivanova (Claustrophobia) 1994, Anna Petrovna (Play Without a Name) 1997, Sonya (Chevengur) 2000, Arcadina (The Seagull) 2001. *Leisure interests:* travelling, books, music. *Address:* Maly Drama Theatre, Rubinstein Str. 18, St Petersburg (office); Michurinskaya St 1-140, St Petersburg, Russia (home). *Telephone:* (812) 113-21-08 (office). *Fax:* (812) 113-33-66 (office); (812) 113-33-66. *E-mail:* mdt@sp.wplus.net (office).

SHETREET, Shimon; Israeli politician, legal scholar and academic; *Professor of Law, Hebrew University of Jerusalem;* b. 1946, Morocco; ed Hebrew Univ., Chicago Univ.; Sec., Council for Public Justice; Chair. Cttee on Broadcasting Authority Law; Chair. Int. Conf. on Legal Matters; Chair. Bd of Dirs Afro-Asian Inst. of the Histadrut; Prof. of Law, Hebrew Univ. 1973–; Minister of Economy, Science and Tech. 1992–95, of Religious Affairs 1995–96; mem. Knesset 1988–96; served on numerous cttees 1988–92, including the Landau Comm. on the Israeli Court System, the Council for Admin. Courts, plenum of the Israel Broadcasting Authority 1984–87; Sr Deputy Mayor of Jerusalem 1998–2003; Dir Leumi Bank; mem. Labour Party; Ethics Prize 1994. *Publications:* numerous books including The Good Land Between Power and Religion, Judges on Trial 1976, Justice in Israel 1994, Women in Law 1998; and articles on legal matters. *leisure interests* Bible study. *Address:* Hebrew University of Jerusalem, Mount Scopus, Jerusalem 91905, Israel (office). *Telephone:* 2-5882534 (office). *Fax:* 2-5883042 (office); 2-5864503 (home). *E-mail:* mshetree@mscc.huji.ac.il (office); shetreet@gmail.com (home). *Website:* mishpatim.mscc.huji.ac.il (office); law.mscc.huji.ac.il/law1/newsite/english.html (office).

SHETTY, Salil, MSc, MBA; Indian international organization official; *Director, Millennium Campaign, United Nations;* b. 3 Feb. 1961, Mumbai; ed Bangalore Univ., Indian Inst. of Man., Ahmedabad, London School of Econs, UK; joined ActionAid 1985, former postings include Africa and India, CEO 1998–2003; Dir UN Millennium Campaign 2003–; Bd mem. The Overseas Devt Inst., London, Agence France-Presse Foundation, Paris; mem. Advisory Council, merican-Indian Foundation, New York, Strategic Planning Group, Amnesty International. *Address:* United Nations Millennium Campaign, 304 E.45th Street, Suite 604, New York, NY 10017, USA (office). *Telephone:* (212) 906-5126 (office). *Fax:* (212) 906-6057 (office). *E-mail:* salil.shetty@undp.org (office). *Website:* www.endpoverty2015.org (office).

SHEVARDNADZE, Eduard; Georgian politician and fmr head of state; b. 25 Jan. 1928, Mamati, Larchkhuti, Transcaucasian SFSR (now in Georgia); s. of Ambrosi Shevardnadze and Sophio Pateishvili; m. Nanuli Tsagareishvili 1950 (died 2004); one s. one d.; ed Party School of the Cen. Cttee, CP of Georgia and Kutaisi Pedagogical Inst.; mem. CPSU 1948–91; Komsomol and party work 1946–56; Second Sec. 1956–57, First Sec., Komsomol in Georgia 1957–61; First Sec., Mtskheti raion 1961–63, Pervomaisky raion, Tbilisi, CP of Georgia 1963–64; First Deputy Minister 1964–65, Minister of Public Order (renamed Ministry of Internal Affairs 1968) 1965–72; First Sec., Tbilisi City Cttee of Cen. Cttee, CP of Georgia 1972; mem. Cen. Cttee, CP of Georgia 1958–64, 1966–91, mem. Politburo 1972–91, First Sec. 1972–85; mem. Cen. Cttee of CPSU 1976–91, Cand. mem. Politburo 1978–85, mem. 1985–90; Deputy to USSR Supreme Soviet 1978; mem. Political Consultative Council 1991; Minister of Foreign Affairs 1985–90, Nov.–Dec. 1991; Head of Soviet Foreign Policy Assen 1991–92; mem. Presidential Council 1990–91; Founder mem. Bd Democratic Reform Movt 1991; Chair. Georgian State Council March–Oct. 1992; Chair. Parl. of Georgia and Head of State 1992–95, Pres. of Georgia 1995–2003 (resgnd); Hon. GCMG 2000; various other decorations; Dr hc from numerous univs. *Publications:* My Choice 1991, The Future Belongs to Freedom 1991, The Great Silk Road 1999, Thoughts About The Past and Future 2006. *Address:* c/o Office of the President, 0134 Tbilisi, P. Ingorovka 7, Georgia.

SHEVCHENKO, Andrei; Ukrainian professional footballer; b. 29 Sept. 1976, Dvrkivshchyna; m. Kristen Pazik; two s.; forward; teams played for include Dynamo Kiev 1994–1999 (118 league appearances, 60 goals), AC Milan, Italy 1999–2006 (debut 29 August 1999 versus Lecce), Chelsea 2006–; first capped by Ukraine 25 March 1995; won Italian Cup (Coppa Italia), Champions League, Supercup with AC Milan 2003, Serie A 2004; 91 Serie A goals from 151 appearances; Ukrainian Footballer of the Year 1997, 1999–2001, 2004–05, Serie A Foreign Footballer of the Year 2000, European Footballer of the Year 2004. *Leisure interests:* pool, tennis, cars. *Address:* c/o Gary Dixon, Wasserman Media Group, LLC 5th Floor, 33 Soho Square, London, W1D 3QU, England. *Telephone:* (20) 7009-6000. *Fax:* (20) 3230-1053. *E-mail:* gdixon@wmgllc.com. *Website:* www.sheva7.com.

SHEVCHENKO, Col-Gen. Yuri Leonidovich, DMed; Russian politician and physician; *President, National Medical-Surgical Centre;* b. 7 April 1947, Yakutsk; m.; two c.; ed Leningrad Acad. of Mil. Medicine; teacher, then Prof., then Head of Chair., Leningrad Mil. Acad. of Medicine 1980–92, Head of Acad. 1992–99; Chief Cardiosurgeon St Petersburg and Leningrad Region, Head, Regional Centre of Cardiac Surgery 1992–99; Minister of Public Health 1999–2004; Rep. of Russian Fed. to WHO Exec. Cttee –2004; Pres. Nat. Medical-Surgical Centre 2004–; Vice-Pres. Russian Acad. of Natural Sciences; Vice-Pres. Peter's Acad. of Sciences and Arts; mem. Bd F. Lang Scientific Soc. of Cardiologists; Corresp. mem. Russian Acad. of Medical Sciences. *Publications:* over 300 articles. *Address:* c/o Ministry of Health, 101431 Moscow, Rakhmanovskii per. 3, Russia (office).

SHEYNIS, Viktor Leonidovich, DrSc; Russian historian, politician and economist; *Chief Research Fellow, Institute of World Economy and International Relations;* b. 16 Feb. 1931, Kiev; s. of Leonid M. Sheynis and Liah O. Kimelfeld; m. Alla K. Nazimova 1953; ed Leningrad Univ.; history teacher in secondary school 1953–56; manual worker, Kirov factory, Leningrad 1958–64; teacher, Leningrad Univ. 1966–75; on staff as researcher at Inst. of World Economy and Int. Relations (IMEMO) 1975–92, Chief Research Fellow 2000–; co-author of Russian Constitution and electoral laws 1993–99; People's Deputy 1990–93, mem. State Duma (Parl.) 1993–99; mem. Supreme Soviet of Russia 1991–93; Co-Founder Consent in Name of Progress faction 1992–93; mem. Council of Reps of 'Democratic Russia' Movt 1990–93, Yabloko Movt 1993–95, Yabloko Party 1995–, Political Bureau and Fed. Council; mem. Cttee on Legislation and Reform of the Judicial System; Imre Nagy Medal (Hungary) 1993. *Publications:* over 250 including Developing Nations at the Turn of the Millennium 1987, Capitalism, Socialism and Economic Mechanism of Present-day Production 1989, Die Präsidentenwahlen in Russland: Ergebnisse und Perspektiven, Osteuropa 1996, O caminho histórico da Revolução de Outubro visto sob a prisma de 1997 1997, Il tormentato cammino della Constituzione russa 1998, Wie Russland gewaklt hat: Osteuropa 2000, The Constitution: In Between Dictatorship and Democracy 2004, The Rise and Fall of Parliament: Watershed Years in Russian Politics 1985–93 (two vols) 2005. *Leisure interests:* tourism, cinematography, reading. *Address:* Institute of World Economy and International Relations, Profsoyuznaya str. 23, 117859 Moscow (office); Vavilova str. 91, corp. 1, Apt 41, 117335 Moscow, Russia (home). *Telephone:* (495) 128-56-46 (office); (495) 128-81-54 (office); (495) 132-73-15 (home). *Fax:* (495) 120-65-75 (office). *E-mail:* nazimova@mtu-net.ru (home). *Website:* www.imemo.ru (office).

SHI, Dahua; Chinese railway industry executive; *Chairman and Executive Director, China Railway Group Limited;* ed Southwest Jiaotong Univ., Cen. Communist Party School; joined China Railway Group Ltd 1997, Deputy Sec. to CCP Cttee, China Railway Construction Corpn 1995–97, Deputy Sec. to

CCP Cttee, China Railway Eng Corpn (CRECG) 1997–98, Sec. 1998–2007, Deputy Gen. Man. CRECG 2002–06, Chair. 2006–, Chair. and Exec. Dir China Railway Group Ltd 2007–; Alt. mem. 16th CCP Cen. Cttee 2002–07, 17th CCP Cen. Cttee 2007–; Dir of Transportation Professionals Co-operation Cttee of Consultant Council for the Promotion of Econ. and Tech. Cooperation of China-Spain Forum; Deputy Dir Steering Cttee of Nat. Construction Enterprise Career Man. Certification and Construction Enterprises Qualifications Admin and Research; recognized as a sr economist by Ministry of Personnel 2007. *Address:* China Railway Group Ltd, 26 Lianhuachi Nanli, Beijing 100055, People's Republic of China (office). *E-mail:* info@crecg.com (office). *Website:* www.crecg.com (office).

SHI, Dazhen; Chinese electrical engineer and government official; b. 1932, Wuxi City, Jiangsu Prov.; ed Shandong Inst. of Tech. 1955; joined CCP 1978; Vice-Minister of Energy and Resources 1988–93, Minister of Electric Power Industry 1993–98; Gen. Man. State Electric Power Corpn 1997–98; mem. Standing Cttee 9th CPPCC Nat. Cttee 1998–2003, Vice-Chair. Econ. Sub-cttee 1998–2003; Alt. mem. 13th Cen. Cttee CCP 1988–92, 14th Cen. Cttee CCP 1992–97. *Address:* c/o National Committee of Chinese People's Political Consultative Conference, 23 Taipingqiao Street, Beijing, People's Republic of China (office).

SHI, Guangsheng; Chinese politician; b. Sept. 1939, Changli, Hebei Prov.; ed Beijing Inst. of Foreign Trade; joined CCP 1965; clerk, Deputy Section Dir, later Deputy Gen. Man. China Metals and Minerals Import and Export Corpn 1974–86; Special Commr Ministry of Foreign Econ. Relations and Trade, Shanghai 1986–88; Dir Import and Export Dept, Ministry of Foreign Trade 1988–91, Asst Minister of Foreign Econ. Relations and Trade 1991–93; Vice-Minister of Foreign Trade and Econ. Co-operation 1993–98, Minister 1998–2003; fmr Exec. Vice-Chair. World Econ. Devt Declaration Conf. *Address:* c/o Ministry of Commerce, 2 Dongchangan Jie, Dongcheng Qu, Beijing 100731, People's Republic of China (office).

SHI, Jiliang; Chinese economist and banker; *Chairman, Board of Supervisors, China Merchants Bank Co., Ltd;* b. Feb. 1945; Vice-Pres. Heilongjiang br., Agricultural Bank of China 1983–88, Vice-Pres. Tianjing br. 1988–91, Pres. Tianjing br. 1991–94, Pres. Agricultural Bank of China 1994–97; Vice-Pres. People's Bank of China 1997–2003; Vice-Chair. China Banking Regulatory Comm. 2003–05; currently Chair. Bd of Supervisors China Merchants Bank Co. Ltd; mem. 10th Nat. Cttee CPPCC. *Address:* China Merchants Bank Co., Ltd, China Merchants Bank Tower, 7088 Shennan Blvd, Shenzhen 518040, People's Republic of China (office). *Telephone:* (755) 83198888 (office). *Fax:* (755) 83195112 (office). *E-mail:* office@cmbchina.com (office). *Website:* www.cmbchina.com (office).

SHI, Jiuyong, MA; Chinese lawyer and professor of international law; *Judge, International Court of Justice;* b. 9 Oct. 1926, Zhejiang; m. Zhang Guoying 1956; one s.; ed St John's Univ., Shanghai and Columbia Univ., New York, USA; Asst Research Fellow, Inst. of Int. Relations, Beijing 1956–58; Sr Lecturer, Assoc. Prof. of Int. Law, Foreign Affairs Coll. Beijing 1958–64; Research Fellow in Int. Law, Inst. of Int. Law, Beijing 1964–73, Inst. of Int. Studies, Beijing 1973–80; Prof. of Int. Law, Foreign Affairs Coll. Beijing 1984–93, Foreign Econ. Law Training Centre of Ministry of Justice; Legal Adviser, Ministry of Foreign Affairs 1980–93, Chinese Centre of Legal Consultancy, Office of Chinese Sr Rep. Sino-British Jt Liaison Group (on question of Hong Kong) 1985–93; Adviser to Chinese Soc. of Int. Law –2003; mem. American Soc. of Int. Law; mem. Standing Cttee Beijing Cttee of CPPCC 1988–93, mem. 8th Nat. Cttee 1993–98; mem. Int. Law Comm. 1987–93, Chair. 1990; Judge, Int. Court of Justice 1994–, Vice-Pres. 2000–03, Pres. 2003–06; mem. Advisory Bd, The Global Community Yearbook of Int. Law and Jurisprudence; Pres. Curatorium Xiamen Acad. of Int. Law 2005–; Hon. Prof. Eastern China Univ. of Political Science and Law 2001–, Hon. Pres. Chinese Soc. of Int. Law 2004–. *Publications:* numerous publs on int. law. *Leisure interest:* classical music. *Address:* International Court of Justice, Peace Palace, Carnegieplein 2, 2517 KJ The Hague, Netherlands (office). *Telephone:* (70) 302-23-23 (office). *Fax:* (70) 364-99-28 (office). *E-mail:* information@icj-cij .org (office). *Website:* www.icj-cij.org (office).

SHI, Xiushi; Chinese politician; b. July 1942, Shangqiu, Henan Prov.; ed Beijing Civil Eng Inst.; joined CCP 1978; technician and engineer, later Deputy Dir Building Materials Research Inst. 1964–80; Engineer and Deputy Chief, Building Materials Industry Div., Heavy Industry Bureau, State Econ. Comm. 1980–86; Deputy Div. Chief, later Div. Chief, Office of Tourist Industry Coordination 1986–88; Deputy Dir, later Dir Bureau of the State Council 1988–96; Deputy Sec.-Gen. State Council 1996–2000; Vice-Gov. of Guizhou 2001, Gov. 2001–; Deputy Sec. Guizhou Prov. Cttee 2000–06; mem. 16th CCP Cen. Cttee 2002–07; Deputy Dir 10th Financial and Econ. Cttee of NPC 2006–. *Address:* c/o Guizhou Provincial People's Government, Guiyang 550004, Guizhou Province, People's Republic of China (office).

SHI, Adm. Yunsheng; Chinese naval officer (retd); b. Jan. 1940, Fushun City, Liaoning Prov.; ed PLA Air Force Aviation School and PLA Navy Acad.; joined PLA 1956, CCP 1960; pilot, Squadron Leader, Deputy Group Commdr and Deputy Regt Commdr Naval Aviation 1962–70; Deputy Commdr Naval Fleet Aviation 1976–81; Div. Commdr Naval Aviation 1981–83; Commdr Naval Fleet Aviation 1983–90; Deputy Commdr PLA Naval Aviation Dept 1990–92; Deputy Commdr PLA Navy 1992–96, Commdr 1996–2003; rank of Adm. 2000; Del. 13th CCP Nat. Congress 1987–92; mem. 15th CCP Cen. Cttee 1997–2002, 16th CCP Cen. Cttee 2002–07. *Address:* c/o Ministry of National Defence, Jingshanqian Jie, Beijing, People's Republic of China (office). *Telephone:* (1) 6370000 (office).

SHI, Zhengrong, BSc, MSc, PhD; Chinese/Australian electrical engineer, research scientist and business executive; *Chairman and CEO, Suntech Power Holdings Company Ltd;* b. 1963, Jjiangsu Prov.; m.; two c.; ed Jilin Univ., Chinese Acad. of Sciences, Univ. of NSW, Australia; Sr Research Scientist and Leader, Thin Film Solar Cells Research Group, Centre of Excellence for Photovoltaic Eng, Univ. of NSW, Australia 1992–95; Research Dir and Exec. Pacific Solar Pty, Australia 1995–2001; Founder, CEO and Chair. Suntech Power Holdings Co., Ltd (manufacturer of photovoltaic cells for use in solar panels), Wuxi, China 2001–; Wuxi Prize for Excellence in Innovation and Pioneering, Nat. Prize for Excellent Achievements by Homecoming Chinese, named by Time magazine one of its 'Heroes of the Environment'. *Publications:* numerous scientific papers. *Address:* Suntech Power Holdings Company Ltd, 17-6 Changjiang South Road, New District, Wuxi 214028, Jiangsu Province People's Republic of China (office). *Telephone:* (86510) 85318888 (office). *Fax:* (86510) 85343049 (office). *E-mail:* ir@suntech -power.com (office). *Website:* www.suntech-power.com (office).

SHI, Zhong-ci; Chinese computer scientist and academic; *Chairman of the Academic Committee, Laboratory of Scientific and Engineering Computing, Chinese Academy of Sciences;* b. 5 Dec. 1933, Ningpo Co., Zhejiang Prov.; ed Fudan Univ., Steklov Inst. of Math., Moscow; Chair. Dept of Math. and Dir of Computer Center, Univ. of Science and Tech. 1984-88; Dir Inst. of Computational Math. and Scientific/Engineering Computing (fmrly Computer Center), Chinese Acad. of Sciences 1987–91, Sr Research Fellow 1987–94; currently Chair. of Academic Cttee, Lab. of Scientific and Eng Computing (LSEC); Vice-Pres. Chinese Math. Soc. 1988-1995; Vice-Pres. Chinese Soc. of Computational Math. 1985-1989, Pres. 1994–; mem. Chinese Sciences Acad. 1992–. *Leisure interests:* travel, classical music. *Address:* State Key Laboratory of Scientific and Engineering Computing (LSEC), Room 208, Institute of Computational Mathematics, Chinese Academy of Sciences, POB 2719, Beijing 100080, People's Republic of China (office). *Telephone:* 62587583 (office). *Fax:* 62542285 (office). *E-mail:* shi@lsec.cc.ac.cn (office). *Website:* www .cc.ac.cn (office); lsec.cc.ac.cn/~shi/homepage.html.

SHI, Zongyuan; Chinese politician; *Chairman, Guizhou Provincial People's Congress Standing Committee;* b. July 1946, Baoding, Hebei Prov.; ed Northwest Ethnic Inst.; worker, People's Govt, Hezheng Co., Gansu Prov. 1968–80, CCP Co. Cttee 1978–80; joined CCP 1978; fmrly clerk in various govt offices in Hezheng Co., Gansu Prov.; Deputy Magistrate Hezheng Co. (Dist) People's Court 1981–82, Magistrate 1981–84; Deputy Chief Magistrate Linxia Hui Autonomous Pref., Gansu Prov., Deputy Sec. and then Sec. CCP Linxia Hui Autonomous Pref. Cttee 1984–93; Dir Propaganda Dept of CCP Gansu Prov. Cttee 1993–98; Dir Propaganda Dept of CCP Jilin Prov. Cttee, also Vice-Sec. CCP 1998–2000; Dir Press and Publications Admin and Dir State Bureau of Copyrights 2000–05; Sec. Guizhou Provincial CCP Cttee 2005–; Chair. Provincial People's Congress Standing Cttee, Guizhou Prov. 2008–; Alt. mem. 14th CCP Cen. Cttee 1992–97, 15th CCP Cen. Cttee 1997–2002, mem. 16th CCP Cen. Cttee 2002–07; mem. 17th CCP Cen. Cttee 2007–. *Address:* Guizhou Provincial People's Congress, Guizhou, People's Republic of China (office).

SHIBATA, Ai; Japanese swimmer; b. 14 May 1982, Fukuoka Prefecture; ed Nat. Inst. of Fitness and Sports, School of Physical Educ.Univ.; gold medal 800m. freestyle, Athens Olympics 2004; silver medal 400 m. freestyle, bronze medal 800 m. freestyle, World Championships, Montreal 2005; bronze medal 400 m. freestyle, bronze medal 1500 m. freestyle, World Championships, Melbourne 2007; swims for Team Arena Club. *Address:* c/o Japan Amateur Swimming Federation, Kishi Memorial Hall, 1-1-1 Jinnan, Shibuya-Ku -50, Tokyo, Japan. *Telephone:* (3) 34 8123 06. *Fax:* (3) 34 81 0942. *Website:* www .descente.co.jp/arena-jp/fan/ai.html.

SHIEH, Samuel C.; Taiwanese banker and academic; *Member, Advisory Committee, Research Center for Taiwan Economic Development;* ed Univ. of Minnesota; fmr Prof.; Gov. Cen. Bank of China 1989–94; Nat. Policy Adviser to Pres. 1994–2000; Chair. Industrial Bank of Taiwan 1999–2002; Sec.-Gen. Vice-Chair. Straits Exchange Foundation 1997–2002, fmr Sec.-Gen.; mem. Advisory Cttee Research Center for Taiwan Econ. Devt, Nat. Cen. Univ. *Address:* Research Center for Taiwan Economic Development, No. 38, Wuchuan Li, Chung-li, Tao-yuan 320, Taiwan (office). *Telephone:* (3) 4277491 (office). *Fax:* (3) 4263067 (office). *E-mail:* rcted@cc.ncu.edu.tw (office).

SHIELDS, Brooke Christa Camille, BA; American actress and model; b. 31 May 1965, New York; d. of Francis Shields and Teri Schmon; m. Andre Agassi (q.v.) 1997 (divorced 1999); m. Chris Henchy 2001; two d.; ed Princeton Univ.; began modelling in Ivory Soap commercials 1966, later for Calvin Klein jeans and Colgate toothpaste. *Theatre includes:* Grease (Broadway) 1994–95, Wonderful Town (Broadway) 2004, Chicago (Adelphi Theatre, London) 2005. *Films:* Communion (aka Alice, Sweet Alice) 1976, Pretty Baby 1977, King of the Gypsies 1978, Wanda Nevada 1978, Just You and Me, Kid 1978, Tilt 1979, The Blue Lagoon 1979, Endless Love 1980, Sahara 1983, The Muppets Take Manhattan 1984, Brenda Starr 1986, Speed Zone! 1988, Backstreet Dreams (aka Backstreet Strays) 1989, Running Wild 1992, Freaked 1993, The Seventh Floor 1993, Freeway 1996, The Misadventures of Margaret 1998, The Weekend 1999, Black and White 1999, The Bachelor 1999, After Sex 2000, Mariti in affitto 2004, The Easter Egg Adventure 2005, Bob the Butler 2005, The Midnight Meat Train 2008. *Television:* After the Fall (film) 1974, The Prince of Central Park (film) 1977, Wet Gold (film) 1984, The Diamond Trap (film) 1988, I Can Make You Love Me (film) 1993, Un Amore americano (film) 1994, Nothing Lasts Forever (mini series) 1995, Suddenly Susan (series) 1996, The Almost Perfect Bank Robbery (film) 1998, What Makes a Family (film) 2001, Widows (mini series) 2002, Miss Spider's Sunny Patch Kids (film, voice) 2003, Gone But Not Forgotten (mini series) 2004. *Publication:* Down Came the Rain: A Mother's Story of Depression and Recovery 2005. *Address:* c/o Christa Inc., 10061 Riverside Drive, Suite 1013, Toluca Lake, CA 91602, USA.

SHIELDS, Hon. Margaret Kerslake, QSO, BA, MP; New Zealand politician; *Chairwoman, Greater Wellington Regional Council;* b. 18 Dec. 1941, Wellington; d. of Ernest Blake Porter and Dorothy Bessie Porter (née Levy); m. Patrick John Shields 1960; two d.; ed Victoria Univ., Wellington; researcher, Consumers' Inst. and Dept of Statistics; MP for Kapiti 1981–; Minister of Customs and of Consumer Affairs 1984–87, of Women's Affairs, Consumer Affairs and Statistics 1987–88, 1989–90, of Customs 1988–89, Assoc. Minister of Educ. 1989–90; mem. Wellington Regional Council 1995–, Deputy Chair. 1998–2001, Chair. 2001–; Vice-Pres. Local Govt, NZ; Co-founder, Pres. and Nat. Sec., Soc. for Research on Women; Dir UN Int. Research and Training Inst. for the Advancement of Women (INSTRAW) 1991–94; Co-convenor of Second UN Women's Convention 1975; mem. Wellington Hosp. Bd 1977–80, Complaints Review Tribunal of NZ Human Rights Comm. 1994–2000, Council of Victoria Univ. of Wellington 1996–99; Deputy Chair. Hutt Valley Dist Health Bd 2000–01; Chair. Plenary Session, Int. Conf. of Women Mayors and Elected Councillors, Phitsanulok, Thailand 2001; Govt Del. to UN Int. Women's Year Conf. Mexico 1975, participated in IPU Conf., Seoul 1983, speaker, IPU Conf., Geneva 1989; mem. Labour. *Leisure interests:* hiking, gardening, music, drama. *Address:* Greater Wellington Regional Council, 142–146 Wakefield Street, Wellington (office); 23 Haunui Road, Pukerua Bay, Porirua, New Zealand (home). *Telephone:* (4) 802-0346 (office); (4) 239-9949 (home). *Fax:* (4) 239-9084 (home). *E-mail:* margaret.shields@gw.govt.nz (office); marg.shields@xtra.co.nz (home).

SHIGEHARA, Kumiharu, BL; Japanese economist; *President, International Economic Policy Studies Association;* b. 5 Feb. 1939, Maebashi; s. of Seizaburo Shigehara and Rutsu Tanabe; m. Akiko Yoshizawa 1965; one s. one d.; ed Maebashi High School, Univ. of Tokyo and Univ. of Poitiers; economist, Bank of Japan 1962–70; admin. OECD 1970–71, Prin. Admin. 1971–72, Head, Monetary Div. 1972–74; Councillor for Policy Planning, Bank of Japan 1974–76, Man. Int. Affairs 1976–80; Deputy Dir Gen. Econs Branch, OECD 1980–82; Gen. Man. Bank of Japan 1983–87; Dir Gen. Econs Branch, OECD 1987–89; Dir-Gen. Inst. for Monetary and Econ. Studies and Chief Economist, Bank of Japan 1989–92; Head, Econs Dept and Chief Economist, OECD 1992–97, Deputy Sec.-Gen. 1997–99; Special Adviser Int. Friendship Exchange Council 2001; Head, Int. Econ. Policy Studies Group 2002–08; Pres. Int. Econ. Policy Studies Asscn 2008–; Hon. PhD; Dr hc (Liège) 1998; Hozumi Special Award, Univ. of Tokyo 1960. *Publications:* The Role of Monetary Policy in Demand Management (co-author) 1975, Europe After 1992 1991, The Problems of Inflation in the 1990s (ed.) 1992, Evolving International Trade and Monetary Regimes 1992, Causes of Declining Growth in Industrialised Countries 1992, Price Stabilization in the 1990s 1993, Long-term Tendencies in Budget Deficits and Debt 1995, The Options regarding the Concept of a Monetary Policy Strategy 1996, Monetary and Economic Policy: Then and Now 1998, Causes and Implications of East Asian Financial Crises 1998, International Aspects of Competition Policy 1999, Monetary Policy and Economic Performance 2001, Looking for Models in Pursuit of Economic Prosperity 2002, Managing the International Economic Crisis 2008. *Leisure interests:* golf, tennis, hiking. *Address:* 4-7-11-802, Seta, Setagaya-ku, Tokyo, Japan (office). *Telephone:* (3) 3709-7969 (office). *Fax:* (3) 3709-7969 (office). *E-mail:* office.shigehara@online.fr (office). *Website:* office.shigehara.online.fr (office).

SHIH, Chi-Yang, LLM, DJur; Taiwanese politician; b. 5 May 1935, Taichung City; m. Jeanne Tchong-Koei Li 1968; ed Nat. Taiwan Univ. and Univ. of Heidelberg; Asst Dept of Law, Nat. Taiwan Univ. 1959–62, Assoc. Prof. 1967–71, Prof. (part-time) 1971–84; Research Asst Inst. of Int. Relations, Nat. Chengchi Univ. 1967–69, Research Fellow 1969–71; Deputy Dir 5th Section, Cen. Cttee, Kuomintang 1969–72, Deputy Dir Dept of Youth Activities 1972–76; Admin. Vice-Minister, Ministry of Educ. 1976–79; Political Vice-Minister, Ministry of Educ. 1979–80, Ministry of Justice 1980–84; Minister of Justice 1984–88; Vice-Premier 1988–93; Sec.-Gen. Nat. Security Council 1993–94; Pres. Judicial Yuan 1994–99. *Address:* c/o Judicial Yuan, 124 Chungching S Road, Sec. 1, Taipei, Taiwan.

SHIH, Choon Fong, MSc, PhD; Singaporean scientist and university administrator; *President, National University of Singapore;* ed Singapore Polytechnic, Harvard Univ., USA; Research Fellow, Harvard Univ. 1973–74; Leader, Fracture Research Group, Corporate Research Lab., General Electric, NY 1974–81; Visiting Assoc. Prof., Brown Univ. 1981–83, Assoc. Prof. 1983–86, Prof. 1986–97; Founding Dir, Inst. of Materials Research and Eng, Singapore 1996–99; Founding Pres., Materials Research Soc. of Singapore; Deputy Vice-Chancellor, Nat. Univ. of Singapore 1997–2000, Vice-Chancellor and Pres. 2000–; Chair. Asscn of Pacific Rim Univs (APRU); fmr consultant to NASA, Oak Ridge Nat. Lab., Nuclear Regulatory Comm.; Dir Agency for Science, Tech. and Research, Biomedical Research Council, Science and Eng Research Council, Inst. of Policy Studies, Singapore Int. Fed.; Foreign Assoc., Nat. Acad. of Eng (USA); several awards including Swallow Award, George Rankin Irwin Medal (American Soc. for Testing and Materials). *Publications:* over 200 papers in academic journals. *Address:* Office of the President, National University of Singapore, 21 Lower Kent Ridge Road, Singapore 119077, Singapore (office). *Telephone:* 6516-2432 (office). *Fax:* 6779-5481 (office). *E-mail:* uprshih@nus.edu.sg (office). *Website:* www.nus.edu.sg/president (office).

SHIH, Jonney, BSc, MBA; Taiwanese business executive; *Chairman, ASUSTeK Computer Inc.;* b. 1951; ed Nat. Taiwan Univ., Nat. Chao-Tung Univ.; fmr research and devt engineer at Acer Inc.; Chair. and CEO ASUSTeK Computer Inc. 1993–2008, Chair. 2008–; Outstanding Tech. Man. Award, Chinese Soc. for Man. of Tech. 2006, Outstanding Entrepreneur Award, Chinatimes and Taiwan DHL 2006. *Address:* ASUSTeK Computer Inc., 15 Li-Te Road, Peitou, Taipei 112, Taiwan (office). *Telephone:* (2) 2894-3447 (office). *Fax:* (2) 2892-6140 (office). *E-mail:* info@asus.com (office). *Website:* www.asus.com (office).

SHIH, Ming-Teh; Taiwanese politician; m. Linda Gail Arrigo; fmr political prisoner in Taiwan; Leader, Taiwan Democratic Progressive Party 1993; mem. Taiwan Legis. Council; initiated Million Voices Against Corruption-Chen Must Go campaign 2006. *Address:* Room 601, 10 Tsingtao E Road, Taipei, Taiwan.

SHIH, Stan; Taiwanese business executive; b. 18 Dec. 1944, Taiwan; m. Carolyn Yeh; two s. one d.; ed Nat. Chiao Tung Univ.; with Unitron Industrial Corpn 1971–72, Qualitron Industrial Corpn 1972–76; Chair. and CEO The Acer Group (electronics co.) –2004 (retd); Pres.'s Special Rep. to APEC Econ. Leaders Meeting, Australia 2007; title of Dato (Malaysia) 1994; Asian Star of the Year, Businessweek magazine 2004, named as one of Asian Heroes, Time magazine 2006. *Publications:* more than 100 articles on man., marketing etc. *Address:* c/o Acer Inc., 21/F, 88 Hsintaiwuh Road, Sec. 1, Hsih Chih Cheng, Taipei, Taiwan (office).

SHIHAB, Hussain, MSc; Maldivian politician and diplomatist; *Ambassador to Saudi Arabia;* b. 1949; m.; six c.; ed Kuban Agric. Inst., Russia; Under-Sec., Ministry of Home Affairs and Social Services 1975, Ministry of Agric. 1976–78; Man. TV Maldives 1978–81, Deputy Dir, then Dir 1985; Dir of Environmental Affairs, Ministry of Home Affairs and Social Services 1986–88, Dir of Environmental Affairs, Ministry of Planning and the Environment 1988–93, Deputy Minister 1993–95, July–Sept. 1998; Dir South Asia Co-operative Environment Programme 1995–98; apptd Perm. Rep. to the UN 1998; del. to numerous UN meetings on the environment, including Conf. on Environment and Devt 1992 and Global Conf. on the Sustainable Devt of Small Island Developing States 1994; fmr Deputy Minister of Foreign Affairs; fmr Minister of State for the Arts; Amb. to Saudi Arabia 2007–; formulated Maldives' first nat. environment action plan; Silver Pen Award 1987. *Films:* Fidhaa 1985, Hadmiya 1993, Rihun 2002, Vissaradmuni 2005. *Publications:* Ochid Eyanarse Maa (short stories) 1983; papers on the environment and sustainable devt presented at int. confs. *Leisure interests:* film, reading, writing. *Address:* Ministry of Foreign Affairs, Boduthakurufaanu Masu, Malé 20-02, Maldives (office). *Telephone:* 3323400 (office). *E-mail:* hshihab@foreign.gov (office).

SHIHAB, Mohamed, BEcons; Maldivian economist and politician; *Speaker of the People's Majlis;* b. 2 Oct. 1957, Male'; s. of Ibrahim Shihab and Jameela Ibrahim; ed James Cook Univ. of N Queensland, Australia; Project Officer, Nat. Planning Agency, Male' 1980–81, Asst Dir 1981–82; Under-Sec., Ministry of Planning and Devt 1982–85, Sr Under-Sec. 1985–89, Dir of External Resources 1989–94; Dir Maldives Transport and Contracting Co. Ltd 1994–99; MP for Dhaal atoll 1985–2005, for Male' 2005–; Man. Dir Maldives Post Ltd 2006–; mem. Bd of Dirs Maldives Transport and Contracting Co. Ltd 1991–99, Bank of Maldives 1994–96, Maldives Tourism Devt Corpn PLC 2007–08. *Address:* Bageechaage, Male' 2191, Maldives (office). *Telephone:* (960) 777-1014 (office). *Website:* www.majlis.gov.mv/pm/english (office).

SHIHAB-ELDIN, Adnan, BSc, MSc, PhD; Kuwaiti engineer and international organization official; *Senior Research Advisor, Oxford Institute for Energy Studies;* b. 1943; ed Univ. of Calif., Berkeley, USA; trained as nuclear engineer; Asst Prof. of Physics, then Vice-Rector of Academic Affairs, Kuwait Univ. 1970–80; Dir-Gen. Kuwait Inst. for Scientific Research 1976–86; Dir of UNESCO Regional Office for Science and Tech. and UNESCO Rep. in Egypt, Sudan and Yemen 1991–99; Dir Africa, E Asia and Pacific Div., Dept of Tech. Cooperation, Int. Atomic Energy Agency (IAEA) 1999–2001; Dir Research Div., OPEC 2001–06, Acting Sec.-Gen. 2005; currently Sr Research Advisor, Oxford Inst. for Energy Studies, UK; serves as consultant to numerous public and pvt. orgs; mem. UN Advisory Cttee on Science and Tech. for Devt, NY, Arab Thought Forum, Amman, Jordan, Int. Scientific Council for Science and Tech. Policy Devt, UNESCO; mem. numerous professional socs. *Address:* Oxford Institute for Energy Studies, 57 Woodstock Road, Oxford, OX2 6FA, England (office). *Telephone:* (1865) 311377. *Fax:* (1865) 310527 (office). *E-mail:* information@oxfordenergy.org (office). *Website:* www.oxfordenergy.org (office).

SHIKAPWASHA, Lt-Gen. Ronnie; Zambian politician and fmr air force officer; *Minister of Information and Broadcasting Services;* b. 25 Dec. 1948; fmr Amb. to UN; mem. of Parl. for Keembe constituency; Minister of Home Affairs 2003–05, 2006–08, of Foreign Affairs 2005–06, of Information and Broadcasting Services 2008–, Acting Health Minister 2006. *Address:* Ministry of Information and Broadcasting Services, Independence Avenue, POB 32245, Lusaka, Zambia (office). *Telephone:* (21) 1228202 (office). *Fax:* (21) 1253457 (office). *Website:* www.mibs.gov.zm (office).

SHIKLOMANOV, Igor A.; Russian hydrologist and research institute director; *Director, State Hydrological Institute;* b. 28 Feb. 1939, Tver Region; ed Leningrad Hydrometerological Inst.; joined State Hydrological Inst. as Engineer 1961, Deputy Dir for Science 1972–81, Dir 1981–; Chair. Water Resources Working Group, World Meteorological Org. 2000–; Deputy Chair. Russian Nat. Cttee, UNESCO/Int. Hydrological Programme (IHP) 1990–; mem. Scientific Steering Cttee for the Global Energy and Water Cycle Experiment (GEWEX) World Climate Research Program 1992–; Chair. Intergovernmental Council of UNESCO's IHP 1992–94, Working Group on Water Resources of the WMO Comm. for Hydrology 2000–; a lead author of Intergovernmental Panel on Climate Change (IPCC) working group third Assessment Report 1998–2000; Vice-Pres. Int. Comm. on Surface Water 1999–; Corresp. mem. Russian Acad. of Natural Sciences 1991, Academician 2001; Int. Hydrology Prize (co-recipient) 2001, Tyler Prize for Environmental Achievement (co-recipient) 2006. *Publications:* World Water Resources at the Beginning of the Twenty-First Century, Water Resources as a Challenge of the Twenty-First Century; more than 200 publs on problems of water man., hydrological computations and ecological studies of water systems, large inter-basin water transfers and assessments of the impact of climate variability and change on water resources. *Address:* State Hydrological Institute, St Petersburg 199053, Russia (office). *Telephone:* (812) 213-35-17 (office). *Fax:* (812) 213-10-28 (office). *E-mail:* support@hydrology.ru (office). *Website:* www.hydrology.ru (office).

SHILLER, Robert James, BA, SM, PhD; American economist and academic; *Stanley B. Resor Professor of Economics, Yale University;* b. 29 March 1946, Detroit, Michigan; ed Univ. of Michigan, Mass. Inst. of Tech.; Asst Prof. of Econs, Univ. of Minn. 1972–74; Assoc. Prof. of Econs, Univ. of Pa 1974–80; Research Fellow Nat. Bureau of Econs Research, Cambridge, Mass. 1980–81; Visiting Prof. MIT 1981–82; Stanley B. Resor Prof. of Econs, Yale Univ. 1982–, also Prof., School of Man.; Co-founder Case Shiller Weiss Inc., Cambridge, Mass. 1991, Macro Securities Research LLC 1999; research in behavioural finance and behavioural macroecons at Nat. Bureau of Econ. Research; Guggenheim Fellowship 1991, Paul Samuelson Award 1996, Commonfund Prize 2000. *Publications:* Market Volatility 1989, Macro Markets: Creating Institutions for Managing Society's Largest Economic Risks 1993, Irrational Exuberance 2000, The New Financial Order 2003, Animal Spirits: How Human Psychology Drives the Economy, and Why It Matters for Global Capitalism 2009. *Address:* Department of Economics, Yale University, PO Box 208281, New Haven, CT 06520-8281, USA (office). *Telephone:* (203) 432-3708 (office). *Fax:* (203) 432-6167 (office). *E-mail:* robert.shiller@yale.edu (office). *Website:* www.econ.yale.edu/~shiller (office).

SHILOV, Aleksandr Maksovich; Russian artist; b. 6 Oct. 1943, Moscow; s. of Ludmila Sergeevna Pazhenova; ed V. I. Surikov Inst. of Fine Arts, Moscow; painted series of portraits of contemporary village people, social and political leaders, astronauts, intellectuals and clergy, also present-day social phenomena, genre paintings, landscapes and still lifes; f. Moscow State A. Shilov Picture Gallery 1997, now Art Dir; mem. Acad. of Social Sciences 1997–, Council for Culture and Art 1999–; Corresp. mem. Russian Acad. of Arts 1997–2001, mem. 2001–; Order for Services to the Motherland (Fourth Degree) 1997, (Third Degree) 2004, Order of Francisk Skorina (Belarus) 2003; Lenin Komsomol Prize 1977, People's Artist of RSFSR 1981, People's Artist of USSR 1985; asteroid named after him 1992. *Address:* Romanov per. 3, Apt 71, 103009 Moscow, Russia. *Telephone:* (495) 203-42-08. *Fax:* (495) 203-69-75 (office). *E-mail:* shilov_gallery@mail.ru (office). *Website:* www.shilov.su (office).

SHILTON, Peter Leslie, MBE, OBE; British fmr professional football player; b. 18 Sept. 1949, Leicester; s. of Les Shilton and May Shilton; m. Sue Shilton 1970; ed King Richard III School, Leicester; played for English Youth team; played for Leicester City 1966–74, Stoke City 1974–77, Nottingham Forest 1977–82, Southampton 1982–87, Derby Co. 1987–92, Plymouth Argyle 1992–94, Bolton 1995, Leyton Orient 1996–97; Man. Plymouth Argyle FC 1992–95; became first England goalkeeper to win more than 100 caps at European Championships 1988; record English league appearances (1,005); record English cap holder (125), conceding only 80 goals. *Address:* c/o Champions PR Ltd, Meadow End, Leake Road, Costock, Loughborough, LE12 6XA, England. *Telephone:* (8453) 313031. *Website:* www.petershilton.com.

SHIMADA, Masao, LLD; Japanese university chancellor (retd); *Professor Emeritus, Meiji University;* b. 29 Sept. 1915, Tokyo; m. Tsumae Shimada 1945; ed Univs of Tokyo and Beijing; mem. Inst. of Oriental Culture, Tokyo Univ. 1941–47; Prof., Meiji Univ. 1947–84, Chancellor 1984–92, Prof. Emer. 1992–. *Publications:* Study on Social History of Liao 1951, Study on the Constitution of Liao 1954, Study of Official Systems of Liao 1978, Study on the History of Liao Dynasty 1979, Compilation of Modern Codes at the Late Ch'ing Period 1980, Study of the Northern Eurasian Legal System 1981, Study of the Special Laws for Mongolia in the Ch'ing Dynasty 1982, Studies on the Mongolian Laws 1986, History of Liao 1991, Studies in the Effectiveness of the Ch'ing Mongol Laws 1992, North Asian Legal History 1995, Preliminary Study of Shisha Code 2003. *Address:* No. 601, Mansion-Ichigaya, 82, Ichigaya Yakuoji, Shinjuku, Tokyo, Japan. *Telephone:* (3) 3268-0290.

SHIMALI, Mustafa Jassem ash-; Kuwaiti civil servant and politician; *Minister of Finance;* served in several sr govt posts, including Under-Sec. for Econ. Affairs 1986–2006 and Under-Sec. for Finance 2006–07; Minister of Finance 2007–, Acting Minister of Commerce and Industry 2008–. *Address:* Ministry of Finance, PO Box 9, 13001 Safat, al-Morkab Street, Ministries Complex, Kuwait City, Kuwait (office). *Telephone:* 2480000 (office). *Fax:* 2404025 (office). *E-mail:* webmaster@mof.gov.kw (office). *Website:* www.mof.gov.kw (office).

SHIMAMURA, Yoshinobu; Japanese politician; b. 27 March 1934; ed Gakushuin Univ.; with Nippon Oil Corpn 1956–71; fmr Parl. Vice-Minister of Agric., Forestry and Fisheries; mem. House of Reps (LDP) for Tokyo 16th Dist., fmr Chair. Cttee on Transport; Minister of Educ. 1995–96, of Agric., Forestry and Fisheries 1997–98, 2004–05; fmr Chair. LDP Diet Affairs Cttee. *Address:* c/o Liberal-Democratic Party—LDP, 1-11-23, Nagata-cho, Chiyoda-ku, Tokyo 100-8910, Japan. *Telephone:* (3) 3581-6211. *E-mail:* koho@ldp.jimin.or.jp. *Website:* www.jimin.jp.

SHIMELL, William; British singer; b. 23 Sept. 1952, Ilford, Essex; s. of W. Shimell and F.E. Shimell; m. Olga Slavka 1996; ed Westminster Abbey Choir School, St Edward's School, Oxford, Guildhall School of Music and Drama, Nat. Opera Studio, London; best known for interpretations of Don Giovanni, Count Almaviva (Marriage of Figaro) and Don Alfonso (Così fan Tutte), has sung in opera houses worldwide including La Scala, Milan, Metropolitan Opera House, New York, Paris Opéra, Rome Opera, Vienna Staatsoper, Covent Garden, London; Assoc. Guildhall School of Music and Drama; numerous recordings. *Leisure interests:* sailing, cooking. *Address:* IMG Artists, The Light Box, 111 Power Road, London, W4 5PY, England (office). *Telephone:* (20) 7957-5800 (office). *Fax:* (20) 7957-5801 (office). *E-mail:* salmansi@imgartists.com (office). *Website:* www.imgartists.com (office).

SHIMIZU, Kayoko; Japanese nurse and politician; *Vice-Chairman, Asian Population and Development Association;* b. 1936; ed Faculty of Medicine, Univ. of Tokyo; fmr Dir Nursing Div., Health and Welfare Ministry; elected mem. House of Councillors (LDP) 1989, Chair. House of Councillors Cttee on Educ.; Parl. Vice-Minister for Labour; Dir-Gen. Environment Agency 1999–2000; Sec.-Gen. Secr. of Japan Parliamentarians Fed. for Population; Vice-Chair. Asian Population and Devt Asscn. *Address:* Asian Population and Development Association, da Vinci Shinjuku-gyoen, Bldg. 3F, 1-5-1 Shinjuku, Shinjuku-Ku, Tokyo 160-0022, Japan (office). *Telephone:* (3) 33582211 (office). *Fax:* (3) 33582233 (office).

SHIMIZU, Masataka; Japanese business executive; *President, Tokyo Electric Power Company, Inc. (TEPCO);* ed Keio Univ.; joined Tokyo Electric Power Co., Inc. (TEPCO) 1968, served as Head of Supplies Div., Man. Dir 2004–06, Vice-Pres. 2006–08, Pres. 2008–; Vice Chair. of the Bd Nippon Keidanren. *Address:* Tokyo Electric Power Co., Inc., 1-1-3 Uchisaiwai-cho, Chiyoda-ku, Tokyo 100-8560, Japan (office). *Telephone:* (3) 4216-1111 (office). *Fax:* (3) 4216-2539 (office). *E-mail:* info@tepco.co.jp (office). *Website:* www.tepco.co.jp (office).

SHIMIZU, Shinobu; Japanese transport industry executive; m.; ed Dept of Econs, Hitotsubashi Univ.; joined Tokyu Corpn 1953, Pres. Tokyo Express Electric Railway 2001, Chair. and Rep. Dir –2005, currently mem. Bd of Dirs; Sr Vice-Pres. Japan Airline System Corpn 2002; apptd Chair. Asscn of Japanese Pvt. Railways 2001; mem. Man. Council, Devt Bank of Japan 2004. *Address:* Tokyu Corporation, 5-6 Nanpeidai-cho, Shibuya-ku, Tokyo 150-8511, Japan (office). *Telephone:* (3) 3477-6111 (office). *Fax:* (3) 3462-1690 (office). *Website:* www.tokyu.co.jp (office).

SHIMIZU, Yasuyuki; Japanese mining executive; *Chairman and Representative Director, Nippon Mining Holdings Inc.;* Exec. Vice-Pres. Nippon Mining and Metals Co. 1999; Exec. Vice-Pres. Toho Titanium Co. 1999–2000, Pres. 2000–01; Sr Man. Dir and Chief Div. Officer, Corp. Support Div., Nippon Mining Holdings, Inc. (fmrly Japan Energy Co.) 1998–2001, Chair. and Rep. Dir 2001–03, CEO 2003, Pres. and Rep. Dir 2003–06, Chair. and Rep. Dir 2006–; Chair. Japan Titanium Soc. *Address:* Nippon Mining Holdings, Inc., 10-1, Toranomon 2-chome, Minato-ku, Tokyo 105-0001, Japan (office). *Telephone:* (3) 5573-5170 (office). *Fax:* (3) 5573-6784 (office). *E-mail:* info@shinnikko-hd.co.jp (office). *Website:* www.shinnikko-hd.co.jp (office).

SHIMOGAICHI, Yoichi; Japanese business executive; *Adviser, JFE Holdings Inc.;* b. 26 Aug. 1934; two s.; ed Univ. of Tokyo; joined NKK Corpn 1958, Gen. Man. Sales Co-ordination, Export and Corp. Planning Depts 1981–86, mem. Bd of Dirs, Gen. Man. Corp. Planning Dept 1987, Man. Dir 1989, Sr Man. Dir, Deputy Dir Steel Div. 1991, apptd Exec. Vice-Pres., Exec. Dir Steel Div. 1994, Exec. Vice-Pres. 1997, apptd Pres. 1997, Pres., CEO 2000–02, Chair. of Bd 2002, Pres., Co-CEO and Rep. Dir JFE Holdings Inc. (jt holding co. of NKK Corpn and Kawasaki Steel) 2002–05, Adviser 2005–; exec. mem. Bd of Dirs Japan Fed. of Econ. Orgs 1997; mem. Export and Import Transaction Council 1996–98, Coal Mining Council 1997; Dir Japan Iron and Steel Fed. 1997. *Address:* JFE Holdings, Inc., 1-1-2 Marunouchi, Chiyoda-ku, Tokyo, 100-0005, Japan. *Telephone:* (3) 3217-4049 (office). *Fax:* (3) 3214-6110 (office). *Website:* www.jfe-holdings.co.jp (office).

SHIMOMURA, Osamu, BS, MS, PhD; Japanese organic chemist and marine biologist; *Senior Scientist Emeritus, Woods Hole Marine Biological Laboratory;* b. 27 Aug. 2008, Kyoto; m. Akemi Shimomura; two c.; ed Nagasaki Univ., Nagoya Univ.; Asst, Faculty of Pharmaceutical Sciences, Nagasaki Univ. 1958–60; Research Biochemist, Dept of Biology, Princeton Univ. 1960–82; Adjunct Assoc. Prof., Boston Univ. Medical School 1982–84, Adjunct Prof. of Physiology and Biophysics 1984, now Prof. Emer.; Sr Scientist, Woods Hole Marine Biological Lab. 1982–2001, Sr Scientist Emer. 2001–; Pearse Prize, Royal Soc. for Microscopy 2004, Emile Chamot Award, Microscopy Soc. of Ill. 2005, Asahi Award 2006, Nobel Prize for Chem. (jtly) 2008. *Address:* c/o Marine Biological Laboratory, 7 MBL Street, Woods Hole, MA 02543, USA (office). *Telephone:* (508) 548-3705 (office). *Fax:* (508) 289-7423 (office). *E-mail:* oshimomura@mbl.edu (office). *Website:* www.mbl.edu (office).

SHIMOMURA, Setsuhiro; Japanese business executive; *Representative Executive Officer, President and CEO, Mitsubishi Electric Corporation;* b. 1945, Tottori Pref.; joined Mitsubishi Electric Corpn in 1969, first served as an engineer in Himeji Works, named to Mitsubishi Electric's Bd of Dirs 2001–, Exec. Vice-Pres. and Group Pres. of Building Systems 2004–06, Rep. Exec. Officer, Pres. and CEO Mitsubishi Electric Corpn 2006–. *Address:* Mitsubishi Electric Corpn, Tokyo Bldg, 2-7-3, Marunouchi, Chiyoda-ku, Tokyo 100-8310, Japan (office). *Telephone:* (3) 3218-2111 (office). *E-mail:* info@mitsubishi.com (office). *Website:* www.mitsubishi.com (office).

SHIN, Heon-cheol, BA, MBA; South Korean business executive; *Vice-Chairman and Co-CEO, SK Corporation;* ed Busan Nat. Univ., Yonsei Univ.; joined SK Corpn as Head Man. of Business Team, Pres.'s Office 1985–89, Sr Man. in charge of developing man. skills 1989–91, Dir 1991, Head, Metropolitan Marketing Br. SK Telecom Co. Ltd 1995–98, Sr Man. Dir 1998, Pres. and CEO SK Telink Co. Ltd 1998–2002, Man. Dir SK Gas Co. Ltd 2002–05, Pres. and CEO SK Corpn 2005–06, Vice-Chair.and Co-CEO 2006–, mem. Bd of Dirs 2004–; mem. Bd of Dirs Korea YMCA. *Address:* SK Corporation, 99 Seorin-dong, Jongno-gu, Seoul 110-110, Republic of Korea (office). *Telephone:* (2) 2121-5114 (office). *Fax:* (2) 2121-7001 (office). *Website:* www.skcorp.com (office).

SHIN, In-ryung, PhD, LLM; South Korean professor of law and fmr university president; *Professor, Ewha Women's University;* ed Coll. of Law, Ewha Women's Univ.; Exec. Sec. in charge of Educ., Korea Dialogue Acad. 1971–80, Dir 2003–; part-time Lecturer in Labor Law, Coll. of Law, Lecturer in Women's Studies, Dept of Women's Studies, Ewha Women's Univ. 1974–84, Asst Prof. Coll. of Law 1985–87, Assoc. Prof. 1987–92, Prof. 1992–, Dean 2000–02, Dir Law Div. 1992–94, Pres. Ewha Women's Univ. 2002–06; Visiting Research Prof. Hitotsubasi Univ., Japan 1994–95; Visiting Scholar, Univ. of Wash. School of Law, USA 1998–99; Exec. Dir Korean Soc. of Labor Law 1990–97, Deputy Pres. 1998–2001, Pres. 2001–02; Dir Korean Public Law Asscn 1991–96, Korea Law Profs Asscn 1995–, Korea Asscn of Labor Studies 1995–, Korea Labour and Soc. Inst. 1995–, Korean Inst. for Labor Studies and Policies 1996–, Korean Constitutional Law Asscn 1997–98, Korea Democracy Foundation 2001–03, Korea Advanced Inst. of Science and Tech. 2003–, Sungkok Acad. and Cultural Foundation 2004–; Deputy Pres. Korean Industrial Relations Research Asscn 1995–96; mem. Deliberation Cttee of Employment Policy, Ministry of Labor 1994–2000, Examination Cttee of Industrial Accident Insurance 2000–02; Co-Pres. Korean Fed. for Environmental Movement 2003–; rep. Korean Legal Center 1995–97; Chair. Cttee of Women's Affairs, Advisory Council on Democratic and Peaceful Unification 2003–; mem. Comm. for the Prevention of Corruption, Bd of Audit and Inspection of Korea 1999, Lawyers Disciplinary Cttee, Ministry of Justice 2000–02, Comm. for the Evaluation of Unification Policy, Ministry of Unification 2001–02; non-exec. mem. Nat. Labor Relations Comm. 1997–98, 1999–2002; Adviser Constitutional Court of Korea 2003–, Presidential Advisory Council on Korea Unification 2003–05; mem. Bd Korea Dialogue Acad. 2003–, Korea Advanced Inst. of Science and Tech. 2003–, Sungkok Acad. and Cultural Foundation 2004–, Korea Inst. of Science and Tech. 2004–, I-Sang Yoon Peace Foundation 2005–, Korea Research Foundation 2005–; mem. Commrs Bd Korea Independent Comm. against Corruption 2004–; mem. Presidential Cttee on Judicial Reform 2005–, Prosecutor's Office Policy Advisory Bd 2005–. *Publications:* Women Labor Law 1985, A Research on Fundamental Rights of Labor 1985, Labor Law and Labor Campaigns 1987, The Overcoming of the Division of the Korean Peninsula, and Korean Women Emancipation Campaigns 1989, Law and Women Studies 1989, Law and Modern Society 1992, Law and Social Justice 1992, A Research on Labor Law Cases – Cases on Labor Union Campaigns 1995, Human Rights of Labor and the Law of Labor 1996, An Introduction to Korean Law 1998, The Historical Development of Korean Labor Legislations 1999, The Globalization and Women's Rights of Labor 2002. *Address:* 11-1 Daehyun-dong, Seodaemun-gu, Seoul 120-750, Republic of Korea (office). *Telephone:* (2) 3277-2011 (office). *Website:* www.ewha.ac.kr (office).

SHIN, Kyuk-ho; South Korean business executive; *Chairman, Lotte Group;* b. 1922, Ulsan, S Kyungsang Prov.; m.; three c.; ed Waseda Univ.; went to Japan in 1941 to study while working as paper boy and milk boy; est. factory to manufacture cutting oil in 1944, factory destroyed in World War II; f. Lotte Group in Japan 1948 as maker of bubble gum; f. Lotte Confectionery Co. Ltd 1967, now a leading food and leisure group spanning hotels, confectionary and an amusement park, currently Chair. *Address:* Lotte Confectionery Co. Ltd, 23,4-ga, Yangpyeong-dong, Yeongdeungpo-gu, Seoul, Republic of Korea (office). *Telephone:* (2) 670-6114/5 (office). *Fax:* (2) 6672-6600 (office). *Website:* www.lotte.com (office); www.lottetown.com (office).

SHIN, Yoshiaki; Japanese business executive; *Chairman, Mitsui Sumitomo Insurance Company;* Sr Man. Dir and Sr Exec. Officer, Mitsui Sumitomo Insurance Co. –2006, Rep. Dir, Pres. and Co-CEO 2006–08, Chair. 2008–. *Address:* Mitsui Sumitomo Insurance Co. Ltd, 27-2 Shinkawa 2-chome, Chuo-ku, Tokyo 104-8252, Japan (office). *Telephone:* (3) 3297-1111 (office). *Fax:* (3) 3297-6888 (office). *E-mail:* info@ms-ins.com (office). *Website:* www.ms-ins.com (office).

SHINDE, Sushilkumar Sambhaji Rao, BA, LLB; Indian politician and lawyer; *Minister of Power;* b. 4 Sept. 1941, Solapur, Maharashtra; m.; three d.; ed Law Coll., Pune; Boy Peon, then Court Peon and then Court Clerk, Sessions Court Solapur 1956–65; officer, Mumbai Police CID 1965–71; mem. Rajya Sabha 1992–98, 2006–; elected to Lok Sabha 1998, re-elected 1999; fmr Minister of Finance and Planning, of Industry, of Urban Devt and of Youth and Social Welfare, Maharashtra; Chief Minister of Maharashtra 2003–04; Gov. of Andhra Pradesh 2004–06 (resgnd); Minister of Power 2006–; mem. Congress Party. *Address:* Ministry of Power, Shram Shakti Bhavan, New Delhi 110 001, India (office). *Telephone:* (11) 23710271 (office). *Fax:* (11) 23721487 (office). *E-mail:* razdana@ias.nic.in (office). *Website:* powermin.nic.in (office).

SHINDO, Kaneto; Japanese film director and screenwriter; b. 28 April 1912, Hiroshima; entered film business 1934 as screenwriter for Kenji Mizoguchi and Keisuke Kinoshita; Asst Dir to Mizoguchi at Shochiku 1936–47; first film Aisai monogatari (Story of a Beloved Wife) 1951; left Shochiku to make ind. films 1950; int. renown followed his film Hadaka no shima 1960. *Films directed:* Genroku chushmgura (Chief Asst Dir) (47 Samurai) 1941; Aisai monogatari (Story of a Beloved Wife) 1951, Nadare (Avalanche) 1952, Gembaku no ko (Children of Hiroshima) 1952, Shukuzu 1953, Onna no issho 1953, Dobu 1954, Okami (Wolf) 1955, Gin shinju 1956, Ryûri no kishi 1956, Joyu (An Actress) 1956, Umi no yarodomo 1957, Kanashimi wa onna dakeni 1958, Daigo Fukuryu-Maru (Lucky Dragon No. 5) 1958, Hanayome-san wa sekai-ichi 1959, Hadaka no shima (Naked Island 1962) 1960, Ningen 1962, Haha (Mother, USA) 1963, Onibaba (The Demon) 1964, Akuto (The Conquest) 1965, Honnou (Lost Sex, USA 1968) 1966, Sei no kigen (Libido) 1967, Yabu no naka kuroneko (Black Cat from the Grove) 1968, Tsuyomushi onna to yowamushi (Strong Women, Weak Men) 1968, Kagerou (Heat Wave Island, USA) 1969, Shokkaku 1970, Hadaka no Jukyu-sai (Live Today, Die Tomor-

row!, USA 1971) 1970, Kanawa 1972, Sanka 1972, Kokoro (The Heart) 1973, Waga michi (My Way), Aru eiga-kantoku no shogai (Kenji Mizoguchi: The Life of a Film Director, USA 1981) 1975, Chikuzan hitori tabi (The Life of Chikuzan) 1977, Kôsatsu 1979, Hokusai manga (Edo Porn, USA 1982) 1981, Chihei-sen (The Horizon, USA 1985) 1984, Black Board 1986, Raku-yo-ju (Tree Without Leaves) 1986, Sakura-tai Chiru 1988, Bokuto kidan (The Strange Story of Oyuki) 1992, Gogo no Yuigon-jo (A Last Note) 1995, Ikitai (Will to Live) 1999, Sanmon yakusha (By Player) 2000, Fukuro (Owl) 2003. *Films produced:* Ashizuri misaki (Cape Ashizuri) 1954, Honnou (Lost Sex, USA 1968) 1966, Kokoro no sanmyaku 1966, Kanawa 1972, Sanka 1972, Kokoro (The Heart) 1973, Kôsatsu 1979. *Screenplays:* Josei no shôri (The Victory of Women) 1946, Kekkon 1947, Anjo-ke no Butokai (The Ball at the Anjo House) 1947, Yuwaku 1948, Waga shogai no kagayakeru hi (The Bright Day of My Life) 1948, Waga koi wa moenu (Flame of My Love) 1949, Ojôsan kanpai (Here's to the Girls) 1949, Mori no Ishimatsu 1949, Senka no hate 1950, Nagasaki no Kane (The Bells of Nagasaki) 1950, Akatsuki no tsuiseki (Police and Small Gangsters) 1950, Itsuwareru seiso 1951, Jiyu gakkou 1951, Dare ga watashi o sabaku no ka 1951, Maihime (Dancing Girl) 1951, Aisai monogatari 1951, Genji monogatari (the Tale of Genji) 1951, Ashura hangan 1951, Rakki-san 1952 (Mr Lucky) 1952, Nadare (Avalanche) 1952, Nishijin no shimai (Sisters of Nishijin) 1952, Gembaku no ko (Children of Hiroshima) 1952, Boryoku 1952, Senba zuru 1953, Onna hitori daichi o iku 1953, Mura hatibu 1953, Shukuzu 1953, Yokubo 1953, Chi no hate made 1953, Onna no issho 1953, Yoake mae (Before Dawn, USA 1966) 1953, Dorodarake no seishun 1954, Wakai hitotachi 1954, Dobu 1954, Ashizuri misaki (Cape Ashizuri) 1954, Ai sureba koso (segment 1) 1955, Ginza no onna 1955, Okami (Wolf) 1955, Haha naki-ko 1955, Bijo to kairyu (Beauty and the Dragon) 1955, Gin shinju 1956, Ryûri no kishi 1956, Yonju hassai no teiko 1956, Joyu (An Actress) 1956, Ako roshi 1956, Ôyasu kichibi 1957, Hikage no musume 1957, Umi no yarodomo 1957, Bitoku no yoromeki 1957, Chijo 1957, Kanashimi wa onna dakeni 1958, Hyoheki (The Precipice, USA) 1958, Yoru no tsuzumi (The Adulteress) 1958, Futeki no took (A Daring Man) 1958, Yoru no sugao1958, Hadaka no taiyo (Naked Sun) 1958, Daigo Fukuryu-Maru (Lucky Dragon No. 5) 1958, Hanayome-san wa sekai-ichi 1959, Ôinaru tabiji 1960, Kunisada Chui (The Gambling Samurai, USA 1960), Robo no ishi (The Wayside Pebble, USA 1962) 1960, Onna no saka 1960, Gambare! Bangaku (Master Fencer Sees the World or Perils of Bangaku) 1960, Ôinaru bakushin 1960, Hadaka no shima (Naked Island 1962) 1960, Ai to honoho to (Challenge to Live) 1961, Onna no kunshô 1961, Netsuai sha 1961, Haitoku no mesu 1961, Katei no jijou (A Family Matter) 1962, Tadare (Indulgence) 1962, Kurotokage (Black Lizard) 1962, Aobe ka monogatari (This Madding Crowd) 1962, 63. Kujira gami (Killer Whale) 1962, Ningen 1962, Shitoyakana kedamono (The Graceful Brute) 1962, Kiru (Destiny's Son) 1962, Uso (Lies, segment 'San jyokyo') 1963, Haha (Mother, USA) 1963, Kizudarake no sanga 1964, Manji (All Mixed Up) 1964, Onibaba (The Demon) 1964, Suruga yûkyôden: Toba arashi 1964, Nikutai no seisô 1964, Seisaku no tsuma (Seisaku's Wife, USA) 1965, Akuto (The Conquest) 1965, Irezumi 1966, Zatôichi umi o wataru (Zatoichi's Pilgrimage) 1966, Honnou (Lost Sex, USA 1968) 1966, Kenka erejii (Elegy to Violence) 1966, Tsuma futari (Two Wives) 1967, Sei no kigen (Libido) 1967, Hanaoka Seishu no tsuma (The Wife of Seishu Hanaoka, USA 1970) 1967, Nemureru bijo (The House of the Sleeping Virgins, USA 1969) 1968, Yabu no naka no kuroneko (Black Cat from the Grove) 1968, Tsuyomushi onna to yowamushi otoko (Strong Women, Weak Men) 1968, Senba zuru (Thousand Cranes) 1969, Kagerou (Heat Wave Island, USA) 1969, Oni no sumu yakata (Devil's Temple) 1969, Shokkaku 1970, Hadaka no Jukyu-sai (Live Today, Die Tomorrow!, USA 1971) 1970, Yami no naka no chimimoryo (Chimimoryo: A Soul of Demons) 1971, Gekido no showashi: Okinawa kessen (The Battle of Okinawa) 1971, Kanawa 1972, Sanka 1972, Gunki hakameku motoni (Under the Flag of the Rising Sun) 1972, Kokoro (The Heart) 1973, Waga michi (My Way) 1974, Aru eiga-kantoku no shogai (Kenji Mizoguchi: The Life of a Film Director, USA 1981) 1975, Shôwa karesusuki 1975, Chikuzan hitori tabi (The Life of Chikuzan) 1977, Kiken na kankei 1978, Jiken (The Incident, USA) 1978, Kôsatsu 1979, Haitatsu sarenai santsu no tegami (The Three Undelivered Letters, USA 1980) 1979, Jishin retto (Death Quake) 1980, Haru kanaru sôro 1980, Hokusai manga (Edo Porn, USA 1982) 1981, Tsumiki kuzushi 1983, Chihei-sen (The Horizon, USA 1985) 1984, Matsumoto Seicho special – Kuroi fukuin: Shinpu no giwaku (TV) 1984, Black Board 1986, Raku-yo-ju (Tree Without Leaves) 1986, Eiga joyu (Film Actress) 1987, Hachiko monogatari 1987, Sakura-tai Chiru 1988, Bokuto kidan (The Strange Story of Oyuki) 1992, Toki rakujitsu (The Distant Setting Sun, also novel) 1992, Gogo no Yuigon-jo (A Last Note) 1995, Miyazawa Kenji sono ai 1996, Kanzen-naru shiiku (The Perfect Education) 1998, Omocha (The Geisha House, USA) 1999, Ikitai (Will to Live) 1999, Sanmon yakusha (By Player, also novel Sanmon yakusha no shi) 2000, Taiga no itteki 2001, Fukuro (Owl) 2003, Battleship on the Ground 2007. *Other films:* as himself: Aru eiga-kantoku no shogai (The Life of a Film Director, USA 1981) 1975, Ikite wa mita keredo – Ozu Yasujirô den (I Lived, But…) 1983.

SHINEFIELD, Henry Robert, BA, MD; American pediatrician; *Clinical Professor of Pediatrics and of Dermatology, University of California, San Francisco;* b. 11 Oct. 1925, Paterson, NJ; s. of Louis Shinefield and Sarah Shinefield (née Kaplan); m. Jacqueline Walker 1983; one s. three d.; ed Columbia Univ.; Asst Resident Pediatrician, New York Hosp. (Cornell) 1950–51, Pediatrician Outpatients 1953–59, Instructor in Pediatrics 1959–60, Asst Prof. 1960–64, Assoc. Prof. 1964–65; Chief of Pediatrics, Kaiser-Permanente Medical Center, San Francisco 1965–89, Chief Emer. 1989–; Co-Dir Kaiser Permanente Pediatric Vaccine Study Center, Calif.; currently Adjunct Investigator, Div. of Research, Kaiser Permanente N Calif.; Assoc. Clinical Prof. of Pediatrics, Univ. of Calif., San Francisco 1966–68, Clinical Prof. of Pediatrics 1968–, Clinical Prof. of Dermatology 1970–; mem. Inst. of Medicine, NAS 1980, American Bd of Pediatrics; Fellow, American

Acad. of Pediatrics. *Leisure interests:* skiing, tennis, travel. *Address:* Kaiser Permanente Vaccine Study Center, Oakland, CA 94612; Kaiser Permanente, 4131 Geary Boulevard, San Francisco, CA 94118 (office); 2705 Larkin Street, San Francisco, CA 94109, USA (home). *Telephone:* (415) 202-3597 (office); (415) 771-5372 (home). *E-mail:* henry.shinefield@kp.org (office). *Website:* www.dermatology.ucsf.edu (office).

SHINKAI, Seiji, PhD; Japanese chemist and academic; *Professor, Department of Chemistry and Biochemistry, Kyushu University;* b. 1944, Fukuoka; ed Kyushu Univ.; Lecturer, Kyushu Univ., Fukuoka City 1972, Asst Prof. 1975, 1987, Prof. 1988, Leader, Kyushu Univ. Centre of Excellence (COE) Project 'Design and Control of Advanced Molecular Assembly Systems' 1998–2002, 21st Century COE Project 'Functional Innovation of Molecular Informatics' 2002–06; Postdoctoral Fellow, Dept of Chem., Univ. of California, Santa Barbara, USA 1972–74; Asst Prof., Nagasaki Univ. 1976; Project Leader, Research Devt Corpn of Japan/Exploratory Research for Advanced Tech. Project (ERATO) 'Shinkai Chemirecognics Project', Kawaguchi City 1990–95; Research Dir Japan Science and Tech. Corpn/Int. Collaboration Project (ICORP) 'Chemotransfiguration' 1997–2001, Japan Science and Tech. Corpn/Solution Oriented Research for Science and Tech. (SORST) 'Gene Manipulators Based on the Polysaccharide-Polynucleotide Interactions' 2002–04; mem. Editorial Bd Bioorganic Chemistry 1986–, Journal of the Chemical Society, Perkin Transactions 1992–2001, Supramolecular Chemistry 1992–, Nanotechnology 1993–, Current Opinion in Chemical Biology 1997–, Angewandte Chemie 1999–, European Journal of Organic Chemistry 2000–; Chemical Soc. of Japan Award for Advanced Research 1978, Soc. of Polymer Science Award 1985, Izatt-Christensen Int. Award, ISMC Cttee 1998, Backer Lecture Award, Univ. of Groningen 1999, Vielberth Lectureship Award, Univ. of Regensburg 2002. *Publications:* more than 750 articles in scientific journals and more than 131 book chapters and reviews on host/guest chem., molecular recognition, liquid crystals/organic gelators, sugar sensing/sugar-based combinatorial chem., polysaccharide-polynucleotide interactions, sol-gel transcription and inorganic combinatorial chem. *Address:* Department of Chemistry and Biochemistry, Kyushu University, Graduate School of Engineering, 6-10-1 Hakozaki, Higashi-ku, Fukuoka-shi, Fukuoka 819-0395, Japan (office). *Telephone:* (92) 642-3583 (office). *Fax:* (92) 642-3611 (office). *E-mail:* seijitcm@mbox.nc.kyushu-u.ac.jp (office). *Website:* www.cstm.kyushu-u.ac.jp/shinkai (office).

SHINMACHI, Toshiyuki; Japanese airline executive; *Resident Adviser, Japan Airlines (JAL) International Co. Ltd;* b. 20 Jan. 1943; ed Gakushuin Univ.; joined Japan Airlines Corpn 1965, Deputy Dir Cargo Export, Tokyo Regional Cargo Sales Office 1987–88, Dir 1988–89, Regional Man. Cargo Sales, New York Regional Cargo Sales Office 1989–91, Gen. Man., Admin, JAL Cargo 1991–93, Vice-Pres. JAL Cargo, Tokyo Regional Cargo Sales Office 1993–95, Vice-Pres. JAL Cargo Sales, Japan Region 1995–97, Sr Vice-Pres. Japan Airlines 1997–2000, mem. Bd of Dirs 1997–, Man. Dir 2000–01, Sr Man. Dir 2001–03, Sr Man. Dir Japan Airlines System Corpn 2002–03, Exec. Vice-Pres. Japan Airlines and Japan Airlines System Corpn 2003–04, Pres. Japan Airlines and Japan Airlines Corpn 2004–05, CEO JAL Group 2005–06, Chair. JAL Group 2006–08 (retd), Resident Adviser, JAL International Co. Ltd 2008–. *Address:* Japan Airlines International Co. Ltd, 4-11, Higashi-shinagawa 2-chome, Shinagawa-ku, Tokyo 140-8637, Japan (office). *Telephone:* (3) 5460-6600 (office). *E-mail:* info@jal.com (office). *Website:* www.jal.com/en/corporate/gaiyo/gaiyo_i.html (office).

SHINODA, Masahiro; Japanese film director; b. 1931, Gifu Pref.; ed Waseda Univ., Tokyo; began working as Asst Dir at Ofuna Studio, Shochiku 1953; worked as asst to Ozu 1957; began directing career 1960. *Films directed:* Koi no katamichi kippu (One-Way Ticket for Love) 1960, Kawaita mizummi (Dry Lake) 1960, Yuhi ni akai ore no kao (My Face Red in the Sunset) 1961, Waga koi no tabiji (Epitaph to My Love) 1961, Watakushi-tachi no kekkon (Our Marriage) 1961, Shamisen to otobai (Love Old and New or Shamisen and Motorcycle) 1961, Namida o shishi no tategami ni (Tears on the Lion's Mane) 1962, Yama no sanka: moyuru wakamono tachi (Glory on the Summit: Burning Youth) 1962, Kawaita hana (Pale Flower) 1964, Ansatsu (The Assassin) 1964, Utsukushisa to kanashimi to (With Beauty and Sorrow, UK) 1965, Ibun sarutobi sasuke (Samurai Spy) 1965, Shokei no shima (Punishment Island) 1966, Akane-gumo (Clouds at Sunset, USA) 1967, Shinjû: Ten no amijima (Double Suicide) 1969, Buraikan (The Scandalous Adventures of Buraikan) 1970, Chinmoku (Silence) 1971, Sapporo Orinpikku (Sapporo Winter Olympics) 1972, Kaseki no mori (The Petrified Forest) 1973, Himiko 1974, Sakura no mori no mankai no shita (Under the Cherry Blossoms) 1975, Hanre Goze Orin (Ballad of Orin, USA, Melody in Gray) 1977, Yashagaike (Demon Pond) 1979, Akuryo-To (Akuryo Island) 1981, Setouchi shonen yakyu dan (MacArthur's Children) 1984, Yari no gonza (Gonza the Spearman) (Silver Bear Award, Berlin) 1986, Maihime (The Dancer) 1989, Shonen jidai (Childhood Days) (several prizes at Japanese Acad. Awards) 1990, Sharaku 1995, Setouchi munraito serenade (Setouchi Moonlight Serenade) 1997, Fukuro no shiro (Owls' Castle, USA) 1999, Spy Sorge 2003. *Films produced:* Himiko 1974. *Screenplays:* Waga koi no tabiji (Epitaph to My Love) 1961, Watakushi-tachi no kekkon (Our Marriage) 1961, Namida o shishi no tategami ni (Tears on the Lion's Mane) 1962, Kawaita hana (Pale Flower) 1964, Shinjû: Ten no amijima (Double Suicide) 1969, Himiko 1974, Hanre Goze Orin (Ballad of Orin, USA or Melody in Gray) 1977, Maihime (The Dancer) 1989, Sharaku 1995, Spy Sorge 2003. *Other films:* Music for the Movies: Tom Takemitsu (as himself) 1994.

SHINOHARA, Yoshiko; Japanese business executive; *President, Tempstaff Co. Ltd;* b. Kanagawa Prefecture; ed Takamizu High School of Commerce, studied languages and secretarial work in Switzerland and UK; with Mitsubishi Heavy Industries Ltd 1953–57; spent time in Japan before moving to Australia in 1971; joined P.A.S.A. Inc. (marketing co.) as asst to Pres. 1971–73; Founder, Rep. Dir and Pres. Tempstaff Co. Ltd 1973–; mem. Bd of Dirs Japan Staffing Business Asscn 1986–; Flower Award, 14th Econ. Awards 1989, Veuve Clicquot Business Woman of the Year 1992, Venture of The Year in Female Entrepreneurs 1993, one of 50 World-Class Eexecutives 1996, selected by Nat. Foundation for Women Business Owners as one of Leading Women Entrepreneurs of the World 1997, Harvard Business School's Business States Woman of the Year 2001, ranked by Fortune magazine amongst 50 Most Powerful Women in Business outside the US (30th) 2001, (28th) 2002, (39th) 2003, (34th) 2004, (38th) 2005, (36th) 2006, (39th) 2007. *Address:* Tempstaff Co. Ltd, Shinjyuku Maynds Tower, 2-1-11, Yoyogi, Shibuya-ku, Tokyo 151-0053, Japan (office). *Telephone:* (3) 5350-1212 (office). *Fax:* (3) 5350-1219 (office). *Website:* www.tempstaff.co.jp (office).

SHINSEKI, Gen. (retd) Eric Ken, BS, MA; American army officer (retd) and government official; *Secretary of Veterans Affairs;* b. 28 Nov. 1942, Lihue, Kauai, Hawaii; m. Patricia Shinseki; two c.; ed US Mil. Acad., Duke Univ., Nat. War Coll., Fort Lesley J. McNair, Washington, DC; commissioned 2nd Lt in US Army 1965, Forward Observer B battery 2nd Battalion, 9th Artillery, 3rd Brigade, 25th Infantry Div., Viet Nam 1965–66; Asst S1 Base Defense Command, XXIV Corps, Viet Nam 1969–70, Commdr A Troop, 3rd Squadron, 5th Cavalry, 9th Infantry Div., Viet Nam 1970 Personnel Staff Officer US Army Pacific, Fort Shafter, Hawaii 1971–74, Instructor, Dept of English, US Mil. Acad., West Point 1976–78, Commdr 3rd Squadron, 7th Cavalry, 3rd Infantry Div. then Asst Chief of Staff, G-3, US Army Europe and 7th Army, Germany 1982–85, Commdr 2nd Brigade, 3rd Infantry Div. then Asst Chief of Staff G3 VII Corps, US Army Europe and 7th Army 1987–90, Deputy Chief of Staff, Admin/Logistics, Allied Land Forces, Southern Europe, Germany 1990–92, Asst Div. Commdr, 3rd Infantry Div., US Army and 7th Army Europe, Germany 1992–93, Commanding Gen. 1st Cavalry Div., Fort Hood, Tex. 1994–95, Asst Deputy Chief of Staff for operations and plans then Deputy Chief of Staff, US Army, Washington, DC 1995–97, Commdr in Chief and Commdr Stabilization Force, US Army Europe and 7th Army in Bosnia-Herzegovina 1997–98, Vice Chief of Staff, Washington, DC 1998–99, Chief of Staff 1999–2003 (retd); Sec. of Veterans Affairs, Washington, DC 2009–; Defense Distinguished Service Medal, Distinguished Service Medal, Legion of Merit with oak leaf cluster, Bronze Star with V device with three oak leaf clusters, Purple Heart with oak leaf cluster, Meritorious Service Medal with two oak leaf clusters, Air Medal, Army Commendation Medal with oak leaf cluster, Army Achievement Medal. *Address:* Department of Veterans Affairs, 810 Vermont Ave, NW, Washington, DC 20420, USA (office). *Telephone:* (202) 273-6000 (office). *Website:* www.va.gov (office).

SHINWARI, Fazulhadi; Afghan judge and Islamic scholar; b. 1929, Huskamena Dist, Nangarhar Prov.; ed Darul-Auloon Maddrassa, Kabul, Dewband Maddrassa, India; teacher of religious subjects Ibnisina School 1959–73; exiled in Pakistan 1973–2001, founded Islamic Maddrassa, Dara Ademkhil, Peshawar; fmr Islamabad leader of United Front Del.; Chief Justice and Head of Supreme Court of Afghanistan 2001–06; currently Head Council of Clergies and Scholars; POHANA 1972. *Publications:* Sharhe Shamel Termizi 1978, Kashfushshubhat 1978, Islam 1982, Faith 1982, This World and the Next World 1982. *Leisure interest:* researching Fiqa, Islamic law and jurisprudence. *Address:* c/o Supreme Court of Afghanistan, Airport Highway, Kabul, Afghanistan.

SHIOKAWA, Masajuro; Japanese politician; b. 1922; mem. House of Reps for Osaka 4th Dist; fmr Minister of Transport, of Educ., Chair. Cttee on Commerce and Industry; Minister of Home Affairs 1991–92, of Finance 2001–03 (resgnd); mem. LDP, Sec.-Gen. 1995, fmr Deputy Chair. Gen. Council; fmr Pres., Toyo Univ. *Address:* c/o Office of the President, Toyo University, 28-20 Hakusan 5-chome, Bunkyo-ku, Tokyo 112-8606, Japan (office).

SHIOZAKI, Yasuhisa, MPA; Japanese politician; b. 7 Nov. 1950; m.; two s.; ed Univ. of Tokyo, John F. Kennedy School of Govt, Harvard Univ.; with Bank of Japan 1975–86; Political Asst to Minister of State for Econ. Planning Agency 1982–83, to Minister of State for Man. and Coordination Agency 1990; mem. House of Reps (Ehime 1st Dist) 1993–95, 2000–, Dir Standing Cttee on Judicial Affairs 2001–, Chair. Standing Cttee on Judicial Affairs 2004–; mem. House of Councillors (Ehime Dist) 1995–, Dir Standing Cttee on the Budget 1996–, Standing Cttee on Audit 1996–97, Chief Dir Standing Cttee on Justice 1999–2000; Parl. Vice-Minister of Finance 1997–98; Sr Vice-Minister for Foreign Affairs 2005–; Chief Cabinet Sec. and Minister of State for the Abduction Issue 2006–07; Chair. LDP Judicial Affairs Div., Policy Research Council (PRC) 1999–2000, Foreign Affairs Div. 2000–, Treasury and Finance Div. 2002–, Deputy Chair. LDP PRC 2003–, Chief Sec. Party Reform and Task Force HQ, Man. Admin. Reform HQ, Vice-Chair. Research Cttee on the Financial Issues, Chair. Sub-cttee on Int. NGOs, Sub-cttee on Corp. Accounting, Sub-cttee on Commercial Law, Man. Research Cttee on the Tax System, PRC; Sec.-Gen. Japan-Thailand Parliamentarians' Friendship League, Japan-Singapore Parliamentarians' Friendship League; Pres. KSG Club of Japan. *Address:* Liberal-Democratic Party (Jiyu-Minshuto), 1-11-23, Nagata-cho, Chiyoda-ku, Tokyo 100-8910, Japan (office). *Telephone:* (3) 3581-6211 (office). *E-mail:* koho@ldp.jimin.or.jp (office); shiozaki@y-shiozaki.or.jp (home). *Website:* www.jimin.jp (office); www.y-shiozaki.or.jp (home).

SHIPLEY, Rt Hon. Jennifer Mary (Jenny), DCNZM, FNZIM; New Zealand politician, fmr prime minister and company director; b. (Jennifer Mary Robson), 4 Feb. 1952, Gore; d. of Leanord Cameron Robson and Adele Doreen Goodall; m. Burton Shipley 1973; one s. one d.; fmr primary school teacher; farmer 1973–88; joined Nat. Party 1975; fmr Malvern Co. Councillor; MP for Ashburton (now Rakaia) 1987–; Minister of Social Welfare 1990–93 and of Women's Affairs 1990–98, of Health 1993–96, of State Services 1996–97, also of State Owned Enterprises, of Transport, of Accident Rehabilitation and Compensation Insurance, Minister Responsible for Radio New Zealand; Minister in Charge of NZ Security Intelligence Service 1997–99; Prime Minister of NZ 1997–99; Leader of the Opposition 1999–2001; Fellow, NZ Inst. of Man.; Distinguished Companion NZ Order of Merit. *Leisure interests:* family, int. affairs, gardening, sailing. *Address:* PO Box 6636, Auckland, New Zealand (home). *Telephone:* (9) 358-5360 (office). *E-mail:* jenny@jsnz.com (office). *Website:* www.national.org.nz (office).

SHIPLEY, Walter Vincent, BS; American business executive (retd); b. 2 Nov. 1935, Newark, NJ; s. of L. Parks and Emily Shipley (née Herzog); m. Judith Ann Lyman 1957; one s. four d.; ed Williams Coll., New York Univ.; with Chemical Bank 1956–96, Exec. Vice-Pres. Int. Div., New York 1978–79, Sr Exec. Vice-Pres. –1981, Pres. 1982–83, Chair. Bd 1983–92, Pres., COO 1992–93, Chair., CEO 1994–96; Chair. Chase Manhattan Banking Co. 1996–99, CEO 1996–99 (cr. after merger of Chomzal Banking Corpn with Chase Manhattan Corpn); retd 2000; mem. Bd of Dirs Wallace Foundation 1991–2007, Chair. 2002–07; mem. Bd Dirs Exxon Mobil Corpn, Verizon Communications, Wyeth; fmr Dir Champion Int. Corpn, NYNEX Corpn, Atlantic Corpn; mem. Bd Dirs Japan Soc., Lincoln Center for the Performing Arts Inc., NY City Partnership Inc., NY Chamber of Commerce and Industry, Goodwill Industries of Greater NY Inc., United Way of Tri-State; Trustee American Museum of Natural History; mem. The Business Council, Business Roundtable, Council for Foreign Relations, Pilgrims of US, English-Speaking Union. *Address:* c/o The Wallace Foundation, 5 Penn Plaza, 7th Floor, New York, NY 10001, USA.

SHIRAISHI, Kazuko; Japanese poet; b. 1931, Vancouver, BC, Canada; m.; one d.; mem. VOU avant-garde literary group 1948–53; with Kazuo Ono mounted series of poetry/dance productions; has received many major Japanese poetry and literary prizes including Yomiuri Literary Prize, Purple Ribbon Medal (Shijuhosho). *Publications:* poetic works include Seasons of Sacred Lust (in English) 1978.

SHIRAISHI, Takashi, PhD; Japanese economist and academic; *Professor Emeritus, Keio University;* b. 1921, Tokyo; m. Toshiko Shiraishi; one d.; ed Keio Univ., Harvard Business School; Lecturer, Keio Univ. 1947–49, Asst Prof. 1949–58, Prof. 1958–86, Vice-Pres. 1965–77, Dean, Faculty of Business and Commerce 1975–77, Prof. Emer. 1986–; Prin. Keio High School 1964–65; Dean Faculty of Social Sciences, Kyorin Univ. 1984–92; Dir Japan Soc. of Int. Econs 1974–; Dir and Pres. Union of Nat. Econ. Asscns in Japan 1975–90; mem. Int. Exchange Program Cttee of Japan Soc. for the Promotion of Science 1982–84; mem. Exec. Cttee, Int. Econ. Asscn 1984–89. *Publications:* Economic Development and Direct Investment 1978, History of Economic Growth and Policy of Japan since the Second World War 1983, Japan's Trade Policies 1989, Reformation of World Economy and Japan 1991, History of Japan's Machine Export 1992, New Age of Asia and Japan 1993, Foreign Exchange Rates and the Japanese Economy 1996. *Address:* 1-19-10, Jiyugaoka, Meguroku, Tokyo, Japan. *Telephone:* (3) 3717-7118.

SHIRAKAWA, Hideki, PhD; Japanese scientist and academic; *Professor Emeritus, Institute of Materials Science, University of Tsukuba;* b. 1936; ed Tokyo Inst. of Tech.; pioneered work on conductive polymers; Prof. Inst. of Materials Science, Univ. of Tsukuba, now Prof. Emer.; elected mem. Council for Science and Tech. Policy, Japanese Cabinet Office 2001; Nobel Prize for Chem. (jt recipient) 2000. *Address:* Institute of Materials Science, University of Tsukuba, 1-1-1 Ten-nodai, Tsukuba, Ibaraki 305-8573, Japan (office). *Telephone:* (298) 53-2111 (office). *Fax:* (298) 53-6012 (office). *E-mail:* hideki@ims.tsukuba.ac.jp (office). *Website:* www.ims.tsukuba.ac.jp/Eng/Eims.html (office).

SHIRAKAWA, Masaaki, BA, MA; Japanese politician and central banker; *Governor, Nippon Ginko (Bank of Japan);* b. 27 Sept. 1949, Kitakyushu; ed Univ. of Tokyo, Univ. of Chicago, USA; joined Nippon Ginko (Bank of Japan) 1972, held various positions including Dir and Head Financial System 1990–93, Head Planning Div, Policy Planning Office 1993–94, Gen. Man. Oita Br. 1994–95, Gen. Man. for the Americas, New York 1995–96, Deputy Dir-Gen. Inst. for Monetary and Econ. Studies 1996–97, Deputy Dir-Gen. Int. Dept 1997, Adviser to the Gov. Credit and Market Man. Dept. 1997, Adviser to Gov. Financial Markets Dept 1998, Adviser to Gov. Policy Planning Office 2000–02, Exec. Dir 2002–06, Deputy Gov. 2008–, Gov. 2008–; Prof., Kyoto Univ. School of Govt 2006–08. *Publications include:* numerous papers on Japanese monetary policy. *Address:* Nippon Ginko (Bank of Japan), 2-1-1, Hongoku-cho, Nihonbashi, Chuo-ku, Tokyo 100-8630, Japan (office). *Telephone:* (3) 3279-1111 (office). *Fax:* (3) 5200-2256 (office). *E-mail:* prd@info.boj.or.jp (office). *Website:* www.boj.or.jp (office).

SHIRAYANAGI, HE Cardinal Peter Seiichi, DCnL; Japanese ecclesiastic; *Archbishop Emeritus of Tokyo;* b. 17 June 1928, Tokyo; s. of Peter Hisazo Shirayanagi and Maria Kura Shirayanagi; ed Gyosei Stella Maris School, Major Seminary, Tokyo, Sophia Univ., Urban Univ., Rome; ordained priest 1954; Sec. Archbishop's House 1954–66, in Rome 1957–60; Auxiliary Bishop of Tokyo 1966; Coadjutor with right of succession 1969; Archbishop of Tokyo 1970–2000; cr. Cardinal 1994; Cardinal-Priest of S. Emerenziana a Tor Fiorenza 1994–; Vice-Pres. Bishops' Conf. of Japan 1975, Pres. 1983–92; Pres. Episcopal Comm. for Social Action 1975. *Leisure interest:* piano. *Address:* Shinjukuku, Shimoochiai 3-2-11-301, Tokyo 161-0033, Japan. *Telephone:* (3) 5988-7817. *Fax:* (3) 5988-7818. *E-mail:* pshira@nifty.com.

SHIRE, Bare Adan; Somali politician; commdr Marehan Somali National Front during civil war; fmr Minister of Reconstruction and Resettlement and fmr Minister of Defence in Transitional Fed. Govt 2004; Chair. Juba Valley Alliance (JVA) 1998–2006. *Address:* c/o Ministry of Defence, Mogadishu, Somalia.

SHIRKOV, Dmitrii Vasilevich, PhD, DrSci; Russian physicist; *Honorary Director, Bogoliubov Laboratory of Theoretical Physics, Joint Institute for Nuclear Research;* b. (Dmitry Vasilevich Shirkov), 3 March 1928, Moscow; s. of Vasili Shirkov and Elizaveta Makushina; m. Svetlana Rastopchina 1950; two s. one d.; ed Moscow State Univ., Steklov Math. Inst., Moscow; attached to Inst. of Chemical Physics, Acad. of Sciences, Moscow 1948–50, Sarov (Arzamas-16) Nuclear Weapon Centre 1950–54, Steklov Math. Inst. of Acad. of Sciences, Moscow 1954–58 and Jt Inst. for Nuclear Research, Dubna 1958–60, 1971–; worked at Inst. of Math., Siberian Div. of Acad. of Sciences, Novosibirsk 1960–70; Prof., Univ. of Novosibirsk 1963–69; Nobel Guest Prof., Lund Univ., Sweden 1970–71; Prof., Moscow State Univ. 1972–2001, Prof. Emer. 2001–; Corresp. mem. USSR (now Russian) Acad. of Sciences 1960, mem. 1994; Foreign mem. Saxonian Acad. of Sciences; Hon. Dir Bogoliubov Lab. at Jt Inst. for Nuclear Research; Orders of USSR, Bulgaria and Russian Fed.; USSR Lenin Prize 1958, USSR State Prize 1984, Bogoliubov Gold Medal, Russian Acad. of Sciences 2005. *Publications:* co-author: Introduction to the Theory of Quantized Fields 1957, A New Method in the Theory of Superconductivity 1958, Dispersion Theories of Strong Interactions at Low Energies 1967, Quantum Fields 1980, Theory of Particle Interactions 1986; more than 200 published papers mainly on the theory of fundamental interactions and particles. *Leisure interests:* tourism, skiing, photography. *Address:* Bogoliubov Laboratory of Theoretical Physics, Joint Institute for Nuclear Research, Joliot Curie str. 6, 141980 Dubna, Moscow Region, Russia (office). *Telephone:* (49621) 65088 (office). *Fax:* (49621) 65084 (office). *E-mail:* shirkovd@theor.jinr.ru (office). *Website:* theor.jinr.ru (office).

SHIRLEY, Donna Lee, BA, BS, MS; American aeronautical engineer, academic and consultant; *President, Managing Creativity;* b. 1941, Wynnewood, Okla; m. (divorced); one d.; ed Univ. of Oklahoma, Univ. of Southern Calif.; specifications writer, McDonnell Aircraft, St Louis, Mo. 1963; joined NASA Jet Propulsion Lab. 1966, mission analyst for Mariner 10 mission to Venus and Mercury 1970–74, Energy and Environmental System Man. 1974–79, Task Man. 1979–81, Man. Mission Design Section 1981–82, Man. Space Station Program Office 1982–85, Man. Automation and Robotics Office 1985–87, Man. Rover Concept Team 1987–90, Leader, Surface Transportation Vehicle Systems Eng 1989–91, Man. Exploration Initiative Studies 1990–91, project engineer, Cassini Mission 1991–1992; Man. Mars Pathfinder Microrover Flight Experiment 1992–94, Man. Mars Exploration Program 1994–98; Asst Dean of Eng for Advanced Program Devt, Coll. of Eng, Univ. of Oklahoma 1999–2002, now mem. Bd of Visitors; Pres. Managing Creativity (consulting firm) 1997–; Sr Fellow, School of Public Policy, UCLA 1997;; NASA Group Achievement Awards, including for Telerobotics Tech. Team 1991 and Pathfinder Mars Rover Devt Team 1997, NASA Outstanding Leadership Medal 1997, Pres.'s Award, Soc. for Tech. Technical Communication 1997, Holley Medal for Lifetime Achievement, ASME 1998, Judith Resnick Award, Soc. of Women Engineers 1998, Wernher Von Braun Memorial Award, Nat. Space Soc. 2000, Washington Award for Eng Achievement, Western Engineer Soc. 2000, inducted into Women in Tech. Int. Hall of Fame 1997. *Publication:* Managing Martians – The Extraordinary Story of a Woman's Lifelong Quest to Get to Mars and of the Team Behind the Space Robot That Has Captured the Imagination of the World (memoir) 1998. *Leisure interests:* acting, painting, playing the guitar, sailing. *Address:* Managing Creativity, 1517 Oklahoma Avenue, Norman, OK 73071-0466, USA (office). *Telephone:* (405) 307-0313 (office). *Fax:* (405) 307-0331 (office). *E-mail:* dshirley@earthlink.net (office). *Website:* www.managingcreativity.com (office).

SHIRLEY, George Irving, BEd; American singer (tenor) and academic; *Joseph Edgar Maddy Distinguished University Emeritus Professor of Music (Voice), University of Michigan School of Music, Theatre & Dance;* b. 18 April 1934, Indianapolis, Ind.; s. of Irving E. Shirley and Daisy Shirley (née Bell); m. Gladys Lee Ishop 1956; one s. one d.; ed Wayne State Univ.; New York City premiere with Amato Opera in Verdi's Aroldo 1961; debuts with Metropolitan Opera, New York Opera, Festival of Two Worlds (Spoleto, Italy), Santa Fé Opera 1961, Teatro Colón, Buenos Aires 1965, La Scala, Milan 1965, Glyndebourne Festival 1966, Royal Opera, Covent Garden, Scottish Opera 1967, Vienna Festival 1972, San Francisco Opera 1977, Chicago Lyric Opera 1977, Théâtre Municipal d'Angers 1979, Edin. Festival 1979, Nat. Opera Ebony, Philadelphia 1980, Spoleto Festival, Charleston, SC 1980, Tulsa Opera, Okla 1980, Ottawa Festival 1981, Deutsche Oper 1983, Guelph Spring Festival 1983, Bregenz Festival, Austria 1998; Glimmerglass Opera, Cooperstown, NY 1999, Eugene Opera, Ore. 2009; Prof. of Voice, Univ. of Md 1980–87; Prof. of Music, Univ. of Mich. School of Music, Theatre & Dance 1987–2007, Joseph Edgar Maddy Distinguished Univ. Prof. of Music (Voice) 1992–2007, Emer. Prof. 2007–, also Dir Emer., Vocal Arts Div.; mem. Univ. of Mich. Soc. of Fellows 1989, American Acad. of Teachers of Singing 1990; Hon. HDH (Wilberforce Univ.) 1967, Hon. LLD (Montclair State Coll.) 1984, Hon. DFA (Lake Forest Coll.) 1988, Hon. DHumLitt (Northern Iowa) 1997; numerous awards including Nat. Arts Club Award 1960, Concorso di Musica e Danza (Vercelli, Italy) 1960, Distinguished Scholar-Teacher Award, Univ. of Md 1985–86, Univ. of Mich. School of Music Alumni Asscn Distinguished Achievement Award 2005, Opera Noire Grazioso Award, New York 2005, Dr. Charles H. Wright Legacy Award for Excellence in Fine Arts, Detroit 2006, Nat. Asscn for the Study and Performance of African American Music Trail Blazer Award 2007; various citations from the City of Detroit and State of Mich.; GRAMMY Award for recording of Mozart's Così fan tutte 1968. *Leisure interests:* golf, sketching and cartoons, photography, writing. *Address:* University of Michigan School of Music, Ann Arbor, MI 48109-2085, USA. *Telephone:* (734) 665-7821 (office). *Fax:* (734) 763-5097 (office). *E-mail:* gis@umich.edu (office); geotenor@fastmail.fmt (home). *Website:* www.music.umich.edu (office).

SHIRLEY-QUIRK, John, CBE, BSc; British/American singer and teacher; *Member of Voice Faculty, Peabody Conservatory, Johns Hopkins University;* b. 28 Aug. 1931, Liverpool; s. of Joseph Stanley and Amelia Shirley-Quirk; m. 1st Dr Patricia Hastie 1952 (died 1981); one s. one d.; m. 2nd Sara Watkins 1981 (died 1997); one s. two d. (one d. died 2001); ed Holt School, Liverpool and Liverpool Univ.; Flying Officer, RAF (Educ. Br.) 1952–55; Asst Lecturer, Acton Tech. Coll. 1956–60; Vicar Choral, St Paul's Cathedral 1960–61; professional singer 1961–; mem. Voice Faculty, Peabody Conservatory, Johns Hopkins Univ., Baltimore, Md, USA 1992–; mem. Voice Dept, Coll. of Fine Arts, Carnegie-Mellon Univ., Pittsburgh, Pa 1994–98; many recordings and first performances, notably works of Benjamin Britten and Michael Tippett; Hon. RAM 1972; Hon. DMus (Liverpool) 1976; Hon. DUniv (Brunel) 1981. *Music:* first performances of Benjamin Britten's last five operas 1964–73, The Ice Break (Michael Tippett) 1977. *TV appearances include:* Carmen, The Marriage of Figaro, Billy Budd, Messiah, Owen Wingrave, Death in Venice. *Films:* Death in Venice (dir Tony Palmer) 1981. *Leisure interests:* clocks, canals, trees. *Address:* 6062 Red Clover Lane, Clarksville, MD 21029, USA. *Telephone:* (410) 531-1315 (home). *Fax:* (410) 531-3335 (home). *E-mail:* jssq@peabody.jhu.edu (home). *Website:* www.peabody.jhu.edu (office).

SHIRO, Hiruta; Japanese business executive; *President, Asahi Kasei Corporation;* b. 1942; joined Asahi Kasei Corpn 1964, held several sr positions including Man. Dir, Sr Man. Dir, Exec. Vice-Pres. 2002–03 Pres. 2003–; apptd Dir Asahi Chemical Industry Co. Ltd 1998; Pres. Petrochemical Industry Asscn; mem. Bd of Dirs Japan Chemical Innovation Inst. (JCII). *Address:* Asahi Kasei Corporation, Hibuya-Mitsui Building, 1-1-2 Yurakucho, Chiyoda-ku, Tokyo 100-8440, Japan (office). *Telephone:* (3) 3507-2060 (office). *Fax:* (3) 3507-2495 (office). *Website:* www.asahi-kasei.co.jp (office).

SHIRVINDT, Alexander Anatolyevich; Russian actor; *Artistic Director, Moscow Academy Theatre of Satire;* b. 19 July 1934, Moscow; m. Natalya Belousova; one s.; ed Shchukin School of Theatre Art; actor, Moscow Theatre of Lenin's Comsomol 1957–70, actor, Moscow Acad. Theatre of Satire 1957–, Artistic Dir 2000–; teacher, Shchukin School of Theatre Art; mem. Union of Cinematographers; People's Artist of Russia 1989. *Films include:* Cossack Chieftain Kodr, Come Tomorrow, Major Vikhr, Facts of the Passed Day, Winter Evening in Gagry, Blackmailer, Once Again About Love, Crankies, A Station for Two, Irony of the Fate, Three in a Boat Not to Mention a Dog, Imaginary Invalid. *Stage appearances include:* Trigorin (The Seagull), Dobchinsky (The Government Inspector), King Louis (Bondage of Hypocrites), Akhmed Ryza (Crank), Count Almaviva (The Marriage of Figaro), Press Secretary (Burden of Decisions), Molchalin (Misfortune from Intellect), Nehrish (Red Horse with Small Bells), President of the Reportage (Bug). *Plays produced include:* Small Comedies of a Big House, Melancholy, Shut Up, Wake Up and Sing; two-man variety shows with M. Derzhavin. *Leisure interest:* fishing. *Address:* Moscow Academic Theatre of Satire, Triumfalnaya pl. 2, 103050 Moscow (office); Kotelnicheskaya nab. 1/15, korp. A, Apt. 50, 109240 Moscow, Russia (home). *Telephone:* (495) 299-63-05 (office); (495) 916-49-82 (home). *Website:* www.satire.ru (office).

SHISLER, Arden L.; American insurance industry executive; *Chairman, Nationwide Mutual Insurance Company;* b. 1941, Massillon, Ohio; ed Ohio State Univ.; COO K&B Transport Inc. 1986–92, Pres. and CEO 1992–2003; mem. Bd of Dirs Nationwide Mutual Insurance Co. 1984–, Chair. 1992–, mem. Bd of Dirs Nationwide Financial Services Inc., Chair. 2003–; Trustee Gartmore Variable Insurance Trust 2002–; fmr Pres. Ohio Agricultural Marketing Asscn; mem. Bd of Dirs Ohio 4-H Foundation; mem. Advisory Cttee, Ohio State Univ. Agric. Tech. Inst.; mem. Wayne Co. Farm Bureau, Cornerstone Community Church. *Address:* Nationwide Mutual Insurance Company, 1 Nationwide Plaza, Columbus, OH 43215-2220, USA (office). *Telephone:* (614) 249-7111 (office). *Fax:* (614) 249-7705 (office). *Website:* www.nationwide.com (office).

SHIVY, Sylvia Massey; American record producer; *Head, RadioStar Studios;* producer Zoo Records; worked with Johnny Cash, Cowboy Mouth, Cyclefly, The Deadlights, Deftones, Dig, Econoline Crush, Firewater, Glueleg, Green Jelly, Greta, Horsehead, Insolence, Luscious Jackson, Lollipop Lust Kill, Loudermilk, Love & Rockets, Lustra, Machines of Loving Grace, Oingo Boing, Powerman 5000, Artist formerly known as Prince, Red Hot Chili Peppers, R.E.M., Seigmen, Sevendust, Skunk Anansie, System Of A Down, Tallman, Tom Petty and the Heartbreakers, Tool, Toyshop, Virgos; f. RadioStar Studios. *Address:* RadioStar Studios, Weed Palace Theater, 180 Main Street, Weed, CA 96094, USA (office). *E-mail:* sylvia@radiostarstudios.com (office). *Website:* www.radiostarstudios.com (office).

SHKOLNIK, Vladimir Sergeyevich; Kazakhstani mining engineer and politician; *Vice-Chairman, President's Administration;* b. 17 Feb. 1949, Serpukhov, Moscow Region; m.; two c.; ed Moscow Inst. of Physics and Math.; mem. Kazakhstan Acad. of Sciences; various posts from engineer to Deputy Dir Mangistauz Energy Complex 1973–92; Dir-Gen. Agency of Atomic Energy Repub. of Kazakhstan 1992–94; Minister of Science and New Tech. 1994–96; Minister of Science 1996–99; Pres. Kazakhstan Acad. of Sciences 1996–; Minister of Energy and Mineral Resources 1999–2001, 2005, of Industry and Trade –2007; Vice-Chair. Pres.'s Admin. 2007–. *Address:* Office of the President, 010000 Astana, Beibitshilik 11, Kazakhstan (office). *Telephone:* (7172) 32-13-99 (office). *Fax:* (7172) 32-61-72 (home). *Website:* www.akorda.kz (office).

SHMAKOV, Mikhail Viktorovich; Russian trade union official; *Chairman, Federation of Independent Trade Unions of Russia;* b. 12 Aug. 1949, Moscow; m.; one s.; ed Bauman Moscow Higher Tech. School; engineer in defence industry factories 1972–75, 1977–86; army service 1975–77; Head, Moscow Trade Union of Workers of Defence Industry 1986–90; Chair. Moscow City Council of Trade Unions, later transformed into Moscow Fed. of Trade Unions 1990–93; Chair. Fed. of Ind. Trade Unions of Russia 1993–; Pres. Gen. Confederation of Trade Unions 2004–; mem. Organizational Cttee Otechestvo Movt. *Leisure interest:* sports. *Address:* Federation of Independent Trade Unions of Russia, Leninsky pr. 42, 117119 Moscow, Russia (office). *Telephone:* (495) 938-86-52 (office). *Website:* www.fnpr.org.ru (office).

SHMAROV, Valery Nikolayevich, PhD; Ukrainian politician; b. 14 Aug. 1945, Zholobi, Vinnitsa; m. Olga Viktorivna Shmarova; one s. one d.; ed Kiev Coll. of Radioelectronics, Kiev State Univ.; radio equipment mechanic, Head of lab., Kiev Radiozavod 1966–72; head of lab., chief of div., chief of workshop, chief of Dept 1973–87, Dir Zhulyany Machine Construction Factory 1987–92; First Deputy Dir-Gen. Nat. Space Agency of Ukraine 1992–93; Deputy Prime Minister on problems of mil.-industrial complex 1993–94; Deputy Prime Minister and Minister of Defence 1994–96; Pres. Asscn of State Aviation Industry Ukraviaprom (Asscn of Aviation Enterprises of Ukraine) 1996–2001; mem. Verhovna Rada (Parl.) 1998–; Dir-Gen. Ukrspetsexport (state co. for export and import of mil. equipment and arms), Kiev 2002–04; Prof., Kiev Int. Univ. of Civil Aviation; mem. Cttee for Nat. Security and Defence 1998; mem. Ukrainian Tech. Acad. *Leisure interests:* history, literature, swimming. *Address:* Bastionna str. 9, 01014 Kiev, Ukraine (office). *Telephone:* (44) 294-81-00 (office); (44) 294-88-49 (home). *Fax:* (44) 294-81-47 (office). *E-mail:* avia@iptelecom.net.ua (office).

SHMATKO, Sergei Ivanovich; Russian politician; *Minister of Energy;* b. 26 Sept. 1966, Stavropol; ed Faculty of Political Economy, Ural State Univ., Mil. Acad., Jt Staff VS of Russia; worked as auditor in BDO Binder 1992–94; Dir RFI GmbH (official rep. of Russian Fed. Property Fund in EU) 1994–95; scientific employee, Inst. of Problems of Investment 1995–97, supervised man. of external relations of All-Russia devt bank of regions; Head of Analytical Centre of Econ. Strategy, Rosenergoatom 1997–99; adviser on econ. strategy to Gen. Dir All-Russian Scientific Research Inst. for Nuclear Power Plant Operation (VNIIAES) 1999–2001; Chair. State fund of conversion 2002–05; adviser to Chair. Gazprombank Feb.–June 2005; adviser to Vice-Pres. Atomstroyexport (jt stock co.) Feb.–June 2005, Pres. Atomstroyexport 2005–08; Minister of Energy 2008–. *Address:* Ministry of Energy, 103074 Moscow, Kitaigorodskii proyezd 7/191, Russia (office). *Telephone:* (495) 220-42-88 (office). *Fax:* (495) 220-56-56 (office). *E-mail:* abs@cdu.oilnet.ru (office). *Website:* www.mte.gov.ru (office).

SHMELEV, Geliy Ivanovich; Russian economist; b. 11 June 1927; m. (wife deceased); ed Rostov State Univ.; Head of Div. Rostov Inst. of Railway Eng 1952–54; Sr Teacher, Black Sea Inst. of Mechanization and Electrification of Agric. 1954–59; Sr Teacher and Docent, Lipetsk br. Moscow Inst. of Steel and Alloys 1962–70; Sr Researcher, Inst. of Econ. USSR Acad. of Sciences 1970–72; Head of Div. Inst. of Int. Econ. and Political Studies, USSR Acad. of Sciences; Sr Researcher, Inst. of Econs, Russian Acad. of Sciences 1998; Corresp. mem. USSR (now Russian) Acad. of Sciences and Russian Acad. of Agric. Sciences 1990. *Publications:* Distribution and Usage of Labour in the Collective Farms 1964, Subsidiary Smallholding and its relations with Public Production 1971, Subsidiary Smallholding: Possibilities and Prospects 1983, Social and Economic Problems to Develop Agriculture in Socialist European Countries 1996, A Reform in American and Russian Scientists' Eyes 1996. *Address:* Institute of Economics, Russian Academy of Sciences, Nakhimovsky prosp. 32, 117 28 Moscow, Russia (office). *Telephone:* (495) 332-45-54 (office).

SHMELYEV, Nikolai Petrovich, DEconSc; Russian economist and author; *Director, Institute of Europe, Russian Academy of Sciences;* b. 18 June 1936, Moscow; s. of Petr Shmelyev and Maria Shmelyeva; m. Gulia Shmelyeva 1965; one d.; ed Moscow Univ.; mem. CPSU 1962–91; researcher, Inst. Econ., USSR Acad. of Sciences 1958–61; Prof., Head of Dept, Inst. of Econ. of World Socialist System (IEMSS), USSR Acad. of Sciences 1961–68, 1970–82; Sr scientific researcher, Inst. of USA and Canada 1982–92; Sr Researcher, Head CIS-Europe Dept, Russian Acad. of Sciences Inst. of Europe 1992–, Dir 2000–; researcher, Slavic Research Centre, Hokkaido Univ., Japan 1995; USSR People's Deputy 1989–91; Corresp. mem. Russian Acad. of Sciences 1994–, mem. 2000–; Lecturer, Stockholm Inst. of Econ. of East European Countries 1992; Lecturer, Middlebury Coll. Vt, USA 1993. *Publications:* books and articles on econ. problems, World Economic Tendencies, Progress and Contradictions 1987, Advances and Debts 1989, The Turning Point 1990; novels and stories include Pashkov House 1987, Performance for Mr. Prime Minister 1988, Pirosmani 1988, Silvestr 1991, V Puti Ya Zanemog 1995, Bezumnaya Greta 1995, Curriculum Vitae (o sebe) 2001. *Leisure interests:* books, travelling. *Address:* Institute of Europe, Mokhovaya 11/3, 125993 Moscow (office); 3-d Frunzenskaya 7, Apt 61, 119270 Moscow, Russia (home). *Telephone:* (495) 629-45-07 (office); (495) 242-13-06 (home). *Fax:* (495) 200-42-98. *E-mail:* europe@ieras.ru (office). *Website:* www.ieras.ru (office).

SHNAIDER, Alexander, BA; Canadian (b. Russian) business executive; *Co-Founder and Director, Midland Group;* b. 1969, St Petersburg; m.; three c.; ed York Univ., Toronto; est. steel-trading business in Belgium, expanded business by trading with steel mills in Soviet Union; Co-f. (with Eduard Shifrin) Midland Resources (later Midland Group) 1994, bought large stakes in Zaporizhstal steel mill, Ukraine, nat. electricity grid, Armenia and now has interests in steel, shipping, construction, real estate in Russia, Ukraine and worldwide; Chair. Royal Laser Corpn 2006–; bought Jordan Grand Prix racing team 2005, renamed Midland Racing, sold team 2006. *Address:* c/o Talon International Development Inc., 77 King Street West, Royal Trust Tower, Toronto-Dominion Centre, Suite 4400, Toronto, ON M5K 1G8, Canada; Midland Group, POB 646, Havelet House, South Esplanade, St Peter Port, Guernsey GY1 3JS, Channel Islands (office). *Telephone:* (1481) 746770 (office). *Fax:* (1481) 746780 (office). *E-mail:* info@mrh.gg (office). *Website:* www.midland.gg (office).

SHOCHAT, Avraham, BSc; Israeli construction engineer, company director and fmr politician; b. 14 June 1936, Tel-Aviv; ed Haifa Technion; fmr paratrooper in Israel Defence Forces; Br. Dir Solel Boneh (Histadrut construction co.); Co-f. City of Arad, Mayor of Arad 1967–89, Chair. Citizens' Cttee Arad, Devt Towns Council, Econ. Cttee, Finance Cttee, Deputy Chair. Union of Local Authorities; mem. Knesset (Parl.) 1988–2003; Minister of Finance 1992–96, 1999–2001, of Nat. Infrastructure 2000–01; mem. Bd of Dirs Alon USA Energy Inc., Israel Chemicals Ltd, Bank Mizrahi Tefahot Ltd, Direct Insurance Financial Investments Ltd; fmr mem. Bd of Dirs Israel Aircraft Industries; headed govt cttee on higher educ. reforms 2007; mem. Labour Party. *Address:* c/o Board of Directors, Bank Mizrahi Tefahot Ltd, 7 Jabotinsky Street, Ramat Gan, 52520, Israel.

SHOCK, Sir Maurice, Kt, MA; British academic; b. 15 April 1926; s. of Alfred Shock and Ellen Shock; m. Dorothy Donald 1947 (died 1998); one s. three d.; ed King Edward's School, Birmingham and Balliol and St Antony's Colls, Oxford; served in Intelligence Corps 1945–48; Lecturer in Politics, Christ Church and Trinity Coll. Oxford 1955–56; Fellow and Praelector in Politics, Univ. Coll. Oxford 1956–77; Estates Bursar 1959–74; Vice-Chancellor, Univ. of Leicester 1977–87; Rector, Lincoln Coll. Oxford 1987–94, Hon. Fellow 1995; Chair. Nuffield Trust 1988–2003; mem. Franks Comm. of Inquiry into Univ. of Oxford 1964–66; mem. Hebdomadal Council, Univ. of Oxford 1969–75; Chair. Cttee of Vice-Chancellors and Prins 1985–87, Rand Health Bd of Advisors 1999–; mem. Gen. Medical Council 1989–95; Hon. Vice-Pres. Political Studies Asscn 1989; Hon. FRCP 1989; Hon. LLD (Leicester) 1987. *Publications:* The Liberal Tradition; articles on politics and recent history. *Leisure interests:* gardening, theatre. *Address:* 4 Cunliffe Close, Oxford, OX2 7BL, England.

SHOEMAKER, Sydney, PhD; American academic; *Susan Linn Sage Professor of Philosophy, Emeritus, Cornell University;* b. 29 Sept. 1931, Boise, Idaho; s. of Roy Hopkins Shoemaker and Sarah Anderson Shoemaker; m. Molly McDonald 1960; one s.; ed Reed Coll., Edinburgh Univ., Cornell Univ.; instructor, Ohio State Univ. 1957–60; Santayana Fellow, Harvard Univ. 1960–61; Asst then Assoc. Prof., Cornell Univ. 1961–67, Prof. 1970–, Susan Linn Sage Prof. 1978–, now Prof. Emer.; Assoc. Prof., Rockefeller Univ. 1967–70; ed. The Philosophical Review, many terms 1964–; Gen. Ed. Cambridge Studies in Philosophy 1982–90; Vice-Pres. Eastern Div. American Philosophical Asscn 1992–93, Pres. 1993–94; John Locke Lecturer, Univ. of Oxford 1972; Josiah Royce Lecturer, Brown Univ. 1993; Fulbright Scholar 1953–54, Fellow Center for Advanced Study in Behavioral Sciences 1973–74, Nat. Endowment for the Humanities Fellowship 1980–81, Guggenheim Fellow and Fellow, Nat. Humanities Center 1987–88; mem. American Acad. of Arts and Sciences, American Philosophical Asscn. *Publications:* Self-Knowledge and Self-Identity 1963, Identity, Cause and Mind 1984, Personal Identity (with Richard Swinburne) 1984, The First Person Perspective 1996. *Leisure interests:* music, reading, gardening. *Address:* Sage School of Philosophy, 227 Goldwin Smith Hall, Cornell University, Ithaca, NY 14850 (office); 104 Northway Road, Ithaca, NY 14850, USA (home). *Telephone:* (607) 255-6817 (office); (607) 257-7382 (home). *Fax:* (609) 255-8177 (office). *E-mail:* ss56@cornell.edu (office). *Website:* www.arts.cornell.edu/phil/faculty/shoemaker (office).

SHOEMATE, Charles Richard, MBA; American business executive; b. 10 Dec. 1939, LaHarpe, Ill.; s. of Richard Osborne Shoemate and Mary Jane Shoemate (née Gillette); m. Nancy Lee Gordon 1962; three s.; ed Western Ill. Univ. and Univ. of Chicago; Comptroller, Corn Products Unit, CPC Int. 1972–74, Plant Man. 1974–76, Vice-Pres. of Operations 1976–81, Corpn Vice-Pres. 1983–88, Pres. 1988–98, Chair. and CEO 1990–98, Chair., Pres., CEO Bestfoods (fmrly CPC Int.) 1998–2000; Pres. Canada Starch Co. 1981–83, mem. Bd of Dirs 1981–88; mem. Bd of Dirs Chevron-Texaco, Inc. (now Chevron Corpn) 1998–, Corn Refiners Asscn 1985–88; fmr mem. Bd of Dirs CIGNA Corpn, Int. Paper Co.; Advisory Dir Unilever –2003; fmr Chair. The Conference Board; mem. Business Roundtable, Cttee for Econ. Devt. *Address:* c/o Board of Directors, Chevron Corporation, 6001 Bollinger Canyon Road, San Ramon, CA 94583, USA (office).

SHOIGU, Col-Gen. Sergei Kuzhugetovich; Russian politician; *Minister of Civil Defence, Emergencies and Clean-up Operations;* b. 21 May 1955, Chadan, Tuva ASSR (now Republic of Tyva), Russian Fed.; m.; two d.; ed Krasnoyarsk Polytech. Inst.; engineer, Sr master construction trust in Krasnoyarsk 1977–78; man. construction trusts Achinskamulinstroi, Cayantyazhstroi, Abakanvagonstroi 1979–88; Second Sec. Abakan City CP Cttee, insp. CP Cttee KrasnoyarskKrai 1989–90; Deputy Chair. State Cttee on Architecture and Construction RSFSR 1990–91; Chair. State Cttee of Russian Fed. on Civil Defence, Emergencies and Natural Disasters 1991–94; Minister of Civil Defence, Emergencies and Clean-up Operations 1994–; Deputy Prime Minister Jan.–May 2000; mem. Security Council of Russia; Co-fournder and leader pre-election bloc (then party) Yedinstvo (Unity) 1999–; mem. State Duma 1999; Co-Chair. of Unity and Fatherland-United Russia (later United Russia), 2001–; Hero of Russian Fed. 1999. *Leisure interests:* singing, playing guitar. *Address:* Ministry of Civil Defence, Emergencies and Clean-up Operations, 109012 Moscow, Teatralnyi proezd 3, Russia (office). *Telephone:* (495) 926-39-01 (office); (495) 923-57-45 (office). *E-mail:* info@mchs.gov.ru (office). *Website:* www.mchs.gov.ru (office).

SHOISMATOV, Ergash R.; Uzbekistani politician; *Deputy Prime Minister, responsible for Machine-construction, Metallurgy, Petroleum and Natural Gas, Geology, Electrical Energy, Chemical Production, Standardization and Metrology and State Reserves;* apptd Minister of Power Eng. and Electrification 2000; Chair. Uzbekenergo (state energy co.) –2006; Deputy Prime Minister, responsible for Machine-construction, Metallurgy, Petroleum and Natural Gas, Geology, Electrical Energy, Chemical Production, Standardization and Metrology and State Reserves 2006–. *Address:* Office of the Cabinet of Ministers, 100078 Tashkent, Mustaqillik maydoni 5, Uzbekistan (office). *Telephone:* (71) 139-82-95 (office). *Fax:* (71) 139-84-63 (office). *Website:* www .gov.uz (office).

SHOKHIN, Aleksandr Nikolayevich, DrEcSc; Russian politician; *President, Russian Union of Industrialists and Entrepreneurs;* b. 25 Nov. 1951, Savinskoye, Arkhangelsk Region; m. Tatyana Valentinovna Shokhina; one s. one d.; ed Moscow Univ.; on staff, Inst. of Econ., State Planning Cttee, Inst. of Labour, State Cttee of Labour 1974–82; researcher, Cen. Econ.-Math. Inst. and Inst. for Industrial Prognostics, USSR Acad. of Sciences 1982–87; adviser, Head of Dept of Int. Econ. Relations, Ministry of Foreign Affairs 1987–91; Dir Inst. of Employment Problems May–Aug. 1991; Russian Minister of Labour Aug.–Nov. 1991; Deputy Chair. of Russian Govt 1991–94; Minister of Labour and Employment 1991–92, of Foreign Econ. Relations 1992–93, of Econs 1994; Man. for Russia, IMF and IBRD 1992–94; mem. Bd State Specialized Export-Import Bank 1995–; Pres. Higher School of Econs 1995–; mem. Bd Russian Party of Unity and Consent 1993–95; Co-ordinator pre-election Union 'Our Home Russia' 1995, Chair. 1997–98; mem. State Duma (Parl.) 1993–97, First Deputy Chair. 1996–97; Deputy Prime Minister Sept. 1998 (resgnd); Chair. Interdepartmental Comm. of Security Council for Econ. Security 1998–99; Ind. mem. Cttee of Credit Org. and Financial Markets 1999–, now Chair.; Pres. Bureau of Russian Union of Industrialists and Entrepreneurs 2003–; mem. Nat. Council of Corp. Governance 2003–; Chair. Observational Council IG Renessans Capital 2002–, Expert Council, Fed. Comm. on Securities Market 2003–. *Publications:* several books including Social Problems of Perestroika 1989, Consumer's Market 1989, Interactive of Powers in the Legislative Process 1997; over 200 scientific articles. *Address:* Russian Union of Industrialists and Entrepreneurs, 103070 Moscow, Staraya Square, d. 10 / 4, Russia (office). *Telephone:* (495) 748-41-11 (office). *Fax:* (495) 606-11-29 (office). *E-mail:* rspp@rspp.ru (office). *Website:* www.rspp.ru (office).

SHOKIN, Yurii Ivanovich; Russian mathematician and academic; *Director, Institute of Computational Technologies, Russian Academy of Sciences;* b. 9 July 1943, Kansk; m. 1968; two d.; ed Novosibirsk State Univ.; Sr Researcher, Head of Lab. Computers, Cen. Siberian br., USSR Acad. of Sciences 1969–76, Head of Lab., Inst. Theoretical and Applied Mechanics (Siberian br.) 1976–83, Dir Computers, Cen. Siberian br. in Krasnoyarsk 1983–90; Dir Inst. of Computational Technologies (Siberian br.), Russian Acad. of Sciences 1990–, Gen. Scientific Sec. (Siberian br.) 1992–97, Gen. Dir United Inst. of Informatics 1997–; Dir Technopark, Novosibirsk 1998–; Corresp. mem. USSR (now Russian) Acad. of Sciences 1984, mem. 1994; research in computational math., numerical methods of mechanics, applied math., informatics; Order of Merit 1982, Order of Friendship 1999, Badge of Repub. of Kazakhstan for services in Devt of Science 2002, Order of Honour 2004, Medal For Belief and Good 2006. *Publications:* Interval Analysis 1981, Numerical Modelling of Tsunami Waves 1983, Method of Differential Approximation: Application in Gas Dynamics 1985, Methods of Interval Analysis 1986, Fortran 90 for the Fortran Programmer 1995, Numerical Simulation of Environmental Problems 1997, Modelling of Jet Flows in Steel Converters 2000, Numerical Modelling of Fluid Flows with Surface Waves 2001, Methods of Riemann's Geometry in Construction Problems of Computational Meshes 2005, numerous scientific articles. *Address:* Lavrentyev av. 6, 630090 Novosibirsk 90 (office); Voevodskogo 10, 630090 Novosibirsk 90, Russia (home). *Telephone:* (3832) 34-11-50 (office). *Fax:* (3832) 34-13-42 (office). *E-mail:* shokin@ict.nsc.ru (office). *Website:* www.ict.nsc.ru/eng/shokin (office).

SHOMAN, Lisa M., LLM; Belizean diplomatist and lawyer; b. 1964; ed Univ. of the West Indies, Norman Manley Law School; admitted to Bar, Belize 1988; Crown Counsel, Office of Dir of Public Prosecutions 1988–89; Assoc., Musa & Balderamos law firm 1989–90; Assoc. Young's Law Firm 1992–98; Founder and Pnr, Shoman & Chebat law firm; fmr Chair. Belize Telecommunications Ltd 2000; Amb. to USA, Perm. Rep. to OAS and High Commr to Canada 2002–07; Minister of Foreign Affairs and Foreign Trade 2007–08; mem. Bar Asscn of Belize, Exec. Cttee mem. 1993–95, Pres. 1996–97, mem. Gen. Legal Council and Disciplinary Cttee 1994–97, 1999–2000. *Address:* Shoman and Chebat, 53 Barrack Road, Belize City, Belize. *Telephone:* 223-4160 (office). *Fax:* 223-4222 (office). *E-mail:* attorney@btl.net (office). *Website:* www .shomanchebat.com (office).

SHONEKAN, Chief Ernest Adegunle Oladeinde, LLB; Nigerian lawyer, business executive, politician and fmr head of state; b. 9 May 1936, Lagos; m. Beatrice Oyelayo Oyebola 1965; two s. three d.; ed Church Missionary Soc. (CMS) Boys' School, Lagos, CMS Grammar School, Lagos and Univ. of London, UK; legal asst, UAC of Nigeria Ltd 1964–67, Asst Legal Adviser 1967–73, Deputy Legal Adviser 1974–75, Legal Adviser 1975–78, Dir 1976, Chair. 1980; Gen. Man. Bordpak Premier Packaging Co. 1978–79; Chair. Transitional Council of Nigeria Jan.–Aug. 1993; Pres. of Nigeria and Head of Interim Govt Aug.–Nov. 1993. *Address:* 12 Alexander Avenue, Ikoyi, Lagos, Nigeria (home). *Telephone:* 681437 (home).

SHONO, Kanji; Japanese business executive; *Chairman, Mitsubishi Chemical Corporation;* b. 1937; Pres. and CEO Mitsubishi Chemical Corpn 1999–2002, Chair. and Dir 2002–04; fmr Chair. Japan Petrochemical Industry Asscn; Chair. Mitsubishi Kagaku Inst. of Life Sciences (MITILS) 2002; fmr mem. Bd of Councilors, Int. Centre for the Study of E Asian Devt (ICSEAD), Kitakyushu. *Address:* c/o Mitsubishi Chemical Corporation, 33-8 Shiba 5-chome, Minato-ku, Tokyo 108-0014, Japan (office).

SHOOMBE, Pashukeni; Namibian fmr politician; b. 12 Dec. 1936, Okadiva, Oshana Region; m.; five c.; ed Okahao Training Coll., UN Inst. for Namibia, Lusaka, Zambia; teacher 1958–74; Prin. Oshigambo Girls' School 1960–63; mem. South-West Africa People's Org. (SWAPO) 1963–, joined mil. arm abroad 1974, elected mem. SWAPO Women's Council Cen. Cttee and Exec.

Cttee 1980, SWAPO Cen. Cttee 1982, 1991; rep. SWAPO as Exec. Sec. for Information and Publicity, Pan-African Women's Org., Algeria and Angola 1985–89; apptd Election Deputy Commr for Northern Region, Oshakati 1989; mem. Constitutional Ass. 1989, Nat. Ass. 1990, Chair. Nat. Ass. Select Cttee on Human Resources, mem. Cttee on Standing Rules and Orders, Public Accounts Cttee; SWAPO Sec. for Finance 1991; mem. nat. group of IPU; UNESCO Int. Award for work in SWAPO refugee camps 1980–85. *Leisure interests:* fighting against the oppression of women, reading, cooking, baking. *Address:* PO Box 1971, Windhoek, Namibia. *Telephone:* 258994. *Fax:* 232368.

SHOR, Peter Williston, BS, PhD; American mathematician and academic; *Professor, Department of Mathematics, Massachusetts Institute of Technology;* b. 14 Aug. 1959, New York; ed California Inst. of Tech., Massachusetts Inst. of Tech.; Post-doctoral Fellow, Math. Sciences Research Inst., Berkeley, Calif. 1985; mathematician, AT&T Bell Labs 1986, with Information Sciences Research Lab., AT&T Fellow 1998; currently Prof., Dept of Math., MIT; specialises in algorithms, quantum computing and quantum information theory; Nevanlinna Award 1998, Quantum Communications Award 1998, Goedel Prize (shared) 1999, Dickson Prize in Science 1999, MacArthur Fellowship 1999, King Faisal Int. Prize in Science (shared) 2002. *Publications:* frequent contribs to professional journals. *Address:* Room 2-284, Massachusetts Institute of Technology, 77 Massachusetts Avenue, Cambridge, MA 02139, USA (office). *Telephone:* (617) 253-4362 (office). *E-mail:* shor@math.mit .edu (office). *Website:* math.mit.edu/~shor (office).

SHORE, Howard; Canadian film score composer; b. 18 Oct. 1946, Toronto, Ont.; ed Berklee Coll. of Music, Boston; f. band Lighthouse; Musical Dir Saturday Night Live TV comedy show 1970s; began composing film music 1978; has collaborated on films by David Cronenberg, Peter Jackson; composed title music for Late Night with Conan O'Brien TV show 1993; mem. ASCAP; ASCAP Lifetime Achievement Award 2004. *Film scores include:* I Miss You, Hugs and Kisses 1978, The Brood 1979, Scanners 1980, Videodrome 1983, Nothing Lasts Forever 1984, After Hours 1985, Fire with Fire 1986, The Fly 1986, Heaven 1987, Nadine 1987, Dead Ringers 1988, Big 1988, Signs of Life 1989, She-Devil 1989, The Local Stigmatic 1989, An Innocent Man 1989, Made in Milan 1990, The Lemon Sisters 1990, Naked Lunch 1991, The Silence of the Lambs 1991, A Kiss Before Dying 1991, Prelude to a Kiss 1992, Single White Female 1992, Philadelphia 1993, Mrs Doubtfire 1993, Guilty As Sin 1993, Sliver 1993, M. Butterfly 1993, Nobody's Fool 1994, The Client 1994, Ed Wood (Los Angeles Film Critics' Asscn Award) 1994, Se7en 1995, Moonlight and Valentino 1995, White Man's Burden 1995, Before and After 1996, The Truth About Cats and Dogs 1996, Striptease 1996, Looking For Richard 1996, Crash 1996, That Thing You Do! 1996, The Game 1997, Cop Land 1997, Gloria 1999, Existenz 1999, Dogma 1999, Analyze This 1999, The Yards 2000, High Fidelity 2000, Esther Kahn 2000, The Cell 2000, Camera 2000, The Score 2001, The Lord of the Rings: The Fellowship of the Ring (Acad. Award for Best Original Score 2002, Grammy Award for Best Soundtrack) 2001, Spider 2002, Panic Room 2002, The Lord of the Rings: The Two Towers 2002, Gangs of New York 2002, The Lord of the Rings: The Return of the King (Golden Globe Award for Best Original Score 2004, Acad. Award for Best Song, for 'Into the West' 2004) 2003, The Aviator (Golden Globe Award for Best Original Score 2005) 2004, The Departed 2006, The Last Mimzy 2007, Eastern Promises 2007. *Opera:* The Fly. *Address:* Gorfaine/ Schwartz Agency Inc, 13245 Riverside Drive, Suite 450, Sherman Oaks, CA 91423, USA (office). *Website:* www.gsamusic.com (office).

SHORT, Rt Hon. Clare, PC, BA; British politician; b. 15 Feb. 1946, Birmingham; d. of Frank Short and Joan Short; m. 1st 1964 (divorced 1974); one s.; m. 2nd Alex Lyon 1981 (died 1993); ed Univs of Keele and Leeds; with Home Office 1970–75; Dir All Faith for One Race 1976–78, Youthaid and Unemployment Unit 1979–83; MP for Birmingham Ladywood 1983–; Shadow Employment Spokesperson 1985–89, Social Security Spokesperson 1989–91, Environment Protection Spokesperson 1992–93, Spokesperson for Women 1993–95; Shadow Sec. of State for Transport 1995–96, for Overseas Devt 1996–97; Sec. of State for Int. Devt 1997–2003; resgnd from the Govt 2003, resgnd Labour whip, now sits as Ind.; Vice-Chair. All-Party Parl. Group on Trafficking of Women and Children; Chair. All Party Group on Race Relations 1985–86, Int. Advisory Bd of Cranfield Masters in Security Sector Man. Programme, Working Group on Mining in the Philippines; mem. Advisory Cttee of Int. Lawyers for Africa; mem. Parl. Network for Nuclear Disarmament; mem. Nat. Exec. Cttee Labour Party 1988–98, Chair. Women's Cttee 1993–97; Vice-Pres. Socialist Int. Women 1992–97; mem. Select Cttee on Home Affairs 1983–95; mem. UNISON; mem. Policy Advisory Bd Cities Alliance 2006–. *Publication:* An Honourable Deception? New Labour, Iraq and the Misuse of Power 2005. *Leisure interests:* books, family, swimming. *Address:* House of Commons, Westminster, London, SW1A 0AA, England (office). *Telephone:* (20) 7219-4264 (office). *Fax:* (20) 7219-2586 (office). *E-mail:* shortc@parliament.uk (office). *Website:* www.epolitix.com/EN/MPWebsites/ Clare+Short.

SHORT, Rt Hon. Edward Watson (see Glenamara, Baron).

SHORT, Nigel David; British chess player, writer, coach and commentator; b. 1 June 1965, Leigh, Lancs.; s. of David Short and Jean Gaskell; m. Rea Karageorgiou 1987; one s. one d.; ed Bolton School, Leigh Coll.; at age of 12 beat Jonathan Penrose in British championship; Int. Master 1980, Grandmaster 1984; British Champion 1984, 1987, 1998, English Champion 1991; Pres. Grandmasters' Asscn 1992; defeated Anatoly Karpov 1992; defeated by Kasparov 1993; chess columnist, The Daily Telegraph 1991, The Sunday Telegraph 1996–2006; stripped of int. ratings by World Chess Fed. June 1993, reinstated 1994; resgnd from Fédération Internationale des Echecs (FIDE) and est. Professional Chess Asscn (PCA) with Garry Kasparov 1993, left PCA 1995; Commonwealth Champion 2004, 2006, 2008; EU Champion 2006; Pres.

Commonwealth Chess Asscn 2006–08; Hon. Fellow, Univ. of Bolton 1993–; Hon. MBE 1999. *Publication:* Learn Chess with Nigel Short 1993. *Leisure interests:* guitar playing, cricket, history, olive farming, swimming. *E-mail:* nigelshort@gmail.com (office).

SHORT, Roger Valentine, AM, ScD, FAA, FRS, FRSE, FRCVS, FRCOG, FAAS, FRCPE, FRANZOG; Australian/British professor of reproductive biology; *Professorial Fellow, Faculty of Medicine, University of Melbourne;* b. 31 July 1930, Weybridge; s. of F. A. Short and M. C. Short; m. 1st Dr Mary Bowen Wilson 1958 (divorced 1981); one s. three d.; m. 2nd Prof. Marilyn Bernice Renfree 1982; two d.; ed Sherborne School, Univs of Bristol and Cambridge, Univ. of Wisconsin, USA; mem. ARC Unit of Reproductive Physiology and Biochemistry, Cambridge 1956–72; Lecturer, then Reader, Dept of Veterinary Clinical Studies, Univ. of Cambridge 1961–72, Fellow, Magdalene Coll. 1961–72; Dir MRC Unit of Reproductive Biology, Edinburgh, Scotland 1972–82; Prof. of Reproductive Biology, Monash Univ., Australia 1982–95; currently Professorial Fellow, Faculty of Medicine, Univ. of Melbourne; J. D. White Visiting Prof., Cornell Univ., USA 2002–, Regent's Prof., Univ. of California 2001; Chair. Family Health Int., NC 1985–95 (mem. Bd 1983–97); Fellow, American Acad. of Arts and Sciences; Hon. Prof., Univ. of Edin. 1976–82; Hon. DSc (Guelph, Bristol, Edin.). *Achievements include:* holder of patents for use of melatonin to control jet lag 1983, 1986, 1987. *Publications include:* Reproduction in Mammals, Vols 1–8 (with C. R. Austin) 1972–86, Contraceptives of the Future 1976, Ever Since Adam and Eve: The Evolution of Human Sexuality (with M. Potts) 1999; contrib. to numerous scientific journals. *Leisure interests:* gardening, wildlife, history of biology. *Address:* Level 4, 766 Elizabeth Street, University of Melbourne, Vic. 3010 (office); 18 Gwingana Crescent, Glen Waverley, Vic. 3150, Australia (home). *Telephone:* (3) 8344-3370 (office); (3) 9561-8873 (home). *Fax:* (3) 9347-8939 (office). *E-mail:* r.short@unimelb.edu.au (office).

SHORTER, Wayne, BA; American jazz musician (saxophone); b. 25 Aug. 1933, Newark, NJ; ed New York Univ.; served US Army 1956–58; played saxophone with Art Blakey 1959–63, Miles Davis 1964–70, Weather Report 1970–86, Miles Davis Tribute Band 1992; solo artist 1962–, and with Wayne Shorter Quartet; winner numerous Down Beat Magazine Awards, Best Soprano Sax 1984, 1985. *Recordings include:* albums: solo: Blues á la Carte 1959, Introducing Wayne Shorter 1959, Second Genesis 1960, Free Form 1961, Wayning Moments 1962, Search for a New Land 1964, Night Dreamer 1964, Some Other Stuff 1964, JuJu 1964, Speak No Evil 1964, The Soothsayer 1965, Et Cetera 1965, The Collector 1965, The All Seeing Eye 1965, Adam's Apple 1966, Schizophrenia 1967, Super Nova 1969, Moto Grosso Felo 1970, Odyssey of Iska 1970, Shorter Moments 1972, Wayne Shorter 1974, Native Dancer 1974, Atlantis 1985, Phantom Navigator 1986, Joy Ryder 1988, High Life 1994, Portrait 2000, All or Nothing at all 2002, Footprints Live! 2002, Alegría 2003, Footprints 2005, Beyond the Sound Barrier (Grammy Award for Best Jazz Instrumental Album by an Individual or Group 2006) 2005; with Weather Report: Weather Report 1971, I Sing the Body Electric 1972, Sweetnighter 1973, Mysterious Traveler 1974, Tail Spinnin' 1975, Black Market 1976, Black Market/Heavy Weather 1978, Mr Gone 1978, 8.30 1979, Night Passage 1980, Procession 1983, Domino Theory 1984, Sportin' Life 1985, This is This! 1986. *Address:* International Music Network, 278 Main Street, Gloucester, MA 01930, USA (office); c/o Verve Music Group, Jai St Laurent-Smyth, 1755 Broadway, Third Floor, New York, NY 10019, USA. *Telephone:* (978) 283-2883 (office); (212) 331-2047. *Fax:* (978) 283-2330 (office); (212) 331-2062. *E-mail:* jai.stlaurent-smyth@umusic.com. *Website:* www .vervemusicgroup.com.

SHOSTAKOVICH, Maksim Dmitriyevich; American (b. Russian) conductor; b. 10 May 1938, Leningrad (now St Petersburg); s. of the late Dmitriy Shostakovich; m. 1st; one s.; m. 2nd Marina Tisie 1989; one s. one d.; ed Cen. Music School, Moscow Conservatory; studied conducting under Rabinovich, Gauk, Rozhdestvensky (q.v.); Asst Conductor, Moscow Symphony Orchestra; Conductor, State Academic Symphony Orchestra; piano debut age 19 in father's Second Piano Concerto; Prin. Conductor and Artistic Dir USSR Radio and TV Symphony Orchestra; requested and granted political asylum in USA while on tour with USSR Radio and TV Symphony Orchestra, Nuremberg April 1981; conducted Nat. Symphony Orchestra, Capitol steps, Washington, DC, USA May 1981; Prin. Guest Conductor Hong Kong Philharmonic 1982–; Music Dir New Orleans Symphony Orchestra 1986–91; Hon. Music Dir Louisiana Philharmonic Orchestra 1993–94. *Performances:* Touring Western Europe with USSR Radio and TV Symphony Orchestra, Japan, USA 1971–81; has conducted all maj. N American orchestras and many in Europe, Asia, S America; conducted premiere of father's 15th Symphony and recorded virtually all father's symphonies in USSR; has performed with leading soloists, incl. Emil Gilels, Oistrakh, Rostropovich. *Address:* PO Box 273, Jordanville, NY 13361, USA.

SHOWALTER, Elaine, MA, PhD; American academic, literary critic and writer; *Professor Emerita of English, Princeton University;* b. 14 Jan. 1941, Cambridge, Mass.; d. of Paul Cottler and Violet Cottler (née Rottenberg); m. English Showalter 1963; one s. one d.; ed Bryn Mawr Coll., Brandeis Univ.; Teaching Asst, Dept of English, Univ. of Calif. 1964–66, teaching posts in Dept, later Assoc. Prof. 1967–78; Prof. of English, Rutgers Univ. 1978–84; Avalon Foundation Prof. of Humanities, Princeton Univ., NJ 1984–2003, Prof. Emer. 2003–; writer, The Guardian newspaper, London 2003; R. Stanton Avery Distinguished Fellow, Huntington Library, Calif. 2004–05; Visiting Prof. of English and Women's Studies, Univ. of Del. 1976–77; Visiting Prof., School of Criticism and Theory, Dartmouth Coll. 1986; Guggenheim Fellow 1977–78; Rockefeller Humanities Fellow 1981–83; fmr Visiting Prof. at several univs abroad; numerous TV and radio appearances; Chair. Man Booker Int. Prize jury 2007 mem. Modern Language Asscn; Howard Behrman

Humanities Award (Princeton Univ.) 1989. *Publications:* A Literature of Their Own 1977, The Female Malady 1985, Sexual Anarchy 1990, Sister's Choice 1991, Hysteria Beyond Freud (jt author) 1993, Hystories 1997, Faculty Towers: The Academic Novel and Its Discontents 2005, A Jury of Her Peers 2009; also ed. of several feminist publs and writer of numerous articles and reviews. *Address:* c/o Department of English, Princeton University, 22 McCosh Hall, Princeton, NJ 08544, USA.

SHOYAMA, Etsuhiko, BS; Japanese electronics industry executive; *Chairman, Hitachi Ltd;* b. 9 March 1936, Niigata Pref.; ed Tokyo Inst. of Tech.; began career as power plant engineer, Hitachi Works 1959–82, Deputy Gen. Man. Hitachi Works 1982–85, Gen. Man. Kokubu Works 1985–87, Gen. Man. Tochigi Works 1987–90, Gen. Man. Household Appliances Div. 1990–1991, elected to Bd of Dirs Hitachi Ltd 1991, Gen. Man. Consumer Electronics Div. 1991–93, Exec. Man. Dir 1993–95, Sr Exec. Man. Dir 1995–97, Exec. Vice-Pres. and Rep. Dir 1997–99, Pres. and Rep. Dir 1999–2003, Pres. and CEO 2003–06, Chair. and Dir 2006–07, Chair. and Advisor 2007–; Chair. Information and Communications Council, Ministry of Internal Affairs and Communications 2005–; mem. Council for Science and Tech., Policy Cabinet Office 2006–; Officier, Légion d'honneur 2007. *Address:* Hitachi Ltd, 6-6 Marunouchi, 1-chome, Chiyoda-ku, Tokyo 100-8280, Japan (office). *Telephone:* (3) 3258-1111 (office). *Fax:* (3) 3258-2375 (office). *E-mail:* service@cm.hbi.co.jp (office). *Website:* www.hitachi.com (office).

SHPAK, Col-Gen. Georgy Ivanovich, CandPedSc; Russian army officer and politician; b. 6 Sept. 1943, Osipovichi, Mogilev Region, Ukraine; m.; one s. (deceased) one d.; ed M. Frunze Mil. Acad., Mil. Acad. of Gen. Staff; commdr paratroopers' regt, head of staff, deputy commdr paratroopers' div., commdr of div. 1978–88; Deputy Commdr of Army Odessa Mil. Command 1988–89; Army Commdr, First Deputy Commdr Turkestan Mil. Command 1989–92; First Deputy Commdr Volga Mil. Command; Commdr Paratrooper Forces of Russian Army 1996; Gov. Ryazan Oblast 2004–08; mem. State Duma 2004; three orders, ten medals. *Leisure interests:* countryside, fishing. *Address:* c/o Office of the Head of the Regional Administration (Governor), ul. Lenina 30, 39000 Ryazan, Russia (office).

SHPEK, Roman Vasilyevich; Ukrainian economist and diplomatist; *Ambassador and Head of Mission to European Union;* b. 10 Nov. 1954, Broshniv, Ivano-Frankivsk Region; m. Maria Romanivna Shpek; one s. one d.; ed Forestry Eng Inst., Lviv, Int. Inst. of Wood Man., Kiev, Dalover Univ.; processing engineer and head of woodworking manufacturing plant, Ivano-Frankivsk Region 1976–78, Chief Engineer, wood and woodworking plant 1978–81, Dir 1981–89; Deputy Minister of Forestry, Woodworking and Furniture Industry, Ukrainian SSR 1989–92; Minister of Privatization, Ukraine April–Oct. 1992; First Deputy Minister of the Economy of Ukraine 1992–93, Minister 1993–95, Deputy Prime Minister on Econ. Policy 1995–96; Head Nat. Agency for Devt and European Integration 1996–2000; Co-Chair. Ukrainian-German Council on Econ. Co-operation, Ukrainian-Italian Council on Econ. Co-operation, Comm Kuchma-Gor on Econ. Devt Cttee; Acting Gov., then Gov. for Ukraine, World Bank Group; Chair. Currency and Finance Council to Cabinet of Ministers of Ukraine; Nat. Co-ordinator of Tech. Assistance Programme for Ukraine 1993–2000; Ukrainian Rep. to UNDP 1996–; Amb. and Head of Mission of Ukraine to EU 2000–; Order for Merits, 3rd Degree (Ukraine). *Leisure:* oil painting, classical music, travelling, sport (football, boxing). *Address:* 99–101 Avenue Louis Lepoutre, 1050 Brussels (office); 29 Avenue de Saturne, 1180 Brussels, Belgium (home). *Telephone:* (2) 340-98-70 (office); (2) 379-09-87 (home). *Fax:* (2) 340-98-79 (office). *E-mail:* roman.shpek@gmail.com (home). *Website:* www.ukraine-eu.mfa.gov.ua (office).

SHRESTHA, Indra Bahadur; Nepalese business executive; *Chairman, Hetauda Cement Industries Ltd;* fmr Pres. CCI Makawanpur; Chair. Hetauda Cement Industries Ltd; Pres. Lalitpur Chamber of Commerce and Industry; mem. Nat. Exec. Cttee, Amnesty Int. Nepal 2004. *Address:* Hetauda Cement Industries Ltd, PO Box 24, Hetauda, Makawanpur (office); Lalitpur Chamber of Commerce and Industry, Mangal Bazar, PO Box 26, Lalitpur, Nepal (office). *Telephone:* (1) 5521740 (office). *Fax:* (1) 5530661 (office). *E-mail:* lcci@mos.com.np (office).

SHREVE, Anita; American writer; fmr high school teacher, journalist in Nairobi, Kenya and USA; teacher of writing Amherst Coll.; O. Henry Prize 1975, New York Newspaper Guild Page One Award, PEN/L. L. Winship Award 1998, New England Book Award for fiction 1998. *Publications:* non-fiction: Remaking Motherhood: How Working Mothers are Shaping Our Children's Future 1987, Women Together, Women Alone: The Legacy of the Consciousness-Raising Movement 1989; fiction: Eden Close 1989, Strange Fits of Passion 1991, Where or When 1993, Resistance 1995, The Weight of Water 1997, The Pilot's Wife 1998, Fortune's Rocks 2000, The Last Time They Met 2001, Sea Glass 2002, All He Ever Wanted 2002, Light on Snow 2004, A Wedding in December 2005, Body Surfing 2008; contrib. to Quest, US, Newsweek, New York Times Magazine. *Address:* c/o Author Mail, Little, Brown and Company, 237 Park Avenue, New York, NY 10017, USA (office). *E-mail:* askanita@hbgusa.com (office). *Website:* www.anitashreve.com.

SHREVE, Susan Richards, MA; American writer and academic; *Professor of English Literature, George Mason University;* b. 2 May 1939, Toledo, OH; d. of Robert Richards and Helen Richards; m. 1st Porter Shreve (divorced 1987); m. 2nd Timothy Seldes 1987; two s. two d.; ed Univs of Pennsylvania and Virginia; Prof. of English Literature, George Mason Univ., Fairfax, Va 1976–; Visiting Prof., Columbia Univ., New York 1982–, Princeton Univ. 1991, 1992, 1993; fmr Pres. PEN/Faulkner Foundation; producer, The American Voice for TV 1986–; Essayist, MacNeil/Lehrer Newshour; George Washington Univ. Jenny Moore Award 1978, Guggenheim Fellowship 1980, Nat. Endowment for the Arts Fellowship 1982. *Publications:* A Fortunate Madness 1974, A Woman Like That 1977, Children of Power 1979, Miracle Play 1981, Dreaming of Heroes 1984, Queen of Hearts 1986, A Country of Strangers 1989, Daughters of the New World 1992, The Train Home 1993, Skin Deep: Women and Race 1995, The Visiting Physician 1995, The Goalie 1996, Narratives on Justice (co-ed.) 1996, Outside the Law 1997, How We Want to Live (co-ed.) 1998, Plum and Jaggers 2000, A Student of Living Things 2006, Warm Springs: Traces of a Childhood at FDR's Polio Haven 2007; juvenile: Jonah, The Whale 1997, Ghost Cats 1999, The End of Amanda, The Good 2000. *Address:* Graduate Creative Writing Program, Department of English, George Mason University, 4400 University Drive, Fairfax, VA 22030 (office); 3319 Newark Street, NW, Washington, DC 20008, USA (home). *E-mail:* writing@gmu.edu (office). *Website:* creativewriting.gmu.edu (office); www.susanshreve.com (home).

SHRIVER, Duward F., BS, PhD; American scientist and academic; *Morrison Professor Emeritus of Chemistry, Northwestern University;* b. 20 Nov. 1934, Glendale, Calif.; s. of D. L. Shriver and J. S. Shriver; m. Shirley A. Clark 1957; two s.; ed Univ. of California, Berkeley, Univ. of Michigan; instructor, Northwestern Univ., Evanston, Ill. 1961–62, Asst Prof. 1962–67, Assoc. Prof. 1967–71, Prof. 1971–78, Morrison Prof. of Chem. 1988–, now Prof. Emer., Chair. Chem. Dept 1992–95; Alfred P. Sloan Research Fellow 1967–69; Guggenheim Fellow 1983–84, mem. Inorganic Syntheses Inc. 1974–, Pres. 1982–85; ACS Award for Distinguished Service in Inorganic Chem. 1987, Materials Research Soc. Medal 1990. *Publications:* five books, including Inorganic Chemistry (jtly) 1990; 295 scientific papers. *Address:* Department of Chemistry, Tech K124, Northwestern University, 2145 Sheridan Road, Evanston, IL 60208 (office); 1100 Colfax Street, Evanston, IL 60201, USA (home). *Telephone:* (847) 491-5655 (office). *Fax:* (847) 491-7713 (office). *E-mail:* shriver@chem.northwestern.edu (office). *Website:* www.chem.northwestern.edu (office).

SHRIVER, (Robert) Sargent, Jr, AB, LLD; American public servant, politician and international organization official; *Chairman Emeritus, Special Olympics International;* b. 9 Nov. 1915, Westminster, Md; s. of Robert Sargent and Hilda Shriver; m. Eunice Kennedy 1953; four s. one d.; ed Yale Univ.; admitted to NY Bar 1941; served USN (Lt Commdr) 1941–45; Asst Ed. Newsweek 1945–46; Adviser The Joseph P. Kennedy, Jr Foundation 1955–; Asst Gen. Man. The Merchandise Mart 1948–61; mem. Chicago Bd of Educ. 1955–60, Pres. 1956–60; Dir The Peace Corps 1961–66, Office of Econ. Opportunity 1964–68; Special Asst to the Pres. 1964–68; Amb. to France 1968–70; Democratic Vice-Presidential Cand. 1972; Pnr, Fried, Frank, Harris, Shriver & Jacobson (law firm) 1971–86; mem. American Comm. on East-West Accord 1978, Americans for SALT 1979; Dir The Arms Control Asscn 1983–, American Council on Germany; Pres. Special Olympics Int. 1986–90, CEO and Chair. 1990–96, Chair. Bd 1996–2003, Chair. Emer. 2003–; Golden Heart Presidential Award (Philippines), Médaille de Vermeil (City of Paris), US Presidential Medal of Freedom 1994, Distinguished American Award from John F. Kennedy Library and Foundation 2001, and many other nat. and int. awards more than 24 hon. degrees including Yale Univ., Brandeis Univ., Boston College, Yeshiva Univ., Univ. of Liberia, Chulalongkorn Univ., Bangkok. *Publication:* Point of the Lance 1964. *Address:* Special Olympics International, 1133 19th Street, NW, Washington, DC 20036, USA (office). *Telephone:* (202) 628-3630 (office). *Fax:* (202) 824-0200 (office). *Website:* www.specialolympics.org (office).

SHTAUBER, Zvi Meir, PhD; Israeli diplomatist, academic and fmr military officer; *Director, Institute for National Security Studies, Tel-Aviv University;* b. 15 July 1947; s. of Yisrael Shtauber and Jaffa Shtauber; m. Nitza Rousso; two s. one d.; ed Harvard Business School, Fletcher School of Law and Diplomacy, Tufts Univ., USA; with Israel Defence Forces 1970–95, Head of Strategic Planning Div. 1995, retd with rank of Brig.-Gen. 1995; Vice-Pres. Ben-Gurion Univ. of the Negev 1996–99; Foreign Policy Adviser to Prime Minister Ehud Barak (q.v.) 1999–2000; Amb. to UK 2001–04; Head, Jaffee Center for Strategic Studies, Tel-Aviv Univ. 2005, now Dir Inst. for Nat. Security Studies (incorporated Jaffee Center). *Address:* Institute for National Security Studies, 40 Haim Levanon Street, Tel-Aviv 61398, Israel (office). *Telephone:* 3-6400401 (office). *E-mail:* zvis@inss.org.il (office). *Website:* www.inss.org.il (office).

SHU, Huiguo; Chinese politician and agronomist; b. July 1938, Jing'an Co., Jiangxi Prov.; ed Zhejiang Agricultural Coll.; joined CCP 1980; Dir Dept of Agric., Animal Husbandry and Fishery, Jiangxi Prov.; Vice-Gov. Jiangxi Prov. 1991–2001; Vice-Sec. CCP Jiangxi Prov. Cttee 1995, Sec. 1997–2001; Chair. Standing Cttee Jiangxi Prov. People's Congress 1998–2001; Vice-Minister of Personnel 2001; mem. 15th CCP Cen. Cttee 1997–2002. *Address:* c/o Ministry of Personnel, 12 Hepingli Central Street, Beijing 100716, People's Republic of China (office). *Telephone:* (1) 84201114 (office).

SHU, Shengyou; Chinese politician; b. Dec. 1936, Yushan Co., Jiangxi Prov.; joined CCP 1959; Mayor of Jingdezhen City; Vice-Gov. Jiangxi Prov. 1991, Gov. 1996–2001; Vice-Sec. CCP Jiangxi Prov. Cttee 1995–2001; mem. 15th CCP Cen. Cttee 1997–2002; mem. Standing Cttee 9th CPPCC Nat. Cttee 1998–2003. *Address:* c/o Jiangxi Provincial Government, Nanchang, Jiangxi Province, People's Republic of China (office).

SHU, Ting; Chinese poet and writer; b. (Gong Peiyu), 1952, Shima, Zhangzhou City, Fujian Prov.; d. of Shi Mo Gang and Xiu Zhen Yong; m. Chen Zhongyi 1981; one s.; sent to work in countryside during Cultural Revolution –1973, then worked on construction sites and in factories; published poems in Today (underground literary magazine); mem. Writers' Asscn Fujian 1983– (Vice-Chair. 1985–), Council of Writers' Asscn of China 1985–; Dir Chinese Writers' Union; Nat. Poetry Award 1981, 1983. *Publications:* Shuangweichuan 1982, Shu Ting Shuqing Shixuan 1984, Poesiealbum

Shu Ting 1989, Selected Poems of Seven Chinese Poets 1993, Selected Poems: An Authoritative Collection 1994, Mist of my Heart: Selected Poems of Shu Ting 1995. *Address:* 13 Zhonghua Road, Gulangyu, Xiamen City, Fujian Province, 361002, People's Republic of China.

SHUE, Elisabeth; American actress; b. 6 Oct. 1963, Wilmington, Del.; d. of James Shue and Anne Wells; m. Davis Guggenheim 1994 (divorced 1996); one s.; ed Wellesley Coll., Harvard Univ.; studied with Sylvie Leigh, Showcase Theater; appeared in Broadway plays including Some Americans Abroad, Birth and After Birth. *Films include:* The Karate Kid 1984, Link 1986, Adventures in Babysitting 1987, Cocktail 1988, Body Wars 1989, Back to the Future Part II 1989, Part III 1990, Soapdish 1991, The Marrying Man 1991, Twenty Bucks 1993, Heart and Souls 1993, Radio Inside 1994, Blind Justice 1994, The Underneath 1995, Leaving Las Vegas 1995, The Trigger Effect 1996, The Saint 1996, Palmetto 1997, Deconstructing Harry 1997, Cousin Bette 1997, Molly 1998, Hollow Man 2000, Amy and Isabelle 2001, Leo 2004, Mysterious Skin 2004, Hide and Seek 2005, Gracie 2007. *Television films include:* The Royal Romance of Charles and Diana 1982, Double Switch 1987, Hale the Hero 1992, Blind Justice 1994, Dreamer: Inspired by a True Story 2005,. *Television series:* Call to Glory 1984. *Address:* c/o Creative Arts Agency, 9830 Wilshire Boulevard, Beverly Hills, CA 90212, USA.

SHUKLA, Vidya Charan, BA; Indian politician; b. 2 Aug. 1929, Raipur; s. of Ravi Shanker and Bhawani Shukla; m. Sarala Devi 1951; three d.; ed Morris Coll. and Univ. Coll. of Law, Nagpur; mem. Lok Sabha 1957–62, 1962–67, 1967–70, 1971–77; Deputy Minister of Communications and Parl. Affairs Jan.–Feb. 1966; Deputy Minister for Home Affairs 1966–67; Minister of State in Ministry of Home Affairs 1967–70; Minister of Revenue and Expenditure in Ministry of Finance 1970–71, Minister of Defence Production 1971–74, Minister of Planning 1974–75, for Information and Broadcasting 1975–77, for Civil Supplies 1980–81, for Foreign Affairs 1990–91, for Water Resources and Parl. Affairs 1991–96; Pres. Special Organising Cttee, 9th Asian Games, Delhi; Pres. All-India Council of Sports 1981–83; Chair. Nat. Insts. of Physical Educ. and Sports 1981–85; Pres. Indian Olympic Asscn 1984–88; expelled from Congress (I) Party 1987; f. Jan Monha (People's Front) 1987; f. Chhattisgarh Sangharsh Morcha and was instrumental in creation of new State of Chhattisgarh in Union of India 2000; helped defeat state govt 2003; currently head Chattisgarh Sangharsh Parishad (NGO). *Leisure interests:* hunting, tracking and photography. *Address:* Radheshyam Bhavan, Krishak Nagar, G.E. Road, Raipur, Chattisgarh; 502, Taj Apartments, 2 Ring Road, Near Safderjung Hospital, New Delhi, India. *Telephone:* (771) 423841 (Raipur); (11) 6196738 (New Delhi). *Fax:* (771) 2425100 (Raipur); (11) 26191525 (New Delhi). *E-mail:* vdshukla@rediffmail.com.

SHUKRI, Ibrahim; Egyptian politician; *Leader, Socialist Labour Party;* b. 22 Sept. 1916; joined Misr al-Fatat (Young Egypt) Party 1935; shot in Cairo strike 1935; managed Sharbeen (family estate); Sec.-Gen. Misr al-Fatat 1946; elected Vice-Pres., then Pres. Socialist Party (fmrly Misr al-Fatat) 1947–53; mem. for Kahaliyya, People's Ass. 1949–52; imprisoned for opposing the monarchy 1952, released after revolution 1952, returned to estate; joined Arab Socialist Union on its formation 1962, elected to Exec. Cttee 1964; re-elected mem. for Kahaliyya 1964–68; Pres. Farmers' Union and Sec. Professional Asscn 1965–66; Gov. Wadi al-Gadeed 1968–76; elected to People's Ass. 1976; Minister of Agric. and Agrarian Reform 1977–98, of Land Improvement May–Oct. 1978; Chair. Socialist Labour Party 1978–99, currently Leader; fmr Man. Ed. Al-Sha'b (party newspaper); Leader of the Opposition, People's Ass. 1979–86. *Address:* c/o Socialist Labour Party, 12 Sharia Awali el-Ahd, Cairo, Egypt.

SHULEVA, Lidiya Santova, BE, MA; Bulgarian economist, business executive and politician; b. 23 Dec. 1956, Velingrad; m. (widowed); two c.; ed Tech. Univ., Sofia, Univ. of Nat. and World Economy, Sofia; specialised in marketing and finance, Man. Acad., Munich, Germany; worked in man. and finance, Japan; fmr man. consultant, EEC, Greece; Owner and Man. Business Intellect EOOD 1992–96; Exec. Man. Albena Invest Holding AD 1996–2000; Chair. Asscn of Industrial Capital 2000–; Minister of Labour and Social Policy 2001; Deputy Prime Minister and Minister of the Economy 2001–05; mem. Governing Bd Assistance to Charity Foundation 2000–; mem. Nat. Ass. 2005–, mem. Econ. Policy Cttee 2005–, Budget and Finance Cttee 2005–; mem. Bulgarian New Democracy Parl. Group 2007–; Observer in European Parl. 2005–06, mem. European Parl. Jan.-May 2007. *Address:* National Assembly, 2 Narodno sabranie Square, 1169 Sofia, Bulgaria (office). *Telephone:* (2) 939-39 (office). *Fax:* (2) 981-31-31 (office). *E-mail:* infocenter@parliament.bg (office). *Website:* www.parliament.bg (office).

SHULMAN, Alexandra, OBE; British journalist; *Editor, British Vogue;* b. 13 Nov. 1957, London; d. of Milton Shulman and Drusilla Beyfus; ed St Paul's Girls' School and Univ. of Sussex; Sec. Over-21 magazine; Writer and Commissioning Ed., later Features Ed. Tatler 1982–87; Ed. Women's Page, Sunday Telegraph 1987, later Deputy Ed. 7 Days current affairs photo/reportage; Features Ed. Vogue 1988; Ed. GQ 1990; Ed. British Vogue 1992–; Dir Condé Nast Publications 1997–2002; Trustee Nat. Portrait Gallery, London 1999–. *Address:* Condé Nast Publications, Vogue House, Hanover Square, London, W1R 0AD, England (office). *Telephone:* (20) 7499-9080.

SHULMAN, Lawrence Edward, MD, PhD, FACP; American biomedical research administrator and rheumatologist; *Director Emeritus, National Institute of Arthritis and Musculoskeletal and Skin Diseases;* b. 25 July 1919, Boston, Mass; s. of David Herman Shulman and Belle Shulman (née Tishler); m. 1st Pauline K. Flint 1946, m. 2nd Reni Trudinger 1959; one s. two d.; ed Harvard and Yale Univs; Research Assoc., John B. Pierce Foundation, New Haven, Conn. 1942–45; Intern, Resident and Fellow in Internal Medicine, Johns Hopkins Hospital and Univ. 1949–53; Dir Connective Tissue Div. Johns Hopkins Univ. Medical School 1955–75; Assoc. Prof. of Medicine, Johns Hopkins Univ. 1964–; Assoc. Dir for Arthritis, Musculosceletal and Skin Diseases, NIH 1976–82, Dir 1982–86; Dir Nat. Inst. of Arthritis and Musculoskeletal and Skin Diseases 1986–94, Dir Emer. 1994–; NIH Emissary for Clinical Research 1994–; several awards. *Publications:* more than 100 articles in scientific journals. *Leisure interests:* music, politics. *Address:* c/o NIAMS/NIH, Bldg 31, Rm 4C32, 31 Center Drive, MSC 2350, Bethesda, MD 20892-2350; 6302 Swords Way, Bethesda, MD 20817, USA (home).

SHULMAN, Robert Gerson, MA, PhD; American biophysicist; *Sterling Professor Emeritus of Molecular Biophysics and Biochemistry, Yale University;* b. 3 March 1924, New York; s. of Joshua S. Shulman and Freda Shulman (née Lipshay); m. 1st Saralee Deutsch 1952 (died 1983); three s.; m. 2nd Stephanie S. Spangler 1986; ed Columbia Univ.; Research Assoc., Columbia Univ. Radiation Lab., New York 1949; AEC Fellow in Chem., Calif. Inst. of Tech. 1949–50; Head, Semiconductor Research Section, Hughes Aircraft Co. Culver City, Calif. 1950–53; mem. tech. staff, Bell Labs, Murray Hill, NJ 1953–66, Head, Biophysics Research Dept 1966–79; Prof. of Molecular Biophysics and Biochemistry, Yale Univ. 1979–94, Dir Div. of Biological Sciences 1979–94, Sterling Prof. of Biophysics and Biochemistry 1994–, now Prof. Emer. and Sr Research Scientist, Diagnostic Radiology, fmr Emissary for Clinical Research; mem. NAS, Inst. of Medicine; Guggenheim Fellow, Cambridge 1961–62. *Address:* Yale University MR Center, Department of Molecular Biophysics and Biochemistry, PO Box 208024, New Haven, CT 06520-8024, USA (office); (203) 432-1333 (home). *Telephone:* (203) 785-6201 (office). *Fax:* (203) 785-7979 (office). *E-mail:* robert.shulman@yale.edu (office). *Website:* xbeams.chem.yale.edu/GradBroch/html/shulman.htm (office).

SHULTZ, George Pratt, BA, PhD; American fmr government official, economist and academic; *Thomas W. and Susan B. Ford Distinguished Fellow, Hoover Institution, Stanford University;* b. New York; s. of Birl E. Shultz and Margaret Lennox Pratt Shultz; m. 1st Helena M. O'Brien 1946; two s. three d.; m. 2nd Charlotte Mailliard Swig 1997; ed Princeton Univ. and MIT; Assoc. Prof. of Industrial Relations, MIT 1955–57; Sr Staff Economist, Pres.'s Council of Econ. Advisers 1955–56; Prof. of Industrial Relations, Grad. School of Business, Univ. of Chicago 1957–68, Dean, Grad. School of Business 1962–68; Pres. Industrial Research Asscn 1968; US Sec. of Labor 1969–70; Dir Office of Man. and Budget, Exec. Office of the Pres. 1970–72; US Sec. of Treasury 1972–74; Chair. Council on Econ. Policy 1973–74; Sec. of State 1982–89; Exec. Vice-Pres. Bechtel Corpn 1974–75, Pres. 1975–77, Vice-Chair. 1977–81, Pres. Bechtel Group Inc. 1981–82; Prof. of Man. and Public Policy, Grad. School of Business, Stanford Univ. 1974–82, of Int. Economy 1989–91, Prof. Emer. 1991–; Chair. JP Morgan Chase Int. Council, Accenture Energy Advisory Bd 2003–07, Advisory Council Inst. of Int. Studies, Stanford, Govs'. Econ. Policy Advisory Bd, Calif., Gov.'s Council of Econ. Advisors 2004–; mem. Bd Bechtel Group Inc. 1989–2007, Accretive Health; Chair. Pres. Reagan's Econ. Policy Advisory Bd 1981–82; Chair. Advisory Bd Precourt Inst. for Energy Efficiency; Chair. External Advisory Bd MIT Energy Initiative; mem. Bd of Trustees, Center for Advancement of Study in the Behavioral Sciences, Stanford, Calif.; Distinguished Fellow, Hoover Inst., Stanford Univ. 1989–; Thomas W. and Susan B. Ford Distinguished Fellow, Hoover Inst. 2001–, Distinguished Fellow American Econ. Asscn 2005; Grand Cordon, Order of the Rising Sun 1989; Jefferson Award 1989, Presidential Medal of Freedom 1989, Seoul Peace Prize 1992, Eisenhower Medal 2001, Reagan Distinguished American Award 2002, Ralph J. Bunche Award for Diplomatic Excellence 2002, Nat. World War II Museum American Spirit Award 2006, George Marshall Award 2007, Truman Medal for Econ. Policy 2007, American Acad. of Arts and Sciences Rumford Prize 2008. *Publications include:* Pressures on Wage Decisions, Labor Problems,The Dynamics of a Labor Market, Management Organization and the Computer, Strategies for the Displaced Worker, Guidelines, Informal Controls and the Market Place, Workers and Wages in the Urban Labor Market, Leaders and Followers in an Age of Ambiguity, Economic Policy beyond the Headlines, Turmoil and Triumph: My Years as Secretary of State 1993, Putting Our House in Order: A Guide to Social Security and Health Care Reform (with John Shoven) 2008. *Leisure interests:* golf, tennis. *Address:* Hoover Institution, Stanford, CA 94305-6010, USA (office). *Telephone:* (650) 725-3492 (office). *Fax:* (650) 723-5441 (office). *Website:* www-hoover.stanford.edu (office).

SHUMEIKO, Vladimir Filippovich, CTechSc DEcon; Russian economist and politician; *Founder and Chairman, Reforms-New Course Movement;* b. 10 Feb. 1945, Rostov Don; m.; two d.; ed Krasnodar Polytech. Inst.; worked in factories as foreman, engineer, chief engineer, Dir-Gen. Concern Krasnodar Factory of Measuring Instruments –1991; People's Deputy of Russia 1990–92; Vice-Chair. Supreme Soviet of Russia 1991–92, First Deputy Prime Minister of Russia 1992–93; Pres. Confed. of Entrepreneurs' Unions of Russia 1992–93; mem. Council of Fed. (Upper House of Parl.) 1993–96, Chair. 1994–96; Founder and Chair. Reforms-New Course Movt 1996–; Lecturer, Acad. of Border Service; Chair. Bd of Dirs Interregional Auction and Stock Corpn 1998–, Moskva Bank 2002–. *Publication:* Russian Reforms and Federalism 1995, Pelmeny po Protocoly 2001. *Leisure interests:* fishing, woodworking, collecting small bells. *Address:* , Novi Arbat 19, Moscow; Moskva Bank, Bolshoi Znamenski per. 6, bldg 9, 121019 Moscow, Russia. *Telephone:* (495) 203-33-47 (Movt); (495) 777-97-97 (Bank). *Fax:* (495) 916-72-07 (Bank). *E-mail:* office@moscow-bank.ru.

SHUSHKIEVICH, Stanislau Stanislavavich, DSc; Belarusian physicist and politician; b. 15 Dec. 1934, Minsk; m. Irina Kuzminichna Shushkevich; one s. one d.; ed Belarus Univ.; CPSU 1967–91; researcher, Inst. of Physics, Belarus Acad. of Sciences 1959–60; engineer Minsk Radio Plant 1960–61; Chief Engineer, Head of Section Belarus Univ. 1961–67; Prof.-Rector Minsk Radiotechnical Inst. 1966–69; Head of Chair., Belarus Univ. 1969–86, Pro-

Rector 1986–90; began involvement in politics 1989 as critic of Govt negligence in aftermath of Chernobyl accident; mem. Supreme Soviet (backed by opposition Belarus Popular Front) 1990–91; Chair. Supreme Soviet 1991–94, mem. –1996; Dir Centre of Political and Econ. Studies, European Humanitarian Inst. 1994–; mem. Civil Action faction; cand. in presidential elections 1994; fmr Leader, Belarusian Social-Democratic Hramada party, merged with Belarusian Social Democratic Party (Nat. Hramada) 2005; Corresp. mem. Belarus Acad. of Sciences 1991–; Belarus State Prize, Council of Ministers of USSR Prize, Int. Phylip Orlik Prize. *Publications:* Belarus – Self-Identification and Statehood, Belorussian Newcommunism; more than 60 articles and papers on problems of nuclear electronics and political problems. *Address:* c/o Belarusian Social-Democratic Party 'Hramada' (Assembly) (Belaruskaya Satsyal-demakratychnaya Partya 'Hramada'), 220035 Minsk, vul. Drozda 8/52; Masherova ave. 78-14, 220035 Minsk, Belarus (home). *Telephone:* (17) 226-70-71 (home). *Fax:* (17) 226-70-71 (home). *E-mail:* stastashu@mail.ru (home).

SHUVALOV, Igor Ivanovich; Russian politician and lawyer; *First Deputy Chairman of the Government;* b. 4 Jan. 1967, Bilibino, Magadan Oblast (now Chukotka Autonomous Okrug), Russia; m.; one s. two d.; ed Moscow State Univ.; lab. worker, EKOS Research Inst., Moscow 1984–85; army service 1985–87; attaché Ministry of Foreign Affairs, Russian Fed. 1993; Sr Legal Adviser, Stock Co. (ALM) Consulting Moscow 1993–95; Dir Advocates' Bureau (ALM) 1995–97; Head, Dept of State Cttee on Man. of State Property Russian Fed. 1997–98; Deputy Minister of State Property 1998; Chair. Russian Foundation of Fed. Property 1998–2000; Head of Govt Admin and Minister Without Portfolio 2000–2002, Deputy Head of Presidential Admin 2003–08; First Deputy Chair. of the Govt, in charge of external econ. relations and foreign trade, WTO negotiations and small business 2008–. *Address:* Office of the Government, 103274 Moscow, Krasnopresnenskaya nab. 2, Russia (office). *Telephone:* (495) 205-57-35 (office). *Fax:* (495) 205-42-19 (office). *Website:* www .government.ru (office).

SHUVALOV, Vladimir A., DrBiol; Russian biologist; *Director, Institute of Soil Science and Photosynthesis, Russian Academy of Sciences;* b. 13 Oct. 1943, Moscow; m.; two c.; ed Moscow State Univ.; Sr Lab Worker, then Jr Researcher, Bach Inst. of Biochem. 1968–72; Sr Researcher, Inst. of Soil Science and Photosynthesis, USSR (now Russian) Acad. of Sciences 1972–79, Head of Lab. 1979, now Dir; State Prize of the Russian Federation 1991. *Publications include:* author of 156 scientific papers on primary light energy transformation at photosynthesis, including The Primary Photoreactions in the Complex P-890-bacteriophophylin 760 1976, Burning of a Narrow Spectral Note at 1.7 K in the Absorption Band of the Primary Electron of Rhodosendomous Vividis Reaction Centres with Blocked Electron Transfer 1988. *Address:* Institute of Photosynthesis, Russian Academy of Sciences, Pushchino 142292, Moscow region, Russia (office). *Telephone:* (9627) 73-36-01 (office); (495) 939-10-92 (office).

SHVYDKOI, Mikhail Yefimovich, PhD, DFA; Russian theatre scholar and politician; *Head, Federal Agency of Culture and Cinematography;* b. 5 Sept. 1948, Kyrgyzia; m. Marina Shvydkaya; two s.; ed Moscow Lunacharsky Inst. of Theatre Art; reviewer, Radio Co., Deputy Ed.-in-Chief Theatr magazine 1973–90; Ed.-in-Chief Publrs Co. Kultura, Russian Fed. Ministry of Culture 1990–93; Deputy Minister of Culture 1993–97; Prof. of Foreign Theatre, Acad. of Humanitarian Sciences; commentator on cultural problems on Russian TV; Deputy Chair. Russian TV and Radio Co., Ed.-in-Chief Cultura TV Channel 1997–98; Chair. All-Russian State Radio and TV Holding 1998–2000; Minister of Culture 2000–04; Head, Fed. Agency of Culture and Cinematography 2004–; Chair. Nat. Comm. World Decade of Culture at UNESCO, mem. Bd of Dirs Pervyi Kanal 2004–; Govt Award of the Russian Fed. for Literature and Art 1999; numerous awards, prizes and decorations from France, Poland, Ukraine, Kazakhstan and Russian Fed. *Television:* broadcaster on Cultural Revolution (Cultura TV channel) 2002–, Life is Wonderful (STS TV channel) 2004–. *Publications:* Dramatic Composition: Theatre and Life, Secrets of Lonely Comedians, Sketches on Foreign Theatre of the Late 20th Century; numerous articles on history and contemporary state of theatre in Russian and foreign periodicals. *Address:* c/o 7/6 Maliy Gnezdnikovskiy per., Moscow 125009, Russia (office). *Telephone:* (495) 629-23-11 (office). *Fax:* (495) 629-22-48 (office). *Website:* www.rosculture.ru/en (office).

SHWAYRI, Ramzi; Lebanese chef; b. Beirut; m. Tanya Jamous; ed Univ. of Lyon; son of Greek Orthodox parents; studied econs and law in France; Lebanon's first TV chef, live programmes three times weekly on Future Television; Pres. Al-Kafaàt Foundation (f. by his father, gives training in vocational skills to disabled or troubled young people). *Publication:* Chef Ramzi. *Address:* Al-Kafaàt Foundation, PO Box 47, Hadath, Lebanon (office). *Telephone:* (961) 1879301 (office). *Fax:* (961) 1879307 (office). *E-mail:* foundation@al-kafaat.org (office). *Website:* www.al-kafaat.org (office).

SHYAMALAN, M. Night; Indian film director, screenwriter, actor and producer; b. (Manoj Nelliyattu Shyamalan), 6 Aug. 1970, Pondicherry, Tamil-Nadu Prov.; m. Bhavna 1993; two c.; ed New York Univ. *Films:* Praying with Anger (writer, dir, actor, producer) 1992, Wide Awake (writer, dir) 1998, The Sixth Sense (writer, dir, actor) 1999, Stuart Little (screenplay writer) 1999, Unbreakable (writer, dir, actor, producer) 2000, Signs (writer, dir, producer) 2002, The Village (writer, dir, producer) 2004, Lady in the Water (writer, dir, producer) 2006, The Happening 2008. *Publications:* juvenile: Stuart Finds His Way Home (with Kitty Richards) 1999, Stuart and the Stouts (with Greg Brooker) 2001, Stuart and Snowbell (with Greg Brooker) 2001. *Address:* United Talent Agency, 9560 Wilshire Blvd, Suite 500, Beverly Hills, CA 90212, USA.

SIALE BILEKA, Silvestre; Equatorial Guinean lawyer and politician; fmr Minister of Justice and Religion; Prime Minister and Head of Govt of Equatorial Guinea 1991–93, 1993–95; Minister of Foreign Affairs and Francophone Affairs 1991–92; Pres. Supreme Tribunal; mem. Partido Democrático de Guinea Ecuatorial. *Address:* Siale Bileka Law Firm, Malabo, Equatorial Guinea (office). *Telephone:* (09) 35-34.

SIAZON, Domingo L., Jr, BA, BSc, MPA; Philippine diplomatist and international civil servant; *Ambassador to Japan;* b. 1939, Aparri, Cagayan; m.; ed Ateneo de Manila Univ., Tokyo Univ., Japan, Harvard Univ., USA; interpreter and trans., then Attaché and Third Sec. and Vice-Consul, Embassy in Tokyo 1964–68; Acting Resident Rep. to IAEA, Alt. Perm. Rep. to UNIDO, Third, Second, then First Sec., Embassy in Berne 1968–73; First Sec. and Consul-Gen., Embassy in Vienna, then Amb. to Austria, also Perm. Rep. to IAEA, UNIDO and UN at Vienna 1973–85; Dir-Gen. UNIDO 1985–93; Minister of Foreign Affairs 1995–2000; Amb. to Japan 2002–. *Address:* Embassy of The Philippines, 5-15-5, Roppongi, Minato-ku, Tokyo 106-8537, Japan (office). *Telephone:* (3) 5562-1600 (office). *Fax:* (3) 5562-1603 (home). *E-mail:* info@tokyope.org (office). *Website:* www.tokyope.org (office).

SIBBETT, Wilson, CBE, PhD, FRS, FRSE; British physicist and academic; *Professor of Natural Philosophy, University of St Andrews;* b. 15 March 1948, Portglenone, Co. Antrim, Northern Ireland; s. of John Sibbett and Margaret Sibbett (née McLeister); m. Barbara Anne Brown 1979; three d.; ed Ballymena Tech. Coll., Queen's Univ. Belfast, Imperial Coll.; Post-doctoral Research Fellow, Imperial Coll., London, later Lecturer and Reader in Physics; Prof. of Natural Philosophy, Univ. of St Andrews 1985–; Chair. Scottish Science Advisory Cttee 2002–06; Fellow, Optical Soc. of America 1998, European Optical Soc. 2007; Schardin Gold Medal 1978, Inst. of Physics Boys Medal and Prize 1993, Rank Prize for Optoelectronics 1997, Royal Soc. Rumford Medal 2000, European Physical Soc. Quantum Electronics Prize 2002. *Publications:* approx. 330 papers published in scientific journals. *Leisure interests:* golf, DIY, gardening. *Address:* School of Physics and Astronomy, University of St Andrews, North Haugh, St Andrews, Fife, KY16 9SS (office); 1 Lawhead Road East, St Andrews, Fife, KY16 9ND, Scotland (home). *Telephone:* (1334) 463100 (office); (1334) 472778 (home). *Fax:* (1334) 463104 (office). *E-mail:* ws@st -andrews.ac.uk (office). *Website:* www.st-andrews.ac.uk/physics (office).

SIBLEY, Dame Antoinette, CBE, DBE; British ballerina; *President, Royal Academy of Dance;* b. 27 Feb. 1939, Bromley, Kent; d. of Edward G. Sibley and Winifred Smith; m. 1st Michael Somes 1964 (divorced 1973, died 1994); m. 2nd Panton Corbett 1974; one s. one d.; joined the Royal Ballet 1956, Soloist 1959, Prin. Ballerina 1960–; Vice-Pres. Royal Acad. of Dance 1989–91, Pres. 1991–. *Ballets:* leading roles in: Swan Lake, Sleeping Beauty, Coppelia, The Nutcracker, La Fille Mal Gardée, Romeo and Juliet, Jabez and the Devil (cr. role of Mary), The Dream (cr. Titania), Jazz Calendar (cr. Friday's Child), Enigma Variations (cr. Dorabella), Thais (cr. Thais), Triad (cr. the Girl), Manon (cr. Manon), Soupirs (cr. pas de deux), Symphonic Variations, Daphnis and Chloë, Varii Capricci (cr. La Capricciosa), The Good-Humoured Ladies, A Month in the Country, L'Invitation au Voyage (cr. a lead role), Anastasia (cr. Kschessinska pas-de-deux), Pavane (cr. pas-de-deux). *Films:* The Turning Point 1978, Mime Matters (video). *Publications:* Sibley and Dowell 1976, Antoinette Sibley 1981, Reflections of a Ballerina 1985. *Leisure interests:* doing nothing, opera, cinema, reading. *Address:* c/o Royal Academy of Dance, 36 Battersea Square, London, SW11 3RA, England (office). *Website:* www.rad .org.uk.

SIDDHI, Air Chief Marshal Savetsila, BS, MS; Thai politician and air force officer; b. 7 Jan. 1919, Bangkok; s. of Phraya Wanapruksapijarn and Khunying Wanapruksapijarn; m. Khunying Thida Savetsila 1952; two s. two d.; ed Chulalongkorn Univ. and MIT; fmr pilot officer, Royal Thai Air Force and Adviser to Royal Thai Air Force; mem. Nat. Ass. 1973, Nat. Reform Council 1976; Minister, Prime Minister's Office 1979–80, Second Kriangsak Govt; Sec.-Gen. Nat. Security Council 1975–80; Minister of Foreign Affairs 1980–90; mem. Parl. 1983–90; Leader, Social Action Party 1986–90; Deputy Prime Minister 1986; Special ADC to HM the King 1986, currently mem. Privy Council; Hon. LLD (Philippines) 1983, (Nat. Univ. Singapore) 1985; Knight Grand Cordon of the Most Noble Order of the Crown of Thailand, Knight Grand Cordon (Special Class) of the Most Exalted Order of the White Elephant, Knight Commander (Second Class, Lower Grade) of the Most Illustrious Order of Chulachomklao, Knight Grand Commander (Second Class, Higher Grade) of the Most Illustrious Order of Chulachomklao. *Leisure interests:* reading, exercise. *Address:* c/o Ministry of Foreign Affairs, Saranrom Palace, Bangkok 10200, Thailand. *Telephone:* 225-6312.

SIDDIQI, Nazim Hussain, BA, LLM; Pakistani judge; b. 30 June 1940; s. of the late Mukarram Hussain Siddiqi; ed Univs of Hyderabad and Karachi; lawyer, Hyderabad 1961–67; fmr Civil Judge, Sr Civil Judge, Customs Judge, Special Judge; apptd Judge, High Court of Sindh 1992, Chief Justice 1999–2000; Judge, Supreme Court 2000–05, Chief Justice 2004–05 (retd); Chair. Cen. Zakat Council of Pakistan; mem. Selection Bd, Quaid-i-Azam Univ. *Address:* c/o Supreme Court, Constitution Avenue, Islamabad, Pakistan (office).

SIDDIQI, Suhaila, MD, PhD; Afghan surgeon and politician; b. 1931, Kabul; studied in Afghanistan and Russia; practising surgeon 1970s–; joined mil. during Soviet occupation of Afghanistan, first and only woman to attain rank of Gen. during communist Najibullah regime; worked two decades in Kabul's 400-bed mil. hosp. then Chief of Surgery, Wazir Akbar Khan Hosp., Kabul; Minister of Public Health, Interim Govt of Afghanistan 2001–02, Transitional Authority 2002. *Address:* c/o Ministry of Public Health, Micro-Rayon, Kabul, Afghanistan (office).

SIDEROV, Volen; Bulgarian politician; *Leader, Attack Party;* b. 19 April 1956, Yambol; worked as photographer at Nat. Literature Museum –1989; mem. Movt for Human Rights 1990; Ed.-in-Chief Democracy (official newspaper of Democratic Party) 1990–92; journalist, 168 Hours (weekly newspaper); press attaché for Sasho Donchev, (Srpska Radikalna Stranka) Topenergy and Overgas mid-1990s; journalist, Monitor (newspaper) –2003; hosted talk show on cable TV channel SKAT 2003–05; Founder and Leader, Attack Nat. Union (later Attack Party) 2005–, mem. Parl. 2005–; unsuccessful cand. for Pres. 2006; Union of Bulgarian Journalists Award 2000. *Address:* Attack Party (Partiya Ataka), 1784 Sofia, bul. Tsargradsko shose 113, Bulgaria (office). *Telephone:* (2) 846-51-31 (office). *Fax:* (2) 846-51-31 (office). *E-mail:* volenataka@abv.bg (office). *Website:* www.atakabg.com (office).

SIDHU, Shivinder Singh, MA (Econ.), PhD; Indian civil servant and government official; *Governor of Goa;* b. 13 Oct. 1929; ed Delhi School of Econs, Univ. of Kanpur; joined Indian Admin. Service 1952, fmr Sec. to three Chief Ministers of UP and Dist Magistrate, Kanpur, fmr Div. Commr, Agra; fmr Sec. to Govt of India, Ministry of Health and Family Welfare, fmr Advisor to the Gov., Punjab, fmr Sec. to Govt of India, Ministry of Industrial Devt, fmr Sec. to Govt of India, Ministry of Tourism and Civil Aviation, fmr Chair. Air India and Indian Airlines, fmr Advisor to the Gov., Tamil Nadu; Sec. Gen. Int. Civil Aviation Org., Montreal, Canada 1988–91; Evaluation of Commonwealth Fund for Tech. Devt in Islands of South Pacific Ocean June–Aug. 1994; Pres. Foundation for Aviation and Sustainable Tourism 1992–2004; Gov. of Manipur 2004–08, of Goa 2008–. *Publications:* Steel Industry in India: Problems & Perspective, Aviation & Sustainable Tourism: Emerging Trends, New Horizons in Travel & Tourism: Asian Approach, Flight into the Millennium: Aviation & Tourism Symbiosis, Tourism & Aviation: Airborne for Progress, Aviation and Tourism: Synergy for Success. *Address:* Office of the Governor of Goa, Rajbhavan, Dona Paula, 404 004, Goa, India (office). *Telephone:* (832) 2453506 (office); (832) 2453507 (office). *Fax:* (832) 2453510 (office). *E-mail:* gv.goa@nic.in (office). *Website:* goagovt.nic.in (office).

SIDHWA, Bapsi; American/Pakistani writer and academic; b. 11 Aug. 1939, Karachi; d. of Peshotan Bhandara and of Tehmina Bhandara; m. Nosher Rustam Sidhwa; two d. one s.; ed Kinnaird Coll. for Women, Lahore; self-published first novel The Crow Eaters 1978; Asst Prof., Creative Writing Program, Univ. of Houston, Tex., USA 1985; Bunting Fellowship, Radcliffe Coll., Harvard Univ. 1986; Asst Prof., Writing Div., Columbia Univ., New York 1989; Visiting Scholar, Rockefeller Foundation Centre, Bellagio, Italy 1991; Prof. of English and Writer-in-Residence, Mount Holyoake Coll., South Hadley, Mass 1997; Fannie Hurst Writer-in-Residence, Brandeis Univ., Mass 1998–99; Postcolonial Teaching Fellowship, Univ. of Southampton, UK 2001; Chair. Commonwealth Writers' Prize 1993; mem. Advisory Cttee to Prime Minister Benazir Bhutto on Women's Devt –1996, Punjab Rep., Asian Women's Conf., Alma Ata; Sec. Destitute Women's and Children's Home, Lahore; Sitara-I-Imtiaz 1991, Lila Wallace Reader's Digest Award 1993, Nat. Award for English Literature, Pakistan Acad. of Letters 1991, Patras Bokhari Award for Literature 1992, Excellence in Literature Award, Zoroastrian Congress 2002. *Plays:* Sock 'em With Honey 1993. *Films:* Earth (film of Ice-Candy-Man aka Cracking India) 1999. *Publications include:* The Crow Eaters 1978 (commercially published 1980), The Bride 1982, Ice-Candy-Man (aka Cracking India) (Notable Book of the Year, New York Times) 1991, An American Brat 1993, Bapsi Sidhwa Omnibus 2001; numerous short stories and reviews. *Leisure interest:* reading, theatre, cinema, cooking, bridge. *Address:* c/o Sterling Lord Literistic, Inc., 65 Bleecker Street, New York, NY 10012, USA (office); 5442 Cheena Drive, Houston, TX 77096, USA (home); c/o Oxford University Press, Banglore Town, Shahrah-e-Faisal, Karachi, Pakistan. *Telephone:* (212) 780-6050 (office); (713) 283-0811 (Houston) (office); (21) 45290259 (Karachi); (42) 6660618 (Lahore). *Fax:* (212) 780-6095 (office). *E-mail:* info@sll.com (office). *Website:* www.sll.com (office); hometown.aol.com/bsidhwa; bapsisidhwa.com.

SIDI, Baba Ould; Mauritanian politician; b. 1946, Méderdra; fmr Man. Soc. Mauritanienne de Commercialization de Produits Petroliers; fmr Dir Banque Int. pour la Mauritanie; Minister for Fisheries and Maritime Economy 1996, for Public Works, Employment, Youth and Sports 2000–02, for Nat. Defence 2003–07; mem. Al Jamiya al-Wataniyah (Nat. Ass.). for Méderdra. *Address:* c/o Ministry of National Defence, BP 184, Nouakchott, Mauritania.

SIDIBÉ, Malick; Malian photographer; b. 1935, Soloba (then French Sudan); ed Ecole des Artisans Soudanais, Bamako; trained to be designer and goldsmith; switched to photography apprenticeship 1955–58; f. Studio Malick 1958; Hasselblad Foundation Int. Prize for Photography, Sweden 2003, Golden Lion Lifetime Achievement Award, Venice Biennale 2007, ICP Infinity Award for Lifetime Achievement 2008. *Publications:* Malick Sidibé Monograph 1998, The 1960's in Bamako: Malick Sidibé and James Brown 2001, You are looking beautiful like that 2001, Chemises de Malick Sidibé 2008, Malick Sidibé Bagadadji 2008. *Address:* FIFTY ONE Fine Art Photography, Zirkstraat 20, 2000 Antwerp, Belgium. *Telephone:* (3) 289-84-58. *Fax:* (3) 289-84-59. *E-mail:* info@gallery51.com. *Website:* www.gallery51.com.

SIDIBÉ, Mandé; Malian economist, banker and fmr politician; *Chairman, Ecobank Group;* b. 1939; economist, IMF, Cen. Bank of W African States; Econ. Adviser to Pres. Alpha Oumar Konare –2000; Prime Minister of Mali and Minister of Integration 2000–02; unsuccessful cand. for Pres. of Mali 2002; Chair. Ecobank Group, Togo 2006–. *Address:* Ecobank Group, 2, Rue du Commerce, BP 3261, Loma, Togo (office). *Telephone:* 221-03-03 (office). *Fax:* 221-51-19 (office). *E-mail:* info@ecobank.com (office). *Website:* www.ecobank.com (office).

SIDIBÉ, Modibo, LLM; Malian politician; *Prime Minister;* b. 4 Nov. 1952, Bamako; m.; five c.; ed Univ. of Reims, Univ. of Aix-en-Provence, France; fmr police commr; Chef de Cabinet for Minister Del. of Nat. Defence 1989–91; Cabinet Dir for Minister Del. of Internal Security 1991; Cabinet Dir for Pres. of Transitional Cttee for Health 1991–92; Minister of Health, Solidarity and the Elderly 1992–97, of Foreign Affairs and Malians Abroad 1997–2002; Sec.-Gen., Office of the Pres. 2002–07; Prime Minister 2007–; Pres. Foreign Affairs Council, ECOWAS (Econ. Community of West African States) 1999–2001, Pres. Mediation and Peace Council 1999–2001; Commandeur, Ordre National du Mali, Commandeur, Légion d'Honneur. *Address:* Office of the Prime Minister, Quartier du Fleuve, BP 790, Bamako, Mali (office). *Telephone:* 223-06-80 (office). *Fax:* 222-85-83 (office).

SIDIMÉ, Lamine; Guinean politician and judge; *President, Supreme Court;* Prime Minister of Guinea, Co-ordinator of Govt Affairs 1999–2004; Pres. Supreme Court 2005–. *Address:* Supreme Court, Corniche-Sud, Camayenne, Conakry, Guinea (office). *Telephone:* 30-41-29-28 (office).

SIDLIN, Murry, MM; American conductor and academic; *Dean, Benjamin T. Rome School of Music, Catholic University of America;* b. 6 May 1940, Baltimore, Md; ed Academia Chigiana, Siena, Cornell Univ.; Asst Conductor, Baltimore Symphony Orchestra 1971–73; Dir of Maryland Ballet Co. 1971–73; Prin. Conductor Baltimore Chamber Players 1971–73; Resident Conductor Nat. Symphony Orchestra under Dorati 1973–77, Wolf Trap American Univ. Music Acad. 1974; Host and Conductor Children's TV series Music is... 1977; Music Dir Tulsa Philharmonic Orchestra 1978–80; Music Dir New Haven Symphony 1977–88, Long Beach Symphony 1980–88, Resident Conductor Aspen Music Festival 1978–93; Resident Conductor Oregon Symphony Orchestra 1994–2002; Dean, School of Music, Catholic Univ., Washington, DC 2002–; Assoc. Dir and Program Coordinator, American Acad. of Conducting, Aspen; Artistic Dir Cascade Festival of Music; guest conductor with numerous orchestras in N America, also performances in Europe and at Festival Casals, Puerto Rico; Carnegie Hall debut 1975; Winner, Baltimore Symphony Orchestra Young Conductor's Competition 1962, Educator of the Year, Nat. Assocn of Ind. Schools of Music in America 1997. *Address:* Benjamin T. Rome School of Music, 111 Ward Hall, Catholic University of America, 620 Michigan Avenue, NE, Washington, DC 20064, USA (office). *Telephone:* (202) 319-5414 (office). *Fax:* (202) 319-6280 (office). *E-mail:* cua-music@cua.edu (office). *Website:* music.cua.edu (office).

SIDOROV, Vasily Sergeyevich; Russian diplomatist; b. 2 Jan. 1945, Moscow; m.; three c.; ed Moscow Inst. of Int. Relations; on staff, Ministry of Foreign Affairs 1967–; fmr Amb. to Greece; Deputy Head, Dept of Int. Orgs 1990–91; Deputy, First Deputy Perm. Rep. to UN, New York 1991–95, Deputy Minister of Foreign Affairs 1995–98; Perm. Rep. to UN, Geneva 1998–2001; Head, Russian del. to UN Comm. on Human Rights 1999–2001; Russian Rep. to Conf. on Disarmament, Geneva 2001–2003. *Address:* Ministry of Foreign Affairs, Smolenskaya-Sennaya 32/34, 119200 Moscow, Russia (office). *Telephone:* (495) 244-16-06 (office). *Fax:* (495) 230-21-30 (office). *E-mail:* ministry@mid.ru (office). *Website:* www.mid.ru (office).

SIDOROV, Yevgeniy Yurievich, DSc; Russian politician and literary critic; b. 11 Feb. 1938, Sverdlovsk (now Ekaterinburg); s. of Yuri Sidorov and Natalia Sidorova; m. Vera Indurskaya 1972; two s.; ed Moscow State Univ., Acad. of Social Sciences of Cen. Cttee of CPSU; mem. CPSU 1962–92; Head, Dept Moskovski Komsomolets 1962–65, Literaturnaya Gazeta 1965–67, Yunost 1967–72; maj. works devoted to analysis of Russian contemporary literature; Prof., Pro-rector, Moscow Gorky Literary Inst. 1978, Rector 1987–92; Minister of Culture 1994–97; mem. State Duma (Parl.) 1993–95; Perm. Rep. to UNESCO 1998–2003; Vice-Pres. European Union of Writers, Scientists, Artists; several nat. and int. literary prizes including Mediterranium Golden Oliva (Palermo, Italy) 1991. *Publications:* On the Stylistic Variety of Soviet Prose, Time to Write, On the Way to Synthesis, Yevgeniy Yevtushenko, The Flow of Poetry Days, Pages and Fates; articles on cinema and theatre. *Leisure interests:* friends, chess, travelling.

SIDORSKY, Syarhey Syarheyovich, DEngSci; Belarusian politician; *Prime Minister;* b. 13 March 1954, Gomel; m.; two d.; ed Belarus Inst. of Railway Transport Engineers; worked as electrical fitter and electrician; foreman of assembly shop, head of lab., head of dept, Deputy Dir Gomel Radio Equipment Plant 1976–91, Dir 1991–92; Gen. Man. Gomel Scientific Production Asscn RATON 1992–98; Deputy Chair. and First Deputy Chair. Gomel Oblast Admin 1998–2001; Deputy Prime Minister 2001–02, First Deputy Prime Minister 2002–03, Acting Prime Minister July–Dec. 2003, Prime Minister Dec. 2003–; Academician, Int. Eng Acad.; Honoured Workman of Industry (Belarus). *Publications include:* more than 40 scientific publs and monographs. *Address:* Office of the Prime Minister, 220010 Minsk, vul. Savetskaya 11, Belarus (office). *Telephone:* (17) 222-69-05 (office). *Fax:* (17) 222-66-65 (office). *E-mail:* timoshenko@government.by (office). *Website:* www.government.by (office).

SIDQI, Atif; Egyptian politician and fmr professor of law; fmr Prof., Cairo Univ. Law School; fmr adviser on econ. affairs to Vice-Pres. Mubarak; mem. Shura; fmr Cultural Attaché, Embassy in Paris; Head, Cen. Auditing Agency 1981–86; Prime Minister of Egypt 1986–96, also fmr Minister of Int. Co-operation; mem. Nat. Democratic Party. *Address:* c/o Office of the Prime Minister, Cairo, Egypt.

SIEBERT, Horst, PhD; German economist; *President Emeritus, Kiel Institute of World Economics;* b. 20 March 1938, Neuwied; s. of Fritz Siebert and Anna Heini; m. Christa Causemann 1965; ed Univ. of Cologne, Wesleyan Univ., Conn., Univ. of Münster; Asst Prof. of Econs Texas A&M Univ.; Prof. of Econs and Chair. of Econs and Int. Trade, Univ. of Mannheim 1969–84; Prof. of Econs and Chair. of Int. Econs, Univ. of Konstanz 1984–89; Chair of Theoretical Econs and Pres. Inst. of World Econs, Kiel Univ. 1989–2003, now Pres. Emer.; Prof. of Int. Econs, Johns Hopkins Univ., Bologna, Italy;

mem. Council of Govt Econ. Advisers 1990–2003, Group of Econ. Analysis of EU 2001–04, Group of Econ. Policy Analysis of EU 2005–; Bundesverdienstkreuz; Dr hc (Ghent) 2000; Karl Bräuer Prize 1999, Ludwig Erhard Prize for Wirtschaftspublizistik 1999. *Publications:* Aussenwirtschaft 2000, Der Kobra-Effekt. Wie man Irrwege der Wirtschaftspolitik vermeidet 2001, The World Economy 2002, Economics of the Environment: Theory and Policy 2005, The German Economy: Beyond the Social Market 2005, Jenseits des sozialen Marktes 2005. *Address:* Institute of World Economics, Kiel University, Düsternbrooker Weg 120, 24105 Kiel, Germany (office); Johns Hopkins University School of Advanced International Studies Bologna Center, Via Belmeloro 11, 40126 Bologna, Italy (office). *Telephone:* (431) 8814567 (Kiel) (office); (51) 2917821 (Bologna) (office). *Fax:* (431) 8814501 (Kiel) (office). *E-mail:* hsiebert@ifw.uni-kiel.de (office). *Website:* www.uni-kiel.de/ifw/staff/siebert.htm (office); www.jhubc.it (office).

SIEGEL, Ira Theodore, MBA; American publishing executive; b. 23 Sept. 1944, New York City; s. of David A. Siegel and Rose Minsky; m. Sharon R. Sacks 1965; three d.; ed New York and Long Island Univs; Business Man. Buttenheim Publishing Co., New York 1965–72; Corp. Vice-Pres. (research) Cahners Publishing Co. (Div. Reed Publishing Co. USA, Boston) 1972–86; Pres. R.R. Bowker Publishing Co. (Div. Reed Publishing, USA, New York) 1986–91, Martindale-Hubbell Div. NJ 1990–91, Reed Reference Publishing 1991–95, Pres., CEO 1993–95; Pres. and CEO Lexis-Nexis 1995–97; mem. Bd of Dirs edata.com (now Seisint) 1999–2004. *Address:* 16589 Senterra Drive, Delray Beach, FL 33484, USA. *Telephone:* (561) 499-6457 (home).

SIEGELMAN, Don Eugene, JD; American politician; b. 24 Feb. 1946, Mobil, Ala; m. Lori Allen; one s. one d.; ed Univs of Alabama, Georgetown and Oxford; called to Bar Ala 1972; Sec. of State of Ala 1979–87, Attorney-Gen. 1987–94, Lt-Gov. 1996–99, Gov. of Alabama 1999–2003; Democrat. *Address:* c/o Office of the Governor, State Capitol, 600 Dexter Avenue, Suite N104, Montgomery, AL 36130, USA (office).

SIEGERT, Theo, MBA, PhD; German business executive; *Member, Supervisory Board, Merck KGaA;* b. 1947, Düsseldorf; m.; two c.; ed Univ. of Munich; joined Franz Haniel & Cie. GmbH 1975, held several sr positions including in Controlling Dept, then Head of Strategic Planning Dept, Dir of Finance and Mergers & Acquisitions, Deputy Mem. Managing Bd 1994–96, mem. 1996–2005, Chair. 2005; Chair. Supervisory Bd Metro AG 2004-05; mem. Supervisory Bd Merck KGaA 2006–, Deutsche Bank AG 2006–; mem. Bd of Pnrs E. Merck OHG 2006–; mem. Bd of Dirs DKSH; Chair. Foundation Council, Stiftung Marktwirtschaft; Hon. Prof. of Financial Analysis and Co. Man., Ludwig-Maximilians Univ. of Munich. *Address:* Merck KGaA, Frankfurter Str. 250, 64293 Darmstadt, Germany (office). *Telephone:* (6151) 72-0 (office). *Fax:* (6151) 72-2000 (office). *Website:* www.merck.de (office).

SIELICKI, Tomasz, BEcons; Polish business executive; *Vice-President, Supervisory Board, Sygnity Group;* ed Warsaw Univ. of Tech.; joined ComputerLand 1991, Pres., Man. Bd 1992–2005, Pres. ComputerLand Group (now Sygnity Group after merger with Emax 2007) 2005, currently Vice-Pres. Supervisory Bd, also mem. Man. Bd; mem. Supervisory Bd Agora SA, Budimex SA, ARAM Sp. z o. o. *Address:* Sygnity Group, Al. Jerozolimskie 180, 02–486 Warsaw, Poland (office). *Telephone:* (22) 5711000 (office). *Fax:* (22) 5711001 (office). *E-mail:* bdrzewicz@sygnity.pl (office). *Website:* www.sygnity.pl (office).

SIEMIĄTKOWSKI, Zbigniew, DH; Polish politician; b. 8 Oct. 1957, Ciechanów; m.; one d.; ed Warsaw Univ.; Sr Asst, Warsaw Univ. 1981–; Deputy to Sejm (Parl.) 1991–2005, mem. Comm. for Nat. and Ethnic Minorities, Comm. of Justice; mem. Polish United Workers' Party (PZPR) 1978–90; mem. Social Democracy of Polish Repub. (SDRP) 1990–99; Minister of Internal Affairs 1996; mem. Council of Ministers 1997; mem. Democratic Left Alliance (SLD) 1999–; Sec. of State in Chancellery of Prime Minister 2001–; Acting Head, Office of State Protection (Urzad Ochrony Panstwa—UOP) 2001–02, Head, Foreign Intelligence Agency (Agencji Wywiadu—AW) (following absorption of UOP into AW and Interior Security Agency (Agencja Bezpieczenstwa Wewnetrznego—AWB)) 2002–04 (resgnd). *Leisure interest:* family, tourism. *Address:* c/o Democratic Left Alliance (SLD), 00-419 Warsaw, ul. Rozbrat 44a, Poland.

SIEVERT, Frederick J., BA, MA; American insurance industry executive (retd); m.; five c.; ed Amherst Coll., Wayne State Univ.; fmr secondary school teacher; joined New York Life Insurance Co. as Sr Vice-Pres. and Chief Financial Officer with responsibility for Financial Man. Dept of Individual Operations 1992–95, also responsible for Individual Life, Individual Annuity and Disability Income Depts 1994, Exec. Vice-Pres. 1995–97, Vice-Chair. 1997–2004, Pres. 2000–07 (retd), fmr mem. Bd of Dirs Max New York Life Insurance Co. (jt venture co. in India); Fellow, Soc. of Actuaries; mem. American Acad. of Actuaries. *Address:* c/o New York Life Insurance Company, 51 Madison Avenue, New York, NY 10010, USA (office).

SIEVERTS, Thomas C. W., DiplIng; German architect and town planner; b. 8 June 1934, Hamburg; s. of Rudolf Sieverts and Elisabeth Sieverts (née Ronnefeldt); m. Heide Pawelzick 1966; one s. two d.; ed in Stuttgart, Liverpool and Berlin; with Kossak and Zimmermann f. Freie Plannungsgruppe Berlin 1965; Prof. of Town Planning Dept of Architecture, Hochschule der Künste, Berlin 1967–70; Guest Prof., Grad. School of Design, Harvard Univ., USA 1970–71; Prof. of Town Planning, Dept of Architecture, Tech. Hochschule, Darmstadt 1971–99, now Prof. Emer.; Special Prof. of Urban Design, Inst. of Planning Studies, Univ. of Nottingham, UK 1978–88; in practice as architect and town planner, Bonn 1978–; Fellow Inst. for Advanced Study, Berlin 1995–96; Regent's Prof. Univ. of Berkeley 2005; mem. Scientific Advisory Council World Exhbn, 'Expo 2000', Hanover 1989–99, Sächsische Akad. der Künste; Deubau Prize (Essen) 1969, Verdienstzeichen in Gold (Vienna) 1988,

Bauherren Prize 1992, Deutsche Städtebau Prize 1993. *Buildings:* town planning consultant to the City of Vienna, planning Danubia area 1973–78, the Gürtel area 1984–88; Dir of Int. Bldg Exhbn Emscher Park (Ruhr) 1989–94. *Publications:* Zwischenstadt (3rd edn) 1999 (English edn: Cities Without Cities – An Interpretation of the Zwischenstadt 2004), Fünfzig Jahre Städtebau – Reflektion und Praxis 2001; many contribs to periodicals and books. *Leisure interest:* drawing. *Address:* skt umbaukultur, Thomas-Mann-Strasse 41, 53111 Bonn, Germany. *Telephone:* (228) 22723620 (office). *Fax:* (228) 22723629 (office). *E-mail:* info@umbaukultur.eu (office). *Website:* www .skt-umbaukultur.eu (office).

SIEW, Vincent C., LLM; Taiwanese diplomatist, fmr government official and research institute administrator; *Vice President;* b. 3 Jan. 1939, Chiayi City, Taiwan; m.; three d.; ed Nat. Chengchi Univ., Georgetown Univ.; Vice-Consul, Kuala Lumpur, Malaysia 1966–69, Consul 1969–72; Section Chief, Asia Pacific Affairs Dept, Ministry of Foreign Affairs 1972; Deputy Dir 4th Dept Bd of Foreign Trade, Ministry of Econ. Affairs 1972–74, Dir 1974–77, Deputy Dir-Gen. Bd of Foreign Trade 1977–82, Dir-Gen. 1982–88; Vice-Chair. Council for Econ. Planning and Devt, Exec. Yuan 1988–89; Dir-Gen. Dept of Organizational Affairs, Kuomintang Cen. Cttee 1989–90, Vice-Chair. Kuomintang 2000–05; Minister of Econ. Affairs 1990–93; Minister of State, Chair. Council for Econ. Planning and Devt, Exec. Yuan 1993–94; Minister of State, Chair. Mainland Affairs Council, Exec. Yuan 1994–95; legislator 1996–97; Premier of Taiwan 1997–2000; Vice Pres. of Taiwan 2008–; Eisenhower Fellow, USA 1985; Chair. Chung-Hua Inst. for Econ. Research, Convenor Presidential Econ. Advisory Panel 2003–04; fmr Chair. Cross-Straits Common Market Foundation; Prof. Nat. Chengchi Univ.; Hon. D.Man (Nat. Chia-Yi Univ.), Hon. DEcon (Sung Kyun Kwan Univ., Seoul), Hon. PhD (Rangsit Univ., Thailand), Hon. Dr Public Service (Ohio State Univ., USA). *Publications:* One Plus One is Greater than Two: The Road to the Cross-Straits Common Market, To Govern the Nation with Expertise. *Address:* Office of the President, 122 Chungking South Rd, Sec. 1, Taipei 10048, Taiwan (office). *Telephone:* (2) 23113731 (office). *Fax:* (2) 23311604 (office). *E-mail:* public@mail.oop.gov.tw (office). *Website:* www.president.gov.tw (office).

SIFAKIS, Joseph, PhD; Greek/French computer scientist, institute director and consultant; *Founder, Verimag Laboratory and Research Director, Centre National de la Recherche Scientifique;* b. 1946, Heraklion, Crete; ed Nat. Technical Univ. of Athens, Univ. of Grenoble, France; Research Dir, CNRS, Founder Verimag Lab., Grenoble, Dir 1993–2006; Scientific Coordinator European Network of Excellence ARTIST2 on Embedded Systems Design; Chair. Chamber B (Public Research Orgs) of ARTEMISIA (industrial asscn within the ARTEMIS European Tech. Platform on Embedded Systems); mem. Bd Dirs CARNOT Inst. 'Intelligent Software and Systems', Grenoble; Co-founder Int. Conf. on Computer Aided Verification (CAV); mem. Steering Cttee EMSOFT (Embedded Software) Conf.; mem. editorial bds of several journals; CNRS Silver Medal 2001, Turing Award for his work on model checking (co-recipient) 2007. *Achievements include:* developed theory and tech. for the SCADE tool used for design and validation of critical real-time systems, de facto standard for aeronautics; recognized for pioneering work on both theoretical and practical aspects of Concurrent Systems Specification and Verification. *Publications:* numerous scientific papers in professional journals on component-based design, modelling, and analysis of real-time systems with focus on correct-by-construction techniques. *Address:* Verimag Laboratory, Centre Equation, 2 avenue de Vignate, 38610 Gieres, France (office). *Telephone:* (4) 56-52-03-51 (office). *Fax:* (4) 56-52-04-46 (office). *E-mail:* joseph.sifakis@imag.fr (office). *Website:* www-verimag.imag.fr/~sifakis (office).

SIGALOVA, Alla Mikhailovna; Russian choreographer, ballet dancer and academic; *Professor, Chekhov Moscow Art Theatre (MKhAT);* b. 28 Feb. 1958, Volgograd; d. of Stalov Mikhail Petrovich and Viogina Tamara Aleksandrovna; m. Kozak Roman Yefimovich; one s. one d.; ed Leningrad Vaganova School of Choreography, Russian Acad. of Theatre Arts; teacher Russian Acad. of Theatre Arts 1983–87; choreographer Theatre Satirikon 1987–89; Artistic Dir Theatre Ind. Troupe of Alla Sigalova 1989–97, Choreography Theatre of Alla Sigalova 2001–; Prof. and Head, Faculty of Eurhythmics, Studio School of Chekhov Moscow Art Theatre (MKhAT) 2004–; choreographer of New Year TV shows for ORT and NTV channels 1996–99; Honoured Artist of Russia. *Dance:* Othello 1990, Queen of Spades 1991, Salomea 1991. *Productions choreographed include:* Moscow Mayakovsky Theatre: Diary of an Ordinary Girl 1984, Bed-Bug 1986; Moscow Satirikon Theatre: Serving Girls 1988; Moscow Mossoviet Theatre: Banana 1994. *Address:* Chekhov Moscow Art Theatre (MKhAT), 3 Kamergerskiy Pereulok, Moscow 103 (office); Prechistenka str. 25/13, apt. 10, Moscow, Russia (home). *Telephone:* (495) 629-87-60 (office); (495) 201-44-36 (home). *Fax:* (495) 201-44-36 (home). *E-mail:* mhat@theatre.ru (office); asigalova@mail.ru (home). *Website:* art.theatre.ru (office).

SIGFÚSSON, Steingrímur J., BSc; Icelandic politician; *Minister of Finance and Minister of Fisheries and Agriculture;* b. 4 Aug. 1955, Thistilfjordur; ed Univ. of Iceland; mem. Althingi (Parl.) 1983–, Chair. People's Alliance Parl. Group 1987–88, mem. Cttee on Fisheries 1991–98 (Chair. 1995–98), on Economy and Trade 1991–99, on Social Affairs 1999–2003, on Foreign Affairs 1999–, Special Cttee on Constitutional Affairs 2004–05, mem. Del. to W Nordic Council 1991–95, to Nordic Council 1996–2005, 2006–07, to Parl. Ass. of the Council of Europe 2007–, Chair. PACE Cttee on Equal Opportunities 2008–; Chair. Left-Green Movement 1999–; Minister of Agric. and Communications 1988–91, of Fisheries and Agric. 2009–, of Finance 2009–. *Address:* Ministry of Finance, Arnarhvoli við Lindargötu, 150 Reykjavík, Iceland (office). *Telephone:* 5459200 (office). *Fax:* 5628280 (office). *E-mail:* postur@fjr.stjr.is (office). *Website:* www.fjarmalaraduneyti.is (office).

SIGUA, Tengiz Ippolitovich, DTechS; Georgian politician; b. 9 Nov. 1934, Lentekhi; s. of Ipolite Sigua and Lidia Schavdia; m. Nina Iwania 1975; one d.; ed Georgian Polytechnical Inst.; engineer and Dir Metallurgy Inst. Georgian Acad. of Sciences 1962–90, now mem. Georgian Acad. of Sciences; fmr leading mem. Round Table—Free Georgia Alliance, Chair. All-Georgia Rustaveli Soc.; apptd Head of Govt by Zviad Gamsakhurdia, Nov. 1990, resigned Aug. 1991 and joined the opposition; mem. State Council March–Oct. 1992; mem. Supreme Soviet 1992–95; apptd Prime Minister by Mil. Council 1992–93 (resgnd), now in Parl. Opposition; Vice-Pres. Georgian Rustaveli Soc. 1989, Pres. 1992–93; arrested with Tengiz Kitovani after an attempted march of armed Georgian refugees on Abkhazia to retak breakaway region 1995, later released. *Leisure interests:* sport, art. *Address:* Phanaskerteli str. 16, Apt. 31, 380094 Tbilisi, Georgia (home).

SIGURÐARDÓTTIR, Jóhanna; Icelandic politician; *Prime Minister;* b. 4 Oct. 1942, Reykjavík; m. 1st Torvaldur Jóhannesson 1970 (divorced); two s.; m. 2nd Jonina Leosdóttir 2002; ed Commercial Coll. of Iceland; fmr flight attendant, Loftleiðir; fmr office worker; elected Social Democratic Party mem. of Althing (Parl.)(Social Democratic Party) 1978, Deputy Speaker 1979, 1983–84, Party Vice-Chair. 1984–93, Minister of Social Affairs and Social Security 1987–94; f. Þjóðvaki party 1994–2000; mem. Social Democratic Alliance 2000–, Deputy Speaker, Althing 2003–07, Minister of Social Affairs and Social Security 2007–09, Prime Minister 2009–; Bd mem. Commercial Workers' Union 1976–83. *Address:* Prime Minister's Office, Stjórnarráðshúsinu við Lækjartorg, 150 Reykjavík, Iceland (office). *Telephone:* 5458400 (office). *Fax:* 5624014 (office). *E-mail:* johanna@althing.is (office); postur@for.stjr.is (office). *Website:* www.forsaetisraduneyti.is (office); www .althingi.is/johanna (office).

SIGURDSSON, Jón, MSc(Econ); Icelandic politician and economist; b. 17 April 1941, Ísafjörður; s. of Sigurdur Gudmundsson and Kristin Gudjona; m. Laufey Thorbjarnardóttir; four c.; ed Akureyri Coll., Univ. of Stockholm, Sweden and London School of Econs, UK; Econ. Inst. of Iceland 1964–71 (Dir Econ. Research 1970–71); Chief Econ. Research Div. Econ. Devt Inst. 1972–74; Man. Dir Nat. Econ. Inst. and Econ. Adviser to Govt 1974–80, 1983–86; Exec. Dir for Nordic Countries IMF 1980–83, Alt. Gov. IMF for Iceland 1974–87; Assoc. Jt IBRD/IMF Devt Cttee 1974–80; IBRD Gov. for Iceland 1987–; EBRD Gov. for Iceland 1991–; mem. Althing (SDP) 1987–; Minister of Justice and Ecclesiastical Affairs 1987–88, of Commerce 1987–93, of Industry 1988–93, of Nordic Co-operation 1988–89; Chair. OECD Council of Ministers 1989, Nordic Council of Ministers 1989; mem. Salaries Arbitration Court 1970–80; Rep. for Iceland Econ. and Devt Review Cttee OECD 1970–80, 1983–86; Gov. and Chair. Bd of Dirs, Cen. Bank of Iceland 1993–94; Pres. and CEO Nordic Investment Bank 1994–2005, mem. Bd of Dirs 1976–87, Chair. 1984–86; currently financial and econ. consultant. *Address:* c/o Nordic Investment Bank, Fabianinkatu 34, PO Box 249, 00171 Helsinki, Finland.

SIGURDSSON, Niels P.; Icelandic diplomatist (retd); b. 1926, Reykjavik; s. of Sigurdur B. Sigurdsson and Karitas Einarsdóttir; m. Olafia Rafnsdóttir; two s. one d.; ed Univ. of Iceland; joined Diplomatic Service 1952; First Sec. Paris Embassy 1956–60; Deputy Perm. Rep. to NATO and OECD 1957–60; Dir Int. Policy Div. Ministry of Foreign Affairs, Reykjavik 1961; Del. to the UN Gen. Ass. 1965; Amb. and Perm. Rep. of Iceland to N Atlantic Council; Amb. to Belgium and the EEC 1968; Amb. to UK. 1971–76, to FRG 1976–78, to Holy See 1977–95, Amb.-at-Large 1979–84, to Norway 1985–89; Chair. Icelandic Del. to Madrid Conf. 1980–83; with Ministry of Foreign Affairs 1990–96. *Leisure interests:* swimming, riding. *Address:* Naustabryggja 55, Reykjavik 110, Iceland.

SIIMANN, Mart; Estonian fmr politician; *President, Estonian Olympic Committee;* b. 1946, Killingi-Nomme; m.; two c.; ed Tartu State Univ.; psychologist, Deputy Head Lab. of Scientific Org. of Work and Man. 1971–75; Sr research Asst Tartu State Univ. 1975–82; broadcaster, Deputy Dir-Gen., Ed.-in-Chief Estonian TV 1982–87, Dir-Gen. 1989–92; Dir-Gen. Estonian Radio 1987–89; Man. Dir commercial TV station ReklamTV 1992–95; mem. Riigikugu (Parl.) 1998–; Chair. Coalition Party Faction, mem. Constitutional Cttee 1995–98; Chair. Coalition Party 1997–99; Prime Minister of Estonia 1997–99; mem. Riigikugu 1998–2003; fmr Counsellor to Pres. of Estonia on Domestic Policy; Pres. Estonian Olympic Cttee 2001–. *Leisure interests:* sport, literature, fishing, philosophy. *Address:* Estonian Olympic Committee (EOK), Pirita tee 12, 10127 Tallinn, Estonia (office). *Telephone:* (2) 6031500 (office). *Fax:* (2) 6031501 (office). *E-mail:* mart@eok.ee (office). *Website:* www.eok.ee (office).

SIKANDER IQBAL, Rao; Pakistani politician; b. 1943; m.; ed Punjab Univ.; Sec. Gen. Punjab Univ. 1963–64; Founder-mem., Dist Pres. Pakistan People's Party; Minister of Food, Agric. and Co-operatives 1988, of Sports, Culture and Tourism 1993; mem. Nat. Ass. (NA144 constituency) 2002–; Sr Minister of Defence 2002–07; mem. Nat. Security Council. *Address:* c/o Ministry of Defence, Pakistan Secretariat, No. II, Rawalpindi 46000, Pakistan. *Telephone:* (51) 9271107.

SIKATANA, Mundia; Zambian lawyer and government official; Minister of Agric. and Cooperatives –2006, of Foreign Affairs 2006–07. *Address:* c/o Ministry of Foreign Affairs, POB RW50069, Lusaka, Zambia.

SIKORSKI, Radosław, BA, MA; Polish journalist and politician; *Minister of Foreign Affairs;* b. 1963, Bydgoszcz; m. Anne Applebaum; two s.; ed Univ. of Oxford, UK; Chair. student strike cttee Bydgoszcz 1981; political refugee in UK 1981–89; journalist reporting on wars in Afghanistan and Angola 1986–89; adviser to Rupert Murdoch on Polish investment 1990; Deputy Minister of Nat. Defence 1992; Under-Sec. of State in Ministry of Foreign Affairs 1998–2002; Fellow, American Enterprise Inst. and Exec. Dir New Atlantic Initiative 2002–05; elected to Senate for Bydgoszcz (Law and Justice Party), Minister of Nat. Defence 2005–07 (resgnd), of Foreign Affairs 2007–; fmr commentator on Polish and int. affairs for numerous TV and radio networks; World Press Photo Prize 1988. *Television:* cr. TV programme Wywiad Miesiąca (interview of the month). *Publications:* Prochy Siętych-podróż do Heratu w czas wojny (Ashes of the Saints- a journey to Herat during the war), The Polish House: An Intimate History of Poland; ed. of series of analytical publs entitled European Outlook. *Address:* Ministry of Foreign Affairs, Al. Szucha 23, 00-580 Warsaw, Poland (office). *Telephone:* (22) 5239000 (office). *Fax:* (22) 6290287 (office). *E-mail:* dsi@msz.gov.pl (office). *Website:* www.msz.gov.pl (office).

SIKUA, David Derek, DipEd, BEd, MEPA, PhD; Solomon Islands educator and politician; *Prime Minister;* b. 10 Sept. 1959; ed Univ. of the South Pacific, Suva, Fiji, Univ. of Southern Queensland, Australia, Monash Univ., Univ. of Waikato, New Zealand; teacher and Deputy Headmaster Pawa Secondary School 1982–84; teacher and Deputy Prin. Waimapuru, Nat. Secondary School 1984–86; Prin. Educ. Officer, Implementation and Planning Unit, Ministry of Educ. and Human Resources Devt 1986–87, Dir Implementation and Planning Unit 1988–90, Dir Secondary School Div. Jan. 1993–Feb. 1993, Under Sec. Minister of Educ. and Human Resources Devt 1993–94, Perm. Sec. 1994–97; Perm. Sec., Ministry of Forests, Environment and Conservation 1997–98; Perm. Sec. (Special Duties), Ministry of Educ. and Human Resources Dev May 2003–Sept. 2003, Perm. Sec. 2003–05; mem. Parl. for North East Guadalcanal 2006–; Minister for Educ. and Human Resources Devt 2006–07; Prime Minister 2007–; Chair. Solomon Islands Nat. Comm. for UNESCO 2006–; Chair. Nat. Educ. Planning Cttee 1989–90, Nat. Library Bd 1993–94; Deputy Chair. Solomon Islands Coll. of Higher Educ. (SICHE) Council 1994–97; mem. USP Council Exec. Cttee 2007–. *Leisure interests:* reading, writing, soccer, cricket, rugby, bushwalking, bird watching. *Address:* Office of the Prime Minister, PO Box G1, Honiara, Solomon Islands (office). *Telephone:* 22202 (office). *Fax:* 28649 (office). *Website:* www.parliament.gov.sb (office).

SILAJDŽIĆ, Haris, PhD; Bosnia and Herzegovina academic and politician; *Member of the Tripartite State Presidency;* b. 1 Oct. 1945, Sarajevo; m.; one s.; ed Garyounis Univ., Libya; has held several academic positions including the Arabic Language Prof., Univ. of Prishtina, Prof., Faculty of Philosophy and Dept of History, Univ. of Sarajevo, Andrew D. White Prof. at Large, Cornell Univ., New York, Guest Lecturer, Harvard Univ. and Univ. of Maryland, Chatham House (fmrly Royal Inst. for Int. Affairs), London, Carnegie Foundation, Woodrow Wilson Center, and other univs; Minister of Foreign Affairs, Repub. of Bosnia and Herzegovina 1991–93, Prime Minister 1993–96, Co-Chair. Council of Ministers of Bosnia and Herzegovina 1996–2000; Bosniak mem. Tripartite State Presidency 2006–, Chair. March–Nov. 2008; fmr mem. and Vice Pres. Party of Democratic Action; Founder and Pres. Party for Bosnia and Herzegovina; Rabbi Marc H. Tanenbaum Memoral Lecturer 1997. *Publications:* several books and papers on int. relations, including relations between USA and Albania. *Address:* Office of the State Presidency, 71000 Sarajevo, Musala 5, Bosnia and Herzegovina (office). *Telephone:* (33) 664941 (office). *Fax:* (33) 472491 (office). *Website:* www.predsjednistvobih.ba (office).

SILAPA-ARCHA, Banharn, LLM; Thai politician; *Leader, Chart Thai;* b. 20 July 1932; s. of Sengkim and Sai-eng sae Ba; ed Ramkhamhaeng Univ.; elected to Suphan Buri Municipal Council 1973; Co-Founder Chart Thai party 1975, Sec.-Gen. 1976, Party Leader 1994–; mem. Legis. Ass. 1973–; Deputy Minister of Industry 1976; Minister of Agric. 1980; Senator 1986; Minister of Communications 1986, of Industry 1989, of Finance 1990, of Interior 1990–91, of Communications 1992; Leader of Opposition 1992–95; Prime Minister 1995–96, also Minister of the Interior. *Address:* Chart Thai, 1 Thanon Pichai, Dusit, Bangkok 10300, Thailand (office). *Telephone:* (2) 243-8070 (office). *Fax:* (2) 243-8074 (office). *E-mail:* chartthai@chartthai.or.th (office). *Website:* www .chartthai.or.th (office).

SILAS, Cecil Jesse, BS; American business executive; b. 15 April 1932, Miami; s. of David Edward Silas and Hilda Videll Silas (née Carver); m. Theodosea Hejda 1965; three s. one d.; ed Miami Sr High School, Georgia Inst. of Tech.; joined Phillips Petroleum Co. 1953; Pres. Phillips Petroleum Co. Europe-Africa, Brussels and London 1968–74, Pres. and COO (also Dir and Chair. Exec. Cttee) Phillips Petroleum Co. 1982–85, Chair. and CEO 1985–94; Man. Dir NRG Europe-Africa, London 1974–76; Vice-Pres. Gas and Gas Liquids, NRG, Bartlesville, Okla 1976–78; Sr Vice-Pres. Natural Resources Group, Bartlesville 1978–80, Exec. Vice-Pres. 1980–82; Chair. Bd American Petroleum Inst. –1993, Bd US Chamber of Commerce; mem. Bd of Dirs Ethics Resource Centre; Trustee Emer. Georgia Tech Foundation; Commdr, Royal Order of St Olav, Norway 1976. *Leisure interests:* golf, fishing, hunting. *Address:* 2400 Terrace Drive, Bartlesville, OK 74004, USA (home). *Telephone:* (918) 333-8577 (home).

SILAYEV, Ivan Stepanovich; Russian politician; b. 21 Oct. 1930; m.; two c.; ed Kazan Aviation Inst.; mem. CPSU 1959–91; foreman, shop supt, deputy chief engineer, chief engineer, plant dir in Gorky 1954–74; Deputy Minister of Aircraft Industry of USSR 1974–77, First Deputy Minister 1977–80, Minister 1981–85; Minister of Machine Tool and Instrument-Making Industry of USSR 1980–81; mem. CPSU Cen. Cttee 1981–91; Deputy Pres. Council of Ministers of USSR 1985–89; Pres. Council of Ministers of RSFSR 1989–91; Pres. Inter-Republican Econ. Cttee of USSR 1991; Russian Perm. Rep. to EC (now EU) 1992–94; Pres. Bd of Dirs Ecology of Russia Consortium 1995–; Chair. Bd Moscow Interregional Commercial Bank 1996–, Int. Union of Mechanical Engineers 1997–; Deputy to USSR Supreme Soviet 1981–89; Hero of Socialist Labour 1975; Lenin Prize 1972. *Address:* c/o International Union of Mechanical Engineers, Bolskaya Dmitrovka 5, Moscow, Russia (office).

SILBER, John Robert, PhD, LHD, LLD EdD, LittD, FRSA; American professor of philosophy and law and university administrator; *President Emeritus, Boston University;* b. 15 Aug. 1926, San Antonio, Tex.; s. of Paul G. Silber and Jewell Joslin; m. Kathryn Underwood 1947 (died 2005); one s. (deceased) six d.; ed Trinity, Northwestern and Yale Univs; Instructor in Philosophy, Yale Univ. 1952–55; Asst Prof., Univ. of Texas 1955–59, Assoc. Prof. 1959–62, Prof. of Philosophy 1962–70, Chair. Dept of Philosophy 1962–67, Chair. Comparative Studies Program 1967, Univ. Prof. of Arts and Letters 1967–70, Dean, Coll. of Arts and Sciences 1967–70; Univ. Prof. and Prof. of Philosophy and Law, Boston Univ. 1971–, Prof. of Int. Relations 1996–, Pres. 1971–96, Chancellor 1996–2003, Pres. Emer. 2003–; mem. Bd of Dirs Americans for Medical Progress 1992–, Chair. 1994–95, mem. Exec. Cttee 1995–; mem. Bd of Dirs Northeast Savings Bank 1988–95, US Surgical Corpn 1994–98, Mutual of America Institutional Funds Inc. 1996–; Vice-Chair. US Strategic Inst.; Chair. Mass. Bd of Educ. 1996–99; mem. Bd of Dirs Nat. Humanities Faculty 1968–72, Exec. Bd, Nat. Humanities Inst. 1975–78, Bd of Dirs New England Holocaust Memorial Cttee; mem. Bd of Trustees Boston Univ. 1971–, Coll. of St Scholastica 1973–85, Univ. of Denver 1985–89, Adelphi Univ. 1989–97; mem. Pres.'s Advisory Bd, Radio Broadcasting to Cuba 1985–92; Pres. Southwestern Philosophy Soc. 1966–67; Fulbright Research Fellow 1959–60; Guggenheim Fellow 1963–64; Wilbur Lucius Cross Medal, Yale Univ. 1971, Ehrenmedaille, Univ. of Heidelberg 1986. *Publications:* The Ethical Significance of Kant's "Religion" 1960, Democracy: Its Counterfeits and Its Promise 1967, The Tuition Dilemma 1978, Straight Shooting: What's Wrong with America and How to Fix It 1989, Ist Amerika zu Retten? 1992; Ed. Kant's "Religion Within the Limits of Reason Alone" 1960, Works in Continental Philosophy 1967; Assoc. Ed. Kant-Studien 1968–87, From Thebes to Auschwitz 1998, The Betrayal of Liberalism 1999, Architecture of the Absurd: How 'Genius' Disfigured a Practical Art 2007; syndicated weekly column; articles in nat. press and philosophical journals. *Address:* Boston University, 73 Bay State Road, Boston, MA 02215, USA (office). *Telephone:* (617) 353-4300 (office). *Fax:* (617) 353-9674 (office). *E-mail:* jhorgan@bu.edu (office). *Website:* www.bu.edu (office).

SILBERMAN, Laurence Hirsch, LLB; American judge, banker, diplomatist and academic; *Senior Judge, United States Court of Appeals for the DC Circuit;* b. 12 Oct. 1935, York, Pa; s. of William Silberman and Anna Hirsch; m. Rosalie Gaull 1957; one s. two d.; ed Dartmouth Coll., Harvard Law School; with Moore, Torkildson & Rice, Quinn & Moore (law firm) 1961–64; Pnr, Moore, Silberman & Schulze 1964–67; lawyer, Nat. Labor Relations Bd 1967–69; solicitor, Labor Dept 1969–70, Under-Sec. for Labor Affairs 1970–73; Pnr, Steptoe & Johnson 1973–74; Deputy Attorney-Gen., Dept of Justice 1974–75; Amb. to Yugoslavia 1975–77 (withdrawn); Man. Pnr, Morrison and Foerster, Washington, DC 1978–79, 1983–85; Exec. Vice-Pres. Legal and Govt Affairs Div., Crocker Nat. Bank 1979–83; Sr Fellow, American Enterprise Inst. for Public Policy Research, Washington, DC 1977–78, Visiting Fellow 1978–85; Vice-Chair. Advisory Council on Gen. Govt, Republican Nat. Comm. 1977–80; mem. US Gen. Advisory Cttee on Arms Control and Disarmament 1981–85; Assoc. Prof. of Admin. Law, Georgetown Univ., Washington, DC 1987–94, 1999–2001, currently Adjunct Prof. and Distinguished Visitor from the Judiciary; Assoc. Prof., New York Univ. 1995–96, Harvard Univ. 1998; Judge, US Court of Appeals, DC Circuit 1985–2000, Sr Judge 2000–; Co-Chair. Pres.'s Comm. on Intelligence Capabilities of the US Regarding Weapons of Mass Destruction 2004–05. *Address:* US Court of Appeals, DC Circuit, 333 Constitution Avenue, NW, Washington, DC 20001, USA. *Website:* www.cadc.uscourts.gov (office).

SILBERSTON, (Zangwill) Aubrey, CBE, MA; British economist and academic; *Professor Emeritus and Senior Research Fellow, Tanaka Business School, Imperial College London;* b. 26 Jan. 1922, London; s. of Louis Silberston and Polly Silberston (née Kern); m. 1st Dorothy Marion Nicholls 1945 (divorced); one s. and one d. deceased); m. 2nd Michèle Ledić 1985; ed Hackney Downs School, London, Jesus Coll., Cambridge; Economist, Courtaulds Ltd 1946–50; Research Fellow, St Catharine's Coll. Cambridge 1950–53, Univ. Lecturer in Econs, Cambridge 1951–71, Fellow, St John's Coll. 1958–71, Chair. Faculty Bd of Econs and Politics 1966–70; Official Fellow in Econs, Nuffield Coll. Oxford 1971–78, Dean 1972–78; Prof. of Econs, Imperial Coll. London 1978–87, now Prof. Emer. and Sr Research Fellow, Business School 1987–; mem. Monopolies Comm. 1965–68, Bd British Steel Corpn 1967–76, Royal Comm. on the Press 1974–77, Restrictive Practices Court 1986–92, Royal Comm. on Environmental Pollution 1986–96; Sec.-Gen. Royal Econ. Soc. 1979–92, Vice-Pres. 1992–; Pres. Confed. of European Econ. Asscns 1988–90, Vice-Pres. 1990–92. *Publications:* Education and Training for Industrial Management 1955, The Motor Industry 1959, Economic Impact of the Patent System 1973, The Multi-Fibre Arrangement and the UK Economy 1984, The Future of the Multi-Fibre Arrangement 1989, Technology and Economic Progress (ed.) 1989, Environmental Economics (ed.) 1995, Beyond the Multifibre Arrangement 1995, The Changing Industrial Map of Europe 1996; articles in Economic Journal, Oxford Economic Papers etc. *Leisure interests:* opera, ballet. *Address:* Tanaka Business School, Imperial College, London, SW7 2AZ, England. *Telephone:* (20) 7594-9354. *Fax:* (20) 7594-9353. *Website:* www.imperial.ac.uk/P1327.htm (office).

SILES DEL VALLE, Juan Ignacio; Bolivian politician, diplomatist and academic; ed Univ. of Chile, Univ. of Ga, USA; Univ. Prof. of Literature, Greater Univ. of San Andrés; Head of Educative Reform 1994–95; Alternating Perm. Rep. to UN, Vienna, Austria and Rome, Italy; Vice-Pres. UN Comm. for Drug Control, representing Latin American and Caribbean Countries, Vienna 2001; Dir Summit Coordination in charge of Cooperation of Latin American Summits 2002; Nat. Coordinator of XIIIth Latin American Summit of Heads of State and Govt 2003; fmr Dir Diplomatic Acad.; fmr Dir Cultural Subjects, Minister of Foreign Affairs and Culture 2003–05. *Publications include:* Canción de Cuna para la Muerte de mi madre (poetry) 1995, La guerrilla de Che y la narrative boliviana (monograph) 1997, Que el sueño era tan grande (novel) 2001, 2003. *Address:* c/o Ministry of Foreign Affairs, Calle Ingavi, esq. Junin, La Paz, Bolivia (office).

SILIÉ VALDEZ, Rubén Arturo; Dominican Republic international organization official, sociologist and administrator; fmr prof. at several univs and insts; fmr Vice-Rector Nat. Univ. of Santo Domingo; Dir Latin American Faculty for Social Sciences (FLACSO), Dominican Repub. 1996–; Adviser to Vice-Pres. and Sec. of State on Educ. 2001–; apptd Amb., Ministry of Foreign Affairs 2001; Sec.-Gen. Asscn of Caribbean States 2004–08; mem. Bd Batey Relief Alliance. *Address:* c/o Secretariat of State for External Relations, Avda Independencia 752, Santo Domingo, DN, Dominican Republic.

SILJA, Anja; German singer (soprano) and producer; b. 17 April 1940, Berlin; m. Christoph von Dohnanyi; one s. two d.; ed studied with Egon van Rijn; began concert career aged ten at Berlin Titania Palace; stage debut Brunswick 1956, as Rosina; mem., Stuttgart and Frankfurt operas 1958–59; sang the Queen of Night at Aix 1959; sang at Bayreuth Festival 1960–67, as Senta, Elsa, Eva, Elisabeth and Venus; London debut at Sadler's Wells Theatre as Leonore/Fidelio 1963; Covent Garden debut as Leonore 1969, returned as Cassandre in Les Troyens, Senta, Marie in Wozzeck, Kostelnicka in Jenůfa; Metropolitan Opera debut 1972, returned as Salome, Marie and Kostelnicka; Vienna Staatsoper 1959–, in roles including Queen of Night, Salome, Elektra, Lulu; Paris Opéra 1964–, as Salome and Brünnhilde; Glyndebourne Opera debut as Kostelnicka 1989; sang the Nurse in Die Frau ohne Schatten at San Francisco 1989; debut as opera producer at Brussels with Lohengrin 1990; sang Emilia Marty at Glyndebourne 1995; season 1997 in The Makropulos Case at Glyndebourne and as Herodias at Covent Garden; Geschwitz in Lulu at Düsseldorf 2000; Clytemnestra at Madrid, Geschwitz and Herodias at Amsterdam, The Makropulos Case at Aix and The Bassarids in Amsterdam, Pierrot Lunaire by Schoenberg at Aix 2003; season 2004 as Madame de Croissy in Milan and Mère Marie in Hamburg and Paris (both in Dialogues des Carmelites), Emilia Marty in Berlin, Clytemnestra (Elektra) in Oviedo, Gräfin Geschwitz (Lulu) in Munich, Madame de Croissy in Dialogues des Carmélites; season 2005 as Kostelnicka in Lyon and Barcelona, Emilia Marty in Lyon and Berlin, Janáček's Osud in Vienna, and Gräfin Geschwitz in Munich; Kammersängerin; Bundesverdienstkreuz 1988; Janacek Medal. *Recordings include:* Der fliegende Holländer, Tannhäuser, Lohengrin and Parsifal from Bayreuth, Lulu, Wozzeck, Jenůfa, Pierrot Lunaire, Salome, Erwartung, The Makropoulos Case. *Publication:* Die Sehnsucht nach dem Unerreichbaren (autobiog.) 1999. *Address:* Artists Management Zürich, Rütistrasse 52, 8044 Zürich-Gockhausen, Switzerland (office). *Telephone:* (1) 8218957 (office). *Fax:* (1) 8210127 (office). *E-mail:* schuetz@artistsman.com (office). *Website:* www.artistsman.com (office).

SILLARD, Yves; French aerospace engineer; b. 5 Jan. 1936, Coutances, Manche; s. of Roger Sillard and Madeleine Sillard (née Guerrand); m. 1st Annick Legrand 1966 (divorced); m. 2nd Hélène Benech-Badiou 1982 (divorced); m. 3rd Martine Gautry 1999; ed Ecole Massillon, Ecole Polytechnique, Ecole nat. Supérieure de l'Aéronautique; Test. Eng and then Head of Colomb-Béchard unit of Centre d'Essais en Vol 1960–62, Tech. Dir of Cazeaux annex 1963–64; Head of Concorde Programme at Secrétariat général à l'Aviation civile 1965; Head of Div. setting up French Guiana Space Centre, Kourou 1966–68; Tech. Dir and then Dir Space Centre, Kourou 1968–72; Dir of Launchers, Centre Nat. des Etudes Spatiales 1973–76, Man. Dir 1976–82; Chair. and Man. Dir Centre nat. pour l'exploitation des océans 1982–; Chair. Conseil d'administration de l'institut français de recherche pour l'exploitation de la mer 1985–89; French Nat. Co-ordinator for EUREKA Programme 1986–89; Gen. Del., Armaments 1989–93; mem. Atomic Energy Cttee 1989–93; Chair., Man. Dir Cogepag 1993–, Défence conseil international 1993–97; Asst Sec. Gen. for Scientific Affairs and Environment, NATO 1998–2001; Vice-Chair. Nat. Acad. for Aeronautics and Space; Commdr, Légion d'honneur; Chevalier, Ordre nat. du Mérite; Médaille de l'Aéronautique; Commdr Merit (FRG). *Address:* 8 rue de la Forge, 17800 Brives sur Charente, France. *Telephone:* (5) 46-95-01-56 (home). *E-mail:* ysillard@club-internet.fr (home).

SILLITOE, Alan; British author; b. 4 March 1928, Nottingham; s. of Christopher Sillitoe and Sabina Burton; m. Ruth Fainlight 1959; one s. one d.; ed elementary school, Radford, Nottingham; worked in various factories including Raleigh Bicycles, Nottingham 1942–45; air traffic control asst 1945–46; served as wireless operator, RAF, Malaya 1946–49; lived six years in France and Spain; professional writer 1958–; Visiting Prof. of English, DeMontfort Univ., Leicester 1993–97; Fellow, Royal Geographical Soc., Royal Inst. of Navigation; Hon. Fellow, Manchester Polytechnic, De Montfort Univ. 1998; Dr hc (Nottingham Polytechnic) 1990, (Nottingham Univ.) 1994; Hawthornden Prize 1960. *Film screenplays:* Saturday Night and Sunday Morning, The Loneliness of the Long Distance Runner, The Ragman's Daughter, Counterpoint. *Publications:* novels: Saturday Night and Sunday Morning 1958, The General 1960, Key to the Door 1961, The Death of William Posters 1965, A Tree on Fire 1967, A Start in Life 1970, Travels in Nihilon 1971, Raw Material 1972, The Flame of Life 1974, The Widower's Son 1976, The Storyteller 1979, Her Victory 1982, The Lost Flying Boat 1983, Down From The Hill 1984, Life Goes On 1985, Out of the Whirlpool 1987, The Open Door 1989, Last Loves 1990, Leonard's War: A Love Story 1991, Snowstop 1993, Alligator Playground 1997, The Broken Chariot 1998, The German Numbers Woman 1999, Birthday 2001, A Man of His Time 2004; short story collections: The Loneliness of the Long Distance Runner 1959, The Ragman's Daughter 1963, Guzman, Go Home 1968, Men, Women and Children 1973, The Second Chance 1981, The Far Side of the Street 1988, Collected Stories 1995, New Collected Stories 2004; essays: Mountains and Caverns 1975, The

Mentality of the Picaresque Hero 1993, A Flight of Arrows 2004; poetry: The Rats and Other Poems 1960, A Falling Out of Love 1964, Love in the Environs of Voronezh 1968, Barbarians and Other Poems 1974, Storm and Other Poems 1974, Snow on the North Side of Lucifer 1979, Sun Before Departure 1984, Tides and Stone Walls (with Victor Bowley) 1986, Collected Poems 1993; travel writing: Road to Volgograd 1964, Leading the Blind: A Century of Guide Book Travel 1815–1914 1995, The Saxon Shore Way (with Fay Godwin) 1983, Nottinghamshire (with David Sillitoe) 1986, Gadfly in Russia 2007; plays: Three Plays 1978; All Citizens are Soldiers 1969 (trans. of Lope de Vega's Fuenteovejuna, with Ruth Fainlight); children's books: The City Adventures of Marmalade Jim 1967, Big John and the Stars 1977, The Incredible Fencing Fleas 1978, Marmalade Jim on the Farm 1980, Marmalade Jim and the Fox 1985, Alligator Playground 1998; autobiography: Life Without Armour 1995. *Leisure interests:* geography, navigation, radio communications, travel. *Address:* 14 Ladbroke Terrace, London, W11 3PG, England.

SILNOV, Andrey Alexandrovich; Russian athlete; b. 9 Sept. 1984, Shakhty, Rostov Oblast; men's high jumper; Gold Medal, European Championships, Gothenburg 2006 (jump of 2.36m); jumped 2.37m in Monaco a week later (world leading jump in 2006); Silver Medal, World Athletics Final, Stuttgart 2006, World Cup, Athens 2006; jumped new personal best of 2.38m in London Grand Prix July 2008; Gold Medal, Olympic Games, Beijing 2008 (jump of 2.36m); coached by Sergey Starykh and Yevgeniy Zagorulko. *Address:* c/o All-Russia Athletic Federation, Moscow 119992, 8 Luzhnetskaya nab., Russia. *Telephone:* (495) 7254693. *Fax:* (495) 2428538. *E-mail:* info@rusathletics.ru. *Website:* www.rusathletics.ru.

SILUNGWE, Hon. Mr Justice Annel Musenga, LLM; Zambian judge and barrister; *Judge of High Court and Acting Judge of Supreme Court, Namibia;* b. 10 Jan. 1936, Mbala; s. of Solo Musenga Silungwe and Janet Nakafunda Silungwe; m. Abigail Nanyangwe Silungwe 1960; one s. four d.; ed Univs of Zambia and London, Inner Temple, London; Resident Magistrate 1967, Sr Resident Magistrate (Class II) 1968, (Class I) 1970; Judge of the High Court 1971; nominated MP and apptd Minister of Legal Affairs and Attorney-Gen. 1973; State Counsel 1974; Chief Justice 1975–92; Judge, Court of Appeal, Seychelles 1992–2003; Judge of High Court and Acting Judge of Supreme Court, Namibia 1999–; Dir Justice Training Centre, Namibia 1994–99; Chair. Judicial Services Comm. 1975–92, Council of Legal Educ. 1975–92, Council of Law Reporting 1975–92; Regional Chair. Southern African Region of Nat. Cheshire Int. Homes and Foundations 1998–; Dist Gov. Rotary Int. 1982–83; mem. Council World Jurist Asscn of World Peace Through Law Center 1985–; mem. Bd Dirs The Commonwealth Judicial Educ. Inst., Halifax, Canada 1997–; Rotary Int. Award for Community Service 1989. *Leisure interests:* music, golf, photography. *Address:* High Court, Private Bag 13179, Windhoek, Namibia. *Telephone:* (61) 2277927 (office); (61) 2921275 (office); (61) 242705 (home). *Fax:* (61) 221686 (office); (61) 235421 (home).

SILVA, Artur; Guinea-Bissau politician; *Minister of Defence;* Sec. of State for Int. Co-operation 2008–09; Minister of Defence 2009–; mem. Partido Africano da Independência da Guiné e Cabo Verde (PAIGC). *Address:* Ministry of National Defence, Amura, Bissau, Guinea-Bissau (office). *Telephone:* 223646 (office).

SILVA, Hon. Sarath Nanda, LLM; Sri Lankan judge; *Chief Justice of the Supreme Court;* ed Univ. of Brussels, Belgium; Advocate of the Supreme Court of Sri Lanka 1967; Crown Counsel, Attorney Gen.'s Dept 1968, Sr State Counsel 1975, Deputy Solicitor Gen. 1979; Lecturer, Sri Lanka Law Coll. 1981–87; Judge, Court of Appeal 1987–1994, Pres. 1994; Judge of the Supreme Court 1995–99, Chief Justice 1999–; Lecturer in Civil Law, Sri Lanka Law Coll. 1981–87; Attorney Gen. 1996; Pres.'s Counsel 1996. *Address:* Supreme Court of Sri Lanka, Superior Courts Complex, Colombo 12, Sri Lanka (office). *Telephone:* (1) 328651 (office). *Fax:* (1) 435446 (office).

SILVA, Tilwin; Sri Lankan politician; *General Secretary, Janatha Vimukthi Peramuna (JVP);* b. 26 Feb. 1956; Gen. Sec. Janatha Vimukthi Peramuna (People's Liberation Front) 1995–. *Address:* Janatha Vimukthi Peramuna, 198/19 Panchikawattha Road, Colombo 10, Sri Lanka (office). *Telephone:* (11) 4400511 (office). *Fax:* (11) 2786050 (office). *E-mail:* contact@jvpsrilanka.com (office). *Website:* www.jvpsrilanka.com (office).

SILVA BARBEIRO, Marciano; Guinea-Bissau politician; Minister of Educ. 2004–05, Minister of Nat. Defence 2007–09; mem. Partido Africano da Independência da Guiné e Cabo Verde (PAIGC). *Address:* Partido Africano da Independência da Guiné e Cabo Verde, CP 106, Bissau, Guinea-Bissau (office). *Website:* www.paigc.org (office).

SILVA-CALDERÓN, Alvaro; Venezuelan international organization executive and government official; b. 9 June 1929, Teresén, Monagas State; m. Judith Pérez; one s. one d.; ed Universidad Cen. de Venezuela; Lecturer, Dept of Mining and Hydrocarbons Law, Law School, Universidad Cen. de Venezuela, now Prof. Emer.; mem. advisory team of Juan Pablo Pérez Alfonso; fmr Pres. Regional Legislature, Monagas State; fmr mem. Nat. Congress, Pres. Int. Treaties Sub-Cttee and mem. Energy and Mines Cttee; Minister of Energy and Mines 2000–02; Sec.-Gen. OPEC 2002–03; currently Special Envoy of Pres. Hugo Chavez to OPEC; fmr External Dir Bd Petróleos de Venezuela, SA; fmr Dir Supreme Electoral Council of Venezuela; fmr Chief Legal Advisor to Ministry of Energy and Mines (also Dir-Gen. and Vice-Minister of Mines); fmr columnist for El Globo nat. daily newspaper; mem. and del. Venezuelan Chapter at World Oil Congress; mem. Nat. Energy Council; Order Francisco de Miranda (First Class), Order Juan Pablo Pérez Alfonso (First Class), Merit Order Ambrosio Plaza (First Class), Order Sol de Carabobo (Chief Official), Order Farten de Bie Faire (Portugal), Merit Order Honor y Gloria (Portugal); OPEC Second Summit Diploma. *Address:* c/o Ministry of Energy and Petroleum, Edif. Petróleos de Venezuela, Torre Oeste, Avda Libertador con Avda Empalme, La Campiña, Porroquia El Recreo, Caracas, Venezuela. *Telephone:* (212) 708-1299. *Fax:* (212) 708-7014. *Website:* www.mem.gov.ve.

SILVA ROSA, Sérgio Ricardo; Brazilian banker and mining industry executive; *Chairman, Vale;* ed Universidade de São Paulo; joined Caixa de Previdência dos Funcionários do Banco do Brasil (PREVI) (investment fund) 2000, Pres. 2003–; mem. Bd of Dirs Companhia Vale do Rio Doce (CVRD) 2003– (now called Vale), Chair. 2003–; Pres. Confederação Nacional dos Bancários (CNB/CUT) 1994–97, 1997–2000; Dir Brasil Telecom –2003, Associação Brasileira das Entidades de Previdência Privada (ABRAPP); mem. Exec Cttee UN's 'Principles for Responsible Investment' programme. *Address:* Vale, Avenida Graça Aranha # 26, 19th Floor, 20030-900 Rio de Janeiro, Brazil (office). *Telephone:* (21) 3814-4477 (office). *Fax:* (21) 3814-4040 (office). *E-mail:* info@vale.com (office). *Website:* www.vale.com (office).

SILVEIRA GODINHO, José António da; Portuguese fmr politician, economist and business executive; *Member, Board of Directors, Banco de Portugal;* b. 16 Oct. 1943, Lisbon; s. of Raul Catarino Godinho and Angela da Silveira Godinho; m. Isabel Maria Canhoto Segura de Faria 1972; three s.; ed Lisbon Tech. Univ.; Asst Prof. Lisbon School of Econs 1967–77; Sr Vice-Pres. Banco de Portugal 1975–79, mem. Bd of Dirs 2004–; mem. Man. Bd Banco Pinto & Sotto Mayor 1979–82; Sec. of State for Finance 1980–81; mem. Exec. Bd Banco Espírito Santo 1982–93; Sec. of State for Nat. Defence 1986–87; Minister of Internal Affairs 1987–90; Amb. to OECD 1993–96; mem. Bd of Dirs Espírito Santo, Ca. de Seguros SA 1996–, AdvanceCare, SA 1999–; mem. Gen. Council Asscn of Portuguese Economists 1999–. *Leisure interests:* reading, travelling, music, sport. *Address:* c/o Board of Directors, Banco de Portugal, R. do Ouro, 27, 1100-150 Lisbon, Portugal (office). *Telephone:* (21) 3213273 (office); (21) 3905236 (home). *Fax:* (21) 3431133 (office). *E-mail:* sgodinho@bportugal.pt (office).

SILVER, Casey; American film producer and film industry executive; began career as screenwriter; Asst to Adrian Lyne (q.v.); fmr Vice-Pres. Production, Sr Vice-Pres. Production TriStar Pictures, Dir of Devt and Production Simpson-Bruckheimer; joined Universal Pictures as Exec. Vice-Pres. Production 1987, Pres. 1989, Pres. Universal Pictures 1994, Chair. 1995–99; f. Casey Silver Productions 1999–. *Films:* Gigli 2003, Hidalgo 2004, Rebels 2004, Ladder 49 2004, Leatherheads 2008, The Forbidden Kingdom 2008. *Address:* Casey Silver Productions, 506 Santa Monica Blvd, Suite 322, Santa Monica, CA 90401, USA. *Telephone:* (310) 566-3750.

SILVER, Joan Micklin, BA; American film and theatre director and screenwriter; b. 24 May 1935, Omaha, Neb.; d. of Maurice Micklin and Doris Shoshone; m. Raphael Silver 1956; three d.; ed Sarah Lawrence Coll.; began career as writer for educational films; original screenplay for Limbo purchased by Universal Pictures; commissioned by Learning Corpn of America to write and direct short narrative film The Immigrant Experience 1972 and wrote and dir two children's films for same co.; Dir plays: Album and Maybe I'm Doing it Wrong; also Dir for TV. *Films include:* Hester Street (dir and screenplay), Bernice Bobs Her Hair (dir and screenplay), Between the Lines (dir), On the Yard (producer), Head Over Heels (dir and screenplay, retitled Chilly Scenes of Winter), Crossing Delancey (dir), Loverboy (dir), Big Girls Don't Cry, They Get Even (dir), In the Presence of Mine Enemies (dir) 1996, Fish in the Bathtub 1997, Invisible Child (dir) 1998, Charms for the Easy Life (dir) 2002, Hunger Point (dir) 2003. *Radio:* Great Jewish Short Stories from Eastern Europe and Beyond (dir) 1995. *Address:* Silverfilm Productions Inc., 510 Park Avenue, Suite 9B, New York, NY 10022-1105, USA (home). *Telephone:* (642) 282-0312 (home). *Fax:* (212) 421-8254 (home). *E-mail:* jmicksil@aol.com (office).

SILVER, Joel; American film producer; b. 14 July 1952, South Orange, NJ; ed New York Univ.; fmrly Asst to Lawrence Gordon, Pres. Lawrence Gordon Productions; producer, Vice-Pres. Universal Pictures; currently runs Silver Pictures 1985– and (with Robert Zemeckis) Dark Castle Entertainment 1999–. *Films:* The Warrior 1979, Xanadu 1980, 48 Hours 1982, Jekyll & Hyde... Together Again 1982, Streets of Fire 1984, Brewster's Millions 1985, Weird Science 1985, Commando 1985, Jumpin' Jack Flash 1986, Lethal Weapon 1986, Predator 1987, Action Jackson 1988, Die Hard 1988, Lethal Weapon 2 1989, Roadhouse 1989, Ford Fairlane 1990, Die Hard 2 1990, Predator 2 1990, Hudson Hawk 1991, Ricochet 1991, The Last Boy Scout 1991, Lethal Weapon 3 1992, Demolition Man 1993, The Hudsucker Proxy, Richie Rich 1994, Demon Knight 1994, Assassins 1995, Fair Game 1995, Executive Decision 1996, Conspiracy Theory, Father's Day, Lethal Weapon 4 1998, Romeo Must Die 1999, Made Men 1999, The Matrix 1999, The House on Haunted Hill 1999, Romeo Must Die 2000, Dungeons & Dragons 2000, Ritual 2001, Exit Wounds 2001, Proximity 2001, Swordfish 2001, Thir13en Ghosts 2001, Ghost Ship 2002, Cradle 2 the Grave 2003, The Animatrix: Final Flight of the Osiris 2003, The Matrix Reloaded 2003, The Matrix Revolutions 2003, Gothika 2003, Kiss, Kiss, Bang, Bang 2005, V for Vendetta 2005, The Reaping 2007, The Invasion 2007, The Brave One 2007, Fred Claus 2007, Speed Racer 2008. *Television:* Tales from the Crypt, Two Fisted Tales, Parker Can, W.E.I.R.D. World, Freedom, Next Action Star, Veronica Mars 2004–07, Moonlight 2007–08. *Address:* Silver Pictures, c/o Warner Bros Pictures, 4000 Warner Boulevard, Building 90, Burbank, CA 91522-0001, USA.

SILVERMAN, Bernard Walter, BTh, MA, PhD, DPhil, DSc, ScD, FRS; British professor of statistics and college president; *Master, St Peter's College, Oxford;* b. 22 Feb. 1952; s. of Elias Silverman and Helen Silverman; m. Rowena Fowler 1985; one s.; ed City of London School, Jesus Coll., Cambridge; Research Fellow, Jesus Coll., Cambridge 1975–77; Calculator Devt Man., Sinclair Radionics 1976–77; Weir Fellow, Univ. Coll., Oxford 1977–78, also Jr Lecturer, Univ. of Oxford; Lecturer, then Reader, then Prof. of Statistics,

Univ. of Bath 1978–93, Head of School of Math. Sciences 1988–91; Prof. of Statistics, Univ. of Bristol 1993–99, Head of Statistics Group 1993–97, 1998–99, Henry Overton Wills Prof. of Math. 1999–2003, Provost Inst. for Advanced Studies 2000–03; Master, St Peter's Coll. Oxford and Prof. of Statistics, Univ. of Oxford 2003–; visiting appointments, Dept of Statistics, Princeton Univ., USA 1978, 1979, Univ. of Paris VI 1979, Sonderforschungsbereich 123, Univ. of Heidelberg 1980, Math. Research Center, Univ. of Wisconsin-Madison 1981, Dept of Statistics, Johns Hopkins Univ. 1981, Depts of Statistics and Biostatistics, Univ. of Washington 1984, Univ. of Frankfurt 1984, Univ. of California, San Diego 1985, CSIRO Div. of Math. and Statistics, Canberra, Sydney, Melbourne and Perth, Australia 1985, Math. Sciences Research Inst., Berkeley, Calif. 1991; Fellow, Center for Advanced Study in the Behavioral Sciences, Stanford, Calif. 1997–98; Chartered Statistician, Royal Statistical Soc., mem. Research Section Cttee 1979–82, mem. Council 1982–90, Hon. Sec. 1984–90, mem. Working Party on Official Statistics, Chair. Research Section 1991–93; Fellow, Inst. of Math. Statistics 1987, mem. Council 1991–94, 1997–2000, Pres. 2000–01; Fellow, Int. Statistical Inst./Bernoulli Soc. 1986, mem. Bernoulli Soc. European Regional Cttee 1986–92 Chair. 1988–90, mem. Bernoulli Soc. Council 1999–2003; Fellow, Royal Soc. 1997, mem. several cttees, including Research Grants Cttee A 1997–2000 (Chair. 1999–2000), Sectional Cttee 1 1998–2001 (Chair. 2001), Conf. Grants Cttee 1998–2001, Dorothy Hodgkin Fellowships Cttee A 1999–2004 (Chair. 2003), Wolfson Merit Awards Cttee 2006–; Ed. Oxford University Press Statistical Science Series 1983–87, International Statistical Review 1991–96, Chapman & Hall Monographs on Statistics and Applied Probability 1985–97, Interdisciplinary Statistics Series 1993–97, Wiley Statistics Series 1997–2001, IMS Bulletin 2002–06, Cambridge University Press Statistics Series 2003– Annals of Statistics 2007–(09); Assoc. Ed. Annals of Statistics 1982–85, Journal of the Royal Statistical Society, Series B 1980–84; Sr Ed. Statistics and Computing 1990–; mem. Editorial Bd Inverse Problems 1998–2000; external examiner for numerous BA, BSc and MSc degree examinations and PhD and research MSc theses world-wide; mem. Science and Eng Research Council Statistics Panel 1990–94; frequent reviewer for US NSF, Natural Sciences and Eng Research Council of Canada, Australian Research Council, etc. Eng and Physical Sciences Research Council Math. Coll. 1994–97, 2000–03; mem. Scientific Cttee, EURANDOM, Netherlands 1997–2003, Statistics Research Assessment Panel for Higher Educ. Funding Council for England (HEFCE) Research Assessment Exercise 2001, Scientific Steering Cttee, Isaac Newton Inst. 2003–06, Steering Group, Int. Review of UK Math. 2003–04 (Chair. Subpanel 22 (Statistics) and mem. Panel F (Math.)), HEFCE Research Assessment Exercise 2008; Patron Royal Inst. Wessex Math. Master Classes; Chair. Jt Math. Council of the UK 2003–06, UK Math. Trust 2004–08; consultant to UK Govt Inquiry (the 'Lessons Learned' Inquiry) into the Foot and Mouth Epidemic 2002, Statistics Commission 2003; consultancies with Nuclear Electric, Nat. Audit Office, Ministry of Defence, Agilent Technologies, Mass Spec Analytical Ltd; consultancy on statistical aspects of legal cases (especially financial and forensic), statistical advice to the press and advice to police in criminal cases; radio and TV programmes on statistics; mem. Advisory Bd Statistics Dept, Carnegie-Mellon Univ. 2002, Academic Chair. 2006; mem. GM Science Review Panel 2002–03, Owner's Advisory Bd (non-exec. dir) Defence Analytical Services Agency 1998–2009; Chair. Peer Review Panel on the Project for the Sustainable Devt of Heathrow 2005–06; mem. Academia Europaea 2001; ordained deacon (Church of England) 1999–, priest 2000–; Hon. Fellow, Jesus College Cambridge 2003; First Prize, Int. Math. Olympiad 1970, Mayhew Prize for Math. Tripos Part III, Univ. of Cambridge 1974, Smith's Prize, Univ. of Cambridge 1976, Guy Medal in Bronze, Royal Statistical Soc. 1984, Guy Medal in Silver 1995, Special Invited Paper, Inst. of Math. Statistics 1985, Technometrics Special Discussion Paper, American Statistical Asscn 1988, Pres.' Award, American Statistical Asscn, Inst. of Math. Statistics, Biometric Soc. (ENAR and WNAR) and Statistical Soc. of Canada for "the outstanding statistician under forty" (COPSS Award) 1991, Fulkerson Lecturer, Cornell Univ. 1993, Special Invited Paper, Inst. of Math. Statistics 1999, Henri Willem Methorst Medal, Int. Statistical Inst. 1999, Corcoran Lecturer, Univ. of Oxford 2000, Original Mem. Highly Cited Researchers database, Information Sciences Inst. 2002. *Publications include:* Density Estimation for Statistics and Data Analysis 1986, Industrial Quality and Productivity with Statistical Methods: A Joint Symposium of the Royal Society and the Royal Statistical Society (co-ed.) 1989, Nonparametric Regression and Generalized Linear Models: A Roughness Penalty Approach (with P. J. Green) 1994, Functional Data Analysis (with J. O. Ramsay) 1997, (revised and expanded second edn 2005), Wavelets: The Key to Intermittent Information? (co-ed.) 2000, Applied Functional Data Analysis (with J. O. Ramsay) 2002; more than 80 papers in peer-reviewed journals and numerous research contribs and govt reports. *Address:* St Peter's College, Oxford, OX1 2DL, England (office). *Telephone:* (1865) 278862 (office); (1865) 278911 (PA) (office). *Fax:* (1865) 278855 (office). *E-mail:* master@spc.ox.ac.uk (office). *Website:* www.bernardsilverman.com (office).

SILVERMAN, Fred, MA; American producer and broadcasting executive; *President, Fred Silverman Company;* b. 13 Sept. 1937, New York; m. Cathy Kihn; one s. one d.; ed Syracuse Univ., Ohio State Univ.; with WGN-TV Chicago; exec. position WP1X-TV New York; Dir Daytime Programmes CBS-TV New York, Vice-Pres. Programmes 1970–75; Pres. ABC Entertainment 1975–78; Pres. NBC 1978–81; ind. film producer 1981–; Pres. The Fred Silverman Co. 1986–. *Address:* Fred Silverman Company, 1648 Mandeville Canyon Road, Los Angeles, CA 90025, USA (office). *Telephone:* (310) 471-4676 (office). *Fax:* (310) 471-3295 (office).

SILVERMAN, Henry Richard, BA, JD; American lawyer and business executive; *Chairman, Realogy Corporation;* b. 2 Aug. 1940, New York; s. of Herbert Silverman and Roslyn (née Moskowitz) Silverman; m. 1st Susan H. Herson 1965 (divorced 1977); two d.; m. 2nd Nancy Ann Kraner 1978; one d.; ed Hackley School, Tarrytown, NY, Williams Coll., Univ. of Pennsylvania Law School; with USNR 1965–73; called to Bar NY 1965; with US Tax Court 1965; with US Court of Appeals 1965; law practice 1965–66; with White, Weld & Co. 1966; Gen. Pnr, Oppenheimer & Co. 1966–70; Pres., CEO ITI Corpn 1970–72; f., Pres. Trans-York Securities Corpn 1972; CEO Vavasseur America Ltd 1974–75; Gen. Pnr,Brisbane Pnrs 1976–77; prin. in various investment groups 1977–, Silverman Energy Co. 1977, NBC Channel 20 1977–83, ABC Channel 9 1977–81, Delta Queen Steamboat 1977–86, also Dir; apptd Pres., CEO Reliance Capital Corpn (subsidiary Reliance Group Holdings Inc.) 1982, Sr Vice-Pres. Business Devt Reliance Group Holdings Inc. 1982–90; Gen. Pnr, Blackstone Group 1990–91; Founder, Chair., CEO HFS Inc. 1990–97; CEO Cendant Corpn 1997–2005, Pres. 1997–2004, Chair. 1998–2005 (co. split into four separate cos including Realogy); Chair. and CEO Realogy Corpn, Parsippany, NJ 2004–07, Chair. (non-exec.) 2007–; Chair. Business Roundtable's Fiscal Policy Task Force; Dir NY Univ. Hosp. 1987–, NYU Child Study Center; Commr Port Authority of New York and New Jersey, Chair. Finance Cttee; Trustee New York Univ. and its School of Medicine and Medical Center; Univ. of Pennsylvania; mem. JP Morgan's Nat. Advisory Bd, G-100; American Heritage Award, Anti-Defamation League 1998, Jackie Robinson Foundation award 2001, US Hispanic Chamber of Commerce award 2003. *Leisure interest:* tennis. *Address:* Realogy, 1 Campus Drive, Parsippany, NJ 07054, USA (office). *Telephone:* (973) 407-2000 (office). *Website:* www.realogy.com (office).

SILVERMAN, Marcia, MEconSc; American business executive; *CEO, Ogilvy Public Relations Worldwide;* one s.; ed Univ. of Pennsylvania; fmr employee Nat. Labour Relations Bd; worked in Public Relations Div., J. Walter Thompson 1978–81; joined Washington office, Ogilvy & Mather Public Affairs 1981, Head of Washington Office 1990–2000; Pres. of the Americas, Ogilvy Public Relations Worldwide 2000–02, CEO 2002–. *Address:* Ogilvy Public Relations Worldwide, 909 Third Avenue, New York, NY 10022, USA (office). *Telephone:* (212) 880-5200 (office). *Fax:* (212) 697-8250 (office). *E-mail:* silverman.marcia@ogilvypr.com (office). *Website:* www.ogilvypr.com (office).

SILVERS, Robert Benjamin, AB; American literary editor; *Editor, The New York Review of Books;* b. 31 Dec. 1929, Mineola, NY; ed Univ. of Chicago, Sorbonne, Ecole Polytechnique, Paris, France; Press Sec. to Gov. of Connecticut 1950; served in US Army 1950–53; Man. Ed. Paris Review 1954–58; Assoc. Ed. Harper's Magazine 1958–63; Co-founder and Co-Ed. New York Review of Books 1963–2006, Ed. 2006–; mem. Council of Foreign Relations, Century Asscn; Chevalier, Légion d'honneur, mem. Ordre National du Mérite; Hon. DLit (Harvard) 2007; Award for Distinguished Service to the Arts from the American Academy of Arts and Letters 2006, National Book Foundation Literarian Award 2006; Robert B. Silvers annual lectures at New York Public Library established 2002. *Address:* New York Review of Books, 1755 Broadway, 5th Floor, New York, NY 10019-3743, USA (office). *Telephone:* (212) 757-8070 (office). *Fax:* (212) 333-5374 (office). *E-mail:* nyrev@nybooks.com (office). *Website:* www.nybooks.com (office).

SILVERSTONE, Alicia; American actress; b. 4 Oct. 1976, San Francisco, Calif.; d. of Monty Silverstone and Didi Silverstone; m. Christopher Jarecki 2005; stage debut in play Carol's Eve at Met Theatre, LA; starred in three Aerosmith videos including Cryin'; f. First Kiss Productions (production co.). *Films:* The Crush 1993, The Babysitter 1995, True Crime 1995, Le Nouveau Monde 1995, Hideaway 1995, Clueless 1995, Batman and Robin 1997, Excess Baggage (also producer) 1997, Free Money 1998, Love's Labour's Lost 1999, Blast from the Past 1999, Rock My World 2002, Scorched 2003, Scooby Doo 2: Monsters Unleashed 2004, Beauty Shop 2005. *Television:* Torch Song 1993, Shattered Dreams 1993, The Cool and the Crazy 1994, The Wonder Years 1997, Miss Match (series) 2003. *Address:* First Kiss Productions, c/o Columbia Pictures, 10202 Washington Boulevard, Culver City, CA 90232; c/o Premiere Artists Agency, Suite 510, 8899 Beverly Boulevard, Los Angeles, CA 90048, USA.

SILVESTRINI, HE Cardinal Achille; Italian ecclesiastic; *Prefect Emeritus, Congregation for Oriental Churches, Roman Curia;* b. 25 Oct. 1923, Brisighella; ordained priest 1946, consecrated Bishop 1979, elected Archbishop of Novaliciana, Mauritania 1979; Sec. Council for Public Affairs of the Church 1979; cr. Cardinal-Deacon of S. Benedetto fuori Porta S. Paolo 1988–99, Cardinal-Priest of S. Benedetto fuori Porta S. Paolo 1999–; Prefect of the Supreme Tribunal of the Apostolic Signatura 1988–91; Prefect of the Congregation for Oriental Churches, 1991–2000, Prefect Emer. and Grand Chancellor of the Pontifical Eastern Inst. 2000–; mem. Congregation for the Doctrine of the Faith, for the Oriental Churches, for the Causes of the Saints, for the Bishops, for the Evangelization of Peoples, for Catholic Educ.; mem. Pontificial Council for the Interpretation of Legislative Texts, for Inter-Religious Dialogue. *Address:* Palazzina della Zecca, 00120 Vatican City, Italy (home). *Telephone:* (06) 69884838 (home). *Fax:* (06) 69881311. *E-mail:* asilvestrini@org.va (office).

SILVESTROV, Valentin Vasilyevich; Ukrainian composer; b. 30 Sept. 1937, Kiev; ed Kiev State Conservatory (pupil of B. Lyatoshinsky); author of compositions performed in USSR and many countries of Europe and in USA; S. Koussevitsky Prize (USA) 1967, Prize of Gaudeamus Soc. (Netherlands) 1970. *Compositions include:* 5 symphonies for large symphony orchestra 1963–82, Symphony for baritone with orchestra Echo Momentum on verses of A. Pushkin 1987, string quartets 1978, 1988, Dedication – symphony for violin and orchestra 1991, Mertamusica for piano and orchestra 1992, numerous chamber ensembles, piano pieces, vocal cycles, choruses. *Address:* Entuziastov str. 35/1, Apt. 49, 252147 Kiev, Ukraine (home). *Telephone:* (44) 517-04-47 (home).

SILVIA, HM The Queen of Sweden; b. (Silvia Renate Sommerlath), 23 Dec. 1943, Heidelberg, Germany; d. of the late Walther Sommerlath and Alice Toledo; m. King Carl XVI Gustaf 1976; two d., Crown Princess Victoria Ingrid Alice Désirée b. 14 July 1977, Princess Madeleine Thérèse Amelie Josephine b. 10 June 1982; one s., Prince Carl Philip Edmund Bertil b. 13 May 1979; ed Munich School of Interpreting; lived in Sao Paulo, Brazil 1947–57, returned to FRG 1957; fmr mem. staff Argentine Consulate, Munich; mem. Organizing Cttee, Munich Olympics 1971–73, Deputy Head of Protocol, Organizing Cttee, Winter Olympics, Innsbruck, Austria 1973; Chair. Royal Wedding Fund, Jubilee Fund; est. Silvia Home, Drottningholm; Patron First World Congress Against Commercial Sexual Exploitation of Children, Stockholm 1996; f. World Childhood Foundation; Hon. mem. Menton Foundation, Swedish Amateur Athletic Asscn, Children's Cancer Foundation of Sweden, Swedish Save the Children Fed.; Dr hc (Åbo Univ.) 1990, (Karolinska Institutet) 1993, (Univ. of Linköping) 1994, (Göteborg Univ.) 1999; Deutsche Kulturpreis 1990, Chancellor's Medal, Univ. of Mass, ranked by Forbes magazine amongst 100 Most Powerful Women (68th) 2004. *Leisure interests:* theatre, opera, concerts, skiing. *Address:* Royal Court of Sweden, Royal Palace, Stockholm 111 30, Sweden. *Telephone:* (8) 4026000. *Fax:* (8) 4026062. *E-mail:* info@royalcourt.se. *Website:* www.royalcourt.se.

SIM, Wong Hoo; Singaporean business executive; *Chairman and CEO, Creative Technology Ltd;* ed Ngee Ann Polytechnic; f. Creative Technology Ltd, Singapore 1981, currently Chair. and CEO; f. Creative Labs, USA; launched Sound Blaster PC card 1989, Sound Blaster Pro 1991; Chair. Technopreneurship 21 Pvt. Sector Cttee. *Publication:* Chaotic Thoughts from the Old Millennium. *Address:* Creative Technology Ltd, 31 International Business Park, Creative Resource, 609921, Singapore (office). *Telephone:* 6895-4000 (office). *Fax:* 6895-4999 (office). *Website:* www.creative.com (office).

SIMAI, Mihály; Hungarian economist; *Professor of International Economics, University of Economics, Budapest;* b. 4 April 1930, Budapest; s. of Mátyás Simai and Jolán Rosenberg; m. Vera Bence 1953; one d.; ed Univ. of Econs, Budapest; postgraduate studies in Geneva and Paris; Prof. of Int. Econs and Nat. Business, Univ. of Econs, Budapest 1971–, Dir of Grad. Studies in Int. Business and Strategy 1987–, in Int. Relations 1991–; mem. Hungarian Acad. of Sciences 1979–, Deputy Dir of Research, Inst. for World Econs, Hungarian Acad. of Sciences, Budapest 1973–87, Dir 1987–91, now Research Prof.; Pres. Hungarian UN Ass., Hungarian Nat. Cttee for UNICEF 1981–; Chair. Council UN Univ. 1990–92; Vice-Pres. Int. Studies Asscn 1988–; fmr Pres. Ed. Cttee Acta Oeconomica; Dir UN Univ. World Inst. for Devt Econs Research 1993–96; mem. Governing Council, Nat. Studies Asscn 1984–, Governing Bd Karl Polanyi Inst. 1988–, Advisory Bd for UN TNCs 1990–, Editorial Bd Environmental Econs 1991–, Advisory Bd Global Governance 1993–; Peace Fellow, US Inst. for Peace 1991–92; Hon. Pres. World Fed. of UN Asscns 1982–; Labour Order of Merit (Golden Degree), Order of the Star of Hungary (Golden Degree), Order of the Flag of the Hungarian Repub. 1990. *Publications:* Capital Export in the Contemporary Capitalist System 1962, The World Economic System of Capitalism, 1965, View from the 26th Floor 1969, Joint Ventures with Foreign Partners 1971, The United States before the 200th Anniversary 1974, Planning and Plan Implementation in the Developing Countries 1975, The United Nations and the Global Problems 1977, Interdependence and Conflicts in the World Economy 1981, Economic Decolonization and the Developing Countries 1981, The United Nations Today and Tomorrow 1985, Power, Technology and the World Economy of the 1990s 1990, Foreign Direct Investments in Hungary 1991, The Future of Global Governance: Managing Risk and Change in the International System 1994, International Business Policy 1996, The Democratic Process and the Market (ed.) 1999, The Reintegration of the Former Socialist Countries in Europe, China and Vietnam into the Global Economy 2000, The Ages of Global Transformations 2001; more than 250 articles on int. econ. and political issues. *Leisure interests:* hiking, skiing. *Address:* Institute for World Economics, Hungarian Academy of Sciences, Országház utca 30, 1014 Budapest, Országház utca 30 (office); Budapest University of Economic Sciences and Department of World Economy, Fővám tér 8, 1093 Budapest, Hungary. *Telephone:* (1) 224-6762 (office); (1) 218-2313. *Fax:* (1) 224-6761 (office). *E-mail:* msimai@vki.hu (office). *Website:* www.vki.hu (office).

SIMELANE, Constance, BA, MBA; Swazi politician; *Deputy Prime Minister;* ed Roosevelt Univ., Chicago, American Univ., Washington, DC, Inst. of Civic Educ., USA, Izburg Int. School, Austria; worked as credit researcher, Chicago, USA; worked at UN Secr., New York, UN Econ. Comm. for Africa, Addis Ababa, Ethiopia; fmr Asst Sec., Deputy Prime Minister's Office, Swaziland; fmr Senator; Minister of Educ. 2003–06; Deputy Prime Minister 2006–. *Address:* Office of the Deputy Prime Minister, POB 433, Swazi Plaza, Mbabane, Swaziland (office). *Telephone:* 4042723 (office). *Fax:* 4044085 (office). *E-mail:* sec-tocab@realnet.co.sz (office). *Website:* www.gov.sz (office).

SIMEON, Yvon; Haitian economist, politician and diplomatist; *Ambassador to Italy;* ed France; fmr consultant; fmr Chargé d'Affaires in France and Belgium; Democratic Convergence rep., Paris; Minister of Foreign Affairs 2004–05; Amb. to Italy 2005–, Perm.Rep. to FAO 2006–. *Address:* Embassy of Haiti, Via di Villa Patrizi 7/7a, 00161 Rome, Italy (office). *Telephone:* (06) 44254106 (office). *Fax:* (06) 44254208 (office). *E-mail:* amb.haiti@tiscali.it (office).

SIMHON, Shalom, BA; Israeli politician and social worker; *Minister of Agriculture and Rural Development;* b. 1956; m.; two c.; ed Univ. of Haifa; Sergeant Maj. in Israel Defence Forces; Exec. Dir Youth Section, Moshav Movt 1985–91, Chair. Social Dept 1991–93, Pension Fund 1993–2001; Sec.-Gen. Moshad Movt 1993–2001; mem. Knesset (Labour Party) 1996–; Chair. Agric. Cttee 1996; mem. Econ. Cttee and Finance Cttee 1996–2002; Chair. Finance Cttee 2000; Minister of Agric. and Rural Devt 2001–02, 2006–, of the Environment 2005–06; Sec.-Gen. Agricultural Centre 1997–2001; fmr Chair. Bd of Tnuva. *Address:* Ministry of Agriculture and Rural Development, PO Box 30, Beit Dagan, Tel-Aviv 50250 (office); The Knesset, HaKiryah, Jerusalem, 91950, Israel. *Telephone:* 3-9485571 (office); 2-6753333. *Fax:* 3-9485870 (office). *E-mail:* regeva@moag.gov.il (office); ssimhon@knesset.gov.il (office). *Website:* www.moag.gov.il (office).

SIMIC, Charles, BA; American poet, writer and academic; *Professor of English, University of New Hampshire;* b. 9 May 1938, Belgrade, Yugoslavia; s. of George Simic and Helen Matijevich; m. Helen Dubin 1965; one s. one d.; ed Oak Park High School, Chicago, Univ. of Chicago and New York Univ.; arrived in USA 1954; army service 1961–64; worked for Chicago Sun-Times as proofreader; later business Man. Aperture Magazine 1966–69; Lecturer, Calif. State Univ., Hayward 1970–73; Assoc. Prof., later Prof. of English, Univ. of New Hampshire 1973–; first vol. of poems published 1967; elected a Chancellor of The Acad. of American Poets 2000; Poet Laureate of USA 2007–08; PEN Int. Award for Translation 1970, 1980, Guggenheim Fellowship 1972, Nat. Endowment for the Arts Fellowships 1974, 1979, Edgar Allan Poe Award 1975, American Acad. of Arts and Letters Award 1976, Harriet Monroe Poetry Award 1980, Fulbright Fellowship 1982, Ingram Merrill Foundation Fellowship 1983, John D. and Catherine T. MacArthur Foundation Fellowship 1984, Acad. of American Poets Fellowship 1998, Wallace Stevens Award 2007. *Publications include:* poetry: What the Grass Says 1967, Somewhere Among Us A Stone Is Taking Notes 1969, Dismantling the Silence 1971, White 1972, Return to a Place Lit by a Glass of Milk 1974, Biography and a Lament 1976, Charon's Cosmology 1977, Brooms: Selected Poems 1978, School for Dark Thoughts 1978, Classic Ballroom Dances 1980, Shaving at Night 1982, Austerities 1982, Weather Forecast for Utopia and Vicinity: Poems 1967–82 1983, The Chicken Without a Head 1983, Selected Poems 1985, Unending Blues 1986, The World Doesn't End (prose poems) (Pulitzer Prize for Poetry 1990) 1989, In the Room We Share 1990, The Book of Gods and Devils 1990, Selected Poems: 1963–83 1990, Hotel Insomnia 1992, A Wedding in Hell 1994, Walking the Black Cat 1996, Jackstraws 1999, Night Picnic 2001, The Voice at 3:00AM 2003, Selected Poems 1963–2003 (Griffin Int. Poetry Prize) 2005, That Little Something 2008; prose: The Uncertain Certainty 1985, Wonderful Words, Silent Truth 1990, Dimestore Alchemy 1992, The Unemployed Fortune Teller 1994, Orphan Factory (essays) 1997, A Fly in the Soup 2000, The Renegade: Writings on Poetry and a Few Other Things 2009; ed.: Another Republic: 17 European and South American Writers (with Mark Strand) 1976, The Essential Campion 1988, The Best American Poetry 1992; many trans of French, Serbian, Croatian, Macedonian and Slovenian poetry. *Address:* Department of English, University of New Hampshire, PO Box 192, Durham, NH 03824 (office); PO Box 192, Stafford, NH 03884, USA. *E-mail:* csimic@cisunix.unh.edu (office). *Website:* www.unh.edu/english (office).

SIMION, Eugen Ioan, PhD; Romanian literary critic; *President, Department of Literature and Philology, Romanian Academy;* b. 25 May 1933, Chiojdeanca, Prahova Co.; s. of Dragomir Simion and Sultana Simion; m. Adriana Manea 1957; one d.; ed I. L.Caragiale High School, Ploiesti, Faculty of Philology, Bucharest Univ.; researcher, Romanian Acad. 1957–62, Corresp. mem. 1991, mem. 1992, Vice-Pres. 1994–98, Pres. 1998–2006, Pres. Dept of Literature and Philology 2006–; Ed. Gazeta literară 1962–68; Asst Lecturer, Bucharest Univ. 1964, Assoc. Prof. 1971, Prof. of Romanian Literature 1990–; Visiting Prof., Sorbonne, Paris 1970–73; Dir Caiete critice (cultural review) 1991–; mem. Bd Romanian Writers' Union; Vice-Pres. Intergovernmental Cttee for the World Decade for Cultural Devt— UNESCO 1992, currently Pres.; Pres. Nat. Council for the Certification of Diplomas and Univ. Certificates; mem. Academia Europaea 1992–, Acad. of Sciences of Moldavia 1999, Int. Union of Literary Critics; Dr hc (Jassy, Galati, Târgoviste, Arad); prizes of Romanian Writers' Union (five times), Prize of Romanian Acad. 1977. *Publications include:* Eminescu's Fiction 1964, Trends in Today's Literature 1965, E Lovinescu the Sceptic Saved 1971, The Romanian Writers Today Vol. I 1974, Vol. II 1976, Vol. III 1983, Vol. IV 1989; A Time to Live, a Time to Confess (Paris Diary), The Morning of Poets 1980, Defying Rhetoric 1985, Mercutio's Death 1993, Talking to Petru Dumitriu 1994, Mircea Eliade, A Spirit Amplitude 1995, The Return of the Author 1996, Critical Fragments I–IV 1998–2000; more than 3000 articles. *Address:* Romanian Academy, Calea Victoriei 725, Bucharest (office); Dr Lister 8, Bucharest, Romania (home). *Telephone:* (1) 3122760 (office); (1) 4109748 (home). *Fax:* (1) 3120209 (office); (1) 3365855 (home). *E-mail:* esimion@acad.ro (office); mdc@rnc.ro (home).

SIMITIS, Constantine (Costas), DJur; Greek lawyer and politician; b. 23 June 1936, Athens; s. of George Simitis and Fani Cristopoulou; m. Daphne Arkadiou; two c.; ed Univ. of Marburg and London School of Econs; lawyer at Supreme Court 1961–; taught in W German univs 1971–75; Prof. of Commercial Law, Univ. of Athens 1977; mem. Nat. Council of Panhellenic Liberation Movt (PAK) during colonels' dictatorship, mem. Pasok 1974–, mem. Cen. Cttee of Pasok, Pres. 1996–2004; mem. Parl. 1985–2004; Minister of Agric. 1981–85, of Nat. Economy 1985–87, of Educ. and Religious Affairs 1989–90, of Industry, Energy, Tech. and Trade 1993–95; Prime Minister of Greece 1996–2004. *Publications include:* Politics is a Creative Greece 1996-2004 2005, Objectives, Strategies and Prospects 2007, Democracy in Crisis? 2007; numerous articles on legal and econ. topics. *Address:* Academy 35, Athens 10672, Greece. *Telephone:* (210) 3624981. *Fax:* (210) 3616527. *E-mail:* contact@costas-simitis.gr. *Website:* www.costas-simitis.gr.

ŠIMKO, Ivan, IngEcon, DIur; Slovak politician; *Founder, Free Forum Party;* b. 1 Jan. 1955, Bratislava; m.; four c.; ed Univ. of Econs, Bratislava, Comenius Univ., Bratislava; mem. staff Inst. for Planning, Bratislava 1978–79; mem. staff Dept of Chief Architect, Bratislava 1979–89; Adviser to Deputy Prime Minister 1990; mem. Parl. 1990–; Vice-Chair. Legis. Council 1992; Minister of Justice 1992; Deputy Prime Minister 1994; mem. Nat. Council for the Slovak

Repub. 1994–; Minister of the Interior 2001–02, of Defence 2002–03; Founder Free Forum Party (Slobodné fórum—SF) 2003–; mem. Nat. Council Cttee for Constitutional Law. *Leisure interests:* sport, literature. *Address:* Slobodné fórum, Bazová 9, 821 08 Bratislava, Czech Republic (office). *Telephone:* (2) 55642494 (office). *Fax:* (2) 55642487 (office). *E-mail:* sf@slobodneforum.sk (office). *Website:* www.slobodneforum.sk (office).

SIMMA, Bruno, DJur; German professor of law and judge; *Judge, International Court of Justice;* b. 29 March 1941, Quierschied, Saar; ed Univ. of Innsbruck; called to the Bar, Innsbruck 1967; Asst, Faculty of Law, Univ. of Innsbruck 1967–72; Expert, Directorate of Legal Affairs, Council of Europe 1972; Prof. of Int. Law and EC Law, Univ. of Munich 1973–, Dir Inst. of Int. Law 1973–, Dean Faculty of Law 1995–97; Dir of Studies, Hague Acad. of Int. Law 1976, 1982, Lecturer 1995; Lecturer in Int. Law, Training Centre for Jr Diplomats, Ministry of Foreign Affairs 1981–89; Visiting Prof., Univ. of Siena, Italy 1984–85; Visiting Prof., Univ. of Michigan Law School, USA 1986, 1995, Prof. of Law 1987–92, mem. Affiliate Overseas Faculty 1997–; mem. UN Cttee on Econ., Social and Cultural Rights 1987–96, UN Int. Law Comm. 1996–2003; Judge, Int. Court of Justice, The Hague 2003–; Co-Founder and Ed. European Journal of Int. Law; Founding Pres. European Soc. of Int. Law; Assoc. Institut de Droit international; Counsel for Germany in various legal cases 1994–2003; consultant, mem. numerous legal advisory bds and professional asscns; Certificate of Merit, American Soc. of Int. Law 1996; Dr hc (Univ. of Macerata, Italy) 2006. *Publications:* articles in professional journals. *Address:* International Court of Justice, Peace Palace, 2517 KJ The Hague, The Netherlands (office). *Telephone:* (70) 3022323 (office). *Fax:* (70) 3022409 (office). *E-mail:* information@icj-cij.org (office). *Website:* www.icj-cij.org (office).

SIMMEN, Jeannot, PD, DrPhil; Swiss art critic and curator; *Director, Club Bel Etage;* b. 14 Sept. 1956, Zürich; s. of Georges Simmen and Clara Brüngger; m. Dr Brigit Blass 1988; two d.; ed Univ. of Zürich, Free Univ. of Berlin; exhbn projects include: Licht: Objekt/Medium, Telematic, Net-Modern-Navigation; Prof., Univs of Wuppertal, Kassel, Essen 1990–; Curator Schwerelos (exhbn), Grosse Orangerie, Charlottenburg Palace, Berlin 1991–92, Die Macht des Alters – Strategien der Meisterschaft (exhbn), Kronprinzen-Palais, Berlin 1998; Dir media future project Ars Digitalis, Acad. of Fine Arts, Berlin 1996; Dir Club Bel Etage 2005–; Design-Preis Schweiz 01 für 'Interaction Design', Design Center Langenthal, Switzerland. *Publications:* Kunst – Ideal oder Augenschein 1980, Der Fahrstuhl 1983, Vertigo 1990, Schwerelos 1991, Vertikal 1994, Kasimir Malewitsch 1998, 1999, Kidai Shôran (CD) 2000, Telematik 2002. *Leisure interests:* art and the media. *Address:* Goethe-Strasse 45, 14163 Berlin, Germany. *Telephone:* (30) 80907145. *Fax:* (30) 80907146. *E-mail:* simmen@snafu.de. *Website:* www.ars-digitalis.de; www.club-bel-etage .de.

SIMMONDS, Rt Hon. Kennedy Alphonse, PC; Saint Christopher and Nevis physician and politician; b. 12 April 1936; s. of the late Arthur Simmonds and of Bronte Clarke; m. Mary Camella Matthew 1976; three s. two d.; ed Basse-Terre Boys' School, St Kitts-Nevis Grammar School and Univ. of the West Indies; Intern, Kingston Public Hosp., Jamaica 1963; Registrar in Internal Medicine, Princess Margaret Hosp., Bahamas 1966–68; Resident in Anaesthesiology, Pittsburgh 1968–69; medical practice in St Kitts and Anguilla 1964–66, in St Kitts 1969–80; Founder mem. People's Action Movt 1965, Pres. 1976, unsuccessfully contested elections 1966, 1971, 1975; elected to Parl. 1979; Premier 1980–83; Minister of Home and External Affairs, Trade, Devt and Industry 1980–84, of Finance, Home and Foreign Affairs 1984–95; Prime Minister 1983–95; Fellow, American Coll. of Anaesthesiologists. *Leisure interests:* cricket, tennis, football. *Address:* P.O. Box 167, Earle Morne Development, Basse-Terre, St Kitts, West Indies.

SIMMONS, David, BA, MEd; Australian politician; b. 7 Nov. 1947, Broken Hill, NSW; m. Kaye Simmons; one s. one d.; ed Univ. of New England, NSW; Head of Social Science Dept, Bathurst High School, NSW; Alderman, Bathurst City Council 1978–83; MP for Calare, NSW 1983–96; mem. House of Reps Cttee on Finance and Public Admin. 1985–89; Minister for Defence, Science and Personnel 1989–90, for Arts, Tourism and Territories 1990–91, for Local Govt and Family Support 1991–93; Chair. House of Reps. Cttee on Banking, Finance and Public Admin. 1994; Exec. Dir Hunter Regional Tourism Org. 1996–97; Gen. Man. Newcastle Regional Chamber of Commerce 1997–98; currently Pres. Heart Foundation (NSW), also Dir Nat. Bd. *Leisure interests:* golf, stamp collecting, arts, travel. *Address:* c/o Heart Foundation, Level 3, 80 William Street, Sydney NSW 2011, Australia.

SIMMONS, Hardwick (Wick), AB, MBA; American business executive; b. 1940; m. Sloan T. Miller; five c.; ed Harvard Univ., Harvard Business School; with US Marine Corps Reserve 1960–66; Financial Adviser, Hayden Stone 1966–69, Vice-Pres. Data Processing and Communications Div. 1969–70, Man. Boston office 1970–73, Exec. Vice-Pres. for Shearson Hayden Stone Retail Sales and Admin. 1973–77, Sr Exec. Vice-Pres. for Marketing and Sales, Shearson/American Express 1977, Pres. Pvt. Client Group, Shearson Lehman Brothers, Inc. –1991; Pres. and CEO Prudential Securities, Inc. 1991–2001; CEO, Chair. Nasdaq Stock Market Inc. 2001–03; Dir New York City Partnership and Chamber of Commerce, Inc.; mem. Bd Nat. Acad. Foundation; mem. Bd of Dirs Raymond James Financial Inc. 2003–, Lead Dir 2006; Co-founder Longwing, mem. Bd of Advisers 2003–06; mem. Bd of Dirs Geneva Acquisition Corpn 2006–; mem. and fmr Chair. Securities Industry Asscn; fmr Dir Chicago Bd Options Exchange; mem. and fmr Pres. Bond Club of New York, Inc.; mem. NY City Public/Pvt. Initiatives (PPI) Bd; mem. Harvard Univ. John King Fairbank Center for E Asian Research; Trustee and Devt Cttee mem. South Street Seaport Museum; Pres. Bd of Trustees Groton School, Mass.; Trustee Woods Hole Oceanographic Inst., Groton School, Rippowan Cisqua School, Mt. Kisco, NY. *Address:* c/o Board of Directors, Geneva Acquisition Corporation, 400 Crown Colony Drive, Suite 104, Quincy, MA 02169, USA. *Telephone:* (617) 933-7100.

SIMMONS, Jean, OBE; British actress; b. 31 Jan. 1929, London; d. of Charles Simmons and Winifred Ada Simmons (née Loveland); m. 1st Stewart Granger 1950 (divorced 1960); one d.; m. 2nd Richard Brooks 1960 (divorced 1977, died 1992); one d.; ed Orange Hill School, Burnt Oak, London; in films from 1943; stage appearance, Philadelphia and on tour in A Little Night Music 1974–75; appeared in TV series The Dain Curse 1978, Down at the Hydro 1982; BFI Fellowship 1994; Commdr des Arts et Lettres 1990; Homage Award (Cannes Film Festival) 1988, Lake Como Italian Film Award 1989. *Films include:* Great Expectations 1946, Black Narcissus 1946, Hamlet 1948, Adam and Evelyne 1949, So Long at the Fair 1950, Young Bess 1953, The Robe 1953, The Actress 1953, Guys and Dolls 1956, The Big Country 1958, Home Before Dark 1958, Elmer Gantry 1960, Spartacus 1960, The Grass is Greener 1961, All the Way Home 1963, Life at the Top 1965, Tough Night in Jericho 1967, Divorce American Style 1967, The Happy Ending 1969, Dominique 1979, The Dawning 1988, How To Make an American Quilt 1996, Hauru no ugoku shiro (Howl's Moving Castle) (voice – English version) 2004, Thru the Moebius Strip (voice) 2005. *Television includes:* The Thornbirds (Emmy Award) 1982, Great Expectations 1989, People Like Us 1990, December Flower, Daisies in December 1995, Ancient Mysteries 1996, Mysteries of the Bible III 1998, Her Own Rules 1998, Winter Solstice 2003. *Address:* 1145 Gayley Avenue, Suite 303, Los Angeles, CA 90024, USA.

SIMMONS, Richard D., AB, LLB; American newspaper publisher; b. 30 Dec. 1934, Cambridge, Mass.; m. Mary DeWitt Bleecker 1961; two s.; ed Harvard and Columbia Univs; admitted to New York Bar; Assoc. Satterlee, Warfield & Stephens 1958–62; Gen. Counsel Giannini Science Corpn 1962–64; Vice-Pres. and Gen. Counsel Southeastern Publishing Service Corpn 1964–69; Counsel Dun & Bradstreet Inc., New York 1969–70, Vice-Pres. and Gen. Counsel 1970–72; Pres. Moody's Investors Service 1973–76, Dun & Bradstreet Inc. 1975–76; Exec. Vice-Pres. Dun & Bradstreet Corpn, New York 1976–78, Dir and Vice-Chair. Bd 1979–81; Pres. and COO The Washington Post Co. 1981–91, Dir 1981–; Pres. Int. Herald Tribune 1989–96. *Address:* c/o The Washington Post Company, 1150 15th Street NW, Washington, DC 20071, USA (office). *E-mail:* twcoreply@washpost.com (office). *Website:* www .washpostco.com (office).

SIMMONS, Robert Malcolm, PhD, FRS; British biophysicist and academic; *Professor Emeritus, Randall Centre for Molecular Mechanisms of Cell Function, King's College London;* b. 23 Jan. 1938, London; s. of Stanley Laurence Simmons and Marjorie Simmons (née Amys); m. Mary Ann (Anna) Ross 1967; one s. one d.; ed King's Coll. London, Royal Inst., Univ. Coll. London; lecturer Univ. Coll., London Univ. 1967–81; MRC Staff Scientist King's Coll., Univ. of London 1981–83, Prof. of Biophysics 1983–2002, Dir Randall Inst. 1995–99, Randall Centre 1999–2001, Prof. Emer. 2002–. *Publication:* Muscular Contraction 1992. *Leisure interests:* music, fishing. *Address:* Edmunds Ground, 1 Woodborough Road, Pewsey, Wilts. SN9 5NH, England (home). *Telephone:* (1672) 562281 (home). *E-mail:* robert.simmons@ tiscali.co.uk (office).

SIMMONS, Ruth J., PhD; American academic and university president; *President, Brown University;* b. 3 July 1945, Grapeland, Tex.; two c.; ed Dillard Univ., New Orleans, Harvard Univ.; Asst Prof. of French Univ. of New Orleans, Asst Dean Coll. of Liberal Arts –1977; Visiting Assoc. Prof. of Pan-African Studies, Acting Dir Int. Programmes, Calif. State Univ., Northridge 1977–79; Asst, then Assoc. Dean of Grad. Studies, Univ. of Southern Calif. 1979–83; Dir Afro-American Studies Princeton Univ., Assoc. Dean 1983, Vice-Provost 1992–95; Provost Spelman Coll., Atlanta 1990–91; Pres. Smith Coll. 1995–2001, Brown Univ., Providence, RI 2001–; 25 hon. doctorates; numerous awards including Danforth Fellowship, Fulbright Fellowship, Eleanor Roosevelt Val-Kill Medal, ROBIE Humanitarian Award. *Address:* Office of the President, Brown University, 1 Prospect Street, Providence, RI 02912, USA (office). *Telephone:* (401) 863-2234 (office). *Fax:* (401) 863-7737 (office). *E-mail:* president@brown.edu (office). *Website:* www.brown.edu (office).

SIMMS, David John, PhD, MRIA; Irish mathematician and academic; *Fellow Emeritus, Trinity College Dublin;* b. 13 Jan. 1933, Sankeshwar, India; s. of John Gerald Simms and Eileen Mary Simms (née Goold-Verschoyle); m. Anngret Erichson 1965; three s.; ed Berkhamstead School, Trinity Coll., Dublin and Peterhouse, Cambridge, England; Asst in Math., Univ. of Glasgow 1958–60, Lecturer in Math. 1960–64; Instructor in Math., Princeton Univ., NJ 1962–63; Lecturer in Math., Univ. of Dublin 1964–73, Assoc. Prof. 1973–, Fellow, Trinity Coll., Dublin 1972–2002, Sr Fellow 2002–03, Fellow Emer. 2003–; Visiting Prof., Univ. of Bonn 1966–67, 1972–73, 1978–80; mem. Royal Irish Acad. 1978–, Vice-Pres. 1983–84, 1987–88, 1995–96; Gold Medal in Math., Univ. of Dublin 1955. *Publications include:* Lie Groups and Quantum Mechanics 1968, Lectures on Geometric Quantization (with N. M. Woodhouse) 1974. *Address:* School of Mathematics, Trinity College, Dublin 2, Ireland (office). *Telephone:* (1) 8961944 (office). *Fax:* (1) 6082282 (office). *E-mail:* simms@maths.tcd.ie (office). *Website:* www.maths.tcd.ie/~simms (office).

SIMMS, Sir Neville Ian, Kt, BSc, MEng, FREng, FRSA, FICE; British business executive and civil engineer; *Chairman, International Power plc;* b. 11 Sept. 1944, Glasgow; s. of the late Arthur Neville Simms and of Anne Davidson Simms (née McCulloch); ed Queen Elizabeth Grammar School, Crediton, Univs. of Newcastle-upon-Tyne and Glasgow; structural engineer Ove Arup and Partners 1966–69; joined Tarmac PLC 1970, Chief Exec. Tarmac Construction Ltd 1988–92, Group Chief Exec. Tarmac PLC 1992–99, (Deputy Chair. 1994–99); Group Chair. Carillion PLC 1999–2004; mem. Bd of Dirs International Power PLC 1998–, Chair. 2000–; Dir Bank of England 1995–2002; Chair. BITC West Midlands 1998–2001; Chair. (non-exec.)

Courtaulds 1994–98, Pvt. Finance Panel Ltd 1994–99, Nat. Power 1998–2000, Sustainable Procurement Task Force 2006; mem. New Deal Task Force 1999–2001; Gov. Stafford Grammar School 1997–, Ashridge Man. Coll. 2000–; Fellow, Chartered Inst. of Bldg; Hon. DTech (Wolverhampton) 1997; Dr hc (Edin.) 2000; Hon. DEng (Glasgow) 2001; Pres.'s Medal, Chartered Inst. of Bldg 1995; Prince of Wales Ambassador Award 2001. *Publications:* Building Towards 2001; numerous speeches and articles on industry-related topics. *Address:* International Power plc, Senator House, 85 Queen Victoria Street, London, EC4V 4DP, England (office). *Telephone:* (20) 7320-8600 (office). *Fax:* (20) 7320-8700 (office). *Website:* www.ipplc.com (office).

SIMON, Carly; American singer, songwriter and musician (piano, guitar); b. 25 June 1945, New York, NY; d. of Richard Simon; m. 1st James Taylor 1972 (divorced 1983); one d. one s.; m. 2nd James Hart 1987; ed Sarah Lawrence Coll.; solo artist and composer 1971–; Grammy Award for Best New Artist 1971, Acad. Award (for Let The River Run) 1989, Golden Globe Award. *Film appearance:* No Nukes 1980. *Compositions:* Romulus Hunt (opera) 1993; film scores for Heartburn 1986, Working Girl 1988, Postcards From the Edge 1990, This Is My Life 1992; theme tunes for Torchlight 1985, Phenom (TV) 1993; contrib. songs to other films. *Recordings include:* albums: Carly Simon 1971, Anticipation 1972, No Secrets 1973, Hotcakes 1974, Playing Possum 1975, Another Passenger 1976, Boys In The Trees 1978, Spy 1979, Come Upstairs 1980, Torch 1981, Hello Big Man 1983, Spoiled Girl 1985, Coming Around Again 1987, My Romance 1990, Have You Seen Me Lately? 1991, This Is My Life 1992, Letters Never Sent 1994, Clouds In My Coffee 1965–95 1996, Film Noir 1997, The Bedroom Tapes 2000, This Kind of Love 2008. *Publications:* juvenile: Amy the Dancing Bear 1989, The Boy of the Bells 1990, The Fisherman's Song 1990, The Nighttime Chauffeur 1993, Midnight Farm 1997, Basket Full of Rhymes 2000. *Address:* c/o Lee Phillips, Manatt Phelps and Phillips, 11355 W Olympic Blvd, Los Angeles, CA 90064, USA (office). *Website:* www.carlysimon.com.

SIMON, Josette, OBE; British actress; d. of Charles Simon and Eileen Petty; m. Mark Padmore 1996; ed Cen. School of Speech Training and Dramatic Art; appeared in TV series Blake's 7; joined RSC; Hon. MA (Leicester) 1995; appeared as Isabella in Measure for Measure 1988, as Maggie in Arthur Miller's After the Fall, Nat. Theatre, in The White Devil, Nat. Theatre 1991, as Ellida Wangel in Ibsen's The Lady from the Sea, Lyric Theatre, Hammersmith 1994, The Taming of the Shrew, Leicester 1995, The Maids, Donmar Warehouse 1997, Titania in A Midsummer Night's Dream 1999, several concert performances. *Films include:* Cry Freedom 1987, Milk and Honey (Best Actress Atlantic Film Festival 1988, Paris Film Festival 1990) 1988. *Television includes:* Henry IV, Parts 1 and 2, Bodyguards, Kavanagh QC, Bridge of Time 1997, Dalziel and Pascoe: Bones and Silence 1998, Polterguests (series) 1999, Poirot: The Mystery of the Blue Train 2005. *Leisure interests:* cinema, gardening, travel, learning languages. *Address:* c/o Conway van Gelder Ltd, 18–21 Jermyn Street, London, SW1Y 6HP, England. *Telephone:* (20) 7287-0077. *Fax:* (20) 7287-1940.

SIMON, Lou Anna Kimsey, PhD; American university president; *President, Michigan State University;* ed Indiana State Univ., Mich. State Univ.; joined faculty of Mich. State Univ. (MSU) 1974, Asst Dir Office of Institutional Research, then Asst Provost for Gen. Academic Admin, Assoc. Provost, Provost (also for MSU Coll. of Law), Vice-Pres. for Academic Affairs 1993, Interim Pres. MSU May–Sept. 2003, Pres. 2005–, has taught seminars at Coll. of Educ.; mem. Exec. Cttee, Cttee on Institutional Cooperation (CIC) 1999– (Chair. 2000–05). *Publications include:* Serving Children and Families through Community-University Partnerships, Universities and Communities: Remaking Professional and Interprofessional Education for the Next Century, Learning to Serve: Promoting Civil Society through Service Learning (co-ed.) 2002. *Address:* Office of the President, Michigan State University, 450 Administration Building, East Lansing, MI 48824-1046, USA (office). *Telephone:* (517) 355-6560 (office). *Fax:* (517) 355-4670 (office). *E-mail:* presmail@msu.edu (office). *Website:* president.msu.edu (office).

SIMON, Neil; American playwright; b. 4 July 1927, New York; s. of Irving Simon and Mamie Simon; m. 1st. Joan Baim 1953 (deceased); two d.; m. 2nd Marsha Mason 1973 (divorced); m. 3rd Diane Lander 1987; one d.; ed New York Univ.; wrote for various TV programmes including The Tallulah Bankhead Show 1951, The Phil Silvers Show 1958–59, NBC Special, The Trouble with People 1972; Hon. DHumLitt (Hofstra Univ.) 1981, (Williams Coll.) 1984; Evening Standard Award 1967, Writers' Guild Screen Award for The Odd Couple 1969, Writers' Guild Laurel Award 1979, American Comedy Award for Lifetime Achievement 1989, Pulitzer Prize (for Lost in Yonkers) 1991, Kennedy Center Mark Twain Prize for American Humor 2006. *Plays:* Come Blow Your Horn 1961, Little Me (musical) 1962, Barefoot in the Park 1963, The Odd Couple 1965, Sweet Charity (musical) 1966, The Star-Spangled Girl 1966, Plaza Suite 1968, Promises, Promises (musical) 1968, Last of the Red Hot Lovers 1969, The Gingerbread Lady 1970, The Prisoner of Second Avenue 1971, The Sunshine Boys 1972, The Good Doctor 1973, God's Favorite 1974, California Suite 1976, Chapter Two 1977, They're Playing Our Song 1979, I Ought to be in Pictures 1980, Fools 1981, Little Me (revised version) 1982, Brighton Beach Memoirs 1983, Biloxi Blues 1985, The Odd Couple Female Version 1985, Broadway Bound 1986, Rumors 1988, Lost in Yonkers 1991, Jake's Women 1992, The Goodbye Girl (musical) 1993, Laughter on the 23rd Floor 1993, London Suite 1995. *Screenplays:* After the Fox 1966, Barefoot in the Park 1967, The Odd Couple 1968, The Out-of-Towners 1970, Plaza Suite 1971, The Last of the Red Hot Lovers 1972, The Heartbreak Kid 1973, The Prisoner of Second Avenue 1975, The Sunshine Boys 1975, Murder By Death 1976, The Goodbye Girl 1977, The Cheap Detective 1978, California Suite 1978, Chapter Two 1979, Seems Like Old Times 1980, Only When I Laugh 1981, I Ought to Be in Pictures 1982, Max Dugan Returns 1983, Lonely Guy (adaptation) 1984, The Slugger's Wife 1984, Brighton Beach Memoirs 1986, Biloxi Blues 1988, The Marrying Man 1991, Broadway Bound (TV film) 1992, Lost in Yonkers 1993, Jake's Women (TV film) 1996, London Suite (TV film) 1996; other motion pictures adapted from stage plays: Come Blow Your Horn 1963, Sweet Charity 1969, The Star-Spangled Girl 1971; mem. Dramatists Guild, Writers' Guild of America; many awards including Emmy Award 1957, 1959; Antoinette Perry (Tony) Awards for The Odd Couple 1965, Biloxi Blues 1985 (Best Play), Lost in Yonkers 1991 (Best Play). *Publications:* Rewrites: A Memoir 1996; individual plays. *Address:* c/o Albert DaSilva, 502 Park Avenue, New York, NY 10022, USA.

SIMON, Paul F., BA; American singer and composer; b. 13 Oct. 1941, Newark, NJ; s. of Louis Simon and Belle Simon; m. 1st Peggy Harper (divorced); one s.; m. 2nd Carrie Fisher 1983 (divorced); m. 3rd Edie Brickell 1992; two s. one d.; ed Queens Coll., Brooklyn Law School; mem. singing duo Simon & Garfunkel (with Art Garfunkel) 1964–71; solo artist 1972–; Hon. DMus (Berklee Coll.) 1986, (Yale) 1996, (Queens Coll.) 1997; Emmy Award (for Paul Simon Special, NBC) 1977, Kennedy Center Honor 2002, Library of Congress Gershwin Prize 2007. *Compositions:* The Capeman (musical) (Antoinette Perry Award for Best Original Score Written for the Theatre 1998) 1997. *Film appearances:* Annie Hall 1977, The Rutles (TV) 1978, All You Need Is Cash 1978, One-Trick Pony 1980. *Recordings include:* albums: as Simon & Garfunkel: Wednesday Morning 3AM 1964, Sounds Of Silence 1966, Parsley, Sage, Rosemary And Thyme 1966, The Graduate (film soundtrack) (two Grammy Awards) 1968, Bookends 1968, Bridge Over Troubled Water (six Grammy Awards 1971) 1970, Concert In Central Park (live) 1982, Early Simon & Garfunkel 1993, Old Friends 1997; solo: The Paul Simon Songbook 1965, Paul Simon 1972, There Goes Rhymin' Simon 1973, Live Rhymin': Paul Simon In Concert 1974, Still Crazy After All These Years (two Grammy Awards) 1975, One-Trick Pony 1980, Hearts And Bones 1983, Graceland (Grammy Award 1987) 1986, Negotiations And Love Songs 1988, Rhythm Of The Saints 1990, Paul Simon's Concert In The Park 1991, Songs From The Capeman 1997, You're The One 2000, Surprise 2006. *Publications:* The Songs of Paul Simon 1972, New Songs 1975, One-Trick Pony (screenplay) 1980, At The Zoo (juvenile) 1991. *Address:* c/o C. Vaughn Hazell, Paul Simon Music, Suite 500, 1619 Broadway, New York, NY 10019, USA (office). *Website:* www.paulsimon.com.

SIMON MUNARO, Yehude; Peruvian politician and fmr teacher; *Prime Minister;* b. 18 July 1947, Lima; ed Univ. Nacional Pedro Ruiz Gallo; teacher, Colegio San Vicente de Paul 1966–72; Pres. Fed. of Teachers, Univ. Nacional Pedro Ruiz Gallo 1981–85; Sec. –Gen. United Left, Lambayeque 1984; Pres. Lambayeque Defence Front 1984–90; Deputy for Lambayeque 1985–90; Pres. Movimiento Humanista Peruano 2000; Regional Pres. for Lambayeque 2003–06; Prime Minister of Peru 2008–. *Address:* Office of the President of the Council of Ministers, Avda 28 de Julio 878, Miraflores, Lima, Peru (office). *Telephone:* (1) 6109800. *Fax:* (1) 4449168 (office). *E-mail:* webmaster@pcm.gob.pe (office). *Website:* www.pcm.gob.pe (office).

SIMON OF HIGHBURY, Baron (Life Peer), cr. 1997, of Canonbury in the London Borough of Islington; **David Alec Gwyn Simon,** Kt, CBE, MA, MBA; British business executive; b. 24 July 1939, London; s. of the late Roger Simon and of Barbara Hudd; m. 1st Hanne Mohn 1964; two s.; m. 2nd Sarah Smith 1992; ed Gonville and Caius Coll., Cambridge; joined BP 1961, Marketing Dir, Holland 1972–75, Marketing Co-ordinator, European Region 1975–80, Marketing Dir, Oil UK 1980–82, Man. Dir, Oil Int. Ltd 1982–85, Man. Dir BP Co. PLC 1986–95, Deputy Chair. 1990–95, Group Chief Exec. 1992–95, Chair. 1995–97; Dir Bank of England 1995–97; Minister of State Responsible for Trade and Competitiveness in Europe (attached to Dept of Trade and Industry and Treasury) 1997–99; Dir (non-exec.) and Deputy Chair. Unilever 2000–04, 2005–09; Dir Centre for European Policy Studies 2002–; Sr Adviser Morgan Stanley Europe 2000–, SUEZ 2001–; Lay mem. and Deputy Chair., Univ. Council, Univ. of Cambridge; mem. Int. Advisory Bd Dana Gas Corpn 2006–, Advisory Bd Montrose Assocs 2008–; Trustee Hertie Foundation; Trustee Cicely Saunders Int. 2001–; Grand Commdr, Order of Leopold II (Belgium); Hon. DEcon (Hull) 1993, (Birmingham) 2003; Dr hc (Univ. of N London) 1995; Hon. LLD (Bath) 1998. *Leisure interests:* golf, books, music. *Address:* House of Lords, Westminster, London, SW1A 0PW, England (office).

SIMONDS-GOODING, Anthony James Joseph; British business executive; *Chairman, OMG plc;* b. 10 Sept. 1937, Dublin; s. of Maj. and Mrs. Hamilton Simonds-Gooding; m. 1st Fiona Menzies 1961 (divorced 1982); three s. two d. (one s. deceased); m. 2nd Marjorie A. Pennock 1982, one step-s.; ed Ampleforth Coll. and Britannia Royal Naval Coll., Dartmouth; served RN 1953–59; with Unilever 1960–73; Marketing Dir Whitbread & Co., PLC 1973, subsequently Man. Dir (UK), latterly Group Man. Dir until 1985; Chair. and Chief Exec. Saatchi PLC 1985–87; Chief Exec. British Satellite Broadcasting 1987–90; Chair. S. P. Lintas 1994–95, Ammirati Puris Lintas 1994–96; Chair. Designers and Art Dirs Asscn 1992–; Dir ICA Devt Cttee 1992–94, Cancer Relief Macmillan Fund 1992–, Robinsons PLC 1993–, D&AD 1993–, Brixton Prison 1994–97, Community Hosps Group PLC 1995–2000, Interbrand Newell & Sorrell 1996–98, Clark & Taylor 1996–99, Blick PLC 1997–, Kunick PLC 1997–, CLK MPL 1999–, Rainbow Children's Trust 2001–, Sea Cadets Asscn 2001, OMG plc 2002– (non-exec. Chair. Dec. 2002–). *Leisure interests:* oil painting, walking, opera, travel, tennis. *Address:* c/o Board of Directors, OMG plc, 14 Minns Business Park, West Way, Oxford, OX2 0JB; Burchetts Brook, Holmbury St Mary, Surrey, RH5 6NA, England. *Telephone:* (1306) 621266 (home). *Fax:* (1865) 240527 (office). *E-mail:* anthony@simonds-gooding.net. *Website:* www.simonds-gooding.net.

SIMONETI, Marko, BA, MA, PhD; Slovenian economist, stock exchange executive and academic; *President and CEO, Ljubljanska Borza d.d. (Ljubljana Stock Exchange);* b. 8 July 1958; m.; ed Univ. of Ljubljana, Cornell

Univ., USA; Sr Research Fellow, Inst. for Econ. Research 1982–90; Under-Sec. of State in Fed. Govt 1989; Man. Dir Agency for Privatization, Ljubljana 1990–93; Co-founder CEEPN (Cen. and Eastern European Privatization Network) 1993, Chair. Steering Cttee 1991–92, Exec. Dir 1993–2004; served as Vice-Chair. Board of the Securities and Exchange Comm., mem. Supervisory Bd of Ljubljana Stock Exchange and Chair. Govt Comm. for privatization of largest bank in Slovenia; served as pvt. sector devt adviser to various int. orgs (IBRD, EBRD, OECD, UNDP, UN-ECE); Prof. of Finance, Law School, Univ. of Ljubljana 1997–; Pref. and CEO Ljubljanska Borza d.d. (Ljubljana Stock Exchange) 2005–; mem. Econ. Asscn of Slovenia, European Asscn for Comparative Econ. Studies. *Publications include:* Investment Funds as Intermediaries of Privatization (CEEPN Workshop Series, Vol. 5) (co-ed.) 1994, Bank Rehabilitation and Enterprise Restructuring (CEEPN Workshop series, Vol. 6) (co-ed.) 1995, The Governance of Privatization Funds: Experiences of the Czech Republic, Poland and Slovenia (co-ed.) 1999; numerous book chapters, reports and articles in professional journals. *Address:* Ljubljanska Borza d.d., Slovenska 56, 1000 Ljubljana, Slovenia (office). *Telephone:* (1) 4710211 (office). *Fax:* (1) 4710213 (office). *E-mail:* info@ljse.si (office). *Website:* www.ljse.si (office).

SIMONETTA; Italian fashion designer; b. (Duchess Simonetta Colonna di Cesaró), 10 April 1922, Rome; d. of Duke Giovanni Colonna di Cesarò and Countess Barbara Antonelli; m. 1st Count Galeazzo Visconti di Modrone 1944; one d.; m. 2nd Alberto Fabiani (fashion designer) 1952; one s.; presented first collection in Rome in 1946; opened fashion Atelier, Rome 1946; transferred fashion business to Paris 1962; Hon. Citizen of Austin, New Orleans and Las Vegas; Philadelphia Fashion Group Award 1953, Davison Paxon Award, Atlanta 1959, Fashion Oscar from Filene's of Boston 1960, after five consecutive years in list of world's best dressed women is in "Hall of Fame". *Publication:* A Snob in the Kitchen 1967. *Address:* 8 Via Cadore, 41012 Caroi, Italy.

SIMONIA, Nodari Aleksandrovich, CandEconSc, DHist; Russian political economist; *Director, Institute of World Economy and International Relations (IMEMO), Russian Academy of Sciences;* b. 30 Jan. 1932, Tbilisi, Georgia; m.; one d.; ed Moscow Inst. of Int. Relations; Corresp. mem. Russian Acad. of Sciences 1990, mem. 1997–; Acad. Sec., Dept of Int. Relations, Jr Researcher, Sr Researcher, Prof. and Head of Sector, Head of Div., Deputy Dir, Inst. of Oriental Studies 1955–86; Deputy Dir Inst. of World Econ. and Int. Relations, Russian Acad. of Sciences 1986–2000, Dir 2000–; Prof., Centre of Slavic Studies, Hokkaido Univ.; main research in comparative studies: Russia and developing countries; mem. Presidium, Russian Acad. of Sciences, Scientific Council Ministry of Foreign Affairs, European Acad. of Sciences, Arts and Literature; Special Rep. of Pres. of Russian Fed. for Relations with African States' Leaders. *Publications:* over 250 scientific works, including 16 books and articles and papers on the devt of capitalism in modern Russia. *Address:* IMEMO, Profsoyuznaya str. 23, 117997 Moscow, GSP-7, Russia (office). *Telephone:* (495) 120-84-50 (office); (495) 434-15-68 (home). *Fax:* (495) 310-70-27 (office). *E-mail:* imemoan@imemo.ru (office). *Website:* www.imemo.ru/eng (office).

SIMONIS, HE Cardinal Adrianus Johannes; Dutch ecclesiastic; *Archbishop of Utrecht and President, Netherlands Bishops' Conference;* b. 26 Nov. 1931, Lisse; ed Hageveld (high school) and Warmond seminaries, Haarlem, Biblicum (Papal Inst. for the Bible), Rome and Jerusalem; ordained priest, Rotterdam 1957; consecrated Bishop of Rotterdam 1971; apptd Coadjutor Archbishop of Utrecht 1983, Archbishop of Utrecht 1983–; cr. Cardinal (Cardinal-Priest of S. Clemente) 1985; currently Pres. Netherlands Bishops' Conf., mem. Perm. Council; Chair. Nat. Episcopal Doctrinary Comm., Episcopal Comm. on Educ.; mem. Congregation for the Catholic Educ., Congregation for the Insts of the Consecrated Life and the Societies of Apostolic Life, Pontifical Council for the Promotion of the Unity Among Christians, Conf. of European Bishops. *Address:* Nederlandse Bisschoppenconferentie, Biltstraat 121, PO Box 13049, 3507 LA Utrecht (office); Aartsbisdom, BP 14019, Maliebaan 40, 3508 SB Utrecht, Netherlands. *Telephone:* 2334244 (office); (30) 2338030. *Fax:* 2332103 (office); (30) 2311962. *E-mail:* secrbk@rkk.nl (office). *Website:* www.rkkerk.nl (office); www.aartsbisdom.nl.

SIMONIS, Heide, MA; German politician; b. 4 July 1943, Bonn; d. of Dr Horst Steinhardt and Sophia Brück; m. Prof. Udo E. Simonis 1967; tutor in German, Univ. of Zambia 1967–69, Goethe Inst. and Nat. TV and Radio Service, Tokyo 1970–72; mem. Bundestag 1976–88; Minister of Finance, Schleswig-Holstein 1988–93, Minister-Pres. 1993–2005; Head of UNICEF Deutschland 2005–08; mem. Social Democratic Party (SPD). *Leisure interests:* music, literature. *Address:* Büro Heide Simonis, Kleiner Kuhberg 28-30, 24103 Kiel; Düsternbrooker Weg 70, 24105 Kiel, Germany. *Telephone:* (431) 9882000. *Fax:* (431) 9881960. *E-mail:* heide.simonis@stk.landsh.de. *Website:* www.heide-simonis.de.

SIMONITI, Vasko, PhD; Slovenian historian, academic and politician; *Minister of Culture;* b. 23 March 1951, Ljubljana; ed Univ. of Ljubljana; Lecturer in History, Ljubljana Univ. 1989–2000, now Prof.; mem. Slovenian Democratic Party 2000–; Minister of Culture 2004–. *Publications:* Vojaška organizacija 1991, Slovenska zgodovina do razsvetljenstva 1995, Turki so v deželi že, Turški vpadi na slovensko ozemlje 1996, Fanfare nasilja 2003, Slovenska povjest do prosvetiteljstva 2004 (co-author). *Address:* Ministry of Culture, 1000 Ljubljana, Maistrova 10, Slovenia (office). *Telephone:* (1) 3695900 (office). *Fax:* (1) 3695901 (office). *E-mail:* gp.mk@gov.si (office). *Website:* www.mk.gov.si (office).

SIMONOV, Aleksey Kirillovich; Russian film director and human rights activist; *President, Glasnost Defence Foundation;* b. 8 Aug. 1939, Moscow; s. of Konstantin Simonov (writer and poet); m.; two s.; ed Inst. of Oriental Languages at Moscow State Univ.; worked in lab. at Inst. of Permafrost Studies 1956–58; translator, USSR State Cttee for Int. Econ. Relations in Indonesia 1963–64; Ed., Khudozhestennaya Literatura 1964–67; film Dir EKRAN TV Studio 1970–91; lecturer All-Russian Inst. of Cinematography 1991–93; Sec. USSR Union of Cinematographists 1991; f. Konf 1991; Co.-Chair. Licence Cttee of Russian Fed. 1992–93; mem. Movt of Democratic Reforms 1991–93; mem. Public Chamber of Russian Presidency; Co-founder Movt for Mil. Reform 1995; Pres. Glasnost Defence Foundation 1991–; mem. Editorial Bd, Sovyetsky Ekran (magazine) 1988–92, Rossia (weekly) 1992–96; mem. Moscow Helsinki Group; Founder Dossier on Censorship (quarterly) 1997–, Law and Practice (monthly) 1995–; Moscow Int. Press Club 1997. *Films:* directed over 20 feature films and documentaries including Team 1985. *Publications:* Private Collection 1999 (prose); numerous articles in newspapers and magazines Yunost, Ogonyok, Moskva; translator of English plays, Indonesian and African poetry. *Leisure interest:* collecting turtles. *Address:* 119021 Moscow, Box 536; 119121 Moscow, Zubovski blvd. 4, apt. 432 (office); Moscow, Leningradski prosp. 60-A, apt. 2, Russia (home). *Telephone:* (495) 637-44-20 (office); (495) 152-18-39 (home). *Fax:* (495) 637-49-47 (office). *E-mail:* fond@gdf.ru (office). *Website:* www.gdf.ru (office).

SIMONOV, Mikhail Petrovich; Russian design engineer and academic; b. 1929, Rostov-on-Don; m.; one s. one d.; ed Kazan Inst. of Aviation; teacher, Prof., Head of Dept Kazan Inst. of Aviation –1959; Founder and Head of Construction Bureau of Sports Aviation 1959–69; Deputy Chief Constructor, Chief Constructor, First Deputy Constructor Gen. P. Sukhoy Special Construction Bureau 1969–76; Deputy Minister of Aviation Industry 1979–83; Constructor Gen., Dir-Gen. P. Sukhoy Special Construction Bureau 1983–99; mem. Russian Govt's Council on Industrial Policy and Business 1994–; mem. Int. and Russian Acad. of Eng; took part in devt of supersonic bombers, fighters-interceptors, low-flying attack aircraft and tactical bombers; Hero of Russia 1999, Lenin's Prize. *Address:* c/o P. Sukhoy Special Construction Bureau, 125284 Moscow, Polikarpova str. 23A, Russia (office).

ŠIMONOVIĆ, Ivan, DJur; Croatian diplomatist, civil servant, academic and politician; *Minister of Justice;* b. 2 May 1959, Zagreb; m.; two c.; ed Univ. of Zagreb; staff mem. Social Research Inst., Zagreb; mem. Faculty of Law, Univ. of Zagreb 1986–93, Asst Prof., then Assoc. Prof. in Dept for Theory of Law and State; Guest Lecturer at univs in Graz, Austria, Kraków, Poland and Yale Univ., Pittsburg, Montana and N Dakota, USA; Fulbright Scholar, Yale Univ. Law School 1993–94; with Ministry of Foreign Affairs, serving as Asst Minister of Foreign Affairs in charge of Consular and Int. Legal Affairs 1992–93, Multilateral Affairs 1994–95, First Asst Minister and Deputy Minister of Foreign Affairs 1995–96, mem. Croatian Del. at Dayton Peace Talks 1995, Deputy Minister of Foreign Affairs 2003–04; Minister of Justice 2008–; mem. numerous Govt comms including Jt Comm. on Search for Missing Persons and Mortal Remains under auspices of ICRC, Comm. for Detained and Missing Persons, State Comm. for UN Protection Force (UNPROFOR); Perm. Rep. to UN, New York 1997–2003; Co-Chair. Hungarian-Croatian Jt Cttee 2003–; apptd Agent of Govt of Croatia to Int. Court of Justice in its case against Fed. Repub. of Yugoslavia for alleged genocide 2000; Sr Vice-Pres. ECOSOC 2001–02, Pres. 2002–03; Vice-Pres. Bureau of Preparatory Cttee of Int. Conf. on Financing for Devt 2002; Officier, Légion d'honneur 2004. *Publications include:* author and ed. of more than 50 publs including books, book chapters and articles in scholarly journals, in Croatian and English. *Address:* Ministry of Justice, 10000 Zagreb, ul. Dežmanova 10, Croatia (office). *Telephone:* (1) 3710666 (office). *Fax:* (1) 3710602 (office). *E-mail:* nmikulin@pravosudje.hr (office). *Website:* www.pravosudje.hr (office).

SIMONS, Elwyn LaVerne, MA, PhD, DPhil, DSc; American professor of anthropology and anatomy; *James B. Duke Professor of Biological Anthropology, Director of Division of Fossil Primates and Senior Primate Biologist, Duke University Primate Center, Duke University;* b. 14 July 1930, Lawrence, Kan.; s. of Verne Franklin Simons and Verna Irene Simons (née Cuddeback); m. 1st Mary Hoyt Fitch 1964; one s.; m. 2nd Friderun Annursel Ankel 1972; one s. one d.; ed Rice and Princeton Univs, Univ. of Oxford, UK; Lecturer in Geology, Princeton Univ. 1958–59; Asst Prof. of Zoology, Univ. of Pennsylvania 1959–61; Visiting Assoc. Prof. of Geology and Curator of Vertebrate Paleontology, Yale Univ. 1960–61, Assoc. Prof. and Head Curator 1961–65; Prof. of Geology and Curator in Charge, Div. of Vertebrate Paleontology, Peabody Museum 1965–77; Prof. of Anthropology and Anatomy, Duke Univ., 1977–82, James B. Duke Prof. of Biological Anthropology 1982–, Prof. of Zoology and Dir Duke Primate Center 1977–91, Scientific Dir 1991–2001, Head of Div. of Fossil Primates and Sr Primate Biologist 2001–, Dir Div. of Fossil Primates, Duke Lemur Center 2004–; mem. Exec. Cttee, Center for Tropical Conservation 1991–; mem. Steering Cttee, Madagascar Fauna Group 1990–; mem. NAS, American Philosophical Soc.; Hon. Citizen of Fayum Prov., Egypt; Chevalier, Ordre Nat., Madagascar; Hon. MA (Yale) 1967; Hon. DSc (Oxford) 1996; public school scholarship, Houston Art Museum 1938–46, numerous awards including Annandale Medal, Asiatic Soc. of Calcutta, Charles R. Darwin Award, Asscn of Physical Anthropology 2000. *Achievements include:* has directed over 80 expeditions to Wyoming, Iran, India and Madagascar and 38 to the Egyptian Fayum in search of fossil primates and associated fauna; discovered Gigantopithecus in India, discovered and named Aegyptopithecus, Catapithecus, Arsinoea and Proteopithecus in Egypt. *Publications:* more than 300 scientific articles, abstracts and books including A SImons Family History in England and America 1975, Caudebec in England and France 2005. *Leisure interests:* drawing and painting, folk singing, genealogy. *Address:* Division of Fossil Primates, Duke University Lemur Center, 1013 Broad Street, Durham, NC 27705-4143 USA (office). *Telephone:* (919) 416-8420 ext. 21, 27 (office). *Fax:* (919) 416-8584 (office). *E-mail:*

esimons@duke.edu (office). *Website:* www.fossils.duke.edu (office); www.baa.duke.edu/FacPages/simons (office).

SIMONS, John P., PhD, FRS; British chemist and academic; *Professor Emeritus of Chemistry, University of Oxford;* fmr Prof. of Chem., Univ. of Oxford, now Prof. Emer. *Publications:* numerous scientific papers in professional journals on structures of biologically important molecules in the gas phase. *Address:* Physical and Theoretical Chemistry Laboratory, University of Oxford, South Parks Road, Oxford, OX1 3QZ, England (office). *Telephone:* (1865) 275973 (office). *Fax:* (1865) 275410 (office). *E-mail:* john.simons@chem.ox.ac.uk (office). *Website:* www.chem.ox.ac.uk/researchguide/jpsimons.html (office).

SIMONYI, András, PhD; Hungarian economist, consultant and diplomatist; b. 16 May 1952, Budapest; s. of Denes Simonyi and Maria Balazs; m. Nada Pejak; one s. one d.; ed Karl Marx Univ. of Econs (now Budapest Univ.); worked in 1980s with different orgs in field of youth exchange, particularly promoting East–West contacts, including programmes with American Council of Young Political Leaders; mem. staff Foreign Relations Dept, Socialist Workers Party 1984–89; Head of Nordic Dept, Ministry of Foreign Affairs 1989–91; Deputy Chief of Mission Embassy of Hungary, The Hague 1991–92, Hungarian Mission to EC and NATO, Brussels 1992–95; Head, Hungarian NATO Liaison Office, Brussels 1995–99; Perm. Rep. to NATO Council (first Hungarian Perm. Rep.) 1999–2001, rep. on North Atlantic Council during Kosovo campaign; Amb. to USA 2002–07; ran own consulting co. Danison Ltd 2001–02; Imre Nagy Award, Hungary–Ohio Partnership for Educ. *Publications include:* numerous articles on the accession process to NATO, trans-Atlantic relations and European security and the war on terror. *Leisure interest:* blues music (plays electric guitar). *Address:* c/o Ministry of Foreign Affairs, 1027 Budapest, Bem rkp. 47, Hungary.

SIMOR, András; Hungarian commercial banker, financial consultant and central banker; *Governor, Magyar Nemzeti Bank (MNB);* b. 1954; ed Budapest Univ. of Econs; Exec. Foreign Exchange Man. Dept, Magyar Nemzeti Bank (MNB) 1976–79, with Hungarian Int. Bank Ltd, London (subsidiary) 1979–85, Gov. MNB 2007–; CEO Creditanstalt Értékpapír Rt, Budapest 1989–97; Exec. Chair. CA IB Investmentbank AG, Vienna 1997–98; Chair. Budapest Stock Exchange 1998–2002; Chair. Deloitte Hungary 1999–2007, Chair. and Office Man. Partner Deloitte & Touche Rt, Budapest 2000–07, also mem. Bd of Dirs Deloitte & Touche Cen. Europe 2002–06. *Address:* Magyar Nemzeti Bank, Szabadság tér 8–9, 1850 Budapest, Hungary (office). *Telephone:* (1) 428-2600 (office). *Fax:* (1) 428-2500 (office). *E-mail:* info@mnb.hu (office). *Website:* www.mnb.hu (office).

SIMPSON, Alan Kooi, BS, JD; American lawyer and fmr politician; *Attorney and Shareholder, Burg Simpson Eldredge Hersh & Jardine, P.C;* b. 2 Sept. 1931, Cody, Wyo.; s. of Milward Lee Simpson and Lorna (née Kooi) Simpson; m. Ann Schroll 1954; two s. one d.; ed Univ. of Wyoming; called to Wyo. Bar 1958, US Supreme Court 1964; Asst Attorney Gen. Wyo. State 1959; Attorney for Cody 1959–69; mem. Wyo. House of Reps 1964–77; Senator from Wyoming 1978–97, Asst Majority Leader 1985–87, Asst Minority Leader 1987–97; Pnr Simpson, Kepler, Simpson & Cozzens, Cody; Attorney and Shareholder Burg, Simpson, Eldredge, Hersh & Jardine; consultant Tongour, Simpson, Holsclaw Group, Washington, DC; Visiting Lecturer, Lambard Chair., Shorenstein Center, Harvard Univ. 1997–2000; Visiting Lecturer, Univ. of Wyo. 2000–; mem. Iraq Study Group, US Inst. of Peace 2006; Trustee Buffalo Bill Historical Center (now Chair.), Cody, Gottsche Foundation Rehabilitation Center; mem. Wyo. Bar Asscn, ABA, Asscn of Trial Lawyers of America; Hon. LLD (Calif. Western School of Law) 1983, (Colo Coll.) 1986, (Notre Dame Univ.) 1987; Hon. JD (Rocky Mountain Coll.) 1996, (Wyo.) 1999; Centennial Alum Award (Wyo. Univ.) 1987, Thomas Jefferson Award in Law, Univ. of Va 1998. *Publication:* Right in the Old Gazoo: A Lifetime of Scrapping with the Press 1997. *Address:* Burg, Simpson, Eldredge, Hersh & Jardine, 1135 14th Street, P.O. Box 490, Cody, WY 82414, USA (office). *Telephone:* (307) 527-7891 (office). *E-mail:* asimpson@burgsimpson.com (office). *Website:* www.burgsimpson.com (office).

SIMPSON, (Alfred William) Brian, QC, JP, MA, DCL, FBA; British legal scholar; *Charles F. and Edith J. Clyne Professor of Law, University of Michigan;* b. 17 Aug. 1931, Kendal; s. of Rev. B. W. Simpson and M. E. Simpson; m. 1st Kathleen Seston 1954 (divorced 1968); one s. one d.; m. 2nd Caroline E. A. Brown 1969; one s. two d.; ed Oakham School, Rutland and Queen's Coll., Oxford; Jr Research Fellow, St Edmund Hall, Oxford 1954–55; Fellow, Lincoln Coll., Oxford 1955–73, Jr Proctor 1967–68; Dean Faculty of Law, Univ. of Ghana 1968–69; Prof. of Law, Univ. of Kent 1973–85, Prof. Emer. 1985–; Prof. of Law, Univ. of Chicago 1983–86; Charles F. and Edith J. Clyne Prof. of Law, Univ. of Michigan 1987–; Goodhart Visiting Prof., Univ. of Cambridge, UK 1993–94; Fellow, American Acad. of Arts and Sciences; Barrister-at-law, Gray's Inn. *Publications:* A History of the Common Law of Contract 1975, Cannibalism and the Common Law 1984, A Biographical Dictionary of the Common Law (Ed.) 1984, A History of the Land Law 1986, Legal Theory and Legal History 1987, Invitation to Law 1988, In the Highest Degree Odious: Detention Without Trial in Wartime Britain 1992, Leading Cases in the Common Law 1995, Human Rights and the End of Empire. Britain and the Genesis of the European Convention 2001. *Leisure interest:* sailing. *Address:* University of Michigan Law School, 409 Hutchins Hall, Ann Arbor, MI 48109-1215, USA (office); 3 The Butchery, Sandwich, Kent, CT13 9DL, England. *Telephone:* (734) 763-0413 (office); (1304) 612783 (Kent). *Fax:* (734) 763-9375 (office). *E-mail:* bsimpson@umich.edu (office). *Website:* www.law.umich.edu (office).

SIMPSON, Derek, BSc; British trade union official; *General Secretary, Unite;* b. Sheffield; m. (divorced, then reunited); three c.; apprenticeship at age of 15 in local eng firm; became involved in union work and attended eng union's youth conf.; shop steward, then convenor, later Sheffield Dist sec. 1981; Amicus union official in Derby –2002; Gen. Sec. Eng Section, Amicus (after merger of Amalgamated Electrical and Eng Union (AEEU) with Manufacturing, Science and Finance Union (MSF) 2002) July 2002–04; Gen. Sec. Unite (Amicus section) 2004–mem. Labour Party; fmr mem. Communist Party. *Leisure interests:* chess, computers, listening to music. *Address:* General Secretary, 35 King Street, Covent Garden, London, WC2E 8JG, England (office). *Website:* www.amicustheunion.org (office).

SIMPSON, Joanne (Gerould), PhD; American meteorologist and academic; *Chief Scientist Emerita for Meteorology, NASA Goddard Space Flight Center;* b. 23 March 1923, Boston, Mass.; d. of Russell Gerould and Virginia Vaughan; m. 1st Victor Starr 1944; m. 2nd William Malkus 1948; two s. one d.; m. 3rd Robert Simpson 1965; ed Univ. of Chicago, Dartmouth Univ.; Instructor, later Asst Prof., New York Univ., Univ. of Chicago, Ill. Inst. of Tech. 1943–51; meteorologist, Woods Hole Oceanographic Inst. 1951–60; Prof. of Meteorology, UCLA 1960–64; Dir Experimental Meteorology Lab., Nat. Oceanic and Atmospheric Admin (NOAA), Coral Gables, Fla 1965–74; Prof. of Environmental Sciences, Univ. of Va 1974–76, William W. Corcoran Prof. 1976–81; Chief Scientist Simpson Weather Assocs 1974–79; Affiliate Prof. of Atmospheric Science, Colo State Univ. 1980–; Head, Severe Storms Branch, Goddard Lab. for Atmospheres, Goddard Space Flight Center, NASA 1979–88, Chief Scientist for Meteorology 1988, now Chief Scientist Emer., also Sr Fellow; Study Scientist for Tropical Rainfall Measuring Mission, Goddard Space Flight Center 1986–89, Project Scientist 1986–98; mem. Bd on Geophysical and Environmental Data 1993–96, on Atmospheric Sciences and Climate 1991–93; Guggenheim Fellow 1954; Fellow, American Meteorological Soc. 1968 (Pres. 1989, Hon. mem. 1995); mem. Nat. Acad. of Eng, American Geophysical Union (Fellow 1994), The Oceanography Soc.; Hon. mem. American Meteorological Soc. 1995–, Royal Meteorological Soc. 1999–; Hon. DSc (State Univ. of New York) 1991; Meisinger Award 1962, Silver Medal US Dept of Commerce 1967, Gold Medal US Dept of Commerce 1972, NASA Exceptional Scientific Achievement Medal 1982, Rossby Research Medal 1983, Charles Franklin Brooks Award from American Meteorological Soc. (AMS) 1992, NASA Nordberg Award 1994, NASA Outstanding Leadership Medal 1999, Charles E. Anderson Award 2001, Int. Meteorological Org. Prize 2002, and numerous other prizes and awards. *Publications:* more than 190 papers on tropical meteorology, tropical cloud systems and modelling, tropical storms and tropical rain measurement from space. *Leisure interests:* sailing, reading, travel. *Address:* NASA/GSFC, Center for Earth Sciences, Greenbelt, MD 20771 (office); 540 North Street, SW, Washington, DC 20024, USA (home). *Telephone:* (301) 614-6310 (office). *Fax:* (301) 614-5484 (office). *E-mail:* simpson@agnes.gsfc.nasa.gov (office). *Website:* earthsciences.gsfc.nasa.gov (office).

SIMPSON, John Cody Fidler-, CBE, MA, FRGS; British broadcaster and writer; *World Affairs Editor, BBC;* b. 9 Aug. 1944, Cleveleys; s. of Roy Fidler-Simpson and Joyce Leila Vivien Cody; m. 1st Diane Petteys 1965 (divorced 1996); two d.; m. 2nd Adèle Krüger 1996; one s.; ed St Paul's School, London, Magdalene Coll. Cambridge; joined BBC 1966, Foreign Corresp. in Dublin, Brussels, Johannesburg 1972–78, Diplomatic Corresp., BBC TV 1978–80, Political Ed. 1980–81, Diplomatic Ed. 1982–88, Foreign Affairs Ed. (now World Affairs Ed.) 1988–; Contributing Ed. The Spectator 1991–95; columnist, Sunday Telegraph 1995–; Chancellor Roehampton Univ. 2005–; Hon. Fellow, Magdalene Coll., Cambridge 2000; Hon. DLitt (De Montfort) 1995, (Univ. of E Anglia) 1998; Dr hc (Nottingham) 2000; Golden Nymph Award Cannes 1979, BAFTA Reporter of the Year 1991, 2001, Royal TV Soc. Dimbleby Award 1991, Peabody Award 1998, Emmy Award (for coverage of the fall of Kabul) 2002, Bayeux War Correspondents' Prize 2002, Int. Emmy Award, New York 2002. *Publications:* The Best of Granta 1966, The Disappeared 1985, Behind Iranian Lines 1988, Despatches from the Barricades 1990, From the House of War 1991, The Darkness Crumbles 1992, In the Forests of the Night 1993, Lifting the Veil: Life in Revolutionary Iran 1995, The Oxford Book of Exile 1995, Strange Places, Questionable People (autobiog.) 1998, A Mad World, My Masters 2000, News from No Man's Land: Reporting the World 2002, Days from a Different World: A Memoir of Childhood (autobiog.) 2005, Twenty Tales from the War Zone 2007, Not Quite World's End 2007. *Leisure interests:* travel, scuba diving, book collecting. *Address:* c/o BBC World Affairs Unit, Television Centre, Wood Lane, London, W12 7RJ, England. *Telephone:* (20) 8743-8000. *Fax:* (20) 8743-7591.

SIMPSON, Louis Aston Marantz, PhD CD; American writer and academic; *Distinguished Professor Emeritus, State University of New York at Stony Brook;* b. 27 March 1923, Kingston, Jamaica, West Indies; s. of Aston Simpson and Rosalind (Marantz) Simpson; m. 1st Jeanne Rogers 1949 (divorced 1954); one s.; m. 2nd Dorothy Roochvarg 1955 (divorced 1979); one s. one d.; m. 3rd Miriam Bachner (née Butensky) 1985 (divorced 1998); ed Munro Coll., Jamaica, Columbia Univ., New York; Assoc. Ed. Bobbs-Merrill Publishing Co., New York 1950–55; Instructor, Asst Prof. Columbia Univ. 1955–59; Prof., Univ. of Calif. at Berkeley 1959–67; Prof. State Univ. of New York at Stony Brook 1967–91, Distinguished Prof. 1991–93, Prof. Emer. 1993–; Hon. DHL (Eastern Mich. Univ.) 1977; Hon. DL (Hampden-Sydney Coll.) 1991; Prix de Rome American Acad. of Rome 1957, Hudson Review Fellowship 1957, Edna St Vincent Millay Award 1960, Guggenheim Fellowships 1962, 1970, ACLS Grant 1963, Pulitzer Prize for Poetry 1964, Columbia Univ. Medal for Excellence 1965, Commonwealth Club of Calif. Poetry Award 1965, American Acad. of Arts and Letters Award 1976, Inst. of Jamaica Centenary Medal 1980, Jewish Book Council Award for Poetry 1981, Elmer Holmes Bobst Award for Poetry 1987, Harold Morton Landon Award for Translation 1997. *Publications:* poetry: The Arrivistes: Poems 1940–49 1949, Good News of Death and Other Poems 1955, The New Poets of England and America (ed.)

1957, A Dream of Governors 1959, At the End of the Open Road 1963, Selected Poems 1965, Adventures of the Letter I 1971, Searching for the Ox 1976, Armidale 1979, Out of Season 1979, Caviare at the Funeral 1980, People Live Here: Selected Poems 1949–83; The Best Hour of the Night 1983; Collected Poems 1988, Wei Wei and Other Poems 1990, In the Room We Share 1990, There You Are 1995, Nombres et poussière 1996, Modern Poets of France (trans.) 1997, Kaviar pä begravningen 1998, The Owner of the House – New Collected Poems 1940–2001 2003; prose: James Hogg: A Critical Study 1962, Riverside Drive 1962, An Introduction to Poetry (ed.) 1967, North of Jamaica 1971, Three on the Tower: The Lives and Works of Ezra Pound, T. S. Eliot and William Carlos Williams 1975, A Revolution in Taste 1978, A Company of Poets 1981, The Character of the Poet 1986, Selected Prose 1989, Ships Going Into the Blue 1994, The King My Father's Wreck 1995, François Villon – The Legacy and the Testament (trans.) 2000. *Leisure interests:* dogs, fishing. *Address:* c/o English Department, Stony Brook University, Humanities Bldg., Stony Brook, NY; PO Box 119, Setauket, NY 11733, USA.

SIMPSON, N(orman) F(rederick); British playwright; b. 29 Jan. 1919, London; s. of George Frederick Simpson; m. Joyce Bartlett 1944; one d.; ed Emanuel School, London and Birkbeck Coll., Univ. of London; teacher in adult educ. –1963; full-time playwright 1963–. *Publications:* plays: A Resounding Tinkle 1958, The Hole 1958, One Way Pendulum (also film) 1959, The Form 1961, The Cresta Run 1965, Some Tall Tinkles 1968, Playback 625 1970, Was He Anyone? 1972, Whither the Ancient Burial Mounds of Old New Brunswick 1978, If So, Then Yes 2007; co-author Diamonds for Breakfast (film) 1968, Was He Anyone? 1973; novel: Harry Bleachbaker 1976. *Leisure interests:* reading, walking. *Address:* c/o Samuel French Ltd, 52 Fitzroy Street, London, W1T 5JR, England.

SIMPSON, Patricia Ann, BSc (Hons), PhD, FRS; British research scientist; *Wellcome Trust Principal Fellow and Professor of Comparative Embryology, Department of Zoology, University of Cambridge;* b. 9 Dec. 1945, Poona, India; d. of James Simpson and Peggy Simpson; ed Univ. of Southampton, Univ. Pierre et Marie Curie, Paris; ind. researcher, CGM, Gif sur Yvette 1975–80; Research Dir CNRS Strasbourg 1981–2000; Wellcome Trust Prin. Fellow, Dept of Zoology, Univ. of Cambridge 2000–, Prof. of Comparative Embryology 2002–; Silver Medal, CNRS, France 1993, Waddington Medal, British Soc. for Developmental Biology 2008. *Publication:* The Notch Receptors 1994. *Leisure interests:* woodwork, boating, hiking, travel, gardening. *Address:* Department of Zoology, Downing Street, Cambridge, CB2 3EJ (office); 25 Temple End, Great Wilbraham, Cambs., CB21 5JF, England (home). *Telephone:* (1223) 336669 (office); (1223) 880664 (home). *Fax:* (1223) 336676 (office). *E-mail:* pas49@cam.ac.uk (office). *Website:* www.zoo.cam.ac.uk/zoostaff/simpson.htm (office).

SIMPSON-MILLER, Most Hon. Portia Lucretia, BPA; Jamaican politician; *President, People's National Party;* b. 12 Dec. 1945, Wood Hall, St Catherine; m. Errald Miller; ed St Martin's High School, Union Inst., Miami, Fla; Councillor in Kingston, People's Nat. Party (PNP) 1974, 1976; Vice-Pres. PNP 1978–2006, Pres. 2006–, mem. Exec. Council and Nat. Exec. Council PNP; PNP Spokesperson on Women's Affairs, Pensions, Social Security, Consumer Affairs 1983–89; MP for SW St Andrew 1989–; fmr Parl. Sec., Ministry of Local Govt, later in Office of the Prime Minister; Minister of Labour, Welfare and Sports 1989–93, of Labour and Welfare 1993–95, of Labour, Social Security and Sports 1995–2000, of Tourism and Sports 2000–02, of Local Govt and Sport 2002–06; Prime Minister (first woman) 2006–07; Jamaican Order of the Nation 2006; Dr hc (Union Inst.); World Women and Sport Trophy, IOC 2007, ranked by Forbes magazine amongst 100 Most Powerful Women (81st) 2007. *Address:* People's National Party, 89 Old Hope Road, Kingston 5, Jamaica (office). *Telephone:* 978-1337 (office). *Fax:* 927-4389 (office). *E-mail:* information@pnpjamaica.com (office). *Website:* www.pnpjamaica.com (office).

SIMPSON OF DUNKELD, Baron (Life Peer), cr. 1997, of Dunkeld in Perth and Kinross; **Rt Hon. George Simpson,** FCIS, FCCA, FRSA; British business executive and company director; b. 2 July 1942, Scotland; s. of William Simpson and Eliza Jane Simpson (née Wilkie); m. Eva Chalmers 1963; one s. one d.; ed Morgan Acad., Dundee, Dundee Inst. of Technology; Sr Accountant Scottish Gas 1964–68; Cen. Audit Man. British Leyland 1969–73, Financial Controller, Leyland Truck and Bus Div. 1973–76, Dir of Accounting, Leyland Cars 1976–78, Finance and Systems Dir, Leyland Trucks 1978–80; Man. Dir Coventry Climax Ltd 1980–83, Freight Rover Ltd 1983–86; CEO Leyland DAF 1986–88; Man. Dir Rover Group 1989–91, Chair. 1991–94, CEO 1991–92; Dir BAe 1990–94, Deputy CEO 1992–94; Chair. Ballast Nedam Construction Ltd 1992–94, Arlington Securities 1993–94; CEO Lucas Industries PLC 1994–96; Man. Dir Marconi PLC (fmrly GEC PLC) 1996–99, CEO 1999–2001; mem. Supervisory Bd and Dir (non-exec.) Pilkington PLC 1992–99, Northern Venture Capital 1992–2000, Pro Share 1992–4, ICI PLC 1995–2001, Nestlé SA 1999–2003; mem. Bd of Dirs Triumph Group Inc. 2003–; Dir (non-exec.) Alstom SA 1997–2004, Bank of Scotland 2000–02; mem. Exec. Cttee SMMT 1986– (Vice-Pres. 1986–95, Pres. 1995–96); Industrial Prof., Univ. of Warwick 1991–; Gov. Nat. Inst. of Econ. and Social Research 1997–; Fellow, Univ. of Abertay; mem. European Round Table of Businessmen 1997–2001, Mayor of Shanghai's Business Advisory Council 1998–2000; Hon. Fellow, London Business School; hon. degrees from Univs of Warwick and Aston. *Leisure interest:* golf. *Address:* House of Lords, London, SW1A 0PW, England (office). *E-mail:* lordsimps@aol.com (home).

SIMS, Geoffrey Donald, OBE, MSc, PhD, ARCS, DIC, FIET, FCGI, FREng; British fmr university vice-chancellor; b. 13 Dec. 1926, London; s. of Albert Sims and Jessie Sims; m. Pamela Richings 1949; one s. two d.; ed Wembley Co. Grammar School and Imperial Coll. London; Research Physicist, GEC, Wembley 1948–54; Sr Scientific Officer, UKAEA, Harwell 1954–56; Lecturer,

Sr Lecturer, Dept of Electrical Eng, Univ. Coll. London 1956–63; Prof. and Head of Dept of Electronics, Univ. of Southampton 1963–74, Dean of Faculty 1967–70, Sr Deputy Vice-Chancellor 1970–72; Vice-Chancellor, Univ. of Sheffield 1974–90; Chair. Council for Educ. in the Commonwealth 1991–96, Sheffield Church Burgess Educ. Foundation 1990– (Chair. 1992–), Sheffield Church Burgesses Trust 1984– (Chair. 1987, 1999); Hon. Fellow, Sheffield City Polytechnic 1989; Hon. DSc (Southampton) 1979, (Huddersfield) 2001; Hon. ScD (Allegheny) 1989; Hon. DScEng (Belfast) 1990; Hon. LLD (Dundee) 1990, (Sheffield) 1991; Symons Medal, Asscn of Commonwealth Univs) 1991. *Publications:* Microwave Tubes and Semiconductor Devices (with I. M. Stephenson) 1963, Variational Techniques in Electromagnetism (trans.) 1965; numerous papers on microwaves, electronics and education. *Leisure interests:* golf, music, travel. *Address:* Ingleside, 70 Whirlow Lane, Sheffield, S11 9QF, England (home). *Telephone:* (114) 2366196. *Fax:* (114) 2366196.

ŞİMŞEK, Mehmet; Turkish economist and politician; *Minister of Finance;* b. 1967, Batman; worked for UBS Bank, New York 1997, for Bender Securities, Istanbul 1998–2000; joined Merrill Lynch, London, UK 2000, Head, Europe, Middle East and Africa region, Econ. and Strategic Research Div. 2005–07; Minister of State and Head of Treasury 2007–09, Minister of Finance 2009–; mem. AKP (Adalet ve Kalkinma Partisi/Justice and Devt Party). *Address:* Ministry of Finance, Maliye Bakanlığı, Dikmen Cad., Ankara, Turkey (office). *Telephone:* (312) 4250018 (office). *Fax:* (312) 4250058 (office). *E-mail:* bshalk@maliye.gov.tr (office). *Website:* www.maliye.gov.tr (office).

SIMŠIČ, Danica; Slovenian politician; b. 22 Feb. 1955, Ljubljana; mem. Nat. Ass. 1992–96, Chair. Comm. for the Disabled, Pres. Para-Olympic Fund of Slovenia, involved in OSCE Women Network and Stability Pact; re-elected to Nat. Ass. 2000, Chair. Cttee on Health, Labour, Family, Social Policy and the Disabled, mem. Cttee on Defence, Del. to Jt Parl. Cttee EU–Slovenia; City Councillor in Ljubljana 1998; Mayor of Ljubljana 2003–06. *Address:* c/o Mestna obcina Ljubljana, Mestni trg 1, 1000 Ljubljana, Slovenia (office).

SIMSON, Wilhelm, PhD; German business executive; *Member of the Supervisory Board, E.ON;* b. 16 Aug. 1938, Cologne; m.; ed Univ. of Munich; with Diamalt AG, Munich 1968; man. responsible for automobile paints, ICI, Lacke-Farben, Hilden 1971, mem. Bd of Man. 1978, Chair. 1982; Visiting Dir, ICI Paints, UK 1984, Exec. Dir, Paints Div. 1987–89; mem. Bd of Man., SKW Trostberg AG 1989–91, Chair. and Personnel Dir 1991–98; Chair. Bd of Man., VIAG AG (now E.ON), Munich 1998–, now mem. Supervisory Bd; Chair. Supervisory Bd, Bayernwerk AG, Th. Goldschmidt AG; mem. Supervisory Bd, RAG AG; Pres. German Paint-makers Asscn 1982–86, Asscn of the Chemical Industry (Bavaria Section) 1993–; Trustee, Chemical Industry Fund 1992–97; mem. Bd of Dirs, Fed. of German Chemical Industry 1997–, Chair. Cttee for Trade Policy 1998–, then Pres.; Hon. Prof. of Tech. Chem., Ludwig-Maximilians-Univ., Munich 1998. *Address:* c/o E.ON, E.ON-Platz 1, 40479 Dusseldorf, Germany. *Website:* www.eon.com (office).

SINAI, Yakov G., PhD; Russian mathematician and academic; *Professor of Mathematics, Princeton University;* b. 21 Sept. 1935, Moscow; s. of Gregory Sinai and Nadezda Kagan; m. Elena Vul; one s.; ed Moscow State Univ.; Scientific Researcher, Lab. of Probabilistic and Statistical Methods, Moscow State Univ. 1960–71, Prof. of Math. 1971–93; Prof. of Math., Princeton Univ., NJ, USA 1993–, Thomas Jones Prof. 1997–98; Sr Researcher, Landau Inst. of Theoretical Physics, Russian Acad. of Sciences 1971–; Chair. Fields Medal Cttee, Int. Math. Union 2001; Foreign mem. Hungarian Acad. of Sciences 1993, Brazilian Acad. of Sciences 2000, Foreign Assoc. NAS 1999, Academia Europaea 2008; Foreign Hon. mem. American Acad. of Arts and Sciences 1983; Hon. mem. London Math. Soc. 1992; Dr hc (Warsaw) 1993, (Budapest Univ. of Tech. and Econs) 2002, (Hebrew Univ. of Jerusalem) 2005; Loeb Lecturer, Harvard Univ. 1978, Plenary Speaker, Int. Congress on Math. Physics, Berlin 1981, Marseilles 1986, Boltzman Gold Medal 1986, Distinguished Lecturer, Israel 1989, Heineman Prize 1989, Markov Prize 1990, S. Lefshetz Lecturer, Mexico 1990, Plenary Speaker, Int. Congress of Mathematicians, Kyoto 1990, Dirac Medal, Int. Centre for Theoretical Physics, Trieste 1992, Landau Lecturer, Hebrew Univ. of Jerusalem 1993, Wolf Foundation Prize in Math. 1997, Plenary Speaker, First Latin American Congress in Math. 2000, Brazilian Award of Merits in Sciences 2000, Andreewski Lecturer, Berlin 2001, Jürgen Moser Lecture Prize, Soc. for Industrial and Applied Math. 2001, Bowen Lecturer, Univ. of Calif., Berkeley 2001, Alaoglu Lecturer, Calif. Inst. of Tech. 2002, Frederic Esser Nemmers Prize in Math. 2002, Lagrange Prize 2008. *Publications:* Probability Theory: An Introductory Course 1992, Classical Nonintegrability, Quantum Chaos (jtly) 1997, Selected Works of Eberhard Hopf with Commentaries (co-ed.) 2003; more than 140 articles in math. journals on dynamical systems (Kolmogorov-Sinai entropy). *Address:* Department of Mathematics, Princeton University, 708 Fine Hall, Washington Road, Princeton, NJ 08544-1000, USA (office). *Telephone:* (609) 258-4200 (office); (609) 258-4199 (office). *Fax:* (609) 258-1367 (office). *E-mail:* sinai@math.princeton.edu (office). *Website:* www.math.princeton.edu (office).

SINAI, Yakov Grigoryevich, D.PHYS.MATH.SC.; Russian physicist; *Professor, Department of Mathematics, Princeton University;* b. 21 Sept. 1935; m.; one s.; ed Moscow State Univ.; Jr, Sr Researcher, Prof. Moscow State Univ. 1960–71; Sr, Chief Researcher L. Landau Inst. for Theoretical Physics USSR Acad. of Sciences 1971–; Prof. Dept of Mathematics, Princeton Univ., USA 1993–; mem. USSR (now Russian) Acad. of Sciences 1991; research in ergodic theory of dynamic systems, math. problems of statistical physics and probability theory; mem. Ed. Bd Uspekhi Matematicheskyh nauk, Ed. Bd Theoretical and Math. Physics, Russian Acad. of Natural Sciences; Foreign mem. American Acad. of Arts and Sciences; Hon. mem. St Petersburg Math. Soc., American Acad. of Science and Art in Boston; Hon. degree (Hebrew Univ.) 2005; Moore Distinguished Scholar (Calif. Inst. of Tech.) 2005; Leonardo da Vinci Lecture, Milan 2006; Galileo Chair., Pisa 2006; Kolmogorov

Lecture and Medal, Univ. of London 2007; John Lewis Lecture Series, Dublin 2007; Porter Lecture Series, Rice Univ., Texas 2007; shared Wolf Prize 1997, Heinemann Prize of American Math. Soc., Boltzmann Prize, P. M. Dirac Medal, Mozer Prize, SIAM 2001, Nemmers Prize in Mathematics 2002. *Publications include:* Dynamic Systems with Elastic Mappings 1970, Math. Theory of Phase Transitions 1981; numerous articles in scientific journals; more than 160 papers. *Address:* L. Landau Institute for Theoretical Physics, Russian Academy of Sciences, Kosygin str. 2, 117940 Moscow, Russia (office); Department of Mathematics, Princeton University, Princeton, NJ 08544, USA (office). *Telephone:* (495) 137-32-44 (Moscow). *E-mail:* sinai@math.princeton .edu (office). *Website:* www.math.princeton.edu (office).

SINAISKY, Vassily Serafimovich; Russian conductor; *Principal Conductor, Malmö Symphony Orchestra;* b. 20 April 1947, Abez, Komi Autonomous Repub., Russia; m. Tamara Grigoryevna Sinayskaya; one s.; ed Leningrad State Conservatory; Artistic Dir and Chief Conductor Novosibirsk State Symphony 1971–73; Latvian State Symphony 1975–89; Moscow State Philharmonic Orchestra 1991–96; State Symphony Orchestra of Russia 2000–02; Prin. Guest Conductor BBC Philharmonic 1996–; worked with Orchestre Nat. de France, Berlin Philharmonic Orchestra, Orchestre Philharmonic du Luxembourg, Royal Scottish Nat. Orchestra and Finnish Radio Symphony; Prin. Conductor Malmö Symphony Orchestra 2007–; Golden Medal and 1st Prize Karayan Competition, Berlin 1973, People's Artist of Latvia 1981. *Address:* Malmö Symphony Orchestra, Konserthuset, 205 80 Malmö, Sweden (office). *Telephone:* (40) 630-45-00 (office). *Fax:* (40) 611-75-05 (office). *E-mail:* info@mso.se (office). *Website:* www.mso.se (office).

SINAMENYE, Mathias; Burundian politician and central banker; Second Vice-Pres. of Burundi for Econ. and Social Affairs 1998–2002; Head of Del. to UN Gen. Ass. Special Session on HIV/AIDS, New York June 2001; fmr Gov. Banque de la République du Burundi. *Address:* c/o Banque de la Republique du Burundi, Avenue du Gouvernement, BP 705, Bujumbura, Burundi (office).

SINANKWA, Denise; Burundian politician; Minister of Trade and Industry 2005–06, of Finance 2006–07; mem. Conseil national pour la défense de la démocratie–Force pour la défense de la démocratie (CNDD—FDD). *Address:* c/o Ministry of Finance, BP 1830, Bujumbura, Burundi (office).

SINCKLER, Christopher Peter, BA, MA; Barbadian civil servant, politician and academic; *Minister of Social Care, Constituency Empowerment and Urban Development;* m. Arlyn Mayers; two s. one d.; ed Univ. of the West Indies; worked on econ. policy issues with IBRD (World Bank), IMF, IDB, WTO, CARICOM, African, Caribbean and Pacific Group of States, EU, among others; Lecturer in Small Economies and Contemporary Trade Policy Issues, Masters in Int. Trade Policy Programme, Univ. of the West Indies Cave Hill Campus; Exec. Dir Caribbean Policy Devt Centre (coalition of Caribbean non-governmental orgs) –2008; mem. Democratic Labour Party, currently Gen. Sec.; MP for St Michael NW; Minister of Foreign Affairs, Foreign Trade and Int. Business 2008, of Social Care, Constituency Empowerment and Urban Devt 2008–. *Address:* Ministry of Social Care, Constituency Empowerment and Urban Development, 4th Floor, Warrens Office Complex, St Michael, Bardados, BB 14018, West Indies (office). *Telephone:* 310-1604 (office). *Fax:* 424-2908 (office). *E-mail:* info@socialtransformation.gov.bb (office); csinckler@sunbeach.net.

SINCLAIR, Charles James Francis, CBE, BA, FCA; British business executive; *Chief Executive, Daily Mail and General Trust plc;* b. 4 April 1948; s. of Sir George Sinclair and the late Lady Sinclair; m. Nicola Bayliss 1974; two s.; ed Winchester Coll. and Magdalen Coll., Oxford; Voluntary Service Overseas, Zambia 1966–67; with Deardon Farrow, chartered accountants 1970–75; with Associated Newspapers Holdings Ltd 1975, Man. Dir 1988, Group Chief Exec. Daily Mail and Gen. Trust plc (after merger with Associated Newspapers) 1989–; mem. Bd of Dirs (non-exec.) Euromoney Institutional Investor PLC 1985–, SVG Capital 2005–, Schroders PLC 1990–2005, Reuters Group PLC 1994–2005; Chair. Bd of Trustees Minack Theatre Trust, Porthcuno, Cornwall. *Leisure interests:* opera, fishing, skiing. *Address:* Daily Mail and General Trust plc, Northcliffe House, 2 Derry Street, London, W8 5TT, England (office). *Telephone:* (20) 7938-6000 (office). *Fax:* (20) 7938-3909 (office). *Website:* www.dmgt.co.uk (office).

SINCLAIR, Sir Clive Marles, Kt; British inventor; *Chairman, Sinclair Research Ltd;* b. 30 July 1940, London; s. of the late George William Carter Sinclair and of Thora Edith Ella Sinclair (née Marles); m. Ann Trevor-Briscoe 1962 (divorced 1985, died 2004); two s. one d.; ed St George's Coll., Weybridge; Ed. Bernards Publrs Ltd 1958–61; Chair. Sinclair Radionics Ltd 1962–79, Sinclair Research Ltd 1979–, Sinclair Browne Ltd 1981–85, Cambridge Computer 1986–90; Chair. British Mensa 1980–98, Hon. Pres. 2001–; Visiting Fellow, Robinson Coll., Cambridge 1982–85; Visiting Prof., Imperial Coll., London 1984–92; Dir Shaye Communications Ltd 1986–91, Anamartic Ltd; Hon. Fellow, Imperial Coll., London 1984; Hon. DSc (Bath) 1983, (Warwick, Heriot Watt) 1983, (UMIST) 1984; Royal Soc. Mullard Award 1984. *Publications:* Practical Transistor Receivers 1959, British Semiconductor Survey 1963. *Leisure interests:* music, poetry, mathematics, science, poker. *Address:* Sinclair Research Ltd, 1A Spring Gardens, Trafalgar Square, London, SW1A 2BB, England (office). *Telephone:* (20) 7839-6868 (office); (20) 7839-7744 (home). *Fax:* (20) 7839-6622 (office). *E-mail:* clivesinclair@sinclair-research.co .uk (office). *Website:* (office).

SINCLAIR, Rt Hon. Ian McCahon, AC, PC, BA, LLB; Australian consultant, lawyer, farmer and fmr politician; *President, Murray-Darling Basin Commission;* b. 10 June 1929, Sydney; s. of George Sinclair and Hazel Sinclair; m. 1st Margaret Tarrant 1956 (died 1967); one s. two d.; m. 2nd Rosemary Edna Fenton 1970; one s.; ed Knox Grammar School, Wahroonga and Sydney Univ.; barrister 1952–; mem. Legis. Council in NSW Parl. 1961–63, House of Reps 1963–98; Minister for Social Services 1965–68; Minister Assisting Minister for Trade and Industry 1966–71; Minister for Shipping and Transport 1968–71, for Primary Industry 1971–72; Deputy Leader Country Party (now Nat. Party) 1971–84, Fed. Parl. Leader 1984–89, Party Spokesman on Defence, Foreign Affairs, Law and Agric. 1973–75, Opposition Spokesman on Agric., Leader of Opposition in House of Reps 1974–75; Minister for Agric. and Northern Australia Nov.–Dec. 1975, for Primary Industry 1975–79, for Communications 1980–82, for Defence 1982–83; Leader of Govt in House of Reps 1975–82; Leader of Opposition in House of Reps 1983–87, Opposition Spokesman for Defence 1983–87, for Trade and Resources 1987–89; Shadow Special Minister of State 1994; mem. Jt Cttee of Foreign Affairs, Defence and Trade 1991–98, Chair. 1996–98; Chair. Australian Constitutional Convention 1998; Speaker, House of Reps, Fed. Parl. 1998; Adjunct Prof. of Political Science, Univ. of New England 2000–; Man. Dir Sinclair Pastoral Co. 1953–, Grazier 1953–; Dir Farmers' and Graziers' Co-operative Co. Ltd 1962–65; Chair. Australian Rural Summit 1999, Australia Taiwan Business Council 2000–, Foundation for Rural and Regional Renewal 2000–, CRC for Sheep 2001–, Good Beginnings Australia; Pres. Austcare 2000–; Nat. Party, Pres. Scouts Australia (NSW) 2001–, Pres. Murray-Darling Basin Comm. 2003–, Chair. NSW Native Vegetation Reform Implementation Group 2003–06; Co-Chair. NSW Health Care Advisory Council 2005–; Hon. DUniv (Univ. of New England); Hon. DLitt (Southern Cross Univ.). *Leisure interests:* surfing, walking, farming. *Address:* PO Box 27, Cundletown, NSW 2430 (home); Mulberry Farm, Dumaresq Island, NSW 2430, Australia (home). *Telephone:* (2) 65538276 (home). *Fax:* (2) 65538358 (home). *E-mail:* iansinclair@ozemail .com.au (home).

SINDEN, Sir Donald Alfred, Kt, CBE, DLitt, FRSA; British actor and author; b. 9 Oct. 1923, Plymouth; s. of Alfred E. Sinden and Mabel A. Sinden (née Fuller); m. Diana Mahony 1948 (died 2004); two s.; entered theatrical profession with Charles F. Smith's Co., Mobile Entertainments Southern Area 1942; with Leicester Repertory Co. 1945; with Memorial Theatre Co., Stratford-upon-Avon 1946–47; with Old Vic and Bristol Old Vic 1948–50; film actor 1952–60; Chair. British Theatre Museum Asscn 1971–77, Theatre Museum Advisory Council 1973–80; Pres. Fed. of Playgoers Socs 1968–93, Royal Theatrical Fund 1983–; Vice-Pres. London Appreciation Soc. 1960–; Assoc. Artist, RSC 1967–; mem. Council, British Actors Equity Asscn 1966–77 (Trustee 1988–2004), Council, RSA 1972, Advisory Council, V&A Museum 1973–80, Arts Council Drama Panel 1973–77, Leicestershire Educ. Arts Cttee 1974–2004, BBC Archives Advisory Cttee 1975–78, Council, London Acad. of Music and Dramatic Art 1976–, Kent and E Sussex Regional Cttee, Nat. Trust 1978–82, Arts Council 1982–86; Drama Desk Award (for London Assurance) 1974, Variety Club of GB Stage Actor of 1976 (for King Lear), Evening Standard Drama Award Best Actor (for King Lear) 1977. *Stage appearances include:* The Heiress 1949–50, Red Letter Day 1951, Odd Man In 1957, Peter Pan 1960, Guilty Party 1961, as Richard Plantagenet in Henry VI (The Wars of the Roses), as Price in Eh!, etc. (RSC) 1963–64, British Council tour of S. America in Dear Liar and Happy Days 1965, There's a Girl in My Soup 1966, as Lord Foppington in The Relapse (RSC) 1967, Not Now Darling 1968, as Malvolio, Henry VIII 1969, as Sir Harcourt Courtly in London Assurance 1972 RSC, (toured USA 1974), In Praise of Love 1973, as Stockmann in An Enemy of the People 1975, Habeas Corpus (USA) 1975, as Benedick in Much Ado About Nothing, King Lear (RSC) 1976–77, Shut Your Eyes and Think of England 1977, Othello (RSC) 1979–80, Present Laughter 1981, Uncle Vanya 1982, The School for Scandal 1983 (European tour 1984), Ariadne auf Naxos (ENO) 1983, Two into One 1984, The Scarlet Pimpernel 1985, Major Barbara 1988, Over My Dead Body 1989, Oscar Wilde 1990, Out of Order 1990 (Australian tour 1992), Venus Observed 1991, She Stoops to Conquer 1993, Hamlet 1994, That Good Night 1996, Quartet 1999, The Hollow Crown (tour to Australia and NZ 2002–03, Canada 2004); Dir The Importance of Being Earnest 1987. *Films:* appeared in 23 films including The Cruel Sea, Doctor in the House 1952–60. *Radio includes:* Doctor Gideon Fell (series). *Television series include:* Our Man from St Marks, Two's Company, Discovering English Churches, Never the Twain, Judge John Deed. *Publications:* A Touch of the Memoirs 1982, Laughter in the Second Act 1985, The Everyman Book of Theatrical Anecdotes (ed.) 1987, The English Country Church 1988, Famous Last Words (ed.) 1994. *Leisure interests:* theatrical history, architecture, ecclesiology, genealogy, serendipity. *Address:* Rats Castle, Tenterden, TN30 7HX, England. *Fax:* (1797) 270230 (office).

SINEGAL, James D. (Jim); American retail executive; *President and CEO, Costco Wholesale Corporation;* b. 1936; ed San Diego State Univ.; held several exec. positions at Fed-Mart Corpn including Exec. Vice-Pres. Merchandising and Operations; fmr Exec. Vice-Pres. The Price Club; Pres. Sinegal, Chamberlain & Assocs –1983; Co-founder (with Jeff Brotman), Pres. and COO Costco 1983–93, CEO 1988–93, merged with The Price Club 1993, mem. Bd Dirs, Pres. and CEO Costco Wholesale Corpn 1993–; mem. Educ. Cttee, Washhington Business Roundtable; Trustee, Seattle Univ.; LCB Visionary Award – Trendsetter of the Year, Lundquist School of Business, Univ. of Oregon 2000, Business Achievement Award, Seattle Univ. 2002. *Address:* Costco Wholesale Corporation, 999 Lake Drive, Issaquah, WA 98027, USA (office). *Telephone:* (425) 313-8100 (office). *Fax:* (425) 313-8103 (office). *E-mail:* info@costco.com (office). *Website:* www.costco.com (office).

SINFELT, John Henry, PhD; American scientist and engineer; *Senior Scientific Advisor Emeritus, Exxon Research and Engineering Company;* b. 18 Feb. 1931, Munson, Pa; s. of Henry Gustave Sinfelt and June Lillian McDonald; m. Muriel Jean Vadersen 1956; one s.; ed Pennsylvania State Univ. and Univ. of Illinois; Scientist, Exxon Research and Eng Co. 1954–, Sr Research Assoc. 1968–72, Scientific Adviser 1972–79, Sr Scientific Adviser 1979–96, Sr Scientific Adviser Emer. 1996–; Consulting Prof., Dept of Chemical Eng, Stanford Univ. 1996–; active in catalysis research, formulated and developed the concept of bimetallic clusters as catalysts, applied the concept in petroleum refining for production of lead-free petrol; mem. NAS, American Philosophical Soc., Nat. Acad. of Eng; Fellow, American Acad. of Arts and Sciences; Hon. ScD (Univ. of Ill.) 1981; Nat. Medal of Science 1979, Perkin Medal in Chem. 1984, NAS Award for the Industrial Application of Science 1996 and many other awards and prizes. *Publications:* Bimetallic Catalysts: Discoveries, Concepts and Applications 1983; 185 articles in scientific journals; 48 patents. *Leisure Interests:* history of science, evolution of scientific concepts and theories. *Address:* PO Box 364, Oldwick, NJ 08858, USA (home). *Telephone:* (908) 439-3603 (home). *Fax:* (908) 730-3301.

SINGAY, Lyonpo Jigme, MBBS, MPH; Bhutanese politician; b. 5 May 1954, Themnangbi, Mongar Dist; ed Delhi Univ., India, San Diego State Univ., USA; Deputy Dir Public Health Div., Dept of Health Services 1987–89, Jt Dir, Dept of Health Services 1989–1993, Dir Div. of Health Services 1994–98; Sec. Royal Civil Service Comm. 1998–2003; Minister of Health 2003–07 (resgnd); mem. People's Democratic Party; Red Scarf 1997, Orange Scarf 2003. *Address:* c/o People's Democratic Party, Drizang Lam, Lower Motithang, Thimphu; Tshogdu Chenmo, Secretariat, Gyelyong Tshokhang, POB 139, Thimphu (office); Themnangbi, Mongar Dzongkhag, Bhutan. *Telephone:* (2) 322729 (office); (2) 322136 (home). *Fax:* (2) 324210 (office). *Website:* www.nab.gov.bt (office).

SINGER, Isadore Manuel, PhD; American mathematician and academic; *Institute Professor, Department of Mathematics, Massachusetts Institute of Technology;* b. 3 May 1924, Detroit, Mich.; s. of Simon Singer and Freda Rose; m. Sheila Ruff 1961; five c.; ed Univs of Michigan and Chicago; C.L.E. Moore Instructor at MIT 1950–52; Asst Prof., UCLA 1952–54; Visiting Asst Prof., Columbia Univ. 1954–55; Visiting mem. Inst. for Advanced Study, Princeton 1955–56; Asst Prof., MIT 1956, Assoc. Prof. 1958, Prof. of Math. 1959, Norbert Wiener Prof. of Math. 1970–79, John D. MacArthur Prof. of Math. 1983–, Inst. Prof. 1987–; Visiting Prof. of Math., Univ. of Calif., Berkeley 1977–79, Prof. 1979–83, Miller Prof. 1982–83; mem. NAS, American Math. Soc., Math. Asscn of America, American Acad. of Arts and Sciences, American Philosophical Soc., American Physical Soc.; Sloan Fellow 1959–62, Guggenheim Fellow 1968–69, 1975–76; Bôcher Memorial Prize 1969, 1975–76, Nat. Medal of Science 1985, Wigner Prize, Int. Congress of Mathematicians 1989, Abel Prize (jtly with Sir Michael Atiyah) 2004. *Publications:* Lecture Notes on Elementary Topology and Geometry; author of research articles in functional analysis, differential geometry and topology. *Leisure interests:* literature, hiking, tennis. *Address:* Department of Mathematics, Massachusetts Institute of Technology, Room 2-387, 77 Massachusetts Avenue, Cambridge, MA 02139, USA (office). *Telephone:* (617) 253-5601 (office). *Fax:* (617) 253-8000 (office). *E-mail:* ims@math.mit.edu (office). *Website:* www-math.mit.edu (office).

SINGER, Maxine, PhD; American biochemist; *President Emerita, Carnegie Institution of Washington;* b. 15 Feb. 1931, New York; d. of Hyman Frank and Henrietta Perlowitz Frank; m. Daniel M. Singer 1952; one s. three d.; ed Swarthmore Coll. and Yale Univ.; Research Chemist, Enzymes and Cellular Biochemistry Section, Nat. Inst. of Arthritis and Metabolic Diseases, NIH, Bethesda, Md 1958–74, Chief, Nucleic Acid Enzymology Section, Lab. of Biochemistry, Div. of Cancer Biology and Diagnosis, Nat. Cancer Inst. 1974–79, Chief, Lab. of Biochem. 1979–87, research chemist 1987–88, Scientist Emer. 1988–; Pres. Carnegie Inst., Wash. 1988–2002, now Pres. Emer., Sr Scientific Advisor and mem. Bd of Trustees; Visiting Scientist, Dept of Genetics, Weizmann Inst. of Science, Rehovot, Israel 1971–72; Dir Foundation for Advanced Educ. in Sciences 1972–78, 1985–86; mem. Yale Corpn 1975–90; Chair. Smithsonian Council 1992–94 (mem. 1990–94); Chair. Comm. on the Future of the Smithsonian 1994–96; mem. Editorial Bd Journal of Biological Chem. 1968–74, Science 1972–82; Chair. Editorial Bd Proceedings of NAS 1985–88; Scientific Council Int. Inst. of Genetics and Biophysics, Naples 1982–86, Bd of Govs of Weizmann Inst., Human Genome Org. 1989–, Cttee on Science, Eng and Public Policy, NAS 1989–91, Int. Advisory Bd Chulabhorn Research Inst. 1990–; mem. Bd Dirs Johnson & Johnson; mem. NAS, American Soc. of Biological Chemists, American Soc. of Microbiologists, ACS, American Acad. of Arts and Sciences, Inst. of Medicine of NAS, American Philosophical Soc., New York Acad. of Sciences; Trustee Wesleyan Univ., Middletown, Conn. 1972–75, Whitehead Inst. 1985–94; Hon. DSc (Wesleyan Univ.) 1977, (Swarthmore Coll.) 1978, (Univ. of Md) 1985, (Brandeis Univ.) 1988, (Radcliffe Coll.) 1990, (Williams Coll.) 1990, (Franklin and Marshall Coll.) 1991, (George Washington Univ.) 1992, (New York Univ.) 1992, (Lehigh Univ.) 1992, (Dartmouth) 1993, (Yale) 1994, (Harvard) 1994; Dir's Award, NIH 1977, Nat. Medal of Science 1992, NAS Public Welfare Medal 2007. *Publications:* molecular biology textbooks (with Paul Berg), Why Aren't Black Holes Black? (with Robert Hazen) and numerous articles in major scientific journals. *Leisure interests:* scuba diving, cooking, literature. *Address:* 5410 39th Street, NW, Washington, DC 20015, USA (home). *Telephone:* (202) 387-6404.

SINGER, Peter Albert David, BPhil, MA; Australian philosopher, academic and writer; *DeCamp Professor of Bioethics, Princeton University;* b. 6 July 1946, Melbourne, Vic.; s. of Ernest Singer and Cora Oppenheim; m. Renata Diamond 1968; three d.; ed Scotch Coll., Univ. of Melbourne and Univ. Coll., Oxford; Radcliffe Lecturer, Univ. Coll., Oxford 1971–73; Visiting Asst Prof., Dept of Philosophy, New York Univ. 1973–74; Sr Lecturer, Dept of Philosophy, La Trobe Univ., Bundoora, Vic., Australia 1974–76; Prof., Dept of Philosophy, Monash Univ., Clayton, Vic. 1977–99, Dir Centre for Human Bioethics 1981–91, Deputy Dir 1992–99; DeCamp Prof. of Bioethics, Princeton Univ., NJ, USA 1999–; Laureate Prof., Centre for Applied Philosophy and Public Ethics, Univ. of Melbourne 2005; various visiting positions in USA, Canada and Italy. *Publications:* Democracy and Disobedience 1973, Animal Rights and Human Obligations (ed. with Thomas Regan) 1975, Animal Liberation: A

New Ethics for Our Treatment of Animals 1975, Practical Ethics 1979, Marx 1980, The Expanding Circle: Ethics and Sociobiology 1981, Test-Tube Babies (ed. with William Walters) 1982, Hegel 1983, The Reproduction Revolution: New Ways of Making Babies (with Deane Wells, aka Making Babies: The New Science and Ethics of Conception) 1984, In Defence of Animals (ed.) 1985, Should the Baby Live?: The Problem of Handicapped Infants (with Helga Kuhse) 1985, Applied Ethics (ed.) 1986, Animal Liberation: A Graphic Guide (with Lori Gruen) 1987, Animal Factories (with Jim Mason) 1990, Embryo Experimentation (ed.) 1990, Companion to Ethics (ed.) 1991, How Are We to Live? 1993, The Great Ape Project: Equality Beyond Humanity (ed. with Paola Cavalieri) 1993, Rethinking Life and Death 1994, Ethics (ed.) 1994, The Greens 1996, Ethics into Action 1998, A Companion to Bioethics (with Helga Kuhse) 1998, A Darwinian Left 1999, Writings on an Ethical Life 2000, One World 2002, Pushing Time Away: My Grandfather and the Tragedy of Jewish Vienna 2003, The President of Good and Evil: Taking George W. Bush Seriously 2004, The Moral of the Story (co-ed.) 2005, Eating: What We Eat and Why it Matters (with Jim Mason) 2006, The Life You Can Save 2009. *Leisure interests:* bushwalking, reading, swimming. *Address:* University Center for Human Values, 5 Ivy Lane, Princeton, NJ, 08544-1013, USA (office). *Telephone:* (609) 258-2202 (office). *Fax:* (609) 258-1285 (office). *Website:* www.princeton.edu/~psinger (office).

SINGH, Lt-Gen. (retd) Ajai, MSc; Indian army officer and government official; b. 20 Nov. 1935, Rajasthan; s. of the late Raj Dalpat Singh; ed Mayo Coll., Ajmer, Madras Univ.; joined Indian Army, Tank Commdrs Course, Czechoslovakia 1966, Defence Services Staff Course, Wellington 1972, Higher Command Course, Coll. of Combat, Mhow 1979–80, Royal Coll. of Defence Studies, London, UK 1983, Discussions at RAND Co-operation, USA 1983, 1989, saw action in Indo-Pak wars 1965, 1971; Commdr Ind. Armed Brigade, Ambala 1980–82, BGS I-Corps, Mathura 1982–84, Dir-Gen. WE, Army HQ, New Delhi 1985–87, GOC 31 Armoured Div., Jhansi 1987–89, Dir-Gen. Mechanised Forces, Army HQ, New Delhi 1989–90, GOC 4 Corps, Tezpur, Assam 1990–92, Dir-Gen. Combat Vehicles, Army HQ, New Delhi 1992–93, CCR&D, Defence Research & Devt Org., Ministry of Defence 1993–95; Gov. of Assam 2003–08; Chair. North Eastern Council; Indian Mil. Acad. Sword of Honour and Silver Medal, (Best All Round Gentleman Cadet of June 1956 Batch), Mentioned in Despatches for Gallantry, Indo-Pak War 1965, Ati Vishist Seva Medal for Gallantry 1986, Param Vishist Seva Medal for Gallantry (Highest Distinguished Service Award of India) 1992. *Leisure interests:* tennis, squash, hockey, football, cricket, polo, golf, oil and crayon painting, landscaping, music, wildlife and Environment, time and personnel management techniques and resource optimization. *Address:* c/o Raj Bhawan, Kharguli, Guwahati 781 004, Assam, India (office). *Telephone:* (361) 2540250 (home).

SINGH, Capt. Amarinder; Indian politician and fmr army officer; b. 11 March 1942; s. of HH Late Maharaja Yadavindra Singh of Patiala; officer in Indian army 1963–66; mem. Lok Sabha (Parl.) 1980–84; mem. Legis. Ass. 1985; f. Shiromani Akali Dal (Panthik) 1991; Chief Minister of Punjab 2002–07. *Address:* New Motibagh Palace, Patiala, 147001; c/o Office of the Chief Minister, Government of Punjab, 45, Sector 2, Chandigarh, India (office).

SINGH, Ashni Kumar, PhD; Guyanese government official; *Minister of Finance;* ed Queens Coll., Lancaster Univ., UK; fmr Commr Gen. Guyana Revenue Authority; Budget Dir –2006; Minister of Finance 2006–. *Address:* Ministry of Finance, Main Street, Kingston, Georgetown, Guyana (office). *Telephone:* 225-6088 (office). *Fax:* (office). *E-mail:* asingh@inetguyana.net (office). *Website:* www.finance.gov.gy (office).

SINGH, Bhishma Narain, BA; Indian politician; b. 13 July 1933, Palamau, Bihar; m. Ram Kumari Devi 1950; two s. two d.; ed Takeya High School, Sasaram, Bihar and Banaras Hindu Univ.; active Congress worker 1953–; mem. All Indian Congress Cttee; mem. Bihar Legis. Ass. 1967–69, 1969–72, 1972–76; Minister, State Gov. of Bihar 1971, 1972–73, 1973–74; mem. Rajya Sabha 1976, 1982, Deputy Chief Whip, Congress Parl. Party 1977, later Chief Whip; Minister of Parl. Affairs 1980–83, of Communications Jan.–March 1980, of Works and Housing, Labour, Supply and Food and Civil Supplies 1980–83; Gov. of Assam and Meghalaya 1983–89, of Sikkim 1985–86, of Arunachal Pradesh 1987, of Tamil Nadu 1991–93; Deputy Chair. Cen. Cooperative Bank, Daltonganj 1964; Dir Bihar State Co-operative Mktg. Union 1967; Chair. Bihar State Co-operative Housing Construction Finance Soc. 1974–75, Bihar State Credit and Investment Corpn 1974. *Leisure interests:* horse riding, marksmanship, music, dance and drama, especially tribal folk dances. *Address:* Hamid Ganj, PO Daitonganj, Palamau District, Bihar, India.

SINGH, Lt-Gen. (retd) Bhopinder; Indian army officer (retd) and government official; *Lieutentant-Governor of Andaman and Nicobar Islands;* b. 20 March 1946, Allahabad, UP; s. of the late Brig. Rajmohan Singh; m. Bhawanee Singh; ed Nat. Defence Acad.; commissioned into Rajput Regt 1965, held several command, staff and instructional appointments, commanded troops in Indo-Pak wars 1965, 1971, led counter-insurgency operations in Jammu and Kashmir, Mizoram and Assam, has been an Instructor at Indian Mil. Acad., held Gen. Staff tenures at Kargil and Kashmir Valley, commanded 17 Rajput Bn, commanded Rajput Regimental Centre, Fategarh, UP; fmr Mil., Naval and Air Attaché in Addis Ababa; as Maj.-Gen. was Additional Dir-Gen. of Org. (AG's Br.), Army HQ; Mil. Sec. to Pres. of India and Col of Pres.'s Bodyguard 1997–; Col, Rajput Regt 2002; Lt-Gov. of Andaman and Nicobar Islands 2006–, of Puducherry 2008; Param Vishisht Seva Medal (PVSM), Ati Vishisht Seva Medal (AVSM); Army Commdr's Commendation, Ethiopian Govt Commendation Certificate. *Leisure interests:* sports, outdoor adventure activities. *Address:* Office of the Governor, Andaman and Nicobar Administration, Port

Blair, Andaman and Nicobar Islands, India (office). *Telephone:* 233333 (office); 233300 (home). *E-mail:* lg@and.nic.in (office); lgandaman@hotmail.com; lgandaman@yahoo.com. *Website:* www.and.nic.in (office).

SINGH, Buta; Indian politician; b. 21 March 1934, Jalandhar Punjab; s. of Sardar Bir Singh; ed Lyallpur Khalsa Coll., Jalandhar and Guru Nanak Khalsa Coll., Bombay; elected to Lok Sabha 1962, 1967, 1971, 1980, 1984, 1999; Union Deputy Minister for Railways 1974–76, for Commerce 1976–77; Minister of State in Ministry of Shipping and Transport 1980–81; Minister of Supply and Rehabilitation 1981–82, of Sport 1982–83, Cabinet Minister in charge of several ministries 1983–84, Minister of Agric. 1984–86, of Home Affairs 1986–89, of Civil Supplies, Consumer Affairs and Public Distribution 1995–96, of Communications 1998; mem. Planning Comm. 1985, Gen. Sec. Indian Nat. Congress 1978–80; Pres. Amateur Athletic Fed. of India 1976–84. *Address:* 9 Lodi Estate, New Delhi 110003, India. *Telephone:* (11) 4699797.

SINGH, Chaudhary Randhir, MA, LLB; Indian politician; b. 1 July 1924, Bayanpur, Haryana; s. of the late Chaudhary Chandgi Ram and Chhoti Devi; m. Vijay Lakshmi Chaudhary 1939; four s. three d.; ed St Stephen's Coll., Delhi, Univ. of Delhi; fmr mem. Parl. (Lok Sabha), All India Congress Cttee, several parl. cttees, Exec. Congress Party in Parl.; mem. Nat. Comm. on Agric. 1970–76; mem. Agric. Prices Comm., Govt of India 1976–79, 1980–83, 1987–89; Gov. Sikkim 1996–2001; Chair. or mem. numerous Govt working groups on land reform and agricultural devt issues; fmrly Chair. Punjab Praja Socialist Party, mem. Nat. Exec. of Punjab Praja Socialist Party of India, Sec.-Gen. United Front of Opposition Parties Punjab, Chair. AICC Land Reforms Panel, Sr Vice-Chair. and Sec.-Gen. Farmers' Parl. Forum of India; active in social work in Haryana; recipient of numerous awards for work on behalf of peasant families and minority groups; Int Man of the Year 2003, Son of India Award, Eminent Personality of India Award, Man of the Year Award, several other nat. and int. awards and honours. *Publications:* 18 books on agricultural devt and problems of rural peoples 1967–. *Leisure interests:* listening to and reading Urdu poetry, especially by Md Iqbal and Ghalib, folk songs and dances. *Address:* G-11 Tara Apartments, Alaknanda, New Delhi 110 019, India. *Telephone:* (11) 26020048 (also fax) (home); (93) 13770764 (Mobile).

SINGH, Dayanita; Indian photographer; b. 1961; ed National Inst. of Design, Ahmedabad, Int. Center of Photography, New York, USA; work has been exhibited widely both in India and abroad; lives and works in Delhi and London; Palm Beach Photographic Museum Rising Star of Photography Award 1996, Andreas Frank Foundation Grant Award for Urban Families Project 1996, Canon India's Top Ten Photographers' Award 1997, Award, Queens Museum of Art, New York 1997. *Address:* c/o Frith Street Gallery, 59–60 Frith Street, London, W1D 3JJ, England (office). *Telephone:* (20) 7494-1550 (office). *Fax:* (20) 7287-3733 (office). *E-mail:* info@frithstreetgallery.com (office). *Website:* www.frithstreetgallery.com (office).

SINGH, Dharam, LLB, MA; Indian politician; b. 25 Dec. 1936, Nelogi, Jewargi; ed Osmania Univ.; fmr advocate; Councillor, Gulbarga City Municipal Council 1968; mem. Karnataka Legis. Ass. 1972–; fmr Karnataka State Minister of Urban Devt, of Home Affairs, of Social Welfare, of Revenue, of Public Works; Chief Minister of Karnataka 2004–06 (resgnd). *Address:* c/o Office of the Chief Minister, Room 323, 3rd Floor, Vidhana Soudha, Bangalore 560 001, India (office).

SINGH, Digvijay, BEng; Indian politician; b. 28 Feb. 1947, Indore; s. of Balbhadra Singh; elected to Ass. 1977, 1980; Gen. Sec. Madhya Pradesh Youth Congress 1978–79; fmr Minister of State for Agric., Arjun Singh Ministry, later Cabinet Minister for Irrigation; elected to Lok Sabha 1991; Pres. Madhya Pradesh Congress Cttee 1980, Council 1984, 1992; Chief Minister of Madhya Pradesh 1993–98, 1998–2003. *Address:* c/o Chief Minister's Secretariat, Ballabh Bhavan, Bhopal (office); 1 Shamla Hill, Bhopal, India (home). *Telephone:* (755) 2540500 (home).

SINGH, Gopal, PhD; Indian politician, poet and writer; b. 29 Nov. 1919, Serai Niamat Khan, NW Frontier Prov.; s. of Atma Singh and Nanaki Devi; m. 1950; one d.; nominated MP 1962–68; Amb. to Bulgaria and Caribbean countries 1970–76; Chair. High Power Comm. of Minorities, Scheduled Castes, Scheduled Tribes and other Weaker Sections 1980–84; Gov. Goa, Daman and Diu 1984, of Nagaland 1989; has lectured at univs in UK, USA, Thailand, Egypt, Iran and India; fmr Sec.-Gen. Indian Council for Africa; Chair. Presidium, World Punjabi Congress; many awards and decorations. *Publications:* first free-verse English trans. of the Sikh Scripture, five books of Punjabi verse, A History of the Sikh People 1469–1978, The Religion of the Sikhs, A History of Punjabi Literature; The Unstruck Melody (poems), The Man Who Never Died (poems), collection of short stories, children's books, an English-Punjabi lexicon, several biogs and books of literary criticism. *Leisure interests:* reading, walking.

SINGH, Harpal, BA, BS, MPA; Indian business executive; *Chairman, Ranbaxy Laboratories Limited;* ed The Doon School, St Stephen's Coll., New Delhi, CSCH, Calif., USA; has held sr positions in Tata Admin. Service, Hindustan Motors, Telco, and Bd-level responsibility at Shaw Wallace; Sr Advisor (Corp. Projects), Mahindra and Mahindra; Chair. Fortis Healthcare Ltd, Fortis Financial Services Ltd, Fortis Securities Ltd; Chair. (non-exec.) Ranbaxy Labs Ltd 2007–. *Address:* Ranbaxy Laboratories Ltd, Corporate Office, Plot 90, Sector 32, Gurgaon 122001, Haryana, India (office). *Telephone:* (124) 4135000 (office). *Fax:* (124) 4135001 (office). *E-mail:* seema.ahuja@ranbaxy.com (office). *Website:* www.ranbaxy.com (office).

SINGH, Harsha Vardhana, MEcon, MPhil, PhD; Indian economist and international organization executive; *Deputy Director-General, World Trade Organization;* b. 30 Aug. 1956, Delhi; m. Veena Jha; two c.; ed Delhi Univ., Univ. of Oxford, UK (Rhodes Scholar); worked as consultant with Bureau of Industrial Costs and Prices, New Delhi and with ILO and UNCTAD, Geneva; worked in GATT/WTO Secr. in various capacities, including Econ. Research and Analysis Unit 1985–89, Trade Policy Review Div. 1989–91, Rules Div. 1991–95, Trade and Environment and Tech. Barriers to Trade Div. 1995–96, Office of WTO Dir-Gen. 1996–97, served as Chair. of dispute settlement panels, Deputy Dir-Gen. WTO 2005–; Econ. Advisor, Telecom Regulatory Authority of India (TRAI) 1997–2001, Sec. cum Prin. Advisor and Head of TRAI Secr. 2001–05; fmr mem. various trade advisory cttees of Indian Govt; mem. Visiting Faculty, TERI School of Advanced Studies for their Masters programme in Regulatory Studies; Hon. Prof., Indian Council for Research on Int. Econ. Relations. *Publications:* several papers on trade policy and regulatory issues. *Address:* World Trade Organization, Centre William Rappard, rue de Lausanne 154, 1211 Geneva 21, Switzerland (office). *Telephone:* (22) 739-51-11 (office). *Fax:* (22) 731-42-06 (office). *E-mail:* enquiries@wto.org (office). *Website:* www.wto.org (office).

SINGH, Jaswant, BA, BSc; Indian politician and army officer; b. 3 Jan. 1938, Jasol, Rajasthan; s. of the late Thakur Sardar Singhji and of Kunwar Baisa; m. Sheetal Kumari 1963; two s.; ed Mayo Coll., Ajmer, Jt Services Wing, Clement Town, Dehradun, Indian Mil. Acad., Dehradun; commissioned Cen. India Horse 1957; resgnd his comm. and elected to Rajya Sabha 1980; Minister of Finance and Company Affairs 1996, 2002–04; Deputy Chair., Planning Comm. 1998–99; Minister of External Affairs 1999, 2001–02, of Electronics Feb.–Oct. 1999, of Surface Transport Aug.–Oct. 1999; Chair. Consultative Cttee for the Ministry of External Affairs 2000–01; Leader of the House, Rajya Sabha 1999–2004, Leader of the Opposition 2004. *Publications:* National Security – An Outline of Our Concerns 1996, Shauryo Tejo 1997, Defending India 1999, District Diary 2001, Khankhananama (Hindi) 2001; numerous articles on int. affairs, security and devt issues to Indian and foreign magazines, newspapers and journals. *Leisure interests:* horses, equestrian sports, reading, music, golf, chess. *Address:* c/o Ministry of Finance, North Block, New Delhi 110 001, India.

SINGH, Gen. Joginder Jaswant, PVSM, AVSM, VSM, ADC; Indian army officer; b. 17 Sept. 1945, Bahawalpur (now in Pakistan); m. Anupama Singh; one s. one d.; ed Nat. Defence Acad.; joined Ninth Maratha Light Infantry (LI) 1964, served in Jammu and Kashmir, Nagaland, Arunachal Pradesh, Uttaranchal Pradesh, Col, Fifth Maratha LI, Defence Attaché to Algeria 1987–1990, Commdr 79th (Ind.) Mountain Brigade, Baramula Sector, Jammu and Kashmir 1991–92, Deputy Dir-Gen. Operational Logistics, Army HQ 1993, Commdr Ninth Infantry Div. 1996–98, Additional Dir-Gen. Mil. Operations, Mil. Operations Directorate, Army Headquarters 1998, Commdr One 'Strike' Corps, Mathura, Gen. Officer Commanding-in-Chief, Army Training Command 2003, Western Command 2004, Chief of Army Staff 2005–07, fmr Chair. Jt Chiefs of Staff Cttee; Vishisht Seva Medal, War Wound Medal, Chief of Army Staff's Commendation, Param Vishisht Seva Medal 2004. *Leisure interests:* basketball, squash, golf, mountaineering. *Address:* c/o Office of the Chief of Army Staff, Army Headquarters, Sena Bhawan, DHQ PO, New Delhi 110 011, India.

SINGH, K. Natwar, BA; Indian diplomatist, politician and writer; b. 6 May 1931; s. of Shri Govind Singhji and Shrimati Prayag Kaur; m. Shrimati Heminder Kumari 1967; one s.; ed Univ. of Delhi, Univ. of Cambridge, UK, Peking Univ., People's Repub. of China; joined Foreign Service 1953; served in Peking 1956–58; Perm. Mission to UN 1961–66; mem. Bd UNICEF 1962–66, rapporteur 1963–65; mem. Prime Minister's Secr. 1966–71; Amb. to Poland 1971–73; Deputy High Commr to UK 1973–77; High Commr to Zambia 1977–80; Amb. to Pakistan 1980–82; mem. Lok Sabha 1984–89; Union Minister of State Dept of Steel, Dept of Fertilizers 1985–86; with Ministry of External Affairs 1986–89; mem. Cttee on External Affairs, on Public Accounts 1998–99; elected to Rajya Sabha 2002; mem. Cttee on External Affairs 2002–04; Minister of External Affairs 2004–05, Minister without Portfolio 2005 (resgnd); mem. Bd Dirs Air India 1982–84; Pres. UN Conf. on Disarmament and Devt, New York 1987; Padma Bhushan 1984, E. M. Forster's Literary Award 1989. *Publications:* E. M. Forster: A Tribute 1964, The Legacy of Nehru 1965, Tales from Modern India 1966, Stories from India 1971, Maharaja Suraj Mal: 1707–63 1981, Curtain Raisers 1984, Profiles and Letters 1997, The Magnificent Maharaja Bhupinder Singh of Patiala: 1891–1938 1997, Heart to Heart 2003; contribs to numerous newspapers and journals. *Address:* 'Govind Niwas', Bharatpur, Rajasthan, 321001, India (home). *Telephone:* (11) 23013855 (home). *Fax:* (11) 23793704 (home).

SINGH, Karan, MA, PhD; Indian politician; b. 9 March 1931, Cannes, France; s. of Lt-Gen. HH Maharaja Sir Hari Singh, GCSI, GCIE, GCVO and Maharani Tara Devi, CI; m. Princess Yasho Rajya Lakshmi of Nepal 1950; two s. one d.; ed Doon School, Univ. of Jammu and Kashmir and Delhi Univ.; appointed Regent of Jammu and Kashmir 1949; elected Sadar-i-Riyasat (Head of State) by Jammu and Kashmir Legis. Ass. Nov. 1952, recognized by Pres. of India and assumed office 17 Nov. 1952, re-elected 1957 and 1962, Gov. 1965–67; Union Minister for Tourism and Civil Aviation 1967–73, for Health and Family Planning 1973–75, 1976–77, for Educ. 1979–80; re-elected mem. of Parl. 1977, 1980; Amb. to USA 1989–91; mem. Rajya Sabha Upper House of Parl. 2005–, Deputy Leader Congress Parl. Party, Chair. Ethics Cttee; Vice-Pres. Indian Council for Cultural Relations; Pres. Delhi Music Soc.; led Indian Del. to World Population Conf., Bucharest; Vice-Pres. World Health Ass. 1975–76; fmr Chancellor Jammu and Kashmir Univ., Banaras Hindu Univ.; currently Chancellor Jawaharlal Nehru Univ.; Chair. Auroville Foundation; Vice-Chair. Jawaharlal Nehru Memorial Fund; fmr Chair. Indian Bd for Wild Life, Life Trustee of the India Int. Centre; Hon. Maj.-Gen. Indian Army; Hon. Col Jammu and Kashmir Regt 1962; Padma Vibhushan 2005; Dr hc (Aligarh Muslim Univ.) 1963, (Banaras Hindu Univ., Soka Univ., Tokyo). *Publications include:* Varied Rhythms (essays and poems) 1960, Shadow and Sunlight (folk songs) 1962, Prophet of Indian Nationalism: The Political Thought of Sri Aurobindo Ghosh 1893–1910 1963, Welcome the Moonrise (poems) 1965, Population, Poverty and the Future of India 1975, In Defence of Religion 1978, Religions of India 1983, One Man's World 1986, Bridge to Immortality 1987, Humanity at the Crossroads 1988, Autobiography 1989, Essays on Hinduism 1990, Brief Sojourn 1991, Hymn to Shiva and Other Poems 1991, The Mountain of Shiva (novel) 1994, India and the World 1995, Hinduism: the Eternal Religion 1999, The Earth has No Corners 2001; and several books on political science, philosophical essays, travelogues, trans. of Dogra-Pahari folksongs and poems in English. *Leisure interests:* reading, writing, music. *Address:* 3 Nyaya Marg, Chanakyapuri, New Delhi 110021, India. *Telephone:* (11) 6115291; (11) 6111744. *Fax:* (11) 6873171. *E-mail:* karansingh@karansingh.com (home). *Website:* www.karansingh.com (home).

SINGH, Khushwant, LLB; Indian author; b. Feb. 1915; m. Kaval Malik; one s. one d.; ed Government Coll., Lahore, King's Coll. and Inner Temple, London, UK; practised at High Court, Lahore 1939–47; joined Indian Ministry of External Affairs 1947; press attaché, Canada then Public Relations Officer, London 1948–51; Ministry of Information and Broadcasting; edited Yojana; Dept of Mass Communication, UNESCO 1954–56; commissioned by Rockefeller Foundation and Muslim Univ., Aligarh, to write a history of the Sikhs 1958; MP 1980–; Ed.-in-Chief The Hindustan Times, New Delhi 1980–83; Visiting Lecturer Hawaii, Oxford, Princeton, Rochester, Swarthmore; numerous TV and radio appearances; Ed. The Illustrated Weekly of India 1969–78; Grove Press Award; Mohan Singh Award; Padma Bhushan 1974, Punjab Rattan Award 2006, Padma Vibhushan 2007. *Publications:* Mark of Vishnu 1949, The Sikhs 1951, Train to Pakistan 1954, Sacred Writings of the Sikhs 1960, I Shall Not Hear the Nightingale 1961, Umrao Jan Ada—Courtesan of Lucknow (trans.) 1961, History of the Sikhs (1769–1839) Vol. I 1962, Ranjit Singh: Maharaja of the Punjab 1962, Fall of the Sikh Kingdom 1962, The Skeleton (trans.) 1963, Land of the Five Rivers (trans.) 1964, History of the Sikhs (1839–Present Day) Vol. II 1965, Khushwant Singh's India 1969, Indira Gandhi Returns 1979, Editor's Page 1980, Iqbal's Dialogue with Allah (trans.) 1981, Punjab Tragedy (with Kuldip Nayar) 1984, Delhi 1990, Roots of Dissent 1992, Train to Pakistan 1998, and others. *Leisure interest:* bird watching. *Address:* 49E Sujan Singh Park, New Delhi 110003, India (home). *Telephone:* (11) 4620159.

SINGH, Lalji, MSc, PhD; Indian molecular biologist and academic; *Director, Centre for Cellular and Molecular Biology;* b. 5 July 1947, Jaunpur Dist, Uttar Predesh; ed Banaras Hindu Univ.; Research Assoc. Dept of Zoology Banaras Hindu Univ. 1970–72; Commonwealth Fellowship to carry out research Univ. of Edinburgh 1974–76, Research Assoc. 1977–79, 1979–87; sr scientist Centre for Cellular and Molecular Biology 1987–, Dir 1998–; Officer on Special Duty f. Centre for DNA Fingerprinting and Diagnostics 1995; mem. Scientific Advisory Cttee Inst. of Cytology & Preventive Oncology, New Delhi, Nat. Inst. of Virology, New Delhi, Inst. of Immunohaemotology, Mumbai; Fellow Nat. Acad. of Sciences, Nat. Science Acad.; mem. Soc. of Cell Biology, Soc. of Biological Chemists of India, Soc. of Human Genetics; Hon. Prof. (Hyderabad) 1998; Dr S.P. Basu Memorial Medal Calcutta Zoological Soc. 1973, Nat. Science Acad. Medal for Young Scientists 1974, Council of Scientific and Industrial Research Technology Award 1992, Jagdish Chandra Bose Award for research in Life Sciences Hari Om Ashram Trust, Delhi 1995, VASVIK Research Award 1995, Prof. Vishwanath Memorial Lecture Award Nat. Science Acad., New Delhi 1995, Sri Om Prakash Bhasin Award for Science & Technology 1996, Padmabhushan Dr P. S. Siva Reddy Endowment Award 1997, Joy Govind Law Memorial Medal The Asiatic Soc., Kolkata 1997, Scroll of Honour – Outstanding Forensic Expert Award 1998, Padma Shri 2004. *Publications:* more than 80 research papers in nat. and inter nat. journals. *Address:* Centre for Cellular and Molecular Biology, Uppal Road, Hyderabad 500 007, India (office). *Telephone:* (40) 27160222 (office). *Fax:* (40) 27160591 (office). *E-mail:* lalji@ccmb.res.in (office). *Website:* www.ccmb.res.in (office).

SINGH, Manmohan, BA, MA, DPhil; Indian economist and politician; *Prime Minister and Minister-in-charge of Personnel, Public Grievances and Pensions, of Planning, of Atomic Energy, of Space, of Coal, of the Environment and Forests and of Finance;* b. 26 Sept. 1932, Gah, Punjab (now Pakistan); s. of Gurumukh Singh and Amrit Kaur; m. Smt. Gursharan Kaur 1958; three d.; ed Panjab Univ., Chandigarh, Univs of Cambridge and Oxford, UK; Sr Lecturer in Econs, Panjab Univ. 1957–59, Reader in Econs 1959–63, Prof. of Econs 1963–65; Econ. Affairs Officer, UNCTAD, UN Secr., New York, USA 1966, Chief, Financing for Trade Section 1966–69; Prof. of Int. Trade, Delhi School of Econs, Delhi Univ. 1969–71; Econ. Adviser, Ministry of Foreign Trade 1971–72; Chief Econ. Adviser, Ministry of Finance 1972–76; Dir Reserve Bank of India 1976–80, Gov. 1982–85; mem. Econ. Advisory Council to the Prime Minister 1983–84; Mem.-Sec. Planning Comm. 1980–82, Deputy Chair. 1985–87; Sec.-Gen., Commr South Comm. 1987–90; econ. adviser to Prime Minister 1990–91; Chair. Univ. Grants Comm. March–June 1991; Minister of Finance 1991–95, Gov. of India on Bd of Govs of IMF and IBRD (World Bank) 1991–95; mem. Rajya Sabha (Parl.) 1991–, Chair. Parl. Standing Cttee on Commerce 1996–97, Leader of Opposition 1998–2004; Prime Minister of India and Minister-in-charge of Personnel, Public Grievances and Pensions, of Planning, of Atomic Energy, of Space 2004–, also Minister of External Affairs 2005–06, Minister of Coal and of the Environment and Forests 2007–, Minister of Finance 2008–; Chair. India Cttee of Indo-Japan Jt Study Cttee 1980–83; Pres. Indian Econ. Asscn 1985; apptd by UN Sec.-Gen. mem. Group of Eminent Persons to advise him on Financing for Devt 2000; Leader of Indian del. to Aid India Consortium Meetings 1977–79, to Indo-Soviet Monitoring Group Meeting 1982, to Indo-Soviet Jt Planning Group Meeting 1980–82, to Commonwealth Heads of Govt Meeting, Cyprus 1993, to Human Rights World Conf., Vienna 1993, and mem. numerous other dels; Distinguished Fellow, LSE Centre for Asia Economy, Politics and Society 1994; Fellow, Nat. Acad. of Agricultural Sciences, New Delhi 1999; Hon. Prof., Jawaharlal Nehru Univ., New Delhi 1976, Delhi School of Econs, Univ. of Delhi 1996; Hon. Fellow, Indian Inst. of Bankers 1982, St John's Coll., Cambridge 1982, All India Man. Asscn 1994, Nuffield Coll., Oxford 1994; Padma Vibhushan Award, Pres. of India 1987; Hon. DLitt (Panjab Univ., Chandigarh, Guru Nanak Univ., Amritsar, Delhi Univ., Sri Venkateswara Univ., Tirupathi, Univ. of Bologna, Italy, Univ. of Mysore, Chaudhary charan Singh Haryana, Kurukshetra Univ., Nagarjuna Univ., Nagarjunanagar, Osmania Univ., Hyderabad, Dr Bhimrao Ambedkar Univ. (fmrly Agra Univ.), Pt Ravishankar Shukla Univ., Raipur); Hon. DScS (Univ. of Roorkee); Hon. LLD (Univ. of Alberta, Edmonton); Hon. DSc (Agricultural Univ., Hisar, Thapar Inst. of Eng and Tech., Patiala, Indian School of Mines, Dhanbad (Deemed Univ.)); Dr hc (Univ. of Cambridge) 2006; Univ. Medal, Panjab Univ. 1952, Uttar Chand Kapur Medal, Panjab Univ. 1954, Wright's Prize for distinguished performance, St John's Coll., Cambridge 1955, Adam Smith Prize, Univ. of Cambridge 1956, Wrenbury Scholar, Univ. of Cambridge 1957, Nat. Fellow, Nat. Inst. of Educ. (NCERT) 1986, Finance Minister of the Year, Asiamoney Awards 1993, 1994, Finance Minister of the Year, Euromoney Awards 1993, Jawaharlal Nehru Birth Centenary Award, Indian Science Congress Asscn for 1994–95 1995, Nikkei Asia Prize for Regional Growth, Nihon Keizai Shimbun Inc. (NIKKEI) 1997, Justice K.S. Hegde Foundation Award for the Year 1996 1997, Lokmanya Tilak Award, Tilak Smarak Trust, Pune 1997, H.H. Kanchi Sri Paramacharya Award for Excellence from Shri R. Venkataraman (fmr Pres. of India) 1999, Annasaheb Chirmule Award, W.L.G. alias Annasaheb Chirmule Trust 2000. *Publication:* India's Export Trends and Prospects for Self-Sustained Growth 1964; numerous articles in econ. journals. *Address:* Prime Minister's Office, South Block, Raisina Hill, New Delhi 110 011 (office); 7 Safdarjung Lane, New Delhi 110011, India. *Telephone:* (11) 23012312 (office); (11) 3018668. *Fax:* (11) 23019545 (office). *E-mail:* manmohan@sansad.nic.in (home). *Website:* www.pmindia.nic.in (office).

SINGH, Rajnath, MSc; Indian politician and farmer; *President, Bharatiya Janata Party;* b. 10 July 1951, Bhabhora village, Tehsil Chakia of Varanasi dist, UP; s. of the late Ram Badan Singh and Gujarati Devi; m. Savitri Singh; two s. one d.; ed Gorakhpur Univ.; Lecturer in Physics, K.B. Postgraduate Coll., Mirzapur, UP; served in various capacities with Rashtriya Swayamsevak Sangh (Nat. Volunteers' Union—Hindu nationalist org.) since 1964; Org. Sec. Akhil Bharthiya Vidyarthi Parishad (Gorakhpur Div.) 1969–71; apptd Sec. Bharatiya Jana Sangh's Mirzapur Unit 1974; joined JP Movt and was apptd its Dist Convenor; apptd Dist Pres. Jana Sangh 1975; jailed during Emergency 1975, remained in jail until elections 1977; elected as mem. Legis. Ass. from Mirzapur constituency 1977; held several positions in Bharatiya Janata Yuva Morcha (BJYM), UP State Unit as well as in Nat. Exec., BJP Sec. in UP 1983–84, State Pres. BJYM 1984–86, Nat. Gen. Sec. BJYM 1986–88, Nat. Pres. BJYM 1988, Vice-Pres. BJP, UP 1990, Pres. 1997–99, mem. Nat. Exec. BJP, Gen. Sec. Cen. BJP org. 2002–05, Pres. BJP 2005–; mem. UP Legis. Council 1988–94; Minister of Educ. 1991–94; elected to Rajya Sabha 1994, mem. Advisory Cttee on Industry 1994–96, Consultative Cttee for Ministry of Agric., Business Advisory Cttee, House Cttee, Cttee on Human Resource Devt, Chief Whip of BJP in Rajya Sabha; Union Minister for Surface Transport 1999–2000; Chief Minister of UP 2000–02; Union Minister of Agric. 2002. *Publication:* book on the causes of and solutions to unemployment problems. *Leisure interests:* reading books on history, culture and science and tech. *Address:* BJP Central Office, 11 Ashoka Road, New Delhi 110 001, India (office). *Telephone:* (11) 23382234 (office). *Fax:* (11) 23782163 (office). *E-mail:* bjpco@vsnl.com (office). *Website:* www.bjp.org (office).

SINGH, Raman, BSc, BAMS; Indian medical practitioner and politician; *Chief Minister of Chhattisgarh;* b. 15 Oct. 1952, Thathapur, Kawardha Dist; s. of Vighnaharan Singh; m. Smt. Beena Singh; one s. one d.; ed Univ. of Ravishankar, Raipur; Ayurvedic medical practitioner; MLA 1990–92, 1993–98; mem. Bharatiya Janata Party (BJP) (Pradesh Mantri) 1996–; Pres. BJP Legislature Party 2003–; mem. Lok Lekha Samitti Public Accounts Samitti, Legis. Cttee; mem. Lok Sabha for Rajnandgaon 1990–, later BJP Chief Whip; Union Minister of State for Commerce and Industry 1999–2003; Chief Minister of Chhattisgarh 2003–. *Leisure interests:* sports, tourism, public welfare. *Address:* Government of Chhattisgarh, Mantralaya, Raipur 492 001, Chhattisgarh, India (office). *Telephone:* (771) 2221000 (office). *E-mail:* cmcg@nic.in (office). *Website:* chhattisgarh.nic.in (office).

SINGH, Shilendra Kumar, BA, LLB, MA; Indian diplomatist, government official and academic; *Governor of Rajasthan;* b. 24 Jan. 1932; m. Manju Singh; two s.; ed St John's Coll., Agra, Agra Univ., Trinity Coll., Cambridge, UK; joined Indian Foreign Service 1954, Third Sec. in Tehran and concurrently attended Tehran Univ. to study Persian 1956–59, assigned to various desks in Foreign Office, Delhi 1959–64, mem. Perm. Mission to UN, New York 1962–68; Dir Foreign Trade, Ministry of Commerce 1968–69; Official Spokesman of Govt of India 1969–74; Amb. to Jordan (also accred to Lebanon and Cyprus) 1974–77, to Afghanistan 1977–79; Additional Foreign Sec. 1979–82; Amb. to Austria 1982–85, to Pakistan 1985–89; Foreign Sec. of India 1989–95; monitored gen. elections for Commonwealth and UN in SA, Kenya, Algeria, Lesotho, Malawi and Sierra Leone and presidential election in Sri Lanka; mem. 19 Indian dels to UN Gen. Ass., ECOSOC and Human Rights Comm.; fmr Pres. G77; also served as India's Gov. on Bd of Govs IAEA, Vienna; taught History at Agra Univ.; fmr Visiting Prof. and mem. Academic Council Jawaharlal Nehru Univ., Delhi; holds personal rank of Grade-1 Amb.; Sec.-Gen. Univ. of Pennsylvania Inst. for the Advanced Study of India, Delhi 1995–2004; Gov. of Arunachal Pradesh 2004– 07, of Rajasthan 2007–; trustee and mem. bd of dirs of numerous cultural, academic and corp. orgs. *Publications:* has contributed articles to many journals and newspapers in India and abroad on int. relations, geopolitics and current developments.

Address: Raj Bhawan, Civil Lines, Jaipur, Rajasthan, India (office). *Telephone:* (141) 2228716 (office); (141) 2228732. *E-mail:* webmaster@rajasthan.gov.in (office). *Website:* www.rajasthan.gov.in/governor.sthm (office).

SINGH, Sukhmander, MS, PhD; American civil engineer and academic; *Wilmot J. Nicholson Professor, Department of Civil Engineering, Santa Clara University;* b. 15 Sept. 1939, Lambi; s. of Mahla Singh and Jangir Kaur; m. Charanjit Kaur 1967; one s. one d.; ed Punjabi Univ., Patiala, Punjab, Indian Inst. of Tech., Delhi, Univ. of Ottawa and Carleton Univ., Ottawa, Canada, Rice Univ., Houston, Tex. and Univ. of Calif., Berkeley, USA; Assoc. Lecturer, Indian Inst. of Tech., Delhi, India 1966–67; Teaching Asst, Univ. of Ottawa 1967–68; Visiting Lecturer, Univ. of Alaska, Anchorage 1975, San Jose State Univ., Calif. 1978; Assoc. Prof. of Civil Eng, Calif. State Univ., LA 1983–86; Assoc. Prof. of Civil Eng, Santa Clara Univ., Calif. 1986–90, Wilmot J. Nicholson Professor, Chair. Dept of Civil Eng and Chair. Eng Mechanics 1990–; professional work as engineer with John V. Lowney & Assocs, Palo Alto, Calif. 1969, Dames & Moore, San Francisco, London, Houston, Anchorage and Seattle offices 1969–83, as Consultant 1983–; Consultant with Purcell, Rhoades and Assocs, Hayward, Calif. 1987–, with Calpine/Kaiser 1989–; mem. numerous cttees on soil dynamics and geotechnical eng; research on liquefaction of silts and geotechnology of cold regions. *Publications:* numerous scientific papers. *Leisure interests:* reading, hiking, volleyball playing. *Address:* Department of Civil Engineering, EC 238, Santa Clara University, Santa Clara, CA 95053, USA. *Telephone:* (408) 554-6869 (office). *Fax:* (408) 554-5474 (office). *E-mail:* ssingh@scu.edu (office). *Website:* www.scu.edu/engineering/ce/people/singh.cfm (office).

SINGH, Vijay; Fijian professional golfer; b. 22 Feb. 1963, Lautoka; m. Ardena Seth; one c.; ed Univ. of N Carolina; turned professional 1982, joined PGA Tour 1983; PGA Tour victories: Buick Classic 1993, 1995, 2004, Phoenix Open 1993, Memorial Tournament 1997, Buick Open 1997, 2004, PGA Championship 1998, 2004, Sprint Int. 1998, 2004, Honda Classic 1999, Masters Tournament 2000, Shell Houston Open 2002, Phoenix Open 2003, Byron Nelson Championship 2003, John Deere Classic 2003, 2004, FUNAI Classic 2003, Pebble Beach Nat. Pro-Am 2004, New Orleans Classic 2004, Deutsche Bank Championship 2004, Canadian Open 2004, 84 Lumber Classic 2004, Chrysler Championship 2004, Sony Open 2005; int. victories: Malaysian PGA Championship 1984, Nigerian Open 1988, Swedish PGA 1988, Volvo Open di Firenze 1989, Ivory Coast Open 1989, Nigerian Open 1989, Zimbabwe Open 1989, El Bosque Open 1990, King Hassan Trophy, Morocco 1991, Turespaña Masters Open de Andalucía 1992, Malaysian Open 1992, Volvo German Open 1992, Bells Cup 1993, Scandinavian Masters 1994, Trophée Lancôme 1994, Passport Open 1995, South African Open 1997, Toyota World Match Play Championship 1997, Johnnie Walker Taiwan Open 2000, Singapore Masters 2001, Malaysian Open 2001; ranked number one in world; first player to win US$10 million in one year 2004; PGA Arnold Palmer Award 2003, PGA Tour Player of the Year 2004. *Leisure interests:* snooker, cricket, rugby, soccer, James Bond movies. *Address:* c/o International Management Group (IMG), 420 West 45th Street, New York, NY 10036, USA (office). *Telephone:* (212) 541-5640 (office). *Fax:* (212) 265-5483 (office). *Website:* www.imgworld.com (office).

SINGH, Virbhadra, BA, MA; Indian agriculturist, horticulturist and politician; b. 23 June 1934, Sarahan, Shimla Dist; s. of Sir Padam Singh; m.; ed St Stephen's Coll. Delhi; mem. Indian del. to Gen. Ass. of UN, New York 1976; elected to Lok Sabha 1962, 1967, 1972, 1980, Deputy Minister of Tourism and Civil Aviation 1976–77, Minister of State for Industries 1982–83; mem. Himachal Pradesh Legis. Ass. 1983–, Leader of Opposition 1998–2003, Chief Minister of Himachal Pradesh 1983–1990, 1993–98, 2003–07 (resgnd); Pres. State Congress Cttee 1992–94; Hon. Capt., Indian Army. *Leisure interests:* reading, meeting people. *Address:* c/o Office of the Chief Minister, H.P. Vidhan Sabha, Council Chamber, Shimla, Himachal Pradesh. *Telephone:* (177) 2625400. *Fax:* (177) 2625011. *E-mail:* cm@hp.nic.in (office).

SINGLETON, William Dean; American newspaper executive; *Vice-Chairman and CEO, MediaNews Group Inc.;* b. 1 Aug. 1951, Tex.; s. of the late William Hyde Singleton and of Florence E. Myrick Singleton; m. Adrienne Casale 1983; two s. one d.; Pres. Gloucester Co. Times, N J.; Vice-Chair. and CEO MediaNews Group, Inc. 1988–; Pres., Chair. The Houston Post 1988–95, The Denver Post; Vice-Chair. 27 daily newspapers and 55 non-daily publications including Houston Post, Denver Post, with daily circulation in excess of 1.1 million in 10 states. *Leisure interest:* skiing. *Address:* MediaNews Group Inc., 101 W. Colfax Avenue, Suite 1100, Denver, CO 80202, USA (office). *Telephone:* (303) 563-6360 (office). *Fax:* (303) 954-6320 (office). *E-mail:* contact@medianewsgroup.com (office). *Website:* www.medianewsgroup.com (office).

SINGSON, Gabriel C., LLM; Philippine lawyer, banker and business executive; *Director and Senior Adviser, JG Summit Holdings Inc.;* b. 18 March 1929, Lingayen, Pangasinan; m. Moonyeen Retizos; two s. one d.; ed Pangasinan Prov. High School, Ateneo de Manila and Univ. of Michigan Law School, Ann Arbor; Assoc. Attorney, Law Office of Justice Jose Bengzon 1952–55; Prof. of Commercial Law and Civil Law, Ateneo de Manila Law School 1956–72; Legal and Evaluation Officer, Cen. Bank 1955–60, Tech. Asst Monetary Bd 1960–62, Asst to Deputy Gov. 1963–66, 1968–70; Legal Officer, Asian Devt Bank 1967–68; Asst to Gov. (with rank of Dir), Cen. Bank 1970–73, Special Asst to Gov. 1973–74, Gen. Counsel 1974–75, Deputy Gov. and Gen. Counsel 1975–80, Sr Deputy Gov. 1980–92; Pres. Philippine Nat. Bank 1992–93; Chair. Monetary Bd and Gov. Bangko Sentral ng Pilipinas 1993–98; Chair. PR Holdings Inc. (holding co. of Philippine Airlines); Vice-Chair., then Chair. Philippine Airlines; Chair. Great Pacific Life Insurance; Dir and Sr Adviser JG Summit Holdings Inc. 1999–, Chair. and Pres. JG Summit Capital Markets Corpn; mem. Bd of Dirs United Industrial Corpn 1999–, Multinational Finance Group Ltd., Summit Forex Brokers Corpn, Summit Point Corpn; mem. Advisory Bd Consultative Constitutional Comm.; Trustee Gokongwei Brothers Foundation Inc., Tan Yan Kee Foundation. *Publications:* articles on Asian Devt Bank, foreign loans, foreign investments and foreign exchange regulations. *Leisure interest:* golf. *Address:* JG Summit Holdings Inc., 42/F Robinsons Equitable Tower, ADB Avenue, cor. Poveda Road, Ortigas Center, Pasig City (office); 28 Polk Street, Greenhills, San Juan, Metro Manila, Philippines (home). *Website:* www.jgsummit.com.ph (office).

SINHA, Ashok, BEng, MBA; Indian petroleum industry executive; *Chairman and Managing Director, Bharat Petroleum Corporation Ltd;* ed Kanpur Tech. Inst., Indian Inst. of Man., Bangalore; joined Bharat Petroleum Corpn 1977, Finance Dir 1996–2005, Chair. and Man. Dir 2005–; mem. Bd of Dirs Kochi Refineries, Numaligarh Refinery, Petronet LNG, Bharat Shell; Econ. Intelligence Unit/American Express India CFO Award 2001. *Address:* Bharat Petroleum Corpn Ltd, 4–6 Currimbhoy Road, Mumbai 400001, India (office). *Telephone:* (22) 2271-3000 (office). *E-mail:* info@bharatpetroleum.com (office). *Website:* www.bharatpetroleum.com (office).

SINHA, Lt-Gen. (retd) Shreenivas Kumar, BA; Indian army officer; b. 7 Jan. 1926, Gaya; s. of M. K. Sinha and Radha Sinha; m. Premini Sinha; one s. three d.; ed Patna Univ, Officers Training School, Belgaum; commissioned 1944, saw combat service during Second World War in Burma and Indonesia and after Independence in Kashmir, served two tenures in Nagaland and Manipur taking part in counter-insurgency operations, transferred to 5 Gorkha Rifles after Independence, fmr Col of Regt (5GR); fmr instructor, Infantry School, Mhow and Defence Services Staff Coll., Wellington; fmr Dir of Mil. Intelligence and Deputy Adjutant-Gen.; fmr Adjutant-Gen., Army HQ; Sec. Del. to UN Comm. for India and Pakistan for Kashmir 1949; Leader Del. UN Conf. on Application of Human Rights to Warfare 1972; Gen. Officer C-in-C, W Command 1981–82; Vice-Chief of Army Staff 1983 (retd); Amb. to Nepal 1990; Gov. of Assam 1997–2003, of Jammu and Kashmir 2003–08; Hon. ADC to Pres. of India 1979; fmr Pres. Gorkha Brigade; Param Vishist Sewa Medal 1973. *Publications:* books: Operation Rescue (on the Jammu and Kashmir operation of 1947–48), A Soldier Recalls (autobiog.), Of Matters Military, Pataliputra, Past to Present, Veer Kuer Singh; 300 articles in nat. newspapers. *Leisure interest:* golf. *Address:* c/o Raj Bhawan, Guwahati, India (office).

SINHA, Yashwant, MA; Indian politician, teacher and civil servant; b. 6 Nov. 1937, Patna, Bihar; m. Nilima Sinha 1961; two s. one d.; ed Patna Coll., Patna Univ. Bihar; Lecturer in Political Science, Patna Univ. 1958–60; joined IAS 1960; Deputy Comm. Santhal Paraganas; Chair. Drafting Cttee of the UNCTAD Conf. on Shipping, Geneva; Consul-Gen. of India, Frankfurt; Prin. Sec. to Chief Minister, Bihar; Jt Sec. to Govt of India, Ministry of Shipping and Transport; retd from IAS and joined Janata Party 1984, Gen. Sec. 1986–88; mem. Rajya Sabha 1988, mem. Cttee on Petitions 1989; joined Janata Dal (Samajwadi) after split in Janata Dal 1990; Minister of Finance 1998–99, 2001–02, of External Affairs 2002–04; mem. Lok Sabha 1998–; mem. Parl. Pay Cttee 1998–99. *Leisure interests:* reading, travelling, listening to music, watching films. *Address:* Jasol House, Paotabarea, Jodhpur (home); Vill. Hupad, Post-Morangi, Demotandh, Thana Muffassil, Hazaribagh (Bihar), India (home). *Telephone:* (11) 23012380.

SINIORA, Fouad, MBA; Lebanese banking executive and government official; *Prime Minister;* b. 19 July 1943, Sidon; m.; three c.; ed Nat. Evangelical Inst., American Univ. of Beirut; various positions at First Nat. City Bank, including clerk 1967, Head Credit Dept 1970–71, Credit Account Officer, Marketing Officer, mem. Credit Cttee 1970–72; lecturer Lebanese Univ., American Univ. Beirut 1971–77; concurrently several positions at Finance Bank including Man. Industry and Tourism loans, mem. Credit Cttee, Sec. Bd of Dirs 1972–75; Financial Adviser Intra Investment 1975–77; Asst Gen. Man. Middle East Cement Co. 1975–77; Banking Control Commr Central Bank 1977–82; Dir, Arab Universal Insurance 1982–92; exec. positions at several cos including Al Mal, IRAD, Méditerranée Investors Group, Méditerranée Group Sevices, Banque de la Méditerranée, Saudi Lebanese Bank 1982–92; Minister of State for Financial Affairs, Acting Minister of Finance 1992–98; Minister of Finance –2004; Prime Minister 2005–. *Address:* c/o Office of the President of the Council of Ministers, Grand Sérail, place Riad es-Solh, Beirut, Lebanon (office).

SINISCALCO, Domenico, LLB, PhD; Italian economist, business executive, writer and fmr government official; *Managing Director and Vice-Chairman, Morgan Stanley International;* b. 15 July 1954, Turin; m.; two c.; ed Univ. of Turin, Univ. of Cambridge, UK; Prof. of Econs, Univ. of Turin 1990–2006 (on leave of absence); Dir-Gen. Treasury, Rome Oct. 2001–04, Minister of Economy and Finance 2004–05; Man. Dir and Vice Chair. Morgan Stanley International, London 2006–; fmr teaching posts at LUISS, Rome, Univ. of Cagliari, Johns Hopkins Univ., USA, Univ. of Cambridge, UK, Univ. Catholique de Louvain, Belgium; Chair. Collegio Carlo Alberto, Turin 2006–; mem. Steering Cttee journals Equilibri, Mercato, Concorrenza and Regole; mem. Royal Swedish Acad. of Sciences, Beijer Inst. *Publications include:* New Directions in Economic Theory of the Environment (co-ed.), The Challenges of Privatization: An International Analysis 2004; more than 90 publs on privatization, environmental and industrial econs. *Address:* Morgan Stanley International, 25 Cabot Square, Canary Wharf, London, E14 4QA, England (office). *Telephone:* (20) 7425-8000 (office). *Fax:* (20) 7425-8990 (office). *E-mail:* domenico.siniscalco@morganstanley.com (office). *Website:* www.morganstanley.com (office).

SINIVASAN, Marimutu; Indonesian business executive; *Chairman, Texmaco Group;* b. 1937, Medan, N Sumatra; ed Universitas Islam Sumatera Utara; began career as English teacher, later clerk in British firm; est. textile trading business (later Texmaco Group, conglomerate of 20 cos) late 1950s, Chair. Texmaco Group; went into exile 2006 after being accused of misappropriating govt funds, turned himself in to authorities 2008; nominated by Pres. Suharto to People's Consultative Ass. 1997. *Address:* Texmaco Group, Sentra Mulia Building, 9th floor, Suite 901, Jl. HR. Rasuna Said Kav. X6 No. 8, Jakarta 12940, Indonesia (office). *Telephone:* (21) 2520656 (office). *Fax:* (21) 2525069 (office). *E-mail:* contacts@texmaco.co.id (office). *Website:* www.texmaco.com (office).

SINN, Hans-Werner, Dr rer. pol; German economist; *President, Ifo Institute for Economic Research;* b. 7 March 1948, Brake; m. Gerlinde Sinn (née Zoubek) 1971; two s. one d.; ed Helmholtz-Gymnasium, Bielefeld, Univ. of Münster, Univ. of Mannheim; Lecturer, Univ. of Münster 1972–74, Univ. of Mannheim 1974–78, Sr Lecturer 1979–83, Assoc. Prof. 1983–84; Visiting Asst Prof., Univ. of Western Ont. 1978–79; Prof. of Econs and Insurance, Univ. of Munich 1984–94, Dir Centre for Econ. Studies 1991–, Prof. of Econs and Public Finance 1994–; mem. Council of Econ. Advisers, Fed. Ministry of Econs 1989–; Chair. Verein für Socialpolitik (German Econ. Asscn) 1997–2000; Pres. Ifo Inst. for Econ. Research 1999–; Pres. Int. Inst. of Public Finance 2006–(09); Order of Merit (Germany) 1999, 2005; Hon. Dr rer. pol (Univ. of Magdeburg) 1999; Venia Legendi 1983, Yrjö Jahnsson Lecturer, Univ. of Helsinki 1999, Stevenson Lecturer on Citizenship, Univ. of Glasgow 2000, Prize of Advisory Council of the Union 2003, Econ. Book Prize, Financial Times Deutschland 2003, Int. Book Prize CORINE 2004. *Publications:* Economic Decisions under Uncertainty 1980, Capital Income Taxation and Resource Allocation 1985, Jumpstart: The Economic Unification of Germany 1991, The German State Banks – Global Players in the International Financial Markets 1999, The New Systems Competition 2002, Ist Deutschland noch zu retten? 2003–05; numerous articles on public finance and other subjects; Ed. several journals including Economic Policy. *Address:* Ifo Institute for Economic Research, Poschingerstr. 5, 81679 Munich (office); Centre for Economic Studies, University of Munich, Schackstr. 4, 80539 Munich, Germany (office). *Telephone:* (89) 92241276 (office). *Fax:* (89) 92241901 (office). *E-mail:* sinn@ifo.de (office). *Website:* www.cesifo-group.de/hws (office).

SINNOTT, Kevin, MA; British artist; b. 4 Dec. 1947, Bridgend, Wales; s. of Myles Vincent Sinnott and Honora Burke; m. Susan Forward 1969; three s. one d.; ed St Robert's School, Royal Coll. of Art; teacher Canterbury Coll. of Art 1981–88, St Martin's School of Art, London 1981–93; solo exhbns at Bernard Jacobson Gallery 1986, 1988, 1990, Bernard Jacobson, New York 1987, 1989, Flowers East 1992, 1994, 1996, 1998, Flowers West, Los Angeles 1999, Caldwell/Snyder, New York 2000; work in numerous public collections (including Arts Council of GB, British Museum, British Council, Nat. Museum of Wales, Metropolitan Museum of Art, New York). *Publications:* Behind the Canvas (autobiog.) 2008. *Leisure interests:* cinema, books, walks, opera. *Address:* Tyr Santes Fair, Pont-y-Rhyl, Bridgend, CF32 8LJ, Wales. *Telephone:* (1656) 871854 (home). *Fax:* (1656) 871854 (home). *E-mail:* mail@kevinsinnott.co.uk (home). *Website:* www.kevinsinnott.co.uk (home).

SINSHEIMER, Robert Louis, SB, SM, PhD; American biologist and academic; *Professor Emeritus, Department of Molecular, Cellular and Developmental Biology, University of California, Santa Barbara;* b. 5 Feb. 1920, Washington, DC; s. of Allen Sinsheimer and Rose Davidson Sinsheimer; m. 1st Flora Joan Hirsch 1943 (divorced 1972); one s. two d.; m. 2nd Kathleen Mae Reynolds 1972 (divorced 1980); m. 3rd Karen B. Keeton 1981; ed MIT; Research Assoc., Biology, MIT 1948–49; Assoc. Prof. of Biophysics, Iowa State Coll. 1949–55, Prof. 1955–57; Prof. of Biophysics, Calif. Inst. of Tech. 1957–77, Chair. Div. of Biology 1968–77, Visiting Prof. of Biology 1987–88; Prof. Dept of Biological Sciences, Univ. of Calif., Santa Barbara 1988–90, Prof. Emer. 1990–; Chancellor, Univ. of Calif., Santa Cruz 1977–87; mem. NAS, mem. Council 1970–73; Pres. Biophysical Soc. 1970–71; Chair. Bd of Ed., NAS Proceedings 1972–80; Calif. Scientist of the Year Award 1968, Beijerinck Medal of the Royal Netherlands Acad. of Sciences 1969, Univ. of Calif. Presidential Medal 2001. *Publications:* The Strands of Life (memoirs) 1994; more than 250 scientific papers 1946–. *Leisure interests:* travel, hiking and photography. *Address:* MCD Biology, University of California, Santa Barbara, CA 93106 (office); 4606 Via Cavente, Santa Barbara, CA 93110, USA (home). *Telephone:* (805) 893-8038 (office); (805) 683-2247 (home). *Fax:* (805) 893-4724 (office). *E-mail:* sinsheim@lifesci.ucsb.edu (office). *Website:* www.lifesci.ucsb.edu/mcdb (office).

SINT, Marjanne; Dutch health administrator and fmr politician; *Chairman, Isala Klinieken;* b. 24 July 1949, Amsterdam; ed Univ. of Amsterdam and IMEDE Business School; mem. staff, Ministry of Econ. Affairs 1974–77, Ministry of Culture, Health and Social Affairs 1977–79; Econ. Ed., Intermediair 1979–80, Chief Ed. 1980–81; Publisher, VNU Business Publs 1981–87; Pres. Dutch Labour Party (PvdA) 1987–91; mem. staff Ministry of Interior 1991–95; Chief Exec. City of Amsterdam 1995; Sec.-Gen., Ministry of Housing, Spatial Planning and the Environment 2000–06; currently Chair. Isala Klinieken (pvt. hosp. group). *Publications:* Tussen wal en schip, etnische minderheden in Nederland 1980, Economen over crisis 1982. *Leisure interests:* literature, poetry, music, modern art and architecture. *Address:* Office of the Chairman, Isala Klinieken, Postbus 10400, 8000 GK Zwolle, Netherlands (office). *Telephone:* (38) 4245000 (office). *Fax:* (38) 4247676 (office). *Website:* www.isala.nl (office).

SINUNGURUZA, Térence; Burundian politician; b. 1937; Minister of Justice 1996–2001; Minister of External Relations and Co-operation 2001–05. *Address:* c/o Ministry of External Relations and Co-operation, Bujumbura, Burundi (office).

SINYAVSKAYA, Tamara Ilyinichna; Russian singer (mezzo-soprano); b. 6 July 1943, Moscow; m. Muslim Magovaev 1974; ed Moscow Music Coll. and

State Theatre Art Inst.; soloist with Bolshoi Theatre 1964–; studied at La Scala, Milan 1973–74; Order of Merit 2001, Order of Lomonosov First Degree 2004; First Prize Int. Singing Competition, Sofia 1968, Grand Prix Int. Singing Competition, Belgium 1969, First Prize at Int. Tchaikovsky Competition, Moscow 1970, People's Artist of RSFSR 1976, People's Artist of USSR 1982, Irina Arkhipova Prize 2004. *Opera roles include:* Olga in Tchaikovsky's Eugene Onegin, Carmen, Blanche and Frosya in Prokofiev's Gambler and Semyon Kotko, Vanya in Glinka's A Life for the Tsar, Ratmir in Glinka's Ruslan and Lyudmila, Lyubasha in Rimsky-Korsakov's The Tsar's Bride, Varvara in Not Love Alone. *Address:* c/o Bolshoi Theatre, 103009 Moscow, 1, Teatralnaya Ploshad, Russia.

SIOUFAS, Dimitris; Greek lawyer and politician; *President, Vouli (Parliament);* b. 15 Aug. 1944, Ellinopyrgos, Karditsa; m. Kaity Anagnostaki; two s. one d.; ed Panteion Univ. of Athens, Univ. of Thessaloníki; attorney-at-law; mem. Nea Demokratia (New Democracy—ND), mem. Cen. Cttee 1979–85, 1994–97, 1997–, mem. Exec. Cttee 1997–2001, mem. Political Council 2001–04; mem. Parl. for Karditsa 1981–, Parl. Spokesman for ND 1990–91, 1993–96, first Parl. Spokesman 1997–2000, Chair. Parl. Cttee on Public Enterprises, Banks and Public Utilities, Cttee on Parl. Procedure, Sec.-Gen. ND Parl. Group 2000–04; Deputy Minister of Social Security 1991–92, Minister of Health, Welfare and Social Services 1992–93, of Devt 2004–07; Pres. (Speaker) of Vouli (Parl.) 2007–; Co-founder Konstantinos Karamanlis Inst. of Democracy 1997; Gen. Dir Hellenic Org. of Small-Medium Sized Enterprises & Handicrafts (EOMMEX) 1977–81; Deputy Chair. Consignment, Deposits & Loans Fund 1980–81. *Address:* Vouli (Parliament), Parliament Building, Leoforos Vassilissis Sofias 2, 100 21 Athens (office); Vas. Konstantinou 25, 106 74 Athens (office); P. Ioakeim 3, 106 73 Athens, Greece (home); Roufou 21, 431 00 Karditsa. *Telephone:* (210) 3707000 (Parl.) (office); (210) 3614562 (office); (24410) 25591. *Fax:* (210) 3692170 (Parl.) (office). *E-mail:* dimgsioufas@parliament.gr (office). *Website:* www.parliament.gr/sioufas (office).

SIPINEN, Arto Kalevi; Finnish architect; b. 20 April 1936, Helsinki; s. of Veikko Emil Sipinen and Tuovi Maria Heino; m. 2nd Sinikka Rossi 1986; one s. one d.; ed Helsinki Univ. of Tech.; worked with Alvar Aalto 1959–61, Viljo Revell 1961–63; f. architectural practice, Espoo 1963–; Lecturer, Helsinki Univ. of Tech. 1964–67, Acting Prof. of Architecture 1991–92; mem. Finnish Architects' Asscn (SAFA) Community Planning Dept Bd 1964–66; Chair. SAFA Competition Cttee 1964–66; SAFA competition judge 1965–; work includes Imatra City Hall 1970, Jyväskylä Univ. Library and Admin Bldg 1974, Music and Art Bldg 1976, Raisio City Hall 1981, Imatra Cultural Centre 1986, Mikkeli Concert Hall 1988, Espoo Cultural Centre 1989, Lahti Main Library 1990, Tammela Town Hall 1991, Mäntsälä Town Hall 1992, Kuusamo Cultural Centre 1995 and planning projects in Helsinki city centre; more than 40 prizes in architectural competitions; other awards include SL Pro Finlandia Medal 1990, Concrete Structure of the Year Prize 1990, Prof. 1995, State Award for Architecture 1999. *Address:* Sipinen Architects Ltd, Tiistilänkuja 5 C, 02230 Espoo (office); Munkkiniemenranta 39, 00330 Helsinki, Finland (home). *Telephone:* 45200811 (office). *Fax:* 45200820 (office). *E-mail:* arto.sipinen@arksipinen.fi (office). *Website:* www.arksipinen.fi (office).

SIRAT, René-Samuel, Dr de Recherches; French rabbi; *Vice-President, Conference of European Rabbis;* b. 13 Nov. 1930, Bône (now Annaba), Algeria; s. of Ichoua Sirat and Oureida Atlan; m. 1st Colette Salamon 1952; one s. two d.; m. 2nd Nicole Holzman 1978; ed Lycée St Augustin, Bône, Univs of Strasbourg and Paris (Sorbonne), Hebrew Univ. of Jerusalem, Ecole Nat. des Langues Orientales (ENLOV); Rabbi, Toulouse 1952–55; Chaplain, Jeunesse juive 1955–63; Prof. Emer., Institut Nat. des Langues et Civilisations Orientales (INALCO, fmrly ENLOV), Dir of Hebrew Studies 1965–96; Prof., Ecole Rabbinique de France 1965–70, 1977–80; Insp.-Gen. of Hebrew, Ministry of Educ. 1972–80; Pres. Hebrew Examining Bd, Certificate of Professional Aptitude and Higher Studies 1973–78; Dir Centre de Documentation et Recherches des Etudes Juives modernes et contemporaines 1974–; Pres. Hebrew Examining Bd, Agrégation 1978–80; Dir Ecole Hautes Etudes de Judaïsme 1985–; Pres. Centre Universitaire Rachi, Troyes 1989; Chief Rabbi of France 1981–87; Chief Rabbi, Consistoire Central 1988; Vice-Pres. Conférence des Rabbins européens 1989–; Pres. Acad. Hillel 1989–, Inst. des connaissances des religions du livre 1996–; Chevalier, Légion d'honneur, Commdr, Ordre nat. du Mérite, Commdr des Palmes Académiques, Commdr des Arts et des Lettres; Dr hc (Yeshiva Univ., USA) 1985, (Université Laval, Canada) 1992; Prix de Jérusalem. *Publications:* Omer Hasikha (co-ed.) 1973, Mélanges A. Neher (co-ed.) 1974, Mélanges Vajda 1974–80 (co-ed.), La joie austère 1990, La tendresse de Dieu 1996, Héritages de Rachi (proceedings of the int. scientific colloquium organized in Troyes in June 2005 on the occasion of the 900th anniversary of the disappearance of Rabbi Shelomo Itshaqie (Rachi) 2006, Chrétiens, Juifs, Musulmans: Lectures qui rassemblent lectures qui séparent (co-author) 2007. *Address:* Université juive européenne, 11 rue Ancelle, 92200, Neuilly-sur-Seine (office); 51 rue de Rochechouart, 75009 Paris, France (home). *Telephone:* 1-46-24-88-50 (office). *Fax:* 1-46-24-88-50 (office). *E-mail:* univ.je@wanadoo.fr (office).

SIRCAR, Muhammad Jamiruddin; Bangladeshi barrister and politician; *Speaker of Jatiya Sangsad (Parliament);* b. 1 Dec. 1931; mem. Bangladesh Jatiyatabadi Dal (Bangladesh Nationalist Party); MP for Panchagarh-1, Seat-1, currently Speaker of Jatiya Sangsad (Parl.); Acting Pres. of Bangladesh June–Sept. 2002. *Address:* Jatiyo Sangshad Bhaban, Dhaka (office); 21 Baily Road, Ramna, Dhaka - 1000, Bangladesh (home). *Telephone:* (2) 8111499 (office); (2) 933480 (home). *E-mail:* info@parliament.gov.bd (office). *Website:* www.parliament.gov.bd (office); www.parliamentofbangladesh.org (office).

SIREN, Heikki; Finnish architect; b. 5 Oct. 1918, Helsinki; s. of Prof. J.S. Siren and Sirkka Siren; m. Kaija Siren 1944 (died 2001); two s. two d.; started pvt. practice with Kaija Siren, Siren Architects Ltd 1949–; mem. Finnish Acad. of Tech. Sciences 1971–; Foreign mem. Académie d'Architecture, Paris 1983; Hon. FAIA; Hon. mem. Finnish Architects' Asscn (SAFA) 1992; Hon. Citation and Medal São Paulo Biennal 1957, Medal São Paulo Biennal 1961, Hon. Citation 'Auguste Perret', Union Int. des Architectes 1965; Prof. hc 1970; Officier Ordre nat. du Mérite 1971, SLK (Finland) 1974, Grand Silver Order of Austria 1977; Hon. DTech 1982; Camillo Sitte Prize, Vienna 1979, Grande Médaille d'Or d'Académie d'Architecture, Paris 1980, Architectural Prize of the State of Finland 1980, Grand Golden Order of the City of Vienna 1982, Prize of Finnish Cultural Foundation 1984, Cultural Prize of City of Helsinki 1988. *Major works include:* Little Stage of Nat. Theatre, Helsinki 1954, Concert House, Lahti 1954, Chapel in Otaniemi 1957, Church in Orivesi 1960, Office Buildings, Helsinki 1965, Housing Area in Boussy St Antoine, Paris 1970, "Round Bank" Kop, Helsinki, schools, sports centres, offices, industrial bldgs., housing, holiday centres, etc., Brucknerhaus Concert Hall, Linz, Austria 1974, Golf complex, Karuizawa, Japan 1974, Golf Club, Onuma, Hokkaido, Japan 1976, Reichsbrücke, Vienna, Austria, Conference Palace, Baghdad, Iraq. *Publication:* Kaija and Heikki Siren, Architects 1978. *Leisure interests:* boat planning, theatre. *Address:* Tiirasaarentie 35, 00200 Helsinki 20, Finland. *Telephone:* 6811680 (office).

SIRIWIT, Cherdpong, MA; Thai energy industry executive and fmr government official; *Chairman, Thai Oil Public Company Ltd;* b. 1 Sept. 1946; ed Thammasat Univ., Nat. Defence Coll., Georgetown Univ., USA; held positions in govt successively as Sec.-Gen. Office of the Cane and Sugar Bd, Deputy Dir-Gen., then Dir-Gen. Office of Industrial Econs, Dir-Gen. Dept of Mineral Resources, Sec.-Gen. Thai Industrial Standards Inst., Deputy Perm. Sec. Ministry of Industry, then Perm. Sec., Ministry of Energy; fmr Chair. PTT Public Co. Ltd, Ratchaburi Electricity Generating Holding Public Co. Ltd; mem. Bd of Dirs Thai Oil Public Co. Ltd, Chair. 2005–, mem. Bd of Dirs Thaioil Power Co. Ltd, PTT Exploration and Production Public Co. Ltd 2002–; mem. Council of Trustees, Petroleum Inst. of Thailand (PTIT). *Address:* Thai Oil Public Company Ltd, Suntowers Bldg. B, 16th Floor, 123 Vibhavadi Rangsit Road, Chomphon, Chatuchak, Bangkok, 10900, Thailand (office). *Telephone:* 2299-0000 (office). *Fax:* 2299-0024 (office). *Website:* www.thaioil.co.th (office).

SIRRINGHAUS, Henning, PhD; Swiss physicist, business executive and academic; *Hitachi Professor of Electron Device Physics, Optoelectronics Group, Cavendish Laboratory, University of Cambridge;* ed Institute of Solid State Physics, ETH Zurich; Postdoctoral Research Fellow, Dept of Electrical Eng, Princeton Univ. 1995–97; postdoctoral research at Cavendish Lab., Univ. of Cambridge 1998, Royal Society University Research Fellowship 1998, Lecturer, Cavendish Lab. 2000–02, Reader 2002–04, Hitachi Prof. of Electron Device Physics, Optoelectronics Group and head Microelectronics Research Centre 2004–; Co-founder and Chief Scientist, Plastic Logic Ltd. (tech. start-up co. commercialising printed organic transistor tech.) 2000–; Balzers Prize, Swiss Physical Soc. 1995, Silver Medal, ETH, Zurich 1996, Descartes Prize, EC 2000, Mullard Award, Royal Soc. 2003. *Publications:* over 70 publs and 20 patents/patent applications. *Address:* Optoelectronics Group, Cavendish Laboratory, University of Cambridge, JJ Thomson Avenue, Cambridge, CB3 0HE (office); Plastic Logic Limited, 34 Cambridge Science Park, Milton Road, Cambridge, CB4 0FX, England (office). *Telephone:* (1223) 337557 (office); (1223) 706000 (Plastic Logic) (office). *Fax:* (1223) 337706 (office); (1223) 706006 (Plastic Logic) (office). *E-mail:* hs220@phy.cam.ac.uk (office); info@plasticlogic.com (office). *Website:* www-oe.phy.cam.ac.uk (office); www.plasticlogic.com (office).

SISOWATH SIRIRATH, Prince; Cambodian politician; fmr Jt Minister of Defence; fmr Perm. Rep. to UN, New York; mem. FUNCINPEC Party (United National Front for an Independent, Neutral, Peaceful and Co-operative Cambodia Party), Second Vice-Pres. 2006–. *Address:* FUNCINPEC Party (United Nat. Front for an Ind., Neutral, Peaceful and Co-operative Cambodia Party), 11 blvd Monivong (93), Sangkat Sras Chak, Khan Daun Penh, BP 1444, Phnom-Penh, Cambodia (office). *Telephone:* (23) 428864 (office). *Fax:* (23) 218547 (office). *E-mail:* funcinpec@funcinpec.org (office). *Website:* www.funcinpec.org (office).

SISSOKO, Cheick Oumar, BA; Malian politician and filmmaker; *Leader, Parti de la solidarité africaine pour la démocratie et l'indépendance;* b. 1945, San Dist, Bamako; ed Ecole nat. de cinématographie Louis Lumière, Ecole des hautes études en sciences sociales; began career in Mali Civil Service; Minister of Culture 2002–; Asst Dir-Gen., later Dir-Gen. Centre nat. de la production cinématographique; f. Kora Films (producers' Asscn); Pres. Kayira (ind. radio station); Leader, Parti de la solidarité africaine pour la démocratie et l'indépendance. *Films include:* Nyamanton ou la leçon des ordures 1987, Finzan 1991, Guimba le tyran, une époque (Grand Prize, Fespaco Festival, Ouagadougou 1995) 1993, La Genèse 1999, Battu 2000. *Documentaries include:* Africa is Moving 1992, Etre jeune à Bamako (Youth in Mali) 1992, Building a Nation – Eritrea 1996, Malnutrition in the Sahel Region 1997. *Radio includes:* L'Afrique en question (producer, weekly programme for Kayira). *Address:* Parti de la solidarité africaine pour la démocratie et l'indépendance, Djélibougou, rue 246, porte 559, BP 3140, Bamako, Mali. *Telephone:* 224-10-04 (office).

SISSONS, Peter George, MA; British television news presenter; b. 17 July 1942, Liverpool; s. of the late George Sissons and Elsie Evans; m. Sylvia Bennett 1965; two s. one d.; ed Liverpool Inst. High School for Boys and Univ. Coll., Oxford; grad. trainee, Independent TV News 1964, gen. reporter 1967, industrial corresp. 1970, industrial ed. 1972–78; presenter, News at One 1978–82, Channel Four News 1982–89; presenter, BBC TV news 1989– (6 O'Clock News 1989–94, 9 O'Clock News 1994–2000, 10 O'Clock News 2000–03, BBC News 24 2003–), Chair. BBC TV Question Time 1989–93; Hon. Fellow, Liverpool John Moores Univ. 1997; Hon. LLD (Liverpool); Broadcasting Press Guild Award 1984, Royal Television Soc. Judges' Award 1988, Television and Radio Industries Club Newscaster of the Year 2000. *Address:* BBC Television Centre, Wood Lane, London, W12 7RJ, England (office). *Website:* www.bbc.co.uk (office).

SISSOUMA, Mamadou Clazié; Malian politician; b. 6 Nov. 1950; Dir of Cabinet, Ministry of Justice 1994–95, Gen. Sec., 1995–98; Admin. Décennal Project for Judicial Reform 1998–99; Adviser, Supreme Court 1999–2003; Minister of Defence and Veterans 2004–07. *Address:* c/o Ministry of Defence and Veterans, route de Koulouba, BP 2083, Bamako, Mali (office).

SISTANI, Grand Ayatollah Sayyid Ali Husaini; Iraqi (b. Iranian) religious leader; b. 1929, Mashhad, Iran; s. of Sayyid Mohammad Baqir; joined Islamic seminary, Qom 1949; fmr lecturer in jurisprudence, Najaf Ashraf; after religious training in Iran moved to Iraq to become most sr Shia cleric; apptd head of network of schools, Najaf 1992. *Publications:* numerous religious works and treatises. *Address:* Office of Grand Ayatollah Sistani, Muallim Street, POB 3514\37185, Qom, Iran. *Telephone:* 251-7741415. *Fax:* 251-7741421. *E-mail:* sistani@sistani.org. *Website:* www.sistani.org.

SISULU, Albertina Nontsikelelo; South African politician; b. 21 Oct. 1918, Tsomo, Transkei; m. Walter Max Ulyate Sisulu 1944 (died 2003); five c.; trained as a nurse, Johannesburg NE Hosp.; joined Fed. of South African Women 1954, Pres. 1984; mem. Women's League, African Nat. Congress (ANC) 1948; participated in women's protest against introduction of Women's Pass; under continual banning orders (including house arrest) 1964–82; Transvaal Pres. United Democratic Front (UDF) 1983–91; tried and sentenced to four years' imprisonment for furthering aims of ANC 1984, successful appeal 1987; elected to Nat. Council, Women's Congress, UDF 1987; Leader UDF Del. to USA and to England July 1989; apptd Co-Convenor (with Gertrude Shope) ANC Women's League Task Force 1990; Deputy Pres. ANC 1991; mem. Nat. Exec. Cttee of ANC 1991–; elected ANC MP 1994; Pres. World Peace Council 1993. *Address:* POB 61884, Marshalltown 2107, South Africa.

SISULU, Sheila Violet Makate, BA; South African diplomatist and UN official; *Deputy Executive Director for Hunger Solutions, United Nations World Food Programme;* d.-in-law of Walter Max Ulyate Sisulu and Albertina Nontsikelelo Sisulu (q.v.); m. Mlungisi Sisulu; one s. two d.; ed Univ. of Witwatersrand; various sr positions, South African Comm. for Higher Educ. 1978–88; Educ. Co-ordinator, African Bursary Fund, South African Council of Churches 1988–91; Dir Jt Enrichment Project 1991–94; Special Adviser, Ministry of Educ. 1994–97; Consul-Gen., South African Consulate-Gen., New York 1997–99; Amb. to USA 1999–2002; Deputy Exec. Dir UN World Food Programme 2003–08, Deputy Exec. Dir for Hunger Solutions 2008–; mem. ANC Nat. Educ. Cttee, USA–South Africa Leadership Training Program, Community Bank Foundation; Council mem. Univ. of Witwatersrand; Trustee, Equal Opportunity Foundation, Women's Devt Foundation, Women's Devt Bank, South African Broadcasting Corpn; Dr hc (Maryland, CUNY). *Address:* UN World Food Programme, Via C.G. Viola 68, Parco dei Medici, 00148 Rome, Italy (office). *Telephone:* (06) 65131 (office). *Fax:* (06) 65132840 (office). *E-mail:* wfpinfo@wfp.org (office). *Website:* www.wfp.org (office).

SITAULA, Krishna Prasad; Nepalese politician; Spokesperson for Nepali Congress, arrested several times and ordered to be released by Supreme Court Feb. 2006; Minister of Home Affairs 2006–07, Interim Minister of Home Affairs 2007; chief govt negotiator at peace talks with Maoist rebels 2006. *Address:* c/o Ministry of Home Affairs, Singha Durbar, Kathmandu, Nepal (office).

SITHANEN, Ramakrishna, BSc, MSc, PhD; Mauritian politician and economist; *Vice Prime Minister and Minister of Finance and Economic Empowerment;* b. 21 April 1954; ed London School of Econs, Brunel Univ.; fmr Research Officer, Centre for Labour Econs, LSE; fmr Research Officer, OECD, Paris; Educ. Officer 1979–80; Econ. Consultant, De Chazal Du Mee & Co. 1980–82; Transport Economist, Air Mauritius 1982–87, Dir of Planning 1987–90; Gen. Man., Planning and Devt, Rogers & Co. Ltd 1990–91; MP for Belle Rose/Quatre Bornes Constituency 1991–; Minister of Finance 1991–95, Vice Prime Minister and Minister of Finance and Econ. Empowerment 2005–; Academic Achievement Prize, LSE, named one of 100 Global Leaders for Tomorrow, World Econ. Forum 1994. *Leisure interests:* reading, football. *Address:* Government House, Ground Floor, Port Louis, Mauritius (office). *Telephone:* 201-2431 (office). *Fax:* 208-6450 (office). *E-mail:* rsithanen@mail.gov.mu (office); secminof@mail.gov.mu (office). *Website:* www.mof.gov.mu (office).

SITHOLE, Majozi; Swazi politician; *Minister of Finance* Minister, Econ. Planning and Devt 1999–2001; Minister Finance 2001–; mem. House of Ass. *Address:* Ministry of Finance, POB 443, Mbabane, Swaziland (office). *Telephone:* 4048148 (office). *Fax:* 4043187 (office). *E-mail:* minfin@realnet.co.sz (office).

SITKOVETSKY, Dmitry; American/British violinist and conductor; *Music Director, Greensboro Symphony Orchestra;* b. 27 Sept. 1954, Baku, USSR (now Azerbaijan); s. of Julian Sitkovetsky and Bella Davidovich; m. Susan Roberts; ed Moscow Conservatory, Juilliard School of Music, New York; debut with Berlin Philharmonic 1980; appearances with Vienna Symphony Orchestra, Orchestre de Paris and the Amsterdam, Rotterdam, Munich and Royal Philharmonic Orchestras in Europe and the Chicago, Cincinnati, Detroit, Montréal and Toronto Symphony Orchestras in N America, Carnegie Hall debut 1986; Artistic Dir Korsholm Festival, Finland 1983–93, Seattle Int. Music Festival 1992–97; Music Dir and Prin. Conductor Ulster Orchestra, NI 1996–2001; Music Dir Tuscan Sun Festival, Cortona, Italy 2003–06; Artist-in-

Residence, Orchestra de Castilla & Leon, Valladolid, Spain 2006–; currently Music Dir Greensboro Symphony Orchestra, Greensboro, N Carolina; First Prize, Fritz Kreisler Competition, Vienna 1979, Avery Fisher Career grant 1983. *Television:* role of Arkady Greenberg in film Heavy Sand (Russian Moscow TV) 2007. *Publications:* transcriptions: Bach – Goldberg Variations for String Trio 1985, Dohnányi – Serenade for string orchestra 1990, Shostakovich – String Symphony Op. 73 1991. *Leisure interests:* movies, football. *Address:* c/o Sulivan Sweetland, 28 Albion Street, London, W2 2AX, England (office). *Telephone:* (20) 7262-0333 (office). *Fax:* (20) 7402-5851 (office). *E-mail:* info@sulivansweetland.co.uk (office). *Website:* www.sulivansweetland.co.uk (office); www.greensborosymphony.org (office).

SITRUK, Joseph; French rabbi; b. 16 Oct. 1944, Tunis; m. Danielle Azoulay 1965; nine c.; ed Seminary rue Vauquelin, Paris; Asst to Rabbi Max Warsharski, Lower Rhine region 1970–75; Rabbi, Marseilles 1975–87; Chief Rabbi of France 1987–2008; mem. Nat. Cttee of Human Rights; Pres. Conf. of European Rabbis 2000–; Chevalier, Ordre Nat. du Mérite, Officier, Légion d'honneur 2001, Commdr Ordre Nat. du Mérite 2003, Légion d'honneur 2007. *Publications:* Chemin faisant 1999, Dix Commandements 2000, Rien ne vaut la vie 2006. *Address:* Consistoire Central Union des Communautés Juives de France, 19 rue Saint Georges, 75009 Paris, France. *Telephone:* 1-49-70-88-00. *Fax:* 1-40-16-06-11. *E-mail:* spgrf@free.fr.

SITTHIPHONG, Norkun, BEng (Mech), MS (MechEng), PhD; Thai business executive; *Chairman, PTT Public Co. Ltd;* m. Bularat Sitthiphong; two d.; ed Chulalongkorn Univ., Oregon State Univ., USA, Nat. Defense Coll., Capital Market Acad.; Dean of Eng. Chiang Mai Univ. 1989–2001, Vice-Pres. for Academic Affairs 2001–03; Deputy Perm. Sec., Ministry of Energy 2003–; currently Chair. PTT Public Co. Ltd; fmr Chair. Electricity Generating Public Co. Ltd; fmr Dir Electricity Generating Authority of Thailand; elected to Acad. of Distinguished Engineers, Oregon State Univ. 2005. *Address:* PTT Public Co. Ltd, 555 Vibhavadi Rangsit Road, Chatuchak, Bangkok 10900, Thailand (office). *Telephone:* 2537-2000 (office). *Fax:* 2537-3499 (office). *E-mail:* info@pttplc.com (office). *Website:* www.pttplc.com (office).

SIWIEC, Marek Maciej; Polish politician and journalist; b. 13 March 1955, Piekary Śląskie; m.; one s. one d.; ed Acad. of Mining and Metallurgy, Kraków; Asst Acad. of Mining and Metallurgy, Kraków 1980–82; trainee Gas and Fuel Corpn of Victoria, Australia 1981–82; Ed.-in-Chief 'Student' (weekly) 1985–87, ITD (weekly) 1987–90, Trybuna (daily) 1990–91; Deputy to Sejm (Parl.) 1991–97; mem. Nat. Broadcasting Council 1993–96; Sec. of State in Chancellery of Pres. of Poland 1996–2004, Head Nat. Security Bureau, Nat. Security Adviser to the Pres. of Poland 1997–2004; mem. European Parl. 2004–; mem. Polish del. to Parl. Ass., Council of Europe; mem. Polish United Workers' Party (PZPR); mem. Social Democracy of Polish Repub. 1990–93, presidium of Head Council 1991–93. *Leisure interests:* jogging, cycling, tennis. *Address:* ASP 126305, 60 rue Wiertz, 1097 Brussels, Poland (office). *Telephone:* (2) 284-76-53 (office). *Fax:* (2)284-36-53 (office). *E-mail:* msiwiec@europarl.eu.int (office). *Website:* www.mareksiwiec.pl (office).

SIZA, Alvaro (Joaquim de Meio); Portuguese architect; b. 25 June 1933, Matosinhos; m. Maria Antonia Marinho Leite 1962 (died 1973); two c.; ed Univ. of Porto; in pvt. practice 1954–; Lecturer, Univ. of Porto 1966–69, Prof. of Construction 1976–; Gold Medal, Alvar Aalto Foundation 1988, Gold Medal, Colegios de Arquitectos, Spain 1988, Pritzker Architecture Prize 1992, Berlage Prize 1994, Gubbio Prize 1994, Nara World Architecture Exhbn Gold Medal 1995, Imperial Prize, Japan Arts Asscn 1998, Wolf Foundation Prize in Arts 2001, Royal Gold Medal, Royal Inst. of British Architects 2008. *Address:* Faculdade de Arquitectura, Universidade do Porto, Rua do Gólgota 215, 4150-755 Porto, Portugal (office). *Telephone:* (226) 057100 (office). *Fax:* (226) 057199 (office). *Website:* www.arq.up.pt (office).

SIZOVA, Alla Ivanovna; Russian ballet dancer; b. 22 Sept. 1939, Moscow; d. of Ivan Sizov and Ekaterina Sizova; m. Mikhail Serebrennikov 1965; one s.; ed Leningrad School of Ballet; joined Leningrad Kirov Theatre of Opera and Ballet 1958–; a frequent pnr of Mikhail Baryshnikov (q.v.); teacher, A. Vagnova Choreography School 1987–91; apptd Ballet Mistress Universal Ballet School 1991; Gold Medals Youth Festival, Vienna 1959, 1st Int. Ballet Contest, Varna; Anna Pavlova Diploma, Paris 1964, People's Artist of the RSFSR 1983. *Major roles include:* Masha (Nutcracker), Mirta (Giselle), Pas de trois (Le Corsaire), Katerina (Stone Flower), Waltz and Mazurka (Chopiniana), Pas de trois (Swan Lake), Aurora (Sleeping Beauty), Maria (Fountain of Bakhchisarai), Juliet (Romeo and Juliet), Cinderella (Cinderella), Kitri (Don Quixote), Girl (Leningrad Symphony). *Address:* Universal Ballet School, 4301 Harewood Road, NE, Washington, DC 20017, USA (office).

SJAASTAD, Anders Christian, PhD; Norwegian politician; *Senior Adviser, Norwegian Institute of International Affairs;* b. 21 Feb. 1942, Oslo; s. of Andreas Sjaastad and Ingrid Sjaastad; m. Torill Oftedal Sjaastad 1969 (died 2000); one d.; ed Univ. of Oslo; Pres. Norwegian Students' Asscn, Univ. of Oslo 1967; Research Asst, Inst. of Political Science, Univ. of Oslo 1968–70; Research Assoc. Norwegian Inst. of Int. Affairs (NUPI) 1970–81, Dir of Information 1973–81, Dir European Studies 1998–2004, Sr Adviser 2004–; mem. Høyre (Conservative Party), Vice-Chair. Oslo Høyre 1977–88, Chair. 1996–2000; mem. Storting (Parl.) 1981–2001; Minister of Defence 1981–86; Pres. European Movt in Norway 1989–92; Chair. Defence and Security Cttee (North Atlantic Ass.) 1994–97; Vice-Chair. Standing Cttee on Justice (Stortinget) 1993–97; mem. Norwegian Nat. Defence Comm. 1974–78, Norwegian Cttee on Arms Control and Disarmament 1976–81, 2002–06, N Atlantic Ass. 1989–97; proxy mem. Nobel Peace Prize Cttee 2004–06. *Publications:* Departmental Decision Making (co-author) 1972, Politikk og Sikkerhet i Norskehavsområdet (with J. K. Skogan) 1975, Norsk Utenrikspolitisk Arbok (ed.) 1975, Deterrence and Defence in the North (co-ed. and contrib.) 1985, Arms Control in a Multipolar World (contrib.) 1996, Maritime Security in Southeast Asia (contrib.) 2007. *Address:* NUPI – Norwegian Institute of International Affairs, C.J. Hambros plass 2D, PO Box 8159, Dep 0033, Oslo, Norway (office). *Telephone:* 22-99-40-00 (office). *Fax:* 22-36-21-82 (office). *E-mail:* internet@nupi.no (office). *Website:* www.nupi.no (office).

SKALICKÝ, Jiří; Czech politician; b. 26 April 1956, Kolín; m.; three s. one d.; ed Coll. of Advanced Chemical Tech., Prague; research worker with Astrid (state enterprise), Prague 1981–90; mem. Civic Democratic Alliance (CDA) 1990–98, Deputy Chair. 1990–92; Deputy to House of Nations, Fed. Ass. of ČSFR 1990–92; mem. Plan and Budget Cttee, House of Nations, Fed. Ass. 1990–92; Minister for Nat. Property Admin. and Privatization 1992–96, for the Environment 1996–98; Chair. Presidium of Nat. Property Fund 1992–96; Deputy Chair. Civic Democratic Alliance 1995–97, Chair. 1997–98; Deputy Prime Minister 1997; Senator 1998–2004. *Address:* Zahradnickova 1220, 150 00 Prague 5, Czech Republic (home). *E-mail:* jiriskalicky@volny.cz (home).

SKÁRMETA, Antonio, BA, MA; Chilean writer and diplomatist; b. 7 Nov. 1940, Antofagasta; m. Cecilia Boisier; two s.; ed Universidad de Chile, Columbia Univ., New York; Prof. of Philosophy, Instituto Nacional 1966–68, Universidad de Chile 1968–75; escaped military dictatorship in Chile, lived in Argentina, Portugal, West Germany, Nicaragua; Distinguished Prof. of Literature and Romance Languages, Washington Univ. of St Louis, Missouri, USA 1988; Amb. to Germany 2000–03; Chevalier, Order des Arts et des Lettres (France) 1986, Commendatore dell'Ordine (Italy) 1996, Goethe Medal (Germany) 2002, Grand Cross of Merit (Germany) 2003; Fulbright Scholarship, Guggenheim Fellowship, Premio Excelencia, Universidad de Artes y Ciencias de la Comunicación 1998, Premio Neruda 2004. *Radio:* Voy y Vuelo 2000. *Publications:* El entusiasmo 1967, Desnudo en el Tejado (Premio Casa de Las Americas) 1969, Tiro Libre 1973, Soné que la nieve ardía 1975, No Pasó Nada (Boccaccio Europa Prize 1986) 1980, La Insurreción 1982, Ardiente paciencia (made into film Il Postino) 1985, Match Ball 1989, La Composición (Jane Adams Prize 2001, Premio Las Américas 2001, Gustav-Heinemann Peace Prize 2004) 1998, La Boda del Poeta (Premio Altazor 2000, Grinzane Cavour Prize 2000, Prix Médicis 2001) 1999, La Chica del Trombón (Premio Elsa Morante 2002, Premio de Narrativa José María Arguedas 2003) 2001, El Baile de la Victoria (Premio Planeta 2003, Premio Municipal de Literatura de la ciudad de Santiago 2004) 2003; trans.: An American Dream, Norman Mailer 1968, The Pyramid, William Golding 1968, Typee, Herman Melville 1968, Visions of Gerard, Jack Kerouac 1969, Love, Roger, Charles Webb 1969, The Last Tycoon, F. Scott Fitzgerald 1969. *E-mail:* cordillero@gmail.com (office). *Website:* www.antonio-skarmeta.com.

SKARPHÉÐINSSON, Össur, BS, PhD; Icelandic journalist and politician; *Minister of Foreign Affairs and External Trade and Minister of Industry;* b. 10 June 1953, Reykjavík; ed Univ. of Iceland, Univ. of East Anglia, UK; ed., Þjóðviljinn newspaper 1984–87, Alþýðublaðið newspaper 1996–97, DV newspaper 1997–98; Asst Prof., Univ. of Iceland 1987–88; Deputy Dir Reykjavík Reinsurance 1989–91; mem. Althingi (Parl.) 1991–, Chair. Social Democratic Party Parl. Group 1991–93, Vice-Chair. 1995–96, Chair. Social Democratic Alliance Parl. Group 2006–07, mem. Cttee on Fisheries 1991–93, on Gen. Affairs 1991–93, on Industry 1991–93, on Agric. 1992–93, on Health and Social Security 1995–99 (Chair.) 1995–99, on Foreign Affairs 1995–99 (Vice-Chair. 1998–99), 2005–07, on the Environment 1999–2000, on the Budget 1999–2001, on Credentials 1999–2003, on Economy and Trade 2001–05, Chair. Del. to NATO Parl. Ass. 2005–07, Vice-Chair. Del. to WEU Ass. 1995–99, mem. Del. to EFTA and EEA Parl. Cttees 1991–93, 1999–2004, Parl. Ass. of the Council of Europe 2003–05; Minister for the Environment 1993–95, for Nordic Co-operation 2007–08, of Industry 2007–, of Foreign Affairs and External Trade 2009–. *Address:* Ministry for Foreign Affairs, Rauðarárstíg 25, 150 Reykjavík, Iceland (office). *Telephone:* 5459900 (office). *Fax:* 5622373 (office). *E-mail:* external@utn.stjr.is (office). *Website:* www.utanrikisraduneyti.is (office).

SKARSGÅRD, J. Stellan; Swedish actor; b. 13 June 1951, Göteborg; s. of J. Skarsgård and Gudrun Skarsgård; m. My Günther 1976; five s. one d.; with Royal Dramatic Theatre, Stockholm 1972–87; Best Actor, Berlin Film Festival 1982; twice Best Film Actor in Sweden; Best Actor, Rouen Film Festival 1988, 1992, Best Actor, Chicago Film Festival 1991, Jury's Special Prize, San Sebastián Film Festival 1995, European Film Award. *Films include:* Simple Minded Murderer 1982, Serpent's Way 1986, Hip Hip Hurrah 1987, The Unbearable Lightness of Being 1988, Good Evening Mr Wallenberg 1990, The Ox 1992, Wind 1992, The Slingshot 1993, Zero Kelvin 1994, Breaking the Waves 1995, Insomnia 1997, Amistad 1997, Good Will Hunting 1997, Ronin 1998, Deep Blue Sea 1998, Passion of Mind 1999, Kiss Kiss (Bang Bang) 2000, Signs & Wonders 2000, Timecode 2000, Dancer in the Dark 2000, Aberdeen (also assoc. producer) 2000, The Hire: Powder Keg 2001, Taking Sides 2001, The House on Turk Street 2002, City of Ghosts 2002, Dogville 2003, King Arthur 2004, Eiffeltornet 2004, Exorcist: The Beginning 2004, Pirates of the Caribbean: Dead Man's Chest 2006, Goya's Ghosts 2006, Pirates of the Caribbean: At World's End 2007, W Delta Z 2007, Arn-Tempelriddaren 2007, Mamma Mia! 2008, Arn-Riket vid vägens slut 2008. *Television includes:* Hamlet 1984, Harlan County War 2000, Helen of Troy 2003, God on Trial 2008. *Address:* Hogbergsgatan 40, 118 26 Stockholm, Sweden.

SKARŻYŃSKI, Henryk, DMedHab, PhD, DSc; Polish medical scientist; *Director, Institute of Physiology and Pathology of Hearing;* b. 3 Jan. 1954, Rosochate Koscielne; s. of Józef Skarzynski and Janina Skarzynska; m. Bozena Bruska; two s.; ed Warsaw Medical Univ.; researcher, Oto-rhinolaryngology Clinic, Warsaw Medical Univ. 1979–2000, Head Ward 1986–96, Asst Prof. 1991–93, Assoc. Prof. 1993–95, Full Prof. 1995–; Dir Diagnostic Treatment Rehabilitation Centre for the Deaf and Hearing-Impaired 1993–95; Dir Inst. of Physiology and Pathology of Hearing 1996–; Head,

Otology Clinic, Warsaw 1999–2003, Int. Centre of Hearing and Speech 2003–; Chair of Audiology and Phoniatrics Dept, F. Chopin Acad. of Music, Warsaw 2002–; mem. American Acad. of Audiology 1994–, Collegium of Oto-Rhino-Laryngologicum Amicitiae Sacrum 1994–, New York Acad. of Sciences 1995–, American Tinnitus Asscn 1995–, Int. Evoked Response Audiometry Study Group 1997–, European Acad. of Otology and Neuro-Otology 1998–; Hon. mem. Slovak Asscn of Otolaryngology and Head and Neck Surgery 1998–; Hon. Prof. Audiology and Speech Therapy Dept, Brigham Young Univ., USA 1998–99; Prize of the Prime Minister 2000, Prize of the Minister of Health and Social Welfare 2000, 2001, Prof. Jan Miodonski Award 1983, Stockholm Challenge Award 2000, Gold Medal of the Acad. of Polish Success 2001, Gold Medal, Brussels Eureka 2002, Award of Chair. of State Cttee for Scientific Research 2003, Golden Medal awarded during Lepine Competition, Paris 2003, Special Prize on behalf of Warsaw City Council 2003, Irlandia Award, High-Level Conf. on eHealth, Cork (Ireland) 2004. *Achievements:* pioneer work in developing first Polish Programme for the Treatment of Hearing Disorders, Cochlear and Brainstem Implants Programme. *Publications include:* co-author: Urazy kosci skroniowej (Damages of the Temporal Bone) 1999, Anatomia topograficzna kosci skroniowej dla potrzeb otochirurgii (Topographical Anatomy of the Temporal Bone for Otosurgery) 2000, Technika komputerowa w audiologii, foniatrii i logopedii (Informatic Techniques in Audiology Phoniatrics and Speech and Language Therapy) 2002, Objawy laryngologiczne w rzadkich zespolach chorobowych (Laryngological Symptoms in Rare Diseases) 2002; monographs: Kryteria kwalifikacji do zabiegów wszczepiania implantów slimakowych i program rehabilitacji calkowitej utraty sluchu u dzieci 1994, Implant nadziei. Nowe szanse dla osób nieslyszacych. Pytania i odpowiedzi (Implant of Hope. New Chances for the Hearing Impaired. Questions and Answers) 1994. *Leisure interests:* football, breeding doves. *Address:* Institute of Physiology and Pathology of Hearing, ul. Pstrowskiego 1, 01-943 Warsaw, Poland (office). *Telephone:* (22) 8356670 (office). *Fax:* (22) 8355214 (office). *E-mail:* sekretariat@ifps.org.pl (office). *Website:* www.ifps.org.pl (office); www.ifps.org.pl/O_nas/profesor_e .html (office).

SKATOV, Nikolai Nikolayevich, DLit; Russian linguist; b. 2 May 1931; m.; one d.; ed Kostroma State Pedagogical Inst.; Sr Teacher, Acting Head, Chair of Literature, Kostroma State Pedagogical Inst. 1956–62; Sr Teacher, Sr Researcher, Docent, Prof., Head of Dept of Literature, Leningrad State Pedagogical Inst. 1962–; Dir Inst. of Russian Literature (Pushkin House) 1987–; Chair., Comm. on Literature and Educ., Russian Acad. of Sciences, Deputy Chair., Comm. on Russian Literature, Presidium Russian Acad. of Sciences, corresp. mem. Russian Acad. of Sciences 1997–; Ed.-in-Chief Russkaya Literature (magazine). *Publications:* 12 books and over 200 scientific works. *Address:* Institute of Russian Literature, Makarova nab. 4, 199034 St Petersburg, Russia (office). *Telephone:* (812) 218-19-01 (office); (812) 311-49-58 (home). *Fax:* (812) 328-11-40 (office). *E-mail:* irli@mail.ru (office). *Website:* spbrc.nw.ru/!english/org/irli.htm (office).

SKEGG, David C. G., OBE, BMedSc, MB, ChB, DPhil, FRSNZ; New Zealand medical researcher, academic and university administrator; *Vice-Chancellor, University of Otago;* b. 1947, Auckland; ed King's Coll., Univ. of Otago, Balliol Coll., Univ. of Oxford, UK; Lecturer in Epidemiology, Univ. of Oxford 1976–79; Chair of Preventive and Social Medicine, Univ. of Otago 1980–, Vice-Chancellor 2004–; known for his work on cancer and reproductive health; Adviser to WHO's Special Programme of Research, Devt and Research Training in Human Reproduction; fmr Chair. NZ Public Health Comm.; Health Research Council of NZ; NZ Commemoration Medal 1990, Sir Charles Hercus Medal, Royal Soc. of NZ 1999, Distinguished Research Medal, Otago Univ. 2003. *Publications:* over 140 papers in academic journals. *Address:* University of Otago, POB 56, Dunedin 9015, New Zealand (office). *Telephone:* (3) 479-1100 (office). *Fax:* (3) 479-8544 (office). *E-mail:* vice-chancellor@otago .ac.nz (office). *Website:* www.otago.ac.nz (office).

SKEHEL, Sir John James, Kt, PhD, FRS; British research scientist; b. 27 Jan. 1941, Blackburn, Lancs.; s. of Joseph Skehel and Ann Skehel; m. Anita Varley 1962; two s.; ed St Mary's Coll. Blackburn, Univ. Coll. of Wales, Aberystwyth and UMIST; Postdoctoral Fellow, Marischal Coll. Aberdeen 1965–68; Fellow, Helen Hay Whitney Foundation 1968–71; mem. Scientific Staff and Head, Infection and Immunity, MRC Nat. Inst. for Medical Research 1971, Dir 1987–2006; Dir World Influenza Centre 1975–94; mem. Academia Europea 1992; Fellow and Vice-Pres. Acad. of Medical Science; Hon. Prof. of Virology, Glasgow Univ. 1997–, Hon. Prof., Liverpool John Moores Univ. 2007–, Univ. Coll. London; Feldberg Prize 1986, Koch Prize 1987, Prix Louis Jeantet de Médecine 1988, ICN Int. Prize in Virology 1993, Royal Soc.'s Royal Medal 2003, Imperial Coll. Ernst Chain Prize 2004, Int. Union of Microbiological Socs Stuart Mudd Award for Basic Microbiology 2005, Int. Louis D, Institut de France Grand Prize (jtly) 2007. *Publications:* numerous articles in scientific journals. *Address:* 49 Homewood Road, St Albans, Herts., AL1 4BG, England (home). *Telephone:* (1727) 860603 (home).

ŠĶĒLE, Andris; Latvian politician; *Chairman, Tautas Partija (People's Party);* b. 16 Jan. 1958, Aluksne District; m. Dzintra Škele; two c.; ed Latvian Acad. of Agric.; Head of Sector, Sr research Asst, Deputy Dir Research Assoc. Inst. of Latvian Agricultural Mechanization and Electrification 1981–90; First Deputy Minister of Agric. 1990–93; Prime Minister of Latvia 1995–97, 1999–2000; Founder and Chair. Tautas Partija (People's Party) 1998–; mem. Saeima (Parl.) 1998–; mem. several Parl. Comms; Chair. several bds of holding cos. *Address:* Tautas Partija, Dzir navu iela 68, Rīga, Latvia (office). *Telephone:* 6728-6441 (office). *Fax:* 6728-6405 (office). *E-mail:* koord1@tautas .lv (office). *Website:* www.tautaspartija.lv (office).

SKELEMANI, Phandu; Botswana lawyer and politician; *Minister of Foreign Affairs and International Co-operation;* mem. Parl. for Francistown East,

mem. Botswana Democratic Party (BDP) (Domkrag); fmr Attorney-Gen.; Minister of Presidential Affairs and Public Admin. 2004–07, of Justice, Defence and Security 2007–08, of Foreign Affairs and Int. Co-operation 2008–. *Address:* Ministry of Foreign Affairs and International Co-operation, Private Bag 00368, Gaborone, Botswana (office). *Telephone:* 3600700 (office). *Fax:* 3913366 (office). *E-mail:* csmaribe@gov.bw (office). *Website:* www.gov.bw/ government/ministry_of_foreign_affairs.html (office).

SKELTON, Carol; Canadian politician; b. 12 Dec. 1945, Biggar, Sask.; m. Noel; three c.; fmr Co-ordinator Canadian Blood Services, Family Services Officer Canadian Red Cross; mem. Parl. (Conservative) for Saskatoon-Rosetown-Biggar 2000–; fmr Deputy Health Critic, Critic for Social Devt, for Public Health, for Human Resources and Skills Devt (Social Economy), Sr Critic for Western Econ. Diversification; fmr Deputy House Leader, later Leader of the Official Opposition; Vice-Chair. Cttee for Persons with Disabilities; Minister of Nat. Revenue and of Western Economic Diversification 2006–07; fmr mem. Bd Sask. Research Council, Canadian 4-H Council; fmr mem. Man. Cttee Sask. Party; fmr mem. Advisory Cttee on Alcohol. *Address:* 356 Confederation Bldg, House of Commons, Ottawa, ON K1A 0A9, Canada (office). *Telephone:* (613) 995-1551 (office). *Fax:* (613) 943-2010 (office). *Website:* www.carolskelton.ca (office).

SKELTON, H. Jay; American retail executive; b. 1938; began career with KPMG Peat Warwick, Jacksonville, Fla 1962; various positions including Man.-Pnr 1979–89; Pres. and CEO DDI Inc. (diversified holding co.) 1989–2004; Chair. Winn-Dixie Stores Inc. 2004–06; fmr mem. Bd of Dirs Patriot Transportation Holding Inc., Consolidated-Tomoka Land Co. *Address:* c/o Winn-Dixie Stores Inc., 5050 Edgewood Court, Jacksonville, FL 32254-3699, USA (office).

SKERRIT, Roosevelt, BA; Dominican politician; *Prime Minister, Minister of Finance, Planning, Foreign Affairs and Social Security;* b. 1972; ed Univ. of Mississippi, USA, New Mexico State Univ.; fmr high school teacher; Lecturer, Dominica Community Coll. –1999; mem. Dominica Labour Party; mem. House of Ass. 2000–; Minister of Educ., Sports and Youth Affairs –2004; Prime Minister of Dominica, Minister of Finance and Planning 2004–, also of Social Security and Foreign Affairs 2007–. *Address:* Office of the Prime Minister, Government Headquarters, Kennedy Avenue, Roseau, Dominica (office). *Telephone:* 4482401 (office). *Fax:* 4485200 (office).

SKHIRI, Neji; Tunisian banker; b. 15 Feb. 1934, Monastir; m. Slimane Nebiha 1962; one s. three d.; ed Univ. of Tunis, Centre for Educ. of Bankers, Paris; Gen. Man. Cen. Bank of Tunisia 1958–80; Deputy Chair., Chair. Banque du Sud 1980–84; Deputy Chair. Union of Arab Banks 1980–89, Chair. 1989–92; Chair. Soc. Tunisienne de banque 1984–87, Union Int. de Banques 1987–89, Banque du Maghreb Arab 1989–91, Banque Tunisio-Qatari d'investissement 1991–95, NSK Finances 1996–, Tunisian-Italian Chamber of Commerce and Industry; Mayor of Monastir 1985–90; Officer Order of the Repub., Kt Order of Independence. *Leisure interests:* science and literature. *Address:* 3 rue Hamidi, Menzah I, 1004 Tunis, Tunisia. *Telephone:* 751-584. *Fax:* 232-363. *E-mail:* fmsk@hexabyte.tn (office).

SKIDELSKY, Baron (Life Peer), cr. 1991, of Tilton in the County of East Sussex; **Robert Jacob Alexander Skidelsky,** MA, DPhil, FBA, FRHistS, FRSL; British professor of political economy; *Professor of Political Economy, University of Warwick;* b. 25 April 1939; s. of the late Boris Skidelsky and Galia Sapelkin; m. Augusta Hope 1970; two s. one d.; ed Brighton Coll. and Jesus Coll., Oxford; Research Fellow, Nuffield Coll. Oxford 1965; Assoc. Prof., Johns Hopkins Univ., USA 1970; Prof. of Political Economy, Univ. of Warwick 1990–; Chair. Social Market Foundation 1991–2001; Chair. Hands Off Reading Campaign 1994–97; Conservative Front Bench Spokesman on Culture, Media and Sport 1997–98, on Treasury Affairs 1998–99; mem. Lord Chancellor's Advisory Council on Public Records 1988–93; mem. Schools Examination and Assessment Council 1992–93; mem. Bd Manhattan Inst. 1994–, Moscow School of Political Studies 1999–, Janus Capital Group Inc. 2001–; mem. House of Lords Select Cttee on Econ. Affairs 2003–; Gov. Brighton Coll. 1998–; Chair. Wilton Park Academic Council 2004–; Hon. DLitt (Buckingham) 1997; Wolfson History Prize 1993, Duff Cooper Prize 2000, Lionel Gelber Prize 2001, Council on Foreign Relations Prize 2002, James Tait Black Memorial Prize 2002. *Publications:* Politicians and the Slump 1967, English Progressive Schools 1970, Oswald Mosley 1975, John Maynard Keynes, Vol. 1 1983, Vol. 2 1992, Vol. 3 2000, (single-vol. abridgement) 2003, Interests and Obsessions 1993, The World After Communism 1995, Beyond the Welfare State 1997, The Politics of Economic Reform 1998. *Leisure interests:* music, tennis. *Address:* House of Lords, London, SW1A 0PW (office); Tilton House, Firle, East Sussex, BN8 6LL, England. *Telephone:* (20) 7219-8721 (office); (1323) 811570. *Fax:* (1323) 811017. *E-mail:* skidelskyr@ parliament.uk (office).

SKILBECK, Malcolm, MA, PhD, FAASS; Australian educational researcher and consultant; b. 22 Sept. 1932, Northam, WA; s. of Charles Harrison Skilbeck and Elsie Muriel Nash Skilbeck; m. 1st Elizabeth Robbins; one s. three d.; m. 2nd Dr Helen Connell 1984; one d.; ed Sydney Univ., Univ. of Ill. and Univ. of London; Prof. and Dean of Educ., Univ. of Ulster 1971–75; Foundation Dir, Australian Curriculum Devt Centre 1975–81; Dir of Studies, Schools Council for Curriculum and Examinations for England and Wales 1981–83; Prof. of Curriculum Studies, Inst. of Educ., Univ. of London 1981–85; Vice-Chancellor and Prin. Deakin Univ. 1986–91; Deputy Dir for Educ., Directorate of Educ., Employment, Labour and Social Affairs, OECD 1991–97; Dir Connell Skilbeck Int. Educ. Consultants 1997–; Consultant to OECD, UNESCO, nat. govts, British Council, Australian Int. Devt Assistance Bureau; Hon. DLitt. *Publications:* Culture and the Classroom 1976, A Core Curriculum for the Common School 1982, School Based Curriculum Development 1984, Evaluating the Curriculum for the Eighties 1984, Curriculum Reform 1990, The Vocational Quest 1994, Redefining Tertiary Education 1998, Access and Equity in Higher Education 2000, The University Challenged 2002. *Leisure interests:* gardens, books, art. *Address:* PO Box 278, Drysdale, Vic. 3222, Australia. *Telephone:* 3525-33340. *Fax:* 3525-33340; 3525-33340 (office). *E-mail:* skilbeck.connell@deakin.edu.au (office).

SKINNER, James (Jim) A.; American food industry executive; *Vice-Chairman and CEO, McDonald's Corporation;* began career with McDonald's as trainee restaurant man. 1971, then numerous man. positions including dir of field operations, market man., regional Vice Pres., US Sr Vice Pres.; joined McDonald's int. man. team as Sr Vice Pres. and Relationship Pnr for Cen. Europe, the Middle East, Africa and India 1992, Exec. Vice Pres. and Relationship Pnr 1995–97, Pres. McDonald's Europe 1997–2001, fmr Pres. and COO for Europe/Asia/Pacific and Middle East, fmr Pres. and COO McDonald's Restaurant Group, Vice-Chair. and CEO McDonald's Corpn 2004–; mem. Bd Ronald McDonald House Charities. *Address:* McDonald's Corpn, McDonald's Plaza, Oak Brook, IL 60523, USA (office). *Telephone:* (630) 623-3000 (office). *Fax:* (630) 623-5004 (office). *E-mail:* info@mcdonalds.com (office). *Website:* www.mcdonalds.com (office).

SKINNER, Paul, BA (Law), DpBA; British mining industry executive; b. 1944; m.; two s.; ed Univ. of Cambridge, Manchester Business School; joined The Royal Dutch/Shell Group of Cos 1966, sr appointments in UK, Greece, Nigeria, NZ and Norway, CEO Global Oil Products Business 1999–2003, Man. Dir Shell Transport and Trading Co. PLC 2000–03, also Group Man. Dir; Dir Rio Tinto plc and Rio Tinto Ltd 2001–09, Group Chair. 2003–09; Dir (non-exec.) Standard Chartered PLC 2003–, Tetra Laval Group 2005–, L'Air Liquide SA 2006–; Chair. Governing Body ICC (UK) 2004–08, Commonwealth Business Council 2007–; mem. (non-exec.) Defence Man. Bd, UK Ministry of Defence 2006–; Pres. UK Chamber of Shipping 1997–98; mem. Bd INSEAD Business School 1999–. *Leisure interests:* skiing, other outdoor sports, opera, modern history. *Address:* c/o Rio Tinto plc, 5 Aldermanbury Square, London, EC2V 7HR England (office).

SKINNER, Quentin Robert Duthie, MA, FBA; British historian and academic; *Barber Beaumont Professor of the Humanities, Queen Mary, University of London;* b. 26 Nov. 1940, Oldham; s. of Alexander Skinner and Winifred Skinner (née Duthie); m. 2nd Susan James 1979; one s. one d.; ed Bedford School, Gonville and Caius Coll., Cambridge; Fellow, Christ's Coll., Cambridge 1962–2008, Vice-Master 1997–99, Hon. Fellow 2008–; Lecturer in History, Univ. of Cambridge 1967–78, Prof. of Political Science 1978–96, Regius Prof. of Modern History 1996–2008, Pro-Vice-Chancellor 1999; Barber Beaumont Prof. of the Humanities, Queen Mary, Univ. of London 2008–; mem. Inst. of Advanced Study, Princeton, NJ 1974–75, 1976–79; mem. Academia Europaea 1989; Foreign mem. American Acad. of Arts and Sciences 1986, American Philosophical Soc. 1997, Royal Irish Acad. 1999, Accademia Nazionale del Lincei 2007; Hon. DLitt (Chicago) 1992, (E Anglia) 1992, (Helsinki) 1997, (Oxford) 2000, (Leuven) 2004, (St Andrews) 2005, (Athens) 2007, (Aberdeen) 2007; Wolfson Literary Award 1979, Balzan Prize 2006, Sir Isaiah Berlin Prize 2006. *Publications:* The Foundations of Modern Political Thought, Vol. I The Renaissance 1978, Vol. II The Age of Reformation 1978, Machiavelli 1981, Philosophy in History (co-ed. and contrib.) 1984, The Return of Grand Theory in the Human Sciences (ed. and contrib.) 1985, The Cambridge History of Renaissance Philosophy (co-ed. and contrib.) 1988, Machiavelli: The Prince (ed. and introduction) 1988, Meaning and Context: Quentin Skinner and His Critics (ed. James Tully) 1988, Machiavelli and Republicanism (co-ed. and contrib.) 1990, Political Discourse in Early-modern Britain (co-ed. and contrib.) 1993, Milton and Republicanism (co-ed.) 1995, Reason and Rhetoric in the Philosophy of Hobbes 1996, Liberty before Liberalism 1998, Visions of Politics, Vol. I Regarding Method 2002, Vol. II Renaissance Virtues 2002, Vol. III Hobbes and Civil Science 2002, Republic-anism: A Shared European Heritage (co-ed. and contrib.) Vol. I Republicanism and Constitutionalism in Early Modern Europe 2002, Vol. II The Values of Republicanism in Early Modern Europe 2002, States and Citizens (co-ed. and contrib.) 2003, Thomas Hobbes: Writings on Common Law and Hereditary Right (co-ed.) 2005, Hobbes and Republican Liberty 2008. *Address:* Department of History, Queen Mary, University of London, Mile End Road, London, E1 4NS, England (office). *Telephone:* (20) 7882-8325 (office). *Fax:* (20) 8980-8400 (office). *E-mail:* q.skinner@qmul.ac.uk (office). *Website:* www.history.qmul.ac.uk (office).

SKOKOV, Yuri Vladimirovich, C.TECH.SC.; Russian politician; b. 16 June 1938, Vladivostok; ed Leningrad Electrotech. Inst.; mem. CPSU 1967–91; researcher then Deputy Dir Kalinin Research Inst. of Electric Sources, USSR Ministry of Defence 1969–75, Dir 1975–76; Deputy Dir-Gen. Research Production Union Quant 1977–86, Dir 1986–90; USSR People's Deputy 1989–91; People's Deputy of Russian Fed. 1990–; Chair. Bd of Concern Quantemp 1988–90, First Deputy Chair. Council of Ministers of RSFSR 1990–91; Econ. Counsellor to Pres. of Russia 1990–91; Sec. Council on Problems of Fed. and Territories 1991–92; Sec. Security Council 1992–93; Head of Fed. of Community Producers of Russian Fed. 1994; Chair. Bd Centre for Int. and Inter-regional Econ. Problems 1994; Chair. Bd Congress of Russian Communities 1995–99; f. AMBI-Bank 1998; Dir-Gen. Scientific Production Union Kvant-Co-operation 2000.

SKOL, Michael, BA; American diplomatist and business executive; *President, Skol and Associates, Inc.;* b. 15 Oct. 1942, Chicago, Ill.; s. of Ted Skol and Rebecca Skol; m. Claudia Serwer 1973; ed Yale Univ.; joined US Foreign Service 1965; served in Buenos Aires, Saigon, Santo Domingo, Naples, Rome, San José and Bogotá (Deputy Chief of Mission) and as Desk Officer for Costa Rica, Paraguay and Uruguay; Deputy Dir for Policy Planning and Dir Andean Affairs, State Dept Bureau of Inter-American Affairs; Deputy

Asst Sec. of State for S America, 1988–90; Amb. to Venezuela 1990–93; Prin. Deputy Asst Sec. Latin American/Caribbean Dept of State 1993–95; Founding Chair. US-Colombia Business Partnership 1996–99; Sr Vice-Pres. Diplomatic Resolutions Inc., Washington, DC 1996–97; founder and Pres. Skol and Assocs, Inc., Washington DC 1998–; Sr Man. Dir for Latin America, DSFX, Washington DC 1998–2005; Founder and Pres. Skol, Ospina & Serna LLC, Bogotá, Colombia 2000–03; Sr Assoc. Manchester Trade Ltd; Prin., Skol and Serna, Washington, DC and Bogota 2003–; mem. Council on Foreign Relations; Order of the Liberator (Venezuela) 1993, Order of Nat. Merit (Paraguay) 1995. *Television includes:* co-creator and first co-host 'Choque de Opiniones', CNN Spanish TV network 1997. *Address:* Skol and Associates, Inc., 1710 Rhode Island Avenue, NW, Suite 300, Washington, DC 20036 (office); PO Box 596, Dennis, MA 02638, USA (home). *Telephone:* (202) 331-9464 (office). *Fax:* (202) 785-0376 (office). *E-mail:* mikeskol@aol.com (office). *Website:* ssadvisors.net (office).

ŠKOLČ, Jožef; Slovenian politician; b. 19 Aug. 1960, Breginj; ed Ljubljana Univ.; active in Socialist Youth League of Slovenia (ZSMS) 1979–84; mem. of Pres. Republican Conf. of Socialist Youth League (RKZSMS) 1984–, Pres. 1988–92; Chair. Cttee for Constitution 1990; Deputy Nat. Ass. for Ljubljana Moste-Polje (6) 1992–, Pres. Nat. Ass. 1994–96; Leader of ZSMS Deputies' Club (later Liberal Democratic Party) 1990–94; Co-ordinator of Liberal Democracy of Slovenia; Minister of Culture 1997–2000; Chair. Comm. for Mandates and Elections 2000–. *Address:* National Assembly, Šubičeva str. 4, 1000 Ljubljana, Slovenia (office). *Telephone:* (1) 4789400 (office). *Fax:* (1) 4789845 (home). *E-mail:* infodz-rs.si (office). *Website:* www.dz-rs.si (office).

SKOLIMOWSKI, Jerzy; Polish film director, artist and actor; b. 5 May 1938, Warsaw; m. Joanna Szczerbic; ed Warsaw Univ. and State Superior Film School, Łódź; wrote scripts for Wajda's Innocent Sorcerers, Polanski's Knife in the Water and Łomnicki's Poślizg; Special Prize, Venice Film Festival 1985. *Films:* Rysopis (Identification Marks: None) (also designer, author, editor, actor) 1964, Walkover (also screenwriter and actor) 1965, Bariera (Barrier) (also screenwriter) (Grand Prix, Int. Film Festival, Bergamo 1966) 1966, Le Départ 1967 Dialogue 20-40-60 1968, The Adventures of Gerard 1969, The Deep End 1971, King, Queen, Knave 1972, Lady Frankenstein (or Terminus) 1976, The Shout (Silver Palm, Cannes Film Festival 1978) 1978, Rece do góry (Hands Up!) (also screenwriter and actor) 1981, Moonlighting (British Film Award 1982) 1982, Success is the Best Revenge 1984, The Lightship 1985, Mesmerized (screenwriter) 1986, Torrents of Spring (screenwriter) 1989, Before and After Death 1990, 30 Door Key 1991, The Hollow Men, America 2008; as actor: Niewinni czarodzieje 1960, Boks 1961, Rysopis 1964, Walkower 1965, Sposób bycia 1966, Deep End 1971, Poslizg 1972, Rece do góry 1981, Die Fälschung 1981, White Nights 1985, Big Shots 1987, Torrents of Spring 1989, Mars Attacks! 1996, L.A. Without a Map 1998, Before Night Falls 2000, Eastern Promises 2007, Cztery noce z Anna (Four Nights with Anna) 2008. *Publications:* poetry: Gdzieś blisko siebie (Somewhere Close to Oneself); play: Ktoś się utopił (Somebody Got Drowned). *Address:* c/o Film Polski, ul. Mazowiecka 6/8, 00-048 Warsaw, Poland.

SKOLL, Jeffrey (Jeff) S., BS, MBA; American/Canadian business executive, foundation executive and film producer; *Chairman, Skoll Foundation;* b. 16 Jan. 1965, Montréal; ed Univ. of Toronto, Stanford Univ. Grad. School of Business; first job as gas pump attendant in North York, Ont.; f. Skoll Eng (consulting firm), Toronto 1987, Micros on the Move Ltd (computer hire firm) 1990; Man. Knight-Ridder Information (online news information) internet distribution channels 1995; Co-founder and Pres. eBay Inc. 1996–98, then Vice Pres., Strategic Planning and Analysis 1998; mem. Bd of Dirs eBay Foundation 1998–; Founder and Chair. Skoll Foundation 1999–; Founder and CEO Participant Productions (film production co.), Los Angeles 2004–; f. Gandhi Project 2005; mem. Bd of Dirs Capricorn Man., Community Founda-tion Silicon Valley; mem. Advisory Bd Stanford Grad. School of Business; Hon. LLD (Univ. of Toronto) 2003; Leafy Award (Canada) 1999, Software Devt Forum Visionary Award 2001, Asscn of Fundraising Professionals Silicon Valley Chapter Outstanding Philanthropist Award 2002, Int. Asscn of Fundraising Professionals Outstanding Philanthropist Award 2003, Nat. Leadership Award for Commonwealth Club Silicon Valley 2004, Wired Magazine's Rave Award 2006. *Films produced:* House of D 2004, Good Night, and Good Luck 2005, North Country 2005, American Gun 2005, Syriana 2005, An Inconvenient Truth 2006, Fast Food Nation 2006, The World According to Sesame Street 2006, Chicago 10 2007. *Publications include:* numerous articles in popular and professional journals. *Address:* Skoll Foundation, 250 Univer-sity Avenue, Suite 200, Palo Alto, CA 94301, USA (office). *Telephone:* (650) 331-1031 (office). *Fax:* (650) 331-1033 (office). *E-mail:* media@skollfoundation.org (office). info@participantproductions.com (office). *Website:* www.skollfoundation.org (office); www.participantproductions.com.

SKOMOROKHA, Viktor Yehorovych, Cand. of Law; Ukrainian judge; b. 1941, Matrosove Village, Solonyansk Dist, Dnipropetrovsk Region; m. Liudmyla Vasylivna; one s. one d.; ed Kharkiv Law Inst. (now Yaroslav Mudry Nat. Law Acad. of Ukraine); Judge, Krasny Luch Municipal Court, Luhansk Region 1967–70; mem. Luhansk Municipal Court 1970–76; Judge, Supreme Court of Ukraine 1976–96; Judge, Constitutional Court of Ukraine 1996, Chair. 1999–2002; Prof. 2003–; Order for Merits, Second Class 2000, First Class 2002; Cross of Honour for the Renaissance of Ukraine 2002; Veteran of Work Medal 1983, Distinguished Lawyer of Ukraine 1995. *Publications:* publs on Ukrainian constitutional issues, human rights and admin. reform. *Leisure interests:* history books, poetry, gardening. *Address:* c/o Constitutional Court, vul. Zhylianska 14, Kiev, Ukraine (office).

SKORTON, David J., BA, MD; American cardiologist, university adminis-trator, computer scientist and jazz musician; *President, Cornell University;* ed Northwestern Univ.; worked as jazz and R&B musician in Chicago area;

medical residency and cardiology fellowship, UCLA; Instructor, Univ. of Iowa 1980, Asst Prof. of Internal Medicine 1981, Asst Prof. of Electrical and Computer Eng 1982–84, Assoc. Prof. 1984–88, Prof. 1988–2003, Co-founder and Co-dir Adolescent and Adult Congenital Heart Disease Clinic, Univ. of Iowa Hosps and Clinics, Vice-Pres. for Research 1992, Interim Vice-Pres. for External Relations 2000–02, Vice-Pres. for Research and External Relations 2002–03, Pres. Univ. of Iowa 2003–06; Pres. Cornell Univ. 2006–, holds faculty appointments in Internal Medicine and Pediatrics at Weill-Cornell Medical Coll., New York City and in Biomedical Eng at Coll. of Eng on Ithaca campus; Charter Past-Pres. Asscn for Accreditation of Human Research Protection Programs, Inc.; has served on bds and cttees of many other nat. orgs, including American Coll. of Cardiology, American Heart Asscn, American Inst. of Ultrasound in Medicine, American Soc. of Echocardiography, Asscn of American Univs, Council on Competitiveness, Korea America Friendship Soc. 2006–; Vice-Chair. Business of Higher Educ. Forum 2006–; mem. Council on Foreign Relations. *Radio:* studied and played saxophone and flute in Iowa City and hosted a weekly jazz program, As Night Falls, on KSUI (Univ. of Iowa's public FM radio station). *Publications:* numerous articles, reviews, book chapters, and two major texts on cardiac imaging and image processing. *Address:* Office of the President, 300 Day Hall, Cornell University, Ithaca, NY 14853, USA (office). *Telephone:* (607) 255-5201 (office). *Fax:* (607) 255-9924 (office). *E-mail:* president@cornell.edu (office). *Website:* www.cornell.edu/president (office).

SKOTHEIM, Robert Allen, PhD; American historian and academic administrator; *President, Occidental College;* b. 31 Jan. 1933, Seattle, Wash.; s. of Sivert O. Skotheim and Marjorie F. Skotheim (née Allen); m. Nadine Vail 1953; one s. two d.; ed Univ. of Wash.; Prof. of History, Univ. of Wash., Wayne State Univ., UCLA, Univ. of Colorado 1962–72; Provost and Faculty Dean Hobart and William Smith Colls 1972–75; Pres. Whitman Coll. 1975–88; Dir Huntington Library, Art Collections, Botanical Gardens 1988–90, Pres. 1990–2001, now Pres. Emer.; Pres. Occidental Coll. 2008–; mem. Advisory Bd Thomas C. Wales Foundation; Guggenheim Memorial Fellowship 1967–68; numerous hon. degrees. *Publications:* American Intellectual Histories and Historians 1966, co-ed. Historical Scholarship in the United States and Other Essays 1967; ed. The Historian and the Climate of Opinion 1969, Totalitarianism and American Social Thought 1971, co-ed. American Social Thought: Sources and Interpretations (two vols) 1972. *Address:* Office of the President, Occidental College, 1600 Campus Road, Los Angeles, CA 90041, USA (office). *Telephone:* (323) 259-2691 (office). *Fax:* (323) 259-2907 (office). *E-mail:* rskotheim@oxy.edu (office). *Website:* www.oxy.edu (office).

SKOTNIKOV, Leonid Alekseyevich; Russian diplomatist and judge; *Judge, International Court of Justice;* b. 26 March 1951, Kalinin; m.; one s.; ed Moscow State Inst. of Int. Relations; mem. staff, Consular Dept Ministry of Foreign Affairs 1974–77; attaché, Perm. Mission to the UN 1977–81; mem. staff, Legal Dept, Ministry of Foreign Affairs 1981–91, Dir 1991–92, 1998–2001; Amb. to the Netherlands 1992–98; Amb. and Perm. Rep. to UN Office and other Int. Orgs in Geneva, the Disarmament Conf. 2001–05; Judge, Int. Court of Justice 2006–; Order of Friendship 2002. *Address:* International Court of Justice, Peace Palace, 2517 KJ The Hague, Netherlands (office). *Telephone:* (70) 3022323 (office). *Fax:* (70) 3649928 (office). *Website:* www.icj-cij.org (office).

SKOU, Jens Christian, MD; Danish biophysicist and academic; *Professor Emeritus of Biophysics, University of Århus;* b. 8 Oct. 1918, Lemvig; s. of Magnus Martinus Skou and Ane Margrethe Skou; m. Ellen Margrethe Nielsen 1948; two d.; ed Univ. of Copenhagen; clinical appointments in surgery and orthopaedics 1944–47; Asst Prof. Inst. of Physiology, Univ. of Århus 1947, Assoc. Prof. 1954, Prof. and Chair. of Dept 1963, Prof. of Biophysics 1978–88, Prof. Emer. 1988–; mem. Royal Danish Acad. of Sciences, Deutsche Akad. der Naturforscher, Leopoldina, European Molecular Biology Org.; Foreign Assoc. NAS, Academia Europaea, Int. Acad. of Humanism; Hon. mem. Japanese Biochemical Soc., American Physiological Soc., American Acad. of Arts and Sciences; Hon. DrMed (Copenhagen) 1986; Leo Prize 1959, Novo Prize 1964, Consul Carlsen Prize 1973, Anders Retzius Gold Medal 1977, Erik K. Fernström's Nordic Prize 1985, shared Nobel Prize for Chemistry 1997 (for identifying the first ion transporting enzyme, the Na,K-ATPase). *Publications:* scientific papers on the mechanism of action of local anaesthetics 1946–57; scientific publs on structure and function of the Na, K-pump, the transport system in the cell membrane responsible for the exchange of cations across membranes 1957–. *Leisure interests:* classical music, yachting, skiing. *Address:* Institute of Biophysics, Ole Worms Allé 185, Universitetsparken, 8000 Århus C. (office); Rislundvej 9, Risskov, 8240, Denmark (home). *Telephone:* 89-42-29-50 (office); 86-17-79-18 (home). *Fax:* 86-12-95-99 (home). *E-mail:* jcs@biophys.au.dk (office). *Website:* www.biophys.au.dk (office).

SKOURAS, Thanos, PhD, FBIM; Greek economist and academic; *Professor, Athens University of Economics and Business;* b. 21 Dec. 1943, Athens; s. of Spyros D. Skouras and Ismini Xanthopoulos; m. 1st Gella Varnava 1966 (divorced 1987); two s.; m. 2nd Savina Ioannides 1998; ed Athens Coll., King's Coll., Durham Univ. and London School of Econs, UK; Asst Lecturer, Lecturer, Sr Lecturer, Middlesex Polytechnic at Enfield, UK 1967–73; Prin. Lecturer and Head Econs Div., Thames Polytechnic 1974–77; Head Dept of Applied Econ. Studies, NE London Polytechnic (now Univ. of E London) 1978–86; Prof., Athens Univ. of Econs and Business 1986–, Deputy Chair. Econs Dept 1987–89, Vice-Rector 1989–92, Pres. Research Centre 1989–92; fmr Visiting Lecturer, Architectural Asscn School, London, Cambridge Univ., CEMI Beijing, Fudan Univ. Shanghai, Katholieke Univ. Leuven; Adviser to Deputy Minister of Nat. Economy, Athens; mem. Council of Econ. Advisers 1986–88; Ed. The Thames Papers in Political Economy 1974–86, The British Review of Econ. Issues 1976–85; Assoc. Ed. Greek Econ. Review 1985–90; mem. Editorial Bd Int. Review of Applied Econs 1993–; Councillor Royal Econ. Soc., London 1982–86; mem. Governing Council Greek Centre of Planning and Econ. Research 1987–88; Chair. Cttee for Financing of Major Infrastructure Projects 1988; Council mem. Euro-China Research Asscn for Man. 1989–92; mem. Supreme Disciplinary Council, Econ. Chamber of Greece 1990–92; Consultant intra muros European Comm. DG XVI 1992–94; Chair. Bd Abax Stockbroking 1991–94; mem. Bd Ergose 1996–97, Commercial Bank 1997, Greek Econ. Soc. 1998–99, Hellenic Centre for European Studies 2001–; Hon. Research Fellow, Polytechnic of E London 1986–91. *Publications:* Land and its Taxation in Recent Economic Theory 1977, Post-Keynesian Economic Theory (co-ed.) 1985, The Greek Economy: Economic Policy for the 1990s (ed.) 1991, Production or Importation of Advanced Technology Manufactures? – The Case of Telecommunications Equipment (co-author) 1993, Economic Priorities on the Threshold of the 21st Century (co-ed.) 2000, The Economic Dimension of Mass Communication Media 2003; about 60 articles in professional journals. *Address:* Athens University of Economics and Business, 76 Patission Street, 104 34 Athens (office); 8 Chlois Street, 145 62 Athens, Greece. *Telephone:* 8203651 (office). *Fax:* 8082543. *E-mail:* chlois@aueb.gr (office). *Website:* www.aueb.gr/gb (office).

SKOURIS, Vassilios; Greek judge; *President, Court of Justice of the European Communities;* b. 1948; ed Free Univ., Berlin, Hamburg Univ., Germany; Asst Prof., Hamburg Univ. 1972–77; Prof. of Public Law, Bielefeld Univ. 1978, Univ. of Thessaloniki 1982; Minister of Internal Affairs 1989, 1996; Judge, Court of Justice of the European Communities 1999–, Pres. 2003–; Dir Centre for Int. and European Econ. Law, Thessaloniki 1997–; mem. Acad. Council, Acad. of European Law, Trier 1995–; mem. Greek Nat. Research Cttee 1993–95, Scientific Cttee, Ministry of Foreign Affairs 1997–99; mem. Admin. Bd, Univ. of Crete 1983–87, Higher Selection Bd for Greek Civil Servants 1994–96, Admin. Bd, Greek Nat. Judge's Coll 1995–96; Pres. Greek Asscn for European Law 1992–94, Greek Econ. and Social Council 1998. *Address:* Court of Justice of the European Communities, Palais de la Cour de Justice, blvd Konrad Adenauer, 2925 Luxembourg (office). *Telephone:* 4303-1 (office). *Fax:* 4303-2600 (office). *E-mail:* info@curia.eu.int (office). *Website:* www.curia.eu.int/en/index.htm (office).

SKOVHUS, Bo; Danish singer; b. 22 May 1962, Ikast; s. of Freddy Jorgensen and Birthe Skovhus; one d.; ed Music Acad., Århus, Royal Music Acad. and Opera School, Copenhagen, and in New York; debut in Don Giovanni, Vienna Volksoper 1988, debut as Silvio, Pagliacci Vienna Staatsoper 1991; regular guest singer with all major orchestras and opera cos including Metropolitan, New York, San Francisco, Houston, Munich State Opera, Hamburg State Opera, Berlin, Cologne, Covent Garden, Dresden, etc.; many recitals in Europe, USA and Japan; numerous lieder recitals with Helmut Deutsch, Stefan Vladar, Yefim Bronfman, Lief Ove Andsnes, Christoph Eschenbach and Daniel Barenboim; repertoire includes Don Giovanni, Almaviva in Le Nozze di Figaro, Guglielmo in Così fan tutte, Wolfram in Tannhauser, Olivier in Capriccio, Barber in Schweigsame Frau, Wozzeck, Hamlet, Billy Budd, Eugene Onegin, Yeletsky in Pique Dame, Danilo in Lustige Witwe, Eisenstein in Die Fledermaus; Kammersänger (Austria) 1997. *Recordings include:* Don Giovanni (twice), Le Nozze di Figaro, The Merry Widow, Britten's War Requiem, Carmina Burana, Fidelio, Das Lied von der Erde, Wozzeck, Mirror of Perfection (Blackford), I Pagliacci, Der Waffenschmied (Lortzing), Maskarade (Nielsen), Venus (Schoek), Die Schöne Müllerin, Schwanengesang (Schubert), Dichterliebe (Schumann), Liederkreis Op. 24 (Schumann), Eichendorff Lieder (Wolf), Faust (Spohr), Oberon (Weber), Die Orchesterlieder (Strauss), Lyrische Sinfonie (Zemlinsky) (twice), Lieder (Zemlinski) and recording of arias by Britten, Gounod, Korngold, Verdi, Wagner, Thomas, Massenet and Tschaikowsky. *Address:* Balmer & Dixon Management AG, Kreuzstrasse 82, 8032 Zürich, Switzerland (office). *Telephone:* (43) 244-8644 (office). *Fax:* (43) 244-8649 (office). *Website:* www.badix.ch (office).

SKRINSKY, Aleksandr Nikolayevich, DSc; Russian physicist; b. 15 Jan. 1936, Orenburg; s. of Nikolay Alexandrovich Skrinsky and Galina Stepanovna Skrinskaya; m. Lydia Borisovna Golovanova; one s. one d.; ed Moscow State Univ.; Research Worker, Inst. of Nuclear Physics, Siberian Dept, USSR (now Russian) Acad. of Sciences, Head of Lab. 1959–, Deputy Dir 1971–77, Dir Budker Inst. of Nuclear Physics 1977–; Prof. Novosibirsk Univ. 1967–85; Corresp. mem. USSR (now Russian) Acad. of Sciences 1968–70, mem. 1970, Academician-Sec. Nuclear Physics Dept 1988–2002; mem. Int. Cttee for Future Accelerators (ICFA) 1983–90 (Chair. 1990–93), CERN Scientific Policy Cttee 1985–91; mem. Royal Swedish Acad. of Science 2002; Fellow American Physical Soc. 1999–; Lenin Prize 1967, USSR State Prize 1989, Robert R. Wilson Prize 2002, Karpinsky Prize 2002. *Publications:* more than 200 scientific works in the field of accelerator physics and technology, elementary particle physics. *Leisure interests:* ski-running, swimming, music. *Address:* Russian Academy of Sciences, Department of Physics, 117334 Moscow, Leninsky prosp. 32A, Russia. *Telephone:* (495) 938-07-53. *Fax:* (495) 938-54-24. *E-mail:* A.N.Skrinsky@inp.nsk.su; skrinsky@npd.ac.ru.

SKROWACZEWSKI, Stanisław; Polish/American conductor and composer; *Principal Conductor, Yomiuri Nippon Symphony Orchestra;* b. 3 Oct. 1923, Lwów (now in Ukraine); s. of Paweł Skrowaczewski and Zofia Skrowaczewska (née Karszniewicz); m. Krystyna Jarosz 1956; two s. one d.; ed Lwów Conservatoire and State Higher School of Music, Kraków; Conductor, Wrocław Philharmonic Orchestra 1946–47; further composition studies with Nadia Boulanger and P. Klecki, Paris 1947–49; Artistic Dir and First Conductor, Silesian Philharmonic Orchestra, Katowice 1949–54; First Conductor, Kraków Philharmonic Orchestra 1955–56; Dir Nat. Philharmonic Orchestra, Warsaw 1957–59; Musical Dir Minnesota Orchestra 1960–79; tours in Europe, N and S America, Israel, Japan, Australia; Prin. Conductor and Musical Adviser, Hallé Orchestra 1984–91; Musical Adviser St Paul Chamber Orchestra 1986–88, Milwaukee Symphony 1992–94; Prin. Conductor Yomiuri Nippon Symphony Orchestra, Tokyo 2007–; Commdr Cross of Polonia Restituta Order; Hon. DHL (Hamline Univ., St Paul, Minnesota) 1961; Hon. DMus (Macalester Coll., St Paul, Minn.) 1977; Dr hc (Univ. of Minnesota) 1979; Second Prize for 'Overture 1947', Szymanowski Competition, Warsaw 1947, Second Prize, Int. Competition for String Quartet, Liège, Belgium 1953, State Prize (3rd Class) 1956, First Prize, Int. Conductor's Competition, Rome 1956, Conductor's Award of Columbia Univ., New York 1973, Third Prize, Kennedy Center Friedheim Award Competition (for Ricercari Notturni) 1978; 5 ASCAP Awards for imaginative programming with Minneapolis Symphony 1961–79, Gold Medal, Bruckner-Mahler Soc. 1999, McKnight Distinguished Artist Award 2004. *Compositions include:* Symphony for String Orchestra, three other symphonies, Muzyka Nocą (Music by Night, suite of nocturnes), four string quartets, two overtures, Cantique des Cantiques (voice and orch.), Prelude, Fugue, Post-Ludium (orch.), English Horn Concerto 1969, Ricercari Notturni (orchestral), Clarinet Concerto, Violin Concerto 1985, Fanfare for Orchestra 1987, Sextet 1988, String Trio 1990, Triple Concerto 1992, Chamber Concerto 1993, Passacaglia Immaginaria 1995, Musica a quattro 1998, Concerto for Orchestra 1999, Trio for piano, clarinet and bassoon, six piano sonatas; also music for opera, ballet, film and theatre; recordings for Mercury, Philips, Angel, RCA Victor, IMP, Erato, Arte Nova, Vox, Albany. *Leisure interests:* alpinism, skiing, books, film, theatre. *Address:* c/o Intermusica Artists Management Ltd, 16 Duncan Terrace, London, N1 8BZ, England (office); Yomiuri Nippon Symphony Orchestra, 7F Daiichi Nurihiko Bldg, 2-9-2 Kyobashi, Chuo-ku, Tokyo 104-0031, Japan (office). *Telephone:* (20) 7278-5455 (office); (3) 3562-1540 (office). *Fax:* (20) 7278-8434 (office); (3) 3562-1544 (office). *E-mail:* mail@intermusica.co.uk (office). *Website:* www.intermusica.co.uk (office); yomikyo.yomiuri.co.jp (office).

SKRZYPEK, Sławomir, MBA; Polish central banker; *President, National Bank of Poland;* b. 1963; m.; three c.; ed Silesian Univ. of Tech., Gliwice, Warsaw School of Econs (SGH), Univ. of Wisconsin, La Crosse, Georgetown Univ., Kraków Univ. of Econs, Faculty of Law and Admin, Silesian Univ.; worked in Supreme Chamber of Control 1993–97; Vice-Pres. Nat. Fund for Environmental Protection and Water Man. 1997–2000; mem. advisory group PZU Życie S.A. (insurance co.) 2000–01; financial adviser and Lecturer in Man., Warsaw Univ., Warsaw Agric. Univ. and Higher School of Man. and Marketing 2001–07; mem. Bd of Dirs IX Nat. Investment Fund April–May 2001, Polish Railways (PKP SA) May 2001–Jan. 2002; Deputy Mayor of Warsaw 2002–05; Vice Pres. Man. Bd Powszechna Kasa Oszczędności Bank Polski (PKO BP) 2005–07, Acting Pres. 2006–07; Chair. Supervisory Bd Bank Pocztowy SA 2006, Polish Television (TVP SA) 2006–07; Pres. Nat. Bank of Poland (cen. bank) 2007–. *Address:* National Bank of Poland (Narodowy Bank Polski), 00-919 Warsaw, Swiętokrzyska 11/21, Poland (office). *Telephone:* (22) 6531000 (office). *Fax:* (22) 6208518 (office). *E-mail:* nbp@nbp.pl (office). *Website:* www.nbp.pl (office).

SKUBISZEWSKI, Krzysztof Jan, DrIur, LLM; Polish politician and lawyer; *President, Iran–US Claims Tribunal;* b. 8 Oct. 1926, Poznań; s. of Ludwik Skubiszewski and Aniela Skubiszewska (née Leitgeber); ed Poznań Univ., Université de Nancy, France and Harvard Univ., USA; mem. staff, Poznań Univ. (renamed Adam Mickiewicz Univ.) 1948–73, Voluntary Asst, Jr Asst, Lecturer 1948–56, Asst Prof. 1956–61, Dozent, Dept of Int. Law 1961–73, Pro-Dean Law Faculty 1961–63; Prof., Inst. of State and Law, Polish Acad. of Sciences, Warsaw 1973–96; Minister of Foreign Affairs 1989–93; Pres. Iran–US Claims Tribunal, The Hague 1994–; Judge ad hoc, Int. Court of Justice 1994–; mem. Curatorium, Hague Acad. of Int. Law 1994–, Bureau, Court of Conciliation and Arbitration, OSCE, Geneva 1995–2000; Chair., Council for Foreign Policy 1996–, Dutch–French Arbitration Tribunal 2000–; Pres. Tribunal of Arbitration in Application of the Convention of December 3, 1976 on the Protection of the Rhine against Pollution by Chlorides, Perm. Court of Arbitration 2001–04; Visiting Scholar, School of Int. Affairs, Columbia Univ., New York 1963–64, Prof. invité, Geneva Univ. 1971, 1979; Visiting Fellow, All Souls Coll. Oxford 1971–72; Curator, Student Asscn of UN Friends, Poznań 1960–73; mem. Poznań Friends of Learning Soc. 1951–, West Inst. in Poznań 1961–, Inst. de Droit Int. 1971–, Polish Group of Int. Law Asscn 1971–, American Soc. of Int. Law, Oxford Soc., Soc. Française pour le Droit Int.; mem. Legal Sciences Cttee, Polish Acad. of Sciences 1981–, Advisory Bd European Journal of Law Reform; Corresp. mem. Polish Acad. of Sciences, Warsaw 1989–, Inst. de France 1995–; mem. Polish Acad. of Arts and Sciences, Kraków 1994–; mem. Primatial Social Council 1981–84, Consultative Council attached to Chair. of Council of State 1986–89; Hon. Prof. (Bucharest); Hon. Bencher, Gray's Inn 1990; Grand Cross of Polonia Restituta; Order of the White Eagle; Grand Officier, Légion d'honneur and other decorations; Dr hc (Ghent, Turin, Liège, Mainz, Geneva, Warsaw); Alexander von Humboldt Foundation Award 1984, R. Schuman Gold Medal 2000. *Publications:* Pieniądz na terytorium okupowanym 1960, Uchwały prawotwórcze organizacji międzynarodowych 1965, Zachodnia granica Polski 1969, Individual Rights and the State in Foreign Affairs (co-author) 1977, Resolutions of the General Assembly of the United Nations 1985, Polityka zagraniczna i odzyskanie niepodległości 1997; over 110 articles on int. law and int. relations. *Address:* Iran–United States Claims Tribunal, Parkweg 13, 2585 JH The Hague (office); Parkweg, 3B, 2585 JG The Hague, Netherlands (home). *Telephone:* (70) 3520064 (office); (70) 3585195 (home). *Fax:* (70) 3502456 (office). *E-mail:* milas@iusct.nl (office).

SKULACHEV, Vladimir Petrovich; Russian biologist and academic; *Director, A. Belozersky Institute of Physico-Chemical Biology, Moscow State University;* b. 21 Feb. 1935, Moscow; s. of Petr Stepanovich Skulachev and Nadezhda Aronovna Skulacheva; m. Severina Inna Isaakovna; four s. one d.; ed Moscow State Univ.; jr researcher, Head of Div., Head of Lab. Moscow State Univ., Dir A. Belozersky Inst. of Physico-Chemical Biology, Dean Faculty of Bioengineering Bioinformatics; Corresp. mem. USSR (now Russian) Acad. of Sciences 1974, mem. 1990–; research in biochemistry, bioenergetics, investigation of molecular mechanisms of energy transformation in membranes of bacteria, mitochondria and chloroplasts; USSR State Prize. *Publications:* Energy Accumulation in Cells 1969, Energy Transformation in Biomembranes 1972, Membranes Bioenergies 1988; numerous other books and articles. *Leisure interests:* badminton, skiing. *Address:* A. N. Belozersky Institute of Physico-Chemical Biology, Moscow State University, 119992 Moscow, Russia (office). *Telephone:* (495) 939-55-30 (office); (495) 939-01-47 (office). *Fax:* (495) 939-03-38 (office). *E-mail:* skulach@belozersky.msu.ru (office). *Website:* www.genebee.msu.su (office).

SKURATOV, Yuri Ilyich, DJur; Russian lawyer and civil servant; b. 3 July 1952, Ulan-Ude; s. of Ilya I. Skuratov and Raisa G. Skuratova; m. Elena D. Besedina 1976; one s. one d.; ed Sverdlovsk Inst. of Law; teacher, Dean Sverdlovsk Inst. of Law 1977–89; Deputy Head of Div. on legis. initiatives and legal issues, CPSU Cen. Cttee 1989–91; Sr Consultant, Russian Ministry of Security 1991–92; Dir Research Inst. of Problems of Justice, Gen. Prosecutor's Office of Russia 1993–95; apptd Gen. Prosecutor 1995; dismissed by Pres. Yeltsin, but reinstated by Council of Fed.; dismissed again 1999; unsuccessful cand. for Pres. 2000. *Publications:* over 90 scientific works on problems of civil and criminal law. *Leisure interests:* chess, swimming.

ŠKVORECKÝ, Josef Václav, PhD, FRSC; Czech/Canadian writer, poet and translator; *Professor Emeritus of English, University of Toronto;* b. 29 Sept. 1924, Náchod; m. Zdena Salivarová 1958; ed Charles Univ., Prague; worked as teacher, Secondary Social School; Ed., Anglo-American Dept, Odeon Publishers, Prague 1953–56; Asst Ed.-in-Chief, World Literature Magazine, Prague 1956–59; Chair., Editorial Bd of journal The Flame –1968; emigrated to Canada 1968; founder (with Zdena Škvorecký) and Ed., Sixty-Eight Publishers, Toronto 1972–95; Visiting Lecturer, Univ. of Toronto 1968, 1970, writer-in-residence 1970, Assoc. Prof. 1971–75, Prof. of English and American Literature 1975–90, Prof. Emeritus 1990–; mem. Bd of Consultants to President Havel 1990–91; f. Literary Acad. Josef Škvorecký, Czech Rep. 2000; mem. Authors League of America, Crime Writers of Canada, Int. PEN Club, MWA, Writers' Union of Canada; Hon. Citizen of Prague 1990, Hon. mem., Czechoslovak Soc. of Arts and Sciences; Order of the White Lion (3rd Grade) Czechoslovakia 1990; Dr hc (Masaryk Univ., Brno) 1991; Guggenheim Fellowship 1980, Neutstadt Int. Prize for Literature 1980, Gov.-Gen.'s Award for Fiction 1984, City of Toronto Book Award 1985, Echoing Green Foundation Literature Award 1990, State Prize for Literature, Czech Repub. 1999, Pangea Foundation Prize, Czech Repub. 2001. *Publications:* The Cowards (novel) 1958, The Legend of Emöke (novel) 1963, The Bass Saxophone (two novellas) 1965, Reading Detective Stories 1965, The Seven-Armed Candlestick, The End of the Nylon Age (story) 1967, The Little Lion (novel), They – Which is We 1968, Miss Silver's Past (novel) 1969, The Tank Battalion (novel) 1969, A Tall Tale About America 1970, The Miracle Game (novel) 1972, All the Bright Young Men and Women 1972, Priest Knox's Sins, The End of Lieutenant Borůvka (novel) 1972, The Swell Season 1975, The Engineer of Human Souls (novel) 1977, The New Men and Women (play) 1977, Working Overtime 1979, Do Not Despair (poems) 1979, The Return of Lieutenant Borůvka (novel) 1980, God in Your House (play) 1980, The Girl from Chicago (poems) 1980, Jiri Menzel and the History of the Closely Watched Trains 1982, Scherzo Capriccioso (novel) 1984, Dvořák in Love 1986, Talkin' Moscow Blues 1988, Sadness of Lieutenant Borůvka (novel) 1988, Bitter Jazz (dramatized stories) 1990, The Bride from Texas (novel) 1992, Headed for the Blues (memoir) 1996, Two Murders in My Double Life (novel) 1996, Short Meeting with Murder (with Zdena Škvorecký) 1999, Life and Work 1999, An Inexplicable Story, or the Narrative of Questus Firmus Siculus (novel) 2002, When Eve Was Naked: Stories of a Life's Journey 2002, Pulchra (novel) 2003, Ordinary Lives (novel) 2004; five full-length film screenplays. *Address:* 487 Sackville Street, Toronto, Ont. M4X 1T6, Canada (home). *Website:* www.skvorecky.com.

SKWEYIYA, Zola Sidney Themba, LLD; South African politician and civil servant; *Minister of Social Development;* b. 14 April 1942, Cape Town; s. of Winnie Skweyiya; one c.; ed Lovedale High School, Univ. of Fort Hare; mem. African Nat. Congress (ANC) 1956, mil. training, Lusaka 1965; Chief ANC Rep. at OAU, Addis Ababa 1980–85, ANC Rep. UN Comm. on Human Rights 1984–93; f. ANC Legal and Constitutional Dept 1985, Head 1985–94; mem. ANC Nat. Exec. Cttee 1991–; Minister of Public Services and Admin., Govt of Nat. Unity 1994–99, of Welfare and Population Devt 1999–2000, of Social Devt 2000–; Chair., Trustee Nat. Children's Rights Comm. 1990–; Trustee SA Legal Defence Fund 1991–. *Leisure interests:* listening to jazz and classical music, reading. *Address:* Ministry of Social Development, Hallmark Building, Vermeulen Street, Pretoria 0002, South Africa (office). *Telephone:* (12) 3284600 (office). *Fax:* (12) 3257071 (office). *E-mail:* welso57@welspta.pwv.gov.sa (office). *Website:* www.welfare.gov.za (office).

SKYRMS, Brian, PhD; American academic; *UCI Distinguished Professor of Social Science, University of California, Irvine;* b. 11 March 1938, Pittsburgh, Pa; s. of Frederick John Skyrms and Marie Margaret Skyrms (née Schlipf); m. Pauline Jenkins 1972; two s.; ed Lehigh Univ., Univ. of Pittsburgh; Asst Prof., Calif. State Univ., Northridge 1964–65, Univ. of Del. 1965–66; Visiting Asst Prof., Univ. of Mich. 1966–67; Asst Prof. then Assoc. Prof., Univ. of Ill., Chicago 1967–70, Prof. 1970–80; Prof. of Philosophy, Univ. of Calif., Irvine 1980–97, Distinguished Prof. of Philosophy and Prof. of Econs 1997–, Dir Program in History and Philosophy of Science, UCI Distinguished Prof. of Social Sciences 1998–; mem. Governing Bd American Philosophical Asscn 1987–90, Philosophy of Science Asscn 1990–91, Pres.-elect 2003–; mem. several editorial bds including American Philosophical Quarterly and Philosophy of Science; Ed. Cambridge Studies in Probability, Induction and Decision Theory; Fellow Center for Advanced Study in the Behavioral Sciences 1993–94, American Acad. of Arts and Sciences 1994, NAS 1999; Guggenheim Fellow 1987–88; numerous science fellowships; Univ. of Calif. Pres.'s Research in the Humanities 1993–94; Pres. Pacific Div. American Philosophical Asscn 2000–01, Philosophy of Science Asscn 2005–07; FAAS 2004–; Lakatos Prize 1999. *Publications:* Choice and Chance: An Introduction to Inductive Logic 1966, Causal Necessity 1980, Pragmatics and Empiricism 1984, The Dynamics of Rational Deliberation 1990, Evolution of the Social Contract 1996, The Stag Hunt and the Evolution of the Social Structure 2004; ed. or co-ed. seven books; numerous articles in learned journals. *Address:* School of Social Sciences, Office 767 SST, 3151 Social Science Plaza, University of California, Irvine, Irvine, CA 92697-5100, USA (office). *Telephone:* (949) 824-6565 (office). *Fax:* (949) 824-2379 (office). *E-mail:* bskyrms@uci.edu (office). *Website:* www.humanities.uci.edu/philosophy (office).

SLABBERT, Frederik van Zyl, DPhil; South African business executive and fmr politician; *Chairman, Adcorp Holdings;* b. 2 March 1940, Pretoria; m. 1st Mana Jordaan; one s. one d.; m. 2nd Jane Stephens 1984; ed Pietersburg High School, Univs of Witwatersrand and Stellenbosch; Lecturer in Sociology, Univ. of Stellenbosch 1964–68, Sr Lecturer 1970–71; Sr Lecturer and Acting Head, Dept of Sociology, Rhodes Univ., Grahamstown 1969, Univ. of Cape Town 1972–73; Prof. and Head Dept of Sociology, Univ. of Witwatersrand 1973–74; Visiting Prof. WBS Business School 1988–; MP for Rondebosch 1974–86; Nat. Leader Progressive Fed. Party and Leader of the Opposition 1979–86; Chair. Cen. Witwatersrand Metropolitan Chamber 1991–94; Co-Chair. Task Group for Local Govt Elections 1994–; Co-f. Inst. for Democratic Alternatives 1988; Co-f. Khula (investment trust) 1990; Dir Adcorp Holdings 1994–, Chair. 1998–; Chair. CTP Caxton; Dr hc (Simon Fraser Univ., Canada), (Univ. of Natal), (Univ. of Orange Free State). *Publications:* South Africa's Options; Strategies for Sharing Power (with David Welsh) 1979, The Last White Parliament 1986, The System and The Struggle 1989, The Quest for Democracy: South Africa in Transition 1992 and various articles on SA politics. *Leisure interests:* squash, tennis, swimming. *Address:* Adcorp Holdings, PO Box 70635, Bryanston 2021, South Africa (office). *Telephone:* (11) 2445300 (office). *Fax:* (11) 2445309 (office). *E-mail:* Info@adcorp.co.za (office). *Website:* www.adcorp.co.za (office).

SLACK, Paul Alexander, DPhil, FBA; British historian and academic; *Professor of Early Modern Social History and Principal, Linacre College, University of Oxford;* b. 23 Jan. 1943, Bradford; s. of Isaac Slack and Helen Slack (née Firth); m. Diana Gillian Manby 1965 (deceased); two d.; ed Bradford Grammar School, St John's Coll., Oxford; Jr Research Fellow, Balliol Coll., Oxford 1966–69; Lecturer in History, York Univ. 1969–72; Fellow and Tutor in Modern History, Exeter Coll. Oxford 1973–96, Reader in Modern History, Univ. of Oxford 1990–96, Chair. Gen. Bd of Faculties 1995–96, Prin., Linacre Coll. Oxford 1996–, Prof. of Early Modern Social History, Oxford Univ. 1999–, Pro-Vice-Chancellor 1997–2000, Pro-Vice-Chancellor (Academic Services) 2000–05. *Publications:* The Impact of Plague in Tudor and Stuart England 1985, Poverty and Policy in Tudor and Stuart England 1988, The English Poor Law 1531–1782 1990, From Reformation to Improvement: Public Welfare in Early Modern England 1999. *Leisure interests:* opera, fell-walking. *Address:* Linacre College, Oxford, OX1 3JA, England (office). *Telephone:* (1865) 271650 (office). *Fax:* (1865) 271668 (office).

SLADE, Rt Hon. Sir Christopher John, Kt; British judge (retd); b. 2 June 1927, London; s. of the late George Penkivil Slade, KC and Mary A. A. Slade; m. Jane G. A. Buckley 1958; one s. three d.; ed Eton Coll. (Scholar) and New Coll., Oxford (Scholar); called to Bar 1951, QC 1965; in practice at Chancery Bar 1951–75; Judge, High Court of Justice, Chancery Div. 1975–82; Judge of Restrictive Practices Court 1980–82, Pres. 1981–82; Lord Justice of Appeal 1982–91; mem. Gen. Council of Bar 1958–62, 1965–69; mem. Senate of Four Inns of Court 1966–69; Bencher, Lincoln's Inn 1973; mem. Lord Chancellor's Legal Educ. Cttee 1969–71; Treas. Lincoln's Inn 1994. *Leisure interests:* multifarious. *Address:* 16 Elthiron Road, London, SW6 4BN, England (home). *Telephone:* (20) 7731-0938 (home).

SLADE, Tuiloma Neroni, LLB; Samoan diplomatist, judge and lawyer; *Secretary-General, Pacific Islands Forum;* b. 8 April 1941; m.; one d.; ed Hague Acad. of Int. Law; qualified as solicitor and barrister, worked in law practice in Wellington, NZ 1967–68; legal counsel, Office of Attorney-Gen., Wellington 1969–73; Parl. Counsel 1973–75; Head of Del. UN Conf. on the Law of the Sea 1973–76; Attorney-Gen. of Western Samoa 1976–82, also Chief Justice for periods between 1980–82; Asst Dir Legal Div. Commonwealth Secr., London 1983–93; Amb. to USA 1993–2003, also Perm. Rep. to the UN, New York and High Commr to Canada; Chair. Alliance of Small Island States 1997–2003; Leader, Samoan del. to Preparatory Comm. for Int. Criminal Court, New York 1999–2002; Distinguished Diplomat in Residence, Temple Univ., Philadelphia 2003; Judge, Int. Criminal Court 2003–06; Sec.-Gen. Pacific Islands Forum 2008–; Chair. first S Pacific Law Conf. 1986; legal consultant S Pacific Forum Fisheries Agency 1989; UNITAR Fellowship, Hague Acad. of Int. Law and UN Legal Office; Order of Samoa (Poloaiga Sili a Samoa) 2005. *Address:* Secretary General, Pacific Islands Forum Secretariat, Private Mail Bag, Suva, Fiji (office). *Telephone:* 3312600 (office). *Fax:* 3220230 (office). *E-mail:* info@forumsec.org.fj (office). *Website:* www.forumsec.org (office).

SLAKTERIS, Atis; Latvian agricultural engineer and politician; b. 21 Nov. 1956, Code Pagasts, Bauska Dist.; m.; two c.; ed Latvian Acad. of Agric., Univ. of Minnesota, USA; began career as mechanic, later Chief Engineer Code Co. 1980–89; First Deputy Man. Bauskas Lauktehnika (state-owned co.) 1989–90; Chief Engineer, Bauska Agric. Dept 1990–94, Head, Agric. Consultation Bureau 1994–96; Minister of State for Cooperation, Ministry of Agric.

1996–97; mem. 7th Saeima 1998–2002, serving as Chair. Cttee on Economy, Agricultural Environment and Regional Policies 1998–99, Chair. Cttee on Privatisation 1999–2000; Parl. Sec., Ministry of Agric. 2000, Minister for Agric. 2000–02; Chair. People's Party 2002–08; Minister of Defence 2004, 2006–07, of Finance 2007–09. *Address:* c/o People's Party, Dzirnavu iela 68, Rīga 1919, Latvia (office).

SLANEY, Sir Geoffrey, Kt, KBE, MSc, ChM, FRCS; British surgeon and academic; *Professor Emeritus of Surgery, Queen Elizabeth Hospital, Birmingham;* b. 19 Sept. 1922, West Hallam; s. of Richard Slaney and Gladys L. Slaney; m. Josephine M. Davy 1956; one s. two d.; ed Univs of Birmingham, London and Illinois; House Surgeon and Surgical Registrar, Gen. Hosp., Birmingham 1947–48; Capt., RAMC 1948–50; Surgical Registrar, Coventry, London and Hackney Hosps 1950–53; Surgical Registrar, Lecturer in Surgery and Surgical Research Fellow, Queen Elizabeth Hosp., Birmingham 1953–59; Hunterian Prof., Royal Coll. of Surgeons 1961–62; Prof. of Surgery, Univ. of Birmingham 1966–87; Barling Prof., Head Dept of Surgery, Queen Elizabeth Hosp., Birmingham 1971–86, now Emer.; Pres. Royal Coll. of Surgeons of England 1982–86, James IV Asscn Surgeons 1984–87, Int. Surgical Group 1985–86, Vascular Surgical Soc. 1974–75; Chair. Asscn Profs of Surgery 1979–81, Confed. of Royal Colls and Faculties in the UK 1984–86; Fellow, Asscn of Surgeons of GB and Ireland, American Surgical Asscn; Hon. Consulting Surgeon, United Birmingham Hosps and Regional Hosp. Bd 1959–, Royal Prince Alfred Hosp., Sydney 1981–; Hon. Consulting Surgeon Emer.; City of London and Hackney Health Authority 1983–; Hon. FRACS, FACS, FRCA, FCSSL, FCSSA; Hon. Fellow, Royal Coll. of Surgeons in Ireland, Royal Coll. of Surgeons of Canada; Jacksonian Prize and Medal, Royal Coll. of Surgeons 1959, Pybus Memorial Medal 1978, Miles Memorial Medal 1984, Vanderbilt Univ. Medal 1987, Brooke Medal, Ileostomy Asscn of GB and Ireland 1990. *Publications:* Metabolic Derangements in Gastrointestinal Surgery (with B. N. Brooke) 1967, Cancer of the Large Bowel (co-author) 1991; numerous contribs to medical and surgical journals. *Leisure interests:* family, fishing. *Address:* Hill Crest, Collins Green, Knightwick, Worcester, WR6 5PT, England. *Telephone:* (1886) 822024.

SLATER, Christian; American actor; b. (Christian Michael Leonard Hawkins), 18 Aug. 1969, New York City; s. of Michael Gainsborough and Mary Jo Slater; m. Ryan Haddon 2000 (divorced 2006); one s. one d.; ed LaGuardia High School of Music, Art and Performing Arts; appeared at age of seven in TV series One Life to Live; professional stage debut at age of nine in touring production of The Music Man. *Stage appearances include:* Macbeth, David Copperfield, Merlin, Landscape of the Body, Side Man, One Flew Over the Cuckoo's Nest (Edinburgh Festival then Gielgud Theatre, London, Garrick Theatre, London 2006) (Theatregoers' Choice Award for Best Actor 2005) 2004–05, The Glass Menagerie (Ethel Barrymore Theatre, Broadway) 2005, Swimming with Sharks (Vaudeville Theatre, London) 2007. *Television appearances include:* Sherlock Holmes (film) 1981, Living Proof: The Hank Williams Jr. Story (film) 1983, The Haunted Mansion Mystery (film) 1983, Ryan's Hope (series) 1975, Secrets (film) 1986, Desperate for Love (film) 1989, Merry Christmas, George Bailey 1997, Prehistoric Planet (series) 2002, The West Wing (series) 2003, 2004, A Light Knight's Odyssey (film) 2004. *Films include:* The Legend of Billie Jean 1985, The Name of the Rose 1986, Twisted 1986, Tucker: The Man and his Dream 1988, Gleaming the Cube 1989, Heathers 1989, Beyond the Stars 1989, The Wizard 1989, Tales from the Darkside: The Movie 1990, Young Guns II: Blaze of Glory 1990, Pump up the Volume 1990, Robin Hood: Prince of Thieves 1991, Mobsters 1991, Star Trek VI: The Undiscovered Country 1991, Kuffs 1992, Ferngully: The Last Rainforest 1992, Where the Day Takes You 1992, Untamed Heart 1993, True Romance 1993, Jimmy Hollywood 1994, Interview with a Vampire 1994, Murder in the First 1995, Bed of Roses 1996, Broken Arrow 1996, Austin Powers: International Man of Mystery 1997, Julian Po 1997, Hard Rain (also prod.) 1998, Basil (also co-prod.) 1998, Very Bad Things (also prod.) 1998, Love Stinks 1999, The Contender 2000, 3000 Miles to Graceland 2001, Who is Cletis Tout? 2001, Run for the Money 2002, Windtalkers 2002, Masked and Anonymous 2003, The Good Shepherd 2004, Mindhunters 2004, Churchill: The Hollywood Years 2004, Pursued 2004, Alone in the Dark 2005, The Deal (also prod.) 2005, Hollow Man II 2006, Bobby 2006, Slipstream 2007, He Was a Quiet Man 2007, The Ten Commandments 2007, Igor (voice) 2008. *Address:* c/o CAA, 9830 Wilshire Blvd., Beverly Hills, CA 90212, USA.

SLATER, James (Jim) Derrick, FCA; British company director and author; b. 13 March 1929, Wirral, Cheshire; s. of Hubert Slater and Jessica Slater; m. Helen Wyndham Goodwyn 1965; two s. two d.; ed Preston Manor County School; Dir, AEC Ltd 1959; Deputy Sales Dir, Leyland Motor Corpn 1963; acquired (with assocs) H. Lotery and Co., Ltd, later renamed Slater, Walker Securities Ltd, and apptd Chair. and Man. Dir 1964–72, Chair., CEO 1972–75; Dir, BLMC 1969–75; Chair., Salar Properties Ltd 1983. *Publications:* Return to Go (autobiog.) 1977; on investment: The Zulu Principle 1992, Investment Made Easy 1994, Pep Up Your Wealth 1994, Beyond the Zulu Principle 1996, How to Became a Millionaire 2000; children's books: Goldenrod, Goldenrod and the Kidnappers, Grasshopper and the Unwise Owl, The Boy Who Saved Earth, A. Mazing Monsters, Grasshopper and the Pickle Factory 1979, Roger the Robot Series 1980, Grasshopper and the Poisoned River 1981. *Leisure interests:* chess, backgammon, bridge, salmon fishing. *Address:* Field House, Alder Brook, Smithwood Common, Cranleigh, Surrey, GU6 8QU, England (home).

SLATER, Adm. Sir Jock (John) Cunningham Kirkwood, GCB, LVO, DL; British naval officer; b. 27 March 1938, Edinburgh, Scotland; s. of James K. Slater, OBE, MD, FRCPE and M. C. B. Slater (née Bramwell); m. Ann Frances Scott 1972; two s.; ed Edinburgh Acad., Sedbergh School, Royal Naval Coll. Dartmouth; Lt, HMS Soberton 1965; Lt Commdr, Equerry to HM The Queen

1968–71; Commdr HMS Jupiter 1972–73; Capt., HMS Kent 1976–77; with Royal Coll. of Defence Studies 1978; Capt. HMS Illustrious 1981–83; Capt. School of Maritime Operations, HMS Dryad 1983–85; Rear Adm., Asst Chief of Defence Staff 1985–87; Flag Officer, Scotland, NI, Naval Base Commdr Rosyth 1987–89; Vice-Adm., Chief of Fleet Support 1989–91; Adm., C-in-C of Fleet, Allied C-in-C Channel and Eastern Atlantic 1991–92; Vice-Chief of Defence Staff 1993–95, Chief of Naval Staff and First Sea Lord 1995–98; Dir Vosper Thornycroft Holdings 1999–2004; Dir and Sr Mil. Adviser to Lockheed Martin (UK) Ltd 1999–2008; consultant, Bristow Helicopters Ltd 2001–04; Chair. Imperial War Museum 2001–06, RN Club 1765–1785 2001–04, White Ensign Asscn 2002–05, Royal Nat. Lifeboat Inst.; Gov. Sedbergh School 1997–2002; Freeman of the City of London; Warden, Shipwrights' Co.; Elder Brother, Trinity House; Commdr, Legion of Merit 1997; DL Hants. 1999; Hon. DSc (Cranfield) 1998, (Univ. of Southampton) 2008; Sword of Honour and The Queen's Telescope, BRNC Dartmouth 1958, Cheetham Hill Memorial Prize, HMS Dryad 1966. *Achievements:* mem. Nat. Youth Orchestra 1955. *Publications:* articles in professional publs. *Leisure interest:* outdoor. *Address:* c/o Naval Secretary, Leach Building, Whale Island, Portsmouth, PO2 8BY, England (home). *E-mail:* jock.slater@talk21.com (home).

SLATER, Kelly; American professional surfer; b. 11 Feb. 1972, Cocoa Beach, Fla; s. of the late Steve Slater and of Judy Slater; one d.; joined professional surfing ranks in 1990; eight times world champion 1992 (age 21, youngest ever), 1994, 1995, 1996, 1997, 1998, 2005, 2006; winner Mountain Dew Pipe Master, Hawaii 1999, Gotcha Tahiti Pro, Tahiti 2000, The Quiksilver, Hawaii 2002; starred in TV series Baywatch early 1990s and in numerous surf movies; inspiration for Kelly Slater Pro Surfer video game. *Leisure interests:* golf, fishing, music. *Address:* c/o Shelby Meade, Fresh and Clean Media, 12701 Venice Boulevard, Los Angeles, CA 90066, USA. *Telephone:* (310) 313 7200. *Fax:* (310) 313 0277. *E-mail:* shelby@freshcleanmedia.com. *Website:* www.freshcleanmedia.com.

SLATER, Rodney E., BS, JD; American lawyer and fmr government official; *Partner, Patton Boggs LLP;* b. 23 Feb. 1955, Tutwyler, Miss.; m. Cassandra Wilkins; one c.; ed Eastern Mich. Univ., Univ. of Ark.; Asst Attorney-Gen., Ark. 1980–82; Special Asst to Gov. of Ark. for community and minority affairs 1983–85, Exec. Asst for econ. and community programs 1985–87, Dir Intergovernmental Relations Ark. State Univ. 1987–93; Admin. Fed. Highway Admin. US Dept of Transportation, Washington, DC 1993–97; US Sec. of Transportation 1997–2001; Ark. Liaison Martin Luther King Jr Fed. Holiday Comm. 1983–87; Pnr Patton Boggs LLP (law firm) 2001–; mem. Ark. Sesquicentennial Comm. 1986, Ark. State Highway and Transportation Comm. 1987–93, Chair. 1992–93; Pres. W. Harold Flowers Law Soc. 1985–92; Sec., Treasurer Ark. Bar Asscn 1989–93; Deputy Campaign Man., Sr Travelling Adviser Clinton for Pres. Campaign 1992; Deputy then Chair. Clinton/Gore Transition Team 1992–93; mem. Bd of Dirs Africane 2001–, Jt Center for Political and Econ. Studies 2001–. *Address:* Patton Boggs LLP, 2550 M Street, NW, Washington, DC 20037, USA (office). *Telephone:* (202) 457-5265 (office). *Fax:* (202) 457-6315 (office). *E-mail:* rslater@pattonboggs.com (office). *Website:* www.pattonboggs.com/rslater (office).

SLATKIN, Leonard Edward; American conductor and pianist; *Music Director, Detroit Symphony Orchestra;* b. 1 Sept. 1944, Los Angeles, CA; s. of Felix Slatkin and Eleanor Aller; m. Linda Hohenfeld 1986; one s.; ed Indiana Univ., Los Angeles City Coll., Juilliard School; studied violin, piano, viola, composition, conducting; debut Carnegie Hall 1966; founder, Music Dir and Conductor St Louis Symphony Youth Orchestra 1979–80, 1980–81; Asst Conductor Youth Symphony of New York, Carnegie Hall 1966, Juilliard Opera, Theater and Dance Dept 1967, St Louis Symphony Orchestra 1968–71, Assoc. Conductor 1971–74, Music Dir and Conductor 1979–96; Prin. Guest Conductor Minn. Orchestra 1974–, Summer Artistic Dir 1979–80; Music Dir New Orleans Philharmonic Symphony Orchestra 1977–78; Music Dir Nat. Symphony Orchestra, Washington, DC 1996–2008; Prin. Conductor BBC Symphony Orchestra 2000–04; Prin. Guest Conductor Royal Philharmonic Orchestra 2005–, Pittsburgh Symphony Orchestra 2008–; Music Dir Detroit Symphony Orchestra 2008–; guest conductor with orchestras worldwide, including most major US orchestras, Montréal, Toronto, Vienna, Vienna State Opera, London Symphony, London Philharmonia, English Chamber, Concertgebouw, Royal Danish, Stockholm, Scottish Nat., NHK Tokyo, Israel, Berlin, Stuttgart Opera; festivals include Tanglewood, Blossom, Mann Music Center, Mostly Mozart and Saratoga; five hon. degrees; four Grammy Awards. *Address:* Columbia Artists' Management Inc., 1790 Broadway, New York, NY 10019-1412, USA (office); Detroit Symphony Orchestra, Max M. Fisher Music Center, 3711 Woodward Avenue, Detroit, MI 48201, USA (office). *Telephone:* (212) 841-9512 (office); (313) 576-511 (office). *Fax:* (212) 841-9734 (office); (313) 576-5109 (office). *E-mail:* info@cami.com (office). *Website:* www.cami.com (office); www.detroitsymphony.com (office); www.leonardslatkin.com.

SLATYER, Ralph Owen, AC, AO, DSc, FRS, FAA; Australian research scientist and academic; *Professor Emeritus, Research School of Biological Sciences, Institute of Advanced Studies, Australian National University;* b. 16 April 1929, Melbourne; s. of Thomas H. Slatyer and Jean Slatyer; m. June H. Wade 1953; one s. two d.; ed Univ. of Western Australia; Research Scientist, later Chief Research Scientist, CSIRO Div. of Land Research 1951–67; Prof. of Biology Research School of Biological Sciences, ANU 1967, Dir Research School of Biological Sciences 1984–89, now Prof. Emer.; Amb. to UNESCO, Paris 1978–81; Chair. (part-time) World Heritage Cttee 1981–83, Australian Nat. Comm. for UNESCO, Australian Science and Tech. Council, Canberra 1982–87; Chief Scientist, Dept of Prime Minister and Cabinet, Canberra 1989–92; Chair. (part-time) Co-operative Research Centre for Rainforest Ecology 1992–2005; Chair. Australian Foundation for Science 1992–94; Visiting Fellow, Prof. Emer., Ecosystem Dynamics Group, Inst. of Advanced Studies, ANU 1994–; Fellow, Australian Acad. of Technological Sciences and Eng; Foreign Assoc. American Nat. Acad. of Sciences; Foreign mem. Korea Acad. of Science and Tech.; Hon. DSc (Western Australia, Queensland, Duke Univ., Charles Sturt Univ.), (Univ. of Newcastle), (James Cook Univ.); Edgeworth David Medal, Royal Soc. of NSW 1968; Australian Medal of Agric. Science 1968, Medal of Australia and NZ Asscn for the Advancement of Science 1991, Clunies Ross Medal for Lifetime Contrib. to Science and Tech. *Publications include:* Practical Micro-climatology (jtly with I.C. McIlroy) 1961, Plant-Water Relationships 1967, Man and the New Biology 1970; ed. of several books and author of numerous scientific publs. *Leisure interests:* reading, bush-walking. *Address:* Research School of Biological Sciences, Institute of Advanced Studies, Australian National University, Canberra, ACT 0200 (office); 54 Musgrave Street, Yarralumla, ACT 2600, Australia (home). *Telephone:* (612) 6125-5041 (office); (612) 6285-1728 (home). *Fax:* (612) 6125-5095 (office); (612) 6185-1738 (home). *E-mail:* ralph.slatyer@anu.edu.au (office). *Website:* www.rsbs.anu.edu.au (office).

SLAVESKI, Trajko, PhD; Macedonian politician and academic; *Minister of Finance;* b. 1960, Ohrid; m.; two c.; ed SS Cyril and Methodius Univ., Skopje, State Univ. of Calif. and Harvard Univ., USA; Prof., Econs Faculty, SS Cyril and Methodius Univ., Skopje; Visiting Prof., Arizona State Univ. 1997, Nat. and Capodistrian Univ., Athens 1999–; Minister of Devt 1999–2000; Adviser to Minister of Finance and Nat. Co-ordinator for Poverty Reduction Strategy 2000–02; mem. Parl. 2006–; Minister of Finance 2006–; mem. Exec. Cttee Internal Macedonian Revolutionary Organization—Democratic Party for Macedonian National Unity (VMRO—DPMNE) 2003–, Vice-Pres. 2005–. *Address:* Ministry of Finance, 1000 Skopje, Dame Gruev 14, Former Yugoslav Republic of Macedonia (office). *Telephone:* (2) 3117288 (office). *Fax:* (2) 3117280 (office). *E-mail:* finance@finance.gov.mk (office). *Website:* www.finance.gov.mk (office).

SLAVITT, David Rytman, (David Benjamin, Henry Lazarus, Lynn Meyer, Henry Sutton), MA; American writer, poet, translator and lecturer; b. 23 March 1935, White Plains, NY; s. of Samuel Slavitt and Adele Slavitt; m. 1st Lynn Meyer 1956 (divorced 1977); two s. one d.; m. 2nd Janet Lee Abrahm 1978; ed Yale and Columbia Univs; Instructor in English, Georgia Inst. of Technology, Atlanta 1957–58; writer, Assoc. Ed., Newsweek 1958–65; Visiting Lecturer, Univ. of Maryland 1977; Visiting Assoc. Prof. Temple Univ. 1978–80; Lecturer in English and Comparative Literature, Columbia Univ. 1985–86; teacher of creative writing, Rutgers Univ. 1987; Lecturer in English and Classics, Univ. of Pennsylvania 1991–97; Visiting Lecturer in Creative Writing, Princeton Univ. 1996; Lecturer in English, Bennington Coll. 2000–; Assoc. Fellow, Trumbull Coll. Yale Univ.; has lectured widely at US univs and other academic insts; Pennsylvania Council on the Arts Award 1985, Nat. Endowment for Arts Fellowship in Translation 1988, Nat. Acad. and Insts. of Arts and Letters Award 1989, Rockefeller Foundation Artist's Residence, Bellagio 1989. *Publications:* fiction: Rochelle, or Virtue Rewarded 1967, King Saul (play) 1967, Feel Free 1968, The Cardinal Sins (play) 1969, Anagrams 1970, ABCD 1972, The Outer Mongolian 1973, The Killing of the King 1974, King of Hearts 1976, Jo Stern 1978, Cold Comfort 1980, Ringer 1982, Alice at 80 1984, The Agent 1986, The Hussar 1987, Salazar Blinks 1988, Lives of the Saints 1990, Short Stories Are Not Real Life 1991, Turkish Delights 1993, The Cliff 1994, Get Thee to a Nunnery: Two Divertimentos from Shakespeare 1999, Aspects of the Novel: A Novel 2003; as Henry Sutton: The Exhibitionist 1967, The Voyeur 1968, Vector 1970, The Liberated 1973, The Proposal 1980, Kid's Stuff 2003; as Lynn Meyer: Paperback Thriller 1975; as Henry Lazarus: That Golden Woman 1976; as David Benjamin: The Idol 1979; poetry: Suits for the Dead 1961, The Carnivore 1965, Day Sailing 1968, Child's Play 1972, Vital Signs: New and Selected Poems 1975, Rounding the Horn 1978, Dozens 1981, Big Nose 1983, Adrien Stoutenburg: Land of Superior Mirages: New and Selected Poems (ed.) 1986, The Walls of Thebes 1986, Equinox 1989, Eight Longer Poems 1990, Crossroads 1994, A Gift 1996, Epic and Epigram 1997, A New Pléiade: Seven American Poets 1998, PS3569.L3 1998, Falling from Silence: Poems 2001, Change of Address: Poems, New and Selected 2005, William Henry Harrison and Other Poems 2006; non-fiction: Understanding Social Life: An Introduction to Social Psychology (with Paul F. Secord and Carl W. Backman) 1976, Physicians Observed 1987, Virgil 1991, The Persians of Aeschylus 1998, Three Amusements of Ausonius 1998, The Book of Lamentations 2001, Re Verse: Essays on Poets and Poetry 2005; translator: The Eclogues of Virgil 1971, The Eclogues and the Georgics of Virgil 1972, The Tristia of Ovid 1985, Ovid's Poetry of Exile 1990, Seneca: The Tragedies 1992, The Fables of Avianus 1993, The Metamorphoses of Ovid 1994, The Twelve Minor Prophets 1999, The Voyage of the Argo of Valerius Flaccus 1999, Sonnets of Love and Death of Jean de Sponde 2001, The Elegies of Propertius 2001, The Poetry of Manuel Bandeira 2002, The Regrets of Joachim du Bellay 2004, The Phoenix and Other Translations 2004, Re Verse: Essays on Poets and Poetry 2005, Blue State Blues: A Republican in Cambridge 2006; contrib. book reviews, articles in journals and magazines. *Address:* 35 West Street, #5, Cambridge, MA 02139, USA (home). *Telephone:* (617) 497-1219 (home). *E-mail:* drslavitt@comcast.net (home).

SLEEP, Wayne, OBE; British dancer, actor and choreographer; b. 17 July 1948, Plymouth; ed Royal Ballet School (Leverhulme Scholar); joined Royal Ballet 1966, Soloist 1970, Prin. 1973; roles in: Giselle, Dancers at a Gathering, The Nutcracker, Romeo and Juliet, The Grand Tour, Elite Syncopations, Swan Lake, The Four Seasons, Les Patineurs, Petroushka (title role), Cinderella, The Dream, Pineapple Poll, Mam'zelle Angot, 4th Symphony, La Fille Mal Gardée, A Month in the Country, A Good Night's Sleep, Coppelia; also roles in operas: A Midsummer Night's Dream, Aida; choreography and lead role, The Point: co-starred in Song and Dance 1982, 1990, Cabaret 1986; f. DASH co. 1980; dancer and jt choreographer, Bits and Pieces 1989; numerous TV appearances including series The Hot Shoe Show 1983, 1984; Show

Business Personality of the Year 1983. *Films include:* The Virgin Soldiers, The First Great Train Robbery, The Tales of Beatrix Potter. *Theatre includes:* Ariel in the Tempest, title role in Pinocchio, Genie in Aladdin, Soldier in The Soldier's Tale, Truffaldino in the Servant of Two Masters, Mr Mistoffelees in Cats. *Publications:* Variations on Wayne Sleep 1983, Precious Little Sleep (autobiog.) 1996. *Leisure interest:* entertaining. *Address:* c/o Nick Thomas Artists, Event House, Queen Margaret's Road, Scarborough, YO11 2SA; 22 Queensberry Mews West, London, SW7 2DY, England. *Telephone:* (1723) 500038.

SLEIMAN, Gen. Michel, BA, MA; Lebanese politician, head of state and fmr army commander; *President;* b. 21 Nov. 1948, Amchit; m. Wafaa Sleiman; three c.; ed Lebanese Univ.; Chief Intelligence Br., Mount Lebanon 1990–91; Army Staff Sec.-Gen. 1991–93; Commdr 11th Infantry Brigade 1993–96, Sixth Infantry Brigade 1996–98; Commdr Lebanese Armed Forces 1998–2008; Pres. of Lebanon 2008–; Kt and Grand Cordon, Nat. Order of the Cedar, First, Second, Third and Extraordinary Grade, Lebanese Order of Merit, Grade of Excellence, Syrian Order of Merit, Medal of King Abdul Aziz, Grand Cross, Italian Order of Merit, Collar of Moubarak the Great; Decoration of Mil. Pride (Silver), Medal of War, Decoration of Mil. Valor (Silver), Decoration of Nat. Unity, Decoration of the Dawn of the South, Internal Security Forces Medal, Gen. Security Medal, Commemorative Medal of Confs 2002. *Address:* Presidential Palace, Baabda, Lebanon (office). *Telephone:* (5) 920900 (office). *Fax:* (5) 922400 (office). *E-mail:* president_office@presidency.gov.lb (office). *Website:* www.presidency.gov.lb (office).

ŚLEPOWROŃSKA, Małgorzata Izabela, MBA; Polish business executive; *Chair, Supervisory Board, PKN Orlen;* b. 1973; ed Nicolas Copernicus Univ., Toruń, Warsaw Univ. of Tech., Warsaw School of Econs; Admin. Integrated Informatics System, ZEP- Info 1997, becoming Supervisor Marketing and Man. Dept, Dir of Business Devt, Vice-Pres. Man. Bd, and Devt and Sales Dir –2006; Dir IT Dept, Chemical Group CIECH (Grupa Chemiczna CIECH) 2006–; Pres. Man. Bd CHEMIA.COM 2007–; Chair. Supervisory Bd PKN Orlen 2007–; mem. Bd of Dirs PLL LOT, IZCH SODA MĄTWY. *Address:* PKN Orlen, ul. Chemikow 7, 09-411 Plock, Poland (office). *Telephone:* (24) 3650000 (office). *Fax:* (24) 3654040 (office). *Website:* www.orlen.pl (office).

SLESARENKO, Yelena; Russian track and field athlete; b. 28 Feb. 1982, Volgograd; competes in high jump; gold medal Athens Olympics 2004, World Indoor Championships, Budapest 2004, Moscow 2006, silver medal Valencia 2008. *Address:* c/o All Russia Athletic Federation, Luzhnetskaya nab. 8, Moscow 119871, Russia.

ŠLESERS, Ainārs; Latvian politician; *Minister of Transport;* b. 22 Jan. 1970, Riga; m.; two c.; ed Riga Secondary School No. 25, Riga Industrial Polytechnics, Christian Folk Coll., Norway, Latvian Christian Acad.; Pres. Latvian-Norwegian jt venture Latvian Information and Commerce Centre, Norway 1992–96; Pres. Skandi Ltd 1993–96; Dir Gen. Varner Baltija Ltd 1994–98; Chair. Bd and Pres. JSC Supermarket Centres 1995–96, 1996–98; Dir Gen. Rimi Baltija Ltd 1996–97, Varner Hakon Invest Ltd 1996–98; mem. Parl. Oct.–Nov. 1998, 1999–2002, 2002–; Minister for Econs 1998–99; Deputy Prime Minister Nov. 2002–Jan. 2004, March–Dec. 2004; Minister of Transport Dec. 2004–; mem. Bd Latvian First Party (LPP) 2002–; mem. Bd Baltic Stability Fund 1996–; mem. Bd 'For Spiritual Renaissance in Latvia' 2001–. *Address:* Ministry of Transport, Gogoļa iela 3, Rīga 1743, Latvia (office). *Telephone:* 722-6922 (office). *Fax:* 721-7180 (office). *E-mail:* satmin@sam.gov.lv (office). *Website:* www.sam.gov.lv (office).

ŠLEŽEVIČIUS, Adolfas; Lithuanian politician; b. 1948, Mirziskes, Šiauliai Region; ed Acad. of Nat. Econ., USSR Council of Ministers; Sr Engineer-Constructor, Chief Mechanic, Chief Engineer, Kaunas dairy factory 1971–77; Vice-Minister of Dairy and Meat Industry of Lithuania 1977–81; Chair. dairy production enterprise Pienocentras 1989–90; Vice-Minister of Agric. 1990–91; Pres. Lithuanian-Norwegian Jt Venture C. Olsen-Baltic 1991–93; Pres. Lithuanian Dairy Producers Assen 1992–; mem. Democratic Labour Party; Prime Minister of Lithuania 1993–96, resgnd following corruption scandals; consultant to pvt. cos.

SLICHTER, Charles Pence, BA, MA, PhD; American physicist and academic; *Research Professor of Physics and Center for Advanced Study Professor Emeritus of Physics and Chemistry, University of Illinois;* b. 21 Jan. 1924, Ithaca, NY; s. of Sumner Huber Slichter and Ada Pence Slichter; m. 1st Gertrude Thayer Almy 1952 (divorced 1977); three s. one d.; m. 2nd Anne FitzGerald 1980; two s.; ed Browne and Nichols School, Cambridge, Mass. and Harvard Univ.; Instructor, Univ. of Illinois 1949–51, Asst Prof. of Physics 1951–54, Assoc. Prof. 1954–55, Prof. of Physics 1955–97, mem. Center for Advanced Study, Univ. of Illinois 1968–, Prof. of Chem. 1986–97, Center for Advanced Study Prof. Emer. of Physics and Chem. 1997–, Research Prof. of Physics 1997–; mem. Bd of Dirs Polaroid Corpn 1975–97; Morris Loeb Lecturer, Harvard Univ. 1961; mem. Pres.'s Science Advisory Cttee 1965–69, Cttee on the Nat. Medal of Science 1969–74, Pres.'s Cttee on Science and Tech. 1976; Alfred Sloan Fellow 1957–63; mem. Corpn of Harvard Univ. 1970–95; mem. Comm. on Physical Sciences, Math. and Applications, Nat. Research Council 1993–96; Fellow, American Physical Soc., Int. EPR Soc. 1998; mem. NAS, American Acad. of Arts and Sciences, American Philosophical Soc., Nat. Science Bd 1975–84; mem. Int. Soc. of Magnetic Resonance (ISMAR), Vice-Pres. 1983–86, Pres. 1987–90; Hon. mem. Corpn, Woods Hole Oceanographic Inst.; Hon. DSc (Univ. of Waterloo) 1993; Hon. LLD (Harvard) 1996; Langmuir Prize of American Physical Soc. 1969, ISMAR Award 1986, Comstock Prize, NAS 1993, Buckley Prize, American Physical Soc. 1996, Nat. Medal of Science 2007, and other awards. *Publications:* Principles of Magnetic Resonance 1963, 1978, 1989, 1990, 1996; articles on solid state physics, chemical physics and magnetic resonance. *Address:* Department of Physics, Univ. of Illinois at Urbana-Champaign, 1110 West Green Street, Urbana, IL 61801-3080 (office); 61 Chestnut Court, Champaign, IL 61822, USA (home). *Telephone:* (217) 333-3834 (office); (217) 352-8255 (home). *Fax:* (217) 244-7559 (office). *E-mail:* cslichte@uiuc.edu (office). *Website:* www.physics.uiuc.edu/People/Faculty/profiles/Slichter (office).

SLIM DOMIT, Patrick; Mexican telecommunications executive; *Chairman, América Móvil SA de CV;* s. of Carlos Slim Helú and Soumaya Domit; ed Univ. Anáhuac; Chair. América Móvil SA de CV 2004–; Vice-Pres. Grupo Carso SA de CV (fmr CEO); Vice-Chair. America Telecom –2004; fmr CEO Industrias Nacobre SA de CV; Chair. Ferrosur SA de CV; mem. Bd of Dirs Carso Global Telecom SA de CV, Teléfonos de México SA de CV (Telmex), Hoteles Calinda SA de CV, Grupo Condumex SA de CV, Empresas Frisco SA de CV, Sears Roebuck de México SA de CV, Cigarros La Tabacalera de México SA de CV, Promotora Inbursa SA de CV, Industrias Nacobre SA de CV. *Address:* América Móvil SA de CV, Lago Alberto 366, Colonia Anáhuac, 11320 Mexico DF, Mexico (office). *Telephone:* (55) 2581-3947 (office). *Fax:* (55)2581-3948 (office). *E-mail:* info@americamovil.com (office). *Website:* www.americamovil.com (office).

SLIM HELÚ, Carlos; Mexican telecommunications industry executive; *Chairman, Teléfonos de México SA de C.V. (Telmex);* b. 28 Jan. 1940, Mexico City; m. Soumaya Domit Gemayel (deceased); six c.; ed Universidad Autónoma de México; f. Grupo Carso 1961, expanded co. through series of acquisitions including Jarritos de Sur (bottling co.) 1970, Galas de México (cigarette manufacturer) 1976, Cigarrera La Moderna 1981, and many other cos, Chair. Teléfonos de México SA (Telmex) 2002–, Grupo Financiero Inbursa; Hon. Lifetime Chair. Grupo Carso, América Móvil; fmr mem. Bd of Dirs Altria, SBC Communications –2004, Alcatel SA 2000–06; f. Fundación del Centro Histórico de la Ciudad de México A.C. 2000; f. Instituto Carso para la Salud 2007. *Address:* Teléfonos de México SA de C.V., Parque Vía 190, Col Cuahtémoc, 06599 México DF , Mexico (office). *Telephone:* (1) 5222-1212 (office). *Fax:* (1) 5545-5550 (office). *Website:* www.telmex.com.mx (office).

SLIPMAN, Sue, OBE, BA; British consumer representative; *Director, Foundation Trust Network;* b. 3 Aug. 1949; d. of Mark Slipman and Doris Barham; one s.; ed Stockwell Manor Comprehensive School, Univs of Wales, Leeds and London; Sec. and Nat. Pres. Nat. Union of Students 1975–78; mem. Advisory Council for Adult and Continuing Educ. 1978–79; area officer Nat. Union of Public Employees 1979–85; Dir Nat. Council for One Parent Families 1985–95; Dir London Training and Enterprise Council 1995–96; Dir Gas Consumer Council 1996–98; Dir for Social Responsibility, Camelot Group PLC 1998–2001, Bd mem., Dir External Relations and Compliance 2001–03; Chair. Financial Ombudsman Service 2003–05; Dir Foundation Trust Network, NHS Confed. 2004–05; Chair. Women for Social Democracy 1983–86, Advice Guidance and Counselling Lead Body 1992–, Better Regulation Task Force 1997–2001, Schools Project Working Group; Deputy Chair. Corp. Responsibility Group 2002; Dir (non-exec.) Thames Water Utilities Ltd; mem. RSA Council; Dr hc (Oxford Brookes) 1994. *Publications include:* Helping Ourselves to Power: A Handbook for Women on the Skills of Public Life 1986, Helping One-Parent Families to Work 1988, Maintenance: A System to Benefit Children 1989, Making Maintenance Pay 1990. *Address:* Foundation Trust Network, 29 Bressenden Place, London, SW1E 5DD, England (office). *Telephone:* (20) 7074-3231 (office). *E-mail:* sue.slipman@nhsconfed.org (office). *Website:* www.foundationtrustnetwork.org (office).

SLISKA, Lyubov Konstantinovna; Russian lawyer and politician; *First Deputy Chairman, State Duma;* b. 15 Oct. 1953, Saratov; m.; ed Saratov Inst. of Law; lawyer, Soyuzpechat Saratov 1977–89; on staff, regional trade cttee of heavy machine construction industry workers 1992–96; Perm. Rep. of Govt in Regional Duma, Deputy Chair. Regional Govt 1996–2000; mem. State Duma (Yedinstvo Movt List) 1999; First Deputy Chair. (Speaker) of State Duma 2000–; Order for Service to Motherland; Hon. PhD. *Leisure interests:* countryside, fishing. *Address:* State Duma, 103265 Moscow, Okhotny Ryad 1, Russia (office). *Telephone:* (495) 292-55-52 (office). *Fax:* (495) 292-86-00 (office). *E-mail:* sliska@duma.gov.ru (office). *Website:* www.duma.gov.ru (office).

SLIVA, Anatoly Yakovlevich, Cand.Jur.; Russian politician and judge; b. 10 Feb. 1940, Slavgorod, Belarus; m.; ed Moscow State Univ.; teacher and Dean, All-Union Juridical Inst. by correspondence; Sr Scientific Consultant, Deputy Head of Div. of local soviets, USSR Supreme Soviet 1988–92; Deputy Head of State Law Dept at Russian Presidency, concurrently Head of Div. on Interaction with Organs of Rep. and Exec. Power 1992–94; Official Rep. of Russian Pres. on legal problems to Supreme Soviet Russian Fed. 1992; mem. State Duma, Chair. Cttee on problems of local man. 1993–95; Rep. of Russian Pres. to Fed. Council 1996–98; Justice, Constitutional Court of Russian Fed. 1998–. *Address:* Constitutional Court, 103132, Moscow, Ilyinka str. 21, Russia. *Telephone:* (495) 206-92-25. *Website:* www.ksrf.ru.

SLOMAN, Sir Albert Edward, Kt, CBE, MA, DPhil; British university administrator; b. 14 Feb. 1921, Launceston, Cornwall; s. of Albert Sloman, CC and L. F. Brewer; m. Marie B. Bergeron 1948; three d.; ed Launceston Coll. and Wadham Coll., Oxford; Lecturer, Univ. of Calif., Berkeley 1946–47; Reader in Spanish, Univ. of Dublin 1947–53; Fellow, Trinity Coll., Dublin 1950–53; Prof. of Spanish, Univ. of Liverpool 1953–62; Vice-Chancellor Univ. of Essex 1962–87; Pres. Conf. of European Rectors and Vice-Chancellors 1969–74; Vice-Pres. Int. Assen of Univs 1970–75; Chair. Cttee of Vice-Chancellors and Prins 1981–83; Chair. Bd of Govs Centre for Information on Language Teaching and Research 1979–86; Chair. British Acad. Studentship Selection Cttee (Humanities) 1965–87, Overseas Research Students Fees Support Scheme 1980–87, Univs Council for Adult and Continuing Educ. 1984–87, Selection Cttee Commonwealth Scholarships Comm. 1986–94;

Chair. Int. Bd United World Colls 1988–93; Vice-Chair. Council of Asscn of Commonwealth Univs 1984–87; mem. Econ. and Social Cttee EEC 1973–82, Cttee for Int. Co-operation in Higher Educ. 1981–88 (Chair. 1985–88), Cttee of Man., British Inst. in Paris 1982–96, Bd of Govs Univ. of Guyana 1966–92; Inspection of Ruskin Coll., Oxford 1986–87; Pres. Penzance Library 1990–96; Dir Close Bros. Bessa Cos 1992–98; Dr hc (Nice) 1974, (Essex) 1988, (Liverpool) 1989. *Publications:* The Sources of Calderón's El Príncipe Constante 1950, The Dramatic Craftsmanship of Calderón 1958, Calderón, La Vida Es Sueño (ed.) 1960, Bulletin of Hispanic Studies (ed.) 1953–62, A University in the Making 1964. *Leisure interest:* travel. *Address:* 19 Inglis Road, Colchester, Essex, CO3 3HU, England. *Telephone:* (20) 7225-0972 (office); (1206) 547270 (home).

SLONIMSKI, Piotr, DSc, MD; French/Polish biologist and academic; *Professor Emeritus, Faculté des Sciences, Université P. et M. Curie;* b. 9 Nov. 1922, Warsaw, Poland; s. of Piotr Waclaw Slonimski; m. Hanna Kulagowska 1951 (deceased); one d. (deceased); ed Lycée Stephane Batory, underground Univ. of Warsaw, Jagiellonian Univ. of Kraków and Faculté des Sciences, Paris; served in Polish underground army 1939–45; Asst, Univ. of Kraków 1945–47; Attaché, CNRS 1947, Chargé 1952, Maître 1956, Dir 1962; Prof. of Genetics, Faculté des Sciences and Université P. et M. Curie 1965–91, Prof. Emer. 1992–; Dir Centre de Génétique Moléculaire, CNRS 1971–91, Hon. Dir CNRS, Gif-sur-Yvette br. 1992–; Dir-Gen. Groupement de Recherches et d'Etudes sur les Genomes (GREG) 1993–96; Visiting Prof. Univs of Calif., Chicago and Louvain; mem. Acad. des Sciences (Inst. de France), Bavarian, Polish and Belgian Acads, Academia Europaea, American Acad. of Arts and Sciences; Chevalier, Légion d'honneur, Mil. Cross (Poland), Officier, Ordre nat. du Mérite, Commdr with Star of Merit of the Repub. (Poland); Dr hc (Wrocław, Louvain, Warsaw, Bratislava, Kraków); CNRS Gold Medal 1985, Hansen Gold Medal 1987, G.J. Mendel Hon. Medal 2001, A. Drawicz Prize 2004, and other awards. *Publications:* scientific publs on cellular respiration, genetics and biogenesis of mitochondria, structure and function of genes, computational biology. *Leisure interest:* mushroom hunting. *Address:* Centre de Génétique Moléculaire du CNRS, avenue de la Terrasse, 91190 Gif-sur-Yvette Cedex (office); Institut de France, 23 quai Conti, 75006 Paris (office); Le Haut Chantemesle, 72150 Courdemanche, France (home). *Telephone:* 1-69-07-54-90 (home). *Fax:* 1-69-82-33-07 (office). *E-mail:* slonimski@cgm.cnrs-gif.fr (office).

SLONIMSKY, Sergey Michailovich, PhD; Russian composer, teacher and pianist; *Professor, St Petersburg Conservatoire;* b. 12 Aug. 1932, Leningrad (now St Petersburg); s. of Michail Slonimsky and Ida Slonimskaya (née Kaplan); m. Raisa Slonimskaya (née Zankisova) 1973; one s. one d.; ed Leningrad Conservatoire; mem. of Teaching Faculty, Music Theory and Composition, Leningrad (now St Petersburg) Conservatoire 1958–, Prof. 1976–; mem. Bd CIS Composers' Union (also mem. St Petersburg Br.); Cavalier of Commdr's Cross of Poland; RSFSR Glinka State Prize 1983, RSFSR People's Artist 1987, State Prize of Russia 2002. *Works include:* 13 symphonies 1958–2004, orchestral and vocal works, chamber works, opera, ballet, songs and choral pieces, including Carnival Overture 1957, Concerto Buffa, chamber orchestra 1966, Antiphones (string quartet) 1969, Virinea opera 1969, Icarus (ballet in three acts) 1973, Master and Margarita (chamber opera in three acts) 1970–85, Merry Songs for piccolo, flute and tuba 1971, Sonata for violoncello and piano 1986, Mary Stuart (opera performed at 1986 Edinburgh Festival, USSR and abroad), Hamlet (opera) 1990–94, Cerch: dell'Inferno secondo Dante 1992, 24 Preludes and Fugues for piano 1994, Ivan the Terrible 1994 (opera premiered at Samara 1998), 24 Preludes and Fugues for piano 1995, King Lear (opera after Shakespeare) 2001, The Magic Nut (ballet) 2005. *Recordings:* Requiem 2003, Magic Nut (ballet, libretto by Mihail Shemiakin) 2005. *Publications:* musicological study of Prokofiev's symphonies 1964, Burlesques, Elegies, Dithyrambs 2000, Free Dissonance 2005. *Leisure interest:* poetry, literature, painting. *Address:* St Petersburg Conservatoire of Music, 190000 St Petersburg, 3, Teatralnaya Square (office); 191186 St Petersburg, Canal Griboedova 9-97, Russia (home). *Telephone:* (812) 571-85-85 (home). *Fax:* (812) 571-58-11 (office). *E-mail:* sloh@rambler.ru (home). *Website:* eng.conservatory.ru (office).

SLOTA, Ján; Slovak politician; *Leader, Slovak National Party;* b. 14 Sept. 1953; Founder Slovak Nat. Party (Slovenská národná strana—SNS) 1990, Leader 1994–99, 2003–; Mayor of Žilina 1990–2006; mem. Parl. 2006–, mem. Cttee for Review of Decisions of Nat. Security Authority 2006–, Cttee on Human Rights, Minorities and Status of Women 2006–, Special Control Cttee of Activities of Slovak Intelligence Service 2006–. *Address:* Slovak National Party (Slovenská národná strana), Šafárikovo nám. 3, 814 99 Bratislava, Slovakia (office). *Telephone:* (2) 5292-4260 (office). *Fax:* (2) 5296-6188 (office). *E-mail:* jan_slota@nrsr.sk (office); sns@sns.sk (office). *Website:* www.sns.sk (office).

SLOVES, Marvin, BA; American advertising agency executive (retd); b. 22 April 1933, New York; s. of John H. Sloves and Evelyn S. Sloves (née Wishan); ed Brandeis Univ. and Oriental Inst., Univ. of Chicago; Staff Researcher, Leo Burnett Co., Chicago 1962; Dir of Research, Earle Ludgin Co., Chicago 1963–64; Account Exec. Ted Bates Co., New York 1965–67; Pres. and CEO, Scali, McCabe, Sloves, Inc., New York 1967–81, Chair. and CEO 1981–93; Vice-Chair. The Lowe Group 1993–95; Co-Chair. Lowe & Pnrs/Scali, McCabe, Sloves 1995–99 (retd). *Leisure interests:* boxing, memorabilia collecting. *Address:* PO Box 1745, Santa Fe, NM 87504, USA.

SMALE, John G., BS; American business executive (retd); b. 1 Aug. 1927, Listowel, Ont., Canada; s. of Vera G. Gray and Peter J. Smale; m. Phyllis Anne Weaver 1950 (died 2007); two s. two d.; ed Miami Univ. (Ohio); worked for Vick Chemical Co., New York 1949–50; with Bio-Research Inc., New York 1950–52; with Procter and Gamble Co. 1952, Dir 1972, Pres. 1974–86, CEO 1981–90, Chair. 1986–90; Dir Gen. Motors Corpn, Detroit 1992–95, Chair. Exec. Comm.

of Bd 1996–2000 and Bd of Dirs (retd); Hon. LLD (Kenyon Coll.) 1974, (Miami Univ.) 1979, Hon. DSc (DePauw Univ.) 1983; Hon. D.Iur (St Augustine's Coll.) 1985 Advertising Hall of Fame, American Advertising Fed. 2002. *Address:* Marathon, FL 33050, USA.

SMALE, Stephen, PhD; American mathematician and academic; *Distinguished University Professor, Department of Mathematics, City University of Hong Kong;* b. 15 July 1930, Flint, Mich.; ed Univ. of Mich.; Instructor, Univ. of Chicago 1956–58; NSF Postdoctoral Fellowship, Inst. for Advanced Study, Princeton, NJ and Instituto de Mathematica Pura e Aplicada Rio de Janeiro, Brazil 1958–60; Alfred P. Sloan Research Fellow 1960–62; Assoc. Prof. of Math., Univ. of Calif, Berkeley 1960–61, Prof. 1964–94, Prof. without Stipend, Dept of Econs 1976–, Faculty Research Lectureship 1983, Prof. of Math. Emer. 1994–; Distinguished Univ. Prof., City Univ. of Hong Kong 1995–; Professorship, Columbia Univ., New York 1961–64; Research Prof., Miller Inst. for Basic Research in Science, Berkeley 1967–68, 1979–80, 1990; visiting mem. Institut des Hautes Etudes Scientifiques, Paris 1969–70, 1972–73, 1976; Visiting Prof., Univ. of Paris 1972–73, Yale Univ. 1974, Instituto de Matematica Pura e Aplicada, Rio de Janeiro 1976, 1988, 1994, Columbia Univ. 1987; Visiting Scientist, IBM Corpn, Yorktown Heights 1987; Visiting Corpn, Collège de France, Paris 1962; Foreign mem. Brazilian Acad. of Science 1964; mem. American Acad. of Arts and Sciences 1967, NAS 1970; Fellow, The Econometric Soc. 1983, Japan Soc. for the Promotion of Science 1993; hon. mem. Instituto de Matematica Pura e Aplicada, Rio de Janeiro 1990, Trinity Math. Soc., Dublin 1991–92, Moscow Math. Soc. 1997, London Math. Soc. 1998;; Hon. Prof., Univ. of Yunnan, Kunming 1997; Class of the Grand Cross of the Brazilian Nat. Order of Scientific Merit 1994; Hon. DSc (Univ. of Warwick, UK) 1974, (Queen's Univ., Kingston, Ont.) 1987, (Univ. of Mich.) 1996, (City Univ. of Hong Kong) 1997, (Rostov State Univ.) 1999; Dr hc (Université Pierre et Marie Curie, Paris) 1997; Veblen Prize for Geometry, American Math. Soc. 1965, Fields Medal, Int. Congress of Mathematicians, Moscow 1966, Univ. of Mich. Sesquicentennial Award 1967, American Math. Soc. Colloquium Lecturer 1972, Chauvenet Prize, Math. Asscn of America 1988, Von Neumann Award, Soc. for Industrial and Applied Math. 1989, Bishop Berkeley Lecturer, Trinity Coll., Dublin 1991, Distinguished Lecturer, Fields Inst., Waterloo, Canada 1992, Nat. Medal of Science 1996, Wolf Foundation Prize in Math. 2007. *Publications:* more than 100 articles in math. journals. *Address:* Department of Mathematics, City University of Hong Kong, 83 Tat Chee Avenue, Kowloon, Hong Kong Special Administrative Region, People's Republic of China (office). *Telephone:* (852) 2788 8646 (office). *Fax:* (852) 2788 8561 (office). *E-mail:* mago@cityu.edu.hk (office). *Website:* www.cityu.edu.hk (office).

SMALLMAN, Raymond Edward, CBE, PhD, DSc, FRS, FREng, FIMMM; British professor of metallurgy and materials science; *Professor Emeritus of Metallurgy and Materials, University of Birmingham;* b. 4 Aug. 1929, Wolverhampton; s. of David Smallman and Edith French; m. Joan D. Faulkner 1952; one s. one d.; ed Rugeley Grammar School and Univ. of Birmingham; Sr Scientific Officer, AERE Harwell 1953–58; Lecturer, Dept of Physical Metallurgy, Univ. of Birmingham 1958–63, Sr Lecturer 1963–64, Prof. of Physical Metallurgy 1964–69, Head, Dept of Physical Metallurgy and Science of Materials 1969–81, Feeney Prof. and Head, Dept of Metallurgy and Materials 1969–88, Prof. of Metallurgy and Materials 1988–93, Hon. Prof. 1993–2001, Prof. Emer. 2001–; Deputy Dean, Faculty of Science and Eng 1981–84, Dean 1984–85, Dean of Eng 1985–87, Vice-Prin. Univ. of Birmingham 1987–92; Pres. Birmingham Metallurgical Asscn 1972–73; Vice-Pres. Metals Soc. 1980–84; Vice-Pres. Fed. of European Materials Socs 1992–94, Pres. 1994–96; Council mem., Science and Eng Research Council 1992–94, (Materials Comm. 1988–91); mem. Council Inst. of Materials (Chair. Int. Affairs Cttee 1993–97), Vice-Pres. 1995–99; Visiting Prof., Univ. of Pa 1961, Stanford Univ. 1962, NSW 1974, Cape Town 1976, Hong Kong 1990–; Van Horn Distinguished Lecturer, CASE Western Reserve Univ. 1978; Distinguished Lecturer, Hong Kong Univ. 1999; Warden Birmingham Assay Office 1994–98, Guardian 1997–2000; Foreign Assoc. Nat. Acad. of Eng, USA; mem. Lunar Soc. 1991–99; Hon. Foreign mem. China Ordnance Soc., Metal Science Soc. Czech Repub.; Hon. DSc (Wales) 1990, (Novi Sad) 1990, (Cranfield) 2001; Sir George Beilby Gold Medal, Inst. of Metals and Chemical Soc. 1969, Rosenhain Medal Inst. of Metals 1972, Elegant Work Prize, Metals Soc. 1979, Platinum Medal, Inst. of Metals 1989, Gold Medal and Prize, Acta Materialia 2004. *Publications:* Modern Physical Metallurgy 1961, Modern Metallography (jtly) 1968, Structure of Metals and Alloys (jtly) 1969, Defect Analysis in Electron Microscopy (jtly) 1975, Metals and Materials: Science, Processes and Applications (jtly) 1994, Modern Physical Metallurgy and Materials Engineering (jtly) 1999, Metals and Materials: The Development and History of the Department in the University of Birmingham 2006; over 300 scientific papers on relationship of microstructure of materials and properties in learned journals. *Leisure interests:* writing, travel, friendly golf, bridge, gardening. *Address:* Department of Metallurgy and Materials, School of Engineering, University of Birmingham, Edgbaston, Birmingham, B15 2TT (office); 59 Woodthorne Road South, Tettenhall, Wolverhampton, WV6 8SN, England (home). *Telephone:* (121) 414-5223 (office); (1902) 752545 (home). *Fax:* (121) 414-7368 (office); (1902) 752545 (home). *E-mail:* r.e.smallman@bham.ac.uk (office); ray.smallman@btopenworld.com (home).

SMART, George M.; American energy industry executive; *Chairman, FirstEnergy Corporation;* b. 1946; Chair. and Pres. Phoenix Packaging Corpn 1993–2001; Pres. Sonoco-Phoenix Inc. 2001–04; Dir FirstEnergy Corpn 1997–, Chair. (non-exec.) 2004–; mem. Bd of Dirs Ball Corpn, Unizan Financial Corpn 2000–, Ohio Edison Co. 1988–97. *Address:* FirstEnergy Corporation, 76 Main Street, Akron, OH 44308, USA (office). *Telephone:* (800) 646-0400 (office). *Fax:* (330) 384-3866 (office). *Website:* www.firstenergycorp.com (office).

SMART, John Jamieson Carswell, AC, MA, BPhil, FAHA; Australian academic; *Professor Emeritus of Philosophy, Australian National University;* b. 16 Sept. 1920, Cambridge, England; s. of William M. Smart and Isabel M. Carswell; m. 1st Janet Paine 1956 (died 1967); one s. one d.; m. 2nd Elizabeth Warner 1968; ed King's Coll. Choir School, Cambridge, The Leys School, Cambridge, Univ. of Glasgow and Queen's Coll., Oxford; served in Royal Signals 1940–45; Jr Research Fellow, Corpus Christi Coll. Oxford 1948–50; Hughes Prof. of Philosophy, Univ. of Adelaide 1950–72, Prof. Emer. 1972–; Reader in Philosophy, La Trobe Univ. 1972–76; Prof. of Philosophy, Research School of Social Sciences, ANU 1976–85, Prof. Emer. 1986–; Fellow, Center for Advanced Study in the Behavioral Sciences, Stanford, USA 1979; Visiting Prof., Princeton Univ. 1957, Harvard Univ. 1963, Yale Univ. 1964, Stanford Univ. 1982, Univ. of Alabama at Birmingham 1990; G. D. Young Lecturer, Univ. of Adelaide 1987; Hon. Fellow, Corpus Christi Coll. Oxford 1991; Hon. Research Fellow, Monash Univ. 2002; Hon. DLitt (St Andrews) 1983, (La Trobe) 1992, (Glasgow) 2001. *Publications:* An Outline of a System of Utilitarian Ethics 1961, Philosophy and Scientific Realism 1963, Problems of Space and Time (ed.) 1964, Between Science and Philosophy 1968, Ethics, Persuasion and Truth 1984, Essays Metaphysical and Moral 1987, Our Place In the Universe 1989, Atheism and Theism (with J. J. Haldane) 1996. *Leisure interest:* walking. *Address:* 159/101 Whalley Drive, Wheelers Hill, Vic. 3150, Australia (home). *Telephone:* (3) 9795-8075 (home). *E-mail:* john.smart@arts.monash.edu.au (home).

SMART, Stephen Bruce, Jr, AB, SM; American business executive and fmr government official; b. 7 Feb. 1923, New York; s. of Stephen Bruce Smart and Beatrice Cobb; m. Edith Minturn Merrill 1949; one s. three d.; ed Harvard Coll. and Mass. Inst. of Tech.; US Army 1943–46, 1951–53; Sales Engineer, Permutit Co., New York 1947–51; joined Continental Group (fmrly Continental Can Co.) 1951, various sales and gen. man. posts 1951–62, Vice-Pres. Cen. Div. 1962–65, Marketing and Corpn Planning 1965–68, Exec. Vice-Pres. Paper Operations 1969–73, Vice-Chair. 1973–75, Pres. and COO 1975–81; Chair. and CEO Continental Group 1981–85; Under-Sec. for Int. Trade US Dept of Commerce 1985–88; Consultant, Dept of State, Washington 1988; Sr Fellow, World Resources Inst. 1989–95; Dir World Resources Inst. 1993–2001, League of Conservation Voters 1995. *Publications:* Beyond Compliance: A New Industry View of the Environment (ed.) 1992, Indian Summer: A Memoir 1999, A Community of the Horse: Partnerships 2003. *Leisure interests:* fishing, sailing, American decorative arts, thoroughbred horse breeding. *Address:* 20561 Trappe Road, Upperville, VA 20184, USA (home). *Telephone:* (540) 554-8302 (home).

SMEAL, Eleanor, MA; American feminist leader, political analyst and author; *President, Feminist Majority and Feminist Majority Foundation;* b. (Eleanor Marie Cutri), 30 July 1939, Ashtabula, OH; d. of Peter Anthony Cutri and Josephine E. Agresti; one s. one d.; ed Strong Vincent High School, Duke Univ., Durham, NC, Univ. of Florida; joined Nat. Org. for Women 1970, Pres. 1977–82, 1985–87, led drive to ratify Equal Rights Amendment; Founder and Pres. Feminist Majority Foundation 1986–; Publr Ms. magazine (owned and published by Feminist Majority Foundation) 2001–; led first nat. abortion rights march of more than 100,000 activists to Washington, DC 1986; launched Feminist Majority Foundation Online (www.feminist.org) 1995; held first-ever nat. feminist exposition, Expo 96 for Women's Empowerment, Washington, DC 1996; organized Feminist Expo 2000; launched int. Campaign to Stop Gender Apartheid in Afghanistan to counter the Taliban's abuse of women 1997, campaign helped stop US and UN from officially recognizing the Taliban; Hon. LLD (Duke Univ.); named by TIME Magazine as one of the "50 Faces for America's Future" 1979, chosen by The World Almanac as the fourth most influential woman in the USA 1983, featured as one of the six most influential Washington lobbyists in U.S. News and World Report. *Achievements include:* involved in several legislative initiatives, including Free Access to Clinic Entrances legislation (influenced by Madsen v. Women's Health Center) 1994, defeat of Proposition 209 in Calif., Pregnancy Discrimination Act, Equal Credit Act, Civil Rights Restoration Act, Violence Against Women Act, Freedom of Access to Clinic Entrances Act, Civil Rights Act 1991, and fight to amend Equal Rights Amendment. *Films:* co-author and co-producer of two videos, Abortion for Survival, Abortion Denied: Shattering Women's Lives. *Publications include:* How and Why Women Will Elect the Next President 1984. *Address:* Feminist Majority Foundation, 1600 Wilson Boulevard, Suite 801, Arlington, VA 22209 (office); Feminist Majority Foundation, 33 S Beverly Drive, Beverly Hills, CA 90212, USA (office). *Telephone:* (703) 522-2214 (Arlington) (office); (310) 556-2500 (Beverly Hills) (office). *Fax:* (703) 522-2219 (Arlington) (office); (310) 556-2509 (Beverly Hills) (office). *E-mail:* info@feminist.org (office). *Website:* www.feminist.org (office).

SMEDEGAARD ANDERSEN, Nils, MSc; Danish business executive; *Partner and Group CEO, A.P. Møller-Maersk A/S;* b. 8 July 1958, Århus; ed Århus Univ.; began career as Sales Dir Tuborg International, becoming Man. Dir of several Carlsberg and Tuborg cos, mem. group man. 1999–2007, CEO Carlsberg A/S 2001–07; mem. Bd Dirs A.P. Møller-Maersk A/S 2005–, Pnr and Group CEO 2007–; mem. European Round Table of Industrialists 2001–; Co-Chair. EU-Russia Industrialists' Round Table 2007–; mem. Bd Dirs William Demant Holding A/S, Oticon A/S. *Address:* A.P. Møller-Mærsk A/S, Esplanaden 50, 1098 Copenhagen K, Denmark (office). *Telephone:* 33-63-33-63 (office). *Fax:* 33-63-41-08 (office). *E-mail:* info@maersk.com (office). *Website:* www.maersk.com (office).

SMIDT, Kristian, PhD; Norwegian academic; *Professor Emeritus of English Literature, University of Oslo;* b. 20 Nov. 1916, Sandefjord; s. of Bishop Johannes Smidt and Jofrid Smidt (née Grimstvedt); m. 1st Aagot Karner 1940 (divorced 1973); m. 2nd Anne Oulie-Hansen 1973; one s. two d.; ed Aske's Hatcham, London, Univ. of Oslo; Reader in English Literature Univ. of Oslo 1953–55, Prof. 1955–85, Prof. Emer. 1985–, Dir British Inst. 1955–73; Prof. of English Literature (temporary) Univ. of Tromsø 1973–76; Rockefeller Fellowship, Princeton Univ. 1951–52; Folger Shakespeare Library Fellowship, Washington, DC 1960–61; Visiting Fellowship, Clare College, Cambridge Univ. 1984; mem. Norwegian Acad. of Science and Letters, Vetenskapssocieten, Lund, Sweden, Norwegian Acad. of Language and Literature; Hon. OBE 1985; Nansen Award 1994. *Publications:* James Joyce and the Cultic Use of Fiction 1959, Poetry and Belief in the Work of T.S. Eliot 1961, Unconformities in Shakespeare's Plays (4 Vols) 1982–93, Shakespeare i norsk oversettelse 1994, Ibsen Translated 2000, Den mangfoldige Shakespeare 2000, The Importance of Recognition and Other Essays on T.S. Eliot 2001; Silent Creditors: Henrik Ibsen's Debt to English Literature 2004; Ed. Shakespeare's Richard III: Parallel Texts 1969. *Address:* Solveien 137, 1167 Oslo, Norway (home). *Telephone:* 22-28-86-42 (home).

SMILEY, Jane Graves, MFA, PhD; American writer and academic; b. 26 Sept. 1949, Los Angeles; d. of James La Verne Smiley and Frances Nuelle (née Graves); m. 1st John Whiston 1970 (divorced); m. 2nd William Silag 1978 (divorced); two d.; m. 3rd Stephen Mark Mortensen 1987 (divorced 1997); one s.; ed Vassar Coll. and Univ. of Iowa; Asst Prof., Iowa State Univ. 1981–84, Assoc. Prof. 1984–89, Prof. 1989–90, Distinguished Prof. 1992–96; Visiting Prof., Univ. of Iowa 1981, 1987; Fulbright Grant 1976, Nat. Endowment for the Arts grants 1978, 1987; Friends of American Writers Prize 1981, O. Henry Awards 1982, 1985, 1988, Distinguished Alumni Award Univ. of Iowa 2003. *Publications:* Barn Blind 1980, At Paradise Gate 1981, Duplicate Keys 1984, The Age of Grief 1987, Catskill Crafts: Artisans of the Catskill Mountains (non-fiction) 1987, The Greenlanders 1988, Ordinary Love and Goodwill 1989, A Thousand Acres (Pulitzer Prize in Fiction 1992, Nat. Book Critics Circle Award 1992, Midland Authors Award 1992, Heartland Prize 1992) 1991, Moo: A Novel 1995, The All-True Travels and Adventures of Lidie Newton 1998, Horse Heaven 2000, Dickens (biog.) 2002, Good Faith 2003, A Year at the Races 2004, Thirteen Ways of Looking at the Novel (non-fiction) 2006, Ten Days in the Hills 2007. *Leisure interests:* cooking, swimming, playing piano, quilting. *Address:* c/o Molly Friedrick, Department of English, 708 Third Avenue, Floor 23, New York, NY 10017, USA (office).

SMIRNOV, Andrei Sergeyevich; Russian actor, film director and scriptwriter; b. 12 March 1941, Moscow; ed All Union State Inst. of Cinematography; numerous prizes at int. film festivals. *Films:* dir: Hey, Anybody! (with B. Yashin) 1962, An Inch of Land (with B. Yashin) 1964, A Little Joke (TV film with B. Yashin) 1966, Somebody Else's Pain (TV film) 1966, Jacqueline Francois Sings (TV film) 1966, Angel 1987, Belorussian Railway Station 1970, Fall 1974, By Trust and Truth 1979, Unwillful Striptease 1983; actor: Following, Chernov, Dreams of an Idiot, Mania of Giselle, Dnevnik ego zheny (Diary of His Wife) 2000, Persona non grata 2005; scriptwriter: Autumn, Sentimental Journey, My Dear Relatives. *Television includes:* actor: Idiot (miniseries) 2003, Moskovskaya saga 2004, Master i Margarita (miniseries) 2005. *Plays directed:* Late Supper (Moscow Art Theatre) 1994, Turgenev's Month in a Village (Comedy Francaise) 1997. *Publications include:* plays: Autumn, Sentimental Journey; My Dear Relative. *Address:* 121019 Moscow, Suvirivski boulevard 8, Apt, Russia (office). *Telephone:* (495) 299-34-93 (office).

SMIRNOV, Igor Nikolayevich, DEconSc; Moldovan politician; *'President', 'Transnistrian Moldovan Republic';* b. 23 Oct. 1941, Petropavlovsk-Kamchatskii, Russian SFSR, USSR; s. of Nikolai Stepanovich Smirnov and Zinaida Grigor'evna Smirnova; m. Zhannetta Nikolaevna Lotnik; two s.; ed Zaporizhzhya Machine Construction Inst., Ukrainian SSR; mem. CPSU 1963–90; early career as engineer, chief engineer, chief of shop; Deputy Dir Novo-Kakhova Electromash plant, Ukrainian SSR; Dir Tiraspol Electromash plant 1987–1990, Moldovan SSR; Dir Tiraspol Jt Trade Union 1989–91, Chair. City Soviet and Tiraspol City Exec. Cttee 1990–91; 'Pres.' Self-Declared 'Transnistrian Moldovan Repub.' (expelled from CPSU for separatism 1990) 1991–; People's Deputy of Moldova 1990–92; Academician, Ukranian Economical-Cybernetics Acad.; mem. Int. Acad. of Informatization, Russian Acad. of Natural Sciences; Order of Republic 1995, Medal, Order of Prince Daniyl of Moscow 1998, Order of Sergei Radonejski 1999, Order for Benefit of Motherland, Russian Acad. of Sciences, Order of World Distributing Univ., Cross for Faith and Motherland (3rd Degree), Cross for Defence of 'Transnistrian Moldovan Repub.', Cross for Service to the Cossacks, Order of Lenin, Star of Hero, Order of Glory of Russia 2000, Order for Personal Courage 2001; Medal for Labour Prowess, Medal on 10th anniversary of 'Transnistrian Moldovan Repub.'. *Publications:* Human Beings, Science and Technical Progress in a Century of Information 2000, In Favour of the Republic 2000, To Live on Our Land (Sholohov Prize) 2004. *Leisure interest:* hunting. *Address:* 'Office of the President of the Transnistrian Moldovan Republic', 3300 Tiraspol, ul. 25 Oktyabrya 45, Moldova (office). *Telephone:* (30) 30-70-78 (office). *E-mail:* president@presidentpmr.org (office). *Website:* presidentpmr.org (office).

SMIRNOV, Igor Pavlovich, DPhilSc; Russian literary scholar; *Professor Emeritus, University of Konstanz;* b. 19 May 1941, Leningrad (now St Petersburg); s. of Pavel Smirnov and Valentina Lomakina; m. Johanna Renate Döring 1979; ed Leningrad Univ.; Research Assoc., Leningrad Inst. of Russian Literature; left USSR 1981; Prof., Univ. of Konstanz, Germany 1981–2006, Prof. Emer. 2006–; Vjazemski Prize 1998, Andrey Bely Prize 2000. *Publications include:* Meaning in Art and the Evolution of Poetic Systems 1977, Diachronic Transformations of Literary Genres and Motifs 1981, Essays on the History of the Typology of Culture (with Johanna Smirnov) 1982, The Emergence of the Inter-text 1985, Towards a Theory of Literature 1987, Being and Creating 1990, On Old Russian Culture, Russian National Specificity and the Logic of History 1991, Psychohistory of Russian Literature from Romanticism to the Present Day 1995, A Novel of Secrets – Dr. Zhivago 1996, Homo homini philosophus 1999, Megahistory 2000, Philosophy for Everyday 2003, Philosophical Sociology of Revolution 2004, Genesis 2006. *Address:* Department of Russian, University of Konstanz, 78457 Konstanz (office); Kornblumenweg 14, 78465 Konstanz, Germany (home). *Telephone:* (7531) 882682 (office); (7531) 43583 (home). *Fax:* (7531) 4852 (office). *E-mail:* igor.smirnov@uni-konstanz.de (office).

SMIRNOV, Stanislav Alekseyevich, DEcon SC.; Russian business executive and academic; *Professor of Sociology, State Technical University;* b. 18 April 1954, Mashok, Vladimir Region; m.; two c.; ed Moscow Inst. of Motor Car Transport; Sec. Moscow City Comsomol Cttee 1982–85, First Sec. 1985–89; Sec., Second Sec. Cen. Comsomol Cttee 1989–90; Peoples' Deputy of Russian Fed.; mem. Supreme Soviet; Chair. Comm. on Problems of Youth 1990–93; expelled from CPSU 1991; mem. of Presidium, Fed. of Mfrs of Russia; mem. Council on Industrial Policy and Business of Russian Presidency; mem. Co-ordination Council Round Table of Russian Business 1994; Corresp. mem. Russian Acad. of Sciences 1997–; Pres. Russian Chamber of Commerce and Industry 1991–2001; Prof. of Sociology, State Tech. Univ. GTU–MADI 2000–. *Publications:* over 100 scientific works. *Address:* State Technical University, Avtomotornaya str. 2, 125438 Moscow, Russia (office). *Telephone:* (495) 155-03-71 (office). *E-mail:* info@madi.ru.

SMIRNOV, Vitaly Georgiyevich; Russian sports official; b. 14 Feb. 1935, Khabarovsk; m. Irina Aleksandrovna Smirnova; three s.; ed Cen. State Inst. of Physical Culture; instructor, Head Div. of Sports Moscow Comsomol Cttee 1958–60; First Sec. Kuntzevo Regional Comsomol Cttee; Moscow Region 1960; Chair. Moscow Regional Council, Union of Sports Socs. and Orgs. 1960–62; Second Sec., First Sec. Moscow Regional Comsomol Cttee 1962–68; First Sec. City Cttee of CPSU 1968–70; Deputy Chair., First Deputy Chair. USSR Cttee of Sports and Physical Culture 1970–75, Chair. Water Polo Fed. 1962–72; First Deputy Chair. Org. Cttee of Olympic Games 1980 in Moscow 1975–81; Chair. State Cttee on Sports and Physical Culture of Russian Fed. 1981–90; Participant IOC EB 1974–78, 1986–90, Vice-Pres. IOC 1978–82, 1991–95, 2001–05, mem. Int. Relations Comm. 2002–Remuneration Working Group 2004–, 2009 Congress 2006–; Chair. USSR Olympic Cttee 1990–92; Pres. Olympic Cttee of Russia 1992–2001, Hon. Pres. 2001–; mem. Acad. of Creativity 1994–, Int. Acad. of Informatization, Peter's Acad. of Sciences and Arts; Order Sign of Honour 1966, 1970, 1976, Order Friendship of Nations 1980, Order Labour Red Banner 1985, Order of Honour 1994, Order For Services to Motherland 3rd degree 1966, Order for Services to Motherland 2nd degree 2001; orders and awards of international sports federations. *Publications:* numerous articles and papers on the devt of sports in Russia and the Olympic movt. *Leisure interests:* hunting, fishing, tennis. *Address:* c/o Russian Olympic Committee, 119992 Moscow, Luzhnetskaya emb. 8, Russia. *Telephone:* (495) 725-45-01 (office). *Fax:* (495) 248-36-11 (office). *E-mail:* pr@olympic.ru (office). *Website:* www.roc.ru (office).

SMIRNOV, Vladimir Nikolaevich; Russian biochemist; b. 17 May 1937, Cheliabinsk; m. 1st Valeriana Kreier 1956 (divorced 1973); m. 2nd Galina Chernonsova 1976; one s.; ed Leningrad Univ.; mem. CPSU 1976–91; postgraduate 1959–64; Jr, Sr Research Fellow at USSR Acad. of Med. Science Inst. of Medical Radiology 1964–68; Head of Biochemical Section, Ministry of Health 1968–72; Corresp. mem. of USSR (now Russian) Acad. of Sciences 1981; Prof. of Biological Science 1977; Head of Lab. at All-Union Scientific Centre for Cardiology (br. of USSR (now Russian) Acad. of Medical Science) 1973–76, Dir 1976–82; Dir of Inst. of Experimental Cardiography of Acad. of Medical Sciences 1982–; Corresp. mem., then mem. Acad. of Medical Sciences 1984–; USSR State Prize 1978. *Publications:* works on molecular biology, biochem. of the heart, cellular and molecular athero- and trombogenesis. *Leisure interests:* hunting, fishing. *Address:* Institute of Experimental Cardiology, Cardiology Research Centre, 112552 Moscow, 3rd Cherepkovskaya 15A, Russia. *Telephone:* (495) 415-00-35 (office); (495) 203-84-83 (home). *Fax:* (495) 415-29-62.

SMISEK, Jeffery A., AB, JD; American airline industry executive; *President, Continental Airlines Inc.;* b. 17 Aug. 1954, Washington; m.; two c.; ed Princeton Univ., Harvard Law School; Pnr and Exec. Vice-Pres. Vinson & Elkins LLP, Houston 1983–95; Sr Vice-Pres. and Gen. Counsel Continental Airlines Inc. 1995–96, Exec. Vice-Pres., Gen. Counsel and Sec. 1996–2001, Exec. Vice-Pres., Corp. 2001–03, Exec. Vice-Pres. 2003–04, Dir 2004–, Pres. 2004–; mem. Bd of Dirs National Oilwell Varco Inc., Varco International Inc., Orbitz Inc. *Address:* Continental Airlines Inc., PO Box 4607, Houston, TX, 77210, USA (office). *Telephone:* (713) 324-2950 (office). *Fax:* (713) 324-2687 (office). *Website:* www.continental.com (office).

SMITH, Ali; British writer; b. 1962, Inverness, Scotland; ed Univ. of Aberdeen, Univ. of Cambridge; fmr Lecturer, Univ. of Strathclyde; gave lecture on Angela Carter, Nat. Portrait Gallery, London 2004; Scottish Arts Council Award 1995. *Publications:* Free Love and Other Stories (Saltire First Book Award) 1995, Like (novel) 1997, Other Stories and Other Stories 1999, Hotel World (novel) (Encore Prize, Scottish Arts Council Book Award, Scottish Arts Council Book of the Year 2002) 2001, The Whole Story and Other Stories 2003, The Accidental (novel) (Whitbread Novel of the Year 2005) 2004, The Reader 2006, Girl Meets Boy 2007, The First Person and other stories 2008; contrib. to TLS, The Scotsman, Guardian. *Address:* c/o Hamish Hamilton, c/o Penguin Books, 80 Strand, London, WC2R 0RL, England.

SMITH, Andrew David; British politician; b. 1 Feb. 1951; m.; one step-s.; ed Reading Grammar School and St John's Coll., Oxford; joined Labour Party 1973; mem. Oxford City Council 1976–87; MP for Oxford East 1987–; Opposition Spokesman on Higher Educ. 1988–92, on Treasury and Econ. Affairs 1992–94; Shadow Chief Sec. to HM Treasury 1994–96; Shadow Transport Sec. 1996–97; Minister of State, Dept for Educ. and Employment 1997–99; Chief Sec. to HM Treasury 1999–2002; Sec. of State for Work and Pensions 2002–04 (resgnd); Chair. Bd Oxford Brookes Univ. (fmrly Oxford Polytechnic) 1987–93. *Address:* House of Commons, London, SW1A 0AA (office); 4 Flaxfield Road, Blackbird Leys, Oxford, OX4 5QD, England (home). *Telephone:* ; (1865) 305080 (constituency office). *Fax:* (1865) 305089. *E-mail:* andrewsmith.mp@virgin.net. *Website:* www.andrewsmithmp.org.uk.

SMITH, Anthony David, CBE, MA; British administrator; b. 14 March 1938; s. of Henry Smith and Esther Smith; ed Brasenose Coll., Oxford; Current Affairs Producer, BBC 1960–71; Fellow, St Antony's Coll., Oxford 1971–76; Dir British Film Inst. 1979–88; Pres. Magdalen Coll., Oxford 1988–2005; mem. Bd of Dirs Channel Four TV 1980–84; mem. Acton Soc. Trust 1978–90; Chair. Writers and Scholars Educational Trust (Index on Censorship) 1989–99, Hill Foundation 1999–, Oxford-Russia Fund 2004–; mem. Arts Council 1990–94; Trustee, Prince of Wales Inst. of Traditional Arts 2005–; Bd mem. The Sixteen Choir 2006–; mem. Council Royal Acad. of Dramatic Art 2007–; Hon. Fellow, Brasenose Coll. Oxford 1994, Magdalen Coll. Oxford 2005–. *Publications:* The Shadow in the Cave: The Broadcaster, The Audience and the State 1973, British Broadcasting 1974, The British Press since the War 1976, Subsidies and the Press in Europe 1977, The Politics of Information 1978, Television and Political Life 1979, The Newspaper: An International History 1979, Newspapers and Democracy 1980, Goodbye Gutenberg – The Newspaper Revolution of the 1980s, The Geopolitics of Information 1980, The Age of the Behemoths 1991, From Books to Bytes 1993, The Oxford Illustrated History of Television 1995, Software for the Self: Culture and Technology 1996. *Address:* Albany, Piccadilly, London, W1J 0AX, England (home). *Telephone:* (20) 7734-5494 (home).

SMITH, Bernard William, PhD; Australian academic; b. 3 Oct. 1916, Sydney; s. of Charles Smith and Rose Anne Tierney; m. 1st Kate Challis 1941 (died 1989); one s. one d.; m. 2nd Margaret Forster 1995; ed Univ. of Sydney, Courtauld and Warburg Inst., London and Australian Nat. Univ., Canberra; school teacher, NSW 1935–44, Educ. Officer, Art Gallery, NSW 1944–52; Lecturer, Sr Lecturer, Univ. of Melbourne 1955–63, Reader 1964–66; Art Critic The Age, Melbourne 1963–66; Prof. of Contemporary Art and Dir Power Inst. of Fine Arts, Univ. of Sydney 1967–77, Sr Assoc., Dept of Fine Arts 1977–; Assoc. Prof., Dept Fine Arts, Classical Studies and Archaeology, Univ. of Melbourne 1994–; Pres. Australian Acad. of the Humanities 1977–80; Chevalier, Ordre des Arts et Lettres 1977. *Publications:* The Advance of Lot and his Brethern 1940, Pompeii 1940, Place, Taste and Tradition 1945, European Vision and the South Pacific 1960, Australian Painting 1962, The Boy Adeodatus 1985, The Art of Captain Cook's Voyages (jt author) 1985–87, The Death of the Artist as Hero 1988, The Critic as Advocate 1989, Imagining the Pacific 1992, Noel Counihan 1994, Poems 1938–1993 1996, Modernism's History 1998, A Pavane for Another Time 2002. *Leisure interests:* swimming, walking, reading. *Address:* c/o 37 Gertrude Street, Fitzroy, Vic. 3065, Australia (home). *Telephone:* (3) 9419-5595 (home). *E-mail:* kc@workwell.com.au (office). *Website:* www.arts.usyd.edu.au/departs/arthistory/power/institute (office); www.historical-studies.unimelb.edu.au/bernardsmith (office).

SMITH, Brian (see Smith, Sir E. Brian).

SMITH, Brian (see Smith, Sir (Norman) Brian).

SMITH, Bruce Alfred, BS, MBA; American energy industry executive; *Chairman, President and CEO, Tesoro Corporation;* b. 12 Oct. 1943, Coffeyville, Kan.; s. of George Alfred Smith and Isabel Smith (neé Andrews); m. 1st Cynthia Denton Smith (neé Doughat) 1969, divorced 1987; five s.; m. 2nd Gail Smith (neé Hutchison) 1990; ed Westminster Coll., Univ. of Kansas; served in US Army; worked as Financial Analyst, Ford Motor Co., Dearborn, Mich. 1967–69; Banking Officer, Metropolitan Div. Continental Ill. Nat. Bank and Trust Co., Chicago 1971–73, 2nd Vice-Pres. Multinational Div. 1973–75, Vice-Pres. Mining Div. 1975–77, Vice-Pres. and Section Man., Chicago and London 1977–80, Vice-Pres. and Man. Int. Energy Div., Chicago 1980–82, Vice-Pres. and Man. Southwest Group and Commercial Banking Houston 1983–86; Vice-Pres. and Treas. Valero Energy Corpn 1986–92; Chief Financial Officer Tesoro Corpn 1992–95, Exec. Vice-Pres. 1993–95, Pres. and CEO 1995–96, mem. Bd of Dirs 1995–, Chair., Pres. and CEO 1996–; mem. Bd of Dirs Noble Energy Inc., Nat. Petrochemical and Refiners Asscn. *Address:* Tesoro Corporation, 300 Concord Plaza Drive, San Antonio, TX 78216-6999, USA (office). *Telephone:* (210) 828-8484 (office). *Fax:* (210) 283-2045 (office). *E-mail:* info@tsocorp.com (office). *Website:* www.tsocorp.com (office).

SMITH, Carsten, DJur; Norwegian judge (retd); b. 13 July 1932, Oslo; s. of Oscar Smith and Julie Høyer; m. Lucy Dahl 1958; three d.; ed Univ. of Oslo; practised as attorney 1956–60; Deputy Judge 1960; Asst Prof., Univ. of Oslo 1957, Assoc. Prof. 1960, Prof. of Law 1964–91; Dir Inst. of Pvt. Law 1972–73, Dean, Faculty of Law 1977–79; Temporary Supreme Court Justice 1987, 1989–90; Chief Justice, Supreme Court of Norway 1991–2002; Chair. Saami Rights Comm. 1980–85, Comm. on Human Rights in Norwegian Legislation 1989–91, Comm. for reviewing Norwegian Court system 1996–99, Comm. on Nordic Saami Rights Convention 2003–05, Comm. on fishing rights in the ocean north of Norway for Saami People and other citizens 2006–08; mem. Permanent Court of Arbitration 1996–2004; mem. Norwegian Acad. of Science and Letters, Pres. 1991; mem. UN Perm. Forum on Indigenous Issues 2008–; Grand Cross of Royal Norwegian Order of St Olav 2003. *Publications include:* Law of Torts and Social Security (co-author) 1953, Law of Guarantees (Vols I–III) 1963–81, State Practice and Legal Theory 1978, Banking Law and State Regulations 1980, Contemporary Legal Reasoning 1992, The Law and the Life 1996; other books and articles in fields of int. law, constitutional law, admin. law and pvt. law. *Address:* c/o Secretariat of the Permanent Forum on

Indigenous Issues, United Nations, 2 UN Plaza, Room DC2-1772, New York, NY, 10017, USA; Høyesterett, PO Box 8016 Dep, 0030 Oslo, Norway. *Telephone:* 22-03-59-05. *Fax:* 22-33-23-55.

SMITH, Dan F., BSc; American petrochemical industry executive; *Chairman, President and CEO, Lyondell Chemical Company;* m. Sandy Smith; two c.; ed Lamar Univ.; Engineer ARCO (Atlantic Richfield Co.) 1968–82, Planning Man. 1982–84, Vice-Pres., Planning and Control, ARCO Metals Co. 1984–85, Exec. Vice-Pres. and COO 1991–93; Vice-Pres., Control and Admin Lyondell Chemical Co. 1985, Vice-Pres. then Pres. of Mfg Operations 1985–88, Exec. Vice-Pres. and Chief Financial Officer 1988–91, 1993–94, Pres. 1994–, CEO 1996–, Chair. 2007–, CEO Partnership Governance Cttee, Equistar Chemicals LP 1997–, Millennium Chemicals Inc. 2004– (subsidiaries of Lyondell Chemical Co.); mem. Bd of Dirs Cooper Industries; mem. Lamar Univ. Coll. of Eng Advisory Council. *Address:* Lyondell Chemical Company, 1221 McKinney Street, Suite 700, Houston, TX 77010, USA (office). *Telephone:* (713) 652-7200 (office). *Website:* www.lyondell.com (office).

SMITH, Sir David Cecil, Kt, FRS, FRSE; British academic; b. 21 May 1930, Port Talbot; s. of William Smith and Elva Smith; m. Lesley Mutch 1965; two s. one d.; ed Colston's School, Bristol, St Paul's School, London and Queen's Coll. Oxford; Browne Research Fellow, Queen's Coll. Oxford 1956–59; Harkness Fellow, Univ. of Calif., Berkeley 1959–60; Univ. Lecturer, Dept of Agric. Science, Univ. of Oxford 1960–74; Fellow and Tutor, Wadham Coll. Oxford 1964–74; Melville Wills Prof. of Botany, Univ. of Bristol 1974–80; Sibthorpian Prof. of Rural Econ. Univ. of Oxford 1980–87; Prin. and Vice-Chancellor, Univ. of Edin. 1987–94; Pres. Wolfson Coll., Oxford 1994–2000; Commdr Order of Merit (Italy), Commdr Order of Merit (Poland); Hon. DSc (Aberdeen) 1990, (Edin.) 1994 and numerous other hon. degrees. *Publication:* Biology of Symbiosis (with A. E. Douglas) 1987. *Leisure interest:* writing. *Address:* 13 Abbotsford Park, Edinburgh, EH10 5DZ, Scotland. *Telephone:* (131) 446-0230. *Fax:* (131) 446-0230. *E-mail:* smithsymbiosis@aol.com (home).

SMITH, Delia, OBE, FRTS; British cookery writer and broadcaster; b. 18 June 1941; m. Michael Wynn Jones; creator and presenter of several TV series; cookery writer, Evening Standard newspaper 1972–85; columnist, Radio Times; Consultant Food Ed., Sainsbury's Magazine; Dir Norwich City Football Club; Hon. Fellow, St Mary's Coll., Univ. of Surrey 1996, John Moores Univ., Liverpool 2000; Dr hc (Nottingham) 1996, (East Anglia) 1999; Special Award, Andre Simon Memorial Fund 1994. *Publications:* How to Cheat at Cooking 1971, Country Fare 1973, Recipes from Country Inns and Restaurants 1973, Family Fare: Book 1 1973, Book 2 1974, Evening Standard Cookbook 1974, Country Recipes from Look East (regional TV programme) 1975, More Country Recipes from Look East 1976, Frugal Food 1976, Book of Cakes 1977, Recipes from Look East 1977, Food for Our Times 1978, Cookery Course: Part 1 1978, Part 2 1979, Part 3 1981, The Complete Cookery Course 1982, A Feast for Lent 1983, A Feast for Advent 1983, One is Fun 1985, Food Aid Cookery Book (ed.) 1986, A Journey into God 1988, Delia Smith's Christmas 1990, Delia Smith's Summer Collection 1993, Delia Smith's Winter Collection 1995, Delia's Red Nose Collection 1997, How to Cook: Book 1 1998, How to Cook: Book 2 1999, How to Cook Book 3 2001, Delia's Chocolate Collection (for Comic Relief) 2001, Delia's Vegetarian Collection 2002, The Delia Collection: Soup, Fish, Chicken, Chocolate 2003, The Delia Collection: Pork, Italian 2004, The Delia Collection: Baking 2005, The Delia Collection: Puddings 2006, How to Cheat at Cooking (completely rewritten) 2007. *Address:* c/o Deborah Owen Ltd, 78 Narrow Street, Limehouse, London, E14 8BP, England. *Telephone:* (20) 7987-5119. *Fax:* (20) 7538-4004. *E-mail:* do@deborahowen.co.uk (office).

SMITH, Sir E. Brian, Kt, MA, PhD, DSc, FRSC; British scientist and university vice-chancellor (retd); b. 10 Oct. 1933, Mold, North Wales; s. of Eric Smith and Dilys Olwen Hughes; m. 1st Margaret Barr 1957 (divorced 1978); two s. one d.; m. 2nd Regina Arvidson Ball 1983; two step-d.; ed Alun Grammar School, Mold, Wirral Grammar School, Univ. of Liverpool; Fellow St Catherine's Coll. Oxford and Lecturer in Physical Chem., Univ. of Oxford 1960–88; Master St Catherine's Coll. 1988–93; Vice-Chancellor Cardiff Univ. 1993–2001; Dir ISIS Innovation Network 1988–97; mem. Bd Welsh Devt Agency 1998–2001, Wales European Centre 2001–03, Higher Educ. Funding Council for Wales 2002–; Gov. Univ. of Glamorgan 2002–06. *Publications:* Virial Coefficients of Pure Gases and Mixtures 1969, Basic Chemical Themodynamics 1973, Intermolecular Forces 1981, Forces Between Molecules 1986; papers in scientific journals. *Leisure interest:* mountaineering. *Address:* c/o Cardiff University, Park Place, Main Building, Cardiff, CF10 3AT, Wales (office). *Website:* www.cf.ac.uk (office).

SMITH, Edwin, PhD, FRS; British engineer; *Consultant and Professor Emeritus, University of Manchester;* b. 28 July 1931, Staveley, Derbyshire; s. of the late Albert Edwin Smith and Sarah Ann Smith (née Toft); m. Patricia Georgina Gale 1958; ed Chesterfield Grammar School, Univs of Nottingham and Sheffield; mem. staff, Assoc. Electrical Industries Research Lab., Aldermaston 1955–61, Cen. Electrical Generating Bd Research Lab., Leatherhead 1961–68; Prof. of Metallurgy, Univ. of Manchester 1968–88, Dean of Science 1983–85, Pro-Vice-Chancellor 1985–88, Prof. Emer. and Consultant 1988–. *Publications:* numerous publs in tech. journals. *Leisure interests:* sport (ran 14 marathons; personal best 2 hrs 47 mins 1958). *Address:* Materials Science Centre, University of Manchester, Grosvenor Street, Manchester, M1 7HS, England (office). *Telephone:* (161) 200-3556 (office). *Fax:* (161) 200-3586 (office).

SMITH, Elizabeth Jean, OBE, MA; British broadcasting executive and international organization official; *Secretary-General, Commonwealth Broadcasting Association;* b. 15 Aug. 1936, Ajmer, India; d. of Sir Robert Hay and Lady Hay; m. Geoffrey Smith 1960; one s. one d.; ed Univ. of Edinburgh; Producer, Radio News, BBC 1960; Asst Head, Cen. Talks and Features, BBC World Service 1980, Head, Current Affairs 1984, Controller, English Programmes 1987–94; Sec.-Gen. Commonwealth Broadcasting Asscn 1994–; Fellow, Radio Acad. *Publication:* Sambo Sahib (as Elizabeth Hay). *Address:* Commonwealth Broadcasting Association, 17 Fleet Street, London, EC4Y 1AA, England (office). *Telephone:* (20) 7583-5550 (office). *Fax:* (20) 7583-5549 (office). *E-mail:* elizabeth@cba.org.uk (office). *Website:* www.cba.org.uk (office).

SMITH, Emil L., BS, PhD; American biochemist, biophysicist and academic; *Professor Emeritus of Biological Chemistry, UCLA;* b. 5 July 1911, New York City; s. of Abraham and Esther Smith; m. Esther Press 1934; two s.; ed Columbia, Cambridge and Yale Univs; Instructor, Columbia Univ. 1936–38; Fellow, Rockefeller Inst. 1940–42; Sr Biochemist and Biophysicist, E. R. Squibb & Sons 1942–46; Assoc. Prof. and Prof., Univ. of Utah 1946–63; Prof. and Chair. Dept of Biological Chem., UCLA 1963–79, Prof. Emer. 1979–; Foreign mem. Russian Acad. of Sciences; mem. NAS, American Acad. of Arts and Sciences, American Philosophical Soc., etc.; Guggenheim Fellow (Cambridge and Yale) 1938–40; Stein-Moore Award (Protein Soc.) 1987. *Publications:* Principles of Biochemistry (co-author) 1954; many articles on biochem. and biophysics. *Leisure interests:* music, literature, art. *Address:* c/o Department of Biological Chemistry, University of California, School of Medicine, Los Angeles, CA 90095-1737, USA (office).

SMITH, Francis Barrymore, PhD, FAHA; Australian historian and academic; b. 16 May 1932, Hughesdale; s. of Francis John Smith and Bertha Smith; m. Ann Stokes 1965; two s. two d.; ed Univ. of Melbourne and Cambridge Univ.; Lecturer in History, Univ. of Melbourne 1962–66; Professorial Fellow in History, Inst. of Advanced Studies, ANU 1974–94, Hancock Prof. of History 1995–98; Ed. Historical Studies 1963–67; Pres. Australian Historical Asscn 1978–80. *Publications:* Making of the Second Reform Bill 1966, Radical Artisan: William James Linton 1973, The People's Health 1830–1910 1979, Florence Nightingale: Reputation and Power 1982, Retreat of Tuberculosis 1987, 'Agent Orange': The Australian Aftermath 1994, G. G. Achilli versus J. H. Newman 2000. *Address:* History Program, Research School of Social Sciences, Australian National University, Canberra 0200, Australia (office). *Telephone:* (2) 6125-2358 (office). *Fax:* (2) 6125-3969 (office).

SMITH, Sir Francis Graham (See Graham-Smith, Sir Francis).

SMITH, Frank Thomas, DPhil, FRS; British mathematician and academic; *Goldsmid Professor of Applied Mathematics, University College London;* b. 24 Feb. 1948, Bournemouth; s. of Leslie Maxwell Smith and Catherine Matilda Smith; m. Valerie Sheila Hearn 1972; three d.; ed Bournemouth School, Jesus Coll. Oxford, Univ. Coll. London; Research Fellow, Southampton Univ. 1972–73; Lecturer in Math., Reader then Prof., Imperial Coll. London 1973–84; Goldsmid Prof. of Applied Math., Univ. Coll. London 1984–; Visiting Prof., Univ. of Western Ont., Canada 1978–79, Ohio State Univ. 1990. *Publications:* Boundary-Layer Separation (co-ed.); numerous scientific papers, mostly on theoretical and computational fluid dynamics, industrial and biomedical applications and math. modelling. *Address:* Mathematics Department, University College, Gower Street, London, WC1E 6BT (office); 9 Woodham Park Road, Woodham, Addlestone, Surrey, KT15 3ST, England (home). *Telephone:* (20) 7679-2837 (office); (1932) 352394 (home). *Fax:* (20) 7383-5519 (office). *E-mail:* frankmath@ucl.ac.uk (office). *Website:* www.ucl.ac.uk/Mathematics (office).

SMITH, George David William, MA, DPhil, FRS, FRSA, FIM, FInstP, FRSC, CEng, CPhys; British metallurgist, materials scientist and academic; *Professor of Materials Science, University of Oxford;* b. 28 March 1943, Aldershot; s. of George Alfred William Smith and Grace Violet Hannah Dayton Smith; m. Josephine Ann Halford 1968; two s.; ed Corpus Christi Coll., Oxford; SRC Research Fellow, Dept of Materials, Univ. of Oxford 1968–70, Research Fellow 1970–75, Sr Research Fellow 1975–77, Lecturer 1977–92, George Kelley Reader in Metallurgy 1992–96, Prof. of Materials Science 1996–, Head of Dept 2000–05; Man. Dir Kindbrisk Ltd (renamed Oxford Nano-science Ltd 2000) 1987–2002, Chair. 2002–04; Chair. Polaron plc 2004–06; mem. Council Inst. of Materials 1998–2002 (Vice-Pres. 2002), UK Materials Foresight Panel 1998–2001, Council Inst. of Materials, Minerals and Mining 2003–05, Council Royal Soc. 2002–04, Scientific Advisory Panel, UK Environment Agency 2004, British Library Advisory Council 2004–; Fellow, Trinity Coll., Oxford 1991–, St Cross Coll., Oxford 1977–91 (Fellow Emer. 1991–); mem. European Acad. of Sciences and Arts 2005; Liveryman of the Armourers' and Brasiers' Co.; Freeman of the City of London 1999; Beilby Medal and Prize 1985, Rosenhain Medal and Prize 1991, Nat. Award for Innovative Measurement 2004, Acta Materialia Gold Medal 2005, Inst. of Materials Platinum Medal 2006. *Publications:* Atom Probe Microanalysis (with M. K. Miller) 1989, Atom Probe Field Ion Microscopy (co-author) 1996; numerous contribs to scientific journals. *Leisure interests:* walking, fishing, bird watching, travel. *Address:* Department of Materials, Oxford University, Parks Road, Oxford, OX1 3PH, England (office). *Telephone:* (1865) 273700 (office). *Fax:* (1865) 273738 (office). *E-mail:* george.smith@materials.ox.ac.uk (office).

SMITH, George E., BA, MS, PhD, FIEEE; American physicist and inventor (retd); b. White Plains, NY; ed Univs of Pennsylvania and Chicago; began career at Bell Labs in 1959, Head of Device Concepts Dept 1964, Head of VLSI Device Dept –1986 (retd); mem. Nat. Acad. of Eng; Fellow, American Physical Soc.; Co-inventor (with Willard S. Boyle) charged-coupled device (CCD) 1970; IEEE Electron Devices Soc. Distinguished Service Award 1997, Stuart Ballentine Medal, Franklin Inst. (co-recipient) 1973, IEEE Morris N. Liebmann Memorial Award 1974, Progress Medal, Photographic Soc. of America 1986, IEEE Device Research Conf. Breakthrough Award 1999, Edwin H. Land Medal, Soc. for Imaging Science and Tech. 2001, C&C Prize (Computer and Communications), NEC Foundation, Tokyo 1999, Draper

Prize (co-recipient) 2006. *Achievement:* completed a world cruise aboard his sailing vessel, Apogee 2006. *Publications:* holds 31 US patents; more than 40 papers in professional journals on junction lasers, semiconducting ferro-electrics, electroluminescence, transition-metal oxides, the silicon-diode-array camera tube and charge-coupled devices.

SMITH, Hon. Godfrey, BL; Belizean politician, lawyer and writer; *Deputy Leader, People's United Party;* m. Valerie Woods; two c.; ed Univ. of the W Indies; Assoc. Attorney, Barrow & Williams, Belize City 1994–97; Sec-Gen. People's United Party, Belize City 1997–98, Deputy Leader 2005–; Chief of Staff Office of the Prime Minister 1998–99; Attorney-Gen. 1999–2006, concurrently Minister of Information, then Minister of Foreign Affairs and Co-operation –2006; Minister of Tourism, and Nat. Emergency Man. 2006–08, of Information 2006–07; Founding Ed. Belize Law Reports, Belize Law Review, Belize Foreign Policy Yearbook; currently Lecturer, Univ. Coll. Belize; columnist Belize Times 2006–. *Publications include:* Belize Law Report (ed.), Practical Guide to Gross Receipt Tax. *Address:* People's United Party, 3 Queen St, Belize City, Belize (office). *Telephone:* 223-2428 (office). *Fax:* 223-3476 (office). *Website:* www.pupbelize.bz (office); www.flashpointbelize.com.

SMITH, Gordon Harold, BA, JD; American fmr politician; b. 25 May 1952, Pendleton, Ore.; s. of Milan Dale Smith and Jessica Smith (née Udall); m. Sharon Lankford; two s. one d.; ed Brigham Young Univ. and Southwestern Univ.; law clerk to Justice H. Vern Payne, New Mexico Supreme Court; pvt. practice in Ariz.; Owner, Smith Frozen Foods; mem. Ore. State Senate 1992–95, Pres. 1995–96; Senator from Ore. 1997–2009, mem. Budget Cttee, Chair. Sub-Cttee on Water and Power, mem. Sub-Cttee on Forests and Public Land Man., Sub-Cttee on Energy Rescheduling, Devt, Production and Regulation, mem. Energy and Natural Resources Cttee, Chair. Sub-Cttee on European Affairs, mem. Sub-Cttee on Near Eastern and S Asian Affairs, mem. Foreign Relations Cttee, mem. Sub-Cttee on E Asian and Pacific Affairs. *Address:* c/o 404 Russell Senate Office Building, Washington, DC 20510-3704, USA (office).

SMITH, Gordon Scott, PhD; Canadian diplomatist, academic and consultant; *Executive Director, Centre for Global Studies and Adjunct Professor of Political Science, University of Victoria;* b. 19 July 1941, Montreal, Que.; s. of the late G. Meredith Smith and Helen Scott; m. Lise G. Lacroix; three s. one d.; ed Lower Canada Coll. Montréal, McGill Univ., Univ. of Chicago and Massachusetts Inst. of Tech.; joined Defence Research Bd 1966, transferred to Dept of External Affairs 1967; mem. Canadian Del. to NATO 1968–70; Special Adviser to Minister of Nat. Defence 1970–72; joined Privy Council Office 1972; Deputy Sec. to Cabinet (Plans) 1978–79; Deputy Under-Sec. Dept of External Affairs 1979; Assoc. Sec. to Cabinet, Privy Council Office 1980–81; Sec. Ministry of State for Social Devt 1981–84; Assoc. Sec. to Cabinet and Deputy Clerk of Privy Council 1984; Deputy Minister for Political Affairs, Dept of External Affairs 1985; Amb. and Perm. Rep. of Canada to NATO 1985–90; Sec. to the Cabinet for Fed.-Provincial Relations, Govt of Canada 1990–91; Amb. to the EC 1991–94; Deputy Minister of Foreign Affairs 1994–97; Chair. Int. Devt Research Centre 1997–2007; Exec. Dir Centre for Global Studies and Adjunct Prof. of Political Science, Univ. of Vic. 1997–; Visiting Prof., Diplomatic Acad. of the Univ. of Westminster, London; mem. Int. Advisory Bd Centre for Int. Governance Innovation, Waterloo, Ont.; Trudeau Mentor, Pierre Elliott Trudeau Foundation, Montréal; Pres. Gordon Smith Int. *Publication:* Altered States. *Leisure interests:* squash, tennis, sailing, skiing, antiques. *Address:* Centre for Global Studies, University of Victoria, POB 1700, STN CSC, Victoria, BC V8W 2Y2 (office); 2027 Runnymede Avenue, Victoria, BC V8S 2V5, Canada. *Telephone:* (250) 472-4726 (office). *Fax:* (250) 472-4830 (office). *E-mail:* gssmith@uvic.ca (office). *Website:* www.globalcentres.org (office).

SMITH, Hamilton O., MD; American academic and medical scientist; *Founder and Co-Chief Scientific Officer, Synthetic Genomics, Inc.;* b. 23 Aug. 1931, New York City; s. of Tommie Harkey and Bunnie Othanel Smith; m. Elizabeth Anne Bolton 1957; four s. one d.; ed Univ. of Illinois, Univ. of California at Berkeley, Johns Hopkins Univ. School of Medicine, Baltimore, Md; Internship, Barnes Hosp., St Louis, Mo. 1956–57; Lt in USNR, Sr Medical Officer 1957–59; Resident, Henry Ford Hosp., Detroit, Mich. 1960–62; Postdoctoral Fellow, Dept of Human Genetics, Univ. of Mich. 1962–64, Research Assoc. 1964–67; Asst Prof. of Microbiology, Johns Hopkins Univ. School of Medicine 1967–69, Assoc. Prof. 1969–73, Prof. of Microbiology 1973–81, Prof. of Molecular Biology and Genetics 1981, now Prof. Emer.; conducted work at Inst. for Genomic Research –1998; joined Celera Genomics 1998–2002; Scientific Dir Synthetic Biology and Biological Energy Groups, Venter Inst. 2002–; Founder and Co-Chief Scientific Officer Synthetic Genomics, Inc. 2005–; sabbatical year with Inst. für Molekular-Biologie, Zürich Univ. 1975–76; Guggenheim Fellow 1975–76; shared Nobel Prize for Physiology and Medicine 1978 with Prof. Werner Arber (q.v.), and Dr Daniel Nathans for work on restriction enzymes; mem. NAS 1980, AAAS. *Leisure interests:* piano, classical music. *Address:* Synthetic Genomics, Inc., 9601 Blackwell Road, Suite 200, Rockville, MD 20850 (office); 8222 Carrbridge Circle, Baltimore, MD 21204, USA (home). *Telephone:* (240) 238-0800 (office); (301) 821-5409 (home). *Fax:* (240) 238-0888 (office). *E-mail:* info@syntheticgenomics.com (office). *Website:* www.syntheticgenomics.com (office).

SMITH, Hans J., BSc, SMP; South African business executive; b. 15 Jan. 1941, Krugersdorp; s. of the late Hendrik C. Smith and Johanna Smith; m. Lydia Minnaar 1969; two d.; ed Kensington High School, Univ. of Pretoria, Univ. of the Witwatersrand, Univ. of SA and Harvard Univ.; with Gold Fields of SA 1965–70; Sr Investment Analyst, Gencor 1970, Asst Gen. Man. Buffalo Fluorspar Mine 1972, Gen. Man. Msuali Asbestos 1973, Operations Man. Chrome Div. Corp. HQ 1974, Man. Dir Zululand Titanium 1978; Tech. Dir Octha Diamonds 1981; rejoined Gencor as Man. Strategic Planning, Corp. Mining Div. 1985, Sr Man. Marketing, Coal Div. 1985; Chief Consultant, Safety and Health, Genmin 1988; Man. Dir Trans-Natal Coal Corpn Ltd 1988; Man. Dir Samancor Ltd 1989; Chief Exec. New Business, Group Co. Gencor 1993; CEO and Man. Dir Iscor Ltd 1993–2002, Exec. Chair. 1995–2002, Chair. Kumba Resources 2002; Chair. AST (GijimaAst) 2003–07 (resgnd); mem. Bd of Dirs Guma Group 2007–; Great Silver Medal of Honour (Austria) 1996; Hon. DEcon (Univ. of Transkei) 1998; Communicator of the Year Award 1996. *Leisure interests:* tennis, golf, jogging, scuba diving, underwater photography. *Address:* c/o Board of Directors, Guma Group, Fleet House, Peter Place Park, 54 Peter Place Road, Bryanston, Johannesburg, South Africa. *E-mail:* info@guma.co.za.

SMITH, Harvey (see Smith, (Robert) Harvey).

SMITH, Henry Sidney, MA, FBA, DLit; British academic; *Professor Emeritus of Egyptology, University College London;* b. 14 June 1928, London; s. of Sidney Smith and Mary W. Smith (née Parker); m. Hazel Flory Leeper 1961 (died 1991); ed Merchant Taylors School, Sandy Lodge, Middx and Christ's Coll., Cambridge; Asst Lecturer in Egyptology, Faculty of Oriental Studies, Cambridge 1954–59, Lecturer 1959–63; Wallis Budge Fellow in Egyptology, Christ's Coll., Cambridge 1955–63; Field Dir Egypt Exploration Soc. Archaeological Survey of Nubia, Epigraphist at Nubian sites 1959–65; Reader in Egyptian Archaeology, Univ. Coll. London 1963–70, Edwards Prof. of Egyptology 1970–86, Prof. Emer. 1986–; Prin. Epigraphist and Site Supervisor, Egypt Exploration Soc., Saqqara, Egypt 1964–70, Field Dir, Sacred Animal Necropolis 1971–76, Anubieton 1976–81, Dir Memphis Project in Egypt 1981–88; Corresp. mem. Deutsches Archäologisches Institut; Medallist, Collège de France, Paris 1984. *Publications:* Preliminary Reports of the EES Archaeological Survey of Egyptian Nubia 1961, A Visit to Ancient Egypt: Memphis and Saqqara, c. 600–30 BC 1974, The Fortress of Buhen, II: The Inscriptions 1976, I: The Archaeological Report (with W. B. Emery and A. Millard) 1979, Saqqara Demotic Papyri I (with W. J. Tait) 1984, The Anubieton at Saqqara, Vols I and II (with D. G. Jeffreys and Lisa L. Giddy) 1988, 1992, The Sculpture from the Sacred Animal Necropolis at North Saqqara 1964–76 (with Elizabeth Anne Hastings) 1997, The Sacred Animal Necropolis at North Saqqara: The Falcon Complex and Catacomb: The Archaeological Report (with Sue Davis); excavation reports, text publications and historical articles in int. journals. *Leisure interests:* varied. *Address:* Ailwyn House, High Street, Upwood, Huntingdon, Cambridgeshire, PE26 2QE, England (home). *Telephone:* (1487) 812196 (home).

SMITH, Ian William Murison, PhD, FRS, FRSC; British chemist and academic; *Research Fellow Emeritus, Department of Chemistry, University of Cambridge;* b. 15 June 1937, Leeds; s. of William Murison Smith and Margaret Moir Smith; m. Susan Morrish 1961; two s. two d.; ed Giggleswick School, Christ's Coll., Cambridge; Fellow, Christ's Coll., Cambridge 1963–85, Demonstrator in Physical Chem., Univ. of Cambridge 1966–71, Lecturer in Physical Chem. 1971–85, Tutor, Christ's Coll., Cambridge 1968–76, Dir of Studies 1972–85, Research Fellow Emer., Dept of Chem. 2002–; Prof. of Chem., Univ. of Birmingham 1985–91, Head, School of Chem. 1989–93, Mason Prof. of Chem. 1991, now Prof. Emer.; Millar Research Professorship, Univ. of California, Berkeley 1996; Stauffer Lectureship, Univ. Southern California 2000; Fellowship, Jt Inst. for Lab. Astrophysics, Univ. of Colorado 2000; Pres. Faraday Div. RSC 2001–03; RSC Tilden Medal and Lectureship, RSC Special Award for Reaction Kinetics, Polanyi Medal 1990, EU Descartes Prize 2000, RSC Livesidge Lecturer 2002, Wilhelm Jost Memorial Lectures, Germany 2003. *Publications:* Kinetics and Dynamics of Elementary Gas Reactions 1980, Modern Gas Kinetics (ed.) 1987; more than 250 contrib. to scientific journals. *Leisure interests:* occasional golf, even more occasional tennis, theatre, walking, gardening under supervision. *Address:* The University Chemical Laboratory, University of Cambridge, Lensfield Road, Cambridge, CB2 1EW (office); 36 Grantchester Road, Cambridge, Cambs., CB3 9ED, England (home). *Telephone:* (1223) 763926 (office). *Fax:* (1223) 336362 (office). *E-mail:* iwms2@czam.ac.uk (office); i.w.m.smith@bham.ac.uk (office). *Website:* www.chem.bham.ac.uk/staff/smith (office).

SMITH, Ivor, MA, LLD, AA Dipl., RIBA; British architect; b. 27 Jan. 1926, Leigh-on-Sea, Essex; s. of H. S. Smith and F. E. Smith; m. Audrey Lawrence 1947; one s. three d.; ed Bartlett School of Architecture, Univ. Coll. London, Univ. of Cambridge School of Architecture, Architectural Assn School of Architecture, London; with City Architects Dept, Sheffield 1951–61; in pvt. architectural practice 1961–87; Prof., Univ. Coll. Dublin 1969–73, Univ. of Bristol 1975–82, Heriot Watt Univ. 1982–90; Educational Consultant, Caribbean School of Architecture 1998–2001; Hon. LLD. *Leisure interests:* walking, drawing. *Address:* 28 Victoria Park, Cambridge, CB4 3EL, England (home). *Telephone:* (1223) 360365 (home). *E-mail:* ivor.arch@btinternet.com (home).

SMITH, Jack; British artist; b. 18 June 1928, Sheffield; s. of John Edward Smith and Laura Smith; m. Susan Craigie Halkett 1956; ed Sheffield Coll. of Art, St Martin's School of Art and Royal Coll. of Art; 1st Prize, John Moores, Liverpool 1957, Nat. Prize, Guggenheim Int. 1960. *Address:* 29 Seafield Road, Hove, East Sussex, BN3 2TP, England. *Telephone:* (1273) 738312.

SMITH, Rt Hon Jacqueline (Jacqui); British teacher and politician; *Secretary of State for the Home Department;* b. 3 Nov. 1962, London; m.; two s.; ed Hertford Coll., Oxford; Business Studies and Econs teacher, Arrow Vale High School, Redditch 1986, Head, Econs Dept, Haybridge High School, Hagley –1997; Councillor, Redditch Borough Council 1991–97; MP for Redditch, Inkberrow and Cookhill 1997–; Parliamentary Under-Sec. of State, Dept for Educ. and Employment 1999–2001; Minister of State with Responsibility for Social Services, Dept of Health 2001–03; Minister of State for Industry and the Regions and Deputy Minister for Women and Equality, Dept of Trade and Industry 2003–05; Minister of State for Schools and 14–19

Learners, Dept for Educ. and Skills 2005–06; Perm. Sec. to the Treasury and Chief Whip 2006–07; Sec. of State for the Home Dept 2007–; mem. Treasury Select Cttee 1998–99; mem. Labour Departmental Cttees for Educ. and Employment 1997–2001, for Treasury 1997–2001; mem. British East-West Centre. *Address:* Home Office, 50 Queen Anne's Gate, London, SW1H 9AT (office); 67 Birmingham Road, West Bromwich, West Midlands, B70 6PY, England (office). *Telephone:* (20) 7035-4848 (Home Office) (office); (1527) 523355 (constituency) (office). *Fax:* (20) 7035-4745 (Home Office) (office); (1527) 523355 (constituency) (office). *E-mail:* public.enquiries@homeoffice.gsi.gov.uk (office); smithjj@parliament.uk (office). *Website:* www.homeoffice.gov.uk (office); www.jacquismithmp.labour.co.uk (home).

SMITH, Hon. James Herbert, MA; Bahamian politician and banker; b. 26 Oct. 1947, Nassau; s. of the late Bertram A. Smith and Rosalie B. Smith; m. Portia M. Campbell 1973 (deceased); two s. one d.; ed Ryerson Polytechnical Coll., Toronto and Univs of Windsor and Alberta, Canada; Deputy Perm. Sec., Ministry of Econ. Affairs 1977–79; Under-Sec., Cabinet Office 1980–84; Sec. for Revenue, Ministry of Finance 1984–85, Perm. Sec. 1985–86; fmr Chair. Bahamas Devt Bank; Gov. Cen. Bank of the Bahamas 1987–97; Amb. for Trade, Chief Negotiator, Free Trade Area of the Americas discussions 1997–2002; Minister of State for Finance 2002–07; fmr Chair. Bahamas Maritime Museum; Hon. doctorate. *Address:* c/o Ministry of Finance, Cecil V. Wallace Centre, West Bay Street, POB N-3017, Nassau, The Bahamas (office). *E-mail:* jp28451@hotmail.com (home).

SMITH, Jean Kennedy, BA; American foundation executive and diplomatist; b. 20 Feb. 1928, Massachusetts; d. of the late Joseph P. Kennedy and Rose Kennedy (née Fitzgerald); m. Stephen E. Smith 1956 (died 1990); two s. two d.; ed Manhattanville Coll., Purchase, NY; mem. Bd trustees Joseph P. Kennedy Jr Foundation 1964–, John F. Kennedy Center for the Performing Arts 1964– (Chair. Educ. Cttee 1964–74 and Founder of Center's children's programs); fmr mem. Bd IRC; f. Very Special Arts (int. program for people with disabilities) 1974; Amb. to Ireland 1993–98; Hon. Irish Citizen; several hon. degrees; Jefferson Award for Outstanding Public Service, American Inst. for Public Service, Margaret Mead Humanitarian Award, Council of Cerebral Palsy Auxiliaries, Irish American of the Year Award, Irish America Magazine 1995, Rotary One Int. Award, Rotary Club of Chicago 1997, Terence Cardinal Cooke Humanitarian Award 1997, Hadassch Volunteer of the Year Award 2003. *Publication:* Chronicles of Courage: Very Special Artists 1993. *Leisure interests:* the arts, tennis, golf, sailing, reading. *Address:* 4 Sutton Place, New York, NY 10022, USA. *Telephone:* (212) 758-3610. *Fax:* (212) 813-1871.

SMITH, Jennifer M., DBE; Bermudian politician; *Deputy Speaker, House of Assembly;* b. 14 Oct. 1947; d. of the late Eugene O. Smith and of Lillian E. Smith; began career as journalist; reporter, Bermuda Recorder 1970–74, Ed. 1974; on staff of Fame magazine, later Ed.; joined ZBM Radio and TV; art teacher at Sr Training School (attached to Bermuda Prison Service) for eight years; represented Bermuda as an artist at CARIFESTA in Jamaica; last exhbn in 1996; contested St George's N seat for Progressive Labour Party (PLP) in House of Ass. elections 1972, 1976, 1980; mem. Senate 1980–; Shadow Minister for Educ.; mem. House of Ass. (PLP) 1989, 1993, 1998–, Deputy Speaker 2003–; Leader of PLP 1996–; Prime Minister of Bermuda 1998–2003; fmr Exec. mem. Commonwealth Parl. Asscn; Hon. DHumLitt (Mount St Vincent, Morris Brown Coll., Art Inst. of Pittsburgh) Outstanding Woman in Journalism Award 1972 and several other awards. *Publications:* Voice of Change 2003. *Leisure interests:* painting, dancing, reading, working with young people, writing, collecting match-book covers and first day stamp covers. *Address:* c/o The House of Assembly, 21 Parliament Street, Hamilton HM 12 (office); POB HM 2191, Hamilton HMHX, Bermuda (home). *Website:* voiceofchange.bm (home).

SMITH, John (Jack) Francis, Jr, MBA; American business executive; b. 6 April 1938, Worcester, Mass.; s. of John Francis Smith, Sr and Eleanor C. Sullivan; m. 1st Marie Roberta Halloway 1962 (divorced); two s.; m. 2nd Lydia G. Sigrist 1988; one step-d.; ed Boston Univ. and Univ. of Massachusetts; Divisional Man., Gen. Motors Corpn, Framingham, Mass. 1961–73, Asst Treas., New York 1973–80, Comptroller, Detroit 1980–81, Dir Worldwide Planning 1981–84, Pres. and Gen. Man., Gen. Motors Canada, Oshawa 1984–86, Vice-Pres. Gen. Motors Corpn and Pres. Gen. Motors Europe 1986–88, Exec. Vice-Pres. Int. Operations, Gen. Motors Corpn, Detroit 1988–90, Vice-Chair. 1990, Pres. Gen. Motors 1992–2003, COO April–Nov. 1992, also Chair. and CEO, Chair. 1996–2000, Chair. Bd 1996–2003; Dir Delta Air Lines Inc. 2000–07, Chair. 2004–07; mem. Bd of Govs Jr Achievement Canada, Ltd 1984; mem. Bd of Dirs Procter & Gamble, Swiss Reinsurance Co.; Chair. Advisory Bd AlixPartners LLC/Questor Partners Funds; mem. Bd of Dirs Swiss Reinsurance Co., Proctor & Gamble 1995–2008; mem. Bd of Govs The Nature Conservancy 1997–; Trustee Boston Univ., mem. School of Man.'s Dean's Advisory Council; fmr mem. Bd Detroit Renaissance; mem. Business Council. *Address:* c/o Delta Air Lines Inc., Hartsfield Atlanta International Airport, 1030 Delta Boulevard, Atlanta, GA 30320-6001, USA.

SMITH, Lt-Gen. (retd) Joseph Henry; Ghanaian army officer and politician; *Minister of Defence;* b. 9 Jan. 1945, Takoradi; m.; five c.; ed Ghana Mil. Acad.; Commdt Mil. Acad. and Training School 1992–93; Commdr 2nd Infantry Brigade Group 1993–96; Special Task Force Commdr to restore law and order in Northern Ghana 1994; Co. Commdr UNEF 1996; Commdr Ghana Army 1996–2001; Minister of Defence 2009–; fmr Chair. Bd of Dirs Nat. Insurance Comm.; mem. Nat. Security Bd 1996–2001, Ghana Armed Forces Command and Staff Coll. Control Bd 1996–2001; Companion of the Order of the Volta 2001, Legion of Merit (USA); Ghana/UN Peace Keeping Award 1976. *Address:* Ministry of Defence, Burma Camp, Accra, Ghana (office). *Telephone:* (21) 777611 (office). *Fax:* (21) 778549 (office). *E-mail:* kaddok@internetghana.com (office).

SMITH, Gen. Lance L., BA, MA; American army officer (retd); ed Virginia Polytechnic Inst., Cen. Michigan Univ., Air Command and Staff Coll., Ala, Army War Coll., Pa, Advanced Exec. Program, J.L. Kellogg Grad. School of Man., Northwestern Univ., Evanston, Ill.; entered USAF in 1970, commanded two fighter wings and led two air expeditionary force deployments to SW Asia: AEF III and the 4th Air Expeditionary Wing, served as Commdr of 7th Air Force, Pacific Air Forces, Air Component Commdr Repub. of Korea and US Combined Forces Command, Korea, Deputy Commdr US Forces, Korea, served two tours at the Pentagon and was Commdt of the NATO School at Supreme HQ Allied Powers Europe, Commdt of Air War Coll. and Commdr Air Force Doctrine Center, Deputy Commdr US Cen. Command, MacDill Air Force Base, Fla, Commdr US Jt Forces Command (USJFCOM) and NATO Supreme Allied Commdr for Transformation (ACT), Norfolk, Va 2005–07, retd 2008; flew more than 165 combat missions in SE and SW Asia in the A-1 Skyraider and the F-15E Strike Eagle, command pilot with more than 3,000 hours in the T-33, T-37, T-38, A-1, A-7, A-10, F-111F, F-15E and F-16 aircraft; rank of Second Lt 1970, First Lt, Capt. 1973, Maj. 1978, Lt-Col 1982, Col 1989, Brig.-Gen. 1995, Maj.-Gen. 1998, Lt-Gen. 2002, Gen. 2005; Defense DSM, DSM, Silver Star with two oak leaf clusters, Defense Superior Service Medal, Legion of Merit with oak leaf cluster, DFC with two oak leaf clusters, Purple Heart, Meritorious Service Medal with three oak leaf clusters, Air Medal with one silver and four bronze oak leaf clusters, Aerial Achievement Medal with oak leaf cluster, Air Force Commendation Medal, Army Commendation Medal, Humanitarian Service Medal, Honor Cross of the Bundeswehr Medal (FRG), Order of Nat. Security Merit Gukseon Medal (Repub. of Korea), Order of Nat. Security Merit Cheonsu Medal (Repub. of Korea), Repub. of Viet Nam Gallantry Cross with Palm. *Address:* c/o NATO Supreme Allied Command Transformation, Public Information Office (ACT PIO), Suite 100, 7857 Blandy Road, Norfolk, VA 23551-2490, USA (office).

SMITH, Lanty Lloyd, BS, LLB; American lawyer and banking executive; *Chairman, Wachovia Corporation;* b. 11 Dec. 1942, Sherrodsville, Ohio; m. Margaret Smith; three d.; ed Wittenberg Univ., Duke Univ.; Assoc. Jones, Day, Cockley & Reavis (law firm), Cleveland 1967–73, Pnr, Jones Day, Reavis & Pogue 1974–77; Exec. Vice-Pres. and Sr Gen. Counsel Burlington Industries, Greensboro, N Carolina 1977–86, Pres. 1986–88; Chair. Precision Fabrics Group Inc. (est. to purchase existing businesses of Precision Fabrics Div. of Burlington Industries) 1988–; mem. Bd of Dirs Wachovia Corpn, Charlotte, N Carolina 1987–, lead Ind. Dir 2000–08, Chair. and interim CEO June–July 2008 Chair. July 2008–, Exec. Chair. Audit Cttee, Corp. Governance and Nominating Cttee; Co-founder and Chair. Exec. Cttee of Bd of Dirs The Greenwood Group, Inc. 1992–; Chair. and CEO Tippet Capital (merchant banking firm), Raleigh, NC 2007–; Founder and Chair. Scion Neurostim (medical device devt co) 2007–; Pres. and CEO MediWave Star Tech Inc. 1999–; mem. Bd of Dirs Piedmont Pharmaceuticals 2007–, N Carolina Inst. of Medicine; f. Piedmont Angel Network; mem. Advisory Cttee Triad Health Project, Cen. N Carolina Chapter of Multiple Sclerosis Soc., Reading Connections; Americanism Award from Anti-Defamation League, Greensboro Outstanding Community Service Award, Class of 1914 Award, Wittenberg Univ. 2007. *Address:* 3105 Cone Manor Lane, Raleigh, NC 27613 (home); Wachovia Corpn, 301 South College Street, Suite 4000, One Wachovia Center, Charlotte, NC 28288-0013, USA (office). *Telephone:* (704) 590-0000 (office). *E-mail:* info@wachovia.com (office). *Website:* www.wachovia.com (office).

SMITH, Dame Maggie Natalie, DBE; British actress; b. 28 Dec. 1934, Ilford, Essex; d. of Nathaniel Smith and Margaret Little; m. 1st Robert Stephens 1967 (divorced 1975, died 1995); two s.; m. 2nd Beverley Cross 1975 (died 1998); ed Oxford High School for Girls; first appeared with Oxford Univ. Dramatic Soc. (OUDS) in Twelfth Night 1952; appeared in revue New Faces NY 1956, Share My Lettuce 1957, The Stepmother 1958; with Old Vic Co. 1959–60 playing in The Double Dealer, As You Like It, Richard II, The Merry Wives of Windsor, What Every Woman Knows; other appearances include Rhinoceros 1960, Strip the Willow 1960, The Rehearsal 1961, The Private Ear and The Public Eye 1962, Mary, Mary 1963; with Nat. Theatre played in The Recruiting Officer 1963, Othello (Desdemona) 1964, The Master Builder 1964, Hay Fever 1964, Much Ado About Nothing 1965, Miss Julie 1965, A Bond Honoured 1966, The Beaux' Stratagem 1970, Hedda Gabler 1970, Three Sisters, Design for Living (Los Angeles) 1971, Private Lives London 1972, USA 1974–75, Peter Pan 1973, Snap 1974; played 1976, 1977, 1978 and 1980 seasons, Stratford, Ont., Canada, Night and Day 1979, Virginia, London 1981, The Way of the World, Chichester Festival and London 1984–85, Interpreters, London 1985, The Infernal Machine 1986, Coming in to Land 1987, Lettice and Lovage, London 1987, New York 1990, The Importance of Being Earnest 1993, Three Tall Women 1994–95, Talking Heads 1996, A Delicate Balance 1997, The Lady in the Van 1999, The Breath of Life 2002, Talking Heads (Australian tour) 2004, The Lady from Dubuque 2007; Dir United British Artists 1992–; Hon. DLit (St Andrew's, Leicester) 1982, (Cambridge) 1993; Hon. DLitt (Bath) 1986; Evening Standard Best Actress Award 1962, 1970, 1982, 1985, 1994; Variety Club Actress of the Year 1963; LA Critics Award Best Actress 1970; Variety Club Award Best Stage Actress 1972 (plays); Acad. Award for Best Actress 1969, for Best Supporting Actress 1979; Best Actress Award from Soc. of Film and Television Arts (UK) 1969; Best Actress Award from Film Critics' Guild (USA) 1969 (films), BAFTA Award for Best Actress 1984, 1987, 1989, BAFTA Award for Lifetime Achievement 1992, BAFTA Award for Best Supporting Actress (for Tea with Mussolini); Tony Award 1990; Shakespeare Prize, FVS Foundation, Hamburg 1991. *Films include:* Child in the House (uncredited) 1956, Nowhere to Go 1958, Go to Blazes 1962, The V.I.P.s 1963, The Pumpkin Eater 1964, Young Cassidy 1965, Othello 1965, The Honey Pot 1967, Hot Millions 1968, The Prime of Miss Jean Brodie 1969,Oh! What a Lovely War 1969, Travels with My Aunt 1972, Love and Pain and the Whole Damn Thing 1973, Murder by Death 1975, Death on the Nile

1978, California Suite 1978, Quartet 1981, Clash of the Titans 1981, Better Late Than Never 1982, Evil Under the Sun 1982, Ménage à Trois 1982, The Missionary 1982, Lily in Live 1984A Private Function 1984, A Room with a View 1985, The Lonely Passion of Judith Hearn 1987, Paris by Night 1988, Romeo-Juliet (voice) 1990, Hook 1991, Sister Act 1992, The Secret Garden 1993, Sister Act 2: Back in the Habit 1993, Richard III 1995, The First Wives Club 1996, Washington Square 1998, Tea with Mussolini 1999, Curtain Call 1999, The Last September 1999, Harry Potter and The Philosopher's Stone 2001, Gosford Park 2002, Divine Secrets of the Ya-Ya Sisterhood 2002, Harry Potter and the Chamber of Secrets 2002, Ladies in Lavender 2004, Harry Potter and the Prisoner of Azkaban 2004, Harry Potter and the Goblet of Fire 2005, Keeping Mum 2005, Becoming Jane 2007, Harry Potter and the Order of the Phoenix 2007. *Television includes:* Kraft Television Theatre (Night of the Plague) 1957, Hay Fever 1960, Much Ado About Nothing 1967, Play of the Month (Man and Superman 1968, The Seagull 1968, The Merchant of Venice 1972, The Millionairess 1972), Mrs. Silly 1983, Talking Heads (mini-series) 1987, Memento Mori 1992, Suddenly, Last Summer 1993, All the King's Men 1999, David Copperfield 1999, My House in Umbria (Emmy Award for Best Actress) 2003, Capturing Mary 2007. *Leisure interest:* reading. *Address:* 41 Warbeck Road, London, W12 8NS, England.

SMITH, Martin William Cruz, BA; American writer; b. 3 Nov. 1942, Reading, PA; s. of John Smith and Louise Lopez; m. Emily Arnold 1968; two d. one s.; ed Univ. of Pennsylvania; fmr newspaper reporte and ed.; CWA Golden Dagger Award 1981. *Publications:* The Indians Won 1970, Gypsy in Amber 1971, Canto for a Gypsy 1972, Gorky Park 1972, Nightwing 1977, Analog Bullet 1981, Stallion Gate 1986, Polar Star 1989, Red Square 1992, Rose 1996, Havana Bay 1999, December 6 (aka Tokyo Station) 1999, Death by Espionage: Intriguing Stories of Betrayal and Deception 2001, Wolves Eat Dogs 2005, Stalin's Ghost 2007. *Address:* c/o Publicity Department, Simon & Schuster, Inc., 1230 Avenue of the Americas, New York, NY 10020, USA. *E-mail:* MCSmith@literati.net. *Website:* literati.net/MCSmith.

SMITH, Michael, TD; Irish politician and fmr farmer; b. Nov. 1940, Roscrea, Co. Tipperary; m. Mary T. Ryan; one s. six d.; ed Univ. Coll. Cork; mem. Irish Farmers' Asscn 1969–; mem. Tipperary North Riding Co. Council 1967–88, Chair. 1986–87; mem. Dáil 1969–73, 1977–82 1987–2007; Minister of State, Dept of Agric. 1980–81; Senator 1982–87, Agric. Panel 1982–83, Culture and Educ. Panel 1983–87; Minister of State, Dept of Energy 1987–88; Minister for Energy 1988–89; Minister of State, Dept of Industry and Commerce 1989–91; Minister for the Environment 1992–94, for Defence 1997–2004; mem. Fianna Fáil. *Address:* Lismackin, Roscrea, Co. Tipperary, Ireland (home). *Telephone:* (505) 43157 (home).

SMITH, Michael Roger Pearson, BSc; British banker; *CEO, Australia and New Zealand Banking Group Ltd (ANZ);* b. 10 Sept. 1956; m.; three c.; ed City Univ., London; joined HSBC Group 1978, Man. Planning, Hongkong and Shanghai Banking Corpn Ltd, Hong Kong 1984–85, Man. Wholesale Banking, Australia 1985–87, State Man., New South Wales 1987–90, with Planning Dept, Midland Bank (now HSBC Bank), UK 1990–93, Man. Dir Int., Midland Bank 1993–95, Exec. Dir and Deputy CEO Hongkong Bank Malaysia Berhad (now HSBC Bank Malaysia Berhad) 1995–97, CEO HSBC Argentina Holdings SA 1997–2000, Chair. 2000–03, HSBC Group Gen. Man. 2000–07, Pres. and CEO Hongkong and Shanghai Banking Corpn Ltd 2004–07, Chair. HSBC Bank Malaysia Berhad 2004–07, Chair. Hang Seng Bank Ltd 2005–07; Exec. Dir and CEO Australia and New Zealand Banking Group Ltd (ANZ) 2007–; fmr mem. Bd Dirs Visa International Asia Pacific 2005–07; mem. Chongqing Mayor's Int. Econ. Advisory Council 2006–; Fellow, The Hong Kong Man. Asscn 2005–. *Leisure interests:* viniculture, golf, classic cars, art, antiques. *Address:* ANZ, 100 Queen Street, Melbourne 3000, Australia (office). *Telephone:* (3) 9273-6717 (office). *Fax:* (3) 9273-6707 (office). *E-mail:* media .relations@anz.com (office). *Website:* www.anz.com.au (office).

SMITH, Patti; American singer, songwriter, musician (guitar), poet and artist; b. 30 Dec. 1946, Chicago; d. of Grant Smith and Beverly Smith; m. Fred 'Sonic' Smith 1980 (died 1994); two s.; ed Glassboro State Teachers' Coll., NJ; avant-garde poet, singer and artist; performed in and co-wrote Cowboy Mouth with Sam Shepard 1971; fmr rock critic for Creem, Rock, Crawdaddy and Rolling Stone magazines 1970s; solo artist 1972–, forming Patti Smith Group 1974–; nat. and int. tours of USA, Europe etc.; Artistic Dir, Meltdown Festival, South Bank Centre, London 2005; Commdr, Ordre des Arts et des Lettres 2005. *Recordings include:* albums: Horses 1975, Radio Ethiopia 1976, Easter 1978, Wave 1979, Dream Of Life 1988, Gone Again 1996, Peace And Noise 1997, Gung Ho 2000, Land 1975–2002 2002, Twelve 2007, The Coral Sea (with Kevin Shields) 2008. *Publications:* Seventh Heaven (poems) 1971, Kodak (poems) 1972, Cowboy Mouth (play, with Sam Shepard) 1972, Witt (poems) 1973, Babel 1978, Early Work 1970–1979 (poems) 1980, Woolgathering (short stories) 1993, The Coral Sea (prose poems in memory of Robert Mapplethorpe) 1996, Auguries of Innocence (poems) 2006. *Address:* Primary Talent International, Fifth Floor, 2–12 Pentonville Road, London, N1 9PL, England (office). *Telephone:* (20) 7833-8998 (office). *Fax:* (20) 7833-5992 (office). *Website:* www.pattismith.net (office).

SMITH, Sir Paul Brierley, Kt, CBE; British fashion designer and retailer; b. 5 July 1946, Nottingham; s. of the late Harold B. Smith and Marjorie Smith; ed Beeston Fields School, Nottingham; first Paul Smith Shop opened, Nottingham 1970, others in London 1979, 1982, 1983, 1987, 1998, 2001, New York 1987, first Paul Smith franchise shop in Hong Kong 1990, flagship store Tokyo, Japan 1991 (now over 220 shops in Japan), first Milan shop 2001, first stand-alone accessories shop, London 2001, shop at London Heathrow Terminal 3 2002; first Paul Smith Collection Show, Paris 1976; launched Paul Smith for Women 1994; designed limited edn Mini 1998; launched fragrances range for men and women 2000, two fragrances 'Paul Smith

Extreme' 2002, collection of furniture with Cappellini 2002; designed collection of rugs for The Rug Company 2002–03; launched collection of Swiss-made watches 2003, collection of writing instruments 2003; Royal Designer for Industry RCA 1991; Hon. MDes (Nottingham Polytechnic) 1991; Queen's Award for Industry 1995. *Address:* Paul Smith Ltd, 20 Kean Street, London, WC2B 4AS, England. *Telephone:* (20) 7836-7828. *Fax:* (20) 7379-0241. *E-mail:* press@paulsmith.co.uk. *Website:* www.paulsmith.co.uk.

SMITH, Ransford, MA, MBA; Jamaican diplomatist and international organization official; *Deputy Secretary-General (Economic), Commonwealth;* b. 1949; served in several sr posts in Jamaican Foreign Service, including posts in NY, Washington,m DC and Geneva; participated in WTO Uruguay Round of multilateral trade negotiations, late 1980s; Perm. Sec., Ministry of Industry and Investment and Ministry of Commerce and Tech. –1999; Perm. Rep. of Jamaica to UN, Geneva 1999–2005; Chair. WTO Cttee on Trade and Devt 2000–01, Commonwealth Group of Developing Countries, Geneva 2001–02; led Jamaican dels to int. confs, including the Doha Ministerial Conf. of WTO; Chief Negotiator and Spokesperson for the Group of 77 and China at UNCTAD XI 2004; Pres. Trade and Devt Bd, UNCTAD 2005–06; Deputy Sec.-Gen. (Econ.), Commonwealth 2006–; Commr, Order of Distinction (Jamaica) 2005. *Publications:* Developing Countries, the WTO and a New Round: A Perspective 2001. *Address:* Commonwealth Secretariat, Marlborough House, Pall Mall, London, SW1Y 5HX, England (office). *Telephone:* (20) 7747-6500 (office). *Fax:* (20) 7930-0827 (office). *E-mail:* e.delbuey@ commonwealth.int (office). *Website:* www.thecommonwealth.org (office).

SMITH, Richard, CBE; British artist; b. 1931, Letchworth, Herts.; m. Betsy Scherman; two s.; ed Luton School of Art, St Albans School of Art and Royal Coll. of Art; lived in New York 1959–61, 1963–65; teacher, St Martin's School of Art, London 1961–63; Artist-in-Residence, Univ. of Virginia 1967; Grand Prix São Paulo Bienal 1967; solo exhbns at the Kasmin Gallery 1963, 1967, Whitechapel Gallery 1966; participated in the Pittsburgh Int. 1961, New Shapes in Colour, Amsterdam, Berne and Stuttgart 1966–67 and in exhbns at Guggenheim Museum, Tate Gallery, etc.; works represented in Tate Gallery, Stuyvesant Foundation, Contemporary Art Soc., the Ulster Museum, Belfast, the Walker Art Centre, etc. *Address:* c/o Flowers East, 82 Kingsland Road, London E2 8DP, England (office). *Telephone:* (20) 7920-7777 (office). *Fax:* (20) 7920-7770 (office). *E-mail:* gallery@flowerseast.com (office).

SMITH OF KELVIN, Baron (Life Peer), cr. 2008, of Kelvin in the City of Glasgow; **Rt Hon. Robert Haldane Smith,** Kt, CA; British business executive; *Chairman, Scottish & Southern Energy PLC;* b. 8 Aug. 1944; m. Alison Marjorie Bell 1969; two d.; ed Allan Glen's School, Glasgow; accountant Robb Ferguson & Co., Glasgow 1963–68; with ICFC (later 3i Group PLC) 1968–82; with Royal Bank of Scotland 1983–85; Man. Dir Charterhouse Devt Capital Ltd 1985–89; BBC Nat. Gov. for Scotland and Chair. Broadcasting Council for Scotland 1999–2004; Chair. and CEO Morgan Grenfell Private Equity 2001, also CEO Morgan Grenfell Asset Man. (renamed Deutsche Asset Man. 1999), Chair. Deutsche Asset Man. 2000–02; Exec. Dir Scottish & Southern Energy PLC 2003–, Deputy Chair. 2003–05, Chair. 2005–, Chair. Nomination Cttee, mem. Remuneration Cttee; Chair. The Weir Group PLC 2002–; Chancellor Paisley Univ. 2003– (named changed to Univ. of the West of Scotland following merger with Bell Coll., Hamilton 2007); Chair. Bd of Trustees, Nat. Museums of Scotland 1993–2002; Dir (non-exec.) 3i Group PLC, Standard Bank Group Ltd, Aegon UK PLC; fmr mem. Bd of Dirs MFI Furniture Group PLC, Stakis PLC (also Chair. 1998–99), Bank of Scotland, Tip Europe PLC, Network Rail; Pres. British Asscn of Friends of Museums 1995–; fmr Pres. Inst. of Chartered Accountants of Scotland; mem. Financial Services Authority 1997–2000, Financial Reporting Council, Judicial Appointments Bd for Scotland, Bd of Trustees, The British Council; mem. Museums and Galleries Comm. 1988–98 (Vice-Chair. 1996–98); Patron of the Scottish Community Foundation; Dr hc (Glasgow, Edinburgh and Paisley). *Address:* Scottish & Southern Energy PLC, Inveralmond House, 200 Dunkeld Road, Perth, PH1 3AQ, Scotland (office). *Telephone:* (1738) 456000 (office). *E-mail:* info@scottish-southern.co.uk (office). *Website:* www.scottish-southern.co.uk (office).

SMITH, Robert Clinton, BA; American organization official and fmr politician; *President, Everglades Foundation;* b. 30 March 1941; s. of Donald Smith and Margaret Eldridge; m. Mary Jo Hutchinson 1966; two s. one d.; ed Lafayette Coll. and Long Beach State Univ.; owner/man. Yankee Pedlar Realtors, Wolfeboro, New Hampshire 1975–85; mem. US 99th Congress from 1st Dist. of NH 1985–91; Senator from New Hampshire 1990–2002, fmr Chair. Cttee on Environment and Public Works, Cttee on Armed Services, Cttee on the Judiciary, Select Cttee on Ethics; unsuccessful campaign for Republican nomination for Senator from Fla 2004; Pres. Everglades Foundation 2004–; Republican. *Address:* The Everglades Foundation, Inc, 1645 Palm Beach Lakes Boulevard, Suite 480, West Palm Beach, FL 33401, USA (office). *Telephone:* (561) 684-1061. *E-mail:* info@saveoureverglades.org (office). *Website:* www.saveoureverglades.org (office).

SMITH, Roberta, BA; American art critic; *Senior Art Critic, The New York Times;* b. New York City; d. of the late Thomas R. Smith and Eleanor Smith; ed Lawrence High School, Grinnell Coll.; participated in Whitney Museum's Ind. Study Program; became a studio asst to sculptor Donald Judd; also worked with Paula Cooper during early years of SoHo gallery devoted to contemporary art; began working as a professional art critic 1970s, writing for journals such as Arts, Artforum and Art in America 1976–80; Art Critic for the Village Voice 1981–85, for New York Times 1986–, now Sr Art Critic; served as guest curator and catalogue essayist for exhbn Four Artists and the Map at Kansas Univ.'s Spencer Museum of Art 1981; Frank Jewett Mather Award for Art Criticism, Coll. Art Asscn 2003, Franklin D. Murphy Lecturer, Spencer Museum of Art and Kress Foundation Dept of Art History at Univ. of Kansas together with Nelson-Atkins Museum of Art, Kansas City 2004. *Address:* The New York Times, 620 Eighth Avenue, New York, NY 10018, USA (office). *Telephone:* (212) 556-1234 (office). *Fax:* (212) 556-7389 (office). *E-mail:* the-arts@nytimes.com (office). *Website:* www.nytimes.com (office); topics.nytimes.com/top/reference/timestopics/people/s/roberta_smith/index.html (office).

SMITH, Roland Hedley, CMG, MA; British fmr diplomatist; *Clerk, Wakefield & Tetley Trust;* b. 11 April 1943, Sheffield; s. of Alan Hedley Smith and Elizabeth Louise Smith; m. Katherine Jane Lawrence 1971; two d.; ed King Edward VII School, Sheffield, Keble Coll. Oxford; joined Diplomatic Service 1967; Second Sec. Moscow 1969–71; Second, later First Sec., UK Del. to NATO, Brussels 1971–74; at FCO, London 1974–78; First Sec. and Cultural Attaché, Moscow 1978–80; at FCO 1980–83; mem. staff Int. Inst. for Strategic Studies 1983–84; Political Adviser, British Mil. Govt, Berlin 1984–88; at FCO 1988–92; Minister, UK Del. to NATO, Brussels 1992–95; Dir Int. Security, FCO 1995–98; Amb. to Ukraine 1999–2002; Dir St Ethelburga's Centre for Reconciliation and Peace, London 2002–04; Clerk Wakefield (now Wakefield & Tetley) Trust 2004–. *Leisure interests:* music, especially choral singing, football (Sheffield United), trams. *Address:* Wakefield & Tetley Trust, Attlee House, 28 Commercial Street, London, E1 6LR, England (office). *Telephone:* (20) 7377-6614 (office). *E-mail:* roland.smith@wakefieldtrust.org.uk (office). *Website:* www.wakefieldtrust.org.uk (office).

SMITH, Gen. Sir Rupert Anthony, Kt, KCB, DSO, OBE, QGM; British army officer; b. 13 Dec. 1943; with Parachute Regt 1964; Deputy Commdt, Staff Col, Camberley 1989–90; Commdr 1st Armoured Div. BAOR, Gulf 1990–92; Asst Chief of Defence Staff (Operations) 1992–94; Commdr UN Protection Force, Bosnia-Herzegovina 1995; GOC and Dir of Mil. Operations, NI 1996–98; Deputy Supreme Allied Commdr in Europe 1998–2002; ADC Gen. to the Queen 2000–02. *Publication:* The Utility of Force: The Art of War in the Modern World 2005. *Address:* c/o RHQ The Parachute Regiment, Colchester, Essex, CO2 7SW, England (office).

SMITH, Stephen Francis, LLM; Australian politician; *Minister for Foreign Affairs;* b. 12 Dec. 1955, Narrogin, WA; ed Univ. of Western Australia, London Univ., UK; solicitor, lecturer and tutor 1978–83; Prin. Pvt. Sec. to State Attorney-Gen., WA 1983–87; mem. Australian Labor Party Nat. Exec. 1987–90, Jr Vice-Pres. 1989–90; Adviser to Treas. P. J. Keating 1991, to Minister for Science and Tech. R. V. Free 1991, to Prime Minister P. J. Keating 1991–92; MP for Perth 1993–, Shadow Minister for Trade 1996–97, for Resources and Energy 1997–98, for Communications 1998–2001, for Health and Ageing 2001–04, for Industry, Infrastructure and Industrial Relations 2004–06, for Educ. and Training 2006–07, Minister for Foreign Affairs 2007–. *Address:* Department of Foreign Affairs and Trade, R. G. Casey Building, John McEwen Crescent, Barton ACT 0221, Australia (office). *Telephone:* (2) 6261-1111 (office). *Fax:* (2) 6261-3111 (office). *Website:* www.dfat.gov.au (office).

SMITH, Vernon L., BSEE, MA, PhD, FAAS; American economist and academic; *Professor of Economics and Law, George Mason University;* b. 1 Jan. 1927, Wichita; m. Candace Smith; ed Calif. Inst. of Tech., Univ. of Kansas and Harvard Univ.; Instructor in Econs Univ. of Kansas 1951–52; Economist, Harvard Econs Research Project 1954–55; mem. Man. Sciences Research Group, Purdue Univ. 1955–56, Asst Prof. 1956–58, Assoc. Prof. 1958–61, Prof. 1961–67, Krannert Outstanding Professorship 1964–67; Research Consultant Rand Corpn 1957–59; Contrib. Ed. Business Scope 1957–62; Visiting Prof. Stanford Univ. 1961–62; Prof. of Econs Brown Univ. 1967–68; Prof. of Econs Univ. of Mass. 1968–75; Visiting Prof. Univ. of Southern Calif. and Calif. Inst. of Tech. 1974–75; Prof. of Econs Univ. of Ariz. 1975–2001, Regents Prof. of Econs 1988–2001, McClelland Prof. of Econs 1998–; Research Dir Econ. Science Lab. 1986–2001; Prof. of Econs and Law George Mason Univ. (GMU), Arlington, Va 2001–, Dir and Research Scholar, Interdisciplinary Center for Econ. Science 2001–, Research Fellow Mercatus Center 2001–; Fellow Econometric Soc. 1988–, American Acad. of Arts and Sciences 1991; Distinguished Fellow American Econ. Asscn 1992; mem. Editorial Bd American Econ. Review 1969–72, The Cato Journal, Journal of Economic Behavior and Organization (Assoc. Ed. 1985–), Journal of Risk and Uncertainty, Science 1988–91, Economic Theory, Economic Design 1994–, Games and Economic Behavior, Journal of Economic Methodology 1995–; mem. NAS 1995–; mem. Acad. Advisory Council, Inst. of Econ. Affairs, UK 1993–; Pres. Public Choice Soc. 1988–90, Econ. Science Asscn (Founding Pres. 1986–87), Western Econ. Asscn 1990–91, Asscn for Pvt. Enterprise Educ. 1997, Int. Foundation for Research in Experimental Econs 1997; fmr Ford Foundation Faculty Research Fellow, Fellow Center for Advanced Study in the Behavioral Sciences 1972–73, Sherman Fairchild Distinguished Scholar, Calif. Inst. of Tech. 1973–74; Blue Ribbon Panel Mem. Nat. Electricity Rehabilitation Council 1997; consultant on privatization of electric power in Australia and NZ and participated in numerous pvt. and public discussions on energy deregulation in the USA; Hon. DrMan (Purdue) 1989; Andersen Consulting Prof. of the Year 1993, Asscn for Pvt. Enterprise Educ. Adam Smith Award 1995, Distinguished Alumni Award, Calif. Inst. of Tech. 1996, Nobel Prize for Econs 2002. *Publications include:* Economics: An Analytical Approach (jtly with K. Davidson and J. Wiley) 1958, Investment and Production 1961, Economics of Natural and Environmental Resources 1977, Papers in Experimental Economics (collected works) 1991, Experiments in Decision, Organization and Exchange 1993, Bargaining and Market Behavior: Essays in Experimental Economics (collected works) 2000; Research in Experimental Economics, Vols. 1–3 (ed.) 1979, 1982, 1985; Schools of Economic Thought: Experimental Economics (ed.) 1990; over 200 articles on capital theory, finance, natural resource econs and experimental econs. *Address:* Department of Economics, Interdisciplinary Center for Economic Science, George Mason University, 4400 University Blvd., MSN 1B2, Fairfax, VA 22030, USA (office). *Telephone:* (703) 993-4842 (office). *Fax:* (703) 993-4851 (office). *E-mail:* vsmith2@gmu.edu (office). *Website:* www.gmu.edu/departments/economics/facultybios/smith (office).

SMITH, Wilbur Addison, BComm; British novelist; b. 9 Jan. 1933, Zambia; m. 1st Danielle Antoinette Smith 1971 (died 1999); two s. one d.; m. 2nd Mokhiniso Rakhimova 2000; ed Michaelhouse, Natal and Rhodes Univ.; business exec. 1954–58; factory owner 1958–64; professional author 1961–. *Publications:* When the Lion Feeds 1964, The Dark of the Sun 1965, The Sound of Thunder 1966, Shout at the Devil 1968, Gold Mine 1970, The Diamond Hunters 1971, The Sunbird 1972, Eagle in the Sky 1974, The Eye of the Tiger 1975, Cry Wolf 1976, A Sparrow Falls 1977, Hungry as the Sea 1978, Wild Justice 1979, A Falcon Flies 1980, Men of Men 1981, The Angels Weep 1982, The Leopard Hunts in Darkness 1984, The Burning Shore 1985, Power of the Sword 1986, Rage 1987, The Courtneys 1987, The Courtneys in Africa 1988, A Time to Die 1989, Golden Fox 1990, Elephant Song 1991, River God 1993, The Seventh Scroll 1995, Birds of Prey 1997, Monsoon 1999, Warlock 2001, Blue Horizon 2003, The Triumph of the Sun 2005, The Quest 2007, Assegai 2009; contrib. to numerous journals and magazines. *Leisure interests:* fishing, wildlife, skiing, wing shooting. *Address:* c/o Charles Pick Consultancy Ltd, 21 Dagmar Terrace, London, N1 2BN, England (office). *Telephone:* (20) 7226-2779 (office). *Fax:* (20) 7226-2779 (office). *Website:* www.wilbursmithbooks.com; www.wilbursmith.net.

SMITH, Will; American actor and singer; b. (Willard Christopher Smith II), 25 Sept. 1968, Philadelphia, Pa; s. of Willard Smith, Sr and Caroline Smith; m. 1st Sheree Zampino 1992 (divorced); one s.; m. 2nd Jada Pinkett 1997; one s. one d.; ed Overbrook High School, Winfield, Pa; formed duo DJ Jazzy Jeff and the Fresh Prince; f. Overbrook Entertainment (production co.); developer and owner The Boom Boom Room (recording studio); with DJ Jazzy Jeff: Grammy Awards Best Rap Performance 1988, 1991; as solo artist: Grammy Awards Best Rap Solo Performance 1998, MTV Music Video Awards Best Male Video, Best Rap Video 1998, American Music Awards Favorite Pop/Rock Male Artist, Favorite Album, Favorite Male Soul/R&B Artist 1998, Favorite Pop/Rock Male Artist 2000; César d'honneur 2005, American Music Award for Favorite Male Pop/Rock Artist 2005, Kora All African Music Award for Best African American Diaspora Artist (for song, Switch) 2005. *Films include:* Where the Day Takes You 1992, Made in America 1993, Six Degrees of Separation 1993, Bad Boys 1995, Independence Day 1996, Men in Black 1997, Enemy of the State 1998, Wild Wild West 1999, Legend of Bagger Vance 2000, Ali 2002, Men in Black II: Alien Attack 2002, Bad Boys II 2003, Shark Tale (voice) 2004, I, Robot 2004, Hitch 2005, The Pursuit of Happyness 2006, I Am Legend 2007, Hancock 2008, Seven Pounds 2009. *Television includes:* The Fresh Prince of Bel Air (series) 1990–96, Happily Ever After: Fairy Tales for Every Child (episode 'Pinocchio'; voice) 1997, All of Us Johnny (three episodes) 2003–04, Nur die Liebe zählt (episode) 2008. *Recordings include:* albums: as The Fresh Prince with DJ Jazzy Jeff: He's the DJ, I'm the Rapper 1988, And in This Corner... 1989, Homebase 1991, Rock the House 1991, Code Red 1993; solo: Big Willie Style 1997, Willennium 1999, Born to Reign 2002, Lost and Found 2005. *Publication:* Just the Two of Us (juvenile) 2005. *Address:* c/o Overbrook Entertainment, 450 North Roxbury Drive, 4th Floor, Beverly Hills, CA 90210, (office); c/o Ken Stovicz, Creative Artists Agency, 9830 Wilshire Boulevard, Beverly Hills, CA 90212, USA (office). *Telephone:* (310) 432-2400 (Overbrook) (office). *Fax:* 9310) 432-2410 (Overbrook) (office). *Website:* www.overbrookent.com (office).

SMITH, Zadie, FRSL; British writer and poet; b. (Sadie Smith), 27 Oct. 1975, London; m. Nick Laird 2004; ed Hampstead Comprehensive, Cricklewood and King's Coll., Cambridge; writer-in-residence Inst. of Contemporary Arts, London; Radcliffe Fellow Harvard Univ. 2002–03; Rylands Prize, King's Coll. London, Betty Trask Prize 2001. *Publications:* White Teeth (novel) (Guardian First Book Award 2001, Whitbread First Novel Award and Book of the Year 2001, James Tait Memorial Prize for Fiction 2001, Commonwealth Writers' Best First Book Prize 2001) 2000, Piece of Flesh (ed.) 2001, The May Anthologies (ed.) 2001, The Autograph Man (novel) 2002, The Burned Children of America (ed.) 2003, On Beauty (novel) (Commonwealth Writers' Regional Award (Eurasia) for Best Book 2006, Orange Prize for Fiction 2006, Soc. of Authors Somerset Maugham Award 2006) 2005, The Book of Other People (short stories, Ed.) 2007; contribs to anthologies and periodicals. *Address:* c/o A. P. Watt Ltd, 20 John Street, London, WC1N 2DR, England (office). *Telephone:* (20) 7405-6774 (office). *Fax:* (20) 7831-2154 (office). *E-mail:* zsmith@literati.net (office).

SMITH BASTERRA, Jaime, BA, MA; Spanish business executive; *CEO, Telefónica O2 Germany GmbH & Co;* b. 6 Sept. 1965; ed Univ. Comercial Deusto, Spain, Exeter Univ., UK; began career as telecommunications industry and Dir of Equity Research, Benito & Monjardin SVB SA, Madrid 1989–98; fmr Dir of Global Equities, Banesto (Banco Santander Group) 1989–99; Dir of Financial Planning, Telefónica Internacional 1999, Chief Financial Officer 1999–2000, Controller, Telefónica Group 2000–02, Chief Financial Officer, Telefónica de Espana 2002–05, Chair., Pres. and CEO Český Telecom a.s. 2005–07; CEO Telefónica O2 Germany GmbH & Co., Munich 2007–; Exec. Dir O2 plc, Telefónica Europe 2006–; mem. Bd of Dirs I+D, Telyco, TTP, Telfisa; mem. Presiding Cttee BITKOM. *Address:* Telefónica O2 Germany GmbH & Co., Georg-Brauchle-Ring 50, 80992 Munich, Germany (office). *Telephone:* (89) 24420000 (office). *Website:* www.o2online.de (office).

SMITH OF CLIFTON, Baron (Life Peer), cr. 1997, of Mountsandel in the County of Londonderry; **Trevor Arthur Smith,** Kt, BSc (Econ.), FRHistS, AcSS; British university vice-chancellor (retd) and business executive; b. 14 June 1937, London; s. of the late Arthur J. Smith and Vera G. Cross; m. 1st Brenda Eustace 1960 (divorced 1973); two s.; m. 2nd Julia Bullock 1979; one d.; ed

London School of Econs; schoolteacher, London 1958–59; Asst Lecturer in Politics, Univ. of Exeter 1959–60; Research Officer, Acton Soc. Trust 1960–62; Lecturer in Politics, Univ. of Hull 1962–67; Lecturer, Queen Mary Coll. London 1967, Sr Lecturer, Head Dept 1972–85, Dean of Social Studies 1979–82, Prof. of Politics 1983–91, Pro-Prin. 1985–87, Sr Pro-Prin. 1987–89, Sr Vice-Prin., Queen Mary & Westfield Coll. 1989–91; Vice-Chancellor, Univ. of Ulster 1991–99 and Hon. Prof.; Visiting Prof., Univ. of York 1999–2003, Univ. of Portsmouth 2000–01; Dir Joseph Rowntree Reform Trust Ltd 1975– (Chair. 1987–99); Chair. Political Studies Asscn UK 1988–89, Vice-Pres. 1989–91, Pres. 1991–93; Dir Job Ownership Ltd 1978–85, New Society Ltd 1986–88, Statesman and Nation Publishing Co. Ltd 1988–90, Bell Educ. Trust Ltd 1988–93, Gerald Duckworth Ltd 1990–95; Deputy Pres. Inst. for Citizenship 1991–01; Dir Irish Peace Inst. 1992–99; Pres. Belfast Civic Trust 1995–99; mem. Admin. Bd Int. Asscn of Univs 1995–96, Editorial Bd Government and Opposition journal 1995–, Bd A Taste of Ulster 1996–99; mem. N Yorks Health Authority 2000–02; Academician Coll. of Learned Socs in the Social Sciences 2000; Liberal Democrat Spokesman on NI 2000–; Chair. Lords Select Cttee on Animals in Scientific Procedures 2001–02; Trustee Stroke Asscn 2002–; Hon. mem. of Senate (Fachhochschule Augsburg) 1994; Hon. Fellow Queen Mary London 2003; Hon. LLD (Dublin) 1992, (Hull) 1993, (Belfast) 1995, (Nat. Univ. of Ireland) 1996; Hon. DHL (Alabama) 1998; Hon. DLitt (Ulster) 2002. *Publications:* Training Managers (with M. Argyle) 1962, Town Councillors (with A. M. Rees) 1964, Town and County Hall 1966, Anti-Politics 1972, The Politics of the Corporate Economy 1979, The Fixers (with Alison Young) 1996; contributed to numerous other publs. *Leisure interest:* water-colour painting. *Address:* House of Lords, Westminster, London, SW1A 0PW, England (office). *Telephone:* (20) 7219-5353 (office). *Fax:* (20) 7219-5979 (office); (1347) 824109 (home). *E-mail:* smitht@parliament.uk (office); sirtas@jrrt.org.uk (home).

SMITH OF FINSBURY, Baron (Life Peer), cr. 2005; **Rt Hon. Chris(topher) Robert Smith,** PC, PhD; British politician; *Chairman, Environment Agency;* b. 24 July 1951, Barnet, London; s. of Colin Smith and Gladys Smith (née Luscombe); ed George Watson's Coll., Edinburgh, Pembroke Coll., Cambridge, Harvard Univ. (Kennedy Scholar 1975–76), USA; Devt Sec., Shaftesbury Soc. Housing Asscn 1977–80; Devt Co-ordinator Soc. for Co-operative Dwellings 1980–83; Councillor, London Borough of Islington 1978–83, Chief Whip 1978–79, Chair. Housing Cttee 1981–83; Labour MP for Islington S and Finsbury 1983–2005, mem. Cttee on Standards in Public Life 2001–05; Opposition Spokesman on Treasury and Econ. Affairs 1987–92; Prin. Opposition Spokesman on Environmental Protection 1992–94, on Nat. Heritage 1994–95, on Social Security 1995–96, on Health 1996–97; Sec. of State for Culture, Media and Sport 1997–2001; Chair. Labour Campaign for Criminal Justice 1985–88, Tribune Group of MPs 1988–89; Life Peer in House of Lords 2005–, Vice-Chair. British Museum Group 2005–; Pres. Socialist Environment and Resources Asscn 1992–2007; mem. Exec. Fabian Soc. 1990–97; Pres. SERA (Labour Environment Campaign) 1992–2007, Ramblers' Asscn 2004–08; Chair. Wordsworth Trust 2001–, Classic FM Consumer Panel 2001–07, Donmar Warehouse Theatre 2003–, Judges, Man Booker Prize for Fiction 2004, London Cultural Consortium 2004–08, Advertising Standards Authority 2007–, Environment Agency 2008–; Dir Clore Cultural Leadership Programme 2003–08; Dir (non-exec.) PPL (Phonographic Performance Ltd) 2006–; Sr Assoc. Judge Inst. in Man. Studies, Univ. of Cambridge 2001–07; Visiting Prof., Univ. of the Arts London 2002–; Visiting Fellow, Ashridge Business Coll. 2007; Sr Fellow, RCA 2007; Companion, Chartered Marketing Inst. 2005–; Patron The Food Chain, London; Hon. FRIBA 2001; Hon. Fellow, Pembroke Coll. Cambridge 2004, King's Coll., London 2008–; Dr hc (City Univ.) 2003. *Publications:* Creative Britain 1998, Suicide of the West (jtly) 2006. *Leisure interests:* mountaineering (first MP to climb all the 3,000ft 'Munros' in Scotland), literature, theatre, music, art. *Address:* House of Lords, Westminster, London, SW1A 0PW (office); Environment Agency, Millbank Tower, 25th Floor, 21–24 Millbank, London, SW1P 4XL, England (office). *Telephone:* (20) 7863-8720 (office). *Fax:* (20) 7863-8722 (office). *E-mail:* benedicta.moxon@environment-agency.gov.uk (office). *Website:* www.environment-agency.gov.uk (office).

SMITH PERERA, Roberto, PhD; Venezuelan politician and business executive; b. 1958, Barquisimeto; s. of Roberto Smith Camacho; m. Marina Pocaterra; three d.; ed Universidad Simón Bolívar and Harvard Univ., USA; early career working for telecommunications cos.; Coordinator of Govt's 8th Plan for the Nation 1989–90; Minister of Transport and Communications 1990–92; Amb. to EU, Belgium and Luxembourg 1992–95; Pres. Digitel Venezuela (telecoms co.) 1997–2002, f. Digicel in El Salvador and Guatemala (subsidiaries of Digitel) 1999; f. Microjuris.com (internet service); unsuccessful cand. in Vargas state gubernatorial elections 2004; Founder and Pres. Venezuela de Primera Party (Venezuela First) 2005–; unsuccessful cand. in presidential elections 2006. *Publications:* Venezuela, Vision or Chaos 1995. *Address:* c/o Microjuris.com Venezuela, Ave Las Acacias con Abraham Lincoln, Torre Lincon, PH –A Plaza Venezuela, Caracas, D.M., Venezuela. *Website:* www.venezueladeprimera.org.ve; www.robertosmith.org.

SMITHIES, Oliver, DPhil; American (b. British) biomedical scientist and academic; *Excellence Professor, Department of Pathology and Laboratory Medicine, School of Medicine, University of North Carolina;* b. 23 June 1925, Halifax; m. Nobuyo Maeda; ed Univ. of Oxford; Postdoctoral Fellowship, Univ. of Wisconsin 1951–53, Asst Prof., later Prof. Genetics and Medical Genetics 1960–63, Leon J. Cole Prof. 1971–80, Hilldale Prof. 1980–88; Excellence Prof. of Pathology and Lab. Medicine, Univ. of North Carolina 1988–; Pres. Genetics Soc. of America; Foreign mem. Royal Soc. 1998; Hon. DSc (Chicago); Gairdner Foundation Int. Award 1990, 1993, Bristol-Myers Squibb Award for Distinguished Achievement in Cardiovascular/Metabolic Disease Research, CIBA Award for Hypertension Research 1996, jt recipient of American Heart

Foundation Research Achievement Award for Distinguished Research in the Biomedical Sciences 1998, Int. Okamoto Award, Japan Vascular Disease Research Foundation 2000, Albert Lasker Award for Basic Medical Research 2001, Wolf Foundation Prize in Medicine 2002, Nobel Prize for Medicine (with Mario Capecchi and Sir Martin Evans) 2007 for the discovery of principles for introducing specific gene modifications in mice by the use of embryonic stem cells. *Publications:* over 240 publs. *Address:* Department of Pathology and Laboratory Medicine, School of Medicine, University of North Carolina, Chapel Hill, NC 27599, USA (office). *Telephone:* (919) 966-6913 (office). *E-mail:* oliver.smithies@pathology.unc.edu (office). *Website:* www.pathology.unc.edu/common/smithies.htm (office).

SMOOT, George Fitzgerald, III, BS, PhD; American astrophysicist and cosmologist; *Professor of Physics and Director, Berkeley Center for Cosmological Physics, University of California, Berkeley;* b. 20 Feb. 1945, Yukon, Fla; ed Stetson Univ., Georgetown Univ., Massachusetts Inst. of Tech.; Postdoctoral researcher, MIT 1970; Research Physicist, Univ. of California, Berkeley Space Sciences Lab. 1971–74, jt appointment, Research Physicist, Lawrence Berkeley Nat. Lab. 1974–, Prof., Physics Dept, Univ. of California, Berkeley 1994–, Dir Berkeley Center for Cosmological Physics 2007–; mem. American Physical Soc. Cttee on Safety of Commercial Nuclear Reactors 1974–75, Man. and Operations Working Group for Shuttle Astronomy 1976–80, Steering Group on Cosmic Background Explorer Satellite (Prin. Investigator on isotropy experiment—NASA) 1975, White Mountain Research Station Advisory Cttee 1982, Superconducting Magnet Facility for the Space Station Study Team 1985, Center for Particle Astrophysics at Univ. of California, Berkeley 1988, Radio Astronomy Lab. Advisory Cttee 1990; mem. American Physical Soc., American Astronomical Soc., AAAS, Int. Astronomical Union; Dr hc (Univ. of Marseille, Reiko Univ., Miguel Hernandez Univ.); NASA Medal for Exceptional Scientific Achievement 1991, Popular Science Award 1992, Aerospace Laureate, Aviation Week & Space Technology 1993, Distinguished Scientist, ARCS Foundation, Inc. 1993, Kilby Award 1993, Gravity Research Foundation Essay First Award 1993, Productivity Group Award, Goddard Space Flight Center, NASA 1993, Golden Plate Award 1994, Lawrence Award 1995, Nobel Prize in Physics (with John C. Mather) 2006, Oersted Medal 2009. *Publications:* Wrinkles in Time (co-author) 1993; more than 220 scientific papers in professional journals on the cosmic background radiation. *Address:* Physics Department, University of California, Berkeley, 437 Old LeConte Hall, Berkeley, CA 94720-7300 (office); Ernest Orlando Lawrence Berkeley National Laboratory, 1 Cyclotron Road, Mail Stop 50R5005, Berkeley, CA 94720, USA (office). *Telephone:* (510) 486-5505 (office); (510) 486-5237 (office); (510) 642-9389 (office). *Fax:* (510) 486-7149 (office). *E-mail:* GFSmoot@lbl.gov (office). *Website:* www.physics.berkeley.edu/research/faculty/Smoot.html (office); cosmos.lbl.gov (office); bccp.lbl.gov (office).

SMOUT, Thomas Christopher, CBE, MA, PhD, FRSE, FBA, FSA (Scot.); British historian and academic; *Professor Emeritus of Scottish History, University of St Andrews;* b. 19 Dec. 1933, Birmingham; s. of Sir Arthur J. G. Smout and Lady Smout (Hilda Smout, née Follows); m. Anne-Marie Schøning 1959; one s. one d.; ed Leys School, Cambridge, Clare Coll., Cambridge; joined staff Edinburgh Univ. 1959, Prof. of Econ. History 1970–79; Prof. of Scottish History, Univ. of St Andrews 1980–91, Prof. Emer. 1991–; Dir St John's House Inst. for Advanced Historical Studies, Univ. of St Andrews 1992–97; Founder and Dir Inst. for Environmental History, Univ. of St Andrews 1992–2000; Visiting Prof., Univ. of Strathclyde 1991–95, Univ. of Dundee 1993–, Univ. of Stirling 1997–, Univ. of York 1998–99; Deputy Chair. Scottish Nat. Heritage 1992–97, mem. Bd 1992–98; Historiographer Royal in Scotland 1993–; mem. Bd Royal Comm. Ancient and Historical Monuments of Scotland 1986–2000, Nature Conservancy Council (Scotland) 1991–92, Royal Comm. on Historical Manuscripts 1999–2003, Advisory Council on Nat. Records and Archives 2003–04; Trustee Nat. Museums of Scotland 1991–94, Woodland Trust 1998–2004; Chair. Scottish Coastal Archaeology and the Problem of Erosion 2001–; Patron Scottish Native Woods 2004–; Hon. Fellow, Trinity Coll. Dublin 1994–; Dr hc (Queen's Univ., Belfast) 1995, (Edin.) 1996, (St Andrews) 1999, (Glasgow) 2001, (Stirling) 2002. *Publications:* Scottish Trade on the Eve of the Union 1963, History of the Scottish People, 1560–1830 1969, State of the Scottish Working Class in 1843 (with Ian Levitt) 1979, Scottish Population History from the 17th Century to the 1930s (with M. W. Flinn) 1976, Century of the Scottish People, 1830–1950 1986, Scottish Voices (with S. Wood) 1990, Prices, Food and Wages in Scotland (with A. Gibson) 1995, Nature Contested 2000, People and Woods in Scotland (ed.) 2002, History of the Native Woods of Scotland (with A.R. MacDonald and F. Watson) 2005. *Leisure interests:* birdwatching and other natural history, conservation, architecture. *Address:* Chesterhill, Shore Road, Anstruther, Fife, KY10 3DZ, Scotland. *Telephone:* (1333) 310330. *Fax:* (1333) 311193. *E-mail:* tcs1@st-andrews.ac.uk.

SMURFIT, Anthony P. J., BSc; Irish business executive; *President and Group Chief Operations Officer, Smurfit Kappa Group;* b. 19 Dec. 1963, Wigan; s. of Michael Smurfit; ed Univ. of Scranton, Pennsylvania, USA; mem. Bd Jefferson Smurfit Group (now Smurfit Kappa Group), Chief Exec. Smurfit France 1996, later Deputy Chief Exec. Smurfit Europe, then Chief Exec. Smurfit Europe –2002, Group COO 2002–05, Pres. and Group Chief Operations Officer Smurfit Kappa Group 2005–; Dir Irish Nat. Stud Co.; Hon. Consul of Mexico to Ireland 2003, Chevalier de la Légion d'honneur 2004. *Leisure interests:* golf, horse breeding. *Address:* Smurfit Kappa Group, Beech Hill, Clonskeagh, Dublin 4, Ireland (office). *Telephone:* (1) 202-7157 (office). *Fax:* (1) 202-7183 (office). *E-mail:* info@smurfitkappa.com (office). *Website:* www.smurfitkappa.com (office).

SMURFIT, Michael, Jr, MBA; Irish business executive; s. of Michael Smurfit; ed Michael Smurfit Grad. Business School, Univ. Coll. Dublin; fmr

Vice-Pres. World Purchasing, Jefferson Smurfit Group, Pres. and Chief Exec., Smurfit Packaging Corpn (now Smurfit-Stone Container Corpn) 1996; currently CEO SF Investments (pvt. investment co.), Dublin; mem. Bd of Dirs CNG Travel Group plc, Irish Youth Foundation; mem. Irish Advisory Bd Michael Smurfit Grad. Business School, Univ. Coll. Dublin. *Address:* c/o Irish Advisory Board, UCD Michael Smurfit Graduate Business School, University College Dublin, Carysfort Avenue, Blackrock, Co. Dublin, Ireland.

SMURFIT, Sir Michael William Joseph, KBE; Irish business executive; b. 1936, St Helens, Lanc., England; m. 1st Norma Treisman (divorced); two s. two d.; m. 2nd Birgitta Beimark; two s.; joined Jefferson Smurfit & Sons Ltd 1955; f. Jefferson Smurfit Packaging Ltd (Lancashire) 1961; rejoined Jefferson Smurfit Group, Dir 1964, Jt Man. Dir 1967, Deputy Chair. 1979; Chair. and CEO Jefferson Smurfit Group PLC, Dublin 1977–2002, Chair. 2002–07, also Chair. Jefferson Smurfit Corpn & Container Corpn of America; mem. Irish Advisory Bd Michael Smurfit Grad. Business School, Univ. Coll. Dublin; fmr Chair. Telecom Eireann; Hon. LLD (Trinity Coll. Dublin), (Univ. of Scranton, Pa). *Address:* c/o Smurfit Kappa Group, Beech Hill, Clonskeagh, Dublin 4, Ireland.

SNEGUR, Mircea, DrAgriSc; Moldovan politician; b. 17 Jan. 1940, V. Trifăneşti, Soroca Dist; s. of Ion Snegur and Ana Snegur; m. Georgeta Snegur 1960; one s. one d.; ed Kishinau Inst. of Agric.; mem. CPSU 1964–90; work as agronomist, man. state and collective farms 1961–68, Chair. of Experimental Station 1968–73, Chief of Section Ministry of Agric. 1973–78; Dir-Gen. Research Production Asscn 'Selektsia', Balts 1978–81; Sec. CP Cttee, Yedinetsky Dist 1981–85; Sec. Cen. Cttee of CP of Moldavia 1985–89, Chair. Presidium of Supreme Soviet of Moldavia 1989–90; Pres. of Moldova 1990–96; Chair. Party of Resurrection and Accord (later Democratic Convention) 1995–2001; mem. of Parl. 1998, Constant Bureau of Parl. 1998–2001; Hon. Chair. Liberal Party 2002–; Order of the Repub. 2000. *Publications:* more than 100 articles on phytotechnical matters and the application of scientific procedures to production, Memories in Two Parts (monograph). *Leisure interests:* billiards, history and detective fiction, sports programmes, sport fishing. *Address:* 62A Puschin Street, Kishinau, Moldova. *Telephone:* 21-10-05 (office). *Fax:* 54-39-22 (office).

SNEH, Brig.-Gen. Ephraim, MD; Israeli politician, physician and army officer (retd); *Chairman, Strong Israel Party;* b. 19 Sept. 1944, Tel-Aviv; s. of Dr Moshe Sneh; m.; two c.; ed Tel-Aviv Univ. Medical School; Research Fellow, Walter Reed Army Medical Center; rank of Brig.-Gen., army service includes Medical Officer of Paratroops Brigade 1972–74; Chief Medical Officer of the Paratroops and Infantry Corps 1974–78; Commdr of the Medical Teams during the Entebbe Rescue Operation 1976; Commdr Israel Defense Forces (IDF) elite unit 1978–80; Chief Medical Officer IDF Northern Command 1980–81; Commdr of Security Zone in S Lebanon 1981–82; Head of the Civil Admin. of the West Bank 1985–87; mem. Knesset (Parl.) 1992– (Labor Party); Minister of Health 1994, of Transportation 2001–04; Deputy Minister of Defence 1999–2001, 2006–07; est. Strong Israel Party 2008. *Publication:* Navigating Perilous Waters 2005. *Address:* 7 La guardia Street, Tel Aviv (office); 12 Hapalmach Street, Herzelia 46793, Israel (home). *Telephone:* (3) 6878761 (office). *Fax:* (9) 9511766 (office). *E-mail:* esneh@netvision.net.il (home). *Website:* www.sneh.org.il.

SNELLGROVE, David Llewelyn, LittD, PhD, FBA; British academic and author; b. 29 June 1920, Portsmouth; s. of Lt-Commdr Clifford Snellgrove, R.N. and Eleanor M. Snellgrove; ed Christ's Hosp., Horsham, Southampton Univ. and Queen's Coll. Cambridge; war service in India –1946; Lecturer in Tibetan, SOAS, Univ. of London 1950–60, Reader in Tibetan, Univ. of London 1960–74, Prof. of Tibetan 1974–82, Prof. Emer. 1982–; has undertaken numerous expeditions to India and the Himalayas; Co-founder Inst. of Tibetan Studies (now Inst. of Buddhist Studies), Tring, Herts. 1966, fmr Chair. of Trustees; expeditions in Indonesia 1987–94, in Cambodia 1995–; Rockefeller Grant 1961–64; Leverhulme Grant 1978–81; The Burton Medal 2004. *Publications:* Buddhist Himalaya 1957, Himalayan Pilgrimage 1961, The Hevajra Tantra (2 vols) 1959, The Nine Ways of Bon 1967, Four Lamas of Dolpo (2 vols) 1967, A Cultural History of Tibet (with H. E. Richardson) 1968, The Cultural Heritage of Ladakh (with T. Skorupski) (two vols) 1979–80, Indo-Tibetan Buddhism, Indian Buddhists and their Tibetan Successors 1986, Asian Commitment 2000, Khmer Civilization and Angkor 2001, Angkor Before and After, A Cultural History of the Khmers 2004; Gen. Ed. and major contrib. to The Image of the Buddha 1978. *Address:* Via Matteo Gay 26/7, 10066 Torre Pellice, Italy (home); Villa Bantay Chah, Krom 11, no. 0718, Siem Reap, Cambodia (home). *Telephone:* (121) 932925 (home). *E-mail:* snellgrove@virgilio.it (home).

SNIDER, Stacey, BA, JD; American film industry executive; *Co-Chairman and CEO, DreamWorks SKG;* b. 29 April 1961, Phila, Pa; m.; two c.; ed Univ. of Pennsylvania, Univ. of Calif., Los Angeles; began career in post room, Triad Agency, later Asst; Asst, Simpson-Bruckheimer Productions; joined Guber-Peters Entertainment Co. as Dir of Devt 1986–90, Exec. Vice-Pres. 1990–92; Production Pres. TriStar Pictures 1992–96; Co-Pres. of Production, Universal Pictures 1996–98, Head of Production April–Nov. 1998, Pres. of Production and Co-Chair. 1998–, Chair. and CEO Universal Pictures 1999–2006; Co-Chair. and CEO DreamWorks SKG 2006–; named No. 2 on Power List in Women in Entertainment Report, The Hollywood Reporter 2003, ranked by Fortune magazine amongst 50 Most Powerful Women in Business in the US (20th) 2002, (18th) 2003, (28th) 2004, (33rd) 2005, (50th) 2006, ranked by Forbes magazine amongst 100 Most Powerful Women (60th) 2004, (59th) 2005, (94th) 2006, (87th) 2007. *Address:* DreamWorks SKG, 1000 Flower Street, Glendale, CA 91201, USA (office). *Telephone:* (818) 733-7000 (office). *Fax:* (818) 695-7574 (office). *Website:* www.dreamworks.com (office).

SNIPES, Wesley; American actor and producer; b. 31 July 1962, Orlando, Fla; one s.; ed High School for the Performing Arts, New York and State Univ. of New York, Purchase; fmr telephone repair man, New York; appeared in Martin Scorsese's video Bad 1987; Co-Founder Struttin Street Stuff puppet theatre mid-1980s; indicted on eight counts of US tax fraud Oct. 2006, convicted and sentenced to three years in prison 2008; ACE Award for Best Actor for Vietnam War Stories (TV) 1989, Best Actor for One Night Stand, Venice Film Festival. *Films:* Wildcats, Streets of Gold, Major League, Mo Better Blues 1990, Jungle Fever 1991, New Jack City, White Men Can't Jump, Demolition Man, Boiling Point, Sugar Hill, Drop Zone, To Wong Foo, Thanks for Everything, Julie Newmar 1995, The Money Train, Waiting to Exhale, The Fan 1996, One Night Stand, Murder at 1600, Blade (also producer) 1997, U.S. Marshals 1998, Down in the Delta (also producer) 1998, The Art of War 2000, Blade 2 2002, Undisputed 2002, Nine Lives 2004. *Broadway stage appearances:* Boys of Winter, Execution of Justice, Death and King's Horsemen. *Address:* c/o Amen Ra Films, 301 N Canon Drive, Beverly Hills, CA 90210, USA (office).

SNODGRASS, Anthony McElrea, DPhil, FBA, FSA, FRSA; British archaeologist and academic; *Professor Emeritus of Classical Archaeology, Faculty of Classics, University of Cambridge;* b. 7 July 1934, London; s. of Maj. W. M. Snodgrass and Kathleen M. Snodgrass; m. 1st Ann Vaughan 1959 (divorced 1978); three d.; m. 2nd Annemarie Künzl 1983; one s.; ed Marlborough Coll. and Worcester Coll., Oxford; Nat. Service, RAF 1953–55; Lecturer in Classical Archaeology, Univ. of Edin. 1961–68, Reader 1968–75, Prof. 1975–76; Laurence Prof. of Classical Archaeology, Univ. of Cambridge 1976–2001, now Prof. Emer.; Sather Prof. in Classics, Univ. of Calif. at Berkeley 1984–85; Geddes-Harrower Prof. Univ. of Aberdeen 1995–96; Fellow, Clare Coll. Cambridge 1977–; Vice-Pres. British Acad. 1990–92; mem. Humanities Research Bd 1994–95; Chair. British Cttee for the Reunification of the Parthenon Marbles 2002–; Foreign mem. Russian Acad. of Sciences 2002; Hon. Fellow, Worcester Coll., Oxford 2000. *Publications:* Early Greek Armour and Weapons 1964, Arms and Armour of the Greeks 1967, The Dark Age of Greece 1971, Archaeology and the Rise of the Greek State 1977, Archaic Greece: the Age of Experiment 1980, An Archaeology of Greece 1987, Homer and the Artists 1998. *Leisure interests:* mountaineering, skiing. *Address:* Clare College, Cambridge, CB2 1TL, England (office). *Telephone:* (1223) 313599 (home). *Fax:* (1223) 313599 (home). *E-mail:* ams1002@cam.ac.uk (office). *Website:* www.classics.cam.ac.uk/Faculty/faculty (office); www.classics.cam.ac.uk/ark (office).

SNOOK, Hans; German business executive; b. 1948; m. Etta Lai Yee Lau; worked in hotel industry and in real estate sales in Canada; joined Young Generation paging group, Hong Kong 1984; co. bought by Hutchinson Whampoa 1986; Founder and CEO Orange 1994–2001; Chair. (non-exec.) Carphone Warehouse PLC 2002–05, Monstermob Group PLC 2005–07; Dir (non-exec.) DDD Group PLC 2006–. *Address:* c/o Board of Directors, DDD Group PLC, 3000 Ocean Park Blvd., Suite 1025, Santa Monica, CA 90405, USA (office).

SNOUSSI, Ahmed, PhD; Moroccan diplomatist; b. 22 April 1929, Meknès; m. Farida Snoussi; three c.; ed Faculté de Droit, Univ. de Paris and Inst. des Hautes Etudes Politiques; Dir of Public Information, Govt of Morocco and ed. various publs on foreign affairs 1958–60; Sec.-Gen. Ministry of Tourism, Information and Fine Arts 1963; Minister of Information 1967–71 (Moroccan Commr-Gen. Expo '67, Montréal); Amb. to Nigeria 1965, to Cameroon 1966, to Tunisia 1971, to Algeria 1973, to Mauritania and Envoy of the King to Heads of State 1978–79; Head of Moroccan del. UN Security Council 1992–94; Amb. and Perm. Rep. to UN, New York 1997–2001; fmr Chair. Exec. Bd Somathon Tuna Fishing and Packing Corpn, Lafarge Maroc Group; fmr Pres. Cinouca Corpn, Asscn of Deep Sea Fishing Fleets, Nat. Producers Asscn. *Address:* 3 Avenue de la Victoire, Rabat, Morocco (office).

SNOW, David B., Jr, BSc, MS; American health care industry executive; *Chairman and CEO, Medco Health Solutions Inc.;* b. 1955; ed Bates Coll., Duke Univ.; began career working for Creighton Univ. Medical School, Memorial Hosp. of Burlington Co. then US Healthcare Inc.; Sr Vice-Pres. American Int. Healthcare 1988–89; Co-Founder, Pres. and CEO Managed Health Care Systems (later renamed AmeriChoice) 1989–93; Exec. Vice-Pres. Oxford Health Plans 1993–98; Pres. and COO WellChoice Inc. (fmrly named Empire BlueCross BlueShield) 1999–2003; Pres. and CEO Medco Health Solutions Inc. March–June 2003, Chair. and CEO June 2003–. *Address:* Medco Health Solutions Inc., 100 Parsons Pond Drive, Franklin Lakes, NJ 07417-2604, USA (office). *Telephone:* (201) 269-3400 (office). *Fax:* (201) 269-1109 (office). *E-mail:* info@medcohealth.com (office). *Website:* www.medcohealth.com (office).

SNOW, John W., LLB, PhD; American business executive and fmr government official; *Chairman, Cerberus Capital Management LP;* b. 2 Aug. 1939, Toledo, Ohio; ed Kenyon Coll., Univ. of Toledo, Univ. of Virginia, George Washington Univ.; Asst Prof. of Econs, Univ. of Maryland 1965–67; with Wheeler & Wheeler (law firm), Washington, DC 1967–72; Asst Gen. Counsel, US Dept of Transportation 1972–73; Adjunct Prof. of Law, George Washington Univ. Law School 1972–75; Deputy Asst Sec. for Policy, Plans and Int. Affairs 1973–74; Asst Sec. for Govt Affairs, US Dept of Transportation 1974–75, Deputy Under-sec. 1975–76; Admin., Nat. Highway Traffic Safety Admin. 1976–77; Visiting Prof. of Econs, Univ. of Virginia, 1977; Vice-Pres. of Govt Affairs, Chessie System Inc. (later part of CSX Corpn) 1977–80, Sr Vice-Pres. Corp. Services, CSX Corpn Richmond 1980–84, Exec. Vice-Pres. 1984–85, COO 1988–89, Pres. 1988–2001, CEO 1989–2003, Chair. 1991–2003; US Sec. of the Treasury 2003–06; Chair. Cerberus Capital Man. LP 2006–; Co-Chair. Nat. Comm. on Financial Inst. Reform, Recovery and Enforcement 1992–93; Chair. Business Roundtable 1995–96, now mem.; mem. Bd of Dirs Sapient Corpn, Verizon,

Johnson & Johnson, US Steel, Asscn of American Railroads, Carmax; mem. Bd of Trustees Johns Hopkins Univ., The Business Council, Va Business Council, Nat. Coal Council; Co-Chair. Conf. Bd Blue-Ribbon Comm. on Public Trust and Pvt. Enterprise; Chair. Kennedy Center Corp. Fund Bd; Hon. LLD (Kenyon Coll.) 1993; Marco Polo Award, US–China Foundation for Int. Exchanges 2001. *Address:* Cerberus Capital Management LP, 299 Park Avenue, New York, NY 10171, USA (office). *Telephone:* (212) 891-2100 (office). *E-mail:* media@cerberuscapital.com (office). *Website:* www.cerberuscapital.com (office).

SNOW, Jonathan (Jon) George; British television journalist; b. 28 Sept. 1947; s. of the late Rt Rev. George Snow and Joan Snow; pnr Madeleine Colvin; two d.; ed St Edward's School, Oxford, Univ. of Liverpool; Voluntary Service Overseas, Uganda 1967–68; Co-ordinator New Horizon Youth Centre, London 1970–73 (Chair. 1986–); journalist, Independent Radio News, LBC 1973–76; reporter, ITN 1977–83, Washington Corresp. 1983–86, Diplomatic Ed. 1986–89; presenter, Channel Four News 1989–; Visiting Prof. of Broadcast Journalism, Nottingham Trent Univ. 1992–2001, Univ. of Stirling 2002–; Chair. New Horizon Youth Centre 1986–, Prison Reform Trust 1992–96, Media Trust 1995–, Tate Modern Council 1999–; Trustee Noel Buxton Trust 1992–, Nat. Gallery 1999–; Chancellor Oxford Brookes Univ. 2001–; Hon. DLitt (Nottingham Trent) 1994, Hon. DLitt (Open Univ.); Monte Carlo Golden Nymph Award, for Eritrea air attack reporting 1979, TV Reporter of the Year, for Afghanistan, Iran and Iraq reporting, Royal Television Soc. (RTS) 1980, Valiant for Truth Award, for El Salvador reporting 1982, Int. Award, for El Salvador reporting, RTS 1982, Home News Award, for Kegworth air crash reporting, RTS 1989, RTS Presenter of the Year 1994, 2002, BAFTA Richard Dimbleby Award 2005, RTS Journalist of the Year 2006. *Publications:* Atlas of Today 1987, Sons and Mothers 1996, Shooting History: A Personal Journey 2004; articles in The Guardian, Financial Times, Independent, Telegraph, New Statesman. *Leisure interests:* water colours, cycling. *Address:* Channel Four News, ITN, 200 Gray's Inn Road, London, WC1X 8HB, England. *Telephone:* (20) 7430-4237; (20) 7833-3000 (office). *Fax:* (20) 7430-4607. *E-mail:* jon.snow@itn.co.uk (office). *Website:* www.channel4.com/news (office).

SNOW, Peter John, CBE; British television presenter, reporter and author; b. 20 April 1938, Dublin, Ireland; s. of Brig. John F. Snow, CBE and Peggy Pringle; m. 1st Alison Carter 1964 (divorced 1975); one s. one d.; m. 2nd Ann MacMillan 1976; one s. two d.; ed Wellington Coll. and Balliol Coll. Oxford; Second Lt, Somerset Light Infantry 1956–58; newscaster and reporter, ITN 1962–79, Diplomatic and Defence Corresp. 1966–79; Presenter BBC Newsnight 1979–97, Tomorrow's World 1997–2001, BBC Election Programmes 1983–2005, BBC Radio 4 Mastermind 1998–2000, Radio 4 Random Edition 1998–, Radio 4 Masterteam 2001–05, Battlefield Britain (BBC 2, jtly with son Dan Snow) 2004, 20th Century Battlefields (BBC, jtly with son Dan Snow) 2007; Judges' Award, Royal TV Soc. 1998. *Publications:* Leila's Hijack War (jtly) 1970, Hussein: A Biography 1972, Battlefield Britain 2004, The World's Greatest 20th Century Battlefields (with Dan Snow) 2007. *Leisure interests:* sailing, skiing, model railways, photography. *Address:* BBC TV Centre, Wood Lane, London, W12 7RJ, England (office). *Telephone:* (20) 8752-4646 (office). *E-mail:* peter.snow@bbc.co.uk (office).

SNOWDON, 1st Earl of, cr. 1961, Baron Armstrong-Jones, cr. 1999; **Antony Charles Robert Armstrong-Jones,** GCVO, FRSA, RDI; British photographer; b. 7 March 1930, London; s. of the late Ronald Owen Lloyd Armstrong-Jones, MBE, QC, DL and the Countess of Rosse; m. 1st HRH The Princess Margaret 1960 (divorced 1978, died 2002); one s. one d.; m. 2nd Lucy Lindsay-Hogg 1979; one d.; ed Eton Coll. and Jesus Coll., Cambridge; Consultant, Council of Industrial Design 1962–89; in charge of design of Investiture of HRH the Prince of Wales, Caernarfon 1969; Editorial Adviser, Design Magazine 1961–87; Artistic Adviser to The Sunday Times and Sunday Times Publs Ltd 1962–90; photographer Telegraph Magazine 1990–96; Constable of Caernarfon Castle 1963–; sits as Lord Armstrong-Jones in the House of Lords 1999–; Pres. Civic Trust for Wales, Contemporary Art Soc. for Wales, Welsh Theatre Co.; Vice-Pres. Univ. of Bristol Photographic Soc.; Sr Fellow, Royal Coll. of Art 1986, Provost 1995–2003; Fellow, Inst. of British Photographers, British Inst. of Professional Photography, Chartered Soc. of Designers, Royal Photographic Soc., Royal Soc. of Arts, Manchester Coll. of Art and Design; mem. Faculty Royal Designers for Industry; Hon. mem. North Wales Soc. of Architects, South Wales Inst. of Architects; Chair. Snowdon Report on Integrating the Disabled 1972; mem. Council, Nat. Fund for Research for the Crippled Child; Founder Snowdon Award Scheme for Disabled Students 1980; Pres. (England) Int. Year of Disabled People 1981; Patron British Disabled Water Ski Asscn; mem. The Prince of Wales Advisory Group on Disability 1983; Metropolitan Union of YMCAs, British Water Ski Fed., Welsh Nat. Rowing Club, Circle of Guide Dog Owners; designed Snowdon Aviary, London Zoo 1965 (Listed Grade II 1998), Chairmobile 1972; Dr hc (Bradford) 1989, (Portsmouth) 1993; Hon. LLD (Bath) 1989; Art Dirs Club of New York Certificate of Merit 1969, Soc. of Publication Designers Certificate of Merit 1970, The Wilson Hicks Certificate of Merit for Photocommunication 1971, Soc. of Publication Designers' Award of Excellence 1973, Design and Art Dirs' Award 1978, Royal Photographic Soc. Hood Award 1979, Silver Progress Medal, Royal Photographic Soc. 1986. *Television documentaries:* Don't Count the Candles (six awards, including two Emmys) 1968, Love of a Kind 1970, Born to be Small 1971, Happy being Happy 1973, Mary Kingsley 1975, Burke and Wills 1975, Peter, Tina and Steve 1977, Snowdon on Camera (presenter) 1981. *Publications:* London 1958, Malta (in collaboration with Sacheverell Sitwell) 1958, Private View (with John Russell and Bryan Robertson) 1965, Assignments 1972, A View of Venice (with Derek Hart) 1972, Inchcape Review 1977, Pride of the Shires (jointly) 1979, Personal View 1979, Tasmania Essay 1981, Sittings: 1979–83 1983, Israel: A First View 1986, My Wales (with Viscount Tonypandy) 1986, Stills 1983–87, 1987, Public Appearances 1987–1991 1991, Wild Flowers 1995, Snowdon on Stage 1996, Wild Fruit 1997, London Sight Unseen by Snowdon 1999, Photographs by Snowdon: A Retrospective 2000. *Leisure interests:* photography, gardening. *Address:* 22 Launceston Place, London, W8 5RL, England. *Telephone:* (20) 7937-1524 (office). *Fax:* (20) 7938-1727 (office). *E-mail:* lordsnowdon@aol.com (office).

SNOWE, Olympia J., BA; American politician; *Senator from Maine;* b. 21 Feb. 1947, Augusta, Me; d. of George Bouchles and Georgia Goranites Bouchles; m. John McKernan 1969; ed Edward Little High School, Auburn, Univ. of Maine; mem. Maine House of Reps 1973–76, Maine Senate 1976–78; mem. 96th–103rd Congresses from 2nd Maine Dist 1979–95; Deputy Republican Whip; Senator from Maine 1995–; Counsel to Asst Majority Leader 1997; Hon. LLD (Husson Coll.) 1981, (Maine) 1982, (Bowdoin Coll.) 1985, (Suffolk) 1994, (Colby Coll.) 1996, (Bates Coll.) 1998; ranked by Forbes magazine amongst 100 Most Powerful Women (58th) 2004, (54th) 2005, numerous other awards and distinctions. *Address:* 154 Russell Senate Building, Washington, DC 20510, USA (office). *Telephone:* (202) 224-5344 (office). *Fax:* (202) 224-1946 (office). *E-mail:* olympia@snowe.senate.gov (office). *Website:* snowe.senate.gov (office).

SNOWMAN, (Michael) Nicholas, MA; British music administrator; *General Director, Opera National du Rhin;* b. 18 March 1944, London; s. of the late Kenneth Snowman and Sallie Snowman (née Moghilevkine); m. Margo Michelle Rouard 1983; one s.; ed Hall School and Highgate School, London, Magdalene Coll., Cambridge; Asst to Head of Music Staff, Glyndebourne Festival 1967–69; co-founder and Gen. Man. London Sinfonietta 1968–72; Admin. Music Theatre Ensemble 1968–71; Artistic Dir Institut de Recherche et de Coordination Acoustique/Musique (IRCAM), Centre d'Art et de la Culture Georges Pompidou 1972–86; co-founder and Artistic Adviser Ensemble InterContemporain 1975–92, mem. Bd 1992–, Vice-Chair. 1998–; mem. Music Cttee Venice Biennale 1979–86; Artistic Dir Projects in 1980, 1981, 1983, Festival d'Automne de Paris; Programme Consultant Cité de la Musique, La Villette, Paris 1991–92; Gen. Dir (Arts) South Bank Centre, London 1986–92, Chief Exec. 1992–98; Gen. Dir Glyndebourne Opera 1998–2000, Opera Nat. du Rhin, Strasbourg 2002–(09); Chair. Wartski; mem. British Section, Franco-British Council 1995–; Trustee New Berlioz Edn 1996–; Gov. Royal Acad. of Music 1998–; Chevalier, Ordre nat. du Mérite, Officier, Ordre des Arts et des Lettres, Polish Order of Cultural Merit. *Publications:* The Best of Granta (co-ed.) 1967, The Contemporary Composers (series ed.) 1982–; papers and articles on music, cultural policy and France. *Leisure interests:* films, eating, spy novels. *Address:* c/o Wartski, 14 Grafton Street, London, W1X 4DE, England; 9 rue de Bain Finkwiller, 67000 Stasbourg, France (home). *Telephone:* (3) 88-75-48-64 (office); (6) 64-77-81-30 (home). *Fax:* (3) 88-25-52-59 (office). *E-mail:* wartski@wartski.com; nsnowman@onr.fr. *Website:* www.wartski.com; www.onr.fr.

SNOY, Bernard, DIur, PhD; Belgian economist and international organization executive; ed Catholic Univ. of Louvain, Harvard Univ., USA; worked for World Bank 1974–86, Exec. Dir representing Austria, Belgium, Luxembourg, Turkey and countries in transition (Belarus, Czech Repub., Hungary, Kazakhstan, Slovakia and Slovenia) 1991–94; Econ. Advisor, EC 1986–88; Chief of the Cabinet, Belgian Minister of Finance, Philippe Maystadt 1988–91; mem. Bd of Dirs EBRD, London, representing Belgium, Luxembourg and Slovenia 1994–2002; Dir Working Table II (Econ. Reconstruction, Devt and Co-operation), Stability Pact for South Eastern Europe 2002–05; Co-ordinator OSCE Econ. and Environmental Activities 2005–08. *Publications include:* Taxes on Direct Investment Income in the E.E.C.: A Legal and Economic Analysis 1975, Fragility of the International Financial System: How Can We Prevent New Crises in Emerging Markets? (International Financial Relations) (co-author) 2002. *Address:* c/o Office of the Co-ordinator of OSCE Economic and Environmental Activities, Kärntner Ring 5–7, 1010 Vienna, Austria. *Telephone:* (1) 514-36-151.

SNYDER, Allan Whitenack, DSc, FRS; American/Australian optical scientist; *Foundation Director, Centre for the Mind, Australian National University and University of Sydney;* b. 28 Nov. 1940; s. of E. H. Snyder and Zelda Cotton; ed Cen. High School, Pa State Univ., MIT, Harvard Univ. and Univ. Coll. London, UK; Greenland Ice Cap Communications Project 1961; Consultant, Gen. Telecommunications and Electricity Research Lab. 1963–67, British Post Office and Standard Telecommunications Lab. 1968–70; Sr Research Fellow, later Prof. Fellow, ANU 1971–79, Chair. Optical Physics and Visual Sciences Inst. for Advanced Studies 1978–, Head Applied Math. 1979–82, Founder and Head Optical Sciences Centre 1983–, Foundation Dir Centre for the Mind 1997, Peter Karmel Professorial Chair of Science and the Mind 1998–; Aniv Prof. of Science and the Mind, Univ. of Sydney 2000–; NSF Fellowship, Dept of Applied Physics, Yale Univ. Medical School, USA 1970–71; Guggenheim Fellow 1977, Foundation Fellow, Nat. Vision Research Inst. of Australia 1983, Royal Soc. Quest Research Fellow, Univ. of Cambridge, UK 1987; 150th Anniversary Chair of Science and the Mind, Univ. of Sydney; Assoc. Ed. Journal of Optical Soc. of America 1981–83; Clifford Patterson Lecturer, Royal Soc., London 2001; Research Medal, Royal Soc. of Vic. 1974, Thomas Rankin Lyle Medal, Australian Acad. of Science 1985, Edgeworth David Medal, Royal Soc. of NSW, Sutherland Memorial Medal, Australian Acad. of Technological Sciences 1991, CSIRO Research Medal 1995, Harrie Massey Medal and Prize, British Inst. of Physics 1996, Arthur E. Mills Oration and Medal, RACP 1966, Int. Australia Prize 1997, Marconi Int. Fellowship and Prize 2001, Centenary Medal 2003. *Publications include:* Photoreceptors Optics (jtly) 1975, Optical Waveguide Sciences (jtly) 1983, Optical Waveguide Theory (jtly) 1983, What Makes a Champion! (ed.). *Leisure interests:* art, thought and mind. *Address:* Centre for Mind, Main Quadrangle (A14), University of Sydney, Sydney, NSW 2006, Australia (office). *Telephone:* (2) 6125-2626 (office); (2) 9351-8531 (office). *Fax:* (2) 6125-

5184 (office); (2) 9351-8534 (office). *E-mail:* allan@centreforthemind.com (office). *Website:* www.centreforthemind.com (office).

SNYDER, Barbara, BA, JD; American lawyer, academic and university administrator; *President, Case Western Reserve University;* b. 23 July 1955; m. Michael Snyder; two s. one d.; ed Ohio State Univ., Univ. of Chicago Law School; called to the Bar in Illinois 1980; Legal Clerk, US Court of Appeals for Seventh Circuit, Chicago 1980–82; with Sidley & Austin (law firm), Chicago –1983; Asst Prof., Case Western Reserve School of Law, Cleveland 1983–86, Assoc. Prof. 1986–88, Pres. Case Western Reserve Univ. 2007–; Assoc. Prof., Moritz Coll. of Law, Ohio State Univ. 1988–90, Prof. 1990–2000, Joanne W. Murphy Prof. 2000–07, Interim Exec. Vice Pres. and Provost Ohio State Univ. 2003–04, Exec. Vice Pres. and Provost 2004–07; mem. American Law Inst. 2007–; Moritz Coll. of Law Outstanding Professor Award 1997. *Publications:* co-author: Ohio Evidence 1996, The Ohio Rules of Evidence Handbook (annual 1996–2005). *Address:* Office of the President, Case Western Reserve University, 10900 Euclid Avenue, Cleveland, OH 44106-7001, USA (office). *Telephone:* (216) 368-4344 (office). *Fax:* (216) 368-4325 (office). *E-mail:* barbara.snyder@case.edu (office). *Website:* www.case.edu/president (office).

SNYDER, Richard E.; American publisher; b. 6 April 1933, New York; s. of Jack Snyder and Molly Rothman; m. 1st Otilie Freund 1963 (divorced); one s. one d.; m. 2nd Laura Yorke 1992; two s; ed Tufts Univ., Medford; sales rep. Simon & Schuster 1961, Vice-Pres. Marketing 1966–69, Vice-Pres. Trade Books 1969–73, Exec. Vice-Pres. Trade and Educ. Admin 1973–75, Pres. and COO 1975–78, Pres. and CEO 1978–86, Chair. and CEO 1986–94, consultant 1994–95; Chair., CEO Golden Books Family Entertainment 1996–2001; Chair. PEN, NY Area 1988; Dir Reliance Group Holdings, Children's Blood Foundation; Trustee NY Presbyterian Hosp.; Founder-mem. Nat. Book Foundation, Nat. Book Awards; mem. Council on Foreign Relations, Wildlife Conservation Soc., Econ. Club of NY.

SO, Augusto Ussumane; Guinea-Bissau politician; ed in USA; Minister, Ministry of Economy and Finance 2002–07; Pres. Asscn of Guineans, Bissau. *Address:* c/o Ministry of the Economy and Finance, CP 67, Avda 3 de Agosto, Bissau, Guinea-Bissau (office).

SO, Rt Hon. the Lord Mayor John; Australian business executive and politician; *Lord Mayor of the Melbourne City Council;* ed Univ. of Melbourne; fmr JP; Councillor, City of Melbourne 1991–96, 1999–2001; Lord Mayor of Melbourne City Council 2001–; mem. Cttee for Melbourne Bd, Cancer Council Bd, Shrine of Remembrance Bd, Victorian Community Council on Crime and Violence; fmr Vice-Pres. Melbourne Chinatown Traders Asscn; Patron Melbourne Jr Chamber of Commerce. *Address:* Town Hall, 90–120 Swanston Street, Melbourne 3000, Vic., Australia (office). *Telephone:* (3) 9658-9825 (office). *Fax:* (3) 9654-2628 (office). *E-mail:* lordmayor@melbourne.vic.gov.au (office). *Website:* www.melbourne.vic.gov.au (office).

SOAMES, Nicholas; British politician; b. 12 Feb. 1948; s. of the late Baron and Lady Soames and grandson of Sir Winston Churchill; m. 1st Catherine Weatherall 1981 (divorced 1988, 2nd Serena Smith 1993; two s. one d.; ed St Aubyns, Sussex and Eton Coll.; commissioned into 11th Hussars, served in Germany and UK, subsequently Equerry to HRH The Prince of Wales; worked as stockbroker 1972–74; Personal Asst to Sir James Goldsmith 1974–76; legislative asst on staff of US Senator Mark Hatfield, Washington DC 1976–78; Asst Dir Sedgwick Group 1979–81; joined firm of Lloyds Brokers as a Dir; MP (Conservative) for Crawley 1983–97, for Mid-Sussex 1997–; Parl. Sec. and Minister of Food, Ministry of Agriculture, Fisheries and Food 1992–94; Minister of State for the Armed Forces 1994–97; served on Countryside and Rights of Way Bill Cttee, Hunting Bill Cttee; fmr mem. Exec. of 1922 Committee; fmr Chair. Conservative Middle East Council; Shadow Sec. of State for Defence 2003–05; Pres. Rare Breeds Survival Trust, East Grinstead Target Shooting Club, Haywards Heath Dist Scout Council, Haywards Heath Rugby Football Club, Staplefield Cricket Club, South of England Hound Show; Vice-Pres. St Catherine's Hospice, Youth Clubs Sussex Ltd; Deputy Vice-Pres. Sussex Cattle Soc.; mem. Commonwealth War Graves Comm., Council of Nat. Trust, Council of Royal United Services Inst., Court of Univ. of Sussex, Council of the South of England Agricultural Soc., Council for the Protection of Rural England, West Sussex Design Comm., Burgess Hill Business Parks Asscn; Trustee Amber Foundation; Patron No. 24 Burgess Hill Detachment, Sussex Army Cadet Force; Hon. Pres. 172 Haywards Heath Squadron (air cadets). *Leisure interests:* reading, music, horse racing, country pursuits. *Address:* House of Commons, Westminster, London, SW1A 0AA (office); Mid-Sussex Conservative Association, 5 Hazelgrove Road, Haywards Heath, West Sussex, RH16 3PH, England (office). *Telephone:* (20) 7219-4143 (London) (office); (1444) 452590 (Haywards Heath) (office). *Fax:* (20) 7219-2998 (London) (office); (1444) 415766 (Haywards Heath) (office). *E-mail:* soamesn@parliament.uk (office); midsussexconassocn@lineone.net (office). *Website:* www.nicholassoames.org.uk (office).

SOARES, Eugénio Lourenço; São Tomé and Príncipe politician and central banker; *Vice-Governor, Banco Central de São Tomé e Príncipe;* fmr MP from Mé-Zochi; Gov. São Tomé e Príncipe, ADB; Minister of Planning and Finance 2003–04; Vice-Gov. and mem. Council of Admin, Banco Central de São Tomé e Príncipe 2006–. *Address:* Banco Central de São Tomé e Príncipe, Praça da Independência, CP 13, São Tomé, São Tomé and Príncipe (office). *Telephone:* 221300 (office). *Fax:* 222777 (office). *E-mail:* bcstp@bcstp.st (office). *Website:* www.bcstp.st (office).

SOARES, Maj. Lúcio; Guinea-Bissau politician; fmr Minister of Defence; Minister of the Interior 2009–. *Address:* Ministry of Internal Administration, Av. Unidade Africana, Bissau, Guinea-Bissau (office). *Telephone:* 203781 (office).

SOARES, Mário Alberto Nobre Lopes, LèsL, DenD; Portuguese politician, lawyer, historian and fmr head of state; *President, Mário Soares Foundation;* b. 7 Dec. 1924, Lisbon; s. of João Lopes Soares and Elisa Nobre Soares; m. Maria Barroso Soares 1949; one s. one d.; ed Univ. of Lisbon, Faculty of Law, Sorbonne, Paris; active opponent to Salazar's dictatorship; joined Anti-Facist Nat. Unity Movt 1943, f. Youth Movt of the Democratic Unity Movt 1946; mem. Presidential Candidature Cttee for Gen. Norton de Matos 1949, Gen. Humberto Delgado 1958; f. Portuguese Socialist Action 1964; deported to São Tomé March–Nov. 1968; rep. of Portuguese socialists at various European socialist congresses and 11th Congress of Socialist Int., Eastbourne, UK 1969; Portuguese rep. Int. League of Human Rights; imprisoned 12 times on political grounds; in exile in Paris 1970–74, returned to Portugal after coup April 1974; f. Partido Socialista 1973, Sec.-Gen. 1973–86; Vice-Pres. Socialist Int. 1976–86, Hon. Pres. 1986–; Minister of Foreign Affairs 1974–75; in charge of negotiations leading to independence of Portuguese colonies; Minister without Portfolio March–Aug. 1975; Deputy, Constituent Ass. 1975, Legis. Ass. 1976; mem. Council of State; Prime Minister of Portugal 1976–78, 1983–85; initiated negotiations in 1977 leading to Portugal joining EC, as Prime Minister signed Treaty of Accession June 1985; Leader of the Opposition 1978–83; Pres. of Portugal 1986–96; mem. European Parl. 1999–2005; Pres. Ind. World Comm. on the Oceans 1995–98, Portugal Africa Foundation 1997–, European Movt 1997–99 (Hon. Pres. 1999–), Steering Cttee World Water Contract 1997–, Cttee of Experts of the Council of Europe 1997–98, IPS Inter Press Int., Rome 2001–07, Inter-Parl. Del. for Relations with Israel 2002, Comm. for Religious Freedom 2007; Founder and Pres. Soares Foundation 1996–; mem. Club of Rome 1998, Euroamerica Foundation 1999–, Gen. Foundation of Salamanca Univ. 2000, Acad. of Latinity, Rio de Janeiro 2000, Foro Mundial de Redes, Barcelona 2001, Club of Madrid 2001, Club of Monaco 2002, World Political Forum 2002, Green Cross Int. 2003, Grupo de Biarritz 2003, Nat. Org. for the Blind, Madrid, Groupement d'etudes et de Recherches: Notre Europe (UNESCO), Peres Centre for Peace, Tel Aviv, Int. Project XXI Century: A Century of Global Challenges (Gorbachev Foundation); fmr Pres. Council of Europe; State Councillor; Corresp. mem. Portuguese Soc. of Writers, Lisbon Acad. of Sciences; mem. Academia Brasileira de Letras, Acad. of the Kingdom of Morocco, Marine Acad. of France, Overseas Acad. of Sciences, France; Dr hc (Rennes, Hankuk, Lancaster, São Paulo, Brown, Salamanca, Princeton, Bologna, Turin, Sorbonne, Univ. Libre Bruxelles, Oxon., Leicester); Joseph Lemaire Prize 1975, Int. Prize of Human Rights 1977, Robert Schuman Prize 1987, Prince of Asturias Prize 1995, "Together" Prize of the Peace Foundation (Rome) 1997, Louis Weiss Prize 1997, Adolph Bentinck Prize 1997, Int. Simón Bolivar Prize 1998, Pres.'s Medal, George Washington Univ. 1998, Stresemann Inst. Gold Medal 1999, Guy Trophy 2000, Univ. of California, Berkeley Gold Medal 2000, Schuman Foundation Honour Medal 2000, North-South Prize 2000, Roma per il Dialogo Prize 2001, Int. Special Press Prize 2001, Troféu Latino Prize 2005, Latinity Prize 2005, Portuguese Parl. Gold Medal for Human Rights 2008. *Publications:* As ideias político-sociais de Teófilo Braga 1950, Escritos Políticos 1969, Portugal's Struggle for Liberty 1972, Destruir o Sistema, Construir uma Vida Nova 1973, Caminho Difícil, do Salazarismo ao Caetanismo 1973, Escritos do Exílio 1975, Liberdade para Portugal (with Willy Brandt and Bruno Kreisky) 1975, Portugal, quelle Révolution? 1976, O Futuro será o Socialismo Democrático 1979, Resposta Socialista para o Mundo em Crise 1983, Persistir 1983, A Árvore e a Floresta 1985, Intervenções Vols I–VI 1987–92, Vols VII–VIII 1994, Moderador e Árbitro 1995, Democracia 1996, O Presidente 1996, Dois anos depois 1998, O mundo em português: um diálogo (with Pres. Fernando Henrique Cardoso) 1998, Português e Europeu 2000, Porto Alegre e Nova Iorque: um mundo dividido? 2002, Mémoire Vivante 2002, A Incerteza dos Tempos 2003, Incursões Literárias 2003, Um Mundo Inquietante 2003, Diálogo de Gerações (with Sérgio Sousa Pinto) 2004, Os Poemas da Minha Vida 2004, A Crise. E agora? 2005, O Que Falta Dizer 2005, Um Diálogo Ibérico no Contexto Europeu e Mundial (with Federico Mayor Zaragoza); contribs. to República, Seara Nova, Ibéria (New York) etc. *Leisure interests:* books and collecting contemporary Portuguese paintings. *Address:* Rua Dr João Soares, 2-3, 1600 Lisbon, Portugal (home). *Website:* www .fmsoares.pt (office).

SOARES ALVES, Francisco José, MA; Portuguese archaeologist; b. 18 April 1942, Lisbon; s. of José Augusto Ferreira Alves and Margaret Hellen Libbie Mason Soares; m. (divorced) João Gachet Alves; ed D. João de Castro High School, Lisbon, Univ. of Paris, DEA—Institut d'Art et d'Archéologie, Paris; Prof. of Nautical and Underwater Archaeology, Universidade Nova de Lisboa, Faculdade de Ciências Sociais e Humanas; Dir archaeological campus, Braga (Bracara Augusta) 1976–80; Dir Portuguese Dept of Archaeology 1980–82; Dir Nat. Museum of Archaeology 1980–96; Dir Portuguese Centre for Underwater and Nautical Archaeology 1997–2007; Dir of underwater archaeology on the sites of L'Océan (French flagship sunk in 1759) 1984, 15th Century shipwreck Ria de Aveiro A 1996–99, Senhora dos Mártires shipwreck (Indiaman lost in Tagus bar 1606) 1997–1998, Lima river dugouts (3rd century BC) 2003, Colab of the rescue of the 16th century Portuguese Oranjemund, Namibia shipwreck 2008; Franco Papo Award, 8th Rassegna di Archeologia, Italy. *Leisure interest:* diving. *Address:* c/o Instituto Português de Arqueologia, Avenida da Índia 136, 1300 300 Lisbon, Portugal (office). *E-mail:* fa.cnans@ipa.min-cultura.pt.

SOBEL, Clifford M.; American business executive and diplomatist; *Ambassador to Brazil;* m. Barbara Sobel; two s. one d.; ed Univ. of Vermont and New York Univ. School of Commerce; f. Norcrown Bank of Roseland, NJ, mem. Bd 1985–91; Chair. Net2Phone –2001; Amb. to the Netherlands 2001–06, to Brazil 2006–; Co-Chair. ADIR; Chair. and Pres. SJJ Investment Corpn, CMS Realty Co.; mem. US Govt Industry Sector Int. Trade Bd 1987–89, US Holocaust Memorial Council 1994–98; mem. Bd New Jersey Performing Arts

Center, Lexington Inst.; mem. Council of American Ambs; fmr Chair. Bd of Overseers, Alexis de Tocqueville Inst.; mem. Advisory Bd Empower America, Bd Business Execs for Nat. Security; Dr hc (Kean Univ.) 1999; ICT (Information and Communication Tech.) Personality of the Year Award 2004. *Address:* Embassy of USA, SES Avenida das Nações, Quadra 801, Lote 03, 70403-900 Brasilia, DF, Brazil (office). *Telephone:* (61) 3312-7000 (office). *Fax:* (61) 3225-9136 (office). *E-mail:* ircbsb@state.gov (office). *Website:* brasilia.usembassy.gov (office).

SOBEL, Dava; American science writer; b. 1947; m. 1st Arthur Klein (divorced); one s. one d.; m. 2nd Alfonso Triggiani; ed State Univ. of NY at Binghamton; fmr science reporter, New York Times; reported for several journals including Audubon, Discover, Life, The New Yorker; fmr Contributing Ed. Harvard Magazine; has lectured at The Smithsonian Inst., The Explorers Club, NASA Goddard Space Flight Center, Folger Shakespeare Library, Los Angeles Public Library, NY Public Library, Royal Geographical Soc. (London); numerous radio and TV appearances; mem. American Asscn of Univ. Women, Planetary Soc.; Fellow, American Geographical Soc.; Hon. DLit (Middlebury Coll., Vt) 2002, (Bath, UK) 2002; Nat. Media Award American Psychological Foundation 1980, Lowell Thomas Award Soc. of American Travel Writers 1992, Gold Medal Council for the Advancement and Support of Educ. 1994, Christopher Award 1999, Los Angeles Times Book Prize 2000, Nat. Science Bd Public Service Award 2001, Bradford Washburn Award Boston Museum of Science 2001, Nathaniel Bowditch Maritime Scholar 2003, Harrison Medal, Worshipful Co. of Clockmakers (UK) 2004. *Publications:* Is Anyone Out There? The Scientific Search for Extraterrestrial Intelligence (with Frank D. Drake) 1992, Longitude (several awards including Harold D. Vursell Memorial Award American Acad. of Arts and Letters 1996, UK Book of the Year 1996, Prix Faubert du Coton, Premio del Mare Circeo) 1995, Galileo's Daughter: A Historical Memoir of Science, Faith, and Love 1999, Letters to Father 2001, The Planets 2005. *Address:* c/o Michael Carlisle, InkWell Management, 521 Fifth Avenue, 26th Floor, New York, NY 10175, USA (office). *Telephone:* (212) 922-3500 (office).

SOBERANES FERNÁNDEZ, José Luis, LicenDer, LLD; Mexican lawyer and academic; *President, Comisión Nacional de los Derechos Humanos (National Commission for Human Rights);* b. 10 Jan. 1950, Santiago de Querétaro, Querétaro; ed law degree from Universidad Nacional Autónoma de México (UNAM), Universidad de Valencia, Spain; Sec.-Gen. Latin American univs' asscn 1985–90; Dir Instituto de Investigaciones Jurídicas, UNAM 1990–98, full-time researcher at UNAM; Prof., Nat. Univ. of San Marcos (Peru); Visiting Prof. of the Social Sciences, Univ. of Toulouse, France; apptd by Congress Pres. Comisión Nacional de los Derechos Humanos (Nat. Comm. for Human Rights) 1999–; Academician and fmr Fellow, Royal Acad. of Jurisprudence, Spain; an expert on the origins of the Supreme Court in Mexico, religion and the law, and the colonial judicial system; Great Cross of San Raimundo de Peñafort (Spain). *Publications:* more than 20 books, including Los tribunales de la Nueva España 1980, Sobre el origen de la Suprema Corte de Justicia de la Nación 1987, Historia del sistema jurídico mexicano 1990, Los bienes eclesiásticos en la historia constitucional de México 1999; numerous papers in academic journals. *Address:* Edificio 'Héctor Fix Zamudio', Blvd Adolfo López Mateos 1922, 6° piso, Col. Tlacopac San Ángel, Delegación Álvaro Obregón, CP 01040, Mexico City, Mexico (office). *Telephone:* (55) 1719-2000 (office). *E-mail:* info@cndh.org.mx (office). *Website:* www.cndh.org.mx (office).

SOBERÓN VALDÉS, Francisco, PhD; Cuban politician; *Minister-President, Central Bank of Cuba;* b. 18 April 1945; fmr Prof. of Social Sciences and Econ. Planning; Founder and Leader, Unión de jóvenes Party (UJC) 1962–64; mem. Cen. Cttee CP Party of Cuba 1970–; Deputy in Nat. Ass. of People's Power; Minister-Pres. Nat. Bank of Cuba (became Cen. Bank of Cuba 1997) 1995–. *Address:* Banco Central de Cuba, Calle Cuba, No 402, Aguiar 411, Habana Vieja, Havana, Cuba (office). *Telephone:* (7) 866-8003 (office). *Fax:* (7) 866-6601 (office). *E-mail:* plascncia@bc.gov.cu (office). *Website:* www.bc.gov.cu (office).

SOBERS, Sir Garfield (Gary) St Aubrun, Kt; Barbadian fmr cricketer; b. 28 July 1936, St Michael; s. of Thelma Sobers and Shamont Sobers; m. Prudence Kirby 1969 (divorced 1985); two s. one d.; ed Bay St School, Barbados; left-hand batsman, left-arm bowler, using all kinds of bowling; outstanding all-rounder; teams: Barbados 1952–74 (Capt. 1965–71), S Australia 1961–64, Notts. 1968–74 (Capt. 1968–71, 1973); 93 Tests for W Indies 1953–74, 39 as Capt., scoring 8,032 runs (average 57.7) with 26 hundreds, including record 365 not out (record 1958–94), taking 235 wickets (average 34.0) and holding 109 catches; scored 28,315 runs (86 hundreds), took 1,043 wickets and held 407 catches in first-class cricket; hit 6 sixes in an over, Notts. v. Glamorgan at Swansea 1968; toured England 1957, 1963, 1966, 1969, 1973; Special Consultant Barbados Tourism Authority 1980; apptd tech. consultant to West Indies cricket coach 2004; Hon. Life mem. MCC 1981; Order of the Caribbean Community 1998; Wisden Cricketer of the Year 1964, Barbados National Hero 1998. *Publications:* Cricket Advance 1965, Cricket Crusader 1966, King Cricket 1967 (with J. S. Barker), Cricket in the Sun (with J. S. Barker) 1967, Bonaventure and the Flashing Blade 1967, Sobers: Twenty Years at the Top 1988, Sobers: The Changing Face of Cricket (with Ivo Tennant) 1995. *Leisure interest:* golf. *Address:* 23 Highgate Gardens, St Michael, Barbados (home).

SOBIROV, Ilgizar Matiakubovich, CandIur; Uzbekistani politician; *Chairman of the Senate;* b. 20 Feb. 1959, Urtaiap Kushkupir dist, Khorezm Prov.; ed Law Faculty, Tashkent State Univ.; began career as mem. law collective, Kurshkupir dist; completed mil. service 1980; carried out pedagogical work in criminal law 1986–94; apptd Pro-Rector Tashkent Legal Inst. 1994; then legal worker, Philosophy and Law Inst., Uzbek Acad. of Sciences; then worked in Supreme Court, later as Plenum Sec. and mem. Supreme Econ. Court; directed prov. admin of justice in Khorezm Prov.; Deputy, Oliy Majlis

2000–03, Deputy Chair. Cttee on Questions of Defence and Security, then Chair. Cttee on Legislation and Legal Questions; Hokim of Kushkupir dist, Khorezm Prov. 2003–05; elected Senator 2005–, Chair. Cttee on Questions of Defence and Security, Chair. Senate 2006–. *Address:* Office of the Chairman of the Senate, 100029 Tashkent, Mustaqillik maydoni 6, Uzbekistan (office). *Telephone:* (71) 238-26-66 (office). *Fax:* (71) 238-29-01 (office). *E-mail:* info@senat.uz (office). *Website:* www.senat.uz (office).

SOBOTKA, Bohuslav, BLL; Czech lawyer and politician; b. 23 Oct. 1971, Telnice nr Brno; ed Masaryk Univ., Brno; mem. Czech Social Democrats—CSSD 1989–, Chair. Deputies Club 2001–02; mem. Parl. 1996–2002, 2002–06, 2006–; mem. Mandate (Proxy) and Immunity Cttee 1996–98; Chair. Sub Cttee for Financial and Capital Markets, Budget Cttee 1998–2001; mem. Municipal Council of Slavkov, nr Brno 1998–; Chair. Interim Comm. for Pension Reform 2001; Minister of Finance 2002–06; First Deputy Prime Minister 2005–06. *Leisure interests:* history, literature, science fiction, film, travel. *Address:* Czech Social Democratic Party, Lidový dům, Hybernská 7, 110 00 Prague 1, Czech Republic (office). *Telephone:* 296522111 (office). *Fax:* 224222190 (office). *E-mail:* info@bohuslavsobotka.cz (home); info@socdem.cz (office). *Website:* www.bohuslavsobotka.cz (home); www.socdem.cz (office).

SOBOTKA, Přemysl, MUDr; Czech doctor and politician; *Chairman, Senát (Senate);* b. 18 May 1944, Mladá Boleslav; s. of Zdeněk Sobotka and Eliška Sobotka; ed Charles Univ., Prague; physician 1968–; councillor, Liberec 1990–96; Chief Physician, Hosp. Liberec 1990–98; mem. Civic Democratic Party (Občanská demokratická strana—ODS); Senator, Vice-Chair. of Senát (Senate) 1996–2002, Chair. 2004–, mem. Cttee on Agenda and Procedure, Sub-cttee on Bestowing Decorations, Civic Democratic Party Caucus. *Publications:* papers in medical journals. *Leisure interests:* tennis, volleyball, travel. *Address:* Senát PČR, Valdštejnské nám. 4, 11801 Prague 1 (office); Nezvaolova 658, 460 16 Liberec, Czech Republic (home). *Telephone:* (2) 57072331 (office); (6) 02348371 (home). *Fax:* (2) 57534509 (office). *E-mail:* sobotkap@senat.cz (office). *Website:* www.mfcr.cz (office); www.premyslsobotka.cz.

SOBYANIN, Sergei Semenovich, PhD; Russian politician; *Deputy Chairman of the Government (Deputy Prime Minister);* b. 21 June 1958, Nyaksumvol, Beryozovsky Dist, Khanty-Mansii Autonomous Okrug; m. Irina Sobyanina; two d.; ed Kostroma State Inst. of Tech.; metalworker and then foreman at Chelyabinsk Pipe Plant 1980–82; Head of Admin. Dept Leninskii Dist Komsomol, Chelyabinsk 1982–84; party and admin. work in Khanty-Mansii Autonomous Okrug, Tyumen Region 1984–90; Head of State Tax Inspection Office, Kogalym in Khanty-Mansii Autonomous Okrug 1990–91; Mayor of Kogalym 1991–93; First Deputy Head Khanty-Mansii Autonomous Okrug 1993–94; Chair. Khanty-Mansii Autonomous Okrug Duma, mem. Fed. Council and Chair. Fed. Council Cttee on Constitutional Legislation and Judicial-Legal Matters 1994–2000; First Deputy to Presidential Plenipotentiary Envoy in Urals Fed. Dist 2000–01; Gov. of Tyumen Region 2001–05; Chief of Staff, Presidential Exec. Office 2005–08; Deputy Chairman of the Govt, in charge of co-ordinating Fed. Agencies 2008–; Chair. Bd of Dirs TVEL (state nuclear power co.) 2006–; Order of Merit, Medal For Services to the Fatherland (Second Degree), Church Second Stage Order of St Kniaz Danil Moscowskiy, Medal of Honour in Educ., Ordre du Mérite Agricole (France) 2003; Russia's Man of the Year: Politician Prize 2003. *Address:* Office of the Government, 103274 Moscow, Krasnopresnenskaya nab. 2, Russia (office). *Telephone:* (495) 205-57-35 (office). *Fax:* (495) 205-42-19 (office). *Website:* www.government.ru (office).

SÓCRATES CARVALHO PINTO DE SOUSA, José; Portuguese politician; *Prime Minister;* b. 6 Sept. 1957, Vilar de Maçada; divorced; two c.; Chair. Castelo Branco Fed., Partido Socialista (Socialist Party) 1983–96, mem. Partido Socialista Secr. 1991–, Spokesperson on Environmental Affairs 1991–95, Sec.-Gen. 2004–; mem. Parl. 1987–95; mem. Covilha Municipal Ass. 1989–96; Deputy Minister to the Prime Minister 1995–99; Minister of Environmental Affairs 1999–2002; mem. Parl. Comm. on National Defence 2002–; Prime Minister of Portugal 2005–; Pres. World Conf. of Ministers Responsible for Youth 1998. *Address:* Office of the Prime Minister, Presidency of the Council of Ministers, Rua da Imprensa á Estrela 4, 1200-888 Lisbon; Partido Socialista, Largo do Rato 2, 1269-143 Lisbon, Portugal (office). *Telephone:* (213) 923500 (office); (21) 3822000 (office). *Fax:* (21) 3822016 (office). *E-mail:* relacoes.publicas@pcm.gov.pt (office); info@ps.pt (office). *Website:* www.portugal.gov.pt (office); www.ps.pt (office).

SODANO, HE Cardinal Angelo, STD, JCD; Italian ecclesiastic; *Dean, College of Cardinals, Roman Curia;* b. 23 Nov. 1927, Isola d'Asti; s. of Hon. Giovanni Sodano and Delfina Brignolo; ed Pontifical Gregorian Univ., Rome, Pontifical Lateran Univ., Rome and Pontifical Ecclesiastical Acad., Rome; ordained priest, Asti 1950; Sec. Apostolic Nunciatures in Ecuador, Uruguay and Chile 1961–68; official, Council for Public Affairs of Church, Vatican City State 1968–77; apptd Titular Archbishop of Nova Caesaris 1977; Apostolic Nuncio to Chile 1978–88; Sec. Council for Public Affairs of the Church 1988–89; Sec. for Relations with States of Secr. of State 1989–90; Pro-Sec. of State to His Holiness Pope John Paul II 1990–91; cr. Cardinal-Priest of S. Maria Nuova 1991; Sec. of State 1991–2005 (resgnd), re-apptd 2005–06 (resgnd); apptd Cardinal-Bishop of Albano 1994–, Cardinal-Bishop of Ostia 2005–; mem. Congregations for the Doctrine of the Faith, for the Bishops, Pontifical Comm. for Vatican City State; Vice-Dean Coll. of Cardinals 2002–05, Dean 2005–; numerous honours and awards. *Address:* 00120 Vatican City, Rome, Italy (office).

SØDERBERG, Jess, MBA; Danish business executive; b. 1944; ed Copenhagen Business School; joined A.P. Møller 1970, various positions finance in USA and Denmark, Pnr 1986–93, Pnr and Group CEO A.P. Møller-Mærsk A/S 1993–2007; Vice-Chair. Mærsk Olie og Gas A/S 2004; Chair. Dansk Supermarked A/S, F. Salling A/S, Ejendomsaktieselskabet; mem. Advisory Council, Danske Bank; Kt, Order of Dannebrog, Order of Bernardo O'Higgins (Chile). *Address:* c/o A.P. Møller-Mærsk A/S, Esplanaden 50, 1098 Copenhagen K, Denmark (office).

SODERBERG, Nancy E., BA, MS; American academic, international organization official, fmr diplomatist and fmr government official; *Distinguished Visiting Scholar, Department of Political Science and Public Administration, University of North Florida;* b. 13 March 1958, San Turce, Puerto Rico; d. of Lars Olof Soderberg and Nancy Soderberg (née MacGilvrey); ed Vanderbilt Univ., Georgetown Univ. School of Foreign Service; budget and reports analyst, Bank of New England, Boston 1980–82; Research Asst Brookings Inst., Washington, DC 1982–83; Research Asst, US Agency for Int. Devt, Washington, DC 1983; Del. Selection Asst, Mondale-Ferraro Cttee, Washington, DC 1983, Foreign Policy Adviser 1984 (unsuccessful US presidential camgaign); Deputy Issues Dir, Foreign Policy, Dukakis for Pres. Cttee, Boston 1988; Foreign Policy Adviser to Senator Edward Kennedy, Washington, DC 1985–88, 1989–92; Foreign Policy Dir Clinton/Gore Transition, Little Rock 1992–93; Special Asst to Pres. for Nat. Security Affairs, Staff Dir Nat. Security Council, Washington, DC 1993–95, Deputy Asst to Pres. for Nat. Security Affairs 1995–2001; Alt. Rep. to UN with rank of Amb. 1997–2001; Vice-Pres. (Multilateral Affairs), Int. Crisis Group, New York 2001–05; Distinguished Visiting Scholar, Univ. of North Fla, Jacksonville 2006–; Adjunct Prof. Columbia Univ. School of Int. and Public Affairs 2004; foreign policy analyst for MSNBC; mem. Council for Foreign Relations; mem. Bd of Dirs Concern Worldwide; mem. Advisory Bd Nat. Cttee on American Foreign Policy, Tannenbaum Center; Pres. Sister Cities Program of the City of New York 2002–06. *Publications:* The Superpower Myth: The Use and Misuse of American Might 2005; numerous articles in professional journals. *Address:* 121 Lantern Wick Place, Ponte Vedra Beach, FL 32082; University of North Florida, Department of Political Science and Public Administration, Jacksonville, FL 32224-2645, USA. *Telephone:* (904) 620-3926; (904) 620-1000 (office). *E-mail:* nsoderberg@aol.com; n00445553@unf.edu (office). *Website:* www.unf.edu/coas/polsci-pubadmin (office).

SODERBERGH, Steven; American film director and film producer; b. 14 Jan. 1963, Atlanta; s. of Peter Andrew Soderbergh and Mary Ann Bernard; m. Elizabeth Jeanne Brantley 1989 (divorced 1994); ed high school and animation course at Louisiana State Univ.; aged 15 made short film Janitor; briefly ed. Games People Play (TV show); made short film Rapid Eye Movement while working as coin-changer in video arcade; produced video for Showtime for their album 90125; co–founder Section Eight Productions 2001-07; signed six-film deal with 2929 Entertainment, releasing films simultaneously in cinemas, on DVD and on cable television 2005–. *Films:* Winston (dir, screenplay) 1987, Sex, Lies and Videotape (dir, screenplay) (Cannes Palme d'Or) 1989, Kafka (dir) 1991, King of the Hill (dir, screenplay) 1993, Suture (exec. prod.) 1993, Underneath (dir, screenplay) 1995, Gray's Anatomy (dir) 1996, Schizopolis (dir, screenplay) 1996, The Daytrippers (prod.) 1996, Nightwatch (screenplay) 1997, Pleasantville (prod.) 1998, Out of Sight (dir) 1998, The Limey (dir) 1999, Erin Brockovich (dir) 2000, Traffic (dir) (Acad. Award for Best Dir) 2000, Ocean's Eleven (dir) 2001, Who is Bernard Tapie? (exec. prod.) 2001, Tribute (exec. prod.) 2001, Welcome to Collinwood (prod.) 2002, Far from Heaven (exec. prod.) 2002, Naqoyqatsi (exec. prod.) 2002, Confessions of a Dangerous Mind (exec. prod.) 2002, Insomnia (exec. prod.) 2002, Full Frontal (dir) 2002, Solaris (dir, screenplay) 2002, Criminal (screenplay) 2004, Eros (dir, screenplay) 2004, Ocean's Twelve (dir) 2004, Able Edwards (exec. prod.) 2004, Criminal (prod.) 2004, Keane (prod.) 2004, Bubble (dir, prod.) 2005, The Big Empty (exec. prod.) 2005, The Jacket (prod.) 2005, Good Night and Good Luck (exec. prod.) 2005, Rumor Has It (exec. prod.) 2005, Syriana (prod.) 2005, A Scanner Darkly (exec. prod.) 2006, The Half Life of Timofey Berezin (prod.) 2006, The Good German (dir, prod.) 2006, Wind Chill (exec. prod.) 2007, Ocean's Thirteen (exec. prod.) 2007, Che 2008. *Television as Director:* Fallen Angels (episode, The Quiet Room) 1993, K Street (series, also exec. prod.) 2003, Unscripted (series pilot episode, also exec. prod.) 2005. *Address:* c/o Dollard Management & Productions, 21361 Pacific Coast Highway, #3, Malibu, CA 90265, USA.

SÖDERSTROM, Elisabeth Anna; Swedish singer (soprano); b. 7 May 1927, Stockholm; m. Sverker Olow 1950; three s.; studied singing under Andrejewa de Skilonz and Opera School, Stockholm; engaged at Royal Opera, Stockholm 1950–; appearances at Salzburg 1955, Glyndebourne 1957, 1959, 1961, 1963, 1964, 1979, Metropolitan Opera, New York 1959, 1960, 1962, 1963, 1983, 1984, 1986, 1987, 1999; frequent concert and TV appearances in Europe and USA; toured USSR 1966; Artistic Dir Drottningholm Court Theatre 1993–97; Hon. mem. RAM, Hon. Prof. 1996; Singer of the Court (Sweden) 1959; Hon. CBE; Stelle della Solidarietà dell'Italia; Commdr of the Order of Vasa 1973, Commdr des Arts et Lettres 1986; Prize for Best Acting, Royal Swedish Acad. 1965, 'Litteris et Artibus' Award 1969, Ingmar Bergman Award 1988. *Recordings include:* complete Rachmaninov songs with Vladimir Ashkenazy, Janáček's operas Katya Kabanova, Jenufa and the Makropoulos Case conducted by Sir Charles Mackerras. *Roles include:* Fiordiligi in Così fan tutte, Countess and Susanna in Figaro, Countess in Capriccio, Christine in Intermezzo; sang three leading roles in Der Rosenkavalier 1959. *Publications:* I Min Tonart 1978, Sjung ut Elisabeth 1986. *Leisure interests:* sailing, literature, embroidery. *Address:* Drottningholms Slottsteater, Box 15417, 10465 Stockholm (office); Hersbyvägen 19, 18142 Lidingo, Sweden. *Telephone:* (8) 765-22-89 (home). *Fax:* (8) 566-931-01.

SOEHARTO (see **SUHARTO**).

SÕERD, Aivar; Estonian business executive and fmr government official; *Managing Director, Tallink Hotels;* b. 22 Nov. 1964; pnr; two s.; ed Univ. of Tartu, Univ. of Oulu; Dir of Tartu Agency, AS Eesti Kindlustus 1990–93; Acting Head of Tax Policy Dept, Ministry of Finance 1993–96; Acting, then Perm. Gen. Dir Estonian Tax Bd 1996–2004; CEO AS Vaba Maa 2004; Minister of Finance 2005–07, also Gov. of EIB for Estonia; Man. Dir Tallink Hotels 2007–; Order of The White Star (Fourth Class) 2003; The Global Finance Minister of the Year (Financial Times Group magazine The Banker Award) 2007. *Leisure interests:* classical music, jogging, sauna club. *Address:* AS Tallink Grupp, Tartu mnt. 13, 10145 Tallinn, Estonia (office). *Telephone:* 640-9800 (office). *Fax:* 640-9810 (office). *E-mail:* info@tallink.ee (office). *Website:* www.tallink.ee (office).

SOEUF, Mohamed El Amine; Comoran diplomatist; Amb. to Egypt 1995–98; Minister of State, Minister of Foreign Affairs, Co-operation, Francophone Affairs, with Responsibility for Comorans Abroad 1999-2005; Deputy Union Ass. 2004; Perm. Rep. to UN, New York 2006; living in exile in Paris since 2006. *Publication:* Les Comores en mouvement 2008. *Address:* c/o Les éditions De La Lune, 11, rue de Bretagne, 92300, Levallois-Perret, France.

SOEWANDI, Rini Mariani Soemarno, BEcons; Indonesian politician and financial executive; b. 9 June 1958, Bethesda, Md., USA; m. Didik Soewandi; three c.; ed Wellesley Coll., Mass, USA; with Departemen Keuangan AS 1981; trainee, US Treasury Dept, Washington, DC 1991–82; economist, Citibank 1982–89; Gen. Man. Finance Div. Astra Int. (car assembler) 1989, Dir 1990–98, Exec. Dir 1990–2000; Commr Jakarta Stock Exchange 1995–2001; Deputy Chair. Indonesian Banking Restructuring Agency 1998; fmr Econ. Adviser to Minister of Finance; Minister of Industry and Trade 2001–04; mem. Bd of Dirs Komisaris Bank Universal 1990, United Tractors 1993, Astra Agro Lestari 1995, Agrakom 2000, Citra Motorindo 2000. *Address:* c/o Ministry of Industry and Trade, Jalan Jenderal Gatot Subroto, Kav. 52–53, 2nd Floor, Jakarta Selatan, Indonesia (office).

SOFAER, Abraham David, LLD; American lawyer, judge and academic; *George P. Shultz Senior Fellow in Foreign Policy and National Security Affairs, Hoover Institution, Stanford University;* b. 6 May 1938, Bombay, India; m. Marian Bea Scheuer 1977; five s. one d.; ed Yeshiva Coll. and New York Univ.; called to New York Bar 1965; law clerk, US Court of Appeals 1965–66, to Hon. J. Skelly and Hon. William J. Brennan, Jr, US Supreme Court 1966–67; Asst US Attorney, South Dist, New York 1967–69; Prof. of Law, Columbia Univ. 1969–79; Judge, US Dist Court for South Dist, New York 1979–85; Legal Adviser, State Dept, Washington, DC 1985–90; Pnr, Hughes Hubbard and Reed 1991–94; George P. Shultz Distinguished Scholar, Sr Fellow, Hoover Inst., Stanford Univ. 1994–, Prof. of Law (by Courtesy), Stanford Univ. 1996–; Distinguished Service Award, US State Dept 1988. *Publications:* War, Foreign Affairs and Constitutional Power: The Origins 1976; articles in legal journals. *Address:* Hoover Institution, Stanford University, Stanford, CA 94305-6010 (office); 1200 Bryant Street, Palo Alto, CA 94301, USA (home). *Telephone:* (650) 725-3763 (office). *Fax:* (650) 723-2103 (office). *E-mail:* sofaer@hoover.stanford.edu (office). *Website:* www-hoover.stanford.edu (office).

SOGAVARE, Manasseh; Solomon Islands politician; *Leader, Social Credit Party;* b. 1954; m. Emmy Sogavare; mem. Nat. Parl. for East Choiseul 1997–, Minister of Finance 1998, Prime Minister of the Solomon Islands 2000–01, 2006–07; Leader, Social Credit Party. *Address:* Social Credit Party, c/o National Parliament, POB G19, Honiara, Solomon Islands (office).

SOGLO, Dieudonné Nicéphore, BA; Benin politician; *Honorary President, La Renaissance du Bénin (RB);* b. 29 Nov. 1934, Lomé, Togo; two c.; ed Univ. of Paris (Sorbonne) and Ecole nat. d'admin, Paris, France; fmr Inspector-Gen. of Finances, Tech. Adviser, Finance Ministry; Head Finance Dept 1963; fmr Chair. Nat. Monetary Comm., other financial insts; Gov. IMF 1964; Prime Minister of Benin 1990–91, Pres. of Benin 1991–96; Leader Parti de la Renaissance de Benin (renamed La Renaissance du Bénin), now Hon. Pres.; Mayor of Cotonou 2003–; Commander, Nat. Order of the Lion, Senegal 1986, Grand Croix, Légion d'Honneur 1995; Hon. DLitt (Clark Atlanta Univ.) 1995. *Address:* Zone Résidentielle, Lot G20, Les Cocotiers, Cotonou, Benin (home). *Telephone:* 21-32-36-76 (office). *Fax:* 21-32-40-23 (office). *E-mail:* ndsoglo@yahoo.fr (home); ndsoglo@hotmail.com (home); nicephore.soglo@wanadoo.fr (home).

SOHLMAN, Staffan A.R., BA; Swedish diplomatist and consultant; b. 21 Jan. 1937, Rome, Italy; s. of Rolf R. Sohlman and Zinaida Jarotskaja; m. Åsa Maria Carnerud 1961; one s. one d.; ed Sigtuna Humanistiska Laroverk, Washington and Lee Univ., Stockholm and Lund Univs; Nat. Inst. for Econ. Research 1962–65; Ministry of Finance 1965–68; mem. Swedish Del. to OECD 1968–70; Ministry for Foreign Affairs, Dept for Devt Co-operation 1970–75, Head Multilateral Dept 1972, Project Leader Secr. for Futures Studies 1975–77, Head Transport Div. 1977–78; Deputy Dir-Gen. Nat. Bd of Trade 1978–84; Head Multilateral Dept of Ministry for Foreign Affairs Trade Dept 1984–88; Co-ordinator for Econ. Co-operation with Cen. and Eastern Europe, Ministry for Foreign Affairs 1989–90; Dir Cen. Bank 1989; Amb., Perm. Rep. Swedish Del. to OECD 1991–95, Acting Sec.-Gen. OECD Oct.–Nov. 1994; Chair OECD Steel Cttee 1986–88, OECD Liaison Cttee with Council of Europe 1992, OECD Council Working Party on Shipbuilding 1993–95, Wassenaar Arrangement on Export Control for Conventional Arms and Dual-Use Goods and Technologies 1996–99; Amb. and Insp. Gen. of Mil. Equipment, Ministry for Foreign Affairs 1995, Amb. and Insp. Gen., Head Nat. Inspectorate of Strategic Products 1996; Amb. and Defence Co-ordinator, Ministry of Defence 2000–03; currently manages Sohlman Senior Consultants. *Publications:* Swedish Exports and Imports 1965–70, Resources, Society and the Future 1980, Swedish Defence Materials Administration 1996–2003, A Russian Family in Letters and memoirs 1886-1961. *Leisure interests:* music, art, architecture, literature. *Address:* Hornsgatan 51, 118 49 Stockholm, Sweden (home). *Telephone:* (8) 668-53-81. *E-mail:* staffan.sohlman@comhem.se (office); sasohlman@privat.utfors.se (office).

SOILIHI, Mohamed Ali; Comoran politician; *Minister of Finance, the Budget and Planning;* Gov. World Bank 1997; Minister of Finance, Economy, Budget and Home Trade 1997, of Interior Jan.–March 2002, of Finance, Economy, Planning and Employment 2002–06, of Finance, Budget and Planning 2007–. *Address:* Ministry of Finance, the Budget and Planning, BP 324, Moroni, The Comoros (office). *Telephone:* (74) 4140 (office). *Fax:* (74) 4141 (office).

SOIRON, Rolf, PhD; Swiss business executive; *Chairman, Holcim Ltd;* b. 31 Jan. 1945; ed Univ. of Basel, Harvard Business School, USA; served in several positions in human resources, finance and man. at Sandoz Group 1972–83, Group Vice-Pres. Agribusiness USA 1988–92, COO 1992–93; CEO and Pres. Protek Group 1983–88; joined Jungbunzlauer Group, Basel 1993, Man. Dir 2002–03; mem. Bd of Dirs Holcim Ltd 1994–, Chair. 2003–, Chair. Governance, Nomination and Compensation Cttee, Chair. Advisory Bd Holcim Foundation for Sustainable Construction; mem. Bd of Dirs Synthes-Stratec 1995–; Chair. Nobel Biocare 2003–, Lonza Group Ltd 2005–; Pres. (part-time) Univ. of Basel 1996–2005. *Address:* Holcim Ltd, Hagenholzstrasse 83, 8050 Zurich, Switzerland (office). *Telephone:* (58) 850-68-68 (office). *Fax:* (58) 850-68-69 (office). *E-mail:* info@holcim.com (office). *Website:* www.holcim.com (office).

SOISSON, Jean-Pierre Henri Robert, LenD; French politician; *Regional Counsellor for Burgundy;* b. 9 Nov. 1934, Auxerre; s. of Jacques Soisson and Denise Soisson (née Silve); m. Catherine Lacaisse 1961; two s.; ed Lycée Jacques-Amyot, Auxerre, Faculté de Droit, Paris, Ecole nationale d'admin; auditor, Audit Office 1961; with del. to Algeria 1961–62; Lecturer, Institute d'Études Politiques de Paris 1962–68; tech. adviser to Sec.-Gen. of Merchant Navy 1964–65, to Sec. of State for Information, later for Foreign Affairs 1966–67, to Minister of Agric. 1967–68; Conseiller référendaire, Audit Office 1968–; Deputy to Nat. Assembly for Yonne 1968–74, 1978, 1981–88, 1993–; Deputy Sec.-Gen. Fédération nationale des républicains indépendants 1969–75, Vice-Pres. 1975–78; fmr Sec.-Gen. Parti Republicain; Co. Councillor, Auxerre sud-ouest 1970–76, Mayor 1971–98; Pres. Caisse d'Aide à l'équipement des collectivités locales 1973–74; fmr Pres. parl. group for rural Devt; Sec. of State for Univs. 1974–76, for Professional Training 1976, to Minister of the Quality of Life (Youth and Sport) 1976–78; Minister for Youth, Sport and Leisure 1978–81, of Labour, Employment and Professional Training 1988–91, of State for the Civil Service and Admin. Reform 1991–92, of Agric. and Forests 1992–93; Vice-Pres., Conseil Général de l'Yonne 1982–88; Vice-Pres. Regional Council for Burgundy 1986–92, Pres. 1992–93, 1998–2004, Regional Counsellor 2004–;; Pres. Comm. de surveillance de La Caisse des dépots et consignations; Sec.-Gen. United France 1991, Mouvement des Réformateurs 1992–2002; mem. Union pour un Mouvement Populaire 2002–; Croix de la valeur militaire; Commdr du Mérite agricole, des Palmes académiques, des Arts et Lettres; Grand Cross, German Order of Merit; Officer of various foreign orders. *Publications:* Le Piège (with Bernard Stasi and Olivier Stirn) 1973, La victoire sur l'hiver 1978, L'enjeu de la formation professionnelle 1987, Mémoires d'ouverture 1990, Politique en jachère 1992, #3, Voyage en Norvège 1995, Charles le Téméraire 1997, Charles Quint 2000, Marguerite, Princesse de Bourgogne 2002, Philibert de Chalon 2005. *Leisure interests:* tennis, skiing. *Address:* Conseil Régional de Bourgogne, 17 Boulevard de la Trémouille, BP 1602, 21035, Dijon Cedex (office); Assemblée Nationale, 75355 Paris; 2 place Robillard, 89000 Auxerre, France (home). *Telephone:* (3) 80-30-30-05 (office). *E-mail:* jpsoisson@cr-bourgogne.fr (office); jpsoisson@assemblee-nationale.fr (home); jp.soisson@wanadoo.fr (home). *Website:* www.cr-bourgogne.fr (office); www.assemblee-nationale.fr (office).

SOJO GARZA-ALDAPE, Eduardo, PhD; Mexican economist, academic and government official; *Secretary of the Economy;* b. 9 Jan. 1956, León, Guanajuato; ed Monterrey Inst. of Tech. and Advanced Studies, Univ. of Pennsylvania; fmr Researcher and Prof., Monterrey Inst. of Tech. and Advanced Studies, León; has held numerous positions in Fed. Public Admin including Tech. Dir and Short-Term Statistics Dir INEGI (Nat. Geography and Statistics Inst. and Analyst Gen. Econ. and Social Policy Bureau 1979–82; Coordinator Guanajuato State Govt Econ. Cabinet during Vicente Fox Quesada admin 1995–2000; Advisors Coordinator during Fox's presidential electoral campaign, then Pres. Elect's Transition Team Econ. Coordinator –2000, Chief Econ. Advisor and Chief, Presidential Office for Public Policy 2000–06; fmr Research Analyst, Univ. of Pa Link Project. *Publications include:* Guanajuato, Century XXI Study (co-author); numerous articles in professional journals and research on combined time series and econometric modeling. *Address:* Secretariat of State for the Economy, Alfonso Reyes 30, Col. Hipódromo Condesa, 06170 México DF, Mexico (office). *Telephone:* (55) 5729-9100 (office). *Fax:* (55) 5729-9320 (office). *E-mail:* fcanales@economia.gob.mx (office). *Website:* www.economia.gob.mx (office).

SOK, An, BSc; Cambodian diplomatist and politician; *Deputy Prime Minister and Minister in Charge of the Council of Ministers;* b. 16 April 1950, Kirivong Dist, Takeiv; m. Lok Chumteav Anny Sok An; four s. one d.; ed Royal Univ. of Phnom Penh, Nat. Sr Admin. School of Diplomacy; Sec.-Gen. and Cabinet Chief, Ministry of Foreign Affairs 1981–83; Sec.-Gen. Cambodian Nat. Peace Cttee 1983–85; Amb. to India 1985–88; Sec. of State, Ministry of Foreign Affairs 1988–91, Ministry of the Interior 1991; Co-Minister, Council of Ministers 1992–98, Sr Minister 1998–2004, Deputy Prime Minister and Minister in Charge of Council of Ministers 2004–; mem. Nat. Ass. for Takeiv 1993–; mem. Cambodian People Party, Cabinet Chief, Cen. Cttee 1991; Vice-Chair. Centralist Democratic Inst.; Head of Council of Admin. Reform, Apasara Authority, Nat. Cambodia Petroleum Authority, Nat. Land Dispute Authority, Cambodia Training Bd, Royal Acad., Khmer Rouge Tribunal, State

Investment Bd on Rubber Enterprise; Hon. mem. Russian Acad. of Sciences 2002; Sena Medal, Thebdint Medal, Mohasena Medal, Mohasereyvathn Medal of Munisaraphond, Mohasereyvathn Medal of Suvathara, Cheatubkar Medal; Dr hc (Wesleyan Coll., Iowa) 1996, (Jeonú Univ., South Korea) 2005, (Kampuchea Univ.) 2006. *Address:* 70, Street 214, Sangkat Beung Rang, Khan Chamkarmom, Phnom Penh, Cambodia (office). *Telephone:* (23) 880628 (office).

SOKHONA, Sidney; Mauritanian diplomatist; *Minister in charge of Relations with Parliament and Civil Society;* b. 1952; early career as film-maker; fmr Dir Nat. Soc. of Cinema and Dir of African Soc. of Production and Distribution of Cinema; joined foreign service, held several positions including Counselor to Dir of Nouakchott Port, Adviser on Human Rights to Pres. Maaouya Ould Taya, Amb. to France (also accred to Switzerland and Portugal), State Counsellor on issues related to Human Rights and Int. Orgs; MP 2006–; currently Minister in charge of Relations with Parl. and Civil Soc.. *Films include:* Nationalité: Immigré (Nationality: Immigrant) 1974, Safrana ou le droit à la parole (Safrana or The Right to Speak) 1977, Remobe: Childhood in Mauritania 1984. *Address:* c/o Office of the President, BP 184, Nouakchott, Mauritania. *Telephone:* 525-26-36.

SOKOLOFF, Louis, MD; American physician and research scientist; *Scientist Emeritus, National Institute of Mental Health;* b. 14 Oct. 1921, Philadelphia; s. of Morris Sokoloff and Goldie Sokoloff; m. Betty Jane Kaiser 1947; one s. one d.; ed Univ. of Pennsylvania; Research Fellow, Instructor and Assoc. in Physiology and Pharmacology, Graduate School of Medicine, Univ. of Pa 1949–53; Assoc. Chief, Section on Cerebral Metabolism, Lab. of Neurochemistry, Nat. Inst. of Mental Health, Bethesda, Md 1953–56, Chief, Section on Cerebral Metabolism, Lab. of Clinical Science 1956–57, Chief 1957–68, Chief, Lab. of Cerebral Metabolism 1968–2004, Scientist Emer., Nat. Inst. of Mental Health, NIH 2004–; mem. NAS 1981, American Acad. of Arts and Sciences 1982, American Philosophical Soc. 2005; Hon. DSc (Yeshiva) 1982, (Glasgow) 1989, (Pennsylvania) 1997; Hon. ScD (Georgetown) 1992, (Mich. State) 1993; Hon. MD (Lund) 1980, (Rome) 1992; Dr hc (Philipps Univ. of Marburg) 1990; F. O. Schmitt Medal in Neuroscience 1980, Albert Lasker Clinical Medical Research Award 1981, Karl Spencer Lashley Award 1987, Distinguished Grad. Award, Univ. of Pennsylvania 1987, NAS Award in Neuroscience 1988, Cerebrovascular Disorder Research Promotion Award, Georg Charles de Hevesy Nuclear Medicine Pioneer Award 1988, Mihara 1988, Ralph Gerard Award, Soc. of Neuroscience 1996. *Publications:* The Action of Drugs on the Cerebral Circulation (Pharmacological Review 11) 1959, The [14C] Deoxyglucose Method for the Measurement of Local Cerebral Glucose Utilization: Theory, Procedure and Normal Values in the Conscious and Anaesthetized Albino Rat (Journal of Neurochemistry, Vol. 28) 1977, The Relationship Between Function and Energy Metabolism: Its Use in the Localization of Functional Activity in the Nervous System (Neurosciences Research Program Bulletin 19 (2)) 1981, Metabolic Probes of Central Nervous System Activity in Experimental Animals and Man (Magnes Lecture Series, Vol. I) 1984, Brain Imaging and Brain Function (Proceedings of the Asscn for Research in Nervous and Mental Disease, Vol. 63) 1985, Imaging of Regional Functional Activities in the Nervous System (Bulletin of the American Acad. of Arts and Scientists) 1993, Energetics of Functional Activation in Neural Tissues (Neurochemical Research) 1999. *Leisure interests:* music, tennis, literature, history, travel. *Address:* Laboratory of Cerebral Metabolism, National Institute of Mental Health, Building 36, Room 1A05, 36 Convent Drive, MSC 4030, Bethesda, MD 20892, USA (office). *Telephone:* (301) 496-1371 (office). *Fax:* (301) 480-1668 (office). *E-mail:* louissokoloff@mail.nih.gov (office). *Website:* intramural.nimh.nih.gov/research/lcm (office).

SOKOLOV, Aleksandr Sergeyevich, DFA; Russian politician and musicologist; b. 8 Aug. 1949, Leningrad; m. Larisa Sokolov; one d.; ed Moscow State Tchaikovsky Conservatory; Lecturer, Moscow State Tchaikovsky Conservatory 1977, Prof. of Musical Theory 1992, Prorector 1992–2001, Rector 2001–04; Minister of Culture and Mass Communications 2004–08; mem. Composers' Union of Russia; Order of the Hungarian Repub. with Star 2006, Order of St Sergiy Radonejsky 2006; Nat. Prize 2004. *Publications:* Music Around Us 1996, Musical Composition of the XX Century: Dialectic of Creation 2002 (Spanish trans. 2005), Introduction to the Musical Composition of the XX Century 2004. *Leisure interests:* music, hunting, tourism. *Address:* c/o Ministry of Culture and Mass Communications, Kitaigorodskii proyezd 7, build. 2, Moscow 109074, Russia (office).

SOKOLOV, Aleksandr (Sasha) Vsevolodovich; Russian writer; b. 6 Nov. 1943, Ottawa, Canada; s. of Vsevolod Sokolov and Lidia Sokolova; m. 2nd Johanna Steindl 1975; one s.; one d. from previous m.; ed Moscow Univ.; left USSR 1975 for Austria, USA, Canada, France, Greece; returned to USSR 1989 (first emigré writer to do so); now lives in Moscow, retaining Canadian citzenship; works published in USSR 1989–. *Publications include:* School for Fools 1976, Entre Chien et Loup 1979, Palisandriia 1985, Vozhidanii nobeliia (Waiting for the Nobel) 1993. *Address:* c/o Ardis Publishers, One Overlook Drive, Woodstock, NY 12498, USA (office).

SOKOLOV, Boris Sergeyevich; Russian palaeontologist and geologist; b. 9 April 1914, Vyshny Volochek, Tver Region; ed Leningrad State Univ.; Laboratory State Asst, Asst Lecturer, Leningrad (now St Petersburg) State Univ. 1937–41, Lecturer 1945–60, Prof. 1964–; Chief of Geological search party, Sr Research Worker, Head of Dept, All-Union Oil Research Geological Inst. 1943–60; Head of Dept, Inst. of Geology and Geophysics, Siberian Dept of USSR (now Russian) Acad. of Sciences 1960–78; Scientific Head of Lab., Moscow Palaeontological Inst. 1979–; apptd Vice-Pres. Int. Palaeontological Asscn 1972; Pres. All-Union Palaeontological Soc. of USSR (now Russian) Acad. of Sciences 1974–; mem. USSR (now Russian) Acad. of Sciences 1975, Acad. Sec., section of Geology, Geophysics and Geochemistry and mem. of

Presidium of USSR (now Russian) Acad. of Sciences 1975–91, Councillor to Pres. 1991–; mem. French, Bulgarian and Chinese Geological Socs; corresp. mem. USSR (now Russian) Acad. of Sciences 1958–68, mem. 1968–; Hon. mem. Swedish Geological Soc. 1968–, Czechoslovak Acad. of Sciences; Hero of Socialist Labour 1984, Order of Lenin (twice) and other decorations; Lenin Prize 1967. *Publications:* works on biosphere of the Earth etc. *Address:* Palaeontological Institute, Profsoyuznaya str. 113, 117 647 Moscow, Russia (office). *Telephone:* (495) 339-95-66 (office); (495) 146-84-44 (home).

SOKOLOV, Grigory Lipmanovich; Russian pianist; b. 18 April 1950, Leningrad (now St Petersburg); ed Leningrad Conservatory (pupil of Moisey Halfin); numerous guest appearances in London, Paris, Vienna, Berlin, Madrid, Salzburg, Munich, Rome and New York; has worked with leading conductors including Myung-Whun Chung, Neeme Järvi, Herbert Blomstedt, Valery Gergiev, Sakari Oramo, Trevor Pinnock, Andrew Litton, Vassilly Sinajskij, Jukka-Pekka Saraste, Alexander Lazarev, John Storgards, Moshe Atzmon, Walter Weller and Evgeny Svetlanov; has performed with orchestras including New York Philharmonic, Montreal Symphony, Münchner Philharmoniker, Leipzig Gewandhaus, Philhannonia, Amsterdam Concertgebouw and Detroit Symphony; Prof., Leningrad (St Petersburg) Conservatory 1975–; Second Prize, All-Union Competition of Musicians 1965, First Prize, Int. Tchaikovsky Competition 1966, People's Artist of Russia 1988. *Recordings:* several live recordings including works by Bach, Beethoven, Brahms, Chopin, Rachmaninoff, Prokofiev, Schubert, Schumann, Scriabin and Tchaikovsky; DVD of 2002 Paris recital directed by Bruno Monsaingeon. *Address:* c/o Artists Management Co., Piazza R. Simoni 1, 37122 Verona, Italy (office). *Telephone:* (45) 8014980 (office). *E-mail:* office@amcmusic.com (office). *Website:* www .amcmusic.com (office).

SOKOLOV, Maksim Yur'yevich; Russian journalist; b. 1959, Moscow; m.; ed Moscow State Univ.; worked as programmer in All-Union Centre of Transport, USSR State Cttee on Science and Tech. 1981–83; All-Union Research Inst. of Patent Information 1983–84; All-Union Research Inst. for Man. of Coal Industry 1985–87; Research Inst. of Gen. Plan of Moscow 1988–89; journalist since late 1980s; contrib. Commersant (weekly) 1989–97; political observer, Izvestiya 1998–; publs in newspapers Nezavisimaya Gazeta, Atmoda, Segodnya, magazines Vek XX i Mir, Oktyabr, Soviet Analyst (UK); broadcaster Russian Public TV Co. ORT; commentator, TV programmes; special corresp., Soviet analyst; Gong 94 Journalism prize; Medal for the Defence of Free Russia 1991. *Leisure interests:* travelling, cooking, reading fiction, mushroom hunting. *Address:* Izvestiya, 103791 Moscow, Tverskaya str. 18, Russia. *Telephone:* (495) 299-21-22 (office).

SOKOMANU, George; Ni-Vanuatu politician; b. (George Kalkoa), 13 Jan. 1937, Vanuatu; m. Leitak Matautava 1960; four s. one d.; fmr Deputy Chief Minister and Minister of the Interior of New Hebrides; Pres. of Vanuatu 1980–88; arrested Dec. 1988; sentenced to six years' imprisonment March 1989, released April 1989; Sec.-Gen. South Pacific Comm. 1992–95; Deputy Prime Minister, Minister of Home Affairs, Local Govt, Police and Defence 1994–95; currently Chair. Red Cross Vanuatu; Patron, Pacific Peacebuilding Initiatives. *Address:* c/o Pacific Peacebuilding Initiatives, 6 Lincluden Place, Oatlands, NSW 2117, AustraliaAUSTRALIA (office). *E-mail:* office@ppbi.org .au (office). *Website:* www.ppbi.org.au (office).

SOKUROV, Alexander Nikolayevich; Russian film director; b. 14 June 1951, Irkutsk; ed Gorky (now Nizhny Novgorod) Univ., All-Union Inst. of Cinematography; worked in Gorky (now Nizhny Novgorod) TV, Lenfilm Studio, directed feature and documentary films; Founder and Dir Experimental School of Young Cinema Vanguard; various prizes at int. film festivals. *Films include:* A Solitary Voice of a Man (Bronze Leopard, Locarno Int. Festival 1978), Mournful Callousness, Days of Eclipse (FIPRESSI Prize—Montreal Int. Festival), A Sonata for Hitler, Second Round, Elegy (about F. Shalyapin), Moscow Elegy (dedicated to A. Tarkovsky) Soviet Elegy, Russian Elegy, The Quiet Pages, The Spiritual Voices (Sony Prize, Locarno Int. Festival 1995), Oriental Elegy (Grand Prix Oberhausen Festival 1996), Mother and Son (prizes at Int. Festivals of Berlin, Moscow 1997), The Knot: Solzhenitsyn 1998, Moloch 1999, Sonata for Hitler 2000, Calf 2001, Russian Ark 2003, The Sun (Best Director Eurasia Int. Film Festival) 2005, Alexandra 2007. *Address:* 199048 St Petersburg, Smolenskaya nab. 4, Apt. 222, Russia.

SULAGH, Baqir, (Bayan Jabr); Iraqi politician; *Minister of Finance;* ed Baghdad Univ.; Sr Official Supreme Council for the Islamic Revolution in Iraq (SCIRI), fmr Head Damascus office; Minister of Construction and Housing 2003–04, of the Interior 2005–06, of Finance 2006–; mem. United Iraqi Alliance. *Address:* Ministry of Finance, Khulafa St, nr ar-Russafi Square., Baghdad, Iraq (office). *Telephone:* (1) 887-4871 (office).

SOLANA MADARIAGA, Javier, PhD; Spanish politician and international organization official; *Secretary-General, Council, Western European Union; Secretary-General and High Representative for Common Foreign and Security Policy, Council of the European Union;* b. 14 July 1942, Madrid; brother of Luis Solana Madariaga; m. Concepción Giménez; two c.; ed Colegio del Pilar, Universidad Complutense de Madrid; joined Spanish Socialist Party 1964; won Fulbright scholarship to study physical sciences in USA until 1968; Asst to Prof. Nicolas Cabrera, Univ. of Va 1968–71, then at Universidad Autónoma de Madrid (where contract was cancelled allegedly for political reasons); mem. Exec., Federación Socialista Madrileña and Federación de Trabajadores de la Enseñanza, Unión General de Trabajadores; Prof. of Solid State Physics, Universidad Complutense de Madrid 1977; mem. Congress of Deputies for Madrid; mem. Fed. Exec. Comm., Partido Socialista Obrero Español, fmr Press Sec. and Sec. for Research and Programmes; Minister of Culture 1982–88; Govt Spokesman 1985–88; Minister of Educ. and Science 1988–92, of Foreign Affairs 1992–95; Sec.-Gen. NATO 1995–99, responsible for NATO

Defence and Foreign Policy 1999–; Sec.-Gen. and High Rep. for Common Foreign and Security Policy, Council of the EU 1999–; Sec.-Gen. WEU 1999–; Pres. European Defence Agency 2004–; Pres. Madariaga European Foundation 1998–; mem. Spanish Chapter of Club of Rome; Hon. KCMG 1999, Grand Cross of Isabel the Catholic (Spain); Manfred Wörner Medal, Ministry of Defence (Germany), Vision for Europe Award 2003, Statesman of the Year Award, EastWest Inst. 2003, Premio Carlomagno 2006, Carnegie-Wateler Peace Prize 2006, Charlemagne Prize 2007. *Publications:* more than 30 publs in field of solid-state physics. *Address:* General Secretariat, Council of the European Union, rue de la Loi 175, 1048 Brussels, Belgium (office). *Telephone:* (2) 285-61-11 (office). *Fax:* (2) 285-73-97 (office). *E-mail:* public.relations@ consilium.eu.int (office). *Website:* www.ue.eu.int (office).

SOLBERG, Monte; Canadian politician; *Minister of Human Resources and Social Development;* b. 17 Sept. 1958, Calgary; m. Debra LeClaire; two s.; fmr broadcaster and businessman; mem. Parl. for Medicine Hat, Alberta (Reform Party 1993–2001, Canadian Alliance 2001, then Conservative Party of Canada) 1993–, parl. positions held include Critic for Foreign Affairs, Nat. Revenue, Human Resources Devt, Vice-Chair. standing cttees on Finance, Human Resources Devt, Status of Persons with Disabilities, Foreign Affairs, Int. Trade, Minister of Citizenship and Immigration 2006–07, of Human Resources and Social Devt 2007–08; fmr mem. Exec. Cttee Canada–USA Parl. Asscn; mem. Bd of Dirs Alberta Asscn of Broadcasters. *Address:* Conservative Party of Canada, 130 Albert Street, Suite 1204, Ottawa, ON K1P 5G4, Canada (office). *Telephone:* (613) 755-2000 (office). *Fax:* (613) 755-2001 (office). *Website:* www.conservative.ca (office).

SOLBES MIRA, Pedro, DPolSci; Spanish politician; b. 31 Aug. 1942, Pinoso, Alicante; m.; three c.; ed Univ. of Madrid, Inst. of European Studies of Free Univ., Brussels; civil servant, Ministry of Trade 1968–73, Commercial Counsellor to Spain's Perm. Mission to the EC 1973–78, Special Adviser to Minister for Relations with the EC 1978–79; Dir Gen. Commercial Policy, Ministry of Econs and Trade 1979–82; Gen. Sec. Ministry of Econs and Finance and mem. of task force for Spanish Accession negotiations to EC 1982–85; Sec. of State for Relations with the EC 1985; Pres. Internal Market Council during first Spanish presidency of EC 1989; Minister of Agric., Food and Fisheries 1991–93, of Economics and Finance 1993–96; Pres. Ecofin Council during Spanish presidency of EU 1995; mem. Spanish Parl. 1996; Pres. Jt Cttee of Spanish Parl. on EU 1996; European Commr for Econ. and Monetary Affairs 1999–2004; Second Deputy Prime Minister and Minister of the Economy and Finance 2004–09. *Address:* c/o Ministry of the Economy, Alcalá 9, 28014 Madrid, Spain.

SOLBRIG, Otto Thomas, PhD; American biologist and academic; *Bussey Professor of Biology, Emeritus, Herbaria, Harvard University;* b. 21 Dec. 1930, Buenos Aires, Argentina; s. of Hans Solbrig and Rose Muggleworth; m. Dorothy Crosswhite 1969; one s. one d.; ed Colegio Nacional de Mar de La Plata, Univ. Nacional de La Plata and Univ. of Calif., Berkeley; Research Asst Univ. of La Plata 1951–54; Teaching Fellow, Univ. of Calif., Berkeley 1956–58; Asst then Assoc. Curator, Gray Herbarium, Harvard Univ. 1960–66, Dir 1963–78; Assoc. Prof., Prof. Univ. of Mich. Ann Arbor 1966–69; Bussey Prof. of Biology Harvard Univ. 1969–, now Prof. Emer.; numerous professional appointments and affiliations etc.; Fellow, American Acad. of Arts and Sciences, AAAS; Guggenheim Fellow 1975–76; Hon. MA (Harvard) 1969; Extraordinary Prof. hc (Univ. of La Plata) 1991; Distinguished Prof. hc (Univ. of Buenos Aires) 1994; Cooley Prize 1961, Congressional Antarctic Medal 1967, Willdenow Medal, Berlin Botanical Gardens 1979. *Publications:* author or co-author of 16 books and more than 210 articles and chapters in books on plant population biology, cytology, ecology, evolution and taxonomy. *Leisure interest:* sailing. *Address:* Harvard University Herbaria, 22 Divinity Avenue, Cambridge, MA 02138, USA (office). *Telephone:* (617) 495-4302 (office). *Fax:* (617) 495-9484 (office). *E-mail:* solbrig@husc.harvard.edu (office). *Website:* www.huh.harvard.edu/research/staff/solbrig/solbrig (office).

SOLE TURA, Jordi, DLaw; Spanish politician; b. 23 May 1930, Mollet del Vallés, Barcelona; ed Cen. Univ. of Barcelona; Prof. of Constitutional Law, Cen. Univ. of Barcelona 1982–; mem. United Catalonian Socialist Party (PSUC) 1956–64; Founder Bandera Roja 1970 (rejoined PSUC 1974); mem. Cen. Cttee Spanish CP; Deputy PSUC for Barcelona and Spokesman and Vice-Pres. Parl. Communist Group 1977–, mem. Perm. Deputation of Congress; Deputy PSC-PSOE for Barcelona and Pres. Constitutional Comm. of Congress 1989–; Minister of Culture 1991–93; Pres. Foreign Affairs Comm. of Congress 1993–96; Senator 2000–; mem. Ass. Council of Europe; mem. WEU; mem. group of deputies who drafted the Spanish Constitution of 1978; Order of Isabel la Católica; Order of Carlos III; Order of Constitutional Merit. *Publications:* several books including Introduction to the Spanish Political Regime, Constitutions and Constitutional Periods in Spain, International Politics and Class Conflicts. *Leisure interests:* sports cross-country skiing, mountaineering, opera, books, movies. *Address:* The Senate, Plaza de la Marina Española 8, 28013 Madrid (office); Pedró de la Creu, 21, ático 0803Y Barcelona, Spain (home). *Telephone:* (1) 5381298 (office). *Fax:* (3) 2803545 (home). *E-mail:* jotec@intercom.es (home).

SOLEHOV, Mahmadnazar; Tajikistani government official; *Minister of Internal Affairs;* Chair. Constitutional Court 1998–2002; Minister of Internal Affairs 2002–03, 2006–; Chair. Council of Justice 2003–04; Head of Exec. Office of the Pres. 2004–06. *Address:* Ministry of Internal Affairs, 734025 Dushanbe, ul. Tekhron 29, Tajikistan (office). *Telephone:* (372) 21-17-40 (office). *Fax:* (372) 21-26-05 (office).

SOLERI, Paolo, D.Arch.; American architect and urban planner; *President, Cosanti Foundation;* b. 21 June 1919, Turin, Italy; m. Corolyn Woods 1949 (died 1982); two d.; ed Turin Polytechnic, Frank Lloyd Wright Fellowship,

SOL THE INTERNATIONAL WHO'S WHO 2010 SOL

Taliesin, Ariz.; went to USA 1947 to study; returned to Italy 1949; commissioned to design and build ceramics factory, Ceramica Artistica Solimene; resident in USA 1955–; Pres. Cosanti Foundation (for research into urban planning) 1965–, developing Arcosanti as an Urban Lab. in Cen. Ariz. 1970–; Prin. Paolo Soleri Assocs Inc., Architects; exbhns of work have appeared in over 70 public and private museums, colls and univs, USA; exhbns at Corcoran Gallery, Washington, DC 1970, NY Acad. of Sciences 1989–90; currently Distinguished Visiting Lecturer, Coll. of Architecture, Ariz. State Univ.; Dr hc (Dickinson Coll., Moore Coll. of Art, Ariz. State Univ.); Gold Medal, World Biennale of Architecture, Sofia, Bulgaria 1981, Gold Medal, American Inst. of Architects, Utopis Award 1989, Nat. Design Award 2006. *Publications:* Sketchbooks of Paolo Soleri 1970, Arcology: City in the Image of Man 1970, Matter becoming Spirit 1971, Fragments 1981, Omega Seed 1981, Arcosanti: an Urban Laboratory? 1983, Paolo Soleri's Earth Casting (with Scott M. Davis) 1984, Space for Peace 1984, Technology and Cosmogenesis 1986. *Address:* Cosanti Foundation, 6433 East Doubletree Ranch Road, Scottsdale, AZ 85253 (office); Arcosanti, HC 74, PO Box 4136, Mayer, AZ 86333, USA (office). *Telephone:* (480) 948-6145 (Cosanti) (office); (620) 632-7135 (Arcosanti) (office). *Website:* www.arcosanti.org (office).

SOLIS, Hilda Lucia, BA, MA; American politician and government official; *Secretary of Labor;* b. 20 Oct. 1957, Los Angeles; d. of Raul Solis and Juana Solis; m. Sam H. Sayyad 1982; ed California State Polytechnic Univ., Univ. of Southern California; interpreter, US Immigration and Naturalization Service, LA 1977–79; Ed.-in -Chief Office of Hispanic Affairs, White House, Washington, DC 1980–81; Man. Analyst, Civil Rights Div., Office of Man. and Budget 1981–82; Field Rep. Office of Assemblyman Art Torres, LA 1982; Dir Calif. Student Opportunity and Access Program 1982; mem. Rio Hondo Community Coll. Bd of Trustees 1985; mem. Calif. State Ass. for 57th Dist 1992–94; mem. Calif. State Senate from 24th Dist 1994–2000; mem. US House of Reps from 32nd Dist 2001–08, mem. Resouces Cttee, Energy and Commerce Cttee (Vice-Chair. Environment and Hazardous Materials Sub cttee, Select Cttee on Energy Independence and Global Warming; Co-Vice Chair. Democratic Steering and Policy Cttee, Sr Whip and Regional Whip for Southern California; Chair. Congressional Hispanic Caucus Task Force on Health and the Environment; mem. Comm. on Security and Cooperation in Europe 2007–08, Vice Chair. Gen. Cttee on Democracy, Human Rights and Humanitarian Questions; US Sec. of Labor, Washington, DC 2009–; Democrat; Meritorious Service Award, US Dept of Defense 1981, Profile in Courage Award, John F. Kennedy Library Foundation 2000. *Address:* Department of Labor, Frances Perkins Bldg, 200 Constitution Ave, NW, Washington, DC 20210, USA (office). *Telephone:* (202) 693-6000 (office). *Fax:* (202) 693-6111 (office). *Website:* www.dol.gov (office).

SOLIS, Otton, MA; Costa Rican politician; b. 31 May 1954; m. Shirley Sanchez 1994; four c.; ed Univ. of Costa Rica, Univ. of Manchester, UK; has taught at Univs of Manchester and Reading, UK, Costa Rican univs, UN Univ. for Peace; Pres. Interamerican Econ. and Social Council, OAS 1987–88; Researcher Sustainable Devt Research Centre, Univ. of Costa Rica 2000; fmr Economist Cen. Bank of Costa Rica, Ministry of Planning and Econ. Policy; fmr Consultant ECLA, UNDP, SIDA; Founding Pres. Citizens Action Party 2000, unsuccessful presidential cand. 2006; Bacardi Family Eminent Scholar, Center for Latin American Studies, Univ. of Florida 2008; mem. Univ. Bd Open Univ. of Costa Rica 1990–93; mem. Special Cttee, La Amistad Park Trust Fund 1999, Cttee of Experts on Public Admin, UN 2002; mem. Team, Millennium Ecosystem Assessment 2001. *Address:* c/o Partido Acción Ciudadana (PAC), 25 San Pedro, 425 m sur del Templo Parroquial, San José, Costa Rica (office). *Telephone:* 281-2727 (office). *Fax:* 280-6640 (office). *E-mail:* pac2002@racsa.co.cr (office). *Website:* www.pac.or.cr (office).

SOLLERS, Philippe, (pseudonym of Philippe Joyaux); French author; b. 28 Nov. 1936, Bordeaux; s. of Octave Joyaux and Marcelle Molinié; m. Julia Kristeva 1967; one s.; ed Lycées Montesquieu and Montaigne, Bordeaux and Ecole Sainte-Geneviève, Versailles; Dir L'Infini (review) 1983–; mem. reading Cttee Editions Gallimard 1990–, Asscn of French Museums 1998–; Chevalier Légion d'honneur; Officier, Ordre nat. du Mérite, des Arts et des Lettres; Prix Médicis 1961, Grand Prix du Roman de la Ville de Paris 1988, Prix Paul-Morand (Académie française) 1992, Prix littéraire de la fondation Prince Pierre de Monaco 2006. *Publications:* Une Curieuse Solitude 1958, Le Parc 1961, Drame 1965, Nombres, Logiques 1968, Lois 1972, H 1973, Paradis, Vision à New York 1981, Femmes 1983, Portrait du joueur 1985, Théorie des exceptions 1986, Paradis 2 1986, Le Coeur absolu 1987, Les Surprises de Fragonard 1987, Les Folies françaises 1988, De Kooning, vite 1988, Le Lys d'or 1989, Carnet de nuit 1989, La Fête à Venise 1991, Improvisations 1991, Le Secret 1993, Venise Éternelle 1993, La Guerre du Goût 1994, Femmes, Mythologies (jtly) 1994, Les Passions de Francis Bacon 1996, Sade contre l'Etre Suprême 1996, Picasso, le héros 1996, Studio 1997, Casanova, L'admirable (Prix Elsa-Morante 1999) 1998, L'Année du Tigre, Journal de l'année 1998, 1999, L'Oeil de Proust, les dessins de Marcel Proust 1999, Passion fixe 2000, La Divine Comédie 2000, Eloge de L'Infini 2001, L'Etoile des amants 2002, Illuminations à travers les textes sacrés 2003, Dictionnaire amoureux de Venise 2004, Le Saint-Ane 2004, Logique de la fiction 2006, Fleurs 2006, Guerres secrètes 2007, Une Vie Divine 2007, Un vrai roman: Mémoires 2007. *Address:* L'Infini, 5 rue Sébastien-Bottin, 75007 Paris, France (office). *Website:* www.philippesollers.net.

SOLOMIN, Yuri Mefod'yevich; Russian actor and theatre director; *Artistic Director, Maly Drama Theatre (National Theatre of Russia);* b. 18 June 1935, Chita; s. of Mefody Solomin and Zinaida Ryabtseva; m. Olga Nikolayevna Solomina; one d.; ed Shchepkin Higher School of Theatre Art; actor Maly Drama Theatre 1959–; Artistic Dir 1988–; teacher, then Prof. Shchepkin Theatre Coll. 1960–; Minister of Culture of Russian Fed. 1990–92; Pres. Asscn of Russian Drama Theatres; mem. Int. Acad. of Creative Arts; corresp. mem. Russian Acad. of Educ.; master-classes in USA, Japan, S Korea; Order For Service to Motherland (Fourth and Third Class), Order Friendship of Peoples, Order of Russian Orthodox Church, Order for Contrib. to Int. Culture (Japan), Int. K.S. Stanislavsky Prize; State Prize of Russian Fed., Prize Golden Aries, A. D. Popov Gold Medal, USSR Peoples' Artist, People's Artist of Russia and Kyrghyzia. *Film roles include:* Sleepless Night, Adjutant of His Highness, Dersu Ursala, Blockade, Ordinary Miracle, Dreams of Russia, There was Evening, There was Morning, Walking Through the Torments (serial), The Bat, The Farewell in June, Penitential Love, Native Land Waits, Moscow's Saga. *Plays include:* Inspector, Tsar Fedor Ioannovich, The Deep, Uncle Vanya, Cyrano de Bergerac, Seagull, Lady Windermere's Fan, Alive Corps. *Plays produced:* Forest (produced in Bulgaria and Russia), Perfidy and Love, Misfortune from Wit, Three Sisters, A Mysterious Box (vaudeville). *Publications:* From Adjutant to His Highness. *Leisure interest:* dogs and cats. *Address:* State Academic Maly Theatre of Russia, Teatralnaya pl. 1/6, Moscow, Russia (office). *Telephone:* (495) 925-98-68 (office). *Fax:* (495) 925-54-36 (office); (495) 921-03-50 (office). *E-mail:* theatre@maly.ru (office). *Website:* www.maly.ru (office).

SOLOMON, David H., MD; American professor of medicine; *Professor Emeritus, Geriatrics Center on Aging, UCLA;* b. 7 March 1923, Cambridge, Mass.; s. of Frank Solomon and Rose Roud Solomon; m. Ronda Markson 1946; two d.; ed Brown Univ. and Harvard Medical School; Medical House Officer, Peter Bent Brigham Hospital 1946–47; Research Fellow in Medicine, Peter Bent Brigham Hospital and Harvard Medical School 1947–48; Sr Asst Surgeon, US Public Health Service and Investigator, Gerontology Section, Nat. Heart Inst. 1948–50; Sr Asst Resident Physician, Peter Bent Brigham Hospital 1950–51; Fellow in Endocrinology, New England Center Hospital 1951–52; Instructor, School of Medicine, UCLA 1952–54, Asst Prof. 1954–60, Assoc. Prof. 1960–66, Prof. of Medicine 1966, Chief of Medicine (Harbor-UCLA Medical Center) 1966–71, Chair. Dept of Medicine 1971–81, Assoc. Dir Multicampus Div. of Geriatric Medicine 1982–89, Dir UCLA Geriatrics Center on Aging 1991–96, Prof. Emer. UCLA 1993–; Consultant, Wadsworth Hosp., LA 1952–, Sepulveda Hosp. 1971–, RAND Corpn 1997–; several awards including John Phillips Memorial Award, American Coll. of Physicians 2002. *Publications:* co-author of three books, author of 202 scientific papers, 44 book chapters, 11 review articles and 122 published abstracts. *Leisure interests:* golf, running, reading, hiking, bridge. *Address:* 2103 Ridge Drive, Los Angeles, CA 90049, USA (home). *Telephone:* (310) 471-6346 (office); (310) 471-5256 (home). *Fax:* (310) 471-6346 (home). *E-mail:* davidsolomon@rand.org (office); d.solomon4@verizon.net (home).

SOLOMON, Edward I., PhD; American chemist and academic; *Monroe E. Spaght Professor in the School of Humanities and Sciences, Stanford University;* b. 20 Oct. 1946, New York; s. of Mordecai L. Solomon and Sally S. Solomon; m. Darlene J. Spira 1984; one s. one d.; ed Rensselaer Polytechnic Inst., Tory, New York, Princeton Univ.; Research Assoc., Princeton Univ., NJ 1972–73; Postdoctoral Fellow H.C. Ørsted Inst. 1973–74, Calif. Inst. of Tech. 1974–75; Asst Prof., MIT 1975–79, Assoc. Prof. 1979–81, Prof. 1981–82; Prof., Stanford Univ. 1982–, Spaght Prof. of Chem. 1991–; Invited Prof., Univ. of Paris, Tokyo Inst. of Tech., Tata Inst., India, Xiamen Univ., China, La Plata Univ., Argentina; First Glen Seaborg and other lectureships; Fellow AAAS, American Acad. of Arts and Sciences; Sloan Fellowship, NIH Merit Award., Japan Soc. for Promotion of Science Invitation Fellow, Dean's Award for Distinguished Teaching, Westinghouse Foundation Nat. Talent Search Award, Remsen Award 1994. *Publications:* three books; over 320 papers in scientific journals. *Leisure interests:* tennis, running, gourmet dining, int. travel. *Address:* Department of Chemistry, Stanford University, Stanford, CA 94305-5080, USA. *Telephone:* (650) 723-9104 (office). *Fax:* (650) 725-0259 (office). *E-mail:* Edward.Solomon@stanford.edu (office). *Website:* www.stanford.edu/dept/chemistry/faculty/solomon (office); www.stanford.edu/group/solomon (office).

SOLOMON, Sir Harry, Kt; British solicitor and entrepreneur; b. 20 March 1937, Middlesbrough; s. of Jacob Solomon and Belle Solomon; m. Judith D. Manuel 1962; one s. two d.; ed St Alban's School and Law Soc. School of Law; qualified solicitor 1960; in pvt. practice 1960–75; Man. Dir Hillsdown Holdings PLC 1975–84, Jt Chair. 1984–87, Chair. 1987–93, Dir (non-exec.) 1993–97; Chair. Harveys Holdings PLC 1994–2000; Dir Princedale Group PLC 1993–2000; mem. Bd of Dirs (non-exec.) Charterhouse European Holding Ltd 1993–2001, Frogmore Estates PLC 1993–2001, US Industries Inc. (now Jacuzzi Brands Inc.) 1995–2004, Falkland Islands Holdings PLC 1999–, Consolidated Land Investments Ltd 2000–, The Portland Trust 2002–, Westcity Plc 2007–; fmr Dir Maple Leaf Foods Inc., Portland Capital 2007–; Hon. FRCP. *Leisure interests:* jogging, tennis, theatre, collector of historical autographed letters. *Address:* Hillsdown House, 32 Hampstead High Street, London, NW3 1QD, England (office). *Telephone:* (20) 7431-7739 (office). *Fax:* (20) 7431-7740 (office). *E-mail:* harry@heathside.co.uk (office).

SOLOMOS, Alexis; Greek stage director (retd) and author; b. 9 Aug. 1918, Athens; s. of John Solomos and Aspasia Eliopoulos; m. Catherine Spathis 1953; two d.; ed Athens Univ., Athens Nat. Theatre Dramatic School, Royal Acad. of Dramatic Art, London, UK and Yale Univ. Piscator New School, USA; stage dir in USA and UK; Stage Dir Athens Nat. Theatre 1950–80; Founder and Dir Proscinio Theatre 1964; Dir Festival of Greek Classical Theatre, Ypsilanti, Mich., USA 1965–66; Prof., Athens Nat. Dramatic School; Asst Man. Dir Hellenic Broadcasting Foundation; Deputy Dir Greek TV 1978; Dir Athens Nat. Theatre 1980, 1991, Athens TV; Hon. Prof., Univ. of Athens; four prizes for Best Author and Dir from Mayor of Athens and Greek Acad.; honours from Czech Acad. and other insts. *Plays:* directed a total of 160 plays in London, New York and at Nat. Theatre, Athens, including works by

Aeschylus, Sophodes, Euripides and Aristophanes at Epidaurus Ancient Theatre; two of his own plays produced in Athens at the Epidaurus Ancient Theatre. *Radio:* many programmes about the history of theatre art. *Publications include:* Living Aristophanes 1961, Saint Bacchus 1964, The Age of Theatre 1973, My Good Thalia 1984, Theatrical Dictionary 1989, Euripides 1995, Cinema Century 2000; trans. of more than 30 foreign plays into Greek. *Leisure interests:* travel, crossword puzzles, being at home with wife, daughters and cats. *Address:* 13 Fokilidou Street, 106 73 Athens, Greece (home). *Telephone:* (210) 3626730 (home); (210) 3626677 (home).

SOLOVTSOV, Col-Gen. Nikolai; Russian army officer; *Commander, Strategic Missile Command;* b. 1 Jan. 1949, Zaysan, USSR Kazakh Repub.; m.; two c.; ed Rostov Higher Eng and Command School, Dzerzhinskiy Acad., Command Dept and General Staff Acad.; First Deputy Strategic Missile Command 1998–2001, Commdr 2001–; fmr Dean SMC Acad.; Order of Honours, Distinguished Service (3rd grade), Military Merits and ten medals. *Address:* Strategic Missile Command, Ministry of Defence, 105175 Moscow, ul. Myasnitskaya 37, Russian Federation (office). *Telephone:* (495) 293-38-54 (office). *Fax:* (495) 296-84-36 (office). *Website:* www.mil.ru/eng/1862/12068/ 12088/12223/index.shtml (office).

SOLOVYEV, Sergey Aleksandrovich; Russian film director and scriptwriter; b. 25 Aug. 1944, Kem, Karelia; m. Tatyana Drubich (divorced); ed All-Union Inst. of Cinematography with Leningrad TV 1960–69; film dir Mosfilm Studio 1969–, artistic Dir Krug Film Union 1987–; Sec. USSR Union of Cinematographers 1986–90; Chair. Moscow Union of Cinematographers 1990–97; Co-Chair. Russian Union of Cinematographers 1990–92; Prof. All-Russian Inst. of Cinematography; debut as scriptwriter Look into the Face 1966, as film dir Family Happiness; worked as stage dir in Maly Theatre (Uncle Vanya) and Taganka Theatre (The Seagull). *Films include:* Yegor Bulychev and Others 1971, Station Inspector 1972, A Hundred Days After Childhood 1975 (Silver Bear, Berlin, Prize of All-Union Festival, Tunes of A White Night 1977), Rescuer 1980, Direct Heir 1982, Strange, White and Speckled 1986, Assa 1987, Black Rose: an Emblem of Sadness, Red Rose: an Emblem of Love 1989, The House Under the Starry Sky 1991, Three Sisters 1994, The Tender Age 2001. *Address:* Akademika Pilyugina, 117393 Moscow, str. 8, korp. 1, Apt. 330, Russia (home). *Telephone:* (495) 132-36-95 (home).

SOLOW, Robert Merton, PhD; American economist and academic; *Institute Professor Emeritus, Massachusetts Institute of Technology;* b. 23 Aug. 1924, Brooklyn, NY; s. of Milton Solow and Hannah Solow; m. Barbara Lewis 1945; two s. one d.; ed Harvard Univ.; Asst Prof. of Statistics, Mass. Inst. of Technology 1950–53, Assoc. Prof. of Econs 1954–57, Prof. of Econs 1958–73, Inst. Prof. 1973–95, Inst. Prof. Emer. 1995–; W. Edwards Deming Prof., New York Univ. 1996; Sr Economist, Council of Econ. Advisers 1961–62; Marshall Lecturer, Univ. of Cambridge, UK 1963–64; De Vries Lecturer, Rotterdam 1963, Wicksell Lecturer, Stockholm 1964; Eastman Visiting Prof., Univ. of Oxford, UK 1968–69; Killian Prize Lecturer, MIT 1978; Geary Lecturer, Univ. of Dublin, Ireland 1980; Overseas Fellow, Churchill Coll., Cambridge 1984; Mitsui Lecturer, Birmingham 1985; Nobel Memorial Lecture, Stockholm 1987 and numerous others in int. academic insts; mem. Nat. Comm. on Tech., Automation and Econ. Progress 1964–65; Presidential Comm. on Income Maintenance 1968–69; mem. Bd of Dirs Fed. Reserve Bank of Boston 1975–81, Chair. 1979–81; Fellow, Center for Advanced Study in Behavioral Sciences 1957–58, Trustee 1982–95; Vice-Pres. American Econ. Asscn 1968, Pres. 1979, Vice-Pres. AAAS 1970; Pres. Econometric Soc. 1964; Trustee Woods Hole Oceanographic Inst. 1988–, Alfred P. Sloan Foundation 1992–, Resources for the Future 1994–96, Urban Inst. 1994–, German Marshall Fund of US 1994–; Pres. Int. Econ. Asscn 1999–2002; mem. Nat. Science Bd 1995–2000; Fellow American Acad. of Arts and Sciences, mem. of Council, NAS 1977–80, mem. 1972–; Corresp. mem. British Acad.; mem. American Philosophical Soc.; Fellow Acad. dei Lincei (Rome); Foundation Fellow, Russell Sage Foundation 2000–; Orden pour le mérite, Germany 1995; Hon. LLD (Chicago) 1967, (Lehigh) 1977, (Brown) 1972, (Wesleyan) 1982; Hon. LittD (Williams Coll.) 1974, (Rensselaer Polytechnic Inst.) 2003; Dr hc (Paris) 1975, (Geneva) 1982, (Conservatoire Nat. des Arts et Métiers, Paris) 1994, (Buenos Aires) 1999; Hon. DLitt (Warwick) 1976, (Colgate) 1990, (Glasgow) 1992, (Harvard) 1992; Hon. ScD (Tulane) 1983; Hon. DScS (Yale) 1986, (Univ. of Mass., Boston) 1989, (Helsinki) 1990, (Boston Coll.) 1990, (Chile) 1992, (Rutgers Univ.) 1994; Hon. DSc in Business Admin. (Bryant Coll.) 1988; Hon. DEng (Colorado School of Mines) 1996; Hon. DHumLitt (New York) 2006; David A. Wells Prize, Harvard Univ. 1951, John Bates Clark Medal, American Econ. Asscn 1961, Killian Award, MIT 1977, Seidman Award in Political Econ. 1983, Nobel Prize for Econs 1987, Nat. Medal of Science 2000. *Publications:* Linear Programming and Economic Analysis 1958, Capital Theory and the Rate of Return 1963, Sources of Unemployment in the United States 1964, Price Expectations and the Behavior of the Price Level 1970, Growth Theory: An Exposition 1970, The Labor Market as a Social Institution 1989, Learning from "Learning by Doing" 1994, A Critical Essay On Modern Macroeconomic Theory (with Frank Hahn) 1995. *Leisure interest:* sailing. *Address:* Department of Economics, Massachusetts Institute of Technology E52-383, Cambridge, MA 02139 (office); 528 Lewis Wharf, Boston, MA 02110, USA (home). *Telephone:* (617) 253-5268 (office); (617) 227-4436 (home). *Fax:* (617) 253-0560 (office). *Website:* econ-www.mit.edu (office).

SOLT, Pál; Hungarian judge; b. 3 Oct. 1937, Szentendre; m.; one c.; ed Univ. of Eötvös Lóránd, Budapest; Asst Court Clerk, Cen. Dist Court of Pest 1960–63, Judge 1964–66; Head, Secr. of Supreme Court of Justice 1966–71, Judge 1980–87, Chair. Panel 1987–89, 2002–, Pres. Supreme Court of Justice 1990–2002; Asst, Legal Dept, Secr. of Ministry of Finance 1971–80; mem. Constitutional Court 1989–; Pres. Nat. Council of Justice 1997–2002; Hon. LLD (San Beda Coll. of Law, Manila) 2001. *Address:* Supreme Court, Markó

utca 16, 1055 Budapest, Hungary (office). *Telephone:* (1) 268-4575 (office). *Fax:* (1) 268-4603 (office). *E-mail:* solt@legtelsobb.birosag.hu. *Website:* www.lb.hu.

SOLTANI, Boudjerra, LèsL, DESS, PhD; Algerian academic and politician; *Minister of State;* b. 12 Jan. 1954, Chréa; m.; five c.; ed Constantine Univ.; Lecturer, Faculty of Humanities, Constantine Univ. 1980–94, Dept of Communications, Emir AbdelKader Univ. 1990–94; Ed.-in-Chief Al Tadhamoun magazine 1990–94; Chair. Consultative Cttee Hamas (now Mouvement de la société pour la paix–MSP) 1992–93, Pres. MSP 2003–; Sec. of State in charge of fishing 1992–93; mem. Nat. People's Ass. for Tébessa 1998–; Minister of Small and Medium-sized Enterprises and Handicrafts 1998–2000, of Labour and Social Security 2000–01; Minister of State 2005–. *Publications:* novel: La vache des orphelins 1970; poetry: L'épée de Al Hajjaj, Regards sur le liens entre le bien et le mal, Roses et Épines; essays: Feuillets Islamique 1979–89, Les écorces de la confrontation 1997, Les racines de la confrontation 1999, L'Algérie nouvelle- L'avancée vers la démocratie. *Address:* Mouvement de la société pour la paix, 63 rue Ali Haddad, Algiers (office); c/o Office of the Prime Minister, rue Docteur Saâdane, Algiers, Algeria (office). *Telephone:* (21) 73-23-40 (office). *Fax:* (21) 71-79-27 (office). *E-mail:* info@hmsalgeria.net (office). *Website:* www.hmsalgeria.net (office); www.cg.gov.dz (office).

SOLVAY, Jacques Ernest; Belgian business executive; *Honorary Chairman, Solvay Cie;* b. 4 Dec. 1920, Ixelles; s. of Ernest-John Solvay and Marie Graux; m. Marie-Claude Boulin 1949; one s. three d.; ed Univ. of Brussels; joined Solvay Cie 1950, mem. Bd 1955, Chair. 1971, currently Hon. Chair.; Chair. Int. Solvay Insts for Physics and Chem., Brussels; apptd Dir Soc. Générale de Banque 1965; apptd Chair. Soltex Polymer Corpn 1974; Pres. Belgo-British Union; mem. European Advisory Council, Tenneco Inc. 1986–; Hon. Pres. Fédération des Industries Chimiques de Belgique; Chevalier de l'Ordre de Leopold, Hon. KBE. *Leisure interest:* orchid growing. *Address:* c/o Solvay Cie SA, rue de Prince Albert 33, 1050 Brussels, Belgium (office).

SOLYMAR, László, MA, PhD, FRS, FIEE; British engineer and academic; *Visiting Professor, Department of Electrical and Electronic Engineering, Imperial College London;* b. 24 Jan. 1930, Budapest, Hungary; s. of Pál Solymar and Aranka Gold; m. Marianne Klopfer 1955; two d.; ed Tech. Univ., Budapest, Hungarian Acad. of Sciences; Lecturer, Tech. Univ., Budapest 1952–53; research engineer, Research Inst. for Telecommunications, Budapest 1953–56, Standard Telecommunications Labs Ltd, Harlow, Essex 1956–65; Lecturer, Dept of Eng Science, Univ. of Oxford 1966–86, Fellow Brasenose Coll. 1966–86, Donald Pollock Reader in Eng Science 1986–92, Fellow Hertford Coll. 1986–, Prof. of Applied Electromagnetism 1992–97, Leverhulme Emer. Fellow 1997–2001; Visiting Prof., Physics Lab., Ecole Normale Supérieure, Univ. of Paris 1965–66, Tech. Univ. of Denmark 1972–73, Dept of Physics, Univ. of Osnabrück 1987, Optical Inst., Tech. Univ., Berlin 1990, Dept of Materials, Autonomous Univ. of Madrid 1993, 1995, Tech. Univ., Budapest 1994, Dept of Electrical and Electronic Eng, Imperial Coll. London 2003–; Faraday Medal, IEE 1992. *Three plays for radio:* Anaxagoras; Archimedes; Hypatia (with John Wain). *Publications:* various research and text books and papers in learned journals; a book on the history of communications. *Leisure interests:* history, bridge, chess, swimming. *Address:* Department of Engineering Science, University of Oxford, Parks Road, Oxford, OX1 3PJ (office); Department of Electrical and Electronic Engineering, Imperial College, Exhibition Road, London, SW7 2BT (office); 62 Hurst Rise Road, Oxford, OX2 9HQ, England (home). *E-mail:* laszlo.solymar@ eng.ox.ac.uk (office).

SOLYOM, Janos Paul; Hungarian/Swedish concert pianist and conductor; b. 26 Oct. 1938, Budapest; s. of Dr I. Solyom and M. Weill; m. Camilla Lundberg 1987; ed Franz Liszt Acad. of Music, Budapest; pvt. studies with Ilona Kabos in London and with Nadia Boulanger in Paris; int. concert career 1958–; mem. Royal Swedish Acad. of Music; Royal Swedish Medal for Outstanding Artistic Merit 'Litteris et Artibus'. *Leisure interests:* architecture, hypnotherapy. *Address:* Norr Mälarstrand 54, VII 112 20 Stockholm, Sweden. *Telephone:* (8) 652-42-72 (home). *Fax:* (8) 652-42-72 (home). *E-mail:* pianos@solyom.com (home). *Website:* www.solyom.com (home).

SÓLYOM, László, LLD; Hungarian academic, judge, politician and head of state; *President;* b. 3 Jan. 1942, Pécs; m. Erzsébet Nagy; one s. one d.; ed Univ. of Pécs, Friedrich Schiller Univ., Jena, Hungarian Acad. of Sciences; Lecturer in Civil Law, Univ. of Jena 1966–69; Research Fellow, Hungarian Acad. of Sciences 1969–82; Prof. of Law, Univ. of Budapest 1982–2002, Catholic Univ. of Budapest 1996–, Univ. of Cologne 1999–2000; Pres. Constitutional Court 1990–98; legal adviser to environmental groups and other civic movts 1982–89; Pres. of Hungary 2005–; mem. Int. Comm. of Jurists, Geneva 1994–2001, scientific council, Wissenschaftskolleg zu Berlin Inst. for Advanced Study, Berlin 1995–2001, European Comm. for Democracy Through Law (The Venice Comm.) 1998–2001; Corresp. mem. Hungarian Acad. of Sciences 2001; Grand Cross of Merit with Star (Germany) 1998; Grand Cross of Merit (Hungary) 1999; Hon. DJur (Cologne) 1999; Humboldt Research Award 1998, Nagy Imre Prize (Hungary) 2003. *Publications:* The Decline of Civil Law Liability 1980, Die Persönlichkeitsrechte: Eine vergleichendhistorische Studie über ihre Grundlagen 1984, Verfassungsgerichtsbarkeit in Ungarn: Analysen und Entscheidungssammlung 1990–93 (with Georg Brunner) 1995, Constitutional Judiciary in a New Democracy: The Hungarian Constitutional Court (with Georg Brunner) 2000, The Beginnings of Constitutional Justice in Hungary (in Hungarian) 2001, The Role of Constitutional Courts in the Transition to Democracy, 18(1) Int. Sociology 2003, Politican Parties and Trade Unions in the Constitution (in Hungarian) 2004. *Address:* Office of the President, 1014 Budapest, Szent György tér 1–2, Hungary (office). *Telephone:* (1) 224-5010 (office). *Fax:* (1) 224-5002 (office). *Website:* www.keh.hu (office).

SOM, Peter; American fashion designer; *Creative Director, Women's Collection, Bill Blass;* ed Connecticut Coll., Parsons School of Design, New York; apprenticed with Michael Kors and Calvin Klein at Parson's School of Design, then worked Bill Blass design room; debut at Seventh on Sixth in Bryant Park tents with Spring 2001 Collection; returned to Bill Blass as Creative Dir Women's Collection 2007–; has designed for Scarlett Johansson, Claire Danes, Camilla Belle, Mandy Moore and Ginnifer Goodwin, among others; CFDA Scholarship Competition winner 1997, Parsons Gold Thimble for his work in the school's Designer Critic program, Lord & Taylor's Dress Competition winner. *Address:* Peter Som, Inc., 260 West 39th Street, 5th Floor, New York NY 10018, USA (office). *Telephone:* (212) 221-5991 (office). *Fax:* (212) 221-1936 (office). *E-mail:* info@petersom.com (office). *Website:* www.petersom.com (office).

SOMARE, Rt Hon. Sir Michael Thomas, PC, CH, GCMG; Papua New Guinea politician; *Prime Minister, Minister of Autonomy and Autonomous Regions;* b. 9 April 1936, Rabaul, East New Britain Prov.; s. of Sana Ludwig Somare and Painari Betha; m. Veronica Bula Kaiap 1965; three s. two d.; ed Sogeri Secondary School, Admin. Coll.; teacher various schools 1956–64; Asst Area Educ. Officer, Madang 1962–63; Broadcasts Officer, Dept of Information and Extension Services, Wewak 1963–66, radio broadcaster and journalist 1966–67; mem. House of Ass. for East Sepik Regional 1968–; Parl. Leader Pangu Party 1968–88; Deputy Chair. Exec. Council 1972–73, Chair. 1973–75; Chief Minister Papua New Guinea 1974–75, Prime Minister 1975–80, 1982–85, 2002–; Minister for Nat. Resources 1976–77, for Public Service Comm. and Nat. Planning 1977–80; Acting Minister for Police 1978–80; Leader of the Opposition 1980–82; Minister of Foreign Affairs 1988–94, 2000–01, 2006–07, also of Bougainville Affairs 2000–01, of Defence (acting) 2007, of Autonomy and Autonomous Regions 2007–; Gov. E Sepik Prov. 1995–; Chair. Bd of Trustees, PNG; mem. Second Select Cttee on Constitutional Devt 1968–72, Australian Broadcasting Comm. Advisory Cttee; Ancient Order of Sikatuna, Title of Rajah (Philippines) 1976, Grand Cross of Equestrian Order of St Gregory the Great 1993; six hon. degrees; Queen's Silver Jubilee Medal 1977, Pacific Man of the Year Award 1983. *Publication:* Sana: An Autobiography. *Leisure interests:* reading, golf, soccer, cricket, fishing. *Address:* Office of the Prime Minister, POB 639, Waigani, NCD (office); Karan, Murik Lakes, East Sepik, Papua New Guinea (home). *Telephone:* 3276544 (office). *Fax:* 3277380 (office). *E-mail:* primeminister@pm.gov.pg (office). *Website:* www.pm.gov.pg/pmsoffice/PMsoffice.nsf (office).

SOMAVÍA, Juan O.; Chilean lawyer, diplomatist and international organization official; *Director-General, International Labour Organization;* b. 21 April 1941; m. Adriana Santa Cruz; two c.; ed Catholic Univ. of Chile, Univ. of Paris; various posts in Ministry of Foreign Relations; Founder and Exec. Dir Latin American Inst. for Trans nat. Studies, Mexico; Co-ordinator Third World Forum; mem. Bd of Dirs and Vice-Pres. for Latin America of Inter-Press Service 1976–87; Sec.-Gen. South American Peace Comm. 1987; Pres. Int. Comm. of Chilean opposition No Campaign for Referendum 1988–89; Perm. Rep. to UN, New York 1990–99; Dir-Gen. ILO 1999–; fmr consultant to GATT and UNDP; mem. Bd of Dirs Int. Foundation for Devt Alternatives, mem. MacBride Comm. on communication problems; Laurea hc (Univ. of Turin) 2001; Dr hc (Connecticut Coll.) 1994, (Catholic Univ. of Lima) 1999, (Univ. of Paris I, Panthéon-Sorbonne) 2003; Leonidas Proaño Prize, Latin American Human Rights Asscn for contrib. to peace and regional security. *Address:* International Labour Organization, 4 route des Morillons, 1211 Geneva 22, Switzerland (office). *Telephone:* (22) 799-6111 (office). *Fax:* (22) 799-8533 (office). *E-mail:* cabinet@ilo.org (office). *Website:* www.ilo.org (office).

SOMCHAI, Wongsawat, BL, MPA; Thai judge and politician; b. 31 Aug. 1947; m.; ed Thammasat Univ., Nat. Defence Coll. of Thailand, Nat. Inst. of Devt Admin; Asst Judge, Ministry of Justice 1974–75, Judge 1975–76; Judge, Chiangmai-Kwaeng Court 1976–77, Chiangmai Court 1977–83, Chiangrai Court 1983–86; Chief Justice, Pang-nga Court 1986–87, Rayong Juvenile Court 1987–88, Chonburi Court 1988–89, Nonthaburi Court 1989–90, Thonburi Criminal Court 1990–93; Justice, Court of Appeal Region II 1993–97, Chief Justice 1997–98; Deputy Perm. Sec., Ministry of Justice 1998–99, Perm. Sec. 1999–2006; Perm. Sec., Ministry of Labour March–Sept. 2006; mem. House of Reps 2007–08; Deputy Leader People Power Party 2007–08; Minister of Educ. Feb.–Sept. 2008; Prime Minister of Thailand 2008, also Minister of Defence, banned by Consitutional Court from holding public office for five years, Court also dissolved People Power Party after finding it committed electoral fraud; Kt Commdr, Most Noble Order of the Crown of Thailand (second class) 1980, (first class) 1986, (special class) 1992, Most Exalted Order of the White Elephant (second class) 1984, (first class) 1989, (special class) 1997; Chakrabarti Mala Medal 1999. *Address:* c/o Office of the Prime Minister, Government House, Thanon Nakhon Pathom, Bangkok 10300, Thailand (office).

SOMDY, Duangdy; Laotian government official; *Minister of Finance;* fmr Vice-Minister of Finance, Minister of Finance 2007–; fmr Vice-Chair. and Standing Mem. Poverty Reduction Fund Admin. Bd. *Address:* Ministry of Finance, rue That Luang, Ban Phonxay, Vientiane, Laos (office). *Telephone:* (21) 412401 (office). *Fax:* (21) 412415 (office).

SOMERVILLE, Christopher Roland, BSc, PhD, FRS, FRSC, FAAS; American (b. Canadian) biochemist and academic; *Professor of Plant and Microbial Biology, University of California, Berkeley;* b. 11 Oct. 1947; ed Univ. of Alberta; naturalized US citizen 1995; Research Assoc., Dept of Agronomy, Univ. of Illinois 1978-81; Asst Prof., Dept of Genetics, Univ. of Alberta 1981; Assoc. Prof., Dept of Botany and Plant Pathology, Michigan State Univ. (MSU) and MSU-DOE Plant Research Lab. 1982–86, Prof. 1986–93; Prof. of Biological Sciences, Stanford Univ. 1994–2007, Dir Dept of Plant Biology, Carnegie Inst. of Washington 1994–2007; Prof. of Plant and Microbial Biology, Univ. of California, Berkeley 2007–, Dir Energy Biosciences Inst. 2007–; Visiting Prof., Univ. of Glasgow, UK 1998–; mem. numerous editorial boards, advisory panels for NSF, NIH, US Dept of Agric. and other agencies and insts; consultant to many cos, including Unilever, DuPont, Monsanto, Eli Lilly, Pioneer, Dow, Mendel, Biotechnology, LS9; mem. Academia Europaea 2002, NAS 1996; Fellow, AAAS 2006; Hon. DSc (Queens) 1993, (Alberta) 1997, (Wageningen) 1998, Guelph (2006); NSF Young Presidential Investigator Award 1984, Schull Award, American Soc. of Plant Biologists 1987, MSU Distinguished Faculty Award 1992, Alexander von Humboldt US Sr Scientist Award 1992, Gibbs Medal, American Soc. of Plant Physiology 1993, Kumho Award Kumho Cultural Foundation 2001, Hopkins Award and Memorial Lecturer, Biochemical Soc. 2004, Mendel Medal, Genetics Soc. 2004, Balzan Prize, Int. Balzan Foundation (co-recipient) 2006. *Achievements include:* has pioneered the use of the small mustard plant, *Arabidopsis thaliana*, as model species for plant molecular genetics. *Publications:* Biochemistry and Molecular Biology of Membrane and Storage Lipids of Plants (co-ed.) 1993, Arabidopsis (co-ed.) 1994, The Arabidopsis Book (co-ed.) 2002; numerous papers in professional journals on plant genomics, embryo devt and the synthesis of structural and storage components of plant cells. *Address:* Energy Biosciences Institute, 130 Calvin Laboratory, University of California, Berkeley, CA 94720-5230 (office); 161 Avenida Drive, Berkeley, CA 94708, USA (home). *Telephone:* (510) 643-6265 (office); (510) 665-6069 (office). *Fax:* (650) 325-6857 (office). *E-mail:* crs@berkeley.edu (office). *Website:* www.energybiosciencesinstitute.org (office); plantbio.berkeley.edu (office).

SOMERVILLE, Jane, MD, FRCP, FACC, FESC; British cardiologist; *Professor of Cardiology, University College Hospital;* est. Grown-Up Congenital Heart Disease (GUCH) Unit, Nat. Heart Hosp. (first specialist GUCH service in UK, led to new discipline in cardiology) 1975; currently Prof. of Cardiology, GUCH, Middlesex Hosp. and Univ. Coll. Hosp., London; Fellow, European Soc. of Cardiology, American Coll. of Cardiology. *Address:* 81/83 Harley Street, London, W1G 8PP (office); University College Hospital, Cecil Flemming House, Grafton Way, London, WC1E 6DB (office); c/o Middlesex Hospital, Mortimer Street, London, W1T 3AA, England (office). *Telephone:* (20) 7387-9300 (office). *E-mail:* somerville.jane@btinternet.com.

SOMMARUGA, Cornelio, LLD; Swiss diplomatist and international organization official; b. 29 Dec. 1932, Rome, Italy; s. of Carlo Sommaruga and Anna-Maria Valagussa; m. Ornella Marzorati 1957; two s. four d.; ed Rome, Paris, Univ. of Zürich; bank trainee, Zürich 1957–59; joined Diplomatic Service 1960; Attaché, Swiss Embassy, The Hague 1961; Sec., Swiss Embassy, Bonn 1962–64, Rome 1965–68; Deputy Head of Del. to EFTA, GATT and UNCTAD, Geneva 1969–73; Asst Sec.-Gen. EFTA 1973–75; Minister Plenipotentiary, Div. of Commerce, Fed. Dept of Public Economy, Berne 1976, Amb. 1977; del. to Fed. Council for Trade Agreements 1980–84; State Sec. for External Econ. Affairs 1984–86; Pres. ICRC 1987–99; Pres., UN Econ. Comm. for Europe 1977–78; Pres. Initiatives of Change Int., Caux 2000; Chair. J. P. Morgan (Suisse) SA, Geneva 2000–03 (mem. Bd 2003–), Geneva Int. Centre for Humanitarian Demining 2000, Karl Popper Foundation 2000; mem. Panel on UN Peace Operations, Int. Comm. on Intervention and State Sovereignty; Hon. mem. ICRC 2000; Commdr, Légion d'honneur; several other state honours from Italy, Belgium, The Holy See, Luxembourg, Lithuania, Iceland, Sweden; Hon. MD; Dr hc (Fribourg) 1985, (Minho) 1990, (Nice-Sophia Antipolis, Seoul Nat. Univ.) 1992; (Bologna) 1991, (Geneva) 1997, (Webster, St Louis) 1998; North-South Prize of the Council of Europe 2001; numerous awards from Red Cross Socs. *Address:* 7bis, avenue de la Paix, 1202 Geneva, Switzerland (office); 16 chemin des Crêts-de-Champel, 1206 Geneva, Switzerland (home). *Telephone:* (22) 906-16-97 (office); (22) 347-45-52 (home). *Fax:* (22) 906-16-90 (office); (22) 347-45-55 (home). *E-mail:* c.sommaruga@gichd.org (office); cornelio.sommaruga@bluewin.ch (home). *Website:* www.gichd.ch (office); www.chaux.ch.

SOMMER, Alfred, MD, MHS; American epidemiologist and academic; *Dean Emeritus and Professor, Bloomberg School of Public Health, Johns Hopkins University;* b. New York; m. Jill Sommer; one s. one d.; ed Union Coll., Schenectady, NY, Harvard Medical School, Hopkins School of Public Health; Medical Intern and Resident, Beth Israel Hosp., Harvard Univ., Boston, Mass 1967–69; Attending Physician, Grady Memorial Hosp., Atlanta, Ga 1969–70; Fellow in Epidemiology, Johns Hopkins School of Hygiene and Public Health, Baltimore, Md 1972–73, Resident and Fellow in Ophthalmology, Wilmer Eye Inst. 1973–76, Instructor in Ophthalmology 1976–80, Active Staff, Ophthalmology 1980–, Asst Prof., Ophthalmology, Epidemiology, and Int. Health 1980–81, Assoc. Prof. 1981–85, Prof. 1985–, Prof. of Ophthalmology, Wilmer Eye Inst., Founding Dir Dana Center for Preventive Ophthalmology 1980–90, Dean, Johns Hopkins School of Hygiene and Public Health (now Bloomberg School of Public Health) 1990–2005, Dean Emer. 2005–; Visiting Prof. of Ophthalmology, Univ. of Padjadjaran; Dir Nutritional Blindness Prevention Research Program, Bandung, Indonesia 1976–79; Surgeon, Cicendo Eye Hosp., Bandung 1976–79; Visiting Fellow, Inst. of Ophthalmology, Univ. of London, UK 1979–80; Dir WHO Collaborating Center for the Prevention of Blindness 1980–90; Medical Adviser, Helen Keller Int., New York 1980–; Consulting Ophthalmologist, Loch Raven Veterans' Admin Hosp., Baltimore 1981–93; Corp. Dir Becton Dickenson & Co. 1998–, T. Rowe Price Group; mem. Bd of Dirs Int. Trachoma Initiative 2003– (also Trustee), Int. Council of Ophthalmology Foundation, 2002–; mem. Exec. Cttee Acad. for Educational Devt 1997–2007 (also Trustee); Chair. Advisory Bd Epidemiologic Reviews 1990–2005; Chair. Bd of Overseers American Journal of Epidemiology 1990–2005; Editorial positions American Journal of Ophthalmology, Archives Ophthalmology, American Journal of Epidemiology, Ophthalmology (TAAOO), New England Journal of Medicine, American Journal of Clinical Nutrition, Investigative Ophthalmology and Visual Science, Experimental Eye Research, American Journal of Public Health, Current Eye Research

Journal of the American Medical Asscn, Milbank Quarterly, Journal of the Royal Soc. of Medicine, Current Issues in Public Health, 1993–; mem. Editorial Advisory Bd EyeNet Magazine 1999–; mem. Royal Soc. of Medicine, UK 1979, Asscn for Research in Vision and Ophthalmology 1981, Soc. for Epidemiologic Research 1981, American Public Health Asscn 1982, American Ophthalmological Soc. 1983, American Glaucoma Soc. 1988, American Inst. of Nutrition/FASEB 1989, American Soc. for Clinical Nutrition 1989, Inst. of Medicine 1992, Academia Ophthalmologica Internationalis (19th Chair. 1997) 1997, NAS 2001, Int. Council of Ophthalmology 2002–; Trustee Foundation of the Int. Council of Ophthalmology; Fellow, American Acad. of Ophthalmology 1978, American Coll. of Preventive Medicine 1982; at forefront of research into vitamin A deficiency; Hon. Prof. of Ophthalmology, Peking Union Medical College, Beijing 1993; Hon. Prof. of Public Health, Sun Yat-sen Univ. of Medical Sciences, People's Repub. of China, 1998; First Hon. Prof., King Carlos III Nat. Inst. of Health, School of Public Health, Madrid; Helen Keller Blindness Prevention Award 1980, Honor Award 1986, Sr Honor Award 1996, American Acad. of Ophthalmology 1986, Charles A. Dana Award for Pioneering Achievements in Health 1988, First Dean's Alumni Award, Johns Hopkins Univ. School of Hygiene and Public Health 1988, Distinguished Service Award for Contribs to Vision Care, American Public Health Asscn 1988, Nat. Merit Award for Contribs to Public Health, Delta Omega (Public Health Honor Soc.) 1988, Award for Distinguished Contribs to World Ophthalmology, XXIVth Int. Congress of Ophthalmology, Int. Fed. of Ophthalmological Societies 1990, ACAM Achievement Award in Preventive Medicine 1990, Gold Medal for Contribs to World Ophthalmology, Saudi Ophthalmological Soc. 1991, Mericos H. Whittier Award in Ophthalmology, Mericos Eye Inst., Scripps Insts of Medicine and Science 1992, Joseph E. Smadel Award, Infectious Diseases Soc. of America 1992, 1st Recipient, Gesellschaft für angewandte Vitaminforschung Prize (Germany) 1995, Distinguished Alumnus Award, Johns Hopkins Univ., 1995, Albert Lasker Award for Clinical Medical Research 1997, Helmut Horten Medical Research Award 1997, Prince Mahidol Award for Int. Contribs to Medicine and Public Health (Thailand) 1997, Int. Gold Medal for Contribs to Ophthalmology, Singapore Nat. Eye Centre 1997, Int. Duke Elder Gold Medal, Int. Council of Ophthalmology 1998, Int. Blindness Prevention Award, American Acad. of Ophthalmology 1998, E. H. Christopherson Award, American Acad. of Pediatrics 2000, F. Parke Lewis Lifetime Achievement Professional Service Award, Prevent Blindness America 2001, Gold Jose Rizal Medal, Asia Pacific Acad. of Ophthalmology 2001, Bristol-Myers Squibb/Mead Johnson Award for Distinguished Achievement in Nutrition Research 2001, Danone Int. Prize for Nutrition 2001, Special Recognition Award for Leadership, Asscn for Research in Vision and Ophthalmology 2002, George Gehrmann Lecturer, American Coll. of Occupational and Environmental Medicine, Baltimore 2002, Howard S. Brode Lecturer in Science, Whitman Coll., Walla Walla, Washington 2002, Sir John Wilson Lecturer, Int. Congress of Ophthalmology, Sydney 2002, Pollin Prize in Pediatric Research 2004, Helen Keller Prize for Vision Research 2005, Gonin Medal 2006. *Publications:* Field Guide to the Detection and Control of Xerophthalmia 1978, Epidemiology and Statistics for the Ophthalmologist 1980, Nutritional Blindness: Xerophthalmia and Keratomalacia 1982, Periodic, Large Oral Doses of Vitamin A for the Prevention of Vitamin A Deficiency and Xerophthalmia (co-author) 1984, Vitamin A Deficiency: Health, Survival, and Vision (co-author) 1996; more than 80 book chapters and reviews and more than 200 articles in scientific journals. *Address:* Johns Hopkins Bloomberg School of Public Health, 615 N Wolfe Street, Baltimore, MD 21205-2179, USA (office). *Telephone:* (410) 502-4167 (office). *Fax:* (410) 502-4169 (office). *E-mail:* asommer@jhsph.edu (office). *Website:* www.jhsph.edu (office).

SOMMER, Elke; German actress and painter; b. (Elke Schletz), 5 Nov. 1940, Berlin; d. of Friedrich Schletz and Renate Schletz; m. Joe Hyams (twice); Wolf Walther 1993; first film, L'Amico del Giaguaro 1958; since then has made more than 70 films including The Prize, The Victors, Shot in the Dark, The Oscar, Himmelsheim, Neat and Tidy, Severed Ties; hosted TV show Painting with Elke (PBS) 1985; Golden Globe Award 1965, Jefferson Award, Merit of Achievement Award 1990. *Leisure interests:* riding, art. *Address:* 540 N Beverly Glen Boulevard West, Los Angeles, CA 90024, USA. *Telephone:* (310) 724-8990. *Fax:* (310) 724-8993.

SOMMER, Ron; German business executive; b. 1949, Haifa, Israel; ed Univ. of Vienna, Austria; began career with Nixdorf Group in New York, Paris and Paderborn, Germany; Man. Sony Deutschland 1980, Chair. 1986; Pres., CEO Sony USA 1990; Pres., CEO Sony Europe 1993; CEO Deutsche Telekom AG 1995–2002; mem. Bd of Dirs Motorola Inc. 2004–, Muenchener Rueckversicherung, AFK Sistema, Tata Consultancy Services, Weather Industries; mem. Int. Advisory Bd Blackstone Group; mem. Supervisory Bd Celanese AG 2004–. *Address:* c/o Board of Directors, Motorola Inc., 1303 East Algonquin Road, Schaumburg, IL 60196, USA (office).

SOMMER, Theo, DPhil; German journalist; *Editor-at-Large, Die Zeit;* b. 10 June 1930, Constance; s. of Theo Sommer and Else Sommer; m. 1st Elda Tsilenis 1952; two s.; m. 2nd Heide Grenz 1976; two s.; m. 3rd Sabine Grewe 1989; one d.; ed Univ of Tübingen, Chicago and Harvard Univs; Local Ed. Schwäbisch-Gmünd 1952–54; Foreign Ed. Die Zeit 1958, Deputy Ed. 1968, Ed.-in-Chief 1973–92, Publr 1992–, Ed.-at-Large 2000–; Lecturer in Int. Relations, Univ. of Hamburg 1967–70; Chief of Planning Staff, Ministry of Defence 1969–70; mem. Deutsche Gesellschaft für Auswärtige Politik; mem. Council IISS 1963–76, 1978–87, German Armed Forces Structure Comm. 1970–72, Int. Comm. on the Balkans 1995–96, Ind. Int. Comm. on the Balkans 1999–2000; Deputy Chair. Comm. on the Future on the Bundeswehr 1999–2000; Chair. Comm. Investigating Effects of DU Ammunitions, Radar and Asbestos on German Armed Forces 2002; mem. Indo-German Consultative Group 1992– (Co-Chair. 1996–), German-Japanese Dialogue Forum

1993–; mem. Bd Deutsche Welthungerhilfe 1992–, Max-Bauer Preis 1992–, German-Turkish Foundation 1998–; mem. German Foreign Policy Asscn, IISS, Königswinter Conf., Advisory Council, Mil. History Inst.; Contributing Ed. Newsweek Int. 1968–90; regular contrib. to American, British, Japanese and Korean publs; commentator German TV, radio and moderator of monthly programmes; Hon. mem. Asscn of Anciens, NATO Defense Coll. 1971, Trilateral Comm. 1993; Fed. Order of Merit (First Class) 1998, Gold Honor Cross, German Armed Forces 2002; Hon. LLD (Univ. of Maryland, USA) 1982; Theoder-Wolf Prize 1966, Int. Communications Award, People's Repub. of China 1991, Columbus Prize 1993. *Publications:* Deutschland und Japan zwischen den Mächten (Germany and Japan Between the Powers) 1935–40 1962, Vom Antikominternpakt zum Dreimächtepakt 1962, Reise in ein fernes Land 1964, Ed. Denken an Deutschland 1966, Ed. Schweden-Report 1974, Die chinesische Karte (The Chinese Card) 1979, Allianz in Umbruch (Alliance in Disarray) 1982, Blick zurück in die Zukunft (Look Back into the Future) 1984, Reise ins andere Deutschland (Journey to the Other Germany) 1986, Europa im 21. Jahrhundert 1989, Geschichte der Bonner Republik 1949–99 1999, Der Zukunft entgegen (Toward the Future) 1999, Phoenix Europe. The European Union: Its Progress, Problems and Prospects 2000, Hamburg 2004, 1945: Biographie eines Jahres 2005. *Address:* Die Zeit, Pressehaus, Speersort 1, 20079 Hamburg (office); 17 Zabelweg, 22359 Hamburg, Germany (home). *Telephone:* (40) 3280240 (office); (40) 6037300 (home). *Fax:* (40) 3280407 (office); (40) 6030044 (home). *E-mail:* sommer@zeit.de (office); tsommer01@aol.com (home). *Website:* www.zeit.de (office); www.theosommer.de.

SOMOGYI, Ferenc, MA, PhD; Hungarian diplomatist, business executive and politician; *Ambassador to USA;* b. 1 Sept. 1945, Hartkirchen, Austria; m.; one d. two s.; ed Univ. of Econs, Coll. of Political Sciences, Budapest; Desk Officer, Ministry of Foreign Affairs 1968–69, Attaché, Embassy in Rangoon 1969–71, Second Sec., Lagos 1971–73, Sr Officer, Ministry for Foreign Affairs 1973–80, Deputy Perm. Rep. to UN, New York 1980–84, Head of Dept, Ministry of Foreign Affairs 1984–89, State Sec. 1989–90, Admin. State Sec. 1990–92, 1994–96, State Sec. for Euro-Atlantic Integration 1996–98; Chair. Exportgarancia Ltd 1992–94; Dir for Integration, Matáv Hungarian Telecommunications Co. 1998–2001; CEO Stonebridge Communications, Skopje 2001–04; Minister of Foreign Affairs 2004–06; Dir for Int. Relations Magyar Telekom, Budapest 2007; Amb. to USA 2007–; Pres. Hungarian Atlantic Council 1998–2003; mem. Bd of Trustees, McDaniel Coll., Westminster, MD, USA, Inst. for European Studies Univ. of Columbia, NY 2000–; mem. Bureau of Atlantic Treaty Asscns 2000–03. *Address:* Embassy of Hungary, 3910 Shoemaker Street, NW, Washington, DC 20008, USA (office). *Telephone:* (202) 362-6730 (office). *Fax:* (202) 966-8135 (office). *E-mail:* ambassador.was@kum.hu (office). *Website:* www.huembwas.org (office).

SOMOGYI, Peter, PhD, FRS, FMedSci, FHAS; Hungarian/British professor of neurobiology; *Director, Medical Research Council Anatomical Neuropharmacology Unit, University of Oxford;* b. 27 Feb. 1950, Szentendre; ed Loránd Eötvös Univ., Budapest; research training in neurocytology and neuroanatomy at Semmelweis Univ. of Medicine, Budapest, in biochemistry and immunocytochemistry at the Univ. of Oxford, UK; postdoctoral fellowship at Flinders Medical Centre, South Australia; has trained research students since 1978; Assoc., later Co-Dir Anatomical Neuropharmacology Unit, MRC, Oxford, 1995–98, Dir 1998–; Prof. of Neurobiology, Univ. of Oxford 1996–; Distinguished Visiting Prof., Kyoto Univ., Japan 1998; Visiting Prof., Nat. Inst. of Physiological Sciences, Okazaki, Japan 2002; Nicholas Kurti Sr Research Fellow, Brasenose Coll., Oxford 2004–; Fellow, Acad. of Medical Sciences 2006–; Corresp. mem. Hungarian Acad. of Sciences 2004–; Assoc. of the Neuroscience Research Program, The Neuroscience Inst., San Diego, USA 2008–; Hon. PhD (József Attila Univ., Szeged) 1990; M. Lenhossek Prize, Asscn of Hungarian Anatomists and Embryologists 1982, Charles Judson Herrick Award, Asscn of American Anatomists 1984, Moruzzi Lecturer, European Neuroscience Asscn, Stockholm 1990, Krieg Cortical Discoverer Award, Cajal Club, American Anatomical Soc. 1991, Julian Tobias Memorial Lecture, Univ. of Chicago 1995, Yngve Zotterman Prize, Swedish Physiological Soc. 1995, Jerzy Olszewski Lecture, Montreal Neurological Inst. 2001, Janos Szentagothai Memorial Lecture, Budapest 2002, Wenner-Gren Foundation Distinguished Lecturer, Sweden 2003, Segerfalk Award Lecture, Lund, Sweden 2003, Special Plenary Lecture, 16th IFAA Conference, Kyoto, Japan 2004, 1st Janos Szentagothai Memorial Lecture, Univ. of California, Irvine 2005, Quastel Lecure, Otto Loewi Conference, Eilat, Israel 2006, Servier Conf. Lecture, Neuroscience Research Centre, Univ. of Montreal 2006, János Arany Medal, Hungarian Acad. of Sciences, Presidential Cttee for Contribution to Hungarian Science from Abroad 2006, István Báthory Award, Hungarian Nat. Council of Transylvania 2006, The IBRO Lecture Univ. of Debrecen, Hungary 2008, The 1st Hans Kosterlitz Lecture, Univ. of Aberdeen, Scotland 2008, The Feldberg Prize and Lectures, Feldberg Foundation, London 2009. *Address:* MRC Anatomical Neuropharmacology Unit, Mansfield Road, Oxford, OX1 3TH, England (office). *Telephone:* (1865) 271865 (office). *Fax:* (1865) 271648 (office). *E-mail:* peter.somogyi@pharm.ox.ac.uk (office). *Website:* mrcanu.pharm.ox.ac.uk (office).

SOMORJAI, Gabor Arpad, PhD, FAAS; American chemist and academic; *Professor of Chemistry, University of California, Berkeley;* b. 4 May 1935, Budapest, Hungary; s. of Charles Somorjai and Livia Ormos; m. Judith Kaldor 1957; one s. one d.; ed Tech. Univ., Budapest, Univ. of Calif. at Berkeley; mem. Research Staff IBM, New York 1960–64; at Faculty of Dept of Chem., Univ. of Calif., Berkeley 1964–, Asst Prof. 1964–67, Assoc. Prof. 1967–72, Prof. 1972–; Faculty Sr Scientist, Materials Science Div. and Dir Surface Science and Catalysis Program, Lawrence Berkeley Lab., Berkeley, Calif. 1964–; Univ. Prof., UC System 2002–; numerous awards and visiting professorships in USA and UK including Visiting Fellow, Emmanuel Coll., Univ. of Cambridge 1969; Centenary Lecturer Royal Soc. of Chem., UK 1983; Hinshelwood Lecturer,

Univ. of Oxford 1994; Linnett Lecturer, Univ. of Cambridge 1994; mem. NAS 1979–, ACS, American Physical Soc., American Acad. of Arts and Sciences 1983; Hon. mem. Hungarian Acad. of Sciences 1990; Hon. Fellow, Cardiff Univ. 2006; Dr hc (Tech. Univ., Budapest) 1989, (Univ. Pierre et Marie Curie) 1990, (Univ. Libre de Bruxelles) 1992, (Ferrara) 1998, József Attila Univ., Hungary) 1999 (Royal Inst. of Tech., Stockholm) 2000, (Manchester) 2001, (ETH Zürich) 2003; Emmett Award American Catalysis Soc. 1977, ACS Colloid and Surface Chem. Award 1981, ACS Peter Debye Award 1989, ACS Adamson Surface Chemistry Award 1994, Von Hippel Award, Materials Research Soc. 1997, Wolf Prize 1998, ACS Catalysis Award 2000, Pauling Medal, Hungarian Acad. of Sciences 2000, Nat. Medal of Science 2002, Cotton Award 2003, Remsen Award, Md Section of ACS 2006, Langmuir Prize, American Physical Soc. 2007, Priestley Medal 2008. *Publications:* Principles of Surface Chemistry 1972, Chemistry in Two Dimensions 1981, Introduction to Surface Chemistry and Catalysis 1994, serves editorial bds of numerous scientific publs, more than 900 publs in major scientific journals. *Leisure interests:* swimming, walking. *Address:* Department of Chemistry, D56 Hildebrand, University of California, Berkeley, Berkeley, CA 94720-1460 (office); 665 San Luis Road, Berkeley, CA 94707, USA (home). *Telephone:* (510) 642-4053 (office). *Fax:* (510) 643-9668 (office). *E-mail:* somorjai@berkeley.edu (home). *Website:* www.cchem.berkeley.edu/gasgrp (office); chem.berkeley.edu/people/faculty/somorjai/somorjai (office).

SOMPONG, Amornvivat, BBA, MA; Thai politician; b. 3 July 1941, Bangkok; m.; ed Curry Coll., Milton, Mass, USA, Chiangmai Univ.; mem. Exec. Cttee, Nat. Democracy Party 1981–82, Deputy Sec.-Gen. 1983–84, Sec.-Gen. 1984–88; Sec.-Gen. Ruam Thai Party 1988–89; Deputy Leader Unity Party 1988–89; Deputy Leader Chart Pathana Party 1992–93, mem. People's Power Party 1998–; mem. Parl. for Chonburi Prov. 1986–89, for Chiangmai Prov. 1992–93, 1994–96, 1999–2000; Vice-Chair. Industry Cttee, Nat. Ass. 1988–89; Deputy Minister of Agric. and Cooperatives 1990–91, of Transport and Communications 1997; mem. Nat. Ass. 1991–; Minister of Industry 1992–93, of Labour and Social Welfare 1994–95, 1997, Minister to Prime Minister's Office 1996, Minister of Justice 2008, Deputy Prime Minister and Minister of Foreign Affairs 2008; adviser to Prime Minister 2001–05. *Address:* People's Power Party, 1770 Thanon Petchaburi Tat Mai, Bang Gapi, Huay Kwang, Bangkok 10310, Thailand (office). *Telephone:* (2) 686–7000 (office). *Website:* www.ppp.or.th (office).

SOMSAVAT, Lengsavad; Laotian politician; *Deputy Prime Minister;* b. 16 June 1945, Luangphrabang; m. Bounkongmany Lengsavad; one s. two d.; ed Nat. Org. for the Study of Policy and Admin; Head of the Secr., Cabinet of the Lao People's Revolutionary Party (LPRP) Cen. Cttee. 1975–82; Deputy Chief, Council of Ministers; fmr Deputy Minister; First Vice-Chair. LPRP History Research Comm. 1982–88, Chief of the Cabinet of LPRP and Cabinet of Ministers 1991–93; Amb. to Bulgaria 1989–91; Minister of Foreign Affairs 1993–2006; Deputy Prime Minister 1998–; Chair. Vientiane Cttee for Flood Control; Dr rer. pol (Ramkhamheang Univ., Thailand) 2000; Medal of Liberty Issara, Medal of Labour, Anti-Imperialist Cross, Revolutionary Medal, People's Repub. of Korea, Medal of Friendship Govts of Cuba and Bulgaria. *Leisure interests:* reading, golf, singing. *Address:* c/o Office of the Prime Minister, Ban Sisavat, Vientiane, Laos (office). *Telephone:* (21) 213653 (office). *Fax:* (21) 213560 (office).

SON, Kil-seung, BA; South Korean business executive; b. 1941; ed Seoul Nat. Univ.; joined Sunkyong Textiles Corpn (renamed SK Corpn) 1965, various Exec. Man. positions in Office of Corp. Man. and Planning, Group Pres. 1991, Pres. Daehan Telecom –1998, Chair. and CEO SK Corpn 1998–2003 (resgnd after conviction for accounting irregularities), also fmr Chair. and CEO SK Telecom, SK Shipping; Chair. Korean Business Council for the Arts, Korean Business Messena Asscn; fmr Chair. Fed. of Korean Industries (FKI); mem. Bd Dirs Forum Council; Hon. Citizen of China Award 2001, CEO of Korea Award, Korean Chamber of Commerce and Industry (KCCI) 2002, 2003, Korean Man. Award, Top Business Man. of Korea Award, KCCI. *Address:* c/o SK Group, 99 Seorin-dong, Jongru-Gu, Seoul 110-110, Republic of Korea (office).

SON, Masayoshi; Japanese business executive; *Chairman and CEO, Softbank Corporation;* b. 11 Aug. 1957, Tosu; m.; two; ed Univ. of California, Berkeley, USA; started by importing used video games from Japan (to USA); co-developed pocket electronic translator bought by Sharp; f. Softbank Corpn 1981, now Chair. and CEO, now more than 165 subsidiaries covering financial services, internet infrastructure, information tech.-related distribution services, publishing and marketing, tech. services. *Address:* Softbank Corpn, Tokyo Shiodome Building, 1-9-1, Higashi-shimbashi, Minato-ku, Tokyo 105-7303, Japan (office). *Telephone:* (3) 5642-8000 (office). *Fax:* (3) 5543-0431 (office). *E-mail:* info@softbank.co.jp (office). *Website:* www.softbank.co.jp (office).

SONDECKIS, Saulius; Lithuanian conductor; b. 11 Oct. 1928, Šiauliai; s. of Jackus Sondeckis and Rozalija Sondeckienė; m. Silvija Sondeckienė; three s.; ed Lithuanian Conservatory as violinist, Moscow State Conservatory; Founder, Conductor and Artistic Dir Lithuanian Chamber Orchestra 1960–2004; tours fmr USSR, Europe, USA and Japan 1960–; teacher, Vilnius M. Čiurlionis School of Arts 1955–85, f. Youth Orchestra; Founder and Artistic Dir St Petersburg Camerata Chamber Orchestra (now Orchestra of Hermitage Museum) 1989–; Prof., Vilnius Conservatory (now Lithuanian Acad. of Music and Theatre) 1957–96, Chair. Strings Dept 1959–87; Prof., St Petersburg Conservatory 1989–91; f. (with G. Kremer) Kremerata Baltica Chamber Orchestra 1996; Chief Conductor Hellos Orchestra of Patras, Greece 1999–2004; conducted various European and Canadian orchestras; worked together with Rostropovich and many other distinguished soloists; first performance of chamber music by Alfred Schnittke, Sergey Slonimsky, Arvo Pärt, contemporary Lithuanian composers; Hon. Prof. N. A. Rimsky-Korsakov Conservatory, St Petersburg; Lithuanian Grand Duke First and Fifth Order of Gediminas Cavalier, First Grade Hon. Cross of Austria for Science and Arts 2003; Dr hc Lithuanian Acad. of Music and Theatre 2003; Lithuanian State Prize 1971, winner of Gold Medal at Herbert von Karajan Stiftung Competition in Berlin 1976, USSR People's Artist 1980, USSR State Prize 1987, State Prize of Lithuanian Govt 1998, WIPO Creativity Award, Gold Medal 2004. *Address:* Čiurlionio 28, Vilnius 03104, Lithuania (home). *Telephone:* (5) 2331557 (home). *Fax:* (5) 2332768 (home). *E-mail:* silvija@studiapro.lt (home).

SONDHEIM, Stephen Joshua, BA; American composer and lyricist; b. 22 March 1930, New York, NY; s. of Herbert Sondheim and Janet Fox; ed George School, Newtown, Pa, Williams Coll., Williamstown, Mass, private instruction; Pres. Dramatists' Guild 1973–81, Council mem. 1981–; Visiting Prof. of Drama and Musical Theatre, Univ. of Oxford Jan.–June 1990; mem. American Acad. and Inst. of Arts and Letters 1983–; Antoinette Perry Awards for Company 1971, Follies 1972, A Little Night Music 1973, Sweeney Todd 1979; Drama Critics' Awards 1971, 1972, 1973, 1976, 1979; Evening Standard Drama Award 1996; Grammy Awards 1984, 1986; Nat. Medal of Arts 1997, Praemium Imperial 2000. *Compositions:* television: Topper (co-author) 1953, Evening Primrose (music and lyrics) 1967; lyrics: West Side Story 1957, Gypsy 1959, Do I Hear a Waltz? 1965, Candide 1973; music and lyrics: A Funny Thing Happened on the Way to the Forum 1962, Anyone Can Whistle 1964, Evening Primrose 1966, Company 1970, Follies 1971, A Little Night Music 1973, The Frogs 1974, Pacific Overtures 1976, Sweeney Todd 1978, Merrily We Roll Along 1981, Sunday in the Park with George 1984, Into the Woods (Drama Critics' Circle Award 1988) 1986, Follies 1987, Assassins 1991, Passion 1994, Wise Guys 2001; anthologies: Side by Side by Sondheim 1976, Marry Me a Little 1980, You're Gonna Love Tomorrow 1983, Putting It Together 1993; screenplays: (with Anthony Perkins) The Last of Sheila 1973, Birdcage 1996, Getting Away Murder 1996; film scores: Stavisky 1974, Reds 1981, Dick Tracy 1989; incidental music: The Girls of Summer 1956, Invitation to a March 1961, Twigs 1971. *Address:* c/o John Breglio, 1285 Avenue of the Americas, New York, NY 10019, USA (office).

SONENBERG, Nahum, BSc, MSc, PhD, FRSC; Israeli biochemist and academic; *James McGill Professor, Department of Biochemistry, McGill University;* m.; two d.; ed Tel-Aviv Univ., Weizman Inst. of Science; early research position at Roche Inst. of Molecular Biology, NJ, USA; joined faculty at McGill Univ., Montreal, Canada 1979, currently James McGill Prof., Dept of Biochemistry, also Dir Sonenberg Lab.; Int. Research Scholar, Howard Hughes Medical Inst.; Distinguished Scientist, Canadian Insts of Health Research; Robert L. Noble Prize, Nat. Cancer Inst. of Canada 2002, Killiam Prize for Health Sciences 2005. *Publications:* numerous papers in scientific and medical journals. *Address:* McGill University, Room 807, McIntyre Medical Building, 3655 Promenade Sir William Osler, Montreal, Quebec H3G 1Y6, Canada (office). *Telephone:* (514) 398-7274 (office). *Fax:* (514) 398-7384 (office). *E-mail:* nahum.sonenberg@mcgill.ca (office). *Website:* www.med.mcgill.ca/nahum (office).

SONG, Baorui; Chinese politician; *Deputy Director-General, CPPCC Subcommittee for Handling Proposals;* b. Dec. 1937, Shunyi Dist, Beijing; ed Tsinghua Univ., Beijing; joined CCP 1958; fmr Deputy Dir, Chief Engineer China Welding Rod Plant, Dir China Welding Rod Plant Inst. 1975–82; Man. China Welding Materials Manufacture Co. 1982–83; Deputy Sec. then Sec. CCP Zigong City Cttee 1983–86; fmr mem. Standing Cttee CCP Sichuan Prov. Cttee; Chair. Sichuan Prov. Comm. for Restructuring the Economy 1986–89, Exec. Deputy Sec. CCP Sichuan Prov. Cttee 1989–99; Gov. Sichuan Prov. 1996–99; Deputy Dir State Comm. for Restructuring Economy 2001–; Deputy Dir-Gen. CPPCC Sub-cttee for Handling Proposals 2003–; Alt. mem. 14th CCP Cen. Cttee 1992–97, mem. 15th CCP Cen. Cttee 1997–2002; Deputy 8th NPC. *Address:* Subcommittee for Handling Proposals, CPPCC, Beijing, People's Republic of China (office).

SONG, Fatang; Chinese politician; b. Dec. 1940, Tancheng, Shandong Prov.; ed Qufu Teachers' Univ.; joined CCP 1961; Cadre, Supervision Cttee, CCP Shandong Prov. Cttee 1964; Sec. Org. Dept, CCP Revolutionary Cttee, Shandong Prov. 1967; Deputy Div. Chief, Org. Dept, CCP Shandong Prov. Cttee 1973; Deputy Sec. CCP Tai'an Co. Cttee, Deputy Sec. CCP Tai'an Municipal Cttee, Shandong Prov. 1979–84, Sec. 1984, Mayor of Taian 1985–89; Vice-Gov. Shandong Prov. 1989–2000; Deputy Sec. CCP Shandong Prov. Cttee 1998–99; Deputy Gov., then Gov. Heilongjiang Prov. 2000–03; Sec. CCP Heilongjiang Prov. Cttee 2003–; Chair. Standing Cttee Heilongjiang Prov. People's Congress 2003–05; Alt. mem. 15th CCP Cen. Cttee 1997–2002, mem. 16th CCP Cen. Cttee 2002–07; Deputy, 9th NPC 1998–2003; Vice-Chair. Education, Science, Culture and Public Health Cttee, NPC 2005–. *Address:* Education, Science, Culture and Public Health Committee, National People's Congress, Beijing, People's Republic of China (office).

SONG, Jian, DSc; Chinese state official and academic; b. 29 Dec. 1931, Rongcheng Co., Shandong Prov.; s. of the late Song Zengjin and Jiang Yuxian; m. Wang Yusheng 1961; one s. one d.; ed Harbin Tech. Univ., Beijing Foreign Languages Inst., Bauman Eng Inst., Moscow and Moscow Univ., USSR; joined CCP 1947; Dir and Head, Lab. of Cybernetics, Inst. of Math., Acad. Sinica 1960–70; Dir Guided Missile Control Lab., 7th Ministry of Machine Bldg Industry 1962–70; Head, Chief Scientist, Space Science Div., Acad. of Space Tech. 1971–78, Vice-Pres., Deputy Science Dir, Acad. of Space Tech. 1978–81; Vice-Minister and Chief Eng Scientist, Ministry of Astronautics 1981–84; Researcher, China Aviation Industry Corpn; Research Prof., Beijing Inst. of Information and Control 1983–; Visiting Prof., MIT, Harvard, Univ. of Minn. 1980; Prof., Tsinghua Univ., Fudan Univ., Harbin Univ. of Tech. 1986–; Chair. State Science and Tech. Comm. 1984–98; State Councillor 1986–98, Chair. Environmental Protection Cttee; Vice-Chair. Three Gorges Project Construction Cttee; Head, State Leading Group for Man. of Intellectual Property Rights; mem. State Steering Group of Science, Tech. and Educ. 1998; Vice-Chair. State Academic Degrees Cttee 1999; Vice-Pres. China Soc. of Demographic Science 1982–86; Assoc. Chief Ed. System & Control Letters 1983–85; Chief Ed. Automatic Control & System Eng, Encyclopaedia of China 1983–; mem. Ed. Bd Encyclopaedia of China 1984–; Council mem. Int. Fed. of Automatic Control 1984–87; Vice-Pres. China System Eng Soc. 1985–87; Vice-Chair. Chinese People's Political Consultative Conf. 1998–; Pres. China-Japan Friendship Asscn 1998–; Alt. mem. 12th CCP Cen. Cttee 1982–87, mem. 13th CCP Cen. Cttee 1987–92, 14th CCP Cen. Cttee 1992–97, 15th CCP Cen. Cttee 1997–2002; Vice-Chair. 9th CPPCC Nat. Cttee 1998–2003; mem. Chinese Acad. of Sciences 1991–, Chinese Acad. of Eng 1994– (Pres. 1998–2002); Foreign mem. Russian Acad. of Sciences 1994, Royal Swedish Acad. of Eng Sciences 1994, Nat. Acad. of Eng, USA 2000, Argentine Acad. of Eng 2001, Yugoslav Acad. of Eng 2002; Corresp. mem. Nat. Acad. of Eng of Mexico 1985; Hon. Distinguished Visiting Prof. Washington Univ. 1986–; Hon. Pres. Chinese Asscn of Environmental Protection; Hon. DHumLitt (Houston) 1996; Nat. Natural Sciences Award, Nat. Award for Advancements in Science and Tech. 1987, Albert Einstein Award 1987, Int. Asscn for Mathematics 1987 and numerous other nat. and int. awards. *Publications:* Reference Frames in Space Flight 1963, Engineering Cybernetics (co-author) 1980, China's Population: Problems and Prospects 1981, Recent Development in Control Theory and Its Applications 1984, Population Projections and Control 1981, Population Control Theory 1985, Population Control in China: Theory and Applications 1985, Population System Control 1988, Science and Technology and Social System 1988; numerous articles. *Leisure interest:* swimming. *Address:* National Committee of Chinese People's Political Consultative Conference, 23 Taipingqiao Street, Beijing, People's Republic of China (office).

SONG, Lin, BEng; Chinese business executive; *President, China Resources National Corporation;* b. 1963, Shanghai; ed Tongji Univ.; joined China Resources Holdings Co. 1986, fmr Deputy Gen. Man. China Resources Petrochemical Co., currently Pres. and mem. Bd of Dirs China Resources Nat. Corpn, China Resources Holdings Co., Chair. China Resources Enterprise Ltd, China Resources Power Holdings, China Resources Logic Ltd; Deputy Chair. China Vanke Co. Ltd; mem. Bd of Dirs Geely Automobile Holdings Ltd 2004–, Bank of East Asia (China) Ltd. *Address:* China Resources National Corporation, Floor 49, CRC Building, 26 Harbour Road, Wanchai, Hong Kong Special Administrative Region, People's Republic of China (office). *Telephone:* 28797888 (office). *Fax:* 25988453 (office). *E-mail:* crc@crc.com.hk (office). *Website:* www.crc.com.hk (office).

SONG, Min-soon; South Korean diplomatist; b. 28 July 1948, Jinyang; m. Young Sook 1977; one s. one d.; ed Seoul Nat. Univ.; joined diplomatic service 1975, served in numerous posts including Vice-Consul, Consulate in West Berlin, served in Embassy in New Delhi, First Sec. Embassy in Washington, DC 1986–89, served in Embassy in Singapore, Dir N America Div., American Affairs Bureau 2000–01, Amb. to Poland 2001–03, Deputy Minister of Foreign Affairs and Trade and lead negotiator in six-party talks with Democratic People's Repub. of Korea 2004–05, Chief Presidential Sec. for Security 2006, Minister of Foreign Affairs and Trade 2006–08. *Address:* c/o Ministry of Foreign Affairs and Trade, 95-1, Doryeom-dong, Jongno-gu, Seoul 110-787, Republic of Korea (office).

SONG, Ping; Chinese party official; b. 1917, Juxian Co., Shandong Prov.; ed Inst. Marxism-Leninism, Yan'an; joined CCP 1937; Vice-Minister, Labour 1953; Vice-Chair. State Planning Comm. 1957–63; Sec. CCP Gansu and Vice-Chair. Gansu Revolutionary Cttee 1972, First Sec. CCP Gansu, Chair. Gansu Revolutionary Cttee, Second Political Commissar, PLA Lanzhou Mil. Region and First Political Commissar, Gansu Mil. Dist, PLA 1977–80; First Vice-Chair. State Planning Comm. 1981–83; Minister in charge of State Planning Comm. 1983–87; Chair. Family Planning Asscn 1990–; Deputy Sec.-Gen., First Session of the 7th NPC March 1988; Deputy Dir Leading Group for Co-ordinating Nat. Scientific Work 1983; State Councillor 1983–88; Vice-Chair. Environmental Protection Cttee State Council 1984–87, Nat. Agric. Zoning Cttee 1983–; Deputy Head Leading Group for Scientific Work, State Council 1983–92; Head Leading Group for Econ. Information Man., State Council 1986–92; Head Org. Dept Cen. Cttee CCP 1988–90; visited Pakistan 1991; mem. 11th Cen. Cttee CCP 1977, 12th Cen. Cttee CCP 1982–87, Political Bureau 1987–92, 13th Cen. Cttee (mem. Standing Cttee 1989–92); mem. Presidium 14th CCP Nat. Congress 1992; Hon. Pres. Chinese Asscn for Promotion of the Population Culture; Hon. Dir-in-Chief China Welfare Fund for the Handicapped; Hon. Adviser 'Happiness Project' Org. *Address:* Central Committee of CCP, Zhang Nan Hai, Beijing, People's Republic of China (office).

SONG, Gen. Qingwei; Chinese army officer and party official; b. 1929, Lingxian Co., Shandong Prov.; joined CCP 1945; Political Commissar of PLA Jinan Mil. Area Command 1987–95; rank of Lt-Gen. 1988, of Gen. 1994; mem. 14th CCP Cen. Cttee 1992–97; Vice-Chair. Foreign Affairs Cttee 9th NPC 1998. *Address:* c/o Standing Committee of National People's Congress, Beijing, People's Republic of China (office).

SONG, Ruixiang; Chinese politician; b. 1939, Jintan Co., Jiangsu Prov.; joined CCP 1959; Gov. of Qinghai Prov. 1985–93; Minister of Geology and Mineral Resources 1993–98, Party Group Sec. Ministry of Geology and Mineral Resources; Chair. Nat. Mineral Reserves Comm. 1995–96; Vice-Chair. Nat. Mineral Resources Cttee 1996–98; Deputy Dir State Gen. Admin. of Environment Protection 1998–2003; Dir China Seismological Bureau 2003–04; mem. 15th CCP Cen. Cttee 1997–2002; Del., 13th CCP Nat. Congress 1987–92. *Address:* c/o China Seismological Bureau, Beijing, People's Republic of China (office).

SONG, Sang-hyun, LLM, JSD; South Korean professor of law and judge; *Judge, International Criminal Court;* b. 21 Dec. 1941; ed Seoul Nat. Univ., Tulane Law School, New Orleans and Cornell Law School, Ithaca, NY, USA, Univ. of Cambridge, UK; called to the Bar, Repub. of Korea 1964; Mil. Prosecutor then Judge, Judge Advocate Office, Korean Armed Forces 1964–67; Attorney Haight, Gardner, Poor & Havens, New York 1970–72; Prof. of Law, Seoul Nat. Univ. 1972–, Dean Law School 1996–98; Lecturer in Law, Nat. Police Coll., Seoul 1983–; Judge, Int. Criminal Court, The Hague 2003–; Vice-Pres. UNICEF Korea 1998–; Pres. Korea Childhood Leukemia Foundation 1999–; Nat. Decoration of 2nd Highest Order (Moran), Govt of Repub. of Korea 1997; Most Distinguished Alumni Medal, Cornell Univ. 1994; Legal Culture Award, Korean Fed. Bar Asscn 1998. *Publications:* books: Introduction to the Law and Legal System of Korea 1983, An Introduction to Law and Economics 1983, Korean Law in the Global Economy 1996, The Korean Civil Procedure 2004; numerous articles in professional journals. *Address:* International Criminal Court, Maanweg 174, 2516 The Hague AB, Netherlands (office); 1629-19 Seocho-dong, Seoul 137-879, Republic of Korea (home). *Telephone:* (70) 5158208 (office). *Fax:* (70) 5158789 (office); (2) 34719502 (home). *E-mail:* pio@icc-cpi.int (office). *Website:* www.icc-cpi.int (office).

SONG, Zhaosu; Chinese politician; *Vice-Chairman, Environment and Resources Protection Committee, National People's Congress;* b. March 1941, Nanyang, He'nan Prov.; ed Zhengzhou Univ.; joined CCP 1965; Section Chief, Org. Dept, CCP Zhoukou Prefectural Cttee, He'nan Prov., later Deputy Sec. Zhoukou Prefectural Cttee; Deputy Sec. CCP Shangshui Co. Cttee, He'nan Prov.; Magistrate, Shangshui Co. (Dist) People's Court, He'nan Prov.; Sec. CCP Taikang Co. Cttee, He'nan Prov.; Sec. CCP Xuchang Prefectural Cttee, He'nan Prov.; Vice-Gov. He'nan Prov. 1988; Deputy Sec. CCP He'nan Prov. Cttee 1993–98, Sec. Political Science and Law Cttee; Acting Gov. Gansu Prov. 1998–99, Gov. 1999–2001; Deputy Sec. CCP Gansu Prov. Cttee 1998–2001, Sec. 2001–03; Chair. Standing Cttee, Gansu Prov. People's Congress 2003–04; Alt. mem. 15th CCP Cen. Cttee 1997–2002, mem. 16th CCP Cen. Cttee 2002–07; Vice-Chair. Environment and Resources Protection Cttee of NPC 2003–. *Address:* Environment and Resources Protection Committee, National People's Congress, Beijing, People's Republic of China (office).

SONN, Franklin Abraham; South African diplomatist and academic; *Chancellor, University of the Free State;* b. 11 Oct. 1939, Vosburg Dist; s. of Pieter (Pat) Sonn and Magdalene Klein; m.; two c.; ed UNISA and Univ. of Western Cape; fmr Rector, Peninsula Technikon; fmr Chair. Comm. of Technikon Prins, Chair. Western Cape Foundation for Community Work, Mobil Foundation of S Africa, Inst. for Distance Educ.; Chair. Bd Trustees, Die Suid-Afrikaan Magazine, Nat. Educ. and Training Forum 1994–; Vice-Chair. Urban Foundation; Dir Metropolitan M-Net 1994–; mem. Bd Corp. Africa; Vice-Pres. Jt Council of Teachers Asscn of S Africa; Amb. to USA 1995–98; Chancellor Univ. of the Free State 2002–. *Publications include:* A Decade of Struggle 1986; numerous papers and official documents. *Leisure interests:* reading, walking, mountaineering, squash. *Address:* Office of the Chancellor, University of the Free State, POB 339, Bloemfontein 9300, South Africa (office). *Telephone:* (51) 401-9111 (office). *Fax:* (51) 401-2117 (office). *E-mail:* info@stiq.uovs.ac.za (home). *Website:* www.uovs.ac.za (office).

SONNENFELD, Barry; American cinematographer, film director and film producer; b. 1 April 1953, New York. *Films as cinematographer include:* Blood Simple 1984, Compromising Positions 1985, Three O'Clock High 1987, Raising Arizona 1987, Throw Momma from the Train 1987, Big 1988, When Harry Met Sally 1989, Miller's Crossing 1990, Misery 1990. *Films directed include:* The Addams Family 1991, For Love or Money 1993, Addams Family Values 1993, Get Shorty 1995, Men in Black 1997, Wild Wild West 1999, Big Trouble 2002, Men in Black II 2002, RV 2006,. *Films produced include:* Get Shorty 1995, Out of Sight 1998, Wild Wild West 1999, The Crew 2000, Big Trouble 2002, The Ladykillers 2004, Lemony Snicket's A Series of Unfortunate Events 2004, Enchanted 2007, Space Chimps 2008. *Television:* Out of Step 1984 (Emmy Award for best cinematography 1984), Fantasy Island 1998, Secret Agent Man 2000, The Crew 2000, The Tick 2001, Karen Sisco 2003, Pushing Daisies 2007. *Address:* c/o CAA, 9830 Wilshire Boulevard, Beverly Hills, CA 90212; United Talent Agency, 9560 Wilshire Boulevard, Beverly Hills, CA 90212, USA.

SONNENFELDT, Helmut, MA; American international business consultant and fmr government official; *Guest Scholar, Brookings Institution;* b. 13 Sept. 1926, Berlin, Germany; s. of Dr Walther H. Sonnenfeldt and Dr Gertrud L. Sonnenfeldt; m. Marjorie Hecht 1953; two s. one d.; ed Univ. of Manchester, Johns Hopkins Univ.; went to USA 1944; mem. Counterintelligence Corps, US Army, Pacific and European Theaters; with Dept of State 1952–69, Policy Officer, US Disarmament Admin. 1960–61, Dir Office of Research and Analysis for the USSR and E Europe 1966–69; Sr Staff mem. for Europe and East–West Relations, Nat. Security Council 1969–74; Counselor of Dept of State 1974–77; Lecturer on Soviet Affairs, Johns Hopkins Univ. School of Advanced Int. Studies 1957–69; Trustee, Johns Hopkins Univ. 1974–, Visiting Scholar, School of Advanced Int. Studies, Johns Hopkins Univ. 1977–78; Guest Scholar, Brookings Inst., Washington, DC 1978–; Consultant Washington Center for Foreign Policy Research; Gov. and Dir UN Asscn of USA 1980; Dir Atlantic Council of USA 1978–; mem. IISS, London 1977–99, (mem. Exec. Cttee 1986–98), Council of Foreign Relations, Royal Inst. of Int. Affairs, London, Int. Advisory Council, Credit-Anstalt-Bankverein, Vienna 1983–98, Defense Policy Bd 2001–; Editorial Bd Politique Internationale (Paris) 1978–, Foreign Policy 1980–; Govt rep. to numerous confs and meetings abroad; consultant to int. investments firms and banks. *Publications:* Soviet Policy in the 1980s 1985, articles on int. issues in American and European journals. *Leisure interests:* tennis, music, reading biography. *Address:* Brookings

Institution, 1775 Massachusetts Avenue, NW, Washington, DC 20036 (office); 5600 Wisconsin Avenue, #1505, Chevy Chase, MD 20815, USA (home). *Telephone:* (202) 797-6028 (office). *Fax:* (202) 797-6004 (office); (310) 656-6706 (home). *E-mail:* hsonnenfeldt@brookings.edu (office); sonnenfeldt@cs.net (home). *Website:* www.brookings.edu/fp/fp_hp.htm (office).

SONOKROT, Mazen, BEng; Palestinian business executive and fmr government minister; *CEO, Sinokrot Global Group;* b. 30 Nov. 1954, Jerusalem; s. of Mohammad Tawfique Sonokrot and Fatimah Sonokrot; four s.; ed Univ. of Nottingham, UK; Chair. and CEO Sinokrot Global Group 1982–2005, CEO 2006–; Regional Dir Arab Food Industries Fed., Arab League 1982–97; Founder and fmr Chair. Palestinian Food Industries Asscn; Chair. Palestinian Fed. of Industries, Universal Group for Eng and Consulting, Industrial Modernization Center; Minister of Nat. Economy 2005–06; Chair. Palestinian Investment Promotion Agency, Palestinian Industrial Estates and Free Zones Area, Palestinian Standards Inst.; Sec. Pvt. Sector Coordinating Council; mem. Bd and Head, Investment Cttee, Palestine Investment Fund; mem. Palestinian Businessmen Asscn, Bd of Palestinian Economic Task Force, Bd Nat. Reform Cttee, Public-Pvt. Jt Econ. Cttee, Bd of Registry and Sanction, Ministry of Higher Educ.; mem. Higher Council of High Council for Tech. and Vocational Educ.; Assoc. mem. of all cttees in charge of formulating laws and legislation relating to the Palestinian economy; rep. of Palestinian pvt. sector in many local, regional and int. activities; contrib. to econ. trade agreements between Palestinian National Authority and USA, EU, Turkey, Arab and EFTA countries. *Address:* Sinokrot Global Group, PO 1410, Betuniah, Industrial Zone, Ramallah, Palestinian Autonomous Area (office). *Telephone:* (2) 2955701 (office). *Fax:* (2) 2955702 (office). *Website:* www.sinokrot.net (office).

SONOMPIL, Mishigiyn; Mongolian politician; b. 27 Jan. 1965; m.; two c.; fmr Commdr mil. unit; Dir Zaluu Mongol Corpn 1991–2004; mem. Democratic Party; mem. Parl. 2004–; Minister of Defence 2006–07. *Address:* c/o Democratic Party, Chingisiin, Örgön Chölöö 1, Ulan Bator, Mongolia (office).

SOOMRO, Mohammad Mian, BSc, MSc; Pakistani banker and politician; *Acting President and Chairman of the Senate;* b. 19 Aug. 1950, Sindh; s. of the late Ahmed Mian Soomro; ed Forman Christian Coll., Lahore, Punjab Univ., Northrop Univ., USA; Head of Soomro tribe; mem. Pakistan Muslim League (PML); held various positions in nat. and int. orgs, including Bank of America; fmr Gen. Man. and CEO Int. Bank of Yemen, Faysal Islamic Bank of Bahrain, Muslim Commercial Bank, Agriculture Devt Bank of Pakistan, Fed. Bank of Cooperatives, Nat. Bank of Pakistan; Chair. Pakistan Banks Asscn 1997–2000; mem. Governing Council Inst. of Bankers in Pakistan 1997–2000; mem. Bd of Dirs Shell Pakistan Ltd, Pakistan Int. Airlines Corpn, Pakistan Refinery Ltd (Shell Petroleum Jt Venture), Pak Arab Refinery, Pak Arab Fertilizer, Bank Al-Jazira (Jeddah, Saudi Arabia), Nat. Investment Trust, Investment Co-operation of Pakistan, Nat. Discounting Services Ltd, Nat. Exchange Co. (Abu Dhabi), Nat. Bank Modaraba Man. Co. Ltd, First Women Bank Ltd, Consolidated Leasing Co., Nat. Construction Co., Pakistan Tourism Devt Corpn (all 1997–2000); helped establish micro-credit banking in Pakistan; Gov. of Sindh 2000–02; Senator 2003–, Chair. of the Senate 2003–; Chair. Finance Cttee; Acting Pres. 2008–. *Address:* Office of the President, Aiwan-e-Sadr, Islamabad (office); Senate of Pakistan, Parliament House, Islamabad, Pakistan (office). *Telephone:* (51) 9206060 (office); (51) 9223475 (office). *Fax:* (51) 9208046 (office); (51) 9223477 (office). *E-mail:* chairman@senate.gov.pk (office). *Website:* www.presidentofpakistan.gov.pk (office); www.senate.gov.pk (office).

SOONG, James Chu-yul, PhD; Taiwanese politician; *Chairman, People First Party (PFP);* b. 16 March 1942, Hunan; m. Viola Chen; one s. one d.; ed Nat. Chengchi Univ., Taipei and Univ. of Calif., Berkeley, Catholic Univ. of America, Georgetown Univ., Washington, DC, USA; Sec. Exec. Yuan, Taiwan 1974–77; Deputy Dir-Gen. Govt Information Office 1977–79; Assoc. Prof., Nat. Taiwan Univ. 1975–79; Research Fellow, Inst. of Int. Relations, Nat. Chengchi Univ. 1974–; Personal Sec. to the Pres. 1978–89; Dir-Gen. Govt Information Office, Govt Spokesman 1979–84; mem. Cen. Cttee Kuomintang 1981–2000, Dir-Gen. Dept of Cultural Affairs, Kuomintang 1984–87; Deputy Sec.-Gen., Cen. Cttee Kuomintang 1987–89, Sec.-Gen. 1989–93; mem. Cen. Standing Cttee 1988–2000; Gov., Taiwan Prov. Govt 1993–98; unsuccessful presidential cand. (ind.) 2000, then f. People First Party (PFP), Chair. 2000–; unsuccessful vice presidential cand. (PFP) 2004; Man. Dir China TV Co. 1984–93, Taiwan TV Enterprise 1984–93; Chair. Hua-hsia Investment Corpn; Distinguished Visiting Fellow Inst. of East Asian Studies, Univ. of Calif. 1999; Eisenhower Fellowship 1982; several decorations. *Publications:* A Manual for Academic Writers, How to Write Academic Papers, Politics and Public Opinions in the United States, Keep Free China Free. *Address:* People First Party, 1/F, 63 Chang-an East Road, Sec. 2, Taipei 10455, Taiwan (office). *Telephone:* (2) 25068555 (office). *Website:* www.pfp.org.tw (office).

SOPE, Barak; Ni-Vanuatu politician and diplomatist; *Chairman, Melanesian Progressive Party;* leading mem. Vanuaaku Pati (VP), Roving Amb.; mem. govts 1980–87; defected from VP, f. Melanesian Progressive Party 1987, Chair. 1987–; mem. coalition govts 1993–96; Prime Minister of Vanuatu 1999–2001 (resgnd); convicted of forgery and sentenced to three years in prison 2002, pardoned in 2003; Minister of Foreign Affairs 2004; Minister of Agric., Quarantine, Forestry and Fisheries 2004-06. *Address:* Melanesian Progressive Pati, PO Box 39, Port Vila, Vanuatu (office). *Telephone:* 23485 (office). *Fax:* 23315 (office).

SOPHUSSON, Fridrik; Icelandic lawyer, politician and business executive; *Managing Director, Landsvirkjun (National Power Company);* b. 18 Oct. 1943, Reykjavik; m. Dr Sigridur Duna Kristmundsdottir 1990; one d. (and five c. from first m.); ed Reykjavik Higher Secondary Grammar School and Univ. of

Iceland; lawyer, part-time teacher Hlídaskóli School, Reykjavik 1963–67; Man. Icelandic Man. Asscn 1972–78; mem. Radio Council Icelandic State Broadcasting Service 1975–78; Nat. Research Council and Exec. Cttee of State Hosps. 1984–87; Cen. Cttee Independence Party 1969–77, 1981–99, Vice-Chair. 1981–89, 1991–99; Pres. Independence Party's Youth Fed. 1973–77; MP for Reykjavik 1978–98; Minister of Industry and Energy 1987–88, of Finance 1991–98; mem. Bd of Dirs Nat. Bank of Iceland 1990–92, Icelandic Church Aid 1990–92, Enex 2001–, Pharmaco 2002–03, Samorka (Fed. of Electricity and Waterworks) 2001–, Icelandic Int. Chamber of Commerce 2001–, Nordel 2001–03, Icelandic Chamber of Commerce 2002–; Man. Dir Landsvirkjun (Nat. Power Co.) 1999–. *Address:* Landsvirkjun, Haaleitisbraut 68, 103 Reykjavik, Iceland. *Telephone:* 5159000 (office). *Fax:* 5159007 (office). *E-mail:* fridrik@lv.is (office). *Website:* www.lv.is (office).

SOPOANGA, Saufatu; Tuvaluan politician; fmr Special Ministerial Adviser, Ministry of Works, Communication and Transport; fmr Minister of Finance; Prime Minister of Tuvalu, Minister of Foreign Affairs and Labour 2002–04; Deputy Prime Minister and Minister of Works and Energy and of Communications and Transport 2004–06. *Address:* c/o Ministry of Works and Energy PMB, Vaiaku, Funafuti, Tuvalu (office).

SOPONRONNARIT, Somchart, PhD; Thai scientist and academic; *Professor of Energy Technology, King Mongkut's University of Technology Thonburi;* currently Prof. of Energy Tech., King Mongkut's Univ. of Tech., Thonburi Campus; mem. Academic Review Cttee, Sirindhorn Int. Inst. of Tech., Thammasat Univ.; mem. Asian Inst. of Tech.; Fellow, Royal Inst. of Thailand; UNESCO Science Prize 2003. *Publications:* Drying Grains and Some Types of Foods (seventh edn, in Thai) 1997; book chapters, research reports and more than 150 scientific papers in professional journals on thermal processes such as thermal application of solar energy, drying and storage of foods and cereal grains. *Address:* School of Energy, Environment and Materials, King Mongkut's University of Technology, Thonburi Campus, Suksawat 48 Road, Bangkok 10140 (office); 152 Banmore Road, Bangkok 10200, Thailand (home). *Telephone:* (2) 4708624 (office); (2) 4270039 (ext. 8624) (office); (2) 263838 (home). *Fax:* (2) 4279062 (office). *E-mail:* somchart.sop@kmutt.ac.th (office). *Website:* www2.kmutt.ac.th (office).

SORABJI, Richard Rustom Kharsedji, CBE, BPhil, MA, FBA; British academic; *Cyprus Global Distinguished Professor in the History and Theory of Justice, University of Texas;* b. 8 Nov. 1934, Brighton; s. of late Prof. Richard Kakushru Sorabji and Mary Katherine Sorabji (née Monkhouse); m. Margaret Anne Catherine Taster 1958; one s. two d.; ed Charterhouse, Pembroke Coll., Oxford Univ.; Assoc. Prof., Sage School of Philosophy, Cornell Univ. 1962–69; joined Dept of Philosophy, King's Coll. London 1970, Prof. of Ancient Philosophy 1981–2000, British Acad./Wolfson Research Prof. 1996–99, now Prof. Emer., Designer, First Dir King's Coll. Centre for Philosophical Studies 1989–91; Gresham Prof. of Rhetoric and mem. Sr Common Room, Pembroke Coll. 2000–03; Supernumerary Fellow, Wolfson Coll. Oxford 1996, now Hon. Fellow; Ranieri Distinguished Visiting Scholar, New York Univ. 2000–03, Cyprus Global Distinguished Prof. in the History and Theory of Justice 2008–; Adjunct Prof., Philosophy Dept, Univ. of Texas 2000–; Visiting Prof., CUNY 2004–07; Pres. Aristotelian Soc. 1985–86; Founder and organizer of int. project to translate ancient commentators on Aristotle in 50 vols 1985–; Dir Inst. of Classical Studies, London Univ. 1991–96; Foreign Hon. mem. American Acad. of Arts and Sciences 1997–. *Publications:* Aristotle on Memory 1972, Necessity, Cause and Blame 1980, Time, Creation and the Continuum 1983, Matter, Space and Motion 1988, Animal Minds and Human Morals 1993, Emotion and Peace of Mind 2001, Self: Ancient and Modern Insights about Individuality, Life and Death 2006, The Ethics of War: Shared Problems in Different Traditions (co-ed.) 2006, Greek and Roman Philosophy 100 BC to 200 AD (co-ed.) 2007; ed. numerous vols on commentators on Aristotle. *Leisure interests:* archaeology, architecture. *Address:* Wolfson College, Oxford, OX1 4LJ, England; Graduate School of Arts and Science, New York University, 6 Washington Square North, New York, NY 10003, USA (office). *Telephone:* (1865) 274100. *Fax:* (1865) 274125. *E-mail:* richard.sorabji@philosophy.oxford.ac.uk (office). *Website:* www.kcl.ac.uk/kis/schools/hums/philosophy/staff/r_sorabji (office).

SOREN, Shibu; Indian politician; b. 11 Jan. 1944, Nemra dist., Bihar; s. of the late Shobaran Soren; m. Rupi Devi; three s. one d.; elected to Rajya Sabha 1989, 1991, 1996, 1998; Minister of Coal May–July 2004 (resgnd), reinstated Nov. 2004, resgnd March 2005; Chief Minister of Jharkhand March 2005–06; Minister for Coal 2004–06 (resgnd); Leader Jharkhand Mukti Morcha; sentenced to life imprisonment on abduction and murder charges 2006, acquitted 2007; Chief Minister of Jharkhand 2008–09 (resgnd). *Address:* c/o Jharkhand Mukti Morcha, Bariatu Road, Ranchi 834 008, India (office).

SØRENSEN, Bengt Algot, DPhil; Danish academic; *Professor Emeritus of German Literature, University of Odense;* b. 24 Nov. 1927, Aarhus; s. of Christian Sørensen and Selma Mellquist; m. Agnes M. Pedersen 1954 (died 2005); one s. two d.; ed Århus, Hamburg and Tübingen Univs; Lecturer in Scandinavian Languages and Literature, Bonn, Germany 1955–60; Lecturer in German Literature, Århus Univ. 1962–66; Prof. of German Literature, Odense Univ. 1966–97, Prof. Emer. 1997–; Visiting Prof. Univ. of Calif. at Irvine 1980, Univ. of Kiel 1983; Pres. Danish Research Council for the Humanities 1971–73; mem. Exec. Council European Science Foundation 1983–89; Vice-Pres. IVG (Int. Vereinigung der Germanistik) 1995–2000; mem. Royal Danish Acad. 1978–, Göttinger Akad. der Wissenschaften 1996–; Gold Medal, Univ. of Århus 1953. *Publications:* Symbol und Symbolismus 1963, Allegorie und Symbol 1972, Herrschaft und Zärtlichkeit 1984, Jens Peter Jacobsen 1990, Geschichte der deutschen Literatur Bd I, II 1997, Funde und Forschungen. Ausgewählte Essays 1997; numerous articles about Danish and German literature. *Leisure interests:* fishing, gardening. *Address:* University of Odense, 5230 Odense M (office); Frederiksberg Alle 100, 1820 Frederiksberg, Denmark (home). *Telephone:* 65-50-32-16 (office); 66-17-64-99 (home). *Fax:* 65-93-16-64. *Website:* www.humaniora.sdu.dk (office).

SÓRENSEN, Jórgen Haugen; Danish sculptor; b. 1934; ed Coll. of Art and Design, Copenhagen; began as apprentice plasterer and potter; debut in Charlottenborg's Spring Exhibition 1953; exhbns at Museum of Modern Art New York, Yorks. Sculpture Park; works in collections in Denmark, England, Italy, Slovenia, Turkey, Olympic Sculpture Park, Seoul; Dir film JHS late 1960s; Prix de la Critique for JHS (Paris Biennale) 1963. *Address:* Galleri Veggerby, Ny Østergade 34, 1101 København K, Denmark. *E-mail:* haugensorensen@FJRN-DETTEhotmail.com. *Website:* www.haugen-sorensen.dk.

SORENSEN, Theodore (Ted) Chaikin, BSL, LLB; American government official and lawyer; *of Counsel (retired Senior Partner), Paul, Weiss, Rifkind, Wharton & Garrison LLP;* b. 8 May 1928, Lincoln, Nebraska; s. of Christian A. Sorensen and Annis Chaikin; m. Gillian Martin 1969; one d.; three s. from previous m.; ed Univ. of Nebraska; attorney, Fed. Security Agency 1951–52; Staff Researcher, Jt Cttee on Railroad Retirement 1952–53; Asst to Senator John F. Kennedy 1953–61; Special Counsel to Pres. Kennedy and Pres. Johnson 1961–64; of Counsel (retd Sr Pnr), Paul, Weiss, Rifkind, Wharton & Garrison, New York 1966–; Ed.-at-Large Saturday Review 1966–69; mem. Advisory Cttee for Trade Negotiations 1979–81; Chair. Task Force on Political Action Cttees; mem. Task Force on Foreign Policy 1986, Int. Trade Round Table 1986, Democratic Nat. Cttee 1981–82, Comm. on White House Fellows 1996–; Dir The Twentieth-Century Fund 1984– (Chair. 1994–99), Council on Foreign Relations 1993–, Nat. Democratic Inst. for Int. Affairs 1993–99, Cen. Asian-American Enterprise Fund 1995–99; Chair. US-Japanese Program Cttee of Japan Soc. 1990; Trustee, The New York Acad. of Medicine 1991–97; Democrat. *Publications:* Decision-Making in The White House 1963, Kennedy 1964, The Kennedy Legacy 1970, Watchmen in the Night: Presidential Accountability After Watergate 1975, A Different Kind of Presidency 1984, A Widening Atlantic? Domestic Change and Foreign Policy (co-author with Ralf Dahrendorf) 1986, Let the World go Forth: The Speeches, Statements and Writings of John F. Kennedy (ed.) 1988, Why I Am a Democrat 1996, Counselor: A Life at the Edge of History 2008. *Address:* Paul, Weiss, Rifkind, Wharton & Garrison, 28th Floor, 1285 Avenue of the Americas, New York, NY 10019-6064, USA (office). *Telephone:* (212) 373-3790 (office). *Fax:* (212) 492-0790 (office). *E-mail:* tsorensen@paulweiss.com (office). *Website:* www.paulweiss.com (office).

SORENSTAM, Annika; Swedish fmr professional golfer; b. 9 Oct. 1970, Stockholm; d. of Tom Sorenstam and Gunilla Sorenstam; m. David Esch; ed Univ. of Arizona, USA; World Amateur Champion 1992; 72 career wins on LPGA tour including 10 major championships; victories include US Women's Open 1995, 1996, Safeway Classic 2003, Mizuno Classic 2003, LPGA Championship 2003, 2004, 2005, Women's British Open 2003, Kraft Nabisco Championship 2005; played on eight European Solheim Cup teams; first woman to shoot 59 in an LPGA Tour tournament 2001; first woman to win US $13 million in golf prize money, is LPGA career earnings leader with more than US$22 million; finished first on LPGA money list 2001–05 and eight times overall; first woman for 58 years to participate in a men's professional tour event, Bank of America Colonial Tournament, Fort Worth, Tex., May 2003; first int. player to be inducted into World Golf Hall of Fame, St Augustine, USA 2003; announced retirement 2008; f. Annika Course Design, ANNIKA Academy; Rookie of the Year 1994, Sports Personality of the Year, Sweden 1995, Vare Trophy Award 1995, 1996, 1998, 2001, 2002, Rolex Player of the Year Award 1995, 1997, 1998, 2001–05; Patty Berg Award 2003, Jerring Prize 2004; inducted into LPGA Hall of Fame 2003. *Leisure interests:* sports, music, cooking, skiing. *Address:* c/o Annika Sorenstam, IMG Center, Suite 100, 1360 East 9th Street, Cleveland, OH 44114, USA; c/o IMG Stureplan, 4C, 114 35 Stockholm, Sweden. *Website:* www.annikasorenstam.com; www.theannikaacademy.com.

SORHAINDO, Crispin Anselm, OBE; Dominican business executive and fmr head of state; b. 23 May 1931, Vieille Case; s. of Clive Sorhaindo and Rosa Frederick; m. Ruby Etheldreda Allport 1956; two s. four d.; Speaker House of Ass. –1993; fmr Vice-Pres., Bank Sec. Caribbean Devt Bank; Pres. of Dominica 1993–98; fmr Chair. Dominica Agricultural and Industrial Devt Bank, Nat. Commercial Bank Dominica Ltd, Dominica Port Authority; mem. Eastern Caribbean Securities Regulatory Comm. 2001– (fmr Chair); Kt Commdr of the Order of St Sylvester; Dominica Award of Honour (DAH). *Leisure interests:* reading, gardening. *Address:* Eastern Caribbean Securities Regulatory Commission, ECCB Financial Complex, PO Box 1855, Basseterre, St Kitts (office); Morne Prosper, PO Box 572, Roseau, Dominica. *Telephone:* 448-8787. *Fax:* 449-8920. *E-mail:* info@ecsrc.com (office). *Website:* www.ecsrc.com (office).

SORINAS BALFEGÓ, Mateo, MSc; Spanish teacher and international organization executive; *Secretary-General of the Parliamentary Assembly, Council of Europe;* b. 13 March 1946, Tarragona; m.; two c.; ed Universidad Complutense, Madrid; Deputy Dir Boarding School, Universidad Laboral de Alcalá de Henares, Madrid 1967–69; teacher, Agüimes High School, Las Palmas, Gran Canaria 1969–70; mil. service 1970–71; teacher, Isabel de España High School, Las Palmas 1971–77, Pérez Galdós High School, Las Palmas 1977–78; Co-Sec. Cttee on Environment, Regional Planning and Local Authorities, Council of Europe 1978–86, Sec. Cttee on Migration, Refugees and Demography 1986–92, Sec. Political Affairs Cttee 1992–94, Political Counsellor, Pvt. Office of the Pres. 1992–96, Head of Cen. Div. 1994–97, Dir Political and Legal Affairs Dept 1997–2002, Dir-Gen. 2002–06, Sec.-Gen. Parl. Ass. 2006–; mem. Nat. Cttee of Juventud Estudiante Católica (Young Catholic Students), Madrid 1963–67, Governing Bd Professional Asscn of Teachers on Sciences and Humanities, Las Palmas 1974–78; Orden del Mérito Civil: Cruz de Caballero 1988, Encomienda 1995; Cavaliere Grand'Ufficiale, Ordine di Sant'Agata (San Marino) 2007. *Address:* Secretariat of the Parliamentary Assembly, Council of Europe, avenue de l'Europe, 67075 Strasbourg Cedex, France (office). *Telephone:* 3-88-41-20-33 (office). *Fax:* 3-88-41-27-45 (office). *E-mail:* webmaster.assembly@coe.int (office). *Website:* www.coe.int (office); assembly.coe.int (office).

SORO, Guillaume Kigbafori; Côte d'Ivoirian fmr rebel leader and government official; *Prime Minister;* b. 8 May 1972, Diawala; two c.; ed univ. studies in France; Leader Ivorian Students' Fed. 1995–98; fmr Sec.-Gen. Mouvement patriotique de Côte d'Ivoire (MPCI); Leader, New Forces Rebels 2000–, led rebellion against Pres. Laurent Gbagbo that triggered Civil War 2002, controlled Northern Prov. of Côte d'Ivoire 2002; Minister of State for Communications 2003–05, of Reconstruction and Reinsertion 2005–07; Prime Minister 2007–. *Address:* Office of the Prime Minister, blvd Angoulvant 01, BP 1533, Abidjan 01 (office); Forces Nouvelles, Bouaké, Côte d'Ivoire. *Telephone:* 20-20-04-04; 20-31-50-00 (office). *Fax:* 20-22-18-33 (office). *E-mail:* senacom@fnci.info; pm@primature.gov.ci (office). *Website:* www.fnci.info.

SOROKIN, Vladimir Georgiyevich; Russian author, screenwriter and painter; b. 7 Aug. 1955, Bykovo, Moscow Region; m. Irina Igorevna Sorokina; two d.; ed Moscow Inst. of Oil and Gas; worked as artist and writer in Moscow underground; not published in USSR until 1987; mem. Russian PEN Centre; scholarship of Deutsche Akademische Austauschung Dienst 1992; Liberty Prize, USA 2005. *Plays:* wrote 10 plays 1986–95. *Screenplays:* Moskva 1995, Kopejka 1997, The Four 2000, Cashfire 2002, The Thing 2003, Exit 2004. *Libretto:* opera 'The Children of Rosenthal' by Leonid Desyatnikov (performed at Bolshoi Theatre, Moscow) 2005. *Publications include:* Thirties Love of Marina 1982–84, The Queue (novel) 1983, The Norm 1984, Obelisk (short stories) 1980–84, Roman 1989, Four Stout Hearts (novel) 1991, Blue Lard 1999, The Feast 2001, The Ice (novel) 2002, Bro 2004, Trilogy 2005. *Leisure interests:* chess, cooking, ping-pong. *Address:* 119333 Moscow, ul. Gubkina, d4 kv 47, Russia (home). *Telephone:* (495) 135-90-76 (home). *E-mail:* sornorma@mtu-net.ru (home). *Website:* www.srkn.ru; www.vladimirsorokin.ru.

SOROS, George; American (b. Hungarian) investment banker and philanthropist; *Chairman, Soros Fund Management LLC;* b. 12 Aug. 1930, Budapest; m.; five c.; ed London School of Econs; moved to England 1947; much influenced by work of philosopher Karl Popper; with Singer & Friedlander (merchant bankers), London; moved to Wall Street, New York 1956; set up pvt. mutual fund, Quantum Fund, registered in Curaçao 1969; since 1991 has created other funds, Quasar Int., Quota, Quantum Emerging Growth Fund (merged with Quantum Fund to form Quantum Endowment Fund 2000), Quantum Realty Trust; Pres. and Chair. Soros Fund Man. LLC, New York 1973–; philanthropist since 1979, provided funds to help black students attend Cape Town Univ., SA; Founder Open Soc. Fund (currently Chair. Open Soc. Inst.) 1979, Soros Foundations, Cen. European Univ., Budapest 1992; f. Global Power Investments 1994; Dr hc (New School for Social Research, Univ. of Oxford, Budapest Univ. of Econs, Yale Univ.); Laurea hc (Univ. of Bologna) 1995. *Publication:* The Alchemy of Finance 1987, Opening the Soviet System 1990, Underwriting Democracy 1991, Soros on Soros – Staying Ahead of the Curve (jtly) 1995, The Crisis of Global Capitalism – Open Society Engendered 1998, Open Society – Reforming Global Capitalism 2000, George Soros on Globalization 2002, The Bubble of American Supremacy – Correcting the Misuse of American Power 2004, Soros on Freedom 2006; numerous essays on politics, society and econs in major int. newspapers and magazines. *Address:* Soros Fund Management LLC, 888 7th Avenue, 33rd Floor, New York, NY 10106, USA (office); Open Society Institute, 400 West 59th Street, New York, NY 10019. *Telephone:* (212) 548-0600. *Website:* www.georgesoros.com; www.soros.org.

SOROUR, Ahmed Fathi, BSc, MA, LLM, PhD; Egyptian politician and academic; *Speaker, Majlis Ash-sha'ab (People's Assembly);* b. 9 July 1932, Kena; s. of Mostafa Kamel Surur and Fatma Ali Hassan; m. Zeinab El-Housseiny; one s. two d.; ed Cairo Univ., Univ. of Mich; Deputy Attorney Gen. 1953–59; Prof. of Criminal Law, Cairo Univ. 1959–, Head of Dept 1978–83, Dean of Faculty of Law 1983–85, Vice-Rector Cairo Univ. 1985–86; Chair. Supreme Council of Univs 1986–90; Cultural Attaché, Embassy in Switzerland 1964, Cultural Counsellor, Embassy in France 1965–67; Minister of Educ. 1986–90; Mem. Majlis Ash-sha'ab (People's Ass.) 1987–, Speaker 1990–; mem. Political Bureau Nat. Democratic Party 1990–; Pres. Union of African Parls 1990–91; Pres. Inter-parl. Union 1994–97; Pres. Arab Parl. Union 1998–2000; Pres. Union of Islamic Parls. 2000–; Chair. Egyptian Soc. for Criminal Law 1989–, Egyptian Soc. of Francophone affiliated Jurists 1992–, Int. Inst. for Law in the totally or partially Francophone countries, Paris 1994–, Conf. of Euro-Mediterranean Speakers, Alexandria 2000–; Vice Chair. Int. Soc. for Criminal Law, Paris 1989–; Hon. Chair. Inst. for Higher Studies in Criminal Science, Sicily 2000–; Dr hc (Constantin Univ., USA) 2001; Sciences and Art Medal 1964, 1983, Highest Homala Decoration of Alawi Throne, Morocco 1987, Ordre de la Pleiade, Assemblée Internationale des Parlementaires des Francophones 1992; Highest Distinction Award in Social Sciences 1993. *Publications:* Theory of Nullity 1959, Offences Against Public Interest 1963, Penal Law (parts I and II) 1980, Criminal Procedures Law 1993, Constitutional Legality and Human Rights 1995, Constitutional Protection of Rights and Liberties 2000, Criminal Constitutional Law 2001. *Address:* 11583 Maglis Al-Shaab, Cairo, Egypt (office). *Telephone:* (2) 7943130 (office). *Fax:* (2) 7943116 (office). *E-mail:* parli@idsc.gov.eg (office). *Website:* www.parliament.gov.eg.

SOROUSH, Abdolkarim, BSc; Iranian academic; *Researcher, Institute for Iranian Contemporary Historical Studies;* b. 1945, Tehran; ed Mortazavi High School, Alavi High School, Univ. of London and Chelsea Coll., London, UK; studied pharmacy and passed nat. entrance exams; left for London following graduation to continue studies; returned to Iran in 1979, and published book Knowledge and Value (Danesh va Arzesh); apptd Dir Islamic Culture Group, Teacher Training Coll., Tehran 1979; mem. Cultural Revolution Inst. 1980–83 (resgnd); Researcher, Inst. for Cultural Research and Studies (now the Inst. for Iranian Contemporary Historical Studies) 1983–; adviser to govt bodies; became more critical of political role played by Iranian clergy 1990s; co-founder monthly magazine Kiyan, and published his most controversial articles on religious pluralism, hermeneutics, tolerance, clericalism etc., magazine suppressed by direct order of supreme leader of Islamic Repub. 1998; more than 1,000 audio tapes of his speeches on various social, political, religious and literary subjects circulated world-wided, became subject to harassment and state censorship; Visiting Prof. teaching Islam and Democracy, Quranic Studies and Philosophy of Islamic Law, Harvard Univ., USA 2000–; Scholar-in-Residence, Yale Univ., USA; taught Islamic Political Philosophy at Princeton Univ. 2002–03; Visiting Scholar, Wissenschaftkolleg, Berlin, Germany 2003–04. *Publications:* Dialectical Antagonism (in Persian) 1978, Philosophy of History (in Persian) 1978, What is Science, What is Philosophy (in Persian) (11th edn) 1992, The Restless Nature of the Universe (in Persian and Turkish) 1980, Satanic Ideology (in Persian) (fifth edn) 1994, Knowledge and Value (in Persian), Observing the Created: Lectures in Ethics and Human Sciences (in Persian) (third edn) 1994, The Theoretical Contraction and Expansion of Religion: The Theory of Evolution of Religious Knowledge (in Persian) (third edn) 1994, Lectures in the Philosophy of Social Sciences: Hermeneutics in Social Sciences (in Persian) 1995, Sagaciousness, Intellectualism and Pietism (in Persian) 1991, The Characteristic of the Pious: A Commentary on Imam Ali's Lecture About the Pious (in Persian) (fourth edn) 1996, The Tale of the Lords of Sagacity (in Persian) (third edn) 1996, Wisdom and Livelihood: A Commentary on Imam Ali's Letter to Imam Hasan (in Persian) (second edn) 1994, Sturdier than Ideology (in Persian) 1994, The Evolution and Devolution of Religious Knowledge in: Kurzman, Ch. (ed.), Intellectualism and Religious Conviction (in Persian), The World We Live (in Persian and Turkish), The Tale of Love and Servitude (in Persian), The Definitive Edition of Rumi's Mathnavi (in Persian) 1996, Tolerance and Governance (in Persian) 1997, Straight Paths, An Essay on Religious Pluralism (in Persian) 1998, Liberal Islam 1998, Political Letters (two vols) (in Persian) 1999, Expansion of Prophetic Experience (in Persian) 1999, Reason, Freedom and Democracy in Islam, Essential Writings of Adbolkarim Soroush (translated, ed with a critical introduction by M. Sadri and A. Sadri) 2000. *Address:* The Institute for Iranian Contemporary Historical Studies, PO Box 19395-1975, 128 Fayyazi (Fereshteh) Avenue, Elahieh, Tehran 19649, Iran (office). *Telephone:* (21) 264037-8 (office); (21) 2003490 (office). *Fax:* (21) 262096 (office). *E-mail:* info@drsoroush.com (office). *Website:* www.drsoroush.com (office); www.iichs.org.

SORRELL, Sir John William, Kt, CBE, FCSD, FRSA; British designer; *Co-Founder, The Sorrell Foundation;* b. 28 Feb. 1945, London; s. of the late John William Sorrell and of Elizabeth Jane Sorrell (née Taylor); m. Frances Mary Newell (q.v.) 1974; two s. one d.; ed Hornsey Coll. of Art; Designer Maine Wolff & Pnrs 1964; Pnr, Goodwin Sorrell 1964–71; Design Man. Wolff Olins 1971–76; Founder and Co-Chair. Newell and Sorrell 1976–97, Chair. Newell and Sorrell (now Interbrand Newell and Sorrell) 1983–2000; Vice-Pres. Chartered Soc. of Designers 1989–92; Chair. DBA 1990–92, Design Council 1994–2000; mem. British Rail Architecture and Design Panel 1991–93, RSA Design Advisory Group 1991–93, D & AD Strategic Planning Soc., Inst. of Design, New Millennium Experience Co. Creative Review Group 1998–2000 (and 'Godparent' for Identity Zone), Panel 2000, Dept of Trade & Industry's Encouraging Competitiveness Working Party 1998; Co-Founder and Chair. The Sorrell Foundation 1999–; Gov. Design Dimension 1991–93; Chair. NHS London Design Advisory Group 2000–, Comm. for Architecture and the Built Environment 2004–, London Design Festival; Co-Chair. British Abroad Task Force 2000–; hon. mem. Romanian Design Centre, Hon. Fellow RIBA 2002–; Hon. DDesign (De Montfort) 1997, Dr hc (London Inst.) 1999; RSA's Bicentenary Medal 1998, D&AD Pres.'s Award 2008. *Publications:* Secret of Design Effectiveness 1995, Utopian Nights 1996, Utopian Papers 1996–, Creative Island 2002. *Leisure interests:* arboriculture, Arsenal Football Club, art, film. *Address:* The Sorrell Foundation, Somerset House, Strand, London WC2R 1LA, England (office). *Telephone:* (20) 7845-5860 (office). *Fax:* (20) 7845-5872 (office). *E-mail:* info@thesorrellfoundation.com (office). *Website:* www.thesorrellfoundation.com (office).

SORRELL, Sir Martin Stuart, Kt, MA, MBA; British advertising executive; *Chief Executive, WPP;* b. 14 Feb. 1945, London; ed Haberdashers' Aske's School, Christ's Coll. Cambridge and Harvard Business School, USA; consultant, Glendinning Assocs, Westport, Conn. 1968–69; Vice-Pres. Mark McCormack Org. 1970–74; Dir James Gulliver Assocs. 1975–77; Group Financial Dir Saatchi and Saatchi Co. PLC 1977–84; Founder and Group Chief Exec. WPP 1986–; Dir Storehouse PLC 1994–97; Dir (non-exec.) Colefax and Fowler Group PLC 1997–; mem. Advisory Bd Int. Grad. School of Man., Univ. of Navarra 1989–, Judge Inst. for Man. Studies, Univ. of Cambridge 1990–, IBM 1997–, Advisory Bd, ATP 2001–; mem. Bd Dirs of Assocs, Harvard Business School 1998–, Bd Dean's Advisors 1998–; Dir (non-exec.) Colefax & Fowler; FCO Amb. for British Business 1997–99, mem. Panel 2000 2000–; mem. Council for Excellence in Man. and Leadership; mem. Bd and Cttee Special Olympics 2000–, Corp. Advisory Group, Tate Gallery 2000–, Bd Nat. Asscn of Securities Dealers Automated Quotation System (NASDAQ) 2001–, Advisory Bd IESE, Spain, Dean's Advisory Council, Boston Univ., Bd Indian School of Business; Deputy Chair. and Gov. London Business School 1990–; Trustee Cambridge Foundation, Royal Coll. of Art Foundation; Patron Cambridge Alumni in Man., Queen Charlotte's Appeal at Hammersmith Hosp.; Hon. DBA (London Guildhall Univ.) 2001. *Leisure interests:* family, skiing, cricket. *Address:* WPP, 27 Farm Street, London, W1J 5RJ, England. *Telephone:* (20) 7408-2204 (office). *Fax:* (20) 7493-6819 (office). *Website:* www.wpp.com (office).

SORU, Renato; Italian entrepreneur and politician; *President, Sardinia Region;* b. 16 Aug. 1957, Sanluri, Sardinia; ed Bocconi Univ., Milan; fmr derivatives trader; Founder, Chair. and CEO Tiscali internet service provider (ISP) 1998–2004, bought six small telecoms cos and ISPs in Germany, France, Switzerland, Belgium and Czech Repub.; Pres. Sardinia Region (Partito Democratico Sardo) with centre-left coalition 2004–. *Address:* Tiscali SpA, Sa Illetta, 09122 Cagliari, Italy (office). *Telephone:* 02309011 (office). *E-mail:* info@tiscali.com (office); info@pdsardo.it (office). *Website:* www.tiscali.com (office); www.pdsardo.it (office).

SORVINO, Mira, AB; American actress; b. 28 Sept. 1968; d. of Paul Sorvino; m. Christopher Backus 2004; one s.; ed Harvard Univ. *Film appearances include:* Amongst Friends 1993 (also assoc. producer), The Second Greatest Story Ever Told 1993, Quiz Show 1994, Parallel Lives 1994, Barcelona 1994, Tarantella 1995, Sweet Nothing 1995, Mighty Aphrodite (Acad. Award Best Supporting Actress 1996) 1995, The Dutch Master 1995, Blue in the Face 1995, Beautiful Girls 1996, Norma Jean and Marilyn 1996, Jake's Women 1996, Romy and Michele's High School Reunion 1997, The Replacement Killers 1997, Mimic 1997, Summer of Sam 1999, At First Sight 1999, Joan of Arc: The Virgin Warrior 2000, Lisa Picard is Famous 2001, The Great Gatsby 2001, The Triumph of Love 2001, Wisegirls 2002, The Grey Zone 2002, Gods and Generals 2003, The Final Cut 2004, Leningrad 2007, Reservation Road 2007,. *Television includes:* The Great Gatsby 2000, Human Trafficking 2005, Covert One: The Hades Factor 2006. *Address:* c/o Michelle Stern, The William Morris Agency, 1325 Avenue of the Americas, New York, NY 10019, USA.

SOTKILAVA, Zurab Lavrentievich; Georgian singer (tenor); b. 12 March 1937, Sukhumi; m.; two d.; ed Tbilisi Polytech. Inst., Tbilisi Conservatory; fmr professional football player in Dynamo, Tbilisi; soloist Tbilisi Opera Theatre 1965–74; Prof., Tbilisi Conservatory 1976–88; with Bolshoi Theatre 1974–; toured with Bolshoi and independently in Europe and America; Hon. Academician, Boston Acad. of Arts; People's Artist of USSR and Georgia; Grand Prize Gold Orpheus Festival (Bulgaria) 1986, Second Prize Int. Tchaikovsky Competition (1970), Grand Priz Barcelona Competition 1970. *Operatic roles include:* Vodemon (Iolanthe), Absalom (Absalom and Eteri), Cavaradossi (Tosca), Richard (Un Ballo in Maschera), Manrico (Il Trovatore), Radames (Aida), José (Carmen), Otello and others. *Address:* Bolshoi Theatre, Teatralnaya pl. 1, Moscow, Russia. *Telephone:* (495) 244-07-31 (home). *Website:* www.bolshoi.ru.

SOTOMAYOR, Javier; Cuban fmr athlete; b. 13 Oct. 1967, Limonar; m. María del Carmen García; first man to jump over 8 ft; set world indoor record (7 ft 11.5 in.) 1989 and world outdoor record (8 ft 0.5 in.) 1993; has cleared above 2.30m in 227 events; World Indoor Championships gold medallist 1989, 1993, 1995, 1999; Olympic gold medallist 1992, silver medallist 2000; World Championships gold medallist 1993, 1997, silver medallist 1991, 1995; achieved best height Pan-American Games, Winnipeg 1999; disqualified after failing cocaine test and prevented from competing again until Aug. 2000 by Int. Asscn of Athletics Feds. (IAAF); finished 5th in World Indoor Championships March 2001; retd Oct. 2001; voted Best Cuban Athlete of the Century.

SOUHAIBI, Noman Taher as-, BA; Yemeni politician; *Minister of Finance;* b. 1965, Al-Sadda, Ibb; ed San'a Univ.; Deputy Chair. Tax Authority 2001–05, Chair. 2005–07; Minister of Finance 2007–. *Address:* Ministry of Finance, PO Box 190, San'a, Yemeni (office). *Telephone:* (1) 260370 (office). *Fax:* (1) 263040 (office).

SOULAGES, Pierre; French painter; b. 24 Dec. 1919, Rodez; m. Colette Llaurens 1942; ed Lycée de Rodez; exhibited abstract painting since 1947 in Salon des Surindépendants, Salon de Mai et Réalités Nouvelles; exhibited in int. festivals including Biennales of Venice and São Paulo and the itinerary of the Guggenheim Collection, the Carnegie Inst., Pittsburgh, The New Decade at the Museum of Modern Art, New York, Tate Gallery, London, etc.; also décors for theatres and ballet; and lithographs and engravings; works in Museums of Modern Art, Paris and NY, Tate Gallery, London, Guggenheim Museum, NY, Phillips Gallery, Washington, Museum of Modern Art, Rio de Janeiro, museums in many American cities, in Europe, Australia and Japan; retrospective solo exhbns Hanover, Essen, The Hague, Zürich 1960–61, Ljubljana 1961, MIT 1962, Copenhagen Glyptothek 1963, Fine Arts Museum, Houston 1966, Musée Nat. d'Art Moderne, Paris 1967; Carnegie Inst., Pittsburgh, Albright Knox Art Gallery, Buffalo, Musée de Québec, Musée d'Art Contemporain, Montréal 1968, Oslo, Aalborg, Neuchâtel, Charleroi 1973, Musée Dynamique, Dakar 1974, Gulbenkian Foundation, Lisbon, Museo de arte contemporáneo, Madrid, Musée Fabre, Montpellier, Museo de Arte Moderno, Mexico City 1975, Museu de Arte Moderna, Rio de Janeiro, Museo de Arte Moderno, Caracas 1976, Museu de Arte Contemporâneo, São Paulo 1976, Centre Georges Pompidou, Paris 1979, Museé du Parc de la Boverie, Liège 1980, Kunstlerhaus, Salzburg 1980, Kunstbygning, Århus; Kunstpavillon, Esbjerg; Palais de Charlottenborg, Copenhagen 1982; Musée d'Unterlinden, Colmar 1983; Museum Seibu, Tokyo 1984; Pulchri Studio, The Hague 1985, Galerie de France 1986, Museum Fridecianum, Kassel, IVAM, Valencia, Musée des Beaux-Arts, Nantes 1989, Galleries Tollarno, Melbourne 1989, Galerie Fandos, Valencia, Galerie Pauli, Lausanne 1990, Museum Moderner Kunst, Vienna 1991, Nat. Museum of Contemporary Art, Seoul, Nat. Palace of Fine Arts, Beijing, Nat. Museum of Fine Arts, Taiwan 1993, Musée d'art moderne de la Ville de Paris 1996, Fine Arts Museum, Montréal 1996, Museu de Arte, São Paulo 1996, Deichtorhallen, Hamburg 1997, Centro de Exposiciones y Congresos, Saragossa 1997, Sala Cultural Rioja, Logroño 1998, Kunstmuseum, Berne 1999, Musée Fabre, Montpelier 1999, Les Abattoirs, Toulouse 2000, The Hermitage, St Petersburg 2001, Galerie

Tretiakof, Moscow 2001, Bibliothèque Nationale de France, Paris 2003; Hon. mem. American Acad. of Arts and Letters; Commdr Légion d'honneur, des Arts et Lettres; Grand Croix, Ordre nat. du Mérite; Grand Prix, Tokyo Biennale 1957, Carnegie Prize, Pittsburgh, USA 1964, Grand Prix des Arts de la Ville de Paris 1975, Rembrandt Prize, Germany, 1976, Prix Nat. de Peinture, Paris 1986, Praemium Imperiale, Tokyo 1992. *Publication:* subject of book 'Soulange, l'œuvre complet: Peintures' by P. Encrevé (three vols). *Address:* 12 rue Monge, 75005 Paris, France. *Website:* www.pierre-soulages.com (office).

SOULÉ MANA, Lawani; Benin government official; previously worked in West African Devt Bank; Minister of Finance 2007–. *Address:* Ministry of Finance And Economy Planning, BP 302, Cotonou, Benin (office). *Telephone:* 229-30-12-47 (office). *Fax:* 229-30-18-51 (office). *E-mail:* sgm@finance.gouv.bj (office). *Website:* www.finance.gouv.bj (office).

SOULEY, Hassane (Bonto); Niger politician; Minister of Youth 2001–02, of Nat. Defence 2002–07. *Address:* c/o Ministry of National Defence, BP 626, Niamey, Niger (office).

SOULEZ-LARIVIÈRE, Daniel Joseph; French lawyer and writer; b. 19 March 1942, Angers (Maine-et-Loire); s. of Furcy Soulez-Larivière and Suzanne Soulez-Larivière (née Larivière); m. Mathilde-Mahaut Nobecourt 1988; one s. with Michèle Abbaye; ed Lycée Janson-de-Sailly, Collège Stanislas, Paris, Garden City High School, New York, USA, Faculty of Law, Paris and Institut d'Etudes Politiques, Paris; lawyer in Paris 1965–; Chargé de mission, Ministry of Equipment and Housing 1966–67; Second Sec. Conférence du stage 1969; mem. Conseil de l'Ordre 1988–90; mem. Consultative Comm. for Revision of the Constitution 1992–93; mem. Advisory Bd Centre de prospective de la gendarmerie; Municipal Counsellor for Chambellay 1995–; mem. Soc. of French Jurists; Chevalier, Légion d'honneur, Ordre nat. du Mérite. *Publications include:* L'avocature 1982, Les juges dans la balance 1987, La réforme des professions juridiques et judiciaires, vingt propositions 1988, Justice pour la justice 1990, Du cirque médiatico-judiciaire et des moyens d'en sortir 1993, Paroles d'avocat 1994, Grand soir pour la justice 1997, Dans l'engrenage de la justice 1998, Lettres à un jeune avocat 1999, La justice à l'épreuve (with Jean-Marie Coulon) 2002, Notre justice 2002, Le temps des Victimes (with Caroline Eliacheff) 2007. *Leisure interest:* hunting. *Address:* 22 avenue de la Grande Armée, 75858 Paris Cedex 17 (office); 6 rue des Fougères, 92140 Clamart (home); le Prieuré, 49220 Chambellay, France (home). *Telephone:* 1-47-63-37-22 (office); 1-45-34-56-50 (home). *Fax:* 1-42-67-83-05 (office); 1-46-26-23-65 (office). *E-mail:* dsl@soulezlariviere.com (office).

SOULIOTI, Stella; Cypriot politician and barrister; b. (Cacoyannis), 13 Feb. 1920, Limassol; d. of Panayiotis Cacoyannis and Angeliki Cacoyannis; sister of Michael Cacoyannis (q.v.); m. Demetrios Souliotis 1949 (died 2002); one d.; ed Cyprus, Egypt and Gray's Inn, London; joined Women's Auxiliary Air Force, Nicosia and served in Middle East 1943–46; called to the Bar, London 1951; law practice, Limassol 1952–60; Minister of Justice 1960–70, concurrently Minister of Health 1964–66; Law Commr 1971–84; Attorney-Gen. 1984–88; Co-ordinator of Foreign Aid to Cyprus Refugees 1974–; Adviser to Pres. of Cyprus on Cyprus Problem 1976–; Chair. Cyprus Overseas Relief Fund 1977–82; Visiting Fellow, Wolfson Coll. Cambridge 1982–83; Pres. Cyprus Red Cross 1961–2004, Hon. Pres. 2004–; Chair. Cyprus Scholarship Board 1962–1985, Cyprus Town and Country Planning Cttee 1967–70; Vice-Pres. Cyprus Anti-Cancer Soc. 1971–; Trustee Cambridge Commonwealth Scholarship Trust for Cyprus 1983–; mem. Exec. Bd UNESCO 1987–91; Hon. Vice-Pres. Int. Fed. of Women Lawyers 1967–; Hon. LLD (Nottingham) 1972; Second World War Medal (1939–1945), Certificate of Good Service RAF, Medal of the Order of the Knights of St Katherine (1967), Officer of Cedars (Lebanon) 1975, Second World War Veterans Medal (Russian Fed.) 1995. *Publications:* Fettered Independence: Cyprus 1878–1964 The Narrative (Vol. 1) 2006, The Documents (Vol. 2) 2006. *Leisure interests:* reading, writing, music, theatre. *Address:* Flat 71, Arethusa House, 3 Kerkyras Street, 3107, Limassol, Cyprus (home). *Telephone:* (22) 666955 (office); (25) 587227 (home). *Fax:* (22) 666956 (office); (25) 587227 (home).

SOUMARÉ, Cheikh Hadjibou; Senegalese politician; b. 1951, Dakar; ed Ecole Nationale d'Administration et de Magistrature, Univ. of Dakar; served as municipal tax officer Kaolack, Sédhiou and Bambey 1981–85; Head Statistics Div., State Treasury 1985–90; Provisional Admin. Bank of Credit and Commerce Int., Senegal 1991–95; adviser to Minister for Finance 1995–96; Dir of the Budget 1996–2000; Dir-Gen. of Finance 2000–01; Deputy Minister for the Budget 2001–07; Prime Minister 2007–09 (resgnd). *Address:* c/o Prime Minister's Office, Building Administratif, BP 4029, Dakar, Senegal (office).

SOUSA, Manuel Inocêncio, MSc; Cape Verde politician; *Minister of State and of Infrastructure, Transport and the Sea;* b. 1951; ed IST, Lisbon, Portugal, IHE, Delft, Netherlands; fmr Minister of the Communities; Minister of Foreign Affairs, Co-operation and Communities 2001–02; Sr Minister of Infrastructure and Transport (now Minister of State and of Infrastructure, Transport and the Sea) 2002–. *Address:* Ministry of Infrastructure and Transport, Ponta Belém, Praia, Santiago (office); CP 376, Santo Vicente, Cape Verde (home). *Telephone:* (261) 5699 (office); (261) 9249 (home). *Fax:* (261) 1595 (office). *E-mail:* msousa@mih.gov.cv (office); inocenciosousa@hotmail.com (home).

SOUTER, Brian; British business executive; *CEO, Stagecoach Group PLC;* b. 1954; s. of Iain Souter and Catherine Souter; m. Elizabeth McGoldrick 1988; three s. one d.; ed Univs of Dundee and Strathclyde; fmrly trainee accountant; f. Stagecoach Selkent bus co. with sister Ann Gloag (q.v.); Chair. Stagecoach Group PLC 1980–2002, CEO 2002–; fmr Chair. ScotAirways Group Ltd; Businessman of theYear, Insider Elite Awards 2004. *Address:* Stagecoach Group PLC, 10 Dunkeld Road, Perth, PH1 5TW, Scotland (office). *Telephone:* (1738) 442111 (office). *Fax:* (1738) 443076 (office). *E-mail:* info@stagecoachgroup.com (office). *Website:* www.stagecoachgroup.com (office).

SOUTER, David Hackett, AB, MA, LLB; American lawyer and judge; *Associate Justice, Supreme Court;* b. 17 Sept. 1939, Melrose, Mass; s. of Joseph A. Souter and Helen A. Hackett; ed Harvard Univ., Univ. of Oxford, UK, Harvard Univ. Law School; admitted to NH Bar 1967; Assoc., Orr & Reno, Concord 1966–68; Asst Attorney-Gen. of NH 1968–71, Deputy Attorney-Gen. 1971–76, Attorney-Gen. 1976–78; Assoc. Justice, NH Superior Court 1978–83, NH Supreme Court 1983–90; Judge US Court of Appeals, 1st Circuit 1990; Assoc. Justice US Supreme Court, Washington, DC 1990–; mem. ABA, NH Bar Asscn; Trustee Concord Hosp. 1972–85, NH Historical Soc. 1976–85; Fellow, American Acad. of Arts and Sciences. *Address:* United States Supreme Court, One First Street, NE, Washington, DC 20543, USA (office). *Telephone:* (202) 479-3211 (office). *Website:* www.supremecourtus.gov (office).

SOUTHERN, Sir Edwin, FRS; British molecular biologist and academic; *Whitley Professor of Biochemistry, University of Oxford;* b. 1938; initiated some of the earliest DNA sequencing at MRC Mammalian Genome Unit, Edinburgh 1967–79; Assoc. Dir MRC Clinical and Population Cytogenetics Unit, where in 1979 he set up first project to map human genome using molecular methods; Whitley Prof. of Biochemistry, Univ. of Oxford 1985–; f. Oxford Gene Technology 1995; f. The Kirkhouse Trust; Gairdner Foundation Int. Award 1990, Royal Medal, Royal Soc. of London 1998, Lasker Prize for Clinical Medical Research (jtly) 2005, Asscn of Biomolecular Resource Facilities Award 2005. *Inventions include:* the Southern Blot, now a common laboratory procedure used in DNA analysis for genetic fingerprinting and paternity testing. *Publications:* numerous articles in professional journals. *Address:* Oxford Gene Technology, The Hirsch Building, Begbroke Science Park, Sandy Lane, Yarnton, Kidlington, OX5 1PF (office); Department of Biochemistry, University of Oxford, South Parks Road, Oxford OX1 3QU, England (office). *Telephone:* (1865) 275282 (office). *Fax:* (1865) 275283 (office). *E-mail:* contact@ogt.co.uk (office); ed.southern@bioch.ox.ac.uk/~southern (office). *Website:* www.ogt.co.uk (office); www.bioch.ox.ac.uk (office).

SOUTHGATE, Sir Colin, Kt; British business executive; b. 24 July 1938, New Malden, Surrey; s. of Cyril Alfred Southgate and Edith Isabelle Southgate; m. Sally Southgate 1962; two s. two d.; ed City of London School; began career with NPI; later worked in computers with ICT then ICL; launched own firm Software Sciences 1970; business sold to Thorn EMI 1982; Dir Thorn EMI 1984, Man. Dir 1985, Chief Exec. 1987, Chair. 1989–99; Chair. Thorn PLC (after de-merger of Thorn EMI) 1996–98, Royal Opera House 1998–2003, Nettrain 2001–; Dir (non-exec.) Bank of England 1991–99, PowerGen 1990–96 (Chair. 1993–96), Terence Chapman Group 1997–99 (Chair. 1999–); Deputy Pres. CBI 1995–96; Dir (non-exec.) Whitehead Mann Group PLC 1997–2003, Chair. 2003–06; Chair. Sibelius Software Ltd 2000; Chair. Adeptra Ltd 2000–; Trustee Nat. Gallery 1998–; Gov. The Man. Coll., Henley 1991–97; mem. World Business Council for Sustainable Devt 1994–96. *Address:* Adeptra Ltd, 200 Brook Drive, Green Park, Reading, RG2 6UB, England (office). *Website:* www.adeptra.net (office).

SOVERN, Michael Ira, BA, LLB; American legal scholar, academic and fmr university president; *President Emeritus and Chancellor Kent Professor of Law, Columbia University;* b. 1 Dec. 1931, New York; m. 2nd Eleanor Lean 1963 (divorced 1974); m. 3rd Joan Wit 1974 (died 1993); m. 4th Patricia Walsh 1995; two s. one d. from first m.; one d. from second m.; ed Columbia Coll., Columbia School of Law; called to the Bar 1956; mem. Faculty, Columbia Law School 1957–, Prof. of Law 1960–, Dean, Law School 1970–79, Chancellor Kent Prof. in Law 1977–, Univ. Provost 1979–80, Pres. 1980–93, now Pres. Emer.; Chair. Japan Soc. 1993–, American Acad., Rome 1993–, nat. advisory council Freedom Forum Media Studies Center 1993–, Sotheby's 2000–; Pres. Schubert Foundation 1996–, also Dir Schubert Org.; mem. Bd of Dirs Comcast Corpn 2002–, Chemical Bank 1981–96; fmr mem. Bd of Dirs AT&T, GNY Insurance Group, Orion Pictures Corpn, Asian Cultural Corpn; Fellow, American Acad. of Arts and Sciences; mem. American Law Inst.; Hon. DPhil (Tel-Aviv), Hon. LL.D (Columbia) 1980, Commendatore, Order of Merit (Italy) 1991, Alexander Hamilton Medal, Columbia Coll. 1993, Ctizens Union Civic Leadership Award. *Publications:* Legal Restraints on Racial Discrimination in Employment 1966, Law and Poverty 1969. *Address:* Office of the President, The Shubert Foundation, 234 West 44th Street, New York, NY 10036; School of Law, Columbia University, 435 West 116th Street, New York, NY 10027, USA (office). *Telephone:* (212) 854-2640 (office). *Website:* www.shubertfoundation.org; www.law.columbia.edu (office).

SOW, Ahmedou Mostapha; Senegalese academic and physician; *Professor Emeritus of Medicine, Dakar University;* b. 5 May 1931, Saint Louis; m.; ten c.; ed Ecole Normale W. Ponty, Dakar, Dakar Univ.; studied medicine in Paris and Sarajevo; Asst Lecturer in Histology and Embryology, Dakar Univ. 1963–66, Prof. of Medicine 1976, Prof. Emer. 1988–; Head Physician, Diabetic Centre, Dakar, Head Internal Medicine 1978–97; Dir urban centre for non-transmissible chronic diseases; Consultant to OAU on Blood and Liver Diseases, to WHO on the Elderly and Diabetes; Fellow Islamic Acad. of Sciences; Officer Palmes Académiques Sénégalaises, Chevalier Ordre nat. du Lion, Commdr Ordre du Mérite, Senegal Commdr Ordre des Palmes académiques, Commdr Ordre nat. du Mérite (France), Distinction Prize in Medicine 1962. *Address:* Islamic Academy of Sciences, P.O. Box 830036, Amman, Jordan (office). *Telephone:* 5522104 (office). *Fax:* 5511803 (office).

SOWRY, Hon. Roger; New Zealand fmr politician; b. 1958, Palmerston North; m.; four c.; ed Victoria Univ. of Wellington; fmr Distribution Man., R. Hannah & Co.; Nat. Party MP 1990–; apptd Jr Whip, then Sr Govt Whip

1993–96; Minister of Social Welfare, Minister in Charge of War Pensions, Assoc. Minister of Health 1996–98 and Minister in Charge of Social Services, Work, Income, Welfare, Housing, Employment and Leader of the House 1998–2000; Deputy Divisional Chair. Wellington Young Nationals 1979–80, Electorate Chair. Pencarrow 1982–86, Divisional Councillor 1985–96, Deputy Chair. Wellington Div. 1988–90, Wellington Rep. on NZ Nat. Exec. 1989–90; Deputy Leader Nat. Party 2001–03, Spokesman on Energy and Labour and Industrial Relations 2003–; mem. Commerce Select Cttee 2003–. *E-mail:* roger .sowry@xtra.co.nz (home).

SOYINKA, Akinwande Oluwole (Wole), BA; Nigerian playwright and academic; *Professor Emeritus of Comparative Literature, Obafemi Awolowo University;* b. 13 July 1934, Abeokuta; s. of Ayo Soyinka and Eniola Soyinka; m.; several c.; ed Univ. of Ibadan, Nigeria and Univ. of Leeds, UK; worked at Royal Court Theatre, London; Research Fellow in Drama, Univ. of Ibadan 1960–61; Lecturer in English, Univ. of Ife 1962–63; Sr Lecturer in English, Univ. of Lagos 1965–67; political prisoner 1967–69; Artistic Dir and Head, Dept of Theatre Arts, Univ. of Ibadan 1969–72; Research Prof. in Dramatic Literature, Univ. of Ife 1972, Prof. of Comparative Literature and Head of Dept of Dramatic Arts 1976–85; Goldwin Smith Prof. of Africana Studies and Theatre Cornell Univ. 1988–92; passport seized Sept. 1994, living in France; charged with treason March 1997 in absentia; Woodruff Prof. Emer. of the Arts, Emory Univ., Atlanta 2004–; Prof. Emer. of Comparative Literature, Obafemi Awolowo Univ. 2007–; Ed. Ch'Indaba (fmrly Transition) Accra; Artistic Dir Orisun Theatre, 1960 Masks; Literary Ed. Orisun Acting Editions; Pres. Int. Theatre Inst. 1986–; Fellow, Churchill Coll. Cambridge 1973–74; mem. American Acad. of Arts and Letters, Int. Theatre Inst., Union of Writers of the African Peoples, Nat. Liberation Council of Nigeria; Fellow, Ghana Asscn of Writers, Pan-African Writers Asscn; Commdr, Légion d'honneur; Commdr, Fed. Repub. of Nigeria 1986; Commdr, Order of Merit (Italy) 1990; Hon. DLitt (Leeds) 1973, (Yale) 1981, (Morehouse), (Paul Valéry), (Bayreuth), (Ibadan), (Harvard); Hon. DScS (Edin.) 1977; Rockefeller Foundation Grant 1960, John Whiting Drama Prize 1966, Prisoner of Conscience Award, Amnesty Int., Jock Campbell-New Statesman Literary Award 1969, Nobel Prize for Literature 1986, George Benson Medal, RSL 1990, Writers Guild Lifetime Achievement Award 1996, Distinguished Scholar-in-Residence, New York Univ. 1999, and numerous other awards. *Plays:* The Invention 1955, The Lion and the Jewel 1959, The Swamp Dwellers 1959, A Dance of the Forests 1960, The Trials of Brother Jero 1961, The Strong Breed 1962, The Road 1964, Kongi's Harvest 1965, Madmen and Specialists 1971, Before the Blackout 1971, Jero's Metamorphosis 1973, Camwood on the Leaves 1973, The Bacchae of Euripides 1974, Death and the King's Horsemen 1975, Opera Wonyosi 1978, A Play of Giants 1984, Six Plays 1984, Requiem for a Futurologist 1985, From Zia, with Love 1991, A Scourge of Hyacinths (radio play) 1992, The Beatification of Area Boy 1995, King Baabu 2003. *Radio:* BBC Reith Lectures 2004. *Publications:* novels: The Interpreters 1964, The Forest of a Thousand Daemons (trans.), Season of Anomy 1973; poetry: Idanre and Other Poems 1967, Poems from Prison 1969, A Shuttle in the Crypt 1972, Poems of Black Africa (ed.) 1975, Ogun Abibman 1977, Mandela's Earth and Other Poems 1988, Samarkand and Other Markets I Have Known 2002; non-fiction: The Man Died (prison memoirs) 1972, Myth, Literature and the African World (lectures) 1972, Aké, The Years of Childhood (autobiog.) 1982, Art, Dialogue and Outrage 1988, Isara: A Voyage Round Essay 1990, Continuity and Amnesia 1991, Ibadan: The Pentelemes Years (memoir) 1994, The Open Sore of a Continent, A Personal Narrative of the Nigerian Crisis 1996, The Burden of Memory, The Muse of Forgiveness 1999, Conversations with Wole Soyinka 2001, You Must Set Forth at Dawn: A Memoir 2006. *Address:* c/o Deborah Rogers, Rogers, Coleridge & White, 20 Powis Mews, London, W11 1JN, England (office); c/o PO Box 935, Abeokuta, Ogun State, Nigeria. *E-mail:* deborahr@rcwlitagency.demon.co.uk (office).

SPACEK, Mary Elizabeth (Sissy); American actress; b. 25 Dec. 1949, Quitman, Tex.; d. of Edwin A. Spacek and Virginia Spacek; m. Jack Fisk 1974; two d.; ed Lee Strasberg Theater Inst. *Films:* Prime Cut 1972, Ginger in the Morning 1972, Badlands 1974, Carrie (Best Actress Nat. Soc. Film Critics) 1976, Three Women (Best Supporting Actress New York Film Critics) 1977, Welcome to LA 1977, Heart Beat 1980, Coal Miner's Daughter (Acad. Award for Best Actress, Best Actress New York and Los Angeles Film Critics, Foreign Press Asscn, Nat. Soc. Film Critics) 1980, Raggedy Man 1981, Missing 1982, The River 1984, Marie 1985, Violets are Blue 1986, Crimes of the Heart 1986, 'night Mother 1986, JFK 1991, The Long Walk Home, The Plastic Nightmare, Hard Promises 1992, Trading Mom 1994, The Grass Harp 1995, Streets of Laredo 1995, If These Walls Could Talk 1996, Affliction 1998, Blast From the Past 1999, In the Bedroom (Golden Globe for Best Actress 2002) 2001, Verna: USO Girl 2002, Tuck Everlasting 2002, Last Call 2003, A Home at the End of the World 2004, An American Haunting 2005, The Ring II 2005, Nine Lives 2005, Summer Running: The Race to Cure Breast Cancer 2005, North Country 2005, Gray Matters 2007, Hot Rod 2007, Lake City 2008. *Television:* The Girls of Huntington House 1973, The Migrants 1973, Katherine 1975, Verna, USO Girl 1978, A Private Matter 1992, A Place for Annie 1994, The Good Old Boys 1995, Pictures of Hollis Woods 2007. *Music includes:* Album of the Year Award (Country Music Asscn) for Coal Miner's Daughter 1980. *Address:* c/o Steve Tellez, CAA, 9830 Wilshire Boulevard, Beverly Hills, CA 90212, USA.

SPACEY, Kevin; American actor and theatre director; *Artistic Director, The Old Vic Theatre;* b. 26 July 1959, S Orange, NJ; ed Chatsworth High School, LA, Juilliard Drama School, NY; stage debut in Henry IV, Part I; Broadway debut in Ghosts 1982; mem. Bd of Trustees, Old Vic Theatre, London, Artistic Dir 2003–, also appearing there several productions; Co-Dir The Bridge Project, (theatre co. est. with Sam Mendes at Old Vic Theatre, London and Brooklyn Acad. of Arts, NY) 2007–; Cameron Mackintosh Visiting Prof. of Contemporary Theatre, St Catherine's Coll., Oxford 2008–; Dr hc London South Bank Univ. 2005; Evening Standard Special Theatre Award 2008. *Films:* Working Girl 1988, See No Evil, Hear No Evil 1989, Dad 1989, Henry and June 1990, Glengarry Glen Ross 1992, Consenting Adults 1992, Hostile Hostages 1994, Outbreak 1995, The Usual Suspects (Acad. Award for Best Supporting Actor) 1995, Se7en 1995, Looking for Richard 1996, A Time to Kill 1996, LA Confidential 1997, Midnight in the Garden of Good and Evil 1997, American Beauty (Acad. Award for Best Actor) 1999, Pay it Forward 2000, The Shipping News 2001, K-PAX 2001, The Life of David Gale 2003, Beyond the Sea (also dir) 2004, Superman Returns 2006, Fred Claus 2007, 21 2008, Recount 2008; Dir Albino Alligator 1997. *Plays:* theatre appearances include: Hurlyburly 1985, Long Day's Journey into Night, London 1986, Yonkers, NY (Tony Award), The Iceman Cometh, London 1998, National Anthems (Old Vic) 2005, Richard II (Old Vic) 2005, The Philadelphia Story (Old Vic) 2006, A Moon for the Misbegotten (Old Vic and Broadway) 2007, Speed the Plow (Old Vic) 2007. *Address:* Polaris PR, 8135 West Fourth Street, Second Floor, Los Angeles, CA 90048, USA (office); c/o The Old Vic Theatre, The Cut, Waterloo, London, SE1 8NB, England (office). *Telephone:* (20) 7928-2651 (office). *Website:* www.oldvictheatre.com (office).

SPADER, James; American actor; b. 7 Feb. 1960, Boston; ed Phillips Acad. *Films include:* Endless Love 1981, The New Kids 1985, Pretty in Pink 1986, Baby Boom 1987, Less Than Zero 1987, Mannequin 1987, Jack's Back 1988, The Rachel Papers 1989, Sex, Lies and Videotape 1989, Bad Influence 1990, The Music of Chance 1993, Dream Lover 1994, Wolf 1994, Stargate 1994, Two Days in the Valley 1996, Crash 1997, Keys to Tulsa 1997, Critical Care 1997, Curtain Call 1998, Supernova 1998, Slow Burn 1999, Curtain Call 1999, Secretary 2002, I Witness 2003, Alien Hunter 2003, Shadow of Fear 2004. *Television:* The Pentagon Papers 2003, The Practice 2003–04, (Emmy Award for Outstanding Lead Actor in a Drama Series 2004), Boston Legal 2004– (Emmy Award for Outstanding Lead Actor in a Drama Series 2005, 2007). *Address:* c/o ICM, 8942 Wilshire Boulevard, Beverly Hills, CA 90211, USA.

SPALDING, Alistair; British theatre executive; *Artistic Director and CEO, Sadler's Wells;* b. 25 Aug. 1957, Stotfold, Herts.; programmer of film, classical music and visual arts, Hawth Theatre, Crawley 1988–94; Head of Dance and Performance, South Bank Centre, London 1994–2000; Dir of Programming, Sadler's Wells, London 2000–03, Interim Artistic Dir 2003–04, Artistic Dir 2004–, CEO 2004–; External Advisor, Validation Bd for Laban Centre degree courses, City Univ., London; Chair. Dance UK; mem. advisory panel, Arts Council England Dance 1995–2003; Chevalier des Artes et Lettres 2005. *Address:* Sadler's Wells, Rosebery Avenue, London EC1R 4TN, England (office). *Telephone:* (20) 7863-8198 (office). *Fax:* (20) 7863-8199 (office). *Website:* www.sadlerswells.com (office).

SPALDING, D. Brian, ScD, PhD, FRS, FIMechE, FInstF, FREng; British scientist, academic and business executive; *Managing Director, Concentration, Heat and Momentum Ltd. (CHAM);* b. 9 Jan. 1923, New Malden, Surrey; s. of Harold Spalding and Kathleen Spalding; m. 1st Eda Ilse-Lotte Goericke; two s. two d.; m. 2nd Colleen King; two s.; ed King's Coll. School, Wimbledon, The Queen's Coll. Oxford and Pembroke Coll. Cambridge; Bataafsche Petroleum Matschapij 1944–45; Ministry of Supply 1945–47; ICI Research Fellow at Cambridge Univ. 1948–50, Demonstrator in Eng 1950–54; Reader in Applied Heat, Imperial Coll. of Science and Tech., London 1954–58, Prof. of Heat Transfer 1958–88, Prof. Emer. 1988–, Head of Computational Fluid Dynamics Unit 1981–88; Man. Dir Conduction Heat and Mass Transfer Ltd 1970–75, Concentration, Heat and Momentum Ltd 1975–; Chair. CHAM of N America Ltd 1977–91; mem. Royal Norwegian Soc., Russian Acad. of Sciences 1994, Ukrainian Nat. Acad. of Sciences 1994; Max Jakob Award 1978, Medaille d'Or 1980, Bernard Lewis Combustion Medal 1982, Luikov Medal 1986. *Publications:* Numerical Prediction of Flow, Heat Transfer Turbulence and Combustion (selected works) 1983, Heat Exchanger Design Handbook (jtly) 1982, Combustion and Mass Transfer 1979, GENMIX: A General Computer Program 1978, Mathematical Models of Turbulence (jtly) 1972, Heat and Mass Transfer in Recirculating Flows (co-author) 1967, Convective Mass Transfer (co-author) 1963, Engineering Thermodynamics (co-author) 1958, Some Fundamentals of Combustion 1955, Postscripts to Pushkin 2002; numerous scientific papers. *Leisure interests:* music, poetry reading. *Address:* Concentration, Heat and Momentum Ltd (CHAM), Bakery House, 40 High Street, Wimbledon, SW19 5AU, England (office). *Telephone:* (20) 8947-7651 (office). *Fax:* (20) 8879-3497 (office). *Website:* www.cham.co.uk (office).

SPALL, Timothy, OBE, FRSA; British actor; b. 27 Feb. 1957, London; s. of Joseph Spall and Sylvia Spall; m.; one s. two d.; ed Battersea Co. Comprehensive, Kingsway and Princeton Coll. of Further Ed., Royal Acad. of Dramatic Art, London. *Television:* The Brylcream Boys 1978, Auf Wiedersehen Pet 1983, 1985, Roots 1993, Frank Stubbs Promotes 1994, 1995, Outside Edge 1994, 1995, Neville's Island 1997, Our Mutual Friend 1997, Shooting the Past 1999, The Thing About Vince 2000, Vacuuming Completely Nude in Paradise 2001, Perfect Strangers 2001, Auf Wiedersehen Pet (third series) 2002, My House in Umbria 2003, Cherished 2005, Mr Harvey Lights a Candle 2005, Mysterious Creatures 2006, A Room with a View 2007, The Street 2006–07, Oliver Twist 2007. *Plays:* Merry Wives of Windsor, Nicholas Nickleby, The Three Sisters, The Knight of the Burning Pestle (RSC 1978–81), St Joan 1985, Mandragola 1985, Le Bourgeois Gentilhomme 1993, A Midsummer Night's Dream 1994 (Royal Nat. Theatre), This is a Chair 1996 (Royal Court). *Films include:* Quadrophenia 1978, Gothic 1986, The Sheltering Sky 1989, Life is Sweet 1990, Secrets and Lies 1996, The Wisdom of Crocodiles 1998, Still Crazy 1998, Topsy Turvy 1999, Clandestine Marriage 1999, Love's Labour's Lost 2000, Intimacy 2001, Lucky Break 2001, Rock Star 2001, Vanilla Sky 2001, All or Nothing 2002, Nicholas Nickleby 2002, Gettin' Square 2003, The Last Samurai 2003, Harry Potter and the Prisoner of

Azkaban 2004, Lemony Snickett's A Series of Unfortunate Events 2004, Harry Potter and the Goblet of Fire 2005, Pierrepoint 2005, Enchanted 2007, Sweeney Todd 2007, Death Defying Acts 2008, Harry Potter and the Half Blood Prince 2008, Apaloosa 2008. *Leisure interests:* boating, drinking fine wines, reading. *Address:* c/o Markham & Froggatt, 4 Windmill Street, London, W1P 1HF, England (office); c/o Hofflund Palone, Suite 420, 9465 Wilshire Blvd, Beverley Hills, CA 90212, USA (office). *Telephone:* (20) 7636-4412 (London) (office); (310) 859-1971 (Beverley Hills) (office). *Fax:* (20) 7637-5233 (London) (office); (20) 8699-1657 (London) (office). *E-mail:* admin@markhamfroggatt.co.uk (office). *Website:* www.markhamfroggatt.com (office).

SPANIER, Graham B., BS, MS, PhD; American university administrator, sociologist and academic; *President, Pennsylvania State University;* m. Sandra Spanier (neé Whipple) 1971; one s. one d.; ed Iowa State Univ., Northwestern Univ.; Prof. and Assoc. Dean, Pennsylvania State Univ. 1973–82, Pres. 1995–; Vice-Provost for Undergraduate Studies, State Univ. of NY at Stony Brook 1982–86; Provost and Vice-Pres. for Academic Affairs, Oregon State Univ. 1986–91; Chancellor Univ. of Nebraska 1991–95; Chair. Nat. Asscn of State Univs and Land-Grant Colls (Co-Chair. Cttee on Higher Educ. and the Entertainment Industry), Nat. Security Higher Educ. Advisory Bd (mem. Nat. Counterintelligence Working Group), Big Ten Conf. Council of Pres/Chancellors; Vice-Chair. Worldwide Univs Network; fmr Chair. Christian Children's Fund; fmr Pres. Nat. Council of Family Relations; mem. Bd of Dirs Jr Achievement Int. *Publications:* ten books and more than 100 scholarly publs. *Leisure interests:* magic, music, racquetball. *Address:* Office of the President, Pennsylvania State University, University Park, PA 16802, USA (office). *Telephone:* (814) 865-2507 (office). *E-mail:* president@psu.edu (office). *Website:* www.psu.edu (office).

SPANTA, Rangin Dadfar, PhD; Afghan academic and government official; *Minister of Foreign Affairs;* b. 15 Dec. 1953, Herat prov.; m.; one s. one d.; ed Kabul Univ., Aachen Univ., Germany; began living in Germany 1982; Prof., Inst. of Political Science, Tech. Univ. of Aachen 1992–2005, Dir Third World Studies Inst.; returned to Afghanistan to teach at Kabul Univ. 2005; Spokesperson Alliance for Democracy; advisor to Pres. on int. affairs 2005; Minister of Foreign Affairs 2006–. *Address:* Ministry of Foreign Affairs, Malak Azghar Road, Kabul, Afghanistan (office). *Telephone:* (70) 104024 (office). *Fax:* (20) 2100360 (office). *E-mail:* contact@mfa.gov.af (office). *Website:* www.mfa.gov.af (office).

SPARGO, Peter Ernest, FRSSAF; South African academic; *Honorary Research Associate, Department of Physics, University of Cape Town;* b. 7 June 1937, Johannesburg; s. of Alfred Hugh Spargo and Lilias McCall (née Fisher) Spargo; m. Celia Rosamunde Key 1964; four d.; ed Jeppe High School, Univ. of the Witwatersrand, Johannesburg and Magdalene Coll. Cambridge, UK; Science Teacher, Jeppe High School, Johannesburg 1961–63; Lecturer in Science Educ., Johannesburg Coll. of Educ. 1964–71; Science Educ. Planner, Pretoria 1972–75; with School of Educ., Univ. of Cape Town 1976–97, Dir Science Educ. Unit 1980–97, Hon. Research Assoc., Dept of Physics 1999–; Nat. Chair. SA Asscn of Teachers of Physical Science 1975–82; Trustee and Dir S African Science Educ. Project 1977–; Educ. Consultant to Shell Oil Co. (SA) 1977–89, Rössing Uranium Co. (Namibia) 1982–90; Nat. Pres. Fed. of Science and Math. Teachers Asscns of SA 1977–79, 1984–85; Gen. Sec. Royal Soc. of S Africa 1986–89; Hon. Nat. Pres. S African Spelaeological Asscn 1996–; Fed. of Science and Math. Teachers Asscns of SA Medal of Honour 1981. *Publications:* numerous publs in the fields of science education, history of science and technology, author of science textbooks. *Leisure interests:* walking, reading, gardening. *Address:* PO Box 211, Rondebosch 7701; Department of Physics, University of Cape Town, Rondebosch 7701 (office); 10 Lochiel Road, Rondebosch, Cape Town, South Africa (home). *Telephone:* (21) 6864289 (home). *Fax:* (21) 6503343 (office). *E-mail:* peter@spargo.wcape.school.za (home). *Website:* www.uct.ac.za/depts/physics (office).

SPARKS, Robert Stephen John, PhD, FRS; British geologist, volcanologist and academic; *Channing Willis Professor of Geology, Department of Earth Sciences, University of Bristol;* b. 15 May 1949, Harpenden, Herts.; s. of Kenneth Grenfell Sparks and Ruth Joan Rugman; m. Ann Elizabeth Talbot 1971; two s.; ed Imperial Coll. London; Fellow of Royal Comm. of Exhbn of 1851, Univ. of Lancaster 1974–76; NATO Post-doctoral Fellow, Univ. of Rhode Island, USA 1976–78; Lecturer, Univ. of Cambridge 1978–89, Fellow, Trinity Hall Cambridge 1980–89; Prof. of Geology, Univ. of Bristol 1989–, Channing Willis Prof. of Geology 1990–; Chief Scientist, Montserrat Volcano Observatory 1997–99; Prof. of Earth Sciences, Nat. Environment Research Council 1998–; Pres. Geological Soc. of London 1994–96, Int. Asscn of Volcanology and Chem. of Earth's Interior 1999–, VGP Section, American Geophysical Union 2008–(10); Chair. of Environmental Sciences, Research Assessment Exercise 2008; Fellow, American Geophysical Union 1998; Hon. DSc (Lancaster) 2000; Dr hc (Univ. Blaise Pascal) 1999, (Univ. of Paris) 2003; Bakerian Lecture, Royal Soc. 2000; Bigsby Medal, Geological Soc. of London, Murchison Medal, Geological Soc. of London 1998, Arthur Day Medal, Geology Soc. of America 2000, Royal Soc. Wolfson Merit Award 2002, Arthur Holmes Medal, European Union of Geosciences 2004, Chiba Univ. Science Prize, Japan 2006. *Publications:* Volcanic Plumes 1997 and more than 330 scientific articles and papers on volcanology (especially physics of volcanic eruptions), fluid mechanics, petrology and other geological topics. *Leisure interests:* music, tennis, football, squash, travel, family. *Address:* Department of Earth Sciences, Wills Memorial Building, Room G17, Queen's Road, Bristol University, Bristol, BS8 1RJ (office); Walnut Cottage, 19 Brinsea Road, Congresbury, Bristol, BS49 5JF, England (home). *Telephone:* (117) 9545419 (office); (1934) 834306 (home). *Fax:* (117) 9253385 (office). *E-mail:* steve.sparks@bristol.ac.uk (office). *Website:* gfd.gly.bris.ac.uk (office); www.gly.bris.ac.uk/www/admin/personnel/RSJS.html (office).

SPASSKIY, Nikolay Nikolayevich, DPolSc; Russian diplomatist and government official; *Deputy Director-General, Rosatom;* b. 1961, Sevastopol; s. of Nikolay Spasskiy and Rimma Spasskiy; ed Moscow Inst. of Int. Relations; with USSR (later Russian) Ministry of Foreign Affairs 1983–; Deputy Head, First Deputy, Dept of N America 1992–94; Dir 1994–97; mem. Advisory Council, Ministry of Foreign Affairs 1995; Amb. to Italy (also accred to San Marino) 1997–2004; Deputy Sec., Nat. Security Council 2004–06, Deputy Dir Gen. Rosatom (Fed. Atomic Energy Agency) 2006–. *Publications:* La Fine del Mondo e Altri Racconti Romani 1999, Il Complotto 2000, Il Bizantino 2002, Le Reliquie di San Cirillo 2004. *Leisure interests:* art, travel. *Address:* Rosatom, 119180 Moscow, Staromonetnyy per., 26, Russia (office). *Website:* www.rosatom.ru/en (office).

SPASSKY, Boris Vasiliyevich; French/Russian chess player and journalist; b. 30 Jan. 1937, Leningrad (now St Petersburg); m. 1st Marina Shcherbacheva; m. 2nd; m. 3rd; ed Faculty of Journalism, Leningrad State Univ.; in Leningrad Section of Voluntary Sport Soc., Trud 1959–61; Trainer, Leningrad Section of Voluntary Sport Soc., Locomotiv 1964–79; played in numerous individual and command int. chess tournaments; USSR Grandmaster, Int. Grandmaster and World Chess Student Champion 1956, USSR Chess Champion 1962, World Chess Champion 1969–72 (when lost to Bobby Fischer); left USSR 1976; lost to Bobby Fischer in Yugoslavia 1992; works as a chess journalist; involved with World Chess Network; Hon. Pres. Kilkenny Chess Club, Ireland; several decorations including Honoured Master of the Sport 1965. *Website:* www.worldchessnetwork.com.

SPASSKY, Igor Dmitriyevich, DrTechSc; Russian engineer and academic; *Head, Central Design Bureau for Marine Engineering (RUBIN);* b. 2 Aug. 1926, Noginsk, Moscow Region; m.; one s. one d.; ed Dzerdjinsky Higher Naval Eng Coll.; service in Black Sea marine forces 1949–50; worked in enterprises of Ministry of Vessel Construction, Leningrad (now St Petersburg) 1950–; Head of Sector, Cen. Design Bureau for Marine Eng (RUBIN), then Deputy Chief Designer, Head and Chief Designer 1974–, Gen. Designer 1983–; Scientific and Tech. Leader of Kursk submarine recovery project; USSR Peoples' Deputy 1990–91; mem. USSR (now Russian) Acad. of Sciences 1987–; Hon. Citizen of St Petersburg; Red Banner of Labour 1963, Hero of Socialist Labour 1978, Order of Lenin 1970, 1978, Orders of October Revolution 1986, Order of Merit for Services to the Motherland 2002; 16 medals; Lenin Prize 1965, USSR State Prize 1983. *Publications:* ed. and contrib.: The Kurst 2000, Five Colours of Time, Submarines of the Tzarist Navy, History of National Shipbuilding (five vols), Submarines of Russia (three vols), Submarine Deisgn (collection of articles); more than 100 scientific works on designing atomic submarines, tech. of machine construction, construction mechanics, reliability and special energetics; articles in magazines Shipbuilding, Military Parade, Naval History, USA Naval Institute Proceedings. *Leisure interest:* fishing. *Address:* Central Design Bureau for Marine Engineering (RUBIN), 191119 St Petersburg, Marata str. 90, Russia (office). *Telephone:* (812) 113-51-32 (office). *Fax:* (812) 113-31-15 (office). *E-mail:* neptun@ckb-rubin.spb.su (office). *Website:* www.ckb-rubin.com (office).

SPÄTH, Lothar; German politician; b. 16 Nov. 1937, Sigmaringen; s. of Friedrich Späth and Helene Späth (née Lillich); m. Ursula Heinle 1962; one s. one d.; ed Gymnasium, Heilbronn, State School of Man., Stuttgart; mem. Landtag 1968–91; Chair. CDU group in Stuttgart Landtag 1972–78, Hon. Leader 1991–; Rep. of CDU for Baden-Württemberg 1977–91; Sec. of Interior Feb.–Aug. 1978, Minister-Pres. of Baden-Württemberg 1978–91; Pres. Bundesrat 1985–86; Chair. Jenoptik AG, Jena 1991–2003; Royal Norwegian Consul-Gen. of Thuringia and Saxony-Anhalt 1992–2003; Dr hc (Karlsruhe) 1984, (Pecs); Winner, John J. McCloy Prize 2000. *Publications:* Wende in die Zukunft 1985, 1992– Der Traum von Europa 1989, Natur und Wirtschaft 1992, Sind die Deutschen noch zu retten? 1993, Countdown für Deutschland 1995, Blühende Phantasien und harte Realitäten 1997, Die zweite Wende 1998, Die Stunde der Politik 1999, Jenseits von Brüssel 2001, Was jetzt getan werden muß 2002. *Leisure interests:* modern painting and graphics, card games, tennis. *Address:* Riedwiesenstrasse 1, 71229 Leonberg, Germany. *Telephone:* (7152) 907444. *Fax:* (7152) 907446. *E-mail:* mmueller@lotharspaeth.de (office).

SPAULDING, Winston, QC; Jamaican lawyer and fmr politician; b. 26 Aug. 1939; m.; five c.; called to the Bar, Inner Temple, London 1966; worked briefly in Jamaican and British civil service and practised law in the Bahamas; subsequently established legal practice in Jamaica; fmr mem. Nat. Exec. People's Nat. Party; Deputy Leader Jamaica Labour Party 1977–83; Senator and Opposition Spokesman on Security and Justice 1977–80; MP for Cen. St James 1980–83 and for SE St Andrew 1983–89; Minister of Nat. Security and Justice and Attorney-Gen. 1980–86; Chair. Defence Bd 1980–86, Legislation Cttee 1980–86, Statute Law Commrs under the Law Revision Act 1980–86; mem. Council of Legal Educ. 1980–86; Founder-mem. Jamaica Council for Human Rights; Founder and First Chair. Human Rights Bureau of Jamaica Labour Party; as Minister of Justice initiated review of Gun Court Act which included abolition of mandatory life sentence; as Minister of Security initiated establishment of Police Staff Coll. *Address:* 21 Balmoral Avenue, Kingston 10, Jamaica (office). *Telephone:* 9298601. *Fax:* 9296196.

SPAVENTA, Luigi; Italian economist and academic; *Professor Emeritus of Economics, University of Rome;* b. 5 March 1934, Rome; s. of Renato Spaventa and Lydia De Novellis; m. Margaret Royce 1962; three c.; ed Univ. of Rome, King's Coll., Cambridge, UK; Prof. of Econ. Policy, Univ. of Palermo 1963–64; Prof. of Econs, Univ. of Perugia 1964–70, Univ. of Rome 1970–, now Prof. Emer.; mem. Italian Parl. (on leave from univ.) 1976–83; Visiting Fellow, All Souls' Coll., Oxford 1968–69; Visiting Scholar, IMF 1984; Luigi Einaudi Prof., Cornell Univ. 1989; Minister of the Budget 1993–94; Chair. Bd Finanza & Futuro SpA, Banca Monte dei Paschi di Siena SpA 1997–98; Chair. Consob

(Securities Comm.) 1998–2003; Fellow, Centre for Econ. Policy Research; mem. Bd Acea SpA; mem. Int. Advisory Council, Chinese Securities Regulatory Comm.; Kt Grand Cross, Order of Merit (Italy). *Publications:* essays and articles in specialized journals and books. *Leisure interest:* mountaineering. *Address:* Via G.B. De Rossi 29, 00161 Rome, Italy (home). *Telephone:* (06) 44238191 (home). *Fax:* (06) 44236225 (home). *E-mail:* l.spaventa@capitalia-am.com (office); Luigi.Spaventa@fastwebnet.it (home).

SPEAKES, Larry Melvin; American business executive and fmr government official; *Manager of Advertising, United States Postal Service;* b. 13 Sept. 1939, Cleveland, Miss.; s. of Harry Speakes and Ethlyn Fincher; m. Laura Crawford 1968; two s. one d.; ed Univ. of Mississippi; news ed. Oxford (Miss.) Eagle 1961–62, Bolivar Commercial, Cleveland 1962–63; Man. Ed. Bolivar Commercial 1965–66; Gen. Man. Progress Publs Leland, Miss. 1966–68; Ed. Leland Progress, Hollandale Herald, Bolivar Co. Democrat, Sunflower Co. News; Press Sec. to Senator for Mississippi 1968–74; Staff Asst Exec. Office of Pres. of USA March–May 1974, Press Asst to Special Counsel to Pres. May–Aug. 1974; Asst to White House Press Sec. 1974–76, Asst Press Sec. to Pres. 1976–77; Press Sec. to Gerald R. Ford 1977; Vice-Pres. Hill & Knowlton, Inc., Washington 1977–81; Prin. Deputy Press Sec. and Asst to Pres. of USA 1981–87; Sr Vice-Pres. Merrill Lynch & Co., Inc., New York 1987–88; corp. communications consultant and lecturer on politics and the presidency 1988–91; Vice-Pres., Communications, Northern Telecom Ltd, Washington and Toronto 1991–93; Senior Vice-Pres. Corp. and Legis. Affairs, US Postal Service 1994–98; Sr Adviser to Postmaster Gen. 1998–, now Man. of Advertising; Hon. LittD (Ind. Cen. Univ.); Presidential Citizens' Medal 1987 and several achievement awards. *Publication:* Speaking Out (biog.) 1988. *Address:* United States Postal Service, 475 L'Enfant Plaza, SW, Washington, DC 20260, USA (office). *Website:* www.usps.com (office).

SPEAR, Laurinda Hope, MA, FAIA; American architect; *Founding Principal, Arquitectonica;* b. 23 Aug. 1951, Rochester, Minn.; d. of Harold Spear; m. Bernardo Fort-Brescia 1976; five s. one d.; ed Columbia and Brown Univs; Founding Prin. Arquitectonica; faculty mem. in charge of design studio, Univ. of Miami School of Architecture; lecturer to professional, civil and academic groups; numerous exhbns throughout USA and Europe including Paris Biennale 1982, Inst. of Contemporary Art, Philadelphia 1986, Buenos Aires Biennale 1987, Inst. Français d'Architecture, Paris 1988, Centrum voor Architectuur en Stedebouw, Brussels 1991, Gallery MA, Tokyo 1993, Philips Arena, Atlanta 1999, Miami Int. Airport; Nat. Academician Nat. Acad. of Design 2002–; mem. Int. Cttee AIA; mem. Bd of Trustees Brown Univ., Ransom Everglades School; mem. Editorial Bd Harvard Design Magazine; Rome Prize in Architecture, AIA Silver Medal for Design Excellence 1999, Salvadori Center Founder's Award 2000. *Major projects include:* low-income housing, high-rise condominiums, residential additions and renovations, office towers, medical office bldgs, retail complexes and hotels in USA, France, Luxembourg and Peru, Festival Walk, Hong Kong 1998. *Address:* Arquitectonica, 550 Brickell Avenue, Suite 200, Miami, FL 33131, USA (office). *E-mail:* lspear@arquitectonica.com (office). *Website:* www.arquitectonica.com (office).

SPEARMAN, Thomas David, PhD, MRIA; Irish mathematician, academic and university vice-provost; *Fellow Emeritus, Trinity College Dublin;* b. 25 March 1937, Dublin; s. of Thomas Spearman and Elizabeth Leadbeater; m. Juanita Smale 1961; one s. two d.; ed Greenlanes and Mountjoy Schools, Dublin, Trinity Coll. Dublin and St John's Coll. Cambridge; Research Fellow, Univ. Coll. London 1960–61; Research Assoc., Univ. of Illinois 1962–64; Lecturer in Theoretical Physics, Univ. of Durham 1964–66; Univ. Prof. of Natural Philosophy, Trinity Coll. Dublin 1966–97, Fellow 1969–94, Senior Fellow 1994–97 (Fellow Emer. 1997–), Bursar 1974–77, Vice-Provost 1991–97; Prof. Associé, Univ. of Montpellier 1985–; Chair. Trustee Savings Bank, Dublin 1989–92; mem. Council, European Physical Soc. 1979–82; mem. European Space Science Cttee 1984–89; Vice-Pres. European Science Foundation 1983–89; Treas. Royal Irish Acad. 1980–88, Pres. 1999–2002; mem. Academia Europaea, Treas. 1989–2000; mem. European Science and Tech. Ass. 1994–98; mem. Bd Nat. Gallery of Ireland 1999–2002; mem. Governing Council European Science Foundation 2000–02; Chair. European Acads Science Advisory Council 2004–07. *Publications:* Elementary Particle Theory (with A. D. Martin) 1970; numerous papers and articles on aspects of elementary particle physics, inverse problems and history of science. *Leisure interests:* walking, gardening, reading, listening to music, looking at pictures. *Address:* House No. 25, Trinity College, Dublin 2 (office); St Elmo, Marlborough Road, Glenageary, Co. Dublin, Ireland (home). *Telephone:* (1) 8962360 (office). *E-mail:* david.spearman@tcd.ie (office).

SPEARS, Britney Jean; American singer; b. 2 Dec. 1981, Kentwood, La; m. Kevin Federline 2004 (divorced 2007); two s.; presenter, Mickey Mouse Club; solo artist 1998–; numerous tours, television and radio appearances; owner of southern grill restaurant, Nyla; MTV Europe Music Awards for Best Female Artist 1999, 2004, for Best Song (for Baby One More Time) 1999, Best Breakthrough Act 1999, Best Pop Act 1999, several MTV Video Music Awards 1999, and Best Female Pop Vocal Performance 2000, Billboard Music Award 2000, American Music Award for Favourite New Artist 2000, Grammy Award for Best Dance Recording (for Toxic) 2005, MTV Video Music Award for Best Female Video (for Piece of Me) 2008. *Film:* Crossroads 2002. *Recordings include:* albums: Baby One More Time 1999, Oops! I Did It Again 2000, Britney 2001, In The Zone 2003, My Prerogative 2004, Blackout 2007, Circus 2008. *Address:* Jive Records, Zomba Recording Corporation, 137–39 West 25th Street, New York, NY 10001, USA (office). *Website:* www.britneyspears.com (office); www.britney.com.

SPECTER, Arlen; American politician; *Senator from Pennsylvania;* b. 12 Feb. 1930, Wichita, Kan.; s. of Harry Specter and Lillie Shanin Specter; m. Joan Lois Levy 1953; two s.; ed Univ. of Oklahoma, Univ. of Pennsylvania,

Yale Univ.; served in USAF 1951–53; Asst Dist Attorney, Phila, Pa 1959–63; Dist Attorney 1966–74; Asst Counsel, Warren Comm., Washington, DC 1964; Special Asst Attorney-Gen., Pa Dept of Justice 1964–65; Del. Republican Nat. Convention 1968, 1972, Alt. Del. 1976; Senator from Pennsylvania (Republican 1981–2009, Democrat 2009–) 1981–, Chair. Select Cttee on Intelligence, Special Cttee on Ageing and Veterans Affairs; mem. Nat. Advisory Cttee on Peace Corps 1969–; Lecturer in Law, Univ. of Pa Law School 1969–72, Temple Univ. Law School 1972–76; mem. White House Conf. on Youth 1971, Gov. Justice Comm., Regional Planning Council, Nat. Advisory Comm. on Criminal Justice Standards and Goals, Criminal Rules Cttee of Pa Supreme Court and Judicial Council of Phila; mem. American, Pa and Phila Bar Asscns, Nat. Council on Alcoholism; Hon. LLB (Phila Coll. of Textiles and Science) 1968; Sons of Italy Award, Alessandroni Lodge. *Publications:* articles in law reviews. *Address:* 711 Senate Hart Building, Washington, DC 20510, USA (office). *Telephone:* (202) 224-4254 (office). *Fax:* (202) 228-1229 (office). *E-mail:* arlen_spector@spector.senate.gov (office). *Website:* spector.senate.gov (office).

SPEDDING, Sir Colin Raymond William, Kt, CBE, BSc, MSc, PhD, DSc, CBiol, FRSA; British agricultural scientist and academic; *Professor Emeritus, University of Reading;* b. 22 March 1925, Cannock; s. of Robert Spedding and Ilynn Spedding; m. Betty N. George 1952 (died 1988); two s. (one deceased) one d.; ed London Univ. (external); Allen & Hanbury 1947; Grassland Research Inst. 1949–75, Deputy Dir 1972–75; Visiting, then part-time Prof. of Agric. Systems, Univ. of Reading 1970–75, Prof. 1975–90, now Prof. Emer.; Head, Dept of Agric. and Horticulture 1975–83, Dean, Faculty of Agric. and Food 1983–86, Dir Centre for Agricultural Strategy 1981–90, Pro-Vice-Chancellor 1986–90; Pres. Inst. of Biology 1992–94; Chair. UK Register of Organic Food Standards 1987–99, Farm Animal Welfare Council 1988–98, Apple and Pear Research Council 1989–97, Council of Science and Tech. Insts (now The Science Council) 1994–2000; Deputy Chair. People's Dispensary for Sick Animals (PDSA) 1996–2003 (mem. Council of Man. 1988–2007); Vice-Pres. Inst. of Biology 1997–2000 (now Hon. FIBiol), Royal Soc. for Prevention of Cruelty to Animals 2002–; Advisory Dir World Soc. for the Protection of Animals 1998–2003, Special Scientific Adviser to Dir Gen. 2003–; Adviser Companion Animal Welfare Council 1999–; Chair. Nat. Equine Forum 1992–, Assured Chicken Production Ltd (ACP) 2000–, now Chair. Poultry Sector Bd (after ACP transfer to Assured Food Standards in 2004), Trustees Farm Animal Welfare Trust 2003–; Fellow Inst. of Horticulture, Royal Agricultural Soc. of England, Royal Agricultural Socs; Hon. Assoc. Royal Coll. of Veterinary Surgeons; Hon. DSc (Reading); George Hedley Memorial Award 1971; Hawkesbury Centenary Medal of Honour, Univ. of W Sydney, Victory Medal, Central Veterinary Soc. 2000 and other honours and distinctions. *Publications:* 16 books and about 200 scientific papers. *Address:* Vine Cottage, Orchard Road, Hurst, Reading, RG10 0SD, England. *Telephone:* (118) 934-1771. *Fax:* (118) 934-2997. *E-mail:* sircolin@crwspedding.fsnet.co.uk (office).

SPEED, Malcolm Walter; Australian lawyer and sports administrator; b. 14 Sept. 1948; s. of Walter Speed and Audrey Speed; m. Alison Cutter 1971; three d.; ed Melbourne Univ.; solicitor 1971–81, called to Victoria Bar 1981, barrister 1981–94, Melbourne; Exec. Chair. Basketball Australia 1994–97; CEO Australian Cricket Bd 1997–2001, Int. Cricket Council 2001–08. *Leisure interests:* cricket, reading, walking, golf, history.

SPEIRN, Sterling, BSc, DIur; American foundation executive; *President and CEO, W. K. Kellogg Foundation;* b. 7 Feb. 1948, Detroit; m. Diana Aviv 2005; two s. (from previous m.); ed Stanford Univ., Univ. of Mich. Law School; taught high school in Cleveland, Ohio; law clerk, US Dept of Interior; practised as lawyer; led Apple Computer's nat. computer grants program 1986–90; joined Peninsula Community Foundation, San Mateo, Calif. 1990, Pres. Chief Exec. 1992–2005; Pres. CEO W. K. Kellogg Foundation, Battle Creek, Mich. 2006–; fmr Chair. League of Calif. Community Foundations; mem. Bd of Advisors Pacific Community Ventures, Global Philanthropy Forum, mem. Bd of Dirs Northern Calif. Grantmakers; taught seminar on philanthropy at Stanford Graduate School of Business 2000, 2001. *Address:* W. K. Kellogg Foundation, One Michigan Avenue, East Battle Creek, MI 49017-4012, USA (office). *Telephone:* (269) 968-1611 (office). *Website:* www.wkkf.org (office).

SPENCE, A. Michael, MA, PhD; American economist and academic; *Philip H. Knight Professor Emeritus, Graduate School of Business, Stanford University;* ed Princeton Univ., Oxford Univ., UK, Harvard Univ.; Assoc. Prof., Harvard Univ. 1973–75, Chair. Advisory Cttee on Shareholder Responsibility 1978–79, Prof. 1979–86, Chair. Project in Industry and Competitive Analysis 1980–85, Chair. Business Econs PhD Program 1981–83, Chair. Dept of Econs 1983–84, Dean of Faculty 1984–90; Philip H. Knight Prof., Stanford Univ. 1990–2000, Dean 1990–99, Prof. Emer. 2000–; Pnr, Oak Hill Venture Pnrs, Menlo Park 1999–; Chair. Nat. Research Council Bd on Science, Tech. and Econ. Policy 1991–97; mem. Bd of Dirs Gen. Mills, Inc., Nike, Inc. 1995–2004, Siebel Systems, Inc. 1995–2004, Exult, Inc. 1999–2004, Blue Martini Software, Torstar, ITI Educ.; mem. American Econ. Asscn; Fellow, AAAS, Econometric Soc.; John Bates Clark Medal, American Econ. Asscn 1981, Nobel Prize in Econs 2001 (jt recipient); numerous other awards and prizes. *Address:* Oak Hill Venture Partners, 2775 Sand Hill Road, Menlo Park, CA 94025-7085; Graduate School of Business, 518 Memorial Way, Stanford University, Stanford, CA 94305-5015, USA (office). *Telephone:* (650) 723-2146 (office). *Website:* www.gsb.stanford.edu/news/spence_resume.html (office).

SPENCE, Jonathan Dermot, PhD, CMG; American historian, academic and writer; *Sterling Professor of History, Yale University;* b. 11 Aug. 1936, Surrey, England; s. of Dermot Spence and Muriel Crailsham; m. 1st Helen Alexander 1962 (divorced 1993); two s.; m. 2nd Chin Annping 1993; ed Univ. of Cambridge, UK and Yale Univ.; Asst Prof. of History, Yale Univ. 1966–71, Prof. 1971–, now Sterling Prof. of History; Visiting Prof. Univ. of Beijing 1987;

Pres. American Historial Asscn 2004–[05]; mem. Bd of Govs Yale Univ. Press 1988–; mem. American Acad. of Arts and Sciences, American Philosophical Soc.; Guggenheim Fellow 1979–80; MacArthur Fellow 1987–92; Hon. LHD (Knox Coll.) 1984, (New Haven) 1989; Hon. LittD (Wheeling Coll.) 1985, (Chinese Univ. of Hong Kong) 1996, (Gettysburg) Coll. 1996, (Union Coll.) 2000, (Beloit Coll.) 2000, (Conn. Coll.) 2000; William C. DeVane Medal, Yale Chapter of Phi Beta Kappa 1978, Los Angeles Times History Prize 1982, Vursell Prize, American Acad. and Inst. of Arts and Letters 1983, Comisso Prize (Italy) 1987; Gelber Literary Prize (Canada) 1991. *Publications:* Ts'Ao Yin and The K'Ang-Hsi Emperor 1966, To Change China 1969, Emperor of China 1974, The Death of Woman Wang 1978, The Gate of Heavenly Peace 1981, The Memory Palace of Matteo Ricci 1984, The Question of Hu 1988, The Search for Modern China 1990, Chinese Roundabout 1992, God's Chinese Son 1996, The Chan's Great Continent 1998, Mao Zedong 1999, Return to Dragon Mountain: Memories of a Late Ming Man 2007. *Address:* Department of History, Yale University, P.O. Box 208324, New Haven, CT 06520 (office); 691 Forest Road, New Haven, CT 06515, USA (home). *Telephone:* (203) 432-0759 (office). *E-mail:* jonathan.spence@yale.edu (office). *Website:* www.yale.edu/history/faculty/spence.html (office).

SPENCE, Michael J., BA, LLB, DPhil; Australian professor of law and university administrator; *Vice-Chancellor and Principal, University of Sydney;* b. 10 Jan. 1962; m. Beth Spence; five c.; ed Univ. of Sydney, Univ. of Oxford, UK; began career as lawyer with Mallesons Stephens Jacques, Sydney; Fellow, St Catherine's Coll., Oxford and Lecturer, Univ. of Oxford 1992, becoming Head of Social Sciences Div.; trained for priesthood at St Stephen's House, Oxford; Vice-Chancellor and Prin. Univ. of Sydney 2008–. *Address:* Office of the Vice-Chancellor, University of Sydney, Sydney, NSW 2006, Australia (office). *Telephone:* (2) 9351-5051 (office). *Fax:* (2) 9351-4596 (office). *E-mail:* Vice-Chancellor@vcc.usyd.edu.au (office). *Website:* www.usyd.edu.au/vice-chancellor (office).

SPENCER, Baldwin; Antiguan politician and trade union official; *Prime Minister and Minister of Foreign Affairs;* b. 8 Oct. 1948; m.; one s. one d.; Leader United Progressive Party; fmr Leader of the Opposition; Prime Minister of Antigua and Barbuda and Minister of Foreign Affairs 2004–. *Leisure interests:* football, cricket, basketball, listening to steel band music, reading, dancing. *Address:* Office of the Prime Minister, Queen Elizabeth Highway, St John's; United Progressive Party, Nevis Street, St John's (office); Cooks Estate, St John's, Antigua (home). *Telephone:* 462-4956 (office); 562-1049 (office); 462-1818; 461-4657 (home). *Fax:* 462-3225 (office); 462-5937 (office); 562-1065 (home). *E-mail:* pmo@candw.ag (office); upp@candw.ag (office). *Website:* www.antiguabarbuda.net/pmo (office); www.uppantigua.com (office).

SPENCER, Elizabeth, AB, MA; American writer; b. 19 July 1921, Carollton, Miss.; d. of James L. Spencer and Mary James McCain; m. John A. B. Rusher 1956 (died 1998); ed Belhaven Coll. and Vanderbilt Univ.; Writer-in-Residence, Univ. of N Carolina 1969, Hollins Coll. 1973, Concordia Univ. 1977–78, Adjunct Prof. 1981–86; Visiting Prof., Univ. of N Carolina, Chapel Hill 1986–92; Vice-Chancellor Fellowship of Southern Writers 1993–97; mem. American Acad. of Arts and Letters; Hon. LittD (Southwestern Univ., Memphis) 1968, (Concordia Univ.) 1987, (Univ. of the South) 1992, (Univ. of NC) 1998, (Belhaven Coll.) 1999; Guggenheim Foundation Fellow 1953, Rosenthal Foundation Award, American Acad. of Arts and Letters 1957, McGraw-Hill Fiction Award 1960, Award of Merit for short story, American Acad. of Arts and Letters 1983, Salem Award for Literature 1992, Dos Passos Award for Fiction 1992, NC Gov.'s Award for Literature 1994, Fortner Award for Literature 1998, Mississippi State Library Asscn Award for Non-fiction 1999, Thomas Wolfe Award, Univ. of NC 2002, NC Hall of Fame 2002, William Faulkner Award for Literary Excellence 2002. *Publications:* Fire in the Morning 1948, This Crooked Way 1952, The Voice at the Back Door 1956, The Light in the Piazza 1960, Knights and Dragons 1965, No Place for an Angel 1967, Ship Island and Other Stories 1968, The Snare 1972, The Stories of Elizabeth Spencer 1981, Marilee 1981, The Salt Line 1984, Jack of Diamonds and Other Stories 1988, For Lease or Sale (play) 1989, On the Gulf 1991, The Night Travellers 1991, Landscapes of the Heart (memoir) 1998, The Southern Woman: New and Selected Fiction 2000; contrib. short stories in magazines and collections. *Leisure interests:* movies, theatre, travel. *Address:* 402 Longleaf Drive, Chapel Hill, NC 27517, USA (home). *Telephone:* (919) 929-2115 (home). *E-mail:* elizabeth0222@earthlink.net (home). *Website:* www.elizabethspencerwriter.com.

SPERBER, Dan; French social sciences researcher; *Researcher, Institut Jean Nicod;* b. 20 June 1942, Cagnes; s. of the late Manes Sperber; ed Univ. of the Sorbonne, Paris and Univ. of Oxford, UK; researcher, CNRS 1965–, Dir of Research 1983, now Research Prof. and Researcher, Institut Jean Nicod; Co-f. EURO-EDU Asscn; Visiting Prof., LSE, Van Leer Inst., Jerusalem, Inst. for Advanced Study, Princeton Univ., Univ. of Michigan, Duxx School, Univ. of Hong Kong, Univ. of Cambridge, Univ. of Bologna; Annual Fellow, Templeton Research Lectures, Vanderbilt Univ. 2007–08; Rivers Memorial Medal, Royal Anthropological Inst. 1991. *Publications:* Rethinking Symbolism 1975, On Anthropological Knowledge 1982, Relevance: Communication and Cognition (with Deirdre Wilson) 1986, Explaining Culture 1996. *Address:* Institut Jean Nicod (EHESS/CNRS), 1bis av. Lowendal, 75007 Paris, France. *Telephone:* 1-53-59-32-89 (office). *E-mail:* dan@sperber.com (home). *Website:* www.institutnicod.org (office); www.dan.sperber.com.

SPERLICH, Peter Werner, PhD; American political scientist, academic and legal consultant; *Professor Emeritus of Political Science, University of California, Berkeley;* b. 27 June 1934, Breslau, Germany (now Wrocław, Poland); s. of Max Otto and Anneliese Gertrud Sperlich (née Greulich); ed Minnesota State Univ. at Mankato, Univ. of Michigan; arrived in USA 1956, naturalized 1961; joined faculty of Univ. of Calif., Berkeley 1963, Prof., Law School 1963–, Prof. of Political Science 1980–, now Prof. Emer.; has served as consultant to courts and law firms; Social Science Research Council Fellow 1966, Ford Foundation Fellow 1968; mem. American Legal Studies Asscn, Law and Soc. Asscn, Nat. Asscn for Dispute Resolution, Int. Soc. of Political Psychology, Soc. for Psychological Study of Social Issues, American, Int. and Western Political Science Asscns, Conf. Group on German Politics; research on law and politics in USA, Germany, Austria, Denmark, the Netherlands, Switzerland, the UK, Canada, Mexico, the USSR, Japan, Thailand, Hong Kong. *Achievements:* work cited by US Supreme Court and various state courts. *Publications:* Conflict and Harmony in Human Affairs 1971, Single Family Defaults and Foreclosures 1975, Trade Rules and Industry Practices 1976, Over-the-Counter Drug Advertisements 1977, Residing in a Mobile Home 1977, An Evaluation of the Emergency School Aid Act Nonprofit Organization 1978, Rotten Foundations – The Conceptual Basis of the Marxist-Leninist Regimes of East Germany and Other Countries of the Soviet Bloc 2002; also numerous articles. *Address:* Department of Political Science, University of California, 581 Barrows Hall, Berkeley, CA 94720 (office); 35503 Vista del Luna, Rancho Mirage, CA 92270, USA (home). *Telephone:* (760) 770-0899 (office). *E-mail:* pws34@yahoo.com. *Website:* www.polisci.berkeley.edu (office).

SPERO, Nancy, BFA; American artist; b. 24 Aug. 1926, Cleveland, Ohio; d. of Henry Spero and Polly Spero; m. Leon Golub 1951; three s.; ed Chicago Art Inst., Atelier André l'Hôte, École des Beaux Arts, Paris; Hon. DFA (Chicago) 1991; Hiroshima Art Prize 1996. *Permanent installations include:* R. C. Harris Water Filtration Plant (Toronto) 1988, Well Woman Centre and exterior mural (Londonderry) 1990, Inst. of Contemporary Art (Philadelphia) 1991, Von der Heydt Museum (Wuppertal) 1991, Círculo de Bellas Artes (Madrid) 1991; also rep. in perm. collections including Art Gallery of Ont. (Toronto), Australian Nat. Gallery, Centro Cultural (Mexico), Museum of Fine Arts (Hanoi), Ulmer Museum (Germany), Musée des Beaux-Arts de Montréal; CAPS Fellow NY State Council on the Arts 1976–77. *Address:* c/o Jeanette Ingberman, Exit Art, 475 10th Avenue, New York, NY 10018; 530 La Guardia Place, New York, NY 10012, USA.

SPETH, James Gustave (Gus), BA, MLitt, JD; American lawyer, scientist and academic; *Carl W. Knobloch, Jr Dean of the School of Forestry and Environmental Studies and Sara Shallenberger Brown Professor in the Practice of Environmental Policy, Yale University;* b. 4 March 1942, Orangeburg, SC; s. of James Gustave and Amelia St Clair Albergotti; m. Caroline Cameron Council 1964; two s. one d.; ed Yale Univ. and Univ. of Oxford, UK (Rhodes Scholar); barrister, Washington, DC 1969, Clerk, Supreme Court 1969–70; Sr Staff Attorney Nat. Resources Defence Council, Washington, DC 1977–79, mem. Bd of Dirs 1981–82, now Trustee; Chair. Council for Environmental Quality 1977–79; Prof. of Law, Georgetown Univ. 1981–82; Pres. and Founder World Resources Inst. 1982–93; joined UNDP 1982, Admin. 1993–99; Carl W. Knobloch, Jr Dean of the School of Forestry and Environmental Studies and Sara Shallenberger Brown Prof. in the Practice of Environmental Policy, Yale Univ. 1999–; mem. Bd of Dirs Center for Humans and Nature, World Resources Inst., Population Action International; Trustee, Rockefeller Brothers Fund; mem. India Council for Sustainable Devt; Hon. DIur (Clark Univ.) 1995, Vermont Law School 2005; Hon. Master of Philosophy (Coll. of the Atlantic) 2001; Hon. DS (Middlebury Coll.) 2007; Hon. DHumLitt (Univ. of South Carolina 2008); Resource Defense Award, Nat. Wildlife Fed. 1975, Nat. Leadership Award, Keystone Center 1991, Barbara Swain Award, Nat. Resources Council of America 1992, Special Recognition Award, Soc. for Int. Devt 1997, Special Leadership Award, Alliance for UN Sustainable Devt Programs 1998, Lifetime Achievement Award, Environmental Law Inst. 1999, Blue Planet Prize 2002, Global Environmental Award, Int. Asscn for Impact Assessment 2005, DeVane Lecturer, Yale Univ. 2007. *Publications:* Worlds Apart: Globalization and the Environment 2003, Red Sky at Morning: America and the Crisis of the Global Environment 2004, Global Environmental Governance (with Peter Haas) 2006, The Bridge at the Edge of the World: Capitalism, the Environment, and Crossing from Crisis to Sustainability 2008. *Address:* Yale School of Forestry and Environmental Studies, 195 Prospect Street, Sage Hall, New Haven, CT 06511 (office); 986 Forest Road, New Haven, CT 06515, USA (home). *Telephone:* (203) 432-5109 (office). *Fax:* (203) 432-3051 (office). *E-mail:* gus.speth@yale.edu (office). *Website:* www.yale.edu/forestry (office).

ŠPIDLA, Vladimír, PhD; Czech politician; *Commissioner for Employment, Social Affairs and Equal Opportunities, European Commission;* b. 22 April 1951, Prague; s. of Václav Špidla and Dagmar Špidlová; m. 1st; two s.; m. 2nd Viktorie Špidlová; one s. one d.; ed Charles Univ., Prague; fmr archaeologist, worker at historical monuments, sawmill, dairy and livestock industry; Vice-Pres. for Educ., Health Service, Social Affairs and Culture, Dist Cttee, Jindřichův Hradec 1990–91; Dir Labour Office, Jindřichův Hradec 1991–96; mem. Chamber of Deputies 1996–2004; Deputy Prime Minister and Minister of Labour and Social Affairs 1998–2002; Prime Minister of the Czech Repub. 2002–04 (resgnd); EU Commr for Employment, Social Affairs and Equal Opportunities 2004–; Founding mem. Czech Social Democratic Party Br. in S Bohemia 1989, joined party leadership 1992, Vice-Chair. 1997–2001, Chair. 2001–04. *Leisure interests:* jogging, poetry, sports in nature, cross-country running, history and prehistory. *Address:* European Commission, 200 Rue de la Loi, 1040 Brussels, Belgium (office). *Telephone:* (2) 299-11-11 (office). *E-mail:* Vladimir.Spidla@ec.europa.eu (office). *Website:* ec.europa.eu/commission_barroso/spidla (office).

SPIEGLER, Marc, MJ; American/French journalist; b. 1968; m.; ed Medill School of Journalism, Univ. of Chicago; moved to Switzerland 1998, freelance art journalist and columnist writing for magazines and newspapers including

The Art Newspaper, Monopol, Art and Auction Magazine, ARTnews Magazine, Artworld Salon, Neue Zürcher Zeitung, New York Magazine; Dir of Strategy and Devt, Art Basel 2008–. *Address:* Art Basel, c/o MCH Swiss Exhibition (Basel) Ltd, 4005 Basel, 10011, Switzerland. *Telephone:* (58) 2062704 (office). *Fax:* (58) 2063130 (office). *E-mail:* info@artbasel.com (office); marc@marcspiegler.com (office). *Website:* www.artbasel.com (office); www.marcspiegler.com (office).

SPIELBERG, Steven, BA; American film director and film producer; b. 18 Dec. 1947, Cincinnati, OH; s. of Arnold Spielberg and Leah Spielberg (née Posner); m. 1st Amy Irving (q.v.) 1985 (divorced 1989); two s.; m. 2nd Kate Capshaw; two d. (one adopted); ed Calif. State Coll., Long Beach; won film contest with war film Escape to Nowhere 1961; Dir episodes of TV series, including Night Gallery, Marcus Welby, MD, Columbo; directed 20-minute short Amblin'; Dir TV films Duel 1971, Something Evil 1972; Dirs Guild of America Award Fellowship 1986; Co-founder and Partner, Dreamworks SKG 1995–2005; Founder and Chair. Emer. Starbright Foundation; Artistic Adviser, 2008 Olympic Games in Beijing 2007–08 (resgnd); Hon. KBE (UK), Grosses Bundesverdienstkreuz 1998, Legion d'honneur 2004; Dr hc (Univ. of Southern California) 1994, Hon. DLitt (Sussex) 1997; Irving G. Thalberg Award 1987, Golden Lion Award (Venice Film Festival) 1993, BAFTA Award 1994, Acad. Award for Schindler's List 1994, David Lean (BAFTA), John Huston Award for Artists Rights 1995, American Film Inst. Lifetime Achievement Award 1995, James Smithson Bicentennial Medal 1999, Lifetime Achievement Award, Dir's Guild of America 1999, Britannia Award 2000, Lifetime Achievement Award, David di Donatello Awards 2004, Kennedy Center Honor 2006, Golden Globe Cecil B. DeMille Award 2009. *Films directed:* The Sugarland Express 1974, Jaws 1975, Close Encounters of the Third Kind 1977, 1941 1979, Raiders of the Lost Ark 1981, E.T. (The Extra Terrestrial) 1982, Indiana Jones and the Temple of Doom 1984, The Color Purple (also produced) 1985, Empire of the Sun 1988; I Wanna Hold Your Hand (produced) 1978, Poltergeist (co-wrote and produced) 1982, Gremlins (produced) 1984, Young Sherlock Holmes 1985 (exec. producer), Back to the Future (co-exec. producer), The Goonies (writer and exec. producer) 1986, Batteries Not Included (exec. producer) 1986, The Money Pit (co-produced) 1986, An American Tail (co-exec. producer) 1986, Always 1989, Gremlins II (exec. producer), Dad (exec. producer), Joe versus the Volcano (exec. producer), Hook 1991, Cape Fear (co-exec. producer) 1992, Jurassic Park 1992, Schindler's List 1993 (Acad. Award for Best Dir), Casper (producer) 1995, Some Mother's Son 1996, Twister 1996 (exec. producer), The Lost World: Jurassic Park 1997, Amistad 1997, Deep Impact 1998, Saving Private Ryan 1998 (Acad. Award for Best Dir), The Last Days (documentary) 1999, AI: Artificial Intelligence 2001, Minority Report 2002, Catch Me If You Can 2003, The Terminal 2004, War of the Worlds 2005, Munich 2005, Indiana Jones and the Kingdom of the Crystal Skull 2008. *Television includes:* Band of Brothers (series) 2000, Semper Fi 2000, Taken 2002, Burma Bridge Busters 2003, Into the West 2006. *Publication:* Close Encounters of the Third Kind (with Patrick Mann). *Address:* CAA, 9830 Wilshire Boulevard, Beverly Hills, CA 90212, USA (office). *Website:* www.starlight.org.

SPIELMANN, Alphonse, DenD; Luxembourg judge; b. 23 May 1931, Brattert; m. Catherine Hildgen 1961; three s.; ed Faculté de Droit and Inst. de Criminologie, Univ. of Paris and Centre Universitaire de Luxembourg; Attorney-Gen., Grand Duchy of Luxembourg; Judge, European Court of Human Rights 1985–98; numerous int. activities. *Publications:* Liberté d'expression ou censure? 1982, La Convention européenne des droits de l'homme et le droit luxembourgeois 1991. *Leisure interest:* history of the Second World War. *Address:* 12 Côte d'Eich, 1450 Luxembourg (office); 108 rue des Muguets, 2167 Luxembourg, Luxembourg (home).

SPIELVOGEL, Carl, BA; American advertising executive; *Chairman and CEO, Carl Spielvogel Associates Inc.;* b. 27 Dec. 1928, New York City; s. of Joseph Spielvogel and Sadie Spielvogel (née Tellerman); m. Barbara Lee Diamonstein 1981; two s. one d.; ed Baruch Coll.; reporter and columnist, New York Times 1950–60; with McCann Erickson, Inc., Interpublic Group of Cos, Inc., New York City 1960–74; Vice-Chair., Chair. Exec. Cttee and Dir Interpublic Group of Cos, Inc. 1974–80; Chair. and CEO Backer & Spielvogel Inc. 1980–87, Backer Spielvogel Bates Worldwide Inc. New York 1987–94; Chair., CEO United Auto Group 1994–97, Consultant –2000; Amb. to the Slovak Repub. 2000–01; currently Chair. and CEO Carl Spielvogel Assocs Inc., New York; mem. Bd of Dirs Apollo Investors Inc., Data Broadcasting Corpn (now Interactive Data Corpn) 1996–2000, 2001–, Asia Soc., Columbia Univ. Inst. for Study of Europe; fmr mem. Bd of Dirs Hasbro Inc., Barney's Inc.; Chair. Cttee Div., WNET-Public Broadcasting, Business Cttee; Trustee State Univ. of New York 2008–, Metropolitan Museum of Art, Lincoln Center for the Performing Arts; fmr Trustee Mount Sinai Hosp., Philharmonic Symphony Soc. of New York; mem.Council on Foreign Relations; mem. Exec. Cttee Council of American Ambs; fmr Fellow, John F. Kennedy School of Govt, Harvard Univ. *Address:* c/o Board of Directors, Interactive Data Corporation, 32 Crosby Drive, Bedford, MA 01730, USA (office).

SPIERKEL, Gregory M. E., BA, MBA; American electronics industry executive; *CEO, Ingram Micro Inc.;* ed Carleton Univ., Canada, Georgetown Univ., Institut Européen d'Admin des Affaires (INSEAD), Fontainebleau, France; Man. Dir Mitel Telecom, UK 1986–89, Gen. Man. for Far East, Hong Kong 1989–90, Pres. Mitel Inc., USA 1992–96, Vice-Pres. Global Sales and Marketing 1996–97; Pres. Ingram Micro Asia-Pacific 1997–99, Exec. Vice-Pres. Ingram Micro Inc. and Pres. Ingram Micro Europe 1999–2004, Corp. Pres. Ingram Micro Inc. 2004–05, CEO 2005–; mem. Bd Dirs PACCAR Inc.; mem. Dean's Advisory Bd School of Business, Univ. of California, Irvine; mem. Bd of Counselors, George L. Argyros School of Business, Chapman Univ., Orange, Calif. *Address:* Ingram Micro Inc., 1600 East St Andrew Place, PO Box 25125, Santa Ana, CA 92799-5125, USA (office). *Telephone:* (714) 566-1000 (office). *E-mail:* info@ingrammicro.com (office). *Website:* www.ingrammicro.com (office).

SPIERS, Ronald Ian, BA, MA; American diplomatist (retd); b. 9 July 1925, Orange, NJ; s. of Thomas Hoskins Spiers and Blanca Spiers (née De Ponthier); m. Patience Baker 1949; one s. three d.; ed Dartmouth Coll., Princeton Univ.; USN 1943–46; mem. US Del. to UN 1955–58; Dir Disarmament Affairs, State Dept, Washington 1958–62, NATO Affairs 1962–66; Political Counsellor, US Embassy in London 1966–69, Minister 1974–77; Asst Sec. of State for Political-Mil. Affairs 1969–73; Amb. to the Bahamas 1973–74, to Turkey 1977–80; Asst Sec. for Intelligence and Research, Dept of State 1980–81; Amb. to Pakistan 1981–83; Under-Sec. for Man., Dept of State 1983–89; Under-Sec.-Gen. for Political and Gen. Ass. Affairs, UN, New York 1989–92; consultant to State Dept 1992–; mem. Council on Foreign Relations; Fellow, Nat. Acad. of Public Admin., American Acad. of Diplomacy; Presidential Distinguished Service Award 1984, 1986. *Leisure interests:* gardening, furniture making, classical music, opera. *Address:* 1320 Middletown Road, S Londonderry, VT 05155, USA (home). *Telephone:* (802) 824-6482 (home). *E-mail:* rispiers@comcast.net (home).

SPILIOTOPOULOS, Spilios P., LLM, MPhil; Greek politician; b. Oct. 1946, Patras; m. Maria Tsouni; ed Univ. of Athens, Hellenic Air Force Acad., Inst. of S Florida, USA; mil. service with air force, becoming Aide de Camp to Pres. Constantine Caramanlis 1980–85, retd from air force with rank of Lt-Col; mem. Parl. (Nea Demokratia Party, NDP) for Achaia Dist 1989–; Deputy Minister for Nat. Defence 1992–93, also Deputy Sec.-Gen., NPD Parl. Ass. and mem. Educational Affairs Parl. Cttee, Foreign Affairs and Defence Parl. Cttee, Inter-parl. Cttee of Greece-Cyprus, Minister of Nat. Defence 2004–06, Chair. NDP Nat. Defence Cttee, NDP Political Council; fmr Dir Foundation of Political Studies and Educ.; fmr Head, Greek Del. to N Atlantic Ass. and mem. Political Cttee; fmr mem. Ass. WEU, OSCE, Org. for Black Sea Econ. Co-operation, Special Mediterranean Group; Grand Decoration of Honour in Silver (Austria), Commdr, Order of Merit (Cyprus, Egypt, Italy), Chevalier, Légion d'honneur, Commdr, Order of Merit and Golden Cross of Honour (Greece), Commdr, Mil. Order of Aviz (Portugal). *Publication:* Responsibilities of the National Air Carrier 1985; several articles. *Leisure interests:* sailing, sports, music. *Address:* Charitos 31, 10675, Athens, Greece (home). *E-mail:* info@e-spilios.gr. *Website:* www.e-spilios.gr.

SPINDELEGGER, Michael, DIur; Austrian politician; *Federal Minister for European and International Affairs;* b. 21 Dec. 1959, Mödling; m.; two c.; ed Univ. of Vienna; Asst Lecturer and Researcher, Inst. of Criminal Law, Univ. of Vienna 1982–83; Judges' Asst at several Courts of Law in Vienna 1983–84; civil servant, Fed. State Lower Austria 1984–87; mem. Cabinet of the Minister of Defence 1987–90; employed within the Secr. of the Bd, Strategic Man., GiroCredit (Austrian bank) 1993–94; speaker on European Relations, Employees' Asscn of the Austrian People's Party (ÖAAB) 1989–91, Deputy Head ÖAAB 1991–; mem. Fed. Chamber, Austrian Parl. 1992–93; mem. Nat. Ass. 1993–95; MEP (ÖVP-EVP), mem. of Parl. Cttee on Econs, Currency Issues and Industrial Policy, Deputy mem. Cttee for Social Issues and Employment 1995–96; ÖAAB Speaker on Foreign Affairs and Head of Parl. Cttee on Foreign Affairs 1996–2006; Chair. NÖAAB (ÖAAB of Lower Austria) 1998–; mem. Parl. Ass., Council of Europe 2000–07; Deputy Parl. Group Leader of the Austrian Peoples Party 2000–06; Head of the Austrian Del. to the Parl. Ass. of the Council of Europe 2002–2006; Second Pres. Austrian Nat. Council 2006–08; Fed. Minister for European and Int. Affairs 2008–. *Address:* Federal Ministry for European and International Affairs, Minoritenplatz 8, 1014 Vienna, Austria (office). *Telephone:* (5) 011-50-0 (office). *Fax:* (5) 011-59-0 (office). *E-mail:* post@bmeia.gv.at (office). *Website:* www.bmeia.gv.at (office).

SPINETTA, Jean-Cyril, LLB, BSc; French airline executive; *Chairman and CEO, Air France Group;* b. 4 Oct. 1943, Paris; s. of Adrien Spinetta and Antoinette Brignoll; m. Nicole Spinetta (née Ricquebourg); two s. two d.; ed Institut d'études politiques and Ecole nationale d'admin., Paris; entered French civil service 1972, Head of Investments and Planning Dept, Ministry of Educ. 1972–76; Head of Information Dept, Office of the Prime Minister 1981–83, Chief of Staff for Michel Delebarre 1984–90; successively Minister of Labour and Vocational Training, Minister of Social Affairs and Employment and Minister of Planning and Devt, Housing and Transport; joined Air Inter 1990, Pres. and CEO 1990–93; advisory posts to Pres. of France (including industrial matters) 1993–95; Admin. in charge of Public Service 1995–96; joined staff of Edith Cresson, European Commr for Science, Research and Educ. 1996–97; Chair. and CEO Air France 1997–, CEO Group Air France-KLM 2004–; Chair. Asscn European Airlines 2001–; Scientific Council, Inst. of Public Admin and Econ. Devt 2002–, Bd of Govs IATA 2004–05; mem. Bd Dirs Saint-Gobain, Alcatel Lucent; Officier de la Légion d'honneur, des Palmes Académiques; Commdr, Ordre nat. du Mérite; Commdr, Order of Orange-Nassau (Netherlands). *Leisure interests:* tennis, skiing. *Address:* Groupe Air France, 45 rue de Paris, 95747 Roissy CDG Cedex, France (office). *Telephone:* 1-41-56-61-65 (office). *Fax:* 1-41-56-61-59 (office). *E-mail:* jcspinetta@airfrance.fr (office). *Website:* www.airfrance.com (office).

ŠPIRIĆ, Nikola, PhD; Bosnia and Herzegovina academic and politician; *Chairman of the State Council of Ministers;* b. 4 Sept. 1956, Drvar; ed Univ. of Sarajevo; fmr Pres. Democratic Party for Banja Luka and Krajina; currently mem. Alliance of Ind. Social Democrats (SNSD); mem. Econs Dept, Banja Luka Univ.; Vice-Pres., Bosnia and Herzegovina Parl. 2001–04, Speaker of the House 2004–07, Chair. State Council of Ministers Jan.–Nov. 2007 (resgnd in protest over imposition of parl. reforms), Dec. 2007– (renominated and confirmed by presidency and parl. following resolution of crisis). *Address:* Office of the Chairman of the Council of Ministers, 71000 Sarajevo, trg Bosne i Hercegovine 1 (office); Alliance of Independent Social Democrats (Savez nezavisnih socijaldemokrata, SNSD), 78000 Banja Luka, Petra Kočića 5, Bosnia and Herzegovina. *Telephone:* (33) 211581 (Sarajevo) (office); (51) 318492 (Banja Luka). *Fax:* (33) 205347 (Sarajevo) (office); (51) 318495 (Banja Luka). *E-mail:* mmicevska@vijeceministara.gov.ba (office); snsd@inecco.net. *Website:* www.vijeceministara.gov.ba (office); www.snsd.org.

SPIRIDONOV, Yurii Alekseyevich, Cand.Tech.Sc; Russian politician; b. 1 Nov. 1938, Poltavka, Omsk Region; m.; one d.; ed Sverdlovsk Mining Inst., Higher CP School at Cen. Cttee CPSU; early career as mining engineer, Gorny Magadan Region 1961–69; master, head of section, chief engineer, Dir Yager oil mine Komi Autonomous Repub. 1969–75; party functionary with different posts in Ukhta City CP Cttee 1975–85; Second Sec., First Sec. Komi Regional CP Cttee 1985–89; USSR Peoples' Deputy 1989–92; Chair. Supreme Soviet Komi Autonomous Repub. 1990–94, Chair. of Komi Repub. Govt, Head of Repub. 1994–2002; mem. Russian Council of Fed. 1993–2001; Peoples' Deputy of Komi Autonomous Repub.; mem. Russian Acad. of Natural Sciences, Acad. of Mining Sciences. *Address:* c/o House of Government, Kommunisticheskaya str. 9, 167010 Syktyvkar, Komi Republic, Russia (office).

SPIRIN, Aleksandr Sergeyevich, PhD, DSc; Russian biochemist and molecular biologist; *Head of Laboratory of Protein Synthesis, Institute of Protein Research, Russian Academy of Sciences;* b. 4 Sept. 1931, Kaliningrad (now Korolev), Moscow Region; s. of Sergey Stepanovitch Spirin and Elena Abramovna Spirina (née Kalabekova); m. Tatiana Nikolayevna Fokina; ed Moscow State Univ.; mem. staff, Bakh Inst. of Biochemistry 1958–62, Head of Lab. 1962–73; Prof., Moscow State Univ. 1964–92, Prof. Emer. 1992–, Prof. and Chair of Molecular Biology 1973–; Head of Lab. of Protein Biosynthesis Mechanisms, Inst. of Protein Research 1967–, Dir Inst. 1967–2001; Chair. Bd Pushchino Scientific Centre 1990–2000; Corresp. mem. USSR (now Russian) Acad. of Sciences 1966–70, mem. 1970–, mem. Presidium 1988–2001, Adviser Presidium 2001–; mem. Deutsche Akad. der Naturforscher Leopoldina (now German Nat. Acad. of Sciences) 1974, Czechoslovak Acad. of Sciences 1988, Academia Europaea 1990, European Molecular Biology Org. 1991, Royal Physiographic Soc. (Lund) 1996, American Philosophical Soc. 1997, AAAS 1997, American Soc. for Biochemistry and Molecular Biology 2003; Two Orders of Lenin and other decorations; Dr hc (Granada) 1972, (Toulouse) 1999; Sir Hans Krebs Medal 1969, Lenin Prize 1976, State Prize of the USSR for Science 1988, Ovchinnikov Prize, Russian Acad. of Science 1992, Karpinskij Prize of FVS for Achievements in Science (Hamburg) 1992, State Prize of Russian Fed. for Science 2000, Belozersky Prize, Russian Acad. of Sciences 2000, Big Gold Lomonosov Medal, Russian Acad. of Sciences 2001, Science Prize, Russian Ind. Charity Foundation 'Triumph' 2005. *Publications:* Macromolecular Structure of Ribonucleic Acids 1964, The Ribosome 1969, Ribosome Structure and Protein Biosynthesis 1986, Ribosomes 1999, Cell-Free Translation Systems (ed.) 2002. *Leisure interests:* hunting, breeding cats. *Address:* Institute of Protein Research, Russian Academy of Sciences, 142290 Pushchino, Moscow Region, Russia (office). *Telephone:* (495) 632-78-71 (office); (499) 137-39-20 (home). *Fax:* (495) 632-78-71 (office). *E-mail:* spirin@vega.protres.ru (office). *Website:* www.protres.ru (office); spirin.protres.ru (office).

SPIROIU, Lt-Gen. Niculae, PhD; Romanian international organization official, fmr government official and fmr army officer; *Executive Director, Euro-Atlantic Council Romania, NATO;* b. 6 July 1936, Bucharest; s. of Constantin Spiroiu and Paulina Spiroiu; m. 1963 (wife died 1991); one s. one d.; ed Tech. Mil. Acad.; scientific researcher with the Centre of Studies and Tests for Tanks and Autos Deputy Chief and Tech. Dept Chief; State Sec. and Head of the Army Supply Dept; Minister of Nat. Defence 1992–94; Counsellor Minister to UN 1994–2000; Sr Counsellor to Minister of Water and Environment Protection 2001–02; Exec. Dir Euro-Atlantic Council of Romania—Casa NATO 2005–; also currently Sr Research Fellow, EURISC Foundation; Co-Chair. US Action Comm., Center of Strategic and Int. Studies, Washington, DC 1997–99;. *Leisure interests:* reading, symphonic music, motor cycling, motoring. *Address:* Euro-Atlantic Council Romania—Casa NATO, 82-88 M. Eminescu Str., ap. 19, Sector 2, Bucharest (office); EURISC Foundation, 82-88 Mihai Eminescu Street, Entrance B, app 19, Sector 2, Bucharest, Sector 2, PO Box 2-101, Romania (office). *Telephone:* (21) 3193278 (Casa NATO) (office); (21) 2122102 (office). *Fax:* (21) 3193279 (Casa NATO) (office); (21) 3193279 (office). *E-mail:* office@casanato.org (office). *Website:* www.casanato.org (office); www.eurisc.org (office).

SPITERI, Lino, MA, DipSocStud; Maltese writer, journalist and fmr politician; *Chairman, Borlex Group;* b. 21 Sept. 1938, Qormi; s. of the late Emanuel Spiteri and of Pauline Spiteri (née Calleja); m. Vivienne Azzopardi 1964; two s. two d.; ed Lyceum, Plater Coll. and St Peter's Coll. Oxford; teacher 1956–57; Clerk UK Mil. Establishment 1957–62; Deputy Ed. Il-Helsien (daily) 1962–64, It-Torca (weekly) 1964–66; Ed. Malta News 1967–68; Research Officer Malta Chamber of Commerce 1968–70; with Cen. Bank of Malta as Sr Research Officer, then Asst Head of Research 1971, Head of Research 1972, Deputy Gov. and Chair. Bd of Dirs 1974–81; Minister of Finance 1981–83, of Econ. Planning and Trade 1983–87; Opposition Spokesman on Econs and Finance 1989–96; Chair. Public Accounts Cttee 1995–96, Co-Chair, Malta-EU Jt Parl. Cttee 1996–98; Minister for Econ. Affairs and Finance 1996–97; mem. Malta Labour Party Gen. Exec. 1958–66; Gen. Sec. Labour League of Youth 1961–62; MP 1962–66; Malta Corresp. for Observer, Observer Foreign News Service, Guardian 1967–71; mem. Malta Broadcasting Authority 1968–70; mem. Comm. on Higher Educ. 1977–79; Chair. Students Selection Bd 1978–79; Pres. Qormi Football Club 1977–79; Chair. Borlex Group of Cos 2004–; columnist, Sunday Times of Malta and others. *Publications:* Studies: The Development of Tourism in Malta 1968, The Development of Industry in Malta 1969; Fiction and poetry: Tad-Demm u L-Laham (short stories) 1968, Hala taz-Zghozija (short stories) 1970, Anatomija (short stories) 1978, Iz-Zewgt Ihbieb (short stories) 1979, Stqarrija (verses) 1979, Il-Halliel (short stories) 1979, Rivoluzzjoni do minore (novel) 1980, Jien Nimxi Wahdi (verses) 1987, Mal-Hmura tas-silla (short stories) 1993, Fejn Jixrob il-Qasab fis-sajf (short stories) 1996, Stejjer ghal Valentina (short stories) 1997, Ghaliex ix-Xewk (verses) 1998, Honourable People (short stories), Moods and Angles (collected articles) 1998, A Gentle Child 2004, Meta Idelled il Qamar (short stories) 2005, Jien u Ghaddej fil-Politika (autobiog.) 2007. *Leisure interests:* listening to other people's views, reading, writing. *Address:* "Aurora", Triq Il-Linja, H'Attard, BZN 05, Malta. *Telephone:* 21239894 (office); 21435089 (home). *E-mail:* biba@borlexgroup.com (office); lspiteri@onvol.net (home).

SPITLER, Kenneth F., BA; American business executive; *President and CEO, SYSCO Corporation;* b. 1949; ed Univ. of Tulsa; joined SYSCO Corpn 1986, Exec. Vice-Pres., Dallas 1986–92, Pres., Detroit 1992–95, Pres. and CEO, Houston 1995–2000, Sr Vice-Pres. of Operations, NE Region 2000–02, Exec. Vice-Pres. Redistribution and NE Region 2002–03, Exec. Vice-Pres. Foodservice Operations 2003–05, Exec. Vice-Pres. and Pres. N American Foodservice Operations 2005–07, Pres. and CEO 2007–. *Address:* SYSCO Corpn, 1390 Enclave Parkway, Houston, TX 77077-2099, USA (office). *Telephone:* (281) 584-1390 (office). *Fax:* (281) 584-2721 (office). *Website:* www.sysco.com (office).

SPITZ, Lewis, MB, ChB, PhD, FRCS, FRCSE; British paediatric surgeon and academic; *Nuffield Professor Emeritus of Paediatric Surgery, Institute of Child Health, University College London;* b. 25 Aug. 1939, Pretoria, S Africa; s. of Woolf Spitz and Selma Spitz; m.; one s. one d.; ed Univs of Pretoria and Witwatersrand; Consultant Paediatric Surgeon, Sheffield 1974–79; Nuffield Prof. of Paediatric Surgery, Inst. of Child Health, Univ. Coll. London 1979–2004, Nuffield Prof. Emer. of Paediatric Surgery 2004–; Consultant Paediatric Surgeon, Great Ormond St Hosp. for Children, London 1979–2006; Hunterian Prof., Royal Coll. of Surgeons (England) 2001–02; Fellow, Royal Coll. of Paediatrics and Child Health; Hon. Fellow, American Acad. of Pediatrics, Royal Coll. of Surgeons in Ireland, Coll. of Medicine, SA, Royal Coll. of Paediatric and Child Health; Hon. MD (Sheffield) 2002, (Univ. of the Witwatersrand South Africa); James Spence Medal, Royal Coll. of Paediatrics 2004, Clement-Price Thomas Award, Royal Coll. of Surgeons (England) 2004, Denis Browne Gold Medal, British Asscn of Paediatric Surgeons 2004, Rehbein Medal, German Asscn of Pediatric Surgeons. *Publication:* Paediatric Surgical Diagnosis (co-ed. with M. Steiner and R. B. Zachary) 1981, Pediatric Surgery (co-ed. with A. G. Coran) 1995, 2006, Great Ormond Street Colour Handbook of Paediatrics and Child Health Papers of Oesophageal Atresia and Replacement and Conjoined Twins 2006. *Leisure interests:* sport, food, drink. *Address:* c/o Paediatric Surgery, Great Ormond Street Hospital for Children, Great Ormond Street, London, WC1N 3JH; c/o Institute of Child Health, 30 Guilford Street, London, WC1N 1EH (office); 78 Wood Vale, London, N10 3DN, England (home). *Telephone:* (20) 8444-9985 (home). *Fax:* (20) 8883-6417 (home). *E-mail:* L.Spitz@ich.ucl.ac.uk (office).

SPITZ, Mark (Andrew); American fmr swimmer; b. 10 Feb. 1950, Modesto, Calif.; s. of Arnold Spitz; m. Suzy Weiner; two s.; ed Indiana Univ.; won two gold medals in the team relay races (4×100m and 4×200m), Olympic Games, Mexico City 1968; became first athlete to win seven gold medals in a single Olympic Games, Munich 1972, in the 100m and 200m freestyle, 100m and 200m butterfly and as a team mem. of the 4×100m relay, 4×200m relay and 4×100m medley relay (all world records); unsuccessful comeback 1991; corporate spokesman, TV broadcaster, real-estate co. owner, now works as stock broker; mem. Int. Swimming Hall of Fame Selection Cttee; World Swimmer of the Year 1969, 1971, 1972, James E. Sullivan Award (for America's Outstanding Amateur Athlete) 1971, Associated Press Male Athlete of the Year 1972, Athlete of the Century (Water Sports) 1999; mem. Laureus World Sports Acad. *Leisure interests:* sailing, travel. *Address:* c/o Laura Cutler, Corporate Communications, Premier Management Group, LLC, 200 Merry Hill Drive, Cary, NC 27511, USA (office). *Telephone:* (919) 363-5105 (office). *E-mail:* laura@pmgsports.com (office). *Website:* www.markspitzusa.com (office).

SPITZER, Eliot Laurence, BA, JD; American lawyer, fmr government official and fmr politician; b. 10 June 1959; m. Silda Spitzer (née Wall); three d.; ed Princeton Univ. and Harvard Law School; fmr Ed. Harvard Law Review; Law Clerk for Hon. Robert W. Sweet, US Dist Court, Southern Dist of New York 1984–85; Assoc. Paul Weiss, Rifkind, Wharton & Garrison 1985–86; Asst Dist Attorney, Manhattan 1986–92, Chief Labor Racketeering Unit 1991–92; Assoc. Skadden, Arps, Slate, Meagher & Flom 1992–94; Pnr Constantine & Pnrs 1994–98; Attorney-Gen. State of New York 1999–2007; Gov. of New York 2007–08 (resgnd); Democrat; named one of World's Most Influential People by Time magazine 2005; Paul H. Douglas Ethics in Govt Award, Univ. of Ill. 2004, Jacob J. Javits Public Service Award, American Psychiatric Asscn 2005. *Address:* c/o Office of the Governor, State Capitol, Albany, NY 12224, USA (office).

SPIVAK, Gayatri Chakravorty, MA, PhD; Indian literary theorist, academic and rural literacy and ecological agriculture activist; *University Professor and Director, Center for Comparative Literature and Society, Columbia University;* b. 24 Feb. 1942, Kolkata, W Bengal; m. Talbot Spivak (divorced); ed Univ. of Kolkata, Univ. of Cambridge, Cornell Univ.; Asst Prof., then Prof. of Comparative Literature, Iowa Univ. 1965–77; Prof., Univ. of Texas 1978–83; Longstreet Prof. of English, Emory Univ. 1983–86; Andrew W. Mellon Prof. of English, Univ. of Pittsburgh 1986–91; Avalon Foundation Prof. in the Humanities, Columbia Univ., New York 1991–2007, Univ. Prof. 2007–, also Dir, Inst. for Comparative Literature and Soc.; Visiting Prof., Brown Univ., Univ. of Texas, Univ. of California, Santa Cruz, Berkeley, Irvine, Université Paul Valery, Jawaharlal Nehru Univ., Stanford Univ., Univ. of British Columbia, Goethe Inst., Frankfurt, Riydah Univ.; Y. K. Pao Distinguished Visiting Prof. in Cultural Studies, Hong Kong Univ. of Science and Tech. 2001;

translated the work of French philosopher Jacques Derrida 1976, Bengali writer Mahasweta Devi 2003; Distinguished Faculty Fellow, Maharaja Sayajirao Univ. of Baroda, India; fmr Fellow, Nat. Humanities Inst., Center for the Humanities at Wesleyan, Humanities Research Center, ANU, Canberra, Australia, Centre for the Study of the Social Sciences, Kolkata, Davis Center for Historial Studies, Princeton Univ., Rockefeller Foundation, Bellagio, Guggenheim Foundation; mem. Editorial Bd Cultural Critique, Diaspora, ARIEL, Re-thinking Marxism, Public Culture, Parallax, Interventions; Hon. PhD (Univ. of Toronto) 2000, (Univ. of London) 2003; Guggenheim Fellowship, Sahitya Akademi Translation Prize, India 1997. *Publications include:* Myself I Must Remake: The Life and Poetry of W. B. Yeats 1974, Of Grammatology (trans. of Jacques Derrida) 1976, In Other Worlds: Essays in Cultural Politics 1987, Selected Subaltern Studies (co-ed.) 1988, The Post-Colonial Critic: Interviews, Strategies, Dialogues 1990, Outside in the Teaching Machine 1993, The Spivak Reader 1996, Don't Call Me Post-Colonial: from Kant to Kawakubo 1998, A Critique of Post-Colonial Reason: Toward a History of the Vanishing Present 1999, Death of a Discipline 2003, Other Asias 2005; chapters in books and articles in professional journals. *Address:* 516 Interchurch Center, Columbia University, 475 Riverside Drive, New York, NY 10115, USA (office). *Telephone:* (212) 870-3990 (office). *Fax:* (212) 870-3989 (office). *E-mail:* gcs4@columbia.edu (office). *Website:* www.columbia.edu/cu/english (office).

SPIVAKOV, Vladimir Teodorovich; Russian violinist and conductor; *Artistic Director and Principal Conductor, National Philharmonic of Russia;* b. 12 Sept. 1944, Ufa, Bashkiria; m. Satinik Saakyants; three d.; ed Moscow State Conservatory, postgraduate with Yury Yankelevich; studied violin since age of six with B. Kroger in Leningrad; prize winner in several int. competitions including Tchaikovsky, Moscow; Founder and Conductor Chamber Orchestra Virtuosi of Moscow 1979–; Founder and Artistic Dir Music Festival in Colmar, France 1989–; Artistic Dir and Chief Conductor Russian Nat. Symphony Orchestra 1999–2003; Founder, Artistic Dir and Prin. Conductor Nat. Philharmonic of Russia 2003–; Guest Conductor of several orchestras including Chicago Symphony Orchestra, LA Philharmonic, London Symphony Orchestra, English and Scottish Chamber Orchestras; f. Int. Charity Foundation 1994; Les Insignes de Chevalier de la Légion d'Honneur 1994 USSR State Prize 1989, USSR People's Artist 1990, Triumph Prize, Nat. Cultural Heritage Award, Russia's Artist of the Year 2002, First Prize Montreal Competition, Marguerite Long St Jacques Thibaud Competition, Paris, Nicolo Paganini Int. Violin Competition, Genoa, Int. Tchaikovsky Competition, Moscow. *Recordings:* more than 20 CDs on Capriccio, RCA Victor Red Seal and BMG Classics including works by Brahms, Berg, Chausson, Franck, Prokoviev, Ravel, Tchaikovsky, Richard Strauss, Schubert, Sibelius, Shostakovich. *Leisure interest:* collecting paintings. *Address:* c/o Columbia Artists Management, 1790 Broadway, New York, NY 10019, USA (office); National Philharmonic of Russia, Moscow 115054, Office 208, 52/8 Kosmodamianskaya Embankment; Vspolny per. 17, Apt 14, Moscow, Russia. *Telephone:* (495) 290-23-24 (Moscow); 1-45-25-50-85 (Paris); (495) 730-1367 (Nat. Philharmonic). *Fax:* 1-45-25-04-60 (Paris); (495) 730-3778 (Nat. Philharmonic). *Website:* www.nfor.ru/eng.

SPOERRI, Philip, PhD; German lawyer and international organization executive; *Director for International Law and Co-operation within the Movement, International Committee of the Red Cross;* b. 1963; m.; one s.; ed Göttingen, Munich and Bielefeld Univs, Geneva Univ., Switzerland; worked as lawyer in pvt. firm in Munich; began career with ICRC in 1994, carried out first mission for ICRC in Israel (Occupied Territories), continued with missions in Kuwait and Yemen, Afghanistan and Democratic Repub. of Congo, headed legal advisers to Dept of Operations, Geneva, returned to Afghanistan as Head of Del. 2004–06, Dir for Int. Law and Co-operation within the Movt 2006–. *Address:* International Committee of the Red Cross, 9 avenue de la Paix, 1202 Geneva, Switzerland (office). *Telephone:* (22) 734-60-01 (office). *Fax:* (22) 733-20-57 (office). *E-mail:* press.gva@icrc.org (office). *Website:* www.icrc.org (office).

SPOGLI, Ronald P., AB, MBA; American diplomatist and investment banker; *Ambassador to Italy;* b. 1948, Los Angeles; m. Georgia Spogli; one d. one steps.; ed Stanford Univ., Harvard Univ.; researcher, Stanford Univ. based in Milan, Italy 1972–73; fmr Man. Dir Investment Banking Div. Dean Witter Reynolds Inc.; Co-founder and Pnr, Freeman Spogli & Co. 1983–; Amb. to Italy 2005–; apptd to US State Dept's Fulbright Foreign Scholarship Bd 2002; mem. Bd of Visitors, Stanford Univ.'s Inst. for Int. Studies 2000–; mem. Bd AFC Enterprises, Regents Bancshares, Winebow. *Address:* United States Embassy, via Vittorio Veneto 119/A, 00187 Rome, Italy (office). *Telephone:* (06) 46741 (office). *Fax:* (06) 46742356 (office). *Website:* rome.usembassy.gov (office).

SPOHR, Arnold Theodore, CC; Canadian ballet director, teacher and choreographer; b. 26 Dec. 1927, Rhein, Canada; ed St John's High School and Winnipeg Teachers' Coll.; piano teacher 1946–51; Prin. Dancer Royal Winnipeg Ballet 1947–54; CBC TV choreographer and performer 1955–57; choreographer, Rainbow Stage 1957–60; Artistic Dir Royal Winnipeg Ballet 1958–88, also Dir-Teacher Royal Winnipeg Ballet School, Artistic Dir Emer. 1988–; Dir Nelson School of Fine Arts Dance Dept 1964–67; Artistic Dir Dance Dept Banff School of Fine Arts 1967–81; mem. Bd of Dirs Canadian Theatre Centre; Hon. LLD (Univ. of Manitoba) 1970; numerous awards including Molson Prize, Canada Council 1970, Centennial Medal, Gov. of Canada 1967, Royal Bank Award 1987. *Choreography:* Ballet Premier 1950, Intermed 1951, E Minor 1959, Hansel and Gretel 1960 and 18 musicals for Rainbow State. *Leisure interests:* sports, piano, travel-research for study of every type of dancing. *Address:* c/o Canada's Royal Winnipeg Ballet, 380 Graham Avenue, Winnipeg, Man., R3C 4K2, Canada.

SPONG, Rt Rev. John Shelby, AB, MDiv; American ecclesiastic and writer; b. 16 June 1931, Charlotte, NC; s. of John Shelby Spong and Doolie Griffith Spong; m. 1st Joan Lydia Ketner 1952 (died 1988); three d.; m. 2nd Christine Mary Bridger 1990; ed Univ. of North Carolina, Virginia Theological Seminary; Rector St Joseph's, Durham, NC 1955–57, Calvary Church, Tarboro, NC 1957–65, St John's Church, Lynchburg, Va 1965–69, St Paul's Church, Richmond, Va 1969–76, Bishop, Diocese of Newark, NJ 1976–2000; Pres. NJ Council of Churches; Quatercentenary Fellow, Emmanuel Coll. Cambridge, UK 1992; William Belden Noble Lecturer, Harvard Univ. 2000; Visiting Lecturer, Univ. of The Pacific, Stockton, Calif. 2003; mem. of Faculty, Grad. Theological Union, Berkeley, Calif.; columnist for Beliefnet.com 1999–2000, AgoraMedia 2002–, Waterfront Media 2002–; Hon. DD (Va Theological Seminary), (St Paul's Coll.); Hon. DHL (Muhlenberg Coll.), (Holmes Inst., Chicago) 2004; Quartercentenary Scholar, Emmanuel Coll., Cambridge, UK 1992, David Frederick Strauss Award, Jesus Seminar 1999, Humanist of the Year, New York City 1999, John A. T, Robinson Award 2004. *Radio:* Play by Play sportscaster in Tarboro NC and Lynchburg, Va 1960–65. *Publications:* Honest Prayer 1973, This Hebrew Lord 1974, 1988, Dialogue: In Search of Jewish-Christian Understanding 1975, Christpower 1975, Life Approaches Death: A Dialogue on Medical Ethics 1976, The Living Commandments 1977, The Easter Moment 1980, Into the Whirlwind 1983, Beyond Moralism 1986, Consciousness and Survival 1987, Living in Sin? 1988, Rescuing the Bible from Fundamentalism 1991, Born of a Woman – A Bishop Rethinks the Virgin Birth and the Place of Women in a Male-Dominated Church 1992, Resurrection: Myth or Reality? 1994, Liberating the Gospels: Reading the Bible with Jewish Eyes 1996, Why Christianity Must Change or Die: A Bishop Speaks to Believers in Exile 1998, Here I Stand: My Struggle for a Christianity of Integrity, Love and Equality 2000, The Bishop's Voice 1999, A New Christianity for a New World 2001, Crossroads – The Sins of Scripture 2005. *Leisure interests:* hiking, reading. *Address:* c/o Julie Rae Mitchell, HarperSanFrancisco, 353 Sacramento Street, Suite 500, San Francisco, CA, 94111, USA (office); 24 Puddingstone Road, Morris Plains, NJ 07950, USA (home). *Telephone:* (973) 538-9825 (home). *Fax:* (973) 540-9584 (home). *E-mail:* johnsspong@aol.com (home); cmsctm@aol.com (home). *Website:* www.johnshelbyspong.com.

SPONHEIM, Lars, MSc; Norwegian politician; *Leader, Liberal Party;* b. 23 May 1957, Halden; m.; three c.; consultant 1981–84; teacher, Statens Gartnerskule Hjeltnes 1984–88, Prin. 1992–; mem. local council, Ulvik Municipality 1984–95, Mayor 1988–91; mem. County Council, Hordaland Co. 1992–93; Dir of Agric., Ulvik and Granvin Municipalities 1993; mem. Parl. for Hordaland Co. to Storting (Parl.) 1993–, mem. Parl. Finance Cttee; Leader Liberal Party 1996–; Minister of Trade and Industry 1997–2000; Minister of Food and Agric. 2001–05; mem. Parl. Foreign Cttee 2005–. *Address:* Venstre, Stortinget, 0026 Oslo, Norway. *Telephone:* 23-31-33-62 (office). *Fax:* 23-31-38-72 (office). *E-mail:* lars.sponheim@stortinget.no (office); lars@venstre.no (office). *Website:* www.venstre.no (office).

SPORBORG, Christopher Henry, CBE; British banker; *Chairman, Chesnara PLC;* b. 17 April 1939; s. of the late Henry Nathan Sporborg and of Mary Rowlands; m. Lucinda Jane Hanbury 1961; two s. two d.; ed Rugby School, Emmanuel Coll. Cambridge; served as officer, Coldstream Guards; joined Hambros Bank 1962, Dir 1970, Exec. Dir Corp. Finance Dept 1975, Deputy Chair. 1983–9, Vice-Chair. Hambros PLC 1986–90, Deputy Chair. 1990–98; Founder and Chair. Countrywide PLC (fmly Countrywide Assured Group PLC) 1986–2007; Chair. Atlas Copco (UK) Holdings Ltd, Chesnara PLC 1986–, Hambros Insurance Services Group 1993–; mem. Horserace Totalisator Bd 1993–96; Chair. Racecourse Holdings Trust 1998–; mem. Bd of Dirs Getty Images Inc. 1996–98, Lindsey Morden Ltd (now Cunningham Lindsey Group Inc.) 1999–; Steward Jockey Club 2001–. *Leisure interests:* riding, racing. *Address:* Brooms Farm, Upwick Green, Albury, Ware, Herts., SG11 2JX, England. *Telephone:* (1279) 771444.

SPRATT, Sir Greville Douglas, Kt, GBE, TD, JP, DL, DLitt, FRSA, FRGS; British business executive (retd); b. 1 May 1927, Westcliff-on-Sea; s. of Hugh D. Spratt and Sheelah I. Stace; m. Sheila F. Wade 1954 (died 2002); three d.; ed Leighton Park, Charterhouse and Sandhurst; served Coldstream Guards 1945–46; Commissioned Oxfordshire and Bucks Light Infantry 1946; seconded to Arab Legion 1946–48; joined HAC Infantry Bn 1950, CO 1962–65, Regimental Col 1966–70, mem. Court of Assistants 1960–70 and 1978–95; ADC to HM The Queen 1973–78; Lloyd's of London 1948–61, Underwriting Mem. 1950–; Man. Dir J. & N. Wade group 1972–76; Liveryman, Ironmongers' Co. 1977–, Master 1995–96; Alderman, Castle Baynard Ward 1978–95; Sheriff of City of London 1984–85; Lord Mayor of London 1987–88; Chancellor, City Univ. 1987–88; Dir Williams Lea Group, Craigie Taylor Int. Ltd; Chair. Governing Body, Charterhouse 1989–95; Chair. Forest Mere Ltd, Charterhouse Enterprises Ltd. 1992–95, Action Research for the Crippled Child 1989–99; Claremont and Kingsmead Underwriting Agency 1994–99; Regional Chair. Nat. Westminster Bank 1992–93; Vice-Pres. British Red Cross 1993–, Greater London TAVRA 1994–; holder of numerous civic, educational and charitable positions; Trustee Chichester Theatre and Cathedral; Hon. Col London Army Cadet Force 1983–98, Queen's Fusiliers 1988–92, London Regt 1992–95; Légion d'honneur, Ordre nat. du Mérite (France); Commdr Order of Lion (Malawi), Order of Aztec Eagle (Mexico), Order of Olav (Norway), Order of Merit (Senegal); KStJ; Hon. DLitt (City Univ.) 1988. *Leisure interests:* tennis, music, mil. history; stamp, coin and bank-note collecting.

SPRING, Richard (Dick), BA, BL; Irish business executive and fmr politician; *Executive Vice-Chairman, Fexco Ltd;* b. 29 Aug. 1950, Tralee, Co. Kerry; s. of Dan Spring and Anna Laide; m. Kristi Lee Hutcheson 1977; two s. one d.; ed Mount St Joseph Coll., Roscrea, Co. Tipperary, Trinity Coll. Dublin, King's Inns, Dublin; mem. Dáil Éireann (House of Reps) for Kerry North

1981–2002; Leader of Labour Party 1982–97; Tanaiste (Deputy Prime Minister) 1982–87 and Minister for the Environment 1982–83, for Energy 1983–87, Tanaiste and Minister for Foreign Affairs 1993–97; Chair. Gulliver Ireland; Exec. Vice-Chair. Fexco 2002–; Dir Realta (Irish Global HIV/AIDS Foundation); chair. or dir numerous public and pvt. cos; fmr Irish rugby union int.; Assoc. Fellow, Kennedy School of Govt, Harvard Univ. 1998–; Fellow, Salzburg Seminar 1998; mem. Council on Foreign Relations; Dr hc (Hartwick Coll., NY) 1998, (Misericordia Coll., Pa) 1999. *Leisure interests:* sport, reading, golf, swimming. *Address:* Fexco Ltd, 12 Ely Place, Dublin 2 (office); Fexco Ltd, Iveragh Road, Killorglin, Co. Kerry, Ireland (office). *Telephone:* (1) 6611800 (Dublin) (office); (66) 9761258 (Killorglin) (office); (87) 2391200 (mobile) (home). *E-mail:* dspring@fexco.com (office). *Website:* www.fexco.com (office).

SPRINGER, Timothy Alan, BA, PhD; American immunologist and academic; *Latham Family Professor of Pathology, Harvard Medical School;* b. 23 Feb. 1948, Fort Benning, Ga; ed Univ. of California, Berkeley, Harvard Univ. Mass; Biochemistry 10 Teaching Asst, Harvard Univ. 1972–74, Biochemistry 111 Teaching Asst 1974–75; NIH Research Fellow, Univ. of Cambridge, UK and MRC Lab. of Molecular Biology, Cambridge 1976–77; Asst Prof., Harvard Medical School 1977–83, Assoc. Prof. 1983–89, Latham Family Prof. of Pathology 1989–, mem. Faculty Council, Harvard Univ. 1996–; Chief of Lab. of Membrane Immunochemistry, Dana Farber Cancer Inst. 1981–88; Vice-Pres. Center for Blood Research 1988–92; Councillor, Int. Leukocyte Workshop 1989–; mem. Scientific Review Bd, Howard Hughes Medical Inst. 1996–2000; Overseer, Bd of Overseers, CBR Inst. for Biomedical Research, Inc. 2002–; Visiting Prof., Univ. of Michigan 1990; Wellcome Visiting Prof., Wayne State Univ. 1997; consultant, Boehringer-Ingelheim 1989–95, LeukoSite, Inc. (Founder and Chair. Scientific Advisory Bd) 1992–99, Scientific Advisory Bd, Molecular Applications Group, Inc. 1997–, Millennium Pharmaceuticals 1999–2001, Sunesis Pharmaceuticals 2003–; Scientific Advisor, Canadian Vaccines and Immunotherapeutics Network 2001; Assoc. Ed. Journal of Immunology 1981–85, Molecular Biology of the Cell 1992–96; Advisory Ed. Journal of Experimental Medicine 1985–95; mem. Editorial Bd, Hybridoma 1981–, Regional Immunology 1988–, Cellular Immunology 1988–93, Journal of Clinical Immunology 1988–92, New Biologist 1989–92, Cell Regulation (Molecular Biology of the Cell) 1989–92, Immunological Reviews 1996–2001; mem. American Asscn of Immunologists 1979– (mem. Nomination Cttee 1993), Reticuloendothelial Soc. 1981–94 (Membership Chair. 1986, Chair. Program Cttee 1989), American Soc. of Biological Chemists 1982–, American Asscn of Pathologists 1989–, Soc. for Leukocyte Biology 1995–, NAS 1996– (Chair. Section 29, Biophysics and Computational Biology 2004–07); Fellow, American Acad. of Arts and Sciences 2001–; Nat. Merit Scholar 1966, Biochemistry Departmental Citation (awarded to most outstanding grad.) 1971, American Cancer Soc. Jr Faculty Research Award 1981, American Cancer Soc. Faculty Research Award 1984, NIH MERIT Grant Award 1988, 2004, Distinguished Lectureship, Vanderbilt School of Medicine 1992, American Heart Asscn Basic Research Prize 1993, Royal Soc. of Medicine Medal and Visiting Prof., UK 1994, William B. Coley Medal for Distinguished Research in Fundamental Immunology, Cancer Research Inst. 1995, Marie T. Bonazinga Award for Excellence in Leukocyte Biology Research, Soc. for Leukocyte Biology 1995, Crafoord Prize in Polyarthritis, Royal Swedish Acad. of Sciences (co-recipient) 2004, Fellowship, John Simon Guggenheim Memorial Foundation 2004. *Publications:* numerous scientific papers in professional journals on adhesion receptors of the immune system. *Address:* The CBR Institute for Biomedical Research, Inc., 200 Longwood Avenue, Room 251, Boston, MA 02115, USA (office). *Telephone:* (617) 278-3200 (office). *Fax:* (617) 278-3232 (office). *E-mail:* springer@cbr.med.harvard.edu (office). *Website:* www.cbrinstitute.org/labs/springer/tim_cv.html (office).

SPRINGS, Alice, (pseudonym of June Browne); Australian actress and photographer; b. June 1923, Melbourne; m. Helmut Newton 1948; fmrly professional actress; professional photographer 1970–; clients have included Jean-Louis David, Fashion Magazine Dépêche Mode, Elle, Marie-Claire, Vogue, Vogue Homme, Nova, Mode Int., Absolu, London Cosmoplitan; contrib. to Egoiste, Vanity Fair, Interview, Passion, Stern, Decoration Internationale, Tatler, Photo, Les Cahiers de l'Energumène. *Catalogues:* Alice Springs Portraits, Musée Sainte Croix, Poitiers 1985, Espace Photo, Paris 1986, Musée d'Art Moderne de la Ville de Paris 1988, Centro Cultural Arte Contemporaneo, Mexico City 1991, Rheinisches Landesmuseum, Bonn 1991/92. *Film:* TV documentary 'Helmut by June' for Canal Plus 1995. *Publications:* Alice Springs Portraits 1983, 1986, 1991.

SPRINGSTEEN, Bruce; American singer, songwriter and musician (guitar); b. 23 Sept. 1949, Freehold, NJ; s. of Douglas Springsteen and Adele Springsteen; m. 1st Julianne Phillips 1985 (divorced 1990); m. 2nd Patti Scialfa 1991; two s. one d.; ed community coll.; performed in New York and NJ nightclubs; solo artist 1972–; numerous tours of USA and Europe; formed backing group the E-Street Band 1974; Grammy Award for Best Male Vocalist 1984, 1987, for Best Rock Performance by a Duo (jtly) 2004, BRIT Award for Best Int. Solo Artist 1986, Acad. Award for Best Original Song in a Film (for Streets of Philadelphia) 1994, MTV Best Video from a Film Award (for Streets of Philadelphia) 1994, Grammy Awards for Best Solo Rock Vocal Performance (for Devils & Dust) 2006, (for Radio Nowhere) 2008, for Best Rock Instrumental Performance (for Once Upon a Time in the West) 2008, for Best Rock Song (for Radio Nowhere) 2008, (for Girls in Their Summer Clothes) 2009, Golden Globe Award for Best Original Song (for The Wrestler) 2009. *Recordings include:* albums: Greetings from Asbury Park, New Jersey 1973, The Wild, The Innocent And The E-Street Shuffle 1973, Born To Run 1975, Darkness On The Edge Of Town 1978, The River 1980, Nebraska 1982, Born In The USA 1984, Bruce Springsteen And The E Street Band Live 1975–85 1986, Tunnel Of Love 1987, Chimes of Freedom 1988, Human Touch 1992, Lucky Town 1992, The Ghost Of Tom Joad 1995, The Rising (Grammy Award

for Best Rock Album 2003) 2002, Roll Of The Dice 2003, Devils & Dust 2005, We Shall Overcome: The Seeger Sessions (Grammy Award for Best Traditional Folk Album 2007) 2006, Magic 2007, Working on a Dream 2009. *Address:* Premier Talent Agency, 3 East 54th Street, New York, NY 10022, USA (office). *Website:* www.brucespringsteen.net.

SPRINKEL, Beryl Wayne, BS, MBA, PhD; American economist, consultant and fmr government official; b. 20 Nov. 1923, Richmond, Mo.; s. of Clarence Sprinkel and Emma Sprinkel (née Schooley); m. 1st Esther Pollard (deceased); m. 2nd Barbara Angus Pipher (deceased); two s.; m. 3rd Lory Reid (née Kiefer) 1993; ed NW Missouri State Univ., Univs of Missouri, Oregon and Chicago; served with US Army 1943–45; Instructor in Econs and Finance, Univ. of Missouri, Columbia 1948–49, Univ. of Chicago 1950–52; with Harris Trust and Savings Bank, Chicago 1952–81, Vice-Pres., economist 1960–68, Dir Research 1968–81, Exec. Vice-Pres. 1974–81; Under-Sec. for Monetary Affairs, Dept of the Treasury 1981–85; Chair. Pres.'s Council of Econ. Advisors 1985–89; mem. Pres.'s Cabinet 1987–89; Consulting Economist 1989–; Pres. Homewood-Flossmoor (Ill.) Community High School 1959–60; seven hon. degrees; Distinguished Alumnus Award, Univ. of Chicago Graduate School of Business 1986, Univ. of Missouri 2001, Distinguished Service Award, Northwest Mo. State Univ., Alexander Hamilton, US Treasury 1985. *Publications:* Money and Stock Prices 1964, Money and Markets – A Monetarist View 1971, Winning with Money (co-author) 1977. *Leisure interests:* reading, writing, golf, tennis, fishing, travel. *Address:* 20140 St Andrew's Drive, Olympia Fields, IL 60461 (office); 16625 Waters Edge, CT 101, Fort Myers, FL 33908, USA (office). *Telephone:* (708) 481-9384 (Ill.) (office); (239) 482-7593 (Fla) (office). *Fax:* (708) 283-1205 (Ill.) (office); (239) 482-7593 (Fla) (office). *E-mail:* sprinkelec@comcast.net (office).

SPURDZIŅŠ, Oskars; Latvian government official; b. 22 Aug. 1963, Aizpute; m.; two c.; ed Aizpute Secondary School, Univ. of Latvia; Chair. Deputies' Council and Bd Valmiera City Council 1990–94; consultant Latvian Asscn of Local Self-Govts 1994; Adviser, Ministry of Finance 1994–96; Adviser, Admin of Local Govt Affairs 1996–97; Man. Municipal Projects, Latvian Environmental Investment Fund 1997–99; Parl. Sec., Ministry of Educ. and Science 1999–2000, Ministry of Finance 2000–02, 2004–07; mem. 7th Saeima (Parl., People's Party, TP) 1999–2002; Project Man. Hipoteku Banka 2002–04. *Address:* People's Party, Basteja Bulvāris 1, Rīga 1050, Latvia (office). *Telephone:* 750-8808 (office). *Fax:* 750-8684 (office). *E-mail:* maija@tautaspartija.lv (office). *Website:* www.tautaspartija.lv (office).

SPYROU, Nicholas M., PhD; British physicist and academic; *Professor of Radiation and Medical Physics and Chairman of Medical Physics, University of Surrey;* currently Prof. of Radiation and Medical Physics and Chair. of Medical Physics, Univ. of Surrey, Dir for MSc Course in Medical Physics and BSc course in Physics with Medical Physics; mem. numerous int. cttees, including Int. Cttee of Activation Analysis, Nat. Health Group Knowledge Group-Network; Exec. mem. Biology and Medicine Div., American Nuclear Soc.; Hevesy Medal, Journal of Radioanalytical and Nuclear Chemistry 2005. *Publications:* more than 220 scientific publs. *Address:* Room 05BC04, School of Electronics and Physical Sciences, University of Surrey, Guildford, GU2 7XH, England (office). *Telephone:* (1483) 686802 (office). *Fax:* (1483) 686781 (office). *E-mail:* n.spyrou@surrey.ac.uk (office). *Website:* www.ph.surrey.ac.uk (office).

SQUIRE, Air Chief Marshal Sir Peter (Ted), GCB, DFC, AFC, DSc, FRAeS; British air force officer; *Chairman, Imperial War Museum;* b. 7 Oct. 1945; s. of the late Wing Commdr Frank Squire and Margaret Pascoe Squire (née Trump); m. Carolyn Joynson 1970; three s.; ed King's School, Bruton; with 20 Squadron, Singapore 1968–70, 4 FTS, Anglesey 1970–73, 3 (F) Squadron, Germany 1975–78; OC1 (F) Squadron 1981–83; Personal Staff Officer to Air Officer Commanding-in-Chief, Strike Command 1984–86; Station Commdr RAF Cottesmore 1986–88; Dir Air Offensive 1989–91; SASO, RAF Strike Command 1991–93; Air Officer Commdg No. 1 Group 1993–94; ACAS 1994–96, DCDS (Programmes and Personnel), Ministry of Defence 1996–99; Air Officer Commanding-in-Chief, Strike Command and Commdr Allied Air Forces Northwestern Europe 1999–2000; Air ADC to HM The Queen 1999–2005; Chief of the Air Staff 2000–03; Commr Commonwealth War Graves Comm. 2003–, Vice Chair. 2005–; Deputy Chair. Imperial War Museum 2004–06, Chair. 2006–; Sr Warden King's School, Bruton 2004–. *Leisure interests:* golf, cricket. *Address:* c/o National Westminster Bank, 5 South Street, Wincanton, Somerset, BA9 9DJ, England (office).

SQUYRES, Steven W., BA, PhD; American astronomer and academic; *Goldwin Smith Professor of Astronomy, Cornell University;* b. 1957, Wenonah, NJ; ed Gateway Regional High School, Woodbury Heights, NJ, Cornell Univ., Ithaca, NY; Postdoctoral Assoc. and Research Scientist at NASA Ames Research Center 1981–86; returned as faculty mem. to Cornell Univ. 1986, currently Goldwin Smith Prof. of Astronomy; has participated in several planetary space flight missions; Assoc. of Voyager imaging science team 1978–81, participated in analysis of imaging data from encounters with Jupiter and Saturn; radar investigator on Magellan mission to Venus; mem. Mars Observer gamma-ray spectrometer flight investigation team; co-investigator on Russian Mars '96 mission; currently Scientific Prin. Investigator for Mars Exploration Rover Project; co-investigator on Mars Express mission 2003, Mars Reconnaissance Orbiter's High Resolution Imaging Science Experiment 2005; mem. Gamma-Ray Spectrometer Flight Investigation Team for Mars Odyssey mission, imaging team for Cassini mission to Saturn; fmr Chair. NASA Space Science Advisory Cttee; mem. NASA Advisory Council; H.C. Urey Prize, Planetary Div. of American Astronomical Soc. 1987, ABC News Person of the Week 9 Jan. 2004, Carl Sagan Memorial Award 2004, World Tech. Award in Space, The World Tech. Network 2005, Wired Rave Award for Science for overseeing creation of Spirit and Opportunity that had, at the time, lasted 13 times longer than expected (1174 vs 90 martian days)

2005, Benjamin Franklin Medal in Earth and Environmental Science, Franklin Inst. 2007. *Publications:* Roving Mars: Spirit, Opportunity, and the Exploration of the Red Planet 2005; numerous scientific papers in professional journals on planetary sciences. *Address:* 428 Space Sciences Building, Cornell University, Ithaca, NY 14853, USA (office). *Telephone:* (607) 255-3508 (office). *Fax:* (607) 255-6918 (office). *E-mail:* squyres@astro.cornell .edu (office). *Website:* www.astro.cornell.edu (office).

ŠRAMKO, Ivan; Slovak central banker; *Governor, National Bank of Slovakia;* b. 3 Sept. 1957, Bratislava; m.; three c.; ed Univ. of Econs, Bratislava; worked in finance depts in several cos 1981–90; Deputy Dir VUB-ING Banking Co. 1990–91; Head VUB-Credit Lyonnais joint venture task force 1991–92; Gen. Man., then Deputy Chair., then Chair., Istrobanka 1992–98; Man. Tatra Banka 1998–2000, mem. Bd of Dirs 2000–02; Deputy Gov. Nat. Bank of Slovakia; 2002–04, Gov. 2005–; mem. Gen. Council of European Cen. Bank; Gov. IMF; Alt. Gov. EBRD; mem. Bd Slovak-Austrian Chamber of Commerce 1998–; Chair. Man. Bd Univ. of Econs, Bratislava 2003–; Banker magazine European Central Banker of the Year 2006, Emerging Markets (newspaper) Central Bank Governor of the Year 2006, 2008. *Address:* National Bank of Slovakia, Imricha Karvaša 1, 813 25 Bratislava, Slovakia (office). *Telephone:* (2) 5787-1111 (office). *Fax:* (2) 5787-1100 (office). *E-mail:* webmaster@nbs.sk (office). *Website:* www.nbs.sk (office).

SRINIVASAN, Krishnan, MA; Indian diplomatist and writer; b. 15 Feb. 1937, Madras; s. of the late Capt. C. Srinivasan and Rukmani Chari; m. Brinda Srinivasan 1975; one s.; ed Bedford School, Christ Church, Oxford, UK; Chargé d'affaires, Libya 1969–71; High Commr in Zambia (also accred to Botswana) 1974–77, in Nigeria (also accred to Benin and Cameroon) 1980–82, in Bangladesh 1989–92; Amb. to Netherlands 1986–89; Perm. Sec. Foreign Ministry 1992–94, Foreign Sec. 1994–95; Deputy Sec.-Gen. (Political) Commonwealth 1995–2002; Visiting Fellow, Wolfson Coll., Cambridge, Centre of Int. Studies, Cambridge; Sr Fellow, Inst. of Commonwealth Studies, Univ. of London; Fellow, Netherlands Inst. of Advanced Study 2003–04, Maulana Azad Inst. of Asian Studies, Calcutta 2006–08, Swedish Collegium for Advanced Studies 2008; Hon. Mem. Christ Church Sr Common Room, Hon. Visiting Prof., Admin. Staff, Coll. of India; Hind Ratna (India) 2001, Chevalier (Cameroon) 2007; Ramsden Sermon, Univ. of Oxford 2002, Rajiv Gandhi Memorial Lecture 2006. *Publications:* The Rise, Decline and Future of the British Commonwealth 2005, The Jamdani Revolution 2008, The New Horizon: World Order in the 21st Century 2009; several novels, short stories and articles on int. affairs. *Leisure interests:* reading, music, watching sports. *Address:* Flat 8, Courtleigh, 126 Earls Court Road, London, W8 6QL, England (home). *Telephone:* (20) 7370-0339. *E-mail:* ksrinivasanuk@yahoo.co.uk (home).

SSEMOGERERE, Paul Kawanga, DipEd, MPA; Ugandan politician; *President, Democratic Party;* b. 11 Feb. 1932, Bumangi Ssese Islands, Kalangala Dist; s. of Yozefu Kapere and Maria Lwiza Nakirya; m. Dr Germina N. Ssemogerere; one s. four d.; ed St Mary's Coll., Kisubu, Makerere Univ. and Syracuse Univ., USA; teacher 1959–60; Leader Democratic Party (DP); fmr Leader of Opposition in Nat. Ass.; Minister of Internal Affairs 1986–88, Second Deputy Prime Minister and Minister of Foreign Affairs 1988–94, of the Public Service 1994, of Regional Co-operation 1989; Chair. OAU Council of Ministers 1993–94; Pres. Democratic Party; Cand. in 1996 Presidential elections; mem. Bd of Migration Policy Group 1999–; Hon. LHD (Alleghony Coll., USA) 1989. *Publications:* two book chapters on democracy and human rights in Africa. *Leisure interests:* seminars on politics and economics, eco-tourism, human rights advocacy, farming. *Address:* Democratic Party, P.O. Box 7098, Kampala (office); 401 Streicher Road, Cathedral Lubaga-Kampala, P.O. Box 548, Kampala, Uganda (home). *Telephone:* (41) 344155 (home). *E-mail:* ssemo2@africaonline.com (home).

SSENDAULA, Gerald; Ugandan politician; *Chairman, Board of Directors, Private Sector Foundation Uganda;* mem. Bd of Govs African Capacity Building Foundation (ACBF); fmr Gov. Bank of Uganda; Minister of Finance, Planning and Econ. Devt –2005; Sr Presidential Adviser on Financial Affairs 2005–; Chair. Bd of Dirs Pvt. Sector Foundation Uganda 2008–. *Address:* Private Sector Foundation Uganda, Plot 43, Nakasero Hill Road, PO BOX 7683, Kampala, Uganda (office). *Telephone:* (31) 2263850 (office). *Fax:* (41) 259109 (office). *E-mail:* psfu@psfuganda.org.ug (office). *Website:* www .psfuganda.org.ug (office).

STAAB, Heinz A., Dr rer. nat, DrMed; German scientist and academic; *Professor Emeritus of Chemistry, University of Heidelberg;* b. 26 March 1926, Darmstadt; m. Dr. Ruth Müller 1953; one s. one d.; ed Univs of Marburg, Tübingen and Heidelberg; research assoc., Max Planck Inst., Heidelberg 1953–59; Asst Prof. of Chem., Univ. of Heidelberg 1956–61, Assoc. Prof. 1961–62, Prof. 1963–, now Prof. Emer.; Dir Inst. of Organic Chem., Univ. of Heidelberg 1964–74; Dir Max Planck Inst. for Medical Research 1974–; Pres. Max Planck Soc. for the Advancement of Science, Munich 1984–90; mem. German Science Council 1976–79; Senator, Deutsche Forschungsgemeinschaft 1976–82 and 1984–90; mem. Bd of Govs Weizmann Inst. of Science, Israel 1977–; Pres. Gesellschaft Deutscher Naturforscher und Ärzte 1981–82; Pres. German Chem. Soc. 1984–85; mem. Heidelberg Acad. of Sciences (Pres. 1994–96), Acad. Leopoldina, Academia Europaea; Corresp. mem. Austrian Acad. of Sciences 1988, Bavarian Acad. of Sciences 1991; Hon. Prof., Chinese Acad. of Sciences 1992; Foreign mem. Russian Acad. of Sciences 1994; Hon. mem. Senate Max-Planck Soc. 1990, German Chem. Soc. 1998, Hon. Fellow Indian Acad. of Sciences 1988; Hon. PhD (Weizmann Inst. of Science) 1984; Adolf von Baeyer Award (German Chem. Soc.) 1979. *Publications:* Einführung in die theoretische organische Chemie 1959 (translations), Azolides in Organic Synthesis and Biochemistry (co-author); about 370/400 publications in professional journals. *Leisure interests:* travel, history,

classical music. *Address:* Max-Planck-Institut für Medizinische Forschung, Jahnstrasse 29, 69120 Heidelberg (office); Schlosswolfsbrunnenweg 43, 69118 Heidelberg, Germany (home). *Telephone:* (6221) 4860 (office); (6221) 803330 (home). *Fax:* (6221) 486585 (office). *E-mail:* heinz.staab@mpimf-heidelberg .mpg.de (office). *Website:* www.chemgeo.uni-hd.de/indexengl (office).

STAATS, Elmer Boyd, PhD; American economist and government official; b. 6 June 1914, Richfield, Kan.; s. of Wesley F. Staats and Maude Staats (née Goodall); m. Margaret S. Rich 1940; one s. two d.; ed McPherson Coll. and Univs of Kansas and Minnesota; Research Asst, Kansas Legis. Council 1936; mem. Staff, Public Admin. Service, Chicago 1937–38; Fellow, Brookings Inst. 1938–39; Staff mem. Bureau of the Budget 1939–47, Asst to Dir 1947, Asst Dir (Legis. Reference) 1947–49, Exec. Asst Dir 1949–50, Asst Dir 1958–59, Deputy Dir 1950–53, 1959–66; Research Dir, Marshall Field & Co., Chicago 1953; Exec. Officer Operations Co-ordinating Bd, Nat. Security Council 1953–58; Comptroller Gen. of the United States 1966–81; fmr mem. Bd of Dirs of several corpns; fmr mem. numerous public orgs including Pres. American Soc. for Public Admin. 1961–62; Pres. Harry S. Truman Scholarship Foundation 1981–84, Chair. Bd of Trustees 1984–; Chair. Govt Procurement Round Table 1984–; mem. Bd of Dirs of American Acad. of Political and Social Science 1966, Bd of Govs Int. Org. of Supreme Audit Insts 1969–81, Visiting Cttee John F. Kennedy School of Govt, Harvard Univ. 1974–80, Visiting Cttee, Graduate School of Man., Univ. of Calif. at LA 1976–85, Visiting Cttee to the Cttee in Public Policy Studies, Univ. of Chicago 1976–; President's Comm. on Budget Concepts 1967–68; mem. Bd of Govs Int. Center on Election Law and Admin. 1985–87; Dir George C. Marshall Foundation 1984–; mem. Bd of Visitors, Nat. Defense Univ. 1981–90; Trustee, Cttee for Econ. Devt 1981–, Nat. Planning Asscn 1981–; Hon. Certified Internal Auditor (Inst. of Internal Auditors) 1973, Hon. mem. Soc. of Mfg Engineers 1978; Hon. Life mem. Municipal Finance Officers Asscn of USA and Canada 1980; Dr Publ Service (George Washington Univ.) 1971, Dr Admin. (Univ. of S Dak.) 1973; Hon. LLD (McPherson Coll.) 1966, (Duke Univ.) 1975, (Nova Univ.) 1976, (Lycoming Coll.) 1982, (Univ. of Penn.); Hon. DHumLitt (Ohio State Univ.) 1982; Rockefeller Public Service Award 1961, Productivity Award, American Productivity Cen. 1980, Medal of Honor AICPA 1980, Presidential Citizens Medal 1981, Accounting Hall of Fame 1981, Inst. of Internal Auditors Thurston Award 1988. *Publication:* Personnel Standards in the Social Security Program 1939. *Address:* 5011 Overlook Road, NW, Washington, DC 20016, USA.

STABENOW, Deborah (Debbie) Ann, BS, MSW; American politician; *Senator from Michigan;* b. 29 April 1950, Gladwin, Mich.; d. of Robert Lee Greer and Anna Merle Greer (née Hallmark); one s. one d.; ed Mich. State Univ.; with Special Services, Lansing School Dist 1972–73; Co. Commr Ingham Co., Mason, Mich. 1975–78; State Rep. for Mich., Lansing 1979–2002; mem. Agric. Cttee, Science Cttee 105th–106th Congress from 8th Mich. Dist; Senator from Mich. 2003–; founder Ingham Co. Women's Comm.; Co-Founder Council Against Domestic Assault; mem. Democratic Business and Professional Club, Mich. Democratic Women's Political Caucus, Grance United Methodist Church (fmr lay preacher, Chair. Social Concerns Task Force, Sunday School Music teacher), Lansing Boys' Club, Professional Advisory Cttee Lansing Parents Without Partners, Advisory Cttee Center for Handicapped Affairs, Mich. Council Family and Divorce Mediation Advisory Bd, Nat. Council for Children's Rights, Big Brothers/Big Sisters Greater Lansing Advisory Bd, Mich. Child Study Asscn Bd Advisers, Mich. Women's Campaign Fund; mem. Nat. Asscn for the Advancement of Colored People (NAACP), Lansing Regional Chamber of Commerce; awards include Service to Children Award, Council for Prevention of Child Abuse and Neglect 1983, Outstanding Leadership Award, Nat. Council of Community Mental Health Centers 1983, Snyder-Kok Award, Mental Health Asscn Mich., Awareness Leader of the Year Award, Awareness Communications Team Developmentally Disabled 1984, Communicator of the Year Award, Woman in Communications 1984, Lawmaker of the Year Award, Nat. Child Support Enforcement Asscn 1985, Distinguished Service Award, Lansing Jaycees 1985, Distinguished Service in Govt Award, Retarded Citizens of Mich. 1986. *Address:* 133 Hart Senate Office Building, Washington, DC 20510 (office); 2709 South Deerfield Avenue, Lansing, MI 48911-1783, USA (home). *Telephone:* (202) 224-4822 (home). *Fax:* (202) 224-2066 (office). *E-mail:* senator@stabenow.senate.gov (office). *Website:* stabenow.senate.gov (office).

STABREIT, Immo Friedrich Helmut, DJur; German diplomatist (retd) and business consultant; b. 24 Jan. 1933, Rathenow/Havel; s. of Kurt Stabreit and Johanna Maria Stabreit (née Groeger); m. Barbara Philippi 1962; two s. one d.; ed Princeton Univ., USA, Free Univ. of Berlin, Univ. of Heidelberg and Harvard Univ., USA; jr law clerk 1957–61; with Financial Dept ECSC, Luxembourg 1959; entered Foreign Service 1962; served Embassy in Moscow 1962–63, 1966–71; with Soviet Desk, Ministry of Foreign Affairs 1964–66, 1971–74; Fellow, Center for Int. Affairs, Harvard Univ., USA 1974–75; Head of Consumer Producer Relations Div., Int. Energy Agency, Paris 1975–78; European Corresp., Ministry of Foreign Affairs 1978–83; Head of Sub-Dept of Foreign Affairs, Fed. Chancellery 1983–87; Amb. to South Africa 1987–92, to USA 1992–95, to France 1995–98; Exec. Vice-Pres. German Soc. for Foreign Affairs 1998–2002; currently business consultant. *Leisure interests:* sport, reading. *Address:* Wundtstr. 18, 14059 Berlin-Charlottenburg (winter) (home); Petersbergstr. 8, 53604 Bad Honnef, Germany (summer) (home). *Telephone:* (30) 25798160 (Berlin) (home); (2224) 900935 (Bad Honnef) (home). *Fax:* (30) 25798162 (Berlin) (home); (2224) 987717 (Bad Honnef) (home).

STADEN, Berndt von; German diplomatist; b. 24 June 1919, Rostock; s. of Richard von Staden and Camilla von Voigt; m. Wendelgard von Neurath 1961; two s. one d.; ed Bonn and Hamburg Univs; mil. service 1940–45; jr barrister 1948–51; with Foreign Ministry 1951–86; served in Brussels 1953–55; Dir, Soviet Affairs Desk, Bonn 1955–58; Staff mem., EEC Comm., Brussels, Head of Office of Pres. of Comm. 1958–63; Counsellor, Embassy, Washington, DC 1963–68; Deputy Asst State Sec., Foreign Office 1968–70, Asst State Sec., Head of Political Dept 1970–73; Amb. to USA 1973–79; Head of Dept for Foreign Relations and Security, Fed. Chancery 1979–81; State Sec., Foreign Office 1981–83; Co-ordinator for German-American Co-operation 1982–86; Prof. of Diplomacy, Georgetown Univ., Washington, DC 1985, 1988, 1990; Order of Merit (FRG), Order of Terra Mariana, First Class (Estonia). *Publications:* Erinnerungen aus der Vorzeit: Eine Jugend im Baltikum 1919–1939 1999, Ende, Anfang: Errinerungen 1939–1963 2001, Zwischen Eiszeit und Tauwetter 2005. *Leisure interests:* music, horse riding. *Address:* Leinfelderhof, 71665 Vaihingen, Germany (home). *Telephone:* (7042) 5440 (home). *Fax:* (7042) 98994 (home).

STADLER, Sergey Valentinovich; Russian violinist and conductor; b. 20 May 1962, Leningrad (now St Petersburg); s. of Valentin Raymundovich Stadler and Margarita Petrovna Stadler; m. Ilza Liepa (divorced); ed Leningrad State Conservatory, studied with Mikhail Vaiman, Boris Gutnikov in Leningrad Conservatory, with Leonid Kogan, Viktor Tretyakov in Moscow State Conservatory; prize winner at several int. competitions; has toured more than 50 countries since 1976; first performed music by Russian composers Rodion Shchedrin, Sergey Slonimsky, Boris Tishchenko and others; Prof., St. Petersburg State Conservatory 1984–89, fmr Artistic Dir and Chief Conductor N.A. Rimsky-Korsakov Saint-Petersburg State Conservatory of Opera and Ballet; began conducting 1996; Head of Competition Jury, Paganini Moscow Int. Violin Competition 2003–; Founder Hermitage Acad. of Music; People's Artist of Russia. *Address:* c/o Competition Jury, Paganini Moscow International Violin Competition, 107045 Moscow, Daev pereulok, 20, office 204, Russia. *E-mail:* info@violin-fund.ru. *Website:* www.violin-fund.ru.

STADTMAN, Thressa (Terry) Campbell, BS, MS, PhD; American biochemist; *Section Head, Laboratory of Biochemistry, National Heart, Lung and Blood Institute, National Institutes of Health (NIH);* b. 12 Feb. 1920, Sterling, New York; d. of Earl Campbell and Bessie Campbell (née Waldron); m. Earl R. Stadtman 1943 (died 2008); ed Cornell Univ. and Univ. of California, Berkeley; Research Assoc., Univ. of California, Berkeley 1942–47; Research Assoc., Harvard Medical School, Boston 1949–50; Biochemist, Nat. Heart, Lung and Blood Inst., NIH 1950–, Section Head, Lab. of Biochemistry 1974–; Ed.-in-Chief Bio Factors (IUB-sponsored journal) 1987–; Senior Exec. Service 1988–; Pres. Int. Soc. of Vitamins and Related Bio Factors 1995; Helen Haye Whitney Fellow, Oxford Univ., England 1954–55; Rockefeller Foundation Grantee, Univ. of Munich, FRG 1959–60; mem. NAS, American Acad. of Arts and Sciences, Burroughs-Welcome Fund Toxicology Advisory Cttee 1994–97; Hillebrand Award, Chemical Soc. of Washington 1979, Rose Award, American Soc. of Biological Chemists 1987, Klaus Schwarz Medal 1988, Public Health Service Special Recognition Award 1991, L'Oréal-UNESCO Women in Science Lifetime Achievement Award 2000, Gabriel Bertrand Award, Fed. of European Socs of Trace Elements and Minerals 2001. *Publications:* original research papers in fields of Methane Biosynthesis, Amino Acid Metabolism, Vitamin B12 biochemistry, selenium biochemistry. *Leisure interests:* travel, gardening, skiing. *Address:* National Institutes of Health, Building 50, Loius B. Stokes Labs, Room 2120, Bethesda, MD 20892 (office); 16907 Redland Road, Derwood, MD 20855, USA (home). *Telephone:* (301) 496-3002 (office); (301) 869-1747 (home). *Fax:* (301) 496-0599 (office). *E-mail:* tcstadtman@nih.gov (office); stadtmat@nhlbi.nih.gov (office). *Website:* www.nhlbi.nih.gov (office).

STAEHELIN, Jenö C. A., Lic.Iur., LLM; Swiss lawyer and fmr diplomatist; *Partner, Brock Partners LLP;* b. 1940, Basel; ed Univ. of Berne, Harvard Law School; called to the Bar, Zurich 1968; fmr Clerk, Zurich Court then pvt law practice, Zurich 1968–69; joined Foreign Service 1969, overseas postings included at Embassies in Berne, Geneva and Stockholm 1969–71; Legal Adviser, Ministry of Foreign Affairs 1971–76; mem. Del. to OECD, Paris 1976–77; Vice-Pres. European Patent Office, Munich 1977–84; Minister and Deputy Dir for Int. Orgs, Ministry of Foreign Affairs 1984–87, Amb. in charge of European and N American Affairs 1987–93, also Amb. to Holy See 1991–93, Amb. to Japan 1993–97; Perm. Observer to UN, New York 1997–2002, Perm. Rep. to UN 2002–04; Pres. UNICEF 2003–04, Chair. UN Mine Action Support Group 2004; Pnr Brock Partners LLP (law firm), New York; f. Dr. Jenö Staehelin Foundation. *Address:* Brock Partners LLP, 622 Third Avenue, 12th Floor, New York, NY 10017, USA (office); Dr. Jenö Staehelin Foundation, Kantonsstrasse 46c, 8807 Freienbach, Switzerland. *Telephone:* (212) 209-3000 (office). *E-mail:* jstaehelin@brockfirm.com (office). *Website:* www.brockfirm.com (office).

STAFF, Joel, MBA; American business executive; *Chairman, Reliant Resources Inc.;* ed Univ. of Tex., Tex. A&M Univ.; began career with Baker Hughes Inc. (oil and gas industry supplier) 1976, served in various financial man. positions including Sr Vice-Pres. parent co. and Pres. Drilling and Production Groups –1993; Chair., Pres. and CEO Nat. OilWell Inc. 1993–2001; joined Reliant Resources Inc. 2002, mem. Bd Dirs 2002–, Interim Pres. Reliant Energy Retail Group, Chair. and CEO Reliant Resources 2003–07, Chair. 2007–; mem. Bd of Dirs Nat. OilWell Inc., Ensco Int. Inc.; Advisory Dir King Chapman & Broussard, Boys and Girls Club of Greater Houston; mem. Devt Bd Univ. of Tex. Health Science Center, Houston. *Address:* Reliant Resources Inc., 111 Louisiana, Houston, TX 77002, USA (office). *Telephone:* (715) 497-3000 (office). *Fax:* (713) 497-2319 (office). *Website:* www.reliant.com (office).

STAFFORD, Godfrey Harry, CBE, MA, MSc, PhD, FRS; British physicist; b. 15 April 1920, Sheffield; s. of Henry Stafford and Sarah Stafford; m. Helen Goldthorp 1950 (died 2003); one s. twin d.; ed Rondebosch Boys' High School, Univ. of Cape Town, Gonville and Caius Coll., Cambridge; South African Naval Forces 1941–46; AERE, Harwell 1949–51; Head of Biophysics Subdivision, Council for Scientific and Industrial Research, Pretoria 1951–54; Cyclotron Group, AERE 1954–57; Head of Proton Linear Accelerator Group, Rutherford Lab. 1957, Head of High Energy Physics Div. 1963, Deputy Dir 1966, Dir 1969–79; Dir of Atlas and Rutherford Lab. 1975–79, Dir-Gen. 1979–81; UK Del. IUPAP Comm. on Particles and Fields 1975–81; Vice-Pres. Inst. of Physics Meetings Cttee 1976–79; Chair. CERN Scientific Policy Cttee 1978–81; Master of St Cross Coll. Oxford 1979–87; Pres. European Physical Soc. 1984–86, Inst. of Physics 1986–88; Visiting Fellow, St Cross Coll. 1971–79, Hon. Fellow 1987; Vice-Pres. European Physical Soc. 1982; Gov. Westminster Coll.; Ebden Scholar, Univ. of Cape Town; Hon. Scientist Rutherford Appleton Lab. 1986; Hon. DSc (Birmingham) 1980; Glazebrook Prize and Medal, Inst. of Physics 1981. *Publications:* papers and articles in learned journals on biophysics, nuclear physics and high energy physics. *Leisure interests:* music, foreign travel, walking. *Address:* Ferry Cottage, North Hinksey Village, Oxford, OX2 0NA, England (home). *Telephone:* (1865) 247621 (home). *E-mail:* godfreystafford@onetel.com (home).

STAFFORD, HE Cardinal James Francis; American ecclesiastic; *Major Penitentiary of Apostolic Penitentiary, Roman Curia;* b. 26 July 1932, Baltimore; s. of F. Emmett Stafford and Mary Dorothy Stafford; ordained priest 1957; Auxiliary Bishop of Baltimore 1976–82; Bishop of Memphis 1982–86; Archbishop of Denver 1986–96, now Archbishop Emer.; cr. Cardinal (Cardinal-Deacon of Gesù Buon Pastore alla Montagnola) 1998–; Pres. Pontifical Council for the Laity 1998–; Major Penitentiary of Apostolic Penitentiary, Roman Curia 2003–. *Address:* Palazzo della Cancelleria, Piazza della Cancelleria, 1, 00186 Rome, Italy (office). *Telephone:* (06) 69887526 (office). *Fax:* (06) 69887557 (office). *E-mail:* vati877@apostpnt.va (office).

STAFFORD, John Rogers, AB, JD; American lawyer and business executive; b. 24 Oct. 1937, Harrisburg, Pa; s. of Paul Henry Stafford and Gladys Lee Sharp; m. Inge Paul 1959; four d.; ed Montgomery Blair High School, Dickinson Coll., George Washington Univ. Law School; Assoc., Steptoe and Johnson 1962–66; Gen. Attorney, Hoffman-LaRoche 1966–67, Group Attorney 1967–70; Gen. Counsel, American Home Products Corpn (now Wyeth) 1970–74, Vice-Pres. 1974–77, Sr Vice-Pres. 1977–80, Exec. Vice-Pres. 1980–81, Pres. 1981–2001, Chair., Pres. and CEO 1986–2001, Chair. 2001–02; mem. Bd of Dirs Verizon 1997– (Dir NYNEX Corpn 1989–97), Honeywell Int. Inc., J.P. Morgan Chase & Co 1982–2005; fmr Dir Mfrs Hanover Corpn, Metropolitan Life Insurance Co., Cen. Park Conservancy, Pharmaceutical Mfrs Asscn, Project Hope, American Paralysis Asscn; mem. Bd of Trustees US Council for Int. Business; mem. ABA, DC Bar Asscn; mem. Advisory Bd Christopher Reeve Paralysis Foundation; Order of the Coif; Outstanding Achievement Alumnus Award 1981. *Leisure interests:* boating, golf. *Address:* c/o Board of Directors, Verizon Communications Inc., 1095 Avenue of the Americas, New York, NY 10036, USA.

STAFFORD-CLARK, Max; British theatre director; *Artistic Director, Out of Joint Theatre Company;* b. 17 March 1941; s. of David Stafford-Clark and Dorothy Stafford-Clark; m. 1st Carole Hayman 1971; m. 2nd Ann Pennington 1981; one d.; m. 3rd Stella Feehily; one d.; ed Felsted School, Riverdale Country Day School, New York and Trinity Coll. Dublin; Artistic Dir Traverse Theatre, Edin. 1968–70; Dir Traverse Workshop Co. 1970–74; Founder and Artistic Dir Joint Stock Theatre Group 1974–79, English Stage Co. at Royal Court Theatre 1979–93; Founder and Artistic Dir Out of Joint Theatre Co. 1993–; Visiting Prof. Royal Holloway and Bedford Coll., Univ. of London 1993–94; Maisie Glass Prof. Univ. of Sheffield 1995–96; Visiting Prof., Univ. of Herts. 1999–, Univ. of York 2002–; Hon. Fellow, Rose Bruford Coll. 1996; Hon. DLitt (Oxford Brookes) 2000, (Herts.) 2000, (Warwick) 2006; Special Award, Evening Standard Theatre Awards 2004. *Principal productions:* Fanshen 1975, Top Girls 1982, Tom and Viv, Rat in the Skull, Serious Money, Our Country's Good, The Steward of Christendom, Shopping And Fucking, Blue Heart, Some Explicit Polaroids, Rita Sue and Bob Too/A State Affair 2000, A Laughing Matter 2002 The Permanent Way 2003, O Go My Man 2006, The Convicts Opera 2008. *Publications:* Letters to George 1989, Taking Stock 2007. *Address:* Out of Joint, 7 Thane Works, Thane Villas, London N7 7PH (office); 11G Beaux Arts Building, 10–18 Manor Gardens, London N7 6JT, England. *Telephone:* (20) 7609-0207 (office). *E-mail:* ojo@outofjoint.co.uk (office). *Website:* www.outofjoint.co.uk (office).

STAGNO UGARTE, Bruno, BSc, MSc; Costa Rican politician; *Minister of Foreign Relations;* b. 8 April 1970, Paris, France; m. Laetitia Stagno; two c.; ed Princeton and Georgetown Univs, USA and Sorbonne, France; Consul-Gen. and Minister-Counsellor, Embassy in France 1994–98; Chef de Cabinet, Minister of Foreign Relations and Worship, San Jose 1998–2000; Prof., Universidad Latina 1999; Prof., School of Political Science, Univ. of Costa Rica 2000–02; adviser to legislative ass. 2000–02; Perm. Rep. to UN, New York 2002–06; Minister of Foreign Relations 2006–; Vice-Chair. Bureau of CSD-11 (Comm. on Sustainable Devt), mem. CSD-12; mem. Inst. for Democracy and Electoral Assistance 1999–2000; Pres. Ass. of State Parties, Int. Criminal Court 2005–08; mem. Advisory Bd Parliamentarians for Global Action 2005–06; Del. Bureau Int. des Expositions, 29th session of UNESCO Gen. Conference 1995–98. *Address:* Ministry of Foreign Relations, Avda 7 y 9, Calle 11 y 13, Apdo 10027, 1000 San Jose, Costa Rica (office). *Telephone:* 223-7555 (office). *Fax:* 257-6597 (office). *E-mail:* despacho.ministro@rree.go.cr (office). *Website:* www.rree.go.cr (office).

STAHL, Heinrich Georg, PhD; Austrian business executive; b. 1947; ed Univ. of Vienna; began career with Zellstoffabrik Frantschach AG 1970–75; Chief Financial Officer, Bunzel & Biach AG 1976–88; Chief Financial Officer, Papierfabrik Laakirchen AG 1980–88; Chief Financial Officer, SCA Laakirchen AG, SCA Ortmann AG 1989–91; Chief Financial Officer, Austria Metall AG 1992–95; Chief Financial Officer, OMV AG 1996–2000; Dir and Chief Financial Officer, Heinzel Holding GmbH 2000–, Dir and Chief Financial Officer, Heinzel, Bunzl Immobilien GmbH 2003–, Heinzel, Bunzl

Service GmbH 2003–; mem. Bd of Dirs CE Oil & Gas Beteiligung und Verwaltung AG 2000–, TVK CE Holding AG 2002–05, Chair. BorsodChem, Hungary 2005 (after acquisition by CE Holding). *Address:* Borsodchem, Bolyai tér 1, 3700 Kazincbarcika, Hungary (office). *Telephone:* (48) 511–211 (office). *Fax:* (48) 511–511 (office). *E-mail:* bcrt@borsodchem.hu (office). *Website:* www.borsodchem.hu (office).

STALLKAMP, Thomas J., BS, MBA; American business executive; *Industrial Partner, Ripplewood Holdings LLC;* b. 1946; ed Miami Univ., Ohio; with Chrysler Corpn, Detroit (now Chrysler LLC) for 20 years in various man. positions including Pres., mem. Man. Bd, then Vice-Chair. 1999; Vice-Chair. and CEO MSX Int. 2000–04; Industrial Pnr, Ripplewood Holdings LLC 2004–; mem. Bd of Dirs Baxter Int. Inc., Visteon, MSX Int.; mem. Bd of Advisors, McDonough School of Business, Georgetown Univ.; Adjunct Prof. in Entrepreneurship, Babson Coll.; Trustee Babson Coll. *Address:* Ripplewood Holdings LLC, One Rockefeller Plaza, 32nd Floor, New York, NY 10020, USA (office). *Telephone:* (212) 582-6700 (office). *Fax:* (212) 582-4110 (office). *E-mail:* tstallkamp@babson.edu.

STALLONE, Sylvester Enzio; American actor and film director; b. 6 July 1946, New York; s. of Frank Stallone and Jacqueline Labofish; m. 1st Sasha Czach 1974 (divorced); two s.; m. 2nd Brigitte Nielsen 1985 (divorced 1987); m. 3rd Jennifer Flavin 1997; two d.; ed American Coll. of Switzerland, Univ. of Miami; has had many jobs including usher, bouncer, horse trainer, store detective, physical educ. teacher; now actor, producer and dir of own films; f. White Eagle Co.; Dir Carolco Pictures Inc. 1987–; mem. Screen Actors Guild, Writers Guild, Directors' Guild; Hon. mem. Stuntmans' Asscn; Acad. Award for best film 1976, Golden Circle Award for best film 1976, Donatello Award 1976, Christopher Religious Award 1976; Officier Ordre des Arts et des Lettres. *Films include:* Lords of Flatbush 1973, Capone 1974, Rocky 1976, F.I.S.T. 1978, Paradise Alley 1978, Rocky II 1979, Nighthawks 1980, Escape to Victory 1980, Rocky III 1981, First Blood, Rambo 1984, Rocky IV 1985, Cobra 1986, Over the Top 1986, Rambo II 1986, Rambo III 1988, Lock Up 1989, Set Up 1990, Tango and Cash 1990, Rocky V 1990, Isobar 1991, Stop or My Mom Will Shoot 1991, Oscar 1991, Cliffhanger 1992, Demolition Man 1993, Judge Dredd 1994, The Specialist 1994, Assassins 1995, Firestorm 1996, Daylight 1996, Cop Land 1997, An Alan Smithee Film: Burn Hollywood Burn 1998, Get Carter 2000, Driven (also screenwriter and producer) 2001, D-Tox 2002, Avenging Angelo 2002, Shade 2003, Spy Kids 3-D: Game Over 2003, Rocky Balboa 2006; films directed: Paradise Alley 1978, Rocky II 1979, Rocky III 1982, Staying Alive 1983, Rocky IV 1985, Rocky Balboa 2006, Rambo 2008. *Publications:* Paradise Alley 1977, The Rocky Scrapbook 1997. *Address:* William Morris Agency, One William Morris Place, Beverly Hills, CA 90212, USA. *Website:* www.sylvesterstallone.com.

STALS, Christian Lodewyk, DComm; South African central banker and academic administrator; b. 13 March 1935; s. of Petrus J. Stals and Lilian Barnard; m. Hester Barnard 1958; three s. one d.; ed Afrikaans Hoër, Germiston and Univ. of Pretoria Extramural Div.; joined South African Reserve Bank 1955, Gen. Man. 1975, Deputy Gov. 1976, Sr Deputy Gov. 1981; Dir-Gen. Dept of Finance 1985; Special Econ. Adviser to Minister of Finance 1989; Gov. South African Reserve Bank 1989–99; Chancellor, Univ. of Pretoria 1997–2006; State President's Decoration for Distinguished Service. *Leisure interest:* golf. *Address:* c/o Office of the Chancellor, University of Pretoria, Pretoria 0002, South Africa (office).

STAMP, Gavin Mark, PhD, FSA; British architectural historian, writer and academic; b. 15 March 1948, Bromley, Kent; s. of Barry Hartnell Stamp and Norah Clare Stamp (née Rich); m. Alexandra Artley 1982 (divorced 2006); two d.; ed Dulwich Coll., London, Gonville and Caius Coll., Cambridge; freelance writer and teacher –1990; Lecturer, Mackintosh School of Architecture, Glasgow School of Art 1990–99, Sr Lecturer and Hon. Prof. 1999–2003; Mellon Sr Fellow and Bye Fellow, Gonville and Caius Coll., Cambridge 2003–04; ind. scholar 2004–; Chair. The Twentieth Century Soc. (fmrly The Thirties Soc.) 1983–2007; Founder and Chair. Alexander Thomson Soc. 1991–2003; Hon. Fellow, Royal Incorporation of Architects of Scotland 1994; Hon. FRIBA 1998. *Publications:* Robert Weir Schultz and his work for Marquesses of Bute 1981, The Great Perspectivists 1982, The Changing Metropolis 1984, The English House 1860–1914 1986, Telephone Boxes 1989, Greek Thomson (co-ed.) 1994, Alexander 'Greek' Thomson 1999, Edwin Lutyens' Country Houses 2001, An Architect of Promise: George Gilbert Scott Junior and the Late Gothic Revival 2002, Lutyens Abroad (co-ed.) 2002, The Memorial to the Missing of the Somme 2006, Britain's Lost Cities 2007. *Address:* 15 Belle Vue Court, 122d Devonshire Road, London, SE23 3SY, England (home). *E-mail:* gavin.stamp@btopenworld.com (home).

STAMP, Terence; British actor; b. 22 July 1938, Bow, London; s. of Thomas Stamp and Ethel Esther Perrott; ed Plaistow Co. Grammar School, Webber–Douglas Dramatic Acad.; theatre work before film debut in Peter Ustinov's film adaptation of Herman Melville's novel Billy Budd 1962; Hon. Dr of Arts (Univ. of East London) 1993; Amhurst Webber Memorial Scholarship 1957. *Music:* The Airborne Symphony (narrator). *Theatre:* Dracula, The Lady from the Sea. *Other films include:* Term of Trial 1962, The Collector 1965, Modesty Blaise 1966, Far From the Madding Crowd 1967, Poor Cow 1967, Blue 1968, Theorem 1968, Tales of Mystery 1968, The Mind of Mr. Soames 1969, A Season in Hell 1971, Hu-man 1975, The Divine Creature 1976, Striptease 1977, Meetings With Remarkable Men 1978, Superman 1978, Superman II 1979 (Superman II: The Richard Donner Cut 2006), Death in the Vatican 1980, The Bloody Chamber 1982, The Hit 1984, Link 1985, Legal Eagles 1986, The Sicilian 1986, Wall Street 1988, Alien Nation 1988, Young Guns 1988, Prince of Shadows 1991, The Real McCoy 1992, The Adventures of Priscilla Queen of the Desert 1994, Limited Edition 1995, Tiré à part 1996, Bliss 1997, Love Walked In 1997, The Limey 1999, Star Wars: Episode I – The Phantom

Menace 1999, Bowfinger 1999, Kiss the Sky 1999, Red Planet 2000, My Wife is an Actress 2000, Revelation 2001, Full Frontal 2002, My Boss's Daughter 2003, The Kiss 2003, The Haunted Mansion 2003, Dead Fish 2004, These Foolish Things 2004, Elektra 2005, Mr. & Mrs. Smith (scenes deleted) 2005, The Elder Scrolls IV: Oblivion (video game; voice) 2006, 9/11: The Twin Towers (narrator) 2006, September Dawn 2007, Wanted 2008, Get Smart 2008. *Television includes:* Mindbender 1996, The Hunger – Anais 1997, Static Shock – Blast from the Past (voice) 2003, Smallville 2003–06. *Publications:* Stamp Album (memoirs, Vol. 1) 1988, Coming Attractions (memoirs, Vol. 2) 1988, Double Feature (memoirs, Vol. 3) 1989, The Night (novel) 1992, Stamp Collection Cookbook (jtly) 1997, The New Testament (audio book). *Leisure interest:* still tap dancing. *Address:* c/o Markham and Froggatt, 4 Windmill Street, London, W1P 1HF, England. *Telephone:* (20) 7636-4412. *Fax:* (20) 7637-5233. *E-mail:* admin@markhamfroggatt.co.uk. *Website:* www.markhamfroggatt.com.

STAMPFER, Meir J., MD, DrPH; American nutritionist, epidemiologist and academic; *Professor of Nutrition and Epidemiology and Chairman, Department of Epidemiology, Harvard School of Public Health;* b. Lincoln, NE; ed Columbia Coll., New York Univ. School of Medicine, Harvard School of Public Health; Intern in Internal Medicine, Maimonides Hosp., Brooklyn, NY 1977–78; Resident, Community Medicine (Environmental), Mount Sinai School of Medicine, New York 1978–79; Resident, Preventive Medicine, Harvard School of Public Health, Boston, Mass 1979–81, Instructor in Medicine, Harvard Medical School 1982–85, Teaching Fellow, Dept of Epidemiology, Harvard School of Public Health 1982–85, Assoc. Physician, Brigham and Women's Hosp., Boston 1982–91, Consultant Physician, Veteran's Admin Hosp., Brockton, Mass 1984–85, Asst Prof. of Medicine, Harvard Medical School 1985–93, Assoc. Prof. of Epidemiology, Harvard School of Public Health 1988–93, Faculty mem. Div. of Biological Sciences, Harvard School of Public Health 1989–, Physician, Brigham and Women's Hosp. 1991–, Prof. of Nutrition and Epidemiology, Harvard School of Public Health 1993–, Assoc. Prof. of Medicine, Harvard Medical School 1993–2001, Chair. Dept of Epidemiology, Harvard School of Public Health 2000–, mem. Dana-Farber/Harvard Cancer Center 2000–, Prof. of Medicine, Harvard Medical School 2001–; Adjunct Prof., Karolinska Institutet, Stockholm, Sweden 2003–; Dozer Visiting Prof., Ben Gurion Univ., Israel; Assoc. Ed. American Journal of Epidemiology 1991–92, 1997, 2003–, Ed. 1992–97; mem. Editorial Bd American Fertility Soc. Menopause Publication 1992–94, Menopause (The Journal of the North American Menopause Soc.) 1993–, Journal of the American College of Nutrition 1994–, European Menopause Journal 1994–98, Journal of Women's Health 1998, American Journal of Medicine 1998; Tech. Reviewer, New England Journal of Medicine 1987–96; Int. Editorial Advisor, Journal of the British Menopause Soc. 2002–; mem. Soc. for Epidemiologic Research 1980–, Int. Soc. and Fed. of Cardiology, Council of Epidemiology and Prevention 1981–, American Epidemiological Soc. 1993–, American Asscn of Cancer Research 1999; Fellow, American Heart Asscn (Council of Epidemiology 1984, Council on Nutrition, Physical Activity and Metabolism 2003), American Coll. of Nutrition 1986; Jones Prize for Logic and Philosophy of Science, Columbia Univ. 1973, NIH Nat. Research Service Award 1979–82, Distinguished Alumnus Speaker, Maimonides Hosp. 1989, Duphar Lecturer, British Menopause Soc., UK 1994, Sr Investigator Award in Antioxidant Research, Comité Français de Coordination des Recherches sur l'Atherosclerose et le Cholesterol (France) 1994, Most-Cited Researchers in Clinical Medicine 1981–1998, Rank #1 in Epidemiology, #3 Overall Science-Watch, Inst. for Scientific Information 1999, Frost Award, American Public Health Asscn 2000; Most-cited Scientist in Clinical Medicine 1995–2005, first overall, Inst. for Scientific Information 2005. *Publications:* more than 617 articles in medical journals on nutrition and chronic disease. *Address:* Department of Epidemiology, Harvard School of Public Health, Kresge Building, Room 904, 677 Huntington Avenue, Boston, MA 02115, USA (office). *Telephone:* (617) 432-6477 (office). *Fax:* (617) 566-7805 (office). *E-mail:* mstampfe@hsph.harvard.edu (office). *Website:* www.hsph.harvard.edu/faculty/meir-stampfe (office).

STANBURY, Hon. Robert Douglas George, PC, QC, BA, LLB, FID; Canadian executive, lawyer and fmr politician; *Integrity Commissioner, Nunavut;* b. 26 Oct. 1929, Exeter, Ont.; s. of James George Stuart Stanbury and Elizabeth Jean Stanbury (née Hardy); m. Miriam Voelker 1952; two s. two d.; ed Exeter and St Catharines public schools, St Catharines Coll. Inst., Univ. of Western Ontario, Osgoode Hall Law School and York Univ.; Account Exec., Public & Industrial Relations Ltd., Toronto 1950–51; Pres. Canadian Univ. Liberal Fed. 1954; Pnr, Hollingworth & Stanbury, Barristers and Solicitors, Toronto 1955–65; mem. North York Bd of Educ. 1961–64, Vice-Chair. 1962, Chair. 1963–64; mem. Metropolitan School Bd, Toronto 1963–64 and Metropolitan Toronto Planning Bd 1963; MP 1965–77; Chair. House of Commons Standing Cttee on Broadcasting, Films and Assistance to the Arts 1966–68; Parl. Sec. to Sec. of State of Canada 1968–69; Minister without Portfolio responsible for Citizenship 1969–71, for Information Canada 1970–71; Minister of Communications 1971–72, of Nat. Revenue 1972–74; Queen's Counsel 1974–; Del. to UN Gen. Ass. 1974, 1975, 1976, to UNESCO Conf., Paris 1969, UN Conf. on Crime, Kyoto 1970, UN Conf. on Apartheid, Lagos 1977, IDB meeting, Kingston 1977; Chair. Canadian Group IPU 1974–77; Founding Chair. Canadian Parl. Helsinki Group 1977; Pres. Hamilton Foundation 1982–83; Vice-Pres. Gen. Counsel and Dir, Firestone Canada Inc. 1977–83, Chair. and CEO 1983–85; Counsel, Inch Easterbrook & Shaker 1986–2000; Dir Art Gallery of Hamilton (Vice-Pres. 1982–86, Pres. 1986–87), mem. Bd of Govs 1988–2004, Dir Art Gallery of Hamilton Foundation 1996–2004; Dir Hamilton and Dist Chamber of Commerce 1980–85 (Pres. 1983–84), Dayton Tire Canada Ltd 1977–85, Canadian Chamber of Commerce 1982–86, Chedoke-McMaster Hosps 1983–92, (Vice-Chair. 1987–89), Workers' Compensation Bd of Ont. 1985–88, 1991–94 (Vice-Chair. 1991–94); mem. Canadian Broadcast Standards Council (Ont.) 1990– (Vice-Chair. 1996–99, Chair. 1991–), Nunavut Arbitration Bd 1994–2005, Advisory Council, Grad. School of Journalism, Univ. of Western Ont. 1994–97; Pres. Inst. of Corp. Dirs in Canada 1987–88; Chair. McMaster Univ. Business Advisory Council 1987–88, Employers' Council on Workers' Compensation 1996–98, Employers' Council of Ont. 1998–2000; Pres. and CEO Canadian Council for Native Business 1989–91; Conflict of Interest Commr, Territory of Nunavut 2000–01, Integrity Commr of Nunavut 2001–; mem. Law Soc. of Upper Canada, Canadian Council of Admin. Tribunals, Int. Comm. of Jurists, UNA in Canada; Fellow, Inst. of Dirs 1985–; Canadian Centennial Medal 1967, Queen's Silver Jubilee Medal 1977, Confederation Medal 1993, Meredith Medal 1994, Queen's Golden Jubilee Medal 2002. *Address:* 607 Edgewater Crescent, Burlington, ON L7T 3L8, Canada (home). *Telephone:* (905) 637-6576 (office); (905) 632-9394 (home). *Fax:* (905) 637-6576 (office). *E-mail:* rstanbury@assembly.nu.ca (office); robert.stanbury@sympatico.ca (home). *Website:* www.integritycom.nu.ca (office).

STANCLIFFE, Rt Rev. David Staffurth, MA, DD, FRSCM; British ecclesiastic; *Bishop of Salisbury;* b. 1 Oct. 1942, Devizes, Wilts.; s. of the late Very Rev. Michael Stancliffe and Barbara Tatlow; m. Sarah Smith 1965; one s. two d.; ed Westminster School, Trinity Coll. Oxford and Cuddesdon Theological Coll.; ordained deacon 1967, priest 1968; Asst Curate, St Bartholomew's, Armley, Leeds 1967–70; Chaplain, Clifton Coll. Bristol 1970–77; Canon Residentiary, Portsmouth Cathedral 1977–82, also Dir of Ordinands and Lay Ministry Adviser, Diocese of Portsmouth 1977–82; Vicar, St Thomas of Canterbury, Portsmouth and Provost of Portsmouth 1982–93; Bishop of Salisbury 1993–; mem. Gen. Synod 1985–, Liturgical Comm. 1986–2005 (Chair. 1993–2005), Cathedral's Fabric Comm. 1991–; Pres. Council, Marlborough Coll. 1994–; Fellow, Royal School of Church Music; Hon. DLitt (Portsmouth) 1993. *Publications include:* Liturgy for a New Century 1990 (contrib.), The Identity of Anglican Worship 1991, Enriching the Christian Year 1992, Celebrating Common Prayer—Pocket Version 1994, The Sense of the Sacramental 1995, New Soundings 1997 (contrib.), Flagships of the Spirit 1998 (contrib.), The Pilgrim Prayer Book 2003, God's Pattern 2003. *Leisure interests:* old music, travel, Italy. *Address:* South Canonry, 71 The Close, Salisbury, Wilts., SP1 2ER, England. *Telephone:* (1722) 334031. *Fax:* (1722) 413112 (office). *E-mail:* dsarum@salisbury.anglican.org (office). *Website:* www.salisbury.anglican.org (office).

STANCZYK, Janusz, PhD; Polish diplomatist; *Ambassador to the Netherlands;* m.; two c.; ed Jagiellonian Univ., Kraków, Saint Louis Univ. and Univ. of Michigan, USA, Inst. of Legal Sciences, Polish Acad. of Sciences; Dir Legal and Treaties Dept, Foreign Ministry, Poland 1992–95, Dir Gen. for Legal Affairs 1995–97, Under-Sec. of State for Legal and Econ. Affairs and for relations with int. orgs (also responsible for ministry contact with nat. parl.) 1997–2000; mem. Del. UN Gen. Ass. 1992–96, 1998–2000; Perm. Rep. to UN, New York 2000–04; Deputy Minister for Foreign Affairs and Under-Secretary of State 2004–07; Amb. to Netherlands 2007–, also Perm. Rep. to Org. for the Prohibition of Chemical Weapons. *Address:* Embassy of Poland, Alexanderstraat 25, 2514 JM, The Hague, Netherlands (office). *Telephone:* (70) 7990100 (office). *Fax:* (70) 7990137 (office). *E-mail:* ambhaga@polamb.nl (office); opcw@polamb.nl (office). *Website:* www.polamb.nl (office).

STANDLEY, John T., BS; American business executive; *President and COO, Rite Aid Corporation;* m.; two c.; ed Pepperdine Univ.; fmr Sr Vice-Pres. Smith's Food and Drug, Salt Lake City; fmr CFO Smitty's Supervalu Inc., Phoenix; Sr Vice-Pres. and CFO Ralphs Grocery Co. 1996–98; Sr Vice-Pres. Fred Meyer, Inc. Inc., Portland, Ore. 1998–99; Exec. Vice-Pres. and CFO Fleming Co., Inc., Oklahoma City May–Dec. 1999; joined Rite Aid Corpn 1999, Sr Exec. Vice-Pres. and Chief Admin. Officer 2002, Chief Financial Officer 2003–05, Pres. and COO Rite Aid Corpn 2008–; CEO Pathmark Stores 2005–07. *Address:* Rite Aid Corpn, PO Box 3165, Harrisburg, PA 17105 (office); Rite Aid Corpn, 30 Hunter Lane, Camp Hill, PA 17011, USA (office). *Telephone:* (717) 761-2633 (office). *Fax:* (717) 975-5871 (office). *E-mail:* contacttheboard@riteaid.com (office). *Website:* www.riteaid.com (office).

STANISHEV, Sergey, PhD; Bulgarian politician; *Prime Minister;* b. 5 May 1966, Kherson, Ukraine; s. of Dimitar Stanishev; ed Moscow State Univ., Moscow School for Political Studies, LSE; freelance journalist 1994–95; staff member Foreign Affairs Dept Bulgarian Socialist Party (BSP) 1995, Chief Foreign Policy and Int. Relations Dept 1996–2001, elected mem. BSP Supreme Council (Chair. 2001–) and mem. Exec. Bureau 2000; mem. Bulgarian Nat. Ass. (for Rousse) 2001–, Prime Minister Aug. 2005–; mem. of the presidency of Party of European Socialists 2004–. *Publications:* more than 50 publs on foreign policy issues. *Address:* Office of the Council of Ministers, 1194 Sofia, bul. Dondukov 1 (office); Bulgarian Socialist Party (Bulgarska Sotsialisticheska Partiya), 1000 Sofia, ul. Positano 20, Bulgaria (office). *Telephone:* (2) 940-27-70 (office). *Fax:* (2) 980-20-56 (office). *E-mail:* gis@government.bg (office); info@bsp.bg (office). *Website:* www.government.bg (office); www.bsg.bg (office).

STANISLAUS, Lamuel A., CBE, BSc, DDS; Grenadian/American diplomatist (retd) and oral surgeon; b. 22 April 1921, Petite Martinique; s. of Nathaniel Stanislaus and Margaret Belmar; m. Beryl R. Staniislaus; five c.; ed Howard Univ., USA; asst teacher, Petite Martinique RC School and St Patrick's RC School 1939–41; statistical clerk, Harbour and Wharves Dept, Port-of-Spain, Trinidad 1941–45; est. dental practice in New York 1956, now retd; Perm. Rep. to UN, New York 1985–90, 1998–2004; Founding mem. Grenada Nat. Party; mem. New Nat. Party, Mayor of New York's Advisory Council; mem. Bd of Advisers, Millennium Devt Goals Global Watch; Hon. Bd mem. and Advisor, West Indian-American Day Carnival Asscn; Hon. DHumLitt (Univ. of St George's); Brooklyn Historical Soc. Award, District Attorney's Man of the Year

Award, American Foundation of the Univ. of the West Indies Luminary Award, Trey Whitfield Award 2008. *Leisure interests:* swimming, public speaking, reading, writing. *Address:* 189 Montague Street, Suite 800D, Brooklyn, New York, NY 11225 (office); 22 Rutland Road, Brooklyn, New York, NY 11225-5313, USA (home). *Telephone:* (718) 857-6639 (office); (718) 282-9150 (home). *E-mail:* estanislausdds@msn.com (office).

STĂNIŞOARĂ, Mihai; Romanian engineer and politician; *Minister of Defence;* b. 11 June 1962, Craiova, Dolj co.; m.; two c.; ed Polytechnic Inst. of Timisoara, Nat. Defence Coll., Higher Coll. of Nat. Security, NATO Defence Coll., Rome; worked as engineer at measurement and control devices factory 1986–89; Asst. Tech. Univ. of Timisoara 1988–90; design engineer, Centre of Appliances Research and Technological Eng 1989–90; Sec. Gen., Chamber of Commerce and Industry, Mehedinti co. 1992–94, Chair. 1994–96; Sec. Gen. Ministry of Defence 2000; mem. Chamber of Deputys 2000– (Democratic Party 2000–08, Democratic Liberal Party 2008–), Pres. Parl. Del. to OSCE Parl. Ass. 2000–04, mem. Foreign Policy Cttee 2000–04, Chair. Defence, Public Order and Nat. Security Cttee 2004–07; Vice-Pres. Parl. Del. to NATO Parl. Ass. 2004–07; Presidential adviser on Nat. Security 2007–08; Minister of Defence 2008–; mem. Democratic Liberal Party (DLP). *Address:* Ministry of Defence, 050561 Bucharest 5, Str. Izvor 3–5, Sector 5, Romania (office). *Telephone:* (21) 4023400 (office). *Fax:* (21) 3195698 (office). *E-mail:* drp@mapn.ro (office). *Website:* www.mapn.ro (office).

STANKEVIČIUS, Česlovas Vytautas; Lithuanian politician, engineer and diplomatist; *Adviser to the Minister of Foreign Affairs;* b. 27 Feb. 1937, Vilkaviskis Region; s. of Jonas Stankevičius and Uršulė Dubickaitė; m. Jadvyga Litvinaitė 1962; two s.; ed Kaunas Polytech. Inst.; engineer, Chief of Design, Chief Engineer, Kaunas Inst. of Urban Planning and Designing 1965–89; Chair. Kaunas Bd Sajūdis Movt 1989–90; elected Deputy and Vice-Pres. of Supreme Council, Repub. of Lithuania; signatory to March 11th Act on Re-establishment of Independence; Head official del. in negotiations with Russia 1990–93; Head, Lithuanian Parl. del. to N Atlantic Ass. 1991–92; mem. Seimas, Parl. Group of Christian Democrats 1996–2000; Minister of Defence 1996–2000; Amb. to Norway 2001–05; Adviser to the Minister of Foreign Affairs 2005–; co-author projects on nat. security and defence concept of Lithuania 1996, Law on Defence Org. 1997, Lithuanian defence strategy 2000; Order of Gediminas 2000. *Publications:* Enhancing Security of Lithuania and Other Baltic States in 1992–94 (monograph), Negotiations with Russia on Troop Withdrawal 2002. *Leisure interests:* literature, the arts. *Address:* Ministry of Foreign Affairs, J. Tumo-Vaizganto 9.2, 01511 Vilnius, Lithuania (office). *Telephone:* (5) 2362861 (office). *Fax:* (5) 2362405 (office). *E-mail:* ceslovas.stankevicius@urm.lt (office); cestan@takas.lt (home). *Website:* www.urm.lt (office).

STANKOVIĆ, Zoran, BA MA PhD; Serbian pathologist and politician; b. 9 Nov. 1954, Tegoviste, Vladicin Han Municipality; m.; two c.; ed Univ. of Niš, Mil. Medical Acad.; head of garrison first aid station, Peč 1982–85; commissioned Medical Corps Lt 1983; specialized training 1985–88; Forensic Assessor 1987; pathologist 1988–90, Head of Tissue Culture Dept 1990–96, Pathology and Forensic Medicine Inst., Mil. Medical Acad.; extraordinarily commissioned Maj. 1991; mem. Vukovar Ad Hoc Group, ICRC 1992–93; extraordinarily commissioned Lt-Col 1993; mem. Comm. Expert on Tracing Missing Persons of Republika Srpska Govt 1994; Prof., Faculty of Medicine, Banja Luka 1994–95; Visiting Prof. King's Coll., Cambridge 1995–; Prof. of Criminological Medicine, Belgrade Police Acad. 1996–; Head of Forensic Medicine Inst., Pathology and Forensic Medicine Inst. 1996–2001; commissioned Col 1997; Expert Officer, Comm. on Humanitarian Issues and Missing Persons of Fed. Repub. of Yugoslavia Govt 1997–; Expert Witness, The Hague Tribunal 1998–; extraordinarily commissioned Maj.-Gen. 2001 (retd in rank, 2005); Head of Pathology and Forensic Medicine Inst., Mil. Medical Acad. 2001–02; Pres. of the Cttee on Data Collection on Crimes Against Humanity and Int. Law of Fed. Repub. of Yugoslavia Govt 2002–03; mem. of Truth Comm. 2002; Head of Mil. Medical Acad. 2002–05; Minister of Defence 2005–06; Mil. Merits Medal 1988, "Bela Povelja" Award, Serbian Asscn of Doctors 1993, Public Health Service Org. Annual Award 1993, Cvijiceva Medal 1999. *Publications:* author or coauthor of over 40 scientific papers. *Address:* c/o Ministry of Defence, 11000 Belgrade, Birčaninova 5, Serbia (office).

STANLEY, Eric Gerald, MA, PhD, FBA; British academic; *Professor Emeritus, University of Oxford;* b. 19 Oct. 1923; m. Mary Bateman, MD, FRCP 1959; one d.; ed Queen Elizabeth's Grammar School, Blackburn, Univ. Coll., Oxford; Lecturer in English Language and Literature, Univ. of Birmingham 1951–62; Reader in English Language and Literature, Univ. of London, Queen Mary Coll. 1962–64; Prof. 1964–75; Prof. of English, Yale Univ. 1975–76; Rawlinson and Bosworth Prof. of Anglo-Saxon, Univ. of Oxford and Fellow Pembroke Coll. Oxford 1977–91, Prof. Emer. 1991–; mem. Mediaeval Acad. of America 1975–; Corresp. mem. Fryske Akad. 1991–, Bavarian Acad. of Sciences 1994–; Sir Israel Gollancz Memorial Lecturer, The British Acad. 1984; Hon. DSLitt (Trinity Coll., Toronto) 2008, Hon. LLD (Toronto) 2008. *Publications:* books and academic articles, some of them in A Collection of Papers with Emphasis on Old English Literature 1987, In the Foreground: Beowulf 1994, Die angelsächsische Rechtspflege und wie man sie später aufgefasst hat 1999, Imagining the Anglo-Saxon Past 2000. *Leisure interest:* travel. *Address:* Pembroke College, Oxford, OX1 1DW, England.

STANNARD, Robert William, CMG, BCom (NZ); New Zealand business executive; b. 16 Sept. 1926, Gisborne; s. of William C. Stannard and Clara Stannard; m. Shirley M. Sparkes 1956; one s. (deceased), two d.; ed Horowhenua Coll., Levin and Victoria Univ., Wellington; J. L. Arcus & Sons (chartered accountants), Wellington 1944–49; Peat, Marwick, Mitchell & Co. (chartered accountants), London and Singapore 1949–53; Pnr, Bowden, Bass

& Cox (now KPMG), Wellington 1954–87; Statutory Man., Cornish Group 1974–90, Public Service Investment Soc. 1979–87; mem. Nat. Parks Centennial Comm. 1983–88; Chair., Databank Systems Ltd 1985–93, NZ Fishing Industry Bd 1988–93, Nat. Australia Bank (NZ) Ltd 1991–92, Overseas Investment Comm. 1978–97, Milburn NZ Ltd 1987–97, Trustees Executors 1991–2000, Bank of NZ 1993–96; Dir, Fiordland Travel Ltd 1973–97, Tower Trust Ltd (Local Bd) 1991–2002, Commercial Fisheries Services Ltd 1998–2003, Tower Safe Ltd 1999–2002; Distinguished Fellow, NZ Inst. of Dirs 2000; Rotary Paul Harris Fellow 1998; Trustee, Chatham Islands Enterprise Trust 1991–94; NZ 1990 Medal. *Leisure interests:* lawn bowls, mountain tramping, travel. *Address:* 36, Spencer Street, Crofton Downs, Wellington 6035, New Zealand (home). *Telephone:* (4) 479-3057 (home).

STANSFIELD SMITH, Sir Colin, Kt, CBE, MA, DipArch, ARIBA; British architect and academic; *Professor Emeritus of Architectural Design, University of Portsmouth;* b. 1 Oct. 1932, Manchester; s. of Stansfield Smith and Mary Simpson; m. Angela Jean Earnshaw 1961; one s. one d.; ed William Hulmes Grammar School, Manchester and Univ. of Cambridge School of Architecture; London Co. Council (Schools Div.) 1958–60; Sr Asst then Assoc. Partner, Emberton Frank & Tardrew (architects) 1960–65; Pnr, Emberton Tardrew & Pnrs 1965–71; Deputy Co. Architect, Cheshire Co. Council 1971–73; Co. Architect, Hampshire Co. Council 1973–92, Consultant Co. Architect 1992–2000; Prof. of Architectural Design Studies, Portsmouth Univ. (fmrly Polytechnic) School of Architecture 1990–, now Prof. Emer.; RIBA Gold Medal 1991. *Publications:* Hampshire Architecture 1974–84 1985, Schools of Thought, Hampshire Architecture 1974–91; articles in Architects' Journal and Architectural Review. *Leisure interests:* golf, painting. *Address:* 8 Christchurch Road, Winchester, Hants., SO23 9SR, England (home). *Telephone:* (1962) 851970 (home). *Website:* www.port.ac.uk/departments/academic/architecture (office).

STANZEL, Franz-Karl, DrPhil; Austrian academic; *Professor Emeritus of English, Karl-Franzens-Universität Graz;* b. 4 Aug. 1923, Molln; s. of Franz Stanzel and Luise Stanzel; m. Ina v. Navarini 1992; one d.; ed Univ. of Graz and Harvard Univ., USA; Lecturer in English, Univ. of Graz 1949–50, 1951–57; Asst Prof., Univ. of Göttingen 1957–59; Prof., Univ. of Erlangen 1959–62; Prof. of English, Univ. of Graz 1962–93, Prof. Emer. 1993–, Dean, Faculty of Arts and Sciences 1967–68, Head, Dept of English 1962–78; mem. Austrian Acad.; Dr hc (Fribourg). *Publications include:* Typische Erzählsituationen im Roman 1955, Typische Formen des Romans 1964, Narrative Situations in the Novel 1969, Der literarische Aspekt unserer Vorstellungen vom Charakter fremder Völker 1974, Theorie des Erzählens 1979, A Theory of Narrative 1984, Englische und deutsche Kriegsdichtung, Sprachkunst 1987, Intimate Enemies (ed.) 1993, Europäer: Ein imagologischer Essay 1997, Europäischer Völkerspiegel (ed.) 1999, Unterwegs Erzähltheorie für Leser 2002. *Leisure interests:* cross-country skiing, gardening, travel. *Address:* Karl-Franzens-Universität Graz, Universitäts-platz 3, 8010 Graz (office); 511 Institut für Anglistik, Heinrichstrasse 36/II, 8010 Graz; Am Blumenhang 31/5, 8010 Graz, Austria (home). *Telephone:* (316) 380-2476 (office); (316) 47-55-56 (home). *Fax:* (316) 47-55-56 (home). *E-mail:* franzkarl.stanzel@kfunigraz.ac.at (office); franzkarl.stanzel@uni-graz.at (office). *Website:* www-gewi.uni-graz.at (office).

STANZEL, Volker, PhD; German diplomatist; *Political Director, Ministry of Foreign Affairs;* b. 1948, Frankfurt; ed Frankfurt Univ., Kyoto Univ., Cologne Univ.; joined Foreign Service 1979, worked in Embassies in Rome, Tokyo, Aden, Beijing; Head of Press and Information Dept, Embassy in Beijing 1990–93; Head of Operation Center, Foreign Office in Bonn 1993–95, Head of Dept for Non-Proliferation and Civilian Use of Nuclear Energy 1999–2001; Foreign Policy Advisor to SPD, Bundestag 1995–98; Visiting Fellow, German Marshall Fund, Washington, DC 1998–99; Dir for Asian and Pacific Affairs, Ministry of Foreign Affairs 2001–02; Dir-Gen. for Political Affairs 2002–04; Amb. to People's Repub. of China 2004–07; Political Dir Ministry of Foreign Affairs 2007–; Hon. Prof. (Zhengzhou Univ.) 2006. *Publications:* Japan: Head of the Earth 1982, Winds of Change: East Asia's New Revolution 1997, A World of Warring States: China's Perception and Possibilities of Its International Role 1997, NATO after Enlargement 1998, Dealing with the Backwoods: New Problems in Transatlantic Relations 1999, Remembering and Forgetting: But Will the Past Forget About Us? 2001, China's Foreign Policy 2001, Germany's Defense at the Hindukush: The Experiment of Afghanistan 2005. *Address:* Federal Ministry of Foreign Affairs, Werderscher Markt 1, 10020 Berlin Germany (office). *Telephone:* (30) 50002677 (office). *Fax:* (30) 500052677 (office). *E-mail:* z-d@diplo.de (office). *Website:* www.diplo.de (office).

STAPLE, George Warren, CB, QC; British lawyer; *Consultant, Clifford Chance LLP;* b. 13 Sept. 1940, Bristol; s. of Kenneth Staple and Betty Staple; m. Olivia Lowry 1968; two s. two d.; ed Haileybury; qualified as solicitor 1963; Assoc., Condon & Forsyth, New York 1963; Pnr, Clifford-Turner, later Clifford Chance 1967–92, 1997–2001, consultant to Clifford Chance LLP 2001–; Dir, Serious Fraud Office 1992–97; Legal Assessor, Disciplinary Cttee Stock Exchange 1978–92; Dept of Trade & Industry Insp., Consolidated Goldfields 1986, Aldermanbury Trust 1988; a Chair., Authorization and Disciplinary Tribunals of Securities Asscn 1987–91, Securities and Futures Authority 1991–92; mem. Commercial Court Cttee 1977–92; mem. Council, Law Soc. 1986–2000; mem. Law Advisory Cttee of British Council 1998–2001; mem. Sr Salaries Review Body 2000–04; Chair., Review Bd for Govt Contracts 2002–; Chair. Govs, Haileybury 2000–08; mem. Accountancy and Actuarial Disciplinary Tribunal; Gov., London Guildhall Univ. 1982–94; Fellow, Chartered Inst. of Arbitrators 1986, Soc. for Advanced Legal Studies 1997; Trustee, Royal Humane Soc. 2007–; Hon. Bencher, Inner Temple 2000. *Leisure interests:* cricket, hill walking, gardening. *Address:* Clifford Chance, 10 Upper Bank Street, London, E14 5JJ, England. *Telephone:* (20) 7006-1000. *Fax:* (20) 7006-5555. *Website:* www.cliffordchance.com (office).

STAPLETON, Nigel John, MA; British business executive and government regulator; *Chairman, Postal Services Commission;* b. 1 Nov. 1946, London; s. of Frederick E J. Stapleton and Katie M. Tyson; m. Johanna Molhoek 1982; one s. one d.; ed Univ. of Cambridge; internal auditor, Unilever Ltd 1968–70; Group Man. Internal Audit, Unilever Ltd 1970–73, Sr Auditor 1973–75; Corp. Planning Man. BOCM Silcock 1975–77, Devt Dir 1977–80; Commercial mem. N American office, Unilever PLC 1980–83; Vice-Pres. Finance, Unilever US Inc. 1983–86; Finance Dir Reed Int. PLC, London 1986–96, Deputy Chair. 1994–97, Chair. 1997–99, CEO 1999; Chair. Uniq PLC 2001–07; Deputy Chair., Chief Financial Officer, Reed Elsevier 1994–97, Co-Chair. 1996–98; Chair. Veronis, Suhler Int. Ltd 1999–2002; Dir (non-exec.) GEC 1997–99, Marconi PLC 1999, Axa UK PLC 2000–02, London Stock Exchange PLC 2001–, Reliance Security PLC 2002–; Chair. (non-exec.) Cordiant 2003; Chair. Postal Services Comm. 2004–; Fellow, Chartered Inst. of Man. Accountants; Liveryman of the Worshipful Company of Stationers and Newspaper Makers; Hon. Fellow, Fitzwilliam Coll., Univ. of Cambridge 1997; Freedom of the City of London 1999. *Leisure interests:* gardening, classical music, opera, food and wine. *Address:* Postal Services Commission, 6 Hercules Road, London, SE1 7DB, England (office). *Telephone:* (20) 7593-2102 (office). *Fax:* (20) 7593-2142 (office). *E-mail:* nigel.stapleton@psc.gov.uk (office); nigel.stapleton@btinternet.com (home). *Website:* www.psc.gov.uk (office).

STARCK, Christian, DrIur; German legal scholar, academic and judge; *Judge, Constitutional Court of Lower Saxony;* b. 9 Jan. 1937, Breslau; s. of Walter Starck and Ruth Hubrich; m. Brigitte Edelmann 1965; one s. two d.; ed Univs of Kiel, Freiburg and Würzburg; clerk, Fed. Constitutional Court 1964–67; Govt official 1968–69; Lecturer, Univ. of Würzburg 1969–71; Prof. of Public Law, Univ. of Göttingen 1971–; Rector Univ. of Göttingen 1976–77; Judge, Constitutional Court of Lower Saxony 1991–; Ed. Studien und Materialen zur Verfassungsgerichtsbarkeit 1973–; co-Ed. Juristenzeitung 1978–, Staatswissenschaften und Staatspraxis 1990–98, Beiträge zum ausländischen und vergleichenden öffentlichen Recht 1989–, Zeitschrift für Staats- und Europawissenschaften 2003–05; mem. TV Bd Zweites Deutsches Fernsehen 1978–92; mem. Asscn of German Profs of Public Law 1969– (Exec. Cttee 1988, 1989, Pres. 1998, 1999), Exec. Cttee Int. Asscn of Constitutional Law 1981–2004, Exec. Cttee German Asscn of Comparative Law 1985–; Pres. Societas Juris Europaei 2003–; Visiting Prof., Paris I (Panthéon-Sorbonne) 1987; mem. Acad. of Sciences of Göttingen 1982–; Fellow Inst. for Advanced Study, Berlin 1990–91; Hon. Pres. Int. Asscn of Constitutional Law 2004. *Publications include:* Der Gesetzesbegriff des Grundgesetzes 1970, Rundfunkfreiheit als Organisationsproblem 1973, Das Bundesverfassungsgericht im politischen Prozess 1976; Bundesverfassungsgericht und Grundgesetz (two vols) (ed.) 1976, Vom Grund des Grundgesetzes 1979, El Concepto de Ley en la Constitución Alemana 1979, La Constitution, cadre et mesure du droit 1994, Praxis der Verfassungsauslegung 1994, Die Verfassungen der neuen deutschen Länder 1994, Der demokratische Verfassungsstaat 1995, Constitutionalism, Universalism and Democracy – A Comparative Analysis (ed.) 1999, Grundgesetz Kommentar, 5th edn, Vol. I–III 2005, Vol. II 2000, Vol. III 2001, Freiheit und Institutionen 2002. *Leisure interests:* architecture, literature, walking. *Address:* Platz der Göttinger Sieben 6, 37073 Göttingen (office); Schlegelweg 10, 37075 Göttingen, Germany (home). *Telephone:* (551) 397412 (office). *Fax:* (551) 4882891 (home). *E-mail:* cstarck@gdwg.de (office). *Website:* www.jura.uni-goettingen.de/privat/c.starck.

STARCK, Philippe-Patrick; French designer; b. 18 Jan. 1949, Paris; s. of André Starck and Jacqueline Lanourisse; m. 1st Brigitte Laurent 1977 (deceased); two c.; m. 2nd Nori Vaccari-Starck; ed Inst. Notre-Dame de Sainte-Croix, Neuilly-sur-Seine, Ecole Nissim de Camondo, Paris; f. Starck Products 1979; Interior architecture: La Main-Bleue 1976, Les Bains-Douches 1978, pvt. apartments in Elysée Palace 1982, Le Café Costes 1984, La Cigale, Paris 1987, restaurants, housing and offices in Tokyo 1986–88, Royalton Hotel, New York 1988, Paramount Hotel, New York 1990, Teatriz Restaurant, Madrid 1990, Groningen Museum 1994, Peninsula Restaurant, Hong Kong 1994, Delano Hotel, Miami 1995, Theatron Restaurant, Mexico 1995, Mondrian Hotel, LA 1996, Asia de Cuba Restaurant, New York 1997, St Martin's Hotel, London 1999, Mikli glasses shop, Paris 1999, Restaurant BON, Paris 2000, Sanderson Hotel, London 2000, Hudson Hotel, New York 2000, Clift Hotel, San Francisco 2001, Miramar Hotel, Santa Barbara (in progress); architecture includes knife factory, Laguiole 1988, Nani Nani Bldg, Tokyo 1989, bldgs in USA, Japan, France, Spain, Ecole Nat. des Arts Décoratifs, Paris 1995, air traffic control tower for Bordeaux Airport 1997, incineration plant, Paris/Vitry (2004); cr. furniture for Pres. of the Repub. 1982, for French, Italian, Spanish, Japanese and Swiss cos; designed boats for Bénéteau, vases for Daum, luggage for Vuitton, toothbrush for Fluocaril, urban furniture for Jean-Claude Decaux, Olympic Flame 1992, children's toys, Aprilia scooters, etc.; Worldwide Artistic Dir Thomson Consumer Electronics Group 1993–96; Artistic Dir Eurostar train 2001; Prof., Domus Acad., Milan, Italy, Ecole des Arts Décoratifs de Paris; Artistic Dir Int. Design Yearbook; exhbns at Georges Pompidou Museum and Decorative Arts Museum, Paris, Villa Medici, Italy, Deutsches Museum, Munich, Kunstmuseum, Düsseldorf, Museum of Modern Art, Kyoto, Japan, Design Museum, London and in Switzerland and USA; Vanity Case Exhbn travelling around the world; Commdr des Arts et des Lettres 1998, Chevalier Légion d'honneur 2000; numerous prizes, including Oscar du Luminaire 1980, three 1st prizes at Neocon, Chicago 1986, Delta de Plata, Barcelona 1986, Platinum Circle Award, Chicago 1987, Grand prix nat. de la Création Industrielle 1988; three awards for hotels in USA 1990, 1991, one for Hotel Paramount 1992, Disseny Barcelona 1995, Design-Zentrum Nordrhein Westfalen Award (Germany) for Duraint bathroom design 1995, Harvard Excellence in Design Award 1997, Prath Inst. Black Alumni Award

2001. *Leisure interest:* sailing. *Address:* Ubik, 18/20 rue de Faubourg du Temple, 75011 Paris; Starck-Ubik, 27 rue Pierre Poli, 92130 Issy les Moulineaux, France. *Telephone:* 1-48-07-54-54 (office); 1-41-08-82-82. *Fax:* 1-48-07-54-64 (office); 1-41-08-96-65. *E-mail:* press@starcknetwork.com (home); starck@starckdesign.com (office). *Website:* www.philippe-starck.com (office).

STARFIELD, Barbara, MD, MPH; American physician and academic; *University Distinguished Professor, Bloomberg School of Public Health, Johns Hopkins University;* b. 18 Dec. 1932, New York; d. of Martin Starfield and Eva Starfield (née Illions); m. Neil A. Holtzman 1955; three s. one d.; ed Swarthmore Coll., State Univ. of New York, The Johns Hopkins Univ.; teaching asst (anatomy), Downstate Med. Center, New York 1955–57; intern. and resident in Pediatrics, Johns Hopkins Univ. Hosp. 1959–62, Dir, Pediatric Medical Care Clinic 1963–66; Dir Pediatric Clinical Scholars Program, Johns Hopkins Univ. 1971–76, Asst Prof., Assoc. Prof. 1967–76, Prof. and Div. Head, Health Policy, Johns Hopkins Bloomberg School of Public Health 1976–94, Dir Primary Care Policy Center 1996–, Univ. Distinguished Prof., Johns Hopkins Univ. 1994–; mem. Nat. Advisory Council for Health Care Policy, Research and Evaluation, US Dept of Health and Human Services 1990–93, Nat. Cttee Vital and Health Statistics (USDHHS) 1994–; mem. Inst. of Medicine, NAS; Hon. Fellow, Royal Coll. of Gen. Practitioners (UK) 2000; Dave Luckman Memorial Award 1958, Career Devt Award 1970–75, Armstrong Award, Ambulatory Pediatric Asscn 1983, Annual Research Award, Ambulatory Pediatric Asscn 1990, Pew Primary Care Achievement Award 1994, Martha May Eliot Award (APHA) 1994, Maurice Wood Award for Lifetime Contrib. to Primary Care Research 2000, Lifetime Achievement Award, Ambulatory Pediatric Asscn 2002, Morehouse School of Medicine Excellence in Primary Care Award 2002. *Publications:* Effectiveness of Medical Care 1985, Primary Care: Concept, Evaluation and Policy 1992, Primary Care: Balancing Health Needs, Services and Technology 1998; over 200 scientific articles. *Address:* Johns Hopkins Bloomberg School of Public Health, 624 N Broadway, Baltimore, MD 21205, USA (office). *Telephone:* (410) 955-9725 (home); (410) 955-3737 (office). *Fax:* (410) 614-9046 (office). *E-mail:* bstarfie@jhsph.edu (office). *Website:* www.jhsph.edu/dept/hpm (office).

STARKER, Janos; American cellist and academic; *Distinguished Professor of Cello, School of Music, Indiana University;* b. 5 July 1924, Budapest, Hungary; s. of Margit Starker and Sandor Starker; m. 1st Eva Uranyi 1944 (divorced); one d.; m. 2nd Rae Busch 1960; three d.; ed Franz Liszt Acad. of Music, Budapest; Solo Cellist, Budapest Opera House and Philharmonic Orchestra 1945–46; Solo Cellist, Dallas Symphony Orchestra 1948–49, Metropolitan Opera Orchestra 1949–53, Chicago Symphony Orchestra 1953–58; Resident Cellist, Indiana Univ. 1958–, Prof. of Music 1961, now Distinguished Prof. of Cello; inventor of Starker bridge for orchestral string instruments; worldwide concert tours; Hon. mem. American Fed. of Musicians, Royal Acad. of London 1981, Indiana Acad. of Arts and Sciences, American Acad. of Arts and Sciences; Chevalier Ordre des Arts et Lettres 1997; Hon. DMus (Chicago Conservatory) 1961, (Cornell Coll.) 1978, (East West Univ.) 1982, (Williams Coll.) 1983, (Lawrence Univ.) 1990; Grand Prix du Disque 1948, George Washington Award 1972, Sanford Fellowship Award, Yale 1974, Herzl Award 1978, Ed Press Award 1983, Kodály Commemorative Medallion, New York 1983, Arturo Toscanini Award 1986, Indiana Univ. Tracy Sonneborn Award 1986, Indiana Gov.'s Award 1995, Medal of Paris 1995, Grammy Award 1998, Indiana Univ. Pres.'s Medal for Excellence 1999, Pres. of Hungary's Gold Medal 1999. *Publications:* Method 1964, Bach Suites 1971, Concerto Cadenzas, Schubert-Starker Sonatina, Bottermund-Starker Variations, Beethoven Sonatas, Beethoven Variations, Dvořák Concerto; numerous magazine articles, essays and record cover notes. *Leisure interests:* writing, swimming. *Address:* Colbert Artists, 111 West 57th Street, New York, NY 10019, USA (office); c/o Department of Music, Office MA155, Indiana University, Bloomington, IN 47405-2200, USA (office). *Telephone:* (212) 757-0782 (office). *Fax:* (212) 541-5179 (office). *E-mail:* nycolbert@colbertartists.com (office); starker@indiana.edu (office). *Website:* www.colbertartists.com (office); www.music.indiana.edu (office).

STARKEY, David Robert, CBE, MA, PhD, FSA, FRHistS; British historian, academic and broadcaster; b. 3 Jan. 1945, Kendal; s. of Robert Starkey and Elsie Lyon; ed Kendal Grammar School, Fitzwilliam Coll. Cambridge; Research Fellow, Fitzwilliam Coll. Cambridge 1970–72, Visiting Fellow 1998–2001, Bye-Fellow 2001–06, Hon. Fellow 2006–; Lecturer in History, Dept of Int. History, LSE 1972–98; Visiting Vernon Prof. of Biography, Dartmouth Coll., NH, USA 1987, 1989; British Council Specialist Visitor, Australia 1989; contribs to various newspapers; mem. Editorial Bd History Today 1980–, Commemorative Plaques Working Group, English Heritage 1993–2006; Pres., Soc. for Court Studies 1995–2005; Patron, Tory Group for Homosexual Equality 1994–; Historical Adviser to Henry VIII Exhbn, Nat. Maritime Museum, Greenwich 1991; Guest Curator, Elizabeth I Exhbn, Nat. Maritime Museum 2003, Lost Faces – Identity and Discovery in Tudor Royal Portraiture Exhbn, Philip Mould Gallery 2006, Henry VIII: Man and Monarch Exhbn, British Library 2009; mem. Fitzwilliam Soc. (Pres. 2003–04); Hon. Assoc., Rationalist Press Asscn 1995–; Freeman, Worshipful Co. of Barbers 1992, Liveryman 1999; Hon. DLitt (Lancaster) 2004, (Kent) 2006; Medlicott Medal 2001. *Radio:* panellist, The Moral Maze (BBC Radio 4) 1992–2001, presenter, Talk Radio 1995–98. *Television:* presenter/writer, This Land of England (Channel 4) 1985, Henry VIII (Channel 4) (Indie Documentary Award 2002) 1998, Elizabeth (Channel 4) 2000, The Six Wives of Henry VIII (Channel 4) (New York Festival for int. TV programming and promotion silver medal) 2001, The Unknown Tudors (Channel 4) 2002, Re-Inventing the Royals 2002, Monarchy (Channel 4) 2004–07, Starkey's Last Word (More 4) 2006, Henry VIII: Mind of a Tyrant (Channel 4) 2009. *Publications:* This Land of England (with David Souden) 1985, The Reign of Henry VIII: Personalities and Politics 1985–86, Revolution Reassessed: Revisions in the History of Tudor Government and Administration (ed. with Christopher Coleman) 1986, The English Court from the Wars of the Roses to the Civil War (ed.) 1987, Rivals in Power: the Lives and Letters of the Great Tudor Dynasties (ed.) 1990, Henry VIII: A European Court in England 1991, The Inventory of Henry VIII, Vol. 1 (with Philip Ward) 1998, Elizabeth: Apprenticeship 2000 (WHSmith Award for Biog./Autobiog. 2001), Six Wives: The Queens of Henry VIII 2003, Monarchy: the early kings 2004, The History of England: Jane Austen and Charles Dickens 2006, Monarchy: From the Middles Ages to Modernity 2006, Henry: Virtuous Prince 2008; numerous articles in learned journals. *Leisure interests:* decorating, gardening. *Address:* Fitzwilliam College, Cambridge, CB3 0DG, England (office). *Telephone:* (1223) 332000 (office). *Website:* www.fitz.cam.ac.uk (office).

STARKOV, Vladislav Andreyevich; Russian journalist; *Editor, Argumenty i Fakty;* b. 28 Feb. 1940, Tomsk; s. of Andrei Nikolayevich Starkov and Maria Mikhailovna Starkova; m. Yulia Fedorovna Kuznetsova; one d.; ed Rostov State Univ.; researcher and computer engineer, USSR Meteorology Centre 1962–73; corresp. Radio Moscow 1973–76; Znaniye Publishing House 1976–79; Ed. Mezhdunarodnye Otnosheniya (journal) 1979–80; Ed.-in-Chief Argumenty i Fakty (weekly) 1980–, Ed. Argumenty i Fakty (weekly newspaper) 1995–; RSFSR People's Deputy 1990–93. *Leisure interests:* reading fiction, swimming. *Address:* AiF, Myasnitskaya str. 42, 101000 Moscow, Russia. *Telephone:* (495) 921-02-34 (office). *Fax:* (495) 925-61-82 (office). *E-mail:* into@aif.ru (office). *Website:* www.aif.ru (office).

STAROBINSKI, Jean, PhD, MD; Swiss academic and writer; b. 17 Nov. 1920, Geneva; s. of Aron Starobinski and Szayndla Frydman; m. Jaqueline H. Sirman 1954; three s.; ed Univs of Geneva and Lausanne; Asst Prof. Johns Hopkins Univ. 1953–56, Prof. of French Literature, History of Ideas 1958–85; Pres. Rencontres Int. de Geneva 1965–; mem. Acad. Lincei, British Acad., American Acad. of Arts and Sciences, Deutsche Akad.; Assoc. mem. Acad. des Sciences Morales et Politiques (France), Acad. Royale de Belgique; Soc. of Fellows, Johns Hopkins Univ.; Officier, Légion d'honneur 1980; hon. degrees from Univs of Lille 1973, Brussels, Lausanne 1979, Chicago 1986, Columbia (New York) 1987, Montréal 1988, Strasbourg 1988, Neuchâtel 1990, Nantes 1992, Oslo 1994, Turin 1994, Urbino 1995, Cluj 1995, ETH, Zürich 1998; Prix Européen de L'Essai 1983, Balzan Prize 1984, Monaco Prize 1988, Goethe Prize 1994. *Publications:* Jean Jacques Rousseau: la transparence et l'obstacle 1957, The Invention of Liberty (in trans.) 1964, La Relation critique 1970, Words upon Words (in trans.) 1971, 1789: Les Emblemes de la raison 1973, Montaigne en mouvement 1983, Le Remède dans le mal 1989, La Mélancolie au miroir 1989, Largesse 1994, Action et Réaction 1999, Les Enchanteresses 2005; contrib. to newspapers and journals. *Leisure interest:* music. *Address:* 51 avenue de Champel, 1206 Geneva, Switzerland (home). *Telephone:* (22) 3209864 (home).

STARODUBOV, Vladimir Ivanovich; Russian politician and surgeon; *Deputy Minister of Health and Social Development;* b. 17 May 1950, Kosobrodsk, Kurgan Region; m.; two d.; ed Sverdlovsk State Medical Inst.; surgeon, Head, Surgery Dept, Nizhny Tagil Hosp., Sverdlovsk Region 1973–77; Asst, Chair of Surgery, Sverdlovsk State Inst. of Medicine 1977–80; Chief, Sverdlovsk town clinic 1980–81; instructor, Sverdlovsk Regional CP Cttee 1981–87; Deputy Head, Sverdlovsk Regional Dept of Public Health 1987–88; First Deputy Head, Main Dept of Public Health, Sverdlovsk, Regional Soviet 1988–89; Head, Main Dept of Treatment and Prophylactics, Ministry of Public Health RSFSR 1989–90; Deputy Minister of Public Health Russian Fed. 1990–94; Head, Prof., Chair of Econs of Man., Russian Medical Univ. 1994–96; Deputy Minister of Public Health and Medical Industry 1996–98, Minister of Public Health 1998–99; Rep. of the Russian Fed. to WHO 1999–2001, 2004; Deputy Minister of Health and Social Devt 2005–, (acting Minister of Health and Social Devt 2007); Prof., Russian State Medical Univ. 1999–, Dir Cen. Public Health Research Inst. 1999–2004; Ed. Physician and Information Technology, Health Care Manager 2003–; mem. Russian Acad. Medical Sciences 2004; Honored Physician, Russian Federation 1999. *Publications:* articles: Methodological basics and mechanisms for health care quality assurance, (with O. Shchepin, A. Lindenbraten, G. Galanova) Moscow Medicine 2002, Clinical Management: theory and practice (with T. Lugovkina) 2003, Epidermilogy of tuberculosis (with I. Son, V. Litvinov, P. Seltsovsky) 2003, Health of Russian Population in social context of 1990s: problems and perspectives (ed with Y. Mikhailova, A. Ivanova) 2003; more than 250 publications. *Address:* Ministry of Health and Social Development 127994 Moscow, Rakhmanovskii per. 3/25 (office); 117587 Moscow, 9 Kirovogradskaya str., block 2 Apartment 169, Russia (home). *Telephone:* (495) 927-28-48 (office); (495) 315-39-26 (home). *Fax:* (495) 928-58-15 (office). *Website:* www.mzsrrf.ru (office).

STARODUBTSEV, Vasily Aleksandrovich, PhD; Russian politician; b. 25 Dec. 1931, Volovchik, Lipetsk Region; one s. one d.; ed Nat. Agric. Inst. of the USSR; machinist of mining machines 1955–64; Chair. Lenin Kolkhoz 1964–97; Chair. Council of Kolkhozes of the Russian Fed. 1986; USSR People's Deputy 1989–91; Chair. Agrarian Union of Russia 1990; Chair. Peasants' Union of the USSR 1990; mem. Cen. Cttee Communist Party of the Soviet Union 1990–91; mem. State Cttee for Nat. Emergency; Bd Agric. Party 1993; Gov. of Tula Region 1997–2005; mem. Council of Fed. 1997–2001; mem. Cen. Cttee of the CP of the Russian Fed. 1997; mem. Presidium of the Coordination Council of the Popular Patriotic Union; mem. Int. Acad. of Information Process and Technologies; Corresp. mem. Acad. of Agric. Sciences; Order of the Sign of Honour 1965, Order of October Revolution 1971, Order of Lenin 1973, 1976, 1980, Hero of Socialist Labour 1976, USSR State Prize 1979, Appreciation of Pres. of Russian Fed. 2001, Diploma of Honour, Govt of Russian Fed. 2001. *Publications:* more than 50 scientific works. *Leisure interest:* chess. *Address:* c/o 300600 Tula, pl. Lenina 2, Russia.

STAROSTENKO, Vladimir Ivanovich; Russian government official; *Director, Moscow Railway;* b. 2 Sept. 1948, Tatarsk, Novosibirsk Region; m.; one s.; ed Tomsk Higher School of Railway Transport, Novosibirsk Inst. of Railway Eng; mem. of station staff, Tatarskaya W Siberian railway 1966–79, Station Man. 1970–75, inspector, Omsk Div. 1975–80, Station Man. Karbyshevo 1980–83, Head of Div. of Cargo, then Head of Div. of Transportation, Omsk Div. 1983–88, First Deputy Head of Omsk Div. 1988–90, Head of Novosibirsk Div. 1990–95, Deputy Head of West Siberian Railway 1995–96, Head 1997–99, Sept. 1999; Head of Kemerovo Railway 1996–97; Minister of Railways May–Sept. 1999; currently Dir Moscow Railway. *Address:* Moscow Railway, 107996 Moscow, 20 Krasnoprudnaya ul., Russia (office). *Telephone:* (495) 266-20-50 (office). *Fax:* (495) 264-51-77 (office). *E-mail:* press@mzd.ru (office). *Website:* www.mzd.ru (office).

STAROVOITOV, Gen. Aleksander Vladimirovich, DTechSc; Russian communications engineer; b. 18 Oct. 1940, Balashov, Saratov Region; m.; one s.; ed Penza Polytech. Inst., Higher Courses of Gen. Staff; numerous positions at Penza Research Electrotechnical Inst. 1962–86, including engineer, deputy head of workshop, sr engineer, head of lab., head of div., Prof., Deputy Dir, Dir-Gen., Kristall, Dir; Deputy Head, Dept of Govt Telecommunications 1986–91; Chair. Cttee on Govt Telecommunications of Pres. Gorbachev 1991; Dir-Gen. Fed. Agency of Govt Telecommunications and Information (FAPSI) 1991–98; Chair. Co-ordination Council of CIS on Security of System of Govt Telecommunications; Constructor-Gen. of Integrated State System of Confidential Telecommunications of Russia; mem. Vice-Pres. Acad. of Eng Sciences; mem. Vice-Pres. Acad. of Electrotechnical Sciences; mem. Acad. of Cryptography. *Publications:* over 150 articles and papers on problems of communications; several patents. *Address:* c/o FAPSI, 103031 Moscow, Bolshoi Kiselny per. 4, Russia.

STAROWIEYSKI, Franciszek; Polish surrealist painter and poster designer; b. 8 July 1930, Bratkówka; ed Acad. of Fine Arts, Kraków and Warsaw; Prof., European Acad. of Art 1993–; Visiting Prof., Berliner Hochschule der Künste, W Berlin 1980; about 300 film and theatre posters and about 2000 paintings and drawings, film and theatre scenography; works in many museums and pvt. collections in Poland and abroad; presenter own TV shows on art; mem. Union of Polish Artists and Designers, Int. Graphic Asscn (Gawędy o sztuce) 1996–99; Prizewinner, Biennale of the Arts, São Paulo 1973, Award, Cannes Film Festival 1974, Silver Medal, Int. Poster Bienale, Warsaw 1974, 1978, Bronze Medal 2000, Film Poster Gold Plaque, Int. Film Festival Chicago 1979, Silver Hugo 1982, and many other awards. *Leisure interest:* collecting Baroque art. *Address:* ul. Bernardyńska 23 m.75, 02-901 Warsaw, Poland (home). *Telephone:* (22) 8403894 (home).

STARR, Albert, MD; American cardiovascular surgeon and academic; *Medical Director, Providence Heart and Vascular Institute;* b. 1 June 1926, New York City; ed Columbia Coll. (now Columbia Univ.), Columbia Coll. of Physicians and Surgeons; completed internship at Johns Hopkins Hosp. and residency in gen. and thoracic surgery at Bellevue and Presbyterian Hosps of Columbia Univ.; Asst in Surgery, Columbia Univ. –1957; worked at Crippled Children's Div., Univ. of Oregon Medical School (now Oregon Health and Science Univ.) from 1957, later Instructor in Surgery, moved to Providence St Vincent Medical Center 1964; currently Medical Dir Providence Heart and Vascular Inst.; Dir Bioscience Research and Devt, Providence Health System, Ore.; Chair Holder, Albert Starr Academic Center for Cardiac Surgery; mem. Starr-Wood Cardiac Group of Portland; hon. degrees from Columbia Univ., Univ. of London, Reed Coll., Lewis and Clark Coll., American Coll. of Surgeons; Int. Heart Pioneer Award, Soc. de Chirurgie Thoracique Cardio-Vasculaire de Langue Francaise 2000, Albert Lasker Award for Clinical Medical Research, Lasker Foundation (co-recipient) 2007. *Achievements include:* co-inventor of first artificial heart valve (Starr heart valve), which he successfully implanted in 1960. *Publications:* numerous papers in professional journals. *Address:* Starr Wood Group, Suite 240, 9155 S.W. Barnes Road, Portland, OR 97225-6625, USA (office). *Telephone:* (503) 296-4027 (office). *Fax:* (503) 216-2488 (office). *E-mail:* astarr@starrwood.com (office). *Website:* www.starrwood.com (office); www.providence.org (office).

STARR, Gregory B., BSc, MSc; American international organization official; *Under-Secretary-General for Safety and Security, United Nations;* b. 3 Feb. 1953; m.; two c.; ed George Washington Univ.; Sr Regional Security Officer, Embassy in Tel-Aviv 1997–2000; also served as Regional Security Officer at embassies in Tunis, Dakar and Kinshasa; Dir Office of Physical Security Programs, US Dept of State, Washington, DC 2000–04, Deputy Asst Sec. of State for Countermeasures 2004–07, Acting Asst Sec. for Diplomatic Security and Acting Dir of Office of Foreign Missions 2007–08, Dir Diplomatic Security Service and Prin. Deputy Asst Sec. for Diplomatic Security 2008–09; Under-Sec.-Gen. for Safety and Security, UN 2009–. *Address:* Office of the Under-Secretary-General for Safety and Security, United Nations, New York, NY 10017, USA (office). *Website:* dss.un.org/dssweb (office).

STARR, Kenneth Winston, MA; American lawyer and academic; *Professor and Dean, School of Law, Pepperdine University;* b. 21 July 1946, Vernon, Texas; s. of W. D. Starr and Vannie M. Starr (née Trimble); m. Alice J. Mendell 1970; one s. two d.; ed George Washington, Brown and Duke Univs; law clerk, Court of Appeals (5th Circuit), Miami 1973–74, Supreme Court 1975–77; Assoc. Gibson, Dunn & Crutcher, LA 1974–75, Assoc. Pnr, 1977–81; counsellor to Attorney-Gen., US Justice Dept, Washington, DC 1981–83, Solicitor Gen. 1989–93; Judge Court of Appeals (DC Circuit) 1983; Pnr, Kirkland & Ellis, Washington, DC 1993–94; apptd ind. counsel for Whitewater Investigation as well as any collateral matters arising out of any investigation of such matters including obstruction of justice or false statements 1994; Prof. and Dean, Pepperdine Univ. School of Law 2004–. *Publications:* contrib. articles to legal journals. *Address:* Pepperdine University School of Law, 24255 Pacific Coast Highway, Malibu, CA 90263, USA (office). *Website:* law.pepperdine.edu (office).

STARR, Ringo, MBE; British musician (drums); b. (Richard Starkey), 7 July 1940, Dingle, Liverpool; m. 1st Maureen Cox 1965 (divorced 1975); two s. one d.; m. 2nd Barbara Bach 1981; ed Dingle Vale Secondary Modern School; fmrly an apprentice engineer; played with Rory Storme and The Hurricanes 1959–62; mem., The Beatles 1962–70; numerous performances and tours world-wide; attended Transcendental Meditation Course at Maharishi's Acad., Rishikesh, India Feb. 1968; formed Apple Corps Ltd, parent org. of The Beatles Group of Companies 1968; solo artist 1969–; BPI Award for Best British Group 1977. *Film appearances:* with The Beatles: A Hard Day's Night 1964, Help! 1965, Magical Mystery Tour (TV film) 1967, Yellow Submarine (animated film) 1968, Let it Be 1970; solo: Candy 1968, The Magic Christian 1969, 200 Motels 1971, Blindman 1971, That'll be the Day 1973, Born to Boogie (also dir and prod.) 1974, Son of Dracula (also prod.) 1975, Lisztomania 1975, Ringo Stars 1976, Caveman 1981, The Cooler 1982, Give My Regards to Broad Street 1984. *Television:* narrator of Thomas the Tank Engine (children's programme) 1980s. *Recordings:* albums: with The Beatles: Please, Please Me 1963, Introducing... The Beatles 1963, With The Beatles 1963, Meet The Beatles! 1964, A Hard Day's Night 1964, Something New 1964, Beatles For Sale 1965, Help! 1965, Rubber Soul 1966, Yesterday... And Today 1966, Revolver 1966, Sgt. Pepper's Lonely Hearts Club Band (BPI Award for Best British Album) 1967, Magical Mystery Tour 1967, The Beatles (White Album) 1968, Yellow Submarine 1969, Abbey Road 1969, Let It Be 1970, At The Beeb 1994, 1 2000; solo: Sentimental Journey 1969, Beaucoups Of Blues 1970, Ringo 1973, Goodnight Vienna 1974, Blasts From Your Past 1975, Ringo's Rotogravure 1976, Ringo The 4th 1977, Bad Boy 1977, Stop And Smell The Roses 1981, Old Wave 1983, All-Starr Band 1990, Time Takes Time 1992, Live From Montreaux 1994, Vertical Man 1998, I Wanna Be Santa Claus 1999, Ringo Starr & His All-Star Band: The Anthology 2001, King Biscuit Flower Hour 2002, Ringorama 2003, Anthology... So Far 2004, Choose Love 2005, Liverpool 8 2008. *Address:* Primary Talent International, Fifth Floor, 2–12 Pentonville Road, London, N1 9PL, England (office). *Telephone:* (20) 7833-8998 (office). *Fax:* (20) 7833-5992 (office). *Website:* www.ringostarr.com.

STARSKI, Allan Mieczysław; Polish filmmaker and production designer; b. 1 Jan. 1943, Warsaw; m.; ed Fine Art Acad., Warsaw; mem. Acad. of Motion Picture Arts and Sciences, Polish Film Asscn; Gdańsk Film Festival Award 1979, Los Angeles Critics' Asscn Award, Polish Film Award for Polish Eagles 2000. *Films include:* The Shadow Line 1976, Man of Marble 1977, The Young Ladies of Wilko 1979, The Conductor 1979, Man of Iron 1981, Danton 1982, Eine Liebe in Deutschland 1983, Escape From Sobibor 1986, Korczak 1990, Europa, Europa 1990, Daens 1992, Papierowe malzenstwo (Paper Marriage) 1992, Schindler's List (Acad. Award 1994) 1993, Wielki tydzien (Holy Week) 1995, Historie milosne (Love Stories) 1997, Washington Square 1997, Pan Tadeusz (Pan Tadeusz: The Last Foray in Lithuania) 1999, Prawo ojca 2000, The Body 2000, The Pianist 2002, The I Inside 2003, EuroTrip 2004, Oliver Twist 2005, Hannibal Rising 2007. *Leisure interests:* cinema, ice skating.

STARZEWSKI, Tomasz; British/Polish fashion designer; b. 1961, London; ed St Martin's School of Design, London; began career designing eveningwear for royals and celebrities 1981; built up large business with distribution over UK, USA and Middle East; collections shown around the world as part of British Collections, group he f. in 1987; opened his first ready-to-wear boutique on Old Brompton Road, London 1989; opened House of Tomasz Starzewski, London 1991; American debut, New York 1999. *Address:* Tomasz Starzewski Studio, 97 Pimlico Road, London, SW1W 8PH, England (office). *Telephone:* (20) 7730-5559 (office). *Fax:* (20) 7730-5977 (office). *Website:* www.starzewski.com (office).

STARZL, Thomas E., BS, MS, MD, PhD; American neurophysiologist, physician and surgeon (retd); *Distinguished Service Professor of Surgery, School of Medicine, University of Pittsburgh;* b. 11 March 1926, LeMars, Ia; ed Westminster Coll., Fulton, Mo., Northwestern Univ. Medical School, Chicago; known as "Father of Transplantation"; postgraduate work at Johns Hopkins Hosp., Baltimore, Md; fellowship and residencies at Johns Hopkins Hosp., Univ. of Miami and Veterans' Admin Research Hosp., Chicago; mem. faculty, Northwestern Univ. 1958–61; Assoc. Prof. of Surgery, Univ. of Colorado School of Medicine 1962–64, Prof. 1964, Chair. Dept of Surgery 1972–80; Prof. of Surgery, Univ. of Pittsburgh School of Medicine 1981, now Distinguished Service Prof. of Surgery, Univ. of Pittsburgh School of Medicine, Chief of Transplantation Services, Presbyterian Univ. Hosp. (now UPMC Presbyterian), Children's Hosp. of Pittsburgh and Veterans' Admin Hosp., Pittsburgh 1981–91, Dir Univ. of Pittsburgh Transplantation Inst. 1991, Inst. renamed Thomas E. Starzl Transplantation Inst. 1996, Dir Emer. 1996–; Pres. The Transplantation Soc.; Founding Pres. American Soc. of Transplant Surgeons, Transplant Recipients Int. Org.; mem. editorial boards of 40 professional publs; mem. more than 60 professional and scientific orgs; mem. Nat. French Acad. of Medicine 1992; has given more than 1,300 presentations at major meetings throughout the world; 24 hon. doctorates from univs in USA and abroad; more than 200 awards and honours, including Markle Scholar in Medical Science, David M. Hume Memorial Award, Nat. Kidney Foundation, Brookdale Award in Medicine, American Medical Asscn Bd of Trustees and Brookdale Foundation, Bigelow Medal, Boston Surgical Soc., City of Medicine Award, Medallion for Scientific Achievement, American Surgical Asscn, William Beaumont Prize, American Gastroenterological Asscn, Peter Medawar Prize, The Transplant Soc., Jacobson Innovation Award, American Coll. of Surgeons, Lannelongue Int. Medal, Acad. Nationale de Chirurgie (France) 1998, King Faisal Int. Prize for Medicine 2001, Rhoads Medal, American Philosophical Soc., Prince Mahidol Award 2002, Presidential Nat. Medal of Science 2004. *Achievements include:* successfully combined azathioprine

(Imuran) and corticosteroids in allogenic kidney transplants performed in 1962 and 1963, leading to the largest series of kidney transplants and invigorating clinical attempts throughout the world; performed world's first human liver transplant in 1963 and first successful liver transplant in 1967, both at Univ. of Colorado; he and his transplant team went on to perform approximately 1,000 kidney and 200 liver transplants at Colorado Gen. and Denver Veterans' Admin Hosps. *Publications:* The Puzzle People: Memoirs of a Transplant Surgeon 1992; author or co-author of four books, 300 book chapters and more than 2,200 scientific articles. *Address:* Thomas E. Starzl Transplantation Institute, UPMC Montefiore, 7 South 3459 Fifth Avenue, Pittsburgh, PA 15213, USA (office). *Telephone:* (412) 647-5800 (office). *Fax:* (412) 647-5070 (office). *E-mail:* sticlinic@upmc.edu (office). *Website:* www .upmc.com/Services/TransplantationServices/StarzlInstitute (office); sti .upmc.com (office).

STASHEVSKYI, Stanislav Telisforovych; Ukrainian politician and electrical engineer; b. 1943, Mar'yanivka, Vasylkivsky dist., Kiev region; ed Kiev Polytechnic Inst.; mil. service 1962–65; electrician, Specialized Planning Dept, Kyivelectromontazh Trust of Kyivmiskbud 1962, then Repairman, Foreman, Sr Foreman, Chief Engineer, Head of Dept 1965–79, then Deputy Head of co. and Chief Engineer 1979–87; Deputy Head, Holovkyivmiskbud 1987–92; First Vice-Pres. Kyivmiskbud Corpn (later Kyivmiskbud Holding Co.) 1992–96; First Deputy Head, Kyiv City Admin 1996–2001, Minister of Fuel and Energy 2001; People's Deputy, Verkhovna Rada (Parl.) 2002–05, Chair. Foreign Relations Cttee, Co-Chair. Inter-Parl. Comm. for Cooperation between Verkhovna Rada (Parl.) and Ass. of Russian Fed.; Head of Verkhovna Rada Perm. Del. to GUAM Parl. Ass., Chair. GUAM Parl. Ass. Cttee on Political and Legal Issues; mem. Ukraine-EU Co-operation Cttee, Deputy Chair., Exec. Cttee of Nat. Parl. Group of Ukraine at Inter-Parl. Union 2002–05; First Deputy Prime Minister 2005–06; mem. Kiev City Council and Nat. Political Council; Head of Pechersk Regional Org.; mem. Our Ukraine Party; I, II, and III Class Orders of Merit, II and III Class Orders of St Prince Volodymyr the Great, Arhistratig Michael Order; Diploma of the Verkhovna Rada. *Leisure interests:* riding, tennis. *Address:* Verkhovna Rada (Supreme Council), 01008 Kyiv, vul. M. Hrushevskoho 5, Ukraine (office). *Telephone:* (44) 255-21-15 (office). *Fax:* (44) 253-32-17 (office). *E-mail:* Stashevskyi .Stanislav@rada.gov.ua (office). *Website:* www.rada.gov.ua (office).

STASI, Bernard, LenD; French politician; b. 4 July 1930, Reims; s. of Mario Stasi and Mercédès Stasi (née Camps); m. Danièle Beaugier 1979; ed Institut d'Etudes Politiques, Paris and Ecole Nat. d'Admin; attached to the Cabinet of the Pres. of the Nat. Ass. 1955; served in army 1955–57; Civil Admin., Ministry of Interior 1959; Chef de Cabinet to the Prefect of Algiers 1959–60; Head of Section, Directorate-Gen. of Political Affairs and Territorial Admin., Ministry of Interior 1960–62; Tech. Adviser, Cabinet of the Sec. of State for Youth and Sports 1963–65; Directeur de Cabinet to the Sec. of Overseas Depts. 1966–68; Deputy for Marne, Nat. Ass. 1968–73, 1978–93; mem. European Parl. 1994–98; charged with missions to Israel, GB, Cuba and Chile; Mayor of Epernay 1970–77, 1983–2000; Médiateur de la République (Ombudsman) 1998–2004; Vice-Pres. Centre Démocratie et Progrès 1969–75, Centre des Démocrates Sociaux 1976–84 (first Vice-Pres. 1984); Minister for Overseas Depts and Territories 1973–74; Fed. Sec. Féd. des Réformateurs 1975–78; mem. Regional Council of Champagne-Ardenne 1976–88, Pres. 1981–88; Pres. Fédération française de course d'orientation 1970–88; Pres. Nat. Council for Regional Econs and Productivity 1986–88; Founder, Groupe d'études parlementaires pour l'aménagement rural 1970; Founder and Pres. Cités Unies France 1975–2004, Hon. Pres. 2004–; Vice-Pres. Co-operative and Devt Comm., Christian Democrat Int. 1993–; Sec.-Gen. Asscn. of Ombudsmen and Mediators of French-speaking Communities 1998–2004; mem. Bd of Dirs Association des Maires de France; mem. various municipal orgs; Officier, Légion d'honneur; Chevalier Ordre nat. du Mérite, du Mérite agricole, Ordre des Palmes académiques; Grand Croix de l'Ordre du Croissant vert et de l'Etoile d'Anjouan (Comoros) and other decorations. *Publication:* Le Piège (with J. P. Soisson and O. Stirn) 1973, Vie associative et démocratie nouvelle 1978, L'Immigration: une chance pour la France 1984, La Politique au coeur 1993, Tous Français: l'immigration, la chance de la France 2007. *Leisure interests:* football, tennis, sailing. *Address:* c/o Cités Unies France, 9 rue Christiani, 75018 Paris, France (office).

STASIAK, Władysław; Polish government official; *Chief, Biuro Bezpieczeństwa Narodowego (National Security Bureau);* b. 15 March 1966, Wrocław; ed Univ. of Wrocław and Nat. School of Public Admin. (KSAP); worked at Cen. Auditing Office (NIK) 1993–2002, positions included Deputy Dir Dept of Defense and Internal Security, in charge of audits concerning examination and evaluation of operational efficiency of police, border guards and fire service; Deputy Mayor of Warsaw 2002–05; Deputy Minister of Internal Affairs 2005–06; Chief Biuro Bezpieczeństwa Narodowego (Nat. Security Bureau) 2006–07, Nov. 2007–; Minister of Internal Affairs and Admin. Aug.–Nov. 2007. *Address:* Biuro Bezpieczeństwa Narodowego, ul. Karowa 10, 00-909 Warsaw 60, Poland (office). *Telephone:* (22) 6951800 (office). *Fax:* (22) 6951801 (office). *E-mail:* bbn@bbn.gov.pl (office). *Website:* www.bbn.gov.pl (office).

STASSE, François; French civil servant and economist; *Senior Member, Council of State;* b. 11 Jan. 1948, Neuilly-sur-Seine; s. of Roger Stasse and Christiane Stasse (née Deveaux); m. Nathalie Duhamel 1978; ed Inst. of Political Studies, Paris; with Ministry of Industry 1972–73; joined Gen. Bd of Planning 1974, Dir Commr's Office 1979–81; Tech. Adviser to Pres. of Rep. on Econs and Finance 1981–84; Counsel Council of State 1984, Sr mem. 1996–; Dir State Hosp. Paris 1989–93; Dir-Gen. Bibliothèque nationale de France 1998–2001. *Publications include:* La Morale de l'histoire 1994, La Véritable

Histoire de la Grande Bibliotheque 2002, L'Heritage de Mendés France 2004. *Address:* Conseil d'État, place du Palais Royal, 75100 Paris, France.

STAUDINGER, Ulrich; German publisher; b. 30 May 1935, Berlin; s. of Wilhelm Staudinger and Elfriede Poth; m. Irmengard Ehrenwirth 1960 (died 1989); one s. two d.; ed Volksschule and Realgymnasium; publishing training 1954–57; Lingenbrinck Barsortiment, Hamburg 1957–58; Publicity and Sales, Ensslin & Laiblin, Jugendbuchverlag, Reutlingen 1958–59; Production, Carl Hanser Verlag, Munich 1959–60; Dawson & Sons, London 1960; Franz Ehrenwirth Verlag, Munich 1960; partner, Ehrenwirth Verlag, Munich 1964; responsible for purchase of Franz Schneekluth Verlag KG, Darmstadt by Ehrenwirth Verlag 1967 and amalgamation of two companies into single firm 1976; purchased parts of Philosophia Verlag GmbH, Düsseldorf 1978; various professional appointments. *Address:* Asgardstrasse 34, 8000 Munich 81, Germany (home). *Telephone:* (89) 98-63-67 (home).

STAUNTON, Imelda Mary Philomena Bernadette; British actress; b. 9 Jan. 1956; d. of Joseph Staunton and Bridie McNicholas; m. Jim Carter 1983; one d.; ed La Sainte Union Convent, Highgate, London, RADA; repertory Exeter, Nottingham, York 1976–81; Olivier Award 1985, 1990, Screen Actors' Guild Award 1999. *Stage appearances include:* Guys and Dolls 1982, 1996, Beggar's Opera 1985, She Stoops to Conquer, Chorus of Disapproval 1985 (Olivier Award, Best Supporting Actress), The Corn is Green 1985, Fair Maid of the West 1986, Wizard of Oz 1986, Uncle Vanya 1988, Into the Woods 1990, Phoenix 1990 (Olivier Award, Best Actress in a Musical), Life x 3 2000, There Came a Gypsy Riding 2007. *Television appearances include:* The Singing Detective 1986, Yellowbacks 1990, Sleeping Life, Roots, Up the Garden Path 1990, Antonia and Jane, David Copperfield 1999, Victoria Wood Xmas Special 2000, Murder 2001, Cambridge Spies 2002, Strange 2002, Fingersmith 2005, A Midsummer Night's Dream 2005, Little Britain 2005, My Family and Other Animals 2005, Cranford (series) 2007, Clay 2008. *Film appearances include:* Comrades 1987, Peter's Friends 1992, Much Ado About Nothing 1993, Deadly Advice 1994, Sense and Sensibility, Twelfth Night, Remember Me 1996, Shakespeare in Love 1998, Another Life 1999, Rat 1999, Crush 2000, Bright Young Things 2002, Virgin of Liverpool 2002, Blackball 2002, Family Business 2002, Vera Drake (Best Performance by an Actress, British Ind. Film Awards, Best Actress, European Film Awards, Los Angeles Film Critics' Asscn, New York Film Critics' Circle, Evening Standard British Film Awards 2005, Best Actress in a Leading Role, BAFTA Awards 2005) 2004, Nanny McPhee 2005, 3 & 3 2005, Freedom Writers 2007, Harry Potter and the Order of the Phoenix 2007, Where Have I Been All Your Life? 2007, Three and Out 2008. *Address:* c/o ARG, 4 Great Portland Street, London, W1W 4PA, England.

STAVRAKIS, Charilaos, BA, MBA; Cypriot politician; *Minister of Finance;* b. 1956; ed Univ. of Cambridge, UK, Harvard Univ. Grad. School of Business Admin, USA; more than 25 years' experience in banking sector; undertook two-month consulting position at World Bank 1989; held various positions at Bank of Cyprus, including Head of Strategic Planning and Business Devt and Sr Man. of Treasury and Int. Services, Group Gen. Man. Int. Banking 1988–2004, Gen. Man. Cyprus Investment & Securities Corpn Ltd (CISCO) (investment banking arm of the Group) 2003–08; mem. Bd Dirs Cyprus Oil Refinery, Bank of Cyprus Australia, Bank of Cyprus (Channel Islands) Ltd, Bank of Cyprus (AEDAK), Bank of Cyprus Mutual Funds Ltd, BOC Ventures Ltd, CEO-Cyprus and Deputy Group CEO 2005–08, assumed additional duties involving man. of subsidiary cos of the Group: BOC Factors, Bank of Cyprus Finance Corpn, General Insurance of Cyprus, Eurolife, The Cyprus Investment and Securities Corpn Ltd (CISCO), BOC Mutual Funds Ltd, Bank of Cyprus UK and the setting up of banks in Russia and Ukraine; Chair. Electricity Authority Cyprus 2005–08, Cyprus Bankers Employers' Asscn 2005–08; Minister of Finance (Ind.) 2008–; mem. Chartered Inst. of Bankers (ACIB) 1988. *Address:* Ministry of Finance, Cnr M. Karaolis Street and G. Afxentiou Street, 1439 Nicosia, Cyprus (office). *Telephone:* 22601192 (office). *Fax:* 22602750 (office). *E-mail:* registry@mof.gov.cy (office). *Website:* www.mof .gov.cy (office).

STAVROPOULOS, William S., PhD; American chemical company executive (retd); b. 12 May 1939, Bridgehampton; m. Linda Stavropoulos; one s. one d.; ed Fordham Univ., Univ. of Washington; research chemist, Pharmaceutical Research Div., Dow Chemical Co. 1967, Diagnostics Product Research Div. 1970, Research Man. 1973, Diagnostic Products Business Man. 1976, Business Man. for polyolefins 1977, Dir of Marketing, Dow USA Plastics Dept 1979, Commercial Vice-Pres. Dow Latin America 1980, Pres. 1984, Commercial Vice-Pres. Dow USA, Basics and Hydrocarbons 1985, Group Vice-Pres. 1987, Pres. Dow USA 1990, Vice-Pres. The Dow Chemical Co. 1990, Dir 1990–, Sr Vice-Pres. 1991, Pres., COO 1993–95, Pres., CEO 1995–2000, 2002–04, Chair. 2002–06 (retd); mem. Bd of Dirs Dow Corning Corpn 1991, Marion Merrell Dow Inc. 1992, Dowell Schlumberger 1992, Chemical Bank; Trustees Midland Community Center and other bodies; Dr hc (Northwood Univ.) 1998; Man of the Year Award from American Hellenic Education Progressive Association 1995, Man of the Year Award from Hellenic American Bankers Association 1997, Ellis Island Medal of Honor in 1998, CEO of the Year Kavaler Award 1999, Man of the Year Award from Hellenic American Chamber of Commerce 2000, Société de Chimie Industrielle's Palladium Medal Award 2001, Chemical Industry Medal Award, Soc. of Chemical Industry 2001, Institutional Investor magazine's award as one of Best CEOs in America in Chemicals/Commodity category (1998, 2003 and 2004), Soc. of Plastic Engineers Annual Business Man. Award 2003, Northwood Univ. 2004, Outstanding Business Leader Award, Junior Achievement of Central Michigan Business Hall of Fame 2005. *Address:* 8865 Bay Colony Drive, Naples, FL 34103, USA.

STEAD, Christian Karlson (C. K.), ONZ, CBE, MA, PhD, LittD, FRSL; New Zealand writer and academic; *Professor Emeritus of English, University of*

Auckland; b. 17 Oct. 1932, Auckland; s. of James Walter Ambrose Stead and Olive Ethel Stead (née Karlson); m. Kathleen Elizabeth Roberts 1955; one s. two d.; ed Mt Albert Grammar School, Auckland Univ. Coll. and Auckland Teachers' Coll., Univ. of Bristol, UK; Lecturer in English, Univ. of New England, NSW, Australia 1956–57; Michael Hiatt Baker Scholar, Univ. of Bristol 1957–59; Lecturer, Sr Lecturer, Assoc. Prof., Univ. of Auckland 1960–67, Prof. of English 1967–86, Prof. Emer. 1986–; writer 1986–; Nuffield Fellow, Univ. of London 1965, Hon. Fellow, Univ. Coll. London 1977, Sr Visiting Fellow, St John's Coll. Oxford 1996–97; Chair. NZ Literary Fund Advisory Cttee 1972–75, NZ Authors' Fund Cttee 1989–91; mem. NZ PEN (Chair. Auckland br. 1986–89, Nat. Vice-Pres. 1988–90), Creative New Zealand 1999; Fellow, English Asscn; Hon. DLitt (Bristol) 2001; Katherine Mansfield Prize 1960, Jessie Mackay Award for Poetry 1972, Katherine Mansfield Menton Fellowship 1972, New Zealand Book Award for Poetry 1976, New Zealand Book Award for Fiction 1985, 1995, Queen Elizabeth II Arts Council Scholarship in Letters 1988–89, Queens' Medal for Services to NZ Literature 1990, Michael King Fellowship 2005–06. *Publications:* fiction: Smith's Dream 1972, All Visitors Ashore 1984, The Death of the Body 1986, Sister Hollywood 1989, The End of the Century at the End of the World 1992, The Singing Whakapapa 1994, Villa Vittoria 1997, Talking about O'Dwyer 2000, The Secret History of Modernism 2002, Mansfield: a novel 2004, My Name Was Judas 2006; poetry: Whether the Will is Free 1964, Crossing the Bar 1972, Quesada 1975, Walking Westward 1978, Geographies 1982, Poems of a Decade 1983, Paris 1984, Between 1986, Voices 1990, Straw into Gold 1997, The Right Thing 2000, Dog 2002, The Red Tram 2004, The Black River 2007, Collected Poems 1951–2006 2008; short story collections: Five for the Symbol 1981, The Blind Blonde with Candles in Her Hair 1998; non-fiction: The New Poetic: Yeats to Eliot 1964, In the Glass Case: Essays on New Zealand Literature 1981, Pound Yeats Eliot and the Modernist Movement 1986, Answering to the Language: Essays on Modern Writers 1990, The Writer at Work 2000, Kin of Place: Essays on 20 New Zealand Writers 2002, Book Self: the reader as writer and the writer as critic 2008; editor: Oxford New Zealand Short Stories (2nd series) 1966, Measure for Measure, a Casebook 1971, Letters and Journals of Katherine Mansfield 1977, Collected Stories of Maurice Duggan 1981, The Faber Book of Contemporary South Pacific Stories 1994, Werner Forman's New Zealand 1994. *Leisure interests:* music, politics. *Address:* 37 Tohunga Crescent, Parnell, Auckland 1001, New Zealand (home). *Telephone:* (649) 379-9420 (home). *Fax:* (649) 379-9420 (home).

STEADMAN, Alison, OBE; British actress; b. 26 Aug. 1946, Liverpool; d. of the late George Percival Steadman and Margorie Evans; m. Mike Leigh (q.v.) (divorced 2002); two s.; ed East 15 drama school, Loughton, Essex; began career in repertory theatre in Lincoln, Bolton, Liverpool, Worcester and Nottingham; Hon. MA (Univ. of E London); Dr hc (Essex) 2003; Evening Standard Best Actress Award 1977, Olivier Award for Best Actress 1993. *Stage appearances include:* Beverley in Abigail's Party, Mae-Sister Woman in Cat on a Hot Tin Roof, Nat. Theatre (NT) 1988, Uncle Vanya, Mari Hoff in The Rise and Fall of Little Voice, NT, David Edgar's Maydays, RSC, Tartuffe, RSC, Joking Apart, Kafka's Dick, Royal Court, Marvin's Room 1993, The Plotters of Cabbage Patch Corner, The Provok'd Wife, Old Vic 1997, When We Are Married, Chichester and Savoy Theatres, The Memory of Water, Vaudeville Theatre, Entertaining Mr Sloane, Arts Theatre, The Woman Who Cooked Her Husband, New Ambassador Theatre, Losing Louis, Hampstead Theatre and Trafalgar Studios, London. *Films:* Champions 1984, A Private Function 1984, Coming Through 1985, Clockwise 1986, Stormy Monday 1988, The Adventures of Baron Munchausen 1988, Wilt 1989, Shirley Valentine 1989, Life is Sweet 1990, Blame It On the Bellboy 1992, Secrets and Lies 1996, Topsy-Turvy 1999, Chunky Monkey 2001, Happy Now 2001, D.I.Y. Hard 2002, The Housewife 2005, Confetti 2006, Dead Rich 2006. *Radio includes:* Bette in Cousin Bette. *Television includes:* Hard Labour 1973, Frost's Weekly (series) 1973, Girl 1974, The Wackers (series) 1975, Tarbuck and All That! (series) 1975, Through the Night 1975, Nuts in May 1976, Esther Waters 1977, Abigail's Party 1977, The Tartuffe or Imposter 1983, P'tang Yang Kipperbang 1984, Number One 1985, The Singing Detective (series) 1986, The Short and Curlies 1987, Virtuoso 1988, Monster Maker 1989, A Small Mourning 1989, The Finding 1990, Newshounds 1990, Gone to the Dogs (series) 1991, Selling Hitler (series) 1991, Gone to Seed (series) 1992, The Wimbledon Poisoner (series) 1994, Pride and Prejudice (series) 1995, The Snow Queen's Revenge (voice) 1996, No Bananas (series) 1996, Cold Lazarus (series) 1996, Karaoke (series) 1996, The Ugly Duckling (voice) 1997, The Missing Postman 1997, Crapston Villas (series, voice) 1998, Stressed Eric (series, voice) 1998, Santa's Last Christmas (voice) 1999, Let Them Eat Cake (series) 1999, Jack and the Beanstalk (voice) 2000, Fat Friends (series 1–4) 2000, Hans Christian Andersen: My Life as a Fairy Tale 2001, Adrian Mole: The Cappuccino Years 2001, Dalziel and Pascoe 2002, The Last Detective 2003, Comic Relief 2003: The Big Hair Do 2003, The Worst Week of My Life (series) 2004–06, Dalziel and Pascoe – Soft Touch 2004, Bosom Pals (voice) 2004, The Life and Death of Peter Sellers 2004, Twisted Tales – Fruitcake of the Living Dead 2005, Who Gets the Dog? 2006, The Worst Christmas of My Life: Part 1 2006, Part 2 2006, Part 3 2006, Marple: Ordeal by Innocence 2007. *Address:* United Agents, 12–26 Lexington Street, London, W1F 0LE, England (office). *Telephone:* (20) 3214-0800 (office). *Fax:* (20) 3214-0801 (office). *E-mail:* info@unitedagents.co.uk (office). *Website:* unitedagents.co.uk (office).

STEADMAN, Ralph Idris; British cartoonist, writer and illustrator; b. 15 May 1936; s. of Raphael Steadman and Gwendoline Steadman; m. 1st Sheila Thwaite 1959 (divorced 1971); two s. two d.; m. 2nd Anna Deverson 1972; one d.; ed London School of Printing and Graphic Arts; with de Havilland Aircraft Co. 1952; cartoonist, Kemsley (Thomson) Newspapers 1956–59; freelance for Punch, Private Eye, Daily Telegraph during 1960s; political cartoonist, New Statesman 1978–80; designed set of stamps depicting Halley's Comet 1986; Artist-in-Residence, Leviathan (series of films, BBC 2) 1999; designer of set and costumes, The Crucible, Royal Ballet 2000; Hon. DLitt (Kent) 1995; Designers and Art Dirs' Asscn Gold Award 1977, Silver Award 1977, Lifetime Achievement Award – Milton Caniff Award, Nat. Cartoonists Soc. (USA) 2005. *Written and illustrated:* Alice in Wonderland 1967, Alice Through the Looking Glass 1972, Sigmund Freud 1979, A Leg in the Wind and Other Canine Curses 1982, I, Leonardo 1983, That's My Dad 1986, The Big I Am 1988, No Room to Swing a Cat 1989, Near the Bone 1990, Tales of Weirrd 1990, Still Life with Bottle, Whisky According to Ralph Steadman 1994, Jones of Colorado 1998, Gonzo: The Art 1998, little.com 2000, The Joke's Over 2006. *Illustrator:* many books from 1961, including Friendship 1990 (in aid of John McCarthy), Adrian Mitchell, Heart on the Left, Poems 1953–84 1997, Roald Dahl, The Mildenhall Treasure 1999, Doodaa: The Balletic Art of Gavin Twinge 2002. *Publications:* Jelly Book 1968, Still Life with Raspberry: collected drawings 1969, The Little Red Computer 1970, Dogs Bodies 1971, Bumper to Bumper Book 1973, Two Donkeys and the Bridge 1974, Flowers for the Moon 1974, The Watchdog and the Lazy Dog 1974, America: drawings 1975, America: collected drawings 1977 (r.e. Scar Strangled Banger 1987), Between the Eyes 1984, Paranoids 1986, The Grapes of Ralph 1992, Teddy Where Are You? 1994, Bruised Memories: Gonzo, Hunter Thompson and Me 2006, The Joke's Over 2007, The Devil's Dictionary (with Ambrose Bierce) 2008. *Leisure interests:* gardening, sheep husbandry, fishing, guitar, trumpet. *Address:* c/o Nat Sobel, Sobel Weber Associates, Inc., 146 East 19th Street, New York, NY 10003-2404, USA (office). *Telephone:* (212) 420-8585 (office). *Website:* www.sobelweber.com (office); www.ralphsteadman.com.

STEBBINS, Donald J., BSc, MBA; American business executive; *President and CEO, Visteon Corporation;* b. 1958; ed Miami Univ., Oxford, Ohio, Univ. of Michigan; fmrly with Bankers Trust Co. and Citibank; joined Lear Corpn as Vice-Pres. Treas. 1992, then Sr Vice-Pres. Chief Financial Officer 1997, then COO Americas, Co-COO Europe, Asia and Africa; Pres. and COO Visteon Corpn 2005–08, Pres. and CEO 2008–; mem. Bd of Dirs WABCO Holdings Inc.; mem. Business Advisory Council, Miami Univ.; Trustee Detroit Country Day School. *Address:* Visteon Corporation, One Village Center Drive, Van Buren Township, MI 48111, USA (office). *Telephone:* (734) 710-7400 (office). *Fax:* (734) 710-7402 (office). *Website:* www.visteon.com (office).

STEEDS, John Wickham, PhD, FRS, FInstP; British physicist and academic; *Henry Overton Wills Professor of Physics, University of Bristol;* b. 9 Feb. 1940, London; s. of John Henry William Steeds and Ethel Amelia Steeds (née Tyler); m. Diana Mary Kettlewell 1969; two d.; ed Haberdashers' Aske's School, Univ. Coll. London, Univ. of Cambridge; Mullard Research Fellow, Selwyn Coll. Cambridge 1964–67; Lecturer, Physics Dept, Univ. of Bristol 1967–77, Reader 1977–85, Prof. of Electron Microscopy 1985–, Head of Dept 2001–05, Henry Overton Wills Prof. 2002–; fmr mem. Council European Pole Univ. of Lille; Chair. Emersons Innovations Ltd; Holweck Medal (Soc. Française de Physique and Inst. of Physics) 1996. *Publications:* Introduction to Anistropic Elasticity Theory of Dislocations 1973, Electron Diffraction of Phases in Alloys (with J. F. Mansfield) 1984, Thin Film Diamond (co-ed.) 1994. *Leisure interest:* tennis. *Address:* H.H. Wills Physics Laboratory, Room 3.20, Royal Fort Tyndall Avenue, University of Bristol, Bristol, BS8 1TL (office); 21 Canynge Square, Clifton, Bristol, BS8 3LA, England (home). *Telephone:* (117) 928-8730 (office); (117) 973-2183 (home). *Fax:* (117) 925-5624 (office). *E-mail:* J.W.Steeds@bristol.ac.uk (office). *Website:* www.phy.bris.ac.uk (office).

STEEL, Danielle Fernande Schüelein; American writer; b. 14 Aug. 1950, New York; d. of John Steel and Norma Schüelein-Steel (née Stone); m. 2nd Bill Toth 1977; m. 3rd John A. Traina Jr; four s. five d.; ed Lycée Français, Parsons School of Design, New York, Univ. of New York; worked as public relations and advertising exec., Manhattan, New York; published first novel 1973, then wrote advertising copy and poems for women's magazines; wrote first bestseller, The Promise 1979; Officier, Ordre des Arts et Lettres. *Publications:* Going Home 1973, Passion's Promise 1977, Now and Forever 1978, Season of Passion 1978, The Promise 1979, Summer's End 1980, The Ring 1980, To Love Again 1981, Palomino 1981, Loving 1981, Remembrance 1981, Love: Poems 1981, A Perfect Stranger 1982, Once in a Lifetime 1982, Crossings 1982, Thurston House 1983, Changes 1983, Full Circle 1984, Having a Baby (contrib., non-fiction) 1984, Family Album 1985, Secrets 1985, Wanderlust 1986, Fine Things 1987, Kaleidoscope 1987, Zoya 1988, Star 1989, Daddy 1989, Heartbeat 1991, Message from Nam 1991, No Greater Love 1991, Jewels 1992, Mixed Blessings 1992, Vanished 1993, Accident 1994, The Gift 1994, Wings 1995, Lightning 1995, Five Days in Paris 1995, Malice 1995, Silent Honor 1996, The Ranch 1996, The Ghost 1997, Special Delivery 1997, His Bright Light (non-fiction) 1998, The Ranch 1998, The Long Road Home 1998, The Klone and I 1998, Mirror Image 1998, Bittersweet 1999, Granny Dan 1999, Irresistible Forces 1999, The Wedding 2000, The House on Hope Street 2000, Journey 2000, Leap of Faith 2001, The Kiss 2001, Lone Eagle 2001, The Cottage 2002, Sunset in San Tropez 2002, Answered Prayers 2002, Dating Game 2003, Johnny Angel 2003, Safe Harbour 2003, Echoes 2004, Toxic Bachelors 2005, The House 2006, Impossible 2006, Miracle 2006, Coming Out 2006, HRH 2006, Bungalow 2 2007, Amazing Grace 2007, Sisters 2007, Honor Thyself 2008, Rogue 2008, One Day at a Time 2009; eight children's books, one book of poetry. *Leisure interest:* my children. *Address:* c/o Random House Publicity Department, 1745 Broadway, New York, NY 10019 (office); PO Box 1637, New York, NY 10156, USA (home). *E-mail:* atrandompublicity@randomhouse.com (office). *Website:* daniellesteel.com.

STEEL, Robert (Bob) K., BA, MBA; American banking executive and fmr government official; *President and CEO, Wachovia Corporation;* b. 3 Aug. 1951; m. Gillian Steel; three d.; ed Duke Univ., Univ. of Chicago; joined Goldman Sachs 1976, held several exec. positions including first as individual and institutional salesperson, then Man. Dir and Co-head of Equity Sales and Trading, Pnr, Head of Equities Div., New York, Co-Chief Operating Officer, Equities Div., Man. Dir and Head of Equities Div., Goldman Sachs Equities Europe 1988–94, Vice-Chair., Co-head of Equities Div. and Fixed Income 1998–2001, Head of Equities Div. 2001–02, Vice-Chair. 2002–04, Advisory Dir and Chair. (non-exec.) Securities 2004–06; Sr Fellow, John F. Kennedy School of Govt, Harvard Univ. 2004–06; Under-Sec. for Domestic Finance, US Dept of the Treasury, Washington, DC 2006–08; Pres. and CEO Wachovia Corpn 2008–; Chair. Bd of Trustees, Duke Univ.; fmr mem. Bd of Dirs Barclays Bank PLC, Barclays PLC. *Address:* Wachovia Corpn, 301 South College Street, Suite 4000, One Wachovia Center, Charlotte, NC 28288-0013, USA (office). *Telephone:* (704) 590-0000 (office). *E-mail:* info@wachovia.com (office). *Website:* www.wachovia.com (office).

STEEL OF AIKWOOD, Baron (Life Peer), cr. 1997, of Ettrick Forest in the Scottish Borders; **David Martin Scott Steel,** KT, KBE, PC, MA, LLB, DL; Scottish politician, journalist and broadcaster; b. 31 March 1938, Kirkcaldy; s. of Very Rev. Dr David Steel; m. Judith Mary MacGregor 1962; two s. one d.; ed Prince of Wales School, Nairobi, Kenya, George Watson's Coll. and Univ. of Edinburgh; Pres., Edin. Univ. Liberals 1959; Past Pres., Students' Rep. Council 1960; Asst Sec., Scottish Liberal Party 1962–64; MP for Roxburgh, Selkirk and Peebles 1965–83, for Tweeddale, Ettrick and Lauderdale 1983–97; Scottish Liberal Whip 1967–70, Liberal Chief Whip 1970–75; Leader of Liberal Party 1976–88; Co-Founder, Social and Liberal Democrats 1988; Vice-Pres., Liberal Int. 1978–93, Pres. 1994–96; mem. Parl. del. to UN Gen. Ass. 1967; Sponsor, Pvt. Member's Bill to reform law on abortion 1966–67; Pres., Anti-Apartheid Movt of UK 1966–69; Chair., Shelter, Scotland 1969–73, Countryside Movt 1995–97; BBC TV Interviewer in Scotland 1964–65; Presenter of weekly religious programme for Scottish TV 1966–67, for Granada 1969, for BBC 1971–76; Dir, Border TV 1991–99; Rector, Univ. of Edin. 1982–85; MSP 1999–2003, Presiding Officer of Scottish Parl. 1999–2003; Chubb Fellow, Yale Univ., USA 1987; DL Ettrick and Lauderdale and Roxburghshire; Freedom of Tweeddale 1989, of Ettrick and Lauderdale 1990; Grand Cross of Order of Merit (Germany); Chevalier de la Légion d'honneur; Dr hc (Stirling) 1991, (Heriot Watt) 1996; Hon. DLitt (Buckingham) 1994; Hon. LLD (Edin.) 1997, (Strathclyde) 2000, (Aberdeen) 2001, (St Andrews) 2003, (Glasgow Caledonian) 2004; Hon. DUniv (Open Univ.) 2001; Bronze Medal London-Cape Town Classic Car Rally 1998. *Publications:* Boost for the Borders 1964, No Entry 1969, A House Divided 1980, Border Country 1985, Partners in One Nation 1985, The Time Has Come (with David Owen) 1987, Mary Stuart's Scotland (with Judy Steel) 1987, Against Goliath (autobiography) 1989. *Leisure interests:* angling, classic cars. *Address:* House of Lords, Westminster, London, SW1A 0PW (office); Aikwood Tower, Ettrick Bridge, Selkirkshire, Scotland (home). *Telephone:* (20) 7219-4433 (office).

STEELE, John Hyslop, DSc, FRS, FRSE, FAAS; American mathematician and scientist; *President Emeritus, Woods Hole Oceanographic Institution;* b. 15 Nov. 1926, Edinburgh, Scotland; s. of Adam Steele and Annie Hyslop Steele; m. Margaret Evelyn Travis 1956; one s.; ed George Watson's Boys' Coll., Edinburgh, Univ. Coll., London; Marine Lab., Aberdeen, Scotland, UK 1951–77, Marine Scientist 1951–66, Sr Prin. Scientific Officer 1966–73, Dir Dept 1973–77; Dir Woods Hole Oceanographic Inst., Mass 1977–89, Pres. 1986–91, Pres. Emer. 1991–; Dir Exxon Corpn 1989–97; Trustee, Robert Wood Johnson Foundation 1990–2001; mem. Nat. Geographic Soc. Cttee Research and Exploration 1987–2000; Fellow, American Acad. of Arts and Sciences 1980; Hon. Prof., Univ. of Aberdeen 1993–; Hon. DSc (Aberdeen) 2001; NAS Agassiz Medal 1973. *Publications:* Structure of Marine Ecosystems 1974; more than 100 articles in oceanographic and ecological journals. *Leisure interest:* sailing, golf. *Address:* Woods Hole Oceanographic Institution, Woods Hole, MA 02543, USA (office). *Telephone:* (508) 289-2220 (office). *Fax:* (508) 457-2184 (office). *E-mail:* jsteele@whoi.edu (office). *Website:* www.whoi.edu (office).

STEELE, Tommy, OBE; British actor and singer; b. (Thomas Hicks), 17 Dec. 1936, Bermondsey, London; s. of Thomas Walter Hicks and Elizabeth Ellen Bennett; m. Ann Donoughue 1960; one d.; ed Bacon's School for Boys, Bermondsey; entered Merchant Navy 1952; first stage appearance Empire Theatre, Sunderland 1956, London debut 1957; roles include Buttons (Cinderella), London 1958/59, Tony Lumpkin (She Stoops to Conquer) 1960, Arthur Kipps (Half A Sixpence) 1963/64, New York 1965/66, Truffaldino (The Servant of Two Masters) 1968, title role in Hans Andersen, London 1974/75, 1977/78, 1981, Don Lockwood (Singin' in the Rain), London (also dir) 1983–85, 1989 Some Like it Hot (also dir) 1991, What a Show! 1995; film debut in Kill Me Tomorrow 1956; sculpted tribute to the Beatles' Eleanor Rigby 1982; Hon. DLitt (South Bank) 1998. *Films include:* The Tommy Steele Story, The Duke Wore Jeans 1957, Tommy the Toreador 1959, Light Up the Sky 1963, Its All Happening 1966, The Happiest Millionaire 1967, Half A Sixpence, Finian's Rainbow 1968, Where's Jack 1971; TV debut in Off the Record 1956, cabaret debut, Caesar's Palace, Las Vegas 1974; composed and recorded musical autobiog. My Life, My Song 1974. *Live performances:* An Evening with Tommy Steele 1979, Tommy Steele in Concert 1998, lead role in Bill Kenwright's stage production of Scrooge (UK tour) 2003–04; Quincy's Quest (TV) 1979. *Publications:* Hans Andersen (co-author, stage version), Quincy 1981, The Final Run 1983, Bermondsey Boy (autobiog.) 2006. *Leisure interests:* tennis, painting, sculpture. *Address:* c/o Laurie Mansfield, International Artistes, 4th Floor, 193–197 High Holborn, London, WC1V 7BD, England (office). *Telephone:* (20) 7025-0600 (office). *Fax:* (20) 7404-9865 (office).

STEELE-PERKINS, Christopher Horace, BSc; British photographer; b. 28 July 1947, Burma; s. of Alfred Steele-Perkins and Mary Lloyd; m. 1st Jacqueline de Gier 1984 (divorced 1999); two s.; m. 2nd Miyako Yamada 1999; ed Christ's Hospital, Horsham, Sussex, Univ. of Newcastle; mem. Exit Group, London 1974–82; Assoc. Viva Agency, Paris 1976–79; mem. Photography Cttee, Arts Council of GB 1977–79; mem. Magnum Photos 1983–, Pres. 1996–98; Visiting Prof., Mushishino Art Univ., Tokyo 2000; World Press Oskar Barnack 1988, Tom Hopkinson Award for Photo-journalism 1988, Robert Capa Gold Medal 1989, Cooperative Award, One World Award (both for film Dying for Publicity) 1994, Naçion-Premier Photojournalism Award, World Press Daily Life First 2000. *Television films:* Dying for Publicity 1993, Afghan Taliban 1995. *Publications:* The Teds 1979, About 70 Photographs 1980, Survival Programmes 1982, Beirut: Frontline Story 1982, The Pleasure Principle 1989, St Thomas' Hospital 1992, Afghanistan 2000, Fuji 2002, Echoes 2004. *Leisure interests:* boxing, chess, photography, film, music, literature. *Address:* 49 St Francis Road, London, SE22 8DE,; Magnum Photos, 63 Gee Street, London, EC1V 3RS, England (office). *Telephone:* (20) 7490-1771 (office); (20) 8693-1114. *E-mail:* chrissteeleperkins@hotmail.com. *Website:* www.magnumphotos.com; chrissteeleperkins.com.

STEENBURGEN, Mary; American film actress; b. 8 Feb. 1953, Newport, Ariz.; m. 1st Malcolm McDowell 1980 (divorced); one s. one d.; m. 2nd Ted Danson (q.v.) 1995; ed Neighborhood Playhouse. *Films include:* Goin' South 1978, Time After Time 1979, Melvin and Howard (Acad. Award for Best Supporting Actress) 1980, Ragtime 1981, A Midsummer Night's Sex Comedy 1982, Romantic Comedy 1983, Cross Creek 1983, Sanford Meisner – The Theatre's Best Kept Secret 1984, One Magic Christmas 1985, Dead of Winter 1987, End of the Line (also exec. producer) 1987, The Whales of August 1987, The Attic: The Hiding of Anne Frank 1988, Parenthood 1989, Back to the Future Part III 1989, Miss Firecracker 1989, The Long Walk Home 1990, The Butcher's Wife 1991, What's Eating Gilbert Grape 1993, Philadelphia 1993, Pontiac Moon 1994, Clifford 1994, It Runs in the Family 1994, My Family, Powder, The Grass Harp, Nixon, About Sarah 1995, Picnic (TV) 2000, Wish You Were Dead 2001, The Trumpet of the Swan 2001, Sunshine State 2002, Life as a House 2001, Nobody's Baby 2002, Casa de Los Babys 2003, Elf 2003, Hope Springs 2003, Marilyn Hotchkiss Ballroom Dancing & Charm School 2005, Inland Empire 2006, The Dead Girl 2006, Elvis and Anabelle 2007, Nobel Son 2007, Numb 2007, The Brave One 2007, Honeydripper 2007, Step Brothers 2008. *Television includes:* Joan of Arcadia (series) 2003–05. *Theatre appearances include:* Holiday (Old Vic, London) 1987, Candida (Broadway) 1993. *Address:* c/o Ames Cushing, William Morris Agency Inc., One William Morris Place, Beverly Hills, CA 90212, USA.

STEENSGAARD, Niels Palle, DPhil; Danish academic; *Professor, Faculty of the Humanities, Københavns Universitet;* b. 7 March 1932, Rødovre; s. of Knud Steensgaard and Kirstine Steensgaard (née Knop); m. Illa Frilis 1954; two d.; ed Univ. of Copenhagen, School of Oriental and African Studies, London, UK; Assoc. Prof., Inst. of History, Univ. of Copenhagen 1962, Dean, Faculty of Humanities 1974–76, Prof. 1977–; mem. Danish Research Council for the Humanities 1980–88, Chair. 1985–87; mem. Nordic Cttee Humanities Research Councils 1983–88, Chair. 1985–87; Danish Rep., Standing Cttee for the Humanities, European Science Foundation 1983–88; mem. Swedish Council for Research in the Humanities and Social Sciences 1992–96; Chair. Nat. Cttee of Danish Historians 1989; mem. Royal Danish Acad. of Sciences and Letters 1982, Academia Europaea 1989, Royal Historical Soc. 1997. *Publications:* The Asian Trade Revolution of the Seventeenth Century 1973, Verden På Opdagelsernes tid 1984, Verdensmarked og kulturmøter 1985. *Leisure interests:* losing my way in large books or towns. *Address:* Faculty of Humanities, Københavns Universitet, Njalsgade 80, 2300 Copenhagen (office); Lemnosvej 19, Copenhagen 2300 S, Denmark (home). *Telephone:* 35-32-80-60 (office). *Fax:* 35-32-80-52 (office). *E-mail:* hum-fak@fak.hum.ku.dk (office). *Website:* www.hum.ku.dk (office).

ŞTEFĂNESCU, I. Ştefan, PhD; Romanian historian; b. 24 May 1929, Goicea, Dolj Co.; s. of Ion Ştefănescu and Dumitra Ştefănescu; m. Teodora Ştefănescu 1958; one s. one d.; ed Coll. of History, Bucharest Univ. Lomonosov Univ. Moscow; researcher in history 1951–65; Head Romanian Medieval History Dept of the N Iorga Inst. of History of the Romanian Acad. 1965–66, Deputy Dir 1966–70, Dir 1970–90; Dean of the Coll. of History and Philosophy, Bucharest Univ. 1977–85; mem. Romanian Acad. of Social and Political Sciences 1970–90; corresp. mem. Romanian Academy 1974, mem. 1992; mem. Romanian Soc. for Historical Sciences (on main Bd), Int. Comm. for Hist. of State Ass., Comm. int. des études slaves; Vice-Chair. of the Nat. Cttee of Historical Sciences; Chair. of the Dept of History and Archaeology, Romanian Acad. of Social and Political Sciences 1970–90; mem. European Acad. of History 1981–; Deputy Nat. Ass. 1975–80, 1985–90; Order of Scientific Merit 1966, Star of the Repub. 1971; Prize of the Romanian Acad. 1967, Romanian Acad. Silver Medal 2003. *Works include:* The History of the Romanian People 1970, Medieval Wallachia from Basarab I the Founder until Michael the Brave, 1970, History of Dobrudja, Vol. III (with I. Barnea) 1971, Demography – a Dimension of History 1974, Encyclopedia of Romanian Historiography 1978, The Romanian Nation 1984, The Beginnings of Romanian Principalities 1991, The Romanian Principalities in the 14th–16th Centuries 1992, Romania's Economic History (co-author) 1994, History of the Romanians in the 17th Century 1996, Romania: Historical-Geographic Atlas (co-author) 1996, The Illustrated History of Craiova (co-author) 1996, The Romanian Principalities in the Eighteenth Century 1998, Studies of Economic History and History of Economic Thought (co-author) 1998, A History of the Romanians (Medieval History), Vol. III (co-author), Vol. IV (Ed.) 2001, Romania: Historical Landmarks (co-author) 2004. *Address:* 125 Calea Victoriei, 010071 Bucharest (office); 214 Calea Victoriei, Apt. 44, 010098 Bucharest, Romania (home). *Telephone:* (1) 2128640 (office); (1) 6593932 (home). *Fax:* (1) 2116608 (office). *E-mail:* msimionescu@acad.ro (office). *Website:* www.academiaromana.ro (office).

STEFANIUK, Franciszek Jerzy; Polish economist, politician and farmer; b. 4 June 1944, Drelów, Biała Podlaska Prov.; m.; five c.; ed Economic Tech. School, Międzyrzec Podlaski; manages own farm; Chair. Cooperative of Agricultural Circles, Drelów 1978–82; mem. United Peasant Party (ZSL) 1963–89, Polish Peasant Party (Polskie Stronnictwo Ludowe—PSL) 1989–, Chair. Party Commune Cttee, Drelów 1982–89; Chair. Party Voivodship Cttee, Biała Podlaska 1990–98, Vice-Chair. Bd Supreme Exec. Cttee 1992–97, Chair. Supervisory Bd PSL 2000–; Deputy to Sejm (Parl.) 1989–; Deputy Chair. PSL Parl. Caucus 1991–93; Vice-Marshal (Deputy Speaker) Sejm 1997–2001. *Leisure interests:* folklore, folk poetry, bee-keeping. *Address:* Biuro Poselskie w Białej Podlaskiej, 21-500 Biała Podlaska, ul. Janowska 3; Kancelaria Sejmu RP, 00-902 Warsaw, ul. Wiejska 4/6/8, Poland (office). *Telephone:* (22) 6942321 (office). *E-mail:* Franciszek.Stefaniuk@sejm.pl (office). *Website:* stefaniuk.sejm.pl.

STEFFEN, Will, PhD; Australian environmental scientist and academic; *Executive Director, Climate Change Institute, Australian National University;* ed Univ. of Florida, USA; began career as research chemist; fmr Researcher, Div. of Environmental Mechanics, CSIRO, Canberra; Exec. Dir Int. Geosphere-Biosphere Programme, Stockholm, Sweden 1998–2004; Visiting Fellow, Bureau of Rural Sciences, Dept of Agric., Fisheries and Forestry 2004–05; Dir Fenner School of Environment and Soc., also Pro Vice-Chancellor (Research), ANU, becoming Exec. Dir ANU Climate Change Inst.; Science Adviser to Australian Dept of Climate. *Address:* Climate Change Institute, Australian National University, Room 4027, Coombs Building, Canberra, ACT 0200, Australia (office). *Telephone:* (2) 6125-6599 (office). *E-mail:* will.steffen@anu.edu.au (office). *Website:* www.anu.edu.au/climatechange (office).

STEFFLER, John Earl, BA, MA; Canadian poet, writer and academic; *Parliamentary Poet Laureate;* b. 13 Nov. 1947, Toronto, Ont.; one s. one d.; ed Univ. of Toronto, Univ. of Guelph; Prof. of English, Sir Wilfred Grenfell Coll., Memorial Univ. of Newfoundland, Corner Brook Campus 1975–; Parl. Poet Laureate 2006–08; Scholar in Residence, Concordia Univ. 2007; mem. League of Canadian Poets, PEN, Writers' Alliance of Newfoundland and Labrador; Newfoundland Arts Council Artist of the Year Award 1992, Joseph S. Stauffer Prize 1993, Newfoundland and Labrador Poetry Award 1998, 2003. *Publications:* An Explanation of Yellow 1980, The Grey Islands 1985, The Wreckage of Play 1988, The Afterlife of George Cartwright (novel) (Smithbooks/Books in Canada First Novel Award 1992, Thomas Raddall Atlantic Fiction Award 1992) 1991, That Night We Were Ravenous (poems) (Atlantic Poetry Award) 1998, Helix 2003; contrib. to journals and periodicals. *Address:* Department of English, Memorial University of Newfoundland, Corner Brook, NL A2H 6PN, Canada (office). *E-mail:* steffler@swgc.mun.ca (office).

ŠTEFKA, Maj.-Gen. Pavel; Czech army general; *Chief of the General Staff;* b. 15 Sept. 1954, Ruda nad Modravou; s. of Ludevít Štefka and Irena Štefka; m. Jirina; three d.; ed Mil. Coll., Vyskov, Mil. Acad., Warsaw, European Business School, Prague and American Nat. War Coll., Washington DC, USA; Chief of Staff of motorized bn., then Deputy Chief of Staff of motorized Regt, E Mil. Dist; Chief of Staff, later Commdr of motorized Regt, Bratislava; Chief of Operations in an armoured div.; tutor Mil. Acad. Brno 1991–94; Commdr 6th Mechanized Brigade, Brno 1994; Deputy Commdr 2nd Army Corps and Chief of Staff HQ Ground Forces, Olomouc 1994–98; Chief of Operations Section of the Gen. Staff, Army of the Czech Repub. 1998–99, Chief of the Gen. Staff 2002–; Cross of Merit of Minister of Defence (Czech Republic), Medal for Service to the Nation, NATO Medal for Service for Peace and Freedom, Commemorative Medal of Minister of Defence (Slovakia), Silver Medal of Polish Army, Commemorative Medal of Auxiliary Tech. Bns, Hon. Remembrance Badge of Fifty Years of NATO. *Leisure interests:* sport, film, travel. *Address:* c/o Ministry of Defence, Tychonova 1, 160 01 Prague 6, Czech Republic (office). *Telephone:* (2) 33041111 (office). *Fax:* (2) 3116238 (office). *E-mail:* stefkap@army.cz (office). *Website:* www.army.cz (office).

STEGER, Joseph A., PhD; American academic and fmr university administrator; b. 17 Feb. 1937, Philadelphia, Pa; s. of Joseph A. Steger and Georgianna Kirby; m. Carol R. Steger 1977; one s. one d.; ed Gettysburg Coll. and Kansas State Univ.; Sr Research Analyst, Prudential Insurance Co. 1964–66; Asst Prof., Assoc. Prof. Dept of Psychology, State Univ. of New York 1966–71; Prof., School of Man., Rensselaer Polytechnic Inst. 1971–74, Dean, School of Man. 1974–79, Dean and Vice-Pres. for Admin. and Budget 1977–78, Dean and Acting Provost 1978–79; Dir Organizational Devt and Human Resources, Colt Industries Inc. 1979–82; Sr Vice-Pres. and Provost, Univ. of Cincinnati 1982–84, Pres. 1984–2003; public comm. to review Cincinnati school finances 2004–; fmr Chair. Bd of Trustees Drake Center. *Publication:* Readings in Statistics for the Behavioral Scientist 1971. *Leisure interests:* sailing, golf. *Address:* c/o Office of the President, University of Cincinnati, PO Box 210063, Cincinnati, OH 45221-0063, USA.

STEHELIN, Dominique Jean Bernard, PhD; French research scientist; *Director of Research, Institute of Biology, Le Centre national de la recherche scientifique (CNRS);* b. 4 Sept. 1943, Thoisy; s. of Robert Stehelin and Berthe Zimmermann; m. 1st Liliane Fachan 1969 (divorced 1975); one d.; m. 2nd Monique Braun 2001; ed Lycée Fustel, Strasbourg and Univ. Louis Pasteur, Strasbourg; Perm. Researcher, sponsored by CNRS, at Louis Pasteur Univ. 1969–71; Post-doctoral studies at Institut de la Recherche Scientifique sur le Cancer with Dr A. Lwoff, Villejuif 1970–71; Visiting Scientist with J. M. Bishop at Univ. of Calif. Medical Center, San Francisco, USA 1972–75; Head of Molecular Oncology Research Unit, Institut Pasteur, Lille 1979–84, Prof. 1984–; Dir of Research CNRS 1985–; Founding Dir CNRS Inst. of Biology, Lille 1994–2000; Corresp. mem. Acad. of Sciences 1990–; mem. American Soc. of Microbiology, European Molecular Biology Org., Editorial Bd Oncogene; Chevalier de l'Ordre nat. du Mérite; Officier, Légion d'honneur; Grand Prix, Acad. des Sciences 1975, Louis Jeantet Award (Medicine), Geneva 1987 and four other awards. *Publications:* more than 300 int. publs on cancer research (cancer genes, retrovirus, angiogenesis). *Leisure interests:* skiing, diving, music. *Address:* CNRS Institut de Biologie, 1 rue Calmette, 59021 Lille (office); 36 rue Jacquemars Gielée, 59800 Lille, France (home). *Telephone:* (3) 20-87-11-08/09 (office); (3) 20-07-63-35 (home). *Fax:* (3) 20-87-11-11 (office). *E-mail:* dominique.stehelin@ibl.fr (office).

STEICHEN, René, DenD; Luxembourg business executive and fmr politician; *Chairman, SES Global;* b. 27 Nov. 1942; m.; three c.; ed Lycée Classique, Diekirch, Cours Supérieurs, Luxembourg, Faculties of Law, Aix-en-Provence and Paris and Inst. d'Etudes Politiques, Paris; lawyer, Diekirch 1969–84; mem. Diekirch Town Council 1969, Mayor 1974–84; Christian Social Deputy in Parl. 1979; Sec. of State for Agric. and Viticulture 1984, of Agric., Viticulture and Rural Devt and Minister-Del. for Cultural Research and Scientific Research 1989–93; Commr for Agric. and Rural Devt, EC 1993–95; Chair. Soc. Européenne des Satellites 1996–2000, SES Global 2001–. *Address:* SES Global SA, Château de Betzdorf, 6815 Betzdorf, RCS LuxembourgB 81267 (office). *Telephone:* 7107251 (office). *Fax:* 710725227 (office). *Website:* www.ses.com (office).

STEIGER, Paul E., BA; American journalist and editor; *Editor-in-Chief, President and CEO, ProPublica;* b. 15 Aug. 1942, Bronx, NY; ed Yale Univ.; staff writer, LA Times 1968, Econ. Corresp., Washington, DC Bureau 1971–78, apptd Business Ed. 1978; with Wall Street Journal, reporter for San Francisco Bureau 1966–68, Asst Man. Ed. 1983–85, Deputy Man. Ed. 1985–91, Man. Ed. 1991–2007, Ed.-at-Large 2007–, also Vice-Pres. Dow Jones & Co.; Ed.-in-Chief, Pres. and CEO ProPublica (ind. non–profit newsroom) 2008–; Chair. Cttee to Protect Journalists; Trustee John S. and James L. Knight Foundation; mem. Pulitzer Prize Bd 1998–2007 (Chair. 2007), Columbia Grad. School of Journalism Bd of Visitors; Poynter Fellow, Yale Univ. 2001–02; George Beveridge Ed. of the Year Award 2001, American Soc. of Newspaper Eds' Leadership Award 2002, Gerald Loeb Award 2002, John Hancock Award 2002, Columbia Journalism Award 2002, Goldsmith Career Award for Excellence in Journalism, Harvard Univ. Joan Shorenstein Center on Press, Politics and Public Policy 2008. *Publications include:* The '70s Crash and How to Survive It 1970. *Address:* ProPublica, One Exchange Plaza, 55 Broadway, 23rd Floor, New York, NY 10006, USA (office). *Telephone:* (212) 514-5250 (office). *E-mail:* info@propublica.org (office). *Website:* www.propublica.org (office).

STEILMANN, Britta; German retail executive; *Founder, Britta Steilmann Design;* b. 1966, Wattenscheid; d. of Prof. Klaus Steilmann; one d.; Marketing and Product Man. Klaus Steilmann GmbH & Co. KG 1987–89, Chief Exec., Environment and Communications Dept 1993–96, Chair. Bd Dirs and CEO 2001–03; opened internet shop and launched website for services including living and interior design www.brittasteilmann.com 2003; f. B.S.S.D. GmbH & Co. KG 1992; Man. SG Wattenscheid 09 professional soccer team 1995; mem. Factor 10 Club, 100 Global Leaders for Tomorrow, World Econ. Forum, Innovation in Deutschland, Curator's Bd Fachhochschule für Technik und Wirtschaft Coll., Dresden Cultural Foundation, Curator's Bd Art of Nature, Bd German Fashion Institute DMI; Patron and Consultant, Big Sisters, AIESEC Meets EXPO 2000; Bundesverdienstkreuz; Capital Magazine Man. of the Year 1993, World-Wide Fund for Nature Eco-Manager of the Year 1993, Forbes Magazine Jr Man. of the Year 1994, Bavarian Communication Asscn Ecology and Communication First Prize 1995, ranked 40th by Fortune magazine amongst 50 Most Powerful Women in Business outside the US 2002. *Publication:* Millenium Moral. *Leisure interests:* hiking, horseback riding. *Address:* B.S.S.D. GmbH & Co. KG, Britta Steilmann | Design, Postfach 101011, 40839 Ratingen, Germany (office). *Telephone:* (2102) 875-0 (office). *Fax:* (2102) 87525 (office). *E-mail:* britta.steilmann@bssd.com (office); britta.steilmann@brittasteilmann.com (office). *Website:* www.brittasteilmann.com (office).

STEIN, Cyril; British business executive; b. 20 Feb. 1928; s. of the late Jack Stein and Rebecca Selner; m. Betty Young 1949; two s. one d.; Chair. and Jt Man. Dir Ladbroke Group PLC 1967–93, Dir (non-exec.) –1994; Chair. St James's Club Ltd 1995–2005; f. Cyril and Betty Stein Charitable Trust.

STEIN, Elias M., AB, MA, PhD; American mathematician and academic; *Professor, Department of Mathematics, Princeton University;* b. 13 Jan. 1931, Antwerp, Belgium; s. of Elkan Stein and Chana Goldman Stein; m. Elly Intrator 1959; one s. one d.; ed Univ. of Chicago; Instructor MIT 1956–58; Asst Prof. Univ. of Chicago 1958–61, Assoc. Prof. 1961–63; mem. Inst. for Advanced Study, Princeton 1962–63, 1984–85; Prof. Princeton Univ. 1963–, Chair. of Dept of Math. 1968–70, 1985–87; Guggenheim Fellow 1976–77, 1984–85; mem. American Acad. of Arts and Sciences, NAS, American Mathematical Soc.; Dr hc (Peking Univ.) 1988; Hon. DSc (Univ. of Chicago) 1992; AMS Steele Prize 1984, 2002, von Humboldt Award 1889–90, Shock Prize, Swedish Acad. of Sciences 1993, Wolf Prize for Math. (jtly) 1999, Nat. Medal of Science 2002. *Publications:* Singular Integrals and Differentiability Properties of Functions 1970, Topics in Harmonic Analysis Related to the Littlewood-Paley Theory 1970, Introduction to Fourier Analysis on Euclidean Spaces (with G. Weiss) 1971. *Address:* Department of Mathematics, Princeton University, 802 Fine Hall, Washington Road, Princeton, NJ 08544 (office); 132 Dodds Lane, Princeton, NJ 08544, USA (home). *Telephone:* (609) 452-3497 (office); (609) 924-9335 (home). *E-mail:* stein@math.princeton.edu (office). *Website:* www.math.princeton.edu (office).

STEIN, Peter Gonville, FBA; British legal scholar and academic; *Professor Emeritus and Fellow, Queens' College, Cambridge;* b. 29 May 1926, Liverpool; s. of Walter O. Stein and Effie D. Walker; m. 1st Janet Chamberlain 1953, three d.; m. 2nd Anne Howard 1978; one step-s.; ed Liverpool Coll., Gonville and Caius Coll. Cambridge and Univ. of Pavia, Italy; served RN 1944–47;

admitted solicitor 1951; Prof. of Jurisprudence, Univ. of Aberdeen 1956–68; Regius Prof. of Civil Law, Univ. of Cambridge 1968–93; Prof. Emer. and Fellow Queens' Coll., Cambridge 1968–; mem. Univ. Grants Cttee 1971–76; JP, Cambridge 1970–; Fellow, Winchester Coll. 1976–91; Pres. Soc. of Public Teachers of Law 1980–81; mem. US–UK Educational Comm. 1985–91; Fellow Academia Europaea 1989; Foreign Fellow, Accad. Nazionale dei Lincei, Accad. di Scienze Morali e Politiche di Napoli, Accad. degli Intronati di Siena, Kon. Akad. v. Wetenschappen, Brussels; Hon. Fellow, Gonville and Caius Coll., Cambridge; Hon. QC 1993; Hon. DrJur (Göttingen) 1980; Dott.Giur. hc (Ferrara) 1990, (Perugia) 2001; Hon. LLD (Aberdeen) 2000; Dr hc (Paris II) 2001. *Publications:* Regulae Iuris: from juristic rules to legal maxims 1966, Legal Values in Western Society (with J. Shand) 1974, Legal Evolution 1980, Legal Institutions 1984, The Character and Influence of the Roman Civil Law: essays 1988, The Teaching of Roman Law in England around 1200 (with F. de Zulueta) 1990, Notaries Public in England since the Reformation (ed. and contrib.) 1991, Römisches Recht und Europa 1996, Roman Law in European History 1999. *Leisure interest:* gardening. *Address:* Wimpole Cottage, 36 Wimpole Road, Great Eversden, Cambridge, CB3 7HR, England (home). *Telephone:* (1223) 262349 (home). *E-mail:* gonville@waitrose.com (home).

STEIN BARILLAS, Eduardo; Guatemalan politician; m. Myrna Coronado; five d.; ed Univ. of St. Louis, Northwestern Univ., USA; teaching positions at Universidad Rafael Landívar, Guatemala 1971–72, Universidad Centroamericana José Simeón Cañas, El Salvador 1972–80), Florida State Univ. Panama campus 1985–87; Resident Rep., Int. Org. for Migration (IOM), Panama 1993–95; Minister of Foreign Affairs 1996–2000; Vice-Pres. 2004–08; fmr Pres. Foundation of the Americas, Washington, DC; apptd by OAS to Head of Electoral Observation Mission, Presidential Elections in Peru 2000, resgnd, then returned as Head of Electoral Observation Mission 2001; consultant to IOM, Guatemala and UNDP, Panama; mem. Int. Crisis Group, Brussels, Inter-American Dialogue, Washington, DC; fmr mem. UN Int. Comm. on Intervention and State Sovereignty 2001; participated in several presidential and vice-presidential summits on Cen. American regional peace process including Esquipulas I and the San José Dialogue with EU. *Address:* c/o Inter-American Dialogue, 1211 Connecticut Avenue, NW, Suite 510, Washington, DC 20036, USA (office).

STEINBERG, Donald K., BA, M.Econ., MA; American diplomatist and international organization official; *Deputy President (Policy), International Crisis Group;* b. 25 March 1953, Los Angeles; s. of Warren Linnington and Beatrice Blass; ed Reed Coll., Portland, Ore., Univ. of Toronto, Canada, Columbia Univ.; joined Foreign Service, rising to rank of Minister-Counselor; postings in Brazil, Malaysia, Mauritius and Cen. African Repub.; acting Chief Textile Negotiator, Office of US Trade Rep. 1988–89; first Dir House Task Force on Trade and Competitiveness 1989, Sr Policy Adviser for Foreign Affairs and Defense to Leader of House of Reps 1989–90; Officer-in-Charge and Counselor for Econ. and Commercial Affairs, US Embassy, Pretoria 1990–93; Deputy Press Sec. for Nat. Security Affairs, White House 1993; Special Asst to fmr Pres. Clinton for W African Affairs and Sr Dir for African Affairs, Sr Dir for Public Affairs, Nat. Security Council; Amb. to Angola 1995–98; Special Haiti Coordinator, Dept of State 1999–2001, Special Rep. of Pres. and Sec. of State for Global Humanitarian Demining 1998, Deputy Asst Sec. of State for Population, Refugees and Migration 2000–01, Prin. Deputy Dir . for Policy Planning 2001–03, Dir Jt Policy Council 2003–05; Sr Fellow, Jennings Randolph Fellowship Program, US Inst. of Peace 2004–05; Vice Pres. for Multilateral Affairs and Dir, New York office, Int. Crisis Group 2005, currently Deputy Pres. (Policy), Brussels; Pulitzer Fellowship and fellowships from American Political Science Asscn, Univ. of Toronto, Uma Chapman Fox Foundation and US Dept of State; Presidential Meritorious Honor Award 1994, Hough Award for Excellence in Print, three Superior Honor Awards, Distinguished Service Award 2002, Hunt Award for Advancing Women's Role in Policy Formation 2003 US Dept of State. *Publications;* many publs on US trade policies, Africa, landmines and the role of Congress in foreign affairs. *Address:* International Crisis Group, 149 Avenue Louise, Level 24, 1050 Brussels, Belgium (office). *Telephone:* (2) 502-90-38 (office). *Fax:* (2) 502-50-38 (office). *Website:* www.crisisgroup.org (office).

STEINBERG, Leo, PhD; American historian, writer and academic; *Benjamin Franklin and University Professor Emeritus, University of Pennsylvania;* b. 9 July 1920, Moscow, USSR; ed Slade School of Art, Univ. of London, Inst. of Fine Arts, New York Univ.; Prof. of Art History, Hunter Coll. & Grad. Center, City Univ., New York 1961–75; Benjamin Franklin and Univ. Prof., Univ. of Pa 1975–91, Prof. Emer. 1991–; Norton Visiting Prof., Harvard Univ. 1995–96; Fellow, American Acad. of Arts and Sciences 1978, Univ. Coll. London 1979, MacArthur Foundation 1986; Mellon Lectures, Nat. Gallery, Wash. 1982; Dr hc (Phila Coll. of Art) 1981, (Parsons School of Design) 1986, (Mass. Coll. of Art) 1987, (Bowdoin Coll.) 1995, (Columbia Univ.) 2004, (Harvard Univ.) 2006; Mather Award for Art Criticism 1956, 1984, Award in Literature, American Acad. and Inst. of Arts and Letters 1983. *Publications:* Other Criteria 1972, Michelangelo's Last Paintings 1975, Borromini's San Carlo alle Quattro Fontane 1977, The Sexuality of Christ in Renaissance Art and in Modern Oblivion 1983, Encounters with Rauschenberg 2000, Leonardo's Incessant Last Supper 2001; articles on the history of art in various journals. *Address:* 165 West 66th Street, New York, NY 10023, USA (home).

STEINBERGER, Jack, PhD; American physicist; b. 25 May 1921, Germany; s. of Ludwig Steinberger and Bertha Steinberger (née May); m. 1st Joan Beauregard 1943; m. 2nd Cynthia Eve Alff 1962; three s. one d.; ed Univ. of Chicago; Visiting mem., Inst. of Advanced Study, Princeton 1948–49; Research Asst, Univ. of Calif., Berkeley 1949–50; Prof., Columbia Univ., New York 1950–71, Higgins Prof. 1967–71; staff mem., CERN 1968–; mem. NAS 1967–2002, Heidelberg Acad. of Sciences 1967–, American Acad. of Arts and Sciences 1969–, Acad. Nazionale dei Lincei 1997; Hon. Prof., Univ. of Heidelberg 1968; Hon. DLitt (Glasgow) 1990; Dr hc (IU Inst. of Tech., Dortmund, Columbia, Barcelona, Univ. Blaise Pascal); Nobel Prize in Physics (jtly) 1988; Pres.'s Science Medal, USA 1988, Mateuzzi Medal, Società Italiana delle Scienze 1991. *Publications:* Muon Decay 1949, Pi Zero Meson 1950, Spin of Pion 1951, Parity of Pion 1954, 1959, Σ° Hyperon 1957, Properties of 'Strange Particles' 1957–64, Two Neutrinos 1962, CP Violating Effects in K° Decay 1966–74, High Energy Neutrino Physics 1975–83, Preparation of Lep Detector 1981, 3 Families of Matter 1989, Electroweak physics experiments 1989–97. *Leisure interests:* mountaineering, flute, cruising. *Address:* CERN, 1211 Geneva 23; 25 chemin des Merles, 1213 Onex, Geneva, Switzerland (home). *Telephone:* (22) 7678125 (office); (22) 7934612 (home). *Fax:* (22) 7679425 (office).

STEINBRUCH, Benjamin; Brazilian business executive; *Chairman and CEO, Companhia Siderúrgica Nacional ADS;* b. 28 June 1953, Rio de Janeiro; s. of Mendel Steinbruch and Dorothéa Steinbruch; m. Carolina Steinbruch; four c.; ed Getulio Vargas Business Foundation; started work at Vicunha Siderurgia (family textiles and telecoms conglomerate) 1983, now Supt Officer; Chair. Companhia Siderúrgica Nacional ADS (steel producer) 1995–, CEO 2002–; Pres. Companhia Vale do Rio Doce (iron ore co.) 1997–; First Vice-Pres. Fiesp (Federação das Indústrias do Estado de São Paulo); regular columnist for Folha de São Paulo (newspaper); Vice Pres. Treasury, Albert Einstein Society 2001–04; Admin. Emer., Regional Admin. Council of São Paulo 1997; mem. Superior Council for Infrastructure 2006–. *Leisure interests:* racehorse training. *Address:* Companhia Siderúrgica Nacional, Avenida Brigadeiro Faria Lima, 3400, 20°Andar, Itaim Bibi, 04538-132 São Paulo, Brazil (office). *Telephone:* (11) 3049-7591 (office). *Website:* www.csn.com.br (office).

STEINBRÜCK, Peer; German politician; *Minister of Finance;* b. 10 Jan. 1947, Hamburg; m.; three c.; ed Christian-Albrechts-Univ. zu Kiel; worked for Fed. Ministry of Planning 1974–76, Fed. Ministry of Research and Tech. 1976–77, Personal Asst to Minister 1977; mem. SPD Party; Chief of Staff for Minister-Pres., State of Nordrhein-Westfalen 1986–90; State Sec., Ministry of Natural Conservation, Environmental Protection and Regional Devt, State of Schleswig-Holstein 1990–92, State Sec., Ministry of Econs, Tech. and Transport 1992–93, State Minister of Econs, Tech. and Transport 1993–98; State Minister of Econs, Small Businesses, Tech. and Transport, State of Nordrhein-Westfalen 1998–2000, State Finance Minister 2000–02, Minister-Pres. 2002–05; Fed. Minister of Finance 2005–. *Address:* Ministry of Finance, Wilhelmstr. 97, 10117 Berlin, Germany (office). *Telephone:* (30) 22420 (office). *Fax:* (30) 22423260 (office). *E-mail:* poststelle@bmf.bund.de (office). *Website:* www.bundesfinanzministerium.de (office).

STEINEM, Gloria, BA; American writer, journalist and feminist activist; *Consulting Editor, Ms Magazine;* b. 25 March 1934, Toledo; d. of Leo Steinem and Ruth (née Nuneviller) Steinem; m. David Bale 2000; ed Smith Coll.; Chester Bowles Asian Fellow, India 1957–58; Co-Dir, Dir Ind. Research Service, Cambridge, Mass. and New York 1959–60; editorial asst, contributing, ed., freelance writer various nat. and New York publs 1960–; co-founder New York Magazine, contrib. 1968–72; co-founder Ms Magazine 1972 (Ed. 1971–87, columnist 1980–87, consulting ed. 1987–); feminist lecturer 1969–; active various civil rights and peace campaigns including United Farmworkers, Vietnam War Tax Protest, Cttee for the Legal Defense of Angela Davis and political campaigns of Adlai Stevenson, Robert Kennedy, Eugene McCarthy, Shirley Chisholm, George McGovern; co-founder and Chair Bd Women's Action Alliance 1970–; Convenor, mem. Nat. Advisory Cttee Nat. Women's Political Caucus 1971–; Co-Founder, Pres. Bd Dirs Ms Foundation for Women 1972–; founding mem. Coalition of Labor Union Women; Woodrow Wilson Int. Center for Scholars Fellow 1977, Women's Media Center 2004; mem. advisory bd Feminist.com; Penney-Missouri Journalism Award 1970, Ohio Gov.'s Award for Journalism 1972, named Woman of the Year, McCall's Magazine 1972, Missouri Honor Medal for Distinguished Service in Journalism 2004. *Publications:* The Thousand Indias 1957, The Beach Book 1963, Outrageous Acts and Everyday Rebellions 1983, Marilyn 1986, Revolution From Within: A Book of Self-Esteem 1992, Moving Beyond Words 1994, Doing Sixty and Seventy 2006; contribs to various anthologies. *Address:* The Women's Media Center, 350 Fifth Avenue, Suite 901, New York, NY 10118, USA (office). *E-mail:* kathy@womensmediacenter.com (office). *Website:* www.womensmediacenter.com (office).

STEINER, Achim, BA, MA; German international organization executive; *United Nations Under-Secretary General and Executive Director, United Nations Environment Programme;* b. 1961, Brazil; ed Univs of Oxford and London, UK, German Devt Inst., Berlin, Harvard Business School, USA; Sr Policy Advisor, Global Policy Unit, Int. Union for the Conservation of Nature and Natural Resources (IUCN—The World Conservation Union), Washington, DC mid-1990s, worked in SE Asia as Chief Tech. Advisor on a programme for sustainable man. of Mekong River watersheds and community-based natural resources man., worked in IUCN's Southern Africa Regional Office, Dir-Gen. IUCN 2001–06; Sec.-Gen. World Comm. on Dams, based in South Africa 1998–2001; UN Under-Sec.-Gen. and Exec. Dir UNEP 2006–; Founding mem. Institut du developpement durable et des relations internationales (France); mem. several int. advisory bds including China Council for Inst. Cooperation on Environment and Devt, Environmental Advisory Council (ENVAC) of EBRD, UN Sec.-Gen.'s Advisory Council for the Global Compact, Int. Advisory Cttee of Global Environmental Action (Japan), Bd of Global Public Policy Inst. (Germany). *Address:* United Nations Environment Programme, United Nations Avenue, Gigiri, PO Box 30552, 00100 Nairobi, Kenya (office). *Telephone:* (20) 7621234 (office). *Fax:* (20) 7624275 (office). *E-mail:* executiveoffice@unep.org (office). *Website:* www.unep.org (office).

STEINER, Barbara; Austrian curator and art historian; *Director, Galerie für Zeitgenössische Kunst Leipzig;* fmr Dir Ludwigsburg and Wofsburg museums; Dir Galerie für Zeitgenössische Kunst Leipzig 2001–; Guest Prof., Univ. of Applied Art, Vienna. *Leisure interests:* city walks, cooking, jogging, yoga. *Address:* Galerie für Zeitgenössische Kunst, Karl-Tauchnitz-Strasse 11, 04107 Leipzig, Germany (office). *Telephone:* (341) 140810 (office). *Fax:* (341) 1408111 (office). *E-mail:* office@gfzk.de (office). *Website:* www.gfzk.de (office).

STEINER, David P., BA, LLB; American lawyer and business executive; *CEO and Director, Waste Management Inc.;* ed Louisiana State Univ., UCLA; began legal career with Jones, Walker, Waechter, Poitevent, Carrere & Denegre, New Orleans, La; fmr Assoc. Gibson, Dunn & Crutcher, San Jose, Calif.; Assoc. Phelps Dunbar, New Orleans –2000; Vice-Pres. and Deputy Gen. Counsel, Waste Man. Inc., Houston 2000–01, Sr Vice-Pres., Gen. Counsel and Corp. Sec. 2001–03, Chief Financial Officer 2003–04, CEO and Dir 2004–; mem. La and Calif. Bar Asscns. *Address:* Waste Management Inc., 1001 Fannin Street, Suite 4000, Houston, TX 77002, USA (office). *Telephone:* (713) 512-6200 (office). *Fax:* (713) 512-6299 (office). *Website:* www.wm.com (office).

STEINER, (Francis) George, DPhil, FBA, FRSL; British writer and scholar; b. 23 April 1929, Paris, France; s. of Dr Steiner and Mrs F. G. Steiner; m. Zara Shakow 1955; one s. one d.; ed Univ. of Paris, Univ. of Chicago, Harvard Univ., USA and Balliol Coll. Oxford, UK; editorial staff, The Economist, London 1952–56; Fellow, Inst. for Advanced Study, Princeton 1956–58; Gauss Lecturer, Princeton Univ. 1959–60; Fellow and Dir of English Studies, Churchill Coll. Cambridge 1961–69, Extraordinary Fellow 1969–, Pensioner Fellow 1996–; Albert Schweitzer Visiting Prof., New York Univ. 1966–67; Visiting Prof., Yale Univ. 1970–71; Prof. of English and Comparative Literature, Univ. of Geneva 1974–94, Prof. Emer. 1994–; Visiting Prof., Collège de France 1992; First Lord Weidenfeld Visiting Prof. of Comparative Literature, Univ. of Oxford 1994–95; Charles Eliot Norton Prof. of Poetry, Harvard Univ. 2001–02; Pres. The English Asscn 1975–76; Corresp. mem. German Acad., Harvard Club, New York; Hon. mem. American Acad. of Arts and Sciences 1989; Hon. RA (London) 2004; Hon. Fellow, Balliol Coll., Oxford, St Anne's Coll., Oxford; Chevalier, Légion d'honneur; Commdr, Ordre des Arts et des Lettres 2001; Hon. DLitt (East Anglia) 1976, (Louvain) 1979, (Bristol) 1989, (Glasgow, Liège) 1990, (Ulster) 1993, (Kenyon Coll., USA) 1995, (Trinity Coll. Dublin) 1995, (Rome) 1998, (Sorbonne) 1998, (Salamanca) 2002, (Athens) 2004, (London) 2006, (Bologna) 2006; O. Henry Award 1958, Jewish Chronicle Book Award 1968, Zabel Prize of Nat. Inst. of Arts and Letters 1970, Le Prix du Souvenir 1974, Massey Lecturer 1974, Ransom Memorial Lecturer 1976, King Albert Medal of the Royal Belgian Acad. 1982, F.D. Maurice Lecturer, Univ. of London 1984, Leslie Stephen Lecturer, Univ. of Cambridge 1985, Robertson Lecturer, Courtauld Inst., London 1985, W.P. Ker Lecturer, Univ. of Glasgow 1986, Page-Barbour Lecturer, Univ. of Virginia 1987, Gifford Lecturer 1990, Priestley Lecturer, Univ. of Toronto 1995, Prince of Asturias Prize 2001, 2002, Alfonso Reyes Prize (Mexico) 2007. *Publications:* Tolstoy or Dostoevsky: An Essay in the Old Criticism 1958, The Death of Tragedy 1960, Homer: A Collection of Critical Essays (co-ed. with Robert Flagles) 1962, Anno Domini: Three Stories 1964, The Penguin Book of Modern Verse Translation (ed.) 1966, Language and Silence 1967, Extraterritorial 1971, In Bluebeard's Castle: Some Notes Towards the Re-Definition of Culture 1971, The Sporting Scene: White Knights in Reykjavík 1973, Fields of Force 1974, A Nostalgia for the Absolute (Massey Lectures) 1974, After Babel: Aspects of Language and Translation 1975, Heidegger 1978, On Difficulty and Other Essays 1978, The Portage to San Cristóbal of A.H. 1981, Antigones 1984, George Steiner: A Reader 1984, Real Presences: Is There Anything in What We Say? 1989, Proofs and Three Parables 1992, The Deeps of the Sea 1996, Homer in English 1996, No Passion Spent 1996, Errata: An Examined Life 1998, Grammars of Creation 2001, Lessons of the Masters: The Charles Eliot Morton Lectures 2001–2002 2004, My Unwritten Books 2008. *Leisure interests:* chess, music, mountain walking. *Address:* 32 Barrow Road, Cambridge, CB2 8AS, England.

STEINER, Michael; German diplomatist and fmr government officer; *Ambassador to Italy;* b. 1949, Munich; ed Munich Univ. Law School; joined Diplomatic Service 1981, served at Perm. Mission to UN, New York, in Embassy in Prague and later Amb. to Czech Repub.; Head of Office of German Humanitarian Aid, Zagreb, Croatia 1991–92; Head of Foreign Office Special Task Force for Peace Efforts in Bosnia and Herzegovina; Nat. Rep. at Int. Contact Group on the Balkans; Contrib. Dayton Peace Talks 1995; Prin. Deputy High Rep. in Sarajevo; apptd Foreign Policy and Security Adviser to Chancellor 1998; Special Rep. for Kosovo and Head of UN Interim Admin. Mission in Kosovo (UNMIK) 2002–03; Perm. Rep. to UN, Geneva 2003–07; Pres. Governing Council of the UN Compensation Comm. for Iraq 2004; Amb. to Italy 2007–. *Address:* Embassy of Germany, Via San Martino della Battaglia 4, 00185 Rome, Italy (office). *Telephone:* (06) 492131 (office). *Fax:* (06) 49213319 (office). *E-mail:* info@rom.diplo.de (office). *Website:* www.rom.diplo.de (office).

STEINER, Sylvia Helena de Figueiredo, LLM; Brazilian judge; *Judge, International Criminal Court;* b. 19 Jan. 1953, São Paulo; m. (divorced); ed Univ. of São Paulo, Univ. of Brasilia; lawyer –1982; mem. Fed. Public Ministry 1982–95; fmr mem. and Vice-Pres. Penitentiary Council of São Paulo; Fed. Judge Regional, Court of Appeal of São Paulo 1995–2003; elected Judge Int. Criminal Court (ICC) 2003–; mem. Brazilian Del. to Preparatory Comm. of ICC 1999–2001, to Experts' Conf. on Implementation of Humanitarian Law 2001, to Meeting on Implementation of ICC Statute 2001, to First Ass. of State Parties of ICC 2002; Founding Assoc. mem. Brazilian Inst. of Criminal Sciences; Deputy Dir Brazilian Criminal Sciences Journal; mem. Admin. Council Asscn of Judges for Democracy, Exec. Council Brazilian Section of Int. Legal Comm., São Paulo Comm. for Peace and Justice; guest lecturer at numerous orgs, univs and insts. *Publications include:* articles in professional journals. *Address:* International Criminal Court, Maanweg 174, 2516 AB The Hague, Netherlands (office); Rua Estado de Israel, No. 181, Apt. 13, Vila Mariana, CEP 04022-000, São Paulo, Brazil (home). *Telephone:* 70 5158515 (office); (11) 3311-4412 (home). *Fax:* 70 5158555 (office); (11) 5572-3897 (home). *E-mail:* pio@icc-cpi.int (office); sylstein@uol.com.br, ssteiner@trf3.gov.br (home). *Website:* www.icp-cpi.int (office).

STEINHOFF, Janusz Wojciech, DTech; Polish politician; *Leader, Centre Party (Partia Centrum);* b. 24 Oct. 1946, Gliwice; m.; one d.; ed Silesian Tech. Univ., Gliwice; with Coal Industry Construction and Mechanization Plants, Gliwice 1974–75; Mining Dept Silesian Tech. Univ., Gliwice 1976–89, 1994–97; Chair. Higher Mining Office 1990–94; adviser, State Hard Coal Agency 1994–95; Vice-Chair. Regional Chamber of Commerce, Katowice 1996–97; Minister of the Economy 1997–2001, also Deputy Prime Minister; Co-Founder Solidarity Trade Union, Silesian Tech. Univ. 1980; underground Solidarity activist during martial law 1981–89; Solidarity expert on mining and protection of environment during Round Table debates, 1989; Deputy to Sejm (Parl.) 1989–93, 1997–2001; mem. Presidium Citizens Parl. Caucus (OKP) 1989–91; mem. Solidarity Election Action (AWS) Parl. Caucus 1997–2001; author of AWS programme for restructuring the mining sector; Co-Founder and Vice-Leader Christian Democratic Party; currently Leader Centre Party (Partia Centrum). *Address:* Centre Party (Partia Centrum), 00-057 Warsaw, pl. Dąbrowskiego 5, Poland (office). *Telephone:* (22) 8278442 (office). *Fax:* (22) 8278441 (office). *E-mail:* centrum@centrum.org.pl (office).

STEINITZ, Yuval, BA, MA, PhD; Israeli academic and politician; *Minister of Finance;* b. 10 April 1958; m.; three c.; ed Hebrew Univ., Jerusalem, Tel-Aviv Univ.; mil. serviced in Golani Brigade, reservist in Alexandroni Brigade; fmr mem. Peace Now movt; Prof. of Philosophy, Haifa Univ. –1999; mem. Knesset (Likud Party) 1999–, Chair. Sub-Cttee for Defence, Planning and Policy 1999–2003, Sub-Cttee for Intelligence and Secret Services 2003–06, Cttee for Examination of Intelligence Services Following the War in Iraq 2003–06, Co-Chair. Jt Security Cttee between Knesset and US Congress 2003–, Sub-Cttee for State of Alert and Field Security 2006–, Sub-Cttee on Intelligence and Secret Services 2006–, mem. Foreign Affairs and Defence Cttee 1993– (Chair. 2003–06), Constitution Law and Courts Cttee 1999–2003; Minister of Finance 2009–; Pres. Asscn for the Public's Right to Know 1999–2004. *Publications:* Invitation to Philosophy 1994, In Defense of Metaphysics 1995; articles in Israeli and Int. academic journals. *Address:* Ministry of Finance, POB 13195, 1 Kaplan Street, Kiryat Ben-Gurion, Jerusalem 91008, Israel (office). *Telephone:* 2-5317111 (office). *Fax:* 2-5637891 (office). *E-mail:* ysteinitz@knesset.gov.il (office). *Website:* www.mof.gov.il (office); yuvalsteinitz.ning.com.

STEINKÜHLER, Franz; German trade union official; b. 20 May 1937, Würzburg; m.; one c.; trained as toolmaker and became Chief of Production Planning 1951–60; joined IG Metall 1951, mem. Youth Group 1952, Chair. Youth Del. 1953, numerous local exec. positions 1953–63, Sec. Regional Exec. Bd, Stuttgart 1963–72, Dir Stuttgart Region 1972–83, Vice-Pres. IG Metall 1983–86, Pres. 1986–93; Pres. Int. Metalworkers' Fed. June 1987; mem. SPD 1951–, Vice-Pres. in Baden-Württemberg 1975–83, mem. Programme Cttee of Exec. Bd 1984; Workers' Rep. VW-AG, Wolfsburg Mannesmann AG, Supervisory Bd, Daimler Benz AG Supervisory Bd –1993, Thyssen AG; fmr Deputy Chair. Supervisory Bd Volkswagen AG; mem. State Tribunal of Baden-Württemberg 1983; currently business consultant; Hon. Senator Univ. of Konstanz 1983.

STEINMAN, Ralph M., BS, MD; Canadian physician, immunologist and academic; *Henry G. Kunkel Professor and Senior Physician, Laboratory of Cellular Physiology and Immunology, The Rockefeller University;* b. 14 Jan. 1943, Montréal; m. fmr Claudia Hoeffel; three c.; ed McGill Univ., Harvard Medical School; completed internship and residency at Massachusetts Gen. Hosp. –1970; Post-doctoral Fellow, Lab. of Cellular Physiology and Immunology, The Rockefeller Univ., New York 1970–72, Asst Prof. 1972–76, Assoc. Prof. 1976–88, Prof. 1988–, Henry G. Kunkel Prof. 1995–, Dir Christopher H. Browne Center for Immunology and Immune Diseases 1998–, also Sr Physician, The Rockefeller Univ. Hosp.; Ed. Journal of Experimental Medicine; Advisory Ed. Human Immunology, Journal of Clinical Immunology, Journal of Immunological Methods, Proceedings of the National Academy of Sciences; scientific adviser to several orgs, including the Charles A. Dana Foundation, a European consortium on devt of HIV vaccines, Campbell Family Inst. of Breast Cancer Research, Toronto, M.D. Anderson Cancer Center for Immunology Research, Houston, Tex., RIKEN Center for Allergy and Immunology Research, Yokohama, Japan, CHAVI Center for HIV/AIDS Vaccine Immunology, Durham, NC; mem. NAS, Inst. of Medicine, American Soc. of Clinical Investigation, American Soc. of Cell Biology, American Asscn of Immunologists, Harvey Soc., Kunkel Soc., Practitioner's Soc., Soc. for Leukocyte Biology; Corresp. FRSE; Trustee, Trudeau Inst., Saranac Lake, NY; hon. degrees from Univ. of Innsbruck, Free Univ. of Brussels, Erlangen Univ., Mount Sinai School of Medicine; Freidrich-Sasse Prize, Emil von Behring Prize, Robert Koch Prize, Rudolf Virchow Medal, Coley Medal, Debrecen Award in Molecular Medicine, Gairdner Foundation Int. Award 2003, New York City Mayor's Award for Excellence in Science and Tech. 2004, Albert Lasker Award for Basic Medical Research, Lasker Foundation 2007. *Achievements include:* co-discovered, with Zanvil A. Cohn, dendritic cells, which are pivotal to adaptive and innate branches of immune system. *Publications:* numerous scientific papers in professional journals on mechanisms employed by dendritic cells to regulate lymphocyte function in tolerance and resistance, as well as use of dendritic cells to understand devt of immune-based diseases and design of new therapies and vaccines. *Address:* Laboratory of Physiology and Immunology, The Rockefeller University, Box 176, 1230 York Avenue, New York, NY 10021, USA (office). *Telephone:* (212) 327-8106 (office). *Fax:* (212) 327-8875 (office). *E-mail:* steinma@rockefeller.edu (office). *Website:* www.rockefeller.edu/labheads/steinman/drSteinman.php (office).

STEINMEIER, Frank-Walter; German politician and lawyer; *Vice Chancellor and Minister of Foreign Affairs;* b. 5 Jan. 1956, Detmold (Dist of Lippe); m.; one d.; ed secondary school in Blomberg and Justus Liebig Univ., Giessen; mil. service 1074–76; law internships in Frankfurt and Giessen 1983–86; Research Asst to Chair for Public Law and Political Science, Dept of Law, Univ. of Giessen 1986–91; mem. SPD; Head of Section for Media Law and Media Policy, Lower Saxony State Chancellery 1991; Chief-of-Staff, Office of the Premier, State of Lower Saxony 1993–94; Head of Directorate for Policy Guidelines, Inter-departmental Coordination and Planning 1994–96; State Sec. and Chief-of-Staff, Lower Saxony State Chancellery 1996–98; State Sec., Federal Chancellery and Commr for the Intelligence Services 1998; Fed. Chancellery Chief-of-Staff 1999–2005; Minister of Foreign Affairs 2005–, Vice Chancellor 2007–; Pres. European Council 2007–. *Address:* Ministry of Foreign Affairs, Werderscher Markt 1, 10117 Berlin, Germany (office). *Telephone:* (30) 50000 (office). *Fax:* (30) 50003402 (office). *E-mail:* poststelle@auswaertiges-amt.de (office). *Website:* www.auswaertiges-amt.de (office).

STEINMETZ, Pierre; French lawyer and politician; *Member, Conseil Constitutionnel;* b. 23 Jan. 1943, Sainte-Colombe (Rhône); s. of Emile Steinmetz and Marguerite Frossard; m. Daniele Sebi 1968; two s.; ed Ecole Nationale d'Administration, Institut d'études politiques de Paris; Civil Admin. second class Ministry of Depts and Territories Overseas, also with Ministry of Public Health and Social Security 1970; Dir Office of High Commr in Noumea 1972; Chargé de mission Gen. Secretariat 1975; Special Adviser in cabinet of Prime Minister Raymond Barre 1979–82; Special Adviser Ministry of Urban Devt and Housing 1982; Chief Office of the Sec. Gen. of City of Paris 1982–87; Dir Econ. and Social Devt, Regional Council of Ile-de-France 1987; apptd to assess situation and restore dialogue in New Caledonia 1988; Prefect of Haute-Marne 1988; Chief, Office of Minister of Int. Cooperation and Devt 1989–91; Prefect of Pyrenees-Orientales 1992, of Haute-Savoie 1993, Reunion 1994; Dir of Cabinet by Minister of Public Service, Reform of the State and Decentralization 1995; Prefect of Burgundy region, Prefect of defence zone of Cen. East, Prefect of Côte d'Or 1996, Prefect of Poitou-Charentes region, Prefect of Vienna 1997; Dir Nat. Gendarmerie 2000–02; Chief of Staff Prime Minister's Office 2002–03; Mem. Conseil Constitutionnel 2004–; Chevalier de la légion d'honneur, Officier de l'ordre national du Mérite. *Leisure interests:* tennis, skiing. *Address:* Conseil Constitutionnel, 2 rue de Montpensier, 75001 Paris, France (office). *Telephone:* 1-40-15-30-00 (office). *Fax:* 1-40-20-93-27 (office). *E-mail:* relations-exterieures@conseil-constitutionnel.fr (office). *Website:* www.conseil-constitutionnel.fr (office).

STEINNES, Eiliv, DPhil; Norwegian environmental scientist and academic; *Professor Emeritus of Environmental Science, Norwegian University of Science and Technology;* b. 21 Sept. 1938, Elverum; s. of Eirik Steinnes and Aslaug Steinnes; m. Randi Surdal 1962; three d.; ed Univ. of Oslo; scientist, Norwegian Inst. for Atomic Energy 1964–68, Research leader 1969–79; Prof. of Environmental Science, Univ. of Trondheim Coll. of Arts and Science (now Norwegian Univ. of Science and Tech.) 1980–2008, Prof. Emer. 2008–, Rector 1984–90; mem. Norwegian Acad. of Tech. Sciences, Norwegian Acad. of Science and Letters, Royal Norwegian Soc. of Science and Letters; Hon. Prof., Univ. of Iasi, Romania 2000; Dr hc (Moldova State Univ.) 2002; Hevesy Medal (co-recipient) 2001. *Publications:* three books and more than 570 scientific papers. *Leisure interests:* outdoor life, in particular cross-country skiing and mountain tours. *Address:* Department of Chemistry, Norwegian University of Science and Technology, 7491 Trondheim (office); Sloreåsen 17A, 1257 Oslo, Norway (home). *Telephone:* 73-59-62-37 (office); 22-75-43-20 (home). *Fax:* 73-55-08-77 (office). *E-mail:* eiliv.steinnes@chem.ntnu.no (office). *Website:* www .chem.ntnu.no/english (office).

STEITZ, Joan Argetsinger, BS, PhD, FRSE; American biophysicist, biochemist and academic; *Sterling Professor of Molecular Biophysics and Biochemistry, School of Medicine, Yale University;* ed Antioch Coll., Harvard Univ.; NSF and Jane Coffin Childs Postdoctoral Fellowships, MRC Lab. of Molecular Biology, Cambridge, UK 1967–70; joined faculty, Yale Univ., New Haven, Conn. in 1970, currently Sterling Prof. of Molecular Biophysics and Biochemistry, School of Medicine, also Investigator, Howard Hughes Medical Inst. 1986–, and Dir Molecular Genetics Program, Boyer Center for Molecular Medicine; mem. Jury of 2004 L'Oréal USA Fellowships 2002, 2004; mem. American Acad. of Arts and Sciences 1982, NAS 1983, American Philosophical Soc. 1992; Fellow, American Acad. of Microbiology, Academia Europaea 2002; Hon. ScD (Brandeis Univ.) 2002, (Brown Univ.) 2003, (Princeton Univ.) 2003, (Watson School of Biological Sciences, Cold Spring Harbor Lab.) 2004; Passano Foundation Young Scientist Award 1975, Eli Lilly Award in Biological Chemistry 1976, US Steel Foundation Award in Molecular Biology 1982, Lee Hawley, Sr Award for Arthritis Research 1983, Nat. Medal of Science 1986, Radcliffe Grad. Soc. Medal for Distinguished Achievement 1987, Dickson Prize for Science, Carnegie-Mellon Univ. 1988, Warren Triennial Prize 1989, Christopher Columbus Discovery Award in Biomedical Research 1992, first Weizmann Women and Science Award 1994, City of Medicine Award 1996, Novartis Drew Award in Biomedical Research 1999, L'Oréal-UNESCO For Women in Science Award 2001, Lewis S. Rosensteil Award 2002, FASEB Excellence in Science Award 2003, Howard Taylor Ricketts Award, Univ. of Chicago 2004, Caledonian Research Foundation Prize Lectureship 2004, RNA Soc. Lifetime Achievement Award 2004, Gairdner Award 2006. *Publications:* Molecular Biology of the Gene (Vol. II, 4th edn) (co-autor) 1987; numerous articles on molecular genetics, especially RNA

structure and function. *Address:* Howard Hughes Medical Institute, Yale University, BCMM 136E, 295 Congress Avenue, PO Box 9812, New Haven, CT 06536-0812, USA (office). *Telephone:* (203) 737-4418 (office). *Fax:* (203) 624-8213 (office). *E-mail:* joan.steitz@yale.edu (office). *Website:* www.mbb.yale .edu/faculty/pages/steitzj.html (office).

STELLE, Kellogg Sheffield, PhD, FInstP; American physicist and academic; *Professor of Physics, Imperial College London;* b. 11 March 1948, Washington, DC; s. of Charles C. Stelle and Jane E. Kellogg; ed Phillips Acad. Andover, Mass., Harvard Coll. and Brandeis Univ.; Field Observer, Bartol Research Foundation, S Pole, Antarctica 1970–72; Lecturer in Math., King's Coll. London 1977–78; Research Fellow, Imperial Coll. London 1978–80, Advanced Fellow 1982–87, Lecturer in Physics 1987–88, Reader 1988–95, Prof. 1995–, Head of Theoretical Physics Group 2002–; mem. Inst. for Advanced Study, Princeton, NJ 1986; Scientific Assoc., CERN, Geneva 1980–81, 1987, 1997–98; Programme Dir Institut Henri Poincaré, Paris 2000–01; Humboldt Visiting Prof., Albert Einstein Inst., Potsdam 2007–08; Ed. Classical and Quantum Gravity 1984–93; mem. Fed. of American Scientists, AAAS, Save British Science; Fellow, American Physical Soc.; Humboldt Research Award, Alexander von Humboldt Foundation 2006. *Publications:* numerous articles in scientific journals. *Address:* The Blackett Laboratory, Imperial College, H/519 Huxley Building, South Kensington Campus, Prince Consort Road, London, SW7 2AZ, England (office). *Telephone:* (20) 7594-7826 (office). *E-mail:* k.stelle@imperial.ac.uk (office). *Website:* www3.imperial.ac.uk/people/k.stelle (office).

STELMACH, Ed; Canadian politician; *Premier of Alberta;* b. 11 May 1951, Andrew, Alberta; m. Marie Stelmach 1973; four c.; ed Univ. of Alberta; cut short his univ. educ. after death of brother and returned home to take over family homestead near Vegreville, Alberta; elected Lamont Co. Council 1986, apptd Reeve 1987; fmr Chair. Vegreville Health Unit Bd and mem. Archer Memorial Hosp. and Lamont Auxiliary Hosp. and Nursing Home Bds; MLA for Vegreville-Viking (now Fort Saskatchewan-Vegreville) 1993–, Deputy Whip, then Govt Caucus Whip 1995–97, Minister of Agric. 1997–99, of Infrastructure 1999–2001, of Transportation 2001–04, of Int. and Intergovernmental Affairs 2004–06; Leader, Progressive Conservative Party of Alberta 2006–; Premier of Alberta 2006–; fmr Chair. Alberta Agric. Research Inst.; fmr Leader Andrew 4-H Beef Club; fmr Pres. Lamont and District 4-H. *Address:* Office of the Premier, Room 307, Legislature Building, 10800 97th Avenue, Edmonton, Alberta T5K 2B6 (office); Progressive Conservative Association of Alberta, 9919 106 Street NW, Edmonton, Alberta T5K 1E2, Canada. *Telephone:* (780) 427-2251 (office). *Fax:* (780) 427-1349 (office). *Website:* www.gov.ab.ca/premier (office); www.albertapc.ab.ca.

STELMAKH, Volodymyr, PhD; Ukrainian economist and central banker; *Governor, National Bank of Ukraine;* b. 18 Jan. 1939; joined Nat. Bank of Ukraine 1992, First Vice-Gov. 1993–2000, Gov. 2000–02, 2004–. *Address:* National Bank of Ukraine (Natsionalny Bank Ukrainy), 01008 Kyiv, vul. Institutska 9, Ukraine (office). *Telephone:* (44) 253-44-78 (office). *Fax:* (44) 230-20-33 (office). *E-mail:* postmaster@bank.gov.ua (office). *Website:* www .bank.gov.ua (office).

STEMBERG, Thomas G. (Tom), AB, MBA; American business executive and venture capitalist; *Managing General Partner, Highland Consumer Fund, Highland Capital Partners LLC;* b. 18 Jan. 1949, New Jersey; s. of Oscar Stemberg and Erika Ratzer Stemberg; pnr Katherine Chapman; six c.; ed Harvard Univ., Harvard Business School, Nichols Coll.; began career as corp. trainee, Jewel's Star Market 1973, Vice-Pres. Sales and Marketing –1980; joined First Nat. Supermarkets 1980, various sr man. positions including Pres. Edwards-Finast Div. –1986; f. Staples Inc. 1986, CEO 1986–2002, Chair. Bd of Dirs 1988–2002, Exec. Chair. 2002–04, Chair. (non-exec.) and Assoc. (part-time) 2004–05, Chair. Emer. 2005–; Man. Gen. Pnr, Highland Consumer Fund, Highland Capital Pnrs LLC 2005–; founder Olly Shoes; mem. Bd of Dirs CarMax, Inc., Guitar Center, lululemon athletica, PETsMART, Inc., Pharmaca; Co-Chair. Friends of Harvard Basketball; mem., Harvard Business School Bd of Dean's Advisers, mem. Faculty of Arts and Sciences Financial Aid Task Force; Trustee Boston Symphony Orchestra; George F. Baker Scholar, Harvard Business School 1972; Hon. DBA; inducted into Babson Coll. Entrepreneurial Hall of Fame, SPARC Retail Hall of Fame 2005, Harvard Business School Alumni Achievement Award. *Publication:* Staples for Success 1996. *Leisure interests:* skiing, squash. *Address:* Highland Capital Partners LLC, 92 Hayden Avenue, Lexington, MA 02421, USA (office). *Telephone:* (781) 861-5500 (office). *Fax:* (781) 861-5499 (office). *E-mail:* tstemberg@hcp.com (office). *Website:* www.hcp.com/highland_consumer_fund (office).

STEMPLOWSKI, Ryszard Maria, LLM, PhD, DHabil(Hist); Polish academic, lawyer, historian and diplomatist; *Professor of History and Politics, Jagiellonian University;* b. 25 March 1939, Wygoda, Witwica; s. of Kazimierz Stemplowski and Eugenia Białecka; m. Irena Zasłona 1975; two d.; ed Tech. Lycée, Bydgoszcz, Dept of Ecological Eng, Wrocław Univ. of Tech., Dept of Law, Wrocław Univ., Inst. of History, Polish Acad. of Sciences, Warsaw; Research Fellow, Inst. of History, Polish Acad. of Sciences 1973–90; Chief, Chancellery of Sejm (Parl.) 1990–93; Amb. to UK 1994–99; Dir Polish Inst. of Int. Affairs 1999–2004; Prof., Warsaw School of Econs 2001–04; Prof. of History and Politics, Jagiellonian Univ., Kraków 2005–; Ed. Polish Diplomatic Review 2000–04; mem. Polish History Soc. 1975–, Sec.-Gen. 1976–78; Co-founder and mem. Polish Soc. of Studies of Latin America 1978–; Visiting Fellow, St Antony's Coll. Oxford 1974; Alexander von Humboldt Research Fellow, Univ. of Cologne 1981–82; Gran Croce di Merito del Ordine Constantiniano di S. Giorgio 1997; Kt, Order of Polonia Restituta 2000; Interfaith Gold Medallion Peace Through Dialogue, Int. Council of Christians and Jews 1999. *Publications:* over 150 articles; 13 books, including (in Polish) Argentina and the Rivalries among the United States, United Kingdom and

Germany 1930–46 1975, State Socialism in the Actually Existing Capitalism: Chile 1932 1996, An Introduction to the Polish Foreign Policy Analysis (two vols) 2006, Government Proposals and Theoretical Concepts of Integration of European States in the 20th and 21st Centuries 2007, Normative Rules of Conducting Foreign Policy 2008. *Leisure interests:* music, cosmology, fiction. *Address:* Uniwersytet Jagielloński, ul. Gronostajowa 7A, pok. nr 3.016, 30-387 Kraków (office); ul. Sulkowskiego 4 M. 3, 01-602, Warsaw, Poland (home). *E-mail:* ryszard.stemplowski@uj.edu.pl (office); ryszard@stemplowski.pl (home). *Website:* www.uj.edu.pl (office); www.stemplowski.pl (home).

STENBÄCK, Pär Olav Mikael, MA; Finnish international administrator and fmr politician; *Vice-President for Europe, International Youth Foundation;* b. 12 Aug. 1941, Porvoo (Borgå); s. of Arne Mikael Stenbäck and Rakel Stenbäck (née Granholm); m. Liv Sissel Lund 1970; two s.; ed Helsinki Univ.; Ed. with Finnish Broadcasting Co. 1962–68; Chair. Svensk Ungdom (youth org. of Swedish People's Party of Finland) 1967–70; mem. Parl. 1970–85; Chair. Swedish People's Party 1977–85; Minister of Educ. 1979–82, of Foreign Affairs 1982–83; Man. Dir Hanaholmen Swedish-Finnish Culture Centre 1974–85; Sec.-Gen. Finnish Red Cross 1985–88, Pres. 1996–99; Sec.-Gen. Int. Fed. (fmrly League) of Red Cross and Red Crescent Socs, Geneva 1988–92; Sec.-Gen. Nordic Council of Ministers, Copenhagen 1992–96; Pres. Foundation for Swedish Culture in Finland 1996–2002; Chair. Norwegian-Swedish Comm. preparing new Reindeer Grazing Convention 1998–2001; Vice-Pres. for Europe, Int. Youth Foundation, USA 1996–; Chair. Finnish Children and Youth Foundation 2001–; mem. Esbo City Council 2005–08; mem. Bd Int. Crisis Group 1995–, Mehiläinen Pvt. Hosp. Corpn 2001–, Deutsche Kinder- und Jugendstiftung 2001–, Finnish Church Aid 2005–; numerous other professional appointments; Hon. Minister (Finland); Grand Cross, Royal Order of Northern Star (Sweden), Grand Cross of the Falcon (Iceland), Grand Cross St Olav (Norway), Grand Cross of Dannebrog (Denmark), Commdr of the Order of the Lion, Order of the White Rose (Finland), Grand Cross of Santa Miranda (Venezuela) and numerous other foreign decorations; Dr hc (Petrozavodsk State Univ.) 2000. *Publication:* Vision och verklighet (Vision and Reality) 2003. *Leisure interests:* literature, fishing, history. *Address:* Finnish Children and Youth Foundation, Georgsgatan 29 A 3, 00100 Helsinki (office); Hirbolebågen 15B, 02160 Esbo, Finland (home). *Telephone:* (9) 61821211 (office); (9) 4128725 (home); 50-5252060 (mobile). *Fax:* (9) 61821200 (office); (9) 4128725 (home). *E-mail:* pst@slns.org (office); par@stenback.fi (home). *Website:* www.slns.org (office); www.stenback.fi (home).

STENBECK, Cristina; Swedish business executive; *Chairman, Investment AB Kinnevik;* worked for Polo Ralph Lauren, New York, USA for two years; mem. Bd Invik & Co. AB 1997–, Vice-Chair. Invik & Co. AB and Industriförvaltnings AB Kinnevik 2003–2007, Chair. 2007–, cos merged to form Investment AB Kinnevik 2003; mem. Bd Metro International SA, Millicom International Cellular SA, Modern Times Group MTG AB, Tele2, Transcom WorldWide SA, Emesco AB; ranked by the Financial Times amongst Top 25 Businesswomen in Europe (11th) 2005, (13th) 2006, (12th) 2007. *Address:* Investment AB Kinnevik, PO Box 2094, 103 13 Stockholm, Sweden (office). *Telephone:* (8) 56200000 (office). *Fax:* (8) 203774 (office). *E-mail:* info@kinnevik.se (office). *Website:* www.kinnevik.se (office).

STENFLO, Jan Olof, MS, PhD; Swedish/Swiss astronomer; b. 10 Nov. 1942, Sweden; s. of Carl Stenflo and Signe Rödén; m. Joyce E. Tucker 1971; two s.; ed Univ. of Lund; Asst Prof., Univ. of Lund 1969–75; Research Scientist, Swedish Natural Science Research Council 1975–80; Prof. of Astronomy, ETH, Zürich and Univ. of Zürich 1980–2007, Dir Inst. of Astronomy, ETH 1980–2006; Pres. LEST Foundation 1983–97; mem. Royal Swedish Acad. of Sciences, Norwegian Acad. of Science and Letters, Royal Physiographic Soc. Lund; Edlund Prize, Royal Swedish Acad. of Sciences 1974. *Publications:* Solar Magnetic Fields 1994; around 250scientific papers on astronomy in int. journals. *Leisure interests:* classical music, mountain hiking, skiing. *Address:* Institute of Astronomy, ETH, 8092 Zürich (office); Haldeweg 4, 5436 Würenlos, Switzerland (home). *Telephone:* (44) 6323804 (office); (56) 4242886 (home). *Fax:* (44) 6321205 (office). *E-mail:* stenflo@astro.phys.ethz.ch (office). *Website:* www.astro.phys.ethz.ch (office).

STENLUND, Bengt Gustav Verner, MSc (Eng), DTech; Finnish professor of polymer technology (retd); b. 17 Aug. 1939, Kristinestad; s. of Gustav Stenlund and Linda Hofman; m. Kerstin Ottosson 1964; one s.; Research Assoc. The Finnish Pulp and Paper Research Inst. 1965–77; Acting Prof. of Polymer Tech., Åbo Akad. 1977–79, Prof. 1979–2002, Dean. Faculty of Chemical Eng 1982–85, Vice-Rector 1985–88, Rector 1988–97; mem. Research Council of Tech. Finish Acad. of Sciences 1983–85, Chair. and Bd mem. 1986–88; Chair. Finnish Rectors' Council 1990–92; Chair. LC Working Group on EC Research Policy 1993–95; Chair. Steering Group, Baltic Univ. Programme 1995–98; Head of Lab. of Polymer Tech. 1997–2002; mem. Scientific Del. of Finnish Chemical Industry 1985–90; mem. Bd Nordic Foundation of Tech. 1987–90; mem. Steering Cttee Finnish Centres of Expertise 1996–98; mem. Bd CRE 1994–98; Chair. Swedish Acad. of Eng of Finland 2001–04, Evaluation Cttee The Bank of Sweden Tercentenary Foundation 2002–04; mem. European Univ. Evaluation Team 1998–, Int. Selection Cttee, The Millenium Tech. Prize 2003–06, Int. Expert Cttee of Vinnova, Sweden 2006, Bd Resource Centre of Math., Science and Tech. 2006–; mem. European Science and Tech. Asscn 1994–97, Finnish Acad. of Eng, Finnish Soc. of Science and Letters, Royal Swedish Acad. of Eng, ACS 1997–2001, Japanese Inst. of Finland 1997–2002; Hon. Mem. Swedish Acad. of Eng Sciences of Finland; Commdr, Order of The White Rose of Finland; Hon. DTech (Karlstad) 2000. *Publications:* Gel Chromatography of Lignosulfonates 1970; about 50 publs about natural and synthetic polymers. *Leisure interests:* art, skiing, sailing, cycling. *Address:* Peltolantie 6 B 61, 20700 Åbo (home); Åbo Akademi University, Biskopsgatan 8, 20500 Åbo, Finland (office). *Telephone:* (400) 521556 (home). *E-mail:* bengt.stenlund@abo.fi (office). *Website:* www.abo.fi/fak/tkf (office).

STEPANIUC, Victor, DHist; Moldovan politician; *Deputy Prime Minister;* b. 13 July 1958, Ialoveni; m.; three c.; ed State Univ. of Moldova, Free Int. Univ. of Moldova; teacher of Russian language and literature, Hansca Village School, Ialoveni 1975–86, Dir of School 1986–96; mem. Parl. 1996–, mem. Juridical Comm. on Nominations and Immunities 1996–98, Chair. Parl. Comm. for Youth, Sport and Tourism 1998–2001, for Culture, Science, Educ., Sport, Tourism and Media 2005–08, Chair. CP Parl. Group 1998–2005, mem. Perm. Bureau 1998–; Deputy Prime Minister of Moldova 2008–. *Address:* Office of the Council of Ministers, 2033 Chişinău, Piaţa Marii Adunări Naţionale 1, Moldova (office). *Telephone:* (22) 25-01-04 (office). *Fax:* (22) 24-26-96 (office). *E-mail:* anteprim@moldova.md (office). *Website:* www.gov.md (office).

STEPANKOV, Valentin Georgievich; Russian lawyer; b. 17 Sept. 1951, Perm; s. of Georgii Vassilyevich Stepankov and Antonina Andreyevna Klopova; m. 2nd Irina Vasilevna Martynova 2000; one s. from first m.; ed Perm State Univ.; investigator, Office of Public Prosecutor, Sverdlovsk Dist 1975–76, Perm Region 1976–77; Public Prosecutor of town of Gubakh Perm Region 1977–81; instructor, Div. of Regional Cttee of CPSU 1981–83; Public Prosecutor of Perm 1983–87; Deputy-Dir Investigation Dept Office of Public Prosecutor of USSR 1987–88; Public Prosecutor of Khabarovsk Region 1986–90; First Deputy Public Prosecutor of RSFSR 1990–91; Procurator-Gen. of Russia 1991–93; Deputy Head of Admin., Perm Region 1994–96; mem. State Duma (Parl.) 1996–99; Deputy Rep. of Russian Pres. to Volga Fed. Dist 2000; Deputy Sec. Security Council of Russia 2003; Deputy Minister of Natural Resources 2004–06; mem. Bd of Dirs Permskiye Motory (Perm Engines) 1999–2000; Honoured Lawyer of Russian Fed. 2001–. *Publications:* monograph on Kremlin conspiracy and numerous articles. *Leisure interests:* painting, reading, walks in the forest. *Address:* c/o Ministry of Natural Resources, ul. B. Gruzinskaya 4/6, 123812 Moscow, Russia (office).

STEPASHIN, Col-Gen. Sergey Vadimovich, CandHist, LLD; Russian security official; *Chairman, Accounts Chamber of the Russian Federation;* b. 2 March 1952, Port Arthur; m.; one s.; ed Higher Political Coll., USSR Ministry of Internal Affairs, Mil. Acad., Financial Acad. under Russian Fed. Govt; service in Interior Forces 1973–90; Lecturer, Higher Political Coll., Leningrad 1981–90; Deputy to RSFSR Supreme Soviet 1990–93; after attempted coup Aug. 1991 Head of Cttee on Defence and Security of the Russian Fed. Supreme Soviet; author programme of reorganization of state security system; Chief, Leningrad Fed. Security Agency; Admin. and Deputy Chair. Russian Fed. Security Agency 1991–92; First Deputy Dir Fed. Counter-Intelligence Service (later Fed. Security Service) 1993–94, Dir 1994–95; Head of Admin, Dept of Govt 1995–97; Minister of Justice 1997–98, of Internal Affairs 1998–99; First Deputy Chair. of Govt April–May 1999, Chair. of Govt (Prime Minister) May–Aug. 1999; Chair. Exec. Council of Russia and Belarus Union May–Aug. 1999; joined Yabloko Movt 1999; mem. State Duma (Parl.) 1999–2000; Chair. Accounts Chamber of Russian Fed. 2000–; Pres. European Org. of Supreme Audit Insts 2002–; Prof., Russian Fed. State Counsellor of Justice; Order of Fortitude 1998, Order 'For Merits Before Fatherland', Third Degree 2002, Légion d'honneur, Commodore degree 2005. *Publication:* Personal and Social Security (Political and Legal Issues) 1994. *Leisure interests:* sports, literature, theatre. *Address:* Accounts Chamber of the Russian Federation, 119992 Moscow, Zubovskaya Str. 2, Russia. *Telephone:* (495) 986-05-09 (office). *Fax:* (495) 986-09-52 (office). *E-mail:* info@ach.gov.ru (office). *Website:* www.ach.gov.ru (office).

STEPHANOPOULOS, George Robert, AB,MA; American broadcast journalist and fmr government official; *Host and Chief Political Analyst, This Week with George Stephanopoulos;* b. 10 Feb. 1961, Fall River, Mass.; s. of Robert Stephanopoulos and Nikki C. Stephanopoulos; ed Columbia Univ., Univ. of Oxford, UK (Rhodes Scholar); fmrly admin. asst to US Rep. Edward Feighan, Washington, DC; Deputy Communications Dir, Dukakis-Bentsen Presidential Campaign 1988; fmr Exec. Floor Man. to US Rep. Richard Gephardt (later House Majority Leader); Sr Adviser to Pres. of USA 1993–96; Communications Dir, Clinton-Gore Presidential Campaign 1992; Communications Dir, The White House 1992–96, also Sr Adviser for Policy and Strategy; Visiting Prof. of Political Science, School of Int. and Public Affairs, Columbia Univ. 2001–02; contrib. and corresp., ABC News 1997–2002, Host and Chief Political Analyst, This Week with George Stephanopoulos (public affairs TV programme) 2002–; Medal of Excellence, Columbia Univ. 1993. *Publication:* All Too Human 1999. *Address:* ABC News This Week, 1717 DeSales Street, NW, Washington, DC 20036, USA (office). *Telephone:* (202) 222-7100 (office). *Website:* abcnews.go.com/Sections/ThisWeek (office).

STEPHANOPOULOS, Konstantinos; Greek lawyer, politician and fmr head of state; b. 1926, Patras; s. of Demetrius Stephanopoulos and Vrisiis Stephanopoulos; m. Eugenia El. Stounopoulou 1959; two s. one d.; ed Univ. of Athens; pvt. law practice 1954–74; mem. Parl. for Achaia (Nat. Radical Union) 1964, (New Democracy) 1974, 1977, 1981, 1985, (Democratic Renewal) 1989; Under-Sec. of Commerce July–Nov. 1974; Minister of the Interior 1974–76, of Social Services 1976–77; in Prime Minister's Office 1977–81; Pres. of Greece 1995–2005; Parl. Rep., New Democracy Party 1981–85, Pres. Party of Democratic Renewal 1985–94; American Hellenic Inst. Hellenic Heritage Nat. Public Service Award 2005. *Address:* Valaoritou 9B, 10671 Athens (office); Dafnis 0, 15452 Psyhico, Greece (home). *Telephone:* (210) 3602212 (office); (210) 6773190 (home). *Fax:* (210) 3602212 (office). *E-mail:* stephan@otenet.gr (office).

STEPHEN, Marcus; Nauruan politician, head of state and fmr weightlifter; *President;* b. 1 Oct. 1969; participated as weightlifter for Samoa at Olympic

Games in Barcelona 1992, for Nauru at Olympic Games in Atlanta 1996 and in Sydney 2000; in Commonwealth Games won one gold and two silver medals at Auckland 1990, three gold medals in Victoria 1994, three gold medals in Kuala Lumpur 1998, three silver medals at Manchester 2002; retd from sport in 2002; mem. Parl. from Ewa and Anetan 2003–07, held positions of Minister of Finance, for Sport, Telecommunications and Transport, Pres. (after vote of no confidence in Parl. against Pres. Ludwig Scotty) 2007–; Rep. at Int. Whaling Comm. 2005. *Address:* Office of the President, Yaren, Nauru (office). *Telephone:* 444-3772 (office). *Fax:* 444-3776 (office). *E-mail:* the.president@naurugov.nr. *Website:* www.naurugov.nr (office).

STEPHEN, Rt Hon. Sir Ninian Martin, KG, AK, GCMG, GCVO, KBE; Australian lawyer and international official; b. 15 June 1923, Oxford, England; s. of the late Frederick Stephen and Barbara Stephen (née Cruickshank); m. Valery Mary Sinclair 1949; five d.; ed George Watson's School, Edinburgh Acad., St Paul's School, UK, Chillon Coll., Switzerland, Scotch Coll., Melbourne, Melbourne Univ.; served World War II, Australian Army; admitted as barrister and solicitor, Victoria 1949; QC 1966; Judge, Supreme Court, Victoria 1970; Justice, High Court, Australia 1972–82; Gov.-Gen. of Australia 1982–89; Chair. Nat. Library of Australia 1989–94; Amb. for the Environment 1989–92; Chair. Strand Two, Northern Ireland Talks 1992, UN Group of Experts on Cambodia, Australian Citizenship Council; Judge, Int. Criminal Tribunals for Yugoslavia 1993–97, for Rwanda 1995–97; mem. Ethics Comm. Int. Olympic Cttee 2000–; Chair. ILO High Level Team to Myanmar 2001; Hon. Bencher Gray's Inn 1981; KStJ 1982; Commdr Légion d'honneur 1993. *Address:* 4 Treasury Place, Melbourne, Vic. 3002 (office); Flat 13/1, 193 Domain Road, South Yarra, Vic. Australia (home). *Telephone:* (3) 9650-0266 (office); (3) 9820-2787 (home). *Fax:* (3) 9650-0270 (office). *E-mail:* ninian.stephen@dpmc.gov.au.

STEPHENS, Toby; British actor; b. 21 April 1969, London; s. of the late Sir Robert Stephens and Dame Maggie Smith; m. Anna-Louise Plowman 2001; ed London Acad. of Music and Dramatic Art. *Plays:* Measure for Measure (RSC), A Midsummer Night's Dream (RSC), Unfinished Business (playing Young Beamish, RSC), Wallenstein (RSC), All's Well That Ends Well (playing Bertram, RSC), Anthony and Cleopatra (playing Pompey, RSC), Coriolanus (playing Coriolanus, RSC) (Sir John Gielgud Award for Best Actor 1994, Ian Charlson Award 1995), Britannicus, Phedre (Almedia & Brooklyn Acad., New York), A Streetcar Named Desire (The Haymarket), Tartuffe (playing Damis, Playhouse Theatre), Ring Around the Moon (Lincoln Center Theater, New York) 1999, Betrayal (Donmar Warehouse, London) 2007. *Films:* Orlando 1992, Twelfth Night 1996, Sunset Heights 1997, Photographic Fairies 1997, Cousin Bette 1998, Onegin 1999, The Announcement 2000, Space Cowboys 2000, Possession 2002, James Bond: Die Another Day 2002, Terkel in Trouble (voice) 2004, The Rising Ballad of Mangal Pandey 2005, Midsummer Dream (voice) 2005, Severance 2006, Dark Corners 2006, One Day 2007. *Television:* The Camomile Lawn 1992, Tenant of Wildfell Hall 1996, The Great Gatsby 2000, Perfect Strangers 2001, Napoléon 2002, Cambridge Spies 2003, Poirot (episode, Five Little Pigs) 2003, London 2004, The Queen's Sister 2005, The Best Man 2005, Sharpe's Challenge 2006, Jane Eyre (miniseries) 2006, Robin Hood (series). *Address:* c/o ICM, Oxford House, 76 Oxford Street, London, W1N 0AX, England. *Telephone:* (20) 7636-6565. *Fax:* (20) 7223-0101.

STEPHENSON, Hugh; British journalist and academic; *Professor Emeritus, Department of Journalism, City University London;* b. 18 July 1938, Simla, India; s. of the late Sir Hugh Stephenson and Lady Stephenson; m. 1st Auriol Stevens 1962 (divorced 1987); two s. one d.; m. 2nd Diana Eden 1990; ed New Coll. Oxford, Univ. of California, Berkeley, USA; in diplomatic service, London and Bonn 1964–68; with The Times, London 1969–81, Ed., The Times Business News 1971–81; Ed. The New Statesman 1982–86; Prof. of Journalism, City Univ. 1986–2003, Prof. Emer. 2003–; Dir History Today Ltd 1981–; Dir European Journalism Centre, Maastricht 1992–2008, Chair. 1995–2002. *Publications:* The Coming Clash 1972, Mrs. Thatcher's First Year 1980, Claret and Chips 1982, Libel and the Media (with others) 1997, Secrets of the Setters 2005. *Address:* Department of Journalism, City University, Northampton Square, London, EC1V 0HB, England (office). *E-mail:* h.stephenson@city.ac.uk (office). *Website:* www.city.ac.uk/journalism (office).

STEPHENSON, Randall L., BSc, MA; American telecommunications executive; *Chairman and CEO, AT&T Inc.;* b. 22 April 1960, Oklahoma City; m. Lenise H. Stephenson; ed Central State Univ., Okla, Univ. of Okla; began career with Southwestern Bell Telephone, Oklahoma City (later SBC) 1982, various man. roles in finance, becoming Dir of Finance SBC International, Mexico City 1992–96, Controller SBC Communications, San Antonio 1996–97, Sr Exec. Vice-Pres. and Chief Financial Officer 2001–04, COO SBC Communications Inc. 2004–05, COO AT&T Inc. (following merger of SBC and AT&T Corpn 2005) 2005–07, mem. Bd of Dirs AT&T Inc. 2005–, Chair. and CEO 2007–; Dir Cingular Wireless 2001–06, Chair. 2003–04; Dir Emerson Electric 2006–; Vice-Chair. The White House Nat. Security Telecommunications Advisory Cttee; Dir San Antonio Metropolitan Missions Bd; mem. San Antonio United Way Exec. Cttee and Audit Cttee; mem. Nat. Exec. Bd, Boy Scouts of America. *Address:* AT&T Inc., 175 East Houston, San Antonio, TX 78205-2233, USA (office). *Telephone:* (210) 821-4105 (office). *Fax:* (210) 351-2071 (office). *E-mail:* info@att.com (office). *Website:* www.att.com (office).

STEPIN, Vyacheslav Semenovich; Russian academic; *Director, Institute of Philosophy, Russian Academy of Sciences;* b. 19 Aug. 1934, Bryansk; s. of Semen Nikolaievich Stepin and Antonina Grigorievna (née Petrova) Stepina; m. Tatiana Ivanovna Vagranova 1957; ed Belorussia State Univ.; Prof., Chair.; Dir Inst. of History of Natural Sciences and Tech. 1987–88; Dir Inst. of Philosophy, Russian Acad. of Sciences 1988–; Corresp. mem. USSR (now Russian) Acad. of Sciences 1987, mem. 1994; research in theory of cognition, philosophy of science and tech., history of science; Vice-Pres. Philosophy Soc.; Pres. Asscn For Humanitarian Dialogue; foreign mem. Nat. Acad. of Sciences, Repub. of Belarus 1998, Ukraine 2000; Hon. Consulting Prof., Inst. of Int. Law and Econs, Hong Kong 1994, Hon. mem. Acad. of Sciences and Educ., Karlsruhe, Germany; Dr hc (Univ. of Karlsruhe) 1999. *Publications include:* Contemporary Positivism and Science 1963, Practical Nature of Cognition and Methodical Problems of Contemporary Physics 1970, Methods of Scientific Cognition 1974, Scientific Revolutions in Dynamics of Culture 1987, Philosophical Anthropology and Philosophy of Science 1992, Scientific Picture of the World in the Culture of Technogenic Civilization 1994, Philosophy of Science and Technics 1995, Age of Changes and Scenarios of the Future 1996, Civilization. Science. Culture 2002. *Address:* Institute of Philosophy, Russian Academy of Sciences, 199991 Moscow, Volkhonka str. 14 (office); DM Ulianov str. 3, Ap. 130, Moscow, Russia (home). *Telephone:* (495) 203-95-69 (office). *Fax:* (495) 200-32-50. *E-mail:* stepin@iph.ras.ru. *Website:* ru.philosophy.kiev.ua.

STERLING, Michael John Howard, PhD, DEng, FREng, FIEE, FRSA, CCMI; British engineer, academic and university vice-chancellor; *Vice-Chancellor and Principal, University of Birmingham;* b. 9 Feb. 1946, Paddock Wood, Kent; s. of Richard Howard Sterling and Joan Valeria Sterling (née Skinner); m. Wendy Karla Anstead 1969; two s.; ed Hampton Grammar School, Middx, Univ. of Sheffield; student apprentice, AEI 1964–68; GEC Research Engineer 1968–71; Lecturer in Control Eng, Univ. of Sheffield 1971–78, Sr Lecturer 1978–80; Prof. of Eng, Univ. of Durham 1980–90; Vice-Chancellor and Prin., Brunel Univ. 1990–2001; Vice-Chancellor, Univ. of Birmingham 2001–; mem. Council IEE 1991–93, Vice-Pres. 1997–2001, Deputy Pres. 2001–02, Pres. 2002–03; Chair. OCEPS Ltd 1990–, Higher Educ. Statistics Agency 1992–, Higher Educ. Funding Council Steering Cttee on Performance Indicators 1992–95 (mem. Quality Assessment Cttee 1992–95), WASMACS Ltd 1994–, MidMAN 2001; Dir COBUILD Ltd 2001–, UCAS 2001–, Universitas 21 2001–; mem. Science & Eng Research Council Eng Bd 1989–92, Electricity Research Council 1987–89, Royal Acad. of Eng Standing Cttee for Educ., Training and Competence to Practise 1993–97, Cttee 2 for Int. Co-operation in Higher Educ., British Council 1991–96, AWM Broadband Steering Group 2002–, Bd WMHEA 2001–; Fellow, Inst. of Measurement and Control (Pres. 1988, Council mem. 1983–91); Pres. Elmhurst School for Dance 2002–; Trustee Barber Inst. of Fine Art 2001–; Gov. Burnham Grammar School 1990–, Hampton School 1991– (Chair. of Govs 1997–); Freeman City of London 1996; Liveryman Worshipful Co. of Engineers 1998; Hon. DEng (Sheffield) 1995; Hon. DUniv (Tashkent, Uzbekistan) 1999; Dr hc (West Bohemia, Czech Repub.) 2001; Inst. of Measurement and Control ICI Prize 1980, IEE Hartree Premium 1985, Commemorative Medal 2000. *Publications:* Power Systems Control 1978; over 200 tech. papers and book contribs. *Leisure interests:* gardening, DIY, computers, model eng. *Address:* Vice-Chancellor's Office, Birmingham University, Edgbaston, Birmingham, B15 2TT, England (office). *Telephone:* (121) 414-3344 (office). *Fax:* (121) 414-3971 (office). *Website:* www.bham.ac.uk (office).

STERLING OF PLAISTOW, Baron (Life Peer), cr. 1990; **Jeffrey Maurice Sterling,** Kt, GCVO, CBE; British business executive; b. 27 Dec. 1934, London; s. of Harry Sterling and Alice Sterling; m. Dorothy Ann Smith 1985; one d.; ed Reigate Grammar School, Preston Manor County School and Guildhall School of Music, London; Paul Schweder & Co. (Stock Exchange) 1955-57; G. Eberstadt & Co. 1957–62; Financial Dir General Guarantee Corpn 1962–64; Man. Dir Gula Investments Ltd 1964–69; Chair. Sterling Guarantee Trust PLC 1969–85 (merged with P&O 1985), P&O Steam Navigation Co. 1983–, P&O Asia 1992–, P&O Princess Cruises 2000–03; Special Adviser to Sec. of State for Industry 1982–83, to Sec. of State for Trade and Industry 1983–90; mem. British Airways Bd 1979–82; mem. Exec., World Org. for Rehabilitation by Training Union 1966–, Chair. Org. Cttee 1969–73, Chair. ORT Tech. Services 1974–, Vice-Pres. British ORT 1978–; Pres. Gen. Council of British Shipping 1990–91, EC Shipowners' Asscns 1992–94; Deputy Chair. and Hon. Treasurer London Celebrations Cttee Queen's Silver Jubilee 1975–83; Chair. Young Vic Co. 1975–83; Vice-Chair. and Chair. of Exec. Motability 1977–94, Chair. 1994–; Chair. of the Govs. Royal Ballet School 1983–99; Chair. Queen's Golden Jubilee Weekend Trust 2001–02; Fellow, ISVA 1995; Gov. Royal Ballet 1986–99; Hon. Capt. RNR 1991–; Elder Brother Trinity House 1991; Hon mem. Royal Inst. of Chartered Surveyors 1993; Freeman City of London; Hon. Fellow Inst. of Marine Engineers 1991, Inst. of Chartered Shipbrokers 1992, Royal Inst. of Chartered Shipbrokers 1992, Royal Inst. of Naval Architects 1997; KStJ 1998; Hon. DBA (Nottingham Trent) 1995; Hon. DCL (Durham) 1996. *Leisure interests:* music, swimming, tennis. *Address:* The Peninsular and Oriental Steam Navigation Company, 79 Pall Mall, London, SW1Y 5EJ, England. *Telephone:* (20) 7930-4343 (office). *Fax:* (20) 7930-8572 (office).

STERN, Ernest, MA, PhD; American economist and academic; b. 25 Aug. 1933, Frankfurt, Germany; s. of Henry Stern; m. Zina Gold 1957; ed Queens Coll., New York and Fletcher School of Law and Diplomacy; Economist, US Dept of Commerce 1957–59; Program Economist, US Agency for Int. Devt (USAID) 1959–63; Instructor, Middle East Tech. Univ. 1960–61; Economist, Office of Pakistan Affairs, USAID 1963–64, Officer in Charge of Pakistan Affairs 1964–64, Asst Dir for Devt Policy USAID India 1965–67, Deputy Dir USAID Pakistan 1967–68, Deputy Staff Dir Comm. on Int. Devt (Pearson Comm.) 1968–69; Lecturer, Woodrow Wilson School of Public and Int. Affairs, Princeton 1971; Sr Staff mem. Council on Int. Econ. Policy, White House 1971; joined World Bank 1972, various posts including Deputy Chair. Econ. Cttee, Sr Adviser on Devt Policy, Dir Devt Policy, then Vice-Pres. S Asia until 1978, Vice-Pres. Operations, World Bank July 1978, Sr Vice-Pres., Operations 1980–87, Sr Vice-Pres., Finance 1987, Man. Dir 1991–95 (retd); fmr Man. Dir JP Morgan Chase; mem. Bd Advisors Inst. for Int. Econs, Washington, DC; mem. Bd of Overseers, Int. Center for Econ. Growth, Calif.; fnr mem. Bd of Dirs Center for Global Devt, US-Russian Business Council, Commonfund;

mem. Council on Foreign Relations, Group of Thirty; William A. Jump Memorial Foundation Meritorious Award 1964, 1966.

STERN, Fritz, PhD; American historian and academic; *University Professor Emeritus, Columbia University;* b. 2 Feb. 1926, Breslau, Germany; s. of Rudolf A. Stern and Catherine B. Stern; m. 1st Margaret J. Bassett 1947 (divorced 1992); one s. one d.; m. 2nd Elisabeth Niebuhr Sifton 1996; ed Bentley School, New York, Columbia Univ.; Lecturer and Instructor Columbia Univ. 1946–51; Acting Asst Prof. Cornell Univ. 1951–53; Asst Prof. Columbia Univ. 1953–57, Assoc. Prof. 1957–63, Full Prof. 1963–67, Seth Low Prof. 1967–92, Univ. Prof. 1992–96, Univ. Prof. Emer. 1997–, Provost 1980–83; Visiting Prof. Free Univ. of Berlin 1954, Yale Univ. 1963, Fondation Nationale des Sciences Politiques, Paris 1979; Perm. Visiting Prof. Konstanz Univ. 1966–; Consultant US State Dept 1966–67; Guggenheim Fellowship 1969–70; mem. OECD team on German Educ. 1971–72; Netherlands Inst. for Advanced Study 1972–73; Trustee German Marshall Fund 1981–99, Aspen Inst. Berlin 1983–2000; Sr Adviser, US Embassy, Bonn 1993–94; mem. American Acad. of Arts and Sciences 1969–, Trilateral Comm. 1983–90, American Philosophical Soc. 1988, German-American Academic Council 1993–97; Corresp. mem. Deutsche Akad. für Dichtung und Sprache 1988; Senator, Deutsche Nationalstiftung 1993–; Hon. Senator, Deutsche Nationalstiftung 2008–; Orden pour le Mérite (Germany) 1994, Knight Commdr's Cross (Germany) 2004; Hon. DLitt (Oxford) 1985; Hon. LLD (New School for Social Research, New York) 1997, (Columbia Univ.) 1998, (Wrocław) 2002; Hon. DHumLitt (Princeton) 2007; Lionel Trilling Book Award 1977, Lucas Prize (Tübingen) 1984, Kulturpreis Schlesien (Wrocław) 1996, Peace Prize of the German Book Trade 1999, Alexander-von-Humboldt Research Prize 1999, Bruno Snell Medal, Univ. of Hamburg 2002, Lifetime Achievement Award, American Historical Asscn 2007, Jacques Barzun Prize, American Philosophical Soc. 2007, Annual Prize for Tolerance and Reconciliation, Jewish Museum, Berlin 2007, Lifetime Achievement Award, American Historical Asscn 2007. *Publications:* The Politics of Cultural Despair: A Study in the Rise of the Germanic Ideology 1961, Gold and Iron: Bismarck, Bleichroeder and the Building of the German Empire 1977, The Failure of Illiberalism: Essays in the Political Culture of Modern Germany 1972, Dreams and Delusions: The Drama of German History 1987; ed. The Varieties of History from Voltaire to the Present 1956, Der Nationalsozialismus als Versuchung, in Reflexionen Finsterer Zeit 1984, Verspielte Grösse: Essays zur deutschen Geschichte 1996, Das Feine Schweigen: Historische Essays 1999, Einstein's German World 1999, Grandeurs et Defaillances de l'Allemagne du XXème Siècle 2001, Five Germanys I Have Known 2006, Der Westen im 20. Jahrhundert: Selbstzerstörung, Wiederaufbau, Gefährdungen der Gegenwart 2008. *Leisure interests:* reading, hiking, cross-country skiing. *Address:* 15 Claremont Avenue, New York, NY 10027, USA (home). *Telephone:* (212) 666-2891 (home). *Fax:* (212) 316-0370 (home). *E-mail:* fs20@columbia.edu (home).

STERN, Howard Allan, BA; American radio broadcaster; b. 12 Jan. 1954, Roosevelt, NY; s. of Ben Stern and Rae Stern; m. Alison Berns 1978 (divorced 2001); three d.; ed Boston Univ.; disc jockey with WRNW, Briarcliff Manor, NY 1976–78, WCCC, Hartford, Conn. 1978–79, WWWW, Detroit 1979–80, WWDC, Washington, DC 1980–82, WNBC, New York 1982–85, WXRK, New York 1985–2005; syndicated in several other radio markets with Clear Channel 1986, with Infinity Broadcasting Corpn 1998–2005; The Howard Stern Show, Sirius Satellite Radio 2006–; Libertarian cand. for Gov. of NY 1994. *TV includes:* The Howard Stern Show (WOR-TV) 1990–92, The Howard Stern Show (E!) 1994, The Howard Stern Radio Show 1998; as producer: Son of the Beach 2000 (also writer), Doomsday 2002 (also writer), Howard Stern: The High School Years 2003. *Recordings include:* 50 Ways to Rank Your Mother 1982, Crucified by the FCC 1991. *Publications:* Private Parts 1993, Miss America 1995. *Address:* c/o Don Buchwald & Associates, 10 East 44th Street, New York, NY 10017, USA (office). *Website:* www.howardstern.com.

STERN, Jacques, MSc; French business executive; b. 21 March 1932, Paris; m. Janine Riemer 1956; three s.; ed Ecole Polytechnique, Ecole Nationale supérieure de l'Aéronautique, Harvard Univ., USA; in charge of devt of air defence computer system, French Air Force 1958–64; Founder and Pres. Société d'Etudes des Systèmes d'Automation (SESA) 1964; apptd Chair. and CEO Bull 1982, Chair. Honeywell Bull Inc. 1987, Hon. Pres. Bull 1989–; Founder and Pres. Sycomore 1989–; Founder and consultant Stern Systèmes d'information 1998–; Founder and Pres. Synesys 1998–2001; Vice-Pres. Fyssen Foundation 1994; mem. Acad. of Tech.; Officier, Ordre nat. du Mérite; Chevalier, Légion d'honneur. *Publications:* several tech. books. *Address:* 1 rue Le Notre, 75016 Paris, France (home). *Telephone:* 1-45-27-35-11 (office). *E-mail:* jacques@stern-si.fr (office). *Website:* www.stern-si.fr (office).

STERN, Klaus, DrIur; German legal scholar, academic and judge; *Professor Emeritus, Institute für öffentliches Recht und Verwaltungslehre, University of Cologne;* b. 11 Jan. 1932, Nuremberg; m. Helga Stern 1976; ed Humanistisches Gymnasium, Nuremberg and Univs. of Erlangen and Munich; Dozent, Univ. of Munich 1961; Prof. Berlin Univ. 1962; Prof. and Dir Inst. für öffentliches Recht und Verwaltungslehre, Univ. of Cologne 1966–, now Prof. Emer., Rector 1971–73, Pro-Rector 1973–75; Head of Studies Verwaltungs- und Wirtschaftsakademie Düsseldorf 1966–; Judge, Constitutional Court, Nordrhein-Westfalen 1976–2000; mem. Rheinland-Westfalische Akademie der Wissenschaften 1978–; Hon. mem. Japan Acad. 2006; Dr hc (Univ. of Breslau, Poland) 1987, (Fed. Univ. Ceara of Fortaleza, Brazil) 1991, (Univ. of Verona) 2005; Grosses Bundesverdienstkreuz 1989, Austrian Ehrenkreuz for Research and Art 1998, Verdienstorden (NRW) 2000, Verdienstorden (City of Düsseldorf) 2002. *Publications:* Staatsrecht der Bundesrepublik Deutschland (4 vols); many other books and articles on constitutional and admin. law. *Address:* Institut für Rundfunkrecht an der Universität zu Köln, Aachener Straße 197-199, 50931 Cologne (office); Universität Cologne, Institut für öffentliches Recht und Verwaltungslehre, Albertus-Magnus-Platz, 50931 Cologne, Germany. *Telephone:* (221) 9415465 (office). *Fax:* (221) 9415466 (office). *E-mail:* klaus.stern@uni-koeln.de; mail@klaus-stern.net. *Website:* www.klaus-stern.net; www.uni-koeln.de/jur-fak/instoerv/index.htm (office).

STERN, Robert Arthur Morton, BA, MArch, FAIA; American architect and academic; *J.M. Hoppin Professor of Architecture and Dean, School of Architecture, Yale University;* b. 23 May 1939, New York; s. of Sidney Stern and Sonya Stern (née Cohen); m. Lynn G. Solinger 1966 (divorced 1977); one s.; ed Columbia and Yale Univs.; Program Dir Architectural League New York 1965–66; designer, Richard Meier, architect, New York 1966; consultant Small Parks Program, Dept of Parks, New York 1966–70; urban designer, Housing and Devt Admin. New York 1967–70; partner Robert AM Stern & John S. Hagmann, Architects, New York 1969–77, Prin. Robert AM Stern Architects 1977–89, Sr Partner 1989–; lecturer to Prof. of Architecture, Columbia Univ. 1970–72, Prof. 1982–98; J.M. Hoppin Prof. of Architecture and Dean, School of Architecture, Yale Univ. 1998–; Acting Dir Historical Preservation Program, Columbia Univ. School of Architecture 1991–98; mem. Bd of Regents American Architecture Foundation 1989–91, Bd of Dirs Chicago Inst. for Architecture and Urbanism 1990–93, Bd of Dirs. Preservation League of NY, Exec. Cttee, Architectural League of New York 1977– (Pres. 1973–77); Dir (non-exec.) Walt Disney Co. 1992–2003; numerous awards including AIA Nat. Honor awards 1980, 1985, 1990; President's Medal from Architectural League of NY 2002. *Television:* hosted Pride of Place: Building the American Dream, an eight-part, eight-hour documentary series on PBS 1986. *Publications include:* New Directions in American Architecture 1969, The House that Bob Built 1991, The American Houses of Robert A. M. Stern 1991, New York 1960 (with Thomas Mellins and David Fishman) 1995; also co-authored series New York 1880, New York 1900, New York 1930, New York 1960. *Address:* Office of the Dean, Yale School of Architecture, 180 York Street, New Haven, CT 06511 (office); Robert A.M. Stern Architects, 460 West 34th Street, New York, NY 10001, USA (office). *Telephone:* (203) 432-2279 (Yale) (office); (212) 967-5100 (NY) (office). *Fax:* (203) 432-7175 (Yale) (office); (212) 967-5588 (NY) (office). *Website:* www.architecture.yale.edu (office); www.ramsa.com (office).

STERN OF BRENTFORD, Baron (Life Peer), cr. 2007, of Elsted in the County of West Sussex and of Wimbledon in the London Borough of Merton; **Nicholas Herbert Stern,** PhD; British economist, academic and fmr government official; *IG Patel Chair in Economics and Government, London School of Economics;* b. 1946, London; m. Susan Stern; three c.; ed Latymer Upper School, Peterhouse Coll., Univ. of Cambridge; taught at Univ. of Oxford, Univ. of Warwick, LSE, Sorbonne, MIT; Chief Economist, EBRD 1993–99; Sr Vice-Pres. and Chief Economist, World Bank 2000–03; Second Perm. Sec., Man. Dir, Budget and Public Finances, Treasury of the UK 2003–04, Head of Govt Econ. Service 2003–07 (retd); commissioned to compile Stern Review on the Economics of Climate Change 2005, published 2006; IG Patel Chair in Econs and Govt, LSE 2007–, Dir India Observatory, Asia Research Centre; Fellow, British Acad., Econometrics Soc.; Hon. Fellow, American Acad. of Arts and Sciences; Hon DSc (Warwick) 2006. *Publications:* Palanpur: The Economy of an Indian Village (with C. J. Bliss) 1982, The Theory and Practice of Tax Reform in Developing Countries (with E. Ahmad) 1991, A Strategy for Development 2002. *Leisure interests:* reading, travelling, watching Wimbledon Football Club. *Address:* House of Lords, London, SW1A 0PW; Asia Research Centre, 10th Floor, Tower 2, London School of Economics, Houghton Street, London, WC2A 2AE, England. *Telephone:* (20) 7219-5353 (House of Lords). *Fax:* (20) 7107-5285. *E-mail:* arc@lse.ac.uk. *Website:* www.lse.ac.uk/collections/IndiaObservatory (office); www.lse.ac.uk/collections/asiaResearchCentre.

STERNBERG, Seymour G. (Sy); American insurance executive; *Chairman, New York Life Insurance Company;* b. 1943, New York City, NY; Sr Vice-Pres. Insurance Dept, New York Life Insurance Co. 1989–91, Exec. Vice-Pres. and Vice-Chair. Bd 1991–95, Pres. and COO 1995–97, Chair. and CEO 1997–2001, Chair., Pres. and CEO 2001–03, Chair. and CEO 2003–08, Chair. 2008–; mem. Bd Dirs Express Scripts Inc. 1992–; US Rep. to Asia-Pacific Econ. Co-operation Business Advisory Council 2001; Pnr and mem. New York City Partnership and Chamber of Commerce, Co-Chair. Breakthrough for Learning Initiative; Vice-Chair. Kennedy Center Corp. Fund; mem. The Business Roundtable, Lincoln Center Consolidated Corp. Fund Leadership Cttee, Bd Govs United Way of Tri-State; mem. Bd Trustees Big Brothers and Big Sisters of New York City; New Yorker for New York Award, Citizens Cttee of New York 2001. *Address:* New York Life Insurance Company, 51 Madison Avenue, New York, NY 10010, USA (office). *Telephone:* (212) 576-7000 (office). *Fax:* (212) 576-8145 (office). *E-mail:* info@newyorklife.com (office). *Website:* www.newyorklife.com (office).

STERNBERG, Sir Sigmund, Kt, FRSA, JP; British business executive; *Chairman, Martin Slowes Estates Limited;* b. 2 June 1921, Budapest, Hungary; s. of the late Abraham Sternberg and Elizabeth Sternberg; m. Hazel Everett Jones 1970; one s. one d. and one s. one d. from a previous m.; Chair., Martin Slowe Estates Ltd 1971–; Deputy Chair., Labour Finance and Industry Group 1972–93, Hon. Life Pres. 2002–; Sr Vice-Pres., Royal Coll. of Speech and Language Therapists 1995–2002, Life Vice-Pres. 2002–; Life Pres., Sternberg Centre for Judaism 1996–; Founder, Three Faiths Forum (Christians, Muslims and Jews Dialogue Group) 1997; Pres., Reform Synagogues of GB 1998–; Pres., British-Hungarian Soc. 2005–; Co-ordinator, Religious Component of World Econ. Forum 2002–; Life mem. Magistrates' Asscn 1965; mem. Bd of Deputies of British Jews, John Templeton Foundation 1998–; Paul Harris Fellow, Rotary Foundation of Rotary Int. 1989; Gov., Hebrew Univ. of Jerusalem; Patron, Int. Council of Christians and Jews, Forum Against Islamaphobia & Racism 2003–, Anne Frank Trust UK; Freeman, City of London; Hon. Fellow, Univ. Coll. London 2001, Hon. Pres.,

Royal Coll. of Speech and Language Therapists 2002–, Life mem. Royal Soc. of Medicine 2002, Hon. Life-; DUniv (Essex) 1996, (Open Univ.) 1998, (Hebrew Union Coll., Cincinnati) 2000, Hon. DHumLitt (Richmond American Int. Univ.) 2008; KCSG 1985, OStJ 1988, Order of the Gold Star (Hungary) 1990, Commdr, Order of Civil Merit (Spain) 1993, Commdr, Order of Honour (Greece) 1996, Commdr, Royal Order of Polar Star (Sweden) 1997,Commdr'sCross with Star, Order of Merit (Poland) 1999, Order of Commendatore (Italy) 1999, Gran Oficial, Orden de Mayo al Merito (Argentina) 1999, Grand Cross, Order of Bernardo O'Higgins (Chile) 2000, Václav Havel Memorial Medal (Ukraine) 2001, Commdr, Order of Merit (Portugal) 2000, Order of the White Two-Armed Cross (Slovakia) 2003, Officier de la Légion d'honneur (France) 2003, Order of the Madara Horseman (Bulgaria) 2003, Order of Francisco de Miranda (Venezuela) 2004, Commdr's Cross, Order of Merit (Hungary) 2004, Knight Grand Cross, Royal Order of Francis I 2005, KnightCommdr'sCross, Order of Merit (Germany) 2006, Order Pentru Merit (Romania) 2007, Alawite Officer Wissam (Morocco) 2009, and numerous other decorations; Medal of Merit, Warsaw Univ. 1995, Rotary Int. Award of Honour 1998, Templeton Prize 1998, Wilhelm Leuschner Medal, Wiesbaden 1998, (jtly) St Robert Bellarmine Medal, Gregorian Univ. 2002, (jtly) Distinguished Service Award, Int. CCJ 2005, St Mellitus Medal 2008, The FIRST Lifetime Achievement Award 2008. *Leisure interests:* swimming. *Address:* Star House, 104 Grafton Road, London, NW5 4BA, England (office). *Fax:* (20) 7485-4512 (office).

STERZINSKY, HE Cardinal Georg Maximilian; German ecclesiastic; *Archbishop of Berlin;* b. 9 Feb. 1936, Warlack, Warmia; ordained priest 1960; elected Bishop of Berlin 1989, consecrated 1989; cr. Cardinal (Cardinal-Priest of S. Giuseppe all'Aurelio) 1991; Archbishop of Berlin 1994–; mem. Congregation for Catholic Educ., Pontifical Council for the Pastoral Care of Migrants and Itinerant People; Chair. Family Comm., German Bishops' Conf. *Address:* Hinter der Katholischen Kirche 3, 10117 Berlin, Germany (office). *Telephone:* (30) 463097-20 (office). *Fax:* (30) 463097-30 (office). *E-mail:* sekretariat .erzbischof@erzbistumberlin.de (office). *Website:* www.erzbistumberlin.de (office).

STETTER, Karl Otto, Dr rer. nat (habil.); German microbiologist and academic; *Professor Emeritus, University of Regensburg;* b. 16 July 1941, Munich, Bavaria; ed Staatliche Luitpold-Oberrealschule, Munich, Technical Univ., Munich, Ludwig Maximilians Univ., Munich; Postdoctoral Fellow, Dept of Molecular Biology, Max Planck Inst. for Biochemistry, Martinsried 1973–75; Lecturer, Botanical Inst. 1975–77; Asst Prof. ('Privatdozent' and 'Oberassistent'), Faculty of Biology, Ludwig Maximilians Univ., Munich 1977–80; Prof. of Microbiology and Head of Dept of Microbiology ('Ordinarius') and Archaeencenter, Univ. of Regensburg 1980–2002, Prof. Emer. 2002–; mem. (Prof. Above Scale) Dept of Microbiology and Molecular Genetics and Inst. of Geophysics and Planetary Science, Faculty of Life Sciences, UCLA, USA 1989–; Co-founder DIVERSA Corpn, San Diego, Calif., USA 1994 (merged with Celunol to form Verenium Corpn 2007); mem. Editorial Bd Systematic and Applied Microbiology 1992–, Extremophiles – Microbial Life Under Extreme Conditions 1996–, Geobiology 2000–; mem. Gesellschaft für Biologische Chemie 1970–, American Soc. of Microbiology 1974–, Deutsche Gesellschaft für Hygiene und Mikrobiologie 1979–, German Univ. Soc. 1981–, Int. Cttee on Environmental Biogeochemistry (ISEB) 1984–, Vereinigung für Allgemeine und Angewandte Mikrobiologie 1986–, Soc. of German Scientists and Physicians 1986–, Int. Cttee on Systematic Bacteriology 1986–, Int. Inst. of Biotechnology 1992–, Gesellschaft Deutscher Chemiker 1994–, Deutsche Akad. der Naturforscher Leopoldina, 1995–, Int. Soc. for the Study of the Origin of Life 1996–, Royal Netherlands Acad. of Arts and Sciences 1999–, Bayerische Akad. der Wissenschaften 2002–; Hon. Mem. Botanical Soc. of Regensburg 2001; Annual Award, German Soc. of Hygiene and Microbiology 1985, Gottfried Wilhelm Leibniz Award, German Science Foundation (Highest German Award for Research Excellence) 1988, Medal Lecture, Int. Inst. of Biotechnology 1994, Bergey Medal, Bergey's Manual Trust 1999, Leeuwenhoek Medal, Royal Netherlands Acad. of Arts and Sciences (in recognition for the most influential work in microbiology in the previous decade) 2003; approx. 330 invited lectures 1987–2007. *Major discovery: Nanoarchaeum equitans,* an archaeal microorganism containing world's smallest known genome, discovered in hydrothermal vent off coast of Iceland 2002. *Television:* contrib. to and appearance in more than 30 nat. and int. films and documentaries, including Life is Impossible (BBC TV Horizon, UK) 1993, The Secret of Life – The Immortal Thread (WGBH, USA) 1993, The Origin of Life (ARTE, France and Germany) 1994, Planet of Ocean (NHK TV, Japan) 1998, Intimate Strangers (PBS, USA) 1999, Die Jagd nach den Feürzwergen (Hunting the Fire Dwarfs; ZDF, Germany) 2001. *Publications:* author or co-author of more than 330 scientific publs. *Address:* Lehrstuhl für Mikrobiologie, Universität Regensburg, Universitätstraße 31, 93343 Regensburg, Germany (office). *Telephone:* (941) 943-1821 (office); (941) 943-3161 (office); (89) 68096548 (home). *Fax:* (941) 943-3243 (office); (89) 68096580 (home). *E-mail:* karl.stetter@biologie.uni-r.de (office). *Website:* www.biologie.uni -regensburg.de/Mikrobio/Stetter (office).

STEVENS, Anne L., BEng; American business executive; *Chairman, President and CEO, Carpenter Technology Corporation;* b. Reading, Pa; ed Drexel Univ., Phila and Rutgers Univ., New Brunswick, NJ; held various eng, mfg and marketing positions at Exxon Chemical Co.; marketing specialist in Plastic Products Div., Vehicle Exterior Systems, Ford Motor Co. 1990–92, Man. Quality Services Dept, Saline, Mich. 1992–95, Mfg Man., Plastic and Trim Products Operations 1995, Plant Man., Enfield Plant, UK (Ford's first female plant man. in Europe) 1995–97, Asst Vehicle Line Dir Small Car Vehicle Centre, Ford Automotive Operations, Dunton, UK 1997–99, Dir Mfg Business Office for Ford in N America 1999–2001, Exec. Dir Vehicle Operations in N America 2000–01, Vice-Pres. N America Ass. Operations

2001, Vice-Pres. N America Vehicle Operations 2001–03, Group Vice-Pres. Canada, Mexico and S America 2003–06, Exec. Vice-Pres. and COO The Americas 2006 (retd); Chair., Pres. and CEO Carpenter Technology Corpn, Reading, Pa 2006–; mem. Bd of Dirs Lockheed Martin 2002–; mem. Bd Council of the Americas; mem. Advisory Bd Mexico Inst. of the Woodrow Wilson Int. Center for Scholars; mem. Exec. Advisory Bd Juran Center for Leadership in Quality, Univ. of Minnesota; mem. Shingo Prize Bd of Govs; mem. Nat. Acad. of Eng 2004; Trustee, Drexel Univ., Women's Automotive Asscn Int; ranked by Fortune magazine amongst 50 Most Powerful Women in Business in the US (27th) 2000, (41st) 2002, (49th) 2004, (22nd) 2005, Shingo Leadership Award 2000, Soc. of Mfg Engineers Eli Whitney Award 2003, Automotive Hall of Fame Distinguished Service Citation 2003, named by Automotive News as a Leading Woman in the North American Automotive Industry 2005, one of only two women nominated by Motor Trend to the Power List (car magazine's list of the top 50 people in the automotive industry) (41st) 2006. *Leisure interest:* car racing. *Address:* Carpenter Technology Corporation, PO Box 14662, Building #L05, Reading, PA 19612-4662, USA (office). *Telephone:* (610) 208-2000 (office). *Fax:* (610) 208-3716 (office). *Website:* www.cartech.com (office).

STEVENS, Cat (see Islam, Yusuf).

STEVENS, Glenn, BEcons, MA; Australian economist and central banker; *Governor, Reserve Bank of Australia;* b. 23 Jan. 1958, Sydney; m.; two c.; ed Univ. of Sydney, Univ. of Western Ont., Canada; joined Research Dept, Reserve Bank of Australia 1980, Head, Econ. Analysis Dept 1992–95, Head, Int. Dept 1995–96, Asst Gov. (Econ.) 1996–2001, Deputy Gov. 2001–06, Gov. 2006–, also Chair. Payments System Bd; Chair. Council of Financial Regulators, Foundation for Children; Visiting Scholar, Fed. Reserve Bank of San Francisco 1990; mem. Bd of Dirs Anika Foundation; fmr mem. Advisory Bd Melbourne Inst. for Applied Econ. and Social Research, Hong Kong Inst. for Monetary Research. *Publications include:* numerous articles on monetary policy and other econ. matters. *Address:* Reserve Bank of Australia, GPO 3947, Sydney, NSW 2001, Australia (office). *Telephone:* (2) 9551-9507 (office). *Fax:* (2) 9551-8000 (office). *E-mail:* governor@rba.gov.au (office). *Website:* www.rba.gov.au (office).

STEVENS, Sir Jocelyn Edward Greville, Kt, CVO, FRSA; British publisher; b. 14 Feb. 1932, London; s. of Major C.G.B. Stewart-Stevens and Betty Hulton; m. Jane Armyne Sheffield 1956 (dissolved 1979); one s. two d. (one s. deceased); ed Eton Coll., Cambridge Univ.; mil. service Rifle Brigade 1950–52; journalist Hulton Press 1955–56; Chair. and Man. Dir Stevens Press Ltd, Ed. Queen Magazine 1957–68; Personal Asst to Chair. Beaverbrook Newspapers 1968, Dir 1971–81, Man. Dir 1974–77; Man. Dir Evening Standard Co. Ltd 1969–72, Daily Express 1972–74; Deputy Chair. and Man. Dir Express Newspapers 1974–81; Ed. and Publr The Magazine 1982–84; Dir Centaur Communications 1982–84; Gov. Imperial Coll. of Science, Tech. and Medicine 1985–92, Winchester School of Art 1986–89; Rector and Vice-Provost RCA 1984–92; Chair. The Silver Trust 1990–93, English Heritage 1992–2000; Deputy Chair. Independent TV Comm. 1991–96; Dir (non-exec.) The TV Corpn 1996–2002, Asprey & Co. –2002, Garrard & Co. –2002; Pres. The Cheyne Walk Trust 1989–93; Chair. The Prince of Wales's Phoenix Trust; Trustee Eureka! The Children's Museum 1990–2000; Hon. DLitt (Loughborough) 1989, (Buckingham) 1998; Hon. FCSD 1990, Sr Fellow RCA 1990. *Leisure interest:* skiing.

STEVENS, John Paul, AB JD; American lawyer and judge; *Associate Justice, Supreme Court;* b. 20 April 1920, Chicago, Ill.; s. of Ernest James Stevens and Elizabeth Street; m. 1st Elizabeth Jane Sheeren 1942; one s. three d.; m. 2nd Maryan Mulholland Simon 1979; ed Univ. of Chicago, Northwestern Univ. School of Law; served USN (awarded Bronze Star Medal) 1942–45; Co-Ed. of Law Review, Northwestern Univ. School of Law 1947; Law Clerk to Supreme Court Justice Wiley Rutledge 1947; with Poppenhusen, Johnston, Thompson and Raymond (law firm) 1948–51, 1952; Pnr, Rothschild, Stevens, Barry and Myers 1952–70; Circuit Judge, Seventh Circuit Court of Appeals 1970–75; Assoc. Justice, US Supreme Court 1975–; Assoc. Counsel, Monopoly Power Sub-Cttee of US House of Reps Judiciary Cttee 1951; mem. Attorney Gen.'s Nat. Cttee on Antitrust Laws 1953–55; part-time teacher, Northwestern Univ. School of Law, later Univ. of Chicago Law School 1952–56; admitted to Ill. Bar 1949, to US Supreme Court 1954; mem. American Law Inst. *Publications:* numerous articles on commercial monopoly affairs. *Address:* United States Supreme Court, One First Street, NE, Washington, DC 20543, USA (office). *Telephone:* (202) 479-3211 (office). *Website:* www.supremecourtus.gov (office).

STEVENS, Robert Bocking, MA, DCL, LLM; British lawyer and academic; b. 8 June 1933; s. of John S. Stevens and Enid Dorothy Bocking Stevens; m. 1st Rosemary Wallace 1961 (divorced 1983); m. 2nd Katherine Booth 1985; one s. two d.; ed Keble Coll. Oxford and Yale Univ., USA; mem. Essex Court Chambers, Lincoln's Inn Fields 1965–; Midland Circuit 1962–76; Asst Prof. of Law, Yale Univ. 1959–61, Assoc. Prof. 1961–65, Prof. 1965–76, Fellow, Jonathan Edwards Coll. 1963–76; Prof. of Law and Adjunct Prof. of History, Tulane Univ. 1976–78, Provost 1976–78; Pres. Haverford Coll. 1978–87; Prof. of History, Univ. of Calif., Santa Cruz 1987–93, Chancellor 1987–91; Counsel, Covington & Burling (law firm), Washington, DC, London 1991–; mem. Council, Justice (UK Br., Int. Comm. of Jurists) 1992–98; Master, Pembroke Coll. Oxford 1993–2001; Chair. Sulgrave Manor (Home of Washington Family) Bd 2002–; Bencher Gray's Inn 1999; Hon. Fellow, Keble Coll. Oxford 1983, Pembroke Coll. Oxford 2001; several hon. degrees. *Publications include:* Law and Politics: The House of Lords as a Judicial Body 1800–1976 1978, The American Law School: Legal Education in America 1850–1980 1983, The Independence of the Judiciary: The View from the Lord Chancellor's Office 1993, The English Judges 2002, From University to Uni 2004; co-author and ed. of other books on law, history and welfare; articles and monographs. *Leisure interests:* politics, history, talking, claret. *Address:* Covington &

Burling, 265 Strand, London, WC2R 1BH; 19 Burgess Meade, Oxford, OX2 6XP, England (home). *Telephone:* (20) 7067-2000 (London) (home); (1865) 558420 (home). *Fax:* (20) 7067-2222 (London); (1865) 558420. *E-mail:* rstevens@cov.com (office).

STEVENS, Robert J., MEng, MBA; American business executive; *Chairman, President and CEO, Lockheed Martin Corporation;* b. McKeesport, Pa; ed Slippery Rock Univ., Polytechnic Univ. of New York, Columbia Univ., Dept of Defense Systems Man. Coll.; served in US Marine Corps; various man. positions in program man., finance, mfg and operations, Loral Systems Mfg Co., Vice-Pres. and Chief Financial Officer –1988, Gen. Man. 1988–93; Exec. Vice-Pres. and Chief Financial Officer, Lockheed Martin Air Traffic Man. 1993–96, Pres. Lockheed Martin Air Traffic Man. 1996–98, Pres. and COO Lockheed Martin Energy and Environment Sector 1998–99, Vice-Pres. Strategic Devt Org., Lockheed Martin Corpn 1998–99, Chief Financial Officer 1999–2001, Pres. and COO 2001–04, Pres. and CEO 2004–, Chair. 2005–; mem. Bd of Dirs Monsanto Co., Congressional Medal of Honor Foundation; mem. US Pres. Bush's Comm. to examine the Future of the US Aerospace Industry 2001–02; Fellow, American Astronautical Soc., American Inst. of Aeronautics and Astronautics; mem. Advisory Bd British-American Business Council, Exec. Cttee Aerospace Industries Asscn, Council on Foreign Relations; Exec. of the Year, Nat. Man. Asscn 2004. *Address:* Lockheed Martin Corporation, 6801 Rockledge Drive, Bethesda, MD 20817-1877, USA (office). *Telephone:* (301) 897-6000 (office). *Fax:* (301) 897-6704 (office). *E-mail:* info@lockheedmartin.com (office). *Website:* www.lockheedmartin.com (office).

STEVENS, Rosemary Anne, PhD; American professor of political and social sciences; *Professor Emerita, University of Pennsylvania;* b. 18 March 1935, Bourne, England; d. of William E. Wallace and Mary A. Wallace; m. 1st Robert B. Stevens 1961 (divorced 1983); one s. one d.; m. 2nd Jack D. Barchas 1994; ed Oxford and Manchester Univs, UK and Yale Univ., USA; trained in hosp. admin. and worked as hosp. admin. Nat. Health Service, UK; mem. Faculty, Prof. of Public Health, Prof. in Inst. of Policy Studies, Yale Univ., USA 1962–76; Prof., Dept of Health Systems Man. (Chair. 1977-78) and Adjunct Prof. of Political Science, Tulane Univ. 1976–79; Prof. of History and Sociology of Science, Univ. of Pa 1979–, now Prof. Emer., Chair. 1980–83, 1986–91; UPS Foundation Prof. in Social Sciences 1990–91, Dean, Thomas S. Gates Prof. 1991–96; Stanley I. Sheerr Prof. 1997; mem. Inst. of Medicine of NAS; Fellow, American Acad. of Arts and Sciences; (Northeastern Ohio Univ. Coll. of Medicine) 1995; Dr hc (Hahnemann Univ., Philadelphia) 1988, (Medical Coll. of Pa) 1992, (Rutgers) 1995; Rockefeller Humanities Award 1983–84, Guggenheim Award 1984–85, Baxter Foundation Prize for Health Services Research 1990; James A. Hamilton Book Award 1990, Welch Medal 1990, ABMS Special Award 1990. *Publications:* Medical Practice in Modern England 1966, American Medicine and the Public Interest 1971, Foreign Trained Physicians and American Medicine 1972, Welfare Medicine in America 1974, The Alien Doctors: Foreign Medical Graduates in American Hospitals 1978, In Sickness and in Wealth: American Hospitals in the Twentieth Century 1989; various articles. *Leisure interests:* painting, reading, flea markets. *Address:* 1900 Rittenhouse Square, #18A, Philadelphia, PA 19103 (home); 324 Logan Hall, University of Pennsylvania, 249 South 36th Street, Philadelphia, PA 19104, USA (office). *Telephone:* (215) 898-8400. *Fax:* (215) 573-2231. *E-mail:* rstevens@sas.upenn.edu (home).

STEVENS, Theodore (Ted) Fulton, BA, LLB; American politician and lawyer; b. 18 Nov. 1923, Indianapolis, Ind.; s. of George A. Stevens and Gertrude Stevens (née Chancellor); m. 1st Ann Cherrington 1952 (died 1978); three s. two d.; m. 2nd Catherine Chandler 1980; one d.; ed High School, Redondo Beach, Calif., Univ. of California, Los Angeles and Harvard Law School; US Attorney, Fairbanks, Alaska 1953–56; Legis. Counsel, Dept of Interior, Washington, DC 1956–58; Asst to Sec. of Interior 1958–60; Solicitor of Interior Dept 1960; pvt. law practice, Anchorage, Alaska 1961–68; Senator from Alaska 1968–2009, Asst Minority Leader 1977–80, Asst Majority Leader 1981–85, Admin. Co-Chair. Appropriations Cttee 1997–2001, Pres. Pro Tempore 2003, fmr mem. Commerce Cttee, Governmental Affairs Cttee, Rules Cttee; fmr US Senate del. to Canadian–US Inter parl. Conf., to British–US Inter parl. Conf.; Republican. *Address:* PO Box 100879, Anchorage, AK 99510, USA (home).

STEVENS OF KIRKWHELPINGTON, Baron (Life Peer), cr. 2005, of Kirkwhelpington in the County of Northumberland; **John Arthur Stevens,** QPM, MPhil, LLB, CIMgt, FRSA, DL; British police officer (retd) and business executive; *Chairman, Quest Limited;* b. 21 Oct. 1942; s. of C. J. Stevens and S. Stevens; m.; two s. one d.; ed St Lawrence Coll., Ramsgate, Univ. of Leicester, Univ. of Southampton; mem. Metropolitan Police 1963–83, staff Police Staff Coll. 1983–84, Deputy Commr 1998–99, Commr 2000–05 (retd); Asst Chief Constable of Hants. Constabulary 1986–89, Deputy Chief Constable of Cambs. Constabulary 1989–91; Chief Constable of Northumbria 1991–96; HM Inspector of Constabulary 1996–98; currently Chair. Quest Ltd (pvt. security co.); has chaired numerous enquiries including Stevens Enquiry on NI 1989–2003, Operation Paget into deaths of Diana, Princess of Wales and Dodi Fayed 2003–06, inquiry into football corruption 2006; Dir (non-exec.) BAA 2007–; Adviser, Forensic Science Service; Visiting Prof., Univ. of Cambridge 1984–85, City Univ. of New York 1984–85; Chancellor, Univ. of Northumbria 2005–; Visiting Lecturer, Int. Crime Prevention Centre, Canada 1998; Adviser to Prime Minister of Romania 2002–; patron, various charities in Romania and London; DL Greater London 2001; Hon. Fellow, Wolfson Coll. Cambridge 2000; KStJ; Hon. LLD (Leicester) 2000; Hon. DCL (Northumbria) 2001. *Leisure interests:* flying, rugby, walking, cricket, charity work. *Address:* Quest Limited, 8 Frederick's Place, London, EC2R 8HY (office); Quest Limited, Selous House, 5-12 Mandela Street, London, NW1 0DU; House of Lords, London, SW1A 0PW, England. *Telephone:* (20) 7387-7993 (office). *Fax:* (20) 7387-7994 (office). *E-mail:* info@quest.co.uk (office). *Website:* www.quest.co.uk (office).

STEVENS OF LUDGATE, Baron (Life Peer), cr. 1987, of Ludgate in the City of London; **David Robert Stevens,** MA; British business executive; b. 26 May 1936; s. of (Arthur) Edwin Stevens; m. 1st Patricia Rose (divorced 1971); one s. one d.; m. 2nd Melissa Milicevich 1977 (died 1989); m. 3rd Meriza Giori 1990; ed Stowe School and Sidney Sussex Coll. Cambridge; man. trainee, Elliott Automation 1959; Dir Hill Samuel Securities 1959–68, Drayton Group 1968–74; Chair. City & Foreign (now Alexander Proudfoot PLC) 1976–95, Drayton Far East 1976–93, English & Int. 1976–79, Consolidated Venture (fmrly Montagu Boston) 1979–93, Drayton Consolidated 1980–92, Drayton Japan 1980–93, Econ. Devt Cttee for Civil Eng 1984–86; Dir United News & Media PLC (fmrly United Newspapers PLC) 1974–99, Chair. 1981–99; CEO INVESCO MIM 1980–87, Deputy Chair. 1987–89, Chair. 1989–93; Chair. MIM Britannia Ltd (fmrly Montagu Investment Man. Ltd) 1980–92 (CEO 1980–87), Express Newspapers 1985–99, PNC Telecom (fmrly. Personal Number Co.) 1998–. *Leisure interests:* golf, gardening. *Address:* c/o Ludgate House, 245 Blackfriars Road, London, SE1 9UY; House of Lords, London, SW1A 0PW, England.

STEVENSON, Hon. Adlai E., III; American lawyer, investment banker and fmr politician; *Chairman, SC&M Investment Management Corporation;* b. 10 Oct. 1930, Chicago, Ill.; s. of the late Adlai Stevenson II (fmr Gov. of Illinois, presidential candidate and Amb. to UN); great-grandson of Adlai E. Stevenson (Vice-Pres. of USA 1893–97); m. Nancy L. Anderson 1955; two s. two d.; ed Milton Acad., Mass. and Harvard Univ.; law clerk to a justice of Ill. Supreme Court 1957; joined Chicago law firm of Mayer, Brown and Platt 1958–66, pnr 1966–67, 1981–83, of Counsel 1983–91; elected to Ill. House of Reps. 1964; State Treas. of Ill. 1966–70; Senator from Illinois 1970–81; Democratic Cand. for Gov. of Ill. 1982, 1986; Chair. SC&M Int. Ltd (now SC&M Investment Man. Corpn) 1991–95, Pres. 1995–98, Chair. 1998–; Co-Chair. Huamei Capital Co., Inc. 2005–; Co-Chair. Stevenson, Melamed & Assocs; mem. Bd of Dirs Stonewater Control Systems Inc.; Order of the Sacred Treasure, Gold and Silver Stars (Japan); numerous awards, hon. degrees and directorships. *Address:* HuaMei Capital Company, Inc., 71 South Wacker Drive, Suite 2760, Chicago, IL 60606 (office); 4302 South Blandings Road, Hanover, IL 61041, USA (home). *Telephone:* (312) 957-4260 (office). *Fax:* (312) 957-4261 (office). *E-mail:* info@huameicapital.com (office). *Website:* www.huameicapital.com (office).

STEVENSON, Juliet, CBE; British actress; b. 30 Oct. 1956; d. of Michael Guy Stevens and Virginia Ruth Marshall; one s. one d. two step-s.; ed Hurst Lodge School, Berks., St Catherine's School, Surrey, Royal Acad. of Dramatic Art; with RSC (now Assoc. Artist), Royal Nat. Theatre, Royal Court Theatre, film, TV, radio, audiobooks; Bancroft Gold Medal, Royal Acad. of Dramatic Art 1977, Time Out Award for Best Actress 1991, Evening Standard Film Award for Best Actress 1992, Lawrence Olivier Theatre Award for Best Actress 1992. *Plays include:* Midsummer Night's Dream, Henry IV Parts 1 and 2, Measure for Measure, As You Like It, Troilus and Cressida, Les Liaisons Dangereuses, Not I, Footfalls Money, The Witch of Edmonton, Breaking the Silence (all for RSC), Burn This (West End), Death and the Maiden (Royal Court and West End) (Olivier Award 1992), The Duchess of Malfi (Greenwich Theatre and West End), Yerma, Hedda Gabler, The Caucasian Chalk Circle, Private Lives, The Seagull (Nat. Theatre), Other Worlds, The Country (Royal Court), A Little Night Music (New York City Opera). *Films include:* Drowning by Numbers, Ladder of Swords, Truly Madly Deeply, The Trial, The Secret Rapture, Emma, The Search for John Gissing, Who Dealt?, Beckett's Play, Bend It Like Beckham, Food of Love, Nicholas Nickleby, Mona Lisa Smile, Being Julia, Pierrepoint 2006, Breaking and Entering 2006, When Did You Last See Your Father? 2007. *Radio includes:* To the Lighthouse, Volcano, Albertina, House of Correction, Hang Up, Cigarettes and Chocolate, A Little Like Drowning, Victory, The Pallisers, Mary Poppins, The Lovers of Viorne. *Television includes:* Miss Marple, Hear the Silence, The Road From Coorain, Play (Beckett), Trial by Fire, Cider with Rosie, Stone Scissors Paper, The Politician's Wife, A Doll's House (Nora), Life Story, Antigone, The March, Maybury, Thomas and Ruth, Aimée, The Mallens, Living With Dinosaurs; wrote and fronted a BBC documentary Great Journeys. *Publications:* Clamorous Voices (jtly) 1988, Shall I See You Again? (jtly), Players of Shakespeare (jtly). *Leisure interests:* piano, travelling, gardening, reading, tennis. *Address:* c/o Markham and Froggatt Ltd, Julian House, 4 Windmill Street, London, W1P 1HF, England.

STEVENSON, Robert Wilfrid, MA, FCCA; British public affairs consultant; b. 19 April 1947, Lochalsh, Ross-shire, Scotland; s. of James Stevenson and Elizabeth Macrae; m. 1st Jennifer Grace Antonio 1972 (divorced 1979); m. 2nd Elizabeth Ann Minogue 1991; one s. two d.; ed Edinburgh Acad. and Univ. Coll., Oxford; Research Officer, Univ. of Edinburgh Students Asscn 1970–74; Sec. and Acad. Registrar, Napier Polytechnic, Edinburgh 1974–87; Deputy Dir BFI 1987–88, Dir 1988–97; Dir The Smith Inst. 1997–2008; currently Sr Policy Adviser to the Prime Minister; Dr hc (Napier Univ., Edinburgh) 2008. *Publications:* Gordon Brown Speeches 1997–2006 (ed.) 2006, Moving Britain Forward (ed.) 2006. *Leisure interests:* cinema, bee keeping. *Address:* Missenden House, Little Missenden, Amersham, Bucks., HP7 0RD, England. *Telephone:* (1494) 890689. *E-mail:* wilf@wilfstevenson.co.uk (home).

STEVENSON OF CODDENHAM, Baron (Life Peer), cr. 1999, of Coddenham in the County of Suffolk; **Henry Dennistoun Stevenson,** Kt, CBE; British business executive and business consultant; b. 19 July 1945, Edinburgh; s. of Alexander James Stevenson and Sylvia Florence Stevenson (née Ingleby); m. Charlotte Susan Stevenson (née Vanneck); four s.; ed Glenalmond School and King's Coll., Cambridge; Dir Pearson Employee Share Trustees Ltd, Chair. Pearson PLC 1997–2005; mem. Bd Dirs and Chair.

Halifax PLC 1999–2009, Chair. HBOS plc (bank formed after merger of Halifax and Bank of Scotland) 2001–08 (resgnd); Chair. Trustees of the Tate Gallery 1988–98 (Trustee 1998–), Sinfonia 21 1989–99, GPA Group PLC (now AerFi) 1993–2000, Aldeburgh Music Ltd 2000–; mem. Bd of Dirs Manpower Inc. 1988–2006, J. Rothschild Assurance PLC 1991–97, J. Rothschild Holdings PLC 1991–97, English Partnerships 1993–99, British Sky Broadcasting Group PLC 1994–2000, British Council 1996–2003, Cloaca Maxima Ltd 1996–2004, Saxton Bampfylde Int. PLC 1996–98, Lazard Bros & Co. Ltd 1997–2000, St James's Place Capital PLC 1997–2002, Economist Newspapers Ltd 1998–, Glyndebourne Productions Ltd 1998–; Dir (non-exec.) The Western Union Group; Pres. Employers' Forum on Age; Chair. House of Lords Appointments Comm. 2000–08; mem. Take Over Panel 1992–2000; Gov. LSE 1996–2002; Chancellor, Univ. of the Arts London 2000–; Dir Loudwater Investment Pnrs Ltd 2007–. *Publication:* Information and Communications Technology in UK Schools (The Stevenson Report) 1997. *Address:* House of Lords, Westminster, London, SW1A 0PW, England.

STEVER, Horton Guyford, PhD; American scientist and business executive; b. 24 Oct. 1916, Corning, NY; s. of Ralph Raymond Stever and Alma Matt; m. Louise Risley Floyd 1946; two s. two d.; ed Colgate Univ. and California Inst. of Tech.; mem. Staff Radiation Lab. and Instructor, Officers' Radar School, MIT 1941–42; Science Liaison Officer, London Mission, Office of Scientific Research and Devt 1942–45; Asst Prof. of Aeronautical Eng, MIT 1946–51, Assoc. Prof. 1951–56, Prof. 1956–65; Chief Scientist, USAF 1955–56; Assoc. Dean of Eng, MIT 1956–59, Head of Depts of Mechanical Eng, Naval Architecture and Marine Eng 1961–65; Pres. Carnegie-Mellon Univ. 1965–72; Chair. USAF Scientific Advisory Bd 1962–69, Aeronautics and Space Eng Bd 1967–69, Foreign Sec. 1984–88; mem. Exec. Cttee Defense Science Bd, US Dept of Defense 1962–69; mem. Panel on Science and Tech. US House of Reps Comm. on Science and Tech. 1959–72, Science and Tech. Adviser to Pres. 1976–77; Science Consultant, Corp. Trustee 1977–; Trustee, Colgate Univ. 1962–72, Sarah Mellon Scaife Foundation 1965–72, Shady Side Acad. 1967–72, Univ. Research Asscn 1977– (Pres. 1982–84); mem. Bd of Dirs Fisher Scientific Co. 1965–72, Koppers Co. 1965–72, System Devt Corpn 1965–70, United Aircraft Corpn 1966–72, TRW 1977–88, Saudi Arabian Nat. Center for Science and Tech. 1978–80, Schering Plough 1980–89, Goodyear 1981–86; mem. Nat. Acad. of Eng, Nat. Science Bd 1970–72; Dir Nat. Science Foundation 1972–76; Science Adviser to Pres. of USA and Chair. Fed. Council for Science and Tech., Exec. Cttee Nat. Science Bd, Energy R & D Advisory Council; US Chair. US-USSR Jt Comm. on Scientific and Tech. Co-operation 1973–77; mem. Carnegie Comm. on Science, Tech. and Govt 1988–93; mem. NAS 1973–; Foreign mem. Royal Acad. of Eng 1989–, Japan Acad. of Eng 1989–; mem. US-Japan Cttee on Scientific Co-operation, Fed. Council on the Arts and Humanities, Nat. Council on Educational Research and many other Govt bodies; 18 hon. degrees; President's Certificate of Merit 1948, Exceptional Civilian Service Award, USAF 1956, Scott Gold Medal of American Ordnance Asscn 1960, Alumni Distinguished Service Award Calif. Inst. of Tech. 1966, Distinguished Public Service Medal, Dept of Defense 1969, Nat. Medal of Science 1991, Vannevar Bush Award 1997; Commdr, Order of Merit, Poland 1976, Distinguished Public Service Medal, NASA 1988, Arthur M. Bueche Award, Nat. Acad. of Eng 1999. *Publications:* Flight (with J. J. Haggerty) 1965, In War and Peace: My Life in Science and Technology 2002. *Leisure interests:* skiing, fishing, golf, hiking. *Address:* 588 Russell Avenue, Gaithersburg, MD 20877, USA. *Telephone:* (301) 216-5689.

STEWART, Alec James, OBE; British fmr professional cricketer; b. 8 April 1963, Merton, London; s. of Michael James Stewart (fmr Surrey Capt. and Test player) and Sheila Stewart; m. Lynn Blades 1991; one s. one d.; ed Tiffin Boys' School, Kingston upon Thames; right-hand opening batsman; wicket-keeper; Surrey 1981–2003 (Capt. 1992–97); 133 Tests for England 1990–2003, 14 as Capt., scoring 8,463 runs (average 39.54) including 15 hundreds; scored 26,165 first-class runs (48 hundreds); held 11 catches, equalling world first-class record, for Surrey v. Leicestershire, Leicester, 19–22 Aug. 1989; toured Australia 1990–91, 1994–95 and 1998–99 (Capt.); 170 one-over ints; overtook record (118 Tests) of Graham Gooch to become England's most-capped cricketer, Lords July 2002; retd 2003; Dir of Business, Surrey County Cricket Club 2003–; cricket columnist, Daily Mirror; Wisden Cricketer of the Year 1993. *Publications:* Alec Stewart: A Captain's Diary (jtly) 1999, Playing for Keeps 2003. *Leisure interests:* soccer (Chelsea), spending time with his family. *Address:* c/o Surrey County Cricket Club, Kennington Oval, London, SE11 5SS, England (home). *E-mail:* enquiries@surreycricket.com.

STEWART, Sir Brian John, Kt, CBE, MSc, CA; British brewery executive; b. 9 April 1945, Stirling, Scotland; s. of Ian M. Stewart and Christina McIntyre; m. Seonaid Duncan 1971; two s. one d.; ed Perth Acad., Edinburgh Univ.; joined Scottish & Newcastle Breweries (now Scottish and Newcastle PLC) 1976, Corp. Devt Dir 1985–88, Group Finance Dir 1988–91, Group Chief Exec. 1991–2000, Deputy Chair. 1997–2000, Exec. Chair. 2000–03, Chair. (non-exec.) 2003–08 (after acquisition of Scottish & Newcastle by a consortium of Carlsberg and Heineken); Dir (non-exec.) Booker 1993–99; Dir (non-exec.) Standard Life Assurance Co. 1993–2007, Chair. (non-exec.) 2003–07 (retd). *Leisure interests:* skiing, golf. *Address:* c/o Scottish & Newcastle PLC, 33 Ellersly Road, Edinburgh, EH12 6HX, Scotland (office).

STEWART, David (Dave) A.; British musician (guitar, keyboards) and songwriter; b. 9 Sept. 1952, Sunderland; m. 1st Pam Stewart (divorced); m. 2nd Siobhan Fahey 1987 (divorced); two s.; fmr mem., Harrison and Stewart (with Brian Harrison); Founder mem. Longdancer 1973; Founder mem. The Catch 1977, later renamed The Tourists 1979–80; Founder mem. Eurythmics (with Annie Lennox) 1980–89, 1999–, live appearances worldwide; solo artist 1990–; Founder mem. The Spiritual Cowboys 1990–92; mem. Vegas 1992–93; f. record label Anxious Records 1988; produces and directs films, including computer-enhanced films; writes film soundtracks; owner of recording studio, The Church 1992; producer and session musician for artists, including Mick Jagger, Bob Dylan, Tom Petty, Daryl Hall, Bob Geldof, Boris Grebenshikov, Sinead O'Connor, Feargal Sharkey; Hon. DMus (Westminster) 1998; Ivor Novello Award for Songwriter of the Year (for Sweet Dreams, with Annie Lennox) 1984, MTV Music Award for Best New Artist Video (for Sweet Dreams (Are Made Of This)) 1984, Ivor Novello Award for Best Song (for It's Alright (Baby's Coming Back, with Annie Lennox) 1987, Grammy Award for Best Rock Performance (for Missionary Man) 1987, BRIT Awards for Best Producer 1986, 1987, 1990, for Oustanding Contribution 1999, Golden Globe Award for Best Original Song (with Mick Jagger, for Old Habits Die Hard, from the film Alfie) 2005. *Compositions for film and television:* Rooftops 1989, De Kassière (with Candy Dulfer) 1989, Jute City (BBC1) 1991, GFI (TV series, with Gerry Anderson) 1992, Inside Victor Lewis-Smith (TV series) 1993, No Worries 1993, The Ref 1994, Showgirls 1995, Beautiful Girls 1996, Crimetime 1996, TV Offal (TV series title theme) 1997, Cookie's Fortune 1999, Honest 2000, Le Pont du trieur 2000, Chaos 2002, Around the World in 80 Days 2004; contrib. songs to numerous other films. *Film directed:* Honest 2000. *Recordings include:* albums: with The Tourists: The Tourists 1979, Reality Affect 1979, Luminous Basement 1980; with Eurythmics: In The Garden 1981, Sweet Dreams 1982, Touch 1983, Be Yourself Tonight 1985, Revenge 1986, Savage 1987, We Too Are One 1989, Eurythmics Live 1983–89 1992, Peace 1999; with The Spiritual Cowboys: Dave Stewart And The Spiritual Cowboys 1990; with Vegas: Vegas 1992; solo: Greetings From The Gutter 1994. *Address:* 19 Management Ltd, Unit 33, Ransomes Dock, 35–37 Park Gate Road, London, SW11 4NP, England (office). *Telephone:* (20) 7801-1919 (office). *Fax:* (20) 7801-1920 (office). *Website:* www.davestewart.com; www.eurythmics.com.

STEWART, Donald A., BA, FIA, FCIA; British insurance industry executive; *CEO, Sun Life Financial Inc.;* b. Glasgow, Scotland; ed Univ. of Glasgow, Harvard Univ., USA; joined Sun Life Financial, London 1969–74, Head of Canadian Pension Div., Toronto, Canada 1980–86, Head Project Team to Est. Mutual Fund Operation 1986, Pres. Spectrum Investments (mutual funds) 1986–87, Head of Information Tech., Sun Life Financial 1987–92, Chair. and CEO Sun Life Financial Trust 1992–95, Sr Vice-Pres. and Chief Actuary 1995–96, Pres. and COO 1996–98, Pres. and CEO Sun Life Insurance Co. of Canada 1998–99, Chair. and CEO 1999–2000, Chair. and CEO Sun Life Financial Inc. 2000–05, CEO 2005–, Chair. and CEO Sun Life Assurance Co. of Canada 2000, also Chair. Sun Life Insurance and Annuity Co. of NY; benefits consultant, William M. Mercer, Toronto 1974–80; mem. Bd MFS Investment Man.

STEWART, John M.; British banker; joined Woolwich 1977, served in numerous exec. positions, Group Operations Dir 1995–96, CEO 1996–2000, Deputy Group CEO Barclays Bank (after acquisition of Woolwich by Barclays) 2000–03; CEO and Prin. Bd mem. Nat. Australia Group Europe 2003–04, Man. Dir and Group CEO Nat. Australia Bank Ltd 2004–08; Assoc. Chartered Insurance Inst. *Address:* c/o National Australia Bank Ltd, 500 Bourke Street, Melbourne, Victoria 3000, Australia. *Telephone:* (3) 8641-3500. *Fax:* (3) 9208-5695. *Website:* www.nabgroup.com.

STEWART, Sir John Young (Jackie), Kt, KBE; British fmr racing driver; b. 11 June 1939, Milton, Scotland; s. of the late Robert Paul Stewart and Jean Clark Young; m. Helen McGregor 1962; two s.; ed Dumbarton Acad.; mem. British Clay Pigeon Shooting Team 1956–62; first raced 1961; competed in four meetings driving for Barry Filer, Glasgow 1961–62; drove for Ecurie Ecosse and other private entrants, winning 14 out of 23 starts 1963, 28 wins out of 53 starts 1964; drove Formula 1 for British Racing Motors (BRM) 1965–67, for Ken Tyrrell 1968–73; has won Australian, New Zealand, Swedish, Mediterranean, Japanese and many other non-championship major int. Grands Prix; set new world record by winning his 26th World Championship Grand Prix (Zandvoort) 1973, 27th (Nürburgring) 1973; third in World Championship 1965, 2nd in 1968 and 1972, World Champion 1969, 1971, 1973; retd 1973; involved with son, Paul, in operation of Paul Stewart Racing and Stewart Grand Prix (CEO 1989–2000), a Formula One team cr. 1996, sold to the Ford Motor Co. who have run the operation as Jaguar Racing from start of 2000 season; Chair. and CEO Jaguar Racing 1999–2000; Pres. British Racing Drivers' Club 2000–06; Hon. Dr Aut. Eng (Lawrence Inst. of Tech., USA) 1986; Dr hc (Glasgow Caledonian) 1993, (Stirling Univ.) 2001, (Edinburgh Univ.) 2006; Hon. DEng (Heriot-Watt Univ.) 1996, (Glasgow Univ.) 2001; Hon. Prof. (Stirling Univ.) 1998; British Automobile Racing Club Gold Medal 1971, 1973, Daily Express Sportsman of the Year 1971, 1973, BBC Sports Personality of the Year 1973, Scottish Sportsman of the Year 1973, Sports Illustrated American Sportsman of the Year 1973, World Sportsman of the Year 1973, ABC Sports Personality of the Year 1973, Seagrove Trophy 1973, 1999. *Film:* Weekend of a Champion 1972. *Publications:* World Champion (with Eric Dymock) 1970, Faster! (with Peter Manso) 1972, On the Road 1983, Jackie Stewart's Principles of Performance Driving (with Alan Henry) 1986, The Jackie Stewart Book of Shooting 1991, Winning is Not Enough (auto-biog.) 2007. *Leisure interests:* shooting (clay pigeon champion), golf, tennis. *Address:* Clayton House, Butlers Cross, Ellesborough, Bucks., HP17 0UR, England (office). *Telephone:* (1296) 620913 (office). *Fax:* (1296) 620049 (office).

STEWART, Jon; American comedian, actor, writer and producer; b. (Jonathan Stuart Leibowitz), 28 Nov. 1962, New York City; m. Tracey McShane 2000; one s. one d.; ed Coll. of William and Mary; numerous early jobs, including contingency planner for New Jersey Dept of Human Services, contract admin. for CUNY, puppeteer for children with disabilities, and bartender at local Franklin Corner Tavern, stand-up comedian; moved to New York City 1986; began hosting TV network Comedy Central's Short Attention

Span Theater 1989; hosted You Wrote It, You Watch It on MTV 1992; appeared several times in HBO's The Larry Sanders Show 1992–2001; host, The Jon Stewart Show on MTV (first talk show on that network) 1993–95; host, Comedy Central's The Daily Show with Jon Stewart 1999–; host, Acad. Awards ceremony 2006, 2008; Hon. DArts (Coll. of William and Mary) 2004; Peabody Awards for coverage of 2000 and 2004 US presidential elections on The Daily Show, keynote speaker at Commencement Ceremony, Princeton Univ. 2004, named one of "Time 100" 2005, recipient of 10 Emmy Awards. *Films include:* Mixed Nuts 1994, Wishful Thinking 1997, Half Baked 1998, The Faculty 1998, Playing by Heart 1999, Big Daddy 1999, The Office Party 2000, Jay and Silent Bob Strike Back 2001, Death to Smoochy 2002. *Television includes:* as writer: The Sweet Life (series) 1989, The Jon Stewart Show (series) 1993, The Daily Show (series) (also co-exec. producer) 1996–; Since You've Been Gone 1998, The Colbert Réport (series) (exec. producer) 2005. *Publication:* The Daily Show with Jon Stewart Presents America (The Book): A Citizen's Guide to Democracy Inaction 2004. *Address:* Comedy Partners, 1175 Broadway, 10th Floor, New York, NY 10019 USA (office). *Telephone:* (212) 767-8600 (office). *Fax:* (212) 767-8592 (office). *Website:* www.thedailyshow.com (office).

STEWART, Martha Helen Kostyra, BA; American editor, writer and business executive; b. 3 Aug. 1941, Jersey City, NJ; d. of Edward Kostyra and Martha Kostyra (née Ruszkowski); m. Andy Stewart 1961 (divorced 1990); one s.; ed Barnard Univ.; fmr model, stockbroker, caterer; owner, Ed.-in-Chief Martha Stewart Living magazine 1990–; Founder, Chair. and CEO Martha Stewart Living Omnimedia 1997–2003, mem. Bd –2004, Founding Editorial Dir (non-exec.) March 2004–; also appears in cooking feature on Today Show; mem. Bd NY Stock Exchange June–Oct. 2002; mem. Bd Revlon Inc. –2004; under investigation for alleged insider trading June 2002, found guilty of conspiracy, making false statements and obstruction of justice March 2004, sentenced to prison and released March 2005, agreed with Securities and Exchange Comm. to settle insider trading charges and to maximum penalty of about $195,000, to a five-year bar from serving as a dir of a public co. and a five-year limitation on the scope of her service as an officer or employee of a public co. Aug. 2006; ranked by Fortune magazine amongst 50 Most Powerful Women in Business in the US (21st) 2005, (28th) 2006. *Television:* host of TV show Martha 2005–, starred in The Apprentice: Martha Stewart 2005. *Publications include:* (with Elizabeth Hawes) Entertaining 1982, Weddings 1987; (as sole author) Martha Stewart's Hors d'Oeuvres: The Creation and Presentation of Fabulous Finger Food 1984, Martha Stewart's Pies and Tarts 1985, Martha Stewart's Quick Cook Menus 1988, The Wedding Planner 1988, Martha Stewart's Gardening: Month by Month 1991, Martha Stewart's New Old House: Restoration, Renovation, Decoration 1992, Martha Stewart's Christmas 1993, Martha Stewart's Menus for Entertaining 1994, Holidays 1994, The Martha Rules 2005, Martha Stewart's Homekeeping Handbook 2006. *Address:* Martha Stewart Living Omnimedia, 11 West 42nd Street, 25th Floor, New York, NY 10036 (office); Martha Stewart, 19 Newton Toke, Suite 6, Westport, CT 06880; 10 Saugatuck Avenue, Westport, CT 06880, USA (home); c/o Susan Magrino Agency, 40 West 57th Street, 31st Floor, New York, NY 10019. *Telephone:* (212) 827-8000 (office). *Fax:* (212) 827-8204 (office). *Website:* www.marthastewart.com.

STEWART, Patrick; British actor and producer; b. 13 July 1940, Mirfield, W Yorks.; s. of Alfred Stewart and Gladys Stewart; m. 1st Sheila Falconer 1966; one s. one d.; m. 2nd Wendy Neuss 2002; ed Bristol Old Vic Theatre School; began career as junior reporter on local newspaper; acting experience with various repertory cos.; joined Royal Shakespeare Co. (RSC) 1966, Assoc. Artist 1967–87; Founding Dir ACTER (A Centre for Theatre Educ. and Research); Dir Flying Freehold Productions, Paramount Studios, LA 1998–; Cameron Mackintosh Visiting Prof. of Contemporary Theatre, St Catherine's Coll., Oxford 2007–08. *Films:* Hedda, Excalibur, Dune, Lady Jane, Gunmen, Robin Hood – Men in Tights, LA Story, Jeffrey, Star Trek: First Contact, Conspiracy Theory, Dad Savage, Masterminds, Star Trek: Insurrection 1999, X-Men 2000, Moby Dick, Star Trek: Nemesis 2002, X-Men: X2 2003, Boo, Zino and the Snurks (voice) 2004, Chicken Little (voice) 2005, Bambi II (voice) 2006, X-Men: The Last Stand 2006, TMNT (voice) 2007. *Theatre includes:* Antony and Cleopatra (Olivier Award, Soc. of West End Theatre Award) 1979, 2006, Henry IV 1984, Who's Afraid of Virginia Woolf (London Fringe Award) 1987, A Christmas Carol (Drama Desk Award, Olivier Award 1992) 1988–1996, The Tempest 1995, Othello 1997, The Ride Down Mount Morgan 1998, The Master Builder 2003, A Christmas Carol 2005, Macbeth (London Evening Standard Award for Best Actor 2007) 2007. *Television:* Star Trek: The Next Generation, The Mozart Inquest, Maybury, I Claudius, Tinker, Tailor, Soldier, Spy, Smiley's People, The Lion in Winter 2003, Mysterious Island 2005, The Snow Queen (voice) 2005, Eleventh Hour 2006, American Dad 2006. *Music:* narrative on Peter and the Wolf (Grammy Award) 1996. *Address:* c/o William Morris Agency, 1 William Morris Place, Beverly Hills, CA 90212 (office); Flying Freehold Productions, 5555 Melrose Avenue, Clara Bow #120, Los Angeles, CA 90038, USA. *Telephone:* (323) 956-8838 (Flying Freehold).

STEWART, Roderick (Rod) David, CBE; British singer; b. 10 Jan. 1945, London; m. 1st Alana Collins 1979 (divorced 1984), one s. one d.; one d. with Kelly Emberg; m. 2nd Rachel Hunter 1990 (divorced), one d. one s.; m. Penny Lancaster 2007, one s.; singer with Steampacket, Shotgun Express, Jeff Beck Group 1968–69, Faces 1969–75; solo artist 1971–; Rolling Stone Magazine Rock Star of the Year 1971, British Rock and Pop Award for Lifetime Achievement 1992, BRIT Lifetime Achievement Award 1993. *Recordings include:* albums: two with Jeff Beck, four with Faces; solo: Every Picture Tells a Story 1971, Never a Dull Moment 1972, Atlantic Crossing 1975, A Night On The Town 1976, Foot Lose and Fancy Free 1977, Blondes Have More Fun 1978, Foolish Behaviour 1980, Tonight I'm Yours 1981, Camouflage 1984, Love Touch 1986, Out of Order 1988, The Best Of 1989, Downtown Train 1990, Vagabond Heart 1991, Lead Vocalist 1992, Unplugged... and Seated 1993, A Spanner In The Works 1995, When We Were the New Boys 1998, Human 2000, It Had To Be You... The Great American Songbook 2002, The Story So Far: The Best of Rod Stewart 2003, Thanks for the Memory 2005, Still the Same 2006, Some Guys Have All the Luck 2008. *Address:* Solo, Second Floor, 53–55 Fulham High Street, London, SW6 3JJ, England (office). *Telephone:* (20) 7384-6644 (office). *E-mail:* solo@solo.uk.com (office). *Website:* www.rodstewart.com.

STEWART, S. Jay, BS, MBA; American business executive; b. 18 Sept. 1938; s. of Virgil Harvey Stewart and Lena Rivers Repair; m. Judith Daniels 1961; one s. two d.; ed Univ. of West Virginia and Univ. of Cincinnati; Eng Marketing and Mfg, Monsanto Corpn 1961–73; Dir of Devt, Dir of Marketing, Gen. Man. Ventron Div., Thiokol Corpn 1973–79, Pres. Dynachem Div. 1979–82, Group Vice-Pres. for Chemicals 1982; Pres. Thiokol Chemical Div., Morton Thiokol, Inc. 1982–83, Group Vice-Pres. Chemicals 1983–86, Pres., COO and Dir 1986–89; Pres., COO and Dir Morton Int. Inc. 1986–94, Chair. and CEO 1994–99 (Morton Int. acquired by Rohm and Haas Co. 1999); mem. Bd of Dirs Autoliv, Inc. 1997–, Chair. 2001–07; mem. Bd of Dirs HSBC North America Holdings Inc.; mem. Advisory Bd Nat. Foundation for History of Chem. 1991–; mem. ACS, AIChE, Commercial Devt Asscn. *Address:* Autoliv, Inc., World Trade Center, Klarabergsviadukten 70, Section E, 107 24 Stockholm, Sweden. *Telephone:* (8) 587-20-600. *Fax:* (8) 411-70-25. *Website:* www.autoliv.com.

STEWARTBY, Baron (Life Peer), cr. 1992, of Portmoak in the District of Perth and Kinross; **Bernard Harold Ian Halley Stewartby,** PC, LittD, FBA, FRSE; British banker and fmr politician; b. (Stewart), 10 Aug. 1935, London; s. of the late Prof. H. C. Stewart and Dorothy Stewart (née Lowen); m. Deborah Charlotte Buchan 1966; one s. two d.; ed Haileybury Coll. and Jesus Coll., Cambridge; Lt-Commdr RNR; Brown Shipley & Co. Ltd 1960–82; Conservative MP for Hitchin/N Herts. 1974–92; Econ. Sec. to the Treasury 1983–87; Minister of State for the Armed Forces 1987–88, for NI 1988–89; Chair., Throgmorton Trust PLC 1990–2005; Dir, Financial Services Authority 1993–97; Deputy Chair., Standard Chartered PLC 1993–2004; Deputy Chair., Amlin PLC 1995–2006; Chair., Treasure Valuation Cttee 1996–2001; Hon. Fellow, Jesus Coll., Cambridge 1994, Hon. Keeper of Medieval Coins, Fitzwilliam Museum, Cambridge 2008; Medallist, Royal Numismatic Soc. 1996, Royal Naval and Royal Marine Forces Reserve Decoration. *Publications:* The Scottish Coinage 1955, Coinage in Tenth-Century England 1989, English Coins 1180–1551 2009. *Leisure interests:* archaeology, tennis. *Address:* House of Lords, London, SW1A 0PW, England (office); Broughton Green, Broughton, Peeblesshire, ML12 6HQ, Scotland (home). *Telephone:* (20) 7219-6418 (office). *Fax:* (20) 7821-6455 (office).

STEYN, Hon. Jan Hendrik, BA, BLL; South African lawyer; b. 4 March 1928, Cape Town; s. of H.P.M. Steyn and Zerilda Steyn; ed Jan van Riebeeck School, Univ. of Stellenbosch; began practising as lawyer, Cape Town 1950, took Silk 1963, apptd. Justice of Supreme Court, Cape Prov. Div. 1964, retd 1981; apptd First Exec. Dir The Urban Foundation 1977 (on leave of absence from Supreme Court), now Hon. Chair.; Chair. Ind. Devt Trust 1990–94, SA Media Council 1989; Judge, Court of Appeal, Lesotho 1992, Botswana 1994; Acting Judge of Cape Supreme Court; Jt Ombudsman to Life Assurance Industry 1996–2003; Chair. Bd of Investigation into Saldanha Steel Project 1995, Comm. of Enquiry into Remuneration of Election Reps; Dir First Nat. Bank, Anglo-American Corpn, Barlow Rand Ltd, Metropolitan Life of SA Ltd; Founder The Inst. of Criminology, Univ. of Cape Town; Trustee of numerous charitable orgs; four hon. degrees; Businessman of the Year Award, SA Inst. of Housing 1984, Paul Harris Fellowship Award, Rotary Int., Harvard Business School Business Statesman Award 1985. *Publications:* Crime and Punishment in South Africa (co-ed.); numerous publs on crime and its control. *Leisure interest:* golf. *Address:* c/o Court of Appeal, Maseru, Lesotho.

STEYN, Baron (Life Peer), cr. 1995, of Swafield in the County of Norfolk; **Johan Van Zyl Steyn,** PC, QC, MA; British judge; b. 15 Aug. 1932, Stellenbosch, S Africa; s. of Van Zyl Steyn and Janet Steyn (née Blignaut); m. Susan Leonore Lewis; two s. two d. by previous m.; one step-s. one step-d.; ed Jan van Riebeeck School, Cape Town, S Africa, Univ. of Stellenbosch, S Africa, Univ. Coll. Oxford; began practising at S African Bar 1958; Sr Counsel of Supreme Court of S Africa 1970; settled in UK; began practising at English Bar 1973, Bencher, Lincoln's Inn 1985, QC 1979; a Presiding Judge, Northern Circuit 1989–91; Judge of the High Court 1985–91; a Lord Justice of Appeal 1992–95, a Lord of Appeal in Ordinary 1995–2005; mem. Supreme Court Rule Cttee 1985–89; Chair. Race Relations Cttee of the Bar 1987–88; mem. Lord Chancellor's Advisory Cttee on Legal Educ. and Conduct 1994–96; Pres. British Insurance Law Asscn 1992–94; Hon. Fellow, Univ. Coll. Oxford 1995; Hon. mem. American Law Inst.; Hon. LLD (Queen Mary and Westfield Coll., London) 1997, (Univ. of East Anglia) 1997. *Publications:* Democracy Through Law 2004. *Address:* House of Lords, Westminster, London, SW1A 0PW, England. *Telephone:* (20) 7219-5353 (office). *Fax:* (20) 7219-6156 (office). *E-mail:* mundeng@parliament.uk (office).

STICH, Michael; German business executive and fmr professional tennis player; b. 18 Oct. 1968, Pinneberg; m. Jessica Stockmann 1992 (divorced 2003); ed studied history of art; Nat. Jr Champion 1986; turned professional 1988; semi-finalist, French Open 1990; mem. W German Davis Cup Team 1990; won first professional title, Memphis 1990; winner, Men's Singles Championship, Wimbledon 1991; Men's Doubles (with John McEnroe q.v., 1992; won ATP World Championship 1993; retd 1997; won 28 professional titles and over 12 million dollars in prize money; UN Amb. 1999–; German Davis Cup team Capt. Oct. 2001–Sept. 2002; mem. Sr tour; CEO Hanseatik Rückenzentrum, Michael Stich Foundation. *Television:* game show (PRO 7) 2000. *Leisure interests:* golf, horses, sports, painting. *Address:* Magdalenstr. 64B, 22148 Hamburg, Germany.

STICH, Otto, DEcon; Swiss politician; b. 10 Jan. 1927, Dornach, Canton Solothurn; m.; two c.; ed Basle; teacher, –1971; mem. Dornach Accounts Audit Comm. 1953; Communal Councillor and part-time Mayor of Dornach 1953–65; Prefect of Dornach-Thierstein 1961–70; mem. Nat. Council (Fed. Parl.) 1963–83, mem. External Trade Cttee 1965–71 (Chair. 1969–71), Finance Cttee 1971–77, 1982–83, Econ. Affairs Cttee 1978–81, fmr mem. other cttees; Fed. Councillor Dec. 1983, Head Fed. Dept of Finance 1984–95, Vice-Pres. Fed. Council 1987, Pres. of Swiss Confed. Jan.–Dec. 1988, Jan.–Dec. 1994; Chair. of Ministers, IMF Group of 10; joined Swiss SDP 1947, Chair. Solothurn cantonal party 1968–72, mem. Man. Cttee of Swiss SDP 1970–75, Vice-Chair. parl. party 1980; Chair. Trade Union Group of Asscn of Staffs of Pvt. Transport Firms and Swiss Railwaymen's Asscn; Man. Cen. Personnel Dept, Co-op Switzerland 1971–80, Deputy Dir and Head of Personnel and Training Dept 1980. *Address:* c/o Social Democratic Party, Spitalgasse 34, 3001 Bern, Switzerland.

STICH, Stephen Peter, PhD; American professor of philosophy and cognitive science; *Board of Governors Professor, Rutgers University;* b. 9 May 1943, New York; s. of Samuel J. Stich and Sylvia L. Stich; m. Judith Ann Gagnon 1971; one s. one d.; ed Univ. of Pennsylvania, Princeton Univ.; mem. staff, Univs of Michigan 1968–78, Maryland 1978–86, California, San Diego 1986–89; Prof. of Philosophy and Cognitive Science, Rutgers Univ. 1989–, Bd of Govs Prof. 1998–, Dir Research Group on Evolution and Higher Cognition; Adjunct Prof., CUNY Grad. Center 1994–97; Pres. Soc. for Philosophy and Psychology 1982–83; Fulbright Sr Research Scholar 1978–79; Fellow, Center for Advanced Study in the Behavioral Sciences 1983–84; Visiting Fellow, Research School of Social Sciences, ANU 1992; Erskine Fellow, Canterbury Univ., Christchurch, NZ 1996; Clark-Way-Harrison Distinguished Visiting Prof., Dept of Philosophy, Washington Univ. in St Louis 2007; Hon. Prof. of Philosophy, Univ. of Sheffield 2005–; Jean Nicod Prize, Institut Jean Nicod, Paris 2007. *Publications:* From Folk Psychology to Cognitive Science 1983, The Fragmentation of Reason 1990, Philosophy and Connectionist Theory (co-author) 1991, Deconstructing The Mind 1996, Mindreading (co-author) 2003. *Address:* Department of Philosophy, Davison Hall, Douglass Campus, Rutgers University, New Brunswick, NJ 08901 (office); 55 Liberty Street, Apt 8-A, New York, NY 10005, USA (home). *Telephone:* (732) 932-9861 (office). *Fax:* (212) 571-4838 (office); (732) 932-8617 (home). *E-mail:* stich@ruccs.rutgers.edu (office). *Website:* ruccs.rutgers.edu/archivefolder/research%20group/research.html (office); www.rci.rutgers.edu/~stich/ (home).

STIGLITZ, Joseph Eugene, PhD, FBA; American economist and academic; *Professor of Economics and Finance, Graduate School of Business, Columbia University;* b. 9 Feb. 1943, Gary, Ind.; s. of Nathaniel D. Stiglitz and Charlotte Fishman; m. 1st 1978; two s. two d.; m. 2nd Anya Schiffrin 2004; ed Amherst Coll., Mass. Inst. of Tech. and Univ. of Cambridge (Fulbright Scholar); Prof. of Econs, Cowles Foundation, Yale Univ. 1970–74; Visiting Fellow, St Catherine's Coll. Oxford 1973–74; Prof. of Econs, Stanford Univ. 1974–76, Sr Fellow, Hoover Inst. 1988–2001, Joan Kenney Prof. of Econs 1992–2001; Drummond Prof. of Political Econ., Univ. of Oxford 1976–79; Oskar Morgenstern Distinguished Fellow, Inst. of Advanced Studies, Princeton 1978–79; Prof. of Econs, Princeton Univ. 1979–88; Stern Visiting Prof., Columbia Univ. 2000, Prof. of Econs and Finance, Grad. School of Business 2000, Co-Founder and Pres. Initiative for Policy Dialogue 2000–, Univ. Prof. 2000–, Chair. Cttee on Global Thought 2006–; mem. Pres.'s Council of Econ. Advisers 1993–95, Chair. (mem. of cabinet) 1995–97; Special Adviser to Pres. of World Bank, Sr Vice-Pres. and Chief Economist 1997–2000; Chair. Man. Bd and Dir Grad. Summer Programs, Brooks World Poverty Inst., Univ. of Manchester 2006–; Special Adviser, Bell Communications Research, numerous consultancies in public and pvt. sector, editorial bd memberships etc.; Sr Fellow, Brookings Inst. 2000; Fellow, American Acad. of Arts and Sciences, NAS, Econometric Soc., American Philosophical Soc., Inst. for Policy Research (Sr Fellow 1991–93); Hon. DHL (Amherst Coll.) 1974; Dr hc (Univ. of Leuven, Ben Gurion Univ.), (Oxford) 2004; Guggenheim Fellow 1969–70; John Bates Clark Award, American Econ. Asscn 1979, Int. Prize, Accad. dei Lincei, Rome 1988, UAP Scientific Prize, Paris 1989; Nobel Prize for Econs (jt recepient) 2001. *Publications include:* Globalization and its Discontents, Economics of the Public Sector 2000, Principles of Economics 1997, Rethinking the East Asia Miracle (co-ed.) 2001, The Roaring Nineties 2003, Fair Trade for All (co-author), 2005, Making Globalization Work 2006, The Three Trillion Dollar War: The True Cost of the Iraq Conflict (co-author), 2008; other books and more than 300 papers in learned journals. *Address:* Uris Hall, Room 814, Columbia University, 3022 Broadway, New York, NY 10027, USA (office). *Telephone:* (212) 854-1481 (office). *Fax:* (212) 662-8474 (office). *E-mail:* jes322@columbia.edu (office). *Website:* www.josephstiglitz.com (office).

STIGWOOD, Robert Colin; Australian business executive; b. 16 April 1934, Adelaide; s. of Gordon Stigwood and Gwendolyn Stigwood (née Burrows); ed Sacred Heart Coll., Adelaide; est. Robert Stigwood Org. (RSO) 1967; f. RSO Records 1973; Founder, Music for UNICEF; TV producer in England and USA of The Entertainer and The Prime of Miss Jean Brodie; Chair. Stigwood group of cos; Key to cities of Los Angeles and Adelaide; Tony Award 1980 for Evita; Int. Producer of the Year, ABC Interstate Theatres Inc. *Films produced:* Jesus Christ Superstar 1973, Tommy 1975, Bugsy Malone 1976, Saturday Night Fever 1977, Grease 1978, Sergeant Pepper's Lonely Hearts Club Band 1978, Moment by Moment 1978, Times Square 1980, Gallipoli 1980, The Fan 1981, Grease 2 1982, Staying Alive 1983, Evita. *Stage musicals produced:* Hair, Oh! Calcutta, The Dirtiest Show in Town, Pippin, Jesus Christ Superstar, Evita, Grease (London) 1993, Saturday Night Fever. *Leisure interests:* tennis, swimming, sailing, reading. *Address:* c/o Robert Stigwood Organisation, Barton Manor, East Cowes, Isle of Wight, PO32 6LB, England (home).

STIHL, Hans Peter; German business executive; b. 18 April 1932, Stuttgart; s. of Andreas Stihl and Maria Giersch; m.; ed Technische Hochschule, Stuttgart; Chair. and Pnr, Andreas Stihl Fabrik; Pres. Deutsche Industrie und Handelstag, Bonn 1988–2000, Hon. Pres. 2001–; Vice-Pres. Inst. of German Economy, Cologne 1983–88, Treas. 1983–88; Pres. IHK Stuttgart 1990–2001, Hon. Pres. 2001–; Chair. Advisory Bd Stihl Holding AF & Co. KG and Chair. Supervisory Bd Stihl AG 2002–; mem. Man. Bd Verein Deutscher Maschinen- und Anlagenbau (VDMA) –1988; Hon. Consul-Gen. of Singapore 2002–; Grand Cross with Star for Distinguished Service of the Order of Merit of FRG 2002; Hanns Martin Schleyer Award 2003. *Address:* Stihl Holding AG & Co., Badstr. 115, 71336 Dieburg, Germany. *E-mail:* hon.konsulat-singapur.stgt@stihl.de.

STILL, Ray; American oboist; b. 12 March 1920, Elwood, Ind.; s. of Roy R. Still and Lillian Taylor; m. Mary Powell Brock 1940; two s. two d.; ed Juilliard School of Music and privately under Phillip Memoli and Robert Bloom; oboist, Kansas City Philharmonic Orchestra 1939–41; mil. service 1941–46; Buffalo Philharmonic Orchestra 1947–49; Prof. of Oboe and mem. Baltimore Symphony 1949–53; Solo Oboist, Chicago Symphony Orchestra 1953–93; taught at Peabody Inst., Baltimore 1949–53, Roosevelt Univ., Chicago 1954–57; Prof. of Oboe, Northwestern Univ. 1960–2003; Conductor, Stratford Music Festival, Canada 1964–69; mem. of a Quintet for 100th anniversary of Yamaha Co., recordings, Tour of Japan, judge int. oboe competition, Japan 1988; has undertaken coaching of many symphony orchestra wind and brass sections; judges oboe competitions in New York, Toulon, Munich, Toronto and Japan. *Recordings include:* Oboe Quartettes (with Perlman, Zuckermann, Harrel) and Mozart Oboe Concerto with Chicago Symphony Orchestra, conducted by Claudio Abbado, Ray Still – A Chicago Legend – Baroque Oboe Sonatas. *Leisure interests:* collecting classical comedy films, listening to great jazz artists of '20s, '30s and '40s, records of great lieder singers. *Address:* 585 West Hawthorne Place, Chicago, IL 60657, USA. *Website:* www.raystill.com.

STILLER, Ben; American actor and film director; b. 30 Nov. 1965, New York; s. of Jerry Stiller and Ann Meara; m.; one d.; ed UCLA. *Films:* Empire of the Sun 1988, Reality Bites (also dir) 1994, Happy Gilmore 1996, Flirting with Disaster 1996, The Cable Guy (also Dir) 1996, Zero Effect 1998, Your Friends and Neighbors 1998, There's Something About Mary 1998, Permanent Midnight 1998, Mystery Men 1999, Black and White 1999, Meet the Parents 2000, Keeping the Faith 2000, Zoolander (also dir) 2001, The Royal Tenenbaums 2001, Duplex 2003, Nobody Knows Anything 2003, Along Came Polly 2004, Starsky & Hutch 2004, Envy 2004, Dodgeball 2004, Anchorman 2004, Meet the Fockers 2004, Madagascar (voice) 2005, Danny Roane: First Time Director 2006, School for Scoundrels 2006, Tenacious D: The Pick of Destiny 2006, Night at the Museum 2006, The Heartbreak Kid 2007, Tropic Thunder (also dir) 2008. *Television:* The Ben Stiller Show (Emmy Award) 1990–93, Heat Vision and Jack, Freaks and Geeks. *Address:* c/o United Talent Agency, 9560 Wilshire Boulevard, Suite 500, Beverly Hills, CA 90212, USA (office).

STILWELL, Richard Dale, MusB; American singer (baritone); b. 6 May 1942, St Louis; s. of Otho John Clifton and Tressie Stilwell (née Parrish); m. 1st Elizabeth Louise Jencks 1967 (divorced); m. 2nd Kerry M. McCarthy 1983; ed Anderson Coll., Univ. of Indiana; with Metropolitan Opera Co., New York 1970–; appearances in major roles Washington Opera Soc., Marseilles Opera Co., Santa Fe Opera, San Francisco Opera Co., Paris Opera Co., La Scala, Covent Garden, Hamburg State Opera, Glyndebourne Opera Festival, Van. Opera Co., Chicago Opera Co., Tanglewood Festival, Israel Philharmonic, Boston Symphony, LA Philharmonic, etc.; soloist with Nat. Symphony, Washington, Chicago Symphony, American Symphony, Carnegie Hall, Boston Symphony, LA Philharmonic, etc.; mem. American Guild Musical Artists; Nat. Soc. of Arts and Letters Award 1963, Fisher Foundation award Metropolitan Opera Auditions 1965. *Address:* Columbia Artists Management, 1790 Broadway, New York, NY 10019-1412, USA (office). *Telephone:* (212) 841-9500 (office). *Fax:* (212) 841-9744 (office). *E-mail:* info@cami.com (office). *Website:* www.cami.com (office).

STINCO, Antoine; French architect; b. 1934, ; ed Ecole Nationale Supérieure des Beaux-Arts, Paris (studio of Edouard Albert-Paul Herbe, Jean Prouvé); worked on light and mobile architecture and particularly on inflated structures; exhibited inflated structure in ARC (Museum of Modern Arts of Paris) 1968; participated with GAU (Urban Architecture Group) in renewal of urban architecture in France 1974; est. own architectural firm 1984; fashion design artist with Christiane Bailly Assocs 1970–90; taught in Sculpture Dept at Beaux-Art, Paris 1993–99. *Major works include:* Jeu de paume, Nat. Gallery, Jardin de Tuileries, Paris 1991, Musée du Louvre, Paris, six kiosks in Jardin de Tuileries 1995–97, Ecole du Louvre and Aile de Flore, Louvre Museum 1997–98, Musée d'art moderne et contemporain Les Abattoirs, Toulouse (with R. Papillault) 2000, Musée des Beaux Arts, Angers 2003, MC2 Arts Centre extension, Maison de la Culture, Grenoble 2004, Le Théâtre nat. de Bretagne 2008. *Publications:* Le Territoire de L'Architecture – Suivi de Vingt-Quatre Projets et Realisations (with Vittorio Gregotti) 1982, Les Abattoirs, Histoires et Transformation 2000. *Address:* SA Antoine Stinco, 73 boulevard de Sebastopol, 75002 Paris, France (office). *Telephone:* 1-45-08-18-66 (office).

STING, CBE; British singer, musician (bass guitar), songwriter and actor; b. (Gordon Matthew Thomas Sumner), 2 Oct. 1951, Wallsend, Newcastle upon Tyne; s. of the late Ernest Sumner and Audrey Sumner (née Cowell); m. 1st Frances Tomelty 1976 (divorced 1984); one s. one d.; m. 2nd Trudie Styler 1992; two s. two d.; ed St Cuthbert's High School, Newcastle upon Tyne, Univ. of Warwick, Coventry, Northern Counties Coll. of Educ.; worked as bus conductor, construction labourer and tax officer –1971; primary school teacher, St Paul's First School, Cramlington, Newcastle 1975–77; played with local jazz bands, including Phoenix Jazzmen, the Newcastle Big Band, and Last Exit; mem., with Stewart Copeland and Henry Padovani (replaced by Andy Summers), and lead singer of rock group, The Police 1977–84, re-formed to tour 2007–08; solo artist 1985–; numerous tours, TV and radio broadcasts in Europe and USA; Chevalier, Ordre des Arts et Lettres 2007; Hon. DMus (Northumbria) 1992; Ivor Novello Awards for Best Song (for They Dance Alone) 1989, four BMI songwriting awards 1998, BMI Award for Int. Achievement 2002, BRIT Award for Best Male Artist 1994, for Outstanding Contribution to Music 2002, Emmy Award for Best Performance (Sting in Tuscany... All This Time) 2002, 14 Grammy Awards (with The Police and solo), Grammy Award for Best Pop Collaboration with Vocals (for Whenever I Say Your Name, with Mary J. Blige) 2004, MusiCares Foundation Person of the Year 2003, Billboard Music Century Award for Creative Achievement 2003. *Stage appearance:* The Threepenny Opera (Broadway) 1989. *Film appearances include:* Quadrophenia 1979, Radio On 1980, Artemis 81 (BBC TV) 1981, Brimstone and Treacle 1982, Dune 1984, The Bride 1985, Plenty 1985, Bring on the Night 1985, Giulia and Giulia 1987, The Adventures of Baron Munchausen 1988, Stormy Monday 1988, The Grotesque 1995, Lock, Stock and Two Smoking Barrels 1998, The Tulse Luper Suitcases: The Moab Story 2003, Bee Movie 2007. *Recordings include:* albums: with the Police: Outlandos D'Amour 1977, Regatta De Blanc 1979, Zenyatta Mondatta 1980, Ghost In The Machine 1981, Synchronicity 1983, Bring On The Night 1986, Every Breath You Take: The Classics 1995, Sting & The Police—The Very Best Of 1997, 2002, The Police 2007; solo: The Dream of The Blue Turtles 1985, Nothing Like The Sun 1987, The Soul Cages 1991, Ten Summoner's Tales 1994, Mercury Falling 1996, Brand New Day 1999, All This Time 2001, Sacred Love 2003, Songs of Love 2003, My Funny Valentine 2005, Songs From The Labyrinth 2007, Songs for Tibet – The Art of Peace 2008. *Publications:* Jungle Stories: The Fight for the Amazon 1989, Escape Artist (memoir) 2003. *Address:* Kathryn Shenker Associates, 12th Floor, 1776 Broadway, New York, NY 10019, USA (office); c/o Publicity Department, Polydor Records, 72 Black Lane, London, W6, England (office). *Telephone:* (20) 8910-4800 (office). *Website:* www.sting.com.

STINSON, William W.; Canadian insurance industry executive; CEO Canadian Pacific Ltd 1985–96; apptd mem. Bd of Dirs Sun Life Financial Inc. 1985, Lead Dir 1999–2003, Chair. (non-exec.) Sun Life Financial Inc. and Sun Life Assurance Co. 2003–05 (retd); currently Chair. and CEO Westshore Terminals Inc., Chair. Westshore Terminals Income Funds; mem. Bd of Dirs Grant Forest Products Inc. 2003–, CHC Helecopter Corpn 2003–; Trustee Fording Canadian Coal Trust. *Address:* Westshore Terminals Income Fund, 1800-1067 Cordova Street West, Vancouver BC V6C 1C7, Canada (office).

STIPE, (John) Michael; American musician and songwriter; b. 1 April 1960, Decatur, GA; ed Univ. of Georgia; founder mem. and lead singer, R.E.M. 1980–; owner C-00 (film co.) and Single Cell Pictures 1987–; Owner, Grit vegetarian restaurant, Athens, Ga; numerous MTV Music Video Awards, Earth Day Award 1990, Billboard Award for Best Modern Rock Artist 1991, BRIT Awards for Best Int. Group 1992, 1993, 1995, Grammy Awards for Best Pop Performance, Best Music Video 1992, Atlanta Music Awards for Act of the Year, Video of the Year 1992, IRMA Award for Int. Band of the Year 1993, Rolling Stone Critics Award for Best Band 1993. *Recordings:* albums: Chronic Town 1982, Murmur 1983, Reckoning 1984, Fables Of The Reconstruction 1985, Life's Rich Pageant 1986, Dead Letter Office 1987, Document 1987, Eponymous 1988, Green 1988, Out Of Time (Billboard Award for Best World Album, Q Award for Best Album) 1991, Automatic For The People (Grammy Award for Best Alternative Music Album, Atlanta Music Award for Rock Album, Q Award for Best Album, Rolling Stone Critics Award for Best Album 1993) 1992, Monster 1994, New Adventures In Hi-Fi 1996, Up 1998, Star Profiles 1999, Reveal 2001, Bad Day Pt 1 and 2 2003, Glastonbury 1999 2003, Around The Sun 2004, Accelerate 2008. *Address:* REM/Athens Ltd, 250 West Clayton Street, Athens, GA 30601, USA (office). *Website:* www.remhq.com.

STIPRAIS, Eduards; Latvian diplomatist and government official; *Head of the Chancery of the President;* b. 19 Feb. 1969, Rīga; m. Zanda Grauze; ed Univ. of Latvia; Desk Officer, Ministry of Foreign Trade 1992–93; EC Desk Officer, Ministry of Foreign Affairs 1993, Head EC/EFTA Relations Div. 1993–94, Deputy Dir Dept of Int. Econ. Relations 1994–95, Head, task force for preparation of EU accession negotiations 1998–99, Deputy Chief Negotiator EU accession negotiations 1999–2003; overseas posts include Adviser on Secondment to OECD/EU Sigma Programme, Paris 1995, Second Sec. Perm. Mission to EU 1995, First Sec. 1995–98, Deputy Head 2003–04, Deputy Perm. Rep. 2004, Perm. Rep. 2004–07; Head of Chancery of the Pres. of Latvia 2007–; mem. Latvijas Ceļš party 1993–; mem. Latvian European Movt. *Address:* Chancery of the President, Pils lauk. 3, Rīga 1050, Latvia (office). *Telephone:* 6709-2106 (office). *Fax:* 6709-2157 (office). *E-mail:* chancery@president.lv (office). *Website:* www.president.lv (office).

STIRLING, Sir Angus Duncan Aeneas, Kt, FRSA; British arts administrator; b. 10 Dec. 1933, London; s. of the late Duncan Alexander Stirling and Lady Marjorie Stirling; m. Armyne Morar Helen Schofield 1959; one s. two d.; ed Eton Coll., Trinity Coll. Cambridge, Univ. of London; mem. staff, Christie, Manson & Woods Ltd 1954–57, Lazard Bros. and Co. Ltd 1957–66; Asst Dir Paul Mellon Foundation for British Art 1966–69, Jt Dir 1969–70; Deputy Sec.-Gen. Arts Council of GB 1971–79; Deputy Dir-Gen. The Nat. Trust 1979–83, Dir-Gen. 1983–95; Sr Policy Adviser Nat. Heritage Memorial Fund 1996–97; Dir Royal Opera House, Covent Garden 1979–96, Chair. 1991–96, Chair. Friends of Covent Garden 1981–91, Deputy Chair. Royal Ballet Bd 1988–91; Chair. Greenwich Foundation for the Royal Naval Coll. 1996–2003, Policy Cttee, Council for Protection of Rural England (CPRE) 1996–2001, Jt Nature Conservation Cttee 1997–2002; mem. Crafts Council 1980–85, Council of Man. Byam Shaw School of Art 1965–89, Bd of Dirs Courtauld Inst. of Art 1981–83, 2002–, Advisory Council London Symphony Orchestra 1979–, Bd of Govs Live Music Now 1982–89, Govt Task Force on Tourism and the Environment 1991, Court of the Fishmongers' Company 1991– (Prime Warden 2004–05), ICOMOS UK Tourism Cttee 1993–2003 (Chair. IUCN/ICOMOS UK Liaison Cttee 2003–07), Council Royal School of Church Music 1996–98, Bd of Govs Gresham School 1999–2007, Fabric Advisory Cttee, Wells Cathedral 2001–, City & Guilds of London Art School 2003–; Trustee, Theatres Trust 1983–91, Heritage of London Trust 1983–95, Samuel Courtauld Trust 1984–, World Monuments Fund UK 1996–, Stowe House Preservation Trust 1998–; Vice-Patron Almshouses Asscn 1998–; Hon. Fellow, Trinity Coll. of Music; Hon. DLitt (Greenwich, Leicester). *Leisure interests:* music, travel, walking, painting. *Address:* 25 Ladbroke Grove, London, W11 3AY, England (home).

STIRN, Olivier, LenD; French politician; *Executive Adviser, Union pour un Mouvement Populaire;* b. 24 Feb. 1936, Boulogne-Billancourt; s. of Alexandre Stirn and Geneviève Dreyfus; m. Evelyn Toledano 1989; one s. one d. (and two s. from previous m.); ed Univ. of Paris, Institut de Sciences Politiques; Chief of Cabinet for Prefect of La Meuse 1961–64, Chargé de mission 1964; Chief of Cabinet for Minister of State in charge of Overseas Depts and Territories 1964, for Sec. of State for Foreign Affairs 1966–67, for Sec. of State for Social Affairs 1967–68; Deputy for Calvados 1968–73, 1981–86 (Gen. Councillor 1970–88, 1994–2001), for Manche 1986–88; Councillor Gen., Mayor of Vire 1971; Pres., Urban Community of Cherbourg 1989–90; Sec. of State for Parl. Relations 1973–74, for Overseas Territories 1974–78, for Foreign Affairs 1978–81, for Defence 1980–81; Minister Del. for Overseas Territories May–June 1988, Minister Del. attached to Minister of Industry and Territorial Devt 1988–89, to Minister of Industry, Territorial Devt and Tourism (with special responsibility for Tourism) 1989–90; Chair. Dialogue 2000 1988–; Amb. to Council of Europe, Strasbourg 1991–93; Business Consultant 1993–; Consultant to Rothschild & Cie 1998–2001; Editorial Dir Editions du Félin 2005–; Executive Adviser, Union pour un Mouvement Populaire (UMP) 2004–; founder, Mouvement des sociaux-libéraux 1977; Vice-Pres., Parti radical socialiste 1977; co-founder, Carrefour social-démocrate 1977; founder and Pres., Union centriste et républicaine 1984; Nat. Del., Parti socialiste 1986; Chevalier, Légion d'honneur, and many foreign decorations. *Publications:* Le piège (with Bernard Stasi and J. P. Soisson) 1973, Une certaine idée du centre 1985, Tourisme: chance pour l'économie, risque pour les sociétés?, Mes Présidents: 50 ans au service de la 5e Republique 2004. *Leisure interests:* tennis, golf, history. *Address:* 55 rue la Boétie, 75008 Paris (office); 14 Avenue Pierre 1er de Serbie, 75116 Paris, France (home). *Telephone:* 1-47-20-41-93 (office); 1-47-20-41-57 (home). *Fax:* 1-40-76-60-44 (office); 1-47-20-41-93 (home). *E-mail:* evestirn.sic@free.fr (office).

STIRRUP, Air Chief Marshal Sir Graham Eric (Jock), GCB, AFC, ADC, DSc, FRAeS, FCMI, RAF; British air force officer; *Chief of Defence Staff;* b. 4 Dec. 1949; s. of William Hamilton Stirrup and Jacqueline Brenda Stirrup (née Coulson); m. Mary Alexandra Elliot 1976; one s.; ed Merchant Taylors' School, Northwood, RAF Coll., Cranwell, Jt Service Defence Coll., Royal Coll. of Defence Studies; qualified flying instructor 1971–73; loan service, Sultan of Oman's Air Force 1973–75; fighter reconnaissance pilot 1976–78; exchange pilot, USAF 1978–81; Flight Commdr 1982–84; Officer Commdr No. II (Army Co-operation) Squadron 1985–87; Dir Air Force Plans and Programmes, Ministry of Defence 1994–97; Air Officer Commdr No. 1 Group 1997–98; Asst Chief of Air Staff 1998–2000; Deputy C-in-C, Stike Commdr, Commdr NATO Combined Air Operations Centre 9 and Dir European Air Group 2000–02; Deputy Chief of Defence Staff (Equipment Capability) 2002–03; Chief of Air Staff 2003–06, Chief of Defence Staff 2006–. *Leisure interests:* golf, music, theatre, history. *Address:* c/o Ministry of Defence, Main Building, Whitehall, London, SW1A 2HB, England (office). *Website:* www.mod.uk (office).

STITZER, H. Todd; American business executive; *CEO, Cadbury plc;* m. Marenda Stitzer; two c.; ed Harvard and Columbia Univs; Asst Gen. Counsel Cadbury Schweppes Beverages N America 1983, Vice-Pres. and Gen. Counsel, Worldwide Beverages Stream 1988, Group Devt Dir responsible for Strategic Planning and External Devt, UK 1991–93, Vice-Pres. Marketing and Strategic Planning N America 1993–95, COO N America 1995–97; Pres. and CEO Dr Pepper/Seven Up 1997–2000; Chief Strategy Officer Cadbury Schweppes (now Cadbury plc) 2000–02, Deputy CEO 2002–03, CEO 2003–; mem. Bd of Dirs Diageo plc. *Address:* Cadbury plc, Cadbury House, Sanderson Road, Uxbridge Business Park, Uxbridge, London, UB8 1DH, England (office). *Telephone:* (18) 9561-5000 (office). *Fax:* (18) 9561-5001 (office). *Website:* www.cadbury.com (office).

STOCKTON, 2nd Earl of; **Alexander Daniel Alan Macmillan,** FBIM, FRSA; British publisher, farmer and politician; b. 10 Oct. 1943, Oswestry; s. of the late Maurice Victor Macmillan (Viscount Macmillan of Ovenden) and of Dame Katherine Macmillan (Viscountess Macmillan of Ovenden), DBE; grandson of the late 1st Earl of Stockton (fmrly, as Harold Macmillan, Prime Minister of UK 1957–63); m. 1st Hélène Birgitte Hamilton 1970 (divorced 1991); one s. two d.; m. 2nd Miranda Elizabeth Louise Nultall 1995; ed Eton Coll. and Paris and Strathclyde Univs; Sub-Ed., Glasgow Herald 1963–65; Reporter, Daily Telegraph 1965–67, Foreign Corresp. 1967–68, Chief European Corresp., Sunday Telegraph 1968–70; Dir, Birch Grove Estates Ltd 1969–86, Chair. 1983–89; Dir, Macmillan and Co. Ltd 1970–76, Deputy Chair. 1976–80, Chair. 1984–90, Pres. 1990–; Chair., Macmillan Publrs Ltd 1980–90 (Pres. 1990–), St Martin's Press, New York 1983–88 (Dir 1974–90), Sidgwick and Jackson 1989–90; mem. (Conservative) European Parl. for SW of England 1999–2004, Vice Pres. (Defence), European Parl. Foreign Affairs Cttee 2000–04, mem. Convention on the Future of Europe (Rep. of European Peoples' Party) 2003–04; Chair., Cen. London Training & Enterprise Council 1990–95; Pres., Ludwig von Mises Institut UZW 2005–; Dir, Book Trade Benevolent Soc.

1976–88, Chair., Bookrest Appeal 1978–86; Dir, United British Artists Ltd 1984–90 (Chair. 1985–90); mem. Lindemann Fellowship Cttee 1979– (Chair. 1983–), British Inst. of Man. 1981–, Council of Publrs Asscn 1985–88, Carlton Club Political Cttee 1975–88 (Chair. 1984); Gov., Archbishop Tenison's School 1979–86, Merchant Taylor's School 1980–82, 1990–, English Speaking Union 1980–84, 1986–93; Liveryman, Worshipful Co. of Merchant Taylors 1972, Court Asst 1987, of Stationers 1973, Master 1991–92; Hon. DLitt (De Montfort) 1993, (Westminster) 1995; Hon. DUniv (Strathclyde) 1993; Schumann Medal 2004. *Leisure interests:* shooting, fishing, aviation. *Address:* Flat M, 9 Warwick Square, London, SW1V 2AA, England (home). *Telephone:* (20) 7834-6004 (home). *Fax:* (1566) 783568 (home).

STODDART, Brian, BA, MA, PhD; New Zealand university administrator; ed Univ. of Canterbury, Univ. of Western Australia; fmr Pro Vice-Chancellor (Asia), RMIT Univ., Dir of Int. Programmes, RMIT Univ., Pro Vice-Chancellor (Research and Int.), Univ. of New England, Pro Vice-Chancellor (Int.), Victoria Univ., Acting Deputy Vice-Chancellor, Victoria Univ.; joined La Trobe Univ. as Deputy Vice-Chancellor (Research) 2004, Vice-Chancellor and Pres. 2005–06 (resgnd); mem. Australian Vice-Chancellors' Cttee (AVCC); fmr mem. numerojus editorial bds including Journal of Sport and Social Issues, Australian Soc. for Sports History; Australia-New Zealand Foundation Award. *Publications:* Saturday Afternoon Fever: Sport in the Australian Culture 1986, Liberation Cricket: Caribbean Cricket Culture 1995, The A–Z of Australian Cricketers 1997, The Imperial Game: Cricket, Culture and Society 1998, Soundings in Modern Sports Culture 2006; contribs to Sport Report, Pro News, World of Cricket, Action, The Australian, Sunday Herald, The Age, and over 35 articles in refereed journals and collections. *Address:* c/o Office of the Vice-Chancellor, La Trobe University, Plenty Road, Bundoora, Vic. 3086, Australia (office).

STODDART, Sir J. Fraser, Kt, DSc, PhD, FRS, FRSE; British chemist and academic; *Board of Trustees Professor of Chemistry, Northwestern University;* b. 24 May 1942, Edinburgh; two c.; ed Edinburgh Univ.; NRC Postdoctoral Fellow, Queens' Univ., Kingston, Ont., Canada 1967–70; ICI Research Fellow, Univ. of Sheffield 1970, Lecturer in Chem. 1970–78, Reader 1981–90; Researcher, ICI Corp. Lab., Runcorn 1978–81; Prof. of Organic Chem., Univ. of Birmingham 1990–97, Head of School of Chem. 1993–97; Winstein Chair., Dept of Chem. and Biochemistry UCLA 1997–2003, Dir California NanoSystems Inst. 2002–07, Fred Kavli Chair in NanoSystems Sciences, UCLA 2003–08; Board of Trustees Prof. of Chemistry, Northwestern University 2008–; visiting Prof. at numerous int. univs; mem. Editorial Bd Crystal Growth and Design, Journal of Organic Chem., Organic Letters, Angewandte Chemie, Chem.-A European Journal, Synthesis, Bioorganic Chem. Reviews; Pres. Chemical Section, BAAS 1996–; mem. Royal Inst., ACS; Fellow German Acad. of Natural Sciences Leopoldina; Hon. Prof., East China Univ. 2005; hon. lecturer at numerous int. univs; Hon. DSc (Univ. of Birmingham) 2005, (Univ. of Sheffield) 2008; numerous awards including Edinburgh Univ. Hope Prize in Chem. 1964, ACS Cope Scholar Award 1999, UCLA Herbert Newby McCoy Award 2000, Nagoya Gold Medal 2004, Univ. of Edinburgh Alumnus of the Year 2005, King Faisal Intl Prize 2007, Albert Einstein World Prize 2007, Tetrahedron Prize for Creativity 2007, Feynman Prize 2007; Arthur C Cope Award 2008, Davy Medal 2008. *Publications:* over 800 publications in scientific journals. *Address:* Department of Chemistry, Northwestern University 2145 Sheridan Road, Evanston, IL 60304-3114, USA (office). *Telephone:* (847) 491-3793 (office). *Fax:* (847) 491-1009 (office). *E-mail:* stoddart@northwestern.edu (office). *Website:* stoddart.northwestern.edu (office).

STOFILE, Rev. Makhenkesi Arnold, MA, MTheol; South African academic and politician; *Minister of Sport and Recreation;* b. 27 Dec. 1944, Winterburg, Adelaide Dist, Eastern Cape; s. of Simon Stofile and Miriam Stofile; m. Nambita Stofile 1977; one s. (deceased) two d.; ed Univ. of Fort Hare, Princeton Univ., USA; worked as farm labourer and machine operator 1965–68; part-time tutor with African Ind. Churches Asscn Seminary 1971–72; Sr Lecturer in Theology and Philosophy, Univ. of Fort Hare 1973–86; convicted under Ciskeian Internal Security Act and sentenced to 11 years imprisonment 1987; Sr Lecturer in Theology, Univ. of Transkei 1991; MP 1994–96, (Govt Chief Whip 1994–96), 2004–; ANC Treas. Gen. 1995–97; Premier of Eastern Cape 1997–2004; Minister of Sport and Recreation 2004–; Dr hc (Univ. of Port Elizabeth) 2000. *Achievement:* (with wife) Ballroom Dancing Champions for Black S African Univs. *Leisure interests:* rugby, boxing. *Address:* Ministry of Sport and Recreation, Oranje Nassau Bldg, 3rd Floor, 188 Schoeman St, Pretoria Private Bag X896, Pretoria 0001 (office); 143 Queens Road, King Williams Town 5600, South Africa (home). *Telephone:* (12) 3343220 (office). *Fax:* (12) 3264026 (office). *E-mail:* greg@srsa.gov.za (office); Nobulali1@sport1.pwv.gov.za (office). *Website:* www.srsa.gov.za (office).

STOIBER, Edmund, DJur; German lawyer and politician; b. 1941, Oberaudorf; m. Karin Stoiber; three c.; ed Univ. of Munich and Hochschule für Politische Wissenschaft; personal counsellor to Bavarian State Minister for Devt 1972–74, Dir of Ministerial Office 1974; entered Bavarian Parl. 1974; admitted solicitor 1978; Gen. Sec. Christian Social Union (CSU) 1978–83, Chair. CSU 1999–2007, Hon. Chair. 2007–; Campaign Man. for Franz Josef Strauss, Fed. Elections 1980; State Sec. and Dir Bavarian State Chancellery 1982–86, State Minister and Dir 1986–88; Bavarian State Minister for Internal Affairs 1988–93, Minister-Pres. of Bavaria 1993–2007; cand. in Chancellery elections 2002; mem. Bd Bayern Munich (football team); Bayerischer Verdienstorden. *Publications:* Politik aus Bayern 1976, Der Hausfriedensbruch im Licht akt. Probleme 1984. *Leisure interests:* skiing, football. *Address:* Wagmüllerstraße 18, 80538 Munich, Germany. *E-mail:* info@stoiber.de. *Website:* www.stoiber.de.

STOICHEFF, Boris Peter, OC, PhD, FRS, FRSC; Canadian physicist and academic; *Professor Emeritus of Physics, University of Toronto;* b. 1 June 1924, Bitol, Yugoslavia (now Macedonia); s. of Peter Stoicheff and Vasilka Stoicheff (née Tonna); m. Lillian Joan Ambridge 1954; one s.; ed Jarvis Collegiate Inst., Toronto, Canada and Univ. of Toronto; Postdoctoral Fellow, Physics, Nat. Research Council, Ottawa 1951–53, Research Officer 1953–64; Visiting Scientist, MIT, USA 1963–64; Prof. of Physics, Univ. of Toronto 1964–89, Univ. Prof. 1977–89, Prof. Emer. 1989–; Chair., Eng Science 1972–77; I.W. Killam Scholar 1977–79; Visiting Scientist, Stanford Univ., USA 1978; Exec. Dir, Ont. Laser and Lightwave Research Centre 1988–91; UK and Canada Rutherford Lecturer 1989; professional interests include lasers, atomic and molecular spectroscopy and structure, light scattering and two-photon processes, nonlinear optics and generation of ultraviolet radiation; determined structures of many molecules by light scattering and discovered inverse Raman effect and stimulated Brillouin scattering (or the generation of sound by light); mem. Gov. Council of Nat. Research Council, Ottawa 1977–83; Pres. Optical Soc. of America 1976, Canadian Asscn of Physicists 1983; Vice-Pres. IUPAP 1993–96; Co-Foreign Sec. RSC 1995–2000; Hon. Foreign mem. American Acad. of Arts and Sciences 1989; Hon. Fellow, Indian Acad. of Sciences, Macedonian Acad. of Sciences and Arts; Hon. DSc (Skopje) 1982, (York Univ., Canada) 1982, (Univ. of Windsor, Canada) 1989, (Toronto) 1994; Medal of Achievement in Physics, Canadian Asscn of Physicists 1974, William F. Meggers Medal 1981, Frederic Ives Medal, Optical Soc. of America 1983, Henry Marshall Tory Medal, Royal Soc. of Canada 1989, Distinguished Service Award, Optical Soc. of America 2002. *Publications:* Gerhard Herzberg: an Illustrious life in Science, (NRC Press) Ottawa 2002, over 180 scientific publs in int. journals. *Leisure interests:* travel, art, music. *Address:* Department of Physics, University of Toronto, 60 St George Street, Toronto, ON M5S 1A7 (office); 66 Collier Street, Apt 6B, Toronto, ON M4W 1L9, Canada (home). *Telephone:* (416) 978-2948 (office); (416) 923-9622 (home). *Fax:* (416) 978-2537 (office). *E-mail:* bps@physics.utoronto.ca (office). *Website:* www.physics.utoronto.ca (office).

STOKER, Sir Michael George Parke, Kt, CBE, MA, MD, FRS, FRSE, FRCP; British medical researcher (retd); b. 4 July 1918, Taunton, Somerset; s. of S. P. Stoker and D. Stoker (née Nazer); m. Veronica Mary English 1942; three s. two d.; ed Sidney Sussex Coll., Cambridge and St Thomas's Hosp., London; Capt. RAMC 1942–47; Lecturer in Pathology, Univ. of Cambridge 1947–58, Fellow of Clare Coll., Cambridge 1948–58; Prof. of Virology, Univ. of Glasgow 1959–68; Dir Imperial Cancer Research Fund Labs, London 1968–79; Visiting Prof., Univ. Coll., London 1968–79; Fellow, Clare Hall, Cambridge 1978, Pres. 1980–87; Foreign Sec., Vice-Pres. Royal Soc. 1976–81; mem. Council for Scientific Policy, Dept of Educ. and Science 1970–73, Gen. Cttee Int. Council of Scientific Unions 1977–82, Scientific Cttee, Ludwig Inst. for Cancer Research 1985–91; Chair. Governing Body Strangeways Research Lab. 1981–93, UK Coordinating Cttee for Cancer Research 1983–86; Foreign mem. Czech. Acad. of Sciences; Hon. Foreign mem. American Acad. of Arts and Sciences; Hon. DSc (Glasgow) 1982; Royal Soc. Leeuwenhoek Lecturer 1971, Blackett Memorial Lecturer 1980, Mendel Gold Medal 1984. *Publications:* over 150 articles and reviews on virology, oncology and cell biology. *Leisure interest:* painting. *Address:* 7 Grange Court, Cambridge, CB3 9BD, England (home).

STOKER, Richard, FRAM, ARAM, ARCM; British composer, actor, conductor, writer and poet and painter; b. 8 Nov. 1938, Castleford, Yorks.; s. of the late Capt. Bower Morrell Stoker and Winifred Harling; m. Gillian Patricia Stoker 1986; ed Breadalbane House School, Castleford, Univ. of Huddersfield with Harold Truscott, Coll. of Art, Royal Acad. of Music and Drama, composition with Sir Lennox Berkeley, conducting with Maurice Miles, pvt. study with Nadia Boulanger in Paris, Arthur Benjamin, Eric Fenby, Benjamin Britten; performance debut with BBC Home Service 1953, Nat. and Int. Eisteddfods, Wales 1955–58; conducting debut 1956; Asst Librarian, London Symphony Orchestra 1962–63; Prof. of Composition, RAM 1963–87 (tutor 1970–80); composition teacher, St Paul's School 1972–74, Magdalene Coll., Cambridge 1974–76; Ed. The Composer magazine 1969–80; apptd Magistrate, Inner London Comm. 1995–2003, Crown Court 1998–2003; Adjudicator, Royal Philharmonic Soc. Composer's Award, Cyprus Orchestral Composer's Award for the Ministry of Culture 2001–, BBC Composers' Awards; mem. Composers' Guild 1962– (mem. exec. cttee 1969–80); Founder mem. RAM Guild Cttee 1994– (Hon. Treas. 1995–); Founder mem. European-Atlantic Group 1993–; mem. Byron Soc. 1993–2000, Magistrates' Asscn 1995–2003, English and Int. PEN 1996–2005; mem. and Treas. Steering Cttee Lewisham Arts Festival 1990, 1992; Founder mem. Atlantic Council 1993, RSL, Creative Rights Alliance 2001–; concert appearances as pianist including Queen Elizabeth Hall, Purcell Rooms, Leighton House, RAM, Pizza on the Park, Barnet Festival; mem. RAM Guild; BBC Music Award 1952, Eric Coates Award 1962, Dove Prize 1962, Nat. Library of Poetry (USA) Editors' Choice Award 1995, 1996, 1997. *Compositions include:* four symphonies 1961, 1976, 1981, 1991; 12 nocturnes; two jazz preludes; overtures: Antic Hay, Feast of Fools, Heroic Overture; three string quartets, three violin sonatas, Partita for Violin and Harp or Piano, Sonatina for Guitar, two piano sonatas, three piano trios, A York Suite for piano, Piano Variations, Piano Concerto, Partita for Clarinet and Piano, Wind Quintet; organ works: Partita, Little Organ Book, Three Improvisations, Symphony; Monologue, Passacagalia, Serenade, Petite Suite, Nocturnal, Festival Suite; choral works and song cycles: Benedictus, Ecce Homo, Proverb, Psalms, Make Me a Willow Cabin, Canticle of the Rose, O Be Joyful, A Landscape of Truth; piano works: Zodiac Variations, Regency Suite, A Poet's Notebook; vocal works: Music That Brings Sweet Sleep, Aspects of Flight, Four Yeats Songs, Four Shakespeare Songs, Johnson Preserv'd (three-act opera), Thérèse Raquin (in preparation), Chinese Canticle, Birthday of the Infanta; music for film and stage includes Troilus and Cressida, Portrait of a Town, Garden Party, My Friend – My Enemy. *Recordings:* appearances on numerous CDs and records. *Films:* appearances include Red Mercury Rising, Woken, Daddy's Girl, Portrait of a Town, Lear and Goncril, The Shrink,

Bedtime Story, The Usual, The End of the Line, The Queen, The Da Vinci Code, Ancient Cataclysms, Vagabond Shoes, Encounter, Bouquet, Interval, Home Guard Ron. *Television:* Mary Tudor (four-part series), Comment (Channel 4), Europe, Dirty Weekend in Hospital, Happiness (BBC), Troilus and Cressida. *Radio:* interviews and discussions on BBC Radio Three, Four, World Service, Radio Leeds, New York Times Radio, Radio New York, Wall Street Radio, Radio Algonquin. *Publications:* Portrait of a Town 1970, Words Without Music 1974, Strolling Players 1978, Open Window – Open Door (autobiog.) 1985, Tanglewood (novel) 1990, Between the Lines 1991, Diva (novel) 1992, Collected Short Stories 1993, Sir Thomas Armstrong: A Celebration 1998, Turn Back the Clock 1998, A Passage of Time 1999; contrib. to anthologies, including Triumph, Forward, Outposts, Spotlight, Strolling Players, American Poetry Soc. publs, reviews and articles for periodicals, including Records and Recording, Books and Bookmen, Guardian, Performance, The Magistrate, poems in numerous anthologies and internet publs; contrib. to Oxford Dictionary of Nat. Biography (nine entries) 2004, 2006 (adviser 2003–). *Leisure interests:* squash, skiing, tennis, swimming, yoga, golf, windsurfing, judo. *Address:* Ricordi & Co. (London) Ltd, 210 New King's Road, London, SW6 4NZ, England (office). *Telephone:* (20) 7371-7501 (office); (20) 8852-9608 (home); (7906) 843812 (mobile). *Fax:* (20) 7371-7270. *E-mail:* gps5@tutor.open.ac.uk. *Website:* www.britishacademy.com/members/stoker.htm.

STOKES, Kerry Matthew, AO, FAIM; Australian business executive; *Chairman, Seven Network Ltd;* b. 13 Sept. 1940, Vic.; s. of M. P. Stokes; m. 2nd Christine Simpson 2003; two s.; ed St George's CBC, WA Tech. Coll.; Chair. Australian Capital Equity Pty Ltd (Dir 1981–), Austrim Ltd, Golden West Network (TV), Westrac Equipment Pty Ltd; Chair. Canberra Theatre Trust 1981–86, Dir 1989–91; Chair. Art Gallery Foundation, WA 1989–91; Chair. The Fed. Capital Press Pty Ltd (Canberra Times), Seven Network Ltd 1995–, Chair. Seven Network Ltd 1995–99, Exec. Chair. 1999–; Dir 1989–91; Pres. Appeal Campaign for Inst. for Child Health Research; Founder-mem. Council Nat. Gallery of Australia, Chair. 1996–2000; Hon. Life Mem. RSL Australia 1993–, Hon. Fellow, Murdoch Univ. 2000; WA Citizen of the Year Award 1994, Centenary Medal 2003. *Publications:* Boyer Lectures (Advance Australia Where) 1994, Andrew Olle Memorial Lecture 2001. *Leisure interests:* photography, sailing, scuba diving. *Address:* Seven Network Ltd, Wharf 17, Pirrama Road, Pyrmont, NSW 2009 (office); c/o Australian Capital Equity Pty Ltd, Level 3, 30 Kings Park Road, West Perth, WA 6005, Australia. *Telephone:* (2) 87777102 (office). *Fax:* (2) 87777149 (office). *Website:* www.yahoo!7.com.au (office).

STOKES, Patrick T., BS, MBA; American brewery industry executive; *Chairman, Anheuser-Busch Companies, Inc.;* b. 11 Aug. 1942, Washington, DC; m. Anna-Kristina Stokes; ed Boston Coll., Columbia Univ.; Financial Analyst, Shell Oil Co. 1966–67; began career in corp. planning, Anheuser-Busch 1969, held various positions including mem. Policy Cttee 1974, Vice-Pres. Raw Materials Acquisition 1976–81, Vice-Pres. and Group Exec. 1981–86; COO Campbell Taggert Inc. (subsidiary), Dallas 1986–90, CEO 1990–2002; Sr Exec. Vice-Pres. Anheuser-Busch Cos Inc. 2000–02, Pres. and CEO 2002–06, Chair. 2006–, Pres. Anheuser-Busch Int. Inc. 1990–99. *Address:* Anheuser-Busch Companies, Inc., 1 Busch Place, St Louis, MO 63118, USA (office). *Telephone:* (314) 577-2000 (office). *Fax:* (314) 577-2900 (office). *Website:* www.anheuser-busch.com (office).

STOL, Marten; Dutch academic; *Professor Emeritus of Akkadian (Assyriology), Ugaritic and History of Ancient Near East, Free University of Amsterdam;* b. 10 Nov. 1940, Oldekerk; m. Rose C. van Wyngaarden 1968; one s. one d.; ed Gymnasium, Middelburg and State Univ. Leiden; Research Assoc., State Univ. Leiden 1968–70, Asst Prof. 1970–82; Research Assoc., Chicago Assyrian Dictionary, Oriental Inst., Univ. of Chicago 1973–74; Prof. of Akkadian (Assyriology), Ugaritic and History of Ancient Near East, Free Univ. Amsterdam 1983–2005, Prof. Emer. 2005–; Sr Researcher, Nederlands Instituut voor het Nabije Oosten, Leiden 2006–; Gen. Sec., Soc. Ex Oriente Lux 1973–99; mem. Royal Netherlands Acad.; Hon. mem., American Oriental Soc. 1999, Ex Oriente Lux 2003. *Publications:* Studies in Old Babylonian History 1976, On Trees, Mountains and Millstones in the Ancient Near East 1979, Letters from Yale 1981, Letters from Collections in Philadelphia, Chicago and Berkeley 1986, Epilepsy in Babylonia 1993, Langs's Heeren wegen 1997, Birth in Babylonia and the Bible 2000, Die Altbabylonische Zeit 2004. *Address:* Heivlinder 27, 2317 JS Leiden, Netherlands.

STOLER, Andrew L., BS, MBA; American international organization official, government official and research institute administrator; *Executive Director, Institute for International Business, Economics and Law, University of Adelaide;* ed George Washington Univ., Georgetown Univ.'s School of Foreign Service; with Office of Int. Trade Policy, Dept of Commerce 1975–79; Dir for Canada, Australia and New Zealand, US Trade Rep. Office 1980–81, MTN Codes Co-ordinator, Geneva 1982–87, Deputy Asst US Trade Rep. for Europe and Mediterranean, Washington 1988–89, Deputy Chief of Mission, Geneva 1989–99 (concurrently Deputy Perm. Rep. to World Trade Org.); Deputy Dir-Gen. World Trade Org. 1999–2002; Exec. Dir Inst. for Int. Business, Economics and Law, Univ. of Adelaide 2002–, also Adjunct Prof. of Int. Trade; mem. Aid Advisory Council (Australia) 2004–, Advisory Cttee of Shanghai WTO Affairs Consultation Centre; Sr. Advisor, Shenzhen WTO Affairs Centre. *Address:* Institute for International Business, Economics and Law, University of Adelaide, Level 12-10, Pulteney Street, Adelaide, SA 5005, Australia (office). *Telephone:* (8) 8303-6944 (office). *Fax:* (8) 8303-6948 (office). *E-mail:* andrew.stoler@adelaide.edu.au (office). *Website:* www.iibel.adelaide.edu.au (office).

STOLFI, Fiorenzo; San Marino lawyer and politician; *Secretary of State for Foreign Affairs, Political Affairs and Economic Planning;* b. 11 March 1956, San Marino; m. Luana Dorina Console; two s.; ed Univ. degli Studi di Urbino; mem. San Marino Socialist Party 1978–, fmr Vice-Pres. and Sec.-Gen.; mem. Great Council of San Marino (Parl.) 1983–, Chair. 2003–06; Sec. of State for Tourism, Commerce, Sport and Agric. 1983–86, for Industry, Handicrafts and Econ. Co-operation 1992–2000, for Internal Affairs, Posts and Telecommunications, Home Affairs and Civil Defence 2001–02, for Finance and the Budget, Transport and Relations with the Azienda Autonoma di Stato Filatelica e Numismatica (AASFN) June–Dec. 2002, for Foreign and Political Affairs, Planning and Econ. Co-operation Dec. 2002–03, for Foreign Affairs, Political Affairs and Econ. Planning 2006–; Vice-Gov. IMF for San Marino 1993–2000, Gov. 2002–03; Gov. World Bank for San Marino 2001–02. *Address:* Secretariat of State for Foreign and Political Affairs, Planning and Economic Co-operation, Palazzo Begni, Contrada Omerelli, 47890 San Marino (office). *Telephone:* 0549 882302 (office). *Fax:* 0549 882814 (office). *E-mail:* segreteriadistato@esteri.sm (office); fo.sepl@esteli.sm (office). *Website:* www.esteri.sm (office).

STOLL, Jean-François; French civil servant; *Head of General Treasury Office (departement de Seine Saint Denis);* b. 19 Jan. 1950, Isle-Adam; m. Noëlle Nicolas 1976; four c.; ed Institut des Etudes politiques, Paris, Ecole Nat. d'Admin; joined Ministry of Econ., Commercial Attaché Indonesia 1982–84, Tech. Adviser 1982–86, Commercial Adviser Mexico 1987–90, Tech. Adviser for Int. Affairs, Office of the Prime Minister 1990–93, Head Service for Promotion of External Trade 1993, Dir External Econ. Relations 1998, Dir-Gen. Econ. and Trade Dept 2001–; Dir Electricité de France (EDF) 1999–2003, Head, General Treasury Office 2003–; Chevalier, Ordre Nat. du Mérite. *Address:* Ministry of the Economy, Finance and Industry, 139 rue de Bercy, 75572 Paris Cedex 12 (office); 6 rue d'Ulm, 75005 Paris, France (home). *Telephone:* 1-40-04-04-04 (office); 1-48-96-60-01 (home). *Fax:* 1-43-43-75-97 (office); 1-48-96-61-11 (home). *E-mail:* jean-francois.stoll@cp.finances.gouv.fr (office). *Website:* www.minefi.gouv.fr (office).

STOLLEY, Paul David, MD, MPH; American physician and professor of medicine; *Professor Emeritus, University of Maryland;* b. 17 June 1937, Pawling, New York; s. of Herman Stolley and Rosalie Chertock; m. Jo Ann Goldenberg 1959; one s. two d.; ed Lafayette Coll., Cornell Univ. Medical School and Johns Hopkins School of Public Health; medical officer, US Public Health Service 1964–67; Asst and Assoc. Prof. of Epidemiology, Johns Hopkins School of Public Health 1968–76; Herbert C. Rorer Prof. of Medical Science, Univ. of Pa School of Medicine 1976–90; Prof. and Chair. Dept of Epidemiology, Univ. of Md 1991–99, currently Prof. Emer.; fmr mem. Editorial Bd New England Journal, Milbank Quarterly; fmr Assoc. Ed. Clinical Pharmacology and Therapeutics; Pres. American Coll. of Epidemiology 1987–88; mem. Inst. of Medicine, NAS, Soc. for Epidemiologic Research (Pres. 1984), Int. Epidemiology Asscn (fmr Treas.), Johns Hopkins Soc. of Scholars, Science Advisory Cttee to Fed. Drugs. Admin. Commr 1993; Hon. MA (Pennsylvania) 1976. *Publications:* Case Control Studies (co-author) 1982, Foundations of Epidemiology (co-author) 1994, Epidemiology 1994, Investigating Disease Patterns 1995 (received American Medical Writers Asscn Award 1996) and numerous articles on epidemiological subjects. *Leisure interests:* classical music, history, literature. *Address:* 6424 Brass Knob, Columbia, MD 21044, USA (home). *Telephone:* (410) 997-9567 (home). *Fax:* (410) 997-9574 (home). *E-mail:* pstolley@aol.com (home).

STOLOJAN, Theodor Dumitru, PhD, DEcon; Romanian economist and politician; b. 24 Oct. 1943, Tîrgoviste; s. of Theodor Stolojan and Nadejda Stolojan; m. Elena Stolojan; one s. one d.; ed Acad. of Econ. Studies, Coll. of Finances, Credit and Accountancy, Bucharest; worked as economist, Ministry of the Food Industry 1966–72; first as economist and then as Chief of Division, State Budget Dept, Ministry of Finance 1972–82, then Deputy Dir, Dir of Dept Foreign Currencies and Int. Financial Relations 1982–87, Gen. Insp. Dept of State Revenues 1988–89, First Deputy Minister of Finance 1989–90, Minister of Finance 1990–91; Pres. of Nat. Agency of Privatization –1991; Prime Minister of Romania 1991–92; Economist, later Sr Economist, IBRD 1992–98; Pres. Tofan Corporated Finance 1999–2000; Pnr, Strategic Consulting Ltd; Prof., Univ. of Transylvania, Braşov 2002–; Pres. Nat. Liberal Party 2002–04; Adviser to the Pres. 2004–06; Co-founder and Chair. Liberal Democratic Party (Partidul Liberal Democrat) 2006–07, First Vice-Chair. 2008–; MEP 2007–, mem. European People's Party (Christian Democrats) and European Democrats; apptd Prime Minister by Pres. of Romania 10 Dec. 2008, withdrew acceptance 15 Dec.; mem. Bd of Dirs Romanian-American Investment Fund, Bucharest; mem. Int. Inst. of Public Finance 1978–. *Publications:* Integration and European Fiscal Policy 2002; numerous studies. *Leisure interests:* skiing, travelling in mountains, jogging. *Address:* European Parliament, Bât. Willy Brandt 04M121, 60, rue Wiertz, 1047 Brussels, Belgium (office); Liberal Democratic Party (Partidul Liberal Democrat), Bucharest (office); Aurel Vlaicu 42-44, Apt 3, Sector 2, Bucharest, Romania. *Telephone:* (2) 284-56-70 (office). *Fax:* (2) 284-96-70 (office). *Website:* www.europarl.europa.eu (office).

STOLPE, Manfred; German politician; b. 16 May 1936, Stettin, Germany (now Szczecin, Poland); m. Ingrid Ehrhardt; one d.; legal studies in Jena and Berlin; fmly in charge of organizational work of Protestant Church in East Germany; Consistorial Pres. Berlin-Brandenburg Church 1982–90; active in human rights movt; joined SPD 1990; Minister-Pres. of Brandenburg 1990–2002; Fed. Minister of Transport, Building and Housing 2002–05; Order of Merit of the State of Brandenburg 2006; Dr hc (Univ. of Dokkyo, Japan) 1989, (Ernst-Moritz-Arndt Univ., Greifswald) 1989, (Univ. of Zürich) 1991, (Univ. of Szczecin) 1996; Carlo-Schmid Prize 1991. *Address:* c/o Sozialdemokratische Partei Deutschlands, Wilhelmstr. 141, 10963 Berlin, Germany.

STOLTE, Dieter; German television executive, newspaper publisher and academic; b. 18 Sept. 1934, Cologne; ed Univs of Tübingen and Mainz; Head of

Science Dept, Saarländischer Rundfunk 1961–62; Personal adviser to Dir-Gen. of Zweites Deutsches Fernsehen (ZDF) 1962, Controller, Programme Planning Dept 1967, Programming Dir 1976–82, Dir-Gen. ZDF March 1982–2002; publisher Die Welt and Berliner Morgenpost (newspapers) 2002–05; Dir and Deputy Dir Gen., Südwestfunk 1973; Prof. Univ. of Music and Presentation Arts, Hamburg 1980–; mem. Admin. Council, German Press Agency (dpa), Hamburg, European Broadcasting Union (EBU); Chair. Admin. Council TransTel, Cologne; Chair. Bd Dirs DeutschlandRadio, Cologne; mem. Int. Broadcast Inst., London; mem. Council, Nat. Acad. of TV Arts, New York, Int. Acad. of Arts and Sciences, New York; Int. Emmy Directorate Award 1997; Bundesverdienstkreuz, Officer's Cross, Golden Order of Merit (Austria), Bavarian Order of Merit, Hon. Citizen of State of Tenn., USA; Köckritz Prize 1999, Verdienstorden, Berlin 1999, Robert Geissendorfer Prize 2001. Publications: ed. and co-author of several books on programme concepts and function of television, etc.; several essays on subjects relating to the philosophy of culture and the science of communication. Address: c/o Axel Springer Verlag AG, Axel-Springer-Platz 1, 20350 Hamburg, Germany.

STOLTENBERG, Jens; Norwegian politician; Prime Minister; b. 16 March 1959, Oslo; m. Ingrid Schulerud; two c.; ed Univ. of Oslo; journalist, Arbeiderbladet (nat. daily) 1979–81; Information Sec., Oslo Labour Party 1981; Exec. Officer, Statistics Norway 1989–90; Lecturer in Econs, Univ. of Oslo 1989–90; mem. Cen. Bd, Labour Youth League (AUF) 1979–89, Leader, AUF 1985–89; Vice-Pres. Int. Union of Socialist Youth 1985–89; mem. Cen. Bd, Norwegian Labour Party 1985–, Leader Oslo Labour Party 1990–92, Deputy Leader Labour Party 1992–2002, Leader 2002–; Deputy mem. Storting (Parl.) 1989–93, mem. for Oslo 1993–, mem. Standing Cttee Social Afairs 1991–93, on Oil and Energy Affairs 1997–2000, on Foreign Affairs 2001–05; Sec., Ministry of Environment 1990–91; Minister of Trade and Energy 1993–96, of Finance 1996–97; Prime Minister of Norway 2000–01, 2005–; Head Govt Comm. on Male Roles 1986; mem. Norwegian Defence Comm. 1990–92; mem. Bd Global Vaccine Fund 2001–05. Address: Office of the Prime Minister, Akersgt. 42, POB 8001 Dep., 0030 Oslo, Norway (office). Telephone: 22-24-90-90 (office). Fax: 22-24-95-90 (office). E-mail: postmottak@ smk.dep.no (office). Website: www.regjeringen.no/smk; odin.dep.no/smk (office).

STOLTENBERG, Thorvald; Norwegian politician and diplomatist; President, Norwegian Red Cross; b. 8 July 1931, Oslo; s. of Emil Stoltenberg and Ingeborg Stoltenberg; m. Karin Stoltenberg 1957; one s. two d.; joined Foreign Service 1959; served in San Francisco, Belgrade, Lagos and Foreign Ministry; Int. Sec. Norwegian Fed. of Trade Unions 1970–71; Under-Sec. of State, Foreign Ministry 1971–72, 1976–79; Under-Sec. of State, Ministry of Defence 1973–74, Ministry of Commerce 1974–76; Minister of Defence 1979–81, of Foreign Affairs 1987–89, 1990–93; Amb. to UN, New York 1989–90; UN High Commr for Refugees 1989–90; Special Rep. for UN Sec.-Gen. in fmr Yugoslavia 1993–94; Co-Chair. Steering Cttee, Int. Conf. on the Fmr Yugoslavia 1993–96; Amb. to Denmark 1996–99; Pres. Norwegian Red Cross; Chair. Bd of Int. Inst. for Democracy and Electoral Assistance –2003. Address: Norwegian Red Cross, PO Box 1, Groenland, 0133 Oslo, Norway (office). Telephone: 22-05-40-00 (office). Fax: 22-05-40-40 (office). E-mail: thorvald.stoltenberg@redcross.no (office). Website: www.redcross.no (office).

STONE, Francis Gordon Albert, CBE, ScD, FRS; British scientist and academic; Robert A. Welch Distinguished Professor of Chemistry, Baylor University; b. 19 May 1925, Exeter; s. of Sidney Charles Stone and Florence Stone; m. Judith M. Hislop 1956; three s.; ed Christ's Coll., Univ. of Cambridge; Fulbright Scholarship, Univ. of Southern Calif. 1952–54; Instructor and Asst Prof., Harvard Univ. 1954–62; Reader, Queen Mary Coll., Univ. of London 1962–63; Head, Dept of Inorganic Chem. and Prof., Univ. of Bristol 1963–90, Prof. Emer. 1990–; Robert A. Welch Distinguished Prof. of Chem., Baylor Univ., Texas 1990–; Visiting Prof. at numerous univs; Pres. Dalton Div., Royal Soc. of Chem. (RSC) 1981–83; Guggenheim Fellow 1961; Sr Visiting Fellow, Australian Acad. of Sciences 1966; mem. Council, Royal Soc. of Chem. 1968–70, 1981–83, Chem. Cttee, Science and Eng Research Council 1971–74, 1982–85; mem. Council of Royal Soc. 1986–88 (Vice-Pres. 1987–88); Hon. DSc (Exeter, Waterloo) 1992, (Durham, Salford) 1993, (Zaragoza) 1994; RSC Medals for Organometallic Chem. 1972, Transition Metal Chem. 1979, Chugaev Medal and Diploma, Kurnakov Inst., USSR (now Russian) Acad. of Sciences 1978, ACS Award in Inorganic Chem. 1985, Davy Medal of Royal Soc. 1989. Publications: more than 700 articles in scientific journals and books; Advances in Organometallic Chemistry, Vols 1–47 (ed.); Comprehensive Organometallic Chemistry, Vols 1–9 (co-ed.) 1982, Comprehensive Organometallic Chemistry II, Vols 1–13 (co-ed.) 1995. Leisure interest: travel. Address: 88 Hackberry Avenue, Waco, TX 76706, USA. Telephone: (254) 752-3617. E-mail: Gordon_Stone@baylor.edu (office). Website: www.baylor.edu/chemistry/splash.php (office).

STONE, John O., BA (Oxon.), BSc (Hons); Australian politician, financial executive, public servant and columnist; Editor and Publisher, Proceedings of The Samuel Griffith Society; b. 31 Jan. 1929, Perth, WA; s. of Horace Stone and Eva Stone (née Hunt); m. Nancy Hardwick 1954; four s. one d.; ed Univ. of Western Australia and New Coll., Oxford; Rhodes Scholar 1951; Asst to Australian Treasury Rep. in London 1954–56, Australian Treasury Rep. in London 1958–61; in Research and Information Div., Gen. Financial and Econ. Policy Br., Dept of Treasury, Canberra 1956–57, in Home Finance Div. 1961–62, Asst Sec. Econ. and Financial Surveys Div. 1962–66; Exec. Dir for Australia, NZ and S Africa, IMF and IBRD 1967–70; First Asst Sec., Revenue, Loans and Investment Div., Treasury 1971; Sec., Australian Loan Council; Sec., Australian Nat. Debt Comm. 1971; Deputy Sec. (Econ.), Treasury 1971–76, Deputy Sec. Treasury 1976–78, Sec. 1979–84; Visiting Prof., Centre of Policy Studies, Monash Univ., Melbourne 1984; consultant, Potter Pnrs,

Stockbrokers 1985–87; weekly columnist, Melbourne Herald, Sydney Morning Herald 1985–87, The Australian 1987–89, Sunday Telegraph 1989, The Australian Financial Review 1990–98, Adelaide Review 1998–2003; regular contrib. to National Observer quarterly and to Quadrant magazine; Dir Sperry (Australia) Ltd 1985–87, Peko-Wallsend Ltd 1986–87; Chair. J. T. Campbell & Co. Ltd 1994–96; Senator for Queensland, Leader of Nat. Party in the Senate and Shadow Minister for Finance 1987–90; mem. Defence Efficiency Review 1996–97; Sr Fellow, Inst. of Public Affairs, Melbourne 1985–87, 1990–95; Fellow, Acad. of the Social Sciences of Australia 1976–81 (resgnd); mem. Mont Pelerin Soc. 2008–; James Webb Medley Prize, Univ. of Oxford 1953. Publications: Upholding the Australian Constitution, Proceedings of The Samuel Griffith Society, Vols 1–20 1992– (ed. and publr). Leisure interests: reading, wine and food. Address: 17 Fitzsimmons Avenue, Lane Cove, NSW 2066, Australia (home). Telephone: (2) 9428-1311 (home). Fax: (2) 9420-0063 (home). E-mail: j_o_stone@bigpond.com (home).

STONE, Norman, MA; British historian and academic; Professor of International Relations and Director, Center for Russian Studies, Bilkent University; b. 8 March 1941, Glasgow; s. of the late Norman Stone and Mary Robertson Stone (née Pettigrew); m. 1st Marie-Nicole Aubry 1966 (dissolved 1977); two s.; m. 2nd Christine Booker (née Verity) 1982; one s.; ed Glasgow Acad. and Gonville & Caius Coll., Cambridge; research student, Christ's Coll., Cambridge attached to Austrian and Hungarian insts 1962–65; Research Fellow, Gonville & Caius Coll. 1965–67; Asst Lecturer, Faculty of History, Univ. of Cambridge 1967–72, lecturer in History (Russian) 1973–84; Fellow, Jesus Coll., Cambridge and Dir of Studies in History 1971–79; Fellow, Trinity Coll. Cambridge 1979–84; Prof. of Modern History, Univ. of Oxford and Fellow, Worcester Coll. Oxford 1984–97; Prof. of Int. Relations, Bilkent Univ., Ankara 1997–, also Dir Center for Russian Studies; Order of Merit (Poland) 1993; Wolfson Prize 1976. Publications: The Eastern Front 1914–17 1976, Hitler 1980, Europe Transformed 1878–1919 1982, Czechoslovakia: Crossroads and Crises (Ed.) 1989, The Other Russia (with Michael Glenny) 1990, articles in the press. Leisure interests: music, Eastern Europe, languages, Turkey. Address: Center for Russian Studies, Department of International Relations, Bilkent University, 06800 Bilkent, Ankara (office); 22 St Margaret's Road, Oxford, OX2 6RX England (home). Telephone: (312) 2901249 (office); (1865) 439481 (home). Fax: (312) 2664326 (office). E-mail: CRS@bilkent.edu.tr (office). Website: www.bilkent.edu.tr/~crs (office).

STONE, Oliver, BFA; American film director, producer and screenwriter; b. 15 Sept. 1946, New York; s. of Louis Stone and Jacqueline Goddet; m. 1st Najwa Sarkis (divorced); m. 2nd Elizabeth Stone (divorced); ed Yale Univ. and New York Univ. Film School; teacher, Cholon, Viet Nam 1965–66; US Merchant Marine 1966, US Army, Viet Nam 1967–68. Films include: Writer: Midnight Express (Acad. Award for best screenplay adapted from another medium) 1978, Conan the Barbarian 1982, Scarface 1983; Writer and Dir: Seizure 1973, The Hand 1981, Year of the Dragon (with Michael Cimino) 1985, Salvador (co-writer) 1986, Platoon (Acad. Award for Best Film and Best Dir) 1986, Wall Street 1987, Talk Radio (co-writer) 1988, Born on the Fourth of July (Acad. Award for Best Dir 1990) 1989, No One Here Gets Out Alive 1990, The Doors 1991, JFK 1991, Heaven and Earth 1993, Natural Born Killers 1994, Nixon 1995, A Child's Night Dream 1997, U-Turn 1998, Saviour 1998; Producer: Reversal of Fortune, Iron Maze, South Central, Zebrahead, Wild Palms (TV series) 1993, New Age 1994, The People vs Larry Flynt; Writer, Dir and Producer: Any Given Sunday 2000, Comandante (documentary) 2003, Alexander 2004, World Trade Center 2006; as director: W. 2008. Address: Ixtlan Productions, 12233 West Olympic Blvd, Suite 322, Los Angeles, CA 90064, USA (office). Telephone: (310) 826-7080 (office). Fax: (310) 826-7090 (office).

STONE, Roger W., BS (Econ); American business executive; CEO and Chairman, KapStone Paper and Packaging Corporation; b. 16 Feb. 1935, Chicago, Ill.; s. of Marvin Stone and Anita Masover; m. Susan Kessert 1955; three d.; ed Wharton School of Finance, Univ. of Pennsylvania; joined Stone Container Corpn 1957, Vice-Pres. Gen. Man. Container Div. 1970–75, Pres. and COO 1975–79, Pres., CEO 1979–98, Chair. 1983–98, Pres., CEO Smurfit Stone Container Corpn 1998–99; Chair. and CEO Box USA Group, Inc. 2000–04; Man. Stone-Kaplan Investments, LLC (pvt. investment co.) 2004–07; CEO and Chair. KapStone Paper and Packaging Corpn, Northbrook, Ill. 2007–; mem. Bd of Dirs McDonalds Corpn, Autoliv, Inc.; fmr mem. Bd of Dirs Morton Int., Option Care Inc.; mem. Advisory Council for Econ. Devt. Leisure interest: golf. Address: Kapstone Paper and Packaging Corporation, 1101 Skokie Blvd, Suite 300, Northbrook, IL 60062-4124, USA (office). Telephone: (847) 239-8800 (office). Fax: (847) 205-7551 (office). E-mail: information@kapstonepaper.com (office). Website: www.kapstonepaper.com (office).

STONE, Sharon; American actress; b. 10 March 1958, Meadville, Pa; m. 1st Michael Greenburg 1984 (divorced 1987); m. 2nd Phil Bronstein 1998 (divorced 2004); two adopted s.; ed high school in Pennsylvania and Edinboro Coll.; Chevalier, Ordre des Arts et Lettres. Films include: Above the Law, Action Jackson, King Solomon's Mines, Allan Quatermain and the Lost City of Gold, Irreconcilable Differences, Deadly Blessing, Personal Choice, Basic Instinct, Diary of a Hit Man, Where Sleeping Dogs Lie, Sliver, Intersection, The Specialist, The Quick and the Dead, Casino, Last Dance, Diabolique 1996, Sphere, The Mighty 1999, The Muse 1999, Simpatico 1999, Gloria 1999, Beautiful Joe 2000, Cold Creek Manor 2003, A Different Loyalty 2004, Catwoman 2004, Jiminy Glick in La La Wood 2004, Broken Flowers 2005, Alpha Dog 2006, Basic Instinct 2 2006, Bobby 2006, If I Had Known I Was a Genius 2007, When a Man Falls in the Forest 2007, Democrazy 2007, The Year of Getting to Know Us 2008, Five Dollars a Day 2008. Television appearances include: Bay City Blues (series), Tears in the Rain (film), War and Remembrance (mini-series), Calendar Girl Murders (film), The Vegas Strip Wars (film), Huff (series) 2006, and roles in numerous series. *Address:* William Morris Agency, 1 William Morris Place, Beverly Hills, CA 90212; c/o Guy McElwaine, PO Box 7304, North Hollywood, CA 91603, USA.

STONECIPHER, Harry Curtis, BS; American aircraft industry executive (retd); b. May 1936, Scott Co., Tenn.; ed Tenn. Poly tech. Inst.; with General Electric 1960–61, 1962–86, Martin Aircraft Co. 1961–62; Exec. Vice-Pres. Sundstrand Corpn 1987, Pres. and COO 1987–88, Pres. and CEO 1988–94, Chair. 1991–94; Pres. and CEO McDonnell-Douglas Corpn, St Louis 1994–97; apptd Pres. and CEO Boeing Co., Seattle 1997, COO Boeing Corpn (later Boeing Co.) 1997–2002, Pres. and CEO 1997–2002, 2003–05 (resgnd); mem. Bd of Dirs Milacron, Inc.; Fellow, Royal Aeronautical Soc.; John R. Allison Award 1996, Rear Adm. John J. Bergen Leadership Medal Nay League 1996. *Address:* 4973 Bacopa Lane South, St Petersburg, FL 33715-2638 USA (office).

STONEHAM, Marshall, PhD, CPhys, FRS, FInstP, FRSA; British theoretical physicist, materials scientist and academic; *Emeritus Massey Professor of Physics, University College London;* b. 18 May 1940, Barrow in Furness; m. Doreen Stoneham; ed Univ. of Bristol; Group Leader, Solid State and Quantum Physics, Theoretical Physics Div., UKAEA, Harwell 1974–89, Head of Materials Physics and Metallurgy Div., Harwell 1989–90, Dir of Research, AEA Industrial Tech. 1990–93, Chief Scientist, AEA Tech. 1993–97 (part-time 1995–97); Wolfson Industrial Fellow, Univ. of Oxford 1985–95, Fellow, Wolfson Coll. Oxford 1989–95; Massey Prof. of Physics, Dept of Physics and Astronomy, Univ. Coll. London (UCL) 1995–2005, Emer. Massey Prof. of Physics 2005–, Dir Centre for Materials Research, mem. London Centre for Nanotechnology (jt UCL/Imperial Coll. venture); mem. Cambridge/UCL/Bristol Interdisciplinary Research Collaboration in Nanotechnology; Visiting Sr Fellow, Dept of Materials, Univ. of Oxford; Lloyd Braga Prof., Univ. of the Minho, Portugal 2005; fmr Vice-Pres. Inst. of Physics (Chair. Inst. of Physics Publishing –2001); mem. Eng and Physical Sciences Research Council (EPSRC) Coll. since its inception (Chair. EPSRC Materials Modelling Initiative Steering Cttee), mem. Fusion Bd (overseeing Culham Lab.'s programme for EPSRC); Co-founding Dir, (with his wife) Oxford Authentication Ltd; mem. Royal Soc. Working Group on Depleted Uranium; Founding mem. IEE Electronic Materials Steering Cttee; Ed.-in-Chief Journal of Physics: Condensed Matter 2002–06; Fellow, American Physical Soc., Inst. of Materials, Mining and Minerals; Hon. Fellow, Univ. Coll. London; Hon. Mem. Pakistan Soc. for Semiconductor Science and Tech.; Merchant Venturers' Scholar 1958–61, Royal Society Zeneca Prize 1995, Cockroft-Walton Lecturer, Inst. of Physics/Indian Physics Asscn 2004, Guthrie Medal, Inst. of Physics 2006. *Publications:* Theory of Defects in Solids: Electronic Structure of Defects in Insulators and Semiconductors 1975, Defects and Defect Processes in Non-Metallic Solids (co-author) 1985, Reliability of Non-destructive Inspection: Assessing the Assessment of Structures under Stress (co-author) 1987, GeSi Strained Layers and their Applications (co-author) 1995, Materials Modification by Electronic Excitation (co-author) 2001; co-author of two books on music: Wind Ensemble Sourcebook (Oldman Prize, Int. Asscn of Music Librarians 1997) 1997, The Wind Ensemble Catalog 1998; more than 500 scientific papers in professional journals. *Leisure interest:* playing the French horn. *Address:* Centre for Materials Research, Department of Physics and Astronomy, University College London, Gower Street, London, WC1E 6BT, England (office). *Telephone:* (20) 7679-1377 (office). *Fax:* (20) 7679-1360 (office). *E-mail:* a.stoneham@ucl.ac.uk (office); ucapams@ucl.ac.uk (office). *Website:* www.cmmp.ucl.ac.uk/~ak (office).

STONESIFER, Patricia Q. (Patty), BA; American foundation executive; b. 1956, Indianapolis; m. 2nd Michael Kinsley; two c. (from previous m.); ed Ind. Univ.; several sr man. positions with Microsoft Corpn 1988–96, most recently Sr Vice-Pres. Interactive Media Div.; man. consultant 1996–97; Pres. and Chair. Gates Learning Foundation 1997–99, Pres. and Co-Chair. Bill and Melinda Gates Foundation 1999–2006, CEO 2006–08; mem. Bd of Dirs amazon.com 1997–, Viacom 2000–; mem. Bd The Vaccine Fund; mem. Bd of Regents Smithsonian Inst., Washington, DC; fmr mem. US Del. to UN Gen. Ass. Special Session on AIDS; ranked by Forbes magazine amongst 100 Most Powerful Women (52nd) 2004. *Address:* c/o Bill and Melinda Gates Foundation, POB 23350, Seattle, WA 98102, USA (office).

STOPFORD, Michael, MA; American public relations executive and fmr international civil servant; *Group Director, Corporate Reputation, The Coca-Cola Company;* b. 22 June 1953, London; s. of Edward Stopford and Patricia Carrick; m. Susan Navrat; two s. one d.; ed Oxford Univ.; fmr mem. HM Diplomatic Service, served at Perm. Mission to UN, New York, Second Sec. and Press Attaché, Embassy in Vienna; Assoc. then Second Officer, Exec. Office of Sec.-Gen. of UN 1979–83, Special Projects Officer, Dept of Public Information 1983–87, Chef de Cabinet to Dir-Gen., UN Office in Geneva and Under-Sec.-Gen. for Human Rights 1987–91, Chef de Cabinet to Exec. Del. of Sec.-Gen. for Inter-Agency Humanitarian Programme in Iraq, Kuwait and Iraq–Turkey and Iraq–Iran border areas 1991–92, with Dept for Humanitarian Affairs 1992, Special Asst to UnderSec.-Gen. for Public Information, Dept of Public Information, UN, New York 1992, Dir UN Information Center, Washington, DC, 1992–95; Chief of Media and Public Relations, Int. Financial Corpn 1996–97; Sr Asst to Pres. for Int. Affairs, American Univ., Washington, DC 1997; Sr Issues Adviser, Exxon Mobil Corpn, USA 2000–01; Head of Global Public Affairs and Govt Relations, Syngenta International AG, Basel, Switzerland 2002–06; Group Dir, Corp. Reputation, The Coca-Cola Company, Atlanta, Ga 2006–; Hon. LLD (New England Coll.) 1998. *Publication:* The UN and Global Intervention: Delusions of Grandeur (co-author) 1997. *Leisure interests:* opera, art, sailing, skiing. *Address:* The Coca-Cola Company, PO Box 1734, Atlanta, GA 30301 (office); 723 Rock Springs Court, NE, Atlanta, GA 30306-2328, USA (home). *Telephone:* (404) 717-2653 (office). *E-mail:* m.stopford@gmx.ch (home). *Website:* www.thecoca-colacompany.com (office).

STOPPARD, Sir Tom, Kt, OM, CBE, FRSL; British writer; b. (Thomas Straussler), 3 July 1937, Zlin, Czechoslovakia; s. of the late Dr Eugene Straussler and Martha Straussler; step-s. of Kenneth Stoppard; m. 1st Jose Ingle 1965 (divorced 1972); two s.; m. 2nd Dr Miriam Moore-Robinson 1972 (divorced 1992); two s.; ed Pocklington Grammar School, Yorks.; Journalist, Bristol 1954–60; freelance journalist, London 1960–64; mem. Cttee of the Free World 1981–; mem. Royal Nat. Theatre Bd 1989–; Hon. MLitt (Bristol, Brunel Univs.); Hon. LittD (Leeds Univ.) 1979, (Sussex) 1980, (Warwick) 1981, (London) 1982; Dr hc (Kenyon Coll.) 1984, (York) 1984; John Whiting Award, Arts Council 1967, Italia Prize (radio drama) 1968, New York Drama Critics Best Play Award 1968, Antoinette Perry Awards (Tony Awards) 1968, 1976, 2007, Evening Standard Awards 1967, 1972, 1974, 1978, 1982, 1993, 1997, 2006, Sony Award 1991, Olivier Award 1993, Dan David Prize 2008, Sunday Times Award for Literary Excellence 2008. *Publications:* plays: Rosencrantz and Guildenstern are Dead 1967, The Real Inspector Hound 1968, Enter a Free Man 1968, After Magritte 1970, Dogg's Our Pet 1972, Jumpers 1972, Travesties 1975, Dirty Linen 1976, New-Found-Land 1976, Every Good Boy Deserves Favour (with music by André Previn, 1978, Night and Day 1978, Dogg's Hamlet, Cahoots Macbeth 1979, Undiscovered Country 1980, On the Razzle 1981, The Real Thing 1982, Rough Crossing 1984, Dalliance (adaption of Schnitzler's Liebelei) 1986, Hapgood 1988, Arcadia 1993 (Evening Standard Award for Best Play), Indian Ink 1995, The Invention of Love 1997, The Seagull (trans. 1997), The Coast of Utopia (trilogy: Part One: Voyage, Part Two: Shipwreck, Part Three: Salvage) (Tony Award for Best Play 2007) 2002, Rock 'N' Roll (London Critics' Circle Award for Best New Play 2006) 2006; radio plays: The Dissolution of Dominic Boot 1964, M is for Moon Among Other Things 1964, Albert's Bridge 1967, If You're Glad I'll be Frank 1968, Where Are They Now? 1970, Artist Descending a Staircase 1972, The Dog It Was That Died 1983, In the Native State 1991; short stories: Introduction 2 1963; novel: Lord Malquist and Mr Moon 1966; screenplays: The Romantic Englishwoman (co-author) 1975, Despair 1977; film scripts: The Human Factor 1979, Brazil (with Terry Gilliam, and Charles McKeown) 1984, Crown 1987, Empire of the Sun 1987, Rosencrantz and Guildenstern are Dead 1989 (also dir), Russia House 1989, Billy Bathgate 1990, Shakespeare in Love (jtly) 1998 (jt winner Acad. Award Best Original Screenplay 1999), Enigma 2001; television plays: Professional Foul 1977, Squaring the Circle 1984, The Television Plays 1965–84 1993; radio: The Plays for Radio 1964–91, 1994. *Address:* United Agents Ltd, 12–26 Lexington Street, London, W1F 0LE, England (office). *Telephone:* (20) 3214-0800 (office). *Fax:* (20) 3214-0801 (office). *E-mail:* info@unitedagents.co.uk (office). *Website:* www.unitedagents.co.uk (office).

STORARO, Vittorio; Italian cinematographer; b. 24 June 1940, Rome; ed Centro Sperimentale; mem. Italian Asscn of Cinematographers 1971–, Vice-Pres. 1977–78, Pres. 1988–90; mem. Acad. of Motion Picture Arts and Sciences 1980–, American Soc. of Cinematographers 1988–, European Acad. of Motion Picture Arts and Sciences 1999–; teacher, Acad. of Motion Picture Arts and Sciences of Image, L'Aquila, Italy 1994; Lifetime Achievement Award, American Soc. of Cinematographers 2001, Coolidge Award 2005. *Films include:* Giovinezza, Giovinezza 1968, Delitto al Circolo del Tennis, La Strategia del Rango 1969, Il Conformista, L'Eneide 1970, Addio Fratello Crudele 1971, Giornata Nera per l'Ariete 1971, Orlando Furioso 1971, Last Tango in Paris 1972, Bleu Gang…, Malizia 1972, Giordano Bruno 1973, Le Orme 1974, Novecento 1974, Scandalo 1975, Agatha, La Luna 1978, Apocalypse Now (Acad. Award for Best Cinematography 1980) 1979, Reds (Acad. Award for Best Cinematography 1981) 1982, Tarzan, the Ape Man 1980, One from the Heart 1981, Wagner 1982, Ladyhawke 1983, The Last Emperor (Acad. Award for Best Cinematography 1988,) 1987, Tucker: The Man and His Dream 1988, New York Stories (Life Without Zoe) 1989, Dick Tracy 1990, The Sheltering Sky 1990, Tosca (TV) 1992, Little Buddha 1993, Roma!, Imago Urbis, Flamenco (de Carlos Saura) 1995, Taxi 1996, Tango, no me dejes nunca (Cannes Film Festival Award) 1998, Bulworth 1998, Goya en Burdeos (Goya in Bordeaux) 1999, Mirka 2000, Picking up the Pieces 2000, La Traviata (TV) 2000, Zapata: El sueño del héroe 2004, Exorcist: The Beginning 2004, Dominion: Prequel to the Exorcist 2005, All the Invisible Children 2005. *E-mail:* vittorio@storarovittorio.com. *Website:* storarovittorio.com.

STORCH, Marcus, MSc; Swedish business executive; b. 28 July 1942, Stockholm; s. of Hilel Storch and Anna Storch; m. Gunilla Berglund 1972; one d.; ed Royal Inst. of Tech., Stockholm; Dept Head, AGA AB, Welding 1968–72, Pres. Welding Div. AGA AB 1972–75, Pres. Gas Div. 1975–81, Exec. Vice-Pres. AGA AB 1978–81, Pres. and CEO 1981–96; Chair. Nobel Foundation; Vice-Chair. A. Johnson AB, AXFOOD AB, Mekonomen AB; mem. Bd NCC AB, Nordstjernan AB; Hon. MD. *Address:* Linnégatan 8, 114 47 Stockholm, Sweden (office). *Telephone:* (8) 679-97-00 (office). *E-mail:* storch@telia.com (office).

STØRE, Jonas Gahr, BSc; Norwegian politician and diplomatist; *Minister of Foreign Affairs;* b. 25 Aug. 1960; m.; three c.; ed Royal Norwegian Naval Acad., Institut d'Etudes Politiques de Paris, France; Teaching Fellow, Harvard Law School, USA 1986; Researcher, Norwegian School of Man. 1986–89; Special Adviser, Office of the Prime Minister 1989–95, Dir-Gen., Int. Dept 1995–98, State Sec. and Chief of Staff 2000–01; Perm. Rep. to UN, Geneva 1998; Chief of Staff, WHO 1998–2000; Working Chair., ECON Analysis 2002–03; Sec.-Gen., Norwegian Red Cross 2003–05; Minister of Foreign Affairs 2005–; mem. Det norske Arbeiderparti (Norwegian Labour Party). *Address:* Ministry of Foreign Affairs, POB 8114 Dep., 0032 Oslo, Norway (office). *Telephone:* 22-24-36-00 (office). *Fax:* 22-24-95-80 (office). *E-mail:* post@mfa.no (office). *Website:* www.regjeringen.no (office).

STOREY, David Malcolm; British author and playwright; b. 13 July 1933, Wakefield, Yorkshire; s. of Frank Richmond Storey and Lily (née Cartwright) Storey; m. Barbara Hamilton 1956; two s. two d.; ed Queen Elizabeth Grammar School, Wakefield, Wakefield Coll. of Art and Slade School of Art; Fellow, Univ. Coll. London 1974; Los Angeles Drama Critics Award 1969, Writer of the Year Award, Variety Club of GB 1969. *Publications:* novels: This Sporting Life (Macmillan Award) 1960, Flight into Camden (John Llewellyn Rhys Memorial Prize 1961, Somerset Maugham Award 1963) 1960, Radcliffe 1963, Pasmore (Faber Memorial Prize 1972) 1972, A Temporary Life 1973, Edward 1973, Saville (Booker Prize 1976) 1976, A Prodigal Child 1982, Present Times 1984, A Serious Man 1998, As It Happened 2002, Thin-Ice Skater 2004; plays: The Restoration of Arnold Middleton (Evening Standard Award 1967), In Celebration 1969 (also film), The Contractor (New York Critics' Prize 1974) 1969, Home (Evening Standard Award, New York Critics' Prize) 1970, The Changing Room (New York Critics' Prize) 1971, Cromwell 1973, The Farm 1973, Life Class 1974, Night 1976, Mother's Day 1976, Sisters 1978, Dreams of Leaving 1979, Early Days 1980, The March on Russia 1989, Stages 1992; poems: Storey's Lives: Poems 1951–1991 1992. *Address:* A.M. Heath and Co. Ltd, 6 Warwick Court, Holborn, London, WC1R 5DJ, England (office). *Telephone:* (20) 7242-2811 (office). *Fax:* (20) 7242-2711 (office). *Website:* www.amheath.com (office).

STORK, Gilbert, PhD; American chemist and academic; *Eugene Higgins Professor Emeritus of Chemistry, Columbia University;* b. 31 Dec. 1921, Brussels, Belgium; s. of Jacques Stork and Simone Weil; m. Winifred Elizabeth Stewart 1944 (died 1992); one s. three d.; ed Univ. of Wisconsin; Instructor, Harvard Univ. 1946–48, Asst Prof. 1948–53; Assoc. Prof., Columbia Univ. 1953–55, Prof. 1955–67, Eugene Higgins Prof. of Chem. 1967–92, Prof. Emer. 1992–, Chair. of Dept 1973–76; mem. NAS 1961, American Acad. of Arts and Sciences 1962, American Philosophical Soc. 1995; Foreign mem. Royal Soc. of Chem. (UK) 1983, Acad. des Sciences (France) 1989, Royal Soc. 1999, Chemical Soc. of Japan 2002; Hon. DSc (Lawrence Coll.) 1961, (Paris) 1979, (Rochester) 1982, (Emory) 1988, (Columbia) 1993, (Wis.) 1997; ACS Award in Pure Chem. 1957, ACS Baekeland Medal, New Jersey Section 1961, Harrison Howe Award 1962, Edward Curtis Franklin Memorial Award of Stanford Univ. 1966, ACS Award in Synthetic Organic Chem. 1967, Nebraska Award 1973, Roussel Prize 1978, Nichols Medal 1980, ACS Arthur C. Cope Award 1980, NAS Award in Chemical Sciences 1982, Willard Gibbs Medal 1982, Nat. Medal of Science 1983, Tetrahedron Prize 1985, Roger Adams Award 1991, George Kenner Award 1992, Robert Welch Award 1993, Wolf Prize (co-recipient) 1995, first Barton Gold Medal, Royal Soc. of Chem. 2002, Noyori Prize (Japan) 2004, H.C. Brown Award 2005; numerous other awards. *Publications:* Stereospecific Synthesis of Cantharidin 1951, The Enamine Alkylation 1954, Stereochemistry of Polyene Cyclization 1955, Enolate Trapping Alkylation 1965, Stereospecific Synthesis of Reserpine 1989, Stereoselective Synthesis of Quinine 2001. *Leisure interest:* tennis. *Address:* Department of Chemistry, Columbia University, Chandler Hall, New York, NY 10027 (office); 188 Chestnut Street, Englewood Cliffs, NJ 07632, USA (home). *Telephone:* (212) 854-2178 (office); (201) 871-4032 (home). *Fax:* (212) 932-1289 (office). *E-mail:* gjs8@columbia.edu (office); gstork@nj.rr.com (home). *Website:* www.columbia.edu/cu/chemistry (office).

STORM, Kornelis (Kees), MA, CPA; Dutch business executive; b. 6 June 1942, Amsterdam; m.; two c.; ed Univ. of Rotterdam; chartered accountant, Moret & Limperg 1970–76; mem. Exec. Bd Kon. Scholten-Honig NV 1976–78, AGO 1978–83; mem. Exec. Bd AEGON NV 1983–93, Chair. 1993–2002; Chair. Supervisory Bd Koninklijke Wessanen NV; Chair. Laurus NV; mem. Supervisory Bds AEGON NV, KLM NV, PON Holding BV, Interbrew SA, Baxter International Inc.; mem. Bd of Dirs Unilever NV. *Publication:* Management With a Smile. *Address:* c/o Supervisory Board, AEGON NV, Aegonplein 50, PO Box 202, 2501 The Hague (office); Vondellaan 24, 2111 CP Aerdenhout, Netherlands (home). *Telephone:* (70) 3448287 (office); (23) 5242619 (home). *Fax:* (70) 3448593 (office); (23) 5248076 (home). *Website:* www.aegon.com (office).

STÖRMER, Horst Ludwig, PhD; German physicist and academic; *I. I. Rabi Professor of Physics and Professor of Applied Physics, Columbia University;* b. 6 April 1949, Frankfurt am Main; s. of Karl-Ludwig Stormer and Marie Ihrig; m. Dominique A. Parchet 1982; ed Univ. of Stuttgart; with tech. staff AT&T Bell Labs 1977–83, head of Dept 1983–91, Dir Physics Research Lab. 1992–; Prof. of Physics and Applied Physics, Columbia Univ. 1998–, now I. I. Rabi Prof. of Physics and Prof. of Applied Physics; Adjunct Physics Dir Lucent Technologies 1997–; Bell Labs Fellow 1982; Fellow, American Physics Soc., American Acad. of Arts and Sciences; Officier, Légion d'honneur 1999; Buckley Prize, American Physics Soc. 1984, Otto Klug Prize, Germany 1985, Nobel Prize in Physics (jtly) 1998, NYC Mayor's Award 2000. *Address:* Department of Physics, Columbia University, 922 Schapiro CEPSR, MC 5206, New York, NY 10027 (office); Lucent Technologies, 700 Mountain Avenue, New Providence, NJ 07974, USA. *Telephone:* (212) 854-3279 (office); (908) 582-3380 (office). *E-mail:* horst@phys.columbia.edu (office). *Website:* www.ap.columbia.edu (office).

STORR, Robert, MFA; American author, curator and academic; *Professor of Painting / Printmaking and Dean of the School of Art, Yale University;* b. 1949; ed Swarthmore Coll., Pa, School of the Art Inst. of Chicago and studies in Europe and Mexico; Curator of Painting and Sculpture, Museum of Modern Art (MOMA), New York 1990–98, Sr Curator of Contemporary Art 1999–2002; Rosalee Solow Prof. of Modern Art, Inst. of Fine Arts, New York Univ. 2002–06; fmr mem. Faculty, Center for Curatorial Studies, Bard Coll.; Prof. of Painting/Printmaking and Dean of the School of Art, Yale Univ. 2006–; also currently Consulting Curator of Modern and Contemporary Art, Philadelphia Museum of Art; Curator Venice Biennale 2007; Visiting Artist, Critic and Lecturer, Univ. of Pennsylvania, Ruskin School of Drawing, Oxford, UK, School of the Art Inst. of Chicago, Rhode Island School of Design, RCA, London, UK, Grad. Painting Program, Hunter Coll.; Grad. School and Univ. Center, CUNY, Harvard Univ.; Contributing Ed. Art in America, Grand Street; mem. Editorial Bd Art Journal 1985–95; Chevalier des Arts et des Lettres 2000; Dr hc School of the Art Institute of Chicago and the Maine College of Art; First Prize, American Inst. of Commemorative Art 2002, American Chapter of Int. Asscn of Art Critics Award, AICA Award for Distinguished Contribution to the Field of Art Criticism, ICI Agnes Gund Curatorial Award, Lawrence A. Fleischman Award for Scholarly Excellence in the Field of American Art History, Smithsonian Institution's Archives of American Art. *Publications include:* prin. author or ed. of 35 books and monographs, including Philip Guston 1986, Modern Art Despite Modernism 2000, Gerhard Richter: October 18, 1977 2000, Gerhard Richter: 40 Years of Painting 2002; author of essays for exhbn catalogues and books on Louise Bourgeois, Chuck Close, Felix Gonzalez-Torres, Philip Guston, David Hammons, Eva Hesse, Ilya Kabakov, Alex Katz, Ellsworth Kelly, Steve McQueen, Elizabeth Murray, Bruce Nauman, Jim Nutt, Raymond Pettibon, Martin Puryear, Susan Rothenberg, Peter Saul, and Nancy Spero, among others; other publs include articles, interviews, and exhbn reviews for Art in America, Art/Press, Paris, Artforum, Grand Street, Parkett, The Art Journal, Washington Post BookWorld, and other journals and newspapers. *Address:* Yale University School of Art, 1156 Chapel Street, New Haven, CT 06511, USA (office). *Telephone:* (203) 432-2600 (office). *Website:* art.yale.edu/RobertStorr (office).

STOTHARD, Sir Peter M., Kt, MA; British journalist and newspaper editor; *Editor, The Times Literary Supplement;* b. 28 Feb. 1951, Chelmsford, Essex; s. of Wilfred Stothard and Patricia Savage; m. Sally Ceris Emerson 1980; one s. one d.; ed Brentwood School, Essex and Trinity Coll. Oxford; journalist, BBC 1974–77; Shell Petroleum 1977–79; business and political writer, Sunday Times 1979–80; Features Ed. and leader writer, The Times 1980–85; Deputy Ed. The Times 1985–92, US Ed. 1989–92, Ed. 1992–2002; Ed. The Times Literary Supplement 2002–; Hon. Fellow Trinity Coll. Oxford 2000. *Publications:* Thirty Days: A Month at the Heart of Blair's War 2003. *Leisure interests:* ancient and modern literature. *Address:* The Times Literary Supplement, Times House, 1 Pennington Street, London, E98 1BS, England (office). *Telephone:* (20) 7782-5000 (office). *E-mail:* editor@the-tls.co.uk (office). *Website:* www.the-tls.co.uk (office).

STOTT, Kathryn Linda, ARCM; British pianist; *Artistic Director, Manchester Chamber Concerts Society;* b. 10 Dec. 1958, Nelson, Lancs.; d. of Desmond Stott and Elsie Cheetham; m. 1st Michael Ardron 1979 (divorced 1983); m. 2nd John Elliot 1983 (divorced 1997); one d.; ed Yehudi Menuhin School (under Marcel Ciampi, Vlado Perlemuter, Louis Kentner) and Royal Coll. of Music, London (under Kendall Taylor); debut Purcell Room, London 1978; has since performed extensively in recitals and concertos both in UK and in Europe, Far East, Australia, Canada and USA; ten appearances at Henry Wood Promenade concerts; Dir Fauré and the French Connection Festival, Manchester 1995, Piano 2000, Manchester 2000, Piano 2003, Manchester 2003, Chopin and his Legacy, Leeds 2005; Artistic Dir, Manchester Chamber Concerts Soc. 2008–; Martin Scholarship 1976, Churchill Scholarship 1979, Croydon Symphony Award, Chappell Medal, Royal Amateur Orchestral Soc. Silver Medal 1979; Chevalier, Ordre des Arts et Lettres 1996. *Recordings:* 30 recordings, including premieres of concertos by George Lloyd and Michael Nyman. *Leisure interests:* horse-riding, travel, film noir. *Address:* c/o Jane Ward, 60 Shrewsbury Road, Oxton, Merseyside CH43 2HY, England (office). *Telephone:* (151) 513-2716. *Fax:* (151) 513-2716. *E-mail:* jane@kathrynstott.com (office). *Website:* www.kathrynstott.com (office).

STOWE, Madeleine; American actress; b. 18 Aug. 1958, Los Angeles; d. of the late Robert Stone and Mireya Mora; m. Brian Benben 1986; one d.; ed Univ. of Southern California; began acting career at Solari Theatre, Beverly Hills; appeared in TV series The Gangster Chronicles, mini-series Beulah Land and TV films The Nativity, The Deerslayer, Amazons, Blood and Orchids. *Films include:* Stakeout 1987, Tropical Snow 1989, Worth Winning 1989, Revenge 1990, The Two Jakes 1990, Closet Land 1991, Unlawful Entry 1992, The Last of the Mohicans 1992, Short Cuts 1993, Blink 1994, China Moon 1994, Twelve Monkeys 1995, Playing by Heart 1998, The Proposition 1998, The General's Daughter 1999, Imposter 2001, We Were Soldiers 2002, Avenging Angelo 2002, Octane 2003. *Television includes:* The Magnificent Ambersons 2002, Saving Milly 2005, Raines (series) 2007. *Address:* c/o David Schiff, UTA, 9560 Wilshire Boulevard, Suite 500, Beverly Hills, CA 90212, USA.

STOYANOV, Petar Stefanov; Bulgarian lawyer and fmr head of state; b. 25 May 1952, Plovdiv; m. Antonina Stoyanova; one s. one d.; ed St Kliment Ohridski Univ. of Sofia; divorce lawyer 1978–90; became active in politics 1989; mem. Union of Democratic Forces (UtDF), Spokesman in Plovdiv 1990, Pres. UtDF Legal Council 1993, Deputy Chair. UtDF responsible for domestic policy 1995, Chair. 2005–07 (resgnd), mem. Nat. Exec. Council; Deputy Minister of Justice 1992–93; mem. Parl. 1994–96, Chair. UtDF Parl. Group Parl. Comm. on Youth, Sports, and Tourism; presidential cand. 1996; Pres. of Bulgaria 1997–2002. *Address:* Blvd V. Levski 54, 1000 Sofia, Bulgaria (office). *Telephone:* 888-80-10-92 (mobile) (office). *Fax:* (2) 988-40-47 (office).

STOYKOV, Gen. Zlatan Kirilov; Bulgarian military officer; *Chief of General Staff;* b. 17 March 1951, Tsarvaritsa; m.; two d.; ed Vasil Levski Army Acad., Nat. War Coll., Gen. Staff Coll., Russia; Platoon Commdr, 19th Motorrifle Regt 1973–74; Co. Commdr, First Motorrifle Div. 1974–78; Service Support and Guard Battalion Commdr and Commdt, First Army 1980–81, Asst Chief of Operations Dept 1981–82, Sr Asst 1982–83; Asst Chief of Operations Dept, Operations Directorate, Land Forces Command 1983–84, Sr

Asst 1984–87, Deputy Chief 1987–88; Chief of Operations Dept and Deputy Chief of Staff, First Army 1988–92, Deputy Chief of Staff 1992–93; Third Motorrifle Div. Commdr 1995–98; Chief Rapid Reaction Forces HQ 1998–2000; Second Army Corps Commdr 2000–02; Deputy Chief of Gen. Staff, Armed Forces for Resources 2002–03; Chief Land Forces HQ 2003–06; Chief of Gen. Staff 2006–; promoted to Gen. 2006. *Address:* Ministry of Defence, 3 Dyakon Ignatiy ul, 1000 Sofia, Bulgaria (office). *Telephone:* (2) 922-09-22 (office). *Fax:* (2) 987-32-28 (office). *E-mail:* presscntr@mod.bg (office). *Website:* www.md.government.bg (office).

STRAARUP, Peter, BCom; Danish banking executive; *CEO and Chairman of the Executive Board and Committee, Danske Bank Group;* b. 19 July 1951; Arbitrage Dealer, Den Danske Bank 1975; Loan Admin Man. Scandinavian Bank Ltd, London 1976–77; Vice-Pres. Den Danske Bank 1977–81, Rep. Houston Rep. Office 1981–83, Head of Foreign Banking Relations, Copenhagen 1983, Gen. Man. Singapore Br. 1984–85, New York 1985–86, mem. Exec. Bd, Copenhagen 1986, CEO, Chair. Exec. Bd and Chair. Exec. Cttee Danske Bank Group 1998–; Chair. Danica Forsikring Group, Northern Bank, DDB Invest AB, Sampo Bank; mem. Bd of Dirs Int. Chamber of Commerce Denmark, Denmark-America Foundation; mem. Ass. of Reps Danish Employers' Asscn; mem. Int. Monetary Conf., Institut Int. d'Etudes Bancaires. *Address:* Danske Bank Group, Danske Bank A/S, Holmens Kanal 2-12, 1092 Copenhagen, Denmark (office). *Telephone:* (33) 440000 (office). *E-mail:* r3778web@danskebank.dk (office). *Website:* www.danskebank.com (office).

STRÅBERG, Hans, MSE; Swedish business executive; *President and CEO, AB Electrolux;* b. 22 Feb. 1957, Västervik; m.; two c.; ed Chalmers Univ. of Technology, Gothenborg; early position as Asst to Scientific Counsellor, Swedish Embassy in Washington, DC; joined AB Electrolux 1983, held various exec. positions including Exec. Vice Pres. of Operations at American subsidiary Frigidaire Home Appliances –1998, Exec. Vice Pres. Electrolux Group and Pres. Floor Care and Light Appliances Business Sector 1998, Pres. and CEO 2002–; mem. Bd of Dirs Asscn of Swedish Eng. Industries, AB Ph. Nederman & Co., Nederman Holding AB, Roxtec AB. *Leisure interests:* tennis, hunting, cars, family. *Address:* Office of the Chief Executive, AB Electrolux, St Göransgatan 143, Stockholm, Sweden (office). *Telephone:* (8) 7386000 (office). *Fax:* (8) 7387640 (office). *Website:* www.electrolux.com (office).

STRACHAN, Sir Ian Charles, Kt, MA, MPA; British business executive; b. 7 April 1943, Oldham; s. of Dr Charles Strachan and Margaret Craig; m. 1st Diane Shafer 1967 (divorced 1987); one d.; m. 2nd Margaret Auchincloss 1987; one step-s. one step-d.; ed Fettes Coll. Edinburgh, Christ's Coll. Cambridge and Princeton and Harvard Univs; Assoc. Ford Foundation, Malaysia 1967–69; various positions in Exxon Corpn 1970–86; Sr Vice-Pres. and Chief Financial Officer, Johnson & Higgins, New York 1986–87; Finance Dir RTZ Corpn PLC (now Rio Tinto) 1987–91, Deputy Chief Exec. 1991–95; Man. Dir BTR PLC July–Dec. 1995, Chief Exec. 1996–99; Deputy Chair. Invensys PLC 1999–2000; Chair. Instinet Group LLC 2003–05; mem. Bd of Dirs (non-exec.) Transocean Inc. 2000–, Johnson Matthey PLC, Xstrata PLC 2003–, Rolls-Royce Group PLC, Commercial Union 1992–95, Thomson-Reuters PLC 2000–. *Leisure interests:* tennis, golf, reading, oriental antiques. *Address:* c/o Board of Directors, Thomson-Reuters PLC, The Reuters Bldg., South Colonnade, Canary Wharf, London, E14 5EP, England (office). *Website:* www.thomsonreuters.com (office).

STRACHE, Heinz-Christian; Austrian politician; *Chairman, Freiheitliche Partei Österreichs (Freedom Party);* b. 12 June 1969; divorced; two c.; trained as a dental technician; active in local Vienna politics since 1991; Chair. Freiheitliche Partei Österreichs (Die Freiheitlichen) (Freedom Party) 2005–. *Address:* Freiheitliche Partei Österreichs (Die Freiheitlichen), Friedrich-Schmidt Pl. 4, 1080 Vienna, Austria (office). *Telephone:* (1) 512-35-35-0 (office). *Fax:* (1) 513-35-35-9 (office). *E-mail:* bgst@fpoe.at (office). *Website:* www.fpoe.at (office); www.hcstrache.at.

STRAHL, Charles (Chuck); Canadian politician; *Minister of Indian Affairs and Northern Development and Federal Interlocutor for Métis and Non-Status Indians;* b. 1957, British Columbia; m. Deb Strahl 1975; four c.; ed Trinity Western Univ.; fmr Pnr road construction and logging contracting firm; elected MP 1993 as Reform Party mem., re-elected 1997 (Reform Party), 2000 (Canadian Alliance), 2004, 2006 (Conservative Party), has represented constituencies of Fraser Valley, Fraser Valley East and Fraser Canyon, BC; fmr Official Opposition Whip and House Leader; Deputy Speaker of House and Chair., Cttees of the Whole 2004; Minister of Agric. and Agri-Food and Minister for Canadian Wheat Bd 2006–07, of Indian Affairs and Northern Devt and Federal Interlocutor for Métis and Non-Status Indians 2007–. *Address:* Indian and Northern Affairs Canada, Terrasses de la Chaudière, 10 Wellington, North Tower, Gatineau, ON K1A 0H4, Canada (office). *Telephone:* (819) 997-0380 (office). *Fax:* (819) 953-3017 (office). *E-mail:* infopubs@ainc-inac.gc.ca (office); ottawa@chuckstrahl.com (home). *Website:* www.ainc-inac.gc.ca (office); www.chuckstrahl.com (home).

STRAHLMAN, Ellen, MD, MHSc; American ophthalmologist and pharmaceutical industry executive; *Chief Medical Officer, GlaxoSmithKline North American Pharmaceuticals;* ed Harvard Univ., Johns Hopkins Univ. School of Medicine, Bloomberg School of Public Health; fmr CEO Virogen Ltd; fmr Chief Medical Officer and Global Head of Research and Devt, Bausch & Lomb; fmr Sr Medical Officer, Nat. Eye Inst., NIH; fmrly held sr positions at Merck and Novartis; Vice-Pres. of Licensing and Worldwide Business Devt, Pfizer –2008; Chief Medical Officer, GlaxoSmithKline North American Pharmaceuticals 2008–; mem. Columbia Univ. Medical and Science Tech. Council; Bd mem. Foundation of American Acad. of Ophthalmology. *Address:* GlaxoSmithKline North American Pharmaceuticals, One Franklin Plaza, Philadelphia, PA 19102, USA (office). *Telephone:* (215) 751-4638 (office). *Website:* us.gsk.com (office).

STRAKER, Louis, KCMG; Saint Vincent and the Grenadines politician; *Deputy Prime Minister and Minister of Foreign Affairs, Commerce and Trade;* Deputy Prime Minister of Saint Vincent and the Grenadines, Minister of Foreign Affairs, Commerce and Trade –May 2005, Deputy Prime Minister and Minister of Transport, Works and Housing May–Dec. 2005; Deputy Prime Minister and Minister of Foreign Affairs, Commerce and Trade Dec. 2005–. *Address:* Ministry of Foreign Affairs, Administrative Building, 3rd Floor, Bay Street, Kingstown, Saint Vincent and the Grenadines (office). *Telephone:* 456-2060 (office). *Fax:* 456-2610 (home). *E-mail:* office.foreignaffairs@mail.gov.vc (office).

STRAKHOV, Vladimir Nikolayevich, D.Phys.Math.Sc.; Russian physicist; b. 3 May 1932; ed Moscow Inst. of Geological Prospecting; sr engineer, researcher, Head of Lab. Prof. O. Schmidt Inst. of Earth Physics, USSR (now Russian) Acad. of Sciences 1959–89, Dir-Gen. 1989–; Corresp. mem. USSR (now Russian) Acad. of Sciences 1987, mem. 1992; main research in math., geophysics, gravitational and magnetic methods of prospecting mineral deposits, magnetic anomalies of oceans; went on hunger strike in protest at the state of scientific research and its financing 1996; mem. Russian Acad. of Natural Sciences. *Address:* c/o Russian Academy of Sciences, 119991 Moscow, Leninskii avenue, 14, Russia (office). *Telephone:* (495) 938-03-09 (office).

STRAND, Mark, AB, BFA, MA; American poet, writer and academic; *Professor of English and Comparative Literature, Columbia University;* b. 11 April 1934, Summerside, PEI, Canada; m. 1st Antonia Ratensky 1961 (divorced 1973); one d.; m. 2nd Julia Rumsey Garretson 1976 (divorced 1998); one s.; ed Antioch Coll., Yale Univ., Univ. of Iowa; instructor, Univ. of Iowa 1962–65; Fulbright Lecturer, Univ. of Brazil 1965; Asst Prof., Mount Holyoke Coll. 1966; Visiting Prof., Univ. of Washington 1967, Univ. of Virginia 1977, California State Univ. at Fresno 1977, Univ. of California, Irvine 1978, Wesleyan Univ. 1979–80; Adjunct Prof., Columbia Univ. 1968–70, currently Prof. of English and Comparative Literature; Visiting Lecturer, Yale Univ. 1969–70, Harvard Univ. 1980–81; Assoc. Prof., Brooklyn Coll., CUNY 1971; Bain Swiggett Lecturer, Princeton Univ. 1972; Fanny Hurst Prof. of Poetry, Brandeis Univ. 1973; Prof. 1981–86, Distinguished Prof. 1986–94, Univ. of Utah; Poet Laureate of the USA 1990–91; Elliot Coleman Prof. of Poetry, Johns Hopkins Univ. 1994–97; fmr Andrew MacLeish Distinguished Service Prof., Univ. of Chicago; Writer-in-Residence, American Acad., Rome 1982; mem. American Acad. and Inst. of Arts and Letters 1980–, Nat. Acad. of Arts and Sciences 1995–; Fulbright Scholarship to Italy 1960–61, Ingram Merrill Foundation Fellowship 1966, NEA grants 1967–68, 1977–78, Rockefeller Fellowship 1968–69; Edgar Allan Poe Prize 1974, Guggenheim Fellowship 1974–75, Nat. Inst. of Arts and Letters Award 1975, Acad. of American Poets Fellowship 1979, John D. and Catherine T. MacArthur Foundation Fellowship 1987–92, Utah Gov.'s Award in the Arts 1992, Bobbitt Nat. Prize for Poetry 1992, Bollingen Prize for Poetry 1993, Bingham Prize for Poetry 1998, Pulitzer Prize 1999, Wallace Stevens Award 2004. *Publications:* poetry: Sleeping With One Eye Open 1964, Reasons for Moving 1968, Darker 1970, Halty Ferguson: 18 Poems from the Quechua (trans.) 1971, Rafael Alberti: The Owl's Insomnia (trans.) 1973, The Sargentville Notebook 1973, The Story of Our Lives 1973, Carlos Drummond de Andrade: Souvenir of the Ancient World (trans.) 1976, Another Republic: 17 European and South American Writers (co-ed. with Charles Simic) 1976, The Late Hour 1978, Selected Poems 1980, Travelling in the Family: The Selected Poems of Carlos Drummond de Andrade (trans.) 1986, The Continuous Life 1990, The Best American Poetry (ed.) 1991, Dark Harbor 1993, The Golden Ecco Anthology (ed.) 1994, Blizzard of One (Pulitzer Prize in Poetry 1999) 1998, Man and Camel 2006, New Selected Poems 2007; prose: The Monument 1978, The Planet of Lost Things (juvenile) 1982, The Art of the Real 1983, Mr and Mrs Baby (short stories) 1985, The Night Book (juvenile) 1985, Rembrandt Takes a Walk (juvenile) 1986, William Bailey 1987, Hopper 1994; contrib. of poems, book reviews, art reviews, essays on poetry and painting, and interviews in numerous periodicals, contrib. to numerous anthologies. *Address:* 602 Philosophy Hall, Department of English and Comparative Literature, Columbia University, New York, NY 10027 (office); 2700 Broadway (8B), New York, NY 10025, USA (home). *Telephone:* (212) 854-7468 (office); (646) 478-8704 (home). *E-mail:* ms3091@columbia.edu (office). *Website:* www.columbia.edu/cu/english (office).

STRANGE, Curtis Northrop; American professional golfer; b. 30 Jan. 1955, Norfolk, Va; s. of Thomas Wright Strange, Jr and Nancy Neal; m. Sarah Jones; two s.; ed Wake Forest Univ.; turned professional 1976; won Pensacola Open 1979, Sammy Davis Jr Greater Hartford Open 1983, LaJel Classic 1984, Honda Classic, Panasonic-Las Vegas Int. 1985, Canadian Open 1985, Houston Open 1986, Canadian Open, Fed. Express-St Jude Classic, NEC Series of Golf 1987, Sandway Cove Classic, Australia 1988, Ind. Insurance Agent Open, Memorial Tournament, US Open, Nabisco Championships 1988, US Open, Palm Meadows Cup, Australia 1989, Holden Classic, Australia 1993; mem. PGA Tour Charity Team, Michelob Championship, Kingsmill 1996; Capt. US Ryder Cup Team 2002 after playing on five Ryder Cup Teams; golf analyst for ABC Sports 1997–; Golfer of the Year 1986, 1987. *Leisure interests:* hunting, fishing, Harley Davidsons. *Address:* c/o IMG, 1 Erieview Plaza, Suite 1300, Cleveland, OH 44114; PGA America, P.O. Box 109601, 100 Avenue of the Champions, Palm Beach Gardens, FL 33410, USA.

STRANGFELD, John R., Jr, BS, MBA; American business executive; *Chairman, President and CEO, Prudential Financial, Inc.;* b. 27 Dec. 1953; m. Mary Kay Strangfeld; ed Susquehanna Univ., Darden School of Business, Univ. of Virginia; joined Prudential 1977, served in various exec. positions, including Chair. PRICOA Capital Group, London, UK 1989–95, Sr Man. Dir,

Pvt. Asset Man. Group 1995–98, CEO Prudential Investment Man. of Prudential Insurance 1998–2002, Chair. and CEO Prudential Securities (renamed Prudential Equity Group LLC) 2000, Exec. Vice-Pres. Prudential Financial 2001–02, Vice-Chair. Prudential Financial, Inc. 2002–07, Pres. and CEO 2007–, mem. Bd Dirs and Chair. 2008–; mem. Bd of Mans Wachovia Securities Financial Holdings LLC (jt venture of Prudential and Wachovia) 2003–; Vice-Chair. Bd of Trustees, Susquehanna Univ.; Pres. Bd of Trustees, Darden Foundation, Univ. of Virginia. *Address:* Prudential Financial, Inc., 751 Broad Street, Newark, NJ 07102-3777, USA (office). *Telephone:* (973) 802-6000 (office). *Fax:* (973) 802-4479 (office). *E-mail:* info@prudential.com (office). *Website:* www.prudential.com (office).

STRÁNSKÝ, Jiří; Czech writer; b. 12 Aug. 1931, Prague; m. Jitka Balíková; one s., one d.; ed High School; manual worker –1989; political prisoner 1950–58, 1970–72; after 'Velvet Revolution' 1989–, mem. of Confed. of Political Prisoners, Pres. of Czech Centre of Int. PEN 1992–; Chair. M. Havel Foundation; mem. Council for TV, Council for Grants and Devt of Czech Cinematography 2000–; Chevalier, Ordre des Arts et des Lettres 2002; Egon Hostovský Prize 1991, Medal for Merit 2001. *Publications include:* Happiness, Tales 1969, The Land that Became Wild (Zdivočelá země) 1991; prose Auction; script for film Boomerang 1996 (Czech Literary Fund Prize 1998), script for TV play The Uniform 2000. *Leisure interests:* scouting, riding. *Address:* Czech Centre of International PEN, 28 øíjna 9, 110 00 Prague 1, Czech Republic (office). *Telephone:* (2) 24235546 (office). *Fax:* (2) 24221926 (office). *E-mail:* jiri@pen.cz (office). *Website:* www.pen.cz (office).

STRĂTAN, Andrei, DEcon; Moldovan government official; *Deputy Prime Minister and Minister of Foreign Affairs and European Integration;* b. 3 Sept. 1966, Chişinău; m.; two c.; ed Chişinău Polytechnic Inst., Moldova State Univ.; served in Soviet Customs Control Dept 1991–92, Repub. of Moldova Customs Dept 1992–2002, Head of Div. 1992–95, Deputy Dir-Gen. 1995–97, Prime Deputy Dir-Gen. 1997–99, Dir-Gen. 1999–2002; served on special missions with rank of Amb. including Head, Nat. Bureau of Stability Pact, Ministry of Foreign Affairs 2002–03; Deputy Prime Minister and Minister of Foreign Affairs 2003–04; Minister of Foreign Affairs 2004; Deputy Prime Minister and Minister of Foreign Affairs and European Integration 2005–. *Address:* Ministry of Foreign Affairs, 2012 Chişinău, str. 31 August 80, Moldova (office). *Telephone:* (22) 57-82-07 (office). *Fax:* (22) 23-23-02 (office). *E-mail:* secdep@mfa.md (office). *Website:* www.mfa.md (office).

STRATAS, Teresa Anastasia Strataki, OC; Canadian singer; b. (Anastasia Stratakis), 26 May 1938, Toronto, Ont.; d. of Emmanuel Stratas and Argero Stratakis; m. Tony Harrison; ed Univ. of Toronto; began singing career in nightclubs in Toronto; debut at Toronto Opera Festival 1958; won audition to Metropolitan Opera, New York 1959; performances there include Berg's Lulu, Jenny in Brecht and Weill's Mahagonny, Suor Angelica, Lauretta and Giorgetta in Il Trittico; major roles in opera houses worldwide include Paris (Lulu 1979), Brussels (Lulu 1988), Boston (Mimi 1989), Chicago (Mélisande 1992); appeared as Violetta in Zeffirelli's film of La Traviata 1983; appeared in Broadway musical Rags 1986; cr. role of Marie Antoinette in Ghosts of Versailles, premiered Metropolitan Opera, NY 1992; Il Tabarro and Pagliacci at the Met 1994; LLD hc (McMaster Univ.) 1986, (Toronto) 1994, (Rochester) 1998, (Juilliard School of Music), (Royal Conservatory of Music); Canadian Music Council Performer of the Year 1979, Drama Desk Award for Leading Actress in a Musical on Broadway 1986–87, Gemini Award for Best Supporting Actress (for Under the Piano) 1997, three Grammy Awards, Opera Canada Award for Creative Artist 2003. *Address:* Vincent & Farrell Associates, 157 W 57th Street, Suite 502, New York, NY 10019, USA (office).

STRATHCLYDE, 2nd Baron, cr. 1955; **Thomas Galbraith,** PC; British politician; *Leader of the Opposition, House of Lords;* b. 22 Feb. 1960; s. of the late Sir Thomas Galbraith and Simone Galbraith; m. Jane Skinner 1992; three d.; ed Sussex House, London, Wellington Coll., Univs of E Anglia and Aix-en-Provence; insurance broker, Bain Clarkson Ltd (fmrly Bain Dawes) 1982–88; Conservative cand. in European Election, Merseyside E 1984; Govt Whip House of Lords 1988–89; Govt Spokesman for Dept of Trade and Industry 1988–89, Parl. Under-Sec. of State Dept of Employment (Tourism) 1989–90, Dept of Environment July–Sept. 1990, 1992, Scottish Office 1990–92; Minister for Agric., Fisheries, Highlands and Islands 1990–92; Chief Govt Whip 1994–97, Opposition Chief Whip 1997–98, Deputy Speaker 1997–98, Leader of the Opposition 1998–. *Address:* House of Lords, Westminster, London, SW1A 0PW, England (office). *Telephone:* (20) 7219-3236 (office). *Fax:* (20) 7219-0304 (home). *Website:* www.parliament.uk (office).

STRAUB, Elek, BEng; Hungarian telecommunications industry executive; b. 1944; ed Budapest Tech. Univ.; Head of IT Dept, Ministry of Labour 1970–80; Head of IT Div. and later Vice-Pres., Cen. Statistical Office 1980–90, also Govt Adviser, IT Devt Cttee, Hungarian Govt; Gen. Man., IBM Hungary 1990–95; CEO, Matáv 1995–2005, mem. Bd 1995–2005, Chair. 1996–2000, Chair. Man. Cttee 2000–05, (Matáv renamed Magyar Telekom 2005) Chair. and CEO Magyar Telekom 2005–06 (resgnd); mem. Bd of Dirs Graphisoft SE 2007–; currently Pres. Hungarian Yachting Asscn; Chair. German-Hungarian Chamber of Commerce 2004–06; 1st Class Cross of Distinction of Order of FRG 2004, Order of Merit of Repub. of Hungary, Officer's Cross 2004. *Address:* Magyar Vitorlás Szövetség (Hungarian Yachting Association), 1146 Budapest, Istvánmezei út 1-3, Hungary. *Telephone:* (1) 4606925. *Fax:* (1) 4606926. *E-mail:* hunsail@hunsail.hu. *Website:* www.hunsail.hu.

STRAUME, Janis; Latvian politician; b. 1962, Sigulda; m.; one s. two d.; ed Rīga State Medical Inst.; physician, Rīga City clinic, endoscopist, Latvian Diagnostics Centre 1986–90; political activities 1988–; mem. Latvian Human Rights Group Helsinki 86 (Rīga Chapter); Latvian Nat. Independence Movt, Citizen's Congress of Latvian Repub., Union of 18th Nov.; mem. Saeima 1990–, Chair. 1999–2002, Deputy Chair. 2002–, mem. Foreign Affairs Cttee, Nat. Security Cttee; Chair., Union for Fatherland and Freedom Faction (LNNK) 1998–2002, For Fatherland and Freedom Union/Latvian National Independence Movement (TB/LNNK) 2002. *Address:* c/o For Fatherland and Freedom Union/Latvian National Independence Movement (TB/LNNK) (Apvienība 'Tēvzemei un Brīvībai'/Latvijas Nacionālās Neatkarības Kustība), Jēkaba iela 20/22–9, Rīga 1050, Latvia. *Telephone:* 6721-6762. *E-mail:* tb@tb.lv. *Website:* www.tb.lv.

STRAUSS, Botho; German playwright and novelist; b. 2 Dec. 1944, Naumburg; ed Cologne and Munich; moved with family to Remscheid, Ruhr region; on staff of Theater heute, West Berlin; Dramaturg at Schaubühne Theater, West Berlin 1970–75; mem. PEN; Schiller Prize Baden-Württemberg 1977, Literaturpreis, Bayerische Akademie der Schönen Künste 1981, Mülheimer Drama Prize 1982, Jean Paul Prize 1987, Georg Büchner Prize 1989. *Plays include:* Die Hypochonder (first play, 1971, winner Hannover Dramaturgie Award), Trilogie des Wiedersehens 1976, Gross und Klein 1978, Kalldeway Farce 1981, Der Park 1983, Das Gleichgewicht 1994, Theaterstücke in zwei Banden 1994. *Publications:* Bekannte Gesichter, gemischte Gefühle (jtly) 1974, Die Widmung (novel) 1979, Rumor (novel) 1980, Paare, Passanten (novel) 1981, Der Junge Mann (novel) 1984, Diese Erinnerung an einen, der nur einen Tag zu Gast War 1985, Die Fremdenführerin 1986, Niemand Anderes (novel) 1987, Besucher 1988, Kongress: Die Kette der Demütigungen 1989, Wohnen Dammern Lügen 1994, Das Partikular 2000, Der Narr und seine Frau heute abend in Pancomedia 2001. *Address:* Rosica Colin Ltd, 1 Clareville Grove Mews, London Sw7 5AH, England (office). *Telephone:* (20) 7370-1080 (office). *Fax:* (20) 7244-6441 (office).

STRAUSS, Robert Schwarz, LLB; American lawyer, diplomatist and fmr government official; *Partner, Akin, Gump, Strauss, Hauer & Feld LLP;* b. 19 Oct. 1918, Lockhart, Tex.; s. of Charles H. Strauss and Edith V. Strauss (née Schwarz); m. Helen Jacobs 1941; two s. one d.; ed Univ. of Texas Law School; Special Agent for US Fed. Bureau of Investigation (FBI) in Ia, Ohio and Dallas, Tex. 1941–45; admitted to Texas Bar 1941; Founding Pnr, Gump and Strauss (now Akin, Gump, Strauss, Hauer and Feld LLP), Dallas 1945–77, 1981–; Pres. Strauss Broadcasting Co. 1965; mem. Texas State Banking Bd 1963–68; mem. Advisory Cttee Forstmann Little & Co.; mem. Democratic Nat. Cttee 1968–70, Treas. 1970–72; Chair. 1972–77; US Prin. Trade Negotiator (rank of Amb.) 1977–79; Special Envoy of Pres. to Middle East April–Nov. 1979; Chair. Pres. Carter's Campaign Cttee 1979–80; mem. Nat. Bipartisan Comm. of Cen. America 1983–84; Co-Chair. Nat. Econ. Comm. 1988–; Amb. to Russia 1991–93; fmr mem. Bd of Dirs Archer Daniels Midland, Lone Star Industries, MCA, Memorex Telex; fmly held Lloyd Bentsen Chair at LBJ School of Public Affairs, Univ. of Texas; Chair. US-Russia Business Council 1993–2004, Chair. Emer. 2004–; mem. Council on Foreign Relations; Trustee Center for Strategic and Int. Studies; Presidential Medal of Freedom 1981. *Leisure interests:* golf, horse racing. *Address:* Akin, Gump, Strauss, Hauer & Feld, 1700 Pacific Avenue, Suite 4100, Dallas, TX 75201-4675 (office); Akin, Gump, Strauss, Hauer & Feld, Robert S. Strauss Building, 1333 New Hampshire Ave, NW, Washington, DC 20036-1564, USA (office). *Telephone:* (202) 887-4190 (DC) (office); (214) 969-2800 (Dallas) (office). *Fax:* (202) 887-4288 (DC) (office); (214) 969-4343 (Dallas) (office). *E-mail:* washdcinfo@akingump.com (office). *Website:* www.akingump.com (office).

STRAUSS-KAHN, Dominique Gaston André; French economist, lawyer, politician and international organization executive; *Chairman, Executive Board and Managing Director, International Monetary Fund;* b. 25 April 1949, Neuilly-sur-Seine; s. of Gilbert Strauss-Kahn and Jacqueline Fellus; m. 3rd Anne Sinclair 1991; one s. three d. from fmr marriages; ed Paris Inst. for Political Studies, École des Hautes Études Commerciales; Lecturer, Univ. of Nancy II 1977–80; Scientific Counsellor Nat. Inst. of Statistics and Econ. Studies (INSEE) 1978–80; Dir Cerepi (CNRS) 1980–; Prof., Univ. of Paris-X Nanterre 1981; Chief of Financial Services Commissariat Gen., Plan, Asst Commr Plan 1984–86; elected Socialist Deputy Val-d'Oise 1988–91, 1997, 2001–02; Pres. of Comm. on Finances, Assemblée Nationale 1988, Minister Del. of Industry and Foreign Trade to the Minister of State, Minister of the Economy, Finance and Budget 1991–92; Minister of Industry and Foreign Commerce under Minister of Economy, Finance and Budget 1992–93, Minister of Economy, Finance and Industry 1997–99; mem. Socialist Party Cttee of Dirs 1983–, Nat. Sec. 1984–89; mem. Socialist Party Bureau 1995–; Mayor City of Sorcelles (Val d'Oise) 1995–97, apptd First Deputy Mayor 1997; Chair. Scientific Cttee Jean-Jaurès Foundation 2000; Special Councellor to Sec.-Gen. OECD 2000; Visiting Prof., Stanford Univ., USA 2000–01; fmr Dir of Research, Paris Inst. of Political Studies and Prof. of Econs; fmr Prof., École des Hautes Études Commerciales (HEC School of Man.); charged with forgery Oct. 2000; on trial for corruption Oct. 2001; Co-founder and Co-Pres. À gauche en Europe (think-tank) 2003–; Chair. Exec. Bd and Man. Dir IMF 2007–; unsuccessful cand. for Socialist Party nomination in 2007 presidential election. *Publications:* La richesse des Français 1977, Economie de la famille et accumulation patrimoniale 1977, L'epargne et la retraite 1982. *Leisure interests:* piano, cinema, skiing, rugby. *Address:* International Monetary Fund, 700 19th Street, NW, Washington, DC 20431, USA (office). *Telephone:* (202) 623-7000 (office). *Fax:* (202) 623-4661 (office). *E-mail:* publicaffairs@imf.org (office). *Website:* www.imf.org (office); www.blogdsk.net (home).

STRAUSS-LAHAT, Ofra; Israeli business executive; *Chairman, Strauss-Elite Group;* b. 22 Aug. 1960; ed Tel-Aviv Univ.; began career in int. marketing services and training program at Estée Lauder, USA 1987–89; joined family-owned Strauss Ice-cream Co. 1989, Organized Market Man. 1989–90, Marketing Man. 1990–93, Gen. Man. Food Div. 1993–95, Deputy Pres. and CEO 1996–2001, Chair. 2001–04, Chair. Strauss-Elite Group 2004–; mem. Supervisory Bd Numico NV 2006–; Co-Chair Israel, United Jewish Communities Gen. Ass.; mem. Exec. The Jewish Agency for Israel; ranked by Fortune magazine amongst 50 Most Powerful Women in Business outside the US (46th) 2002, (48th) 2003, (45th) 2004, (42nd) 2005, (47th) 2006. *Address:* Strauss-Elite Group, 84 Arlozorov Street, PO Box 19, Ramat Gan 52100, Israel (office). *Telephone:* (3) 6752111 (office). *Fax:* (3) 6752366 (office). *E-mail:* peril@elite.co.il (office). *Website:* www.elite.co.il (office).

STRAW, Rt Hon. John (Jack) Whitaker, PC, MP; British politician and lawyer; *Lord Chancellor and Secretary of State for Justice;* b. 3 Aug. 1946, Buckhurst Hill, Essex; s. of Walter A. W. Straw and Joan S. Straw; m. 1st Anthea L. Weston 1968 (divorced 1978); one d. (deceased); m. 2nd Alice E. Perkins 1978; one s. one d.; ed Brentwood School, Univ. of Essex and Univ. of Leeds School of Law; Pres. Nat. Union of Students 1969–71; mem. Islington Borough Council 1971–78, Inner London Educ. Authority 1971–74 (Deputy Leader 1973–74); called to Bar, Inner Temple 1972, Bencher 1997, practised as barrister 1972–74; special adviser to Sec. of State for Social Services 1974–76, to Sec. of State for Environment 1976–77; on staff of Granada TV (World in Action) 1977–79; MP for Blackburn 1979–; Opposition Treasury Spokesman 1980–83, Environment 1983–87; mem. Parl. Cttee of Labour Party (Shadow Cabinet) 1987–97; Shadow Sec. of State for Educ. 1987–92, for the Environment (Local Govt) 1992–94; Shadow Home Sec. 1994–97; Home Sec. 1997–2001; Sec. of State for Foreign and Commonwealth Affairs 2001–06; Leader of the House of Commons and Lord Privy Seal 2006–07; Lord Chancellor and Sec. of State for Justice 2007–; mem. Council, Inst. for Fiscal Studies 1983–2000, Lancaster Univ. 1989–92; Vice-Pres. Asscn of District Councils; Visiting Fellow, Nuffield Coll. Oxford 1990–98; Gov. Blackburn Coll. 1990–, Pimlico School 1994–2000 (Chair. 1995–98); Fellow Royal Statistical Soc. 1995–; Labour; Hon. LLD (Leeds) 1999. *Publications:* Policy and Ideology 1993; contribs to pamphlets, newspaper articles. *Leisure interests:* walking, cooking puddings, music. *Address:* Ministry of Justice, Selborne House, 54 Victoria Street, London, SW1E 6QW (office); House of Commons, Westminster, London, SW1A 0AA, England. *Telephone:* (20) 7210-8500 (office); (20) 7219-3000; (1254) 52317 (constituency office) (office). *Fax:* (20) 7210-0647 (office). *E-mail:* general.queries@justice.gsi.gov.uk (office). *Website:* www.justice.gov.uk (office).

STREEP, Meryl (Mary Louise), AB, MFA; American actress; b. 22 June 1949, Summit, NJ; d. of Harry Streep, Jr and Mary W. Streep; m. Donald Gummer 1978; one s. three d.; ed singing studies with Estelle Liebling; studied drama at Vassar, Yale School of Drama; stage debut in New York in Trelawny of the Wells; 27 Wagons Full of Cotton, New York; New York Shakespeare Festival 1976 in Henry V, Measure for Measure; also acted in Happy End (musical), The Taming of the Shrew, Wonderland (musical), Taken in Marriage and numerous other plays; Dr hc (Dartmouth) 1981, (Yale) 1983, (Lafayette) 1985; Commdr, Ordre des Arts et des Lettres 2003; Bette Davis Lifetime Achievement Award 1998, Special Award, Berlin Int. Film Festival 1999, American Film Inst. Lifetime Achievement Award 2004. *Films include:* Julia 1976, The Deer Hunter (Best Supporting Actress Award from Nat. Soc. of Film Critics) 1978, Manhattan 1979, The Seduction of Joe Tynan (New York Film Critics Circle Award for Best Supporting Actress) 1979, The Senator 1979, Kramer vs. Kramer (Acad. Award for Best Supporting Actress, New York Film Critics Circle Award for Best Supporting Actress) 1979, The French Lieutenant's Woman 1980, Sophie's Choice (Acad. Award for Best Actress, New York Film Critics Circle Award for Best Actress) 1982, Still of the Night 1982, Silkwood 1983, Plenty 1984, Falling in Love 1984, Out of Africa 1985, Heartburn 1985, Ironweed 1987, A Cry in the Dark (Best Actress Award, New York Critics 1988, Cannes 1989) 1988, The Lives and Loves of a She Devil 1989, Hollywood and Me 1989, Postcards from the Edge 1991, Defending Your Life 1991, Death Becomes Her 1992, The House of the Spirits, The River Wild 1994, The Bridges of Madison County 1995, Before and After, Marvin's Room, One True Thing 1998, Dancing at Lughnasa 1999, Music of the Heart 1999, The Hours 2002, Adaptation (Golden Globe for Best Supporting Actress) 2003, The Manchurian Candidate 2004, Lemony Snicket's A Series of Unfortunate Events 2004, Prime 2005, The Ant Bully (voice) 2006, The Devil Wears Prada (Golden Globe for Best Actress Musical or Comedy 2007) 2006, A Prairie Home Companion (Best Supporting Actress Nat. Soc. of Film Critics 2007, Best Actress, London Film Critics' Circle Awards 2007) 2006, Evening 2007, Rendition 2007, Lions for Lambs 2007, Mamma Mia! 2008. *Plays include:* Alice in Concert 1978, 1980–81, The Seagull 2001, Mother Courage and her Children 2006, Soho Rep Spring Gala 2007. *Television appearances include:* The Deadliest Season, Uncommon Women, Holocaust (Emmy Award), Velveteen Rabbit, First Do No Harm 1997, Angels in America (Golden Globe for Best Actress in a Miniseries or TV Movie 2004, Screen Actors Guild Award for Best Actress in a Miniseries 2004, Emmy Award for Outstanding Lead Actress in a Miniseries or Movie 2004) 2003. *Leisure interests:* peace and anti-nuclear causes, gardening, skiing, raising family, visiting art galleries and museums. *Address:* c/o Creative Artists Agency, 9830 Wilshire Boulevard, Beverly Hills, CA 90212, USA.

STREET, Hon. Anthony Austin; Australian business executive and fmr politician; b. 8 Feb. 1926, Melbourne, Vic.; s. of Brig. the Hon. Geoffrey Austin Street, MC and Evora Francis Street (née Currie); m. Valerie Erica Rickard 1951; three s.; ed Melbourne Grammar; Royal Australian Navy; primary producer; mem. for Corangamite, House of Reps 1966–84; Sec. Govt Mems Defence and Wool Cttees 1967–71; mem. Jt Parl. Cttee on Foreign Affairs 1969; Chair. Fed. Rural Cttee of Liberal Party 1970–74; mem. Fed. Exec. Council 1971–; Asst Minister for Labour and Nat. Service 1971–72; mem. Liberal Party Shadow Cabinet for Social Security, Health and Welfare 1973, for Primary Industry, Shipping and Transport 1973–74, for Science and Tech. and ACT 1974–75, for Labour 1975; Minister for Labour and Immigration Nov.–Dec. 1975; Minister Assisting the Prime Minister in Public Service Matters 1975–77; Minister for Employment and Industrial Relations 1975–78, for Industrial Relations 1978–80, for Foreign Affairs 1980–83; resgnd from Parl. 1984; now Man. and Co. Dir. *Leisure interests:* flying, cricket, golf, tennis. *Address:* 153 The Terrace, Ocean Grove, Vic. 3226, Australia (home).

STREET, Sir Laurence Whistler, AC, KCMG, LLB, QC; Australian lawyer and commerical mediator; b. 3 July 1926, Sydney, NSW; s. of the late Sir Kenneth Street and Jessie Street; m. 1st Susan Gai Watt 1952, two s. two d.; m. 2nd Penelope Patricia Ferguson 1989; one d.; ed Cranbrook School, Sydney, Univ. of Sydney; served in Royal Australian Navy 1943–47; barrister, NSW 1951; Lecturer, Univ. Sydney Law School 1962–65; QC 1963; Commdr and Inaugural Sr Officer RANR Legal Br. 1964–65, Pres. Courts Martial Appeal Tribunal 1971–74; Judge Supreme Court NSW 1965–88; Judge Court of Appeal 1972–74; Chief Judge in Equity 1972–74; Chief Justice of NSW 1974–88; Lt-Gov. NSW 1974–89; Pres. Cranbrook School Council 1966–74, St John Ambulance Australia (NSW) 1974–; Chair. Inaugural Planning Cttee, Australian Commercial Disputes Centre 1985–86; Fellow UTS Sydney 1990; Hon. Col 1st/15th Royal NSW Lancers 1986–96; mem. London Court of Int. Arbitration 1988–2003; Pres. LCIA Asia-Pacific Council 1989–; Chair. Advisory Bd Dispute Resolution Centre, Bond Univ. 1989–99, UTS Centre for Dispute Resolution 1991–2001; Pres. Australian Br. Int. Law Asscn 1990–94, World Pres. 1990–92, Life Vice-Pres. 1992–; Pres. Sydney Univ. Law School Foundation 1990–; Chair. Australian Govt Int. Legal Services Advisory Council 1990–; Dir John Fairfax Holdings Ltd 1991–94, Chair. 1994–97; mem. WIPO Arbitration Consultative Comm., Geneva 1994–2003; Chair. Judiciary Appeals Bd NSW Rugby League 1998–; Australian Govt Designated Conciliator to ICSID, Washington 1995–; ADR Consultant to Australian Defence Legal Office 1999–; Mediator Court of Arbitration for Sport, Lausanne 2000–; Fellow, Chartered Inst. of Arbitrators (UK) 1992, Australian Inst. of Co. Dirs 1992; Hon. Fellow, Inst. of Arbitrators Australia (Grade I) 1989, Australian Inst. of Building 2004; KStJ 1976; Grand Officer of Merit Order of Malta 1977; Hon. LLD (Sydney), (Macquarie), (Univ. of Tech.); Hon. DEcon (New England Univ.) 1996. *Publication:* Mediation – A Practical Outline (5th edn) 2003. *Address:* 233 Macquarie Street, Sydney (office); 1 Wolseley Crescent, Point Piper, NSW 2027, Australia (home). *Telephone:* (2) 9223-0888 (office); (2) 9363-1480 (home). *Fax:* (2) 9223-0588 (office); (2) 9327-8871 (home). *E-mail:* lstreet@laurencestreet.com.au (office). *Website:* www.laurencestreet.com.au (office).

STREET, Robert, AO, PhD, DSc, FAA; Australian physicist and academic; *Honorary Research Fellow, Department of Physics, University of Western Australia;* b. 16 Dec. 1920, Wakefield, England; s. of Joe Street and Edith Elizabeth Street; m. Joan Marjorie Bere 1943; one s. one d.; ed Univ. of London; Scientific Officer, Dept of Supply, UK 1942–45; Lecturer, Dept of Physics, Univ. of Nottingham 1945–54; Sr Lecturer, Dept of Physics, Univ. of Sheffield 1954–60; Foundation Prof. of Physics, Monash Univ., Melbourne, Victoria 1960–74; Dir Research School of Physical Sciences, ANU 1974–77; Vice-Chancellor Univ. of Western Australia 1978–86, Dir Magnetics Group, Research Centre for Advanced Materials and Minerals Processing 1991, now Hon. Research Fellow; fmr Pres. Australian Inst. of Nuclear Science and Eng; mem. and Chair. Australian Research Grants Cttee 1970–76; Chair. Nat. Standards Comm. 1967–78; FAA 1973, Treas. 1976–77; Pres. Int. Inst. of Business and Tech., Perth, WA 1987–90; Chair. Child Health Research Foundation of Western Australia 1988–93; Consultant, CRA Advanced Tech. Devt 1992–96. *Publications:* scientific papers on magnetism in learned journals. *Address:* The University of Western Australia, Department of Physics, 35 Stirling Highway, Crawley, WA 6009, Australia (office). *Telephone:* 6488-2718 (office). *E-mail:* street@physics.uwa.edu.au (office). *Website:* www.physics.uwa.edu.au (office).

STREET-PORTER, Janet, FRTS, FRIBA; British writer, broadcaster and fmr newspaper editor; *Editor-at-Large, The Independent on Sunday;* b. (Janet Bull), 27 Dec. 1946, London, England; m. 1st Tim Street-Porter 1967 (divorced 1975); m. 2nd A. M. M. Elliott 1976 (divorced 1978); m. 3rd Frank Cvitanovich (divorced 1988, died 1995); ed Lady Margaret Grammar School and Architectural Asscn; columnist and fashion writer, Petticoat Magazine 1968, Daily Mail 1969–71, Evening Standard 1971–73; own show, LBC Radio 1973; presenter of youth programmes, late night talk shows and prime time factual series, London Weekend Television (LWT) 1975–83; Head of Youth and Entertainment Features, BBC TV 1988–94, Head of Ind. Production for Entertainment 1994; Head of Live TV, Mirror Group TV 1994–95; Ed. The Independent on Sunday 1999–2001, Ed.-at-Large 2001–; presenter, Bloomberg TV 2001–05; Pres. Ramblers' Asscn 1994–97 (now Vice-Pres.), Globetrotters Club 2003–08; Trustee, Nat. Media Museum 2006, Science Music 2008; Patron ICA; Prix Italia 1992, BAFTA Award for Originality 1988, European Cedefop Award (twice), Food and Farming Industry Award 2008. *Television includes:* as presenter: London Weekend Show, Saturday Night People, Six O'Clock Show 1975–; as series presenter (BBC 2): Design Awards, Travels with Pevsner, Coast to Coast, The Midnight Hour, As The Crow Flies (series), Cathedral Calls; series presenter (Channel 4): J'Accuse, The Internet, Men Talking, Demolition, The F Word; presented two series on teaching and nursing for Channel 5 and two documentaries for Sky; writer and producer: The Vampire (opera for BBC 2); as producer: Get Fresh (ITV network), Network 7 (co-producer, Channel 4) 1987–94. *Publications:* Scandal 1980, The British Teapot 1981, Coast to Coast 1998, As the Crow Flies 1999, Baggage – My Childhood 2004, Fall Out 2006, Life's too F***ing Short 2008. *Leisure interests:* walking, modern art. *Address:* c/o Emma Hardy, Princess Productions, Whiteleys Centre, 151 Queensway, London, W2 4SB, England (office). *Telephone:* (20) 7985-1917 (office). *E-mail:* emma.hardy@princesstv.com (office). *Website:* www.janetstreetporter.com.

STREIFF, Christian; French automotive industry executive; b. 21 Sept. 1954, Sarrebourg; m.; three c.; ed Ecole Nationale Supérieure de Mines, Paris;

joined Saint-Gobain Group 1979, served in various mfg positions and as Corp. Planning Man., Gen. Man. Gevetex GmbH 1988–91, Gen. Man. Vetrerie Italaine SpA, Italy 1991–94, CEO Saint-Gobain Emballage 1994–97, Pres. Pipe Div. and Chair. and CEO Pont-a-Mousson SA 1997–2001, Sr Vice-Pres. Saint-Gobain Group and Pres. Abrasives and Ceramics and Plastics Div. 2001–03, Deputy CEO Saint-Gobain Group 2003–05; Pres. and CEO Airbus S.A.S. July–Oct. 2006; Special Advisor, reporting to Chair. Man. Bd PSA Peugeot Citroën SA 2006–07, Chair. Man. Bd 2007–09; Dir (non-exec.) Thyssen-Krupp AG, Continental AG; mem. Supervisory Bd Prysmian SpA (Italy). *Address:* c/o PSA Peugeot Citroën SA, 75 avenue de la Grande-Armée, 75116 Paris, France (office).

STREISAND, Barbra Joan; American singer and actress; b. 24 April 1942, Brooklyn, New York; d. of Emanuel Streisand and Diana Streisand (née Rosen); m. 1st Elliot Gould 1963 (divorced 1971); one s.; m. 2nd James Brolin 1998; ed Erasmus Hall High School; nightclub debut at Bon Soir 1961; appeared in off-Broadway revue Another Evening with Harry Stoones 1961; appeared at Caucus Club, Detroit and Blue Angel New York 1961; played in musical comedy I Can Get It for You Wholesale 1962; began recording career with Columbia records 1963; appeared in musical play Funny Girl, New York 1964, London 1966; TV programme My Name is Barbra shown in England, Holland, Australia, Sweden, Bermuda and the Philippines, winning five Emmy awards; second programme Color Me Barbra also shown abroad; numerous concert and nightclub appearances; f. Barwood Films (film production co.) 1972; Commdr des Arts et Lettres 1984; New York, Critics Best Supporting Actress Award 1962, Grammy Awards for Best Female Pop Vocalist 1963, 1964, 1965, 1977, 1986, London Critics' Musical Award 1966, American Guild of Variety Artists' Entertainer of the Year Award 1970, Nat. Medal of Arts, Emmy Award for Best Individual Performance in a Music or Variety Programme (for Barbra Streisand: Timeless) 2001, American Film Inst. Lifetime Achievement Award 2001, Kennedy Center Honor 2008. *Recordings include:* albums: The Barbra Streisand Album 1963, The Second Barbra Streisand Album 1963, The Third Album 1964, My Name Is Barbra 1965, People 1965, Color Me Barbra 1966, Je m'appelle Barbra 1967, Barbra Streisand: A Happening In Central Park 1968, What About Me? 1969, Stoney End 1970, Barbra Joan Streisand 1972, Classical Barbra 1974, The Way We Were 1974, Lazy Afternoon 1975, A Star Is Born 1976, Superman 1977, Songbird, 1978, Wet 1979, Guilty (with Barry Gibb) 1980, Memories 1981, Emotion 1984, The Broadway Album 1986, One Voice 1986, Til I Loved You 1989, Just For The Record 1991, Butterfly 1992, Back To Broadway 1993, Barbra Streisand – The Concert 1994, The Concert – Highlights 1995, Mirror Has Two Faces 1996, Higher Ground 1997, A Love Like Ours 1999, Timeless 2000, Christmas Memories 2001, The Essential Barbra Streisand 2002, Duets 2002, The Movie Album 2003, Guilty Pleasures 2005; soundtracks include: Funny Girl 1968, Yentl 1983, Nuts 1987, The Prince of Tides 1991. *Films include:* Funny Girl (Acad. Award (Oscar) 1968) 1968, Hello Dolly 1969, On a Clear Day You Can See Forever 1969, The Owl and the Pussycat 1971, What's up Doc? 1972 Up the Sandbox 1973, The Way We Were 1973, For Pete's Sake 1974, Funny Lady 1975, A Star is Born 1977, Yentl 1983 (also dir and producer), Nuts 1987, Sing 1989, Prince of Tides 1990 (also dir, co-producer), The Mirror Has Two Faces 1996 (also dir), Meet the Fockers 2004. *Address:* The Endeavor Agency, 9601 Wilshire Boulevard, 3rd Floor, Beverly Hills, CA 90210 (office); Barwood Films, 330 West 58th Street, Suite 301, New York, NY 10019, USA (office). *Telephone:* (212) 762-7191 (office). *Website:* www.barbrastreisand.com.

STREISSLER, Erich W., DrIur; Austrian economist and academic; *Professor Emeritus of Economics, Econometrics and Economic History, University of Vienna;* b. 8 April 1933, Vienna; s. of Albert Streissler and Erna Leithe; m. Monika Ruppe 1961; two s. (one deceased) three d.; ed Vienna Law School, Univ. of Vienna, Oxford Univ., UK, Hamilton Coll., New York, USA; studied also in France and Spain; Prof. of Statistics and Econometrics, Univ. of Freiburg Br., Germany 1962–68, twice Dean of Law and Social Science Faculty 1965–67; Prof., Univ. of Vienna 1968, now Prof. Emer., Dean of Law and Social Science Faculty 1973–74; Vice-Pres. Austrian Inst. of Econ. Research 1990–; Distinguished Austrian Visiting Prof., Stanford Univ., USA 1983; Pres. Austrian Econ. Asscn 1988–94, Pres. Confed. of European Econ. Asscns 1990–91; mem. Bd of Control, Vienna Stock Exchange 1990–98; Treas. Int. Econ. Asscn 1992–99; mem. Austrian Acad. of Sciences; hon. mem. Hungarian Acad. of Sciences, Bavarian Acad. of Sciences; various science prizes. *Publications:* numerous articles in scientific journals on econ. growth, distribution, monetary matters, analysis of econ. systems and especially on the history of thought in econs. *Leisure interests:* hiking, history. *Address:* Faculty of Social Sciences and Economics, Vienna University, Hohenstaufeng 9, 1010 Vienna (office); 18 Khevenhuellerstrasse 15, 1180 Vienna, Austria (home). *Telephone:* 4277-374-25 (office); 44-05-770 (home). *Fax:* 4277-9374 (office). *E-mail:* Erich.Streissler@oeaw.ac.at (office).

STREITWIESER, Andrew, Jr, MA, PhD; American scientist and academic; *Professor Emeritus of Chemistry, University of California, Berkeley;* b. 23 June 1927, Buffalo, NY; s. of Andrew Streitwieser and Sophie Streitwieser; m. 1st Mary Ann Good 1950 (died 1965); m. 2nd Suzanne Cope 1967; one s. one d.; ed Stuyvesant High School and Columbia Univ.; Atomic Energy Comm. Postdoctoral Fellow, MIT 1951–52; Instructor in Chem., Univ. of Calif., Berkeley 1952–54, Asst Prof. 1954–59, Assoc. Prof. 1959–63, Prof. of Chem. 1963, Prof. Emer. 1993–, Prof. Grad. School 1995–98; consultant to industry 1957–; Guggenheim Fellow 1969; mem. NAS, American Acad. of Arts and Sciences, Bavarian Acad. of Sciences; ACS awards: Calif. Section 1964, Award in Petroleum Chem. 1967; Humboldt Sr Scientist Award (Bonn) 1976, Humboldt Award (Bonn) 1979, Norris Award in Physical Organic Chem. 1982, Cope Scholar Award 1989, Sr Scientist Mentor, Camille and Henry Dreyfus Foundation 2008, Roger Adams Award in Organic Chem. 2009. *Publications:* Molecular Orbital Theory for Organic Chemists 1961, Solvolytic Displacement Reactions 1962, Supplemental Tables of Molecular Orbital Calculations (with J. I. Brauman) Vols I and II 1965, Progress in Physical Organic Chemistry (co-ed.) Vols I–XI 1963–74, Dictionary of π-Electron Calculations (with C. A. Coulson) 1965, Orbital and Electron Density Diagrams (with P. H. Owens) 1973, Introduction to Organic Chemistry (with C. H. Heathcock) 1976, 1981, 1985, (also with E.L. Kosower) 1992, Solutions Manual and Study Guide for Introduction to Organic Chemistry (with C. H. Heathcock and P. A. Bartlett) 1985 (3rd edn), A Lifetime of Synergy with Theory and Experiment 1996. *Leisure interests:* music (especially opera), wine, photography. *Address:* Department of Chemistry, 325B Lewis, University of California, Berkeley, CA 94720-1960, USA (office). *Telephone:* (510) 642-2204 (home). *Fax:* (510) 642-6072 (home); (510) 643-6232. *Website:* chemistry.berkeley.edu (office).

STRENGER, Hermann-Josef; German business executive; *Honorary Chairman of the Supervisory Board, Bayer AG;* b. 26 Sept. 1928, Cologne; m. Gisela Buchholtz 1956; two s. two d.; joined Bayer AG as commercial trainee 1949; Chemical Sales Dept –1954; assigned to subsidiary, Brazil 1954–57, to Bayer subsidiary, AB Anilin Kemi, Sweden 1958–61; Head, Sales Dept for raw materials for surface coatings, Leverkusen 1961–65; Head, Polyurethanes Dept 1965–69, Dir 1969–70; Commercial Head, Polyurethanes Div. 1970–72; mem. Bd of Man. 1972–; Deputy Chair. Man. Bd Bayer AG 1978–84, Chair. and Chief Exec. 1984–92, Chair. Supervisory Bd, CEO 1992–, now Hon. Chair.; Chair. Supervisory Bd VEBA AG; Chair. Carl Duisberg Gesellschaft 1987–; Chair. Supervisory Bd Linde AG 1996; mem. Supervisory Bd Hapag-Lloyd AG 1983, Karstadt AG 1983. *Address:* c/o Bayer AG, 51368 Leverkusen, Germany.

STRETTON, James, BA, FFA; British business executive; *Chairman, The Wise Group;* b. 16 Dec. 1943; m. Isobel Christine Robertson 1968; two d.; ed Laxton Grammar School, Oundle, Worcester Coll., Oxford; Deputy Man. Dir Standard Life Assurance Co. 1988–94, Chief Exec. UK Operations 1994–2001; Dir Bank of England 1998–2003, Chair. Bank of England Pension Trustee Co. 2001–; Chair. The Wise Group 2002–; mem. Scottish Business Forum 1998–99, Court of Univ. of Edin. 1996–2002 (Rector's Asst 2003–), Franchise Bd of Lloyds 2003–, Disciplinary Bd of Actuarial Profession 2004–; Dir Edin. Int. Festival Ltd 1997–; Trustee Lamp of Lothian Collegiate Trust 2003–. *Address:* The Wise Group Head Office, 72 Charlotte Street, Glasgow, G1 5DW, Scotland (office); 15 Letham Mains, Haddington, EH41 4NW, Scotland (home). *Telephone:* (141) 303 3131 (office). *Fax:* (141) 303 0070 (office). *E-mail:* enquiries@thewisegroup.co.uk (office). *Website:* www.thewisegroup.co.uk.

STRICKLAND, John E., MA, GBS, JP; British business executive; *Chairman, Hong Kong Cyberport Management Co. Ltd;* b. 23 Oct. 1939; s. of William F. Strickland and Nora N. Strickland; m. Anthea Granville-Lewis 1963; three s.; ed Univ. of Cambridge; early positions with IBM in UK and Control Data in USA; Asst Gen. Man. TSV, Hongkong and Shanghai Banking Corpn 1980–82, Gen. Man. TSV 1983–88, Exec. Dir Services 1989–96, Chair. 1996–99; Dir HSBC Holdings PLC 1988, Marine Midland Bank 1991–96, Midland Bank PLC 1993–96; Chair. Hongkong Bank Malaysia Berhad 1996–98; Vice-Chair. Hang Seng Bank Ltd 1996; currently Chair. Hong Kong Cyberport Management Co. Ltd; Pres. Outward Bound Trust of Hong Kong; mem. Bd of Dirs Airport Authority Hong Kong, Hong Kong Exchanges and Clearing Ltd; mem. Council Outward Bound Trust of Hong Kong; Hon. Fellow, Univ. of Hong Kong 2000, Hong Kong Computer Soc., Hong Kong Inst. of Bankers, Hong Kong Man. Asscn; Dr hc (City Univ. of Hong Kong), (Hong Kong Polytechnic Univ.). *Leisure interests:* mountaineering, reading. *Address:* Hong Kong Cyberport Management Co. Ltd, Units 1102-1104, Cyberport 2, 100 Cyberport Road, Hong Kong Special Administrative Region, People's Republic of China (office). *Telephone:* 31663800 (office). *Fax:* 31663118 (office). *E-mail:* enquiry@cyberport.hk (office). *Website:* www.cyberport.hk (office).

STRICKLAND, Theodore (Ted), BA, MA, PhD; American psychologist, politician and state official; *Governor of Ohio;* b. 4 Aug. 1941, Lucasville, Ohio; m. Frances Strickland; ed Asbury Coll., Wilmore, Ky, Univ. of Kentucky, Asbury Theological Seminary; worked as clinical psychologist at maximum security prison at Lucasville, Ohio, as an admin. at Methodist children's home; fmr Prof. of Psychology, Shawnee State Univ., Portsmouth, Ohio; also served as United Methodist Minister; briefly Assoc. Pastor, Wesley United Methodist Church (now Cornerstone United Methodist Church), Portsmouth; cand. for 6th Congressional Dist of Ohio 1976, 1978, 1980; mem. US House of Reps for 6th Congressional Dist of Ohio 1993–96, 1997–2006; Gov. of Ohio 2007–; Democrat. *Address:* Office of the Governor, 30th Floor, 77 South High Street, Columbus, OH 43215-6117, USA (office). *Telephone:* (614) 466-3555 (office). *Website:* governor.ohio.gov (office); www.tedstrickland.com.

STRINGER, Sir Howard, Kt, MA; American/British electronics industry executive and broadcasting executive; *President, Chairman and CEO, Sony Corporation;* b. 19 Feb. 1942, Cardiff, Wales; s. of Harry Stringer and Marjorie Mary Pook; m. Dr Jennifer A. K. Patterson 1978; ed Merton Coll., Oxford; served with US Army in Viet Nam 1965–67; researcher and producer, CBS News 1967–76; Exec. Producer, CBS Reports 1976–81, CBS Evening News 1981–84; Exec. Vice-Pres. CBS News 1984–86, Pres. 1986–88; Pres. CBS Broadcast Group 1988–95; Chair. and CEO Tele-TV 1995–97; Pres. Sony Corpn of America 1997, Chair. and CEO 1998–, Chair. and CEO Sony Corpn 2005–, Pres. 2009–; Vice-Chair. American Film Inst. –1999, Chair. Bd of Trustees 1999–; mem. Bd Six Continents PLC; Gov. Motion Picture and TV Fund Foundation; Trustee Presbyterian Hosp., Museum of TV and Radio; Hon. Fellow, Merton Coll., Oxford 1999. *Address:* Sony Corporation, 1-7-1 Konan, Minato-ku, Tokyo 108-0075, Japan (office). *Telephone:* (3) 6748-2111 (office). *Fax:* (3) 6748-2244 (office). *E-mail:* info@sony.net (office). *Website:* www.sony.net (office).

STRITCH, Elaine; American actress and singer; b. 2 Feb. 1926, Detroit; d. of George J. Stritch and Mildred Stritch (née Tobe); m. John Bay 1973 (died 1982); ed Sacred Heart Convent, Detroit, Drama Workshop, New School for Social Research; Broadway debut as Pamela Brewster in Loco 1946; other performances include Three Indelicate Ladies 1947, Yes M'Lord 1949, Melba Snyder in revival of Pal Joey 1952, Bus Stop 1955, Mimi Paragon in Sail Away, New York 1961, London 1962, Martha in Who's Afraid of Virginia Woolf? 1962 and 1965, Joanne in Company, New York 1970, London 1971, Love Letters, London 1990, Elaine Stritch At Liberty (tour) 2002. *Films include:* The Scarlet Hour 1956, Three Violent People 1956, A Farewell to Arms 1957, The Perfect Furlough 1958, Who Killed Teddy Bear 1965, Pigeons 1971, September 1988, Cocoon: The Return, Cadillac Man 1990, Out to Sea 1997, Screwed 2000, Small Time Crooks 2000, Autumn in New York 2001, Monster-in-Law 2005, Romance & Cigarettes 2005. *Television includes:* My Sister Eileen 1962, Two's Company (British Series) 1975–76 and 1979, Stranded 1986, Life's a Bitch (series) 2003, Elaine Stritch: At Liberty (Emmy Award for Outstanding Individual Performance in a Variety or Music Programme 2004), Paradise 2004, 30 Rock 2007. *Publication:* Am I Blue? – Living With Diabetes and, Dammit, Having Fun 1984. *Address:* c/o The Blake Agency, 23441 Malibu Road, Malibu, CA 90265, USA. *E-mail:* blakeagency@aol.com.

STROHAL, Christian, DrIur; Austrian diplomatist and international organization executive; *Director, Office for Democratic Institutions and Human Rights, Organization for Security and Co-operation in Europe;* b. 1 May 1951, Vienna; m.; three c.; ed schools in Vienna, studies in law, econs and int. relations in Vienna, London and Geneva; voluntary mil. service; with Ministry for Foreign Affairs (MFA) since 1976: Attaché, Office of Legal Adviser and Dept for Int. Orgs, postings to London, Geneva, and as First Sec. and Deputy Head of Mission to Rabat 1981–85, mem. Austrian dels to Madrid and Vienna CSCE follow-up meetings, Head of Human Rights Office, Dept of the Legal Adviser, MFA, del. to UN, Council of Europe and CSCE meetings 1985–88, Minister and Deputy Perm. Rep. at Austrian Mission at UN and int. orgs, Geneva 1988–92, Amb. and Special Rep. for World Conf. on Human Rights 1992–93, Dir for Human Rights, Int. Humanitarian Law, and Minority and Gender Issues, MFA, Austrian Rep. to UN Comm. on Human Rights, del. to UN Gen. Ass., rep. to EU Working Group on Human Rights 1994–2000, Amb. to Luxembourg 2000–03, Amb. and Dir Office for Democratic Insts and Human Rights, OSCE 2003–; del. to numerous int. confs in framework of UN, Council of Europe and OSCE; Co-convener informal East–West human rights consultations, Geneva 1988–90; rep. to Finance and Council Cttees of CERN 1988–92; Chair. Western Human Rights Group, Geneva 1990–92; Vice-Chair. UN Comm. on Human Rights 1997–98; Chair. Council of Europe Working Group for 50th anniversary of Universal Declaration of Human Rights 1997–98, EU Working Group on Human Rights 1998; Moderator OSCE supplementary human dimension meetings on human rights and inhuman treatment or punishment as well as on trafficking in human beings 2000; Lecturer, Diplomatic and Admin. Acads, Vienna, and at EU Masters Programme for Democracy and Human Rights. *Publications:* several publs on int. human rights issues. *Address:* Office for Democratic Institutions and Human Rights, Aleje Ujazdowskie 19, 00-557 Warsaw, Poland (office). *Telephone:* (22) 520-06-00 (office). *Fax:* (22) 520-06-05 (office). *E-mail:* office@odihr.pl (office). *Website:* www.osce.org/odihr (office).

STRØM-ERICHSEN, Anne-Grete; Norwegian computer engineer and politician; *Minister of Defence;* b. 1949; m.; two c.; mem., Bergen City Council 1991–2005, mem. Exec. Bd 1991–2000, Deputy Mayor, City of Bergen 1998–99, Mayor 1999–2000, Chief Commr, City of Bergen 2000–03, Commr 2003–, Councillor and Chair., Standing Cttee on Environmental Affairs and Urban Devt, City of Bergen 2003–05; Deputy Leader, Labour Party in Bergen 1992, Leader, Hordaland Labour Party 1997–99, mem. Det norske Arbeiderparti (Norwegian Labour Party) Cen. Council 2001–; Minister of Defence 2005–. *Address:* Ministry of Defence, POB 8126 Dep., 0032 Oslo, Norway (office). *Telephone:* 23-09-80-00 (office). *Fax:* 23-09-60-51 (office). *E-mail:* postmottak@fd.dep.no (office). *Website:* odin.dep.no/fd (office); www.mod.no.

STRÖMHOLM, Stig Fredrik, LLD, DJur; Swedish university vice-chancellor (retd); b. 16 Sept. 1931, Boden; s. of Major Frederik Strömholm and Gerda Jansson; m. Gunilla M. Forslund 1958; one s. two d.; ed Univs of Uppsala, Cambridge and Munich; clerk, Southern Dist Court of Uppsala 1958–60; Jr Judge, Stockholm Court of Appeal 1961; Asst Prof. of Comparative Law, Uppsala Univ. 1966, Prof. of Jurisprudence 1969, Dean, Faculty of Law 1973–79, Deputy Vice-Chancellor 1978–89, Vice-Chancellor 1989–97; Pres. Royal Swedish Acad. of Letters, History and Antiquities 1985–93, Academia Europaea, London 1997–2002; mem. several Swedish and foreign acads; Orden pour le Mérite (FRG) and other decorations; Dr hc at several Swedish and foreign univs; several prizes. *Publications:* 25 vols of legal science including Le droit moral de l'auteur, three vols 1967–73, A Short History of Legal Thinking in the West 1985; some 20 vols of criticism and fiction. *Leisure interests:* reading, travelling. *Address:* Norra Rudbecksgatan 5, 752 36 Uppsala, Sweden (home). *Telephone:* (18) 515-045 (home); (18) 548-208 (home). *Fax:* (18) 548-208 (home).

STROMINGER, Jack L., MD; American physician, biochemist and academic; *Higgins Professor of Biochemistry, Department of Molecular and Cellular Biology, Harvard University;* b. 7 Aug. 1925, New York; m.; four c.; ed Harvard and Yale Univs; Intern, Barnes Hosp., St Louis 1948–49; Research Fellow, American Coll. of Physicians, Dept of Pharmacology, Washington Univ. School of Medicine, St Louis 1949–50, Research Asst 1950–51; Sr Asst Surgeon, US Public Health Service, Nat. Inst. of Arthritis and Metabolic Diseases, Bethesda 1951–54; leave of absence, Carlsberg Lab., Copenhagen, Denmark and Molteno Inst., Cambridge Univ., England, Commonwealth Fund Fellow 1955; Asst Prof. of Pharmacology, Dept of Pharmacology, Washington Univ. School of Medicine, Markel Scholar in Medical Science 1958–60, Prof., 1960–61, Forsyth Faculty Fellow 1960, Prof. of Pharmacology and Microbiology, Depts of Pharmacology and Microbiology 1961–64; Prof. of Pharmacology and Chemical Microbiology, Univ. of Wis. Medical School, Madison, Chair. Dept of Pharmacology, mem. Univ. Cttee on Molecular Biology 1964–68; Prof. of Biochem., Dept of Biochem. and Molecular Biology, Harvard Univ., Cambridge, Mass. 1968–83, Chair. Dept of Biochem. and Molecular Biology 1970–73, Higgins Prof. of Biochem. 1983–, Dir of Basic Sciences, Sidney Farber Cancer Center 1974–77; Head of Tumor Virology Div., Dana–Farber Cancer Inst., Boston 1977–; mem. Steering Cttee Biomedical Sciences Scientific Working Group, WHO; mem. NAS 1970–, American Acad. of Arts and Sciences, Nat. Inst. of Medicine 1975–, AAAS, American Soc. of Biological Chemists, of Microbiologists, of Pharmacology and Experimental Therapeutics, American Assn of Immunologists, ACS; Hon. DSc (Trinity Coll., Dublin) 1975; Guggenheim Fellowship 1974–75; John J. Abel Award in Pharmacology 1960, Paul-Lewis Labs. Award in Enzyme Chem. 1962, NAS Award in Microbiology in Honour of Selman Waxman 1968, Rose Payne Award, American Soc. for Histocompatibility and Immunogenetics 1986, Pasteur Medal 1990, Albert Lasker Award for Basic Medical Research 1995, Paul Ehrlich Prize 1996, Klemperer Award, New York Acad. of Medicine 1999, Japan Prize, Science and Tech. Foundation of Japan 1999. *Address:* Dana-Farber Cancer Institute, 44 Binney Street, Dana 1410, Boston, MA 02115; Department of Molecular and Cell Biology, Harvard University, Room 407, 7 Divinity Avenue, Cambridge, MA 02138, USA (office). *Telephone:* (617) 632-3083 (office). *Fax:* (617) 632-2662. *E-mail:* jlstrom@fas.harvard.edu (office). *Website:* www.mcb.harvard.edu/Faculty/Strominger.html (office); www.people.fas.harvard.edu/%7Ejlstrom (office).

STRONACH, Hon. Belinda C., PC; Canadian politician and business executive; b. 2 May 1966, Newmarket, Ont.; d. of Frank Stronach; two c.; ed York Univ.; joined family-owned Magna Int. Inc. (automotive components supplier) 1988, mem. Bd of Dirs 1988–, held various sr positions including Vice-Pres. 1995–98, Exec. Vice-Pres. 1998–2001, CEO 2001–02, Pres. and CEO 2002–04; resgnd to run for leadership of Conservative Party of Canada, which she lost, also resgnd as Chair. Bd of Dirs Decoma Int. Inc., Tesma Int. Inc.; Conservative MP for Newmarket-Aurora and trade critic 2004–05, joined Liberal Party as MP May 2005–; Minister of Human Resources and Skills Devt and Minister responsible for Democratic Renewal 2005–06; Critic for Competitivness and the New Economy 2006–07, Chair. Women's Caucus 2006–07; fmr mem. Bd of Dirs Intier Automotive Inc.; Founding mem. Canadian Automotive Partnership Council; Dir Yves Landry Technological Endowment Fund, US Chamber of Commerce 2003–; mem. Dean's Council, John F. Kennedy School of Govt, Harvard Univ., Dean's Advisory Council, Joseph L. Rotman School of Man., Univ. of Toronto; mem. Ont. Task Force on Productivity, Competitiveness and Econ. Progress; Hon. LLD (McMaster Univ.) 2003; ranked by Time Magazine as one of the world's 100 most influential people 2004, ranked 77th by Forbes magazine amongst 100 Most Powerful Women 2004. *Address:* c/o Karen Addison, 14996 Yonge Street, Aurora, ON L4G 1M6, Canada (office). *Telephone:* (905) 727-8874 (office). *Fax:* (905) 727-1308 (office). *E-mail:* belinda@belinda.ca (office). *Website:* www.belinda.ca (office); www.belindastronach.ca (office).

STRONACH, Frank, OC; Canadian automotive industry executive; *Chairman, Magna International Inc.;* b. (Franz Strohsack), 6 Sept. 1932, Weiz, Austria; one d. Belinda C. Stronach (q.v.); one s.; tool and die apprentice in Weiz, Austria; immigrated to Montreal, Canada 1954; various jobs including machinist, dish-washer and golf course asst, Kitchener and Toronto, Ont. 1954–57; Co-founder (with Tony Czapka) Multimatic Investments Ltd 1957, merged with Magna Electronics Co. Ltd 1969, renamed Magna International Inc. 1973, Chair. 1969–; cand. for Liberal Party, Fed. Elections 1988; Pnr, Stronach & Co. (consulting firm); Owner Magna Entertainment Corpn specializing in horse-racing entertainment and owns and operates several US racetracks; Hon. Prof. of Practical Business Man., Graz Univ. of Tech. 2004; Hon. PhD (Haifa Univ.), Hon. LLD (Univ. Coll. of Cape Breton), Hon. DComm (St Mary's Univ., Halifax); inducted into Canadian Business Hall of Fame 1996, Business Leader of the Year Award, Richard Ivey School of Business 1997, Entrepreneur of the Year Award, Univ. of Michigan 1998, Entrepreneur of the Year Lifetime Achievement Award, Ernst & Young 2000, Canadian Int. Exec. of the Year, Canadian Council for Int. Business 2001. *Leisure interest:* horse breeding. *Address:* Magna International Inc., 337 Magna Drive, Aurora, ON L4G 7K1, Canada (office). *Telephone:* (905) 726-2462 (office). *Fax:* (905) 726-7164 (office). *E-mail:* info@magna.com (office). *Website:* www.magna.com (office).

STRONG, David F., PhD, FRSC; Canadian geologist and university president; *President, University Canada West;* b. 26 Feb. 1944, Botwood, Newfoundland; m. Lynda Joan Marshall; two d.; ed Memorial Univ. of Newfoundland, Lehigh Univ., Pa, USA, Univ. of Edinburgh, Scotland; Asst Prof., Dept of Geology, Memorial Univ. of Newfoundland 1970–72, Assoc. Prof. 1972–74, Acting Head of Dept 1974–75, Prof., Dept of Earth Sciences 1974–90, Univ. Research Prof. 1985–90, Special Adviser to Pres. 1986–87, Vice-Pres. (Academic) 1987–90; Pres. and Vice-Chancellor Univ. of Vic. 1990–2000, Pres. Emer. 2000–; Chair. and CEO LearningWise Inc. 2002–; Pres. Univ. Canada West 2005–; Visiting Prof. Université de Montpellier, France 1976–77; W.F. James Prof. of Pure and Applied Sciences, St Francis Xavier Univ., Nova Scotia 1981–82; mem. Bd of Dirs Seabright Corpn Ltd 1986–; Assoc. Ed. Canadian Journal of Earth Sciences 1977–83, Transactions of the Royal Soc. of Edinburgh 1980–; Chair. Natural Sciences and Eng Research Council of Canada 1983–86, mem. 1982–88; mem. Research Council, Canadian Inst. of Advanced Research 1986–, Newfoundland and Labrador Advisory Council on Science and Tech.

1988–, Governing Council, Nat. Research Council of Canada 1999– (mem. Exec. Cttee 2002–); Fellow Geological Asscn of Canada, Geological Soc. of America, Soc. of Econ. Geologists; mem. Canadian Inst. of Mining and Metallurgy, Mineralogical Asscn of Canada; Univ. of Edin. Swiney Lecturer 1981; Hon. Fellow Geological Asscn of Canada; Hon. DSc (Memorial Univ., Newfoundland) 1990; Hon. LLD (St Francis Xavier Univ.) 1992; APICS Young Scientist Award (now the Frazer Medal) 1973, Foreign Exchange Fellowships to Japan 1976, to France 1976–77, Canadian Inst. of Mining and Metallurgy Distinguished Service Award 1979, Geological Asscn of Canada Past Pres.'s Medal 1980. *Publications:* about 200 scientific and technical papers. *Leisure interests:* reading, music, gardening. *Address:* Office of the President, University Canada West, 950 Kings Road, Victoria, BC V8T 1W6 (office); LearningWise Inc., Suite 135A, R-Hut, McKenzie Avenue, PO Box 3075 STN CSC, Victoria, BC V8W 3W2, Canada (office). *Telephone:* (250) 978-1800 (office); (250) 472-4331. *Fax:* (250) 978-1801 (office); (250) 721-6497. *E-mail:* david.strong@universitycanadawest.ca (office); dfstrong@learningwise.com (office). *Website:* www.universitycanadawest.ca (office); www.learningwise .com (office).

STRONG, James Alexander, LLB; Australian business executive; *Chairman, Woolworths Ltd;* b. 31 July 1944, Lismore, NSW; s. of R. J. Strong; m. Laile Strong 1968 (divorced 1993); two s.; ed Univ. of Queensland, Univ. of Sydney; industrial officer, Sugar Producers Asscn, Brisbane 1964–70; industrial officer, Northern Territory, Nabalco Pty Ltd, 1970–74, Chief Industrial Officer 1974–78, Personnel and Legal Man. 1978–80, Admin. Man. Northern Territory and Sydney 1980–81, Site Man. 1981–83; admitted to Bar NSW 1976; Exec. Dir Australian Mining Council 1983–86; CEO Australian Airlines 1986–89; Chair. Bd of Dirs SEAS Sapfor Ltd 1990–92; Dir RGC Ltd 1990–98; Nat. Chair. of Partners Corrs Chambers Westgarth 1991–92 (fmr Man. Partner, CEO Corrs Australia Solicitors); Dir Clarks Shoes Australia Ltd 1991–92; Man. Dir, CEO, DB Group Ltd., Auckland, New Zealand 1992–93; Man. Dir Qantas Airways Ltd 1993–2001 (Dir 1991–2001); Dir (non-exec.) Woolworths Ltd 2000–, Chair. 2001–; Chair. Insurance Australia Group (IAG) 2001–; Chair. Int. Air Transport Asscn 1999–; mem. Law School Advisory Bd, Flinders Univ. of S Australia, Advisory Council Tasman Econ. Research; Trustee Vic. State Opera Foundation. *Leisure interests:* drama, music, opera, reading, tennis. *Address:* Woolworths Limited, 540 George Street, 5th Floor, Sydney, NSW 2000, Australia (office). *Telephone:* (2) 9323-1555 (office). *Fax:* (2) 9323-1599 (office). *Website:* www.woolworthslimited.com.au (office).

STRONG, Liam (Gerald Porter), BA; British business executive; *Chairman, Virtual IT Ltd;* b. 6 Jan. 1945, Enniskillen, Northern Ireland; s. of Gerald James Strong and Geraldine Crozier Strong; m. Jacqueline Gray 1970; one s. one d.; ed Trinity Coll., Dublin; joined Procter & Gamble, Newcastle-upon-Tyne 1967–71; Household Man., Reckitt & Colman 1971, moved to Corp. Planning Unit, London 1973, Marketing and Sales Dir, then Gen. Man. Reckitt & Colman 1975–80, Vice-Pres. Sunset Designs, Calif., USA 1980–82, Head Int. Pharmaceuticals Div., Reckitt & Colman 1982–86, Pres. Durkee French, USA 1986–89; Dir of Marketing, British Airways 1989–90, Dir Marketing and Operations 1990–91; Chief Exec. Sears PLC 1991–97; CEO Worldcom International 1997–2001; Pres. CEO Teleglobe International Holdings Ltd. 2003–06; currently Pnr Cerberus European Capital Advisors LLP; Chair. Virtual IT Ltd, London; Dir Skystream Inc., USA 2000–; mem. Bd of Govs Ashridge (Bonar Law Memorial) Trust. *Leisure interests:* reading, shooting, opera. *Address:* Virtual IT Ltd, The Lime House, Quadrant Business Centre, Salusbury Road, London, NW6 6RJ, England (office). *Telephone:* (20) 7644-2800 (office). *Fax:* (20) 7644-2801 (office). *E-mail:* info@virtualit.biz (office). *Website:* www.virtualit.biz (office).

STRONG, Rt Hon. Maurice F., PC, CC, OM, LLD, FRS, FRSA, FRSC; Canadian environmentalist, international organization official and business executive; b. 29 April 1929, Oak Lake, Man.; s. of Frederick Milton Strong and Mary Fyfe Strong; m. 1st Pauline Olivette Williams 1950 (divorced 1980); two s. two d. one foster d.; m. 2nd Hanne Marstrand 1981; ed Oak Lake High School, Manitoba; served in UN Secr. 1947; Pres. or Dir of various Canadian and int. corpns 1954–66; also involved in leadership of various pvt. orgs in field of devt and int. affairs; Dir-Gen. External Aid Office of Canadian Govt 1966 (now Canadian Int. Devt Agency); Chair. Canadian Int. Devt Bd; Alt. Gov. IBRD, ADB, Caribbean Devt Bank; UN Under-Sec. Gen. with responsibility for environmental affairs 1970–72, Chief Exec. for 1972 Conf. on Human Environment, Stockholm, June 1972; Montague Burton Prof. of Int. Relations, Univ. of Edin. 1973; Exec. Dir UNEP 1973–75; Chair. Petro Canada 1976–78; Pres. Stronat Investments Ltd 1976–80; Chair. Bd of Govs Int. Devt Research Centre 1977–78; Chair. Strovest Holdings Inc., Procor Inc. 1978–79, AZL Resources Inc. 1978–83, Int. Energy Devt Corpn 1980–83, NS Round Table Soc. for Int. Devt, Canadian Devt Investment Corpn 1982–84, Supercritical Combustion Corpn, Int. Advisory Group, CH2M Hill Cos Ltd; Chair. and Dir Tech. Devt Corpn; Dir or mem. numerous business and conservation groups in Canada and internationally including Foundation Bd World Econ. Forum, Leadership for Environment and Devt, Zenon Environmental, Inc., The Humane Soc. of the US; UnderSec.-Gen., UN 1985–87, 1989; Pres. World Fed. UNA 1987, The Baca Corpn; Dir Better World Soc. 1988; Chair., Pres. American Water Devt Inc., Denver 1986–89; Sec.-Gen. UN 1992 Conf. on Environment and Devt; Chair. Ontario Hydro 1992–95, World Resources Inst.; Sr Adviser to Pres. of World Bank 1995–; Under-Sec.-Gen. and Exec. Co-ordinator for UN Reform 1997; Under-Sec.-Gen. and Sr Adviser to Sec.-Gen. of UN 1998–2005 (resgnd); Pres. Council UN Univ. for Peace, San José, Costa Rica 2001–; Chair. Earth Council Foundation; mem. Bd of Dirs UN Foundation, Int. Advisory Bd, Toyota Motor Corpn, Int. Advisory Bd, Center of Int. Devt at Harvard Univ., Int. Advisory Council, Liu Centre for the Study of Global Issues at Univ. of British Columbia, Lamont-Doherty Observatory Advisory Bd; Distinguished Fellow, Int. Inst. for Sustainable Devt; Fellow, Royal Architectural Inst. of Canada; Hon. Bd mem. David Suzuki Foundation; hon. degrees from 49 univs; Nat. Order of the Southern Cross (Brazil), Commander of the Order of the Golden Ark (Netherlands), Royal Order of the Polar Star (Sweden 1996, Henri Pittier Order of Venezuela 1997; Tyler Evironmental Prize 1974, Nat. Audubon Soc. Award 1975, Charles A. Lindbergh Award 1981, Pearson Peace Medal 1989, Alexander Onassis Delphi Prize 1993, Int. St Frances Prize for the Environment 1993, Jawaharlal Nehru Award for Int. Understanding 1994, Blue Planet Prize, Asahi Glass Foundation 1994, IKEA Environmental Award 1995, Millennium Award, The Princes' Award Foundation, Denmark 2000, Global Steering Wheel Int. Prize, Russia 2001, Global Environment Leadership Award 2002, Candlelight Award, Carriage House Center on Global Issues 2002, NAS Public Welfare Medal (first non-US citizen) 2004 and numerous other awards, prizes and decorations. *Publications:* The Great Building Bee (with Jacques Hébert) 1980, A Life for the Planet 1999, Where On Earth Are We Going?; various articles in journals. *Address:* S3 Holdings Inc., 150 Isabella Street, Suite 100, Ottawa, ON K15 1V7, Canada (office). *Telephone:* (613) 232-1222 (office). *Fax:* (613) 569-4667 (office). *E-mail:* info@mauricestrong.org (office). *Website:* www .mauricestrong.net (office).

STRONG, Sir Roy Colin, Kt, PhD, FSA, FRSL; English historian, writer and fmr museum director; b. 23 Aug. 1935, London; s. of George Edward Clement Strong and Mabel Ada Smart; m. Julia Trevelyan Oman 1971 (died 2003); ed Queen Mary Coll., Univ. of London and Warburg Inst.; Asst Keeper, Nat. Portrait Gallery, London 1959–67, Dir 1967–73; Dir, Victoria and Albert Museum, London 1974–87; Vice-Chair., South Bank Bd (now South Bank Centre) 1985–90; Dir, Oman Productions Ltd, Nordstern Fine Art Insurance 1988–2001; organizer of exhbns including The Elizabethan Image (Tate Gallery) 1969, The Destruction of the Country House (Victoria and Albert Museum) 1974, Artists of the Tudor Court (Victoria and Albert Museum) 1983; mem. Arts Council of GB 1983–87 (Chair., Arts Panel 1983–87), Council, RCA 1979–87; Patron, Pallant House, Chichester 1986–; Fellow, Queen Mary Coll., Univ. of London, Royal Soc. of Literature 1999; High Bailiff and Searcher of the Sanctuary of Westminster Abbey 2000; Pres., Garden History Soc. 2000–06; Hon. MA (Worcester) 2004; Hon. DLitt (Leeds) 1983, (Keele) 1984; Shakespeare Prize (FVS Foundation, Hamburg) 1980, President's Award Royal Photographic Soc. of Great Britain 2003. *Television:* Royal Gardens (series) 1992, The Diets Time Forgot 2008. *Publications:* Portraits of Queen Elizabeth I 1963, Leicester's Triumph (with J. A. Van Dorsten) 1964, Holbein and Henry VIII 1967, Tudor and Jacobean Portraits 1969, The English Icon: Elizabethan and Jacobean Portraiture 1969, Elizabeth R (with Julia Trevelyan Oman) 1971, Van Dyck: Charles I on Horseback 1972, Inigo Jones: The Theatre of the Stuart Court (with S. Orgel) 1972, Mary Queen of Scots (with Julia Trevelyan Oman) 1972, Splendour at Court: Renaissance Spectacle and The Theatre of Power 1973, An Early Victorian Album (with Colin Ford) 1974, Nicholas Hilliard 1975, The Cult of Elizabeth: Elizabethan Portraiture and Pageantry 1977, And When Did You Last See Your Father? The Victorian Painter and British History 1978, The Renaissance Garden in England 1979, Britannia Triumphans, Inigo Jones, Rubens and Whitehall Palace 1980, Holbein 1980, The English Miniature (with J. Murdoch, J. Murrell and P. Noon) 1981, The English Year (with Julia Trevelyan Oman) 1982, The English Renaissance Miniature 1983, Artists of the Tudor Court (with J. Murrell) 1983, Glyndebourne, A Celebration (contrib.) 1984, Art and Power, Renaissance Festivals 1450–1650 1984, Strong Points 1985, Henry Prince of Wales and England's Lost Renaissance 1986, C.V. Wedgwood Festschrift (contrib.) 1986, Creating Small Gardens 1986, Gloriana, Portraits of Queen Elizabeth I 1987, The Small Garden Designers Handbook 1987, Cecil Beaton: the Royal Portraits 1988, Creating Small Formal Gardens 1989, Lost Treasures of Britain 1990, A Celebration of Gardens 1991, Small Period Gardens 1992, Royal Gardens 1992, Versace Theatre 1992, William Larkin 1994, A Country Life 1994, Successful Small Gardens 1994, The Tudor and Stuart Monarchy 1995, The Story of Britain 1996, The English Arcadia 1996, Country Life 1897–1997 1997, The Roy Strong Diaries 1967–1987 1997, On Happiness 1997, The Tudor and Stuart Monarchy 1998, The Spirit of Britain 1999, Garden Party 2000, The Artist and the Garden 2000, Ornament in the Small Garden 2001, Feast – A History of Grand Eating 2002, The Laskett – The Story of a Garden 2003, Coronation: A History of Kingship and the British Monarchy 2005, Passions Past and Present 2005, A Little History of the English Country Church 2007; numerous articles in newspapers and periodicals. *Leisure interests:* gardening, cooking, country life. *Address:* The Laskett, Much Birch, Hereford, HR2 8HZ, England.

STROSSEN, Nadine, BA, JD; American lawyer and academic; *President, American Civil Liberties Union;* b. 18 Aug. 1950, Jersey City; d. of Woodrow John Strossen and Sylvia Strossen; m. Eli Michael Noam 1980; ed Harvard Law School, Radcliffe Coll.; assoc. attorney Sullivan and Cromwell 1978–83; pnr Harvis and Zeichner 1983–84; mem. Nat. Bd Dirs American Civil Liberties Union 1983–, Pres. 1991–, mem. advisory Cttee on Reproductive Freedom Project 1983–, Nat. Exec. Cttee 1985–, Nat. Gen. Council 1986–91; Asst Prof. of Clinical Law Univ. of New York 1989–; Adjunct Prof. Grad. School of Business Univ. of Columbia 1990–; mem. Exec. Cttee Human Rights Watch 1989–91; mem. Bd Dirs Coalition to Free Soviet Jewry 1984–; mem. Asia Watch 1987–, Vice-Chair. 1989–91; mem. Nat. Coalition Against Censorship 1988, Middle East Watch 1989–91, The Fund for Free Expression 1990–; mem. Steering Cttee New York Legal Council for Soviet Jewry 1987–. *Publications include:* Regulating Campus Hate Speech – A Modest Proposal? 1990, Recent US and International Judicial Protection of Individuals Rights: A Comparative Legal Process Analysis and Proposed Synthesis 1990, In Defense of Pornography: Free Speech and the Fight for Women's Rights 1995, numerous articles in professional journals. *Leisure interests:* singing, skiing, travel. *Address:* American Civil Liberties Union, 125 Broad Street, 18th Floor,

New York, NY 10004 (office); New York Law School, 57 Worth Street, New York, NY 10013-2960 (office); 450 Riverside Drive, #51, New York, NY 10027, USA (home). *Telephone:* (212) 431-2375 (office). *Fax:* (212) 431-1992 (office). *E-mail:* nstrossen@aclu.org (office). *Website:* www.aclu.org (office).

STROTHOTTE, Willy; German mining industry executive; *Chairman, Xstrata PLC;* b. 23 April 1944; apprentice Frank & Schulte 1961–64; joined C Tennant 1966; various positions trading in metals and minerals in Germany, Belgium and USA 1961–78; joined Glencore International 1978, becoming Head of Metals and Minerals 1984–93, CEO 1993–94, CEO and Chair. 1994–2001, currently Chair. Glencore International AG, also Chair. Xstrata AG 1994–, Xstrata PLC 2002–; mem. Bd of Dirs Century Aluminium Corpn, Minara Resources Ltd 2000–, KKR Financial Holdings LLC 2007–. *Address:* Xstrata PLC, Bahnhofstrasse 2, PO Box 102, 6301 Zug, Switzerland (office). *Telephone:* (41) 726-60-70 (office). *Fax:* (41) 726-60-89 (office). *E-mail:* info@xstrata.com (office). *Website:* www.xstrata.com (office).

STROYEV, Yegor Semyonovich, DEcons; Russian politician; *Governor, Orel Oblast;* b. 25 Feb. 1937, Stroyevo, Khotynetsky, Orel Region; s. of Semyon Fedorovich Stroyev and Anna Ivanovna Stroyeva; m. Nina Semvyovna Stroyeva; one d.; ed I.V. Michurin Horticultural Inst., Acad. of Social Sciences, Moscow; mem CPSU 1958–91; worked at Progress collective farm, Khotynetsky Dist; Sec. Khotynetsky CPSU Dist Cttee, Chair. Exec. Cttee Pokrovsky Dist Soviet of People's Deputies, First Sec. Pokrovsky CPSU Dist Cttee, Sec., First Sec. Orel CPSU Regional Cttee 1985–89; Sec. CPSU Cen. Cttee 1989–91; mem. Politburo of CPSU Cen. Cttee 1990–91; resgnd after Aug. coup d'état; fmr People's Deputy of USSR; mem. Council of Fed. Ass. of Russian Fed. 1995–2001, Chair. 1996–2001, Hon. Chair. 2001–; Chair. Council of Inter parl. Ass. of CIS Mem. States 1996–; Head of Admin. Orel Region 1993–; Dir All-Russia Scientific Research Inst. of Fruit Crop Breeding 1991–93; Academician Russian Acad. of Agricultural Sciences; Hon. mem. Russian Acad. of Literature; Order of the Oct. Revolution 1973; Order of the Red Banner of Labour 1987; Order of St Prince Vladimir 1997 and other awards. *Publications:* Methodology and Practices of Agrarian Restructuring 1994, To Give a Chance to the Peasant 1995, Land Issue 1999, Self-determination of Russia and Global Modernization 2001, In A Rapid River 2003, Agricultural Complex of Russian Chernozem Land 2003. *Leisure interest:* recreation in the countryside. *Address:* Governor's Office, Lenina pl. 1, 30200 Orel, Russia. *Telephone:* (862) 41-63-13. *Fax:* (862) 41-25-30 (office). *Website:* www.adm.orel.ru (office).

STRUBE, Jürgen F., DJur; German business executive; *Chairman of the Supervisory Board, BASF SE;* b. 1939, Bochum; m.; one d.; ed Univs of Freiburg, Geneva, Switzerland and Munich; joined BASF 1969, several posts, then with BASF Brasileira SA, São Paulo 1974–85, Head, Glasurit do Brasil Ltda 1980–, Head, Brazil Regional Div. 1982–, in charge of Information Systems and Fibres Operating Divs. and Regional Divs in N America 1985–88, of Foams, Polyolefins and PVC and Information Systems Operating Divs and Brazil and Latin American Regional Divs 1988–90, mem. Bd Exec. Dirs BASF AG, Ludwigshafen, Germany 1985–, Chair. 1990–2003, Chair. Supervisory Bd BASF AG 2003– (renamed BASF SE Jan. 2008); Chair. Supervisory Bd Fuchs Petrolub AG; mem. Supervisory Bd Allianz Deutschland AG, Bayerische Motoren Werke AG, Bertelsmann AG (Deputy Chair. Supervisory Bd), Commerzbank AG –2008, Hapag-Lloyd AG, Linde AG –2008; Pres. Asscn of Chemical Industry (VCI) 1996–97, UNICE 2003–; mem. Int. Advisory Cttee New York Stock Exchange Euronext, Inc.; mem. Econ. Advisory Bd RWE AG; Hon. Senator, Deutsche Hochschule für Verwaltungswissenschaften, Speyer 1997, Hon. Prof. 1999; Hon. Senator, Univ. of Mannheim 1998, Univ. of Heidelberg 2003; Order of Merit, 1st Class of FRG 2000; Dr hc (Univ. of Maryland) 1995, (European Business School, Oestrich-Winkel) 2003; Centenary Medal, Soc. of Chemical Industry 1999, John J. McCloy Award, American Council on Germany 2001, Rhine-Neckar Regional Award 2003, Medal of Merit (Rhineland-Palatinate) 2003, Int. Palladium Medal Award, Soc. de Chimie Industrielle (American Section) 2005. *Address:* BASF SE, Carl-Bosch-Str. 38, 67056 Ludwigshafen, Germany (office). *Telephone:* (621) 60-0 (office); (621) 60-99938 (office). *Fax:* (621) 60-42525 (office); (621) 60-20129 (office). *E-mail:* presse.kontakt@basf.com (office). *Website:* www.basf.com (office).

STRUCK, Peter, DJur; German lawyer and politician; b. 24 Jan. 1943, Göttingen; m.; three c.; ed Univs of Göttingen and Hamburg; adviser to govt, Hamburg 1971; personal adviser to Pres. of Univ. of Hamburg 1971–72; elected Town Councillor and Deputy Town Mayor of Uelzen 1973; admitted to Bar, 1983; worked in Dist Court of Uelzen and Regional Court of Lueneburg; mem. SDP 1964–, mem. Bundestag (representing Lower Saxony) 1980–, Chair. of Parl. Group 1998–; Minister of Defence 2002–05; mem. ÖTV (Public Workers' Union); mem. Bd Hilden AHG Gen. Hosp., Rockwool Beteiligungs GmbH, Gladbeck. *Address:* Bundestag, Platz der Republik 1, 11011 Berlin; c/o Sozialdemokratische Partei Deutschlands (SPD), Wilhelmstr. 141, 10963 Berlin, Germany (office). *E-mail:* peter.struck@bundestag.de (office). *Website:* www.bundestag.de/~Peter.Struck (office).

STRUGATSKY, Boris Natanovich, (S. Viticky); Russian writer and astronomer; b. 15 April 1933, Leningrad; s. of Natan Strugatsky; m.; one s.; ed Leningrad State Univ.; astronomer's post in Pulkovo Observatory, Leningrad 1955–65; started publishing science-fiction (with his brother) 1957; Victor Hugo Prize (France). *Publications:* with A. N. Strugatsky over 25 novels including: The Land of Purple Clouds 1959, The Return 1962, Escape Attempt 1962, The Far-Away Rainbow 1964, Rapacious Things of the Century 1965, The Inhabited Island 1971, The Ugly Swans 1972, Stories 1975, The Forest 1982, The Lame Fortune 1986, One Billion Years Before the End of the World 1988, Collected Works 1991, Burdened by Evil 1988, The Search of Destination 1994, Collected Works 2001. *Address:* 196070 St Petersburg,

Pobeda Str. 4, Apt 186, Russia. *Telephone:* (812) 291-37-55. *E-mail:* bns@tf.ru (home).

STRUNK, Klaus Albert, DPhil; German professor of linguistics; b. 22 Aug. 1930, Düsseldorf; s. of Albert Strunk and Hedwig Schäfer; m. Marion Kriegeskotte 1957; two s. one d.; ed Univs of Cologne and Bonn; Prof., Univ. of Saarland and Dir, Inst. of Indo-European Linguistics and Indo-Iranian Philology 1967–77; Prof., Univ. of Munich and Dir, Inst. of Gen. and Indo-European Linguistics 1977–98, Dean Dept I (Linguistics and Literature) 1985–87; Ed., Kratylos review 1969–83; Co-Ed., Glotta review 1974–2000, series Studies in Indo-European Language and Culture (Berlin and New York) 1985–, Muenchener Studien zur Sprachwissenschaft review 1992–2002; Pres., Indogermanische Gesellschaft 1983–92; mem. Bayerische Akademie der Wissenschaften 1979–, Sec., Philosophy and History section 1989–2004; mem. Société de Linguistique de Paris 1978–, Philological Soc., London 1993–. *Publications:* Die sogenannten Aeolismen der homerischen Sprache 1957, Nasalpraesentien und Aoriste. Ein Beitrag zur Morphologie des Verbums im Indo-Iranischen und Griechischen 1967, Probleme der lateinischen Grammatik (Ed.) 1973, Lachmanns Regel für das Lateinische 1976, Generative Versuche zu einigen Problemen in der historischen Grammatik indogermanischer Sprachen 1976, Typische Merkmale von Fragesätzen und die altindische Pluti 1983, Zum Postulat 'vorhersagbaren' Sprachwandels bei unregelmässigen oder komplexen Flexionsparadigmen 1991, Kleine Schriften 2005; numerous articles and reviews on Greek, Latin, Indo-Iranian and Indo-European linguistics. *Leisure interests:* reading books on history, literature, classical music, sport. *Address:* Ringbergstrasse 11, 83707 Bad Wiessee, Germany. *Telephone:* (8022) 82198.

STRUZIK, Adam; Polish physician and politician; *Marshal of Mazovian Voivodeship;* b. 1 Jan. 1957, Kutno; m.; one s. one d.; ed Medical Acad., Łódź; Councillor, Municipal Council of Duninów 1986–90, City and Commune of Gąbin 1990–; Dir Voivodeships Jt Hosp. in Płock 1990–97; Marshal (Speaker) of Nat. Regional Council of Territorial Self-Govt 1994–98; Councillor, Regional Council of Mazovian Voivodeship 1998–, Marshal of Mazovian Voivodeship 2001–; mem. Solidarity Trade Union 1980–; mem. Polish Peasant Party (PSL) 1989–, Exec. Council; Senator (Płock Voivodship) 1991–2001, Marshal of Senate 1993–97; Pres. Council of Mazovian Sickness Foundation 1999–2001, Council for Nat. Asscn of Sickness Foundations 1999–2001; Co-founder Aid Foundation for Voivodeship Hosp., Płock; mem. Programming Bd TVP SA; mem. Polish Hunting Asscn, Płock Scientific Soc., Polish Haematology Soc. *Leisure interests:* politics, literature, tourism. *Address:* Urząd Marszałkowski Województwa Mazowieckiego, ul. Brechta 3, 03-472 Warsaw, Poland (office). *Telephone:* (22) 5979104 (office). *Fax:* (22) 5979275 (office). *E-mail:* a.struzik@mazovia.pl (office). *Website:* www.mazovia.pl (office).

STRZEMBOSZ, Adam Justyn, DrIur; Polish lawyer, judge and government official; b. 11 Nov. 1930, Warsaw; s. of Adam Strzembosz and Zofia Strzembosz (née Gadomska); m. Zofia Strzembosz 1957; two s. two d.; ed Jagiellonian Univ., Cracow, Warsaw Univ.; legal adviser, Ministry of Labour and Social Security 1953–56; judge, Co. Court 1956–68, Prov. Court 1968–81; researcher, Research Inst. of Judicial Law 1974–81; Head of Solidarity Group, Ministry of Justice 1980–81; Asst Prof. and Head of Dept of Penal Law, Catholic Univ. of Lublin 1982–89, Prof. 1986–; Vice-Minister of Justice 1989–90; judge and First Pres. Supreme Court 1990–98 (retd); Head of Tribunal of State 1990–98; mem. Bd Solidarity Mazowsze Region 1980; Del. to 1st Solidarity Conf., Jt Leader Appeal Comm., Gdańsk Oliwa 1981; Co-Founder Soc. for Promotion and Propagation of Sciences; mem. Catholic Univ. of Lublin Scientific Asscn, Penal Law Asscn. *Publications:* six books and more than over 200 treatises and articles. *Leisure interests:* cycling, literature. *Address:* ul. Stanisława Augusta 73 m.20, 03-846 Warsaw, Poland (home).

STUART, Sir Kenneth Lamonte, Kt, MD, FRCP, FACP, FFPM, FFPHM; Barbadian physician; b. 16 June 1920, Barbados; s. of Egbert Stuart and Louise Stuart; m. Barbara Cecille Ashby 1958; one s. two d.; ed Harrison Coll., Barbados, Queen's Univ., Belfast, Northern Ireland; Rockefeller Foundation Fellow in Cardiology, Mass. Gen. Hosp., Boston, USA 1956–57; Wellcome Research Fellow, Harvard Univ. 1960–61; Prof. of Medicine, Univ. of West Indies 1966–76, Dean of Medical School 1969–73, Head of Dept of Medicine 1972–76; Commonwealth Medical Adviser 1976–85; Consultant Adviser, Wellcome Tropical Inst. 1985–95; Gresham Prof. of Physics, Gresham Coll., London 1988–94; Trustee Int. Medical Educ. Trust 2000 1998–; mem. Bd of Govs Liverpool School of Tropical Medicine 1980–96, Int. Research Centre of Canada 1985–90; Chair. Court of Govs, London School of Hygiene and Tropical Medicine 1983–86; Chair. Commonwealth Caribbean Medical Research Council 1988; Chair. Errol Barrow Memorial Trust 1989–99; mem. of Council and Trustee The London Lighthouse 1994–2001; mem. of Council Royal Overseas League 1994–2000, United Medical and Dental Schools of Guy's and St Thomas's Hosps 1994–98, Guy's, King's and St Thomas's Hosp. Medical and Dental School 1998, King's Coll. London 1998–2002; Trustee Schools Partnership Worldwide 1990–; Hon. Medical and Scientific Adviser, Barbados High Comm., London 1991–, Freeman of City of London 1992; Hon. DSc (Queen's, Belfast) 1986. *Leisure interests:* tennis, literature. *Address:* 3 The Garth, Cobham, Surrey, KT11 2DZ, England (home). *Telephone:* (1932) 863826 (home). *Fax:* (1932) 860427 (office). *E-mail:* kenstuart@lineone.net (home).

STUBB, Cai-Göran Alexander, BA, MA, PhD; Finnish journalist, politician and academic; *Minister for Foreign Affairs;* b. 1 April 1968, Helsinki; m. Suzanne Innes-Stubb; one s. one d.; ed Mainland High School, Daytona Beach, Fla, USA, Gymnasiet Lärkan, Helsinki, golf scholarship to Furman Univ., S Carolina, USA, Univ. of the Sorbonne, Paris, Coll. of Europe, Belgium, London School of Econs, UK; mil. service; researcher, Ministry of Foreign Affairs 1995–97, Finnish Acad. 1997–99; columnist for various newspapers, including

APU, Ilta-Sanomat, Blue Wings, various papers in Suomen Lehtiyhtymä group, Nykypäivä and Hufvudstadsbladet 1997–; special researcher, Finland's representation to EU, Brussels 1999–2001, mem. Finnish Govt's del. to intergovernmental negotiations for Treaty of Nice; Prof., Coll. of Europe, Brussels 2000–; adviser to Pres. of EC 2001–03, mem. Comm. Task Force on European Convention; mem. Finland's representation to EU as a special expert and to intergovernmental negotiations for European Constitution 2003–04; mem. Nat. Coalition; mem. European Parl. (European People's Party) 2004–08, Vice-Pres. Cttee on Internal Market and Consumer Protection, mem. Cttee on Budgetary Control, substitute mem. Cttee on Constitutional Affairs, substitute mem. Del. to EU-Turkey Jt Parl. Cttee; Minister for Foreign Affairs 2008–. *Publications:* nine books about the EU; several articles in academic journals. *Address:* Ministry of Foreign Affairs, Merikasarmi, Laivastokatu 22, PO Box 176, 00161 Helsinki, Finland (office). *Telephone:* (9) 16005 (office). *Fax:* (9) 629840 (office). *E-mail:* kirjaamo.um@formin.fi (office). *Website:* formin.finland.fi (office); www.alexstubb.com.

STUBBS, Imogen Mary, MA; British actress; b. 20 Feb. 1961, Rothbury; d. of late Robin Stubbs and Heather McCracken; m. Trevor Nunn (q.v.) 1994; one s. one d.; ed St Paul's Girls School, London, Exeter Coll. Oxford and Royal Acad. of Dramatic Art; Gold Medal, Chicago Film Festival. *Plays as actress:* appeared with RSC in The Rover, Two Noble Kinsmen, Richard II 1987–88, Othello 1991, Heartbreak House 1992, St Joan 1994, Twelfth Night 1996, Blast from the Past 1998, Betrayal 1998, The Relapse 2001, Three Sisters 2002, Fallujah 2007. *Play as author:* We Happy Few (Gielgud Theatre, London) 2004. *Television appearances include:* The Browning Version 1985, The Rainbow 1988, Fellow Traveller 1989, Pasternak 1990, Othello 1990, Relatively Speaking 1990, Sandra, c'est la vie 1993, Anna Lee (series) 1993, Mothertime 1997, Blind Ambition 2000, Big Kids (series) 2000. *Films:* Privileged 1982, Nanou 1986, A Summer Story 1988, Deadline 1988, Erik the Viking 1989, True Colors 1991, The Wanderer (voice) 1991, A Pin for the Butterfly 1994, Jack and Sarah 1995, Sense and Sensibility 1995, Twelfth Night: Or What You Will 1996, Collusion 2003, Dead Cool 2004. *Leisure interests:* writing, skiing, collecting junk. *Address:* c/o Nick Hern Books Ltd, The Glasshouse, 49a Goldhawk Road, London, W12 8QP, England.

STUCKY, Steven, BM, MFA, DMA; American composer, conductor and academic; b. 7 Nov. 1949, Hutchinson, Kan.; s. of Victor Eugene Stucky and Louise Doris Trautwein; two c.; ed Baylor Univ., Cornell Univ. with Karel Husa, studied conducting with Daniel Sternberg; mem. of faculty, Cornell Univ. 1980–, Chair. Music Dept 1992–97, currently Given Foundation Prof. of Composition; Composer-in-Residence Los Angeles Philharmonic Orchestra, later consulting composer for new music 1988–2009; Composer-in-Residence Aspen Music Festival and School 2001, Dir Aspen Contemporary Ensemble 2005; Visiting Prof. of Composition, Eastman School of Music 2001–02; Ernest Bloch Visiting Prof. of Music, Univ. of Calif., Berkeley 2003; Co-dir Seal Bay Festival of American Chamber Music, Maine; mem. Bd of Dirs Koussevitzky Foundation, Bogliasco Foundation; Barr Inst. Composer Laureate, Univ. of Missouri at Kansas City 2007; Trustee American Acad. in Rome; Guggenheim Foundation Fellowship 1986; Bogliasco Fellowship 1997; American Acad. of Arts and Letters Goddard Lieberson Fellowship 2002; mem. American Acad. of Arts and Sciences 2006–, American Acad. of Arts and Letters 2007–; Pulitzer Prize for Music 2005. *Compositions include:* Notturno 1981, Two Holy Sonnets of Donne for mezzo, oboe and piano 1982, Sappho Fragments for mezzo and ensemble 1982, Voyages for voice and wind orchestra 1984, Double Concerto for violin, oboe and chamber orchestra 1985, Concerto for Orchestra 1987, Threnos for wind ensemble 1988, Son et Lumière for orchestra 1988, Angelus for orchestra 1989, Serenade for wind quintet 1989, Impromptus for orchestra 1991, Four Poems of A. R. Ammons for baritone and ensemble 1992, Funeral Music for Queen Mary (arrangement of Purcell) 1992, Ancora for orchestra 1994, Fanfares and Arias for wind ensemble 1994, Concerto for two flutes and orchestra 1994, Pinturas de Tamayo for orchestra 1995, Cradle Songs 1997, Concerto Mediterraneo 1998, Ad Parnassum 1998, American Muse 1999, Nell'ombra, nella luce 2000, Partita-Pastorale 2000, Etudes (concerto for recorder and chamber orchestra) 2000, Skylarks 2001, Noctuelles (orchestration of Ravel) 2001, Concerto for percussion and wind orchestra 2001, Album Leaves 2002, Whispers 2002, Colburn Variations 2002, Spirit Voices for percussion and orchestra 2002–03, Second Concerto for Orchestra (Pulitzer Prize for Music 2005) 2003, Jeu de timbres 2003, Sonate en forme de préludes 2003–04, Piano Quartet 2004–05, New Motets 2005, Hue and Cry 2006, Dialoghi 2006, Radical Light 2006–7, August 4, 1964 2007–8, Rhapsodies 2008. *Publications include:* Lutoslawski and his Music (ASCAP-Deems Taylor Prize 1982) 1981. *Address:* 21C Media Group, 162 West 56th Street., Suite 506, New York, NY 10019, USA (office). *Telephone:* (212) 245-2110 (office). *E-mail:* ses6@cornell.edu. *Website:* www.stevenstucky.com.

STUDER, Cheryl; American singer (soprano); b. 24 Oct. 1955, Midland, Mich.; m. 2nd Ewald Schwarz; two d. (one by previous m.); ed Interlochen Arts Acad., Mich., Oberlin Coll. and Univ. of Tennessee; studied singing with Gwendolyn Pike, at Berkshire Music Centre, at Tanglewood with Phyllis Curtin and at Hochschule für Musik, Vienna with Hans Hotter; engaged for concert series with Boston Symphony Orchestra by Seiji Ozawa 1979; opera debut as the First Lady in The Magic Flute, Munich 1980–82; with Darmstadt State Theatre, Germany 1982–84, Deutsche Oper, Berlin 1984–86; US debut as Micaela in Carmen, Lyric Opera of Chicago 1984; debut at Bayreuth 1985, Royal Opera House, Covent Garden 1987, Metropolitan Opera, New York 1988; sings wide variety of roles, especially Wagner, Verdi, Mozart and Strauss; Prof., Hochschule für Musik Würzburg 2003–; Hon. Prof., Beijing Cen. Conservatory; Int. Music Award 1993, Vocalist of the Year (USA) 1994. *Address:* Encompass Arts, LLC, 119 West 72nd Street, New York, NY 10023, USA (office). *Telephone:* (212) 439-8055 (office). *E-mail:* kathy@encompassarts.com (office). *Website:* www.encompassarts.com/soprano/cheryl_studer (office).

STUHR, Jerzy; Polish actor and film director; b. 18 April 1947, Kraków; s. of Tadeusz Stuhr and Maria Stuhr; m. 1971; one s. one d.; ed Jagiellonian Univ. and Ludwik Solski State School of Drama, Kraków; main theatrical roles at Stary Theatre, Kraków with Andrzej Wajda (q.v.), notably Hamlet 1982, Dostoevsky's The Possessed and Crime and Punishment 1984, P. Süskind's Double Bass (actor and dir) 1985–, Le Bourgeois Gentilhomme 1993, Harold Pinter's Ashes to Ashes 1996, Merry Wives of Windsor (dir) 1998; dir, actor and teacher, Italy 1980–; Rector, Ludwik Solski State School of Drama, Kraków 1990–97, 2002–, lecturer 1998–; lecturer Faculty of Radio and TV, Silesia Univ. 1998–; mem. European Film Acad. 1998–; Best Actor, Chicago Festival 1978, Premio della Critica Teatrale 1982, Premio Fipirescii for Love Stories, Venice Film Festival 1997, Grand Prix for Love Stories, Polish Film Festival, Gdynia 1997, Nastro d'Argento 1997, Big Anima Special Jury Prize, Karlovy Vary 2000, Emerging Master, Int. Film Festival, Seattle 2001. *Film roles include:* Zycie za zycie (Life for Life) 1991, Uprowadzenie Agaty (Hijacking of Agata) 1993, Decalogue X, Three Colours – White 1994, Spis cudzoloznic (List of Lovers) 1995, Matka swojej matki 1996, Historie milosne (Love Stories) 1997, Kiler 1997, Kilerów 2-óch 1999, Tydzien z zycia mezczyzny (A Week in the Life of a Man) 1999, Down House 2000, La Vita altrui 2000, Duze zwierze (Big Animal) 2000, Weiser 2001, Show 2003, Pogoda na jutro (Tomorrow's Weather) 2003, Persona non grata 2005, Doskonale popoludnie 2005, Il Caimano 2006, The Making of Parts 2006, Korowód 2007. *Films directed include:* Spis cudzoloznic (List of Lovers) (also screenwriter) 1995, Historie milosne (Love Stories) (also screenwriter) 1997, Tydzien z zycia mezczyzny (A Week in the Life of a Man) (also screenwriter) 1999, Duze zwierze (Big Animal) 2000, Pogoda na jutro (Tomorrow's Weather) (also screenwriter) 2003, Korowód (also screenwriter) 2007. *Publications:* Heart Illness, or My Life in Art (autobiog.) 1992, Big Animal 2000, True Pretender 2000. *Leisure interests:* literature, sport. *Address:* Ludwik Solski State School of Drama, ul. Straszewskiego 22, 31-109 Kraków, Poland (office). *Telephone:* (12) 4228196 (office). *Fax:* (12) 4220209 (office). *E-mail:* jerzy_stuhr@poczta.onet.pl; sekr@pwst.krakow.pl (office). *Website:* www.stuhr.onet.pl (office).

STUIVER, Minze, PhD; American geologist and academic; *Professor Emeritus, Department of Earth and Space Sciences, University of Washington;* b. 25 Oct. 1929, Vlagtwedde, Netherlands; s. of Albert Stuiver and Griet Welles; m. Annie Hubbelmeyer 1956; two d.; ed Univ. of Groningen; Research Assoc., Yale Univ. 1959–62; Sr Research Assoc. and Dir Radiocarbon Lab. 1962–69; Prof. of Geological Sciences and Zoology, Univ. of Washington, Seattle 1969–82, Prof. of Geological Sciences and Quaternary Sciences 1982–98, now Prof. Emer., Dir Quaternary Isotope Lab. 1972–98; Ed. Radiocarbon 1976–88; mem. Geological Soc. of America, American Quaternary Asscn; Alexander von Humboldt Sr Scientist, FRG 1983; Pomerance Award, Archaeological Inst. of America 1993, Distinguished Career Award in Quaternary Science, AMQUA 2000, Penrose Medal, Geological Soc. of America 2005. *Achievements include:* second-most-cited scientist in the field of Geosciences in 1990s, Incities. *Address:* University of Washington, Department of Earth and Space Sciences, 035 QRC/ATG, Seattle, WA 98195-1310, USA (office). *E-mail:* minze@u.washington.edu (office). *Website:* depts.washington.edu/qil (office).

STUMP, Nicholas (Nick) Withrington, BAppSc, MAppSc, F AusIMM; Australian business executive; *Chairman, GroundProbe Pty Ltd;* b. 16 Dec. 1941, Adelaide; s. of Stanley Withrington and Dorothy Ellen; m. Alison Goode 1966; one s. two d.; ed Scotch Coll. Adelaide, Unley High School, Univ. of Adelaide and S Australian Inst. of Tech.; worked for CRA Group 1970–95; held several tech. and operating man. positions with Zinc Corpn Broken Hill 1970–77; transferred to Mary Kathleen Uranium Ltd (CRA subsidiary) 1977; Man. Planning and Evaluation, CRA Group, Melbourne 1980; Gen. Man. CRA's Sulphide Corpn zinc smelter, Cockle Creek, NSW 1983–85; Man. Dir Comalco Rolled Products, Sydney 1985–87; Pres. Commonwealth Aluminum Corpn Ltd USA 1988; Chief Exec. Comalco Ltd and Group Exec. CRA Ltd 1991–95; Chief Exec. MIM Holdings Ltd 1995–2001; Chair. Sustainable Minerals Inst., Univ. of Queensland; Chair. GroundProbe Pty Ltd; mem. Bd of Dirs John Holland Group Pty Ltd, Ludowici Ltd, Australia 21 Ltd; mem. Senate, Univ. of Queensland 1996–; Pres. Minerals Council of Australia 1997–99 (mem. 1995–); Vice-Pres. Queensland Mining Council Ltd 1995; Arthur F. Taggart Award, American Inst. of Mining Engineers 1975 (jtly). *Leisure interests:* cruising and offshore yacht racing. *Address:* GroundProbe Pty Ltd, 8 Hockings Street, South Brisbane QLD 4101, Australia (office). *Telephone:* (7) 3010-8999 (office). *Fax:* (7) 3010-8988 (office). *E-mail:* info@groundprobe.com (office). *Website:* www.australia21.org.au (office).

STUMPF, John G., BA, MBA; American banker; *President and CEO, Wells Fargo & Company;* b. Pierz, Minn.; ed St Cloud State Univ., Univ. of Minnesota; joined Norwest Corpn 1982, served in numerous exec. positions including Sr Vice-Pres. and Chief Credit Officer, Norwest Bank NA, Minneapolis 1982–89, Exec. Vice-Pres. Southwestern Banking 1989–91, Regional Pres. Norwest Banks Colo/Ariz. 1991–94, Regional Pres. Norwest Banks Texas 1994–98, Head of Southwestern Banking Group (after merger of Norwest Corpn and Wells Fargo & Co.) 1998–2000, Head of Western Banking Group 2000–02, Group Exec. Vice-Pres. of Community Banking 2002–05, Pres. Wells Fargo & Co. 2005–, mem. Bd of Dirs 2006–, CEO 2007–; Chair. Visa USA 2005–; mem. Bd of Dirs Visa Int., The Clearing House, Bay Area chapter of Junior Achievement, San Francisco Cttee on JOBS, Financial Services Roundtable, Carlson School of Man. at Univ. of Minnesota; mem. California Business Roundtable; Trustee, San Francisco Museum of Modern Art. *Address:* Wells Fargo & Co., PO Box 63750, San Francisco, CA 94163 (office); Wells Fargo & Co., 420 Montgomery Street, San Francisco, CA 94104, USA (office). *Telephone:* (866) 878-5865 (office). *Fax:* (626) 312-3015 (office). *E-mail:* BoardCommunications@wellsfargo.com (office). *Website:* www.wellsfargo.com (office).

ŠTURANOVIĆ, Željko; Montenegrin politician; b. 31 Jan. 1960, Nikšić; m.; two c.; ed Faculty of Law, Podgorica; early career working at Nikšić Steel Factory as Sr Officer and Head, Legal Dept; Rep. House of Citizens, Fed. Parl. 1993–2001; mem. Parl. of Repub. of Montenegro 2001–06, Minister of Justice 2001–06, Prime Minister 2006–08 (resgnd); Chair. Comm. for Human Resources; mem. Democratic Party of Socialists of Montenegro (DPSM). *Address:* c/o Democratic Party of Socialists of Montenegro (Demokratska Partija Socijalista Crne Gore), 81000 Podgorica, Jovana Tomaševića 33, Montenegro. *Telephone:* (81) 225830. *Fax:* (81) 242101. *E-mail:* webmaster@dps.cg.yu. *Website:* www.dps.cg.yu.

STURRIDGE, Charles; British director; b. 24 June 1951, London; s. of Jerome Sturridge and Alyson Sturridge (née Burke); m. Phoebe Nichols; three c.; ed Univ. Coll., Oxford; fmr mem. Nat. Youth Theatre; fmr Pres. Oxford Univ. Dramatic Soc.; worked as actor and theatre dir; debut as professional dir in musical version of Hard Times, Belgrade Theatre, Coventry; joined Granada TV 1974; freelance dir 1979–; numerous awards for feature films and TV documentaries. *Theatre includes:* Dir and Co-writer Hard Times, Belgrade Theatre, Coventry 1974; Dir own trans. of The Seagull, Queens Theatre, London 1985, Endgame, Gate Theatre 2006; trans. (with Tania Alexander) Uncle Vanya. *TV documentaries and drama include:* Brideshead Revisited (17 awards including BAFTA award for Best Series, two American Golden Globe awards, Grand Award of New York Film and TV Festival), Soft Targets (BBC) 1982, The Storyteller 1988, Gulliver's Travels 1996 (12 int. awards, including Humanitas Prize and five US Primetime Emmys), A Foreign Field, Longitude (writer/dir, Channel 4) 2000 (five BAFTA Awards including Best Series), Shackleton (writer/dir, Channel 4) (BAFTA Award for Best Series and two Emmy Awards), Ohio Impromptu (Beckett on Film, Channel 4) (LWT South Bank Award for Best TV Drama). *Feature films include:* Runners 1982, A Handful of Dust 1988, Where Angels Fear to Tread 1991, Fairytale – A True Story (co-writer) (BAFTA Best Children's Film 1998) 1997, Lassie 2005 (writer/dir); Contrib. Dir to Aria (La Vergine degli angeli from La Forza del Destino). *Address:* United Agents, 12–26 Lexington Street, London, W1F 0LE, England (office). *Telephone:* (20) 3214-0800 (office). *Fax:* (20) 3214-0801 (office). *E-mail:* info@unitedagents.co.uk (office). *Website:* unitedagents.co.uk (office).

STURUA, Robert Robertovich; Georgian theatre director; *Artistic Director, Shota Rustaveli Theatre;* b. 31 July 1938, Tbilisi; s. of the late Robert Ivanovich Sturua; m. Dudana Kveselava 1968; two s.; trained at Georgian Theatre Inst. 1956–61; joined Rustaveli Theatre, Tbilisi 1963, Prin. Dir 1979–80, Artistic Dir 1982–, has staged over 100 productions, including operas; first Guest Dir at Saarbrücken State Theatre; USSR State Prize 1979, Georgian State Prize 1981, USSR People's Artist 1982. *Opera productions include:* Music for Alive (G. Kancheli) 1984, Keto and Kote (V. Dolidze) 1986. *Plays include:* The Crucible (Miller), Italian Straw Hat (Labiche), The Good Woman of Szechuan (Brecht), Caucasian Chalk Circle, Medea (Anouilh), King Lear, Tartuffe (in Tel Aviv) 1989, Three Sisters (in London) 1990, Eugene Onegin (in Bologna) 1991, Comedy of Errors (in Helsinki) 1992, Hamlet (in London) 1992, Richard III (toured theatres around world), Antigone and many Russian and Georgian plays. *Address:* Shota Rustaveli Theatre, Tbilisi, Georgia. *Telephone:* (32) 99-85-87. *E-mail:* mail@rustavelitheatre.ge.

STÜTZLE, Walther K. A., Dr rer. pol; German journalist; *Senior Distinguished Fellow. German Institute for International and Security Affairs;* b. 29 Nov. 1941, Westerland-Sylt; s. of the late Moritz Stützle and of Annemarie Ruge; m. Dr H. Kauper 1966; two s. two d.; ed Westerland High School and Univs of Berlin, Bordeaux and Hamburg; researcher, Inst. for Strategic Studies, London 1967–68, Foreign Policy Inst. Bonn 1968–69; Desk Officer, Ministry of Defence, Planning Staff, Bonn 1969–72, Pvt. Sec. and Chef de Cabinet, 1973–76, Head, Planning Staff, Under-Sec. of Defence, Plans and Policy 1976–82; editorial staff, Stuttgarter Zeitung 1983–86; Dir Stockholm Int. Peace Research Inst. (SIPRI) 1986–91; Ed.-in-Chief Der Tagesspiegel 1994–98; Perm. Sec., Ministry of Defence 1998–2002, Visiting Prof., Potsdam Univ. 2004–; Sr Distinguished Fellow, German Institute for Int. and Security Affairs 2004–. *Publications:* Adenauer und Kennedy in der Berlinkrise 1961–62 1972, Politik und Kräftverhältnis 1983, Europe's Future – Europe's Choices (co-author) 1967, ABM Treaty – To Defend or Not to Defend 1987, SIPRI Yearbook (ed.) 1986–90, From Alliance to Coalition: The Future of Transatlantic Relations (contributor) 2004. *Leisure interests:* history, reading, sailing, mountain walking. *Address:* Stiftung Wissenschaft und Politik, Deutsches Institut für Internationale Politik und Sicherheit, Ludwigkirchplatz 3-4, 10719 Berlin, Germany (office). *Telephone:* (30) 880070 (office). *Fax:* (30) 88007100 (office). *E-mail:* walther.stuetzle@swp-berlin.org. *Website:* www.swp-berlin.org.

STYLIANOU, Petros Savva, PhD; Cypriot politician, journalist and writer; b. 8 June 1933, Kythrea; s. of Savvas and Evanthia Stylianou; m. Voula Tzanetatou 1960; two d.; ed Pancyprian Gymnasium, Univs. of Athens and Salonika; served with Panhellenic Cttee of the Cyprus Struggle (PEKA) and Nat. Union of Cypriot Univ. Students (EFEK), Pres. EFEK 1953–54; co-founder Dauntless Leaders of the Cypriot Fighters Org. (KARI); joined liberation Movt of Cyprus 1955; imprisoned in Kyrenia Castle 1955, escaped; leader, Nat. Striking Group; sentenced to 15 years' imprisonment 1956, transferred to UK prison, released 1959; mem. Cen. Cttee United Democratic Reconstruction Front (EDMA) 1959; Deputy Sec.-Gen. Cyprus Labour Confed. (SEK) 1959, Sec.-Gen. 1960–62; f. Cyprus Democratic Labour Fed. (DEOK) 1962, Sec.-Gen. 1962–73, Hon. Pres. 1974–; mem. House of Reps 1960–70, 1985–91, Sec. 1960–62; Deputy Minister of Interior 1980–82; Special Adviser to Pres. on Cultural Affairs 1982–85; Mayor of Engomi 1992–95; Founder Pancyprian Orgs for Rehabilitation of Spastics, Rehabilitation from Kidney Disease, from Haemophilia and from Myopathy; Pres. Cyprus Historical Museum and Archives, Movement for the Salvation of Cyprus; numerous awards and prizes from Cyprus, Greece and USA. *Publications:* numerous works on poetry, history, etc. *Address:* Kimonos 10, Engomi, Nicosia, Cyprus (home). *Telephone:* (2) 445972 (home).

STYMIEST, Barbara, MBA; Canadian banking executive; *Chief Operating Officer, RBC Financial Group;* ed Richard Ivey School of Business, London, Ont.; Exec. Vice-Pres. and Chief Financial Officer Investment Banking Div., Bank of Montreal –2000; CEO (first woman) TSX (Toronto Stock Exchange) Group 2000–05; COO RBC (Royal Bank of Canada) Financial Group 2005–; mem. or fmr mem. Canadian Inst. for Advanced Research, Royal Ont. Museum, Toronto Rehabilitation Inst. Foundation, Hincks-Dellcrest Children's Centre, United Way Campaign Cabinet; Fellow, Inst. of Chartered Accountants of Ont.; ranked by Fortune magazine amongst 50 Most Powerful Women in Business outside the US (34th) 2005, (27th) 2006, (30th) 2007. *Address:* RBC Financial Group, Royal Bank Plaza, 200 Bay Street, Toronto, ON M5J 2J5, Canada (office). *Fax:* (905) 813-4800 (office). *Website:* www.rbc.com (office).

SU, Chi, PhD; Taiwanese government official and academic; *Secretary General, National Security Council;* b. 1 Oct. 1949, Taichung; s. of Chan-Wu Su and Kuo-Yin Ni; m. Grace Chen; one s. one d.; ed Nat. Chengchi Univ., Johns Hopkins and Columbia Univs, USA; Assoc. Prof., Dept of Diplomacy, Nat. Chengchi Univ. 1984–90, Prof. 1990–, Deputy Dir Inst. of Int. Relations 1990–93; Sec. Gen., Office of the Univ. Pres. 1989–90; mem. Exec., Yuan Research, Devt and Evaluation Comm. 1990–94; Sec.-Gen., China Political Science Asscn 1990–91; Deputy Dir, Kuomintang Cen. Cttee, Dept of Mainland Affairs 1992–93; Vice-Chair Exec., Yuan Mainland Affairs Council 1993–96; Dir-Gen., Govt Information Office 1996–97; mem. Exec., Yuan Minister of State 1997; Nat. Policy Adviser to Pres. of Repub. 1997, Deputy Sec.-Gen. to Pres. 1997–99; Chair., Mainland Affairs Council 1999; Prof., Inst. of China Studies, Tamkang Univ. and Convener, Nat. Security Div., Nat. Policy Foundation 2000–05; Legislator 2005–08; Sec.-Gen. Nat. Security Council 2008–. *Publications:* The Normalization of Sino-Soviet Relations, Taiwan's Relations with Mainland China: A Tail Wagging Two Dogs; over 20 papers and articles. *Address:* 122, Sec. 1, Chung-Ching 5 Road, Taipei 10048, Taiwan.

SU, Guaning, BSc, MS, PhD; Singaporean engineer and university administrator; *President, Nanyang Technological University;* ed Univ. of Alberta, Canada, Calif. Inst. of Tech. (Caltech), Stanford Univ., Harvard Business School; began career as Research and Devt Engineer, Ministry of Defence; CEO Defence Science and Tech. Agency 2000–02; Pres., Nanyang Tech. Univ. 2003–; Adviser, Bitwave Pte Ltd; Dir Singapore Cable Vision, DSO Nat. Labs, Agency for Science, Tech. and Research, Biomedical Research Council; mem. Science and Eng Research Council, Nat. Science and Tech. Bd 1991–2001, Econ. Devt Bd Exec. Cttee; Fellow, Inst. of Engineers, Singapore (Pres. 1994–96); Public Admin Medal (Silver) 1989, Public Service Medal 1997, Public Admin Medal (Gold) 1998, Long Service Medal 1998, Nat. Science and Tech. Medal 2003. *Address:* Nanyang Technological University, Nanyang Avenue, Singapore, 639798, Singapore (office). *Telephone:* 6790-4769 (office). *Fax:* 6791-8494 (office). *E-mail:* ntu@edu.sg (office). *Website:* www.ntu.edu.sg (office).

SU, Rong; Chinese politician; *Secretary, Jiangxi CCP Provincial Committee;* b. Oct. 1948, Taonan, Jilin Prov.; ed Jilin Univ.; joined CCP 1970; Deputy Sec., later Sec. CCP Party Cttee, Najin Commune, Tao'an Co., Jilin Prov. 1974, Sec. Najin Commune 1975, Lingxia Commune 1975; Deputy Sec. CCP Tao'an Co. Cttee 1980; Sec. CCP Fuyu Co. Cttee, Jilin Prov. 1983; mem. Standing Cttee, CCP Baicheng Prefectural Cttee, Jilin Prov. 1983, Deputy Sec. CCP Baicheng Prefectural Cttee 1985–87, Commr Prefectural Admin. Office 1985, Sec. CCP Baicheng Prefectural Cttee 1987; Sec. CCP Siping City Cttee, Jilin Prov. 1989, Chair. Standing Cttee, Siping City People's Congress 1990; mem. Standing Cttee, CCP Jilin Prov. Cttee 1992–93, Sec.-Gen. Jilin Prov. Cttee 1992–93, Deputy Sec. 1996–2001; Sec. Yanbian Korean Autonomous Prefecture Cttee 1995–97, Qinghai Prov. Cttee 2001–03 (mem. Standing Cttee 2001–03), CCP Gansu Prov. Cttee 2003–06; Chair. Standing Cttee, Gansu Prov. People's Congress 2004–06; Exec. Vice-Pres. CCP Cen. Cttee Party School 2006–07; Alt. mem. 14th CCP Cen. Cttee 1992–97, 15th CCP Cen. Cttee 1997–2002, mem. 16th CCP Cen. Cttee 2002–07, 17th CCP Cen. Cttee 2007–; Sec. CCP Jianqxi Prov. Cttee 2007–. *Address:* Jianqxi Provincial People's Government, Jianqxi Province, People's Republic of China (office).

SU, Shaozhi, MA; Chinese research professor; b. 25 Jan. 1923, Peking; s. of Su Xiyi and Jin Yunquan; m. Hu Jianmei; two d.; ed Chongqing Univ. and Nankai Inst. of Econs; Assoc. Prof., Fudan Univ. 1949–63; Ed. Theoretical Dept Renmin Ribao (People's Daily) 1963–79; Deputy Dir Inst. of Marxism-Leninism-Mao Zedong Thought 1979–82, Dir 1982–87; Research Prof., Chinese Acad. of Social Sciences (CASS) 1982–87, mem. Acad. Cttee of CASS 1982–85, Prof., Grad. School of CASS 1982; Ed. Studies of Marxism (quarterly) 1983–; fmr Chair. Princeton China Initiative, USA; mem. Advisory Bd Beijing Spring (magazine). *Publications:* Democracy and Socialism in China 1982, Marxism in China 1983, Democratization and Reform 1988, Marxism and Reform in China 1993; books and articles on politics and economics. *Leisure interests:* calligraphy and paintings, classical music. *Address:* c/o Princeton China Initiative, 226 Brickhouse Rd, Princeton NJ 08540, USA (office).

SU, Shuyang, (Su Yang, Yu Pingfu); Chinese writer; b. 1938, Baoding, Hebei Prov.; ed Renmin Univ.; fmrly teaching asst, Dept of CCP History, Renmin Univ.; Lecturer, Beijing Teachers' Coll.; worker, Baoding Voltage Transformer Factory; Lecturer, Beijing Coll. of Chinese Medicine; currently playwright, Beijing Film Studio; Vice-Chair. China Film Asscn. *Publications:*

Song of Loyal Hearts (play), Wedding, Masquerade, The Death of Lao She, The Moon Goddess, I Am a Zero, Big Family Matter, Flying Moth, Taiping Lake, Sunset Boulevard: Selected Screenplays by Su Shuyang, Homeland (novel), About Love (poetry), A Reader on China 2007. *Address:* Beijing Film Studio, Beijing, People's Republic of China. (office).

SU, Tong; Chinese writer; b. (Tong Zhonggui), 23 Jan. 1963, Suzhou, Jiangsu Prov.; ed Beijing Normal Univ.; fmrly Lecturer, Nanjing Acad. of Arts; Ed. Zhongshan Magazine; writer-in-residence Univ. of Iowa Int. Writing Program 2001; mem. Jiangsu Provincial Writers' Asscn. *Publications include:* (titles in translation) The Eighth Is a Bronze Sculpture, The Escape of 1934, The Mournful Dance, The Lives of Women, Wives and Concubines 1990, Raise the Red Lantern (three novellas) 1991, Blush 1994, Rice 1995, Jasmine Woman 2004, My Life as an Emperor 2005, Binu and the Great Wall 2007. *Address:* c/o Canongate Books, 14 High Street, Edinburgh, EH1 1TE, Scotlanf (office). *Website:* www.canongate.net (office).

SU, Tseng-chang; Taiwanese lawyer and politician; b. 28 July 1947, Pingtung; m. Su Jan Shiow-ling; three d.; ed Nat. Taiwan Univ.; practised as lawyer 1973–83; joined Taipei Jr Chamber 1973, Pres. 1978; Vice-Pres. Jr Chamber Int. Taiwan 1979; elected mem. Taiwan Prov. Ass. 1981; Magistrate, Pingtung County 1989–94, Taipei County 1997–2004; Sec.-Gen. Democratic Progressive Party (DPP), Chair. 2005; Sec.-Gen. Office of the Pres. 2004–05; Premier of Taiwan 2006–07; unsuccessful cand. for Vice-Pres. of Taiwan 2008; Most Outstanding Chapter in Asia Award 1978, Outstanding LOM Pres. of the World Award 1978. *Address:* c/o Democratic Progressive Party, 10/F, 30 Beiping East Rd, Taipei 10051, Taiwan (office). *Telephone:* (2) 23929989. *E-mail:* foreign@dpp.org.tw. *Website:* www.dpp.org.tw.

SUÁREZ PERTIERRA, Gustavo, LLD; Spanish academic and fmr politician; *Chairman, Real Instituto Elcano;* b. 1949, Cudillero, Oviedo; m.; one s. one d.; ed Univs. of Oviedo, Valladolid and Munich; Prof. in Canon Law, Complutense Univ., Madrid 1978, also sometime Vice-Dean of Law and mem. Academic Council of Human Rights Inst.; Dir-Gen. of Religious Matters, Ministry of Justice and Pres. of Advisory Comm. on Religious Freedom 1982; Deputy Sec. Ministry of Defence 1984; Sec. of State for Mil. Admin. 1990–93; Minister of Educ. and Science 1993–95, of Defence 1995–96; Pres. Parl. Comm. for Public Admin. 1996–2000; Prof., Universidad Nacional de Educación a Distancia 2000–; Dir Instituto Universitario General Gutiérrez Mellado 2001–05; Chair. Real Instituto Elcano (research inst.), Madrid 2002–. *Address:* Real Instituto Elcano, Príncipe de Vergara, 51, 28006 Madrid, Spain (office). *Telephone:* (91) 7816770 (office). *Fax:* (91) 4262157 (office). *E-mail:* info@rielcano.org (office). *Website:* www.realinstitutoelcano.org (office).

SUBBA ROW, Raman, CBE, MA; British company director, public relations consultant and fmr cricketer; b. 29 Jan. 1932, Streatham, London; s. of the late Panguluri Venkata Subba Row and of Doris Pinner; m. Anne Harrison 1960; two s. one d.; ed Whitgift School, Croydon and Trinity Hall, Cambridge; Pilot Officer, RAF 1956–58; left-hand opening batsman; played for Univ. of Cambridge 1951–53, Surrey 1953–54, Northants. 1955–61 (Capt. 1958–61); 13 Tests for England 1958–61; toured Australia 1958–59; scored 14,182 first-class runs with 30 hundreds; Assoc. Dir W. S. Crawford Ltd 1963–69; Man. Dir Management Public Relations Ltd 1969–92; Chair. Surrey Co. Cricket Club 1974–79, Test and County Cricket Bd 1985–90; Int. Cricket Council referee 1992–2001; apptd to work with ICC on reform of int. umpiring and refereeing panels; mem. Inst. of Dirs; Wisden Cricketer of the Year 1961. *Leisure interests:* golf, sports generally. *Address:* Leeward, 13 Manor Way, South Croydon, Surrey, CR2 7BT, England (home). *Telephone:* (20) 8688-2991 (home). *Fax:* (20) 8688-2991 (home).

SUBBARAO, Duvvuri, MS, PhD; Indian economist and central banker; *Governor, Reserve Bank of India;* b. 1949; ed Indian Inst. of Tech., Ohio State Univ., USA, Andhra Univ.; Jt Sec., Dept of Econ. Affairs 1988–93; Finance Sec., Govt of Andhra Pradesh 1993–98; Economist, World Bank 1999–2004; Sec. to Prime Minister's Econ. Advisory Council 2004–07; Sec., Dept of Econ. Affairs 2007–08; Gov. Reserve Bank of India 2008–; Humphrey Fellow, MIT 1982–83. *Address:* Reserve Bank of India, Central Office, Shahid Bhagat Singh Road, POB 10007, Mumbai 400 001, India (office). *Telephone:* (22) 22661602 (office). *Fax:* (22) 22658269 (office). *E-mail:* helpprd@rbi.org.in (office). *Website:* www.rbi.org.in (office).

SUBBOTIN, Valery Ivanovich; Russian physicist; b. 12 Dec. 1919, Baku; s. of Ivan Subbotin and Tatiana Subbotin; m. Irina Subbotin 1945; two s. one d.; ed Baku Industrial Inst.; engineer, then chief of section, Kavkazenergomash 1943–48; jr then sr researcher, Energy Inst. Azerbaijan Acad. of Sciences 1952–53; Head of Lab., of Div., Deputy Dir Inst. of Physics and Energy Obninsk 1953–75; Dir Research Production enterprise Energiya 1975–77; Chair. Moscow Inst. of Physics and Eng 1977–88, also Prof.; Scientific Sec., Research Group, Research Construction Inst. of Energy Tech. 1988–; Corresp. mem. USSR (now Russian) Acad. of Sciences 1967, mem. 1987, mem. Presidium 1991–, Chair. Scientific Council 'Physico tech. Analysis of Power Systems', Dept of Power, Mechanical Eng and Process Control, Chair. Comm. on Use of Energy-Accumulating Substances in Mechanics, Power Eng. and Ecology; Lenin Prize 1964. *Publications:* Liquid Metals 1967, Physical-Chemical Basis for Application of Liquid Metal Heat Carriers 1978, Structure of Turbulent Flow and Mechanism of Heat Exchange in Channels 1978, On Thermophysics of Focusing Mirrors of Laser Nuclear Reactors 1983, Interchannel Heat Exchange at Transversal Water Flow Around a Bunch of Pipes 1985, Reflections on Atomic Energetics 1995, 21st Century – Century of Nuclear Energy 1998; articles in scientific journals. *Leisure interest:* literature. *Address:* Leninsky prospect 14, Moscow, 117901; Institute of Mechanical Engineering (IMASH), Haribouevskij per. 4, 101990 Moscow, Russia (office). *Telephone:* (495) 135-61-31 (office); (495) 135-77-69 (home). *E-mail:* subbotin@imash.ru (office). *Website:* www.imash.ru (office).

SUBOLEV, Col Gen. Valentin; Russian government official; *Acting Secretary, Security Council of the Russian Federation;* b. 11 March 1947, Kyzyl-Atrek Dist (Turkmen SSR); ed V. Kuibyshev Inst. of Engineering and Construction, Moscow and Fed. Security Services Acad.; began career as construction worker, Aşgabat 1962; served in KGB; Deputy Dir Fed. Counterintelligence Service 1994–97; First Deputy Dir Fed., Security Service 1997–99; Deputy Sec., Security Council of the Russian Fed. 1999–2007, Acting Sec. 2007–. *Address:* Security Council of the Russian Federation, 123132 Moscow, Ipatyevskii per. 4/10, Russia (office). *Telephone:* (495) 910-31-51 (office). *E-mail:* scrf_sec@gov.ru (office). *Website:* www.scrf.gov.ru (office).

SUBOTNICK, Morton Leon, MA; American composer and academic; b. 14 April 1933, Los Angeles; s. of Jack Jacob Subotnick and Rose Luckerman; m. 1st Linn Pottle 1953 (divorced 1971); one s. one d.; m. 2nd Doreen Nelson 1976 (divorced 1977); m. 3rd Joan La Barbara 1979; one s.; ed Univ. of Denver, Mills Coll.; Co-founder San Francisco Tape Music Center 1961–65; fmr Music Dir Ann Halprin's Dance Co. and San Francisco Actors' Workshop, fmr Music Dir Lincoln Center Repertory Theatre; Dir of electronic music at original Electric Circus, St Mark's Place, New York 1967–68; Artist-in-Residence, New York Univ. School of the Arts 1966–69; Co-Dir Center for Experiments in Art, Information and Tech., Calif. Inst. of Arts, Valencia 1969–, also Co-Chair. Composition Dept; Visiting Prof. in Composition, Univ. of Maryland 1968, Univ. of Pittsburgh 1969, Yale Univ. 1982, 1983; has toured extensively as lecturer and composer/performer; Composer-in-Residence DAAD, West Berlin 1981, MIT 1986; Brandeis Award for Music 1983, American Acad. of Arts and Letters Composer Award, SEAMUS Lifetime Acheivement Award 1998, ASCAP John Cage Award, ACO Lifetime Achievement Award. *Compositions include:* Silver Apples of the Moon, The Wild Bull, Trembling, The Double Life of Amphibians, The Key to Songs, Return: The Triumph of Reason (electronic composition in honour of the return of Halley's Comet) 1986, In Two Worlds 1987–88, And The Butterflies Begin to Sing 1988, A Desert Flowers 1989, All my Hummingbirds have Alibis, Jacob's Room (opera) 1993, Making Music 1996, Intimate Immensity 1997, Echoes from the Silent Call of Girona 1998. *Address:* 25 Minetta Lane, Apt 4B, New York, NY 10012, USA. *E-mail:* morts@creatingmusic.com. *Website:* www.mortonsubotnick.com.

SUBRAMANIAM, A.; Indian social worker and educationalist; b. 18 Oct. 1925, Kodungallur, Kerala State; s. of Ananthanarayanan Ammal and Lakshmi Ammal; jailed for six months in 1942 for participating in Quit India Movt; trade union worker; Tamil Nadu State Sec. of Socialist Party for several years; headed trade unions in textiles, eng, road transport, ports and docks, papermaking, tea plantations, heavy electricals, etc.; Nat. Pres. Hind Mazdoor Sabha for two terms, has represented Hind Mazdoor Sabha on visits to UK, USA, USSR, China, Japan, South Africa, Sri Lanka, Singapore, Malaysia, Germany, France, Italy and Switzerland; Sec. Thiagi N. G. Ramaswarny Memorial Higher Secondary School and Nursery School; mem. of Tamil Nadu Legis. Ass. 1971–76. *Leisure interest:* reading. *Address:* Thiagi NGR Bhavan, 248 (Old 2112) Trichy Road, Singanallur, Coimbatore 641 005 (office); Thamarai, 42 (Old 65) 2nd Street, Lal Bahadur Nagar, Coimbatore 641 004, India (home). *Telephone:* (422) 2573145 (office); (422) 2574460 (home); (422) 2574140. *Fax:* (422) 2574140 (office). *E-mail:* ayess_25@yahoo.co.in (office).

SUBRAMANYAN, Kalpathi Ganapathi; Indian artist and academic; *Professor Emeritus, Kala Bhavana;* b. 5 Feb. 1924, Kerala; s. of K. P. Ganapathi and Alamelu Ammal; m. Susheela Jasra 1951; one d.; ed Univ. of Madras, Kalabhavana, Visvabharati and Slade School of Art, London; Lecturer in Painting, Faculty of Fine Arts, M. G. Univ., Baroda 1951–59, Reader 1961–66, Prof. 1966–80, Dean, Faculty of Fine Arts 1968–74; Prof. of Painting, Kala Bhavana, Visva Bharati, Santiniketan 1980–89, Prof. Emer. 1989–; Deputy Dir (Designs), All India Handloom Bd, Bombay 1959–61, Design Consultant 1961–65; Visiting Lecturer, Canada 1976; Visiting Fellow, Visvabharati, Santiniketan 1977–78; Christensen Fellow, St Catherine's Coll., Oxford 1987–88; JDR III Fund Fellowship, New York 1967–68; Fellow, Lalit Kala Acad. 1984; Hon. DLitt (Rabindra Bharati Univ., Calcutta) 1992, (Banaras Hindu Univ., Varanasi) 1997; Hon. Mention (São Paulo Biennale) 1961, Nat. Award 1965, Gold Medal, 1st Indian Triennale 1968; Padma Shri 1975, Kalidas Samman 1981. *Publications:* Moving Focus (essays on art) 1978, Living Tradition 1985, Creative Circuit (collection of lectures) 1991. *Leisure interests:* reading, handicraft. *Address:* Kala Bhavana, Santiniketan, 731235, West Bengal (office); Kailas, 13 Purvapalli, Santiniketan, 731235, West Bengal, India (home). *Website:* www.visva-bharati.ac.in/map/contents/kalabhavan (office).

SUCHET, David, OBE; British actor; b. 2 May 1946, London; s. of the late Jack Suchet and Joan Suchet (née Jarché); m. Sheila Ferris 1976; one s. one d.; ed Wellington School, Somerset, LAMDA, London; fmr mem. Nat. Youth Theatre, Chester Repertory Co.; joined RSC 1973; Assoc. Artist, Birmingham Rep., Connaught Theatre, Worthing, Northcott Theatre, Exeter, Liverpool Rep., Chichester Festival Theatre, Theatre Royal, Bath; Visiting Prof. of Theatre, Univ. of Neb., USA 1975; mem. Fight Dirs' Asscn; Brown Belt in Aikido; a First Master of Japanese Samurai. *Roles for RSC include:* Tybalt in Romeo and Juliet 1973, Orlando in As You Like It 1973, Tranio in Taming of the Shrew 1973, Zamislov in Summerfolk 1974, 1975, Wilmer in Comrades 1974, The Fool in King Lear 1974, 1975, Pisanio in Cymbeline 1974, Hubert in King John, Ferdinand King of Navarre in Love's Labour's Lost 1975, Shylock in The Merchant of Venice 1978, Grumio in Taming of the Shrew 1978, Sir Nathaniel in Love's Labour's Lost 1978, Glougauer in Once in a Lifetime 1978, Caliban in The Tempest 1978, Sextus Pompey in Antony and Cleopatra 1978, Angelo in Measure for Measure 1979, Iago in Othello, Every Good Boy Deserves Favour, Bolingbroke in Richard II 1981, Achilles in Troilus and

Cressida, Mercutio in Romeo and Juliet, Iago in Othello 1985. *Other stage roles include:* Lucio in Measure for Measure 1977, Thomas Gilthead in The Devil is an Ass 1977, The Kreutzer Sonata 1978, Tsaravitch and George Wochner in Laughter! 1978, Joe Green in Separation 1987, This Story of Yours, Litvanoy in The Wedding Feast, Estragon in Waiting for Godot, John Aubrey in Brief Lives, Mole in Toad of Toad Hall, Timon in Timon of Athens 1991, John in Oleanna (Variety Club Best Actor Award 1994) 1993, Sid Field in What a Performance 1994, George in Who's Afraid of Virginia Woolf? (Critic's Circle Best Actor Award 1997) 1996, Salieri in Amadeus (Variety Club Best Actor Award 1998, South Bank Award and Backstage Theatre Award 2000) 1998–2000, Gregor Antonescu in Man and Boy, Duchess Theatre, London 2005, Once in a Lifetime, Royal Nat. Theatre 2006. *Films include:* Tale of Two Cities 1978, Schiele in Prison 1980, The Missionary 1982, Hunchback of Notre Dame 1982, Red Monarch (Best Actor, Marseilles Film Festival 1983) 1983, Trenchcoat 1983, Greystoke: The Legend of Tarzan, Lord of the Apes 1984, Little Drummer Girl 1984, Song for Europe (video title Cry for Justice) (Best Actor, Royal TV Soc. Performance Awards 1986) 1985, Thirteen to Dinner 1985, Falcon and the Snowman 1985, Gulag 1985, Iron Eagle 1986, Murrow 1986, Big Foot and The Hendersons 1986, Stress (Best Actor Award, British Industry/Scientific Film Asscn 1986) 1986, Crime of Honor 1987, The Last Innocent Man 1987, A World Apart 1988, To Kill a Priest (also known as Popielusko) 1988, The Lucona Affair, When the Whales Came 1990, Executive Decision 1995, Deadly Voyage 1995, Sunday 1996, A Perfect Murder 1997, RKO 1999, Sabotage 1999, Live From Baghdad 2002, The In-Laws 2003, Foolproof 2003, Flood 2006, Flushed Away (voice) 2006, Flood 2007, The Bank Job 2008. *Work for radio includes:* The Kreutzer Sonata (one-man show) (Best Radio Actor of the Year 1979), Shylock in The Merchant of Venice, Bolingbroke in Richard II, First Night Impression, Rosenberg in the Trenches, Chimes at Midnight, The Isaac Babel Stories, Super Cannes (Book at Bedtime) and numerous other parts. *Television includes:* role of Hercule Poirot in dramatization of 63 Agatha Christie Poirot novels (for LWT) Series 1989–2008, 100th Anniversary Special: The Mysterious Affair at Styles 1990, Oppenheimer 1978, Being Normal, Saigon – the Last Days, Time to Die, The Life of Freud (Best Actor, Royal TV Soc. Performance Awards 1986), Blott on the Landscape (Best Actor, Royal TV Soc. Performance Awards 1986), Oxbridge Blues 1986, Playing Shakespeare 1983, Master of the Game 1984, Reilly – Ace of Spies 1984, Mussolini: The Untold Story 1985, James Joyce's Ulysses, Cause Célèbre 1988, The Life of Agatha Christie 1990, Once in a Lifetime, Bingo, Long Ago and Far Away 1989, Days of Majesty 1994, Fighting Fund (episode of The Protectors), Separation 1990, Secret Agent, Kings and Castles, Nobody Here but Us Chickens 1989, The Cruel Train, The Curious 1994, Moses 1995, Solomon 1997, See Saw 1997, The Way We Live Now 2001, National Crime Squad 2001–02, The First Lady 2003, Henry VIII 2003, Space Odyssey (voice) 2004, A Bear Named Winnie 2004, Dracula 2006, Maxwell 2007. *Publications:* essays in Players of Shakespeare 1985. *Leisure interests:* photography, clarinet, ornithology, theology, boating on inland waterways. *Address:* c/o Ken McReddie Associates Ltd, 36-40 Glasshouse Street, London, W1B 5DL, England (office). *Telephone:* (20) 7439-1456 (office). *Fax:* (20) 7734-6530 (office). *E-mail:* email@kenmcreddie.com (office).

SUCHOCKA, Hanna, DrIur; Polish diplomatist, politician and lawyer; *Ambassador to the Holy See;* b. 3 April 1946, Pleszew; ed Adam Mickiewicz Univ., Poznań; scientific worker, Dept of Constitutional Law of Adam Mickiewicz Univ., Poznań 1968–69, 1972–90, Catholic Univ. of Lublin 1988–92, Polish Acad. of Science 1990–; mem. Democratic Party (SD) 1969–84, Democratic Union 1991–94, Freedom Union 1994–; Deputy to Sejm (Parl.) 1980–85, 1989–2001; mem. Civic. Parl. Caucus 1989–91, mem. Democratic Union Parl. Caucus (now Freedom Union) 1991–, Deputy Chair. Parl. Legis. Cttee 1989–92; Chair. Council of Ministers (Prime Minister) 1992–93; Minister of Justice and Attorney-Gen. 1997–99; mem. Pontifical Acad. of Social Sciences, Rome 1994–; Amb. to the Holy See 2001–; Dr hc (Oklahoma Univ.); Max Schmidtheiny Prize 1994, Foyer Prize 2004. *Publications:* author of reports and articles for professional publs and int. confs. *Address:* Polish Embassy, Via dei Delfini 16/3, 00186 Rome, Italy (office). *Telephone:* (06) 6990958 (office). *Fax:* (06) 6990978 (office). *E-mail:* polamb .wat@agora.it (office).

SUCKLING, Charles W., CBE, PhD, DSc, FRSC, FRS; British chemist and business executive; b. 24 July 1920, Teddington; s. of Edward Ernest Suckling and Barbara Suckling (née Thomson); m. Eleanor Margaret Watterson 1946; two s. one d.; ed Oldershaw Grammar School, Wallasey, Univ. of Liverpool; with Imperial Chemical Industries PLC 1942–82, Deputy Chair. Mond Div. 1969–72, Chair. Paints Div. 1972–77, Gen. Man. Research and Tech. 1977–82; Chair. Bradbury, Suckling and Pnrs Ltd 1981–92; Dir (non-exec.) Albright and Wilson 1982–89; Visiting Prof., Stirling Univ. 1969–92; mem. Science Consultative Group, BBC 1979–82; mem. Royal Comm. on Environmental Pollution 1981–92; Treas. Royal Coll. of Art, London 1984–90; mem. Nat. Curriculum Working Parties for English and Modern Foreign Languages 1988–91; numerous other appointments; Hon. DSc (Liverpool) 1980; Hon. DUniv (Stirling) 1985; John Scott Medal of City of Philadelphia for invention of anaesthetic halothane 1973, Leverhulme Prize Soc. Chem. Industry 1942, Gold Medal of Royal Coll. of Anaesthetists 1992. *Publications:* Research in the Chemical Industry 1969, Chemistry Through Models (with C. J. and K. E. Suckling) 1978. *Leisure interests:* music, writing, horticulture, languages. *Address:* 1 Desborough Drive, Tewin, Welwyn, Herts, AL6 0HQ, England. *Telephone:* (1438) 798250 (home). *E-mail:* charles.suckling@dsl.pipex.com (home).

SUDAN, Madhu, BTech., PhD; Indian mathematician and academic; *Fujitsu Chair Professor, Department of of Electrical Engineering and Computer Science, Massachusetts Institute of Technology;* ed Indian Inst. of Tech. and Univ. of California, Berkeley, USA; student researcher, IBM Almaden Research Center 1990, mem. Research Staff, Math. Sciences Dept, IBM Thomas J. Watson Research Center, Yorktown Heights, NY 1992–97; Assoc. Prof., Dept of Electrical Eng and Computer Science, MIT 1997–2002, Prof. 2003–05, Fujitsu Chair Prof. 2005–, mem. Computer Science and AI Lab. (CSAIL), Theory of Computing (TOC) Group, CSAIL, Algorithms, Complexity, and Cryptography and Information Security subgroups, TOC; Fellow, Radcliffe Inst. for Advanced Study 2003–04; Ed. Soc. for Industrial and Applied Math. (SIAM) Journal on Discrete Mathematics 1997–, SIAM Journal on Computing 2000–03, Information and Computation 2000–03; Guest Ed. Journal of Computer and System Sciences (special issue devoted to papers from Complexity '2001) 2001–02; mem. Asscn for Computing Machinery, IEEE, Soc. for Industrial and Applied Math., American Math. Soc.; Sakrison Memorial Award for PhD Thesis, Dept of Electrical Eng and Computer Science, Univ. of California, Berkeley 1993, ACM Doctoral Dissertation Award 1993, Sloan Foundation Fellowship 1998, NSF Career Award 1999, Information Theory Paper Award 2000, Gödel Prize 2001, Nevanlinna Prize 2002. *Publications:* Efficient Checking of Polynomials and Proofs and the Hardness of Approximation Problems 1996, Complexity Classiffications of Boolean Constraint Satisfaction Problems (co-author) 2001; more than 90 articles in scientific journals on theoretical computer science, algorithms, computational complexity, optimization and coding theory. *Address:* Stata Center, Massachusetts Institute of Technology, Room G640, 32 Vassar Street, Cambridge, MA 02139, USA (office). *Telephone:* (617) 253-9680 (office). *Fax:* (617) 258-8682 (office). *E-mail:* madhu@mit.edu (office). *Website:* theory.csail .mit.edu/~madhu (office); people.csail.mit.edu/madhu (office).

SUDARSONO, Juwono, PhD; Indonesian government official, diplomatist and academic; *Minister of Defence;* m.; two s. one d.; ed Univ. of Indonesia, Univ. of Calif., Berkeley, USA, London School of Econs, UK; Visiting Prof., Columbia Univ. 1986–87; Dean of Social and Political Science, Univ. of Indonesia 1988–94; Vice Gov. Indonesian Defence Coll. 1995–98; apptd Minister of Environment 1998, then Minister of Educ.; served as first civilian Minister of Defence 1999; returned to Univ. of Indonesia teaching part-time; fmr Commr Strategic Intelligence; Amb. to UK and Repub. of Ireland 2003–04; Minister of Defence 2004–. *Address:* Ministry of Defence, Jalan Medan Merdeka Barat 13–14, Jakarta Pusat, Indonesia (office). *Telephone:* (21) 3456184 (office). *Fax:* (21) 3440023 (office). *E-mail:* postmaster@dephan.go.id (office). *Website:* www.dephan.go.id (office).

SUDJIC, Deyan, OBE; British architecture critic and arts administrator; *Director, The Design Museum;* b. 6 Sept. 1952, London; s. of the late Miša J. Sudjic and of Ceja Sudjic (née Pavlovic); m. Sarah Miller; one d.; ed Latymer Upper School, London and Univ. of Edin.; chose not to practise as an architect; Architecture Corresp. Sunday Times 1980–85; fmr Critic London Daily News; Critic Sunday Correspondent 1989–90; Architecture Critic The Guardian 1991–97; Visiting Prof. of Design Theory and History, Hochschule für Angewandte Kunst, Vienna 1993–97; Dir Glasgow 1999 UK City of Architecture and Design; Ed. Domus Magazine 2000–04; Architecture Critic The Observer 2000–; Dir 8th Venice Architectural Biennale 2002; Dir The Design Museum, London 2006–; Visiting Prof. of Design, Royal Coll. of Art; Founder Ed., later Editorial Dir Blueprint magazine, also f. Tate and Eye magazines. *Publications include:* Cult Objects 1985, New British Architecture: The Design of Richard Rogers, Norman Foster and James Stirling 1986, Rei Kawakubo: A Monograph of the Japanese Fashion Designer 1990, Cult Heroes: An Investigation of the Mechanics of Celebrity 1990, The Hundred Mile City: A Study of the Rapidly Evolving Modern City 1992, The Architecture of Richard Rogers 1995, The Architecture of Erick van Egeraat 1997, Ron Arad: A Monograph 1999, John Pawson Works 2000, Architecture and Democracy 2001, The Edifice Complex: How the Rich and Powerful Shape the World 2005, The Language of Things 2008. *Address:* The Design Museum, 28 Shad Thames, London, SE1 2YD, England (office). *Telephone:* (870) 909-9009 (office). *E-mail:* info@designmuseum.org (office). *Website:* www .designmuseum.orgus (office).

SUDO, Fumio; Japanese steel industry executive; *President and CEO, JFE Holdings, Inc.;* b. 3 March 1941; ed Hokkaido Univ.; joined Kawasaki Steel Corpn 1964, Gen. Man., Steelmaking, Mizushima 1988, mem. Bd of Dirs 1994–, Exec. Officer 1994–2000, Exec. Vice-Pres. 2001, Pres. and CEO 2001–03; mem. Bd of Dirs JFE Holdings Inc. 2002–, Pres. and CEO 2005–, also Pres. and CEO JFE Steel Corpn 2003–, Pres. Nihon Keizai Shimbun of JFE Holdings, Inc. 2005–, Chair. JFE 21st Century Foundation. *Address:* JFE Holdings, Inc., 1-5-1 Marunouchi, Chiyoda-ku, Tokyo 100-6527, Japan (office). *Telephone:* (3) 3217-4049 (office). *Fax:* (3) 3214-6110 (office). *E-mail:* info@jfe -holdings.co.jp (office). *Website:* www.jfe-holdings.co.jp (office).

SUEBWONGLEE, Surapong; Thai physician and politician; *Secretary General, People's Power Party;* fmr Communist rebel; trained as a medical doctor before entering politics; fmr mem. Thai Rak Thai party; Govt Spokesman 2005; Minister of Information and Communications Tech. –2006 (Govt of Prime Minister Thaksin Sinawatra deposed in mil. coup Sept. 2006); Sec.-Gen. People's Power Party 2007–; Deputy Prime Minister and Minister of Finance Sept. 2008. *Address:* People's Power Party (PPP), 1770 Thanon Petchaburi Tat Mai, Bang Gapi, Huay Kwang, Bangkok 10310, Thailand (office). *Telephone:* (2) 686–7000 (office). *Website:* www.ppp.or.th (office).

SUGA, Yoshihide; Japanese politician; b. 6 Dec. 1948; ed Hosei Univ.; Sec. to Rep. Hikosaburo Okonogi 1975, Sec. to Minister for Int. Trade and Industry 1984–87; mem. Yokohama City Council 1987; mem. House of Reps 1996–, Parl. Sec. for Land, Infrastructure and Transport 2002–03, for Int. Trade and Industry 2003–04; Deputy Sec.-Gen. LDP 2001–, Chair. Diet Affairs Cttee 2004, Sr Vice-Minister for Internal Affairs and Communications 2005–06, Minister of Internal Affairs and Communications and Minister of State for Privatization of Postal Services 2006–07. *Address:* Liberal-Democratic Party

(Jiyu-Minshuto), 1-11-23, Nagata-cho, Chiyoda-ku, Tokyo 100-8910, Japan (office). *Telephone:* (3) 3581-6211 (office). *E-mail:* koho@ldp.jimin.or.jp (office). *Website:* www.jimin.jp (office).

SUGAR, Sir Alan Michael, Kt; British business executive; *Chairman and CEO, Amstrad PLC;* b. 24 March 1947, London; s. of Nathan Sugar and Fay Sugar; m. Ann Simons 1968; two s. one d.; ed Brooke House School, London; Chair. and Man. Dir Amstrad PLC 1968–97, CEO –1993, Chair. 1997–2001, Chair. and CEO 2001–; Owner and Chair. Tottenham Hotspur PLC 1991–2001; Chair. Viglen PLC 1997–; Hon. DSc (City Univ.) 1988; Hon. Fellow, City and Guilds of London Inst. *Television:* star The Apprentice (BBC TV show) 2005–. *Publication:* The Apprentice Revisited 2006. *Leisure interest:* tennis. *Address:* Amstrad PLC, Brentwood House, 169 King's Road, Brentwood, Essex, CM14 4EF, England (office). *Telephone:* (1277) 228888 (office). *Fax:* (1277) 211350 (office). *E-mail:* info@amstrad.com (office). *Website:* www .amstrad.com (office).

SUGAR, Ronald D., BEng, MSc, PhD; American defence industry executive; *Chairman and CEO, Northrop Grumman Corporation;* b. July 1948, Toronto, Ont., Canada; m.; two c.; ed Univ. of California, Los Angeles, Stanford Univ., Univ. of Pennsylvania, Harvard Univ.; began career in tech. and man. positions at Hughes Aircraft Co., Argosystems Inc. and The Aerospace Corpn 1970s; joined TRW Aerospace and Information Systems 1970s, held various sr positions including Vice-Pres. Space Communications Div., Chief Financial Officer, Exec. Vice-Pres., Gen. Man. Global Automotive Electronics –1990s; Pres. and COO Litton Industries 2000-01, Pres. and COO Northrup Grumman Corpn (following acquisition of Litton by Northrup 2001) 2001–03, Chair., Pres. and CEO 2003–06, Chair. and CEO 2006–; mem. Bd Dirs Chevron Corpn 2005–, LA Philharmonic Asscn; apptd by Pres. of USA to Nat. Security Telecommunications Advisory Cttee; Gov. Aerospace Industries Asscn; Nat. Fundraising Chair. Pearl Harbor Memorial Fund; fmr Chair. Aerospace Industries Asscn; Nat. Trustee Boys & Girls Clubs of America; Trustee, Cleveland Inst. of Music, Nat. Defense Industrial Asscn, Univ. of Southern California; Fellow, AIAA; FRAeS; mem. Nat. Acad. of Eng; Engineering Alumnus of the Year, UCLA 1996, Daniel J. Epstein Eng Man. Award, Univ. of Southern Calif. 2003, Semper Fidelis Award, Marine Corps Foundation, John R. Alison Leadership to Nat. Defense Award, Air Force Asscn, Eisenhower Distinguished Citizen Award, Army Distaff Foundation. *Address:* Northrop Grumman Corpn, 1840 Century Park East, Los Angeles, CA 90067-2199, USA (office). *Telephone:* (310) 553-6262 (office). *Fax:* (310) 553-2076 (office). *E-mail:* info@northropgrumman.com (office). *Website:* www .northropgrumman.com (office).

SUGISAKI, Shigemitsu; Japanese financial industry executive, international organization official and fmr civil servant; *Vice Chairman, Goldman Sachs Japan Company, Ltd;* b. 1941, Tokyo; ed Univ. of Tokyo, Columbia Univ.; positions with Ministry of Finance 1964–76, 1979–94 including mem. Minister's Secr., Deputy Vice-Minister of Finance for Int. Affairs 1990–91, Deputy Dir-Gen. Int. Finance Bureau 1991–92, Commr Tokyo Regional Taxation Bureau 1992–93, Sec.-Gen. Exec. Bureau Securities and Exchange Surveillance Comm. 1993–94; Personal Asst to Pres. Asian Devt Bank 1976–79; Special Adviser to Man. Dir IMF 1994–97, Deputy Man. Dir 1997–2004; currently Vice Chair. Goldman Sachs Japan Co. Ltd. *Address:* Goldman Sachs Japan Co. Ltd, Roppongi Hills, Mori Tower, Level 43-48, 10-1, Roppongi 6-chome, Minato-ku, Tokyo 106-6147, Japan (office). *Telephone:* (3) 6437-1000. *Website:* www2.goldmansachs.com/worldwide/japan.

SUGIURA, Seiken, BEcons; Japanese lawyer and politician; b. 26 July 1934, Okazaki-city, Aichi Pref.; m. Toshiko Sugiura; one s. one d.; ed Univ. of Tokyo; began career with Kawasaki Steel Corpn 1957; called to the Bar 1972; Vice-Pres. Tokyo First Bar Asscn 1982; elected to House of Reps 1986, Parl. Vice-Minister, Ministry of Agric., Forestry and Fisheries 1990–92, Parl. Vice-Minister, Nat. Land Agency 1992–96, Chair. House of Reps Judicial Affairs Cttee 1998, Sr Vice-Minister for Foreign Affairs 2001–02, Deputy Chief Cabinet Sec. 2004–06, also Minister of Justice 2005–06; several sr posts in LDP including Deputy Chair. of Gen. Council 1999, Deputy Chair. Policy Research Council 2000. *Leisure interests:* golf, walking, classical music. *Address:* c/o Liberal-Democratic Party (Jiyu-Minshuto), 1-11-23, Nagata-cho, Chiyoda-ku, Tokyo 100-8910, Japan. *Telephone:* (3) 3581-6211. *E-mail:* koho@ ldp.jimin.or.jp. *Website:* www.jimin.jp; www.seiken-s.jp.

SUH, Kyung-suk; South Korean business executive; *President and CEO, GS Holdings;* began career in Ministry of Finance –1991; moved to LG Group as Sr Finance Advisor to Chair. LG Group 1991, later Pres. LG Investment & Securities Co.; Pres. and CEO GS Holdings Corpn (spun off from LG Group in 2004) 2004–, mem. Exec. Bd. *Address:* GS Holdings Corpn, 23 F, GS Tower, 679 Yoksam Dong, Gangnam Gu, Seoul, South Korea (office). *Telephone:* (2) 2005-1114 (office). *Fax:* (2) 2005-8181 (office). *E-mail:* info@gsholdings.com (office). *Website:* www.gsholdings.com (office).

SUHAIBI, Numan Saleh al-; Yemeni politician; currently Minister of Finance. *Address:* Ministry of Finance, PO Box 190, San'a, Yemen (office). *Telephone:* (1) 260370 (office). *Fax:* (1) 263040 (office).

SUHL, Harry, PhD; American physicist and academic; *Professor of Physics, Institute for Pure and Applied Physical Sciences, University of California, San Diego;* b. 18 Oct. 1922, Leipzig, Germany; s. of Bernhard Suhl and Klara Bergwerk; m. 1949 (deceased); ed Univ. Coll., Cardiff and Oriel Coll., Oxford, UK; Temp. Experimental Officer, Admiralty, London 1943–46; Tech. Staff, Bell Labs, NJ 1948–60; Prof. of Physics, Univ. of Calif., San Diego 1961–, now at Inst. for Pure and Applied Physical Sciences; Consultant, Aerospace Corpn 1961–, Exxon Research and Eng, NJ 1977–; Co-Ed. Magnetism 1961–74; Solid State Communications 1961–; Nat. Science Foundation Fellow 1971; Alexander V. Humboldt Sr Fellow 1991; Fellow, American Physics Soc., NAS, American Acad. of Arts and Sciences; Guggenheim Fellow 1968–69. *Publication:* Magnetism – A Treatise on Modern Theory and Materials (with G. T. Rado) 1966. *Address:* Physics Department, University of California, San Diego, 9500 Gilman Drive, La Jolla, CA 92093, USA. *Telephone:* (619) 534-4748. *Fax:* (619) 534-0173 (office). *E-mail:* hsuhl@ucsd.edu (office). *Website:* ipaps.ucsd.edu/faculty/suhl (office).

SUI, Anna; American fashion designer; *Founder and Designer, Anna Sui Corporation;* b. 1955, Dearborn, Mich.; d. of Paul Sui and Grace Sui; ed Parsons School of Design, New York; Founder and Designer Anna Sui Corpn 1988–; brought out first collection 1991; established reputation with 'baby-doll' collection 1993; designer Sui Anna Sui 1995–; launched new line of special-occasion gowns 1997; CFDA Perry Ellis Award for New Fashion Talent 1993. *Address:* c/o KCD Inc., 450 West 15th Street, Suite 604, New York, NY 10011; Anna Sui Corporation, 275 West 39th Street, Floor 9, New York, NY 10018 (office); 113 Green Street, New York, NY 10012, USA (office). *Telephone:* (212) 768-1951 (office). *E-mail:* contactus@annasui.com. *Website:* www.annasui.com.

SUI, Lt-Gen. Mingtai; Chinese army officer; b. 1942, Zhaoyuan Co., Shandong Prov.; ed Political and Mil. Coll. and Univ. of Nat. Defence; joined PLA 1960, CCP 1962; Deputy Political Commissar, later Political Commissar, Zhouqiao Regt 1976–82; Deputy Political Commissar, Eng Corps, PLA Services and Arms 1982–83 (also Dir Political Dept); Deputy Political Commissar, 2nd Artillery Force, PLA Services and Arms 1983–86 (Dir Political Dept 1983–86, 1994–97, Deputy Dir 1990–94), Political Commissar 1997–2007 (retd); mem. 15th CCP Cen. Cttee 1997–2002, 16th CCP Cen. Cttee 2002–07; rank of Maj.-Gen. 1988, Lt-Gen. 1996. *Address:* c/o People's Liberation Army Second Artillery Force Headquarters, Beijing, People's Republic of China (office).

SUI, Gen. Yongju; Chinese army officer; *Political Commissar, Second Artillery Force, Services and Arms, People's Liberation Army;* b. Nov. 1932, Dalian City; engaged in secret communist activities while still at school as mem. New Democratic Youth; joined CCP 1950, PLA 1950; Clerk Luda Garrison Command responsible for Communist Youth League work; Sec. Political Office Public Security Militia Luda Border Defence Regt 1953; Co. Political Guidance Officer Eng Regt Second Artillery, Regt Org. Section Chief, Div. Chief Political Dept 1969, Political Commissar, Dir Base Political Dept, Asst Political Commissar, Base Political Commissar; elected. mil. rep. 7th NPC 1988; selected as activist to study Mao's works 1968; trained Second Artillery Eng Acad. 1985, Dir Political Office Second Artillery 1988; Second Asst Political Commissar, Second Artillery 1985–92, Political Commissar 1992–; mem. Cen. Comm. for Disciplinary Inspection; rank of Maj.-Gen. 1988, Lt-Gen. 1990, Gen. 1996; Del., 15th CCP Nat. Congress 1997–2002; mem. 9th Standing Cttee of NPC 1998–2003. *Address:* People's Liberation Army, c/o Ministry of National Defence, Jingshanqian Jie, Beijing, People's Republic of China (office).

ŠUICA, Dubravka, BA; Croatian teacher and politician; *Mayor of Dubrovnik;* b. (Dubravka Luetić), 20 May 1957, Dubrovnik; m. Capt. Stijepo Šuica; one d.; ed Univ. of Zagreb, Univ. of Buffalo, NY, USA; taught English and German in Lapad Elementary School, Dubrovnik 1981–88, Centar za odgoj i usmjereno obrazovanje High School, Dubrovnik 1988–90; Prof. of English and German, Luka Sorkočević School of Arts, Dubrovnik 1990–92; Asst, Maritime Faculty, Dubrovnik 1992–94; Prof. of English, Polytechnic of Dubrovnik 1994–2000; Prin. Gimnazija Dubrovnik Classical Academic High School 1996–2000; Prof. of German, American Coll. of Man. and Tech., Dubrovnik 1998–2000; mem. Exec. Bd Municipality of Dubrovnik in charge of educ. 1991–93; Mayor of Dubrovnik 2001–; mem. Croatian Democratic Union (HDZ) 1990–, Pres. City Cttee and mem. HDZ's Cen. Cttee 1998–; mem. Croatian Parl. 2000–, mem. Inter-Parl. Cooperation Cttee 2000–04, Cttee on Local and Regional Self-Govt 2000–04, Deputy mem. Del. in OSCE Parl. Ass. 2000–04, Pres. Cttee for Family, Youth and Sport 2000–04; Pres. Croatian Del. to Congress of Local and Regional Authorities of Council of Europe (CLRAE) 2004–, First Vice-Pres. Chamber of Local Authorities of CLRAE 2004–; Councillor, Dubrovnik-Neretva Co. Ass. 1997–2001, 2006–; mem. Bd Union of Asscn of Towns of Repub. of Croatia 2002–, European Asscn of Historic Towns and Regions 2004–, Union of Asscn of Towns and Asscn of Municipalities of Repub. of Croatia 2005–; Kt, Order of European Wine Kts 2005, Croatian Kts' Consulate–Order of European Wine Kts 2005; named Croatia's Mayor of the Year 2005, 'Tourist Flower – Quality for Croatia' Award 2005, named one of Top 10 World Mayors 2006, World Mayor Award, City Mayors 2006. *Address:* Pred Dvorom 1, 20 000 Dubrovnik, Croatia (office). *Telephone:* (20) 351807 (office). *Fax:* (20) 321033 (office). *E-mail:* mayor@dubrovnik.hr (office); dubravka@dubravka-suica.com (office). *Website:* www.dubrovnik.hr (office); www.dubravka-suica.com.

SUISSA, Eliyahu (Eli); Israeli politician; b. 1956, Afula, Morocco; m.; four c.; career officer in Israel Defense Forces (IDF) and Army Chaplain of IDF Northern Command; mem. Knesset (Shas) 1999–2003; joined Ministry of Interior, first in charge of Jerusalem Dist, then as Deputy Dir-Gen.; Minister of the Interior and of Religious Affairs 1996–99, of Nat. Infrastructure 1999–2000; Minister without Portfolio, responsible for Jerusalem Affairs 2001–03. *Address:* c/o Ministry of the Interior, PO Box 6158, 2 Rehov Kaplan, Kiryat Ben-Gurion, Jerusalem 9108, Israel (office).

SUJATHA, Ramdorai, PhD; Indian mathematician and academic; *Professor of Mathematics, Tata Institute of Fundamental Research;* b. 1962, Bangalore; ed Annamalai Univ. and Tata Inst. of Fundamental Research; Research Fellow, Univ. of Regensburg, Germany 1992–93, Ohio State Univ., USA 1993–95; Assoc. Prof. of Math., Tata Inst. of Fundamental Research 2000–06, Prof. of Math. 2006–; Fellow, Indian Acad. of Sciences 2003; Shanti Swarup

Bhatnagar Prize, Council of Scientific & Industrial Research 2004, Ramanujan Prize, Int. Centre for Theoretical Physics 2006. *Address:* School of Mathematics, Tata Institute of Fundamental Research, Homi Bhabha Road, Colaba, 400005 Mumbai, India (office). *Telephone:* (22) 22782283 (office). *E-mail:* sujatha@math.tifr.res.in (office). *Website:* www.tifr.res.in (office).

SUKARNOPUTRI, Megawati (see MEGAWATI SUKARNOPUTRI).

ŠUKER, Ivan, DiplEcon; Croatian politician and economist; *Minister of Finance;* b. 12 Nov. 1957, Livno; m. Andrea Šuker; one s. one d.; ed Univ. of Zagreb; Chief Accountant, City Council, Velika Gorica 1984–86, Financial Dir 1986–1990, Head of Fiscal Office 1990–2000, Deputy Mayor 1990–91, Chief of Gen. Staff, Velika Gorica (during war) 1991–92; mem. City Council, Zagreb 1993–97, Deputy Mayor 1997–2000; elected to Sabor (Parl.) for Croatian Democratic Union (Hrvatska Demokratska Zajednica—HDZ) 2000–, mem. Finance and Budget Cttee, Pres. HDZ, Velika Gorica 2000–03, mem. HDZ Nat. Bureau 2000–, Deputy Chair. HDZ 2002–; Minister of Finance 2003–. *Address:* Ministry of Finance, 10000 Zagreb, ul. Katančićeva 5, Croatia (office). *Telephone:* (1) 4591300 (office). *Fax:* (1) 4922583 (office). *E-mail:* kabinet@mfin.hr (office). *Website:* www.mfin.hr (office).

ŠUKYS, Raimondas, DCL; Lithuanian lawyer and politician; b. 27 Oct. 1966, Šiauliai; m. Adelė Šukys; one s. one d.; ed Janonio Secondary School (now J. Janonio Gymnasium), Šiauliai, Vilnius State Univ. (now Vilnius Univ.); mil. service 1985–87; lawyer, Šiauliu kraštas (daily newspaper) 1991–92; lawyer, Verslo raktas (advisory co.) 1992–94; asst, Civil Law and Civil Process Dept, Law Faculty, Vilnius Univ. 1992–2004; referent, Fraction of Lithuanian Democratic Working Party (LDDP) 1993–94; adviser, Seimas (Parl.) Comm. on Econ. Crimes Investigation 1994–97; mem. Lithuanian Liberal Party 1997–2003, Liberal and Centre Union 2003–; mem. election HQ of cand. for presidency, Valdas Adamkus 1997; solicitor, UAB BNA grupe 1998–99; adviser for civil law, Legal Dept, Office of the Govt 1999–2000; mem. Seimas (Lithuanian Liberal Party) for Fabijoniškes Election Dist No. 5, mem. Cttee on Legal Affairs 2000–04, re-elected to Seimas for Liberal and Centre Union 2004–; mem. Vilnius City Bd 2002–03; Attorney of Pres. Valdas Adamkus for elections 2004; Minister of the Interior 2006–07 (resgnd). *Leisure interests:* gardening, literature, music, fishing. *Address:* Liberal and Centre Union (Liberalų Centro Sąjunga), Vilniaus g. 22/1, 01119 Vilnius, Lithuania (office). *Telephone:* (5) 231-3264 (office). *Fax:* (5) 261-9363 (office). *E-mail:* info@lics.lt (office). *Website:* www.lics.lt (office).

SULAIM, Suliman Abd al aziz as-; Saudi Arabian politician; b. 1941; ed Cairo Univ., Univ. of Southern Calif., Johns Hopkins Univ., USA; Dir Dept of Foreign Relations and Confs, Ministry of Labour; Asst Dir-Gen. Gen. Org. of Social Insurance; Prof. of Political Science, Riyadh Univ. 1972–74; Deputy Minister of Commerce and Industry for Trade and Provisions 1974–75; Minister of Commerce 1975–95; Chair. Bd Saudi Arabian Specifications and Standardization Org., Wheat Silos and Flour Mills Org. *Address:* c/o Ministry of Commerce, P.O. Box 1774, Airport Road, 11162 Riyadh, Saudi Arabia.

SULEYMANOGLU, Naim; Turkish weightlifter; b. (Naim Suleimanov), 1967, Ptchar, Bulgaria; defected to Turkey in 1986; youngest world record breaker (16 years, 62 days) when he set records for clean and jerk (160 kg.) and combined total (285 kg.); triple Olympic gold medallist; 22 gold, one silver and one bronze in Senior World Championships (twice for Bulgaria); retd 1996; fmr Vice-Pres. Int. Weightlifting Fed.; launched clothing and leather goods business; inducted into Int. Weightlifting Hall of Fame 2000, 2004; voted one of the 25 greatest athletes of the 20th century by Int. Sports Journalist Asscn. *Address:* c/o Turkiye Halter Federasyonu, Ulus Ishani A Blok, Ulus 06050 Ankara, Turkey (office).

SULEYMENOV, Olzhas Omarovich; Kazakhstani politician, diplomatist and writer; *Ambassador to United Nations Educational, Scientific and Cultural Organization (UNESCO);* b. 1936; ed Kazak State Univ., Maxim Gorky Inst. of Literature in Moscow; mem. CPSU 1989–90; debut as writer in 1960; Ed.-in-Chief Studio Kazakhfilm 1962–71; head of div. Prostor (magazine) 1971–; Sec. Bd Kazakh Writers' Union 1971–; Chair. Kazakh Cttee on relations with writers of Asia and Africa 1980–; actively participates in ecological movt, actions of protest against nuclear tests in Semipalatinsk since late 1980s; Deputy to USSR Supreme Soviet 1984–89; People's Deputy, mem. USSR Supreme Soviet 1989–91; Founder and Leader of People's Progress Party of Kazakhstan 1992–95; Amb. to Italy 1995–2001; Amb. to UNESCO 2001–; USSR Komsomol Prize, State Abai Prize of Kazakh SSR. *Publications:* collections of poetry including Argamaki 1961, Sunny Nights 1962, The Night of Paris 1963, The Kind Time of the Sunrise 1964, The Year of Monkey 1967, Above White Rivers 1970, Each Day – Morning 1973, Repeating in the Noon 1973, A Round Star 1975, Definition of a Bank 1976 and others. *Address:* Permanent Delegation to UNESCO, 59, rue Pierre Charron, 75008 Paris, France (office). *Telephone:* 1-42-25-02-10 (office). *Fax:* 1-42-25-11-11 (office). *E-mail:* Unescokz@wanadoo.fr (office).

SULLIVAN, Andrew, PhD; British journalist; b. 20 Aug. 1963, Godstone, Surrey; pnr Aaron Tone; ed Magdalen Coll., Oxford Univ., Dept of Govt, Harvard Univ., USA; intern Centre For Policy Studies, London; intern New Republic magazine 1986, returned to Harvard and taught in Govt Dept 1987, returned as Assoc. Ed. New Republic 1987, Deputy Ed. 1990, Acting Ed. 1991, Ed. 1991–96; contributing writer and columnist New York Times Magazine, contrib. New York Times Book Review –2002; weekly columnist for Sunday Times of London; est. andrewsullivan.com's Daily Dish blog 2000 at Time magazine, now with The Atlantic Monthly. *Publication:* Virtually Normal: An Argument About Homosexuality 1995, Love Undetectable: Notes on Friendship, Sex, and Survival 1999, The Conservative Soul 2006. *Address:* c/o The Atlantic Monthly Group, The Watergate, 600 New Hampshire Avenue, NW, Washington, DC 20037, USA (office). *Website:* andrewsullivan.theatlantic.com.

SULLIVAN, Barry F., MBA; American business executive and fmr government official; *Vice Chairman, K Road Acquisition Corporation;* b. 21 Dec. 1930, Bronx, NY; m.; four s. one d.; ed Columbia Univ.; Georgetown Univ. and Univ. of Chicago; served in US Army in Korea; with Chase Manhattan Bank 1957–80, mem. Man. Cttee 1974–80; Chair. and CEO First Chicago Corpn, First Nat. Bank of Chicago 1980–91; apptd Deputy Mayor, Finance and Econ. Devt, New York City 1992; Pres. New York City Partnership and New York Chamber of Commerce and Industry 1993; Vice Chair. Sithe Energies Inc. 1995–2003; Pres. and Chief Operating Officer K Road Power Management LLC (pvt. investment co.) 2003–, Vice Chair. Man. Bd K Road Acquisition Corpn 2003–; Dir and Chief Operating Officer EBG 2006–07; fmr mem. Econ. Devt Comm. of Chicago, Asscn of Reserve City Bankers, Mayor's Airport Study Comm., Chicago Clearing House Cttee, World's Fair Finance Cttee; fmr Vice-Pres. Exec. Cttee, Chicago Asscn of Commerce and Industry; mem. Bd of Dirs Liati Group LLC, Liati Capital LLC, Omega Tools Inc., Perftech Inc., Hilliard Farber & Co. Inc., US Power Generating Co. 2007–; fmr Dir United Way: Crusade of Mercy Chicago, Campaign Dir 1985; mem. Pres.'s Council, Graduate Theological Union; Trustee and mem. Exec. Cttee, Univ. of Chicago, also Chair. of Council of Graduate School of Business; Trustee, Art Inst. of Chicago, Gregorian Univ. Foundation; Dr hc (Univ. of Chicago) 1994; John Jay Award, Columbia Coll. 1996. *Address:* K Road Acquisition Corporation, 330 Madison Avenue, 25th Floor, New York, NY 10017, USA. *Telephone:* (212) 351-0535.

SULLIVAN, Dennis P., BA, PhD; American mathematician and academic; *Einstein Chair, Department of Mathematics, City University of New York;* b. 12 Feb. 1941, Port Huron, Mich.; three s. two d.; ed Rice and Princeton Univs; NATO Fellow, Univ. of Warwick, UK 1966; Miller Fellow, Univ. of California, Berkeley 1967–69; Sloan Fellow of Math., MIT 1969–72, Prof. of Math. 1972–73; Prof. Perm., Institut des Hautes Etudes Scientifiques, Paris, France 1973–96; Einstein Prof. of Sciences, Queens Coll. and CUNY Grad. School, CUNY, New York 1981–; concurrently Distinguished Prof. of Math., State Univ. of NY at Stony Brook; mem. NAS, NY Acad. of Sciences; Fellow, AAAS, American Acad. of Arts and Sciences 1991–; fmr Vice-Pres. American Math. Soc.; Dr hc (Warwick) 1984; Oswald Veblen Prize in Geometry 1971, Elie Cartan Prix en Géométrie, French Acad. of Sciences 1981, King Faisal Int. Prize of Science 1994, New York City Mayor's Award for Excellence in Science and Tech. 1997, Nat. Medal of Science 2004, Steele Prize, American Math. Soc. 2006,. *Publications:* several papers in math. journals. *Leisure interest:* people. *Address:* Mathematics Ph.D. Program, City University of New York, The Graduate Center, 365 Fifth Avenue, Room 4208, New York, NY 10016-4309 (office); Mathematics Department, 5-114 Mathematics Building, SUNY, Stony Brook, NY 11794-3651, USA. *Telephone:* (212) 817-8578 (office); (631)-632-8359 (Stony Brook). *Fax:* (212) 817-1527; (631)-632-7631 (Stony Brook). *E-mail:* dsullivan@gc.cuny.edu (office); dennis@math.sunysb.edu (office). *Website:* math.gc.cuny.edu (office); www.math.sunysb.edu/html/index.shtml (office).

SULLIVAN, Janice; American business executive; *President, Calvin Klein Jeans Division, Warnaco Group Inc.;* fmr exec. with Donna Karan; joined DKNY Jeans and DKNY Active licence divs, Liz Claiborne 1997, Pres. 2005–07, Pres. Narciso Rodriguez LLC 2007; Pres. Calvin Klein Jeans div., Warnaco Group, Inc. 2007–. *Address:* Calvin Klein Jeans Division, Warnaco Group Inc., 501 7th Avenue, New York, NY 10018, USA (office). *Telephone:* (212) 287-8250 (office). *E-mail:* contactus@warnaco.com (office). *Website:* www.warnaco.com (office).

SULLIVAN, Louis Wade, BS, MD; American physician and fmr government official; b. 3 Nov. 1933, Atlanta; s. of Walter Wade Sullivan and Lubirda Elizabeth Sullivan (née Priester); m. Eve Williamson 1955; three c.; ed Morehouse Coll., Atlanta, Boston Univ.; Intern, New York Hosp.-Cornell Medical Centre, New York 1958–59, resident in internal medicine 1959–60; Fellow in Pathology, Mass. Gen. Hosp., Boston 1960–61; Research Fellow, Thorndike Memorial Lab., Harvard Medical School, Boston 1961–63, Instructor of Medicine 1963–64; Asst Prof. Medicine, NJ Coll. Medicine 1964–66; Co-Dir Haematology, Boston Univ. Medical Centre 1966, Assoc. Prof. 1968–74, Prof. of Medicine and Physiology 1974–75; Dir Hematology, Boston City Hosp.; Founder and Dean School of Medicine, Morehouse Coll. 1975–89, Pres. 1981–89, 1993–2002, Pres. Emer. 2002–; Sec., US Health and Human Services Admin., Washington, DC 1989–93; mem. Bd of Dirs Gen. Motors 1993–2002, Points of Light Foundation 2004–; mem. sickle cell anaemia Advisory Cttee, NIH 1974–75, Medical Advisory Bd, Nat. Leukemia Asscn 1968–70, (Chair. 1970); mem. American Soc. of Hematology, American Soc. of Clinical Investigation, Inst. of Medicine; mem. Pres.'s Bd of Advisors on Historically Black Colls and Univs, Presidential Advisory Council on HIV/AIDS; Founding Pres. Asscn of Minority Health Professions Schools. *Publications:* numerous papers on medical matters. *Address:* c/o Office of the President, Morehouse School of Medicine, 720 Westview Drive, SW, Atlanta, GA 30310, USA (office).

SULLIVAN, Martin J.; British insurance executive; m.; two d.; joined Finance Dept, American Int. Underwriters (AIU), part of American Int. Group (AIG) 1971, with Property Dept 1974, Property Man. UK 1983, later Regional Property Man. UK/Ireland, Man. AIU London and Regional Marketing Man. UK/Ireland 1988, Asst Man. Dir AIG Europe (UK) Ltd 1989, COO 1991, Pres. UK/Ireland Div., AIU and Man. Dir AIG Europe (UK) Ltd 1993, Sr Vice-Pres., Foreign Gen. Insurance 1996, Exec. Vice-Pres. 1998, COO AIU New York 1996, Pres. 1997, mem. Bd AIG Inc. 2002–, Vice-Chair. and Co-COO AIG Inc. 2002–05, Pres. and CEO AIG Inc. 2005–08; Dir Int. Insurance Soc., Geneva Asscn, Young Audiences Inc., Friends of London Youth Inc.; mem. Business

Advisory Cttee, St George's Soc., British Memorial Garden Trust; mem. Bd of Trustees, American Assocs of the Royal Acad. Trust; assoc. mem. Chartered Insurance Inst.; mem. Chartered Man. Inst.; Fellow, Inst. of Leadership and Man. *Address:* c/o American International Group Inc., 70 Pine Street, New York, NY 10270, USA (office).

SULLIVAN, Michael J., BSc, JD; American lawyer, diplomatist and fmr politician; *Partner, Rothgerber Johnson & Lyons LLP;* b. 22 Sept. 1939, Omaha; s. of Joseph B. Sullivan and Margaret Hamilton; m. Jane Metzler 1961; one s. two d.; ed Univ. of Wyoming; Assoc., Brown, Drew, Apostolos, Barton & Massey (law firm), Casper, Wyo. 1964–67; Pnr, Brown, Drew, Apostolos, Massey & Sullivan, Casper 1967–; Gov. of Wyo. 1987–95; Amb. to Ireland 1998–2001; Pnr, Rothgerber Johnson & Lyons LLP 2001–; mem. ABA; Democrat. *Leisure interests:* jogging, tennis, golf, fly-fishing, reading. *Address:* Rothgerber Johnson & Lyons LLP, 123 West First Street, Suite 200, Casper, WY 82601-2480, USA (office). *Telephone:* (307) 232-0222 (office). *Fax:* (307) 232-0077 (office). *E-mail:* msullivan@rothgerber.com (home). *Website:* www.rothgerber.com.

SULSTON, Sir John Edward, Kt, PhD, FRS; British scientist; b. 27 March 1942, Fulmer; s. of the late Rev. Canon Arthur Edward Aubrey Sulston and Josephine Muriel Frearson Blocksidge; m. Daphne Edith Bate 1966; one s. one d.; ed Merchant Taylor's School and Pembroke Coll., Cambridge; Postdoctoral Fellowship at the Salk Inst., Calif. 1966–69; staff scientist, MRC Lab. of Molecular Biology, Cambridge 1969–2003; Dir The Sanger Centre 1992–2000; Chair. Inst. for Science Ethics and Innovation, Univ. of Manchester 2007–; mem. Human Genetics Comm. 2001–; mem. European Molecular Biology Org. 1989–, Academia Europaea 2001–; Hon. Fellow, Pembroke Coll., Cambridge 2000, Royal Soc. of Chemisty 2003, Acad. of Medical Sciences 2003, hon. mem. Biochemical Soc. 2002, Physiological Soc. 2002, Freedom of Merchant Taylors' Co. 2004; Hon. DSc (Trinity Coll., Dublin) 2000, (Essex) 2002, (Cambridge) 2003, (Royal Holloway) 2003, (Exeter) 2003, (Newcastle) 2004, Hon. LLD (Dundee) 2005; Officier, Légion d'honneur 2004; W. Alden Spencer Award (jtly) 1986, Gairdner Foundation Award (jtly) 1991, 2002, Darwin Medal, Royal Soc. 1996, Rosenstiel Award (jtly) 1998, Pfizer Prize for Innovative Science 2000, Genetics Soc. of America George W. Beadle Medal 2000, Biochemical Soc. Sir Frederick Gowland Hopkins Medal 2000, Edinburgh Medal 2001, City of Medicine Award, Durham, NC 2001, Prince of Asturias Award, Spain 2001, Robert Burns Humanitarian Award 2002, Daily Mirror Pride of Britain Award 2002, Medical Soc. of London Fothergillian Medal 2002, Tel-Aviv Univ. Dan David Prize 2002, General Motors Sloan Prize 2002, Nobel Prize in Physiology or Medicine (jtly) 2002. *Television:* Royal Inst. Christmas Lectures (Channel 4) 2001. *Publications:* The Common Thread – A Story of Science, Politics, Ethics and the Human Genome (jtly) 2002; papers in scientific journals. *Leisure interests:* gardening, walking. *Address:* 39 Mingle Lane, Stapleford, Cambridge, CB22 5SY, England (home). *Telephone:* (1223) 842248 (home). *E-mail:* jes@sanger.ac.uk (office).

SULTAN, Altoon, BA, MFA; American artist; b. 29 Sept. 1948, Brooklyn, New York; d. of Raymond Sultan and Adele Chalom Sultan; ed Abraham Lincoln High School, Brooklyn and Brooklyn Coll.; work in public collections: Metropolitan Museum of Art, New York, Tate Modern, London, Nat. Gallery of Australia, Canberra, Hunter Museum, Chattanooga, Tenn., Library of Congress, Washington, DC, Museum of Fine Arts, Boston, Nat. Museum of Women in the Arts, Washington, DC, Yale Univ. Art Gallery and Walker Art Center, Minneapolis; mem. Nat. Acad. of Design, New York; Nat. Endowment for the Arts Fellowship Grant 1983, 1989, Karolyi Foundation Fellowship 1984, Acad. Award in Art, American Acad. of Arts and Letters 1999, Prix Duc de Valverde d'Ayala Valva, Fondation Monaco 1999. *Publication:* The Luminous Brush: Painting with Egg Tempera. *Leisure interest:* gardening. *Address:* PO Box 2, Groton, VT 05046, USA (home). *Telephone:* (802) 584-4052 (home). *Fax:* (802) 584-4052 (office). *E-mail:* asultan@fairpoint.net (home).

SULTAN, Donald Keith, BFA, MFA; American painter, printmaker and sculptor; b. 5 May 1951, Asheville, NC; s. of Norman Sultan and Phyllis Sultan; m. Susan Reynolds 1978; one s. one d.; ed Univ. of N Carolina, Art Inst. of Chicago; represented by Willard Gallery 1979–82, Blum Helman Gallery 1982–89, M. Knoedler Gallery New York 1989; work in collections: Art Inst. of Chicago, Hirsh Museum and Sculpture Garden, Washington DC, The Metropolitan Museum of Art, New York, The Museum of Fine Arts, Boston, The Museum of Modern Art, New York, The Solomon R. Guggenheim Museum, New York, Walker Art Center, Minneapolis, Bibliothèque Nationale, Paris 1992; Public Service Grant NY State 1978–79, Nat. Endowments for the Arts 1980–81; Dr hc (Corcoran School of Art, Washington, DC) 2000, (New York Acad. of Art) 2002. *Address:* c/o Jonathan Novak Contemporary Art, 1880 Century Park East, Suite 100, Los Angeles, CA 90067, USA.

SULTAN, Fouad, BSc; Egyptian business executive and fmr government official; *Chairman, Heliopolis Sporting Club;* b. 26 Jan. 1931; s. of Abdel Latif Sultan and Farida Torky; m. Ferial Fikry 1956, one s. one d.; ed Univ. of Cairo; worked for 21 years with Cen. Bank of Egypt; seconded to IMF, North Yemen 1971–74; CEO Misr-Iran Bank 1974–85; head of several cttees in Fed. of Egyptian Banks; Minister of Tourism and Civil Aviation 1985–93; fmr Chair. and CEO El Ahly Development and Investment Co.; Chair. Heliopolis Sporting Club 1989–. *Leisure interests:* rowing, tennis, swimming. *Address:* Heliopolis Sporting Club, 17 El-Merghany St., Heliopolis, 11341 Cairo. *E-mail:* info@hsc.com.eg. *Website:* www.hsc.com.

SULTANGAZIN, Umirzak Makhmutovich, D.Physics and Maths; Kazakhstani scientist and academic; b. 10 April 1936, Kustanai Region; s. of Sultangazy Makhmutov and Nurila Makhmutova; m. Raikhan Meirmanova 1958, two c.; ed Kazakh State Univ. and USSR (now Russian) Acad. of Sciences, Novosibirsk; Asst Prof., Kazakh State Univ. 1958–60, Assoc. Prof. 1960–64, Prof. of Math. 1972–78; Dir Inst. of Math. and Mechanics, Acad. of Sciences of Kazakh SSR 1978–88, Vice-Pres. of Acad. 1986–88, Pres. 1988–94, Dir Space Research Inst. of Kazhakhstan 1991–95; Visiting Prof., Karlov Univ. Czechoslovakia 1972, Kyoto Univ. Japan 1994–95; Chair. Fed. of Cosmonautics 1985, Peace Fund of Kazakh SSR 1987, Math Cttee of Rep. of Kazakhstan 1994; Corresp. mem. Acad. of Sciences of Kazakh SSR 1975, mem. 1983; CPSU 1968–91, Cen. Cttee 1989–91; mem. Parl. Kazakh SSR 1987–89, Parl. of USSR 1989–91; Korolev's Medal 1986, State Prize of USSR for Science and Tech. 1987, Red Banner Order 1987, Prize of Acad. of Sciences of USSR and Czechoslovakia for Nat. Sciences 1988. *Publications:* Concentrated Capacity in the Problems of Heat Physics and Microelectronics 1972, Method of Spherical Harmonics in Kinetic Transport Theory 1979, Mathematical Problems of Kinetic Transport Theory 1986, Discrete Nonlinear Models of Boltzmann Equation 1987, Ecological and Economical Model of Kazakhstan 1995; 150 articles on mathematical physics, numerical mathematics and ecology. *Leisure interests:* history, mountain tourism. *Address:* c/o National Academy of Sciences of the Republic of Kazakhstan, PO 480021, 28 Shevchenko Street, Almaty; Institute of Space Research, 120–33 Maulenov str., 50096 Almaty, Kazakhstan (office). *Telephone:* (727) 262-38-96 (office); (727) 261-68-53. *Fax:* (727) 249-43-55. *E-mail:* usultan@academset.kz.

SULTANOV, Marat Abdyrazakovich; Kyrgyzstani politician; *Minister of Finance;* b. 5 Dec. 1960, Frunze (Bishkek); m.; two d.; ed Moscow State Univ.; Prof., Kyrgyz Nat. Univ. 1987–92; Deputy Chair. Nat. Bank 1992–94, Chair. 1994–98; Minister of Finance Jan.–June 1999, 2009–; mem. Parl. 2000–, Speaker, Zhogorku Kenesh 2006–09; Head, Defence and Security Dept in Presidential Admin 2004. *Address:* Ministry of Finance, 720040 Bishkek, pr. Erkindik 58, Kyrgyzstan (office). *Telephone:* (312) 66-13-50 (office). *Fax:* (312) 66-16-45 (office). *E-mail:* it@minfin.kg (office). *Website:* www.minfin.kg (office).

SULTANOV, Otkir S.; Uzbekistan fmr politician; b. 14 July 1939; m.; one d.; ed Tomsk State Polytech. Inst.; electrician, Tomsk plant of cutting metals 1963; with Tashkent Aviation Production Union 1964–85, numerous positions including Master, Head of Lab., Head of Production Automatization, Deputy Chief Engineer, Deputy Dir-Gen.; Head of Scientific Production Unit, Vostok 1985–91; Chair. State Cttee for Foreign Trade and Int. Relations 1991–92; Minister of External Econ. Relations, Deputy Prime Minister 1992–95; Prime Minister of Uzbekistan 1995–2003; fmr Deputy Prime Minister in charge of Industry; People's Deputy of Uzbekistan; Mekhnat Shukhradi; Merited Engineer Repub. of Uzbekistan. *Address:* c/o Office of the Cabinet of Ministers, Mustaqillik maydoni 5, 100078 Tashkent, Uzbekistan (office).

SULZBERGER, Arthur Ochs; American newspaper executive; *Chairman Emeritus, New York Times Company;* b. 5 Feb. 1926, New York City; s. of Arthur Hays and Iphigene Sulzberger (née Ochs); m. 1st Barbara Grant 1948 (divorced 1956); one s. (Arthur Ochs Sulzberger Jr) one d.; m. 2nd Carol Fox 1956 (died 1995); two d.; m. 3rd Allison Stacey Cowles 1996; ed Columbia Univ.; served in US Marine Corps during Second World War and Korean War; joined The New York Times Co., New York 1951, Asst Treas. 1958–63, Pres. 1963–79, Publr 1963–92, Chair., CEO 1992–97, Chair. Emer. 1997–, mem. Bd of Dirs –2002; Co-Chair. Bd Int. Herald Tribune 1983; Chair. Newspaper Pres. Assen 1988; Dir, Times Printing Co., Chattanooga, Gapesia Pulp and Paper Co. Ltd of Canada; Trustee Columbia Univ., mem. Coll. Council, now Trustee Emer.; Trustee Metropolitan Museum of Art, Chair. Bd of Trustees 1987–99; Hon. LHD (Montclair State Coll.), (Tufts Univ.) 1984; Columbia Journalism Award 1992; Alexander Hamilton Medal 1982, Vermeil Medal (City of Paris) 1992. *Address:* New York Times Co., 620 8th Avenue, New York, NY 10018, USA. *Telephone:* (212) 556-1234. *Fax:* (212) 556-7389. *Website:* www.nytco.com.

SULZBERGER, Arthur Ochs, Jr, BA; American newspaper publisher; *Chairman, The New York Times Company;* b. 22 Sept. 1951, Mount Kisco, NY; s. of Arthur Ochs Sulzberger and Barbara Winslow Grant; m. Gail Gregg 1975; one s. one d.; ed Tufts Univ., Harvard Univ. Business School; reporter, The Raleigh Times, N Carolina 1974–76; corresp., Associated Press, London, UK 1976–78; Washington bureau corresp., The New York Times 1978–81, city hall reporter 1981, Asst Metro Ed. 1981–82, Group Man., Advertising Dept 1983–84, Sr Analyst, Corp. Planning 1985, Production Co-ordinator 1985–87, Asst Publr 1987–88, Deputy Publr 1988–92, Publr 1992–, Chair. The New York Times Co. 1997–; mem. Bd New York City Outward Bound Center; RIT Isaiah Thomas Award in Publishing 2003. *Address:* The New York Times Company, 620 Eighth Avenue, New York, NY 10018, USA (office). *Telephone:* (212) 556-1234 (office). *E-mail:* publisher@nytimes.com (office). *Website:* www.nytco.com (office).

SUMAIDA'IE, Samir Shakir Mahmood, BSc; Iraqi business executive and diplomatist; *Ambassador to USA;* b. 1944, Baghdad; m.; five c.; ed Univ. of Durham, UK; left Iraq after Saddam Hussein seized power 1973; Middle East Man., Nixdorf Computers, Paderborn, Germany 1973–74; Middle East Man., Logica Ltd, London 1974–78; Man. Dir Tenda Ltd, London 1978–82; Man. Dir Turath Ltd, London 1982–90; Man. Dir Samir Design Ltd, London 1991–96; Man. Dir China Business Int., Beijing 1996–2003; returned to Baghdad and was apptd mem. Iraq Governing Council July 2003; Minister of the Interior April–Aug. 2004; Perm. Rep. to UN, New York 2004–06, Amb. to USA 2006–; participant, Beirut and Vienna Opposition Confs 1991, NY Iraqi Opposition Conf. 1992; Co-founder, manifesto, Democratic Party of Iraq 1993; mem. Governing Council of Iraq 2003, fmr Chair. Media Cttee, Cttee on Provs, fmr Deputy Chair. Foreign Affairs Cttee, fmr mem. Security, Finance and Public Service Cttees. *Publication:* The Night of the Long Lament: A Day in the Life of an Iraqi Dissident, Ahmed Al-Habboubi (trans). *Address:* Embassy of Iraq, 1801 P Street, Washington, DC 20036, USA (office). *Telephone:* (202) 483-7500 (office). *Fax:* (202) 462-5066 (office). *E-mail:* admin@iraqiembassy.us (office). *Website:* www.iraqiembassy.us (office).

SUMAYE, Frederick; Tanzanian politician; b. 29 May 1950, Hanang Dist, Arusah; ed Egerton Coll., Kenya, Edward S. Mason Program, Kennedy School of Govt, Harvard Univ., USA; Tutor, MATI–Nyegezi 1973–76; Eng. Section Man. Kilombero Sugar Co. 1976–80; Head of Rural Energy Dept, CARMATEC 1980–82; mem. Parl. for Hanang constituency 1985–2005; Deputy Minister of Agric. 1987–94, Minister of Agric. 1995; Prime Minister of Tanzania 1995–2005; mem. Chama Cha Mapinduzi (Party for Democracy and Progress), mem. Cen. Cttee –2007. *Address:* c/o Chama Cha Mapinduzi (Revolutionary Party of Tanzania), Kuu Street, PO Box 50, Dodoma, Tanzania. *Telephone:* 2180575. *E-mail:* katibumkuu@ccmtz.org. *Website:* www.ccmtz.org.

SUMI, Shuzo, BEng; Japanese insurance executive; *President and Representative Director, Millea Holdings Inc.;* b. 11 July 1947; ed Waseda Univ.; joined Tokio Marine and Fire Insurance Co. Ltd 1970, Gen. Man. Production Dept No. 7 1995–98, Gen. Man. Commercial Lines Underwriting Dept 1998–2000, Dir and Chief Rep. Tokio Marine Overseas Div., London 2000–02, Man. Dir Tokio Marine 2002–04, Man. Dir Tokio Marine & Nichido (following merger 2004) 2004–05, Sr Man. Dir 2005–07, Pres. 2007–, Pres. and Rep. Dir Millea Holdings Inc. (parent co.) 2007–; Dir Gen. Insurance Asscn of Japan. *Address:* Millea Holdings Inc., 1-2-1 Marunouchi, Chiyoda-ku, Tokyo, 100-0005, Japan (office). *Telephone:* (3) 6212-3333 (office). *Fax:* (3) 6212-3711 (office). *E-mail:* info@millea.co.jp (office). *Website:* www.millea.co.jp/en (office).

SUMMER, Donna; American singer and actress; b. (Donna Adrian Gaines) 31 Dec. 1948, Boston, Mass; d. of Andrew Gaines and Mary Gaines; m. 1st Helmut Sommer 1971 (divorced); one d.; m. 2nd Bruce Sudano 1980 (divorced); one s. one d.; singer 1967–; appeared in German stage production Hair; in Europe 1967–75, appearing in Vienna Folk productions of Porgy and Bess and German productions of The Me Nobody Knows; Hon. DFA (Univ. of Massachussetts) 1997; Nat. Acad. of Recording Arts and Sciences Best Rhythm and Blues Female Vocalist 1978, Acad. Award for Best Original Song (for Heaven Knows) 1979, Rolling Stone Magazine Soul Artist of Year 1979, Grammy Awards for Best Rhythm and Blues Vocal Performance 1979, Best Rock Vocal Performance 1980, Best Inspirational Performance 1984, 1985, American Music Awards for Favorite Female Disco Artist, Disco Single, Disco Album 1979, Favorite Female Pop/Rock Artist, Favorite Pop/Rock Single, Favorite Female Soul/R&B Artist 1980, Best Rock Performance, Best of Las Vegas Jimmy Award 1980, Best Dance Recording (for Carry On) 1997. *Film appearance:* Thank God It's Friday 1978. *Recordings:* albums: Lady of the Night 1974, Love to Love You Baby 1975, Four Seasons of Love 1976, Love Trilogy 1976, I Remember Yesterday 1977, Once Upon a Time... 1977, Live and More 1978, Bad Girls 1979, The Wanderer 1980, On The Radio (Ampex Golden Reel Award) 1979, Donna Summer 1982, She Works Hard for the Money 1983, Cats Without Claws 1984, All Systems Go 1987, Another Place and Time 1989, Mistaken Identity 1991, This Time I Know 1993, Endless Summer 1994, Christmas Spirit 1994, Live 1994, Nice to See You 1995, Shout it Out 1995, I'm a Rainbow 1996, Live And More Encore 1999, Crayons 2008. *Address:* Moress Nanas Hart Entertainment, 14945 Ventura Blvd, Suite 228, Sherman Oaks, CA 91403, USA (office). *Telephone:* (818) 379-9516 (office). *Fax:* (818) 379-9517 (office). *Website:* www.donnasummer.com (office).

SUMMERS, Lawrence H., PhD; American economist, academic, fmr government official and fmr university administrator; *Charles W. Eliot University Professor, Department of Economics, Harvard University;* b. 30 Nov. 1954, New Haven, Conn.; s. of Dr Robert Summers and Anita Summers; one s. two d.; ed Mass. Inst. of Tech and Harvard Univ.; domestic policy economist, US Council of Econ. Advisers 1982–83; Prof. of Econs Harvard Univ. 1983–93, 2002, Nathaniel Ropes Prof. of Political Economy 1987, Pres. Harvard Univ. 2002–06, Charles W. Eliot Univ. Prof. 2006–; Chief Economist and Vice-Pres. of Devt Econs IBRD 1991–93; fmr Econ. Adviser to Pres. Bill Clinton; Treasury Under-Sec. for Int. Affairs 1993–95; Deputy Treasury Sec. 1995–99; Sec. of Treasury 1999–2001; Arthur Okun Distinguished Fellow in Econs, Globalization and Governance, Brookings Inst. 2001–02; Pres. Harvard Univ. 2002–06; Fellow, American Acad. of Arts and Sciences; mem. Nat. Acad. of Sciences 2002–; Hon. DJur (Harvard) 2007; Alan T. Waterman Award, Nat. Science Foundation 1987, John Bates Clark Medal 1993, Alexander Hamilton Medal 2001. *Publications:* Understanding Unemployment, Reform in Eastern Europe (co-author), more than 100 articles. *Leisure interests:* skiing, tennis. *Address:* Department of Economics, Harvard University, Littauer Center 242, 1875 Cambridge Street, Cambridge, MA 02138, USA (office). *Telephone:* (617) 495-0436 (office). *Fax:* (617) 495-8550 (office). *E-mail:* lawrence_summers@harvard.edu (office). *Website:* www.economics.harvard.edu (office).

SUMNER, Gordon Matthew (see STING).

SUMPTION, Jonathan Philip Chadwick, QC, MA; British barrister and author; *Judge of Courts of Appeal of Guernsey and Jersey;* b. 9 Dec. 1948, London; s. of A. J. Sumption and Mrs H. Sumption; m. Teresa Mary Whelan 1971; one s. two d.; ed Eton Coll., Magdalen Coll., Oxford; Fellow in History, Magdalen Coll., Oxford 1971–75; called to Bar (Inner Temple) 1975; Recorder 1992–; Judge of Courts of Appeal of Guernsey and Jersey 1995–; mem. Brick Court Chambers. *Publications:* Pilgrimage: An Image of Medieval Religion 1975, The Albigensian Crusade 1979, The Hundred Years War (Vol. 1) 1989, (Vol. 2) 1999. *Leisure interests:* music, history. *Address:* Brick Court Chambers, 7–8 Essex Street, London, WC2R 3LD, England (office). *Telephone:* (20) 7379-3550 (office). *Fax:* (20) 7379-3558 (office). *Website:* www.brickcourt.co.uk (office).

SUN, Fuling; Chinese party official and business executive; b. 1921, Shaoxing City, Zhejiang Prov.; Head, Fuxing Flour Mill, Beijing 1948–54;

Vice-Chair. Beijing Municipal Cttee China Democratic Nat. Construction Asscn 1956–87; Dir Beijing Municipal Services Admin 1958–66; Deputy Dir Beijing Foreign Trade Bureau 1979–83; fmr Dir China Int. Trust and Investment Corpn; Vice-Mayor Beijing 1983–93; Vice-Chair. CPPCC Beijing Municipal Cttee 1988–93; Vice-Chair. Beijing Fed. of Industry and Commerce 1993–97, Hon. Chair. 1997–2001; Hon. Vice-Chair. Exec. Cttee All-China Fed. of Industry and Commerce 1993–2001; mem. 5th CPPCC Nat. Cttee 1978–82, Standing Cttee 6th CPPCC Nat. Cttee 1983–88, Standing Cttee 7th CPPCC Nat. Cttee 1988–93, Vice-Chair. 8th CPPCC Nat. Cttee 1993–98, 9th CPPCC Nat. Cttee 1998–2003; Chair. China-Nepal Friendship Asscn 2004–. *Address:* c/o National Committee of Chinese People's Political Consultative Conference, 23 Taiping Qiao Street, Beijing, People's Republic of China (office).

SUN, Honglie, BSc, MSc; Chinese agronomist; b. 2 Jan. 1932, Puyang, Henan Prov.; m. Wu Huanning 1956; one s. one d.; ed Beijing Agricultural Univ., Shenyang Inst. of Forestry and Soil Science, Chinese Acad. of Sciences; Research Fellow, Comm. for Integrated Survey of Natural Resources (Chinese Acad. of Sciences) 1961–, Dir 1983; Head Multi-disciplinary Expedition of Qinghai-Tibet Plateau 1973; Visiting Scholar Inst. of Alpine and Arctic Research, Colorado Univ. 1981–82; Vice-Pres. Chinese Acad. of Sciences 1984–92; Vice-Pres. Int. Council of Scientific Unions 1993–96. Chair. Academic Cttee of Antarctic Research of China 1986; Chair. Nat. Cttee of China for MAB, UNESCO; Vice-Chair. Int. Mountain Soc., State Antarctic Cttee; a Vice-Pres. Social Devt Science Soc. 1992–; Dir Cttee for Comprehensive Survey of Natural Resources; Fellow, Third World Acad. of Sciences 1987; mem. Gen. Cttee of ICSU 1990; mem. Div. of Earth Sciences, Chinese Acad. of Sciences 1992–; mem. Standing Cttee of 8th Nat. People's Congress 1993–; mem. Credentials Cttee, Environmental and Resources Protection Cttee; mem. 4th Presidium of Depts, Chinese Acad. of Sciences 2000–; mem. 21st Century Cttee for China-Japan Friendship; Special Prize, Chinese Acad. of Sciences 1986, First Prize, State Natural Sciences Awards 1987, Chen Jiagen Prize 1989. *Publications:* The Soil of Heilongjiang River Valley 1960, The Land Resources Assessment of North-East China, Inner Mongolia and West China 1966, The Soils of Tibet 1970, Land Types of Qinghai-Tibet Plateau and the Principles of Agricultural Assessment 1980, Land Resources and Agricultural Utilization in Tibet Autonomous Region, Mountain Research and Development 1983, Integrated Scientific Survey on Tibetan Plateau (series) 1983–89. *Leisure interest:* photography. *Address:* Chinese Academy of Sciences, 52 Sanlihe Road, Beijing 100864, People's Republic of China (office).

SUN, Jiadong; Chinese rocket scientist; b. 7 April 1948, Fuxian, Liaoning Prov.; ed Harbin Univ. of Tech.; USSR Ruchkovski Air Force Eng Inst.; Dir of Design Section, Vice-Dir Overall Design Dept, No. 5 Research Inst. of Ministry of Defence; Vice-Pres. No. 5 Research Inst. of Seventh Ministry of Machine Bldg Industry; Pres. Chinese Space Tech. Research Inst.; Dir Science and Tech. Cttee, Chief Engineer, fmr Vice-Minister of Ministry of Aerospace Industry; Researcher, Sr Science and Tech. Adviser, China Aviation Industry Corpn; Fellow, Chinese Acad. of Sciences; instrumental in devt of China's first atomic bomb and hydrogen bomb; presided over the overall design of China's first medium-range missile, first satellite and first telecommunications satellite; Meritorious Service Medal, CCP Cen. Cttee, State Council and Cen. Mil. Comm. 1999. *Address:* c/o State Commission of Science, Technology and Industry for National Defence, Aimin Daijie, Xicheng Qu, Beijing 100035, People's Republic of China (office). *Telephone:* (10) 66058958 (office). *Fax:* (10) 66673811 (office).

SUN, Jiazheng; Chinese politician; *Vice-Chairman, 11th CPPCC National Committee;* b. March 1944, Siyang, Jiangsu Prov.; ed Nanjing Univ., May 7th Cadre School, Jilin Prov.; joined CCP 1966; sent to do manual labour, Liuhe Co., Jilin Prov.; fmr Deputy Head, Chinese People's Armed Police Force, Fanji Commune; Deputy Head, Work Group, CCP Revolutionary Cttee, Liuhe Co. 1971; Sec. Liuhe Co. Cttee CCP Communist Youth League of China 1971; Sec. CCP Party Cttee, Ma'an Commune, Liuhe Co. 1971, mem. Standing Cttee CCP Liuhe Co. Cttee 1975; Vice-Chair. CCP Revolutionary Cttee, Liuhe Co. 1975; Sec. Jiangsu Prov. Cttee CCP Communist Youth League of China 1978; mem. Standing Cttee CCP Jiangsu Prov. Cttee 1983–89, Sec.-Gen. Jiangsu Prov. Cttee 1983–89, Head, Publicity Dept 1988; Sec. CCP Xuzhou City Cttee, Jiangsu Prov. 1984–86; Minister of Radio, Film and TV 1984–88; Minister of Culture 1998–2007; Pres. China Fed. of Literary and Art Circles 2006–; Alt. mem. 12th CCP Cen. Cttee 1982–87, 13th CCP Cen. Cttee 1987–92, 14th CCP Cen. Cttee 1992–97, mem. 15th CCP Cen. Cttee 1997–2002, 16th CCP Cen. Cttee 2002–07; Vice-Chair. 11th CPPCC Nat. Cttee 2008–; Hon. Chair. Bd of Dirs Beijing Film Coll. *Address:* China Federation of Literary and Art Circles, On Court North, Chaoyang District, Beijing 100029, People's Republic of China. *Telephone:* (10) 64025528. *E-mail:* webmaster@cflac.org.cn. *Website:* .

SUN, Joun-yung; South Korean diplomatist, civil servant and academic; *Chair Professor, Graduate School of North Korean Studies, Kyungnam University;* b. 16 June 1939; m.; two c.; ed Seoul Nat. Univ. Coll. of Law, The American Univ. School of Int. Service, Washington, DC; with Ministry of Foreign Affairs, Dir-Gen. Int. Econ. Affairs Bureau 1987–88, Int. Trade Bureau 1988–90, Deputy Foreign Minister for Econ. Affairs 1993–96; Vice-Minister, Ministry of Foreign Affairs and Trade 1997–2000; Counsellor for Political Affairs, Embassy in London 1978; Minister, Embassy in Brasilia 1981, Minister for Econ. Affairs, Embassy in Washington, DC 1986; apptd Amb. to Czechoslovakia 1990; Minister at Perm. Mission to UN, Geneva 1984, Amb. and Perm. Rep. to Other Int. Orgs 1996–98; Perm. Rep. to UN, New York 2000–04; Amb.-at-Large for Trade Negotiations 1993, Chief Negotiator on Repub. of Korea–EC Framework Agreement for Trade and Co-operation 1994–95; Govt Co-ordinator for Accession to OECD; Co-Chair. Korea's Econ. Jt Cttees with China, Canada, Viet Nam, UK, Germany, Australia and Asscn of SE Asian Nations (ASEAN) 1993–95; Chair. World Trade Org. Council for

Trade Services 1997–98, Int. Textile and Clothing Bureau and also in Geneva Co-ordinator Western Group, Conf. on Disarmament 1997 and Head of Del. at Multi-Fiber Arrangement negotiations 1985–86; currently Chair Prof., Grad. School of North Korean Studies, Kyungnam Univ.; mem. Advisory Council Korean Econ. Inst.; Order of Civil Service Merit (Red Stripes) Civil Service Merit Medal of Honour. *Address:* Graduate School of North Korean Studies, Kyungnam University, 449 Wolyoung-dong, Masan, Kyungnam 631-701, Republic of Korea (office). *Telephone:* (55) 245-5000 (office). *Fax:* (55) 246-6184 (office). *E-mail:* webmaster@kyungnam.ac.kr (office). *Website:* www.kyungnam.ac.kr (office).

SUN, Laiyan, PhD; Chinese engineer; *Administrator, China National Space Administration;* b. Oct. 1957, Beijing; m.; one d.; ed Xian Communication Univ., Univ. de Paris 6ème; Eng Team Leader/Deputy Div. Dir Beijing Inst. of Satellite Environment Eng 1982–87, Acting Deputy Dir, later Dir, Prof. 1993–99; Vice Admin. China Nat. Space Admin (CNSA) 1999–2004, Admin. 2004–; Sec. Gen. Comm. of Science, Tech. and Industry for Nat. Defence (COSTIND) 2001–04, Vice Minister 2004–, also Dir COSTIND State Aerospace Industry Bureau; numerous ministerial and nat. awards. *Address:* COSTIND, 2A Guang'anmen, Xuanwu District, Beijing 100053; China National Space Administration, Beijing, People's Republic of China (office). *Website:* www.cnsa.gov.cn (office).

SUN, Shu; Chinese geologist; b. 1933, Jintan, Jiangsu Prov.; ed Nanjing Univ.; Research Fellow, Inst. of Geology, Chinese Acad. of Sciences, now Dir; Fellow, Chinese Acad. of Sciences; Deputy Dir Nat. Natural Science Foundation of China; mem. 4th Presidium, Chinese Acad. of Sciences 2000. *Publications:* Geological Changes of Precambian Period in the South of North China Fault Block (ed.), The Geology of Xiaoxing'anling, Wandashan and Zhangguangchailing (jtly), over 50 research papers and research reports. *Address:* Institute of Geology, Chinese Academy of Sciences, Beijing, People's Republic of China (office). *E-mail:* suoban@mail.iggcas.ac.cn (office). *Website:* www.igcas.ac.cn (office).

SUN, Weiben; Chinese politician; b. 1928, Yingkou Co., Liaoning; joined CCP 1947; Alt. mem. 12th CCP Cen. Cttee 1982, mem. 1985, mem. 13th Cen. Cttee 1987–92, 14th Cen. Cttee 1992–97; Sec. CCP Cttee, Liaoning Prov. 1983–85; Chair. Heilongjiang 7th Prov. People's Congress Standing Cttee 1988, 8th Cttee 1993–98; 1st Sec. Party Cttee, PLA Heilongjiang Prov. Command 1985–94; Ed.-in-Chief Dictionary of Party Affairs of the CCP 1989–. *Address:* c/o Heilongjiang Provincial 8th People's Congress, Heilongjiang, People's Republic of China.

SUN, Weiyan; Chinese economist; b. 1937, Cixi, Zhejiang Prov.; ed Beijing Foreign Trade Inst.; Pres. Univ. of Int. Business and Econs (UIBE), Beijing 1984–99; mem. China Council for Promotion of Int. Trade; Vice-Pres. China Int. Research Asscn on Transnational Corpns. *Publications:* A Handbook of International Commerce and Trade (Chief Ed.), Multi-National Management Encyclopaedia for Chinese Enterprises (Chief Ed.). *Address:* c/o University of International Business and Economics, Huixin Dong Jie, He Ping Jie N., Beijing 100029, People's Republic of China (office).

SUN, Wenjie; Chinese engineer and construction industry executive; *President, China State Construction Engineering Corporation;* ed Tongji Univ.; joined China State Construction Engineering Corpn (CSCEC) 1968, posted to Hong Kong 1981, subsequently Chair. China Overseas Holdings Ltd, Pres. CSCEC 2001–, also Deputy Sec. Leading Party Mems' Group; Rep. 15th and 16th CCP Cen. Cttees. *Address:* China State Construction Engineering Corporation, CSCEC Mansion, 15 Sanlihe Road, Haidian District, Beijing 100037, People's Republic of China (office). *Telephone:* (10) 88082888 (office). *E-mail:* info@app.cscec.com.cn (office). *Website:* app.cscec.com.cn (office).

SUN, Wensheng; Chinese government official; b. Feb. 1942, Weihai City, Shandong Prov.; ed Shandong Metallurgical Inst. and CCP Cen. Cttee Cen. Party School; joined CCP 1966; workshop dir, Zhuzhou Smeltery 1963–81, Deputy Dir 1981–83; Sec. CCP Zhuzhou City Cttee 1983; Vice-Dir Org. Dept CCP Hunan Prov. Cttee, CCP 1984, Dir 1985, Vice-Sec. 1989; Vice-Sec. CCP Shanxi Prov. Cttee, Vice-Gov., Acting Gov. of Shanxi Prov. 1993–94, Gov. 1994–98; Vice-Minister of Land and Resources 1999–2003, Minister of Land and Resources 2003–07; Deputy Sec. CCP Leading Party Group, Ministry of Land and Resources 1999–2003, Sec. 2003–; mem. Cen. Comm. for Discipline Inspection, CCP Cen. Cttee 2002–; Alt. mem. 12th CCP Cen. Cttee 1982–87, 13th CCP Cen. Cttee 1987–92, mem. 14th CCP Cen. Cttee 1992–97, 15th CCP Cen. Cttee 1997–2002. *Address:* c/o Ministry of Land and Resources, 3 Guanyingyuanxiqu, Xicheng Qu, Beijing 100035, People's Republic of China (office).

SUN, Yafang; Chinese business executive and fmr government official; *Chairwoman, Huawei Technologies Company Ltd;* Co-founder Huawei Technologies 1992, Chair. 1998–; ranked by Fortune magazine amongst 50 Most Powerful Women in Business outside the US (25th) 2006, (27th) 2007. *Address:* Huawei Technologies Co. Ltd, Bantian, Longgang District, Shenzhen, 518129, People's Republic of China (office). *Telephone:* (755) 28780808 (office). *E-mail:* hwtech@huawei.com (office). *Website:* www.huawei.com (office).

SUN, Ying; Chinese politician; b. Nov. 1936, Tianjin, Baodi Co.; ed Shanxi Teachers' Coll. 1958; joined CCP 1956; fmr Deputy Sec. CCP Communist Youth League of China, Shanxi Univ.; fmr Dir Political Dept, Taiyuan Eng Inst., Shanxi Prov.; fmr Deputy Sec. Shanxi Prov. Cttee CCP Communist Youth League of China; fmr Vice-Chair. Shanxi Prov. Science and Tech. Asscn; fmr mem. Standing Cttee CCP Shanxi Prov. Cttee; Deputy Sec. CCP Taiyuan City Cttee, Sec. 1985; Deputy Sec. CCP Gansu Prov. Cttee 1988–98, Sec. 1998–2001, Standing Cttee CCP Gansu Prov. Cttee 1998–2001; Vice-Gov.

Gansu Prov. 1996–97, Gov. 1997–98; Dir Party History Research Centre of CCP Cen. Cttee 2001–; mem. 15th CCP Cen. Cttee 1997–2002; Deputy, 9th NPC 2002–. *Address:* c/o Central Committee of Chinese Communist Party, Beijing, People's Republic of China (office).

SUN, Yuxi; Chinese diplomatist; *Ambassador to Italy;* b. 1951, Heilongjiang Prov.; m.; one d.; ed Beijing Foreign Studies Univ., London School of Econs, UK; Political Officer, Embassy in France 1979–81; various positions in Ministry of Foreign Affairs 1981–88, including Desk Officer, Third Sec., Deputy Dir, First Sec., Dept of Asian Affairs; Chief of Political Section, Embassy in Pakistan 1988–91; Asst Rep., Rep. Office of People's Repub. of China, Cambodian Nat. Supreme Cttee 1991–93; Political Counsellor, Embassy in Cambodia 1991–93; Counsellor and Dir Dept of Asian Affairs 1993–95; Minister Counsellor, Embassy in Repub. of Korea 1995–98; Spokesman and Deputy Dir-Gen., Information Dept, Ministry of Foreign Affairs 1998–2002; Amb. to Afghanistan 2002–04, to India 2004–07, to Italy 2008–, also accred to San Marino; mem. working staff, UN Gen. Ass. 1992, 1999, APEC 1994, ASEAN Regional Forum (ARF) 1994, Asia Europe Meeting (ASEM) 1996, Shanghai Cooperation Org. (SCO) Prime Minister's Meeting 2001. *Publications include:* two books in Chinese on Afghanistan and Indian Affairs; articles on world affairs to magazines and newspapers. *Leisure interests:* golf, tennis, bridge, chess. *Address:* Embassy of the People's Republic of China, Via Bruxelles 56, 00198 Rome, Italy (office). *Telephone:* (06) 8413458 (office). *Fax:* (06) 85352891 (office). *E-mail:* chinaemb_it@mfa.gov.cn (office). *Website:* it.china-embassy.org (office).

SUN, Zhenyu; Chinese economist and diplomatist; *Permanent Representative, World Trade Organization;* b. 1946, Fengrun, Hebei Prov.; ed Beijing Foreign Languages Inst.; joined Ministry of Foreign Trade 1973, served as Deputy Dir, Dir and Deputy Dir-Gen. Regional Policy Dept; fmr Vice-Pres., China Nat. Cereals, Oils and Foodstuffs Import and Export Corpn 1985–90; Dir-Gen., Dept of American and Oceanic Affairs, Ministry of Foreign Trade and Econ. Cooperation 1990–94, Vice-Minister 1994–2002, Perm. Rep., WTO 2002–. *Publications:* Decision Making in the WTO 2004, Multilateralism and Regionalism 2005, China's Performance in the WTO 2007. *Address:* Permanent Mission of China to the World Trade Organization, 228 rue de Lausanne, 1292 Chambéry, Switzerland (office). *Telephone:* (22) 9097615 (office). *Fax:* (22) 9097699 (office). *Website:* http://wto2.mofcom.gov.cn (office).

SUNDERLAND, Eric, CBE, MA, LLD, PhD, FIBiol; British anthropologist and fmr university vice-chancellor; b. 18 March 1930, Ammanford, Carmarthenshire, Wales; s. of Leonard Sunderland and Mary Agnes Davies; m. Jean Patricia Watson 1957; two d.; ed Univ. of Wales, Univ. Coll., London; Prof. of Anthropology, Univ. of Durham 1971–84, Pro-Vice-Chancellor 1979–84; Prin., Univ. Coll. of N Wales, Bangor 1984–95; Vice-Chancellor Univ. of Wales 1989–91, Prof. Emer. 1995–; Sec.-Gen., Int. Union of Anthropological and Ethnological Sciences (IUAES) 1978–98, Pres. 1998–2003; Pres. Royal Anthropological Inst., London 1989–91; Chair. of Dirs, Gregynog Press 1991–; Chair. Local Govt Boundary Comm. for Wales 1994–2001; Chief Counting/Returning Officer, The Referendum on Devolution in Wales 1997; Chair. Comm. on Local Govt Electoral Arrangements in Wales 2001–02; Vice-Pres. Llangollen Int. Music Eisteddfod 1990–; Vice-Pres. Hon. Soc. of Cymmrodorion 1990–; mem. BBC Broadcasting Council for Wales 1995–2000; mem. Bd British Council 1996–2001, Chair. 1996; Chair. Environment Agency Advisory Cttee for Wales 1996–2000; High Sheriff of Gwynedd 1998–99; DL; Pres. Univ. of Wales, Lampeter 1998–2002; Lord-Lt of Gwynedd 1999–2006; Chair. Wetlands for Wales Project 2001–; mem. The Welsh Livery Guild 2001–, Hon. Court Asst 2008–; Chair. National Centre for Languages (CILT) Cymru 2002–05, Gov. CILT UK 2002–07; Regional Chair. Wales, The Art Fund 2005–; Freeman, City of Bangor 2005–; Hon. mem. Gorsedd of Bards, Royal Nat. Eisteddfod of Wales; Hon. Fellow, Univ. of Wales, Lampeter, Univ. of Wales, Bangor; Commdr Brother, Order of St John of Jerusalem 2000; Gold Medal of IUAES, Zagreb XIIth Int. Congress 1988. *Publications:* Elements of Human and Social Geography: Some Anthropological Perspectives 1973, Genetic Variation in Britain (co-ed.) 1973, The Exercise of Intelligence: Biological Pre-conditions for the Operation of Intelligence (co-ed.) 1980, Genetic and Population Studies in Wales (co-ed.) 1986. *Leisure interests:* travelling, book collecting, gardening, paintings. *Address:* Y Bryn, Ffriddoedd Road, Bangor, Gwynedd, LL57 2EH, Wales (home). *Telephone:* (1248) 353265 (home). *Fax:* (1248) 355043 (home).

SUNDERLAND, Sir John Michael, Kt, MA; British business executive; b. 24 Aug. 1945, Oxford; m.; three d. one s.; ed King Edward VII School, Lytham, Lancs., Queen's Coll., Univ. of St Andrews, Scotland; joined Cadbury Ltd 1968, apptd. mem. Bd Cadbury Ireland 1978, Cadbury Schweppes SA 1981, Marketing Dir, then Man. Dir Schweppes Ltd UK 1983, Founding Dir Coca-Cola & Schweppes Beverages 1987, Man. Dir Trebor Bassett 1989, Cadbury Schweppes Confectionery and Cadbury Schweppes Main Bd Dir 1993, Group CEO Cadbury Schweppes PLC (now Cadbury PLC) 1996–2003, Chair. 2003–08; Deputy Pres. CBI 2003, 2007, Pres. 2004–06; mem. Bd of Dirs Financial Reporting Council; Dir (non-exec.) Barclays; adviser, CVC Capital Pnrs (pvt. equity firm), London; mem. Advisory Bd Trinsum Group (fmrly Marakon and IFL); Asscn mem. BUPA; Gov. Court of Henley Man. Coll.; Pres. Chartered Man. Inst. *Leisure interests:* sport, history, theatre. *Address:* c/o CVC Capital Partners Ltd, 111 Strand, London, WC2R 0AG, England (office).

SUNDLUN, Bruce George, LLB; American business executive, academic and fmr politician; b. 19 Jan. 1920, Providence, RI; s. of Walter I. Sundlun and Jane Z. Colitz; m. 2nd Marjorie G. Lee 1985; three s. three d. by previous m.; m. 3rd Susan Dittelman 2000; two step-c.; ed Williams Coll., Harvard Univ. and Air Command and Staff School; served as Capt. in US Army Air Force 1942–45; admitted Bars of RI and DC 1949; Asst US Attorney, Washington, DC 1949–51; Special Asst to US Attorney-Gen. 1951–54; Pnr, Amram, Hahn &

Sundlun, Washington, DC 1954–72, Sundlun, Tirana & Scher 1972–76; Vice-Pres., Dir and Gen. Counsel, Outlet Co., Providence 1960–76, Pres. and CEO 1976–84, Chair. and CEO 1984–91; Pres. Exec. Jet Aviation Inc., Columbus, Ohio 1970–76, Chair. 1976–84; Dir Questech Inc. 1972–91; Incorporator, Dir Communications Satellite Corpn 1962–91; Dir Hal Roach Studios Inc. 1986–91; del. to Democratic Nat. Convention 1964, 1968, 1980, 1990, RI Constitutional Convention 1985; Gov. of Rhode Island 1990–95; Gov-in-Residence, Univ. of Rhode Island 1995–; Dir Nat. Security Educ. Bd 2000–2001, Fort Adams Trust, Sargent Rehabilitation Center; Hon. DSBA (Bryant Coll.) 1980; Hon. DBA (Roger Williams Coll.) 1980; Air medal with oak leaf cluster; Purple Heart; Chevalier, Légion d'honneur; Prime Minister's Medal (Israel); Hall of Fame Univ. of Rhode Island Coll. of Business Admin 2005 DFC;. *Address:* 280 Seaside Drive, Jamestown, RI 02835-3031, USA.

SUNDQUIST, Donald Kenneth (Don), BA; American business executive and fmr politician; *Founding Partner, Sundquist Anthony LLC;* b. 15 March 1936, Moline, Ill.; s. of Kenneth Sundquist and Louise Rohren; m. Martha Swanson 1959; one s. two d.; ed Augustana Coll. Rock Island, Ill.; Div. Man. Josten's Inc. 1961–72; Exec. Vice-Pres. Graphic Sales of America, Memphis 1973, Pres. 1973–82; mem. 98th–103rd Congresses from 7th Tenn. Dist 1983–95; Gov. of Tennessee 1995–2003; Founding Pnr, Sundquist Anthony LLC 2004–; Chair. Medicaid Advisory Comm., US Dept of Health and Human Services 2005–06; Founding mem. and Hon. Co-Chair. Japan-America Soc. of Tenn.; Republican. *Leisure interests:* golf, reading. *Address:* Sundquist Anthony LLC, 51 Louisiana Avenue, NW, Washington DC 20001 (office); c/o Medicaid Commission, Hubert H. Humphrey Building, 200 Independence Avenue, SW, Suite 450G, Washington DC, 20201, USA. *Telephone:* (202) 347-3900 (office). *Fax:* (202) 347-4448 (office). *E-mail:* dh@sundquistanthony.us (office). *Website:* www.sundquistanthony.us (office).

SUNDQVIST, Ulf Ludvig, MPolSc; Finnish business consultant and fmr politician; *Senior Associate, Business Environment Europe;* b. 22 Feb. 1945, Sipoo; s. of Karl Eric Sundqvist and Helga Linnea Lönnkvist; m. Eine Kristiina Joki 1969; one s. one d.; ed Helsinki Univ.; Asst Lecturer, Faculty of Political Science, Helsinki Univ. 1968–70; mem. Parl. 1970–83; Minister of Educ. 1972–75, of Trade and Industry 1979–81; Gen. Sec. Finnish Social Democratic Party 1975–81, Chair. 1991–93; mem. Supervisory Bd Neste Ltd 1970–, Chair. 1976–94; Deputy Chief Gen. Man. STS-Bank Ltd 1981, Chief Gen. Man. 1982–91, mem. Bd 1992–94; pvt. consultant 1993–; Sr Adviser Ergo Consult Oy; Sr Assoc. Business Environment Europe SA, Brussels; Hon. PhD (Kuopio). *Leisure interests:* music, literature. *Address:* Business Environment Europe, Rue d' l'Industrie, 42 bte 16, 1040 Brussels, Belgium (office). *Telephone:* (2) 2308360 (office). *Fax:* (2) 2308370 (office). *E-mail:* info@bee.be (office). *Website:* www.bee.be (office).

SUNG, Chul-yang, PhD; South Korean diplomatist and academic; b. 20 Nov. 1939; m.; one s. one d.; ed Seoul Nat. Univ., Univ. of Hawaii and Univ. of Kentucky, USA; mil. service 1960–62; taught at Eastern Kentucky Univ. and Univ. of Kentucky Fort Knox Center, USA 1970–75, Prof. of Political Science, Lexington 1978; Visiting Prof., Northwestern Univ., Pembroke State Univ., Indiana Univ., USA and Seoul Nat. Univ.; taught at Grad. Inst. of Peace Studies (GIP), Kyung Hee Univ., Seoul 1986, Dean of Academic Affairs at GIP 1987–94; Sec.-Gen. Asscn of Korean Political Scientists in N America; Pres. Korean Asscn of Int. Studies; contrib. to journals and leading newspapers in Repub. of Korea; mem. Advisory Cttee, Ministry of Foreign Affairs, Ministry of Nat. Defence, Nat. Unification Bd; Amb. to USA 2000–03. *Publications include:* numerous articles and essays. *Address:* c/o Ministry of Foreign Affairs and Trade, 77, 1-ga, Sejong-no, Jongno-gu, Seoul, Republic of Korea (office).

SUNGAR, Murat E., MA; Turkish diplomatist and international organization executive; *First Deputy Secretary-General, Organization of the Black Sea Economic Cooperation;* b. 1942, Ankara; m.; one d.; ed School of Political Sciences, Ankara Univ., Univ. of Cincinnati, USA; mil. service 1966–68; joined Ministry of Foreign Affairs (MFA) 1970, Third and Second Sec., NATO Dept 1970–72, Second and First Sec., Turkish Del. to NATO, Brussels 1972–75, First Sec., Embassy in Islamabad 1975–77, Head of Section, NATO Dept, MFA 1977–79, Counsellor, Embassy in Washington, DC 1979–83, Advisor to Under-Sec. of MFA 1983–85, Consul Gen. of Turkey, New York 1985–89, Spokesman of MFA 1989–91, Amb. to India 1991–95, Sr Advisor to Prime Ministry 1995–97, Deputy Under-Sec. of MFA 1997–98, Amb. to UN Office, Geneva 1998–2002, Sec.-Gen. EU Affairs 2002–06; First Deputy Sec.-Gen. Org. of the Black Sea Econ. Co-operation (BSEC) PERMIS 2006–. *Address:* Organization of the Black Sea Economic Co-operation, Sakıp Sabancı Cad., Müşir Fuad Paşa Yalısı, Eski Tersane, 34460 İstinye-İstanbul, Turkey (office). *Telephone:* (212) 229-63-30 (office). *Fax:* (212) 229-63-36 (office). *E-mail:* info@bsec-organization.org (office). *Website:* www.bsec-organization.org (office).

SUNGURLU, Mahmut Oltan; Turkish lawyer and politician; b. 1936, Gümüşhane; m.; one c.; ed Bursa Lycée, Istanbul Univ.; practised law in Gümüşhane; f. Anavatan Partisi (Motherland Party) prov. org. in Gümüşhane; elected Deputy for Gümüşhane 1983; Minister of Justice 1986–87, 1987–88, 1989–92, 1997–98; Deputy Chair. Anavatan Partisi (Motherland Party) June 1988. *Address:* c/o Anavatan Partisi (Motherland Party), 13 Cad. 3, Balgat, Ankara, Turkey.

SUNUNU, John E., MMechEng, MBA; American fmr politician; b. 10 Sept. 1964, Salem, NH; s. of John H. Sununu; m. Kitty Sununu; three c.; ed Salem High School, Massachusetts Inst. of Technology and Harvard Grad. School of Business; worked for REMEC, Inc. 1987; man. and operations specialist with Pittiglio, Rabin Todd & McGrath 1990–92; Chief Financial Officer and Dir of Operations Teltrol Systems, Inc. 1992–96; mem. US House of Reps for First Congressional Dist, NH 1996–2002, mem. Commerce, Science, and Transportation Cttee, Finance Cttee, Homeland Security and Governmental Affairs Cttee, Jt Econ. Cttee; Senator from New Hampshire 2003–09; fmr mem. Republican Policy Cttee; Republican. *Address:* 1589 Elm Street, Suite 3, Manchester, NH 03101, USA.

SUNUNU, John H., PhD; American business consultant and fmr politician; *President, JHS Associates, Ltd;* b. 2 July 1939, Havana, Cuba; m. Nancy Hayes 1958; five s. including John E. Sununu (q.v.) three d.; ed Mass. Inst. of Tech.; Founder and Chief Engineer Astro Dynamics 1960–65; Pres. JHS Eng Co. and Thermal Research Inc., Salem, NH 1965–82; Assoc. Prof. of Mechanical Eng, Tufts Univ. 1966–82, Assoc. Dean Coll. of Eng 1968–73; mem. NH House of Reps 1973–74, Govt Energy Council; Chair. Govt Council on NH Future 1977–78; mem. Govt Advisory Cttee on Science and Tech. 1977–78; Gov. of NH 1983–89; Chair. coalition of NE Govs 1985–86; White House Chief of Staff 1989–91, Counsellor to the Pres. 1991–92; Chair. Task Force on Tech.; Pres. JHS Assoc. Ltd 1992–; host, Crossfire (CNN nightly news/public affairs discussion program) 1992–98; fmr Pnr, Trinity Int. Pnrs; Vice-Chair. Alliance for Acid Rain Control; fmr Chair. Republican Gov.'s Asscn, New England Gov.'s Asscn; Vice-Chair. Advisory Comm. on Intergovernmental Relations. *Address:* JHS Associates Ltd, 49 Linden Road, Hampton Falls, NH 03844 (office); JHS Associates Ltd, 815 Connecticut Avenue, NW, Suite 1200, Washington, DC 20006, USA. *Telephone:* (603) 890-1630 (office). *Fax:* (603) 890-1634 (office). *Website:* www.jhsassociates.com (office).

SUNYAYEV, Rashid Aliyevich; Russian astrophysicist; *Head, Department of High Energy Astrophysics, Institute of Space Studies, Russian Academy of Sciences;* b. 1 March 1943; m.; three s. one d.; ed Moscow Inst. of Physics and Tech.; jr, sr researcher Inst. of Applied Math. USSR Acad. of Sciences; Head of Div., Head Dept of High Energy Astrophysics, Inst. of Space Studies, Russian Acad. of Sciences; Scientific Head Int. Orbital Observatory ROENTGEN on complex space station Mir, Orbital Observatory GRANAT; Dir Max-Planck-Institut for Astrophysics, Garching 1995–; Prof. Moscow Physical-Tech. Inst.; Corresp. mem. USSR (now Russian) Acad. of Sciences 1984, mem. 1992; research in high energy astrophysics, cosmology, theoretical astrophysics, X-ray astronomy; Foreign mem. NAS; mem. European Acad. of Sciences, Int. Acad. of Astronautics; Adjunct Prof., Columbia Univ. (USA); Bruno Rossi Prize, Bruce Medal 2000, Dannie Heineman Prize for Astrophysics 2003, Int. Astronomical Union Gold Medal for Cosmology, Crafoord Prize (jtly) 2008. *Publications:* Black Holes in Double Systems 1973, Observation of Relict Irradiation as Method of Studying the Nature of X-ray Irradiation of Galaxy Clusters 1973, Comptonization of X-ray Irradiation in Plasma Clouds: characteristic spectra 1980; numerous articles. *Address:* High Energy Astrophysics Department (otdel 52), Institute of Space Studies, Russian Academy of Sciences, Profsoyuznaya str. 84/32, 117997 Moscow, Russia (office). *Telephone:* (495) 333-33-73 (office); (495) 331-38-05 (home). *Fax:* (495) 233-53-77. *E-mail:* rs@star.iki.rssi.ru (office); iki@cosmos.ru. *Website:* arc.iki.rssi.ru/eng/index.htm (office).

SUOMINEN, Ilkka Olavi, MPolSc; Finnish business executive and fmr politician; b. 8 April 1939, Nakkila; s. of Leo Suominen and Anna Suominen; m. Riitta Suhonen 1977; one s. two d.; Dept Head, J. W. Suominen Oy 1960–72, Deputy Man. Dir 1972–74, Man. Dir 1975–79, mem. Man. Bd 1982–; mem. Parl. 1970–75, 1983–94; Leader Nat. Coalition Party 1979–91; Vice-Chair. European Democrat Union 1986–93; Speaker of Parl. 1987, 1991–96; Minister of Trade and Industry 1987–91; Pres. CSCE Parl. Ass. 1992–94; MEP 1999–2004; Chair. Admin. Bd Oy Alko AB 1980–88, 1991–94, Gen. Man. 1994; Chair. Bd of Dirs ICL Data (Finland) 1992–; Vice-Chair. Confed. of Finnish Industries 1978–79. *Leisure interests:* hunting, fishing. *Address:* c/o J W Suominen Oy, Lassila & Tikanoja Group, POB 25, 29251 Nakkila, Finland (office).

SUONIO, Kaarina Elisabet, MA, LLM; Finnish cultural centre administrator, politician, psychologist and lawyer; b. 7 Feb. 1941, Helsinki; d. of Prof. Karl Otto Brusiin and Ulla Helena Raassina; m. 1st Reino Kalevi 1961; m. 2nd Kÿosti Kullervo Suonio 1967; m. 3rd Ilkka Tanner 1993; one s. one d.; ed Helsinki Univ.; psychologist, Inst. of Occupational Health 1963–71; Researcher, Ministry of Justice 1971–75; mem. Helsinki City Council 1973–; mem. Parl. 1975–86; Alt. mem. Exec. Finnish Social Democratic Party 1981–84; Second Minister of Educ. (Minister of Culture and Science) 1982–83, Minister of Educ. 1983–86; Deputy Mayor of Tampere 1986–94; Gov. Province of Häme 1994–97; Man. Dir Tampere Hall Conf. and Concert Centre 1997–; Gov. for Finland Asia-Europe Foundation; Hon. DTech (Tampere University of Tech.) 2007; Commdr, Ordre des Arts et Lettres. *Address:* Tampere Hall, c/o Box 16, 33101 Tampere; Lomatic 2, 13720 Parola, Finland (home). *Telephone:* (3) 2434100 (office); (50) 5509401 (home). *Fax:* (3) 2434199 (office); (3) 6372175 (home); (3) 2434199. *E-mail:* kaarina.suonio@tampere-talo.fi (office); kaarina.suonio@mail.htk.fi (home). *Website:* www.tampere-talo.fi (office).

SUPAMONGKOL, Kantathee, MA, PhD; Thai government official; b. 3 April 1952; m.; ed UCLA, Univ. of Southern Calif., American Univ., Washington, DC, USA; fmr Prof. of Law and Int. Relations; joined Ministry of Foreign Affairs 1984; with Perm. Mission to UN, New York 1988–92; Adviser on Foreign Affairs to Speaker of House of Reps 1992; Dir Policy and Planning Div., Ministry of Foreign Affairs 1993–94; mem. Parl. 1995, 2001; Adviser on Foreign Affairs to Prime Minister 1996; Adviser to Minister of Industry; mem. Cttee on Foreign Affairs, Cttee on Tourism, House of Reps; Trade Rep. of Thailand 2001–05; Special Envoy of the Prime Minister; Adviser on Foreign Affairs to Minister of Foreign Affairs; Minister of Foreign Affairs 2005–06; Kt Grand Cordon (Special Class) of the Most Noble Order of the Crown of Thailand. *Address:* c/o Ministry of Foreign Affairs, Thanon Sri Ayudhya, Bangkok 10400, Thailand.

SUPLICY, Marta Teresa, MSc; Brazilian politician and psychologist; b. 18 March 1945, São Paulo; m. 1st Eduardo Suplicy (divorced 2003); three s.; m. 2nd Luís Favre; ed Pontifícia Universidade Católica de São Paulo and Stanford and Michigan State Univs; fmr psychotherapist War Veterans Hosp., Palo Alto, Calif.; TV presenter, Brazil 1980–87, 1999; Fed. Deputy for São Paulo 1995–98; Mayor of São Paulo 2001–04; Minister of Tourism 2007–08; mem. United Cities and Local Govts (Pres. 2004–2005); Assoc. mem. Sociedade Brasileira Psicanalítica de São Paulo 1990–; cand. in São Paulo mayoral elections 2008. *Address:* c/o Partido dos Trabalhadores, Rua Silveira Martins 132, Centro, 01019-000 São Paulo, SP, Brazil (office). *Website:* www .marta13.can.br (office).

SUPPES, Patrick, BS, PhD, FAAS; American philosopher, scientist and academic; *Lucie Stern Emeritus Professor of Philosophy, Stanford University;* b. 17 March 1922, Tulsa, Okla; m. 1st Joan Farmer 1946 (divorced 1970); one s. two d.; m. 2nd Joan Elizabeth Sieber 1970 (divorced 1973); m. 3rd Christine Johnson 1979; one s. one d.; ed Univ. of Chicago and Columbia Univ.; Lecturer (part-time), Columbia Univ. 1948–50; Asst and Assoc. Prof., Dept of Philosophy, Stanford Univ. 1950–59, Prof. 1959–92, Dir, Inst. for Math. Studies in the Social Sciences 1959–92, Prof. (by courtesy), Dept of Statistics 1960–92, Chair., Dept of Philosophy 1963–69, Prof. (by courtesy), School of Educ. 1967–92, Prof. (by courtesy), Dept of Psychology 1973–92, Lucie Stern Prof. of Philosophy 1975–92, Prof. Emer. 1992–, Dir and Faculty Advisor, Educ. Program for Gifted Youth 1992–; Pres. Computer Curriculum Corpn 1967–90; Fellow, American Psychological Asscn, Asscn for Computing Machinery 1994; mem. Nat. Acad. of Educ. (Pres. 1973–77), American Acad. of Arts and Sciences, Finnish Acad. of Science and Letters, NAS, European Acad. of Sciences and Arts; Corresp. mem. Yugoslav Acad. of Sciences and Arts 1990; Foreign mem. USSR (now Russian) Acad. of Pedagogical Sciences, Norwegian Acad. of Science and Letters; Hon. mem. Chilean Acad. of Sciences; Dr hc (Nijmegen) 1979, (Acad. de Paris, Univ. René Descartes) 1982, (Regensburg) 1999, (Bologna) 1999; Palmer O. Johnson Memorial Award, American Educational Research Asscn 1967, Distinguished Scientific Contribution Award, American Psychological Asscn 1972, Columbia Univ. Teachers College Medal for Distinguished Service 1978, E. L. Thorndike Award for Distinguished Psychological Contrib. to Educ., American Psychological Asscn 1979, Nat. Medal of Science 1990, Louis Robinson Award, Educom 1993,. *Publications:* Introduction to Logic 1957, Decision Making: An Experimental Approach (with D. Davidson and S. Siegel) 1957, Axiomatic Set Theory 1960, Markov Learning Models for Multiperson Interactions (with R. C. Atkinson) 1960, First Course in Mathematical Logic (with S. Hill) 1964, Experiments in Second-Language Acquisition (with E. Crothers) 1967, Computer Assisted Instruction: Stanford's 1965–66 Arithmetic Program (with M. Jerman and D. Brian) 1968, Studies in the Methodology and Foundations of Science 1970, A Probabilistic Theory of Causality 1970, Foundations of Measurement (with D. Krantz, R. D. Luce, A. Tversky) Vol. I 1971, Vol. II 1989, Vol. III 1990, Computer-assisted Instruction at Stanford, 1966–68 (with M. Morningstar); Probabilistic Metaphysics 1974, The Radio Mathematics Project: Nicaragua 1974–1975 (with B. Searle and J. Friend) 1976, Logique du Probable 1981, Estudios de Filosofía y Metodología de la Ciencia 1988, Language for Humans and Robots 1991, Models and Methods in the Philosophy of Science 1993, Language and Learning for Robots (with C. Crangle) 1994, Foundations of Probability with Applications (with M. Zanotti) 1996, Representation and Invariance of Scientific Structures 2002; and over 300 articles in professional journals. *Address:* Center for the Study of Language and Information, Ventura Hall, Stanford University, Stanford, CA 94305-4115; 678 Mirada Avenue, Stanford, CA 94305, USA. *Telephone:* (650) 725-6030 (office). *E-mail:* suppes@csli.stanford.edu (office). *Website:* www.stanford.edu/~psuppes (office).

SUPPLE, Barry Emanuel, CBE, PhD, FRHistS, FBA; British economic historian and academic; *Academic Consultant, Lisbet Rausing Charitable Fund;* b. 27 Oct. 1930, London, England; s. of Solomon Supple and Rose Supple; m. 1st Sonia Caller 1958; two s. one d.; m. 2nd Virginia McNay 2003; ed Hackney Downs Grammar School, LSE and Christ's Coll. Cambridge; Asst Prof. of Business History, Grad. School of Business Admin., Harvard Univ., USA 1955–60; Assoc. Prof. of Econ. History, McGill Univ. 1960–62; Lecturer in Econ. and Social History, Univ. of Sussex, Reader, then Prof. 1962–78, Dean, School of Social Sciences 1965–68, Pro-Vice-Chancellor (Arts and Social Studies) 1968–72, Pro-Vice-Chancellor 1978; Reader in Recent Social and Econ. History, Univ. of Oxford 1978–81, Professorial Fellow, Nuffield Coll. 1978–81; Prof. of Econ. History Univ. of Cambridge 1981–93, Prof. Emer. 1993–, Professorial Fellow, Christ's Coll. 1981–83, Hon. Fellow 1984; Master of St Catharine's Coll., Cambridge 1984–93, Hon. Fellow 1993; Dir Leverhulme Trust 1993–2001; Pres. Econ. History Soc. 1992–95, Foreign Sec. British Acad. 1995–99; mem. Social Science Fellowship Cttee, Nuffield Foundation 1974–94; Co-Ed. Econ. History Review 1973–82; Academic Consultant, Lisbet Rausing Charitable Fund (renamed Arcadia) 2001–07; Hon. Fellow, Worcester Coll., Oxford 1986; Hon. FRAM 2001; Hon. DLitt (Sussex) 1998, (Leicester) 1999, (Warwick) 2000, (Bristol) 2001. *Publications:* Commercial Crisis and Change in England, 1600–42, 1959, The Experience of Economic Growth (ed.) 1963, Boston Capitalists and Western Railroads 1967, The Royal Exchange Assurance: a history of British insurance 1720–1970, 1970, Essays in Business History (ed.) 1977, History of the British Coal Industry, Vol. IV (1914–46), The Political Economy of Decline 1987, The State and Economic Knowledge: the American and British Experience (ed.) 1990, The Rise of Big Business (ed.) 1992, articles and reviews in learned journals. *Leisure interests:* tennis, photography. *Address:* 3 Scotts Gardens, Whittlesford, Cambridge, CB22 4NR, England (home). *Telephone:* (1223) 830606 (home). *E-mail:* bes@arcticnet.com (home).

SURANI, Azim, CBE, PhD, FRS, FMedSci; British biologist and academic; *Mary Marshall and Arthur Walton Professor of Physiology and Reproduction, The Wellcome Trust/Cancer Research UK Gurdon Institute, University of Cambridge;* currently Mary Marshall and Arthur Walton Prof. of Physiology and Reproduction, The Wellcome Trust/Cancer Research UK Gurdon Inst. of Cancer and Developmental Biology, Univ. of Cambridge, also Research Group Leader, Div. of Molecular and Developmental Physiology, Dept of Physiology; Assoc., Third World Acad. of Sciences; mem. European Molecular Biology Org., Academia Europaea. *Publications:* Genomic Imprinting (co-ed.) 1997; numerous articles in scientific journals on germ line, epigenetic reprogramming, pluripotent stem cells and transdifferentiation. *Address:* The Wellcome Trust/Cancer Research UK Gurdon Institute, Henry Wellcome Building of Cancer and Developmental Biology, University of Cambridge, Tennis Court Road, Cambridge, CB2 1QN, England (office). *Telephone:* (1223) 334088 (office). *Fax:* (1223) 334089 (office). *E-mail:* a.surani@gurdon.cam.ac.uk (office). *Website:* www.gurdon.cam.ac.uk (office); www.gurdon.cam.ac.uk/ ~suranilab (office).

SURÁNYI, György, PhD, DEcon; Hungarian economist; *Chairman of the Board, Central European International Bank Limited;* b. 3 Jan. 1954, Budapest; m.; two c.; ed Univ. of Econs, Budapest, Hungarian Acad. of Sciences; Research Fellow and Head of Dept, Financial Research Inst., Budapest 1977–86; consultant, World Bank, Washington, DC 1986–87; Counsellor to Deputy Prime Minister, Council of Ministers 1988–89; Sec. of State, Nat. Planning Office 1989–90; Pres. Nat. Bank of Hungary 1990–91; Man. Dir Cen. European Int. Bank Ltd 1992–95, Chair. Bd 2001–; Pres. Nat. Bank of Hungary 1995–2001; Head of Multinational Banking, IntesBci Group, Italy 2001–; Pres. Supervisory Bd Privredna Banka, Zagreb 2001–; mem. Supervisory Bd VUB, Bratislava 2001–; Prof. of Finance, Corvinus Univ. of Economics, Central European Univ., Budapest; mem. Bd of Dirs Bruegel (econ. research inst.), Inst. for East-West Studies; mem. PCG Principles Consultative Group; mem. Bd; Global Leader for Tomorrow, World Econ. Forum 1993, Leadership in Econ. Transition, EastWest Inst. New York 2001. *Publications:* author of several articles and books on monetary and financial issues. *Address:* Central European International Bank Ltd, Medve u. 4-14, 1027 Budapest, Hungary (office). *Telephone:* (1) 423-2924 (office). *Fax:* (1) 489-6226 (office). *E-mail:* gsuranyi@cib.hu (office). *Website:* www.cib.hu (office).

SUREAU, Claude, LèsSc, MD; French obstetrician and gynaecologist; *President, Theramex Institute;* b. 27 Sept. 1927, Paris; s. of Maurice Sureau and Rita Jullian; m. Janine Murset 1956; one s. two d.; ed Paris Univ., Columbia Presbyterian Medical Center; Asst Prof., Paris Univ. 1956–61, Assoc. Prof. 1961–74; Prof. and Chair., Dept of Obstetrics and Gynaecology, St Vincent de Paul Hosp., Paris 1974–76, Univ. Clinique Baudelocque 1976–89; Pres., Int. Fed. of Obstetricians and Gynaecologists 1982–85, Pres., Standing Cttee on Ethical Aspects of Human Reproduction 1985–94; Pres. European Asscn of Gynaecology and Obstetrics 1988–91; Dir Unit 262, Physiology and Physiopathology of Reproduction, Nat. Inst. of Health and Medical Research 1983–90; Active Staff mem. American Hosp. of Paris 1989–93, Chief of Gynaecological Unit 1990–93, Medical Dir American Hosp. of Paris 1994–95; Pres. Theramex Inst. 1996; mem. Nat. Acad. of Medicine of France 1978–, Vice-Pres. 1999, Pres. 2000; mem. High Council on Population and Family 1996–2003, Nat. Ethics Advisory Cttee 2005–; Commdr Ordre nat. du Mérite 1996, Légion d'honneur. *Publications:* Le danger de naître 1978, Ethical Dilemmas in Assisted Reproduction 1996, Alice au pays des clones 1999; Co-Ed.: Clinical Perinatology 1980, Immunologie de la réproduction humaine 1983, Aux débuts de la vie 1990, Ethical Aspects of Human Reproduction 1995, Ethical Problems in Obstetrics and Gynaecology 2000, Fallait-il tuer l'enfant Foucault? et Humanisme médical 2003, Son nom est personne 2005, Contemporary Ethical Dilemmas in Assisted Reproduction, l'Erreur médicale et De la sanction à la prévention de l'erreur médicale 2006. *Address:* Institut Theramex, 38–40 avenue de New York, BP 398-16, 75768 Paris Cedex 16 (office); 16 rue d'Aubigny, 75017 Paris, France (home). *Telephone:* 1-53-67-63-32 (office); 1-42-67-44-08 (home). *Fax:* 1-42-67-35-49 (home); 1-53-67-63-03 (office). *E-mail:* csureau@theramex.mc (office). *Website:* www.institut -theramex.com (office).

SURESH, Subra, MS, ScD; Indian engineer, academic and university administrator; *Ford Professor of Engineering and Dean, School of Engineering, Massachusetts Institute of Technology;* ed Indian Inst. of Tech., Madras, Iowa State Univ., Massachusetts Inst. of Tech.; Postdoctoral Researcher, Univ. of California, Berkeley and Lawrence Berkeley Lab. 1981–83; Asst Prof. of Eng, Brown Univ. 1983–89, Prof. 1989–93; R.P. Simmons Prof. of Materials Science and Eng, MIT 1993, Head of Dept of Materials Science and Engineering 2000–06, Ford Prof. of Eng 2002–, Dean, School of Eng 2007–; Clark B. Millikan Endowed Chair for Visiting Professorship, California Inst. of Tech. 1999–2000; Founding Chair, Program on Advanced Materials, Singapore-MIT Alliance; Founding Dir Global Enterprise for Micromechanics and Molecular Medicine; mem. Nat. Acad. of Eng 2002–, American Acad. of Arts and Sciences 2004–, Indian Nat. Acad. of Eng 2004–, German Acad. of Sciences 2007–; Dr hc (Sweden Royal Inst. of Tech.); Acta Materialia Gold Medal 2006, European Materials Medal, Fed. of European Materials Socs 2007. *Publications:* Fatigue of Materials 1991, Fundamentals of Functionally Graded Materials (co-author) 1998, Thin Film Materials: Stress, Surface Evolution and Failure (co-author) 2003. *Address:* Room 1-206, Massachusetts Institute of Technology, 77 Massachusetts Avenue, Cambridge, MA 02139-4307, USA (office). *Telephone:* (617) 253-3320 (office). *Fax:* (617) 253-8549 (office). *E-mail:* ssuresh@mit.edu (office). *Website:* sureshgroup.mit.edu (office).

SURJÁN, László, MD, PhD; Hungarian politician and physician; b. 7 Sept. 1941, Kolozsvár (now Cluj, Romania); s. of László Surján and Margit Surján (née Göttinger); m. Zsófia Stverteczky 1966; one s. two d.; ed Roman Catholic Theologic Acad. Semmelweis Univ. Medical School, Budapest; specialist in pathology 1973; Lecturer, Semmelweis Medical Univ. 1969–70, Post grad. Medical School 1970–90; joined Hungarian Christian Democratic Party (Chair. 1990–95); mem. Hungarian Parl. (Magyar Polgári Szövetség—Fidesz) 1990–, Deputy Speaker 2000–01; Minister of Welfare 1990–94; Pres. Employment and Labour Affairs Cttee of Parl. 1994–98; Head, Hungarian Del. to Parl. Ass. of Council of Europe and Vice-Chair. Foreign Affairs Cttee 1998–2004; mem. European Parl. (Group of the European People's Party—Christian Democrats and European Democrats) 2004–, mem. Cttee on Budgets, Substitute mem. Cttee on Regional Devt, mem. Temporary Cttee on Policy Challenges and Budgetary Means of the Enlarged Union 2007–2013, Vice-Chair. Del. to EU-Chile Jt Parl. Cttee, Substitute mem. Del. to EU-Romania Jt Parl. Cttee; Chair. WHO Regional Cttee for Europe 1992–93; Vice-Chair. European Union of Christian Democrats 1992–99; mem. numerous socs. *Publications:* author of 48 scientific publs. *Address:* European Parliament, Bâtiment Altiero Spinelli, 12E246, 60 rue Wiertz, 1047 Brussels, Belgium (office). *Fax:* (2) 284-9835 (office). *E-mail:* lsurjan@europarl.eu.int (office).

SURKIS, Grigoriy; Ukrainian politician, business executive and international organization executive; *President, Football Federation of Ukraine;* b. 4 Sept. 1949, Odessa; one s. one d.; ed Kyiv Technological Inst. of Food Industry; worked for Trest Kievzhilstroymontazh 1974–88; held exec. positions with Kiev City Council 1988–91; Pres. Slavutich (holding co.) 1993–98; Owner, Dynamo Kiev Football Club, Pres. 1993–98; Pres. Professional Football League and Vice-Pres. Football Fed. of Ukraine 1996–2000, currently Pres.; mem. Parl. 1998–2006; mem. UEFA Professional Football Cttee 2002–04, mem. UEFA Exec. Cttee 2004–; mem. FIFA Nat. Asscns Cttee; Amb. to Council of Europe for Sport; mem. Nat. Olympic Cttee of Ukraine; mem. Bd of Trustees Jewish Confed. of Ukraine; Order of Merit (Third Degree) 1996, (Second Degree) 1999, (First Degree) 2004, Commdr, Order of the Italian Repub., Order of Prince Yaroslav Mudry The Wise (Fifth Degree) 2006), Order of Ukrainian Orthodox Church 'Apostale Prince Volodymyr' (First Degree) 2006; Businessman of the Year 1996, 1998, Man of the Year 1997. *Leisure interests:* collecting, fitness. *Address:* Football Federation of Ukraine, 7-A Laboratornyi provulok, PO Box 293, Kiev 03150, Ukraine (office). *Telephone:* (44) 521-05-21 (office). *Fax:* (44) 521-05-50 (office). *E-mail:* info@ffu.org.ua (office). *Website:* www.ffu.org.ua (office).

SURKOV, Vladislav Yuryevich, MSc; Russian business executive and government official; *First Deputy Chief of Staff, Presidential Executive Office;* b. ((Vladislav Yuryevich Dudayev)), 21 Sept. 1964; s. of Andarbek (Yuriy) Danil'bekovich Dudayev and Zinaida Antonovna Surkova; m. Yuliya Vishnevskaya; one s.; ed Moscow Inst. of Steel and Alloys, Moscow Inst. of Culture, Moscow Int. Univ.; name changed to Vladislav Surkov 1969; army service 1983–85; Dir Metapress Agency (communications) 1990–92; Head of Advertising Dept Menatep Credit and Financial Enterprises Asscn (later Menatep Bank) 1992–94, Deputy Head of Client Services Dept 1992–94, Deputy Head of Public Relations Dept 1994–96, Vice-Pres. State Orgs Relations Dept 1996–97, mem. Bd of Dirs 1996–97; Deputy Head, Head of Public Relations Rosprom 1996–97; First Deputy Council Chair. Commercial Innovation Bank Alfa Bank 1996–97; First Deputy Dir-Gen., then Public Relations Dir Public Russian TV (ORT) 1998, First Sec., Supervisory Bd 1998–99; Aide to Chief of Staff, Presidential Exec. Office 1999, Deputy Chief of Staff, Presidential Exec. Office 1999–2008, Aide to Pres. 2004–08, First Deputy Chief of Staff, Presidential Exec. Office 2008–. *Leisure interests:* playing the guitar, writing music. *Address:* Office of the President, 103132 Moscow, Staraya pl. 4, Russia (office). *Telephone:* (495) 925-35-81 (office). *Fax:* (495) 206-07-66 (office). *Website:* www.kremlin.ru (office).

SURLYK, Finn C., PhD, DrScient; Danish geologist and academic; *Professor, Geological Institute, University of Copenhagen;* b. 17 March 1943, Copenhagen; s. of C. Surlyk and K. Surlyk; m. Nanna Noe-Nygaard; two s.; Adjunct Prof., Univ. of Copenhagen 1968–69, Assoc. Prof. 1969–80, Prof. 1984–; Head, Dept of Oil Geology, Geological Survey of Greenland, Copenhagen 1981–84; Gen.-Sec. Int. Asscn of Sedimentologists 1986–94; Fellow, Royal Danish Acad. of Arts and Letters; Hon. Fellow, Geological Soc. of London; Kt of the Dannebrog 2001; Gold Medal, Univ. of Copenhagen 1969; Recipient First Jubilee Prize, Danish Nat. Oil and Gas Co. *Publications:* over 100 papers, particularly on the geology of Greenland. *Leisure interests:* jazz, bass-playing, outdoor life. *Address:* Geological Institute, University of Copenhagen, Øster Voldgade 10, 1350 Copenhagen K (office); Islandsvej 11, 2800 Lyngby, Denmark (home). *Telephone:* 35-32-24-53 (office); 45-87-72-09 (home). *Fax:* 33-14-83-22 (office). *E-mail:* finns@geol.ku.dk (office). *Website:* trophy.geol.ku.dk/index_e.htm (office).

SURMA, John P., Jr, BS; American steel industry executive; *Chairman and CEO, United States Steel Corporation;* b. 1954, Pittsburgh, Pa; ed Pennsylvania State Univ.; joined Price Waterhouse LLP 1976–81, Man. 1981–85, Sr Man. 1985–87, Partner 1987–97; Exec. Staff Asst to Vice-Chair. Fed. Reserve Bd (as part of Pres.'s Exec. Exchange Program) 1983; Sr Vice-Pres. Finance and Accounting, Marathon Oil Co. 1997, Pres. Speedway SuperAmerica LLC 1998–2000, Sr Vice-Pres. Supply and Transportation, Marathon Ashland Petroleum LLC 2000, Pres. 2001; Vice-Chair. and Chief Financial Officer United States Steel Corpn 2002–03, Pres. and COO 2003–04, Pres. and CEO 2004–06, Chair. and CEO 2006–; Chair. Int. Iron and Steel Inst. 2006–07, Vice-Chair. 2007–; mem. Bd of Dirs American Iron and Steel Inst. (fmr Chair. and Vice-Chair.); mem. Bd of Dirs The Bank of New York Mellon Corpn, Calgon Carbon Corpn, Nat. Asscn of Mfrs, Int. Iron and Steel Inst., Allegheny Conf. on Community Devt (also mem. Exec. Cttee), Nat. Petroleum Council; Chair. Allegheny County (Pa) Parks Foundation; mem. Bd of Visitors Univ. of

Pittsburgh Katz Grad. School of Business, Bd of Trustees Penn State Univ. (and its Smeal Coll. of Business's Bd of Visitors); mem. American Inst. of Certified Public Accountants. *Address:* United States Steel Corpn, 600 Grant Street, Pittsburgh, PA 15219-2800, USA (office). *Telephone:* (412) 433-1121 (office). *Fax:* (412) 433-5733 (office). *E-mail:* info@ussteel.com (office). *Website:* www.ussteel.com (office).

SURTEES, John, OBE; British fmr racing motorcyclist and driver; b. 11 Feb. 1934, Tatsfield, Surrey; s. of John Norman Surtees and Dorothy Cynthia Calla Surtees; m. Jane Sparrow 1987; one s. two d.; ed Ashburton Secondary School, London; only man to win both world motorcycling and world motor racing championships; began motorcycle road racing 1950, 350cc World Champion 1958, 1959 and 1960, 500cc World Champion 1956, 1958, 1959 and 1960; began car racing 1960, World Champion 1964, runner-up 1966, CanAm Champion 1966; Grand Prix wins (motorcycling): won 32 World Championship motor cycle Grand Prix and six Isle of Man TT races; (motor racing): 1963 German (Ferrari), 1964 German (Ferrari), 1964 Italian (Ferrari), 1966 Belgian (Ferrari), 1966 Mexican (Cooper-Maserati), 1967 Italian (Honda); racing car constructor and team owner (F5000, F2 and F1); closed down racing operation Team Surtees 1978; Founder-mem. Constructers' Asscn; drives for Mercedes Benz and Honda in historic demonstration events; motor sport consultant, journalist and property developer, Man. Dir John Surtees Ltd 1979–; Vice-Pres. British Racing Drivers' Club; mem. Worshipful Co. of Carmen. *Publications:* Speed 1963, John Surtees – World Champion 1991. *Leisure interests:* restoration of period property, Grand Prix motor cycles and cars, antiques, food and wine. *Address:* John Surtees Ltd, Monza House, Fircroft Way, Edenbridge, Kent, TN8 6EJ, England (office). *Telephone:* (1732) 865496 (office). *Fax:* (1732) 866945 (office). *E-mail:* johnsurtees@johnsurtees.com (office).

SURTY, Mohamed Enver, BA, LLM; South African lawyer and politician; *Minister of Justice and Constitutional Development;* b. 15 Aug. 1953; m.; ed Univ. of Durban-Westville, Univ. of South Africa, Univ. of Western Cape; cand. attorney, Johannesburg 1975, gen. practitioner and human rights lawyer 1977–94; Prov. and Programming Whip for NW Prov. 1994–99; mem. Senate, then Nat. Council of Provs 1994–2004, Chief Whip 1999–2004; mem. Man. Cttee, Constitutional Ass., negotiator for African Nat. Congress (ANC) on the Bill of Rights 1994–96; observer mem. Nat. Exec. Council, (ANC) 1999–2007; Deputy Minister of Educ. 2003–04; Minister of Justice and Constitutional Devt 2008–. *Leisure interests:* soccer, cricket, squash reading. *Address:* Ministry of Justice and Constitutional Development, Momentum Centre, 329 Pretorius Street, corner Pretorius and Prinsloo Streets, Pretoria 0001, South Africa (office). *Telephone:* (12) 3151332 (office). *Fax:* (12) 3151749 (office). *E-mail:* znqayi@justice.gov.za (office). *Website:* www.doj.gov.za (office).

SURUMA, Ezra, PhD, MA, BSc; Ugandan economist; b. 11 Nov. 1945; s. of Sulimani Balirenwa and Esiteri; m. Specioza Suruma; four s.; ed Fordham Univ., Univ. of Conn.; previous positions include Dir of Econ. Affairs, Movement Secr., Chair. and Man. Dir, Uganda Commercial Bank, Deputy Gov. and Dir of Research, Bank of Uganda; Minister of Finance, Planning and Econ. Devt 2005–09. *Address:* c/o Ministry of Finance, Planning and Economic Development, Appollo Kaggwa Road, Plot 2/4, POB 8147, Kampala, Uganda (office).

SUSCHITZKY, Wolfgang, BSc; British (b. Austrian) cameraman and photographer (retd); b. 29 Aug. 1912, Vienna, Austria; s. of Wilhelm Suschitzky and Mrs Suschitzky (née Bauer); m. three times; two s. one d.; ed Graphische Lehr- und Versuchsanstalt Vienna; started in documentary films with Paul Rotha 1937; first feature film No Resting Place 1950; freelance cameraman, exhbns London 1982, 1988, 1989, 1995, 1997, 2000, 2001, 2007, Edin. 2002, Amsterdam 1982, 2006, Vienna 1999, 2006; mem. British Soc. of Cinematographers, BAFTA; Hon. mem. Asscn of Cinematograph, Television and Allied Technicians, Royal Photographic Soc., British Soc. of Cinematographers; City of Vienna Gold Medal, The Amateur Photographer's Award for Exceptional Achievement in Photography 2008. *Films as cameraman include:* The Small World of Sammy Lee 1962, Ulysses 1966, Entertaining Mr Sloan 1969, Get Carter 1970, Staying On 1980; numerous documentaries and commercials. *Publications:* Photographing Animals 1941, Photographing Children 1942, Kingdom of the Beasts (with Julian Huxley) 1956, Charing Cross Road in the Thirties 1980, Photos 2006. *Leisure interests:* photography, film, music, literature, travel. *Address:* Flat 11, Douglas House, 6 Maida Avenue, London, W2 1TG, England (home). *Telephone:* (20) 7723-6269 (home).

SUSHCHENYA, Leonid Mikhailovich, DBiolSc; Belarusian scientist; b. 11 Nov. 1929, Maly Luky, Brest Region; m. Nina Nikolayevna Khmeleva; three c.; ed Belarus Univ.; Asst Prof. Byelorussian State Univ., Minsk 1956–59; sr researcher, Inst. of Biology of Southern Seas, Ukrainian Acad. of Sciences 1959–67, Head of Div. of Marine Animal Physiology 1967–71; Head of Div., Dir Inst. of Zoology, Belarus Acad. of Sciences, 1971–95, Academician Sec., Div. of Biological Sciences 1979–92, Head of Div., Hon. Dir Inst. of Zoology 1995–; Pres. Belarus Acad. of Sciences 1992–97; Counsellor Nat. Belarus Acad. of Sciences 1997–; Vice-Pres. Int. Asscn of Acads of Sciences of CIS and other cos 1996–; Ed.-in-Chief Doklady Akademii nauk Belarusi; mem. Belarus and USSR (now Russian) Acads of Sciences; mem. Int. Soc. of Limnology, Hydrobiological Socs of Belarus and Russia (Hon. Pres. –1989); mem. Peace Cttee (Chair. Environmental Protection section); mem. All European Acads Ass.; Foreign mem. Polish and Lithuanian Acads of Sciences 1994; represents Belarus in ICSU; Hon. Scientist of Repub. of Belarus 1978; Order of People's Friendship 1986, Order of Red Banner of Labour USSR 1989, Order of Fatherland of Repub. of Belarus 1999, Order of Friendship of Russian Fed. 2000; Hon. Awards of Supreme Soviet of Repub. of Belarus 1979, 1994. *Publications:* more than 190 articles on hydrobiology, gen. ecology, ecology of animals and environment, including monographs Respiration of Crustacea 1972, Quantitative Regularities of Crustacea Feeding 1975, Growth of Water Animals at Changing Temperatures 1978, Fundamentals of Rational Use of Nature 1980, Biology and Products of Ice-age Relic Crayfish 1985, Ecology of Animals in the Radioactive Contaminated Zone 1993. *Leisure interests:* travelling, reading, music. *Address:* Presidium of the Academy of Sciences of Belarus, Prospekt F. Skoriny 66, 220072 Minsk (office); 15 fl. 41 Kulman Street, 220100 Minsk, Belarus (home). *Telephone:* (2) 84-04-77 (office); (2) 34-44-05 (home). *Fax:* (2) 39-31-63.

SÜSKIND, Patrick; German author; b. 26 March 1949, Ambach, Bavaria; ed Univ. of Munich; fmr teacher; fmr writer for TV. *Publications:* Perfume: The Story of a Murderer (novel) 1979, The Double Bass (play), The Pigeon (novel) 1988, Three Stories and a Reflection, On Love and Death; juvenile: The Story of Mr Summer 1991. *Address:* c/o Diogenes Verlag AG, Sprecherstr. 8, 8032 Zürich, Switzerland. *Telephone:* (1) 2548511. *Fax:* (1) 2528407.

SUŠNIK, Janez; Slovenian transport industry executive and government official; *President, National Council of Slovenia;* b. 18 Sept. 1942, Golnik; m.; two c.; ed Tech. Coll., Ljubljana; Pres. Admin. Bd Alpe Tour (forwarding agency) –2001; Asst Man. Viator–Vektor (forwarding agency) 2002; Pres. Nat. Council of Repub. of Slovenia 2002–; currently Pres. Adria Kombi (intermodal transport co.), Ljubljana; mem. Exec. Cttee Chamber of Commerce and Industry of Slovenia (CCIS), Transport Section 1995–2003, Exec. Cttee Regional Chamber for Gorenska Region at CCIS 1995–2003; Chair. Supervisory Bd Adtla Kaubl (nat. authority for combining traffic) 1990–, Supervisory Bd Automehaniza (road enterprise) 1998–2002; First Prize, Dance Contest, Bled 1959, Silver Plaquette of Community Kranw 1982, Praise of the Fed. Traffic Ministry of Yugoslavia 1984, Acknowledgement of the Presidency of the Yugoslav Repub. Traffic Agency 1988. *Leisure interests:* cycling, skiing, swimming, mountaineering, reading. *Address:* Office of the President, Drzavni Svet, Subiceva 4, 1000 Ljubljana, Slovenia (office). *Telephone:* (1) 4789799 (office); (1) 2345280 (Adria Kombi) (office). *Fax:* (1) 4789851 (office). *E-mail:* janez.susnik@ds-rs.si (office); infor@adriakombi.si (office). *Website:* www.ds-rs.si (office); www.adriakombi.si (office).

SUSSANGKARN, Chalongphob, PhD; Thai government official and economist; b. 16 April 1950; ed Univ. of Cambridge, UK; Lecturer in Econs, Univ. of Calif., Berkeley, USA 1977–79; Economist, World Bank, USA 1979–85; Research Fellow, Macroeconomic Policy Program, Thailand Devt Research Inst. 1985–86, Dir Human Resources and Social Devt Program 1987–95, Pres. 1996–2007; Minister of Finance 2007–08; mem. Bd Econ. Soc. of Thailand, Exec. Cttee Global Devt Network –2005, Exec. Cttee Nat. Centre for Genetic Eng and Biotechnology; Law Devt Cttee, Office of the Council of State; mem. Advisory Bd Asia-Pacific Devt Journal, ASEAN Econ. Bulletin, Asian Devt Review, Asian Econ. Policy Review; Regional Co-ordinator, East Asian Devt Network 2004–; Nat. Outstanding Researcher Award, Nat. Research Council of Thailand 2004. *Publications:* numerous research papers and contribs to professional publs. *Address:* c/o Ministry of Finance, Thanon Rama VI, Samsennai, Phaya Thai, Bangkok, 10400, Thailand (office).

SUSSKIND, Leonard, BS, PhD; American physicist and academic; *Felix Bloch Professor of Physics, Stanford University;* b. 1940, South Bronx, New York City; m. 1st 1960; four c.; m. 2nd; ed City Coll. of New York, Cornell Univ., Ithaca, NY; began working as a plumber aged 16; NSF Post-doctoral Fellow, Cornell Univ. 1965–66; Asst Prof. of Physics, Belfer Grad. School of Science, Yeshiva Univ., New York City 1966–68, Assoc. Prof. of Physics 1968–70, Prof. of Physics 1970–79; Prof. of Physics, Univ. of Tel-Aviv, Israel 1971–72; Prof. of Physics, Stanford Univ., Calif. 1979–, Felix Bloch Prof. of Physics 2000–; Assoc. Faculty mem. Perimeter Inst. for Theoretical Physics, Waterloo, Ont., Canada 2007; Distinguished Prof., Korea Inst. for Advanced Study; mem. NAS, American Acad. of Arts and Sciences; Pregel Award, New York Acad. of Science 1975, Loeb Lecturer, Harvard Univ. 1976, J.J. Sakurai Prize in Theoretical Particle Physics 1997. *Achievements include:* widely regarded as one of the fathers of string theory for his early contributions to the String Theory model of particle physics; one of at least three physicists who independently discovered, during or around 1970, that Veneziano dual resonance model of strong interactions could be described by a quantum mechanical model of strings. *Publications:* The Cosmic Landscape: String Theory and the Illusion of Intelligent Design 2005, The Black Hole War 2008; numerous scientific papers in professional journals on models of internal structure of hadrons, gauge theories, quark confinement, symmetry breaking, instantons, quantum statistical mechanics, baryon production in the universe, model for fermion masses, gravity in lower dimensions and quantum cosmology. *Address:* Room 332, Varian Physics Building, 382 Via Pueblo Mall, Stanford, CA 94305-4060, USA (office). *Telephone:* (650) 723-2686 (office). *Fax:* (650) 723-9389 (office). *E-mail:* susskind@stanford.edu (office). *Website:* www.stanford.edu/dept/physics (office).

SÜSSMUTH, Rita, DPhil; German politician; b. (Rita Kicknuth), 17 Feb. 1937, Wuppertal; m. Prof. Dr. Hans Süssmuth; one d.; ed Univs of Münster, Tübingen and Paris; academic career includes Prof., Int. Comparative Educ. Science, Univ. Bochum 1969; Prof. of Educ., Univ. of Dortmund 1971; Dir Research Inst. Frau und Gesellschaft (Woman and Soc.), Hanover 1982–85; mem. Scientific Advisory Cttee on Family Affairs, Fed. Ministry for Youth, Family Affairs and Health 1971–85; mem. 3rd Comm. on Family Affairs; Head of 7th Comm. on Youth; Fed. Minister for Family Affairs, Youth and Health 1985–88; Fed. Minister for Youth, Family Affairs, Women and Health 1986–88; Pres. German Fed. Parl.; mem. Bundestag representing Göttingen 1987–2002; mem. CDU Bd 1987–1998; Fed. Chair. Women's Union of CDU 1986–2001; Pres. European Movt Germany; Vice Pres. German Asscn of Adult Educ. Centres 1997–; mem. Advisory Council, Bertelsmann Stiftung 1997–; Vice Pres. Parl. Ass. of OSCE 2000–2003; Chair. Ind. Comm. on Migration to Germany 2000–01; Chair. Ind. Council of Experts on Immigration and Integration 2002–; Hon. Prof., Univ. of Göttingen 2003–; Steering Cttee on Intercultural Conflict and Societal Integration, Social Science Research Centre, Berlin 2004; Dr hc (Hildesheim) 1988, (Bochum) 1990, (Veliko Tărnovo, Czech Repub.) 1994, (Timişoara, Romania) 1995, (Sorbonne Nouvelle) 1996, (Johns Hopkins) 1998, (Ben Gurion, Israel) 1998. *Publications:* Frauen: Der Resignation keine Chance 1985, Aids: Wege aus der Angst 1987, Kämpfen und Bewegen: Frauenreden 1989, Wenn der Zeit der Rhythmus ändert 1991, Die planlosen Eliten (jtly) 1993, Wer nicht kämpft, hat schon verloren 2000, Mut zur Macht in Frauenhand. *Leisure interest:* tennis. *Address:* Platz der Republik 1, 11011 Berlin, Germany (office). *Telephone:* (30) 22777998 (office). *Fax:* (30) 22776998 (office). *E-mail:* rita.suessmuth@bundestag.de (office).

SUTALINOV, Murat; Kyrgyzstani politician; *Chair, State Committee for National Security;* b. 24 April 1963, Frunze; ed Higher School of USSR Ministry of Internal Affairs; held numerous positions in USSR Ministry of Internal Affairs in Kyrgyzstan; Deputy Head of Internal Affairs Dept, Bishkek 2000–01; Head of Internal Affairs Dept in Chuy Region 2001–02; Chief Criminal Investigation and Head of Dept of Ministry of Internal Affairs 2002–03; Head of Internal Affairs Dept in Osh Region 2003–04; Head of Defense and Security Dept of Presidential Admin. 2004–05; Attorney-Gen. March–May 2005; Minister of Internal Affairs May 2005–06 (resgnd); Chair. State Cttee for Nat. Security 2006–. *Address:* c/o Ministry of Internal Affairs, 720040 Bishkek, ul. Frunze 469, Kyrgyzstan (office).

ŠUTANOVAC, Dragan; Serbian politician; *Minister of Defence;* b. 1968, Belgrade; m.; two c.; ed Faculty of Mechanical Eng, Univ. of Belgrade, Marshall Centre for Security Studies, Germany; MEP April–May 2000; Deputy, Belgrade City Ass. 2000–; Special Adviser, Ministry of Internal Affairs 2000–01; mem. Parl. 2000–, Pres. Parl. Cttee for Defence and Security 2002–03; Deputy Minister of the Interior 2001–06; Minister of Defence 2007–; mem. Demokratska Stranka, DS (Democratic Party). *Address:* Ministry of Defence, 11000 Belgrade, Birčaninova 5, Serbia (office). *Telephone:* (11) 3006323 (office). *Fax:* (11) 3000328 (office). *E-mail:* minstar.odbrane@mod.gov.yu (office). *Website:* www.mod.gov.yu (office).

SUTCLIFFE, James (Jim), BSc, FIA; British financial services industry executive; b. 20 April 1964, Blantyre, Malawi; m. Sharon Sutcliffe 1977; two s.; ed Univ. of Cape Town, South Africa; COO Jackson Nat. Life, Lansing, Mich. USA 1989–91; joined Prudential UK 1992, various positions including Deputy Man. Dir Prudential Home Service Div. and CEO UK 1995–97, led creation of banking div. 1996, oversaw acquisition of Scottish Amicable 1997; Deputy Chair. Liberty Int. Property and Financial Services Inc. 1998–99; mem. Bd Old Mutual PLC 2000–08, CEO 2001–08 (resgnd); Chair. Försäkringsaktiebolaget Skandia; mem. Bd of Dirs Nedbank Group Ltd –2008 (resgnd); Trustee, Nelson Mandela Legacy Trust (UK). *Leisure interests:* golf, cricket, travelling. *Address:* c/o Old Mutual PLC, 3rd Floor, Lansdowne House, 57 Berkeley Square, London, W1J GER, England (office).

SUTER, Albert Edward, BME, MBA; American business executive; b. 18 Sept. 1935, East Orange, New Jersey; s. of Joseph V. Suter and Catherine Clay; m. Michaela S. Suter 1966; two s. one d.; ed Cornell Univ.; project engineer, Knight & Assocs, Chicago 1959–79, Pres. and CEO 1972–79; Exec. Vice-Pres. for Int. Operations, Emerson Electric Co., St Louis, Mo. 1979–88; Pres. and COO Firestone Tire & Rubber Co., Akron, Ohio 1986–88; Pres. and COO Whirlpool Co. 1988–89; Pres. COO Emerson Electric Co. 1990–92, Sr Vice-Chair. and COO 1992–97, Sr Vice-Chair. and Chief Admin. Officer –2001, Sr Advisor 2001–; mem. Bd of Dirs Furniture Brands International Inc. –2008, DeCrane Aircraft Holdings 2002–; Regional Trustee Boys and Girls Clubs of America; mem. Exec. Cttee of Nat. Bd of Dirs Jr Achievement; Chair. St Louis Community Foundation; mem. Eng. Council Cornell Univ. *Address:* c/o Emerson Electric Co., PO Box 4100, St Louis, MO 63136, USA.

SUTHERLAND, Donald McNichol, OC; Canadian actor; b. 17 July 1935, St John, NB; s. of Frederick McLae and Dorothy Isabel Sutherland (née McNichol); m. 1st Lois May Hardwick 1959; m. 2nd Shirley Jean Douglas 1966 (divorced); one s. Keifer Sutherland (q.v.) one d.; m. 3rd Francine Racette 1971; three s.; ed Bridgewater, NS, High School, Univ. of Toronto; TV Hallmark Hall of Fame; appeared on TV (BBC and ITV) in Hamlet, Man in a Suitcase, The Saint, Gideon's Way, The Avengers, Flight into Danger, Rose Tattoo, March to the Sea, Lee Harvey Oswald, Court Martial, Death of Bessie Smith, Max Dugan Returns, Crackers, Louis Malle, The Disappearance; Pres. McNichol Pictures Inc.; Hon. PhD; Officier, Ordre des Arts et des Lettres. *Films include:* The World Ten Times Over 1963, Castle of the Living Dead 1964, Dr Terror's House of Horrors 1965, Fanatic 1965, The Bedford Incident 1965, Promise Her Anything 1966, The Dirty Dozen 1967, Billion Dollar Brain 1967, Oedipus Rex 1968, Interlude 1968, Joanna 1968, The Split 1968, Start the Revolution Without Me 1969, Act of the Heart 1970, M*A*S*H* 1970, Kelly's Heroes 1970, Little Murders 1970, Alex in Wonderland 1971, Klute 1971, Johnny Got His Gun (as Christ) 1971, Steelyard Blues 1972, Lady Ice 1972, Alien Thunder 1973, Don't Look Now 1973, S*P*Y*S* 1974, The Day of the Locust 1975, 1900 1976, Casanova (Fellini) 1976, The Eagle Has Landed 1977, The Great Train Robbery 1978, Blood Relatives 1978, Bear Island 1979, Ordinary People 1980, Lolita 1981, Eye of the Needle 1981, Threshold 1982, Winter of Our Discontent, Ordeal by Innocence 1984, Revolution 1985, Gauguin 1986, The Wolf at the Door 1987, A Dry White Season 1988, Bethune: The Making of a Hero 1989, Lock Up 1989, Apprentice to Murder 1989, Lost Angels 1989, The Railway Station-man 1991, Scream from Stone 1991, Faithful 1991, JFK 1991, Backdraft, Agaguk, Buffy the Vampire Slayer, Shadow of the Wolf 1993, Benefit of the Doubt, Younger and Younger 1993, Six Degrees of Separation 1993, The Puppet Masters, Disclosure, Outbreak, Hollow Point, The Shadow Conspiracy, A Time to Kill, Virus 1999, Instinct

1999, Toscano 1999, The Art of War 2000, Panic 2000, Space Cowboys 2000, Uprising 2001, The Big Herst 2001, Final Fantasy: The Spirits Within 2001, Big Shot's Funeral 2001, Five Moons Plaza 2003, Italian Job 2003, Baltic Storm 2003, Cold Mountain 2003, Aurora Borealis 2005, Fierce People 2005, Pride and Prejudice 2005, Land of the Blind 2005, An American Haunting 2005, Ask the Dust 2006, Sleepwalkers 2007, Reign Over Me 2007, Puffball 2007, Fool's Gold 2008. *Television includes:* Hamlet, Man in a Suitcase, The Saint, Gideon's Way, The Avengers, Flight into Danger, Rose Tattoo, March to the Sea, Lee Harvey Oswald, Court Martial, Death of Bessie Smith, Max Dugan Returns, Crackers, Louis Malle, The Disappearance, The Path To War (Golden Globe for Best Supporting Actor in a TV series or TV movie 2003) 2002, Salem's Lot 2004, Human Trafficking 2005, Commander in Chief (series) 2005–06, Land of the Blind 2006, Dirty Sexy Money 2007–. *Plays:* Lolita (Broadway) 1981, Enigmatic Variations 2000. *Leisure interests:* sailing, baseball, Montreal. *Address:* c/o Katherine Olin, CAA, 9830 Wilshire Boulevard, Beverly Hills, CA 90212, USA.

SUTHERLAND, Grant Robert, AC, PhD, DSc, FRS, FAA; Australian geneticist and academic; *Geneticist Emeritus, Women's and Children's Hospital, Adelaide;* b. 2 June 1945, Bairnsdale, Victoria; s. of John Sutherland and Hazel Wilson Mason McClelland; m. Elizabeth Dougan 1979; one s. one d.; ed Numurkah High School, Univ. of Melbourne and Univ. of Edinburgh, UK; Dir Dept of Cytogenetics and Molecular Genetics, Women's and Children's Hosp., Adelaide 1975–2002, Foundation Research Fellow 2002–07, Geneticist Emer. 2007–; Affiliate Prof., Dept of Paediatrics, Univ. of Adelaide 1991–, School of Molecular and Biomedical Science 1996–2001, 2006–; Int. Research Scholar, Howard Hughes Medical Inst., Bethesda, Md 1993–97; Pres. Human Genetics Soc. of Australasia 1989–91, Human Genome Org. 1996–97; Co-Founder and Co.-Chair., Scientific Advisory Bd of Bionomics Ltd; mem. Bd of Dirs Thesan PLC, Beef CRC Ltd; Hon. Fellow, Royal Coll. of Pathologists of Australasia 1994, Hon. Mem. European Cytogenetics Asscn 2005; co-recipient Australia Prize in Molecular Genetics 1998, Nat. Australia Day Council Australian Achiever Award 2001, Ramaciotti Medal for Excellence in Biomedical Research 2001, Thompson ISI Australian Citation Laureate 2004, Major Lecture, Annual Scientific Meeting of the Human Genetics Soc. of Australasia (named the Grant Sutherland Lecture 2005–) 2005. *Publications include:* two books and more than 480 papers in medical and scientific journals on human genetics. *Leisure interest:* beef cattle farming. *Address:* Department of Genetic Medicine, Women's and Children's Hospital, Adelaide, S Australia 5006 (office); PO Box 300, Macclesfield, S Australia 5153, Australia (home). *Telephone:* (8) 8388-9524 (home). *E-mail:* grant.sutherland@adelaide.edu.au (office).

SUTHERLAND, Dame Joan, OM, AC, DBE, FRCM; Australian singer (soprano) (retd); b. 7 Nov. 1926, Sydney, NSW; d. of William McDonald Sutherland and Muriel Beatrice Sutherland (née Alston); m. Richard Bonynge (q.v.) 1954; one s.; ed St Catherine's School, Waverley, Sydney; debut as Dido in Purcell's Dido and Aeneas, Sydney 1947; Royal Opera Co., Covent Garden, London 1952–59, with first role as First Lady in The Magic Flute 1952; performed world-wide at Vienna State Opera, La Scala, Milan, Teatro Fenice, Venice, Paris Opera, San Francisco Opera, Chicago Lyric, The Metropolitan, New York, Australian Opera, Sydney, Hamburg, Canadian Opera, Buenos Aires, and at Glyndebourne, Edinburgh, Leeds and Florence Festivals; repertoire included Amelia in Un Ballo in Maschera, Aida, Eva in The Mastersingers, Gilda in Rigoletto, Desdemona in Othello, Agathe in Der Freischütz, Olympia, Giulietta, Antonia, Stella in Les Contes d'Hoffmann, Jenifer in The Midsummer Marriage, lead role in Lucia di Lammermoor, Norma, I Puritani, Dialogues of the Carmelites, Euridice, La Traviata, Adriana Lecouvreur, Lucrezia Borgia, Semiramide, Don Giovanni, Faust, Die Zauberflöte, Dido and Aeneas, The Merry Widow, Die Fledermaus, Les Huguenots; last operatic role as Marguerite de Valois in Les Huguenots for Opera Australia 1990, retd from performing 1991; Hon. Life mem. Australian Opera Co. 1974, Hon. Assoc. Accademia Filarmonica di Bologna 2007; Commdr, Ordre des Arts et des Lettres 1989, Order of Merit 1991; Hon. DMus (Sydney) 1984, (Oxford) 2002; recipient of Kennedy Center Honors 2004, depicted on two Australian postage stamps 2004. *Publications:* The Joan Sutherland Album (autobiography, with Richard Bonynge) 1986, A Prima Donna's Progress: The Autobiography of Joan Sutherland 1997. *Leisure interests:* reading, needlepoint, gardening. *Address:* c/o Ingpen & Williams, 7 St George's Court, 131 Putney Bridge Road, London, SW15 2PA, England (office). *Telephone:* (20) 8874-3222 (office). *Fax:* (20) 8877-3113 (office). *E-mail:* info@ingpen.co.uk (office). *Website:* www.ingpen.co.uk (office).

SUTHERLAND, John Andrew, PhD, FRSL; British academic and writer; *Emeritus Lord Northcliffe Professor of Modern English Literature, University College London;* b. 9 Oct. 1938; s. of Jack Sutherland and Elizabeth Sutherland (née Salter); m. Guilland Watt 1967; one s.; ed Colchester Royal Grammar School, Univs of Leicester and Edinburgh; nat. service, 2nd Lt, Suffolk Regt 1958–60; Lecturer in English, Univ. of Edin. 1965–72; Lecturer in English, Univ. Coll. London 1972–84, Lord Northcliffe Prof. of Modern English Literature 1992–2004, Prof. Emer. 2004–; columnist, The Guardian; Hon. DLitt (Leicester) 1998. *Publications include:* Thackeray at Work 1974, Victorian Novelists and Publishers 1976, Fiction and the Fiction Industry 1978, Bestsellers 1980, Offensive Literature 1982, The Longman Companion to Victorian Fiction 1989, Mrs Humphry Ward 1992, The Life of Walter Scott: A Critical Biography 1995, Victorian Fiction: Writers, Publishers, Readers 1995, Is Heathcliffe a Murderer? 1996, Can Jane Eyre be Happy? 1997, Where Was Rebecca Shot? 1998, Who Betrays Elizabeth Bennet? 1999, Henry V, War Criminal ? 1999, Last Drink to LA 2000, The Literary Detective 2000, Literary Lives 2001, Reading the Decades 2002, Stephen Spender: The Authorised Biography 2004, How to Read a Novel: A User's Guide 2006, Bestsellers: A Very Short Introduction 2007, Curiosities of Literature 2008, Magic Moments 2008. *Leisure interest:* walking. *Address:* c/o Department of English, University College London, Gower Street, London, WC1E 6BT, England. *Telephone:* (20) 7387-7050.

SUTHERLAND, Kiefer; American actor; b. 21 Dec. 1966, London, England; s. of Donald Sutherland (q.v.) and Shirley Douglas; m. 1st Camelia Kath 1987 (divorced 1990); two d.; m. 2nd Kelly Winn 1996 (divorced 2008); two step-s.; debut with LA Odyssey Theatre in Throne of Straw aged 9. *Films include:* Max Dugan Returns 1983, The Bay Boy 1984, At Close Range 1986, Crazy Moon 1986, Stand By Me 1986, The Lost Boys 1987, The Killing Time 1987, Promised Land 1987, Bright Lights, Big City 1988, Young Guns 1988, Renegades 1989, Chicago Joe and the Showgirl 1990, Flashback 1990, Flatliners 1990, The Nutcracker Prince (voice) 1990, Young Guns II 1990, Article 99 1991, Twin Peaks: Fire Walk With Me 1992, A Few Good Men 1992, The Vanishing 1993, The Three Musketeers, The Cowboy Way, Teresa's Tattoo, Eye for an Eye, A Time to Kill 1996, Truth or Consequences NM (also Dir) 1997, Dark City 1997, Ground Control 1998, The Breakup 1998, Woman Wanted 1999, The Red Dove 1999, Hearts and Bones 1999, Beat 2000, Picking up the Pieces 2000, The Right Temptation 2000, Cowboy Up 2001, To End All Wars 2001, Desert Saints 2002, Dead Heat 2002, Behind the Red Door 2002, Phone Booth 2002, Paradise Found 2003, Taking Lives 2004, Jiminy Glick in La La Wood 2004, River Queen 2005, The Sentinel 2006, Mirrors 2008. *Television appearances include:* Amazing Stories, Trapped in Silence, Brotherhood of Justice, Last Light (also Dir), 24 (Golden Globe for Best Actor in a TV Series 2002, Screen Actors Guild Best Actor in a Drama Series Award 2004, 2006) 2001–07. *Address:* c/o William Morris Agency, 1 William Morris Place, Beverly Hills, CA 90212; c/o International Creative Management, 8942 Wilshire Boulevard, Beverly Hills, CA 90211, USA.

SUTHERLAND, Peter Denis, SC, BCL; Irish international civil servant, lawyer, politician and business executive; *Chairman, BP plc; Non-Executive Chairman, Goldman Sachs International;* b. 25 April 1946; s. of W. G. Sutherland and Barbara Sutherland; m. Maria del Pilar Cabria Valcarcel 1971; two s. one d.; ed Gonzaga Coll., Univ. Coll., Dublin and King's Inns; called to Irish Bar (King's Inns), English Bar (Middle Temple) and New York Bar; admitted to Bar of the Supreme Court of the United States; practising mem. of Irish Bar 1968–81; Tutor in Law, Univ. Coll., Dublin 1968–71; apptd. Sr Counsel 1980; Attorney-Gen. 1981–82, 1982–85; mem. Strategy Cttee Fine Gael Party 1978–81, Dir Policy Programme, 1981 Gen. Election; mem. Comm. of the European Communities (responsible for Competition and Relations with the European Parl.) 1985–89; Dir-Gen. GATT (later World Trade Org.) 1993–95; Chair. Allied Irish Banks 1989–93; mem. Bd of Dirs British Petroleum Co. PLC (now BP plc), Deputy Chair. 1995–97, Chair. 1997–; Chair. (non-exec.) Goldman Sachs Int. 1995–; Dir (non-exec.) Royal Bank of Scotland Group PLC 2001–; Special Rep. of UN Sec.-Gen. on Int. Migration 2006–; mem. advisory group to José Manuel Barroso, Pres. of EC, on energy and climate change issues 2007–; Pres. Federal Trust, European Policy Center Advisory Council; Chair. Trilateral Comm. (Europe); Vice-Chair. European Roundtable of Industrialists; Consultor, Admin of the Patrimony of the Holy See; Goodwill Amb. UNIDO; Visiting Fellow, Kennedy School of Govt, Harvard Univ. 1989; Visiting Prof., Univ. Coll. Dublin; mem. Royal Irish Acad., Bar Council of Ireland Action Cttee for Europe, World Econ. Forum's Foundation Bd; Hon. Bencher, King's Inns Dublin 1995, Hon. Fellow, London Business School 1997, Oxford Univ. Inst. of Econs; Hon. KCMG 2004, Hon. KBE (UK) 2004; Grand Cross of Civil Merit (Spain) 1989; Grand Cross of King Leopold II (Belgium) 1989; Chevalier Légion d'honneur; Commdr du Wissam (Morocco) 1994; Order of Rio Branco (Brazil) 1996; Grand Cross of Order of Infante Dom Henrique (Portugal) 1998; Hon. LLD (St Louis, Nat. Univ. of Ireland, Bath, Suffolk Univ. (USA), Open Univ., Trinity Coll. (Dublin), Reading, Nottingham, Exeter); Hon. DPhil (Dublin City Univ.); European Person of the Year 1988, Gold Medal of European Parl. 1988, First European Law Prize Paris 1988, Robert Schuman Medal 1989, NZ Centenary Medal 1990, Consumer for World Trade Annual Award 1994, Dean's Medal, Wharton School, Univ. of Pa 1996, David Rockefeller Int. Leadership Award 1998. *Publications:* 1[er]janvier 1993 – ce qui va changer en Europe 1989; and numerous articles in law journals. *Leisure interests:* reading, sport. *Address:* BP plc, 1 St James's Square, London, SW1Y 4PD (office); Goldman Sachs International, Peterborough Court, 133 Fleet Street, London, EC4A 2BB, England (office). *Telephone:* (20) 7496-4000 (BP) (office); (20) 7774-4141 (Goldman Sachs) (office). *Fax:* (20) 7496-4572 (BP) (office). *Website:* www.bp.com (office).

SUTHERLAND, Dame Veronica Evelyn, DBE, MA; British college president and fmr diplomatist; *President, Lucy Cavendish College, Cambridge;* b. 25 April 1939, York; d. of the late Lt-Col Maurice G. Beckett and of Constance M. Cavenagh-Mainwaring; m. Alex J. Sutherland 1981; ed Royal School, Bath, Univs of London and Southampton; joined diplomatic service 1965, Second Sec., then First Sec. Embassy in Copenhagen 1967–70, Embassy in New Delhi 1975–78; with FCO 1970–75, 1978–80, Counsellor 1981, 1984–87, Asst Under-Sec. of State (Personnel) 1990–95; Perm. Del. to UNESCO 1981–84; Amb. to Côte d'Ivoire 1987–90, to Ireland 1995–99; Deputy Sec.-Gen. of the Commonwealth 1999–2002; Pres. Lucy Cavendish Coll., Cambridge 2001–; Hon. LLD (Trinity Coll., Dublin) 1998. *Address:* Lucy Cavendish College, Cambridge, CB3 0BU, England. *Telephone:* (1223) 332192.

SUTHERLAND OF HOUNDWOOD, Baron (Life Peer), cr. 2001, of Houndwood in the Scottish Borders; **Stewart Ross Sutherland,** Kt, KT, MA, FBA, FRSE; British university vice-chancellor and company director (non-executive); *President, Royal Society of Edinburgh;* b. 25 Feb. 1941, Scotland; s. of George Sutherland and Ethel Masson; m. Sheena Robertson 1964; one s. two d.; ed Woodside School, Robert Gordon's Coll., Univ. of Aberdeen and Corpus Christi Coll. Cambridge; Asst Lecturer in Philosophy, Univ. Coll. of N Wales

1965; Lecturer in Philosophy, Univ. of Stirling 1968, Sr Lecturer 1972, Reader 1976; Prof. of History and Philosophy of Religion, King's Coll. London 1977–85, Vice-Prin. 1981–85, Prin. 1985–90, Fellow 1983; Vice-Chancellor, Univ. of London 1990–94; HM Chief Insp. of Schools 1992–94; Vice-Chancellor and Prin. Univ. of Edin. 1994–2002; non-party political mem. House of Lords 2001–; mem. Council of Science and Tech. 1993–2000; Chair. Royal Comm. on Long-term Care of the Elderly 1997–99; Univ. Grants Cttee (Hong Kong) 1996–2004; Liveryman, Goldsmiths Co. 1991, Courts Assistant 2002; Chair. YTL Education (UK) 2003–; Provost Gresham Coll. 2003–; Hon. Fellow, King's Coll., London 1984, Corpus Christi Coll. Cambridge 1989, Univ. Coll. at Bangor 1991, Inst. of Educ., London 2003, Royal Coll. of Gen. Practitioners 2003, Faculty of Actuaries 2004, Birbeck, London 2004; Hon. LHD (Coll. of Wooster, Ohio) 1986, (Commonwealth Univ. of Va) 1992, (New York Univ.) 1996; Hon. LLD (Aberdeen) 1991, (Nat. Univ. of Ireland) 1992; Hon. DUniv (Stirling) 1993; Hon. DLitt (Richmond Coll.) 1995, (Univ. of Wales) 1996, (Glasgow) 1999, (Warwick) 2001, (St Andrews) 2002, (McGill) 2003, (London) 2004, (Queen Margaret Univ. Coll.) 2004, (Edin.) 2004; Dr hc (Uppsala) 1995. *Publications:* Atheism and the Rejection of God 1977, The Philosophical Frontiers of Christian Theology (ed. with B. L. Hebblethwaite) 1983, God, Jesus and Belief 1984, Faith and Ambiguity 1984, The World's Religions (ed.) 1988, Religion, Reason and the Self (jtly) 1989; articles in books and learned journals. *Leisure interests:* Tassie medallions, theatre, jazz. *Address:* House of Lords, London SW1A 0PD, England (office). *E-mail:* sutherlands@parliament.uk (office).

SUTJIPTO, Adm. (retd) Widodo Adi; Indonesian government official and fmr naval officer; b. 1 Aug. 1944; fmr Head of Armed Forces; Co-ordinating Minister for Political, Legal and Security Affairs 2004–. *Address:* Office of the Co-ordinating Minister for Political, Legal and Security Affairs, Jalan Medan Merdeka Barat 15, Jakarta 10110, Indonesia (office). *Telephone:* (21) 3849453 (office). *Fax:* (21) 3450918 (office).

SUTLEY, Nancy, BA, MA; American government official; *Chair, White House Council on Environmental Quality;* b. 20 April 1962, New York City; ed Cornell Univ., Kennedy School of Govt, Harvard Univ.; fmr Special Asst to Admin. US Environmental Protection Agency (EPA), Washington, DC; Deputy Sec. for Policy and Intergovernmental Relations, Calif. Environmental Protection Agency 1999–2003; Energy Adviser to Calif. Gov. Gray Davis 1999–2003; Deputy Mayor for Energy and Environment, Los Angeles; mem. Calif. State Water Resources Control Bd 2003–05; mem. Bd Metropolitan Water Dist of Southern Calif.; Chair. White House Council on Environmental Quality, Washington, DC 2009–. *Address:* White House Council on Environmental Quality, 722 Jackson Place NW, Washington, DC 20503, USA (office). *Telephone:* (202) 395-5750 (office). *Fax:* (202) 456-6546 (office). *Website:* www.whitehouse.gov/ceq (office).

SUTRESNA, Nana S., MA; Indonesian diplomatist; *Special Envoy of the President of Indonesia on Co-operation between Asian-African Countries and among members of the Non-Aligned Movement;* b. 21 Oct. 1933, Ciamis, Jawa Barat; m. 1973; two s. one d.; ed Acad. for Foreign Affairs, Jakarta, Univ. of Wales, Aberystwyth, UK; foreign news for the Indonesian News Agency, ANTARA 1955–57; joined Dept of Foreign Affairs 1957, Head of Public Relations and Spokesman 1972–76, Dir for European Affairs 1979–81, Dir-Gen. for Political Affairs 1984–88, served at Embassy in Washington, DC and in Mexico City, as Minister Counsellor then Minister in Vienna 1976–79, Head of Indonesian Del. to Disarmament Conf., Geneva 1981–83, Deputy Perm. Rep. to UN, Geneva 1981–84, Perm. Rep. to UN (also accred to Bahamas, Jamaica and Nicaragua) 1988–92, Amb.-at-Large 1992–99, Amb. to UK (also accred to Ireland) 1999–2002, Special Envoy of Pres. of Indonesia to N and S Korea 2002–06, Special Envoy of Pres. on Co-operation between Asian-African Countries and among mems of the Non-Aligned Movt 2006–. *Leisure interest:* golf. *Address:* Ministry of Foreign Affairs, Jalan Taman Pejambon 6, 10th Floor, Jakarta Pusat 10110, Indonesia (office). *Telephone:* (21) 3813453 (office). *Fax:* (21) 3857316 (office). *E-mail:* infomed@deplu.go.id (office). *Website:* www.deplu.go.id (office).

SUTRISNO, Gen. Try; Indonesian army officer (retd) and politician; early career as mil. engineer; ADC to Pres. 1974–78; Army Chief of Staff 1986–88; Commdr of the Armed Forces 1988–93; Vice-Pres. of Indonesia 1993–97; left Golkar Party to join Justice and Unity Party (PKP) 1998; mem. Indonesian-Malaysian Eminent Persons Group (est. by govts of Indonesia and Malaysia to advise on jt issues) 2008–. *Address:* c/o Partai Keadilan dan Persatuan (PKP), c/o Dewan Perwakilan Rakyat, Jalan Gatot Subroto 16, Jakarta, Indonesia (office).

SUTTON, Philip John, RA; British artist; b. 20 Oct. 1928, Poole, Dorset; s. of L. L. Sutton and Anne Sutton; m. Heather Cooke 1954; one s. three d.; ed Slade School of Fine Art and Univ. Coll., London; Lecturer, Slade School of Fine Art, Univ. Coll. 1954–; Artist-in-Residence, Fulham Pottery 1987–; solo exhbns bi-annually at Roland Browse & Delbanco and Browse & Darby 1956–84; Leeds City Art Gallery retrospective 1960; travelled in Australia and Fiji painting landscapes 1963–64; retrospective exhbn, Diploma Gallery, Royal Acad. 1977; toured Israel with 10 British artists 1979; visited Australia 1980; designed Post Office Greeting Stamps 1989. *Publication:* Philip Sutton Life and Art. *Leisure interests:* swimming, running. *Address:* 3 Morfa Terrace, Manorbier, Tenby, Pembrokeshire, SA70 7TH, Wales. *Telephone:* (1834) 871474. *E-mail:* sutton.cooke@dogglemail.com. *Website:* www.philip-sutton.co.uk.

SUWAIDI, Sultan bin Nasser as-, BS; United Arab Emirates business executive and central banker; *Governor, Central Bank of the United Arab Emirates;* joined Abu Dhabi Investment Authority 1978, later Deputy Dir –1982; Gen. Man. Abu Dhabi Investment Co. 1982–84; Gen. Man. Gulf Int. Bank, Bahrain 1984–85; Man. Dir and CEO Abu Dhabi Commercial Bank 1985–91; Gov. Cen. Bank of the UAE 1991–. *Address:* Central Bank of the United Arab Emirates, POB 854, Abu Dhabi, United Arab Emirates (office). *Telephone:* (2) 6652220 (office). *Fax:* (2) 6667494 (office). *E-mail:* admin@cbuae.gov.ae (office). *Website:* www.centralbank.ae (office).

SUZMAN, Janet, BA; British/South African actress and director; b. 9 Feb. 1939, Johannesburg; d. of Saul Suzman and Betty Sonnenberg; m. Trevor Nunn (q.v.) 1969 (divorced 1986); one s.; ed Kingsmead Coll., Univ. of the Witwatersrand, London Acad. of Music and Dramatic Art; moved to UK 1960; The Spencer Memorial Lecture, Harvard Univ. 1987; The Tanner Lectures, Brasenose Coll., Oxford 1995, The Drapers Lecture, Queen Mary and Westfield Coll., Univ. of London 1996, The Morell Lecture, Univ. of York 1999; Vice-Pres. Council of LAMDA; Hon. Assoc. Artist RSC; Hon. Patron the Market Theatre; Queen's Silver Jubilee Medal 1977; Hon. MA (Open Univ.) 1984; Hon. DLit (Warwick) 1990, (Leicester) 1992, (Queen Mary and Westfield Coll.) 1997, (Southampton) 2002, (Middlesex) 2003, (Kingston) 2006; Best Actress, Evening Standard Drama Award 1973, 1976, Plays and Players Award 1976, Barclays TMA Award for Best Director 1997. *Roles for RSC and West End include:* Lady Anne, La Pucelle, Lady Percy, Luciana, (RSC) Ophelia, Beatrice, Rosalind 1962–70, Lulu in The Birthday Party 1963–64, Portia, Rosalind 1965, Carmen in The Balcony, She Stoops to Conquer (Oxford Playhouse) 1966, Katharina, Celia, Berinthia in The Relapse 1967, Cleopatra and Lavinia 1972–73, Hester in Hello and Goodbye (Kings Head) 1973, Masha in Three Sisters (Cambridge Theatre) 1976, The Death of Bessie Smith (Market Theatre, Johannesburg 1976), Shen Te in The Good Woman of Setzuan (Tyneside Theatre Co.) 1976, at Royal Court Theatre 1977; Hedda Gabler (Duke of York's Theatre) 1977, Duchess of Malfi 1978, The Greeks (Aldwych) 1980, Boesman and Lena (Hampstead) 1984, Vassa (Greenwich Theatre) 1985, Andromache (Old Vic) 1987, Another Time (Wyndhams) 1989–90, Hippolytus (Almeida) 1991, The Sisters Rosensweig (Old Vic) 1994, The Retreat from Moscow (Chichester) 1999, The Free State (Birmingham Repertory and tour) 2000, The Hollow Crown (tour of Far East) 2003, Whose Life is it Anyway (Comedy) 2005, Frobishers Gold (The Shaw) 2006, Volumnia in Coriolanus (RSC) 2007. *Directed:* theatre: Othello, (Market Theatre, Johannesburg) 1987, A Dream of People (The Pit) 1990, The Cruel Grasp (Edinburgh Festival) 1991, No Flies on Mr. Hunter (Chelsea Centre) 1992, Death of a Salesman (Theatr Clwyd) 1993, The Deep Blue Sea (Theatr Clwyd) 1996, The Good Woman of Sharkville (Market Theatre, Johannesburg) 1996 and UK tour 1997, The Cherry Orchard (Birmingham Rep.) 1997, The Snow Palace (tour 1998) and Tricycle Theatre 1998, The Free State – A South African Response to The Cherry Orchard (Birmingham Repertory) and UK tour 2000, The Guardsman 2000; television: Othello (Channel 4) 1988, Measure for Measure (Guildhall) 2004, Hamlet (Grahamstown Festival and The Complete Works Festival, Stratford-on-Avon) 2006, Coriolanus (The Complete Works Festival, Stratford-on-Avon) 2007. *Film appearances:* A Day in the Death of Joe Egg 1970, Nicholas and Alexandra 1971, Nijinsky 1978, The Black Windmill 1979, Priest of Love 1981, The Draughtsman's Contract 1981, E la Nave Va 1982, A Dry White Season 1988, Nuns on the Run 1990, Leon the Pig-Farmer 1992, Max 2001, Fairy Story 2002. *Radio:* Latest: Miss Haversham. *Television includes:* The Family Reunion 1967, Saint Joan 1968, The Three Sisters 1969, Macbeth 1970, Hedda Gabler 1972, Twelfth Night 1973, Shakespeare or Bust 1973, Antony and Cleopatra 1974, Miss Nightingale, Clayhanger (serial) 1975–76, Robin Hood (CBS TV) 1983, Mountbatten: The Last Viceroy 1985, The Singing Detective 1986, The Miser 1987, Revolutionary Witness 1989, Masterclass on Shakespearian Comedy 1990, Masterclass from Haymarket Theatre (Sky TV) 2001, White Clouds (BBC) 2002. *Publications:* Hedda Gabler: The Play in Performance 1980, Acting with Shakespeare: Three Comedies 1996, The Free State 2000, A Commentary on Antony and Cleopatra 2001. *Leisure interests:* not climbing Everest or rowing the Atlantic. *Address:* c/o Steve Kenis and Co., Royalty House, 72–74 Dean Street, London, W1D 3SG, England (office). *Telephone:* (20) 7434-9055 (office). *Fax:* (20) 7287-6328 (office). *E-mail:* sk@sknco.com (office).

SUZUKI, David Takayoshi, OC, BA, PhD; Canadian broadcaster, geneticist and academic; *Chairman, David Suzuki Foundation;* b. 24 March 1936, Vancouver, BC; s. of Kaoru Carr Suzuki; m. 2nd Tara Cullis; two c.; ed Amherst Coll., Univ. of Chicago; Biologist, Dept of Lands & Forests, Sudbury, Ont. 1958; Teaching Asst, Dept of Biology, Amherst Coll., Amherst, Mass 1957–58; Research Asst for Dr W. K. Baker, Univ. of Chicago 1958–59, Teaching Asst, Dept of Zoology, Univ. of Chicago 1959–61; Asst Prof., Dept of Genetics, Univ. of Alberta 1962–63; Asst Prof., Dept of Zoology, Univ. of BC 1963–65, Assoc. Prof. 1965–69, Prof. 1969–93, Prof. Emer. 2001–; Visiting Prof., Univ. of Calif., Berkeley 1966, 1969, 1976, 1977, Univ. of Puerto Rico 1972, Univ. of Toronto 1978; f. David Suzuki Foundation 1990, now Chair.; Fellow, Royal Soc. of Canada 1978–84, AAAS 1980–; has produced and hosted many CBC and other TV series and specials on science topics; Order of BC 1995; Hon. LLD (Univ. of Prince Edward Island) 1974, (Trent Univ., Ont.) 1981, (Univ. of Calgary) 1986, (Queen's Univ. in Kingston, Ont.) 1987; Hon. DSc (Univ. of Windsor, Ont.) 1979, (Acadia Univ., NS) 1979, (Lakehead Univ., Ont.) 1986, (McMaster Univ., Ont.) 1987, (Carleton Univ., Ont.) 1987, (Amherst Coll., Mass) 1988, (Griffith Univ., Queensland, Australia) 1997, (Whitman Coll., Washington, DC) 1999, (York Univ., Ont.) 2005, (UQAM, PQ) 2005, (Flinders Univ., S Australia) 2006, (Univ. of Montreal, PQ) 2007, (Univ. of Western Ont.) 2007; Hon. DHL (Governors State Univ., Ill.) 1986; Hon. DDL (Open Univ., Canada) 1998, (Simon Fraser Univ., BC) 2001; Hon. Doctor of Environmental Science (Unity Coll., ME) 2000; Hon. Doctor of Communication (Ryerson Univ., Ont.) 2007; numerous awards including Oustanding Japanese-Canadian of the Year Award 1972, Broadcaster of the Year, Canadian Broadcasters'; League 1976, Sanford Fleming Medal, Royal Canadian Inst. 1981, Japan Times Prize 1983, Medal of Honor, Canadian Assсn 1984, Gold Medal Award, Biological Council of Canada 1986, UNESCO

Kalinga Prize 1986, Wiegand Award for Canadian Excellence, Univ. of Waterloo 1990, Lifetime Achievement Award, Univ. of BC Alumni 2000, John Drainie Award for Excellence in Broadcast Journalism 2002, Queen Elizabeth II Golden Jubilee Medal 2002, Lindbergh Award 2004, voted one of 10 Greatest Canadians by CBC viewers 2004, Bradford Washburn 2006. *Radio includes:* Quirks and Quarks 1974–79, It's a Matter of Survival 1989. *Television includes:* Science Magazine 1974–79, Suzuki on Science 1979, The Nature of Things 1979–, A Planet for the Taking (UNEP Medal) 1985, From Naked Ape to Superspecies. *Publications:* more than 45 books, including An Introduction to Genetic Analysis (with A. F. Griffiths) 1976, The Japan We Never Knew 1996, The Sacred Balance: Rediscovering Our Place in Nature (with A. McConnell) 1997, A Glimpse of Canada's Future 1997, Tree Suitcase 1998, Earth Time 1998, From Naked Ape to Superspecies 1999, You Are the Earth 1999, Eco-Fun 2000, Good News for a Change 2001, When the Wild Comes Leaping Up 2002, Genetics – A Beginner's Guide (co-author) 2002, Sacred Balance – A Visual Celebration 2002, The Salmon Forest 2002, David Suzuki Reader 2003, Tree – A Life Story 2004, Grassroots Rising 2006, David Suzuki: The Autobiography (British Columbia Booksellers' Choice Award in Honour of Bill Duthie 2007) 2006. *Address:* c/o Elois Yaxley, David Suzuki Foundation, Suite 219, 2211 West 4th Avenue, Vancouver, BC V6K 4S2, Canada (office). *Telephone:* (604) 732-4228 (office). *Fax:* (604) 730-9672 (office). *E-mail:* contact@davidsuzuki.org (office). *Website:* www.davidsuzuki.org (office).

SUZUKI, Haruo, LLB; Japanese business executive; b. 31 March 1913, Hayama, Kanagawa Pref.; s. of Chuji and Masu Suzuki; m. Ito Hibiya 1941; two d.; ed Tokyo Imperial Univ.; with Nomura Securities Co. Ltd 1936–38; joined Showa Denko KK 1939, Exec. Vice-Pres. 1959–71, Pres. 1971–81, Chair. 1981–87, Hon. Chair. 1987–2000, Sr Counsellor 2000–; Chair. Japan Chemical Industry Asscn 1976–78, New Materials Study Group 1983, Japan Fine Ceramics Asscn 1986–91; Perm. Trustee Japan Cttee for Econ. Devt 1945; Dir Int. Primary Aluminium Inst. 1974–76, 1980–82; Exec. Dir Fed. of Econ. Orgs. 1972–87; Chair. Japan-Southern US Asscn 1984–90; Dir and Sr Counsellor Japan Econ. Research Inst. 1997–; Chair. Asscn for Corp. Support for the Arts in Japan 1990–94, Hon. Chair. 1994–; Consultant, Village Shonan Inc. 1996–; Industrial Structure Council of Ministry of Int. Trade and Industry (MITI) 1972–92, Legis. Council, Ministry of Justice 1982–92; mem. Industrial Property Council, Patent Office, MITI 1983–91, Comité de réflexion sur l'avenir des relations franco-japonaises, Ministry of Foreign Affairs 1982–84; First Class Order of the Sacred Treasure (Japan) 1989, Officier Légion d'honneur 1995; Hon. DEcon (Humboldt Univ., Berlin) 1975. *Publications:* Chemical Industry 1968, What the Classics Have Taught Me 1979 and others. *Leisure interests:* reading, art appreciation, painting, travelling. *Address:* Showa Denko KK, 13-9, Shiba Daimon 1-chome, Minato-ku, Tokyo, Japan (office). *Telephone:* (3) 5470-3300 (office). *Fax:* (3) 3455-5600 (office).

SUZUKI, Ichiro; Japanese professional baseball player; b. 22 Oct. 1973, Kasugai, m. Yumiko Suzuki; ed Aikoudai Meiden, Aichi Pref.; right fielder; with Japanese Pacific League team Orix Blue Wave 1994–2000; set Japanese records for continuous games and batting average; signed with Seattle Mariners Nov. 2000; set American League record for singles (190) in a season 2001; American League batting champion 2001 (.350 avg.), 2004 (.372 avg.); set major league record for hits (262) 2004; American League Most Valuable Player 2001, American League Rookie of the Year 2001, Gold Glove award 2001, 2002, 2003, 2004. *Address:* c/o The Baseball Club of Seattle LP, 1250 1st Avenue, South, Seattle, WA 98134, USA (office). *Telephone:* (206) 346-4000 (office). *Fax:* (206) 346-4100. *Website:* www.seattle.mariners.mlb.com.

SUZUKI, Kunio; Japanese business executive; *Representative Director and Chairman, Mitsui OSK Lines Limited;* b. 27 Aug. 1939; joined Osaka Shosen Kaisha (renamed Mitsui OSK Lines Ltd 1964) 1962, Gen. Man. Tanker Div. 1988–91, Dir and Gen. Man. Tanker Div. 1991–93, Dir 1993–94, Man. Dir 1994–95, Rep. Dir 1995–, Sr Man. Dir 1995–98, Vice-Pres. 1998–2000, Pres. 2000–04, Chair. and CEO Mitsui OSK Lines Ltd 2004–06, Chair. 2006–; Chair. Japanese Shipowners' Asscn; Dir (non-exec.) Dah Sing Financial Holdings Ltd 2003–. *Address:* Mitsui OSK Lines Ltd, 1-1 Toranomon, 2-chome, Tokyo 105-8688, Japan (office). *Telephone:* (3) 3587-6224 (office). *Fax:* (3) 3587-7734 (office). *E-mail:* info@mol.co.jp (office). *Website:* www.mol.co.jp (office).

SUZUKI, Osamu; Japanese business executive; *Chairman and CEO, Suzuki Motor Corporation;* b. 30 Jan. 1930, Gero, Gifu; s. of Shunzo Suzuki and Toshiko Suzuki; m. Shoko Suzuki 1958; two s. one d.; ed Chuo Univ.; joined Suzuki Motor Co. Ltd 1958, Dir 1963–66, Jr Man. Dir 1967–72, Sr Man. Dir 1973–77, Pres. and CEO 1978–2000 (name changed to Suzuki Motor Corpn 1990), Chair. and CEO 2000–, mem. Bd Dirs Maruti Suzuki India Ltd; Medal of Honour with Blue Ribbon 1987, Mil. Cross of Order of Repub. of Hungary 1993, Middle Cross with Star Order of Merit (Hungary) 2004, Padma Bhushan (India) 2007; Award 'Sitara-i-Pakistan' (Pakistan) 1985. *Leisure interest:* golf.

SUZUKI, Seijun; Japanese film director and actor; b. (Seitaro Suzuki), 24 May 1923, Nihonbashi, Tokyo; after service in Japanese navy during World War II enrolled in film dept, Kamakura Acad.; Asst Dir Shochiku studios –1954, then Dir Nikkatsu studios 1954–1967; after release of Zigeunerweisen 1980 began to receive much critical praise and numerous awards. *Films directed include:* Minato no Kanapi (Harbour Toast) 1956, Hozuna wa utau (Pure Emotions of the Sea) 1956, Akuma no Machi (Satan's Town) 1956, Ukigusa no yado (Inn of the Floating Weeds) 1957, Rajo to Kenju (The Naked Woman and the Gun) 1957, Hachijikan no Kyofu (Eight Hours of Terror) 1957, Kagenaki koe (Voice Without a Shadow) 1958, Fumihazushita Haru (The Boy Who Came Back) 1958, Aoi Chibusa (Young Breasts) 1958, Ankokugai no bijo (Beauty of the Underworld) 1958, Suppadaka no Nenrei (Age of Nudity) 1959, Love Letter 1959, Ankoku no Ryoken (Passport to Darkness) 1959, Subete Ga

Kurutteru (Everything Goes Wrong) 1960, Kutabare Gurentai (Fighting Delinquents) 1960, Kemono no Nemuri (Sleep of the Beast) 1960, Clandestine Zero Line 1960, Tokyo Kishitai (Tokyo Nights) 1961, Toge O Wataru Wakai Kaze (The Wind-of-Youth Group Crosses the Mountain Pass) 1961, Sandanju no Otoko (Man With a Shotgun) 1961, Muteppo-daisho 1961, Hell of a Guy 1961, Blood-Red Water in the Channel 1961, Ore ni Kaketa Yatsura (Guys Who Put Money on Me) 1962, Hai Tiin Yakuza (High-Teen Yakuza) 1962, Yaju no Seishun (Youth of the Beast) 1963, Tantei Jimusho 23 (Detective Bureau 2-3) 1963, Kanto Mushuku (Kanto Wanderer) 1963, Akutaro (The Bastard) 1963, Nikutai no Mon (Gate of Flesh) 1964, Oretachi no chi ga Yurusanai (Our Blood Will Not Forgive) 1964, Hana to Doto (The Flower and the Angry Wave) 1964, Shunpu Den (Story of a Prostitute) 1965, Irezumi ichidai (Tattooed Life) 1965, Akutaroden: Waruihoshi no Shita Demo (Stories of Bastards) 1965, Kawachi Karumen 1966, Tokyo Nagaremono (Tokyo Drifter) 1966, Kenka Erejii (The Born Fighter) 1966, Koroshi no Rakuin (Branded to Kill) 1967, Otoko no Naka ni wa Tori Ga Iru (There's a Bird Inside a Man) 1969, Hishu Monogatari (Tale of Sorrow and Sadness) 1977, Ana no Kiba (The Fang in the Hole) 1979, Tsigoineruwaizen 1980, Kageroza (Heat Shimmer Theatre) 1981, Kapone oi ni Naku (Capone Cries a Lot) 1985, Rupan Sansei: Babiron no Ogon Densetsu (Lupin III: The Golden Legend of Babylon) 1985, Yumeji 1991, Kekkon 1993, Pistol Opera 2001, Princess Raccoon 2005. *Films as actor include:* Yaju no Seishun (Youth of the Beast) 1963, Kuraku naru-made Matenai! 1975, Marilyn ni Aitai (Shiro and Marilyn) 1988, Pachinko Graffiti 1992, Cold Fever 1995, Ki no ue no Sogyo 1997, Fuyajo (Sleepless Town) 1998, Pupu no Monogatari 1998, Kôfuku no Kane (Blessing Bell) 2002.

SUZUKI, Tadashi; Japanese theatre director and producer; *Chairman, Japan Performing Arts Foundation;* b. 20 June 1939, Shimizu City; m. Hiroko Takeuchi 1969; one s.; ed Kitazono High School and Waseda Univ.; f. Waseda Sho-Gekijo 1966; changed name to Suzuki Co. of Toga (SCOT) 1984; apptd. Artistic Dir of Iwanami Hall 1974; built Toga Theatre, Toga Village, Toyama Pref. 1976; Guest Prof. at various schools including Juilliard School, Univ. of Wis. (Milwaukee), Univ. of Calif. (San Diego) and Univ. of Del.; founded Japan Performing Arts Center 1982–99; began annual Toga Int. Arts Festival 1982, Toga Int. Actor Training Programme 1983; apptd Artistic Dir of Acting Co. Mito (ACM) Theatre 1989–94; Gen. Artistic Dir Shizuoka Performing Arts Center 1995–2007; Artistic Dir Suzuki Co. of Toga; Chair. Japan Performing Arts Foundation 2007–; mem. Int. Cttee Theatre Olympics 1994; several awards for services to the arts. *Work includes:* own texts On the Dramatic Passions I 1969, II 1970, III 1970 and Night and Clock 1975, A Greek trilogy and plays by Chekhov and Shakespeare, many of these in theatres around the world. *Publications:* The Sum of the Internal Angles 1973, Dramatic Language 1977, On the Dramatic Passions 1977, Horizon of Deception 1980, Force that Crosses the Border 1984, The Way of Acting 1986, What Theatre Is 1988, The Way of Directing 1994, Dramatic Language II 1999, The Sum of the Internal Angles II 2003. *Leisure interest:* collecting costumes (especially hats). *Address:* Japan Performing Arts Foundation, 3-19-17-402, Takanawa, Minato-ku, Tokyo, 108-0074, Japan. *Telephone:* (3) 3445-8010. *Fax:* (3) 3445-8012 (office). *E-mail:* engekijin@jpaf.or.jp (office). *Website:* www.jpaf.or.jp (office).

SUZUKI, Toshifumi; Japanese retail executive; *Chairman and CEO, Seven & i Holdings Co. Ltd;* b. 1933; opened first convenience store (konbini) 1974; fmr labour union leader; f. Seven-Eleven Japan Co. (imported name and concept from US to Japan 1970s); Pres. Ito Yokado Co. Ltd (supermarket chain) 2000–03, Chair. and CEO 2003–05, Chair. and CEO Seven & i Holdings (holding co. of Ito Yokado, Seven Eleven Japan, Denny's Japan and other operating cos) 2005–, Chair. 7-Eleven Inc. (after acquisition by Seven & i Holdings) 2005–; Pres. Keiranden Cttee on Distribution 2000–. *Address:* Seven & i Holdings Co. Ltd, 8-8 Nibancho, Chiyoda-ku, Tokyo 102-8455, Japan (office). *Telephone:* (3) 6238-3711 (office). *E-mail:* info@7andi.com (office). *Website:* www.7andi.com (office).

SUZUKI, Tsuneo; Japanese politician; *Minister of Education, Culture, Sports, Science and Technology;* b. 10 Feb. 1941; ed Faculty of Political Science and Econs, Waseda Univ.; mem. House of Reps (Kanagawa Pref. 7th Dist) 1986–; joined LDP 1986, Dir Environment Div., LDP 1997, Deputy Chair. Research Comm. on the Educ. System 1998, Research Comm. on Fundamental Environmental Issues 1999, Policy Research Council 2000–01, Vice-Chair. Party Org. HQ 2001, Chair. Special Cttee on Foreign Students 2001–03, Deputy Chair. Diet Affairs Cttee 2003–04, Chair. Cttee on Nat. Capital Area 2004–05, Dir-Gen. Information Research Bureau 2006–07, Chair. Special Cttee on Public Safety 2007; Parl. Sec. of Educ. 1992–96, of Environment 1996–97; Chair. Cttee on Educ., House of Reps 1999, Special Cttee on Political Ethics and Election Law 2005, Cttee on Disasters 2007–08; Sr State Sec. for Educ., Science, Sports and Culture 2000; Minister of Educ., Culture, Sports, Science and Tech. 2008–. *Address:* Ministry of Education, Culture, Sports, Science and Technology, 3-2-2, Kasumigaseki, Chiyoda-ku, Tokyo 100-8959, Japan (office). *Telephone:* (3) 5253-4111 (office). *Fax:* (3) 3595-2017 (office). *E-mail:* info@mext.go.jp (office). *Website:* www.mext.go.jp (office).

SUZUMURA, Kotaro, BA, MA, PhD; Japanese economist and academic; *Professor of Public Economics, Institute of Economic Research, Hitotsubashi University;* b. 7 Jan. 1944, Tokoname, Aichi Pref.; s. of Hidetaro Suzumura and Sumie Suzumura; three d.; ed Hitotsubashi Univ.; Lecturer, Dept of Econs, Hitotsubashi Univ. 1971–73, Prof. of Public Econs, Inst. of Econ. Research 1984–; Assoc. Prof., Inst. of Econ. Research, Kyoto Univ. 1973–82; Lecturer, LSE 1974–76; Visiting Assoc. Prof. of Econs, Stanford Univ. 1979–80; Visiting Fellow, Dept of Econs, Univ. of Pennsylvania 1987, All Souls Coll., Oxford 1988; Dir-Gen. Tokyo Centre for Econ. Research 1990–92; Pres. Japanese Econ. Asscn 1999–2000, Soc. for Social Change and Welfare 2000–01; Chair. Far Eastern Standing Cttee Econometric Soc. 1995–2000,

Fellow 1990–, mem. Council 1995–2000; Ed.-in-Chief Japanese Econ. Review 1995–97; mem. Council Soc. for Social Choice and Welfare, Science Council of Japan 2000–03; Medal with Purple Ribbon 2004, Japan Acad. Prize 2006. *Publications:* Rational Choice, Collective Decisions and Social Welfare (Nikkei Econs Book Prize 1984) 1983, The Economic Analysis of Industrial Policy (Nikkei Econs Book Prize 1988) 1988, Competition, Commitment and Welfare 1995, Social Choice Re-examined (co-ed. two vols) 1996, 1997, Development Strategy and Management of the Market Economy (jtly) 1997, Handbook of Social Choice and Welfare Vol. I (co-ed.) 2002. *Leisure interests:* reading novels. *Address:* Institute of Economic Research, Hitotsubashi University, Naka 2-1, Kunitachi, Tokyo 186-8603 (office); 1-29-3 Asagaya Minami, Suginami-ku, Tokyo, Japan (home). *Telephone:* (42) 580-8353 (office); (3) 3311-5110 (home). *Fax:* (42) 580-8353 (office); (3) 3311-5110 (home). *E-mail:* suzumura@ier.hit-u.ac.jp (office). *Website:* www.ier.hit-u.ac.jp (office).

SVANBERG, Carl-Henric, BSc, MSc; Swedish telecommunications industry executive; *President and CEO, Telefonaktiebolaget L. M. Ericsson;* b. 1952, Porjus; ed Univ. of Uppsala, Linköping Inst. of Tech.; various foreign assignments in project exports, Asea Brown Boveri 1977–85; joined Securitas (security co.) 1986, Exec. Vice-Pres. 1990–94; Pres. and CEO Assa Abloy Group 1994–2003, Deputy Chair. 2003–; Pres. and CEO Telefonaktiebolaget L. M. Ericsson 2003–; mem. Bd Dirs Melker Schörling AB; mem. Bd Confed. of Swedish Enterprise, Bd Univ. of Uppsala; Dr hc (Linköping Univ.) 2006, (Luleå Univ. of Tech.). *Leisure interests:* sailing, working with Boy Scouts. *Address:* Telefonaktiebolaget L. M. Ericsson, Telefonvägen 30, 126 25 Stockholm, Sweden (office). *Telephone:* (8) 719000 (office). *Fax:* (8) 184085 (office). *E-mail:* info@ericsson.com (office). *Website:* www.ericsson.com (office).

SVANHOLM, Poul Johan, LLB; Danish banker and business executive; b. 7 June 1933, Aalborg; s. of Poul Svanholm and Gerda Svanholm (née Stougaard); m. Lise Andersen 1957; one s. one d.; ed Univ. of Copenhagen; Pres., Vingaarden, Odense 1962–72; Pres., Carlsberg A/S, Copenhagen 1972–82, CEO, Carlsberg Group 1982–96; Chair., Danske Bank 1983–2003; mem. Bd, D/S Svendborg (A. P. Moeller Group) 1978–2003, Vice-Chair., A. P. Moeller-Maersk A/S 2003–; mem., European Advisory Cttee to New York Stock Exchange 1986–2005; Chair., Thomas B. Thrige Foundation 1979–2008; Grand Cross of Order of Dannebrog 1997, Hon. CBE 1997. *Leisure interest:* Ravnborg Estate. *Address:* 15 Helleruplund Allé, 2900 Hellerup, Denmark (home). *Telephone:* 39-62-23-45 (home). *Fax:* 39-62-75-46 (home). *E-mail:* poul.svanholm@privat.dk (home).

SVANIDZE, Nikolay Karlovich; Russian television journalist and historian; b. 2 April 1955, Moscow; m. Marina Svanidze; one s.; ed Moscow State Univ.; researcher, Inst. of USA and Canada, USSR (now Russian) Acad. of Sciences 1978–91; on staff, Russian TV 1992–; commentator, program Vesti 1991–94; host program Zerkalo 1996–; Deputy Dir of Information Programmes and Head of Studio Information and Analytical Programmes 1996–97; Deputy Chair., then Chair. All Russian State TV and Radio Co. 1996–98; mem. Public Chamber; Teffi Prize of Russian Acad. of TV for the best information programme. *Publication:* Medvedev 2008. *Address:* c/o All-Russian State Television and Radio Broadcasting Company, 125040 Moscow, ul. 5-aya Yamskogo Polya 19/21, Russia. *Telephone:* (495) 745-39-78. *Fax:* (495) 975-26-11. *E-mail:* info@rfn.ru. *Website:* www.rtr-zerkalo.ru.

ŠVANKMAJER, Jan; Czech stage designer and film director; b. 4 Sept. 1934, Prague; m. Eva Dvořáková 1960; one s. one d.; ed Theatrical Acad. of Performing Arts, Prague 1954–58; freelance artist 1958–; numerous drawings, graphic sheets, collages, stage sets and (with his wife) art pottery; Prix Special ASIFA 1990, Award for Lifetime Work UK 1995, Freedom Prize, Berlin 2001, Czech Lion Prize 2002. *Films directed include:* Dimensions of Dialogue 1982, Down to the Cellar 1982, The Pendulum, The Pit and Hope 1983, Alice 1987, Virile Games 1988, Another Kind of Love 1988, Meat Love 1988, Darkness-Lightness-Darkness 1989, The Death of Stalinism in Bohemia 1990, Food 1992, The Faust Lesson 1994, Conspirators of Pleasure 1996, Otesánek (Little Otik) (Kristián Prize 2002) 2000, Chimaeras (co-dir) 2001, Lunacy 2005. *Publications:* Hmat a imaginace 1994, Animus Anima Animation (co-author) 1998, Power of Imagination 2001, Transmutation of the Senses 2004. *Address:* Studio Athanor, Knovíz, 274 01 Slaný (office); Černínská 5, 118 00 Prague 1, Czech Republic (home). *Telephone:* (2) 20514785 (home). *E-mail:* jansvankmajer@seznam.cz.

SVARTVIK, Jan, PhD; Swedish academic; *Professor Emeritus of English, Lund University;* b. 18 Aug. 1931, Torsby; s. of Gustaf Svartvik and Sigrid Svartvik; m. Gunilla Berner 1958; two s. one d.; ed Uppsala Univ.; Research Asst and Asst Dir Survey of English Usage, Univ. Coll. London 1961–65; Lecturer, Univ. of Gothenburg 1965–70; Visiting Prof., Brown Univ., USA 1969; Prof. of English, Lund Univ. 1970–95, now Prof. Emer.; Pres. Asscn Int. de Linguistique Appliquée 1981–84; Chair. Org. Cttee, Nobel Symposium on Corpus Linguistics 1991; Chair. Steering Cttee for Evaluation of Linguistics in Sweden 1990–92; mem. Royal Acad. of Letters, History and Antiquities, Royal Swedish Acad. of Sciences, Academia Europaea, Societas Scientarum Fennica; Dr hc (Bergen) 1996, (Masaryk Univ.) 1998, (Helsinki) 2000. *Publications:* On Voice in the English Verb 1966, The Evans Statements 1968, A Grammar of Contemporary English (co-author) 1972, A Comprehensive Grammar of the English Language (co-author) 1985, The London-Lund Corpus of Spoken English: Description and Research 1990, Directions in Corpus Linguistics: Proceedings of Nobel Symposium 82 1992 (ed.), Words, Proceedings (ed.) 1996, Engelska – öspråk världsspråk, trendspråk (August Prize for Swedish Non-fiction Book of the Year) 1999, Handbok i engelska (co-author) 2001, Politikens bog om engelsk 2001, A Communicative Grammar of English 2002, English: One Tongue, Many Voices (co-author) 2006. *Leisure interest:* sailing. *Address:* Tumlaregränden 7, 22651 Lund, Sweden (home). *Telephone:* (46) 248412 (home).

SVEDBERG, Bjoern, MSc; Swedish business executive; b. 4 July 1937, Stockholm; s. of Inge Svedberg and Anna-Lisa Svedberg; m. Gunnel Nilsson 1960; four c.; ed Royal Inst. of Tech., Stockholm and Man. Devt Inst. (IMEDE), Univ. of Lausanne; Man. Eng Telephone Exchange Div., L. M. Ericsson Telephone Co. 1972–76, Sr Vice-Pres. Research and Devt 1976–77, Pres. 1977–90, Chair. 1990; Chair. NEFAB AB 1999–; Mo och Domsjo AB, Chair. 1991–92; mem. Bd of Dirs AB Volvo 1994–, ABB Ltd –1999, Stora AB, Investor 1998–2007; fmr Pres. Canada/Sweden Business Asscn; fmr mem. Bd Fed. of Swedish Industry; mem. Royal Swedish Acad. of Eng Sciences (fmr Chair.). *Address:* Prêt à Porter Group AB Visiting address: Petersbergsgatan 19, Borås Postal address: Box 935, SE-501 10 Borås, Sweden Phone: +46 (0) 33 17 60 00 Fax: +46 (0) 33 17 60 97 E-mail: mail@pretaporter.se; http://www.pretaporter.se.

SVEJGAARD, Arne, MD, DSc; Danish scientist, immunologist and academic; *Professor of Clinical Immunology, University of Copenhagan;* b. 13 March 1937, Odense; m. Else Lyngsøe 1960; two s. one d.; ed Univ. of Århus Medical School and Univ. Hosp. of Århus; Dir Tissue Typing Lab., Univ. Hosp. of Copenhagen 1970–87, Dept of Clinical Immunology 1987–; Prof. of Clinical Immunology, Univ. of Copenhagen 1991–; Councillor Int. Histocompatibility Workshops 1975–; Chair. Danish Cttee for Immunology 1985–; mem. Royal Danish Acad. of Sciences and Letters 1981–; Chair. Alfred Benzon Foundation 1996; Danish Medical Research Council 1997–2002; Kt of Dannebrog 1994; Tsuji Memorial Lecture 1981; Gaardon Prize 1980, Novo Prize 1981, Hess Thaysen Prize 1989, Europe and Medicine Senior Prize 2002. *Publications:* Iso-antigenic Systems of Human Blood Platelets 1969, The HLA System (with others) 1975, HLA and Disease (with J. Dausset) 1977, numerous scientific articles. *Address:* Department of Clinical Immunology, Section 7631, University Hospital of Copenhagen, Blegdamsvej 9, 2100 Copenhagen 0 (office); Skovvang 67, 3450 Allerød, Denmark. *Telephone:* 35-45-76-30 (office); 48-17-32-11 (home). *E-mail:* arnesvej@post4.tele.dk (office).

SVENSSON, Åke, MSc; Swedish business executive; *President and CEO, Saab AB;* b. 1952; joined Saab Group 1976, held several exec. positions including Project Man., Gen. Man. Saab Aerosystems, Gen. Man. Future Products and Tech., Sr Vice-Pres. Saab Aerospace 2000–03, Pres. and CEO Saab AB 2003–; mem. Bd of Dirs Gripen International (Saab jt venture), Copenhagen Malmö Port AB 2001–, Asscn of Swedish Eng. Industries; Chair. AeroSpace and Defence Industries Asscn of Europe 2007–; mem. Royal Swedish Acad. of War Sciences. *Address:* Head Office, Saab AB, PO Box 70363, 107 24 Stockholm, Sweden (office). *Telephone:* (8) 463-0000 (office). *Fax:* (8) 463-0152 (office). *Website:* www.saabgroup.com (office).

SVĚRÁK, Jan; Czech film director; b. 6 Feb. 1965, Žatec; m.; three c.; ed Film Acad. of Arts; pnr in film production co. Luxor 1996; Co. Biograf Jan Svěrák Pictures 1996–; mem. Acad. of Motion Picture Arts and Sciences, Czech Film Acad.; numerous awards including Acad. Award for best foreign student film 1989, Czech Lion Awards for Direction 1996, 1997, 2001, Time for Peace Prize 1997. *Film roles:* Kulový blesk (Ball Lightning) (uncredited) 1978, Nejistá sezóna (An Uncertain Season) 1988, Valka barev 1993, Rebelové (The Rebels) 2001, Tmavomodrý svet (Dark World Blue) (uncredited) 2001, Román pro zeny 2005. *Films directed include:* Sbohem, nadrazicko 1984, Vsak su vinar 1985, Ropáci (Oil Gobblers) 1988, Obecná skola (The Elementary School) 1991, Akumulátor 1 1994, Jizda (The Ride) 1994, Kolya (Golden Globe Award, Acad. Award and Czech Lion Award) 1996, Tmavomodrý svet (Dark World Blue) 2001, Tatínek (video) 2004, Vratné lahve 2007. *Leisure interest:* painting. *Address:* c/o Fandango Portobello Sales, Eardley House, 4 Uxbridge Street, Notting Hill Gate, London, W8 7SY, England; PO Box 33, 155 00 Prague 515, Czech Republic. *Telephone:* (20) 7908-9890 (London). *E-mail:* biograf@sverak.cz. *Website:* www.sverak.cz.

SVERDLOV, Yevgeny Davidovich; Russian biochemist; b. 16 Nov. 1938, Dnepropetrovsk; ed Moscow State Univ., Sr lab., Jr, Sr researcher Inst. of Bioorganic Chem. 1965–88; Dir Inst. of Molecular Genetics 1988–; Corresp. mem. USSR (now Russian) Acad. of Sciences 1984, mem. 1994–; Ed.-in-Chief Molekulyarnaya Genetika, Mikrobiologiya i Virusologiya (Molecular Genetics, Microbiology and Virology); mem. Russian Acad. of Agricultural Sciences 1994–; mem. Scientific Council of Biotech., Russian Acad. of Sciences; Lenin Prize; USSR State Prize. *Publications include:* Organic Chemistry of Nucleic Acids 1970, over 300 scientific articles. *Address:* Institute of Molecular Genetics, 123182 Moscow 2, Kurchatov Sq., Russia. *Telephone:* (495) 196-00-00 (office). *Fax:* (495) 196-02-21 (office). *E-mail:* img@img.ras.ru (office).

SVERRISDÓTTIR, Valgerður; Icelandic politician; b. 23 March 1950; m. Arvid Kro; three d.; ed Reykjavík Women's School; Sec., Agricultural Research Labs 1967–68; Sec. to Man. Dir KEA Cooperative 1969–70; Sec., Akureyri Regional Hosp. 1970–71; teacher, Grenivík School, 1972–82; has worked as farmer 1974–; Deputy Mem. Althingi (Parl.) 1984–87, mem. Parl. for NE Iceland constituency 1987–, Second Deputy Speaker 1988–89, 1990–91, Deputy Speaker 1992–95; Minister of Industry and Commerce 1999–2005, for Nordic Cooperation 2004–05, of Foreign Affairs 2006–07; mem. Progressive Party NE Iceland Constituency Cttee 1983–87, Chair. 1985-86, mem. Cen. Cttee 1983–, Deputy Sec. 1990–92, Parl. Group Leader 1995–99; mem. Nordic Council 1987–90, 1995–99, Chair. Parl. Group 1995–99; mem. Bd of Dirs KEA Cooperative 1981–92, SÍS (Fed. of Iceland Cooperative Socs) 1985–92, Akureyri Ship Repair Yard 1989–91, Bifröst Cooperative Coll. 1990–96 (Chair. 1995–96), Nordic Cultural Fund 1991–93, 1995–99 (Chair. 1995). *Address:* c/o Framsóknarflokkurinn (Progressive Party), Hverfisgata 33, POB 453, 121 Reykjavík, Iceland (office). *Telephone:* 5630500 (office). *E-mail:* valgsv@althingi.is. *Website:* www.valgerdur.is.

SVILANOVIČ, Goran, LLM; Serbian politician and lawyer; *Co-ordinator of Economic and Environmental Activities, Organization for Security and Co-*

operation in Europe; b. 22 Oct. 1963, Gnjilane, Kosovo; m.; two c.; ed Belgrade Univ., Inst. of Law, Strasbourg, Saarbrücken Univ., European Univ. of Peace, Austria; worked as Asst Researcher, Belgrade Univ. 1986–98, discharged following protest against controversial univ. law 1998; collaborator with Yugoslavian Forum on Human Rights 1989–93; head of telephone service for rescue of victims of nat., ethnic, religious and other discrimination, Centre for Anti-war Action 1993–97; Chair. Council on Human Rights 1996–98; Official Rep. of Civic Alliance of Serbia (Građanski savez Srbije—GSS) 1997, Vice-Pres. 1998, Pres. 1999, left party 2004; Fed. Minister of Foreign Affairs 2000–04; mem. Parl. (nominated for Democratic Party) 2004–; Chair. Working Table I, Stability Pact for South Eastern Europe 2004–08; Co-ordinator of Econ. and Environmental Activities, OSCE 2008–; mem. Int. Comm. on the Balkans. *Publications:* Civil and Civil Process Law; books and numerous articles on the situation of refugees and problems of citizenship. *Address:* Office of the Co-ordinator of Economic and Environmental Activities, Organization for Security and Co-operation in Europe, Kärntner Ring 5–7, 1010 Vienna, Austria (office). *Telephone:* (1) 514-36-151 (office). *Fax:* (1) 514-36-96 (office). *E-mail:* info@osce.org (office). *Website:* www.osce.org/eea (office).

SVINAROV, Nikolai Avramov, LLB; Bulgarian politician and lawyer; b. 6 May 1958, Shuman; m.; two d.; ed Univ. of Sofia St Kliment Ohridsky; lawyer (penal law), Turgoviste 1984–85; lawyer (civil and commercial law), Sofia 1985–2001; mem. Council, Lawyer's League, Sofia 1992–96; mem. and Chief Sec., Supreme Lawyer's Council 1998–2001; mem. Parl., 39th Nat. Ass. (Nat. Movt Simeon the Second) 2001–; Minister of Defence 2001–05. *Address:* c/o Ministry of Defence, Aksakov Str. 1, 1000 Sofia, Bulgaria.

SVOBODA, Cyril, DJur; Czech politician and lawyer; *Chairman, Government Legislative Council;* b. 24 Nov. 1956, Prague; m. Věnceslava Svoboda; four s.; ed Charles Univ., Prague, Pan American Inst. for Int. Studies, Notre Dame Univ., USA; legal officer, Transgas 1980–93; Adviser to Deputy Prime Minister for Human Rights, Restitution and Relations Between the State and the Church 1990–92; Deputy Chair. Legis. Council, Czech Govt 1992–98; Deputy Minister of Justice 1992–96; Deputy Minister of Foreign Affairs for issues related to accession to the EU 1996–98; Minister of the Interior Jan.–July 1998; Chair. Petition Cttee, Chamber of Deputies 1998–2002; Deputy Prime Minister and Minister of Foreign Affairs 2002–04; Minister of Foreign Affairs 2002–06; mem. Chamber of Deputies 2006–; Chair. Govt Legis. Council 2007–; joined Christian Democratic Union-Czecheslovak People's Party (KDU-ČSL) 1995, First Deputy Chair. 1999–2001, Chair. 2001–03, Deputy Chair. 2003–06; Leader of Coalition of Four Jan.–March 2001; mem. European Comm. for Democracy through Law 1994–, Deputy Chair. 1997–; Chair. Cttee for the Rules of Procedure and Immunity of the Parl. Ass., Council of Europe 2001–; Grosses Verdienstkreuz mit Stern und Schulterband (Germany) 2008. *Publications include:* Annotations on the Constitution of the Czech Republic (co-author), The Act on Out-of-Court Rehabilitation in Questions and Answers; numerous articles and studies on legislation and foreign policy. *Leisure interests:* literature, sport (running, skiing, swimming, cycling). *Address:* Government of the Czech Republic, Nábřeží Edvarda Beneše 4, 118 01 Prague 1, Czech Republic (office). *Telephone:* 224002455 (office). *Fax:* 224002228 (office). *E-mail:* posta@vlada.cz (office). *Website:* www.vlada.cz (office).

SVOBODA, Jiří; Czech film director; *Professor, J.A.Komensky University;* b. 5 May 1945, Kladno; s. of Dr Jiří Svoboda and Bozena Svobodova (née Procházková); m. Milena Niznanska 1973; two d.; ed Film Faculty, Acad. of Performing Arts, Prague; studied drama at Acad. of Performing Arts, Prague, expelled for political reasons 1963; worked as warehouseman and driver 1963–66; Dir and scriptwriter, Film Studios Barrandov 1971–93; freelance film dir and scriptwriter 1994–; mem. CP of Czechoslovakia 1975–90; Deputy Chair. Union of Czech Dramatic Artists 1987–89; Chair. Film Section of Union of Czech Dramatic Artists 1987–89; Chair. CP of the Czechlands and Moravia 1990–93; Deputy to House of Nations, Fed. Ass. of CSFR 1990–92; seriously wounded in attempt on his life Dec. 1992; Sr Lecturer, Acad. of Performing Arts; Prof., Film and TV and New Media, J.A.Komensky Univ. 2000–; Merited Artist 1986, Grand Prize Karlovy Vary 1982, San Remo 1982, Jury Prize Cannes 1983. *Films include:* (as Dir or scriptwriter): Hostage 1975, A Mirror for Christine 1975, House on the Embankment 1976, The Break Time 1977, The Blue Planet 1979, Girl with a Shell 1980, The Chain 1981, A Meeting with Shadows 1982, The End of the Lonely Berhof Farmstead 1983, The Lancet, Please 1985, Papilio 1986, The World Knows Nothing 1987, A Curse on the Hajnůs' House 1988, Only About Family Orders (about political trials in 1950s) 1989, Sametoví vrazi 2005; also directed more than 25 TV films and plays and part of series 10 Centuries of Architecture 1999–2000, Bolt from the Blue 2004, The Wave 2007, Rainbow of God 2007. *Television films:* Blow Up 2001, (Udelení milosti se zamítá) The Act of Grace is Disproved 2002, The Visionary 2003. *Publication:* Killers from the Velvet (novel). *Leisure interests:* philosophy, political theory, literature. *Address:* University of J.A.Komensky, Rohacova 17, Prague 3 (office); Na Balkáně 120, Prague 3, Czech Republic. *Telephone:* 7772113247 (home). *E-mail:* ji.svoboda@centrum.cz (home). *Website:* jiri-svoboda.cz; svobodajiri.euweb.cz.

SWAGER, Timothy M., BS, PhD; American chemist and academic; *John D. MacArthur Professor of Chemistry and Head, Department of Chemistry, Massachusetts Institute of Technology;* b. 7 Jan. 1961, Sheridan, Mont.; m.; two c.; ed Calif. Inst. of Tech., Mont. State Univ.; IBM Graduate Fellow 1984–87; Asst Prof. of Chem., Univ. of Pa 1990–96, Prof. 1996; Prof. of Chem., MIT 1996–2005, John D. MacArthur Prof. and Head, Dept of Chem. 2005–; Founder Iptyx Corpn; Clare Hall Visiting Fellow, Univ. of Cambridge, England 2005; has served on panels for Nat. Research Council, Defense Science Bd, Nat. Science Foundation, US Senate Commerce Cttee; mem. Science Advisory Bd, ICx Technologies, Nomadics Inc., Collegium Pharmaceutical Inc., Plextronics Inc., Nano-C Inc.; Assoc. Ed. Synfacts 2005–; mem. Editorial Advisory Bd Accounts of Chemical Research, Journal of Polymer Science, Supramolecular Chemistry, Advanced Synthesis & Catalysis, Journal of Supramolecular Chemistry, Journal of Materials Chemistry; Alfred P. Sloan Research Fellow 1994–96; Fellow, American Acad. of Arts and Sciences 2006–; mem. Nat. Acad. of Arts and Sciences 2008–; Dr hc (Montana State Univ.) 2007; Merck Index Undergraduate Chem. Award 1983, Most Outstanding Senior Chem. Major, American Inst. of Chemists 1983, Herbert Newby McCoy Award For Outstanding Graduate Research, Calif. Inst. of Tech. 1988, Office of Naval Research Young Investigator 1992–95, DuPont Young Faculty Award 1993–96, ACS Philadelphia Section Award 1996, Union Carbide Innovation Recognition Award 1998, ACS Cope Scholar Award 2000, Vladimir Karapetoff Award, MIT 2000, Carl S. Marvel Creative Polymer Chem. Award, ACS-Polymer Div. 2005, Christopher Columbus Foundation Homeland Security Award 2005, Lemelson-MIT Award for Inventorship 2007. *Publications:* more than 200 publs in scientific books and journals. *Address:* Massachusetts Institute of Technology, Department of Chemistry, Cambridge, MA 02139, USA (office). *Telephone:* (617) 253-4423 (office). *Fax:* (617) 253-7929 (office). *E-mail:* tswager@mit.edu (office). *Website:* web.mit.edu/tswager/www (office).

SWAN, Sir John William David, KBE, BA, JP; Bermudian business executive; *Chairman, Swan Group of Companies;* b. 3 July 1935, Bermuda; s. of John Nicholas and Margaret Swan; m. Jacqueline Roberts 1965; one s. two d.; ed Cen. School and Howard Acad., Bermuda and W. Virginia Wesleyan Coll.; Real-Estate Salesman with Rego Ltd 1960–62; Founder, CEO and Chair. of John W Swan Ltd 1962–, Chair. Swan Group of Cos 1996–; mem. Parl. (United Bermuda Party) 1972–95, Minister for Marine and Air Services, Labour and Immigration 1977–78, Home Affairs 1978–82, Premier of Bermuda 1982–95; fmr Parl. Sec. for Finance, Chair. Bermuda Hosp. Bd, Chair. Dept of Civil Aviation; mem. Chief. Execs. Org. and World Business Council; mem. and Fellow, Senate, Jr Chamber Int. 1992; Eminent Professional Mem. Royal Inst. of Chartered Surveyors 2006–; Trustee Bermuda Inst. of Ocean Sciences; Hon. Freeman City of London 1985; Hon. LLD (Tampa Univ.) 1986, (W Va Wesleyan Coll.) 1987, (Atlantic Union Coll., Mass.) 1991; St Paul's Anniversary Citation 1969, Outstanding Young Man of the Year 1969, Int. Medal of Excellence (first recipient), Poor Richard Club of Phila 1987 and other awards. *Leisure interests:* tennis, sailing, reading. *Address:* Swan Building, 26 Victoria Street, Hamilton, HM12 (home); 11 Grape Bay Drive, Paget PG06, Bermuda (home). *Telephone:* (441) 295-1785 (office); (441) 236-1303 (home). *Fax:* (441) 295-6270 (office); (441) 236-7935 (home). *E-mail:* sirjohn@challengerbanks.bm (office).

SWAN, Wayne Maxwell, BA; Australian academic and politician; *Treasurer of Australia;* b. 30 June 1954, Nambour, Queensland; m. Kim Swan; one s. two d.; ed Nambour State High School, Univ. of Queensland; Lecturer in Public Admin, Queensland Inst. of Tech. 1976–77, 1981–82, 1985–88; Policy Analyst, Office of Youth Affairs 1978; adviser to Leader of the Opposition, Bill Hayden 1978–80, to Fed. Labor Ministers, Mick Young and Kim Beazley 1983, to Minister for Foreign Affairs, Bill Hayden 1984; mem. Australian Labor Party (ALP) Admin. Cttee (Queensland) 1984–90, Del., ALP Nat. Conf. 1986, 1988, 1990, Campaign Dir 1989–, State Sec. Queensland Br. of ALP 1991–93; Treas. and Labor MP for Lilley, Brisbane 1993–96, 1998–; Shadow Minister for Family and Community Services 1998–2000, 2001–04, Man. of Opposition Business in the House 2001–03; Shadow Treas. 2004–07; Treas. of Australia 2007–. *Publication:* Postcode: The Splintering of a Nation 2005. *Address:* Department of the Treasury, Langton Crescent, Parkes, ACT 2600, Australia (office). *Telephone:* (2) 6263-2111 (office). *Fax:* (2) 6273-2614 (office). *E-mail:* wayne.swan.mp@aph.gov.au (office); department@treasury.gov.au (office). *Website:* www.treasury.gov.au (office); www.swanmp.org (office).

SWANK, Hilary; American actress; b. 30 July 1974, Bellingham, Wash.; m. Chad Lowe 1997 (divorced 2006). *Films include:* Buffy the Vampire Slayer 1992, The Next Karate Kid 1994, Sometimes They Came Back . . . Again 1996, Heartwood 1997, Boys Don't Cry (Best Actress, Acad. Awards) 1999, The Gift 2000, Affair of the Necklace 2000, Insomnia 2002, The Core 2003, 11:14 2003, Red Dust 2004, Million Dollar Baby (Best Dramatic Actress, Golden Globe Awards 2005, Best Actress, Screen Actors Guild Awards 2005, Best Actress, Acad. Awards 2005) 2004, Black Dahlia 2006, Freedom Writers 2007, The Reaping 2007, P.S. I Love You 2007, Birds of America 2008. *Television includes:* Terror in the Family 1996, Leaving LA 1997. *Address:* c/o Metropolitan Talent Agency, 4526 Wilshire Boulevard, Los Angeles, CA 90010, USA.

SWANN, Kate E., FCA; British business executive; *CEO, WH Smith PLC;* fmrly in retail marketing, Tesco PLC, Coca-Cola Schweppes, Homepride Foods and Dixons Stores Group; fmr Marketing Dir Currys PLC; Marketing Dir then Man. Dir Homebase, J Sainsbury PLC –2000; Man. Dir Argos PLC 2000–03; CEO WH Smith PLC 2003–, mem. Exec. Bd 2003–; Dir (non-exec.) Lambert Howarth Group PLC 2000–06, The British Land Co. PLC 2006–; ranked by Fortune magazine amongst 50 Most Powerful Women in Business outside the US (tenth) 2004, (20th) 2005, (34th) 2006, (32nd) 2007, ranked by the Financial Times amongst Top 25 Businesswomen in Europe (17th) 2005, (21st) 2006, (17th) 2007. *Address:* WH Smith PLC, Nations House, 103 Wigmore Street, London, W1U 1WH, England (office). *Telephone:* (20) 7409-3222 (office). *Fax:* (20) 7514-9633 (office). *Website:* www.whsmithplc.com (office).

SWANSON, William H., BEng, FRAeS; American business executive; *Chairman and CEO, Raytheon Company;* b. 1949, Calif.; m. Cheryl Swanson; ed Calif. Polytechnic State Univ., Golden Gate Univ.; joined Raytheon Co. 1972, various man. positions including Exec. Vice-Pres. and Chair. and CEO Raytheon Systems Co. 1998–2000, Exec. Vice-Pres. and Pres. Electronic

Systems Div. 2000–02, Pres. 2002–03, Pres., Dir and CEO Raytheon Co. 2003–04, Chair. and CEO 2004–; mem. Bd Congressional Medal of Honor Foundation; mem. Advisory Council Calif. Polytechnic State Univ. School of Eng, Bd of Regents Pepperdine Univ., Bd Visitors Graziadio School of Business and Man.; mem. Bd Dirs Cal Poly Foundation, John F. Kennedy Library Foundation; Vice-Chair. Business-Higher Educ. Forum, Co-Chair. Securing America's Leadership in Science, Tech., Eng and Math.; mem. Editorial Advisory Bd The Journal of Electronic Defense; mem. Nat. Defense Industrial Asscn, the Navy League, Air Force Asscn; a Regent of Pepperdine Univ.; Trustee, Asscn of the US Army; Hon. LLD (Pepperdine Univ.) 2002, Hon. DrSc (California Polytechnic State Univ.); Hon. Alumnus Award, Calif. Polytechnic State Univ. School of Eng 1991. *Address:* Raytheon Co., Mail Stop 2335, 870 Winter Street, Waltham, MA 02451-1449, USA (office). *Telephone:* (781) 522-3000 (office). *Fax:* (781) 522-3001 (office). *E-mail:* info@raytheon .com (office). *Website:* www.raytheon.com (office).

SWAR AD-DAHAB, Field Marshal (see DAHAB, Field Marshal Abdul-Rahman Swar ad-).

SWARAJ, Sushma, BA, LLB; Indian politician; b. 14 Feb. 1952, Ambala Cantonment; m. Swaraj Kaushal 1975; one d.; ed Punjab Univ., Chandigarh; Advocate, Supreme Court of India 1973–; mem. (Janata Party) Haryana Legis. Ass. 1977–82, (Bharatiya Janata Party–BJP) 1987–90; All-India Sec. BJP 1985–87, 1990–92, All-India Gen. Sec. and Official Spokesperson 1992–96; Cabinet Minister 1977–78; Minister for Educ. 1987–89; mem. Parl. (Rajya Sabha) 1990–96, 2000–; Chair. Cttee on Petitions 1994–96; mem. Parl. (Lok Sabha) for S Delhi 1996–98, 1998–2000; mem. Delhi Legis. Ass. 1998; Chief Minister of Delhi 1998; Minister of Information and Broadcasting 1996–98, 2000–03, with additional charge of Ministry of Communications 1998; Minister of Health and Family Welfare and of Parliamentary Affairs 2003–04; Head of BJP 2009 poll campaign cttee. *Address:* Bharatiya Janata Party, 11 Ashok Rd, New Delhi 110 001 (office); Daga House, In front of Raja Bhoj Airport, Bhopal, India (home). *Telephone:* (11) 23382234 (office). *Fax:* (11) 23782163 (office). *E-mail:* swaraj@sansad.nic.in; bjpco@vsnl.com (office). *Website:* www.bjp.org (office).

SWAYZE, Patrick; American actor and dancer; b. 18 Aug. 1954, Houston; s. of Patsy Swayze; m. Lisa Niemi 1976; ed Harkness and Joffrey Ballet Schools; began as dancer in Disney on Parade on tour as Prince Charming. *Theatre:* dancer in Goodtime Charley, Grease (Broadway), as Nathan Detroit in Guys and Dolls (Piccadilly Theatre, London) 2006. *Television appearances include:* North and South: Books I and II, The New Season, Pigs vs. Freaks, The Comeback Kid, The Return of the Rebels, The Renegades, King Solomon's Mines. *Films:* Skatetown USA 1979, The Outsiders, Uncommon Valor, Red Dawn, Grandview USA (also choreographer), Dirty Dancing (co-wrote song and sings She's Like the Wind), Steel Dawn, Tiger Warsaw, Road House, Next of Kin, Ghost, Point Break, City of Joy, Father Hood, Tall Tales, To Wong Foo – Thanks for Everything – Julie Newmar, Three Wishes, Letters from a Killer 1997, Vanished 1998, Black Dog 1998, Without a Word 1999, The Wind-drinker 2000, Forever Lulu 2000, Donnie Darko 2001, Waking Up in Reno 2002, One Last Dance 2003, 11:14 2003, Dirty Dancing: Havana Nights 2004, George and the Dragon 2004, Keeping Mum 2005, Jump! 2007, Christmas in Wonderland 2007. *Address:* c/o Annett Wolf, Wolf Kasteler Van Iden and Associates, 335 N. Maple Drive, Suite 351, Beverly Hills, CA 90210, USA.

SWEENEY, Anne M., BA, EdM; American media executive; *Co-Chair, Media Networks and President, Disney-ABC Television Group, The Walt Disney Company;* b. 4 Nov. 1957, Kingston, NY; m. Philip Miller; two c.; ed The Coll. of New Rochelle, NY and Harvard Univ.; various exec. positions at Nickelodeon/ Nick at Nite 1981–93, most recently Sr Vice-Pres. Program Enterprises; Chair. and CEO FX Networks Inc. 1993–96; Pres. Disney Channel and Exec. Vice-Pres. Disney/ABC Cable Networks, The Walt Disney Co. 1996–2000, Pres. ABC Cable Networks Group and Disney Channel Worldwide 2000–04, Co-Chair. Media Networks and Pres. Disney-ABC Television, The Walt Disney Co. 2004–; mem. Bd Dirs Lifetime Television, The Museum of Radio & Television, Special Olympics, Women in Cable and Telecommunications, Walter Kaitz Foundation; Hon. Chair. Cable Positive; Women in Cable Executive of the Year 1994, American Women in Radio and Television STAR Award 1995, inducted into American Advertising Fed.'s Advertising Hall of Achievement 1996, Women in Cable Woman of the Year 1997, Women in Cable Advocate Leader Award, Southern Calif. chapter 1998, Women in Film's Lucy Award 2002, Cable Television Public Affairs Asscn's Pres.'s Award 2004, New York Women in Film & Television Muse Award 2004, named by The Hollywood Reporter "The Most Powerful Woman in Entertainment", inducted into the Broadcasting & Cable Hall of Fame 2005, ranked by Fortune magazine amongst 50 Most Powerful Women in Business in the US (39th) 2002, (35th) 2003, (18th) 2004, (16th) 2005, (13th) 2006, (15th) 2007, ranked by Forbes magazine amongst The 100 Most Powerful Women (27th) 2004, (33rd) 2005, (15th) 2006, (77th) 2007, (30th) 2008. *Address:* 500 S Buena Vista Street, Burbank, CA 91521-9722, USA (office). *Telephone:* (818) 560-1000 (office). *Fax:* (818) 560-1930 (office). *Website:* www.disneyabctv.com (office).

SWEENEY, John Joseph, BSc; American trade union official; *President, American Federation of Labor and Congress of Industrial Organizations (AFL-CIO);* b. 5 May 1934, Bronx, New York; s. of John Sweeney and Patricia Sweeney; m. Maureen Power; one s. one d.; ed Iona Coll.; with IBM (Int. Business Machines Corpn); researcher, Int. Ladies Garment Workers Union; Contract Dir Building Service Employees Int. Union (later Service Employees Int. Union) New York City Local 32B 1960–80, Pres. 1980; Vice-Pres. AFL-CIO (American Fed. of Labor-Congress of Industrial Orgs) 1980–95, Pres. 1995–. *Publication:* America Needs a Raise 1996. *Address:* AFL-CIO, 815 16th Street, NW, Washington, DC 20006, USA (office). *Telephone:* (202) 637-5000 (office). *Fax:* (202) 637-5058 (office). *Website:* www.aflcio.org (office).

SWEENEY, Ed, BA, MSc; British public servant; *Chairman, Advisory, Conciliation and Arbitration Service;* ed Warwick Univ., LSE; Research Officer Nat. Union of Bank Employees (NUBE) 1977, various roles in Finance Dept, becoming Deputy Gen. Sec. Banking Insurance and Finance Union (BIFU) 1991–96, Gen. Sec. 1996–2000, Gen. Sec. UNIFI 2000–04, Deputy Gen. Sec. Amicus (following merger) 2004–07; Chair. Advisory, Conciliation and Arbitration Service (ACAS) 2007–; mem. TUC Gen. Council, TUC Exec. Cttee; Chair. TUC Int. Devt Group; Jt Chair. DfID/TUC Forum; mem. TUC Superannuation Cttee, TUC Learning and Skills Task Group; TUC Skills for Life Advocate; mem. Trade Union Sustainable Devt Cttee; mem. Council Inst. of Employment Rights; mem. British Del. to WTO Ministerial Confs 2001, 2003; Reviewer on Occupational Pensions De-Regulation Review; Visiting Prof., Leeds Business School. *Address:* Advisory, Conciliation and Arbitration Service, Brandon House, 22nd Floor, Euston Tower, 286 Euston Road, London, NW1 3JJ, England (office). *Website:* www.acas.org.uk (office).

SWENSEN, Joseph Anton; American conductor, composer and violinist; *Principal Conductor, Malmö Opera;* b. 4 Aug. 1960, New York City; m. 2nd Kristina Algot-Sörensen; three s. (one from previous marriage); ed Juilliard School; Prin. Guest Conductor Stockholm Chamber Orchestra 1994–97, Lahti Symphony Orchestra 1995–2000; Prin. Conductor Scottish Chamber Orchestra (SCO) 1996–2005, Conductor Emer. 2005–; Prin. Guest Conductor BBC Nat. Orchestra of Wales 2000–03; Prin. Conductor Malmö Opera och Musiktheater 2006–; toured Japan with SCO 1995, USA 1999; debut at Edinburgh Int. Festival with SCO 1998; cycle of Beethoven performances to mark 25th anniversary of SCO 1999; conducted new production of The Marriage of Figaro at the Royal Danish Opera 1999; guest conductor with City of Birmingham Symphony, Finnish Radio Symphony, Hallé Orchestra, Orchestra Nat. du Capitole de Toulouse, Ensemble Orchestral de Paris; own orchestral works have been performed by various orchestras. *Recordings include:* Mendelssohn, Sibelius, Brahms, Prokofiev, Dvorak. *Address:* c/o Victoria Rowsell Artist Management Limited, 34 Addington Square, London, SE5 7LB, England (office). *Telephone:* (20) 7701-3219 (office). *Fax:* (20) 7701-3219 (office). *E-mail:* management@victoriarowsell.co.uk (office). *Website:* www.victoriarowsell.co.uk (office); www.josephswensen.com (office); www .malmoopera.se (office).

SWETT, Richard Nelson, BA, FAIA; American architect, business consultant and fmr politician; *Senior Counselor, APCO Worldwide Inc.;* b. 1 May 1957, Lower Merion, Pa; s. of the late Philip Eugene Swett Sr and of Ann Parkhurst Swett; m.; three s. four d.; ed Yale Univ.; licensed architect in several states; has worked in real estate devt, alternative energy devt, energy conservation, industrial devt and export promotion; mem. US House of Reps from 2nd Congressional Dist of NH 1990–95, mem. several Congressional Cttees, co-author Congressional Accountability Act, author, Transportation for Livable Communities Act; Amb. to Denmark 1998–2001; currently Sr Counselor, APCO Worldwide Inc. and Pres. Swett Assocs Inc.; mem. Denmark's H.C. Andersen Foundation Board of Advisors; mem. Bd of Peers overseeing design quality issues for US Gen. Services Admin for US Govt bldg portfolio; Founding mem. Advisory Bd European Center of Calif. 2001–06; mem. Bd Sunrise Capital Pnrs 2001–04, CATCH (Concord Area Trust for Community Housing); fmr State Chair. US Olympic Cttee 2001; Fellow, AIA, Sr Fellow, Design Futures Council; Grand-Croix of the Order of the Dannebrog (Denmark) 2001; Hon. LLD (Franklin Pierce Coll.) and several other hon. degrees; Presidential Citation, AIA. *Publications:* A Nation Reconstructed, A Quest to Make Cities All That They Can Be (co-author), Leadership by Design: Creating an Architecture of Trust. *Leisure interests:* tennis, reading, piano, sailing, skiing, running, basketball, golf, painting, travel, family. *Address:* 1 Putney Road, Bow, NH, 03304 (home); APCO Worldwide Inc., 700 12th Street, NW, Suite 800, Washington, DC 20005, USA (office). *Telephone:* (603) 774-1072 (home); (202) 778-1088 (office). *Fax:* (603) 774-1071 (home); (202) 466-6002 (office). *E-mail:* dswett@apcoworldwide.com (office). *Website:* www .swettassociates.com (home); www.apcoworldwide.com (office).

ŚWIĘCICKI, Marcin, DEconSc; Polish politician and economist; *Director, UNDP Blue Ribbon Analytical and Advisory Centre, Kyiv;* b. 17 April 1947, Warsaw; s. of Andrzej Święcicki and Jadwiga Święcicka; m. Joanna Szyr 1969; three s., one d.; ed Warsaw Univ.; Asst, Econ. Sciences Inst., Warsaw Univ. 1971–72; Councillor, then Chief Specialist in Planning Comm. attached to the Council of Ministers 1972–82; Dir for study and analysis matters 1982–87, Gen. Sec. of Consultative Econ. Council 1987–89; mem. PZPR 1974–90, PZPR Cen. Cttee 1989–90, Sec. PZPR Cen. Cttee Aug.–Sept. 1989; participant Round Table debates, mem. group for economy and social policy Feb.–April 1989; Deputy to Sejm (Parl.) 1989–91, 1993–96; Minister for Foreign Econ. Co-operation 1989–91; Deputy Chair. Sejm Cttee on Foreign Econ. Relations 1993–95; Mayor of Warsaw 1994–99; Co-Chair. Govt and Territorial Self-Govt Jt Comm. 1994–99; Adviser to Lithuanian Govt 1993; Co-Founder Tax Reform Movt 1993–; Co-Founder Cen. European Forum 1995–; Pres. Union of Polish Metropolises 1994–99; mem. Polish Econ. Soc. 1978–; Co-Founder Consensus Dialogue Group 1986–90, mem. Secr. 1986–89; Co-Founder and Treas. Polish Asscn for the Club of Rome 1987–91; scientific worker, Inst. of Econ. Sciences, Polish Acad. of Sciences 1991–93; ind. adviser 1991–94; 2001–; Under-Sec. of State, Ministry of the Economy 1999; mem. Negotiating Team, Polish Accession to EU 1999–2000; Adviser to Pres. of Lithuania 1999–2000; Co-ordinator of OSCE Econ. and Environmental Activities 2002–05; Dir UNDP Blue Ribbon Analytical and Advisory Centre, Kyiv, Ukraine 2005–; mem. Democratic Union (now Freedom Union) 1991– (mem. Council, Warsaw br. 1991–93, mem. Nat. Council 1993–); Co-Founder and Vice-Pres. Polish Fulbright Alumni Asscn 1993–96; Pres. Polish Cttee of Support for Museum of the History of Polish Jews 1997–; Fellowship, George Washington Univ., Washington, DC 1975–76, Harvard Univ. 1984–85; Hon. mem. Union of Warsaw Uprising Veterans (Związek Powstańców Warszawskich); Gold and

Bronze Cross of Merit; Labour and Wages Comm. Award 1971, Award of Chair. of Radio and TV Cttee 1988, Daily Trybuna Ludu Award 1989, Bronze Medal in long jump, European Jr Athletic Championship, Odessa 1966. *Publications include:* Perspektywiczne programowanie problemowe w Polsce 1978, Revolution in Social Sciences and Future Studies Movement 1978, Rozwój sytuacji i polityki gospodarczej (Ed.) 1985, Reforma własnościowa 1989, The Economy of Ukraine (with Stanisław Wellisz) 1993. *Leisure interests:* mountain hiking, jogging, volleyball, political books, memoirs, essays. *Address:* Węgrzyna 29, 00-769 Warsaw, Poland (home); UNDP Blue Ribbon Analytical and Advisory Centre, 1/14 Sadova St., 4th floor, 01021 Kyiv, Ukraine (office). *Telephone:* (22) 6423651 (Warsaw) (home); (44) 2535866 (Kyiv) (office). *Fax:* (22) 6422722 (Warsaw) (home); (44) 2535611 (Kyiv) (office). *E-mail:* marcin.swiecicki@undp.org (office); m.swiecicki@melog.com (office). *Website:* www.un.org/brc (office).

ŚWIERZY, Waldemar; Polish graphic designer; b. 9 Sept. 1931, Katowice; ed Acad. of Fine Art, Cracow; lecturer Acad. of Fine Art, Poznań 1965–, Prof. 1987–; Prof. Acad. of Fine Art, Warsaw 1994–; Visiting Prof. Univ. of Mexico 1979–80, Hochschule der Kunste, Berlin 1985–86, Gesamthochschule Kassel 1989–90; has designed over 1,500 posters and 500 book covers; mem. Alliance Graphique Internationale; Hon. Prof. Acad. of Fine Art, Cracow 1997; Gold Cross of Merit 1955; Kt's Cross, Order of Polonia Restituta 1978, Officer's Cross 1989; Lautrec Grand Prix, Toulouse 1959, Minister of Culture and Arts Prize (1st Class) 1961, First Prize, Prix X Biennale di São Paulo 1970, Gold Medal, Int. Posters Biennale, Warsaw 1976, Gold and Bronze Medal, Int. Jazz Poster Exhbn., Bydgoszcz 1985, First Prize, Annual Film Posters Competition of Hollywood Reporter, Los Angeles 1975, 1985. *Address:* ul. Piwna 45/47 m. 14, 00-265 Warsaw, Poland (home). *Telephone:* (22) 8312048 (home). *Fax:* (22) 8312048 (home).

SWIFT, Graham Colin, FRSL; British writer; b. 4 May 1949, London; s. of Lionel Allan Stanley Swift and Sheila Irene Swift (née Bourne); ed Dulwich Coll., Queens' Coll., Cambridge, Univ. of York; Hon. Fellow, Queens' Coll. Cambridge 2005; Hon. LittD (East Anglia) 1998; Hon. DUniv (York) 1998; Hon. DLit (London) 2003; Geoffrey Faber Memorial Prize, Guardian Fiction Prize, RSL Winifred Holtby Award 1983, Premio Grinzane Cavour (Italy) 1987, Prix du meilleur livre étranger (France) 1994, Booker Prize, James Tait Black Memorial Prize 1996. *Publications:* (novels) The Sweet Shop Owner 1980, Shuttlecock 1981, Waterland 1983, Out of This World 1988, Ever After 1992, Last Orders 1996, The Light of Day 2003, Tomorrow 2007; (short stories) Learning to Swim and Other Stories 1982; (anthology) The Magic Wheel (co-ed. with David Profumo) 1986. *Leisure interest:* fishing. *Address:* c/o AP Watt Ltd, 20 John Street, London, WC1N 2DR, England (office). *Telephone:* (20) 7405-6774 (office). *Fax:* (20) 7831-2154 (office). *E-mail:* apw@apwatt.co.uk (office). *Website:* www.apwatt.co.uk (office).

SWINBURNE, Richard Granville, MA, BPhil, FBA; British academic; *Nolloth Professor Emeritus of the Philosophy of the Christian Religion, University of Oxford;* b. 26 Dec. 1934, Smethwick; s. of William H. Swinburne and Gladys E. Swinburne; m. Monica Holmstrom 1960 (separated 1985); two d.; ed Univ. of Oxford; Fereday Fellow, St John's Coll., Oxford 1958–61; Leverhulme Research Fellow in History and Philosophy of Science, Univ. of Leeds 1961–63; Lecturer in Philosophy, Univ. of Hull 1963–72; Prof. of Philosophy, Univ. of Keele 1972–84; Nolloth Prof. of the Philosophy of the Christian Religion, Univ. of Oxford 1985–2002, Prof. Emer. 2002–; Visiting Assoc. Prof., Univ. of Maryland 1969–70; Visiting Prof., Syracuse Univ. 1987, Univ. of Rome 2002, Catholic Univ. of Lublin 2002, Yale Univ. 2003, St Louis Univ. 2003. *Publications:* Space and Time 1968, 2nd edn 1981, The Concept of Miracle 1971, An Introduction to Confirmation Theory 1973, The Coherence of Theism 1977, rev. 1993, The Existence of God 1979, 2nd edn 2004, Faith and Reason 1981, 2nd edn 2005, Personal Identity (with S. Shoemaker) 1984, The Evolution of the Soul 1986, rev. 1997, Responsibility and Atonement 1989, Revelation 1991, 2nd edn 2007, The Christian God 1994, Is There a God? 1996, rev. 2009, Providence and the Problem of Evil 1998, Epistemic Justification 2001, The Resurrection of God Incarnate 2003, Was Jesus God? 2008. *Address:* 50 Butler Close, Oxford, OX2 6JG, England (home). *Telephone:* (1865) 514406 (home). *E-mail:* richard.swinburne@oriel.ox.ac.uk (office). *Website:* users.ox .ac.uk/~orie0087 (office).

SWING, William Lacy, BA, BD; American diplomatist; *Director-General, International Organization for Migration;* b. 11 Sept. 1934, Lexington, N Carolina; s. of Baxter D. Swing and Mary F. Swing (née Barbee); m. Yuen Cheong 1993; one s. one d. from previous marriage; ed Catawba Coll., Yale Univ., Tübingen Univ., Harvard Univ.; Vice-Consul, Port Elizabeth, S. Africa 1963–66; int. economist, Bureau of Econ. Affairs, Dept of State 1966–68; Consul, Hamburg 1968–72; Desk Officer for FRG, Dept of State 1972–74; Deputy Chief of Mission, US Embassy, Bangui, Cen. African Repub. 1974–76; Sr Fellow, Center for Int. Affairs, Harvard Univ. 1976–77; Deputy Dir, Office of Cen. African Affairs, Dept of State 1977–79; Amb. to People's Repub. of Congo 1979–81, to Liberia 1981–85, to S Africa 1989–93, to Nigeria 1992–93, to Haiti 1993–98, to Democratic Repub. of Congo 1998–2001; Special Rep. of UN Sec.-Gen. for Western Sahara 2001–03, Democratic Repub. of Congo 2003–08; Dir-Gen. Int. Org. for Migration 2008–; Dir Office of Foreign Service Assignments and Career Devt 1985–87; Deputy Asst Sec. for Personnel 1987–89; Fellow, Harvard Univ.; Hon. LLD (Catawba Coll.) 1980; Hon. DHumLitt (Hofstra) 1994; Presidential Distinguished Service Award 1985; Distinguished Honor Award 1994, Award for Valor 1995, Presidential Meritorious Service Award 1987, 1990, 1994, 1998, Presidential Certificate of Commendation 1998. *Publications:* Education for Decision 1963, U.S. Policy Towards South Africa: Dilemmas and Priorities 1977, Liberia: The Road to Recovery 1982, Haiti: In Physical Contact with History 1994; book chapter in Challenges of Peace Implementation 2004. *Leisure interests:* tennis, squash,

golf. *Address:* International Organization for Migration, 17 route des Morillons, CP 71, 1211 Geneva 19, Switzerland (office). *Telephone:* 227179111 (office). *Fax:* 227986150 (office). *E-mail:* info@iom.int (office). *Website:* www.iom.int (office).

SWINNERTON-DYER, Sir (Henry) Peter Francis, Bt, KBE, MA, FRS; British mathematician and academic; *Professor Emeritus, Department of Pure Mathematics and Mathematical Statistics, University of Cambridge;* b. 2 Aug. 1927, Ponteland; s. of the late Sir Leonard Dyer; m. Dr Harriet Crawford 1983; ed Eton Coll. and Trinity Coll., Cambridge; Research Fellow, Trinity Coll. 1950–54; Commonwealth Fund Fellow, Univ. of Chicago 1954–55; Coll. Lecturer in Math., Trinity Coll. 1955–71, Dean 1963–70; Lecturer in Math., Cambridge Univ. 1960–71, Prof. of Math. 1971–88, now Prof. Emer., Master of St Catharine's Coll. 1973–83; Vice-Chancellor, Cambridge Univ. 1979–81; Chair. Univ. Grants Cttee 1983–89, Chief Exec. Univs Funding Council 1989–91, European Scientific and Tech. Ass. 1994–; Chair. Sec. of State for Nat. Heritage's Advisory Cttee, Library and Information Services Council 1992–95; mem. Advisory Bd for Research Councils 1977–90; Vice-Pres. Inst. of Manpower Studies 1983; Visiting Prof. Harvard Univ. 1970–71; Chair. Cttee on Acad. Org., Univ. of London 1980–81; mem. Advisory Council on Science and Tech. 1987–89; Hon. Fellow, Worcester Coll., Oxford 1980, St Catharine's Coll., Cambridge 1983, Trinity Coll., Cambridge 1983; Hon. DSc (Bath) 1981, (Wales) 1991; Hon. ScD (Ulster) 1991, (Birmingham) 1992, (Nottingham) 1992; Hon. LLD (Aberdeen) 1991; Hon. DMath (Oslo) 2003. *Publications:* Analytic Theory of Abelian Varieties 1974, A Brief Guide to Algebraic Number Theory 2002 and papers in learned journals. *Leisure interest:* gardening. *Address:* The Dower House, Thriplow, Royston, Herts., SG8 7RJ; c/o Department of Pure Mathematics and Mathematical Statistics, Centre for Mathematical Sciences, University of Cambridge, Wilberforce Road, Cambridge, CB3 0WB, England (office). *Website:* www.dpmms.cam.ac.uk (office).

SWINNEY, John Ramsay, MA; Scottish politician and management specialist; b. 13 April 1964; s. of Kenneth Swinney and Nancy Swinney (née Hunter); m. 1st Lorna Ann King 1991 (divorced 1998); one s. one d.; m. 2nd Elizabeth Quigley 2003; ed Univ. of Edin.; Sr Man. Consultant, Devt Options Ltd 1988–92; Strategic Planning Prin., Scottish Amicable 1992–97; MP for North Tayside 1997–2001; mem. North Tayside, Scottish Parl. 1999–; Nat. Sec. Scottish Nat. Party 1986–92, Vice-Convener for Publicity 1992–97, Treasury Spokesperson 1995–2000, Deputy Leader 1998–2000, Leader 2000–2004; Leader of the Opposition, Scottish Parl. 2000–04; Convener Enterprise and Lifelong Learning Cttee, Scottish Parl. 1999–2000; Convener European and External Relations Cttee 2004–05; Shadow Minister for Finance and Public Services 2005–07; Cabinet Sec. for Finance and Sustainable Growth 2007–. *Leisure interests:* hill walking, cycling. *Address:* 35 Perth Street, Blairgowrie, PH10 6DL, Scotland (office). *Telephone:* (1250) 876576 (office). *Fax:* (1250) 876576 (office). *E-mail:* john.swinney.msp@scottish .parliament.uk (office).

SWINTON, Tilda; British actress; ed New Hall, Cambridge; performance art appearance sleeping in a glass case, Serpentine Gallery, London 1996; Dr hc (Royal Scottish Acad. of Music and Drama, Glasgow) 2006. *Films include:* The Last of England, The Garden 1990, Edward II 1991, Orlando 1993, Wittgenstein 1993, Female Perversions 1996, Love is the Devil 1997, Conceiving Ada 1997, The War Zone 1998, The Beach 2000, The Deep End 2001, Vanilla Sky 2001, Teknolust 2002, Adaptation 2003, Young Adam (Scottish BAFTA Award for Best Actress 2004) 2003, The Statement 2003, Thumbsucker 2004, Broken Flowers 2005, Constantine 2005, The Chronicles of Narnia: The Lion, the Witch and the Wardrobe 2005, Stephanie Daley 2006, Deep Water (voice) 2006, The Man from London 2007, Sleepwalkers 2007, Michael Clayton (Acad. Award for Best Supporting Actress 2008) 2007, Burn After Reading 2008, The Chronicles of Narnia: Prince Caspian 2008, Julia 2008, The Curious Case of Benjamin Button 2008. *Address:* c/o Christian Hodell, Hamilton Hodell Ltd, 66–68 Margaret Street, London, W1W 8SR, England (office). *Telephone:* (20) 7636-1221 (office). *Fax:* (20) 7636-1226 (office). *E-mail:* info@hamiltonhodell.co.uk (office). *Website:* www .hamiltonhodell.co.uk (office).

SWIRE, Sir Adrian (Christopher), Kt, MA; British business executive; *Honorary President, John Swire & Sons;* b. 15 Feb. 1932, London; s. of the late John Kidston Swire and Juliet Richenda Barclay; m. Lady Judith Compton 1970; two s. one d.; ed Eton, Univ. Coll., Oxford; served Coldstream Guards 1950–52; fmrly with RAFVR and Royal Auxiliary Air Force; joined Butterfield & Swire in Far East 1956; Dir, John Swire & Sons Ltd 1961–2004, Deputy Chair. 1966–87, Chair. 1987–97, 2002–04, Exec. Dir 1998–2002, Hon. Pres. 1998–; Dir, Swire Pacific 1978–2008; Pro-Chancellor, Southampton Univ. 1995–2004; Chair., China Navigation Co. Ltd 1968–88; Dir, Cathay Pacific Airways 1965–2005, Brooke Bond Group 1972–82, Navy, Army and Air Force Insts 1972–87, HSBC Holdings PLC 1995–2002; Pres., Gen. Council of British Shipping 1980–81; Chair., Int. Chamber of Shipping 1982–87; mem. Gen. Cttee Lloyds Register 1967–99, Int. Advisory Council, China Int. Trust and Investment Corpn 1995–2005; Chair., RAF Benevolent Fund 1996–2000; Pres., Spitfire Soc. 1996–; Trustee, RAF Museum 1983–91; Hon. Air Commodore Royal Auxiliary Air Force 1987–2000; DL Oxfordshire 1989; Hon. Fellow, Nuffield Coll., Oxford 1998; Hon. DSc (Cranfield) 1995, Hon. DUniv (Southampton) 2002; Air League Founder's Medal 2006. *Address:* Swire House, 59 Buckingham Gate, London, SW1E 6AJ, England (office). *Telephone:* (20) 7834-7717 (office). *Fax:* (20) 7630-0380 (office).

SWITKOWSKI, Zygmunt (Ziggy) Edward, BSc, PhD, FAICD; Australian (b. German) scientist and business executive; *Chairman, Australian Nuclear Science and Technology Organisation;* b. 21 June 1948, Rheine, Germany; m. Jadzia Teresa 1970; one s. one d.; ed St Bernardo's Coll., Univ. of Melbourne; Sr Research Scientist, Eastman Kodak Co., New York 1978–80, Man.

Research and Devt 1980–82, Sales Man. 1982–83, Marketing Man. Consumer Products 1983–85, Dir Business Planning 1985–88; Deputy Man. Dir Kodak (Australasia) Ltd 1988–92, Chair., Man. Dir 1992–96; Dir Amcor Ltd 1995–99; Chair., Acting CEO Optus Vision Pty Ltd 1996–97, CEO Optus Communications Pty Ltd 1996–97; Group Man. Dir Business Int. Div. Telstra Corpn Ltd 1997–99, CEO 1999–2004 (resgnd); Chair. Australian Nuclear Science and Tech. Org. 2007–; Chair. Opera Australia 2008–; fmr Chair. Australian Quality Council; fmr mem. Business Council of Australia. *Address:* Australian Nuclear Science and Technology Organisation, PMB 1, Menai, NSW 2234, Australia (office). *Telephone:* (2) 9717-3111 (office). *Fax:* (2) 9543-5097 (office). *E-mail:* enquiries@ansto.gov.au (office). *Website:* www.ansto.gov.au (office).

SY-COSON, Teresita T.; Philippine retail executive; *Executive Vice-President, SM Prime Holdings Inc.;* b. 1950; d. of Henry Sy, Sr; m.; three c.; Pres. Shoemart 1990, currently Exec. Vice-Pres. SM Prime Holdings Inc., Vice-Chair. Investments Corpn (SM Group's holding co.); fmr Chair. and Chief Exec. Banco de Oro Universal, Chair. Banco de Oro Unibank, Inc. (after merger with Equitable PCI Bank) 2007–; mem. APEC Business Advisory Council; Trustee and Treas. SM Foundation Inc. 2003–; ranked by Fortune magazine amongst 50 Most Powerful Women in Business outside the US (39th) 2002, (45th) 2003, (47th) 2004, (46th) 2005, (46th) 2006, (41st) 2007, selected by Forbes magazine as one of Top 50 International Power Women 2003, Excellence in Retail Banking Award, The Asia Banker 2004. *Leisure interest:* reading business books. *Address:* SM Prime Holdings Inc., Building A, SM Corporate Offices, JW Diokno Blve., Mall of Asia Complex, Pasay City 1300, Philippines 1300 (office). *Telephone:* (632) 831-1000 (office). *Fax:* (632) 833-8991 (office). *E-mail:* info@smprime.com (office). *Website:* www.smprime.com (office).

SYAL, Meera, MBE, BA; British writer and actress; b. 27 June 1963, Wolverhampton; d. of Surendra Syal and Surrinder Syal; m. 1st 1989; one d.; m. 2nd Sanjeev Bhaskar 2005; one s.; ed Queen Mary's High School for Girls, Walsall, Univ. of Manchester; actress in one-woman comedy One of Us after graduation (Nat. Student Drama Award); fmr actress Royal Court Theatre, London; writer of screenplays and novels; actress and comedienne in theatre, film and on TV; contrib. to The Guardian newspaper; Scottish Critics Award for Most Promising Performer 1984, Woman of the Year in the Performing Arts, Cosmopolitan Magazine 1994, Chair.'s Award, Asian Women of Achievement Awards 2002, Women in Film and TV Creative Originality Award 2002. *Plays include:* Serious Money (London and Broadway, New York) 1987, Stitch 1990, Peer Gynt 1990, Bombay Dreams (story to musical) 2001, Rafta Rafta (Royal Nat. Theatre) 2007. *Radio includes:* Legal Affairs 1996, Goodness Gracious Me 1996–98, The World as We Know It 1999. *Film appearances include:* Sammie and Rosie Get Laid 1987, A Nice Arrangement, It's Not Unusual, Beautiful Thing 1996, Girls' Night 1997. *Television appearances include:* The Real McCoy (five series) 1990–95, My Sister Wife (BBC series) 1992, Have I Got News For You 1992, 1993, 1999, Sean's Show 1993, The Brain Drain 1993, Absolutely Fabulous 1995, Soldier Soldier 1995, Degrees of Error 1995, Band of Gold 1995, Drop the Dead Donkey 1996, Ruby 1997, Keeping Mum (BBC sitcom) 1997–98, The Book Quiz 1998, Goodness Gracious Me (first UK Asian TV comedy sketch show; co-writer) 1998–2000, Room 101 1999, The Kumars at No. 42 2002–06, Jekyll 2006,. *Written works include:* A Nice Arrangement (short TV film) 1991, My Sister Wife (TV film; Best TV Drama Award, Comm. for Racial Equality, Awards for Best Actress and Best Screenplay, Asian Film Acad. 1993) 1992, Bhaji on the Beach (film) 1994, Anita and Me (novel and adapted for TV) (Betty Trask Award) 1996, Goodness Gracious Me (comedy sketch TV show; co-writer) 1999, Life isn't all Ha Ha Hee Hee (novel) 1999. *Leisure interests:* singing in jazz quintet, netball. *Address:* c/o Rochelle Stevens, 2 Terretts Place, Islington, London, N1 1QZ, England (office). *Telephone:* (20) 7359-3900 (office).

SYBERBERG, Hans-Jürgen, DrPhil; German film director, film producer, theatre director and writer; b. 8 Dec. 1935, Nossendorf, Pomerania; m.; ed studies in literature and history of art at Munich; made over 80 short TV films 1963–65; later work includes documentaries, feature films and theatre; several Bundesfilmpreise and other awards including Bayerischer Filmpreis. *Films:* Fritz Kortner Rehearses Schiller's Intrigue and Love 1965, Shylock Monolog 1966, The Counts Pocci 1967, How Much Earth Does a Man Need 1968, Sexbusiness Made in Passing 1969, San Domingo 1970, After My Last Removal (Brecht) 1971, Ludwig—Requiem for a Virgin King 1972, Ludwig's Cook 1972, Karl May—In Search of Paradise Lost 1974, The Confessions of Winifred Wagner 1975, Hitler, A Film from Germany 1977, Parsifal (Kritiker Preis, Berlin 1983) 1982, Die Nacht 1984, Edith Clever liest Joyce-Molly 1985, Fräulein Else 1987, Penthesilea 1988, Marquise von O 1990, Ein Traum, was sonst? 1994, Höhle der Erinnerung 1997. *Plays include:* (in collaboration with E. Clever) Die Nacht 1984, Penthesilea 1988, Die Marquise von O... 1989, Ein Traum, was sonst? 1990. *Publications:* The Film as the Music of the Future 1975, Syberbergs Filmbuch 1976, Die Kunst als Rettung aus der deutschen Misere (essay) 1978, Die freudlose Gesellschaft 1981 Der Wald steht schwarz und schweiget 1984, VomUnglück und Glück der Kunst in Deutschland nach dem letzten Kriege 1990, Der verlorene Auftrag 1994. *Address:* Genter Strasse 15A, 80805 Munich, Germany. *Telephone:* (89) 3614882. *Fax:* (89) 3614905. *E-mail:* film@syberberg.de; hjs@syberberg.de. *Website:* www.syberberg.de.

SYCHOV, Alyaksandr; Belarusian diplomatist; *Ambassador to Austria;* b. 19 Sept. 1951, Gomel, Belarus; m. Natalia Vedmedenko 1976; one s. one d.; ed Moscow State Inst. of Int. Relations; Third then Second Sec., Ministry of Foreign Affairs 1979–84; Del. Perm. Mission of the Repub. of Belarus to UN office and other int. orgs., Geneva 1984–90; Head Dept of Foreign Econ. Relations, Ministry of Foreign Affairs 1991–92, Deputy Minister for Foreign Affairs 1992–94; Perm. Rep. to UN, New York 1994–2000; Deputy Minister of Foreign Affairs 2000–05; Amb. to Austria 2005–, also Perm. Rep. to OSCE, JCG, OSCC and other int. orgs in Vienna; Chair. First Cttee of the 51st session of the UN Gen. Ass., 19th Special Session 1996–97; Vice-Pres. ECOSOC 1998–99. *Publications:* numerous articles on Belarus foreign policy and int. affairs. *Leisure interests:* art, opera, tennis, soccer. *Address:* Embassy of Belarus, Hüttelbergstr. 6, 1140 Vienna, Austria (office). *Telephone:* (1) 419-96-30-11 (office). *Fax:* (1) 416-96-30-30 (office). *E-mail:* mail@byembassy.at (office). *Website:* www.austria.belembassy.org (office).

SYDOW, Max von; French (b. Swedish) actor; b. 10 April 1929, Lund, Sweden; s. of Carl W. von Sydow and Greta Rappe; m. 1st Kerstin Olin 1951 (divorced 1979); two s.; m. 2nd Catherine Brelet 1997; two s.; ed Royal Dramatic Theatre School, Stockholm; Norrköping-Linköping Theatre 1951–53, Hälsingborg Theatre 1953–55, Malmö Theatre 1955–60, Royal Dramatic Theatre, Stockholm 1960–74, 1988–94; film work in Sweden 1949–95; int. productions 1962–; Commdr Ordre des Arts et Lettres; Golden Beetle Award for Best Actor 1987, 1996, for Best Dir 1988, Best Actor, European Film Award, Berlin 1988, Litteris et Artibus (Sweden). *Plays acted in include:* Peer Gynt, Henry IV (Pirandello), The Tempest, Le misanthrope, Faust, Ett Drömspel, La valse des toréadors, Les sequestrés d'Altona, After the Fall, The Wild Duck, The Night of the Tribades 1977, Duet for One 1981, The Tempest 1988, Swedenhielms 1990, And Give Us the Shadows 1991, The Ghost Sonata 1994. *Films include:* Bara en mor (Only a Mother) 1949, Fröken Julie (Miss Julie) 1951, Ingen mans kvinna 1953, Rätten att älska 1956, Det sjunde inseglet (The Seventh Seal) 1957, Smultronstället (Wild Strawberries) 1957, Prästen i Uddarbo 1957, Nära livet (So Close to Life) 1958, Spion 503 1958, Ansiktet (The Face) 1958, Jungfrukällan (The Virgin Spring) 1960, Bröllopsdagen (The Wedding Day) 1960, Såsom i en spegel (Through a Glass Darkly) 1961, Nils Holgerssons underbara resa (Wonderful Adventures of Nils) 1962, Älskarinnan (The Mistress) 1962, Nattvardsgästerna (Winter Light) 1963, The Greatest Story Ever Told 1965, 4 × 4 1965, The Reward 1965, Hawaii 1966, The Quiller Memorandum 1966, Här har du ditt liv (This Is Your Life) 1966, Vargtimmen (Hour of the Wolf) 1968, Svarta palmkronor (Black Palm Trees) 1968, Skammen (Shame) 1968, Made in Sweden 1969, En passion (A Passion) 1969, The Kremlin Letter 1970, The Night Visitor 1971, Utvandrarna (The Emigrants) 1971, Beröringen (The Touch) 1971, Äppelkriget (The Apple War) 1971, Embassy 1972, Nybyggarna (The New Land) 1972, The Exorcist 1973, Steppenwolf 1974, Cuore di cane (Dog's Heart) 1975, Ägget är löst! (Egg! Egg! A Hardboiled Story) 1975, Trompe-l'oeil 1975, Three Days of the Condor 1975, The Ultimate Warrior 1975, Cadaveri eccellenti (aka Illustrious Corpses) 1976, Foxtrot (aka The Far Side of Paradise) 1976, Il deserto dei Tartari (The Desert of the Tartars) 1976, Voyage of the Damned 1976, Gran bollito (aka Black Journal) 1977, Exorcist II: The Heretic 1977, March or Die 1977, Brass Target 1978, Hurricane 1979, Bugie bianche (aka Footloose, and Venetian Lies) 1980, La mort en direct (Death Watch) 1980, Flash Gordon 1980, Victory 1981, Jugando con la muerte (aka Hit Man, USA) 1982, Conan the Barbarian 1982, Ingenjör Andrées luftfärd (The Flight of the Eagle) 1982, Le cercle des passions (aka Circle of Passions), The Adventures of Bob & Doug McKenzie: Strange Brew 1983, Never Say Never Again 1983, A Soldier's Tale 1984, The Ice Pirates 1984, Dreamscape 1984, Dune 1984, Code Name: Emerald (aka Deep Cover, USA TV title) 1985, Il pentito (The Repenter) 1985, The Second Victory 1986, Hannah and Her Sisters 1986, Oviri (The Wolf at the Door) 1986, Duet for One 1986, Pelle erobreren (Pelle the Conqueror) 1987, Una vita scellerata (A Violent Life) 1990, Father 1990, Awakenings 1990, Mio caro dottor Gräsler (aka The Bachelor, USA) 1991, A Kiss Before Dying 1991, Europa (voice) 1991, Bis ans Ende der Welt (Until the End of the World) 1991, Oxen 1991, Den goda viljan (The Best Intentions) 1992, Dotkniecie reki (The Silent Touch) 1992, Morfars resa (Grandpa's Journey) 1993, Needful Things 1993, Time Is Money 1994, Dypets ensomhet (Depth Solitude) 1995, Judge Dredd 1995, Truck Stop 1996, Hamsun (Swedish Guldbagge Award for Best Actor 1997) 1996, Jerusalem 1996, What Dreams May Come 1998, Snow Falling on Cedars 1999, Non ho sonno (aka Sleepless, USA) 2001, Vercingétorix 2001, Intacto (Intact) 2001, Les amants de Mogador 2002, Minority Report 2002, Heidi 2005, Le Scaphandre et le papillon 2007, Rush Hour 3 2007, Emotional Arithmetic 2007; Dir Katinka 1987. *Television includes:* Herr Sleeman kommer 1957, Rabies 1958, The Diary of Anne Frank 1967, I havsbandet (mini-series) 1971, Kvartetten som sprängdes (mini-series) 1973, Le dernier civil 1983, Samson and Delilah 1984, Quo Vadis? (mini-series) 1985, The Last Place on Earth (mini-series) 1985, Kojak: The Belarus File 1985, Christopher Columbus (mini-series) 1985, Gösta Berlings saga (mini-series, segments 1–3) 1986, Red King, White Knight 1989, Hiroshima: Out of the Ashes 1990, Den goda viljan (mini-series) 1991, Och ge oss skuggorna 1993, Onkel Vanja 1994, A che punto è la notte 1995, Citizen X 1995, Radetzkymarsch (mini-series) Radetzky March) 1995, Samson and Delilah (voice, uncredited) 1996, Enskilda samtal (Private Conversations) 1996, Profiler (series) 1997, Hostile Waters 1997, La principessa e il povero (The Princess and the Pauper) 1997, Solomon 1997, Nuremberg (mini-series) 2000, La fuga degli innocenti (Hidden Children: The Flight of the Innocents) (mini-series) 2004, Ring of the Nibelungs 2004, L'Inchiesta 2007. *Publication:* Loppcirkus (with Elisabeth Sörenson) 1989. *Leisure interests:* nautical history, environment preservation, Baroque music. *Address:* c/o London Management, 2–4 Noel Street, London, W1V 3RB, England (office); c/o Agence Anne Alvares Correa, 18 rue Troyon, 75017 Paris, France (office).

SYKES, Eric, CBE; British actor, writer and director; b. 4 May 1923, Oldham; s. of Vernon Sykes and Harriet Sykes; m. Edith Eleanor Milbradt; one s. three d.; ed Ward Street Cen. School, Oldham; left school at 14; long-running TV comedy show Sykes (with Hattie Jacques) 1960–79; many other TV appearances; Freeman City of London 1988; Hon. Fellow, Univ. of Lancashire 1999; Writers' Guild Lifetime Achievement Award 1992. *Plays include:* Big Bad Mouse 1977–78, A Hatful of Sykes 1977–78, Run For Your Wife 1992, The

19th Hole 1992, Two of a Kind 1995, Fools Rush In 1996, The School For Wives 1997, Kafka's Dick 1998–99, Caught in the Net 2001–02, Three Sisters 2003, As You Like It 2003. *Films include:* actor: Tommy the Toreador 1959, Watch Your Stern 1960, Very Important Person (aka A Coming-Out Party, USA) 1961, Invasion Quartet 1961, Village of Daughters 1962, Kill or Cure 1962, Heavens Above! 1963, The Bargee 1964, One Way Pendulum 1964, The Liquidator 1965, Those Magnificent Men in Their Flying Machines, or How I Flew from London to Paris in 25 hours 11 minutes 1965, Rotten to the Core 1965, The Spy with a Cold Nose 1966, The Plank 1967, Shalako 1968, Rhubarb 1969, It's Your Move 1969, Monte Carlo or Bust! 1969, Theatre of Blood (aka Much Ado About Murder) 1973, Rhubarb Rhubarb 1980, If You Go Down in the Woods Today 1981, The Boys in Blue 1982, Gabrielle and the Doodleman 1984, Absolute Beginners (uncredited) 1986, The Big Freeze 1993, Splitting Heirs 1993, The Others 2001, Mavis and the Mermaid 2004, Harry Potter and the Goblet of Fire 2005, Son of Rambow 2007. *Radio includes:* as writer: Educating Archie, The Frankie Howerd Show. *Television includes:* The Idiot Weekly, Price 2d (series) 1955, Dress Rehearsal 1956, Opening Night 1956, Pantomania, or Dick Whittington 1956, Closing Night 1957, Gala Opening 1959, Sykes and A… (series) 1960, Clicquot et fils (aka Comedy Playhouse: Clicquot et Fils, UK series title) 1961, Sykes Versus ITV 1967, Curry & Chips (series) 1969, Sykes and a Big Big Show (series) 1971, Sykes: With the Lid Off 1971, Sykes (series) 1972, Eric Sykes Shows a Few of Our Favourite Things 1977, The Plank 1979, The Likes of Sykes 1980, The Eric Sykes 1990 Show 1982, It's Your Move 1982, Mr. H Is Late 1988, The Nineteenth Hole (series) 1989, Teletubbies (series) 1997 Gormenghast (mini-series) 2000. *Publications:* The Great Crime of Grapplewick 1996, UFOs Are Coming Wednesday 1995, Smelling of Roses 1997, Sykes of Sebastopol Terrace 2000, Eric Sykes' Comedy Heroes 2003, If I Don't Write It, Nobody Else Will (autobiog.) 2005. *Leisure interest:* golf. *Address:* 9 Orme Court, London, W2 4RL, England. *Telephone:* (20) 7727-1544. *Fax:* (20) 7792-2110.

SYKES, Lynn R., PhD; American geologist and academic; *Higgins Professor Emeritus of Earth and Environmental Sciences, Lamont-Doherty Geological Observatory, Columbia University;* b. 16 April 1937, Pittsburgh, Pa; s. of Lloyd A. Sykes and Margaret Woodburn Sykes; m. 1st Meredith Henschkel (divorced); m. 2nd Katherine Flanz 1986 (died 1996); m. 3rd Kathleen Mahoney 1998; ed Massachusetts Inst. of Tech. and Columbia Univ.; Research Asst, Lamont-Doherty Geological Observatory, Columbia Univ. 1961–64, Research Assoc. 1964–66, Adjunct Asst Prof. of Geology 1966–68, Head of Seismology Group 1973–83, apptd Higgins Prof. of Earth and Environmental Sciences 1978, now Prof. Emer.; main areas of interest are seismology, tectonics and arms control, earthquake prediction and the detection and identification of underground atomic tests; Chair. Nat. Earthquake Prediction Evaluation Council; mem. NAS, American Acad. of Arts and Sciences, Geological Soc. of London, Arms Control Asscn; Fellow, American Geophysical Union, Geological Soc. of America, Royal Astronomical Soc., AAAS; Walter H. Bucher Medal of American Geophysical Union for original contribs. to basic knowledge of earth's crust 1975, Public Service Award, Fed. of American Scientists 1986, John Wesley Powell Award, US Geological Survey 1990, Vetleson Award for devt and testing of plate tectonics 2000. *Publications:* more than 135 papers in scientific journals. *Leisure interests:* hiking, canoeing, opera, travel. *Address:* Lamont-Doherty Earth Observatory, Columbia University, PO Box 1000, 230C Seismology Building, 61 Route 9W, Palisades, NY 10964-8000 (office); 100 Washington Spring Road, Palisades, NY 10964-8000, USA. *Telephone:* (845) 365-8880 (office). *Fax:* (845) 365-8150 (office). *E-mail:* sykes@ldeo.columbia.edu (office). *Website:* www.ldeo.columbia.edu/~sykes (office).

SYKES, Sir Richard (Brook), Kt, PhD, DSc, FRS, FMedSci; British research microbiologist, business executive and university administrator; *Chairman, NHS London;* b. 7 Aug. 1942, Huddersfield, Yorks.; s. of the late Eric Sykes and of Muriel Mary Sykes; m. Janet Mary Norman 1969; one s. one d.; ed Queen Elizabeth Coll., London, Bristol Univ., London Univ.; Head of Antibiotic Research Unit, Glaxo Research Ltd 1972–77; Asst Dir, Dept of Microbiology, Squibb Inst. for Medical Research, Princeton 1977, Dir of Microbiology 1979, Vice-Pres. Infectious and Metabolic Diseases 1983–86; Deputy Chief Exec., Glaxo Group Research Ltd 1986, Group Research and Devt Dir, Glaxo PLC and Chair. and Chief Exec., Glaxo Group Research Ltd 1987, Deputy Chair. and Chief Exec., Glaxo PLC 1993, Chair., Glaxo Wellcome PLC 1997–2001, CEO 1997; Chair. (non-exec.), GlaxoSmithKline 2001–02; Chair., Metabometrix Ltd 2004–, Merlion Pharmaceuticals Pte Ltd 2005–, Omnicyte Ltd 2006–, Circassia Ltd 2007–; Rector, Imperial Coll. of Science, Tech. and Medicine 2001–08; Chair., NHS London 2008–; Visiting Prof., King's Coll., London and Univ. of Bristol; Pres., British Asscn for the Advancement of Science 1998–99; Dir (non-exec.), Rio Tinto PLC 1997–, Lonza Group Ltd 2003–, Imperial Coll. Healthcare NHS Trust 2007–, Eurasian Natural Resources Corpn 2007–; Chair., UK Stem Cell Foundation 2005–; mem. Council for Science and Tech. 1993–2002; mem. Bd of Trustees Nat. History Museum 1996–2005, Bd Higher Educ. Funding Council for England 2002–, UK India Business Council 2007–; Fellow, Imperial Coll. School of Medicine; Fleming Fellow, Lincoln Coll., Oxford 1992; Hon. mem. Nat. Acad. of Medicine, Brazil; Hon. Fellow Royal Coll. of Physicians, Univ. of Wales, Cardiff, Royal Pharmaceutical Soc.; Hon. FRSC; Hon. Citizen of Singapore 2004; Companion of the Most Admirable Order of Direkgunabhom (Thailand) 2006; Hon. DPharm (Madrid) 1993, Hon. DSc (Brunel, Hull, Herts.) 1994, (Bristol, Newcastle) 1995, (Huddersfield, Westminster) 1996, (Leeds) 1997, (Edin., Strathclyde) 1998, (Cranfield, Leicester, Sheffield, Warwick) 1999, Hon. MD (Birmingham) 1995, Hon. LLD (Nottingham) 1997, Dr hc (Sheffield Hallam, Surrey); Hamao Umezawa Memorial Award (Int. Soc. of Chemotherapy) 1999, Singapore Nat. Day Public Service Star Award 1999. *Leisure interests:* tennis, swimming, opera, skiing. *Address:* NHS London, Southside, 105 Victoria Street, London, SW1E 6QT (office); Flat 11, Hale House, 34 De Vere Gardens, London W8 5AQ, England (home). *Telephone:* (20) 7932-3702 (office). *E-mail:* rsykes@london.nhs.uk (office). *Website:* www.london.nhs.uk (office).

SYLLA, Jacques Hugues, LLB; Malagasy politician and lawyer; *President, National Assembly;* b. 1946, Holy Marie, Toamasina Prov.; m. Yvette Rakoto; four c.; practised as lawyer; Co-founder Toamasina Br. of Nat. Cttee for Observation of the Elections (CNOE), First Foreign Minister of fmr Pres. Albert Zafy 1992–93; Minister of Foreign Affairs 1993–96; Prime Minister of Madagascar 2002–07; Pres. Nat. Ass. 2007–. *E-mail:* poste@assemblee-nationale.mg (office). *Website:* www.assemblee-nationale.mg (office).

SYMON, Lindsay, CBE, TD, MB, ChB, FRCS, FRCSE; British professor of neurological surgery; b. 4 Nov. 1929, Aberdeen, Scotland; s. of William L. Symon and Isabel Symon; m. Pauline Barbara Rowland 1954; one s. two d.; ed Aberdeen Grammar School and Univ. of Aberdeen; House Physician/Surgeon, Aberdeen Royal Infirmary 1952–53, Surgical Registrar 1956–58; Clinical Officer/Jr Specialist in Surgery, British troops in Austria 1953–55; Clinical Research Fellow, MRC 1958–61; Major in charge, No. 2 Mobile Neurosurgical Team, TA, RAMC 1960–68; Rockefeller Travelling Fellow, Wayne State Univ., Detroit, Mich., USA 1961–62; Sr Registrar, Neurosurgery, Nat. Hosps 1962–65, Consultant Neurosurgeon 1965–78, Prof. of Neurological Surgery and Sr Surgeon 1978–95; mem. External Staff MRC 1965–78; Hon. Consultant Neurosurgeon, St Thomas's Hosp., London 1973–95, Hammersmith Hosp., London 1978–95, Royal Nat. Throat, Nose and Ear Hosp. 1979–95, The Italian Hosp. 1981–89; Adjunct Prof., Dept of Surgery, Southwestern Medical School, Dallas, Tex. 1982–95; Civilian Adviser in Neurosurgery, RN 1979–95; Pres. World Fed. of Neurosurgical Socs 1979–93, Hon. Pres. 1993–; Pres. Harveian Soc., London 1997–98, Trustee 1999–; Hon. FACS 1994; Jamieson Medal, Australasian Neurosurgical Soc. 1982, John Hunter Medal, Royal Coll. of Surgeons 1985, Joachim Zulch Prize, Max Planck Inst. 1993, Otfrid Förster Medal, German Soc. Neurosurgery 1998, Medal of Honour, Soc. of British Neurological Surgeons 2008. *Publications:* texts on cerebrovascular surgery, physiology of the cerebral circulation, surgery of acoustic neuroma, general neurosurgical topics. *Leisure interests:* golf, prehistory. *Address:* Maple Lodge, Rivar Road, Shalbourne, nr Marlborough, Wilts., SN8 3QE, England (home). *Telephone:* (1672) 870501 (home). *Fax:* (1672) 870501 (home).

SYMONENKO, Petro Mykolayovych; Ukrainian politician; *Secretary of Central Committee, Communist Party of Ukraine;* b. 1 Aug. 1952, Donetsk; m.; two s.; ed Donetsk State Polytechnical Inst. and Kyiv Inst. of Political Science and Social Admin; joined Komsomol 1975; joined CPSU 1978, fmr Deputy Sec. Donetsk regional CP Cttee; Deputy Dir Ukrvuhlemash machine-building co. 1991–93; Sec. Cen. Cttee of CP of Ukraine 1993–; mem. Verkhovna Rada (Parl.) 1994–, Chair. CP Parl. faction; mem. Parl. Ass. of the Council of Europe 1997–; cand. in presidential elections 1999, 2004. *Address:* Communist Party of Ukraine (Komunistychna Partiya Ukrainy), 04070 Kyiv, vul. Borysohlibska 7, Ukraine (office). *Telephone:* (44) 425-54-87 (office). *E-mail:* Symonenko.Petro@rada.gov.ua (office); press@kpu.net.ua (office). *Website:* www.kpu.net.ua (office).

SYMONETTE, Theodore Brent; Bahamian barrister, real estate developer and politician; *Deputy Prime Minister and Minister of Foreign Affairs;* b. 2 Dec. 1954, Nassau; s. of Sir Roland Symonette (first Prime Minister of the Bahamas) and Lady Margaret Symonette; m. Robin Mactaggart; one s. two d.; ed St Andrew's School, Nassau, Leys School, Cambridge, Brunel Univ., London, UK; called to Bahamas Bar 1978; fmr Senator; mem. House of Ass. for St Anne; fmr Minister of Tourism; fmr Attorney-Gen.; Deputy Leader, Free Nat. Movt; Deputy Prime Minister and Minister of Foreign Affairs 2007–, also responsible for Immigration 2008–; fmr Chair. Hotel Corpn, Airport Authority, Public Accounts Cttee. *Address:* Ministry of Foreign Affairs, East Hill Street, PO Box N-3746, Nassau, The Bahamas (office). *Telephone:* 322-7624 (office). *Fax:* 328-8212 (office). *E-mail:* mfabahamas@batelnet.bs (office). *Website:* www.mfabahamas.org (office).

SYMONS OF VERNHAM DEAN, Baroness (Life Peer), cr. 1996, of Vernham Dean in the County of Hampshire; **Elizabeth Conway Symons,** MA, FRSA; British politician; b. 14 April 1951; d. of Ernest Vize Symons and Elizabeth Megan Symons (née Jenkins); pnr, Philip Alan Bassett; one s.; ed Putney High School for Girls, Girton Coll., Cambridge; Admin. Trainee, Dept of the Environment 1974–77; Asst Sec., Inland Revenue Staff Fed. 1977–88, Deputy Gen. Sec. 1988–89; Gen. Sec., Asscn of First Div. Civil Servants 1989–96; Parl. Under-Sec. of State, FCO 1997–99; Minister of Defence Procurement, Ministry of Defence 1999–2001; apptd Minister of State (Minister for Trade), FCO and Dept of Trade and Industry 2001; Deputy Leader of House of Lords 2001–05; Minister of State for the Middle East, FCO and Dept of Trade and Industry 2003–05; mem. Gen. Council, TUC 1989–96, Council, RIPA 1989–97, Exec. Council, Campaign for Freedom of Information 1989–97, Hansard Soc. Council 1992–97, Advisory Council, Civil Service Coll. 1992–97, Council, Industrial Soc. 1994–97, Council, Open Univ. 1994–97; Employment Appeal Tribunal 1995, Equal Opportunities Comm. 1995–97; Exec. mem. Involvement and Participation Asscn 1992; Gov. Polytechnic of N London 1989–94, London Business School 1993–97; Trustee, Inst. for Public Policy Research 1993; Hon. Assoc. Nat. Council of Women 1989. *Leisure interests:* gardening, reading. *Address:* House of Lords, Westminster, London, SW1A 0PW, England (office).

SYMS, Sylvia, OBE; British actress and director; b. 6 Jan. 1934, London; m. Alan Edney 1957 (divorced 1989); one s. one d.; ed Royal Acad. of Dramatic Art; Founder-mem. and Artistic Dir Arbela Production Co.; numerous lectures, including Dodo White McLarty Memorial Lecture 1986; mem. The Actors' Centre 1986–91, Arts Council Drama Panel 1991–96, Council for

RADA 1992–; Variety Club Best Actress in Films Award 1958, Ondas Award for Most Popular Foreign Actress (Spain) 1966, Manchester Evening News Best Actress Award. *Theatre includes:* Dance of Death, Much Ado About Nothing, An Ideal Husband, Ghosts, Entertaining Mr. Sloane (Best Actress Award, Manchester Evening News) 1985, Who's Afraid of Virgina Woolf? 1989, The Floating Lightbulb 1990, Antony and Cleopatra 1991, For Services Rendered 1993, Funny Money 1996, Ugly Rumours 1998, Mothers and Daughters 1999–2003, Love Lust 2003, We All Make Mistakes 2003. *Films include:* Ice Cold in Alex 1953, The Birthday Present 1956, The World of Suzie Wong 1961, Run Wild Run Free 1969, The Tamarind Seed 1974, Chorus of Disapproval 1988, Shirley Valentine 1989, Shining Through 1991, Dirty Weekend 1992, Staggered 1994, Food for Love 1996, Mavis and the Mermaid 1999, Deep Down 2001, What a Girl Wants 2002, I'll Sleep When I'm Dead 2003, The Queen 2006, Is There Anybody There? 2008. *Television includes:* Love Story 1964, The Saint 1967, My Good Woman 1972–73, Nancy Astor 1982, Ruth Rendell Mysteries 1989, Dr. Who 1989–90, May to December 1989–90, The Last Days of Margaret Thatcher 1991, Natural Lies, Mulberry, Peak Practice, Ruth Randell Mysteries 1993, 1997–98, Ghost Hour 1995, Heartbeat 1998, At Home with the Braithwaites 2000–03, The Jury 2002, Where the Heart Is 2003, Born and Bread 2003, The Poseidon Adventure 2005, Child of Mine 2005. *Radio includes:* Little Dorrit, Danger in the Village, Post Mortems, Joe Orton, Love Story, The Change 2001, 2003. *Plays and television directed:* Better in My Dreams 1988, The Price 1991, Natural Lies 1991–92. *Leisure interests:* gardening, dogs. *Address:* c/o Brown & Simcocks, 1 Bridge House Court, 109 Blackfriars Road, London, SE1 8HW, England (office). *Telephone:* (20) 7928-1229 (office). *Fax:* (20) 7928-1909 (office). *E-mail:* barryandcarrig@lingone.net (office).

SYRON, Richard (Dick) Francis, PhD; American banking executive and economist; b. 25 Oct. 1943, Boston; s. of Dominick Syron and Elizabeth Syron (née McGuire); m. Margaret Mary Garatoni 1972; one s. one d.; ed Boston Coll., Tufts Univ.; Deputy Dir Commonwealth of Mass 1973–74; Vice-Pres., Economist Fed. Reserve Bank of Boston 1974–82, Sr Vice-Pres., Econ. Adviser 1982–85, Pres., CEO 1989–94; Chair. American Stock Exchange 1994–99; Chair. and CEO Thermo Electron, Mass. 1999–2002; Chair. and CEO Freddie Mac (Fed. Home Loan Mortgage Corpn) 2003–08; Exec. Asst to Sec. US Treasury, Washington 1979–80, Deputy Asst to Sec. for Econ. Policy 1980–81; Asst to Chair. Volcker Fed. Reserve, Washington 1981–82; Pres. Fed. Home Loan Bank of Boston 1986–88; mem. Bd of Dirs John Hancock, Thermo Electron, The Dreyfus Corpn, US Stock Exchange; Trustee, Boston Coll. *Address:* c/o Freddie Mac, 8200 Jones Branch Drive, McLean, VA 22102-3110, USA. *Telephone:* (703) 903-2000. *Website:* www.freddiemac.com.

SYRYJCZYK, Tadeusz Andrzej, DTech; Polish politician; b. 9 Feb. 1948, Kraków; m.; ed Acad. of Mining and Metallurgy, Kraków; Lecturer, Acad. of Mining and Metallurgy, Kraków 1971–89; mem. Solidarity Trade Union 1980–89; interned during state of martial law 1981–82; mem. regional authorities, Kraków 1982–84; with ABAKS, Kraków 1987–89; Minister of Industry 1989–91; Chief of Prime Minister's team of advisers and Under-Sec. of State in Council of Ministers 1992–93; Minister of Transport and Maritime Economy 1998–2000; Deputy to Sejm (Parl.) 1991–2001, mem. Parl. Comm. for Privatization, Econ. System and Industry 1991–92, Parl. Comm. for Econ. Policy, Budget and Finances 1993–97, Parl. Comm. for Public Finances 1997–98, Parl. Comm. for Nat. Defence 1998; mem. Democratic Union Parl. Caucus 1991–94, Freedom Union Parl. Caucus 1994–2001, Chair. 1997–98; mem. Democratic Union 1991–94; mem. Presidium Małopolska Region 1981; mem. Freedom Union 1994–, Nat. Council and Regional Council, Kraków 1983–2001; Vice-Pres. Freedom Union 1995–2001; Co-Founder Industrial Soc. of Kraków 1987; mem. Polish Tourist Country-Lovers' Asscn, Polish Informatics Soc. *Publications:* papers on automatics and informatics, articles in nat. magazines. *Leisure interest:* tourism, mountaineering. *Address:* ul. Kazimierza Wielkiego 4 m.9, 30-074 Kraków, Poland (home). *Telephone:* (12) 6336427 (home); (601) 471870. *Fax:* (601) 405999 (home). *E-mail:* tadeusz@syryjczyk.krakow.pl. *Website:* www.syryjczyk.krakow.pl.

SYSUYEV, Oleg Nikolayevich; Russian banker and fmr politician; *First Deputy Chairman of the Board of Directors, Alfa-Bank;* b. 23 March 1953, Kuybyshev (now Samara); m.; one s. one d.; ed Kuybyshev Moscow Aviation Inst.; Master, Head of Tech. Div., engineer and Sec., CP Cttee at Kuibyshev aviation team 1976–87; Sec., Krasnoglinsk Dist CP Cttee of Kuybyshev 1987–91; del. to 18th CP Congress; Head of Samara Admin. 1991–94; Mayor of Samara 1994–97; participant in Russia Our Home movt; Co-Chair. Union of Mayors of Russian Towns 1995–97; Deputy Head of Russian Govt, Minister of Labour and Social Devt 1997–98; Co-ordinator Russian Comm. on Regulation of Trade-Social Relations 1997–98; First Deputy Head of Admin. of Pres. Yeltsin 1998–99; First Deputy Chair. of Bd Alfa-Bank 1999–; Pres. Congress of Municipalities of Russia 2000–; mem. Presidential Council for Local Govt; Deputy Chair. Presidential Cttee for Literature and the Arts. *Leisure interests:* playing guitar, piano, violin. *Address:* Alfa-Bank, 27 Kalanchevskaya Str., 107078 Moscow, Russia (office). *Telephone:* (495) 620-91-91 (office). *E-mail:* mail@alfabank.ru (office). *Website:* www.alfabank.com (office).

SZABAD, György, PhD; Hungarian politician and historian; b. 4 Aug. 1924, Arad, Romania; s. of Erzsébet Blantz; m. Andrea Suján; one d.; ed Loránd Eötvös Univ., Budapest; served in forced labour camp 1944; mem. staff, Nat. Archives 1949, Univ. Asst Lecturer 1954, Lecturer 1956, Prof. 1970; mem. Revolutionary Cttee 1956; Founding mem. and Nat. Bd mem. Hungarian Democratic Forum 1987; Founding mem. Hungarian Democratic People's Party; Speaker of Hungarian Parl. 1990–94, mem. Parl. 1994–98; Pres. Cttee of Hungarian and Polish Historians; Corresp. mem. Hungarian Acad. of Sciences 1982, mem. 1998–; Grand Cross of Honour of the Republic of Hungary 2000; Hungarian Acad. of Sciences Award 1965, 1973, Council of Europe Pro Merito 1991. *Publications include:* Kossuth on the Political System of the United States of America 1975, Hungarian Political Trends between the Revolution and the Compromise 1849–1867 1977, Conceptualization of a Danubian Federation 1998. *Address:* Kelenhegyi ut. 40/B, 1118 Budapest, Hungary (home). *Telephone:* 385-3761 (home). *E-mail:* aszabad@t-online.hu (home).

SZABO, Denis, OC, DèsSc, FRSC, OQ; Canadian/Belgian criminologist and academic; *Professor Emeritus of Criminology and Chairman, International Centre for Comparative Criminology, University of Montreal;* b. 4 June 1929, Budapest, Hungary; s. of Jenö Denes and Catherine Zsiga; m. Sylvie Grotard 1956; two d.; ed Univs of Budapest, Louvain and Paris; Asst Univ. of Louvain 1952–56; lecturer in Sociology, Catholic Univ. of Paris and Lyon 1956–58; Asst Prof. Univ. of Montreal 1958–59, Assoc. Prof. 1959–66, Prof. of Criminology 1966–95, Prof. Emer. 1995–; Founder and Dir School of Criminology, Univ. of Montreal 1960–70; Founder and Dir Int. Center for Comparative Criminology, Univ. of Montreal 1969–84, now Chair. of Bd; founder Quebec Soc. of Criminology; Pres. Asoc. Internationale des Criminologues de Langue Française, Geneva 1989–2002 (Hon. Pres. Liége 2002); consultant to Canadian, US, French, Hungarian and UN comms and bodies on crime prevention; mem. Hungarian Acad. of Sciences 1993–, Romanian Soc. of Criminology 2003–; Corresponding mem. Acad. des Sciences Morales et Politiques, Institut de France 2004; Hon. Pres. Int. Soc. of Criminology, Hon. mem. Basque Inst. of Criminology (Spain) 2003; Commdr Ordre Nat. du Mérite, Côte d'Ivoire 1986, Commdr Ordre du Mérite Répub., Hungary 1996, Chevalier des Arts et des Lettres, France 1996, Officier Ordre nat. du Québec 1998 and other decorations; Dr hc (Siena, Budapest, Aix-Marseille, Panteios-Athens, Bucharest); Sutherland Award, American Soc. of Criminology 1968, Golden Medal Beccaria, German Soc. of Criminology 1970 and other awards. *Publications:* Crimes et villes 1960, Criminologie et politique criminelle 1978, The Canadian Criminal Justice System (with A. Parizeau), Science et crimes 1986, Criminologie empirique au Québec (ed. with Marc Le Blanc), De l'anthropologie à la criminologie comparée 1993, Traité de criminologie empirique (ed. with Marc Le Blanc) 1994, Vols II and III 2002–04. *Leisure interests:* gardening, swimming. *Address:* International Centre for Comparative Criminology, Pav.M.Caron-L.Groulx-3200 J.B., bureau C-4103, University of Montreal, C.P. 6128, Montreal, H3C 3J7 (office); 66, Square Copp, Georgeville, J0B 1T0, Canada (home). *Telephone:* (514) 343-6111 (office); (819) 843-4343 (home). *Fax:* (514) 343-2269 (office); (514) 343-2269 (office). *E-mail:* denis.szabo@umontreal.ca (office). *Website:* www.cicc.umontreal.ca (office).

SZABO, Gabriela; Romanian professional athlete; b. 14 Nov. 1975, Bistrita; m. Gyonyossy Zsolt 1999; fmr indoor European record-holder and outdoor World record-holder in 5,000m; silver medal, 1,500m, Olympic Games, Atlanta 1996; world's fastest at 1,500m, one mile, 2,000m, 3,000m and 5,000m 1998; gold medal, 5,000m Olympic Games, Sydney 2000, bronze medal, 1,500m, Sydney 2000; set new world records for indoor 5,000m in Feb. 1999, 3,000m. Birmingham, England, Feb. 2001; gold medal, 1,500m World Championships 2001; silver medal, European Championships 5,000m 1998, 1,500m 2002; retd 2005; currently Vice-Pres. Romanian Athletics Fed.; first female track athlete to make US $1 million in prize money in one season; European Athlete of the Year 1999, IAAF Athlete of the Year 1999. *Address:* Romanian Athletics Federation, 2, dr. Primo Nebiolo, 71323 Bucharest, Romania (office). *Telephone:* (21) 2232229 (office). *Fax:* (21) 2232227 (office). *E-mail:* gabi@gabiszabo.com; fra.teh@ew.ro (office). *Website:* www.gabiszabo.com; www.fra.ro (office).

SZABÓ, István, DLA; Hungarian film director, writer and academic; b. 18 Feb. 1938, Budapest; s. of Dr István Szabó and Mária Vita; m. Vera Gyürey; ed Budapest Acad. of Theatre and Film Arts; started as mem. Balázs B. Studio, Budapest; leading mem. Hungarian Film Studios; Tutor, Coll. of Theatre and Film Arts, Budapest; mem. Acad. of Motion Picture Arts and Sciences, Akad. der Künste, Berlin; Béla Balázs Prize 1967, Kossuth Prize 1975. *Productions:* short films: Concert 1961, Variations upon a Theme 1961, Te (You) (Grand Prix de Tours) 1963, Budapest, amiért szeretem (Budapest, Why I Love It) 1971; series: Álom a házról (Dream About the House) (Main Prize of Oberhausen) 1971; documentaries: Kegyelet (Piety) 1967, Várostérkép (City Map) (Grand Prix of Oberhausen) 1977, Steadying the Boat 1996; TV plays: Osbemutató (Première) 1974, Katzenspiel (Cat Play) 1982, Bali 1983; TV films: Der grüne Vogel (The Green Bird) 1979, Offenbach 1995; full-length films: Álmodozások kora (The Age of Day-Dreaming) (Silver Prix, Locarno) 1964, Apa (Father) (Grand Prix, Moscow) 1966, Szerelmesfilm (A Film of Love) 1970, Tüzoltó utca 25 (No. 25 Fireman's Street) (Grand Prix of Locarno) 1973, Budapesti mesék (Budapest Tales) 1976, Bizalom (Confidence) (Silver Bear of Berlin 1981) 1979, Mephisto (Acad. Award 1982, David di Donatello Prize (Italy), Italian Critics' Prize, Critics' Prize, UK) 1981, Colonel Redl (BAFTA Award 1986, Best West German Film—Golden Band) 1985, Hanussen 1988, Meeting Venus 1990, Sweet Emma, Dear Böbe (Silver Bear of Berlin, European Acad. Award for Best Screenplay) 1991, Steadying the Boat (BBC) 1996, Sunshine (European Acad. Award for Best Screenplay, Canadian Acad. Award for Best Film) 1999, Taking Sides 2001, Being Julia 2003, Relatives 2005; operas: Tannhäuser, Paris 1987, Boris Godunov, Leipzig 1993, Il Trovatore, Vienna 1993, The Three Sisters, Budapest 2000 (also Kassel 2002). *Address:* I. S. L.-Film, 1149 Budapest, Róna utca 174 (office); 1132 Budapest, Vácí-6, Hungary (home). *Telephone:* (1) 251-9369 (office); (1) 340-5559 (home). *Fax:* (1) 251-9369 (office); (1) 340-5559 (home). *E-mail:* islfilm@t-online.hu (home).

SZABÓ, Miklós, PhD, DSc; Hungarian archaeologist and academic; *Director, Archaeological Institute, Eötvös Loránd University of Arts and Sciences;* b. 3 July 1940, Szombathely; s. of Dezső Szabó and Irén Süle; m. Ágnes Molnár; three s.; ed Eötvös Loránd Univ. of Arts and Sciences (ELTE); with Dept of

Archaeology Hungarian Nat. Museum 1963–66; with Dept of Antiquities Museum of Fine Arts 1966–85, Deputy Dir Gen. 1985–87; Asst Prof., Dept of Classical Archaeology of ELTE 1983–89, Prof. and Head of Dept 1989, Gen. Vice-Rector 1991–93, Rector 1993–99; research into Ancient Greek and Celtic archaeology, involved in excavations in Greece by the French Inst. of Archaeology in Athens 1970–78; in France 1978, led the Hungarian excavation expedition in Bibracte, France 1988–; Visiting Prof., Univ. of the Sorbonne, Paris 1980–81, Ecole normale supérieure, Paris 1985, Coll. de France 1989, 2000–01, Univ. of Burgundy 2003; Pres. Archaeological Cttee Hungarian Acad. of Sciences 1994; Corresp. mem. Hungarian Acad. of Sciences 1995 (mem. 2001), German Archaeological Inst. 1977, Royal Acad. of Barcelona 1997, Acad. française 2002; Ed. Dissertationes Pannonicae; mem. Editorial Bd of Acta Archaeologica and Études Celtiques; Hon. mem. Greek Archaeological Soc. 1998; Chevalier, Ordre nat. du Mérite 1995, Commdr, Légion d'honneur 2001, Ordre des Arts et Lettres 2001; Dr hc (Burgundy) 1997, (Dijon) 1997, (Bologna) 1999; Kuzsinszky Medal 1984, Collège de France Medal 1989, Rómer Flóris Commemorative Medal 1990, City of Dijon Commemorative Medal 1991. *Publications:* The Celtic Heritage in Hungary 1971, Hellász fénykora (The Golden Age of Greece) 1972, Világtörténelem képekben I, (World History in Pictures I, co-author) 1972, A keleti kelta művészet (Eastern Celtic Art, co-author) 1974, Les Celtes (co-author) 1978, Les Celtes en Pannonie. Contribution à l'histoire de la civilisation celtique dans la cuvette des Karpates 1988, I Celti (co-author) 1991, Les Celtes de l'Est: Le second âge du fer dans la cuvette des Karpates 1992, Decorated Weapons of the La Tène Iron Age in the Carpathian Basin (co-author) 1992, Archaic Terracottas of Boeotia 1994, Storia d'Europa II (co-author) 1994, A la frontière entre l'Est et l'Ouest (co-author) 1998, Prähistorische Goldschätze im Ungarischen Nationalmuseum (co-author) 1999, Trésors préhistoriques de Hongrie (co-author) 2001, Celtes de Hongrie (co-author) 2001, Celtas y Vettones (co-author) 2001. *Address:* Eötvös Loránd University of Arts and Sciences, Múzeum krt. 4/B, 1088 Budapest, Hungary (office). *Telephone:* (1) 411-6554 (office); (1) 200-1743 (home). *Fax:* (1) 411-6553 (office). *E-mail:* archinst@ludens.elte.hu (office).

SZASZ, Thomas Stephen, AB, MD; American psychiatrist, psychoanalyst, writer and academic; *Professor Emeritus of Psychiatry, Upstate Medical Center, State University of New York;* b. (Tamas Istvan Szasz), 15 April 1920, Budapest, Hungary; s. of Julius Szasz and Lily Wellisch; m. Rosine Loshkajian 1951 (divorced 1971); two d.; ed Cincinnati Univ. and Medical Coll.; staff mem., Chicago Inst. for Psychoanalysis 1951–56; mil. service with US Naval Hosp., Bethesda (attained rank of Commdr) 1954–56; Prof. of Psychiatry, State Univ. of NY, Upstate Medical Center 1956–90, Prof. Emer. 1990–; Co-founder and Chair. Bd of Dirs American Asscn for the Abolition of Involuntary Mental Hospitalization Inc. 1970–80; mem. Bd of Dirs, Nat. Council on Crime and Delinquency; Consultant, Cttee on Mental Hygiene, NY State Bar Asscn and other advisory positions; mem. AAAS and other asscns, Int. Editorial Bd The Int. Journal of the Addictions, Contemporary Psychoanalysis, Editorial Bd Journal of Humanistic Psychology, The Humanist, also consulting positions with journals; Hon. Pres. Int. Comm. for Human Rights 1974; Hon. DSc (Allegheny Coll.) 1975, (Univ. Francisco Marroquín, Guatemala) 1979, (State Univ., New York) 2001; Hon. DHL (Towson Univ.) 1999; numerous awards including Martin Buber Award, NY 1974, Mencken Award, Free Press Asscn 1981, 1988, George Washington Award, American Hungarian Foundation 2003, Rollo May Award, Saybrook Graduate School, San Francisco 2007. *Publications:* Pain and Pleasure 1957, The Myth of Mental Illness 1961, 1974, Law, Liberty and Psychiatry 1963, Psychiatric Justice 1965, The Ethics of Psychoanalysis 1965, Ideology and Insanity 1970, The Manufacture of Madness 1970, The Age of Madness 1973, The Second Sin 1973, Ceremonial Chemistry 1974, Heresies 1976, Schizophrenia: The Sacred Symbol of Psychiatry 1976, Karl Kraus and the Soul-Doctors 1976, Psychiatric Slavery 1977, The Theology of Medicine 1977, The Myth of Psychotherapy 1978, Sex By Prescription 1980, Sex: Facts, Frauds and Follies 1981, The Therapeutic State 1984, Insanity: The Idea and its Consequences 1987, The Untamed Tongue: A Dissenting Dictionary 1990, Our Right to Drugs 1992, A Lexicon of Lunacy 1993, Cruel Compassion 1994, The Meaning of Mind 1996, Fatal Freedom: The Ethics and Politics of Suicide 1999, Pharmacracy: Medicine and Politics in America 2001, Liberation by Oppression: A Comparative Study of Slavery and Psychiatry, Words to the Wise: A Medical–Philosophical Dictionary 2004, Faith in Freedom: Libertarian Principles in Psychiatric Practices 2004, My Madness Saved Me: The Madness and Marriage of Virginia Woolf 2006, Coercion as Cure: A Critical History of Psychiatry 2007, The Medicalization of Everyday Life 2007, Psychiatry: The Science of Lies 2008. *Leisure interests:* reading, hiking, swimming. *Address:* Department of Psychiatry, State University of New York, Upstate Medical Center, 750 East Adams Street, Syracuse, NY 13210 (office); 4739 Limberlost Lane, Manlius, NY 13104, USA (home). *Telephone:* (315) 464-3106 (office); (315) 637-8918 (home). *Fax:* (315) 464-3163 (office). *Website:* www.upstate.edu (office); www.szasz.com (home).

SZCZYGLO, Aleksander, PhD; Polish politician; b. 27 Oct. 1963, Jeziorany; ed Univ. of Gdańsk and Univ. of Wisconsin, USA; Asst to Senator Lech Kaczyński, Office of Civic Parl. Caucus, Gdańsk 1990–91; Legal Specialist, Nat. Security Office 1991–92; Dir Office of the Pres., Supreme Chamber of Audit 1992–95; Advisor to Chief Inspector, Cen. Labour Inspectorate 1997; Dir European Educ. and Information Dept, Office of Cttee for European Integration 1997–2000; Advisor to Pres., PKO BP SA 2001; mem. Parl. (Law and Justice) 2001–06; Sec. of State for Nat. Defence 2005–07; Chief of Chancellery of the Pres. 2006–07; Minister of Nat. Defence 2007. *Address:* c/o Law and Justice Party, ul. Nowogrodzka 84/86, 02-018 Warsaw, Poland (office). *Telephone:* (22) 6215035 (office). *Fax:* (22) 6216767 (office). *E-mail:* biuro@pis.org.pl (office). *Website:* www.pis.org.pl (office).

SZÉKELY, Gábor, MA, DLA; Hungarian theatre director and academic; *Faculty Director, University of Drama, Film and Television, Budapest;* b. 26 May 1944, Jászberény; s. of late Árpád Székely and of Irma Csuka; m. Erika Székely 1967; one s. two d.; ed Könyves Kalmán Grammar School, Budapest, Budapest Acad. of Dramatic and Cinematic Art; Asst Dir, Szolnoki Szigligeti Theatre 1968–71, Prin. Dir 1971–72, Theatre Man. and Prin. Dir 1972–78; Prin. Dir Budapest Nat. Theatre 1978–82, apptd Theatre Man. 1982; Theatre Man. Budapest Katona József Theatre 1982–89; teacher of dramatic art and theatre direction, Acad. of Dramatic and Cinematic Art 1972–, Head, Theatre Dirs' Faculty 1990–; has directed in Novi Sad, Stuttgart, Prague Nat. Theatre; invited to direct at Deutsches Theater, Berlin, Comédie Française, Paris 1991, Helsinki City Theatre 1993; Dir Új Szinház Theatre 1993–97; univ. prof. 1991–; guest teacher, Paris Acad. of Dramatic and Cinematic Art 1993; Rector Univ. of Drama, Film and TV, Budapest 2001–06, Faculty Dir 2007–; Dr hc (Tirgu Mures Univ.); Jászai Mari Prize, Merited Artist, Outstanding Artist, Kossuth Prize, critics' prize for best theatre performance and best theatre direction, several times. *Plays directed include:* As You Like It, Troilus and Cressida, Timon of Athens (Shakespeare), Georges Dandin, L'impromptu de Versailles, Don Juan (Molière), The Death of Tarelkin (Kobilin), The Death of Danton, Woyzeck (Büchner); guest performances abroad with Budapest Nat. and Katona József theatres (among others): Cat's Play (Orkény), Family Toth (Orkény), Moscow, Bucharest, Prague, Helsinki; Catullus (Fust), Vienna, Paris (Odeon), Zürich; Le Misanthrope (Molière), Moscow; Coriolanus (Shakespeare), Berlin; The Escape (Bulgakov), Prague. *Leisure interests:* architecture, fine arts. *Address:* Jókai u. 36. II/12, 1066 Budapest, Hungary. *Telephone:* (1) 332-4284.

SZEKERES, Imre, PhD; Hungarian engineer and politician; *Minister of Defence;* b. 9 Sept. 1950, Szolnok; m.; two c.; ed Veszprém Univ.; sec. of communist youth org. at Univ.; Asst Lecturer, Cybernetics Inst., Veszprém Univ. 1974–77; mem. Veszprém City Council 1986, later Deputy Chair. responsible for culture and finances; co-f. Reformkömök movt; Chair. Hungarian Socialist Party (HSP) Org. in Veszprém Co. 1989, headed electoral list during first parl. elections 1990, Nat. Sec. 1990, Vice-Chair. 1990–2004, Deputy Chair. 2004–, electoral campaign chief 1994; mem. Parl. 1994–, Head, HSP parl. group 1994–98; Chair. Parl. Budget and Finance Cttee 1998-2002; Political State Sec., Cabinet of Prime Minister 2002–04; Minister of Defence 2006–; Pres. Hungarian Triathlon Asscn 2003–. *Leisure interest:* triathalon. *Address:* Ministry of Defence, 1055 Budapest, Balaton u. 7–11, Hungary (office). *Telephone:* (1) 474-1114 (office). *Fax:* (1) 474-1285 (office). *E-mail:* media@hm.gov.hu (office). *Website:* www.hm.gov.hu (office).

SZENES, Lt-Gen. Zoltán, MSc, PhD, CSc; Hungarian army officer (retd); *Associate Professor, Department of Security and Social Sciences, Zrínyi Miklós National Defence University;* b. 23 July 1951, Köcsk; m. Ibolya Szenes; one d.; ed Mil. Tech. Acad., Budapest, War Coll. of Logistics and Transportation, Leningrad (now St Petersburg), Russia, Hungarian Acad. of Science, Budapest Univ. of Econs, Royal Coll. of Defence Studies, London, UK; joined Hungarian People's Army 1969; assigned to 25th Tank Regt, Tata 1973–74; staff officer, 11th Tank Div. 1974–75; Chief of Staff for Logistics, 9th Mechanized Div., Kaposvár 1979–82; Sr Lecturer, Dept of Security and Social Sciences, Zrínyi Miklós Nat. Defence Univ., Budapest 1985–86, Assoc. Prof. 2005–; Head of Logistics Dept 1986–91; Chief of Supply Services of Defence Staff 1991–92; Fellow, Royal Coll. of Defence Studies, London 1995–96; Head of Educ. and Science Dept, Ministry of Defence 1996–98; Mil. Rep. to NATO and WEU, Brussels, Belgium 1998–99; ACOS Logistics, AFSOUTH HQ, Naples, Italy 1999–2002; Dir of Defence Staff 2002–03, Chief of Defence Staff 2003–05; apptd Maj.-Gen. 2002, Lt-Gen. 2003–05 (retd); Visiting Prof. of NATO Studies, Baltic Defence Coll., Tartu, Estonia; Co-Pres. Budapesti Honvéd Sport Club; mem. Hungarian Acad. of Sciences, Hungarian Logistics Asscn, Hungarian Soc. of Mil. Sciences, Int. Inst. for Strategic Studies, London, Eurodefence, Hungary; Cross of the Legion of Honour (Officer Grade) 2004, Commdr's Cross, Order of Merit (Mil. Div.) 2004; Meritorious Service Award, Pro Scientia Gold Medal, Tanárky Sándor Price Award, Hungarian Asscn of Mil. Sciences, Budapest, Hungarian NATO Enlargement Medal, NATO KFOR and SFOR Medals, Officer Service Medal (First Class), Andrássy Gyula Price Award 2001, NATO Service Award for the Period 1998–2002 2004. *Publications:* The Implications of NATO for Civil-Military Relations in Hungary 2001, Future of NATO (in Academic and Applied Research in Military Science journal) 2005, The Effects of Peacekeeping on the HDF (in Peacekeeping Today and Tomorrow) 2006. *Leisure interests:* photography, reading, squash, running and gardening. *Address:* Zrínyi Miklós Nat. Defence Univ., 1101, Budapest, Hungary (office). *Telephone:* (1) 432-9087 (office); (30) 2428914 (mobile) (office). *Fax:* (1) 432-9217 (office). *E-mail:* szenes .zoltan@zmne.hu (office); szenes@hotmail.com (home). *Website:* www.zmne.hu (office).

SZENTIVÁNYI, Gábor; Hungarian economist and diplomatist; *State Secretary and Political Director, Ministry of Foreign Affairs;* b. 9 Oct. 1952, Vaskút; s. of József Szentiványi and Ilona Fejes; m. Gabriella Gönczi; one s. one d.; ed Univ. of Econ. Sciences, Budapest; joined Foreign Service 1975, positions in Baghdad 1976–81, Washington, DC 1986–91; mem. staff Protocol Dept, Ministry of Foreign Affairs 1982–85, Spokesman and Dir Gen. for Press and Int. Information Dept 1994–97, Deputy State Sec. 2002–06, State Sec. and Political Dir 2007–; Amb. to UK 1997–2002, to the Netherlands 2004–07; Man. Dir Burson-Marsteller's Budapest office 1991–94; mem. Hungarian Foreign Affairs Soc., Hungarian Atlantic Council; Freeman, City of London 2000; Hon. GCVO, Officer, Order of Prince Henry the Navigator 1982, Grand Cross of Merit (Chile) 2002, Middle Cross of the Order of Merit (Hungary) 2004, Kt Grand Cross, Order of Oranje-Nassau (Netherlands) 2007. *Leisure interests:* boating, reading. *Address:* Ministry of Foreign Affairs, Bem rkp. 47, 1027

Budapest, Hungary (office). *Telephone:* (1) 458-1936 (office). *Fax:* (1) 458-1811 (office). *E-mail:* GSzentivanyi@kum.hu (office).

SZILÁGYI, János György, PhD; Hungarian art historian and research curator; b. 16 July 1918, Budapest; s. of Hugo Szilágyi and Adél Braun; m. Mária Rabinovszky; one d.; ed Pázmány Péter Univ. of Arts and Sciences; research fellow at the Classical Dept, Museum of Fine Arts of Budapest 1941, Head of Dept 1952–93; Prof., Budapest Univ. of Arts and Sciences 1952–2003; mem. Cttee on History of Ancient Civilizations of the Hungarian Acad. of Sciences, Istituto Nazionale di Studi Etruschi, Florence, Deutsches Archäologisches Institut, Istituto per la Storia e l'Archeologia della Magna Grecia; Ábel Jenő Commemorative Medal, Móra Ferenc Commemorative Medal, Kossuth Award 1991, Eötvös Wreath 1996, Rómer Flóris Commemorative Medal. *Publications include:* Ceramica etrusco-corinzia figurata I–II 1992–98, In Search of Pelasgian Ancestors 2002, Corpus Vasorum Antiquorum, Hongrie, fasc 1–2 1981–2007; numerous works on Greek and Etruscan art and culture. *Address:* Museum of Fine Arts, PF 463, 1396 Budapest 62 (office); Margit Körut 7, III, 1 Budapest, 1024 Hungary (home). *Telephone:* (1) 469-7123 (office); (1) 335-1298 (home). *Fax:* (1) 469-7171 (office).

SZILI, Katalin, DJur; Hungarian lawyer and politician; *Speaker, Országgyülés (National Assembly);* b. 13 May 1956, Barcs; m. Miklós Molnár 1977; raising two c. of friends who died in an accident; ed Nagy Lajos Grammar School, Pécs, Janus Pannonius, Univ. of Pécs, Eötvös Loránd Univ., Budapest; mem. Hungarian Socialist Workers' Party 1983–89, mem. Hungarian Socialist Party (MSZP) 1989–, Chair. MSZP Nat. Women's Section 2000–02, MSZP Vice-Pres. 2000–04; clerk for guardianship affairs, later group leader, Pécs Council –1985; legal advisor to Southern Transdanubia Water Man. Directorate 1985–92, later dept head Southern Transdunabia Environmental Protection Inspectorate; mem. Pécs Municipal Ass. 1992–94; mem. of Parliament for Pécs Constituency No. 2 1994–; State Sec., Ministry for Environmental Protection and Regional Devt 1994–98; Deputy Speaker of Országgyülés (Nat. Ass.) and mem. Council of Elders 1998–2002, Speaker 2002–; Chair. Council of Elders 2002–06; Co-ordinating Chair. for Chairpersons of European Parl. 2004–05; Grand Cross of Belgium 2003, Grand Cross, Order of Merit (Germany) 2004, Commdr, Légion d'honneur 2005, Grand Gold Service Medal with Ribbon (Austria), Congressional Great Cross of Peru 2005, Commdr's Cross, Order of Merit (Poland), Order of Merit (Mongolia) 2006, Hon. Medal of the Bulgarian Pres. 2007, Spanish Legion of Honour Grand Cross 2007; Dr hc (L. N. Gumilev Eurasian Univ., Kazakhstan) 2007; 18 Trees in the Yad Vashem Memorial Park, Israel 2005, Medal of Honour, Asscn of Displaced Persons 2007. *Leisure interest:* environmental protection. *Address:* Országgyülés (National Assembly), 1055 Budapest, Kossuth Lajos tér 1–3, PO Box 1357, Hungary (office). *Telephone:* (1) 441-4000 (office); (1) 441-4333 (office). *Fax:* (1) 441-4806 (office). *E-mail:* katalin.szili@parlament.hu (office). *Website:* www.szilikatalin.hu; www.mkogy.hu (office).

SZILVÁSY, György, PhD; Hungarian politician; *Minister without Portfolio, in charge of Civilian National Security Services;* b. 29 April 1958, Budapest; ed Karl Marx Univ. of Econs, Loránd Eötvös Univ. of Arts and Sciences; Govt Chief Consultant, Office of Council of Ministers 1989; Deputy Minister, Office of the Prime Minister 1989–90, also Sec., Bd of Supervision of Hungarian TV and Radio; Deputy Sec. of State, Office of the Prime Minister 1990–95; Sec. of State, Ministry of Environment and Regional Devt 1995–98, of Children, Youth and Sports 2002–03, of Culture 2003–04, of the Interior 2004–05; Titular Sec. of State and Chief of Cabinet, Office of the Prime Minister 2005–06, Political Sec. of State 2006, Minister in charge of Prime Minister's Office 2006–07, Minister without Portfolio in charge of Civilian Nat. Security Services 2007–; Dir Altus Investment and Assets Man. Inc. 1998–2000; CEO Perfekt Inc. 2000–02. *Address:* Office of the Prime Minister, 1055 Budapest, Kossuth Lajos tér 1–3, Hungary (office). *Telephone:* (1) 441-4000 (office). *Fax:* (1) 268-3050 (office). *E-mail:* webmaster@meh.hu (office). *Website:* www.meh.hu (office).

SZINETÁR, Miklós; Hungarian theatre and film director; b. 8 Feb. 1932, Budapest; m. Ildikó Hámori, one s. one d.; ed High School of Dramatic Art; producer of Budapest Operetta Theatre, Chief Producer 1953–60; Chief Producer of Hungarian TV, artistic Dir Chief Artistic Dir 1962–, Deputy Chair. of Hungarian TV 1979–90; Man. Dir of Budapest Operetta Theatre 1993–96; Chief Man. Dir of Hungarian State Opera House 1996–2001, Intendant-Gen. Dir 2002–; also Univ. Prof.; Golden Nympha, Monte Carlo 1970, Best Director, Prague TV Festival 1976–79, Silver Asterix, Trieste 1980. *Films include:* Délibáb minden mennyiségben 1961, Janos Háry 1965, Baleset 1967, Csárdás Fürstine (The Csardas Princess, UK) (also adaptation) 1971, Az erőd (The Fortress) (also screenwriter) 1979. *Television:* Éjszakai repülés 1963, Halálnak halála 1969, Az ember tragédiája (The Tragedy of the Man, USA) 1969, Igéző 1969, Rózsa Sándor (mini-series) 1979, A Kékszakállú herceg vára (Bluebeard's Castle) 1981, Der Kronprinz 1988, Così fan Tutte, Fidelio, The Barber of Seville, The Life of Franz Liszt. *Publications:* Kalandsaim 1987, Igy Kell Ezt 2003. *Address:* Magyar Állami Operaház, Andrássy út 22, 1061 Budapest (office); Bethlen Gábor u. 16, 2011 Budakalász, Hungary (home). *Telephone:* (36) 13124642 (office); (36) 26343000 (home). *Fax:* (36) 26540380 (home). *E-mail:* szini1@axelero.hu (home).

SZMAJDZIŃSKI, Jerzy Andrzej; Polish economist and politician; b. 9 April 1952, Wrocław; m.; two s.; ed Acad. of Econs, Wrocław; activist, Fed. of Socialist Unions of Polish Youth, Socialist Union of Polish Youth 1975–89 (Chair. 1986–89); Head of Dept, Cen. Cttee Polish United Workers' Party, (PZPR) 1989–90; mem. Social Democracy of Polish Repub. (SdRP) 1990–99, Sec. Gen. 1993–98, Deputy Chair. 1998–99; mem. Democratic Left Alliance Party 1999–; Deputy to Sejm (Parl.) 1985–89, 1991–, Vice Pres. of Sejm 2007–; Chair. Cttee of Nat. Defence 1993–97, Deputy Chair. 1997–2001; Chair. Sejm Democratic Left Alliance (SLD) 1995–97, Deputy Chair. 1997–; Deputy Chair. Democratic Left Alliance Dec. 1999–; Minister of Nat. Defence 2001–05. *Leisure interests:* history, sport. *Address:* Sejm (Assembly), 00-902 Warsaw, ul. Wiejska 4/6 (office); c/o Democratic Left Alliance (Sojusz Lewicy Demokratycznej), 00-419 Warsaw, ul. Rozbrat 44a, Poland. *Telephone:* (22) 285927 (office). *E-mail:* zjablon@sejm.gov.pl (office). *Website:* www.sejm.gov.pl (office); www.sld.org.pl.

SZOKA, HE Cardinal Edmund Casimir, BA; American ecclesiastic; b. 14 Sept. 1927, Grand Rapids, Mich.; s. of Casimir Szoka and Mary Wolgat; ordained priest 1954, Bishop of Gaylord, Mich. 1971–81; Bishop of Detroit 1981–90, Archbishop Emer. 1990–; Cardinal-Priest of Ss. Andrea e Gregorio al Monte Celio 1988–; Pres. of Pref. of Econ. Affairs of Holy See, Roman Curia 1990–97; Pres. of Governatorate of Vatican City State, Roman Curia 1997–2006, Pres. Emer. 2006–; Pres. of Vatican City State, Roman Curia 2001–06; Second Sec. Council for Relations with States; mem. Congregations for the Causes of Saints, for the Bishops, for the Evangelization of Peoples, for the Clergy, for Insts of Consecrated Life and for Socs of Apostolic Life. *Address:* c/o Secretariat of State, Palazzo Apostolico Vaticano, 00120 Città del Vaticano, Rome, Italy.

SZŐNYI, Erzsébet; Hungarian musician; b. 25 April 1924; d. of Jenő Szőnyi and Erzsébet Piszanoff; m. Dr. Lajos Gémes 1948; two s.; ed Music Acad., Budapest and Paris Conservatoire; teacher of music at a Budapest grammar school 1945–48, Music Acad., Budapest 1948–; leading Prof. of Music Acad. 1960–81; Vice-Pres. Int. Soc. for Music Educ. 1970–74; Co-Chair. Hungarian Kodály Soc. 1978–2003, Chair. 2007–, Co-Chair. Bárdos Soc. 1988–, Forum of Hungarian Musicians 1995–; Hon. Pres. Hungarian Choir Asscn 1990–; Gen. adviser on methodology, Int. Kodály Soc. 1979–; mem. Chopin Soc. of Warsaw, Liszt Soc. of Hungary; mem. Hungarian Acad. of Art 1992–, Hungarian Composers' Soc. 1999–; Dr hc (Duquesne Univ., Pittsburgh) 2006; Erkel Prize 1959, Hungarian Repub. Medal 1993 Apácai Csere János Prize 1994, Bartók-Pásztory Prize 1995, 2004, Prize for Artistic Excellence 2000, Zoltán Kodály Prize 2001, Hungarian Heritage Prize 2004, Hungarian Choir Asscn Medal 2004, Kossuth Prize 2006. *Compositions include:* Concerto for Organ and Orchestra; symphonic works: Musica Festiva, Divertimento 1 and 2, Prelude and Fugue, Three Ideas in Four Movements; operas: Tragedy of Firenze, A Gay Lament, Break in Transmission, Elfrida (madrigal opera) 1987–, several children's operas; chamber music, oratorios, vocal compositions, etc. *Publications:* Methods of Musical Reading and Writing, Kodály's Principles in Practice, Travels in Five Continents, Twentieth-Century Musical Methods. *Leisure interests:* gardening, cooking. *Address:* Ormódi-utca 13, 1124 Budapest XII, Hungary (home). *Telephone:* (1) 356-7329 (home).

SZÖRÉNYI, Levente; Hungarian musician, composer and songwriter; b. 26 April 1945, Gmunden, Austria; m. (divorced); ed Coll. of Music; guitar player; worked with János Bródy 1965–; pop musician with Mediterrán and Balassa 1963–64, with Illés 1965–73; dance participant, Még fáj minden csók (song festival) 1966; Founding mem. Fonográf (band) 1974–81; retd from theatre 1984; First Prize Hungarian Radio Amateur Competition 1965, SZOT (Trade Union) Award 1981, Composer of the Year 1983, Erkel Ferenc Award 1983, KISZ (Youth Org.) Award. *Soundtracks include:* Ezek a fiatalok 1967, Extázis 5-7-ig 1969, Eltávozott a nap, Locsolókocsi, Pókfoci, A Koncert 1982, István a Király 1983, Attila Isten kardja (opera) 1993, Veled Uram! (opera) 2000, Ének a csodaszarvasról 2001. *Compositions include:* Human Rights (Oratory) 1968, Kömíves Kelemen (rock ballad) 1982, István a Király (rock opera) 1983, Fehér Anna (rock ballad) 1988, Fénylő Ölednek édes Örömében (Innin and Dumuzi—oratory) 1989. *Address:* Mátru u. 9, 1029 Budapest, Hungary (office). *E-mail:* szorenyi@c2.hu (office). *Website:* ummagumma.hu/szorenyi.

SZOSTAK, Jack W., BS, PhD; American molecular biologist and academic; *Professor, Department of Genetics, Harvard Medical School;* b. 9 Nov. 1952, London, England; ed McGill Univ., Canada, Cornell Univ.; Asst Prof., Sidney Farber Cancer Inst. and Dept of Biological Chemistry, Harvard Medical School 1979–83, Assoc. Prof., Dana Farber Cancer Inst. and Dept of Biological Chem. 1983–84, Assoc. Prof., Dept of Genetics 1984–87, Prof. 1988–; Assoc. Molecular Biologist, Dept of Molecular Biology, Mass Gen. Hosp. 1984–87, Molecular Biologist 1988–, Alex Rich Distinguished Investigator 2000–; Investigator, Howard Hughes Medical Inst. 1998–; Co-Chair. Nat. Research Council Cttee on the Origin and Evolution of Life 2003–; mem. NAS 1998–; Fellow, New York Acad. of Sciences 1999–; mem. Editorial Bd Chemistry and Biology 1994–; Penhallow Prize in Botany, McGill Univ. 1972, NAS Award in Molecular Biology 1994, Louis Vuitton-Moet Hennesey 'Vinci of Excellence' Award 1996, Hans Sigrist Prize, Univ. of Bern, Switzerland 1997, Genetics Soc. of America Medal 2000, ACS Harrison Howe Award 2003, Albert Lasker Award for Basic Medical Research 2006. *Publications:* over 170 papers in scientific journals. *Address:* Szostak Lab, CCIB 7215, Simches Research Center, 185 Cambridge Street, Boston, MA 02114; Department of Molecular Biology, Massachusetts General Hospital, Wellman 9, Fruit Street, Boston, MA 02114, USA (office). *Telephone:* (617) 726-5981 (office). *Fax:* (617) 726-6893 (office). *E-mail:* szostak@molbio.mgh.harvard.edu (office). *Website:* genetics.mgh.harvard.edu/szostakweb (office).

SZOSTEK, Andrzej Ryszard, BPhil, Dr habil.; Polish ecclesiastic and academic; *Professor of Ethics and Philosophy, Catholic University of Lublin;* b. 9 Nov. 1945, Grudziądz; ed Catholic Univ. of Lublin; ordained priest 1974; with Dept of Ethics, Catholic Univ. of Lublin 1970–, scientific worker 1971–, Extraordinary Prof. 1992–99, Ordinary Prof. of Ethics and Philosophy 2000–, Head of Dept of Ethics, mem. man. team Inst. of John Paul II 1983–98, Pro-Rector 1992–98, Rector 1998–2004; numerous visiting lectureships; Lecturer, Superior Monastic House, Lublin 1987–90; Provincial Councillor Marians 1987–93; mem. Cttee of Formation of Marians 1975–90, Scientific Soc., Catholic Univ. of Lublin 1980–, Polish Philosophical Soc., Lublin 1982, Int.

Cttee of Theology, Vatican Congregation of Religious Studies 1992–98, Lublin Scientific Soc. 1998–2001 (Distinguished mem. 2001–), Pontificia Academia Pro Vita 2001–; Order of Merit 2001, Palmes Académiques (France) 2001, Kawaler Orderu Odrodzenia Polski (2005 r.); Hon. Fellow, St Mary's Coll., London 2000; Medal, Comm. of Nat. Educ. 2001, Brązowe Odznaczenie, Za załugi w obronności kraju 2002, Honorowe Odznaczenie (Premium Honorificum) Lubelskiego Towarzystwa Naukowego 2003, Nagroda naukowa im Wł. Pietrzaka 2003, Nagroda Rektora KUL I stopnia 2005, Wyróżnienie Lubelskiego Towarzystwa Naukowego Resolutio pro Laude Academica 2005. *Publications:* Rules and Exceptions – Philosophical Aspects of the Discussion about Absolute Norms in Contemporary Theology 1980, Nature–Reason–Freedom. Philosophical Analysis of the Concept of Creative Intellect in Contemporary Moral Theology 1989, Talks on Ethics 1993, On Dignity, Truth and Love 1995 and numerous other publs. *Leisure interests:* mountaineering, music, chess. *Address:* Katolicki Uniwersytet Lubelski, Katedra Etyki, Al. Racławickie 14, 20-950 Lublin (office); ul. Bazylianówka 54B, 20-160 Lublin, Poland (home). *Telephone:* (81) 4454039 (office); (81) 7433773 (home). *Fax:* (81) 4454123 (office). *E-mail:* rektorat@kul.lublin.pl (office). *Website:* www.kul.lublin.pl (office).

SZUMSKI, Henryk; Polish army officer; b. 6 April 1941, Potulice; m. Wiesława Jawor; three s. one d.; ed Officer's School, Poznan, Gen. Staff Acad. Polish Armed Forces, Warsaw, Gen. Staff Acad. Armed Forces of USSR, Moscow; career soldier 1964–; commdr section and co. of brigade 1964–68, Chief of Staff and Commdr 1971–76, Chief of Staff and Commdr of 16th Armoured Div. 1976–78, Commdr, 12th Mechanized Div., Szczecin 1980–84, Chief of Staff of Pomeranian Mil. Dist 1984–86, Deputy Chief Gen. Staff for Operational Matters, 1986–87, Commdr Silesian Mil. Dist 1987–89, First Deputy Chief Gen. Staff, 1989–90, Chief Main Bd of Combat Training, 1990–92; Brig.-Gen. 1983, Maj. Gen. 1988, Lt-Gen. 1997; Inspector of Leadership of Gen. Staff 1993–97, Chief of Gen. Staff 1997–2000; mem. Nat. Security Council 2000–05; Commandory Cross with Star, Poland, Legion d'Honneur, France, Legion of Merit, USA. *Leisure interests:* history, literature, sport. *Address:* Kancelaria Prezydenta ZP, 00-902 Warsaw, ul. Uiejska 10 (office); 05-806 Komorów, ul. Bugai 14A, Poland (home). *Telephone:* (22) 6952387 (office); (22) 7989487 (home). *Fax:* (22) 6952969 (office); (22) 6826488 (home).

SZŰRÖS, Mátyás, PhD; Hungarian politician and diplomatist; b. 11 Sept. 1933, Püspökladány; ed Moscow Univ. Inst. of Int. Relations, Budapest Univ. of Econ. Sciences; on staff of Foreign Ministry 1959–65; staff mem. HSWP 1965–74, Deputy Leader Foreign Dept HSWP Cen. Cttee 1974–75, Head 1982–83; Amb. to GDR 1975–78, to USSR 1978–82; mem. Cen. Cttee HSWP 1978, Secr. 1983–89; mem. Parl. 1985–, Chair. Foreign Relations Parl. Cttee 1985–89 (mem. 1998–), Pres. of Parl. March–Oct. 1989, Acting Pres. 1989–90, Deputy Speaker 1990–94; Chair. Hungarian Group of IPU 1989–90, 1994–2002, mem. Exec. Cttee IPU 1994–96; Gen. Pres. SDP 2003–05; Chair. Ópusztaszer Historical Commemorative Cttee 1989–98, Bd Trustees Illyés Foundation 1994–99, Trustee 1999–; mem. Council of Hundreds (World Fed. of Hungarians) 1997–; Freeman of Püspökladány 1996, of Beregszász 1997; Bocskai Award 1996. *Publications:* Hazánk és a nagyvilág (Homeland and World) 1985, Hazánk és Európa (Homeland and Europe) 1987, Magyarságról-Külpolitikáról (On Being Hungarian and on Foreign Policy) 1989, Cselekvő politikával a magyarságért-Politikai portré (1988–96) (Active policy for Hungary, portrait of a politician) 1996, Köztársaság született harangszavú délben (1989. október 23) (The Republic Was Born and the Bells Rang at Noon, 23 October 1989) 1999, National Politics and Joining. Questions of Integration 2001, Hoggan tovább a rőgős utakon (How Much Marching Further on the Thorny Way) 2003. *Address:* Hungarian National Assembly, 1055 Budapest, Kossuth Lajos tér 1-3, Hungary (office). *Telephone:* (1) 441-5067 (office); (1) 441-5068 (office). *Fax:* (1) 441-5972 (office). *E-mail:* secretariate@ipu.parlament.hu (office).

SZYMANCZYK, Michael E., BS; American business executive; *Chairman and CEO, Altria Group, Inc.;* ed Indiana Univ.; joined Proctor & Gamble 1971, served in several sales and marketing positions –1987; Vice-Pres. of Sales, Kraft Inc. 1987–88, Vice-Pres. Retail Operations 1988, Sr Vice-Pres. Swift-Eckrich Inc. 1989; Sr Vice-Pres. of Sales Philip Morris USA, New York 1990–97, COO July-Nov. 1997, Pres. and CEO Nov. 1997–, Chair. 2002–; Chair. and CEO Altria Group Inc. (parent co.) 2008–; mem. Bd Trustees Univ. of Richmond, Virginia Commonwealth Univ. School of Eng Foundation, United Negro Coll. Fund, Richmond Performing Arts Center; fmr Chair. and current mem. Dean's Advisory Council for Indiana Univ. Kelley School of Business; fmr mem. Bd Futures for Children. *Address:* Altria Group, Inc., 120 Park Avenue, New York, NY 10017, USA (office). *Telephone:* (917) 663-4000 (office). *Fax:* (917) 663-2167 (office). *E-mail:* info@altria.com (office). *Website:* www.altria.com (office).

SZYMANEK-DERESZ, Jolanta; Polish government official and lawyer; b. 12 July 1954, Przedbórz; d. of Tadeusz Szymanek and Zenajda Szymanek; m. Pawel Deresz; one d.; ed Warsaw Univ.; worked at Municipal Court, Warsaw 1977–82; judge, Dist Court 1982–87, attorney 1987–; fmr Spokeswoman, Warsaw Attorney Council; mem. Int. League of Right to Competition 1996–; Under-Sec. of State at the Chancellery 2000, Head of the Chancellery 2000–05; Deputy to Sejm 2005–; Vice-Pres. Democratic Left Alliance (Sojusz Lewicy Demokratycznej) 2008–. *Publications include:* articles in Polish press on protection of personal rights, trade marks and patents. *Leisure interests:* tennis, skiing, literature (especially essays of Bohumil Hrabal). *Address:* ul. Stary Rynek 27, 09- 400 Płock, Poland (office). *Telephone:* (24) 3644151 (office). *E-mail:* Jolanta.Szymanek-Deresz@sejm.pl. *Website:* szymanek-deresz.sejm.pl (office).

SZYMBORSKA, Wisława; Polish poet, translator and literary critic; b. 2 July 1923, Kórnik, nr Poznań; ed Jagiellonian Univ., Kraków; first work 'Szukam slowa' (I am Looking for a Word) published in Dziennik Polski daily 1945; Poetry Ed. and columnist, Życie Literackie (weekly) 1953–81; mem. Polish Writers' Asscn 1951–81, 1981–, mem. Gen. Bd 1978–83; poems have been translated into (and published in book form in) English, German, Swedish, Italian, Danish, Hebrew, Hungarian, Czech, Slovakian, Serbo-Croatian, Romanian, Bulgarian and other languages, and have also been published in numerous foreign anthologies of Polish poetry; Gold Cross of Merit 1955; Hon. DLitt (Poznań) 1995; Nobel Prize for Literature 1996, Goethe Award (Frankfurt) 1991, Herder Award 1995, Polish PEN Club Award 1996. *Publications:* poetry: Dlatego żyjemy (That's Why We're Alive) 1952, Pytania zadawane sobie (Questioning Oneself) 1954, Wołanie do Yeti (Calling Out to Yeti) 1957, Sól (Salt) 1962, Sto pociech (No End of Fun) 1967, Wybór wierszy (Selected Poems) 1967, 1973, Poezje 1970, Wszelki wypadek (Could Have) 1972, Wielka liczba (A Large Number) 1976, Poezje wybrane (Selected Poems II), Ludzie na moście (The People on the Bridge) 1986, Koniec i początek 1993, Widok z ziarnkiem piasku (View With a Grain of Sand) 1996, Poems New and Collected 1957–97 1998, Wiersze wybrane (Selected Poems III) 2000, Chwila (A Moment) 2002, Rymowanki dla dużych dzieci 2003, Dwukropek 2005. *Address:* Polish Writers' Association, ul. Kanonicza 7, 31-002 Kraków, Poland.

TABACHNYK, Dmytro Volodimirovych, DS; Ukrainian politician and historian; b. 26 Nov. 1964, Kiev; s. of Volodomir Igorovich Tabachnyk and Alla Viktorovna Tabachnyk; m. Tetyana Evgenyovna Nazarova; ed Kiev State Univ.; fmr copyist, then restorer, Cen. State Archives of Cinematography, Documents of Ukraine; jr researcher, Inst. of History of Ukraine, Ukrainian Acad. of Sciences, leading researcher, Inst. of Politology 1997–; Deputy, Kiev City Soviet 1990–94; Deputy Head Kiev City Exec. Comsomol Cttee 1991–92; Head of Press Service, Cabinet of Ministers 1992–93; First Deputy Head, State Cttee on Publishing, Polygraphy and Book Trade 1993–94; Head of Admin., Presidency 1994–96, Counsellor 1997–98, Head, Constitution Comm. 1994–96; People's Deputy of Ukraine of III, IV Convocations 1998–2003, Deputy of Verkhovna Rada (Party of the Regions), Crimean Autonomous Repub. 2006; Vice-Prime Minister of Ukraine 2002–05, responsible for Humanitarian Issues 2006–07; mem. Verkhovna Rada (Parl.) 2007–; Dir Nat. Expert Inst. of Ukraine 2005–; Prof., Ukrainian Acad. of State Man. 1995–; Corresp. mem. Acad. of Juridical Sciences. *Publications:* over 400 papers. *Leisure interests:* collecting art, theatre, books. *Address:* Verkhovna Rada of Ukraine, 01008 Kiev, vul. Hryshevskogo 5, Ukraine (office). *Telephone:* (44) 255-31-55 (office). *Fax:* (44) 255-31-55 (office). *E-mail:* Tabachnyk.Dmytro@rada.gov.ua (office). *Website:* www.partyofregions.org.ua (office).

TABAI, Ieremia T., CMG; I-Kiribati fmr head of state and international organization official; b. 1950, Nonouti; m.; two c.; ed King George V School, Tarawa, St Andrew's Coll., Christchurch, NZ, Victoria Univ., Wellington, NZ; mem. Gilbert Islands (later Kiribati) House of Ass. 1974–91; fmr Leader of the Opposition; Chief Minister of the Gilbert Islands 1978–79, also Minister of Local Govt; Pres. of Kiribati and Minister of Foreign Affairs (fmrly Gilbert Islands) 1979–91; Sec.-Gen. South Pacific Forum 1991–98; Chair. Commonwealth Observer Group 2001; Co-Owner New Star newspaper; Hon. LLD (Vic. Univ. of Wellington). *Address:* c/o Ministry of Foreign Affairs, PO Box 68, Bairiki, Tarawa, Kiribati.

TABAKOV, Oleg Pavlovich; Russian actor and director; b. 17 Aug. 1935, Saratov; s. of Pavel K. Tabakov and Maria A. Beresovskaya; m. 1st Lyudmila Krilova 1959 (divorced); one s. one d.; m. 2nd Marina V. Zudina 1995; one s.; ed Moscow Arts Theatre Studio-School; Co-founder and actor with Sovremennik Theatre 1957–83; with Moscow Arts Theatre 1983–; stage debut 1956; film debut 1957; mem. CPSU 1965–91; master of theatre training 1976–; Assoc. Prof. State Inst. of Theatre Arts (GITIS) 1976–85; Prof. Moscow Arts Theatre Studio School 1985–, Chancellor 1986–; Founder and Producer, Moscow Theatre Studio (now Oleg Tabakov Theatre) 1974–; Artistic Dir Moscow A. Chekhov Arts Theatre; directed and taught in numerous countries; f. and teacher Stanislavsky Summer School, Cambridge, Mass. 1992–; Founder and Pres. Russian-American Performing Arts Center 1992–; People's Artist of the USSR 1987; State Prize for Acting 1967. *Films include:* The Tight Knot 1956, War and Peace 1967, Noisy Day 1960, Light My Star, Light 1969, Kashtanka 1975, Unfinished Play for Mechanical Piano 1977, A Few Days of I. I. Oblomov's Life (Oxford Int. Festival Prize for best male actor 1980) 1979, Flights of Fancy 1983, The Art of Living in Odessa 1989, The Inner Circle 1991, The Shadows 1991, Shirli-Myrli 1995, Moskovskiye kanikuly 1995, The White Dunes 1996, Three Stories 1997, Sympathy Seeker 1997, Prezident i yego vnuchka 2000, Taking Sides 2001, Statski sovetnik 2005. *Stage roles include:* Misha in Always Alive 1956, Aleksandr in The Same Old Story 1966, Brother Lymon in The Ballad of Sad Café 1966, Klava in Always on Sale 1965, Major in Tooth, Others and Major 1971, Balalaykin in Balalaykin and Co. 1974, Anchugin in Provincial Anecdotes 1975, 1996, Malvolio in Twelfth Night 1975, Peter Stockman in Dr. Stockman 1979, Salieri in Amadeus 1983, Hailmayer in Judgers 1985, Sorin in Seagull 1987, Buton in Cabal of Hippocrates 1989, Tacker in I Ought to be in Pictures 1990, Meyer Volf in My Big Land 1991, Famusov in Woe from Wisdom 1992, Uncle in The Same Old Story 1993, Tallyran in Le Souper 1994, Ivan Kolomiytsev in The Last Ones 1995; has directed Champions, Every Wise Man Has a Fool in his Sleeve, The Same Old Story, Goldoni's Revenge. *Publication:* My Real Life. *Leisure interest:* driving a car. *Address:* Moscow A. Chekhov Arts Theatre, Kamergurskiy per. 3, 103009 Moscow (office); Chernysherskogo 39, Apt. 3, 103062 Moscow, Russia (home). *Telephone:* (495) 229-33-12 (office); (495) 924-76-90 (home). *Fax:* (495) 975-21-96. *E-mail:* tabakov@theatre.ru (office). *Website:* www.tabakov.ru (office).

TABAKSBLAT, Morris; Dutch business executive; b. Rotterdam; m.; two s. one d.; ed Leiden Univ.; joined Unilever 1964, mem. Bd 1984, mem. Unilever Special Cttee 1992–99, Chair. and CEO 1994–99; Chair. Reed Elsevier Group plc and Reed Elsevier plc 1999–2005, Chair. Supervisory Bd 1999–2005; Pres. Aegon NV 2000–; Chair. European Round Table of Industrialists –2001; mem. Bd of Govs., Leiden Univ. Medical Centre, Mauritshuis Museum, The Hague; Vice-Chair. USA Conf. Bd; Chair. Supervisory Bd, AEGON NV, TNT Post Group NV, TPG NV; mem. Int. Advisory Bds. Salomon Smith Barney, Renault Nissan; Hon. KBE.

TABECARU, Nicolae; Moldovan politician and diplomatist; b. 20 Aug. 1955, Nadrechnoye, Odessa Region, Ukraine; m.; two c.; ed Moldovan State Univ., Moscow Diplomatic Acad.; diplomatic service 1989–; Head Protocol Dept, Ministry of Foreign Affairs 1990; First Sec. Perm. Mission of Repub. of Moldova to UN 1991–92; Head, Dept for UN and Disarmament, Ministry of Foreign Affairs 1992–93; Head, Protocol Diplomatic Dept 1993; Counsellor, Minister-Counsellor, Embassy in Belgium (also accred to Luxembourg, UK, NATO and EC) 1993–96; Head, Dept of Europe and N America, Ministry of

Foreign Affairs 1996–97; Adviser on Problems of Foreign Policy to Moldovan Pres. 1997–; Minister of Foreign Affairs 1997–99; fmr Amb. to Germany. *Address:* c/o Ministry of Foreign Affairs, Piaţa Marii Adunari Nationale 1, 2033 Chişinău, Moldova.

TABIANI, Mahmoud, PhD; Iranian electrical engineer and academic; *Professor and Director, Electronics Research Centre, Sharif University of Technology;* b. 1950; ed Sharif Univ. of Tech., Tehran and MIT, USA; Prof., Electrical Eng Dept, Sharif Univ. of Tech. 1979–, Dir Electronics Research Centre; Pres. Iranian Research Org. for Science and Tech. 1982–89; Fellow Islamic Acad. of Sciences. *Address:* Electronics Research Centre, Sharif University of Technology, PO Box 11365-9363, Tehran, Iran (office). *Telephone:* (21) 600-5317 (office). *Fax:* (21) 601-2983 (office). *E-mail:* tabiani@sharif.edu (office). *Website:* sina.sharif.edu (office); sina.sharif.edu/~tabiani (office).

TABINAMAN, John; Papua New Guinea politician; *Acting President, Autonomous Government of Bougainville;* mem. Regional House of Reps 2005–; Vice-Pres. Autonomous Govt of Bougainville 2007–, additional ministerial portfolios for Public Service, Planning and Implementation and Peace and Autonomy 2007–, Acting Pres. Autonomous Govt of Bougainville 2008–. *Address:* Autonomous Bougainville Government, House of Representatives, PO Box 322, Buka, Autonomous Region of Bougainville, Papua New Guinea (office). *E-mail:* abghausparl@datec.net.pg (office).

TABONE, Anton; Maltese politician; *Speaker of the House of Representatives;* b. 15 Nov. 1937; s. of Anton Tabone; m. Margerite Stivala; three s.; ed St Aloysius Coll.; employee, Nat. Bank of Malta 1955–66; mem. Parl. for Gozo (Nationalist Party) 1966–98; mem. Gozo Civic Council 1966–73; Party Spokesman for Agric. and Fisheries, later for Gozo Affairs 1973–87; Minister for Gozo 1987–96; Shadow Minister for Gozo 1996–98; Speaker House of Reps 1998–. *Address:* House of Representatives, The Palace, Valletta, Malta. *Telephone:* (356) 222294. *Fax:* (356) 242552.

TABONE, Vincent, GCB, MD, DO(Oxon), DOMS, DMJ, FRCS(E), FCS, KUOM; Maltese fmr politician and fmr ophthalmic specialist; b. (Censu Tabone), 30 March 1913, Victoria, Gozo; s. of Nicholas Tabone and Elisa Calleja; m. Maria Wirth 1941; four s. (one deceased) five d.; ed St Aloysius Coll., Univ. of Malta, Univ. of Oxford and Royal Coll. of Surgeons of Edin.; served Royal Malta Artillery during World War II; has held sr ophthalmic posts in various hosps in Malta; mem. Exec. Cttee Nationalist Party 1961, Sec.-Gen. 1962–72, First Deputy Leader 1972–77, Pres. 1978–85; mem. Parl. (Nationalist Party) 1966–89; Minister of Labour, Employment and Welfare 1966, of Foreign Affairs 1987–89; Pres. of Repub. of Malta 1989–94; Visiting Prof. Univ. of Malta; Corresp. mem. Accad. Pontificio Pro Vita; Hon. LLD (Univ. of Malta) 1989; UN Testimonial for Service to UN Programme on Aging 1989; Grand Cross, Order of Merit (Fed. Repub. of Germany) 1990, Pro Merito Medal (Council of Europe) 1991, Presidential Gold Medal (Royal Coll. of Surgeons of Edin.) 1991, Cavaliere di Gran Croce 1991, Hon. GCB. *Address:* 33 Carmel Street, St Julians, Malta (home). *Telephone:* 2136994 (home). *Fax:* 21362310 (home). *E-mail:* ctabone@keyworld.net (home).

TABOR, Harry Zvi, PhD, FInstP; British/Israeli fmr research physicist; b. 7 March 1917, London; s. of Charles Tabor and Rebecca Tabor; brother of David Tabor; m. Vivienne Landau 1947; two d.; ed Quintin Hogg School, London, Univ. of London and Hebrew Univ. of Jerusalem; research physicist in UK instrument industry (including defence-related research and devt 1939–45) 1939–49; Research Council of Israel 1949–74; Dir Nat. Physical Lab. of Israel 1950–74; Chair. and Scientific Dir Scientific Research Foundation, Jerusalem 1969–; mem. research cttees Ministry of Science & Tech., Ministry of Energy and Infrastructure 1975–; Pres. Int. Solar Energy Soc. (ISES) 1981–83; guest lecturer NAS 1961 and at numerous univs; consultant to UNESCO and WEC; primarily responsible for widespread use of solar water heating in Israel; Hon. PhD (Weizmann Inst.) 1992; Royal Soc. Gold Medal Energy Award 1975 for pioneering work on exploitation of solar energy; Diesel Gold Medallist 1977; Farrington Daniels Award (ISES) 1981; Alfred Krupp Energy Prize 1981; Quality of Life Award (Knesset, Israel) 1995 and other honours. *Publications:* selected reprints of papers by Harry Zvi Tabor, Solar Energy Pioneer (ed. by Morton B. Prince) 1999, book chapters and some 90 papers in scientific journals. *Leisure interests:* music, theatre, study of social problems (non-party). *Address:* PO Box 3745, Jerusalem 91036, Israel. *Telephone:* 2-6435785. *Fax:* 2-6437470. *E-mail:* taborh@zahav.net.il.

TABUCCHI, Antonio; Italian novelist; b. 1943, Vecchiano, Tuscany; m.; one d. one s.; ed Univ. of Pisa; Chair of Literature, Univ. of Siena; columnist for Italian newspaper, Corriere della Sera, Spanish newspaper, El País; trans. of Fernando Pessoa; Prix Européen Jean Monnet 1994, Prix Médicis Étranger 1987, Leibniz Acad. Nossack Prize 1999, Italian PEN Club Prize, Premio Salento 2003. *Publications include:* Piazza d'Italia (novel) 1975, Il piccolo naviglio (novel) 1978, Il gioco del rovescio (short stories, trans. as Letter from Casablanca) 1981, Donna di Porto Pim (short stories) 1983, Notturno indiano (novel, trans. as Indian Nocturne) 1984, Pessoana minima: escritos sobre Fernando Pessoa (non-fiction) 1984, Piccoli equivoci senza importanza (novel, trans. as Little Misunderstandings of No Importance) 1985, Il filo dell'orizzonte (novel, trans. as The Edge of the Horizon) 1986, I volatili del Beato Angelico (short stories) 1987, Un baule pieno di gente: scritti su Fernando Pessoa (non-fiction) 1990, Requiem, uma alucinação (novel, trans. as Requiem: A Hallucination) 1990, Sogni di sogni (trans. as Dreams of Dreams) 1992, Gli ultimi tre giorni di Fernando Pessoa (trans. as The Last Three Days of Fernando Pessoa) 1994, Sostiene Pereira (novel, trans. as Pereira Declares) 1994, La testa perduta di Damasceno Monteiro (novel, trans. as The Missing Head of Damasceno Monteiro) 1997, Un baule pieno di gente 2000, Si sta facendo sempre più tardi (novel) 2001, Tristano muore (novel) 2004, Il Marinaio 2005, Racconti 2005, Tanti saluti 2006, L'Oca al Passo 2006. *Address:* c/o Giacomo Feltrinelli Editore, via Andegari 6, 21021 Milan, Italy (office). *Website:* www.feltrinellieditore.it (office).

TABUNSCIC, Gheorghe, PhD; Moldovan politician; b. 1 Jan. 1949, Copciac; m.; two c.; ed Chişinău Agricultural Inst.; agronomist and Vice-Chair. Victory collective farm, Taraclia rayon 1962–75; fmr leader Moldovan Communist Party (MPC) Comrat Branch, advocate for autonomy of Gagauz region; elected Başkan (Gov.) of Gagauz-Yeri following attainment of autonomy 1995–99, re-elected 2002–06. *Address:* c/o Office of the Başkan, Gagauz-Yeri, 3800 Comrat, Moldova (office).

TACHI, Ryuichiro; Japanese professor of economics; *Counsellor, Institute for Monetary and Economic Studies, Bank of Japan;* b. 11 Sept. 1921, Yokohama; m. Yoko Shinmel 1951; two s.; ed Univ. of Tokyo; Assoc. Prof. of Econs, Univ. of Tokyo 1950–61, Prof. 1961–82, Prof. Emer. 1982–, Dean Faculty of Econs 1972, Vice-Pres. 1979–81; Prof. of Econs, Aoyama Gakuin Univ. 1984–; Chief Counsellor Inst. for Monetary and Econ. Studies, Bank of Japan 1982–; Dir Inst. of Public Finance 1982–84; Pres. Japan Soc. of Monetary Econs 1982–88, Inst. of Fiscal and Monetary Policy, Ministry of Finance 1985–; mem. Japan Acad. 1986–. *Publications include:* Japan and the United States Today (ed. with Hugh T. Patrick) 1987. *Address:* Bank of Japan, 2-1-1, Hongoku-cho, Nihonbashi, Chuo-ku, Tokyo, Japan. *Telephone:* (3) 3279-1111. *Fax:* (3) 5200-2256. *Website:* www.boj.or.jp.

TADDZHUDDIN, Talgat Safich; Russian (Tartar) ecclesiastic; *Head, Central Spiritual Directorate of Russian Muslims;* b. 12 Oct. 1948, Kazan, Tatarstan, Russia; m.; five c.; ed El-Azkhar Theological Univ., Cairo; First Imam-Khatyb, mufti and Chair. of Sacred Bd Mosque El-Mardjani; Chair. Dept of Int. Relations of Muslim Orgs of the USSR 1990; Supreme Mufti of Russia and European countries of CIS; awarded the sacred title Sheik-iul-Islam; Official Rep. of Muslims of Russia to maj. foreign and public Muslim orgs., Org. of Islam Confed., UNESCO, European League of Muslims; currently Head, Central Spiritual Directorate of Russian Muslims. *Publications:* The Wild East 1999, Limit of Rationality 1998, and numerous scientific works on political and religious culture. *Leisure interest:* foreign languages. *Address:* Vypolzov per. 7, 129090 Moscow, Russia (office). *Telephone:* (095) 281-49-04 (office).

TADIĆ, Boris; Serbian politician, psychologist and head of state; *President;* b. 15 Jan. 1958, Sarajevo, Bosnia and Herzegovina; s. of Ljuba Tadić and Nevenka Tadić; m.; two c.; ed Univ. of Belgrade; convicted for student political activities; several positions as prof. of psychology, army clinical psychologist, researcher on devt and social psychology projects; Prof. of Politics and Advertising, Univ. for Drama and Arts, Belgrade 2003; Founder and Dir Centre for the Devt of Democracy and Political Skills 1997–2002; mem. Democratic Party 1990–, later Sec. of Gen. Cttee, Vice-Pres. Exec. Bd, Acting Pres. Exec. Bd, Vice-Pres. of Democratic Party (twice), Pres. 2004–; Rep. to Nat. Ass 1996–97, 2004–; mem. Council for Science and Tech.; Rep. in Council of Fed. Ass. 2000; Minister of Telecommunications, Fed. Repub. of Yugoslavia 2002–03; Minister of Defence, Council of Ministers of Serbia and Montenegro 2003–04; elected Rep. to Ass. of Serbia and Montenegro 2003, Acting Head of Group of Democratic Party Reps; Pres. of Repub. of Serbia 2004–; mem. Bd for Defence and Security; first Pres. Comm. for the Supervision of Security Service. *Address:* Office of the President, 11000 Belgrade, Andrićev venac 1, Serbia (office). *Telephone:* (11) 3030866 (office). *Fax:* (11) 3030868 (office). *Website:* kontakt.predsednik@predsednik.yu (office); www.boristadic.org (office); www.predsednik.yu (office).

TADLAOUI, Mohammed, BSc; Moroccan engineer; *President, SOCOPLAN;* b. 1939, Meknès; m.; two s. one d.; ed Imperial Coll. London and Inst. of Civil Engineers, UK, Sorbonne, Paris; research engineer, UK 1963, project engineer Arup and Partners 1966; consulting engineer Morocco 1973; Founder, Pres. and Gen. Dir SOCOPLAN (consulting engineers) 1975; co-founder and mem. Moroccan Fed. of Consulting Engineers (FMCI) 1976–; Gen. Sec. Ismailia Asscn of Micro Credit; founding mem. Regional Asscn Grande Ismailia, Meknès; mem. Moroccan Nat. Fed. of Micro-Credit. *Leisure interests:* swimming, tennis, history, literature. *Address:* Residence Al Mansour, Zankat Moulay Slimane, Rabat, Morocco. *Telephone:* (7) 721020 (office). *Fax:* (7) 735663 (office). *E-mail:* socoplan@menara.ma.

TADROS, Tharwat Fouad, MSc, PhD; British/Egyptian scientist, academic and consultant; *Consultant and Visiting Professor, Imperial College London;* b. 29 July 1937, Kena, Egypt; s. of Fouad Tadros Mikhail and Rosa Wasif El-Gouhary; m. Jantina Lodewijka Buter 1969; two s.; ed secondary school, Luxor, Egypt, Alexandria Univ.; Lecturer in Physical Chem., Faculty of Science, Alexandria Univ. 1962–66; Agric. Univ. Wageningen, Netherlands 1966–68; research worker Lab. for Applied Research, Delft, Netherlands 1968–69; Tech. Officer ICI 1969–74, Sr Research Officer 1974–78, Research Assoc. 1978–89, Sr Research Assoc. 1989–; Visiting Prof. Bristol Univ. 1983–84; Consultant and Visiting Prof. Imperial Coll. London 1988–; Industrial Lecturer; past Pres. Int. Asscn of Colloid and Interface Science; Royal Soc. of Chem. Colloid and Surface Chem. Award and Medal, Silver Medal 1990. *Publications:* ed five books, two scientific journals; author of two books and over 250 scientific articles in learned journals. *Leisure interests:* chess, reading, debates. *Address:* 89 Nash Grove Lane, Wokingham, Berks., RG40 4HE, England (home). *Telephone:* (118) 973-2621 (home). *E-mail:* tharwat@tadros.fsnet.co.uk (home).

TAFROV, Stefan; Bulgarian diplomatist; b. 11 Feb. 1958, Sofia; ed Lycée de langue française, Sofia, Univ. of Sofia; staff writer, weekly newspaper ABV, Sofia 1983–87; First Deputy Minister of Foreign Affairs 1991–92, April–Dec. 1997; Amb. to Italy 1992–95, to UK 1995–97, to France 1998–2001; Perm. Rep. to UN, New York 2001–06; Commdr Légion d'honneur (France). *Leisure interests:* literature, philosophy, classical music, history. *Address:* c/o Ministry of Foreign Affairs, ul. Al. Zhendov 2 1040 Sofia, Bulgaria (office). *Telephone:* (2) 971-14-08 (office). *Fax:* (2) 870-30-41 (office). *E-mail:* iprd@mfa.government.bg (office).

TAFT, Robert (Bob), BA, MA, JD; American politician and fmr state official; b. 8 Jan. 1942; s. of the late Robert Taft Jr, fmr Senator from Ohio, grand-s. of the late Robert Taft, fmr Senator from Ohio, great grand-s. of the late William Howard Taft, fmr US Pres.; m. Hope Taft; one d.; ed Yale Univ, Princeton Univ, Univ of Cincinnati Law School; served as volunteer teacher for US Peace Corps in East Africa; mem. Ohio House of Reps 1976–80; Commr Hamilton Co., Ohio 1981–90; Sec. of State of Ohio 1990–99; Gov. of Ohio 1999–2007; pleaded no contest to four criminal misdemeanors for violating state ethics laws 2005. *Address:* c/o Office of the Governor, 30th Floor, 77 South High Street, Columbus, OH 43215, USA (office).

TAGAYEV, Aitibai; Kyrgyzstani economist and politician; *Chairman, Zhogorku Kenesh (Supreme Council);* b. 30 April 1958, Naukat Dist, Osh; m.; three s.; ed Kyrgyz State Univ.; early career as bookkeeper; Deputy, Zhogorku Kenesh (Parl.) 2005–, Chair. 2008–; mem. Bright Road People's Party (Ak Zhol) 2007–. *Address:* Office of the Chairman, Zhogorku Kenesh, 720053 Bishkek, ul. Abdymomunov 207, Kyrgyzstan (office). *Telephone:* (312) 61-16-04 (office). *Fax:* (312) 62-50-12 (office). *E-mail:* zs@kenesh.gov.kg (office). *Website:* www.kenesh.kg (office).

TAGIYEV, Tachberdy; Turkmenistani engineer and politician; *Deputy Prime Minister, responsible for Petroleum and Natural Gas;* b. 1955, Etrek dist; ed Turkmen Polytechnic Inst.; Minister of the Petroleum Industry and Mineral Resources 2002–03; Gov. Balkan Velayat 2003; Head of Turkmenbashi oil refinery 2006–07; Deputy Chair. of the Govt (Deputy Prime Minister), responsible for Petroleum and Natural Gas 2007–, also Dir-Gen. Turkmengaz (state-run gas monopoly). *Address:* Office of the President and the Council of Ministers, 744000 Aşgabat, Turkmenistan (office). *Telephone:* (12) 35-45-34 (office). *Fax:* (12) 35-51-12 (office). *Website:* www.turkmenistan.gov.tm (office).

TAHA, Ali Osman Mohamed; Sudanese politician; *Second Vice-President;* b. 1947, Khartoum; ed Univ. of Khartoum; mem. Khartoum Univ. Student Union (Kusu) 1966–71, Pres. 1969–70; organizer sha'ban movement 1973; in judiciary 1972–76; Minister of Social Planning. 1973; Minister of Foreign Affairs 1996–98; First Vice-Pres. of Sudan 1998–2005; Second Vice-Pres. 2005–. *Address:* People's Palace, POB 281, Khartoum, Sudan (office). *Fax:* 183-771025.

TAHER, Abdul Hadi, PhD; Saudi Arabian government official; b. 1930, Medina; ed Ain Shams Univ., Cairo and Univ. of Calif.; entered Saudi Arabian Govt service 1955; Dir-Gen. Ministry of Petroleum and Mineral Resources 1960; Gov., Gen. Petroleum and Mineral Org. (PETROMIN), Riyadh 1962–86; Man. Dir Saudi Arabian Fertilizers Co. (SAFCO) 1966–76, Jeddah Oil Refinery 1970–; Chair. Arab Maritime Petroleum Transport Co. –1981; Dir Arabian American Oil Co. (ARAMCO), Saudi Govt railways Corpn; Trustee, Coll. of Petroleum and Minerals; mem. Industrial Research and Devt Centre, Saudi Arabia; Hon. mem. American Soc. of Petroleum Engineers. *Publications:* Income Determination in the International Petroleum Industry 1966, Development and Petroleum Strategies in Saudi Arabia (Arabic) 1970, Energy – A Global Outlook 1981; lectures and papers on econ. and petroleum affairs. *Address:* c/o General Petroleum and Mineral Organization (PETROMIN), PO Box 757, Riyadh, Saudi Arabia.

TAHER, Nahed, BS, MA, MSc, PhD; Saudi Arabian banker and economist; *CEO, Gulf One Investment Bank;* ed King Abdulaziz Univ., Jeddah, Univ. of Lancaster, UK; Co-owner and Financial Advisor, Bullhide Liner (polyurethane coating) franchise, Jeddah 1987–97; Financial Advisor, Minara (support services co.), Jeddah 1993–2002; Lecturer, later Asst Prof. of Econs and Head of Accounting Dept, King Abdulaziz Univ.; Sr Strategic Economist and Chair. Portfolio Man. Cttee, Nat. Commercial Bank, Jeddah (first woman to hold such a position in a bank in Saudi Arabia) 2002–05; Founder and CEO Gulf One Investment Bank, Bahrain (first Saudi woman to head a bank in Gulf region) 2005–; consultant to Saudi Cultural Summit; mem. Saudi Econ. Asscn, Center for Strategic Studies of Mekkah Emirate, Businesswomen's Cttee of Jeddah Chamber of Commerce, Saudi Cttee of Eisenhower Fellowship; ranked 72nd by Forbes magazine amongst 100 Most Powerful Women 2006. *Address:* Gulf One Investment Bank BSC, Bahrain Financial Harbour, West Tower, Level 15, PO Box 11172, Manama, Bahrain (office). *Telephone:* 17102555 (office). *Fax:* 17100063 (office). *E-mail:* info@gulf1bank.com (office). *Website:* www.gulf1bank.com (office).

TAIANA, Jorge; Argentine academic, politician and diplomatist; *Minister of Foreign Affairs, International Trade and Worship;* b. 31 May 1950, Buenos Aires; m.; three c.; ed Bachiller Colegio Nacional, Buenos Aires, Univ. of Buenos Aires; Adjunct Prof., Univ. of Buenos Aires 1985–91; Titular Prof., Univ. of Lomas de Zamora 1987; Prof., Univ. Rafael Landívar, Guatemala 1994; Titular Prof., Nat. Univ. of Quilmes 1995–2001; Head of Cabinet, Ministry of Education 1973–74; Under-Sec., Ministry of Economy 1974–75; Regional Dir Servicio Universitario Mundial (non-Govt Org.) 1986–89; advisor to Foreign Affairs Cttee, Chamber of Deputies 1987–89; Under-Sec. for Foreign Policy, Ministry of Foreign Affairs 1989–90, Dir Int. Orgs 1990–91; Amb. to Guatemala and Belize 1992–96; Exec. –Sec. Inter-American Comm. on Human Rights, OAS 1996–2001; Sec. for Human Rights, Govt of Buenos Aires Province 2002–03; Vice-Minister of Foreign Affairs 2003–05, Minister of

Foreign Affairs, Int. Trade and Worship 2005–; Grand Cross, Order of Quetza (Guatemala) 1996, Order of El Sol del Peru (Peru) 2003, Order of Antonio José de Irisarri (Guatemala) 2003, Order of Baron de Rio Branco (Brazil) 2005, Officer, Order of Wissam Al Alaoui (Morocco) 2004. *Publications:* author of several publications on human rights and labour movements. *Address:* Ministry of Foreign Affairs, International Trade and Worship, Esmerelda 1212, 1007 Buenos Aires, Argentina (office). *Telephone:* (11) 4819-7000 (office). *E-mail:* web@mrecic.gov.ar (office). *Website:* www.mrecic.gov.ar (office).

TAILLANDIER, François Antoine Georges, MA; French writer; b. 20 June 1955, Chamalières; s. of Henri Taillandier and Denise Ducher; three c.; teacher 1980–83; full-time writer 1984–, also contrib. Le Figaro (newspaper), La Montagne (newspaper), L'Humanité (newspaper), L'Atelier du Roman (periodical); Admin., Soc. des Gens de Lettres de France; Prix Roger Nimier 1992, Acad. française Prix de la critique 1997. *Publications:* fiction: Personnages de la rue du Couteau 1984, Tott 1985, Benoît ou les contemporains obscurs 1986, Les Clandestins (Prix Jean-Freustié 1991) 1990, Les Nuits Racine 1992, Fan et le jouet qui n'existe pas (with Charles Barat) 1993, Mémoires de Monte-Cristo 1994, Des hommes qui s'éloignent 1997, Anielka (Grand Prix du roman de l'Académie française 1999) 1999, Le cas Gentile 2001, La Grande Intrigue: Vol. 1 Option Paradis 2005, Vol. 2 Telling 2006; non-fiction: Tous les secrets de l'avenir 1996, Aragon 1997, Journal de Marseille 1999, N6, la route de l'Italie 1999, Les Parents lâcheurs 2001, Borges, une restitution du monde 2002, Pour ou contre Jacques Chirac (with Joseph Macé-Scaron) 2002, Un Autre langue 2004, Balzac (biog.) 2005. *Address:* c/o Editions Stock, 31 rue de Fleurus, 75006 Paris, France (office).

TAILLIBERT, Roger René; French architect; *President, L'Académie de Beaux Arts;* b. 21 Jan. 1926, Châtres-sur-Cher; s. of Gaston Taillibert and Melina Benoit; m. Béatrice Pfister 1965; one d.; ed schools in Toulouse, Dreux, Argenton-sur-Creuse, Tours, Vaureal and Ecole Nat. des Beaux-Arts, Paris; own practice 1969–; Chief Architect, Public Buildings for Govt 1967, civil buildings and nat. palaces; Curator Grand Palais des Champs-Elysées 1977–82, Palais de Chaillot 1983–86; Chair. Taillibert Gulf Int., UAE; mem. Acad. d'architecture; mem. Acad. des Beaux-Arts, Pres. 2004–; mem. Inst. de France, Acad. d'Architecture 2000, Acad. des Sports, des Arts des Rues, New Thinking group, RSA; Commdr Légion d'honneur 1983, Ordre nat. du Mérite 1983, des Arts et Lettres 1983, Commdr des Palmes Académiques 1983, Chevalier dans l'Ordre du Mérite pour le Commerce et l'Industrie 2000; Ecole Nat. Supérieure des Beaux-Arts, Diplôme d'Architecture (DPLG) décerné par le Gouvernement Français 1959; Médaille d'argent décerné par l'Acad. d'Architecture pour ses recherches et ses applications pratiques 1971, Grand Médaille du Sport 1972, Prix Nat. des Arts et de la Littérature 1973, Prix Européen 1973, Médaille d'or de la Créatvitié Architecturale 1973, Grand Prix Cembureau 1974–76, Médaille des Structures 1976, Grand Prix Nat. d'Architecture 1976, Premier Prix Nat. d'Architecture 1977, Grand Prix des Arts, Canada 1977, Prix Elphège Baude 1977, Médaille de l'Acad. Nat. des Sports, Italie 1977, Grand Prix du Rayonnement Français 1982, Laureat du Prix Européen d'Architecture Métallique 2000, Médaille de Vermeil de la Ville de Paris 2000, Médaille d'Or du Sport 2000, Grand Prix of Europe Timber Structures. *Main works:* numerous including: sporting facilities: Deauville Swimming-Pool 1966, Parc des Princes Stadium Paris 1972, Olympic Complex, Montréal, Canada 1976, Olympic Complex, Lille, France 1977–81, Sporting and cultural facilities at Kirchberg Luxembourg 1984, Khalifa Stadium, Qatar 2002, Bamenda Stadium Cameroon, Ice Skating-Ring, Abu Dhabi, Stadia for Soccer World Cup 2006, Morocco, velodromes at Bordeaux 1987, Poitiers 1997, Vannes 2001, Astana (Kazasthan) 2004; also: Nat. Geographic Centre, Amman, Jordan; Officers' Club, Abu Dhabi, UAE; sports complex, Baghdad, Guests' Palace, Bahrain, univ. bldgs, Sousse, Gabès, Tunisia, sports and golf club houses, Yamoussoukro and Abidjan, Côte d'Ivoire; in France: School of Pharmacy, Toulouse, Coca-Cola plant, Grigny, pharmaceutical lab. P. Fabre, Castres, DAF plant, Survilliers, skiing and mountaineering nat. school, Chamonix, Nat. Inst. for Sports and Physical Educ., Paris, pre-Olympic centre, Font-Romeu, nuclear plants Penly and Civaux, swimming complex at Nogent-sur-Oise 1995; Lycée Raspail, Paris 1995, Commercial and residential complex, St-Quentin-en-Yvelines 1995; studies for projects in Iraq and Lebanon; feasibility studies for projects in Argentina and Uruguay (hotels, sports facilities, leisure parks, etc.). *Publications:* Montréal – Jeux Olympiques 1976, Construire l'avenir 1977, Roger Taillibert (autobiog.) 1978. *Leisure interests:* painting, photography, music. *Address:* Agence Roger Taillibert, 163 rue de la Pompe, 75116 Paris, France (office); Taillibert Gulf Environment, PO Box 25418, Abu Dhabi 603, Bin Hamoodah Bldg, UAE (office). *Telephone:* 1-47-04-29-92 (office); 2627-3667 (office). *Fax:* 1-42-27-37-71 (office); 2627-4012 (office). *E-mail:* roger.taillibert@free.fr (office); roger.taillibert@online.fr (office); tailgulf@emirates.net.ae. *Website:* www.agencetaillibert.com (office).

TAIPALE, Vappu Tuulikki, DM; Finnish politician and psychiatrist; *Director General, National Research and Development Centre for Welfare and Health;* b. 1 May 1940, Vaasa; m. Ilkka Taipale 1965; two s. two d.; psychiatrist, Aurora Youth Polyclinic 1970–74; Paediatric Clinic 1975–79; Asst Prof. of Child Psychiatry, Kuopio Univ. 1980–83, Tampere Univ. 1983–; First Minister of Social Affairs and Health 1982–83, Second Minister 1983–84; Dir-Gen. Nat. Bd of Social Welfare 1984–90; Dir-Gen. Nat. Agency for Welfare and Health 1991–92, Nat. Research and Devt Centre for Welfare and Health 1992–; Chair. COST A5 Ageing and Tech. Int. Soc. for Gerontechnology, EAG Key Action 6, EU 5th FP; mem. SDP, UNU Council 2001–; Dr hc (Univ. of Vaasa) 1998, (Univ. of Jyväskylä) 2004. *Address:* STAKES National Research and Development Centre for Welfare and Health, Lintulahenkuja 4, PO Box 220, 00531 Helsinki, Finland (office). *Telephone:* (9) 39672011 (office). *Fax:* (9) 39672417 (office). *E-mail:* vappu.taipale@stakes.fi (office). *Website:* www.stakes.fi (office).

TAIT, Alan A., MA, PhD; British international civil servant, academic and consultant; b. 1 July 1934, Edinburgh, Scotland; s. of Stanley Tait and Margaret Anderson; m. Susan Somers 1963; one s.; ed Heriots School, Univs of Edinburgh and Dublin; Lecturer, Trinity Coll., Dublin 1959–70, Fellow 1967, Sr Tutor 1968; Prof. of Money and Finance, Univ. of Strathclyde 1970–76; Visiting Scholar, IMF 1971; Consultant to Sec. of State for Scotland 1972–76; Adviser to Pakistan Taxation Comm. 1973; Chief Fiscal Analysis Div., IMF 1975–82, Deputy Dir Fiscal Affairs Dept 1982–94, Dir of Geneva Office 1994–98; Co-Chair. Working Group, WHO Cttee on Macroeconomics and Health 2000–02; mem. Review Cttee GAVI 2003–04; Hon. Fellow, Trinity Coll. Dublin 1996; Hon. Prof., Univ. of Kent at Canterbury 1999–2007. *Publications:* Taxation of Personal Wealth 1967, Economic Policy in Ireland (ed. with J. Bristow) 1968, Value-Added Tax 1988; contribs to numerous academic journals on public finance, macroecons, econs of health. *Leisure interest:* painting. *Address:* Cramond House, Harnet Street, Sandwich, Kent, CT13 9ES, England (home). *Telephone:* (1304) 621038 (home). *E-mail:* alan@ataits.plus.com (home).

TAIT, James Francis, PhD, FRS; British/American biophysicist, endocrinologist and academic; *Professor Emeritus, University of London;* b. 1 Dec. 1925, Stockton-on-Tees; s. of H. Tait and C. L. Brotherton; m. Sylvia A. S. Wardropper 1956 (died 2003); ed Univ. of Leeds; Lecturer in Medical Physics, Middlesex Hosp. Medical School 1947–57, Joel Prof. of Medical Physics 1970–82, Dir Jt Head Biophysical Endocrinology Unit 1970–82; External Scientific Staff, MRC 1955–58; Sr Scientist, Worcester Foundation, USA 1958–70; Prof. Emer., Univ. of London 1982–; Hon. DSc (Hull) 1979; Reichstein Award, Int. Soc. of Endocrinology 1976, CIBA Award, American Heart Asscn for Hypertension Research 1977, Dale Medal, Soc. for Endocrinology 1979, R. Douglas Wright Lecturer, Melbourne 1989. *Publications:* A Quartet of Unlikely Discoveries (with Sylvia A. S. Tait) 2004; numerous papers on medical physics and endocrinology. *Leisure interests:* photography, listening to music, computing, touring Yorkshire. *Address:* Granby Court, Granby Road, Harrogate, N Yorks., HG1 4SR, England (home). *Telephone:* (1423) 524284 (home). *E-mail:* jftait@globalnet.co.uk (home).

TAIT, Marion, CBE; British ballet mistress and dancer; *Ballet Mistress, Birmingham Royal Ballet;* b. 7 Oct. 1950, London; d. of Charles Tait and Betty Hooper; m. David Morse 1971; ed Royal Acad. of Dancing and Royal Ballet School; joined Royal Ballet School aged 15, graduating to Royal Ballet's touring co. (later known as Sadler's Wells Royal Ballet, now Birmingham Royal Ballet); Prin. Dancer 1974; danced all the classics and other prin. roles including Juliet, Elite Syncopations, Las Hermanas, The Invitation, Hobson's Choice, The Dream, The Burrow, Lizzie Borden in Fall River Legend and Hagar in Pillar of Fire; cr. many roles for Kenneth MacMillan and David Bintley; guest appearances world-wide; Ballet Mistress (to both co. and students), and still performs character roles, Birmingham Royal Ballet 1995–; Dancer of Year 1994, Evening Standard Ballet Award 1994. *Leisure interest:* needlework. *Address:* Birmingham Royal Ballet, Thorp Street, Birmingham, B5 4AU, England (office). *Telephone:* (121) 245-3500 (office). *Website:* www.brb.org.uk (office).

TAITT, Branford Mayhew, LLB, MPA; Barbadian politician; b. 15 May 1938; m. Marjorie C. Taitt (deceased); one s. two d.; ed Univ. of West Indies, New York Univ. and Brooklyn Coll., New York; Cable and Wireless 1954–62; Conf. Officer, UN Secr. 1962–65; US Rep. Barbados Industrial Devt Corpn 1965–67; mem. Barbados Del. to UN 1966–71; Consul-Gen. of Barbados, New York 1967–71; mem. Barbados Senate 1971–76; Minister of Trade, Industry and Commerce, of Tourism and Industry 1986–88, of Health 1988–93, of Foreign Affairs 1993–94; Pres. Democratic Labour Party 1978–84; fmr part-time Lecturer in Law, Univ. of W Indies, Cave Hill, Barbados and visiting or guest lecturer at univs and colls in USA. *Publications:* over 200 articles in newspapers and periodicals. *Address:* 10 Stanmore Crescent, Black Rock, St Michael, Barbados (home). *Telephone:* 424-0363 (office); 424-4113. *Fax:* 424-5436. *E-mail:* hontaitt@cariaccess.com (home).

TAITTINGER, Anne-Claire, MA; French business executive; *Chairman of the Executive Board, Groupe Taittinger;* d. of Jean Taittinger (q.v.) and Corinne Deville; m.; two s.; ed Inst. d'Etudes Politiques de Paris and Centre for Advanced Business Courses; fmr urban planner; fmrly held positions within several Soc. du Louvre cos, Head Soc. du Louvre 1997–2006, Pres. and CEO 2003–06; Chair. Bd Baccarat 1993–2005, Vice-Pres. 2005–06, mem. Bd of Dirs 2006–07; Chair. Exec. Bd Groupe Taittinger 2003–; Dir Dexia 2001–. *Address:* Groupe Taittinger, 9, place Saint-Nicaise, 51100 Reims, France (office). *Telephone:* 3-26-85-45-35 (office). *Fax:* 3-26-50-14-30 (office). *Website:* www.taittinger.fr (home).

TAITTINGER, Jean; French politician and vintner; b. 25 Jan. 1923, Paris; s. of Pierre Taittinger and Gabrielle Guillet; m. Marie Corinne Deville 1948; three s. two d.; ed Coll. Stanislas, Paris; Dir Champagne Taittinger 1946, Vice-Chair. 1958–94, Chair. 1994–; Deputy for Marne, Nat. Ass. 1958–73; Mayor of Rheims 1959–77; Nat. Sec. UNR-UDT (Union Démocratique du Travail) 1967; mem. Exec. Office and Nat. Treas. UDR Feb.-Oct. 1968, Deputy Sec.-Gen. 1974–76; Vice-Pres. Finance Comm. of Nat. Ass. 1967–68, Pres. 1968–71; Sec. of State, Ministry of Finance and Econ. Affairs 1971–73; Minister of Justice 1973–74; Minister of State for Justice March–May 1974; Chair Imprimerie Union Républicaine 1960, Soc. du Louvre 1977, Soc. des Hôtels Concorde 1978–90, Cofidev 1979, Société Deville 1979, Société Hôtelière Martinez 1981, Banque Privée de Dépôt et de Crédit 1987; Vice-Chair. Société Taittinger 1947, Société Hôtelière Lutetia Concorde 1980–; Dir Banque de l'Union Occidentale 1976–85, Banque Worms 1978–82, Etablissements VQ Petersen 1979–84; Pres., Dir-Gen. Banque du Louvre 1987–90 (Hon. Pres. 1990–), Cie Cristalleries de Baccarat 1992–94, Hon. Pres. 1994–; Dir Gen. Compagnie Financière Taittinger 1989–94, Chair. 1994–2000; Pres. Supervisory Council

Euro Disneyland SA 1989–95; Vice-Chair. Deville SA 1993–95. *Leisure interest:* breeding basset hounds. *Address:* Compagnie Financière Taittinger, 58 boulevard Gourion Saint-Cyr, 75017 Paris (office); Cristallerie de Baccarat, 30 bis rue de Paradis, 75010 Paris, France.

TAJ, Lt.-Gen. Nadeem; Pakistani military and intelligence officer; *Director, Inter-Services Intelligence Directorate;* fmr Mil. Sec. to fmr Pres. Musharraf; fmr Dir-Gen. of Mil. Intelligence; fmr Gen. Officer Commdt, Lahore; Commandant Pakistan Mil. Acad., Kakul –2007; Dir, Inter-Services Intelligence Directorate (Pakistan's largest intelligence agency) 2007–, promoted to Lt-Gen. *Address:* c/o Ministry of Defence, Pakistan Secretariat, No. II, Rawalpindi 46000, Pakistan.

TAKABWEBWE, Michael, LLB; I-Kiribati lawyer; b. 11 Nov. 1945, Tabiteuea North; s. of Teababa Taumeang and Nei Ana Neaua; m. Tebaniman Tito 1979; three d.; ed Univ. of Melbourne, Australia; State Advocate 1979–81, Sr State Advocate 1981–83; Attorney-Gen. of Kiribati 1983–2002; prin. legal adviser to Kiribati govt on constitution and all other Kiribati laws 1983–2002; mem. Parl. and Cabinet 1983–2002; Puisne Judge 2002–05; Judge High Court of Kiribati 2002–05; Rep. to Commonwealth Law Ministers Meetings 1986, 1990, 1993, 1996; Rep. to Int. Bar Asscn Meeting, Fiji 2002; mem. Int. Bar Asscn 2004; Rep. to Int. Bar Conference Auckland 2004. *Publications include:* Kiribati, Asia–Pacific Constitutional Yearbook 1995. *Leisure interests:* gardening, listening to pop and classical music, reading. *Address:* c/o Justice's Chambers, High Court of Kiribati, POB 501, Betio, Tarawa, Kiribati (office). *Telephone:* (686) 26007/25043 (office); (686) 21849 (home). *Fax:* (686) 26149 (office). *E-mail:* michael.j@tskl.net.ki (office).

TAKÁCS-NAGY, Gábor; Hungarian violinist and conductor; *Musical Director, Verbier Festival Chamber Orchestra;* b. 17 April 1956, Budapest; s. of László Takács-Nagy and Matild Pataki; m. Lesley (née Townson) de Senger 1991; two d.; ed Béla Bartók Conservatory and Franz Liszt Music Acad. of Budapest; f. Takács String Quartet 1976, Takács Piano Trio 1996, Mikrokosmos String Quartet 1998, Camerata Bellerive 2005; concert tours from 1980 every year throughout Europe, every other year in Australia, USA, Japan, South America; Prof. Conservatoire de Musique, Geneva 1997–; Conductor, Swiss and Hungarian Orchestras 2002–; Musical Dir, Verbier Festival Chamber Orchestra; first prize Evian competition 1977, Menuhin competition (Portsmouth) 1981, Scholarship award, Banff School of Fine Arts, Liszt Prize 1983. *Leisure interests:* sport, theatre, hiking, reading. *Address:* Case postale 186, 1245 Collonge-Bellerive, Switzerland (home). *E-mail:* ldstn@hotmail.com (home). *Website:* www.bellerive-festival.ch (office).

TAKAGAKI, Tasuku; Japanese banker; b. 1928, Tokyo; m.; two d.; ed Univ. of Tokyo; joined The Bank of Tokyo Ltd (merged with Mitsubishi Bank Ltd 1996, now Bank of Tokyo-Mitsubishi Ltd) 1953, Gen. Man. Int. Investment Div. 1975–76, mem. Bd 1979–, Dir and Gen. Man. Planning and Personnel Div. 1979–82, Resident Man. Dir for Europe 1982–84, Man. Dir Head Office 1984, Sr Man. Dir 1986, Deputy Pres. 1989, Pres. 1990–98, Chair. of Bd 1998–, Sr Adviser 2000–; Deputy Treas. Asian Devt Bank 1966–71; Gran Cruz, Orden Nacional al Mérito (Colombia), Medal of Honour with Blue Ribbon (Japan), Grã-Cruz, Ordem do Mérito Agrícola, Comercial e Industrial (Portugal), Commdr Orden del Libertador, Venezuela. *Address:* 7-1 Marunouchi 2-chome, Chiyoda-ku, Tokyo 100-8388, Japan (office). *Telephone:* (3) 3240-1111 (office). *Website:* www.btm.co.jp (office).

TAKAGI, Kunio; Japanese retail executive; *President and CEO, The Daiei Inc.;* b. 1944; mem. Advisory Bd Daiei Inc. –2001, Pres. 2001–03, Pres. and CEO Daiei Inc. 2003–; Dir Nichiai Ltd; mem. Bd of Dirs CIES—The Food Business Forum. *Address:* The Daiei Inc., 4-1-1 Minatojima Nakamachi, Chuo-ku, Kobe 650-0046, Japan (office). *Telephone:* (7) 8302-5001 (office). *Fax:* (7) 8302-5572 (office). *Website:* www.daiei.co.jp (office).

TAKAHAGI, Mitsunori; Japanese business executive; *President and CEO, Nippon Mining Holdings, Inc.;* b. 3 Dec. 1940, Kanagawa Pref.; ed Faculty of Law, Hitotsubashi Univ.; joined Nippon Mining Co. Ltd 1964, Gen. Man. Products Export Dept, Petroleum Group 1988–89, Gen. Man. Marketing Dept, Petroleum Group 1989–91, Deputy Gen. Man., Chita Oil Refinery, Japan Energy Corpn 1991–94 (Nippon Mining Co. merged with Kyodo Oil Co. in 1992 to create Nikko Kyodo, renamed Japan Energy Corpn 1993), Dir in charge of Industry Energy Dept 1994–96, Dir and Gen. Man. Osaka Br. Office 1996–98, Man. Dir and Gen. Man. Tokyo Br. Office 1998–99, Dir, Exec. Corp. Officer, Gen. Man. of Managerial Staff Group 1999–2001, Dir and Sr Exec. Corp. Officer 2001–02, Pres., Rep. Dir and Dir Nippon Mining Holdings, Inc. 2002–06, Pres. and CEO 2006–. *Address:* Nippon Mining Holdings, Inc., 10-1, Toranomon 2-chome, Minato-ku, Tokyo 105-0001, Japan (office). *Telephone:* (3) 5573-5170 (office). *Fax:* (3) 5573-6784 (office). *E-mail:* info@shinnikko-hd .co.jp (office). *Website:* www.shinnikko-hd.co.jp (office).

TAKAHASHI, Genichirō; Japanese writer and critic; b. 1951, Onomichi, Hiroshima; ed Yokohama Nat. Univ.; participated in radical student movt 1960s and early 70s, imprisoned for six months; worked as a labourer until 1981; successful novelist and essayist 1982–; Visiting Fellow Donald Keene Center of Japanese Culture, Columbia Univ., USA 2002. *Publications:* novels: Sayonara Gyangutachi (Gunzō New Writers' Award) (first novel to be translated into English, as Sayonara, Gangsters 2004) 1982, Ōbaa za reinbō (Over the Rainbow) 1984, Oyogu Otoko (The Swimming Man) 1984, Jon Renon tai kaseijin (John Lennon Versus the Martians) 1985, Yūga de kanshōteki Nihon yakkyū (Japanese Baseball: Languid and Happy) (Mishima Yukio Award 1988) 1987, Penguin mura ni hi ga Ochite (Sundown in Penguin Town) 1989, Wakusei P-13 no himitsu (The Secret of Planet 13) 1990, Gosutobasutazu (Ghostbusters) 1997; numerous collections of essays including Bungaku ga konna ni wakatte ii kashira (Is it Okay to Understand Literature So Well?) 1989. *Address:* c/o Vertical, Inc., 257 Park Avenue South, 8th Floor, New York,

NY 10010, USA (office). *Telephone:* (212) 529-2350 (office). *E-mail:* info@ vertical-inc.com (office). *Website:* www.vertical-inc.com (office).

TAKAHASHI, Hiroaki; Japanese energy industry executive; *President and Representative Director, Tohoku Electric Power Company, Inc.;* Pres. and Rep. Dir Tohoku Electric Power Co., Inc.; mem. Bd of Dirs The Energy Conservation Centre, Japan. *Address:* Tohoku Electric Power Company, Inc., 1-7-1 Honcho, Aoba-ku, Sendai, Miyagi 980-8550, Japan (office). *Telephone:* (22) 225-2111 (office). *Fax:* (22) 225-2550 (office). *Website:* www.tohoku-epco.co.jp (office).

TAKAHASHI, Takako; Japanese writer; b. 1932, Kyoto; m. Takahashi Kazumi (died 1971); ed Kyoto Univ.; writer of novels and short stories 1972–1985; trans. of French writers including Mauriac; retd from writing to become a Roman Catholic nun first in Paris, then Japan; returned to writing during 1990s. *Publications:* Sojikei (Congruent Figures) 1972, Sora no hate made (To the End of the Sky) 1973, Botsuraku Fusei (Falling Scenery) 1974, Yuwakusha (The Temptress) 1976, Ningyo no ai (Doll Love) 1976, Ronrii uuman (trans. as Lonely Woman) 1977, Ten no Mizumi 1977, Yomigaeri no ie (The House of Rebirth) 1980, Yosoi seya, waga tamashii yo (Gird up Thyself, Oh My Soul) 1982, Ikari no ko (Child of Wrath; winner Yomiuri Prize) 1985, Tochi no Chikara 1992, Takahashi Kazumi to iu hito: Nijugonen no nochi ni 1997, Kirei na hito 2003, Haka no hanashi 2006. *Address:* c/o Kodansha International Ltd, Otowa Building, 1-17-14 Otowa, Bunkyo-ko, Tokyo, 112-8652, Japan (office). *E-mail:* editorial@kodansha-intl.co.jp (office). *Website:* www.kodansha-intl.com (office).

TAKAHASHI, Toshiyuki, PhD; Japanese physicist and academic; currently Asst Prof., Experimental Nuclear Physics Group, Dept of Physics and Research Center for Neutrino Science, Tohoku Univ. *Publications:* numerous articles in scientific journals. *Address:* Department of Physics, Tohoku University, Sendai 980-8578, Japan (office). *Telephone:* (22) 217-6453 (office). *Fax:* (22) 217-6455 (office). *E-mail:* takahasi@lambda.phys.tohoku.ac.jp (office). *Website:* lambda.phys.tohoku.ac.jp (office).

TAKAKURA, Ken; Japanese actor; b. (Oda Toshimasa), 16 Feb. 1931, Kita Kyushu, Fukuoka; made screen debut 1956, actor in more than 130 films in Japan and USA; Japanese Acad. Awards 1978, 1981, 1982, Best Actor, Montreal World Film Festival 1999. *Films include:* Denko Karate Uchi (Lightning Karate Blow) 1956, Nippon G-men 1956, Gyangu series of films 1961–64, Abashiri Bangaichi (Abashiri Prison) series of films 1963–72, Koya no toseinin (Drifting Avenger) 1968, Gion Matsuri (The Day the Sun Rose) 1968, Too Late the Hero 1970, The Yakuza 1975, Shinkansen daibakhua (Bullet Train) 1975, Hakkodasen 1977, Shiawase no kiiroi hankachi (The Yellow Handkerchief) 1978, Haruka naru yama no yobigoe (Distant Cry from Spring) 1980, Eki Station (Station) 1981, Nankyoku Monogatari (Antarctica) 1983, Umi e (See You) 1988, Black Rain 1989, Mr Baseball 1992, Shiju Shichinin no Shikaku (47 Ronin) 1994, Poppoya (Railroad Man) 1999, Hotaru (The Firefly) 2001, Riding Alone for Thousands of Miles 2005.

TAKAMATSU, Shin, PhD; Japanese architect; b. 5 Aug. 1948, Shimane Pref.; s. of Toshio Takamatsu and Yuriko Takamatsu; m. Toshiko Hariguchi 1970; two d.; ed Ohda High School, Kyoto Univ.; Prin. Architect, Shin Takamatsu Architects and Assocs, Kyoto 1980; mem. Nihon Kenchiku Gakai (Japan Architecture Inst.) 1989–, Japan Inst. of Architecture 1993–; work exhibited at Venice Biennale 1985, Kirini Plaza, Paris 1988, Killing Moon, London 1988, Nîmes 1989, Berlin 1991, San Francisco Museum of Modern Art 1992, Kyoto Municipal Museum of Art 1995; Hon. Fellow AIA 1995; several prizes and awards including Japan Architects Asscn Prize 1984, Venice Biennale Prize 1985, Second Int. Interior Design Award 1987, Architectural Inst. of Japan Prize 1989, Grand Prize, Journal of Japanese Soc. of Commercial Space Designers 1989, Architectural Inst. of Japan Prize 1990, Kyoto Pref. Meritorious Cultural Service Award 1994, Art Encouragement Prize, Ministry of Educ. 1996, Public Architecture Prize 1998. *Publications:* Works-Shin Takamatsu 1984, Architecture and Nothingness 1996, To the Poetic Space 1998. *Leisure interests:* architecture, furniture design. *Address:* Shin Takamatsu Architects and Associates, 195 Jobodaiin-cho Takeda, Fushimi-ku, Kyoto 612, Japan. *Telephone:* (7) 5621-6002 (office). *Fax:* (7) 5621-6079 (office). *E-mail:* syntax@takamatsu.co.jp (office). *Website:* www.takamatsu.co .jp (office).

TAKANO, Toshiyuki; Japanese diplomatist; *Ambassador to Germany;* b. 1944; fmr Counsellor, Embassy in USA; fmr Amb. to Singapore, to S Korea –2005, Amb. to Germany 2005–; fmr Deputy Foreign Minister. *Address:* Embassy of Japan, Hiroshimstr. 6, 10785 Berlin, Germany (office). *Telephone:* (30) 210940 (office). *Fax:* (30) 21094222 (office). *E-mail:* info@botschaft-japan .de (office). *Website:* www.botschaft-japan.de (office).

TAKASHIMA, Tatsuyoshi; Japanese advertising industry executive; *President and COO, Dentsu Inc.;* joined Dentsu Inc. advertising agency 1966, fmr Sr Man. Dir, Exec. Vice-Pres. –2007, Pres., COO and Rep. Dir 2007–. *Address:* Dentsu Incorporated, 1-8-1, Higashi-shimbashi, Minato-ku, Tokyo 105-7001, Japan (office). *Telephone:* (3) 6216-5111 (office). *Website:* www.dentsu.com (office).

TAKASU, Yukio, LLB; Japanese diplomatist; *Permanent Representative, United Nations;* ed Univ. of Tokyo, Merton Coll., Oxford; First Sec., then Counsellor, Perm. Mission to UN, New York 1981–88; Dir W Europe Div., Ministry of Foreign Affairs 1989–92; Deputy Chief of Mission, Embassy in Indonesia 1992–93; Asst Sec.-Gen. and Controller, UN, New York 1993–97; Perm. Rep. to UN, New York 1997–2000, 2007–; Dir-Gen. Multilateral Co-operation Dept 2000–01, Ministry of Foreign Affairs; Perm. Rep. to IAEA and UNIDO 2001–05; Amb. responsible for Human Security, Science and Tech. Co-operation, also Special Envoy for UN Reform 2005–06; Visiting Fellow,

Harvard Univ. 2006–07. *Address:* Permanent Mission of Japan to the United Nations, 866 United Nations Plaza, 2nd Floor, New York, NY 10017, USA (office). *Telephone:* (212) 223-4300 (office). *Fax:* (212) 751-1966 (office). *E-mail:* mission@un-japan.org (office). *Website:* www.un.int/japan (office).

TAKEBE, Tsutomu; Japanese politician; *Secretary-General, Liberal Democratic Party;* ed Waseda Univ.; mem. Hokkaido Ass. 1971–; elected to House of Reps 1986; Vice Minister Hokkaido Devt Agency 1990–92, Vice Minister, Ministry of Transport 1992–94, apptd Chair. Commerce and Industry Cttee 1996, Judicial Affairs Cttee 1999, Rules and Admin Cttee 2003; apptd Dir Transport Div., Liberal Democratic Party (LDP) 1994, Dir Cabinet Div. 1994, Deputy Sec.-Gen. 1998, Deputy Chair. Policy Research 2000, Chief Deputy Chair. Policy Research 2002, Sec.-Gen. 2004–. *Address:* Liberal Democratic Party, 1-11-23 Nagata-cho, Chiyoda-ku, Tokyo 100-8910, Japan (office). *Telephone:* (3) 3581-6211 (office). *E-mail:* koho@ldp.jimin.or.jp (office). *Website:* www.jimin.jp (office).

TAKEGOUCHI, Gen. Shoji; Japanese military officer; *Chairman, Joint Staff Council;* fmr Chief of Staff, Air Self Defence Force; Chair. Joint Staff Council 2001–. *Address:* Joint Staff Council, Self Defence Force, 9-7-45 Akasaka, Minato-ku, Tokyo 107-8573, Japan (office). *Telephone:* (3) 3408-5211 (office). *Website:* www.jda.go.jp (office).

TAKEICHI, Masatoshi, MSc, PhD; Japanese cell biologist and academic; *Director, RIKEN Kobe Institute and Centre for Developmental Biology;* ed Nagoya and Kyoto Univs; Asst Prof., Dept of Biophysics, Faculty of Science, Kyoto Univ. 1970–78, Assoc. Prof. 1978–86, Prof. 1986–99, Head, Centre for Molecular and Developmental Biology 1993–98, Prof., Dept of Cell and Developmental Biology, Grad. School of Biostudies 1999–2002; Visiting Prof., Nat. Inst. for Basic Biology 1992–97; Dir RIKEN Kobe Inst. and Centre for Developmental Biology, Kobe 2000–; Assoc. Ed. Cell Structure and Function 1983–, Neuron 1988–, Molecular Biology of the Cell 1989–97, Development, Growth and Differentiation 1990–, Developmental Biology 1991–95 (mem. Editorial Bd 1995–), Developmental Cell 2001–; Reviewing Ed. Science 1996–99; mem. Advisory Bd Development 1987–; mem. Editorial Bd Differentiation 1988–, Current Opinion in Cell Biology 1989–, Cell 1991–94, Trends in Genetics 1994–, Cell Adhesion and Communication 1994–, Genes and Development 1995–, Molecular and Cellular Neuroscience 1995–, Genes to Cells 1996–, Developmental Dynamics 1996–, Journal of Cell Biology 1998–2000, Journal of Neuroscience 1998–; mem. Japan Acad. 2000–, Japanese Soc. of Developmental Biologists (Pres. 1999–), Japan Soc. for Cell Biology (Bd mem.), Molecular Biology Soc. of Japan, Japan Neuroscience Soc. 2001, Japanese Cancer Asscn (Bd mem. –2000), Japanese Biochemical Soc., Japanese Soc. for Molecular Biology, American Soc. for Cell Biology, Int. Soc. of Developmental Biologists (Bd mem.); Toray Science and Tech. Grant 1984, Asahi Gakujyutsu Grant 1985, Naito Foundation Special Project Grant 1988–90, Tsukahara Nakaakira Award 1989, Chunichi Culture Award 1992, Dunham Lecturer, Harvard Medical School 1993, Osaka Science Award 1993, Keith Porter Lecturer, 33rd Annual Meeting of American Soc. of Cell Biology 1993, Asahi Award, Asahi Shimbun 1994, Jean Brachet Lecturer, 8th Congress of Int. Soc. of Differentiation 1994, Academic Prize, The Princess Takamatsuno-miya Cancer Research Foundation 1995, Japan Acad. Prize 1996, Uehara Award 1996, Ross Harrison Prize, Int. Soc. of Developmental Biologists 2001, Keio Medical Science Prize 2001, Person of Cultural Merits 2004, co-recipient Japan Prize, Science and Tech. Foundation of Japan 2005. *Publications:* numerous articles in scientific journals. *Address:* RIKEN Kobe Institute and Centre for Developmental Biology, 2-2-3 Minatojima-minami-machi, Chuo-ku, Kobe 650-0047, Japan (office). *Telephone:* (78) 306-0111 (office). *Fax:* (78) 306-0101 (office). *E-mail:* contact@cdb.riken.jp (office). *Website:* www.cdb.riken.go.jp (office).

TAKEMURA, Masayoshi; Japanese politician; b. 26 Aug. 1934, Youkaichi City, Shiga Pref.; ed Tokyo Univ.; joined Ministry of Home Affairs 1962, at Saitama Pref. offices 1967–70, Research Counsellor to Minister of Home Affairs 1970–71; Mayor of Youkaichi City, Shiga Pref. 1971–74, Gov. of Shiga Pref. 1974–86; Pres. New Party Sakigake (Harbinger) 1993–96; Minister of State, Chief Cabinet Sec. 1993–94; Minister of Finance 1994–96; mem. House of Reps, Shiga Pref. 1986–2000 (Chair. Environment Cttee).

TAKENAKA, Heizo, PhD; Japanese economist, academic and government official; b. 3 March 1951; ed Hitotsubashi Univ. and Osaka Univ.; joined Japan Devt Bank 1973, Research Inst. of Capital Formation 1977; Visiting Scholar, Harvard Univ., USA 1981, Visiting Assoc. Prof. 1989; Visiting Scholar, Univ. of Pennsylvania 1981; Assoc. Prof., Faculty of Econs, Osaka Univ. 1987; Visiting Fellow, Inst. of Int. Econs 1989; Assoc. Prof., Faculty of Policy Man., Keio Univ. 1990, Prof. 1996; Dir The Tokyo Foundation (fmrly Global Foundation for Research and Scholarship) 1997, Exec. Dir 1998, Pres. 1999; mem. Econ. Strategy Council 1998, IT Strategy Council 2000, IT Strategy HQ 2001; Minister of State for Econ. and Fiscal Policy 2001–05, for Information Tech. Policy 2001–02, for Financial Services Agency 2002–04, for Privatization of the Postal Services 2004–06, of Internal Affairs and Communications 2005–06; mem. House of Councillors, Diet, Tokyo 2004–. *Publications:* in Japanese: The Economics of Business Investment 1984, The Macroeconomic Analysis of External Imbalances 1987, The Economics of US–Japan Friction 1991, The Globalization of the Japanese Economy and Corporate Investment 1993, Wealth of People 1994, The Economy in Which Fast Movers Win 1998; in English: Contemporary Japanese Economy and Economic Policy 1991; popular writing includes a cartoon book explaining economics. *Address:* c/o Ministry of Internal Affairs and Communications 2-1-2, Kasumigaseki, Chiyoda-ku, Tokyo 100-8926, Japan (office).

TAKENAKA, Kyoji; Japanese manufacturing executive; *President and CEO, Fuji Heavy Industries Ltd;* b. 28 Nov. 1946; joined Fuji Heavy Industries Ltd

1969, Staff Gen. Man. Product Planning Office 1998–91, Staff Gen. Man. Product Planning Div. 1991–95, Project Gen. Man. Subara Devt and Eng Div. 1995–99, Vice-Pres., Project Gen. Man. of Product Planning Office and Gen. Man. Special Version Devt Dept 1999–2000, Vice-Pres., Sr Gen. Man. of Corp. Planning Div. and Gen. Man. Alliance Promotion Office 2000–01, Pres. and COO 2001–03, Pres. and CEO Fuji Heavy Industries Ltd 2003–. *Address:* Fuji Heavy Industries Ltd, Subaru Building, 7-2 Nishi-Shinjuku 1-chome, Shinjuku-ku, Tokyo 160-8316, Japan (office). *Telephone:* (3) 3347-2111 (office). *Fax:* (3) 3347-2338 (office). *Website:* www.fhi.co.jp (office).

TAKEYAMA, Minoru, BArch, MArch; Japanese architect and academic; *Professor of Architectural and Urban Design, Musashino Art University;* b. 15 March 1934, Hokkaido; ed Waseda Univ., Harvard Univ.; began career with Josep Lluis Sert, Mass, USA 1960–61, Harrison Abramovitz, NY 1961, Jorn Utzon, Arne Jacobsen and Henning Larsen, Copenhagen, Denmark 1962–64; returned to Japan and set up his own practice Takeyama Minoru and the United Actions 1965, opened second office in Sapporo 1975; co-f. post-modernist group ARCHITEXT 1971; Prof. of Architecture Musashino Art Univ., Tokyo 1975–, currently Prof. of Architectural and Urban Design; Special Prize, First World Biennale of Architecture, Bulgaria 1981, Annual Design Award 1987, Int. Illumination Design Award 1992, Honour Award of Waterfront Design 1993, Tokyo Design Award 1993. *Buildings include:* Ichiban-kan, Number One Bldg 1969, Niban-kan, Number Two Bldg 1970, Hotel Beverley Tom, Hokkaido 1973, Atelier Indigo studio, Sapporo 1976, Nakamura Hospital, Sapporo 1978, Sweet Factory, Nara 1985, Renaissance Bldg, Kyoto 1986, Tokyo Port Terminal 1991, Crematorium, Cemetery and Memorial Complex, Yokohama 2001, Central Railway Station Complex, Seoul 2002. *Publications:* Blue Nirvana 1972, Autobiography of an Architect 1973, Street Semiology 1975, Meaning of Streets 1977, Language in Architecture 1983, Tokyo Urban Language 1984. *Address:* Musashino Art University, 1-736 Ogawa-cho, Kodaira-shi, Tokyo 187-8505, Japan (office). *Website:* www.musabi.ac.jp (office).

TAKHAR, Bonnie; American business executive; *CEO and President, Halston LLC;* has held managerial positions with Donna Karan and Nicole Farhi Group; joined Earl Jean, Inc., CEO of Earl Jean Europe, London 1999–2002, Global Pres. of Earl Jean, New York (following acquisition of Earl Jean, Inc. by Nautica Enterprises) 2002–04; Advisor to CEO of Jimmy Choo Ltd on business devt 2004–06, Chief Commercial Officer, Jimmy Choo Ltd 2006–07; CEO and Pres. Halston LLC 2007–. *Address:* Halston LLC, 1350 Avenue of the Americas, Suite 2025, New York NY 10019, USA (office). *Telephone:* (212) 282-1200 (office). *Fax:* (212) 786-6775 (office). *E-mail:* info@halston.com (office). *Website:* www.halston.com (office).

TAKUMIYA, Osamu; Japanese health care industry executive; *Chairman, Kuraya Sanseido Inc.;* Vice-Pres. Kuraya Sanseido Inc. 2001, Vice-Pres. and Exec. Dir of Sales 2003, Chair. and Rep. Dir Kuraya Sanseido Inc. (following separation of pharmaceutical distribution from purchasing businesses to form new Kuraya Sanseido Inc. and MEDICEO Holdings Co. Ltd, as parts of MEDICEO Group) 2004–. *Address:* Kuraya Sanseido Inc., 7-15 Yaesu 2-chome, Chuo-ku, Tokyo 104-8464, Japan (office). *Telephone:* (3) 3517-5800 (office). *Fax:* (3) 230-5566 (office). *Website:* www.kurayasanseido.co.jp/english/ (office); www.mediceo-gp.com/english/ (office).

TAL, Hisham at-; Jordanian government official; b. 1943, Irbid; ed Damascus Univ.; lawyer –1991; Judge, Higher Court of Justice 1991–94; apptd Minister of Justice 1994; Deputy Prime Minister and Minister of Political Devt and Parl. Affairs 2005. *Address:* c/o Office of the Prime Minister, POB 80, Amman, Jordan (office).

TALABANI, Jalal; Iraqi politician and head of state; *President;* b. 1933, Kelkan; ed high schools in Erbil and Kirkuk; f. secret student asscn at age of 13; mem. Kurdish Democratic Party 1947, elected to Cen. Cttee 1951; denied admission to medical school by govt due to political activities; allowed to enter law school 1953; forced to go into hiding to escape arrest for founding and becoming Sec.-Gen. of Kurdistan Student Union 1956; following overthrow of Hashemite monarchy, returned to law school 1958; pursued career as journalist and ed. of Khabat and Kurdistan; mil. service 1959, later Commdr of tank unit; organized and led Kurdish revolt against Govt in Mawat, Rezan and Karadagh regions 1961; rep. Kurdish leadership on numerous diplomatic missions in Europe and Middle East 1960s; Founder and Sec.-Gen. Patriotic Union of Kurdistan 1975–; apptd mem. Iraqi Governing Council 2003; President of Iraq 2005–. *Address:* Office of the President, Baghdad, Iraq (office).

TALAEI, Mohsen, MA, BA; Iranian diplomatist; *Deputy Foreign Minister for Economic Affairs;* b. 1954; ed Univ. of Tehran; Sr Research Expert, Supreme Inst. of Planning 1977–79; Sr Macro Econ. Programming Expert, Man. and Planning Org. 1980–84, Sec. to State Planning HQ 1980–92, Dir Econ. Planning Office 1984–92, Dir-Gen. Enterprise Coordination Office 1986–92, Adviser to Econ. Deputy 1996–98, Adviser to Head 2002–04; Chief of Secr., Council of Free Trade Areas 1986–92; Head Cttee on Privatization Studies 1986–92; Econ. Counsellor, Embassy in Rome, Italy 1992–96, Deputy Amb. 1994–96; Adviser on Europe and USA to Deputy Minister of Foreign Affairs 1996–98; Dir-Gen. Strategic and Econ. Coordination Office, Ministry of Foreign Affairs 1996–98; Amb. to S Korea 1998–2002; Special Asst to Minister for Foreign Affairs 2002–04; Amb. to Japan 2006–08; Deputy Foreign Minister for Econ. Affairs 2008–. *Address:* Ministry of Foreign Affairs, Shahid Abd al-Hamid Mesri Street, Ferdowsi Avenue, Tehran, Iran (office). *Telephone:* (21) 61151 (office). *Fax:* (21) 66743149 (office). *E-mail:* matbuat@mfa.gov.ir (office). *Website:* www.mfa.gov.ir (office).

TALAGI, Grace Sisilia Tupou, BSc; Niuean civil servant and diplomat; *High Commissioner to New Zealand;* b. 27 Feb. 1952, Niue; m. Takili Talagi;

one s. three d.; food technologist 1976–81, food industry trainer 1981–83; Agric. Projects Man. and Exports Promoter 1983–88; Dir of Agric. and Fisheries 1988–94; Asst Head of External Affairs 1994–99; Sec. to the Govt 1999–2005; High Commr to NZ (first woman diplomat) 2005–. *Leisure interests:* research reading, golf, watching sports. *Address:* High Commission of Niue, Molesworth House, 101 Molesworth Street, Thorndon, Wellington, New Zealand (office); PO Box 175, Alofi, Niue (home). *Telephone:* (4) 499-4515 (office). *Fax:* (4) 499-4516 (office). *E-mail:* komisina@niuhicom.co.nz (office).

TALAGI, Toke Tufukia; Niuean politician; *Premier;* elected to Nat. Ass. 2002; fmr Deputy Prime Minister, Minister of Finance, of Educ.; Premier 2008–, also Chair. of Cabinet and Minister responsible for Premier's Dept, Civil Aviation, Crown Law Office, Planning, Econ. Devt and Statistics, External Affairs, Niue Public Service Comm., Finance, Customs and Revenue, Govt Assets, Police and Nat. Security, Environment, Meteorological Services and Climate Change, Tourism, Immigration and Population, Private Sector Devt, and Youth and Sports; Pres. Niue Rugby Union. *Leisure interests:* . *Address:* Office of the Premier, Alofi, Niue (office).

TALAL, Prince Walid ibn; Saudi Arabian business executive; s. of HRH Prince Talal ibn Abd al-Aziz as-Sa'ud and Princess Mona as-Solh; ed Menlo Coll., Syracuse Univ., New York, USA; Chair. United Saudi Bank 1988–99; f. Kingdom Holding Co.; investments in Citigroup Inc., News Corpn, Euro Disney SCA, Planet Hollywood chain of restaurants, Apple Computers. *Address:* c/o United Saudi Bank, PO Box 25895, Riyadh 11476, Saudi Arabia (office).

TALAT, Mehmet Ali, MSc; Turkish Cypriot politician; *President, 'Turkish Republic of Northern Cyprus';* b. 6 July 1952, Kyrenia; m.; one s. one d.; ed Middle East Tech. Univ., Ankara, Eastern Mediterranean Univ., Famagusta; began career as self-employed electrical engineer; active in Turkish Cypriot orgs, co-founder and first Chair. Cypriots Educ. and Youth Fed. (KÖGEF), Turkey; joined youth div. Republican Turkish Party (Cumhuriyetçi Türk Partisi, CTP), mem. CTP Party Council, and Cen. Exec. Cttee, also CTP Sec., becoming Chair. 1996–; Minister of Educ. and Culture 1994, later Minister of State and Deputy Prime Minister; MP for Nicosia 1998–; Prime Minister of 'Turkish Repub. of Northern Cyprus' 2004–05, Pres. 2005–. *Address:* c/o Office of the President, Lefkosa (Nicosia), Mersin 10 (office); Mersin Cad 12, Kyrenia, Mersin 10, Turkey (home). *Telephone:* 2283444 (office); (392) 8154866 (home). *Fax:* 2272252 (office). *E-mail:* info@kktc-cb.org (office). *Website:* www.tncpresidency.org.

TALBAKOV, Ismoil; Tajikistani economist and politician; *Secretary of Central Committee, Communist Party of Tajikistan;* m.; four c.; ed Tajik State Univ.; fmr officer in Soviet Army; mem. Majlisi Namoyandagon (Parl.); currently Sec., Cen. Cttee, CP of Tajikistan; unsuccessful cand. in presidential elections 2006. *Address:* Communist Party of Tajikistan, 734002 Dushanbe, Kuchai F. Niyazi 37, Tajikistan (office). *Telephone:* (372) 21-14-54 (office). *E-mail:* talbakov_555@mail.ru (office). *Website:* www.kpt.freenet.tj (office).

TALBOTT, Strobe; American journalist and fmr government official; *President, Brookings Institution;* b. 25 April 1946, Dayton, Ohio; s. of Nelson S. Talbott and Josephine Large; m. Brooke Lloyd Shearer 1971; two s.; ed Hotchkiss School, Connecticut, Yale Univ. and Univ. of Oxford, UK; joined Time magazine; Diplomatic Corresp., White House Corresp., Eastern Europe Corresp., Washington Bureau Chief 1984–89, Ed.-at-Large 1989–94; Amb.-at-Large State Dept Feb.–Dec. 1993; Deputy Sec. of State 1994–2001; Pres. The Brookings Inst. 2002–; Rhodes Scholar, Univ. of Oxford 1969; Dir Carnegie Endowment for Int. Peace; mem. Council on Foreign Relations. *Publications:* Khrushchev Remembers 1970, Khrushchev Remembers: The Last Testament (jtly) 1974, Endgame: The Inside Story of Salt II 1979, Deadly Gambits: The Reagan Administration and the Stalemate in Nuclear Arms Control 1984, The Russians and Reagan 1984, Reagan and Gorbachev (jtly) 1987, The Master of the Game: Paul Nitze and the Nuclear Peace 1988, At the Highest Levels: The Inside Story of the End of the Cold War (jtly) 1993, The Age of Terror: America and The World After September 11 (co-ed.) 2001, The Russia Hand: A Memoir of Presidential Diplomacy 2002, Engaging India 2005, The Great Experiment 2008. *Address:* The Brookings Institution, 1775 Massachusetts Avenue, NW, Washington, DC 20036, USA (office). *Telephone:* (202) 797-6000 (office). *Fax:* (202) 797-6004 (office). *E-mail:* communications@brookings.edu (office). *Website:* www.brookings.edu (office).

TALENT, James (Jim) Matthes; American politician; b. 18 Oct. 1956, Des Peres, Mo.; s. of Milton Talent and Marie Talent (née Matthes); m. Brenda Talent 1984; one s. two d.; ed Kirkwood High School, Washington Univ., St Louis and Univ. of Chicago Law School; clerk to Judge of US Court of Appeals 1982–83; elected (Republican) to Mo. House of Reps 1984–92, later Minority Leader –1992; elected to Congress (Second Dist, Mo.) 1992–2000, later Asst Minority Leader; mem. Armed Services Cttee 1992–2000, Small Business Cttee 1992–2000 (Chair. 1997), Educ. Cttee; Senator from Missouri 2003–07; Republican; Arnold J. Lien Prize for Most Outstanding Undergrad. in Political Science, Nat. Asscn of Women Business Owners' Nat. Public Policy Award (first male recipient), named Legislator of the Year by Dept of Missouri Veterans of Foreign Wars, Int. Franchise Asscn and Ind. Electrical Contractors, Vietnam Veterans of America's Lifetime Achievement Award 2000. *Address:* 9433 Olive Blvd, St Louis, MO 63132, USA (home). *Telephone:* (314) 453-0344 (home). *Fax:* (314) 453-0805 (home).

TALIB, Maj.-Gen. Naji; Iraqi fmr politician and soldier; b. 1917; ed Iraqi Staff Coll. and Sandhurst, England; Mil. Attaché, London 1954–55; Commdr Basra Garrison 1957–58; Minister of Social Affairs 1958–59; lived abroad 1959–62; Minister of Industry 1963–64; mem. UAR-Iraq Jt Presidency Council 1964–65; Minister of Foreign Affairs 1964–65; Prime Minister and Minister of Petroleum Affairs 1966–67.

TALIBOV, Vasif Yusif oğlu; Azerbaijani politician; *Chairman, Ali Majlis (Supreme Assembly) of the Autonomous Republic of Naxçıvan;* b. 14 Jan. 1960, Aralig, Ilyich (now Şarur) Dist, Naxçıvan ASSR, Azerbaijan SSR; s. of Yusif Talibov and Minaye Talibova; m. Sevil Sultanova; two s. one d.; ed Naxçıvan State Pedagogical Inst., Baku State Univ.; began career with Sharur Dist Public Educ. Dept 1976; Cadre Inspector Naxçıvan Knitted Goods Factory 1982; Sr Asst Ali Majlis (Supreme Ass.) of the Autonomous Repub. of Naxçıvan 1991–94, First Deputy for Econ. Links 1994–95, Deputy (mem. Parl.) 1995–, Chair. Ali Majlis 2005–; Founder-mem. New Azerbaijan Party (NAP), Chair. 1995–; mem. Co-ordinating Council, Congress of Azerbaijanis Worldwide 2001–. *Address:* Supreme Assembly of the Autonomous Republic of Naxçıvan, 7000 Naxçıvan, Azerbaijan (office). *Telephone:* (136) 44-01-01 (office). *Fax:* (136) 44-01-01 (office). *E-mail:* ali-hasanov@mail.ru (office).

TALLAWY, Mervat; Egyptian diplomatist and international organization official; b. 1 Dec. 1937, Menya; d. of Mehani Tallawy and Soraya Abdel-Hamid; m. Dr Ali Abdel-Rahman Rahmy 1964; one d.; ed American Univ. Cairo, Inst. for Diplomatic Studies, Cairo and Grad. Inst. of Int. Studies, Geneva; joined Ministry of Foreign Affairs 1963; served Geneva, New York and Caribbean countries, Vienna and Tokyo; Deputy Dir UN Inst. for the Advancement of Women 1982–85; Minister Plenipotentiary, Deputy Dir Dept of Int. Orgs. Ministry of Foreign Affairs 1985–88; Amb. to Austria and Resident Rep. to IAEA, UNIDO and UN Centre for Social and Humanitarian Affairs 1988–91; Dir of Int. Econ. Dept, Ministry of Foreign Affairs 1991; Asst Minister for Int. Political and Econ. Affairs 1992–93; Amb. to Japan 1993–97; Minister of Insurance and Social Affairs 1997–99; Asst UN Sec. for UNDP, Arab countries 1997; Sec.-Gen. Nat. Council for Women 2000; Exec. Sec. UN Econ. and Social Comm. for Western Asia (ESCWA) 2000–07; Rapporteur-Gen. UN Conf. on Adoption of Int. Convention on Prevention of Illicit Drug Trafficking, Vienna 1988; mem. UN Cttee on Elimination of Discrimination against Women (CEDAW) (Chair. 1990–92); Chair. UN Comm. on Status of Women 1991–93; Chair. workshop on Women and Violence leading to adoption of UN Declaration on Elimination of Violence Against Women, Vienna 1992; Chair. Working Group on Health, UN Int. Conf. for the Advancement of Women, Beijing 1995; Head Egyptian Del. to Multilateral Middle East Peace Talks Working Group on Econ. Regional Co-operation, Brussels 1992, Paris 1992, Rome 1993 and to Steering Cttee of Multilateral Middle East Talks, Tokyo 1994; Head Egyptian Del. to UN World Conf. on Natural Disasters, Yokohama 1994; Del. to UN Environment Conf., Rio de Janeiro 1992, to UN Int. Conf. on Population and Devt, Cairo 1994; initiator of proposal leading to adoption of UN Declaration for the Protection of Women and Children in Time of Armed Conflicts 1974; mem. Club of Rome; Amb. of the Year (Austria) 1991. *Leisure interests:* theatre, classical music, walking, reading, painting. *Address:* 18 el-Mansour Mohammed Street, Apt 15, Zamalek, 11211 Cairo, Egypt (home). *Telephone:* (2) 735-8102 (home). *Fax:* (2) 735-8102 (home).

TALLING, J(ohn) F(rancis), PhD, FRS; British biologist; b. 23 March 1929, Grange Town; s. of Frank Talling and Miriam Talling; m. Ida Björnsson 1959; one s. one d.; ed Sir William Turner's School, Coatham, Yorks., Univ. of Leeds, Univ. of London; Lecturer in Botany, Univ. of Khartoum 1953–56; Postdoctoral Fellow, Univ. of California, USA 1957; Biologist, Freshwater Biological Asscn 1958–89, Sr Research Fellow 1991–2008; Visiting Prof., Univ. of Lancaster 1992–98. *Publications:* Ecological Dynamics of Tropical Inland Waters (with J. Lemoalle) 1998; about 90 scientific papers. *Leisure interests:* archaeology. *Address:* c/o Freshwater Biological Association, The Ferry Landing, Far Sawrey, Ambleside, Cumbria, LA22 0LP, England (office).

TALMACI, Leonid; Moldovan banker; *Governor, National Bank of Moldova;* b. 26 April 1954; m. Nina Talmaci 1977; one d.; ed Financial Banking Coll., Chişinău, Financial-Econ. Inst. Leningrad (now St Petersburg); Prin. Economist Stroibank USSR 1984–88; Deputy Head Dept, Promstroibank USSR 1988, Chair. Energomash Bank 1988–91; Gov. Nat. Bank of Moldova 1991–. *Address:* National Bank of Moldova, 7 Renaşterii Avenue, 2006 Chişinău, Moldova (office). *Telephone:* (2) 22-16-79 (office). *Fax:* (2) 22-05-91 (office). *Website:* www.bnm.org (office).

TALMI, Igal, DrScNat; Israeli physicist and academic; *Professor Emeritus, Department of Particle Physics, Weizmann Institute of Science;* b. 31 Jan. 1925, Kiev, Ukraine (USSR); s. of Moshe Talmi and Lea Talmi (née Weinstein); m. Chana Talmi (née Kivelewitz) 1949; one s. one d.; ed Herzlia High School, Hebrew Univ. of Jerusalem and Swiss Fed. Inst. of Tech.; served in Israeli Defence Forces 1947–49; Research Fellow Princeton Univ. 1952–54, Visiting Assoc. Prof. 1956–57, Visiting Prof. 1961–62, 1966–67; Prof. of Physics, Weizmann Inst. of Science 1958–, Prof. Emer. 1995–, Head Dept of Nuclear Physics 1967–76, Dean Faculty of Physics 1970–84; mem. Israel Acad. of Sciences and Humanities 1963–, Chair. Div. of Sciences 1974–80; Weizmann Prize of the Tel-Aviv Municipality 1962, Israel Prize (with A. de Shalit) 1965, Rothschild Prize, 1971, Hans A. Bethe Prize, American Physical Soc. 2000, EMT Prize 2003. *Publications:* Nuclear Shell Theory (with A. de Shalit) 1963, Simple Models of Complex Nuclei 1993, numerous publs on theoretical nuclear physics. *Leisure interest:* bird watching. *Address:* Department of Particle Physics, Weizmann Institute of Science, Rehovot 76100, Israel (office). *Telephone:* 8-9342060 (office); 8-9468166 (home). *Fax:* 8-9344106 (office). *E-mail:* igal.talmi@weizmann.ac.il (office). *Website:* www .weizmann.ac.il/particle (office); www.weizmann.ac.il/physics/staff/Talmi.htm (office).

TALPES, Ioan, PhD; Romanian politician and fmr army officer; b. 24 Aug. 1944, Topleţ, Caraş-Severin Co.; m.; one c.; ed Faculty of History and Philosophy and School of Active Officers 'Nicolae Balcescu', Sibiu; scientific research mil. officer, Centre of Historical Studies and Researches and Mil. Theory of the Defence Ministry 1970–88; Ed.-in-Chief Mil. Publishing House 1988–90, Dir March–July 1990; worked for secret service –1989; Presidential

Adviser, Romanian Presidency 1990–92; Dir Foreign Intelligence Service with ministerial rank 1994–97; Amb. to Bulgaria 1997–98; Chief Adviser on Security Matters to the Pres. and Head of Presidental Admin 2000–Minister of State responsible for Defence, European Integration and Justice and Head of Nat. Security Dept 2004; mem. Senatul (The Senate) 2004–. *Publications:* numerous articles, studies and books published in Romania and abroad. *Address:* Senatul (The Senate), 050711 Bucharest 5, Calea 13 Septembrie 1–3, Romania (office). *Telephone:* (21) 4021111 (office). *Fax:* (21) 3121184 (office). *E-mail:* csava@senat.ro (office). *Website:* www.senat.ro (office).

TALU, Umur E., BA (Econ); Turkish journalist; b. 7 Aug. 1957, Istanbul; s. of M. Muvakkar and G. Güzin; m. Şule Talu 1987; two d.; ed Galatasaray High School and Bosphorus Univ.; educ. specialist, Railway Workers' Union 1977–78; Int. Econ. Cooperation Sec. Union of Municipalities 1978–80; Econ. Corresp. Günaydin (newspaper) 1980–82; Chief, Econ. Dept Günes (newspaper) 1982–83; Ed. with Cumhuriyet (newspaper) 1983–85; Chief, Econ. Dept Milliyet (newspaper) 1985–86, News Ed. 1986–87, 1988–92, Ed.-in-Chief 1992–94, columnist 1994–; News Ed. Hürriyet (newspaper) 1987–88; Freedom of the Press Award (Turkish Journalists' Asscn) 1996. *Publications:* Social Democracy in Europe (co-author) 1985, Keynes (trans.) 1986, Mr Uguran's Post Office 1996. *Leisure interests:* sport, music, films. *Address:* Milliyet, Dogan Medya Centre, Bagcilar 344554, Istanbul, Turkey. *Telephone:* (212) 5056111. *Fax:* (212) 5056233.

TALWAR, Rana Gurvirendra Singh, BA; Indian banker; b. 22 March 1948; s. of R. S. Talwar and Veera Talwar; m. 1st Roop Som Dutt 1970 (divorced); one s. one d.; m. 2nd Renuka Singh 1995; one s.; ed Lawrence School, Sanawar, St Stephen's Coll., Delhi; exec. trainee, Citibank 1969–70, numerous operational, corp. and institutional banking assignments, India 1970–76, Group Head for Treasury and Financial Inst. 1976, Regional Man. for Eastern India 1977, Group Head of Treasury and Financial Insts Group, Saudi American Bank, Jeddah 1978–80, Regional Consumer Business Man., Singapore, Malaysia, Indonesia, Thailand and India 1982–88, Div. Exec., Asia Pacific 1988–91, Exec. Vice-Pres. and Group Exec., Consumer Bank, Asia Pacific, Middle East and Eastern Europe 1991–95, Exec. Vice-Pres. Citicorp and Citibank, responsible for USA and Europe 1996–97; Group Exec. Dir Standard Chartered PLC 1997–98, CEO 1998–2001; Dir (non-exec.) Pearson PLC 2000–. *Leisure interests:* bridge, golf, tennis, travel. *Address:* c/o Standard Chartered Bank, 1 Aldermanbury Square, London, EC2V 7SB, England (office).

TAM, Yiu Chung, JP; Chinese trade union official and government official; *Chairman, Democratic Alliance for Betterment of Hong Kong;* b. 15 Dec. 1949, Hong Kong; m. Lai Xiang Ming; two c.; ed Australian Nat. Univ., London School of Econs, UK; trade union officer; Vice-Chair. Hong Kong Fed. of Trade Unions; Chair. Employees' Retraining Bd, Elderly Comm., fmr mem. Preparatory Cttee for Hong Kong Special Admin. Region; mem. Exec. Council Hong Kong Special Admin. Region 1997–2002, Legis. Council Hong Kong Special Admin. Region 1998–; mem. Vocational Training Council, Standing Comm. on Civil Service Salaries and Conditions of Service, Ind. Comm. Against Corruption Complaints Cttee, Services Promotion Strategy Unit; fmr Vice-Chair. Democratic Alliance for Betterment of Hong Kong, Chair. 2007–; Hon. Life Fellow Inst. of Commercial Man., UK; Gold Bauhinia Star. *Address:* 12F SUP Tower, 83 King's Road, North Point, Hong Kong Special Administrative Region (office); Executive Council Secretariat, 1st Floor, Main Wing, Central Government Offices, Central, Hong Kong Special Administrative Region, People's Republic of China. *Telephone:* 25286888 (office). *Fax:* 25282326 (office). *E-mail:* yctam@dab.org.hk (office). *Website:* www.yctam.org (office).

TAMAKOSHI, Ryosuke; Japanese banking executive; *Chairman, Mitsubishi UFJ Financial Group;* b. 10 July 1947; joined Sanwa Bank Ltd 1970, mem. Bd of Dirs 1997–2002, Sr Exec. Officer 1999–2000, Pres. 2000–01; Pres. United Calif. Bank 2001–02; Sr Exec. Officer UFJ Bank Ltd 2002, Deputy Pres. 2002–04, Head, Global Banking and Trading Div. 2003, Chair. 2004, Pres. and CEO UFJ Holdings Inc. 2004, Chair. Mitsubishi UFJ Financial Group (after merger with Mitubishi Tokyo Financial Group, Inc.) 2005–, Deputy Chair. Bank of Tokyo-Mitsubishi UFJ Ltd 2006–08. *Address:* Mitsubishi UFJ Financial Group, Inc., 7-1 Marunouchi 2-Chome, Chiyoda-ku, Tokyo 100-8330, Japan (office). *Telephone:* (3) 3240-8111 (office). *Fax:* (3) 3240-8203 (office). *E-mail:* info@mufg.jp (office). *Website:* www.mufg.jp (office).

TAMARÓN, Marqués de Santiago de Mora-Figueroa, 9th Marqués de Tamarón; Spanish diplomatist; b. 18 Oct. 1941, Jerez de la Frontera; s. of José de Mora-Figueroa, 8th Marqués de Tamarón, and Dagmar Williams; m. Isabelle de Yturbe 1966; one s. one d.; ed Univ. of Madrid and Escuela Diplomática; Lt Spanish Marine Corps 1967; Sec. Embassy, Nouakchott 1968–70, Paris 1970–73; Banco del Noroeste 1974; Counsellor, Copenhagen 1975–80; Minister-Counsellor, Ottawa 1980–81; Pvt. Sec. to Minister of Foreign Affairs 1981–82; Head of Studies and Deputy Dir Escuela Diplomática 1982–88; Dir Inst. de Cuestiones Internacionales y Política Exterior (INCIPE) 1988–96; Dir Instituto Cervantes 1996–99; Amb. to UK 1999–2004; mem. Trilateral Comm. 1989–96; Commdr Order of Carlos III, Officier, Ordre nat. du Mérite (France), Commdr Order of Dannebrog, Commdr Order of Merit (Germany), Gran Cruz Mérito Naval (Spain). *Publications:* Pólvora con Aguardiente 1983, El Guirigay Nacional 1988, Trampantojos 1990, El Siglo XX y otras Calamidades 1993, El Peso de la Lengua Española en el Mundo (co-author) 1995, El Rompimiento de Gloria 2003. *Leisure interests:* philology, mountain walking, gardening.

TAMAZAWA, Tokuichiro; Japanese politician; mem. House of Reps; Dir-Gen. Defence Agency, fmr Parl. Vice-Minister for Agric., Forestry and Fisheries, Minister 1999–2001. *Address:* c/o Ministry of Agriculture, Forestry and Fisheries, 1-2-1, Kasumigaseki, Chiyoda-ku, Tokyo 100-0013, Japan (office).

TAMEN, Pedro, LLB; Portuguese foundation executive and poet; b. 1 Dec. 1934, Lisbon; s. of Mário Tamen and Emília Tamen; m. Maria da Graça Seabra Gomes 1975; two s. two d.; ed Lisbon Univ.; Dir Moraes Publishing House 1958–75; Pres. Portuguese PEN Club 1987–90, Vice Pres. 1991–2002; Trustee Calouste Gulbenkian Foundation, Lisbon 1975–2000; mem. Bd Portuguese Asscn of Writers; D. Diniz Prize 1981; Grand Prix for Translation 1990; Critics Award 1993; INAPA Prize for Poetry 1993, Nicola Prize for Poetry 1998, Press Poetry Prize 2000, PEN Club Poetry Prize 2000. *Publications:* 12 books of poetry since 1958; Tábua das Matérias (Collected Works) 1991, Depois de Ver 1995, Guião de Caronte 1997, Memória Indescritível 2000, Retábulo das Matérias 2001, Analogia e Dedos 2006. *Address:* Rua Luís Pastor de Macedo, lote 25, 5° esq., 1750-157 Lisbon, Portugal (home). *E-mail:* ptamen@mail.telepac.pt (home).

TAMM, Ditlev, DJur, DPhilR; Danish historian, academic and legal scholar; *Professor of Legal History, Faculty of Law, University of Copenhagen;* b. 7 March 1946, Copenhagen; s. of Henrik Tamm and Lizzie Knutzen; m. 1st Maria Pilar Lorenzo 1973 (separated 1987); two d.; m. 2nd Anne-Marie Wivel; ed Univ. of Copenhagen and in Germany and France; Prof. of Legal History, Univ. of Copenhagen 1978–; mem. Royal Danish Acad., Academia Europea and several other Danish and int. scientific bds and cttees; Dr hc (Helsinki) 2000; A. S. Orsted Award 1974, Sarton Medal 2005. *Publications:* Fra lovkyndighed til retsvidenskab 1976, Retsopgøret efter besaettelsen 1984, Roman Law 1997; several books and articles on Danish and European legal history, political history and cultural history. *Leisure interests:* languages, opera, bicycling. *Address:* Studiegården, Studiestraede 6, 1455 Copenhagen (office); Attemovevej 80, 2870 Holte, Denmark (home). *Telephone:* 35-32-31-67 (office); 45-80-43-66 (home); 39-29-93-92 (home). *Fax:* 35-32-32-05 (office). *E-mail:* ditlev.tamm@jur.ku.dk (office). *Website:* www.jur.ku.dk/english (office).

TAMM, Peter; German publisher; b. 12 May 1928, Hamburg; s. of Emil Tamm; m. Ursula Weisshun 1958; one s. four d.; ed Univ. of Hamburg; Shipping Ed., Hamburger Abendblatt 1948–58; Man. Dir Ullstein GmbH (Publr) Berlin 1960–62; Man. Dir Bild-Zeitung Hamburg 1962–64; Man. Dir Verlagshaus Axel Springer and Ullstein Verlag Berlin 1964–68, Chair. and CEO Axel Springer Verlag 1968–82, Chair. Bd 1982–91; Vice-Pres. Bundesverband Deutscher Zeitungsverleger 1982–91; currently Propr Koehler/Mittler-Verlagsgruppe and Schiffahrtsverlages Hansa, Propr and Dir Scientific Inst. for Maritime and Naval History; mem. Royal Swedish Soc. of Maritime Sciences, Stockholm 1999; Bayerischer Verdienstorden 1976, Bundesverdienstkreuz I. Klasse 1986, Grosses Verdienstkreuz des Verdienst-ordens der Bundesrepublik Deutschland 1993, Cavaliere Ufficiale: Orden für die Verdienste um die Italienische Republik 1994, Hamburger Bürgerpreis 1996, Vasco da Gama Naval Medal 1997, Grosses Verdienstkreuz mit Stern 1998, Seewartmedaille in Silber 1998, Bismarckmedaille in Gold 1999, Gold Ehrenkreuz der Bundeswehr 2001, Professoren-Titel durch die Stadt Hamburg 2002, Commdr Order of the White Rose of Finland 2003, Hamburg Citizen of the Year 2004. *Publication:* Maler der See 1980. *Leisure interests:* model ships, marine books, maritime and naval history. *Address:* Elbchaussee 277, 22605 Hamburg, Germany. *Telephone:* (40) 821341 (office). *Fax:* (40) 8226300 (office).

TAMUERA, Tekiree; I-Kiribati politician; b. 16 Feb. 1940, Maiana; s. of Tamuera Timau and Era Iobi; m. Raratu Rouatu; three s.; ed King George V School, Tarawa Teachers Coll., Geelong Teachers Coll., Australia, South Devon Tech. Coll., UK; teacher; admin. officer; Chair. Public Services Comm.; Speaker of Parl. –2003. *Leisure interests:* cutting toddy, fishing. *Address:* Betio, Tarawa, Kiribati (home).

TAMURA, Shigemi; Japanese business executive; *Chairman, Tokyo Electric Power Company Inc.;* b. 1940; Man. Dir Tokyo Electric Power Co. Inc. (TEPCO) 1998, Exec. Vice-Pres. 1999–2003, Chair. 2003–; mem. Bd of Dirs e7 Fund (group of electricity utilities operating in G7 countries) 2003–, AOC Holdings Inc.; mem. Bd of Dirs Japan Productivity Centre for Socio-Econ. Devt (JPC-SED), Business Ethics Research Centre (BERG) 2003, Asscn of Radio Industries and Businesses (ARIB) 2004; Rep. Pres. Greater-Kanto Industrial Advancement Centre 2003. *Address:* Tokyo Electric Power Company Inc., 1-3 Uchisaiwai-cho 1-chome, Chiyoda-ku, Tokyo 100-8560, Japan (office). *Telephone:* (3) 4216-1111 (office). *Fax:* (3) 4216-2539 (office). *Website:* www.tepco.co.jp (office).

TAN, Amy Ruth, MA, LHD; American writer; b. 19 Feb. 1952, Oakland, Calif.; d. of John Yuehhan and Daisy Ching Tan (née Tu); m. Louis M. DeMattei 1974; ed San José State Univ., Calif., Univ. of Calif., Berkeley, Dominican Coll., San Rafael; specialist in language devt Alameda Co. Asscn for Mentally Retarded 1976–80; Project Dir MORE, San Francisco 1980–81; freelance writer 1981–88; Marian McFadden Memorial Lecturer, Indianapolis-Marion Co. Public Library 1996; Best American Essays Award 1991. *Film:* The Joy Luck Club (screenwriter, producer) 1993. *Publications:* The Joy Luck Club (Commonwealth Club and Bay Area Book Reviewers' Best Fiction Award 1990) 1989, The Kitchen God's Wife 1991, The Hundred Secret Senses 1995, The Bonesetter's Daughter 2000, Saving Fish from Drowning 2005; for children: The Moon Lady 1992, The Chinese Siamese Cat 1994; non-fiction: The Opposite of Fate: A Book of Musings (autobiog.); numerous short stories and essays. *Address:* Steven Barclay Agency, 12 Western Avenue, Petaluma, CA 94952, USA (office); c/o Ballantine Publications Publicity, 201 East 50th Street, New York, NY 10022, USA. *Telephone:* (707) 773-0654 (office). *Fax:*

(707) 778-1868 (office). *Website:* www.barclayagency.com (office); www .amytan.net.

TAN, Dun, MA; Chinese composer; b. 18 Aug. 1957, Si Mao, Hunan Province; s. of Tan Xiang Qiu and Fang Qun Ying; m. Jane Huang 1994; ed Cen. Conservatory of Music, Beijing and Columbia Univ., USA; violist, Beijing Opera Orchestra 1976–77; Vice-Pres. Cen. Conservatory of Music 1978–; works performed by major orchestras in China and at festivals world-wide; four recordings of his major orchestral works, oriental instrumental music, chamber music and electronic music issued by China Nat. Recording Co.; works also include 14 film scores for US and Chinese films, six modern ballet scores, music for several stage plays; orchestral piece commissioned by Inst. for Devt of Intercultural Relations Through the Arts, USA for Beijing Int. Music Festival 1988; Artistic Dir Fire Crossing Water Festival Barbican Centre, London 2000; composed music for Olympic Games medal ceremonies, Beijing 2008; commissioned by Google/You tube to compose internet yymphony "Eroica"; second place Weber Int. Chamber Music Composition Competition, Dresden 1983, Suntory Prize 1992, Grawemeyer Award 1998, Musical America Composer of the Year 2003. *Film scores:* Aktion K 1994, Nanjing 1937 1995, Fallen 1997, In the Name of the Emperor 1998, Wo hu cang long (Crouching Tiger Hidden Dragon) (Grammy Award 2001, Acad. Award 2001, British Acad. Film Award 2001, Classical BRIT Contemporary Music Award 2001) 2000, Ying xiong (Hero) 2002. *Compositions:* orchestral works: Li Sao (symphony) 1979, Five Pieces in Human Accent for piano 1980, Feng Ya Song for string quartet 1982, Fu for two sopranos, bass and ensemble 1982, Piano Concerto 1983, Symphony in two movements 1985, On Taoism for orchestra 1985, Traces for piano 1989, Eight Colours for string quartet 1989, Silk Road for soprano and percussion 1989, Orchestral Theatre I: Xun 1990, Soundshape 1990, Silent Earth 1991, Elegy: Snow in June 1991, Jo-Ha-Kyu 1992, Death and Fire: Dialogue with Paul Klee 1992, Orchestral Theatre II: Re 1992, CAGE for piano 1993, Circle for four trios, conductor and audience 1993, The Pink 1993, Autumn Winds for instruments and conductor ad lib 1993, Memorial Nineteen for voice, piano and double paper 1993, Orchestral Theatre III: Red 1993, Yi concerto for cello 1994, Ghost Opera 1994, Marco Polo 1995, A Sinking Love 1995, Heaven, Earth, Mankind symphony for the 'Bian Zhong' bronze bells (composed in celebration of the Hong Kong handover) 1997, Concerto for Six 1997, Heaven Earth Mankind 1997, Peony Pavilion 1998, 2000 Today: A World Symphony for the Millennium: A Musical Odyssey for the Ages 1999, Water Passion after St Matthew 2000, Crouching Tiger Concerto 2000, The Map concerto for cello, video and orchestra 2003, Eight Memories in Watercolor 2003, Secret Land: for Orchestra and 12 Violoncelli 2004; opera: Out of Beijing 1987, Nine Songs 1989, Marco Polo 1994, Peony Pavilion 1998, Tea 2002, Eight Memories in Watercolor 2003, The First Emperor (opera score, libretto co-writer) 2006. *Leisure interests:* painting in ink, calligraphy. *Address:* 367 W 19th Street, Suite A, New York, NY 10011, USA (office). *Telephone:* (212) 627-0410 (office). *Fax:* (917) 606-0247 (office). *E-mail:* tan_dun@hotmail.com (office). *Website:* www .tandunonline.com (office); www.youtube.com/tandun (office).

TAN, Kim, BSc, PhD; Malaysian biotechnology entrepreneur; *Chairman, SpringHill Management Ltd;* Chair. Spring Hill Man. Ltd, Fund Man. Spring Hill Bioventures Sdn Bhd; Dir (non-exec.) Active Capital Investment Trust. *Publications include:* over 40 scientific publs. *Address:* SpringHill Management, PO Box 822, Guildford, Surrey, GU5 0ZR, England (office). *Telephone:* (1483) 890574 (office). *Fax:* (1483) 894333 (office). *E-mail:* info@springhilluk .com (office). *Website:* www.springhilluk.com (office).

TAN, Lucio C., BS; Philippine business executive; *Chairman and CEO, Philippine Airlines Inc.;* b. 17 July 1934, Amoy, Fujian province, China; m.; ed Far Eastern Univ., Manila; f. Fortune Tobacco 1966; f. Asian Breweries 1970s; acquired Allied Banking Corpn 1977; Chair. and CEO Philippine Airlines Inc. 1995–; acquired Philippine National Bank, other cos under Lucio Tan Group of Cos include Foremost Farms Inc., Shareholdings Inc. *Address:* Philippine Airlines Inc., PAL Corporate Communications Department, PAL Center, Ground Floor, Legazpi Street, Legaspi Village, Makati City, Metro Manila, 0750, The Philippines (office). *Telephone:* (2) 8171234 (office). *Fax:* (2) 8136715 (office). *E-mail:* rgeccd@pal.com.ph (office). *Website:* www.philippineairlines .com (office).

TAN, Melvyn, FRCM; British concert pianist; b. 13 Oct. 1956, Singapore; s. of Tan Keng Hian and Wong Sou Yuen; ed Anglo-Chinese School, Yehudi Menuhin School, Royal Coll. of Music; performs on historical keyboard instruments, particularly early pianos, which he has introduced to audiences around the world; has now extended repertory to include modern piano; performs regularly in music festivals in USA, Japan, the Far East, Australia and throughout Europe. *Recordings include:* Debussy Préludes 2005, Beethoven Complete Piano Concertos with London Classical Players under Sir Roger Norrington, Beethoven and Schubert piano works. *Leisure interests:* keeping fit, good cuisine and being able to visit places without having to perform. *Address:* c/o Valerie Barber PR, Suite 2, 9A St John's Wood High Street, London, NW8 7NG, England (office). *Telephone:* (20) 7586-8560 (office). *Fax:* (20) 7586-9246 (office). *E-mail:* vbpr@btclick.com (office). *Website:* www .vbpr.co.uk (office); www.melvyntan.com (home).

TAN, Royston; Singaporean filmmaker; ed Temasek Polytechnic; writer and dir of numerous short films and one feature film 1999–; work has been showcased at over 20 int. film festivals; ASEAN Dir of the Year Award 2001, Young Artist of the Year, Singapore Nat. Arts Council 2002, Asia's Most Promising Talents, Netpac Jury 2003. *Films:* short films: Sons (Best Short Film, Singapore Int. Film Festival 2000) 1999, Hock hiap leong (Merit Award, Tampere Int. Film Festival) 2001, Mother (Voice Award, Singapore Shorts Film Festival) 2001, 24 Hours 2002, 4A Florence Close, AIDS documentary for Channel News Asia; feature film: 15 (Netpac-Frespesci Award, Singapore Int. Film Festival) 2003. *Address:* c/o The Substation, 45 Armenian Street, 179936 Singapore (office).

TAN, Tan Sri Dato' Seri Vincent; Malaysian entrepreneur; *Chairman and CEO, Berjaya Corporation Berhad;* b. (Tan Chee Yioun), 1952; m.; 11 c.; family originated from Yongchun Pref., Fujian Prov., China; began career as McDonald's franchisee; acquired major controlling stake in share capital of Berjaya Kawat Berhad, currently Chair. and CEO Berjaya Corpn Berhad, businesses include golfing, property, resorts and gambling; operates MiTV, pay-TV service in Malaysia launched 2005; Co-owner 289-foot yacht, Asean Lady. *Leisure interest:* scuba diving. *Address:* Berjaya Corporation Berhad, Lot 13-01A, Level 13 (East Wing), Berjaya Times Square, No. 1 Jalan Imbi, 55100 Kuala Lumpur, Malaysia (office). *Telephone:* (3) 2149-1999 (office). *Fax:* (3) 2143-1685 (office). *E-mail:* info@berjaya.com (office). *Website:* www.berjaya .com (office).

TAN, Yuan Yuan; Chinese ballet dancer; b. 1976, Shanghai; ed Shanghai Dancing School, John Cranko School, Stuttgart, Germany; enrolled Shanghai Dance School 1987; briefly studied in Stuttgart, Germany; joined San Francisco Ballet as a soloist 1995, promoted to Prin. Ballerina 1997; Guest Prin. Dancer, Hong Kong Ballet May 2008; Silver Medal, Jr Female Div., Second Int. Ballet Competition, Helsinki 1991, Gold Medal, Jr Female Div., 5th Int. Ballet Competition, Paris 1992, Gold Medal, Jr Female Classical Div. and Nijinsky Award, 1st Japan Int. Ballet and Modern Dance Competition 1993, MOVADO Award for Outstanding Contrib. to Arts and Culture in China 1998, named by Dance magazine as one of Top 100 Elite Dancers of the 20th Century 2000, World Journal Outstanding Youth Award 2003, honoured by Time magazine (Asia edn) as one of Asia's Heroes 20 Under 40 2004, The Bund magazine City of Heart award, Shanghai 2007. *Ballet roles:* Giselle in Giselle (Tomasson), Juliet in Romeo & Juliet (Tomasson), Odette/Odile in Swan Lake (Tomasson), Kitri in Don Quixote (Tomasson/Possokhov), Nanna in Nanna's Lied (Tomasson), cr. role in 7 for Eight (Tomasson), Aurora, Lilac Fairy, and Enchanted Princess in The Sleeping Beauty (Tomasson), cr. lead role in Sylvia (Morris), Desdemona in Othello (Lubovitch), Sugar Plum Fairy and Snow Queen in Nutcracker (Christensen/Tomasson), cr. title role in Chi-Lin, cr. prin. role in Silver Ladders, cr. pas de deux in Pandora Dance, Schoenberg variation prin. in Criss-Cross, pas de deux and second movt prin. in Prism, pas de trois in Tuning Game, Prin. in Handel – a Celebration, Valses Poeticos, and Beads of Memory (Tomasson), second movt prin. in Symphony in C, Angel and Waltz Couple in Serenade, fourth movt prin. in Western Symphony, Prin. in Theme and Variations, Prin. and Soloist in Concerto Barocco, demi-soloist in Ballo Delia Regina, Aria II in Stravinsky Violin Concerto, Siren in Prodigal Son and Prin. in Bugaku, pas de deux in Emeralds, soloist in Rubies, Terpsichore in Apollo, second aria in Stravinsky Violin Concerto, and Prin. in Diamonds (Balanchine), Maninyas, La Cathedrale Engloutie, Spirit in Taiko, and cr. prin. role in Tu Tu (Welch), Thais Pas de Deux (Ashton), cr. role in Continuum and Polyphonia (Wheeldon), cr. role of Princess in Damned (Possokhov), cr. role in Study in Motion (Possokhov), The Waltz Project (Martins), Prin. in Raymonda, Act III (Nureyev after Petipa), Elite Syncopations (MacMillan), La Esmeralda pas de deux (Perrot), first and second pas de deux in Without Words (Duato), Italian Ballerina in Gala Performance (Tudor), Prin. in Etudes (Lander), Prin. and Soloist in Glass Pieces, Mauve and Pink in Dances at a Gathering, and first pas de deux in In the Night (Bobbins), Prin. in Paquita and Nikiya and third variation in La Bayadere, Act II (Makarova after Petipa), cr. prin. role in Magrittomania (Possokhov), Angelo (Adam), Grand Pas Classique (Gsovsky). *Address:* Hong Kong Ballet, G/F 60 Blue Pool Road, Happy Valley, Hong Kong Special Administrative Region, People's Republic of China (office). *Website:* www.hkballet.com (office).

TAN KENG YAM, Tony, PhD; Singaporean academic, banker, government official and business executive; *Chairman, Singapore Press Holdings Ltd;* b. 7 Feb. 1940, Singapore; s. of the late Tan Seng Hwee and of Lim Neo Swee; m. Mary Chee Bee Kiang 1964; four c.; ed St Patrick's School, St Joseph's Inst., Univ. of Singapore, Mass. Inst. of Tech., USA and Univ. of Adelaide, Australia; Lecturer in Math., Univ. of Singapore 1967–69; Sub-Man. Overseas Chinese Banking Corpn 1969, Gen. Man. 1978; MP 1979–; Sr Minister of State (Educ.) 1979; Minister of Educ. 1980, concurrently Vice-Chancellor, Nat. Univ. of Singapore; Minister for Trade and Industry, concurrently Minister in charge of Nat. Univ. of Singapore and Nanyang Tech. Inst. 1981–83; Minister of Finance 1983–85, of Educ. and Health Jan.–April 1985, for Trade and Industry 1985–86, of Educ. 1985–91; Chair. People's Action Party Cen. Exec. Cttee 1993; Chair. and CEO Oversea-Chinese Banking Corpn Ltd 1992; Deputy Prime Minister of Singapore Aug. 1995–, concurrently Minister of Defence 1995–2003, Coordinating Minister for Security and Defence 2003–05; Dir. Singapore Press Holdings Ltd 2005–, currently Chair.; Deputy Chair. and Exec. Dir Govt of Singapore Investment Corpn Pte Ltd (GIC); Chair. Nat. Research Foundation; Deputy Chair. Research, Innovation and Enterprise Council; Chair. Ministry of Educ.'s Int. Academic Advisory Panel. *Leisure interests:* swimming, golf and walking. *Address:* Singapore Press Holdings Ltd, 1000 Toa Payoh North, Singapore 318994 (office); Government of Singapore Investment Corpn Pte Ltd (GIC), 168 Robinson Rd, 37-01 Capital Tower, Singapore 068912, Singapore (office). *Telephone:* 63196319 (office); 68898888 (GIC) (office). *Fax:* 63198282 (office); 68898722 (GIC) (office). *E-mail:* sphcorp@cyberway.com.sg (office); contactus@gic.com.sg (office). *Website:* www.sph.com.sg (office); www.gic.com.sg (office).

TANABE, Makoto; Japanese politician; b. 25 Feb. 1922, Maebashi City, Gunma Pref.; Chair. All Japan Postal Workers Union, Gunma Dist 1949; Pres. Workers Unions Council, Gunma Dist 1951–60; mem. Gunma Pref. Ass. 1955–60; mem. House of Reps 1960–; Vice-Chair. Cen. Exec. Cttee Socialist Party of Japan 1982–83, Gen. Sec. 1983–86, Vice-Chair. 1990–91; Chair. Cen. Exec. Cttee Social Democratic Party of Japan 1991–. *Address:* Social

Democratic Party of Japan, 1-8-1, Nagata-cho, Chiyoda-ku, Tokyo, Japan. *Telephone:* (813) 3592-7512.

TANAHASHI, Yasufumi, BA; Japanese politician; b. 11 Feb. 1963; ed Univ. of Tokyo; joined Ministry of Int. Trade and Industry 1987, Asst Chief Electronic Policy Div. 1992; lawyer 1993–96; elected to House of Reps 1996, re-elected 2000, 2003; Dir Special Parliamentary Cttee on Relocation of the Nat. Diet and Related Orgs Jan. 2001, Standing Cttee on Health, Labour and Welfare Feb. 2001, Standing Cttee on Judicial Affairs Feb. 2002; Acting Dir Economy, Trade and Industry Div., Liberal Democratic Party (LDP) Policy Research Council 2001, Dir LDP Youth Div.; Minister of State for Science and Tech. Policy, Food Safety and Information Tech. 2004–05. *Address:* c/o Liberal-Democratic Party–LDP (Jiyu-Minshuto), 1-11-23, Nagata-cho, Chiyoda-ku, Tokyo 100-8910, Japan (office).

TANAI, Shahnawaz; Afghan politician and fmr army general; *Leader, Da Afghanistan Da Solay Ghorzang Gond (Afghanistan Peace Movement);* b. 1950, Dargai, Khost Prov.; m.; two s. one d.; apptd Chief of Mil. Intelligence 1978, served as Chief of Army Staff and Minister of Defence in Soviet-backed Democratic Repub. of Afghanistan 1988–90; led mil. coup against Pres. Mohammad Najibullah 1990, after failure of coup went into exile in Pakistan 1990–2005; returned to Afghanistan 2005 as Leader, Da Afghanistan Da Solay Ghorzang Gond (Afghanistan Peace Movt). *Address:* Da Afghanistan Da Solay Ghorzang Gond (Afghanistan Peace Movement), Kabul, Afghanistan.

TANAKA, Koichi, BEng; Japanese chemist; *Assistant Manager, Life Science Laboratory, Shimadzu Corporation;* b. 3 Aug. 1959, Toyama City; ed Tohoku Univ.; joined Cen. Research Lab., Shimadzu Corpn 1983, seconded to subsidiary Kratos Group PLC, UK 1992, joined R&D Dept of Analytical Instruments Div., Japan 1992, seconded to Shimadzu Research Lab. (Europe) Ltd, UK 1997, seconded to Kratos Group PLC, UK 1999, Asst Man. Life Science Lab., Shimadzu Corpn, Japan May 2002–; Nobel Prize in Chemistry (co-recipient) 2002. *Address:* Shimadzu Corporation, 1 Nishinkokyo Kuwabaracho, Nakagyou-ku, Kyoto 604-8511, Japan (office). *Website:* www.shimadzu.com (office).

TANAKA, Makiko; Japanese politician; b. 14 Jan. 1944; d. of Kakuei Tanaka (fmr Prime Minister of Japan); m. Naoki Tanaka; ed Waseda Univ.; fmr Deputy Dir-Gen. LDP Int. Bureau; Minister of State, Dir-Gen. Science and Tech. Agency 1994–95; Ministry of Foreign Affairs 2001–02; mem. House of Reps for Nigata –2002 (resgnd), 2003–; mem. House Cttee on Health and Welfare. *Address:* c/o Ministry of Foreign Affairs, 2-2-1, Kasumig aseki, Chiyoda-ku, Tokyo 100-8919, Japan.

TANAKA, Nobuaki, BA, MA; Japanese diplomatist and international organization official; *Ambassador to Turkey;* b. 26 Aug. 1946, Chiba; m.; one s.; ed Tokyo Univ., King's Coll., Cambridge, UK; on staff, Ministry of Foreign Affairs Japan 1970–78, First Sec., Washington, DC 1978–86, Dir Oceania Div., Ministry of Foreign Affairs 1986–88, Dir Policy Planning Div. 1990, Dir First N America Div. 1990–92, Minister, Embassy of Japan to Thailand 1992–94, Deputy Dir-Gen. N American Affairs Bureau and Deputy Press Sec., Ministry of Foreign Affairs 1997–99, Deputy Dir-Gen. Foreign Policy Bureau 1999–2000, Consul-Gen., San Francisco, USA 2000–02, Amb. to Pakistan 2004–06, to Turkey 2008–; Asst Dir-Gen. for Man. and Admin, UNESCO, Paris 1994–97, UN Under-Sec.-Gen. for Disarmament Affairs 2006–07; Lecturer, Waseda Univ. 1986–91; Sr Researcher, Int. Inst. of Peace Studies, Japan (Asst to fmr Prime Minister Nakasone for the Trilateral Comm) 1988–90; Prof., Doshisha Women's Coll., Japan 2002–04. *Address:* Embassy of Japan, Reşit Galip Caddesi 81, GOP 06692, Ankara, Turkey (office). *Telephone:* (312) 4460500 (office). *Fax:* (312) 4371812 (office). *E-mail:* culture@jpn-emb.org.tr (office). *Website:* www.tr.emb-japan.go.jp (office).

TANAKA, Nobuo, MBA; Japanese international organization official; *Executive Director, International Energy Agency;* b. 3 March 1950; m. Gloria Tanaka; two c.; ed Univ. of Tokyo, Case Western Reserve Univ., Ohio, USA; began career with Ministry of Economy, Trade and Industry (METI) 1973, held posts including Deputy Dir Gen. Affairs Div., Machinery and Information Industries Bureau, Personnel Div., Dir of Int. Nuclear Energy Affairs, Natural Resources and Energy Agency; Deputy Dir for Science, Tech. and Industry, OECD 1989–91, Dir for Science, Tech. and Industry 1991–95, 2004–07, also Head Steering Group of Centre for Entrepreneurship 2004–07; Dir for Industrial Finance Div. and Dir for Policy Planning and Coordination Div., METI 1995–98; Minister for Energy, Trade and Industry, Embassy in Washington, DC 1998–2000; Exec. Vice-Pres. Research Inst. of Economy Trade and Industry, Japan 2000–02; Dir-Gen. Multilateral Trade System Dept, METI 2002–04; Exec. Dir IEA 2007–. *Address:* The International Energy Agency, 9 rue de la Fédération, 75015 Paris, France (office). *Telephone:* 1-40-57-65-00 (office). *Fax:* 1-40-57-65-59 (office). *E-mail:* info@iea.org (office). *Website:* www.iea.org (office).

TANAKA, Shoji, PhD; Japanese scientist and academic; *Director, Superconductivity Research Laboratory (SRL);* b. 19 Sept. 1927, Odawara, Kanagawa; m. Kimiko Tanaka 1956; one s.; ed Univ. of Tokyo; lecturer, Faculty of Eng Univ. of Tokyo 1955, Assoc. Prof. 1958, Prof. 1968, Prof. Emer. 1988; Prof. Tokai Univ. 1988–93; Vice-Pres. Int. Superconductivity Tech. Center (ISTEC) 1988–; Dir Superconductivity Research Lab. (SRL) 1988–; Hon. DSc (Purdue Univ., USA) 1999; Purple Ribbon Medal 1990 and other awards. *Publications:* Research of Semiconductor Physics 1950–75, Research of Superconductivity 1975, High-Temperature Superconductivity 1991, Industry Technology are the World of the Future 1994. *Leisure interests:* golf, reading. *Address:* Superconductivity Research Laboratory, 1-10-13, Shinonome, Koto-ku, Tokyo 135-0062 (office); 2-5-26, Ichigaya kaga-cho, Shinjuku-ku, Tokyo 162, Japan (home). *Telephone:* (3) 3536-5700 (office); (3) 3260-5500 (home). *Fax:* (3) 3536-5717 (office); (3) 3260-9398 (home). *E-mail:* tanaka@istec.or.jp (office). *Website:* www.istec.or.jp (office).

TANAKA, Shun-ichi, DEng; Japanese scientist and academic; *Professor of Physics, Science University of Tokyo;* b. 28 May 1926, Tokyo; m. Yuriko Tanaka 1957; two d.; ed The First Higher School, Univ. of Tokyo; Assoc., Univ. of Tokyo 1954–58, Lecturer 1958–60, Assoc. Prof. 1960–71, Prof. 1971–87; Prof., Faculty of Physics, Science Univ. of Tokyo 1987–; Ed.-in-Chief Japanese Journal of Applied Physics 1976–78; Ed. Journal of Modern Optics 1984–97; Postdoctoral Fellow NRC Canada 1963–64; Fellow Optical Soc. of America 1986–; Optics Paper Award 1960 and Micro-optics Award 1991, Japanese Soc. of Applied Physics, Distinguished Service Award, Minister of Int. Trade and Industry 1990. *Publications:* Dictionary of Optical Terms 1981, Handbook of Optical Engineering 1986, Fundamentals and Applications of Lightwave Sensing 1990, Dictionary of Optoelectronic Terms 1996; more than 70 scientific papers on optics, mostly in English. *Address:* Faculty of Sciences, Department of Applied Physics, Science University of Tokyo, 1-3 Kagurazaka, Shinjuku-ku, Tokyo 162-8601 (office); 3-7-7 Zoshigaya, Toshima-ku, Tokyo 171-0032, Japan (home). *Telephone:* (3) 3260-4271 (office); (3) 3982-0023 (home). *Fax:* (3) 3260-4772 (office); (3) 3982-0023 (home). *E-mail:* ystanaka@t.toshima.ne.jp (home).

TANAKA, Yasuo; Japanese writer and politician; b. 1956; ed Univ. of Hitotsubashi; community activist, Kobe, following 1995 earthquake; elected first ind. Gov. of Nagano Pref. 2000–02, 2002–. *Publications:* Nantonaku Kurisutaru (Somehow Crystal, Bungei Prize) 1983. *Address:* Nagano Prefectural Government, 692-2 Habashita Minaminagano, Nagano City, 380-8570, Japan (office).

TANASESCU, Mihai Nicolae; Romanian politician; b. 11 Jan. 1956, Bucharest; m.; two c.; ed Acad. of Econ. Studies, Bucharest, Int. Inst. for Public Admin, Paris, France, Int. Monetary Fund Inst., Vienna, Austria, Harvard Business School, USA; Head of Accounting Dept, ICRAL (Constructions, Repairs and Locative Admin Enterprise), Bucharest 1978–83; Exec., Dept for State Incomes, Ministry of Finance 1990–92, Dept for the State Budget 1992–93, Dept for Public Debt 1993–97; Alt. Exec. Chair. IBRD for group of 12 East European countries, Washington, DC 1997–2000; Minister of Public Finance 2000–04. *Publications:* scientific research papers on econs, financial analysis and forecasting in Romanian and foreign journals. *Address:* c/o Ministry of Public Finance, Str. Apolodor 17, 70663 Bucharest, Romania (office). *Telephone:* (21) 4103400 (office). *Fax:* (21) 3122077 (office).

TANAYEV, Nikolai Timofeyevich; Kyrgyzstani politician; b. 5 Nov. 1945, Penza Oblast, Russia; ed Dzhambul Hydroengineering Inst. (Kazakh SSR); Head of Osh Regional Water Canal Directorate 1984; Head of Chuipromstroi (Chui Industrial Construction) Trust 1985; apptd Chair. State Agency on Architecture and Construction 2000; fmr First Deputy Prime Minister 2001; Head of Special Comm. investigating deaths of demonstrators shot by police March 2002; Acting Prime Minister of Kyrgyzstan May 2002, Prime Minister 2002–05. *Address:* c/o Office of the Prime Minister, 720003 Bishkek, Government House, Kyrgyzstan (office).

TANDJA, Col Mamadou; Niger army officer (retd) and head of state; *President;* b. 1938, Maine-Soroa; m.; 10 c.; participated in mil. junta that ousted Pres. Diori 1974, apptd mem. Supreme Mil. Council; Prefect of Maradi region 1976–79; Minister of the Interior 1979–81, 1990–91; Prefect of Tahoua region 1981–88; Amb. to Nigeria 1988–90; Chair. Mouvement national pour la société de développement—Nassara 1991–; Pres. of Niger 1999– (re-elected 2004); fmr Chair. Econ. Community of West African States. *Address:* Office of the President, BP 550, Niamey, Republic of Niger (office). *Telephone:* 20-72-23-80 (office). *Fax:* 20-72-33-96 (office). *Website:* www.delgi.ne/presidence (office).

TANDJUNG, Akbar; Indonesian politician; *Speaker, House of Representatives;* b. 14 Aug. 1945, Sibolga, N Sumatera; m. R. A. Krissnina Maharani; four d.; ed Univ. of Indonesia; mem. Functional Devt Faction, House of Reps 1977–88, Deputy Chair. 1997–, Speaker House of Reps 1999–; State Minister for Youth and Sports 1988–93, for People's Housing 1993–98, for People's Housing and Settlement 1998, Minister State Sec. 1998; found guilty of embezzling state funds Sept. 2002, conviction dismissed Feb. 2004; mem. People's Consultative Ass. 1992–97; Chair. Cen. Bd GOLKAR Party 1998–2004; Mahaputra Adiprandana Star. *Leisure interest:* swimming. *Address:* House of Representatives, Jalan Gatot Subroto 16, Jakarta, Indonesia (office). *Telephone:* 5734469 (office). *Fax:* 5723635 (office). *E-mail:* akbartandjung@pr.go.id (office). *Website:* www.dpr.go.id (office).

TANFORD, Charles, PhD; American physiologist, biochemist and academic; *Professor Emeritus, Duke University;* b. 29 Dec. 1921, Halle, Germany; s. of Max Tanford and Charlotte Tanford; m. 1st Lucia Brown 1948 (divorced 1969); two s. one d.; m. 2nd Jacqueline Reynolds 1971; ed New York and Princeton Univs; Lalor Fellow, Harvard Univ. 1947–49; Asst Prof., Univ. of Iowa 1949–54, Assoc. Prof. 1954–59, Prof. 1959–60; Prof. Duke Univ. 1960–70, James B. Duke Prof. of Physical Biochem. 1970–80, James B. Duke Prof. of Physiology 1980–88, currently Prof. Emer.; mem. Whitehead Medical Research Inst. 1977–83; George Eastman Visiting Prof., Oxford Univ. 1977–78; Pres. Biophysical Soc. 1979; Walker-Ames Prof. Univ. of Washington 1979, Reilly Lecturer, Univ. of Notre Dame 1979; Guggenheim Fellow 1956–57; mem. NAS; Alexander von Humboldt Prize 1984, Merck Award (American Soc. for Biochem. and Molecular Biology) 1992. *Publications:* Physical Chemistry of Macromolecules 1961, The Hydrophobic Effect 1973, Ben Franklin Stilled the Waves 1989, The Scientific Traveller (with J. A. Reynolds) 1992, Travel Guide to Scientific Sites of the British Isles (with J. A. Reynolds) 1995, Nature's Robots: A History of Proteins (with J. A. Reynolds) 2001; 200 scientific articles in various journals. *Leisure interests:* photography, hiking, travel. *Address:* Tarlswood, Back Lane, Easingwold, York, YO61 3BG, England. *Telephone:* (1347) 821029. *E-mail:* candj@dial.pipex.com (home).

TANG, Gen. Fei; Taiwanese politician and air force officer (retd) and government official; b. 15 March 1932, Jiangsu; m. Chang, Ming-tsan; one s. two d.; ed Air Force Preparatory School, Chinese Air Force Acad.; air force pilot 1953–60, Operations Officer 1960–61, Flight Leader 1961–65, Squadron Commdr 1968–72, Asst Air Attaché, Embassy in USA 1972–75, Chief, Operations Section, 3rd Wing 1975–76, Group Commdr 1976–78, Mil. Attaché, Embassy in S. Africa 1979–83, Wing Commdr 1983–84, C/S/ Planning, GHQ, ROCAF 1984–85, Supt, Air Force Acad. 1985–86, Dir, Political Warfare Dept, GHQ, ROCAF 1986–89, CG, Combat Air Commdr 1989, Vice C-in-C ROCAF 1989–91, Insp.-Gen., MND 1991–92, C-in-C ROCAF 1992–95, Vice Chief of Gen. Staff (Exec.), MND 1995–98, Chief of Gen. Staff, MND 1998–99, Gen., ROCAF (retd); Minister of Defence 1999–2000; Premier of Taiwan 2000; Sr Adviser to Pres. 2000; Visiting Fellow, Hoover Inst., Stanford Univ. 2004.

TANG, Ignacio Milam; Equatorial Guinean politician and diplomatist; *Prime Minister;* fmr Minister for Youth and Sports; fmr Second Vice-Pres. Chamber of People's Reps; Deputy Prime Minister 2001–03; Sec.-Gen. of the Presidency 2003–06; Amb. to Spain 2006–08; Prime Minister 2008–; mem. Democratic Party of Equatorial Guinea. *Address:* Office of the Prime Minister, Malabo, Equatorial Guinea (office).

TANG, Jiaxuan; Chinese diplomatist; b. Jan. 1938, Zhenjiang City, Jiangsu Prov.; ed Fudan Univ., Shanghai, Peking Univ.; intern, State Broadcasting Admin 1962; staff mem., Translation and Interpretation Dept, Ministry of Foreign Affairs 1964–70; mem. Council and Deputy Div. Chief Chinese People's Asscn for Friendship with Foreign Countries 1970–78; mem. Council Sino-Japanese Friendship Asscn 1970–78; joined CCP 1973; Second Sec., then First Sec. Embassy, Tokyo, Japan 1978–83, Minister-Counsellor 1988–91, Minister 1988–91; First Secretary, then Deputy Dir Asian Affairs Dept, Ministry of Foreign Affairs 1983–88; Asst to Minister of Foreign Affairs 1991–93, Vice-Minister 1993–98, Minister 1998–2003; State Councillor 2003–08; mem. 15th CCP Cen. Cttee 1997–2002, 16th CCP Cen. Cttee 2002–07. *Address:* Zhangguo Gongchan Dang (Chinese Communist Party), Beijing, People's Republic of China (office).

TANG, Pan-Pan, MA; Taiwanese broadcasting executive; *President, Chinese Taipei Baseball Association;* b. 3 April 1942, Hunan Prov.; m. Helen Chao; one s. one d.; ed Political Warfare Coll. Taipei and Southern Illinois Univ., Carbondale, Ill.; Chief Ed. Free China Weekly 1968–72; Deputy Dir English Dept Central News Agency, Taipei 1973–79; City Ed. China News 1973–75; Chief Ed. Central Daily News (overseas edn, Chinese) Taipei 1976–77; Deputy Ed.-in-Chief, Cen. Daily News (Chinese-language daily), Taipei 1977–79, Ed.-in-Chief –1996; Dir Dept of Media Research, Govt Information Office 1979–80; News and Overseas Programmes Dir Broadcasting Corpn of China (BCC) 1980–83; Pres. BCC 1986–92; Pres. Chinese Taipei Baseball Asscn 1986–; Founding Commr Chinese Professional Baseball Org. 1990–; Edward R. Mason Fellow, Kennedy School of Govt, Harvard Univ. 1998. *Publications:* more than 500 features, commentaries and analytical articles. *Address:* Chinese Taipei Baseball Association, 16 Floor, 270 Chung Hsiao East Road, sec.4, Taipei City 106, Taiwan (office). *Telephone:* (2) 7118128, ext. 152 (office). *Fax:* (2) 27115487 (office). *E-mail:* ctba@ctba.org.tw (office). *Website:* www .ctba.org.tw (office).

TANG, Pascal Biloa, BA; Cameroonian diplomatist; *Ambassador to France;* b. 20 Nov. 1937, Ebolowa; m.; six c.; ed Univs of Aix-en-Provence and Grenoble, France, Institut Universitaire des Hautes Etudes Internationales, Geneva, Switzerland; Dir Dept of Admin., Consular and Cultural Affairs, Ministry of Foreign Affairs 1965, Dept of African and Asian Affairs 1976–77, Dept of Legal Affairs and Treaties 1985–86; served in Embassy in Addis Ababa and London, then First Counsellor, Embassy in Bonn 1979–81, Chargé d'Affaires, Algiers 1982, First Counsellor, Brussels 1982–85; Chargé de Mission, Presidency of Repub. 1977–79, Diplomatic Adviser to Pres. and Tech. Adviser to Presidency 1986–90; Perm. Rep. of Cameroon to UN, New York 1990–95; currently Amb. to France. *Address:* Embassy of Cameroon, 73 rue d'Auteuil, 75116 Paris, France. *Telephone:* 1-47-43-98-33. *Fax:* 1-46-51-24-52.

TANG, Shubei; Chinese government official; b. Jan. 1931, Shanghai; m. Liang Wenfeng; one s. one d.; joined CCP 1949; fmrly official Shanghai Fed. of Trade Unions; Ed., Head of Reporters Centre, Fujian Daily 1955; Chief, Editorial Dept, New Vietnamese-Chinese News 1955–57; Sec., then Deputy Dir, Dir China News Service 1957–69; Deputy Div. Chief Dept of Consular Affairs 1971–78; First Sec. Tokyo Embassy 1978–82; Div. Chief Dept of Consular Affairs 1982–83; Consul-Gen., San Francisco 1983–86; Amb. to USA 1986–88; Dir Office for Taiwan Affairs of Foreign Ministry 1988–89, Deputy Dir for Taiwan Affairs of State Council 1989–2000; Deputy Dir CCP Cen. Cttee Taiwan Affairs Office 1991–; Exec. Vice-Chair. Asscn for Relations Across the Taiwan Straits 1991–2000; Deputy Dir CPPCC Cen. Cttee Coordinating Cttee for Reunification of the Motherland 1993–98; mem. Standing Cttee 8th CPPCC Nat. Cttee 1993–98, 9th CPPCC Nat. Cttee 1998–2003, Vice-Chair. CPPCC Sub-cttee for Hong Kong, Macao and Taiwan Compatriots and Overseas Chinese 1998–2003; mem. Hong Kong Special Admin. Region Preparatory Cttee 1995–97. *Address:* Office for Taiwanese Affairs, c/o State Council, Beijing, People's Republic of China (office). *Telephone:* (10) 68332419 (office). *Fax:* (10) 68332824 (office).

TANG, Gen. Tianbiao; Chinese army officer; b. Oct. 1940, Shimen Co., Hunan Prov.; ed Harbin Inst. of Mil. Eng., Inst. of PLA Engineer Corps, Propaganda and Theoretical Cadre Training Course of CCP Cen. Cttee Party School and Univ. of Nat. Defence; joined CCP 1961; held various posts in

Guangzhou Mil. Region; Deputy Dir Propaganda Dept Guangzhou Mil. Region 1983; Deputy Office Head and Deputy Dir Cadre Dept of PLA Gen. Political Dept; Deputy Dir PLA Navy's Political Dept; Dir Cadre Dept of Gen. Political Dept; Deputy Dir Leading Group for the Placement of Demobilized Army Officers 1993–; Asst Dir PLA Gen. Political Dept 1993–95, Deputy Dir 1995–; rank of Lt-Gen. 1994, Gen. 2000; Deputy to 8th NPC 1993–98; mem. 15th CCP Cen. Cttee 1997–2002, 16th CCP Cen. Cttee 2002–07. *Address:* c/o Ministry of National Defence, Jingshanqian Jie, Beijing, People's Republic of China (office). *Telephone:* (10) 6370000 (office).

TANG, Truong Nhu; Vietnamese lawyer and politician; b. 1923, Cholon; ed Univ. of Paris; Controller-Gen., Viet Nam Bank for Industry and Commerce; Dir-Gen. Viet Nam Sugar Co., Saigon; Sec.-Gen. People's Movt for Self-Determination 1964–65; mem. Saigon Cttee for Restoration of Peace; Pres. Viet Nam Youth Union 1966–67; imprisoned 1967–68; joined Nat. Liberation Front 1968; Minister of Justice, Provisional Revolutionary Govt of S Viet Nam 1969–76 (in Saigon 1975–76). *Address:* c/o Council of Ministers, Hanoi, Viet Nam.

TANG, Xiaowei; Chinese physicist; b. Oct. 1931, Wuxi Co., Jiangsu Prov.; ed Tsinghua Univ., Beijing; Researcher, later Prof. Inst. of High Energy Physics, Beijing (IHEP) 1981–; Prof. Zhejiang Univ., Univ. of Science and Tech. of China (USTC); mem. Dept Math. and Physics, Academia Sinica 1985–; Del. 12th and 13th CCP Nat. Congress; mem. Chinese Acad. of Sciences 1980–; Nat. Scientific Prize of China. *Publications:* author or co-author of more than 400 papers. *Address:* Institute of High Energy Physics (IHEP), POB 918, Beijing 100039, People's Republic of China (office).

TANG, Yiau-Ming, BSc; Taiwanese army officer (retd) and government official; b. 29 Nov. 1938; m. Liu, Hsiu; two s. one d.; ed Mil. Acad., Army Command and Gen. Staff Coll., Armed Forces Univ., Armed Forces War Coll., Armed Forces Univ.; Div. Commdr in army 1984–86, Corps Commdr 1988–90, Deputy Field Army Commdr 1990–93, Field Army Commdr 1993–95, Deputy C-in-C 1995–96, C-in-C 1996–99; Chief of Gen. Staff, Ministry of Nat. Defense 1999–2002; Minister of Nat. Defense 2002–04; Sr Adviser to Pres. 2004. *Address:* c/o Office of the President, 122 Chungking South Road, Sec. 1, Taipei 100, Taiwan (office).

TANG YING YEN, Henry, JP, GBS; Hong Kong business executive and government official; *Chief Secretary for Administration, Hong Kong Special Administrative Region;* b. 6 Sept. 1952, Hong Kong; m. Lisa Kuo; four c.; ed Univ. of Michigan; Man. Dir Peninsula Knitters Ltd; Chair. Fed. of Hong Kong Industries; Dir Meadville Ltd; Hong Kong Affairs Adviser to Chinese Govt; fmr mem. Legis. Council; mem. Exec. Council Hong Kong Special Admin. Region July 1997–, Sec. for Commerce, Industry and Technology July 2002–Aug. 2003, Financial Sec. Aug. 2003–2007, Chief Sec. for Admin 2007–; mem. Selection Cttee for First Govt of the Hong Kong Special Admin. Region, CPPCC Shanghai Cttee, Hong Kong Trade Devt Council, Liberal Party. *Address:* Central Government Offices, Lower Albert Road, Central, Hong Kong Special Administrative Region, People's Republic of China. *Telephone:* (852) 28102545 (office). *Fax:* (852) 28450176 (office).

TANGAROA, Hon. Sir Tangaroa, Kt, MBE; Cook Islands administrator (retd); b. 6 May 1921; s. of Tangaroa and Mihiau; m. 1939; two s. seven d.; ed Avarua Primary School, Rarotonga; radio operator 1939–54; shipping clerk, Donald and Ingram Ltd 1955–63; MP for Penrhyn 1958–84; Minister of Educ., Works Survey Printing and Electric Power Supply, then Minister of Internal Affairs 1978–80; Minister of Educ. 1980–84; Queen's Rep. Cook Islands 1984–90; Pres. Cook Island Crippled Children's Soc. 1966–; Deacon Cook Islands Christian Church; fmr Pres. Cook Islands Boys Brigade; Del. Islands Sports Asscn; Silver Jubilee Medal 1952–1977, New Zealand Commemoration Medal 1990. *Address:* PO Box 870, Avarua, Rarotonga, Cook Islands. *Telephone:* 21690.

TANGNEY, Lt-Gen. William Patrick, BA, MA; American military commander; b. 7 Oct. 1945, Worcester, Mass.; ed The Citadel, SC, Syracuse Univ., US Naval Coll.; joined US Army 1968, advanced to rank of Lt.-Gen. 1998; Operational Staff Officer G-3 Training Div., US Army John F. Kennedy Center for Military Assistance, Fort Bragg 1972–74; Exec. Officer 2nd Special Forces Bn, 7th Special Forces Group 1974, 5th Special Forces Group 1981–83; Deputy Asst Chief of Staff G-3 1983–85; Commdr 3rd Bn 5th Special Forces Group 1985–87; Chief of Special Forces, US Total Army Personnel Command, Alexandria, VA 1987–88; Commdr 10th Special Forces Group, Fort Devens, Mass. 1990–92; Commanding Gen. Special Operations, MacDill Air Force Base, Fla 1993–94; Deputy Commanding Gen., Chief of Staff, US Army Special Operations Command, Fort Bragg 1994–95; Commanding Gen. US Army Special Forces Command (Airborne), Fort Bragg 1995–97, US Army John F. Kennedy Special Warfare Center, Fort Bragg 1996–98; Deputy Commdr in Chief, Special Operations Command, MacDill Air Force Base, Fla 2000–02; now retd from active duty; Distinguished Service Medal, Defense Superior Service Medal (with Oak Leaf Cluster), Legion of Merit (with Oak Leaf Cluster), Bronze Star Medal with V Device, Bronze Star Medal (with 2 Oak Leaf Clusters), Defense Meritorious Service Medal. *Address:* c/o United States Special Operations Command, 7701 Tampa Point Boulevard, MacDill Air Force Base, FL 33621-5323, USA (office).

TANIGAKI, Sadakazu; Japanese politician; *Minister of Land, Infrastructure, Transport and Tourism, Ocean Policy;* b. 7 March 1945, Kyoto; m.; two d.; ed Univ. of Tokyo; first elected to House of Reps 1983; Vice-Minister for Post and Telecommunications 1988–89, for Defence 1990; Chair. Parl. Cttee on Communications 1991–93, Rules and Admin 1995–96; Minister for Science and Tech. 1997–98; State Sec. for Finance 1998–99; Chair. Financial Reconstruction Comm. 2000; Minister for Food Safety Comm. 2002–03; Chair. Nat. Public Safety Comm. 2002–03; Minister for Industrial Revitalization

Corpn 2002–03, of Finance 2003–06, of Land, Infrastructure, Transport and Tourism, Ocean Policy 2008–; mem. LDP, Chief Policymaker 2007–. *Address:* Ministry of Land, Infrastructure, Transport and Tourism, Ocean Policy, 2-1-3, Kasumigaseki, Chiyoda-ku, Tokyo 100-8918, Japan (office). *Telephone:* (3) 5253-8111 (office). *Fax:* (3) 3580-7982 (office). *E-mail:* webmaster@mlit.go.jp (office). *Website:* www.mlit.go.jp (office).

TANIGUCHI, Ichiro, BSc; Japanese physicist and electronics industry executive; *Chairman, Mitsubishi Electric Corporation;* ed Kyoto Univ.; joined Mitsubishi Electric Corpn (Melco) 1959, specialist in laser devt, then researcher devt of missile, defence and control systems, Cen. Research Lab., Gen. Man. Kamakura Works 1975, oversaw design and devt of ETS-4 (Japan's first independently developed satellite) 1979, Man.-Dir Electronic Products and Systems Group 1995–98, Sr Man. Dir 1997–98, Pres. and CEO 1998–2002, Chair. 2002–; mem. Bd of Dirs Mitsubishi Corpn; Chair. Japan Electronics and Information Tech. Industries Asscn, VCCI (Voluntary Control Council for Interference). *Address:* Mitsubishi Electric Corporation, Mitsubishi Denki Building, 2-3 Marunouchi 2-chome, Chiyoda-ku, Tokyo 100-8310, Japan (office). *Telephone:* (3) 3218-2111 (office). *Fax:* (3) 3218-2185 (office). *Website:* global.mitsubishielectric.com (office).

TANIGUCHI, Makoto, BA, MA; Japanese diplomatist and university professor; *Director, Research Institute of Current Chinese Affairs, Waseda University;* b. 1930, Osaka; s. of Yoshio Taniguchi and Tomiko Tamura; m. Hiroko Kanari 1972; one s.; ed Hitotsubashi Univ., St John's Coll. Cambridge, UK; joined Ministry of Foreign Affairs 1959; specialized in econ. affairs; Dir for UN Specialized Agencies 1972, Dir for UN Econ. Affairs 1973–74, Counsellor of Japanese Mission to Int. Orgs, Geneva, in charge of UNCTAD Affairs 1974–76, Minister and Consul-Gen., Manila 1976–79, Minister, Japanese Mission to UN, in charge of Econ. Matters 1979–83; Amb. to Papua New Guinea 1983–86, to UN, New York 1986–90; Deputy Sec.-Gen. OECD 1990–96; External Auditor Hitachi Metals 1995–; Special Adviser to Sec.-Gen. OECD 1997; Prof. Inst. of Asia-Pacific Studies, Waseda Univ., Tokyo 1998–2000, Dir Research Inst. of Current Chinese Affairs, Waseda Univ. 2000–; Prof., Toyo Eiwa Women's Univ., Tokyo 1997–; Chair. Preparatory Cttee for UN Conf. on New and Renewable Sources of Energy 1980–81, Chair. Cttee I 1981; Chair. Cttee I, UNCTAD VII; Vice-Pres., Pres. Exec. Bd UNICEF 1987–88; Visiting Prof. Univ. of Int. Trade and Econs Beijing 1995; Head Japanese Del. to UN Comm. on Human Rights 1987–89; Second Order of Merit 1999. *Publications:* North-South Issues: A Path to Global Solutions (in Japanese) 1993, North-South Issues in the 21st Century: A Challenge of Globalization (in Japanese) 2001, Japan and Asia in a New Global Age 2001; many articles. *Leisure interests:* music (opera), singing, walking. *Address:* Research Institute of Current Chinese Affairs, Waseda University, Bokusha Building 2F 1-101, Totsuka-machi, Shinjuku-ku, Tokyo 169-0071 (office); Azabu House 901, 1-7-13 Roppongi, Minato-ku, Tokyo 106-0032, Japan (home). *Telephone:* (3) 5286-3987 (office); (3) 3585-2879 (home). *Fax:* (3) 5286-3987 (office); (3) 3585-2879 (home). *E-mail:* xxchiang@mn.waseda.ac.jp (office).

TANIGUCHI, Yoshio; Japanese architect; b. 1937, Tokyo; ed Keio Univ., Tokyo, Grad. School of Design, Harvard Univ., USA; won competition to design expansion of Museum of Modern Art, New York 1998, completed 2004.

TANIN, Zahir, MD; Afghan journalist, physician and diplomatist; *Permanent Representative, United Nations;* b. 1 May 1956; m.; two c.; ed Kabul Medical Univ., BBC Leadership Programme; began career as journalist in Kabul 1980; freelance writer in France 1992–93; fmr Ed.-in-Chief Afkbar-e-Haftah and Sabawoon Magazine; Research Fellow, Int. Relations Dept, LSE, UK 1994–95; Producer, BBC World Service 1995–2000, Sr Producer 2000–01, Ed. Afghanistan and Cen. Asia (Persian Section) 2001–03, Persian/Pashto Section in Afghanistan 2003–06; Perm. Rep. to the UN, New York 2006–. *Radio:* The Oral History of Afghanistan in the 20th Century (29-part series; BBC). *Publications include:* The Communist Regime in Afghanistan (co-author), Afghanistan in the Twentieth Century. *Address:* Permanent Mission of Afghanistan to the United Nations, 360 Lexington Avenue, 11th Floor, New York, NY 10017, USA (office). *Telephone:* (212) 972-1212 (office). *Fax:* (212) 972-1216 (office). *E-mail:* afgwatan@aol.com (office). *Website:* www.mfa.gov.af (office).

TANKARD, Meryl; Australian choreographer, director and designer; b. 8 Sept. 1955, Darwin; d. of (Mick) Clifford Tankard and Margot Tankard; ed Australian Ballet School; dancer with Australian Ballet Co. 1975–78; soloist, Pina Bausch Wuppertal Tanztheater, Germany 1978–84, Guest Performer and Choreographer 1984–89; Artistic Dir Meryl Tankard Co., Canberra 1989–92, Australian Dance Theatre, Adelaide 1993–99, Meryl Tankard Australian Dance Theatre 1993–99, freelance choreographer 1999–; Sidney Myer Performing Arts Award for Individual Achievement 1993, Victoria Green Room Awards 1993, 1994, Betty Pounder Award for Original Choreography 1994, 'Age' Performing Arts Award for Best Collab. (Dance) 1995, Mobil Pegasus Award for Best Production 1997; Australian Dance Awards' Lifetime Achievement Award 2003, Centenary Medal Australia, Australia Council Creative Devt Fellowship. *Major works choreographed include:* Echo Point (Australia) 1984, 1990, Travelling Light (UK and Australia) 1986–87, Two Feet (Australia, NZ, Japan and Germany) 1988–94, VX 18504 (Australia) 1989–95, Court of Flora (Australia) 1990–93, Nuti & Kikimora (Italy, Indonesia, Australia, China and Germany) 1990–94, Chants of Marriage I and II (Australia) 1991–92, Furioso (Australia and overseas) 1993–99, O Let Me Weep (Australia) 1994, Aurora (Australia) 1994–96, Orphée et Eurydice (Australia) 1995–96, Possessed (Australia, France and Germany) 1995–99, The Deep End (Australia) 1996, Bolero (France, USA, Hong Kong) 1999, The Beautiful Game (UK) 2000, Merryland (Netherlands, Switzerland, Germany), The Wild Swans (Australia) 2003, @North (Berlinballet, Berlin) 2004,

Petrushka for Netherlands Dance Theatre I (Den Haag) 2004. *Leisure interests:* designing, drawing. *Address:* PO Box 3129, Bellevue Hill, NSW 2023, Australia (office). *Telephone:* (2) 9300-6817 (office). *Fax:* (2) 9300-6817 (office). *E-mail:* meryltankard@aol.com (office). *Website:* www.meryltankard .com (office).

TANKSLEY, Steven D., BS, PhD; American agronomist, geneticist and academic; *Liberty Hyde Bailey Professor of Plant Breeding and Chairman of the Genomics Initiative Task Force, Cornell University;* b. Hattiesburg, Miss.; ed Colorado State Univ., Univ. of California, Davis; Postdoctoral Fellow, Univ. of California, Davis 1979–81; Asst Prof., New Mexico State Univ., Las Cruces 1981–85; Assoc. Prof. of Plant Breeding, Cornell Univ. 1985–94, Full Prof. 1994–, currently Liberty Hyde Bailey Prof. of Plant Breeding and Chair. Genomics Initiative Task Force; mem. NAS 1995–; Alexander von Humboldt Foundation Award, Martin Gibbs Medal, American Soc. of Plant Biologists, Wolf Prize in Agric., Wolf Foundation (co-recipient) 2004. *Achievement:* mem. team of Cornell scientists who successfully cloned first gene for disease resistance in tomato, using technique known as map-based cloning developed for Human Genome Project 1993. *Publications:* numerous scientific papers in professional journals. *Address:* Department of Plant Breeding and Genetics, 248 Emerson, Cornell University, Ithaca, NY 14853, USA (office). *Telephone:* (607) 255-1673 (office). *Fax:* (607) 255-6683 (office). *E-mail:* sdt4@cornell.edu (office). *Website:* plbrgen.cals.cornell.edu (office).

TANNER, Alain; Swiss film director; b. 1933, Geneva; ed in London; made numerous documentaries before directing feature films. *Films include:* Charles Dead or Alive 1969, The Salamander, The Middle of the World, Jonah Who Will be 25 in the Year 2000, Light Years Away (Special Jury Prize, Cannes Film Festival 1985) 1981, No Man's Land 1985, Une Flamme Dans Mon Coeur 1987, The Woman of Rose Hill 1989.

TANNER, Lindsay, MA; Australian politician; *Minister for Finance and Deregulation;* b. 26 April 1956, Orbost, Vic.; m. Andrea Tanner; two d.; ed Univ. of Melbourne; Articled Clerk and Solicitor, Holding Redlich 1982–85; Electorate Asst for Senator Barney Cooney 1986; Asst Sec., Federated Clerks Union, Vic. 1987–88, State Sec. 1988–93; MP (Australia Labor Party) for Melbourne 1993–, Shadow Minister for Transport 1996–98, for Finance and Consumer Affairs 1998, for Communications 2001–04, for Finance 2005–07, Minister for Finance and Deregulation 2007–. *Publications:* The Politics of Pollution (jt author) 1978, The Last Battle 1996, Open Australia 1999, Crowded Lives 2003; numerous articles in journals and newspapers. *Leisure interests:* reading, playing piano, sport. *Address:* Department of Finance and Administration, John Gorton Building, King Edward Terrace, Parkes ACT 2600, Australia (office). *Telephone:* (2) 6215-2222 (office). *Fax:* (2) 6273-3021 (office). *E-mail:* Lindsay.Tanner.MP@aph.gov.au (office). *Website:* www .finance.gov.au (office); www.lindsaytanner.com.

TANNER, Roger Ian, PhD, FRS, FAA; British academic and engineer; *P. N. Russell Professor of Mechanical Engineering, University of Sydney;* b. 25 July 1933, Wells, Somerset; s. of R. J. Tanner and E. Tanner; m. Elizabeth Bogen 1957; two s. three d.; ed Univs of Bristol and Manchester, Univ. of California at Berkeley, USA; eng apprentice, Bristol Aero Engines 1950–53; Lecturer in Mechanical Eng, Univ. of Manchester 1958–61; Sr Lecturer, Reader, Univ. of Sydney, Australia 1961–66, P. N. Russell Prof. of Mechanical Eng 1975–, Pro-Vice-Chancellor (Research) 1994–97; Prof., Brown Univ. Providence, RI, USA 1966–75; Fellow, Australian Acad. of Tech. Science and Eng 1977; Edgeworth David Medal 1966, Australian Soc. of Rheology Medallion 1993, A.G.M. Michell Medal 1999, British Soc. of Rheology Gold Medal 2000. *Publications:* Engineering Rheology 1985, 2000, Rheology: An Historical Perspective 1998. *Leisure interests:* golf, opera. *Address:* Department of Aerospace, Mechanical and Mechatronic Engineering, University of Sydney, NSW 2006 (office); Marlowe, Sixth Mile Lane, Roseville, NSW 2069, Australia (home). *Telephone:* (2) 9351-7153 (office). *Fax:* (2) 9351-7060 (office). *E-mail:* rit@aeromech.usyd .edu.au (office).

TANTAWI, Field Marshal Muhammad Hussain; Egyptian army officer and government official; *Minister of Defence and Military Production;* served in Suez war 1956, six-days war 1967, October 1973 war; currently Minister of Defence and Mil. Production. *Address:* Ministry of Defence and Military Production, Sharia 23 July, Kobri el-Kobba, Cairo, Egypt (office). *Telephone:* (2) 4032159 (office). *Fax:* (2) 2916227 (office). *E-mail:* mod@idsc.gov.eg (office).

TANTI, Tulsi R., BCom, DipEng; Indian energy industry executive; *Chairman and Managing Director, Suzlon Energy;* b. Rajkot, Gujarat; m.; three c.; ed Rajkot Coll.; began career in textile industry, Gujarat; co-f. Suzlon Energy (wind power venture) 1995, currently Chair. and Man. Dir; Solar Energy Soc. of India (SESI) Business Leadership Award 2002, World Wind Energy Award 2003, SESI Lifetime Achievement Award as Best Renewable Man of the Decade 2006, Time magazine Hero of the Environment 2007. *Address:* Suzlon Energy, 5th Floor, Godrej Millennium 9, Koregaon Park Road, Pune 411 001, Maharashtra, India (office). *Telephone:* (20) 40122000 (office). *Fax:* (20) 40122100 (office). *E-mail:* pune@suzlon.com (office). *Website:* www.suzlon.com (office).

TANZI, Vito, PhD; American/Italian economist; *Senior Consultant in Trade and Integration, Inter-American Development Bank;* b. 29 Nov. 1935, Italy; s. of Luigi Tanzi and Maria Tanzi; m. Maria T. Bernabé 1997; three s.; ed George Washington and Harvard Univs; Chair. of Econs Dept, American Univ. 1971–74, Prof. of Econs 1970–74; Head of Tax Policy Div. IMF 1974–81, Dir Fiscal Affairs Dept 1981–2000; Pres. Int. Inst. of Public Finance 1990–94; Sr Assoc. Carnegie Endowment for Int. Peace 2001; Under-Sec. of State, Ministry of Economy and Finance, Italy 2001–03; Sr Consultant in Trade and Integration, IDB 2003–; Dr hc (Córdoba, Argentina) 1998, (Liège) 1999, (Turin) 2001, (BARI) 2003; Commendatore della Repubblica Italiana. *Publi-*

cations: ten books, over 200 articles in professional journals. *Leisure interests:* naif art, African art, photography, music, travel, collecting old keys and old locks. *Address:* Inter-American Development Bank, 1300 New York Avenue, NW, Washington, DC 20577 (office); 5912 Walhonding Road, Bethesda, MD 20816, USA (home). *Telephone:* (202) 623-3442 (office). *Fax:* (202) 623-3096 (office); (301) 229-4106 (home). *E-mail:* vivot@contractual.iadb.org (office); vitotanzi@msn.com (home). *Website:* www.iadb.org (office).

TAO, Gen. Bojun; Chinese army officer; *Commander, Chengdu Military Region, People's Liberation Army;* b. 1936, Yongji Co., Jilin Prov.; joined PLA 1951, CCP 1961; Chief, Wuhan Mil. Dist (Combat Div., Artillery HQ), PLA Guangzhou Mil. Region 1976–77, Dir Artillery HQ 1983; Deputy Army Commdr PLA Chengdu Mil. Region 1983–85, Chief-of-Staff 1985–92, Commdr 2000–; Chief of Staff Guangzhou Mil. Region 1992, Deputy Commdr 1993–96, Commdr 2000; Commdr Guangdong Mil. Region 1996; rank of Maj.-Gen. 1988, Lt-Gen. 1991, Gen. 2000; Del., 13th CCP Cen. Cttee 1987–92, 14th CCP Cen. Cttee 1992–97, mem. 15th CCP Cen. Cttee 1997–2002. *Address:* People's Liberation Army, c/o Ministry of National Defence, Jingshanqian Jie, Beijing, People's Republic of China (office).

TAO, Dayong; Chinese economist; *Professor of Economics, Beijing Normal University;* b. 12 March 1918, Shanghai; m. Niu Ping-Qing 1942; one s. one d.; ed Nat. Cen. Univ.; Lecturer, Nat. Sun Yat-sen Univ. 1942–43; Assoc. Prof., Nat. Guangxi Univ. 1943–44, Nat. Jiaotong Univ. 1944–45; Prof., Nat. Szechwan Univ. 1945–46; Visiting Prof. (invited by British Council) 1946–48; Prof., Beijing Univ. 1949–51; Prof., Beijing Normal Univ. 1952–; Ed.-in-Chief, New Construction 1951–54, Qunyan 1985–; mem. 5th CPPCC Nat. Cttee 1978–83, Standing Cttee 6th CPPCC Nat. Cttee 1983–88; mem. Standing Cttee 6th, 7th, 8th NPC 1983–98; Vice-Chair. 5th, 6th, 7th Cen. Cttee Chinese Democratic League 1985–97, Hon. Vice-Chair. 8th Cen. Cttee 1997–; Vice-Pres. World Econs Soc. of China 1980–85, Chinese Soc. of Foreign Econ. Theories 1983–; Adviser, Centre for Hongkong and Macao Studies 1982; Int. Order of Merit 1990, Medal of The First Five Hundred 1991, Int. Register of Profiles 1993, 20th Century Award for Achievement 1993. *Publications:* Economic Reconstruction of Post-War Eastern Europe 1948, Post-war Capitalism 1950, History of Socialism 1949, Introduction to World Economy 1951, Studies in Contemporary Capitalistic Economy 1985, A Critique of Henry George's Economic Thought 1982, History of Social Development 1982, A New History of Foreign Economic Thoughts 1990, Selected Works of Tao Dayong (Vols I and II) 1992, (Vol. III) 1998, Outline of New Democratic Economics 2002. *Leisure interests:* reading, travel, music. *Address:* Economics Department, Beijing Normal University, Xinjiekouwai Street 19, Beijing 100875, People's Republic of China (office). *Telephone:* (10) 62200012 (office).

TAO, Ho; Chinese artist and architect; b. 1936; ed Williams Coll. and Harvard Univ., Mass, USA; worked with architect Walter Gropius; in practice as architect in Hong Kong; art work includes acrylic paintings, lithographs, pen-and-ink sketches and sculptures in marble, wood and rusty scrap iron; works exhibited at Hong Kong Univ. Museum; f. TAOHO Design 1968; World Economic Forum Crystal Award 1997. *Buildings include:* Hong Kong Arts Centre 1977. *Designs include:* Bauhinia emblem, flag of Hong Kong Special Administrative Region, Synergy of Dynamic Energy (displayed at West Hall area, Hong Kong International Airport). *Address:* Taoho Design Architects Ltd, 4 Suffolk Road, Kowloon, Hong Kong Special Administrative Region, People's Republic of China (office). *Website:* www.taoho.com (office).

TAO, Siju; Chinese party official; *Commissioner General, Chinese People's Armed Police Force;* b. 1935, Jingjiang Co., Jiangsu Prov.; joined CCP 1949; Vice-Minister of Public Security 1984–90, Minister 1990–98; Vice-Chair. Internal Affairs and Judicial Cttee 9th NPC 1998–; Chair. Nat. Narcotics Control Comm. 1993–; First Political Commissar, Chinese People's Armed Police Force 1990–, Commr-Gen. 1992–; mem. Cen. Comm. of Political Science and Law; mem. 14th CCP Cen. Cttee 1992–97, 15th CCP Cen. Cttee 1997–2002; mem. 9th Standing Cttee of NPC 1998–2003. *Address:* c/o Standing Committee of National People's Congress, Beijing, People's Republic of China (office). *Telephone:* (10) 65122831 (office).

TAO, Terence, BSc, MSc, PhD; Australian mathematician and academic; *Professor of Mathematics, UCLA;* b. 17 July 1975, Adelaide; s. of Dr Billy Tao and Grace Tao; m.; one s.; ed Flinders Univ. of South Australia, Princeton Univ.; began learning calculus aged seven years, progressed to univ.-level calculus aged eleven, apptd Full Prof. aged twenty-four; Hedrick Asst Prof. then Prof. of Math., UCLA 1996–; Visiting Prof., Univ. of New South Wales 2000; Hon. Prof., ANU 2001–03; Bronze, Silver and Gold Medals (youngest ever Gold medallist) Int. Math. Olympiads, Salem Prize 2000, Bocher Prize 2002, Clay Research Award 2003, Australian Math. Soc. Medal 2005, American Math. Soc.'s Levi L. Conant Prize (jtly) 2005, Int. Congress of Mathematicians' Fields Medal 2006, MacArthur Fellowship 2006, SASTRA Ramanujan Prize 2006. *Publications:* Solving Mathematical Problems: A Personal Perspective 2006; has contributed to several books; numerous articles in professional journals including Annals of Mathematics, Acta Mathematica, and American Journal of Mathematics. *Address:* Mathematical Sciences 5622, Department of Mathematics, UCLA, Los Angeles, CA 90095-1596, USA (office). *Telephone:* (310) 206-4844 (office). *Fax:* (310) 206-6673 (office). *E-mail:* tao@math.ucla.edu (office). *Website:* www.math.ucla.edu/~tao (office).

TAPAGARARUA, Willie Jimmy; Ni-Vanuatu politician; fmr Deputy Prime Minister and Minister for Industry and Commerce; fmr Minister for Finance and Econ. Man. *Address:* c/o Ministry of Finance, PMB 058, Port Vila, Vanuatu (office).

TAPIA ROA, Ruth Esperanza; Nicaraguan government official; *Secretary-General, Ministry of National Defence;* b. 21 Nov. 1960, Masaya; ed Centre D' Etudes Diplomatiques et Strategiques, France, Universidad Centroamericana, Managua; First Sec. at Embassy in Paris 1985–90; Spokesperson, Supreme Court of Justice 2002–07; Sec.-Gen. Ministry of Nat. Defence 2007–. *Address:* Ministry of National Defence, Casa de la Presidencia, Managua, Nicaragua (office). *Telephone:* 266-3580 (office). *Fax:* 228-7911 (office). *E-mail:* webmaster@midef.gob.ni (office). *Website:* www.midef.gob.ni (office).

TÀPIES PUIG, Antoni; Spanish painter; *President, Fundació Antoni Tàpies;* b. 13 Dec. 1923, Barcelona; m. Teresa Barba; three c.; ed Inst. Menéndez Pelayo and Univ. of Barcelona; first one-man exhbn, Barcelona 1948, later in Paris, New York, London, Zürich, Rome, Milan, Munich, Stockholm, Hanover, Washington, Pasadena, Buenos Aires, Caracas, Düsseldorf, Bilbao, Madrid and Barcelona; cr. Mural for Saint Gallen Theatre, Switzerland 1971; French Govt Scholarship 1950; Pres. Fundació Antoni Tàpies; Officier des Arts et des Lettres; UNESCO Prize, Venice Biennale and Pittsburgh Int. Prize 1958, Guggenheim Prize 1964, Rubens Prize 1972, City of Barcelona Prize 1979, Rembrandt Prize, Goethe Foundation, Basle 1984, French Nat. Grand Prize for Painting 1985, Prince of Asturias Prize 1990, Praemium Imperiale 1990, Golden Lion Venice Biennale 1993. *Publications:* La pràctica de l'art, L'art contra l'estètica, Memòria personal (autobiog.) 1978, La realitat com a art 1983, Valor de l'Art 1993, L'Art i els seus llocs 1999. *Address:* Fundació Antoni Tàpies, Aragó 255, 08007 Barcelona (office); C. Zaragoza 57, 08006 Barcelona, Spain. *Telephone:* (93) 4870315 (office); (93) 2173398. *Fax:* (93) 4870009 (office). *Website:* www.fundaciotapies.org (office).

TAPLIN, Guy Christie; British artist; b. 5 March 1939, London; s. of George Frederick Taplin and Gladys Lillian Taplin (née Peters); m. Robina Dunkery Jack 1989; one s. one d.; ed Norlington Secondary Modern School, Leyton; self-taught artist (sculptor) 1978–; fmrly worked as window cleaner; Post-Office messenger 1954–58, meat porter 1960, driver 1961, ladies' hairdresser 1961–62, lifeguard 1962–68, cook 1964, birdkeeper Regent's Park 1970–76; also had own fashion business during 1960s. *Publications:* books on his work: Birds of Creation, Bird on Wire (by Ian Collins). *Leisure interests:* life, art, folk art, travel, chance.

TAPPER, Colin Frederick Herbert, MA, BCL; British lawyer and academic; *Fellow, Magdalen College, University of Oxford;* b. 13 Oct. 1934, W Drayton; s. of H. F. Tapper and F. G. Tapper (née Lambard); m. Margaret White 1961; one d.; ed Magdalen Coll. Oxford; teacher LSE 1959–65; barrister Grays Inn 1961; tutor Magdalen Coll. 1965–79, Fellow 1965–, Reader 1979–91, Prof. 1992–2002; Dir Butterworth Group 1979–84, Butterworth Telepublishing 1979–89; consultant to Masons (solicitors) 1990–. *Publications:* Computers and the Law 1973, Computer Law 1978, Cross on Evidence (ed.) 1990, Handbook of European Software Law (ed.) 1995, Cross and Tapper on Evidence (ed.) 1999. *Leisure interests:* computing, reading, writing. *Address:* Magdalen College, Oxford, OX1 4AU (office); Corner Cottage, Woodstock Road, Stonesfield, Witney, Oxon., OX29 8QA, England (home). *Telephone:* (1865) 276055 (office); (1993) 891284 (home). *Fax:* (1865) 276103 (office); (1993) 891395 (home). *Website:* www.admin.ox.ac.uk/gsp/colleges/magd.shtml (office).

TARAND, Andres; Estonian politician; b. 11 Jan. 1940, Tallinn; s. of Helmut Tarand and Leida Tarand; m. Mari (née Viiding) Tarand 1963; two s.; ed Tartu State Univ.; hydrometeorologist 1963; Research Asst, Tallinn Botanical Gardens 1965–68, Sr Engineer 1970–73, Sr Researcher 1973–76, Sector Dir 1976–79, 1981–88, Dir of Research 1979–81, Dir Tallinn Botanical Gardens 1988–90; researcher, Antarctic Expedition 1968–70; Chair. Environment Cttee Supreme Soviet Estonian SSR 1990; mem. Council of Estonia 1990–92; mem. Constitutional Ass. 1991–92; mem. Riigikogu (Parl.) 1992, 1995–2004; Minister for the Environment 1992–94, 1994–95; Prime Minister of Estonia 1994–95; mem. People's Party Moderates (Rahvaerakond Mõõdukad, renamed Sotsiaaldemokraatlik Erakond 2004) 1996–, Chair. 1996–2002, Chair. Cttee of Foreign Affairs 1999–2002; mem. European Parl. (Socialist Group) 2004–, mem. Cttee on Industry, Research and Energy, Del. for Relations with the Korean Peninsula, Substitute mem. Cttee on the Environment, Public Health and Food Safety, Del. for Relations with Australia and NZ; Regional Vice-Pres. Globe International Europe 1999–; mem. Estonian Geographical Asscn 1966–, Bd Estonian Inst. for Sustainable Devt, Stockholm Environment Inst.'s Centre, Tallinn 1988–, Bd Univ. of Tartu 1996–, Bd Estonian Nature Fund 1998–; Badge of the Order of Nat. Coat of Arms (Second Class) 2001, Commdr, Légion d'honneur 2001; Panda Award, Danish Section of WWF 1998. *Publications:* Neljakümne kiri 1991, Cassiopeia 1992, Kiri ei Põle Ära 2005; numerous articles on climatology, urban ecology, politics. *Leisure interests:* chess, ornithology, traditional style gardening. *Address:* European Parliament, Bâtiment Altiero Spinelli, 12G165, 60 rue Wiertz, 1047 Brussels, Belgium (office); Harju 1-1, 10 146 Tallinn Estonia. *Telephone:* (2) 284-5429 (office). *Fax:* (2) 284-9429 (office). *E-mail:* andres.tarand@europarl.europa.eu (office). *Website:* www.europarl.europa.eu (office); www.atarand.eu.

TARANDA, Gediminas Leonovich; Russian/Lithuanian ballet dancer; b. 26 Feb. 1961, Kaliningrad; ed Moscow Acad. of Choreography, Moscow Acad. of Dance; dancer, Bolshoi Theatre 1980–, Soloist 1982, Leading Soloist 1985–93, dismissed after conflict with admin.; Founder (with M. Plisetskaya) and Dir Imperial Russian Ballet of Vienna 1994–; First Prize, USSR Championship Ballet Competition 1980. *Leading roles include:* classical and contemporary Russian repertoire including Espado (Don Quixote), Corregidor (Carmen), Forest Warden (Giselle), Kuman (Prince Igor), Severyan (Stone Flower), Yashka (Golden Age), Kurbsky (Ivan the Terrible), Abderakhman (Raimonda), Vizir (Legend of Love) and others. *Address:* Imperial Russian Ballet, Vienna, Austria (office); Imperial Ballet, Trekhprudny per. 11/13, building 2B, Office 45, 103001 Moscow, Russia. *Telephone:* (095) 299-13-98 (Moscow).

TARANTINO, Quentin; American film director, actor and screenwriter; b. 27 March 1963, Knoxville, Tenn.; s. of Tony Tarantino and Connie McHugh; fmrly worked in Video Archives, Manhattan Beach, Calif.; Career Achievement Award, Casting Soc. of America 2004, Empire Film Award for Icon of the Decade 2005, Golden Eddie Filmmaker of the Year Award, American Cinema Eds 2007, Lifetime Achievement Award, Cinemanila Int. Film Festival 2007; Officier, Ordre des Arts et des Lettres. *Films:* My Best Friend's Birthday (actor, dir, prod.) 1987, Reservoir Dogs (actor, dir) 1992, Past Midnight (assoc. prod.) 1992, Siunin Wong Fei-hung tsi titmalau (prod.) 1993, Eddie Presley (actor) 1993, Sleep With Me (actor) 1994, Killing Zoe (exec. prod.) 1994, Somebody to Love (actor) 1994, Pulp Fiction (actor, dir) (Golden Palm, Cannes Film Festival, Acad. Award for Best Screenplay 1995) 1994, Destiny Turns on the Radio (actor) 1995, Desperado (actor) 1995, Four Rooms (actor, dir, exec. prod.) 1995, Red Rain (prod.) 1995, Girl 6 (actor) 1996, From Dusk Till Dawn (actor, exec. prod.) 1996, Curdled (actor, exec. prod.) 1996, Jackie Brown (dir) 1997, God Said, 'Ha!' (exec. prod.) 1998, 40 Lashes (dir) 2000, Little Nicky (actor) 2000, Kill Bill Vol. I (dir, prod.) 2003, Kill Bill Vol. II (dir, prod.) 2004, Daltry Calhoun (exec. prod.) 2005, Hostel (exec. prod.) 2005, Freedom's Fury (exec. prod.) 2006, Grindhouse (actor) 2007, Death Proof (writer, producer, dir, actor) 2007, Planet Terror (actor) 2007, Sukiyaki Western Django (actor) 2007, Diary of the Dead (voice) 2007. *Film screenplays:* My Best Friend's Birthday 1992, Reservoir Dogs 1992, True Romance 1993, Natural Born Killers 1994, Pulp Fiction 1994, Four Rooms (segment: The Man from Hollywood) 1995, From Dusk Till Dawn 1996, Jackie Brown 1997, 40 Lashes (dir) 2000, Kill Bill (also novel) 2003. *Television:* ER (dir, episode 'Motherhood') 1994, Alias (actor, one episode) 2004, CSI: Crime Scene Investigation (dir, writer two episodes) 2005, Alias (actor, four episodes) 2006. *Address:* William Morris Agency, 1 William Morris Place, Beverly Hills, CA 90212; 6201 Sunset Boulevard, Suite 35, Los Angeles, CA 90028, USA.

ŢĂRANU, Cornel, DMus; Romanian composer and conductor; b. 20 June 1934, Cluj; s. of Francisc Ţăranu and Elisabeta Ţăranu; m. Daniela Mărgineanu 1960; one d.; ed Cluj Conservatory; Prof. of Composition, Cluj Conservatory; Conductor of Ars Nova, contemporary music ensemble; Vice-Pres. Romanian Composers' Union 1990–; Artistic Dir Modern Festival Cluj; mem. Romanian Acad. 1993–; Chevalier, Ordre des Arts et des Lettres 2002; Prize of the Romanian Composers' Union 1972, 1978, 1981, 1982, 2001, Grand Prize 2005, Prize of the Romanian Acad. 1973, The Koussevitsky Prize 1982. *Works include:* Sonatas for flute, oboe, clarinet and percussion, Sonata for double bass solo, viola sonata, one piano concerto, cantatas, four symphonies, Séquences, Incantations, Symmétries, Alternances, Raccords for orchestra, two Sinfoniettas for strings, Garlands for chamber orchestra, Don Giovanni's Secret for chamber opera, Chansons nomades (oratorio), Chansons sans amour (lieder), Sempre Ostinato for saxophone and ensemble, Chansons sans réponse, Hommage à Paul Célan, Memento and Dedications (cantatas), Miroirs for saxophone and orchestra, Prolégomènes for chamber orchestra, Orpheus (cantata), Tombeau de Verlaine for mixed choir, Mosaïques for saxophone and ensemble, Testament for choir 1988, Chansons interrompues for voice and ensemble 1993, Cadenze Concertante for cello and chamber orchestra 1993, Trajectoires for ensemble 1994, Crisalide for saxophone, tape and ensemble, Five Tzara Songs for voice and piano, Remembering Bartók for oboe and ensemble, Enescu's 'Caprice Roumain' for violin and orchestra (new arrangement) 1995, Responsorial for clarinet 1996, Antiphona for flute and orchestra 1996, Flaine Quintette for winds 1997, Laudatio per Clusium for voice and instruments 1997, Saturnalii for baritone and ensemble 1998, Three Labiş Poems for bass and piano 1998, Cadenze per Antiphona for flute and solo 1998, Siciliana Blues for piano and chamber orchestra 1998, Concerto for oboe and strings 1998, Oreste-Oedipe (chamber opera) 1999–2001, Concerto Breve for flute orchestra 2001, Modra Rijeka for choir 2002, Shakespeare Sonnets for voice and ensemble 2003, Baroccoco for baroque ensemble 2004, Rimembranza for orchestra 2004, Sinfonia da Requiem for choir and orchestra 2005, Sax-Sympho for saxophone and orchestra 2006, Madrigals (verse by Blaga, Vinea, Attila, Ady); also film and theatre music. *Publication:* Enesco dans la conscience du présent 1981. *Leisure interest:* chess. *Address:* 'Gh. Dima' Music Academy, str. I. I. C. Bratianu 25, 400079 Cluj (office); Str. Nicolae Iorga 7, 400063 Cluj-Napoca, Romania (home). *Telephone:* (264) 593879 (office); (264) 443283 (home). *Fax:* (264) 593879 (office). *E-mail:* corneltaranu@yahoo.com (office). *Website:* www.corneltaranu.com.

TARAR, Muhammad Rafiq; Pakistani politician and lawyer; b. 2 Nov. 1929, Pir Kot, Gujranwala Dist; m.; three s. one d.; ed Govt Islamia High School, Gujranwala, Guru Nanak Khalsa Coll., Gujranwala, Punjab Univ. Law Coll.; legal practice, Gujranwala; Additional Sessions Judge, Gujranwala, Bahawalnagar, Sargodha; mem. Lahore High Court 1974, Chief Justice of Punjab 1989; mem. Electoral Comm. of Pakistan 1980–89; mem. Supreme Court 1991–94; Senator, Pakistan Muslim League March–Dec. 1997; Pres. of Pakistan 1998–2001. *Address:* House 457, G-3, Johar Town, Lahore, Pakistan.

TARASCON, Jean-Marie, MS, PhD; French physicist and academic; *Professor and Director, CNRS Laboratory of Reactivity and Solid State Chemistry, Amiens;* b. 21 Sept. 1953; ed Univ. of Bordeaux; Post-Doctoral Fellow, Cornell Univ., Ithaca, NY, USA 1980–81; Post-Doctoral Fellow, Bell Labs, Murray Hill, NJ, USA 1982–83; mem. Tech. Staff, Bellcore Solid State Chem. Div., Red Bank, NJ, USA 1983–89, Dir Energy Storage Group 1989–94, Bellcore Fellow 1994–; Prof. and Dir, CNRS Lab. of Reactivity and Solid State Chem., Amiens 1995–; Co-Ed. Journal of Solid State Ionics, Journal of Solid State Electrochemistry, Journal of Materials Chem., International Journal of Inorganic Materials; mem. Academie des Sciences 1999–; mem. ACS, Electrochemical Soc., Materials Research Soc., Institut Universitaire de France 2002–; Bellcore Award of Excellence 1987, Bellcore President Award 1993, Industry Week Best Tech. of the Year Award 1994, R and D 100 Award 1994, 1995, Popular Mechanics Design and Eng Award 1995, Int. Battery Asscn Research Award 1995, Electrochemical Soc. Battery Tech. Award 1997, Thomas Alva Edison Patent Award 2001, Volta Medal Award 2002, ISI Award 2004, Prix du rayonnement français 2004. *Address:* Laboratoire de Réactivité et de Chimie des Solides, Université de Picardie Jules Verne, UMR-CNRS 6007, 33, rue Saint-Leu, 80039 Amiens, Cedex 1, France (office). *Telephone:* (3) 22-82-75-71 (office). *Fax:* (3) 22-82-75-90 (office). *E-mail:* jean-marie.tarascon@sc.u-picardie.fr (office). *Website:* www.u-picardie.fr/labo/lrcs/jean-marie_tarascon.htm (office).

TARASOV, Gennady Pavlovich; Russian diplomatist; *Ambassador to Israel;* b. 14 Sept. 1947; ed Moscow State Inst. of Int. Relations; on staff Ministry of Foreign Affairs 1970–; worked in Egypt, USSR Mission in UN and other posts –1986; Deputy Head of Dept Near E and S African Countries, USSR Ministry of Foreign Affairs 1986–90; Amb. of USSR, then of Russia to Saudi Arabia 1990–96; Dir Dept of Information and Press, Ministry of Foreign Affairs 1996–98; Amb. to Portugal 1998–2001, to Israel 2002–. *Address:* Embassy of Russia, 120 Rehov Hayarkon, Tel Aviv 63753, Israel. *Telephone:* 3-35226736 (office). *Fax:* 3-35226713 (office). *E-mail:* amb_ru@mail.netvision.net.il (office). *Website:* www.israel.mid.ru (office).

TARASSOVA, Elvira; Russian ballet dancer; *Principal Dancer, Kirov Ballet;* b. 5 Aug. 1969, St Petersburg; ed Vaganova Acad.; joined Kirov Ballet 1988–, currently Prin. Dancer; Best Pnr, Moscow Competition 1997. *Repertoire includes:* Cinderella (Coppelia, Krivlaka), Don Quixote (Kitri), Faust (Vakhanka), Giselle (Myrtha), La Bayadère (Gamzatti), Le Corsaire (Medora, Gulnara), Sleeping Beauty (Brilliant Fairy), Symphony in C (Allegro Vivace). *Address:* Kirov Ballet, c/o Maryinsky Theatre, One Theatre Square (Teatralnaya Ploshchad), St Petersburg 190000, Russia (office). *Telephone:* (812) 114-12-11 (office). *Fax:* (812) 314-17-44 (office). *E-mail:* elvira@kirov.com (office). *Website:* www.kirov.com (office).

TARASYUK, Borys Ivanovych; Ukrainian politician and diplomatist; *Chairman, Narodnyi Rukh Ukrainy (People's Movement of Ukraine-Rukh);* b. 1 Jan. 1949, Dzerzhynsk, Zhytomyr Oblast; m.; one s. two d.; ed Kyiv State Univ.; attaché, Third, Second, First Sec., Ukrainian Ministry of Foreign Affairs 1975–81; Second, First Sec., Perm. Mission of Ukrainian SSR to UN, New York 1981–86; First Sec., Div. of Int. Orgs, Ukrainian Ministry of Foreign Affairs 1986–87; instructor, Div. of Foreign Relations, Ukrainian CP Cen. Cttee 1987–90; Head, Dept of Political Analysis and Planning, Ministry of Foreign Affairs 1991–92; Deputy, First Deputy Minister of Foreign Affairs, Head, Nat. Cttee on Disarmament Problems 1992–95; Amb. to Belgium (also accred to Netherlands, Luxembourg) 1995–98; Head, Mission to NATO, Brussels 1997–98; Minister of Foreign Affairs 1998–2000, 2005–07 (resgnd); mem. Nat. Security Defence Council; Chair. Narodnyi Rukh Ukrainy (People's Movt of Ukraine-Rukh) 2003–; mem. Bd of Dirs East-West Inst. 1993–2001; Chair. Cttee on European Integration 2002–; Dir Inst. of Social Studies and Int. Relations 2001–02; Founder and Dir Inst. of Euro-Atlantic Co-operation 2001–; State Order 'For Merits', III Grade 1996, II Grade 1999, I Grade 2005; Dr hc (Rivne Int. Econ. and Humanitarian Univ.) 2000, (Ivan Franko Nat. Univ. of Lviv) 2002, (Int. Personnel Acad.) 2002; state awards from Argentina, Brazil, France, Lithuania, Portugal, Sweden, Venezuela. *Leisure interests:* table tennis, fishing, woodwork. *Address:* Narodnyi Rukh Ukrainy, 01034 Kyiv, vul. O. Honchara 33, Ukraine (office). *Telephone:* (44) 246-47-67 (office). *Fax:* (44) 531-30-42 (office). *E-mail:* org@nru.org.ua (office). *Website:* www.nru.org.ua (office); www.ieac.org.ua.

TARCHER, Jeremy Phillip, BA; American publisher; b. 2 Jan. 1932, New York; s. of Jack D. Tarcher and Mary Breger Tarcher; m. 1st Shari Lewis 1958 (died 1998); one d.; m. 2nd Judith Paige Mitchell 1999; ed St John's Coll., Annapolis, Md; Founder and Pres. Jeremy P. Tarcher Inc., LA 1964–91, Pres. Tarcher/Putnam (after acquisition by Putnam) 1991–96; Vice-Pres. Houghton Mifflin, Boston 1980–83; Chair. Bd Audio Renaissance Tapes, LA 1985–; mem. Bd Trustees The Esalen Inst., Big Sur, Calif. 1986–; Producer Shari Lewis Show, NBC Network 1959–62; Exec. Producer A Picture of U.S. (Emmy Award for Children's Programming) 1976. *Television:* with wife the late Shari Lewis wrote episode (Lights of Zetar) of original Star Trek series 1969. *Leisure interests:* ethnogenic research, travel, reading, primitive Oceanic art. *Address:* 10960 Bellagio Road, Los Angeles, CA 90077-3203, USA (home).

TARFUSSER, Cuno J.; Italian lawyer and judge; *Judge, Pre-Trial Division, International Criminal Court;* Deputy Public Prosecutor, Bolzano (or Bozen, capital of mainly German-speaking prov. of Southern Tyrol) –2001, Chief Prosecutor 2001–08; Judge, Pre-Trial Div., ICC, The Hague, Netherlands 2009–. *Address:* International Criminal Court, PO Box 19519, 2500 CM The Hague, The Netherlands (office). *Telephone:* (70) 515-85-15 (office). *Fax:* (70) 515-85-55 (office). *E-mail:* otp.informationdesk@icc-cpi.int (office). *Website:* www.icc-cpi.int (office).

TARIFA, Fatos, PhD; Albanian diplomatist, academic and editor; b. 21 Aug. 1954; ed Univ. of Tirana and Univ. of N Carolina, USA; Founding Chair. Sociological Research Centre, Univ. of Tirana 1991–93, Dir New Sociological Research Centre 1993–98; Prof. of Sociology, Univ. of N Carolina and Ed.-in-Chief Sociological Analysis (journal) 1997–99; Guest Lecturer, Duke Univ., Stanford Univ. and New York Univ., USA, Univ. of Essex, UK, Univ. of Amsterdam, Netherlands; Amb. to Netherlands 1998–2001, to USA 2001–05; mem. Int. Advisory Bd Journal of Social Sciences 1996–; Fulbright Sr Research Fellow, Univ. of N Carolina. *Publications include:* numerous books and articles on political science and int. relations theory. *Address:* c/o Ministry of Foreign Affairs, Bulevardi Gjergj Fishta Nr. 6, Tirana, Albania.

TARISA, Watanagase, BA, MA, PhD; Thai economist and central banker; *Governor, Bank of Thailand;* b. 30 Nov. 1949; m.; one d.; ed Keio Univ., Japan, Univ. of Washington, AMP program at Harvard Univ., USA; joined Bank of Thailand 1975, economist, Financial Inst. Analysis Section, Dept of Econ.

Research 1975–78, Chief Analyst, Banking Analysis Section, Banking Dept 1979, study leave 1979–83, Section Chief, Policy Section, Dept of Financial Insts Supervision and Examination 1984–85, Deputy Div. Chief, Financial Insts Supervision Div. 1986–87, Asst Dir Dept of Econ. Research 1987, Deputy Dir Dept of Bank Supervision and Examination and Head of Payment System Devt Task Force 1991–93, Dir Payment System Devt Office 1993–96, Dir Payment System Dept 1996–97, Dir Financial Insts Regulations Dept 1997–98, Asst Gov., Financial Insts Regulation and Examination Group 1998–99, Asst Gov., Financial Insts Policy Group 1999–2001, Asst Gov., Financial Markets Operations Group 2001–02, Deputy Gov. Financial Insts Stability 2002–07, also mem. Bd, Financial System Policy Cttee, Monetary Policy Cttee, Gov. Bank of Thailand (first woman) 2006–; economist Cen. Banking Dept, IMF, Washington, DC 1988–91; fmr mem. Bd of Dirs Securities Analysts Asscn; Outstanding Leadership Award, Bank of Thailand 2001, Outstanding Individual Research Award, Nat. Defence Coll. of Thailand 2006. *Leisure interests include:* watercolour painting, yoga. *Address:* Bank of Thailand, 273 Thanon Samsen, Bangkhunprom, Bangkok 10200, Thailand (office). *Telephone:* (2) 283-5010 (office). *Fax:* (2) 280-0609 (office). *E-mail:* TarisaW@bot.or.th (office). *Website:* www.bot.or.th (office).

TARJAN, Robert Endre, PhD, FAAS; American computer scientist and academic; *James S. McDonnell Distinguished University Professor of Computer Science, Princeton University;* b. 30 April 1948, Pomona, Calif.; ed Calif. Inst. of Tech., Pasadena, Stanford Univ., Calif.; Asst Prof. of Computer Science, Cornell Univ., Ithaca, NY 1972–73; Miller Research Fellow, Univ. of California, Berkeley 1973–75; Asst Prof. of Computer Science, Stanford Univ. 1974–77, Assoc. Prof. 1977–80; mem. tech. staff, AT&T Bell Labs, Murray Hill, NJ 1980–89; Adjunct Prof. of Computer Science, New York Univ. 1981–85; James S. McDonnell Distinguished Univ. Prof. of Computer Science, Princeton Univ. 1985–, Co-Dir NSF Center for Discrete Math. and Theoretical Computer Science 1989–94, 2001–; Fellow, NEC Research Inst., Princeton 1989–97; Visiting Scientist, MIT 1996; Chief Scientist, InterTrust and Sr Research Fellow, STAR Labs, InterTrust Technologies Corpn, Sunnyvale, Calif. 1997–2001; Corp. Fellow, Compaq Computer Corpn, Houston, Tex. 2002; Chief Scientist, Hewlett Packard Corpn, Palo Alto, Calif. 2002–03, Sr Fellow 2003–; mem. Nat. Advisory Bd Computer Professionals for Social Responsibility 1987–, Bd of Govs Inst. for Math. and its Applications 1988–91; Ed. Princeton University Press Series in Computer Science 1985–, John Wiley Series in Discrete Mathematics 1987–97, Transactions on Mathematical Software 1978–80, Journal of the Association for Computing Machinery 1979–83, SIAM Journal on Computing 1979–83, Journal of Graph Theory 1985–88, Journal of Algorithms 1983–90, Discrete and Computational Geometry 1985–, Journal of the American Mathematical Society 1986–91, European Journal of Combinatorics 1988–91; Correspondent, Mathematical Intelligencer 1991–; mem NAS 1987, Nat. Acad. of Eng 1988, American Philosophical Soc. 1990; Foundation Fellow, Inst. for Combinatorics and its Applications 1991; Fellow, American Acad. of Arts and Sciences 1985, Asscn for Computing Machinery (ACM) 1994, New York Acad. of Sciences 1994; Miller Research Fellowship, Univ. of California, Berkeley 1973–75, Guggenheim Fellowship 1978–79, Nevanlinna Prize in Information Science 1983, NAS Award for Initiatives in Research 1984, Lanchester Prize (Hon. Mention), Operations Research Soc. of America 1984, 1993, Distinguished mem. of Technical Staff, AT&T Bell Labs 1985, A. M. Turing Award, Asscn for Computing Machinery 1986, ACM Paris Kanellakis Award in Theory and Practice 1999. *Publications:* Data Structures and Network Algorithms 1983, Notes on Introductory Combinatorics 1983; one patent and more than 230 articles and reports in scientific journals. *Address:* Department of Computer Science, Princeton University, 35 Olden Street, Room 324, Princeton, NJ 08544-2087 (office); Hewlett Packard Corporation, 1501 Page Mill Road, Mail Stop 3U-1172, Palo Alto, CA 94304 (office); 4 Constitution Hill East, Princeton, NJ 08540, USA (home). *Telephone:* (609) 258-4797 (Princeton) (office); (650) 857-2497 (Palo Alto) (office); (609) 921-0132 (home). *Fax:* (609) 258-1771 (Princeton) (office). *E-mail:* robert.tarjan@hp.com (office). *Website:* www.cs.princeton.edu/~ret (office).

TARJANNE, Pekka, DTech; Finnish international telecommunications official; *Executive Co-ordinator, United Nations Information and Communication Technologies Task Force;* b. 19 Sept. 1937, Stockholm; s. of P. K. Tarjanne and Annu Ritavuori; m. Aino Kairamo 1962; two s. one d.; ed Helsinki Univ. of Tech.; research and teaching at univs in Denmark and USA 1961–66; Prof. of Theoretical Physics, Univ. of Oulu 1965–66, Univ. of Helsinki 1967–77; mem. Parl. 1970–77; Minister for Transport and Communications 1972–75; Dir-Gen. of Posts and Telecommunications, Finland 1977–89; Sec.-Gen. ITU 1989–98; Vice-Chair. Project Oxygen 1999–2000; Exec. Co-ordinator, UN Information and Communication Technologies Task Force 2001–; Commdr Order of White Rose of Finland; Commdr Légion d'honneur; Grand Cross, Order of Finnish Lion 1998. *Publication:* A Group Theoretical Model for Strong Interaction Dynamics 1962. *Address:* United Nations Information and Communication Technologies Task Force, United Nations Plaza, New York, NY 10017, USA.

TARKOWSKI, Andrzej K., MSc, PhD, DSc; Polish zoologist, embryologist and academic; *Professor, Institute of Zoology, Warsaw University;* b. 4 May 1955, s. of Władysław Tarkowski and Janina Tarkowska de domo Osuchowska; m. Teresa Tarkowska; one d.; ed Warsaw Univ.; a world leader in research on early devt of mammals; Asst and Adjunct, Inst. of Zoology, Warsaw Univ. 1955–64, Assoc. Prof. 1960–61, Head, Dept of Embryology 1964–2003, Dir Inst. of Zoology 1972–81 1987–2003, Prof. 1978–; Visiting Prof. of the Royal Soc., Dept of Zoology, Univ. of Oxford, UK 1984–85; mem. Polish Acad. of Sciences 1974–, Polish Acad. of Arts and Sciences 1990–, Academia Europaea 1991–; Foreign mem. French Acad. of Sciences 1984–; Foreign Assoc. NAS 2003–; Dr hc (Jagiellonian Univ., Kraków) 2000, (Medical Univ., Łódź) 2005; Albert Brachet Prize, Royal Acad. of Belgium 1980, Polish Nat. Award 1980, Alfred Jurzykowski Foundation (USA) Award 1984, Embryo Transfer Pioneer Award, Int. Embryo Transfer Soc. 1991, Japan Prize, Science and Tech. Foundation of Japan 2002. *Publications:* numerous articles in scientific journals. *Leisure interest:* photography. *Address:* Zakład Embriologii, Instytut Zoologii, Miecznikowa 1, 02-096 Warsaw, Poland (office). *Telephone:* (22) 5541208 (office). *Fax:* (22) 5541210 (office). *E-mail:* akt@biol.uw.edu.pl (office). *Website:* www.biol.uw.edu.pl (office).

TARLEV, DTechSci; Moldovan business executive and politician; b. 9 Oct. 1963, Başcalia, Basarabeasca Dist; m.; three c.; ed Chişinău Polytechnical Inst.; worked as tractor driver; served in army of USSR 1981–83; Chief Mechanic, Bucuria confectionery factory, Chief Engineer Bucuria SA 1991–93, First Deputy Dir-Gen. 1993–95, Chair. Bd of Admin., Dir-Gen. 1995–2001; studied int. marketing and trade man. in USA; fmr mem. Supreme Econ. Council of Pres., Econ. Council of Govt; mem. Repub. Comm. on Collective Negotiations between Businessmen and Trade Unions 1998–99; mem. Party of Communists of the Repub. of Moldova; Prime Minister of Moldova 2001–08; fmr Chair. Nat. Asscn of Mfrs 1995–2001; mem. Council Int. Union of Mfrs, Int. Acad. of Sciences and Computing Systems 1998–; mem. Int. Acad. of Sciences and Informational Systems 1998; Order of Work Glory 1997; Businessman of the Year (six times) 1995–2000, Gold Medal for Efficient Man., Int. Acad. of Human Resources 2000, several medals for tech. inventions shown at int. exhbns 1997–. *Achievements include:* holds five patents on tech. inventions. *Publications:* more than 30 scientific publs. *Address:* Party of Communists of the Republic of Moldova, 2012 Chişinău, N. Iorga Str. 11, Moldova (office). *Telephone:* (22) 23-46-14 (office). *Fax:* (22) 23-36-73 (office). *E-mail:* info@pcrm.md (office). *Website:* www.pcrm.md (office).

TARNOPOLSKI, Vladimir Grigor'yevich; Russian composer; *Professor of Composition, Moscow Conservatory;* b. 30 April 1955, Dniepropetrovsk, Ukraine; m. Irinna Ivanovna Snitkova; one s.; ed Moscow State Tchaikovsky Conservatory; freelance composer 1988–; co-f. Moscow Asscn of Contemporary Music 1989; Prof. of Composition, Moscow Conservatory 1992–, Founder and Artistic Dir Centre for Contemporary Music 1993–; f. Studio for New Music Ensemble 1993–, Moscow Forum –Int. Festival of Contemporary Music 1994–; Prof., Dept for Contemporary Music, Tchaikovsky Conservatory 2003–; works performed by Ensemble Modern, Intercontemporain, Schonberg Ensemble, Ensemble Recherche, Bayerische Rundfunk Symphony Orchestra in major European and US festivals; Dmitry Shostakovich Prize, Moscow 1991, Paul Hindemith Prize, Plon 1991, Rostrum. *Compositions include:* operas: Wenn die Zeit ueber die Ufer tritt (Munich 1999), Jenseits der Schatten (Bonn 2006); music parodies: Three Graces 1987, Ah, ces russes... ou l'Elexir Magic (Evian 1993); ballet: Ins Theater 1998; chorus and orchestral/instrumental: 1986 Psalmus poenitentialis for violin, choir and organ 1986, Roald Dahl's Cinderella 2003; orchestral: Cello Concerto 1980, Choral Prelude 'Jesus, Your Deep Wounds' 1987, Impression-Expression for piano and orchestra 1989, Cassandra 1991, The Breath of the Exhausted Time 1994, Landscape after the Battle 1995, ...Le vent des mots qu'il n'a pas dits for cello and orchestra 1996, Feux follets 2003, Foucault's Pendulum 2004, Eastanbul 2008; wind band: Welt voll Irrsinn on texts by K. Schwitters 1993; chamber music: Echoes of the Passing Day for clarinet, cello and piano 1989, Troïsti muziki for piano trio 1989, O, PÄRT – OP ART 1992, Amoretto for soprano and ensemble (text by E. Spenser) 1992, Scenes from the Real Life for soprano and three instruments on texts by E. Jandl 1995, Chevengur for voice and ensemble (text by Andrey Platonov) 2001. *Address:* Centre for Contemporary Music, Tchaikovsky Conservatoire, of. 316, Bolshaya Nikitskaya str. 13, 125009 Moscow (office); Arbat str., N 51, Apt 41-a, 119002 Moscow, Russia (home). *Telephone:* (495) 690-51-81 (office). *Fax:* (495) 690-51-81 (office). *E-mail:* istar-priv@mtu-net.ru (home). *Website:* www.tarnopolski.ru.

TARR, Béla; Hungarian film director, screenwriter and producer; b. 21 July 1955, Pécs; ed Budapest Film Acad.; began making amateur films aged 16 and later worked as caretaker at nat. House for Culture and Recreation; amateur work brought him to attention of Bela Balazs Studios which helped fund his feature debut Családi tűzfészek 1979; founding mem. Tarsulas Film Studio 1981–85, TT Filmmühely Kft 2003–; Commdr, Cross of the Hungarian Repub., Kossuth Decoration of the Hungarian Repub.; Andrzej Wajda Freedom Award, France Culture Award, Lifetime Achievement Award, Jerusalem, Giraldillo Award, Seville. *Films include:* Hotel Magnezit 1978, Családi tüzfészek (Family Nest) (also screenplay) 1979, Szabadgyalog (The Outsider) (also screenplay) 1981, Panelkapcsolat (The Prefab People, USA) (also screenplay) 1982, Őszi almanach (Almanac of Fall) (also screenplay) 1985, Szörnyek évadja (Season of Monsters, USA) (actor) 1987, Kárhozat (Damnation) (also screenplay) 1987, The Last Boat (short feature, also screenwriter) 1989, City Life 1990, Sátántangó (Satan's Tango) (also screenplay) 1994, Journey on the Plain 1995, Szenvedély (Passion) (screenplay) 1998, Werckmeister harmóniák (Werckmeister Harmonies) (also assoc. producer and screenwriter) 2000, Château de sable (artistic supervisor) 2000, Visions of Europe (segment 'Prologue') 2004, A Halál kilovagolt Perzsiából (producer) 2005, The Man from London 2007. *Television includes:* Macbeth (also screenplay) 1982. *Address:* c/o TTF Kft, Ròna u. 174, Budapest 1145, Hungary. *Fax:* (1) 251-9969. *E-mail:* ttfilmmuhely@t-online.hu.

TARSCHYS, Daniel, PhD; Swedish politician and political scientist; *Professor of Political Science and Public Administration, University of Stockholm;* b. 21 July 1943, Stockholm; s. of Bernhard Tarschys and Karin Alexanderson; m. Regina Rehbinder 1970; two d.; ed Univ. of Stockholm, Univ. of Leningrad, USSR, Univ. of Princeton, USA; Prof. of Political Science and Public Admin., Stockholm Univ. 1985–; adviser with Ministry of Finance 1976–78, 1979–83; Sec. of State, Prime Minister's Office 1978–79; Prof. of Soviet and E European Studies, Uppsala Univ. 1983–85; mem. Parl. 1976–82, 1985–94; Chair. Parl.

Social Affairs Cttee 1985–91, Foreign Affairs Cttee 1991–94; Vice-Pres. Liberal Int. 1992–94; mem. Council of Europe Parl. Ass. 1986–94, Alt. mem. 1981–83; Sec.-Gen. Liberal, Democratic and Reformers Group (LDR) 1987–91, Chair. 1991–94; Sec.-Gen. Council of Europe 1994–99; Chair. Bank of Sweden Tercentenary Foundation 2006–; chair. of several insts and govt cttees; Grand Crosses of Germany, Liechtenstein, Romania, San Marino and Spain; King's Medal (Sweden). *Publications:* books and articles on political philosophy, budgetary policy, public admin. and comparative politics. *Address:* University of Stockholm, 10691 Stockholm, Sweden (office). *E-mail:* daniel.tarschys@statsvet.su.se (office).

TARTAKOVSKY, Vladimir Aleksandrovich; Russian chemist; *Director, N. D. Zelinsky Institute of Organic Chemistry;* b. 10 Aug. 1932; m.; one d.; ed Moscow State Univ.; worked as researcher, teacher; Head of Lab., Inst. of Organic Chem., USSR (now Russian) Acad. of Sciences 1955–86; Dir N.D. Zelinsky Inst. of Organic Chem. 1987–; Corresp. mem., USSR (now Russian) Acad. of Sciences 1987, mem. 1992–; main research in organic synthesis, chem. of nitrocompounds; Lenin Prize 1976, AM Butlerov Prize. *Address:* N.D. Zelinsky Institute of Organic Chemistry, Leninsky prosp. 47, 117913 GSP-1 Moscow, Russia. *Telephone:* (495) 137-29-44 (office).

TARTT, Donna; American writer; b. 1963, Greenwood, Miss.; ed Univ. of Miss., Oxford, Bennington Coll., Vt; published first sonnet in a Miss. literary review 1976; WHSmith Literary Award 2003. *Publications:* novels: The Secret History 1992, The Little Friend 2002; short stories include: A Christmas Pageant (Harper's) 1993, A Garter Snake (GQ) 1995, True Crime (audio book) 1996; contrib. articles to magazines. *Address:* c/o Gill Coleridge, Rogers, Coleridge & White Ltd, 20 Powis Mews, London, W11 1JN, England (office). *Telephone:* (20) 7221-3717 (office). *Fax:* (20) 7229-9084 (office). *E-mail:* info@rcwlitagency.com (office). *Website:* www.rcwlitagency.com (office).

TARUTA, Sergey A.; Ukrainian steel industry executive; *Chairman, Industrial Union of Donbass;* fmr Head, Dept of Foreign Econ. Relations, AzovStal Steel Mill; mem. Bd of Dirs Industrial Union of Donbass (ISD) 1995, Chair. 2001–; Chair. Supervisory Bd, JSC Khartsyzsk Pipe Mill; mem. Supervisory Bd OJSC AzovStal; owner Metallurg Donetsk football team. *Address:* Industrial Union of Donbass, Shorsa str. 48, Donetsk 83050, Ukraine. *Telephone:* (62) 381-40-02 (office). *Fax:* (62) 381-40-30 (office). *Website:* www.isd.com.ua (office).

TASCA, Catherine, LenD; French politician and government official; *Senator from Yvelines;* b. 13 Dec. 1941, Lyons; d. of Angelo Tasca and Alice Naturel; one d.; ed Inst. d'Etudes Politiques, Paris and Ecole Nat. d'Admin; civil servant, Ministry of Culture 1967; Dir Maison de la Culture de Grenoble 1973; Gen. Man. Ensemble Intercontemporain 1978; Co-Dir Théâtre de Nanterre-Amandiers 1982; mem. Comm. Nat. de la Communication et des Libertés (CNCL) 1986; Minister Del. attached to the Minister of Culture and Communications 1988–91; Sec. of State for Francophone Countries and External Cultural Relations 1992–93; Minister of Culture and Communications March 2000–02; Conseiller d'Etat en service extraordinaire 2003–04; Senator from Yvelines 2004–; Pres. Admin. Bd Canal+Horizons 1993–97; Deputy to Nat. Ass. from Yvelines 1997–, mem. Socialist Party; Ordre des Arts et des Lettres, Chevalier, Légion d'honneur. *Publication:* Un Choix de vie 2002. *Address:* Sénat, 15 rue de Vaugirard, 75291 Paris (office); 21 rue Saint-Amand, 75015 Paris, France (home). *Telephone:* 42-34-28-18 (office). *E-mail:* c.tasca@senat.fr (office). *Website:* www.senat.fr (office).

TASEER, Salmaan; Pakistani chartered accountant, business executive and politician; *Governor of Punjab;* s. of Mohammadin Din Taseer and Christabel Taseer (née Bilqees); ed qualified as chartered accountant (England and Wales); began business career by setting up two chartered accountancy and man. consultancy firms, KPMG, United Arab Emirates and Taseer Hadi Khalid & Co., Pakistan; est. First Capital Securities Corpn Ltd 1994; currently Chair. and CEO First Capital and Worldcall Group; actively involved in establishing other cos in financial services sector as well as telecommunications, media, insurance and real estate devt sectors in Pakistan; also owns Daily Times newspaper, Business Plus TV channel, Pace shopping malls and Hyatt hotel range in Pakistan; mem. Bd Export Promotion Bureau of Pakistan, Bd USF (Universal Service Fund) Co. Ltd; began political career as student mem. of Zulfikar Ali Bhutto's Pakistan People's Party (PPP) late 1960s; active in Pakistan Youth politics; ran movt for Zulfikar Bhutto's release and against his arrest and death sentence; mem. Nat. Ass. 1988, 1990, resgnd from exec. membership of PPP; returned to politics when selected as Fed. Minister for Industries, Production and Special Initiatives in caretaker govt of Prime Minister Muhammad Mian Soomro 2007–08; Gov. of Punjab 2008–. *Publications:* political biography of Prime Minister Zulfikar Ali Bhutto. *Address:* Governor House, Government of Punjab, Lahore, Punjab (office); First Capital/Worldcall Group, 103-C/II Gulberg III, Lahore, Punjab, Pakistan. *Telephone:* (42) 9203151 (Govt) (office); (42) 111-947-947. *Fax:* (42) 9203154 (Govt) (office); (42) 5757590. *E-mail:* webmaster@punjab.gov.pk (office); info@worldcall.com.pk. *Website:* www.punjab.gov.pk (office); www.worldcall.com.pk.

TASHMUHAMEDOVA, Dilorom Hafurjanovna, MD; Uzbekistani physician and politician; *Speaker, Qoqunchilik palatasi Kengashi (Legislative Chamber);* b. 1962, Tashkent Oblast; m. P. Tashmuhamedov; four c.; ed Tashkent State Medical Inst., Faculty of Intergovernmental Relations and External Econ. Relations, Acad. of State and Social Construction; early career as teacher, Tashkent State Medical Inst.; f. Farmed (pharmaceuticals co.) 1994; Deputy, Oly Majlis (Supreme Ass.) 2001–04, Deputy Qoqunchilik palatasi Kengashi (Legis. Chamber) 2004–, mem. Cttee for Int. Affairs and Inter-parl. Communication, Deputy Speaker 2007–08, Speaker 2008–; mem. Adolat (Justice) Social Democratic Party, First Sec. Political Council 2005–, also leader of parl. faction; unsuccessful cand. in presidential election 2007; Dustlik (Friendship) Order 2006. *Publications include:* series of academic works about medicine; numerous articles abou socio-political reform, the development of a multi-party system and of democratic institutions and the increasing involvement of women in social life. *Address:* Office of the Speaker, Qoqunchilik palatasi Kengashi, 100008 Tashkent, Xalqlar Do'stligi shoh ko'ch. 1, Uzbekistan (office). *Telephone:* (71) 139-87-07 (office). *Fax:* (71) 139-41-51 (office). *Website:* www.parliament.gov.uz (office).

TASMAGAMBETOV, Imangali Nurgaliyevich; Kazakhstani politician; b. 1956; served in various govt positions including Chair. State Cttee on Youth Affairs 1991–93; Asst to Pres. 1993–94; apptd Atyrau oblast akim (Gov.) 1998; Deputy Prime Minister for Cultural Affairs 1991–93, in charge of Social and Ethnic Policy 2000–02; Prime Minister of Kazakhstan 2002–03; State Secretary 2003–04. *Address:* c/o Office of the Prime Minister, 473000 Astana, Beibitshilik 11, Kazakhstan (office).

TATA, Jamshed Rustom, DSc, FRS; British medical research scientist; *Senior Research Scientist, Medical Research Council;* b. 13 April 1930, Bombay, India; s. of Dr Rustom J. Tata and Gool Tata (née Contractor); m. Renée S. Zanetto 1954; two s. one d.; ed Univ. of Bombay, Indian Inst. of Science, Bangalore, Coll. de France, Paris and Univ. de Paris, Sorbonne; Postdoctoral Fellow, Sloan-Kettering Inst., New York 1954–55; Beit Memorial Fellow, Nat. Inst. for Medical Research, London 1956–60; Visiting Scientist, Wenner-Gren Inst., Univ. of Stockholm 1960–62; mem. Scientific Staff, MRC, Nat. Inst. for Medical Research, London 1962–96, Sr Research Scientist 1996–, Head, Lab. of Developmental Biochemistry 1973–96; Visiting Prof., Univ. of Calif., Berkeley 1969–70; Fogarty Int. Scholar, NIH, Bethesda, Md 1983–89, Visiting Scientist 1997; Chair. Cell and Molecular Panel, Wellcome Trust 1990–92, Int. Relations Group 1997–2004; Dir (non-exec.) Biotech Analytic 2000–04; mem. Indian Nat. Acad. of Sciences; Corresp. mem. Soc. de Biologie, France; Fellow, Third World Acad. of Sciences; Chair. and Trustee, Oxford Int. Biomedical Centre 1996–2007; several interviews and reports on BBC Radio and one documentary on BBC TV; various awards. *Publications:* The Thyroid Hormones 1959, Chemistry of Thyroid Diseases 1960, Metamorphosis 1972, The Action of Growth and Developmental Hormones 1983, Metamorphosis 1986, Hormonal Signalling and Post-embryonic Development 1998. *Leisure interests:* gardening, reading, travel, tennis. *Address:* 15 Bittacy Park Avenue, Mill Hill, London, NW7 2HA, England (home). *Telephone:* (20) 8816-2108 (office); (20) 8346-6291 (home). *Fax:* (20) 8906-4477 (office). *E-mail:* jtata@nimr.mrc.ac.uk (office); jtata@clara.co.uk (home).

TATA, Ratan N., BSc; Indian business executive; *Chairman, Tata Sons Ltd;* b. 28 Dec. 1937, nephew of J. R. D. Tata; ed Cornell Univ., Harvard Business School, USA; joined Tata Group 1962, Chair. Tata Industries 1981–, Chair. Tata Sons Ltd (holding co. comprising 80 cos) 1991–; also Chair. various cos in Tata Group, including Tata Steel, Tata Engineering & Locomotive Co. Ltd, Tata Industries Ltd, Tata Chemicals Ltd, The Indian Hotels Co. Ltd, Tata Tea Ltd, Tata IBM Ltd, Information Technology Park Ltd, Tata Lucent Technologies Ltd, Tata Trustee Co. Ltd, Tata International AG Zug, Switzerland, Tata Ltd, London, UK, Tata Inc., New York, USA, Tata Technologies (Pte) Ltd, Singapore, Tata Communications Ltd, Tata Hydro Electric Power Supply Co. Ltd, The Andhra Valley Power Supply Co. Ltd, The Tata Power Co. Ltd, Corus (following acquisition of Corus by Tata Steel in April 2007) 2007–; mem. Bd Dirs The Bombay Dyeing & Mfg Co. Ltd, Haldia Petrochemicals Ltd, Antrix Corpn Ltd, Varuna Overseas Ltd, UK; Chair. Indian Investment Comm.; mem. Indian Prime Minister's Council on Trade and Industry, Nat. Hydrogen Energy Bd, Nat. Mfg Competitiveness Council, Global Business Council on HIV/AIDS, The Reserve Bank of India, Nat. Council of Applied Econ. Research; mem. Int. Advisory Council, Singapore Econ. Devt Bd; mem. Int. Investment Council, Repub. of SA; mem. Int. Advisory Bd Mitsubishi Corpn, American Int. Group, JP Morgan Chase; Trustee, Rand Corpn, Cornell Univ., Univ. of Southern Calif., Foundation Bd, Ohio State Univ.; Hon. DBA (Ohio State Univ.), Hon. DTech (Asian Inst. of Tech., Bangkok), Hon. DS (Warwick Univ.); Padma Bhushan 2000. *Address:* Tata Sons Ltd, Bombay House, 24 Homi Mody Street, Mumbai 400 001 (office); s/o Mr Nowroji Hormusji Tata, Bakhtavar, 163 Lower Colaba Road, Mumbai 400 005, India. *Telephone:* (22) 22049131 (office). *Fax:* (22) 22042333 (office). *E-mail:* info@tata.com (office). *Website:* www.tata.com (office).

TATARINOV, Leonid Petrovich; Russian palaeontologist and zoologist; *Adviser, Russian Academy of Sciences;* b. 12 Nov. 1926, Tula; s. of Petr Lukich Tatarinov and Anna Nikolayevna Tatatrinova; m. Bulat Susanna Gurgenovna 1959; two d.; ed Moscow Univ.; mem. CPSU 1964–91; served in Soviet Army 1943–44; mem. staff USSR Acad. of Sciences Inst. of Palaeontology (jr research fellow, then head of lab. and sr research fellow) 1955–73, Dir 1975–92, Vice-Sec. Dept of Gen. Biology of USSR (now Russian) Acad. of Sciences 1975–, currently Adviser; Chair. Council for Study of Palaeobiology and Evolution 1981; mem. Council Russian Acad. of Sciences 1992–; Scientific Chief of Jt Soviet- (now Russian-) Mongolian Palaeontological Expedition 1975–96; Ed.-in-Chief Palaeontology Journal 1978–88, 1993–2001, Zoological Journal 1988–93; Corresp. mem. USSR (now Russian) Acad. of Sciences 1974, mem. 1981–; Foreign mem. Linnean Soc., London; USSR State Prize 1978, Order of Merit for the Fatherland 1999. *Publications:* Sketches on the Theory of Evolution 1987, Palaeontology and Evolutionary Doctrine 1989, Sketches on the Evolution of Reptiles 2006, and other works on origins and early evolution of tetrapods. *Leisure interests:* music, history. *Address:* Palaeontological Institute, Academy of Sciences, Profsoyunaya str. 123, 117868 Moscow GSP-7, Russia. *Telephone:* (495) 339-07-00 (office); (495) 438-12-94 (home). *Fax:* (495) 339-12-66. *E-mail:* tatarin@paleo.ru (office). *Website:* www.paleo.ru (office).

TATE, Jeffrey Philip, CBE, MA, MB, BChir; British conductor; *Musical Director, Teatro di San Carlo, Naples;* b. 28 April 1943, Salisbury, Wilts.; s. of Cyril H. Tate and Ivy Ellen Naylor (née Evans); ed Farnham Grammar School, Christ's Coll. Cambridge and St Thomas's Hosp. London; trained as medical doctor 1961–67; joined London Opera Centre 1969; joined staff of Royal Opera House, Covent Garden 1970; made recordings as harpsichordist 1973–77; Asst to Pierre Boulez (q.v.) for The Ring, Bayreuth 1976–81; Asst to Sir John Pritchard, Cologne Opera 1977; conducted Gothenburg Opera, Sweden 1978–80; Metropolitan Opera début 1979; Covent Garden debut 1982; Chief Guest Conductor, Geneva Opera 1983–95; Prin. Conductor, English Chamber Orchestra 1985–, Royal Opera House, Covent Garden 1986–91; Prin. Guest Conductor, Royal Opera House, Covent Garden 1991–94, Orchestre Nat. de France 1989–98; Chief Conductor and Artistic Dir Rotterdam Philharmonic Orchestra 1991–94; Chief Conductor Minnesota Orchestra Summer Festival 1997–; Prin. Guest Conductor Teatro La Fenice 1999; Musical Dir Teatro di San Carlo, Naples 2005–; Principal Conductor, Hamburger Symphoniker 2008–; appears with maj. orchestras in Europe and America; numerous recordings with English Chamber orchestra; Pres. Asscn for Spina Bifida and Hydrocephalus 1989–, Music Space Trust 1991–; other charitable positions; Hon. DMus (Leicester) 1993; Hon. Fellow Christ's Coll. Cambridge, St Thomas's and Guy's Hosp. Medical School; Grand Prix du Disque (for complete recording of opera Lulu) 1995, Premio della Critica Musicale 'Franco Abbiati' Spettacolo prize (for Königskinder, with Paul Curran) 2003; Officier, Ordre des Arts et des Lettres 1995, Chevalier, Légion d'honneur 1999. *Leisure interests:* church-crawling, with gastronomic interludes. *Address:* Fondazione Teatro di San Carlo, Via San Carlo 98/F, 80132 Naples, Italy (office). *Telephone:* (081) 7972331 (office). *Fax:* (081) 400902 (office). *Website:* www .teatrosancarlo.it (office).

TATE, John T., PhD; American mathematician and academic; *Sid W. Richardson Foundation Regents Chair in Mathematics, University of Texas;* b. 1925, Minneapolis, Minn.; ed Harvard Coll. and Princeton Univ.; Research Asst and Instructor, Princeton Univ., NJ 1950–53; Visiting Prof., Columbia Univ., New York 1953–54; Prof., Harvard Univ., Cambridge, Mass 1954–90; Prof. and Sid W. Richardson Foundation Regents Chair in Math., Univ. of Texas, Austin 1990–; mem. NAS 1969; Foreign mem. Acad. des sciences (France) 1992; Hon. Mem. London Math. Soc. 1999; Cole Prize, American Math. Soc. 1956, Sloan Fellowship 1959–61, Guggenheim Fellowship 1965–66, Leroy P. Steele Prize for Lifetime Achievement 1995, Wolf Foundation Prize, Israel 2003. *Publications:* numerous articles in math. journals on arithmetic algebraic geometry. *Address:* University of Texas, Mathematics Department, 1 University Station Stop C1200, Austin, TX 78712, USA (office). *Telephone:* (512) 471-7127 (office); (512) 471-7711 (office). *Fax:* (512) 471-9038 (office). *E-mail:* tate@math.utexas.edu (office). *Website:* www.utexas.edu (office).

TATE, Robert Brian, PhD, FBA, FRHistS; British academic; *Professor Emeritus of Hispanic Studies, University of Nottingham;* b. 27 Dec. 1921, Belfast, Northern Ireland; s. of Robert Tate and Jane Grantie Tate; m. Beth Ida Lewis 1951; one s. one d.; ed Royal Belfast Academical Inst., The Queen's Univ., Belfast; Asst Lecturer, Univ. of Manchester 1949–52; Lecturer, The Queen's Univ., Belfast 1952–56; Reader in Hispanic Studies, Univ. of Nottingham 1956–58, Prof. 1958–83, Prof. Emer. 1983–; Visiting Prof., State Univ. of New York (Buffalo), Harvard and Cornell Univs, Univ. of Virginia and Univ. of Texas; Corresp. Fellow, Institut d'Estudis Catalans, Real Acad. de Buenas Letras, Barcelona, Real Acad. de Historia, Madrid; Dr hc (Girona, Spain). *Publications:* numerous publs on Hispanic topics. *Leisure interests:* art, architecture, jazz. *Address:* 11 Hope Street, Beeston, Nottingham, England (home). *Telephone:* (115) 925-1243 (home). *E-mail:* brian@rbtate19 .freeserve.co.uk (home).

TATHAM, David Everard, CMG, BA; British diplomatist (retd) and consultant; b. 28 June 1939, York; s. of the late Lt-Col Francis Everard Tatham and of Eileen Mary Wilson; m. Valerie Ann Mylechreest 1963; three s.; ed St Lawrence Coll., Ramsgate, Wadham Coll. Oxford; entered HM Diplomatic Service 1960, Third Sec., UK Mission to UN, New York 1962–63; Vice-Consul (Commercial), Milan 1963–67; Middle East Centre for Arabic Studies 1967–69; served Jeddah 1969–70, FCO 1971–74, Muscat 1974–77; Asst Head, Middle East Dept, FCO 1977–80; Counsellor, Dublin 1981–84; Amb. to Yemen Arab Repub. (also accred to Djibouti) 1984–87; Head, Falkland Islands Dept, FCO 1987–90; Amb. to Lebanon 1990–92; Gov., Falkland Islands 1992–96, concurrently Commr S Georgia and S Sandwich Islands; High Commr to Sri Lanka (also accred to Maldives) 1996–99; adviser on diplomatic training to Palestinian Authority 2000; Dist Man., UK Census 2000–01; Ed., Dictionary of Falklands Biography Project 2002–08. *Publications:* Dictionary of Falklands Biography (ed.). *Leisure interests:* walking uphill, historical research. *Address:* c/o Foreign and Commonwealth Office, Whitehall, London, SW1A 2AH, England. *Telephone:* (20) 7008-1500.

TATISHVILI, Tsisana Bezhanovna; Georgian singer (soprano); b. 30 Dec. 1939, Tbilisi; m. Giorgi Totibadze; ed V. Sarandzhishvili Conservatoire, Tbilisi; soloist with Tbilisi (now Georgian) State Opera 1963–; has toured Germany, Poland, fmr Czechoslovakia and other countries; roles have included Tatiana in Eugene Onegin, Liza in Queen of Spades, Aida, Leonora in Il Trovatore, Donna Anna in Don Giovanni, Ortrud in Lohengrin, Salome, Desdemona in Otello, Santuzza in Cavalleria Rusticana, Eteri in Paliashvili's Absalom and Eteri; Prof. V. Saradjishvili Tbilisi State Conservatoire 1985–; vocal consultant at Georgian State Opera 1999–; mem. Artistic Council 2001–; Fellow, Georgian Acad. of Humanitarian Sciences; Order of Nat. Merit of Georgia; People's Artist of Georgian SSR 1973, Paliashvili Prize 1979, 1987, People's Artist of USSR 1979; Order of Honour. *Address:* c/o V. Saradjishvili Tbilisi State Conservatoire, 8 Griboedov str., 0108 Tbilisi, Georgia. *Telephone:*

(32) 99-91-44. *Fax:* (32) 98-71-87. *E-mail:* info@conservatoire.edu.ge; Tatishvili@rambler.ru (home).

TATTENBACH-YGLESIAS, Christian, LLB; Costa Rican diplomatist and politician; b. 1924; ed Univ. of Costa Rica; mem. Nat. Wage Bd 1949; Amb. to Guatemala 1951, to Nicaragua 1952; Deputy Legis. Ass. 1962–66, 1978–82, 1986–90, Pres. Legis. Ass. 1981–82; Minister of Interior, Police and Justice 1966–70; Alt. Sec.-Gen. Cen. American Inst. for Extension of Culture and Dir Escuela para Todos publs programme 1970–77; Co-founder and Chair. Union Popular Party 1977; Head Parl. Group of Coalición Unidad 1980–81; Pres. Union Popular 1982–84, now Hon. Pres. Unidad Social Cristiana; Perm. Rep. to UN, New York 1990–94; mem. Bd Inter-American Inst. of Human Rights 1982. *Address:* c/o Ministry of Foreign Affairs, 1000 San José, Costa Rica.

TATUM, Beverley Daniel, MA, PhD; American clinical psychologist, academic and university administrator; *President, Spelman College;* m. Travis Tatum; two s.; ed Wesleyan Univ., Conn., Univ. of Mich., Hartford Seminary, Conn.; clinical psychologist, ind. practice 1988–98; Dissertation Fellow, Center for Black Studies, Univ. of Calif., Santa Barbara 1980–81, Lecturer, Dept of Black Studies 1982–83; Asst Prof. Dept of Psychology, Westfield State Coll., Mass 1983–86, Assoc. Prof. 1986–89; Assoc. Prof. Dept of Psychology and Educ., Mount Holyoke Coll., Mass 1989–96, Prof. 1996–, Dept Chair 1997–98, Dean of Coll. and Vice-Pres. for Student Affairs 1998–2002, Acting Pres. 2002; Pres. Spelman Coll., Atlanta, Ga 2002–; Visiting Scholar, Wellesley Coll., Mass 1991–92; mem. Bd of Dirs Smith Child Care Center at Sunnyside, Mass 1985–92, Equity Inst., Mass 1988–90; mem. Bd of Trustees, Williston Northampton School 1999–; mem. Bd of Incorporators, Hartford Seminary 2000–; Chair. Human Subjects Cttee, Psychology Dept, Mount Holyoke Coll. 1989–90; Chair. Coll. Cttee on Fellowships 1998–; fmr mem. Summer Math Steering Cttee, Frances Perkins Steering Cttee, Faculty Cttee on Appeals, Faculty Affirmative Action Cttee; mem. African-American Studies Steering Cttee, Multicultural Community and College Life Cttee, Academic Policies Cttee; Faculty Adviser, Psychology Club, Mount Holyoke Club 1990–91, Psi Chi Honor Soc. 1993–95; Westfield State Coll. Campus Rep., Mass Teachers Asscn 1986–89; mem. American Psychological Asscn, American Educational Research Asscn, American Coll. Personnel Asscn, American Asscn of Univ. Women, Nat. Asscn of Multicultural Educ.; Elder, Martin Luther King Community Presbyterian Church 1994–97; recipient Mount Holyoke Coll. Faculty Grant 1990, Mount Holyoke African-American Studies Research Grant 1991, Carnegie Corpn Grant 1996, Mellon Foundation Planning Grant 2000, Mellon Foundation Implementation Grant 2000, Braitmayer Foundation Grant 2000; Rackham Opportunity Fellowship, Univ. of Mich. 1975–78; American Psychological Asscn Minority Fellow 1976–79; Ford Foundation Postdoctoral Fellow 1991–92; Nat. Achievement Award 1971–72, Distinguished Service Award, Westfield State Coll. 1986, 1987, Commonwealth Citation for Meritorious Service, Westfield State Coll. 1988, Asscn of Women in Psychology Publ. Award 1994, Nat. Asscn of Multicultural Educ. Book of the Year Award 1998. *Publications:* Assimilation Blues: Black Families in a White Community 1987, Why Are All the Black Kids Sitting Together in the Cafeteria? and Other Conversations About Race 1997. *Address:* Office of the President, Spelman College, 350 Spelman Lane, SW, Atlanta, GA 30314-4399, USA (office). *Telephone:* (404) 270-5001 (office). *Fax:* (404) 270-5010 (office). *E-mail:* btatum@spelman.edu (office). *Website:* www.spelman.edu/administration/office (office).

TAUBMAN, A. Alfred; American entrepreneur; b. 31 Jan. 1925, Pontiac, Mich.; s. of Philip Taubman and Fannie Taubman; m. 1st Reva Kolodney 1949 (divorced 1977); two s. one d.; m. 2nd Judith Mazor 1982; ed Univ. of Michigan, Lawrence Inst. of Tech.; Chair. and CEO The Taubman Co. (now Taubman Centers Inc.), Bloomfield Hills, Michigan (specializing in shopping-centre design, planning and devt) 1950–; Chair. Sothebys Holdings 1983–2000, owner of Sotheby's (art auctioneers) 1983–2000; sentenced to one year and one day's imprisonment for price-fixing 2002, released after 10 months. *Address:* c/o Taubman Centers Inc., 200 E Long Lake Road, Bloomfield Hills, MI 48303-0200, USA.

TAUMOEPEAU TUPOU, Sonatane Tu'akinamolahi; Tongan diplomatist; *Permanent Representative to United Nations;* m.; four c.; ed Newington Coll., Sydney, Australia, East–West Centre, Univ. of Hawaii, USA; commissioned Lt in Tongan Defence Services 1971, attained rank of Capt.; First Sec. in High Comm. to UK 1973, High Commr to UK (also accred to other European countries, EEC and USA) 1979–83; Asst Sec. in Prime Minister's Office 1977; apptd. Deputy Sec. to the Govt 1978; Sec. of Foreign Affairs 1979–83, 1986–2000; Perm. Rep. to UN, New York (also accred as Amb. to USA and High Commr to Canada) 1999–2004, 2009–; Minister of Foreign Affairs 2004–09, Acting Minister of Defence 2005–09; Acting Gov. of Vava'u 2005–09. *Address:* Permanent Mission of Tonga, 250 East 51st Street, New York, NY 10022, USA (office). *Telephone:* (917) 369-1025 (office). *Fax:* (917) 369-1024 (office). *E-mail:* tongaunmission@aol.com (office).

TAURAN, HE Cardinal Jean-Louis Pierre, MA, DCnL; Vatican ecclesiastic, diplomatist and librarian; *Archivist of Vatican Secret Archives and Librarian of Vatican Library;* b. 5 April 1943, Bordeaux; France; ed Gregorian Univ., Rome, Italy, Institut Catholique, Toulouse, France; ordained priest 1969; Parish Priest, Bordeaux 1969–72; joined Diplomatic Service of the Holy See 1975, later serving in Dominican Repub. and Lebanon, joined Council for the Public Affairs of the Church (now Section for Relations with States) Rome 1983, apptd Under-Sec. 1988, Sec. for the Holy See's Relations with States 1990–2003; ordained Titular Archbishop of Thelepte 1991; created Cardinal, of the Deaconry of St Apollonius at the Neronian-Alexandrian Baths 2003; Archivist of Vatican Secret Archives and Librarian of Vatican Library 2003–; Pres.'s Medal, Catholic Univ. of America 1999. *Address:* Vatican Secret Archives, 00120, Vatican City (office). *Telephone:* (06) 69883314 (office). *Fax:*

(06) 69885574 (office). *E-mail:* vati032@relstat-segstat.va (office). *Website:* www.vatican.va/library_archives/vat_secret_archives/index.htm (office).

TAUREL, Sidney, MBA; American (b. Spanish) pharmaceuticals industry executive; *Chairman, Eli Lilly & Company;* b. 9 Feb. 1949, Casablanca, Morocco; ed École des Hautes Études Commerciales, Paris, France, Columbia Univ., New York; joined Eli Lilly Int. Corpn 1971, Marketing Assoc. 1971–72, Marketing Plans Man., Brazil 1971–76, marketing and sales assignments in E Europe and France 1976–81, Gen. Man., Brazil 1981–83, Vice-Pres. Lilly European Operations, London, UK 1983–86, Pres. Eli Lilly Pres. Pharmaceutical Div. 1991–93, mem. Lilly Bd Dirs 1991–, Exec. Vice-Pres. Eli Lilly & Co. and Pres. Pharmaceutical Div. 1993–96, Pres. 1996–2005, COO 1996–98, CEO 1998–99, Chair. 1999–, CEO 1999–2008, Chair. Policy Cttee and Sr Man. Forum; mem. Bd of Dirs IBM Corpn, McGraw-Hill Cos Inc., RCA Tennis Championships; mem. Exec. Cttee Pharmaceutical Research and Mfrs of America (PhRMA), Exec. Cttee Business Council; apptd to Pres.'s Homeland Security Advisory Council 2002–03, to Pres.'s Export Council 2003–06, Advisory Cttee for Trade Policy and Negotiations 2007–; mem. Bd of Overseers Columbia Business School; Trustee, Indianapolis Museum of Art; US citizen 1995; Chevalier, Legion d'honneur 2001. *Address:* Eli Lilly and Company, Lilly Corporate Center, Indianapolis, IN 46285, USA (office). *Telephone:* (317) 276-2000 (office). *Fax:* (317) 277-6579 (office). *E-mail:* info@lilly.com (office). *Website:* www.lilly.com (office).

TAUS, Josef, LLD; Austrian politician, banker and industrialist; b. 8 Feb. 1933, Vienna; s. of Josef Taus and G. Schinko; m. Martha Loibl 1960; ed Univ. of Vienna, Hochschule für Welthandel; journalist; law practice; with Austrian Inst. of Econ. Research; Sec. and Head of Econ. Div., Girozentrale und Bank der Österreichischen Sparkassen AG 1958, mem. Man. Bd 1967–68, Chair. and Man. Dir 1968–75; fmr Man. Sparinvest-Kapitalanlage GmbH; mem. Parl. 1975–91; State Sec. Fed. Ministry of Communications and Nationalized Enterprises 1966–67; Fed. Chair. Austrian People's Party (ÖVP) 1975–79; Man. Partner Constantia Industrieverwaltungs GesmbH. 1979–86; mem. Bd Constantia Industrieholding AG 1986–89; mem. Bd ECO TRUST Holding AG 1989, Man. Trust Holding AG 1989–, Trust Invest AG 1990–; Man. Dir Fremdenverkehrsbetriebe GesmbH and Co. OHG. *Leisure interests:* skiing, music, reading, swimming. *Address:* Zahnradbahnstrasse 17, 1190 Vienna, Austria (home).

TAUTOU, Audrey; French actress; b. 9 Aug. 1978, Beaumont, Puy de Dôme, Auvergne; began acting lessons, Cours Florent, Paris; film debut in Vénus beauté (Institut) 1999; Best Young Actress Award, Jeune Comedien de Cinema Festival, Bezier 1998, Most Promising Young Actress César Award 2000; Golden Swann, Jeune comedienne, Festival de Cabourg 1999, Lumières 2000 (meilleur espoir), Lumières 2002 (meilleure actrice), Trophie Chopard Cannes 2001. *Films include:* Vénus beauté (institut) (Venus Beauty Salon) 1999, Triste à mourir 1999, Épouse-moi 1999, Voyous Voyous (Pretty Devils) 2000, Le Libertin (The Libertine) 2000, Le battement d'ailes du papillon (Happenstance) 2000, Le fabuleux destin d'Amélie Poulain (Amélie) 2001, Dieu est grand, je suis toute petite (God Is Great, And I'm Not) 2001, À la folie... pas du tout (He Loves Me... He Loves Me Not) 2002, L'auberge espagnole (The Spanish Apartment) 2002, Dirty Pretty Things 2002, Pas sur la bouche 2003, Nowhere to Go But Up 2003, Les Marins perdus (Lost Seamen) 2003, Un long dimanche de fiançailles 2004, Les poupées russes 2005, The Da Vinci Code 2006, Hors de prix 2006, Ensemble, c'est tout 2007. *Address:* c/o Claire Blondel, Artmedia, 20 avenue Rapp, 75007 Paris, France (office). *Telephone:* 1-43-17-33-55 (office). *Fax:* 1-44-18-34-60 (office). *E-mail:* bcgpresse@wanadoo.fr (office). *Website:* www.artmedia.fr (office).

TAVENER, Sir John, Kt; British composer; b. 28 Jan. 1944, London; s. of Kenneth Tavener and Muriel Tavener; m. 1st Victoria Marangopoulou 1974 (divorced 1980); m. 2nd Maryanna Schaefer 1991; two d.; ed Highgate School and RAM; Organist St John's Church, London 1960; Prof. of Composition, Trinity Coll. of Music, London 1968–; youngest composer ever performed at Promenade Concert, London 1969, at Royal Opera House, Covent Garden (Thérèse) 1979; works performed in UK, USA, fmr USSR, Greece, Poland, Australia, Germany, Scandinavia, S America and elsewhere; converted to Russian Orthodox Church 1974; works recorded on numerous labels; Hon. FRAM, Hon. Fellow Royal School of Church Music, Hon. Fellow Trinity Coll. of Music, London; Hon. DMus (New Delhi) 1990, (City of London Univ.) 1996; Prince Rainier Int. Prize 1965, First Prize Sacred Music Int. Composition Contest 1972, Gramophone Award (for The Protecting Veil) 1992. *Compositions include:* The Whale, Celtic Requiem, Últimos Ritos, Palintropos, Antigone, Thérèse, Akhmatova-Rekviem, Liturgy of St John Chrysostom, 16 Haiku of Seferis, Sappho – Lyrical Fragments, Great Canon of St Andrew of Crete, Prayer for the World, Kyklike Kinesis, Ikon of Light, A Gentle Spirit, All-Night Vigil Service of the Orthodox Church (commissioned by Orthodox and Anglican Churches, for Christ Church Cathedral, Oxford 1985), Two Hymns to the Mother of God, Trisāgion, Mandelion; Eis Thanaton (a ritual), Ikon of St Cuthbert, God is with Us, Acclamation for Patriarch Demetrios, Akathist of Thanksgiving, Meditation on the Light, Panikhida, Ikon of Saint Seraphim, The Protecting Veil, Resurrection, Magnificat and Nunc Dimittis, The Hidden Treasure, Eonia, Mary of Egypt, The Repentant Thief, We Shall See Him as He Is, The Last Sleep of the Virgin, The Annunciation, Hymns of Paradise, Akhmatova Songs, The Child Lived, The Apocalypse, Let's Begin Again, Wake Up and Die, The Toll Houses, Agraphon, Vlepondas, The Last Discourse, Diodia, Song for Athene (performed at funeral of Diana, Princess of Wales), Nipson Fall and Resurrection, Total Eclipse, A New Beginning, Eternity's Sunrise, The Bridegroom, Lamentations and Praises, Life Eternal, Song of the Cosmos, The Veil of the Temple 2003, Fragments of A Prayer (for film Children of Men) 2006. *Publication:* The Music of Silence – A Composer's Testament. *Leisure interests:* iconography, love of Greece. *Address:* c/o Chester Music, 8–9 Frith Street, London, W1D 3JB, England.

TAVERNE, Suzanna, BA; British company director; b. 3 Feb. 1960; d. of Dick Taverne and Janice Taverne; m.; Marc Vlessing 1993; one s. one d.; ed Pimlico School, Westminster School, Balliol Coll., Oxford; with S. G. Warburg and Co. Ltd 1982–90; Head of Strategic Planning, then Finance Dir, Newspaper Publishing PLC 1990–94; consultant to Saatchi & Saatchi PLC 1994–95; Dir of Strategy and Devt, Pearson PLC then Man. Dir FT Finance, Financial Times Group 1995–98; Man. Dir British Museum, London 1999–2001; Dir of Operations and mem. Exec. Cttee Imperial Coll. London 2002–05; Chair. Nat. Council for One Parent Families 2002–07, One Parent Families | Gingerbread 2007–; Dir (non-exec.) Nationwide Building Society 2005–; Adviser and Trustee, Design Museum 2006–. *Address:* 35 Camden Square, London, NW1 9XA, England (home). *Telephone:* (20) 7284-2421 (office). *E-mail:* taverne@vlessing.com (home).

TAVERNER, Sonia; Canadian ballerina and dance teacher; b. 18 May 1936, Byfleet, Surrey, England; d. of Herbert F. Taverner and Evelyn N. Taverner; ed Elmhurst Ballet School, Royal Ballet School, London and Ballet Arts and American Ballet Theater Schools, New York; joined Royal Ballet 1954, toured USA and Canada; joined Royal Winnipeg Ballet 1956, leading dancer 1957, ballerina 1962–66; appeared with Royal Winnipeg Ballet, Commonwealth Arts Festival, London 1964; joined Les Grands Ballets Canadiens as Prin. Dancer 1966–74; appeared as guest artist with the Boston Ballet Co., in Swan Lake 1967; Guest Teacher, Les Grands Ballets Canadiens Summer School 1970; Prin. Artist, The Pennsylvania Ballet 1971–72; Head of Ballet Div., Grant MacEwan Community Coll. 1975–80; Dir Professional Program Devt, Alberta Ballet School 1981–82; f. School of Classical Ballet, Spruce Grove, Alberta 1982–97; producer, own concert Variations 1977; Guest Artist, Vancouver Opera 1977, Les Grands Ballets Canadiens in Giselle and The Nutcracker 1977, 1978, Alberta Ballet Co. in The Nutcracker and Raymonda 1978, 1979; Guest Teacher, Alberta Ballet Summer School 1975, 1976, Pacific Ballet Theatre Summer School 1979; Guest Artist with Toronto, Winnipeg and Vancouver Symphony Orchestras; Guest Teacher, Penticton, BC 1984–85; Royal Acad. of Dance (RAD) Teaching Diploma 1993; Guest Teacher, Edmonton Dance Centre 1998–2002; has toured extensively in N America, Jamaica and UK; registered mem. RAD (Life mem. 2002–), Actors Equity Asscn, American Guild of Musical Artists, ARAD (Assoc. of the Royal Acad. of Dance) 2003; Dame Adeline Genée Silver Medal 1954, Canada Council Exploration Grant 1977. *Principal roles include:* classical: Swan Lake, Sleeping Beauty, Giselle, Nutcracker, Raymonda and Les Sylphides; Balanchine: Symphony in C, Allegro Brilliante, Theme and Variations, Raymonda Variations; Pas de Deux from Don Quixote. *Leisure interests:* cooking, reading, gardening, sewing, currently writing my memoirs of my life in dance. *Address:* PO Box 2039, Stony Plain, Alberta, T7Z 1X6, Canada (home). *Telephone:* (780) 963-5567 (home). *E-mail:* taverner@telusplanet.net (home).

TAVERNIER, Bertrand René Maurice; French film director; b. 25 April 1941, Lyon; s. of René Tavernier and Geneviève Dumond; m. Claudine O'Hagan 1965; one s. one d.; ed Ecole St-Martin de Pontoise, Lycées Henri-IV, Fénelon, Paris, Univ. de Paris (Sorbonne); press attaché and journalist, then film dir; mem. Société des réalisateurs de films, APR; Pres. Inst. Lumière 1982–. *Films include:* Le baiser de Judas, Une charge explosive, La chance et l'amour, L'horloger de Saint-Paul (Louis Delluc prize 1973), Que la fête commence (César Best Screenplay, Best Direction) 1975, Le juge et l'assassin (César Best Screenplay 1976) 1976, Des enfants gâtés 1977, La mort en direct (Foreign Press Award 1979) 1979, Une semaine de vacances 1980, Coup de torchon 1981, Mississippi Blues 1983, Un dimanche à la campagne (Best Dir Award, Cannes Film Festival, NY Critics Award) 1984, Autour de minuit 1986, La passion béatrice 1987, La vie et rien d'autre 1988 (European Film Festival Special Prize 1989), Daddy nostalgie 1990, La guerre sans nom 1991, L.627 1991, La fille d'Artagnan 1994, L'Appât 1995, De l'autre côté du periph (TV documentary) 1997; jt screenplay La trace 1983; (producer) Veillées d'Armes 1994, Capitaine Conan 1996 (Méliès Prize for Best French Film 1996, César for Best Dir 1997), Ça commence aujourd'hui 1999 (Prix de la Fipresci, Berlin, Prix du Public, San Sebastian and Tübingen, Prix Photogramas de Plata for Best Foreign Language Film, Spain), Histoires de vies brisées 2001, Laissez-passer 2002 (Best Film, Best Dir Fort Lauderdale 2002), Holy Lola 2004, In the Electric Mist 2008. *Publications:* 30 ans de cinéma américain (jtly) 1970, 50 ans de cinéma américain (jtly) 1991, Qu'est-ce qu'on attend? 1993, Amis américains 1994 and other books. *Leisure interests:* jazz, food, literature, movies. *Address:* Institut Lumière, 25 rue du Premier Film, 69008 Lyon (office); Little Bear, 7–9 rue Arthur Groussier, 75010 Paris, France. *Telephone:* 1-42-38-06-55 (office). *Fax:* 1-42-45-00-33 (office). *E-mail:* contac@institut-lumiere.org (office). *Website:* www.institut-lumiere.org (office).

TAVIANI, Paolo; Italian film director; b. 8 Nov. 1931, San Miniato; brother of Vittorio Taviani (q.v.); ed Univ. of Pisa. *Films:* co-dir (with Vittorio Taviani): Un uomo da bruciare 1963, I fuorilegge del matrimonio 1963, Sovversivi 1967, Sotto il segno dello scorpione 1969, San Michele aveva un gallo 1971, Allonsanfan 1974, Padre Padrone 1977, The Meadow 1979, La notte di San Lorenzo (The Night of the Shooting Stars) 1981, Xaos 1984, Good Morning, Babylon 1988, Il Sole anche di Notte 1990, Fiorile 1993, The Elective Affinities, You Laugh.

TAVIANI, Vittorio; Italian film director; b. 20 Sept. 1929, San Miniato; brother of Paolo Taviani (q.v.); ed Univ. of Pisa. *Films:* co-dir Un uomo da Bruciare 1963, I fuorilegge del metraimonio 1963, Sovversivi 1967, Sotto il segno dello scorpione 1969, San Michele aveva un gallo 1971, Allonsanfan 1974, Padre Padrone 1977, The Meadow (Italian-French) 1979, La notte di San Lorenzo (The Night of the Shooting Stars) 1981, Xaos 1984, Good

Morning, Babylon 1988, Il Sole Anche di Notte 1990, Fiorile 1993, The Elective Affinities, Tu Ridi (You Laugh) 1998, Un Altro mondo è possibile (Another World Is Possible) 2001. *Television:* Resurrezione (Resurrection) (film) 2001, Luisa Sanfelice (miniseries) 2004.

TAVOLA, Kaliopate, MAgrSc; Fijian politician and economist; b. 10 Oct. 1946, Dravuni; m. Helen Tavola; two d. one s.; ed Massey Univ., New Zealand, Australian Nat. Univ., Australia; Agric. Officer Ministry of Primary Industries 1973–77, Sr Agric. Officer 1977–79, Prin. Economist 1979, Prin. Agric. Officer Eastern Div./Projects 1980, Chief Economist 1980–81, 1982–84, Dir of Agric. (acting) 1981–82, later Minister of Primary Industries; London Rep. Fiji Sugar Marketing (FSM) Co. Ltd 1984–88, Deputy CEO 1998–2000; Commercial Counsellor Fiji High Comm. 1984–88; Head of Mission, EU, Brussels 1988–98; Amb. to Belgium, Luxembourg, Netherlands, France, Italy, Spain, Portugal, Greece 1988–98; Perm. Rep. to UNESCO, FAO, WTO, WCO, OPCW; responsible for IFAD, MFO, PCA 1988–98; Commr-Gen. S Pacific Pavilion, EXPO '92, Seville, Spain 1992; Minister of Foreign Affairs and External Trade 2000–06; mem. Senate. *Leisure interests:* reading, gardening, music, golf. *Address:* c/o The Senate, Parliament of Fiji Islands, Government Buildings, Suva, Fiji (office). *E-mail:* ktavola@govnet.gov.fj.

TAWARA, Machi, BA; Japanese poet; b. 1962, Osaka; ed Waseda Univ.; worked as a high school teacher 1985–89; bestselling writer of tanka poetry 1987–, over three million copies of first collection in print; 32nd Kadokawa Tanka Award 1986. *Publications:* poetry collections: Sarada kinenbi (Salad Anniversary) (Modern Japanese Poets Asscn Award 1988) 1987, Chokoreeto kakumeri (The Chocolate Revolution) 1997; translations of classic poetry into contemporary Japanese: Man'yoshu (10,000 Leaves), Taketori Monogatori (The Tale of the Bamboo Cutter), Chokoreeto-go yaku midaregami (Tangled Hair in Chocolate Language) 1998; several popular travel and photography books, numerous essays for newspapers and magazines. *Address:* c/o Kodansha International Limited, Otowa YK Building, Bunkyo-ku, Tokyo 112-8652, Japan (office). *Website:* www.gtpweb.net/twr/indexe.htm.

TAXELL, (Lars Evald) Christoffer, LLM; Finnish business executive; *President and CEO, Partek Corporation;* b. 14 Feb. 1948, Turku; s. of Lars Erik Taxell and Elna Hillevi Brunberg; m. Rachel Margareta Nygård 1974; Chair. Youth Org., Swedish People's Party 1970–72, Party Chair. 1985–90; Political Sec. 1970–71; Asst, School of Econ., Åbo Akademi, Turku 1973–75; MP 1975–91; Minister of Justice 1979–87, of Educ. and Science 1987–90; Pres. and CEO Partek Corpn 1990–. *Address:* Partek Corporation, 21600 Pargas, Finland. *Telephone:* 21 74261. *Fax:* 21 742 6340. *Website:* www.partek.fi.

TAY, Simon SC, LLB, LLM; Singaporean academic; *Chairman, Singapore Institute of International Affairs;* s. of the late Tay Seow Huah and of Cheong Keong Hin; m. Siow Jin Hua; one s.; ed Nat. Univ. of Singapore, Harvard Univ., USA; served as Nominated Mem. of Parl. 1997–2001; Chair. Nat. Environment Agency 2002–08; Visiting Prof. Harvard Law School 2003; currently Prof. of Int. Law and Public Policy, Nat. Univ. of Singapore and Visiting Prof., Yale; mem. numerous expert panels, ASEAN Regional Forum, APEC Independent Experts, Energy City Center Int. Advisory Bd; Ind. Bd mem. and adviser to several large cos with regional interests; Fulbright Fellow, Harvard 1993–94; Laylin Prize, Harvard 1994, Singapore Young Artist of the Year 1995, Eisenhower Fellowship 2002, National Day Award PBM 2006. *Publications:* Stand Alone 1993, Asian Dragons and Green Trade 1996, Reinventing ASEAN 2001, The Enemy Within: Combating Corruption in Asia 2003, Sketching Regional Futures 2005, A Mandarin and the Making of Public Policy 2006. *Address:* Singapore Institute of International Affairs, 2 Nassim Road, Singapore, 258370 (office). *Telephone:* 67349600 (office). *Fax:* 67336217 (office). *E-mail:* chairman@siiaonline.org (office). *Website:* www .siiaonline.org (office).

TAYA, Col Maawiya Ould Sid'Ahmed; Mauritanian politician, fmr army officer and fmr head of state; b. 1943; served in Saharan War 1976–78, Chief of Mil. Operations, then commdr garrison at Bir Mogkrein; Minister of Defence 1978–79; Commdr nat. gendarmerie 1979–80; Minister in charge of Perm. Secr., Mil. Cttee for Nat. Recovery 1979–81; Army Chief of Staff 1980–81, March–Dec. 1984; Prime Minister and Minister of Defence 1981–84, 1984–92; Pres. of Mauritania and Chair. Mil. Cttee for Nat. Salvation 1984–92, elected Pres. of Mauritania 1992–2005 (deposed in bloodless coup). *Address:* c/o Présidence de la République, BP 184, Nouackchott, Mauritania.

TAYLOR, Allan Richard, OC; Canadian banker; b. 14 Sept. 1932, Prince Albert, Saskatchewan; s. of Norman Taylor and Anna Lydia Norbeck Taylor; m. Shirley Irene Ruston 1957; one s. one d.; joined Royal Bank of Canada 1949, Dir, Head Int. Div. 1977–83, Pres. and COO 1983–86, CEO 1986–94, Chair. 1986–95; Dir Canadian Inst. for Advanced Research, Toronto, Neuroscience Network, Montréal; Pres. Int. Monetary Conf. 1992–93; Chair. Canadian Bankers Asscn 1984–86; mem. Council of Patrons, Canadian Outward Bound; mem. Advisory Council Canadian Exec. Service Overseas; mem. Advisory Bd, Canadian Journalism Foundation, Advisory Bd, Canadian Foundation for AIDS Research; Exec. Adviser, Public Policy Forum; Hon. DJur (Univ. of Regina) 1987, (Concordia Univ.) 1988, (Queen's Univ.) 1991; Hon. DBA (Laval) 1990; Dr hc (Ottawa) 1992. *Leisure interests:* golf, tennis, fishing. *Address:* Suite 2915, South Tower, Royal Bank Plaza, Toronto, ON M5J 2J5, Canada (office). *Telephone:* (416) 974-4041 (office). *Fax:* (416) 974-8713 (office). *E-mail:* allan.taylor@rbc.com (office).

TAYLOR, Andrew Dawson, OBE, DPhil; British physicist and academic; *Director, ISIS Neutron Scattering Facility, Rutherford Appleton Laboratory;* ed St John's Coll., Oxford; joined Rutherford Lab. as part of team promoting accelerator-based neutrons sources as tools to investigate microscopic structure and dynamics of condensed matter, currently Dir ISIS facility, Science and Tech. Facilities Council Rutherford Appleton Lab., Didcot, Oxon.; also

worked at Los Alamos, NM, USA; Glazebrook Medal, Inst. of Physics 2006. *Publications:* numerous scientific papers in professional journals on pulsed neutron source instrumentation and science. *Address:* Science and Technology Facilities Council, Rutherford Appleton Laboratory, Harwell Science and Innovation Campus, Chilton, Didcot, OX11 0QX, Oxon., England (office). *Telephone:* (1235) 446681 (office). *Fax:* (1235) 445383 (office). *E-mail:* andrew .taylor@stfc.ac.uk (office). *Website:* www.scitech.ac.uk (office).

TAYLOR, Ann (see TAYLOR, Rt Hon. (Winifred) Ann).

TAYLOR, Baroness (Life Peer), cr. 2005, of Bolton in the County of Greater Manchester; **(Winifred) Ann Taylor,** PC; British politician; b. 2 July 1947, Motherwell; m. David Taylor 1966; one s. one d.; ed Bolton School and Univs of Bradford and Sheffield; fmr teacher and part-time tutor, Open Univ.; MP for Bolton West 1974–83, for Dewsbury 1987–2005; Parl. Pvt. Sec. to Sec. of State for Educ. and Science 1975–76, to Sec. of State for Defence 1976–77; an Asst Govt Whip 1977–79; Opposition Spokesman on Educ. 1979–81, on Housing 1981–83, on Home Affairs 1987–90, on Environment 1990–92, on Educ. 1992–94; Shadow Leader of House of Commons 1994–97; Pres. of the Council and Leader of the House of Commons 1997–98; Chief Whip 1998–2001; Chair. Select Cttee on Modernization 1997–98; Spokesperson on Citizen's Charter 1994–95; mem. Select Cttee on Standards and Privileges 1995–97; fmr Deputy Chair. Ind. Football Comm.; Vice-Chair Forestry Group, House of Lords 2005–, Parl. Under-Sec. of State and Govt Spokesperson, Ministry of Defence 2007–; mem. Labour Party; Hon. Fellow, Birkbeck Coll. London. *Address:* House of Lords, London, SW1A 0PW, England (office). *Telephone:* (20) 7219-5183 (office). *E-mail:* taylora@parliament.uk (office).

TAYLOR, Arthur Robert, MA; American business executive and fmr university president; b. 6 July 1935, Elizabeth, NJ; s. of Arthur Earl Taylor and Marion Hilda Scott; m. Marion McFarland 1959 (divorced); three d.; m. 2nd Kathryn Pelgrift; ed Brown Univ.; Asst Dir of Admissions, Brown Univ. 1957–60; with The First Boston Corpn 1961–70, Vice-Pres. Underwriting Dept 1966–70, Dir 1970; Vice-Pres. (Finance), Int. Paper Co. 1970–71, Exec. Vice-Pres. 1971–72, Dir 1971–72; Pres. and Dir CBS Inc. 1972–76; Dir Arthur Taylor & Co., New York 1977– (Chair. 1977–), Travelers Corpn, Rockefeller Center Inc., American Friends of Bilderberg, Pitney Bowes Inc., Louisiana Land and Exploration, Eastern Airlines, Nomura Pacific Basin Fund, etc.; Vice-Chair. Forum Corpn, Boston, Mass 1988–; Dean, Faculty of Business, Fordham Univ. 1985–89; Pres. Muhlenberg Coll., Pa 1992–2002; mem. Council on Foreign Relations, Nat. Cttee on American Foreign Policy, Center for Inter-American Relations, Japan Soc.; Trustee, Brown Univ., Franklin Savings Bank, New York Hosp., William H. Donner Foundation; Commr Trilateral Comm. *Publications:* article in Harvard Review of Business History 1971, chapter in The Other Side of Profit 1975. *Address:* Main Street, Salisbury, CT 06068, USA (home).

TAYLOR, Charles, CC, OQ, BA, MA, DPhil, FRSC; Canadian academic; *Board of Trustees Professor of Law and Philosophy, Northwestern University;* b. 5 Nov. 1931, Montréal; ed McGill Univ., Balliol Coll., Oxford; Fellow, All Souls Coll., Oxford 1956–61; Asst Prof., Dept of Political Science, McGill Univ., Montréal 1961–62, Prof. 1962–97, Prof. Emer. 1998–; Bd of Trustees Prof. of Law, Northwestern Univ. 2002–; Prof., Univ. of Montréal 1962–71; Chichele Prof. of Social and Political Theory, Univ. of Oxford 1976–81; Mills Visiting Prof., Univ. of California, Berkeley 1974, 1983; Alan B. Plaunt Memorial Lecturer, Carleton Univ., Ottawa 1978; Alex Corry Lecturer, Queen's Univ., Kingston, Ont. 1980; B.N. Ganguli Lecturer, Centre for the Study of Developing Socs, Delhi 1981; Suhrkamp Lecturer, Univ. of Frankfurt 1984; Guest Prof., J.W. Goethe Univ., Frankfurt 1984; Visiting Prof. of Political Science and Philosophy, Hebrew Univ. of Jerusalem 1985; Massey Lecturer, CBC 1991; Tanner Lecturer, Stanford Univ. 1992; Max Horkheimer Lecturer, Univ. of Frankfurt 1996; Storrs Lecturer, Yale Univ. 1998; Templeton Prize 2007, Kyoto Prize 2008. *Publications:* The Explanation of Behaviour 1964, The Pattern of Politics 1970, Erklärung und Interpretation in den Wissenschaften vom Menschen 1975, Hegel 1975, Hegel and Modern Society 1979, Social Theory As Practice 1983, Human Agency and Language: Philosophical Papers 1 1985, Philosophy and the Human Sciences: Philosophical Papers 2 1985, Negative Freiheit? Zur Kritik des neuzeitlichen Individualismus 1988, Sources of the Self: The Making of the Modern Identity 1989, The Malaise of Modernity 1991, Multiculturalism and 'The Politics of Recognition' 1992, Rapprocher les solitudes: crits sur le fédéralisme et le nationalisme au Canada 1992, Roads to Democracy: Human Rights and Democratic Development in Thailand 1994, Philosophical Arguments 1995, A Catholic Modernity? 1999, Wieviel Gemeinschaft braucht die Demokratie? Aufsätze zur politische Philosophie 2002, Varieties of Religion Today: William James Revisited 2002, Modern Social Imaginaries 2004, A Secular Age 2007. *Address:* Department of Philosophy, Northwestern University, Kresge Hall, Campus Drive, Evanston, IL 60208-2214, USA (office). *Telephone:* (847) 491-3656 (office). *Fax:* (847) 491-2547 (office). *E-mail:* charles-taylor@law.northwestern .edu (office). *Website:* www.philosophy.northwestern.edu/people/taylor.html (office).

TAYLOR, Charles, CC, OQ, DPhil, FBA; Canadian academic; *Professor of Philosophy, McGill University;* b. 5 Nov. 1931, Montréal; s. of Walter Margrave Taylor and Simone Beaubien; m. Alba Romer 1956 (deceased), five d.; m. 2nd Aube Billard; ed McGill and Oxford Univs; Fellow of All Souls Coll., Oxford 1956–61; Asst Prof. of Political Science and Philosophy 1961, Prof. of Political Science and Prof. of Philosophy 1973–; Prof. of Philosophy, Univ. of Montréal 1962–71; Chichele Prof. of Social and Political Theory, Univ. of Oxford and Fellow of All Souls Coll. 1976–81; Prof. of Political Science, then of Philosophy, McGill Univ. 1982–2006, Emer. 2006–; mem. RSC; Corresp. mem. American Acad. of Arts and Sciences; Grand Officier de l'Ordre Nat. de Québec 2000; John Locke Prize, Oxford 1955, Templeton Prize 2007.

Publications: The Explanation of Behaviour 1964, Hegel 1975, Hegel and Modern Society 1979, Human Agency and Language 1985, Philosophy and the Human Sciences 1985, Sources of Self 1989, The Malaise of Modernity 1991, Philosophical Arguments 1995, Varieties of Religion Today 2002, Modern Social Imaginaries 2004, A Secular Age 2007. *Leisure interests:* skiing, swimming, hiking. *Address:* Department of Philosophy, McGill University, Stephen Leacock Building, Room 908, 855 Sherbrooke Street W, Montréal, Québec, H3A 2T7 (office); 6603 Jeanne Mance, Montréal, Québec, H2V 4L1, Canada (home). *Telephone:* (514) 398-6060 (office). *E-mail:* cmt1111111@aol.com. *Website:* www.mcgill.ca/philosophy (office).

TAYLOR, Charles Ghankay; Liberian fmr head of state; Leader Nat. Patriotic Front of Liberia (NPFL) which was part of combined rebel force which overthrew fmr Pres. Samuel Doe; engaged in civil insurrection 1991–96; mem. Transitional Exec. Council of State 1996–97; Pres. of Liberia 1997–2003; indicted for war crimes 2003; in exile in Nigeria 2003, arrested March 2006.

TAYLOR, Derek H.; Turks and Caicos Islands politician; Leader, People's Democratic Movt; Chief Minister and Minister of Finance, Devt and Commerce 1995–2003. *Address:* c/o Office of the Chief Minister, Government Compound, Grand Turk, The Turks and Caicos Islands (office).

TAYLOR, Dame Elizabeth Rosemond, DBE; British/American actress; b. 27 Feb. 1932, London; d. of Francis Taylor and Sara Sothern; m. 1st Conrad Nicholas Hilton, Jr 1950 (divorced); m. 2nd Michael Wilding 1952 (divorced); two s.; m. 3rd Mike Todd 1957 (died 1958); one d.; m. 4th Eddie Fisher 1959 (divorced); m. 5th Richard Burton 1964 (divorced 1974, remarried 1975, divorced 1976); one adopted d.; m. 7th Senator John Warner (q.v.) 1976 (divorced 1982); m. 8th Larry Fortensky 1991 (divorced 1996); ed Byron House, Hawthorne School and Metro-Goldwyn-Mayer School; active in philanthropic and relief charitable causes internationally including Israeli War Victims Fund for the Chaim Sheba Hosp. 1976, UNICEF, Variety Children's Hosps, medical clinics in Botswana; initiated Ben Gurion Univ.-Elizabeth Taylor Fund for Children of the Negev 1982; supporter AIDS Project LA 1985; Founder, Nat. Chair. Council for AIDS Research (AmFAR) 1985–, int. fund 1985–; Founder Elizabeth Taylor AIDS Foundation 1991–; licensed fragrances: Elizabeth Taylor's Passion, Passion for Men, White Diamonds/Elizabeth Taylor, Elizabeth Taylor's Diamonds and Emeralds, Diamonds and Rubies, Diamonds and Sapphires; jewellery: The Elizabeth Taylor Fashion Jewelry Collection for Avon; Commdr des Arts et Lettres 1985; Légion d'honneur (for work with AmFAR) 1987; Aristotle S. Onassis Foundation Award 1988, Jean Hersholt Humanitarian Acad. Award (for work as AIDS advocate), Life Achievement Award, American Film Inst. 1993, Lifetime Achievement Award, Screen Actors Guild 1998, BAFTA Fellowship 1999; honoured with dedication of Elizabeth Taylor Clinic, Washington 1993, Kennedy Center Honoree 2002, BAFTA Britannia Award for Artistic Excellence in Hollywood 2005. *Films include:* Lassie Come Home 1942, There's One Born Every Minute 1943, The White Cliffs of Dover 1943, Jane Eyre 1943, National Velvet 1944, Courage of Lassie 1946, Life with Father 1946, Cynthia 1947, A Date With Judy 1948, Julia Misbehaves 1948, Little Women 1948, Conspirator 1949, The Big Hangover 1949, Father's Little Dividend 1950, Father of the Bride 1950, A Place in the Sun 1950, Love is Better Than Ever 1951, Ivanhoe 1951, Rhapsody 1954, Elephant Walk 1954, Beau Brummel 1954, The Last Time I Saw Paris 1955, Giant 1956, Raintree Country 1957, Cat on a Hot Tin Roof 1958, Suddenly Last Summer 1959, Butterfield 8 1960, Cleopatra 1962, The VIPs 1963, The Sandpiper 1965, Who's Afraid of Virginia Woolf? 1966, The Taming of the Shrew 1967, The Comedians 1967, Reflections in a Golden Eye 1967, Doctor Faustus 1968, Boom 1968, Secret Ceremony 1968, The Only Game in Town 1969, Under Milk Wood 1971, X, Y and Zee 1972, Hammersmith is Out 1972, Night Watch 1973, Ash Wednesday 1974, The Driver's Seat 1975, Blue Bird 1976, A Little Night Music 1977, The Mirror Crack'd 1980, Between Friends 1983, The Young Toscanini 1988, The Flintstones 1994. *Television appearances include:* Divorce His, Divorce Hers 1973, Victory at Entebbe 1977, Return Engagement 1979, Between Friends 1982, Hotel (series) 1984, Malice in Wonderland 1986, North and South (mini-series) 1986, There Must be a Pony 1986, Poker Alice 1987, Sweet Bird of Youth 1989, The Simpsons (voice) 1992, These Old Broads 2001, God, the Devil and Bob (voice) 2003. *Plays include:* The Little Foxes (New York) 1981, (Los Angeles) 1981, (London) 1982, Private Lives (New York) 1983. *Publications:* World Enough and Time (with Richard Burton) 1964, Elizabeth Taylor 1965, Elizabeth Taylor Takes Off – On Weight Gain, Weight Loss, Self-Esteem and Self Image 1988. *Address:* 12400 Wilshire Blvd, Suite 1275, Los Angeles, CA 00025-1010; c/o Dick Guttman, Guttman Associates, 118 South Beverly Drive, Beverly Hills, CA 90212, USA.

TAYLOR, Grace Oladunni L., PhD; Nigerian biochemist and academic; ed Univ. of London, UK and Univ. of Ibadan; Prof. of Chemical Pathology, Univ. of Ibadan (retd); has taught medicine in Nigeria and other African countries; mem. Third World Org. for Women in Science; L'Oréal-UNESCO For Women in Science Award 1998. *Publications:* numerous articles in scientific journals on lipid metabolism. *Address:* c/o Department of Chemical Pathology, University of Ibadan, Ibadan, Nigeria (office). *Website:* www.ui.edu.ng (office).

TAYLOR, Graham, OBE; British professional football manager; b. 15 Sept. 1944, Worksop; s. of Tommy Taylor; m. Rita Cowling 1965; two d.; ed Scunthorpe Grammar School; player, Grimsby Town 1962–68, Lincoln City 1968–72 (Man. 1972–77); Man. Watford FC 1977–87, 1996–2001, Aston Villa 1987–90, 2001–03, England nat. team 1990–93, Wolverhampton Wanderers FC 1994–95; Dir (non-exec.) Aston Villa 2001–03; Vice-Pres. Scunthorpe United 2003–; football commentator, BBC Radio Five Live, Sky TV 2004–; Patron, Lincoln City FC. *Address:* Scunthorpe United Football Club, Glanford Park, Doncaster Road, Scunthorpe, Lincolnshire DN15 8TD, England (office). *Telephone:* (1724) 848077 (office). *E-mail:* admin@scunthorpe-united.co.uk (office). *Website:* www.scunthorpe-united.premiumtv.co.uk (office).

TAYLOR, Gregory Frank, AO, BEcons; Australian civil servant and diplomatist; b. 1 July 1942, Adelaide; s. of Frank Taylor and Constance Rischbieth; m. Jill Beatrice Bodman 1967; one s. one d.; ed Univ. of Adelaide; Chair. Industries Assistance Comm., Canberra 1988; CEO Dept of Employment Educ. and Training 1989–94, Dept of Primary Industries and Energy 1993–95, Dept of Industry, Tech. and Commerce 1996; Exec. Dir IMF, Washington, DC 1997–2000; Chair. Australian Mathematics Trust Bd. *Leisure interest:* skiing. *Address:* c/o Australian Mathematics Trust, University of Canberra, ACT 2601, Australia.

TAYLOR, Jermain; American professional boxer; b. 11 Aug. 1978, Little Rock, Ark.; m. Erica Smith-Taylor; ed Northern Mich. Univ./USOEC; nicknamed 'Bad Intentions'; began boxing 1992; coached by Al Mitchell, Pat Burns and Ozell Nelson; semi-finalist (twice) US Championships; Bronze Medal, Goodwill Games 1998; Nat. Golden Gloves Champion 1998, 1999; Eastern Trials Champion 2000; Bronze Medal, Olympic Games, Sydney, Australia 2000; defeated previously unbeaten Daniel Edouard via tech knockout 19 Feb. 2005, earned title bout against Middleweight Champion Bernard Hopkins, won fight by close split decision to become new undisputed (WBA, WBC, IBF and WBO) Middleweight champion 16 July 2005, rematch scheduled in Las Vegas, Nev. for 3 Dec. 2005; holds perfect record of 24 wins, 0 losses, 0 draws, with 17 wins coming by way of knockout. *E-mail:* AB@jermaintaylor.com (office). *Website:* jermaintaylor.com (office).

TAYLOR, John B., BA, DEcon; American economist and government official; *Mary and Robert Raymond Professor of Economics, Stanford University;* b. 8 Dec. 1946, Yonkers, NY; m. Allyn Taylor; two c.; ed Princeton Univ., Stanford Univ.; Mary and Robert Raymond Prof. of Econs, Stanford Univ., also Sr Fellow, Hoover Inst., fmr Dir Stanford Inst. for Econ. Policy Research, fmr Dir Introductory Econs Center, fmr Chair. Stanford Cttee on Undergraduate Studies; Sr Staff Economist and mem. Presidential Council of Econ. Advisers under Pres Gerald Ford and George Bush, Sr; Under-Sec. of Treasury for Int. Affairs 2001–05; mem. California Council of Econ. Advisers under Gov. Arnold Shwarzenegger 2005–; Fellow, American Acad. of Arts and Sciences; Medal of Repub. of Uruguay 2005; Hoagland Prize 1992, Lilian and Thomas B. Rhodes Prize 1997, Alexander Hamilton Award 2005, George Shultz Award 2005, Adam Smith Award 2007. *Address:* Stanford University, Department of Economics, Stanford, CA 94305, USA (office). *Telephone:* (650) 723-9677 (office). *E-mail:* JohnBTaylor@stanford.edu (office). *Website:* www.stanford.edu/~johntayl (office).

TAYLOR, Rt Rev. John Bernard, KCVO, MA; British ecclesiastic; b. 6 May 1929, Newcastle upon Tyne; s. of George Taylor and Gwendoline Taylor; m. Linda Courtenay Barnes 1956; one s. two d.; ed Watford Grammar School, Christ's and Jesus Colls Cambridge, Hebrew Univ. of Jerusalem and Ridley Hall, Cambridge; RAF service 1952–54; ordained deacon 1956, priest 1957; Vicar of Henham and Elsenham, Essex 1959–64; Vice-Prin. Oak Hill Theological Coll. London 1964–72; Vicar of All Saints' Woodford Wells, Essex 1972–75; Archdeacon of West Ham 1975–80; Bishop of St Albans 1980–95; Chair. Council, Wycliffe Hall, Oxford 1985–99; Lord High Almoner to HM the Queen 1988–97; Pres. The Bible Soc. 1997–2004; Pres. and Chair. of Council, Haileybury 1980–95; Pres. Hildenborough Evangelistic Trust 1986–2000, Garden Tomb Asscn 1987–, Church's Ministry Among Jewish People 1996–; Chair. Council, Tyndale House, Cambridge 1996–2004; Hon. LLD. *Publications:* Tyndale Commentary on Ezekiel 1969, Preaching through the Prophets 1983, Preaching on God's Justice 1994. *Leisure interests:* bird-watching, walking. *Address:* 22 Conduit Head Road, Cambridge, CB3 0EY, England. *Telephone:* (1223) 313783.

TAYLOR, John Bryan, PhD, FRS; British physicist and academic; *Consultant, Culham Laboratory;* b. 26 Dec. 1928, Birmingham; s. of Frank H. Taylor and Ada Taylor (née Stinton); m. Joan M. Hargest 1951; one s. one d.; ed Oldbury Co. High School and Univ. of Birmingham; served in RAF 1950–52; physicist, Atomic Weapons Research Establishment, Aldermaston 1955–59, 1961–62; Harkness Fellow, Univ. of Calif. 1959–60; on staff of UKAEA, Culham Lab. 1962–89, Head of Theory Div. 1963–81, Chief Physicist, Culham Lab. 1981–89, Consultant 1994–; Fondren Foundation Prof. of Plasma Theory, Univ. of Texas at Austin 1989–94; mem. Inst. for Advanced Study, Princeton, NJ 1969, 1980, 1981; Fellow, American Physical Soc.; Maxwell Medal, Inst. of Physics 1971, Max Born Prize and Medal, German Physical Soc. 1979, Award for Excellence in Plasma Research, American Physical Soc. 1986, James Clerk Maxwell Prize, American Physical Soc. 1999, Hannes Alfvén Prize, European Physical Soc. 2004. *Publications:* contribs to scientific learned journals. *Leisure interests:* gliding, model engineering. *Address:* Radwinter, Winterbrook Lane, Wallingford, Oxon., OX10 9EJ, England (home). *Telephone:* (1491) 837269 (home). *Fax:* (1235) 466435 (office). *E-mail:* bryan.taylor@ukaea.org.uk (office). *Website:* www.ukaea.org.uk (office).

TAYLOR, (John) Maxwell (Percy); British insurance broker; b. 17 March 1948; s. of Harold Guy Percy Taylor and Anne Katherine Taylor (née Stafford); m. Dawn Susan Harling 1970; one s. one d.; joined Willis Faber & Dumas as jr aviation broker 1970; Dir Willis Faber, then Willis Corroon Group PLC, Chair. and Chief Exec. Willis, Faber & Dumas, Group Exec. Dir 1997; elected to Council of Lloyd's 1997, Chair. of Lloyd's 1998–2000; fmr Chair. Lloyd's Insurance Brokers' Cttee, London Insurance Market Network; Vice-Pres. Insurance Inst. of London. *Leisure interests:* music, skiing, golf, travelling. *Address:* c/o Office of the Chairman, Lloyds, 1 Lime Street, London, EC3M 7HA, England (office). *Telephone:* (20) 7327-1000 (office). *Fax:* (20) 7327-5926 (office).

TAYLOR, John Russell, MA; British writer, editor and academic; *Art Critic, The Times;* b. 19 June 1935, Dover, Kent; s. of Arthur Russell Taylor and Kathleen Mary Taylor (née Picker); pnr Ying Yeung Li; ed Dover Grammar School, Jesus Coll. Cambridge, Courtauld Inst. of Art; Sub-Ed., Times Educ. Supplement 1959–60; Editorial Asst, Times Literary Supplement 1960–62; Film Critic, The Times 1962–73; Dir of Film Studies, Tufts Univ. in London 1970–72; Prof., Div. of Cinema, Univ. of Southern Calif., USA 1972–78; Art Critic, The Times 1978–; Ed. Films and Filming 1983–90; Art Critic, Radio Two Arts Programme 1990–2000. *Television:* Feet Foremost 1968, The Imposter 1969, Dracula 1969, Curse of the Mummy 1970, A Letter to David 1971. *Film:* Charles Chaplin Makes The Countess from Hong Kong 1966. *Publications:* Anger and After 1962, Anatomy of a Television Play 1962, Cinema Eye, Cinema Ear 1964, Penguin Dictionary of the Theatre 1966, The Art Nouveau Book in Britain 1966, Art in London 1966, The Rise and Fall of the Well-Made Play 1967, The Art Dealers 1969, The Hollywood Musical 1971, The Second Wave 1971, Directors and Directions 1975, Hitch 1978, Impressionism 1981, Strangers in Paradise 1983, Ingrid Bergman 1983, Alec Guinness 1984, Vivien Leigh 1984, Hollywood 1940s 1985, Portraits of the British Cinema 1986, Orson Welles 1986, Edward Wolfe 1986, Great Movie Moments 1987, Meninsky 1990, Impressionist Dreams 1990, Liz Taylor 1991, Muriel Pemberton 1993, Ricardo Cinalli 1993, Igor Mitoraj 1993, Claude Monet 1995, Bill Jacklin 1997, The World of Michael Parkes 1998, Antonio Saliola 1998, The Sun is God 1999, Peter Coker 2002, Roberto Barnardi 2002, Zsuzsi Roboz 2005, The Art of Michael Parkes 2006, Adrian George 2006, The Michael Winner Collection of Donald McGill 2006, Carl Laubin 2007, The Art of Jeremy Ramsey 2007, The Glamour of the Gods 2008, Philip Sutton 2008, Exactitude 2009; edited: Look Back in Anger: A Casebook 1968, The Pleasure Dome (Graham Greene on Film) 1972, Masterworks of British Cinema 1974. *Leisure interest:* book collecting, DVD collecting, talking to strange dogs. *Address:* c/o The Times, 1 Pennington Street, London, E1 9XN, England (office). *Telephone:* (20) 7782-5167 (office).

TAYLOR, Joseph Hooton, Jr, PhD; American radio astronomer, physicist and academic; *Emeritus James McDonnell Distinguished Professor of Physics, Princeton University;* b. 29 March 1941, Philadelphia; s. of Joseph Taylor and Sylvia Evans; m. Marietta Bisson 1976; one s. two d.; ed Haverford Coll. and Harvard Univ.; Research Fellow and Lecturer, Harvard Univ. 1968–69; Asst Prof. of Astronomy, Univ. of Mass., Amherst 1969–72, Assoc. Prof. 1973–77, Prof. 1977–81; Prof. of Physics, Princeton Univ. 1980–2006, James McDonnell Distinguished Prof. of Physics 1986–2006, Prof. Emer. 2006–, Dean of Faculty 1997–2003; Fellow, American Acad. of Arts and Sciences; mem. NAS, American Astronomy Soc., Int. Scientific Radio Union, Int. Astronomy Union; Hon. DSc (Chicago) 1985, (Mass) 1994; Wolf Prize in Physics 1992, shared Nobel Prize for Physics 1993 and other awards and distinctions. *Publication:* Pulsars 1977. *Address:* Department of Physics, Princeton University, 215 Jadwin Hall, PO Box 708, Princeton, NJ 08544 (office); 272 Hartley Avenue, Princeton, NJ 08540, USA (home). *E-mail:* jtaylor@princeton.edu (office).

TAYLOR, Ken, FRSA; British screenwriter; b. 10 Nov. 1922, Bolton, Lancs.; m. Gillian Dorothea Black 1953; two s. two d.; ed Greshams School; Writers' Guild Best Original Teleplay Award 1964, Guild of TV Producers and Dirs' Writer of the Year Award 1964, Royal Television Soc. Writer's Award 1984. *Plays for TV include:* One of Us, Special Occasion, The Tin Whistle Man, China Doll, Into the Dark, Parkin's Primitives, The Long Distance Blue, The Slaughtermen, The Devil and John Brown, The Seekers, The Magicians, The Edwardians: E. Nesbit, Death or Liberty (Churchill's People), The Pankhursts, Christabel Pankhurst, Sylvia Pankhurst (three plays for BBC's Shoulder to Shoulder), The Poisoning of Charles Bravo, The Devil's Crown (five plays on Henry II), Cause Célèbre 1988, The Camomile Lawn 1992, The Peacock Spring 1995; many adaptations for TV of works by Somerset Maugham, D. H. Lawrence, Jane Austen, Muriel Spark, Rebecca West, Mary Wesley etc., also The Jewel in the Crown from Paul Scott's The Raj Quartet. *Stage plays:* The Strange Affair of Charles Bravo 1979, Staying On 1997. *Films:* Beyond This Place, Lets Get Married, Alfred the Great. *Publication:* Staying On 2001. *Leisure interests:* walking, music, theatre. *Address:* c/o The Agency, 24 Pottery Lane, Holland Park, London, W11 4LZ (office); Churchtown House, Gwithian, Hayle, Cornwall, TR27 5BX, England (home). *Telephone:* (20) 7727-1346 (office); (1736) 752287 (home). *Fax:* (20) 7727-9637 (office); (1736) 752536 (home). *E-mail:* nnorth@theagency.co.uk (office).

TAYLOR, Lance Jerome, BS, PhD; American economist and academic; *Arnhold Professor of International Co-operation and Development, New School University;* b. 25 May 1940, Montpelier, Idaho; s. of W. Jerome Taylor and Ruth R. Taylor; m. Yvonne S. M. Taylor 1963; one s. one d.; ed Calif. Inst. of Tech., Harvard Univ.; Asst then Assoc. Prof., Harvard Univ. 1968–74; Prof., MIT 1974–93; Arnhold Prof. of Int. Co-operation and Devt, New School for Social Research (now New School Univ.), New York 1993–, also Dir Center for Econ. Policy Analysis –2008, now Faculty Research Fellow; Visiting Prof., Univ. of Brasília 1973–74, Delhi School of Econs 1987–88, Stockholm School of Econs 1990; consultant for UN agencies and over 25 govts and agencies; Marshall Lecturer, Univ. of Cambridge 1987; V. K. Ramaswamy Lecturer, Delhi School of Econs 1988. *Publications:* Structuralist Macroeconomics 1983, Varieties of Stabilization Experience 1988, Income Distribution, Inflation and Growth 1991, The Market Meets its Match: Restructuring the Economies of Eastern Europe 1994, Global Finance at Risk 2000, Reconstructing Macroeconomics 2003. *Leisure interest:* raising cashmere goats. *Address:* Center for Economic Policy Analysis, New School University, 80 Fifth Avenue 5th Floor, Room 509, New York, NY 10011 (office); 15 Old County Road, P.O. Box 378, Washington, ME 04574, USA (home). *Telephone:* (212) 229-5901 ext. 352 (office); (207) 845-2722 (home). *Fax:* (212) 229-5903 (office); (207) 845-2589

(home). *E-mail:* taylorl@newschool.edu (office); lance@blacklocust.com (home). *Website:* www.newschool.edu/cepa (office).

TAYLOR, Martin; British banker and retail executive; b. 8 June 1952; m. Janet Davey 1976; two d.; ed Eton Coll. and Balliol Coll. Oxford; joined Reuters news agency, Paris; subsequently ed. Lex comment column, Financial Times; Personal Asst to Chair. of Courtaulds, later Dir Courtaulds Clothing Div.; CEO Courtaulds PLC 1990–93, Chair. 1993; Dir Barclays Bank PLC Nov. 1993–, Chief Exec. 1994–98; Leader New Whitehall Task Force 1997–; Dir (non-exec.) WH Smith Group PLC 1993–98, Chair. 1999–2003. *Address:* c/o WH Smith Group PLC, Nations House, 103 Wigmore Street, London, W1H 0WH, England (office).

TAYLOR, Martin, MBE; British jazz musician (guitar) and composer; b. 20 Oct. 1956, Harlow, Essex; s. of William 'Buck' Taylor; ed Passmore Comprehensive School, Harlow; began playing aged four, playing in local bands aged 12, professional musician 1972–; support act for Count Basie and his Orchestra, QE2; performed and recorded regularly with violinist Stéphane Grappelli; formed Martin Taylor's Spirit of Django 1994–; played and recorded with Bill Wyman's Rhythm Kings 1998, 1999; featured on Prefab Sprout album Andromeda Heights; recordings (with Steve Howe) of guitars from the Chinery Collection; Freeman of the City of London 1998; Dr hc (Paisley) 1999; Music Retailers Asscn Award for Excellence 1985, British Jazz Award for Best Guitarist 1987, 1988, 1989, 1990, 1991, 1993, 1995, 1997, 1999, 2001, British Acad. of Composers & Songwriters Gold Badge of Merit 1999, Pioneer to the Life of the Nation 2003, BBC Radio 2 Jazz Award 2007. *Recordings:* albums: Taylor Made 1978, Skye Boat 1981, Sarabanda (with John Patitucci and Paulinho Da Costa) 1987, Don't Fret 1990, Change Of Heart 1991, Artistry 1993, Reunion (with Stéphane Grappelli) 1993, Spirit of Django (British Jazz Awards for Best Album 1995) 1994, Portraits 1995, Years Apart 1996, Gypsy 1998, Two's Company 1999, I'm Beginning To See The Light 1999, Kiss & Tell 1999, In Concert (live) 2000, Stepping Stones 2000, Nitelife 2001, Solo (Int. Guitar Foundation Award for Best Album) 2002, Valley 2005, Gypsy Journey 2005, Freternity 2007, Double Standards 2008. *Film soundtracks include:* (with Stéphane Grappelli) Milou en Mai, Dirty Rotten Scoundrels. *Publication:* Martin Taylor: Autobiography of a Travelling Musician, The Martin Taylor Guitar Method. *Leisure interests:* cooking, walking, painting, cartoons, caricatures. *Address:* P3 Music Ltd, Incheoch, Alyth, Perthshire PH11 8HJ, Scotland (office). *E-mail:* management@p3music.com (office); martin@martintaylor.com. *Website:* www.p3music.com (office); www.martintaylor.com (home).

TAYLOR, Rev. Michael Hugh, OBE, BD, MA, DLitt, STM; British minister of religion, charity administrator and academic; *Professor Emeritus of Social Theology, University of Birmingham;* b. 8 Sept. 1936, Northampton; s. of Albert Taylor and Gwendolen Taylor; m. Adele May Dixon 1960; two s. one d.; ed Northampton Grammar School, Univ. of Manchester, Union Theological Seminary, New York; Baptist Minister, North Shields, Northumberland and Hall Green, Birmingham 1960–69; Prin. Northern Baptist Coll., Manchester 1970–85; Lecturer in Theology and Ethics, Univ. of Manchester 1970–85; Examining Chaplain to Bishop of Manchester 1975–85; Dir Christian Aid 1985–97; Pres. Selly Oak Colls, Birmingham 1998–99; Prof. of Social Theology, Univ. of Birmingham 1999–2004, Prof. Emer. 2004–; Dir World Faiths Devt Dialogue 2002–04; Chair. Audenshaw Foundation Trustees 1979–93; mem. Comm. on Theological Educ., WCC 1972–91, Vice-Moderator 1985–91; mem. Council, Overseas Devt Inst. 1986–2000; mem. Comm. IV: Sharing and Service WCC; Chair. Asscn of Protestant Devt Agencies in Europe 1991–94; Pres. Jubilee 2000 UK Coalition 1997–2001; Chair. Burma Campaign –2000, Health Unlimited 2002; Chair. Govs Fircroft Coll., Birmingham 2006–; Trustee, Mines Advisory Group 1998 (Chair. 2000–), Responding to Conflict 2005– (Chair. 2007–; Trustee and Vice-Chair. St Philip's Centre, Leicester 2002–; Patron, Jubilee Debt Campaign 2001–, Student Christian Movt 2005–; broadcast talks on radio; Hon. Mem. of Foundation, Worcester Cathedral 2002–07; Fulbright Travel Award 1969. *Publications:* Variations on a Theme 1971, Learning to Care 1983, Good for the Poor 1990, Christianity and the Persistence of Poverty 1991, Not Angels but Agencies 1995, Jesus and the International Financial Institutions 1996, Past their Sell-By Date? The Role of Northern NGOs in the Future of Development 1998, Poverty and Christianity 2000, Christianity, Poverty and Wealth in the 21st Century 2003, Eat Drink and Be Merry for Tomorrow We Live 2005, Border Crossings 2006. *Leisure interests:* walking, theatre, music, cinema, cooking. *Address:* University of Birmingham, Elmfield House, Selly Oak, Birmingham, B29 6LQ, England (office). *Telephone:* (121) 415-8352 (office). *E-mail:* m.h.taylor@bham.ac.uk (office). *Website:* www.globalethics.bham.ac.uk/staff/taylor.shtml (office).

TAYLOR, Paul B.; American dancer and choreographer; b. 29 July 1930, Allegheny Co., Pa; s. of Paul B. Taylor and Elizabeth P. Rust; ed Virginia Episcopal School, Syracuse Univ., Juilliard School, Metropolitan School of Ballet and Martha Graham School of Contemporary Dance; fmr dancer with the cos of Martha Graham, George Balanchine, Charles Weidman, Anna Sokolow, Merce Cunningham, Katherine Litz, James Waring and Pearl Lang; Dancer-Choreographer-Dir The Paul Taylor Dance Co. 1955–; co. has performed in 450 cities in more than 60 countries; choreographed 119 dances, many of them taken up by more than 50 other dance cos world-wide; Guggenheim Fellowship 1961, 1965, 1983; Hon. Mem. American Acad. and Inst. of Arts and Letters 1989; Hon. Dr Fine Arts (Connecticut Coll., Duke Univ.) 1983, (Syracuse Univ.) 1986; Centennial Achievement Award (Ohio State Univ.), 1970; Brandeis Univ. Creative Arts Award gold medal 1978, Dance Magazine Award 1980, Samuel H. Scripps/American Dance Festival Award 1983, MacArthur 'Genius' Award 1985, New York State Governor's Award 1987, New York City Mayor's Award of Honor for Art and Culture

1989, Kennedy Center Honor 1992, Nat. Medal of Arts 1993, Award from Chicago Int. Film Festival 1993, Algur H. Meadows Award for Excellence in the Arts 1995, Emmy Award for Speaking in Tongues 1991; Commdr des Arts et des Lettres 1990, Légion d'honneur 2000. *Choreography includes:* Three Epitaphs 1956, Rebus 1958, Tablet 1960, Junction 1961, Fibers 1961, Insects and Heroes 1961, Tracer 1962, Piece Period 1962, Aureole 1962, Party Mix 1963, Scudorama 1963, Duet 1964, From Sea to Shining Sea 1965, Post Meridian 1965, Orbs 1966, Agathes' Tale 1967, Lento 1967, Public Domain 1968, Private Domain 1969, Churchyard 1969, Foreign Exchange 1970, Big Bertha 1970, Fêtes 1971, Book of Beasts 1971, Guests of May 1972, So Long Eden 1972, Noah's Minstrels 1973, American Genesis 1973, Untitled Quartet 1974, Sports and Follies 1974, Esplanade 1975, Runes 1975, Cloven Kingdom 1976, Polaris 1976, Images 1976, Dust 1977, Aphrodisiamania 1977, Airs 1978, Diggity 1978, Nightshade 1979, Profiles 1979, Le Sacre du Printemps (subtitled The Rehearsal) 1980, Arden Court 1981, Lost, Found and Lost 1982, Mercuric Tidings 1982, Sunset 1983, Snow White 1983, Musette 1983, Equinox 1983, Byzantium 1984, Roses 1985, Last Look 1985, A Musical Offering 1986, Ab Ovo Usted Mala 1986, Syzygy 1987, Kith and Kin 1987, Minikin Fair 1989, Speaking in Tongues 1989, The Sorcerer's Sofa 1989, Of Bright and Blue Birds and The Gala Sun 1990, Company B 1991, Fact and Fancy (3 Epitaphs and All) 1991, Oz 1992, A Field of Grass 1993, Spindrift 1993, Moonbine 1994, Funny Papers 1994, Offenbach Overtures 1995, Eventide 1996, Prime Numbers 1996, Piazzolla Caldera 1997, The World 1998, Oh, You Kid! 1999, Cascade 1999, Arabesque 1999, Fiends Angelical 2000, Dandelion Wine 2000, Black Tuesday 2001, Antique Valentine 2001, Promethean Fire 2002, Dream Girls 2002, In the Beginning 2003. *Television:* eight different programmes on Dance in America (PBS). *Publication:* Private Domain (autobiog.) 1987. *Leisure interests:* gardening, snorkelling. *Address:* Paul Taylor Dance Co., 552 Broadway, New York, NY 10012, USA.

TAYLOR, Philip (Phil); British professional darts player; b. 13 Aug. 1960, Stoke-on-Trent; s. of Douglas and Elizabeth Taylor; m. to Yvonne Taylor; three d. one s.; ed Milfield Middle School, Stanfield Technical High School; fmr sheet metal worker; numerous tournament victories including: Embassy World Championship 1990, 1992, World Master 1990, European Cup Singles Championship 1992, PDC World Championship 1995, 1996, 1997, 1998, 1999, 2000, 2001, 2002, 2004, 2005, 2006, PDC World Matchplay 1995, 1997, 2000, 2001, 2002, News of the World Championship 1997, PDC World Grand Prix 1998, 1999, 2000, 2002, 2003, Quebec Open 2001, North American Cup 2001, 2002, 2003, JP Sports Pro Singles 2002, Montréal Open 2002, Las Vegas Desert Classic 2002, UK Open 2003, Bobby Bourn Memorial Trophy 2003, Stan James World Matchplay 2003; first unranked player to win a major tournament (Canadian Open 1990); unbeaten for nearly two years in televised matches 1999–2001; nine-dart finish at Stan James World Matchplay 2002 (1st since 1990 in televised match). *Publications:* (with Sid Waddell) The Power: My Autobiography 2003. *E-mail:* philtaylor@premiumtv.co.uk. *Website:* www.philthepower.com.

TAYLOR, Richard Edward, CC, PhD, FRS, FRSC; Canadian physicist and academic; *Professor Emeritus, Stanford Linear Accelerator Center;* b. 2 Nov. 1929, Medicine Hat, Alberta; s. of Clarence Richard Taylor and Delia Alena (née Brunsdale) Taylor; m. Rita Jean Bonneau 1951; one s.; ed Univ. of Alberta, Edmonton, Stanford Univ., Calif., USA; Boursier, Laboratoire de l'Accélérateur Linéaire, Orsay, France 1958–61; physicist, Lawrence Berkeley Lab., Berkeley, Calif. 1961–62; staff mem. Stanford Linear Accelerator Center, Calif. 1962–68, Assoc. Prof. 1968–70, Prof. 1970–2003, Prof. Emer. 2003–, Assoc. Dir Research Div. 1982–86, Lewis M. Terman Prof. 1993–99; mem. American Acad. of Arts and Sciences, Canadian Asscn of Physicists; Foreign Assoc. NAS; Fellow, American Physical Soc., AAAS; Hon. DSc (Alberta) 1991, (Lethbridge, Alberta) 1993, (Victoria, BC) 1994, (Liverpool) 1999, (Queen's, Ont.) 2000; Hon. LLD (Calgary, Alberta) 1993; Dr hc (Paris-Sud) 1980, (Blaise-Pascal) 1997, (Carleton Univ., Ont.) 1999; Guggenheim Fellow 1971–72, A. von Humboldt Sr Scientist Award 1982, W.K.H. Panofsky Prize (with H.W. Kendall and J.I. Friedman) 1989, Nobel Prize in Physics (with H. W. Kendall and J. I. Friedman) 1990, Canadian Science and Eng Hall of Fame. *Publications:* numerous scientific papers. *Address:* Stanford Linear Accelerator Center (SLAC), Mail Stop 43, 2575 Sand Hill Road, Menlo Park, CA 94025 (office); 757 Mayfield Avenue, Stanford, CA 94305, USA (home). *Telephone:* (650) 926-2417 (office); (650) 857-1345 (home). *Fax:* (650) 926-2923 (office). *E-mail:* retaylor@slac.stanford.edu (office). *Website:* www.slac.stanford.edu (office).

TAYLOR, Richard Lawrence, BA, PhD, FRS; British mathematician and academic; *Herchel Smith Professor of Mathematics, Harvard University;* b. 19 May 1962; s. of John C. Taylor (physicist); m. Christine Taylor; one s. one d.; ed Clare Coll., Cambridge, Princeton Univ., USA; fmr research student of Andrew Wiles, returned to Princeton Univ. to help Wiles complete proof of Fermat's last theorem 1995; Savilian Chair of Geometry, Univ. of Oxford and Fellow, New Coll. Oxford 1995–96; currently Herchel Smith Prof. of Math., Harvard Univ., USA; Whitehead Prize 1990, Fermat Prize 2001, Ostrowski Prize 2001, Cole Prize, American Math. Soc. 2002, Shaw Prize in Math. Sciences for his work on the Langlands program with Robert Langlands 2007, Clay Research Award, Clay Math. Inst. (co-recipient) 2007. *Publications:* numerous math. papers in professional journals. *Address:* Department of Mathematics, Faculty of Arts and Sciences, Harvard University, One Oxford Street, Cambridge, MA 02138, USA (office). *Telephone:* (617) 495-2171 (office). *Fax:* (617) 495-5132 (office). *E-mail:* rtaylor@math.harvard.edu (office). *Website:* www.math.harvard.edu (office).

TAYLOR, Stuart Ross, MA, PhD, DSc, FAA; New Zealand geochemist; *Visiting Fellow, Australian National University;* b. 26 Nov. 1925; s. of the late T. S. Taylor; m. Noel White 1958; three d.; ed Ashburton High School, NZ, Canterbury Univ. Coll., Univ. of NZ and Indiana Univ., USA; Lecturer in Mineralogy, Univ. of Oxford 1954–58; Sr Lecturer in Geochemistry, Univ. of Cape Town 1958–60; Professorial Fellow, Research School of Earth Science, Australian Nat. Univ. (ANU) 1961–90, Visiting Fellow, Research School of Physical Sciences 1991, 1993–99, and currently; mem. Council, ANU 1971–76; mem. Lunar Sample Preliminary Examination Team, Houston, Tex. 1969–70, Prin. Investigator, Lunar Sample Analysis Program 1970–90; Visiting Prof., Univ. of Vienna 1992, 1996; Foreign Assoc. NAS (USA); Fellow Geochemical Soc., American Geophysical Union; Hon. Fellow, UK and Indian Geological Socs, Royal Soc. of NZ; Hon. AC 2008; Goldschmidt Medal, Geochemical Soc. 1993, Gilbert Award, Geological Soc. of America 1994, Leonard Medal, Meteoritical Soc. 1998, Bucher Medal, American Geophysical Union 2002; Asteroid 5670 named Ross Taylor. *Publications include:* Spectrochemical Analysis (jtly) 1961, Moon Rocks and Minerals (jtly) 1971, Lunar Science: A Post-Apollo View 1975, Planetary Science: A Lunar Perspective 1982, The Continental Crust: Its Composition and Evolution (jtly) 1985, Solar System Evolution: A New Perspective 1992, Destiny or Chance: Our Solar System and Its Place in the Cosmos 1998, Planetary Crusts (with Scott McLennan) 2009; some 240 papers in scientific journals. *Leisure interests:* reading history, gardening, classical music. *Address:* 18 Sheehan Street, Pearce, ACT 2607, Australia.

TAYLOR, Wendy Ann, CBE, LDAD, FZS, FRBS, FRSA; British sculptor; b. 29 July 1945, Stamford, Lincs.; d. of Edward P. Taylor and Lilian M. Wright; m. Bruce Robertson 1982; one s.; ed St Martin's School of Art; mem. Fine Art Bd Council of Acad. Awards 1980–85, Specialist Adviser 1985–93; Specialist Adviser, Cttee for Art and Design 1988–93; mem. Cttee for Art and Design, Council of Nat. Acad. Awards; mem. Royal Fine Art Comm. 1981–99; mem. Council, Morley Coll. 1984–89; mem. Court RCA; design consultant, New Towns Comm. (Basildon) 1985–; design consultant, London Borough of Barking and Dagenham 1989–93, 1997–2003; Advisory Bd, London Docklands Devt Corpn 1989–98; mem. Advisory Group of the Polytechnics and Colls Funding Council 1989–90; mem. Council, Royal Soc. of British Sculptors 1999–2000; Fellow Queen Mary and Westfield Coll. (London Univ.); Trustee, Leicestershire's Appeal for Music and the Arts 1993–; mem. Design Panel, Thames Gateway Area 2005–; Walter Neurath Award 1964, Pratt Award 1965, Sainsbury Award 1966, Arts Council Award 1977, Duais Na Ríochta Gold Medal, Éire 1977. *Leisure interest:* gardening. *Address:* 73 Bow Road, London, E3 2AN, England. *Telephone:* (20) 8981-2037. *Fax:* (20) 8980-3153. *E-mail:* wendy-taylor@fsmail.net. *Website:* wendytaylorsculpture.co.uk (office).

TAYLOR, Sir William, Kt, CBE, BSc (Econ), PhD; British academic; *Visiting Professor, University of Southampton;* b. 31 May 1930, Crayford, Kent; s. of Herbert Taylor and Maud Taylor; m. Rita Hague 1954; one s. two d.; ed London School of Econs; fmr school teacher and deputy head teacher, Kent; later worked in two colls of educ. and Dept of Educ., Univ. of Oxford; Prof. of Educ., Univ. of Bristol 1966; Dir London Inst. of Educ. 1973–83; Prin. Univ. of London 1983–85, Chair. of Convocation 1994–97; Vice-Chancellor Univ. of Hull 1985–91; Vice-Chancellor Univ. of Huddersfield 1994–95, Thames Valley Univ. 1998–99; Visiting Prof., Univ. of Oxford 1991–97, Univ. of Southampton 1998–; Gov. Univ. of Glamorgan 1992–2002, Christ Church, Univ. Coll., Canterbury 1996–2004; Interim Head, Winchester School of Art, Univ. of Southampton 2004; Chair. Council for Accreditation of Teacher Educ. 1984–93; Chair. Bd NFER/Nelson publishing co. 1988–99; Pres. Soc. for Research in Higher Educ. 1996–2001; Specialist Adviser, House of Commons Educ. and Skills Cttee 2000–; Chair. NI Cttee for Teacher Educ. 1994–2003; mem. Council, Hong Kong Inst. of Educ. 1998–2003; Charter Fellow, Coll. of Preceptors; Hon. Fellow, Westminster Coll. Oxford, Thames Polytechnic, Commonwealth Council for Educ. Admin., Inst. of Educ.; Dr hc (Aston, Bristol, Leeds, London, Kent, Loughborough, Open Univ., Huddersfield, Hull, Kingston, Plymouth, Oxford Brookes, Univ. of West of England, Ulster, Queen's Univ. Belfast, Southampton, Leicester, Glamorgan, Essex, Hong Kong Inst. of Educ.). *Publications include:* The Secondary Modern School, Society and the Education of Teachers, Planning and Policy in Post-secondary Education, Heading for Change, Research and Reform in Teacher Education, The Metaphors of Education, Universities under Scrutiny. *Leisure interest:* books and music. *E-mail:* wt@soton.ac.uk (office).

TAYLOR-WOOD, Sam; British artist, photographer and filmmaker; b. 1967; m. Jay Jopling; one d.; ed Hastings Coll. of Art and Tech., Goldsmiths Coll., London; uses highly choreographed photographic sequences; first solo exhbn, London 1994. *Solo exhibitions include:* White Cube^2, London 1995–96, Fundació 'la Caixa', Barcelona 1997, Hirshhorn Museum and Sculture Garden, Washington, DC 1999, Musée d'art contemporain, Montreal, Matthew Marks Gallery, New York, The State Russian Museum, St Petersburg, Kunsthalle, Zurich, Louisiana Museum of Modern Art in Denmark, White Cube^2, London 2001, Stedelijk Museum, Amsterdam 2001, Hayward Gallery, London (retrospective) 2001, White Cube, London 2004. *Works include:* Fuck, Suck, Spank, Wank 1993, Slut 1993, Killing Time (film) 1994, Method in Madness (film) 1994, Five Revolutionary Seconds XI 1997, Atlantic 1997, Five Revolutionary Seconds XIII 1998, Soliloquy I 1998, Soliloquy V 1998, Self Portrait in a Single Breasted Suit with Hare 2001, Hummmm 2001, Mute (film) 2001, Breach (film) 2001, Still Life (film) 2001, Self Portrait as a Tree, Strings (film) 2003, Ascension (film) 2003, David (video portrait) 2004, Crying Men 2004, Self Portrait Suspended 2004. *Publications include:* Contact 2001, Crying Men 2004. *Address:* c/o Regen Projects, 633 North Almont Drive, Los Angeles, CA 90069, USA (office). *Telephone:* (310) 276-5424. *Fax:* (310) 276-7430.

TAZAKI, Masamoto; Japanese manufacturing executive; *President and CEO, Kawasaki Heavy Industries Ltd ;* began career with Kawasaki Heavy

Industries Ltd, various exec. and man. positions including Exec. Man.-Dir and Sr Gen.-Man. Consumer Products and Machinery Group, Pres., currently Pres. and CEO; Chair. Japan Robot Asscn. *Address:* Kawasaki Heavy Industries Ltd, Kobe Crystal Tower, 1-3 Higashikawasaki-cho 1-chome, Chuo-ku, Kobe 650-8680, Japan (office). *Telephone:* (7) 8371-9530 (office). *Fax:* (7) 8371-9568 (office). *Website:* www.khi.co.jp (office).

TAZHIN, Marat Muhanbetkaziyevich, PhD; Kazakhstani politician; *Minister of Foreign Affairs;* b. 8 April 1960, Aktubinsk; ed Almaty Inst. of Nat. Economy, Kazakh State Univ.; began career as scientific researcher –1992; First Deputy Head, then Head of Internal Policy Dept, Deputy Chief of Presidential Apparatus, Head of Information and Analysis Center, Office of the Pres. 1992–94; State Adviser to Pres. 1994–95; Deputy Head, Admin of Pres. and Head, Analysis and Strategic Research Center 1995–99; Nat. Security Asst to Pres. 1999–2001, 2002, 2006–07; Sec. Security Council 1999–2001, Dec. 2001–Aug. 2002, April 2006–Jan. 2007, Chair. Nat. Security Cttee May–Dec. 2001; First Deputy Chief, Admin of Pres. 2002–06; Minister of Foreign Affairs 2007–; Order of Kurmet, Order of Barys. *Address:* Ministry of Foreign Affairs, 010000 Astana, Tauelsizdik 31, Kazakhstan (office). *Telephone:* (3172) 72-05-18 (office). *Fax:* (3172) 72-05-16 (office). *E-mail:* midrk@mid.kz (office). *Website:* www.mfa.kz (office).

TCHAIKOVSKY, Aleksandr Vladimirovich; Russian composer and pianist; b. 19 Feb. 1946, Moscow; m. 1st; one s. one d.; m. 3rd; one d.; ed Moscow State Conservatory; performs as pianist and chamber musician 1967–; teacher Moscow State Conservatory 1976, Prof. 1994–; Artistic Consultant, Mariinski Theatre, St Petersburg 1996–; Artistic Dir Moscow State Philharmonia 2003–; mem. Bd of Dirs Pervyi Kanal; winner Hollybush Festival Prize (USA) 1987; People's Artist of Russia 1998. *Compositions include:* operas Grandfather Is Laughing 1976, Three Sisters (after A. Chekhov) 1994, ballets Inspector 1960, Battleship Potemkin 1988, symphonies 1985, 1991 (Aquarius), two piano concertos, two viola concertos, Distant Dreams of Childhood for violin and viola 1990, Concerto-Buff for violin and marimba 1990, Triple Concerto for piano, violin and cello 1994, folk operas Tsar Nikita and Motya and Savely for two soloists and folk instruments, Quartet (after A. Pushkin) 1997–99, chamber music, incidental music to theatre and film productions. *Leisure interests:* collecting models of cars, table hockey. *Address:* Leningradsky prosp. 14, Apt. 4, 125040 Moscow, Russia (home). *Telephone:* (495) 151-54-18 (home).

TCHONGÓ DOMINGOS, Salvador; Guinea-Bissau politician; m.; two c.; ed Instituto Superior de Economia, Lisbon, Portugal and Universidade Católica, Lisbon; teacher of secondary education, Portugal 1981–92; founding mem., Resistência da Guiné-Bissau—Movimento Bah-Fatah, Sec.-Gen. 1987–92, 1993–95, Vice-Pres. 1992–93, 1995–2002, interim Pres. 2002, elected Pres. 2002; Vice-Pres. Assembléia Nacional Popular 1994–99; presidential candidate 1999; Sec.-Gen. Presidência da República da Guiné-Bissau 2000–05. *Address:* c/o Assembléia Nacional Popular, Bissau, Guinea-Bissau.

TCHUKHONTSEV, Oleg Grigoryevich; Russian poet; b. 8 March 1938, Pavlov Posad, Moscow Region; m. Irina Igorevna Povolotskaya; ed Moscow Pedagogical Inst.; poetry section, mem. Editorial Bd Novy Mir; published in Druzhba Narodov, Yunost, Molodaya Gvardiya, Novy Mir; State Prize of Russia 1993. *Publications:* From Three Notebooks (cycles Posad, Name, Sparrow's Night) 1976, The Dormer Window 1983, Poetry 1989, By Wind and Heat 1989, Passing Landscape 1997 and other books of poetry; translations of Goethe, Warren, Frost, Kits and numerous other poets. *Address:* Bolshoi Tishinsky per. 12, Apt. 10, 123557 Moscow, Russia (home). *Telephone:* (495) 253-51-95 (home).

TCHURUK, Serge; French engineer and business executive; b. 13 Nov. 1937, Marseille; s. of Georges Tchurukdichian and Mathilde Dondikian; m. Hélèna Kalfus 1960; one d.; ed Lycée Thiers à Marseille, Ecole nationale supérieure de l'armement, Ecole Polytechnique, Paris; various refining and research positions Mobil/Oil BV Rotterdam 1964–68, Dir French research centre 1968–70, Dir of Information, France 1971–73, attaché int. planning, New York and dir plans and programmes France 1973–77, Dir social and external relations 1977–79, Pres. and Dir-Gen. 1979–80; Dir-Gen. fertilizer div. Rhône-Poulenc Inc. 1981, Asst Dir-Gen. Rhône-Poulenc Group 1982, Dir-Gen. special chemicals 1983, Dir-Gen. Rhône-Poulenc Group 1983; Pres. Bd Dirs CdF Chimie 1986, Pres. Dir-Gen. 1987–90 (became Orkem 1988); mem. Bd Dirs Total 1989, 1995–, Pres. 1990–95; Chair. and CEO Alcatel Alsthom (later Alcatel) 1995–2006, Chair. Alcatel-Lucent (after Alcatel acquisition of Lucent) 2006–08; mem. Bd of Dirs Inst. Pasteur 2001–, Total, Thales; Officier, Légion d'honneur, Officier, Ordre nat. du Mérite; Manager of the Year Award, Le Nouvel Economiste 2000. *Leisure interests:* music, skiing, tennis. *Address:* c/o Alcatel-Lucent, 54 rue de la Boétie, 75008 Paris, France. *Telephone:* 1-40-76-10-10. *E-mail:* execoffice@alcatel-lucent.com.

TE KANAWA, Dame Kiri Jeanette Claire, ONZ, DBE, AC; New Zealand singer (soprano); b. 6 March 1944, Gisborne; m. Desmond Park 1967 (divorced 1997); one s. one d.; ed St Mary's Coll., Auckland, London Opera Centre; first appearance at Royal Opera, Covent Garden, London 1970, Santa Fe Opera, USA 1971, Lyons Opera, France 1972, Metropolitan Opera, New York, USA 1974; appeared at Australian Opera, Royal Opera House Covent Garden, Paris Opera during 1976–77 season; appeared at Houston Opera, USA and Munich Opera 1977; debut La Scala, Milan 1978; Salzburg Festival 1979; San Francisco Opera Co. 1980; Edinburgh Festival, Helsinki Festival 1980; sang at wedding of HRH the Prince of Wales 1981; sang the premiere of Paul McCartney's Liverpool Oratorio, written by Carl Davis, at Liverpool Cathedral and in London 1991; appeared in 2000 Today on 1 January 2000; Founding Trustee and Chair. Kiri Te Kanawa Foundation 2004–; Hans Christian Andersen Amb. 2005–; Hon. Fellow Somerville Coll. Oxford 1983, Wolfson Coll. Cambridge 1997; Hon. Mem. RAM; Hon. LLD (Dundee) 1982; Hon. DMus (Durham) 1982, (Oxford) 1983, (Nottingham) 1992, (Waikato) 1995, (Cambridge) 1997; Hon. DLitt (Warwick) 1989, (Sunderland) 2003, (Auckland), (Chicago). *Operas:* Boris Godunov 1970–71, Parsifal 1971, The Marriage of Figaro (Countess) 1971, 1972, 1973, 1976, 1979, 1986, 1991, 1997, Otello 1972, 1973, 1974, 1987, 1988, 1991, 1992, Simon Boccanegra 1973, 1974, 1975, 1976, 1977, 1979, 1980, 1986, 1988, 1991, 1995, 1997, Carmen 1973, Don Giovanni 1974, 1975, 1976, (film) 1979, 1981, 1983, 1988, 1996, Faust 1974, The Magic Flute 1975, 1980, La Bohème 1975, 1976, 1977, 1979, 1980, 1989, 1991, Eugene Onegin 1975, 1976, Così fan tutte 1976, 1981, 1986, 1987, 1988, Arabella 1977, 1980, 1981, 1983, 1984, 1990, 1993, 1994, 1995, Die Fledermaus 1978, 1984, 1986, 1987, La Traviata 1978, 1980, 1983, 1984, Der Rosenkavalier 1981, 1984, 1985, Manon Lescaut 1983, Samson 1986, Don Carlos 1984, Capriccio 1990, 1991, 1993, 1998, Vanessa 2001, 2002, 2004. *Recordings include:* Don Giovanni (as Elvira), Così fan tutti (as Fiordiligi), Carmen (as Michela), Mozart Vespers, Mozart C Minor Mass, The Magic Flute (Pamina), Siegfried (Woodbird), The Marriage of Figaro, Hansel and Gretel, La Bohème, Capriccio, Otello, Die Fledermaus, French and German arias and songs, Maori songs 1999, Strauss songs with orchestra, Songs of the Auvergne, West Side Story, The Very Best of .. 2003, Kiri Sings Karl 2006. *Publications:* Land of the Long White Cloud (children's book) 1989, Opera for Lovers (with Conrad Wilson) 1997. *Leisure interests:* golf, swimming, cooking. *Address:* c/o Kiri Te Kanawa Foundation, PO Box 38387, Howick 2014, Auckland 2014, New Zealand (office). *Telephone:* (20) 8332-9829 (office). *Fax:* (20) 8332-7049 (office). *Website:* www.kiritekanawa.org (office).

TEA BANH, Lt-Gen.; Cambodian politician; *Deputy Prime Minister and Minister of Defence;* b. 5 Nov. 1945, Koh Kong Prov.; s. of the late Tea Toek and Nou Pheng Chenda; m. Tao Toeun 1955; three c.; platoon Commdr Koh Kong Prov. 1962–69, Co. Commdr 1969–70, Mil. Commdr and Dir Training 1973–79; Deputy Chief of Staff in charge of Telecommunications and Air Force 1979–80, Deputy Minister of Nat. Defence in charge of Telecommunications and Air Force 1980–82; Minister of Communications Transport and Posts 1982–87; Vice-Chair. Council of Ministers 1984–88; mem. Parl. for Siem Reap Prov. 1988–; Minister of Nat. Defence 1987–88, 1993–94, 2006–, Deputy Minister 1988–93, Co-Minister 1994–2006; Deputy Prime Minister 2006–; Co-Deputy C-in-C Nat. Armed Forces 1994–95. *Leisure interest:* golf. *Address:* blvd Confederation de la Russie, cnr rue 175, Phnom-Penh, Cambodia (office). *Telephone:* (23) 883184 (office). *Fax:* (23) 366169 (office). *E-mail:* info@mond.gov.kh (office). *Website:* www.mond.gov.kh (office).

TEANNAKI, Teatao; I-Kiribati politician; *Leader, National Progressive Party;* mem. Parl. for Abiang; fmr Vice-Pres. of Kiribati; Pres. of Kiribati 1991–94; currently Leader Nat. Progressive Party. *Address:* National Progressive Party, Tarawa, Kiribati.

TEAR, Robert, CBE, MA, FRSA, RCM, RAM; British singer (tenor); b. 8 March 1939, Barry, Wales; s. of Thomas Arthur Tear and Edith Tear; m. Hilary Thomas 1961; two d.; ed Barry Grammar School, King's Coll., Cambridge; embarked on solo career as tenor after singing as mem. of King's Coll. Choir 1957–60 and St Paul's Cathedral Choir; joined English Opera Group 1964; worked with leading conductors (including Karajan, Giulini, Bernstein, Solti) and appeared in numerous operas by Benjamin Britten 1964–68; has appeared at Royal Opera House, Covent Garden on regular basis since his debut in The Knot Garden 1970; US conducting debut in Minneapolis 1985; debut with ENO in The Turn of the Screw 1988–89; debut as Aschenbach in Death in Venice with Glyndeboume Touring Co. 1989–90, later filmed by BBC TV; subsequently worked with BBC Nat. Orchestra of Wales, London Mozart Players, Northern Sinfonia, English Chamber Orchestra, Philharmonia Orchestra, Royal Liverpool Philharmonic, Royal Scottish National Orchestra, Toulouse Chamber Orchestra, Tapiola Sinfonietta and Scottish Chamber Orchestra; opera performances have included Opera Nat. de Paris Bastille (Marriage of Figaro), Los Angeles Opera (Tales of Hoffmann), Royal Opera House (Falstaff), WNO (Eugene Onegin) and Bayerische Staatsoper (Saul); appearances in all major festivals; close asscn with Sir Michael Tippett 1970–97; first Prof. of Int. Singing, Royal Acad. of Music, London 1985–; Hon. Fellow, King's Coll. Cambridge 1989, Welsh Coll. of Music and Drama 1994; Hon. DMus (Royal Scottish Acad. of Music and Drama). *Recordings:* more than 250 records, including premiere recording of Tippett's opera King Priam 1981. *Publications:* Victorian Songs and Duets, Tear Hear (autobiog.) 1990, Singer Beware 1995, 10 Christmas Carols. *Leisure interests:* sport, 18th- and 19th-century English watercolours. *Address:* Askonas Holt Ltd, Lincoln House, 300 High Holborn, London, WC1V 7JH, England (office). *Telephone:* (20) 7400-1751 (office). *Fax:* (20) 7400-1799 (office). *E-mail:* melanie.moult@askonasholt.co.uk (office). *Website:* www.askonasholt.co.uk (office).

TEARE, Andrew, BA; British business executive; b. 8 Sept. 1942; s. of Arthur Hubert Teare and Rosalind Margaret Baker; m. Janet Skidmore; three s.; with Turner and Newall 1964–72, CRH 1972–83, Rugby Group 1983–90; Group Chief Exec. English China Clays 1990–96; Chief Exec. Rank Group. 1996–98; Dir (non-exec.) Heiton Holdings PLC 1984–90, Prudential Insurance Co. 1992–98, Nat. Freight Corpn 1989–96. *Leisure interests:* skiing, opera. *Address:* Flat 2, 34 Craven Street, London, WC2N 5PB, England.

TEBBIT, Baron (Life Peer), cr 1992, of Chingford in the London Borough of Waltham Forest; **Norman Beresford Tebbit,** PC, CH; British politician; b. 29 March 1931, Enfield; s. of Leonard Tebbit and Edith Tebbit; m. Margaret Elizabeth Daines 1956; two s. one d.; ed Edmonton Co. Grammar School; RAF Officer 1949–51; commercial pilot and holder of various posts, British Air Line Pilots' Asscn 1953–70; MP for Epping 1970–74, for Chingford 1974–92; Parl. Pvt. Sec. Dept of Employment 1972–73; Under-Sec. of State, Dept of Trade 1979–81; Minister of State, Dept of Industry Jan.–Sept. 1981; Sec. of State for Employment 1981–83, for Trade and Industry 1983–85; Chancellor of the

Duchy of Lancaster 1985–87; Chair., Conservative Party 1985–87; Life Peer, House of Lords 1992–; Dir, BET PLC 1987–96, British Telecom PLC 1987–96, Sears PLC 1987–99, Spectator Ltd; Co-Presenter, Target, Sky TV 1989–97; columnist, The Sun 1995–97, Mail on Sunday 1997–2001. *Publications:* Upwardly Mobile 1988, Unfinished Business 1991. *Leisure interests:* peace and quiet, shooting, gardening. *Address:* House of Lords, Westminster, London, SW1A 0PW, England (office). *Telephone:* (20) 7219-1635 (office). *Fax:* (20) 7219-3144 (office); (1403) 270727 (home).

TÉCHINÉ, André Jean François; French author and film-maker; b. 13 March 1943, Valence, Tarn-et-Garonne. *Films:* Paulina s'en va 1969, Souvenirs d'en France 1975, Barocco 1976, Les Sœurs Bronté 1979, Hôtel des Amériques 1981, Rendez-vous 1985 (Prize for Best Director, Cannes Int. Film Festival 1985), Le Lieu du crime 1986, Les Innocents 1987, J'embrasse pas 1991, Ma Saison préférée 1993, Les Roseaux sauvages 1994 (Prix Louis-Delluc 1994, César for Best French Film, Best Dir and Best Original Screenplay or Adaptation 1995), Les Voleurs 1996, Alice et Martin 1998, Loin 2001, Les Égarés (Strayed) 2003, Les Temps qui changent 2004, Les Témoins 2007. *Television:* La Matiouette.

TEER, Kees, DSc, FIEEE; Dutch scientist; b. 6 June 1925, Haarlem; m. Jozina A. Kas 1951; three c.; ed Tech. Univ. Delft; joined Philips Research Labs, Eindhoven 1950, Sr Researcher, Deputy Head of Acoustics, 1958, Deputy Dir 1966, Man. Dir 1968, Chair. Man. Cttee 1982–85; Prof. Tech. Univ. Delft 1987–91; mem. Netherlands Scientific Council for Govt 1985–88; mem. Bd of Dirs Royal Dutch PTT 1988–97, Nedap Industries 1985–97; mem. Royal Netherlands Acad. of Sciences 1977; Officer Order of Orange Nassau 1984; C. T. de Groot plaquette 1992. *Publications:* several publs on electro-acoustics, TV systems, electronic principles, information tech. and society, R&D man. etc. *Leisure interests:* philosophy, writing, society versus technology. *Address:* Hoge Duinlaan 3, 5582 KD Waalre, Netherlands. *Telephone:* (40) 2216861. *Fax:* (40) 2219222. *E-mail:* k.teer@wxs.nl.

TEEWE, Natan; I-Kiribati lawyer and politician; *Minister of Finance and Economic Development;* Minister for Communications, Transport and Tourism Devt –2007, of Finance and Econ. Devt 2007–; mem. Boutokaan Te Koaua Party. *Address:* Ministry of Finance and Economic Development, POB 67, Bairiki, Tarawa, Kiribati (office). *Telephone:* 21802. *Fax:* 21307.

TEH, Tan Sri Dato' Hong Piow, PhD; Malaysian banker; *Chairman, Public Bank Berhad;* b. 14 March 1930, Singapore; m. Puan Sri Tay Sock Noy 1956; four c.; ed Anglo-Chinese School, Singapore, Pacific Western Univ., Clayton Univ., Univ. of Malaya; began career as bank clerk in Overseas-Chinese Banking Corpn Ltd 1950, promoted to bank officer 1955–60; Man. Malayan Banking Berhad 1960–64, Gen. Man. 1964–66; est. Public Bank 1966, currently Chair. Public Bank Berhad. *Address:* Public Bank Berhad, Menara Public Bank 146, Jalan Ampang, 50450 Kuala Lumpur, Malaysia (office). *Telephone:* (3) 2176-6000 (office). *Fax:* (3) 2161-9307 (office). *E-mail:* info@publicbank.com.my (office). *Website:* www.pbebank.com (office); www.publicbank.com.my (office).

TEICH, Malvin Carl, PhD; American academic; *Professor of Electrical and Computer Engineering, Biomedical Engineering and Physics, Boston University;* b. 4 May 1939, New York; s. of Sidney R. Teich and Loretta K. Teich; ed Mass. Inst. of Tech. and Stanford and Cornell Univs; Research Scientist, MIT Lincoln Lab., Lexington, Mass. 1966–67; Prof. of Eng Science and Applied Physics, Columbia Univ. 1967–96, Prof. Emer. 1996–, Chair. Dept of Electrical Eng 1978–80, mem. Columbia Radiation Lab.; Prof. of Electrical and Computer Eng, Prof. of Biomedical Eng, Prof. of Physics, Boston Univ. 1995–, mem. Photonics Center, Hearing Research Center, Center for Adaptive Systems; Deputy Ed. Journal of European Optical Soc. B: Quantum Optics 1988–92; mem. Bd of Editors Optics Letters 1977–79, Journal of Visual Communication and Image Representation 1989–92, Jemná Mechanika a Optika 1994–; mem. Scientific Bd Czech Acad. of Sciences Inst. of Physics; Fellow, IEEE, AAAS, American Physical Soc., Optical Soc. of America, Acoustical Soc. of America; IEEE Browder Thompson Memorial Prize 1969, John Simon Guggenheim Memorial Foundation Fellow 1973, Citation Classic Award, Inst. for Scientific Information 1981, Memorial Gold Medal, Palacký Univ. 1992, IEEE Morris E. Leeds Award 1997. *Publications:* Fundamentals of Photonics (with B. E. A. Saleh) 1991, 2007, Fractal-Based Point Processes (with S. B. lowen) 2005; 350 articles in tech. journals; six US patents. *Address:* Department of Electrical and Computer Engineering, Boston University, 8 Saint Mary's Street, Boston, MA 02215, USA (office). *Telephone:* (617) 353-1236 (office). *Fax:* (617) 353-6440 (office). *Website:* www.people.bu.edu/teich (office); www.bu.edu/dbin/bme/people/joint/teich.php (office).

TEISSIER, Guy; French politician; b. 4 April 1945, Marseilles; ed Ecole de Notariat de Marseilles; mem. Parti Républicain (Union pour un Mouvement Populaire from 2002); Conseiller Général for Bouches de Rhône 1982–2004; Mayor 9th and 10th arrondissements, Marseilles 1983–; mem. Conseil Municipal de Marseilles 1983–; elected Deputy to Nat. Ass. for Bouches-du-Rhône 1988 (invalidated by Conseil Constitutionel) re-elected 1993–; Sec. Nat. Ass. 1997–99, 2002), mem. Comm. of Cultural, Family and Social Affairs 1988; mem. Comm. of Nat. Defence 1993–2002, Sec. 1994–95, Pres. 2002–07. *Address:* Mairie des 9e et 10e arrondissements, 150 boulevard Paul-Claudel, 13009 Marseille (office); Assemblée Nationale, 33, rue Saint-Dominique, 75 007 Paris (office); Nouveau Parc Sevigne, 15 place Mignard, 13009 Marseilles, France (home). *Telephone:* 4-91-14-63-50 (office); 1-40-63-73-83 (office); 4-91-23-39-28 (home). *Fax:* 4-91-14-63-44 (office); 1-40-63-79-63 (office); 4-91-23-36-14 (office). *E-mail:* gteissier@assemblee-nat.fr (office). *Website:* www.guyteissier.com (office).

TEITELBAUM, Philip, PhD; American psychologist and academic; *Graduate Research Professor in Psychology, University of Florida;* b. 9 Oct. 1928,

Brooklyn, New York; s. of Bernard Teitelbaum and Betty Schechter; m. 1st Anita Stawski 1955; m. 2nd Evelyn Satinoff 1963; m. 3rd Osnat Boné 1985; five s.; ed Johns Hopkins Univ.; Instructor and Asst Prof. in Psychology, Harvard Univ. 1954–59; Assoc., Full Prof., Univ. of Pa 1959–73; Prof., Univ. of Ill. 1973–85, Emer. Prof. 1985–; Fellow Center for Advanced Studies, Univ. of Ill. 1979–85; Grad. Research Prof. in Psychology, Univ. of Fla 1984–; mem. NAS, AAAS; Guggenheim Fellow; Fulbright Fellow; American Psychology Asscn Scientific Contrib. Award. *Publications:* Fundamental Principles of Physiological Psychology 1967, Vol. on Motivation, Handbook of Behavioral Neurobiology (with Evelyn Satinoff) 1983. *Address:* 2239 NW 17th Avenue, Gainesville, FL 32605 (home); Psychology Department, 337 PSY, University of Florida, Gainesville, FL 32611, USA. *Telephone:* (352) 392-0615 (office); (352) 372-5714 (home). *Fax:* (352) 392-7985 (office). *E-mail:* teitelb@ufl.edu (office); teitelb@hotmail.com (home). *Website:* www.psych.ufl.edu/~teitelb (office).

TEIXEIRA, Jose; Timor-Leste politician; *Minister for Natural Resources, Minerals and Energy Policy;* left East Timor aged 11; worked as lawyer in Brisbane, Australia; returned to East Timor 2002; fmr Sec. of State for Tourism, Environment and Investment; Minister for Natural Resources, Minerals and Energy Policy 2006–. *Address:* Direcção Nacional de Petróleo e Gas, 1st Floor Fomento Building, Mandarin Dili, Dili (office); POB 171, Dili Post Office, Dili, Timor-Leste. *Website:* www.timor-leste.gov.tl (office).

TEIXEIRA DOS SANTOS, Fernando, PhD; Portuguese economist and government official; *Minister of State and Finance;* b. 13 Sept. 1951; m. Maria Clementina Pereira Nunes; ed Univ. of Porto, Univ. of SC, USA; Chair. Exec. Cttee, Int. Org. of Securities Comms 2000–04, Chair. European Regional Cttee 2004–05; Chair. Instituto Iberoamericano de Mercado de Valores, Cttee of European Securities Regulators Expert Group, Portuguese Securities Exchange Comm.; Prof. of Economics, Univ. of Porto 1986–95; Sec. of State for the Treasury and Finance 1995–99; Pres. Comissão do Mercado de Valores Mobiliários 2000–05; Minister of State and Finance 2005–; Gov. for Portugal, EIB; Grand Official of the Order Infante D. Henrique 2005. *Address:* Ministry of Finance and Public Administration, Av. Infante D. Henrique 1, 1149-009 Lisbon, Portugal (office). *Telephone:* (21) 8816800 (office). *Fax:* (21) 816862 (office). *E-mail:* gab.mf@mf.gov.pt (office). *Website:* www.min-financas.pt (office).

TEIXEIRA PINTO, Elsa; São Tomé and Príncipe politician; *Minister of Defence and Internal Order;* Sec. of State for State Reforms and Public Admin 2002–04; fmr Minister for Justice, State Reforms and Public Admin; Minister of Defence and Internal Order 2008–; mem. Movimento de Libertação de São Tomé e Príncipe—Partido Social Democrata. *Address:* Ministry of Defence and Internal Order, Av. 12 de Julho, CP 427, São Tomé, São Tomé and Príncipe (office). *Telephone:* 222041 (office). *E-mail:* midefesa@cstome.net (office). *Website:* www.mindefordInterna.gov.st (office).

TEIXEIRA PINTO, Paulo Jorge; Portuguese banker; *Chairman, Banco Comercial Português SA;* b. 10 Oct. 1960, Angola; m. Paula da Cruz; two c.; ed Univ. of Lisbon, Univ. of Madrid, INSEAD, Fontainebleau; Lecturer in Law, Univ. of Lisbon and Free Univ. 1983–88; Undersec. of State of the Presidency of the Council of Ministers 1991–92, Sec. of State of the Presidency 1992–95; Head of Legal Dept, Banco Comercial Português SA 1995–2000, Gen. Man. 2000–05, Co. Sec. 2000–05, Chair. 2005–; Gen. Sec. Millennium bcp Foundation 2004–05, Chair. 2005–; Vice-Chair. Portuguese Banking Asscn; mem. Opus Dei 1986–; mem. Supervisory Bd Energias de Portugal. *Address:* Banco Comercial Português SA, Praça D. João I, 28, Praça D. João I, 28, 4000-295 Porto, Portugal (office). *Telephone:* (707) 502424 (office). *Fax:* (210) 066858 (office). *Website:* www.millenniumbcp.pt (office).

TEJPAL, Tarun J.; Indian newspaper editor and writer; *CEO and Editor-in-Chief, Tehelka;* over 20 years' experience, including reporter for The Indian Express and The Telegraph, ed. with India Today and India Express Group; has written for numerous int. publications, including The Paris Review, The Guardian, Financial Times and Prospect; co-f. India Ink publishing house; fmr Managing Ed. Outlook news magazine –2000; f., CEO and Ed.-in-Chief Tehelka newspaper 2000–, initially web-only news site, relaunched as nat. weekly newspaper 2004–. *Publication:* The Alchemy of Desire (novel) (Prix Millepages) 2005, The Story of My Assassins 2009. *Address:* Tehelka, M-76, Second Floor, M-Block Market, Greater Kailash Part 2, New Delhi 110048, India (office). *E-mail:* editor@tehelka.com (office). *Website:* www.tehelka.com (office); www.taruntejpal.com.

TEKLE, Afewerk, OM; Ethiopian painter, sculptor and architect; b. 22 Oct. 1932, Ankober, Shoa Prov.; s. of Weizero Feleketch Yematawork and Ato Tekle Mamo; ed Cen. School of Arts and Crafts, London, Slade School of Art, Univ. of London, UK, and Accad. di Michelangelo, Italy; sent to England to become a mining engineer 1947; artistic studies 1947–54; solo exhbns worldwide; has also produced drawings and designs for stamps, playing cards, posters, flags and nat. ceremonial dress; designed his own house, studio and gallery 'Villa Alpha'; exhibited and lectured in fmr USSR, USA, Senegal, Turkey, Zaïre, UAE, Bulgaria, Munich, Germany (XX Olympiad), Kenya and Algeria; mem. French Int. Acad. of Arts 1997, Russian Acad. of Fine Arts 1999; Hon. Citizen of USSR 1989; Grand Order of Cyril and Methodius (Bulgaria)1968, Order of Merit (Senegal), Kt Commdr, Order of St Sylvester (Holy See); Haile Selassie I Prize for Fine Arts 1964, Int. Gold Mercury Award, Italy 1982, American Golden Acad. Award 1992, Cambridge Order of Excellence, UK 1992, Council of the ABI World Laureate, 27th Int. Millennium Congress on the Arts and Communication, Washington, DC 2000, Grand Ambassador of the Fine Arts and Int. Peace Award, Int. World Forum 2008; numerous other awards, medals and decorations by heads of state. *Works include:* King Solomon meets the Queen of Sheba, St George's Cathedral,

Addis Ababa, Equestrian Statue of Ras Makonnen, Harar, The Struggles and Aspirations of the African People (stained glass), Africa Hall, UN Building 1960, Meskel Flower (considered to be his masterpiece) 1961, Mural of St Paul's Hosp. 1972, Last Judgment, Adigrat Cathedral, Tigrai, northern Ethiopia, Unity Triptych: (a) The Disunity of Man, (b) Towards the Unity of Man, (c) Symbol of Human Unity (Gold Medal, Algiers Int. Festival 1977), Self Portrait (first African painting to be included in perm. collection of Uffizi Gallery, Florence, Italy) 1981, The Victory of Ethiopia over Evil Forces 1992, The Chalice and the Cross in the Life of the African People (First Prize, Biennale of Aquitaine 1997) 1997, The Sun of Senegal 1997, Mother Ethiopia, The Simien Mountains. *Leisure interests:* reading, fencing, walking, mountaineering. *Address:* Villa Alpha 22, Yetebeb Godanna, P.O.BOX 5651, Addis Ababa, Ethiopia (office). *Telephone:* 71-59-41 (office). *Fax:* 71-59-41 (office). *E-mail:* hmal.afewerk.tekle@telecom.net.et (office). *Website:* www .afewerktekle.org (office).

TELEFONI RETZLAFF, Misa, LLB, CPA; Samoan politician and lawyer; *Deputy Prime Minister and Minister of Commerce, Industry and Labour;* b. 21 May 1952; ed King's Coll., Auckland and Auckland Univ., NZ; with Jackson Russell Tunks and West, Auckland, NZ 1974–76; admitted to Bar as Barrister and Solicitor of the Supreme Court, NZ 1975, Western Samoa 1976; pvt. legal practice as H. T. Retzlaff, Apia, Western Samoa 1976–92 (closed office on appointment as Minister of State); apptd Attorney-Gen. 1986–88, resgnd on running as MP; elected MP for Falelatai and Samatau Dist 1988–, served as Opposition MP 1988–91; Minister of State with portfolios of Agric., Forests, Fisheries and Meteorology and Minister of Shipping 1992–96, of Health 1996–2001; Deputy Prime Minister and Minister of Finance 2001–06; Deputy Prime Minister and Minister of Commerce, Industry and Labour 2006–; Vice-Pres. WHO 1999; Chair. FAO Asia/Pacific Regional Conf. and Inaugural Meeting, FAO Ministers 1995; admitted as CPA Samoa 1977, apptd Pres. of Samoa Chamber of Commerce 1977–79; Dir Retzlaff Group of Cos 1975–86, also of eight cos in Western Samoa, one in NZ and Suva, Fiji (resgnd from all 1992); Pro-Chancellor Nat. Univ. of Samoa 1986–98; elected to Komiti Tumau (Standing Cttee) of Methodist Church of Samoa 1996–; mem. Inaugural Council of Piula Theological Coll. 1998–; Signatory Latimer House Rules on Good Governance, The Commonwealth; spoke at numerous univs and int. confs including ESCAP 1994, Commonwealth Law Conf., Kuala Lumpur 1999; Order of Merit, Chile 1994; Kelliher Econs Scholarship, NZ 1969, Sr Prize in Law, Auckland Univ., World Food Day Medal 2005. *Publications:* Love and Money 2005. *Address:* Department of Trade, Industry and Commerce, POB 862, Apia, Samoa. *Telephone:* (685) 20471 (office); (685) 24363 (home). *Fax:* (685) 21646 (office); (685) 21721 (home). *E-mail:* tipu@tci.gov.ws (office). *Website:* www.tradeinvestsamoa.ws.

TELIČKA, Pavel; Czech diplomatist, lawyer and university teacher; *Partner, BXL Consulting;* b. 24 Aug. 1965, Washington, USA; m. Eva Teličková; one s. one d.; ed Charles Univ., Prague; joined Ministry of Foreign Affairs 1986, mem. of del. for talks on Czech membership of EU 1991, with Czech Standing Mission to EU 1991–95, Deputy Amb. to Brussels 1993–95; Dir of Dept in Ministry of Foreign Affairs 1995–98, Dir-Gen. Dept for EU and NATO 1998; Deputy Chair. Comm. for Czech Integration to EU 1998, Chief Negotiator 1998–99; Deputy Minister for Foreign Affairs 1998–99; apptd State Sec. for European Affairs 1999; Amb. and Head, Perm. Mission of Czech Repub. to European Communities 2003–04, EU Commr without Portfolio 2004; currently Co-founder and Pnr, BXL Consulting (consults on EU affairs); Sr External Adviser, European Policy Centre; mem. Admin. Council, Notre Europe Foundation, Paris; mem. Europe-USA-Asia Trilateral Comm.; Hon. mem. Man. Bd Nat. Training Fund 1999–2003, Centre of Good Will 2001–; mem. Bd Govs Univ. of Tomase Bati 2001–03; mem. Tomáš Baťa Foundation 1997–; Pres. Václav Havel Commemorative Medal 2003, Commemorative Medal of King Jiří z Poděbrad 2003. *Publications:* (with K. Barták) How Were We Entering the EU? 2003. *Leisure interests:* playing rugby and squash, fitness, cross-country skiing, biking, roller-skating, music, travel, driving. *Address:* BXL Consulting, Rond-Point Schuman 11, 1040 Brussels, Belgium (office). *Telephone:* (2) 256-75-15 (office). *Fax:* (2) 256-75-18 (office). *E-mail:* office@bxl.cz (office). *Website:* www.bxl.cz (office).

TELITO, Rev. and Rt Hon. Sir Filoimea, GCMG, MBE; Tuvaluan government official; *Governor-General;* b. Vaitupu Island; fmr school prin. and church pastor; Gov.-Gen. of Tuvalu 2005–. *Address:* Office of the Governor-General, Private Mail Bag, Vaiaku, Funafuti, Tuvalu (office). *Telephone:* 20715 (office). *Website:* www.tuvaluislands.com (office).

TELLEM, Nancy; American media executive; *President, CBS Paramount Network Television Entertainment Group;* b. 1954; m. Arn Tellem; three c.; ed Univ. of California; began career as TV industry lawyer; with Warner Bros TV (then Lorimar TV) 1987–97, Exec. Vice-Pres. of Business and Financial Affairs; Exec. Vice-Pres. of Business Affairs for CBS Entertainment and Exec. Vice-Pres. CBS Productions 1997–98, Pres. CBS Entertainment 1998–2004, Pres. CBS Paramount Network Television Entertainment Group 2004–; Dir ThirdAge Media Inc. 2000–, Artful Style Inc. 2000–; ranked by Forbes Magazine amongst 100 Most Powerful Women (75th) 2006, (49th) 2007, (32nd) 2008. *Address:* CBS Paramount Network Television Entertainment Group, 5555 Melrose Avenue, Hollywood, CA 90038, USA (office). *Telephone:* (323) 956-5000 (office). *Website:* www.cbs.com (office); www.cbscorporation.com/ our_company/divisions/paramount_tv/tellem.php (office).

TELLEP, Daniel Michael, MS; American business executive (retd); b. 20 Nov. 1931, Forest City, Pa; m. Pat Tellep; six c.; ed Univ. of Calif., Berkeley and Harvard Univ.; with Lockheed Missiles & Space Co. 1955–, Chief Eng Missile Systems Div. 1969–75, Vice-Pres., Asst Gen. Man. Advanced Systems Div. 1975–83, Exec. Vice-Pres. 1983–84, Pres. 1984–; Pres. Lockheed Missiles and Space Group 1986–; Chair. and CEO Lockheed Corpn 1989–95 (merged

with Martin Marietta to form Lockheed Martin 1994), Chair., CEO Lockheed Martin 1996–97; now consultant; mem. Interstate Bancorp Bd 1991–, Bd of Govs Music Center LA Co. 1991–95, Calif. Business Round Table 1992–; Fellow, AIAA, American Astronautical Soc.; mem. Nat. Acad. of Eng; James V. Forrestal Award 1995, Calif. Mfrs Award 1996, Nat. Eng Award 1996, Karman Wings Award 1997 and numerous other awards. *Address:* c/o Lockheed Martin Corporation, 6801 Rockledge Drive, Bethesda, MD 20817, USA.

TELLER, Juergen; German photographer; b. 28 Jan. 1964, Erlangen; partner Venetia Scott; one d.; ed Bayerische Staatslehranstalt für Photographie, Munich; living and working in London 1986–; Citibank Photography Prize 2003. *Publications:* Go Sees 1999, Tracht 2001, More, Stephanie Seymour 2001. *Address:* 1 Telford Road, London, W10 5SH, England (office). *Telephone:* (20) 8964-0966 (office). *Fax:* (20) 8964-0790 (office). *E-mail:* juergenteller@ukf.net (office).

TELLIER, Paul M., PC, CC; Canadian business executive and former public official; b. 1939, Joliette, Québec; ed Université Laval and Univ. of Oxford, UK; admitted to Bar, Québec 1963; Deputy Minister for Indian Affairs and Northern Devt 1979–82; Deputy Minister of Energy, Mines and Resources 1982–85; Clerk of the Privy Council and Sec. to Cabinet of Govt of Canada 1985–92; Pres. and CEO Canadian Nat. Railway Co. (CN) 1992–2003; Pres. and CEO Bombardier Inc. 2003–04; Chair. GCT Global Container Terminals Inc. 2007–; Dir Alcan Aluminium Ltd, Bell Canada Enterprises Inc./Bell Canada 1999–, McCain Foods Ltd; fmr Chair. Conf. Bd of Canada, Co-Chair. Canada–Japan Business Council; Vice-Chair. Canadian Council of Chief Execs, Co-Chair. N America Policy Cttee; mem. Bd Dans la rue 2000–03; Hon. LLD (Univ. of Alberta) 1996; Hon. PhD (Univ. of Ottawa) 2000; Hon. DComm (St Mary's Univ.) 2001; Public Policy Forum Outstanding Performance Award 1988, Gov. Gen.'s Outstanding Achievement Award 1990, Transportation Person of the Year Award, Nat. Transportation Week 1997, Grand Montréalais 1998, Canada's Outstanding CEO of the Year 1998, B'nai Brith Canada Award of Merit 2000, Les Affaires newspaper Personality of the Year 2000, McCullogh Logistics Exec. of the Year Award, Nat. Industrial Transportation League and Logistics Management & Distribution Report 2001, Industry Achievement Award, Canadian Railway Hall of Fame 2002, Fellowship Award, Inst. of Corp. Dirs 2003, Distinguished Canadian Leadership Award 2004; second St Clair tunnel named in his honour 2004. *Address:* Bell Canada Enterprises, 1000 de La Gauchetière Ouest, Bureau 3700, Montréal, Québec H3B 4Y7, Canada (office). *Telephone:* (888) 932-6666 (office). *Fax:* (514) 870-4385 (office). *E-mail:* bcecomms@bce.ca (office).

TELLO, Manuel, BA; Mexican diplomatist (retd); b. 15 March 1935, Mexico City; s. of Manuel Tello and Guadalupe M. de Tello; m. Rhonda Mosesman 1983; three step-d.; ed Georgetown Univ., Washington, DC, USA, Escuela Libre de Derecho, Mexico City; Dir-Gen. for Int. Orgs, Ministry of Foreign Affairs 1970–72, Head of Div. of Int. Orgs 1972–74, of Political Affairs 1975–76; Amb. to the UK 1977–79; Vice-Minister of Multilateral Affairs 1979–82; Perm. Rep. of Mexico to Geneva-based int. orgs 1983–88, Rep. to GATT 1986–88; Amb. to France 1989–92; Perm. Rep. of Mexico to UN, New York 1993–94, 1995–2001; Minister of Foreign Affairs 1994–95; Alt. Rep. on Council of Agency for Prohibition of Nuclear Weapons in Latin America 1970–73; Rep. to Third UN Conf. on Law of the Sea 1971–82; several foreign decorations. *Publications:* various papers and articles on Mexico's foreign policy, the law of the sea etc. *Leisure interests:* reading, tennis. *Address:* c/o Secretary of State for Foreign Affairs, Avda Ricardo Flores Magón 2, 4°, Col Vonoalce Tlatelolco, 09600 México, DF, Mexico (office).

TELMER, Frederick Harold, MA; Canadian business executive; b. 28 Dec. 1937, Edmonton, Alberta; s. of Ingar Telmer and Bernice Telmer; m. Margaret Goddard Hutchings; three s.; ed Garneau High School, Edmonton, Univ. of Alberta; joined Industrial Relations Dept, Stelco Inc. 1963, various man. positions in Marketing Div., subsequently Gen. Man. Field Sales, apptd Gen. Man. Corp. Affairs and Strategic Planning 1984, Vice-Pres. 1985, Pres. Stelco Steel 1988, Dir Stelco Inc. 1989, Chair. and CEO 1991–97, Chair. 1997–2003; Founding Dir Japan Soc. *Leisure interests:* golf, tennis, skiing. *Address:* 4451 Lakeshore Road, Burlington, Ont., L7L 1B3, Canada (home).

TELTSCHIK, Horst; German fmr politician and business executive; *President, Boeing Germany;* b. 14 June 1940, Klantendorf; s. of Richard Teltschik and Anja Teltschik; m. Gerhild Ruff 1967; one s. one d.; ed Gymnasium Tegernsee and Freie Univ. Berlin; fmrly held various positions in CDU offices and in State Govt of Rhineland-Palatinate; then Ministerial Dir Dept 2, Fed. Chancellery; CEO Bertelsmann Foundation, Herbert Quandt Foundation 1993; Chair. Teltschik Assocs. GmbH 2002; Pres. Boeing Germany 2003–; mem. Bd of Man. BMW AG 1993–2000, BMW Rep. Bd for Eastern Europe, Asia and Middle East; organizer Munich Conf. on Securities Policy; fmr Hon. Gen. Consul of India for Bavaria and Thuringia; Diplompolitologe; Hon. DUniv (Budapest) 1991, (Sogang, Seoul) 1997; Bundesverdienstkreuz, First Class; Commdr, Légion d'honneur; Grande Ufficiale (Italy), Commdr (Luxembourg), Bavarian Verdienstorden. *Publication:* 329 Tage – Innenansichten der deutschen Einigung. *Leisure interests:* literature, tennis. *Address:* Boeing International Corpn, Pariser Platz 4a, 10117 Berlin (office); Karl-Theodor Strasse 38, 83700 Rottach-Egern, Germany (home). *Telephone:* (30) 77377100 (office); (8022) 26677 (home). *Fax:* (30) 77377102 (office); (8022) 662849 (home). *E-mail:* horst.m.teltschik@ boeing.com (office).

TEMARU, Oscar Manutahi; French Polynesian politician and head of state; *President;* b. 1 Nov. 1944, Faa'a Dist, Tahiti; m. Marie Temaru; seven c.; in French Navy 1961–63; customs officer 1964–99; f. Front de Libération de la Polynésie—FLP (Polynesia Liberation Front) 1977 (changed party name to

Tavini Huiraatira no te ao maohi—Serve the Polynesian People 1983); Mayor of Faa'a 1983; elected mem. Territorial Ass. 1986; mem. UPD Party (Union for Democracy); Pres. of French Polynesia June–Oct. 2004, 2005–06, 2007–08, 2009–. *Leisure interest:* golf. *Address:* Office of the President of the Government, BP 2551, 98713 Papeete, French Polynesia (office). *Telephone:* 472121 (office). *Fax:* 472210 (office). *Website:* www.presidence.pf (office).

TEMBO, Akihiko; Japanese oil industry executive; *President and Representative Director, Idemitsu Kosan Company;* joined Idemitsu Kosan Co. Ltd 1964, later Dir of Accounting, Man. Dir and Sr Man. Dir, Pres. and Rep. Dir 2002–; Vice-Pres. Petroleum Asscn of Japan. *Address:* Idemitsu Kosan Co. Ltd, 1-1, Marunouchi 3-chome, Chiyoda-ku, Tokyo 100-8321, Japan (office). *Telephone:* (3) 3213-3115 (office). *Fax:* (3) 3213-9354 (office). *E-mail:* info@ idemitsu.co.jp (office). *Website:* www.idemitsu.co.jp (office).

TEME, Jorge; Timor-Leste diplomatist; b. 24 June 1964, Oe-cusse; ed Seminary of the Immaculate Conception Catholic School, São José, Dili, Christian Univ. of Satya Wacana Salatiga, Indonesia, Massey Univ., Palmerston North, New Zealand; Chief of Seminary Students, Diocese of Dili em Laalian, Indonesai 1985–86; Chief of External Political Agitation for RENETIL 1988, 1993; Chief of Timorese Students in Salatiga, Indonesia 1990, 1992; teacher of English Language, Univ. of Timor and Seminary De Nossa Senhora de Fatima, Batilde, East Timor 1993–98; Vice-Dean for East Timorese Students' Asscn, Univ. of Timor 1996–98; Rep. of Nat. Council of Timorese Resistance (CNRT), NZ 1998–2000; Programme Officer, UNDP April–Sept. 2001; teacher, Faculty of Social Sciences and Politics, Univ. of East Timor April–Sept. 2001; elected mem. Constituent Ass. (Fretilin Party) 2001–; Vice-Minister of Foreign Affairs and Cooperation 2001–03; Amb. to Australia 2003–06; Chair. Fundacao Solenusat (business foundation), Oecussi Enclavei. *Address:* Fundacao Solenusat, Oecussi Enclave, Timor-Leste.

TEMERLIN, (Julius) Liener, BFA; American advertising executive; *President, Temerlin Consulting;* b. 27 March 1928, Ardmore, Okla; s. of S. Pincus Temerlin and Julie Kahn Temerlin; m. Karla Samuelsohn 1950; two d.; ed Ardmore, Okla High School, Univ. of Oklahoma; COO Glenn Advertising 1970–74; Pres. Glenn, Bozell & Jacobs 1974–79; Chair. of Bd Bozell & Jacobs 1979–85; Chair. Bozell, Jacobs, Kenyon & Eckhardt 1985–88, Bozell 1989–92; Chair. Temerlin McClain Advertising 1992–2001, Chair. Emer. 2001–; Founder and Pres. Temerlin Consulting, Dallas; consultant, The Richards Group 2005–; Founder, Chair. and Festival Dir AFI Dallas Int. Film Festival 2007–08; Algur H. Meadows Distinguished Prof. of Advertising, Meadows School of the Arts, Southern Methodist Univ.; Chair. Dallas Museum of Art Devt Cttee 1993–96; Pres. Council Dallas Symphony Asscn 1989–; Chair. Lieberman Research Bldg, Baylor Medical Center, Fundraising Campaign 1997–; mem. Bd of Dirs, Madison Council, Library of Congress 1991–; East-West Inst. 1999–; mem. Steering Cttee for Capital Campaign, KERA (Public TV Council) 2000–01; Trustee, American Film Inst. 1992–2000, Hon. Trustee 2000–; Bill D. Kerss Award, Dallas Advertising League 1983, Nat. Conf. of Christians and Jews Brotherhood Award 1984, Susan G. Komen Foundation for Breast Cancer Research 1989, Community Service Award, Jas. K. Wilson Silver Cup Award, Dallas 1990, Linz Award for civic service 1990, Volunteer Fundraiser of the Year 1991, Silver Medal Award, Dallas Advertising League 1991, Father of the Year 1991, Best Man in Advertising Award 1992, Servant Leader Award, Volunteer Center of Dallas 2001, Advertising Hall of Fame 2004. *Address:* Temerlin Consulting, 8401 North Central Expressway, Suite 390, Dallas, TX 75225, USA (office). *Telephone:* (972) 739-7480 (office). *Fax:* (972) 739-7483 (office). *E-mail:* connie.beebe@temerlinconsulting.com (office).

TEMIRKANOV, Yuri Khatuyevich; Russian conductor; *Music Director and Principal Conductor, St Petersburg Philharmonic Orchestra;* b. 10 Dec. 1938, Nalchik; s. of Khatu Sagidovich Temirkanov and Polina Petrovna Temirkanova; m. Irina Guseva (deceased); one s.; ed Leningrad Conservatoire; First Violinist with Leningrad Philharmonic Orchestra 1961–66; Conductor for Maly Theatre and Opera Studio, Leningrad 1965–68; Chief Conductor, Leningrad Philharmonic Orchestra 1968–76, Kirov Opera and Ballet Co. 1976–88; Prof. Leningrad Conservatoire 1979–88; Artistic Dir State Philharmonia 1988–; Prin. Guest Conductor Royal Philharmonic Orchestra and Philadelphia Orchestra; Chief Conductor London Philharmonic Orchestra 1992–97; Prin. Guest Conductor, Danish Radio Orchestra 1997–2008; Music Dir Baltimore Symphony Orchestra 1999–2007, Music Dir Emer. 2007–; Music Dir and Prin. Conductor, St Petersburg Philharmonic Orchestra 2007–; guest conductor in a number of countries, including Scandinavia (Sweden 1968), USA and UK (Royal Philharmonic Orchestra 1981–); USSR People's Artist 1981, Glinka Prize, USSR State Prize 1976, 1985. *Opera productions include:* Porgy and Bess (at Maly), Peter the Great (at Kirov), Shchedrin's Dead Souls (at Bolshoi and Kirov), Tchaikovsky's Queen of Spades and Eugene Onegin (Kirov) 1979. *Address:* c/o IMG Artists, The Light Box, 111 Power Road, London, W4 5PY, England (office). *Telephone:* (20) 7957-5800 (office). *Fax:* (20) 7957-5801 (office). *E-mail:* nmathias@imgartists.com (office). *Website:* www.imgartists.com (office).

TEMÍSTOCLES MONTÁS, Juan, PhD; Dominican Republic politician; *Secretary of State for the Economy, Planning and Development;* ed Univ. Autónoma de Santo Domingo, Univ. Politécnica de Madrid, Spain; Admin. Corporación Dominicana de Electricidad (now Corporación Dominicana de Empresas Eléctricas Estatales) 1996–98; Tech. Sec. to the Presidency 1998–2000, 2004–06; Exec. Dir Global Foundation for Democracy and Devt 2000–04; Sec. of State for Economy, Planning and Devt 2007–; mem. Partido de la Liberación Dominicana. *Address:* Secretariat of State for the Economy, Planning and Development, Palacio Nacional, Avda México, esq. Dr Delgado, Bloque B, 2°, Santo Domingo, Dominican Republic (office). *Telephone:* 695-8028 (office). *Fax:* 695-8432 (office). *E-mail:* informacion@economia.gov.do (office). *Website:* www.economia.gov.do (office).

TEMPEST, Brian W., PhD; British pharmaceuticals executive; *Strategy Advisor, Hale & Tempest Company Ltd;* b. 13 June 1947, Morecambe, Lancs.; s. of Bill Tempest and Joan Tempest; m. Jasmin Tempest; three s.; ed Univ. of Lancaster; fmrly with Beecham and GD Searle, various positions in sales, marketing and man.; Regional Dir for Africa, Far East and Middle East, Glaxo Holdings 1985–93; Worldwide Commercial Operations Dir, Fisons plc 1993–95; Regional Dir for Europe, CIS and Africa, Ranbaxy Laboratories Ltd 1995–2000, Worldwide Pres., Pharmaceuticals 2000–04, CEO and Man. Dir July 2004–Dec. 2005, Chief Mentor and Exec. Vice Chair. 2006–07; Strategy Advisor, Hale & Tempest Co. Ltd 2008–; mem. Advisory Bd JM Financials India Fund, Bombay 2008–; mem. Editorial Bd Journal of Generic Medicine 2007–; Hon. Prof., Lancaster Univ. 2007–. *Address:* Tanglewood, St Leonards Hill, Windsor, Berks., SL4 4AL England (office). *Telephone:* 98-10091192 (India; mobile) (office). *Fax:* (1753) 850849 (office). *E-mail:* brian .tempest@clara.co.uk (home). *Website:* www.briantempest.com (home).

TEMPLE, Shirley (see Black, Shirley Temple).

TEMPLEMAN, Baron (Life Peer), cr. 1982, of White Lackington in the County of Somerset; **Sydney William Templeman,** PC, QC, MBE, MA; British fmr judge; b. 3 March 1920, London; s. of Herbert W. Templeman and Lilian (née Pheasant) Templeman; m. 1st Margaret Rowles 1946 (died 1988); two s.; m. 2nd Sheila Barton Edworthy 1996 (died 2009); ed Southall Grammar School and St John's Coll. Cambridge; served 4/1st Gurkha Rifles 1941–46; mem. Middle Temple 1946–, Treas. 1987–; mem. Bar Council 1961–65, 1970–72; QC 1964; Attorney-Gen., Duchy of Lancaster 1970; Judge, Chancery Div., 1972; Pres., Senate of Inns of Court and Bar 1974; mem., Royal Comm. on Legal Services 1976; Lord Justice of Appeal 1978–82; Lord of Appeal in Ordinary 1982–95; Visitor, Essex Univ. 1990; Pres., Bar European Group 1987–95, Asscn of Law Teachers 1997–; Hon. Fellow, St John's Coll. Cambridge 1982; Hon. mem. Canadian Bar Asscn 1976, American Bar Asscn 1976, Newfoundland Law Soc. 1984; Hon. DLitt (Reading) 1980, Hon. LLD (Birmingham) 1986, (Exeter) 1991, (Huddersfield Polytechnic) 1989, (West of England) 1993, (Nat. Law School of India) 1994. *Address:* House of Lords, London, SW1A 0PW, England. *Telephone:* (1392) 275428 (home).

TEMPLETON, Richard (Rich) K., BSc; American electronics industry executive; *President and CEO, Texas Instruments Inc.;* b. 1958; m.; three c.; ed Union Coll., NY; joined Texas Instruments Inc. (TI) 1980, held various positions including Exec. Vice-Pres. semiconductor business 1996–2004, COO TI 2000–04, mem. Bd of Dirs 2003–, Pres. and CEO 2004–; Dir Semiconductor Industry Asscn; mem. Business Roundtable, Dallas Chief Exec. Roundtable. *Address:* Texas Instruments Inc., 12500 TI Boulevard, Dallas, TX 75266-4136, USA (office). *Telephone:* (972) 995-2011 (office). *Website:* www.ti.com (office).

TEN HOLT, Friso; Dutch painter and etcher; b. 6 April 1921, Argelès-Gazost, France; m. A. Taselaar 1946; two s. one d.; ed Rijksakademie van Beeldende Kunsten, Amsterdam; paintings mainly of swimmers, landscapes and nudes, portraits and figures; Prof. of Painting, Rijksakademie van Beeldende Kunsten, Amsterdam 1969–83; one-man exhbns in Netherlands since 1952, London 1959, 1962, 1963, 1965, 1969, 1973; group exhbns at Beaverbrook Art Gallery, Canada and Tate Gallery, London 1963, Biennale Salzburg 1964, Carnegie Inst., Pittsburgh 1964, Netherlands travelling exhbn 1957–58; works in collections in Netherlands, Sweden, UK, France and America. *Major works:* stained-glass windows for churches in Amsterdam and The Hague and for Haarlem Cathedral. *Leisure interest:* reading. *Address:* Keizersgracht 614, Amsterdam, Netherlands. *Telephone:* 022481727 (Studio); 6230736 (home).

TENDULKAR, Sachin Ramesh; Indian professional cricketer; b. 24 April 1973, Mumbai; s. of the late Ramesh Tendulkar; m. Anjali Mehta; one s. one d.; right-hand batsman, right-arm off-break, leg-break bowler (over 100 One Day Ints (ODI) wickets); teams: Bombay 1988–96 (renamed Mumbai) 1997–, Yorkshire 1992, India 1989–; first-class debut for Bombay cricket team aged 14, scored a century on debut; Test debut (cap 187) v. Pakistan, Karachi 15 Nov. 1989, in 151 Tests (25 as Capt.) scored 11,953 runs (average 55.57), 39 centuries, 49 fifties; set new record for most runs scored by a batsman in Test cricket, Oct. 2008; ODI debut (cap 74) v. Pakistan 18 Dec. 1989, 412 ODIs (73 as Capt.) for 16,088 runs (average 44.07), 41 centuries, 87 fifties; first player to reach 13,000 runs in ODIs; 19,894 first-class runs (average 59.38), including 63 hundreds, 91 fifties; top scores: 248 (test), 186 (ODI); balls bowled: 3742 (test), 7895 (ODI); wickets taken: 42 (test), 154 (ODI); bowling average: 51.02 (test), 43.71 (ODI); best bowling 3/10 (test), 5/32 (ODI); catches: 98 (test), 120 (ODI); statistics as of 20 Oct. 2008; Padma Vibhushan 2008; Arjuna Award 1994, Wisden Cricketer of the Year 1997, Rajiv Gandhi Khel Ratna Award 1998, Padma Shri Award 1999, Maharashtra Bhushan Award, rated by Wisden as the second greatest Test batsman after Sir Donald Bradman, and the second greatest ODI batsman behind Sir Vivian Richards 2002 (ratings revised to leave Tendulkar ranked No. 1 and Richards at No. 2 2003). *Address:* 7 Ushakkal, Sahitya Sahawas Colony, Bandra (East), Mumbai 400051 (office); 10/11 La Mer, Mistry Park, Kadeshwari Road, Brandra (West), Mumbai 400 050, India (home). *E-mail:* ast1@vsnl.net (home). *Website:* tendulkar@cricinfo .com (office).

TENET, George J., MIA; American fmr government official and academic; *Distinguished Professor in the Practice of Diplomacy, Edmund A. Walsh School of Foreign Service and Senior Research Associate, Institute for the Study of Diplomacy, Georgetown University;* b. New York; m. A. Stephanie Glakas; one s.; ed Georgetown Univ. School of Foreign Service, School of Int. Affairs, Columbia Univ.; Legis. Asst, Legis. Dir, staff of US Senator John Heinz 1982–85; fmr head of supervision of arms control negotiations between USSR and USA, subsequently Staff Dir, Senate Select Cttee on Intelligence; fmr Special Asst to Pres. and Sr Dir for Intelligence Programs, Nat. Security

Council; Deputy Dir of CIA 1995–96, Acting Dir 1996–97, Dir 1997–2004 (resgnd); Distinguished Prof. in the Practice of Diplomacy, Edmund A. Walsh School of Foreign Service and Sr Research Assoc., Inst. for the Study of Diplomacy, Georgetown Univ. 2004–; mem. Bd of Dirs QinetiQ Group plc, UK 2006–; Egyptian Order of Merit (First Class); Canadian Security Intelligence Service Gold Medal, Presidential Medal of Freedom 2004, America's Democratic Legacy Award from Anti-Defamation League (ADL) 2005. *Publications:* The Ability of US Intelligence to Monitor the Intermediate Nuclear Force Treaty, At the Center of the Storm 2007. *Address:* Edmund A. Walsh School of Foreign Service, 301 InterCultural Center, 37th and O Streets, NW, Washington, DC 20057, USA; c/o Board of Directors, QinetiQ Group plc, Cody Technology Park, Ively Road, Hants., Farnborough, GU14 0LX, England (office). *Telephone:* (202) 687-5696 (Georgetown). *Fax:* (202) 687-1431(Georgetown). *Website:* www.georgetown.edu/sfs.

TENG, Teng; Chinese politician; b. 1930, Jiangyin Co., Jiangsu Prov.; ed Tsinghua Univ., Beijing and in USSR; joined CCP 1948; Deputy Dir Chemical Eng Dept, Tsinghua Univ. 1960–66, Prof., Vice-Pres. Tsinghua Univ. 1980–84; Vice-Minister in charge of State Science and Tech. Comm. 1985–86; Deputy Head, Propaganda Dept CCP Cen. Cttee 1986–87; Vice Minister in charge of State Educ. Comm. 1988–93; Vice-Chair. Exec. Bd UNESCO 1991–93; Dir Sustainable Devt Research Centre; Pres. Chinese Ecological Econs Council; Vice-Pres. Chinese Acad. of Sciences 1986–87, Chinese Acad. of Social Sciences 1993–98; mem. 8th and 9th Standing Cttee NPC 1993–2003, mem. Educ., Science, Culture and Public Health Cttee 1993–98; Pres. Chinese and Ecological Econs Council 1998–2005; Govt Prize of Science and Tech. 1978. *Publication:* Future Outlook for the Environment and Sustainable Development 2002. *Leisure interest:* classical music. *Address:* 5th Jianguomennei Dajie, Beijing 100732 (office); Cuiweisili 1-2-401, Beijing 100036, People's Republic of China (home). *Telephone:* (10) 65137697 (office); (10) 68258097 (home). *Fax:* (10) 65137815 (office); (10) 68252720 (home). *E-mail:* tengteng@cass.org.ch (office); tengcass@yahoo.com (home).

TENG, Wensheng; Chinese writer and politician; b. 1940, Changning Co., Hunan Prov.; ed Chinese People's Univ.; joined CCP 1965; Research Fellow, Research Office, Secr. of CCP Cen. Cttee; Vice-Dir, later Dir Policy Research Office of CCP Cen. Cttee; Deputy Sec.-Gen. CCP Cen. Advisory Comm. 1988–92; Dir CCP Cen. Cttee Literature Research Office 2002–; mem. 15th CCP Cen. Cttee 1997–2002, 16th CCP Cen. Cttee 2002–07; fmr chief speech writer for Pres. Jiang Zemin. *Publication:* book on evolution of Mao Zedong thought. *Address:* Policy Research Office of Chinese Communist Party Central Committee, 1 Zhong Nan Hai, Beijing, People's Republic of China (office).

TENGBOM, Anders, DArch; Swedish architect; b. 10 Nov. 1911, Stockholm; s. of Ivar Tengbom and Hjördis Tengbom; m. Margareta Brambeck 1937 (died 2002); two s. two d.; ed Royal Inst. of Tech. and Royal Acad. of Fine Arts, Stockholm, Cranbrook Acad., Mich., USA; travelled in Europe, USA, Japan, China and USSR 1935–36; architectural practice in Stockholm 1938–; designed bldgs for many different functions in Sweden, Belgium, Venezuela and Saudi Arabia; Asst Prof. of Architecture, Royal Inst. of Tech., Stockholm 1947; Pres. Nat. Asscn of Swedish Architects (SAR) 1963–65; mem. Bd Swedish Hosps Fed. 1962–70; Pres. Swedish Asscn of Consulting Architects 1972–75; mem. Royal Acad. of Fine Arts, Stockholm 1973–, Pres. 1980–86; Hon. Corresp. mem. RIBA 1963: Hon. Fellow AIA 1978. *Address:* Canton 2, 178 93 Drottningholm, Sweden (home). *Telephone:* (8) 759-01-75 (home).

TENNANT, Sir Anthony John, Kt, BA; British business executive (retd); b. 5 Nov. 1930, London; s. of the late Maj. John Tennant and of Hon. Antonia (later Viscountess) Radcliffe; m. Rosemary Violet Stockdale 1954; two s.; ed Eton Coll., Trinity Coll. Cambridge; with Mather and Crowther 1953–66, Dir 1960–66; Marketing Consultancy 1966–70; Marketing Dir then Deputy Man. Dir, Truman Ltd 1970–72; Sales and Marketing Dir then Deputy CEO, Watney, Mann and Truman Brewers 1972–76; Deputy Man. Dir, later CEO, then Chair. Int. Distillers and Vintners Ltd 1976–87; Dir, later Group Man. Dir, then Deputy Chief Exec., Grand Metropolitan 1977–87; CEO, Guinness PLC 1987–89, Chair. 1989–92; Dir (non-exec.), Christie's Int. PLC 1993–98, (non-exec. Chair. 1993–96); Chair. Priorities Bd 1992–93; Deputy Chair. (non-exec.), Wellcome PLC 1994–95, Arjo Wiggins Appleton PLC 1996–2000; Dir (non-exec.), Guardian Royal Exchange 1989–99, Guardian Royal Exchange Assurance 1989–94, Banque Nat. de Paris 1990–91, BNP UK Holdings Ltd 1991–2002, London Stock Exchange 1991–94; Deputy Chair., Forte PLC 1992–96; Sr Adviser, Morgan Stanley UK Group 1993–2000; Dir (non-exec.), Morgan Stanley Dean Witter Bank Ltd 1999–2000; Chair. Bd of Trustees, Royal Acad. Trust 1996–2002 (Trustee 1994–2002), Univ. of Southampton Devt Trust 1994–2002 (Trustee 1992–2002); mem. Supervisory Bd, LVMH, Moët Hennessy Louis Vuitton, Paris 1988–92; Trustee, Cambridge Foundation 1996–2001; Légion d'honneur; Hon. DBA (Nottingham Trent Univ.) 1996; Hon. DUniv (Southampton) 2000; Médaille de la Ville de Paris. *Leisure interest:* gardening. *Address:* 18 Hamilton House, Vicarage Gate, London, W8 4HL, England (home).

TENNANT, Emma Christina, FRSL; British writer; b. 20 Oct. 1937; d. of 2nd Baron Glenconner and Elizabeth Lady Glenconner; one s. two d.; ed St Paul's Girls' School; fmr freelance journalist; Founder, Ed., Bananas 1975–78; Gen. Ed., In Verse 1982–, Lives of Modern Women 1985–; Hon. DLitt (Aberdeen) 1996. *Television includes:* Frankenstein's Baby, Screen One. *Publications:* The Colour of Rain (as Catherine Aydy) 1963, The Time of the Crack 1973, The Last of the Country House Murders 1975, Hotel de Dream 1976, Bananas Anthology (ed.) 1977, Saturday Night Reader (ed.) 1978, The Bad Sister 1978, Wild Nights 1979, Alice Fell 1980, The Boggart (with M. Rayner) 1981, The Search for Treasure Island 1981, Queen of Stones 1982, Woman Beware Woman 1983, The Ghost Child 1984, Black Marina 1985, The Adventures of Robina by Herself (ed.) 1986, Cycle of the Sun: The House of Hospitalities

1987, A Wedding of Cousins 1988, The Magic Drum 1989, Two Women of London 1989, Faustine 1992, Tess 1993, Pemberley 1993, Emma in Love 1996, An Unequal Marriage 1994, Strangers: A Family Romance 1998, Girlitude 1999, Burnt Diaries 1999, The Ballad of Sylvia and Ted (contrib.) 2001, A House in Corfu 2001, Felony 2002, Corfu Banquet 2003, Heathcliff's Tale 2005, The Harp Lesson 2005, The French Dancer's Bastard 2006, The Autobiography of the Queen 2007. *Leisure interest:* walking in Greece. *Address:* c/o Marsh Agency, 12 Dover Street, London, W1S 4LJ, England (office). *Telephone:* (20) 7399-2800 (office). *Fax:* (20) 7399-2801 (office). *Website:* www.marsh-agency.co.uk (office).

TENNEKES, Hendrik, DS (Eng); Dutch meteorologist; b. 13 Dec. 1936, Kampen; s. of the late Cornelis Tennekes and of Harmpje Noordman; m. Olga Vanderpot 1964 (divorced 1998); one s. one d.; ed Delft Tech. Univ.; Asst Prof., Assoc. Prof., Prof. of Aerospace Eng, Pennsylvania State Univ. 1965–77, currently Adjunct Prof.; Dir of Research, Royal Netherlands Meteorological Inst. 1977–90, Dir of Strategic Planning 1990–95; Prof. of Meteorology, Free Univ., Amsterdam 1977–2001; Visiting Prof. Univ. of Washington, Seattle 1976–77; Visiting Sr Scientist, Nat. Center for Atmospheric Research, Boulder, Colo 1987; mem. Royal Netherlands Acad. of Arts and Sciences; mem. Advisory Bd Royal Palace Foundation, Amsterdam 1990–2001. *Publications:* A First Course in Turbulence (with J. L. Lumley) 1972, The Simple Science of Flight 1996; numerous publs on turbulence, predictability, chaos, boundary-layer meteorology and environmental philosophy. *Leisure interests:* poetry, landscape painting. *Address:* Velperweg 30-19, 6824 BJ Arnhem, Netherlands (home). *Telephone:* (30) 379-2247 (home). *E-mail:* henktennekes@kpnplanet.nl (home).

TENORIO, Pedro Pangelinan; American politician (retd); b. 18 April 1934, Saipan, Northern Mariana Islands; s. of the late Blas Pangelinan Tenorio and of Guadalupe Sablan Pangelinan; m. Sophia Pangelinan 1959; four s. four d.; ed George Washington High School, Guam; mem. House of Reps, Congress of Micronesia; Senator Marianas Dist Legislature; Vice-Pres. The Senate, Northern Mariana Commonwealth Legislature 1978–80, Pres. 1980–82; Gov. Commonwealth of the Northern Mariana Islands 1982–91, 1998–2001; Hon. LLD (Univ. of Guam) 1998. *Leisure interest:* golf. *Address:* c/o Office of the Governor, Caller Box 10007, Capitol Hill, Saipan, MP 96950, Commonwealth of the Northern Mariana Islands.

TENYAKOV, Eduard Venyaminovich; Russian business executive; b. 25 Feb. 1952, Chelyabinsk; m.; one d.; ed Chelyabinsk Polytechnic Inst., Moscow Inst. of Finance; with production co. Polyot Chelyabinsk 1971–79; Deputy Dir Gen. on commercial problems 1979–82; Dir Chelyabinsk Factory 1982–85; Dir construction co-operative, Chelyabinsk 1985–87; Chair. Exec. Bd Chelyabinsk Rotorbank, Council of Exchange All-Union Assc n of Commercial Banks and Russian Banking Union 1987–89; one of founders Moscow Cen. Stock Exchange 1989, Pres. 1990–91; Pres. Jt Stock Finance Co. Fininvest, Chelyabinsk 1990–91; Founder and Pres. Chelyabinsk Universal Exchange and Moscow Cen. Stock Exchange 1991–; Co-Chair. Interregional Council of Exchanges and Congress of Exchanges. *Publications:* Optimally Possible Variant 1991, People of the Future 1994. *Leisure interests:* reading, hunting, riding and breeding horses. *Address:* Chelyabinsk Universal Stock Exchange, Chelyabinsk, Russia (office). *Telephone:* (495) 292-85-43 (office).

TEO, Rear-Adm. (retd) Chee Hean, MSc, MPA; Singaporean politician and fmr naval officer; *Minister for Defence;* b. 27 Dec. 1954; m. Chew Poh Yim; one s. one d.; ed St Michael's School, St Joseph's Inst., Singapore Armed Forces Training Inst., UMIST, Manchester, Imperial Coll., London, Kennedy School of Govt, Harvard Univ.; various command and staff appointments in Repub. of Singapore Navy and Jt Staff 1977–86, Chief of Navy 1991, rank of Rear-Adm. 1991, retd 1992; MP for Marine Parade Group Representation Constituency 1992–97, becoming Minister of State in Ministries of Finance, Communications and Defence; Acting Minister for Environment and Sr Minister of State for Defence 1995–96, Minister for Environment and Second Minister for Defence 1996–97, MP for Pasir Ris Group Representation Constituency 1997–, Minister for Educ. and Second Minister for Defence 1997–2001, Minister for Defence 2003–. *Address:* Ministry of Defence, Gombak Drive, off Upper Bukit Timah Road, Mindeg Building, Singapore 669645, Singapore (office). *Telephone:* 67608844 (office). *Fax:* 67646119 (office). *Website:* www .mindef.gov.sg (office).

TEO, Michael Eng Cheng, BBA, MA; Singaporean diplomatist and air force officer (retd); *High Commissioner to UK;* b. 19 Sept. 1947, Sarawak; s. of Teo Thian Lai and Lim Siew Kheng; m. Joyce Teo (née Ng Sinn Toh); one s. one d.; ed Auburn Univ., Fletcher School of Law and Diplomacy, Tufts Univ., USAF War Coll., USA; joined Repub. of Singapore Air Force 1968, Commdr 1985, Brig.-Gen. 1987, Chief of Air Force 1990 (retd); joined Diplomatic Sevice 1993, High Commr to NZ 1994–96, Amb. to Repub. of Korea 1996–2001, High Commr to UK (also accred as Amb. to Ireland) 2002–; The Most Noble Order of the Crown (Thailand) 1981, Legion of Merit, Degree of Commdr (USA) 1991, Order of Diplomatic Service Merit Gwanghwa Medal (Repub. of Korea) 2002; Public Admin Medal (Singapore) 1989, Outstanding Achievement Award (Philippines) 1989, Bintang Swa Bhuana Paksa Utama (Indonesia) 1991. *Leisure interests:* golf, hiking, reading. *Address:* Singapore High Commission, 9 Wilton Crescent, London, SW1X 8SP, England (office). *Telephone:* (20) 7201-5850 (office). *Fax:* (20) 7245-6583 (office). *E-mail:* info@singaporehc.org.uk (office); singhc_lon@sgmfa.gov.sg (office). *Website:* www.mfa.gov.sg/london (office).

TEODORO, Gilberto ('Gilbert') Cojuangco, Jr, BSc, LLB, LLM; Philippine lawyer, politician and air force officer; *Secretary of National Defense;* b. 14 June 1964, Manila; s. of Gilberto Teodoro, Sr and Mercedes Cojuangco; m. Monica Prieto-Teodoro; one s.; ed Xavier School, De La Salle Univ., Univ. of

the Phillipines (UP), Harvard Law School, USA, Air Command and Staff Coll. of the Philippine Air Force, Jt Command and Staff Coll.; Pres. Kabataang Barangay for Cen. Luzon 1980–85, for Prov. of Tarlac 1980–85; mem. Sanguniang Panlalawigan, Prov. of Tarlac 1980–86; called to the Phillipines Bar 1989; lawyer, EP Mendoza Law firm 1990–97; admitted to State Bar of NY, USA 1997; Congressman of First Dist of Tarlac 1998–, Asst Majority Leader (11th Congress), Head of Nationalist People's Coalition House mems and mem. House contingent to Legis.-Exec. Devt Advisory Council; Sec. of Nat. Defense (youngest Sec. to hold Defense portfolio) 2007–; licensed commercial pilot; Col, Philippine Air Force, 0-133104 E (Reserve Force); Asst Faculty mem. Command and Gen. Staff Course; Lecturer, Air Command Staff Coll.; Chair. Philippine Nat. Police Foundation Inc.; mem. Integrated Bar of the Philippines, UP Alumni Asscn, UP Law Alumni Asscn, Harvard Alumni Asscn, Harvard Law Alumni Asscn; Lifetime mem. Armor-Cavalry Asscn of the Philippines; Hon. Command Pilot, Philippine Air Force; Hon. mem. PMA Alumni Asscn Sponsoring Class – '76, Philippine Air Force Aviation Cadet Alumni Asscn Sponsoring Class – '80, Asscn of Chiefs of Police of the Philippines, Inc.; Mil. Merit Medal, Philippine Air Force Gen. Staff Course Badge, Presidential Flight Crew Badge, Mil. Civic Action Medal (Plain), Mil. Civic Action Medal with Bronze Service Star, Mil. Civic Action Medal with Second Service Star; Dean's Medal for Academic Excellence, Univ. of the Phillipines 1989, Leadership and Seminar Academic Excellence Awardee, Air Command and Staff Coll. of the Philippine Air Force 2001, Leadership Award, Jt Command and Staff Coll. 2003; numerous mil. awards and commendations, including Basic RASS Aeronautical Badge, Caliber .45 Pistol Expert Marksmanship Badge, M-16 Rifle Marksmanship Badge. *Address:* Department of National Defense, DND Building, 3rd Floor, Camp Aguinaldo, Quezon City, 1100 Metro Manila, The Phillipines (office). *Telephone:* (2) 9113300 (office). *Fax:* (2) 9116213 (office). *E-mail:* webmaster@dnd.gov.ph (office). *Website:* www.dnd.gov.ph (office).

TEPPERMAN, Jonathan D., BA, MA, LLM; Canadian journalist; *Assistant Managing Editor, Newsweek International;* b. 10 Aug. 1971, Windsor, Ont.; s. of Bill and Rochelle Tepperman; ed Yale Univ., Univ. of Oxford, UK, NYU School of Law; fmr speechwriter for US Amb. to UN 1994–95; journalist writing for Forward 1996, Jerusalem Post 1997; Assoc. Ed. and Production Man. Foreign Affairs (journal of Council on Foreign Relations) 1998–2001, Sr Ed. 2001–04, Deputy Man. Ed. 2004–07; Asst Managing Ed. Newsweek International, New York 2007–. *Publications:* numerous contributions to publications including New York Times, Newsweek, LA Times, Christian Science Monitor, Wall Street Journal, New Republic. *Address:* Newsweek Inc., 251 West 57th Street, New York, NY 10019, USA (office). *Telephone:* (212) 445-5818 (office). *Fax:* (212) 445-5764 (office). *E-mail:* jonathan.tepperman@newsweek.com (office). *Website:* www.newsweekeurope.com (office).

TER-MINASSIAN, Teresa, MS (Econs); Italian economist and international organization official; *Director, Fiscal Affairs Department, International Monetary Fund;* ed Univ. of Rome, Harvard Univ., USA; began career in Research Dept, Cen. Bank of Italy 1967–78; seconded to IMF as economist in Fiscal Affairs Dept 1971, Deputy Dir 1988–97, Dir 2001–, also fmr Chief, Southern European Div., European Dept and Deputy Dir Western Hemisphere Dept 1997–2001. *Publication:* Fiscal Federalism in Theory and Practice 1997. *Address:* International Monetary Fund, 700 19th Street, NW, Washington, DC 20431, USA (office). *Telephone:* (202) 623-8844 (office). *Fax:* (202) 623-4259 (office). *E-mail:* tterminassian@imf.org (office). *Website:* www.imf.org (office).

TER-PETROSYAN, Levon Akopovich, DLit; Armenian politician and philologist; b. 9 Jan. 1945, Aleppo, Syria; m. Lyudmila Pletnitskaya; one s.; ed Yerevan State Univ., Leningrad Inst. of Orientology; family moved to Armenia in 1946; jr researcher Armenian Inst. of Literature 1972–78, sr researcher, then Scientific Sec. Matenadaran Archive 1978–90; took part in dissident movt, arrested 1966, 1988–89; mem. Chair. Karabakh Cttee in Matenadaran 1988; Deputy Supreme Soviet of Armenian SSR 1989, Chair. 1990–91; mem. Bd, Chair. Armenian Nat. Movt; Pres. of Armenia 1991–98. *Publications:* six books and over 70 papers on the history of Armenia. *Leisure interests:* reading, chess. *Address:* 19a Koyun str., 375009, Yerevan (office); 10 Tsitsernakaberd road, Yerevan, Armenia (home). *Telephone:* (10) 52-09-74; (10) 52-09-57. *E-mail:* aladtp@arminco.com (office).

TERASAWA, Yoshio, BA (Econs); Japanese banker and business executive; *Chairman, Tokyo Star Bank;* b. 3 Oct. 1931, Tokyo; s. of Tsunesaburo Terasawa and Kura Terasawa; m. 1960; one s. three d.; ed Waseda Univ., Wharton Business School, Univ. of Pennsylvania, USA; Pres. Nomura Securities Int. 1970–80, Chair. 1980–85, Exec. Vice-Pres. Nomura Securities, Tokyo 1985–88; Dir-Gen. Econ. Planning Agency May–June 1994; Chair. Foreign Policy Cttee 1996–97; Sr Adviser Price Waterhouse 1998–99; Chair. Lone Star Japan Acquisitions 1999–2001; Chair. Tokyo Star Bank, 2001–; Exec. Vice-Pres. Multilateral Investment Guarantee Agency 1988–; Dir English-Speaking Union of Japan; fmr Fulbright Scholar; mem. New York Stock Exchange 1971–; Hon. Citizen New York City 1972. *Publications:* Night and Day on Wall Street, Windblown on Wall Street, Think Big!!, From the Window of Washington, DC.

TEREKHOVA, Margarita Borisovna; Russian actress and filmmaker; b. 25 Aug. 1942, Turinsk, the Urals; d. of Galina Stanislavovna Tomashevich and Boris Ivanovich Terekhov; one s. one d.; ed Tashkent Univ. and Mossoviet Studio School; with Mossoviet Theatre 1964–83; Founder and Dir of Theatre Studio (Balaganchik) 1987–; film debut 1966; RSFSR Artist of Merit 1976, K. Stanislavsky Prize 1992. *Films include:* Hi! It's Me! 1966, Byelorussian Station 1971, My Life 1972, Monologue 1973, Mirror 1975, Day Train 1976, Who'll go to Truskovets? 1977, Dog in a Manger 1977, Kids, Kids, Kids 1978, D'Artagnan and the Three Musketeers 1978, Let's get Married 1983, Only for

Crazy 1991 (San Remo Int. Film Festival Prize), Forbidden Fruit 1993, The Way 1995, The Seagull 2002–2004 (also dir and scriptwriter). *Theatre:* (dir and actress) When Five Years Elapse, The Tsar's Hunt, Mossoviet Theatre, Bel Ami. *Radio:* A Game for Two, adaptations from the Bible. *Television:* Players, Manon Lescaut, Childhood. *Leisure interest:* son's upbringing and educ. *Address:* Mossovet Theatre, B. Sadovaya Str. 16, Moscow (office); Bolshaya Gruzinskaya Str. 57, Apt. 92, 123056 Moscow, Russia. *Telephone:* (495) 254-96-95. *Fax:* (495) 254-96-95 (home); (495) 299-44-37. *E-mail:* terekh.m@mail.ru.

TERENGGANU, HM The Sultan of; Tuanku Mizan Zainal Abidin; Malaysian; *Yang di-Pertuan Agong (Supreme Head of State);* b. 22 Jan. 1962, Kuala Terengganu; s. of the late Sultan Mahmud Al Muktafi Billah Shah and Bariah binti Hishamuddin Alam Shah; m. Permaisuri Nur Zahirah Cik Puan Seri Rozita Adil Bakeri 1996; one s. one d.; apptd Heir Apparent Yang di-Pertuan Muda of Terengganu 1979; 16th Sultan of Terengganu 1998–; Timbalan Yang di-Pertuan Agong (Deputy Supreme Head of State) 1999–2006; Col-in-Chief Royal Armoured Corps; elected as 13th Yang di-Pertuan Agong (Supreme Head of State) 13 Dec. 2006, crowned 26 April 2007. *Address:* Istana Badariah, 20500 Kuala Terengganu, Malaysia (office).

TERENIUS, Lars Yngve, PhD; Swedish medical research scientist and academic; *Professor of Experimental Alcohol and Drug Dependence Research, Karolinska Institute;* b. 9 July 1940, Örebro; s. of Yngve Terenius and Margareta Hallenborg; m. 1st Malin Åkerblom 1962 (divorced 1986); m. 2nd Mona Hagman 1989; two s.; ed Faculties of Science and Medicine, Uppsala Univ.; Asst Prof. of Pharmacology, Medical Faculty, Uppsala Univ. 1969–79, Prof. of Pharmacology, Faculty of Pharmacy 1979–89; Prof. of Experimental Alcohol and Drug Dependence Research, Karolinska Inst. 1989–; Visiting Scientist Nat. Inst. for Medical Research, London 1972–73, Univ. of Aberdeen, Scotland 1975, Hebrew Univ., Jerusalem 1983, 1986; Fogarty Scholar, NIH, USA 1988–89; mem. Royal Swedish Soc. of Sciences, Royal Swedish Acad. of Sciences, Academia Europaea, American Acad. of Arts and Sciences, IPSEN Award 2000; Dr hc (Uppsala) 1981, (Trondheim) 1983; Olof Rudbeck Prize 1999; Pacesetter Award 1977, Gairdner Award 1978, Jahre Award 1980, Björkén Award of Uppsala Univ. 1984, IPSEN Award 2000. *Publications:* 400 papers on experimental endocrinology, cancer research, neurobiology. *Address:* Department of Experimental Drug Dependence Research, L8: 01, Karolinska Institute, 17176 Stockholm (office); Kyrkogårdsgatan 29, 75312 Uppsala, Sweden (home). *Telephone:* (8) 5177-48-60 (office). *Fax:* (8) 34-19-39 (office). *E-mail:* lars.terenius@cmm.ki.se (office). *Website:* www.ki.se (office).

TERENTYEVA, Nina Nikolayevna; Russian singer (mezzo-soprano); b. 9 Jan. 1946, Kusa, Chelyabinsk Region; d. of Nikolai Fedorovich and Tatyana Vladimirovna Terentyev; one d.; ed Leningrad State Conservatory (class of Olga Mshanskaya); soloist Kirov (now Mariinsky) Theatre 1971–77, Bolshoi 1979; leading solo mezzo-soprano; People's Artist of Russia. *Russian repertoire includes:* Marta in Khovanshchina, Lubasha in Tsar's Bride, Lubava in Sadko, Marina Mnishek in Boris Godunov, also Amneris in Aida, Azucena in Il Trovatore, Delila in Samson and Delila, Eboli in Don Carlos, Santuzza in Cavalleria Rusticana and others; participated in productions of maj. theatres of the world including Covent Garden (Amneris 1995), Metropolitan-Opera (Eboli 1993), La Scala (oratorio Ivan Grozny with R. Muti 1994), also in Deutsche Oper and Staatsoper Berlin, Munich, Hamburg, Bordeaux, Los Angeles opera houses; participated in int. festivals; concert repertoire comprises Russian classics. *Leisure interest:* driving. *Address:* Bolshoi Theatre, Teatralnaya pl. 1, 103009 Moscow, Russia (office). *Telephone:* (495) 971-67-61 (home).

TERESHCHENKO, Sergei, BSc; Kazakhstani politician; *Chairman, Otan (Fatherland) Party;* b. 30 March 1951, Lesozavodsk, Primorskiy Region; s. of Aleksandr Ivanovich Tereshchenko and Tamara Ivanovna Tereshchenko; m. Yevgenya Tsykunova; two d.; ed Alma-Ata Inst. of Agric., Moscow Univ. of Commerce; held offices in state power organs of Chimkent Region 1986–89, Chair. of the Exec. Cttee of Chimkent Region 1990–91; First Deputy-Chair. Council of Ministers of Kazakh Soviet Repub. 1989–90; Vice-Pres. of Kazakhstan April–May 1991; Prime Minister of Kazakhstan 1991–94; Minister of Foreign Affairs 1994–95; Chair. Bd of Dirs Integrazia Fund 1994–; Vice-Chair. Republican (Otan) Party 1999–2002, Deputy Chair. Ass. of the Peoples of Kazakhstan Oct. 2002–; Order of Dostyk (First Class) 1999; State Prize for Peace and Spiritual Content 1999. *Publications include:* Kazakh Land is My Cradle 1999, Kazakhstan, Reforms, Market 2000. *Leisure interests:* hunting, swimming, fashion, travelling. *Address:* 92 Maoulenov str., 480012 Almaty (office); 121-18 Kounaev str., 480100 Almaty, Kazakhstan (home). *Telephone:* (727) 262-40-57 (office); (727) 263-36-18 (home). *Fax:* (727) 262-14-96 (office). *E-mail:* tyelena@nursat.kz (home).

TERESHKOVA, Maj.-Gen. Valentina Vladimirovna, CandTechSc; Russian politician and fmr cosmonaut; *Head, Russian Centre for International Scientific and Cultural Co-operation;* b. 6 March 1937, Maslennikovo, Yaroslavl Region; d. of the late Vladimir Aksyonovich Tereshkov and Elena Fyodorovna Tereshkova; m. 1963 (divorced); one d.; ed Yaroslavl Textile Coll. and Zhukovsky Air Force Engineering Acad.; fmr textile worker, Krasny Perekop textile mill, Yaroslavl; Textile Mill Sec., Young Communist League 1960; joined Yaroslavl Air Sports Club 1959 and started parachute jumping; mem. CPSU 1962–91, Cen. Cttee CPSU 1971–90; began cosmonaut training March 1962; made 48 orbits of the Earth in spaceship Vostok VI 16–19 June 1963; first woman in world to enter space; Deputy to USSR Supreme Soviet 1966–90; USSR People's Deputy 1989–91; Chair. Soviet Women's Cttee 1968–87; mem. Supreme Soviet Presidium 1970–90; Head Union of Soviet Socs. for Friendship and Cultural Relations with Foreign Countries 1987–92; Chair. then Dir of Presidium, Russian Asscn of Int. Co-operation (now Russian Centre of Int. Scientific and Cultural Co-operation) 1992–; Pres. Moscow

House of Europe 1992–; Head Russian Centre for Int. Scientific and Cultural Co-operation 1994–; visit to UK 1977; Pilot-Cosmonaut of USSR, Hero of Soviet Union, Joliot-Curie Gold Medal, World Peace Council 1966, Order of the Nile (Egypt) 1971 and other decorations. *Address:* Russian Centre of International Co-operation, 103885 Moscow, Vozdvizhenka Str. 14–18, Russia. *Telephone:* (495) 290-12-45.

TERFEL, Bryn, CBE; British singer (bass-baritone); b. (Bryn Terfel Jones), 9 Nov. 1965, Pantglas, Snowdonia, Wales; s. of Hefin Jones and Nesta Jones; m. Lesley Halliday 1987; three s.; ed Ysgol Dyffryn Nantlle, Penygroes, Gwynedd and Guildhall School of Music and Drama; debut, WNO as Guglielmo 1990; sang Mozart's Figaro at Santa Fe Opera and ENO 1991; Royal Nat. Opera, Covent Garden debut as Masetto in Don Giovanni 1992, repeated on tour to Japan; sang at Salzburg Festival as the Spirit Messenger in Die Frau ohne Schatten, and as Jochanaan in Salome 1992, returning as Leporello in Patrice Chéreau's production of Don Giovanni 1994; further appearances at Vienna Staatsoper as Mozart's Figaro 1993, at Chicago as Donner in Das Rheingold, debuts at New York Metropolitan Opera 1994, Sydney Opera House 1999, and frequent guest soloist with Berlin Philharmonic Orchestra; sang in the Brahms Requiem under Colin Davis and at Salzburg Easter Festival under Abbado (Herbert von Karajan In Memoriam) 1993; sang Nick Shadow in The Rake's Progress for WNO 1996, Figaro at La Scala 1997, Scarpia for Netherlands Opera 1998, Falstaff at the reopening of the Royal Opera House, Covent Garden 1999; four male roles in Les Contes d'Hoffmann, and Don Giovanni, both at Metropolitan Opera, New York, and Nick Shadow in The Rake's Progress for San Francisco Opera 1999–2000; BBC London Proms 2002; baritone roles in Les Contes d'Hoffmann at the Opéra Bastille, Sweeney Todd in Chicago, and Falstaff and Don Giovanni at Covent Garden 2002–03; Mephistopheles in Faust, Wotan in Das Rheingold and Die Walküre at Covent Garden 2004; many concert appearances in Europe, USA, Canada, Japan and Australia; Pres. Nat. Youth Choir of Wales, Festival of Wales; Vice-Pres. Llangollen Int. Eisteddfod; Founder, Faenol Festival 2000–; Hon. Fellow, Univ. of Wales, Aberystwyth, Welsh Coll. of Music and Drama, Univ. of Wales, Bangor; Hon. DMus (Glamorgan) 1997; White Robe, Gorsedd, recipient Kathleen Ferrier Scholarship 1988, Gold Medal Award 1989, Lieder Prize Cardiff Singer of the World Competition 1989, Gramophone magazine Young Singer of the Year 1992, British Critics Circle Award 1992, Int. Classical Music Awards Newcomer of Year 1993, Classical BRIT Award for Male Artist of the Year 2004, 2005, Nordoff-Robbins Silver Clef Classical Award 2006, Queen's Medal for Music 2006. *Recordings include:* Salome, Le nozze di Figaro, An Die Musik, Wagner Arias, Britten's Gloriana, Beethoven's Ninth Symphony, Brahms' Requiem, Schwanengesang, Cecilia and Bryn, If Ever I Would Leave You, Handel Arias, Vagabond (Caecillia Prize 1995, Gramophone People's Award 1996) 1995, Opera Arias (Grammy Award for best classical vocal performance) 1996, Something Wonderful (Britannia Record Club Members' Award) 1997, Don Giovanni 1997, Bryn (Classical BRIT Award for Best Album 2004) 2003, Simple Gifts (Grammy Award for Best Classical Crossover Album 2007) 2005, Tutto Mozart! 2006, First Love: Songs from the British Isles 2008. *Leisure interests:* golf, collecting fob watches, supporting Manchester United. *Address:* c/o Harlequin Agency, 203 Fidlas Road, Cardiff, CF14 5NA, Wales (office). *Telephone:* (29) 2075-0821 (office). *Fax:* (29) 2075-5971 (office).

TEROKHIN, Serhiy Anatolijovych; Ukrainian politician; b. 29 Sept. 1963, Kyiv; ed Nat. Taras Shevchenko Univ. of Kyiv, Vienna Univ. of Econs, Austria, Aspen Inst.; joined Army 1986–88; Asst Head of Admin, Head of Marketing, Ukrainian Republican Bank, State Bank of USSR 1988–91; Head Monetary and Financial Dept, Minister of External Econ. Relations 1991–92; Chief Dept of Monetary and Financial Policy, Econ. Bd, State Duma June–Nov. 1992; Deputy Minister of the Economy and Head Dept of Financial and External Econ. Activity 1992–93; Dir Ukrainian Fund on Support of Reforms 1993–94; mem. Parl. 1994–; Scientific Researcher Harvard Univ. 1995; Minister of the Economy 2005; mem. Reforms and Order party; Co-Dir Open Soc. Inst.; Head Asscn of Tax Payers of Ukraine 1999–. *Publications:* over 100 works. *Address:* c/o Ministry of the Economy, vul. M. Hrushevskoho 12/2, 01008 Kyiv, Ukraine (office).

TERRAGNO, Rodolfo H., DJur; Argentine politician; b. 16 Nov. 1945, Buenos Aires; m. Sonía Pascual Sánchez; two s.; ed Univ. de Buenos Aires; Asst Prof. Univ. de Buenos Aires 1973–80; researcher Inst. of Latin American Studies, London 1980–82, LSE 1980–82; Pres. Terragno SA de Industrias Químicas 1970–76; Exec. Vice-Pres. El Diario de Caracas SA 1976–80; Vice-Pres. Alas Enterprises Inc., NY 1982–86; Dir Letters SAR, Luxembourg 1982–86, Latin American Newsletters Ltd, London and Paris 1982–86; also columnist on several newspapers; rep. at int. conferences, including dispute with UK over Falkland Islands 1983–85; Sec. to Cabinet 1987, Minister of Works and Public Services 1987–89; Pres. Fundación Argentina Siglo 21 1986–87. *Publications:* Los dueños del poder 1972, Los 400 días de Perón 1974–75, Contratapas 1976, Muerte y resurrección de los políticos 1981, La Argentina del Siglo 21 1985–87, also numerous research papers.

TERRAZAS SANDOVAL, HE Cardinal Julio; Bolivian ecclesiastic; *Archbishop of Santa Cruz de la Sierra;* b. 7 March 1936, Vallegrande; ed Emacas Univ.; ordained priest 1962; consecrated Titular Bishop of La Paz 1978–82; Bishop of Oruro 1982–91; Archbishop of Santa Cruz 1991–; cr. Cardinal 2001, apptd Cardinal-Priest of S. Giovanni Battista de' Rossi; elected Pres. Bolivian Episcopal Conf. 1985, re-elected 1988, 2001; named one of the 100 most important people in the world by El Pais newspaper 2008. *Address:* Arzobispado, Casilla 25, Calle Ingavi 49, Santa Cruz, Bolivia (office). *Telephone:* (3) 32-4286 (office). *Fax:* (3) 33-0181 (office). *E-mail:* asc@scbbs-bo.com (office).

TERRY, John Quinlan, AADip, FRIBA; British architect; b. 24 July 1937, London; s. of the late Philip Terry and Phyllis Terry; m. Christina de Ruttié 1961; one s. four d.; ed Bryanston School, Architectural Asscn; joined late Raymond Erith RA 1962–73; work includes Kingswalden Bury, the New Common Room Bldg at Gray's Inn, the restoration of St Mary's Church on Paddington Green; Partner Erith and Terry 1967–; in pvt. practice (latterly under name Quinlan and Francis Terry) 1973–, work includes large classical pvt. houses in stone erected in England, USA and Germany including six pvt. villas in Regent's Park for Crown Estate Commrs, offices, shops and flats at Richmond Riverside, new Lecture Theatre, Jr Common Room, Library and residential bldgs for Downing Coll. Cambridge, Brentwood Cathedral, restoration of the three State Rooms at No. 10 Downing Street, restoration of St Helen's Church, Bishopsgate, new commercial bldg 20–32 Baker Street, new retail bldg at Merchant Square, Colonial Williamsburg, Va; mem. Royal Fine Art Comm. 1994–97; Rome Scholar 1969, Prix Int. de la Reconstruction 1983, Building of the Year Award 1994, Georgian Groups' Award for Best Modern Classical House 2005, Richard H. Driehaus Prize 2005. *Publications:* Architectural Monographs 1991, Architects Anonymous 1993, Radical Classicism 2006. *Leisure interest:* theology. *Address:* Old Exchange, High Street, Dedham, Colchester, Essex, CO7 6HA, England (office). *Telephone:* (1206) 323186 (office); (1206) 322370 (office). *Fax:* (1206) 322862 (office). *E-mail:* quinlan@qftarchitects.com (office). *Website:* www.qftarchitects.com (office).

TERZIĆ, Adnan, BA; Bosnia and Herzegovina politician; b. 1960, Zagreb; ed Univ. of Sarajevo; mem. Party of Democratic Action 1991–, Vice-Chair. 2001; served in army 1992–95; Gov. Cen. Bosnia canton 1997–98, 2000–01; Prime Minister 2002–2007, Head SDA Club of Reps, House of Reps 2000–02, concurrently Minister of European Integration. *Address:* Party of Democratic Action, Mehmeda Spahe 14, 71000 Sarajevo, Bosnia and Herzegovina (office). *Telephone:* (33) 472192 (office). *Fax:* (33) 650429 (office). *Website:* www.sda.ba (office).

TERZIEFF, Laurent Didier Alex; French actor and theatre director; b. 27 June 1935, Toulouse; s. of Jean Terzieff and Marie Terzieff (née Lapasset); ed Lycée Buffon, Paris; Officier Ordre nat. du Mérite, Commdr des Arts et des Lettres; numerous prizes and awards including Prix du disque français 1975, Grand prix nat. du théâtre (Ministry of Culture) 1984, Pirandello Prize (Italy) 1989. *Theatre includes:* as dir and actor: Zoo Story 1964, Tango 1968, Fragments 1978, Le Pic du bossu 1979, Le Philanthrope 1979, Les Amis 1981, L'Ambassade 1982, Guérison americaine 1984–85, Témoignage sur Ballybeg 1986, A pied 1987, Henri IV 1989, Ce que voit Fox 1988 (Molière Prize) 1990, Richard II 1991, Temps contre temps 1993 (Molière Prize); as actor: Meurtre dans la cathédrale 1994, Le Bonnet de fou 1997, Brulés par la glace 1999, Brecht, poète 2000, Le Regard 2002, Florilège 2003. *Cinema includes:* Les tricheurs 1958, Les régates de San Francisco, Le bois des amants 1960, Tu ne tueras point, Les garçons 1961, Les 7 péchés capitaux, Les culottes rouges 1962, Kapo 1966, La prisonnière 1967, Vanina Vanini 1967, La voie lactée 1968, Les gémeaux 1971, Medea 1973, Le désert des tartares 1977, Noces de sang 1980, La flambeuse 1981, Détective 1984, Diésel 1984, Rouge baiser 1985, Hiver 54 1989, Germinal 1993, Fiesta 1994, Pianiste 1997, Le manuscrit du prince 1999, Sur la plage 1999, Territori d'omba 2000, Peau d'ange 2002, Rien, voilà l'ordre 2003, Pontormo 2004, Mon petit doigt m'a dit 2005, J'ai toujours rêvé d'être un gangster 2007. *Television includes:* Bérénice, Le Beau françois, Moïse, Hedda Gabler, Rimbaud, Le Martyre de Saint Sébastien, La Flèche dans le coeur 1985, La Fille aux lilas 1985. *Address:* 8 rue du Dragon, 75006 Paris, France.

TESAURO, Giuseppe; Italian professor of international law; *President, Autorità Garante della Concorrenza e del Mercato;* b. 15 Nov. 1942, Naples; m. Paola Borrelli 1967; three c.; ed Liceo Umberto, Naples, Univ. of Naples, Max Planck Inst. Volkerrecht-Heidelberg; Asst Prof. of Int. Law, Univ. of Naples 1965–71; Prof. of Int. Law and Int. Org., Univs of Catania, Messina, Naples, Rome 1971–88; Dir EEC Law School, Univ. of Rome 1982–88; mem. Council Legal Affairs, Ministry of Foreign Affairs 1986–; Judge, First Advocate Gen. European Court of Justice 1988–98; Pres. Italian Competition Authority 1998–. *Publications:* Financing International Institutions 1968, Pollution of the Sea and International Law 1971, Nationalizations and International Law 1976, Movements of Capital in the EEC 1984, Course of EEC Law 1988. *Leisure interests:* tennis, football, sailing. *Address:* Autorità Garante della Concorrenza e del Mercato, Piazza Verdi 6/A, 00198 Rome, Italy (office). *Telephone:* (06) 858211 (office). *Fax:* (06) 85821256 (office). *E-mail:* antitrust@agcm.it (office). *Website:* www.agcm.it (office).

TESCH, Emmanuel Camille Georges Victor; Luxembourg iron and steel company executive and engineer; b. 9 Dec. 1920, Hespérange; s. of Georges Tesch and Marie-Laure Weckbecker; m. Thérèse Laval 1949; one s.; ed Technische Hochschule, Aachen and Eidgenössische Technische Hochschule, Zürich; engineer, Manufacture de Tabacs Heintz van Landewyck 1948–51; fmr Man. Dir Soc. Générale pour le Commerce de Produits Industriels (SOGECO); joined ARBED as auditor 1958, Dir 1968, Chair. Bd of Dirs 1972–91; Chair. Bd of Dirs ARBED Finance SA –1992, Electro Holding Co., SA Luxembourgeoise d'Exploitations Minières; Dir SIDMAR SA, Compagnie Maritime Belge, SOGECO SA, LE FOYER SA, Banque Générale du Luxembourg SA; Adviser Soc. Générale de Belgique, Companhia Siderurgica Belgo-Mineira; mem. Internationaler Beraterkreis der Allianz-Versicherungs-Gesellschaft, Conseil Economique et Social (Luxembourg); Pres. Chambre de Commerce du Grand-Duché de Luxembourg; Médaille de la Résistance (France); Grand Officer Ordre de la Couronne de Chêne (Luxembourg); Commdr avec Couronne dans l'Ordre de mérite civil et militaire d'Adolphe de Nassau (Luxembourg); Ordre de la Couronne (Belgium); Commdr Order of Orange-Nassau (Netherlands); Cavaliere di Gran Croce (Italy); Order of Tudor Vladimirescu (Romania); Hon. KBE;

Grosses Goldenes Ehrenzeichen mit Stern des Verdienstordens der Republik Österreich; Grosses Verdienstkreuz mit Stern des Verdienstordens der Bundesrepublik Deutschland; Encomienda de numero, Mérito Civil, Spain. *Leisure interests:* fishing, literature. *Address:* La Cléchère, 45 Route de Bettembourg, 1899 Kockelscheuer, Luxembourg (home). *Telephone:* 47-921 (office); 36-81-68 (home).

TESHABAEV, Fatikh G., PhD; Uzbekistan diplomatist; *Special Adviser in Uzbekistan, United Nations Development Programme (UNDP);* b. 18 Oct. 1939, Tashkent; s. of Gulam Ahmad Teshabaev and Hajiniso Teshabaev; m. Mauluda Teshabaev 1966; two s. one d.; ed Univs. of Tashkent and Delhi; First Deputy Minister for Foreign Affairs 1991–93; Amb. to USA and Perm. Rep. to UN 1993–96; Amb.-at-Large 1996–97; Amb. to UK 1997–99; Special Adviser, UNDP in Uzbekistan 2000–; Nehru Award. *Publications:* articles on political thought in oriental countries. *Leisure interest:* tennis. *Address:* United Nations Development Programme, 4 T. Shevchenko Street, 100029 Tashkent; Birinchitor Kucha Topqairagoch 12, 100081 Tashkent, Uzbekistan (home). *Telephone:* (71) 2791786 (home); (71) 1055860. *E-mail:* fatih.teshabaev@undp.org (office); teshabaev2002@yahoo.com.

TESSON, Philippe, DèsSc; French journalist; b. 1 March 1928, Wassigny (Aisne); s. of Albert Tesson and Jeanne Ancely; m. Dr Marie-Claude Millet 1969; one s. two d.; ed Coll. Stanislas, Inst. of Political Studies, Paris; Sec. of Parl. Debates 1957–60; Ed.-in-Chief, Combat 1960–74; candidate in legis. elections 1968; Diarist and Drama Critic, Canard Enchaîné 1970–83; Co-Man. and Dir Soc. d'Editions Scientifiques et Culturelles 1971, Pres. 1980; Dir and Ed.-in-Chief, Quotidien de Paris 1974; Dir Nouvelles Littéraires 1975–83; Drama Critic, L'Express Paris 1986; Dir and Co.-Man. Quotidien du Maire 1988; Animator (TV programme with France 3) A Quel Titre 1994–96; Ed. Valeurs actuelles 1994–; Drama Critic Revue des deux Mondes 1990–, Figaro Magazine 1995–; literary and theatre Corresp. Rive Droite/Rive Gauche (TV) 1997–2004; Dir Avant-scène Théâtre 2001–; Chevalier, Légion d'honneur. *Publication:* De Gaulle 1er 1965, Où est passée l'autorité? 2000. *Address:* L'Avant-scène Théâtre, 75 rue des Saints-Pères, 75006 Paris, France (office). *Telephone:* 1-53-63-80-60 (office). *Fax:* 1-53-63-88-75 (office). *E-mail:* contact@avant-scene-theatre.com (office). *Website:* www.avant-scene-theatre.com (office).

TESTER, Jonathan (Jon), BS; American politician and organic farmer; *Senator from Montana;* b. 21 Aug. 1956, Havre, Mont.; m. Sharla Tester; one s. one d.; ed Univ. of Great Falls; worked as custom butcher operator; fmr music teacher, Big Sandy School Dist; fmr Chair. Sandy School Bd of Trustees; served on Big Sandy Soil Conservation Service Cttee, Chouteau Co. Agricultural Stabilization and Conservation Service Cttee; elected to Mont. State Senate 1998, Minority Whip 2001, Minority Leader 2003, Pres. Mont. Senate 2005–06; Senator from Mont. 2007–, mem. Banking, Housing and Urban Affairs Cttee, Energy and Natural Resources Cttee, Homeland Security and Govt Affairs Cttee, Veterans' Affairs Cttee, Small Business and Entrepreneurship Cttee, Indian Affairs Cttee; Democrat. *Address:* Senate Dirksen Building, Room B40E, Washington, DC 20510, USA (office). *Telephone:* (202) 224-2644 (office). *Fax:* (202) 224-8594 (office). *Website:* tester.senate.gov (office); www.testerforsenate.com (office).

TESTINO, Mario; Peruvian fashion photographer; b. 1954, Lima; portfolio includes Madonna for Versace, Princess of Wales for Vanity Fair 1997, advertising campaign for Gucci, Sir Hardy Amies, John Galliano, Jade Jagger, Naomi Campbell, Devon Aoki and Alexander McQueen for Vogue's Millennium souvenir issue 2000; work exhibited in Nat. Portrait Gallery, London 2001–02. *Publications include:* Visionaire 35: Man 2000, Mario Testino: Portraits 2003, Mario Testino: Kids 2003, Let Me In 2007. *Address:* c/o Art Partner New York, 155 Sixth Avenue, 15th Floor, New York, NY 10013, USA (office). *Telephone:* (212) 343-9889 (office). *Fax:* (212) 343-9891. *Website:* info@artpartner.com (office).

TETANGCO, Amando M., Jr, AB (Econ), MA; Philippine central banker; *Governor, Bangko Sentral ng Pilipinas (Central Bank of the Philippines);* m. Elvira Ma. Plana; one s. two d.; ed Ateneo de Manila Univ., Univ. of Wisconsin-Madison, USA (Central Bank scholar); worked with Man. Services Div. of SGV & Co. 1973–74; joined Bangko Sentral ng Pilipinas (BSP— Cen. Bank of the Philippines) 1974, Deputy Gov. BSP in-charge of Banking Services Sector, Econ. Research and Treasury –2005, represented BSP at Nat. Econ. and Devt Authority Bd, Nat. Food Authority Council, Industrial Guarantee and Loan Fund Review Cttee, also served as Alt. Exec. Dir IMF, Washington, DC 1992–94, closely involved with various int. and regional orgs including Exec. Meeting of East Asia and Pacific Cen. Banks, ASEAN and ASEAN +3, South East Asia Cen. Banks (SEACEN) and APEC, Gov. BSP 2005–. *Address:* Bangko Sentral ng Pilipinas, A. Mabini Street, cnr Pablo Ocampo Street, Malate, 1004 Metro Manila, Philippines (office). *Telephone:* (2) 5247011 (office). *Fax:* (2) 5236210 (office). *E-mail:* bspmail@bsp.gov.ph (office). *Website:* www.bsp.gov.ph (office).

TETTAMANZI, HE Cardinal Dionigi; Italian ecclesiastic; *Archbishop of Milan;* b. 14 March 1934, Renate; ordained priest 1957; consecrated Bishop 1989; Metropolitan Archbishop of Ancona-Osma 1989–1991; Pres. Episcopal Conf., Marche region 1989; Pres. Bishops' Comm., CEI 1990, Sec.-Gen. CEI 1991, Vice-Pres. 1995–2000; Metropolitan Archbishop of Genoa 1995–2002; cr. Cardinal 1998; Archbishop of Milan 2002–. *Address:* Piazza Fontana 2, 20122 Milan, Italy. *Website:* www.diocesi.milano.it.

TEUFEL, Erwin; German politician; *Minister-President of Baden-Württemberg;* b. 4 Sept. 1939, Rottweil; m.; four c.; Dist Admin. Rottweil and Trossingen municipality 1961–64; Mayor of Spaichingen 1964–72; mem. State Parl. of Baden-Württemberg 1972–; Leader CDU Parl. Group 1978–91; Minister-Pres. of Baden-Württemberg 1991–; Chair. CDU-Baden-Württemberg 1991–; mem. Fed. Cttee of CDU. *Address:* Landtag von Baden-Württemberg, Haus des Landtags, Konrad-Adenauer-strasse 3, 70173 Stuttgart (office); Dreifaltigkeitsbergstrasse 44, 78549 Spaichingen, Germany (home). *Telephone:* (711) 20630 (office). *Fax:* (711) 2063299 (office). *E-mail:* post@lantag-bw.de. *Website:* www.landtag-bw.de (office).

TEVES, Margarito B., BA, MSc; Philippine government official and economist; *Secretary of Finance;* ed Universidad Cen. de Madrid, Spain, Williams Coll., USA; mem. Congress 1987–98, Chair. Cttee on Rural Devt, on Econ. Affairs; Chair. and CEO Think Tank Inc. 1998–2000; Pres. and CEO Land Bank of the Philippines 2000–05; Sec. of Finance 2005–; Chair. People's Credit and Finance Corpn, Philippine Crop Insurance Corpn; mem. Bd Manila Electric Co., PhilEquity Fund Inc.; mem. Council, Nat. Food Authority, Food Terminal Inc.; f. Corporate Planning Soc. of the Philippines; fmr Pres. Philippine Econ. Soc.; fmr Trustee Philippine Futuristics Soc. *Address:* Department of Finance, DOF Building, Roxas Boulearvd, cnr Pablo Ocampo Street, 1004 Metro Manila, Philippines (office). *Telephone:* (2) 4041774 (office). *Fax:* (2) 5219495 (office). *E-mail:* hotline@dof.gov.ph (office). *Website:* www.dof.gov.ph (office).

TÉVOÉDJRÈ, Albert, LèsL; Benin politician and international civil servant; *Ombudsman, Presidential Mediation Board;* b. 10 Nov. 1929, Porto Novo; s. of Joseph Tévoédjrè and Jeanne Singbo Tévoédjrè; m. Isabelle Ekué 1953; three s.; ed Toulouse Univ., France, Fribourg Univ., Switzerland, Institut Universitaire de Hautes Etudes Internationales, Geneva, Sloan School of Management and MIT, USA; teaching assignments include Lycée Delafosse, Dakar, Senegal 1952–54, Ecole Normale d'Institutrices, Cahors, France 1957–58, Lycée Victor Ballot, Porto Novo 1959–61, Geneva Africa Inst. 1963–64, Georgetown Univ., Washington, DC 1964; Sec. of State for Information 1961–62; Sec.-Gen. Union Africaine et Malgache (UAM) 1962–63; Research Assoc., Center for Int. Affairs, Harvard Univ. 1964–65; joined Int. Labour Office 1965, Regional Dir for Africa March 1966, Asst Dir-Gen. 1969–75, Deputy Dir-Gen. 1975; Dir Int. Inst. for Labour Studies 1975–84; Sec.-Gen. World Social Prospects Asscn (AMPS) 1980–; fmr Chief Ed. L'Etudiant d'Afrique Noire; Minister of Planning and Employment Promotion 1997–99; Chair. Millennium for Africa Comm. –2002; Special Envoy of the UN Sec.-Gen. in Ivory Coast 2003–05; Ombudsman, Presidential Mediation Bd (OPM) 2006–; Founding mem. Promotion Africaine (soc. to combat poverty in Africa); Founding mem. Nat. Liberation Movt and mem. Cttee 1958–60; Deputy Sec.-Gen. of Nat. Syndicate of Teachers, Dahomey 1959–60; Visiting Prof., Sorbonne, Paris 1979–, Univ. des Mutants, Dakar 1979–, Nat. Univ. of Côte d'Ivoire 1979–, Northwestern Univ. 1980; Int. Humanitarian Medal 1987. *Publications:* L'Afrique revoltée 1958, La formation des cadres africains en vue de la croissance économique 1965, Pan-Africanism in Action 1965, L'Afrique face aux problèmes du socialisme et de l'aide étrangère 1966, Une stratégie du progrès social en Afrique et la contribution de l'OIT 1969, Pour un contrat de solidarité 1976, La pauvreté—richesse des peuples 1978, etc. *Address:* Place de la République, 01BP, 1501 Port-Novo, Benin (office). *Telephone:* 20-21-20-22 (office). *Fax:* 20-21-44-36 (office). *E-mail:* webmaster@mediateur.gouv.bj (office). *Website:* www.mediateur.gouv.bj (office).

THABANE, Motsoahae Thomas, BA; Lesotho politician and civil servant; *Minister of Home Affairs and Public Safety;* b. 28 May 1939, Maseru; m.; two s. two d.; ed Univ. of South Africa (UNISA); worked as civil servant for 26 years, First Clerk Asst to Senate and Deputy to Clerk of the Senate, Parl. of Lesotho 1966–70, Asst Sec. (Admin), Ministries of Health and Education 1970–72, Prin. Sec. in various govt ministries including Justice 1972–76, Health 1978–83, Foreign Affairs 1983–85 and Interior 1985–86, Sec. to ruling Mil. Council and also political adviser to the Mil. 1986–88, Govt Sec. 1988–90; Minister of Foreign Affairs, Information and Broadcasting 1990–91; escaped to South Africa following mil. coup in April 1991, worked as devt consultant; following April 1993 democratic elections, re-opened an office as devt consultant and commodities broker 1994–95; joined Ind. Electoral Comm. as Prov. Office Admin. for Free State region, South Africa March–June 1994; Special Political Adviser to Prime Minister Dr Ntsu Mokhehle 1995–98; elected mem. Parl. (Abia constituency) 1998; Minister of Foreign Affairs 2001–02, of Home Affairs and Public Safety 2002–. *Leisure interests:* politics, reading, physical fitness, walking, light classic and traditional music, jazz rhythm and blues. *Address:* Ministry of Home Affairs and Public Safety, POB 174, Maseru 100, Lesotho (office). *Telephone:* 323771 (office). *Fax:* 310319 (office).

THAÇI, Hashim, PhD; Kosovo politician and fmr guerrilla leader; *Prime Minister;* b. 24 April 1968, Burojë; m.; one s.; ed Univ. of Zurich, Switzerland; fmr Commdr Kosovo Liberation Army, fmr Dir Political Group; Chair. Partia Demokratike e Kosovës (PDK—Democratic Party of Kosovo–fmrly Party for the Democratic Progress of Kosovo) 2000–, mem. Parl. Group 2006–; mem. and Prime Minister, Interim Admin. Council, Kosovo 1999–2001, Prime Minister of Kosovo 2008–. *Address:* Office of the Government of Kosovo, 10000 Prishtina, Rruga Nënë Terezë (office); Partia Demokratike e Kosovës, 10000 Prishtina, Rruge Nënë Terezë 20; Arbëria, Rruge Metush Krasniqi 22, 10000 Prishtina, Kosovo. *Telephone:* (38) 224262. *Fax:* (38) 223769. *E-mail:* webmaster@ks-gov.net (office); pdk@pdk-ks.org. *Website:* www.ks-gov.net/pm (office); www.pdk-ks.org.

THACKERAY, Balashaheb Keshav (Bal); Indian politician; *President, Shiv Sena;* b. 23 Jan. 1927; fmr cartoonist, Free Press Journal Mumbai and int. dailies; est. Marmik cartoon weekly 1960, Daily Saamana newspaper 1989, Dopahar ka Saamana; Founder-Pres. Shiv Sena. *Address:* Shiv Sena, Shiv Sena Bhavan, Ram Ganesh Gadkari Chowk, Dadar, Mumbai, 400 028, India (office). *Telephone:* (22) 24309128 (office). *E-mail:* shivalay@shivsena.org (office). *Website:* www.shivsena.org (office).

THADATHAMRONGVECH, Suchart, BSc, MSc, PhD; Thai politician; b. 8 Aug. 1952; ed Thammasat Univ., London School of Econs, UK, McMaster Univ., Canada, Nat. Defence Coll.; Vice Chancellor of Int. Relations and Research Div., Ramkhamhaeng Univ. 1991–93; mem. Prov. Waterworks Authority 1992–95; mem. Audit Cttee, Bangkok Metropolitan Bank PLC 1998–2002; mem. Bd of Dirs Bank for Agric. and Agricultural Cooperatives 2001; mem. Metropolitan Waterworks Authority 2001–02; adviser to Minister for Commerce 2003, to Minister for Energy 2003–05; Deputy Minister of Finance 2008, Minister of Finance 2008; fmr mem. Securities and Exchange Comm.; fmr mem. and Chair. Examination Cttee Ratchaburi Electricity Generating PLC, PTT PLC, Siam City Bank PLC, Pan Asia Footwear PLC. *Address:* c/o Ministry of Finance, Thanon Rama VI, Samsennai, Phaya Thai, Rajatevi, Bangkok 10400, Thailand (office). *Website:* www.mof.go.th (office).

THAHANE, Timothy T., BComm, MA; Lesotho government official and diplomatist; *Minister of Finance and Development Planning;* b. 2 Nov. 1940, Leribe; s. of Nicodemus Thahane and Beatrice Thahane; m. Dr Edith Mohapi 1972; one s. one d.; ed Lesotho High School, Univs of Newfoundland and Toronto, Canada; Asst Sec., Prin. Asst Sec., Cen. Planning Office 1968–70, Dir of Planning 1968–73; Amb. to EEC for Negotiations of Lomé Convention 1973–74; Alt. Exec. Dir (Africa Group 1) World Bank 1974–76, Exec. Dir 1976–78, representing 15 African countries and Trinidad and Tobago; Vice-Chair. and Chair., Jt Audit Cttee of World Bank Group 1976–78; Amb. to the USA 1978–80; Vice-Pres. UN Affairs, IBRD 1990–96; Deputy Gov. South African Reserve Bank 1996–2002; Minister of Finance and Devt Planning 2002–; Vice-Pres. and Sec., IBRD 1980–96; Dir Bd of Global Coalition for Africa, Washington 1992–; mem. Bd of Lesotho Bank (Vice-Chair. 1972–73), Third World Foundation, Centre for Econ. Devt and Population Activities, Washington, DC. *Publications:* articles on econ. planning and investment in Lesotho, Southern Africa and Africa in general. *Leisure interests:* reading, music. *Address:* Ministry of Finance and Development Planning, POB 395, Maseru 100, Lesotho (office). *Telephone:* 22310826 (office). *Fax:* 22310411 (office). *E-mail:* hmf@finance.gov.ls (office); thahanet@finance.gov.ls (office). *Website:* www.finance.gov.ls (office).

THAIN, John A., BS, MBA; American business executive; ed Massachusetts Inst. of Tech., Harvard Univ.; Chief Financial Officer and Head of Operations, Tech. and Finance The Goldman Sachs Group LP 1994–99, also Co-CEO for European Operations 1995–97, Dir 1998–2003, Pres. and Co-COO 1999, Pres. and Co-COO Goldman Sachs Inc. 1999–2003, Pres. and COO 2003; CEO New York Stock Exchange (NYSE) 2004–07 (NYSE Euronext, Inc. following merger of NYSE Group and Euronext NV in June 2006); Chair. and CEO Merrill Lynch & Co., Inc. 2007–09 (resgnd); mem. Bd Dirs Blackrock Inc.; mem. several visiting cttees at MIT Sloan School of Management, Int. Advisory Panel of Monetary Authority of Singapore, US Nat. Advisory Bd of INSEAD (Institut Européen d'Admin des Affaires), Bd of Mans of New York Botanical Garden, Bd of Mans of New York-Presbyterian Hosp., Harvard Business School Bd of Dean's Advisors, Partnership for New York City. *Address:* c/o Merril Lynch & Co., Inc., Global Headquarters, 4 World Financial Center, 250 Vesey Street, New York, NY 10080, USA (office).

THAKSIN SHINAWATRA, PhD; Thai politician and police officer; b. 26 July 1949, Chiangmai; m. Pojaman Shinawatra (divorced 2008); three c.; ed Police Cadet Acad., Eastern Kentucky Univ., Sam Houston State Univ., USA; joined Royal Thai Police Dept 1973, Lt-Col 1987, resgnd 1987; Chair. Shinawatra Computer and Communications Group 1987–94; Minister of Foreign Affairs 1994–95; Leader Palang Dharma Party 1995–96; Deputy Prime Minister in charge of Traffic and Transportation in Bangkok 1995–96, Deputy Prime Minister 1997; Prime Minister of Thailand 2001–06 (re-elected 2005, briefly resigned position 4 April–23 May 2006, ousted in bloodless coup by army generals led by Gen. Sonthi Boonyaratglin for alleged "corruption and devisiveness" while abroad visiting UN Gen. Ass. in New York 19 Sept. 2006); Founder and Leader Thai Rak Thai Party 1998–2006; Founder and Vice-Chair. THAICOM Foundation for Secondary Educ. 1993–; Pres. North-erners' Asscn of Thailand 1998–; Chair. Manchester City Football Club 2007–08; found guilty by Thai court of corruption in Oct. 2008 and sentenced in absentia to two years imprisonment; Hon. (External) mem. Police Cadet Acad. Council 1996–, Hon. mem. Asscn Ex-Mil. Officers 1998–; 1992 ASEAN Businessman of the Year Award, Lee Kuan Yew Exchange Fellowship 1994 and other awards. *Address:* c/o Manchester City Football Club, City of Manchester Stadium, SportCity, Manchester, M11 3FF, England (office).

THAKUR, Rameshwar, LLB, MA, FCA; Indian chartered accountant and politician; *Governor of Karnataka;* b. 28 July 1927, Thakur Gangti village, Godda Dist, Jharkhand; m. Narmada Thakur; two s. two d.; ed Bhagalpur, Patna Univ., Calcutta Univ., Inst. of Chartered Accountants of India, New Delhi; actively participated in Quit India Movt 1942, remained underground for nearly six months in Raj Mahal Hills, Santhal Parganas, arrested and detained in Cen. Jail, Dum Dum, Calcutta in connection with nat. movt 1946; took active part in health care, educational upliftment, social reforms and rural reconstruction activities, particularly in Santhal Parganas, Jharkhand; chartered accountant since 1953; Lecturer, City Coll., Calcutta Univ. 1955–60; Visiting Prof., Delhi Univ. 1960–73; mem. Rajya Sabha (Indian Nat. Congress) 1984–96; Union Minister of State for Finance (Revenue), Rural Devt and Parl. Affairs 1991–94; Gov. of Orissa 2004–07, of Andhra Pradesh (Additional Charge) 2006–07, of Karnataka 2007–; Pres. Inst. of Chartered Accountants of India 1966–67; Nat. Pres. All India Bharat Scouts & Guides 1998–2001, 2004–; Chair. Study Group on Banking Costs, Banking Comm., Govt of India 1978–82, Associated Journals Ltd 1987–91, Thakur Research Foundation, New Delhi, Rajenda Bhawan Trust, New Delhi; Director, Unit Trust of India four years, Export Credit and Guarantee Corpn three years, Punjab Nat. Bank 1978–82, Punjab, Haryana and Delhi Chambers of Commerce three years, Bd Govs Man. Devt Inst., Gurugaon, Haryana; Sec. Sanjay Gandhi Memorial Trust, Amethi, UP; Group Leader Indian Del. to World Congress of Scouts, Brussels 1964, Int. Congress of Accountants, Mexico 1982; Deputy Leader Indian Parl. Union Conf., Geneva 1984; Leader, 15th Asia Pacific Gathering, Colombo 1984, Indian Del. to 17th Gen. Ass., Coventry, UK 1987; Chair. World Congress of Scouts & Guides Fellowship 1999; Trustee Hari Devi Smarak Nidhi and Gadadhar Mishra Smarak Nidhi public charitable trusts; engaged in Khadi & Village Industries, Rural Devt Programmes, Godda Dist, Jharkhand since 1965. *Address:* Raj Bhavan, Raj Bhavan Road, Bangalore 560 001, Karnatka, India (office). *Telephone:* (80) 2254101 (office); (80) 2253555 (office); (80) 2254102 (home). *Fax:* (80) 2258150 (office). *E-mail:* rbblr@vsnl.com (office). *Website:* rajbhavan.kar.nic.in (office).

THALER, Zoran; Slovenian business executive and fmr politician; *CEO, Si.mobil;* b. 21 Jan. 1962, Kranj; m.; one c.; ed Univ. of Ljubljana; with Yugoslavian Foreign Ministry 1987; took part in various int. confs; Deputy Minister of Foreign Affairs Slovenian Repub. 1990–93; mem. of Parl. 1990–97; mem. Liberal Democracy of Slovenia 1992; Chair. Parl. Cttee for Foreign Affairs 1993–95; Pres. Slovenian Inter parl. Group; Minister of Foreign Affairs 1995–96, 1997; in pvt. business 1996–; retd from politics 1997; Founder and Owner Int. Consulting Ltd 1997–; currently CEO Si.mobil. *Leisure interests:* sailing, skiing, gardening, travelling. *Address:* Si.mobil, Šmartinska cesta 134b, Ljubljana, Slovenia.

THAN, Field Marshall Shwe; Myanma politician, army officer and head of state; *Chairman of the State Peace and Development Council;* b. 2 Feb. 1933, Kyaukse; m. Daw Kyaing Kyaing; joined army aged 20; positions included time spent in dept of psychological warfare; several other positions in army after mil. coup that ousted Prime Minister U Nu in 1962, including promotion to Lt-Col 1972, to Col 1978, to Commdr of Mil. Dist of South West 1983, Asst Man. of Gen. Staff of the Army, Brig.-Gen. and Vice-Minister of Defence 1985, Maj.-Gen. 1986; mem. Cen. Exec. Cttee 1986; Prime Minister 1992–2003, Minister of Defence 1992–; Chair. State Law and Order Restoration Council (SLORC) 1992–97, Chair. State Peace and Devt Council (SDP) 1997–. *Address:* Ministry of Defence, Ahlanpya Phaya Street, Yangon; Office of the Chairman of the State Peace and Development Council, 15–16 Windermere Park, Yangon, Myanmar. *Telephone:* (1) 281611 (Ministry); (1) 282445.

THANAJARO, Gen. Chettha; Thai politician; *Leader, Ruam Jai Thai Chart Pattana (Thais United National Development);* fmr Deputy Army Com-mander, later C-in-C; fmr Minister of Science and Tech.; Minister of Defence 2004–05; currently Leader, Ruam Jai Thai Chart Pattana (Thais United Nat. Devt); Pres. Olympic Cttee of Thailand. *Address:* Ruam Jai Thai Chart Pattana (Thais United National Development), c/o House of Representatives, Bangkok, Thailand (office).

THANH, Lt-Gen. Phung Quang; Vietnamese military officer and govern-ment official; *Minister of Defence;* b. 2 Feb. 1949, Vin Phuc Prov.; ed Univ. of Mil. Science; fmr Commdr First Mil. Zone; fmr Chief of Gen. Staff, People's Army of Viet Nam and Deputy Minister of Defence; Minister of Defence 2006–; mem. CP of Viet Nam Central Cttee (CPVCC); mem. Politburo. *Address:* Ministry of National Defence, 1a Hoang Dieu, Ba Dinh District, Hanoi, Viet Nam (office). *Telephone:* (4) 069 882041 (office). *Fax:* (4) 069 532090 (office).

THANHAWLA, Lal, BA; Indian politician; *Chief Minister of Mizoram;* b. 19 May 1942, Durtlang, Aizawl, Mizoram; s. of H. P. Sailo and Lalsawmliani; m. Lal Riliani 1970; one s. two d.; ed Gauhati Univ.; joined Indian Nat. Congress 1967, mem. All India Congress Cttee 1973–, Pres. Mizoram Pradesh Congress Cttee 1973–2009; mem. Mizoram Legis. Ass. 1978, 1979, 1984, 1989, 1994, 2003–08, Chief Minister 1984–87, 1989–98, 2008–, Leader of Opposition 1978–84, 1987–89, 2003–08; mem. Congress Working Cttee; mem. 9th Finance Comm. of India; Chair. NE Olympic Comm.; Founder-Ed. Remna Arsi & Mizo Aw (daily newspaper); Chair. Literary Cttee of Nat. Devt Council; Pres. Mizoram Olympic Asscn; mem. Nat. Interpretation Council; Life mem. YMCA, Evangelical Fellowship of India, Bible Soc. of India; 12 nat. and int. awards for contribs to peace and social work. *Leisure interests:* gardening, reading. *Address:* Chief Minister's Office, McDonald Hill, Zarkawt, Aizawl 796001, Mizoram (office); A/14 Zarkawt, Aizawl, Mizoram, India (home). *Telephone:* (389) 2322150 (office); (389) 2343461 (home) *Fax:* (389) 2322245 (office); (389) 2342898 (home). *E-mail:* cm-mizoram@nic.com (office); hawla19@yahoo.com (office). *Website:* mizoram.nic.in (office).

THANI, Sheikh Abdul Aziz ibn Khalifa ath-, BS; Qatari politician, international official and petroleum industry executive; *Chairman, State of Qatar Investment Board;* b. 12 Dec. 1948, Doha; one s. three d.; ed Northern Indiana Univ., USA; Deputy Minister of Finance and Petroleum June–Dec. 1972, Minister of Finance and Petroleum, State of Qatar 1972; Chair. State of Qatar Investment Bd 1972–, Qatar Nat. Bank 1972, Qatar Gen. Petroleum Corpn 1973–; Gov. IMF and IBRD (World Bank) 1972; rep. at numerous int. confs including OPEC, OAPEC and Arab, Islamic and non-aligned summit confs. *Leisure interest:* scuba diving. *Address:* c/o Qatar General Petroleum Corporation, PO Box 3212, Doha, Qatar.

THANI, Sheikh Abdullah bin Khalifa ath-; Qatari politician; b. 25 Dec. 1959, Doha; ed Royal Military Acad., Sandhurst UK; various positions within Qatar Armed Forces 1976–89; Minister of the Interior 1989–96; Deputy Prime Minister 1995–96; Prime Minister of Qatar 1996–2007 (resgnd); Chair. Qatari Olympic Cttee 1979–89. *Address:* c/o Office of the Prime Minister, PO Box 923, Doha, Qatar.

THANI, Abdullah Saud Al-, BA, MBA; Qatari banking official; *Governor, Qatar Central Bank;* worked in Foreign Exchange Dept, Qatar Cen. Bank 1982–89, Deputy Gov. 1990–2001, Gov. 2006–; Chair. Qatar Industrial Devt Bank 1996–; Chair. State Audit Bureau 2001–06; Pres. Gen. Retirement and

Pension Authority 2006–; mem. Bd of Dirs Coll. of Business and Economy, Qatar Univ. 2006–. *Address:* Qatar Central Bank, POB 1234, Doha, Qatar (office). *Telephone:* 4456400 (office); 4456456 (office). *Fax:* 4415587 (office). *E-mail:* g@qcb.gov.qa (office). *Website:* www.qcb.gov.qa (office).

THANI, Sheikh Hamad bin Jasim bin Jaber ath-; Qatari politician; *Prime Minister and Minister of Foreign Affairs;* b. 1959; Dir Office of the Minister of Municipal Affairs and Agric. 1982–89, Minister of Municipal Affairs and Agric. 1989–92; Deputy Minister of Electricity and Water 1990–92; Minister of Foreign Affairs 1992–; First Deputy Prime Minister 2003–07; Prime Minister 2007–; Head Perm. Cttee for the Support of Al Quds 1998–; mem. Supreme Defence Council 1996–, Parl. Constitution Cttee 1999–, Ruling Family Council 2000–; CEO Supreme Council for the Investment of the Reserves of State (Qatar Investment Authority) 2000–; fmr Chair. Qatar Electricity and Water Co.; fmr Pres. Cen. Municipal Council, Special Emiri Projects Office; fmr Dir Special Emiri Projects Office; fmr mem. Bd of Dirs Qatar Petroleum, Supreme Council for Planning. *Address:* Ministry of Foreign Affairs, POB 250, Doha (office); Qatar Investment Authority, PO Box 23224, Doha, Qatar. *Telephone:* 4334334 (office). *Fax:* 4442777 (office). *E-mail:* webmaster@mofa.gov.qa (office). *Website:* www.mofa.gov.qa (office).

THANI, Sheikh Hamad bin Khalifa ath-, (Amir of Qatar); b. 1952, Doha; s. of Sheikh Khalifa bin Hamad ath-Thani; m. Sheikha Mozah bint Nasser al-Missned; five s. (including Sheikh Tamim bin Hamad bin Khalifa ath-Thani) two d.; ed Royal Mil. Coll., Sandhurst, UK; apptd Heir-Apparent May 1977; Commdr First Mobile Bn (now Hamad Mobile Bn); Maj., then Maj.-Gen., C-in-C Armed Forces of Qatar; Minister of Defence May 1977–; Amir of Qatar 27 June 1995–; Prime Minister 1995–96; Supreme Pres. Higher Planning Council; Pres. Higher Youth Council 1979–91; f. Mil. Sports Fed.; mem. Int. Mil. Sports Fed.; Pres. Qatari Nat. Olympic Cttee 2000–; mem. IOC (mem. Sports for All Cttee.); Chair. Organizing Cttee. 15th Asian Games 2006; Head, Upper Council of Environment and Natural Sanctuaries; Orders of Merit from Egypt, France, Indonesia, Lebanon, Morocco, Oman, Saudi Arabia, UK, Venezuela. *Address:* The Royal Palace, PO Box 923, Doha, Qatar.

THANI, Sheikh Khalifa bin Hamad ath-, (fmr Amir of Qatar); b. 1932, Doha; s. of the late Heir Apparent Sheikh Hamad bin Abdullah bin Jassim ath-Thani; son, Sheikh Hamad bin Khalifa ath-Thani; ed Royal Mil. Coll., Sandhurst, UK; apptd Heir Apparent 1948; served successively as Chief of Security Forces, Chief of Civil Courts, Minister of Educ., Finance and Petroleum; Deputy Ruler 1960–72, also Minister of Educ. 1960–70; Prime Minister 1970–72, Minister of Finance 1970–72; Chair. Investment Bd for State Reserves 1972; deposed his cousin Sheikh Ahmad and took office as Amir of Qatar 1972, deposed by his son June 1995.

THANI, HH Sheikh Tamim bin Hamad bin Khalifa ath-; Qatari; *Heir Apparent and Commander-in-Chief of the Armed Forces;* b. 3 June 1980, Doha; s. of Sheikh Hamad bin Khalifa ath-Thani and Sheikha Mozah bint Nasser al-Missned; m. Sheikha Jawahar bint Hamad bin Sohaim ath-Thani 2005; ed Sherborne School and Royal Mil. Acad., Sandhurst, UK; proclaimed Heir Apparent 8 Aug. 2003; Officer Qatar Armed Forces 1997– (now C-in-C of the Armed Forces); Head Upper Council of the Environment and Natural Sanctuaries; Pres. as-Sadd Sports Club 1999–2000; Chair. Qatar Nat. Olympic Cttee 2000–, Organizing Cttee Asian Games, Doha 2006; mem. IOC, Supreme Educ. Council; Chair. ictQATAR programme 2005–; Sheikh Zayed bin Sultan al-Nahyan Medal of Honor, UAE 2004, Issa bin Salman al-Khalifa Order of Merit – Excellence Class, Bahrain 2004. *Address:* The Royal Palace, POB 923, Doha, Qatar (office). *Website:* www.diwan.gov.qa.

THANIN KRAIVICHIEN (see Kraivichien, Thanin).

THAPA, Bhek Bahadur; Nepalese diplomatist and politician; fmr Amb. to USA, Amb. to India 1997–2003; Special Rep. for Foreign Affairs 2003–04, Minister of Foreign Affairs 2004; Amb.-at-Large 2004–. *Address:* Shital Niwas, Maharaganj, Kathmandu, Nepal (office). *Telephone:* (1) 4416011 (office). *Fax:* (1) 4416016 (office). *E-mail:* mofa@mos.com.np (office). *Website:* www.mofa.gov.np (office).

THAPA, Gen. Pyar Jung, BA; Nepalese army officer; b. 15 Sept. 1946; ed St Xavier High School, Tribhuvan Univ., Royal Mil. Acad., Sandhurst, UK, US Army War Coll., USA; joined Royal Nepalese Army 1964, Second Lt Singh Nath Battalion, promoted to rank of Maj.-Gen. 1998, Asst Chief of Army Staff 1998–2002, Dir Integrated Security and Devt Program, promoted to rank of Lt-Gen. 2001, Chief of Army Staff 2002–06; Battalion Commdr UN Interim Force in Lebanon 1986, Deputy Sector Commdr Sector West, UN Protection Forces in Fmr Yugoslavia 1992. *Address:* c/o Army Headquarters, Singha Durbar, Kathmandu, Nepal (office).

THAPA, Ram Bahadur, (Badal); Nepalese politician and fmr guerrilla commander; *Minister of Defence;* b. 1955; s. of Karn Bahjadur Thapa Magar and Nanda Kumari Thapa Magar; mem. Cen. Cttee CP of Nepal (Maoist), coordinator of cen. advisory council of Magar Nat. Liberation Front; coordinator of cand. selection cttee for Constituent Ass. election 2008; Minister of Defence 2008–. *Address:* Ministry of Defence, Singha Durbar, Kathmandu, Nepal (office). *Telephone:* (1) 4211290 (office). *Fax:* (1) 4211294 (office). *Website:* www.cpnm.org.

THAPA, Surya Bahadur; Nepalese politician; *President, Rashtriya Janashakti Party;* b. 20 March 1928, Muga, East Nepal; s. of Bahadur Thapa; m. 1953; one s. three d.; ed Allahabad Univ., India; House Speaker, Advisory Ass. to King of Nepal 1958; mem. Upper House of Parl. 1959; Minister of Forests, Agric., Commerce and Industry 1960, of Finance and Econ. Affairs 1962; Vice-Chair. Council of Ministers, Minister of Finance, Econ. Planning, Law and Justice 1963; Vice-Chair. Council of Ministers, Minister of Finance, Law and Gen. Admin. 1964–65; Chair. Council of Ministers, Minister of Palace Affairs

1965–69; Prime Minister of Nepal and Minister of Palace Affairs 1979–83; Minister of Finance 1979–80, of Defence 1980–81, 1982–83, of Foreign Affairs 1982; Prime Minister of Nepal 1997–98, Prime Minister and Minister of Royal Palace Affairs, of Defence, of Home Affairs, of Foreign Affairs, of Industry, Commerce and Supplies, of Law, Justice and Parl. Affairs, of Agric. and Co-operatives, of Population and the Environment, of Water Resources, of Land Reforms and Man., of Women, Children and Social Welfare, of Forest and Soil Conservation, of Science and Tech., of Labour and Transport Man., of Gen. Admin., of Local Devt and of Health, Interim Govt 2003–04 (resgnd); Pres. Rashtriya Prajatantra Party 1990–2002; Pres. Rashtriya Janashakti Party (split from Rashtriya Prajatantra Party Nov. 2004) 2005–; mem. Royal Advisory Cttee 1969–72; arrested and released 1972, 1975; Hon. DLitt (Kurukshetra Univ.); Tri-Sahkti-Patta 1963, Gorkha Dakshinbahu I 1965, Om Rama Patta 1980; several Nepalese and foreign awards. *Address:* Rashtriya Janashakti Party (National People's Power Party), Ramalphokhari, Kathmandu, Nepal (office). *Telephone:* (1) 4437063 (office). *Fax:* (1) 4437064 (office). *E-mail:* rjpnepal@info.com.np (office).

THAPAR, Gautam; Indian business executive; *Vice-Chairman and Managing-Director, Ballapur Industries Limited (BILT);* nephew of Lalit Mohan Thapar; ed Doon School, St Stephen's Coll., Delhi, Pratt Inst., USA; trained as chemical engineer; joined family co. Ballapur Industries Ltd (BILT) 1986, held positions successively in paper mills and pulp unit, chemicals and foods businesses, Head of Finance 1997–98, CEO 1998–99, Man.-Dir Andra Pradesh Rayons (APR) Ltd 1999, Jt Man.-Dir BILT 1999, Vice-Chair. and Man.-Dir BILT 1999–; Chair. Crompton Greaves Ltd 2004–; mem. Bd of Dirs Asahi India Safety Glass Ltd 2002–, Pratham India Educ. Initiative 2003–. *Address:* Northern Region, Ballapur Industries Limited (BILT), Thapar House, 124 Janpath, New Delhi 110 001 (office); Ballapur Industries Limited, First India Place, Tower C, Mehrauli – Gurgaon Road, Gurgaon, Haryana 122 002, India (office). *Telephone:* (11) 23368332 (office); (124) 280424243 (office). *Fax:* (11) 23368729 (office); (124) 280426061 (office). *E-mail:* gthapar@vsnl.com (office); corpcom@bilt.com (office). *Website:* www.bilt.com (office).

THAROOR, Shashi, MA, MALD, PhD; Indian international organization official and writer; b. 9 March 1956, London, UK; s. of Chandran Tharoor and Lily Tharoor; divorced; twin s; ed St Stephen's Coll., Delhi Univ., Tufts Univ. Fletcher School of Law and Diplomacy, USA; int. civil servant and professional author; joined UN 1978; with UNHCR, served at Geneva HQ, Head of Office in Singapore; Special Asst for UN Peace-keeping operations; Exec. Asst to UN Sec.-Gen. 1997–98, Dir Communications and Special Projects, Office of the Sec.-Gen. 1998–2000; Interim Head of Dept of Public Information 2001–02, Head and Under-Sec.-Gen. for Public Information 2002–07; mem. Bd of Overseers Fletcher School of Law and Diplomacy, Bd of Trustees Aspen Inst. India, Advisory Bd World Policy Journal, Advisory Bd Virtue Foundation, Advisory Bd Breakthrough (human rights org.); Fellow, New York Inst. of the Humanities; Hon. DLitt; Pravasi Bharatiya Samman 2004; Commonwealth Writers' Prize, several journalism and literary awards; named Global Leader of Tomorrow by World Econ. Forum, Davos, Switzerland 1998. *Publications:* Reasons of State 1981, The Great Indian Novel 1989, The Five Dollar Smile and Other Stories 1990, Show Business 1992, India: From Midnight to the Millennium 1997, Riot 2001, Kerala: God's Own Country 2002, Nehru: The Invention of India 2003, Bookless in Baghdad 2005. *Leisure interests:* cricket, theatre, literature, cinema. *Address:* c/o Department of Public Information, United Nations, New York, NY 10017; c/o Editorial Offices, Arcade Publishing, 141 Fifth Avenue, New York, NY 10010, USA. *E-mail:* tharoor@un.org (office). *Website:* www.shashitharoor.com.

THARP, Twyla, BA; American dancer and choreographer; b. 1 July 1941, Portland, Ind.; m. 1st Peter Young (divorced); m. 2nd Robert Huot (divorced); one s.; ed Pomona Coll., American Ballet Theatre School, Barnard Coll.; studied with Richard Thomas, Merce Cunningham, Igor Schwezoff, Louis Mattox, Paul Taylor, Margaret Craske, Erick Hawkins; with Paul Taylor Dance Co. 1963–65; freelance choreographer with own modern dance troupe Twyla Tharp Dance and various other cos, including Joffrey Ballet and American Ballet Theater 1965–87, The Paris Opera Ballet, The Martha Graham Dance Company; Artistic Assoc. Choreographer American Ballet Theatre, New York 1988–91; re-formed Twyla Tharp Dance 1991, numerous int. tours 1999–; Hon. mem. American Acad. of Arts and Letters 1997; has received 15 hon. degrees, two Emmy Awards and numerous other awards including Dance Magazine Annual Award 1981, Laurence Olivier Award 1991, Doris Duke Awards for New Work 1999, Astaire Award 2003, The Drama League Award for Sustained Achievement in Musical Theatre, the Outer Critics Circle Award for Outstanding Choreography, Kennedy Center Honor 2008. *Major works choreographed include:* Tank Dive 1965, Re-Moves 1966, Forevermore 1967, Generation 1968, Medley 1969, Fugue 1970, Eight Jelly Rolls 1971, The Raggedy Dances 1972, As Time Goes By 1974, Sue's Leg 1975, Push Comes to Shove 1976, Once More Frank 1976, Mud 1977, Baker's Dozen 1979, When We Were Very Young 1980, The Catherine Wheel (with music by David Byrne) 1981, Nine Sinatra Songs 1982, Amadeus 1984, White Nights 1985, Singin' in the Rain 1985, In the Upper Room 1986, Rules of the Game 1989; choreographed Cutting Up 1993 for US tour, Demeter and Persephone 1993, 1994, Waterbaby Bagatelles 1994, Red White and Blues 1995, How Near Heaven 1995, Mr. Worldly Wise 1996, Movin' Out (Tony Award 2003), Even the King 2003, The Times They Are A Changin' 2006, Armenia 2008, Nightspot 2008, Rabbit and Rogue 2008; films Hair 1979, Ragtime 1980, Amadeus 1984, White Nights 1985, I'll Do Anything 1994; videotape Making Television Dance (Chicago International Film Festival Award) 1977, CBS Cable Confessions of a Corner Maker 1980, Baryshnikov by Tharp (two Emmy Awards, Director's Guild for America Award for Outstanding Director of Achievement. *Publications:* Push Comes to Shove (autobiog.) 1992, The Creative Habit: Learn it and Use it for Life 2003. *Address:* Tharp

Productions, 720 10th Avenue, #2, New York, NY 10019, USA (office). *E-mail:* jah@twylatharp.org (office). *Website:* www.twylatharp.org (office).

THATCHER, Baroness (Life Peer), cr. 1992, of Kesteven in the County of Lincolnshire; **Margaret Hilda Thatcher,** LG, OM, PC, BSc, MA, FRS; British fmr politician and fmr barrister; b. 13 Oct. 1925; d. of the late Alfred Roberts and Beatrice Ethel Stephenson; m. Denis Thatcher (later Sir Denis Thatcher, Bt) 1951 (died 2003); one s. one d. (twins); ed Grantham High School and Somerville Coll. Oxford; research chemist 1947–51; called to the Bar, Lincoln's Inn 1953; MP for Finchley 1959–92; Parl. Sec. Ministry of Pensions and Nat. Insurance 1961–64; Chief Opposition Spokesman on Educ. 1969–70; Sec. of State for Educ. and Science 1970–74; Leader of Conservative Party 1975–90; Leader of HM Opposition 1975–79; Prime Minister 1979–90; First Lord of the Treasury and Minister for the Civil Service 1979–90; retd from public life 2002; Pres. No Turning Back Group 1990–; Dir Tiger Man. 1998–; Vice-Pres. Royal Soc. of St George 1999–; Hon. Pres. Bruges Group 1991–; Chair. Advisory Bd Univ. of London's Inst. of US Studies 1994–; Hon. Bencher, Lincoln's Inn 1975; Hon. Master of the Bench of Gray's Inn 1983; Chancellor Univ. of Buckingham 1992–98, William and Mary Coll., Va 1994–2000; mem. Worshipful Co. of Glovers 1983–, Int. Advisory Bd British-American Chamber of Commerce 1993–; Conservative Companion of Guild of Cambridge Benefactors 1999–; Hon. Fellow, Royal Inst. of Chem. 1979, Freedom of Royal Borough of Kensington and Chelsea 1979, of London Borough of Barnet 1980, of Falkland Islands . 1983, of City of London 1989, of the City of Westminster 1990, Hon. Citizen of Gorasde 1993; Hon. LLD (Univ. of Buckingham) 1986; Dr hc (Rand Afrikaans Univ.) 1991, (Weizmann Inst. of Science) 1992, (Mendeleyev Univ.) 1993, (Brunel Univ.) 1996; MacArthur Foundation Fellowship 1992, Presidential Medal of Freedom (USA) 1991, Order of Good Hope (SA) 1991, Hilal-i-Imitaz 1996, ranked by Forbes magazine amongst 100 Most Powerful Women (21st) 2004. *Publications:* In Defence of Freedom 1986, The Downing Street Years 1979–1990 1993, The Path to Power 1995, The Collected Speeches of Margaret Thatcher 1997, Statecraft 2002. *Address:* House of Lords, Westminster, London, SW1A 0PW; POB 1466, London, SW1X 9HY, England.

THAWLEY, Michael; Australian fmr diplomatist; joined Foreign Affairs Dept 1972, served in Rome, Moscow, Tokyo; Foreign Policy Adviser to the Prime Minister 1996–99; fmr staff mem. Office of Nat. Assessments, Dept of Prime Minister and Cabinet; Amb. to USA 1999–2005; Sr Vice-Pres. Capital Strategy Research Inc, Washington, DC 2005–. *Address:* c/o Australian Embassy, 1601 Massachusetts Avenue, NW, Washington, DC 20036, USA (office).

THÉ, Guy Blaudin de (see DE THÉ, Guy Blaudin).

THEEDE, Steven M., BS; American oil industry executive; *CEO, OAO NK Yukos;* b. 1952, Hutchison, Kan.; ed Kan. State Univ.; trained as mechanical engineer; joined Conoco, Houston, TX 1974, worked in production, pipelines, refining, marketing, and int. relations, held positions successively as Gen. Dir Assessment and Tech. Devt, Gen. Dir Planning and Admin, Int. Refining and Marketing, Pres. Conoco Pipeline Co., CEO and Gen. Dir Conoco Ltd (UK), Gen. Dir Exploration & Production (E&P) for S and N America, Vice-Pres. Human Resources, Pres. of E&P for Europe (following merger of co. to form ConocoPhilips 2002) 2002–03, for Europe, Russia and the Caspian 2002–03; COO OAO NK Yukos (Yukos Oil Co.), Moscow, Russian Fed. 2003–04, CEO 2004–; Chair. Energy Cttee, US —Russia Business Council (USRBC) 2003. *Address:* OAO NK Yukos, 31A Dubininskaya Street, 115054 Moscow, Russia (office). *Telephone:* (095) 232-31-61 (office). *Fax:* (095) 232-31-60 (office). *Website:* www.yukos.com (office).

THEIN SEIN, Gen. U; Myanma army officer and politician; *Prime Minister;* m. Daw Khin Khin Win; ed Defence Services Academy 9; held positions of Second and First Sec. in ruling State Peace and Devt Council junta; also serves as Chair. govt-sponsored Nat. Convention Convening Comm.; Acting Prime Minister April–Oct. 2007, Prime Minister Oct. 2007–; promoted to rank of full Gen. from Lt-Gen. (Myanmar's fourth-highest ranking gen.) 2007. *Address:* Prime Minister's Office, Theinbyu Street, Botahtaung Township, Yangon, Myanmar (office). *Telephone:* (1) 283742 (office).

THÉMEREAU, Marie-Noëlle; New Caledonian politician; b. 1949; m.; two c.; served as Rep. in Southern Prov. and Congrès 1989–2001, 2004–07, Vice-Pres. Congrès 1999–2001; Vice-Pres. Southern Prov. 1996–99; also fmr Head of Admin; Pres. New Caledonia 2004–07 (resgnd); mem. L'Avenir Ensemble party. *Address:* c/o L'Avenir Ensemble, 2 bis blvd Vauban, Nouméa, New Caledonia. *Telephone:* 281179. *Fax:* 281011. *E-mail:* avenirensemble@lagoon .nc. *Website:* www.avenirensemble.nc.

THEOCHARIS, Reghinos D., PhD; Cypriot economist and academic; *Professor Emeritus, Athens University of Economics and Business;* b. 10 Feb. 1929, Larnaca; s. of Demetrios Theocharis and Florentia Theocharis; m. Madeleine Loumbou 1954; one s. one d.; ed Athens School of Econs, Univ. of Aberdeen and London School of Econs; Insp. of Commercial Educ., Cyprus 1953–56; at LSE 1956–58; Bank of Greece, Athens 1958–59; Minister of Finance in Cyprus Provisional Govt 1959–60; Minister of Finance 1960–62; Gov. of Bank of Cyprus 1962–75; Prof., Athens Univ. of Econs and Business 1975–96, Prof. Emer. 1996–; Dir-Gen. Centre of Planning and Econ. Research (KEPE), Athens 1978–81; Hon. Fellow, LSE 1971. *Publications:* On the Stability of the Cournot Solution on the Oligopoly Problem 1960, Early Developments in Mathematical Economics 1983, The Development of Mathematical Economics: From Cournot to Jevons 1993. *Leisure interests:* chess, gardening. *Address:* 2 Raidestou Street, Kessariani, Athens, 16122, Greece (home). *Telephone:* 2107214531 (home).

THEODORAKIS, Mikis; Greek composer; b. 29 July 1925, island of Chios; s. of Georges Michel Theodorakis and Aspasia Poulaki; m. Myrto Altinoglou 1953; one s. one d.; ed Athens Conservatoire and Paris Conservatoire; joined resistance against German occupation of Greece 1942; arrested and deported during civil war 1947–52; moved to Paris 1953 and studied under Olivier Messiaen; first public concert Sonatina (for pianoforte), Paris 1954; set to bouzouki music the poem Epitaphios by Iannis Ritsos 1958–59 and subsequently wrote numerous other successful songs; Ballet music for Antigone (first performed in London by Dame Margot Fonteyn), Stuttgart Ballet, etc.; returned to Greece 1962; leader Lambrakis youth movt; MP 1963; imprisoned for political activities 1967, released April 1970; lived in Paris 1970–74; resgnd from CP March 1972; MP 1981–1986 (resgnd), 1989–93 (resgnd), Minister of State 1990–92 (resgnd); f. Cttee for Greek-Turkish Friendship 1986; Gold Medal, Moscow Shostakovich Festival 1957, Copley Prize, USA 1957, First Prize Athens Popular Song Festival 1961, Sibelius Award, London 1963, Gold Medal for Film Music, London 1970, Socrates Prize, Stockholm 1974, First Literary Prize, Athens 1987; Lenin Int. Peace Prize 1982. *Works include:* Sinfonia (oratorio) 1944, Love and Death (voice, strings) 1945–48, Assi-Gonia (orchestra) 1945–50, Sextet for Flute 1946, Oedipus Tyrannus (strings) 1946, Greek Carnival (ballet suite) 1947, First Symphony (orchestra) 1948–50, Five Cretan Songs (chorus, orchestra) 1950, Orpheus and Eurydice (ballet) 1952, Barefoot Battalion (film) 1953, Suite No. 1 (four movements, piano and orchestra) 1954, Poèmes d'Eluard (Cycle 1 and Cycle 2) 1955, Suite No. 2 (chorus, orchestra) 1956, Suite No. 3 (five movements, soprano, chorus, orchestra) 1956, Ill Met by Moonlight (film) 1957, Sonatina No. 1 (violin, piano) 1957, Les amants de Teruel (ballet) 1958, Piano Concerto 1958, Sonatina No. 2 (violin, piano) 1958, Antigone (ballet) 1958, Epitaphios (song cycle) 1959, Deserters (song cycle) 1958, Epiphania (song cycle) 1959, Honeymoon (film) 1960, Phoenician Women – Euripides (theatre music) 1960, Axion Esti (pop oratorio) 1960, Electra-Euripides (film), Phaedra (film) 1962, The Hostage (song cycle) 1962, The Ballad of the Dead Brother (musical tragedy) 1962, Zorba the Greek (film), The Ballad of Mauthausen (song cycle) 1965, Romiossini (song cycle) 1965, Lisistrata – Aristophanes (theatre music) 1966, Romancero Gitano (Lorca) (song cycle) 1967, Sun and Time (song cycle) 1967, Arcadias Nos. 1–10 (song cycles) 1968–69, Canto General (Pablo Neruda) (pop oratorio) 1972, Z (film), Etat de Siège (film) 1973, Ballads (song cycle) 1975, Symphony No. 2 (orchestra and piano) 1981, Messe Byzantine (Liturgie) 1982, Symphony No. 3 (orchestra, chorus, soprano) 1982, Sadoukeon Passion (cantata for orchestra, chorus, soloists) 1983, Liturgie No. 2 1983, Symphony No. 7 (orchestra, chorus, soloists) 1983, Requiem 1985, Kostas Kariotakis (opera in two acts) 1985, Beatrice (song cycle) 1987, Faces of the Sun (song cycle) 1987, Symphony No. 4 1987, Memory of Stone (song cycle) 1987, Like an Ancient Wind (song cycle) 1987, Canto Olympico (symphony) 1991, Medea (opera) 1990, Electra (opera) 1993. *Publications include:* La Dette, Journals of Resistance 1972, Ballad of the Dead Brother, Culture et dimensions politiques 1973, Star System, Antimanifeste, Les chemins de l'Archange (autobiog.), 4 vols 1986–92. *Address:* Epifanous 1, Akropolis, 117 42 Athens, Greece. *Telephone:* (1) 9214863. *Fax:* (1) 9236325.

THÉODORE, Jean-François; French stock exchange executive; *Deputy CEO, NYSE Euronext;* b. 5 Dec. 1946, Paris; s. of Charles Théodore and Aimée Chevallier; m. Claudine Lefèbvre 1976; one s. two d.; ed Lycées Montaigne and Louis-le-Grand, Faculty of Law, Paris, Institut d'études politiques de Paris; Ecole nat. d'admin 1971–74; civil servant, Ministry of Econ. and Finance 1974–78, Crédit nat. 1978–80, Head, Bureau des états africains et de la zone franc 1980–82, Head, Bureau des investissements étrangers en France et français à l'étranger 1982–84, Asst Dir Etablissements de crédit 1984–86, Deputy Dir, Head of Funding and Investment Dept, Treasury 1986–90; Gen. Man. Soc. des bourses françaises 1990–91, Chair. and CEO 1991–; Pres. Int. Fed. of Stock Exchanges 1993–94, Fed. of European Stock Exchanges 1998–; Vice-Pres. Soc. interprofessionnelle de compensation des valeurs mobilières (Sicovam) 1992, Chair. 1993–; Pres. Matif SA 1998–; Chair. Euronext 2000–07, Deputy CEO NYSE Euronext (after acquisition of Euronext by New York Stock Exchange) 2007–; Chevalier, Ordre nat. du Mérite, Légion d'honneur; Prix Andese du financier 2000. *Leisure interests:* opera, American cinema, theatre. *Address:* NYSE Euronext, Société des bourses françaises, 39 rue Cambon, 75001 Paris, France (office). *Telephone:* 1-49-27-10-00 (office). *Fax:* 1-49-27-14-33 (office). *E-mail:* d.lande@euronext.fr (office). *Website:* www .euronext.fr (office); www.nyse.com (office).

THEOPHILOS, Theophilou V., MA; Cypriot lawyer and fmr diplomatist; b. 9 Sept. 1946, Limnia, Famagusta; ed Athens Univ., Stanford Univ., USA; lawyer in Famagusta 1971–73; Attaché, Cultural Div., Ministry of Foreign Affairs 1974, Head of EEC Desk 1974–76, Sec., Political Affairs Div. (Question of Cyprus) 1977–78, Head of Cyprus Question Desk 1979–81, Deputy Dir Political Div. 1985–86, Dir Office of Minister of Foreign Affairs 1993, Dir European Div. 1993–96; Consul Gen., New York, USA 1981–84; in charge of Orgs of NAM Foreign Ministers Conf., Nicosia 1987–88; High Commr to India with concurrent accreditation to nine other countries 1989–93; Amb. to Germany (also accred to Poland and the Holy See) 1996–2000; Perm. Rep. to EU 2000–04; mem. Bd of Dirs Laiki Group 2005; mem. Cyprus Bar Asscn. *Publications:* numerous articles in Cypriot newspapers and magazines. *Address:* 16 Panteli Katelari, Diagoras Bldg, Nicosia 1306, Cyprus (office). *Telephone:* 22660767 (office). *Fax:* 22678777 (office). *E-mail:* montanios@ montanioslaw.com.cy (office).

THEOPHILUS III, His Beatitude Patriarch of the Holy City of Jerusalem and all Palestine, Syria, beyond the Jordan river, Cana of Galilee and Holy Zion (Ilija Jannopoulos); Greek ecclesiastic; b. 1952, Messinia, Greece; ed Univ. of Athens, Durham Univ.; entered Brotherhood of Holy Sepulchre 1964; attended Patriarchal school in Jerusalem 1964–70; tonsured monk withe name of Theophilus 1970; ordained deacon 1970;

ordained priest 1975; attended Athens Univ. and later worked in Jerusalem at Gen. Secr. of the Holy Synod, Patriarchal School, and St Charalampy's Monastery; elevated to rank of archimandrite 1978; apptd mem. Editorial Bd Nea Zion journal 1981; sent to UK to study at Durham Univ. 1981; Sec. for Foreign Relations, Holy Synod of the Patriarchate of Jerusalem 1986–88; Rep. Patriarchate of Jerusalem in Cen. Cttee, World Council of Churches 1988–91; hegumen, Monastery of St George the Victorious, Cana Galilee 1991–96; Rep. of Patriarchate of Jerusalem with Patriarch of Moscow and All Russia and Rector, Jerusalem Representation Church, Moscow 2001–03; Patriarchal epitrop, Doha Qatar 2003–04; Senior Custodian Holy Sepulchre and mem. Holy Synod of Patriarchate of Jerusalem 2004–05; Archbishop of Mount Tabor Feb. 2005; elected Patriarch of Jerusalem Aug., enthroned Nov. 2005;*Website:* www.jerusalem-patriarchate.org (office).

THERON, Charlize; South African actress; b. 7 Aug. 1975, Benoni, SA; trained as ballet dancer; went to Milan aged 16 to become a model; moved to New York to dance with Joffrey Ballet; knee injury ended dancing career; moved to Los Angeles to take up acting; appointed UN Messenger of Peace 2008–; Los Angeles Film Festival Spirit of Independence Award 2006. *Films include:* Children of the Corn III 1994, Two Days in the Valley 1996, That Thing You Do! 1996, Trial and Error 1997, Hollywood Confidential 1997, Devil's Advocate 1997, Cop Land/The Yards 1997, Mighty Joe Young 1998, Celebrity 1998, The Cider House Rules 1999, The Astronaut's Wife 1999, The Yards 2000, Reindeer Games 2000, Men of Honor 2000, The Legend of Bagger Vance 2000, Navy Diver 2000, Sweet November 2001, The Curse of the Jade Scorpion 2001, 15 Minutes 2001, The Yards/Nightwatch 2002, Waking Up in Reno 2002, Trapped 2002, 24 Hours 2002, Sweet Home Alabama (exec. producer) 2002, The Italian Job 2003, Monster (Golden Globe Award, Best Dramatic Actress 2004, Critics' Choice Award, Best Actress 2004, Screen Actors Guild Best Actress Award 2004, Acad. Award, Best Actress 2004) 2003, The Life and Death of Peter Sellers 2004, Head in the Clouds 2004, North Country 2005, Aeonflux 2005, In the Valley of Elah 2007, Battle in Seattle 2007, Hancock 2008, The Burning Plain 2008. *Address:* c/o Spanky Taylor, 3727 West Magnolia, Burbank, CA 91505 (office); c/o United Talent Agency, Inc., 9560 Wilshire Blvd., Suite 500, Beverly Hills, CA 90212, USA.

THEROUX, Paul Edward, BA, FRSL, FRGS; American writer; b. 10 April 1941, Medford, MA; s. of Albert Eugene Theroux and Anne Dittami Theroux; m. 1st Anne Castle 1967 (divorced 1993), two s.; m. 2nd Sheila Donnelly 1995; ed Univ. of Massachusetts; lecturer, Univ. of Urbino, Italy 1963, Soche Hill Coll., Malawi 1963–65, Makerere Univ., Kampala, Uganda 1965–68, Univ. of Singapore 1968–71; Writer-in-Residence, Univ. of Va 1972; Hon. DLitt (Tufts Univ., Trinity Univ.) 1983, (Univ. of Mass.) 1988; Playboy magazine Editorial Awards 1972, 1976, 1977, 1979. *Play:* The White Man's Burden 1987. *Screenplay:* Saint Jack 1979. *Publications:* fiction: Waldo 1967, Fong and the Indians 1968, Girls at Play 1969, Murder in Mount Holly 1969, Jungle Lovers 1971, Sinning with Annie 1972, Saint Jack 1973, The Black House 1974, The Family Arsenal 1976, The Consul's File 1977, Picture Palace (Whitbread Award) 1978, A Christmas Card 1978, London Snow 1980, World's End 1980, The Mosquito Coast (James Tait Black Memorial Prize 1982, Yorkshire Post Best Novel Award 1982) 1981, The London Embassy 1982, Doctor Slaughter 1984, O-Zone 1986, My Secret History 1988, Chicago Loop 1990, Dr. DeMarr 1990, Millroy the Magician 1993, My Other Life 1996, Kowloon Tong 1997, Collected Stories 1997, Collected Short Novels 1998, Hotel Honolulu 2000, The Stranger at the Palazzo d'Oro (short stories) 2002, Telling Tales (contrib. to charity anthology) 2004, Blinding Light 2005, The Elephanta Suite 2007; non-fiction: V. S. Naipaul (criticism) 1973, The Great Railway Bazaar (travel) 1975, The Old Patagonian Express (travel) 1979, The Kingdom by the Sea (travel) 1983, Sailing through China (travel) 1983, Sunrise with Sea Monsters (travel) 1985, Riding the Iron Rooster: By Train Through China (travel) (Thomas Cook Prize for Best Literary Travel Book 1989) 1988, Travelling the World (travel) 1990, The Happy Isles of Oceania: Paddling the Pacific (travel) 1992, The Pillars of Hercules (travel) 1995, Sir Vidia's Shadow: A Friendship Across Five Continents (travel) 1998, Fresh-Air Fiend (travel) 1999, The Worst Journey in the World 2000, Nurse Wolf and Dr Sacks 2000, Dark Star Safari: Overland from Cairo to Cape Town (travel) 2002, Ghost Train to the Eastern Star (travel) 2008. *Leisure interest:* rowing. *Address:* Hamish Hamilton Ltd, 80 Strand, London, WC2, England (office); The Wylie Agency, 250 West 57th Street, New York NY 10107, USA (office).

THEVENOUX, Sophie; Monegasque politician; *Government Councillor for Finance and the Economy;* m.; two c.; Head of Admin and Finance, Seigneurie Caraïbes, Elf Group, Guadeloupe 1981–82; Financial Officer, Gen. Mills Toys and Games, France 1982–86; Deputy Dir of the Budget and Treasury 1995–99, Dir 1999–2005, Dir-Gen. Dept of Finance and the Economy 2005–09, Govt Councillor for Finance and the Economy 2009–. *Address:* Department of Finance and the Economy, Ministère d'Etat, place de la Visitation, Monte Carlo, MC 98000, Monaco (office). *Telephone:* 98-98-82-56 (office). *E-mail:* dfin@troisseptsept.mc (office).

THEWLIS, David; British actor; b. 20 March 1963; s. of Alec Raymond Wheeler and Maureen Wheeler (née Thewlis); m. Sara Jocelyn Sugarman 1992; ed Highfield High School, Blackpool, St Anne's Coll. of Further Educ., Guildhall School of Music and Drama, London. *Theatre includes:* Buddy Holly at the Regal, Ice Cream, Lady and the Clarinet (winner Edin. Fringe First), The Sea. *Television includes:* Valentine Park (series) 1985, The Singing Detective (miniseries) 1986, The Short and Curlies (film) 1987, Skulduggery (film) 1989, Bit of a Do (series) 1989, Oranges Are Not the Only Fruit (film) 1990, Journey to Knock (film) (Best Actor, Rheims Film Festival 1992) 1991, Filipina Dreamgirls (film) 1991, Prime Suspect 3 1993, Dandelion Dead (miniseries) 1994, Endgame (film) 2000. *Films include:* Road 1987, Vroom 1988, Little Dorrit 1988, Resurrected 1989, Life is Sweet 1990, Afraid of the

Dark 1991, Damage 1992, The Trial 1993, Naked (Best Actor, Cannes Film Festival) 1993, Black Beauty 1994, Total Eclipse 1995, Restoration 1995, James and the Giant Peach (voice) 1996, Dragonheart 1996, The Island of Dr Moreau 1996, Seven Years in Tibet 1997, Divorcing Jack 1998, The Big Lebowski 1998, Besieged 1998, Whatever Happened to Harold Smith 1999, Gangster No. 1 2000, Timeline 2003, Harry Potter and the Prisoner of Azkaban 2004, Kingdom of Heaven 2005, All the Invisible Children 2005, The New World 2005, Basic Instinct 2 2006, The Omen 2006, The Inner Life of Martin Frost 2007, Harry Potter and the Order of the Phoenix 2007, The Boy in the Striped Pyjamas 2008. *Publication:* The Late Hector Kipling (novel) 2007. *Leisure interest:* painting.

THEWS, Gerhard, Dr rer. nat, DrMed; German academic; *Professor of Physiology, University of Kiel;* b. 22 July 1926, Königsberg; m. Dr. Gisela Bahling 1958; three s. one d.; ed Univ. of Kiel; Research Fellow Univ. of Kiel 1957–61, Asst Prof. 1961–62, Assoc. Prof. 1962–63, Prof. 1964–, Dir Physiological Inst. 1964–, Dean Faculty Medicine 1968–69; Vice-Pres. Acad. Science and Literature 1977–85, Pres. 1985–93; Pres. German Physiological Soc. 1968–69; mem. German Scientific Council 1970–72; Pres. Int. Soc. for Oxygen Transport 1973–75; Wolfgang Heubner Prize (Berlin) 1961, Feldberg Prize (London) 1964, Carl Diem Prize 1964, Adolf Fick Prize (Würzburg) 1969, Ernst von Bergmann Medal (Germany) 1986. *Publications:* Human Anatomy, Physiology and Pathophysiology 1985, Autonomic Functions in Human Physiology 1985, Human Physiology 1989. *Address:* Weidmannstrasse 29, 55131 Mainz, Germany.

THIAM, Habib, LenD; Senegalese politician; b. 21 Jan. 1933, Dakar; ed Ecole Nat. de la France d'Outre-mer; Sec. of State for the Devt Plan 1963; Minister of Planning and Devt 1964–67, of Rural Econ. 1968–73; mem. Nat. Ass. 1973–, Pres. 1983–84; Prime Minister 1981–83, 1991–96; Press Sec. Union progressiste sénégalaise (now Parti socialiste sénégalais—PS); Pres. Parl. Group PS 1978; Chair. Bd Banque Int. pour le Commerce et l'Industrie du Sénégal; Dir Ethiopique 1976–, L'Unité Africaine 1976–.

THIBAUDET, Jean-Yves; French pianist; b. 7 Sept. 1961, Lyon; ed Paris Conservatoire, Lyon Conservatory of Music; now based in LA and Paris; appears with major orchestras in USA and Europe including Royal Concertgebouw, London Philharmonic, Royal Philharmonic, Orchestre Nat. de France etc.; regular visitor to major US and European music festivals; in recital has collaborated with mezzo-sopranos Brigitte Fassbaender and Cecilia Bartoli, Renee Fleming and cellist Truls Mørk; debut, BBC Promenade Concerts 1992, continuing to 2001; records exclusively for Decca (over 20 recordings); Chevalier, Ordre des Arts et des Lettres 2001; Prix du Conservatoire, Paris Conservatory 1976, winner, Young Concert Artists Auditions 1981, Echo Award 1990, 1998, Schallplattenpreis 1992, Gramophone Award 1998, Edison Prize 1998, Choc de la Musique 1999, 2003, Diapason d'Or for his recordings of works by Debussy 2000, Premio Pegasus 2002, Echo Classical Music Awards 2002. *Films:* Portrait of a Lady 1997, Bride of the Wind 2001. *Television:* Piano Grand! (PBS/Smithsonian Special) 2000. *Leisure interests:* tennis, swimming, riding, water-skiing, museums, movies, racing cars. *Address:* c/o Mastroianni Associates, 161 West 61st Street, Suite 17E, New York, NY 10023 (office); c/o M. L. Falcone Public Relations, 155 West 68th Street, Suite 1114, New York, NY 10023, USA (office). *Telephone:* (212) 580-4302 (office). *Fax:* (212) 787-9638 (office).

THIBAULT, Bernard; French trade union official; *Secretary-General, Confédération Générale du Travail (CGT);* b. 2 Jan. 1959, Paris; m.; two c.; apprentice Société Nationale des Chemins de fer Français (SNCF) 1974–76; Sec.-Gen. Confédération Générale du Travail (CGT) 1999–. *Address:* Confédération Générale du Travail, 263, rue de Paris, 93 516 Montreuil cedex, France (office). *Telephone:* 1-48-18-80-00 (office). *Fax:* 1-49-18-18-57 (office). *E-mail:* info@cgt.fr (office). *Website:* www.cgt.fr (office).

THIBAULT, Paul, MA; Canadian international organization official (retd); b. April 1945; m. Denyse Dufresne; one d.; ed Univ. of Ottawa, Carlton Univ., Ecole nationale d'administration, Paris, France; with Dept of External Affairs 1968–85, various positions in Ottawa and abroad including Geneva, Tehran and Paris; Dir of Operations, Priorities and Planning Secr., Privy Council Office 1985–88; Asst Sec. to the Cabinet (Security and Intelligence) 1988–92; Asst Sec. Program Br. (Govt Operations, Foreign and Defence), Treasury Bd Secr. 1992–96; Acting Deputy Sec. Program Br. 1996; Exec. Dir Immigration and Refugee Bd 1997–98; Fed. Coordinator, Year 2000 Nat. Contingency Planning for Dept of Nat. Defence 1998–2000; Assoc. Deputy Minister of Industry 2000–01, of Foreign Affairs 2001–03; Pres. Canadian Int. Devt Agency 2003–05. *Address:* c/o Canadian International Development Agency, 200 Promenade du Portage, Gatineau, PQ K1A 0G4, Canada (office).

THIEBAUD, Wayne, MA; American artist; *Professor Emeritus, University of California, Davis;* b. 15 Nov. 1920, Mesa, Ariz.; m. 1st Patricia Patterson 1945 (divorced 1959); two d.; m. 2nd Betty Jean Carr 1959; one s. one step s.; ed Frank Wiggins Trade School, Long Beach Jr Coll., San. José State Coll. (now San José State Univ.), California State Coll. (now California State Univ.); worked as commercial artist and freelance cartoonist from 1938; served USAAF 1942–45; started career as painter 1947; Asst Prof., Dept of Art, Univ. of Calif., Davis 1960, Assoc. Prof. 1963–67, apptd Prof. 1967, Faculty Research Lecturer 1973–, currently Prof. Emer.; co-founder Artists Co-operative Gallery (now Artists Contemporary Gallery), Sacramento 1958; numerous one-man exhbns in USA since 1950; one-man exhbn Galleria Schwarz, Milan, Italy 1963; represented USA at São Paulo Bienal, Brazil 1968; commissioned to do paintings of Wimbledon tennis tournament, England 1968; selected as Nat. Juror for Nat. Endowment for the Arts, Washington, DC 1972; commissioned by US Dept of Interior to paint Yosemite Ridge Line for Bicentennial Exhbn, America 1976; mem. American Acad., Inst. of Arts and

Letters, New York City 1985, Nat. Acad. of Design, New York City; Award of Distinction, Nat. Art Schools Asscn and Special Citation Award, Nat. Asscn of Schools of Art and Design 1984, Nat. Medal of the Arts 1994. *Publication:* Wayne Thiebaud: Private Drawings—The Artist's Sketchbook 1987. *Address:* Department of Art, University of California, 1 Shields Avenue, Davis, CA 95616, USA. *Telephone:* (530) 752-1011. *Fax:* (530) 752-6363. *Website:* www .ucdavis.edu (office).

THIELEN, Gunter, DEng; German business executive; *Chairman, Supervisory Board, Bertelsmann AG;* b. 4 Aug. 1942, Quierschied, Saarland; ed Tech. Univ. of Aachen; various man. positions with BASF, Ludwigshafen 1970; Tech. Dir Wintershall Refinery, Kassel 1976; joined Bertelsmann AG as CEO Maul Belser printing co., Nuremberg 1980, mem. Exec. Bd Bertelsmann AG 1985, Head Print and Industrial Operations Div. (renamed Bertelsmann Arvato AG) 1985–2002, Chair. and CEO 2002–07, mem. Bertelsmann AG Supervisory Bd 2002–, Chair. 2007–; Chair. Bertelsmann Stiftung (Foundation) 2001, 2007–; Chair. Bertelsmann Verwaltungsgesellschaft mbH (BVG) 2001; Johns Hopkins Univ. Global Leadership Award 2005. *Address:* Supervisory Board, Bertelsmann AG, Carl-Bertelsmann-Strasse 270, 33311 Gütersloh, Germany (office). *Telephone:* 5241800 (office). *Fax:* 5241809662 (office). *E-mail:* info@bertelsmann.de (office). *Website:* www.bertelsmann.de (office).

THIEME, Reiner; German business executive; *Chairman of the Supervisory Board, ZF Friedrichshafen AG;* Chair. Keiper Recaro Group 1979–87; joined Wilhelm Karmann GmbH, Osnabrück 1987, Chair. Bd of Man. 1990–2003; Chair. Supervisory Bd ZF Friedrichshafen AG 2003–; fmr Vice-Pres. German Automobile Industry Asscn (VDA). *Address:* ZF Friedrichshafen AG, Graf-von-Soden-Platz 1, 88046 Friedrichshafen, Germany (office). *Telephone:* (7541) 77-0 (office). *Fax:* (7541) 77-908000 (office). *E-mail:* postoffice@zf.com (office). *Website:* www.zf.com (office).

THIER, Samuel Osiah, MD; American physician and academic; *Emeritus Professor of Medicine and Health Care Policy, Harvard Medical School;* b. 23 June 1937, Brooklyn, New York; s. of Sidney Thier and May H. Kanner Thier; m. Paula Dell Finkelstein 1958; three d.; ed Cornell Univ., State Univ. of New York, Syracuse; Intern Mass. Gen. Hosp. 1960–61, Asst Resident 1961–62, 1964–65, Postdoctoral Fellow 1965; Clinical Assoc. Nat. Inst. of Arthritis and Metabolic Diseases 1962–64; Chief Resident in Medicine, Mass. Gen. Hosp. 1966; Instr. to Asst Prof. Harvard Medical School 1967–69; Assoc. Prof. then Prof. of Medicine, Univ. of Pa Medical School 1969–74; Prof. and Chair. Dept of Medicine, Yale Univ. School of Medicine and Chief of Medicine, Yale-New Haven Hosp. 1975–85; Pres. Inst. of Medicine, NAS 1985–91; Pres. and Prof. Brandeis Univ. 1991–94; Pres. Mass. Gen. Hosp. 1994–97; Pres. Partners Healthcare System Inc. 1994–2002, CEO 1996–2002; Prof. of Medicine and Health Care Policy, Harvard Medical School 1994–2007, Prof. Emer. 2008–. *Publications:* numerous articles and chapters in medical journals and textbooks. *Address:* Massachusetts General Hospital, 55 Fruit Street, Bulfinch 370, Boston, MA 02114, USA (office). *Telephone:* (617) 726-1811 (office). *Fax:* (617) 726-1900 (office). *E-mail:* sthier@partners.org (office). *Website:* whitepages.med.harvard.edu/hms/home.asp (office).

THIERSE, Wolfgang; German politician; *Vice-President of Bundestag;* b. 22 Oct. 1943, Breslau; ed Humboldt Univ., Berlin; fmr typesetter; teaching asst, Dept of Cultural Theory and Aesthetics, Humboldt Univ. Berlin 1964; mem. staff Ministry of Culture, GDR 1975–76, Cen. Inst. for History of Literature, Acad. of Sciences, GDR 1977–90; Chair. Social Democratic Party, GDR (which later factioned) 1990; mem. Bundestag (Parl.) 1990–, Pres. 1998–2005, Vice-Pres. 2005–. *Publications:* The Right Life in a False System, The Future of the East. *Address:* Hagenauer Straße 3, 10435 Berlin; Bundestag, Platz der Republik 1, 11011 Berlin, Germany. *Telephone:* (30) 22777023 (office). *Fax:* (30) 22776023 (office). *E-mail:* wolfgang.thierse@bundestag.de (office). *Website:* www.bundestag.de (office); www.thierse.de.

THIESSEN, Gordon, OC, BA, MA, PhD; Canadian banker and economist; *Chairman, Canadian Public Accountability Board;* b. 14 Aug. 1938, South Porcupine, Ont.; m. Annette Hillyar 1964; two c.; ed Univ. of Saskatchewan, London School of Econs, UK; joined Bank of Canada 1963; Visiting Economist, Reserve Bank of Australia 1973–75; Adviser to Gov. Bank of Canada 1979, Deputy Gov. responsible for econ. research and financial analysis 1984, Sr Deputy Gov. 1987, Chair. Bd Dirs, mem. Exec. Cttee 1987, Gov. 1994–2001; fmr Exec.-in-Residence, Univ. of Ottawa School of Man.; Chair. Canadian Public Accountability Bd 2003–; mem. Bd Dirs Manulife Financial Corpn, IPSCO Inc., Inst. for Research on Public Policy, Univ. of Saskatchewan; Swedish Order of the Polar Star, Commdr, Order of the North Star; Dr hc (Univ. of Saskatchewan, Univ. of Ottawa). *Leisure interests:* skiing, sailing. *Address:* Canadian Public Accountability Board, 150 York Street, Suite 200, PO Box 90, Toronto, ON M5H 3S5, Canada (office). *Telephone:* (416) 913-8260 (office). *Fax:* (416) 850-9235 (office). *Website:* www.cpab-ccrc.ca (office).

THINLEY, Lyonchhen Jigmi Yozer, MA; Bhutanese politician; *Prime Minister and Chairman;* b. 1952, Bumthang; ed St Stephen's Coll., India, Pennsylvania State Univ., USA; mem. civil service 1954–1983, Head, Royal Civil Service Comm. Secr., Dir Educ. Dept; fmr Perm. Rep. to UN, New York; fmr Chair. Council of Ministers; Minister of Foreign Affairs 1998–2003; Prime Minister, Chair. and Minister of Home and Cultural Affairs 2003–04; Minister of Home and Cultural Affairs 2004–07 (resgnd), Prime Minister and Chair. 2008–; Founder and Pres. Druk Phuensum Tshogpa (DPT) party 2007–; Red Scarf 1987, Druk Thuksey and Coronation Medals 1999. *Address:* Cabinet Secretariat, Tashichhodzong, Thimphu (office); Druk Phuensum Tshogpa (DPT), Thimphu; Druk Phuensum Tshogpa (DPT), Chang Lam, Thimphu, Bhutan (office). *Telephone:* (2) 321437 (office); (2) 336336 (DPT) (office). *Fax:* (2) 321438 (office); (2) 335845 (DPT) (office). *E-mail:* cabinet@druknet.bt (office); dpt@druknet.bt (office). *Website:* www.dpt.bt (office).

THINOT, Dominique Pierre; French painter, teacher and diplomatist; *Professor, École Nationale Supérieure des Arts Décoratifs;* b. 3 Oct. 1948, Paris; s. of Y. Hervé and Pierre Thinot; m. Claire Moreau 1977; two s.; ed Diplôme d'études supérieures, Paris; Prof., École Nationale Supérieure des Arts Décoratifs, Paris 1972–; has taught at various univs in Asia 1980–; leader of several cultural missions to Japan, Singapore, Korea and China 1985–; Pres. Asscn of Artists of the Bateau-Lavoir, Paris; mem. Gruppe Sieben, Germany 1975–; currently Chargé de Misson pour l'Asie, International Relations; Conseiller pour les enseignements artistiques auprès des universités; Prof., Xi'an Acad. of Fine Arts, China; Prix de la Création Artistique, Ministry of Cultural Affairs 1971, 1974, Prix de l'Acad. des Beaux-Arts 1983, Distinction du Govt de la République Arabe d'Egypte 1996. *Television:* numerous reports for TV networks in France, Japan, Korea and China. *Leisure interests:* music, oenology. *Address:* Bateau-Lavoir, 13 place Emile Goudeau, 75018 Paris; 13 route des Vieilles-Vignes, 17880 Les Portes, Ile-de-Ré, France. *Telephone:* 1-78-11-30-08 (home). *Fax:* 1-42-57-33-58 (office). *E-mail:* dominique.thinot@ensad.fr (office); dominique.thinot@club-internet .fr (home). *Website:* www.ensad.fr (office).

THIRSK, (Irene) Joan, CBE, PhD, FBA, FRHistS; British historian and academic (retd); b. (Irene Joan Watkins), 19 June 1922, London; d. of William Henry Watkins and Daisy Watkins (née Frayer); m. James Wood Thirsk 1945; one s. one d.; ed Camden School for Girls, London and Westfield Coll., Univ. of London; war service in Auxiliary Territorial Service (ATS), Intelligence Corps, Bletchley Park 1942–45; Asst Lecturer in Sociology, LSE 1950–51; Sr Research Fellow in Agrarian History, Dept of English Local History, Leicester Univ. 1951–65; Reader in Econ. History, Oxford Univ. 1965–83, Professorial Fellow of St Hilda's Coll. 1965–83, Hon. Fellow 1983–; mem. Royal Comm. on Historical Monuments of England 1977–86, Historical Manuscripts 1989–96; Pres. British Agricultural Hist. Soc. 1983–86, 1995–98, British Asscn for Local History 1986–92, Kent History Fed. 1990–99, Vice-Pres. Past and Present Soc. 2003–; Gen. Ed. Agrarian History of England and Wales 1975–2000; Mellon Sr Fellow, Nat. Humanities Center, NC, USA 1986–87; Foreign mem. American Philosophical Soc.; Corresp. mem. Colonial Soc. of Massachusetts; Hon. Fellow, Queen Mary and Westfield Coll. London 1997, Kellogg Coll. Oxford 1998; Hon. DLitt (Leicester) 1985, (East Anglia) 1990, (Kent) 1993, (Sussex) 1994, (Southampton) 1999, (Greenwich) 2001; Hon. DUniv (Open Univ.) 1991; Hon. Dr of Agricultural and Environmental Sciences (Agricultural Univ., Wageningen, Netherlands) 1993. *Publications:* ed. and contrib. The Agrarian History of England and Wales, IV 1500–1640 1967, V 1640–1750 1985; Seventeenth-Century Economic Documents (with J. P. Cooper) 1972, The Restoration 1976, Economic Policy and Projects: The Development of a Consumer Society in Early Modern England 1978, The Rural Economy of England: Collected Essays 1984, England's Agricultural Regions and Agrarian History 1500–1750 1987, Alternative Agriculture: a History from the Black Death to the Present Day 1997, The English Rural Landscape 2000, Food in Early Modern England: Phases, Fads, Fashions 2007, Hadlow: Life, Land and People in a Wealden Parish, 1460–1600 2007. *Leisure interests:* gardening, sewing and machine knitting. *Address:* 1 Hadlow Castle, Hadlow, Tonbridge, Kent, TN11 0EG, England. *Telephone:* (1732) 850708. *Fax:* (1732) 850708. *E-mail:* jthirsk@onetel.com.

THOMAS, Betty; American film director and actress; b. 27 July 1948, St Louis, Mo.; ed Ohio Univ., Chicago Art Inst., Roosevelt Univ.; fmr mem. Second City improvisation group, Chicago; performed at the Comedy Store, LA. *Films:* actress: Tunnelvision 1976, Chesty Anderson: US Navy 1976, Jackson County Jail 1976, Loose Shoes 1980, Used Cars 1980, Homework 1982, Troop Beverly Hills 1989; director: Only You 1992, The Brady Bunch Movie 1995, Private Parts 1997, Dr Dolittle 1998, 28 Days 2000, I Spy (also producer) 2002, R3 2003, John Tucker Must Die 2006; producer: Can't Hardly Wait 1998, Surviving Christmas 2004; exec. producer: Charlie's Angels 2000. *Television:* director: (series) Doogie Howser MD, Dream On (Emmy Award 1993), Hooperman, Mancusco FBI, Arresting Behavior, Couples; (film) My Breast; (documentary drama) The Late Shift (Directors' Guild of America Award 1997); (actress) (series) Hill Street Blues (Emmy Award 1985); (films) Outside Chance, Nashville Grab, When Your Lover Leaves, Prison for Children. *Address:* 10201 West Pico Blvd, Bldg 43, Los Angeles, CA 90069, USA (office).

THOMAS, Chantal; French essayist; *Director of Research, Centre National de la Recherche Scientifique (CNRS);* b. 1945, Lyon; specialist in eighteenth century history; biographical publs on Sade, Casanova, Thomas Berhard and Marie-Antoinette; debut novel Adieux à la Reine sold over 110,000 copies and translated into German, English, Korean, Greek, Italian, Japanese, Dutch and Portugese 2002; currently Dir of Research, CNRS. *Publications include:* Marquis de Sade: L'Oeil de la letter 1978, Casanova: Un Voyage libertine 1985, The Wicked Queen: The Origins of the Myth of Marie-Antoinette 2001, Coping with Freedom: Reflections on Ephemeral Happiness 2001, Adieux à la Reine (Farewell to the Queen, Prix Femina 2002) 2002, Le Lectrice-Adjointe 2003, Lîle flottante 2004, Apolline ou L'école de la Providence 2005, Le Palias de la Reine 2005, Chemins de sable 2006, Jardinière Arlequin 2006, Cafés de la Mémoire 2008. *Address:* CNRS Headquarters, 3, rue Michel-Ange, 75794 Paris cedex 16 (office); c/o Éditions du Seuil, 27 rue Jacob, 75006 Paris, France (office). *Telephone:* 1-44-96-40-00 (CRNS) (office); 1-40-46-50-50 (office). *Fax:* 1-44-96-53-90 (CRNS) (office); 1-40-46-43-00 (office). *E-mail:* contact@seuil .com (office). *Website:* www.cnrs.fr (office).

THOMAS, Clarence, BA, JD; American judge; *Associate Justice, Supreme Court;* b. 23 June 1948, Pinpoint, Savannah, Ga; ed Conception Seminary, Conception Junction, Mo., Holy Cross Coll. and Yale Law School; admitted to bar in Mo. 1974, served as Asst Attorney-Gen. Mo. 1974–77; pvt. legal practice as an attorney for Monsanto Co. 1977–79; Legislative Asst to Mo. Senator John Danforth, US Senate 1979–81; Asst Sec. for Civil Rights, US Dept of Educ. 1981–82; Chair. US Equal Employment Comm. 1982–90; Judge US Court of Appeals for DC Circuit 1990–91; Assoc. Justice US Supreme Court 1991–. *Publication:* My Grandfather's Son 2007. *Address:* United States Supreme Court, One First Street, NE, Washington, DC 20543, USA (office). *Telephone:* (202) 479–3211 (office). *Website:* www.supremecourtus.gov (office).

THOMAS, (David) Craig Owen, MA; British writer; b. 24 Nov. 1942; s. of late John Brinley George Thomas and Gwendoline Megan Thomas (née Owen); m. Jill Lesley White 1967 (died 1987); ed Cardiff High School, Univ. Coll. Cardiff; schoolteacher 1966–77; full-time novelist 1977–; mem. Bd Lichfield Int. Arts Festival; mem. Soc. of Authors. *Publications:* Rat Trap 1976, Firefox 1977, Wolfsbane 1978, Snow Falcon 1979, Sea Leopard 1981, Jade Tiger 1982, Firefox Down 1983, The Bear's Tears 1985, Winter Hawk 1987, All the Grey Cats 1988, The Last Raven 1990, There to Here – Ideas of Political Society 1991, A Hooded Crow 1992, Playing with Cobras 1993, A Wild Justice 1995, A Different War 1997, Slipping into the Shadow 1998; (as David Grant) Moscow 5000 1979, Emerald Decision 1980. *Leisure interests:* history, philosophy, jazz, classical music, gardening, cricket.

THOMAS, David; British singer (bass); b. 26 Feb. 1943, Orpington, Kent, England; m. Veronica Joan Dean 1982; three d.; ed St Paul's Cathedral Choir School, London, King's School, Canterbury, Choral Scholar, King's Coll. Cambridge; began singing as boy chorister in St Paul's Cathedral Choir, London; repertoire ranges from Baroque and Classical, and includes works by Walton, Tippet, Britten, Stravinsky, Schoenberg and Schnittke; tours to Europe, USA and Japan; appearances at int. festivals, including Tanglewood, Salzburg, Edingburgh, Luzerne, Stuttgart, Aldeburgh and BBC Promenade Concerts; has appeared with many of the major symphony orchestras and ensembles in UK, including City of Birmingham Symphony, London Philharmonic, Royal Philharmonic, Philharmonia, Hallé, Royal Liverpool Philharmonic, Chamber Orchestra of Europe, London Classical Players, Scottish Chamber Orchestra, Manchester Camerata, Northern Sinfonia, Taverner Consort, Acad. of Ancient Music and London Baroque, and has worked regularly with conductors including Simon Rattle, John Eliot Gardiner, Nicholas McGegan and Christopher Hogwood; notable engagements in UK include TV recording of Beethoven's 9th Symphony with London Classical Players conducted by Roger Norrington, Handel's Orlando at BBC Proms conducted by Christopher Hogwood and Die Schöpfung' with Chamber Orchestra of Europe and Frans Bruggen; regular concerts with soprano Emma Kirkby and lutenist Anthony Rooley; sang Sarasto in Covent Garden Festival's production of Die Zauberflöte and the Commendatore in Don Giovanni and General Spork in Cornet Cristoph Rilke's Song of Love and Death for Glyndebourne Touring Opera; other engagements have included performances of the Christmas Oratorio in Leipzig and Berlin, a series of Messiahs in Italy and concerts with the Orchestre de la Swiss Romande, Fundaçao de Sao Carlos in Lisbon, Wiener Akademie, with Kammerchor Stuttgart in concerts in Göttingen, and Handel's Serse and Resurrezione in Brighton and Göttingen; engagements in USA have included Messiah with Los Angeles Philharmonic in the Hollywood Bowl, Haydn's Creation with Boston Symphony Orchestra and Simon Rattle, Messiah at Lincoln Center with Acad. of Ancient Music, Schubert's Winterreise at Cornell University and Handel's Judas Maccabaeus, Susanna and Theodora with Philharmonia Baroque and Nicholas McGegan; teaches at Trinity Coll. of Music, London. *Recordings include:* more than 100 records, including Handel's Serse (Hanover Band/Nicholas McGegan), Handel's Susanna, Apollo and Daphne and Judas Maccabeus (Philharmonia Baroque/Nicholas McGegan), Handel's Semele, Purcell's Fairy Queen and Bach's Magnificat (Monteverdi Choir/English Baroque Soloists/John Eliot Gardiner), Handel's Messiah, Orlando, Athalia, etc. (Acad. of Ancient Music/Christopher Hogwood), Handel's Acis, Galatea e Polifemo (London Baroque/Charles Medlam), Handel's Messiah and Israel in Egypt, Bach's B Minor Mass and St John Passion (Taverner Consort & Players/Andrew Parrot), Handel's Messiah (Bach Collegium, Japan/Masaaki Suzuki), Coffee Cantata with Emma Kirkby, Mozart's Requiem (Hanover Band/Roy Goodman), Stravinsky's Pulcinella (City of London Sinfonia/Richard Hickox) and The Creation (City of Birmingham Orchestra/Simon Rattle), Bethoven Choral Symphony (American Bach Soloists/Jeffrey Thomas); solo record Arias for Montagnana, Handel. *Leisure interests:* the island of Dominica, Koi carp. *Address:* Allied Artists, 42 Montpelier Square, London, SW7 1JZ (office). *Telephone:* (20) 7589-6243 (office). *Fax:* (20) 7581-5269 (office). *Website:* www.alliedartists.co.uk (office). *E-mail:* davidthomas@london.com (home).

THOMAS, Sir Derek Morison David, KCMG, MA; British fmr diplomatist and business consultant; b. 31 Oct. 1929, London; s. of K. P. D. Thomas and Mali Thomas; m. Lineke Van der Mast 1956; one s. one d.; ed Radley Coll. and Trinity Hall, Cambridge; articled apprentice, Dolphin Industrial Developments Ltd 1947; entered HM Foreign Service 1953; RNVR 1953–55; appointments overseas included Moscow, Manila, Sofia, Ottawa, Paris, Washington; Deputy Under-Sec. of State for Europe and Political Dir FCO 1984–87; Amb. to Italy 1987–89; European Adviser to NM Rothschild and Sons Ltd 1990–2003, Dir 1991–99; Dir Rothschild Italia 1990–97, Christow Consultants Ltd 1990–99, Rothschild Europe 1991–97; Dir, Assoc. CDP Nexus 1990–92; Dir New Court Int. Ltd, Moscow, Consilium Spa, Prague 1994–2001; mem. Export Guarantees Advisory Council 1991–97; Chair. British Invisibles Lotis Cttee 1992–96, Council S.O.S. Sahel 1991–2000, Council Royal Inst. of Int. Affairs 1994–97, Council Reading Univ. 1990–99; Chair. British Inst. of Florence 1996–2002; Hon. Fellow, Trinity Hall, Cambridge 1998; Hon. LLD (Leicester) 2003. *Leisure interests:* exploring the past and present, music, theatre, wines, reading when there is time, grandchildren, gardening.

Address: Flat 1, 12 Lower Sloane Street, London, SW1W 8BJ, England (home); Ferme de l'Epine, 14490 Planquery, France (home). *Telephone:* (20) 7730-1473 (home). *E-mail:* derek@thomas.fsnet.co.uk (home).

THOMAS, Donald Michael, MA; British novelist and poet; b. 27 Jan. 1935, Redruth, Cornwall; s. of Harold Redvers Thomas and Amy Thomas (née Moyle); m. Angela Thomas; two s. one d.; ed Redruth Grammar School, Univ. High School, Melbourne, New Coll., Oxford; English teacher, Teignmouth, Devon 1959–63; Lecturer, Hereford Coll. of Educ. 1963–78; full-time author 1978–; Gollancz/Pan Fantasy Prize, PEN Fiction Prize, Cheltenham Prize, Los Angeles Times Fiction Prize, Cholmondeley Award for Poetry, Orwell Prize for Biography. *Play:* Hell Fire Corner 2004. *Publications:* Two Voices 1968, Logan Stone 1971, Love and Other Deaths 1975, Honeymoon Voyage 1978, The Flute-Player 1978, Birthstone 1980, The White Hotel 1981, Dreaming in Bronze 1981, Ararat 1983, Selected Poems 1983, Swallow 1984, Sphinx 1986, Summit 1987, Memories and Hallucinations 1988, Lying Together 1989, Flying in to Love 1992, The Puberty Tree (new and selected poems) 1992, Pictures at an Exhibition 1993, Eating Pavlova 1994, Lady with a Laptop 1996, Alexander Solzhenitsyn (biog.) 1998, Charlotte 2000, Dear Shadows 2003, Not Saying Everything 2006, Bleak Hotel 2008. *Leisure interests:* travel, Russia, Cornwall, the life of the imagination. *Address:* The Coach House, Rashleigh Vale, Truro, Cornwall, TR1 1TJ, England (home). *Telephone:* (1872) 261724 (home). *E-mail:* dmthomas@btconnect.com (home). *Website:* www.dmthomasonline.com; www.don-whitehotel.blogspot.com.

THOMAS, Edward Donnall, MD; American physician; *Professor Emeritus, University of Washington Medical School;* b. 15 March 1920, Mart, Tex.; s. of Edward E. Thomas and Angie Hill Donnall Thomas; m. Dorothy Martin 1942; two s. one d.; ed Univ. of Tex., Harvard Univ.; US Army 1948–50; Chief Medical Resident, Sr Asst Resident, Peter Bent Brigham Hosp. 1951–53; Research Assoc., Cancer Research Foundation Children's Medical Centre, Boston 1953–55; Instructor in Medicine, Harvard Medical School 1953–55; Physician-in-Chief, Mary Imogene Bassett Hosp., Cooperstown, NY 1955–63; Assoc. Clinical Prof. of Medicine, Coll. of Physicians and Surgeons, Columbia Univ. 1955–63; Prof. of Medicine, Univ. of Wash. Medical School, Seattle (Head, Div. of Oncology 1963–85), Attending Physician, Univ. of Wash. Hosp., Seattle 1963–90, Prof. Emer. 1990–; mem., Fred Hutchinson Cancer Research Centre, Seattle 1974–, Dir, Medical Oncology 1974–89, Assoc. Dir, Clinical Research Programs 1982–89; mem., Haematology Study Section, Nat. Insts of Health 1965–69; mem. Bd of Trustees and Medical Science Advisory Cttee, Leukaemia Soc. America, Inc. 1969–73; mem., Clinical Cancer Investigation Review Cttee, Nat. Cancer Inst. 1970–74; mem. numerous editorial bds; numerous guest lectures; Hon. MD (Cagliari) 1981, (Verona) 1991, (Parma) 1992, (Barcelona) 1994; hon. mem. numerous socs; received McIntyre Award 1975, Levine Award 1979, Kettering Prize 1981, de Villiers Award 1983, Landsteiner Award 1987, Fox Award 1990, Gairdner Foundation Award 1990, Nat. Medal of Science 1990, shared Nobel Prize for Medicine and Physiology 1990 for pioneering bone marrow transplants in leukaemia patients, Kober Medal 1992. *Publications:* numerous articles. *Address:* Fred Hutchinson Cancer Center, 1100 Fairview Avenue North, D5-100, P.O. Box 19024, Seattle, WA 98109, USA.

THOMAS, Eric Jackson, MD, FRCOG, FMedSci, FRCP; British physician, academic and university administrator; *Vice-Chancellor, University of Bristol;* b. 24 March 1953, Hartlepool; s. of Eric Jackson Thomas and Margaret Mary Murray; m. Narell Marie Ronnard 1976; one s. one d.; ed Ampleforth Coll., Univ. of Newcastle upon Tyne; Lecturer in Obstetrics and Gynaecology, Univ. of Sheffield 1985–87; Sr Lecturer in Obstetrics and Gynaecology, Univ. of Newcastle upon Tyne 1987–90; Prof. of Obstetrics and Gynaecology, Univ. of Southampton 1991–2001, Head School of Medicine 1995–98, Dean Faculty of Medicine, Health and Biological Sciences 1998–2000; Vice-Chancellor Univ. of Bristol 2001–; Consultant Obstetrician and Gynaecologist, Newcastle Gen. Hosp. 1987–2000, Southampton Univ. Hosps Trust 1991–2001; Dir (non-exec.) Southampton Univ. Hosps Trust 1997–2000, Southampton and SW Hants. Health Authority 2000–01; Exec. Sec. Council of Heads of Medical Schools 1998–2000; mem. Council Royal Coll. of Obstetricians and Gynaecologists 1995–2001; mem. Bd South West Regional Devt Agency 2003–08; mem. Bd Universities UK 2006– (also Chair. Research Policy Cttee 2006–); mem. South West Regional Sports Bd 2003–06; Hon. DSc, Hon. LLD; William Blair Bell Memorial Lecturer, Royal Coll. of Obstetricians and Gynaecologists 1987. *Publications:* Modern Approaches to Endometriosis (jtly) 1991; publs on endometriosis and reproductive medicine. *Leisure interests:* keeping fit, golf, Newcastle United. *Address:* Office of the Vice-Chancellor, University of Bristol, Senate House, Tyndall Avenue, Bristol, BS8 1TU, England (office). *Telephone:* (117) 928-7499 (office). *Fax:* (117) 930-4263 (office). *Website:* www.bris.ac.uk (office).

THOMAS, Gareth, PhD; American scientist and academic; *Professor, University of California, Berkeley;* b. 9 Aug. 1932, Maesteg, Wales; s. of David Basset Thomas and Edith May Gregory; m.; one s.; ed Univ. of Wales, Univ. of Cambridge, UK; with Univ. of Calif., Berkeley 1960–, Prof. 1967–; Assoc. Dean, Grad. Div. 1968–69, Asst to Chancellor 1969–72, Acting Vice-Chancellor, Acad. Affairs 1971–72, Chair. Faculty of Coll. of Eng 1977–78, Sr Faculty Scientist, Materials and Molecular Research Div., Scientific Dir, Nat. Center for Electron Microscopy, Prof., Dept of Materials and Mineral Eng 1982–93; mem. NAS, Nat. Acad. of Eng and numerous cttees; Hon. ScD (Cambridge) 1969, (Lehigh Univ.) 1978, (Kraków Univ., Poland) 1999 and numerous other awards. *Publications:* several books and 600 research papers. *Leisure interests:* squash, skiing, cricket. *Address:* Department of Materials Science and Mineral Engineering, University of California, 561 Evans Hall, Berkeley, CA 94720, USA. *Telephone:* (510) 486-5696. *Fax:* (510) 643-0965.

THOMAS, Harvey, CBE, FRSA; British international public relations consultant; b. 10 April 1939, London; s. of the late John Humphrey Kenneth Thomas and Olga Rosina Thomas; m. Marlies Kram 1978; two d.; ed Westminster School, London, Northwestern Coll., Minn., USA, Univ. of Minnesota, Univ. of Hawaii, Honolulu; articled in law 1957–60; Billy Graham Evangelistic Asscn 1960–75, N of England Mission 1960–61, Direct Mail, Minneapolis 1961–63, Press Relations, Southern California Mission 1963, KAIM Radio, Honolulu 1963–64, London Missions 1965–67, World Congress on Evangelism, Berlin 1966, Australasian Missions 1967–69, Dir Euro 70 Crusades 1969–70, Dir European Congress on Evangelism, Amsterdam 1970–71, research in 80 countries for 1974 Int. Congress on World Evangelization Lausanne 1971–72, SPRE-E 73, London 1973, Dir Billy Graham LAUSTADE Rally, Lausanne 1974, Gen. Sec. EUROFEST Brussels 1975; int. public relations and presentation consultant 1976–; Co-ordinator Int. Exposition for Tech. Transfer 1984; Public Relations, Luis Palau Mission to London 1984; Dir of Presentation, Conservative Party 1978; Field Dir Prime Minister's Election Tour 1987; Chair. Fellowship of European Broadcasters; mem. Bd London Cremation Co. PLC; Chair. Trans World Radio UK; Fellow, Chartered Inst. of Public Relations, Chartered Inst. of Journalists; mem. Inst. of Dirs; int. political consultant; conf. speaker and moderator; broadcaster and commentator on politics, religion and media; exec. coach; Individual Achievement Int. Broadcasting Award 2000. *Publications:* In the Face of Fear 1985, Making an Impact 1989, If They Haven't Heard It – You Haven't Said It 1995. *Leisure interests:* family, travel, broadcasting, public speaking, trains. *Address:* 23 The Service Road, Potters Bar, Herts., EN6 1QA, England (home). *Telephone:* (1707) 649910 (home). *Fax:* (1707) 662653 (home). *E-mail:* harvey@hthomas.net (office). *Website:* www.hthomas.net (office).

THOMAS, Iwan, MBE, BSc; British athlete; b. 5 Jan. 1974, Farnborough, Hants.; ed Stamford School, Brunel Univ.; fourth-ranked BMX rider, Europe 1988; Fifth, Olympic Games 400m 1996, Silver Medal 4×400m relay; Gold Medal, Amateur Athletics Asscn Championships 400m 1997 (British record, 44.36 seconds), 1998; Silver Medal, World Championships 4×400m relay 1997; Gold Medal, European Championships 400m 1998, World Cup 400m 1998, Commonwealth Games 400m 1998; Patron Norwich Union Startrack Scheme; after-dinner speaker; British Athletics Writers' Male Athlete of the Year 1998. *Leisure interests:* music, Playstation, socializing with friends. *Address:* Nuff Respect (Agent), 107 Sherland Road, Twickenham, Middx, TW1 4HB, England (office). *Telephone:* (20) 8891-4145 (office). *Fax:* (20) 8891-4140 (office). *E-mail:* nuff_respect@msn.com (office). *Website:* www.nuff-respect.co.uk (office); www.iwanthomas.com.

THOMAS, Dame Jean Olwen, CBE, DBE, SCD., FRS, CChem, FMedSci; British scientist and academic; *Professor of Macromolecular Biochemistry and Master, St Catharine's College, University of Cambridge;* b. 1 Oct. 1942; d. of John Robert Thomas and Lorna Prunella Thomas (née Harris); ed Llwyn-y-Bryn High School for Girls, Swansea, Univ. Coll., Swansea, Univ. of Wales; Beit Memorial Fellow 1967–69, Univ. of Cambridge 1967–69, demonstrator in Biochemistry 1969–73, Lecturer 1973–87, Reader in the Biochemisry of Macromolecules 1987–91, Prof. of Macromolecular Biochemistry 1991–, Chair. Cambridge Centre for Molecular Recognition 1993–2003, Fellow, New Hall 1969–2006, tutor 1970–76, Vice-Pres. 1983–87, Master, St Catharine's Coll. 2007–; Fellow, Royal Soc. 1986–, mem. Council 1990–02, Biological Sec. and Vice-Pres. 2008–; Pres. Biochemical Soc. 2000–05; mem. European Molecular Biology Org. 1982–, Academia Europaea 1991–, Council and Scientific Advisory Cttee Imperial Cancer Research Fund 1994–2000, Scientific Advisory Cttee Lister Inst. 1994–2000, Internal Merit Promotion Panel of Research Councils (Chair. 2006–), Royal Soc. of Chem.; Fellow, Acad. of Medical Sciences 2002–; Gov. Wellcome Trust Ltd 2000–; Trustee British Museum 1994–2004; Hon. Fellow, UCW Swansea 1987, Cardiff Univ. 1998, Hon. Mem. Biochemical Soc. 2008; Hon. DSc (Wales) 1992, (East Anglia) 2002; Ayling Prize 1964, Hinkel Research Prize 1967, K. M. Stott Research Prize, Newnham Coll., Cambridge 1976. *Publications:* Companion to Biochemistry: Selected Topics for Further Study Vol. 1 1974, Vol. 2 1979 (jt and contrib.); numerous papers in scientific journals. *Leisure interests:* reading, music, walking. *Address:* St Catharine's College, Trumpington Street, Cambridge, CB2 1RL (office); Department of Biochemistry, 80 Tennis Court Road, Cambridge, CB2 1QW (office); 26 Eachard Road, Cambridge, CB3 0HY, England (home). *Telephone:* (1223) 338347 (St Catharine's) (office); (1223) 333670 (office); (1223) 362620 (home). *E-mail:* master@caths.cam.ac.uk (office). *Website:* www.caths.cam.ac.uk (office).

THOMAS, Jeremy, CBE; British film producer; b. 26 July 1949, London; s. of Ralph and Joy Thomas; m. 1st Claudia Frolich 1977 (divorced 1981); one d.; m. 2nd Vivien Coughman 1982; two s.; began work in film-processing lab., later worked as asst and in cutting room; worked with Dir Philippe Mora, editing Brother Can You Spare a Dime; went to Australia where he produced first film Mad Dog Morgan 1974, then returned to England in 1976 to produce Jerzy Skolimowski's The Shout; f. Recorded Picture Co. Ltd 1975; Chair. BFI 1992–97; set up own film distribution co. Recorded Releasing 1985; f. Hanway Films 1998; Vittorio de Sica Prize 1986, Special Award, Evening Standard Film Awards 1991, Michael Balcon BAFTA Award 1991, BFI Fellowship, Screen International Prize for World Cinema Achievement, European Film Awards 2006. *Films:* Mad Dog Morgan 1976, The Shout (Grand Prix de Jury, Cannes Film Festival) 1978, The Great Rock'n'Roll Swindle 1979, The Kids are Alright (Special Consultant) 1979, Bad Timing 1980, Eureka 1982, Merry Christmas Mr Lawrence 1982, The Hit 1983, Insignificance 1984, The Last Emperor 1987 (winner of nine Acad. Awards including Best Picture), Everybody Wins 1990, The Sheltering Sky 1990, The Naked Lunch 1991, Let Him Have It (Exec. Producer) 1991, Little Buddha 1993, Rough Magic (Exec. Producer) 1994, Victory (Exec. Producer) 1994, Stealing Beauty 1995, The Ogre (Exec. Producer) 1996, The Brave (Exec. Producer) 1996, Crash

(Exec. Producer) (Grand Prix de Jury, Cannes Film Festival) 1996, Blood and Wine 1996, All The Little Animals (Dir) 1998, The Cup (Exec. Producer) 1999, Gohatto 2000, Brother 2000, Sexy Beast 2001, Rabbit Proof Fence (Exec. Producer) 2002, Triumph of Love (Exec. Producer) 2002, Young Adam 2003, Travellers and Magicians (Exec. Producer) 2003, The Dreamers (Producer) 2003, Dreaming Lhasa (Exec. Producer) 2004, Heimat 3 (Exec. Producer) 2004, Don't Come Knocking (Exec. Producer) 2004, Tideland 2004, Glastonbury (Exec. Producer) 2005, Fast Food Nation 2005, Mister Lonely (Exec. Producer) 2006, Joe Strummer: The Future is Unwritten (Exec. Producer) 2007, Franklyn 2008, Creation 2009. *Address:* Recorded Picture Company Ltd, 24 Hanway Street, London, W1T 1UH, England (office). *Telephone:* (20) 7636-2251 (office). *Fax:* (20) 7636-2261 (office). *E-mail:* kp@recordedpicture.com (office). *Website:* www.recordedpicture.com (office).

THOMAS, (John David) Ronald, (J. D. R. Thomas), DSc, CSci, CChem, FRSC; British chemist and academic; *Professor Emeritus of Chemistry and Applied Chemistry, University of Wales and Cardiff University;* b. 2 Jan. 1926, Carnaugwynion, Gwynfe, Wales; s. of John Thomas and Betty Thomas (née Watkins); m. Gwyneth Thomas 1950; three d.; ed Llandovery Grammar School and Univ. of Wales, Cardiff; RAMC blood transfusion training, Clifton Coll. and Southmead Hosp., Bristol 1944; served in RAMC, India 1944–47; Tech. Asst British Resin Products Ltd Tonbridge 1948; analytical chemist, Spillers Ltd, Cardiff 1950–51, Glamorgan Co. Council 1951–53; Asst Lecturer, Cardiff Coll. of Tech. 1953–56; Lecturer, South East Essex Tech. Coll. 1956–58; Sr Lecturer, Newport and Monmouthshire Coll. of Tech. 1958–61; Sr Lecturer and Reader, Univ. of Wales Inst. of Science and Tech. (UWIST) and Univ. of Wales, Cardiff 1961–90; Counsellor, Open Univ. 1970–71; Prof., Univ. of Wales, Cardiff (now Cardiff Univ.) 1990–93, Prof. Emer. 1994–; mem. Court Univ. of Wales 1989–2001, 2002–08, Council 1997–2001; mem. Council UWIST, Cardiff 1976–79, Univ. of Wales Coll. of Medicine 1993–99; mem. Court Aberystwyth Univ. 1995–; Royal Soc. sponsored invitee to Iranian Chemical Soc. Third Int. Congress and Iranian univs 1975; British Council sponsored invitee to Asian Chemical Congress '87, Seoul and univs at Taejon and Ulsan, S Korea 1987; Foreign Expert, Academia Sinica (Nanjing), Hunan (Changsha), North West (Xian) and Shanghai Teachers Univs 1983, 1985; Visiting Prof., Japan Soc. for the Promotion of Science 1985, NEWI (now Glyndwr Univ.), Wrexham 1995–96; Assessor, Univ. Pertanian Malaysia 1992–94, 1997–99, Univ. Sains Malaysia 1996–98, Universidade Nova de Lisboa and Universidade do Porto 1998–99, Hong Kong Research Grants Council 1996–2009; RSC Schools Lecturer in Analytical Chem. 1985–86; Distinguished Visiting Fellow, La Trobe Univ., Australia 1989; mem. Govt High-Level Mission on Analytical Instrumentation to Japan 1991; Adviser to RSC on privatization of UK Lab. of Govt Chemist 1995–97; Vice-Pres. Soc. for Analytical Chem. and Analytical Div. Chem. Soc. 1974–76, mem. Council Chem. Soc. 1976–79; Hon. Sec. Analytical Div. RSC 1987–90, Pres. 1990–92, mem. Council RSC 1990–2005; Chair. Analytical Editorial Bd RSC 1985–90; Sec. Baptist Union of Wales Superannuation Appeal 1976–78; mem. Council, Baptist Union of Wales 1994–97; lectured widely in UK, Europe, Middle and Far East, Australia, USA; famed for PVC-based ion sensors and electrochemical sensors for biomedical and technological roles; Hon. Ed. Newsletter, Analytical Div., RSC 1995–2007; Hon. Prof., Univ. 'Politehnica', Bucharest, Romania 1996–; Hon. Course Adviser, Hong Kong Baptist Univ. 1991–2009; Hon. Mem. Romanian Soc. of Analytical Chem. 1994–, Romanian Chem. Soc. 1999–; Commonwealth Foundation Lecturer, CSMC Research Inst., Bhavnagar, India 1978, RSC Electroanalytical Chem. Medal and Award 1981, E.A. Moelwyn-Hughes Lecturer, Univ. of Cambridge 1988, J. Heyrovsky Centenary Medal, Czechoslovak Acad. of Sciences 1990, RSC symposium in his honour, Cardiff 1994, White Robe, Gorsedd of Bards 2000, RSC L.S. Theobald Lectureship, 2001, Enric Casassas Memorial Lecturer, Univ. of Barcelona 2002, Most Visited Article Award of Inst. d'Estudis Catalans 2005, Distinguished Service Award Analytical Div. RSC 2006. *Publications:* ed.: Selective Electrode Reviews, Vols 1–14 1979–92; Trans. Ed.: Membrane Electrodes in Drug Substances Analysis (Cosofret) 1982; author: History of the Analytical Division, Royal Society of Chemistry 1999; co-author: Calculations in Advanced Physical Chemistry 1962–83 (Hungarian trans. 1979), Noble Gases and Their Compounds 1964, Selective Ion-Sensitive Electrodes 1971 (Chinese trans. 1975, Japanese 1977), Dipole Moments in Inorganic Chemistry 1971 (Spanish trans. 1974), Practical Electrophoresis 1976, Chromatographic Separations and Extraction with Foamed Plastics and Rubbers 1982; more than 300 articles in scientific journals on chemical and bio-sensors, reaction kinetics, separation chem. and environmental matters. *Leisure interests:* travel, reading (current affairs and history), browsing and things of Wales, genealogy. *Address:* 4 Orchard Court, Gresford, Wrexham, LL12 8EB, Wales (home). *Telephone:* (1978) 856771 (home). *E-mail:* jdrthomas@aol.com (home).

THOMAS, Sir John Meurig, Kt, MA, DSc, LLD, FRS; British scientist and academic; *Professorial Research Fellow, Davy Faraday Research Laboratory;* b. 15 Dec. 1932, Llanelli, Wales; s. of David J. Thomas and Edyth Thomas; m. Margaret Edwards 1959 (died 2002); two d.; ed Gwendraeth Grammar School, Univ. Coll., Swansea, Queen Mary Coll., London; Scientific Officer, UKAEA 1957–58; Asst Lecturer, Lecturer, Sr Lecturer then Reader, Dept of Chem., Univ. Coll. of N Wales, Bangor 1958–69; Prof. and Head Dept of Chem., Univ. Coll. of Wales, Aberystwyth 1969–78; Head of Dept of Physical Chem., Univ. of Cambridge, Professorial Fellow of King's Coll. 1978–86, Master of Peterhouse 1993–2002, Distinguished Hon. Research Fellow, Dept of Materials Science, 1993–2002, Hon. Prof. in Solid State Chem. 2002–; Cabinet Office Advisory Cttee on Applied Research and Devt 1982–85; Dir Royal Inst. of GB 1986–91, Resident Prof. 1986–88, Fullerian Prof. of Chem. 1988–94, Prof. of Chem. and Professorial Research Fellow 1994–; Deputy Pro-Chancellor Univ. of Wales 1991–94; Dir Davy Faraday Research Labs 1986–91; Chair. Chem. Research Applied to World Needs, IUPAC 1987–95; Pres. Chem. Section, BAAS

1988–89; Hon. Visiting Prof. of Physical Chem., Queen Mary Coll., London 1986–, Prof. of Chem., Imperial Coll., London 1986–91, Miller Prof., Univ. of Calif., Berkeley 1998; Distinguished Visiting Prof., Ecole Nat. Supérieure de Chimie Paris 1991; Visiting Prof., Scuola Normale Superiore Pisa 2003; Trustee British Museum (Natural History) 1986–91, Science Museum 1989–95; Commr, 1851 Royal Exhbn 1995– (Chair. Scientific Research Cttee 1996–2005); Tetelman Fellow, Yale Univ. 1997; mem. Academia Europaea 1989; Rutherford Memorial Lecturer of Royal Soc. in New Zealand 1997; Hon. Professorial Fellow Academia Sinica (Shanghai), Imperial Coll. London, Queen Mary Coll. London; Hon. FREng; Hon. FRSE; Hon. Fellow, Indian Acad. (Bangalore), Indian Acad. (Delhi), UMIST, Univ. Coll. Swansea, American Acad. of Arts and Science, American Philosophical Soc., Venezuelan Acad. of Sciences, Russian Acad. of Sciences, Inst. of Physics; Hon. Foreign Fellow, Eng Acad. Japan 1991, Hungarian and Polish Acad. of Sciences 1998, Royal Spanish Acad. of Sciences 1999, Göttingen Acad. of Sciences 2003–, Hon. Bencher, Gray's Inn 1986; Hon. DSc (Heriot-Watt Univ.) 1989, (Birmingham) 1991, (Claude Bernard Univ., Lyon) 1994, (Complutense Univ., Madrid) 1994, (Western Univ., Ont.) 1995, (Eindhoven Univ., Netherlands, Hull Univ.) 1996, (Aberdeen, Surrey) 1997, (American Univ. Cairo) 2002, (Sydney, Clarkson, NY) 2005, (Osaka) 2006; Hon. DUniv (Open Univ.) 1992; laureate hc (Turin Univ.) 2004; Baker Lecturer, Cornell Univ. 1983, Bakerian Prize Lectureship, Royal Soc. 1990, Rutherford Lecturer, Royal Soc. NZ 1997, Centennial Karl Ziegler Lecturer Max Planck Inst. Mülheim 1998, Linus Pauling Lectureship, Calif. Inst. of Tech. 1999, John C. Polanyi Nobel Laureate Lecturer, Univ. of Toronto 2000, Dreichamer Lecturer, Univ. of Illinois–Urbana 2004, Ipatieff Lecturer, Northwestern Univ. 2004, Golden Jubilee Distinguished Lecturer, Hong Kong Baptist Univ. 2006, Woodward Lecturer, Yale Univ. 2006; numerous awards including Faraday and Longstaff Medals, RSC 1990, Messel Gold Medal, Soc. of Chemical Industry 1992, Davy Medal, Royal Soc. 1994, ACS Willard Gibbs Gold Medal 1995, Hon. Medal, Polish Acad. of Sciences, Warsaw 1996, Semonov Centenary Medal, Russian Acad. of Sciences 1996, ACS Award for Creative Research in Catalysis 1999, Linus Pauling Gold Medal for Advances in Science, Stanford Univ. 2003, Giulionatta Gold Medal for Contributions to Catalysis, Italian Chem. Soc. 2003; new mineral meurigite named in his honour 1995; symposium in his honour organized by Microscopy and Microanalysis Soc. of America, Philadelphia 2000 and by RSC London 2002, Sir George Gabriel Stokes Gold Medal for Analytical Science, Royal Soc. of Chem. 2005. *Television:* Royal Inst. Christmas Lectures on Crystals 1987–88; many Welsh language broadcasts. *Radio:* BBC Annual Lecture in Welsh 1978. *Publications:* Principles of Heterogeneous Catalysis 1967, Characterization of Catalysts 1980, Heterogeneous Catalysis: Principles and Practice 1997, Michael Faraday and the Royal Institution: The Genius of Man and Place 1991, Perspectives in Catalysis (with K. I. Zamaraev) 1992; Pan Edrychwyf ar y Nefoedd (Welsh Radio Lecture) 1978; Founding Co-Ed.-in-Chief Catalysis Letters 1988–, Topics in Catalysis 1992–; Current Opinion in Solid State and Materials Science; over 950 articles on catalysis solid-state and surface science. *Leisure interests:* walking, Welsh literature, ancient civilizations, birdwatching, popularization of science, listening to music. *Address:* Dept of Materials Science, Cambridge, CB2 3QZ (office); Davy Faraday Research Laboratory, The Royal Institution, 21 Albemarle Street, London, W1S 4BS, England (office). *Telephone:* (1223) 334300 (Cambridge) (office); (20) 7670-2928 (London) (office). *Fax:* (1223) 740360 (Cambridge) (home); (20) 7670-2958 (London) (office). *E-mail:* jmt@ri.ac.uk (office). *Website:* www.ri.ac.uk/DFRL (office).

THOMAS, Sir Keith Vivian, Kt, MA, FBA; British historian and academic; *Fellow, All Souls College, Oxford;* b. 2 Jan. 1933, Wick, Glamorgan, Wales; s. of Vivian Thomas and Hilda Thomas; m. Valerie June Little 1961; one s. one d.; ed Barry Co. Grammar School and Balliol Coll., Oxford (Brackenbury Scholar); nat. service in Royal Welch Fusiliers 1950–52; Fellow, All Souls Coll., Oxford 1955–57, 2001–, St John's Coll. Oxford 1957–86, Tutor 1957–85; Reader in Modern History, Univ. of Oxford 1978–85, Prof. 1986, Pres. Corpus Christi Coll. 1986–2000, Pro-Vice-Chancellor, Univ. of Oxford 1988–2000, Fellow, All Souls Coll. 2001–; Del., Oxford Univ. Press 1980–2000; mem. Econ. and Social Research Council 1985–90, Reviewing Cttee on Export of Works of Art 1990–92, Royal Comm. on Historical Manuscripts 1992–2002; Trustee, Nat. Gallery 1991–98, British Museum 1999–; Pres. British Acad. 1993–97; Chair. Supervisory Cttee, Oxford Dictionary of Nat. Biography 1992–2004, British Library Advisory Cttee for Arts, Humanities and Social Sciences 1997–2002, Advisory Cttee, Warburg Inst., Univ. of London 2000–; mem. Academia Europaea 1993; Hon. Fellow, Balliol Coll. Oxford 1984, St John's Coll. Oxford 1986, Corpus Christi Coll. Oxford 2000; Hon. Vice-Pres. Royal Historical Soc. 2001–; Foreign Hon. mem. American Acad. of Arts and Sciences 1983; Cavaliere Ufficiale, Ordine al Merito della Repubblica Italiana 1991; Hon. DLitt (Kent) 1983, (Wales) 1987, (Hull) 1995, (Leicester) 1996, (Sussex) 1996, (Warwick) 1998, (London) 2006; Hon. LittD (Sheffield) 1992, (Cambridge) 1995; Hon. LLD (Williams) 1988, (Oglethorpe, Atlanta, Ga) 1996; Wolfson Literary Award for History 1971, G.M. Trevelyan Lecturer, Univ. of Cambridge 1979, Ford's Lecturer, Univ. of Oxford 2000, Norton Medlicott Medal, Historical Asscn 2003. *Publications:* Religion and the Decline of Magic 1971, Puritans and Revolutionaries (co-ed with Donald Pennington) 1978, Man and the Natural World 1983, The Oxford Book of Work (ed.) 1999, Roy Jenkins: A Retrospective (co-ed with Andrew Adonis) 2004, Changing Conceptions of National Biography 2005, The Ends of Life: Roads to Fulfilment in Early Modern England 2009. *Leisure interest:* visiting secondhand bookshops. *Address:* All Souls College, Oxford, OX1 4AL (office); The Broad Gate, Broad Street, Ludlow, Shropshire, SY8 1NJ, England (home). *Telephone:* (1865) 279379 (office); (1584) 877797 (home). *Fax:* (1865) 279299 (office). *E-mail:* keith.thomas@all-souls.oxford.ac.uk (home).

THOMAS, Michael Tilson (see Tilson Thomas, Michael).

THOMAS, Robert Kemeys, MA, DPhil, FRS; British chemist and academic; *Professor, Physical and Theoretical Chemistry Laboratory, University of Oxford;* b. 25 Sept. 1941, Harpenden; s. of Rev. Herbert Thomas and Agnes Thomas (née McLaren); m. Pamela H. Woods 1968; one s. two d.; ed St John's Coll., Oxford; researcher Univ. of Oxford 1968–78, Fellow Merton Coll. 1975–78, Lecturer in Physical Chemistry 1978–, Fellow and tutor Univ. Coll. 1978–; Tilden Lecturer, Royal Soc. of Chemistry; Hon. Prof. Inst. of Chemistry, Chinese Acad. of Sciences, Beijing 1999–. *Publications:* papers in scientific journals. *Leisure interests:* music, flora, fungi, Chinese language. *Address:* Physical and Theoretical Chemistry Laboratory, South Parks Road, Oxford, OX1 3QZ, England (office); University College, High Street, Oxford, OX1 4BH. *Telephone:* (1865) 275422 (office); (1865) 276602 (office). *Fax:* (1865) 275410 (office). *E-mail:* robert.thomas@chem.ox.ac.uk (office). *Website:* physchem.ox.ac.uk/~rkt (office); www.chem.ox.ac.uk/researchguide/rkthomas .html (office).

THOMAS, Tillman, BEcons; Grenadian lawyer and politician; *Prime Minister;* b. 13 June 1945, Hermitage, St Patrick; ed Fordham Univ., USA, Univ. of the West Indies, Hugh Woodling Law School, Trinidad; fmr political prisoner under govt of Maurice Bishop in early 1980s; mem. House of Reps for St Patrick E 1984–90, 2003–; Jr Minister, Ministry of Legal Affairs 1984–90; Founder mem. Nat. Democratic Congress Party 1987, Asst Gen. Sec. 1987–90, Leader 2000–; Leader of Opposition 2003–08; Prime Minister 2008–. *Address:* Office of the Prime Minister, Ministerial Complex, 6th Floor, Botanical Gardens, St George's, Grenada (office). *Telephone:* 440-2255 (office). *Fax:* 440-4116 (office). *E-mail:* pmoffice@gov.gd (office). *Website:* www.pmoffice.gov.gd (office).

THOMAS-GRAHAM, Pamela, BA, MBA, JD; American business executive and author; *Managing Director, Angelo, Gordon and Company;* b. 1963, Detroit, Mich.; m. Lawrence Otis Graham; one s.; ed Detroit Lutheran West High School, Harvard-Radcliffe Coll., Harvard Business School, Harvard Law School; fmr Ed. Harvard Law Review; joined McKinsey & Co. 1989, Pnr 1995–99, leader of Media and Entertainment practice –1999; Pres. and CEO CNBC.com 1999–2001, Pres. and CEO CNBC 2001–05, Chair. 2005; Group Pres. Better and Moderate Apparel, Liz Claiborne Inc. 2006–07; Man. Dir Angelo, Gordon and Co. (pvt. investment man. firm), New York 2008–; mem. Bd of Dirs Clorox Co. 2005–, Idenix Pharmaceuticals Inc. 2005–; fmr mem. US Sec. of State Condoleezza Rice's Advisory Cttee on Transformational Diplomacy; Capt. Jonathan Fay Prize. *Publications:* A Darker Shade of Crimson 1998, Blue Blood 2000, Orange Crushed 2004. *Address:* Angelo, Gordon and Company, 245 Park Avenue, New York, NY 10167, USA (office). *Telephone:* (212) 692-0242 (office). *E-mail:* pthomas-graham@angelogordon.com (office). *Website:* www.angelogordon.com (office).

THOMAS OF SWYNNERTON, Baron (Life Peer), cr. 1981, of Notting Hill in Greater London; **Hugh Swynnerton Thomas,** MA, FRHistS; British historian; b. 21 Oct. 1931, Windsor; s. of Hugh Whitelegge and Margery (née Swynnerton) Thomas; m. Vanessa Jebb 1962; two s. one d.; ed Sherborne School, Queens' Coll., Cambridge and Sorbonne, Paris; Foreign Office 1954–57; Sec. UK Del. to UN Disarmament Sub-cttee 1955–56; Lecturer, Royal Mil. Acad., Sandhurst 1957; worked for UNA 1959–61; Prof. of History, Univ. of Reading 1966–76; Chair. Grad. School of European Studies 1973–76, Centre for Policy Studies 1979–91; King Juan Carlos I Prof. New York Univ. 1995; Visiting Prof. of History, Boston Univ. 1996, Univ. Prof. 1997–; Corresp. mem. Real Academia de la Historia, Madrid; Order of the Aztec Eagle 1995, Grand Cross, Order of Isabel la Católica, Spain 2001; Somerset Maugham Prize 1962, Arts Council Nat. Book Award for History 1980. *Publications include:* The Spanish Civil War 1961, The Suez Affair 1966, Cuba or the Pursuit of Freedom 1971, Goya and the Third of May 1808 1973, John Strachey 1973, An Unfinished History of the World 1979, A Case for the Round Reading Room 1983, Havannah! (novel) 1984, Armed Truce: The Beginnings of the Cold War 1945–46 1986, Klara (novel) 1988, Madrid: A Traveller's Companion (ed.) 1988, Ever Closer Union: Britain's Destiny in Europe 1991, The Conquest of Mexico 1993, The Slave Trade 1997, The Future of Europe 1998, Who's Who of the Conquistadors 2000, Rivers of Gold 2003, Beaumarchais in Seville 2007, Don Eduardo 2007. *Address:* 29 Ladbroke Grove, London, W11 3BB, England.

THOMPSON, Alan Eric, MA, PhD, FRSA, FSA (Scot); British economist and academic; *Professor Emeritus of Economics, Heriot-Watt University;* b. 16 Sept. 1924; s. of Eric Thompson and Florence Thompson; m. Mary Heather Long 1960; three s. one d.; ed Univ. of Edin.; Lecturer in Econs, Univ. of Edin. 1953–59, 1964–71; Labour MP for Dunfermline 1959–64; Econ. Consultant, Scotch Whisky Asscn 1965–70; Visiting Prof., Graduate School of Business, Stanford Univ., Calif. 1966, 1968; A. J. Balfour Prof. of Econs of Govt, Heriot-Watt Univ., Edin. 1972–87, Prof. of Econs, School of Business and Financial Studies 1987–88, Prof. Emer. 1988–; mem. Scottish Council for Adult Educ. in HM Forces 1973–98; mem. Local Govt Boundaries Comm. for Scotland 1975–82; mem. Joint Mil. Educ. Cttee, Edin. and Heriot-Watt Univs 1975–2004; mem. Court, Heriot-Watt Univ. 1980; Chair. Northern Offshore Maritime Resources Study 1974–84; BBC Nat. Gov. for Scotland 1976–79; mem. Royal Fine Art Comm. for Scotland 1975–80, Scottish-Russian Co-ordinating Cttee for Trade and Industry 1985–90; Parl. Adviser to Scottish TV 1966–76, to Pharmaceutical Gen. Council (Scotland) 1985–99; Adviser, Robert Burns Memorial Trust 1995–97; Chair. Bd of Govs, Newbattle Abbey Coll. 1980–82; mem. Bd of Dirs Scottish AIDS Research Foundation 1991–96; Hon. Vice-Pres. Asscn of Nazi War Camp Survivors 1960–. *Publications:* The Development of Economic Doctrine (with Alexander Gray) 1980; contributions to learned journals. *Leisure interests:* writing children's stories and plays, croquet, bridge. *Address:* 11 Upper Gray Street, Edinburgh, EH9 1SN,

Scotland (home). *Telephone:* (131) 667-2140 (Edinburgh); (1764) 685275 (Perthshire).

THOMPSON, Sir Clive Malcolm, Kt, BSc; British business executive; b. 4 April 1943, Bristol; s. of H. L. Thompson and P. D. Thompson (née Stansbury); m. Judith Howard 1968; two s.; ed Clifton Coll., Bristol and Birmingham Univ.; Marketing Exec. Royal Dutch Shell Group 1964–67; Marketing Exec. and Gen. Man. Boots Co. PLC 1967–70; Gen. Man. Jeyes Group Ltd 1970–78; Man. Dir Health and Hygiene Div., Cadbury Schweppes 1978–82; Chief Exec. Rentokil Initial PLC 1983–2003, Chair. (non-exec.) 2003–04; Pres. CBI 1998–2000; Deputy Chair. Financial Reporting Council; fmr Dir (non-exec.) Wellcome PLC, Sainsbury PLC, Seeboard PLC, Caradon PLC, BAT Industries PLC; fmr Chair. Kleeneze PLC, European Home Retail (EHR) 2002–06; mem. Hampel Cttee on Corp. Governance 1998; Hon. DSc (Birmingham) 1999. *Leisure interests:* the stock market, current affairs, walking, golf.

THOMPSON, Daley (Francis Morgan), CBE; British fmr athlete; b. 30 July 1958, Notting Hill, London; m. Tisha Quinlan 1987; one c.; Sussex Schools 200 m title 1974; first competitive decathlon, Welsh Open Championship June 1975; European Junior Decathlon Champion 1977; European Decathlon silver medallist 1978, gold medallist 1982 and 1986; Commonwealth Decathlon gold medallist 1978, 1982 and 1986; Olympic Decathlon gold medallist 1980 (Moscow) and 1984 (LA); World Decathlon Champion 1983; est. new world record for decathlon (at Olympic Games, LA), set four world records in all and was undefeated between 1978 and 1987; retd July 1992; invited to run leg of the Olympic Torch relay at the opening of the Sydney Olympic Games 2000. *Publications:* Going for Gold 1987, The Greatest 1996. *Address:* Church Row, Wandsworth Plain, London SW18, England.

THOMPSON, David; Barbadian lawyer and politician; *Prime Minister and Minister of Finance, Economic Affairs and Development, Labour, Civil Service and Energy;* ed Combermere School, Hugh Wooding Law School, Trinidad and Tobago, Univ. of the W Indies; in pvt. law practice 1986–91; Pnr, Thompson & Patterson 1994–; mem. House of Ass.; Minister of Community Devt and Culture 1991; Minister of Finance 1992–93; Leader of Democratic Labour Party 1994–2001, fmr Leader of the Opposition; Prime Minister and Minister of Finance, Econ. Affairs and Devt, Labour, Civil Service and Energy 2008–; mem. Barbados Bar Asscn, Barbados Museum and Historical Soc. *Address:* Office of the Prime Minister, Government Headquarters, Bay Street, St. Michael (office); Democratic Labour Party, George Street, Belleville, St Michael, Barbados (office). *Telephone:* 436-6435 (office); 429-3104 (office). *Fax:* 436-9280 (office); 427-0548 (office). *E-mail:* info@primeminister.gov.bb (office); dlp@sunbeach.net (office). *Website:* www.primeminister.gov.bb (office).

THOMPSON, Emma; British actress and screenwriter; b. 15 April 1959; d. of Eric Thompson and Phyllida Law; m. 1st Kenneth Branagh 1989 (divorced); m. 2nd Greg Wise 2003; one d.; ed Camden Girls' School and Newnham Coll. Cambridge; appeared with Cambridge Footlights; Chair. Bd of Trustees Helen Bamber Foundation; Int. Amb. ActionAid (charity). *Stage appearances include:* The Cellar Tapes, Edin. Festival 1981–82 (Perrier Pick of the Fringe Award 1981), A Sense of Nonsense (revue tour) 1983, Short Vehicle, Edin. Festival 1984, Me and My Girl, Adelphi 1984–85, Look Back in Anger, Lyric 1989, A Midsummer Night's Dream (world tour) 1990, King Lear (world tour) 1990. *Films:* The Tall Guy 1988, Henry V 1989, Impromptu 1989, Howards End 1991 (eight awards for Best Actress, including New York Critics, LA Critics, Golden Globe, Acad. Award, BAFTA, Nat. Bd of Review; David di Donatella Award for Best Foreign Actress (Italy)), Dead Again 1991, Cheers 1992, Peter's Friends 1992, Much Ado About Nothing 1993, Remains of the Day 1993 (David di Donatella Award for Best Foreign Actress (Italy)), In the Name of the Father 1993, Junior 1994, Carrington 1995, Sense and Sensibility (nine awards for Best Screenplay, including Acad. Award, Golden Globe, LA Film Critics, New York Film Critics, Writers Guild of America, Evening Standard British Film Award; awards for Best Actress from BAFTA and Nat. Bd of Review), The Winter Guest 1996 (Panisetti Award for Best Actress, Venice Film Festival), Primary Colors 1997, Judas Kiss 1997, Imagining Argentina 2003, Love Actually 2003, Harry Potter and the Prisoner of Azkaban 2004, Nanny McPhee (also screenplay writer) 2005, Stranger Than Fiction 2006, Harry Potter and the Order of the Phoenix 2007, Brideshead Revisited 2008. *Television appearances include:* Emma Thompson Special, Channel 4 1983, Alfresco (two series), Granada 1983–84, The Crystal Cube, BBC 1984, Tutti Frutti, BBC (BAFTA Award for Best Actress) 1986, Fortunes of War, BBC (BAFTA Award for Best Actress) 1986–87, Thompson 1988, Knuckle, BBC 1988, The Winslow Boy, BBC 1988, Look Back in Anger, Thames 1989, Blue Boy, BBC Scotland 1994, Ellen, Touchstone TV/ABC (Emmy Award for Outstanding Guest Actress in a Comedy Series) 1998, Wit (Best Actress Award, Semana Internacional de Cine de Valladolid) 2000, Angels in America (miniseries) 2003. *Address:* c/o Hamilton Hodell Ltd, 5th Floor, 66–68 Margaret Street, London, W1W 8SR, England (office). *Telephone:* (20) 7636-1221 (office). *Fax:* (20) 7636-1226 (office). *E-mail:* info@hamiltonhodell.co.uk (office). *Website:* www.hamiltonhodell.co.uk (office).

THOMPSON, Francis Michael Longstreth, CBE, DPhil, FBA; British historian and academic; *Professor Emeritus of History, University of London;* b. 13 Aug. 1925, Purley, Surrey; s. of Francis Longstreth-Thompson; m. Anne Challoner 1951; two s. one d.; ed Bootham School, York and The Queen's Coll., Oxford; Lecturer in History, Univ. Coll. London 1951–63, Reader in Econ. History 1963–68; Prof. of Modern History, Univ. of London and Head of Dept of History, Bedford Coll. London 1968–77, Prof. of History and Dir, Inst. of Historical Research 1977–90, Prof. Emer. 1990–; Ford's Lecturer, Univ. of Oxford 1993–94; Pres., Econ. History Soc. 1983–86, Hon. Vice-Pres. 1986–; British mem., Standing Cttee for Humanities, European Science Foundation 1983–93; Pres., Royal Historical Soc. 1988–92; Pres., British Agric. History Soc. 1989–92. *Publications:* English Landed Society in the 19th Century 1963,

Chartered Surveyors: The Growth of a Profession 1968, Victorian England: The Horse-Drawn Society 1970, Hampstead: Building a Borough, 1650–1964 1974, Countrysides (in The Nineteenth Century; ed. Asa Briggs) 1970, Britain (in European Landed Elites in the Nineteenth Century; ed. David Spring) 1977, Landowners and Farmers (in The Faces of Europe; ed. Alan Bullock) 1980, The Rise of Suburbia (ed.) 1982, Horses in European Economic History (ed.) 1983, The Rise of Respectable Society: A Social History of Victorian Britain 1988, The Cambridge Social History of Britain 1750–1950, three vols (ed.) 1990, The University of London and the World of Learning 1836–1986 (ed.) 1990, Landowners, Capitalists and Entrepreneurs (ed.) 1994, Gentrification and the Enterprise Culture: Britain, 1780–1980 2001. *Leisure interests:* gardening, walking, carpentry. *Address:* Holly Cottage, Sheepcote Lane, Wheathampstead, Herts., AL4 8NJ, England (home). *Telephone:* (158) 283-3129 (home).

THOMPSON, Fred Dalton, BA, JD; American politician, actor and lawyer; *Visiting Fellow, American Enterprise Institute;* b. 19 Aug. 1942, Sheffield, Ala; m. (divorced); three c.; ed Vanderbilt Univ., Memphis State Univ.; practiced law 1967–69; Asst US District Attorney 1969–72; Minority Counsel, Senate Select Cttee on Presidential Campaign Activities ('Watergate Cttee') 1973–74; Special Counsel to Tenn. Gov. Lamar Alexander 1980; Special Counsel, Senate Cttee on Foreign Relations 1980–81; Special Counsel, Senate Cttee on Intelligence 1982; mem. Tenn. Appellate Court Nominating Comm. 1985–87; Senator from Tenn. 1994–2003; Chair. Senate Cttee to Investigate Fund Raising during 1996 Presidential Election 1997; Chair. Senate Governmental Affairs Cttee 1997–2001; campaign chair. for John McCain in 2000 Republican presidential primary; currently Visiting Fellow, American Enterprise Inst.; Special Program Host and Sr Analyst for ABC News Radio; Republican; cand. for Republican nomination for US Pres. 2007. *Films include:* No Way Out 1987, Feds 1988, Fat Man and Little Boy 1989, Hunt for Red October 1990, In the Line of Fire 1993, Days of Thunder 1990, Die Hard 2 1990, Class Action 1991, Necessary Roughness 1991, Curly Sue 1991, Cape Fear 1991, Aces: Iron Eagle III 1992, Thunderheart 1992, Born Yesterday 1993, In the Line of Fire 1993, Baby's Day Out 1994, and others. *Television includes:* Law and Order 2002–07. *Publication:* At That Point in Time: The Inside Story of the Senate Watergate Committee 1975. *Address:* American Enterprise Institute, 1150 17th Street, NW, Washington, DC 20036, USA (office). *Telephone:* (615) 256-2702 (office). *Fax:* (202) 862-7177 (office). *E-mail:* fthompson@aei.org (office). *Website:* www.aei.org (office).

THOMPSON, G. Kennedy (Ken), BA, MBA; American business executive; b. 25 Nov. 1950, Rocky Mount, NC; ed Univ. of NC, Wake Forest Univ.; joined First Union Corpn 1976, various man. and exec. positions including Pres. First Union Ga, Sr Vice-Pres. and Head First Union Human Resources, Pres. First Union Fla, Vice-Chair. of Corpn and Head Global Capital Markets 1998–99, Chair., Pres. and CEO First Union Corpn 1999–2001, Pres. and CEO Wachovia Corpn (after merger of First Union and Wachovia) 2001–08; mem. Bd of Dirs Fla Rock Industries Inc., Carolinas Healthcare System; mem. Financial Services Forum, The Business Council, Bd Financial Services Roundtable; Vice-Chair. NY Clearing House; mem. Bd Teach for America, NC Blumenthal Performing Arts Center, Charlotte Latin School, YMCA Metropolitan Bd, United Way of Cen. Carolinas Inc., Charlotte Inst. for Tech. Innovation; Co-Chair. Advantage Carolina; mem. Bd Trustees Wake Forest Univ. *Address:* c/o Wachovia Corporation, 301 South College Street, Suite 4000, Charlotte, NC 28288-0013, USA (office).

THOMPSON, Gregory (Greg) Francis, BA, BEd; Canadian politician; *Minister of Veterans Affairs;* b. 28 March 1947, St Stephen, NB; m. Linda Thompson; two s.; ed St Thomas Univ.; fmr teacher and financial planner; MP (Conservative) for NB Southwest Riding 1988–, has served as Critic for Atlantic Canada Opportunities Agency, Public Accounts, Health, Regional Devt, Treasury Bd and Human Resources Devt, fmr mem. cttees for Fisheries and Oceans, Health, Public Accounts and subcommittees for Whistleblowing, Non-Medicinal use of Drugs, Combatting Corruption, Agenda and Procedure; Co-Chair. Canada–US Inter-Parl. Group 2004–06; Minister of Veterans Affairs 2006–; mem. Bd of Dirs Theatre New Brunswick, Charlotte County Hosp., New Brunswick Drug and Alcohol Dependency Comm. *Address:* Veterans Affairs Canada, 161 Grafton Street, POB 7700, Charlottetown, PE C1A 8M9 (office); House of Commons, Ottawa, ON K1A 0A6, Canada. *Telephone:* (902) 566-8888 (Charlottetown) (office); (613) 995-5550 (office). *Fax:* (902) 566-8508 (Charlottetown) (office); (613) 995-5226 (office). *E-mail:* information@vac-acc.gc.ca (office); Thompson.G@parl.gc.ca (office). *Website:* www.vac-acc.gc.ca (office).

THOMPSON, Harold Lindsay, MB, BS, FRACGP, AM; Australian medical practitioner; b. 23 April 1929, Aberdeen, Scotland; s. of Harold Thompson and Johan D. Thompson; m. 1st Audrey J. Harpur 1957 (died 1996); three s. two d.; m. 2nd Jennifer Manton 1997; ed Aberdeen, Melbourne and Sydney Grammar Schools and postgrad. training in UK; Surgeon-Lt Royal Australian Navy 1956–60; now in gen. practice in Lakemba, NSW; Exec. Dir Canterbury Div. of Gen. Practice 1996–2002; Assoc. Prof., Faculty of Medicine, Univ. of Sydney 1996–; fmr Chair. Diagnostic Medical Cooperative Ltd; Fellow Australian Medical Asscn 1973, Pres. 1982–85; Pres. Confed. of Medical Asscns. of Asia and Oceania 1985–87, Immediate Past Pres. 1987–89; Chair. Australian Urban Divs of Gen. Practice 1995–2000; Vice-Chair. Australian Council on Healthcare Standards 1985–89; Vice-Pres. Australian Council of Professions 1985–87, Pres. 1989–91; mem. Council, World Medical Asscn 1984–90, Pres. 1988–89; mem. Econ. Planning Advisory Cttee 1989–91, Bd Southern Sydney Area Health Service 1991–95; Chair. Council Confed. of Medical Asscns of Asia and Oceania 1989–95, GP Advisory Cttee NSW Health 1997–2002, Chair. 1998–2002; Gold Medal, Australian Medical Asscn 1986; Medal, Australian Council on Healthcare Standards 1990, Distinguished Service Award, Confed.

of Medical Asscns of Asia and Oceania 1987, Award of Merit 1989, 1995. *Leisure interests:* croquet, fishing, bridge. *Address:* 601/2 Roseby Street, Drummoyne, NSW 2047 (office); 4/100 Milsom Road, Cremorne, NSW 2090, Australia (home). *Telephone:* (2) 9719-8391 (office); (2) 9908-2980 (home). *E-mail:* hlthompson@iprimus.com.au.

THOMPSON, James R., LLD; American politician and lawyer; *Partner and Chairman of the Executive Committee, Winston & Strawn LLP;* b. 8 May 1936, Chicago, Ill.; s. of Dr J. Robert Thompson and Agnes Thompson; m. Jayne Carr 1976; one d.; ed Univ. of Illinois, Washington Univ., St Louis, Missouri, Northwestern Univ. Law School; admitted to Illinois Bar 1959; Prosecutor, State Attorney's Office, Cook County, Ill. 1959–64; Assoc. Prof. Northwestern Univ. Law School, Ill. 1964–69; Chief, Dept of Law Enforcement and Public Protection, Office of Ill. Attorney-Gen. 1969–70, First Asst US Attorney 1970–71, US Attorney for Northern Dist of Ill. 1971–75; Counsel, Winston & Strawn law firm, Chicago 1975–77, pnr, Chair. Exec. Cttee 1991–; Gov. of Ill. 1977–91; mem. Exec. Cttee Nat. Govs' Asscn (NGA) 1980–82, Chair. 1983–84; Co-Chair. Attorney-Gen.'s Task Force on Violent Crime 1981; Chair./President's Intelligence Oversight Bd 1989–93; mem. Presidential Advisory Cttee on Federalism 1981, Advisory Bd of Fed. Emergency Man. Agency 1991–93; Chair. Republican Govs' Asscn, Midwestern Govs' Conf., NGA Task Force on Job Creation and Infrastructure 1982; Chair. Council of Great Lakes Govs 1985; Vice-Chair. Martin Luther King Jr Nat. Holiday Cttee 1985; Chair. Ill. Math. and Science Foundation; Commr Nat. Comm. on Terrorist Attacks Upon the US (9-11 Comm.) 2003–04; Republican; Hon. LLD (Lincoln Coll.) 1975, Hon. DHumLitt (Roosevelt Univ.) 1979, Hon. DJur (Northwestern Univ. and Illinois Coll.) 1979, Hon. LLD (Monmouth Coll.) 1981, (Marshall Law School) 1984, (Elmhurst Coll.) 1985, Dr hc (Pratt Inst.) 1984; Justice in Legislation Award, American Jewish Congress 1984; Distinguished Public Service Award, Anti-Defamation League 1984, Swedish-American of the Year, Vasa Order of America 1985. *Publications:* co-author of four textbooks incl. Cases and Comments on Criminal Procedure; numerous articles in professional journals. *Address:* Winston & Strawn LLP, 35 W Wacker Drive, Suite 4200, Chicago, IL 60601-9703, USA (office). *Telephone:* (312) 558-7400 (office). *Fax:* (312) 558-5700 (office). *E-mail:* jthompson@winston.com (office). *Website:* www.winston.com (office).

THOMPSON, Jennifer (Jenny), BSc, MD; American physician and fmr swimmer; b. 26 Feb. 1973, Danvers, Mass; ed Stanford Univ., Columbia Univ.; mem. Badger Swim Club, NY 2001–; won 19 Nat. Collegiate Athletic Asscn (NCAA) titles, most in NCAA female swimming history; 26 nat. medals, 85 medals from int. competition including 14 from World Championships; competed at Olympic Games 1992, 1996, 2000, 2004 (third female swimmer to qualify for four Olympics); most decorated swimmer in Olympic history with 12 medals (eight gold medals); most Olympic gold medals among US women; holds world records 100m. butterfly, 50m. butterfly, 100m. individual medley; intern, Memorial Sloan-Kettering Cancer Center, New York; currently resident anesthesiologist, Brigham and Women's Hosp., Boston; US All-Star swimming team 1989, 1992–95, 1997–2000, 2002–04, USA Swimming Swimmer of the Year 1993, 1998, Female Swimmer of the Meet, World Short Course Championships 1999, Female Swimmer of the Meet, Pan Pacific Championships 1999, Sports Foundation's Sportswoman of the Year 2000. *Address:* Department of Anesthesiology, Perioperative and Pain MedicineBrigham and Women's Hospital, 75 Francis Street, Boston, MA 02115, USA (office). *Telephone:* (617) 732-8210 (office). *Website:* www.brighamandwomens.org/anesthesiology (office).

THOMPSON, John Griggs, PhD, FRS; American mathematician and academic; *Graduate Research Professor, Department of Mathematics, University of Florida;* b. 13 Oct. 1932, Ottawa, Kan.; ed Yale Univ., Univ. of Chicago; with Inst. of Defense Analysis 1959–60; Asst Prof., Harvard Univ., 1961–62; Prof., Univ. of Chicago 1962–68; Fellow, Univ. Coll., Cambridge, UK 1968–70, Rouse Ball Prof. of Pure Math. 1970–93; Grad. Research Prof., Univ. of Florida 1993–; mem. NAS 1971; Dr hc (Illinois) 1968, (Yale) 1980, (Chicago) 1985, (Oxford) 1987; Cole Prize, American Math. Soc. 1965, Fields Medal, Int. Congress of Mathematicians, Nice 1970, American Math. Soc. Colloquium Lecturer 1974, Berwick Prize, London Math. Soc. 1982, Sylvester Medal, Royal Soc. 1985, Wolf Prize (Israel) 1992, Poincaré Prize, Acad. des sciences (France) 1992, Nat. Medal of Science (jtly) 2000. *Publications:* numerous articles in math. journals on group theory. *Address:* Department of Mathematics, University of Florida, 358 Little Hall, corner of SW 13th Street and SW 2nd Avenue, PO Box 118105, Gainesville, FL 32611-8105, USA (office). *Telephone:* (352) 392-0281 (office). *Fax:* (352) 392-8357 (office). *E-mail:* department@math.ufl.edu (office). *Website:* www.math.ufl.edu (office).

THOMPSON, John M.; Canadian banker and business executive; *Chairman, Toronto-Dominion Bank;* ed Univ. of Western Ont., Richard Ivey Business School at Univ. of Western Ont. and Kellogg Grad. School at Northwestern Univ., USA; joined IBM Canada Ltd 1966, systems engineer, marketing man., Pres. and CEO 1986; Corp. Vice-Pres. marketing and services IBM Corpn 1991, Head AS/400 Server business, Sr Vice-Pres. and Group Exec. IBM Software Group 1995, Vice-Chair. 2000–02; mem. Bd Dirs Toronto-Dominion Bank 1988–, Chair. (non-exec.) 2003–. *Address:* Toronto-Dominion Bank, Toronto-Dominion Centre, King Street West and Bay Street, Toronto, ON M5K 1A2, Canada (office). *Telephone:* (416) 982-8222 (office). *Fax:* (416) 982-5671 (office). *E-mail:* td.capa@td.com (office). *Website:* www.td.com (office).

THOMPSON, Mark John, BA, FRTS, FRSA; British broadcasting executive; *Director-General, British Broadcasting Corporation;* b. 31 July 1957; s. of Duncan John Thompson and Sydney Columba Corduff Thompson; m. Jane Emilie Blumberg 1987; two s. one d.; ed Stonyhurst Coll., Merton Coll. Oxford; Research Asst Trainee, BBC TV 1979–1980, Asst Producer Nationwide 1980–1982, Producer Breakfast Time 1982–84, Output Ed. London Plus 1984–85, Newsnight 1985–87, Ed. Nine O'Clock News 1988–90, Panorama 1990–92, Head of Features 1992–94, Head of Factual Programmes 1994–96, Controller BBC2 1996–98; Dir of Nat. and Regional Broadcasting 1998–2000; Dir of TV, BBC 2000–02; CEO Channel 4 2002–04; Dir-Gen. BBC 2004–. *Leisure interests:* walking, cooking. *Address:* British Broadcasting Corporation, Broadcasting House, Portland Place, London W1A 1AA, England (office). *Telephone:* (20) 7580-4468 (office). *Fax:* (20) 7765-1181 (office). *Website:* www.bbc.co.uk (office).

THOMPSON, Sir Michael Warwick, Kt, DSc, FInstP; British physicist and university vice-chancellor; *Emeritus Professor, University of Birmingham;* b. 1 June 1931; s. of Kelvin W. Thompson and Madeleine Walford; m. 1st Sybil N. Spooner 1956 (died 1999); two s.; m. 2nd Jenny Mitchell 2000; ed Rydal School and Univ. of Liverpool; research scientist, AERE, Harwell, Reactor Physics and Metallurgy 1953–65; Prof. of Experimental Physics, Univ. of Sussex 1965–80, Pro-Vice-Chancellor 1972–78; Vice-Chancellor, Univ. of E Anglia 1980–86; Vice-Chancellor and Prin. Univ. of Birmingham 1987–96, Emer. Prof. 1996–; Chair. Council John Innes Research Inst. 1980–86, British Council Cttee for Academic Research Collaboration with Germany 1988–; mem. SRC Physics Cttee (also Chair.) 1972–79, E Sussex Educ. Cttee 1973–78, E Sussex Area Health Authority 1973–80, W Midlands Regional Health Authority 1987–90 (non-exec. Dir 1990–96), Council for Nat. Academic Awards 1988–91, Council of Asscn of Commonwealth Univs 1990–95, Council for Industry and Higher Educ. 1991–96; Dir (non-exec.) Alliance Bldg Soc. 1979–85 (Alliance and Leicester Bldg Soc., now Alliance & Leicester PLC) 1985–2000, Deputy Chair. 1995–2000; COBUILD Ltd 1987–96, TPIC Ltd 1987–, Council of the Cttee of Vice-Chancellors and Prins 1989–96 (Chair. Medical Cttee 1994–); Trustee Barber Inst. of Fine Art 1987–, St Bartholomew's Medical Coll. 1998–; Hon. LLD (Birmingham) 1997; Hon. DSc (Sussex) 1998; CV Boys Prize, Inst. of Physics; Grosses Bundesverdienstkreuz 1997. *Publications:* Defects and Radiation Damage in Metals 1968; over 100 papers in scientific journals on the interaction of radiation with solids. *Leisure interests:* sailing, the arts. *Address:* The University of Birmingham, Edgbaston, Birmingham, B15 2TT (office); Stoneacre, The Warren, Polperro, Cornwall, PL13 2RD, England (home). *Telephone:* (121) 414-4536 (office).

THOMPSON, (Rupert) Julian (de la Mare), MA; British art consultant; b. 23 July 1941; s. of Rupert Spens Thompson and Florence Elizabeth (de la Mare) Thompson; m. Jacqueline Julie Ivimy 1965; three d.; ed Eton Coll. and King's Coll., Cambridge; joined Sotheby's 1963, Dir 1969–, Chair. 1982–86, Deputy Chair. 1987–92, Chair. Sotheby's Asia 1992–2003. *Address:* Crossington Farm, Upton Bishop, Ross-on-Wye, Herefordshire, HR9 7UE, England. *Telephone:* (1989) 780-471. *E-mail:* rjdlmthompson@hotmail.com (office).

THOMPSON, Tommy George, BS, JD; American lawyer and fmr politician; *Partner, Akin Gump Strauss Hauer & Feld LLP;* b. 19 Nov. 1941, Elroy, Wis.; s. of Allan Thompson and Julie Dutton; m. Sue Ann Mashak 1969; one s. two d.; ed Univ. of Wisconsin; political intern, US Rep. Thomson 1963; legis. messenger, Wis. State Senate 1964–66; sole practice, Elroy and Mauston, Wis. 1966–87; self-employed real estate broker, Mauston 1970–; mem. Dist 87 Wis. State Ass. 1966–87, Asst Minority Leader 1972–81, Floor Leader 1981–87; Gov. of Wisconsin 1987–2001; Sec. Health and Human Services 2001–05; Partner, Akin Gump Strauss Hauer & Feld LLP, Washington, DC 2005–; Chair. Republican Govs' Asscn 1991–92; Chair. Bd of Dirs Amtrak 1998–99; fmr mem. Exec. Cttee Nat. Govs' Asscn; mem. ABA; Nature Conservancy Award 1988, Thomas Jefferson Freedom Award (American Legis. Exchange Council) 1991; Leadership in Natural Energy Conservation Award, US Energy Asscn 1994, Horatio Alger Award, and numerous other awards. *Leisure interests:* hunting, fishing, sports. *Address:* Akin Gump Strauss Hauer & Feld LLP, Robert S. Strauss Building, 1333 New Hampshire Avenue, NW, Washington, DC 20036-1564, USA (office). *Telephone:* (202) 887-4000 (office). *Fax:* (202) 887-4288 (office). *E-mail:* tthompson@akingump.com (office). *Website:* www.akingump.com (office).

THOMPSON-MAALOUM, Julie Dawn, PhD; British biologist, biochemist and academic; *Senior Researcher, Institut de Génétique et de Biologie Moléculaire et Cellulaire;* with Vickers Shipbuilding and Eng Ltd 1984–86; with Singer Link Miles Ltd 1986–88; with Rediffusion Simulation Ltd 1988–90; European Molecular Biology Lab., Heidelberg, Germany 1991–94; Sr Researcher, Institut de Génétique et de Biologie Moléculaire et Cellulaire (CNRS/Institut Nat. de la Santé et de la Recherche Médicale—INSERM/Université Louis Pasteur), Illkirch, France 1995–; collaborated in creation of CLUSTAL W program for nucleic acid sequencing; Cristal du CNRS 2005, prix Madeleine Lecoq 2007. *Publications:* numerous articles in scientific journals on nucleic acid multiple sequence alignment programs. *Address:* Institut de Génétique et de Biologie Moléculaire et Cellulaire, 1 rue Laurent Fries, BP10142, 67404 Illkirch Cedex, France (office). *Telephone:* (3) 88-65-32-00 (office). *Fax:* (3) 88-65-32-00 (office). *E-mail:* julie@igbmc.u-strasbg.fr (office). *Website:* www-igbmc.u-strasbg.fr (office).

THOMSEN, Niels Jørgen, DPhil; Danish historian and academic; b. 21 April 1930, Copenhagen; s. of the late Sigurd Thomsen and Gudrun Kirkegaard; m. Birgit Nüchel Petersen 1953; two s.; ed Univ. of Copenhagen; Dir Danish Press Museum, Århus 1958–65; Lecturer, School of Journalism, Århus 1962–65; Asst Prof. of Econ. History, Univ. of Copenhagen 1965–71, Asst Prof. of Political Science 1971–73, Prof. of Modern History 1973–2000; Danish Ed. Pressens Årbog 1968–82; Chair. Soc. for History and Econs, Copenhagen 1980–83; Chair. Soc. for Contemporary History 1982–; mem. Royal Danish Acad. of Science and Letters. *Publications:* Partipressen 1965, Dagbladskonkurrencen 1870–1970 I–II 1972, Københavns Universitet 1936–66 1986, De danske aviser 1634–1989 (with Jette Søllinge) I–III 1987–91, Industri, stat og samfund 1870–1939 1991, Hovedstrømninger 1870–1914 1998; about 80 articles on political and media history in professional journals. *Address:* Institute of History, University of Copenhagen, Njalsgade 102, 2300 Copenhagen S (office); Vitus Berings Allé 15, 2930 Klampenborg, Denmark (home). *Telephone:* 35-32-82-43 (office); 39-64-33-16 (home). *Fax:* 35-32-82-41 (office). *E-mail:* n.thomsen@mail.tele.dk (home). *Website:* www.hum.ku.dk (office).

THOMSON, Brian Edward, AM; Australian film, theatre and opera designer; b. 5 Jan. 1946, Sydney; s. of Austin Thomas Thomson and Adoree Gertrude Thomson; ed Applecross Sr High School, Perth Tech. Coll., Univ. of New South Wales; Supervising Designer, closing ceremony of Olympic Games, Sydney 2000; Production Designer, Centennial of Fed. Ceremony 2001; Designer, opening and closing ceremonies, Rugby World Cup 2003; Australian Film Inst. Award for production design, Rebel 1985, Ground Zero 1987, Sydney Theatre Critics' Award for Best Designer 1989, 1992, 1993, 1994, Mo Award 1994, 1995, Tony Award for The King and I 1996. *Musicals:* Hair, Jesus Christ Superstar (London and Australia), The Rocky Horror Show (original London production and worldwide), Chicago, The Stripper, Company, Chess, The King and I (Broadway production 1996, London Palladium), How to Succeed in Business Without Really Trying, South Pacific, Hello, Dolly!, Merrily We Roll Along, Grease, Happy Days. *Theatre:* Housewife Superstar!!! (London and New York); The Threepenny Opera (opening season, Drama Theatre, Sydney Opera House); Big Toys (the Old Tote); A Cheery Soul, Chinchilla, Macbeth, The Doll Trilogy, The Ham Funeral, A Midsummer Night's Dream, The Crucible, The Homecoming, Uncle Vanya, Death and the Maiden, Coriolanus, Falsettos, King Lear, Arcadia, Medea, Mongrels, Third World Blues, After the Ball, White Devil (also at Brooklyn Acad. of Music), Up for Grabs (all for Sydney Theatre Co.); Arturo Ui, Rock-Ola (Nimrod); Lulu, Shepherd on the Rocks Crow (State Theatre Co. of S Australia); Ghosts, The Tempest, The Master Builder, Buzz, Frogs, Aftershocks, Radiance, Up the Road, Burnt Piano, The Laramie Project (Company B Belvoir); Angels in America (Melbourne Theatre Co.); Soulmates, One Day of the Year (Sydney Theatre Co.), My Zinc Bed, Buried Child (Company B Belvoir), Dame Edna Back With A Vengeance, Broadway 2004, Three Furies, Sydney Festival 2005. *Film and television:* Barlow and Chambers, Shadow of the Cobra (both mini-series); Shirly Thompson vs. the Aliens, The Rocky Horror Picture Show, Starstruck, Rebel, Night of Shadows (also dir), Ground Zero, Turtle Beach, Frauds. *Dance:* Synergy, Fornicon (Sydney Dance Co.), Tivol (Sydney Dance Co. and Australian Ballet). *Opera:* Death in Venice, The Makropulos Affair (Adelaide Festival); Turandot, Aida, Summer of the Seventeenth Doll (Vic. State Opera); Voss, Death in Venice, Tristan und Isolde, Katya Kabanova, The Eighth Wonder (The Australian Opera); Billy Budd (Welsh Nat. Opera, Opera Australia, Canadian Nat. Opera), Sweeney Todd (Lyric Opera of Chicago). *Leisure interests:* movies, sport (Aussie rules, cricket, tennis). *Address:* 5 Little Dowling Street, Paddington, NSW 2021, Australia. *Telephone:* (2) 9331-1584 (office); (4) 1164-3323 (home). *E-mail:* bt@brianthomson.biz (office). *Website:* www.brianthomson.biz (office).

THOMSON, James Alan, BS, MS, PhD; American business executive and security expert; *President and CEO, RAND Corporation;* b. 21 Jan. 1945, Boston, Mass.; ed Univ. of New Hampshire and Purdue Univ.; Research Fellow, Univ. of Wisconsin, Madison 1972–74; Systems Analyst, Office of Sec. of Defense, US Dept of Defense, Washington, DC 1974–77; staff mem. Nat. Security Council, Washington, DC 1977–81; Vice-Pres. RAND Corpn, Santa Monica, Calif. 1981–88, Pres. and CEO 1989–; Dir LA World Affairs Council, Object Reservoir Inc., AK Steel Holdings Corpn, Encysive Pharmaceuticals Inc.; mem. Int. Inst. for Strategic Studies (UK), Council on Foreign Relations 1985–, Bd Los Angeles World Affairs Council; Hon. DSc (Purdue) 1992, (New Hampshire); Hon. LLD (Pepperdine) 1996. *Publications:* Conventional Arms Control and the Security of Europe 1988; articles on defence issues. *Address:* RAND Corporation, 1776 Main Street, Santa Monica, CA 90401, USA (office). *Telephone:* (310) 451-6936 (office). *Fax:* (310) 451-6972 (office). *E-mail:* thomson@rand.org (office). *Website:* www.rand.org (office).

THOMSON, James (Jamie) Alexander, BS, DVetMed, PhD; American developmental biologist and academic; *Professor, Department of Anatomy, University of Wisconsin;* b. 20 Dec. 1958, Oak Park, Ill.; ed Univs of Illinois and Pennsylvania; board certified in veterinary pathology 1995; Post-doctoral Research Fellow, Primate In Vitro Fertilization and Experimental Embryology Lab., Ore. Nat. Primate Research Center 1988–90; joined Univ. of Wisconsin-Madison 1990, currently John D. MacArthur Prof. of Anatomy, Univ. of Wisconsin-Madison School of Medicine and Public Health, faculty mem. Genome Center of Wis., has conducted pioneering work in isolation and culture of non-human primate and human embryonic stem cells; Chief Pathologist, Wis. Nat. Primate Research Center. *Publications:* several patents and numerous articles in professional journals. *Address:* Department of Anatomy, Genome Center of Wisconsin, 425 Henry Mall, University of Wisconsin-Madison Medical School, Madison, WI 53706, USA (office). *Telephone:* (608) 263-3585 (office). *Fax:* (608) 265-8984 (office). *E-mail:* thompson@primate.wisc.edu (office). *Website:* www.anatomy.wisc.edu (office); ink .primate.wisc.edu/~thomson (office).

THOMSON, Jennifer Ann, PhD; South African microbiologist, molecular biologist and academic; *Professor of Microbiology, Department of Molecular and Cell Biology, University of Cape Town;* ed Univ. of Cape Town, Univ. of Cambridge, UK, Rhodes Univ.; Post-doctoral Fellow, Harvard Univ., USA; Visiting Scientist, MIT –1983; Lecturer, later Assoc. Prof., Dept of Genetics, Univ. of Witwatersrand 1983; Dir Lab. for Molecular and Cell Biology, CSIR; Head, Dept of Microbiology, Univ. of Cape Town 1988, Prof. of Microbiology, Dept of Molecular and Cell Biology (formed by merger of Depts of Biochemistry and Microbiology) 2001–; expert adviser, WHO; addressed UN Gen. Ass. on theme of genetically modified crops for developing countries 2002; Co-founder South African Women in Science and Eng; fmr Vice-Pres. Acad. of Science of South Africa; fmr mem. African Acad. of Sciences Policy Cttee; Fellow, Royal Soc. of South Africa; L'Oréal-UNESCO For Women in Science Award 2004. *Publications:* Genes for Africa 2002; numerous articles in scientific journals on biological control of plant pests and diseases, genetically modified plants to improve agricultural productivity and food quality in developing countries and molecular genetics of industrially and medically important anaerobic bacteria. *Address:* Department of Molecular and Cell Biology, University of Cape Town, Private Bag Rondebosch, 7701 Cape Town, South Africa (office). *Telephone:* (21) 650-3256 (office). *Fax:* (21) 689-7573 (office). *E-mail:* jat@science.uct.ac.za (office). *Website:* www.mcb.uct.ac.za// Staff/jat.htm (office).

THOMSON, Sir John Adam, GCMG, MA; British diplomatist (retd); b. 27 April 1927, Aberdeenshire; s. of the late Sir George Thomson, FRS and Kathleen Smith; m. 1st Elizabeth Anne McClure 1953 (died 1988); three s. one d.; m. 2nd Judith Ogden Bullitt 1992; ed Philips Exeter Acad., NH, USA, Aberdeen Univ., Trinity Coll., Cambridge; Third Sec., Embassy in Jeddah 1951, Damascus 1954; Foreign Office 1955; Private Sec. to Perm. Under-Sec. 1958; First Sec., Embassy in Washington, DC 1960; Foreign Office 1964; Acting Head of Planning Staff 1966; Counsellor, Head of Planning Staff 1967; seconded to Cabinet Office as Chief of Assessment Staff 1968; Minister, Deputy Perm. Rep. to NATO 1972; Asst Under-Sec. of State, Foreign and Commonwealth Office 1973; High Commr in India 1977–82; Perm. Rep. to UN 1982–87; Leader CSCE Humanitarian Mission to Bosnia-Herzegovina 1992; Prin. Dir, 21st Century Trust 1987–90; Chair. Minority Rights Group Int. 1991–99, Flemings Emerging Markets Investment Trust 1991–98; int. adviser, ANZ Grindlays Bank 1996–97 (Dir 1987–96); mem. Council IISS, Governing Body Inst. of Devt Studies, Sussex, Council Overseas Devt Inst., London, Howie Cttee for Secondary Educ. in Scotland 1990–92; Trustee Nat. Museums of Scotland 1991–99 (Dir 1987–96); Assoc. mem. Nuffield Coll., Oxford 1988–91; Hon. LLD (Ursinus Coll.) 1984, (Aberdeen) 1986. *Publication:* Crusader Castles (with Robin Fedden) 1956. *Leisure interests:* castles, oriental carpets, walking. *Address:* c/o Minority Rights Group International, 54 Commercial Street, London, E1 6LT, England (office).

THOMSON, Peter William, AO, CBE; Australian professional golfer; b. 23 Aug. 1929, Melbourne; m. Stella Mary 1960; one s. three d.; turned professional 1949; British Open Champion 1954, 1955, 1956, 1958, 1965 (only player to win three successively since Open became 72-hole event 1892); won British PGA Match-Play Championship four times and 16 major tournaments in Britain; Australian Open Champion 1951, 1967, 1972, NZ Open Champion nine times; won open titles of Italy, Spain, Hong Kong, Philippines, India and Germany; played 11 times for Australia in World Cup (won twice); won World Seniors Championship 1984, PGA Seniors Championship of America 1984; Capt. Pres.'s Cup Int. Team 1996, 1998, 2000; fmr Pres. Professional Golfers' Asscn of Australia; Dir Thomson, Wolveridge, Perrett; mem. James McGrath Foundation, Vic.; Hon. DBA (Queen Margaret Univ. Coll. Edin.) 2002, Hon. DIur (St Andrews) 2005, Dr hc (Victoria) 2006. *Leisure interests:* classical music, literature, discussing politics. *Address:* Kerkin Court, 1–107 Mathoura Road, Toorak, Vic. 3142, Australia (home). *Telephone:* (3) 9654-4100 (office). *E-mail:* peter@thomsonperrett.com.au (office).

THOMSON, Richard Murray, OC, BASs(Eng), MBA; Canadian banker; b. 14 Aug. 1933, Winnipeg, Man.; s. of H. W. Thomson and Mary Thomson; m. Heather Lorimer 1959; ed Univ. of Toronto, Harvard Business School, Queen's Univ., Kingston, Ont.; joined Toronto-Dominion Bank, Head Office 1957, Senior Asst Man., St James & McGill, Montreal 1961, Asst to Pres., Head Office 1963, Asst Gen. Man. 1965, Chief Gen. Man. 1968, Vice-Pres., Chief Gen. Man., Dir 1971, Pres. 1972–79, Pres. and CEO 1977–79, CEO 1978–97, Chair. 1978–98; Dir Canada Pension Plan Investment Bd., Nexen Inc., Ontario Power Generation Inc., INCO Ltd, S. C. Johnson & Son Inc., Prudential Financial Inc., The Thomson Corpn, The Toronto-Dominion Bank, Trizec Hahn Corpn, Stuart Energy Systems Inc. *Leisure interests:* golf, tennis, skiing. *Address:* c/o Toronto-Dominion Bank, P.O. Box 1, Toronto-Dominion Centre, 55 King Street, P.O. Box 1, Toronto, Ont., M5K 1A2, Canada. *Telephone:* (416) 982-8354 (office). *Fax:* (416) 983-9607 (office).

THOMSON, Robert; Australian journalist and newspaper editor; *Managing Editor, Wall Street Journal;* b. 11 March 1961, Torrumbarry; m. Ping Wang; two s.; financial and gen. affairs reporter, then Sydney Corresp. The Herald, Melbourne 1979–83; sr feature writer Sydney Morning Herald 1983–85; corresp. for the Financial Times, Beijing 1985–89, Tokyo 1989–94, Foreign News Ed., London 1994–96, Asst Ed. Financial Times and Ed. Weekend FT 1996–98, US Man. Ed. Financial Times 1998–2002; Ed. The Times (UK) 2002–07; Publisher, Wall Street Journal 2007–08, Managing Ed. 2008–; Ed.-in-Chief, Dow Jones 2008–; mem. Knight-Bagehot Fellowship Bd, Columbia Univ.; Dir and Chair. Arts International 2000–02; Business Journalist of the Year, The Journalist and Financial Reporting Group (TJFR) 2001. *Television:* regular appearances on ABC News, CNN, Fox News Channel. *Publications:* The Judges – A Portrait of the Australian Judiciary, The Chinese Army, True Fiction (ed.). *Leisure interests:* cinema, tennis, reading. *Address:* The Wall Street Journal, 200 Liberty Street, New York, NY 10281, USA (office). *Telephone:* (212) 416-2000 (office). *Website:* www.wsj.com (office).

THOMSON, Sir Thomas James, Kt, CBE, OBE, MB, ChB, FRCP, FRCPE, FRCP (Glasgow), FRCPI; British gastroenterologist (retd) and consultant physician; b. 8 April 1923, Airdrie; s. of Thomas Thomson and Annie Jane Grant; m. Jessie Smith Shotbolt 1948; two s. one d.; ed Airdrie Acad. and Univ. of Glasgow; posts in clinical medicine continuously 1945–87, teacher 1948–87; posts as Lecturer in Dept Materia Medica, Univ. of Glasgow 1953–87, Hon. Lecturer 1961–87; Consultant Physician and Gastroenterologist, Stobhill Gen. Hosp.,

Glasgow 1961–87; Postgraduate Clinical Tutor to Glasgow Northern Hosps 1961–80; Chair. Greater Glasgow Health Bd 1987–93; mem. Court, Univ. of Strathclyde 1992–97, Chair. Staff Cttee 1993–97; Sec. Specialist Advisory Cttee for Gen. Internal Medicine for UK 1970–74; Chair., Medico-Pharmaceutical Forum 1978–80; Conf. of Royal Colls and Faculties in Scotland 1982–84, Nat. Medical Consultative Cttee for Scotland 1982–87; Hon. Sec., Royal Coll. of Physicians and Surgeons, Glasgow 1965–73, Pres. 1982–84; Hon. Fellow, American Coll. of Physicians; Hon. LLD (Glasgow) 1988; Hon. DUniv (Strathclyde) 1997. *Publications:* Dilling's Pharmacology (jt author) 1969, Gastroenterology: An Integrated Course 1972. *Leisure interests:* swimming and golfing. *Address:* 1 Varna Road, Glasgow, G14 9NE, Scotland (home). *Telephone:* (141) 959-5930 (home).

THOMSON, William Cran, CA, CBIM; British business executive; b. 11 Feb. 1926, Glasgow; s. of William Thomson and Helen Cran; m. Jessie Wallace 1951; four s.; ed Hutchesons (Boys) Grammar School; joined Royal Dutch/Shell Group 1951, Shell Co. of Egypt 1951–54, of Sudan 1954–56, of Aden 1956–58, Finance Dir P.T. Shell Indonesia 1961–64, Finance Co-ordinator Shell Int. Chemical Co. 1966–70, Chemical Co-ordinator Shell Int. Chemical Co. 1970–79, Chair. Shell Chemicals UK 1974–79, Finance Dir Shell Petroleum Co. 1979–86, Man. Dir Royal Dutch/Shell Group 1979–86, Man. Dir Shell Transport and Trading 1979–86 (Dir 1986–), Chair. Shell Holdings (UK) 1981–86; Chair. Shell Pensions Trust Ltd 1986–, (Dir 1976–); Chair. The Nickerson Group 1990– (Dir 1986–); Dir Coats Viyella PLC 1986–, Romaga AG 1986–. *Leisure interests:* golf, shooting. *Address:* c/o Royal Dutch/Shell Group, Shell Centre, London, SE1 7NA, England.

THOMSON, William Reid, BSc, MSc, MPhil; American/British international economist, financial adviser and writer; *Chairman, Private Capital Ltd., Hong Kong;* b. 10 Aug. 1939, London; s. of the late Wing-Commdr W. Thomson and Nellie Hendry Thomson; m. 1st Mary Cormack 1967 (divorced 1986); m. 2nd Jeannette Vinta 1987; two s. one d.; ed George Washington Univ., Univ. of Washington, Univ. of Manchester, UK; economist and operations analyst various cos 1961–72; investment analyst, Legg Mason & Co. 1973–74; Sr Economist, US Treasury Dept 1974–85, Office of Debt Analysis and Office of Int. Devt Banks; Exec. Dir African Devt Bank 1982–83; Alt. Exec. Dir Asian Devt Bank 1985–90, Vice-Pres. 1990–94, Sr Counsellor to Pres. 1994–95; Sr Adviser Franklin Templeton Investments Asia 1995–2008; Chair. Yamamoto Int. Co (Japan) (venture capital) 1996–, Siam Recovery Fund 1997–2005, PEDCA LLC 1997–, Momentum Asia Ltd (hedge funds) 1998–2003, Private Capital Ltd Hong Kong 2005–; Dir Finavestment Ltd, London 2008–; adviser, Axiom Alternative Fund 2004–; Visiting Prof., Nihon Univ., Tokyo; writer on Asian political/econ. affairs, Asia and Pacific Review, Asia Times, The Standard Hong Kong and also for many websites. *Publication:* Confidential Inside Asia Report 1996–2001, Asia Asset Management 2003–; many others. *Leisure interests:* jogging, cricket, reading, writing. *Address:* 184 London Road, Guildford, GU1 1XR, England (home); Private Capital Ltd. 16/F Shun Ho Tower, 24-30 Ice House Street, Central, Hong Kong Special Administrative Region, People's Republic of China (office). *Telephone:* 2869-1996 (Hong Kong) (office); 811-8181 (Manila) (office); (1483) 440825 (home). *Fax:* 28110-9521 (Hong Kong) (office); 814-0130 (Manila) (office); (1483) 440825 (home). *E-mail:* wrthomson@btconnect.com; bill_thomson2003@yahoo.com. *Website:* www .private-capital.com.hk (office); www.axiomfunds.com (office).

THONDAMAN, Arumugam Ramanathan; Sri Lankan politician; *Minister of Youth Empowerment and Socio-Economic Development;* b. 29 May 1964; fmr Minister of Livestock Devt and Estate Infrastructure; Minister of Housing and Plantation Infrastructure –2004; Pres. and Gen. Sec. Ceylon Workers' Congress; Minister of Youth Empowerment and Socio-Economic Development 2007–. *Address:* Ministry of Youth Empowerment and Socio Economic Development, 15a, Flower Terrace, Colombo 7 (office); No. 09 2/2, Rajakeeya Mawatha, Mayfair Flats, Colombo 7, Sri Lanka (home).

THONEMANN, Peter Clive, MSc, DPhil; British (b. Australian) physicist and academic; *Professor Emeritus, University of Wales, Swansea;* b. 3 June 1917, Melbourne, Australia; s. of Frederick Emil Thonemann and Mabel Jessie Thonemann; one s. one d.; ed Univs of Melbourne and Sydney and Trinity Coll., Oxford; Commonwealth Research Scholar, Sydney Univ. 1944–46; ICI Fellow, Clarendon Lab., Oxford; proposed principles and initiated research for a fusion reactor, 1946–49; Head of Research on Controlled Thermonuclear Reactions, AERE, Harwell 1949–60, designed and built prototype fusion reactor Zeta, Deputy Dir, Culham Lab. of the Atomic Energy Authority 1965–66; Prof. of Physics and Head of Dept, Univ. Coll. of Swansea (now Univ. of Wales Swansea) 1968–84, Prof. Emer. 1984–. *Leisure interests:* physics, musical composition. *Address:* 130 Bishopston Road, Swansea, SA3 3EU, Wales.

THONGLOUN, Sisolit; Laotian politician; *Deputy Prime Minister and Minister of Foreign Affairs;* b. 10 Nov. 1945; ed Pedagogical Coll., Neo Lao Hak Sat, Houaphanh, Pedagogical Inst., St Petersburg, Russia, Acad. of Social Science, Moscow; Staff Officer, Educational Div., Neo Lao Hak Sat (Lao Nat. Patriotic Front), Houaphanh Prov. 1967–69; Staff Officer, Rep. Office, Neo Lao Hak Sat (LNPE), Hanoi 1969–73; Instructor, Vientiane Univ. 1978–79; Sec. to Ministry of Educ. and Chief, External Relations Div., Ministry of Educ. 1979–81; Dir Public Research Dept, Minister Council Bd, Office of the Prime Minister 1985–86; Vice-Minister, Ministry of Foreign Affairs 1987–92; Minister of Labour and Social Welfare 1993–97; mem. Parl. 1998–2000; Deputy Prime Minister of Laos 2001–, Minister of Foreign Affairs 2006–; Pres. Cttee for Planning and Cooperation, Cttee for Investment and Cooperation, Lao Nat. Cttee for Energy; Hon. Pres., SOS of Lao PDR1–. *Address:* Ministry of Foreign Affairs, rue That Luang 01004, Ban Phonxay, Vientiane, Laos (office). *Telephone:* (21) 413148 (office). *Fax:* (21) 414009 (office). *E-mail:* souknivone@mofa.gov.la (office). *Website:* www.mofa.gov.la (office).

't HOOFT, Gerardus; Dutch physicist and academic; *Professor of Theory of Solids, University of Utrecht;* b. 5 July 1946, Den Helder; s. of H. 't Hooft and M. A. van Kampen; m. Albertha A. Schik 1972; two d.; ed Dalton Lyceum Gymnasium beta, The Hague, Rijks Universiteit, Utrecht; Fellow CERN (Theoretical Physics Div.), Geneva 1972–74; Asst Prof., Univ. of Utrecht 1974–77, Prof. of Theory of Solids 1977–; mem. Koninklijke Acad. van Wetenschappen, Letteren en Schone Kunsten v. België, Koninklijke Nederlandse Acad. van Wetenschappen; Foreign Assoc. NAS; Foreign Hon. mem. American Acad. of Arts and Sciences, Acad. des Sciences; Fellow and CPhys, Inst. of Physics (London) 2000; Asteroid 9491 Thooft is named in his honour; Dr hc (Chicago) 1981, (Leuven) 1996, (Bologna) 1998; W. Prins Prize 1974, Akzo Prize 1977, Dannie Heineman Prize 1979, Wolf Foundation Prize in Physics, 1981, Spinoza Premium 1995, Pius XI Medal 1983, Lorentz Medal 1986, Franklin Medal 1995, G. C. Wick Medal 1997, High Energy Physics Prize (European Physical Soc.) 1999, Nobel Prize for Physics (jtly) 1999. *Publications:* Under the Spell of the Gauge Principle 1994, In Search of the Ultimate Building Blocks 1996; papers on Renormalization of Yang-Mills Fields, magnetic monopoles, Instantons, Gauge theories, quark confinement, quantum gravity and black holes. *Address:* Faculty of Physics and Astronomy, University of Utrecht, Prinetonplein 5, 3584 CC Utrecht (office); University of Utrecht, Spinoza Institute, PO Box 80.195, 3508 TD Utrecht, Netherlands (office). *Telephone:* (30) 2533284 (office); (30) 2537549 (office); (30) 2535928 (office). *Fax:* (30) 2539282 (office); (30) 2535937 (office). *Website:* www.phys.uu .nl/~thooft (office).

THORBURN, Clifford Charles Devlin (Cliff), CM; Canadian snooker player; b. 16 Jan. 1948, Victoria, BC; s. of James Thorburn and Adel Hanna Thorburn; m. 1981; two s.; World Professional Champion 1980; 27 tournament wins (worldwide); winner 13 Canadian Championships; first player in World Professional Championship to make a 147 break (Crucible Theatre, Sheffield) 1983; Canadian Snooker Hall of Fame 1990, mem. Canada's Sports Hall of Fame. *Publications:* Cliff Thorburn's Snooker Skills, Playing for Keeps (autobiog.). *Leisure interests:* golf, chess, reading. *Address:* 31 West Side Drive, Markham, Ontario, Canada. *Website:* www.thorburn-wych-.on.ca (office).

THORENS, Justin Pierre, DenD; Swiss professor of law and attorney; *President, Latsis International Foundation;* b. 15 Sept. 1931, Collonge-Bellerive; s. of Paul L. Thorens and Germaine Falquet; m. Colette F. Vecchio 1963; one s. one d.; ed Univ. of Geneva, Freie Univ. Berlin and Univ. Coll. London; attorney-at-law, Geneva Bar 1956–; Alt. Pres. Jurisdictional Court, Geneva 1971–78; Lecturer, Faculty of Law, Univ. of Geneva 1967, Assoc. Prof. 1970, Prof. 1973–96, Dean 1974–77, Hon. Prof. 1996–; Rector, Univ. of Geneva 1977–83; Visiting Scholar, Stanford Univ. 1983–84, Univ. of Calif., Berkeley 1983–84; Guest Prof., Univ. of Munich, Germany 1984; mem. Cttee European Centre for Higher Educ. (CEPES), Bucharest 1981–95, Pres. 1986–88; mem. Admin. Council Asscn des Universités Partiellement ou Entièrement de Langue Française (AUPELF), Montreal 1978–87, Vice-Pres. 1981–87, Hon. Vice-Pres. 1987–, mem. Gov. Council 1987–; Pres. Bd Int. Asscn of Univs (AIU), Paris 1985–90, Hon. Pres. 1990–; mem. Council UN Univ. Tokyo 1986–92, Pres. 1988–89; mem. UNESCO Swiss Nat. Comm. 1989–2001, Int. Acad. of Estate and Trust Law; Pres. Latsis Int. Foundation 1989–; various prizes, awards and distinctions. *Publications:* publs on pvt. law, civil procedure, arbitration, Anglo-American property law, univ. politics, cultural questions. *Leisure interests:* history and all its aspects, both European and the rest of the world; interaction of cultures of various times and regions. *Address:* 18 chemin du Nant d'Aisy, 1246 Corsier (Geneva), Switzerland. *Telephone:* (22) 7518081 (office); (22) 7511262 (home). *Fax:* (22) 7518082 (office); (22) 7518082 (home). *E-mail:* etude.jthorens@bluewin.ch (office); justin.thorens@ bluewin.ch (home).

THORNBURGH, Richard (Dick) Lewis, BEng, LLB; American lawyer and fmr politician; *Counsel, Kirkpatrick & Lockhart Nicholson Graham LLP;* b. 16 July 1932, Pittsburgh; s. of Charles G. Thornburgh and Alice Sanborn; m. Virginia W Judson 1963; four s.; ed Yale Univ. and Univ. of Pittsburgh; admitted to Pa Bar 1958, US Supreme Court Bar 1965; attorney, Kirkpatrick & Lockhart LLP (now Kirkpatrick & Lockhart Nicholson Graham LLP), Pittsburgh 1959–79, 1977–79, 1987–88, 1994– (in Washington, DC); US attorney for Western Pa, Pittsburgh 1969–75; Asst Attorney-Gen. Criminal Div. US Justice Dept 1975–77; Gov. of Pennsylvania 1979–87; Dir Inst. of Politics, J.F. Kennedy School of Govt, Harvard Univ. 1987–88; Attorney-Gen. of USA 1988–91; UnderSec. Gen. for Admin. and Man. UN 1992–93; Chair. State Science and Tech. Inst., Legal Policy Advisory Bd, Washington Legal Foundation; Vice-Chair. World Cttee on Disability; Fellow, American Bar Foundation; mem. American Judicature Soc., Council on Foreign Relations; Trustee Urban Inst., Nat. Acad. of Public Admin.; Lifetime Nat. Assoc., Nat. Acads of Science and Eng 2001–; Republican; 31 hon. degrees; Special Medallion Award, Fed. Drug Enforcement Admin. 1973, Distinguished Service Medal, American Legion 1992, Wiley E. Branton Award, Washington Lawyers' Cttee 2002, American Lawyer Magazine Lifetime Achievement Award 2006. *Publications:* Where the Evidence Leads (autobiog.) 2003, Report of the Independent Review Panel on the September 8, 2004 '60 Minutes Wednesday' Segment "For the Record" Concerning President Bush's Texas Air National Guard Service (with Louis D. Boccardi) 2005. *Address:* Kirkpatrick & Lockhart Nicholson Graham LLP, 1800 Massachusetts Avenue, NW, Washington, DC 20036-1221, USA (office). *Telephone:* (202) 778-9080 (office). *Fax:* (202) 778-9100 (office). *E-mail:* dick.thornburgh@klgates.com (office). *Website:* www.klng.com (office).

THORNE, Kip Stephen, BS, PhD; American research physicist, academic and writer; *Richard P. Feynman Professor of Theoretical Physics, California Institute of Technology;* b. 1940, Logan, UT; s. of David Wynne Thorne and

Alison Comish; m. 1st Linda Jeanne Peterson 1960 (divorced 1977); one s. one d.; m. 2nd Carolee Joyce Winstein 1984; ed Calif. Inst. of Tech. and Princeton Univ.; Postdoctoral Fellow, Princeton Univ. 1965–66; Research Fellow in Physics, Calif. Inst. of Tech. 1966–67, Assoc. Prof. of Theoretical Physics 1967–70, Prof. 1970–, William R. Kenan Jr Prof. 1981–91, Richard P. Feynman Prof. of Theoretical Physics 1991–; Adjunct Prof. of Physics, Univ. of Utah 1971–98; Fulbright Lecturer, France 1966; Visiting Prof., Moscow Univ. 1969, 1975, 1978, 1981, 1982, 1986, 1988, 1990, 1998; Andrew D. White Prof.-at-Large, Cornell Univ. 1986–92; Chair. Topical Group on Gravity of American Physical Soc. 1997–98; Alfred P. Sloan Research Fellow 1966–68; Guggenheim Fellow 1967; mem. Int. Cttee on Gen. Relativity and Gravitation 1971–80, 1992–, Cttee on US-USSR Co-operation in Physics 1978–79, Space Science Bd, NASA 1980–83; Foreign mem. Russian Acad. of Sciences 1999; mem. American Philosophical Soc. 1999; mem. NAS 1973; Fellow, American Acad. of Arts and Sciences, American Physical Soc., AAAS; Hon. DSc (Illinois Coll.) 1979, (Utah State Univ.) 2000, (Glasgow) 2001; Dr hc (Moscow State Univ.) 1981; Hon. DHumLitt (Claremont Grad. Univ.) 2002; American Inst. of Physics Science Writing Award in Physics and Astronomy 1969, 1994, Priroda (USSR) Readers' Choice Award 1989, 1990, Phi Beta Kappa Science Writing Award 1994, Julius Edgar Lilienfeld Prize, American Physical Soc. 1996, Karl Schwarzschild Medal, German Astronomical Soc. 1996, 24th Annual Award for Excellence in Teaching, Associated Students of the California Inst. of Tech. (undergraduates) 1999–2000, Robinson Prize in Cosmology, Univ. of Newcastle 2002, California Scientist of the Year 2004, Student Council Mentoring Award 2004, Commonwealth Award in Science 2005. *Publications:* co-author: Gravitation Theory and Gravitational Collapse 1965, High Energy Astrophysics, Vol. 3 1967, Gravitation 1973, Black Holes: The Membrane Paradigm 1986; sole author: Black Holes and Time Warps: Einstein's Outrageous Legacy 1994. *Address:* California Institute of Technology, MS 130-33 Theoretical Astrophysics, 1200 East California Boulevard, Pasadena, CA 91125-0001, USA (office). *Telephone:* (626) 395-4598 (office). *Fax:* (626) 796-5675 (office). *E-mail:* kip@tapir.caltech.edu (office). *Website:* www.its.caltech.edu/~kip (office).

THORNING-SCHMIDT, Helle, MA, MSc; Danish politician; *Leader, Socialdemokraterne (Social Democrats);* b. 14 Dec. 1966, Rødovre; d. of Holger Thorning-Schmidt Grete Thorning-Schmidt; m. Stephen Kinnock; ed Univ. of Copenhagen, Coll. of Europe, Bruges; Int. Consultant, Danish Trades Union Congress (LO) 1997–99; Head, Socialdemokraterne (Social Democrats) Secr., European Parl. 1994–97, MEP 1999–2004; Leader, Socialdemokraterne 2005–; mem. Bd of Dirs Danmarks Nationalbank 2005–. *Publications:* En dollar om dagen (A Dollar a Day) (co-author) 2001, Forsvar for Fællesskabet (In Defence of Fellowship) (co-author) 2002. *Address:* Socialdemokraterne (Social Democrats), Danasvej 7, 1910 Frederiksberg C, Denmark (office). *Telephone:* 72-30-08-00 (office). *Fax:* 72-30-08-50 (office). *E-mail:* s@socialdemokraterne.dk (office). *Website:* www.socialdemokraterne.dk (office); www.thorning-schmidt.dk.

THORNTON, Billy Bob; American actor, director and writer; b. 4 Aug. 1955, Hot Springs, Ark.; m. 1st Melissa Lee Gatlin (divorced 1980); one d.; 2nd Toni Lawrence (divorced 1988); 3rd Cynda Williams (divorced 1992); 4th Pietra Dawn Chernak (divorced 1997); two s.; 5th Angelina Jolie (q.v.) 2000 (divorced 2003); one adopted s.; one d. with Connie Angland. *Films include:* Sling Blade (also dir, screenplay; Acad. Award for Best Adapted Screenplay 1996, Chicago Film Critics Award for Best Actor, Independent Spirit Awards), U-Turn 1997, A Thousand Miles 1997, The Apostle 1997, A Gun A Car A Blonde, Primary Colors 1997, Homegrown 1998, Armageddon 1998, A Simple Plan 1998, Pushing Tin 1998, The Man Who Wasn't There 2001, Bandits 2001, Monster's Ball 2001, Love Actually 2003, Intolerable Cruelty 2003, Bad Santa 2003, The Alamo 2004, Friday Night Lights 2004, Bad News Bears 2005, The Ice Harvest 2005, School for Scoundrels 2006, The Astronaut Farmer 2007, Mr Woodcock 2007. *Television:* The 1,000 Chains, Don't Look Back (actor, writer), The Outsiders (series), Hearts Afire. *Address:* c/o William Morris Agency, 1 William Morris Place, Beverly Hills, CA 90212, USA (office).

THORNTON, Clive Edward Ian, CBE, LLB, BA, FCIB; British lawyer and business executive; b. 12 Dec. 1929, Newcastle upon Tyne; s. of Albert Thornton and Margaret Thornton; m. Maureen Crane 1956; one s. one d.; ed St Anthony's School and Coll. of Commerce, Newcastle upon Tyne and Coll. of Law, London; articled, Kenneth Hudson, Solicitor, London 1959; solicitor to Cassel Arenz (merchant bankers), London 1964; Chief Solicitor, Abbey Nat. Bldg Soc. 1967, Deputy Chief Gen. Man. 1978, Chief Gen. Man. 1979–83, Dir 1980–83; Chair. Commerce and Industry Group, The Law Soc. 1974–75; mem. Council, Bldg Socs Asscn 1979–83, Housing Corpn 1980–86; Chair. Shelter Housing Aid Centre 1983–86, Mirror Group of Newspapers Jan.–July 1984, Thorndale Farm 1984–, Financial Weekly Ltd 1984–87, Thamesmead Town Ltd 1986–90, Gabriel Communications Ltd 1986–96, Universe Publs 1986–96, Armstrong Capital Holdings Ltd 1988–; Dir Investment Data Services 1986–90, Melton Mowbray Building Soc. 1988–, (Chair. 1991–), LHW Futures 1988–96, Burgon Hall Ltd 1988–96; Council mem., St Mary's Hosp. Medical School 1986–96; Partner, Stoneham Langton and Passmore (int. lawyers) 1984–88; Solicitor of Supreme Court. *Publications:* Building Society Law: Cases and Materials 1975, 1989, History of Devon Cattle 1999. *Leisure interests:* antique collecting, music, reading, breeding Devon cattle. *Address:* Lansbury House, 3 St Mary's Place, Stamford, Lincs., PE9 2DN; Keythorpe Grange, East Norton, Leics., LE7 9XL; Belford Hall, Belford, Northumberland, England. *Telephone:* (1162) 598201 (East Norton); (1668) 213667 (Belford).

THORNTON, Janet Maureen, CBE, PhD, FRS; British molecular biologist and academic; *Director, European Bioinformatics Institute;* b. 23 May 1949; d. of Stanley James McLoughlin and Kathleen Barlow; m. Alan Thornton 1970; one s. one d.; ed Nottingham Univ., King's Coll. London, Nat. Inst. of Medical Research; tutor, Open Univ. 1976–83; molecular pharmacologist, Nat. Inst. of Medical Research 1978; Science and Eng Research Council Advanced Fellow 1979–83, Lecturer 1983–89, Sr Lecturer 1989–90, Bernal Chair. of Crystallography 1996–; Dir Biomolecular Structure and Modelling Unit, Univ. Coll. London 1990–, Prof. of Biomolecular Structure 1990–; consultant, European Molecular Biology Lab., European Bioinformatics Inst. (EMBL-EBI) 1994–2000, Dir EMBL-EBI 2000–; Head Jt Research School in Molecular Sciences, Univ. Coll. London and Birkbeck Coll. 1996–2000; Fellow, Churchill Coll. Cambridge; Hon. Prof., Dept of Chem., Univ. of Cambridge; Hans Neurath Award, Protein Soc., USA 2000. *Publications:* numerous articles in scientific journals. *Leisure interests:* reading, music, gardening, walking. *Address:* EMBL-EBI, Wellcome Trust Genome Campus, Hinxton, Cambridge, CB10 1SD, England (office). *Telephone:* (1223) 494648 (office); (1223) 494444 (office). *Fax:* (1223) 494468 (office). *E-mail:* director@ebi.ac.uk (office); thornton@ebi.ac.uk (office). *Website:* www.ebi.ac.uk/Thornton/index.html (office).

THORNTON, John L.; American business executive and academic; *Professor and Director of Global Leadership, Tsinghua University;* b. 2 Jan. 1954, New York; ed Hotchkiss School, Harvard Coll., Oxford Univ., Yale School of Org. and Man.; joined Goldman Sachs 1980, f. and built merger and acquisition business for co. in Europe 1983–91, partner 1988 with exec. responsibility for operations in Europe, Middle East and Africa, mem. Bd of Dirs. 1996, Pres., Co-COO 1999–2003; Prof. and Dir of Global Leadership Tsinghua Univ., China 2003–; mem. Audit Cttee, Org. Review and Nominating Cttee; mem. Bd Dirs Intel Corpn, Goldman Sachs Group, Inc., Ford Motor Co., British Sky Broadcasting, Laura Ashley Holdings PLC, Hughes Electronics Corpn, Pacific Century Group Inc.; Chair. Brookings Inst. Bd of Trustees; mem. Council on Foreign Relations; mem. Advisory Bd Asia Society, Goldman Sachs Foundation, Hotchkiss School, Morehouse Coll., Tsinghua Univ. School of Econs and Man. (Beijing), Yale Univ. Investment Cttee, Yale School of Man. *Address:* Tsinghua University, 1 Qinghuayuan, Beijing 100084, People's Republic of China (office). *Telephone:* (10) 62782015 (office). *Fax:* (10) 62770349 (office). *E-mail:* info@tsinghua.edu.cn (office). *Website:* www.tsinghua.edu.cn/eng/index.htm (office).

THORP, Holden, BSc, DSc; American chemist, academic and university administrator; *Chancellor, University of North Carolina;* b. 16 Aug. 1964, Fayetteville, NC; m. Patti Worden Thorp; one s. one d.; ed Univ. of North Carolina, California Inst. of Tech.; Postdoctoral Asst, Yale Univ. 1989–90; Asst Prof. of Chem., North Carolina State Univ. 1990–92; Asst Prof. of Chem., Univ. of North Carolina 1992–99, Prof. 1999–, Kenan Prof. and Chair. Dept of Chem. 2005, Dean Coll. of Arts and Sciences 2007–08, Chancellor Univ. of North Carolina 2008–; Dir Morehead Planetarium and Science Center 2001–05; co-f. Viamet Pharmaceuticals Inc. 2005; numerous awards including Ruth and Philip Hettleman Prize for Artistic and Scholarly Achievement 1996, Tanner Award for Excellence in Undergraduate Teaching, Nat. Science Foundation's Presidential Young Investigator Award. *Publications:* more than 130 scholarly publications on the electronic properties of DNA and RNA. *Leisure interests:* playing jazz bass and keyboard. *Address:* Office of the Chancellor, 103 South Building, Campus Box 9100, Chapel Hill, NC 27599-9100, USA (office). *Telephone:* (919) 962-1365 (office). *Fax:* (919) 962-1647 (office). *E-mail:* chancellor@unc.edu (office). *Website:* www.unc.edu/chan (office).

THORPE, Ian James; Australian swimmer; b. 13 Oct. 1982, Sydney; s. of Kenneth William Thorpe and Margaret Grace Thorpe; ed East Hills Boys Technical High School; winner three Olympic gold medals, two silver medals 2000; set new world record in 400m freestyle and 4×200m relay; winner 11 World Championship gold medals 1998–2003; won ten gold medals and broke own 400m freestyle world record Commonwealth Games; won nine titles including five gold medals Pan-Pacific Games; winner two gold medals, one silver medal, one bronze medal Olympic Games, Athens 2004; world-record holder for 200m and 400m freestyle; retd from competitive swimming 2006; numerous awards including NSW Athlete of the Year 1998, three times Australian Swimmer of the Year, four times World Swimmer of the Year, Swimming World Magazine 1998, 1999, Male Athlete of the Year, Australian Sports Awards 2000, Young Australian of the Year 2000, The Sport Australia Hall of Fame's 'Don Award' 2000, Jesse Owens American Int. Athlete Trophy Award 2001, China Sports Daily's Most Popular World Athlete 2002. *Achievements:* Ian Thorpe's Fountain for Youth Trust launched by Australian Prime Minister John Howard. *Publications:* The Journey, Live Your Dreams. *Leisure interests:* surfing, cooking, movies, dinner, water skiing, computer games, music, TV. *Address:* c/o Grand Slam International Pty Ltd, PO Box 402, Manly, NSW 1655, Australia (office). *Telephone:* (2) 9976-0844 (office). *Fax:* (2) 9976-0767 (office). *E-mail:* gsi@grandslamint.com (office). *Website:* www.grandslamint.com (office).

THORPE, Rt Hon. (John) Jeremy, PC; British politician; b. 29 April 1929; m. 1st Caroline Allpass 1968 (died 1970); one s.; m. 2nd Maria (Marion) Stein, fmr Countess of Harewood, 1973; ed Rectory School, Eton Coll. and Trinity Coll., Oxford; barrister, Inner Temple 1954; MP for N Devon 1959–79; Treas. UN Parl. Group 1962–67; Hon. Treas. Liberal Party 1965–67, Leader 1967–76; Pres. N Devon Liberal Asscn 1987–; Consultant, Stramit; Chair. Jeremy Thorpe Assocs Ltd 1984–; Hon. Fellow, Trinity Coll., Oxford Univ.; Hon. DCL (Exeter). *Publications:* To All Who Are Interested in Democracy 1951, Europe: The Case for Going In 1971, In My Own Time (autobiography) 1999. *Leisure interests:* collecting Chinese ceramics, music. *Address:* 2 Orme Square, Bayswater, London, W2 4RS, England.

THORPE, Nigel James, CVO, BA; British diplomatist (retd); b. 3 Oct. 1945; three d.; ed East Grinstead Co. Grammar School, Cardiff Univ.; joined

Diplomatic Service 1969, with Embassy, Warsaw 1970–72, High Comm., Dhaka 1973–74; at FCO, London 1975–79, High Comm., Ottawa 1979–81; seconded to Dept of Energy, London 1981–82; Deputy Head Southern Africa Dept, FCO 1982–85; Deputy Head of Mission, Warsaw 1985–88; Deputy High Commr, Harare 1989–92; Head Cen. European Dept, FCO 1992–96; Sr Directing Staff, Royal Coll. of Defence Studies, London 1996–98; Amb. to Hungary 1998–2003. *Publication:* Harmincad Utca 6: A Twentieth Century History of Budapest. *Leisure interests:* family, his dog, music. *Address:* c/o Foreign and Commonwealth Office, King Charles Street, London, SW1A 2AH, England.

THOULESS, David James, PhD, FRS; American (b. British) physicist and academic; *Professor Emeritus of Physics, University of Washington;* b. 21 Sept. 1934, Bearsden, Scotland; s. of Robert Thouless and Priscilla (née Gorton) Thouless; m. Margaret Scrase 1958; two s. one d.; ed Winchester Coll., Trinity Hall, Cambridge, Cornell Univ., USA; physicist, Lawrence Radiation Lab., Berkeley 1958–59; ICI Research Fellow, Univ. of Birmingham 1959–61, Prof. of Math. Physics 1965–79; Lecturer, Univ. of Cambridge and Fellow of Churchill Coll. 1961–65, Royal Soc. Research Prof. and Fellow of Clare Hall, Cambridge 1983–86; Prof. of Applied Science, Yale Univ. 1979–80; Prof. of Physics, Univ. of Washington 1980–2003, currently Prof. Emer.; mem. NAS 1995; Fellow American Physical Soc. 1987; Maxwell Prize 1973, Holweck Medal 1980, Fritz London Award 1984, Wolf Prize for Physics 1990, Dirac Prize 1993, Onsager Prize 2000. *Publications:* Quantum Mechanics of Many-Body Systems 1961, Topological Quantum Numbers in Nonrelativistic Physics 1998. *Address:* Department of Physics, Box 351560, University of Washington, Seattle, WA 98195, USA. *Telephone:* (206) 685-2393 (office). *E-mail:* thouless@uwashington.edu (office). *Website:* www.phys.washington .edu/~thouless/ (office).

THRUSH, Brian Arthur, MA, ScD, FRS; British scientist and academic; *Professor Emeritus of Physical Chemistry, University of Cambridge;* b. 23 July 1928, London; s. of late Arthur Thrush and Dorothy Thrush; m. Rosemary C. Terry 1958; one s. one d.; ed Haberdashers' Aske's Hampstead School and Emmanuel Coll., Cambridge; Univ. Demonstrator, Asst Dir of Research, Lecturer, Reader in Physical Chem. Univ. of Cambridge 1953–78, Prof. of Physical Chem. 1978–95, now Prof. Emer.; Head Dept of Chem., Univ. of Cambridge 1988–93; Fellow, Emmanuel Coll., Cambridge 1960–, Vice-Master 1986–90; mem. Natural Environment Research Council 1985–90; Visiting Prof. Chinese Acad. of Sciences 1980–; mem. Council, Royal Soc. 1989–91, Academia Europaea 1992–98; Tilden Lecturer (Royal Soc. of Chem.) 1965; M. Polanyi Medal (Royal Soc. of Chem.) 1980, Rank Prize for Opto-Electronics 1992. *Publications:* papers on spectroscopy, gas reactions and atmospheric chemistry in learned journals. *Leisure interests:* wine, gardens. *Address:* Department of Chemistry, University of Cambridge, Lensfield Road, Cambridge, CB2 1EW (office); Brook Cottage, Pemberton Terrace, Cambridge, CB2 1JA, England (home). *Telephone:* (1223) 336458 (office); (1223) 357637 (home). *Fax:* (1223) 336362.

THUBRON, Colin Gerald Dryden, CBE, FRSL; British writer; b. 14 June 1939, London; s. of Brig. Gerald Ernest Thubron and Evelyn Kate Dryden; ed Eton Coll.; mem. editorial staff, Hutchinson & Co. Publishers Ltd 1959–62; freelance documentary film maker 1963–64; Production Ed., The Macmillan Co., USA 1964–65; freelance author 1965–; Vice-Pres., Royal Soc. of Literature; Hon. DLitt (Warwick) 2002; Silver Pen Award of PEN 1985, Thomas Cook Award 1988, Hawthornden Prize 1988, Mungo Park Medal, Royal Scottish Geographical Soc. 2000, Lawrence of Arabia Medal, Royal Soc. of Asian Affairs 2001. *Scenario:* The Prince of the Pagodas (ballet at The Royal Opera House, Covent Garden). *Publications:* Mirror to Damascus, The Hills of Adonis, Jerusalem, Journey into Cyprus, Among the Russians, Behind the Wall, The Lost Heart of Asia, In Siberia, Shadow of the Silk Road 2006; novels: The God in the Mountain, Emperor, A Cruel Madness, Falling, Turning Back the Sun, Distance, To the Last City. *Address:* 28 Upper Addison Gardens, London, W14 8AJ, England. *Telephone:* (20) 7602-2522.

THULASIDAS, V., MA; Indian airline industry executive; b. 25 March 1948, Allepey dist, Kerala; ed Inst. of English, Thiruvananthapuram; fmr lecturer, Kerala; various positions in Tripura including Commr of Taxes, Dir of Settlement and Land Records, of Food and Civil Supplies; fmr Under-Sec., Ministry of Civil Aviation; fmr Jt Sec. (Air), Ministry of Defence; Chief Sec. of Tripura –2003; Chair. and Man. Dir Air-India 2003–08. *Address:* c/o Air-India Ltd, Air India Building, Nariman Point, Mumbai 400 021; 22B Sterling Apartments, 38 Peddar Road, Mumbai 400 026, India (home). *Telephone:* (22) 22796666. *Fax:* (22) 22024897.

THUN, Matteo; Italian architect and designer; b. 1952, Bolzano; ed Salzburg Acad. under Oskar Kokoschka, Univ. of Florence; moved to Milan 1978; Co-Founder and fmr Partner, Sottsass Associati, Milan; co-f. Memphis Group 1981; Chair of Product Design and Ceramics, Vienna Acad. for Applied Arts 1982; f. Matteo Thun studio 1984; Creative Dir Swatch 1990–93; Applied Art Chair, Vienna; mem. RIBA; ADI Compasso d'Oro Award (three times), Design of the Year Award for Via col Vento 1987, Forum Design Award 1989, Design Award, North Rhine-Westphalia 1994, Baden Württemberg Int. Design Award for 'O Sole Mio' 1997, Good Design Award 2000, IF Contract world Award for Missoni Shop System 2000, Industrial Design Forma Forum for 'Heidis' 2000, IF Contract world Award for Fila Shop 2000, Side Hotel in Hamburg chosen as Hotel of the Year 2001, Red Dot Award for 'Isy' 2002, Architecture and Tech. Innovation Prize and Good Design Award for 'Thun' 2003, ADI Design System: Architecture and Tech. Int. Prize for 'Girly' 2004, ADI Design System: Architecture and Tech. Int. Prize for 'Isy' 2004, Vigilius mountain resort won the Wallpaper Design Award 2004, inducted into Interior Hall of Fame, New York 2004, Red Dot Award for Product Design for Porsche Design Store 2005, Radisson SAS, Frankfurt chosen as the best hotel opened in the year, Worldwide Hospitality Awards 2005, Panda d'oro Award for Vigilius Mountain Resort 2005, Neue Horizonte/Ideenpool Holz 21: "Elf gute Ideen zu Holz" for Strategic Business Unit of Hugo Boss 2006, Design Plus Award for 'Archetun' 2006, IF Product Design Award for 'Roma' 2006, Legambiente/Regione Lombardi Award for Viglius Mountain Resort 2006, Good Design Award for 'Roma' 2007, Prix Acier Construction for Strategic Unit by Hugo Boss 2007, New Classic Award for 'Isy', Schöner Wohnen Magazine 2007, Bronze Medal for 'Valverde' 2008, Water Innovation Award 2008, IF Product Design Award for 'Muse' 2008, IF Contract world Award for 'Architektur und Boden' 2008. *Address:* Via Appiani 9, 20121 Milan, Italy (office). *Telephone:* (02) 655691 (office). *Fax:* (02) 6570646 (office). *E-mail:* info@matteothun.com (office). *Website:* www.matteothun.com (office).

THUNE, John, MBA; American politician; *Senator from South Dakota;* m. Kimberley Weems; two d.; ed Univ. of S Dakota; started career in Washington DC working for Senator Jim Abdnor; served in Small Business Admin; returned to S Dakota as Exec. Dir of local Republican Party 1989; State Railroad Dir 1991–93; Exec. Dir S Dakota Municipal League 1993–96; mem. Congress 1996–2004, served on House Transportation and Agric. Cttees; Senator from S Dakota 2005–. *Address:* United States Senate SR-383, Washington, DC 20510, USA (office). *Telephone:* (202) 224-2321 (office). *Fax:* (202) 228-5429 (office). *Website:* thune.senate.gov (office).

THUNELL, Lars H., PhD; Swedish international organization executive; *Executive Vice-President, International Finance Corporation, World Bank Group;* ed Univ. of Stockholm; fmr Research Fellow, Harvard Univ. Center for Int. Affairs, USA; fmr CEO Trygg-Hansa insurance co.; fmr Deputy CEO Nordbanken; fmr Pres. and CEO Securum (asset man. co.), Stockholm; CEO Skandinaviska Enskilda Banken AB 1997–2005; Chair. Bd IBX Integrated Business Exchange AB; mem. or fmr mem. Bd of Dirs Svenska Cellulosa AB, Swedish Bankers Asscn, Akzo Nobel NV, Mentor Foundation; worked at ABB Zurich and American Express, New York; has also held numerous non-exec. bd positions with int. cos and non-governmental orgs; Exec. Vice-Pres. IFC (pvt. sector arm of World Bank Group) 2006–. *Publications:* author of books and articles on risk and risk man. in int. business. *Address:* International Finance Corporation, 2121 Pennsylvania Avenue, NW, Washington, DC 20433, USA (office). *Telephone:* (202) 473-1000 (office). *Website:* www.ifc.org (office).

THURAU, Klaus Walther Christian, MD; German physiologist; b. 14 June 1928, Bautzen; s. of Walther Thurau and Helene Engel; m. Antje Wiese 1957; two s.; ed High School, Berlin and Univs of Erlangen and Kiel; Lecturer in Physiology, Univ. of Göttingen 1955–65; Chair. Dept of Physiology, Univ. of Munich 1968–; Visiting Prof. American Heart Asscn 1964; Gilman Prof., Dartmouth Medical School 1968; Visiting Prof., American Kidney Foundation 1980; Pres. Int. Soc. of Nephrology; Treas. and Councillor Int. Union of Physiological Science; mem. Exec. Bd Int. Council of Scientific Unions; Chair. Verum-Foundation, German UNESCO Comm. on Natural Sciences; mem. German Physiological Soc., Soc. for Clinical Investigation, American Soc. of Physiology, Int. Soc. for Hypertension, Int. Soc. of Nephrology; Emer. Ed. European Journal of Physiology (Pflügers Archiv.); Hon. mem. Australian Soc. of Nephrology, S African Soc. of Nephrology, Int. Soc. of Nephrology, Heidelberg Acad. of Sciences, Acad. Europaea, London; Dr hc; Civil Service Cross 1st Class, Germany, Homer Smith Award. *Publications:* various papers on renal function (in medical journals). *Leisure interest:* music. *Address:* Department of Physiology, University of Munich, 12 Pettenkoferstr., 80336 Munich (office); Josef-Vötterstrasse 6, 81545 Munich, Germany (home). *Telephone:* (89) 218075558 (office); (89) 6422618 (home). *Fax:* (89) 218075532 (office); (89) 64254517 (home). *E-mail:* thurau@physiol.med.uni -muenchen.de (office).

THURLEY, Simon John, MA, PhD; British foundation executive and museum administrator; *Chief Executive, English Heritage;* b. 29 Aug. 1962; s. of the late Thomas Manley Thurley and Rachel Thurley (née House); ed Kimbolton School, Bedford Coll., London, Courtauld Inst.; Insp. of Ancient Monuments, Crown Buildings and Monuments Group, English Heritage 1988–90; Curator Historic Royal Palaces 1990–97; Dir Museum of London 1997–2002; CEO English Heritage 2002–; Chair. Cttee Soc. for Court Studies 1996–; Pres. City of London Archaeological Soc. 1997–2002, Huntingdonshire Local History Soc.; Visiting Prof. of Medieval History and Hon. Fellow, Royal Holloway Coll., Univ. of London; mem. Council St Paul's Cathedral, RIBA; Fellow Soc. of Antiquaries, Royal Historical Soc.; Hon. Mem. RICS . *Television:* Lost Building's of Britain (Channel 4) 2004, The Buildings that Made Britain (Channel 5) 2006. *Publications:* Henry VIII: Images of a Tudor King (co-author) 1989, The Royal Palaces of Tudor England 1993, Whitehall Palace 2000, Lost Buildings of Britain 2004, Hampton Court 2004; frequent contribs to historical publs. *Leisure interest:* ancient buildings. *Address:* English Heritage, 1 Waterhouse Square, 138–142 Holborn, London, EC1N 2ST, England (office). *Telephone:* (20) 7973-3000 (office). *E-mail:* chief .executive@english-heritage.org.uk (office). *Website:* www.english-heritage .org.uk (office).

THURLOW, 8th Baron, cr. 1792; **Francis Edward Hovell-Thurlow-Cumming-Bruce,** Kt, KCMG; British diplomatist (retd); b. 9 March 1912, London; s. of 6th Baron Thurlow and Grace Catherine Trotter; m. Yvonne Diana Aubyn Wilson 1949 (died 1990); two s. (one deceased) two d.; ed Shrewsbury School and Trinity Coll., Cambridge; Asst Prin., Dept of Agric. for Scotland 1935–37, Dominions Office 1937; Asst Sec. Office of UK High Commr in New Zealand 1939–44, in Canada 1944–46; Prin. Pvt. Sec. to Sec. of State 1946–48; Asst Sec. Commonwealth Relations Office (CRO) 1948; Head of Political Div., UK High Commr in India 1949–52; Establishment Officer, CRO 1952–54, Head of Commodities Dept 1954–55; Adviser on External Affairs to Gov. of Gold Coast 1955–57, Deputy High Commr for UK in Ghana 1957–58;

Asst Under-Sec. of State, CRO 1958; Deputy High Commr for UK in Canada 1958–59, High Commr in New Zealand 1959–63, in Nigeria 1964–66; Deputy Under-Sec. of State Foreign & Commonwealth Office (FCO) 1968; Gov. and C-in-C Bahamas 1968–72; KStJ. *Address:* 102 Leith Mansions, Grantully Road, London, W9 1LJ, England (home). *Telephone:* (20) 7289-9664 (home). *E-mail:* f.thurlow@btinternet.com (home).

THURMAN, Uma; American actress; b. 29 April 1970, Boston; d. of Robert Thurman and Nena Schlebrugge; m. 1st Gary Oldman (q.v.) 1991 (divorced 1992); m. 2nd Ethan Hawke (q.v.) 1997 (divorced 2004); one d. one s.; worked as model; Chevalier, Ordre des Arts et des Lettres 2006. *Films:* The Adventures of Baron Munchhausen 1988, Dangerous Liaisons 1988, Even Cowgirls Get the Blues, Final Analysis, Where the Heart Is, Henry and June, Mad Dog and Glory 1993, Pulp Fiction 1994, Robin Hood, Dylan, A Month by the Lake 1995, The Truth About Cats and Dogs 1996, Batman and Robin 1997, Gattaca 1997, The Avengers 1998, Les Misérables 1998, Vatel 2000, The Golden Bowl 2001, Chelsea Walls 2002, Kill Bill Vol. I 2003, Kill Bill Vol. II 2004, Be Cool 2005, The Producers: The Movie Musical 2005, Prime 2005, My Super Ex-Girlfriend 2006, The Life Before Her Eyes 2008, The Accidental Husband (also prod.) 2008. *Television includes:* Hysterical Blindness (Golden Globe for Best Actress in a mini-series or TV movie 2003) 2002. *Address:* c/o Brian Lourd, CAA, 9830 Wilshire Boulevard, Beverly Hills, CA 90212, USA.

THURSTON, William Paul, PhD; American mathematician and academic; *Professor of Mathematics, Cornell University;* b. 30 Oct. 1946, Washington, DC; ed New Coll., Sarasota, Fla, Univ. of California, Berkeley; at Inst. for Advanced Study, Princeton NJ 1972–73; Asst Prof. of Math., MIT 1973–74; Prof. of Math., Princeton Univ. 1974–96, Univ. of California, Davis 1996–2003, Cornell Univ., Ithaca, NY 2003–; Alfred P. Sloan Foundation Fellowship 1974–75, Oswald Veblen Geometry Prize, American Math. Soc. 1976, Alan T. Waterman Award 1979, Fields Medal, Gen. Ass. of Int. Math. Union, Warsaw 1982 (presented 1983), American Math. Soc. Colloquium Lecturer 1989. *Publications:* numerous articles in math. journals on topology. *Address:* Department of Mathematics, 533 Malott Hall, Cornell University, Ithaca, NY 14853-4201, USA (office). *Telephone:* (607) 255-2334 (office). *Fax:* (607) 255-7149 (office). *E-mail:* wpt@math.cornell.edu (office). *Website:* www.math.cornell.edu (office).

THUY, Le Duc, PhD; Vietnamese central banker; *Vice-Chairman, National Financial, Monetary Policy Advisory Council;* b. 1948, cen. Ha Tinh Prov.; ed Nat. Econs Univ., Hanoi, postgraduate studies in USSR; mem. Party Cen. Cttee; Asst in Econs to Prime Minister and to Gen. Sec. of CP early 1990s; joined State Bank of Viet Nam 1996, Deputy Gov. –1999, Gov. 1999–2007, Gov. for Viet Nam, IMF, Washington, DC; Vice-Chair. Nat. Financial, Monetary Policy Advisory Council 2007–; Visiting Scholar, Harvard Inst. for Int. Devt 1991–92. *Address:* National Financial, Monetary Policy Advisory Council, Ministry of Finance, 28 Tran Hung Dao, Hoan Kiem District, Hanoi, Viet Nam (office). *Telephone:* (4) 2202828 (office). *Fax:* (4) 2208129 (office). *E-mail:* support@mof.gov.vn (office). *Website:* www.mof.gov.vn (office).

THWAITE, Anthony Simon, OBE, MA, DLitt, FRSL, FSA; British writer and poet; b. 23 June 1930, Chester, Cheshire; s. of Hartley Thwaite and Alice Thwaite (née Mallinson); m. Ann Barbara Thwaite (née Harrop) 1955; four d.; ed Kingswood School, Bath, Christ Church, Oxford; Visiting Lecturer in English Literature, Univ. of Tokyo 1955–57; radio producer, BBC 1957–62; Literary Ed., The Listener 1962–65; Asst Prof. of English, Univ. of Libya, Benghazi 1965–67; Literary Ed., New Statesman 1968–72; Co-Ed., Encounter 1973–85; Editorial Dir, Editorial Consultant, André Deutsch 1986–95; Hon. Lay Canon, Norwich Cathedral 2005; Hon. DLitt (Hull) 1989, (East Anglia) 2007; Richard Hillary Memorial Prize 1968, Cholmondeley Award 1983. *Publications:* poetry: Home Truths 1957, The Owl in the Tree 1963, The Stones of Emptiness 1967, Inscriptions 1973, New Confessions 1974, A Portion for Foxes 1977, Victorian Voices 1980, Poems 1953–1983 1984, revised edn as Poems 1953–1988 1989, Letter from Tokyo 1987, The Dust of the World 1994, Selected Poems 1956–1996 1997, A Different Country: New Poems 2000, A Move in the Weather 2003, The Ruins of Time (ed.) 2006, Collected Poems 2007; other: Contemporary English Poetry 1959, The Penguin Book of Japanese Verse (co-ed. with Geoffrey Bownas) 1964, Japan (with Roloff Beny) 1968, The Deserts of Hesperides 1969, Poetry Today 1973, The English Poets (co-ed. with Peter Porter) 1974, In Italy (with Roloff Beny and Peter Porter) 1974, New Poetry 4 (co-ed. with Fleur Adcock) 1978, Twentieth Century English Poetry 1978, Odyssey: Mirror of the Mediterranean (with Roloff Beny) 1981, Larkin at Sixty (ed.) 1982, Poetry 1945 to 1980 (co-ed. with John Mole) 1983, Six Centuries of Verse 1984, Philip Larkin: Collected Poems (ed.) 1988, Selected Letters of Philip Larkin (ed.) 1992, Philip Larkin: Further Requirements (ed.) 2001, Poet to Poet: John Skelton 2008. *Leisure interests:* archaeology, antiquarian beachcombing. *Address:* The Mill House, Low Tharston, Norwich, Norfolk, NR15 2YN, England (home). *Telephone:* (1508) 489569 (home). *Fax:* (1508) 489221 (home).

THYS, Willy Lucien Ghislain; Belgian trade union official and international organization official; b. 18 July 1943, Le Roeulx; m. Micheline Berteau; three c.; ed FOPES/UCL Inst. for Adult Educ.; shop steward, ACV-CSC at Belgian Rail 1963, mem. Exec. Cttee railway workers' fed. in ACV-CSC 1970; Sec.-Gen. Belgian Christian Fed. of Communication and Cultural Workers 1976–87; Nat. Sec. ACV-CSC 1987; Sec.-Gen. World Confed. of Labour (WCL) 1996–2006 (after WCL merged with Int. Confed. of Free Trade Unions and eight nat. trade union orgs to form Int. Trade Union Confed. — ITUC). *Address:* c/o International Trade Union Confederation (ITUC), 5 blvd Roi Albert II, 1210 Brussels, Belgium.

TIAN, Chengping; Chinese politician; b. 1940, Daming, Hebei Prov.; s. of Tian Ying; ed Tsinghua Univ., Beijing; joined CCP 1964; sent to do manual labour, Huoqiucheng (Xihu Army Farm), Anhui Prov. 1968; Sec. Publicity Section, Shengli Chemical Plant, Shandong Prov. 1970; Sec. CCP Communist Youth League of China, Beijing Gen. Petrochemical Works 1970; Deputy Sec. CCP Party Cttee, Qianjin Chemical Plant, Beijing Yanshan Petrochemical Corpn 1974; Deputy Sec. CCP Party Cttee, Beijing Yanshan Petrochemical Corpn 1983; Sec. CCP Xicheng Dist Cttee, Beijing 1984; Deputy Sec. CCP 8th Qinghai Prov. Cttee 1988–97, Sec. 1997–99; Gov. of Qinghai Prov. 1993–97; Chair. Standing Cttee Qinghai Prov. People's Congress 1998–99; mem. Standing Cttee CCP Shanxi Prov. Cttee 1999–2005, Sec. CCP Shanxi Prov. Cttee 1999–2005; Chair. Standing Cttee Shanxi Prov. People's Congress 2003–05; Minister of Labour and Social Security 2005–07; Alt. mem. 13th Cen. Cttee CCP 1987–91, 14th CCP Cen. Cttee 1992–97, mem. 15th CCP Cen. Cttee 1997–2002, 16th CCP Cen. Cttee 2002–07, 17th CCP Cen. Cttee 2007–; Deputy, 8th NPC 1993–98, 9th NPC 1998–2003. *Address:* c/o Ministry of Labour and Social Security 12 Hepinglizhong Jie, Dongcheng Qu, Beijing 100716, People's Republic of China (office).

TIAN, Congming; Chinese politician; b. May 1943, Fugu, Shaanxi Prov.; ed Beijing Normal Univ.; joined CCP 1965; clerk, Political Department, Bayannur League, Inner Mongolia Autonomous Region People's Govt 1970–74; corresp., Xinhua News Agency Nei Monggol Br. 1974–80; Deputy Dir Policy Research Office, CCP Inner Mongolia Autonomous Regional Cttee 1980–83, mem. Standing Cttee CCP Inner Mongolia Autonomous Regional Cttee 1983–84, Sec.-Gen. CCP Inner Mongolia Autonomous Regional Cttee 1983–84, Deputy Sec. CCP Inner Mongolia Autonomous Regional Cttee 1984–88; Deputy Sec. CCP Tibetan Autonomous Regional Cttee 1988–90; Vice-Minister of Radio, Motion Picture and TV 1990–98 (Deputy Sec. CCP Leading Party Group 1990–98); Dir State Gen. Admin of Radio, Motion Picture and TV 1998–2000 (Sec. CCP Leading Party Group 1998–2000); Pres. Xinhua News Agency 2000–08; mem. 14th CCP Cen. Cttee 1992–97 (mem. Cttee for Discipline Inspection 1992–97), 15th CCP Cen. Cttee 1997–2002, 16th CCP Cen. Cttee 2002–07. *Address:* c/o Xinhua News Agency, 57 Xuanwumen Xidajie, Beijing 100803, People's Republic of China (office). *Telephone:* (10) 63071114 (office). *Fax:* (10) 63071210 (office). *Website:* www.xinhuanet.com (office).

TIAN, Fengshan; Chinese fmr politician; b. Oct. 1940, Zhaoyuan Co., Heilongjiang Prov.; ed Second Artillery Tech. Coll., Xi'an City, Shaanxi Prov.; joined CCP 1970; teacher, Zhaoyuan Co.; Sec. CCP Party Cttee, Zhaoyuan People's Commune; Chair. CCP Revolutionary Cttee, Zhaoyuan Co.; Deputy Sec. CCP Zhaoyuan Co. Cttee; Deputy Magistrate, later Magistrate Zhaoyuan Co. (Dist) People's Court; Deputy Commr Suihua Prefectural Admin. Office, Heilongjiang Prov. 1983–85, Commr 1985–88 (Deputy Sec. CCP Party Cttee); Sec. CCP Mudanjiang Municipal Cttee 1988–89; Vice-Gov. Heilongjiang Prov. 1989–94, Acting Gov. 1994–95, Gov. 1995–2000; Sec. CCP Leading Party Group, Ministry of Land and Resources 1999–2003, Minister of Land and Resources 2000–03 (removed from post); Deputy Sec. CCP Heilongjiang Prov. Cttee; Sec. CCP Harbin Municipal Cttee 1992; Alt. mem. 13th CCP Cen. Cttee 1987–92, 14th CCP Cen. Cttee 1992–97, mem. 15th CCP Cen. Cttee 1997–2002, 16th CCP Cen. Cttee 2002–04 (expelled from CCP 2004); Deputy to 8th NPC from Heilongjiang Prov. 1996; sentenced to life imprisonment for accepting bribes Dec. 2005.

TIAN, Jiyun; Chinese politician; b. June 1929, Feicheng Co., Shandong Prov.; joined CCP 1945; teacher, Guiyang People's Revolutionary Univ., Guizhou Prov.; Admin. Cadre, Prov. Training Class for Financial Cadres, Guizhou Prov.; Section Chief, later Div. Chief, later Deputy Dir Finance Dept, Guizhou Prov.; Deputy Dir, later Dir Financial Bureau, Sichuan Prov. 1969; Deputy Sec.-Gen. State Council 1981–83, Sec.-Gen. 1983–88; Dir Nat. Afforestation Cttee; Chair. China Cttee of the Int. Decade for Natural Disaster Reduction 1983–87; Vice-Premier, State Council 1983–93; Head, Commodity Prices Group, State Council 1984–93; mem. Secr. CCP Cen. Cttee 1985–87; Dir State Flood Control and Drought Relief HQ 1988–93, Cen. Forest Fire Prevention HQ 1987–93; mem. 12th CCP Cen. Cttee 1982–87, 13th CCP Cen. Cttee 1987–92, 14th CCP Cen. Cttee 1992–97, 15th CCP Cen. Cttee 1997–2002, mem. Politburo 1985–2002, Politburo Secr. 1985–87; Vice-Chair. 8th Standing Cttee of NPC 1993–98, 9th Standing Cttee of NPC 1998–2003. *Address:* c/o Standing Committee of National People's Congress, Beijing, People's Republic of China (office).

TIAN, Zengpei; Chinese diplomatist and politician; b. 1930, Raoyang Co., Hebei Prov.; ed Nankai Univ.; joined CCP 1947; joined Ministry of Foreign Affairs, becoming Section Chief and Dir, Political Dept, later Deputy Dir, Dir, and Deputy Dir-Gen. Dept of Soviet Union and Eastern Europe Affairs, Counsellor, Chinese Embassy, Moscow, USSR 1976–81; Minister-Counsellor, Embassy in Yugoslavia 1982–84, Amb. to Czechoslovakia 1984–85, to Yugoslavia 1986–88, Vice-Minister of Foreign Affairs 1988–96; mem. 14th CCP Cen. Cttee 1992–97; Del., 15th CCP Nat. Congress 1997–2002; mem. Standing Cttee 9th CPPCC Nat. Cttee 1998–2003, Chair. Foreign Affairs Sub-cttee 1998–2003. *Address:* c/o National Committee of Chinese People's Political Consultative Conference, Taipingqiao Street, Beijing, People's Republic of China (office). *Telephone:* (10) 553831 (office).

TIAN, Zhaowu; Chinese scientist and university administrator; b. 1927, Fuzhou City, Fujian Prov.; ed Xiamen Univ., Fujian Prov.; Prof., Xiamen Univ., Pres. 1982–89; Pres. China Chem. Asscn 1986; Vice-Pres. Int. Electrochemistry Asscn 1996; mem. Dept of Chem., Academia Sinica 1980–, Third World Acad. of Sciences 1996–; advanced the Feature Current idea of multi-hole electrode polarization and the Uneven Liquid Film model; also promoted electrochemical tech., including a new generation of ion chromatogram suppressers, corrosion measurement systems, and the first domestic electrochemical comprehensive testers; mem. Standing Cttee 8th CCP Nat. Cttee 1993–98; Dr hc (Univ. of Wales, UK) 1984; Hon. Nat. Prize of Sciences

1987. *Address:* c/o Xiamen University, Xiamen, Fujian Province, People's Republic of China.

TIBAIJUKA, Anna Kajumulo, DSc; Tanzanian agricultural economist and United Nations official; *Under-Secretary-General and Executive Director, United Nations Centre for Human Settlements (UN-HABITAT);* m. Wilson Tibaijuka (died 2000); five c. (one adopted); ed Swedish Univ. of Agricultural Sciences, Uppsala; Assoc. Prof. of Econs, Dar-es-Salaam Univ. 1993–98; Founding Chair. Tanzanian Nat. Women's Council; UNCTAD Special Coordinator for Least Developed Countries, Landlocked and Small Island Developing Countries 1998–2000; Exec. Dir UN Centre for Human Settlements (UN-HABITAT) 2000–, Under-Sec.-Gen. 2002–, Dir-Gen. UN Office, Nairobi (UNON) 2006–; mem. Tanzanian Govt del. to several UN Summits, including World Summit for Social Devt, Copenhagen 1995, Fourth World Conf. on Women, Beijing 1995, UN Conf. on Human Settlements, Istanbul 1996, World Food Summit, Rome 1996 (elected Coordinator for Eastern Africa in Network for Food Security, Trade and Sustainable Devt—COASAD); mem. Bd Int. Scientific Advisory Bd, UNESCO 1997–; Exec. Sec. for Third UN Conf. on Least Developed Countries, Brussels, Belgium 2001; mem. Comm. for Africa 2004–05; apptd UN Special Envoy to study impact of Zimbabwean Govt's campaign (known as Operation Murambatsvina) to evict informal traders and people deemed to be squatting illegally in certain areas 2005. *Address:* UN-HABITAT, PO Box 30030, GPO, Nairobi 00100, Kenya (office). *Telephone:* (20) 7621234 (office). *Fax:* (20) 7624266 (office). *E-mail:* infohabitat@unhabitat.org (office). *Website:* www.unhabitat.org (office).

TIBERI, Jean, LenD; French politician; *Deputy, National Assembly;* b. 30 Jan. 1935, Paris; s. of Charles Tiberi and Hélène Pallavicini; m. Xavière Casanova; one s. one d.; ed Coll. Sainte-Barbe, Lycées Montaigne and Louis-le-Grand and Faculté de Droit, Paris; Acting Judge, Colmar 1958; Deputy Public Prosecutor, Metz 1959, Meaux 1959; Judge, Beauvais 1959, Nantes 1960; Chancellery 1960–63; Dir of Studies, Faculté de Droit, Paris 1961–; Conseiller de Paris 1965–; First Vice-Pres. Conseil de Paris 1983–95; Deputy to Mayor of Paris 1977–83, First Deputy 1983–95; Deputy to Nat. Ass. 1968–; fmr Sec. of State at Ministries of Agric., Industry and Research; Mayor of 5th arrondissement of Paris 1983–95; Sec. Paris RPR 1985–2000; Mayor of Paris 1995–2000; Deputy of Paris 2002–; Mayor of 5th arrondissement of Paris 2000–. *Publications:* Le quartier latin, Paris capitale des siècles 1988, La nouvelle Athènes, Paris capitale de l'esprit 1992. *Address:* Assemblée Nationale, 126 rue de l'Université, 75007 Paris (office); 1 place du Panthéon, 75005 Paris, France (home). *Telephone:* 1-40-63-62-84 (office). *Fax:* 1-40-63-62-96 (office). *E-mail:* jtiberi@assemblee-nationale.fr (office). *Website:* www.assemblee-nationale.fr/12/tribun/fiches_id/2816.asp (office).

TICKELL, Sir Crispin (Charles Cervantes), GCMG, KCVO; British university chancellor and fmr diplomatist; *Director, Policy Foresight Programme, The James Martin 21st Century School, University of Oxford;* b. 25 Aug. 1930, London; s. of the late Jerrard Tickell and Renée Haynes; m. 1st Chloë Gunn 1954 (divorced 1976); two s. one d.; m. 2nd Penelope Thorne-Thorne 1977; ed Westminster School and Christ Church, Oxford; entered HM Diplomatic Service 1954; served at The Hague 1955–58, Mexico 1958–61, Paris 1964–70; Pvt. Sec. to Chancellor of Duchy of Lancaster 1970–72; Head, Western Orgs Dept FCO 1972–75; Fellow, Center for Int. Affairs Harvard Univ. 1975–76; Chef de Cabinet to Pres. of Comm. of EC 1977–81; Visiting Fellow, All Souls Coll. Oxford 1981; Amb. to Mexico 1981–83; Deputy Under-Sec. of State FCO 1983–84; Perm. Sec. Overseas Devt Admin. 1984–87; Perm. Rep. to UN 1987–90; Warden Green Coll. Oxford 1990–97; Dir Green Coll. Centre for Environmental Policy and Understanding 1992–; Chancellor Univ. of Kent 1996–; Chair. Trustees, St Andrew's Prize for the Environment 1998–; Dir Policy Foresight Programme, The James Martin 21st Century School, Univ. of Oxford 2006–; Adviser at Large to Pres. of Arizona State Univ. 2004–; Dir (non-exec.) IBM UK 1990–95 (mem. IBM Advisory Bd 1995–2000), Govett Mexican Horizons Investment 1991–96, Govett American Smaller Companies Trust 1996–98, Govett Enhanced Income Investment Trust 1999–; mem. Friends Provident Stewardship Cttee of Reference 1999–; Dir BOC Foundation 1990–2003; Pres. Royal Geographical Soc. 1990–93 (Vice-Pres. 1993–2002, Hon. Vice-Pres. 2002), Marine Biological Asscn 1990–2001 (Vice-Pres. 2001–), Earth Centre 1996–2000, Nat. Soc. for Clean Air 1997–99, South East England Climate Change Partnership 2005–; Chair. Int. Inst. for Environment and Devt 1990–94, Earthwatch Europe 1990–97, Climate Inst. of Washington, DC 1990–2002 (Chair. Emer. 2002–), Advisory Cttee on Darwin Initiative for the Survivial of Species 1992–99, Gaia Soc. 1998–2001, Advisory Cttee on the Environment of Int. Council for Science 1999–2004, Gaia Special Interest Group of Geological Soc. of London 2000–; Convenor Govt Panel on Sustainable Devt 1994–2000; mem. Govt Task Force on Urban Regeneration 1998–99, on Potential Risks from Near Earth Objects 2000; Trustee, Nat. History Museum 1992–2001, World Wildlife Fund (UK) 1993–99, Royal Botanic Garden, Edinburgh 1997–2001, Reuters Foundation 2000–, TERI Europe 2003–; Sr Inaugural Visiting Fellow, Harvard Univ. Center for the Environment 2002–03; Hon. Fellow, Anglo American School, New York 1990, Westminster School 1993, St Edmund's Coll., Cambridge 1995, Green Coll., Oxford 1997; Hon. Fellow, Royal Scottish Geographical Soc. 1992, Chartered Inst. of Water and Environmental Man. 1996, Royal Inst. of GB 2002; Hon. FRIBA 2000; Hon. Sr mem. Darwin Coll., Cambridge 1997; Officer, Order of Orange-Nassau (Netherlands) 1958, Chevalier, Nat. Order of Mali 1979, Orden Academica del Derecho, de la Cultura, y de la Paz 1989, Order of Aztec Eagle with Sash (Mexico) 1994; Dr hc (Academia Mexicana de Derecho Internacional) 1983, (Univ. of Stirling) 1990, (Sheffield Hallam Univ.) 1996, (Univ. of East London) 1998; Hon. LLD (Univ. of Massachusetts, USA) 1990, (Univ. of Birmingham) 1991, (Univ. of Bristol) 1991; Hon. DSc (Univ. of East Anglia) 1990, (Univ. of Sussex) 1991, (Cranfield Univ.) 1992, (Loughborough Univ. of Tech.) 1995, (Univ. of Exeter) 1999, (Univ. of Hull) 2001, (Univ. of Plymouth) 2001, (Univ. of St Andrews) 2002, (Univ. of Southampton) 2002, (Oxford Brookes Univ.) 2002, (Université du Littoral Cote d'Opale) 2002; Hon. DLitt (Polytechnic of Cen. London (now Univ. of Westminster)) 1990; Hon. DCL (Univ. of Kent at Canterbury) 1996; Hon. DHumLitt (American Univ. of Paris) 2003; Hon. DJur (Univ. of Nottingham) 2003; Hon. Dr of The Open Univ. 2006; Hon. DrScs (Univ. of Brighton) 2006; mem. The Global 500: Roll of Honour for Environmental Achievement of UNEP 1991, Global Environmental Leadership Award, Climate Inst. of Washington, DC 1996, Distinguished Lecturer, British Geological Survey 1994, Centennial Lecturer, Arizona State Univ. 1995, Melchett Medallist, Inst. of Energy 1996, Kelvin Medallist, Royal Philosophical Soc. of Glasgow 1996, first Happold Medallist, Nat. Construction Industry Council 1998, Patron's Medal, Royal Geographical Soc. 2000, Distinguished Environmental Lecturer, Harvard Univ. 2001, Award for Int. Cooperation on Environment and Devt, China Council for Int. Cooperation on Environment and Devt 1996, Award for Int. Cooperation on Environmental Protection, Chinese State Environmental Protection Agency (SEPA) 2003, CAB Int. Bioscience Fellow 2004, Friendship Award, Govt of People's Repub. of China 2004, Minor Planet named No. 5971 Tickell 2006. *Publications:* Climatic Change and World Affairs 1977, Mary Anning of Lyme Regis 1996; contribs to many books and papers. *Leisure interests:* climatology, palaeohistory, art (especially pre-Colombiana, mountains). *Address:* Ablington Old Barn, Ablington, Cirencester, Glos., GL7 5NU (home); Policy Foresight Programme, The James Martin 21st Century School, University of Oxford, Old Indian Institute, 34 Broad Street, Oxford, OX1 3BD, England (office). *Telephone:* (1285) 740569 (home); (1865) 287430 (office). *Fax:* (1285) 740671 (home); (1865) 287435 (office). *E-mail:* ct@crispintickell.net (office); info@21school.ox.ac.uk (office). *Website:* www.crispintickell.com (office).

TICKNER, Robert, LLM, BEcons; Australian organization official and fmr politician; *CEO, Australian Red Cross;* b. 24 Dec. 1951, Sydney; m. Jody Tickner; one c.; ed Univ. of Sydney; Lecturer, Faculty of Business Studies, NSW Inst. of Tech. 1974–78, Faculty of Law 1978–79; Prin. Solicitor, Aboriginal Legal Service, Redfern, Sydney 1979–83; Alderman Sydney City Council 1977–84; MP for Hughes, NSW 1984–96; Minister for Aboriginal and Torres Strait Islander Affairs 1990–96; CEO Job Futures Ltd 2000–; CEO Australian Red Cross 2005–; Office holder Fed. Electorate Council and other Australian Labor Party bodies; Pres. NSW Soc. of Labor Lawyers; Cttee mem. NSW Council for Civil Liberties; Founding Cttee mem. Citizens for Democracy; Convenor Labor Parliamentarians for Nuclear Free Australia; fmr Chair. Parl. Group of Amnesty Int. *Leisure interests:* golf, tennis. *Address:* Australian Red Cross National Office, PO Box 196, Carlton, Vic. 3053, Australia (office). *Telephone:* (3) 9345-1800 (office). *Fax:* (3) 9348-2513 (office). *E-mail:* redcross@nat.redcross.org.au (office). *Website:* www.redcross.org.au (office).

TIDIANE SOUARÉ, Ahmed; Guinean politician; *Prime Minister;* b. 1951; mem. Cttee for Implementation of Econ., Financial and Admin. Reforms of Presidency 1989–90, Coordinator, Office for Monitoring and Evaluation of Presidency 1990–94; Head of Cabinet, Ministry of Econ. and Financial Control 1994–96, Ministry Del. to the Prime Minister in charge of the budget 1996–97, Ministry of Economy and Finance 1997–2002; Insp. Gen. of Finances 2002–05; Minister of Mines and Geology 2005–06, also Chair. Bd of Dirs Compagnie des Bauxites de Guinée; Minister of State for Higher Educ. and Scientific Research 2006–07; Prime Minister of Guinea 2008–. *Address:* Office of the Prime Minister, BP 5141, Conakry, Guinea (office). *Telephone:* 30-41-51-19. *Fax:* 30-41-52-82 (office).

TIE, Ning; Chinese writer; *Chairman, Chinese Writers Association;* b. 1957, Beijing; d. of Tie Yang and Xu Zhi-ying; Council mem. of Chinese Writers' Asscn 1985–, Vice-Chair. 2001–06, Chair. (first woman) 2006–; Alt. mem. 16th CCP Cen. Cttee 2002–07. *Publications:* Path in the Night 1980, Xiangxue (Nat. Short Story Prize) 1982, Red Shirt With No Buttons (Nat. Fiction Prize) 1984, Rose Gate 1988, Cotton Stack 1988, Hay Stack (short stories) 1991, Women's White Night (non-fiction) 1991, Straw Ring (non-fiction) 1992, For Ever and Ever 1999, The Great Bather 2000. *Leisure interests:* music, gourmet cooking. *Address:* 40-2-201 Luo Si-zhuang, Baoding City, Hebei Province, People's Republic of China. *Telephone:* (312) 34341. *Website:* www.chinawriter.com.cn.

TIEFENSEE, Wolfgang; German politician; *Federal Minister of Transport, Building and Urban Affairs;* b. 1955, Gera; skilled telecommunications worker 1974; mil. service 1975, as a conscientious objector served in a construction unit; graduated as an industrial electronics engineer 1979; Research and Devt Engineer, VEB Communications Works, Leipzig 1979–86; studied part-time for a postgraduate degree in computer science in the construction industry 1982; Devt Engineer, Technische Hochschule Leipzig 1986–90; studied part-time for a degree in electrical eng 1988; engaged in politics with Leipzig Round Table, Deputy Mayor without portfolio and mem. City Council 1989–90, Head of School Admin Office 1990, Deputy Mayor for Schools and Educ. 1992–94, Deputy Mayor for Youth, Schools and Sport and Vice-Mayor 1994, Mayor of Leipzig 1998–2005; mem. SPD 1995–; Fed. Minister of Transport, Building and Urban Affairs and Fed. Govt Commr for the New Fed. States 2005–; Vice-Pres. Saxon Asscn of Cities and Towns 2001–; Pres. Eurocities 2002–04; mem. Exec. Cttee German Asscn of Cities. *Address:* Federal Ministry of Transport, Building and Urban Affairs, Invalidenstr. 44, 10115 Berlin, Germany (office). *Telephone:* (30) 182008-0 (office). *Fax:* (30) 182008-1920 (office). *E-mail:* buergerinfo@bmvbs.bund.de (office). *Website:* www.bmvbs.de (office); www.wolfgang-tiefensee.de.

TIEMANN, Susanne, DJur; German lawyer, politician and academic; b. 20 April 1947, Schwandorf; d. of Hermann Bamberg and Anna-Maria Bamberg; m. Burkhard Tiemann 1969; one s. two d.; ed Ludwig-Maximilian Univ. Munich; called to the Bar, Munich 1975; served as lawyer in Cologne 1980;

currently Prof. for Social and Admin. Law, Univ. of Bonn, Catholic Univ. of Cologne; mem. Bundestag (CDU/CSU) 1994–; mem. Econ. and Social Cttee of EC 1987–, Chair. 1992–94; Hon. Prof. Katholische Fachhochschule Nordrhein-Westfalen 1998–; mem. Bd German Fed. of Liberal Professions 1988–; mem. Exec. Bd and Vice-Pres. European Secr. of the Liberal, Intellectual and Social Professions (SEPLIS) 1988, Pres. 1989–95; Chair. German Taxpayers' Asscn 1992–94; Frauen für Europa Prize 1993. *Address:* Stefan-Lochner-Straße 11, 50999 Cologne, Germany. *Telephone:* (221) 2807871 (office). *Fax:* (221) 2807872 (office).

TIEN, Chang-Lin, PhD; Chinese/American academic; *NEC Distinguished Professor of Engineering, University of California, Berkeley;* b. 24 July 1935, Wuhan, China; s. of Yun Chien and Yun Di (Lee) Tien; m. Di-Hwa Liu 1959; one s. two d.; ed Nat. Univ. of Taiwan, Univ. of Louisville, USA, Univ. of Princeton, USA; acting Asst Prof. Dept of Mechanical Eng Univ. of Calif., Berkeley 1959–60, Asst Prof. 1960–64, Assoc. Prof. 1964–88, Prof. 1968–88, 1990–, A. Martin Berlin Prof. 1987–88, 1990–97, NEC Distinguished Prof. of Eng 1997–, Univ. Prof. 1999–, Dept Chair. 1974–81, Vice-Chancellor for Research 1983–85, Chancellor 1990–97; Exec. Vice-Chancellor Univ. of Calif. at Irvine 1988–90; Chair. Int. Advisory Panel, Univ. of Tokyo Inst. of Ind. Science 1995; Gov. Bd of Dirs, Cttee of 100 1991–; mem. Bd of Dirs Wells Fargo Bank 1991–, AAAS 1992–96, Berkeley Community Foundation 1993–97, Raychem Corpn 1996–; mem. Bd of Trustees, Chiang Industrial Charity Foundation Ltd, Hong Kong 1991–, Princeton Univ. 1991–95, Asia Foundation 1993– (Chair. 1998–), Carnegie Foundation for the Advancement of Teaching 1994–97, US Cttee on Econ. Devt 1994–, Council on Foreign Relations 1996; mem. Aspen Inst. Domestic Strategy Group 1992–97; mem. Nat. Advisory Council, American Soc. for Eng Educ. 1993, Int. Advisory Panel, Nat. Univ. of Singapore 1993; Ed. Int. Journal of Heat and Mass Transfer 1981–, Int. Communications in Heat and Mass Transfer 1981–; Ed.-in-Chief Experimental Heat Transfer 1987–, Microscale Thermophysical Eng 1997–; consultant for numerous industrial, governmental and educational orgs; Guggenheim Fellow 1965; Fellow Academia Sinica (Taiwan) 1988, AAAS 1989, American Acad. of Arts and Sciences 1991; Hon. Prof. at 12 leading univs in China since 1981; Hon. mem. or Fellow of numerous socs including mem. Nat. Acad. of Eng 1976; 12 hon. doctor's degrees; Heat Transfer Memorial Award 1974, Gustus L. Larson Memorial Award 1975, Thermophysics Award 1977, Max Jakob Memorial Award 1981; asteroid Tien Chang-Lin Star named in his hon. by Int. Astronomy Union 1999; mega oil tanker named in his hon. 2000. *Publications:* Statistical Thermodynamics (co-author) 1971; ed. of 16 titles, author of 312 research papers. *Address:* Department of Mechanical Engineering, University of California, 6101 Etcheverry Hall # 1740, Berkeley, CA 94720, USA. *Telephone:* (510) 643-3886 (office). *Fax:* (510) 643-3887 (office). *E-mail:* nancie@newton.berkeley.edu (office). *Website:* www.me.berkeley.edu/faculty/tien/index.html (office).

TIEN, Hung-Mao, MA, PhD; Taiwanese academic and diplomatist; *Representative to UK;* b. 7 Nov. 1938, Tainan; m. Amy Tien; one s. one d.; ed Tunghai Univ. and Univ. of Wisconsin, USA; fmr Prof. of Political Science, Univ. of Wisconsin; Pres. Inst. for Nat. Policy Research 1991–; mem. Nat. Unification Research Council, Office of Pres. of Taiwan 1994–; Nat. Policy Adviser to Pres. of Taiwan 1996–; Dir Foundation for Int. Co-operation and Devt 1996–, Minister of Foreign Affairs 2000–02; Rep. to UK 2002–. *Publications include:* Government and Politics in Kuomintang China 1927–37, The Great Transition, Social and Political Change in the Republic of China, Taiwan's Electoral Politics and Democratic Transition: Riding the Third Wave 1995. *Leisure interests:* golf, tennis, table-tennis. *Address:* Taipei Representative Office in the UK, 50 Grosvenor Gardens, London, SW1W 0EB, England (office); #225, Tung-shih Street, Hsi-chih, Taipei County, Taiwan (home). *Telephone:* (20) 7881-2650 (office); (2) 660-0145 (home). *Website:* www.taiwanembassy.org/uk (office).

TIEN, Ping-King, MS, PhD; Chinese research engineer; b. 2 Aug. 1919, Checkang Prov.; s. of N. S. Tien and C. S. (Yun) Tien; m. Nancy Chen 1952; two d.; ed Nat. Cen. Univ., China and Stanford Univ., USA; Vice-Pres. Tien-Sun Industrial Co. 1942–47; Research Assoc., Stanford Univ. 1948–52; mem. Tech. Staff, AT&T Bell Labs (now Bell Labs) 1952–61, Head, Electronics Physics Research 1961–80, Head, Microelectronics Research 1980–84, Ed.-in-Chief High Speed Electronics and Systems; Fellow, Bell Labs 1984 (Fellow Emer. 1990–), IEEE, Optical Soc. of America; mem. Nat. Acad. of Eng, NAS, Third World Acad. of Sciences, NAS (Taiwan); Chinese Inst. of Eng Achievement Award 1966, Morris N. Liebmann Award, IEEE 1979. *Publications:* numerous technical publs. *Address:* c/o Bell Laboratories, Lucent Technologies, Room 4B-433, 101 Crawfords Corner Road, Holmdel, NJ 07733 (office); 9 Carolyn Court, Holmdel, NJ 07733, USA (home). *Telephone:* (201) 949-6925 (office). *E-mail:* pkt@bell-labs.com (office).

TIETMEYER, Hans, Dr rer. pol; German banker, economist and civil servant; *Senior Adviser, Lazard Asset Management (Deutschland) GmbH;* b. 18 Aug. 1931, Metelen; s. of Bernhard Tietmeyer and Helene Tietmeyer; m. 1st Marie-Luise Tietmeyer (died 1978); m. 2nd Maria-Therese Tietmeyer 1980; one s. one d.; ed Univs of Münster, Bonn and Cologne; Sec. Bischöfliche Studienforderung Cusanuswerk 1959–62; Fed. Ministry of Econs 1962–82, Head of Div. of Gen. Econ. Policy 1973–82; mem. Econ. Policy Cttee of EC and OECD 1972–82; Sec. of State, Ministry of Finance 1982–89; mem. Bd of Dirs, Bundesbank 1990, Vice-Pres. 1991–93, Pres. 1993–99; Hon. Prof. of Public Econ. of Halle-Wittenberg 1996–; Monetary Policy Adviser to IMF 2002; Sr Adviser, Lazard Asset Man., Frankfurt 2003–; Grosses Bundesverdienstkreuz; Dr hc (Münster) 1994, (Maryland) 1997. *Publications:* The Social Market Economy and Monetary Stability 1999; more than 100 articles on economics. *Leisure interests:* sport, rambling. *Address:* Lazard Asset Management (Deutschland) GmbH, Alte Mainzer Gasse 37, 60311 Frankfurt, Germany (office). *Telephone:* (69) 506060 (office). *Fax:* (69) 50606100 (office). *Website:* www.lazardnet.com (office).

TIGERMAN, Stanley, MArch, FAIA; American architect; *Partner, Tigerman McCurry Architects;* b. 20 Sept. 1930, Chicago, Ill.; s. of Samuel B. Tigerman and Emma L. Stern; m. Margaret I. McCurry 1979; one s. one d.; ed Yale Univ.; architectural draughtsman, George Fred Keck, Chicago 1949–50; Skidmore Owings & Merrill, Chicago 1957–59; Paul Rudolph, New Haven 1959–61; Harry Weese 1961–62; Pnr Tigerman & Koglin, Chicago 1962–64; Prin. Stanley Tigerman & Assoc. Chicago 1964–82; Pnr Tigerman Fugman McCurry, Chicago 1982–88, Tigerman McCurry Architects, Chicago 1988–; Co-Founder Archeworks Design Lab. Chicago 1993; Prof. of Architecture Univ. of Ill., Chicago 1967–71, 1980–93, Dir School of Architecture 1985–93; Davenport Prof. of Architecture, Yale Univ. 1979, 1993, Bishop Prof. 1984; Architect-in-Residence, American Acad. Rome 1980; Visiting Prof. Univ. of Cincinnati 1980, Univ. of Houston 1981, Tulane 1981, Univ. of Nebraska 1981, Univ. of North Carolina, Charlotte 1982, Harvard 1982, Iowa State 1985 Univ., Univ. of Rotterdam 1985; Visiting Scholar, American Acad. in Rome 1985; mem. Advisory Cttee Princeton Univ. 1997; 55 nat.,and local AIA awards, 96 various other awards, AIA Illinois Gold Medal in recognition of outstanding lifetime service 2008, AIA/ACSA Topaz Medallion for Excellence in Architectural Educ. 2008. *Publications:* Chicago's Architectural Heritage: A Romantic Classical Image... & Work of the Current Generation of Chicago Architects 1979, VERSUS: An American Architect's Alternatives 1982, Stanley Tigerman Architoons 1988, The Architecture of Exile 1988, Stanley Tigerman, Buildings & Projects 1966–89 1989. *Leisure interests:* drawing, reading. *Address:* Tigerman McCurry Ltd, 444 North Wells Street, Suite 206, Chicago, IL 60654, USA (office). *Telephone:* (312) 644-5880 (office). *Fax:* (312) 644-3750 (office). *E-mail:* tma@tigerman-mccurry.com (office). *Website:* www.tigerman-mccurry.com (office).

TIGYI, József; Hungarian biophysicist; b. 19 March 1926, Kaposvár; s. of András Tigyi and Julianna Mátrai; m. Anna Sebes; two s.; ed Medical Univ. of Pécs; Prof. and Dir of Biophysical Inst. Medical Univ. Pécs 1971–91, Vice-Rector 1967–73, Rector 1973–79; corresp. mem. Hungarian Acad. of Sciences 1967–76, mem. 1976–, Vice-Pres. 1988, Pres. Regional Cttee, Pécs 1996–; Pres. Acad. Section No. 8 (Biological Sciences) 1980–88; Pres. Hungarian Biophysical Soc. 1972–91, Hon. Pres. 1991–; Pres. UNESCO European Collaboration in Biophysics 1976–86; Chief Ed. Acta Biochimica et Biophysica 1981–91; mem. Royal Soc. of Medicine, New York Acad. of Sciences 1980–, European Acad. of Arts, Sciences and Humanities, Paris 1990–, WHO Exec. Bd 1972–75, Int. Council of Scientific Unions (ICSU) Gen. Cttee, Cttee on the Teaching of Science 1986–93, Gesellschaft für mathematische u. physikalische Biologie (GDR), Biophysical Soc. of Romania, of India; Gen. Sec. Int. Union of Pure and Applied Biophysics (IUPAB) 1984–93, Co-Chair. Special Cttee on Radiation and Environmental Biophysics 1993–; Labour Order of Merit (Silver) 1966, (Gold) 1970, 1979. *Publications:* Application of Radioactive Isotope in Experimental Medicine 1965, Biophysics: Theory of Bioelectric Phenomena, Biological Semi-conductors, Energetics of Cross-Striated Muscle 1977, Physical Aspects of the Living Cell 1991. *Address:* Biophysical Institute of the Medical University, Szigeti ut 12, 7643 Pécs, Hungary (office). *Telephone:* (72) 536-264 (office). *Fax:* (72) 536-261 (office). *E-mail:* jozsef.tigyi@aok.pte.hu (office). *Website:* www.aok.pte.hu (office).

TIHIĆ, Sulejman; Bosnia and Herzegovina politician; *Chairman, Party of Democratic Action (PDA) (Stranka Demokratske Akcije) (SDA);* b. 26 Nov. 1951, Bosanski Šamac; m.; two s. one d.; ed Univ. of Sarajevo; judge and public prosecutor, Bosanski Samac 1975–83, lawyer 1983–92; imprisoned for three months by Bosnian Serb forces in Bosanski Samac and other towns during Bosnian War of 1992–95; Head Consular Dept, Embassy of Bosnia and Herzegovina, Berlin, Germany 1994–96; Adviser to Minister of Foreign Affairs on Consular Affairs 1996–99; mem. Parl. Republika Srpska 1996–2002, Deputy Speaker 2000–02, nominated by UN High Rep. in Bosnia and Herzegovina as mem. of Parl. Cttee on Constitutional Issues 2001; Founding mem. Party of Democratic Action, Chair. 2001–; mem. of the Presidency (tripartite) 2002–06, Chair. Presidency March–Oct. 2004, Feb.–Oct. 2006. *Address:* Party of Democratic Action (PDA) (Stranka Demokratske Akcije) (SDA), 71000 Sarajevo, Mehmeda Spahe 14, Bosnia and Herzegovina (office). *Telephone:* (33) 472192 (office). *Fax:* (33) 650429 (office). *E-mail:* centrala@sda.ba (office). *Website:* www.sda.ba (office).

TIHIPKO, Serhiy Leonidovych; Ukrainian banker and politician; b. 13 Feb. 1960; m.; one d.; ed Dnipropetrovsk Metallurgical Inst.; Head Dept of Agitation and Propaganda, Young Communist League during late 1980s; Chair. Bd Privatbank 1992–97; Deputy Prime Minister responsible for Privatization and Econ. Devt 1997–99, apptd Minister of Economy 1999; elected to Verkhovna Rada (Parl.) June 2000; elected Leader Working Ukraine party Nov. 2000; Gov. Nat. Bank of Ukraine 2002–05 (resgnd); campaign man. for Viktor Yanukovich during 2004 presidential election. *Address:* c/o Working Ukraine (Trudova Ukraina), vul. Shovkovychna 4, 01021, Kyiv, Ukraine (office). *Telephone:* (44) 229-89-03 (office). *E-mail:* inform@tu.privat-online.net (office). *Website:* www.trud.org.ua (office).

TIINGA, Beniamina; I-Kiribati politician; Vice-Pres. of Kiribati 2000–03; also Minister of Finance and Econ. Planning. *Address:* c/o Ministry of Finance and Economic Planning, PO Box 67, Bairiki, Tarawa, Kiribati (office).

TIJDEMAN, Robert; Dutch mathematician and academic; *Professor of Mathematics, University of Leiden;* b. 30 July 1943, Oostzaan; ed Univ. of Amsterdam; scientific worker, Univ. of Amsterdam 1967–70; Reader, Univ. of Leiden 1970–75, Prof. of Math. 1975–; mem. Royal Netherlands Acad. of Sciences 1987; Dr hc (Debrecen, Hungary) 1999. *Publication:* Exponential diophantine equations (with T. N. Shorey) 1986. *Address:* Mathematical

Institute, University of Leiden, POB 9512, 2300 RA Leiden, Netherlands. *Telephone:* (71) 5277138. *Fax:* (71) 527 7101. *E-mail:* tijdeman@math .leidenuniv.nl (office). *Website:* www.math.leidenuniv.nl/~tijdeman (office).

TIKHVINSKY, Sergej Leonidovich; Russian historian and academic; *President, National Committee of Russian Historians;* b. 1 Sept. 1918, Petrograd; s. of Leonid Tikhvinsky and Kira Tikhvinsky; m. Vera Nikitichna Tikhvinskaya 1940; one s. one d.; ed Oriental Inst., Moscow; mem. CPSU 1941–91; diplomatic service in China, UK and Japan 1939–57; Head of Asian Dept of USSR State Cttee with Council of Ministers for Foreign Cultural Relations 1957–60; Prof., Moscow Univ. 1959; Dir USSR Acad. of Sciences Inst. of Sinology 1960–61; Deputy Dir of Acad. of Sciences Inst. of the Peoples of Asia 1961–63; Deputy Dir of Acad. of Sciences Inst. of World Socialist Economies 1963–65; Corresp. mem. of Acad. of Sciences 1968–81, mem. 1981–; Chief of History of Diplomacy Dept, Head of Asia Section in Foreign Policy Planning Dept USSR Ministry of Foreign Affairs 1965–80; Rector of Diplomatic Acad. of USSR Ministry of Foreign Affairs 1980–86; Academician-Sec. of Historical Section of USSR Acad. of Sciences 1982–88; Pres. Nat. Cttee of Soviet (now Russian) Historians 1980–; Chair. Scientific Council for The History of Russia's Foreign Policy and Int. Relations 1987–; Adviser to the Presidium of Acad. of Sciences 1988–; Hon. Chair. All-Russia Asscn of Sinologues 1988; Hon. mem. Accad. Fiorentina delle Arti 1984. *Publications include:* The Reform Movement in China and K'ang Youwei 1959, Sun Yatsen Foreign Affairs Theories and Practice 1964, Manchu Rule in China 1966, History of China and Present Time 1976, The Reform Movements in China at the end of the 19th Century 1980, China and her Neighbours 1980, China and World History 1988, China: History through Personalities and Events 1991, China in My Life 1992, China's Road to Unity and Independence 1996, Eternal Sleep in China's Earth: Memorial Album 1996, Russia–Japan, Doomed to Good Neighbourhood 1996, My Return to Tiananmen Square 2002, The Age of Rapid Changes 2005, Selected Works (five vols) 2006; numerous articles on Soviet and Russian foreign policy and int. affairs. *Leisure interest:* angling. *Address:* National Committee of Historians, Leninsky prosp. 32A, 117334 Moscow, Russia. *Telephone:* (495) 938-00-87 (office); (495) 124-07-24 (office); (495) 915-45-20 (home).

TILEY, John, CBE, LLD, MA, BCL; British lawyer and academic; *Professor of Law of Taxation, University of Cambridge;* b. 25 Feb. 1941, Leamington Spa; s. of the late William Tiley and Audrey Tiley; m. Jillinda Draper 1964; two s. one d.; ed Winchester Coll. and Lincoln Coll. Oxford; called to the Bar, Inner Temple 1964, Hon. Bencher 1993; Recorder 1989–97; Lecturer, Lincoln Coll. Oxford 1963–64, Univ. of Birmingham 1964–67; Fellow, Queens' Coll. Cambridge 1967–; Asst Lecturer, Univ. of Cambridge 1967–72, Lecturer 1972–87, Reader 1987–90, Prof. of Law of Taxation 1990–, Chair. Faculty Bd of Law 1992–95, currently Dir Centre for Tax Law; Pres. Soc. of Public Teachers of Law 1995–96; Visiting Prof., Dalhousie Univ., Canada 1972–73, Univ. of Auckland 1973, Univ. of Western Ontario 1978–79, Univ. of Melbourne 1979, Case Western Reserve Univ. 1985–86, 1996, 2002. *Publications:* Revenue Law 1976, fifth edn 2005; ed. of various works on taxation and contribs to legal journals. *Leisure interests:* walking, visits to art galleries, listening to music. *Address:* Queens' College, Cambridge, CB3 9ET, England (office). *Telephone:* (1223) 335511 (office). *Website:* www.queens.cam.ac.uk (office).

TILGHMAN, Shirley Marie, BSc, PhD; Canadian university president, biologist and academic; *President, Princeton University;* b. 17 Sept. 1946; one s. one d.; ed Queen's Univ., Kingston, Ont., Canada, Temple Univ., Philadelphia, USA; secondary school teacher, Sierra Leone 1968–70; Fogarty Int. Fellow, NIH 1975–77; Asst Prof., Fels Research Inst., Temple Univ. School of Medicine 1978–79; mem., Inst. for Cancer Research 1979–86; Adjunct Assoc. Prof. of Human Genetics and Biochemistry and Biophysics, Univ. of PA 1980–86; Howard A. Prior Prof. of the Life Sciences, Princeton Univ. 1986–; investigator, Howard Hughes Medical Inst. 1988–; Adjunct Prof., Dept of Biochemistry, Univ. of Medicine and Dentistry of NJ (UMDNJ) – Robert Wood Johnson Medical School 1988–; Chair., Council on Science and Tech., Princeton Univ. 1993–2000; Dir, Lewis-Sigler Inst. for Integrative Genomics, Princeton Univ. 1998–, Pres., Princeton Univ. 2001–; foreign assoc., US Nat. Acad. of Sciences; mem. American Acad. of Arts and Sciences; mem. Nat. Advisory Council, Nat. Center for Human Genome Research 1991–96; mem. Editorial Bd, Genes and Development (journal); mem. Bd of Dirs, Rockefeller Univ., NIH, Jackson Laboratory, Whitehead Inst. for Biomedical Sciences of MIT, Google Inc. 2005–; Princeton Pres.'s Award for Distinguished Teaching 1996, L'Oréal-UNESCO Women in Science Award 2002, Lifetime Achievement Award, Soc. of Developmental Biology 2003. *Address:* Office of the President, One Nassau Hall, Princeton University, Princeton, NJ 08544, USA (office). *Telephone:* (609) 258-6101 (office). *Website:* www.princeton.edu (office).

TILL, James Edgar, OC, MA, PhD, FRS, FRSC; Canadian biophysicist; *Senior Scientist Emeritus and University Professor Emeritus, Prevention/Statistics, Ontario Cancer Institute;* b. Lloydminster, Sask.; ed Univ. of Sask. and Yale Univ.; post-doctoral fellowship, Connaught Medical Research Labs; mem. Faculty, Dept of Medical Biophysics, Univ. of Toronto 1958, Univ. Prof. 1984–97, Assoc. Dean (Life Sciences) School of Grad. Studies for three years, Sr Scientist Ontario Cancer Inst. 1957–96, Sr Scientist Emer., Prevention/ Statistics 1996–, Univ. Prof. Emer. 1997–; mem. Nat. Bd Canadian Breast Cancer Foundation, Bd of Ethics Cttee, Stem Cell Network, Editorial Bd Journal of Medical Internet Research, Editorial Bd BMC Medical Informatics and Decision Making, Coll. of Reviewers, Canada Research Chairs Program; Pres. (Volunteer) Nat. Cancer Inst. of Canada 1998–2000, Past Pres. (Volunteer) 2000–01; Chair. Man. Cttee Cancer Information Service, Canadian Cancer Soc. 1998–99, Knowledge Man. Cttee Stem Cell Network

2001–04; Vice-Chair. Institutional Advisory Bd Inst. of Cancer Research, Canadian Insts of Health Research 2001–04; mem. Research Advisory Cttee Canadian Breast Cancer Research Alliance 2001–05, Clinical Trials Network Advisory Cttee, Ontario Cancer Research Network 2002–03, Research Action Group, Canadian Strategy for Cancer Control 2002–05, Jt Preventive Oncology and Research Bd Cttee, Cancer Care Ontario 2002–05; Hon. DSc (Toronto) 2004; co-recipient Gairdner Foundation Int. Award 1969, co-recipient RSC Thomas W. Eadie Medal 1991, Robert L. Noble Prize, Nat. Cancer Inst. of Canada 1993, Ernest McCulloch & James Till Award est. by American Soc. for Blood and Marrow Transplantation for the best scientific paper by a new investigator published in its journal 1999, R. M. Taylor Medal, Canadian Cancer Soc./Nat. Cancer Inst. of Canada 2001, inducted into The Canadian Medical Hall of Fame 2004, co-recipient Albert Lasker Basic Medical Research Award, Albert and Mary Lasker Foundation 2005, co-recipient Biomedical Science Ambassador Award, Partners in Research 2005, co-recipient Centenary Medal, Royal Soc. of Canada 2005. *Publications:* numerous articles in scientific journals. *Address:* Princess Margaret Hospital, 9th Floor Room 416, 610 University Avenue, Toronto, ON M5G 2M9, Canada (office). *Telephone:* (416) 946-2948 (office). *Fax:* (416) 946-2024 (office). *E-mail:* till@uhnres.utoronto.ca (office). *Website:* medbio.utoronto.ca/faculty/till.html (office); myprofile.cos.com/tillj16 (office).

TILL, Jeremy, MA, Dip Arch, RIBA; British architect and academic; *Dean, School of Architecture and the Built Environment, University of Westminster;* b. 5 April 1947, Cambridge; s. of Barry Till and Shirley Philipson; ed Univ. of Cambridge, Polytechnic of Cen. London, Middlesex Univ.; Pnr, Peter Currie Architects 1985–92; Dir Sarah Wigglesworth Architects 1992–; Sr Lecturer, Kingston Univ. 1986–92; Sr Lecturer and Sub-Dean of Faculty, The Bartlett School of Architecture, Univ. Coll. London 1992–98; Prof. of Architecture and Head School of Architecture Univ. of Sheffield 1999–2008; Dean, School of Architecture and the Built Environment, Univ. of Westminster 2008–; Curator British Pavilion, Venice Architecture Biennale 2006; Fulbright Arts Fellowship 1990, Civic Trust Award 2002, RIBA Award 2004, RIBA Sustainability Prize 2004, RIBA Pres.'s Award for Research 2007. *Radio includes:* Shaping Our Spaces (two-part series), BBC Radio 4. *Television includes:* Grand Designs 2002. *Publications include:* Architecture and the Everyday 1997, 9 Stock Orchard Street: A Guidebook 2002, Architecture and Participation 2005, Flexible Housing 2007, Architecture Depends 2008. *Leisure interests:* cooking, eating, drinking. *Address:* School of Architecture and the Built Environment University of Westminster, 35 Marylebone Road, London, NW1 5LS (office); 9 Stock Orchard Street, London, N7 9RW, England (home). *Telephone:* (20) 7911-5130 (office). *Fax:* (20) 7911-5171. *E-mail:* j.till@ westminster.ac.uk (office). *Website:* www.wmin.ac.uk (office).

TILLERSON, Rex W., BS; American energy industry executive; *Chairman and CEO, Exxon Mobil Corporation;* b. Wichita Falls, Tex.; ed Univ. of Texas at Austin; joined Exxon Co. as Production Engineer 1975, held several eng, tech. and supervisory roles 1975–87, including Business Devt Man., Natural Gas Dept 1987–89, Gen. Man. Cen. Production Div. 1989–92, moved to Dallas, Tex. as Production Advisor to Exxon Corpn and then to Florham Park, NJ as Coordinator of Affiliate Gas Sales, Exxon Corpn Int. 1992–95; Pres. Exxon Yemen Inc. and Esso Exploration and Production Khorat Inc. 1995–98, Vice-Pres. Exxon Ventures (CIS) Inc. and Pres. Exxon Neftegas Ltd 1998–99, Exec. Vice-Pres. ExxonMobil Devt Co. 1999–2001, Sr Vice-Pres. Exxon Mobil Corpn 2001–04, Pres. and mem. Bd of Dirs 2004–06, Chair. and CEO 2006–; mem. Bd of Dirs American Petroleum Inst. (Chair. Exec. Cttee and Policy Cttee), US-Russia Business Council, United Negro Coll. Fund; mem. Exec. Bd Boy Scouts of America; mem. Nat. Petroleum Council, Business Roundtable (and its Energy Task Force), Emergency Cttee for American Trade; mem. Eng Advisory Bd for Univ. of Texas at Austin and Soc. of Petroleum Engineers; Vice-Chair. Ford's Theatre Soc.; Trustee, Center for Strategic and Int. Studies; Hon. Trustee Business Council for Int. Understanding. *Address:* ExxonMobil Corporation, 5959 Las Colinas Blvd, Irving, TX 75039-2298, USA (office). *Telephone:* (972) 444-1000 (office). *Fax:* (972) 444-1350 (office). *Website:* www.exxonmobil.com (office).

TILLMAN, Robert (Bob) L.; American retail executive; began career as store man., Lowe's 1962, various man. positions including Exec. Vice-Pres. and COO, Exec. Vice-Pres. Merchandising, Sr Vice-Pres. Merchandising and Marketing, mem. Bd of Dirs 1994–, Pres. and CEO 1996–98, Chair. and CEO Lowe's Cos Inc. 1998–2005 (retd), Chair. and CEO Emer. 2005–; mem. Bd of Dirs Bank of America 2005–. *Address:* c/o Lowe's Companies Inc., 1000 Lowe's Boulevard, Mooreville, NC 28117, USA (office).

TILLMANS, Wolfgang; German artist; b. 1968, Remscheid; s. of Karl A. and Elisabeth Tillmans; ed Bournemouth and Poole Coll. of Art and Design; Turner Prize 2000. *Publications:* Wolfgang Tillmans, 1995, For When I'm Weak I'm Strong, exhbn catalogue 1996, Burg 1998, Soldiers: The Nineties 1999, Portraits 2001, View from Above, If one thing matters, everything matters 2002, Freischwimmer 2004, Truth Study Center 2005, Manual 2007. *Address:* c/o Maureen Paley, 21 Herald Street, London, E2 6JT, England (office). *Telephone:* (20) 7729-4112 (office). *Fax:* (20) 7729-4113 (office). *E-mail:* info@maureenpaley.com (office). *Website:* www.maureenpaley.com (office).

TILMANT, Michel; Belgian banking executive; b. 21 July 1952; ed Univ. of Louvain, Louvain School for European Affairs; with Morgan Guaranty Trust Co., New York 1977–91, held various positions including Head of European Investor Services, Paris and London, Head of Operations Services, New York, Gen. Man., Brussels br.; Vice-Chair. and COO, Banque International à Luxembourg 1991–92; mem. Exec. Cttee, Bank Brussels Lambert (BBL) 1992–2000, CEO 1997–2000; mem. Exec. Bd, ING Groep NV (after acquisition of BBL by ING) 1998–2009, Chair., ING Barings 1998–99, Vice-Chair., ING Groep 2000–04, Chair. Exec. Cttee, ING Europe 2000–04, Chair. Exec. Bd,

ING Groep 2004–09; Chair., European Financial Services Round Table, Institut Int. d'Etudes Bancaires; mem. Bd, Belgian Governance Inst., Koninklijk Concertgebouworkest, Inst. of Int. Finance, Inc., Geneva Asscn; Trustee, Univ. of Louvain.

TILSON, Joseph (Joe), ARCA, RA; British artist; b. 24 Aug. 1928, London; s. of Frederick Albert Edward Tilson and Ethel Stapley Louise Saunders; m. Joslyn Morton 1956; one s. two d.; ed St Martin's School of Art, Royal Coll. of Art, British School, Rome; Visiting Lecturer, Slade School, Univ. of London, 1962–63, King's Coll., Univ. of Durham 1962–63, exhibited at Venice Biennale 1964; Lecturer, School of Visual Arts, New York 1966, Staatliche Hochschule, Hamburg 1971–72; Rome Prize 1955, Grand Prix Fifth Biennale, Kraków 1974, Henry Moore Prize, Bradford 1984, Grand Prix, 15th Biennale, Ljubljana 1985 and 21st Biennale 1995. *Art exhibitions:* retrospective exhbn, Boymans van Beuningen Museum, Rotterdam 1973, Sackler Galleries, Royal Acad., London 2002. *Address:* c/o Alan Cristea Gallery, 31 Cork Street, London, W1X 2NU, England; c/o Waddington Galleries, 11 Cork Street, London, W1S 3LT, England. *Telephone:* (20) 7439-1866; (20 7851-2200; (20) 7259-0024 (home). *Fax:* (20) 7734-4146; (20) 7734-1549. *E-mail:* info@alancristea.com; mail@waddington-galleries.com. *Website:* www.alancristea.com; www.waddington-galleries.com.

TILSON THOMAS, Michael; American conductor, pianist and composer; *Music Director, San Francisco Symphony Orchestra;* b. 21 Dec. 1944, Los Angeles, CA; s. of Theodor Thomas and Roberta Thomas; ed Univ. of S Calif.; conductor, Young Musicians' Foundation Orchestra, Los Angeles 1963–67; conductor and pianist, Monday Evening Concerts 1963–68; musical Asst Bayreuth 1966–67; Asst Conductor, Boston Symphony Orchestra 1969, Assoc. Conductor 1970–71, Prin. Guest Conductor 1972–74; New York debut 1969; London debut with London Symphony Orchestra (LSO) 1970; Dir Young People's Concerts, New York Philharmonic 1971–77; Music Dir Buffalo Philharmonic 1971–79; Prin. Guest Conductor, Los Angeles Philharmonic 1981–85; Music Dir Great Woods Inst. 1985, Music Dir Great Woods Festival 1987–88; Prin. Conductor, LSO 1988–95, Prin. Guest Conductor 1995–; founder and Artistic Dir, New World Symphony 1988–; Music Dir San Francisco Symphony Orchestra 1995–; Artistic Dir Pacific Music Festival; Dir YouTube Symphony Orchestra 2009–; guest conductor with orchestras and opera houses in USA and Europe; Tanglewood Koussevitzky Prize 1968, Ditson Award for contrib. to American music 1994, Musical America Conductor of the Year 1994, American Music Center Award 2001, two Gramophone Awards, five Grammy Awards including Best Classical Album 2004, 2007, Classic FM Gramophone Award for Artist of the Year 2005. *Compositions include:* Poems of Emily Dickinson, premiered by Renée Fleming and San Francisco Symphony Orchestra. *Recordings include:* Mahler Symphonies 1, 3 and 6 (with San Francisco Symphony Orchestra), four-hand version of Stravinsky's Rite of Spring (with Ralph Grierson), Charles Ives' 2nd Symphony (with Concertgebouw Orchestra), complete works of Carl Ruggles (with Buffalo Philharmonic), various musicals by Weill and Gershwin, works of Bach, Beethoven, Prokofiev, Reich and Cage, Mahler's Seventh Symphony (with San Francisco Symphony Orchestra) 2007. *Address:* c/o Van Walsum Management Ltd, 4 Addison Bridge Place, London, W14 8XP, England (office); c/o San Francisco Symphony, Davies Symphony Hall, 201 Van Ness Avenue, San Francisco, CA 94102, USA. *Telephone:* (20) 7371-4343 (office). *Fax:* (20) 7371-4344 (office). *E-mail:* chouse@vanwalsum.co.uk (office). *Website:* www.vanwalsum.co.uk (office); www.sfsymphony.org; www.youtube.com/symphony.

TILTON, Glenn F.; American airline industry executive; *Chairman, President and CEO, United Airlines Corporation and United Airlines;* b. 1948; joined Texaco Inc. 1970, served in various marketing, corp. planning and European downstream assignments, Pres. US Refining and Marketing –1989, Vice-Pres. Texaco Inc. 1989–91, Chair. Texaco Ltd 1991–92, Pres. Texaco Europe 1992–95, Pres. Texaco USA 1995, Sr Vice-Pres. Texaco Inc. 1995–97, apptd Pres. Texaco Global Business Unit 1997, Chair. and CEO Texaco Inc. 2001, Vice-Chair. ChevronTexaco Corpn (following merger between Texaco and Chevron) 2001–02; Chair. Dynegy Inc. 2002; Chair., Pres. and CEO United Airlines (UAL) Corpn and United Airlines 2002–; mem. Bd of Dirs Abbott Laboratories, Air Transport Asscn; mem. US Travel & Tourism Advisory Bd; mem. Bd of Dirs Economic Club of Chicago, Executives' Club of Chicago, After School Matters; mem. Civic Cttee of Commercial Club of Chicago, Int. Relations Advisory Council of Chicago 2016; Trustee, Field Museum, Museum of Science and Industry. *Address:* UAL Corpn, World Headquarters, PO Box 66100, Chicago, IL 60666 (office); UAL Corpn, 77 W. Wacker Drive, Chicago, IL 60601, USA (office). *Telephone:* (312) 997-8000 (office). *E-mail:* info@united.com (office). *Website:* www.united.com (office).

TIMBERLAKE, Justin Randall; American singer, songwriter and actor; b. 31 Jan. 1981, Memphis, Tenn.; started vocal training aged eight; guest appearance at Grand Ole Opry 1991; early TV appearances include Star Search 1992, The Mickey Mouse Club 1993–94; mem. *NSYNC vocal quintet 1995–, first headline US tour 1998; also solo artist 2002–; f. Justin Timberlake Foundation, a charity to fund music and art programmes in schools; founder, Chair. and CEO Tennman Records 2007–; presented with keys to City of Orlando 2000, American Music Award for Favorite Pop/Rock Band, Duo or Group 2002, for Favorite Pop/Rock Male Artist 2007, MOBO Award for Best R&B Act 2003, MTV Award for Best Pop Video (for Cry Me A River) 2003, BRIT Award for Best Int. Male Solo Artist 2004, 2007, Grammy Award for Best Male Pop Vocal Performance (for Cry Me A River) 2004, (for What Goes Around...Comes Around) 2008, for Best Dance Recording (for Sexy Back) 2007, (for LoveStoned/I Think She Knows) 2008, for Best Rap/Sung Collaboration (with T.I.) 2007, MTV Europe Music Award for Best Male Artist, for Best Pop Act 2006, Meteor Ireland Music Award for Best Int. Male Artist 2007, MTV Video Music Award for Best Male Artist 2007. *Film appearances:* Longshot 2000, Model Behavior (TV) 2000, On the Line 2001, Edison 2005, Alpha Dog 2006, Southland Tales 2006, Black Snake Moan 2006, Shrek the Third (voice) 2007. *Recordings include:* albums: with *NSYNC: *NSYNC 1998, Home For The Holidays 1998, The Winter Album 1998, No Strings Attached 2000, Celebrity 2001; solo: Justified (Grammy Award for Best Pop Vocal Album, BRIT Award for Best Int. Album 2004) 2002, FutureSex/LoveSounds (American Music Award for Favorite Soul/R&B Album 2007) 2006. *Publication:* Justin Timberlake (autobiography) 2004. *Address:* Wright Entertainment Group, PO Box 590009, Orlando, FL 32859-0009, USA (office). *Website:* www.justintimberlake.com; www.nsync.com.

TIMMS, Rt Hon. Stephen C., MA, MPhil; British business consultant and politician; *Financial Secretary, HM Treasury;* b. 29 July 1955, Oldham; s. of Ronald James Timms and Margaret Joyce Timms (née Johnson); m. Hui-Leng 1986; ed Farnborough Grammar School, Emmanuel Coll., Cambridge; worked as consultant in computer and telecommunications industries for Logica then Ovum 1978–94; Councillor, London Borough of Newham 1984–97, Chair. Planning Cttee 1987–90, Leader Newham Council 1990–94; MP for Newham North East (by-election) 1994–97, for East Ham 1997–; Parl. Pvt. Sec. to Andrew Smith MP as Minister of State, Dept for Educ. and Skills 1997–98; joint Parl. Pvt. Sec. to Marjorie Mowlam MP as Sec. of State for NI 1998; Parl. UnderSec. of State, Dept of Social Security 1998–99, Minister of State 1999; Financial Sec. HM Treasury 1999–2001, 2004–05, 2008–; Minister of State for School Standards, Dept for Educ. and Skills 2001–02; Minister of State for Energy, E-Commerce and Postal Services, Dept of Trade and Industry 2002–04; Minister of State (Pensions Reform), Dept for Work and Pensions 2005–06; Chief Sec. to the Treasury 2006–07; Minister for Competitiveness, Dept for Business, Enterprise and Regulatory Reform 2007–08; Minister of State for Employment, Dept for Work and Pensions 2008; mem. Commons Select Cttees for Treasury 1996–97 and Public Accounts 2004–05; Sec., Parl. Labour Party Treasury Cttee 1997–98; mem. Labour Party Departmental Cttees for Educ. and Employment 1997–2001, Environment, Transport and the Regions 1997–2001, the Treasury 1997–2001, Vice-Chair. for faith groups and adviser to the Govt on faith 2007–; Jt Vice-Chair. Christian Socialist Movt 1995–98; mem. Bd E London Partnership (now E London Business Alliance) 1990–2006; mem. Stratford Devt Partnership 1992–94; Dr hc (Univ. of East London) 2002; Computing Magazine Award for Outstanding Contrib. to UK IT 2007. *Publication:* Broadband Communications: The Commercial Impact 1986. *Address:* House of Commons, Westminster, London, SW1A 0AA, England (office). *Telephone:* (20) 7219-3000 (office). *E-mail:* stephen@stephentimms.org.uk (office). *Website:* www.stephentimms.org.uk (office).

TIMON, Clay S., BS; American business executive (retd); b. 20 May 1943, Chicago, Ill.; m. Barbara Timon; two c.; ed Leed School of Business Univ. of Colo; fmr Bd Dir, Man. Supervisor (Paris) McCann-Erickson, Man. Services Dir (Tokyo), Sr Vice-Pres./Man. Supervisor; fmr Sr Vice-Pres. Int. Doyle Dane Bernbach; fmr Vice-Pres./Dir Worldwide Advertising Colgate-Palmolive; fmr Regional Vice-Pres. Saatchi & Saatchi, Paris; Chair., Pres., CEO Landor Assocs 1994–2004 (retd); World Pres. Int. Advertising Asscn 1988–90; fmr Chair. Int. Cttee of American Asscn of Advertising Agencies; mem. Business Advisory Council Leeds School of Business, Univ. of Colorado; mem. Bd of Dirs LifeMasters Supported SelfCare, Inc. 2006–, Music in the Vineyards (the Napa Valley Summer Chamber Music Festival); fmr mem. Bd of Dirs WebWare Corpn (now ClearStory Systems) 2001; Outstanding Speaker Award, Leeds School of Business, Univ. of Colo 2002. *Leisure interests:* travel, reading, tennis, vintage automobiles.

TINDEMANS, Leo; Belgian politician; b. 16 April 1922, Zwyndrecht; s. of Frans Tindemans and Margaret Vercruyssen; m. Rosa Naesens 1960; two s. two d.; ed State Univ. of Ghent, Catholic Univ. of Louvain, Univ. of Antwerp; mem. Chamber of Deputies 1961–89; Mayor of Edegem 1965–76; Minister of Community Affairs 1968–71; Minister of Agric. and Middle Class Affairs 1972–73; Deputy Prime Minister and Minister for the Budget and Institutional Problems 1973–74; Prime Minister 1974–78; Minister of Foreign Affairs 1981–89, Minister of State 1992; Vice-Pres. European Union of Christian Democrats, Leader 1992–94; Pres. European People's Party 1976–85; mem. European Parl. 1979–81, 1989–99; Pres. Group of European People's Party, European Parl. 1992–94; Pres. Belgian Christian People's Party (CVP) 1979–81; Pres. Antwerp Business School; Hon. Prof., Faculty of Social Sciences, Catholic Univ., Louvain; Christian Democrat; Hon. DLitt (City Univ., London) 1976, Dr hc (Heriot-Watt Univ., Edin.) 1978, (Georgetown Univ.) 1984, (Deusto Univ., Bilbao) 1991; Charlemagne Prize 1976, St-Liborius-Medaille für Einheit und Frieden 1977, Stresemann Medal 1979, Robert Schuman Prize 1980. *Publications:* Ontwikkeling van de Benelux 1958, L'autonomie culturelle 1971, Regionalized Belgium, Transition from the Nation State to the Multinational State 1972, Een handvest voor woelig België 1972, Dagboek van de werkgroep Eyskens 1973, European Union 1975, Europe, Ideal of Our Generation 1976, Open Brief aan Gaston Eyskens 1978, Atlantisch Europa 1980, Europa zonder Kompas 1987, L'Europe de l'Est vue de Bruxelles 1989, Duel met de Minister 1991, De toekomst van een idee 1993, Cain in the Balkans 1996. *Leisure interests:* reading, writing, walking. *Address:* Jan Verbertlei 24, 2650 Edegem, Belgium (home). *Fax:* (3) 455-66-58.

TINDLE, David, RA; British artist; b. 29 April 1932, Huddersfield, Yorks; m. 1st Jillian Evans 1953 (divorced) 1957); one s. one d.; m. 2nd Sheila Pratt 1957 (divorced 1969); three s. one d.; m. 3rd Janet Trollope 1969 (divorced 1992); one s. two d.; ed Coventry School of Art; worked as scenic artist for theatre until moving to London in 1951; numerous exhbns in London and provinces since 1952; works in many public and private collections including Tate Gallery, Nat. Portrait Gallery; designed and painted set for Iolanta (Tchaikovsky), Aldeburgh Festival 1988; Visiting Tutor, Royal Coll. of Art

1973–83, Fellow 1981, Hon. Fellow 1984; Ruskin Master of Drawing, St Edmund Hall, Oxford 1985–87; lives and works in Italy; Hon. Fellow St Edmund Hall, Oxford 1988–; Hon. mem. Royal Birmingham Soc. of Artists; Hon. MA (St Edmund Hall, Oxford) 1985; Critics Award 1962, RA Johnson Wax Award 1983. *Television:* contrib. on egg tempura to A Feeling for Paint 1980. *Leisure interests:* music, films, cats and dogs, visiting the towns and museums of Italy. *Address:* c/o The Redfern Gallery, 20 Cork Street, London, W1S 3HL, England. *Telephone:* (20) 7734-1732. *E-mail:* art@redfern-gallery .com. *Website:* www.redfern-gallery.com.

TING, Samuel Chao Chung, BSE, PhD; American physicist and academic; *Thomas Dudley Cabot Professor of Physics, Massachusetts Institute of Technology;* b. 27 Jan. 1936, Ann Arbor, Mich.; s. of Prof. Kuan Hai Ting and Prof. Tsun-Ying Wang; m. 2nd Susan Carol Marks 1985; one s. two d.; two d. (from previous marriage); ed primary and secondary schools in China, Univ. of Michigan; Ford Foundation Fellow, European Org. for Nuclear Research (CERN), Geneva 1963; Instructor, Columbia Univ., NY 1964, Asst Prof. 1965–67; Group Leader, Deutsches Elektronen Synchrotron (DESY), Hamburg, Fed. Repub. of Germany 1966; Assoc. Prof. of Physics, MIT, Cambridge 1967–68, Prof. 1969–, Thomas Dudley Cabot Inst. Prof. 1977–; Programme Consultant, Div. of Particles and Fields, American Physical Soc. 1970; Hon. Prof. Beijing Normal Coll., China 1984, Jiatong Univ., Shanghai, China 1987; Assoc. Ed. Nuclear Physics B 1970; mem. Editorial Bd Nuclear Instruments and Methods 1977, Mathematical Modelling, Chinese Physics; worked chiefly on physics of electron or muon pairs, investigating quantum electro-dynamics, production and decay of photon-like particles, searching for new particles which decay to electron or muon pairs, studying physics and astrophysics phenomena in space; Fellow, American Acad. of Arts and Sciences 1975; mem. American, Italian and European Physical Socs.; Foreign mem. Academia Sinica, Taiwan 1975, Pakistani Acad. of Science 1984, USSR (now Russian) Acad. of Science 1989, Hungarian Acad. of Science 1993; mem. NAS 1977–, Deutsche Akademie der Naturforscher Leopoldina 1996; Hon. ScD (Michigan) 1978, (Chinese Univ. of Hong Kong) 1987, (Bologna) 1988, (Columbia) 1990, (Univ. of Science and Tech., China) 1990, (Moscow State Univ.) 1991, (Bucharest) 1993, (Tsinghua Taiwan) 2002, (Nat. Tiaotong Univ. Taiwan) 2003; Ernest Orlando Lawrence Award 1976, Nobel Prize for Physics (jtly with Burton Richter q.v.) for discovery of the heavy, long-lived 'J' (or 'psi') particle 1976, Eringen Medal, Soc. of Eng Scientists 1977, De Gasperi Gold Medal for Science, Italy 1988, Gold Medal for Science, City of Brescia, Italy 1988, Forum Engelberg Prize 1996, NASA Public Service Award 2001. *Address:* Department of Physics, Room 44-114, Massachusetts Institute of Technology, 51 Vassar Street, Cambridge, MA 02139, USA. *Telephone:* (617) 253-8326. *E-mail:* ting@lns.mit.edu (office). *Website:* web.mit.edu/physics/facultyandstaff/faculty/samuel_ting.html (office).

TINKHAM, Michael, MS, PhD; American physicist and academic; *Rumford Professor Emeritus of Physics and Gordon McKay Professor Emeritus of Applied Physics, Harvard University;* b. 23 Feb. 1928, nr Ripon, Wisconsin; s. of Clayton H. Tinkham and Laverna Krause Tinkham; m. Mary S. Merin 1961; two s.; ed Ripon Coll., Ripon, Wis., Mass Massachusetts Inst. of Tech. and Univ. of Oxford; Research Asst, Univ. of California, Berkeley 1955–57, Asst Prof. of Physics 1957–59, Assoc. Prof. of Physics 1959–61, Prof. of Physics 1961–66, Visiting Miller Research Prof.; Gordon McKay Prof. of Applied Physics, Harvard Univ. 1966–2006, Prof. Emer. 2006–, Prof. of Physics 1966–80, Rumford Prof. of Physics 1980–2006, Prof. Emer. 2006–, Chair. Dept of Physics 1975–78; Richtmyer Lecturer (of American Physical Soc. and American Asscn of Physics Teachers) 1977; Visiting Prof., Delft Univ. of Tech. 1993; mem. NAS; Fellow, American Acad. of Arts and Sciences; Hon. DrScNat (ETH, Zürich) 1997; Guggenheim Fellow 1963–64, Buckley Prize 1974, Alexander von Humboldt Foundation Award 1978–79. *Publications:* Group Theory and Quantum Mechanics 1964, Superconductivity 1965, Introduction to Superconductivity 1996 (second edn); numerous articles in journals. *Address:* Department of Physics, Lyman 447, Harvard University, 17 Oxford Street, Cambridge, MA 02138 (office); 98 Rutledge Road, Belmont, MA 02478, USA (home). *Telephone:* (617) 495-3735 (office). *E-mail:* tinkham@physics .harvard.edu (office). *Website:* physics.harvard.edu/tinkham.htm (office).

TINY, Carlos Alberto Pires; São Tome and Príncipe politician; *Minister of Foreign Affairs, Co-operation and Communities;* fmr Minister of Health; fmr Pres. Assembleia Nacional; unsuccessful cand. for Pres. 2001; Minister of Foreign Affairs, Co-operation and Communities 2008–; mem. Movimento de Libertação de São Tomé e Príncipe—Partido Social Democrata. *Address:* Ministry of Foreign Affairs, Co-operation and Communities, Av. 12 de Julho, CP 111, São Tomé, São Tomé and Príncipe (office). *Telephone:* 221017. *Fax:* 222597 (office). *E-mail:* minecoop@cstome.net (office). *Website:* www.mnecc .gov.st (office).

TIONG, Tan Sri Datuk Hiew King; Malaysian/Chinese business executive; *Executive Chairman, Rimbunan Hijau Group;* m.; four c.; Founder and Chair. Rimbunan Hijau Group (timber co.) 1975–, with logging operations in Papua New Guinea and Russia, also controls Sin Chew Jit Poh and Guang Ming Daily (Chinese nat. daily newspapers in Malaysia), The National Daily, Papua New Guinea, and Ming Pao Holdings Ltd, Hong Kong; mem. Sarawak United People's Party (major party of ruling coalition govt in Sarawak). *Address:* Rimbunan Hijau Group, PO Box 454, No. 66–78 Pusat Suria Permata, Jalan Upper Lanang, Sibu 96000, Sarawak, Malaysia (office). *Telephone:* (84) 216155 (office). *Fax:* (84) 215217 (office). *E-mail:* info@rhg.com.my (office). *Website:* www.rhg.com.my (office).

TIRIMO, Martino, FRAM, FRSAMD, Dip RAM; British concert pianist and conductor; *Professor, Trinity College of Music, Middlesex University;* b. 19 Dec. 1942, Larnaca, Cyprus; s. of Dimitri Tirimo and Marina Tirimo; m. Mione J. Teakle 1973; one s. one d.; ed Bedales School, England (Cyprus Govt

Scholarship), Royal Acad. of Music, London, Vienna State Acad.; first public recital, Cyprus 1949; conducted seven performances of La Traviata with singers and musicians from La Scala, Milan, at Cyprus Opera Festival 1955; prizewinner Int. Beethoven Competition, Vienna 1965; London début Wigmore Hall 1965; jt winner Munich Int. Piano Competition 1971; winner Geneva Int. Piano Competition 1972; gave first public performance of complete Schubert sonatas (including unfinished ones with own completions), London 1975; first public performance of Beethoven piano concertos cycle directed from keyboard in two consecutive evenings, Dresden 1985, London 1986; first performance Tippett piano concerto in several European countries 1986–87; concerto performances with major orchestras worldwide as well as recitals, radio and TV appearances Europe, USA, Canada, SA and Far East 1965–; four series of performances of complete Beethoven piano sonatas 2000, two series devoted to the maj. piano works of Robert and Clara Schumann 2001; six-concert series devoted to the major piano works of Chopin 2002; began Mozart piano concertos series, directing from keyboard 2001–; f. Rosemunde Trio with violinist Ben Sayevich and cellist Daniel Veis 2002; performed with Vienna Philharmonic during Olympics, Athens Festival 2004, Olympic Games torch bearer 2004; performed complete Mozart solo piano works in several series of eight concerts, including at Cadogan Hall, London 2006; composed film score The Odyssey 1998; Prof., Trinity Coll. of Music 2003–; Hon. Prof., Middlesex Univ. 2004–; Visiting Prof., Royal Scottish Acad. of Music and Drama; Liszt Scholarship, Boise Foundation Scholarship, Gulbenkian Foundation Fellowship 1967–69; mem. jury in various int. piano competitions 1995–; Gold Medal, Associated Bd of Royal Schools of Music 1959, Macfarren Medal, Royal Acad. of Music 1964, Silver Disc 1988 and Gold Disc 1994 for recording of Rachmaninov 2nd Concerto and Paganini Rhapsody and other prizes and awards. *Recordings include:* Brahms piano concertos, Chopin concertos, Tippett piano concerto, Rachmaninov concertos, complete Debussy piano works, complete Mozart piano works, complete Beethoven works, complete Schubert piano sonatas, complete Janacek piano works, complete Mendelssohn works for piano and cello, Tchaikovsky and Shostakovich piano Trios (Rosamunde Trio), several other recordings with mixed repertoire. *Television:* live performance of Tippett piano concerto from Coventry Cathedral for BBC TV in celebration of composer's 90th birthday and the 50th birthday of the UN. *Publications include:* urtext edn of complete Schubert piano sonatas in 3 vols 1997–99. *Leisure interests:* chess, reading, self-knowledge, theatre, badminton. *Address:* 1 Romeyn Road, London, SW16 2NU, England (home). *Telephone:* (20) 8677-4847 (home). *Fax:* (20) 8677-6070 (home). *E-mail:* martino@tirimo.fslife.co.uk (home). *Website:* www .martinotirimo.com (office).

TIRKEY, Dilip; Indian professional field hockey player; b. 24 Nov. 1977, Sawnamara, Sundergarh, Orissa; s. of Vincent Tirkey; ed Bhanwani Shankar School; belongs to Oraon tribe of Chota Nagpur; fmr Asst Man., Indian Airlines; trained in NIS Patiala under coach A. K. Basal; started his career as inside forward but developed into defender; int. debut in Test Series vs Australia 1994; Vice-Capt. Jr World Cup, Milton Keynes, UK 1997, selected in World XI Team; Gold Medal, SAF Games, Chennai 1995, Bangkok Asian Games 1998, Prime Minister's Gold Cup 2001; Silver Medal, Asian Games, Busan 2002; Bronze Medal, Asia Cup, Kuala Lumpur, Malaysia 1999; first Adivasi captain of ind. Indian nat. team and second in Indian history; youngest Olympian when capped at Atlanta, USA 1996; signed to play with Klein Zwitserland hockey club, Netherlands 2005; currently Capt. with Orissa Steelers; Ekalavya Puraskar 1996, ONGC-Hockey Year Book Award 1998, Arjuna Award 2002, Padma Shri 2004. *Leisure interests:* music, dance.

TIROLE, Jean, PhD; French economist and academic; *Scientific Director, Institut d'Économie Industrielle (IDEI);* b. 9 Aug. 1953; ed Université Paris IX–Dauphine, MIT; researcher, CERAS, École Nationale des Ponts et Chaussées 1981–84; Prof. of Econs, MIT 1984–91; Sr Fellow, Inst. for Policy Reform 1990–95; Prof., Ecole Polytechnique 1994–96; Dir of Accumulative Studies, Ecole des Hautes Etudes en Sciences Sociales 1995–; mem. Conseil d'Analyse Économique (Prime Minister's Council of Econ. Advisors) 1999–2006; currently Dir Fondation Jean-Jacques Laffont, Toulouse School of Econs; also currently Scientific Dir Institut d'Économie Industrielle (IDEI), Toulouse; Founder mem. and Fellow, European Corp. Governance Inst. 2002–; visiting prof. at Harvard, Stanford, Princeton, Lausanne, Wuhan univs; mem. Econometric Soc. (mem. Exec. Cttee 1993–99, Pres. 1998); Pres. European Econ. Asscn 2001; mem. French High Council for Science and Tech. 2006–, European Research Council panel 2007–; Foreign Hon. Mem., American Acad. of Arts and Sciences 1993, American Econ. Asscn 1993; Chevalier de la légion d'honneur 2007; Dr hc (Université Libre de Bruxelles) 1989; Yrjo Jahnsson prize, European Econ. Asscn 1993, Center for Econ. Studies Prize 1996, Public Utility Research Center Distinguished Service Award, Univ. of Fla 1997, John von Neumann Award, Budapest Univ. 1998, Distinguished Fellow Award, Industrial Org. Soc. 1999, Gold Medal, CNRS 2002, 2007, Prix Dargélos de l'Ecole Polytechnique 2002, Thomson Prize in Econs, Inst. of Scientific Information 2004. *Publications:* The Theory of Industrial Organization, Game Theory (with Drew Fudenberg), A Theory of Incentives in Procurement and Regulation (with Jean-Jacques Laffont), The Prudential Regulation of Banks (with Mathias Dewatripont), Competition in Telecommunications (with Jean-Jacques Laffont), Financial Crises, Liquidity and the International Monetary System, The Theory of Corporate Finance; more than 180 articles in journals. *Address:* IDEI, Université des Sciences Sociales, Manufacture des Tabacs, Aile Jean-Jacques Laffont, Accueil MF 404, 21 allée de Brienne, 31000 Toulouse, France (office). *Telephone:* 5-61-12-86-42 (office). *Fax:* 5-61-12-86-37 (office). *E-mail:* tirole@cict.fr (office). *Website:* idei.fr (office).

TISCH, Andrew H., BS, MBA; American business executive; *Chairman of the Executive Committee, Member of the Office of the President and Co-Chairman*

of the Board, Loews Corporation; b. 14 Aug. 1949, Asbury Park, NJ; s. of the late Laurence and Wilma Tisch; m. Ann Tisch (née Rubenstein); four c.; ed Cornell and Harvard Univs; joined Loews Corpn 1971, mem. Bd of Dirs 1985–, Chair. Exec. Cttee, mem. Office of the Pres. and Co-Chair. Bd 2006–; Pres. Bulova Corpn 1979–90, currently Chair.; CEO and Chair. Lorillard Inc. 1990–95; mem. Bd of Dirs Canary Wharf Group PLC, Zale Corpn, K12 Inc., CNA Financial Corpn 2006–. *Address:* Loews Corpn, 667 Madison Avenue, New York, NY 10021-8087, USA (office). *Telephone:* (212) 521-2000 (office). *Fax:* (212) 521-2525 (office). *E-mail:* info@loews.com (office). *Website:* www.loews.com (office).

TISCH, James S., MBA; American business executive; *President, CEO and Member of the Office of the President, Loews Corporation;* b. 2 Feb. 1953, Atlantic City, NJ; s. of the late Lawrence Tisch and Wilma Tisch; m. Merryl Tisch (neé Hiat); two s. one d.; ed Cornell Univ., Wharton Business School, Univ. of Pennsylvania; joined Loews 1977 (hotel chain est. by Lawrence Tisch 1946), various exec. positions including Dir Loews Corpn, Pres. 1998–, COO 1998–99, CEO 1999–, also Mem. Office of the Pres.; Chair. and CEO Diamond Offshore Drilling Inc.; Dir, Educational Broadcasting Corpn 2003–, Chair. 2006–; mem. Bd of Dirs CAN Financial Corpn, Vail Resorts Inc.; mem. Bd of Overseers Univ. of Pennsylvania; mem. Council on Foreign Relations. *Address:* Loews Corpn, 667 Madison Avenue, New York, NY 10021-8087, USA (office). *Telephone:* (212) 521-2000 (office). *Fax:* (212) 521-2525 (office). *E-mail:* info@loews.com (office). *Website:* www.loews.com (office).

TISCH, Jonathan Mark, BA; American business executive; *Co-Chairman and Member of the Office of the President, Loews Corporation;* b. 7 Dec. 1953, Atlantic City, NJ; s. of the late Preston Robert Tisch and Joan T. Tisch (née Hyman); cousin of James Tisch (q.v.) and Andrew Tisch (q.v.); m. Lizzie Rudnick 2007; ed Tufts Univ.; worked as cinematographer and producer at WBZ-TV, Boston 1976–79; Sales Man. Loews Hotels, New York 1980–81, Dir of Devt 1981–82, Vice Pres. 1982–85, Exec. Vice-Pres. 1985–86, Pres. 1986, CEO 1989–, also Chair., mem. Bd of Dirs Loews Corpn 1986–, mem. Office of the Pres. 1998–, Co-Chair. 2006–; Chair. Travel Business Roundtable 1995–; Co-Chair. NYC & Co. tourism agency; Treas. and mem. Bd of Dirs, NY Giants football team 1991–; mem. Bd of Dirs Elizabeth Glaser Paediatric AIDS Foundation, Tribeca Film Inst., Business Council for the Metropolitan Museum of Art; mem. Bd of Trustees and Patron, Jonathan M. Tisch Coll. of Citizenship and Public Service, Tufts Univ.; mem. US Dept of Commerce US Travel and Tourism Advisory Bd 2003–; fmr Chair. New York Rising, American Hotel and Lodging Asscn; fmr Vice-Chair. Welfare to Work Partnership; Travel Agent magazine Hotel Person of the Year, Business Travel Industry's Most Influential Executives, Business Travel News, 25 Most Influential People in the Meetings Industry, Meeting News magazine, Tufts Alumni Asscn Distinguished Alumni Award 1996. *Television:* host, Open Exchange: Beyond the Boardroom. *Publications:* The Power of We: Succeeding Through Partnerships 2004, Chocolates on the Pillow Aren't Enough: Reinventing the Customer Experience 2007. *Address:* Loews Corpn, 667 Madison Avenue, New York, NY 10021-8087, USA (office). *Telephone:* (212) 521-2000 (office). *Fax:* (212) 521-2525 (office). *E-mail:* info@loews.com (office). *Website:* www.loews.com (office).

TISCH, Thomas J., BA, LLB; American business executive and university administrator; *Chancellor, Brown University;* b. 1955; ed Brown Univ., New York Univ.; Man. Pnr, Four Partners (pvt. investment co.) 1992–; mem. Bd of Trustees, Brown Univ. 2002–, Chancellor 2007–; mem. Bd of Dirs Sears Holdings Corpn, Infonxx Inc.; mem. Bd of Trustees New York Univ. Medical Center, KIPP Acad., Manhattan Inst. for Public Policy Research. *Address:* Office of the Chancellor, Brown University, One Prospect Street, Campus Box 1860, Providence, RI 02912, USA (office). *Telephone:* (401) 863-2234 (office). *Fax:* (401) 863-7737 (office). *Website:* www.brown.edu/Administration (office).

TISHCHENKO, Boris Ivanovich; Russian composer; b. 23 March 1939, Leningrad; s. of Ivan I. Tishchenko and Zinaida A. Tishchenko; m. Irina A. Donskaya 1977; three s.; ed Leningrad Conservatory, with post-grad. course under Shostakovich; Prof. at St Petersburg Conservatory; Russian Order of Merit for the Homeland, Fourth Class 2002; 1st Prize, Int. Contest of Young Composers, Prague 1966, RSFSR State Prize (Glinka) 1978, People's Artist of RSFSR 1987, Prize of Mayor of St Petersburg 1995, Pushkin Gold Medal 2000, Union of Composers of Russia Prize 2002, Prize of Honour of Russian Author's Society 2003. *Compositions include:* vocal works and ballets: Lenin Lives (cantata) 1959, The Twelve (ballet) 1963, Requiem (words by A. Akhmatova) 1966, Fly-bee (ballet) 1968, A Cockroach (operetta) 1968, The Stolen Sun (opera) 1968, Yaroslavna (The Eclipse, ballet) 1974, Beatriche (ballet) 2005; symphonies: French Symphony 1958, Sinfonia Robusta 1970, Violin Symphony (2nd Violin Concerto) 1981, The Siege Chronicle 1984, Pushkin's Symphony 1998, 7 symphonies 1961–94; other works: 10 piano sonatas 1957–97, violin and cello solo sonatas, Sonata for family of flutes and organ 1999, Rondo, Capriccio and Fantasy for violin and piano, also concertos for violin, piano, cello, flute and harp 1962–77, Concerto alla marcia for 16 soloists 1989, The Dog's Heart – Novels for chamber ensemble based on M. Bulgakov 1988, Concerto for clarinet and piano trio 1990, Piano Quintet 1985, String quartets 1957–84, Twelve Inventions and Twelve Portraits for Organ 1964, 1994, Double Concerto for violin, piano and strings 2006, orchestral and instrumental suites and pieces, vocal cycles and ensembles, choral works, music for drama productions and films; edns and instrumentations of some works by Monteverdi, Grieg, Mahler, Prokofiev and Shostakovich. *Leisure interest:* reading. *Address:* Rimsky-Korsakoff Avenue 79, Apt 10, 190121 St Petersburg, Russia (home). *Telephone:* (812) 714-75-16 (home). *E-mail:* boristishchenko@rambler.ru (home).

TISHKOV, Valery Aleksandrovich, DHist; Russian historian and anthropologist; *Director, Institute of Ethnology and Anthropology, Russian Academy of Sciences;* b. 6 Nov. 1941; m.; one s.; ed Moscow State Univ.; teacher, Magadan State Pedagogical Inst. 1964–66; aspirant, Moscow State Pedagogical Inst. 1966–69; docent, Dean, Magadan State Pedagogical Inst. 1969–72; researcher, Inst. of Gen. History USSR (now Russian) Acad. of Sciences, Scientific Sec., Div. of History, USSR Acad. of Sciences, also Head of Dept, Inst. of Ethnography; Deputy Dir, Inst. of Ethnology and Anthropology Russian Acad. of Sciences 1972–89, Dir 1989–; Fed. Minister for Nationalities, Russian Govt 1992; Vice-Pres. Int. Union of Ethnological and Anthropological Sciences 1993 (re-elected 1998); mem. Russian Acad. of Sciences; mem. Public Chamber of Russia, Chair. Cttee on Tolerance and Freedom of Faith; Order of Honour 2009; Distinguished Scholar of the Russian Fed. 1998, State Prize in Science and Art 2001. *Publications:* Ethnicity, Nationalism and Conflict in and after the Soviet Union. The Mind Aflame 1997, Peoples and Religions of the World (Russian Encyclopaedia) 1998, Chechnya: Life in a War-Torn Society 2004, Tundra and Sea: Chukotka Ivory Art 2008. *Leisure interests:* fishing, collection of Arctic ivory art. *Address:* Institute of Ethnology and Anthropology, Russian Academy of Sciences, Leninsky prosp. 32A, 119334 Moscow, Russia. *Telephone:* (495) 938-17-47 (office). *Fax:* (495) 938-06-00 (office). *E-mail:* tishkov@orc.ru (home). *Website:* www.valerytishkov.ru (office).

TITARENKO, Mikhail Leontyevich, PhD; Russian academic; *Director, Institute of Far East Studies, Russian Academy of Sciences;* b. 27 April 1934, Bryansk region; s. of the late Leonty Titarenko and Maria Titarenko; m. Galina Titarenko 1957 (died 1997); two s.; ed Moscow State Univ., Beijing Univ., Fudan Univ., Shanghai; diplomatic service 1961–65; researcher and consultant in govt bodies 1965–85; Dir Inst. of Far East Studies, Russian Acad. of Sciences 1985–; mem. Editorial Bd, Far Eastern Affairs 1986–; Chair. Academic Council on Problems of Modern China, Russian Acad. of Sciences 1987–; Pres. All-Russian Asscn of Sinologists 1988–; Corresp. mem. Russian Acad. of Sciences 1997–, Academician 2003–; mem. Russia Acad. of Natural Sciences, Int. Acad. of Informatization; Honour of the Russian Fed. 1994, Merited Scholar of Russia 1995, 200 Years of Russian Foreign Service Medal 2002. *Publications:* Anthology of Ancient Chinese Philosophy (two vols), Ancient Chinese Philosopher Mo Di 1985, Development of Productive Forces in China 1989, History of Chinese Philosophy 1989, Economic Reform in China: Theory and Practice 1990, Russia and East Asia: Issues of International and Cross-Civilization Relations 1994, Russia Towards Asia 1998, China: Civilization and Reforms 1999, Russia's Co-operative Security: East Asian Vector 2003; and numerous articles. *Leisure interests:* collecting stamps, matchboxes, skiing, mushroom hunting. *Address:* Institute of Far East Studies, Russian Academy of Sciences, 32 Nakhimovsky pr., 117218 Moscow, Russia (office). *Telephone:* (495) 124-01-17 (office); (495) 198-55-38 (home). *Fax:* (495) 718-96-56 (office). *E-mail:* ifes@cemi.rssi.ru (office). *Website:* www.ifes-ras.ru (office).

TITHERIDGE, John Edward, PhD, FRSNZ, FInstP; New Zealand physicist and academic; *Honorary Research Fellow, Physics Department, University of Auckland;* b. 12 June 1932, Auckland; s. of Leslie Edward Titheridge and Clarice Muriel Barnes; m. Patricia Joy Brooker 1970; one s. one d.; ed Avondale Coll., Univ. of Auckland and Univ. of Cambridge; Research Fellow, Univ. of Auckland 1960–, Sr Research Fellow 1961, Assoc. Prof. 1967–, now Hon. Research Fellow; Fellow, NZ Inst. of Physics; Cheeseman-Pond Memorial Prize 1962, Michaelis Memorial Prize 1972, NZ Geophysics Prize, Wellington Br. Royal Soc. of NZ 1977. *Publications:* more than 120 refereed scientific papers 1959–. *Leisure interests:* music, photography, reading, woodwork, electronics. *Address:* Physics Department, University of Auckland, Auckland (office); 1500 Dominion Road, Auckland 1041, New Zealand (home). *Telephone:* (9) 373-7599, ext. 88866 (office); (9) 620-6231 (home). *Fax:* (9) 373-7445 (office). *E-mail:* j.titheridge@auckland.ac.nz (office). *Website:* www.phy.auckland.ac.nz (office).

TITO, Teburoro, BSc; I-Kiribati politician and fmr head of state; b. 25 Aug. 1953, Tabiteuea North; m. Nei Keina; one c.; ed King George V Secondary School, Univ. of South Pacific, Suva, Papua New Guinea Admin. Coll.; student co-ordinator, Univ. of South Pacific Students' Asscn 1977–79; scholarship officer, Ministry of Educ. 1980–82, Sr Educ. Officer 1983–87; mem. Maneaba ni Maungatabu (Parl.) and Leader of Opposition 1987–94; mem. Parl. Public Accounts Cttee 1987–90; Pres. of Kiribati 1994–2003, also Minister of Foreign Affairs; and Int. Trade mem. CPA Exec. Cttee for Pacific Region 1989–90; Chair. Kiribati Football Asscn 1980–94; Dr of World Peace (Maharishi Univ. of World Peace) 2001. *Leisure interests:* sports, especially soccer, tennis and table tennis. *Address:* c/o Office of the President, PO Box 68, Bairiki, Tarawa (office); Tabuarorae, Eita Village, South Tarawa, Kiribati (home). *Telephone:* 21183. *Fax:* 21145.

TITOV, Konstantin Alekseyevich, CandEconSc; Russian politician; b. 30 Oct. 1944, Moscow; m. Natalia Borisovna Titova; one s.; ed Kuybyshev (now Samara) Aviation Inst., Kuybyshev Inst. of Planning; milling-machine operator, Kuybyshev aviation factory 1962–63, flight engineer 1968–69, Deputy Sec. Komsomol Cttee 1969–70; Deputy Head Students Div., Kuybyshev City Komsomol Cttee 1970–73; Sec. Komsomol Cttee, Jr, Sr Researcher, Head of Group, Head Research Lab. Kuybyshev Inst. of Planning 1973–88; Deputy Dir Research Cen. Informatika (Samara br.) 1988–90; Chair. Samara City Council 1990–91; Head of Admin. Samara Region 1991–96; Gov. Samara Region 1996–2007; mem. Council of Fed. of Russia 1993–2001, Chair. Cttee on Budget, Taxation Policy, Finance and Customs Regulation 1996–2001; Pres. Interregional Asscn of Econ. Interaction 'Bolshaya Volga' 1994; Deputy Chair. 'Our Home Is Russia' political movt 1995; Chair. of Council, Union of Right Forces 1998–; Cand. for Pres. of Russian Fed. 2000; Chair. Russian Party of Social Democracy 2000, Co-Founder Union of Social Democratic Parties 2001; mem. Russian Acad. of Natural Sciences; Golden Mask Prize, Russian Theatre

Artists Union; Order of St Faithful Prince Daniil Moskovsky (3rd Degree), Order of St Grand Duke Vladimir (2nd Degree); Order of Friendship, Green Man of the Year, Russian Ecological Union 1996, Honoured Economist of the Russian Fed., Gov. of the Year 1998, National Prize of Peter the Great 2002, Order Glory of Russia 2002, National Olympus Laureate 2003. *Leisure interests:* football, photography, music, painting, reading. *Address:* c/o Office of the President, 103132 Moscow, Staraya pl. 4, Russia (office). *Website:* www.kremlin.ru (office).

TITOV, Col. Vladimir Georgievich; Russian cosmonaut; *Director for Space and Communications, Russia and the Commonwealth of Independent States, Boeing Corporation;* b. 1 Jan. 1947, Sretensk, Chita Region; s. of Georgie Titov (deceased) and Vera Titova; m. Alexandra Kozlova; one s. one d.; ed Chernigov Higher Mil. Aviation School, Yuriy Gagarin Air Force Acad.; pilot instructor, Commdr of aviation unit 1970–76; mem. cosmonauts' team since 1976; Commdr of space flights on spacecraft Soyuz T-8 1983 and record-breaking flight on Soyuz TM-4 and space station MiR; Deputy Head Dept of Man. Centre of Cosmonauts' Training 1988–99; Dir for Space and Communications, Russia and CIS, Boeing Corpn, Moscow 1999–; Hero of the Soviet Union, Order of Lenin 1983, 1988, Commdr Légion d'honneur 1988; US Harmon Prize 1990. *Address:* Yuriy Gagarin Centre for Cosmonauts' Training, Zvezdny Gorodok, Moscow Region, Russia. *Telephone:* (495) 797-34-00 (Boeing) (office). *Fax:* (495) 797-34-01 (Boeing) (office). *Website:* www.boeing.ru (office).

TITOV, Yuriy Evlampievich; Russian fmr gymnast; b. 27 Nov. 1935, Omsk; s. of Evlampiy Titov and Marina Titova; m. Valerie Kouzmenko 1960; one s. one d.; ed Kiev Inst. of Physical Culture; all-round champion of USSR 1958, 1961, of Europe 1959 and the world 1962; Honoured Master of Sports 1956; Olympic gymnastics champion 1956; won 13 gold medals at European, World Championships and Olympic Games; int. class judge 1968; mem. CPSU 1969–91; Vice-Pres. Int. Gymnastic Fed. 1972–76, Pres. 1976–96, Hon. Life Pres. 1996–; Head Dept of Gymnastics, USSR State Sports Cttee 1968–87; lecturer Moscow Acad. of Physical Culture 1980–, Leningrad (now St Petersburg) Acad. of Physical Culture 1988–, Prof. 1993–; Sec. Nat. Olympic Cttee 1987–88, mem. Int. Olympic Cttee (IOC) Working Group on Women and Sport 1995–, ex officio mem. IOC 1995–96; Olympic Order 1992, inducted into Int. Gymnastics Hall of Fame 1999. *Publications:* The Sum of Points 1971, The Ascent 1982, The Notes of the President 1984, Rhythmic Gymnastics (jtly) 1998; works on methodology of gymnastics. *Leisure interests:* history, carpentry, doing nothing with pleasure. *Address:* Kolokolnikov per. 6, Apt. 19, 103045 Moscow, Russia. *Telephone:* (495) 208-46-57. *Fax:* (495) 208-46-57.

TITS, Jacques Léon, DrSc; French mathematician and academic; *Honorary Professor of Mathematics, College of France;* b. 12 Aug. 1930, Uccle, Belgium; s. of Léon Tits and Louisa Tits (née André); m. Marie-Jeanne Dieuaide 1956; ed Univ. of Brussels; with Belgian Nat. Fund for Scientific Research 1948–56; Asst, Univ. of Brussels 1956–57, Assoc. Prof. 1957–62, Prof. 1962–64; Prof., Univ. of Bonn 1964–74; Assoc. Prof., Coll. de France, Paris 1973–74, Prof. of Group Theory 1975–2000, Hon. Prof. 2000–; Visiting Teacher and Prof., Eidgenössische Technische Hochschule, Zürich, Switzerland 1950, 1951, 1953, Inst. for Advanced Study, Princeton, USA 1951–52, 1963, 1969, 1971–72, Univ. of Rome, Italy 1955, 1956, Univ. of Chicago, USA 1963, Univ. of California, Berkeley, USA 1963, Univs of Tokyo and Kyoto, Japan 1971, Yale Univ., USA 1966–67, 1976, 1980, 1984, 1990, 1995, 2002; mem. editorial bds of periodicals and scientific collections; Ed.-in-Chief Math. Publs of IHES 1980–99; Guest Speaker at Int. Congresses of Mathematicians, Stockholm 1962, Nice 1970, Vancouver 1974; lecture tours in USA, UK, Israel, etc.; mem. Deutsche Akad. der Naturforscher Leopoldina 1977, American Acad. of Arts and Sciences 1992, NAS 1992; founding mem. Academia Europaea; Corresp. mem. Acad. des Sciences, Paris 1977, mem. 1979; Foreign mem. Royal Netherlands Acad. of Arts and Sciences 1988; Foreign Assoc. Royal Belgian Acad. 1991; Hon. mem. London Math. Soc. 1993; Chevalier, Légion d'honneur, Commdr des Palmes académiques, Officier, Ordre Nat. du mérite; Dr hc (Utrecht) 1970, (Ghent) 1979, (Bonn) 1987, (Louvain) 1992; Prix scientifique Interfacultaire L. Empain 1955, Prix Wettrems, Acad. de Belgique 1958, Grand Prix des Sciences mathématiques et physiques, Acad. des Sciences 1976, Wolf Prize 1993, Cantor Medal, Deutsche Mathematiker-Vereinigung (German Math. Soc.) 1996, Prix Abel 2008. *Publications:* more than 150 scientific papers. *Leisure interests:* languages, literature, arts. *Address:* College de France, 11, place Marcelin Berthelot, 75231 Paris Cedex 05, France (office). *Fax:* 1-44-27-17-04 (office). *E-mail:* jacques.tits@college-de-france.fr (office).

TIWARI, Shri Narayan Dutt, LLB, MA; Indian politician, social worker and journalist; *Governor of Andhra Pradesh;* b. 18 Oct. 1925, Balyuti, Nainital Dist, Uttaranchal; s. of the late Shri Poornanand Tiwari; m. Dr (Smt.) Sushila Tiwari 1954 (deceased); ed M.B. School, Haldwani, E.M. High School, Bareilly, C.R.S.T. High School, Nainital, Allahabad Univ., Uttar Pradesh (UP); joined Indian Freedom Movt aged 13; joined 'Quit India' Movt 1942; imprisoned for 15 months; Pres. Allahabad Univ. Students' Union 1947; Sec. Political Sufferers' Distress Relief Soc.; mem. Uttar Pradesh Legis. Ass. 1952–62, 1969–79 1984–85, 1988–89, 1991–92, mem. Finance Cttee, Estimates Cttee, Privileges Cttee 1952–54, 1954–60, Leader of the Opposition 1960–61, 1977–79, 1988–89, 1990–91; Chair. Public Accounts Cttee 1961–62, mem. UP Police Comm. and Panchayati Raj Comm. 1961–62; Pres. Indian Youth Congress 1965–69; Minister of Labour, Planning and Panchayati Raj, UP 1969, of Finance and Parl. Affairs 1970, of Finance, Power, Heavy Industries, Irrigation, Labour, Sugarcane, Excise, Panchayati Raj and Parl. Affairs 1971, of Finance, Industry, Irrigation, Labour, Sugarcane, Excise and Parl. Affairs 1973, of Finance, Heavy Industries, Hill Devt and Planning 1974–75; Chief Minister of UP 1976–77, 1984–85, 1988–89; elected to Lok Sabha 1980, re-elected 1996, elected to 13th Lok Sabha from Nainital Constituency 1999, Chair. Public Accounts Chair. 2000–02; Union Minister of Planning and Deputy Chair. Planning Comm. (held additional Charge of Labour Ministry) 1980–81; Union Minister for Industry (held additional charge of Ministry of Steel and Mines) 1981–84 (1982–83); Union Minister for Industry (held additional charge of Ministry of Petroleum & Natural Gas) 1985–86 (June–Oct. 1986); mem. Rajya Sabha 1985–88; Union Minister for External Affairs 1986–87; Leader Congress (I) Party in Rajya Sabha May–June 1987; Union Minister of Finance and Commerce and mem. Cabinet Cttee on Political Affairs 1987–88; Pres. All India Indira Congress (Tiwari) 1995–96; Leader Parl. Party, AIIC (T) May–Dec. 1996, party merged with Indian Nat. Congress 1997; first elected Chief Minister of newly created Uttaranchal State (now Uttarakhand) 2002–07; Gov. of Andhra Pradesh 2007–; Ed. Prabhat (monthly); Special Corresp., National Herald; est. Jana Vidyapeeth (People's Coll.) in Haldwani 1962, Jawahar Lal Nehru Nat. Youth Centre 1967. *Publications:* European Miscellany (collection of articles) 1964; contributed numerous articles in Amrit Bazar Patrika, Leader, Deshdoot, National Herald, Pioneer, Blitz etc. *Leisure interests:* music, reading books on modern topics, econs, planning, int. relations and socio-economic reforms in the Indian/world perspective, technological/industrial/integrated devt. *Address:* c/o Office of the Chief Minister, Government of Andhra Pradesh, 'C' Block, 4th Floor, AP Secretariat, Hyderabad, India (office); Mohalla Ganj, Kashipur, Distt. Udham Singh Nagar, Uttaranchal; B-315, Dr Sushila Tiwari Marg, Mahanagar, Lucknow, Uttar Pradesh, India. *Telephone:* (522) 2384854. *E-mail:* webmaster_aponline@ap.gov.in (office). *Website:* www.aponline.gov.in/apportal/index.asp (office).

TIZARD, Dame Catherine (Anne), ONZ, GCMG, GCVO, DBE, QSO; New Zealand fmr public official; b. 4 April 1931, Auckland; d. of Neil Maclean and Helen Montgomery Maclean; m. Robert James Tizard 1951 (divorced 1983); one s. three d.; ed Matamata Coll. and Auckland Univ.; Tutor in Zoology, Univ. of Auckland 1963–83; mem. Auckland City Council 1971–83, Auckland Regional Authority 1980–83, Mayor of Auckland (first woman) 1983–90; JP 1980–86; Gov.-Gen. of New Zealand (first woman) 1990–96; Chair. NZ Worldwide Fund for Nature 1996–2000, NZ Historic Places Trust 1996–2002, Sky City Charitable Trust 1996–2002; Dir NZ Symphony Orchestra Trust Bd; occasional radio, TV and newspaper commentator and columnist; public speaker and debater; numerous community activities including roles with Auckland War Memorial Inst. and Museum, Library Council of NZ, Auckland Univ. Council, Local Govt Assen of NZ, Royal NZ Ballet Trust, etc; Dir XIV Commonwealth Games Ltd; Hon. Fellow, Lucy Cavendish Coll. Cambridge, UK and Winston Churchill Fellow 1981; Hon. Freeman,Worshipful Co. of Butchers 1990; Freedom, City of London 1990; Hon. Capt. RNZN 1997; Hon. Col Auckland (Countess of Ranfurly's Own) and Northland Bn Group 2007; D St J 1990, Additional Mem.; Hon. LLD (Auckland) 1992; New Zealand Medal 1990, Suffrage Centennial Medal 1995. *Leisure interests:* music, reading, drama, scuba diving. *Address:* 12A Wallace Street, Herne Bay, Auckland 1, New Zealand. *Telephone:* (9) 376-2555. *Fax:* (9) 360-0656. *E-mail:* cath.tizard@xtra.co.nz (home).

TJEKNAVORIAN, Loris-Zare; American/Armenian composer and conductor; b. 13 Oct. 1937; s. of Haikaz and Adriné Tjeknavorian; m. 1st Linda Pierce 1964 (divorced 1979); one s.; m. 2nd Julia Cory Harley-Green 1986; ed Vienna Acad. of Music, Salzburg Mozarteum; studied with the late Carl Orff 1963–64; worked in USA until 1970; fmr Teaching Fellow, Univ. of Michigan; fmr Composer-in-Residence, Concordia Coll., Minnesota; Composer-in-Residence, Ministry of Culture and Fine Arts; Prin. Conductor, Tehran Opera 1972–79; artist with RCA 1976–; Composer-in-Residence American-Armenian Int. Coll., La Verne Univ., Calif. 1979–; Prin. Conductor and Artistic Dir Armenian Philharmonic Orchestra, Yerevan, Armenia 1989–; principally associated with London Symphony Orchestra with whom he has recorded; Chair. Bd of Trustees, Inst. of Armenian Music, London 1976–80; Order of Homayoun; several int. tours as a conductor. *Works include:* Requiem for the Massacred 1975, Simorgh (ballet music), Lake Van Suite, Erebouni for 12 strings 1978, a piano concerto, several operas, several chamber works, Credo Symphony Life of Christ (after medieval Armenian chants) 1976, Liturgical Mass, Violin Concerto, oratorios Lucifer's Fall and Book of Revelation, Mass in Memoriam 1985, Othello (ballet), ballet suites for orchestra, five symphonies. *Address:* Thea Dispeker Artist Representative, 59 E 54th Street, New York, NY 10022, USA (office); c/o State Philharmonia, Mashtotsi Prospekt 46, Yerevan, Armenia (office); 347 W 57th Street, Apt 37C, New York, NY 10019, USA (home). *Telephone:* (212) 421-7676 (office).

TKACHENKO, Oleksander Mikolayevich, CandTechSc; Ukrainian politician; b. 7 March 1939, Shpola, Cherkassy Region; m. Larissa Mitrofanivna Tkachenko; one d.; ed Belotsekivski Agric. Inst., Higher Party School, CPSU Cen. Cttee; worked as First Sec., Tarashansk Comsomol Cttee 1966–70, then Ukrainian CP functionary in agric. sector 1970–82; State Minister, Head Cttee on Agric. Policy and Food Ukrainian SSR 1985–91; Head, Agric. Asscn Zemlya i Lyudi 1992–94; leader Ukrainian Farmers' Party; mem. Verkhovna Rada (Parl.) 1994–; First Vice-Chair. Verkhovna Rada 1994–98, Chair. (Speaker) 1998–99, Pres. Cand. 1991. *Address:* Verkhovna Rada, M. Hrushevskoga str. 5, 252008 Kiev, Ukraine. *Telephone:* (381) 226-28-25 (office).

TKESHELASHVILI, Davit, LLM; Georgian politician; *Minister of Regional Development and Infrastructure;* b. 16 Oct. 1969, Tbilisi; m.; one c.; ed Tbilisi State Univ., Emory Univ., USA; mil. service 1987–89; Head of Regional Dept of the Citizens' Union's Youth Arm 1993–95, also Political Sec. and Deputy Chair., Press Sec. 1994–95, Chair. Youth Arm of Citizens' Union 1998–2002; elected to Parl. 1995, served as Deputy Majority Leader (re-elected 1999, (for Nat. Movt-Democrats) 2004), Chair. Sub-cttee for Relations with the Media and Non-governmental orgs of the Human Rights Cttee 1999–2003; Minister of Environmental Protection and Natural Resources 2006–07, of Health, Labour and Social Welfare 2007–08, of Regional Devt and Infrastructure 2008–; Edmund Muskie Scholarship 2005. *Address:* Ministry of Regional Development and Infrastructure, Tbilisi, Al. Kazbegi av. 12, Georgia (office). *Telephone:* (32) 37-05-08 (office).

TKESHELASHVILI, Ekaterine (Eka), LLM; Georgian lawyer and government official; *Secretary, National Security Council;* b. 23 May 1977, Tbilisi; m.; four c.; ed Tbilisi State Univ., Univ. of Notre Dame, USA; field officer, Int. Cttee of Red Cross 1998–2000; intern, Appeals Office, Int. Tribunal of fmr Yugoslavia 2001–02; lawyer and Dir Institutional Reform and Non-governmental Sector, IRIS Georgia 2002–04; Deputy Minister of Justice 2004–05; Deputy Minister of Internal Affairs 2005–06; Chair. Tbilisi Court of Appeals 2006–07; Minister of Justice 2007; Gen. Prosecutor Jan.-May 2008; Minister of Foreign Affairs May–Dec. 2008; Sec. Nat. Security Council 2009–. *Address:* National Security Council of Georgia, 0134 Tbilisi, Ingorokva str.7, Georgia (office). *Telephone:* (32) 28-77-11 (office).

TLASS, Lt-Gen. Mustafa el; Syrian politician and army officer; b. 11 May 1932, Rastan City, Mouhafazat, Homs; m. Lamyaa al-Jabri 1958; two s. two d.; ed Mil. and Law Colls. and Voroshilov Acad., Moscow; active mem. Baath Arab Socialist Party 1947–, Sec. of Rastan Section 1951; Sports teacher, Al-Kraya School, Mouhafazat al-Soueda 1950–52; attended Mil. Coll. 1952–54; seconded to Egyptian army 1959–61; Insp. Ministry of Supply 1962; mem. Free Officers' Movement 1962–63, detained 1962–63; Commdr Tank Bn and Chief of Cen. Region of Nat. Security Court 1963; Chief of Staff, 5th Armoured Brigade 1964–66; mem. Regional Command, Regional Congress of Baath Arab Socialist Party 1965, 1968, 1969, 1975, of Politbureau 1969–, of Nat. Council of Revolution 1965–71; participated in movt of 23 Feb., promoted to Commdr of Cen. Region and of 5th Armoured Brigade; rank of Maj.-Gen. 1968, Chief of Staff of Armed Forces 1968–70, First Deputy Minister of Defence 1968–72; participated in coup installing Pres. Hafez Al-Assad Nov. 1970; First Deputy C-in-C Armed Forces 1970–72, Deputy C-in-C 1972; mem. People's Council 1971–; Minister of Defence 1972–2004, also Deputy Prime Minister; Deputy Chief of Jt Supreme Mil. Council of Syrian and Egyptian Armed Forces 1973; rank of Lt-Gen. 1978; 33 orders and medals. *Publications include:* Guerilla War, Military Studies, An Introduction to Zionist Strategy, The Arab Prophet and Technique of War, The Armoured Brigade as an Advanced Guard, Bitter Memories in the Military Prison of Mezzah, The Fourth War between Arabs and Israel, The Second Chapter of the October Liberation War, Selections of Arab Poetry, The Steadfastness Front in Confrontation with Camp David, The Algerian Revolution, Art of Soviet War, American Policy under the Carter Regime, The Technological Revolution and Development of the Armed Forces. *Leisure interests:* reading and writing books, military and historical studies, photography. *Address:* c/o Ministry of Defence, Place Omayad, Damascus, Syria.

TLOU, Thomas, MA, PhD, MAT; Botswana historian, academic and diplomatist; *Chairman, Botswana Institute of Development Policy Analysis;* b. 1 June 1932, Gwanda, Southern Rhodesia (now Zimbabwe); s. of Malapela Tlou and Moloko Nare; m. Sheila Dinotshe 1977; two s. one d.; ed schools in Rhodesia, Luther Coll., Decorah, Iowa, Johns Hopkins Univ., Baltimore and Univ. of Wisconsin; primary school teacher, Rhodesia 1957–62; Lecturer in History, Luther Coll. 1969, Univ. of Wis. 1970–71; Lecturer in History, Univ. of Botswana, Lesotho and Swaziland (UBLS) 1971, later Prof., Dean of Faculty of Humanities and Head of History; mem. Bd Nat. Museum and Art Gallery of Botswana 1974–76, 1981–; mem. Univ. Senate and Council of UBLS 1974–76; Acting Dir Nat. Research Inst. 1976; Perm. Rep. to UN 1977–80; Deputy Vice-Chancellor Univ. of Botswana 1980, Vice-Chancellor 1984–98, mem. Senate and Council of Univ. of Botswana and Swaziland (now Univ. of Botswana) 1980–, mem. Nat. Archives Advisory Council, mem. Univ. of Botswana Review Comm.; mem. Pres.'s Comm. on Incomes Policy 1989–90; mem. Namibian Pres. Comm. on Higher Educ. 1991, Univ. of Botswana Review Comm. 1990, UNESCO Bd 1992–95; Chair. SADCC Consultancy on Human Resources Devt 1991, Asscn of Eastern and Southern African Univs 1992–93; Vice-Chair. Asscn of Commonwealth Univs 1993, Chair. 1994; mem. Bd Botswana Tech. Centre; mem. Nat. Employment, Manpower and Incomes Council; Chair. Asscn of Eastern and Southern Africa Univs; mem. Exec. Bd Asscn of African Univs 1993–96, Botswana Inst. of Devt Policy Analysis (Chair. 1999–), Botswana Nat. Council on Educ. (Chair. 1999–2003); mem. Council, Univ. of Swaziland 1993–95; mem. American-African Studies Asscn; Life mem. Botswana Soc.; mem. Bd Lutheran World Fed. (LWF) 1998–2002; mem. LWF Study Group on African Religion 1998–2000; Chair. Tertiary Educ. Council 2002–; mem. Evangelical Lutheran Church 2003–; Chevalier des Palmes académiques 1982, Presidential Order of Honour 1994; Hon. DLitt (Luther Coll.) 1978, Hon. LLD (Ohio) 1986. *Publications:* History of Botswana (co-author) 1984, A History of Ngamiland 1750–1906: The Formation of an African State 1985, Biography of Seretse Khama 1995; and several articles and book chapters on history of Botswana and Ngamiland. *Leisure interest:* swimming, reading, walking. *Address:* PO Box 1004, Gaborone, Botswana. *Telephone:* 3927645 (office); 3927645 (home). *Fax:* 3185098. *E-mail:* tlout@mopipi.ub.bw (office).

TLUSTÝ, Vlastimil; Czech politician; b. 19 Sept. 1955; early career as Researcher, Agricultural Machinery Research Inst.; Asst Lecturer, Agricultural Univ. of Prague 1990; mem. Parl. 1991–, mem. Civic Democratic Party (Občanská demokratická strana—ODS), Deputy Chair., Chair. ODS Parl. Club, Vice Chair. Finance Cttee; Chair. Supervisory Bd ČKA (Czech Consolidation Agency) –2006; Minister of Finance June–Oct. 2006 (resgnd); fmr Chair. Union of Land Owners and Pvt. Farmers of Czech Repub. *Address:* c/o Ministry of Finance, Letenská 15, 118 00 Prague 1, Czech Republic (office).

TOAFA, Maatia; Tuvaluan politician; Deputy Prime Minister of Tuvalu, Minister for Works, Communications and Transport –2004; acting Prime Minister Aug.–Oct. 2004, Prime Minister and Minister of Foreign Affairs and Labour, Oct. 2004–06. *Address:* c/o Office of the Prime Minister, Private Mail Bag, Vaiaku, Funafuti, Tuvalu (office).

TOAN, Barrett A., MA; American business executive; b. 1947, Briarcliff Manor, NY; m. Polly Toan; one d. one s.; ed Kenyan Coll., Wharton School, Univ. of Pa; began career in Bureau of the Budget, Office of the Gov. of Ill.; fmr consultant to state and local govts Price Waterhouse & Co., Washington, DC; budgetary adviser to Ark. Attorney-Gen. Bill Clinton, 1979; Commr Ark. Div. of Social Services 1980–81; Dir Mo. Dept of Social Services 1982; Exec. Dir and COO Sanus Corp. Health Systems Inc. (renamed GenCare) 1985–1991; joined Express Scripts Inc. (pharmacy benefit man. co.) 1992, mem. Bd of Dirs 1992–, Pres. and CEO –2000, Chair., Pres. and CEO 2000–05, Chair. 2005–06 (retd); mem. Bd of Dirs US Cellular, Olin School of Business, Mo. Historical Soc., Mentor St Louis, Kenyon Coll.; mem. Investors Council and Leadership Circle, Regional Chamber and Growth Asscn. *Leisure interests:* history, literature. *Address:* c/o Express Scripts Inc., 13900 Riverport Drive, Maryland Heights, MO 63043, USA (office).

TOAN, Tran Trong, MA; Vietnamese diplomatist and international organization official; *Vice-Chairman, Committee for Overseas Vietnamese, Ministry of Foreign Affairs;* b. 12 Oct. 1952, Ha Tay Prov.; s. of Tran Trong An and Pham Thi Lan; m. Le Thi Lai; two d.; ed Oriental Faculty, Tashkent State Univ., Uzbekistan; official, S Asia Dept, Ministry of Foreign Affairs 1975–80, Embassy of Viet Nam, New Delhi 1980–83, Foreign Ministry's Secr. and Asst Dir Foreign Ministry's Secr. 1984–89, Acting Dir-Gen. S Asia Dept 1990–92, Minister Counsellor, New Delhi 1992–95, Dir-Gen. Dept of Econ. Affairs 1996–2000, Vice-Chair. Viet Nam Nat. Cttee for the Pacific Econ. Cooperation Council 1996–2000, 2004–05, Viet Nam Sr Official to APEC Secr. 1999; Amb. to Viet Nam, to Malaysia 2000–03, Dir-Gen. Foreign Minister's Advisory Bd, then Dir-Gen. Dept of Multilateral Econ. Cooperation, Ministry of Foreign Affairs 2003–04, mem. Govt Negotiation Team for Int. Econ. Integration, Amb. and Deputy Exec. Dir APEC Secr. 2005, Amb. and Exec. Dir 2006; currently Standing Vice-Chair. Cttee for Overseas Vietnamese, Ministry of Foreign Affairs. *Publications:* several books and a series of articles, including The Asia-Pacific Economic Cooperation Forum (APEC) (author and Chief Ed.) 1998, Globalization and Vietnam's International Economic Integration (author and Chief Ed.) 1999, APEC Glossaries 2006. *Leisure interests:* volleyball, badminton, table tennis. *Address:* No. 32 Ba Trieu Str., Ha Noi, Viet Nam (office). *Telephone:* 4.8 261 602 (office). *Fax:* 4.8 259 211 (office). *E-mail:* kt.toantt@mofa.gov.vn (office).

TOBEN, Doreen A., AB, MBA; American telecommunications industry executive; *Executive Vice-President, Verizon Communications Inc.;* b. 1949, Curaçao, Netherlands Antilles; m. Ed Toben; two c.; ed Rosemont Coll. and Fairleigh Dickinson Univ.; raised in Harding Township, NJ; began career at AT&T in Treasury, later named Dir of Corp. Planning; joined Bell Atlantic, Pa 1986, held several leadership positions in equipment eng, operations, and small business and consumer market man., Asst Vice-Pres.-Comptroller Bell Atlantic-New Jersey 1992–93, Chief Financial Officer 1993, Vice-Pres. Corp. Finance, Bell Atlantic Inc. –1995, Vice-Pres. Finance and Controller 1995–97, Vice-Pres. and Chief Financial Officer Telecom/Network 1997–99, Vice-Pres. and Controller Verizon Communications (formed by merger of Bell Atlantic and GTE) 1999–2000, Sr Vice-Pres. and Chief Financial Officer, Domestic Telecom Group 2000–02, Exec. Vice-Pres. and Chief Financial Officer Verizon Communications Inc. 2002–07, Exec. Vice-Pres. 2007–; mem. Nat. Advisory Bd J.P. Morgan Chase & Co. 2003–, Bd of Dirs The New York Times Co. 2004–, Citymeals-on-Wheels 2004–, Lincoln Center 2004–, Verizon Wireless; ranked by Fortune magazine amongst 50 Most Powerful Women in Business in the US (25th) 2002, (17th) 2003, (17th) 2004, (32nd) 2005, (36th) 2006. *Address:* Verizon Communications Inc., 1095 Avenue of the Americas, New York, NY 10036, USA (office). *Telephone:* (212) 395-2121 (office). *Fax:* (212) 869-3265 (office). *Website:* www.verizon.com (office).

TOBGYE, Lyonpo Sonam; Bhutanese judge; currently Chief Justice, High Court; Chair. Nat. Judicial Comm. 2003–. *Address:* High Court (Thrimkhang Gongma), Thimphu, Bhutan (office). *Telephone:* 322344 (office). *Fax:* 322921 (office). *E-mail:* judiciary@druknet.bt (office). *Website:* www.judiciary.gov.bt (office).

TOBIA, Maguid, BSc; Egyptian writer; b. 25 March 1938, Minia; teacher of math. 1960–68; mem. Higher Council of Arts and Literature 1969–78; mem. staff Ministry of Culture 1978–; mem. Writers' Union, Chamber of Cinema Industry, Soc. of Egyptian Film Critics, Fiction Cttee of Supreme Council of Culture; Medal of Science and Arts (First Class); several literary prizes. *Film scripts include:* Story of Our Country 1967, Sons of Silence 1974, Stars' Maker 1978, Harem Cage 1981. *Play:* International Laugh Bank 2001. *Television:* Friendly Visit (series) 1980. *Publications:* (collections of short stories): Vostock Reaches the Moon 1967, Five Unread Papers 1970, The Coming Days 1972, The Companion 1978, The Accident Which Happens 1987, 23 Short Stories 2001; (novels): Circles of Impossibility 1972, The They 1973, Sons of Silence 1974, The Strange Deeds of Kings and the Intrigues of Banks 1976, The Room of Floor Chances 1978, The Music Kiosk 1980, Hanan 1981, West Virgin 1986, The Emigration to the North Country of Hathoot's Tribe (3 vols: To the North Country 1987, To the South Country 1992, To the Lakes Country 2005), The Story of Beautiful Reem 1991, The Great History of Donkeys 1996, Amosis Case 2005; contribs to Al Ahram and several Arabic magazines. *Leisure interests:* reading, travel. *Address:* 15 El-Lewaa Abd El Aziz Aly, Heliopolis 11361, Cairo, Egypt. *Telephone:* 2917801. *Fax:* 2917801.

TOBIAS, Phillip Vallentine, PhD, DSc, MBBCh, FRS, FRCP, FLS; South African professor of anatomy and anthropologist; *Professor Emeritus and Honorary Professorial Research Fellow, University of the Witwatersrand;* b. 14 Oct. 1925, Durban; s. of the late Joseph Newman Tobias and Fanny Rosendorff; ed St Andrew's School, Bloemfontein, Durban High School, Univ. of the Witwatersrand, Emmanuel Coll., Cambridge, UK; Lecturer in Anatomy, Univ. of Witwatersrand 1951–52, Sr Lecturer 1953–58, Dir Palaeo-anthropology Research Unit 1966–96, Prof. and Head of Anatomy Dept 1959–90, Dean of Faculty of Medicine 1980–82, Hon. Professorial Research Fellow 1994–, Prof. Emer. 1994–, fmr Dir Sterkfontein Research Unit, now Hon. mem. of staff; fmr Visiting or Hon. Prof. Univs of Cambridge, Pennsylvania, Cornell, Vienna, Palma de Mallorca, Florence, Nanjing Normal, IVPP, Acad. Sinica, Beijing; Founder-Pres. Inst. for the Study of Mankind in Africa, Anatomical Soc. of Southern Africa, S African Soc. for Quaternary Research; Hon. mem. and mem. numerous int. asscns; Foreign Assoc. NAS; sometime Vice-Pres. and acting Exec. Pres. S African Asscn for the Advancement of Science; Pres. Royal Soc. of S Africa 1970–72. Int. Asscn of Human Biologists 1994–98; Perm. Council mem. Int. Union of Prehistoric and Protohistoric Sciences, Pan-African Congress of Prehistory and Quaternary Studies, Int. Asscn of Human Biologists; Trustee, Leakey Foundation, Pasadena, Calif.; Vice-Pres. World Cultural Council 2001–04; Hon. Prof. of Palaeo-anthropology, Bernard Price Inst. for Palaeontological Research; Hon. Prof. of Zoology; Hon. Corresp. mem., Austrian Acad. of Sciences 1978; Hon. Fellow, Royal Anthropological Inst. of Great Britain and Ireland, Coll. of Medicine of S Africa, American Philosophical Soc.; Hon. FRSSA; Foreign Hon. mem. American Acad. of Arts and Sciences 1986–; Order for Meritorious Service (Gold Class) (S Africa) 1992, Commdr, Ordre nat. du Mérite 1998, Order of Southern Cross, Silver Class (S Africa) 1999, Commdr, Order of Merit (Italy) 2000, Hon. Cross for Science and Arts (First Class) (Austria) 2002, Commander of Order of St John; Hon. DSc (Natal) 1980, (Cambridge) 1988, (Univ. of Western Ont.) 1986, (Alberta) 1987, (Cape Town) 1988, (Guelph) 1990, (Univ. S Africa) 1990, (Durban-Westville) 1993, (Pennsylvania) 1994, (Witwatersrand) 1994, (Musée Nat. d'Histoire Naturelle, Paris) 1996, (Barcelona) 1997, (Turin) 1998, (Charles Univ., Prague) 1999, (Stellenbosch) 1999, (Transkei) 2003, (Fribourg) 2003; British Asscn Medal 1952, Simon Biesheuvel Medal 1966, South Africa Medal 1967, Sr Captain Scott Medal 1973, Rivers Memorial Medal 1978, Anisfield-Wolf Award for Race Relations 1978, Rotary Int. Paul Harris Award 1981, 1991, Percy Fox Foundation Award 1983, Phillip Tobias Medal 1983, Certificate of Honour, Univ. of Calif. 1983, Balzan Prize 1987, John F.W. Herschel Medal 1990, Silver Medal, Medical Asscn of S Africa 1990, 1st John Grant Distinguished Lecturer Award, Univ. of Toronto 1991, 1st L.S.B. Leakey Prize 1991, Carmel Merit Award (Haifa) 1992, Huxley Memorial Medal of Royal Anthropological Inst. 1996, Wood Jones Medal of the Royal Coll. of Surgeons 1997, Charles R. Darwin Lifetime Achievement Award, American Asscn of Physical Anthropologists 1997, Gold Medal, Charles Univ. 1999, Hrdlicka Memorial Medal 1999, Gold Medal of Simon van der Stel Foundation (S Africa) 1999, Plaque of Honour, Univ. of S Amaro, São Paulo 2001, UNESCO Medal 2001, Medal of Honour, Univ. of Cagliari 2001, Siriraj Foundation Sangvichien Medal, Thailand 2002, Nat. Treasure of South Africa 2003, Walter Sisulu Award 2006. *Television:* Tobias's Bodies (Idée Suisse Prize 2003) documentary series. *Achievements:* only person at Witwatersrand Univ. to hold three chairs simultaneously (anatomy, palaeoanthropology, zoology). *Publications:* Chromosomes, Sex-cells and Evolution 1956, Olduvai Gorge Vol. II 1967, Man's Anatomy (with M. Arnold) 1963, The Brain in Hominid Evolution 1971, The Meaning of Race 1972, The Bushmen 1978, Dart, Taung and the Missing Link 1984, Hominid Evolution: Past, Present and Future 1985, Olduvai Gorge Vol. IV *A* and *B* 1991, Images of Humanity 1991, Paleo-antropologia 1992, Il Bipede Barcollante 1992, The Origins and Past of Modern Humans 1998, Humanity from African Naissance to Coming Millennia 2001; more than 1,100 scientific and other publs. *Leisure interests:* people, books, music, philately, art, writing. *Address:* School of Anatomical Sciences, University of the Witwatersrand Medical School, 7 York Road, Parktown, Johannesburg 2193 (office); 409 Summerhill, Sally's Alley, Kentview, Johannesburg 2196, South Africa (home). *Telephone:* (11) 7172516 (office); (11) 8852748 (home). *Fax:* (11) 7172773 (office). *E-mail:* phillip.tobias@wits.ac.za (office). *Website:* web.wits.ac.za/Academic/Health/AnatomicalSciences/Staff/PhillipTobias.htm (office).

TOBIAS, Randall L., BS; American business executive and government official; b. 20 March 1942, Lafayette, Ind.; m. 1st Marilyn Jane Salyer 1966 (died 1994); one s. one d.; m. 2nd Marianne Williams 1995; one step-s. one step-d.; ed Indiana Univ.; served US Army 1964–66; numerous positions Ind. Bell 1964–81, Ill. Bell 1977–81; Vice-Pres. (residence marketing, sales and service) AT & T 1981–82; Pres. American Bell Consumer Products 1983–84, Sr Vice-Pres. 1984–85, Chair. and CEO AT & T Communications, New York 1985–91, AT & T Int., Basking Ridge, NJ 1991–93, Vice-Chair. Bd AT & T, New York and Chair. Bd of Dirs 1986–93; Chair., Pres. and CEO Eli Lilly & Co., Indianapolis 1993–98, Chair. Emer. 1999–; Amb. and Coordinator US Govt Activities to Combat HIV/AIDS Globally 2003–06; Dir of Foreign Assistance and Admin., Agency for Int. Devt 2006–07; fmr mem. Bd of Dirs Eli Lilly & Co., Kimberly-Clark, Knight-Ridder, Phillips Petroleum; fmr Chair. Bd of Trustees Duke Univ.; fmr Vice-Chair. Colonial Williamsburg Foundation; mem. Council on Foreign Relations, numerous other appointments; Dr hc (Indiana Univ.), (Wabash Coll.), (Butler Univ.), (Gallaudet Univ.), (Ball State Univ.); Hon. Dr of Eng (Rose-Hulman Inst. of Tech.) Pharmaceutical Industry CEO of the Year 1995, CEO of the Year by Working Mother magazine 1996, one of Top Twenty-Five Mans of the Year by Business Week Magazine 1997, Norman Vincent Peale Humanitarian of the Year 1997, Indiana Univ.-Purdue Univ.-Indianapolis (IUPUI) Urban Univ. Medal. *Publications:* Put The Moose On The Table (with Todd Tobias) 2003. *Leisure interests:* skiing, shooting. *Address:* c/o Department of State, 2201 C Street, NW, Washington, DC 20520, USA (office).

TOBIN, Brian V., PC; Canadian politician; *Senior Business Advisor, Fraser Milner Casgrain LLP;* b. 21 Oct. 1954, Stephenville, Newfoundland; s. of Patrick Tobin and Mary Frye; m. Jodean Smith 1977; two s. one d.; ed Memorial Univ., St. John's, Newfoundland; worked as a journalist; MP for Humber-St Barbe-Baie Verte 1980–96; MP for Bonavista-Trinity-Conception 2000–02, Parl. Sec. to Minister of Fisheries and Oceans 1980; Minister of Fisheries and Oceans 1993; Premier of Newfoundland 1996–2000; Minister of Industry and Minister responsible for the Atlantic Canada Opportunities Agency and for Western Econ. Diversification and Francophonie and for the Econ. Devt Agency of Canada for the Regions of Québec 2000–02; currently Sr Business Advisor, Fraser Milner Casgrain LLP, Toronto; Sr Fellow, Fraser Inst. 2006–; Chair. Nat. Liberal Caucus 1989; mem. numerous House of Commons Cttees; Chair. New Flyer Industries; Vice-Chair. Consolidated Thompson Iron Mines; mem. Bd of Dirs Lions Gate Entertainment, Aecon Group Inc., Sonnen Energy Group, Canpages; Special Adviser, Canadian Youth Business Foundation. *Address:* Fraser Milner Casgrain LLP, 1 First Canadian Place, 39th Floor, 100 King Street West, Toronto, ON M5X 1B2, Canada (office). *Telephone:* (416) 863-4511 (office). *Fax:* (416) 863-4592 (office). *Website:* www.fmc-law.com (office).

TODD, Damian Roderic (Ric), BA; British diplomatist; *Ambassador to Poland;* b. 29 Aug. 1959, Crawley, Surrey; s. of George Todd and Annette Todd; m. Alison Todd; one s. two d.; ed Worcester Coll., Oxford; FCO 1980–81, Third then Second Sec., Cape Town and Pretoria 1981–84, EC Dept, FCO 1984–87, First Sec. and Consul, Prague 1987–89, Econ. Relations Dept 1989–91, First Sec. (Econ.), Embassy in Bonn 1991–95; seconded to HM Treasury, London 1995–97; Head, Agricultural Team 1996–97; Head, EU Coordination and Strategy Team 1998–2001; Amb. to Slovakia 2001–04, to Poland 2007–; Finance Dir FCO 2004–07; Head, Agric. Spending Team, HM Treasury 1995–97,. *Leisure interests:* history, family life, looking at buildings. *Address:* British Embassy, Aleje Róż 1, Warsaw 00-556, Poland (office). *Telephone:* (22) 3110000 (office). *Fax:* (22) 3110311 (office). *E-mail:* info@britishembassy.pl (office). *Website:* www.britishembassy.pl (office).

TODD, Sir David, Kt, CBE, MD, FAM, FRCP, FRCPE, FRCPGlas, FRACP, FRCPath; British professor of medicine; *Professor Emeritus, University of Hong Kong;* b. 17 Nov. 1928, China; s. of Paul J. Todd and Margaret S. Todd; ed Univ. of Hong Kong; Prof. Dept of Medicine, Univ. of Hong Kong 1972–96, Head, Dept of Medicine 1974–89, Sub-Dean, Faculty of Medicine 1976–78, Pro-Vice-Chancellor 1978–80, now Prof. Emer.; consultant (medicine) to Govt of Hong Kong 1974–89; Pres. Hong Kong Acad. of Medicine 1992–96, Council for AIDS Trust Fund, Hong Kong 1993–96; Hon. Mem. Chinese Medical Asscn 1995; Hon. DSc (Chinese Univ. of Hong Kong) 1990, (Hong Kong Univ.) 1992, Hon. LLD (Lingnan Univ. Hong Kong). *Publications:* numerous articles in professional journals. *Leisure interests:* classical music, stamp collecting, swimming. *Address:* D12 Breezy Court, 2A Park Road, Mid-levels, Hong Kong Special Administrative Region, People's Republic of China (home). *E-mail:* dtodd@hkucc.hku.hk (office).

TODD, Olivier René Louis, LèsL, MA; French writer; b. 19 June 1929, Neuilly; s. of Julius Oblatt and Helen Todd; m. 1st Anne-Marie Nizan 1948; m. 2nd France Huser 1982; two s. two d.; ed Sorbonne, Corpus Christi Coll., Cambridge; teacher, Lycée Int. du Shape 1956–62; Univ. Asst, St-Cloud 1962–64; reporter, Nouvel Observateur 1964–69; Ed. TV Programme Panorama 1969–70; Asst Ed. Nouvel Observateur 1970–77; columnist and Man. Ed. L'Express 1977–81; worked for BBC (Europa, 24 Hours) and ORTF 1964–69; Chevalier, Légion d'honneur, Commdr, Ordre des Arts et des Lettres; Hon. PhD (Stirling, Bristol), Hon. DLitt (Edinburgh) 2005; Prix Cazes 1981, Prix France Télévision 1997, Prix du Mémorial 1997. *Publications:* Une demi-campagne 1957, La traversée de la Manche 1960, Des trous dans le jardin 1969, L'année du Crabe 1972, Les canards de Ca Mao 1975, La marelle de Giscard 1977, Portraits 1979, Un fils rebelle 1981, Un cannibale très convenable 1982, Une légère gueule de bois 1983, La balade du chômeur 1986, Cruel Avril 1987, La négociation 1989, La Sanglière 1992, Albert Camus, une vie 1996, André Malraux, une vie 2001, Catre d'identités, souvenirs 2005. *Leisure interests:* walking, Luxembourg Gardens. *Address:* 21 rue de l'Odéon, 75006 Paris (home); 8 rue du Pin, 83310 La Garde Freinet, France. *Telephone:* 1-43-29-55-26 (home).

TODD, Richard Andrew Palethorpe, OBE; British actor, producer and author; b. 11 June 1919, Dublin, Ireland; s. of Major A. W. Palethorpe Todd and Marvilla Palethorpe Todd (née Agar-Daly); m. 1st Catherine Stewart Crawford Grant-Bogle 1949 (divorced 1970); one s. one d.; m. 2nd Virginia Anne Rollo Mailer 1970 (divorced 1992); two s. (one deceased); ed Shrewsbury, privately; began theatrical career, London 1937; Founder-mem. Dundee Repertory Co. 1938–39, rejoined 1947; served in King's Own Yorkshire Light Infantry and Parachute Regt 1940–46; entered film industry in For Them That Trespass 1948; returned to London stage as Lord Goring (An Ideal Husband) 1965, Nicholas Randolph (Dear Octopus), Haymarket 1967; formed Triumph Theatre Production 1970, appeared in numerous productions in Britain, as the Comte (The Marquise), USA 1972, as Andrew Wyke (Sleuth), Australia and NZ 1972–73, English tour 1976, RSC productions of The Hollow Crown and Pleasure and Repentance, Canada and USA 1974, as Martin Dysart (Equus) for Australian Nat. Theatre Co., Perth Festival 1975, toured as John (Miss Adams Will Be Waiting) 1975, toured SA in On Approval 1976, in Quadrille 1977, The Heat of the Moment 1977, appeared in Double Edge in UK and Canada 1978, in Nightfall, South Africa 1979, in This Happy Breed, UK 1980; The Business of Murder (Duchess Theatre 1981, Mayfair Theatre 1981–88), The Woman in Black (Sydney Opera House) 1991; as Lord Caversham (An Ideal Husband), Old Vic 1996, Albery Theatre, Theatre Royal

Haymarket 1998, Lyric Theatre 1999; Past Grand Steward, Grand Lodge of England, Past Master Lodge of Emulation No. 21; Pres. Birmingham Age Concern 1990–; British Nat. Film Award, Picturegoer Award, Hollywood Golden Globe. *Other films include:* Good Morning, Boys (uncredited) 1937, The Interrupted Journey 1949, For Them That Trespass 1949, The Hasty Heart 1949, Flesh and Blood 1950, Stage Fright 1950, Portrait of Clare 1950, Lightning Strikes Twice (USA) 1951, 24 Hours of a Woman's Life, The Story of Robin Hood and His Merrie Men 1952, Venetian Bird 1953, The Sword and the Rose 1953, The Dam Busters 1954, Rob Roy, the Highland Rogue 1954, Secrets d'alcove 1954, A Man Called Peter 1955, The Virgin Queen (USA) 1955, Marie-Antoinette reine de France 1956, D-Day the Sixth of June 1956, Chase a Crooked Shadow 1957, Saint Joan 1957, Yangtse Incident: The Story of H.M.S. Amethyst 1957, The Naked Earth 1958, Intent to Kill 1958, Danger Within 1959, The Long and the Short and the Tall 1960, Don't Bother to Knock (for own film co. Haileywood Films Ltd) 1960, Never Let Go 1960, The Hellions 1961, The Very Edge 1962, Le crime ne paie pas 1962, The Longest Day 1962, The Boys 1962, Death Drums Along the River (aka Sanders, USA) 1963, Coast of Skeletons 1964, Operation Crossbow 1965, The Battle of the Villa Fiorita 1965, Blood Bath (uncredited) 1966, The Love-Ins 1967, Last of the Long-Haired Boys 1968, Subterfuge 1969, Dorian Gray 1970, Asylum 1972, Secret Agent 008 1976, No. 1 of the Secret Service 1977, The Big Sleep 1978, Home Before Midnight 1979, Las flores del vicio (aka Bloodbath, USA) 1979, House of the Long Shadows 1983, Murder One 1988, The Olympus Force 1988. *Television includes:* Wuthering Heights (mini-series) 1953, Edmund Gurney and the Brighton Mesmerist 1967, The Next Scream You Hear 1974, Boy Dominic (series) 1974, Dominic (mini-series) 1976, The Last Place on Earth (mini-series) 1985, Jenny's War 1985, Incident at Victoria Falls 1991, Dr. Who, Virtual Murder, as H.G. Wells in Beautiful Lies, Carrington V.C., Silent Witness, Murder She Wrote, Midsomer Murders 2002, The Royal, Holby City, Songs of Praise 2005, Heartbeat 2006. *Publications:* Caught in the Act (Vol. I of autobiography) 1986, In Camera (Vol. II of autobiography) 1989. *Leisure interests:* game shooting, fishing, gardening. *Address:* Chinham Farm, Faringdon, Oxon., SN7 8EZ (home); c/o Richard Stone Partnership, 2 Henrietta Street, London, WC2E 8PS, England (office). *Telephone:* (20) 7497-0849 (office). *Fax:* (20) 7497-0869 (office). *E-mail:* rap.todd@btinternet.com (home).

TODMAN, Michael, BSBA; American business executive; *President, Whirlpool North America;* b. St Thomas, US Virgin Islands; ed Georgetown Univ.; various man. roles with Wang Laboratories Inc. and Price Waterhouse & Co. –1993; Finance Dir Whirlpool UK 1993, later Gen. Man. N Europe and Vice-Pres. Consumer Services, Whirlpool Europe, Controller N America 1995, Vice-Pres. Product Man. 1996, Vice-Pres. Sears Sales and Marketing 1997, Sr Vice-Pres. Sales and Marketing, N America 1999, Exec. Vice-Pres. N America, also mem. Exec. Cttee Whirlpool Corpn 2001, Exec. Vice-Pres. and Pres. Whirlpool Europe 2001, Pres. Whirlpool International 2005, mem. Bd of Dirs Whirlpool Corpn 2006–, Pres. Whirlpool N America 2007–. *Address:* Whirlpool Corporation, 2000 North M-63 States, Benton Harbor, MI 49022-2692, USA (office). *Telephone:* (269) 923-5000 (office). *Fax:* (269) 923-3722 (office). *Website:* www.whirlpoolcorp.com (office).

TODORIĆ, Ivica, BEcons; Croatian business executive; *President, Agrokor Group;* b. 1951; m. Vesna Bašic; two s. one d.; ed Zagreb Univ.; f. Agrokor as private co. trading in flowers 1976 (jt stock co. from 1989), now Pres., Agrokor Group; founder and first Pres., Croatian Employers' Assen 1993. *Address:* Agrokor d.d., Trg D. Petrovića 3, 10000 Zagreb, Croatia (office). *Telephone:* (1) 4894000 (office). *Fax:* (1) 48444363 (office). *E-mail:* agrokor@agrokor.hr (office). *Website:* www.agrokor.hr (office).

TODOROVSKY, Piotr Yefimovich; Russian film director, cameraman and scriptwriter; b. 26 Aug. 1925; m. Myra Grigoryevna Todorovskaya; one s.; ed All-Union Inst. of Cinematography; started as cameraman at film studios of Kishinev (Moldovafilm) and Odessa in films Moldavian Tunes 1955, Spring in the Zarechnaya Street 1956, Two Fyodors 1958, Thirst 1960; debut as film Dir Never 1962; numerous prizes All-Union and Int. Festivals in Tokyo, Venice, Berlin, San Remo and others; Nica Prize 1992, State Prize 1995; People's Artist of Russia 1985. *Film productions include:* Faithfulness 1965 (Prize of Int. Festival in Venice), Juggler 1968, City Romance 1971, Our Own Land 1973, The Last Victim 1976, On Holiday 1979, The Beloved Woman of Mechanic Gavrilov 1982, Wartime Romance 1984, Intergirl 1988, Encore, Encore 1993, What a Wonderful Game 1995, Retro for Three Together 1998; frequently author of scripts and music for his own films. *Leisure interests:* composition and performance of guitar music. *Address:* Vernadskogo prospect 70A, Apt. 23, 117454 Moscow, Russia (home). *Telephone:* (495) 193-52-06 (home).

TODOROVSKY, Valery Petrovich; Russian film-maker; b. 8 May 1962, Odessa; s. of Piotr Yefimovich Todorovsky and Maiya Grigoriyevna Todorovskaya; ed All-Union Inst. of Cinematography; began career as scriptwriter; producer several TV series. *Films include:* A Man of the Retinue, Cynics, Live (UNICEF Prize, Chicago Film Festival), Moscow Nights (Green Apple Prize, Golden Leaf), Katafalk (dir) 1990, Lyubov (Love) (writer, dir) 1991, Otdushina (A Vent) (writer) 1991, Hearse (dir) (Mannheim Film Festival Prize 1991), Nad tyomnoy vodoy (Above Dark Water) 1993, Katya Ismailova (dir) 1994, Strana glukhikh (Country of the Deaf) (writer, dir) 1998, Lyubovnik (The Lover) (dir) 2002, Moy svodnyy brat Frankensteyn (My Step Brother Frankenstein) (dir) 2004. *Television includes:* Kamenskaya, Morskoy volk (The Sea Wolf) (writer) 1991. *Address:* Ramenki str. 11, korp. 2, Apt. 272, 117607 Moscow, Russia. *Telephone:* (495) 931-56-63.

TOELLE, Michael, BS; American business executive and farmer; *Chairman, CHS;* ed Minnesota State Univ., Moorhead; served on Bd of Country Pnrs Cooperative, Browns Valley, Minn. for 15 years, Chair. for 10 years; first elected to Bd of Dirs of CHS to represent Minnesota mems 1992, Chair. CHS 2002–, fmr mem. Finance and Investment Cttee CHS Cooperatives Foundation; actively involved in numerous agric. and commodity groups. *Address:* CHS, PO Box 64089, St Paul, MN 55164-0089 (office); CHS, 5500 Cenex Drive, Inver Grove Heights, MN 55077, USA (office). *Telephone:* (651) 355-6000 (office). *E-mail:* michael.toelle@chsinc.com (office). *Website:* www.chsinc.com (office).

TOENNIES, Jan Peter, PhD; German physicist and academic; *Director Emeritus, Max-Planck-Institut für Dynamik und Selbstorganization;* b. 3 May 1930, Philadelphia, Pa, USA; s. of Dr Gerrit Toennies and Dita Jebens; m. Monika Zelesnick 1966; two d.; ed Amherst Coll., Brown Univ.; Asst, Bonn Univ., FRG 1962–65, Privat Dozent 1965–67, Dozent 1967–69; Scientific mem. and Dir Max-Planck-Inst. für Strömungsforschung (now Max-Planck Inst. für Dynamik und Selbstorganisation) 1969–98, Acting Dir 1998–2002, now Dir Emer., Emer. Scientific Mem., Max-Planck-Soc. 2002–05, Admin. Dir 2001–02; Assoc. Prof., Dept of Physics, Göttingen Univ. 1971–; Visiting Miller Prof. of Chem. and Physics, Univ. of California, Berkeley 2005; Corresp. mem. Acad. of Sciences, Göttingen; mem. German Acad. of Natural Sciences 'Leopoldina'; Hon. Prof., Bonn Univ. 1971–; Hon. DPhil (Gothenburg) 2000; Hon. DSci (Amherst Coll.) 2007; Physics Prize, Göttingen Acad. of Sciences 1964, Gold Heyrovsky Medal of the Czechoslovak Acad. of Sciences 1991, Hewlett-Packard Europhysics Prize (for outstanding achievement in condensed matter research) 1991, Max Planck Prize, Alexander von Humboldt Foundation 1992, Stern-Gerlach Medal, German Physical Soc. 2002, Kotos Medal, Univ. of Warsaw 2005, Benjamin Franklin Medal for Physics (co-winner with Giacinto Scoles) 2006. *Publications:* Chemical Reactions in Shock Waves (with E. F. Greene) 1964, A Study of Intermolecular Potentials with Molecular Beams at Thermal Energies (with H. Pauly) in Advances in Atomic and Molecular Physics 1965, Molecular Beam Scattering Experiments, contribution in Physical Chemistry, An Advanced Treatise 1974, Rotationally and Vibrationally Inelastic Scattering of Molecules (Chem. Soc. Review) 1974, Scattering Studies of Rotational and Vibrational Excitation of Molecules (with M. Faubel) 1977, Advances in Atomic and Molecular Physics 1977, The Study of the Forces between Atoms of Single Crystal Surfaces 1988, Annual Review of Physical Chemistry, Serendipitous Meanderings and Adventures with Molecular Beams 2004, Angewaudte Chemie (Int. Ed.), Superfluid Helium Droplets: A Uniquely Cold Nanomatrix for Molecules and Molecular Complexes 2004; more than 600 publs in scientific journals. *Leisure interest:* sailing. *Address:* Max-Planck-Institut für Dynamik und Selbstorganisation, Bunsenstrasse 10, 37073 Göttingen (office); Ewaldstrasse 7, 37085 Göttingen, Germany (home). *Telephone:* (551) 5176600 (office); (551) 57172 (home). *Fax:* (551) 5176607 (office). *E-mail:* jtoenni@gwdg.de (office). *Website:* wwwuser.gwdg.de/~mpisfto (office).

TOEWS, Vic, BA; Canadian politician; *President of the Treasury Board;* b. 10 Sept. 1952, ; m. Lorraine; two c.; ed Univs of Winnipeg and Manitoba; Dir of Constitutional Law, Prov. of Manitoba 1987; apptd Queen's Counsel 1991; mem. Legis. Ass. for Rossmere 1995; fmr Minister of Labour; Attorney Gen. and Minister of Justice, Prov. of Manitoba 1997–99; mem. Parl. 2000–, fmr Vice-Chair. Subcttee on the Process for Appointment to the Judiciary, fmr mem. several subcttees including Nat. Security, Agenda and Procedure; Justice Critic 2001; Minister for Justice and Attorney Gen. 2006–07; Pres. of Treasury Bd 2007–. *Address:* Treasury Board, Corporate Communications, West Tower, 10th Floor, l'Esplanade Laurier, 300 Laurier Avenue West, Ottowa, ON K1A 0R5, Canada (office). *Telephone:* (613) 957-2400 (office). *Fax:* (613) 998-9071 (office). *E-mail:* info@tbs-sct.gc.ca (office). *Website:* www.tbs-sct.gc.ca (office); www.victoews.com.

TOH, Chin Chye, PhD; Singaporean politician and physiologist; b. 10 Dec. 1921, Malaya; s. of Toh Kim Poh and Tan Chuan Bee; m. Yeapp Sui Phek; one d.; ed Raffles Coll., Singapore, Univ. Coll., London Univ. and National Inst. for Medical Research, London; Founder, People's Action Party, Chair. 1954–; Reader in Physiology, Univ. of Singapore 1958–64; Research Assoc., Univ. of Singapore 1964; Deputy Prime Minister of Singapore 1959–68; Minister for Science and Tech. 1968–75, for Health 1975–81; MP Singapore 1959–88; Chair. Bd of Govs, Singapore Polytechnic 1959–75; Vice-Chancellor, Univ. of Singapore 1968–75; Chair. of Bd of Govs Regional Inst. for Higher Educ. and Devt 1970–75; Chair. Applied Research Corpn 1973–75; Hon. DLitt (Univ. of Singapore) 1976;Nila Utama, First Class 1990. *Leisure interests:* orchids, reading. *Address:* 23 Greenview Crescent, Singapore 289332, Singapore.

TOHÁ MORALES, Carolina Montserrat, PhD; Chilean government official; *Government Spokesperson;* b. 12 May 1965; d. of the late José Tohá (fmr Vice-Pres. of Chile under Salvador Allende); m. Fulvio Rossi; ed Universidad de Chile, Univ. of Milan, Italy; played role in re-establishment of Federación de Estudiantes de la Universidad de Chile (FECH) 1984, Vice-Pres. 1987; mem. Partido por la Democracia (PPD), Vice-Pres. 1999; worked on presidential campaign of Ricardo Lagos 1999; Under-Sec. to Govt Spokesperson 2000–06; mem. Nat. Congress (PPD) for Santiago 2001–09 (re-elected 2005), has served on Legis., Educ. and Security Cttees and on Special Cttee on the Freedom of Expression and the Media; apptd to Presidential Advisory Council on Educ. 2006; apptd Govt Spokesperson (first woman) 2009–. *Address:* Office of the Minister, Secretary-General of the Government, Palacio de la Moneda, Santiago, Chile (office). *Telephone:* (2) 690-4160 (office). *Fax:* (2) 697-1756 (office). *E-mail:* cmladini@segegob.cl (office). *Website:* www.segegob.cl (office).

TÓIBÍN, Colm; Irish journalist and writer; b. 1955, Enniscorthy, Co. Wexford; s. of Michéal Tóibín; ed Christian Brothers School, Enniscorthy, Univ. Coll., Dublin; in Spain 1975–78; Features Ed., In Dublin 1981–82; Ed. Magill (political and current affairs magazine) 1982–85; journalist and columnist, Dublin Sunday Independent 1985–; American Acad. of Arts and

Letters E. M. Forster Award 1995, Center for Scholars and Writers Fellowship, New York Public Library, Soc. of Authors Travelling Scholarship 2004. *Play:* Beauty in a Broken Place 2003. *Publications:* fiction: Infidelity (contrib.), The South (Irish Times First Novel Award 1991) 1990, The Heather Blazing (Encore Award) 1993, The Story of the Night 1996, The Blackwater Lightship 1999, Finbar's Hotel (contrib.) 1999, The Master (Int. IMPAC Dublin Literary Award 2006) 2004, Mothers and Sons 2006, Brooklyn 2009; non-fiction: Seeing is Believing: Moving Statues in Ireland 1985, Walking Along the Border (with T. O'Shea) 1987, Homage to Barcelona 1990, Dubliners 1990, The Trial of the Generals: Selected Journalism 1980–90 1990, Bad Blood 1994, Sign of the Cross 1994, The Kilfenora Teaboy 1997, The Irish Famine 1999, Love in a Dark Time 2001, Lady Gregory's Toothbrush 2002; editor: SOHO Square VI: New Writing from Ireland 1993, Enniscorthy: History & Heritage 1998, Penguin Book of Irish Fiction 1999, The Modern Library 1999, New Writing II 2002; contrib. articles. *Address:* c/o Rogers, Coleridge and White Ltd, 20 Powis Mews, London, W11 1JN, England (office). *Telephone:* (20) 7221-3717 (office). *Fax:* (20) 7229-9084 (office). *E-mail:* info@rcwlitagency.co.uk (office). *Website:* www.rcwlitagency.co.uk (office); www.colmtoibin.com.

TOIVO, Andimba Toivo ya; Namibian politician; b. 22 Aug. 1924, Omangundu, Ovamboland; s. of Andimba Toivo ya Toivo and Nashikoto Elizabeth; m. 2nd Vicki Lynn Erenstein 1990; three s. two d.; ed St Mary's Mission School, Odimbo; taught at St Mary's Mission School, Odimbo; served in SA Army 1942–43; worked in SA gold mines and on railways; mem. African National Congress and Modern Youth Soc.; deported to Ovamboland 1958; f. (with Sam Nujoma) SW African People's Org. (SWAPO), mem. Politburo –2007; arrested 1966; sentenced to 20 years' imprisonment, Robben Island 1968; released in Windhoek, Namibia 1984; mem. Politburo and Sec.-Gen. SWAPO 1984–91; Minister of Mines and Energy 1990–98, Minister of Labour 1999–2003; Minister of Prisons and Correctional Services 2003–06; Leader SWAPO del. to UN 1984. *Leisure interests:* volleyball, tennis, jogging, swimming and reading. *Address:* c/o SWAPO Party of Namibia (SWAPO), POB 1071, Windhoek, Namibia.

TOKAREVA, Victoria Samoilovna; Russian writer and screenwriter; b. 20 Nov. 1937, Leningrad; ed All-Union Inst. of Cinematography; literary debut 1969; freelance writer; mem. Russian Writers' Union 1971. *Film scripts include:* Dzhentlmeny udachi (Gentlemen of Luck) 1972, Mimino 1977, Shla sobaka po royalyu (A Dog Was Walking on the Piano) 1978, Tayna zemli (The Earth's Secret) 1985, Tu es... 1995, Vmesto menya 2000, Lavina 2001. *Publications:* A Day Without Lies 1967, About What That Has Never Been 1969 (collected stories), Flying Swing (collected stories) 1978, Nothing Particular 1983; numerous works of prose 1994–97. *Address:* 119590 Moscow, Dovzhenko str. 12, korp. 1, apt. 148, Russia (home). *Telephone:* (495) 147-99-71 (home).

TOKAYEV, Kasym-Zhomart Kemelevich; Kazakhstani diplomatist and politician; *Chairman (Speaker), Senat (Senate);* b. 17 May 1953, Almaty, Kazakhstan; s. of the late Kemel Tokaev and of Turash Shabyrbayeva; m. Nadeyda Tokayeva (née Poznanskaya) 1983; one s.; ed Moscow Inst. of Int. Relations, Diplomatic Acad., USSR Ministry of Foreign Affairs, Inst. of the Chinese Language, Beijing; with USSR Ministry of Foreign Affairs 1975; served at Embassy in Singapore 1975–79; Attaché, Third Sec. Ministry of Foreign Affairs 1979–83; Second Sec. of Dept 1984–85; Second, then First Sec., Embassy in Beijing 1985–91; attained rank of Amb. of Kazakhstan 1994; Deputy Minister, then First Deputy Minister of Foreign Affairs Repub. of Kazakhstan 1992–94, State Sec. and Minister 1994–99; Deputy Prime Minister March–Oct. 1999, Prime Minister of Kazakhstan 1999–2002; Minister of Foreign Affairs 2002–06; Chair. (Speaker) Senat (Senate) 2007–; Parasat (Nat. Award) 1996, Astana Medal. *Publications:* How it Was... Disturbance in Beijing 1993, United Nations: Half a Century of Serving for Peace 1995, Under the Banner of Independence 1997, Kazakhstani Foreign Policy in the Context of Globalisation 2000, Diplomacy of the Republic of Kazakhstan 2001. *Leisure interests:* reading, playing tennis. *Address:* Office of the Chairman, Senat, 010000 Astana, pr. Abaya 33, Parliament House, Kazakhstan (office). *Telephone:* (7172) 15-33-76 (office). *Fax:* (7172) 33-31-18 (office). *E-mail:* smimazh@parlam.kz (office). *Website:* www.parlam.kz (office).

TŐKÉS, Very Rev. László; Romanian ecclesiastic; b. 1 April 1952, Cluj/Kolozsvár; s. of István Tőkés and Erzsébet Vass; m. Edit Joó 1985; two s. one d.; ed Protestant Theological Inst. Cluj; asst minister at Brașov/Brassó, then at Dej/Dés 1975–84; discharged for political reasons and suspended from church service 1984–86; reinstalled as chaplain then pastor, Timișoara/Temesvár 1986–89; banished to small parish of Mineu/Menyő, threatened with eviction; demonstration by supporters was beginning of revolution that overthrew Communist Govt 1989; Oradea Bishop of Királyhágómellék Diocese, Nagyvárad 1990–; mem. Temporary Nat. Salvation Council; Co-Chair. Hungarian Reformed Synod of Romania; Hon. Pres. Hungarian Democratic Alliance of Hungarians in Romania; Hon. Pres. Hungarian World Fed.; Pres. Reformed Hungarian World Fed.; Freeman Cities of Sárospatak amd Székelyudvarhely and of 5th and 11th dists of Budapest; Kt of Johannit Order; Dr hc (Theological Acad. of Debrecen) 1990, (Regent Univ., Va Beach, USA) 1990, (Hope Coll., Holland, Mich.) 1991; Berzsenyi Prize, Hungary 1989, Roosevelt Prize of The Netherlands 1990, Bethlen Gábor Prize, Hungary 1990, Geuzenpenning Prize, Netherlands 1991, Pro Fide Prize, Finland 1993, Bocskay Prize, Hungary 1995, Hungarian Heritage Prize 1996, Minority Prize of Catalan CIEMEN Centre, Spain 1996, Leopold Kunschak Prize, Austria 1998. *Publications:* Where the Lord's Soul, there Freedom (selections of sermons) 1990, The Siege of Timișoara '89 1990, With God for the People 1990, There is a Time to Speak (with David Porter) 1993, A Phrase – And What is Behind 1993, In the Spirit of Timișoara – Ecumenism and Reconciliation 1996, Hope and Reality – Selected Writings 1999, Timișoara Memento – Self

Confessions 1999, Timișoara Siege 1999; sermons, articles in ecclesiastical and secular publs. *Address:* Str. Craiovei 1, 3700 Oradea, Romania (office). *Telephone:* (991) 131708 (office).

TOKHI, Hamidullah; Afghan politician; Gov. of Zabul Prov. 2002–03, of Wardak Prov. –Aug. 2003; mem. Hizb-i-Islami party; currently mem. Parl.

TOKIWA, Toshiji; Japanese retail executive; ed Keio Univ.; Dir and Gen. Man., New York Br., Dai-Ichi Kangyo Bank, Ltd 1993–95, Sr Man. Dir Dai-Ichi Kangyo Bank, Ltd 1995–96; Pres. and CEO Chuo Real Estate Co., Ltd. 1996–2000; Chair. AEON Co. Ltd 2000–06, Dir (non-exec), Vice-Chair. then Chair. Jusco Stores (Hong Kong) Co. Ltd (subsidiary) 2003–06; mem. Bd of Dirs Talbots Inc. 2000–. *Address:* c/o AEON Company Ltd, 1-5-1 Nasake, Mihami-ku, Chiba 261-8515, Japan (office).

TOKODY, Ilona; Hungarian soprano; b. Szeged; d. of András Tokody and Ilona Nagy; ed Liszt Ferenc Music Acad., Budapest; won Kodály singing competition 1972, Erkel competition of Inter-konzert Agency 1973, Ostend competition operatic category 1976; joined State Opera, Budapest 1976; regular guest performer Staatsoper Wien and Deutsche Oper West-Berlin; appearances in opera houses and concert halls worldwide, including Metropolitan Opera House, Royal Opera House Covent Garden, Vienna State Opera, San Francisco Opera, Teatro Colón, Buenos Aires, Liceo, Barcelona, Bavarian State Opera, San Carlo, Naples, Rome Opera, Bolshoi, Carnegie Hall, New York, Musikverein, Vienna, Royal Opera, Copenhagen. *Operatic roles include:* leading roles in La Forza del Destino, Don Carlos, Suor Angelica, Madama Butterfly, Il Trovatore, Aida, La Juive, La Bohème, Manon Lescaut, Nedda in I Pagliacci, Micaela in Carmen, Alice in Falstaff, Giselda in I Lombardi, Desdemona in Otello. *Recordings include:* Suor Angelica, Nerone, La Fiamma, Brahms Requiem, Il Tabarro, Guntram, Iris, Ilona Tokody – Portrait Of The Artist 1995, Beethoven – Symphony No. 9 2000. *Leisure interests:* cooking, badminton, gymnastics, table tennis, reading. *Address:* c/o Hungarian State Opera, Andrássy ut 22, 1062 Budapest, Hungary. *Telephone:* (1) 312-550.

TOKURA, Yoshinori, PhD; Japanese physicist and academic; *Professor, Department of Applied Physics, University of Tokyo;* ed Univ. of Tokyo; Assoc. Prof., Dept of Physics, Univ. of Tokyo 1986–93, Prof. 1994–95, Prof., Dept of Applied Physics 1995–; mem. Physical Soc. of Japan, American Physical Soc., Japan Soc. of Applied Physics; Nishina Memorial Prize 1990, IBM Japan Science Prize 1990, Bernd Matthias Prize 1991, Nissan Science Prize 1998, Asahi Prize 2001, James C. McGroddy Prize for New Materials, American Physical Soc. 2005. *Publications:* more than 500 articles in scientific journals. *Address:* Department of Applied Physics, School of Engineering, University of Tokyo, Hongo 7-3-1, Bunkyo-ku, Tokyo 113-8656, Japan (office). *Telephone:* (3) 5841-6870 (office). *Fax:* (3) 5841-6839 (office). *E-mail:* octo@t-adm.t.u-tokyo.ac .jp (office). *Website:* www.ap.t.u-tokyo.ac.jp (office).

TOLEDANO, Sidney; French fashion industry executive; *CEO, Christian Dior SA;* b. Morocco; m. Katia Toledano; one s. two d.; ed École Centrale Paris; began career as researcher, A.C. Nielsen; joined Lancel (handbag mfr) 1983; joined Christian Dior SA 1993, Pres. 1998, CEO 2003–, also responsible for overseeing strategy at Fendi, also currently Pres. and CEO Christian Dior Couture, Acting Pres. Galliano 2006; Chevalier, Légion d'honneur 2005. *Address:* Christian Dior SA, 30 avenue Montaigne, 75008 Paris, France (office). *Telephone:* 1-44-13-24-98 (office). *Fax:* 1-44-13-27-86 (office). *E-mail:* info@dior.com (office). *Website:* www.dior.com (office).

TOLEDO, Francisco; Mexican artist; b. 1940, Juchitán, Tehuantepec; worked in Paris until 1965; returned to Mexico 1965; worked at Casa de la Cultura, Juchitán and Inst. de Artes Gráficas, Oaxaca; associated with Museo de Arte Contemporaneo de Oaxaca, Jorge Luis Borges Library for the Blind, Cine El Pochote, Centro Cultural de Santo Domingo.

TOLEDO MANRIQUE, Alejandro ('Cholo'), PhD; Peruvian economist and politician; b. 28 March 1946, Cabana, Ancash Prov.; m. Eliane Karp; ed Univs of Stanford and San Francisco, USA; fmr mem. staff World Bank; adviser to UN, World Bank, IDB, ILO and OECD; Research Fellow, Inst. for Int. Devt, Harvard Univ., 1991–94; Perm. Prof. of ESAN, Univ. Lima; Visiting Prof., Univ. of Waseda and Japan Foundation, Tokyo; Founder-mem. and Leader Perú Posible party (opposition alliance); presidential cand. 2000, subsequently boycotted election; Pres. of Peru 2001–06. *Publications:* Las Cartas sobre la Mesa, Social Inversion for Growth, Economic Structural Reforms, Peru's Challenge: The Transition to Sustained Economic Growth; and several books on econs and devt. *Address:* Perú Posible, Bajada Balta 131, Miraflores, Lima. *Telephone:* (1) 2419307 (pp). *Fax:* (21) 2419307.

TOLGFORS, Sten, BSc; Swedish politician; *Minister of Defence and of Foreign Trade;* b. 17 July 1966, Forshaga; ed Karlberg Upper Secondary School and Örebro Univ.; mem. Örebro City Ass. 1991–94; Special Adviser, Ministry of Defence 1992–93, Ministry of Industry and Commerce 1992–94; mem. Nat. Bd Moderate Party Youth Org. 1990–95, Nat. Exec. 2002–, Spokesperson for Social Insurance 2002–03, Spokesperson for Educ. 2003–06; mem. Riksdag (Parl.) 1994–, Alt. mem. Cttee on Educ. 1994–2002, Cttee on Foreign Affairs 1994–98, Cttee on Industry and Trade 1998–2002, Del. to OSCE Parl. Ass. 1998–2002; mem. Del. to Nordic Council 1998–2002, Cttee on Foreign Affairs 1998–2002, Cttee on Social Insurance 2002–03, Cttee on Educ. 2003–06, Advisory Council on Foreign Affairs 2006; Minister for Foreign Trade 2006–, of Defence 2007–. *Address:* Ministry of Defence, Jakobsgt. 9, 103 33 Stockholm, Sweden (office). *Telephone:* (8) 405-10-00 (office). *Fax:* (8) 723-11-89 (office). *E-mail:* registrator@defence.ministry.se (office). *Website:* forsvar.regeringen.se (office).

TOLLI, Abbas Mahamat; Chadian politician; Sec. of State –2005; Minister of Finance and Information Tech. 2005–08. *Address:* c/o Ministry of Finance, BP 816, N'Djamena, Chad (office).

TOLNAY, Lajos, PhD; Hungarian business executive; *President, Hungarian Chamber of Commerce and Industry;* b. 27 Sept. 1948, Sajószentpéter; m.; four c.; ed Heavy Industries Tech. Univ., Miskolc and Budapest Univ. of Econs; various positions DIMAG Co. Ltd 1971–92, Gen. Dir 1989–92; Man. Dir Dunaferr Trading House Ltd 1992–93; Pres.-Man. Dir PTW Investment Co. Ltd 1993–95; Man. Dir Rákóczi Bank 1994, Pres. 1994–; Pres. Hungarian Chamber of Commerce 1990–93, Hungarian Chamber of Commerce and Industry 1994–; Man. Dir Inota Aluminium Co. Ltd 1996–; Chair. Bd Magyar Aluminium Inc. 1997–; Chair. Controlling Cttee Életút First Nat. Pension Fund; Chair. NAT Hungarian Accreditation Bd; mem. Exec. Bd ICC, Hon. Chair. ICC Hungary; mem. Supervisory Bd Hungexpo Co. Ltd, Bankár Investment Co. Ltd; various awards and decorations. *Address:* Magyar Kereskedelmi és Iparkamara, Kossuth Lajos tér 6–8, 1055 Budapest, Hungary (office). *Telephone:* (1) 353-3333 (office). *Fax:* (1) 269-4628 (office). *E-mail:* mkik@mail.mkik.hu (office). *Website:* www.mkik.hu (office).

TOLSTAYA, Tatyana Nikitichna; Russian writer; b. 3 May 1951, Leningrad (now St Petersburg); d. of Mikhail Lozinsky; great-grandniece of Leo Tolstoy and granddaughter of Alexei Tolstoy; m. Andrey V. Lebedev; two s.; ed Univ. of Leningrad; Ed. of Eastern Literature Nauka Publishing, Moscow 1987–89; fmr Assoc. Prof. of English, Skidmore Coll., NJ, USA; co-host The School for Scandal TV interview show (Telekanal Kultura); Triumph Prize 2001. *Publications:* On the Golden Porch (short story) 1983, Sleepwalker in a Fog 1992, Night 1995, Day 1997, Kys 1998, Two of Them 2001, The Slynx 2007, White Walls 2007. *Address:* c/o Telekanal Kultura (Television Channel Culture), 123995 Moscow, ul. M. Nikitskaya 24, Russian Federation (office). *Telephone:* (495) 780-56-01 (office). *E-mail:* web@tv-culture.ru (office). *Website:* www.tvkultura.ru (office).

TOMALIN, Claire, MA, FRSL; British writer; b. 20 June 1933, London; d. of Emile Delavenay and Muriel Emily Herbert; m. 1st Nicholas Osborne Tomalin 1955 (died 1973); two s. three d. (one d. and one s. deceased); m. 2nd Michael Frayn (q.v.) 1993; ed Hitchin Girls' Grammar School, Dartington Hall School, Newnham Coll., Cambridge; publr's reader and Ed. 1955–67; Asst Literary Ed. New Statesman 1968–70, Literary Ed. 1974–77; Literary Ed. Sunday Times 1979–86; Vice-Pres. English PEN 1997, Royal Literary Fund 2000; mem. London Library Cttee 1997–2000, Advisory Cttee for the Arts, Humanities and Social Sciences, British Library 1997–2000, Council RSL 1997–2000; Trustee, Nat. Portrait Gallery 1992–2002, Wordsworth Trust 2004; Hon. Fellow, Lucy Cavendish Coll. Cambridge 2003, Newnham Coll. Cambridge 2003; Hon. DLitt (East Anglia) 2005, (Birmingham) 2005, (Greenwich) 2006, (Cambridge) 2007; Whitbread Prize 1974, James Tait Black Prize 1990, NCR Book Award 1991, Hawthornden Prize 1991, Samuel Pepys Award 2003, Rose Mary Crawshay Prize 2003. *Play:* The Winter Wife 1991. *Publications:* The Life and Death of Mary Wollstonecraft 1974, Shelley and his World 1980, Katherine Mansfield: A Secret Life 1987, The Invisible Woman 1990, The Winter Wife 1991, Mrs Jordan's Profession 1994, Jane Austen: A Life 1997, Maurice by Mary Shelley (ed.) 1998, Several Strangers: Writing from Three Decades 1999, Samuel Pepys: The Unequalled Self (Whitbread Awards for Book of the Year and Best Biog.) 2002, Thomas Hardy: The Time-Torn Man 2006, Selected Poems of Thomas Hardy 2006. *Leisure interests:* music, gardening, walking. *Address:* c/o David Godwin, David Godwin Associates, 55 Monmouth Street, London, WC2H 9DG, England (office). *Telephone:* (20) 7240-9992 (office). *Fax:* (20) 7395-6130 (office). *E-mail:* assistant@davidgodwinassociates.co.uk (office). *Website:* www .davidgodwinassociates.co.uk (office).

TÓMASSON, Tómas Ármann, MA; Icelandic diplomatist; b. 1 Jan. 1929, Reykjavik; s. of Tómas Tómasson and Gudrun Thorgrimsdóttir; m. Heba Jónsdóttir 1957 (divorced); three s. one d.; ed Reykjavik Grammar Schoo and Univ. of Illinois, Fletcher School of Law and Diplomacy and Columbia Univ., USA; entered Icelandic foreign service 1954; Sec. Moscow 1954–58; Ministry for Foreign Affairs 1958–60; Deputy Perm. Rep. to NATO and OECD 1960–66; Chief of Div., Ministry for Foreign Affairs 1966–69, Deputy Sec.-Gen. of Ministry 1970–71; Amb. to Belgium and EEC and Perm. Rep. on N Atlantic Council 1971–77, 1984–86, also accred to Luxembourg 1976–77, 1984–86; Perm. Rep. to UN 1977–82, 1993–94; Amb. to France (also accred to Portugal, Spain, Cape Verde) 1982–84, to USSR (also accred to Bulgaria, GDR, Hungary, Mongolia and Romania) 1987–90; Amb., Head of Del. to CSBMs and CFE negotiation, Vienna 1990; Amb. to USA (also accred to Canada) 1990–93; Amb., Head of Del. to CSCE Review Conf. and Summit, Budapest Oct.–Dec. 1994; mem. staff, Ministry for Foreign Affairs, Reykjavik 1994–; Order of the Falcon (Iceland) and decorations from France, Belgium, Luxembourg, Portugal and Sweden. *Address:* Ministry for Foreign Affairs, 150 Reykjavik; Espigerdi 4/9H, 108 Reykjavik, Iceland (home). *Telephone:* 5459900 (office); 5534918 (home). *Fax:* 5526247 (office); 5623152 (office). *E-mail:* tomas.a.tomasson@utn.stjr.is (office); tat@islandia.is (home).

TOMBRELLO, Thomas Anthony, Jr, BA, MA, PhD; American physicist and academic; *William R. Kenan Jr Professor of Physics, California Institute of Technology;* b. 20 Sept. 1936, Austin, Tex.; s. of the late Thomas A. Tombrello and Jeanette M. Tombrello; m. Stephanie Merton Tombrello; one s. three d. (one deceased); ed Rice Univ.; joined Physics Dept, Calif. Inst. of Tech. (Caltech) 1961, Prof. of Physics 1971–, William R. Kenan Jr Prof. of Physics 1997–, Tech. Assessment Officer 1996–, and Chair., Div. of Physics, Math. and Astronomy 1998–2008; fmr faculty mem., Yale Univ.; Vice-Pres. and Dir of Research, Schlumberger-Doll Research 1987–89; fmr mem. Vice-Pres.'s Space Policy Advisory Bd; mem. US Nuclear Physics Del. to People's Repub. of China; mem. NAS Panel on Future of Nuclear Science; Assoc. Ed. Nuclear Science Applications; fmr Assoc. Ed. Radiation Effects; mem. Visiting Cttees, Lawrence Livermore Nat. Lab.; mem. Scientific Advisory Bd Rice Univ. Center for Nanoscience and Tech.; Consultant, Applied Minds Inc., Arrowhead Research, Trillience Research, Form Factor Inc., Schlumberger Ltd, Glenair Inc.; Distinguished Alumnus, Rice Univ. 1998; Hon. DSc (Uppsala) 1997; Von Humboldt Award 1983, Feynman Prize. *Address:* Department of Physics, California Institute of Technology, 201 Sloan Annex, Pasadena, CA 91125, USA (office). *Telephone:* (626) 395-4581 (office). *Fax:* (626) 577-8442 (office). *E-mail:* tat@caltech.edu (office). *Website:* www.aph.caltech.edu/ people/tombrello_t.html (office).

TOMBS, Baron (Life Peer), cr. 1990, of Brailes in the County of Warwickshire; **Francis Leonard Tombs,** BSc, LLD, DSc, FREng; British business executive; b. 17 May 1924, Walsall; s. of Joseph Tombs and Jane Tombs; m. Marjorie Evans 1949; three d.; ed Elmore Green School, Walsall, Birmingham Coll. of Tech.; with British Electricity Authority 1948–57; Gen. Man., Gen. Electric Co. Ltd 1958–67; Dir and Gen. Man. James Howden and Co. 1967–68; Dir of Eng, South of Scotland Electricity Bd 1969–73, Deputy Chair. 1973–74, Chair. 1974–77; Chair. Electricity Council for England and Wales 1977–80; Dir N. M. Rothschild and Sons Ltd 1981–94; Chair. The Weir Group Ltd 1981–83; Chair. T&N PLC 1982–89; Dir Rolls-Royce Ltd 1982–92, Chair. 1985–92; Chair. Old Mutual SA Fund 1994–99; Dir Shell (UK) Ltd 1983–94; Chancellor Univ. of Strathclyde 1991–97; Chair. Eng Council 1985–88; Hon. FICE; Hon. FIMechE; Hon. FIChemE; Hon. FIEE (and fmr Pres.); Hon. FRSE 1996; Papal Knighthood of the Order of St Gregory 2002; Hon. DSc (Aston) 1979, (Lodz, Poland) 1980, (Cranfield Inst. of Tech.) 1985, (City Univ., London) 1986, (Bradford) 1986, (Queen's Univ., Belfast) 1988, (Surrey) 1988, (Nottingham) 1989, (Cambridge) 1990, (Warwick) 1990; Hon. DUniv (Strathclyde) 1991; Hon. DTech (Loughborough) 1979; Dr hc (CNAA) 1988. *Publications:* Nuclear Energy Past, Present and Future—Electronics and Power 1981, Reversing the Decline in Manufacturing Industry (Mountbatten Lecture 1993). *Leisure interest:* music. *Address:* Honington Lodge, Honington, Shipston on Stour, Warwicks., CV36 5AA, England (home).

TOMČIĆ, Zlatko, BSc (Eng); Croatian politician; *President, Croatian Peasants' Party;* b. 10 July 1945, Zagreb; ed Belgrade Univ.; f. underground Croatian Peasants' Party (Hrvatska seljačka stranka—HSS), Zagreb 1984, mem. re-est. HSS 1990–, Pres. 1994–; mem. Sabor (Ass.), Pres. 2000–03 (Acting Pres. Repub. of Croatia following death of Franjo Tuđman Feb. 2000), also Pres. Chamber of Reps 2000–. *Address:* Sabor, trg sv. Marka 617, 10000 Zagreb (office); Croatian Peasants' Party, ul. Kralja Zvonimira 17, 10000 Zagreb, Croatia. *Telephone:* (1) 4569444 (office); (1) 4553624. *Fax:* (1) 6303010 (office); (1) 4553631. *E-mail:* predsjednik@sabor.hr (office); hss@hss.hr. *Website:* www.hss.hr.

TOMÉ, Carol B., BA, MBA; American business executive; *Executive Vice-President and Chief Financial Officer, Home Depot, Inc.;* b. Wyo.; ed Univ. of Wyoming, Univ. of Denver, Colo; began career as commercial lender with United Bank of Denver (now Wells Fargo); spent several years as Dir of Banking for Johns-Manville Corpn; Vice-Pres. and Treas. Riverwood Int. Corpn –1995; joined Home Depot, Inc., Atlanta, Ga in 1995, Chief Financial Officer 2001–, Exec. Vice-Pres. of Corp. Services 2007–; mem. Bd of Dirs United Parcel Service (UPS, Chair. Audit Cttee) 2003–, High Museum of Art and Atlanta Botanical Garden, Fed. Reserve Bank of Atlanta 2008–; Chair. Advisory Bd Metropolitan Atlanta Arts Fund; mem. The Committee of 200; named by The Wall Street Journal as one of 50 Women to Watch 2007, ranked by Forbes magazine amongst 100 Most Powerful Women (16th) 2008. *Address:* Home Depot Inc., 2455 Paces Ferry Road NW, Atlanta, GA 30339, USA (office). *Telephone:* (770) 433-8211 (office). *Fax:* (770) 384-2805 (office). *E-mail:* info@homedepot.com (office). *Website:* www.homedepot.com (office).

TOMEING, Litokwa; Marshall Islands politician and head of state; *President;* b. Ratak Chain; m.; traditional tribal chief; apptd Minister for Ratak 1997; mem. Nitijela (Parl.) for Wotje Atoll, fmr Vice-Speaker, later Speaker –2007; fmr mem. United Democratic Party, now mem. United People's Party 2007–; Pres. Marshall Islands 2008–. *Address:* Office of the President, Government of the Republic of the Marshall Islands, POB 2, Majuro MH 96960, Marshall Islands (home). *Telephone:* (625) 3445 (office). *Fax:* (625) 4021 (office). *E-mail:* pressoff@ntamar.net (office). *Website:* www .rmigovernment.org (office).

TOMESCU, Constantina; Romanian athlete; b. (b. Constantina Diță), 23 Jan. 1970, Turburea, Gorj Co.; m. Valeriu Tomescu (her coach); long-distance runner, specializes mainly in half marathon and marathon; competed at World Half Marathon Championships, Palermo 1999; finished 10th in marathon at World Championships, Edmonton 2001; finished seventh in 10,000m at European Championships Munich 2002; finished fifth at World Half Marathon Championships, Vilamoura, Portugal 2003, third at World Half Marathon Championships, New Delhi 2004; won Chicago Marathon 2004 (personal best time of 2:21:30); Bronze Medal, marathon, World Championships, Helsinki 2005; won women's half marathon at World Half Marathon Championships, Edmonton 2005; finished second in 20km at World Road Running Championships, Debrecen, Hungary 2006; finished third in London Marathon 2007; Gold Medal, women's marathon, Olympic Games, Beijing 2008 (time of 2:26:44, oldest Olympic marathon champion in history). *Address:* c/o Federatia Romana de Atletism, 2 dr. Primo Nebiolo, 71323 Bucharest, Romania. *Telephone:* (21) 2232229. *Fax:* (21) 2232227. *E-mail:* fra.teh@ew.ro. *Website:* www.fra.ro.

TOMIĆ, Dragan; Serbian politician, engineer and business executive; b. 9 Dec. 1935, G. Bukovica; s. of Boško Tomić and Mitra Tomić; m. Milica Tomić 1964; two d.; ed Belgrade Univ.; various positions, Rekord Rubber Works, Rakovica 1962–86, Gen. Dir 1986; Pres. Eng Soc. of Yugoslavia; Gen. Dir NIS

– Jugopetrol Co.; Chair. Man. Bd RTV Politika Co. 1993–; mem. Nat. Parl. (Skupština) of Serbia 1994–, Chair. 1994–97; Chair. Union of Yugoslav Engineers and Technicians 1993–. *Leisure interests:* chess, walking with his dog. *Address:* Skupština Srbije, Srpskih Vladara 14, 11000 Belgrade, Serbia (office). *Telephone:* (11) 324-8604 (office). *Fax:* (11) 685-092 (office).

TOMIZAWA, Ryuichi; Japanese chemical industry executive; *Chairman, Mitsubishi Chemical Holdings Corporation;* b. Tokyo; m.; two s.; ed Tokyo Univ. Faculty of Law; began career with Mitsubishi Chemical Corpn (MCC), assignments in Malaysia 1990–92, Germany 1992–95, involved in cr. of Mitsubishi Tokyo Pharmaceuticals, various positions including Gen. Man., Dir, Exec. Vice-Pres. Mitsubishi Pharma Corpn –2002, Pres. and CEO MCC 2002–07, Dir 2007–, Chair. Mitsubishi Chemical Holdings Corpn 2007–. *Leisure interest:* golf. *Address:* Mitsubishi Chemical Holdings, 14-1 Shiba 4-chome, Minato-ku, Tokyo 108-0014, Japan (office). *Telephone:* (3) 6414-4870 (office). *Website:* www.mitsubishichem-hd.co.jp (office).

TOMKA, Peter, LLM, PhD; Slovak diplomatist, lawyer, arbitrator and judge; *Judge, International Court of Justice;* b. 1 June 1956, Banska Bystrica; s. of Ján Tomka and Kornélia Tomková; m. Zuzana Halgasová 1990; one s. one d.; ed Charles Univ., Prague; Asst, Faculty of Law, Charles Univ., Prague 1980–84, Lecturer 1985–86, Adjunct Lecturer 1986–91; Asst Legal Adviser, Ministry of Foreign Affairs, Czechoslovakia 1986–90, Head of Public Int. Law Div. 1990–91; Counsellor and Legal Adviser, Czechoslovakian Mission to the UN 1991–92; Deputy Perm. Rep. of Slovakia to the UN 1993–97, Perm. Rep. 1999–2003; Agent of Slovakia before the Int. Court of Justice 1993–2003, Judge, Int. Court of Justice 2003–; Legal Adviser to Slovak Ministry of Foreign Affairs 1997–99; Chair. UN Legal Cttee 1997, Cttee of Advisers on Public Int. Law, Council of Europe 2001–02; mem. Perm. Court of Arbitration, The Hague 1994–, UN Int. Law Comm. 1999–2003; Arbitrator in the Iron Rhine case (Belgium/Netherlands) 2003–05, in Annex VII to the UN Convention on the Law of the Sea 2004–, and in Int. Centre for Settlement of Investment Disputes 2005–. *Address:* International Court of Justice, Peace Palace, 2517 KJ The Hague, Netherlands (office). *Telephone:* (70) 3022323 (office). *Fax:* (70) 3649928 (office). *E-mail:* mail@icj-cij.org (office). *Website:* www.icj-cij.org (office).

TOMKO, HE Cardinal Jozef, DTheol, DrIur, DScS; Slovak ecclesiastic; *President of the Pontifical Committee, International Eucharistic Congresses;* b. 11 March 1924, Udavské, Humenné; s. of Andrej Tomko and Anna Tomko; ordained priest 1949; consecrated Bishop (Titular See of Doclea) 1979; cr. Cardinal (Cardinal-Deacon of Gesù Buon Pastore alla Montagnola) 1985 (Cardinal-Priest of S. Sabina) 1996; Sec.-Gen. of Synod of Bishops; mem. Comm. for Admin. of State of Vatican 1985–2004; Prefect of the Congregation for the Evangelization of Peoples 1985–2001; Adviser, Sec. of Vatican State 1996–2004; Pres. Pontifical Cttee for Int. Eucharistic Congresses (retd) 2001–07; numerous missions world-wide; Gran Cruz de la Orden del Libertador San Martín (Argentina) 1989, Order of the White Double Cross, First Class (Slovak Repub.) 1995; Prize of Grand Duchy of Luxembourg 1988. *Publications include:* Light of Nations 1972, Christianity and the World 1974, Christ Yesterday and Today 1976, Ecumenism 1977, Sinodo dei Vescori 1985, La Missione verso il terzo millennio 1998. *Address:* 00120 Citto del Vaticano (office); Via della Conciliazione 44, 00193 Rome, Italy (home). *Telephone:* (06) 698-873-66 (office); (06) 698-824-24 (home). *Fax:* (06) 698-871-54 (office); (06) 698-823-53 (home). *E-mail:* jozef.tomko@tin.it (home).

TOMKYS, Sir (W.) Roger, Kt, KCMG, DL, MA; British diplomatist and academic; *Chairman, Arab-British Chamber of Commerce;* b. 15 March 1937, Bradford; s. of Arthur Tomkys and Edith Tomkys; m. Margaret Abbey 1963; one s. one d.; ed Bradford Grammar School and Balliol Coll., Oxford; entered HM Diplomatic Service 1960; served Amman, Benghazi, Athens, Rome; Amb. to Bahrain 1981–84, to Syria 1984–86; Asst Under-Sec., later Deputy Under-Sec. of State, FCO 1986–90; High Commr in Kenya 1990–92; Master of Pembroke Coll., Cambridge 1992–2004, Chair. Arab-British Chamber of Commerce 2004–; Commendatore dell'Ordine al Merito, Order of Bahrain. *Leisure interests:* travel, books, golf, shooting. *Address:* Croydon House Farm, Lower Road, Croydon, Royston, Cambs., SG8 0EF, England (home). *Telephone:* (20) 7659-4853 (office); (1223) 207343 (home). *Fax:* (20) 7245-6688 (office); (1223) 207339 (home). *E-mail:* r.tomkys@abcc.org.uk (office); r.tomkys@btinternet.com (home).

TOMLINSON, Sir John Rowland, CBE; British singer (bass); b. 22 Sept. 1946, Accrington, Lancs.; s. of Rowland Tomlinson and Ellen Greenwood; m. Moya Joel 1969; one s. two d.; ed Accrington Grammar School, Manchester Univ. and Royal Manchester Coll. of Music; debut at Glyndebourne Festival 1972, ENO 1974, Royal Opera House, Covent Garden 1976; since then has appeared in many operas throughout Europe and N America, including Parsifal, Tristan und Isolde and Lohengrin; has sung role of Wotan/Wanderer in The Ring Cycle, Bayreuth Festival 1988–98; other significant roles include Boris in Boris Godunov, ENO (Manchester) 1982, Don Basilio in Il Barbiere di Siviglia, Covent Garden 1985, Moses, ENO 1980, Fiesco in Simon Boccanegra, ENO 1988, Mephistopheles in Damnation of Faust, Santiago, Chile 1990, Attila, Opera North 1990, Filippo II in Don Carlos, Opera North 1992, König Marke in Tristan and Isolde, Bayreuth Festival 1993, Mephistopheles in Damnation of Faust, La Fenice, Venice 1993, Claggart in Billy Budd, Covent Garden 1994, Hans Sachs in Die Meistersinger, Berlin Staatsoper 1995, Kingfisher in Midsummer Marriage, Covent Garden 1996, Bluebeard in Bluebeard's Castle, Berlin Philharmonic 1996, Four Villains in Tales of Hoffmann, ENO 1998, Moses in Moses and Aaron, New York Metropolitan Opera 1999, Golaud in Pelléas et Mélisande, Glyndebourne 1999, Mephistopheles in Damnation of Faust, Munich Staatsoper 2000, Hagen in Götterdämmerung, Bayreuth 2000, Baron Ochs in Rosenkavalier, Staatsoper Dresden 2000, Borromeo in Palestrina, Covent Garden 2001, Gurnemanz in Parsifal, New York Metropolitan 2001; numerous broadcasts, recordings, opera videos and concert performances; Hon. FRNCM; Hon. DMus (Sussex) 1997, (Manchester) 1998; Singer of the Year, Royal Philharmonic Soc. 1991, 1998, 2008, Evening Standard Opera Award 1998, Soc. of London Theatre's Special Award, Olivier Awards 2007. *Address:* Music International, 13 Ardilaun Road, Highbury, London, N5 2QR, England (office). *Telephone:* (20) 7359-5183 (office).

TOMLINSON, Lindsay Peter, OBE, MA, FIA; British financial executive; *Vice Chairman, Europe, Barclays Global Investors Ltd.;* b. 7 Oct. 1951, Derby; s. of P. Tomlinson and J. M. Tomlinson; m. Sarah Caroline Anne Martin 1973; four s. one d.; ed Clifton Coll., St John's Coll., Cambridge; actuarial student Commercial Union Assurance Co. 1973–77; sr pensions consultant Metropolitan Pensions Asscn 1977–81; Sr Investment Man. Provident Mutual Managed Pension Funds 1981–87; CEO (Europe) Barclays Global Investors (fmrly BZW Investment Man.) 1987–2003, now Vice Chair. *Address:* Barclays Global Investors Limited, Murray House, 1 Royal Mint Court, London, EC3N 4HH (office); Investment Management Association, 65 Kingsway, London, WC2B 6TD, England (office). *Telephone:* (20) 7668-8866 (office). *Fax:* (20) 7668-6866 (office). *Website:* www.barclaysglobal.com (office); www.investmentuk.org (office).

TOMLINSON, Mel Alexander, BFA; American dancer; b. 3 Jan. 1954, Raleigh, NC; s. of Tommy W. A. Tomlinson and Marjorieline Henry Tomlinson; ed F. J. Carnage Jr High School, J. W. Ligon High School, NC Gov.'s School and NC School of the Arts; Prin., Agnes DeMille's Heritage Dance Theater 1973, Dance Theatre of Harlem Inc. 1974–77, Alvin Ailey American Dance Theatre 1977–78, Dance Theatre of Harlem Inc. 1978–81; mem. corps de ballet, New York City Ballet 1981, soloist 1982–; guest appearance, DeMille Tribute, Joffrey Ballet. *Leisure interests:* knitting, swimming, gymnastics, reading, sewing, games. *Address:* New York City Ballet, Lincoln State Theater, New York, NY 10023; 790 Riverside Drive, Apt. 6B, New York, NY 10032; 1216 Bunche Drive, Raleigh, NC 27610, USA. *Telephone:* (212) 234-3320; (919) 834-7010.

TOMNITZ, Donald, BA, MBA; American real estate executive; *Vice-Chairman, President and CEO, D. R. Horton Inc.;* b. 1948, St Louis; m. Sharon Tomnitz; two c.; ed Westminster Coll., Western Ill. Univ.; served as capt. in US Army; fmr Vice-Pres. Republic Bank of Dallas, Crow Development Co.; joined D. R. Horton Inc. as Vice-Pres. 1983, Pres. Homebuilding Div. 1996–98, CEO and Vice-Chair. 1998–, Pres. 2000–. *Address:* D.R. Horton, Inc., 301 Commerce Street, Suite 500, Fort Worth, TX 76102, USA (office). *Telephone:* (817) 390-8200 (office). *Fax:* (817) 436-6717 (office). *Website:* www.drhorton.com (office).

TOMOS; Chinese artist; b. 26 Nov. 1932, Tumed Banner, Inner Mongolia (Nei Monggol); s. of Yun Yao and Xing Yu; m. Xiahe-xiou 1967; two s.; ed Cen. Inst. of Fine Arts, Beijing; Assoc. Prof. of Fine Arts, Inner Mongolia Normal Coll.; Dean of Fine Arts, Inner Mongolia Teachers' Training Coll. 1984–; Adviser on Fine Arts to Children's Palace, Huhehot, Inner Mongolia; Vice-Chair. Inner Mongolian Branch of Chinese Artists' Asscn 1980–; Dir Standing Cttee, Chinese Artists' Asscn 1985–, mem. Oil Art Cttee 1985–; mem. Selection Cttee for Sixth Nat. Art Exhbn of oil paintings; mem. Art Educ. Cttee of Nat. Educ. 1986–; Dir Inner Mongolia branch of China External Culture Exchange Asscn; Dir Cheng's Style Tai-Chi Chuan Asscn 1993–; Chair. Judges' Cttee for 8th Annual Chinese Art Exhbn, Inner Mongolia 1994, 8th Annual Best Chinese Artwork Exhbn 1994; Consultant, The Watercolour Asscn, Inner Mongolia 1994; Dir China Oil Painting Asscn 1995–; Chair. Inner Mongolian Artists' Asscn 1996–; Head of Del. of Inner Mongolian painters to Hong Kong 1993; First Prize for Art, Inner Mongolia, Merit of Art Educ. Award, Wu Zuo Ren Int. Art Foundation 1990, Expert and Scholar award of Govt 1991 and medals awarded for individual paintings. *Works include:* Mine, Wind on the Grasslands, Having a Break, Dawn, Milkmaid, A Woman Hay-making, At Dusk, Polo, Spring Wind, White Horse and Wind, At Dark and many others. *Publications:* Selection of oil-paintings, Tomos's Album of Paintings (sketches and oil paintings) 1993, The Techniques of Oil Painting 1999. *Leisure interests:* Chinese Gongfu, Peking opera, Chinese medicine. *Address:* Art Department, Normal College, Nei Monggol Autonomous Region, People's Republic of China (office).

TOMOWA-SINTOW, Anna; Austrian singer (soprano); b. 22 Sept. 1943, Stara Zagora, Bulgaria; m. Albert Sintow; one d.; ed Nat. Conservatory of Sofia with Zlatew Tscherkin and Katja Spiridonowa; debut at Leipzig Opera 1967; joined Deutsche Staatsoper, Berlin 1973; guest engagements at all leading European and US opera houses, with conductors including Karajan, Böhm, Haitink, Kleiber, Solti, Abbado, Muti, Maazel, Mehta, Levine, Chailly, Davis, Barenboim, Thielemann; N America debut in San Francisco 1974, at Met, New York 1978, Chicago 1981; numerous tours in Japan, also with La Scala and Berlin Philharmonic under von Karajan; regular guest at Salzburg Festival 1973–1991; Dr hc; Kammersängerin, Vienna and Berlin, two Grammies for Ariadne and Don Giovanni/Donna Anna, three Orphée d'Or awards. *Recordings include:* Lohengrin, Le Nozze di Figaro, Don Giovanni, Die Zauberflöte, Der Rosenkavalier, Ariadne auf Naxos, Madame Butterfly, La Traviata, Tosca, Eugene Onegin, Aida, Otello, Capriccio, Andrea Chenier, Simon Boccanegra, Prince Igor, Mozart Coronation Mass, Mozart Requiem, Bach Magnificat,Brahms German Requiem, Verdi Requiem, Strauss Four Last Songs (Orphée d'Or) and Capriccio monologue, Beethoven Missa Solemnis and 9th Symphony, recitals of Verdi arias and of Italian and German arias. *Major roles include:* Arabella, Ariadne, Marschallin, Salome, Madelaine in Capriccio, Ägyptische Helena, Countess Almaviva, Fiordiligi, Donna Anna, Elsa in Lohengrin, Elisabeth in Tannhäuser, Sieglinde, Aida, Traviata, Leonora in La Forza del Destino, Amelia in Ballo, Simone Boccanegra, Elisabetta in Don Carlo,Yaroslavna in Prince Igor, Tatjana in

Onegin, Tosca, Madama Butterfly, Turandot, Manon Lescaut, Norma, Santuzza, Das Wunder der Heliane, etc. *Leisure interests:* nature, reading books, singing. *Address:* c/o Silvana Sintow-Behrens International Promotions, Schleibingerstrasse 8, 81669 Munich, Germany (office). *Telephone:* (89) 44218900 (office). *Fax:* (89) 44218903 (office). *E-mail:* ats@sintow-behrens.com (office); office@sintow-behrens.com (office). *Website:* www.sintow-behrens.com (office).

TOMUR, Dawamat; Chinese party official; b. 1927, Toksun, Xinjiang Uygur Autonomous Region; s. of Ziweidihan Dawamat; m. Gulzirahan 1944; five s. two d.; ed Cen. Nationalities Coll., Beijing; village chief 1950–54; joined CCP 1952; Magistrate, County (Dist) People's Court, Toksun, Xinjiang Uygur Autonomous Region 1954–64; Sec. CCP Cttee, Toksun Cttee, Tunpan Basin 1956, First Sec. 1960; Vice-Chair. Xinjiang Autonomous Region 1964–78; Deputy for Xinjiang, 3rd NPC; mem. Standing Cttee, Autonomous Regional Revolutionary Cttee, Xinjiang 1968; Deputy for Xinjiang, 5th NPC 1978; Deputy Sec. CCP Cttee Xinjiang 1978–; Vice-Minister of State Nationalities Affairs Comm., State Council 1979–89; Chair. Autonomous Regional People's Congress, Xinjiang 1978–85; mem. 12th Cen. Cttee, CCP 1982; Gov. Xinjiang Autonomous Region 1986–93; Vice-Sec. Xinjiang Autonomous Regional CCP Cttee 1985; mem. 13th Cen. Cttee, CCP 1987–92, 14th Cen. Cttee CCP 1992–97; mem. Standing Cttee 5th NPC 1978–83, Vice-Chair. Standing Cttee 8th NPC 1993–98, 9th NPC 1998–2003. *Publications:* Footprints of my Life (poetry) 2005. *Leisure interests:* writing poetry, playing Chinese Checkers. *Address:* Standing Committee of National People's Congress, Beijing, People's Republic of China (office).

TONEGAWA, Susumu, PhD; Japanese immunologist, neuroscientist and academic; *Director, Picower Center for Learning and Memory, Massachusetts Institute of Technology;* b. 5 Sept. 1939, Nagoya; s. of Tsutomu Tonegawa and Miyuko Tonegawa; m. Mayumi Yoshinari 1985; three c.; ed Kyoto Univ. and Univ. of Calif., San Diego; postgraduate work at Dept of Biology, Univ. of Calif., San Diego 1968–69, The Salk Inst., San Diego 1969–70; mem. Basle Inst. for Immunology, Basle, Switzerland 1971–81; Prof. of Biology, Center for Cancer Research and Dept of Biology, MIT 1981–, now Picower Prof. of Biology and Neuroscience, Depts of Brain and Cognitive Sciences and Biology; investigator Howard Hughes Medical Inst. 1988–; Dir Picower Center for Learning and Memory, MIT 1994–; mem. American Acad. of Arts and Sciences; Foreign Assoc. mem. NAS; Hon. mem. American Asscn of Immunologists, Scandinavian Soc. for Immunology; numerous awards and prizes including Avery Landsteiner Prize 1981, Gairdner Foundation Int. Award 1983, Robert Koch Prize 1986, Lasker Prize 1987, Nobel Prize for Medicine 1987; Bunkakunsho Order of Culture 1984. *Address:* Picower Center for Learning and Memory, Room E17-353, Massachusetts Institute of Technology, 77 Massachusetts Avenue, Cambridge, MA 02139, USA. *Telephone:* (617) 253-1000. *Fax:* (617) 253-8000. *Website:* web.mit.edu/picowercenter/faculty/tonegawa.html (office).

TONELLI, Gilles; Monegasque civil servant and politician; *Government Counsellor for Facilities, the Environment and Urban Planning;* m.; three c.; ed Ecole des Travaux Publiques; engineer in Paris 1983–84, section head at public works service 1984–87; Official Rep. at Dept of Public Works and Social Affairs 1987–90, Dir of Urban Planning and Construction 1990–93, Dir-Gen. Dept Public Works and Social Affairs 1993–95, 1995–99; Tech. Advisor, Dept of Finance 1995; Gen. Controller of Expenditure 1999–2000; Sec.-Gen. Ministry of State 2000–05; Govt Counsellor for Facilities, the Environment and Urban Planning 2005–06, 2009–, for Finance and the Economy 2006–09. *Address:* Department of Facilities, the Environment and Urban Planning, Ministère d'Etat, place de la Visitation, Monte Carlo, MC 98000, Monaco (office). *Telephone:* 98-98-85-67 (office).

TONG, Anote, MSc; I-Kiribati head of state and politician; *President and Minister for Foreign Affairs and Immigration;* b. 1952; s. of Chinese migrant who settled in Gilbert Islands following World War II; m. Meme Bernadette Tong; eight c.; ed Univ. of Canterbury, Christchurch, NZ, LSE, UK; Sr Asst Sec., Ministry of Educ. 1976–77; Sec. Ministry of Communication and Works 1980–82; Minister for Natural Resources Devt 1994–96; mem. Parl. for Maiana Island 1996–2003; Sr mem. Boutokaan Te Koaua Party 1996–2003; Beretitenti (Pres.) of Kiribati and Minister for Foreign Affairs and Immigration 2003–; fmr Chair. National Fishing Co., Development Bank of Kiribati, Otintai Hotel Ltd, Air Tungaru Co-operative. *Address:* Office of the President (Beretitenti), POB 68, Bairiki, Tarawa, Kiribati (office). *Telephone:* 21183 (office). *Fax:* 21145 (office).

TONG, Yin Chu; Chinese politician; b. 1915, Hefei City, Anhui Prov.; ed Shanghai Jiaotong Univ.; lived in Indonesia 1938–47; joined China Democratic Construction Asscn 1948; Chair. Cen. Cttee China Zhi Gong Dang (political party) 1988–97, Hon. Chair. 1997; Vice-Chair. 8th Nat. Cttee CPPCC 1993–98; Adviser, China Council for Promotion of Peaceful Nat. Reunification, All China Fed. of Returned Overseas Chinese. *Address:* c/o National Committee of Chinese People's Political Consultative Congress, 23 Taiping Qiao Street, Beijing, People's Republic of China (office).

TONG, Zengyin; Chinese banker; b. 1934, Yinxian, Zhejiang Prov.; joined CCP 1954; Vice-Gov. People's Bank of China –1993; fmrly Vice-Chair. China Securities Regulatory Cttee; Founding Pres. Minsheng Bank (China's first privately owned nat. bank) 1996; currently Chair. TRAC Financial Talents Cttee. *Address:* TRAC Financial Talents Committee, No.6-302 Famous Garden 77, Fucheng RD, Haidian District, Beijing 100006, People's Republic of China (office). *Website:* www.ft.org.cn/en/ (office).

TONG, Zhiguang; Chinese international official and professor of economics; *Chairman, Research Society of China, World Trade Organization;* b. 21 Jan. 1933, Hebei Prov.; ed Beijing Inst. of Foreign Trade and Univ. of Int. Business and Econs, Bombay Univ., India; joined CCP 1973; Deputy Head State Council Leading Group for Right to Intellectual Property 1991–; Vice-Minister of Foreign Trade and Econ. Co-operation 1991–93; Chair. Bd The Export-Import Bank of China 1994–99; Chair. WTO Research Soc. of China 2001–; Vice-Chair. China-UK Friendship Group; mem. China-US Inter-parliamentarian Exchange Group of the NPC; fmr Chief Negotiator and Del. Leader for China's accession to GATT/WTO and Sino-US Trade Negotiations; fmr sr diplomatist to India, Myanmar, USA and UN; fmr Adviser to Chinese Del. of UN Gen. Ass.; fmr Pres. and CEO of China Resources (Holdings) Co. Ltd, Hong Kong; mem. 8th Standing Cttee NPC 1993–98, mem. NPC Foreign Affairs Cttee, del. of Hebei Prov. to 8th NPC 1993–98, 9th Standing Cttee NPC 1998–2003; Del., 15th CCP Nat. Congress 1997–2002. *Publications:* several articles on foreign trade, int. econs and the WTO. *Leisure interests:* golf, classical music, Chinese calligraphy. *Address:* 2212, 28 Dong Holi Xiang, Anwai Beijing 100710 (office); 7202 Yin Zha Hu Tong, Xicheng Qu, Beijing (home); c/o The Export-Import Bank of China, 75 Chongnei Street, Beijing 100005, People's Republic of China (office). *Telephone:* (10) 84255121 (office); (10) 64259703 (home). *Fax:* (10) 84255122 (office). *E-mail:* wtori@sina.com.cn (office); info@chinawto.org.cn (office). *Website:* (office).

TONG SANG, Gaston, DipEng; French Polynesian engineer, politician and fmr head of state; b. 7 Aug. 1949, Bora Bora; two c.; ed Collège La Mennais, Papeete, Lycée Montaigne, Bordeaux, Ecole des Hautes études industrielles (HEI), Centre des Hautes Etudes de la Construction, Paris; engineer, Road Infrastructure Dept, Polynesian Dept of Works 1976–80, Head, Maritime Works Dept 1980–82; Cabinet Dir for Govt Counsellors 1982–84; Cabinet Dir for Minister of Works 1984–86; Minister of Works, Supplies, Energy and Mines 1986–89; Mayor of Bora Bora 1989–91; Regional Councillor for Iles sous le Vent and Minister of Supplies, Urban Areas, Works and Energy 1991–95; Minister of Works, Energy and Ports 1995–96, of Housing, Territories, Urban Areas and Real Estate 1996–98, of Property Affairs, Land Man. and Urban Areas 1998–2000, of Land Man. and Land Redistribution 2001–04, of Energy, Commerce, Industry and Small Businesses 2004–07; Pres. of French Polynesia 2007, 2008–09 (resgnd), also Minister for External Relations, Int. Transport and Communication; mem. To Tatou Ai'a party; Chevalier de l'ordre Nat. du Mérite 1996, Chevalier des Palmes académiques 2000, Chevalier de la Légion d'honneur 2004. *Address:* c/o Office of the President of the Government, BP 2551, 98713 Papeete, French Polynesia (office).

TONKIN, Peter Frederick, BSc (Arch)(Hons), BArch (Hons); Australian architect; *Director, Tonkin Zulaikha Greer Architects;* b. 10 Jan. 1953, Blayney, NSW; s. of John Ebenezer Tonkin and Veronica Mariea Tonkin (née Perry); m. Ellen Claire Woolley; one s. one d.; ed Univ. of Sydney; in practice with Lawrence Nield and Partners 1979–81; ind. practice 1981–, Co-founder Tonkin Zulaikha 1987, Tonkin Zulaikha Greer 1988–; Visiting Design Tutor, Sydney Univ., Univ. of NSW, Univ. of Tech., Sydney; Adjunct Prof. of Architecture, Univ. of Queensland; mem. Royal Australian Inst. of Architects (fmr Vice-Pres. and Chair. of Practice and Design Bds), Historic Houses Trust Exhbns Cttee; Trustee, Historic Houses Trust NSW; numerous awards and prizes, including Royal Australian Inst. of Architects Merit Awards 1988, 1991, 1993, 1996, 2000, 2001, 2003, 2007, 2008, winner, Vietnam Memorial Competition 1990, Tomb of the Unknown Soldier Competition 1993, Master Builders Asscn Merit Award 1993, ACEA Engineering Excellence Award 1999, Property Council of NSW Devt of the Year 1999, Int. Royal Inst. of Chartered Surveyors Award for Conservation 2000; winner, Nat. Gallery of Australia Competition 2000, winner, Australian War Memorial London Competition 2003, winner, Canberra Int. Arboretum Competition 2005. *Achievements:* design projects include refurbishment of Sydney Customs House, Fed. Museum and Library, Tenterfield, Royal Blind Soc. Library, Nat. Memorial to Australian Vietnam Forces, Tomb of the Unknown Australian Soldier, Canberra, Australian War Memorial, London, Craigieburn Bypass, Hume Freeway, Melbourne, Carriageworks Performing Arts Centre, Sydney. *Publications:* numerous articles, papers and essays. *Leisure interests:* mountain sports, motorcycling. *Address:* Tonkin Zulaikha Greer Architects, 117 Reservoir Street, Surry Hills, NSW 2010, Australia (office). *Telephone:* (2) 9215-4900 (office). *Fax:* (2) 9215-4901 (office). *E-mail:* peter@tzg.com.au (office). *Website:* www.tzg.com.au (office).

TØNNESSON, Stein, CandPhil, DPhil; Norwegian research institute director; *Director, International Peace Research Institute, Oslo;* b. 2 Dec. 1953, Copenhagen, Denmark; m.; one c.; ed Univ. of Århus, Denmark, Univ. of Oslo; taught Norwegian and History at Univ. of Oslo 1983; historian for Norwegian Asscn of Sports 1983–85; wrote doctoral thesis on Vietnam Revolution of 1945 1986–92; Research Fellow, Int. Peace Research Inst., Oslo (PRIO) 1990–92, Dir 2001–09; Research Prof. Nordic Inst. of Asian Studies 1992–95, Sr Research Fellow 1995–98; consultant to Statoil 1996–2000; Prof. of Human Devt Studies, Univ. of Oslo; mem. Advisory Bd Norwegian Forum for Research in US; mem. Bd CARE Norway, Swedish School of Advanced Asia Pacific Studies, Bd NORFUND 2007–. *Publications include:* The Vietnamese Revolution of 1945 1991, Imperial Policy and Southeast Asian Nationalism 1930–1957 (co-ed.) 1995, Asian Forms of the Nation (co-ed.) 1996, Vietnam 1946: How the War Began 2008; book chapters and articles in scholarly journals. *Address:* Jacob Aalls gt. 13, 0368 Oslo (home); International Peace Research Institute, Fuglehauggata 11, 0260 Oslo, Norway (office). *Telephone:* 22-54-77-31 (office). *Fax:* 22-54-77-01 (office). *E-mail:* stein@prio.no (office). *Website:* www.prio.no (office).

TONOMURA, Hitoshi; Japanese banker; fmr Pres. and Chair. Nomura Int., apptd Head of Overseas Operations 1995, currently Sr Adviser; Chair. Investment Trusts Asscn. *Address:* 2-1-14, Nihombashi, Chuo-ku, Tokyo, 103-8260, Japan (office). *Telephone:* (3) 3241-9500 (office). *Fax:* (3) 3241-9599 (office).

TOOLEY, Sir John, Kt, MA; British arts administrator and arts consultant; b. 1 June 1924, Rochester, Kent; s. of the late H. R. Tooley; m. 1st Judith Craig Morris 1951 (divorced 1965); three d.; m. 2nd Patricia J. N. Bagshawe 1968 (divorced 1990); one s.; m. 3rd Jennifer Anne Shannon 1995 (divorced 2003); ed Repton School and Magdalene Coll., Cambridge; Sec. Guildhall School of Music and Drama 1952–55; Asst to Gen. Admin., Royal Opera House, Covent Garden 1955–60, Asst Gen. Admin. 1960–70, Gen. Admin. 1970–80, Gen. Dir 1980–88; Chair. Almeida Theatre 1990–97, Fabric Advisory Cttee Salisbury Cathedral 1992–2005, Salisbury Cathedral Girl Choristers Trust 1995–2006, Nureyev Foundation 1995–; Pres. Salisbury Festival 1988–2005; Chair. Monument Insurance Brokers Ltd 1997–2002; consultant, Int. Man. Group 1988–97, Ballet Opera House, Toronto 1989–90, Istanbul Foundation for Culture and Arts 1993–, Antelope Films 1993–; Dir London Philharmonic Orchestra 1998–, Britten Estate 1989–96, South Bank Bd 1991–97, Compton Verney Opera Project 1991–97, Welsh Nat. Opera 1992–2000, David Gyngell Holdings Ltd 1996–97; Gov. Royal Ballet 1994–97; adviser, Borusan Philharmonic Orchestra, Istanbul 2005–; Trustee Britten Pears Foundation 1988–99, Walton Trust 1988–2000, Wigmore Hall 1989–2001, Almeida Theatre 1990–2002, Performing Arts Labs 1992–97, Cardiff Bay Opera House 1995–96, Sidney Nolan Trust 1995–, Mozartfest, Bath 2001–; Hon. FRAM; Hon. GSM; Hon. mem. Royal Northern Coll. of Music; Hon. ISM; Hon. Fellow, Magdalen Coll. Cambridge 2005; Commendatore of Italian Repub. 1976; Hon. DUniv (Univ. of Central England) 1996; Queen Elizabeth II Coronation Award 2005. *Publication:* In House 1999. *Leisure interests:* walking, theatre. *Address:* 18 Grange Court, Cambridge, CB3 9BD, England (home). *Telephone:* (1223) 358737 (office); (1223) 351995 (home). *Fax:* (1223) 358737 (office). *E-mail:* tooley@btinternet.com (home).

TOON, Malcolm, MA, LLD; American diplomatist (retd); b. 4 July 1916, Troy, NY; s. of George Toon and Margaret Broadfoot; m. Elizabeth J. Taylor 1943; one s. two d.; ed Tufts Univ., Fletcher School of Law and Diplomacy and Harvard Univ.; Research Technician, Nat. Resources Planning Bd 1939–41; Ensign, Lt.-Commdr, USNR 1942–46; in US Foreign Service 1946–79; Amb. to Czechoslovakia 1969–71, to Yugoslavia 1971–75, to Israel 1975–76, to USSR 1976–79; Dir McKesson Corpn, San Francisco; mem. Bd of Trustees Tufts Univ., Bd of Visitors, Fletcher School of Law and Diplomacy 1992; Co-Chair. US–Russian Jt Comm. on POWs and MIAs 1992–98; Hon. LLD (Tufts Univ.) 1977, (Middlebury Coll.) 1978, (Drexel Univ.) 1980, (American Coll. of Switzerland) 1985, (Grove City Coll.); degree of Prof., Acad. of Natural Sciences of the Russian Fed. 1996; Superior Honor Award, Dept of State 1965; Distinguished Honor Award, Dept of State 1979; Freedom Leadership Award, Hillsdale Coll., Mich. 1980, Freedom Award 1981, Wallace Award 1984, Gold Medal, Nat. Inst. of Social Sciences 1987. *Leisure interests:* golf, tennis, hunting, fishing. *Address:* 375 Pee Dee Road, Southern Pines, NC 28387, USA (home). *Telephone:* (910) 692-5992 (home).

TOOPE, Stephen J., LLB, BCL, PhD; Canadian university administrator; *President and Vice-Chancellor, University of British Columbia;* m. Paula Rosen; three c.; ed Trinity Coll., Cambridge, UK, McGill Univ., Harvard Univ., USA; served as Law Clerk to Chief Justice of Canada 1986–87; Research Dir, Office of the Special Rep., Royal Comm. on Aboriginal Peoples 1991; Asst Prof. of Law, McGill Univ. 1987–93, Assoc. Prof. 1993–99, Prof. 1999–2006, Assoc. Dean (Grad. Studies and Research), Faculty of Law 1991–94, Dean 1994–99; Pres. and Vice-Chancellor Univ. of British Columbia 2006–; consultant on int. law, int. human rights and legal reform to Depts of Foreign Affairs and Justice, Int. Devt Agency 1988–; Dir World Univ. Service of Canada 2004–; mem. Bd of Dirs Canadian Human Rights Foundation (now Equitas) 2001–06; mem. UN Working Group on Enforced or Involuntary Disappearances (Chair. and Rapporteur 2004–06) 2003–07; mem. Int. Advisory Bd, Faculty of Law, Nat. Univ. of Singapore 2001–, Journal of Int. Law and Int. Relations 2004–; mem. Academic Council, Inst. for Transnational Arbitration, USA 2001–, Research Council, Canadian Inst. for Advanced Research 2004–, Advisory Council, Minister of Justice 2005–06, Social Sciences and Humanities Research Council 2005–; Fern Gertrude Kennedy Prize in Jurisprudence (jtly) 1982, F. R. Scott Prize in Constitutional Law 1983, Casimar Bielski QC Prize in Int. Law 1983, Ballon Medal 1983, Douglas J. Sherbaniuk Distinguished Writing Award, Canadian Tax Foundation (jtly) 1995, Francis Deák Publication Award, American Soc. of Int. Law (jtly) 1998, David L. Johnston Award for Distinguished Service, McGill Alumni Asscn 1997, John W. Durnford Teaching Excellence Award, McGill Univ. 2001, McGill Univ. Scarlet Key Award. *Publications:* Mixed International Arbitration 1990; articles in American Journal of International Law, Columbia Journal of Transnational Law, Harvard Journal of International Law, McGill Law Journal and many other int. journals in N. America and Europe. *Address:* Office of the President, University of British Columbia, 6328 Memorial Road, Vancouver, BC V6T 1Z2, Canada (office). *Telephone:* (604) 822-8300 (office). *Fax:* (604) 822-5055 (office). *E-mail:* presidents.office@ubc.ca (office). *Website:* www.president.ubc.ca (office).

TOPALLI, Jozefina Çoba, MPA; Albanian politician; *Speaker, Kuvendi Popullor (Parliament);* b. 26 Nov. 1963, Shkodra; m.; two c.; ed Luigj Gurakuqi Univ., Shkodra, Univ. of Padova, Italy and Tirana Univ.; civil servant, Chamber of Commerce, Shkodra 1992–95; Lecturer and Chancellor, Luigi Gurakuqi Univ., Shkodra 1995–98; mem. Democratic Party of Albania—Partia Demokratike e Shqipërisë, Vice-Chair. 1997–; mem. Kuvendi Popullor (Parl.) 1996–, Deputy Speaker 1997–2005, Speaker (first woman) 2005–, fmr Deputy Pres. Parl. Children's Cttee, fmr mem. Social Work, Health and Family Cttee; mem. Council of Europe 2002–05; mem. monitoring missions during gen. elections held in Ukraine and Palestine 2004–05. *Address:* Office of the Speaker, Kuvendi Popullor, Bulevardi Dëshmorët e Kombit Nr.4, Tirana, Albania (office). *Telephone:* (4) 237413 (office). *Fax:* (4) 227949 (office). *E-mail:* marlind@parlament.al (office). *Website:* www.parlament.al (office).

TOPALOV, Veselin; Bulgarian chess master; b. 15 March 1975, Rousse; winner, World Under-14 Chess Championship, Puerto Rico 1989, silver medal, World Under-16 Championship, Singapore 1990; named Grandmaster 1992; reached last 16 in FIDE World Chess Championship 1999, quarter-finals 2000, last 16 2001, semi-finals 2004, World Champion 2005; losing finalist, Cands Tournament, Dortmund 2002; jt first place with Gary Kasparov, Linares 2005; winner, M-tel Masters 2005, 2006; lost title reunification match against Vladimir Kramnik 2006;*Website:* www.veselintopalov.net.

TOPBAŞ, Kadir, PhD; Turkish politician; *Mayor of Istanbul;* b. 1945, Artvin; ed Univ. of Istanbul; worked as architect, Istanbul metropolitan municipality; fmr Mayor of Beyoğlu; Mayor of Istanbul 2004–; served as Deputy Pres., Istanbul Architecture Cttee, Ministry of Culture. *Address:* Istanbul Büyükşehir Belediye Başkanlığı, Kasım Sok. 34010–MERTER, Istanbul, Turkey (office). *Telephone:* (212) 4494101 (office). *Fax:* (212) 4494158 (office). *E-mail:* baskan@ibb.gov.tr (office).

TOPCHEYEV, Yuriy Ivanovich, DTech Sc; Russian cyberneticist; *Emeritus Professor, International G. Soros Science Education Programme;* b. 26 Sept. 1920, Yaroslavl; s. of Ivan Yakovlevich Topcheyev and Vera Aleksandrovna Topcheyeva; m. Inna Ivanovna Smirnova 1965; one s.; ed Moscow Aviation Inst.; mem. CPSU 1948–91; Chief Dept of Scientific Research Inst. of Automatic Systems 1943–72; mem. staff and Prof., Inst. of Physical Eng, Moscow 1968–89, Chief of Faculty 1972–88; Prof. Int. G. Soros Science Educ. Programme 1996–97, Emer. Prof. 1997–; mem. Comm. of Co-ordination Cttee on Computers of USSR (now Russian) Acad. of Sciences 1978–85, Co-ordination Cttee on Robotics 1980–87; Chair. Council on Systems of Automated Design, Ministry of Higher Educ. 1977–87; mem. Council Specialized Scientific and Technological Activities of USSR (now Russian) Acad. of Sciences 1989–, Russian Cosmonautics 1992–, World Innovation Foundation 2001–, Prof. and Grand Doctor of Philosophy, Acad. Européenne d'Informatisation (Belgium) 2003–; Order of Labour Banner 1950, State Prize 1972, Korolev Medal 1977, Gagarin Medal 1981, Gold Medal, Russian Exhbn Centre 2005. *Publications include:* Encyclopaedia for Automatic Regulation Systems Design 1989; (co-author) Basics of Automatic Regulation 1954, Modern Methods of Automatic Control System Design (ed. and co-author) 1967, Technical Cybernetics (4 Vols) 1967–89, Philosophy of Nonlinear Control Systems 1990, Nonlinear Systems of Automatic Control (Vols 1–9) 1970–92, People and Robotics (Vol. 1) 1995, (Vol. 2) 1998, Development of Robotics 2000, Robotics: A Historical Overview 2001, Robotics – History and Perspectives 2002, Robotic Assisted Human's Activity (A History of Development) 2004, Biography of Mstislav Vsevolodovich Keldysh 2002, biographies of Vladimir Mikhailovich Myasischev and Pavel Osypovich Sukhoi 2003, Robotics – Assisted Human's Activity (A History of Development) (co-author) 2005, Biography of Vladimir Mikhailovich Petlyakov 2005, History of Domestic Aviation Arms 2005; over 310 articles, including 12 on great contemporary Russian scientists in A History of Science Engineering 2002, and 2 pieces on contemporary biosphere ecology. *Leisure interests:* nonlinear systems design, the history of the development of automatic systems and robotics. *Address:* Leningradskoye sch. 31, Apt. 147, 125212 Moscow, Russia. *Telephone:* (495) 156-63-06. *E-mail:* fsg100@yandex.ru (home).

TÖPFER, Klaus, PhD; German politician and international organization official; b. 29 July 1938, Waldenburg, Silesia; m.; three c.; ed Univs of Mainz, Frankfurt am Main and Munster; family expelled from Silesia, settled in Höxter/Weser 1945; Head, Political Economy Dept, Inst. of Devt Planning, Munster 1970–71; Head, Planning and Information Section, Saarland State Chancellery, Saarbrücken; lecturer, Coll. of Admin., Speyer 1971–78; Prof. Ordinarius, Hanover Univ., Dir Inst. of Environmental Research and Regional Planning 1978–79; Hon. Prof. Mainz Univ. 1985–; joined Christian Democratic Union (CDU) 1972, CDU Dist Chair., Saarbrücken, mem. CDU State Exec., Saar 1977–79; State Sec., Rhineland Palatinate Ministry of Social Affairs, Health and Environment, Mainz 1978–85; Deputy Chair. CDU Fed. Cttee of Experts on the Environment 1983; Minister of Environment and Health, Rhineland Palatinate 1985–87; CDU Dist Chair., Rhein-Hunsrück 1987–; Fed. Minister for the Environment, Nature Conservation and Nuclear Safety 1987–94, of Regional Planning, Housing and Urban Devt 1994–98; Exec. Dir UNEP, Nairobi 1998–2006; Acting Dir UN Centre for Human Settlements (Habitat) 1998–2000; TÜV Environment Prize 2000, German Environment Prize 2002.

TOPI, Bamir, PhD, DrSc; Albanian biologist, politician and head of state; *President;* b. 24 April 1957, Tirana; m. Teuta Topi; two d.; ed Veterinary Medicine Faculty, Agricultural Univ. of Tirana; Scientific Researcher, Inst. for Veterinary Studies, Tirana 1984–87, Dir 1990–96; elected to Nat. Ass. 1996, re-elected twice; Minister of Agric. and Food 1996–97; Pres. of Albania 2007–; fmr Deputy Chair. Democratic Party, resgnd on taking office 2007. *Address:* Office of the President, Bulevardi Dëshmorët e Kombit, Tirana, Albania (office). *Telephone:* (4) 228437 (office). *Fax:* (4) 236925 (office). *E-mail:* info@president.al (office). *Website:* www.president.al (office).

TOPOL, Chaim; Israeli actor, producer and director; b. 9 Sept. 1935, Tel-Aviv; s. of Yaakov Topol and Rela Goldman; m. Galia Finkelstein 1956; one s. two d.; joined entertainment unit during army service 1953; f. The Green Onion satirical theatre 1956, Municipal Theatre of Haifa 1959; starred in stage productions of Fiddler on the Roof in London 1967, 1983, 1994, on Broadway NY, 1990 in Melbourne 1998, in Sydney 2005, in Wellington, New Zealand 2007, USA tour 2009, in Ziegfield 1988, in The Caucasian Chalk Circle, Romanov and Juliet, Othello, A View From The Bridge, Chichester Festival Theatre; actor, producer, director for the Genesis Project, filming the Bible, New York; Golden Globe Award 1972, San Francisco Film Festival Winner 1972, David Donatello Award 1972. *Films include:* Cast A Giant

Shadow 1965, Sallah 1966, Before Winter Comes 1969, A Talent for Loving, Fiddler on the Roof 1971, The Public Eye 1972, Galileo 1974, Flash Gordon 1972, For Your Eyes Only 1980, The Winds of War 1981, A Dime Novel, Ervinka, Left Luggage 1997; several TV films. *Albums include:* Fiddler on the Roof (cast album), It's Topol, War Songs, Topol 68, Fiddler on the Roof (film album), Topol's Israel. *Publication:* Topol by Topol (autobiog.) 1981, To Life! (A Treasury of Jewish Wisdom, Wit and Humour) 1995. *Leisure interests:* book illustrations and portrait drawings. *Address:* 22 Vale Court, Maida Vale, London, W9 1RT, England (home). *Fax:* (20) 7266-2155 (home).

TOPOL, Eric J., MD; American cardiologist and academic; *Provost, Chief Academic Officer and Chairman, Department of Cardiovascular Medicine, Cleveland Clinic Foundation;* b. 26 June 1954, Queens, NY; ed Univ. of Virginia, Charlottesville, Univ. of Rochester School of Medicine and Dentistry, NY; Univ. of Rochester School of Medicine and Dentistry 1975–79; Intern in Medicine, Moffitt Hosp., Univ. of California, San Francisco 1979–80, Asst and Sr Resident in Medicine 1980–82; Fellow in Cardiovascular Medicine, Johns Hopkins Hosp., Baltimore, Md 1982–85; Sr Fellow, Coronary Angioplasty, San Francisco Heart Inst. 1984; Asst Prof. of Internal Medicine, Univ. of Mich. School of Medicine, Ann Arbor 1985–87, Assoc. Prof., 1987–90, Prof. 1990–91; Consulting Prof. of Medicine, Duke Univ. School of Medicine, Durham, NC 1991–2002; Prof. of Medicine, Cleveland Clinic Health Sciences Center, Ohio State Univ. School of Medicine 1991–2002; Provost and Prof. of Medicine, Cleveland Clinic Lerner Coll. of Medicine, Case Western Reserve Univ. 2002–; Co-Dir, Cleveland Clinic Heart Center 1991–, Chair. Dept of Cardiovascular Medicine, Cleveland Clinic Foundation 1991–, Provost, Chief Academic Officer and mem. Bd of Govs Cleveland Clinic Foundation 2001–; Vice-Chair. Dept of Molecular Cardiology, Cleveland Clinic Research Institute 1991–, Dir Joseph J. Jacobs Center for Thrombosis and Vascular Biology 1991–; Amon G. Carter Professorship, Univ. of Texas Health Science Center 1988; Donald and Lois Roon Visiting Professorship, Scripps Clinic and Research Foundation 1992; Barnet Berris Visiting Professorship, Univ. of Toronto 1992; Goldberg Visiting Professorship, Cedars-Sinai Medical Center 1994; Edward Massie Visiting Professorship, Washington Univ. School of Medicine 1995; Simon Dack Visiting Professorship, Mount Sinai Cardiovascular Inst. 1995; Marjorie and Gaye Grollman Visiting Professorship, Univ. of Virginia 1995; Isadore Rosenfeld Visiting Professorship, Cornell Univ. Medical School 1995; John J. Sampson Visiting Professor, Univ. of California, San Francisco Medical Center 1998; mem. Bd of Dirs Rhone-Poulenc-Rorer, Inc. 1997, Quintiles Transnational, Inc. 1997–; Ed. Current Opinion in Cardiology 1994–96, Scientific American Medicine 1995–98, Cardiology Website: TheHeart.Org 2000–; mem. Editorial Bd American Journal of Cardiology 1988–, Journal of the American College of Cardiology 1989–93, 1995–99, 2001–03, Coronary Artery Disease 1989–, International Journal of Cardiac Imaging 1990–, Cardiology 1990–, Trends in Cardiovascular Medicine 1990–, Choices in Cardiology 1990–, Clinical Cardiology 1990–, Circulation 1991– (Consulting Ed. 2001–), Cardiology in the Elderly 1991–, British Heart Journal 1992–, Journal of Myocardial Ischemia 1992–, Current Literature 1993–, Cardiovascular Drug Therapy 1993–, Primary Cardiology 1994–, Clinics in Interventional Cardiology 1995–, Journal of Women's Health 1995–, European Heart Journal 1996–, Seminars in Interventional Cardiology 1996–, Revista Espanola de Cardiologia 1996–, American Heart Journal 1996–, Journal of Clinical and Experimental Cardiology 1997–, Acute Coronary Syndromes 1997–, American Journal of Medicine 1998–, Journal of Clinical and Basic Cardiology 1998–, Current Treatment Options in Cardiovascular Diseases 1998–, Heart Disease: A Journal of Cardiovascular Medicine 1998–, Current Opinion in Cardiovascular, Renal and Pulmonary Investigational Drugs 1998–, International Journal of Cardiology 1999–, Heart Drug Journal 1999–, Cardiovascular Therapeutics 2000–, ASEAN Heart Journal 2001–; editorial consultant/manuscript reviewer for numerous journals; mem. AAAS, American Soc. of Clinical Investigation 1990, Best Doctors in America 1992–2003, American Asscn of Physicians 1995, Johns Hopkins Soc. of Scholars 1999, Int. Soc. for Fibrinolysis and Thrombolysis, American Fed. for Clinical Research, Asscn of Univ. of Cardiologists, Asscn of Profs in Cardiology, Inst. of Medicine (NAS) 2004; Fellow, American Heart Asscn 1983–85, American Coll. of Chest Physicians, Soc. of Cardiac Angiography and Interventions (also Trustee), European Soc. of Cardiology, American Coll. of Cardiology, American Coll. of Physicians; Hon. mem. Columbian Soc. of Cardiology, Polish Cardiac Soc.; Outstanding Medical Specialist in the US, Town and Country 1989, Sir William Osler Award, Univ. of Miami School of Medicine 1989, 4th Annual Virginia Heart Center Award, Virginia Heart Center 1992, Distinguished Teacher Award, Cleveland Civic Foundation 1992, Best Doctors in America, American Health Magazine 1996, Distinguished Teacher Award, Cleveland Civic Foundation 1997, Most Cited Researchers in Cardiology, Science Watch 1999, Top Docs-Medicine's Most Cited, Science Watch 1999, Scientific Achievement in Clinical Research, Cleveland Clinic Foundation 2000, Innovator of the Year, American Coll. of Cardiovascular Administrators and Alliance of Cardiovascular Professionals 2001, Top 0.5% Cited Researcher, Inst. for Scientific Information 2001, America's Top Doctors, Castle Connolly Medical Publishers 2001, American Heart Asscn's Top Ten Research Advances 2001, Gill Heart Inst. Award for Outstanding Contribs to Cardiovascular Medicine 2002, Dr William Beaumont Award in Medicine, American Medical Asscn 2002, Andreas R. Gruntzig Award, Swiss Soc. of Cardiology 2002, one of Top 10 Most Cited Researchers in Medicine, In-Cites, ISI 2003, Silver Medal for Outstanding Physician/Scientist, European Soc. of Cardiology 2004. *Publications:* ed. of 30 medical books and author of more than 1,600 articles in medical and scientific journals. *Leisure interests:* family, golf, travel, reading. *Address:* Department of Cardiovascular Medicine, Cleveland Clinic Foundation, Building F-25, 2062 Clinic Drive, Cleveland, OH 44195, USA (office). *Telephone:* (216) 445-9490 (office). *Fax:* 216) 445-9595

(office). *E-mail:* topole@ccf.org (office). *Website:* www.clevelandclinic.org/staff/getstaff.asp?StaffId=123 (office).

TOPOLÁNEK, Mirek; Czech politician; b. 15 May 1956, Vsetín; m.; three c.; ed Brno Univ. of Tech.; Project Designer, later Ind. Designer, OKD Ostrava 1980–87; Head Designer Specialist, Energoproject Praha, Ostrava Works 1987–91; Exec. Dir then Man. Dir VAE Ltd (later VAE Inc.) 1991–96, Chair. 1996; active in citizens forum 1989; mem. Municipal Corpn of Ostrava-Poruba 1990–94; Senator 1995–2004; mem. Civil Democratic Party (ODS) 1994–, Vice-Chair. 1996–98, Chair. 2002–; mem. Cttee for Economy, Agric. and Transport, Org. Cttee and Chair. Sub-cttee for Power Eng, Vice-Pres. of Senate 2002–04; Chair. ODS Senate Club 1990–2002; Prime Minister June–Oct. 2006 (resgnd), reinstated Jan. 2007–09 (resgnd); mem. Bd Asscn for Restoration and Devt of Northern Moravian Region and Silesia, Mining Coll., Univ. of Tech., Ostrava, Jagello Asscn. *Address:* Civic Democratic Party (Občanská demokratická strana), Jánský vršek 13, 110 00 Prague 1, Czech Republic (office). *Telephone:* 234707188 (office). *Fax:* 234707103 (office). *E-mail:* hk@ods.cz (office). *Website:* www.ods.cz (office); www.topolanek.cz (office).

TOPORNIN, Boris Nikolayevich; Russian legal specialist; *Director, Institute of State and Law, Russian Academy of Sciences;* b. 29 Dec. 1929; m.; two s.; ed Moscow Inst. of Int. Relations; jr, sr researcher, Scientific Sec. Inst. of Law USSR (now Russian) Acad. of Sciences 1955–62; Deputy Chief Scientific Sec. Presidium of USSR Acad. of Sciences 1962–67; Head of Div., First Deputy Dir Inst. of State and Law, USSR Acad. of Sciences 1967–89, Dir 1989–; Corresp. mem. USSR (now Russian) Acad. of Sciences 1987, mem. 1991, Acad. Sec. Dept of Philosophy and Law; research in constitutional law and state law 1991–; Deputy Pres. Int. Asscn of Constitutional Law; Mem. Int. Acad. of Law; Humboldt Inst. Prize 1999, Femida Prize 2000. *Publications include:* Political Foundation of Socialism 1972, New Constitution of USSR 1980, Development of Socialist Democracy 1985, Foreign Policy and Science 1990. *Publications:* Federalismus zwischen Integration und Sezession. Chancen und Risiken bundesstaatlicher Ordnung 1993, Legal Foundation of Russian Economy 2000. *Address:* Institute of State and Law, Russian Academy of Sciences, Znamenka str. 10, 119841 Moscow, Russia (office). *Telephone:* (495) 291-87-56; (495) 203-92-12. *Website:* www.igpran.ru/engl (office).

TOPOROV, Col-Gen. Vladimir Mikhailovich; Russian politician and army officer; b. 7 Feb. 1946, Baranovichi; ed Odessa Artillery School, Frunze Mil. Acad., Gen. Staff Acad.; Commdr of platoon, battery 1968–75, Deputy Commdr of Regt, Commdr 1976–79, Deputy Commdr of Div., Commdr 1979–84, First Deputy Commdr, Commdr of army 1987–89; Head of Staff, First Deputy Commdr of troops of Far East Mil. Dist 1989–92; Commdr of troops of Moscow Mil. Dist 1991–92; Deputy Minister of Defence 1992–2000; C-in-C of airborne (expeditionary) forces 1995–98. *Address:* c/o Ministry of Defence, Znamenka 19, Moscow, Russia.

TOPOYEV, Maj.-Gen. Esen; Kyrgyzstani politician and army officer; fmr Minister of Defence. *Address:* c/o Ministry of Defence, 26 Logvinenko str., Bishkek, 710001, Kyrgyzstan.

TOPPO, HE Cardinal Telesphore Placidus, DD; Indian ecclesiastic; *Archbishop of Ranchi;* b. 15 Oct. 1939, Jhargaon, Gumla Dist, Jharkhand; s. of Ambrose Toppo and Sofia Xalxo; ed Lievens Barway Boys' Secondary School, Chainpur, St Xavier's Coll., Ranchi, Pontifical Urban Univ., Rome, Italy, Univ. of Ranchi; ordained priest 1969; f. apostolic school for cands to priesthood from Munda Tribe; Prof. and Asst to Dir of St Joseph's High School, Torpa; Bishop of Dumka 1978; Coadjutor Archbishop of Ranchi 1984, Archbishop of Ranchi 1985–; attended Eighth Ordinary Ass. of World Synod of Bishops, Vatican City 1990, Special Ass. for Asia of World Synod of Bishops, Vatican City 1998, Second Special Ass. for Europe of World Synod of Bishops, Vatican City 1999, Tenth Ordinary Ass. of World Synod of Bishops, Vatican City 2001; cr. Cardinal (Cardinal Priest of Sacro Cuore di Gesù agonizzante a Vitinia) (first tribal cardinal of India—Oraon of Kurukh tribe) 2003; Pres.-Del. 11th Gen. Ordinary Ass. of World Synod of Bishops 2005; fmr Vice-Pres. Conf. of Catholic Bishops of India, Pres. 2004–06, mem. Special Comm. for Evangelization, Comm. for Inter-religious Dialogue; mem. Pontifical Council for Inter-Religious Dialogue, Bishops' Friends of the Focalare Movt, Cen. Cttee Fed. of Asian Bishops' Confs, Advisory Council Margareta Weisser Foundation for Indigenous Tribal Peoples in Asia, Governing Body Indo-German Social Service Soc., New Delhi, Nat. Educ. Group; Chair. Regional Bishops' Council, Jharkhand Bishops and Major Superiors Forum; fmr Chair. Office of Peace and Harmony of the FABC; Chancellor Faculty of Theology, Ranchi; mem. Governing Body Vikas Maitri, Ranchi, St Xavier's Coll., Ranchi, Nirmala Coll., Hinoo, Ursuline BEd Coll., Lohardaga; Pres. Chotanagpur Catholic Mission Co-operative Credit Soc., Catholic Charities, Ranchi; Patron Sarva Dharma Milan Parishad, Ranchi, Citizens' Forum, Ranchi; Managing Trustee Jharkhand Antyodaya Public Charitable Trust; Jharkhand Ratan, Lok Sewa Samity, Ranchi 2002. *Address:* Archbishop's House, PO Box 5, Purulia Road, Ranchi 834 001, Jharkhand, India (office). *Telephone:* (651) 204728 (office). *Fax:* (651) 304844 (office). *E-mail:* rca_ranch@hotmail.com; telestoppo@rediffmail.com. *Website:* www.ranchiarchdiocese.org (office).

TOPTAN, Köksal; Turkish politician; *Speaker, Büyük Millet Meclisi (Grand National Assembly);* b. 1943, Rize; m.; three c.; ed Law Faculty, Istanbul Univ.; fmr mem. Dogru Yol Party and mem. Parl. from Bartin, now mem. Justice and Development Party (AKP) and mem. Parl. from Zonguldag, fmr Chair. Parl. Justice Cttee; fmr State Minister; fmr Minister of Educ. and Minister of Culture; Speaker, Büyük Millet Meclisi (Grand Nat. Ass.) 2007–. *Address:* Office of the Speaker, Büyük Millet Meclisi (Grand National Assembly), 06543 Bakanlýklar, Ankara, Turkey. *Telephone:* 4205323 -

4205324. *E-mail:* koksal.toptan@tbmm.gov.tr; info@koksaltoptan.net. *Website:* www.tbmm.gov.tr; www.koksaltoptan.com.

TORIBIONG, Johnson, LLM, DIur; Palauan lawyer, diplomatist, politician and head of state; *President;* b. 1946; ed Univ. of Washington Law School, USA; fmr Amb. to Taiwan; Pres. of Palau 2009–. *Address:* Office of the President, POB 6051, Koror, PW 96940, Palau (office). *Telephone:* 488-2403 (office). *Fax:* 488-1662 (office). *E-mail:* pres@palaunet.com (office).

TORKUNOV, Anatoly Vassilyevich, Cand Hist, DrPolSci; Russian academic and diplomatist; b. 26 Aug. 1950, Moscow; m.; one d.; ed Moscow State Inst. of Int. Relations; teacher Moscow State Inst. of Int. Relations 1974–, Pro-Rector 1977–, Dean Chair. of Int. Relations, then First Pro-Rector 1986–; diplomatic service in People's Democratic Repub. of Korea 1971–72, in USA 1983–86; Rector Moscow State Inst. of Int. Relations 1992–; Pres. Russian UN Asscn; mem. Expert Analytical Council, Attestation Bd Ministry of Russian Asscn of Int. Studies, Scientific Council of Security Council of Russian Fed., Russian Acad. of Nat. Sciences, Acad. of Sciences of Higher Schooling, Nat. Russian Cttee on problems of UNESCO; mem. Editorial Bd journals Global Gov. (USA), Mezhdunarodnaya Zhizn, Moscovsky Zhurnal Mezhdunarodnogo Prava, Bisnes i Politika; Medals for Labour Merit, 850th Anniversary of Moscow, 300 Years of Russian Navy, Order of Friendship between Peoples, Order of Merit, Order of Honour, Order of Diplomatic Merit (Repub. of Korea). *Publications:* seven monographs and over 170 scientific publs on int. relations, problems of Russian foreign policy, Asian-Pacific Region, Korea including: The War in Korea 1950–1953 Tokyo 2000, History of Korea, Moscow 2003, Contemporary International Relations and Russian Foreign Policy, Moscow 2004. *Leisure interests:* theatre, music. *Address:* Moscow State Institute of International Relations, Vernadskogo prosp. 76, 117454 Moscow, Russia (office). *Telephone:* (495) 434-00-89 (office). *Fax:* (495) 434-90-61 (office). *E-mail:* tork@mgimo.ru (office). *Website:* www.mgimo.ru (office).

TÖRMÄLÄ, Pertti, BMS, DPhil; Finnish scientist and academic; *Chief Scientific Officer and Chairman, Bioretec Limited;* b. 26 Nov. 1945, Tampere; s. of Matti Törmälä and Elma Virtanen; m. 1st Kirsti Miettinen 1967 (dissolved); two d.; m. 2nd Mirja Talasoja 1995; Assoc. Prof. of Non-Metallic Materials, Tampere Univ. of Tech. 1975, Prof. of Fibre Raw Materials, Prof. of Plastics Tech. and Head Inst. of Plastics Tech. 1985–95; fmr Research Prof., Acad. of Finland, Acad. Prof. and Head of Inst. of Biomaterial Tech. 1995–2005; Chief Scientific Officer and Chair. Bioretec Ltd 2005–; Hon. DMed; Nat. Inventor Prize 1986, Nordic Tech. Prize 1988. *Publications:* eight textbooks, 150 patents and more than 800 scientific papers. *Leisure interests:* exercise, music. *Address:* Bioretec Limited, Saarchkarjenknja 5, 33300 Tampere, Finland (office). *Telephone:* (40) 5146944 (office). *E-mail:* pertti .tormala@bioretec.com (office). *Website:* www.bioretec.com (office).

TORNATORE, Giuseppe; Italian film-maker; b. 27 May 1956, Bagheria, Palermo, Sicily; debut as dir at age 16, with short film Il Carretto. *Television films include:* Ritratto di un Rapinatore, Incontro con Francesco Rosi, Scrittori Siciliani e Cinema: Verga, Pirandello, Brancati and Sciascia and Il Diario di Guttuso. *Feature films include:* writer and dir: Il Camorrista (The Professor) 1987, Cinema Paradiso (Special Jury Prize, Cannes Festival 1989) 1988, Stanno Tutti Bene (Everybody's Fine) 1991, Una Pura formalità (A Pure Formality) 1994, Uomo delle Stelle (Starmaker) 1995, La Leggenda del pianista sull'oceano (The Legend of the Pianist on the Ocean) 1998, Malèna 2000. *Documentaries include:* Ethnic Minorities in Sicily (Best Documentary, Salerno Film Festival 1982).

TÖRNUDD, Klaus, PhD; Finnish diplomatist and academic; b. 26 Dec. 1931, Helsinki; s. of Allan Törnudd and Margit Niininen; m. Mirja Siirala 1960; one s. one d.; ed Univ. of Helsinki, Univ. of Paris and School of Advanced Int. Studies, Johns Hopkins Univ., Washington DC; entered Finnish Foreign Service 1958, served at Finnish Mission to UN 1961–64, Cairo Embassy 1964–66, Moscow Embassy 1971–73, CSCE 1973–74; Prof. of Int. Politics, Univ. of Tampere, Finland 1967–71; Deputy Dir of Political Affairs in the Ministry for Foreign Affairs 1974–77, Dir 1977–81, Under-Sec. of State for Political Affairs 1983–88; Perm. Rep. to the UN 1988–91; Fellow, Harvard Univ., USA 1991–92; Sr Adviser, Ministry for Foreign Affairs 1992–93; Amb. to France and to UNESCO 1993–96; mem. Sr Faculty, Geneva Centre for Security Policy 1997–98; Visting Prof. Nat. Defence Coll. of Finland 1998–2003; Ed. Co-operation and Conflict (Nordic Journal of Int. Politics) 1968–70, mem. Editorial Bd 1976–79; mem. Editorial Bd of Ulkopolitiikka-Utrikespolitik 1983–87; Chair. of Bd Tampere Peace Research Inst. 1978–82; Chair. UN Study Group on Nuclear Weapon-Free Zones 1983–85; mem. Bd of Trustees UNITAR 1984–88; mem. of Bd of Govs IAEA 1985–87; mem. UN Sec.-Gen.'s Advisory Bd on Disarmament Matters 1991–96; Dr hc (Åbo Akademi Univ., Finland) 2002. *Publications:* several books on Finnish politics and int. affairs. *Address:* Tempelgatan 8A, 00100 Helsinki, Finland (home). *Telephone:* (9) 490159 (home). *Fax:* (9) 448849 (home). *E-mail:* klaus .toernudd@kolumbus.fi (home).

ToROBERT, Sir Henry Thomas, KBE, BEcons; Papua New Guinea banker; b. 1942, Kokopo; ed Univ. of Sydney; Asst Research Officer, Reserve Bank of Australia, Port Moresby 1965, Deputy Man. 1971, Man. 1972; Gov. and Chair. of Bd Bank of Papua New Guinea 1973–93; Chair. Papua New Guinea Inst. of Applied Social and Econ. Research 1975–82; Chair. Man. Bd Bankers' Coll. 1973–; Pnr, Deloitte Touche Tohmatsu 1993–; Chair. Credit Corpn (PNG) Ltd 1993–2007 (resgnd); Chair. Govt Super Task Force on Project Implementation 1994–; Pres. Amateur Sports Fed. and PNG Olympic and Commonwealth Games Cttee 1980–. *Address:* c/o Credit Corporation (PNG) Ltd, PO Box 1787, Port Moresby, Papua New Guinea.

TÖRÖK, László, DTech; Hungarian archaeologist and academic; *Research Professor, Archaeological Institute, Hungarian Academy of Sciences;* b. 13 May 1941, Budapest; s. of László Török and Mária Giesz; m. Erzsébet Szódy 1984; ed Budapest Univ. of Tech. Sciences, Eötvös Loránd Univ.; Research Fellow, Archaeological Inst., Hungarian Acad. of Sciences 1964, Sr Research Fellow 1985, Adviser 1991, Research Prof. 2004–; Lecturer, Eötvös Loránd Univ. of Arts and Sciences, Dept of Egyptology 1972, Hon. Prof. 1992–; Visiting Prof., Dept of Classics, Univ. of Bergen, Norway 1980, 1989–92, 1994–99; Overseas Visiting Scholar, St John's Coll. Cambridge 1998; Vice-Pres. of the Int. Soc. for Nubian Studies 1990–2002; Gen. Ed. of Antaeus (periodical) 1984–99; mem., Norwegian Acad. of Science and Letters 1994; mem., Hungarian Acad. of Science 2004; Albert Reckitt Archaeological Lecture, British Acad. 1995; research into ancient history and archaeology of Middle Nile Region and Hellenistic and late antique art of Egypt; Dr hc (Univ. of Bergen, Norway) 2000. *Publications:* Economic Offices and Officials in Meroitic Nubia 1978, Der meroitische Staat 1986, The Royal Crowns of Kush 1987, Late Antique Nubia 1988, Coptic Antiquities I–II 1993, Fontes Historiae Nubiorum I 1994, II 1996, III 1998, IV 2000 (with co-authors), Hellenistic and Roman Terracottas from Egypt 1995, The Birth of an Ancient African State 1995, Meroe City: An Ancient African Capital 1997, The Kingdom of Kush: Handbook of the Napatan-Meroitic Civilization 1997, The Hunting Centaur 1998, The Image of the Ordered World in Ancient Nubian Art 2002, Transfigurations of Hellenism: Aspects of Late Antique Art in Egypt AD 250–700 2005, Between Two Worlds: The Frontier Region Between Ancient Nubia and Egypt 3700 BC – 500 AD 2009; over 100 articles. *Leisure interest:* reading (belles-lettres). *Address:* MTA Régészeti Intézete, 1014 Budapest, Úri utca 49, Hungary (office). *Telephone:* (1) 224-6700. *Fax:* (1) 224-6719 (office).

TOROSSIAN, Tigran, PhD, DPolSci; Armenian engineer and politician; *Deputy Chairman, Republican Party of Armenia;* b. 14 April 1956, Yerevan; m.; one d.; ed Yerevan Polytechnic Inst.; Engineer, then Leading Engineer, Yerevan Scientific Research Inst. of Math. Machines 1978–88, Subdivision Head, then Scientific Assoc. 1988–95; mem., Cen. Electoral Comm. 1996–98; Ed.-in-Chief, Republican Party newspaper 1997–98; Deputy, Nat. Ass. (Republican Party of Armenia) 1999–, Vice-Chair. Azgayin Zhoghov (Nat. Ass.) 1999–2006, Chair. 2006–08, Chair. ad hoc Cttee on Constitutional Amendments 2001–03, ad hoc Cttee on Matters of Integration in European Structures 2003–08; Head of Armenian Del., Parl. Ass. of Council of Europe, Vice-Chair. Parl. Ass. of the Council of Europe European Democrat Group 2004–; Vice-Chair. Cttee on the Honouring of Obligations and Commitments by Mem. States of Council of Europe 2006–; mem. Party Bd Republican Party of Armenia 1993–, Deputy Chair. 1998–2005, Deputy Chair. Republican Party of Armenia 2005–; Medal for Exceptional Services to Motherland 2006. *Achievements include:* holder of 10 eng patents. *Publications:* more than 30 scientific studies in math., one monograph and more than 20 scientific studies in political science and about 200 articles. *Address:* Haiastani Hanrapetakan Kusaktsutiun, 0010 Yerevan, Melik-Adamian Str. 2, Armenia (office). *Telephone:* (10) 58-00-31 (office). *Fax:* (10) 50-12-59 (office). *E-mail:* toros@ parliament.am (office); hhk@hhk.am (office). *Website:* www.hhk.am (office).

TORP, Niels A., DipArch; Norwegian architect; *Principal, Niels Torp Arkitekter MNAL;* b. 8 March 1940, Oslo; s. of Ernst Torp and Nini Torp (née Butenschøn); m. Bente Poulsson; one s. three d.; ed Norges Tekniske Høgskole, Trondheim, The Norwegian Inst. Rome; joined Torp & Torp Arkitekter MNAL 1965, Pnr 1970, Man. 1974, Man., Prin. Niels Torp Arkitekter MNAL 1984–; visiting lecturer at architectural schools in Norway and other European countries; A. C. Houens Legacy, Sundts Prize for Architectural Merits, Awards from the Stone Asscn, Fine Art Award (Oslo City Council), Carl M. Egers Legacy, Europa Nostra Awards, Prize for Built Environment (Norwegian Dept of Environment), Kasper Salin Prize (Sweden), European Award for Steel Structures, Swedish Stone Asscn Award, Concrete Award (Norway), British Construction Industry Award 1998, Brunel Award 1998, Aesthetic Counsel Diploma, Bærum, Norway 1998, Parelius Scholarship 1998, Glulam Award 1999 (with Aviaplan), RIBA Award for Architecture 1999, Jacob Award for Design 1999. *Major works:* Giskehagen residential homes 1986, Scandinavian Airlines System (SAS) HQ, Stockholm 1987, Aker Brygge (dockland devt Oslo) 1988, HQ Den Norske Bank 1988, Hamar Olympiahall 1991, Alna Shopping Centre, Oslo 1996, railway station/bus terminal, Gothenburg 1996, Christiania Qvartalet 1996, BA HQ, London 1997, Colosseum Park, Oslo 1997, Oslo Airport Gardermoen (with Aviaplan) 1998, airport control tower and airport hotel, Oslo 1998, Papendrop – Utrecht, The Netherlands, five office bldgs 1999, NSB (Norwegian Railway) HQ, Oslo 1999, devt plans for towns Larvik, Sandefjord, Drammen, Ås, Elverum, Hamar and Bodø. *Leisure interests:* music, playing piano, sailing. *Address:* Industrigaten 59, PO Box 5387, 0304 Oslo, Norway (office). *Telephone:* 23-36-68-00 (office). *Fax:* 23-36-68-01 (office). *E-mail:* firmapost@ntorp.no (office). *Website:* www.ntorp.no (office).

TORRANCE, Sam, MBE, OBE; British professional golfer; b. 24 Aug. 1953, Largs; s. of Bob Torrance and June Torrance; m. Suzanne Torrance 1995; one s. two d.; professional golfer 1970–; has played in eight Ryder Cups (European Capt. 2002) and represented Scotland on numerous occasions; winner Scottish PGA Championship 1978, 1980, 1985, 1991, 1993; mem. Dunhill Cup team (eight times), World Cup team (11 times), Hennessy Cognac Cup team (five times), Double Diamond team (three times); Capt. winning European team in Asahi Glass Four Tours Championship, Adelaide 1991; Capt. winning British Ryder Cup Team 2002; winner of 28 tournaments worldwide since 1972 including Italian Open 1987, Germany Masters 1990, Jersey Open 1991, Kronenbourg Open 1993, Catalan Open 1993, Honda Open 1993, Hamburg Open 1993, British Masters 1995, French Open 1998; played US Sr Tour 2003–04, returned to European Sr Tour 2004–, winner Travis Perkins Senior Masters 2004, Irvine Whitlock Seniors Classic 2005, De Vere PGA Seniors Championship 2005, Bendinat London Seniors Masters 2005, Sharp Italian

Seniors Open 2006, AIB Irish Seniors Open 2006, PGA Seniors Championship 2006, Scottish Seniors Open 2006; winner European Seniors Tour's Order of Merit 2005, 2006. *Publications:* Sam: The Autobiography of Sam Torrance 2003. *Leisure interests:* snooker, tennis. *Address:* c/o CSA, 90 High Street, Burnham, Bucks., SL1 7JT, England (office).

TORRICELLI, Robert G., JD, MPA; American fmr politician; b. 26 Aug. 1951, Paterson, NJ; ed Rutgers and Harvard Univs; called to bar, NJ 1978; Deputy legis. counsel, Office of Gov. of NJ 1975–77; counsel to Vice-Pres. Mondale, Washington, DC 1978–81; pvt. practice, Washington, DC 1981–82; mem. 98th-104th Congresses 1983–97; Senator from New Jersey 1996–2002; Democrat.

TORRIJOS ESPINO, Martin; Panamanian business executive, politician and fmr head of state; b. 18 July 1963, Panama City; s. of Gen. Omar Torrijos; m. Vivian de Torrijos; one s.; ed Texas A&M Univ., USA; fmr man. McDonald's, Chicago, USA; Sec.-Gen. Democratic Revolutionary Party (PRD) 1999–; cand. for presidential elections 1999; Pres. of Panama 2004–09; Vice-Pres. Conference of Political Parties of Latin America and the Caribbean (COPPAL) 2002–. *Address:* c/o Partido Revolucionario Democrático (PRD), Calle 42 Bella Vista, entre Avda Perú y Avda Cuba, bajando por el teatro Bella Vista, Panamá 9, Panama (office).

TORRINI, Emilíana; Icelandic singer and songwriter; b. 16 May 1977, Kópavogur; fmr mem. Spoon, GusGus; solo artist 1995–; songs recorded by artists including Kylie Minogue, Thievery Corporation; Icelandic Music Award for Singer of the Year, for Video of the Year (for Sunny Road) 2005. *Recordings include:* albums: Crouçie d'où là 1995, Merman 1996, Love in the Time of Science 1999, Fisherman's Woman (Icelandic Music Award for Pop Album of the Year) 2005, Me and Armini 2008. *Address:* c/o Rough Trade Records, 66 Golborne Road, London, W10 5PS, England (office). *Website:* www.roughtrade.com (office); www.emilianatorrini.com.

TORSHIN, Aleksander Porfiryevich; Russian politician; *Deputy Chairman, Council of Federations;* b. 27 Nov. 1953, Mitoga, Kamchatsk region; m. Nina Valer'yevna Torshina; two d.; ed All Union Inst. of Law, Moscow State Univ.; teacher, Docent, Acad. of Public Sciences, then functionary, Cen. CPSU Cttee; Deputy Head Div. on Public Relations with Chambers, Factions and Public Orgs, Fed. Ass. of Russian Fed. 1993–95; Statistics Sec., Deputy Chair. Cen. Bank 1995–98; Deputy Chair. Admin of Russian Fed. Govt, Rep. of Russian Fed. Gov. to State Duma (Parl.) 1998–99; Deputy Dir-Gen. Statistics-Sec., State Corp. Agency on Restructuring of Credit Orgs (ARKO) 1999–2001; mem. Council of Feds representing Mari-El Repub. 2001–, Deputy Chair. 2002–; mem. Cttee on Agrarian-Food Policy, Comm. on Regulation and Organization of Parl. Activities, Comm. on Controlling Council of Fed. Activities; Rep. of Govt of Mari-El Repub. to Fed. Ass. *Address:* Leninsky prosp. 29, office 114, Yoshkar-Ola, 424001 Republic of Mari-El (office); Council of Federations, Bolshaya Dmitrovka str. 26, 103426 Moscow, Russia (office). *Telephone:* (88326) 12-68-04 (office); (495) 292-59-21 (office). *Fax:* (495) 292-76-03 (office).

TORSTENDAHL, Rolf, PhD; Swedish historian and academic; *Professor Emeritus of History, Uppsala University;* b. 9 Jan. 1936, Jönköping; s. of Torsten Torstendahl and Ragnhild Torstendahl (née Abrahamsson); m. 1st Anna-Maria Ljung 1960 (died 1987); two s.; m. 2nd Tamara A. Salycheva 1996; ed Uppsala Univ.; Lecturer, Dept of History, Uppsala Univ. 1964–67, Assoc. Prof. 1968–78, Sven Warburg Prof. of History 1978–80, Stockholm Univ.; Prof., Uppsala Univ. 1981–2000, Prof. Emer. 2001–; Prof., Mälardalen Univ. 2002–03; Dir Swedish Collegium for Advanced Study in the Social Sciences 1985–90, Dean of Faculty 1994–99; mem. Royal Swedish Acad. of Letters, History and Antiquities 1982, Norwegian Acad. of Science and Letters 1989, Academia Europaea 1989, Russia Acad. of Sciences, Urals Div. 1995; Björnstiernas Prize, Royal Swedish Acad. of Letters, History and Antiquities 1976. *Publications include:* Teknologins nytta 1975, Dispersion of Engineers in a Transitional Society 1975, Professions in Theory and History (ed.) 1990, The Formation of Professions (ed.) 1990, Bureaucratization in Northwestern Europe 1880–1985 1991, State Theory and State History (ed.) 1992, History-making (ed.) 1996, State Policy and Gender System (ed.) 1999, An Assessment of Twentieth-Century Historiography (ed.) 2000, Zarozhdenie demokraticheskoi kultury 2005. *Address:* Department of History, Uppsala University, PO Box 628, 751 26 Uppsala (office); St Olofsgatan 4, 75312 Uppsala, Sweden (home). *Telephone:* (18) 12-52-98 (home). *E-mail:* rolf.torstendahl@hist.uu.se (office). *Website:* www.hist.uu.se (office).

TORTELIER, Yan Pascal; French conductor and violinist; *Principal Guest Conductor, Pittsburgh Symphony Orchestra;* b. 19 April 1947, Paris; s. of the late Paul Tortelier and of Maud Tortelier; m. Sylvie Brunet-Moret 1970; two s.; ed Paris Conservatoire and Berks. Music Centre, music studies with Nadia Boulanger, studies in conducting with Franco Ferrara; debut as concert violinist, Royal Albert Hall 1962; has since toured extensively world-wide; Konzertmeister, Assoc. Conductor of Orchestre du Capitole de Toulouse 1974–82; Prin. Conductor and Artistic Dir, Ulster Orchestra 1989–92; Prin. Conductor BBC Philharmonic 1992–2003, Conductor Laureate 2003–; Principal Guest Conductor, Pittsburgh Symphony Orchestra 2006–; Hon. DLitt (Ulster) 1992; Dr hc (Lancaster) 1999; First Prize for Violin, Paris Conservatoire 1961. *Publication:* première orchestration of Ravel's Piano Trio (world première concert 1992). *Leisure interests:* skiing, windsurfing, scuba diving, nature. *Address:* c/o IMG Artists, The Light Box, 111 Power Road, London, W4 5PY, England (office); c/o Pittsburgh Symphony Orchestra, Heinz Hall, 600 Penn Avenue, Pittsburgh, PA 15222-3259, USA (office). *Telephone:* (20) 7957-5800 (office). *Fax:* (20) 7957-5801 (office). *E-mail:* nmathias@imgartists.com (office). *Website:* www.imgartists.com (office); www.pittsburghsymphony.org (office).

TORVALDS, Linus; Finnish computer software developer; *OSDL Fellow, Open Source Development Labs Inc.;* b. 1969; m. Tove Torvalds; two d.; ed Univ. of Helsinki; fmr teacher and research asst; creator of Linux operating system; with Transmeta 1997, now Transmeta Fellow (on leave 2003-); OSDL Fellow Open Source Devt Labs Inc. 2003–. *Publication:* Just for Fun (with David Diamond) 2001. *Address:* c/o OSDL Headquarters, 12725 SW Millikan Way, Suite 400, Beaverton, OR 97005, USA (office). *Website:* www.osdl.org (office).

TORVILL, Jayne, OBE; British ice skater; b. 7 Oct. 1957; d. of George Torvill and Betty Torvill (née Smart); m. Philip Christensen 1990; ed Clifton Hall Grammar School for Girls; insurance clerk 1974–80; British Pair Skating Champion (with Michael Hutchinson) 1971; British Ice Dance Champion (with Christopher Dean q.v.) 1978–83, 1994; European Ice Dance Champion (with Christopher Dean) 1981–82, 1984, 1994; World Ice Dance Champion (with Christopher Dean) 1981–84; World Professional Ice Dance Champion (with Christopher Dean) 1984, 1985, 1990, 1995, 1996; Olympic Ice Dance Champion (with Christopher Dean) 1984; Olympic Ice Dance Bronze Medal (with Cristopher Dean) 1994; Tours include: Australia and NZ 1984, Royal Variety Performance London 1984, world tour with own co. of int. skaters 1985, guest artists with IceCapades 1987, world tour with co. of skaters from Soviet Union 1988, Australia as guests of S Australian Govt 1991, GB with co. of skaters from Ukraine 1992, Torvill & Dean, Face the Music, World Tour, UK, Australia and N America 1994, Stars on Ice tour in USA and Canada 1997, Torvill & Dean Ice Adventures in UK 1997–98, Stars on Ice Tour in USA and Canada 1997–98; choreography includes Stars on Ice in USA 1998–99, 1999–2000, O'Connor and O'Dougherty 1999–2000, GB Nat. Champion Synchronized Skating Team 1999–2000; Hon. MA (Nottingham Trent) 1994; BBC Sportsview Personality of the Year (with Christopher Dean) 1983–84; Figure Skating Hall of Fame (with Christopher Dean) 1989. *Television:* Path of Perfection (Thames Television video) 1984, Fire & Ice (also video) 1986, World Tour (video) 1988, Bladerunners (BBC documentary) 1991, Great Britain Tour (TV special and video) 1992, The Artistry of Torvill and Dean (ABC) 1994, Face the Music (video) 1995, Torvill & Dean: The Story So Far (video) 1996, Bach Cello Suite (with Yo-Yo Ma) 1996, Dancing on Ice. *Publications:* (with Christopher Dean) Torvill and Dean: An Autobiography 1984, Torvill and Dean: Fire on Ice (with Christopher Dean) 1984, Torvill and Dean: Face the Music and Dance 1995, Facing the Music (with Christopher Dean) 1995. *Leisure interests:* theatre, ballet, dogs. *Address:* POB 32, Heathfield, East Sussex, TN21 0BW, England. *Telephone:* (1435) 867825.

TOSATTI, Erio, PhD; Italian physicist and academic; *Professor and Head, Condensed Matter Theory Group, International School For Advanced Studies (SISSA);* ed Univ. of Modena, CERN, Geneva, Scuola Normale Superiore, Pisa; served as Second Lt, Weather Forecast Service, Italian Air Forces 1970–71; staff mem. Italian Research Council, Univ. of Rome 1971–77; Royal Soc./NATO Fellow, Cavendish Lab., Univ. of Cambridge, UK 1972–73; Deutsche Forschungsgemeinschaft Visitor, Univ. of Stuttgart, Germany 1974; Sr NATO Fellow, Stanford Univ., USA 1977; sr staff mem. Italian Research Council and Lecturer, Univ. of Trieste 1977–80; Co-founder and consultant Condensed Matter Programme, Int. Centre for Theoretical Physics, Trieste 1977–, Deputy Head 1990–, Permanent Bd Mem., Trieste and Adriatico Research Confs; Prof. and Head, Condensed Matter Theory Group, Int. School For Advanced Studies (SISSA), Trieste 1980–; Visiting Scientist, RCA Zürich and IBM Zürich Research Labs 1984–85; Visiting Prof., Universite' Pierre et Marie Curie, Paris 1994, 1996, 2002, 2003, Univ. of NSW, Australia 1999, Donostia Int. Physics Centre, San Sebastian, Spain 2001; mem. Scientific Advisory Cttee, Elettra Synchrotron, Trieste 2002–; mem. Italian Physical Soc., American Physical Soc.; Eli Burstein Lecture Award, Univ. of Pa 1994, Francesco Somaini Triennial Physics Prize 1997, Lamina Aurea di Redu' 1999, US Physics Medal for Int. Leadership 2006. *Publications:* co-ed.: Physics of Intercalation Compounds 1981, Fractals in Physics 1986, High-Temperature Superconductors 1987, Towards the Theoretical Understanding of High-Temperature Superconductors 1988, Strongly Correlated Electron Systems I 1990, Strongly Correlated Electron Systems II 1991, Strongly Correlated Electron Systems III 1993, Clusters and Fullerenes 1993, The Physics of Sliding Friction 1996; contrib.: over 380 articles and reviews in int. journals. *Address:* International School For Advanced Studies (SISSA), via Beirut 2–4, Trieste 34014, Italy (office). *Telephone:* (40) 3787438 (office). *Fax:* (40) 3787528 (office). *Website:* www.sissa.it/~tosatti (office).

TOSHKOVA, Emel Etem, MEng; Bulgarian engineer and politician; *Deputy Prime Minister and Minister of Emergency Situations;* b. 4 March 1958, Isperih; m.; one c.; ed Angel Kanchev Univ. of Ruse; technologist at Naiden Kirov Co. 1981–92; Founding mem. Movt for Rights and Freedoms, Head of Ethics Cttee Movt for Rights and Freedoms 1993–96, elected mem. of cen. operational office 1996, Deputy Chair. of Cen. Council 2000–; Founding mem. Podkrepa (trade union), Rousse 1990, elected confederate sec. 1992; mem. Rousse Municipality Man. 1990–91; Councillor, Council of Rousse 1991–94; mem. Parl. 1997–, Deputy Chair. Parl. Media Cttee 2001, mem. Ad-hoc Parl. Cttee studying alleged funding of Bulgarian Socialist Party by Saddam Hussein's regime 2004, mem. Ad-hoc Parl. Cttee on Treaty of Accession of Bulgaria to EU 2005; mem. Parl. Culture Cttee, Del. Cen. Europe Initiative 2005; Deputy Prime Minister and Minister of Emergency Situations 2005–; Hon. mem. Bd of Trustees Angel Kanchev Univ., Ruse. *Address:* Ministry of Emergency Situations, 1000 Sofia, pl. Sv. Nedelya 6, Bulgaria (office). *Telephone:* (2) 940-14-01 (office). *Fax:* (2) 940-15-35 (office). *E-mail:* press@mdpba.government.bg (office). *Website:* www.mes.government.bg (office).

TOSIC, Momir, BEcons; Bosnia and Herzegovina politician and economist; ed Univ. of Belgrade; Head of Investments, Sipad Planinski, Han Pijesak 1979–83; Man. OOUR Dept, Centrotrans (transport co.) 1983–87; Chair. Exec.

Bd, Han Pijesak municipality 1987–93; Gen. Dir Sipad Komerc, Sokolac 1993–95; Pres. Bd of Dirs Elektroprivreda Republika Srpska 1995; Dir Srpske Sume (Serb Forests) 1992–98; Rep., Ass. of Bosnia and Herzegovina, also Nat. Ass. of Republika Srpska; Del. and First Chair. House of People (Parl. Ass.); mem. Bosnia and Herzegovina parl. del. to Council of Europe, Strasbourg; mem. SDS (Serbian Democratic Party) Main Bd –2004, conditionally removed from office by High Rep. Paddy Ashdown 30 June 2004; Deputy Minister of Foreign Trade and Econ. Relations 2003–04, conditionally removed from office by High Rep. Paddy Ashdown 30 June 2004. *Address:* c/o Ministry of Foreign Trade and Economic Relations, trg Oktobra bb, 71000 Sarajevo, Bosnia and Herzegovina (office). *Telephone:* (33) 445750 (office).

TOŠOVSKÝ, Josef, BCom; Czech banker; *Chairman, Financial Stability Institute;* b. 28 Sept. 1950, Náchod; m. Bohdana Světlíková; two d.; ed Univ. of Econs Prague; Assoc. Prof. Univ. of Econs, Prague; banker with Czechoslovak State Bank 1973–, Deputy Dir 1978–, consultant to Bank Chair. 1982; Chief Economist, Živnostenská banka, London 1984–85, Deputy Dir June–Dec. 1989; Consultant to Bank Chair., Prague 1986–89; Chair. Czechoslovak State Bank 1989–92, Gov. 1992, for Czech Nat. Bank 1993–97, 1998–2000; Prime Minister of Czech Repub. 1997–98; Chair. Financial Stability Inst., BIS, Basel, Switzerland 2000–; Dr hc (Mendelova Univ. Brno) 2002; Cen. Banker of the Year, IMF 1993, European Man. of the Year, European Business Press Fed. 1994, Karel Engliš Prize 1994, European Banker of the Year, Group 20+1 1996, East-West Inst. Award for Leadership in Transition (USA) 2001. *Publications:* numerous articles in professional press. *Leisure interest:* tennis. *Address:* Financial Stability Institute, Bank for International Settlements, Centralbahnplatz 2, 4002 Basel, Switzerland (office). *Telephone:* (61) 2808074 (office). *Fax:* (61) 2809100 (office). *E-mail:* josef.tosovsky@bis.org (office). *Website:* www.bis.org (office).

TOSUNYAN, Garegin A., CandPhys, Math, Sciences, DrJur; Russian banker; *President, Association of Russian Banks;* b. 1955, Yerevan; m.; two d. one s.; ed Moscow State Univ., All-Union Jurist Inst. (by correspondence), Acad. of Nat. Economy, Govt of Russian Fed.; worked in United Inst. of Nuclear Studies in Dubna Moscow region; Researcher, All-Union Electrotechnology Inst., Moscow 1977–88, later Sr Researcher, Head of Div.; Chief Expert, Head of Div., Head of Dept, Chief of Dept on Sciences and Tech., Moscow City Council of Deputies 1988–90; Founder and Pres. Technobank 1990–98; first Vice-Pres. Asscn of Russian Banks 1990, Pres. 2002–; Chair. Bd of Dirs Interbanking Finance Corpn 1992–; Head of Dept, Acad. of Nat. Economy 1997–; Head, Banking Law Centre, Inst. of State and Law, Russian Acad. of Sciences 1999–; mem. Council of Banking Reps, Office of Mayor of Moscow 1994–; mem. Consultative Council on Banking Activities, Govt of Russian Fed. 1996–; adviser to Mayor of Moscow on financial and banking problems 1997–, to Chair. of Fed. Council of Fed. Ass. of Russian Fed. 2004–; Adviser to Chair. Govt of Russian Fed. 1998–2000. *Publications include:* more than 170 scientific works and articles on problems of the banking system and banking law, and 37 studies, including Banking Business and Banking Law in Russia: Experience, Problems, Perspectives 1995, State Management in the Field of Finance and Credits in Russia (textbook) 1997, Money and Power 2000, Banking Law of the Russian Federation 1999–2002, Market of Self Regulation 2004. *Address:* Association of Russian Banks, Skatertny per. 20 bldg 1, PO Box 41, Moscow 121069, Russia (office). *Telephone:* (495) 291-66-30 (office). *Fax:* (495) 291-66-66 (office). *E-mail:* arb@arb.ru (office). *Website:* www.arb.ru (office).

TÓTH, Július, CSc; Slovak politician and engineer; b. 6 May 1935, Zvolen; m. Mária Tóthová; held numerous positions in various iron-processing plants, participated in the privatization of these plants 1990; Minister of Finance 1992–94; Chair. Econ. Council of Slovak Repub. 1992–98, Council for Regional Devt 1992–; Vice-Premier, Govt of Slovakia –March 1994; Alt. Gov. IMF 1992–98; mem. Party for Democratic Slovakia 2000–; Chair. Bd of Supervisors, E Slovak Iron Works, Košice 1994–99; Deputy Chair. Bd of Dirs Industrial Bank, Košice 1994–. *Address:* Party for a Democratic Slovakia, Tomášikova 32/A, Bratislava, Slovakia (office). *Telephone:* (2) 43330144 (office).

TOTSKY, Gen. Konstantin Vasilyevich; Russian army officer and diplomatist; b. 23 Feb. 1950, Kagan, Uzbekistan; m.; two d.; ed Higher Frontier Mil. School, Frunze Mil. Acad., Gen. Staff Mil. Acad.; army service in Pacific, Cen. Asian, Transcaucasian, NW Border Dist 1977–89; participated in mil. operations in Afghanistan; Head, Acad. of Fed. Border Service of Russian Fed. 1996–; Dir Fed. Border Service 1998; Chair. Council of Border Forces of CIS Countries 1998–2003; Head of the Mission of Russian Fed. to NATO 2003–08. *Address:* Avenue de Fre 66, 1180 Brussels, Belgium (office). *Telephone:* (2) 374-20-25 (office). *Website:* www.nato.int.

TÖTTERMAN, Richard Evert Björnson, DPhil, JurLic; Finnish diplomatist; b. 10 Oct. 1926, Helsinki; s. of B. Björn Tötterman and Katharine Clare Wimpenny; m. Camilla S. Veronica Huber 1953; one s. one d.; ed Univ. of Helsinki and Brasenose Coll. Oxford, UK; entered Ministry for Foreign Affairs 1952; diplomatic posts in Stockholm 1954–56, Moscow 1956–58, at Ministry of Foreign Affairs 1958–62, Berne 1962–63, Paris 1963–66; Deputy Dir, Ministry of Foreign Affairs 1966; Sec.-Gen., Office of Pres. of Finland 1966–70; Sec. of State, Ministry of Foreign Affairs 1970–75; Amb. to UK 1975–83, to Switzerland 1983–90, concurrently to the Holy See 1988–90; Chair., Multilateral Consultations preparing CSCE 1972–73; Hon. Fellow, Brasenose Coll. Oxford 1982; Hon. GCVO, Hon. OBE; Kt Commdr Order of the White Rose (Finland); Grand Cross, Order of Dannebrog (Denmark), Order of Merit (Austria), Order of Orange-Nassau (Netherlands), Order of the Pole Star (Sweden), Order of the Falcon (Iceland); Grand Officier, Ordre de la Couronne (Belgium), Order of St Olav (Norway), Order of Merit (Poland), Order of the Lion (Senegal), Order of the Banner (Hungary), Commdr, Ordre nat. du Mérite (France). *Leisure interests:* music, international relations. *Address:* Parkgatan 9A, 00140 Helsinki, Finland (home). *Telephone:* (9) 627721 (home).

TOTTI, Francesco; Italian footballer; b. 27 Sept. 1976, Rome; s. of Enzo Totti and Fiorella Totti; forward; mem. AS Roma 1993–; 38 caps for Italy (debut 10 Oct. 1998 versus Switzerland); leading all-time scorer for AS Roma; won Serie A with AS Roma 2001; Good-Will Amb., UNICEF 2003–. *Address:* c/o AS Roma, Via di Trigoria Km 3,600, 00128 Rome, Italy. *Telephone:* (06) 501911. *Fax:* (06) 5061736. *E-mail:* info@asromaweb.com. *Website:* www.asromacalcio.it; wwwfrancescototti.com.

TOTTIE, Thomas, FilLic; Swedish librarian; b. 3 July 1930, Waxholm; s. of the late John Tottie and Gerda Tottie (née Willers); m. 1st; two d.; m. 2nd Marianne Sandels 1972; two s.; ed Stockholm Univ.; Asst Librarian, Royal Library, Stockholm 1961; Sec. Swedish Council of Research Libraries 1966–73; Deputy Dir Stockholm Univ. Library 1975–76; Dir Library of Royal Carolingian Medico-Chirurgical Inst., Stockholm 1977; Chief Librarian, Uppsala Univ. 1978–96; mem. and official of various professional orgs; Dr hc (Uppsala) 1994. *Publications:* 2 books and numerous articles and reports on librarianship. *Leisure interests:* biography, sailing. *Address:* University Publications from Uppsala, Uppsala University Library, PO Box 510, 751 20 Uppsala (office); Kyrkogardsgatan 5A, 753 10 Uppsala, Sweden. *Telephone:* (18) 471-20-39 (office); (18) 12-32-00 (home). *E-mail:* thomas.tottie@ub.uu.se (office). *Website:* www.ub.uu.se/upu (office).

TOUADÉRA, Faustin-Archange, BSc, MSc, PhD; Central African Republic mathematician, university vice-chancellor and politician; *Prime Minister;* b. 21 April 1957, Bangui; ed Barthelemy Boganda Coll., Bangui, Univ. of Bangui, Univ. of Abidjan, Côte d'Ivoire, Lille Univ. of Science and Tech. (Lille I), France, Univ. of Yaoundé I, Cameroon; Asst Lecturer in Math., Faculty of Science, Univ. of Bangui 1987, Vice-Dean Faculty of Science 1989–92, apptd Dir Coll. for Training of Teachers (ENS) 1992, Vice-Chancellor Univ. of Bangui 2004–08; mem. Inter-state Cttee for Standardization of Math. Programmes in French-speaking countries and Indian Ocean (CIEHPM) 1992–2002, Pres. CIEHPM 2001–03; mem. African Network of Math. and Applications for Devt (RAMAD) 2001–; Vice-Pres. Math. Union of Cen. African Repub. (UMAC) 2003–; Prime Minister of Cen. African Repub. 2008–; Chevalier of the Order, Officer of the Order, Kt of the Order (all for services to educ.). *Address:* Office of the Prime Minister, c/o Office of the President, Palais de la Renaissance, Bangui, Central African Republic (office). *Telephone:* 61-46-63 (office).

TOUBERT, Pierre Marcel Paul, PhD; French academic; *Professor of Medieval History, Collège de France;* b. 29 Nov. 1932, Algiers; s. of André Toubert and Paola Garcia y Planes; m. Hélène Poggioli 1954; one s.; ed Ecole Normale Supérieure, Paris, Ecole des Hautes-Etudes, Paris, Univ. of Paris and Ecole Française d'Archéologie, Rome; mem. Ecole Française, Rome 1958–61; Dir of Studies, Ecole des Hautes-Etudes 1964–92; Prof. Dept of History, Univ. of Paris (Sorbonne) 1969–92; Prof. Coll. de France 1991–; mem. Nat. Council for Scientific Research, CNRS 1992–; mem. Acad. des Inscriptions et Belles-Lettres, Inst. de France, Academia Europaea 1989–, Nat. Cttee of Evaluation of Univs 1996–, High Council of Technological Research 1999–; Officier, Légion d'honneur, Ordre nat. du Mérite, Ordre des Arts et Lettres; Commdr des Palmes académiques; Dr hc (Siena) 1999, (Liège) 2002. *Publications include:* Les structures du Latium médiéval, 2 vols 1973, Etudes sur l'Italie médiévale 1976, Histoire du haut Moyen Age et de l'Italie médiévale 1987, Castillos señores y campesinos en la Italia medieval 1990, Dalla terra aì castelli nell'Italia medioevale 1994, L'Europe dans sa première croissance 2004; many other books and publs on medieval Italy, econ. and social history of the Middle Ages. *Address:* Collège de France, 11 place Marcelin Berthelot, 75231 Paris Cedex 05 (office); 34 rue Guynemer, 75006 Paris, France (home). *Telephone:* 1-44-27-10-32 (office). *Fax:* 1-44-27-11-09 (office). *E-mail:* pierre.toubert@college-de-france.fr (office).

TOUBON, Jacques, LenD; French politician; *President, Eurimages,, Council of Europe;* b. 29 June 1941, Nice; s. of Pierre-Constant Toubon and Yolande (Molinas) Toubon; m. 1st Béatrice Bernascon; m. 2nd Lise Weiler 1982; ed Lycée Masséna, Nice, Lycée Jean Perrin, Lyon, Faculté de Droit, Lyon, Inst. d'Etudes Politiques, Lyon and Ecole Nat. d'Admin; civil servant 1965–76, Chef de Cabinet, to Minister of Agric. 1972–74, to Minister of Interior 1974, Tech. Adviser, Office of Prime Minister 1974–76; Asst Sec.-Gen. Rassemblement pour la République (RPR) 1977–81, Sec.-Gen. 1984–88; Deputy to Nat. Ass. 1981–93; Mayor 13th Arrondissement, Paris 1983–2001, Deputy Mayor of Paris 1983–2001; Pres. Club 89 1993–; Minister of Culture and the French Language 1993–95, of Justice 1995–97; adviser to Pres. Jacques Chirac 1997–98; mem. European Parl. 2004–; Pres. Eurimages, Council of Europe 2002–; Dir Fondation Claude Pompidou 1970–77; Chevalier du Mérite Agricole. *Publication:* Pour en finir avec la peur 1984. *Leisure interests:* collecting modern art, volleyball, tennis. *Address:* Eurimages, Conseil de l'Europe, 67075 Strasbourg Cedex, France (office). *Telephone:* 3-88-41-26-40 (office). *Fax:* 3-88-41-27-60 (office). *Website:* www.coe.int/t/dg4/eurimages (office).

TOUKAN, Umayya Salah, MBA; Jordanian economist, diplomatist and banking official; *Governor and Chairman, Central Bank of Jordan;* b. 1946, Amman; ed American Univ., Beirut, Univ. of Oxford, UK, Columbia Univ., USA; joined Cen. Bank of Jordan 1967, fmr Head Econ. Research Dept, Gov. and Chair. 2001–; Perm. Rep. to UN, New York 1973–78; Amb. to Netherlands, Belgium, Luxembourg and the EU 1996–2000; fmr Econ. Adviser to the Prime Minister; fmr Dir-Gen. Jordan Stock Exchange; fmr Sr Economist, Arab Monetary Fund, Abu Dhabi; Grand Order of Al-Istiklal (Independence) 1995, Grand Order of Al-Kawkab 2001, Belgian Grand Cross, Order of the Crown 2001. *Address:* Central Bank of Jordan, POB 37, King Hussein Street, Amman

11118, Jordan (office). *Telephone:* (6) 4630301 (office). *Fax:* (6) 4638889 (office). *E-mail:* info@cbj.gov.jo (office). *Website:* www.cbj.gov.jo (office).

TOULOUSE, Gérard, DSc; French scientist; *Research Scientist, Laboratoire de Physique de l'Ecole Normale Supérieure, Le Centre national de la recherche scientifique (CNRS);* b. 4 Sept. 1939, Vattetot-sur-mer; s. of Robert Toulouse and Thérèse Toulouse (née Tiret); m. Nicole Schnitzer 1970; one s. one d.; ed Ecole Normale Supérieure, Ulm, Orsay; research scientist, CNRS 1965–, Laboratoire de Physique de l'Ecole Normale Supérieure 1976–; Post-doctoral Fellow, Univ. of California, San Diego, La Jolla 1969–71; Vice-Pres. Cttee of Exact and Natural Sciences (French nat. comm. for UNESCO) 1997 (Pres. 1999); Sec.-Gen. Foundation La Ferthé 1996; Vice-Pres. Pugwash France 1998; Visitor, Ecole Supérieure de Physique et Chimie, Paris 1985–86; Fellow, Inst. for Advanced Studies, Jerusalem 1987–88; Vice-Pres. European Acad. of Sciences, Arts and Letters 2004; mem. Acad. of Sciences, Paris 1990; Founding mem. French Nat. Acad. of Tech., Paris 2000; Foreign Hon. Mem. American Acad. of Arts and Sciences 1996; Hon. Mem. Palestine Acad. of Science and Tech.; Chevalier, Ordre nat. du Mérite; Langevin Prize 1976, Triossi Prize 1979, Holweck Prize 1983, CEA Prize 1989; Cecil Powell Medal 1999. *Publications:* Introduction au groupe de renormalisation 1975, Biology and Computation: a Physicist's Choice 1994, Regards sur l'éthique des sciences 1998, Les scientifiques et les droits de l'homme 2003, Quelle éthique pour les sciences? 2005. *Address:* Laboratoire de physique de l'Ecole Normale Supérieure, 24 rue Lhomond, 75231 Paris, France (office). *Telephone:* 1-44-32-34-87 (office). *Fax:* 1-43-36-76-66 (office). *E-mail:* toulouse@physique.ens.fr (office). *Website:* www.lpt.ens.fr/~toulouse (office).

TOUMI-MESSAOUDI, Khalida; Algerian politician; *Minister of Culture;* b. 1958; ed Univ. of Algiers; Co-founder Algerian League of Human Rights 1985, Asscn for Equality of Men and Women Before the Law 1985, Ind. Asscn for the Triumph of Women's Rights (also Pres.) 1990, SOS Women in Distress 1991, Asscn of Solidarity and Support to Families of Victims of Terrorism 1992; mem. Nat. Consultative Comm. 1992–93; Co-founder Mouvement pour la République 1992, Vice-Pres. 1992–97; mem. Rassemblement pour la Culture et la Démocratie (RCD) 1997–2001, Vice-Pres. 1998–2000; Deputy for Algiers 1997–2001, Head of RCD Parl. Group 2000; Vice-Pres. Nat. Comm. for Educ. Reform 2000; Minister of Communication and Govt Spokesperson 2002–, of Culture 2004–; Hon. Citizen Commune de Caltabellotta, Italy 1997; Dr hc (Catholic Univ. of Louvain, Belgium) 1998; Alexander Langer Int. Prize 1997, Freedom Prize 1998, Pisa Donna Prize 1998, Telamone Peace Prize 1998, City of Ferrarra Prize 1999, Liberty Prize (Sociéta Libera, Milan) 2004, Gamayung Award 2004. *Address:* Ministry of Culture, BP 100, Palais de la Culture 'Moufdi Zakaria', Plateau des Annassers, Kouba, Algiers, Algeria (office). *Telephone:* (21) 29-10-00 (office). *Fax:* (21) 29-20-89 (office). *E-mail:* contact@m-culture.gov.dz (office). *Website:* www.m-culture.gov.dz (office).

TOUNGUI, Paul; Gabonese politician; *Minister of Foreign Affairs, Co-operation, Francophonie and Regional Integration;* s.-in-law of Pres. Omar Bongo; fmr Univ. Prof. of Math.; Minister of Mines, Energy Resources, Oil and Hydro Resources 2001; Minister of State for Econ. Affairs, Finance, the Budget and Privatization 2002–08; Minister of Foreign Affairs, Co-operation, Francophonie and Regional Integration 2008–; First Vice-Chair. IMF Intergovernmental Group of 24 on Int. Monetary Affairs and Devt; mem. Bd of Govs African Devt Bank, Islamic Devt Bank. *Address:* Ministry of Foreign Affairs, Co-operation and Francophone Affairs, BP 2245, Libreville, Gabon (office). *Telephone:* 72-95-21 (office). *Fax:* 72-91-73 (office).

TOURAINE, Agnès, LenD, MBA; French business executive; *Founder and Partner, Act III Consultants;* b. 18 Feb. 1955, Neuilly-sur-Seine; d. of René Touraine and Eliane Touraine (née Bertolus); m. Joël Cordier 1987; one s. one d.; ed Institut d'Études Politiques, Paris, Columbia Univ., New York, USA; consultant then Project Man., McKinsey & Co. 1981–85; Sr Vice-Pres. for Strategy then Head of Consumer Publishing Div., Hachette 1985–95; Founding Pres. and CEO Liris Interactive 1995–97, renamed Havas Interactive 1997, Exec. Vice-Pres. Consumer Products 1998–2000, Vice-Chair. and CEO Havas 2000–01, renamed Vivendi Universal Publishing 2001, Chair. and CEO Vivendi Universal Publishing 2001–03; f. Act III Consultants (man. consultancy), Paris 2003; Dir Cable and Wireless, London, Fondation de France, Liberation newspaper; Chevalier, Ordre du Merite; ranked 26th by Fortune magazine amongst 50 Most Powerful Women in Business outside the US 2002. *Leisure interests:* contemporary art, reading, skiing, tennis. *Address:* Act III Consultants, 44 avenue des Champs Elysées, 75008 Paris, France (office). *Telephone:* 1-58-56-19-04 (office); 1-46-33-38-66 (home). *Fax:* 1-58-56-18-78 (office). *E-mail:* atouraine@act3consultants.com (office). *Website:* www.act3consultants.com (office).

TOURAINE, Alain Louis Jules François, DèsSc; French sociologist; *Founder and Director of Studies, Centre d'Analyse et d'Intervention Sociologiques;* b. 3 Aug. 1925, Hermanville; s. of Albert Touraine and Odette Cleret; m. Adriana Arenas 1957 (deceased); one s. one d.; ed Lycées Montaigne and Louis-le-Grand, Paris and Ecole Normale Supérieure; Dir of Studies, Ecole Pratique des Hautes Etudes (now Ecole des Hautes Etudes en Sciences Sociales) 1960–, Founder and Dir of Studies, Centre d'Analyse et d'Intervention Sociologiques (CADIS) 1980–; Prof. Faculté des Lettres de Paris-Nanterre 1966–69; f. Lab. de Sociologie Industrielle (now Centre d'Etude des Mouvements Sociaux) 1958–80; mem. Haut Conseil à l'Intégration 1994–96; mem. Acad. Europaea, American Acad. of Arts and Sciences, Polish Acad. of Sciences 1991, Mexican Acad. of Sciences 1998, Brazilian Acad. of Letters 1998; Officier Légion d'honneur, Officier des Arts et Lettres. *Publications:* Sociologie de l'Action 1965, La Société post-industrielle 1969, Production de la société 1973, Pour la sociologie 1974, La voix et le regard 1978, Mort d'une gauche 1979, L'après-socialisme 1980, Solidarité 1982, Le mouvement ouvrier (with Dubet and Wieviorka) 1984, Le retour de l'acteur 1984, La parole et le sang. Politique et société en Amérique Latine 1988, Critique de la modernité 1992, Qu'est-ce que la démocratie? 1994, Lettre à Lionel, Michel, Jacques, Martine, Bernard, Dominique . . . et vous 1995, Le Grand refus, réflexion sur la grève de décembre 1995 (with Dubet, Khosrokhavar, Lapeyronnie and Wieviorka), Pourrons-nous vivre ensemble? Egaux et différents 1997, Comment sortir du libéralisme? 1999, La recherche de soi. Dialogue sur le sujet (with F. Khosrokhavar) 2000. *Leisure interest:* Latin America. *Address:* CADIS, 54 blvd Raspail, 75006 Paris (office); 32 blvd de Vaugirard, 75015 Paris, France (home). *Telephone:* 1-49-54-24-57 (office); 1-43-20-04-11 (home). *Fax:* 1-42-84-05-91 (office); 1-45-38-54-05 (home). *E-mail:* touraine@ehess.fr (office). *Website:* www.ehess.fr/centres/cadis (office).

TOURAY, Omar Alieu, MA, PhD; Gambian diplomatist; *Secretary of State for Foreign Affairs;* b. Farafenni; m.; three c.; ed Grad. Inst. of Int. Studies, Univ. of Geneva; joined diplomatic corps as Sr Asst Sec., Ministry of External Affairs 1995, served at Embassy in Brussels and at Mission to EU 1995–2002; Amb. to Ethiopia, Perm. Rep. to African Union and High Commr to South Africa and Kenya 2002–07; Perm. Rep. to UN, New York 2007; Sec. of State/Minister for Foreign Affairs 2008–. *Publications:* The Gambia and the World: A History of the Foreign Policy of Africa's Smallest State, 1965–1995 2000; numerous papers on int. econ. relations. *Address:* Department of State for Foreign Affairs, 4 Marina Parade, Banjul, Gambia (office). *Telephone:* 4223577 (office). *Fax:* 4223578 (office).

TOURÉ, Lt-Col Amadou Toumani; Malian army officer and head of state; *President;* b. 4 Nov. 1948, Mopti; m.; two d.; ed Ecole Normale Secondaire de Badalabougou, Bamako; with Armed Forces of Mali, Lt 1974–78, Capt. 33rd Parachute Bn 1978–84, Commdr 1984–88, rank of Lt-Col 1988, Brigade General 1992–96, Army General 1996–; Commdr Presidential Guard 1981–84; led coup which overthrew Gen. Moussa Traoré (q.v.) March 1991; Leader Nat. Reconciliation Council 1991–92; Chair. Transition Cttee for the Salvation of the People (acting Head of State) 1991–92; participated in diplomatic initiatives in Rwanda, Burundi, Togo 1996, Cen. African Repub. 1997; Head Inter-African Mission to Monitor the Implementation of the Bangui Agreements 1997–; Pres. of Mali 2002–; Rotary Int. Paul Harris Fellow; Chevalier, National Order of Mali 1981, Grand Cross 1993, Gold Medal of Independence, Mali 1992, Commander, Légion d'Honneur 1994, Grand Officier 1998, Grand Officier, Central African Order of Merit 1996, Grand Officer, Order of Merit of Chad 1997, Grand Medal, Int. Order of Lawyers 2005; Laureate Prize for the Promotion of Democracy in Africa, Observatoire Panafricain de la Démocratie (OPAD) 1996, Prix du Ciwara d'Exception 1997, Prix Chaba Sangare 2001. *Address:* Office of the President, B.P. 1463, Koulouba, Bamako, Mali. *Telephone:* 222-25-72 (office). *Fax:* 223-00-26 (office). *E-mail:* presidence@koulouba.pr.ml (office). *Website:* www.koulouba.pr.ml (office).

TOURÉ, Hamadoun, PhD; Malian electrical engineer and international organization official; *Secretary-General, International Telecommunication Union (ITU);* m.; four c.; ed Tech. Inst. of Electronics and Telecommunications of Leningrad, Univ. of Electronics, Telecommunications and Informatics, Moscow, Russia; early positions at Office des Postes et Télécommunications du Mali 1979–85; Group Dir and Regional Dir Int. Telecommunications Satellite Org. (INTELSAT), Washington, DC 1985–96; Dir Gen. Africa Region, ICO Global Communications 1996–98; Dir Telecommunications Devt Bureau (BDT), Int. Telecommunication Union (ITU), Geneva 1999–2006, Sec.-Gen. ITU 2006–; mem. IEEE 1986–, Asscn of Satellite Professionals 1990–, Int. Telecommunications Acad. 1999–; Chevalier, Ordre Nat. du Mali. *Address:* International Telecommunication Union (ITU), Place des Nations, 1211 Geneva 20, Switzerland (office). *Telephone:* 7305111 (office). *Fax:* 7337256 (office). *E-mail:* itumail@itu.int (office). *Website:* www.itu.int (office).

TOURÉ, Modibo, BSc, MBA; Malian international organization official; *Secretary General, African Development Bank;* m.; three c.; ed Ecole Nationale d'Admin, Bamako, Vanderbilt Univ., USA; consultant with Shell Oil, Mali 1982–84; Inspecteur des Finances, Bamako 1984–87; Man. United Parcel Service, Nashville, Tenn., USA 1989–90; UNDP Program Officer and later Asst Resident Rep., Burkina Faso 1991–94, Deputy Resident Rep., Djibouti 1994–97, Program Man., New York 1997–98, Sr Deputy Resident Rep., Rwanda 1998–99, Sr Country Program Man., New York 1999–2001, Special Advisor to Dir, Regional Bureau for Africa, New York 2000–01, UN Resident Coordinator, Humanitarian Coordinator and UN Resident Rep., Chad 2001–04, UNDP Resident and Humanitarian Coordinator, Ethiopia 2004–05, mem. UNDP Transition Team 2005–06; Dir UN Mine Action Service 2005–06; Sec. Gen. African Devt Bank (ADB) 2006–. *Address:* African Development Bank, 15 avenue du Ghana, angle des rues Pierre de Coubertin et Hedi Nouira, BP 323, 1002 Tunis Belvédère, Tunisia (office); ADB Headquarters, Rue Joseph Anoma, 01 BP 1387, Abidjan 01, Côte d'Ivoire. *Telephone:* (71) 333-511 (Tunis) (office). *Fax:* (71) 351-933 (Tunis) (office). *E-mail:* afdb@afdb.org (office). *Website:* www.afdb.org (office).

TOURÉ, Sanoussi, PhD; Malian politician; *Minister of the Economy and Finance;* ed Univ. of Paris X, France; Dir-Gen. of Finance Control, Ministry of Economy and Finance 1978–87, Dir-Gen. of Budget 1987–91, tech. adviser to Minister of the Economy and Finance 1991–94; consultant to the World Bank, Canadian Co-operation, US-Aid 1995–2000; Dir of Public Finances, W African Econ. and Monetary Union 2001–05, consultant 2005–; Minister and Dir of Cabinet Office 2008–09; Minister of Economy and Finance 2009–; Lecturer in Finance and Fiscal Studies, Univ. of Mali 1980–2000. *Address:* Ministry of the Economy and Finance, Bamako, Mali (office). *Website:* www.finances.gov.ml (office).

TOURÉ, Sidia; Guinean politician; *President, Union des forces républicaines;* fmr Dir Office of the Prime Minister of Côte d'Ivoire; Prime Minister of Guinea

1996–99, Minister of Economy, Finance and Planning 1996–97; Pres. Union des forces républicaines. *Address:* Union des forces républicaines (UFR), Immeuble 'Le Golfe', 4e étage, BP 6080, Conakry, Guinea (office). *Telephone:* 45-42-38 (office). *Fax:* 45-42-31 (office). *E-mail:* ufrguinee@yahoo.fr (office). *Website:* www.ufrguinee.net (office).

TOURÉ, Younoussi; Malian politician; *Acting President, Union pour la République et la démocratie (URD);* b. 27 Dec. 1941, Niodougou, Timbuktu Region; s. of Singoro Touré and Santadji Tamoura; m. Alimata Traore 1970; two s. three d.; studied in Dakar, Senegal and Abidjan, Côte d'Ivoire; joined Cen. Bank of Mali 1969, Dir Gen. 1983; rep. at Banque Centrale des états de l'Afrique de l'ouest (BCEAO); Prime Minister 1992–93; Special Adviser to Gov. of BCEAO 1993–94; Commissaire, Union Economique et Monétaire Ouest Africaine (UEMOA) 1994; currently Acting Pres. Union pour la République et la démocratie. *Leisure interests:* reading, sport. *Address:* Union pour la République et la démocratie (URD), Bamako, Mali.

TOURET, Jacques Léon Robert; French geologist and academic; *Guest Scientist, ABC Mines (Ecole des Mines), Paris;* b. 2 Jan. 1936, Fumay; s. of the late Martial Touret and Suzanne Gouilly; m. 1st Christiane Poinsignon 1960 (divorced 1972); one s. two d.; m. 2nd Lydie Mohammed 1974; one d.; ed Lycée Chanzy, Charleville, Ecole Nat. Supérieure de Géologie Appliquée, Nancy and Univ. of Nancy; Asst, Ecole Nat. Supérieure de Géologie, Nancy 1958–64, Asst Lecturer in Geology 1964–69; Lecturer in Geology, Univ. of Nancy 1969–74; Prof., Univ. of Paris 7 1974–80; Prof., Earth Science Inst., Free Univ., Amsterdam, Netherlands 1980–2001, Prof. Emer. 2001–; currently Guest Scientist, ABC Mines (Ecoles des Mines), Paris; Invited Prof., Ecole Normale Supérieure, Paris 1994–97; Chargé de mission, CNRS, Paris 1978–80; mem. Royal Netherlands Acad. of Sciences, Norwegian Acad. of Science and Letters, Academia Europaea; Hon. Fellow, European Union of Geologists; Chevalier, Ordre nat. du mérite; Dr hc (Liège Univ., Belgium) 2001; Prix Carrière, Acad. des Sciences, Paris 1970, Dumont Medal (Belgian Geological Soc.) 1992, Van Waterschoot van der Gracht Medal (Netherlands) 1996. *Publications include:* Le Socle précambrien de Norvège méridionale 1969, The deep Proterozoic Crust in the North Atlantic province (with A. C. Tobi) 1985. *Leisure interests:* classical music, French literature. *Address:* Musée de Minéralogie (ABC Mines), 60 blvd Saint Michel, 75006 Paris, France (office). *Telephone:* 1-40-51-92-90 (office). *E-mail:* jacques.touret@ensmp.fr (office).

TOURNIER, Michel, LèsL, LenD, DPhil; French writer; b. 19 Dec. 1924, Paris; s. of Alphonse Tournier and Marie-Madeleine Tournier (née Fournier); ed Saint-Germain-en-Laye, Univ. of Paris (Sorbonne), Univ. of Tübingen (Germany); radio and TV production 1949–54; press attaché, Europe No. 1 1955–58; head of literary services, Editions Plon 1958–68; contrib. to Le Monde, Le Figaro; mem. Acad. Goncourt 1972–; Officier, Légion d'honneur, Commdr, Ordre nat. du Mérite; Dr hc (Univ. Coll. London) 1997; Goethe Medal 1993. *Publications:* fiction: Vendredi, ou les limbes du Pacifique (trans. as Friday) 1967 (Grand Prix de l'Acad. Française), Le Roi des Aulnes (trans. as The Ogre) (Prix Goncourt) 1970, Vendredi, ou la vie sauvage (trans. as Friday and Robinson: Life on Esperanza Island) 1971, Les Météores 1975, Le Coq de bruyère 1978, Pierrot, ou les secrets de la nuit 1979, Gaspard, Melchior et Balthazar (trans. as The Four Wise Men) 1980, Gilles et Jeanne 1983, Le Vagabond immobile 1984, Journal de voyage au Canada 1984, La Goutte d'or (trans. as The Golden Droplet) 1986, Le Médianoche amoureux (trans. as The Midnight Love Feast) 1989, La Couleuvrine 1994, Eléazar, ou la source et le buisson 1996, Barbedor 2003, La Famille Adam 2003, Telling Tales (contrib. to charity anthology) 2004, Journal extime 2004, Mephisto 2006, Vendredi ou la vie sauvage: D'après Vendredi ou les limbes du Pacifique 2007; non-fiction: Le Vent paraclet (trans. as The Wind Spirit: An Autobiography) 1977, Des clefs et des serrures 1979, Le Vol du vampire 1981, Le Tabor et le Sinaï 1989, Le Crépuscule des masques 1992, Le Miroir des idées 1994, Le Pied de la lettre 1994, Célébrations 1999, Les vertes lectures 2006, Le bonheur en Allemagne? 2004. *Leisure interest:* photography. *Address:* Le Presbytère, Choisel, 78460 Chevreuse, France. *Telephone:* 1-30-52-05-29.

TOUSIGNANT, Claude, OC; Canadian artist; b. 23 Dec. 1932, Montreal; s. of Alberic Tousignant and Gilberte Hardy-Lacasse; m. Judith Terry 1968; two d.; ed School of Art and Design, The Montreal Museum of Fine Arts; numerous solo and group nat. and int. exhbns 1956–; works included in major N American public and pvt. collections; 1st Prize, Salon de la jeune peinture 1962, 1st Prize, Painting, Art Gallery of Ont. 1967, Canadian Inst. in Rome Award 1973, Prix Paul-Emile Borduas 1989. *Address:* 181 Bourget Street, Montreal, Québec, H4C 2M1(Studio); 460 Avenue Bloomfield, Outremont, Québec, H2V 3R8, Canada (home). *Telephone:* (514) 934-3012 (Studio); (514) 948-1463 (home).

TOVAR FAJA, Roberto; Costa Rican politician; b. 1945; ed Univ. of Barcelona, Spain; Deputy 1978–82, 1990–94; Pres. Legis. Ass. 1992–93; Head of Faction, Unidad Social Cristiana (USC—Christian Social Unit) 1991–92, fmr Sec.-Gen.; Pres. Comm. of Econ. Subjects 1978–79; mem. Bd of Dirs Consultant Inter-American Inst. of Human Rights; fmr Minister of the Presidency and Planning; Minister of Foreign Relations 2002–06. *Address:* c/o Ministry of Foreign Affairs, Avda 7 y 9, Calle 11 y 13, Apdo 10027, 1000 San José, Costa Rica (office).

TOWNE, Robert; American scriptwriter; b. 23 Nov. 1934, Los Angeles; m. Luisa Towne; two c.; ed Pomona Coll. *Screenplays include:* The Tomb of Ligeia 1964, Villa Rides 1967, The Last Detail 1967, Chinatown 1974, Shampoo (with Warren Beatty) 1974, The Yazuka (jtly) 1975, Personal Best (also producer-dir 1984), Greystoke 1984, Tequila Sunrise 1988, Days of Thunder, The Two Jakes, The Firm (co-screenwriter) 1993, Love Affair (co-screenwriter), Mission Impossible (co-screenwriter), Without Limits (also dir) 1998, Mission Impos-

sible 2 2000, Ask the Dust (also dir) 2006. *Address:* c/o CAA, 9830 Wilshire Boulevard, Beverly Hills, CA 90212, USA.

TOWNES, Charles Hard, PhD; American physicist and academic; *Professor Emeritus of Physics, University of California, Berkeley;* b. 28 July 1915, Greenville, S Carolina; s. of Henry Keith Townes and Ellen Sumter Hard; m. Frances H. Brown 1941; four d.; ed Furman and Duke Univs, California Inst. of Tech.; Asst, Calif. Inst. of Tech. 1937–39; mem. Tech. staff, Bell Telephone Labs 1939–47; Assoc. Prof. of Physics, Columbia Univ., New York 1948–50, Prof. 1950–61; Exec. Dir Radiation Lab. 1950–52, Chair. Dept of Physics 1952–55; Vice-Pres. and Dir of Research, Inst. for Defense Analyses 1959–61; Provost and Prof. of Physics, MIT 1961–66, Inst. Prof. 1966–67; Univ. Prof., Univ. of California 1967–86, Prof. Emer. 1986–94, Prof. in the Grad. School 1994–; Trustee, Carnegie Inst. of Washington 1965–, Bd of Dirs Perkin-Elmer Corpn 1966–85, Gen. Motors 1973–86, Bulletin of the Atomic Scientists 1964–69; Chair. Science and Tech. Advisory Comm. for Manned Space Flight, NASA 1964–69; Chair. Space Science Bd, NAS 1970–73; Guggenheim Fellow 1955–56; mem. Bd of Trustees Rand Corpn 1965–70; Trustee, Calif. Inst. of Tech. 1979–; mem. Pres.'s Science Advisory Cttee 1966–70, Vice-Chair. 1967–69; Trustee, Pacific School of Religions 1983–93; mem. Bd Dirs Grad. Theological Union 1993–96, Center for Theology and the Natural Sciences 1989–; mem. Bd of Advisers, Templeton Foundation Humility Theology Center 1993–; mem. Editorial Bd Review of Scientific Instruments 1950–52, Physical Review 1951–53, Journal of Molecular Spectroscopy 1957–60, etc.; mem. Astronomical Soc. of the Pacific 1989–, American Acad. of Arts and Sciences, American Philosophical Soc., American Astronomical Soc., Space Program Advisory Council, NASA, NAS (Council mem. 1967–72, 1978–81), Pontifical Acad. of Science 1983, Russian Acad. of Sciences 1993, Nat. Acad. of Eng; Fellow, American Physical Soc. (Council mem. 1959–62, 1965–71, Pres. 1967), IEEE, Californian Acad. of Sciences; Foreign mem. Royal Soc. 1976, Nat. Acad. of Sciences, India, Indian Nat. Science Acad.; holder of patents in electronics, including fundamental patents on masers and lasers, etc.; Hon. mem. Optical Soc. of America; Hon. Fellow, Rozhdestvensky Optical Soc. of Russia 1995; Officier, Légion d'honneur; hon. degrees include DLitt, ScD, DottIng, LLD, LHD, DMedSc; Fulbright Lecturer, Paris 1955–56, Tokyo 1956; Richtmeyer Lecturer, American Physical Soc. 1959, Scott Lecturer, Cambridge 1963, Centennial Lecturer, Univ. of Toronto 1967, Jansky Lecturer, Nat. Radio Astronomy Observatory 1971, Lincoln Lecturer 1972–73, Halley Lecturer, Oxford 1976, Schiff Memorial Lecturer, Stanford 1982, Michelson Memorial Lecturer, US Naval Acad. 1982, Faculty Research Lecturer, Univ. of Calif., Berkeley 1986, Beckman Lecturer, Univ. of Illinois 1986, Schultz Lecturer, Yale Univ. 1987, Fulbright Fellow Lecturer, Collège de France 1987, Darwin Lecturer, Univ. of Cambridge 1988, Houston Memorial Lecturer, Rice Univ., Houston 1990, VanVleck Lecturer, Univ. of Minnesota 1990, K.S. Krishnan Memorial Lecture, Nat. Physical Lab., India 1992, Golden Jubilee Lecture, Council of Scientific and Industrial Research, India 1992, Nishina Lecturer, Tokyo, Japan 1992, Rajiv Gandhi Lecture, New Delhi, India 1997, Weinberg Lecture, Oak Ridge Nat. Lab., Tenn. 1997, Henry Norris Russell Lectureship, American Astronomical Soc. 1998, Sackler Lecturer, Univ. of Leiden 1999, Loeb Lecturer, Harvard Univ. 2000, Hamilton Lecturer, Princeton Univ. 2000, Bunyan Lecturer, Stanford Univ. 2000, Ford/Nobel Lecture, MIT 2001, Karl Schwarzschild Lecture, Astronomische Gesellschaft 2002, Schroedinger Lecture, Centre for Philosophy and Foundations of Science, New Delhi 2003, Birla Lecture, Birla Science Centre, Hyderabad 2003; awards include NAS Comstock Award 1959, Stuart Ballantine Medal, Franklin Inst. 1959, 1962, Rumford Premium, American Acad. of Arts and Sciences 1961, AIEE David Sarnoff Award in Electronics 1961, NAS John A. Carty Medal 1962, Thomas Young Medal and Prize, Inst. of Physics and Physical Soc., UK 1963, Nobel Prize for Physics 1964, NASA Distinguished Public Service Medal 1969, IEEE Medal of Honor 1967, Wilhelm Exner Award 1970, Plyler Prize, American Physical Soc. 1977, Niels Bohr Int. Gold Medal 1979, LeConte Medal 1980, Nat. Medal of Science 1982, L.W. Frolich Award 1986, Berkeley Citation 1986, Nat. Inventors' Hall of Fame 1976, Eng and Science Hall of Fame 1983, Commonwealth Award 1993, ADION Medal, Observatory of Nice 1995, Frederick Ives Medal, Optical Soc. of America 1996, Frank Annunzio Award 1999, Rabindranath Tagore Centenary Plaque 1999, Founder's Award, Nat. Acad. of Eng 2000, Author of Best Science Book of the Year, American Physical Soc. 2000, Lomonosov Gold Medal, Russian Acad. of Sciences 2001, Karl Schwarzschild Medal, Astronomische Gesellschaft 2002, Templeton Prize 2005, Vannevar Bush Medal 2006. *Publications:* Microwave Spectroscopy 1955, Quantum Electronics 1960, Quantum Electronics and Coherent Light 1964, Making Waves 1995, How the Laser Happened; Adventures of a Scientist 1999; other scientific papers on microwave spectroscopy, molecular and nuclear structures, radio and infra-red astronomy, masers and lasers, etc. *Leisure interest:* natural history. *Address:* University of California, Department of Physics, 366 LeConte, # 7200, Berkeley, CA 94720, USA (office). *Telephone:* (510) 642-1128 (office). *Fax:* (510) 643-8497 (office). *E-mail:* cht@ssl.berkeley.edu (office). *Website:* physics.berkeley.edu/research/faculty/Townes.html (office); isi.ssl.berkeley.edu/team.htm (office).

TOWNSEND, Susan (Sue) Lilian, FRSL; British writer; b. 2 April 1946, Leicester; m. (divorced); four c.; started writing professionally early 1980s; mem. Writers' Guild, PEN; Hon. MA (Leicester) 1991. *Plays:* Bazaar and Rummage 1984, Groping for Words 1984, Womberang 1984, The Great Celestial Cow 1985, Ten Tiny Fingers, Nine Tiny Toes 1990, The Secret Diary of Adrian Mole Aged 13¾ 1992, Dayroom, The Ghost of Daniel Lambert, Captain Christmas and the Evil Adults, Are You Sitting Comfortably?. *Television:* Think of England (writer, narrator and presenter) 1991. *Publications:* The Secret Diary of Adrian Mole Aged 13¾ 1982, The Growing Pains of Adrian Mole 1984, Rebuilding Coventry 1988, Mr Bevan's Dream 1989, True

Confessions of Adrian Albert Mole, Margaret Hilda Roberts and Susan Lilian Townsend 1989, Adrian Mole from Minor to Major 1991, The Queen and I 1992, Adrian Mole: The Wilderness Years 1993, Adrian Mole, The Lost Years 1994, Ghost Children 1997, Adrian Mole, The Cappuccino Years 1999, The Public Confessions of a Middle-Aged Woman Aged $55^3/_4$ 2001, Number 10 2002, Adrian Mole and the Weapons of Mass Destruction 2004, Queen Camilla 2006, The Lost Diaries of Adrian Mole 1999–2001 2008; contribs to London Times, New Statesman, Observer, Sainsbury's Magazine. *Leisure interests:* canoeing, reading. *Address:* The Sale Agency, 11 Jubilee Place, London, SW3 3TD (office); Curtis Brown Group Ltd, 28–29 Haymarket, London, SW1Y 4SP, England (office); c/o Reed Books, Michelin House, 81 Fulham Road, London, SW3 6RB, England (office). *E-mail:* kate50@fsmail.net.

TOWNSHEND, Peter (Pete) Dennis Blandford; British composer, musician (guitar), publisher and author; b. 19 May 1945, Isleworth, London; s. of Clifford Townshend and Betty Townshend; m. Karen Astley 1968; one s. two d.; ed Acton Co. Grammar School and Ealing Art Coll.; mem. rock group, The Detours, renamed The Who 1964– (various reunion tours and recordings); solo artist 1979–; appearances include: Nat. Jazz and Blues Festival 1965, 1966, 1969, Monterey Pop Festival 1967, Woodstock 1969, Rock at the Oval 1971, Farewell tour 1982–83, Live Aid, Wembley 1985, Reunion tour 1989, Quadrophenia 1996/1997, Concert for NYC 2001, Live8 2005; owner Eel Pie Recording Productions Ltd and Eel Pie Publishing Ltd 1972–; est. Eel Pie (bookshops and publishing co.) 1976–83; est. Meher Baba Oceanic (UK archival library) 1976–; Ed., Faber & Faber (publrs) 1983–; Gold Ticket Madison Square Garden 1979, Ivor Novello Award for Contribution to British Music 1982, British Phonographic Industry Award 1983, BRIT Lifetime Achievement Award 1983, BRIT Award for Contribution to British Music 1988, International Rock Living Legend Award 1991, Q Lifetime Achievement Award 1997, Ivor Novello Lifetime Achievement Award 2001, BMI Pres.'s Award 2002, BMI TV Music Awards 2004, 2005, 2006, 2007, Silver Clef Award 2005, The Who were inducted into the UK Music Hall of Fame in 2005, Q Legend Award 2006, South Bank Show Outstanding Achievement Award 2007, Kennedy Center Honor 2008. *Compositions include:* Tommy (rock opera) (Tony Award for score 1993, Grammy Award for original cast recording 1993, Dora Mavor Moore Award 1994, Olivier Award 1997) 1969, Quadrophenia (rock opera) 1973, The Boy Who Heard Music (rock opera) 2007. *Recordings include:* albums: with The Who: My Generation 1965, A Quick One 1966, Happy Jack 1967, The Who Sell Out 1967, Magic Bus 1968, Tommy 1969, Live At Leeds 1970, Who's Next 1971, Meaty Beefy Big And Bouncy 1971, Quadrophenia 1973, The Who By Numbers 1975, The Story Of The Who 1976, Who Are You 1978, The Kids Are Alright (live) 1979, Face Dances 1981, Hooligans 1982, It's Hard 1982, Rarities Vols. 1 and 2 1983, Who's Last (live) 1984, Two's Missing 1987, Join Together (live) 1990, Live At The Isle Of Wight Festival 1970 1996, The BBC Sessions 2000, Moonlighting 2005, Endless Wire 2006; solo: Who Came First 1972, Rough Mix 1977, Empty Glass 1980, All The Best Cowboys Have Chinese Eyes 1982, Scoop 1983, White City: A Novel 1985, Another Scoop 1987, The Iron Man: A Musical 1989, Psychoderelict 1993, Pete Townshend Live 1999, Lifehouse Chronicles 2000, The Oceanic Concerts 2001, Live: La Jolla 2001, Live: Sadler's Wells 2001. *Films:* music for: Tommy 1975, Quadrophenia 1979, The Kids Are Alright 1979. *Television:* music for CSI Miami and CSI Crime Scene Investigation. *Publications:* The Story of Tommy (with Richard Barnes), Horse's Neck 1985, Tommy: The Musical 1995, London 1996. *Leisure interest:* sailing. *Address:* Trinifold Management, 12 Oval Road, Camden, London, NW1 7DH, England (office); Eel Pie Publishing Limited, 4 Friars Lane, Richmond, Surrey, TW9 1NL, England (office). *Telephone:* (20) 7419-4300 (office); (20) 8940-8171 (office). *Fax:* (20) 7419-4325 (office); (20) 8940-8172 (office). *E-mail:* trinuk@globalnet.co.uk (office); nic@eelpie.com (office). *Website:* www.trinifold.co.uk (office); www.eelpie.com (office); www.thewho.com.

TOYE, Wendy, CBE; British theatrical director, film director, choreographer, actress and dancer; b. 1 May 1917, London; d. of Ernest W. Toye and Jessie Crichton Toye (née Ramsay); ed privately, trained as dancer with Euphan MacLaren, Tamara Karsavina, Anton Dolin, Morosoff, Legat, Marie Rambert, Ninette de Valois; first performance aged 3 years, Albert Hall; first professional appearance as Cobweb (Midsummer Night's Dream), Old Vic 1929; prin. dancer Hiawatha, Albert Hall 1931; played Marigold and Phoebe and produced dances, Toad of Toad Hall, Royalty 1931–32; masked dancer Ballerina, Gaiety 1933; danced and choreographed for Carmargo Soc. of Ballet; mem. Ninette de Valois' original Vic Wells Ballet, danced in C. B. Cochran's The Miracle, Lyceum 1932, prin. dancer The Golden Toy, Coliseum 1934; toured with Anton Dolin's Ballet (choreographer for divertissements and short ballets) 1934–35; Tulip Time, Alhambra, then prin. dancer and choreographer, Markova-Dolin Ballet 1935; arranged dances and ballets for many shows and films 1935–42, including most of George Black's productions notably Black Velvet (also prin. dancer) 1939; Shakespearean season, Open Air Theatre 1939; musicals, variety, cabaret; Guest Artist with Sadler's Wells Ballet and Mme Rambert's Ballet Club; prin. dancer with British Ballet organized by Adeline Genée, Denmark 1932; lectured in Australia 1977; Adviser, Arts Council Training Scheme 1978–; mem. Grand Council, Royal Acad. of Dancing, Council LAMDA, Wavendon All Music scheme, Richard Stilgoe Award scheme, original Accreditation Bd, Nat. Council of Drama Training for Acting Courses; Dir Royal Theatrical Fund; Vice-Pres. TACT; Pres. Vic Wells Asscn; Patron Millennium 2000 Dance; Hon. DLitt (City) 1997; The Queen's Silver Jubilee Medal. *Theatre productions:* Big Ben, Bless the Bride, Tough at the Top (for C. B. Cochran), Adelphi, The Shepherd Show, Prince's, Peter Pan (co-dir and choreographer), New York, And So To Bed, New Theatre, Feu d'Artifice (co-dir and choreographer), Paris, Night of Masquerade, Queen, Second Threshold, Vaudeville, Three's Company (choreographer) in Joyce Grenfell Requests the Pleasure, Fortune, Wild Thyme, Duke of York's, Lady at the Wheel and Robert and Elizabeth, Lyric, Hammersmith, Majority of One, Phoenix, Magic Lantern and On the Level, Saville, As You Like It, Old Vic, Virtue in Danger, Mermaid and Strand, A Midsummer Night's Dream, Shakespeare quatercentenary, Latin American tour 1964, Soldier's Tale, Edin. Festival 1967, Boots and Strawberry Jam, Nottingham Playhouse 1968, The Great Waltz, Drury Lane 1970, Showboat, Adelphi 1971, She Stoops to Conquer, Young Vic 1972, Cowardy Custard, Mermaid 1972, Stand and Deliver, Roundhouse 1972; at Chichester R. Loves J 1973, The Confederacy 1974, Follow The Star 1974, Made in Heaven 1975, Make Me a World 1976, Once More with Music 1976, Oh Mr. Porter, Mermaid 1977, Gingerbread Man, Watermill Theatre 1981, This Thing Called Love, Watermill Theatre 1982, Ambassadors Theatre 1983, Singing in the Rain (Assoc. Producer), Palladium 1983, Noel and Gertie, Monte Carlo 1983, Birds of A Feather 1984, Barnum (Assoc. Producer) 1985, Madwoman of Chaillot, Torville and Dean World Tour (Assoc. Producer) 1985, Once Upon A Mattress, Watermill Theatre 1985, Kiss Me Kate, Copenhagen 1986, Laburnham Grove, Palace Theatre, Watford 1987, Miranda, Chichester Festival Theatre 1987, Get the Message, Molecule 1987, Songbook, Watermill 1988, Mrs Dot, Watford 1981, When that I was, Manitoba 1988–89, Cinderella, Watford 1989, Penny Black, Wavendon 1990, Moll Flanders, Watermill 1990, Heaven's Up, Playhouse 1990, Bernard Shaw and Mrs Patrick Campbell (musical), Wavendon 1990, Mrs Pat's Profession, Wavendon 1991, The Drummer, Watermill 1991, Sound of Music 1992, See How They Run, Watermill 1992, Vienna 1992, The Kingfisher, Vienna 1993, Under Their Hats, King's Head 1994, Vienna 1995, The Anastasia File, Watermill 1994, Der Apotheker, Menton, France 1995, Warts and All, Watermill 1996, Sadler's Wells Finale Gala 1996, Rogues to Riches, Watermill 1996. *Opera productions:* Bluebeard's Castle (Bartók), Sadler's Wells and Brussels, The Telephone (Menotti), Rusalka (Dvořák) and La Vie Parisienne, Sadler's Wells, Die Fledermaus, Coliseum and Sadler's Wells, Orpheus in the Underworld, Sadler's Wells and Australia, The Abduction from the Seraglio, Bath Festival 1967, The Impresario, Don Pasquale (for Phoenix Opera Group) 1968, The Italian Girl in Algiers, Coliseum 1968, Orpheus 1978, Merry Widow 1979–80, Orpheus 1981, Mikado (Turkey) 1982, The Italian Girl in Algiers 1982, Serva Padrona and the Apothecary Operas for Aix-en-Provence Festival 1991. *Films directed:* The Stranger Left No Card 1952, The Teckman Mystery, Raising a Riot, The Twelfth Day of Christmas, Three Cases of Murder 1954, All for Mary 1955, True as a Turtle 1956, We Joined the Navy 1962, The King's Breakfast, Cliff in Scotland, A Goodly Manor for a Song, Girls Wanted – Istanbul; retrospective of films, Paris Film Festival 1990, Nat. Film Theatre 1995. *Television productions include:* Chelsea at 8 and Chelsea at 9 and Orpheus in the Underworld (dir) for Granda TV; directed Esmi Divided 1957, Follow the Star 1979, Tales of the Unexpected 1981, Trial by Jury 1982 for the BBC; choreographed many revues for the BBC. *Leisure interests:* embroidery, gardening. *Address:* c/o Diamond Management, 31 Percy Street, London W1T 2DD; 5 Wedderburn House, 95 Lower Sloane Street, London, SW1W 8BZ, England (home). *Telephone:* (20) 7631-0500.

TOYODA, Akio, MBA; Japanese automotive industry executive; *President, Toyota Motor Corporation;* b. 3 May 1956, Nagoya; grandson of Kiichiro Toyoda; m. Hiroko Toyoda; two c.; ed Keio Univ., Tokyo, Babson Coll., Mass, USA; joined Toyota Motor Corpn 1984, Vice-Pres. New United Motor Manufacturing Inc., Calif., USA, mem. Bd of Dirs Toyota Motor Corpn 2000–, Man. Dir 2002–03, Sr Man. Dir and Chief Asia and China Operations Officer 2003–05, Exec. Vice-Pres. 2005–09, Pres. 2009–, Head of team that developed Gazoo.com (Toyota web site) 1996. *Address:* Toyota Motor Corporation, 1 Toyota-Cho, Toyota City, Aichi Prefecture 471-8571, Japan (office). *Telephone:* (5) 6528-2121 (office). *Fax:* (5) 6523-5800 (office). *Website:* www.toyota.co.jp (office).

TOYODA, Kanshiro; Japanese automotive industry executive; *Chairman, Aisin Seiki Company Ltd;* s. of Eiji Toyoda and Kazuko Toyoda; m. Akiko Toyoda; fmr Man. Shinkawa Seiki Co. Ltd; fmr Pres. Aisin Seiki Co. Ltd (automotive component mfr), Chair. 2005–, Dir Aisin AW Co. Ltd.

TOYODA, Shoichiro, DEng; Japanese automotive industry executive; *Honorary Chairman, Toyota Motor Corporation;* b. 27 Feb. 1925, Nagoya; s. of Kiichiro Toyoda and Hatako Toyoda; m. Hiroko Mitsui 1952; one s. one d.; ed Nagoya and Tohoku Univs; joined Toyota Motor Corpn 1952, Man. Dir 1961, Sr Man. Dir 1967, Exec. Vice-Pres. 1972, Pres. Marketing Org. 1981, Pres., Toyota Motor Corpn 1982, Chair. 1992–99, Hon. Chair. 1999–, Sr Adviser and mem. Bd 1996–; Chair., Japanese Automobile Mfrs Asscn 1986–90; Vice-Chair., Keidanren (Fed. of Econ. Orgs) 1990–94, Chair. 1994–2002, Hon. Chair. 2002–; Chair., Japan Asscn for 2005 World Exposition 1997–2006, Pres., Kaiyo Acad. 2006–; Hon. KBE 1995, Commdr, Légion d'honneur (France) 1998, Order of Merit (Turkey) 1998, Commdr's Cross of the Order of Merit (Germany) 2001, Grand Cordon of the Order of the Rising Sun (Japan) 2002, Knight Grand Cordon (First Class) of the Most Admirable Order of the Direkgunabhorn (Thailand) 2004, Grand Cordon, Order of the Paulownia Flowers (Japan) 2007, Cavaliere di Gran Croce decorato di Gran Cordone (Italy) 2007, numerous other hons; Deming Prize (Japan) 1980, Medal with Blue Ribbon for Outstanding Public Service (Japan) 1984, FISITA Medal (France) 2000. *Leisure interests:* traditional Japanese music, gardening, golf. *Address:* Toyota Motor Corporation, 1 Toyota-cho, Toyota, Aichi 471-8571, Japan (office).

TOYODA, Tetsuro, BMechEng, MBA; Japanese automotive industry executive; *President, Toyota Industries Corporation;* b. 1 June 1929, Nagoya; s. of Kiichiro Toyoda and Hatako Iida; m. Shimizu Ayako; one s. one d.; ed Univ. of Tokyo, New York Univ., USA; joined Toyota Motor Corpn 1953, apptd Dir 1974, supervised creation of New United Motor Mfg Inc. (NUMMI), jt venture with General Motors in Calif., USA 1984, Pres. NUMMI 1984–86; Sr Man. Dir

Toyota 1986–88, Exec. Vice-Pres. 1988–92, Pres. 1992–95, Vice-Chair 1995–96, Sr Adviser to the Bd 1996–, Pres. and Rep. Dir, Toyota Industries Corpn 2005–; fmr Chair. Japan Automobile Mfrs' Asscn; Vice-Chair. Japan Asscn of Corp. Execs (Keizai Doyukai); Grand Cordon of the Orders of the Sacred Treasure 1999. *Leisure interest:* listening to music. *Address:* Toyota Industries Corpn, 2-1, Toyota-cho, Kariya-shi, Aichi 448-8671, Japan (office). *Telephone:* (566) 222511 (office). *Fax:* (566) 275650 (office). *E-mail:* info@toyota-industries.com (office). *Website:* www.toyota-industries.com (office).

TOZAKA, Milner, OBE; Solomon Islands politician and fmr diplomatist; *Minister for Public Service;* b. 21 Oct. 1951; m. Jane Tozaka; ed Univ. of South Pacific, Suva, Fiji; Chair. Nat. Disaster Council 1984–85; UNDP Consultant, Ministry of Prov. Govt 1995; Chair. Prov. Govt Review Cttee 1999; High Commr to Australia 2000–05; mem. Parl. for North Vella Lavella Constituency 2006–, Chair. Constitution Review Cttee 2006–07; Minister for Public Service April–May 2006, 2007–. *Address:* Ministry of Public Service, Honiara, Solomon Islands (office). *Telephone:* 28617 (office). *Fax:* 25559 (office). *E-mail:* pspublic@pmc.gov.sb (office).

TOZOUN, Biossey Kokou; Togolese politician; *Keeper of the Seals, Minister of Justice;* Minister of Foreign Affairs and Co-operation 2003–05, of Communication and Civil Affairs 2005–06, Keeper of the Seals, Minister of Justice 2007–; also currently Pres. Société Nationale des Editions du Togo (publr). *Address:* Ministry of Justice, ave de la Marina, rue Colonel de Roux, Lomé (office); Société Nationale des Editions du Togo (EDITOGO), BP 891, Lomé, Togo. *Telephone:* 221-26-53 (office); 221-61-06 (EDITOGO). *Fax:* 222-29-06 (office).

TRA, Lt-Gen. Pham Van; Vietnamese politician; Minister of Nat. Defence –2006; mem. Politburo, Vice-Sec. Party Cen. Cttee Mil. Comm. *Address:* c/o Ministry of National Defence, 1a Hoang Dieu, Ba Dinh District, Hanoi, Viet Nam (office).

TRABER, Peter G., BS, MD; American gastroenterologist and college administrator; *President Emeritus, Baylor College of Medicine;* m. Bobbi Traber; one s. one d.; ed Univ. of Michigan, Wayne State Univ. Medical School, Detroit, Northwestern Univ. School of Medicine, Chicago; mem. of faculty, Univ. of Michigan School of Medicine, Ann Arbor 1987–92; Chief of Gastroenterology, Univ. of Pennsylvania School of Medicine 1992–97, Chair., Dept of Internal Medicine 1997–2000, also CEO Univ. of Pennsylvania Health System and Interim Dean; Sr Vice-Pres. for Clinical Devt and Medical Affairs and Chief Medical Officer, GlaxoSmithKline 2000–03; Pres. and CEO Baylor Coll. of Medicine 2003–08, Pres. Emer. 2008–; Fellow, AAAS 2003–; mem. American Soc. of Clinical Investigation; Dir Alkek Foundation, BCM Technologies, BioHouston, Federal Reserve Bank of Dallas (Houston Br.), Greater Houston Partnership, Houston Tech. Center, Nat. Space Biomedical Research Inst.; Sr Ed. Handbook of Gastroenterology; Assoc. Ed. Kelly Textbook of Internal Medicine; Wayne State Univ. School of Medicine Distinguished Alumnus Award 1999, American Gastroenterological Asscn Outstanding Service Award 2006. *Address:* Baylor College of Medicine, One Baylor Plaza, Houston, TX 77030, USA (office). *Telephone:* (713) 798-4951 (office). *E-mail:* pgtraber@bcm.tmc.edu (office). *Website:* www.bcm.edu (office).

TRACHTENBERG, Stephen Joel, JD, MPA; American lawyer and academic administrator; *President and Professor of Public Administration, George Washington University;* b. 14 Dec. 1937, Brooklyn; s. of Oscar Trachtenberg and Shoshana Weinstock; m. Francine Zorn 1971; two s.; ed Columbia, Yale and Harvard Univs; admitted New York Bar 1964, US Supreme Court Bar 1967; attorney, Atomic Energy Comm. 1962–65; Special Asst to US Educ. Comm., Health, Educ. and Welfare, Washington, DC 1966–68; Assoc. Prof. of Political Science, Boston Univ. 1969–77, Assoc. Dean 1969–70, Dean 1970–74, Assoc. Vice-Pres., co-Counsel 1974–76, Vice-Pres. Academic Services 1976–77; Pres., Prof. of Law, Univ. of Hartford, Conn. 1977–88; Pres. and Prof. of Public Admin George Washington Univ., Washington, DC 1988–; Dir NationsBank, Greater Washington Bd of Trade, Nat. Educ. Telecommunications Org., Washington Research Library Consortium, DC Tax Revision Comm., Newcomen Soc.; numerous awards including Sabin Vaccine Institute Prize 2005; several hon. degrees. *Address:* Office of the President, George Washington University, 2121 Eye Street, NW, Washington, DC 20052, USA (office). *Telephone:* (202) 994-1000 (office). *Fax:* (202) 994-9025 (office). *Website:* www.gwu.edu/~gwpres (office).

TRAHAR, Anthony (Tony) John, BComm, CA (SA); South African business executive; b. 1 June 1949, Johannesburg; m. Patricia Trahar; one s. one d.; ed St. John's Coll., Univ. of the Witwatersrand; qualified CA 1973; man. trainee, Anglo American Corpn 1974–76, Personal Asst to Chair. of Exec. Cttee 1976–77, Exec. Dir 1991–2000, CEO 2000–07 (retd), Chair. Anglo Forest Products, Anglo Industrial Minerals Div., Financial Dir Anglo American Industrial Corpn 1982–92, Deputy Chair. 1992–2007; Man. Dir Mondi 1986–89, Exec. Chair. 1989, Chair. Mondi Europe 1993–2003; Chair. Anglo American Corpn of SA, Paleo Anthropological Scientific Trust; Dir Anglo Platinum, Anglo Gold, DB Investments; Kt Grand Commdr, Gold Cross with Star (First Class) (Austria) 2004. *Leisure interests:* shooting, fishing, gym, classic cars and music. *Address:* c/o Anglo American PLC, 20 Carlton House Terrace, St James's, London, SW1Y 5AN, England (office). *Telephone:* (20) 7968-8888 (office). *Fax:* (20) 7968-8500 (office). *E-mail:* ajtrahar@angloamerican.co.za (office). *Website:* www.angloamerican.co.uk (office).

TRAILL, Sir Alan, KStJ, GBE, QSO, MA, DMus; British arbitrator and insurance consultant; b. 7 May 1935, London; s. of George Traill and Margaret (Matthews) Traill; m. Sarah Jane Hutt 1964; one s.; ed Charterhouse and Jesus Coll., Cambridge; Dir Morice Tozer Beck (insurance brokers) 1960; Underwriting mem. Lloyd's 1963–89; Founder Dir Traill Attenborough (Lloyd's brokers) 1973, Chair. 1980; Man. Dir Colburn Traill Ltd 1989–96; Div. Dir First City Insurance Brokers Ltd 1996–2000; Dir City Arts Trust Ltd, Grandactual Ltd 1993–97, Int. Disputes Resolution Centre (IDRC) 2002–, Cayman Islands Monetary Authority 2003–; Bd mem. ARIAS (Insurance Arbitration Soc.) 1997–; mem. Pathfinder Team Consulting 1992–; mem. Advisory Council and Educ. Cttee, London Symphony Orchestra 1997–; Chair. UK/NZ 1990 Cttee 1989–90; Chair. Trustees, Waitangi Foundation 1991–99; Trustee, St Paul's Cathedral Choir School Foundation 1985–, Morden Coll. 1995–; Gov. Christ's Hosp. 1980–, Chair. Gov. Menuhin School 2000–; Patron Lord Mayor Treloar Trust 1985–; mem. Court of Common Council (of City of London) 1970–2005, Alderman 1975–2005, Sheriff 1982–83, Lord Mayor of London 1984–85; Master Worshipful Co. of Musicians 2000; Vice-Pres. Bridewell Royal Hosp. 2003–06; Commemorative Medal NZ 1990. *Leisure interests:* DIY, travel, opera, music, assisting education. *Address:* Wheelers Farm, Thursley, Godalming, Surrey, GU8 6QE, England (home). *Telephone:* (7714) 328204 (mobile); (1252) 703271 (home). *Fax:* (1252) 703271 (home). *E-mail:* atraill.granary@btinternet.com (office).

TRAINOR, Richard Hughes (Rick), MA, DPhil, FRHistS; American historian, academic and university administrator; *Principal, King's College London;* b. 1948; m. Marguerite Dupree; one s. one d.; ed Brown Univ. and Princeton Univ., USA, Univ. of Oxford, UK; joined Dept of Econ. History, Glasgow Univ. 1979, later becoming Prof., Dean of Social Sciences and Vice-Prin.; Vice Chancellor and Prof. of Social History, Univ. of Greenwich 2000–04; Prin. and Prof. of Social History, King's Coll. London 2004–; Chair. Advisory Council, Inst. of Historical Research; Pres. Univs UK; mem. Arts and Humanities Research Council, UK-US Fulbright Comm.; mem. Acad. of Social Sciences; Hon. Fellow, Merton Coll. Oxford, Trinity Coll. of Music. *Address:* Office of the Principal, King's College London, Strand, London, WC2R 2LS, England (office). *Telephone:* (20) 7848-3434 (office). *Fax:* (20) 7848-3430 (office). *E-mail:* principal@kcl.ac.uk (office). *Website:* www.kcl.ac.uk/about/structure/principal/trainor.html (office).

TRAN TAM TINH, Rev., PhD, FRSC; Vietnamese/Canadian professor of classical archaeology; b. 16 April 1929, Nam Dinh; ed Séminaire Pontifical, Università Laterano, Université de Fribourg, Ecole Pratique des Hautes Etudes, Paris, CNRS; ordained priest 1956; excavations at Soli, Cyprus 1965–74, Pompeii and Herculaneum 1969–76; Co-Founder Fraternité Vietnam 1976; Prof. of Classical Archaeology, Laval Univ. 1964–, Sr Prof. 1971–94; Tatiana Warscher Award for Archaeology (American Acad. at Rome) 1973, Prix G. Mendel (Académie des Inscriptions et Belles-Lettres, France) 1978. *Publications:* Le culte d'Isis à Pompéi 1964, Le culte des divinités orientales à Herculaneum 1971, Le culte des divinités orientales en Campanie 1972, Isis lactans 1973, Catalogue des peintures romaines au musée du Louvre 1974, I cattolici nella storia del Vietnam 1975, Dieu et César 1978, Sérapis debout 1983, Soloi I, La Basilique 1985, La casa dei Cervi à Herculaneum 1988, Tôi vê Hanoi 1974, Tro vê nguôn 1974, Corpus des lampes antiques conservées au Québec I 1991, Corpus des lampes à sujets asiatiques du musée gréco-romain d'Alexandrie 1993; and numerous articles on classical iconography and religion. *Address:* Université Laval, Cité Universitaire, Québec, G1K 7PQ (office); 2995 Maricourt, Suite 300, Ste.-Foy, Québec, G2W 4T8, Canada. *Telephone:* (418) 653-3513. *Website:* www.ulaval.ca (office).

TRAORÉ, Abou-Bakar; Malian government official; Minister of the Economy and Finance 2004–07, of Finance 2007–09. *Address:* c/o Ministry of the Economy and Finance, BP 234, Koulouba, Bamako, Mali (office).

TRAORÉ, Col Diara; Guinean politician and army officer; Prime Minister of Guinea April–Dec. 1984, Minister of Nat. Educ. 1984–85; mem. Comité militaire de redressement nat. 1984–85; staged abortive coup d'état July 1985; arrested and sentenced to death; sentence commuted to life imprisonment; released Dec. 1988.

TRAORÉ, Lassana; Malian politician; Minister of Foreign Affairs and Int. Co-operation –April 2004. *Address:* c/o Ministry of Foreign Affairs and International Co-operation, Koulouba, Bamako, Mali (office).

TRAORÉ, Gen. Moussa; Malian politician and army officer; b. 25 Sept. 1936, Kayes; ed Training Coll., Fréjus, Cadets Coll., Kati; became NCO in French Army; returned to Mali 1960; promoted Lt 1964, Col 1971, Brig.-Gen. 1978; at Armed Forces Coll., Kati until 1968; led coup to depose Pres. Modibo Keita Nov. 1968; Pres. Mil. Cttee for Nat. Liberation (Head of State) and C-in-C of the Armed Forces 1968–91, also Prime Minister 1969–80; Pres. of Mali 1979–91; Minister of Defence and Security 1978–86, of the Interior 1978–79, of Nat. Defence 1988–90 (overthrown in coup, under arrest); Chair. OAU 1988–89; Sec.-Gen. Nat. Council Union Démocratique du Peuple Malien 1979–80, fmr mem. Cen. Exec. Bureau; Pres. Conf. of Heads of State, Union Douanière des Etats de l'Afrique de l'Ouest 1970; overthrown March 1991; stood trial Nov. 1992; sentenced to death for mass murder Feb. 1993; sentence commuted to life imprisonment 1997; charged with embezzlement Oct. 1998; sentenced to death Jan. 1999; sentence commuted to life imprisonment Sept. 1999; officially pardoned 2002.

TRAPATTONI, Giovanni; Italian professional football manager; b. 17 March 1939, Milan; player AC Milan; 17 caps for Italy; coach 2000–; fmr Man. Juventus (won six Serie A titles), Inter (won one Serie A title), Bayern Munich (won one Bundesliga title), Italy nat. team 2000–04; Head Coach, Benfica, Portugal 2004–05, Head Coach VfB Stuttgart 2005–06, Red Bull Salzburg, Austria 2006-08; Man. Repub. of Ireland nat. team 2008–; winner of numerous other trophies including the World Club Cup, European Cup, Cup Winner's Cup, European Supercup, UEFA Cup (three times). *Publication:* Fischia il Trap (biog.). *Address:* Football Association of Ireland, National Sports Campus, Abbotstown, Dublin 15, Ireland. *Telephone:* (1) 8999500. *Fax:* (1) 8999501. *Website:* www.fai.ie.

TRAUNER, Sergio; Italian business executive and lawyer; b. 9 March 1934, Athens, Greece; s. of Livio Trauner and Nada Mandich; m. (divorced); ed Univ. of Trieste; lawyer in pvt. practice; counsellor to Trieste Municipality 1962–75, 1982–, to Friuli Venezia Giulia Region 1964–78; Dir Finmare Co. (IRI Group) 1981–84, EFIM 1984–87; mem. Presidential Cttee and Bd of Dirs IRI 1986–91; Pres. ILVA SpA 1991–; Commendatore of Italian Repub., Officer, Order of Merit of Italian Repub. *Publications:* books on art and history. *Leisure interests:* reading, travel.

TRAUTMAN, Andrzej; Polish theoretical physicist and academic; *Professor Emeritus, Warsaw University;* b. 4 Jan. 1933, Warsaw; s. of Mieczysław Trautman and Eliza Trautman (née André); m. Róża Michalska 1962; two s.; ed Warsaw Univ. of Tech., Warsaw Univ.; asst, Inst. of Radiolocation, Warsaw Univ. of Tech. 1952–53, Inst. of Applied Math. 1953–55; postgraduate studies, Inst. of Physics, Polish Acad. of Sciences (PAN) 1955–58, doctorate 1959; lecturer 1959; scientific training, Imperial Coll., King's Coll., London, Univ. of Syracuse, USA 1959–61; scientist, Inst. of Theoretical Physics, Warsaw Univ. 1961–, Asst Prof. and Head of Dept Electrodynamics and Theory of Relativity 1962–68, Extraordinary Prof. 1964–71, Ordinary Prof. 1971–2004, Prof. Emer. 2004–; Deputy Dir Inst. of Theoretical Physics 1968–74, Dir 1975–85; Corresp. mem. Polish Acad. of Sciences 1969–76, mem. 1977–, mem. Presidium 1972–83, Vice-Pres. 1978–80, Chair. Cttee of Physics; Corresp. mem. Polish Acad. of Arts and Science, Kraków; Deputy Chair. Gen. Bd of Polish Physics Asscn 1970–73, Foreign mem. Czechoslovak Acad. of Sciences 1980–90; mem. Int. Cttee of Theory of Relativity and Gravitation 1965–80, Int. Journal of Theoretical Physics, Journal of Geometry and Physics; Visiting Prof., American Math. Soc., Santa Barbara 1962, Coll. de France, Paris 1963 and 1981, Brandeis Univ., USA 1964, Univ. of Chicago 1971, Univ. of Pisa, Italy 1972, The Schrödinger Professorship, Univ. of Vienna 1972, State Univ. of NY at Stony Brook 1976–77, Univ. of Montreal 1982, 1990, Univ. of Tex. at Dallas 1985, 1986; Gold Cross of Merit, Officer's Cross of Order of Polonia Restituta; Dr hc (Silesian Univ., Czech Repub.) 2001; State Prize 1st Class 1976, Alfred Jurzykowski Foundation Award in Physics 1984. *Publications:* Differential Geometry for Physicists 1984, The Spinorial Chessboard (with P. Budinich) 1988, Space Time and Gravitation (with W. Kopczyński) 1992; and numerous works on theory of gravitational waves, energy of gravitation field, modern methods of differential geometry and their application in physics, Einstein-Cartan's Theory, Dirac operator and spin structures on manifolds. *Leisure interest:* chess. *Address:* Instytut Fizyki Teoretycznej UW, ul. Hoża 69, 00-681 Warsaw, Poland (office). *Telephone:* (22) 5532295 (office). *Fax:* (22) 6219475 (office). *E-mail:* Andrzej.Trautman@fuw.edu.pl (office). *Website:* www.fuw.edu.pl (office).

TRAUTZ, Volker; German business executive; *CEO, LyondellBasell Industries;* joined BASF 1974, served several man. positions, including 14 years in S America, Pres. BASF's Consumer Products Div. 1991–95, mem. Bd Exec. Dirs BASF 1995–2000, responsible for all polymers, including eng resins, PVC and polyurethanes, and for BASF's activities in Asia; CEO Basell (renamed LyondellBasell Industries following acquisition by Basell of Lyondell Chemical Co. Dec. 2007) 2000–. *Address:* LyondellBasell Industries, PO Box 2416, 3000 CK Rotterdam (office); LyondellBasell Industries, Weena 737, 3013 Rotterdam, The Netherlands (office). *Telephone:* (10) 275-55-00 (office). *E-mail:* info@lyondellbasell.com (office). *Website:* www.lyondellbasell.com (office).

TRAVIESO, Federico Brevé, MSc MA; Honduran politician; b. Tegucigalpa; ed McGill Univ. Montréal, Canada and INAE, Managua, Nicaragua; began working for Hogares de Honduras (construction co.), later mem. Bd, currently Exec. Pres.; Dir Empresa Nacional de Energia Eléctrica (ENEE); mem. Bd. of Dirs various cos including Cámera Hondureña de la Construcción, Instituto Centroamericano de Administración de Empresas, Comité Nacional Scout en Desarrollo e Inversiones Nacionales SA, Supermercado La Colonia; Minister Nat. Defence –2006; mem. Nat. Anti-Corruption Council; Order Merit in Labour 1st Class from Govt Venezuela; Incahista Notable, INCAE. *Address:* c/o Ministry of National Defence, 5a Avda, 4a Calle, Tegucigalpa, Honduras (office).

TRAVIS, Randy; American country singer, songwriter and musician (guitar); b. (Randy Bruce Traywick), 4 May 1959, Marshville, NC; m. Lib Hatcher (Mary Elizabeth Robertson) 1991; played local clubs with brothers; resident Charlotte nightclub (owned by Lib Hatcher) 1977; early recordings as Randy Traywick; resident singer, as Randy Ray, Nashville Palace 1992; solo artist as Randy Travis 1985–; Acad. of Country Music Top Male Vocalist 1985, 1986, 1987, 1988, Grammy Award for Best Country Newcomer 1986, CMA Horizon Award 1986, Acad. of Country Music Song of the Year (for On the Other Hand) 1986, (for Forever and Ever Amen) 1987, (for Three Wooden Crosses) 2004, CMA Single of the Year (for Forever and Ever Amen) 1987, Music City News Male Artist of the Year, Star of Tomorrow and Single of the Year (for On the Other Hand) 1987, CMA Male Vocalist of the Year 1987, 1988, Music City News Entertainer of the Year, Male Artist of the Year, Single of the Year (for Forever and Ever Amen) and Entertainer of the Year 1989, Grammy Award for Best Album Collaboration (for Same Old Train 1998, CMA Song of the Year (for Three Wooden Crosses) 2003, also awards from Performance magazine, AMOA Jukebox, Country Music Round Up, NECMA, TNN Viewers Choice Awards, Rolling Stone magazine, Playboy magazine, Billboard Music Awards, BBC Radio Two, Dove Awards, Christian Country Music Awards. *Recordings include:* albums: Storms Of Life (Acad. of Country Music Album of the Year 1986, Music City News Album of the Year 1986) 1986, Always And Forever (Grammy Award 1987, CMA Album of the Year 1987, Music City News Album of the Year 1988) 1987, Old 8x10 (Grammy Award 1988) 1988, An Old Time Christmas 1989, No Holdin' Back 1989, Heroes And Friends 1990, High Lonesome 1991, Wind In The Wire 1993, This Is Me 1994, Full Circle 1996, You And You Alone 1998, A Man Ain't Made Of Stone 1999, Inspirational Journey 2000, Randy Travis Live 2001, Anthology 2002, Rise And Shine (Grammy Award 2004) 2002, Worship & Faith (Grammy Award 2005) 2003, Passing Through 2004, Glory Train (Grammy Award for Best Southern, Country, Or Bluegrass Gospel Album 2007) 2005, Songs of the Season 2007, Around the Bend 2008. *Address:* Elizabeth Travis Management, 1610 16th Avenue S, Nashville, TN 37212, USA (office). *Telephone:* (615) 383-7258 (office). *Fax:* (615) 269-7828 (office). *E-mail:* webmaster@randytravis.com. *Website:* www.randytravis.com.

TRAVKIN, Nikolai Ilyich; Russian politician; b. 19 March 1946, Novo-Nikolskoe, Moscow region; m.; two s.; ed Kolomna Pedagogical Inst., Higher Party School; mem. CPSU 1970–90; worker, brigade-leader, Head of the Dept of "Glavmosstroi"; initiator self-financing and self-man. into construction industry 1969–; Deputy Head of construction union 1967–89; mem. of the movt "Democratic Russia" 1988–; People's Deputy of the USSR 1989–91; People's Deputy of Russia 1990–93; a founder and Chair. Democratic Party of Russia 1990–94; Chair. of the Sub cttee, Supreme Soviet of the USSR (supervising local soviets and devt of self-man.) 1989–90; Chair. Cttee Supreme Soviet of Russia; supervising local soviets and devt of self-man. May–Dec. 1990; head of local admin. Shakhovskoy Dist 1991–96; co-leader Civic Union coalition 1992–93; mem. State Duma (Parl.) Yabloko group (now Union of Right Forces faction) 1993–2003; Minister without Portfolio 1994–96; mem. Cttee on Problems of Fed. and Regional Politics 1996–; Pres. Fund in Support of Farmers; Hero of Socialist Labour 1986. *Leisure interests:* theatre, literature. *Address:* Yabloko Party, Novy Arbat 21, 18th Floor, 121019 Moscow, Russia (office). *Telephone:* (495) 202-80-72 (office). *Fax:* (495) 202-73-99 (office). *E-mail:* info@yabloko.ru (office).

TRAVOLTA, John; American actor; b. 18 Feb. 1954, Englewood, NJ; s. of Salvatore Travolta and the late Helen (née Burke) Travolta; m. Kelly Preston 1991; one s. one d.; TV series Welcome Back Kotter 1975–77; l.p. records 1976, 1977; Billboard Magazine Best New Male Vocalist Award 1976; Best Actor Award, Nat. Bd of Review 1978; Male Star of the Year, Nat. Asscn of Theatre Owners 1983, Alan J. Pakula Prize 1998, Lifetime Achievement Award, Palm Springs Int. Film Festival 1999. *Films:* Carrie 1976, The Boy in the Plastic Bubble (for TV) 1976, Saturday Night Fever 1977, Grease 1978, Moment by Moment 1978, Urban Cowboy 1980, Blow-Out 1981, Staying Alive 1983, Two of a Kind 1983, Perfect 1985, The Experts 1988, Chains of Gold 1989, Look Who's Talking 1989, Look Who's Talking Now 1990, The Tender 1991, All Shook Up 1991, Look Who's Talking 3 1994, Pulp Fiction 1994, White Man's Burden 1995, Get Shorty 1995, Broken Arrow 1996, Phenomenon 1996, Michael 1997, Face Off 1997, She's So Lovely 1997, Primary Colors 1998, A Civil Action 1998, The General's Daughter 1999, Battlefield Earth 2000, Lucky Numbers 2000, Swordfish 2001, Domestic Disturbance 2001, Basic 2003, The Punisher 2004, A Love Song for Bobby Long 2004, Ladder 49 2004, Be Cool 2005, Lonely Hearts 2006, Wild Hogs 2007, Hairspray 2007. *Publications:* Staying Fit 1984, Propeller One-Way Night Coach (juvenile) 1998. *Leisure interest:* flying. *Address:* William Morris Agency, One William Morris Place, Beverly Hills, CA 90212, USA (office); William Morris Agency, 1 William Morris Place, Beverly Hills, CA 90212; 1504 Live Oak Lane, Santa Monica, CA 93105. *Telephone:* (310) 859-4000 (office). *Fax:* (310) 859-4462 (office). *Website:* www.wma.com (office).

TREACY, Philip, MA, RCA; Irish milliner; b. 26 May 1967, Ballinsoe, Co. Galway; s. of the late James Vincent Treacy and Katie Agnes Treacy; ed Nat. Coll. of Art and Design, Dublin, Royal Coll. of Art, London; while still a student, worked for designers including Rifat Ozbek, John Galliano and Victor Edelstein; f. Philip Treacy Millinery, London 1991; house milliner for Marc Bohan at Hartnell and for Victor Edelstein; has collaborated with Karl Lagerfeld, Chanel's couture and ready-to-wear shows 1991–; his own ready-to-wear range sold in New York and London 1991–; designed head dresses for Pola John's production of My Fair Lady 1992; presented own show, London 1993; launched accessory range 1997; first show in New York 1997; Interior Design Dir The G (hotel) 2005; British Accessory Designer of the Year award 1991, 1992, 1993, 1996, 1997, Irish Fashion Oscar 1992, Haute Couture Paris 2000, Moet & Chandon Award 2002, Int. Designer of the Year, China Fashion Awards 2004. *Address:* Philip Treacy London Head Office, 1 Havelock Terrace, London, SW8 4AS, England (office). *Telephone:* (20) 7738-8080 (office). *Fax:* (20) 7738-8545 (office). *E-mail:* admin@philiptreacy.co.uk (office). *Website:* www.philiptreacy.co.uk (office).

TRECHSEL, Stefan, DIur, Priv Doz; Swiss lawyer; *Judge ad litem, International Criminal Tribunal for the former Yugoslavia;* b. 25 June 1937, Berne; s. of Manfred F. Trechsel and Steffi Friedlaender; m. Franca Julia Kinsbergen 1967; two d.; ed Univ. of Berne and Georgetown Univ., Washington, DC; Asst and Main Asst for Criminal Law, Univ. of Berne 1964–71; Swiss Fed. Dept for Tech. Cooperation 1966–67; Public Prosecutor, Dist of Bern-Mittelland 1971–75; Guest Prof. of Criminal Law and Procedure, Univ. of Fribourg 1975–77; Prof., Hochschule St Gallen 1979–99; Prof. of Criminal Law and Legal Instruction, Univ. of Zurich 1999–2004, Prof. Emer. 2004–; Judge ad litem, Int. Criminal Tribunal for the fmr Yugoslavia, The Hague, Netherlands 2004–; mem. European Comm. of Human Rights 1975–99, 2nd Vice-Pres. 1987, Chamber Pres. 1993–94, Pres. 1995–99; Council of Europe Medal pro merito 2004; Dr hc (New York Univ. Law School) 1975; ASIL award for Human Rights in Criminal Proceedings 1995. *Publications:* Der Strafgrund der Teilnahme 1967, Die Europäische Menschenrechtskonvention, ihr Schutz der persönlichen Freiheit und die Schweizerischen Strafprozessrechte 1974, Strafrecht Allgemeiner Teil I (6th edn of textbook by Peter Noll) 1994, Schweizerisches Strafgesetzbuch, Kurzkommentar 1997, Human Rights in Criminal Proceedings 2005, Praxiskommentar StGB 2008. *Leisure interests:* skiing, music, literature, psychology, chamber music (cello). *Address:*

Statenlaan 77, NL 2582 GE The Hague, Netherlands (home). *Telephone:* (3170) 306-15-11 (home). *Fax:* (3170) 512-52-52 (office). *E-mail:* trechsel@gmx .net (office). *Website:* www.un.org/icty (office).

TREDE, Michael, MB, BChir, MD; German surgeon; b. 10 Oct. 1928, Hamburg; s. of Hilmar Trede and Gertrud (née Daus) Trede; m. Ursula Boettcher 1956; one s. four d.; ed The Leys School, Cambridge and Univ. of Cambridge; Surgeon-in-training, Freie Universität, Berlin 1957–62, Heidelberg Univ. 1962–72; Prof. and Chair. Dept of Surgery, Klinikum Mannheim, Univ. of Heidelberg, now Prof. Emer. and Chair.; Pres. Deutsche Gesellschaft für Chirurgie, Int. Surgical Soc. 1993–95; Hon. mem. Austrian, American, Swiss, Italian and Portuguese Surgical Asscns; Hon. FRCS (England, Ireland, Glasgow, Edin.); Hon. FACS; Dr hc (Edin.) 1995. *Publications:* Surgery of the Pancreas (with D. C. Carter), The Art of Surgery 1999, Der Rückkehrer. Skizzenbuch eines Chirurgen 3rd edn 2003; 500 articles on surgery in scientific journals. *Leisure interests:* painting, violin-playing, mountaineering, skiing. *Address:* Nadlerstrasse 1A, 68259 Mannheim, Germany. *Telephone:* (621) 383-2728 (office); (621) 796301.

TREGLOWN, Jeremy Dickinson, BLitt, MA, PhD, FRSL; British academic, writer and journalist; *Professor of English, University of Warwick;* b. 24 May 1946, Anglesey, N Wales; s. of late Rev. G. L. Treglown and of Beryl Treglown; m. 1st Rona Bower 1970 (divorced 1982); one s. two d.; m. 2nd Holly Eley (née Urquhart) 1984; ed Bristol Grammar School, St Peter's Coll., Oxford; Lecturer in English Literature, Lincoln Coll., Oxford 1973–76, Univ. Coll., London 1976–79; Asst Ed. The Times Literary Supplement 1979–81, Ed. 1982–90; Prof. of English, Univ. of Warwick 1993– (Chair. Dept of English and Comparative Literary Studies 1995–98); Chair. of Judges, Booker Prize 1991, Whitbread Book of the Year Award 1998; Co-ed. Liber, a European Review of Books 1989; Contributing Ed., Grand Street magazine, New York 1991–98; Visiting Fellow, All Souls Coll., Oxford 1986; Fellow Huntington Library 1988; Mellon Visiting Assoc., Calif. Inst. of Tech. 1988; Ferris Visiting Prof., Princeton Univ. 1992; Jackson Brothers Fellow, Beinecke Library, Yale Univ. 1999; Leverhulme Research Fellow 2001–03; Margaret and Herman Sokol Fellow, Cullman Center for Scholars and Writers, New York Public Library 2002–03; Hon. Research Fellow, Univ. Coll. London 1991–. *Publications:* The Letters of John Wilmot, Earl of Rochester (ed.) 1980, Spirit of Wit: Reconsiderations of Rochester (ed.) 1982, Roald Dahl: A Biography 1994, Grub Street and the Ivory Tower: Literary Journalism, and Literary Scholarship from Fielding to the Internet (ed. with Bridget Bennett) 1998, Romancing: The Life and Work of Henry Green 2000, VS Pritchett: a Working Life 2004, Essential Stories/V.S. Pritchett (ed.) 2005, Roald Dahl: Collected Stories (ed.) 2006; contrib. introductions to recent edns of R. L. Stevenson's In the South Seas, Robert Louis Stevenson's The Lantern Bearers, the complete novels of Henry Green; contrib. various articles on poetry, drama and literary history. *Address:* English and Comparative Literary Studies, Room H526, University of Warwick, Coventry, CV4 7AL, England (office). *Telephone:* (24) 7652-3323 (office). *Fax:* (24) 7652-4750 (office). *E-mail:* jeremy.treglown@ warwick.ac.uk (office). *Website:* www2.warwick.ac.uk/fac/arts/english (office).

TREICHL, Andreas; Austrian banking executive; *Chairman of the Management Board,, Erste Bank Group;* b. 1952; ed studied econs in Vienna; began career with Chase Manhattan Bank, New York 1977; joined Erste Bank in 1983 for three years, rejoined bank 1994, apptd to Man. Bd, Chair. Man. Bd 1997–, responsible for Group Communication, Group HR, Strategic Group Devt, Group Secr., Group Audit, Group Marketing, Group Investor Relations. *Address:* Erste Bank der oesterreichischen Sparkassen AG, Graben 21, 1010 Vienna, Austria (office). *Telephone:* (50) 100-10100 (office). *Fax:* (50) 100-13112 (office). *E-mail:* investor.relations@erstebank.at (office). *Website:* www .erstebank.com/investorrelations (office).

TREICHL, Heinrich; Austrian business executive; *President, F.A. v Hayek Institute;* b. 31 July 1913, Vienna; s. of Dr Alfred Treichl and Dorothea Treichl (née Baroness Ferstel); m. Helga Ross 1946; two s.; ed Univs of Frankfurt, Germany and Vienna; Dir, Banque des Pays de l'Europe Centrale, Paris, Mercur Bank AG and Länderbank Wien AG, Vienna 1936–39; Pnr, Ullstein and Co., Vienna 1946–55; Dir, Österreichische Industrie- und Bergbauver- waltungs GmbH, Vienna 1956–58; Dir, Creditanstalt-Bankverein, Vienna 1958, Chair. of Man. Bd 1970–81 (merged with Bank Austria 1998); currently Pres. F.A. v Hayek Inst., Vienna; Hon. Pres. Austrian Red Cross Soc.; Hon. Chair. Supervisory Bd Bank für Kärnten und Steiermark AG, Bank für Oberösterreich und Salzburg, Bank für Tirol und Vorarlberg AG; Grande Ufficiale Ordine del Merito (Italy), Commdr, Order Homayoun, Commdr, Légion d'honneur, Kt Commdr, Order of St Gregory, Grand Decoration of Honour in Gold for Services to Repub. of Austria, Grand Decoration in Silver with Star for Services to Repub. of Austria. *Leisure interests:* literature, hunting, skiing. *Address:* Salmgasse 2, 1030 Vienna, Austria (home). *Telephone:* (1) 713-31-50 (home). *Fax:* (1) 713-31-50 (home). *Website:* www .hayek-institut.at.

TREITEL, Sir Guenter Heinz, Kt, QC, MA, DCL, FBA; British academic; *Professor Emeritus of English Law, University of Oxford;* b. 26 Oct. 1928, Berlin, Germany; s. of Dr Theodor Treitel and Hanna Treitel (née Levy); m. Phyllis M. Cook 1957; two s.; ed Kilburn Grammar School and Magdalen Coll., Oxford; came to UK 1939; Fellow of Magdalen Coll., Oxford 1954–79, Fellow Emer. 1979–; All Souls Reader in English Law 1964–79; Vinerian Prof. of English Law, Univ. of Oxford and Fellow of All Souls Coll. 1979–96, Prof. Emer. and Fellow Emer. 1996–; Visiting Lecturer, Univ. of Chicago 1963–64, Visiting Prof. 1968–69, 1971–72; Visiting Prof., Univ. of Western Australia 1976, Univ. of Houston 1977, Southern Methodist Univ. 1978, 1988–89, 1994, Distinguished Visiting Prof. 2000, 2003; Visiting Prof., Univ. of Va 1978–79, 1983–84, Univ. of Santa Clara 1981; Visiting Scholar, Ernst von Caemmerer Gedächtnisstiftung 1990; Clarendon Lecturer in Law, Univ. of Oxford 2001;

consultant to Law Comm. on law of contract 1972–84; Trustee, British Museum 1983–98; mem. Council Nat. Trust 1984–93; Hon. Bencher, Gray's Inn. *Publications:* The Law of Contract 1962, An Outline of the Law of Contract 1975, Remedies for Breach of Contract: A Comparative Account 1988, Unmöglichkeit, "Impracticability" und "Frustration" im anglo-amer- ikanischen Recht 1991, Frustration and Force Majeure 1994, Benjamin's Sale of Goods (co-author) 1974, English Private Law (co-author) 2000, Carver on Bills of Lading (co-author) 2001, Some Landmarks of Twentieth Century Contract Law 2002; ed. of other law books. *Leisure interests:* reading, music. *Address:* All Souls College, Oxford, OX1 4AL, England. *Telephone:* (1865) 279379. *Fax:* (1865) 279299.

TREJOS FERNÁNDEZ, José Joaquín; Costa Rican politician and aca- demic; *Professor Emeritus, School of Statistics, University of Costa Rica;* b. 18 April 1916, San José; s. of Juan Trejos and Emilia F. de Trejos; m. Clara F. de Trejos 1936; five s.; ed Univ. of Chicago; Prof. of Statistical Theory and Dean, Faculty of Econ., Univ. de Costa Rica 1952–56, Dean, Faculty of Sciences and Letters 1957–62, Prof. Emer. School of Statistics 1979–; Pres. of Costa Rica 1966–70; Partido Unidad Social Cristiana. *Publications:* Reflexiones sobre la Educación, 2nd edn 1968, Ocho Años en la Política Nacional – Ideales Políticos y Realidad Nacional, Vol. I 1973, Vol. III 1973, Vol. IV 1973, Vol. II 1974, Ideas Políticas Elementales 1985, Reflexiones Políticas 1995, Por Esfuerzo Propio 1999. *Leisure interests:* music, history. *Address:* Apartado 10.096, San José, Costa Rica. *Telephone:* 224-2411.

TREKY, Ali Abdussalam, PhD; Libyan diplomatist and politician; b. 10 Oct. 1938, Misurata; s. of Abdussalem Treiki and Amna Treiki; m. Aisha Dihoum 1969; one s. three d.; ed Univ. of Benghazi, Libya and Toulouse Univ., France; joined Foreign Ministry 1970; Minister Plenipotentiary 1970, Dir of Political Admin 1970–73, Dir of African Admin 1973–74, Asst Deputy for Political Affairs 1974–76; Sec. of State for Foreign Affairs 1971–77, Foreign Sec. 1977–81, Sec. of Liaison for Foreign Affairs 1981–86; Foreign Minister 1984–86; Head of Libyan del. to UN Gen. Ass. 1977–80; Perm. Rep. of Libya to the UN 1982–84, 1986–91, 2003–07, to League of Arab States, Cairo 1991–93; Amb. to France 1995–2001; Minister of African Affairs –2003; Sec. Libyan Popular Cttee for African Unity 2000–. *Address:* c/o Secretariat of the People's Committee for Foreign Liaison and International Co-operation, Tripoli, Libya (office).

TRELFORD, Donald Gilchrist, MA, FRSA; British journalist; b. 9 Nov. 1937, Coventry; s. of T. S. Trelford and Doris Gilchrist; m. 1st Janice Ingram 1963 (divorced 1978); two s. one d.; m. 2nd Katherine Louise Mark 1978 (divorced 1998); one d.; m. 3rd Claire Elizabeth Bishop 2001; ed Bablake School, Coventry, Selwyn Coll., Cambridge; pilot officer, RAF 1956–58; worked on newspapers in Coventry and Sheffield 1961–63; Ed. Times of Malawi and corresp. in Africa, The Times, Observer, BBC 1963–66; joined Observer as Deputy News Ed. 1966, Asst Man. Ed. 1968, Deputy Ed. 1969–75, Dir and Ed. 1975–93, CEO 1992–93; Dir Optomen Television 1988–97, Observer Films 1989–93, Cen. Observer TV 1990–93; Dir, Prof., Dept of Journalism Studies, Univ. of Sheffield 1994–2000, Visiting Prof. 2001–, Prof. Emer. 2007–; Chair. Soc. of Gentlemen, Lovers of Musick 1996–2002, London Press Club 2002–07 (Pres. 2007–); mem. British Exec. Cttee, Int. Press Inst. 1976–, Asscn of British Eds 1984–, Guild of British Newspaper Eds 1985– (mem. Parl. and Legal Cttee 1987–91); Vice Pres. British Sports Trust 1988–2002; Ind. Assessor BBC TV Regional News 1997; mem. Council, Media Soc. 1981–2003 (Pres. 1999–2002), Judging Panel, British Press Awards 1981– (Chair. 2003–05); Scottish Press Awards 1985, Olivier Awards Cttee, SWET 1984–93, Defence, Press and Broadcasting Cttee 1986–93, Cttee, MCC 1988–91, Competition Comm.'s Newspaper Panel 1999–, Council Advertising Standards Authority 2002–; Vice-Pres. Newspaper Press Fund 1992– (Chair. Appeals Cttee 1991), Acting Ed. The Oldie 1994; Judge, Whitbread Literary Awards 1992, George Orwell Prize 1998; sports columnist Daily Telegraph 1993–; Dir St Cecilia Int. Festival of Music 1995–2002; Freeman City of London 1988; Hon. DLitt (Sheffield); Granada Newspaper of the Year Award 1983, 1993; commended, Int. Ed. of the Year (World Press Review) 1984. *Radio:* presenter, LBC Breakfast News 1994; regular panellist, BBC Radio Five Live. *Television:* presenter sports and current affairs series, Channel 4 and BBC 2. *Publications:* Siege 1980, Snookered 1986, Child of Change (with Garry Kasparov) 1987, Saturday's Boys 1990, Fine Glances 1990; (contrib.) County Champions 1982, The Queen Observed 1986, Len Hutton Remem- bered 1992, World Chess Championships (with Daniel King) 1993, W. G. Grace 1998; Ed.: Sunday Best 1981, 1982, 1983, The Observer at 200 1992; contrib. to Animal Passions 1994. *Leisure interests:* golf, snooker. *Address:* Flat 3, 6 River Terrace, Henley-on-Thames, RG9 1BG, England. *Telephone:* (7850) 131742 (mobile). *E-mail:* donaldtrelford@yahoo.co.uk (home).

TREMAIN, (Edwin) Garrick; New Zealand landscape artist and cartoonist; b. 4 Feb. 1941, Wellington; s. of Edwin Rex Tremain and Linda Joyce Tremain; m. Jillian Mary Butland; two d.; ed Palmerston North Boys' High School; worked as shepherd; fmr artist and art dir for advertising cos in NZ, UK and elsewhere; full-time artist 1973–; syndicated cartoonist 1988–; NZ Commem- orative Medal 1990, Cartoonist of the Year 1996, 1999. *Publication:* Nursery Rhymes Mother Never Read You 2005. *Leisure interests:* golf, piano, jazz music. *Address:* Stonebridge, 188 Domain Road, RDI Queenstown, Otago, New Zealand (home). *Telephone:* (3) 409-8244. *E-mail:* tremain@queenstown .co.nz. *Website:* garricktremain.com.

TREMAIN, Rose, CBE, BA, FRSL; British writer; b. (Rosemary Jane Thomson), 2 Aug. 1943, London; d. of the late Keith Thomson and Viola Mabel Thomson; m. 1st Jon Tremain 1971; one d.; m. 2nd Jonathan Dudley 1982 (dissolved 1990); pnr Richard Holmes; ed Sorbonne, Paris and Univ. of East Anglia; novelist and playwright 1971–; part-time tutor Univ. of East Anglia 1988–95; mem. judging panel, Booker Prize 1988, 2000; Hon. DLitt

(East Anglia) 2001, (Essex) 2005; Univ. of Essex Fellowship 1979–80; one of Granta's Best Young British Novelists 1983, Giles Cooper Award 1985, Angel Literary Award 1986, Sony Award 1996. *Plays for radio include:* Temporary Shelter 1985, Who Was Emily Davison? 1996, The End of Love 1999, One Night in Winter 2001. *Television:* A Room for the Winter 1979, Daylight Robbery 1982. *Publications:* fiction: Sadler's Birthday 1976, Letter to Sister Benedicta 1978, The Cupboard 1981, The Swimming Pool Season 1984, Restoration (Sunday Express Book of the Year Award) 1989, Sacred Country (James Tait Black Memorial Prize 1993, Prix Fémina Etranger 1994) 1992, The Way I Found Her 1997, Music and Silence (Whitbread Novel of the Year) 1999, The Colour 2003, The Road Home (Orange Broadband Prize for Fiction 2008) 2007; for children: Journey to the Volcano 1985; short story collections: The Colonel's Daughter (Dylan Thomas Short Story Prize 1984) 1982, The Garden of the Villa Mollini 1988, Evangelista's Fan 1994, Collected Short Stories 1996, The Darkness of Wallis Simpson and Other Stories 2005; non-fiction: The Fight for Freedom for Women 1971, Stalin: An Illustrated Biography 1974. *Leisure interests:* yoga, gardening. *Address:* 2 High House, South Avenue, Thorpe St Andrew, Norwich, NR7 0EZ, England (home). *Telephone:* (1603) 439682 (home). *Fax:* (1603) 434234 (home).

TREMAINE, Scott Duncan, BSc, MA, PhD, FRS, FRSC; Canadian astrophysicist and academic; *Professor, Institute for Advanced Study, Princeton;* b. 25 May 1950, Toronto, Ont.; s. of Vincent Tremaine and Beatrice (Sharp) Tremaine; ed McMaster Univ., Hamilton, Ont., Princeton Univ., NJ; mem. Inst. for Advanced Study 1978–81; Assoc. Prof., MIT 1981–85; Prof., Univ. of Toronto 1985–97; Dir Canadian Inst. for Theoretical Astrophysics 1985–96; Prof. and Chair. Dept of Astrophysical Sciences, Princeton Univ. 1998–2006; Prof., Inst. for Advanced Study, Princeton 2007–; mem. NAS 2002; Foreign Hon. mem. American Acad. of Arts and Sciences 1992; Hon. DSc (McMaster Univ., St Mary's Univ.). *Publication:* Galactic Dynamics (with J. Binney) 1987. *Address:* School of Natural Sciences, Institute for Advanced Study, Einstein Drive, Princeton, NJ 08540, USA (office). *Telephone:* (609) 734-8191 (office). *Fax:* (609) 924-7592 (office). *E-mail:* tremaine@ias.edu (office). *Website:* www.sns.ias.edu (office).

TREMBLAY, Gérald, MBA; Canadian lawyer and politician; *Mayor of Montréal;* b. 20 Sept. 1942, Ottawa, Québec; ed Harvard Business School, USA; lawyer and mem. Barreau du Québec 1980–; fmr Prin. Assoc. and Dir Gen. consulting firm affiliated to Groupe Sobeco Ernst and Young; Pres. Soc. de développement industriel du Québec 1986–89; fmr mem. Admin. council of the Caisse de dépôt et de placement du Québec; fmr mem. Admin. Council and Exec. Cttee Hydro Québec; Mem. Nat. Ass. MNA (Liberal) and Minister of Industry, Commerce, Science and Tech. 1989–94; Pres. Centre de perfectionnement de l'École des Hautes Études Commerciales 1996; Chair. Comm. consultative sur la politique de consultation publique sur les projets dérogatoires au plan ou aux règlements d'urbanisme de Montréal 2000; Mayor of Montréal and Chair. Montréal Metropolitan Community 2001–. *Address:* Hotel de Ville, 275, Notre-Dame Street East, Montréal, PQ H2Y 1C6, Canada (office). *Telephone:* (514) 872-3101 (office). *Fax:* (514) 872-4059 (office). *E-mail:* geraldtremblay@ville.montreal.qc.ca (office). *Website:* ville.montreal .qc.ca (office).

TREMBLAY, Marc-Adélard, OC, MA, LSA, PhD, FRSC, GOQ; Canadian social anthropologist and academic; *Professor Emeritus of Social Anthropology, Laval University;* b. (Joseph Adélard), 24 April 1922, Les Eboulements; s. of Wellie Tremblay and Lauretta Tremblay; m. Jacqueline Cyr 1949; one s. five d.; ed Montreal, Laval and Cornell Univs; research assoc., Cornell Univ. 1953–56; Asst Prof., Dept of Sociology and Anthropology, Laval Univ. 1956, Prof. of Social Anthropology 1963–93, Prof. Emer. 1994–; Founding Pres., Canadian Sociology and Anthropology Asscn 1965–67; Pres. Canadian Ethnology Soc. 1976–77, Royal Soc. of Canada 1981–84, Asscn of Canadian Univs for Northern Studies 1985–87, Québec Council for Social Research 1987–91; Dir Groupe d'études Inuit et Circumpolaires 1990–94; mem. Nunavik Comm. 1999–2001; Special Adviser Fed. Negotiating Team for Establishment of a Nunavik Govt; mem. many other professional and scientific orgs; Grand Officier Ordre Nat. du Québec 1995; Dr hc (Ottawa) 1982, (Guelph) 1984, (Univ. of N British Columbia) 1994, (Carleton) 1995, (Ste-Anne) 1997, (McGill) 1998; Prix de la Province de Québec 1964, Innis-Gérin Medal, Royal Soc. of Canada 1979, Molson Prize, The Canada Council 1987, Marcel Vincent Prize, French Canadian Asscn for the Advancement of Science 1988. *Publications:* People of Cove and Woodlot: communities from the viewpoint of social psychiatry 1960, Les comportements économiques de la famille salariée 1964, Initiation à la recherche dans les sciences humaines 1968, Famille et Parenté en Acadie 1971, Communities and culture in French Canada 1973, Patterns of Amerindian Identity 1976, L'identité québécoise en péril 1983, Conscience et Enquête 1983, L'Anthropologie à l'Université Laval: Fondements historiques, pratiques, académiques, dynamismes d'évolution 1989, Les Fondements historiques et pratiques de l'anthropologie appliquée 1990; 25 books and monographs and 200 articles. *Leisure interests:* gardening, cross-country skiing, classical music, skating. *Address:* Département d'Anthropologie, Université Laval, Cité Universitaire, Ste-Foy, Québec (office); 835 rue Nouvelle-Orléans, Ste-Foy, Québec, G1X 3J4, Canada (home). *Telephone:* (418) 653-5411 (home). *Fax:* (418) 653-9865. *E-mail:* matremgt@globetrotter .net (home). *Website:* pages.globetrotter.net/matrem (home).

TREMBLAY, Michel; Canadian writer; b. 25 June 1942, Montréal; ed Graphic Arts Inst. of Québec; worked as linotypist 1963–66; Dr hc (Concordia, McGill, Stirling, Windsor); first prize for young writers sponsored by CBC (for play Le Train, written 1959) 1964, Gov.-Gen.'s Performing Arts Award 1999; Officier, Ordre des Arts et des Lettres, France. *Film scripts include:* Françoise Durocher, Waitress 1972, Il était une fois dans l'Est 1973, Parlez-nous d'amour 1976, Le Soleil se lève en retard 1977. *Plays include:* Les Belles sœurs 1968, En pièces detachées 1969, La Duchesse de Langeais 1969, Les Paons 1971, Hosanna 1973, Bonjour Là, bonjour 1974, Ste Carmen de la Main 1976, Damnée Manon, Sacrée Sandra 1977, L'Impromptu d'outremont 1980, Les Grandes vacances 1981, Les Anciennes odeurs 1981, Albertine en cinq temps 1984, Le Vrai monde? 1987, La Maison suspendue 1990, Nelligan (opera libretto, Opéra de Montréal) 1990, Marcel poursuivi par les chiens 1992, Messe solennelle pour une pleine lune d'été 1996, Encore une fois, si vous permettez 1998, L'État des lieux 2002, Le Passé antérieur 2003. *Radio plays include:* Le Cœur découvert 1986, Le Grand Jour 1988, Six Heures au plus tard 1988. *Television:* Le Cœur découvert 2000. *Publications:* Contes pour buveurs attardés 1966, La Cité dans l'oeuf 1969, C't'à ton tour, Laura Cadieux 1973, La Grosse femme d'à côté est enceinte 1973, Thérèse et Pierrette à l'école des Saints-Anges 1980, La Duchesse et le roturier 1982, Des Nouvelles d'Edouard 1984, Le Cœur découvert 1986, Le Premier quartier de la lune 1989, Les Vues animées 1991, Douze coups de théâtre 1992, Le Cœur éclaté 1995, Un Ange cornu avec des ailes de tôle 1996, L'Homme qui entendait siffler une bouilloire 2001, Bonbons assortis 2002, Le Cahier noir 2003, Le Cahier rouge 2004. *Leisure interests:* painting water colours. *Address:* Agence Goodwin, 839 Sherbrooke est, Suite 200, Montréal, QC H2L 1K6, Canada (office). *Telephone:* (514) 598-5252 (office). *Fax:* (514) 598-1878 (office). *E-mail:* artistes@goodwin.agent.ca (office). *Website:* www.agencegoodwin.com (office).

TREMLETT, David Rex; British artist; b. 13 Feb. 1945, Cornwall; s. of Rex Tremlett and Dinah Tremlett; m. Laure Florence 1987; one s. two d.; ed St Austell Grammar School, Falmouth Art Coll. and Royal Coll. of Art; exhibited widely in UK, USA, Europe, Africa, Australia, Mexico, Japan etc.; recent projects include: walls of Law Courts, Amsterdam, Benesse Guesthouse, Naoshima Island, Japan, façade of St Denis Univ., Paris, main hall of BBL Bank Kortrijk, Belgium, walls at Eaton Hall, Chester, UK, walls of castle of Marchese di Barolo, Barolo, Italy, lobby of Central Landesbank, Dresden, Germany, ceiling at Eaton Hall, Chester, Chapel of Barolo, Italy, interior wall at ABN AMRO HQ, Amsterdam, walls of British Embassy Berlin, walls at Obayashi HQ, Tokyo, walls and floor of Palazzo Fantuzzi, Bologna, wall for the Grosvenor Estates, London, walls and floor of the Re Enzo Chapel, Bologna, walls of Rione Alto metro station, Naples, walls, ceiling and floor of Chapel of Santa Maria dei Carcerati Bologna, wall drawings for British Council Centre, Nairobi, Kenya, walls of Esserheem Penitentiary, N Holland, all 25 stained glass windows of St Peter and St Paul Church, Villenauxe-la-Grande, France, ceiling and walls in Eaton Hall, Chester, Villa Caldogno (Palladio) Vicenza, Italy (one room of wall drawings), Zamosc Synagogue wall drawings, Zamosc, Poland, The Qube Atrium wall drawings, Tottenham Court Road, London, Villa Amista (Byblos Hotel) ceilings, Verona, Italy, The Qube (Atrium) Tottenham Court Road, London, 2 Entrance Rooms Castello di Formigine, Formigine, Italy, The Walls of 'Chapelle Notre-Dame des Fleurs', Moric, Brittany, France. *Films:* Non-Improvisation (b/w) 1971, No Title 1995. *Music:* Hand Up/Too Bad (CD), A Journey with David Tremlett (soundtrack). *Television:* A Journey with David Tremlett (satellite) 2003. *Publications:* Some Places to Visit 1974, On the Waterfront 1978, Scrub 1978, On the Border 1979, Restless 1983, Rough Ride 1985, Ruin 1987, Dates/Differents 1987, Sometimes We All Do 1988, Tremlett-West Bengal 1990, Written Form 1990, Internal 1991, From Wall to Wall 1991, Mjimwema Drawings 1991, A Quiet Madness 1992, PAC Catalogue 1993, Abandoned Drawings 1993, Casa de Dibujos 1993, Nouveaux Plans 1994, Rooms in Vienne 1994, Walls at the Palais Jacques Coeur, Bourges 1994, Wall Drawings 1969–1995, Columns 1995, How Far in that Direction 1996, Walls and their Drawings 1997, Pages (Eritrea) 1998, Clear and Fuzzy 1999, Passa Dentro 2000, If Walls Could Talk 2001, If Things Could Talk 2002, Black as Midnight with the Eyes Shut 2002, A New Light 2003, 37 Wall Drawings in Issoire 2003, David Tremlett – British Council Nairobi 2005, David Tremlett-Retrospectve Musée des Beaux Arts, Grenoble France/Pecci Museum, Prato, Italy 2006, Between You and Me (with John Haldane and Laure Genillard) 2006, Lumière – The Stained Glass Windows of St Peter and St Paul Church, Villenauxe-la-Grande, France 2006, Texas 2007, David Tremlett: A Dialogue Between Past and Present 2008. *Leisure interests:* Davidson glass, African music, Saharan architecture, cross-country running. *Address:* Broadlawns, Chipperfield Road, Bovingdon, Herts., England (home). *Telephone:* (1442) 832214 (home). *Fax:* (1442) 832533 (home). *E-mail:* tremlett@tremlett.demon.co.uk (home). *Website:* www.laudanum.net/tremlett (home).

TREMONTI, Giulio; Italian politician and lawyer; *Minister of Finance;* b. 18 Aug. 1947, Sondrio, Lombardy; ed Univ. of Pavia; teacher of tax law, Univ. of Pavia; fmr Sr Teaching Fellow, Inst. of European and Comparative Law, Univ. of Oxford, UK; mem. Camera dei Deputati (Parl.) (Forza Italia) 1994–, mem. Parl. Special Cttee for Reform of Italian Constitution; Minister of Finance 1994–95, 2008–, of Economy and Finance 2001–04 (resgnd), Sept. 2005–06, Deputy Prime Minister 2005–06; Pres. Comm. for Monetary Reform 1994–95; 1994–95; fmr Vice-Pres. Aspen Inst. Italia; mem. Italy/Vatican Cttee for Treaty on Financing of Ecclesiastical Insts, Comm. on Deregulation; Ed. Rivista di Diritto Finanziario e Scienza delle Finanze; regular contrib., Corriere della Sera. *Publications:* several books on tax and public policy. *Address:* Ministry of Finance, Via XX Settembre 97, 00187 Rome, Italy (office). *Telephone:* (06) 476111 (office). *Fax:* (06) 5910993 (office). *E-mail:* pubblicazione.sito@tesoro.it (office). *Website:* www.mef.gov.it (office).

TRENDAFILOVA, Ekaterina Panayotova, PhD; Bulgarian barrister and judge; *Judge, International Criminal Court;* b. 20 June 1953, Sofia; m. Emil Roussev Bachvarov; one d.; ed Sofia Univ. 'St Kliment Ohridski'; legal internship, Sofia City Court 1977–78; Deputy Dist Attorney, Sofia Dist Court 1985–89; specialization at Inst. of State and Law, Moscow, USSR 1983, 1985; Prof., Faculty of Law, Sofia Univ. 'St Kliment Ohridski' 1984–, Assoc. Prof. (Docent) 1996–2001, Full Prof. 2001–; Prof., Faculty of Law, Veliko Turnovo Univ. 'Sts Cyril and Methodius' 1995–; Visiting Prof., Tokai Univ., Japan

1993; called to the Bar of Bulgaria 1995; advised the Ministry of Foreign Affairs on the establishment of the Int. Criminal Court (ICC) and served as an expert to the Ministry of Justice, Ministry of Interior, Constitutional Court, Supreme Court of Cassation and Parl. of Bulgaria where she chaired the Criminal Div. of the Legis. Consultative Council; Judge, Pre-Trial Div., ICC 2003–(12); mem. Intergovernmental Comm. entrusted with the preparation of the ratification of the European Convention on Human Rights and Fundamental Freedoms 1991; Bulgarian Rep. to UN Comm. for Crime Prevention and Criminal Justice, Vienna 1992–94; Chair. Program and Analytical Center for European Law 1999–, Modern Criminal Procedure Foundation 1999–; Vice-Pres. Specialized Scientific Council on Legal Science 2003–04; mem. Comm. for Social Sciences at the Higher Accreditation Agency with the Council of Ministers of Bulgaria 2000–03, Legal Comm. Nat. Higher Attestation Comm. with the Council of Ministers of Bulgaria 2004–05; scientific advisor, Students' Internship Program between the American Govt and Bulgarian Parl. 2000–05; Head, Criminal Div. Legis. Consultative Council with the Speaker of the Bulgarian Parl. 2001–05; Middle-term expert under the PHARE Twinning project (Bulgaria–Austria) 2002–03; mem. Consultative Council Open Soc. Inst. Project "Access to Justice" 2002–05, Advisory Bd Open Soc. Inst. Int. Project "Independence and Accountability of Prosecution" 2003–05; European expert within EC CARDS Regional Project 2004–; Head of Working Group on Judicial Reform, Open Soc. Inst. Project Strategy for the Socio-econ. and Political Devt of Bulgaria 2005–2010 2004–05; mem. Editorial Bd Human Rights Review 2003–; mem. Union of Bulgarian Lawyers 1980–, Union of Bulgarian Scholars 1984– (Chair. legal section 2001–03), Bulgarian Humboldt Soc. 1994–, Bulgarian Fulbright Soc. 1997–, Women with Int. Societal Expertise (WISE), Paris 2004–; Hon. mem. European Correspondents Scientific Cttee, Centre Int. Constats et Prospective, Paris 1991; Best Young Lecturer of the Year Award, Nat. Soc. for Dissemination of Legal Knowledge 1984, Alexander von Humboldt Scholarship, Augsburg Univ., Germany 1993–94, Fulbright Scholarship, Univ. of California, USA 1997, Author of the Year Award for contrib. to the legal literature 2000, Legal Initiative for Training and Devt Award 2004. *Publications:* more than 70 publs in Bulgaria, USA, France, Italy and the Netherlands in the field of human rights law, criminal procedural law, int. criminal procedural law, comparative law and constitutional law. *Address:* International Criminal Court, PO Box 19519, 2500 CM, The Hague (office); International Criminal Court, Maanweg 174, 2516 AB, The Hague, Netherlands (office). *Telephone:* (70) 515-8515 (office). *Fax:* (70) 515-8555 (office). *E-mail:* eptrend@abv.bg (office); pio@icc-cpi.int (office). *Website:* www.icc-cpi.int (office); www.icc-cpi.int/library/asp/ICC-ASP_ej2_bul-cv.pdf (office).

TRENTHAM, David R., PhD, FRS; British medical research scientist and academic; *Honorary Professor, Randall Division of Cell and Molecular Biophysics, King's College London;* b. 22 Sept. 1938, Solihull; s. of John A. Trentham and Julia A. M. Trentham; m. Kamalini Bhargava 1966; two s.; ed Uppingham School and Univ. of Cambridge; Faculty mem., Biochemistry Dept, Bristol Univ. 1972–77; Chair. and Edwin M. Chance Prof., Dept of Biochemistry and Biophysics, School of Medicine, Univ. of Pa, Philadelphia, USA 1977–83; Head, Physical Biochemistry Div., Nat. Inst. for Medical Research, London 1984–2003; Hon Prof., Randall Division, King's Coll London 2001–, Visiting Prof., Dept of Molecular Physiology and Biological Physics, Univ. of Virginia, Charlottesville, USA 2002–; Hon. Prof. King's Coll. London 2003; Colworth Medal, Biochemical Soc. 1974, Wilhelm Feldberg Prize 1990. *Publications:* numerous articles in biochemical and academic journals. *Address:* Randall Division of Cell and Molecular Biophysics, King's College London, School of Biomedical Sciences, New Hunt's House, Guy's Campus, London, SE1 1UL, England (office). *Telephone:* (20) 8959-3666. *E-mail:* dtrenth@nimr.mrc.ac.uk (office). *Website:* www.kcl.ac.uk/depsta/biomedical/randall/index.html (office).

TRESCHOW, Michael, MEng; Swedish business executive; *Chairman, Unilever PLC;* b. 1943, Helsingborg; ed Inst. of Tech., Lund; divisional man. roles in Scandinavia and France with Bahco Ventilation 1970–76; joined Atlas Copco AB 1976, Pres. and CEO 1991–97; Pres. and CEO AB Electrolux 1997–2002, Chair. 2004–07; Chair. Ericsson (Telefonaktiebolaget LM Ericsson) 2002–; Chair. (non-exec.) Unilever NV/Unilever PLC 2007–; mem. Bd of Dirs B-Business Pnrs 2001–, Knut and Alice Wallenberg Foundation; Dir (non-exec.) SKF 1992, Saab 1992, Parker-Hannifin Corp. 1996; mem. Bd Dirs ABB Ltd 2003–; Chair. Swedish Trade Council 1996, Confed. of Swedish Enterprise 2004–07; mem. Royal Acad. of Eng Sciences; King's Medal of 12th Dimension and Ribbon of Order of Seraphims (Sweden) 2000, Gran Cruz de la Orden del Mérito Civil (Spain) 2000, Chevalier, Légion d'honneur 2002, Commr Order of the Crown (Belgium) 2004. *Leisure interests:* golf, hunting. *Address:* Unilever PLC, Unilever House, 100 Victoria Embankment, London, EC4Y 0DY, England (office). *Telephone:* (20) 7822-5252 (office). *Fax:* (20) 7822-5511 (office). *E-mail:* press-office.london@unilever.com (office). *Website:* www.unilever.com (office).

TRETYAK, Vladislav A.; Russian politician and ice hockey player (retd); b. 25 April 1952, Orudyevo, Moscow region; s. of Alexander D. Tretyak and Vera P. Tretyak; one s. one d.; m. Tatyana Ye Tretyak; ed Moscow State Inst. of Physical Culture, Lenin Military Political Acad.; ice hockey player 1967– 84; (13 times USSR champion); hockey goalkeeper Central Army Sports Club and USSR nat. team (10 times world champion, nine times European champion); as a nat. team player played in 117 games in world, European championships and Olympic games; Pres. Int. Sports Acad.; served as goal keeper consultant to Chicago Black Hawks 1990s; mem. State Duma (faction United Russia) 2003–; Hockey Hall of Fame 1989, Best Russian Hockey Player of the 20th century 2000. *Publications include:* four books. *Address:* State Duma, Okhotnyi ryad 1, 103265 Moscow,, Russia (office). *Website:* www.duma.ru (office).

TRETYAKOV, Viktor Viktorovich; Russian violinist; b. 17 Oct. 1946, Krasnoyarsk; m. Natalia Likhopoi; one d.; ed Moscow Conservatory (pupil of Yury Yankelevich); First Prizes, All-Union Competition of Violinists 1965, Int. Tchaikovsky Competition 1966; concert career since mid-1960s, soloist of Moscow Philharmonic 1969; tours Europe, USA, Japan; participant in numerous European music festivals; Artistic Dir and Conductor Moscow (now Russian) Chamber Orchestra 1983–90; Prof., Head of Chair of Violin, Moscow Conservatory 1983–90; Prof., Hochschule für Musik, Cologne 1996–; State Prize of Russia 1981, USSR People's Artist 1987, "Triumph" Prize (Russia) 2003. *Address:* Berliner Konzertagentur Monika Ott, Dramburger, Str. 46, 12683 Berlin (office); Burgblick 9b, 53177 Bonn, Germany (home). *Fax:* (228) 9329641 (home).

TRETYAKOV, Vitaly Toviyevich; Russian journalist; b. 2 Jan. 1953, Moscow; m.; one s.; ed Moscow State Univ.; jr ed. to Ed. Press Agency Novosti (APN) 1976–88; reviewer, political reviewer, Deputy Ed.-in-Chief Moskovskiye Novosti (weekly) 1988–90; f. Nesavisimaya Gazeta (newspaper) 1990, Ed.-in-Chief 1990–2000; Dir-Gen. Indpendent Publishing Group 2001–; mem. Exec. Bd Council on Foreign and Defence Policy. *Publications include:* Philanthropy in Soviet Society 1989, Gorbachev, Ligachev, Yeltsin: Political Portraits on the Perestroika Background 1990, Titus of Sovietologists: Their Struggle for Power: Essays on Idiotism of Russian Policy 1996; numerous articles on political problems. *Leisure interests:* theatre, collecting of art albums. *Address:* Independent Publishing Group, Moscow, Russia (office). *E-mail:* wt1t@narod.ru (office).

TREVES, Vanni E., MA, LLM; British/Italian business executive; b. 3 Nov. 1940, Italy; s. of the late Giuliano Treves and of Marianna Treves; m. Angela Treves; two s. one d.; ed St Paul's, London, Univ. Coll. Oxford, Univ. of Illinois; joined City law firm Macfarlanes as articled clerk 1963, qualified 1965, Asst Solicitor 1965–68, Visiting Attorney White & Case, NY 1968–69, Partner Macfarlanes 1970–2002, Sr. Partner 1987–99; Chair. Equitable Life Assurance Soc. 2001–; Chair. Channel Four Television Corpn 1998–Jan. 2004, Korn Ferry Int. UK, BBA Group PLC 1989–2000, McKechnie PLC 1991–2000; Dir Intertek Testing Services PLC, Amplifin; Chair. NSPCC Justice for Children Appeal 1997–2000; Gov. Coll. of Law 1999–, Sadler's Wells Foundation 1999–; Trustee J. Paul Getty Charitable Trust and many other private cos and pension schemes; mem. Devt Bd, Nat. Art Collections Fund; mem. Law Soc. *Leisure interests:* art, walking, food. *Address:* c/o Macfarlanes, 10 Norwich Street, London, EC4A 1BD, England (office). *Telephone:* (20) 7831-9222 (office). *E-mail:* vet@macfarlanes.com (office). *Website:* www.macfarlanes.com (office).

TREVINO, Lee Buck; American professional golfer; b. 1 Dec. 1939, Dallas, Tex.; s. of Joe Trevino and Juanita Barrett; m. Claudia Bove 1983; three s. three d.; professional 1960–; US Open Champion 1968, 1971; British Open Champion 1971, 1972; Canadian Open Champion 1971 and numerous other championships 1965–80; US PGA Champion 1974, 1984; Champion US Sr Open 1990, PGA Sr Championship 1994; won Australian PGA Sr Championship 1996; Chair. Bd Lee Trevino Enterprises, Inc. 1967–; US PGA Player of the Year 1971, Sr Tour Player of the Year 1990, 1992, 1994. *Publication:* Super Mex (autobiog.) 1983. *Leisure interest:* fishing. *Address:* Senior PGA Tour, 112 Tpc Boulevard, Ponte Vedra Beach, FL 32082, USA (office).

TREVOR, William, CLit, BA; Irish writer; b. 24 May 1928, Mitchelstown, Co. Cork; s. of James William Cox and Gertrude Cox; m. Jane Ryan 1952; two s.; ed St Columba's Coll., Dublin, Trinity Coll., Dublin; mem. Irish Acad. of Letters; Hon. KBE 2002; Hon. DLitt (Exeter) 1984, (Dublin) 1986, (Queen's Univ., Belfast) 1989, (Nat. Univ., Cork) 1990; Hawthornden Prize 1965, Royal Soc. of Literature Prize 1978, Whitbread Prize for Fiction 1978, Allied Irish Banks Award for Services to Literature 1978, Whitbread Prize for Fiction 1983, Whitbread Book of the Year 1994, Sunday Express Book of the Year Award 1994, David Cohen British Literature Prize 1999, PEN Prize for Short Stories 2001, Irish Times Prize for Irish Fiction 2001, Listowel Prize 2002, Int. Nonino Prize 2008. *Publications:* The Old Boys 1964, The Boarding House 1965, The Love Department 1966, The Day We Got Drunk on Cake 1967, Mrs Eckdorf in O'Neill's Hotel 1968, Miss Gomez and the Brethren 1969, The Ballroom of Romance 1970, Elizabeth Alone 1972, Angels at the Ritz 1973, The Children of Dynmouth 1977, Lovers of Their Time 1979, Other People's Worlds 1980, Beyond the Pale 1981, Fools of Fortune 1983, A Writer's Ireland: Landscape in Literature 1984, The News from Ireland 1986, Nights at the Alexandra 1987, The Silence in the Garden 1988, Family Sins and Other Stories 1989, The Oxford Book of Irish Short Stories (ed.) 1989, Two Lives 1991, William Trevor: The Collected Stories 1992, Juliet's Story 1992, Excursions in the Real World (essays) 1993, Felicia's Journey 1994, Ireland: Selected Stories 1995, After Rain 1996, Cocktails at Doney's and Other Stories 1996, Death in Summer 1998, The Hill Bachelors 2000, The Story of Lucy Gault 2002, A Bit on the Side (short stories) 2004, Cheating at Canasta 2007, Love and Summer 2009. *Address:* PFD, Drury House, 34–43 Russell Street, London, WC2B 5HA, England (office). *Telephone:* (20) 7344-1000 (office). *Fax:* (20) 7836-9543 (office). *E-mail:* medwards@pfd.co.uk (office). *Website:* www.pfd.co.uk (office).

TRIANTAFYLLIDES, Michalakis Antoniou; Cypriot judge; b. 12 May 1927, Nicosia; m.; two c.; ed Gray's Inn, London; practised as a lawyer in Cyprus 1948–60, serving for three years as Sec. of Human Rights Cttee of Bar; mem. Greek Cypriot del. to Jt Constitutional Comm. which drafted Cyprus Constitution 1959–60; Greek Cypriot Judge, Supreme Constitutional Court 1960–64, Judge 1964–71, Pres. Supreme Court 1971–88; Attorney Gen. 1988–94; Pres. Council of the Univ. of Cyprus 1997; Chair. Oncology Centre 1998; now practicing privately as lawyer. *Address:* 22 Iras, Flat 2, 1061 Lefkosia, Cyprus.

TRICHET, Jean-Claude, LèsSc (Econ); French banker; *President, European Central Bank;* b. 20 Dec. 1942, Lyon; s. of Jean Trichet and Georgette Vincent-Carrefour; m. Aline Rybalka 1965; two s.; ed Ecole des Mines, Nancy, Univ. of Paris, Inst. d'Etudes Politiques, Paris, Faculté Sciences Economiques, Paris and Ecole Nat. d'Admin; Engineer, competitive sector 1966–68, Insp. of Finances 1971–76; assigned to Gen. Inspectorate of Finance 1974, assigned to Treasury Dept 1975, Sec.-Gen. Business Restructuring Interministerial Cttee 1976–78; Adviser, Minister of Economic Affairs 1978; Adviser to Pres. of Repub. 1978–81; Head of Devt Aid Office and Deputy Dir of Bilateral Affairs, Treasury Dept 1981, Head of Int. Affairs, Treasury Dept 1985; Chief of Staff to Minister of Finance 1986–87; Dir Treasury Dept 1987; Alternate Gov. IMF and World Bank 1987, Under-Sec. of Treas. and Censor Bank of France 1987–93; Gov. Bank of France 1993–2003; Chair. Paris Club 1985–93; mem. Bd of Dirs BIS 1993–2003, EMI 1994–98; a Gov. IBRD 1993–95; Vice-Gov. IMF 1995–2003; Chair. Monetary Cttee of EC 1992–93; Dir European Cen. Bank 1998–2003, Pres. 2003–; Chair. Group of Ten Central Bank Govs 2003–; Officier, Légion d'honneur, Ordre nat. du Mérite; decorations (Commdr) from Austria, Argentina, Belgium, Brazil, Ecuador, Germany, Ivory Coast, Yugoslavia; Policy Maker of the Year, Int. Economy Magazine 1991, Prize Zebilli Marimo, Acad. des Sciences Morales et Politiques 1999, Int. Prize Pico della Mirandola 2002. *Publications:* various articles on finance and economy. *Leisure interest:* poetry. *Address:* European Central Bank, Kaiserstrasse 29, 60311 Frankfurt am Main, Germany (office). *Telephone:* (69) 1344-7301 (office). *Fax:* (69) 1344-7305 (office). *E-mail:* info@ecb.europa.eu (office). *Website:* www.ecb.europa.eu (office).

TRICOIRE, Jean-Pascal, MBA; French business executive; *Chairman and CEO, Schneider Electric SA;* b. 11 May 1963; m.; three c.; ed ESEO Grad. School of Eng, Angers, CESMA Business School, Lyon; began career with Alcatel, Schlumberger and St Gobain 1985–86; joined Merlin Gerin 1986; various exec. roles with Schneider Electric SA 1988–99 including posts in Italy, China and S Africa, becoming Head of Global Strategic Accounts 1999–2001, Exec. Vice-Pres. Int. Div. 2002–03, COO 2003–06, Chair. Man. Bd and CEO 2006–. *Leisure interests:* multicultural teams, commitment, humour, curiosity, travelling off the beaten path, whitewater sports, new technologies. *Address:* Schneider Electric SA, 43–45 boulevard Franklin Roosevelt, 92500 Rueil-Malmaison, France (office). *Telephone:* 1-41-29-70-00 (office). *Fax:* 1-41-29-71-00 (office). *E-mail:* info@schneider-electric.com (office). *Website:* www.schneider-electric.com (office).

TRIESMAN, Baron (Life Peer), cr. 2004, of Tottenham in the London Borough of Haringey; **David Maxim Triesman,** MA, FRSA; British politician and trade union official; *Prime Minister's Special Envoy on Returns;* b. 30 Oct. 1943, Hertfordshire; s. of Michael Triesman and Rita Triesman (née Lubran); m. Lucy Hooberman 2004; ed Stationers' Co. School, London, Univ. of Essex and King's Coll., Cambridge; Sr Research Officer in Addiction, Inst. of Psychiatry 1970–74; secondment to Asscn of Scientific, Tech. and Managerial Staff 1974–75; Sr Lecturer and Co-ordinator Post grad. Research, Poly tech. of South Bank 1975–84; Deputy Sec.-Gen. (Nat. Negotiating Sec.) Nat. Asscn of Teachers in Further and Higher Educ. 1984–93; Gen. Sec. Asscn of Univ. Teachers 1993–2001; Gen. Sec. Labour Party 2001–03, Govt Whip and Lord-in-Waiting 2004–05; Parl. Under-Sec. of State for Foreign and Commonwealth Affairs 2005–07; Govt Spokesman on Higher Educ., Trade and Industry, Foreign Affairs and Aid 2004–; Prime Minister's Special Envoy on Returns 2007–; Visiting Prof. in Social Econs, St Lawrence Univ. 1977; Visiting Fellow in Econs, Wolfson Coll., Cambridge 2000–; Sr Visiting Fellow, Univ. of Warwick 2003–; Visiting Fellow, LSE 2004–; mem. Greater London Manpower Bd 1981–86, Home Office Consultative Cttee on Prison Educ. 1980–83, Burnham Further and Higher Educ. Cttee 1980–84, Univ. Entrance and Schools Exams Bd for Social Science 1980–84, Standing Cttee on Business and the Community, Higher Educ. Funding Council for England 1999–; mem. Kensington, Chelsea and Westminster Area Health Authority 1976–82; mem. Industrial Relations Public Appointments Panel, Dept of Trade and Industry 1996–2001, Ind. Review of Higher Educ. Pay and Conditions 1998–99, Cabinet Office Better Regulation Task Force 2000–03, Treasury Public Services Productivity Panel 2000–03, British N American Cttee 1999–; Chair. (non-exec.) Mortgage Credit Corpn 1978–2001, Vic. Man. Ltd 2000–01; Chair. Usecolor Foundation 2001; mem. Fabian Soc. 1974–, Charles Rennie Mackintosh Soc., Glasgow 1986–, Highgate Literary and Scientific Inst. 1990–; mem. Council Ruskin Coll., Oxford 2000–03; Hon. Fellow, Univ. of Northampton 1995. *Publications include:* The Medical and Non-Medical Use of Drugs 1969, Football Mania (with G. Viani) 1972, Football in London 1985, College Administration (co-author) 1988, Managing Change 1991, Can Unions Survive (Staniewski Memorial Lecture) 1999, Higher Education for the New Century 2000. *Leisure interests:* football, art, reading, blues guitar, hill walking. *Address:* House of Lords, Westminster, London, SW1A 0PW, England (office). *Telephone:* (20) 7219-1114 (office). *E-mail:* triesman@parliament.uk (office).

TRIET, Nguyen Minh, BS; Vietnamese politician and head of state; *President;* b. 8 Oct. 1942, Ben Cat dist., Binh Duong Prov.; ed Nguyen Ai Quoc Party School, Saigon Univ.; active in Sai Gon Students' Movt 1960–63; mem. Cadre of Cen. Cttee of the People's Revolutionary Youth Union and Youth Mobilisation of Party Cen. Cttee's Dept for S Vietnam, also Sec.Agency's Youth Union 1963–73, Deputy Dir.Office of Youth Union and Deputy Chief Youth Union Cen. Cttee's Bd for Voluntary Young People 1974–79; apptd additional mem. Party Cttee of Song Be Prov., Perm. Deputy Sec. 1989–91; mem. Party Cen. Cttee 1991–; Deputy Nat. Ass. 1991–2006; mem. Politburo 1997–; Dir Cen. Party Cttee's Comm. for Mass Mobilisation 1997–2000; Sec. Ho Chi Minh City Party Cttee 1997–2000, Gen. Sec. 2000–06; Pres. of Viet Nam 2006–. *Address:* c/o Dang Cong San Viet Nam (Communist Party of Viet Nam), 1 Hoang Van Thu, Hanoi, Viet Nam. *E-mail:* cpv@hn.vnn.vn. *Website:* www.cpv.org.vn.

TRIGUBOFF, Harry Oscar, AO; Australian property developer; *Chairman and Managing Director, Meriton Apartments Pty Ltd;* b. 3 March 1933, Darien, People's Repub. of China; s. of Moishe Triguboff and Freda Triguboff; m.; two c.; ed Scotts Coll., Sydney, Leeds Univ., UK; immigrated to Australia 1947; early jobs included driving a taxi and owning a milk run; Founder, Chair. and Man. Dir Meriton Apartments Pty Ltd 1963–. *Address:* Meriton Apartments Pty Ltd, Level 11, 528 Kent Street, Sydney, NSW 2000, Australia (office). *Website:* www.meriton.com.au (office).

TRILLO-FIGUEROA MARTÍNEZ CONDE, Federico, PhD; Spanish politician and jurist; b. 23 May 1952, Cartagena; ed Univ. of Salamanca, Univ. Complutense of Madrid; Counsel to State Council 1979–89; lawyer for Coll. of Madrid 1980–; mem. Cuerpo Jurídico de la Armada –1989; Gen. Coordinator of reformation of Partido Popular and Asst Sec. Gen. 1989–90, Nat. Deputy for Alicante 1989–2004, Spokesperson for Justice and Constitution 1991–96; Vice-Speaker of Congress 1988–96; Cttee mem. Constitutional Court 1991–96; Speaker of Congress and Nat. Ass. 1996–2000; Minister of Defence 2000–04. *Publication:* El poder político en los dramas de Shakespeare. *Leisure interests:* opera, Shakespeare. *Address:* c/o Ministry of Defence, Paseo de la Castellana 109, 28071 Madrid, Spain (office).

TRIMBLE OF LISNAGARVEY, Baron (Life Peer), cr. 2006, of Lisnagarvey in the County of Antrim; **David Trimble,** PC, LLB; British politician, barrister and university lecturer; b. 15 Oct. 1944, Belfast; s. of the late William Trimble and of Ivy Jack; m. 1st Heather McComb (divorced); m. 2nd Daphne Orr 1978; two s. two d.; ed Bangor Grammar School and Queen's Univ. Belfast; Lecturer in Law, Queen's Univ. Belfast 1968–77, Sr Lecturer 1977–90; mem. N Ireland Constitutional Convention 1975–76; mem. Parl. for Upper Bann 1990–2005; Leader Ulster Unionist Party (UUP) 1995–2005; First Minister, Northern Ireland Ass. 1998–2000, 2001–02 (Ass. suspended Oct. 2002); mem. N Ireland Ass. for Upper Bann 1998–; Chair. Lagan Valley Unionist Asscn 1985–90, Ulster Soc. 1985–90; left UUP and joined Conservative Party 2007; hon. degrees include Hon. LLD (Queen's) 1999, (New Brunswick) 2000, (Wales) 2002; shared Nobel Peace Prize 1998. *Publications:* To Raise up a New Northern Ireland 2001, Misunderstanding Ulster 2007. *Leisure interests:* music, reading, opera. *Address:* House of Lords, London, SW1A 0PW England (office). *Telephone:* (20) 7219-3000 (office). *Fax:* (20) 7219-5979 (office). *E-mail:* trimbled@parliament.uk (office). *Website:* www.davidtrimble.org (office).

TRINH, Xuan Lang, BA; Vietnamese diplomatist; b. 4 Sept. 1927, Hanoi; m.; three c.; took part in Viet Nam's independence movt 1945–54; joined Ministry of Foreign Affairs 1955, Consul-Gen., Rangoon 1960–64, Counsellor of Embassy in New Delhi 1969–73; Amb. to Indonesia 1981–84; Dir Press and Information Dept and spokesman for Ministry of Foreign Affairs 1984–88; Perm. Rep. to the UN 1988–93. *Address:* c/o Ministry of Foreign Affairs, Hanoi, Viet Nam.

TRINTIGNANT, Jean-Louis (Xavier); French actor; b. 11 Dec. 1930, Piolenc (Vaucluse); s. of Raoul Trintignant and Claire Tourtin; m. 1st Colette Dacheville (the actress Stéphane Audran q.v.) 1954 (divorced); m. 2nd Nadine Marquand (q.v.) 1961 (divorced 1997); one s. two d. (both deceased); ed Faculté de Droit, Aix-en-Provence; theatre début 1951; film roles 1955–; Officier des Arts et des Lettres; Prix d'interprétation de l'Acad. du Cinéma (for Mata Hari, Agent H21) 1965; Prize, Cannes Festival (for Z) 1969; Prix David de Donatello, Taormina Festival 1972;. *Plays include:* Macbeth, Jacques ou la Soumission (Ionesco), Hamlet, Bonheur, impaire et passe (Sagan), Deux sur la balançoire, Art 1998, Poèmes à Lou 1999, Comédie sur un quai de gare 2001, Moins deux 2005. *Films include:* Et Dieu créa la femme 1956, Club de femmes 1956, Les liaisons dangereuses 1959, L'été violent 1959, Austerlitz 1959, La millième fenêtre 1959, Pleins feux sur l'assassin 1960, Coeur battant 1960, Le jeu de la vérité 1961, Horace 62 1961, Les sept péchés capitaux 1961, Il sorpasso 1962, Il successo 1962, Chateau en Suède 1963, La bonne occase 1964, Mata Hari, Agent H21 1964, Angélique marquise des anges 1964, Meurtre à l'italienne 1965, La longue marche 1965, Le 17e ciel 1965, Paris brûle-t-il? 1965, Un homme et une femme 1966, Safari diamants 1966, Trans-Europ-Express 1966, Mon amour, mon amour 1967, L'homme qui ment 1967, Les biches 1968, Le voleur de crimes 1968, Z 1969, Ma nuit chez Maud 1969, Disons un soir à diner 1969, L'Américain 1969, La mort a pondu un oeuf 1969, Le conformiste 1970, Si douces, si perverses 1970, Le grand silence 1971, Une journée bien remplie (author and dir) 1973, Le train 1973, Les violins du bal 1973, Le mouton enragé 1974, Le secret 1974, Le jeu avec le feu 1975, Shattering 1977, Le désert des Tartares 1977, The French Way 1978, L'argent des autres 1978, Le maitre nageur 1979 (also dir), La terrasse 1980, Je vous aime 1980, La femme d'à côté 1981, Un assassin qui passe 1981, Malevil 1981, Passion d'amour 1981, Une affaire d'hommes 1981, Eaux profondes 1981, Le grand-pardon 1982, Boulevard des assassins 1982, Le bon plaisir 1983, Vivement dimanche! 1983, La crime 1983, Le bon plaisir, Femmes de personne 1984, Under Fire, Viva la vie 1984, L'été prochain, Partir, revenir 1985, Rendez-vous, David, Thomas et les autres 1985, L'homme aux yeux d'argent 1985, Un homme et une femme: vingt ans déja 1986, La femme de ma vie 1986, La vallée fantôme 1987, Le Moustachu 1987, Bunker Palace Hotel 1989, Merci la vie 1991, L'Instinct de l'ange 1993, Rouge 1994, Regarde les hommes tomber 1994, Fiesta 1995, C'est jamais loin 1996, Ceux qui m'aiment prendront le train 1998, Janis et John 2003, Immortel (ad vitam) 2004, Galilée ou L'amour de Dieu 2005. *Address:* c/o Artmédia, 20 avenue Rapp, 75007 Paris; 30 rue des Francs-Bourgeois, 75003 Paris, France (home).

TRINTIGNANT, Nadine; French film director, screenwriter and writer; b. 11 Nov. 1934, Nice, Alpes-Maritimes; d. of Jean Marquand and Lucienne Marquand (née Cornillad); m. 1st Jean-Louis Trintignant (q.v.) 1961 (divorced

1997); two d. (both deceased) one s.; m. 2nd Alain Corneau 1998; ed Lycée Molière, Inst. Fénelon and Cours Lamartine, Paris; trainee, LTC Lab. 1952, trainee film ed. 1953–54, Asst Film Ed. 1954–58, Chief Ed. and Continuity Person 1958–64; Dir TV programmes in the Le Cinéma and Les Femmes Aussi series 1965–66; writer and dir of films and TV programmes; Officier Ordre des Arts et Lettres, Chevalier Ordre nat. du Mérite. *Films:* Dir: Fragilité, ton nom est femme (Festival de Hyères Prize, Salonika Festival Prize, Greece) 1965, L'île bleue 2000; Writer and Dir: Mon amour, mon amour 1967, Le voleur de crimes 1969, Ça n'arrive qu'aux autres 1971, La semaine des quatre jeudis 1972, Défense de savoir 1973, Le voyage de noces 1976, Madame le Juge, L'innocent 1977, Premier voyage 1980, Portrait de Mikis Theodorakis, L'été prochain 1984, La maison de jade 1988, Fugueuses 1994, L'insoumise 1996. *Television includes:* film: Le tiroir secret 1985, Lucas 1988, Rêveuse jeunesse 1992, Les inséparables; Dir: Qui c'est ce garçon? (series) 1986, Victoire 1998 (Sept d'or de la mise en scène), L'île bleue 2000, Colette 2003. *Publications:* Ton chapeau au vestiaire 1998, Combien d'enfant 2000, Le jeune-homme de la rue de France 2002, Ma fille Marie 2003, Marie Trintignant 2004, J'ai été jeune un four 2006. *Leisure interests:* music, travelling. *Address:* 30 rue des Francs-Bourgeois, 75003 Paris, France. *Telephone:* (1) 42-74-47-01. *Fax:* (1) 42-74-55-03. *E-mail:* nadine.trintignant@wanadoo.fr.

TRIPPE, Thomas G., PhD; American particle physicist; ed UCLA; with Particle Data Group, Lawrence Berkeley Nat. Lab., Berkeley, Calif. 1970–2008; research work at Bevatron, CERN, SLAC and Fermilab. *Publication:* Particle Physics: One Hundred Years of Discoveries: An Annotated Chronological Bibliography 1996, Review of Particle Physics, biennial 2006. *Leisure interests:* windsurfing, gardening. *Address:* 1551 La Vereda Road, Berkeley, CA 94708, USA (home). *Telephone:* (510) 841-0262 (home). *Fax:* (510) 548-8435 (home). *E-mail:* Trippe@lbl.gov (home). *Website:* www.lbl.gov (office).

TRITTIN, Jürgen; German politician; b. 25 July 1954, Bremen; one d.; worked as journalist 1973; business man. Alternative-Greens-Initiative List (AGIL) group Göttingen City Council 1982–84; press spokesman for Green Party group Lower Saxony Landtag 1984–85, Chair. 1985–86, 1988–90, Deputy Chair. Alliance '90/Greens group 1994–95, spokesman Fed. Exec. 1994–98; mem. Lower Saxony Landtag 1985–90, 1994–95, Lower Saxony Minister for Fed. and European Affairs 1990–94, also head of state mission to fed. insts in Bonn; mem. Bundestag 1998–; Fed. Minister for the Environment, Nature Conservation and Nuclear Safety 1998–2005. *Address:* Bündnis 90/Die Grünen (Alliance 90/Greens), Pl. vor dem Neuen Tor 1, 10115 Berlin, Germany (office).

TRIVEDI, Ram Krishna, MA; Indian state governor (retd); b. 1 Jan. 1921, Myingyan, Burma (now Myanmar); s. of Pandit Mahavir Trivedi and Rama Trivedi; m. Krishna Trivedi 1944 (deceased); four s. one d.; joined civil service 1943; Dist Magistrate, Tehri Garhwal, Faizabad, Allahabad and Kanpur; Vice-Prin., IAS Training School, Delhi 1957–58, Acting Prin. 1958–59, Deputy Dir Nat. Acad. of Admin. 1959–62; Sec. Medical and Health Dept Govt of Uttar Pradesh 1968–70; Commr and Sec. Dept of Finance 1968–71; Commr Allahabad 1970–71; Chair. UP State Electricity Bd 1972–73; Sec. Dept of Civil Supplies and Cooperation 1974–75; Dept of Personnel & Admin. Reforms, Govt of India 1975–77; Chair. and Man. Dir STC 1978; Vice-Chancellor, Bundelkhand Univ. 1979; Adviser to Gov. of Madhya Pradesh; Chair. British India Corpn Kanpur 1980; Central Vigilance Commr Govt of India 1980–82; Chief Election Commr of India 1982–85; Gov. of Gujarat 1986–90; fmr Vice-Pres. Exec. Council, Indian Inst. of Public Admin.; mem. Gov. Body, Asian Centre for Devt Admin. Kuala Lumpur; Pres. Ramkrishna Mission, Lucknow; Hon. DLitt (Lucknow); Hon. LLD (Bundelkhand); Padma Bhushan Award 1986. *Publication:* The Greening of Gujarat. *Leisure interests:* yoga, serious reading, philately, photography. *Address:* Anand Niwas, B-7, Niralanagar, Lucknow, UP 226020, India. *Telephone:* (522) 2787180.

TROE, Jürgen, Dr rer. nat; German chemist and academic; *Director, Max-Planck-Institute for Biophysical Chemistry;* b. 4 Aug. 1940, Göttingen; ed Univ. of Göttingen; Prof. of Physical Chem., Ecole Polytechnique Fédérale de Lausanne, Switzerland 1971–75, Hon. Prof. 1976–; Prof. of Physical Chem., Inst. for Physical Chem., Univ. of Göttingen 1975–, Chair. Lab. for Laser Tech. 1987–, Dir Max-Planck-Inst. for Biophysical Chem., Göttingen 1990–; Pres. Deutsche Bunsen-Gesellschaft für Physikalische Chemie 1999–2002; Editorial Chair. Physical Chem./Chemical Physics 2000–03; mem. Deutsche Akademie der Naturforscher Leopoldina 1980–, Akademie der Wissenschaften zu Göttingen 1982–, Academia Europaea, London 1989–, Berlin-Brandenburgische Akademie der Wissenschaften 2000–; mem. Senate, Deutsche Forschungsgemeinschaft 2002– (Chair. Physical Chem. and Chem. Sections 1984–92); mem. Nat. Science Bd of Germany 1993–98; foreign hon. mem., American Acad. of Arts and Science 1989–; Hon. DSc (Bordeaux) 1995, (Karlsruhe) 1995; Deutsche Bunsen-Gesellschaft für Physikalische Chemie Bodenstein Award 1971, Walther-Nernst-Denkmünze 1998, Royal Soc. of Chem. Centenary Medal 1980, Polanyi Medal 1992, Alexander von Humboldt Foundation Max-Planck Research Award 1993, Deutsche Akademie der Naturforscher Leopoldina Carus Medal 1995, Int. Combustion Inst. Bernard Lewis Gold Medal 1996. *Address:* Institut für Physikalische Chemie, Georg-August-Universität Göttingen, Tammannstrasse 6, 37077 Göttingen, Germany (office). *Telephone:* (551) 39-3121 (office). *Fax:* (551) 39-3150 (office). *E-mail:* shoff@gwdg.de (office). *Website:* 134.76.68.210/Troe/j_troe/j_troe.htm (office).

TROISGROS, Pierre Emile René; French hotelier and restaurateur; b. 3 Sept. 1928, Châlon-sur-Saône; s. of Jean-Baptiste Troisgros and Marie Badaut; m. Olympe Forte 1955; two s. one d.; ed Lycée Bourgneuf, Roanne; worked Roanne-Etretat 1944–45, Armenonville, Paris 1946, St Jean de Luz 1947; mil. service, Tunisia 1948; at Lucas Carton, Paris 1950–52, Point,

Vienne 1954, then Maxim's and Retour à Roanne; now Pres. Supervising Cttee Restaurant Troisgros SA, Roanne; Ordre Nat. du Mérite 1969, Officier des Arts et des Lettres 1985, Chevalier, Légion d'honneur 1987. *Publications:* Cuisiniers à Roanne (with Jean Troisgros) 1977, Toc et Toque 1983, Les Petits Plats des Troisgros (with Michel Troisgros) 1985, Cuisine de famille chez les Troisgros (jtly) 1998. *Leisure interests:* tennis, basketball. *Address:* Place Jean Troisgros, 42300 Roanne; 20 route de Commelle, 42120 Le Coteau, France (office). *Telephone:* 4-77-71-66-97. *Fax:* 4-77-70-39-77 (office). *E-mail:* info@troisgros.com (office). *Website:* www.troisgros.fr (office).

TRØJBORG, Jan; Danish politician; *Mayor of Horsens;* b. 14 Dec. 1955, Horsens; m. Janne Lindgaard Trøjborg; four c.; ed Ealing Coll., London, Horsens Tech. Coll.; bricklayer 1976; engineer A/S Samfundsteknik 1986, Dept Head Horsens br. 1987; Chair. Social Democratic Youth Org. 1973–78; mem. Horsens Town Council 1978–86; Deputy Chair. Social Democratic Party, Horsens 1981–82; mem. Parl. for Horsens 1987–; Chair. Trade and Industry Cttee 1991–93; Minister of Industry 1993–94, of Transport 1994–96, of Business and Industry 1996–98, of Research and Information Tech. 1998–99, of Devt Co-operation 1999–2000, of Defence 2000–01; Personal Rep. of OSCE Chair. for Preventing and Combating Terrorism 2002–; Mayor of Horsens 2006–. *Address:* Horsens Kommune, Rådhustorvet 4, 8700 Horsens, Denmark (office). *Telephone:* 76-29-29-29 (office). *E-mail:* horsens.kommune@horsens.dk (office). *Website:* www.horsenskom.dk (office).

TROLLOPE, Joanna, (Caroline Harvey), OBE, MA, DL; British writer; b. 9 Dec. 1943, England; d. of Arthur Trollope and Rosemary Hodson; m. 1st David Potter 1966; two d.; m. 2nd Ian Curteis 1985 (divorced 2001); two step-s.; ed Reigate Co. School and St Hugh's Coll. Oxford; Information and Research Dept Foreign Office 1965–67; various teaching posts, including Farnham Girl's Grammar School, Daneshill School 1967–79; Chair. Advisory Cttee on Nat. Reading Initiative, Dept of Nat. Heritage 1996–97; mem. Advisory Cttee on Nat. Year of Reading, Dept of Educ. 1998, Council of Soc. of Authors 1997–, Campaign Bd St Hugh's Coll., Oxford; Vice-Pres. Trollope Soc., West Country Writers' Asscn, Advisory Bd Costa Book Awards 2008–; Trustee Joanna Trollope Charitable Trust 1995–; Patron County of Glos. Community Foundation 1994–2004, March Foundation, Mulberry Bush, For Dementia; Deputy Lieutenant for Co. of Gloucestershire 2002–04; Romantic Historical Novel of the Year 1980. *Publications:* as Caroline Harvey: Eliza Stanhope 1978, Parson Harding's Daughter (aka Mistaken Virtues) 1979, Leaves from the Valley 1980, The City of Gems 1981, The Steps of the Sun 1983, The Taverners' Place 1986, Legacy of Love 1992, A Second Legacy 1993, A Castle in Italy 1993, The Brass Dolphin 1997; as Joanna Trollope: Britannia's Daughters: A Study of Women in the British Empire 1983, The Choir 1988, A Village Affair 1989, A Passionate Man 1990, The Rector's Wife 1991, The Men and the Girls 1992, A Spanish Lover 1992, The Best of Friends 1992, The Country Habit: An Anthology (ed.) 1993, Next of Kin 1996, Faith 1996, Other People's Children 1998, Marrying the Mistress 2000, Girl from the South 2002, Brother and Sister 2004, Second Honeymoon 2006, The Book Boy 2006, Britannia's Daughters 2007, Friday Nights 2008; contribs to newspapers and magazines. *Leisure interests:* reading, conversation, very long baths. *Address:* United Agents, 12–26 Lexington Street, London W1F 0LE, England (office). *Telephone:* (20) 3214-0800 (office). *Fax:* (20) 3214-0801 (office). *E-mail:* info@unitedagents.co.uk (office); joanna@joannatrollope.net (office). *Website:* unitedagents.co.uk (office); www.joannatrollope.com.

TRONCHETTI PROVERA, Marco; Italian business executive; *Chairman, Pirelli SpA;* b. 1948, Milan; three c.; ed Bocconi Univ., Milan; worked in family maritime transport business 1973–86; joined Pirelli Group as Partner, Pirelli & C. 1986, Man. Dir and Gen. Man. Soc. Int. Pirelli SA, Basle 1988–92, Man. Dir and Gen. Man. (Finance and Admin. and Gen. Affairs) Pirelli SpA 1991–92, Exec. Deputy Chair. and Man. Dir Pirelli SpA 1992–96, Deputy Chair. Pirelli & C. 1995–99, Chair. and CEO Pirelli SpA 1996–, Chair. Pirelli & C. 1999–; Chair. Olivetti 2001–; Chair. Bd and Exec. Cttee CAMFIN SpA, Milan; Chair. Telecom Italia SpA 2001–06 (resgnd); Chair. Bd Il Sole 24 Ore; Deputy Chair. Confindustria (nat. employers' org.), Chair. 2000–; mem. Bd Mediobanca, Banca Commerciale Italiana, Banca Intesa, GIM, RAS, Università Commerciale Luigi Bocconi; mem. European Round Table of Industrialists, Int. Advisory Bd of Allianz, Int. Council of J. P. Morgan, New York Stock Exchange Advisory Cttee, Italian Group of Trilateral Comm. *Address:* Office of the Chairman, Pirelli SpA, Viale Sarca 202, 20126, Milan (office); CONFINDUSTRIA, Viale dell'Astronomia 30, EVR, 00144 Rome, Italy. *Telephone:* (02) 6442.2650 (office); (06) 59031. *Fax:* (02) 64423733 (office); (06) 5919615. *E-mail:* confindustria@confindustria.it (office). *Website:* www.confindustria.it.

TRONG, Nguyen Phu; Vietnamese politician; *Chairman, National Assembly;* apptd to Politburo 1957 with oversight of ideology, culture, science and educ. matters; Sec. Hanoi CP Cttee –2006; Chair. Nat. Ass. 2006–. *Address:* Office of the Chairman, National Assembly, Ban bien tap Trang tin, Dia chi: so 2, Bac Son, Ba Dinh, Hanoi, Viet Nam. *E-mail:* webmaster@qh.gov.vn. *Website:* www.na.gov.vn.

TROSHANI, Arenca; Albanian politician and academic; b. 20 June 1973, Shkoder; ed Univ. of Trento, Italy, Univ. of Tirana, Univ. of Graz, Austria; Asst in Law Faculty, Luigj Gurakuqi Univ. of Shkoder, 1995–2000, Dean 2000–01, Head of Dept 2001–03, Lecturer 2003–; Deputy, Kuvendi Popullor (Parl.) for electoral zone number 5 2005–; Minister of European Integration 2005–07; mem. Democratic Party of Albania. *Publications:* several publications on human rights and international public rights. *Address:* Kuvendi Popullor (People's Assembly), Bulevardi Dëshmorët e Kombit 4, Tirana (office); Democratic Party of Albania (PDSh), Rruga Punetoret e Rilindjes, Tirana, Albania. *Telephone:* (4) 2264887 (office); (4) 228091. *Fax:* (4) 2221764 (office); (4) 223525. *E-mail:* competitionsecretariat@parlament.al (office). *Website:* www.parlament.al (office); www.dpalbania.org.

TROŠKA, Zdeněk, MA; Czech film and theatre director and scriptwriter; b. 18 May 1953, Strakonice; s. of Václav Troška and Růžena Troška; ed Lycée Carnot, Dijon, France, Acad. of Film and Musical Arts; Prin./Head Prize for Luck From Hell II, St Petersburg, Russia 2002. *Films:* Jak rodí chlap (How a Man Gives Birth) 1980, Bota jménem Melichar (Boot) 1983, Slunce, seno, jahody (The Sun, Hay and Strawberries) 1984, Poklad hrabete Chamaré (The Treasure of Count Chamaré) 1984, O princezne Jasněnce a létajicim sevci (About Princess Jasněnka) 1987, Flying Shoemaker 1987, Slunce, seno a pár facek (The Sun, Hay and Some Slaps) 1989, Zkouškové období (The Time of Examinations) 1990, Slunce, seno, erotika (The Sun, Hay and Erotics) 1991, Princezna ze mlejna (The Princess from the Mill) 1994, Z pekla stestí (Helluva Good Luck) 1999, Princezna ze mlejna 2 2000, Z pekla stestí 2 (Goblins and Good Luck 2) 2001, Andelská tvár 2002, Kamenák 2003, Kamenák 2 2004, Kamenák 3 2005. *Plays:* Don Carlos (Nat. Theatre, Prague) 1989, Rusalka, Hamlet (musical version) 2000, Luck From Hell 2000, Luck From Hell II 2001. *Leisure interests:* literature, music: piano and organ, cooking, mushrooming, hiking. *Address:* Hoštice u Volyně 77, 387 01 Volyně, Czech Republic (office).

TROST, Barry Martin, PhD; American scientist and academic; *Tamaki Professor of Humanities and Science, Department of Chemistry, Stanford University;* b. 13 June 1941, Philadelphia, Pa; s. of Joseph and Esther Trost; m. Susan Paula Shapiro 1967; two s.; ed Univ. of Pennsylvania and MIT; Asst Prof. of Chem., Dept of Chem., Univ. of Wis. 1965–68, Assoc. Prof. 1968–69, Prof. 1969–76, Helfaer Prof. 1976–82, Vilas Prof. 1982–87; Prof. of Chem., Stanford Univ. 1987–, Tamaki Prof. of Humanities and Sciences 1990–; consultant, E.I. du Pont de Nemours and Merck, Sharp & Dohme; mem. ARCO Science Bd; mem. Cttee on Chemical Sciences, NAS 1980–83; mem. and Chair. NIH Medicinal Chem. Study Section 1982–; Commr, Nat. Research Council Comm. on Eng and Tech. Systems; Ed.-in-Chief Comprehensive Organic Synthesis (Vols 1–9) 1991, Chair. 1996–; Ed. Chemical Tracts/ Organic Chem.; mem. NAS, American Chemical Soc., AAAS; Dr hc (Univ. Claude Bernard, Lyon, Technion, Israel); ACS Award in Pure Chem. 1977, for Creative Work in Synthetic Organic Chem. 1981, Backland Award 1981, AIC Chemical Pioneer Award 1983, Alexander von Humboldt Award (Fed. Repub. of Germany) 1984, Cope Scholar Award of ACS 1989, ACS Guenther Award 1990, Dr Paul Janssen Prize for Creativity in Organic Synthesis 1990, Merit Award, NIH 1988, Roger Adams Award 1995, Herbert C. Brown Award 1999, Nichols Medal 2000, Elsevier Boss Award 2000, Yamada Prize 2001, Signature Award for Grad. Educ. in Chem. 2002, ACS Arthur C. Cope Award 2004, John Scott Award 2004. *Publications:* Problems in Spectroscopy 1967, Sulfur Ylides 1974, Organic Synthesis Today and Tomorrow (ed.) 1981, Selectivity: a Goal for Synthetic Efficiency (ed.) 1984; more than 700 scientific articles in leading chemical journals. *Address:* Department of Chemistry, Stanford University, Stanford, CA 94305-5080, USA (office). *Telephone:* (650) 723-3385 (office). *Fax:* (650) 725-0002 (office). *E-mail:* bmtrost@stanford.edu (office). *Website:* www.stanford.edu/dept/chemistry/faculty/trost (office); www .stanford.edu/group/bmtrost (office).

TROTMAN-DICKENSON, Sir Aubrey Fiennes, Kt, DSc; British university vice-chancellor and principal (retd); b. 12 Feb. 1926, Wilmslow, Cheshire; s. of the late Edward Trotman-Dickenson and Violet Murray (née Nicoll); m. Danusia Hewell 1953; two s. one d.; ed Winchester Coll., Balliol Coll. Oxford and Univs of Manchester and Edin.; Fellow, Nat. Research Council, Ottawa, Ont. 1948–50; Asst Lecturer, ICI Fellow, Univ. of Manchester 1950–53; E.I. Du Pont de Nemours, Wilmington, USA 1953–54; Lecturer, Univ. of Edin. 1954–60; Prof. of Chem. Univ. Coll. of Wales, Aberystwyth 1960–68; Prin. Univ. of Wales Inst. of Science and Tech. 1968–88, Univ. Coll. Cardiff 1987–88, Univ. of Cardiff 1988–93; Vice-Chancellor Univ. of Wales 1975–77, 1983–85, 1991–93; Tilden Lecturer 1963; Chair. Kingswood Conservative Asscn 1996–98, Chair. Kingswood Liberal Democrats 2004–; Hon. LLD (Wales). *Publications:* Gas Kinetics 1955, Free Radicals 1959, Tables of Biomolecular Gas Reactions 1967, Comprehensive Inorganic Chemistry (ed. 1973); more than 150 contribs to learned journals. *Address:* Siston Court, Bristol, BS16 9LU, England (home). *Telephone:* (117) 937-2109 (home).

TROVOADA, Miguel dos Anjos da Cunha Lisboa; São Tomé and Príncipe fmr head of state; fmrly in charge of foreign relations for the São Tomé e Príncipe Liberation Movt (MLSTP), fmr mem. Political Bureau; Prime Minister of São Tomé e Príncipe 1975–78, also Minister of Defence and Foreign Affairs July–Dec. 1975, of Econ. Co-ordination, Co-operation and Tourism 1975–78, of Trade, Industry and Fisheries 1978–79; arrested and imprisoned 1979, released 1981, then in exile in Lisbon; Pres. and C-in-C of the Armed Forces of São Tomé e Príncipe 1991–95 (deposed in coup 15 Aug. 1995), reinstalled 1995–2001. *Address:* c/o Office of the President, São Tomé, São Tomé e Príncipe.

TROVOADA, Patrice Emery; São Tomé and Príncipe politician; b. 18 March 1962, Libreville, Gabon; s. of Miguel Trovoada, Pres. of São Tomé and Príncipe 1991–2001; Minister of Foreign Affairs 2001–02; oil adviser to Pres. Fradique de Menezes –2005 (sacked by Pres.); Sec.-Gen. Independent Democratic Action (ADI) Party; cand. in presidential election July 2006; Prime Minister 2008. *Address:* Acção Democrática Independente (ADI), Av. Marginal 12 de Julho, Edif. C. Cassandra, São Tomé, São Tomé and Príncipe (office). *Telephone:* 222201 (office).

TRPEVSKI, Ljube, MSc, PhD; Macedonian banker and politician; *Governor, National Bank of Macedonia;* b. 3 Aug. 1947, Velmej, Ohrid; m.; one s. one d.; ed Univ. of St Cyril and St Methodius, Skopje, Univ. of Tallahassee, Fla; teaching Asst, Faculty of Econs, Univ. of St Cyril and St Methodius, Skopje 1970–77, lecturer 1977–80, Docent 1980–85, Assoc. Prof. 1985–91, Prof. 1991; Deputy Gov. Nat. Bank of Macedonia 1987–91, Gov. 1997–; Minister, Pres. Securities and Exchange Comm. 1992–95; Vice-Pres. of Macedonia 1996. *Publications:* Lexicon of Contemporary Market Economy (co-author, ed.) 1993, Money and Banking 1995, The Republic of Macedonia (co-author) 1996 and numerous articles. *Address:* Office of the Governor, National Bank of the Republic of Macedonia, Kompleks banki bb, P.O. Box 401, *1000 Skopje (office); Mile Pop Jordanov 52, 91000 Skopje, Republic of Macedonia (home). *Telephone:* (2) 112177 (office). *Fax:* (2) 113481 (office). *E-mail:* governorsoffice@nbrm.gov.mk (office). *Website:* www.nbrm.gov.mk (office).

TRUBETSKOI, Kliment Nikolayevich; Russian geochemist; *Chair, Russian State Geological Exploration University;* b. 3 July 1933; m.; two c.; ed Moscow Inst. of Nonferrous Metals and Gold; jr, sr researcher Moscow Inst. for Problems of Complex Utilization of Mineral Resources 1961–81; Head of Lab. 1981–87, Deputy Dir 1987, Dir 1987–2003, Prof. of Geotechnology 2003–; Chair. Russian State Geological Exploration Univ. 2003–; Corresp. mem. USSR (now Russian) Acad. of Sciences 1987, mem. 1991; Vice-Pres. Acad. of Mining Sciences; took part in devt of tech. to save resources in quarries, developed theoretical fundamentals of projecting, prognosis and tech. of complex utilization of mineral deposits; USSR State Prize 1990, N. Melnikov Gold Medal and Prize 1989, 2004, Russian State Prize 1999, 2000, Prize of the Pres. of Russia 2001. *Publications:* author of 30 books and 600 scientific articles in periodicals. *Leisure interests:* chess, swimming, photography, travelling. *Address:* Institute of Problems of Complex Utilization of Mineral Resources, Krukovsky tupik 4, 111020 Moscow, Russia. *Telephone:* (495) 360-89-60 (office); (495) 331-52-55 (home). *Fax:* (495) 360-89-60 (office). *E-mail:* trubetsk@ipkonran.ru (office). *Website:* www.ipkonran.ru (office).

TRUBETSKOV, Dmitry Ivanovich, DPhys-MathSc; Russian physicist and academic; *Head Chair of Electronics, Oscillations and Waves, Saratov State University;* b. 14 June 1938, Saratov; s. of Ivan Trubetskov and Varvara Trubetskova; m. Sofya Vasilyeva 1962; one s.; ed Saratov State Univ.; aspirant 1960–64; teacher 1961–68; docent 1968; Prof., Saratov State Univ. 1981–, Head, Chair of Electronics and Wave Processes 1981–, Rector 1994–2003; mem. IEEE Electron Devices Soc. 1995; Corresp. mem. USSR (now Russian) Acad. of Sciences 1991; Educ. Award of the Pres. of Russian Fed. 2001. *Publications include:* Analytical Methods of Calculation in Microwave Electronics (with V. N. Shevchik) 1970, Electronics of Backward-Wave Tubes 1975, Introduction into the Theory of Oscillations and Waves 1984, Oscillations and Waves in Linear and Non-linear Systems (with M. I. Rabinovich) 1989, Nonlinear Dynamics in Action (with A. A. Koronovsky) 1995, Lectures on Microwave Vacuum Microelectronics (with A. G. Rozjenev and D. V. Sokolov) 1996, Nonlinear Waves (with N. M. Ryskyn) 2000, Linear Oscillators and Waves (with A. G. Rozjenev) 2001, The Trace of Inspiration and Patient Labour 2001, Linear Oscillations and Waves, Problems (with A. P. Kuznetsov and A.G. Rozjenev) 2001, Introduction into the Theory of Self-Organization Open Systems (with E. S. Mchedlova and L. V. Krasichkov) 2002, Lectures on Microwave Electronics for Physicists, Vol. 1 (with A. Hramov) 2003, Introduction to Synergetics, Oscillations and Waves 2003, Lectures on Microwave Electronics for Physicists Vol. 2 (with A. Hramov) 2004, Introduction to Synergetics, Chaos and Patterns 2004, The Way to Synergetics (with B. Bezruchko, A. Koronovsky and A. Hramov) 2005, Synchronization: Scientist and Time 2006, Higher Education in Russia from the Point of Vew of Nonlinear Dynamics (with M. Strikhanov, A. Koronovsky, U. Sharaevsky and A. Hramov) 2007. *Leisure interest:* reading. *Address:* Saratov State University, Astrakhanskaya str. 83, 410071 Saratov, Russia (office). *Telephone:* (8452) 512-107 (office); (8452) 231-993 (home). *Fax:* (8452) 512-107 (office). *E-mail:* trubetskovdi@nonlin.sgu.ru (office).

TRUBNIKOV, Gen. Vyacheslav Ivanovich; Russian security officer, politician and diplomatist; *Ambassador to India;* b. 25 April 1944, Irkutsk; m.; one d.; ed Moscow State Inst. of Int. Relations; served in USSR KGB (First Main Directorate, intelligence) 1967–91; staff mem. HQ of First Main Dept (intelligence) 1977–84; KGB station officer in India (as corresp. Press Agency Novosti) 1971–77; mem. Union of Journalists 1973; resident in Bangladesh and India 1984–90; Head Div. of America KGB 1990–92; First Deputy Dir Russian Intelligence Service 1992–96, Dir 1996–2000; mem. Security Council, Defence Council and Foreign Policy Council of Russia 1996; First Deputy Minister of Foreign Affairs 2000–04; Amb. to India 2004–. *Address:* Embassy of the Russian Federation, Shanti Path, Chanakyapuri, New Delhi, 110 021, India. *Telephone:* (11) 26873799 (office). *Fax:* (11) 26876823 (office). *E-mail:* indrusem@del2.vsnl.net.in (office). *Website:* www.india.mid.ru (office).

TRUDEAU, Garry B., BA, MFA; American cartoonist; b. 21 July 1948, New York; m. Jane Pauley 1980; three c.; ed Yale Univ. School of Art and Architecture; cr. comic strip Doonesbury at Yale 1969, now syndicated nationwide; Fellow American Acad. of Arts and Sciences; Pulitzer Prize for Editorial Cartooning 1975, 12th Annual John S. Knight Lecturer 2000; hon. degrees from Yale Univ., Colgate Univ., Williams Univ., Duke Univ. and 18 other univs. *Plays include:* Doonesbury 1983, Rapmaster Ronnie, A Partisan Review (with Elizabeth Swados) 1984. *Films:* A Doonesbury Special for NBC-TV 1977 (Special Jury Prize at Cannes Film Festival). *Television:* conceived (with Robert Altman) Tanner '88 1988. *Publications include:* Any Grooming Hints for Your Fans, Rollie, But the Pension Fund was Just Sitting There, The Doonesbury Chronicles, Guilty, Guilty, Guilty, We Who are about to Fry, Salute You: selected cartoons in In Search of Reagan's Brain, Vol. 2, Is This Your First Purge, Miss ?, Vol. 2, It's Supposed to be Yellow, Pinhead: selected cartoons from You Ask for Many, Seetle for June, Vol. 1, The Wreck of the Rusty Nail, Dressed for Failure 1983, Confirmed Bachelors are Just So Fascinating 1984, Sir I'm Worried About Your Mood Swings 1984, Doonesbury Dossier: The Reagan Years 1984, Check Your Egos at the Door 1986, Talking 'Bout My G-G-Generation 1988, We're Eating More Beets 1988, Read My Lips,

Make My Day, Eat Quiche and Die 1989, Recycled Doonesbury 1990, You're Smoking Now Mr Butt! 1990, In Search of a Cigarette Holder Man: A Doonesbury Book 1994, Doonesbury Nation 1995, Flashbacks 1995; The Portable Doonesbury 1993; contribs to The People's Doonesbury and many others. *Address:* c/o Universal Press Syndicate, 4520 Main Street, Kansas City, MO 64111-7701, USA. *Website:* www.doonesbury.com.

TRUJILLO, Solomon (Sol) D., BS, MBA; American telecommunications industry executive; *CEO, Telstra Corporation Ltd;* b. 1951, Cheyenne, Wyo.; ed Univ. of Wyoming; began career with Mountain Bar Telephone 1974; Pres. and CEO USWest Dex Inc. 1992–95, Pres. and CEO US est Communications 1995–98, CEO and Chair. USWest Inc. 1999–2000; Chair., Pres. and CEO Graviton Inc., La Jolla, Calif. 2000; mem. Exec. Bd Orange SA 2001–04, CEO 2003–04; mem. Bd of Dirs and CEO Telstra Corpn Ltd, Australia 2005–; mem. Chair.'s Council, Alcatel 2000–03; mem. Bd of Dirs Target, GSMA 2008–; fmr mem. Bd of Dirs Pepsi Co., Gannet, Bank of America, Electronic Data Systems Corpn (EDS), Tomas Rivera Policy Inst.; mem. Advisory Bd UCLA School of Public Affairs; fmr Gov. World Econ. Forum, mem. World Econ. Forum's Steering Cttee on Climate Change 2008; fmr Trustee, Boston Coll., UCLA's School of Public Policy; fmr trade policy adviser in Clinton and Bush admins; Dr hc (Univ. of Wyoming, Univ. of Colorado). *Address:* Telstra Corporation Ltd, 242 Exhibition Street, Melbourne, Vic. 3000, Australia (office). *Telephone:* (3) 9634-6400 (office). *Fax:* (3) 9632-3215 (office). *E-mail:* info@telstra.com.au (office). *Website:* www.telstra.com.au (office).

TRUMAN, Edwin Malcolm, BA, MA, PhD; American economist and academic; *Senior Fellow, Peterson Institute for International Economics;* b. 6 June 1941, Albany, NY; s. of David B. Truman and Elinor G. Truman; m. Tracy P. Truman; one s. one d.; ed Amherst Coll., Yale Univ.; trained as economist; fmr Lecturer, Yale Univ.; joined Div. of Int. Finance, Bd of Govs of Fed. Reserve System 1972, Dir (later Staff Dir) 1977–98; Asst Sec., US Treasury for Int. Affairs 1998–2001; Asst Sec. (Int. Affairs), Senate Finance Cttee 1999–; Sr Fellow, Peterson Inst. for Int. Econs, Washington, DC; mem. G-7 Working Group on Exchange Market Intervention 1982–83, G-10 Working Group on the Resolution of Sovereign Liquidity Crises 1995–96, G-10-sponsored Working Party on Financial Stability in Emerging Market Econs 1996–97, G-22 Working Party on Transparency and Accountability 1998, Financial Stability Forum's Working Group on Highly Leveraged Insts 1999–2000; Hon. LLD (Amherst Coll.) 1988. *Publications:* Inflation Targeting in the World Economy 2003, Chasing Dirty Money: The Fight Against Money Laundering (co-author) 2004, A Strategy for IMF Reform 2006; numerous articles on int. monetary econs, int. debt problems, econ. devt and European econ. integration. *Address:* Peterson Institute for International Economics, 1750 Massachusetts Avenue, NW, Washington, DC 20036-1903, USA (office). *Telephone:* (202) 328-9000 (home). *Fax:* (202) 659-3225 (office). *E-mail:* ttruman@iie.com (office); tnttruman@yahoo.com (home). *Website:* www.iie.com (office).

TRUMKA, Richard Louis, JD; American lawyer and trade union official; *Secretary Treasurer, AFL-CIO;* b. 24 July 1949, Nemacolin, Pa; s. of Frank Richard Trumka and Eola Elizabeth Bertugli; m. Barbara Vidovich 1982; one s.; ed Philadelphia State Univ., Villanova Univ.; served at bar US Dist Court 1974, US Court of Appeals 1975, US Supreme Court 1979; Attorney United Mine Workers of America, Washington 1974–77, 1978–79; Miner-Operator Jones and Loughlin Steel, Nemacolin, Pa 1977–78, 1979–81, mem. Int. Exec. Bd Dist 4, Masontown, Pa 1981–83, Int. Pres., Washington 1982–95, Pres. Emer. 1995–; Sec. Treas. AFL-CIO, Washington 1995–; Dir Nat. Bank, Washington 1983–85, Dinamo Corpn 1983–; mem. Bd of Dirs American Coal Fund 1983–; Trustee Philadelphia State Univ.; Labor Responsibility Award, Martin Luther King Center for Non-Violent Social Change 1990. *Address:* AFL-CIO, 815 16th Street, NW, Washington, DC 20006, USA (office). *Telephone:* (202) 637-5000 (office). *Fax:* (202) 637-5058 (office). *Website:* www.aflcio.org (office).

TRUMP, Donald John, BS; American business executive, property developer and television producer; *Chairman, President and CEO, The Trump Organization;* b. 14 June 1946, New York; s. of Fred C. Trump and Mary Trump; m. 1st Ivana Zelnicek 1977 (divorced 1991); two s. one d.; m. 2nd Marla Maples 1993 (divorced 1999); one d.; m. 3rd Melania Knauss 2005; ed Univ. of Pennsylvania Wharton School of Finance; Pres. Trump Org.; holdings include: (New York) Trump Tower on Fifth Avenue; (Fla) Mar-A-Lago at Palm Beach, Trump Plaza; (Atlantic City) Trump Plaza Hotel Casino, Trump Castle Casino, Trump Taj Mahal Casino Resort; acquired 50 per cent stake in Empire State Bldg 1994; mem. Bd of Dirs Police Athletic League; Advisory Bd mem., Lenox Hill Hosp. and United Cerebral Palsy; Dir Fred C. Trump Foundation; Founder-mem. cttee to complete construction of Cathedral of St John the Divine and Wharton Real Estate Center; fmr Co-Chair. New York Vietnam Veterans Memorial Fund; Hotel and Real Estate Visionary of the Century, from UJA Fed. 2000. *Radio:* Clear Channel Radio broadcasts 2004. *Television:* The Apprentice (star and co-exec. producer) 2004. *Publications:* Trump: The Art of the Deal 1987, Trump: Surviving at the Top 1990, The Art of the Comeback 1997, The America We Deserve 2000, How to Get Rich 2004, Think Like a Billionaire 2004, The Way to the Top 2004, Trump World Magazine 2004. *Address:* Trump Organization, 725 Fifth Avenue, New York, NY 10022, USA. *Telephone:* (212) 832-2000. *Fax:* (212) 755-3230. *Website:* www.trumponline.com.

TRUSZCZYNSKI, Jan; Polish politician and diplomatist; *Deputy Minister of Foreign Affairs;* b. 30 July 1949, Warsaw; m.; two c.; ed Main School of Planning and Statistics, Warsaw; with Ministry of Foreign Affairs (MFA) 1972–93, 1996–, Dept of Human Resources and Training 1972–74, 1975–78, European Integration Desk Officer, Western Europe Dept 1982; Second Sec., Polish Embassy, The Hague 1978–82, Adviser, Brussels 1988–89, Adviser, Mission to EC, Brussels 1989–93, Amb. to EU 1996–2001, Under-Sec. of State,

Ministry of Foreign Affairs, Govt Plenipotentiary for Poland's Accession Negotiations to EU 2001–03, Political Dir MFA 2003–04; Deputy Minister of Foreign Affairs 2004–; Adviser to Chair., Dept Dir Inicjatyw Gospodarczych Bank (BIG) SA 1993–94; Dir Poland Office, Kreditbank NV 1995–96; Under-Sec. of State, Chancellery 2001. *Address:* Ministry of Foreign Affairs, al. J.Ch. Szucha 23, 00-580 Warsaw, Poland (office). *Telephone:* (22) 5239610 (office). *Fax:* (22) 6219614 (office). *E-mail:* jan.truszczynski@msz.gov.pl (office). *Website:* www.negocjacje.gov.pl (office).

TRUTNEV, Yurii Petrovich; Russian politician; *Minister of Natural Resources and Ecology;* b. 1 March 1956; m.; two s.; ed Perm Polytechnic Inst.; engineer, Perm Scientific Research Inst. of Oil 1978–81; instructor Regional Komsomol Cttee and Sport Cttee 1981–88; Pres. E.K.S Int. 1996, Dir 2000–; Deputy, Perm city Duma 1994–96, Chair. Cttee on Econ. Policy and Taxation; Mayor of Perm 1996–2000; Gov. of Perm Oblast 2000–04; Minister of Natural Resources and Ecology 2004–. *Leisure interests:* karate, wrestling, rally racing. *Address:* Ministry of Natural Resources, ul. B. Gruzinskaya 4/6, 123242 Moscow, Russia (office). *Telephone:* (495) 254-48-00 (office). *Fax:* (495) 254-43-10 (office). *E-mail:* admin@mnr.gov.ru (office); admin@cbi-mpr.ru (office). *Website:* www.mnr.gov.ru (office); www.trutnev.ru.

TRZECIAKOWSKI, Witold Mieczysław, DEconSc; Polish economist and politician; b. 6 Feb. 1926, Warsaw; s. of Witold Trzeciakowski and Zofia Trzeciakowska; m. Anna Przedpełska 1951; three s.; ed Cen. School of Planning and Statistics, Warsaw, Harvard Univ., Cambridge, Mass and Columbia Univ., New York, USA; mem. underground Home Army 1942–44, took part in Warsaw uprising 1944; Asst Prof. 1966, Extraordinary Prof. 1972, Ordinary Prof. 1979; Dir Podkowiak Metal Wares Factory, Szydłowiec 1946–49; Vice-Pres. Asscn of Pvt. Producers of Metal Wares 1946–49; designer, Transport Design Office, Warsaw 1949–57; consultant, Inst. of Foreign Trade Conjuncture and Prices, Warsaw 1959–60, Deputy Dir 1960–76, Dir 1976–78, Prof. 1972–81; Prof., Econ. Sciences Inst., Polish Acad. of Sciences (PAN), Warsaw 1981–91; mem. Solidarity Trade Union 1980–, Civic Cttee attached to Chair. of Solidarity Trade Union, Lech Wałęsa (q.v.) 1988–; participant Round Table plenary debates, co-Chair. group for econ. and social policy Feb.–April 1989; Senator 1989–91, Chair. Senate Comm. of Nat. Econ. 1989–91; Minister, mem. Council of Ministers 1989–90, Chair. Econ. Council 1989–91; mem. Primatial Social Council 1983–85; Chair. Church Agric. Cttee 1987–89, mem. 1987–; Hon. Pres. Inst. of Econs, Polish Acad. of Sciences; Commdr's Cross with Star, Officer's Cross and Kt's Cross, Order of Polonia Restituta, Gold Cross of Merit, Cross of Valour; Prime Minister's Prize for achievements in economics of transformation 1995. *Publications include:* Modele pośredniego kierowania gospodarką planową w sterowaniu handlem zagranicznym 1975, Structural Adjustments in Trade-Dependent Small Centrally Planned Economies 1984, Reforma–restruktur-yzacja– zadłużenie 1987, Transition in Poland 1993, Dynamika Transformacji Polskiej Gospodarki 1996. *Leisure interests:* skiing, horse-riding. *Address:* ul. Langiewicza 2 m.2, 02-071 Warsaw, Poland. *Telephone:* (22) 8256615. *Fax:* (22) 6295897. *E-mail:* wtrzecia@staszic.inepan.waw.pl (home).

TSAGOLOV, Maj.-Gen. Kim Makedonovich, PhD; Russian/Ossetian; *Director, Institute of Peoples of Russia;* b. 1930, N Ossetia, Russia; ed School of Fine Arts, Yeysk Mil. School of Marine Aviation; sr mil. adviser Limited Contingent of Soviet armed forces in Afghanistan 1981–84; expelled from army for public criticism of Afghanistan war 1989; headed defence of the N Ossetian Capital during attack of Georgian troops of Pres. Gamsakhurdia 1989–91; Deputy Minister on Problems of Nationalities Russian Fed. 1993–98; Deputy Minister on Nat. Policy of Russian Fed. 1999–2000; Dir Inst. of Peoples of Russia 2000–. *Leisure interest:* painting. *Address:* Institute of Peoples of Russia, Smolenskaya str. 14, 125493 Moscow, Russia (office). *Telephone:* (095) 456-72-13 (home).

TSAI, Eng-Meng; Taiwanese business executive; *Chairman and CEO, Want Want China Holdings Ltd;* m.; one s.; joined Want Want China Holdings Ltd 1976, Gen. Man. I Lan Foods Industrial Co. Ltd (subsidiary), Taiwan –1987, Chair., Exec. Dir and CEO Want Want China Holdings Ltd, Shanghai 1987–, Chair. and CEO Want Want Holdings Ltd 1987–; Chair. and controlling shareholder of San Want; fmr mem. Council Standing Cttee of Taiwan Confectionery, Biscuit and Floury Food Industry Asscn, Food Devt Asscn of Taiwan; Hon. Prof. (Nanjing Normal Univ.) 1995. *Address:* Want Want China Holdings Ltd, 1088 East Hong Song Road, Shanghai 201103, People's Republic of China (office). *Telephone:* (21) 61151111 (office). *Fax:* (21) 61151777 (office). *E-mail:* info@www.want-want.com (office). *Website:* www.want-want.com (office).

TSAI, Hong-tu, BA, JD; Taiwanese insurance industry executive; *Chairman, Cathay Life Insurance Company Ltd;* s. of the late Tsai Wan-lin and the late Tsai Chou Pao-chin; ed National Taiwan Univ., Southern Methodist Univ., USA; Man. Dir and Vice-Chair. Cathay Life Insurance Company Ltd –1980, Chair. 1980–, also Chair. Cathay Financial Holding Co. (parent co. Lin-Yuan Group est. by father Tsai Wan-lin); mem. Life Insurance Asscn of Repub. of China; Chair. Life Insurance Asscn of Repub. of China. *Address:* Cathay Life Insurance Company Ltd, 296 Jen Ai Road, Section 4, Taipei 10639, Taiwan (office). *Telephone:* (22) 755-1399 (office). *Fax:* (22) 704-1485 (office). *E-mail:* info@cathlife.com.tw (office); service@cathayholdings.com.tw (office). *Website:* www.cathlife.com.tw (office).

TSAI, Ing-wen, LLB, LLM, PhD; Taiwanese politician and professor of law; *Chairman, Democratic Progressive Party;* b. 31 Aug. 1956; ed Nat. Taiwan Univ., Cornell Univ., USA and LSE, UK; Assoc. Prof., Law Dept, Nat. Chengchi Univ. 1984–90, Prof., Grad. School of Law 1990–91, Prof. of Law, Grad. Inst. of Int. Trade 1993–2000 (mem. Int. Trade Comm.); Prof., Grad. School of Law, Soochow Univ. 1991–93; Adviser on Int. Econ. Orgs, Ministry of

Econ. Affairs 1992–2000; Convener, Drafting/Research Group on 'Statute Governing Relations with Hong Kong and Macao' 1994–95; mem. Advisory Cttee Mainland Affairs Council, Exec. Yuan 1994–98, Chair. 2000–04; Nat. Policy Adviser to Pres. 2004–06; Vice-Pres. of Exec. Yuan 2006–07 (resgnd); Chair. TaiMedBiologics (biotechnology firm) 2007–08; Chair. Democratic Progressive Party 2008–; mem. Fair Trade Comm., Exec. Yuan 1995–98, Advisory Cttee of Copyright Comm., Ministry of Interior 1997–99; Sr Adviser Nat. Security Council 1999–2000. *Address:* Democratic Progressive Party, 10/F, 30 Beiping East Rd, Taipei 10051, Taiwan (office). *Telephone:* (2) 23929989 (office). *Fax:* (2) 23929989 (office). *E-mail:* foreign@dpp.org.tw (office). *Website:* www.dpp.org.tw (office).

TSAI, Michael Ming-hsien, PhD; Taiwanese politician and diplomatist; ed California Western School of Law, USA; mem. Parl. (Progressive Democratic Party), served as a legislator for two terms and as Deputy Rep. to USA; fmr Vice-Minister of Nat. Defense, adviser to Ministry of Nat. Defense –2008, Minister of Nat. Defense 2008; mem. Democratic Progressive Party. *Publications include:* Defending Taiwan – The Future Vision of Taiwan's Defence Policy and Military Strategy (co-ed.) 2002, Submarines and Taiwan's Defense (co-author) 2004, Taiwan's Security and Air Power (co-author) 2004, (co-author of book on Taiwanese defence reform) 2006. *Address:* Democratic Progressive Party, 10/F, 30 Beiping East Road, Taipei 10051, Taiwan (office). *Telephone:* (2) 23929989 (office). *Fax:* (2) 23929989 (office). *E-mail:* foreign@dpp.org.tw (office). *Website:* www.dpp.org.tw (office).

TSAI, Ming-Liang; Taiwanese film director. *Films include:* Rebels of the Neon God 1992, Vive l'Amour (Venice Golden Lion Award 1994) 1994, The River (Berlin Silver Bear Award 1996) 1996, Tian bian yi duo yun 2005, The Hole, Last Dance, Dong, I Don't Want to Sleep Alone 2006.

TSAI, Wan-tsai; Taiwanese banker; b. 5 Aug. 1929, brother of Tsai Wan-lin; uncle of Tsai Hong-tu; m.; four c.; Founder and fmr Chair. Fubon Group, now retd; fmr legislator of Legis. Yuan (Parl.). *Address:* Fubon Financial Holding Co. Ltd, 237 Chien Kuo South Road Section 1, Taipei, Taiwan (office). *Telephone:* (2) 6636-6636 (office). *Fax:* (2) 6636-0111 (office). *E-mail:* ir@fubon.com (office). *Website:* www.fubongroup.com (office).

TSANG, Sir Donald Yam-kuen, Kt, KBE, JP, MPA; Hong Kong government official; *Chief Executive;* b. (Tsang Yam-kuen), 7 Oct. 1944, Hong Kong; m.; two s.; ed in Hong Kong and Harvard Univ., USA; joined Govt of Hong Kong 1967; served in various govt depts and brs of Govt Secr.; attached to Asian Devt Bank, Manila 1977; Dist Officer, Shatin; Deputy Dir of Trade responsible for trade relations with N America; Deputy Sec. of Gen. Duties Br. responsible for Sino-British Jt Declaration 1985–89; Dir of Admin. Office of Chief Sec. 1989–91; Dir-Gen. of Trade 1991–93; Sec. for the Treasury 1993–95; Financial Sec. 1995–2001; Chief Sec. for Admin. 2001–05, Acting Chief Exec. March–May 2005 (resgnd to campaign for election as Chief Exec.), Chief Exec. 2005–; Grand Bauhinia Medal 2002; Hon. LLD 1999; Hon. DBA 1999; Dr hc (Chinese Univ. of Hong Kong, Hong Kong Polytechnic Univ., Univ. of Hong Kong). *Leisure interests:* hiking, swimming, bird-watching, music. *Address:* Office of the Chief Executive, 5/F Main Wing, Central Government Offices, Lower Albert Rd, Central, Hong Kong Special Administrative Region, People's Republic of China (office). *Telephone:* 28783300 (office). *Fax:* 25090577 (office). *E-mail:* ceo@ceo.gov.hk (office). *Website:* www.ceo.gov.hk (office).

TSANG, John, JP, MPA; Hong Kong ; *Financial Secretary;* b. 1951; m.; two c.; ed La Salle Coll., Hong Kong, Boston State Coll., Massachusetts Inst. of Tech., Kennedy School of Govt, Harvard Univ., USA; began career working in Boston Public Schools, USA; joined Hong Kong civil service 1982, Admin. Asst to the Financial Sec. 1987–91, Asst Dir-Gen. of Trade 1991–95, Pvt. Sec. to Gov. Chris Patten 1995–97, Dir-Gen. Econ. and Trade Office, London 1997–99, Commr of Customs and Excise 1999–2002, Perm. Sec. for Housing, Planning and Lands 2002–03, Sec. for Commerce, Industry and Tech. 2003–06; Dir Office of the Chief Exec. of Hong Kong 2006–07, Financial Sec. 2007–, mem. Exec. Council, Hong Kong Special Admin. Region; Chair. Sixth Ministerial Conference (MC6), WTO 2005. *Address:* Executive Council, Central Government Offices, Lower Albert Road, Central, Hong Kong Special Administrative Region, People's Republic of China (office). *Telephone:* 28102545 (office). *Fax:* 28450176 (office). *Website:* www.gov.hk (office).

TSANG, Yok-Sing; Hong Kong politician; *Legislative Councillor, Hong Kong Special Administrative Region;* Founding Chair. Democratic Alliance for the Betterment of Hong Kong 1992–2003 (resgnd); currently Legis. Councillor, Special Admin. Region of Hong Kong, People's Repub. of China, apptd mem. Exec. Council (Cabinet) 2002, Chair. Cttee on Rules of Procedure, Panel on Educ.; mem. political section, Preparatory Cttee for Hong Kong Special Admin. Region (SAR); mem. Bd of Dirs Airport Authority; mem. Comm. on Strategic Devt, ICAC Complaints Cttee, Disaster Relief Fund Advisory Cttee. *Address:* Executive Council Secretariat, 1/F, Main Wing, Central Government Offices, Lower Albert Road, Central, Hong Kong Special Administrative Region, People's Republic of China (office). *Telephone:* 28102581 (office). *Fax:* 28450176 (office). *E-mail:* ceo@ceo.gov.hk (office). *Website:* www.ceo.gov.hk (office); www.dab.org.hk (office).

TSAO, Robert H.C., MS; Taiwanese electronics industry executive; *Chairman, United Microelectronics Corporation;* b. 24 Feb. 1947, Shantung; ed Nat. Univ. of Taiwan, Nat. Chiao Tung Univ.; Deputy Dir Electrical Research Service Org. 1979–81; Vice-Pres. United Microelectronics Corpn 1980, Pres. 1981–91, Chair. 1991–; Chair. Unipac Microelectronics Corpn 1989–, World Wiser Electrical Inc. 1989–; Vice-Chair. TECO Information System Co. Ltd 1995–; mem. Standing Bd Chinese Nat. Fed. of Industry, Chair. Intellectual Property Protection Cttee 1991–94; Chair. Asscn of Allied Industries in Science-Based Industry Park 1987–93. *Address:* United Microelectronics Corporation Ltd, No. 3, Li-Hsin 2nd Road, Hsinchu Science Park, Hsinchu, Taiwan (office). *Telephone:* (35) 782258 (office). *Fax:* (35) 779392 (office). *E-mail:* foundry@umc.com (office). *Website:* www.umc.com (office).

TSAPOGAS, Makis Joakim, MD, DSc, MCh, PhD, MRCS, LRCP, FACS; Greek professor of vascular diseases, medical scientist and academic; *Professor of Vascular Diseases, New York University and University of London;* m. Lily Philossopoulou; ed Univs of Athens, London and New York; Lecturer, King's Coll. Hosp. Medical School, London 1961–63, Sr Lecturer 1963–67; Hunterian Prof., Royal Coll. of Surgeons, UK 1964; Assoc. Prof., Albany Medical Coll. Union Univ. New York 1967–70, Prof. 1970–75; Adjunct Prof. Rensselear Polytechnic Inst. New York 1970–75; Prof., Rutgers Medical School, NJ 1976; Prof. of Vascular Diseases, State Univ. of New York, Stony Brook 1977–; adviser, WHO 1986–; consultant, UN, New York 1993–; Prof. of Vascular Diseases, Univs of NY and London; Visiting Prof. in many univs in Europe and N America; Physician in charge of the Pres. of Greece and the Ecumenical Orthodox Patriarchate, Constantinople; corresp. mem. Acad. of Athens; Fellow, Archaeological Soc. of Athens; Hon. mem. Parnassos Literary Soc. and over 30 medical, research and bio-medical scientific socs, Hon. citizen of Nea Smyrni and Kos; Hon. MD (Nice Univ.), (Athens Univ.), (Patras Univ.); Hon. PhD; Red Cross Gold Medal, Gold Medal and Cross of the Ecumenical Patriarchate, Medal of the towns of Heraklion and Alexandroupoulis. *Publications include:* Atherosclerosis in the Lower Limb 1959, Treatment of Thrombosis 1965, Management of Vascular Diseases 1985, Medical Education 1992, Venous Thrombosis and Pulmonary Embolism 2001, Biomedical Progress and Society 2004, Hypertension 2006, Lipids and Cardiovascular Disease 2007, Post-Graduate Medical Education 2008, Athersclerosis in Women 2009, Recent Advances in Medicine 2009, Molecular Biology in Medicine (contrib.) 2009, Prevention of Vascular Diseases 2009; over 200 articles in scientific medical journals. *Leisure interests:* classical music, reading, travelling. *Address:* 8 Merlin Street, Kolonaki, 106 71 Athens, Greece (home). *Telephone:* (21) 03390988 (home). *Fax:* (21) 03390989 (home).

TSCHIRA, Klaus; German software industry executive; *Managing Director, European Media Laboratory;* b. Freiburg; with IBM Germany as systems engineer Mannheim –1972; Co-founder of Systemanalyse + Programmentwicklung (later SAP AG) 1972, now mem. Supervisory Bd 1998–; f. Klaus Tschira Foundation 1995; founder and Man. Dir European Media Lab. 1997–; mem. IBM European Software Vendors Advisory Council 1990–92; Chair. Friends of FZI (Forschungszentrum für Informatik) Karlsruhe; mem. Supervisory Bd GMD (Forschungszentrum für Informatik) St. Augustin; mem. GI Praesidium of German Informatics Society 1991–96; Hon. mem. Senate of Heidelberg Univ. 1996, Senate of Mannheim Univ. 1999 Dr hc (Klagenfurt Univ., Austria) 1995. *Address:* Villa Bosch, Schloss-Wolfsbrunnen-Weg 33, 69118 Heidelberg (office); SAP AG, PO Box 1461, 69185 Walldorf, Germany (office). *Telephone:* (6227) 747474 (SAP) (office). *Fax:* (6227) 757575 (SAP) (office). *Website:* www.eml.villa-bosch.de (office); www.kts.villa-bosch.de (office); www.sap.com (office).

TSCHÜTSCHER, Klaus, LLM, DrIur; Liechtenstein politician and academic; *Prime Minister;* b. 8 July 1967; m. Jeanette Tschütscher; two c.; ed Univs of St Gallen and Zurich, Switzerland; Leader Liechtenstein Fiscal Admin Sept. 1995; mem. Exec. Cttee Liechtenstein Steuerwaltung 1996–; Dozent, Univ. of Liechtenstein 1998–; mem. Vaterländische Union (Patriotic Union); mem. Liechtenstein Del. to OECD (Harmful Tax Practices) 1999, to EU (EU tax topics, in particular EU interest taxation) 1999, for legal aid negotiations with USA 2001; Chair. Standing Working Group 'International Developments of the Tax Law' 2001–; mem. MWS Mixed Comm. 2001–; mem. Future Finance Plan Liechtenstein 2002; Deputy Prime Minister and Minister of Econ. Affairs, of Justice and of Sports 2005–09, Prime Minister of Liechtenstein 2009–. *Address:* Regierungsgebäude, Postfach 684, 9490 Vaduz, Liechtenstein (office). *Telephone:* 2366180 (office). *Fax:* 2366022 (office). *E-mail:* office@liechtenstein.li (office). *Website:* www.liechtenstein.li (office).

TSEKOA, Mohlabi Kenneth, BEd, MA; Lesotho politician, educator and diplomatist; *Minister of Foreign Affairs and International Relations;* b. 13 Aug. 1945; m.; two s. one d.; ed Nat. Univ. of Lesotho, Univ. of Botswana, Lesotho and Swaziland, Univ. of Newcastle-upon-Tyne, Univ. of London, UK, Univ. of Mass, USA; teacher, Hlotse High School 1970–74; Deputy Headmaster, St Agnes High School 1974–76; Sr Educ. Officer, Lesotho Distance Teaching Centre 1976–78, Dir 1978–84; Deputy Prin. Sec., Ministry of Educ. 1984–86, Prin. Sec. 1986–89; High Commr to UK and Amb. to Ireland, Spain and Portugal 1989–96; Govt Sec. and Head of the Public Service 1996–2001; Minister of Finance and Devt Planning 2001–02, of Foreign Affairs 2002–04, of Educ. and Training 2004–07, of Foreign Affairs and Int. Relations 2007–. *Address:* Ministry of Foreign Affairs and International Relations, POB 1387, Maseru 100, Lesotho (office). *Telephone:* 22311746 (office). *Fax:* 22310527 (office). *E-mail:* dps@foreign.gov.ls (office). *Website:* www.lesotho.gov.ls/foreign (office).

TSELKOV, Oleg; Russian artist; b. 1934, Moscow; ed Moscow secondary school, Minsk Inst. of Theatre Art and Leningrad Acad. of Art; expelled from both for 'formalism'; later graduated from Leningrad Theatre Inst. as stage-designer 1958; designed numerous productions; mem. of Artists' Union; left USSR 1977; now lives in Paris.

TSEPKALO, Valery V.; Belarusian academic, government official and fmr diplomatist; *Director, High-Tech Park Administration;* b. 22 Feb. 1965, Grodno; m. Veronika Tsepkalo; ed Belarus Technological Inst., Moscow State Inst. of Int. Relations, Russia; mil. service 1984–86; with Embassy of USSR in Finland 1991; joined Ministry of Foreign Affairs, Repub. of Belarus 1992–93, First Deputy Minister for Foreign Affairs 1994–97; Adviser to Exec. Sec. of CIS 1994; lecturer on int. relations, geopolitics and neo-conservatism; Amb. to USA 1997–2002; Sr Adviser to Pres. of Belarus 2002–, Rep. of Pres. to Nat.

Ass. 2005–; currently also Dir High-Tech Park Admin. *Publications include:* By The Road of the Dragon 1994, numerous articles on int. security, foreign policy and world economy. *Address:* Office of the President, vul. K. Marksa 38, Dom Urada, 220016 Minsk, Belarus (office). *Telephone:* (17) 222-60-06 (office). *Website:* www.president.gov.by (office).

TSEPOV, Boris Anatolyevich, CJur; Russian diplomatist; *Ambassador to Lithuania;* b. 13 June 1948; ed Moscow Inst. of Int. Relations, Diplomatic Acad.; entered diplomatic service 1971; posts in USSR Embassy, Kuwait 1971–76; in Third African Div., USSR Ministry of Foreign Affairs 1976–78; Secr. of Deputy Minister 1978–86, with Dept for Int. Humanitarian Cooperation and Human Rights 1986–90; Counsellor Perm. USSR (now Russian) Mission to UN New York 1991–94; Dir of Dept, concurrently Exec. Sec. Russian Ministry of Foreign Affairs 1994–98; Amb. to Kenya (also accred Perm. Rep. to int. orgs, Nairobi) 1998–2001; Dir Dept of Compatriots' Affairs and Human Rights 2001; currently Amb. to Lithuania. *Address:* Embassy of the Russian Federation, Latvių 53/54, Vilnius 2600, Lithuania (office). *Telephone:* (5) 272-1763 (office). *Fax:* (5) 272-3877 (office). *E-mail:* rusemb@rusemb.lt (office).

TSERETELI, Zurab Konstantinovich; Georgian sculptor and artist; *President, Russian Academy of Arts;* b. 4 Jan. 1934, Tbilisi; m. Inessa Andronikashvili (deceased); one d.; ed Dept of Painting, Tbilisi Acad. of Arts; Chief Designer, Ministry of Foreign Affairs 1970–80; Prof. Brockport Univ. New York USA 1979; Chief Designer, Summer Olympic Games, Moscow 1980; Prof. Acad. of Arts, Tbilisi 1981; Deputy, Supreme Council of Georgia 1985–89; Chair. Union of Designers of Georgia 1987–91; Sec. USSR Union of Designers; USSR People's Deputy 1989–91; Pres. Moscow Int. Foundation for Support to UNESCO Russia 1992–; Chief Designer, War Memorial, Moscow 1995; Chief Designer, interior and exterior decoration of Cathedral of Christ the Saviour, Moscow 1995–2000; UNESCO Goodwill Amb. 1996–; Chief Designer, Manezh Square and the underground shopping mall, Moscow 1997; Vice-Pres. Russian Acad. of Informatics 1998; Dir Moscow Museum of Modern Art 1999–; Dir Tsereteli Art Gallery, Moscow 2000–; mem. Russian Acad. of Arts 1989–, Pres. 1997–, Head Dept of Design; mem. Georgian Acad. of Arts 1996, Acad. of World Elite 1997, Acad. of Art of Kyrgyzstan 1998; corresp. mem. Spanish Royal Acad. of Fine Arts, Madrid, Spain 1998, French Acad. of Fine Arts, Paris, France; Vice-Pres. Russian Acad. of Creativity; author of numerous sculptures, mosaics, monumental murals, stained-glass windows, revived old technique of traditional Georgian enamel; author of numerous monuments including Friendship in Moscow (with poet A. Voznesensky), Kindness Wins over Evil (New York, UN Bldg), Happiness for Children of the World (Univ. of Fine Arts, Brockport), Columbus (Miami), Birth of a New Man (London), Moment of Victory (Moscow), Peter the Great (Moscow) and others in Tbilisi, Tokyo, Seville, Osaka, Brasília; Hero of Socialist Labor USSR 1991, Order, Friendship of Peoples, Russia 1994, Order for Services to the Fatherland 3rd Grade (Russia) 1996, Hon. Cross Combattant Voluntaire, Asscn of Veterans, French Resistance, France 2000, Order, Glory of Russia 2003, Int. Peace Prize, Jt Convent of Figures of Culture, USA 2003; Lenin Prize 1976, State Prize of USSR 1978, 1983, People's Artist of Georgia 1978, of USSR 1979, of Russia 1994, Picasso Prize 1994, State Prize of Russia 1996, Vermeil Medal, Paris, France 1998, Prize of Modern Art 2000, Int. Recognition, Golden Hand (France) 2000, Medal for Services and Homeland, Russia 2003. *Leisure interests:* collecting works of art. *Address:* 21 Prechistenka str., 119034, Moscow (office); Bolshaya Gruzinskaya str. 17, 123557, Moscow, Russia (office). *Telephone:* (095) 201-36-65 (office); (095) 254-77-67 (home).

TSHABALALA-MSIMANG, Mantombazana (Manto) Edmie, BA, MSc, MD,; South African medical practitioner and politician; b. 9 Oct. 1940, Durban; m. Mendi Msimang; two d.; ed Univ. of Fort Hare, First Leningrad Medical Inst., USSR, Univ. of Dar es Salaam, Tanzania, Univ. of Antwerp, Belgium, Univ. of Sussex, UK; in exile 1962–90; Registrar, Obstetrics and Gynaecology, Muhimbili Hosp., Dar es Salaam 1970–73; Medical Superintendant, Lobatswe Hosp., Botswana 1973–76; Head, Health Training Programme for Nat. Liberation Movts, OAU/UNDP, Morogoro, Tanzania 1976–79; Deputy Sec. for Human Resource Devt and Deployment of African Nat. Congress (ANC), Dept of Health, Tanzania and Zambia 1979–90; staff mem. Nat. Progressive Primary Care Health Network, Durban 1991–94; mem. of Parl. 1994–, Chair. Parl. Cttee on Health 1994–; Deputy Minister of Justice 1996–99; Minister of Health 1999–2005, 2005–08; Minister in the Presidency 2008–; Nat. Exec., ANC Women's League and Coordinator ANC Health Plan 1991–94. *Publications:* National Directory of Community-based Health Workers 1992, Directory of Community-based Women's Organisations in Natal 1993. *Address:* African National Congress, 54 Sauer Street, Johannesburg 2001, South Agrica (office). *Telephone:* (11) 3761000 (office). *Fax:* (11) 3761134 (office). *E-mail:* nmtyelwa@anc.org.za (office). *Website:* www.anc.org.za (office).

TSHERING, Lyonpo Dago; Bhutanese diplomatist and politician; *Ambassador to India;* b. (Dago Tshering), 17 July 1941, Paro; ed Univ. of Bombay, Indian Admin. Service Training, Mussoorie and Indian Audit and Accounts Service Training, Simla, India, Univ. of Manchester, UK, Nat. Admin, Tokyo; Asst, Ministry of Devt 1961–62; Asst, Office of the Chief Sec. 1962–63; returned to Ministry of Devt 1963, Sec. 1965–71; mem. Nat. Ass. 1968–1990; mem. Royal Advisory Council 1968–70; First Sec., Bhutan Embassy in India 1971–73; Deputy Perm. Rep. to UN 1973–74, Perm. Rep. 1974–80, 1984–85; Amb. to Bangladesh 1980–84; Minister of Home Affairs 1985–98; Amb. to India 1998–; Orange Scarf. *Address:* Embassy of Bhutan, Chandragupta Marg, Chanakyapuri, New Delhi 110 021, India (office). *Telephone:* (11) 26889807 (office). *Fax:* (11) 26876710 (office). *E-mail:* bhutan@vsnl.com (office).

TSHERING, Dozin (Brig.) Goongloen Wogma Batoo; Bhutanese army officer; *Chief Operations Officer, Royal Bhutan Army;* b. Nov. 1951, Toebesa, Thimphu; ed Indian Mil. Acad., Dehradun, Defence Services Staff Coll., Wellington, India; completed Young Officer's Course, Commando Course, Intelligence Staff Officer's Course, Jr Command Course and Sr Command Course; commissioned into Royal Bhutan Army 1971, has held various command posts, apptd Operations and Training Officer 1976, commanded Wing 4 and Wing 7, apptd Commdt of mil. training centre 1988, Deputy Chief Operations Officer 1991, Commdr Command Centre 1997, promoted to rank of Dozin (Brig.) 1997; Deputy Chief Operations Officer Royal Bhutan Army Feb.–Nov. 2005, Chief Operations Officer Nov. 2005–; Druk Yurgyal Medal, Drakpoi Wangyal Medal, Drakpoi Thugsey Medal, Drakpoi Khorlo Medal. *Address:* Royal Bhutan Army Headquarters, Thimphu, Bhutan (office).

TSHERING, Lyonpo Ugyen, BA; Bhutanese politician and diplomatist; *Minister of Foreign Affairs;* b. 8 Aug. 1954, Thimphu; m.; ed Univ. of Calif., Berkeley, USA; joined Govt Planning Comm. 1978, apptd Co-ordinator bilateral and multilateral assistance to Govt 1983, Project Co-ordinator, Computer Support Centre 1984, apptd Sec. Computerization Cttee 1983, Dir Planning Comm. 1986–89, now Vice-Chair.; Perm. Rep. to UN, New York 1989–98; apptd Editorial Adviser to Nat. Ass. 1980; fmr Chair. Asian Devt Bank; apptd Chair. World Bank Projects Implementation Cttee 1984; Chair. Tech. Cttee on Rural Devt, SAARC 1988–89; Sec., Ministry of Foreign Affairs 2001–03; Minister of Labour and Human Resources 2003–07 (resgnd); Minister of Foreign Affairs 2008–; Red Scarf 1998. *Address:* Ministry of Foreign Affairs, Convention Centre, POB 103, Thimphu, Bhutan (office). *Telephone:* (2) 321413 (office). *Website:* www.mfa.gov.bt (office).

TSHISEKEDI, Etienne; Democratic Republic of the Congo politician; *Leader, Union pour la démocratie et le progrès social;* Prime Minister of Zaïre (now Democratic Repub. of the Congo) and C-in-C of Armed Forces Sept.–Oct. 1991, Prime Minister 1992–93 (dismissed by Pres. Mobutu March 1993), April 1997; Leader, Union pour la démocratie et le progrès social. *Address:* Union pour la démocratie et le progrès social (UDPS), Twelfth Street, Limete Zone, Kinshasa, Democratic Republic of the Congo. *E-mail:* udps@globalserve.net. *Website:* www.udps.org/udps.html.

TSHULTIM, Dasho Jigme, BA; Bhutanese diplomatist and politician; *Speaker of the National Assembly;* ed St Joseph's Coll., Darjeeling, India, Univ. of Manchester, UK; served in Govt as Head of Tourism, Dzongda and Zhung Dronyer (Chief of Protocol); Amb. to Bangladesh (also accred to Pakistan, Maldives, Sri Lanka and S Korea) 2004–07; mem. Bhutan People's Unity Party; mem. Parl. for Radhi-Sakteng constituency, Trashigang 2008–, Speaker of Nat Ass. 2008–. *Address:* Office of the Speaker, National Assembly Secretariat, Gyelyong Tshokhang, PO Box 139, Thimphu, Bhutan (office). *Telephone:* (2) 322729 (office). *Fax:* (2) 324210 (office). *E-mail:* jtshultim@nab.gov.bt (office). *Website:* www.nab.gov.bt (office).

TSIEN, Hsue-Shen, PhD; Chinese rocket scientist and engineer; b. 11 Dec. 1911, Hangzhou; m. Jiang Ying 1947; two c.; ed Chiaotung Univ., Massachusetts Inst. of Tech. and California Inst. of Tech. (Caltech), USA; went to USA to study 1935; instrumental in founding of Cal Tech Rocket Research Project (forerunner of the Jet Propulsion Laboratory), Calif., USA; Head Supersonic Research Lab, California Inst. of Tech. 1938; served in US Army with rank of Lt Col; Dir Rocket Section, US Nat. Defense Scientific Advisory Bd during World War II; Prof., MIT 1946, California Inst. of Tech. 1946; Dir Guggenheim Jet Propulsion Laboratory 1949–55; deported to China 1955; f. Inst. of Mechanics 1955; named first Dir Chinese missile programme 1956; mem. CCP 1958–; personal tutor to Mao Zedong 1964; built nat. space and rocketry programme, launched first Chinese-built R-2 in 1960, launched first satellite in 1970; f. Space Flight Medical Research Centre 1968; Pres. China Asscn for Science and Tech.; Vice-Chair. Science and Tech. Cttee, Comm. of Science, Tech. and Industry for Nat. Defence; retd 1991; Caltech Distinguished Alumni Award 1979, inducted into World Level of the Hall of Fame for Eng, Science and Tech., New York, USA 1989, State Scientist of Outstanding Contribution 1991, Aviation Week and Space Technology Person of the Year 2008, named one of 11 most inspiring people in China by China Central TV 2008.

TSIEN, Roger Y., PhD; American chemical biologist and academic; *Professor of Pharmacology, School of Medicine and Professor of Chemistry and Biochemistry, University of California, San Diego;* ed Harvard Coll. and Univ. of Cambridge, UK; Postdoctoral Fellow, Gonville and Caius Coll., Cambridge; fmr Faculty mem., Univ. of California, Berkeley; Prof. of Pharmacology, School of Medicine and Prof. of Chem. and Biochemistry, Univ. of California, San Diego 1989–; Investigator, Howard Hughes Medical Inst. 1989–; mem. Inst. of Medicine, NAS; Searle Scholar 1983, Gairdner Award 1995, Artois-Baillet-Latair Health Prize 1995, ACS Creative Invention Award 2002, Protein Soc. Anfinsen Award 2002, Heineken Prize in Biochemistry 2002, Royal Netherlands Acad. of Sciences Award, Wolf Prize in Medicine (jtly) 2004, Keio Medical Science Prize 2004, Nobel Prize for Chem. (jtly) 2008. *Publications:* numerous articles in scientific journals on signal transduction, especially in neurons and cancer cells, with the help of designed molecules, imaging, and photochemical manipulation. *Address:* Tsien Laboratory, Howard Hughes Medical Insititute, 9500 Gilman Drive, CMM West Room 310, La Jolla, CA 92093-0647, USA (office). *Telephone:* (858) 534-4891 (office). *Fax:* (858) 534-5270 (office). *E-mail:* rtsien@ucsd.edu (office). *Website:* www.tsienlab.ucsd.edu (office).

TSISKARIDZE, Nikolai; Georgian ballet dancer; b. 31 Dec. 1973, Tbilisi; s. of Maxim Tsiskaridze and Lamara Tsiskaridze; ed Tbilisi Ballet School, Bolshoi Ballet Acad., Moscow Choreographic Inst.; joined the Bolshoi Ballet 1992, now prin. dancer; numerous prizes including Silver Medal, 7th Japan World Ballet Competition, Osaka 1995, Soul of Dance Rising Star Nat. Prize 1995, First Prize and Gold Medal, 8th Moscow Int. Ballet Competition 1997,

TSO · THE INTERNATIONAL WHO'S WHO 2010 · TSU

Merited Artist of Russia 1997, La Sylphide Russian Nat. Dance Org. Diploma Dancer of the Year 1997, Gold Mask, Russian Nat. Award for Best Male Role 1999, 2000, Benois de la Danse Int. Award, Dancer of the Year 1999, Mayor of Moscow Prize in Literature and Art 2000. *Dance:* roles in numerous ballets including Sleeping Beauty, Gisèle, Raymonda, La Sylphide, La Bayadère, The Nutcracker, Swan Lake, Romeo and Juliet, Legend of Love, Narcissus, Pharaoh's Daughter, etc. *Leisure interest:* reading. *Address:* Bolshoi Theatre, Teatralnaya Pl. 2, Moscow 103009 (office); Komsomolsky Prospekt 35, Apt. 106, Moscow 119146, Russian Federation (home). *Telephone:* (095) 292-06-55 (office); (095) 242-29-79 (home). *Fax:* (095) 242-47-53 (office).

TSOHATZOPOULOS, Apostolos-Athanasios; Greek politician and civil engineer; b. 1939, Athens; m. Mrs Vassiliki Stamati; two s. one d.; ed Tech. Univ. of Munich, FRG; deprived of citizenship by mil. dictatorship 1969; active in Panhellenic Liberation Movt, mem. Nat. Council during dictatorship; returned to Greece 1974; mem. Cen. Cttee and Exec. Office PASOK 1974–90, Gen. Sec. 1990–95, mem. Exec. Office 1995–; mem. Parl. 1981–; Minister of Public Works 1981–84, to the Prime Minister 1986–87, of the Interior 1987–89, of Transport and Communications 1989, of the Interior 1993–94, 1995–96, of Nat. Defence 1996–2001, of Devt 2002–04. *Address:* Komna Traka 3, 11257 Athens (office); Omirou 8, 10564 Athens, Greece. *Telephone:* (210) 3216059 (office). *Fax:* (210) 3246070 (office). *E-mail:* tsoha-ath@ath.forthnet .gr (office). *Website:* www.akis.gr (office).

TSONEV, Nikolai Georgiev, PhD; Bulgarian economist, academic, politician and fmr army officer; *Minister of Defence;* b. 9 June 1956, Pernik; ed Nat. Artillery Mil. School, Shumen, Vassilyevski Air Defence School, Kyiv, Ukrainian SSR, Univ. for Nat. and World Economy, Sofia, Sofia Univ. St Kliment of Ohrid; officer in Bulgarian Army 1978–92; man. of several limited liability firms 1992–99; Dir Public Procurement Directorate, Ministry of Defence 1999–2000, adviser to Minister of Defence 2001–02, Dir of Social Activities Directorate 2002–08, Minister of Defence 2008–; Prof. of Strategic Planning, Civic Admin and European Integration Inst. 2002–; Prof., Univ. for Nat. and World Economy, Sofia 2004–. *Address:* Ministry of Defence, 1000 Sofia, ul. Dyakon Ignatiy 3, Bulgaria (office). *Telephone:* (2) 922-09-22 (office). *Fax:* (2) 987-32-28 (office). *E-mail:* presscntr@mod.bg (office). *Website:* www .md.government.bg (office).

TSOVOLAS, Dimitris; Greek politician; *Leader, Democratic Social Movement;* b. 1942, Melissourgi, Arta; m. Ekaterini Yoti; one s. one d.; ed Salonika Univ.; practised law at Arta –1977; mem. Parl. 1977–92, mem. Parl. Working Cttees on Labour, Public Order and Premiership 1977–81; elected Sec. of Presidium of Parl.; Minister of Finance 1985–89; Founder and Leader Democratic Social Movt (DHKKI) 1995–; Parl. Deputy (DHKKI) for Athens II 1996–. *Address:* Democratic Social Movement, Odos Halkokondili 9, 106 77 Athens (office); 48 Serifou Street, 112 54, Athens, Greece. *Telephone:* (1) 3801712 (office); (1) 2020469. *Fax:* (1) 3839047 (office). *E-mail:* dikki@otenet .gr (office).

TSUDA, Hiroshi; Japanese automotive industry executive; *President and COO, Suzuki Motor Corporation;* fmr Sr Man. Dir Suzuki Motor Corpn, Pres. and COO 2003–. *Address:* Suzuki Motor Corpn, 300 Takatsuka-cho, Minami-ku, Hamamatsu-shi, Shizuoka 432-8611, Japan (office). *Telephone:* (53) 440-2023 (office). *Fax:* (53) 440-2776 (office). *E-mail:* info@suzuki.co.jp (office). *Website:* www.suzuki.co.jp (office); www.globalsuzuki.com (office).

TSUI, Daniel C., PhD; American (b. Chinese) physicist and academic; *Arthur LeGrand Doty Professor of Electrical Engineering, Princeton University;* b. 1939, Henan, China; ed Univ. of Chicago; Arthur LeGrand Doty Prof. of Electrical Eng, Princeton Univ. 1982–; mem. NAS, Acad. Sinica, American Acad. of Arts and Sciences, Chinese Acad. of Sciences; Fellow American Physics Soc.; Nobel Prize in Physics for discovery of fractional quantum Hall effect (jtly with Robert B. Laughlin and Horst L. Störmer) 1998, Benjamin Franklin Medal 1998. *Publications:* numerous articles in scientific journals. *Address:* Princeton University, Department of Electrical Engineering, Engineering Quadrangle, Olden Street, Princeton, NJ 08544, USA (office). *Telephone:* (609) 258-2544 (office). *Fax:* (609) 258-6279 (office). *E-mail:* tsui@ee .princeton.edu (office). *Website:* www.ee.princeton.edu/people/Tsui.php (office).

TSUI, Lap-Chee, OC, OOnt, PhD, FRSC, FRS; Canadian geneticist, academic and university administrator; *Vice-Chancellor, University of Hong Kong;* b. 21 Dec. 1950, Shanghai, China; s. of Jing Lue Hsue and Hui Ching Wang; m. (Ellen) Lan Fong 1977; two s.; ed The Chinese Univ. of Hong Kong, Univ. of Pittsburgh, USA; staff geneticist, Dept of Genetics and scientist, The Research Inst., Hosp. for Sick Children, Toronto, Canada 1983–88, Sr Research Scientist 1988–89, Sellers Chair in Cystic Fibrosis Research 1989–, Geneticist-in-Chief 1996–2002; Asst Prof. Depts of Medical Genetics and Medical Biophysics, Univ. of Toronto 1983–88, Assoc. Prof. 1988–90, Prof., Dept of Molecular and Medical Genetics 1990–2006, Univ. Prof. 1994–2006, H. E. Sellers Chair in Cystic Fibrosis 1998–2006; Vice-Chancellor, Univ. of Hong Kong 2002–; Howard Hughes Int. Scholar 1991–96; Assoc. Ed. Clinical Genetics 1991–; Ed. Int. Journal of Genome Research 1990, Assoc. Ed. Genomics 1994–; mem. Editorial Bd several scientific journals; Adviser, European Journal of Human Genetics 1992–; Dir American Soc. of Human Genetics, Mon Sheong Foundation, Educ. Foundation, Fed. of Chinese Canadian Professionals; Foreign Assoc., NAS 2004; mem. or fmr mem. numerous scientific cttees; Pres. The Human Genome Org.; Lee Kuan Yew Distinguished Visitor, Singapore 2000; Hon. Pres., Prix Galien 1998; Hon. Mem. World Innovation Foundation 2001, Hon. FRCP, UK 2005, Hong Kong Coll. of Physicians 2005, Hong Kong Coll. of Pathologists 2005; Dr hc (St Francis Xavier Univ., Antigonish, NS) 1994, (York Univ., Toronto) 2001, (Tel Aviv Univ.) 2005; Hon. DSc (Univ. of New Brunswick) 1991, (Chinese Univ. of

Hong Kong) 1992; Hon. DCL (Univ. King's Coll.) 1991; numerous prizes and awards including Scientist Award, Medical Research Council (Canada) 1989–93, Gold Medal of Honor, Pharmaceutical Mftrs Asscn of Canada 1989, Royal Soc. of Canada Centennial Award 1989, Award of Excellence, Genetic Soc. of Canada 1990, Gairdner Int. Award 1990, Canadian Achiever Award 1991, Sarstedt Research Prize 1993, XII San Remo Int. Award for Genetic Research 1993, J. P. Lecocq Prize 1994, Henry Friesen Award, Canadian Soc. of Clinical Investigation and Royal Coll. of Physicians and Surgeons of Canada 1995, Medal of Honour, Canadian Medical Asscn 1996, Distinguished Scientist Award, MRC 2000, Zellers Sr Scientist Award, Canadian Cystic Fibrosis Foundation 2001, Killam Prize, Canada Council 2002, The Queen's Golden Jubilee Medal, Canada 2002, Distinguished Achievement Award, Chinese American Physicians Soc. 2004. *Achievements include:* identified the defective gene (viz. Cystic Fibrosis Transmembrane Regulator (CFTR)) that causes cystic fibrosis. *Publications:* numerous scientific papers and reviews. *Leisure interests:* travel, good food. *Address:* Vice Chancellor's Office, University of Hong Kong, 10/F Knowles Building, Pokfulam Road, Hong Kong Special Administrative Region, People's Republic of China (office). *Telephone:* 28592100 (office). *Fax:* 28589435 (office). *E-mail:* tsuilc@hkucc.hku.hk (office). *Website:* www.hku.hk (office).

TSUJI, Tohru; Japanese business executive; *Chairman, Marubeni Corporation;* Pres. and CEO Marubeni Corpn 1999–2003, Chair. 2003–; Chair. Japan–Pakistan Business Cooperation Cttee (JPBCC) 2004, Japan–Qatar Friendship Asscn; Deputy Leader Japan–China Econ. Asscn Visitation Group 2003; Del. EU–Japan Business Dialogue Round Table 2004; Corp. Auditor, Sompo Japan Insurance Inc. 2003. *Address:* Marubeni Corporation, 4-2 Ohtemachi 1-chome, Chiyoda-ku, Tokyo 100-8088, Japan (office). *Telephone:* (3) 3282-2111 (office). *Fax:* (3) 3282-4241 (office). *Website:* www.marubeni.co.jp (office).

TSUJI, Yoshifumi; Japanese business executive; b. 6 Feb. 1928, Kagawa Pref.; ed Univ. of Tokyo; joined Nissan Motor Co., Ltd 1954, Gen. Man. Tochigi Plant 1984, Dir, mem. Bd and Gen. Man. Tochigi Plant 1985, Man. Dir in charge of Product Planning 1987, Exec. Man. Dir in charge of Plant Operations, Eng Depts 1989, Exec. Vice-Pres. in charge of Product Operation Group, Purchasing Group, Non-Automotive Operations Group, etc. 1990, Exec. Vice-Pres. in charge of Production Operation Group, Non-automotive Operations Group 1991, Pres. 1992–96, Chair. 1996–2000, Consultant 2000–. *Leisure interests:* golf, reading. *Address:* Nissan Motor Co., 17-1 Ginza 6-chome, Chuo-ku, Tokyo 104-23, Japan. *Telephone:* (3) 3543-5523.

TSUJII, Akio; Japanese transport industry executive; *Chairman, Kinki Nippon Railway Company;* Pres. Kinki Nippon Railway Co. Ltd –2003, apptd CEO 2003, Chair. 2003–. *Address:* Kinki Nippon Railway Company Ltd, 6-1-55 Uehommachi Tennoji-ku, Osaka 543-8585, Japan (office). *Telephone:* (6) 6775-3465 (office). *Fax:* (6) 6775-3467 (office). *Website:* www.kintetsu.co.jp (office).

TSUKA, Kohei (Bong Woong Kim); South Korean author and theatre director; b. 24 April 1948, Iizuka City, Fukuoka Pref., Japan; m. Naoko Ikoma; one d.; ed Keio Univ. Tokyo; wrote first play, Red Beret for You 1969; writer and dir for Waseda Univ. Theatre Club 1972; published first play The Murder of Atami 1975; est. Thukakoahei office for plays 1975–82; est. Kitaku Thukakoahei Gekidan 1994, Ôita City Thukakoahei Gekidan 1996; Dir Ginchan Ga Yuku, New Nat. Theatre 1997; Japan Acad. Award for film Kamata March Song 1983, 42nd Yomiuri Literature Prize for play of The Tale of Hiryu '90 1990, and other awards. *Publications:* novels: The Murder of Atami 1975, For the Father Who Couldn't Die in the War 1976, Introduction to Revolution, The Tale of Hiryu 1977, Sun is in Your Mind 1978, Kamata March Song 1981, Town with Well 1985, The Day that they Bombed Hiroshima 1986, A Stripper's Story 1984, Birth of a Star 1986, My Country, Tell it to my Daughter 1990, The Story of Ryoma 1992–2000; many other plays and essays. *Address:* Room 401, Villa Kamimura, Tabata, 6-3-18 Tabata, Kita-ku, Tokyo 114-0014; 4F Kitazono Mahabi-kan, 3-6-1 Akabane-kita, Kita-ku, Tokyo 114-0014, Japan. *Telephone:* (3) 5814-5177; (3) 5924-1126. *Fax:* (3) 5814-5178; (3) 5924-1127. *E-mail:* mail@tsuka.co.jp. *Website:* www.tsuka.co.jp.

TSUKADA, Maki; Japanese judo exponent; b. 5 Jan. 1982; Gold Medal, German World Open, Hamburg 2003; Silver Medal, +78kg Class, World Judo Championship, Osaka, Japan 2003; Gold Medal, +78kg Class, Olympic Games, Athens, Greece 2004; Silver Medal, Olympic Games, Beijing 2008; Bronze Medal, +78kg Class, World Judo Championship, Cairo, Egypt 2005; Gold Medal, Super World Cup, Tournoi de Paris 2005, 2007; Gold Medal, Japanese Nat. Championships, Fukuoka 2006, 2007; Gold Medal, All Japan Judo Championship 2006; Silver Medal, +78kg Class, World Judo Championship, Rio de Janeiro 2007, Gold Medal, Open Class;. *Address:* c/o All-Japan Judo Federation (Zen Nihon Judo Renmei), c/o Kodokan, 1-16-30 Kasuga, Bunkyo-ku, Tokyo 112-0003, Japan. *Telephone:* (3) 3818-4199. *Fax:* (3) 3812-3995. *Website:* www.judo.or.jp.

TSUKAMOTO, Hiroshi; Japanese national organization official and fmr government official; *President, Japan External Trade Organization (JETRO);* b. 10 March 1946; ed Kyoto Univ.; joined Ministry of Int. Trade and Industry (MITI) 1968, First Sec., Embassy in Jakarta 1979–82, Dir for Int. Petroleum Affairs, Petroluem Dept, Natural Resources and Energy Agency April–Dec. 1982, Dir Middle East Office, West Europe-Africa-Middle East Div., Int. Trade Policy Bureau, Nat. Land Agency 1982–84, Office Dir Regional Devt Bureau 1984–86; Visiting Research Fellow, Royal Inst. of Int. Affairs (now Chatham House), London 1986; Dir-Gen. for Gen. Coordination Dept, MITI Osaka Bureau 1987–89, Dir Fiber and Spinning Div., Consumer Goods Industry Bureau 1989–91, Dir Policy Planning Office, Minister's Secr. 1991–92; Pres. Japan External Trade Org. (JETRO), New York 1992–94, Pres. 2002–; Deputy

Dir-Gen. for Global Environment Affairs (MITI) 1994–95; Exec. Dir People's Finance Corpn 1995–97; Pres. Electronic Industries Asscn of Japan (later Japan Electronics and Information Tech. Industries Asscn) 1997–2002. *Address:* Japan External Trade Organization (JETRO), 2-2-5, Toranomon, Minato-ku, Tokyo 105-8466, Japan (office). *Telephone:* (3) 3582-5511 (office). *Fax:* (3) 3587-2485 (home). *Website:* www.jetro.go.jp (office).

TSUKUDA, Kazuo, BS, MS; Japanese engineering industry executive; *Chairman, Mitsubishi Heavy Industries;* b. 1 Sept. 1943; m. Yoshiko Kazuo; ed Univ. of Tokyo; joined Mitsubishi Heavy Industries 1968, engineer 1968–79, liaison to Westinghouse 1979–81, steam-turbine engineer 1982–95, Deputy Gen. Man., Takasago Machinery Works 1995–99, Gen. Man., Nagoya Machinery Works 1999–2000, Gen. Man., Industrial Machinery Div. 2000–02, Man. Dir and Gen. Man., Global Strategic Planning and Operations HQ 2002–03, Pres. Mitsubishi Heavy Industries 2003–08, Chair. 2008–. *Address:* Mitsubishi Heavy Industries, 16-5, Konan 2-chome, Minato-ku, Tokyo 108-8215, Japan (office). *Telephone:* (3) 6716-3111 (office). *Fax:* (3) 6716-5800 (office). *E-mail:* info@mhi.co.jp (office). *Website:* www.mhi.co.jp (office).

TSUMBA, Leonard Ladislas, PhD; Zimbabwean banker; *Chairman, Central African Building Society;* b. 27 June 1943, Harare; s. of Ladislus Million Tsumba and Regina Tsumba; m. Nola Arne Yasinski 1969; two d.; ed Va Tech., Blackburg, VA, USA; Instructor in Econs, Hampton Inst. USA 1970–72; Asst Prof. of Econs, Trinity Coll. USA 1975–77; consultant, Money and Finance Div. UNCTAD 1979; CitiBank NA, USA 1977–81; Exec. Asst to Gov. Reserve Bank of Zimbabwe 1981–82, Gen. Man. 1982–86, Deputy Gov. 1986–87, Group Chief Exec. 1987–83, Gov. 1993–2003; Chief Exec. and Man. Dir Finhold/ Zimbabwe Banking Corpn 1987–93; Chair. Central African Bldg Soc. 2004–. *Leisure interest:* golf. *Address:* Central African Building Society, North Ridge Park, North Close, PO Box 2798, Harare (office); 23 Shawasha Hills, PO Box Ch 147, Chisipite, Harare, Zimbabwe (home). *Telephone:* (4) 883823 (office); (91) 282791 (home). *Fax:* (4) 883804 (office); (4) 582791 (home). *E-mail:* management@cabs.co.zw (office); zwtsumba@zol.co.zw (home).

TSUNG, Christine Tsai-yi, MBA; Taiwanese politician and business executive; *Chairperson, The Grand Hotel, Taipei;* b. 1949; m. Jerome Chen; ed Nat. Taiwan Univ. and Univ. of Missouri, USA; fmr exec. at farm machinery co. in Texas, USA; fmr Budget Man., Columbia Pictures; Consultant, Kaohsiung Mass Rapid Transit System 1999; Pres. and CEO China Airlines 2000–02; Minister of Econ. Affairs Feb.–March 2002 (first woman in position); Chair. The Grand Hotel, Taipei 2002–; ranked 10th by Fortune magazine amongst 50 Most Powerful Women in Business outside the US 2001. *Address:* The Grand Hotel, 1, Chung Shan North Road, Sec. 4, Taipei 104, Taiwan (office). *E-mail:* grand@grand-hotel.org. *Website:* www.grand-hotel.org.

TSURCAN, Vladimir; Moldovan diplomatist and politician; *Chief, Parliamentary Commission for Law, Appointment and Immunity;* fmr Minister of Internal Affairs; Amb. to Russian Fed. –2006; currently Chief of Parl. Comm. for Law, Appointment and Immunity; also currently chief negotiator with Russia regarding Russian banning of Moldovan wine 2006. *Address:* Parliamentary Commission for Law, Appointment and Immunity, Parlamentul, 2073 Chişinău, bd Ştefan cel Mare 105, Moldova. *Telephone:* (22) 23-33-52. *Fax:* (22) 23-30-12. *E-mail:* info@parlament.md. *Website:* www.parliament.md.

TSURUMI, Shunsuke, BS; Japanese writer; b. 25 June 1922, Tokyo; s. of Yusuke Tsurumi and Aiko Tsurumi; m. Sadako Yokoyama 1960; one s.; ed Harvard Coll.; f. The Science of Thought (philosophical journal) 1946; Asst Prof., Univ. of Kyoto 1949, Tokyo Inst. of Tech. 1954; Prof., Doshisha Univ. 1960; freelance author 1970–; Visiting Prof., El Colegio de México 1972–73, McGill Univ. 1979–80; Takano Chōei Prize 1976, Osaragi Jiro Prize 1982, Mystery Writers' Soc. Prize 1989, Asahi Prize 1994. *Publications:* Collected Works (five vols) 1974, An Intellectual History of Wartime Japan 1986, A History of Mass Culture in Postwar Japan 1987, Collected Works (12 vols) 1992, Conversation (ten vols) 1996, Further Collected Works (five vols) 2000. *Leisure interest:* reading. *Address:* 230-99 Nagatanicho, Iwakura, Sakyōku, Kyoto, Japan (home).

TSUSHIMA, Yuko, BA; Japanese writer; b. 30 March 1947, Tokyo; d. of Shuji Tsushima and Michiko Tsushima; one d.; ed Shirayuni Women's Coll., Tokyo; mem. Japan's Writers Asscn, Literary Women's Asscn. *Publications (translations):* Child of Fortune (Women's Literary Award) 1978, Territory of Light (Noma Award for new writers) 1979, By the River of Fire 1983, Silent Trader (Kawabata Literary Award) 1984, Driven by the Night Light (Yomiari Literary Award 1987) 1986, The Shooting Gallery 1989, Woman Running in the Mountains 1991, Watashi 1999. *Address:* The Women's Press, 34 Great Sutton Street, London, EC1V 0DX, England (office); c/o Japan PEN-Club, Room 265, 9-1-7 Akasaka, Minato-ku, Tokyo (office); 6-7-10 Honkomagome, Bunkyo-ku, Tokyo 113, Japan (home).

TSUSHKO, Vasyl P.; Ukrainian economist and politician; b. 1 Feb. 1963, Tarutynsky Dist, Odesa Oblast; m.; one s. one d.; ed Izmayil Tech. School of Agric., Odesa Agric. Inst. and Nat. Univ. of Internal Affairs; served in Soviet Army 1983–85; Deputy Dir and Dir of various state farms 1988–97; Gov. Odesa Regional State Admin 2005–06; Minister of Internal Affairs 2006–07; mem. Parl. and Leader Parl. faction Socialist Party of Ukraine (SPU) (Sotsialistychna Partiya Ukrainy) –2006. *Address:* Socialist Party of Ukraine, 01025 Kiev, vul. Vorovskoho 45 Ukraine (office). *Telephone:* (44) 554-17-13 (office). *Fax:* (44) 573-58-97 (office). *E-mail:* pravozahist2003@ukr.net (home). *Website:* www.socpart.info (office).

TSUZUKI, Kunihiro; Japanese politician; mem. House of Councillors; Chair. House of Councillor's Cttee on Judicial Affairs and Cttee on Oversight of Admin.; Dir-Gen. Man. and Co-ordination Agency 1999–2000. *Address:* c/o Management and Co-ordination Agency, 3-1-1, Kasumigaseki, Chiyoda-ku, Tokyo 100-0013, Japan (office).

TSVANGIRAI, Morgan; Zimbabwean trade union official and politician; *Prime Minister;* b. 1952, Gutu, Masvingo; m. Susan Tsvangirai 1978 (died 2009); six c.; ed Silveria and Gokomere High Schools, Harvard Univ., USA; with Mutare Clothing Co. 1972–74; mem. local textile union; rose from plant operator to foreman Trojan Nickel Mine, Bindura 1974–84; mem. Associated Mine Workers' Union, apptd Br. Chair. 1984; fmr exec. mem. Nat. Mine Workers' Union; elected Sec.-Gen. Zimbabwe Congress of Trade Unions (ZCTU) 1988; charged with being a spy for SA, imprisoned for six weeks 1989; Founder and Chair. Nat. Constitutional Ass.; organized series of anti-Govt strikes against tax rises 1997; Founder and Pres. Movement for Democratic Change (MDC) 1999–; Parl. Opposition Leader 2000–09; Prime Minister 2009–; unsuccessful Presidential cand. 2002, 2008; charged with treason Feb. 2002 and put on trial for allegedly plotting the assassination of Pres. Robert Mugabe (q.v.), acquitted Oct. 2004. *Leisure interests:* reading, spending time with family. *Address:* Movement for Democratic Change, Harvest House, 6th Floor, cnr Angwa St and Nelson Mandela Ave, Harare, Zimbabwe (office). *Website:* www.mdczimbabwe.org (office).

TSVETKOV, Aleksey, PhD; Russian poet and critic; b. 2 Feb. 1947, Stanislaw (now Ivano-Frankivsk), Ukraine; s. of Petr Tsvetkov and Bella Tsvetkov (née Tsyganov); m. Olga Samilenko 1978; ed Odessa and Moscow Univs, Univ. of Mich., USA; journalist in Siberia and Kazakhstan; poetry recitals and participant in Volgin's Moscow Univ. literary soc. Luch 1970–75; emigrated to USA 1974; co-of Russkaya zhizn', San Francisco 1976–77; Prof. of Russian Language and Literature, Dickinson Coll., Pa 1981–85; broadcaster, Voice of America; poetry has appeared in Kontinent, Ekho, Vremya i my, Apollon, Glagol and elsewhere; Dr hc (Univ. of Mich.) 1977. *Publications include:* A Collection of Pieces for Life Solo 1978, Three Poets: Kuzminsky, Tsvetkov, Limonov, 1981, Dream State 1981, Eden 1985, Simply Voice 1991. *Leisure interest:* collecting baroque opera records.

TSZYU, Kostya; Australian (b. Russian) professional super-lightweight boxer; b. 19 Sept. 1969, Serov, Russia; youngest person to win Russian National Championships (aged 16); six times Russian champion, three times European champion; won gold medal World Amateur Championships, Sydney 1991; emigrated to Australia 1991; won International Boxing Federation (IBF) World Super-Lightweight Championship Jan. 1995, lost title to Vince Phillips May 1997; won World Boxing Asscn (WBA) and World Boxing Council (WBC) World Super-Lightweight Championships Feb. 2001 v. Sharmba Mitchell; won Undisputed World Super–Lightweight Championship Nov. 2001 v. Zab Judah, became first in 40 years to unify the division, one of only three undisputed champions, two defences; stripped of WBA title for failing to make mandatory defence June 2004; beat Sharmba Mitchell again to retain WBC and IBF titles; won 30 fights, including 24 knock-outs, one defeat; rated 4th best pound-for-pound boxer by USA Today Oct. 2003; trainer Johnny Lewis. *Address:* c/o Sports Management Australia, POB 66, Miller's Point, NSW 2000, Australia (office). *Fax:* (2) 9548-5789. *E-mail:* webmaster@kostyatszyu.com; mwatt@smagroup.com.au (office). *Website:* www.kostyatszyu.com.

TUBAYYEB, Samir A., BEng, PhD, MBA; Saudi Arabian petroleum industry executive; *CEO, S-Oil Corporation;* ed King Fahad Univ. of Petroleum and Minerals, Univ. of Calif., Berkeley, Harvard Business School; in various positions over 25 years with Saudi Aramco, including Project Man., Jt Venture and Planning; Rep. Dir and CEO S-Oil Corpn 2005–; Maeil Business Economy CEO of the Year 2007. *Address:* S-Oil Corporation, PO Box 758, 60 Yoido-dong, Yeongdungpo-gu, Seoul 150-607, Republic of Korea (office). *Telephone:* (2) 3772-5151 (office). *Fax:* (2) 783-7993 (office). *Website:* www.s-oil.com (office).

TUBMAN, Winston; Liberian diplomatist, lawyer and politician; *Leader, National Democratic Party of Liberia;* ed London School of Econs and Univ. of Cambridge, UK and Harvard Law School, USA; taught law at Univ. of Liberia and at univs in USA 1968–72; est. Tubman Law Firm, Monrovia 1968, Man. and Sr Partner until late 1980s; Prin. Legal Officer, Office of Legal Affairs 1973–75, 1991–96, UNEP 1975–77; served in Ministry of Foreign Affairs and Ministry of Planning and Economic Affairs 1977–79; Amb. to UN, New York (also accred to Cuba and Mexico) 1979–81; Justice Minister 1982–83; Chair. Legal and Constitutional Cttee of the group of Liberian political leaders meeting in Banjul, Gambia that established an interim govt in Liberia (later Foreign Minister and Minister of State) 1990; Exec. Sec. Comm. of Inquiry into ambushing and killing of Pakistani peace-keepers in Mogadishu 1993; assigned to UN Peace Office in Zagreb, Croatia and UN Peace-keeping Mission in Eastern Slavonia (UNTAES) –1998; Sr Adviser to Commdr UN Iraq–Kuwait Observation Mission (UNIKOM) 1998–; Head of UN Political Office for Somalia (UNPOS) 2002–05; Leader and presidential cand. (Nat. Democratic Party of Liberia) 2005; mem. Bar of Supreme Court of Liberia. *Address:* National Democratic Party of Liberia (NDPL), Capital Bye Pass, Monrovia, Liberia (office).

TUCCI, HE Cardinal Roberto; Italian ecclesiastic and broadcasting official; b. 19 April 1921, Naples; ordained priest; fmr Ed. La Civiltà Cattolica; Vice-Pres. Italian Catholic Union of the Press 1961–82; Gen. Sec. Italian Province of the Jesuits 1967–69; consultor to Pontifical Council for Social Communications 1965–89; apptd Gen. Man. Vatican Radio 1973, Chair. Admin. Cttee 1986–2001; cr. Cardinal 2001. *Address:* c/o Radio Vaticana, Palazzo Pio, Piazza Pia 3, 00193 Rome, Italy (office).

TUCKER, Mark, ACA; British business executive; fmr tax consultant, Price Waterhouse UK; joined Prudential 1986, sr positions in UK and USA, Chief

Exec. Prudential Corpn Asia 1993–2003, Exec. Dir Prudential 1999–2003, Exec. Dir and Group Chief Exec. Prudential plc 2005–09; Group Finance Dir HBOS plc and Dir Halifax plc 2004–05. *Address:* c/o Prudential plc, Laurence Pountney Hill, London, EC4R 0HH, England (office).

TUCKER, Paul; British central banker; *Deputy Governor, Bank of England;* ed Trinity Coll., Cambridge; several pvt. banking positions 1980–89, including working as banking supervisor, corp. financier at merchant bank and on projects to reform Hong Kong securities markets and regulatory system following the 1987 crash; Prin. Pvt. Sec. to Bank of England Gov. Leigh-Pemberton 1989–93, Head, Gilt-Edged and Money Markets Div. 1994–97, Head, Monetary Assessment and Strategy Div. 1997-1998, Deputy Dir Financial Stability 1999–2002, Exec. Dir Markets and mem. Monetary Policy Cttee 2002–09, Deputy Gov. 2009–, mem. Secr. of Monetary Policy Cttee 1997–2002. *Address:* Bank of England, Threadneedle Street, London, EC2R 8AH, England (office). *Telephone:* (20) 7601-4444 (office). *Fax:* (20) 7601-5460 (office). *E-mail:* enquiries@bankofengland.co.uk (office). *Website:* www .bankofengland.co.uk (office).

TUCKWELL, Barry Emmanuel, AC, OBE, FRCM, FRSA; Australian horn player and conductor; b. 5 March 1931, Melbourne, Australia; s. of Charles Tuckwell and Elizabeth Hill; m. 1st Sally E. Newton 1958; one s. one d.; m. 2nd Hilary J. Warburton 1971; one s.; m. 3rd Susan T. Levitan 1992; ed Sydney Conservatorium; French horn player with Melbourne Symphony Orchestra 1947, Sydney Symphony Orchestra 1947–50, Hallé Orchestra 1951–53, Scottish Nat. Orchestra 1954–55, Bournemouth Symphony Orchestra, London Symphony Orchestra 1955–68; Horn Prof., RAM 1963–74; f. Tuckwell Wind Quintet 1968; int. soloist and recording artist; Conductor of Tasmanian Symphony Orchestra 1980–83; Music Dir and Conductor Md Symphony Orchestra 1982–98; Pres. Int. Horn Soc. 1969–76, 1993–95; Guest Conductor Northern Sinfonia 1993–; Hon. Professorial Fellow, Univ. of Melbourne Faculty of Music 2006–; mem. Bd of Dirs, London Symphony Orchestra 1957–68, Chair. 1961–68; mem. Chamber Music Soc. of Lincoln Center 1974–81; hon. degrees from RAM, Guildhall School of Music and Drama, Sydney Univ.; Harriet Cohen Int. Award for Solo Instruments 1968, George Peabody Medal for outstanding contribs to music in America. *Publications:* Playing the Horn, 50 1st Exercises 1978, The Horn (Yehudi Menuhin Music Guides) 1981, entire horn repertoire of G. Schirmer Inc. (Ed). *Address:* c/o Faculty of Music, University of Melbourne, Melbourne, Vic. 3010, Australia. *Website:* www.music.unimelb.edu.au.

TUDOR, Corneliu Vadim; Romanian politician; *Leader, Greater Romania Party;* b. 28 Nov. 1949, Bucharest; m.; two d.; ed Univ. of Bucharest; fmr court poet for Ceauşescu family; mem. Parl. 1992–; Leader Greater Romania Party; runner-up in presidential elections 2000. *Address:* Greater Romania Party (Partidul România Mare), 010296 Bucharest, Str. G. Clemenceau 8–10, Romania (office). *Telephone:* (21) 3130967 (office). *Fax:* (21) 3126182 (office). *E-mail:* prm@prm.org.ro (office). *Website:* www.prm.org.ro (office).

TUENI, Ghassan, BA, MA; Lebanese journalist, writer and publishing executive; *Chairman and CEO, An-Nahar newspaper, Les Editions Dar An-Nahar;* b. 5 Jan. 1926, Beirut; s. of Gebran Tueni and Adèle Tueni (née Salem); m. 2nd Chadia El-Khazen; ed American Univ. of Beirut and Harvard Univ.; Lecturer in Political Science, American Univ. of Beirut 1947–48; Ed.-in-Chief An-Nahar daily newspaper 1948, Pres. Annahar Daily –2000, Man. An-Nahar Publishing Co. (now Dar an-Nahar SAL) 1963–, Pres. Dar Annahar Publishing 'Les Editions Dar an-Nahar' SAL 2000–, Chair. and CEO An-Nahar newspaper 2006–; Co-founder Lebanese Acad. of Law and Political Science 1951, Lecturer 1951–54; mem. Parl. for Beirut 1953–57, 2006; mem. Lebanese del. to UN Gen. Ass. 1957; f. Middle East Business Services and Research Corpn 1958, Chair. 1958–70; Founder, Chair. and Man.-Dir Press Co-operative, SAL 1960–; Deputy Prime Minister and Minister of Information and Nat. Educ. 1970–71; arrested Dec. 1973, appeared before mil. tribunal and then released in accordance with press laws; Minister for Social Affairs and Labour, Tourism, Industry and Oil 1975–76; Perm. Rep. to UN 1977–82; Founding Pres. Balamand Univ. 1990–93; Trustee Emer. American Univ. of Beirut; Détenteur des insignes d'Officier de la Légion d'honneur 2005; Hon. DHumLitt (American Univ. of Beirut) 2005. *Publications:* Peace-Keeping Lebanon 1979, Laissez vivre mon peuple! 1984, Une guerre pour les autres 1985, El Bourj (Place de la liberté et porte du Levant) 2000, Un siècle pour rien 2002, Trialogue (with Jean Lacouture and Gérard D. Khoury); several publs in Arabic and English on the Middle East, Palestine and the Lebanese wars 1952–. *Address:* An-Nahar Newspaper, PO Box 11-226, An-Nahar Building, Martyr Square, Beirut (office); Ras Kafra, Beit Mery, Lebanon (home). *Telephone:* (1) 963717 (office); (1) 994888 (office). *Fax:* (1) 970375 (office). *E-mail:* ghs@annahar.com.lb (office).

TUGENDHAT, Baron (Life Peer), cr. 1993, of Widdington in the County of Essex; **Christopher Samuel Tugendhat,** Kt, MA; British company chairman, fmr international official and politician; *Chairman, Lehman Brothers Europe;* b. 23 Feb. 1937, London; s. of the late Dr Georg Tugendhat; m. Julia Lissant Dobson 1967; two s.; ed Ampleforth Coll., Gonville and Caius Coll., Cambridge; Pres. Cambridge Union; Mil. Service, commissioned in The Essex Regt 1955–57; leader and feature writer, The Financial Times 1960–70; Consultant to Wood Mackenzie & Co. Ltd, stockbrokers 1968–77; Conservative MP for Cities of London and Westminster 1970–74, for City of London and Westminster South 1974–76; Dir Sunningdale Oils 1971–77, Phillips Petroleum Int. (UK) Ltd 1972–77, Nat. Westminster Bank PLC 1985–91 (Deputy Chair. 1990–91), BOC Group PLC 1985–96, Commercial Union PLC 1988–91, LWT (Holdings) PLC 1991–94; Dir (non-exec.), Eurotunnel PLC 1991–2003, Rio Tinto PLC 1997–2004; Chair. Civil Aviation Authority 1986–91, Abbey Nat. PLC 1991–2002, Blue Circle Industries PLC 1996–2001; Chair. (non-exec.) Lehman Brothers Europe 2002–; mem. Comm. of EEC with responsibility for Budget and Financial Control, Financial Institutions, Personnel and Admin. 1977–81, Vice-Pres. with responsibility for Budget and Financial Control, Financial Institutions and Taxation 1981–85; Chancellor Univ. of Bath 1998–; Chair. Royal Inst. of Int. Affairs (now Chatham House) 1986–95; Gov. and mem. Council of Man., Ditchley Foundation; Patron and Vice-Pres. British Lung Foundation; Chair. Gonville & Caius Devt Campaign Cttee, Cambridge Univ.; Freeman City of London; Hon. Fellow, Gonville and Caius Coll., Cambridge; Hon. LLD (Bath) 1998; Hon. DLitt (UMIST) 2002; McKinsey Foundation Book Award 1971. *Publications:* Oil: the Biggest Business 1968, The Multinationals 1971, Making Sense of Europe 1986, Options for British Foreign Policy in the 1990s (with William Wallace) 1988; numerous articles. *Leisure interests:* reading, family, conversation. *Address:* Lehman Brothers European Headquarters, 25 Bank Street, London, E14 5LE (office); 35 Westbourne Park Road, London, W2 5QD, England (home). *Telephone:* (20) 7102-1214 (office). *E-mail:* cstug@lehman.com (office). *Website:* www.lehman .com (office).

TUGWELL, Very Rev. Simon Charles ffoster, OP, STM, DD, STD; British ecclesiastic and historian; *Fellow, Istituto Storico Domenicano;* b. 4 May 1943, Brighton, Sussex; s. of Maj. Herbert Tugwell and Mary Brigit Tugwell (née Hutchinson); ed Lancing Coll. and Corpus Christi Coll., Oxford; received into Roman Catholic Church 1964; joined Dominican Order 1965; ordained priest 1971; Lecturer and Tutor, Blackfriars, Oxford 1972–92, Regent of Studies 1976–90; mem. Faculty of Theology, Univ. of Oxford 1982–92; Fellow, Istituto Storico Domenicano 1987– (Pres. 1992–97); Ed., Monumenta Ordinis Praedicatorum Historica 1992–; Visiting Lecturer, Pontifical Univ. of St Thomas, Rome 1977–93; Flannery Prof. of Theology, Gonzaga Univ., Spokane, Wash., USA 1982–83; Read-Tuckwell Lecturer on Human Immortality, Univ. of Bristol 1988; Consultor to Congregation for Causes of Saints 1994–97; has lectured in many countries around the world. *Publications:* The Way of the Preacher 1979, Early Dominicans 1982, Ways of Imperfection 1984, Albert and Thomas 1988, The Apostolic Fathers 1989, Letters of Bede Jarrett (ed.) 1989, Human Immortality and the Redemption of Death 1990, Saint Dominic 1995, Miracula S. Dominici... Petri Calo legendae S. Dominici (ed.) 1997, Bernardi Guidonis: Scripta de Sancto Dominico (ed.) 1998, Humberti de Romanis, Legendae Sancti Dominici (ed.) 2008; articles on aspects of theology and Dominican history, especially sources for the life of St Dominic. *Leisure interests:* music, science fiction, teddy bears, avoiding sightseeing. *Address:* Istituto Storico Domenicano, Largo Angelicum 1, 00184 Rome, Italy (office).

TUITA, Baron Siosaia Aleamotu'a Laufilitonga Tuita, CBE; Tongan government official and civil servant; b. 29 Aug. 1920, Lapaha, Tongatapu; s. of 'Isileli Tupou Tuita and Luseane Halaevalu Fotofili; m. Fatafehi Lapaha Tupou 1949; two s. two d.; ed Tupou Coll., Wesley Coll., Auckland, New Zealand, Univ. of Oxford, UK; Lt Officer, Tonga Defence Service 1942–43; Court Interpreter and Registrar, Supreme Court 1945; Asst Sec. Prime Minister's Office 1954; Acting Gov. of Vava'u 1956, Gov. 1957; Acting Minister of Lands 1962, of Police 1964–65; Chair. Niuafo'ou evacuation 1965; Minister of Lands and Survey and Minister of Health 1965; assumed title of Tuita 1972, awarded title of Baron Tuita of 'Utungake 1980; Deputy Prime Minister and Minister of Lands, Survey and Natural Resources 1972–89; mem. Privy Council; Chair. Town Planning Cttee, Energy Standing Cttee, Royal Land Comm., Tonga Broadcasting Comm.; mem. numerous socs. *Leisure interests:* rugby, cricket, driving, fishing. *Address:* Mahinafekite, Nuku'alofa, Tonga (home). *Telephone:* 22451 (home).

TUIVAGA, Hon. Sir Timoci (Uluiburotu), Kt, BA; Fijian judge; *Chief Justice;* b. 21 Oct. 1931; s. of Isimeili Siga Tuivaga and Jessie Hill; m. Vilimaina Leba Parrott Tuivaga 1958; three s. one d.; ed Univ. of Auckland, New Zealand; native magistrate 1958–61, called to the Bar, Gray's Inn, London 1964, NSW 1968; Crown Counsel 1965–68, Prin. Legal Officer 1968–70, Puisne Judge 1972, Acting Chief Justice 1974, Chief Justice of Fiji 1980–87, 1988–; Acting Gov.-Gen. 1983–87. *Leisure interests:* golf, gardening. *Address:* 228 Ratu Sukuna Road, Suva, Fiji. *Telephone:* 301-782.

TUJU, Hon. Raphael, MA; Kenyan politician, film producer, film director, broadcaster and business executive; b. 30 March 1959, Ndori, Bondo district; m.; three c.; ed Starehe Boys' Centre and School, Univ. of Leicester; producer-dir of numerous films, and radio and TV programmes principally concerned with promotion of health awareness 1992–97; chief public relations consultant Population Services Int. Social Marketing of Condoms Project 1994–95; writer of newspaper column and leader of project to promote AIDS awareness 1995–96; chief communications consultant, STI electronic media intervention in Kenya, The World Bank 1998; communications consultant UNICEF and Ministry of Health 1998; lead public relations consultant, Kenya Re-Insurance Corporation 1998–2000 (resgnd); lead consultant and communications advisor, Int. AIDS Vaccine Initiative (IAVI) 1999–2002; lead consultant, IEC component of DFID funded HIV/AIDS Prevention and Care Project (HAPAC) in Nyanza province 1999–2003; lead consultant, Poverty Reduction Strategy Paper (PRSP) 2000–01; mem. of Parliament for Rarieda; Minister for Tourism and Information 2003–04; Minister for Information and Communications 2004–05; Minister of Foreign Affairs 2005–08; team leader of first African winner ofe Int. Emmy Awards; Dir Ace Communications Md, USA and Nairobi, Kenya; Chair. Kenya AIDS NGOs Consortium (KANCO); Chair. Development Communications Inst.; Dir BITC; mem. Public Relations Soc. of Kenya (PRSK), Int. Mass Communication Soc. (IMCS), African Council for Communication Educ. (ACCE). *Publications:* AIDS: Understanding the Challenge. *Address:* c/o Ministry of Foreign Affairs, Old Treasury Building, Harmbee Avenue, POB 30551, Nairobi, Kenya (office).

TULAFONO, Togiola T. A.; American Samoa government official and lawyer; *Governor;* b. 28 Feb. 1947; m. Mary Tulafono; c.; ed Samoana High School, Chadron State Coll., Neb., Washburn Univ. School of Law, Topeka,

Kan., National Judicial Coll., Reno, Nev., USA; lawyer in pvt. practice for 20 years; fmr policeman; fmr Admin. Asst to Sec. of Samoan Affairs; fmr Samoan Asst to Attorney Gen.; fmr Dist Court Judge; fmr Senator for Saole County for four years, for Sua County for eight years; mem. Democratic Party; Lt Gov. of American Samoa 1997–2003, Gov. 2003–; fmr Chair. Bd of Dirs American Samoa Power Authority; fmr first Chair. Bd of High Educ.; Chair. South Pacific Mini-Games Cttee 1997, American Samoa Centennial Cttee 2000; Deacon of Congregational Christian Church in American Samoa, Sailele for more than 20 years. *Address:* Executive Office Building, Third Floor, Pago Pago, AS 96799, American Samoa (office). *Telephone:* (684) 633–4116 (office). *Fax:* (684) 633–2269 (office). *E-mail:* governorsoffice@asg-gov.com (office). *Website:* www.asg-gov.com (office).

TULEYEV, Aman Gumirovich, (Aman-geldy Moldagazyevich), DPolSc; Kazakhstani politician; *Governor, Kemerovo Region;* b. 13 May 1944, Krasnovodsk, Turkmenistan; s. of the late Tuleyev Moldagazy Kaldybayevich and the late Vlasova Munira Faizovna; m. Elvira Fedorovna; two s.; ed Tikhoretsk Railway Tech. School, Novosibirsk Inst. of Railway Eng, Acad. of Social Sciences at Cen. Cttee CPSU; worked on Krasnodar railway station 1961, Head Mundybash railway station 1969, Mezhdurechensk railway station 1973, Head Novokuznetsk Dept Kemerovo Railway 1978–85; Head Div. of Transport and Communications Regional Cttee CPSU 1985–88; Head Kemerovo Railway 1988; Peoples' Deputy of Russian Fed. for Mountain-Shor region 1990–93; Chair., Kemerovo Regional Soviet 1991; Cand. for Presidency 1991, 1996, 2000; supported coup d'état attempt 1991; mem. CP of Russian Fed. 1993–2003, Yedinaya Rossiya party 2003–; Deputy Fed. Council of Russia 1993–95, 1997–2001; Chair. Legis. Ass. Kemerovo Region 1994–96; Minister of Co-operation with CIS 1996–97; Gov. Kemerovo Region 1997–;; Order of Honour 1999, Order of Mongolia 'Polar Star' 2000, Order of Russian Orthodox Church, Rev. Sergey Radonezhsky II degree 2001, Order for Outstanding Country Service IV degree 2003, III degree 2008, Dostyk Order (Kazakhstan) 2003, Order of Jaroslav the Wise (Ukraine) 2004; Medal for Labour Valour 1976, Medal Labour Veteran of USSR 1992, Medal 300th Anniversary of Russian Navy 1998, Peter the Great Int. Award 2002, Int. Millennium Award for Service to Humanity 2003, Andrey Pervozvanny Int. Award for Faith and Loyalty 2003. *Publications:* 63 publications. *Leisure:* mushrooming, skiing, snow-tractor driving. *Address:* Office of the Governor, Sovetsky prosp. 62, 650000 Kemerovo, Russia (office). *Telephone:* (3842) 36-34-09 (office); (3842) 36-43-33 (office). *Fax:* (3842) 58-31-58 (office). *E-mail:* postmaster@ako.ru (office). *Website:* www.mediakuzbass.ru/tuleev (office); www.ako.ru (office).

TULIN, Dmitri Vladislavovich, MBA, PhD; Russian economist; b. 26 March 1956, Moscow; s. of the late Vladislav Tulin and of Emma S. Tulin; m. Vera Nerod 1977; two s.; ed Moscow Financial Inst. and USSR Inst. of Econs and Finance; economist, Int. Monetary and Econ. Dept USSR State Bank (Gosbank) 1978, Sr Economist 1980, Chief Economist 1985, Man. 1989, Man. Dir, mem. Bd Securities Dept 1990; Deputy Chair. Cen. Bank of Russian Fed. 1991–94; Exec. Dir for Russian Fed. IMF 1994–96; Chair. Bd Vneshtorgbank (Bank for Foreign Trade) 1996–98; Sr Adviser EBRD 1999–2004; Deputy Chair. Cen. Bank of Russian Fed. 2004. *Publications:* articles on monetary econs and banking in Russian professional journals. *Leisure interests:* gardening, chess. *Address:* c/o Central Bank of the Russian Federation, 12 Neglinnaya Street, Moscow, 107016, Russian Federation (office).

TULLY, Daniel Patrick; American finance industry executive; *Chairman Emeritus, Merrill Lynch & Co., Inc.;* b. 2 Jan. 1932, New York; m. Grace Tully; four c.; ed St John's Univ. New York and Harvard Business School; army service 1953–55; joined Merrill Lynch and Co., Inc. 1955; Account Exec., Stamford Office 1959, Man. 1970, Vice-Pres. 1971; Individual Sales Dir, New York HQ 1976; mem. Bd Dirs Merrill Lynch, Pierce, Fenner & Smith 1977, Chair. and CEO 1985; Exec. Vice-Pres. Marketing 1979; Pres. Individual Services Group 1982 and Exec. Vice-Pres. Merrill Lynch & Co. Inc. 1982, Pres. and COO 1985–92, Chair. Bd and CEO 1992–96, Chair., CEO, Pres. 1993–97, now Chair. Emer.; Vice-Chair. American Stock Exchange 1984–86, Securities Industry Asscn 1985–86; Dir New York Stock Exchange. *Address:* Merrill Lynch & Co., Inc., 4 World Financial Center, New York, NY 10080, USA (office). *Website:* www.merrilllynch.com.

TULLY, Sir (William) Mark, Kt, KBE, MA; British journalist; b. 24 Oct. 1935, Calcutta, India; s. of William S. C. Tully and Patience T. Tully; m. Frances M. Butler 1960; two s. two d.; ed Marlborough Coll., Trinity Hall, Cambridge; Regional Dir Abbeyfield Soc. 1960–64; Personnel Officer BBC 1964–65, Asst Rep. then Rep. (a.i.), BBC, Delhi 1965–69, Hindi Programme Organizer BBC External Services, London 1969–70, Chief Talks Writer 1970–71, Chief of Bureau BBC, Delhi 1971–93, BBC South Asia Corresp. 1993–94; now freelance writer, broadcaster, journalist 1994–; Hon. Fellow Trinity Hall, Cambridge 1994; Hon. DLitt (Strathclyde) 1997; Dimbleby Award (BAFTA) 1984, Padma Shri (India) 1992, Padma Bhushan 2005. *Radio:* series: Raj to Rajiv BBC 1987, Something Understood BBC 1995–. *Television:* series: Lives of Jesus BBC 1996. *Publications:* Amritsar: Mrs Gandhi's Last Battle (jtly) 1985, Raj to Rajiv (jtly) 1988, No Full Stops in India 1991, The Heart of India 1995, The Lives of Jesus 1996, India in Slow Motion (with Gillian Wright) 2002. *Leisure interests:* bird watching, reading, railways, theology. *Address:* 1 Nizamuddin East, Delhi 110013, India (office). *Telephone:* (11) 24359687; (11) 24352878. *Fax:* (11) 24359687. *E-mail:* tulwri@ndf.vsnl.net.in (office).

TULYAGANOV, Kozim N.; Uzbekistan politician; fmr Mayor of Tashkent; First Deputy Prime Minister of Uzbekistan 2001; Khokim (Gov.) Tashkent Province 2004–05; sentenced to 20 years' imprisonment 2006.

TŮMA, Zdeněk, CSc, MCom; Czech central banker; *Governor, Czech National Bank;* b. 19 Oct. 1960, České Budějovice; m.; two s. one d.; ed Univ. of Econs, Prague; researcher, Inst. for Forecasting, Prague 1986–90; Lecturer, School of Econs, Prague, Faculty of Social Sciences Charles Univ., Prague 1990–98, mem. Scientific Council 2003–06; Adviser to Minister of Trade and Industry 1993–95; Chief Economist, Patria Finance 1995–98; Exec. Dir EBRD 1998–99; Vice-Gov. Czech Nat. Bank 1999–2000, Gov. 2000–; Pres. Czech Econs Soc. 1999–2001; mem. Editorial Bd Finance a úvěr (Finance and Credit); mem. Bd of Trustees Jan and Meda Mládek Foundation, Univ. of Econs, Prague; Hon. mem. Bd of Trustees US Business School, Prague; mem. Bd of Govs English College, Prague; mem. Scientific Council, Czech Tech. Univ. 2006–. *Publications:* articles and chapters on econ. transition. *Leisure interests:* skiing, squash, tennis, cycling. *Address:* Czech National Bank, Na Příkopě 28, 115 03 Prague 1, Czech Republic (office). *Telephone:* (2) 24411111 (office). *Fax:* (2) 24412404 (office). *E-mail:* governor@cnb.cz (office). *Website:* www.cnb.cz (office).

TUMANOV, Vladimir Aleksandrovich, DJur; Russian lawyer; *Member, European Court of Human Rights;* b. 20 Oct. 1926, Kropotkin, Krasnodar Dist; s. of Aleksandr Tumanov and Serafima Tumanov; m. 1948; one s.; ed Inst. of Foreign Trade, USSR Ministry of Foreign Trade, All-Union Inst. of Law; Scientific Researcher All-Union Inst. of Law 1952–59; Chief Scientific Researcher, Head of Comparative Law Dept, Inst. of State and Law USSR (now Russian) Acad. of Sciences; Pres. Int. Asscn of Legal Science at UNESCO (resgnd); mem. State Duma (Russian Parl.) 1993–94; mem. Constitutional Court of Russian Fed. 1994–, Chair. 1995–97, Adviser 1997–; mem. European Court of Human Rights 1997–, Acad. of Comparative Rights; Pres. Int. Asscn of Legal Sciences; Chair. Council on Problems of Improving Legal System, Admin. of Russian Pres. 2000–. *Publications include:* Force-majeure in Civil Law 1958, Constitutional Law of Foreign Countries (Vols 1, 2) 1987–88, Legal Nihilism and Prospects of the Rule of Law 1991, Constitution of the Russian Federation of 1993 (an encyclopaedic guide) 1994. *Leisure interests:* canoeing, travel. *Address:* 13th Parkovaya str. 25, Korp. 1, Apt. 40, 105215 Moscow, Russia (home). *Telephone:* (495) 206-18-39 (home).

TUMI, HE Cardinal Christian Wiyghan; Cameroonian ecclesiastic; *Archbishop of Douala;* b. 15 Oct. 1930, Kikaikelaki; ordained priest 1966, elected to Yagoua 1979, consecrated Bishop 1980, Coadjutor Bishop 1982, Diocesan Bishop 1984; now Archbishop of Douala; cr. Cardinal 1988. *Address:* Archevêché, BP 179, Douala, Cameroon. *Telephone:* 423714. *Fax:* 421837. *E-mail:* christiantumi@camnet.com (office).

TUMUSIIME-MUTEBILE, Emmanuel, BA; Ugandan economist and government official; *Governor, Bank of Uganda;* b. 27 Jan. 1949; ed Balliol Coll., Oxford, Durham Univ., UK; Visiting Lecturer, Centre for Int. Briefing, Farnham, UK 1977; Lecturer in Industrial Econs, Univ. of Dar es Salaam, Tanzania 1977–79; Deputy Prin. Pvt. Sec. to the Pres. of Uganda 1979–80; Acting Under-Sec., Ministry of Planning and Econ. Devt 1981, Chief Govt Planning Economist 1982, Perm. Sec. and Chair. Agricultural Policy Cttee 1986–92; Perm. Sec. in charge of Econ. Affairs, Prime Minister's Office 1985; Sec. to the Treasury, Ministry of Finance 1992–98; Perm. Sec. to the Treasury and Chair. Agricultural Policy Cttee and Steering Cttee for Agricultural Modernization Plan, Ministry of Finance, Planning and Econ. Devt 1998–2000; mem. Bd of Dirs Bank of Uganda 1992–, Gov. 2001–; has served as consultant to IMF, OECD, World Bank, Macroeconomic and Financial Man. Inst. of Eastern and Cen. Africa, North-South Inst., Canada and the govts of Rwanda, Tanzania, Eritrea, Kenya, Nepal; Fellow, Econ. Devt Inst. of the World Bank; Hon. Prof., Makerere Univ. 2006. *Publications:* numerous articles in professional journals. *Address:* Bank of Uganda, 37–43 Kampala Road, POB 7120, Kampala, Uganda (office). *Telephone:* (41) 2258441 (office). *Fax:* (41) 2255983 (office). *E-mail:* info@bou.or.ug (office). *Website:* www.bou.or.ug (office).

TUNE, Thomas (Tommy) James, BFA; American theatrical performer, director and choreographer; b. 28 Feb. 1939, Witchita Falls, Tex.; s. of Jim Tune and Eva Tune; ed Lamar High School, Houston, Lon Morris Junior Coll., Univ. of Tex. at Austin and Univ. of Houston; began professional career as chorus dancer on Broadway 1963; appeared in films Hello, Dolly! and The Boyfriend; appeared on Broadway in Seesaw (Tony Award, Best Supporting Actor); Off-Broadway Dir The Club, Cloud 9 (Obie and Drama Desk Awards), Stepping Out 1987; Choreographer, A Day in Hollywood/A Night in the Ukraine (Tony Award); Dir The Best Little Whorehouse in Texas, Nine (Tony Award 1982); actor and choreographer, My One and Only (Tony Award 1983), Grand Hotel 1989 (London 1992), The Will Rogers Follies, Bye, Bye Birdie 1991–92; nine Tony Awards, Nat. Medal of Arts. *Publication:* Footnotes: A Memoir 1997. *Leisure interests:* cooking, yoga, painting. *Address:* c/o International Creative Management, 40 W 57th Street, New York, NY 10019; Tommy Tune Inc., 50 East 89th Street, New York, NY 10128, USA (office). *Telephone:* (212) 427-8214 (office).

TUNG, Chee-hwa, BSc; Hong Kong business executive and politician; b. 29 May 1937, Shanghai; m. Betty Chiu Hung Ping 1961; two s. one d.; ed Univ. of Liverpool; with Gen. Electric, USA –1969; Chair. Island Navigation Corpn Ltd, fmr Chair. Orient Overseas (Holdings) Ltd; Dir Sing Tao Newspapers Ltd, Sun Hung Kai Bank Ltd, Hsin Chong Properties Ltd, Mass Transit Railway Corpn; Vice-Chair. Preparatory Cttee for Hong Kong Special Admin. Region; mem. Exec. Council, Hong Kong Govt 1992–96; Chief Exec. of Hong Kong Special Admin. Region 1997–2005 (resgnd); mem. 8th CPPCC Nat. Cttee 1993, Vice Chair. 10th CPPCC Nat. Cttee 2005–08, 11th CPPCC Nat. Cttee 2008–; numerous civic appointments; Hon. Consul of Monaco in Hong Kong 1982–96; Int. Councillor Centre for Strategic and Int. Studies, Washington, DC 1983–97; mem. Advisory Council Inst. for Int. Studies, Stanford Univ. 1995–97, Int. Advisory Bd, Council on Foreign Relations, New York 1995–97.

Leisure interests: reading, hiking, watching sport, Tai Chi, swimming. *Address:* Chinese People's Political Consultative Conference, No.23, Taipingqiao Street, Beijing 100811, People's Republic of China.

TUNLEY, David Evatt, AM, MMus, DLitt, FAHA; Australian musicologist and academic; *Professor Emeritus and Honorary Senior Research Fellow, Department of Music, University of Western Australia;* b. 3 May 1930, Sydney; s. of Leslie Tunley and Marjorie Tunley; m. Paula Patricia Laurantus 1959; one s. two d.; ed The Scots Coll., Sydney, State Conservatorium of Music, Sydney; music master, Fort Street Boys' High School, Sydney 1952–57; joined staff of Dept of Music, Univ. of Western Australia 1958, Personal Chair. of Music 1980–, now Emer., Head Dept of Music 1985–90, Hon. Sr Research Fellow in Music 1994–; studied under Nadia Boulanger with French Govt Scholarship 1964–65; Scholar-in-residence, Rockefeller Foundation, Bellagio, Italy 1987; Fowler Hamilton Visiting Research Fellow, Christ Church, Oxford 1993; Visiting Scholar, Wolfson Coll. Oxford 1996; Founder/Conductor Univ. Collegium Musicum, 1976–83; Founder/Chair. York Winter Music Festival, 1982–; Founder/Dir The Terrace Proms, Perth; Nat. Pres. Musicological Soc. of Australia 1980–81; Chair. Music Bd, Australia Council 1984–85; Hon. FMusA; Chevalier, Ordre des Palmes académiques, Australian Centenary Medal; Hon. DMus (Western Australia). *Compositions include:* Two Preludes for Piano 1962, Concerto for Clarinet and Strings 1966 (revised 2000), A Wedding Masque 1970, Two Carols (words by Gerard Manley Hopkins) 1995, Immortal Fire 1999. *Publications:* The 18th-Century French Cantata 1974, Couperin 1982, Harmony in Action 1984, The French Cantata in Facsimile, 17 Vols 1990, Romantic French Song in Facsimile (6 Vols) 1994, The Bel Canto Violin: the life and times of Alfredo Campoli 1906–1991 1999, Salons, Singers and Songs: A Background to Romantic French Song 1830–70 2002, François Couperin and The Perfection of Music 2004, William James and the Beginnings of Modern Musical Australia; contribs to the New Grove Dictionary of Music and Musicians, the New Grove Dictionary of Opera, the New Oxford History of Music, European Music 1520–1640; numerous articles in major musicological journals. *Leisure interests:* reading, travel, theatre. *Address:* School of Music, University of Western Australia, Nedlands 6009, Western Australia (office); 100 Dalkeith Road, Nedlands 6009, Western Australia, Australia (home). *Telephone:* (8) 9386-1934 (home). *E-mail:* dtunley@westnet.com.au (office).

TUNNEY, John Varick, BA, LLB; American fmr politician and business executive; *Chairman, Armand Hammer Museum of Art and Cultural Center;* b. 26 June 1934, New York City; s. of the late boxer Gene Tunney and Mary Lauder Tunney; m. 2nd Kathinka Osborne 1977; two s. two d.; ed Westminster School, Simsbury, Conn., Yale Univ., Univ. of Virginia School of Law and Acad. of Int. Law, The Hague; practised law, New York City 1959–60, Riverside 1963–; Judge Advocate, US Air Force 1960–63; taught Business Law at Univ. of Calif., Riverside; mem. US House of Reps 1964–70; Senator from California 1971–77; pvt. law practice Manatt, Phelps, Rothenberg and Tunney, LA 1977–83; Chair., Bd of Dirs Cloverleaf Group Inc., LA 1981, Enterprise Plan Inc., Trusted Brands Inc.; Pres. JVT Consultants 1997–; fmr mem. and Vice-Chair. Bd of Dirs Foamex Int.; Pres. Gen. Partner Sun Valley Ventures 1995–; Chair. Armand Hammer Museum of Art and Cultural Center, UCLA; Democrat. *Leisure interests:* tennis, sailing, skiing, handball. *Address:* c/o Armand Hammer Museum of Art and Cultural Center, 10899 Wilshire Blvd., Los Angeles, CA 90024; 1819 Ocean Ave, Santa Monica, CA 90401, USA. *Website:* www.tunney.org.

TUOMIOJA, Erkki Sakari, MBA, Dr rer. pol; Finnish politician; b. 1 July 1946, Helsinki; s. of Sakari Tuomioja and Vappu Wuolijoki; m. Marja-Helena Rajala 1979; reporter 1967–69; econ. researcher Rautaruuki 1975–77; Chief Ed. Ydin magazine 1977–91; MP 1970–79, 1991–; Deputy Mayor of Helsinki 1979–91; Minister of Trade and Industry 1999–2000, of Foreign Affairs 2000–07; Pres. European Council July–Dec. 2006; Chair. Parl. Grand (European Affairs) Cttee 1995–99; lecturer Helsinki Univ. 1997–. *Publications:* 18 books on history, politics and int. affairs. *Leisure interests:* history, literature, running. *Address:* c/o Ministry of Foreign Affairs, Merikasarmi, PO Box 176, 00161 Helsinki, Finland (office). *Website:* www.tuomioja.org (office).

TUPOUTO'A LAVAKA, HRH Crown Prince; Tongan politician and army officer; b. 12 July 1959, Nuku'alofa; s. of HM King Taufa'ahau Tupou IV; m. Nanasipau'u Vaea 1982; three c.; ed in New Zealand, Britannia Royal Naval Coll., Dartmouth, Univ. of New South Wales, Australian Jt Services Staff Coll., US Naval War Coll.; fmrly known as Aho'eitu' Unuaki'otonga Tuku'aho, then HRH Prince 'Ulukalala-Lavaka-Ata; joined Tonga Defence Services 1981, Second-in-Command 1995; CO, Navy 1993; Minister of Foreign Affairs and Defence 1998–06; Prime Minister of Tonga 2000–06, also fmr Minister of Civil Aviation and Telecommunications; proclaimed Crown Prince 11 Sept. 2006.

TURABI, Hassan at-; Sudanese politician; Leader Nat. Islamic Front (NIF) 1986–; established Popular Arab Islamic Conference (PAIC) in Khartoum 1990–; Pres. Nat. Ass. 1996–2000; Sec.-Gen. Nat. Congress Party; arrested and imprisoned 2001, released Oct. 2003, arrested April 2004 in connection with alleged plot to overthrow President Omar al-Bashir. *Address:* National Islamic Front, Khartoum, Sudan.

TURAJONZODA, Haji Akbar; Tajikistani ecclesiastic and politician; b. 16 Feb. 1954, Kafarnikhon; s. of Ishan-e Tourajon; two s. four d.; ed Tashkent Islam Inst., Amman Univ., Jordan, Mir-e Arab School, Buxora; teacher, Tashkent Islam Inst. 1987–88; Head of Office of Qaziate of Tajikistan 1988–90; apptd Chief Qazi of Tajikistan 1990, Qaziate position abolished 1993; elected mem. Supreme Soviet Tajik SSR 1990; participant in democratic movt against Islamic fundamentalists, forced to emigrate to Iran, in hiding 1993; First Deputy Chair. Islamic Renaissance Movt of Tajikistan 1993–99; headed United Tajik Opposition in negotiations with the Govt leading to peace settlement 1995–97; fmr First Deputy Chair. of Tajikistan; currently Senator in Majlisi Milly (Nat. Ass.); Ismael Somoni Medal of Honour, World Islamic Centre Prize for Peace 1999. *Publication:* Between Water and Fire: The Peace Plan. *Leisure interests:* reading, sports. *Address:* Majlisi Milliy (National Assembly), 734051 Dushanbe, Xiyoboni Rudaki 42, Tajikistan (office). *Telephone:* (372) 23-19-33 (office). *Fax:* (372) 21-51-10 (office). *E-mail:* mejparl@parliament.tojikiston.com (office).

TURCHYNOV, Oleksandr Valentynovych, PhD; Ukrainian politician; *First Deputy Prime Minister;* b. 31 March 1964, Dnipropetrovsk; m. Hanna Volodymyrivna Turchynov 1970; one s.; ed Dnipropetrovsk Metallurgic Inst., Dept of Technology; began career working at Kryvorizhstal complex then moved into Komsomol and CP apparatus; worked in Dnipropetrovsk regional admin; Co-founder and mem. All-Ukrainian Hromada Asscn 1993–99; apptd Adviser on Econ. Issues to Prime Minister Leonid Kuchma 1993, then apptd Vice-Pres. Ukrainian Union of Industrialist and Entrepreneurs; Dir Econ. Reforms Inst., Kyiv 1994–98, also Head of Ukrainian Nat. Acad. of Science's Lab. of Shadow Econ. Research; mem. Parl. 1998–; joined Yuliya Tymoshenko's Fatherland (Batkivshchyna) party 1999; Chief of Security Service of Ukraine (SBU) 2004–05; Vice-Chair. Yuliya Tymoshenko Bloc (BYuT) in charge of election campaign HQ 2006–07; First Deputy Prime Minister 2007–; pastor of Baptist church, Kyiv. *Address:* Office of the Cabinet of Ministers, 01008 Kyiv, vul. M. Hrushevskoho 12/2, Ukraine (office). *Telephone:* (44) 254-05-84 (office). *Fax:* (44) 254-05-84 (office). *E-mail:* web@kmu.gov.ua (office). *Website:* www.kmu.gov.ua (office).

TURCO, Livia; Italian politician; b. 13 Feb. 1955, Cuneo; mem. Italian Communist Party (PCI) 1986–2001, Democratici di Sinistra (DC) 2001–07, Partito Democratico 2007–; mem. Camera dei Deputati (Parl.) 1987–, Head, Nat. Comm. for Equal Opportunities 1995–96; Minister of Social Solidarity 1996–98, of Health 2006–08. *Address:* Partito Democratico, Piazza Saint'Anastasia 7, 00186 Rome, Italy (office). *Telephone:* (06) 675471 (office). *Fax:* (06) 67547319 (office). *E-mail:* info@partitodemocratico.it (office). *Website:* www.partitodemocratico.it (office).

TURCOTTE, HE Cardinal Jean-Claude; Canadian ecclesiastic; *Archbishop of Montréal;* b. 26 June 1936, Montréal; ed André-Grasset School, Major Seminary, Montreal, Catholic Faculty, Lille, France; ordained priest 1959; vicar to Parish of St Mathias 1959–61, subsequently Diocesan Asst Chaplain for Christian Working Youth 1961–64; pastoral work, Montreal 1959–64, 1965–81; Diocesan Counsellor of JOC, JICF and Christian Workers' Movt 1965–67; held various posts, including Sec. Comm. des Traitemens, (responsible for studies and perm. formation of clergy), Diocesan Director for Parochial Pastoral, Diocesan Procurator and Cathedral Canon 1967–74; Vicar Gen. and Gen. Coordinator of Diocesan Pastoral Programmes 1981; Titular Bishop of Suas and Auxiliary Bishop of Montréal 1982–90; Archbishop of Montréal 1990–; attended Ninth Ordinary Ass. of World Synod of Bishops, Vatican City 1994; cr. Cardinal (Cardinal Priest of Nostra Signora del SS Sacramento e Santi Martiri Canadesi) 1994; mem. Council of Cardinals for Study of Organizational and Econ. Problems of Holy See 1995; attended Special Ass. for America of World Synod of Bishops, Vatican City 1997; Pres. Canadian Conf. of Catholic Bishops 1997–2000. *Address:* Archdiocese of Montréal, 2000 Rue Sherbrooke Ouest, Montréal, PQ H3H 1G4, Canada (office). *Telephone:* (514) 931-7311 (office). *Fax:* (514) 931-3432 (office).

TÜRK, Danilo, PhD; Slovenian academic, diplomatist, lawyer, politician and head of state; *President;* b. 19 Feb. 1952, Maribor; m. Barbara Miklic Türk; one d.; ed Ljubljana and Belgrade Univs; Lecturer in Public Int. Law, Univ. of Ljubljana 1978–88, Prof. of Int. Law 1988–, Head Inst. of Int. Law and Int. Relations 1983–95; mem. UN Sub-comm. on Prevention of Discrimination and Protection of Minorities 1984–92; Special Rapporteur 1989–92, Chair. 1990; Perm. Rep. of Slovenia to the UN 1992–2000; mem. UN Security Council 1998–99, Pres. Aug. 1998, Nov. 1999; mem. Security Council Mission to Jakarta and East Timor, Indonesia Sept. 1999, Asst Sec.-Gen. of UN for Political Affairs 2000–05; active in the field of human rights with several NGOs; Chair. Int. Law Asscn, Slovenia 1990–; Pres. of Slovenia 2007–. *Publications:* book on the principle of non-intervention in int. relations and int. law and over 100 articles in legal journals and other publs. *Address:* Office of the President, 1000 Ljubljana, Erjavčeva 17 (office); Faculty of Law, University of Ljubljana, Kongresni trg 12, 1000 Ljubljana, Slovenia. *Telephone:* (1) 4781222 (office); (1) 2418500. *Fax:* (1) 4781357 (office); (1) 2418660. *E-mail:* gp.uprs@up-rs.si (office); rektorat@uni-lj.si. *Website:* www.up-rs.si (office); www.uni-lj.si.

TURK, Salem; Jordanian royal court official and military officer; *Chief of the Royal Court;* fmr mil. officer, fmr Deputy Chief of Staff in charge of army investments; Chief of the Royal Court 2005–. *Address:* Office of the Chief of the Royal Court, Royal Hashemite Court, Amman, Jordan (office). *Telephone:* (6) 463-7341 (office).

TURK, Žiga, BSc, MSc, PhD; Slovenian academic and politician; *Minister without Portfolio, responsible for Growth;* b. 1962, Ljubljana; ed Univ. of Ljubljana; Founding Ed. Moj mikro (magazine on microcomputers) 1984–87; Asst Research Engineer, Inst. of Structural Eng and Earthquake and Building Informatics, Univ. of Ljubljana 1986–89, Asst in Computer Science, Dept of Architecture 1989–93, Asst Prof. 1993–98, Assoc. Prof. of Information Tech. and Documentation, Faculty of Civil and Geodetic Eng 1998–2004, Prof. 2004–07; Visiting Lecturer, Royal Inst. of Tech., Stockholm, Sweden 1997–99; Visiting Prof., Istanbul Tech. Univ. 2001–07; Minister without Portfolio, responsible for Growth 2007–; fmr mem. Scientific Council, Slovenia Research Agency; fmr Vice-Pres. Strategic Council for Culture, Educ. and Science; Co-founder and Co-ed. ITcon (int. science magazine); fmr Chair. Supervisory Bd

Telecom Slovenia, Mobitel. *Address:* Government Office for Growth, 1000 Ljubljana, Gregorčičeva 25, Slovenia (office). *Telephone:* (1) 4781180 (office). *Fax:* (1) 4781191 (office). *E-mail:* go.svr@gov.si (office). *Website:* www.svr.gov.si (office).

TURKI, Abdul Aziz al-Abdullah at-, BA; Saudi Arabian international organization official; b. 12 Aug. 1936, Jeddah; m.; two d.; ed Univ. of Cairo; with US Embassy, Jeddah 1953–54, ARAMCO 1954–66; Dir Office of Minister of Petroleum and Mineral Resources 1966–68; Dir of Gen. Affairs, Directorate of Mineral Resources 1968–70; Asst Sec.-Gen. OAPEC 1970–75, Sec.-Gen. 1990–2008; Sec.-Gen. Supreme Advisory Council for Petroleum and Mineral Affairs, Saudi Arabia 1975–90; Saudi Gov. for OPEC 1975–90; Deputy Minister, Ministry of Petroleum and Mineral Resources 1975; Chair. Arab Maritime Petroleum Transport Co., Kuwait 1981–87, Pemref 1982–89; mem. Bd of Dirs Petromin 1975–89, ARAMCO 1980–89. *Leisure interests:* tennis, swimming. *Address:* c/o Organization of Arab Petroleum Exporting Countries, PO Box 20501, Safat 13066, Kuwait (office).

TURKMANI, Lt-Gen. Hasan at-; Syrian government official and politician; *Minister of Defence;* b. 1935, Aleppo; ed Syrian Mil. Acad.; various mil. posts including command of mechanical div. during 1973 War, Chief Commdr Cen. Staff 2002-04; fmr. Vice-Pres., Council of Ministers; Minister of Defence 2004–. *Address:* Ministry of Defence, place Omayad, Damascus, Syria (office). *Telephone:* (11) 7770700 (office). *Fax:* (11) 2237842 (office).

TÜRKMEN, Ilter; Turkish politician and diplomatist; b. 1927, Istanbul; s. of Behçet Türkmen and Nuriye Türkmen; m. Mina Türkmen 1953; one s. one d.; ed Galatasaray Lycée, Istanbul, Faculty of Political Sciences, Ankara; Dir-Gen. of Policy Planning Dept, Ministry of Foreign Affairs 1964, Asst Sec.-Gen. for Political Affairs 1967; Amb. to Greece 1968, to USSR 1972, to France 1988–90; Perm. Rep. to UN in New York 1975–78, 1985–88, in Geneva 1983–85; Special Rep. to UN Sec.-Gen. for Humanitarian Affairs in South East Asia 1979–80; Minister of Foreign Affairs 1980–83; Commr-Gen. UNRWA 1991–96; fmr Adjunct Prof. Galatasaray Univ.; founding mem. Turkish Armenian Reconciliation Comm. (TARC); mem. Bd of Advisors Model UN Turkey (MUN-TR).

TURKSON, HE Cardinal Peter Kodwo Appiah, MTh., MDiv; Ghanaian ecclesiastic; *Archbishop of Cape Coast;* b. 11 Oct. 1948, Nsuta, Wassaw; ed St Teresa's Minor Seminary, Amisano, St Peter's Regional Seminary, Pedu, Seminary of St Anthony-on-Hudson, Rensaleer, New York, USA, Pontifical Biblical Inst., Rome, Italy 1976–80; ordained priest 1975; staff mem., St Teresa's Minor Seminary 1975–76, 1980–81; staff mem. and lecturer of Sacred Scripture, St Peter's Major Seminary; pastoral work in parish annexed to seminary; visiting lecturer, Major Seminary, Anyama Cote d'Ivoire 1983–86; part time lecturer and Chaplain, Univ. of Cape Coast 1984–86; promoted to episcopate while studying in Rome; Archbishop of Cape Coast 1992–; attended Special Ass. for Africa of World Synod of Bishops, Vatican City 1994, Ninth Ordinary Ass. of World Synod of Bishops, Vatican City 1994; cr. Cardinal (Cardinal Priest of S. Liborio) 2003; Pres. Ghana Catholic Bishop's Conference 1997–2004; Chancellor Catholic Univ. College of Ghana, Legon 2002–; Chair., Ghana Chapter of "Conference of Religions for Peace" 2003–, Ghana Nat. Peace Council 2006–; Treasurer Symposium of Episcopal Confs of Africa and Madagascar; mem. Nat. Sustainable Devt Council, Ministry of Environment, Pontificial Comm., Methodist-Catholic Dialogue 1997–2007, Governing Council of Univ. of Ghana 2001–06, Bd of Dirs, Pontificial Council for Christian Unity 2002–, Pontificial Comm. for the Cultural Patrimony of the Church 2002–, Pontificial Congregation for Divine Worship 2005–, Supreme Cttee of the Pontificial Missions Soc. 2006–, Pontifical Council for Justice and Peace 2007–; mem. Bd of Dirs CEDECOM 2002–, Cen. Regional Devt Cttee; Trustee Komenda-Edina-Eguafo-Abrem Educational Fund; Order of the Star, Order of the Rock, Ghana; Dr hc (Univ. of Ghana, Legon), (Univ. of Educ., Winneba, Ghana), (Holy Cross Coll., Notre Dame, USA). *Address:* Archdiocese of Cape Coast, PO Box 112, Cape Coast, Ghana (office). *Telephone:* (42) 33471/2 (office); (42) 33997 (office); (42) 32593 (home). *Fax:* (42) 33473 (office); (42) 32593 (home). *E-mail:* archcape@ghanacbc.org (office); pkturkson@yahoo.com (home).

TURLINGTON, Christy; American fashion model; b. 2 Jan. 1969, Walnut Creek, Calif.; d. of Dwain Turlington and Elizabeth Turlington; m. Edward Burns 2003; two d.; discovered at age 14; with Ford Models Inc. 1985; model for Calvin Klein 1986; model for Revlon, Maybelline 1993; face of Calvin Klein's Eternity Fragrance 1988–; promotes advertisement campaigns for Michael Kors, Camay Soap, Special K Cereal; Spokesperson, Centers for Disease Control (CDC), American Cancer Soc. (ACS). *Film:* Catwalk 1996, appeared in George Michael's video Freedom. *Address:* United Talent Agency, 9560 Wilshire Boulevard, Suite 500, Beverly Hills, CA 90212 (office); 344 East 59th Street, New York, NY 10022, USA (office).

TURNAGE, Mark-Anthony; British composer; b. 10 June 1960, Corringham, Essex; s. of Roy Turnage and Patricia Knowles; m. 1st Susan Shaw 1989 (divorced 1990); m. 2nd Helen Reed 1992; two s.; ed Hassenbrook Comprehensive School, Palmers Sixth Form, Grays, Royal Coll. of Music with Oliver Knussen and John Lambert and Tanglewood, USA with Hans Werner Henze and Gunther Schuller; first opera, Greek, premiered at first Munich Biennale 1988; Composer in Asscn with City of Birmingham Symphony Orchestra, composing three major works 1989–93; Composer in Asscn with ENO 1995–99; Assoc. Composer in Asscn with BBC Symphony Orchestra 2000–03; Momentum, BBC 3 composer weekend dedicated to his music, Barbican Hall, London 2003; composer-in-residence London Philharmonic Orchestra 2005–, Chicago Symphony Orchestra 2006–08; Guinness Prize for Composition 1982, Benjamin Britten Young Composers' Prize 1983, BMW Music Theatre Prize 1988, Laurence Olivier Award 2001. *Compositions include:* Night Dances for orchestra 1980, Lament for a Hanging Man for soprano and ensemble 1983, Sarabande for soprano saxophone and piano 1985, On All Fours for chamber ensemble 1985, Release for eight players 1987, Greek opera in two acts 1987, Three Screaming Popes for orchestra 1988, Greek Suite for mezzo soprano, baritone and ensemble 1989, Kai for solo cello and ensemble 1989, Some Days 1989, Momentum for orchestra 1990, Killing Time television scena 1991, Drowned Out 1992, Your Rockaby saxophone concerto 1992, Blood on the Floor for large ensemble 1994, Dispelling the Fears 1994, Twice Through the Heart for mezzo and 16 players 1997, Country of the Blind 1997, Four-Horned Fandango 1997, The Silver Tassie opera in four acts 1997, Silent Cities for orchestra 1998, About Time for two orchestras 1999, Evening Songs for orchestra 2000, Another Set To for trombone and orchestra 2000, Fractured Lines for two percussionists and orchestra 2000, Scorched for jazz trio and orchestra (with John Scofield) 2000, On Opened Ground concerto for viola and orchestra 2000, Bass Inventions for double bass and ensemble 2001, The Torn Fields for orchestra 2001, Dark Crossing 2001, A Quick Blast 2001, The Game is Over for orchestra 2002, Riffs and Refrains 2005. *Leisure interests:* football, films, theatre. *Address:* Van Walsum Management Ltd, 4 Addison Bridge Place, London, W14 8XP, England (office). *Telephone:* (20) 7371-4343 (office). *Fax:* (20) 7371-4344 (office). *E-mail:* vwm@vanwalsum.co.uk (office). *Website:* www.vanwalsum.co.uk (office).

TURNBERG, Baron (Life Peer), cr. 2000, of Cheadle in the County of Cheshire; **Leslie Arnold Turnberg,** Kt, MB, ChB, MD, FRCP, FMedSci; British professor of medicine; b. 22 March 1934, Manchester; s. of Hyman Turnberg and Dora Bloomfield; m. Edna Barme 1968; one s. one d.; ed Stand Grammar School, Whitefield and Univ. of Manchester; Lecturer, then Sr Lecturer in Gastroenterology, Univ. of Manchester, Manchester Royal Infirmary 1968–73; Prof. of Medicine Univ. of Manchester 1973–97, Dean Faculty of Medicine 1986–89; Hon. Consultant Physician, Hope Hosp. 1973–97; Pres. Royal Coll. of Physicians 1992–97, Asscn of Physicians of GB and Ireland 1996–97; Chair. Conf. of Medical Royal Colls. 1993–95, Strategic Review of London's Health Services 1997; Pres. Medical Protection Soc. 1997–, Medical Council on Alcoholism 1997–2002; Chair. Bd of Public Health Lab. Service 1997–2002; Scientific Adviser Asscn of Medical Research Charities 1997–; Pres. British Soc. of Gastroenterology 1999–2000; Chair. Bd of Health Quality Service 2000–04; Chair. UK Forum on Genetics and Insurance 2000–02; Vice-Pres. Acad. of Medical Sciences 1998–2004; Hon. FRCP (Edin.), FRCP (Glasgow), FRCPI, FRCOG; Hon. Fellow Royal Colls. of Ophthalmologists, Psychiatrists, Surgeons of England; Hon. Fellow Royal Australian Coll. of Physicians, S African Coll. of Medicine, Pakistan Coll. of Physicians, Acad. of Medicine of Hong Kong and of Singapore and several others; Hon. DSc (Salford) 1996, (Manchester) 1998, (Imperial Coll. London) 2000. *Publications:* Intestinal Secretion 1982, Mechanisms of Mucosal Protection in the Upper Gastro-Intestinal Tract 1983, Clinical Gastroenterology 1989. *Leisure interests:* reading, antiquarian books, walking, talking, Chinese ceramics. *Address:* House of Lords, Westminster, London, SW1A 0PW, England. *Telephone:* (20) 7435-8223. *Fax:* (20) 7435-9262 (office).

TURNBULL, Baron (Life Peer), cr. 2005, of Enfield in the London Borough of Enfield; **Andrew Turnbull,** KCB, CVO; British fmr civil servant; b. 21 Jan. 1945, Enfield; s. of Anthony Turnbull and Mary Turnbull; m. Diane Clarke 1967; two s.; ed Enfield Grammar School, Christ's Coll., Cambridge; Overseas Devt Inst. Fellow working as economist to Govt of Zambia 1968–70; Asst Principal HM Treasury 1970, Prin. 1972, seconded to IMF 1976–78, Asst Sec. 1978, Head of Gen. Expenditure Policy Group 1985–88, Deputy Sec. (Public Finance) 1992, Second Perm. Sec. 1993–94; Pvt. Sec. to Prime Minister 1983–85, UnderSec. 1985, Prin. Pvt. Sec. to Prime Minister 1988–92; Perm. Sec. Dept of Environment 1994–97, Dept of Environment, Transport and the Regions 1997–98, HM Treasury 1998–2002, Cabinet Sec. and Head of the Home Civil Service 2002–05 (retd); mem. House of Lords 2005–; Dir (non-exec.) Prudential plc, British Land plc, Frontier Economics Ltd; Sr Adviser, Booz Allen Hamilton UK; Hon. Fellow, Christ's Coll. Cambridge; hon. degrees (Nottingham, Cranfield). *Leisure interests:* walking, opera, golf, sailing. *Address:* House of Lords, Westminster, London, SW1A 0PW, England (office).

TURNBULL, Charles Wesley, PhD; American politician and educationalist; *Governor, US Virgin Islands;* b. 1935, St. Thomas,USVirgin Islands; s. of John W. Turnbull and Ruth Ann Turnbull; ed Charlotte Amalie High School, Hampton Univ. and Univ. of Minn.; elementary school teacher, secondary teacher, Asst Prin., High School Prin.; Prof. of History and Trustee Univ. of the VI; Asst Commr of Educ., Commr Dept of Educ., est. Cultural Educational Div., Chair. VI Bd Educ.; Gov. of US VI 1998–; mem. Territorial Cttee VI Democratic Party; served on all four Constitutional conventions of VI; mem. Bd Roy Lester Schneider Hosp. *Address:* Office of the Governor, Government House, 21–22 Kongens Gade, Charlotte Amalie, 00802 United States Virgin Islands (office). *Telephone:* (340) 774-0001 (office). *Fax:* (340) 774-1361 (office). *E-mail:* rcanton@govhouse.gov.vi (office).

TURNBULL, Lucinda Mary (Lucy), LLB, MBA; Australian lawyer and politician; b. 30 March 1958, Sydney; d. of Thomas Eyre Forrest Hughes and Joanna Fitzgerald; m. Malcolm Bligh Turnbull 1980; one s. one d.; ed Univ. of Sydney, Univ. of New South Wales; Pnr, Turnbull McWilliam (solicitors) 1988–99, Turnbull & Pnrs Ltd 1988–92, Turnbull & Co. 1992–95, Dir Turnbull & Pnrs Pty Ltd 1990–; Dir FTR Holdings Ltd 1997– (Chair. 1997–2001), Melbourne IT Ltd 2006–; Deputy Lord Mayor of Sydney 1999–2003, Lord Mayor (first woman) 2003–04; Deputy Chair. Sydney Cancer Centre Foundation 2002–, Cttee for Sydney; Dir Museum of Contemporary Art 2002–, Centre for Ind. Studies, Nat. Portrait Gallery; Chair. NSW Ministerial Advisory Council on Biotechnology 2001–, WebCentral Group Ltd; mem. Australian Museum Trust 1995–99, Deputy Pres. 1995–99; Pres. Sydney Children's Hosp. Appeal, Sydney Children's Hosp. Foundation Ltd 1996–2000;

Commr Australian Pavilion at Venice Architecture Biennale 2006, 2008; Gov. Woolcock Inst. of Medical Research; mem. Commonwealth of Nations Comm. on Respect and Understanding, NSW Cancer Council 1997–99. *Publications include:* Sydney: Biography of a City 1999. *Leisure interests:* history, politics, contemporary culture, visual arts, urban design, architecture. *Address:* Turnbull &Partners Pty Ltd, Level 38/264 George Street, Sydney, NSW 2000, Australia (office). *Telephone:* (2) 8248-3900 (office).

TURNBULL, Malcolm Bligh, BA, LLB, BCL; Australian banker, lawyer and politician; *Leader, Liberal Party of Australia;* b. 24 Oct. 1954, Sydney; s. of Bruce B. Turnbull and Coral Lansbury; m. Lucinda M. F. Hughes 1980; one s. one d.; ed Sydney Grammar School, Univ. of Sydney and Univ. of Oxford (Rhodes Scholar); State Parl. Corresp. for Nation Review 1976; journalist, The Bulletin 1977–78; Exec. Asst to Chair. Consolidated Press Holdings Ltd 1978; journalist, The Sunday Times, London 1978–79; barrister, Sydney 1980–82; Gen. Counsel and Sec. Consolidated Press Holdings Ltd 1983–85; solicitor in pvt. practice, Turnbull McWilliam, Sydney 1986–87; Prin. Turnbull and Co. (solicitors) 1987; Man. Dir Turnbull & Pnrs Pty Ltd (investment bankers), Sydney 1987–97; Chair. Axiom Forest Resources Ltd (HK) 1991–92; Dir Perseverance Corpn Ltd 1993–94, Star Mining Corpn NL 1993–95, FTR Holdings Ltd 1995–2004; Chair. Oz Email Ltd 1994–99; Dir Australian Republican Movt 1991–93, Chair. 1993–2000; Chair. cttee to advise on changing Australia to Repub.; Chair. and Man. Dir Goldman Sachs Australia 1997–2001, Pnr Goldman Sachs (US) 1998–2001; Chair. Menzies Research Centre 2001–04; Hon. Fed. Treas., Liberal Party 2002–03, Treasury Spokesman 2007–08, Leader 2008–; mem. NSW State Exec. 2002–03, mem. Fed. Finance Cttee 2002–03, mem. Fed. Exec. 2002–03; MP for Wentworth, NSW 2004–, Parl. Sec. to Prime Minister 2006–07; Minister for the Environment and Heritage 2007; Henry Lawson Prize for Poetry 1975, Centenary Medal 2003. *Publications:* The Spycatcher Trial 1988, The Reluctant Republic 1993, Fighting for the Republic 1999. *Leisure interests:* reading, walking, riding, gardening. *Address:* PO Box 6022, House of Representatives, Parliament House, Canberra, ACT 2600 (office); PO Box 1840, Bondi Junction, NSW 1355, Australia. *Telephone:* (2) 6277-7640 (office). *Fax:* (2) 6273-6101 (office). *E-mail:* Malcolm.Turnbull.MP@aph.gov.au (office). *Website:* www.malcolmturnbull.com.au.

TURNBULL, Rt Rev. Michael, CBE, DL, MA, DipTheol, DLitt, DD; British ecclesiastic; b. 27 Dec. 1935, Yorks.; s. of George Turnbull and Adeline Awty; m. Brenda Merchant 1963; one s. two d.; ed Ilkley Grammar School, Keble Coll. Oxford and St John's Coll. Durham; ordained deacon 1960, priest 1961; curate, Middleton 1960–61, Luton 1961–65; Domestic Chaplain to Archbishop of York 1965–69; Rector of Heslington and Chaplain, York Univ. 1969–76; Chief Sec. Church Army 1976–84; Archdeacon of Rochester 1984–88; Bishop of Rochester 1988–94, of Durham 1994–2003; Hon. Asst Bishop, Diocese of Canterbury and of Europe 2003–; mem. Gen. Synod of Church of England 1970–75, 1987–2003; mem. Archbishops' Council 1999–2001, Chair. Ministry Div. 1999–2001; Chair. Archbishops' Comm. on Org. of Church of England; mem. House of Lords 1994–2003; Chair. Foundation for Church Leadership 2002–05; Hon. DLitt 1994; Hon. DD 2003. *Publications:* Unity: the Next Step? (contrib.) 1972, God's Front Line 1979, Parish Evangelism 1980, Learning to Pray 1981, 100 Minute Bible Reflections (ed) 2007; numerous articles in journals. *Leisure interests:* cricket, family life, letcurer with Swan Helenic Criuises, leader Holy Land Pilgrimages. *Address:* 67 Strand Street, Sandwich, Kent, CT13 9HN, England. *Telephone:* (1304) 611389. *E-mail:* bstmt@btopenworld.com (home).

TURNBULL, William; British sculptor, painter and printmaker; b. 11 Jan. 1922, Dundee, Scotland; m. Cheng Kim Lim 1960; two s.; ed Slade School of Fine Art, London; has participated in numerous group exhbns around the world since 1950; works in public collections in UK, USA, Australia and Germany. *Leisure interests:* reading, music. *Address:* c/o Waddington Galleries, 11 Cork Street, London, W1S 3LT, England.

TURNER, Fred L.; American business executive (retd); *Honorary Chairman, McDonald's Corporation;* one of the first employees of McDonald's Corpn in 1956, Operations Vice-Pres. 1958–67, Exec. Vice-Pres. 1967–68, mem. Bd of Dirs, Pres. and Chief Admin. Officer 1968–73, CEO 1973–77, Chair. and CEO 1977–90, Sr Chair. 1990–2004, Hon. Chair. 2004–; Life Trustee, Ronald McDonald House Charities; Hon. LLD (Drake Univ.) 1983, Hon. DBA (Johnson & Wales Univ.) 1991; inducted into Chicago Jr Achievement's Business Hall of Fame 1989, named by Advertising Age magazine as "Ad Man of the Decade" for the 1980s 1990, Horatio Alger Award 1991. *Address:* McDonald's Corpn, McDonald's Plaza, Oak Brook, IL 60523, USA (office). *Telephone:* (630) 623-3000 (office). *Fax:* (630) 623-5004 (office). *E-mail:* info@mcdonalds.com (office). *Website:* www.mcdonalds.com (office).

TURNER, Grenville, MA, DPhil, FRS; British geophysicist and academic; *Research Professor, University of Manchester;* b. 1 Nov. 1936, Todmorden; s. of Arnold Turner and Florence Turner; m. Kathleen Morris 1961; one s. one d.; ed St John's Coll., Cambridge and Balliol Coll., Oxford; Asst Prof., Univ. of California, Berkeley 1962–64; Lecturer, Univ. of Sheffield 1964–74, Sr Lecturer 1974–79, Reader 1979–80, Prof. of Physics 1980–88; Prof. of Isotope Geochemistry, Univ. of Manchester 1988–2002, Research Prof. 2002–; Visiting Assoc. in Nuclear Geophysics, Calif. Inst. of Tech. 1970–71; Fellow, Royal Soc. 1980, Council mem. 1990–92; Fellow, Meteoritical Soc. 1980, European Asscn of Geochemistry 1996, American Geophysical Union 1998; Rumford Medal, Royal Soc. 1996, Leonard Medal, Meteoritical Soc. 1999, Urey Medal European Asscn of Geochemists 2002, Gold Medal Royal Astronomical Soc. 2004. *Achievements:* developed Ar-Ar method for rock dating, used it to determine first ages of Apollo lunar samples and a chronology of lunar evolution; discovered early isotopic evidence leading to discovery of pre-solar material in primitive meteorites; developed ultra-sensitive isotopic analysis

by resonance ionisation mass spectrometry. *Publications:* scientific papers on the application of naturally occurring isotopes to earth science and the evolution of the solar system. *Leisure interests:* photography, walking, theatre. *Address:* School of Earth, Atmospheric and Environmental Sciences, University of Manchester, Manchester M13 9PL, England (office). *Telephone:* (161) 275-0401 (office). *Fax:* (161) 275-3947 (office); (161) 275-3947 (office). *E-mail:* grenville.turner@manchester.ac.uk (office).

TURNER, Rt Hon. John Napier, PC, CC, QC, MA, BCL; Canadian politician and lawyer; b. 7 June 1929, Richmond, Surrey, England; s. of Leonard Turner and Phyllis Turner (née Gregory); m. Geills McCrae Kilgour 1963; three s. one d.; ed schools in Ottawa and Univs of British Columbia, Oxford and Paris; MP 1962–76, 1984–93; Minister without Portfolio 1965; Registrar-Gen. 1967–68; Minister of Consumer and Corp. Affairs Jan.–July 1968; Solicitor-Gen. April–July 1968; Minister of Justice and Attorney-Gen. 1968–72; Minister of Finance 1972–75; Leader Liberal Party of Canada 1984–90; Prime Minister of Canada June–Sept. 1984, Leader of Opposition 1984–90; Partner, McMillan, Binch (law firm), Toronto 1976–84; Partner, Miller Thomson (law firm), Toronto 1990–; mem. Bd Dirs Purolator Courier Ltd. *Publications:* The Senate of Canada 1961, Politics of Purpose 1968. *Leisure interests:* tennis, canoeing, skiing. *Address:* Miller Thomson, 20 Queen Street West, Box 27, Suite 2500, Toronto, Ont., M5H 3S1 (office); 59 Oriole Road, Toronto, Ont., M4V 2E9, Canada (home). *Telephone:* (416) 595-8500 (office). *Fax:* (416) 595-8695 (office). *E-mail:* jturner@millerthomson.ca (office).

TURNER, (Jonathan) Adair, MA; British business executive and political adviser; *Vice Chairman, Merrill Lynch Europe;* b. 5 Oct. 1955; s. of Geoffrey Vincent Turner and Kathleen Margaret Turner; m. Orna Ni Chionna 1985; two d.; ed Hutcheson's Grammar School, Glasgow, Glenalmond School and Gonville & Caius Coll. Cambridge; Pres. Cambridge Union 1977; began career with BP (British Petroleum) PLC 1979; with Chase Manhattan Bank 1979–82; McKinsey & Co. 1982–95, Dir 1994–95; Dir-Gen. CBI 1995–99; Vice-Chair. Merrill Lynch Europe 2000–; Dir (non-exec.) United News and Media 2000–, Netscalibur Ltd 2000–01; mem. British Overseas Trade Bd 1995–99; Visiting Prof. LSE 1999–, Visiting Prof. City Univ. 2004–; Chair. Policy Cttee, Centre for Econ. Performance 1999–; Chair. Low Pay Comm. 2002–; Chair. Pensions Comm. 2003–; Strategic Adviser to British Prime Minister 2001–02; mem. Econ. and Social Research Council; Trustee Worldwide Fund for Nature 2002–. *Publication:* Just Capital: The Liberal Economy 2001. *Leisure interests:* skiing, opera, theatre, gardening. *Address:* Merrill Lynch Europe, 2 King Edward Street, London, EC1A 1HQ (office); Pensions Commission, 4th floor, Adelphi, 1-11 John Adam Street, London WC2N 6HT, England. *Telephone:* (20) 7628-1000 (Merrill Lynch) (office); (20) 7712-2534 (Pensions Commission). *Fax:* (20) 7867-2867 (Merrill Lynch) (office). *Website:* www.ml.com; www.pensionscommission.org.uk.

TURNER, Kathleen, BFA; American actress; b. 19 June 1954, Springfield, Mo.; m. Jay Weiss 1984 (divorced); one d.; ed Cen. School of Speech and Drama, London, SW Missouri State Univ., Univ. of Maryland. *Plays:* various theatre roles including Broadway debut, Gemini 1978, The Graduate, London 2000, Who's Afraid of Virginia Woolf? (London Evening Standard Award for Best Actress 2006, London Critics' Circle Best Actress 2006) 2006, Crimes of the Heart, New York (Dir) 2007–08, The Third Story, New York 2009. *Television series include:* The Doctors 1977, Leslie's Folly (also dir 1994, Friends at Last (also producer) 1995, Style and Substance 1996, Legalese 1998, Love and Action in Chicago 1999. *Films include:* Body Heat 1981, The Man With Two Brains 1983, Crimes of Passion 1984, Romancing the Stone 1984, Prizzi's Honour 1985, The Jewel of the Nile 1985, Peggy Sue Got Married 1986, Julia and Julia 1988, Switching Channels 1988, The Accidental Tourist 1989, The War of the Roses 1990, V.I. Warzhawski 1991, House of Cards, Undercover Blues 1993, Serial Mom 1994, Naked in New York 1994, Moonlight and Valentino 1995, A Simple Wish 1997, The Real Blonde 1997, The Virgin Suicides 1999, Baby Geniuses 1999, Prince of Central Park 2000, Beautiful 2000, Without Love 2004, Monster House 2006; producer Hard Boiled 1990. *Publication:* Send Yourself Roses (auto-biog.) 2008. *Address:* c/o Phil Gersh, The Gersh Agency, 232 N. Canon Drive, Suite 202, Beverly Hills, CA 90210, USA. *Website:* www.kathleen-turner.com.

TURNER, Michael John, CBE, BA, ACIS, FRAeS; British business executive; b. 1948; m. four c.; ed Didsbury Tech. High School, Manchester and Manchester Polytechnic; joined Hawker Siddeley Aviation as undergraduate commercial apprentice 1966, later Contracts Officer; Contracts Man. (Mil.) British Aerospace (BAe) Aircraft Group, Manchester Div. 1978, Admin. Man. 1980, Exec. Dir of Admin. 1981, Divisional Admin. Dir 1982 (led Advanced Turboprop Project Team 1982–84), Divisional Dir and Gen. Man., Kingston 1984, Dir Divisional Man. Cttee and Gen. Man. Mil. Aircraft Div. 1986, Dir Marketing and Product Support, Mil. Aircraft Div. 1987, Exec. Vice-Pres. Defence Marketing, BAe PLC 1988; Chair. and Man. Dir BAe Regional Aircraft Ltd and Chair. Jetstream Aircraft 1992; Chair. Commercial Aerospace 1994 (mem. Main Bd BAe PLC), assumed responsibility for all BAe's defence export business 1996, mem. Airbus Supervisory Bd (renamed AIC) 1998, mem. Shareholders' Cttee AIC, COO BAE Systems (following merger of BAe PLC and Marconi Electronic Systems) 1999, CEO 2002–08; Vice-Pres. Soc. of British Aerospace Cos 1995, Pres. 1996–97; Dir (non-exec.) Babcock Int. Group PLC 1996–; Hon. Doctor of Admin (Manchester Metropolitan Univ.). *Leisure interests:* Manchester United Football Club, golf, cricket, rugby. *Address:* c/o BAE Systems, 6 Carlton Gardens, London, SW1Y 5AD, England.

TURNER, Adm. Stansfield, MA; American naval officer (retd), lecturer and author; b. 1 Dec. 1923, Chicago, Ill.; s. of Oliver Stansfield Turner and Wilhelmina Josephine (née Wagner) Turner; m. 1st Eli Karin Gilbert 1985 (died 2000); m. 2nd Marion Weiss 2002; ed Amherst Coll., US Naval Acad.,

Annapolis, Univ. of Oxford, UK (Rhodes Scholar); active duty, USN, serving minesweeper, destroyers, USS Horne (guided missile cruiser in action in Vietnamese conflict); served in Office of Chief of Naval Operations, then in Office of Asst Sec. of Defense for Systems Analysis; Advanced Man. Program, Harvard Business School; Exec. Asst and Naval Aide to Sec. of the Navy 1968–70; Rear Adm. 1970; CO Carrier Task Group in USS Independence, US Sixth Fleet 1970; Dir Systems Analysis Div. of Office of Chief of Naval Operations, Dept of the Navy 1971–72; Vice-Adm. 1972; Pres. US Naval War Coll., Newport, RI 1972–74; Commdr US Second Fleet and NATO Striking Fleet Atlantic 1974–75; Adm. 1975; C-in-C Allied Forces Southern Europe, NATO 1975–77; Dir Cen. Intelligence (CIA) 1977–81; Sr Research Scholar, Center for Int. and Security Studies, Univ. of Maryland 1991–2007; Hon. Fellow, Exeter Coll., Oxford 1981–; Nat. Security Medal, Legion of Merit, Bronze Star. *Publications:* Secrecy and Democracy: The CIA in Transition 1985, Terrorism and Democracy 1991, Caging the Nuclear Genie: An American Challenge for Global Security 1997, Caging the Genies: A Workable Plan for Nuclear, Chemical and Biological Weapons 1998, Burning Before Reading 2005. *Leisure interests:* tennis, reading. *Address:* 488 River Bend Road, Great Falls, VA 22066, USA (home). *E-mail:* admturner@aol.com.

TURNER, Robert (Ted) Edward, III; American broadcasting executive and yachtsman; b. 19 Nov. 1938; s. of Robert Turner and Frances Rooney; m. 1st Judy Nye (divorced); one s. one d.; m. 2nd Jane S. Smith 1965 (divorced 1988); one s. two d.; m. 3rd Jane Fonda (q.v.) 1991 (divorced 2001); ed McCallie School, Brown Univ.; Gen. Man. Turner Advertising, Macon, Ga 1960–63; Pres. and CEO various Turner cos., Atlanta 1963–70; Chair. Bd and Pres. Turner Broadcasting System (TBS) Inc. 1970–96, est. Cable News Network (CNN) 1980, Headline News Network 1992, CNN Int. 1985, acquired MGM library of film and TV properties 1986, launched Cartoon Network 1992; TBS merged with New Line Cinema 1994; Vice-Chair. Time Warner Inc. (after TBS merger with Time Warner Inc.) 1996–2001, Vice-Chair. AOL Time Warner (after Time Warner Inc. merger with AOL) 2001–03, mem. Bd of Dirs –2006; f. Ted Turner Pictures and Ted Turner Documentaries (film production cos) 2001; f. Ted's Montana Grill restuarant chain 2002; fmr owner and Pres. Atlanta Braves professional baseball team, fmr owner and Chair. Bd Atlanta Hawks professional basketball team; Chair. Better World Soc., Wash., DC 1985–90; f. Turner Foundation, Inc. 1991, UN Foundation 1997, Nuclear Threat Initiative 2001; Dir Martin Luther King Center, Atlanta; sponsor, creator, The Goodwill Games 1985; Man of the Year, Time Magazine 1991, Cable and Broadcasting's Man of the Century 1999, Cable TV Hall of Fame 1999, U Thant Peace Award 1999, World Ecology Award (Univ. of Missouri) 2000, named Yachtsman of Year four times, Fastnet Trophy 1979, Delta Air Lines Prize for Global Understanding (administered by Univ. of Georgia) 2006, Bower Award for Business Leadership, Franklin Inst. 2006. *Yachting achievements include:* successful defense of 1977 America's Cup in yacht Courageous. *Publication:* The Racing Edge 1979. *Leisure interests:* fishing, sailing. *Address:* c/o Ted's Montana Grill, 133 Luckie Street NW, Atlanta, GA 30303, USA (office). *Telephone:* (404) 266-1344 (office). *Fax:* (404) 233-6717 (office). *Website:* www.tedturner.com (office).

TURNER, Tina; American singer and songwriter; b. (Annie Mae Bullock), 26 Nov. 1939, Brownsville, Tenn.; m. Ike Turner 1956 (divorced 1978); four s.; singer with Ike Turner Kings of Rhythm, Ike and Tina Turner Revue 1958–78; numerous concert tours worldwide; solo artist 1978–; Grammy Awards include for Record of the Year, Song of the Year, Best Female Vocal Performance, Best Female Rock Vocal, MTV Music Video Award 1985, American Music Awards for Favorite Soul/R&B Female Artist, for Best Video Artist 1985, for Best Female Pop/Rock Artist 1986, World Music Award for Outstanding Contribution to the Music Industry 1993, Chevalier, Ordre des Arts et des Lettres, Kennedy Center Honor 2005. *Films:* Gimme Shelter 1970, Soul to Soul 1971, Tommy 1975, Mad Max: Beyond Thunderdome 1985, What's Love Got to Do with It (vocals) 1993, Last Action Hero 1993. *Recordings include:* albums: with Ike Turner: River Deep, Mountain High 1966, Outa Season 1969, The Hunter 1969, Proud Mary 1970, Come Together 1970, Workin' Together 1971, 'Nuff Said 1971, Blues Roots 1972, Feel Good 1972, Nutbush City Limits 1974, The Gospel According to Ike and Tina 1974; solo: Let Me Touch Your Mind 1972, Tina Turns the Country On 1974, Acid Queen 1975, Rough 1978, Private Dancer 1984, Break Every Rule 1986, Foreign Affair 1989, Wildest Dreams 1996, Dues Paid 1999, Twenty Four Seven 1999. *Publication:* I, Tina (autobiog.) 1985. *Address:* RD Worldwide Management, 1158 26th Street, Suite 564, Santa Monica, CA 90403 (office); CAA, 9830 Wilshire Boulevard, Beverly Hills, CA 90212, USA (office). *Website:* www.officialtina.com.

TURNER, William Cochrane, BS; American diplomatist and business executive; b. 27 May 1929, Red Oak, Iowa; s. of James Lyman Turner and Josephine Cochrane Turner; m. Cynthia Dunbar 1955; two s.; ed Northwestern Univ.; Vice-Pres. and Dir, Western Man. Consultants Inc. 1955–60, Pres., CEO and Dir 1960–74, Chair. and Dir Western Man. Consultants Europe SA 1969–74; Dir Ryan-Evans Drug Stores Inc. 1964–68, First Nat. Bank of Arizona 1970–74; Trustee Thunderbird American Graduate School of Int. Man. 1972–, Vice-Chair. 1972–86, Chair. 1986–88; mem. Advisory Cttee for Trade Negotiations 1982–84; Amb. and US Rep. to OECD 1974–77; mem. US Advisory Comm. on Int. Educ. and Cultural Affairs 1969–74, Nat. Review Bd, Center for Cultural and Tech. Interchange between East and West 1970–74, Western Int. Trade Group, US Dept of Commerce 1972–74; Pres. and Dir Phoenix Symphony Asscn 1957–72; Gov. Atlantic Inst. for Int. Affairs, Paris 1977–88, Joseph H. Lauder Inst. of Man. and Int. Studies, Univ. of Pa 1983–2001; Chair. and CEO Argyle Atlantic Corpn 1977–, Avon Int. Advisory Council, Avon Products Inc. 1985–98, Int. Advisory Council, Plasma Tech. Inc. 1992–97; Chair Bd GO Wireless Int. Ltd 1995–97; Chair. European Advisory Council, Asia Pacific Advisory Council, AT&T Int. 1981–88; Dir Pullman Inc. 1977–80, Nabisco Brands Inc. 1977–85, Goodyear Tire and Rubber Co. 1978–2001, Salomon Inc. 1980–93, Energy Transition Corpn (also Vice-Chair.) 1979–86, The Atlantic Council of the US 1977–92, AT&T Int. 1980–84, Swensen's Inc. 1981–84, Atlantic Inst. Foundation Inc. 1984–90, Rural/Metro Corpn 1993–, Microtest Inc. 1995–2001; mem. IBM European Advisory Council 1977–80, Gen. Electric of Brazil Advisory Council 1979–81, Caterpillar of Brazil Advisory Council 1979–84, American Asia Pacific Advisory Council 1981–85, Caterpillar Tractor Co. Asia Pacific Advisory Council 1984–90, Spencer Stuart Advisory Council 1984–90; mem. European Community-US Business Council, Washington, DC 1978–79, Advisory Bd Center for Strategic and Int. Studies, Georgetown Univ. 1978–81, Nat. Councils, The Salk Inst. 1978–82, Council of American Ambs 1984–, Council on Foreign Relations 1980–2002, US-Japan Business Council 1987–93, Nat. Advisory Council on Business Educ., Council on Int. Educ. Exchange, New York City 1987–2000, Trade and Environment Cttee Nat. Advisory Council for Environmental Policy and Tech., US Environmental Protection Agency, Washington, DC 1991–95, Gov.'s Strategic Partnership for Econ. Devt, Phoenix 1992–95; Chair. and mem. ASM Int. Advisory Council, Advanced Semiconductor Materials Int. NV, Bilthoven 1985-88; Trustee and mem. Exec. Cttee, US Council for Int. Business 1977–, Heard Museum, Phoenix 1983–85 (mem. Nat. Advisory Bd 1985–93); Nat. Trustee, Nat. Symphony Orchestra Asscn 1973–84; mem. Bd of Govs American Hosp. of Paris 1974–77, Bd of Trustees, American School of Paris, St-Cloud 1975–77, Vestry, American Cathedral, Paris 1976–77, Greater Phoenix Leadership 1979–97; Co-Chair. Int. Advisory Bd, Univ. of Nations 1985–; Dir and fmr Founding Chair. Bd of Dirs Mercy Ships Int., A Ministry of Youth with a Mission, Lindale, Tex. 1986–2000; Dir Ariz. Econ. Council, Phoenix 1989–93, mem. Nat. Council, World Wildlife Fund and The Conservation Foundation, Washington, DC 1989–95; f. mem. Pacific Council on Int. Policy 1995–; Chair. and Dir WorldWideTalk Inc. 1999–; Chair. Advisory Bd Arris Ventures 2001–, One Touch 2002–, Significant Ventures Inc. 2002–; East-West Center Distinguished Service Award 1977; Hon. LLD (Thunderbird American Grad. School of Int. Man.) 1993. *Leisure interests:* tennis, fly fishing, opera, symphonic and chamber music, international political and economic relations. *Address:* 5434 East Lincoln Drive, No. 74, Paradise Valley, AZ 85253, USA. *Telephone:* (480) 998-1890. *Fax:* (480) 948-4674. *E-mail:* wct-aac@mindspring.com (office).

TURNER-WARWICK, Dame Margaret, DBE, BCh, MA, DM, PhD, FRCP, FMedSci, FRCPE, FRACP, FFPHM, FACP, FRSM, FRCS; British consultant physician; b. 19 Nov. 1924, London; d. of William Harvey Moore, QC and Maude Baden-Powell; m. Richard Turner-Warwick 1950; two d.; ed Maynard School, Exeter, St Paul's School for Girls, Univ. of Oxford and Univ. Coll. Hosp.; consultant physician, Royal Brompton Hosp., London Chest Hosp. 1965–72; Prof. of Medicine, Cardiothoracic Inst. 1972–87, Dean 1984–87; Pres. Royal Coll. of Physicians 1989–92; Emer. Prof. of Medicine, London Univ.; Chair. Royal Devon & Exeter Health Care NHS Trust; Fellow Univ. Coll. London 1991; Fellow Royal Coll. of General Practitioners, Faculty of Occupational Medicine, Royal Coll. of Physicians Canada, Royal Coll. of Pathologists, Royal Coll. of Physicians Ireland, Royal Coll. of Physicians and Surgeons (Canada) and others; Founder-mem. Nuffield Bioethics Council, Round Table on Sustainable Devt; Hon. Bencher, Middle Temple; Hon. Fellow Lady Margaret Hall, Oxford, Green Coll., Oxford, Girton Coll., Cambridge, Imperial Coll., London, Univ. Coll., London; Hon. DSc (New York, Sussex, Hull, Exeter, London, Oxford, Cambridge, Leicester); numerous other honours including Osler Medal, Oxford Univ. and President's Medal, British Thoracic Soc. and European Respiratory Soc. *Publications:* Immunology of the Lung 1978, Occupational Lung Disease (jtly) 1981; chapters in textbooks and articles in medical journals on asthma, fibrosing connective tissue disorders and occupational lung diseases. *Leisure interests:* gardening, watercolour painting, violin playing, country life and family. *Address:* Pynes House, Thorverton, Exeter, EX5 5LT, Devon, England (home). *Telephone:* (1392) 861173 (home). *Fax:* (1392) 860940 (home).

TURNQUEST, Orville A. T. (Tommy); Bahamian politician; *Minister of National Security and Immigration;* b. 16 Nov. 1959, Nassau; s. of Sir Orville Turnquist (fmr Gov.-Gen.) and Lady Edith Turnquist; m. Shawn Carey; two s. one d.; ed St Anne's School, Nassau, Malvern Coll., UK and Univ. of Western Ont., Canada; began career with Canadian Imperial Bank of Commerce; mem. Free Nat. Movt (FNM) 1985–, fmr Vice-Pres., Leader 2002–05; mem. Parl. 1992–2002, 2007–; Parl. Sec., Office of the Prime Minister 1992–95; Minister of State for Public Service and Labour 1995–96, for Public Works 1996–97; Minister of Works 1997–98, of Public Service, Immigration and Nat. Insurance 1998–2000, of Tourism 2000–02, of Nat. Security and Immigration 2007–. *Address:* Ministry of National Security and Immigration, Churchill Building, 3rd Floor, PO Box N-3217, Nassau, The Bahamas (office). *Telephone:* 356-6792 (office). *Fax:* 356-6087 (office). *E-mail:* psmns@hotmail.com (office); tommyt@tommyturnquest.org. *Website:* www.tommyturnquest.org.

TURNQUEST, Sir Orville (Alton), GCMG, QC, LLB, JP; Bahamian politician, lawyer and judge; b. 19 July 1929, Grants Town, New Providence; s. of the late Robert Turnquest and Gwendolyn Turnquest; m. Edith Louise Thompson 1955; one s. two d.; ed Govt High School, Univ. of London, Lincoln's Inn, London; articled in chambers of Hon. A. F. Adderley 1947–53; called to The Bahamas Bar 1953, to English Bar (Lincoln's Inn) 1960; Counsel and Attorney of Supreme Court of Bahamas; Notary Public; in pvt. practice 1953–92; stipendiary and circuit magistrate and coroner 1959; law tutor and mem. Examining Bd, The Bahamas Bar 1965–92; Pres-Bahamas Bar Asscn; Chair. Bahamas Bar Council 1970–72; Sec.-Gen. Progressive Liberal Party 1960–62; MP for S Cen. Nassau 1962–67, for Montagu 1982–94; Opposition Leader in Senate 1972–79; Deputy Leader Free Nat. Movt 1987–94; Attorney-Gen. 1992–94, Minister of Justice 1992–93, of Foreign Affairs 1992–94, Deputy Prime Minister 1993–94, currently Leader; Gov.-Gen. The Bahamas

1995–2001; mem. Del. to first Bahamas Constitutional Conf., London 1963, Bahamas Independence Conf., London 1972; Pres. Commonwealth Parl. Asscn 1992–93; Patron The Bahamas Games; Chancellor of Diocese of Nassau and The Bahamas 1965–2002; mem. Anglican Cen. Educational Authority, Nat. Cttee of United World Colls, Bd of Govs St John's Coll., St Anne's High School; fmr mem. Prov. Synod, Anglican Church of West Indies; Life mem. Rotary Int., Salvation Army Advisory Bd; Hon. LLD (Elmira Coll. NY, USA) 1998, (Univ. of West Indies) 2000; Hon. LHD (Sojourner-Douglass Coll., USA) 2002; Hon. Bencher, Lincoln's Inn; President's Assocs (Nova Southeastern Univ. Fla USA). *Leisure interests:* tennis, swimming, music, reading. *Address:* Free National Movement (FNM), POB N-10713, Nassau (office); Library House, Dowdeswell Street, POB N-8181, Nassau, Bahamas (office); Kalamalka, Skyline Drive, POB N-682, Nassau, Bahamas (home). *Telephone:* (242) 3937863 (office); (242) 3232942 (office); (242) 3277951 (home). *Fax:* (242) 3282222 (office); (242) 3274994 (home). *E-mail:* oatchambers@batelnet.bs (office).

TUROK, Neil Geoffrey, PhD; South African/British physicist and academic; *Director, Perimeter Institute for Theoretical Physics;* b. 1958, Johannesburg, S Africa; s. of Ben Turock and Mary Turok; ed Churchill Coll., Univ. of Cambridge, Imperial Coll., London; fmr Assoc. Scientist, Fermilab, Chicago; Prof. of Physics, Princeton Univ. 1994–97; Chair. of Math. Physics, Univ. of Cambridge 1997–2008; f. African Inst. for Math. Sciences, Muizenberg 2003; Dir Perimeter Inst. for Theoretical Physics (ind. research inst.), Canada 2008–; Maxwell Medal, Inst. of Physics 1992, Most Innovative People Award for Social Innovation, World Summit on Innovation and Entrepreneurship 2008, TED (Tech., Entertainment, Design Conf.) Prize 2008. *Publications:* Global Texture 1999, Structure Formation in the Universe (co-author) 2001, Endless Universe: Beyond the Big Bang (co-author) 2007. *Address:* Perimeter Institute for Theoretical Physics, 31 Caroline Street, North Waterloo, ON N2L 2Y5, Canada (office). *Telephone:* (519) 569-7000 (office). *Fax:* (519) 569-7611 (office). *Website:* www.perimeterinstitute.ca (office).

TUROW, Scott F., JD; American writer and lawyer; b. 12 April 1949; s. of David Turow and Rita Pastron; ed Amherst Coll. and Stanford and Harvard Univs; mem. Bar, Ill. 1978, US Dist Court. Ill. 1978, US Court of Appeals (7th Circuit) 1979; Assoc. Suffolk Co. Dist Attorney, Boston 1977–78; Asst US Attorney, US Dist Court, Ill., Chicago 1978–86; partner Sonnenschein, Nath & Rosenthal, Chicago 1986–; mem. Chicago Council of Lawyers. *Publications:* One L.: An Inside Account of Life in the First Year at Harvard Law School 1977, Presumed Innocent 1987, The Burden of Proof 1990, Pleading Guilty 1993, The Laws of our Fathers 1996, Personal Injuries 1999, Reversible Errors 2002, Ultimate Punishment: A Lawyer's Reflections on Dealing with the Death Penalty 2003, Ordinary Heroes 2006, The Best American Mystery Stories (ed.) 2006, Limitations 2007; contribs to professional journals. *Address:* Sonnenschein, Nath & Rosenthal, Sears Tower, Suite 8000, 233 South Wacker Drive, Chicago, IL 60606, USA (office). *Website:* www.scottturow.com.

TURRO, Nicholas John, PhD; American scientist and academic; *William P. Schweitzer Professor of Chemistry, Columbia University;* b. 18 May 1938, Middletown, Conn.; s. of Nicholas J. Turro and Philomena Russo; m. Sandra J. Misenti 1960; two d.; ed Wesleyan Univ., California Inst. of Tech., Harvard Univ.; Instructor Columbia Univ. 1964–65, Asst Prof. 1965–67, Assoc. Prof. 1967–69, Prof. of Chem. 1969–82, William P. Schweitzer Prof. of Chem. 1982–, Chair. Dept of Chem. 1981–84, Co-Chair. Dept of Chemical Eng and Applied Chem. 1997–2000; Prof. of Earth and Environment Eng 1998–; Sloan Fellowship 1966–70; Guggenheim Fellowship, Univ. of Oxford 1984–85; mem. NAS, American Acad. of Arts and Sciences; Fellow, New York Acad. of Science; Hon. DSc (Wesleyan Univ.) 1984, (Univ. of Fribourg) 2004; several awards and distinctions including Gibbs Medal Award 2000, Pimental Award of ACS for Chemical Education 2004. *Publications:* Molecular Photochemistry 1965, Modern Molecular Photochemistry 1978. *Leisure interests:* racquet ball, music, reading. *Address:* Department of Chemistry, Columbia University, 3000 Broadway, New York, NY 10027 (office); 125 Downey Drive, Tenafly, NJ 07670, USA (home). *Telephone:* (212) 854-2175 (office). *Fax:* (212) 932-1289 (office). *Website:* wwwapp.cc.columbia.edu/sws/cucms/chem/build/fac-bios/turro/group/index.html (office).

TURTURRO, John; American actor and film director; b. 28 Feb. 1957, Brooklyn; s. of Nicholas Turturro and Katherine Turturro; m. Katherine Borowitz; one s.; ed State Univ. of New York at New Paltz and Yale Drama School; fmr labourer; Best Actor Award, Cannes Film Festival, for role in Barton Fink 1991; Obie Award for stage appearance in Danny and the Deep Blue Sea. *Films include:* Raging Bull, Desperately Seeking Susan, Exterminator III, The Flamingo Kid, To Live and Die in LA, Hannah and Her Sisters, Gung Ho, Offbeat, The Color of Money, The Italian Five Corners, Do the Right Thing, Miller's Crossing, Men of Respect, Mo' Better Blues, Jungle Fever, Barton Fink, Brain Doctors, Mac (co-author, dir and actor), Being Human, Quiz Show, Fearless, Clockers, Search and Destroy, Unstrung Heroes, Sugartime (dir), Grace of My Heart (dir), Box of Moonlight (dir), The Truce (dir), The Big Lebowski 1997, Animals 1997, Lesser Prophets 1998, Rounders 1998, Illuminata (dir) 1998, The Source 1999, The Cradle Will Rock 1999, Company Man 1999, Two Thousand and None 1999, Oh Brother, Where Art Thou? 1999, The Man Who Cried 1999, The Luzhin Defense 1999, Thirteen Conversations About One Thing (dir) 2000, Collateral Damage (dir) 2001, Mr Deeds 2002, Fear X 2003, Anger Management 2003, 2BPerfectlyHonest 2004, Secret Passage 2004, Secret Window 2004, She Hate Me 2004, Romance and Cigarettes (dir) 2005, Quelques jours en septembre 2006, The Good Shepherd 2006, Slipstream 2007, Transformers 2007, Margot at the Wedding 2007, You Don't Mess with the Zohan 2008, What Just Happened? 2008, Miracle at St. Anna 2008. *Television includes:* The Bronx Is Burning 2007. *Address:* c/o Bart Walker, Creative Artists Agency LLC, 162 5th Avenue, 6th Floor, New York, NY 10010; 16 North Oak Street, 2A Ventura, CA 93001, USA. *Telephone:* (212) 277-9000 (CAA).

TUSA, Sir John, Kt, MA,; British broadcaster and administrator; b. 2 March 1936, Zlín, Czechoslovakia (now Czech Repub.); s. of Jan Tusa and Lydie Sklenarova; m. Ann Hilary Dowson 1960; two s.; ed Gresham's School, Holt, Trinity Coll., Cambridge; joined BBC as general trainee 1960; Producer, Talks and Features, BBC World Service 1964–66; Ed., Forum World Features 1966–67; Presenter, The World Tonight, Radio 4 1970–78, 24 Hours, BBC World Service 1972–78, Newsweek, BBC2 1978–79, Newsnight, BBC2 1979–86, Timewatch, BBC2 1982–84, One O'Clock News BBC 1993–95; Chair. London News Radio 1993–94; Pres. Wolfson Coll., Cambridge Feb.–Oct. 1993; Man. Dir BBC World Service 1986–92; Man. Dir Barbican Centre 1995–2007; Chair. Advisory Cttee, Govt Art Collection 1993–2003, BBC Marshall Plan of the Mind Trust 1992–99; mem. Bd ENO 1994–2005; Freeman, City of London 1997; Trustee, Nat. Portrait Gallery 1988–2000, Design Museum 1998–2000; Vice-Chair. British Museum 2000–; Chair. Wigmore Hall Trust 1999–, Univ. of the Arts, London 2007–, Architecture Club 2007–; Visiting Prof., Dept of Arts Policy and Man., City Univ.; Hon. mem. RAM 1999, Guildhall School of Music and Drama 1999; Order of the White Rose (Finland) 1998; Dr hc (Heriot-Watt) 1993, (Kingston) 2007; Hon. LLD (London) 1993; Hon. DLitt (City Univ.) 1997, (Essex) 2006; Royal TV Soc. (RTS) TV Journalist of the Year 1984, BAFTA Richard Dimbleby Award 1984, Broadcasting Press Guild Award 1991, RTS Presenter of the Year 1995, Broadcasting Press Guild Radio Programme of the Year (for 20/20 – A View of the Century) 1995. *Publications:* The Nuremberg Trial (with Ann Tusa) 1983, The Berlin Blockade (with Ann Tusa) 1988, Conversations with the World 1990, A World in Your Ear 1992, Art Matters 1999, On Creativity 2003, The Janus Aspect: Artists in the 21st Century 2005, Engaged with the Arts: Writings from the Frontline 2007. *Leisure interests:* tennis, string quartets, listening. *Address:* University of the Arts London, 65 Davies Street, London, W1K 5DA, England (office). *E-mail:* jtusa@arts.ac.uk (office). *Website:* www.arts.ac.uk (office).

TUSCHL, Thomas, PhD; German biochemist, molecular biologist and academic; *Associate Professor and Head of Laboratory, The Rockefeller University;* b. 1 June 1966, Altdorf bei Nürnberg; ed Univ. of Regensburg, Max Planck Inst. for Experimental Medicine, Göttingen; Jr Investigator, Max Planck Inst. for Biophysical Chem. 1999–2003; fmr Researcher, Biology Dept, Whitehead Inst. for Biomedical Research, MIT 1995–99; Assoc. Prof. and Head of Lab., Rockefeller Univ. 2003–; Howard Hughes Medical Inst. Investigator; Fellow, New York Acad. of Sciences 2005; Biofuture Award (German Govt) 1999, Young Investigator Award, European Molecular Biology Org. 2001, Otto Klung Weberbank Prize for Chem. and Physics, Berlin 2002, Eppendorf Young Investigator Award, Hamburg 2002, Wiley Prize in Biomedical Sciences 2003, Mayor's Award for Excellence in Science and Tech. 2003, AAAS Newcomb Cleveland Prize 2003, Ernst Schering Prize (for basic scientific research) 2005, Meyenburg Prize 2005, Irma T. Hirschl Career Scientist Award 2005, Dr Albert Wander Gedenk Prize, Bern 2005 Molecular Bioanalytics Prize 2006, Max Delbrück Medal, Berlin 2007. *Publications:* numerous scientific papers in professional journals on studies of RNA interference. *Address:* Howard Hughes Medical Institute Laboratory of RNA, Molecular Biology, The Rockefeller University, 1230 York Avenue, Box 186, New York, NY 10065, USA (office). *Telephone:* (212) 327-7651 (ext. 7651) (office). *Fax:* (212) 327-7652 (office). *E-mail:* ttuschl@rockefeller.edu (office). *Website:* www.rockefeller.edu/labheads/tuschl (office).

TUSK, Donald Franciszek; Polish politician; *Prime Minister;* b. 22 April 1957, Gdańsk; m.; one s. one d.; ed Gdańsk Univ.; journalist Maritime Publishing House, with magazines Pomerania and Samorządność; with Gdańsk Height Services Work Co-operative; Deputy ed. Gazeta Gdańska 1989; mem. Liquidation Cttee RSW Press-Books-Ruch; assoc. Free Trade Unions by the Coast; co.-f. Independent Students Union (NZS); mem. Solidarity Trade Union 1980–89; Founder and Ed. underground Publ Przegląd Polityczny; Leader Programme Council for Liberals Foundation; Leader Congress of Liberals 1989, later the Liberal-Democratic Congress (Kongres Liberalno-Demokratyczny—KLD), Chair. 1991–94; Vice-Chair. Freedom Union (Unia Wolnosci—UW) 1994 following the merger with Democratic Union (UD); Deputy to Sejm (Parl.) (Gdynia/Słupsk constituency) 1991–93, 2001–, Deputy Marshal of Sejm 2001–, mem. Civic Platform Parl. Caucus 2001–; Chair. Parl. Liberal-Democratic Caucus and Special Cttee for Consideration of Constitutional Acts 1991–93; Senator (Gdańsk Voivodship) and Vice-Marshal of Senate 1997–2001; Co-Founder Civic Platform (Platforma Obywatelska—PO) 2001, Leader 2005–; Prime Minister 2007–; unsuccessful cand. in presidential elections 2006; Silver Mouth Award, Radio Three (Sweden) 2004. *Publications:* Kashubian Lake District 1985, Once There Was Gdańsk 1996, Gdańsk 1945, 1998, Old Sopot 1998, Ideas of Gdańsk's Liberalism 1998. *Leisure interests:* football, old photography. *Address:* Chancellery of the Prime Minister, 00-583 Warsaw, Al. Ujazdowskie 1/3 (office); Civic Platform (Platforma Obywatelska), 00-159 Warsaw, ul. Andersa 21, Poland (office). *Telephone:* (22) 8413832 (Prime Minister's Office) (office); (22) 6357879 (Civic Platform) (office). *Fax:* (22) 6284821 (Prime Minister's Office) (office); (22) 6357641 (Civic Platform) (office). *E-mail:* cirinfo@kprm.gov.pl (office); poczta@platforma.org (office). *Website:* www.kprm.gov.pl (office); www.platforma.org (office).

TUSQUETS BLANCA, Oscar; Spanish architect and designer; b. 14 June 1941, Barcelona; m. Eva Blanch; one s. one d.; ed Arts & Crafts School, Barcelona, School of Architecture, Barcelona; with Luis Clotet, Studio Per 1964–84; Co-Founder BD Ediciones de Diseño 1972; Prof., School of Architecture, Barcelona 1975–76, 1979–80; f. Tusquets, Diaz & Assoc. Architects'

Office, with Carlos Diaz 1987; Chevalier des Arts et des Lettres; FAD Architecture Prize (five times), FAD Design prize (six times), Sant Jordi Cross 1987, Ciutat de Barcelona Prize 1988, 1989, Nat. Prize for Design 1988, Fukuoka Beautification Award 1994, Medalla de Oro 1998. *Work includes:* Casa Fullá, Barcelona, Belvedere Regas, Girona, Casa Vittoria, Sala Mae West, Dali Museum, Figueras, remodelling of Music Palace, Barcelona, Pavilion, Parc de la Villette, Paris, Chandon Vinery, Barcelona, dwellings in Kashii, Fukuoka and in Olympic Village, Barcelona, La Coupole, Montpellier, music auditorium, Canary Islands, public square, shopping mall and dwellings, Den Bosch, Netherlands; design of furniture and objects for various producers, bus stop for Hanover, Germany. *Leisure interest:* painting. *Address:* Arquitecturas Oscar Tusquets Blanca, Cavallers 50, 08034 Barcelona, Spain (office). *Telephone:* (93) 2065580 (office). *Fax:* (93) 2804071 (office). *E-mail:* tusquets@tda.es (office). *Website:* www.tusquets.com (office).

TUTKUS, Lt Gen. Valdas; Lithuanian military officer; *Chief of Defence, Armed Forces;* b. 27 Dec. 1960, Vilnius; m.; one s.; ed Frunze Mil. Acad., NATO Defence Coll., Rome; Second Lt Motorised Infantry Battalion 1982; served in Afghanistan 1983–85; promoted to First Lt 1984; Founding mem. Lithuanian Armed Forces 1991; Chief of Jt Staff, Ministry of Defence 1992–94; First Deputy Commdr, Armed Forces 1994–96, Deputy Commdr 1996–99; Mil. Rep. to NATO, Brussels, to EU, to WEU 1999–2001; Commdr Land Forces 2001–04; Chief of Defence 2004–; Officer Order of Vytautas the Great; Commemorative Badge to mark Russian Troops Withdrawal from Lithuania, Honour Award for Merits to Nat. Defence System, Honour Award Iron Wolf, Nat. Defence System Level Medal of Merit, Nat. Defence Minister's Letters of Merit. *Address:* Ministry of National Defence, Totorių 25/3, Vilnius 01121, Lithuania (office). *Telephone:* (5) 278-50001 (office). *Fax:* (5) 212-6082 (office). *E-mail:* vis@kam.lt (office). *Website:* www.kam.lt (office).

TUTT, Leo Edward, FCA, FAIM, FCPA, FAICD; Australian business executive; *Chairman, Promina Group Ltd.;* b. 6 April 1938, Sydney; s. of Leo Edward Tutt and Dorothy Tutt; m. Heather Coombe 1961; two s. one d.; ed Knox Grammar School, Univ. of Sydney and Inst. of Chartered Accountants, Australia; CA 1966–71; Man. Dir Tutt Bryant Ltd 1971–74; CEO Bowater Industries Australia Ltd 1974–96; Chair. Royal and Sun Alliance Insurance Australia Ltd 1994, Promina Group 1996–, MIM Holdings Ltd (Australia) 1998–2003 (Dir 1991–2003), Pirelli Telecom Cables and Systems Australia Ltd 1999–, ITG Ltd 2001–; mem. Bd of Dirs Phoenix Assurance Co. Australia 1974–82, Rexam PLC (fmrly Bowater PLC) 1978–96, Friends Provident 1984–94, Grad. School of Man., Univ. of Sydney 1989–, Australian Grad. School of Man. 1999–, State Rail Authority of NSW 1989–94, Metway Bank Ltd (Australia) 1992–96, Crane Group Ltd 2001– (now Chair.); Hon. Fellow Univ. of Sydney 1996. *Leisure interests:* sailing, golf, reading. *Address:* Promina Group Ltd., 465 Victoria Avenue, Chatswood, NSW 2067 (office); 58 Prince Alfred Parade, Newport, NSW 2106, Australia. *Telephone:* (2) 8275-3998 (office); (2) 9979-5744 (home). *Fax:* (2) 9235-2585 (office); (2) 8275-3104 (office); (2) 9997-3119 (home). *E-mail:* leo_tutt@promina.com.au (office). *Website:* www.promina.com.au.

TUTTLE, Robert Holmes, MBA; American diplomatist and business executive; *Ambassador to UK;* m. Maria Hummer; two d.; ed Stanford Univ., Univ. of Southern Calif.; Asst to Pres. Reagan 1982–85, Dir of Presidential Personnel 1985–89; Co-Man. Pnr Tuttle-Click Automotive Group; Amb. to UK 2005–; fmr mem. Bd Woodrow Wilson Int. Center for Scholars, Ronald Reagan Presidential Library Foundation, Annenberg School of Communication, Univ. of Southern Calif., Los Angeles Museum of Contemporary Art (Chair. 2001–04). *Address:* Embassy of the United States, 24 Grosvenor Square, London, W1A 1AE, England (office). *Telephone:* (20) 7499-9000 (office). *Website:* www.usembassy.org.uk (office); london.usembassy.gov (office).

TUTU, Most Rev. Desmond Mpilo, MTh; South African ecclesiastic (retd) and academic; b. 7 Oct. 1931, Klerksdorp; s. of Zachariah Tutu and Aletta Tutu; m. Leah Nomalizo Tutu 1955; one s. three d.; ed Bantu High School, Bantu Normal Coll., Univ. of South Africa, St Peter's Theological Coll., Rosettenville, King's Coll., Univ. of London; schoolmaster 1954–57; parish priest 1960; Theological Seminary Lecturer 1967–69; Univ. Lecturer 1970–71; Assoc. Dir Theological Educ. Fund, World Council of Churches 1972–75; Dean of Johannesburg 1975–76; Bishop of Lesotho 1977–78, of Johannesburg 1984–86; Archbishop of Cape Town, Metropolitan of the Church of the Prov. of Southern Africa 1986–95, Archbishop Emer. 1995–; Chancellor Univ. of Western Cape 1988–; Chair. Truth and Reconciliation Comm. 1995–99; Pres. All Africa Conf. of Churches 1987–97; Sec.-Gen. South African Council of Churches 1979–84; Visiting Prof. of Anglican Studies, New York Gen. Theological Seminary 1984; elected to Harvard Univ. Bd of Overseers 1989; Dir Coca-Cola 1986–; Visiting Prof., Emory Univ., Atlanta 1998–2000; Visiting Prof. in Post-Conflict Studies, King's Coll., London 2004–; f. Desmond Tutu Peace Centre, Cape Town, supported by Desmond Tutu Peace Trust; mem. Third Order of the Soc. of St Francis; Freedom of Borough of Merthyr Tydfil (Wales), Durham, Hull, Borough of Lewisham (UK), Florence, Lecco (Italy), Kinshasa (Democratic Repub. of Congo), Krugersdorp, Cape Town (SA); Order of Jamaica; Hon. DD, DCL, LLD, ThD (Gen. Theol. Sem. New York, Kent Univ., Harvard Univ., Ruhr Bochum Univ.); Hon. DDiv (Aberdeen) 1981; Hon. STD (Columbia) 1982; Dr hc (Mount Allison Univ., Sackville, NB, Strasbourg) 1988, (Oxford) 1990; Hon. LLD (South Bank Univ.) 1994; Hon. DD (Exeter) 1997; FKC (Fellow of King's Coll. London); numerous awards including Onassis Award, Family of Man Gold Medal 1983, Nobel Peace Prize 1984, Carter-Menil Human Rights Prize 1986, Martin Luther King Jr Humanitarian Award 1986, Third World Prize (jt recipient) 1989, Grand Cross of Merit, Germany 1996, Bill of Rights Award, American Civil Liberation Union Fund 1997, Henry W. Edgerton Civil Liberties Award, American Civil Liberties Union 1997, One Hundred Black Men Award, USA 1997, Peace Prize, Int. Community of UNESCO, Athens 1997, Gandhi Peace Prize 2007. *Publications:* Crying in the Wilderness 1982, Hope and Suffering 1983 (both collections of sermons and addresses), The Rainbow People of God 1994, An African Prayer Book 1996, No Future Without Forgiveness 1999. *Leisure interests* reading, music, jogging. *Address:* c/o Desmond Tutu Peace Trust, PO Box 8428, Roggebaai, 8012 Cape Town, South Africa. *Telephone:* (21) 4257002. *Fax:* (21) 4189468. *E-mail:* info@tutu.org. *Website:* www.tutu.org.

TUWAIJRI, Abdulrahman at-, PhD; Saudi Arabian economist; *Secretary-General, Supreme Economic Council;* b. 23 Feb. 1955, Almajmaah; s. of Abdulaziz Al-Tuwaijri and Hussah Al-Tuwaijri; m. Norah Alabdulatif 1982; three s. two d.; ed King Saud Univ. and Iowa State Univ., USA; grad. asst Dept of Econs, King Saud Univ. 1978–84, Asst Prof. 1985–88; Econ. Adviser Gen. Secr. Cooperation Council for the Arab States of the Gulf 1988–90; Alt. Exec. Dir IMF 1991–95, Exec. Dir 1995–2001; Sec.-Gen., Supreme Econ. Council 2002–. *Leisure interests:* reading, swimming. *Address:* c/o Ministry of Finance and National Economy, Airport Road, Riyadh 11177, Saudi Arabia. *Telephone:* (1) 405-0000. *Fax:* (1) 401-0583.

TUYAA, Nyam-Osoryn, MA; Mongolian politician; b. 1958, Ulan Bator; m.; two s. one d.; ed Moscow State Inst. of Int. Relations, Univ. of Sorbonne, Univ. of Leeds; Ed., later Ed.-in-Chief Foreign Service Broadcasting Dept State Cttee for Radio, TV and Information 1980–90; researcher Strategic Studies Centre 1990–95; Sec. Elections Cttee Mongolian Nat. Democratic Party 1995–96; Head Policy Planning Dept, Ministry of External Relations 1996–98; Minister for External Relations 1998–2000. *Address:* c/o Ministry of External Relations, Government Building 6, Ulan Bator, Mongolia.

TUYAKBAI, Col-Gen. Zharmakhan Aitbaiuly, CandJur; Kazakhstani politician and jurist; *Leader, National Social-Democratic Party (Zhalpyulttyk Sotsial Demokratiyalyk Partiyasy);* b. 22 Nov. 1947; m. Bagilya Aptayeva; two s. one d.; ed Kirov Kazakh State Univ.; worked in prosecutors' bureau in S Kazakhstan –1978; Deputy Prosecutor-Gen. Kazakh SSR 1981; Prosecutor, Mangyshlak region, then Guryev region 1987–90; mem. Supreme Soviet, Repub. of Kazakhstan 1990; Prosecutor-Gen. Repub. of Kazakhstan 1990–95, Deputy Prosecutor-Gen., Chief Mil. Prosecutor 1997–99; Chair. State Investigation Comm. 1995–97; elected mem. Majlis (Parl.) 1999, Chair. 1999–2004; Leader, For a Just Kazakhstan Movt (Social Democrats) 2005–, Leader, Nat. Social Democratic Party, merged with Real Bright Road—Democratic Party of Kazakhstan (Naghyz Ak Zhol—Kazakstanyn Demokratiyalyk Partiyasy) 2007; unsuccessful presidential cand. 2005; Order of Barys 2001, Sodruzhestvo 2002. *Publications:* Development Prosecution in Kazakhstan in the Period of Reforms 1997; numerous articles. *Leisure Interests:* golf, reading. *Address:* National Social Democratic Party (Zhalpyulttyk Sotsial Demokratiyalyk Partiyasy), 050000 Almaty, Kabanbai batyr 58, Kazakhstan (office). *Telephone:* (727) 663-64-06 (office). *Fax:* (727) 266-36-43 (office). *E-mail:* ocdp@mail.ru (office). *Website:* (office).

TUYMANS, Luc; Belgian artist; b. 14 July 1958, Mortsel. *Address:* c/o Zeno X Gallery, Leopold de Waelplaats 16, 2000 Antwerp, Belgium. *E-mail:* info@zeno-x.com. *Website:* www.zeno-x.com.

TVRDÍK, Lt-Col Jaroslav, MSc(Econ); Czech politician and army officer; *Chairman and President, Czech Airlines (CSA);* b. 11 Sept. 1968, Prague; m. Blanka Tvrdíková; one d.; ed Mil. School, Vyškov; Head of Financial Services, Schooling and Training Centre, Ministry of Defence 1990–91, Commanding Sr Officer, Foreign Relations Section 1991–92, Head of Dept 1993–95, Dir Interior Admin. 1996, Deputy Minister of Defence 2000–01, Minister of Defence 2001–03; Dir Mil. Spa and recreations facilities 1996–2000; Chief, Financial Services, Czechoslovak contingent, UNPROFOR 1993–95; mem. Parl. 2002–03; Chair. Bd of Dirs and Pres. CSA (Ceske Aerolinie a.s.) 2003–; UN Medal for Activity in UNPROFOR 1992–93, Anniversary Medal of Honour, NATO 2002. *Publication:* Transformation of the Army 2001. *Leisure interests:* squash, swimming, historical literature. *Address:* c/o Dana Dvorakova, Ceske Aerolinie a.s., Prague Ruzynì Airport, 160 08 Prague 6, Czech Republic (office). *Telephone:* (2) 20116220 (office). *Fax:* (2) 20115397 (office). *E-mail:* dana.dvorakova@csa.cz (office). *Website:* www.csa.cz (office).

TWAIN, Shania; Canadian country singer and songwriter; b. (Eileen Regina Edwards), 28 Aug. 1965, Windsor, Ont.; d. of Gerry Twain and Sharon Twain; m. Robert John Lange 1993 (divorced); one s.; fmr cabaret singer; Country Music Television Europe Rising Video Star of the Year 1993, Female Artist of the Year 1996, Canadian Country Music Award for Female Vocalist 1995, American Music Awards for Favorite New Country Artist 1995, Favorite Female Pop/Rock Artist 2000, Favorite Female Country Artist 2000, Grammy Awards for Best Female Country Vocal Performance, Best Country Song 2000, Juno Award for Songwriter of the Year 2000, Best Country Female Artist 2000, Billboard Award for Top Country Artist 2003. *Recordings:* albums: Shania Twain 1993, The Woman in Me (Grammy Award for Best Country Album 1996) 1995, Come On Over 1997, On The Way 1999, Beginnings 1989–1990 1999, Wild and Wicked 2000, Complete Limelight Sessions 2001, Up! (Billboard Award for Top Country Album 2003) 2002, Greatest Hits 2004; singles: What Made You Say That 1993, Dance With The One That Brought You 1993, You Lay A Whole Lotta Love On Me 1993, Whose Bed Have Your Boots Been Under 1995, Any Man of Mine 1995, Woman In Me 1995, You Win My Love 1996, God Bless The Child 1996, I'm Outta Here 1996, Love Gets Me Every Time 1997, Don't Be Stupid 1997, You're Still The One 1998, From This Moment On 1998, When 1998, That Don't Impress Me Much 1998, Man I Feel Like A Woman 1999, You've Got A Way 1999, Don't Be Stupid (You Know I Love You) 2000, I'm Gonna Getcha Good 2002, Ka-Ching 2003, Up 2003, Forever & Always 2003, Thank You Baby For Making Someday Come So Soon

2003, When You Kiss Me 2003, Party For Two 2005. *Address:* Georgette Pascale, Shore Fire Media, 32 Court Street, Floor 16, Brooklyn, NY 11201, USA (office); c/o Mercury Nashville, 54 Music Square E, Nashville, TN 37203, USA. *Website:* www.shaniatwain.com.

TWEEDIE, Sir David Philip, Kt, BCom, PhD, CA, FRSE; British chartered accountant; *Chairman, International Accounting Standards Board;* b. 7 July 1944; s. of Aidrian Ian Tweedie and Marie Patricia Tweedie (née Phillips); m. Janice Christine Brown 1970; two s.; ed Grangemouth High School, Univ. of Edin.; accountancy training Mann, Judd, Gordon (Glasgow) 1969–72; Lecturer in Accounting, Univ. of Edin. 1973–78; Tech. Dir Inst. of Chartered Accountants, Scotland 1978–81; Pnr, KMG Thomson McLintock 1982–87, KPMG Peat Marwick McLintock 1987–90; Chair. Accounting Standards Bd 1990–2000, Int. Accounting Standards Bd 2001–; Hon. FIA 1999, Hon. FSIP 2004, Hon. FCCA 2005; Hon. DSc (Econ.) (Hull) 1993, Hon. LLD (Lancaster) 1993, (Exeter) 1997, (Dundee) 1998), Hon. DLitt (Heriot-Watt) 1996, Hon. DBA (Napier) 1999, (Oxford Brookes) 2004, Hon. DSc (SocSci) (Edinburgh) 2001; Founding Socs Award, Inst. of Chartered Accountants in England and Wales 1997, Chartered Inst. of Man. Accounting Award 1998. *Publications:* Financial Reporting, Inflation & The Capital Maintenance Concept 1979; co-author of three other books and contribs. to professional and academic journals. *Leisure interests:* athletics, watching rugby, walking, gardening. *Address:* International Accounting Standards Board, 1st Floor, 30 Cannon Street, London, EC4M 6XH, England (office). *Telephone:* (20) 7246-6480 (office). *Fax:* (20) 7246-6411 (office). *E-mail:* dtweedie@iasb.org.uk (office). *Website:* www.iasb.org.uk (office).

TWEGRI, Muhammad Ibrahim at-, PhD; Egyptian academic and international organization executive; *Assistant General Secretary for Economic Affairs, League of Arab States;* Dir-Gen. Arab Admin. Devt Org. (ARADO) –2007; Asst Gen. Sec. for Econ. Affairs, League of Arab States (Arab League) 2007–; Mem.-at-Large Int. Fed. of Training and Devt Orgs; mem. Preparatory Cttee Int. Conf. of Cyberlaw (ICCY) 2005. *Publications:* numerous papers in professional journals. *Address:* League of Arab States, PO Box 11642, Arab League Bldg, Tahrir Square, Cairo, Egypt (office). *Telephone:* (2) 575-0511 (office). *Fax:* (2) 574-0331 (office). *E-mail:* info@arableagueonline.org (office). *Website:* www.arableagueonline.org (office).

TWIGGY (see LAWSON, Lesley).

TWIN, Peter John, OBE, PhD, FRS; British physicist and academic; *Professor Emeritus of Experimental Physics, University of Liverpool;* b. 26 July 1939, London; s. of Arthur James Twin and Hilda Ethel Twin; m. Jean Leatherland 1963; one s. one d.; ed Sir George Monoux Grammar School, Walthamstow, London and Univ. of Liverpool; Lecturer, Univ. of Liverpool 1964, Sr Lecturer 1973, Prof. of Experimental Physics 1987–2001, Sr Fellow and Prof. Emer. 2001–; Head, Nuclear Structure Facility, Daresbury Lab. Cheshire 1983–87; Weatherill Medal, Franklin Inst. USA 1991, Bonner Prize, Americal Physical Soc. 1991, Lisa Meitner Prize, European Physical Soc. 2004. *Publications:* articles in professional journals. *Address:* Department of Physics, University of Liverpool, Liverpool, L69 7ZE, England. *Telephone:* (151) 794-3378 (office). *Fax:* (151) 794-3348 (office). *E-mail:* pjt@ns.ph.liv.ac.uk (office). *Website:* www .ph.liv.ac.uk (office).

TWOMBLY, Cy; American artist; b. 25 April 1929, Lexington, Va; ed Boston Museum School of Fine Arts, Washington & Lee Univ., Art Students League and Black Mountain Coll. with Frank Kline and Robert Motherwell; Head, Art Dept Southern Seminary and Jr Coll. Buena Vista, Va 1955–56; retrospective exhbn Whitney Museum of Art, New York 1979; works in numerous public and pvt. collections in USA and Europe; Fellow American Acad. of Arts and Letters; Imperial Praemium Prize 1996. *Address:* c/o Gagosian Gallery, 980 Madison Avenue, New York, NY 10021, USA.

TWOMEY, Paul, MA, PhD; Australian international organization executive; *President and CEO, Internet Corporation for Assigned Names and Numbers (ICANN);* b. 18 July 1961; ed Univ. of Queensland, Pennsylvania State Univ., USA, Univ. of Cambridge, UK; consultant, McKinsey & Co. –1994; Exec. Gen. Man. for Europe, Austrade-the Australian Trade Comm. 1994–97; Founding CEO Nat. Office for Information Economy 1997; Australian Fed. Govt's Special Adviser for Information Economy and Tech. 1997; Australia's Rep. at int. forums, including WTO, OECD, APEC and Internet Corpn for Assigned Names and Numbers (ICANN); founder Argo P@cific (int. advisory and investment firm); Chair. Govt Advisory Cttee, ICANN 1999–2002, Pres. and CEO ICANN 2003–. *Address:* Internet Corporation for Assigned Names and Numbers, 4676 Admiralty Way, Suite 330, Marina del Rey, CA 90292-6601, USA (office). *Telephone:* (310) 823-9358 (office). *Fax:* (310) 823-8649 (office). *E-mail:* icann@icann.org (office). *Website:* www.icann.org (office).

TYAGACHEV, Leonid Vassilyevich; Russian sports administrator and Ski Coach; *President, Russian Olympic Committee;* b. 1946, Dedenevo, Moscow region; m.; two d.; ed Moscow Pedagogical Inst., Mountain Ski School Kirschberg, Austria; participated in All-Union and int. ski competitions until 1971; fmr USSR Ski Champion; Sr Ski Coach, Moscow region 1971–76; Chief Coach USSR Ski team, has coached numerous skiers including Zhirov, Zelenskaya, Tsyganov, Makeyev, Gladyshev 1976–81; took part in organizing World Cup competitions in Saalbach, Schladming, Saint Anton 1981–95; Minister of Sport and Tourism 1995–99; First Vice-Pres. Russian Olympic Cttee 1991–2001, Pres. 2001–, also Pres. Russian Alpine Ski and Snowboard Fed.; numerous medals. *Address:* Olympic Committee of Russian Federation, Luzhnetskaya nab. 8, 119992 Moscow, Russia (office). *Telephone:* (095) 725-45-23 (office). *Website:* www.olympic.ru (office).

TYAZHLOV, Anatoly Stepanovich; Russian politician; b. 11 Oct. 1942, Kopeisk, Chelyabinsk Region; m.; two c.; ed Chelyabinsk Polytech. Inst.; metalworker, master, head of workshop, head of div., chief engineer Orenburg factory of prefabricated ferro-concrete structures 1959–69; chief engineer Orekhovo-Zuyevo house construction factory, Egoryevsk agric. construction factory 1969–73; chief engineer, man. of div., Head Moscow Region Dept of Construction, Chair. State Production Asscn Mosoblstroimatelialy 1973–82; Head Elektrostal Construction Trust 1982–90; Chair. Exec. Cttee Moscow Region Soviet 1990–91; Head Moscow Region Admin. 1991–; Gov. of Moscow Region 1995–99; mem. Russian Council of Fed. 1993–99; Pres. Int. Asscn of Fraternized Towns; Pres. Asscn of Admin. Heads of Regions and Territories, Chair. Union of Govs of Russia 1992–99; mem. State Duma (Parl.) 1999–2003; mem. Otechestvo faction; mem. Co-ordination Council on Introduction of Privatization Cheques by Russian Govt 1992–; mem. Fed. State Comm. on Problems of Reforms 1993–; mem. Int. Acad. of Ecological Sciences. *Address:* c/o State Duma, Okhotny ryad 1, 103265 Moscow, Russia (office).

TYCZKA, Mieczysław; Polish lawyer; b. 13 April 1925, Witków; s. of Szczepan Tyczka and Maria Tyczka; m. 1956; two d.; ed Adam Mickiewicz Univ., Poznań; with Investment Bank 1950–53, Dist Arbitration Comm., Poznań 1953–61, Adam Mickiewicz Univ., Poznań 1961–; Prof. and Head of Dept of Civil Proceedings Adam Mickiewicz Univ.; Prof., Higher School of Man. and Banking, Dept of Econ., Civil and Labour Law, Poznań 1996; Inst. for Environmental Foundations of Tourism and Recreation of Physical Educ. Acad., Poznan; Pres. Constitutional Tribunal 1989–93; mem. Cttee for Legal Sciences of Polish Acad. of Sciences; mem. Poznań Friends of Learning Soc. (Chair. Comm. for Legal Sciences), Democratic Party (SD) 1963–. *Publications:* Organization of the Polish Judicature, Law-making Procedure in the Polish National Economy Governmental Agencies, Arbitration Proceedings, Proceedings in Law on Inventions and Industrial Designs. *Leisure interest:* tourism. *Address:* Katedra Postępowania Cywilnego Univ. im. Adama, Mickiewicza, ul. Sw. Marcin 90, 61-809 Poznań, Poland (office). *Telephone:* (61) 8536251 (office).

TYLER, Anne, BA; American writer; b. 25 Oct. 1941, Minneapolis, Minn.; d. of Lloyd Parry Tyler and Phyllis (Mahon) Tyler; m. Taghi M. Modarressi 1963 (died 1997); two c.; ed Duke Univ., Columbia Univ.; mem. American Acad. of Arts and Letters, American Acad. of Arts and Sciences. *Publications:* If Morning Ever Comes 1964, The Tin Can Tree 1965, A Slipping-Down Life 1970, The Clock Winder 1972, Celestial Navigation 1974, Searching for Caleb 1976, Earthly Possessions 1977, Morgan's Passing 1980, Dinner at the Homesick Restaurant 1982, The Best American Short Stories (ed. with Shannon Ravenel) 1983, The Accidental Tourist (Nat. Book Critics Circle Award for Fiction) 1985, Breathing Lessons (Pulitzer Prize for Fiction 1989) 1988, Saint Maybe 1991, Tumble Tower (juvenile) 1993, Ladder of Years 1995, A Patchwork Planet 1998, Back When We Were Grown-ups 2001, The Amateur Marriage (Richard & Judy Book Club Choice 2005) 2004, Digging to America 2006; short stories in magazines. *Address:* 222 Tunbridge Road, Baltimore, MD 21212, USA (home). *E-mail:* atmBaltimore@aol.com (home).

TYLER, Liv; American actress; b. 1 July 1977, Portland, Maine; d. of Steve Tyler and Bebe Buell; m. Royston Langdon 2003; one s.; fmr model Eileen Ford Agency. *Film appearances include:* Silent Fall 1994, Empire Records 1995, Heavy 1995, Stealing Beauty 1996, That Thing You Do! 1996, Inventing the Abbotts 1997, Plunkett and Macleane 1999, Armageddon 1998, Cookie's Fortune 1999, Onegin 1999, The Little Black Book 1999, Dr T and the Women 2000, The Lord of the Rings: The Fellowship of the Ring 2001, One Night at McCool's 2001, The Lord of the Rings: The Two Towers 2002, The Lord of the Rings: The Return of the King 2003, Jersey Girl 2004, Lonesome Jim 2005, Reign Over Me 2007, The Strangers 2008, The Incredible Hulk 2008. *Address:* c/o United Talent Agency, 9560 Wilshire Blvd, Suite 500, Beverly Hills, CA 90212-2401, USA (office).

TYMOSHENKO, Yuliya Volodymyrivna, CandEcon; Ukrainian business executive and politician; *Prime Minister;* b. 27 Nov. 1960, Dnipropetrovsk; m. Oleksandr Hennadyovych Tymoshenko; one d.; ed Dnipropetrovsk State Univ.; planning engineer, Dnipropetrovsk Machine-Construction Plant 1984–89; Commercial Dir Dnipropetrovsk Youth Centre Terminal 1989–91; Dir-Gen. Ukraine Benzine Corpn 1991–95; Pres. Union Unified Energy Systems of Ukraine (UES), First Deputy Chair. Bd of Dirs, Head Cttee on Budgetary Issues 1995–97; elected to Verkhovna Rada (parl.) 1996, joined political union Community (Hromada—with Pavlo Lazarenko), left Hromada to form and lead Fatherland (Batkivishchina) faction 1999; Deputy Prime Minister of Ukraine responsible for energy issues 1999–2001 (resgnd); joined opposition Nat. Salvation Forum 2001; arrested on charge of corruption March 2001, released due to pressure of opposition; led Yuliya Tymoshenko Bloc in 2002 and 2006 elections; Prime Minister of Ukraine Jan.–Sept. 2005, 2007–; Higher Order of Orthodox Church St Barbara Great Martyr 1997; ranked by Forbes magazine amongst 100 Most Powerful Women (third) 2005, (17th) 2008. *Publications:* about 50 papers on econs. *Address:* Office of the Cabinet of Ministers, 01008 Kyiv, vul. M. Hrushevskoho 12/2 (office); Fatherland (Batkivshchyna), 01133 Kyiv, bulv. Lesi Ukrainky 26, POB 81, Ukraine. *Telephone:* (44) 293-21-71 (office); (44) 286-65-42. *Fax:* (44) 293-20-93 (office); (44) 285-69-07. *E-mail:* web@kmu.gov.ua (office); sector@byti.org.ua. *Website:* www.kmu.gov.ua (office); www.tymoshenko.com.ua.

TYNDALE-BISCOE, Cecil Hugh, PhD; Australian research scientist and university teacher; b. 16 Oct. 1929, Kashmir, India; s. of Eric Dallas Tyndale-Biscoe and Phyllis Mary (née Long) Tyndale-Biscoe; m. Marina Szokoloczi 1960; two s. one d.; ed Wycliffe Coll., England, Canterbury Univ., NZ, Univ. of Western Australia and Washington Univ., St Louis, USA; Animal Ecology, Dept of Scientific and Industrial Research, NZ 1951–55; lecturer Edwardes Coll., Peshawar, Pakistan 1955–58, Univ. of WA, Perth 1961; Deputy Leader, Biologist, NZ Alpine Club Antarctic Expedition 1959–60; Lecturer, Sr Lecturer, Reader in Zoology, Australian Nat. Univ., Canberra 1962–75,

Adjunct Prof. 1996–2002; Sr Prin. Research Scientist Div. of Wildlife Research, CSIRO, Canberra 1976–78, Chief Research Scientist Div. of Wildlife and Ecology 1978–91; Dir Co-operative Research Centre for Biological Control of Vertebrate Pest Populations 1992–95; Hayward Fellow, Manaaki Whenua Landcare Research, NZ 1996–97; mountaineering in NZ, including first north-south traverse of Mt Cook, first ascent of Torres from the Balfour; in the Karakorum, including first ascents of Falak Sar, Barteen and Buni Zom; Fellow Australian Acad. of Science, Australian Inst. of Biologists; Life mem. Australian Mammal Soc.; Hon. mem. RSNZ 1982; Clarke Medal, Royal Soc. of NSW 1974, Troughton Medal 1982, Aitken Medal 1986, CSIRO Medal 1987, Whitely Medal, Royal Zoological Soc. of NSW 2005. *Publications:* Life of Marsupials 1973, Reproduction and Evolution (Ed.) 1977, Reproductive Physiology of Marsupials (with M. B. Renfree) 1987, Developing Marsupials (Ed. with P. A. Janssens) 1988; about 120 papers in scientific journals of reproduction, ecology and endocrinology. *Leisure interests:* mountaineering, agroforestry, earth houses, woodwork, history of N India. *Address:* 114 Grayson Street, Hackett, ACT 2602, Australia (home). *Telephone:* (2) 6249-8612 (home). *E-mail:* hught@bigpond.com (office).

TYSON, Harvey Wood; South African journalist; b. 27 Sept. 1928, Johannesburg; two s. one d.; ed Kingswood Coll., Rhodes Univ., Grahamstown; Ed.-in-Chief The Star, Sunday Star, Johannesburg 1974–90; Dir Argus Holdings 1991–94, Argus Newspapers 1991–94, Sussens Mann Tyson Ogilvie & Mather, Omni Media Holdings 1994–. *Publication:* Editors Under Fire 1993. *Leisure interests:* writing, golf. *Address:* c/o The Star, 47 Sauer Street, PO Box 1014, Johannesburg 2000, South Africa.

TYSON, John H., BBA; American food industry executive; *Chairman, Tyson Foods;* b. 5 Sept. 1953, Springdale, AR; s. of Don Tyson; grands. of John Tyson; m.; one s. one d.; ed Springdale High School, Southern Methodist Univ., Dallas, TX; began career with Tyson Foods Inc. (family-owned business est. by grandfather John Tyson), various positions including Retail Sales Man. for NE states, Purchasing Man., Complex Man. NC Region, Pres. Beef and Pork Div., Vice-Chair. –1998, Chair. 1998–2000, Chair. Tyson Foods 1998–, Pres. 2000–06, CEO 2000–06; fmr Pres. Ark. Poultry Fed.; mem. Bd of Dirs Nat. Council on Alcoholism and Drug Dependence, Steering Cttee Campaign for 21st Century, Univ. of Ark.; Chair. Corpn and Foundation Relations Cttee, Univ. of Ark.; mem. Walden Woods (non-profit org.), Bridge School Project. *Leisure interests:* golf, deep sea fishing, music, travel, culture, philanthropy. *Address:* Tyson Foods Inc., 2210 West Oakland Drive, Springdale, AR 72762-6999, USA (office). *Telephone:* (479) 290-4000 (office). *Fax:* (479) 290-4061 (office). *Website:* www.tysonfoodsinc.com (office).

TYSON, Keith, MA; British artist; b. Ulverston, Cumbria; s. of David Tyson and Audrey Rigby; ed Dowdales School, Dalton-in-Furness, Carlisle Coll. of Art and Univ. of Brighton; studied mechanical eng craft before taking up art studies; worked as metal turner and draftsman at Vickers shipyard; has exhibited across Europe and N America; Turner Prize 2002. *Group exhibitions include:* Pandemonium Show, Inst. of Contemporary Arts 1996, Venice Biennale 2001, São Paulo Bienal 2002. *Solo exhibitions include:* From The Artmachine, Anthony Reynolds Gallery 1995.

TYSON, Laura D'Andrea, PhD; American economist, academic, fmr government official and fmr university administrator; *Professor, Haas School of Business, University of California, Berkeley;* b. 28 June 1947, New Jersey; m. Erik Tarloff; one s.; ed Smith Coll., Northampton, Mass and MIT; Asst Prof., Princeton Univ. 1974–77; Nat. Fellows Program Fellowship, Hoover Inst. 1978–79; consultant to IBRD 1980–86, Pres.'s Comm. on Industrial Competitiveness 1983–84, Hambrecht & Quist 1984–86, Plan-Econ 1984–86, Western Govs Asscn 1986, Council on Competitiveness 1986–89, Electronics Industry Asscn 1989, Motorola 1989–90; Visiting Prof., Harvard Business School 1989–90; Prof., Dept of Econs and Business Admin. and Dir Inst. of Int. Studies, Univ. of California, Berkeley 1978–98, Dean, Haas School of Business 1998–2001, Prof. 2006–; Dean, London Business School 2001–06; Chair. Council of Econ. Advisers to Pres. Clinton 1993–95, Nat. Econ. Adviser to Pres. US Nat. Econ. Council 1995–97; Visiting Scholar, Inst. of Int. Econs; mem. Bd of Economists, Los Angeles Times; mem. Council on Foreign Relations, numerous other professional and public appointments; mem. Bd of

Dirs SBC Communications, Morgan Stanley, Kodak, Human Genome Sciences, The Brookings Inst.; columnist for Business Week magazine. *Publications:* The Yugoslav Economic System and its Performance in the 1970s 1980, Economic Adjustment in Eastern Europe 1984, Who's Bashing Whom?, Trade Conflict in High Technology Industries 1992; articles in professional journals. *Address:* Haas School of Business, S545, Haas, #1900, 2220 Piedmont Avenue, University of California, Berkeley, CA 94720-1900, USA (office). *Telephone:* (510) 643-2027 (office). *E-mail:* tyson@haas.berkeley .edu (office). *Website:* www.haas.berkeley.edu (office).

TYSON, Michael (Mike) Gerard; American professional boxer; b. 30 June 1966, New York City; s. of the late John Kilpatrick Tyson and Lorna Tyson; m. 1st Robin Givens 1988 (divorced 1989); 2nd Monica Turner 1997 (divorced 2003); two c.; career record of 50 wins, five losses, two no contest; defeated Trevor Berbick to win WBC heavyweight title 1986; winner WBA heavyweight title March 1987, IBF heavyweight title Aug. 1987; fmr undefeated world champion, lost to James Buster Douglas 1990, defeated Donovan Ruddock 1991; Hon. Chair. Cystic Fibrosis Asscn 1987; sentenced to six years' imprisonment for rape and two counts of deviant sexual practice March 1992, appealed against March sentence, appeal rejected by US Supreme Court March 1994, released March 1995; regained title of heavyweight world champion after defeating Frank Bruno (q.v.) March 1996; lost to Evander Holyfield Dec. 1996; licence revoked by Nevada State Athletics Comm. after disqualification from rematch against Holyfield 1996, reinstated on appeal Oct. 1998; sentenced to a year's imprisonment for assault Feb. 1999; released on probation May 1999; fought Lennox Lewis (q.v.) June 2002 for WBC and IBF titles, knocked out in eighth round; defeated Clifford Etienne Feb. 2003; lost to Danny Williams 2004; BBC Sports Overseas Personality of the Year 1989. *Film appearance:* Rocky Balboa 2006.

TZABAN, Yair, BA; Israeli journalist and politician; *Chairman, Association for Modern Jewish Culture (LAMDA), issuing a New Encyclopedia on Jewish Culture in the Era of Modernisation and Secularisation;* b. 1930, Jerusalem; one s. one d.; ed Bar-Ilan and Tel Aviv Univs; Chair. political bureau of Maki (Israeli CP) 1972–75; Co-Founder of Moked 1972–1977, Co-Founder of Sheli Coalition 1977; Political Sec. Mapam (United Workers' Party) 1981–, Chair. Mapam's faction in the Histadrut; Minister of Immigrant Absorption 1992–96; mem. Knesset 1981– (Meretz), served on numerous cttees 1981–92, Lecturer, School for Political Studies, Univ. of Tel-Aviv 1996–2002; fmr Chair. The College of Judaism as Culture (Meitar), mem. Exec. Bd; Founder and Chair. Asscn for Modern Jewish Culture (LAMDA), issuing a New Encyclopedia on Jewish Culture in the Era of Modernisation and Secularisation; Dr hc Hebrew Union Coll. 1996; Itamar Ben-Avi Shield 1984. *Publications:* New Jewish Time 2007; various articles on political, social and econ. topics and on Judaism and Zionism. *Address:* 1A Tarad Street, Ramat-Gan 52503, Israel (home). *Telephone:* 3-6735160 (office); 3-6121495 (home). *Fax:* 3-6727364 (office); 3-6121497 (home). *E-mail:* zabany@netvision.net.il (home).

TZANNETAKIS, Tzannis; Greek politician; b. 13 Sept. 1927, Gytheion; s. of Petros Tzannetakis and Maria Tzannetakis; m. Maria Ragoussi 1954; one s. one d.; ed Naval Acad., War Acad.; served in Greek Navy 1945–67; business exec. 1967–74; Sec.-Gen. Nat. Tourist Org. 1975; elected mem. Parl. 1977, 1981, 1985, 1989, 1990, 1993, 1996, 2000, currently mem. Standing Cttee on Cultural and Educational Affairs, Special Standing Cttee on Insts and Transparency; Minister of Public Works 1980–81; Prime Minister 1989; Minister of Defence 1990; Vice-Premier 1990–91; Deputy Prime Minister 1992–93; Minister of Culture 1990–93; founder of project to restore traditional villages in Greece; has promoted diverse cultural activities including exhbns; Gold Cross of George I, Gold Cross of the Phoenix, Great Cross of Honour, Great Cross of Luxembourg. *Publications:* The Greek Agora: Public Political Space 1994, India: Another Way of Life (First Prize, Fed. of Indian Publrs) 1994; translations into Greek. *Leisure interests:* reading, sailing, travelling. *Address:* Omirou 54, Athens 10672 (office); Odos Pefkon 25, Kifissia, Athens, Greece (home). *Telephone:* (210) 3385374 (office); (210) 8017133 (home). *Fax:* (210) 3385370. *E-mail:* tztz@parliament.gr (office). *Website:* www.parliament .gr/english/synthesh/mp.asp?MPID=401 (office).

U

UBAIDI, Gen. Abd al-Qader Jasim al-; Iraqi army officer and government official; *Minister of Defence;* b. Ramadi; fmr Gen. in Iraqi army under Saddam Hussein, rejoined army 2003, served as Commdr of Operations Centre, then Mil. Commdr in western Iraq, then Commdr infantry commando units; Minister of Defence 2006–. *Address:* Ministry of Defence, Baghdad, Iraq (office). *E-mail:* webmaster@mod.iraqiaf.org (office). *Website:* www.iraqmod.org (office).

UBAIDULLOEV, Mahmadsaid; Tajikistan politician and electrical engineer; *Chairman, Majlisi Milli Majlisi Oli (National Assembly);* b. 1 Feb. 1952, Khatlon region; s. of the late Ubaidullo Mahmudov and Sabagul Nazirova; m. R. Karimova; two s. one d.; ed Tajik Polytechnical Inst., Kharkov Polytechnical Inst., Tashkent Higher CPSU School; Sr Engineer, Kulob Regional Dept of Statistics 1974–75, Main Engineer 1975–76, Dir Computation Centre 1976–79; Instructor, Organizing Dept, CP Cttee of Kulob 1979–81, Head of Organizing Dept 1981–83; Deputy Head of Cen. Dept of Statistics, Dushanbe 1985–86; Head of Dept of Industry, Transport and People's Food Products, CP Cttee of Kulob 1986–88; Head of Khatlon Regional Dept of Statistics, Kurghon-Teppa 1988–90; Deputy Chair. Exec. Cttee, Kulob Regional People's Deputy Council 1990–92; Deputy Chair. Council of Ministers 1992–94; First Deputy Prime Minister 1994–96; Mayor of Dushanbe 1996–; mem. People's Democratic Party; Chair. Majlisi Milli Majlisi Oli (Nat. Ass.) 2000–, Interparliamentary Ass. of EuroAsEC (Euroasian Econ. Cooperation) 2007–; Order of the Dusti (Friendship) 1998, Order of the Ismoili Somoni 1999, Order of the Ismoili Somoni, First Degree 2006; 21st Century Achievement Award 2001, Diploma of UN-HABITAT and World Org. of United Cities and Local Govts 2006, Medal in respect of IBC Leading Engineers of the World 2006, Int. Honour Diploma and Prize, Five Hundred Leaders of Influence, American Bibliographic Inst. 2001. *Publications:* The Foundation of Newest Statehood (ed.) 2002, History of Dushanbe City (from ancient times till our days) (ed.) 2004, Dushanbe: City of Peace (co-author) 2004. *Leisure interests:* politics, logic, dialectics and philosophy. *Address:* Majlisi Milli Majlisi Oli, Rudaki prosp. 42, 734001 Dushanbe (office); M. Kholov Street, Dushanbe, Tajikistan (home). *Telephone:* (372) 21-27-04 (office). *Fax:* (372) 21-85-09 (office); (372) 21-94-38 (office). *E-mail:* majmilli@netrt.org (office). *Website:* www.majmilli.tj (office); www.dushanbe.tj.

UCHIDA, Mitsuko; Japanese pianist; b. 20 Dec. 1948, Tokyo; d. of Fujio Uchida and Yasuko Uchida; ed Vienna Acad. of Music with Prof. R. Hauser; debut Vienna 1963; recitals and concerto performances with all major London orchestras, Chicago Symphony, Boston Symphony, Cleveland Orchestra, Berlin Philharmonic, Vienna Philharmonic, New York Philharmonic, Los Angeles Philharmonic and others; played and directed the cycle of 21 Mozart piano concertos with the English Chamber Orchestra, London 1985–86; gave US premiere of piano concerto Antiphonies by Harrison Birtwistle 1996; Perspectives recital series at Carnegie Hall 2003; Co-Dir Marlboro Music Festival; Artist-in-Residence, Cleveland Orchestra 2002–07, Berlin Philharmonic Orchestra 2008–09, Vienna Konzerthaus 2008–09; Trustee, Borletti-Buitoni Trust; Hon. CBE 2001; First Prize Beethoven Competition Vienna 1969, Second Prize Chopin Competition Warsaw 1970, Second Prize Leeds Competition 1975, Gramophone Award (Mozart Piano Sonatas) 1989, Gramophone Award (Schoenberg Piano Concerto) 2001, Royal Philharmonic Soc.'s Instrumentalist Award 2004. *Recordings include:* Mozart Complete Piano Sonatas and 21 Piano Concertos (English Chamber Orchestra and Jeffrey Tate), Chopin Piano Sonatas, Debussy 12 Etudes, Schubert Piano Sonatas, Beethoven Piano Concertos, Schoenberg Piano Concerto, Beethoven Piano Sonatas Op. 109, 110 and 111, Beethoven: Sonatas Op 101 & 106. *Address:* Victoria Rowsell Artist Management Ltd, 34 Addington Square, London, SE5 7LB, England (office). *Telephone:* (20) 7701-3219 (office). *Fax:* (20) 7701-3219 (office). *E-mail:* management@victoriarowsell.co.uk (office). *Website:* www.victoriarowsell.co.uk (office); www.mitsukouchida.com.

UCHIDA, Tsuneji; Japanese electronics industry executive; *President and COO, Canon Inc.;* has worked with Canon Inc. for over 40 years business 1999–2000, in charge of promotion of digital photo home business 2000–01, Group Exec. Lens Products Group 1995–2001, Deputy Chief Exec. Camera Operations HQ 1995–97, Group Exec. Photo Products Group 1997–99, Chief Exec. Camera Operations HQ April–July 1999, in charge of promotion of digital photo, Man. Dir 2001–03, Sr Man. Dir 2003–06, Vice-Pres. 2006, mem. Bd of Dirs, Pres. and COO 2006–. *Address:* Canon Inc., 30-2, Shimomaruko 3-chome, Ohta-ku, Tokyo 146-8501, Japan (office). *Telephone:* (3) 3758-2111 (office). *Fax:* (3) 5482-5135 (office). *E-mail:* info@canon.com (office). *Website:* www.canon.com (office).

UCHINAGA, Yukako; Japanese business executive; *Technical Advisor, IBM Japan Ltd;* ed Univ. of Tokyo; joined IBM Japan in 1971, several man. positions in devt and marketing, Dir Asia Pacific Products 1989, Gen. Man. AP Cross Industry 1995, mem. Bd Dirs 1995–, Gen. Man. Services Offerings 1998, Vice-Pres. Multi-industry Solutions, IBM Asia Pacific –1999, Vice-Pres. Software Devt Lab., Yamato 1999–2007, Tech. Advisor; Co-leader IBM Asia Pacific Women's Council; mem. Global Workforce Diversity Council; fmr mem. Council for Health Science, Japanese Ministry of Health and Welfare, Council for Gender Equality, Japan Prime Minister's Office; mem. Council for Education, Japanese Ministry of Education and Science 2001–; Women in Technology International (WITI) Hall of Fame (first woman inducted from outside the USA) 1999–, ranked by Fortune magazine amongst 50 Most Powerful Women in Business outside the US (33rd) 2002. *Address:* 3-2-12, Roppongi, Minato-ku, Tokyo 106-8711, Japan (office). *Telephone:* (3) 5563-3213 (office). *Fax:* (3) 5563-4872 (office). *E-mail:* uchinaga@jp.ibm.com (office). *Website:* www.ibm.com (office).

UCHITEL, Aleksei Yefimovich; Russian film director; *Founder and Director-General, Rock Studio;* b. 31 Aug. 1931, Leningrad; s. of Yefim Uchitel; ed All Union State Inst. of Cinematography; with Leningrad Studio of Documentary Films, St Petersburg 1975–90; Founder and Dir-Gen. Rock Studio 1989–; Merited Worker of Arts. *Documentaries:* Its Name is Novgorod 1974, Leningrad: Years of Achievement 1975, Leningrad – Hero City 1975, Ten Thousand I's (Molodost-78 Int. Festival Prize) 1976, Irina Kolpakova, Snow Fantasy 1977, October and Youth 1977, Starting Up: Portrait of An Event (Leipzig Film Festival Prize) 1978, How many faces does the disco have? (Leningrad Komsomol Prize) 1980, Who is for? (Krasnoyarsk All-Union Film Festival Prize) 1982, The Earth is Entrusted to You (Almaty All-Union Film Festival Prize) 1983, Aktsiya (Krakow Int. Film Festival Prize) 1983, Planet Natasha 1986, Rock 1988, Obvodny Kanal (First Prize, Int. Cinema Festival, Bornholm, Denmark) 1990, Butterfly (First Prize, Best Dir, Open Russian Festival of Documentary Cinema, Ekaterinburg) 1993, Elite 1997. *Feature films:* Mania Giseli (Mania of Giselle) (Honfleur Film Festival Prize) 1996, Elite 1997, His Wife's Diary (Grand Prix, Kinotavr Open Russian Cinema Festival) 2000, The Stroll (First Prize, Cleveland Int. Film Festival, Syracuse Int. Film Festival, Special Jury Prize for Outstanding Artistic Concept, FIPRESSI prize and Boulder Prize, 13th Int. Festival of Eastern European Cinema, Kottbus, Best Direction Prize, Window onto Europe Film Festival, Vyborg) 2003. *Address:* Rock Studio, 12 Krukov Canal, 190068 St Petersburg (office); 4th Krasnokararmennaya str. 6–5, Apt 4, 198052 St Petersburg, Russia (home). *Telephone:* (812) 114-2056 (office); (812) 292-59-45 (home). *E-mail:* rockfilmstudio@mail.ru (office). *Website:* www.rockfilm.ru (office); eng.uchitel.info.

UCISIK, Ahmet Hikmet, PhD; Turkish engineer and academic; *Professor of Materials Science, Boğaziçi University;* ed Istanbul Univ.; Assoc. Prof., Istanbul Tech. Univ.; Dir Marmara Scientific and Industrial Research Inst., Turkish Scientific and Tech. Research Council; instructor Metallurgical Eng Dept, Istanbul Tech. Univ.; currently Prof. of Materials Science, Bogazici Univ.; mem. American and Japanese Socs for Dental Materials and Devices; Fellow Islamic Acad. of Sciences. *Address:* Boğaziçi University, 80815 Bebek, Istanbul, Turkey (office). *Telephone:* (212) 263-15-00 (office). *Fax:* (212) 265-63-57 (office). *E-mail:* halkilis@boun.edu.tr (office). *Website:* www.boun.edu.tr (office).

UDALL, Mark Emery, BA; American politician; *Senator from Colorado;* b. 18 July 1950, Tucson, Ariz.; s. of the late Morris Udall and Patricia Emery Udall; nephew of Stewart Udall; m. Maggie Fox; one s. one d.; ed Williams Coll.; Field Organizer, Morris K. Udall for Pres. 1974–75; Course Dir and Educator, Colo Outward Bound School 1975–85, Exec. Dir 1985–95; mem. Colo State House of Reps 1997–98; mem. US House of Reps from 2nd Colo Dist 1999–2009; Senator from Colorado 2009–; mem. American Alpine Club, Parkinson's Action Network; mem. Bd of Dirs Berger Foundation; Democrat. *Leisure interest:* mountaineering. *Address:* Office of Senator Mark Udall, US Senate, Washington, DC, USA (office). *Website:* www.senate.gov (office).

UDALL, Thomas (Tom) S., BA, LLB, JD; American lawyer and politician; *Senator from New Mexico;* b. 18 May 1948, Tucson, Ariz.; s. of Stewart Udall and Lee Udall; m. Jill Cooper; one d.; ed Prescott Coll., Univ. of Cambridge, UK, Univ. of New Mexico School of Law; Legis. Asst, staff of US Senator Joe Biden 1973; clerk to Chief Justice Oliver Seth, US Tenth Circuit Court of Appeals, Santa Fe, New Mexico 1977–78; Asst US Attorney 1978–81; attorney in pvt. practice, Santa Fe 1981–83; Chief Counsel, New Mexico Health and Environment Dept 1983–84; attorney, Miller, Stratvert, Torgerson and Schlenker, Albuquerque 1985–90; State Attorney, New Mexico 1991–99; mem. US House of Reps from 3rd New Mexico Dist 1999–2009, mem. Cttees on Appropriations, Educ. and Related Agencies, Sub-Cttees on Interior, Environment and Related Agencies, on Labor, Health and Human Services, on Legis. Branch; Senator from New Mexico 2009–; Pres. Nat. Assn of Attorney Gens 1996; mem. New Mexico Environmental Improvement Bd 1986–87; mem. Kiwanis Club of Albuquerque Inc., Santa Fe Chamber Music Festival, LAW FUND, Regional Environmental Public Interest Law Firm; Democrat. *Address:* Office of Senator Tom Udall, US Senate, Washington, DC 20510, USA (office). *Website:* www.senate.gov (office).

UDOVENKO, Hennadiy Yosipovich, PhD; Ukrainian diplomatist and politician; *Chairman, Standing Committee on Human Rights, Verkhovna Rada;* b. 22 June 1931, Kryvy Rih; s. of Yosyp Petrovich Udovenko and Maria Maksimivna Kharenko; m. Dina Grigorivna Boutenko 1953; one d.; ed Kiev State Univ.; joined Diplomatic Service 1959, First Sec., Counsellor 1959–64; Sr Recruitment Officer, UN Tech. Assistance Recruitment Service, Geneva 1965–71; Chief of Depts., Ministry of Foreign Affairs 1972–76; Dir Interpretation and Meetings Div., Dept of Conf. Services, UN Secr., New York 1977–80; Deputy Minister for Foreign Affairs of Ukrainian SSR 1980–85; Rep. of Ukrainian SSR on Governing Body of ILO 1981–85; Rep. to UN Security Council 1985; Perm. Rep. of Ukrainian SSR to UN 1985–91; Deputy Minister of Foreign Affairs 1991–92, Minister of Foreign Affairs 1994–98; Ukrainian Amb. to UN 1992; Amb. to Poland 1992–94; Pres. UN Gen. Ass. 1997–98; mem. Verkhovna Rada (Parl.), Head Standing Cttee on Human Rights 1999–, leader RUKH Faction 1999–2002; Head Narodnyy Rukh Ukrainy political party 1999–2003; Hon. DHumLitt (Bridgeport Univ., USA) 1997; Dr. hc (Ukrainian Free Univ., Munich) 1996, (Int. Human Rights Acad., Kiev, Int. Solomon Univ., Kiev) 1998; Diplomatist of the Year 1996, 1998. *Leisure interest:*

jogging. Address: 5 Hrushevskogo Str., 01008 Kiev (office); Desyatynna Str. 10, Apt. 2, 01025 Kiev, Ukraine (home). *Telephone:* (44) 255-40-36 (office); (44) 279-65-08 (home). *Fax:* (44) 255-49-02 (office); (44) 276-28-79 (home). *E-mail:* udovenko@rada.gov.ua (office). *Website:* www.rada.gov.ua (office).

ŪDRE, Ingrīda, MSc; Latvian politician; b. 14 Nov. 1958, Rīga; m. (divorced); two s.; ed Univ. of Latvia, Umeå Univ., Sweden; fmr Chief Accountant SWH Riga; fmr Auditor, Coopers & Lybrand Latvija Ltd; fmr Lecturer, Accountancy Inst., Univ. of Latvia; mem. Saeima (Parl.) for Union of Greens and Farmers 1998–2006, mem. several cttees including Budget and Finance Cttee, Cttee on Supervising the Prevention and Combating of Corruption, Contraband and Organized Crime, Speaker 2002–06; Deputy Chair. Union of Greens and Farmers Parl. Group 2002–06. *Address:* Centre Party Latvian Farmers' Union (Centriskā partija Latvijas Zemnieku Savienība), Republikas lauk. 2, Rīga 1010, Latvia. *Telephone:* 6702-7163. *Fax:* 6702-7467. *E-mail:* lzs@latnet.lv. *Website:* www.lzs.lv.

UDUGOV, Brig.-Gen. Movladi; Russian/Chechen politician; *Chief, Committee of the Information Council, State Defence Council;* b. 9 Feb. 1962, Grozny; m. 1st; m. 2nd; four c.; ed Chechen-Ingush State Univ.; trained as economist; co-founder Soc. Kavkaz, co-founder political org. Bart and newspaper Bart 1987; founder and Ed. Orientir (newspaper) banned by Soviet regime 1988; organizer Mil. Patriotic Union Mansur 1990; participant Congress of Chechen People 1990; Sec. all sessions of Chechen Nat. Congress; Leader Formation Cttee of Nat. Congress of Chechen People, anti-Russian resistance group Nov. 1991; participant in overthrow of Communist leadership of Chechen-Ingushetia 1991; Minister of Information and Press, Dudayev Govt 1991; head of propaganda service of Chechen separatists 1994–; took part in negotiations resulting in resolution of that conflict; First Vice-Minister Coalition Govt Chechen Repub. Ichkeria 1996–97, First Deputy Prime Minister 1997–98, Foreign Minister 1998–99; fmr. Pres. Kavkaz–Center News Agency; currently Chief, External Sub-Cttee of Informational Council, State Defence Council.

UEBERROTH, Peter Victor; American sports administrator and business executive; *Chairman, United States Olympic Committee;* b. 2 Sept. 1937, Evanston, Ill.; s. of Victor Ueberroth and Laura Larson; m. Ginny Nicolaus 1959; one s. three d.; ed Freemont High School, San Jose State Univ.; Operations Man., Trans Int. Airlines 1959, later part owner; f. Transportation Consultants, later First Travel Corpn 1962, sold in 1980; Head, LA Olympic Games Organizing Cttee 1980–84; Maj. League Baseball Commr 1984–89; Head Rebuild LA 1992–93; Co-Chair. Doubletree Hotels Corpn 1993; Chair. and Man. Dir Contrarian Group Inc. (investment co.) 1990–, Pres. Contrarian Center; owner and Co-Chair. Pebble Beach Co. 1999–; currently Chair. US Olympic Cttee; mem. Bd of Dirs Coca-Cola Co., Hilton Hotel Corpn, Adecco S.A., Tiger Woods Learning Center; Chair. Bd Ambassadors International (AMIE) 1995–; mem. Young Pres.'s Org.; 12 honorary degrees Legion déHonneur (France), Time magazine's Man of the Year 1984, Scopus Award 1985, Olympic Order-Gold (Int. Olympic Cttee, Youthlinks Indiana's Nat. Pathfinder Award 2005. *Publication:* Made in America (autobiog.) 1985. *Leisure interests:* reading (especially historical non-fiction), golf. *Address:* United States Olympic Committee, One Olympic Plaza, Colorado Springs, CO 80909, USA (office). *Telephone:* (719) 632-5551 (office). *Website:* www.olympic -usa.org (office).

UEDA, Hideaki; Japanese diplomatist; m.; three c.; ed Tokyo Univ., Harvard Univ., USA; joined Ministry of Foreign Affairs 1967, served at Embassy in Moscow; fmr First Sec., Embassy in Australia; Dir, Press Div., Ministry of Foreign Affairs 1986–88; Counsellor and Minister for Public Affairs, Embassy in Washington, DC 1990–92; Deputy Dir-Gen., Econ. Cooperation Bureau, Ministry of Foreign Affairs, Tokyo 1992–95, Dir-Gen., Multilateral Cooperation Dept 1998–2000; Amb. to Japanese Secr. for Osaka APEC 1995; Consul Gen., Hong Kong 1995–98; Amb. to Poland 2000–03, to Australia 2004–07. *Publication:* Rise and Fall of the Far Eastern Republic 1990. *Address:* c/o Ministry of Foreign Affairs, 2-11-1, Shiba-Koen, Minato-ku, Tokyo 105-8519, Japan.

UEHARA, Haruya; Japanese banking executive; *Chairman, Mitsubishi UFJ Trust and Banking Corporation;* b. 1946; Dir Mitsubishi Trust Bank 1996–98, Man.-Dir 1998–2001, Sr Man.-Dir 2001–02, Deputy Pres. 2002–04, Pres. 2004–; Dir Mitsubishi Tokyo Financial Group Inc. 2003–, Chair. and Co-CEO 2004–05, Deputy Chair. and Pres. Mitsubishi UFJ Trust and Banking Corpn 2005–08, Chair. 2008–; mem. Bd Dirs Japanese Bankers Asscn 2004–. *Address:* Mitsubishi UFJ Trust and Banking Corpn, 4-1 Marunouchi 2-chome, Chiyoda-ku, Tokyo 100-6326, Japan (office). *Telephone:* (3) 3240-8111 (office). *Fax:* (3) 3240-8203 (office). *E-mail:* info@mufg.jp (office). *Website:* www.mufg .jp (office).

UEMATSU, Kunihiko, DEng; Japanese engineer; *Senior Advisor, Japan Atomic Industrial Forum;* b. 1931, Kochi; m.; three c.; ed Kyoto Univ. and MIT; Head of Fuel and Materials Devt for Fast Breeder Reactor Project, Japanese Power Reactor and Nuclear Fuel Devt Corpn (PNC) 1968, Dir Fuel Devt Div. 1982, Exec. Dir 1983–88, Exec. Vice-Pres. 1995–98, Special Tech. Adviser 1998–; Dir-Gen. OECD Nuclear Energy Agency (NEA) 1988–95; currently Sr Adviser, Japan Atomic Industrial Forum and Research Adviser, Cen. Research Inst. of Electric Power Industry. *Publications:* numerous papers on tech. and policy issues in field of nuclear energy. *Address:* NKK Building, 1-1-2, Marunouchi, Chiyoda-ku, Tokyo (office); 1-27-3-611, Nishigahara, Kitaku, Tokyo, Japan (home). *Telephone:* (3) 5220-3311 (office); (3) 5394-8259 (home). *Fax:* (3) 3212-2020 (office); (3) 5394-8259 (home). *E-mail:* uematsu@ jnc.go.jp (office). *Website:* www.jnc.go.jp (office).

UEMURA, Hiroyuki; Japanese insurance executive; b. 1942; Pres. Sumitomo Marine & Fire Insurance Co. Ltd 1999–2001, Pres. Mitsui Sumitomo Insurance Co. Ltd (cr. from merger between Mitsui Marine & Fire Insurance and Sumitomo Marine & Fire Insurance Cos 2001) 2001–03, Pres. and Co-CEO 2003–06, led negotiations with CitiInsurance Int. Holdings Inc. to establish jt venture Mitsui Sumitomo CitiInsurance Co. (variable annuities life insurance business) 2002; mem. Bd of Dirs Japan Telework Asscn, Yamaha Music Foundation, Japan Earthquake Reinsurance Co. Ltd; apptd Chair. Marine and Fire Insurance Asscn of Japan 2001. *Address:* c/o Co. Ltd, 27-2 Shinkawa 2-chome, Chuo-ku, Tokyo 104-8252, Japan. *Telephone:* (3) 3297-1111.

UENO, Chizuko, BA, MA; Japanese sociologist and academic; *Professor of Sociology, Tokyo University;* b. 1948, Toyama; ed Kyoto Univ.; Prof., Grad. School of Humanities and Sociology, Tokyo Univ.; Mori Hamada and Matsumoto Visiting Fellow, Cornell Univ. Law School, USA 2003–04; Suntory Prize for Social Sciences and Humanities. *Publications:* Sekushi Gyaru no Daikenkyu (A Study of Sexy Girls) 1982, Explorations in Structuralism 1986, Pleasure of Womanhood 1986, Patriarchy and Capitalism 1990, The Rise and Fall of the Modern Japanese Family 1994, Nationalism and Gender 2003, Miwa Yanagi (jtly) 2004. *Address:* Department of Sociology, Faculty of Letters, University of Tokyo, 7-3-1 Hongo, Bunkyoku, Tokyo 113-0033, Japan (office). *Telephone:* (3) 5841-3875 (office). *Fax:* (3) 5841-8930 (office). *E-mail:* ueno@l.u-tokyo.ac.jp (office). *Website:* www.l.u-tokyo.ac.jp (office).

UENO, Hirofumi; Japanese banking executive; *President and CEO, Norinchukin Bank;* Dir-Gen. The Food Agency 1994; Vice-Minister of Agric., Forestry and Fisheries –1997; currently Pres. and CEO Norinchukin Bank; mem. Advisory Bd Bank of Japan. *Address:* Norinchukin Bank, 13-2 Yurakucho 1-chome, Chiyoda-ku, CPO Box 364, Tokyo 100-8420, Japan (office). *Telephone:* (3) 3279-0111 (office). *Fax:* (3) 3218-5177 (office). *E-mail:* info@nochubank.or.jp (office). *Website:* www.nochubank.or.jp (office).

UFFEN, Robert James, OC, PhD, DSc, PEng, FRSC, FGSA, FCAE; Canadian geophysicist and academic; *Professor Emeritus of Geophysics, Queen's University;* b. 21 Sept. 1923, Toronto, Ont.; s. of James Frederick Uffen and Elsie May (Harris) Uffen; m. Mary Ruth Paterson 1949; one s. one d.; ed Univ. of Toronto, Western Ontario; war service 1942–45; Lecturer, Univ. of Western Ont. 1951–53, Asst Prof. of Physics and Geology 1953–57, Assoc. Prof. of Geophysics 1957–58, Prof. and Head of Dept of Geophysics 1958–61, Acting Head Dept Physics 1960–61; Prin. Univ. Coll. of Arts and Science, London, Ont. 1961–65; Dean, Coll. of Science, Univ. of Western Ont. 1965–66; Vice-Chair. Defence Research Bd, Ottawa 1966–67, Chair. 1967–69; Chief Science Adviser to the Cabinet 1969–71; Dean, Faculty of Applied Science, Queen's Univ., Kingston, Ont. 1971–80, Prof. of Geophysics 1971–89, Prof. Emer. 1989–; Commr Ont. Royal Comm. on Asbestos 1980–84, on Truck Safety 1981–83; Research Fellowship, Inst. of Geophysics, Univ. of Calif., LA 1953; mem. Council of Regents Colls. of Applied Arts and Tech. 1966–69, 1973–76, Nat. Research Council of Canada 1963–66, Science Council of Canada 1967–71; Dir Canadian Patents and Devt Ltd 1965–70; mem. Club of Rome 1969–83; Chair. Canadian Eng Manpower Council 1973–74; Dir Centre for Resource Studies 1973–76, 1980–83, Ont. Hydro 1974–79, (Vice-Chair. 1975–79); Councillor, Asscn of Professional Engineers of Ont. 1975–78; Chair. Ont. Exploration Tech. Devt Fund 1981–84; Consultant to EEC on energy research 1987–88; Tech. Adviser to AECL on nuclear waste 1988–91; mem. Fisheries Research Bd of Canada 1974–78; Visiting Fellow, Univ. of Sussex 1976–77; Fellow American Asscn for the Advancement of Science 1986, Canadian Acad. of Eng 1988–; Hon. DSc (Queen's Univ.) 1967, (Univ. of Western Ont.) 1970, (Royal Mil. Coll. of Canada) 1978, Hon. DSc (McMaster Univ.) 1983; Centennial Medal, Canada 1967, APEO Public Service Award 1985, Distinguished Service Award, Queen's Univ. 1990, Eng Hall of Distinction, Univ. of Toronto 1990, 1867–1992 Commemorative Medal 1992, John Orr Award (Queen's Univ.) 1993. *Publications:* papers on geophysics, operations research, evolution, science policy and radioactive waste management. *Leisure interests:* painting, boating, old bottles. *Address:* 185 Ontario Street, No. 1504, Kingston, Ont. K7L 2Y7, Canada. *Telephone:* (613) 546-4981.

UGEUX, Georges; Belgian investment banker, lawyer, economist and financier; *Chairman and CEO, Galileo Global Advisors LLC;* b. 20 April 1945, Brussels; m. Francine Godet 1970; two s. two d.; ed Catholic Univ. of Louvain; Lecturer in Econs, Faculty of Law, Univ. of Louvain 1970–72; fmr Gen. Man. Investment Banking & Trust Div., Générale Bank; Man. Dir Morgan Stanley 1985–88; Group Finance Dir Société Générale de Belgique 1988–92; Pres. Kidder Peabody-Europe 1992–95; Chair. Belgian Privatization Comm. 1995–96; Pres. European Investment Fund 1995–96; Group Exec. Vice-Pres., Int., New York Stock Exchange 1996–2003; currently Chair. and CEO Galileo Global Advisors LLC; Officer of the Order of Leopold. *Publication:* Floating Rate Notes 1985. *Leisure interests:* music, arts, philosophy. *Address:* Galileo Global Advisors LLC, Ten Rockefeller Plaza, Suite 1001, New York, NY 10020, USA (office). *Telephone:* (212) 332-6055 (office); (212) 332-6044 (office). *Fax:* (212) 332-6033 (office). *E-mail:* gugeux@galileoadvisors.com (office). *Website:* www.galileoadvisors.com (office).

UGGLAS, Baroness Margaretha af, BA; Swedish foundation executive and fmr politician; *Chairman, Jarl Hjalmarson Foundation;* b. 5 Jan. 1939; ed Harvard-Radcliffe Program in Business Admin., USA, Stockholm School of Econs; leader-writer Svenska Dagbladet 1968–74; mem. Stockholm Co. Council 1971–73; mem. Parl. 1974–95; fmr Moderate Party Spokesman on Foreign Affairs; Chair. Swedish Section, European Union of Women 1981; mem. Parl. Standing Cttee on Foreign Affairs 1982, Advisory Council on Foreign Affairs, Swedish Del. to Council of Europe; Observer, European Parl.; Minister for Foreign Affairs 1991–94; Vice-Pres. European People's Party (EPP) 1996; Chair. Save the Children Fed., Stockholm 1970–76; Chair. Jarl Hjalmarson Foundation (Swedish Moderate Party); mem. Bd of Dirs Karolinska Inst., Becton, Dickinson and Co. 1997–2007; Robert Schuman

Medal 1995. *Leisure interests:* art, walking, sailing, mountains and country-side. *Address:* Jarl Hjalmarson Foundation, PO Box 2080, 103 12 Stockholm, Sweden (office). *Telephone:* (8) 676-80-00 (office). *Fax:* (8) 676-80-86 (office). *E-mail:* stiftelsen@moderat.se (home). *Website:* www.hjalmarsonstiftelsen.se (office).

UGOLINI, S. E. Giovanni Francesco; San Marino politician; b. 28 Feb. 1953, Borgo Maggiore; m. Loredana Mularoni; one d.; industrial chemical expert, technician in state hosp. 1974–81; with family hotel business 1981–; Pres. of San Marino Union of Tourist Hospitality (USOT); joined Partito Democratico Cristiano Sammarinese (PDCS) 1973–, mem. Cen. Council 1993–, Sec. Borgo Maggiore Br. 1989–93; elected Mem. of Govt 2001–; Head of State (Capt. Regent) 2002; mem. Foreign Policy Advisory Comm., Council of the XXII. *Address:* Partito Democratico Cristiano Sammarinese (PDCS), Via delle Scalette 6, 47890 San Marino (office). *Telephone:* (549) 991193 (office). *Fax:* (549) 992694 (office). *E-mail:* pdcs@omniway.sm (office). *Website:* www.pdcs.sm (office).

UHDE, Milan, PhD; Czech politician, journalist and playwright; b. 28 July 1936, Brno; m. Jitka Uhdeová; two c.; ed Masaryk Univ., Brno; Ed. of literary monthly A Guest Is Coming 1958–70; signed Charter 77; published essays in unofficial periodicals and abroad; Reader, Faculty of Philosophy, Masaryk Univ., Brno Dec. 1989–; Ed.-in-chief, Atlantis Publishing House, Brno March–June 1990; Minister of Culture, Czech Repub. 1990–92; Pres. of Foundation for Preservation of Cultural Monuments 1991–; mem. Civic Democratic Party (ODS) 1991–98, Unie Svobody 1998; Deputy to Czech Nat. Council June 1992–; mem. Presidium; Pres. of Parl., Czech Repub. 1992–96; Chair. Civic Democratic Party in Parl. 1996–97; mem. State Radio Council 1999–; Medal for Merit 2000; Czechoslovak Radio Prize 1966. *Plays include:* in trans.: King Vávra 1964, The Tax-Collector 1965, Witnesses 1966, The Tart from the Town of Thebes 1967, The Gang 1969, Ballad for a Bandit 1975, Professional Woman 1975, A May Fairy Tale 1976, A Dentist's Temptation 1976, Lord of the Flames 1977, The Hour of Defence 1978, The Blue Angel 1979, Ave Maria played Softly 1981, The Annunciation 1986, The Bartered and the Bought 1987, Miracle in the Dark House 2004, Depart in Peace 2004, Nana 2005. *Publications:* novels: Like Water off a Duck's Back 1961, A Mysterious Tower in B. 1967. *Address:* Aura-Pont Agency, Radlická 99, 150 00 Prague, Czech Republic (office). *Telephone:* 251554938 (office). *Fax:* 251550207 (office). *E-mail:* aura-pont@aura-pont.cz (office). *Website:* www.aura-pont.cz (office).

UHL, Petr; Czech human rights activist; *Editor, Právo;* b. 8 Oct. 1941, Prague; s. of Bedřich Uhl and Marie Kohoutová; m. Anna Šabatová 1974; three s. one d.; ed Czech. Univ. of Tech., Prague; designer and patent clerk 1964–66; teacher, Coll. of Tech. Prague 1966–69; imprisoned for political activities 1969–73; designer 1974–78; Co-Founder Charter 77; Co-Founder Cttee for Protection of the Unjustly Prosecuted 1978; imprisoned for political activities 1979–84; stoker 1984–89; ed. of East European Information Agency 1988–90; leading rep. of Civic Forum, Prague 1989–90; Dir-Gen., Czechoslovak News Agency 1990–92; Ed. 1992–94; Ed.-in-Chief Listy (magazine) 1994–96; Ed. Právo (daily) 1996–98, 2001–; Commr of Govt of Czech Repub. for Human Rights 1998–2001; Deputy to House of the Nations, Fed. Ass. 1990–92; Chair., Control and Auditing Comm. of Prison Staff Corps, Czech Repub. 1990; mem. Working Group on Arbitrary Detention of UN Comm. on Human Rights 1991–2001, Chair., Cttee for Prevention of Torture of Human Rights Council of Czech Govt 2002–, mem. Council of Czech TV 2003–, mem. Monitoring Centre for Racism and Xenophobia 2004–; State Honours of Czech Repub. 1998, of Poland 2000, of Germany 2001, Order of Merit, France 2002; Press Freedom Award, Reporter without Borders, Austria 2002. *Publications:* The Programme of Social Self-government 1982, On Czechoslovak Prison System (co-author) 1998, Justice and Injustice in the Eyes of Petr Uhl 1999, and numerous articles in Czech and foreign press. *Address:* Právo, Slezská 13, 121 50 Prague (office); Anglická 8, 120 00 Prague 2, Czech Republic (home). *Telephone:* (2) 24228865 (home); (2) 606662279. *Fax:* (2) 21001276 (office). *E-mail:* uhl@seznam.cz (home).

UHLIG, Harald Friedrich Hans Volker Sigmar, PhD; German economist; *Professor of Macroeconomic and Economic Policy, Humboldt University;* b. 26 April 1961, Bonn; s. of Jan Peter Uhlig and Anjuli Sarah Uhlig; ed Technische Univ., Berlin, Univ. of Minnesota; Research Asst, Fed. Reserve Bank of Minneapolis and Inst. for Empirical Macroeconomics 1986–89; teaching asst, Univ. of Minn. 1987; Asst Prof., Dept of Econs, Princeton Univ. 1990–94; Research Prof. for Macroeconomics, Center for Econ. Research, Tilburg Univ., Netherlands 1994–2000; Prof. of Macroecon. and Econ. Policy, Humboldt Univ. 2000–; main field of work macroecons, secondary fields Bayesian time series econometrics and financial econs; assoc. ed., Journal of Econ. Dynamics and Control 1995–98, Macroecon. Dynamics 1997–, Computational Econs 1998–, Econometric Theory 2000–; Asst, Review of Econ. Studies 1998–; co-ed. European Econ. Review 1997–; mem. Econometric Soc., American Econ. Asscn, European Econ. Asscn; Alfred P. Sloan Doctoral Dissertation Fellowship 1989–90, Gossenpreis 2003, Fellow of the Econometric Soc. 2003. *Publications:* numerous articles in econ. journals. *Address:* Department of Business Administration and Economics, Spandauer Str. 1, 10178 Berlin (office); Neidenburger Allee 22, 14055 Berlin, Germany (home). *Telephone:* (30) 20935926 (office). *Fax:* (30) 20935934 (office). *E-mail:* uhlig@wiwi.hu-berlin.de. *Website:* www.wiwi.hu-berlin.de/wpol.

UHRIG, John Allan, AC; Australian business executive; *Chairman, Codan Ltd;* b. 24 Oct. 1928, Newcastle, NSW; s. of L. J. Uhrig; m. Shirley Attwood 1956; two s. two d.; ed Newcastle Tech. High School, Univ. of New South Wales; Man. Dir Simpson Ltd 1975–85; Dir CRA Ltd (now Rio Tinto Australia Ltd) 1983–98, Chair. (non-exec.) 1987–98; Chair. Codan Pty Ltd 1986–, Australian Mineral Devt Laboratories Ltd (Amdel) 1989, Australian Minerals and Energy Environment Foundation 1991–; fmr Chair. Australian Mfg

Council; Dir Westpac Banking Corpn 1989–, apptd Chair. 1992; Deputy Chair. Santos Ltd 1992–94, apptd Chair. 1994 (Dir 1991); Deputy Chair. RTZ 1995–; mem. Remuneration Tribunal of South Australia 1985–89. *Address:* Codan Ltd, 81 Graves Street, Newton, SA 5074, Australia (office). *Telephone:* (8) 8305-0311 (office). *Fax:* (8) 8305-0411 (office). *Website:* www.codan.com.au (office).

UJIIE, Junichi, BA, MEcons, MBA; Japanese business executive; *Chairman, Nomura Holdings Inc.;* ed Univs of Tokyo, Chicago and Ill.; joined Nomura Securities as analyst 1975, Pres. Nomura Bank, Switzerland 1984–87, Gen. Man. Int. Planning Dept 1987–90, Pres. Nomura Securities Int., USA 1990–92, mem. Bd of Dirs Nomura Holdings 1990–, Head US Div. 1992–95, Co-Chair. Nomura Securities Int., USA 1995–97, CEO and Pres. Nomura Securities Co. 1997–2003, Chair. Nomura Holdings Inc. 2003–; Vice Chair. Japan Asscn of Corp. Execs (Keizai Doyukai); Chair. Bd of Govs Tokyo Stock Exchange 2000–; Co-Chair. World Econ. Forum on East Asia. *Address:* Nomura Holdings Inc., 1-9-1, Nihonbashi, Chuo-ku, Tokyo 103-8645, Japan (office). *Telephone:* (3) 3211-1811 (office). *Fax:* (3) 3278-0420 (office). *Website:* www.nomura.com (office).

ULAAN, Chultemiin, MSc; Mongolian economist and politician; *Minister of Finance;* b. 22 April 1954, Baruun, Sukhbaatar Prov.; m. Baldan-Osor Bud; three c.; ed Irkhutsk Inst. of Nat. Economy, Irkhutsk, Acad. of Social Sciences, Moscow, Russia, Acad. of Social Sciences, Sofia, Bulgaria; Officer State Planning Dept 1977–82, Head of Div. 1982–85; Instructor, Cen. Cttee, Mongolian People's Revolutionary Party (MPRP) 1985–89, Deputy Dir 1989–90, Adviser to Sec.-Gen. 1990; Cabinet mem. and Minister, Nat. Devt Bd 1992–96; mem. Parl. 1996–; Minister of Finance and Economy 2000–04; Deputy Prime Minister 2004–06; Minister of Finance 2007–. *Address:* Ministry of Finance, Government Building 2, Negsden Ündestnii Gudmaj 5/1, Chingeltei District, Ulan Bator (office). *Telephone:* (11) 320247 (office). *Fax:* (11) 320247 (office). *E-mail:* webmaster@pmis.gov.mn (office). *Website:* www.pmis.gov.mn (office).

ULLENDORFF, Edward, MA, DPhil, DLitt, FBA; British academic; *Professor Emeritus of Ethiopian Studies and Semitic Languages, University of London;* b. 25 Jan. 1920; s. of Frederic Ullendorff and Cilli Ullendorff; m. Dina Noack 1943; ed Univs of Jerusalem and Oxford; war service in Eritrea and Ethiopia 1941–46; Asst Sec., Govt of Palestine 1946–47; Research Officer, Oxford Univ. Inst. of Colonial Studies 1948–49; Lecturer, later Reader, in Semitic Languages, St Andrews Univ. 1950–59; Prof. of Semitic Languages, Manchester Univ. 1959–64; Prof. of Ethiopian Studies, Univ. of London 1964–79, Prof. of Ethiopian Studies and Semitic Languages 1979–82, Prof. Emer. 1982–; Head of Africa Dept, School of Oriental and African Studies (SOAS) 1972–77; Chair. Asscn of British Orientalists 1963–64, Anglo-Ethiopian Soc. 1965–68, Editorial Bd of Bulletin of SOAS 1968–78; Schweich Lecturer, British Acad. 1967; Pres. Soc. for Old Testament Study 1971; Vice-Pres. Royal Asiatic Soc. 1975–79, 1981–85; Fellow, British Acad. 1965–, Vice-Pres. 1980–82; Foreign Fellow, Accad. Nazionale dei Lincei, Rome 1998–; Hon. Fellow, Oxford Centre of Hebrew Studies 1998–; Hon. DLitt (St Andrews) 1972; Hon. DPhil (Hamburg) 1990; Haile Selassie Prize for Ethiopian Studies 1972, Festschrift in honour of EU 1989, 2005. *Publications:* Exploration and Study of Abyssinia 1945, Catalogues of Ethiopic MSS in the Bodleian Library 1951, The Royal Library, Windsor Castle 1953, Cambridge Univ. Library 1961, The Semitic Languages of Ethiopia 1955, The Ethiopians 1960, 3rd edn 1973, Comparative Grammar of the Semitic Languages 1964, An Amharic Chrestomathy 1965, Ethiopia and the Bible 1968, Solomon and Sheba 1974, translated and annotated Emperor Haile Selassie's autobiography 1976, Studies in Semitic Languages and Civilizations 1977, The Ethiopic Enoch (with M. A. Knibb, two vols) 1978, The Amharic Letters of Emperor Theodore to Queen Victoria (co-author) 1979, The Bawdy Bible, The Hebrew Letters of Prester John (co-author) 1982, A Tigrinya Chrestomathy 1985, Studia Aethiopica et Semitica 1987, The Two Zions 1988, From the Bible to Enrico Cerulli 1990, H. J. Polotsky's Selected Letters 1992, From Emperor Haile Selassie to H. J. Polotsky 1995 and others; articles and reviews in journals of learned socs. *Leisure interests:* music. *Address:* 4 Bladon Close, Oxford, OX2 8AD, England (home). *Telephone:* (1865) 552845 (home).

ULLMAN, Myron (Mike) Edward, III, BS; American retail executive; *Chairman and CEO, J.C. Penney Company Inc.;* b. 26 Nov. 1946, Youngstown, OH; s. of Myron Edward Ullman Jr and June Cunningham; m. Cathy Emmons 1969; six c.; ed Univ. of Cincinnati, Harvard Univ.; Int. Account Man. IBM Corpn 1969–76; Vice-Pres. for Business Affairs Univ. of Cincinnati 1976–81; White House Fellow, The White House 1981–82; Exec. Vice-Pres. Sanger Harris Div., Federated Stores 1982–86; Man. Dir and COO Wharf Holdings Ltd, Hong Kong 1986–88; Man. Dir Lane Crawford Ltd, Hong Kong 1986–88; Chair. and CEO R. H. Macy & Co. 1988–95; Deputy Chair. and Dir Federated Dept Stores Inc.; Chair. Bd of Dirs Mercy Ships Int. 1992–; Chair. and CEO DFS Group Ltd 1995–98, Group Chair. 1999–2000; Dir-Gen. and Group Man. Dir Louis Vuitton Möet Hennessy, Paris 1999–2002; Chair. De Beers LV 2000–02; Co-Chair. Global Crossing Ltd 2002–04; Chair. and CEO J.C. Penney Co. Inc. 2004–; mem. Bd of Dirs Starbucks Coffee, Segway LLC, Polo Ralph Lauren, Nat. Multiple Sclerosis Soc., Brunswick School, Univ. of Cincinnati Foundation, Fed. Reserve Bank of Dallas; Chair. Exec. Council Univ. of California Medical Center Foundation 2002–, Nat. Retail Fed., Mercy Ships International; Int. Vice-Pres. Univ. of Cincinnati Alumni Asscn. *Address:* J.C. Penney Company Inc., 6501 Legacy Drive, Plano, TX 75024-3698, USA (office). *Telephone:* (972) 431-1000 (office). *Fax:* (972) 431-1362 (office). *E-mail:* info@jcpenney.net (office). *Website:* www.jcpenney.net (office).

ULLMAN, Tracey; British actress and singer; b. 30 Dec. 1959, Slough; d. of the late Anthony John Ullman and of Dorin Cleaver; m. Allan McKeown 1984; one s. one d.; ed Italia Conti Stage School, London; British Acad. Award 1983,

Rudolph Valentino Cinema Lifetime Achievement Award 1992, Charlie Chaplin Lifetime Achievement Award, BAFTA 2009. *Films include:* The Rocky Horror Picture Show, Give My Regards to Broad Street, Plenty 1985, Jumpin' Jack Flash 1986, I Love You To Death 1990, Robin Hood: Men in Tights 1993, Household Saints, Bullets over Broadway 1994, Pret-a-Porter 1995, Everybody Says I Love You 1996, C-Scam 2000, Panic 2000, Small Town Crooks 2000, A Dirty Shame 2004, The Cat That Looked at a King (voice) 2004, Corpse Bride (voice) 2005, Kronk's New Groove (voice) 2005, I Could Never Be Your Woman 2007, The Tale of Despereaux (voice) 2008. *Stage appearances include:* Gigi, Elvis, Grease, Four in a Million (London Theatre Critics' Award 1981). *Album* You Broke My Heart in Seventeen Places. *Television appearances include:* The Tracey Ullman Show 1987–90, The Best of the Tracey Ullman Show 1990, Tracey Takes On 1996, Ally McBeal 1998–99, Visible Panty Lines (series) 2001, Tracey Ullman in the Trailer Tales 2003, Once Upon a Mattress 2005, State of the Union (series) 2008–09. *Leisure interests:* hiking, riding. *Address:* 13555 D Este Drive, Pacific Palisades, CA 90272; IFA Talent Agency, 8730 W Sunset Boulevard, Suite 490, Los Angeles, CA 90069, USA; c/o ICM, Oxford House, 76 Oxford Street, London, W1N 0AX, England. *Telephone:* (20) 7636-6565 (London). *Fax:* (20) 7323-0101 (London).

ULLMANN, Liv Johanne; Norwegian actress; b. 16 Dec. 1938, Tokyo, Japan; d. of the late Viggo Ullmann and of Janna (née Lund) Ullmann; m. 1st Dr. Gappe Stang 1960 (divorced 1965); one d.; m. 2nd Donald Saunders 1985; worked in repertory co., Stavanger 1956–59; has appeared at Nat. Theatre and Norwegian State Theatre, Oslo; work for UNICEF as Goodwill Amb. 1980–; Vice-Chair. Int. Rescue Cttee; Pres. Fed. of European Film Dirs; Commdr of Olav 1994, Commdr with Star of the Order of St Olav 2005; 12 hon. doctorates; Best Actress of the Year, Nat. Soc. of Critics in America 1969, 1970, 1974, NY Film Critics Award 1973, 1974, Hollywood Foreign Press Asscn's Golden Globe 1973, Best Actress of the Year, Swedish TV 1973, 1974, Donatello Award (Italy) 1975, Bambi Award (Fed. Repub. of Germany) 1975, nominated for Tony Award as Best Stage Actress, debut on Broadway in A Doll's House 1975, LA Film Critics' Award (Face to Face) 1976, New York Film Critics' Award (Face to Face) 1977, Nat. Bd of Review of Motion Pictures Award (Face to Face) 1977, Peer Gynt Award (Norway), Eleanor Roosevelt Award 1982, Roosevelt Freedom Medal 1984, Dag Hammarskjöld Award 1986. *Films include:* Pan 1965, Persona 1966, The Hour of the Wolf 1968, Shame 1968, The Passion of Anna 1969, The Night Visitor 1971, The Emigrants 1972, Cries and Whispers 1972, Pope Joan 1972, Lost Horizon 1973, 40 Carats 1973, The New Land 1973, Zandy's Bride 1973, Scenes from a Marriage 1974, The Abdication 1974, Face to Face 1975, The Serpent's Egg 1978, Sonate d'automne 1978, Richard's Things 1980, The Wild Duck 1983, Love Streams 1983, Let's Hope It's a Girl 1985, Baby Boy 1984, Dangerous Moves 1985, Gaby Brimmer 1986, Moscow Adieu 1986, Time of Indifference 1987, La Amiga 1987, Mindwalk, The Ox, The Long Shadow; Dir: Sophie 1993, Kristin Lavrandsdatter (wrote screenplay also), Faithless (Dir) 2000, Saraband (TV) 2003, The Danish Poet (voice) 2006. *Plays include:* Brand 1973, A Doll's House 1975, Anna Christie 1977, I Remember Mama 1979, Ghosts 1982, Old Times 1985, The Six Faces of Women (TV), Mother Courage. *Publication:* Changing (autobiog.) 1976, Choices (autobiog.) 1984. *Leisure interest:* reading. *Address:* c/o International Artists Management, 235 Regent Street, London, W1A 2JT, England.

ULLRICH, Jan; German professional cyclist; b. 2 Dec. 1973, Rostock; s. of Werner Ullrich and Marianne Kaatz; m. Sara Ullrich; one s. one d.; ed S.C. Dynamo sports school, Berlin; wins as an amateur include: World Championships (Road) 1993, South Africa Tour (three stage wins) 1994, Lower Saxony Tour (two stage wins); turned professional 1995; wins as a professional include: German Time Trial Champion (50km) 1995, Regio Tour (one stage win) 1996, Tour de France 1997, German Road Championships 1997, silver and gold Olympic medals, Sydney 2000; runner-up Tour de France 1996, 1998, 2000, 2001, 2003, fourth 2004, third 2005; seven stage wins, Tour de France; in 2002 tested positive in dope test and given 6-month suspension by German Cycling Fed.; now lives in Switzerland; German Sportsman of the Year 1997, 2003, World Cyclist of the Year 1997. *Leisure interests:* cars, cinema, music. *E-mail:* jan@janullrich.de. *Website:* www.janullrich.de.

ULLSTEN, Ola; Swedish international organization official, politician and diplomatist; *Co-Chair, World Commission on Forests and Sustainable Development;* b. 23 June 1931, Umeå; s. of C. A. Ullsten and Ştina Ullsten; graduated in social sciences 1956; Sec. Parl. Group Liberal Party 1957–61; journalist Dagens Nyheter 1962–64; mem. Riksdag (Parl.) 1965–84; Chair. Liberal Party Stockholm County 1972–76; Minister of Int. Devt Co-operation 1976–78; Deputy Prime Minister March–Oct. 1978, Prime Minister 1978–79; Minister for Foreign Affairs 1979–82, Deputy Prime Minister 1980–82; Chair. Liberal Party 1978–83; Amb. to Canada 1983–89, to Italy 1989–95; mem. Interaction Council of Former Heads of Govt; Co-Chair World Comm. on Forests and Sustainable Devt 1995–; Chair. Int. Advisory Council, Ontario Agricultural Coll., Univ. of Guelph; Sr Fellow Int. Inst. for Sustainable Devt; mem. Bd of Dirs Woods Hole Research Center, MA; hon. degree (Univ. of Guelph) 1999. *Address:* International Institute for Sustainable Development, 161 Portage Avenue East, 6th Floor Winnipeg, Manitoba R3B 0Y4, Canada (office). *Telephone:* (204) 958-7700 (office). *Fax:* (204) 958-7710 (office). *E-mail:* info@iisd.ca (office). *Website:* www.iisd.org (office).

ULMANIS, Guntis, BEcon; Latvian fmr head of state; b. 13 Sept. 1939, Riga; m. Aina Ulmane (née Stelce); one s. one d.; ed Univ. of Latvia; as a child was exiled to Russia together with his parents, returned to Latvia in 1946; mil. service 1963–65; economist bldg industry and Riga Public Transport Bd; Man. Riga Municipal Community Services 1965–92; fmr Lecturer in Construction Econs, Riga Polytechnic Inst. and Econ. Planning, Latvian State Univ.; mem. CPSU 1965–89; mem. Bd of Cen. Bank of Latvia 1992–93, Deputy to Parl.

(Saeima) June–July 1993; Pres. of Latvia 1993–99; Hon. Chair. Union of Farmers Party 1993–; numerous decorations including Order of St Michael and St George (UK) 1996, Légion d'honneur 1997, Order of Merit (Germany) 1999; Dr hc (Charleston Univ., USA) 1996; Award of US Inst. for East West Studies 1996, Cen. and E European Law Initiative Award, American Bar Asscn 1997, Distinguished Statesman Award, Anti-Defamation League 1998. *Publications:* Autobiography 1995, My Time as President 1999. *Leisure interests:* hunting, reading, playing with grandchildren. *Address:* Brīvības iela 38, Apt 5, 1050 Riga, Latvia (home). *Telephone:* 709 2112 (office); 927 8758. *Fax:* 732 5800. *E-mail:* eva@president.lv (office).

ULOUM, Ibrahim Muhammad Bahr al-, PhD; Iraqi politician; *Minister of Oil;* b. 1954; s. of Muhammad Bahr al-Uloum; ed Univ. of New Mexico, USA; worked for Kuwaiti Oil Ministry and Petroleum Recovery Research Center, New Mexico –1992; ind. consultant, London, UK 1992–2003; Minister of Oil of Iraq 2003–04, 2005–; survived assassination attempts in 2003 and 2005. *Address:* Ministry of Oil, Oil Complex Building, Port Said Street, Baghdad, Iraq (office). *Telephone:* (1) 9143 605134 (office); (1) 7901 913315 (home). *Fax:* (1) 886-9432 (office). *E-mail:* oil@uruklink.net (office). *Website:* www.uruklink.net/oil (office).

ULRICH, Jing, BA, MA; Chinese investment manager and business executive; *Chairman and Managing Director, JPMorgan Chase China Equities;* b. 1967, Beijing; m. Paul Ulrich; ed Harvard and Stanford Univs, USA; worked as fund man. for Greater China at Emerging Markets, Washington, DC, USA 1990–96; led top-ranked team covering China market, Credit Lyonnais Securities Asia 1996–2003; Man. Dir Greater China Equities, Deutsche Bank 2003–05; Chair. and Man. Dir JPMorgan Chase China Equities 2005–; serves as adviser to Chinese insts making investments overseas; chosen by Asiamoney magazine as Best China Strategist, ranked by Institutional Investor magazine as head of the top China team world-wide 2003, 2004, 2005, 2006, 2007, chosen by The South China Morning Post and the American Chamber of Commerce in Hong Kong as Hong Kong's Young Achiever of the Year 2006, ranked by Forbes magazine amongst 100 Most Powerful Women (95th) 2008. *Address:* JF Investment Centre, Walkway Level, Jardine House, 1 Connaught Place, Central, Hong Kong Special Administrative Region, People's Republic of China (office). *Telephone:* 2265-1133 (office). *Fax:* 2868-5013 (office). *E-mail:* comments@jfam.com (office). *Website:* www.jfam.com (office).

ULRICH, Robert (Bob) J., BA; American retail executive; *Chairman, Target Corporation;* b. 1943, Minneapolis, Minn.; ed Univ. of Minn.; began career as merchandising trainee, Dayton Hudson 1967, Pres. and CEO Diamond Dept Stores 1981–82, Pres. Dayton Hudson Dept Store Co. 1982–84, Pres. Target Div. 1984–87, Chair. and CEO Target 1987–94, Chair. and CEO Dayton Hudson Corpn (renamed Target Corpn 2000) 1994–2008, Chair. Target Corpn 2008; mem. Bd of Dirs Yum! Brands, Inc. 1997–; Life Trustee, Minneapolis Inst. of Arts; Discounter of the Year, Discount Store News SPARC (Supplier Performance Award by Retail Category) Award 1992. *Address:* Target Corporation, 1000 Nicollet Mall, Minneapolis, MN 55403, USA (office). *Telephone:* (612) 304-6073 (office). *Fax:* (612) 696-3731 (office). *E-mail:* info@target.com (office). *Website:* www.target.com (office).

'ULUKALALA LAVAKA ATA, HRH Prince; Tongan royal; s. of HRH King Taufa'ahau Tupou IV; m. HRH Princess Nanasipau'u Tuku; Cadet Officer, Tonga Defence Services 1981, Commdg Officer of the Navy 1991–95; Prime Minister of Tonga 2000–06 (resigned); held ministerial posts including Minister for Foreign Affairs and Defence 1999–2000, for Agric. and Forestry, Fisheries, Marine and Ports, Civil Aviation 2001–06, for Communications 2001–06, for Works and Disaster Relief Activities 2004–06; fmr Pres. ACP Council of Ministers. *Address:* POB 901, Nuku'alofa, Tonga (office). *Telephone:* 23565 (office). *Fax:* 24626 (office). *E-mail:* webmaster@parliament.gov.to (office). *Website:* parliament.gov.to (office).

ULUSU, Adm. Bülent; Turkish politician and naval officer; b. 7 May 1923, Istanbul; s. of M. Salih Ulusu and Seniye Ulusu; m. Mizat Erensoy 1951; one d.; ed Naval Acad.; various command posts in navy; rank of Rear-Adm. 1967, Vice-Adm. 1970, Adm. 1974; fmr Commdr of War Fleet; Commdr of Turkish Naval Forces –1980; fmr Under-Sec., Ministry of Defence; Prime Minister of Turkey 1980–83; mem. Parl. 1983–87. *Address:* Ciftehavuzlar Yesilbahar 50K. 8/27, Kadikoy Istanbul, Turkey.

ULVÆUS, Björn Kristian; Swedish songwriter, musician (guitar) and singer; b. 25 April 1945, Gothenburg; m. Agnetha Fältskog 1971 (divorced 1979); songwriter with Benny Andersson 1966–; duo with Andersson as The Hootennanny Singers; partner in production with Andersson at Polar Music 1971; mem. pop group, ABBA 1973–82; winner, Eurovision Song Contest 1974; world-wide tours; concerts include Royal Performance, Stockholm 1976, Royal Albert Hall, London 1977, UNICEF concert, New York 1979, Wembley Arena 1979; reunion with ABBA, Swedish TV This Is Your Life 1986; continued writing and producing with Andersson 1982–; produced musical Mamma Mia! with Andersson, West End, London 1999–; World Music Award for Best Selling Swedish Artist 1993, Ivor Novello Special International Award (with Benny Andersson) 2002. *Film:* ABBA: The Movie 1977. *Compositions include:* ABBA songs (with Benny Andersson); musicals: Chess (with lyrics by Tim Rice) 1983, The Immigrants 1994, Mamma Mia! (with Andersson) 1999. *Recordings:* albums: with Andersson: Happiness 1971; with ABBA: Waterloo 1974, ABBA 1976, Greatest Hits 1976, Arrival 1977, The Album 1978, Voulez-Vous 1979, Greatest Hits Vol. 2 1979, Super Trouper 1980, The Visitors 1981, The Singles: The First Ten Years 1982, Thank You For The Music 1983, Absolute ABBA 1988, ABBA Gold 1992, More ABBA Gold 1993, Forever Gold 1998, The Definitive Collection 2001; singles include: with ABBA: Ring Ring 1973, Waterloo 1974, Mamma Mia 1975, Dancing Queen

1976, Fernando 1976, Money Money Money 1976, Knowing Me Knowing You 1977, The Name Of The Game 1977, Take A Chance On Me 1978, Summer Night City 1978, Chiquitita 1979, Does Your Mother Know? 1979, Angel Eyes/Voulez-Vous 1979, Gimme Gimme Gimme (A Man After Midnight) 1979, I Have A Dream 1979, The Winner Takes It All 1980, Super Trouper 1980, On And On And On 1981, Lay All Your Love On Me 1981, One Of Us 1981, When All Is Said And Done 1982, Head Over Heels 1982, The Day Before You Came 1982, Under Attack 1982, Thank You For The Music 1983. *Publication:* Mamma Mia! How Can I Resist You? (with Björn Ulvaeus and Judy Craymer) 2006. *Address:* Södra Brobänken 41A, 111 49 Stockholm, Sweden. *Website:* www.abbasite.com.

ULYUKAYEV, Alexey Valentinovich, Dr Econ; Russian politician, economist and banker; *First Deputy Chairman, Central Bank of the Russian Federation;* b. 23 March 1956, Russia; m.; one s.; ed Moscow State Univ.; Asst, then Assoc. Prof. Moscow Inst. of Construction Eng 1982–88; Consultant, Head of Div. Communist (journal) 1988–91; political analyst Moskovskiye Novosti (weekly) 1991; econ. adviser to Russian Govt 1991–92; Head Group of Advisers to Chair. of Govt Russian Fed. 1992–93; Asst to First Deputy Chair. of Govt Russian Fed. 1993–94; Deputy Dir Inst. of Econ. Problems of the Transition Period 1994–96, 1998–2000; Deputy Moscow City Duma 1996–98; First Deputy Minister of Finance 2000–04; First Deputy Chair. Central Bank of the Russian Fed. 2004–. *Leisure interests:* tourism, swimming, literature. *Address:* Bank Rossii (Central Bank of the Russian Federation), ul. Neglinnaya 12, 107016 Moscow, Russia (office). *Telephone:* (495) 771-40-46 (office). *Fax:* (495) 921-91-47 (office). *E-mail:* webmaster@www.cbr.ru (office). *Website:* www.cbr.ru (office).

UMAR, Asad, MBA; Pakistani business executive; *Chairman and CEO, Engro Chemical Pakistan Ltd;* ed Inst. of Business Admin, Pakistan; joined Exxon Chemical Pakistan (later renamed Engro Pakistan Ltd) 1985, worked in Karachi, Daharki and Edmonton, Canada in Finance, Manufacturing, Marketing and New Ventures Div., later Sr Vice-Pres. Engro Chemical Pakistan Ltd, Chair. and CEO 2004–, Dir Engro Chemical Pakistan Ltd, Engro Vopak Terminal Ltd, Engro Asahi Polymer & Chemicals Ltd (fmr first Pres.), Port Qasim Authority 2000–01; mem. Bd of Man. Pakistan State Oil; Chapter Chair. Young Presidents' Org. (Pakistan Chapter); mem. Overseas Investors' Chamber of Commerce and Industry's Standing Sub-cttee for Commercial and Industrial Matters 1998–00, Man. Asscn Pakistan's Corp. Excellence Award Sub-cttee 1998–2000; mem. Bd of Dirs Pakistan Centre for Philanthropy. *Address:* Engro Chemical Pakistan Ltd, 8th Floor, PNSC Building, M.T. Khan Road, Karachi, Pakistan (office). *Telephone:* (21) 5611060-69 (office). *Fax:* (21) 5611249 (office). *E-mail:* aumar@engro.com (office). *Website:* www.engro.com (office).

UMAROV, Doku (Dokka) Khamatovich, (Emir Abu Usman); Russian/Chechen construction engineer and rebel leader; b. 13 April 1964, Kharsenoi, Shatoyskii Dist, Checheno-Ingush ASSR (now Chechen—Nokchi Repub.); s. of Khamad Umarov; m.; six c.; ed Construction Faculty, Oil Inst., Grozny; mem. Chechen separatist movt 1994–, field commdr southwestern front 2002–, 'Vice-Pres.' 'Chechen Repub. of Ichkeriya' –2006, 'Pres.' 2006–07, proclaimed Caucasus Emirate and declared himself Emir 2007–; fmr Head of Chechen Security Council; Kioman Syi (Honour of the Nation), Kyoman Turpal (Hero of the Nation).

UMBA DI LUTETE, LenD; Democratic Republic of the Congo diplomatist and former government official; b. 30 June 1939, Kangu; s. of late Umba Julien and Mdbuilu Matsumba; m. Diomi Kiese 1967; three s. three d.; ed Univ. of Lovanium, Univ. Libre de Bruxelles, Belgium; training with US Agency for Int. Devt and with Belgian Parl. and Foreign Ministry; taught at Univ. of Lovanium, at Nat. Univ. of Zaire; Minister at the Presidency 1969–70, of Energy 1970–71, of Mining 1971–74, for Foreign Affairs 1974–75, for Politics 1975–76, for State Affairs, Foreign Affairs and Int. Co-operation 1977–79, for Nat. Guidance, Culture and the Arts 1979–80; mem. Political Bureau of Mouvement populaire de la révolution (MPR), also MPR Perm. Cttee; Perm. Rep. to UN 1976–77, 1982–84; State Commr for Foreign and Int. Affairs 1984–85; fmr leader of dels to UN Gen. Ass. and Security Council, to OAU, OCAM, UNCTAD. *Address:* c/o Ministry of Foreign Affairs, Kinshasa, Democratic Republic of the Congo.

UMEDA, Sadao; Japanese business executive; *Chairman, Kajima Corporation;* Pres. Kajima Corpn (building construction co. providing design, eng, building and real estate devt services) 1996–2005, Chair. 2005–; mem. Keidanren Japan–Hong Kong Business Cooperation Cttee 2000–, Chair. 2002; mem. Bd of Dirs Japan Telework Asscn 2003, Japan Fashion Asscn, Japan Water Forum Advisory Council; Pres. Ethiopian Asscn of Japan, Japanese-Turkish Econ. Council; mem. Japan Cttee, Pacific Basic Econ. Council. *Address:* Kajima Corporation, 2-7 Motoakasaka 1-chome, Minatu-ku, Tokyo 107-8388, Japan (office). *Telephone:* (3) 3403-3311 (office). *Fax:* (3) 3470-1444 (office). *Website:* www.kajima.co.uk (office).

UMEHARA, Makoto; Japanese business executive; *President, Citizen Watch Company Limited;* managed sales, service, and production at Citizen Watch Co. Ltd German subsidiary –1993, Dir Precision Machinery Div. 1993–98, Exec. Dir and Man. Tokorozawa Works 2000–2002, Pres. and CEO Citizen Watch 2002–; Chair. Japan Clock and Watch Asscn. *Address:* Citizen Watch Company Limited, 6-1-2 Tanashi-cho, Nishi Tokyo-shi, Tokyo 188-8511, Japan (office). *Telephone:* (4) 2466-1231 (office). *Fax:* (4) 2466-1280 (office). *Website:* www.citizen.co.jp (office).

UMRI, Gen. Hassan; Yemeni politician; took part in revolution against Imamate 1962; Minister of Transport Sept.–Oct. 1962, of Communications 1962–63; mem. Council of Revolutionary Command 1962–63; Vice-Pres. of Yemen 1963–66; mem. Political Bureau 1963–66; Prime Minister Jan.–April 1965, 1965–66, 1967–68; Mil. Gov.-Gen. of Yemen 1968–69; also C-in-C of Army; Prime Minister Aug.–Sept. 1971; in exile in Lebanon until Jan. 1975; returned to Yemen Arab Repub. Jan. 1975.

UNAKITAN, Kemal; Turkish politician; b. 1946, Edirne; m.; three c.; ed Ankara Econ. and Commerical Sciences Acad.; fmr Financial Comptroller Ministry of Finance, Minister of Finance 2002–09; fmr mem. Exec. Bd SEKA Directorate Gen., Albaraka Türk and Family Finance. *Address:* c/o Ministry of Finance, Maliye Bakanlığı, Dikmen Cad., Ankara, Turkey (office).

UNANUE, Emil Raphael, MD; Cuban immunologist and academic; *Mallinckrodt Professor and Chairman, Department of Pathology and Immunology, School of Medicine, Washington University;* b. 13 Sept. 1934, Havana; ed Inst. of Secondary Educ., Havana, Univ. of Havana School of Medicine; Intern in Pathology, Presbyterian Univ. Hosp., Pittsburgh, Pa 1961–62; Research Fellow, Dept of Experimental Pathology, Scripps Clinic and Research Foundation, La Jolla, Calif. 1962–66, Assoc. 1968–70; Research Fellow, Immunology Div., Nat. Inst. for Medical Research, London, UK 1966–68; Asst Prof. of Pathology, Harvard Medical School, Boston, Mass 1970–71, Assoc. Prof. 1972–74, Mallinckrodt Prof. of Immunopathology 1974–84, Consultant in Pathology, Dept of Pathology, Brigham and Women's Hosp. 1977–84; Visiting Prof., Kuwait Univ. School of Medicine, Kuwait 1982, Royal Postgraduate Medical School, London 1983; Pathologist-in-Chief, Barnes-Jewish Hosp., St Louis, Mo. 1985–; Mallinckrodt Prof. and Chair. Dept of Pathology and Immunology, Washington Univ. School of Medicine, St Louis 1985–; Burroughs Wellcome Visiting Prof. in the Basic Medical Sciences, Tulane Univ., New Orleans, La 2000; Pres. American Asscn of Pathologists 1988–89; Assoc. Ed. Journal of Immunology 1972–77, Clinical Immunology and Immunopathology 1972–89, International Archives of Allergy and Applied Immunology 1973–91, Journal of the Reticuloendothelial Society 1974–77, Laboratory Investigation 1975–90, Immunity 1994–96 (Ed. 1996–2000); Contributing Ed. Sanguinis 1976–77; Transmitting Ed. International Immunology 1992–; mem. Editorial Bd Modern Pathology 1988–97, Molecular Medicine 1994–, Immunological Reviews 1996–; mem. American Soc. of Investigative Pathology 1966, American Asscn of Immunologists 1966, Reticuloendothelial Soc. 1977, American Soc. for Cell Biology 1984, Asscn of Pathology Chairmen 1986, US and Canadian Acad. of Pathology 1986, NAS 1987 (Chair. Section 43—Microbiology and Immunology 1998–), Alpha Omgea Alpha Hon. Medical Soc. 1988, Pew Nat. Advisory Council 1994–98, Inst. of Medicine 1995; Sr Fellow, American Cancer Soc. (Calif. Div.) 1969–70, American Acad. of Arts and Sciences 1989; Hon. mem. Venezuelan Soc. of Allergy and Immunology 1981; Hon. MA (Harvard) 1974; Dr hc (Barcelona) 1999; Helen Hay Whitney Fellowship and T. Ducket Jones Award 1966–69, NIH Research Career Development Award 1971, Parke Davis Award, American Soc. for Experimental Pathology 1973, Guggenheim Fellowship 1980–81, Marie T. Bonzainga Annual Research Award, Reticuloendothelial Soc. 1986, William B. Coley Award, Cancer Research Inst. 1989, Albert Lasker Award for Basic Medical Research 1995, Rous-Whipple Award, American Soc. for Investigative Pathology 1998, Kenneth W. Sell Memorial Lecturer, Emory Univ. 1999, Gairdner Foundation Int. Award 2000. *Publications:* more than 210 articles in scientific journals. *Address:* Department of Pathology and Immunology, School of Medicine, Washington University in St Louis, Room 1751, 660 S Euclid Avenue, 1st Floor, West Building, Campus Box 8118, St Louis, MO 63110, USA (office). *Telephone:* (314) 362-7440 (office). *Fax:* (314) 362-4096 (office). *E-mail:* unanue@wustl.edu (office). *Website:* pathology.wustl.edu (office).

UNCKEL, Per; Swedish civil servant; *Governor of Stockholm;* b. 24 Feb. 1948, Finspång, Östergötland; m. Christina Lagenquist 1977; two s.; ed Uppsala Univ.; Chair. Swedish Young Moderates 1971–76, mem. Parl. (Östergötland) 1976–86, 1994–2002, Moderate Party Spokesman on Energy Questions 1978–82, Nat. Campaign Leader 1980 Referendum on Nuclear Power, Party Spokesman on Educ. and Science 1982–86, Sec.-Gen. Moderate Party 1986–91; Minister of Educ. and Science 1991–94; Spokesman on Employment 1994–98, Chair. Parl. Standing Cttee on the Constitution 1998–2002, Parl. Group Leader Moderate Party 1999–2002; Sec.-Gen. Nordic Council of Ministers 2002–07; Gov. Stockholm Co. 2007–. *Publications:* Knowledge as a Personal Investment 1998, No One Behind 2002. *Leisure interests:* music, carpentry. *Address:* Office of the Governor, Stockholm County Administrative Board, Box 22067, 104 22 Stockholm, Sweden (office). *Telephone:* (8) 785-40-00 (office). *Fax:* (8) 785-40-01 (office). *E-mail:* lansstyrelsen@ab.lst.se (office). *Website:* www.ab.lst.se (office).

UNGARO, Emanuel Mattéotti; French fashion designer; b. 13 Feb. 1933, Aix-en-Provence; s. of Cosimo Ungaro and Concetta Casalino; m. Laura Bernabei; one d.; ed Lycée d'Aix-en-Provence; worked as tailor at Aix-en-Provence then with Camps, Paris, Balenciaga, Paris and Madrid 1958–64, Courrèges, Paris 1964; Couturier, Paris 1965–2004; Chevalier, Légion d'honneur. *Leisure interests:* music, reading, skiing. *Address:* 2 avenue Montaigne, 75008 Paris, France. *Telephone:* 1-53-57-00-00 (office). *Fax:* 1-47-23-82-31 (office). *E-mail:* info@ungaro.fr. *Website:* www.ungaro.com.

UNGER, Felix, DrMed; Austrian surgeon; *Head of Heart Surgery, Salzburg State Hospital;* b. 2 March 1946, Klagenfurt; s. of Carl Unger and Maria Unger; m. Monika von Fioreschy 1971; two s.; Lecturer, Univ. of Vienna 1978–83, Prof., Univ. of Innsbruck 1983–; Head of Heart Surgery, Salzburg State Hosp.; Founder and Pres. European Acad. of Sciences and Arts; Bundesverdienstkreuz 1992; Hon. DrMed (Temeschwar, Budapest, Tokyo, Maribor and Riga) 1990–2003; Dr Karl Renner Prize 1975, Sandoz Prize 1980, Plannsee Prize 1982. *Publications:* 15 books and more than 500 articles in specialist journals. *Leisure interest:* arts. *Address:* European Academy of Sciences and Arts, Mönchsberg 2, 5020 Salzburg (office); Schwimmschulstrasse 31, 5020 Salzburg, Austria. *Telephone:* (662) 841345 (office); (662)

824741 (home). *Fax:* (662) 841343 (office); (662) 8247414 (home). *E-mail:* felix.unger@european-academy.at (office); f.unger@salk.at (office). *Website:* www.european-academy.at (office); www.ehi.at; www.eomed.at.

UNGER, Michael Ronald; British newspaper editor and business executive; b. 8 Dec. 1943, Surrey; s. of Ronald Unger and Joan Stanbridge; m. 1st Eunice Dickens 1966 (divorced 1992); one s. one d. (deceased); m. 2nd Noorah Ahmed 1993; ed Wirral Grammar School, Liverpool Polytechnic; trainee journalist, Stockport 1963–65; Production Ed., Reading Evening Post 1965–67; News Ed., Perth, Australia 1967–71; Deputy Ed. Daily Post, Liverpool 1971–79, Ed. 1979–82; Ed. Liverpool Echo 1982–83; Ed. Manchester Evening News 1983–97; Dir Guardian Media Group 1983–97, Manchester Evening News PLC 1983–97; Communications Consultant 1997–2000; Gen. Man. Jazz FM 2000; Chair. The Lowry Centre 1996, Youth Charter for Sport 1996–2000; mem. Broadcasting Standards Comm. 1999–2000; Trustee Scott Trust 1986–97; various newspaper awards including Newspaper Design 1980, 1981, 1982, 1994; Ed. of the Year 1988. *Publication:* The Memoirs of Bridget Hitler 1979. *Leisure interests:* books, theatre. *Address:* c/o VNXD, PO Box 171, Welwyn Garden City, Herts. AL6 0ZQ, England (office). *E-mail:* vnxd@lineone.net (office). *Website:* www.vnxd.co.uk (office).

UNGERER, Werner, Dr rer. pol; German diplomatist; b. 22 April 1927, Stuttgart; s. of Max Ungerer and Elisabeth (Mezger) Ungerer; m. Irmgard Drenckhahn 1959; one s. two d.; ed Dillman Gymnasium, Stuttgart, Technical Univ. Stuttgart, Univ. of Tübingen and Coll. of Europe, Bruges; Attaché, diplomatic service 1952–54; Vice-Consul, Boston 1954–56; Consul, Bombay 1956–58; Head of Div. Euratom Comm. Brussels 1958–64; Ministry of Foreign Affairs 1964–70; Resident Lecturer on Diplomacy and European Integration, Univ. of Bonn 1965–66; rep. to int. orgs in Vienna 1970–75; Consul-Gen. New York 1975–79; Ministry of Foreign Affairs 1979–85; Dir-Gen. Dept of Econ. Affairs 1984–85; Perm. Rep. to EEC Brussels 1985–89; Rector Coll. of Europe 1990–93; lecturer, Univ. of Bonn 1994–98; Pres. European Co-operation Fund 1994–98; mem. Bd of Trustees, Trier Acad. of European Law 1993–2003; Order Leopold II of Belgium 1989, Medal of Merit, Europa-Union Germany 1989, Bundesverdienstkreuz 1991. *Music:* piano recitals in Carnegie Hall, NY 1979, Brussels Opera 1989. *Publications:* numerous articles on European integration, energy problems and int. orgs in reviews and anthologies. *Leisure interests:* history, religions, playing piano and composing. *Address:* Nachtigallenweg 19, 53343 Wachtberg, Germany. *Telephone:* (228) 325572.

UNGUREANU, Mihai-Răzvan, MA, MPhil, PhD; Romanian academic and politician; b. 22 Sept. 1968, Iasi; m.; ed C. Negruzzi High School of Math.-Physics, Iasi, Al. I. Cuza Univ., Iasi, St Cross Coll., Oxford, UK; Jr Fellow, New Europe Coll. for Advanced Studies, Bucharest, mem. Admin. Bd 2002; teacher, Mihai Eminescu Philology-History High School, Iasi 1992; Univ. Tutor, Faculty of History, Al. I. Cuza Univ., Iasi 1992–96, Univ. Asst 1996–98, Univ. Lecturer 1998, Dir Centre for Jewish Studies 2004, mem. Senate Al. I. Cuza Univ. 1990–92; Guest Scientist, Dept for European History, Albert Ludwig Univ., Freiburg im Breisgau, Germany 1993–97; Assoc. Prof., School of Slavonic and East European Studies, Univ. of London, UK 1996–98; Dir Centre for Romanian Studies, Romanian Cultural Foundation, Iasi 1996–99; Sr Fellow, Oxford Centre for Jewish and Hebrew Studies, St Cross Coll. Oxford 1998; Sr Reader, NATO School (SHAPE), Oberammergau, Germany 2001; Assoc. Univ. Prof., SNSPA, Bucharest 2002; Sr Reader, George C. Marshall Centre for Security Studies, Garmisch-Partenkirchen, Germany 2003; Sec. of State, Ministry of Foreign Affairs 1998–2001, Regional Emissary, Stability Pact for South-Eastern Europe 2001–03; Deputy Coordinator SE European Cooperation Initiative (SECI), Vienna 2003; Minister-Counselor 2003; Minister of Foreign Affairs 2005–07 (resgnd); Coordinator Historia Collection, Polirom Publishing House, Iasi 1998; Ed.-in-Chief Revista de Istorie Sociala 1996; Ed. Dialog Magazine 1988–92, Arhiva Genealogica 1993, Revue des Etudes Roumains 1994, Nat. Council for Educ. Reform, Nat. of National Educ., 1998–2000, Scientific Council, Sever Zotta Inst. for Genealogical and Heraldic Studies, Iasi, 1998; Sec. Exec. Int. Students in History Asscn, Budapest-Brussels 1990–93; mem. Scientific Bd Soros Foundation for an Open Society, Iasi 1996–98; Pres. Romanian Inst. for Strategic Studies, Bucharest 2001; mem. Romanian Soc. for Heraldry, Sealography and Genealogy of the Romanian Acad. (Iasi Br.) 1993, European Asscn for Jewish Studies, Oxford 1997, Scientific Bd Centre for Security Policies, Szeged, Hungary 2003; Commdr (First Rank), Royal Order of the Dannebrog (Denmark) 2000, Grand Officer of Nat. Order for Merits (Romania) 2000; Republican Praiseworthy Scholarship, Al. I. Cuza Univ. 1991, Royal Soc. Mark Rich Scholarship, St Cross Coll., Oxford 1992, Studies and Research Scholarship, Albert Ludwig Univ., Freiburg im Breisgau, Germany 1994–98, NEC Fellowship, New Europe Coll., Bucharest 1996, REX Fellowship IREX, State Dept, USA 1996, Chevening-FCO Fellowship SEES, Univ. of London 1997, Relink Fellowship, New Europe Coll. 1998, Felix Posen Fellowship, Hebrew Univ., Jerusalem, Israel 1998–99, Andrew Mellon Fellowship, Wissenschaftskolleg zu Berlin 1998; Nat. Prize of 22 Magazine, Bucharest 1992, Felix Posen Prize, Hebrew Univ. 1996–97, 1997–98, Vasile Pogor Prize, Iasi City Hall 1998, Corneliu Coposu Prize, Youth Org. of PNT-cd 1999, Dimitrie Onciul Prize, Magazin Istoric Cultural Foundation for the publication of the work Relatiile Romano-sovietice, Documente, 1917–1934, I, Bucharest, 1999 (in collaboration with the Ministry of Foreign Affairs of the Russian Federation). *Publications:* Statistical Documents Regarding the City of Iasi (1755–1828), Vols I–II (co-author) 1996–97, Marea Arhondologie a boierilor Moldovei 1998, The Comprehensive Catalogue of Moldavian Boyars, 1829–1856 1997, Convertire si integrare in societatea romaneasca la inceputul epocii moderne 2004; more than 50 scientific articles and more than 60 publs in magazines and learned reviews including Dialog, Cronica, Timpul, Convorbiri literare, Astra, Romania Literara, 22, Dilema, Tinerama, Contrapunct, Polis, Revue des Etudes Roumaines, The Genealogic Archives, The Romanian Review of Social History, Nepszabadsag 1991–2004. *Address:* c/o Ministry of Foreign Affairs, Aleea Alexandru 31, Sector 1, 71274 Bucharest, Romania (office).

UNO, Ikuo; Japanese insurance executive; *Chairman, Nippon Life Insurance Company;* Pres. Nippon Life Insurance Co. –2005, Chair. 2005–; Vice-Chair. Kansai Econ. Fed. (Kankeiren); mem. Bd of Auditors Odakyu Electric Railway Co. Ltd 2002; Corp. Auditor Tanabe Seiyaku Co. Ltd; Chair. Life Insurance Asscn of Japan 2001–05; mem. Bd of Dirs Int. Insurance Soc. Inc., New York 2003–, Japan Investor Relations Asscn 2003–, Obayashi Foundation 2006–. *Address:* Nippon Life Insurance Co., 3-5-12 Imabashi, Chuo-ku, Osaka 541-8501, Japan (office). *Telephone:* (6) 6209-5525 (office). *Fax:* (3) 5510-7340 (office). *E-mail:* info@nissay.co.jp (office). *Website:* www.nissay.co.jp (office).

UNSWORTH, Barry; British writer; b. 10 Aug. 1930, Wingate, Co. Durham; s. of the late Michael Unsworth and Elsie Unsworth; m. 1st Valerie Irene Moore 1959 (divorced 1991); three d.; m. 2nd Aira Pohjanvaara-Buffa 1992; ed Manchester Univ.; nat. service; taught English in France and at Univs of Athens and Istanbul; Writer-in-Residence, Ambleside, Cumbria 1979, Univ. of Liverpool 1985; Visiting Literary Fellow, Univs of Durham and Newcastle 1982; moved to Helsinki 1987; now lives in Italy; Hon. LittD (Manchester) 1998. *Publications:* The Partnership 1966, The Greeks Have A Word For It 1967, The Hide 1970, Mooncranker's Gift (winner, Heinemann Fiction Prize) 1973, The Big Day 1976, Pascali's Island 1980, The Rage of the Vulture 1982, Stone Virgin 1985, Sugar and Rum 1988, Sacred Hunger 1992 (jt winner, Booker Prize 1992), Morality Play 1995, After Hannibal 1996, Losing Nelson 1999, The Songs of the Kings 2002, The Ruby in her Navel 2006, Land of Marvels 2009. *Leisure interests:* gardening, bird-watching. *Address:* c/o Vivien Green, Sheil Land Associates, 52 Doughty Street, London WC1N 2LS, England (office); Casella Postale 24, 06060 Agello (PG), Italy (home). *Telephone:* (20) 7405-9351 (office). *E-mail:* info@sheilland.co.uk (office); vgreen@sheilland.co.uk (office). *Website:* www.sheilland.co.uk (office).

UNTERMANN, Jürgen, DPhil; German professor of linguistics; *Professor Emeritus, University of Cologne;* b. 24 Oct. 1928, Rheinfelden; ed Univs of Frankfurt and Tübingen; Asst Prof., Univ. of Tübingen 1953–58; pvt. tutor 1962–65; project on Pre-Roman inscriptions in the Iberian Peninsula 1958–62; Full Prof. of Comparative Linguistics, Univ. of Cologne 1965–94, Dean, Faculty of Letters 1971–72, Prof. Emer. 1994–; Dr hc (Salamanca) 1993, (Santiago de Compostela) 2003. *Publications:* Die Venetischen Personennamen 1961, Monumenta Linguarum Hispanicarum, Vol. I 1975, Vol. II 1980, Vol. III 1990, Vol. IV 1997, Einführung in die Sprache Homers 1987, Oskisch-Umbrisches Wörterbuch 2000. *Address:* Pfalzgrafenstrasse 11, 50259 Pulheim, Germany (home). *Telephone:* (2234) 82274 (home). *E-mail:* juergen@untermannonline.de (home).

UNWIN, Eric Geoffrey (Geoff), BSc; British business executive; *Chairman, Halma plc;* b. 9 Aug. 1942, Radcliffe-on-Trent, Notts.; s. of Maurice Doughty Unwin and Olive Milburn (née Watson); m. Margaret Bronia Element 1967; one s. one d.; ed Heaton Grammar School, Newcastle upon Tyne, King's Coll., Durham Univ.; with Cadbury Bros 1963–68; joined John Hoskyns & Co. 1968, Man. Dir Hoskyns Systems Devt 1978, Dir Hoskyns Group 1982, Man. Dir 1984, Exec. Chair. 1988; COO Cap Gemini 1993–2000, CEO and Vice-Chair. Exec. Bd 1996–2000, Chair. Cap Programmator AB 1993–2000, CEO, mem. Bd Cap Gemini Ernst & Young (fmrly Cap Gemini) 2000–02; Dir (non-exec.) Volmac Software Group NV 1990, Gemini Consulting Holding SA 1994–2000, NED United News & Media (now United Business Media) PLC 1995–2007, Chair. 2002–07; Dir (non-voting) CGEY 2002–; Chair. Cloud Networks Ltd 2005–06, Omnibus Systems Ltd 2005–, 3G Lab 2002–05, Taptu 2007–, Alliance Medical 2008–; Pres. Computing Services Asscn 1987–88; Deputy Chair. (now Chair.) Halma plc 2002–, Liberata PLC 2003–, Cloud Networks Ltd 2005–06, Omnibus Systems Ltd 2007; mem. Information Tech. Advisory Bd 1988–91, Palamon Capital Pnrs 2002–; Freeman City of London 1987. *Leisure interests:* golf, riding, skiing, gardening. *Address:* 17 Park Village West, London, NW1 4AE, England (home). *Telephone:* (20) 7378-3727 (office). *Fax:* (20) 7378-3705 (office). *E-mail:* geoff.unwin@gunwin.co.uk (office).

UNWIN, Sir (James) Brian, Kt, KCB, MA; British banker and fmr government official; b. 21 Sept. 1935, Chesterfield; s. of Reginald Unwin and Winifred Walthall; m. Diana Scott 1964; three s.; ed Chesterfield School, New Coll. Oxford and Yale Univ., USA; Asst Prin. Commonwealth Relations Office 1960; Pvt. Sec. to British High Commr Salisbury, Rhodesia 1961–64; First Sec. British High Comm. Accra 1964–65; FCO 1965–68; transferred to HM Treasury 1968; Pvt. Sec. to Chief Sec. Treasury 1970–72, Asst Sec. 1972, Under-Sec. 1976, Deputy Sec. 1983–85; seconded to Cabinet Office 1981–83; Dir European Investment Bank (EIB) 1983–85, Pres. 1993–2000, Hon. Pres. 2000–; Deputy Sec. Cabinet Office 1985–87; Chair. Bd HM Customs & Excise 1987–93; Gov. EBRD 1993–2000; Chair. Supervisory Bd European Investment Fund 1994–2000; mem. Advisory Bd IMPACT 1990–93; mem. Bd of Dirs ENO 1993–94, 2000–08, Fondation Pierre Werner, Centre d'Etudes Prospectives (CEPROS) 1996–2000, Dexia Bank 2000–, European Centre for Nature Conservation 2000– (Pres. 2001–), "Britain in Europe" Council 2002–05; Chair. Assettrust Housing 2003; Dir Fed. Trust for Educ. and Research 2003–; Pres. New College (Oxford) Soc. 2004–; Hon. Pres. Euronem (Athens) 2000–08; Hon. Fellow, New Coll. Oxford 1997, Inst. of Indirect Taxation 2002; Commdr du Wissam Alloui (Morocco) 1999, Grand Officier Ordre de la Couronne (Belgium) 2000, Grand Croix Ordre Grand Ducal de la Couronne de Chêne (Luxembourg) 2001; Gold Medal, Fondation du Mérite Européen. *Publication:* Corporate Social Responsibility and Socially Responsible Investing (co-author) 2002, Britain's Future and the Euro (co-author) 2004. *Leisure interests:* opera, bird-watching, Wellingtoniana, cricket. *Address:* c/o Reform Club, Pall Mall, London, SW1Y 5EW, England.

UOSUKAINEN, Riitta Maria, MA, LicPhil; Finnish politician and teacher; b. 18 June 1942, Jääski; d. of Reino Vainikka and Aune Vainikka; m. Toivo Uosukainen 1968; one s.; ed Univ. of Helsinki; teacher, Imatrankoski Upper Second School 1969–; Prov. Instructor in Finnish Language, Kymi Prov. 1976–83; mem. Imatra Town Council 1977–92, Vice-Chair. 1980–86; mem. Eduskunta (Parl.) 1983–2003, Minister of Educ. 1991–94, Speaker of Parl. 1994–2003; presidential cand. 2003; Commdr Order of White Rose 1992, Commdr Italian Repub. 1993, Order of First Class of White Star (Estonia) 1995, Grand Cross First Class, Order of Merit (Germany) 1996, Grand Cross, Order of the Crown (Belgium) 1996, Commdr Grand Cross, Royal Order of Polar Star (Sweden) 1996, Grand Cross, Order of Honour (Greece) 1996, Commdr Cross, Order of Falcon (Finland) 1997, Valtioneuvos (Councillor of State) 2004; Dr hc (Finlandia Univ., USA) 1997, (Lappeenranta Inst. of Tech.) 1999; Speaker of the Year Award 1985. *Publications:* (as co-author): Clues for Mother Tongue Teaching 1979, Link Exercises in Mother Tongue 1981, Mother Tongue Fountain 1984, Liehuva Liekinvarsi (speeches and letters) 1996. *Leisure interest:* literature. *Address:* Olkinuorankatu 11, 55910 Imatra, Finland (home). *Telephone:* (5) 4337766 (home). *Fax:* (5) 4337700 (home).

UPADHAYA, Kedar Nath; Nepalese judge; Chief Justice, Supreme Court of Nepal –2004. *Address:* c/o Supreme Court of Nepal, POB 20438, Ramashahapath, Kathmandu, Nepal.

URANO, Yasuoki; Japanese politician; fmr Parl. Vice-Minister of Foreign Affairs, of Int. Trade and Industry; mem. House of Reps, Chair. Cttee on Commerce and Industry; Minister of State, Dir-Gen. Science and Tech. Agency 1995–96. *Address:* c/o Science and Technology Agency, 2-2-1, Kasumigaseki, Chiyoda-ku, Tokyo 100, Japan. *Telephone:* (3) 3581-5271.

URBAIN, Robert; Belgian politician; *Minister of State;* b. 24 Nov. 1930, Hornu; three s.; ed Ecole Normale, Mons; math. teacher 1950–58; Deputy for Mons 1971–95; Sec. of State for Planning and Housing 1973, for Econ. Affairs (French region) 1977–78; Minister of Posts and Telephones 1979, of Foreign Trade 1980–81, of Health and Educ. (French sector) 1981–85, of Social Affairs and Health Feb.–May 1988, of Foreign Trade 1988–92, of Foreign Trade and European Affairs 1992–95; mem. Senate 1995–99; Minister of State 1998–; Prés. du Conseil d'Admin. de la Faculté Polytechnique de Mons; Grand-Croix Ordre de Léopold II, Croix civique (1st Class); Officier Ordre de la Pléiade, Grand-Croix Ordre de la Couronne, and numerous foreign awards. *Leisure interests:* cycling, swimming. *Address:* Hôtel de Ville, 7300 Boussu (office); Rue de Bavay 42, 7301 Hornu, Belgium (home). *Telephone:* (65) 71-73-11 (office); (65) 63-07-38 (home). *Fax:* (65) 79-36-14 (office); (65) 65-02-65 (home). *E-mail:* r.urbain@boussu.be (office).

URBAN, Jerzy; Polish journalist; *President, URMA Company Ltd;* b. 3 Aug. 1933, Łódź; s. of Jan Urban and Maria Urban; m. 1st 1957; one d.; m. 3rd Małgorzata Daniszewska 1986; ed Warsaw Univ.; staff writer, weekly Po Prostu, Warsaw 1955–57; head of home section, weekly Polityka, Warsaw 1960–63, 1968–81; columnist of satirical weekly Szpilki, articles written under pen-names including Jan Rem and Jerzy Kibic; Govt Press Spokesman 1981–89; Minister without portfolio, Head Cttee for Radio and Television April–Sept. 1989; Dir and Ed.-in-Chief, Nat. Workers' Agency Nov. 1989–90; Dir and Ed.-in-Chief Unia-Press Feb.–May 1990; Pres. Kier Co. Ltd 1990–; Pres. URMA Co. Ltd, Warsaw 1991–; Ed.-in-Chief, political weekly Nie Oct. 1990–; participant Round Table debates, mem. group for mass media Feb.–April 1990; mem. Journalists' Asscn of Polish People's Repub. 1982–, Polish Writers' Union; Ztoty KrzyżZastTugi, KrzyżKomandorski Polonia Restituta; Victor Prize (TV) 1987. *Screenplays include:* Sekret, Otello. *Publications:* Kolekcja Jerzego Kibica 1972, Impertynencje: Felietony z lat 1969–72 1974, Wszystkie nasze ciemne sprawy 1974, Grzechy chodzą po ludziach 1975, Gorączka 1981, Romanse 1981, Robak w jabłku 1982, Na odlew 1983, Samosądy 1 1984, Felietony dla cudzych zon 1984, Samosądy 2 1984, Z pieprzem i solą 1986, Jakim prawem 1988, Rozkosze podglądania 1988, Cały Urban 1989, Alfabet Urbana 1990, Jajakobyły 1991, Prima aprilis towarzysze 1992, Klątwa Urbana 1995, Druga Klątwa Urbana 2000. *Leisure interest:* social life. *Address:* URMA Co. Ltd, ul. Słoneczna 25, 00 789 Warsaw, Poland (office). *Telephone:* (22) 8485290 (office). *Fax:* (22) 8497258 (office). *E-mail:* NIE@redakcja.nie.com.pl (office); nie@redakcja.nie.com.pl (office).

URBAN, Wolfgang; German business executive; *Chairman, Karstadt Quelle;* b. 1945, Oberbaumgarten, Schleisen; commercial exec. Kaufhof AG, Cologne 1973–83, Dir Accounts Dept and Finance Dept 1983–85, Gen. Man. 1985–87, mem. Finance, Accounts and Tax Cttees 1987–95; Speaker Exec. Bd Kaufhof Holding AG, Cologne 1995–96; mem. Exec. Bd Schickedanz Holding-Stiftung & Co. KG, Fürth 1998–99; mem. Exec. Bd Karstadt Quelle AG, Essen 1999–, Chair. Karstadt Warenhaus AG Jan.–Oct. 2000, Chair. Karstadt Quelle AG Oct. 2000–. *Address:* Karstadt Quelle AG, Theodor-Althoff-Strasse 2, 45133 Essen, Germany (office). *Telephone:* (201) 7271 (office). *Fax:* (201) 7275216 (office). *Website:* www.karstadtquelle.com (office).

URBANOVÁ, Eva; Czech singer (soprano); b. 20 April 1961, Slaný; ed Acad. of Musical Arts; opera debut at Plzeň Josef Kajetan Tyl Theatre 1987; soloist, Plzeň Opera 1988–90; Chief of Opera Singer section, Conservatory Plzeň 1989; soloist, Nat. Theatre Opera, Prague 1990–, Metropolitan Opera, New York 1996–; charity concert tours with Karel Gott, Czech Repub. 1998; concert tours and opera performances in Canada, France, Italy, USA (Dvořák operas), Hong Kong (Janáček operas) and Germany (Verdi opera); charity concerts after floods in Czech Repub. 2002–; Classic Prize for propagation of Czech music in the world 1999. *Recordings:* Duets (with Karel Gott) 1998, Czech Opera Airs 1998, Czech Christmas Carols 2000. *Leisure interests:* cooking, piano. *Address:* Národní divadlo, National Theatre, Ostrovní 1, 110 30 Prague 1, Czech Republic (office). *Telephone:* (2) 24910312 (office). *Fax:* (2) 24911524

(office). *E-mail:* herzeru.jaroslava@quick.cz. *Website:* www.evaurbanova.com/en.

URE, Sir John Burns, Kt, KCMG, LVO, MA; British diplomatist, author and company director; b. 5 July 1931, London; s. of the late Tam Ure; m. Caroline Allan 1972; one s. one d.; ed Uppingham School, Magdalene Coll., Cambridge, Harvard Business School, USA; active service as 2nd Lt, Cameronians (Scottish Rifles), Malaya 1950–51; appointments in British Embassies in Moscow, Léopoldville, Santiago and Lisbon and at Foreign Office, London 1956–79, Asst Under-Sec. of State (Americas), FCO 1981–83; Amb. to Cuba 1979–81, to Brazil 1984–87, to Sweden 1987–91; UK Commr-Gen. for Expo '92, Seville; Dir, Thomas Cook Group 1991–99, CSE Aviation Ltd 1992–94; consultant, Sotheby's Scandinavia Advisory Bd, Robert Fleming (merchant bankers) 1995–98, Ecosse Films 1996–99; Chair., Anglo-Swedish Soc. 1992–96, Brazilian Chamber of Commerce 1994–96, Panel of judges for Travel Book of the Year Award 1991–99; Trustee, Leeds Castle Foundation 1995–2006; Pres., Weald of Kent Protection Soc. 2005–; Commdr, Mil. Order of Christ (Portugal) 1973. *Publications:* Cucumber Sandwiches in the Andes 1973, Prince Henry the Navigator 1977, The Trail of Tamerlane 1980, The Quest for Captain Morgan 1983, Trespassers on the Amazon 1986, Royal Geographical Soc. History of World Exploration (contrib. section on Cen. and S. America) 1991, A Bird on the Wing 1992, Diplomatic Bag 1994, The Cossacks 1999, In Search of Nomads 2003, Pilgrimage: The Great Adventure of the Middle Ages 2006, The Seventy Great Journeys in History (contrib.) 2006; regular book reviews in Times Literary Supplement, Country Life; travel articles for Daily Telegraph and Sunday Telegraph; numerous entries in The New Dictionary of National Biography. *Leisure interests:* travel, writing. *Address:* Netters Hall, Hawkhurst, Kent, TN18 5AS, England (home).

URECHEAN, Serafim, DEcon; Moldovan politician; *Chairman, Alianţă Moldova Noastră (Our Moldova Alliance);* b. 2 Feb. 1950, Larga, Briceni dist; m.; two c.; ed Chişinău Polytechnic Inst., Inst. of Political Studies, Leningrad (now St Petersburg), Russia; Engineer, Briceni Construction Enterprise 1976–78, later Head of Dept for Industrial Devt; Second Sec., Briceni CP Cttee 1978–83; Chair. Anenii Noi CP Exec. Cttee 1985–87; Deputy Chair., First Deputy Chair., then Chair. Fed. of Ind. Trade Unions 1987–94; mem. Parl. 1990–94, 2005–, mem. Standing Bureau of Parl., Cttee for Social Policy, Healthcare and Family, Democratic Moldova electoral bloc; Mayor of Chişinău 1994–2005; Chair. Alianţă Moldova Noastră (Our Moldova Alliance) 2003–; fmr Chair. Fed. of Local and Regional Authorities; Corresp. mem. Inst. for Int. Affairs, Int. Acad. of Informatisation, Int. Acad. of Man.; Hon. mem. Int. Acad. of Eng; Order of the Repub. (USSR), Medal for Public Order Protection (Moldova), St Dumitru Order (Second Class), Sergii Radonejsky Order (Second Class), St Stanislav Order. *Address:* Alianţă Moldova Noastră, 2012 Chişinău, str. M. Eminescu 68A, Moldova (office). *Telephone:* (22) 26-00-07 (office). *Fax:* (22) 21-13-94 (office). *E-mail:* alianta@amn.md (office). *Website:* www.amn.md (office).

UREN, Thomas, AO; Australian politician (retd); b. 28 May 1921, Balmain, NSW; s. of Thomas Uren and Agnes Uren; m. 1st Patricia Uren 1947 (died 1981); one s. one d.; m. 2nd Christine Anne Logan 1992; one d.; served with Royal Australian Artillery 1939, 2nd Australian Imperial Force 1941, in Japanese prisoner-of-war camp 1942–45 (Burma–Siam Railway); Labor MP for Reid 1958–90; mem. Opposition cabinet 1969–72; mem. Fed. Parl. Labor Party Exec. 1969–72, Deputy Leader 1975–77; First Minister of Urban and Regional Devt 1972–75; Fed. Labor Spokesman, Urban and Regional Devt 1976–77, on Urban and Regional Affairs, Decentralization, Local Govt, Housing and Construction 1977–80, on Urban and Regional Affairs 1980–83; Minister for the Territories and Local Govt and Minister assisting Prime Minister for Community Devt and Regional Affairs 1983–84, Minister for Local Govt and Admin Services 1984–87; del. to Australasian Area Conf. of Commonwealth Parl. Asscn, Darwin 1968, to Australian Parl. Mission to Europe 1968, to Commonwealth Parl. Asscn Conf., Canberra 1970; Australian Rep. at Lord Mountbatten's Funeral, Westminster Abbey 1979; del. to IPU 1965, Leader Australian del. to IPU 1987–90, Chair. Asian-Pacific Group 1989–90; brought back Australian hostages from Baghdad 1990; Chair. Australia-Vietnam Soc., Parramatta Park Trust; Pres. H. V. Evatt Foundation; Patron Defenders of Sydney Harbour Foreshores; Life Mem. Australian Labor Party 1993, Australian Nat. Trust 2004; Hon. DUniv (Charles Sturt Univ.) 1997, Hon. DSciArch (Sydney) 2002. *Publication:* Tom Uren Straight Left 1994. *Leisure interests:* gardening, theatre, opera, music, art, environmental issues, photography. *Address:* 8 Gilchrist Place, Balmain, NSW 2041, Australia.

URIBE ECHAVERRÍA, Jorge Alberto; Colombian business executive and politician; b. 30 Oct. 1940, Rionegro, Antioquia; ed Collegio Jorge Robledo Ortiz, Culver Military Acad., Ind., Cheshire Acad., Conn, George Washington Univ., Washington DC, USA, Univ. of Besançon, France; Nat. Dir Compañía de Exportaciones Comex 1963; Nat. Dir Instituto Colombiano de Administración, Incolda 1964–65; joined DeLima Marsh SA (insurance co.), becoming Man., Medellín br., later Gen. Man., Exec. Vice-Pres., Pres. 1991–2003; Minister of Nat. Defence 2003–05 (resgnd); Estrella de Antioquia, Distinción Especial Policía Nacional y Ejecutivo 1973. *Address:* c/o Ministry of National Defence, Centro Administrativo Nacional (CAN), 2, Avda El Dorado, Bogotá, DC, Colombia (office).

URIBE VÉLEZ, Alvaro, LLB; Colombian politician and head of state; *President;* b. 4 July 1952, Medellín; m. Lina Moreno; two s.; ed Univ. of Antioquia, Harvard Univ., USA, Univ. of Oxford, UK; Sec.-Gen. Ministry of Labour 1977–78; Dir of Civil Aviation 1980–82; Mayor of Medellín 1982, Councillor 1984–86, Senator of Antioquia Prov. 1986–90, 1990–94; Gov. of Antioquia 1995–97; Presidential cand. for Movimiento Primero Colombia 2002, Pres. 2002–; Light Unto The Nations Award 2007, US Presidential

Medal of Freedom 2009. *Address:* Office of the President, Palacio de Nariño, Carrera 8A, No. 7–26, Bogotá, Colombia (office). *Telephone:* (1) 562-9300 (office). *Fax:* (1) 286-8063 (office). *E-mail:* primerocolombia@md.impsat.net.co (office). *Website:* web.presidencia.gov.co (office).

URINSON, Yakov Moiseyevich, DEcon; Russian business executive, fmr politician and economist; *Deputy Chairman of the Management Board, Unified Energy System of Russia;* b. 12 Sept. 1944; m.; one s. one d.; ed Moscow Plekhanov Inst. of Nat. Econs; researcher Centre Inst. of Econ. and Math. USSR Acad. of Sciences 1968–72; Deputy Head of Div., Deputy Dir Computation Centre USSR State Planning Cttee 1972–91; Dir Centre of Econ. Conjuncture and Prognosis, Russian Govt 1992–94; First Deputy Minister of Econs 1993–97; Deputy Chair. Russian Govt, Minister of Econs 1997–98; mem. Defence Council 1997–98; Chief Expert on econ. and financial problems United Power Grids of Russia Jan.–Sept. 1999, Deputy Chair. Sept. 1999; Deputy Chair. Man. Bd Unified Energy System (UES) of Russia, Head Corp. Center, UES of Russia, Chair. Bd of Dirs Russian Communal Systems (RCS) 2005–; Chair. Bd of Pvt. Pensions Fund of Energy Industry 2001–. *Publications:* over 50 papers and articles in specialized periodicals. *Leisure interest:* football. *Address:* RAO UES of Russia, 101-3 Vernadskogo Prosp., 119526 Moscow, Russia (office). *Telephone:* (495) 710-40-01 (office). *Fax:* (495) 927-30-07 (office). *E-mail:* rao@elektra.ru (office). *Website:* www.rao-ees.ru (office).

URNOV, Mark Yuryevich, Cand. Econ., PhD; Russian academic and politician; *Dean of Political Science Department, Higher School of Economics;* b. 12 May 1947, Moscow; m.; one d.; ed Moscow State Inst. of Int. Relations; on staff Inst. of Conjuncture USSR Ministry of Foreign Trade 1970–76; researcher Inst. of World Econs and Int. Relations USSR Acad. of Sciences 1976–79; sr researcher Inst. of Culture, Ministry of Culture RSFSR 1979–82; sr researcher Leningrad Inst. of Information and Automatization 1982–86; sr researcher Inst. of Int. Workers' Movt USSR Acad. of Sciences 1986–89; leading researcher USSR Acad. of Nat. Econ. 1989–90; Dir of programmes Foundation of Social Econ. and Political Studies Gorbachev Foundation 1990–94; Head of Div., Deputy Head, Dir Analytical Centre, Russian Presidency 1994–96; mem. Political Council, Russian Presidency 1994–98; Dir Research Centre Ekspertiza 1996–98, 2000–04; First Deputy Head, Centre for Econ. Reforms 1998–2000; currently Dean of Political Science Dept, Higher School of Econs, Moscow. *Leisure interest:* cycling. *Address:* State University–Higher School of Economics, 3, Kochnovsky proezd, Moscow 125319, Russia (office). *Telephone:* (499) 152-12-81 (office). *Fax:* (499) 152-03-01 (office). *E-mail:* murnov@hse.ru (office). *Website:* www.hse.ru/eng (office).

URQUHART, Sir Brian, KCMG, MBE; British international official (retd); b. 28 Feb. 1919, Bridport, Dorset; s. of Murray Urquhart and Bertha Urquhart (née Rendall); m. 1st Alfreda Huntington 1944 (dissolved 1963); two s. one d.; m. 2nd Sidney Howard 1963; one s. one d.; ed Westminster School and Christ Church, Oxford; Army service 1939–45; Personal Asst to Gladwyn Jebb, Exec. Sec. of Preparatory Comm. of UN London 1945–46; Personal Asst to Trygve Lie, First Sec.-Gen. of UN 1946–49; served in various capacities relating to peace-keeping operations in Office of UN Under-Sec.-Gen for Special Political Affairs 1954–71; Exec. Sec. 1st and 2nd UN Int. Confs on Peaceful Uses of Atomic Energy 1955, 1958; Deputy Exec. Sec. Preparatory Comm. of IAEA 1957; Asst to Sec.-Gen.'s Special Rep. in the Congo July–Oct. 1960; UN Rep. in Katanga, Congo, 1961–62; Asst Sec.-Gen. UN 1972–74; Under-Sec.-Gen. for Special Political Affairs UN 1974–86; Scholar-in-residence, Ford Foundation 1986–95; Hon. LLD (Yale Univ.) 1981, (Tufts Univ.) 1985; Dr hc (Essex Univ.) 1981, (Westminster) 1993; Hon. DCL (Oxford Univ.) 1986, (Cambridge) 2005, hon. degrees (City Univ. of New York, Grinnell Coll., State Univ. of New York—Binghamton) 1986, (Univ. of Colorado, Keele) 1987, (Hobart Coll., William Smith Coll.) 1988, (Warwick Univ.) 1989, (Williams Coll.) 1992, (Lafayette Coll.) 1993, (Ohio State Univ.) 2000, (Hamilton Coll.) 2000, (Brown Univ.) 2003; Roosevelt Freedom Medal 1984, Int. Peace Acad. Prize 1985. *Publications:* Hammarskjöld 1973, A Life in Peace and War 1987, Decolonization and World Peace 1989, A World in Need of Leadership: Tomorrow's United Nations (with Erskine Childers) 1990, Ralph Bunche: An American Life 1993, Renewing the United Nations System (with Erskine Childers) 1994, A World in Need of Leadership: A Fresh Appraisal (with Erskine Childers) 1996. *Address:* 50 West 29th Street, New York, NY 10001 (home); Jerusalem Road, Tyringham, MA 01264, USA (home). *Telephone:* (212) 679-6358 (New York) (home); (413) 243-0542 (Tyringham) (home). *E-mail:* bsurq@worldnet .alt.net (home).

URQUHART, Lawrence McAllister, LLB, CA; British business executive; b. 24 Sept. 1935, Liverpool; s. of the late Robert Urquhart and Josephine McEwan Urquhart (née Bissell); m. Elizabeth Catherine Burns 1961; three s. one d.; ed Strathallan School, Perthshire, King's Coll., London Univ., Inst. of Chartered Accountants of Scotland; Price Waterhouse 1957–62; Shell Int. Petroleum 1962–64; PA Man. Consultants 1964–68; Sr Group Exec. Charterhouse Group Ltd 1968–74; Group Finance Dir Tozer Kemsley & Millbourn Holdings 1974–77, Burmah Oil Co. Ltd 1977–82; Chief Exec. Castrol Ltd 1982–85; Group Man. Dir The Burmah Oil PLC 1985–88, Group Chief Exec. 1988–90; CEO Burmah Castrol PLC 1988–93, Chair. 1990–98; Dir (non-exec.) Premier Consolidated Oilfields PLC 1986, English China Clays PLC 1991–99 (Chair. 1995–99), BAA PLC 1993–2002 (Deputy Chair. 1997–98, Chair. 1998–2002), Scottish Widows' Fund and Life Assurance Soc. 1992–2001 (Deputy Chair. 1993–95, Chair. 1995–2001), Kleinwort Benson PLC 1994–98. *Leisure interests:* golf, music.

URRUTIA FERNÁNDEZ, Paulina; Chilean actress and politician; *Minister of the National Commission for Culture and the Arts;* b. 1969, Santiago; ed Pontificia Univ. Católica; Pres. Sindicato de Actores de Chile (Sidarte) 2001–04; mem. Nat. Council of Culture 2004–08; Minister of the Nat. Comm. for Culture and the Arts 2006–. *Films:* Johnny cien pesos 1993 (APES Prize for Best Actress), El Encierro 1996, No tan lejos de Andrómeda 1999, Piel canela 2001, Carga vital 2003, Cachimba 2004, Tendida, mirando las estrellas 2004, Fuga 2006. *Television includes:* Sor Teresa de los Andes 1989, El Milagro de vivir 1990, Volver a empezar 1991, Trampas y caretas 1992, Jaque mate 1993, Champaña 1994, El Amor esta de moda 1995, Marrón Glacé, el regreso 1996, Eclipse de luna 1997, Amandote 1998, Fuera de control 1999, Sabor a ti 2000, Puertas adentro 2003, Cuentos de mujeres 2003, Tentación 2004, Casados 2005, Gatas & tuercas 2005–6. *Address:* National Commission for Culture and the Arts, San Camilo 262, Santiago, Chile. *Telephone:* (2) 589-7824 (office). *Website:* www.consejodelacultura.cl (office).

URRUTIA MONTOYA, Miguel, PhD; Colombian banker; *Professor of Economics, Universidad de los Andes;* b. 20 April 1939, Bogotá; s. of Francisco Urrutia and Genoveva Montoya; m. Elsa Pombo 1963; three c.; ed Univ. de los Andes, Bogotá, Univs of Harvard and Calif., Berkeley, USA; Gen. Sec. Ministry of Finance 1967–68, Adviser to Monetary Bd 1969; Deputy Tech. Man. Banco de la República 1970–74; Dir Nat. Planning Dept 1974–76; Minister of Mines and Energy 1977; Vice-Rector Univ. of the UN, Tokyo 1981–85; Man. Econ. and Social Devt Dept, IDB 1985–89; Exec. Dir Fedesarrollo 1978–81, 1989–91; mem. Bd Dirs Banco de la República (Cen. Bank of Colombia) 1991–93, Gov. Banco de la República 1993–2005; Head of Planning (Minister); has taught various courses at Univ. de los Andes at various times, currently Prof. of Econs; fmr weekly columnist for El Tiempo newspaper; decoration from the Ministry of Culture; Dr hc (Universidad de los Andes). *Publications:* Empleo y Desempleo en Colombia 1968, The Development of the Colombia Labor Movement 1969, Income Distribution in Colombia 1975, Winners and Losers in Colombia's Economic Growth of the 1970s 1985, Development Planning in Mixed Economies (with Setsuko Yukawa) 1988, Financial Liberalization and the Internal Structure of Capital Markets in Asia and Latin America 1988, Economic Development Policies in Resource Rich Countries (with Setsuko Yukawa) 1988, The Political Economy of Fiscal Policy (with Shinichi Ichimura and Setsuko Yukawa) 1989. *Leisure interests:* golf, reading. *Address:* Facultad de Economia, Universidad de los Andes, Carrera 1 N° 18A-70, Bloque C, Bogotá, Colombia (office). *Telephone:* (1) 349-4949 ext. 2056 (office). *Fax:* (1) 332-4492 (office). *E-mail:* murrutia@uniandes.edu.co (office). *Website:* economia.uniandes.edu.co (office).

URSU, Ioan, PhD; Romanian physicist and academic; *Senior Scientist, University of Bucharest;* b. 5 April 1928, Mânăstireni Commune, Cluj Co.; s. of Ioan Ursu and Ana Abrudan; m. Lucia Flămându 1930; two s. one d.; ed Univ. of Cluj and Univ. of Princeton, USA; Asst Prof., Univ. of Cluj 1949, Prof. and Head of Dept 1960–68; Prof. and Head of Dept, Univ. of Bucharest 1968–89, Sr Scientist 1990–; Visiting Prof., ICTP, Italy 1991; Dir-Gen., Inst. for Atomic Physics 1968–76; Pres. State Cttee for Nuclear Energy 1969–76; Pres. Nat. Council for Science and Tech. 1976–79, Vice-Chair. 1979–86, First Vice-Chair. Nat. Cttee for Science and Tech. 1986–89; Corresp. mem. Romanian Acad. 1963, mem. 1974, Pres. Physics Section 1988–; mem. Scientific Council of the Jt Inst. for Nuclear Research, Dubna 1969; mem. Bd of Govs IAEA 1971, Vice-Pres. 1972; mem. Scientific Advisory Cttee, IAEA 1979–90; mem. Exec. Council, European Physical Soc. 1968, Vice-Pres. 1975, Pres. 1976–79; Pres. Balkan Physical Union 1987; Ed. two Romanian journals of physics and int. journals of magnetic resonance, lasers, materials and energy; mem. Romanian Soc. of Physics and Chem., Physical Socs of USA, Belgium, France; mem. Bd of Int. Soc. of Magnetic Resonance; mem. Cttee Atomes et Molécules par Etudes Radioélectriques (AMPERE); mem. American Nuclear Asscn 1976, Canadian Nuclear Asscn 1976; Corresp. mem. Ecuadorian Inst. of Natural Sciences 1976, Centre for Scientific Culture 'Ettore Majorana' (Erice, Italy) 1977; mem. European Acad. of Sciences, Arts and Humanities 1980. *Publications:* Rezonanţa Electronică de Spin 1965, La résonance paramagnétique électronique 1968, Magnetic Resonance and Related Phenomena (ed.) 1971, Energia atomică 1973, Magnetic Resonance in Uranium Compounds 1979, Magnitny Rezonans v Soedynenyah Urana 1982, Fizica şi Tehnologia Materialelor Nucleare 1982, Physics and Technology of Nuclear Materials 1985, Interactiunea Radiaţiei Laser cu Metalele (with others) 1986, Fizika i technologyia iadernyh materialov, Vzaimodeistwie lazernovo iżluchenyia s metallami 1988, Laser Heating of Metals 1990; and about 300 papers on atomic and nuclear physics, nuclear materials, nuclear technologies, solid state physics, interaction of radiation with matter. *Address:* National Institute for Aerospace Research 'Elie Carafoli', B-dul Iuliu Maniu 220, sector 6, 77538 Bucharest (office); Str. Iuliu Tetrat 26, Bucharest 1, Romania (home). *Telephone:* (21) 4340083 (office). *Fax:* (21) 4340082 (office). *E-mail:* incas@aero.incas.ro (office). *Website:* www.incas.ro (office).

URUSEMAL, Joseph J., BA; Micronesian politician and fmr head of state; b. 19 March 1952, Woleai, Yap State; m. Olania Latileilam; three s. one d.; ed Xavier High School, Chuuk State, Rockhurst Coll., Kansas City, MO, USA; worked for Jackson Co. Dept of Correction, USA 1976–82; returned to Micronesia 1982; worked with State Dept of Educ., Yap as teacher and counsellor to Outer Islands High School and mem. Educ. Steering Cttee; elected Yap State's Rep. to Fifth Congress of Federated States of Micronesia (FSM) and mem. Standing Cttees on Health Educ. and Social Affairs, Resources and Devt and External Affairs; mem. Congress Federated States of Micronesia 1987–2003, Floor Leader 1991–2003; mem. Standing Cttees on Health Educ. and Social Affairs, Resources and Devt, Transportation and Communication, and Judiciary and Governmental Operations 1991–2003; Pres. 2003–07; fmr Chair. Jt Cttee on Compact Econ. Negotiations Working Group; fmr Sec. Gen. FSM Nat. Group to Asia-Pacific Parliamentarians' Union. *Address:* c/o Office of the President, POB PS-53, Palikir, Pohnpei, FM 96941, Federated States of Micronesia (office).

URWICK, Sir Alan (Bedford), KCVO, CMG, MA; British fmr parliamentary official and diplomatist (retd); b. 2 May 1930, London; s. of the late Lyndall

Fownes Urwick and Joan Saunders; m. Marta Yolanda (née Montagne) 1960; three s.; ed Dragon School, Oxford, Rugby School, New Coll. Oxford; joined Foreign Service 1952; served in embassies in Belgium 1954–56, USSR 1958–59, Iraq 1960–61, Jordan 1965–67, USA 1967–70, Egypt 1971–73; seconded to Cabinet Office as Asst Sec., Cen. Policy Review Staff 1973–75; Head of Near East and North Africa Dept, Foreign and Commonwealth Office 1975–76; Minister, British Embassy in Madrid 1977–79; Amb. to Jordan 1979–84, to Egypt 1984–87; High Commr in Canada 1987–89; Serjeant at Arms, House of Commons 1989–95; Chair. Anglo-Jordanian Soc. 1997–2001. *Leisure interests:* reading, gardening. *Address:* The Moat House, Slaugham Place, nr Haywards Heath, W Sussex, RH17 6AL, England (home). *Telephone:* (1444) 400458 (home).

URWIN, Roger, CBE, PhD, FREng, FIEE, CEng; British energy industry executive; b. 1946; ed Watford Grammar School, Weston-super-Mare Grammar School, Univ. of Southampton; various positions with Cen. Electricity Generating Bd 1980s; fmr Dir of Eng, Midlands Electricity Bd; CEO London Electricity PLC –1995; apptd Dir The National Grid Group and National Grid Transco PLC 1995, Man.-Dir of Transmission 1999, Group Dir for Europe, Group Chief Exec. National Grid PLC 2001–06 (retd). *Address:* c/o National Grid PLC, 1–3 Strand, London, WC2N 5EH, England (office).

UŠACKA, Anita, DrIur; Latvian professor of law and judge; *Judge, International Criminal Court;* b. 26 April 1952, Rīga; ed Moscow State Univ., Univ. of Latvia; Asst, Dept for Fundamental Legal Studies, Univ. of Latvia 1975–76, Prin. Lecturer 1980–82, Docent 1982–99, Head of Dept 1989–96, Assoc. Prof. 1999–, Prof. Dept for State Law 2002–; Assoc. Prof. Rīga Grad. School of Law 1999–2001; Exec. Dir Latvian Br., UNICEF 1994–96; Judge Constitutional Court of Repub. of Latvia 1996–; Judge, Int. Criminal Court 2003–; mem. Ed. Bd Law and the Rights journal; mem. Bd Lawyers Training Centre of Latvia, Sub-Comm. Constitutional Legal Procedure, Council of Europe, Int. Women Lawyers Asscn 1997–; Hon. LLD (Lewis and Clark Law School, Portland, Oregon). *Publications:* numerous articles in professional journals, reports to int. scientific confs. *Address:* International Criminal Court, Maanweg 174, 2516 AB, The Hague, Netherlands (office). *Telephone:* (70) 5158515 (The Hague) (office). *Fax:* (70) 5158555 (The Hague) (office). *Website:* www.icc-cpi .int (office).

UŠACKAS, Vygaudas, LLB; Lithuanian diplomatist; *Minister of Foreign Affairs;* b. 16 Dec. 1964, Skuodas; m. Loreta Ušackienė-Bilkstyte; one s. one d.; ed Vilnius Univ., Univ. of Oslo, Norway, Århus Univ., Denmark; Counsellor, Lithuanian Mission to EU, Brussels 1992–94, Rep. for Relations with NATO 1994–96, mem. Del. to WEU 1995–96; Political Dir, Ministry of Foreign Affairs 1996–99, Deputy Minister of Foreign Affairs 1999–2000, also served as Chief Negotiator for Lithuania accession to EU; Amb. to USA (also accred to Mexico and for Special Missions at Ministerial Advisory Group) 2001–06, to UK 2006–08; Minister of Foreign Affairs 2008–. *Address:* Ministry of Foreign Affairs, J. Tumo-Vaižganto g. 2, Vilnius 01511, Lithuania (office). *Telephone:* (5) 236-2444 (office). *Fax:* (5) 231-3090 (office). *E-mail:* urm@urm.lt (office). *Website:* www.urm.lt (office).

UŠAKOVS, Nils, BEcons, MSc; Latvian editor, television producer and politician; *Chairman, Saskaņas Centrs/Tsentr soglasiya (Harmony Centre party);* b. 8 June 1976, Rīga; ed Univ. of Latvia, The Southern Univ.; producer, Baltic Div., Russian NTV 1998–99; News Service Corresp., Latvian Public TV 1999–2000; News and Politics Section Ed., Respublika newspaper 2000–01; News and Policy Ed. Teļegraf newspaper 2001–02; Ed. 'Theme Week' weekly programme, TV5 channel 2001–04, also 'The Russian Question', later Ed. and Head of TV5; first Baltic Canal News Service Ed. 2004–05, Evening News Ed. for Lithuania and Estonia 2005–06; mem. Saskaņas Centrs/Tsentr soglasiya (Harmony Centre party), Chair. 2005–; Deputy for Rīga Constituency, 9th Saeima (Parl.) 2006–, mem. Foreign Affairs Cttee, European Affairs Cttee, Substitute mem. Latvian del. to NATO Parl. Ass.; mem. Bd of Dirs Baltic Forum 2002–; Cicerona Award, Latvian Journalists' Union and Univ. of Latvia 2004. *Leisure interests:* sports, especially running and cycling. *Address:* Saskaņas Centrs/Tsentr soglasiya, Rīga, Latvia (office). *Telephone:* 6921-8855 (office). *E-mail:* nils.usakovs@saeima.lv (office). *Website:* www.saskanascentrs .lv (office).

USENOV, Daniyar Toktogulovich; Kyrgyzstani politician; *First Deputy Prime Minister;* b. 1960, Frunze (now Bishkek); m.; two s.; ed Frunze Polytechnic Inst.; served in USSR Armed Forces 1982–84; Engineer, Mechanization and Automation Section, Kara-Balta Ore-Processing Plant 1984–90; First Deputy Chair. Kara-Balta City Exec. Council 1990–92; Deputy in Kara-Balta City Council and Chui Duban Council 1990–95; Asst Head of Chui Duban State Admin 1992–93; Gen. Dir Eridan Corpn 1994–95; Deputy in Legis. Ass. 1995–2000; banned from Parl. Elections 2000; Leader of Poor and Unprotected People's Party; First Deputy Prime Minister, responsible for Econ. Issues, by Pres. Bakiyev 2005–06 (resgnd), reappointed 2007–; Exec. Dir Kyrgyz–British Investment Co. 1992–93. *Address:* c/o Office of the Prime Minister, 720003 Bishkek, Dom Pravitelstva, Kyrgyzstan (office). *Telephone:* (312) 66-12-20 (office). *Fax:* (312) 66-66-58 (office). *E-mail:* www.government .gov.kg (office).

USHAKOV, Yuri Viktorovich, PhD; Russian diplomatist and government official; *Deputy Chief of the Government Office and Foreign Policy Assistant to the Prime Minister;* b. 13 March 1947, Moscow; m.; one d.; ed Moscow State Inst. of Int. Relations, Diplomatic Acad.; joined diplomatic service 1970; trans., expert, attaché USSR Embassy in Denmark 1970–75, Second then First Sec. 1978–82, Minister-Counsellor 1986–92; adviser Gen. Secr. USSR Ministry of Foreign Affairs 1982–86; Head Dept of All-Europe Co-operation, Ministry of Foreign Affairs 1992–96; Perm. Rep. of Russia to Org. for Security and Co-operation in Europe (OSCE) 1996–98; Deputy Minister of Foreign

Affairs 1998; Amb. to USA 1999–2008; Deputy Chief of the Govt Office and Foreign Policy Asst to the Prime Minister 2008–; Hon. Meritorious Diplomat of Russia; several medals and decorations. *Leisure interests:* tennis, alpine skiing. *Address:* Office of the Government of the Russian Federation, Krasnopresnenskaya nab. 2, 103274 Moscow, Russia (office). *Telephone:* (495) 605-51-45 (office). *Fax:* (495) 605-54-21 (office). *E-mail:* ushakov_yv@ aprf.gov.ru (office). *Website:* www.government.ru (office).

USHER, Thomas J., PhD; American business executive; *Chairman, Marathon Oil Corporation;* b. 11 Sept. 1942, Reading, Pa; s. of Paul T. Usher and Mary Leonard; m. Sandra L. Mort 1965; three c.; ed Univ. of Pittsburgh; with Industrial Eng Dept, US Steel Corpn 1965–75, Asst to Gen. Superintendent, Superintendent of Transportation and Gen. Services, South Works 1975, Asst Div. Superintendent, Gary Works 1978–79, Dir Corp. Strategic Planning, Pittsburgh 1979–81, Asst to Pres. 1981, Man. Dir for Facility Planning, Eng, Research and Industrial Eng 1981–82, Vice-Pres. Eng and Research US Steel Mining Co. 1982–83, Pres. 1983–84, Vice-Pres. Eng, Steel 1984, Sr Vice-Pres. Operations, Steel 1984–86, Exec. Vice-Pres. Heavy Products 1986–90, Pres. Steel Div. 1990, mem. Corp. Policy Cttee, USX Corpn 1990, Bd of Dirs 1991, Pres. US Steel Corpn 1991, Pres. and COO USX Corpn 1994, Chair. and CEO 1995–2001, Chair. US Steel Corpn 2001–06 (retd), CEO 2001–04, Pres. 2001–03; Chair. Bd of Dirs Marathon Oil Corpn 1995–; mem. Bd of Dirs H. J. Heinz Co., PPG Industries, PNC Financial Services Group, Boy Scouts of America, Extra Mile Educ. Foundation; mem. Bd of Trustees Univ. of Pittsburgh; Iron and Steel Soc. Steelmaker of the Year 2002. *Leisure interests:* golf, tennis, racquetball, scuba diving, swimming. *Address:* Marathon Oil Corporation, 5555 San Felipe Road, Houston, TX 77056-2723, USA (office). *Telephone:* (713) 629-6600 (office). *Fax:* (713) 296-2952 (office). *Website:* www .marathon.com (office).

USHER ARSÉNE, Assouan, MA; Côte d'Ivoirian politician and lawyer; b. 24 Oct. 1930; ed Dakar, Bordeaux and Poitiers Univ.; Lawyer, Court of Appeals, Poitiers 1955–56; Cabinet attaché of M. Houphouët-Boigny 1956; Asst Dir Caisse des Allocations Familiales 1957–59; Conseiller Général 1957–59; Deputy Vice-Pres. Nat. Ass. 1959–60; Lawyer, Court of Appeals, Abidjan 1959; Head, Ivory Coast (now Côte d'Ivoire) Perm. Mission to UN 1961–67; Minister of Foreign Affairs 1967–77; mem. UN Security Council 1964–67, Political Bureau Parti Démocratique de Côte d'Ivoire responsible for Mass Educ. 1970; Pres. Société des Ananas de la Côte d'Ivoire 1987; Nat. Order of Côte d'Ivoire.

USHERWOOD, Nicholas John, BA; British curator and art critic; *Features Editor, Galleries Magazine;* b. 4 June 1943, Bucks.; s. of Stephen Usherwood and Hazel Usherwood (née Weston); m. 1st Henrietta Mahaffy (dissolved 1990); one s. one d.; m. 2nd Jilly Szaybo 1991; ed Westminster School, Courtauld Inst. of Art, Univ. of London; lecturer in art history, Portsmouth Coll. of Art, Wimbledon Coll. of Art 1965–68; researcher, Pelican History of Art 1966–68; Admin., Press Officer RA 1969–74, Exhbns Sec. 1974–77; Deputy Keeper in charge of exhbns and public relations, British Museum 1977–78; freelance exhbn curator and organizer, art-critic, lecturer, writer 1978–; Features Ed., Galleries Magazine 1998–; Curator, Topolski C Sections 2001–02; Pres. UK Chapter, Int. Asscn of Art Critics (AICA) 2000–03; mem., Critics' Circle 2004–; Trustee, Evelyn Williams Trust 1994–; Chevalier, Order of Léopold II of Belgium. *Publications include:* exhbn catalogues for Algernon Newton 1980, Tristram Hillier 1983, Alfred Munnings 1986, Richard Eurich 1991, 1994, Nolan's Nolans 1997, Julian Trevelyan 1998, Joash Woodrow 2003, Norman Adams 2007, Evelyn Williams 2008. *Leisure interests:* new maps, reading poetry, talking to artists, contemporary music. *Address:* 82 High Street, Hampton Wick, Surrey, KT1 4DQ, England (office). *Telephone:* (20) 8973-0921 (office). *E-mail:* njusherwood@hotmail.co.uk (office).

USMAN, Nenadi E., BSc; Nigerian politician; b. 12 Nov. 1966, Jere, Kaduna State; ed Ahmadu Bello Univ., Univ. of Jos; served as Commr of Health, for Environment and Natural Resources, for Women's Affairs, Youth and Social Devt; fmr Exec. Advisor for Youth, for Information, Home Affairs and Culture; Minister of State for Finance 2003–06, Minister of Finance 2006–07; Chair. Fed. Accounts Allocation Cttee 2003–06; mem. Govt Econ. Man. Team 2003–06; mem. House of Reps for Kachia/Kagarko Fed. Constituency; mem. Kaduna State Caucus, Defunct Nat. Republican Convention; f. Educ. and Empowerment for Women in Kaduna State. *Address:* c/o National Assembly of Nigeria, National Assembly Complex, Three Arms Zone, POB 141, Abuja, Nigeria (office).

USMAN, Shamsudeen, BSc, MSc, PhD; Nigerian economist and government official; *Minister, Chairman of the National Planning Commission;* m. Nenadi Usman; ed Ahmadu Bello Univ., Zaria, LSE, UK; Planning Officer, Kano State Ministry of Econ. Planning 1974–76; Lecturer, Ahmadu Bello Univ., Zaria 1976–81; Controller, Nigerian Industrial Devt Bank 1981–85; Gen. Man. Corp. Banking, NAL Merchant Bank 1985–98; Dir-Gen. Tech. Cttee on Privatization and Commercialization (TCPC) 1989–91; Exec. Dir, United Bank of Africa Plc and later Union Bank of Nigeria 1992–94; Deputy Gov. Cen. Bank of Nigeria 1999–2007; Minister of Finance 2007–08; Minister, Chair. of the Nat. Planning Comm. 2009–; Pres. Nigerian Econ. Soc. 1986–87, Fellow 1995; Officer of the Order of the Fed. Repub. *Address:* National Planning Commission, Old Central Bank Building, 4th Floor, Garki, PMB 234, Abuja, Nigeria (office). *E-mail:* info@nigerianeconomy.com (office). *Website:* www.npc .gov.ng (office).

USMANOV, Alisher; Russian steel industry executive; *Co-Founder and Majority Shareholder, Metalloinvest Management Company LLC;* b. 9 Sept. 1953, Namangan Prov., Uzbekistan; m.; two c.; ed Moscow State Inst. for Int. Relations; Owner, Gallagher Holdings, Ural steel industrial complex, Ormeto-YUMZ mechanical eng corpn; Co-owner Oskol steel plant, Lebedinsky iron-ore mine, Mikhalovsky GOK iron ore mining and processing plant; has major stakes in Nosta steel co., Moldavia Metal, Olenegorsk iron-ore co., Australian Medusa mining, Tulachermet stock co.; Co-founder (with Vasiliy Anisimov) and majority shareholder Metalloinvest Man. Co. LLC; Co-owner Gazmetall steel and mining empire; Owner, Kommersant newspaper, Muz TV; acquired large share-holding in Arsenal football club, UK 2007; mem. Bd of Dirs Gazprominvestholding; fmr Pres. Russian and European fencing asscns. *Address:* Metalloinvest Management Company LLC, 3 Lesnaya St, Moscow 125047, Russia (office). *Telephone:* (495) 981-55-55 (office). *Fax:* (495) 981-99-92 (office). *Website:* www.metinvest.com (office).

USPASKICH, Viktor; Lithuanian (b. Russian) politician and business executive; *President, Vikonda Company;* b. 24 July 1959, Undoma, Russia; one s. one d. from 1st marriage; m. 2nd Jolanta Blazyte; mil. service 1977; welder, Northern Lights Co., worked on projects across USSR including Lithuania 1979–90; attained Lithuanian citizenship 1991; f. Efektas Co. 1990, became component of Vikonda Co. 1993, Pres. Vikonda Co. 1996–; non-party mem. New Union 2000–03; Founder and Chair. Labour Party 2003–06 (resgnd); mem. Seimas (Parl.) 2000–2005; Minister of the Economy 2004–2005 (resgnd following allegations of violating law on combining public and private interests), mem. Cttee on Econs 2004–05, Labour Party Parl. Group 2004–05; Chair. Asscn of Lithuanian Employers 1997–2003; Order of Daniil Moskovsky 1999. *Address:* c/o Koncernas Vikonda, Didzioji g. 22, Kedainiai, Lithuania (office). *Telephone:* (3) 475-0220 (office). *Fax:* (3) 475-6717 (office). *Website:* www.vikonda.lt (office).

USPENSKIJ, Boris Andreyevich, PhD, DLitt; Russian/Italian linguist, philologist, critic, semiotician and historian and academic; *Professor, Dipartimento di Studi dell'Europa Orientale, Universita degli studi di Napoli l'Orientale;* b. 1 March 1937, Moscow; s. of Andrej Uspensky and Gustava Mekler; m. 1st Galina Korshunova 1963 (died 1978); m. 2nd Tatiana Vladyshevskaya 1985; two s.; ed Moscow Univ.; dissertation on structural typology of languages published 1965 and partly translated into English 1968; dissertation on history of Russian church pronunciation partly published 1968; studied under Hjelmslev at Univ. of Copenhagen 1961; expedition to Siberia to study Ket language 1962; research at USSR Acad. of Sciences Inst. of African Languages 1963–65; research mem. of Lab. of Computational Linguistics, Moscow Univ. 1965–77, Prof., Moscow Univ. 1977–92; Fellow Inst. for Advanced Studies, Russian State Univ. for the Humanities 1992–93; Visiting Prof. Vienna Univ. 1988, Harvard Univ. 1990–91, Graz Univ. 1992, Cornell Univ. 1994, Univ. of Italian Switzerland 1997–(2007); Fellow Wissenschaftskolleg (Berlin) 1992–93; Prof., Oriental Univ. of Naples 1993–; major structuralist publs 1962–; Foreign Corresp. mem. Austrian Acad. of Science 1987, Foreign mem. Norwegian Acad. of Science and Letters 1999; mem. Int. Asscn for Semiotic Studies 1976, Academia Europaea 1990, Russian Acad. of Natural Science 1992, Russian PEN Centre 1994, Soc. Royale des Lettres de Lund 1996; Hon. mem. Slavonic and E European Medieval Studies Group 1987, Asscn Int. de sémiologie de l'image 1990, Hon. Cttee, American Friends of the Warburg Inst. 1993; Dr hc (Russian State Univ. for the Humanities) 2001, (Konstantin Preslavsky Univ., Bulgaria) 2003. *Publications include:* Principles of Structural Typology 1962, Structural Typology of Languages 1965, The Archaic System of Church Slavonic Pronunciation 1968, The History of Church-Slavonic Proper Names in Russia 1969, A Poetics of Composition 1970, The First Russian Grammar in the Native Language 1975, The Semiotics of the Russian Icon 1976, Tipologia della cultura (with Yu. M. Lotman) 1975, Philological Investigations in the Field of Slavic Antiquities 1982, The Semiotics of Russian Culture (with Yu. M. Lotman) 1984, The Semiotics of Russian Cultural History (with Yu. M. Lotman and L. Ja. Ginsburg) 1985, The History of the Russian Literary Language of XVIII to early XIX centuries 1985, The History of the Russian Literary Language XI–XVII centuries 1987, Storia e Semiotica 1988, Sémiotique de la culture russe (with Yu. M. Lotman) 1990, Semiotik der Geschichte 1991, Storia della lingua letteraria russa: Dall'antica Rus' a Puškin 1993, Semiotics of Art 1995, Linguistica, semiotica, storia della cultura 1996, Selected Works (three vols) 1996–97, Tsar and Patriarch 1998, Boris and Gleb: The Perception of History in the Old Rus' 2000, "In regem unxit..." 2001, La pala d'altare di Jan Van Eyck a Gand 2001, Studies in the Russian History 2002, Part and Whole in Russian Grammar 2004, Essays in History and Philology 2004, Il segno della croce e lo spazio sacro 2005, Cross and Circle: From the History of Christian Symbolism 2006; numerous articles. *Leisure interest:* travelling. *Address:* Universita degli studi di Napoli l'Orientale, Dipartimento di Studi dell'Europa Orientale, Via Duomo 219, Naples 80138 (office); Via Principe Eugenio 15, Rome 00185, Italy (home); Serebrianicheskij per. 9 Apt. 21, Moscow 109028, Russia (home). *Telephone:* (81) 6909902 (office); (6) 4468157 (Italy); (495) 917-40-67 (Russia). *Fax:* (81) 5630220 (Italy) (office). *E-mail:* buspenskij@union.it (office); borisusp@tiscalinet.it (home); borisusp@gmail.com (home).

USPENSKY, Vladislav Aleksandrovich; Russian composer and academic; *Professor of Composition, Leningrad State Conservatory;* b. 7 Sept. 1937, Omsk; s. of Alexander Grigoryevich Kolodkin and Vera Pavlovna Uspenskaya; m. Irina Yevgenyevna Taimanova 1963; ed Leningrad State Conservatory; postgrad. studies under Dmitri Shostakovich; teacher of music theory Leningrad State Conservatory 1965–67, Dean of Musicology 1967–72, Prof. of Composition 1982–; Guest Composer-in-Residence Seoul Univ., Korea 1995, Lima Univ., Peru 1997, Boston Univ. USA; Chair. Music Council of Cultural Cttee, St Petersburg Govt 1996–; Vice-Pres. Union of Composers of St Petersburg 1972–; Gen. Dir Int. Musical Children's Festival 1995–; People's Artist of Russia, D. Shostakovich Prize 1997, Order of Merit of Homeland 1998, Order of Catherine the Great 2002; music festival in his honour, St Petersburg autumn 2002. *Compositions:* Phantasmagoria, Vepres, Requiem, Liturgie, Temperaments, Toccata, Sonata-Phantasia, States, Sonata for the Violin and Piano, Anna Karenina (musical), Trombone Concertino 1963, Double Piano Concerto 1965, Music for Strings and Percussion 1967, The War

Against Salamanders (opera) 1967, To the Memory of a Hero (ballet) 1969, Intervention (opera) 1970, A Road to the Day (ballet) 1974, Symphonic Frescoes 1977, For You to the Sea (ballet) 1978, Nocturne for low voice and orchestra 1980, Expectation 1982, With You and Without You (oratorio) 1984, Cranes Flying (ballet) 1984, Towards the Light (symphony) 1985, Dedication (symphony) 1988, The Mushroom's Alarm (ballet) 1990, All Night Vigil 1990, The Departure of the Soul (funeral service) 1992, A Dithyramb of Love for two pianos and orchestra 1995, Trombone Concerto 1995, Concerto for low voice and orchestra 1997, Casanova in Russia (musical) 1998, Temptation of Jeanna (musical) 1999; music for plays, including Revizor, over 100 songs, music for films, theatre and TV productions. *Publication:* D. Shostakovich in My Life. *Leisure interest:* love. *Address:* Composers' Union, B. Morskaia 45, St Petersburg (office); Admiralteysky canal 5 Apt. 26, St Petersburg, Russia (home). *Telephone:* (812) 117-35-48 (office); (812) 117-74-35 (home). *Fax:* (812) 117-35-48 (office).

USTINOV, Vladimir Vassilyevich; Russian lawyer and government official; *Presidential Representative in the Southern Federal Okrug;* b. 25 Feb. 1953, Nikolayevsk-on-Amur, Khabarovsk Krai, Russia; m.; one s. one d.; ed Kharkiv Inst. of Law, Ukrainian SSR; prosecutor, Krasnodar Krai 1978–92, Sochi 1992–97; concurrently First Deputy Prosecutor Krasnodar Krai and Deputy Prosecutor-Gen. Russian Fed. 1997–2000; also Head, Dept Office of Prosecutor-Gen., N Caucasus 1998–99; Acting Prosecutor-Gen. Russian Fed. 1999–2000, Prosecutor-Gen. 2000–06; Minister of Justice 2006–08; Presidential Rep. in the Southern Fed. Okrug 2008–; Merited Jurist of Russian Fed. *Publication:* Indictment of Terror 2003. *Address:* Office of the Presidential Representative, 344006 Rostov-on-Don, ul. B. Sadovaya 73, Russia (office). *Telephone:* (863) 249-99-43 (office). *Fax:* (863) 249-99-47 (office). *E-mail:* pppufo@ufo.gov.ru (office). *Website:* www.ufo.gov.ru (office).

USUBOV, Col.-Gen. Ramil Idris oğlu; Azerbaijani politician and government official; *Minister of Internal Affairs;* b. 22 Dec. 1948, Xocalı, Nagornyi Karabakh; m.; three c.; ed N. Rzayev Police School, Acad. of the Ministry of Internal Affairs of the USSR; joined Ministry of Internal Affairs 1970; Head, Criminal Investigation Div., Şuşa district Police Dept 1975-80; Deputy Head, Internal Affairs Dept, Nagornyi Karabakh Autonomous Oblast 1980–84; Head, Ali-Bayramlı Region Police Dept 1984–87; Minister of Internal Affairs, Autonomous Rep. of Naxçıvan 1987–89, 1993–94; Head, Criminal Investigation Dept, then Passport, Visa and Registration Dept, then Human Resources Div., Ministry of Internal Affairs 1989–93; Minister of Internal Affairs 1994–; promoted to Maj.-Gen. 1994, Lt.-Gen. 1995, Col.-Gen. 2002; Azerbaijani Banner Order. *Address:* Ministry of Internal Affairs, 1005 Baku, 7 Azerbaijan Avenue, Azerbaijan (office). *Telephone:* (12) 492-57-54 (office). *Fax:* (12) 498-22-85 (office). *E-mail:* info@mia.gov.az (office). *Website:* mia.gov.az (office).

UTADA, Hikaru (Hikki), (Cubic U); Japanese/American singer and songwriter; b. 19 Jan. 1983, New York, NY; d. of Utada Teruzane and Utada Junko (Keiko Fuji); m. Kazuaki Kiriya 2002 (divorced 2007); ed American School, Tokyo, Columbia Univ., New York; recorded demos in downtime at father's studio, releasing them in USA under pseudonym Cubic U; first Japan releases as Utada Hikaru 1999, while continuing education in Tokyo; simultaneously maintained US and Japanese careers under respective names; World Music Award for Bestselling Asian Artist 2000. *Radio:* hosted own radio shows in Japan, incl. Très Bien Bohemian. *Recordings:* albums: Precious (as Cubic U) 1998, First Love 1999, U3*Star (live) 2000, Distance 2001, Deep River 2002, Singles Collection Vol. I 2004, Exodus (in English) 2005, Ultra Blue 2006, Heart Station 2008, This is the One 2009. *Address:* c/o EMI Music Japan, 3-taku, Room 2–2–17, Akasaka Minato-Ku, Tokyo 107-8510, Japan (office). *Website:* www.utada.com; www.emimusic.jp/hikki/index_e.htm.

UTEEM, Cassam, GCSK, LèsL; Mauritian politician and fmr head of state; b. 22 March 1941, Plaine Verte; m. 1967; two s. one d.; ed Univs of Mauritius and Paris VII; fmr supervisor, Cable & Wireless Ltd; Personnel Man. Currimjee Jeewanjee & Co., Ltd; Sec.-Gen. Mauritius Nat. Youth Council 1971–72; Treas. Mauritius Council of Social Service 1971–73; Rep. of World Ass. of Youth (WAY) to UNESCO 1974–76; municipal councillor, Port Louis 1969, 1977–79, 1986–88; Lord Mayor of City of Port Louis 1986; mem. Legis. Ass. 1976–92; Minister of Employment, Social Security and Nat. Solidarity 1982–83; Opposition Whip 1983–87; Chair. Public Accounts Cttee 1988–90; Deputy Leader, Mouvement Militant Mauricien 1988; Deputy Prime Minister and Minister of Industry and Industrial Tech. 1990–92; Pres. Repub. of Mauritius 1992–2002; mem. Bd Int. Inst. for Democracy and Electoral Assistance; mem. hc Acad. Nationale Malgache 1995; Hon. DCL (Univ. of Mauritius) 1994; Dr hc (Univ. of Marseille III) 1994. *Address:* c/o Board of Directors, International IDEA, Strömsborg, 103 34 Stockholm, Sweden.

UTOIKAMANU, Siosiua Tu'italukua Tupou, MCA, MScS; Tongan politician and economist; b. 1 July 1956; ed Wellington Univ. of Victoria, New Zealand, Univ. of Birmingham, UK; trainee economist, Ministry of Finance 1981, Economist 1981, Deputy Sec. 1984, Acting Dir of Planning, Cen. Planning Dept 1987, Minister of Finance 2001–08 (resgnd); Acting Finance Man. Tonga Commodities Bd 1989; Deputy Gov. Nat. Reserve Bank of Tonga 1989–91, Gov. 1991–2001. *Address:* c/o Ministry of Finance, Treasury Building, POB 87, Vuna Road, Kolofo'ou, Nuku'alofa, Tonga (office).

UTSUDA, Shoei, BS; Japanese business executive; *Representative Director, President and CEO, Mitsui & Company Ltd;* b. 1943; ed Univ. of Tokyo; joined Mitsui & Co. Ltd (general trading co.) 1967, mem. Bd Dirs (Dir, Gen. Man. Machinery, Information Industries Admin. Div.) 1997–, Rep. Dir, Exec. Man. Dir, Gen. Man. Corp. Planning Div. 2000–02, Rep. Dir, Sr Exec. Man. Officer, Chief Strategic Officer (responsible for Admin. Div.), COO Business Process Re-Eng Project April–Oct. 2002, Rep. Dir, Pres. and Oct. CEO 2002–; Chair. Keizai Doyukai Cttee on Asia-Japan Relations 2004–. *Address:* Mitsui &

Company Ltd, 2-1 Ohtemachi 1-chome, Chiyoda-ku, Tokyo 100-0004, Japan (office). *Telephone:* (3) 3285-1111 (office). *Fax:* (3) 3285-9819 (office). *E-mail:* info@mitsui.co.jp (office). *Website:* www.mitsui.co.jp (office).

UTSUMI, Akio; Japanese financial executive; *Chairman and Co-CEO, Mitsubishi Tokyo Financial Group;* b. 7 Sept. 1942; Dir Mitsubishi Trust Bank 1991–, Sr Man.-Dir 1995–98, Deputy Pres. 1998–99, Pres. 1999–; Dir, Chair. and Co-CEO Mitsubishi Tokyo Financial Group Inc. (cr. following merger between Bank of Tokyo-Mitsubishi and Mitsubishi Trust & Banking Corpn 2001) 2001–. *Address:* Mitsubishi Tokyo Financial Group Inc., 10-1 Yurakucho 1-chome, Chiyoda-ku, Tokyo 100-0006, Japan (office). *Telephone:* (3) 3240-8111 (office). *Fax:* (3) 3240-8203 (office). *Website:* www.mtfg.co.jp (office).

UTSUMI, Yoshio, LLB, MA; Japanese civil servant and international organization official (retd); b. 14 Aug. 1942; m. Masako Utsumi 1970; one s. one d.; ed Tokyo Univ. and Univ. of Chicago, USA; joined Ministry of Posts and Telecommunications 1966, Head of Investment Postal Life Insurance Bureau 1986–88, Head Gen. Affairs Div., Broadcasting Bureau 1988, with Communications Policy Bureau, Deputy Minister, Asst Vice-Minister, Dir-Gen. MPT 1988–98; First Sec. Perm. Mission of Japan, Int. Telecommunications Union (ITU), Geneva 1978–81, Chair. ITU Plenipotentiary Conf. 1994, Sec.-Gen. ITU 1998–2006; Prof. of Public Admin., MPT Postal Coll. 1972; del. to numerous int. negotiations. *Address:* c/o Office of the Secretary-General, International Telecommunications Union, Place des Nations, 1211 Geneva 20, Switzerland. *Telephone:* (22) 7305111.

UTTLEY-MOORE, William James, CBE, BSc, FREng, FRAeS; British electrical engineer; b. 19 July 1944, Crayford, Kent; s. of late William Uttley-Moore and of Louisa Clara Dixon; m. Jennifer Benger 1966; one s.; ed Erith Tech. School, London Univ.; student apprentice and devt engineer, Cintel Ltd 1960–68; project leader, Molins Machine Co. Ltd 1968–69; Chief Engineer, Computing Devices Co. Ltd 1969–75, Tech. Dir 1979–85, Chair. and Man. Dir 1985; Founder Dir Southern FM 1989–92, Conqueror Broadcasting Ltd 1996–; Chair. E Sussex Econ. Partnership 1998–; mem. Bd, Defence Scientific Advisory Council 1994–; Fellow Royal Acad. of Eng 1993–. *Publications:* numerous tech. papers on reconnaissance, avionics and digital battlefield. *Leisure interests:* practical eng, farming, running, classical music. *Telephone:* (1424) 426322 (home).

UTZERATH, Hansjörg; German theatre director and author; b. 20 March 1926, Tübingen; m. Renate Ziegfeld 1957; one s. two d.; ed Kepler Oberschule, Tübingen; began as actor, later in theatre man. in Düsseldorf and then in production; Chief Stage Man., Düsseldorfer Kammerspiele 1955–59; Dir 1959–66; Intendant, Freie Volksbühne, Berlin 1967–73; Dir Städtische Bühnen, Nuremberg 1977–92; freelance dir 1993–; guest producer at Staatstheater Stuttgart, Municher Kammerspiele, Schauspielhaus Düsseldorf and Schiller-Theater, Berlin 1959–; Visiting Prof. Universitat Mozarteum, Salzburg. *Productions include:* Tango 1971, Der Vater 1972, Viele heissen Kain (TV), Waiting for Godot 1980, Mother Courage 1981, King Lear 1982, Der Hauptmann von Köpenick 1986, Liebeskonzil 1988, Richard III 1990, Lila 1990, Check-Point-Charly 1996, Besuch der Alten Dame 1998, Nathan der Weise 2002, Der Kaufmann von Venedig 2003, Purpurstaub 2005. *Publications:* Die Grossväter (novel) 2005. *Address:* Knesebeckstr. 98A, 10623 Berlin, Germany (home).

UVAROV, Andrei Ivanovich; Russian ballet dancer; *Soloist, Bolshoi Ballet;* b. 28 Sept. 1971, Moscow; m. Filippova Svetlana; one d.; ed Moscow School of Choreography; soloist Bolshoi Ballet 1989–; Merited Artist of Russian Fed.; Benoit de la Danse Int. Prize 1993, 1st Prize Int. Ballet Competition, Japan 1995. *Ballets:* has danced leading roles with Bolshoi Theatre including Swan Lake, Chopiniana, Ivan the Terrible, Romeo and Juliet, Giselle, La Bayadère, Sleeping Beauty. *Address:* State Academic Bolshoi Theatre, Teatralnaya pl. 1, 103009 Moscow, Russia (office). *Telephone:* (495) 292-99-86 (office). *Website:* www.bolshoi.ru (office).

UYEDA, Seiya, DSc; Japanese geophysicist; b. 28 Nov. 1929, Tokyo; s. of the late Seiichi Uyeda and Hatsuo Uyeda; m. Mutsuko Kosaka 1952; one s. two d.; ed Univ. of Tokyo; Research Fellow, Earthquake Research Inst., Univ. of Tokyo 1955–63, Assoc. Prof., Geophysical Inst. 1963–69, Prof., Earthquake Research Inst. 1969–89; Prof., School of Marine Science and Tech., Tokai Univ. 1990–95; Harris Prof. of Geophysics, Texas A&M Univ. 1990–2008; Dir RIKEN Int. Frontier Program on Earthquake Research 1996–2002; mem. Japan Acad. 1996; Foreign Assoc. NAS 1976; Foreign mem. Russian Acad. of Sciences 1994; Hon. Foreign mem. American Acad. of Arts and Sciences 1981; Tanakadate Prize, Soc. of Terrestrial Electricity and Magnetism 1955; Okada Prize, Oceanographical Soc. of Japan 1968; Alexander Agassiz Medal, Nat. Acad. of Sciences 1972, Japan Acad. Prize 1987, George P. Woollard Award, Geological Soc. of America 1989, Walter H. Bucher Medal, American Geophysical Union 1991. *Publications:* Debate about the Earth 1967, Island

Arcs 1973, The New View of the Earth 1977; 300 scientific papers. *Leisure interest:* skiing. *Address:* 2-39-6 Daizawa, Setagaya-ku, Tokyo 155-0032, Japan (home). *Telephone:* (3) 3412-0237 (home). *E-mail:* sueyeda@st.rim.or.jp (office). *Website:* www.u-tokai.ac.jp (office).

UYS, Pieter-Dirk, BA; South African playwright, performer and producer; b. 28 Sept. 1945, Cape Town; s. of Helga Bassel and Hannes Uys; ed Univ. of Cape Town, London Film School, UK; joined Space Theatre, Cape Town 1973; f. Syrkel Theatre Co.; Dir P. D. Uys Productions, Bapetikosweti Marketing Enterprises; produced and performed 30 plays in revues throughout SA and in UK, USA, Australia, Canada, Netherlands; several videos and TV films and documentaries; Hon. DLitt (Rhodes Univ.) 1997. *Theatre:* cr. Mrs Evita Bezuidenhout – the most famous white woman in South Africa. *Television:* Evita Live and Dangerous, weekly talk/satire show 1999. *Publications:* Die van Aardes van Grootoor 1979, Paradise is Closing Down 1980, God's Forgotten 1981, Karnaval 1982, Selle ou storie 1983, Farce about Uys 1984, Appassionata 1985, Skote! 1986, Paradise is Closing Down and Other Plays 1989, No one's Died Laughing 1986, P.W. Botha: In His Own Words 1987, A Part Hate, A Part Love 1990, Funigalore 1995. *Leisure interests:* films, music, people, South African politics. *Address:* Evita SE Perron Theatre/Cafe/Bar Darling Station, Darling 7345 (office); 17 Station Road, Darling 7345, South Africa. *Telephone:* (22) 4922831 (office); (22) 4923208 (home). *Fax:* (22) 4923208 (home). *E-mail:* evita@africa.com (office); evitadarling@hotmail.com (home). *Website:* millennia.co.za/evita (office).

UZAN, Cem; Turkish media executive and politician; ed Pepperdine Univ.; owner of eight radio channels, four TV channels, two newspapers and Telsim mobile telephone network; f. Youth Party, cand. in parl. elections Nov. 2002. *Address:* Telsim, Ikitelli, Istanbul 38600, Turkey (office).

UZAWA, Hirofumi, PhD; Japanese economist and academic; *Professor Emeritus of Economics, University of Tokyo;* b. 21 July 1928, Tottori Province; s. of Tokio Uzawa and Toshiko Uzawa; m. Hiroko Aoyoshi 1957; two s. one d.; ed Univ. of Tokyo; Research Assoc., Lecturer, Asst Prof., Dept of Econs, Stanford Univ., Calif. 1956–60, Assoc. Prof. of Econs and Statistics 1961–64; Asst Prof. of Econs and Math., Univ. of Calif., Berkeley 1960–61; Prof. of Econs, Univ. of Chicago 1964–68, Univ. of Tokyo 1969–89, Prof. Emer. 1989–; Prof. of Econs, Niigata Univ. 1989–94; Foreign Assoc., NAS; mem., Japan Acad. 1989–; Matsunaga Memorial Prize 1969, Yoshino Prize 1971, Mainichi Prize 1974, desig. as Person of Cultural Merits 1983, Order of Culture 1997. *Publications:* in English: Studies in Linear and Nonlinear Programming (co-author) 1958; in Japanese: Economic Development and Fluctuations (co-author) 1972, Social Costs of the Automobile 1974, A Re-examination of Modern Economic Theory 1977, Transformation of Modern Economics 1986, A Critique of Japanese Economy 1987, Towards a Theory of Public Economics 1987, Preference, Production and Capital 1988, Optimality, Equilibrium and Growth 1988, A History of Economic Thought (in Japanese) 1989, Poverty Amid Economic Prosperity (in Japanese) 1989, Economic Analysis (in Japanese) 1990, Collected Papers of Hirofumi Uzawa (12 vols) 1994–95, Introduction to Mathematics (six vols) 1997–2000, Economic Theory and Global Warming 2003, Economic Analysis of Social Common Capital 2005. *Leisure interest:* walking. *Address:* Kamiyama-cho 20-23, Shibuya-ku, Tokyo, Japan (home).

UZELAC, Slobodan, PhD; Croatian psychologist, academic and politician; *Deputy Prime Minister;* b. 9 Aug. 1947, Kakma; m.; two c.; ed Univ. of Zagreb, Univ. of Belgrade; Asst, Faculty of Defectology, Univ. of Zagreb 1973–82, Asst Prof. 1982–87, Head of Dept of Behavioural Disorders 1982–86, Assoc. Prof., Faculty of Educ. and Rehabilitation 1987–99, Prof. 1999–; Visiting Lecturer, Pennsylvania State Univ. 1991, Univ. of Pittsburgh 1991; Inst. for Russian and E European Studies; External Assoc. Zagreb Center for Social Care 1976–86; mem. Ind. Democratic Serb Party (Samostalna demokratska srpska stranka); Sec. of State for Science –2008; Deputy Prime Minister 2008–; mem. Advisory Bd Vukovar Inst. for Peace Research and Educ. 2000. *Leisure interests:* reading, travel. *Address:* Office of the Prime Minister, 10000 Zagreb, trg sv. Marka 2, Croatia (office). *Telephone:* (1) 4569266 (office). *Fax:* (1) 6303045 (office). *E-mail:* slobodan.uzelac@vlada.hr (office). *Website:* www.vlada.hr (office).

UZUN, Ahmet, BSc; Turkish-Cypriot civil servant and politician; *Minister of Finance, 'Turkish Republic of Northern Cyprus';* b. 1950, Lefkoşa (Nicosia); m.; two c.; ed Ankara Univ.; held various political roles since 1975, including Under-Sec. to Deputy Prime Minister; Minister of Finance, 'Turkish Repub. of Northern Cyprus' 2004–; fmr Pres. Public Officers' Union (KTAMS); mem. Cen. Admin. Council Republican Turkish Party (Cumhuriyetci Turk Partisi). *Leisure interest:* playing the trumpet. *Address:* Ministry of Finance, Lefkoşa (Nicosia), Mersin 10, Turkey (office). *Telephone:* 2283116 (office). *Fax:* 2278230 (office). *E-mail:* bim@kktcmaliye.com (office). *Website:* www.kktcmaliye.com (office).

V

VAAHTORANTA, Tapani, CandPolit, MA, PhD; Finnish research institute director; ed Univ. of Turku, Princeton Univ., USA; Asst Prof., Univ. of Turku 1986–89; Sr Research Fellow, Finnish Inst. of Int. Affairs 1989–90, Research Dir 1990–91, later Dir; mem. faculty, Geneva Centre for Security Policy 1998–2001. *Publications:* Finnish and Swedish Security: Comparing National Policies (co-ed.) 2001, Charting a New Course: Globalisation, African Recovery and the New African Initiative (co-ed.) 2002. *Address:* Finnish Institute of International Affairs, Mannerheimintie 15 A, Helsinki 00260, Finland (office). *Telephone:* (9) 43420722 (office). *Fax:* (9) 43420769 (office). *E-mail:* tapani.vaahtoranta@upi-fiia.fi (office). *Website:* www.upi-fiia.fi.

VĂCĂROIU, Nicolae; Romanian politician and economist; *President of the Senate;* b. 5 Dec. 1943, Bolgrad, Bessarabia; m. Marilena Văcăroiu; one s.; ed Bucharest Acad. of Econ. Studies; Economist, Ilfov Co. Inst. of Design and Systemization; then with State Planning Cttee, promoted to Dir Econ.-Financial Synthesis Dept; apptd Deputy Minister of Nat. Economy 1990; subsequently Head of Price Dept, Ministry of Finance, Sec. of State and Head of Tax Dept, Chair. Interministerial Cttee of Foreign Trade Guarantees and Credits; Prime Minister 1992–96; Senator 1996–, Vice-Pres. of Senate 1999–2000, Pres. 2000–, Chair. Privatization Cttee 1997–99, Vice-Pres. Parl. Group of Social Democratic Party (Partidul Social Democrat—PSD) 1996–2000; Chair. Romania–Brazil Friendship Asscn 1997–. *Publications:* numerous articles on econ. and financial matters. *Address:* Senatul (The Senate), 050711 Bucharest 5, Calea 13 Septembrie 1–3 (office); B-dul Gh. Prezan, nr. 4, 2nd Floor, Apt 3, Sector 1, Bucharest, Romania (home). *Telephone:* (21) 4021111 (office). *Fax:* (21) 3121184 (office). *E-mail:* csava@senat.ro (office). *Website:* www.senat.ro (office).

VACEK, Miroslav; Czech politician and army officer (retd); b. 29 Aug. 1935, Kolín; m. Helena Vacek 1958; one s.; ed A. Zápotocký Mil. Acad. Brno and Mil. Acad. of USSR; Commdr Western Mil. Dist 1985; Chief of Gen. Staff of Czechoslovak Army and First Deputy of Minister of Nat. Defence 1987; Minister of Nat. Defence 1989–90; Adviser to Ministry of Defence 1990–91; Pres. Victoria (business) 1992–; mem. Parl. of Czech Repub. 1996–98; mem. Comm. for Defence and Security in Parl. 1996–98; Communist Party of Bohemia and Moravia (KSČM). *Publications:* Why Should I Keep Silent? 1991, In Fairness 1994, Úsměvy v barvě (Smiles in Khaki) 2002; articles on mil. problems published in mil. press. *Address:* c/o Communist Party of Bohemia and Moravia, Politických vězňů 9, 110 00 Prague 1, Czech Republic.

VACHON, Louis; Canadian banker; *President and CEO, National Bank of Canada;* b. 1962; m.; two c.; ed Fletcher School, USA; Vice-Pres. Capital Markets Levesque Beaubien (later Nat. Bank Financial) 1986–90; with Bankers Trust 1990–96; joined Nat. Bank of Canada 1996, Pres. and CEO Innocap Investment Man. and Sr Vice-Pres. Treasury and Financial Markets, Nat. Bank of Canada 1997, Chair. Nat. Bank Financial Group and Natcan Investment Man. 2004–05, Chair. and CEO Nat. Bank Financial Group 2005–06, COO Nat. Bank of Canada 2006–07, mem. Bd of Dirs 2006–, Pres. and CEO 2007–; fmr Pres. and CEO BT Bank Canada, Innocap; mem. Bd of Dirs Montreal Exchange, Boston Option Exchange, Nat. Bank Discount Brokerage. *Address:* National Bank of Canada, 600 rue de la Gauchetière ouest, Montreal, PQ H3B 4L2, Canada (office). *Telephone:* (514) 394-5000 (office). *Fax:* (514) 394-8434 (office). *Website:* www.nbc.ca (office).

VĂDUVA, Leontina; French singer (soprano); b. 1 Dec. 1960, Rosiile, Romania; d. of Maria Ciobanu; m. Gheorghe Codre; ed Bucharest Conservatoire; gained political asylum in France; debut in Massenet's Manon, Toulouse 1987; appeared as Ninetta in La Gazza Ladra at the Théâtre des Champs Elysées, Paris 1988; Covent Garden debut as Manon 1988; appeared at Covent Garden as Gilda in Rigoletto 1989; sang Drusilla at Théâtre du Châtelet, Paris, and at the Grand Théatre, Geneva; other roles included appearances in Les Pêcheurs de Perles and L'Elisir d'amore at Toulouse, Manon at Montpellier, Bordeaux, Avignon, Paris (Opéra Comique) and Vienna, Rigoletto at Bonn, Donizetti's Il Campanello di Notte at Monte Carlo, Les Contes d'Hoffmann in Paris (Théâtre du Châtelet) and London (Covent Garden), Ismene in Mitridate by Mozart at the Châtelet, Micaela in Carmen at Covent Garden (returned 1996 as Mimi); sang Juliet in Romeo and Juliet at Covent Garden, Adina at Barcelona, Marguerite and Mimi at Los Angeles, Poulenc's Blanche at La Scala, Offenbach's Antonia for Festival d'Orange and Adina at Savonlinna 2000; season 2003–04 as Euridice at Barcelona, as Marguérite in Turin, Alice Ford for Bordeaux Opéra and Mimi on tour of Japan for Catania Opera; Chevalier, Ordre des Arts et des Lettres 1998, Grand Officer Order of Merit (Romania); winner Concours de Chant, Toulouse 1986, Hertogenbosch Competition, Netherlands 1987, Olivier Award for Outstanding Achievement in Opera 1988, Medal of the City of Toulouse. *Recordings include:* Mitridate, Le nozze di Figaro 1993. *Address:* Stafford Law, Candleway, Broad Street, Sutton Valence, Kent ME17 3AT, England (office). *Website:* www.stafford-law.com (office).

VAEA OF HOUMA, Baron; Tongan politician; b. 15 May 1921, Nuku'alofa; s. of Vilai Tupou and Tupou Seini Vaea; m. Hon. Tuputupu-'o-Pulotu Ma'afu 1952; three s. three d.; ed Tupou Coll., Wesley Coll., NZ, St Edmund's Hall, Oxford Univ., Kidlington Air Training School; inherited title 'Vaea' 1942; mil. service with RNZAF 1942–44; joined Tonga Civil Service 1945; Aide-de-Camp to HM Queen Salote Tupou III 1954–59; Gov. of Ha'apai 1960–68; Commr and Consul for Tonga in London 1969–70, High Commr and Consul 1970–72; given title of Baron by HM King Taufa'ahau Tupou IV 1970; Minister for Labour, Commerce and Industries 1973–91; Acting Deputy Prime Minister 1989; Prime Minister, Minister for Agric. and Forestry, for Fisheries 1991–2000, for Telecommunications 1991, for Women's Affairs 1991, of Marines and Ports 1994–2000; mem. Tonga Defence Bd 1973; Chair. Shipping Corpn of Polynesia 1978, Nat. Reserve Bank 1989, Tonga Telecommunications Comm. 1991–2000, Tonga Broadcasting Comm. 1991–2000, Tonga Investments Ltd 1991–; FAO Agricola Medal 2001. *Leisure interests:* tennis, rugby, farming. *Address:* PO Box 262, Nuku'alofa, Tonga. *Telephone:* 24-644. *Fax:* 23-888.

VAGELOS, Pindaros Roy, MD; American pharmaceutical industry executive; *Chairman, Regeneron Pharmaceuticals Inc.;* b. 8 Oct. 1929, Westfield, NJ; s. of Roy John Vagelos and Marianthi Lambrinides; m. Diana Touliatos 1955; two s. two d.; ed Univ. of Pennsylvania and Columbia Univ. Coll. of Physicians and Surgeons; Intern in Medicine, Mass. Gen. Hosp. 1954–55, Asst Resident in Medicine 1955–56; Surgeon, Lab. of Cellular Physiology, NIH 1956–59, Surgeon, Lab. of Biochem. 1959–64, Head, Section on Comparative Biochem. 1964–66; Prof. of Biochem., Chair. Dept of Biological Chem., Washington Univ. School of Medicine, St Louis, Mo. 1966–75, Dir Div. of Biology and Biomedical Sciences 1973–75; Sr Vice-Pres. Research, Merck Sharp & Dohme Research Labs, Rahway, NJ 1975–76, Pres. 1976–84, Corporate Sr Vice-Pres. Merck & Co., Inc. 1982–84, Exec. Vice-Pres. 1984–85, CEO 1985–86, Chair. and CEO 1986–95; Chair Regeneron Pharmaceuticals Inc. 1995–, also mem. Scientific Advisory Bd; Trustee Rockefeller Univ. 1976–94, Univ. of Pa 1988– (Chair. Bd 1994–), Danforth Foundation 1978–; mem. Bd of Dirs Prudential Insurance Co. of America 1989–; fmr mem. Bd of Dirs TRW Inc., PepsiCo Inc.; mem. NAS, American Acad. of Arts and Science; ACS Enzyme Chem. Award 1967, NJ Science/Tech. Medal 1983, Pupin Medal 1995. *Achievements include:* discoverer of acyl-carrier protein. *Leisure interests:* jogging, tennis. *Address:* Regeneron Pharmaceuticals Inc., 777 Old Saw Mill River Road, Tarrytown, NY 10591-6707 (office); 82 Mosle Road, Far Hills, NJ 07931, USA (home). *Telephone:* (914) 347-7000 (office). *Fax:* (914) 347-2113 (office). *Website:* www.regeneron.com (office).

VAGHUL, Narayanan, BCom; Indian banker; mem. of staff, State Bank of India 1957–1974; fmr Dir Nat. Inst. of Bank Man.; Exec. Dir Cen. Bank of India 1978–1981; Chair., Man. Dir Bank of India 1981–84; Chair. (non-exec.) Industrial Credit and Investment Corpn of India Ltd (ICICI) 1985–, fmrly also Man. Dir. *Address:* ICICI Bank, PO Box 18712, Andheri East, Mumbai 400 069, India (office). *E-mail:* info@icicibank.com (office).

VAGNORIUS, Gediminas, DEconSc; Lithuanian politician; *Chairman, Christian-Conservative Social Union;* b. 10 June 1957, Plunge Dist; m. Nijole Vagnorenė; one s. one d.; ed Inst. of Eng and Construction, Vilnius; engineer-economist, jr researcher, then researcher, Inst. of Econs, Lithuanian Acad. of Sciences 1980–90; Deputy to Lithuanian Supreme Soviet, mem. Presidium 1990–91; Chair. Council of Ministers (Prime Minister) of Lithuania 1991–92, 1996–99; mem. Seimas (Parl.) 1992–2004; Chair. Bd Homeland Union/Lithuanian Conservative Party 1993–2000; Chair. Krikščionių Konservatorių Socialinė Sąjunga (Christian-Conservative Social Union) 2000–. *Leisure interest:* jogging. *Address:* Krikščionių Konservatorių Socialinė Sąjunga, Odminių g. 5, 01122 Vilnius, Lithuania (office). *Telephone:* (5) 212-6874 (office). *Fax:* (5) 212-6874 (office). *E-mail:* sekretoriatas@nks.lt (office). *Website:* www.nks.lt (office).

VAGO, Constant, PhD, DSc; French pathologist and academic; b. 2 May 1921, Debrecen, Hungary; s. of Vincent Vago and Françoise Schibl; m. Catherine Sary 1944; one s. one d.; ed Lycée of Debrecen, Univ. of Marseilles; Dir Lab. of Cytopathology, Nat. Inst. for Agron. Research, St-Christol 1958–; Prof. of Pathology and Microbiology, Univ. of Science, Montpellier 1964–; fmr Dir Centre of Comparative Pathology (now UMR Integrative biology and virology of insects— Bivi), Univ. of Montpellier; mem. Acad. of Sciences of France 1971–, Acad. of Agric. of France, New York Acad. of Sciences, Hungarian Acad. of Sciences, Nat. Acad. of Sciences of India, European Acad. of Sciences, Int. Acad. of Sciences; Past Pres. Int. Soc. for Invertebrate Pathology; Pres. Nat. Cttee of Biological Sciences of France; mem. numerous scientific socs; Hon. Prof., Univ. of Cen. China; Légion d'honneur, Ordre nat. du Mérite and other decorations; Dr hc (Medical Univ., Debrecen, Hungary); Int. Ishida Prize of Cytology, Int. El Fasi Great Prize for Science, Int. Pasteur Prize, Int. Great Prize for Scientific Film. *Publications:* Invertebrate Tissue Culture 1972 and about 400 publications on comparative pathology, tissue culture, molecular virology, chlamydial diseases, comparative oncology. *Leisure interests:* sculpture, swimming. *Address:* c/o Institut de France, 23 quai Conti, 75006 Paris; Chemin Serre de Laurian, 30100 Alès, France (home).

VÄHI, Tiit; Estonian politician and business executive; b. 10 Jan. 1947, Valgamaa; m.; two c.; ed Tallinn Polytechnic Inst.; fmr Production Man. Valga Motor Depot, later Deputy Dir, Chief Engineer, Dir, Chair. Transport Cttee; helped organize Estonian Popular Front, led its regional committee in Valga Co.; Minister of Transport and Communications 1989–92; Govt's Special Rep. to NE Estonia 1991; Acting Prime Minister of Estonia Jan.–Oct. 1992, Prime Minister 1995–97; mem. Bd Coalition Party, Chair. 1993–99; attended refresher courses in Germany 1993; Chair. Tallinn City Council 1993–95. *Address:* c/o Office of the Prime Minister, Stenbocki maja, Rahukohtu 3, Tallinn 15161, Estonia. *Telephone:* 631-6701.

VAIL, Peter R., PhD; American oceanographer and academic; *Professor Emeritus of Oceanography, Rice University; President, Peter R. Vail Oil and Gas Consulting and Investing Company;* b. 1930, New York; m. Carolyn Vail; three c.; ed Dartmouth Coll. and Northwestern Univ.; Research Geologist, Exxon Corpn 1956; Research Geologist, Esso Production Research Co. 1965, Sr Research Scientist 1980–86; W. Maurice Ewing Prof. of Oceanography,

Rice Univ. 1986–2001, Prof. Emer. 2001–; Founder and Pres. Peter R. Vail Oil and Gas Consulting and Investing Co. 2001–; FGS (US) 1993–, FGS (UK) 1995–; Fellow, AAAS; mem. Sigma Xi (American Geophysical Union), American Geophysical Inst.; Hon. mem. Gulf Coast Section of the Soc. for Sedimentary Geology, Soc. of Exploration Geologists, Houston Geophysical Soc.; Penrose Medal Award, Geological Soc. of America 2003, Legendary Geoscientist Award, American Geological Inst. 2004, Hollis D. Hedbers Award in Energy, Inst. for the Study of Earth and Man 2005, Benjamin Franklin Medal in Earth Science, The Franklin Inst. 2005. *Publications:* numerous articles in scientific publications. *Address:* Keith-Weiss Geological Laboratories, Room 201, Department of Earth Science, 6100 Main Street, Houston, TX 77005 (office); Peter R. Vail Oil and Gas Consulting and Investing Co., 3745 Del Monte Drive, Houston, TX 77019, USA (office). *Telephone:* (713) 348-4888 (office); (713) 993-0885 (office). *E-mail:* vail@rice.edu (office); prvail@prvail.com (office). *Website:* www.prvail.com (office).

VAILE, Hon. Mark Anthony James; Australian politician; b. 18 April 1956, Sydney; s. of George Strafford Vaile and Suzanne Elizabeth Vaile; m. Wendy Jean Vaile 1976; three d.; worked as jackaroo 1973–76; farm machinery retailer 1976–79; Real Estate and Stock and Station Agent 1979–92; Chair, Wingham Chamber of Commerce 1980–85; fmr Deputy Speaker, then Chair. House of Reps Standing Cttee on Communications, Transport and Micro-Econ. Reform; mem. House of Reps for Lyne (Nat. Party), NSW 1993–; Nat. Party Whip, House of Reps 1994; Minister for Transport and Regional Devt 1997–98, for Agric., Fisheries and Forestry 1998–99, for Trade 1999–2006, for Transport and Regional Services 2006–07; Deputy Leader Nat. Party of Australia 1999–2005, Fed. Parl. Leader 2005–07 (resgnd); Deputy Prime Minister 2005–07. *Leisure interests:* squash, tennis, water skiing, golf. *Address:* National Party of Australia, John McEwen House, National Circuit, Barton, ACT 2600, Australia. *Telephone:* (2) 6273-3822. *Fax:* (2) 6273-1745. *E-mail:* federal.nationals@nationals.org.au (office). *Website:* www.nationals.org.au (office).

VAILLANT, Daniel; French politician; b. 19 July 1949, Lormes (Nièvre); s. of Raymond Vaillant and Germaine Andre; three c.; ed Ecole supérieure de biologie et biochimie; joined Convention des Institutions Républicaines 1966; Parti Socialiste (PS) official, 18th arrondissement Paris 1971–95; Special Asst to François Mitterrand, presidential election campaign 1981; Asst Nat. Sec. for PS Feds 1986, Nat. Sec. for PS Feds 1988–94, Nat. Sec. without specific assignment 1994–95; Campaign Dir, Lionel Jospin's parl. and regional election campaigns 1986, Organizer and Co-ordinator of Lionel Jospin's gen. election campaign 1997; City Councillor 18th arrondissement Paris 1977–95, Mayor of 18th arrondissement 1995–2001, 2003– (First Deputy Mayor 2001–03); Ile-de-France Regional Councillor 1986–89; Nat. Ass. Deputy for 19th Paris constituency 1988–93, 1994–97, 2002–07, 2007–; Minister for Relations with Parl. 1997–2000, of the Interior 2000–02. *Publications:* C'est ça ma gauche 2000, Sécurité, priorité à gauche 2003. *Address:* Mairie, 1 place Jules Joffrin, 75877 Paris cedex 18, France.

VAILLAUD, Pierre; French oil industry executive; b. 15 Feb. 1935, Paris; s. of Marcel Vaillaud and Rose Larrat; m. Geneviève Dreyfus 1960; two s.; ed Lycée Janson-de-Sailly, Paris, Ecole Polytechnique, Ecole des Mines, Ecole Nat. Supérieure du Pétrole et des Moteurs; engineer, Ministry of Industry 1959–63; project man. Technip 1964–68, Dir, Vice-Pres. Eng and Construction Atochem (affiliate of Total) 1968–72; Vice-Pres. Natural Gas Div., Total 1972–74, Vice-Pres. Devt and Construction Div., Vice-Pres. Exploration and Production Operations then Pres., Total Exploration Production 1974–89, Exec. Vice-Pres. Total, Pres. and CEO Total Chimie 1989–92, Chair. and CEO Technip 1992–99, Elf Aquitaine SA 1999–2000; Pres. Asscn des techniciens du pétrole 1985–87; Commdr, Ordre nat. du Mérite, Officier, Légion d'honneur. *Leisure interests:* tennis, sailing, golf. *Address:* 5 villa Madrid, 92200 Neuilly-sur-Seine, France (home). *Telephone:* (6) 03-03-00-70 (Mobile).

VAINIO, Vesa Veikko, LLM; Finnish business executive; *Chairman of the Board, UPM-Kymmene Corporation;* b. 2 Dec. 1942, Helsinki; s. of Veikko Vainio and Aune Vainio; m. Marja-Liisa Harjunen 1968; two s.; ed Univ. of Helsinki; Circuit Court Notary, Rovaniemi Circuit Court 1966–67; Counsellor, Union of Finnish Lawyers 1968; Sec. Finnish Employers' Confed. 1969, Counsellor and Asst Head of Dept 1969–72; Admin. Dir Aaltonen Footwear Factory 1972, Deputy Man. Dir 1974–76; Man. Dir Aaltonen Factories Oy 1976–77; Dir Confed. of Finnish Industries 1977–83, Deputy Man. Dir 1983–85; Exec. Vice-Pres. Kymmene Corpn 1985–91, Pres. 1991–92, mem. Bd of Dirs 1996–, Chair. UPM-Kymmene Corpn 2001–; Pres. and CEO Unitas Ltd 1992–94; Chair. and CEO Union Bank of Finland 1992–94 (after merger with Kansallis-Osake-Pankki into Merita Bank Ltd) Merita Bank Ltd 1995–97, Pres. and CEO of Merita Ltd 1995–97, Pres. Merita PLC 1998–2000, Chair. Bd MeritaNordbanken PLC 1998, Vice-Chair. Nordbanken Holding PLC 1998–2000, Vice-Chair. Bd MeritaNordbanken PLC 1999, Chair. Nordea AB (publrs) 2000–02; mem. Bd of Dirs Nokia Corpn ADS 1993–, Vice-Chair. Bd of Dirs Wärtsilä NSD Oy Ab, Chair. Bd of Dirs Finnish Cen. Chamber of Commerce 1996–2003; Kt, Order of Finnish Lion, Commdr of Finnish White Rose. *Leisure interests:* hunting, fishing. *Address:* UPM-Kymmene Corporation, Eteläsplandadi 2, PO Box 380, 00101, Helsinki, Finland (office). *Telephone:* (204) 15111 (office). *Fax:* (204) 150110 (office). *E-mail:* info@upm-kymmene.com (office). *Website:* www.upm-kymmene.com (office).

VAINSHTEIN, Aleksander Lvovich; Russian media executive; *President, Moscow News;* b. 1 Sept. 1953, Moscow; m. Lia Vainchteine; one s. one d.; ed Moscow Inst. of Radio Tech., Electronics and Automation; worked in light bulb factory, Moscow 1976–86, Dir Club of Moscow factory 1986–89; Commercial Dir Moscow News newspaper 1989–90, Pres. Information-Publishing co. Moscow News 1995–; Dir-Gen. Acad. of Free Press; Exec. Dir Cup of Kremlin tennis tournament 1990–95; mem. Union of Journalists, Exec. Cttee Russian Football Union until 1998; USSR Council of Ministers Prize in the field of science and tech., TEFFI Prize for Best Sports TV Show 1998. *Television:* writer and producer: Century of Football, Football in Dialogues. *Publication:* N. Starostin: Football Through the Years. *Address:* Moscow News Publishing House, Tverskaya str. 16/2, 125009 Moscow, Russia (office). *Telephone:* (495) 200-63-90 (office). *Fax:* (495) 937-45-29 (office). *Website:* www.mn.ru (office).

VAINSHTOK, Semyon Mikhailovich; Russian business executive; b. 5 Oct. 1947, Klimatsy, Moldova; m.; one d.; ed Kiev Inst. of Construction and Eng, Acad. of KGB; engineer in Chernovtsy, Ukraine 1969–74; Head, Chernovtsy regional Dept of Provision and Trade 1974–82; Deputy Head, Povkhneft 1982–86; Deputy Dir-Gen. Bashneft, W Siberia 1986–88; Deputy Head, Kolymneftgas 1988–93; Dir-Gen. LukOil–Kolymneftgas 1993–95, LukOil, W Siberia 1995, Vice-Pres., mem. Bd of Dirs LukOil co. 1995; Pres. Transneft 1999–2007 (retd); apptd to oversee preparations for 2014 Winter Olympics in Sochi 2007–; mem. Acad. of Mining Sciences; Order for Service to Motherland. *Address:* c/o Transneft Co., B. Polyanka str. 57, 119180, Moscow, Russia (office).

VAISEY, David George, CBE, MA, FSA, FRHistS; British librarian and archivist; *Fellow Emeritus, Exeter College, University of Oxford;* b. 15 March 1935; s. of William Thomas Vaisey and Minnie Vaisey (née Payne); m. Maureen Anne Mansell 1965; two d.; ed Rendcomb Coll., Glos., Exeter Coll. Oxford; archivist, Staffordshire Co. Council 1960–63; Asst, then Sr Librarian, Bodleian Library 1963–75, Keeper of Western Manuscripts 1975–86, Bodley's Librarian 1986–96, Bodley's Librarian Emer. 1997–; Deputy Keeper, Oxford Univ. Archives 1966–75, Keeper 1995–2000; Professorial Fellow, Exeter Coll. Oxford 1975–96, Fellow by Special Election 1997–2000, Fellow Emer. 2000–; Visiting Prof. of Library Studies, UCLA 1985; Chair. Nat. Council on Archives 1988–91; mem. Royal Comm. on Historical Manuscripts 1986–98, Advisory Council on Public Records 1989–94; Vice-Pres. British Records Asscn 1999–; Pres. Soc. of Archivists 1999–2002, Expert Panel on Museums, Libraries and Archives, Heritage Lottery Fund 1999–2004; Hon. Fellow, Kellogg Coll. Oxford 1996–; Hon. Research Fellow, Dept of Library, Archive and Information Studies, Univ. Coll. London 1987–; Encomienda, Order of Isabel La Catolica (Spain) 1989. *Publications:* Staffordshire and the Great Rebellion (co-author) 1964, Probate Inventories of Lichfield and District 1568–1680 1969, Victorian and Edwardian Oxford from Old Photographs (co-author) 1971, Oxford Shops and Shopping 1972, Art for Commerce (co-author) 1973, Oxfordshire: A Handbook for Students of Local History 1973, The Diary of Thomas Turner 1754–65 1984; numerous articles in learned journals. *Address:* Bodleian Library, Oxford, OX1 3BG, England (office). *E-mail:* david.vaisey@bodley.ox.ac.uk.

VAITHINGHAM, V.; Indian politician; *Chief Minister of Puducherry;* b. 5 Oct. 1950, Cuddalore, Tamil Nadu; s. of V.Venkatasubba Reddiar; Leader Congress Legis. Party 1991–2000; Chief Minister of Puducherry 1991–96, 2008–, Leader of Opposition 1996–2000. *Address:* Office of the Chief Minister, Puducherry, India (office).

VAITIEKŪNAS, Petras, PhD; Lithuanian diplomatist and politician; b. 26 March 1953; m.; three c.; ed Vilnius Univ., Acad. of Sciences of Repub. of Lithuania, Coll. of Strategic Studies and Defence Econs, Germany; scientific researcher, Inst. of Physics, Acad. of Sciences of Repub. of Lithuania 1976–90; mem. Supreme Council, Restoration Seimas (Parl.) of Repub. of Lithuania 1990–92, adviser to Chair. of Seimas 1992–93; Sr Asst for Foreign Affairs to Pres. 1993–98; Head, Cen. European Div., Political Dept, Ministry of Foreign Affairs 1998; Adviser to Minister of Foreign Affairs 1998–99; Amb. to Latvia 1999–2004; Foreign Affairs Adviser to Pres. 2004; Amb.-at-Large, Foreign Policy and Analysis Planning Dept, Ministry of Foreign Affairs 2004–05; Amb. to Belarus 2005–06; Minister of Foreign Affairs 2006–08. *Address:* c/o Ministry of Foreign Affairs, J. Tumo-Vaižganto g. 2, Vilnius 01511, Lithuania (office).

VAJDA, György, DSc, FIEEE; Hungarian engineer; *President, Science Committee, Hungarian Atomic Energy Authority;* b. 18 June 1927, Budapest; s. of László Vajda and Mária Daróczi; m. 1st Magdolna Krasznai 1969 (died 1987); one s. one d.; m. 2nd Dr Klára Berei 1988; ed Tech. Univ., Budapest; Asst Lecturer 1949–50; on staff of Hungarian Acad. of Sciences 1950–52; Deputy Dir Inst. of Measurements 1952–57, Research Inst. of Electric Energetics 1957–63; Deputy Section Leader, Ministry of Heavy Industry 1963–70; Dir Inst. for Electrical Power Research 1970–93, Prof. 1993–97; Dir Gen. Hungarian Atomic Energy Authority 1994–99 (Vice-Pres. 1979–97), currently Pres. Science Cttee; Pres. European Atomic Energy Soc.; mem. Hungarian Nat. Comm. for Tech. Devt, Hungarian Acad. of Eng; mem. Admin. Comm. Conf. Int. des Grands Reseaux Electriques, Paris; Chair. ECE Electric Power Comm. 1972–76; Corresp. mem. Hungarian Acad. of Sciences 1976–81, mem. 1982, Section Pres. 1985–92; mem. New York Acad. of Sciences, Hungarian Acad. of Engineers; Fellow, Wireless Interconnection Forum; Hon. Pres. Hungarian Electrotechnical Soc.; Hon. Mem. Sigma Kszi; Distinguished Mem. CIGRE (Int. Council on Large Electric Systems); Hungarian Order; State Prize 1975, Szilárd Prize 1999, Széchenyi Award 2000, Renovanda Kult. Hung Grand Award 2002, Helios Award 2004, Prize of Labor (five times). *Publications:* A szigetelések romlása (Deterioration of Insulations) 1964, Szigetelések villamos erőterei (Electric Power Fields of Insulation) 1970, Energia és Társadalom (Energy and Society) 1975, Energetika (Energetics), Vols I–II 1984, Risk and Safety 1998, Energy Policy 2001, Energy Today and Tomorrow 2003, Utilization of Energy 2005; more than 150 papers in int. journals. *Leisure interest:* gardening. *Address:* Országos Atomenergia Hivatal, Fényes Adolf utca 4, 1036 Budapest (office); Bem rkp. 32, 1027 Budapest, Hungary (home). *Telephone:* (1) 436-4809 (office). *Fax:* (1) 436-4804 (office). *E-mail:* vajda@haea.gov.hu (office). *Website:* www.haea.gov.hu (office).

VAJPAYEE, Atal Bihari, MA; Indian politician; b. 25 Dec. 1924, Gwalior, MP; s. of Krishna Bihari Vajpayee; ed Victoria (now Laxmibai) Coll., Gwalior, D.A.V. Coll., Kanpur; mem. Rashtriya Swayamsewak Sangh 1941, Indian Nat. Congress 1942–46; mem. Lok Sabha 1957–62, 1967–84 (for New Delhi 1977–84), 1991–, Rajya Sabha 1962–67, 1986; Founder-mem. Bharatiya Jana Sangh 1951, Parl. Leader 1957–77; Chair. Cttee on Govt Assurance 1966–67, Public Accounts Cttee, Lok Sabha 1967–70, 1991–93; detained during Emergency 1975–77; Founder-mem. Janata Party 1977, Pres. Bharatiya Janata Party 1980–86, Parl. Leader 1980–84, 1986; Minister of External Affairs 1977–79; Leader of Opposition, Lok Sabha 1993–98, Chair. Standing Cttee on External Affairs 1993–96; Minister of External Affairs 1998; Prime Minister of India 15–28 May 1996, 1998–2004, also Minister of Health and Family Welfare, Atomic Energy and Agric. 1998–2004; Chair. Nat. Security Council 1998–2004; mem. Nat. Integration Council 1961–; fmr Ed. Rastradharma (monthly), Panchjanya (weekly), Swadesh and Veer Arjun (dailies); Dr hc (Kanpur Univ.) 1993; Bharat Ratna Pte Govind Ballabh Pant Award 1994, Padma Vibhushan 1992, Lokmanya Tilak Puruskar. *Publications:* New Dimensions of India's Foreign Policy, Jan Sangh Aur Musalmans, Three Decades in Parliament; collections of poems and numerous articles. *Leisure interests:* reading, writing, travelling, cooking. *Address:* c/o Bharatiya Janata Party (BJP) (Indian People's Party), 11 Ashok Rd, New Delhi 110 001 (office); 7 Race Course Road, New Delhi 110011, India (home). *Telephone:* (11) 23018939 (home). *Fax:* (11) 23019545 (home).

VAKHROMEYEV, Geliy Sergeyevich, DGeol; Russian scientist; b. 21 June 1934, Sverdlovsk; ed Sverdlovsk Ore Inst.; participated in geological expeditions with Irkutsk Geology Dept 1957–68; teacher, Head of Chair of Geophysics, Irkutsk State Tech. Univ. 1960–77; Dir Inst. of Ecological Geophysics, Russian Acad. of Natural Sciences 1992–; Ed. Geophysical Searches for Ore and Non-Ore Sources (yearbook) 1976–91; mem. Russian Acad. of Natural Sciences 1996, Scientific Council on Geology and Identification; Hon. Prof. Mongolian Tech. Univ. *Publications:* numerous scientific publications. *Address:* Institute of Ecological Geophysics, Irkutsk, Russia (office). *Telephone:* (3952) 43-08-54 (office).

VAKHROMEYEV, Kyril Varfolomeyevich (see Philaret).

VAKSBERG, Arkady Iosifovich, DJur; Russian writer, journalist and lawyer; b. 11 Nov. 1933, Novosibirsk; m.; one d.; ed Moscow State Univ.; barrister Moscow City Bd of Bar –1973; political observer in Paris, Literaturnaya Gazeta; Vice-Pres. Russian PEN Centre; mem. Russian Writer's Union, Journalist's Union, Union of Cinematography Workers, Int. Cttee of Writers in Prison; Grand-Prix, the Eurasian Teleforum (Moscow). *Screenplays for films:* The Storm Warning, The Provincial Romance, In Broad Daylight. *Plays:* A Shot in the Dark, The Supreme Court, The Alarm. *TV work includes:* The Special Reporter (serial), A Dangerous Zone (actor and scriptwriter), Reprise (Grand-Prix and Best Screenplay, International Telefilm Festival). *Publications:* three books and numerous articles on copyright law; over 40 works of fiction, collections of essays, biogs. and memoirs. *Leisure interests:* collecting reference books and encyclopaedias. *Address:* Krasnoarmeiskaya str. 23, Apt. 65, 125319 Moscow, Russia (home); 17 blvd Garibaldi, 75015 Paris, France. *Telephone:* (495) 151-33-69 (home); 1-45-66-45-31. *Fax:* 1-45-66-45-31. *E-mail:* vaksberg@noos.fr (home).

VALDÉS, Juan Gabriel, PhD; Chilean politician and diplomatist; b. June 1947; m. Antonia Echenique Celis; four c.; ed Catholic Univ. of Chile, Santiago, Univ. of Essex, UK, Princeton Univ., USA; Researcher, Political Science Inst. of Catholic Univ. of Chile, Inst. for Policy Studies, Washington, DC 1972–76; Officer, Latin American Inst. for Transnational Studies, Prof. of Int. Relations, Econ. Research and Devt Centre, Mexico City, Mexico 1976–1984; Research Fellow, Kellogg Inst. of Int. Studies, Notre Dame Univ., USA, Center for Latin American Studies, Princeton Univ. 1984, 1987; Consultant, Econ. Comm. for Latin America 1985; Amb. to Spain 1990–94; Dir Int. Div. and Co-ordinator NAFTA Negotiating Team, Ministry of Finance 1994–96, Lead Negotiator Chile–Canada Free Trade Agreement 1996; Consultant, UN Programme for Devt, Santiago 1994; mem. Nat. TV Council 1995; Vice-Minister Int. Econ. Affairs, Ministry of Foreign Affairs 1996–99, Minister 1999–2000; Perm. Rep. to UN, New York 2000–03, concurrently Amb. to Iran 2001; Amb. to Argentina 2003–04; Sec.-Gen.'s Special Rep., UN Stabilization Mission in Haiti (MINUSTAH) 2004–06; Dir Public Diplomacy Program, Ministry of Foreign Affairs 2006–. *Publications include:* Movimiento Sindical Y Empresas Transnacionales 1979, Chile 2000: Encuentro En Caceres De Politicos E Intelectuales Chilenos 1994, Pinochet's Economists : The Chicago School of Economics in Chile 1995; numerous articles on int. relations. *Address:* Ministry of Foreign Affairs, Catedral 1158, Santiago, Chile (office). *Telephone:* (2) 679-4200 (office). *Fax:* (2) 699-4202 (office). *Website:* www.minrel.gov.cl (office).

VÁLDEZ ALBIZÚ, Héctor, BEconSc; Dominican Republic economist and banker; *Governor, Banco Central de la República Dominicana;* b. 10 Nov. 1947; s. of Hector Manuel Valdez Albizu and Ana Rita Valdez Albizu; m. Fior d'Aliza Martinez 1971; one s.; Tech. Asst (Publs), Cen. Bank of Dominican Repub. 1970–75, Head of Banking and Monetary Div., Tech. Co-ordinator of Econ. Studies 1975–82, Econ. Asst to Gov. 1982–84, Dir Econ. Studies Dept 1984–86, Asst Man., Monetary and Exchange Policy 1986–90, Adviser to Monetary Bd 1987–89, Rep. of Cen. Bank at Banco de Reservas (state commercial bank) 1991–92, Asst Gen. Man. and Gen. Admin. Banco de Reservas 1992–94, Gov. Cen. Bank and Pres. Monetary Bd 1994–2000, 2004–; mem. Bd of Dirs Consejo Estatal del Azucar (State Sugar Council) 1993–94; Prof., Universidad Cen. del Este and Instituto de Estudios Superiores 1975–89. *Publications:* Financial Programs for the Dominican Republic 1976–1990, Dimensions of the National Banking System and its Enhancement 1976, Exchange Emergency Regime 1985. *Address:* Banco Central de la Republica Dominicana, Calle Pedro Henriquez Ureña, Esq. Leopoldo Navarro, Apdo. 1347, Santo Domingo, DN, Dominican Republic (office). *Telephone:* 221-9111 (office). *Fax:* 687-7488 (office). *E-mail:* info@bancentral.gov.do (office). *Website:* www.bancentral.gov.do (office).

VALDIVIESO MONTANO, Luis Miguel, PhD; Peruvian economist and politician; s. of Juan "El Mago" Valdivieso; ed Pontificia Univ. Católica del Perú, Boston Univ., USA; joined IMF 1980, held several exec. positions including Chief of Mission to Cambodia and Laos and Dir Asia-Pacific Region; adviser to Pres. Alberto Fujimori 1990–2000; Minister of Economy and Finance July 2008–Jan. 2009 (resgnd). *Address:* c/o Ministry of Economy and Finance, Jirón Junín 339, 4°, Circado de Lima, Lima, Peru (office).

VALDIVIESO SARMIENTO, Alfonso, LLD; Colombian diplomatist and politician; b. Oct. 1949, Bucaramanga; m.; two s.; ed Javerian Univ., Bogotá, Boston, Toronto and Stanford Univs; Admin. Vice-Rector and Dir of Planning, Autonomous Univ. of Bucaramanga 1978–86; mem. House of Reps 1982–86; mem. Council, Bucaramanga 1988–89, Pres. 1989; Senator 1986–90, 1990–94; Minister for Nat. Educ. 1990–91; Amb. to Israel 1992–93; Attorney-Gen. in charge of criminal investigations 1994–97; presidential cand. 1998; Perm. Rep. to UN 1998–2002. *Address:* c/o Ministry of Foreign Affairs, Palacio de San Carlos, Calle 10a, No. 5-51, Bogotá DC, Colombia (office).

VÁLEK, Vladimír; Czech conductor; b. 2 Sept. 1935, Nový Jičín; m. 1st Jana Adamová; m. 2nd Hana Patočková 1986; two s. one d.; ed Acad. of Musical Arts, Bratislava, Acad. of Performing Arts, Prague; conductor with several Czech orchestras 1962–75; Conductor FOK Prague Symphony Orchestra 1975–87; Chief Conductor Prague Radio Symphony Orchestra 1985–; Conductor Czech Philharmonic 1996–; Prin. Guest Conductor Orchestra Osaka Symphoniker 2003–; Guest Conductor with many orchestras world-wide including The Big Radio Orchestra Leipzig, Tonkuenstler and ORF (Vienna), Israeli and Japan Philharmonics; Music Critics' Award, MIDEM Classic Cannes (for recording of piano concertos by Ervin Schulhoff) 1996. *Performances:* concert tours include Japan, France, Spain, USA and Singapore; has appeared as guest conductor with numerous symphony orchestras in many countries. *Recordings:* more than 100 classical music recordings and more than 1,000 recordings for radio. *Leisure interest:* aviation. *Address:* Český rozhlas, Vinohradská 12, 120 00 Prague 2 (office); Nad údolím 24, 140 00 Prague 4, Czech Republic (home). *Telephone:* (2) 2155-1400 (office); (2) 4177-1463 (home). *Fax:* (2) 2155-1413 (office). *E-mail:* socr@cro.cz (office). *Website:* www.cro.cz/socr (office).

VALENÇA PINTO, Gen. Luis, BEng; Portuguese military officer; *Chief of Defence;* b. Lisbon; m. Maria de Lourdes; two s. one d.; ed Tech. Univ. of Lisbon, NATO Defence Coll., Rome; Engineer Platoon Leader during combat tour in Angola 1971–72, Engineer Co. Commdr 1973–75; Mil. Rep. to NATO, Brussels 1978–84; Mil. Counsellor, Del. to NATO, Brussels 1990–93; Mil. Rep. to SHAPE 1997–2000; Dir Nat. Defence Inst. 2000; Army Logistics Commdr 2001–03; Chief of Staff 2003–06; Chief of Defence 2006–; seven Distinguished Service Medals (five Gold and two Silver), Mil. Merit Medal (three classes). *Publications:* articles on security and defence issues in mil. and academic journals. *Address:* Ministry of National Defence, Av. Ilha de Madeira 1, 1400-204 Lisbon, Portugal (office). *Telephone:* (21) 3038528 (office). *Fax:* (21) 3020284 (office). *E-mail:* gcrp@sg.mdn.gov.pt (office). *Website:* www.mdn.gov.pt (office).

VALENCIA COSSIO, Fabio, LLB; Colombian politician and diplomatist; *Minister of Interior and Justice;* b. 23 March 1948, Medellín; ed Univ. de Antioquia; worked at Land Credit Inst., Bogotá 1974–81; Sec. Gen. Conservative Party 1981–84, Vice-Pres. 1984–96, Pres. Nat. Bd 1996–; mem. House of Reps 1982–91; Senator 1991–99, Pres. of Congress 1998–99; apptd negotiator in peace discussions with FARC guerilla movt 1999–2001; Amb. to Italy 2001–05; High Commr for Competitiveness 2005–08; Minister of Interior and Justice 2008–. *Address:* Ministry of the Interior and Justice, Palacio Echeverry, Carrera 8a, No 8-09, Bogotá, Colombia (office). *Telephone:* (1) 334-0630 (office). *Fax:* (1) 341-9583 (office). *Website:* www.mij.gov.co (office).

VALENCIA RODRÍGUEZ, Luis, LLD; Ecuadorean diplomatist, lawyer and academic; *Professor of Private International Law, Universidad Internacional del Ecuador;* b. 5 March 1926, Quito; s. of Pedro Valencia and María Rodríguez; m. Cleopatra Moreno 1952; two s. three d.; ed Cen. Univ., Quito; entered Ecuadorean Foreign Service 1944; Counsellor, Buenos Aires 1957–59; Minister-Counsellor, UN, New York 1959–64; Minister of Foreign Affairs 1965–66, 1981–84; legal adviser on foreign affairs 1964–65, 1966–69, 1980–81, 1990–94, 2001–03; Amb. to Bolivia 1969–71, to Brazil 1971–74, to Peru 1974–78, to Venezuela 1978–79, to Argentina 1988–91, fmr Amb. to Peru; Perm. Rep. to UN 1994–99; Prof. Cen. Univ., Quito 1984–86, Int. Univ., Quito 2001–; mem. UN Cttee on the Elimination of Racial Discrimination 1974–86, 1992–96; special citation of Ecuadorean Nat. Ass. 1966 and decorations from Ecuador, Italy, Nicaragua, Bolivia, Brazil, Peru, Venezuela, Colombia, Argentina, El Salvador, Dominican Republic and Korea. *Publications:* books on legal matters, foreign affairs etc. *Leisure interests:* swimming, reading. *Address:* Calle Agustin Mentoso 273, N47–153, Quito, Ecuador (home). *Telephone:* (2) 245-8765 (home). *Fax:* (2) 292-2668 (home). *E-mail:* lvalencia@mmree.gov.ec (office). *Website:* www.mmree.gov.ec (office).

VALENTIĆ, Nikica; Croatian business executive and fmr politician; *President, Niva Ltd;* b. 24 Nov. 1950, Gospić; m. Antoneta Valentić; one s. one d.; ed Law School, Zagreb Univ.; journalist for Radio Zagreb 1969–71; Ed. Pravnik (magazine) 1972–74; legal adviser in Zeljko Jurkovič office; Founder and Gen. Man. S2 Stanograd and Stanogradinvest consultancy co. 1978–83; f. legal firm 1984–90; Gen. Man. INA Industria Nafte 1990–93; Prime Minister of Croatia 1993–95; Founder and Pres. Niva Ltd, Zagreb 1995–. *Leisure* *interests:* painting, music. *Address:* Niva Ltd, Vlaška 83/1, 10000, Zagreb (office); Jordanovac 71, 10000, Zagreb, Croatia (home). *Telephone:* (1) 4664751 (office); (1) 4664752 (office). *Fax:* (1) 4664753 (office). *E-mail:* niva-holding@niva.htnet.hr (office).

VALENTINE, Jean, BA; American poet and teacher; b. 27 April 1934, Chicago, IL; m. James Chace 1957 (divorced 1968); two d.; ed Radcliffe Coll.; teacher Swarthmore Coll. 1968–70, Barnard Coll. 1968, 1970, Yale Univ. 1970, 1973–74, Hunter Coll., CUNY 1970–75, Sarah Lawrence Coll. 1974–, 92nd Street Y; Guggenheim Fellowship 1976; Nat. Endowment for the Arts grant 1972, Maurice English Prize, Teasdale Poetry Prize, Poetry Soc. of America Shelley Memorial Prize 2000. *Publications:* Dream Barker and Other Poems (Yale Series of Younger Poets Award) 1965, Pilgrims 1969, Ordinary Things 1974, The Messenger 1979, Home Deep Blue: New and Selected Poems 1989, The River at Wolf 1992, The Under Voice: Selected Poems 1995, Growing Darkness, Growing Light 1997, The Cradle of the Real Life 2000, The Lighthouse Keeper: Essays on the Poetry of Eleanor Ross Taylor (ed.) 2001, Door in the Mountain: New and Collected Poems 1965–2003 (Nat. Book Award for Poetry) 2004. *Address:* 527 W 110th Street, Suite 81, New York, NY 10025, USA. *E-mail:* info@jeanvalentine.com. *Website:* www.jeanvalentine.com.

VALENTINO (see Garavani, Valentino).

VALENZUELA, Luisa; Argentine writer and journalist; b. 26 Nov. 1938, Buenos Aires; d. of Luisa Mercedes Levinson and Pablo F. Valenzuela; m. Théodore Marjak 1958 (divorced); one d.; ed Belgrano Girls' School, Colegio Nacional Vicente Lopez, Buenos Aires; lived in Paris, writing for Argentinian newspapers and for the RTF 1958–61; Asst Ed. La Nación Sunday Supplement, Buenos Aires 1964–69; writer, lecturer, freelance journalist in USA, Mexico, France, Spain 1970–73, Buenos Aires 1973–79; taught in Writing Div., Columbia Univ., New York 1980–83; conducted writers' workshops, English Dept, New York Univ. and seminars, Writing Div. 1984–89; returned to Buenos Aires 1989; Fulbright Grant 1969–70; Guggenheim Fellow 1983; Fellow, New York Inst. for the Humanities; mem. Acad. of Arts and Sciences, Puerto Rico; Dr. hc (Knox Coll., Ill.) 1991; Machado de Assis Medal, Brazilian Acad. of Letters 1997. *Publications:* novels: Hay que sonreír 1966, El gato eficaz 1972, Como en la guerra 1977, Cambio de armas 1982, Cola de largartija 1983, Novela negra con argentinos 1990, Realidad Nacional desde la cama 1990, La travesía 2001, Trilogía de los bajos fondos 2004; short stories: Los heréticos 1967, Aquí pasan cosas raras 1976, Libro que no muerde 1980, Donde viven las águilas 1983, Simetrías (Cuentos de Hades) 1993, Antología Personal 1998, Cuentos Completos y Uno Más 1999, BREVS, microrrelatos completos hasta hoy 2004, Juego de villanos 2008, Tres por cinco 2008, Generosos inconvenientes 2008. *Leisure interests:* masks, anthropology, ceremonies. *Address:* c/o Amy Berkower, Writers House, 21 West 26th Street, New York, NY 10010, USA (office). *Telephone:* (212) 685-2400 (office). *Fax:* (212) 685-1781 (office). *E-mail:* aberkower@writershouse.com (office). *Website:* www.writershouse.com (office); www.luisavalenzuela.com.

VALIANT, Leslie G., DIC, PhD, FRS; British computer scientist and academic; *T. Jefferson Coolidge Professor of Computer Science and Applied Mathematics, Division of Engineering and Applied Sciences, Harvard University;* ed King's Coll., Cambridge, Imperial Coll., London, Univ. of Warwick; taught at Univ. of Leeds, Univ. of Edinburgh and Carnegie-Mellon Univ., Pittsburg, Pa; fmr Gordon McKay Prof. of Computer Science and Applied Math., Div. of Eng and Applied Sciences, Harvard Univ., Cambridge, Mass 1982–2002, T. Jefferson Coolidge Prof. of Computer Science and Applied Math. 2002–; has served on numerous editorial bds and program cttees including Soc. for Industrial and Applied Math. Journal on Computing, Machine Learning Computational Complexity, Neural Computation, Neural Networks, International Journal of Foundations of Computer Science, Symposium on Theory of Computing, Conf. on Computational Learning Theory, EuroColt, Symposium on Parallel Algorithms and Architectures, and others; Fellow, American Asscn for Artificial Intelligence; Nevanlinna Prize, Int. Congress of Mathematicians 1986, Knuth Award 1997. *Publications:* Circuits of the Mind 1994; more than 80 articles in scientific journals on parallel computing, computational complexity theory (and physics), computational learning and cognitive computation, neural computation, large computer systems and data centres. *Address:* Division of Engineering and Applied Sciences, Harvard University, 351 Maxwell Dworkin, 33 Oxford Street, Cambridge MA 02138, USA (office). *Telephone:* (617) 495-5817 (office). *Fax:* (617) 495-9837 (office). *E-mail:* valiant@deas.harvard.edu (office). *Website:* people.seas.harvard.edu/~valiant (office).

VALINSKAS, Arūnas, MA; Lithuanian television producer and politician; *Chairman, Seimas (Parliament);* b. 28 Nov. 1966, Lazdijai; m. Ingrida Valinskas; two s.; ed Vilnius Secondary School No. 12, Faculty of Law, Vilnius Univ.; 22-year career on stage and TV, host and moderator of radio and TV programmes, shows and concerts; writer and producer of popular TV shows, including TV games and quizzes: Taip ir Ne, Šeši nuliai – milijonas, and Žodžių mūšis, as well as TV entertainment show Vakarėlis jums, and music reality show Kelias į žvaigždes; co-writer TV series daily show Dviračio šou; Organizer Lithuanian Music Festival Nida; initiator and organizer of first ever beauty contest Miss Captivity at women's prison; gave more than 1,000 concerts as mem. of comic show team Dviratis; Founder Tautos prisikėlimo partija (Nat. Revival Party) 2008–; mem. Seimas (Parl.) 2008–, Speaker and Chair. Bd of the Seimas 2008–, mem. Ass. of Elders, Group for Inter-parl. Relations with Iraq, Group for Inter-parl. Relations with USA, Del. of Seimas to Ass. of Seimas of Repub. of Lithuania, of Sejm and Senate of Repub. of Poland and of Supreme Rada of Ukraine; first Golden Medal Award, Vilnius Secondary School No. 12. *Address:* Seimas (Parliament), Gedimino pr. 53, Vilnius 01109 (office); Tautos prisikėlimo partija, Laisvės pr. 60, 15A, postcode Vilnius, Lithuania. *Telephone:* (5) 239-6212 (office); (5) 239-6001. *Fax:* (5) 239-

6330 (office). *E-mail:* arunas.valinskas@lrs.lt (office); bustine@prisikelimopartija.lt. *Website:* www.lrs.lt (office); www.prisikelimopartija.lt.

VALIONIS, Antanas, PhD; Lithuanian politician, engineer and diplomatist; b. 21 Sept. 1950, Kedainiai Dist; s. of Antanas Valionis and Stanislova Valioniene; m. Romualda Valionis; two s.; ed Kaunas Polytechnic Inst., Warsaw Univ., Poland; foreman, Kaunas Meat Processing Plant 1974–76, Man. Compressor House, Taurage Meat Processing Plant 1976–80; Chief Instructor, Taurage Regional Cttee, Industry and Transport Dept of Cen. Cttee, Lituanian CP 1980–85, Instructor, Agric. and Food Industry Dept 1985–90; Head of Div. of Perspective Planning and Foreign Relations, Food Industry Dept, Ministry of Agric. 1990–94; Amb. to Poland 1994–2000, to Romania (also accred to Bulgaria) 1996–2000; mem. Seimas (New Union party) 2004–, mem. Cttee on State Admin and Local Authorities 2004–, Cttee on European Affairs 2006–; Minister of Foreign Affairs 2000–06; Commdr's Cross of Order of Lithuanian Grand Duke Gedimmas, Three-star Order of Repub. of Latvia, Chevalier de la Légion d'honeur, Grand Cross of Infante Dom Henriques (Portugal), Commdr's Cross with Star of Order of Merit (Poland); Commemorative Badge for Personal Input in the Development of Trans-Atlantic Relations and on the Occasion of Invitation of Lithuania to join NATO. *Publications:* numerous articles in nat and int press. *Leisure interests:* literature, traditional jazz, swing, rock 'n' roll 1950s–70s, classical music. *Address:* Seimas, Gedimino pr. 53, Vilnius, 01109, Lithuania (office). *Telephone:* (5) 239-6975 (office). *Fax:* (5) 239-6330 (office). *E-mail:* antanas.valionis@lrs.lt (office); www.lrs.lt (office).

VALIYEV, Kamil Akhmedovich; Russian/Tatar physicist; *Director, Institute of Physics and Technology, Russian Academy of Sciences;* b. 15 Jan. 1931, Verkhny Shendar, Tatarstan; m.; two c.; ed Kazan State Univ.; Sr Teacher, then Head of Lab. Kazan State Pedagogical Inst.; Dir Research Inst. of Molecular Physics; Head of Sector Ledebev Inst. of Physics; Deputy Dir, then Dir Inst. of Physics and Tech. (FTIAN), Russian Acad. of Sciences; mem. Russian Acad. of Sciences 1984, Presidium Tatarstan Acad. of Sciences; Ed.-in-Chief Russian Microelectronics (Mikroelektronika); Order of October Revolution, Order of Labour Red Banner; Lenin Prize, State Prize of Azerbaijan. *Publications include:* Microelectronics: Achievements and Ways of Development 1986, Physics of Submicronic Lithography 1990. *Leisure interests:* chess, photography. *Address:* Institute of Physics and Technology, Russian Academy of Sciences, 36/1 Nakhimovskii pr., 117218 Moscow, Russia (office). *Telephone:* (495) 125-77-09 (office). *Fax:* (495) 129-31-41 (office). *E-mail:* valiev@ftian.oivta.ru (office).

VALL, Col Ely Ould Mohamed; Mauritanian government official; b. 1952, Nouakchott; ed coll. and lycée in Aix-en-Provence and Le Mans, France, Mil. Acad. of Meknès; served in mil. campaign on border with Western Sahara 1970s, Commdr mil. stations of Bir-Mogreïn, Ouadane and Aïn-Benteli, Compagnie du Quartier Général, l'Etat-Major Nat. 1979–81, Seventh Mil. Area of Rosso 1982–83, Sixth Mil. Area of Nouakchott 1983–85; Dir Sûreté Nationale (nat. police force) 1985–2005; proclaimed as Pres. Mil. Council for Justice and Democracy (i.e. Pres. of Mauritania) following overthrow of Pres. Maaouya Ould Taya in a coup 2005–07; numerous decorations. *Address:* c/o Office of the President of the Military Council for Justice and Democracy, BP 184, Nouakchott, Mauritania (office).

VALLANCE OF TUMMEL, Baron (Life Peer), cr. 2004, of Tummel in Perth and Kinross; **Iain David Thomas Vallance,** BA, MSc; British business executive; *Chairman, Royal Scottish Academy of Music and Drama;* b. 20 May 1943, London; s. of Edmund Thomas Vallance and Janet Wright Bell Ross Davidson; m. Elizabeth Mary McGonnigill 1967; one s. one d.; ed Edinburgh Acad., Dulwich Coll., Glasgow Acad., Brasenose Coll. Oxford, London Grad. School of Business Studies; Asst Postal Controller, Post Office 1966, Personal Asst to Chair. 1973–75, Head of Finance Planning Div. 1975–76, Dir Cen. Finance 1976–78, Telecommunications Finance 1978–79, Materials Dept 1979–81; mem. Bd for Org. and Business Systems, British Telecommunications (BT) 1981–83, Man. Dir, Local Communications Services Div. 1983–85, Chief of Operations 1985–86, Chief Exec. 1986–95, Chair. 1987–2001, Pres. Emer. 2001–02; Vice-Chair. Royal Bank of Scotland 1994–2005; Liberal Democrat Spokesperson for Trade and Industry/Business, Enterprise and Regulatory Reform, House of Lords 2005–, mem. Select Cttee on Econ. Affairs 2005–; Chair. Royal Scottish Acad. of Music and Drama 2006–; Founding mem. Pres.'s Cttee of European Foundation for Quality Man. 1988; mem. CBI Pres.'s Cttee, Pres. CBI 2000–02; mem. Advisory Council of Business in the Community, Allianz Int. Advisory Bd, Advisory Council of Prince's Youth Business Trust 1988–, Advisory Bd British-American Chamber of Commerce 1991–, Supervisory Bd Siemens AG 2002–; Chair. European Services Forum 2002–; Vice-Chair. European Advisory Cttee to New York Stock Exchange, Chair. 2000–02; Vice-Pres. The Princess Royal Trust for Carers; fmr mem. Bd Scottish Enterprise, Mobil Corpn; Trustee Monteverdi Trust; Fellow London Business School 1989; Liveryman of Worshipful Co. of Wheelwrights; Freeman of the City of London; Hon. Fellow Brasenose Coll.; Hon. Gov. Glasgow Acad. 1993–; Fellow, Chartered Inst. of Bankers in Scotland; Hon. DSc (Ulster) 1992, (Napier) 1994; Hon. DTech (Loughborough) 1992, (Robert Gordon) 1994; Hon. DBA (Kingston) 1993; Hon. DEng (Heriot-Watt) 1995; Hon. DSc (City Univ.) 1996. *Leisure interests:* walking, playing the piano, listening to music. *Address:* House of Lords, London, SW1A 0PW, England; Royal Scottish Academy of Music and Drama, 100 Renfrew Street, Glasgow G2 3D, Scotland. *Telephone:* (20) 7219-2715 (House of Lords). *Website:* www.rsamd.ac.uk.

VALLANCE-OWEN, John, MA, MD, FRCP, FRCPI, FRCPath; British academic and physician; *Visiting Professsor, Imperial College of Science, Technology and Medicine, Hammersmith Hospital;* b. 31 Oct. 1920, London; s. of Edwin Augustine Vallance-Owen and Julia May; m. Renee Thornton 1950; two s. two d.; ed Epsom Coll., Surrey, Univ. of Cambridge, The London Hosp.; various appointments including Pathology Asst and Medical First Asst to Sir Horace Evans, London Hosp. 1946–51; Medical Tutor, Royal Postgrad. Medical School, Hammersmith Hosp., London 1952–55, 1956–58; Consultant Physician and Lecturer in Medicine, Univ. of Durham 1958–64; Consultant Physician and Reader in Medicine, Univ. of Newcastle-upon-Tyne 1964–66; Prof. and Chair., Dept of Medicine, Queen's Univ., Belfast and Consultant Physician to Royal Victoria Hosp., Belfast City Hosp. and Forster Green Hosp., Belfast 1966–82; Dir of Medical Services, The Maltese Islands 1981–82; Foundation Prof. and Chair. Dept of Medicine, The Chinese Univ. of Hong Kong 1983–88, Assoc. Dean 1984–88; Consultant in Medicine to Hong Kong Govt 1984–88, to British Army in Hong Kong 1985–88; Medical Adviser on Clinical Complaints, NE Thames Regional Health Authority 1989–96; Visiting Prof. Imperial Coll. of Science, Tech. and Medicine, Hammersmith Hosp. 1989–; Consultant Physician London Ind. Hosp. 1989–99, Wellington Hosp. 1999–2003; Rockefeller Travelling Fellowship, held at Univ. of Pennsylvania, USA 1955–56; Fellow, Royal Hong Kong Coll. of Physicians; Oliver-Sharpey Prize, Royal Coll. of Physicians 1976. *Publications:* Essentials of Cardiology 1961, Diabetes: Its Physiological and Biochemical Basis 1975; numerous papers in scientific journals on carbohydrates and fat metabolism and the aetiology of diabetes mellitus, with special reference to insulin antagonism. *Leisure interests:* music, tennis, golf. *Address:* 10 Spinney Drive, Great Shelford, Cambridge (home); 17 St Matthews Lodge, Oakley Square, London, NW1 1NB, England; Cuildochart, Killin, Perthshire, Scotland. *Telephone:* (20) 7388-3644 (London); (1223) 842767 (Cambridge) (home); (1567) 820337 (Scotland). *E-mail:* renee@vallance-owen.freeserve.co.uk (office).

VALLARINO BARTUANO, Arturo Ulises, BSc, DJurSc; Panamanian politician and lawyer; b. 15 Dec. 1943, Capiro Dist, Panamá; s. of Ismael Vallarino and María Concepción Bartuano; m. Elka Aparicio de Vallarino; five c.; ed Univ. of Panama, Universidad Nacional Autónoma de México, Univ. of Costa Rica; Legal Adviser Ministry of Foreign Affairs 1966; elected Councillor for Panamá Dist 1968; lawyer pvt. firm Carillo, Villalaz & Muñoz; Sr Pnr, Bufete, Vallarino y Asociados –1999; fmr Prof. of Political Science and Commercial Law Univ. of Panama; fmr Chargé d'affaires for Business, Argentina; fmr Legal Adviser Ministry of Planning and Econ. Politics, Nat. Banking Comm.; fmr Pres. Legis. Ass.; Sec.-Gen. Partido Movimiento Liberal Republicano Nacionalista (MOLIRENA) –2003; First Vice-Pres. of Panama 1999–2003 (retd). *Address:* c/o Oficina del Primer Vice-Presidente, Palacio Presidencial, Valija 50, Panamá 1, Panama (office).

VALLEE, Bert Lester, MD; American biochemist, physician and academic; *Edgar M. Bronfman Senior Distinguished Professor, Harvard Medical School;* b. 1 June 1919, Hemer, Westphalia, Germany; s. of Joseph Vallee and Rosa Vallee (née Kronenberger); m. Natalie Kugris 1947; ed Univ. of Berne, Switzerland and New York Univ. Coll. of Medicine; went to USA 1938, naturalized 1948; Research Fellow, Harvard Medical School, Boston 1946–49, Research Assoc. 1949–51, Assoc. 1951–56, Asst Prof. of Medicine 1956–60, Assoc. Prof. 1960–64, Prof. of Biological Chem. 1964–65, Paul C. Cabot Prof. of Biological Chem. 1965–80, Paul C. Cabot Prof. of Biochemical Sciences 1980–89, Prof. Emer. 1989–, Distinguished Sr Prof. Biochemical Sciences 1989–90, Edgar M. Bronfman Distinguished Sr Prof. 1990–; Research Assoc., Dept of Biology, MIT 1948–; physician, Peter Bent Brigham Hosp., Boston 1961–80; Biochemist-in-Chief, Brigham and Women's Hosp., Boston 1980–89, Emer. 1989–; Scientific Dir Biophysics Research Lab., Harvard Medical School, Peter Bent Brigham Hosp. 1954–80; Head, Center for Biochemical and Biophysical Sciences and Medicine, Harvard Medical School 1980–; Founder and Trustee Boston Biophysics Foundation 1957–; Founder and Pres. Endowment for Research in Human Biology, Inc. 1980–; mem. ACS; Fellow, AAAS, NAS, American Acad. of Arts and Sciences, New York Acad. of Sciences; Hon. mem. Swiss Biochemical Soc. 1976, Japan Soc. for Analytical Chem.; Hon. Foreign mem. Royal Danish Acad. of Sciences and Letters; Hon. Prof., Tsinghua Univ. 1987, Stellenbosch Univ. 1995, Shanghai Inst. of Biochemistry 1997; Order Andres Bello (1st Class) (Venezuela); Hon. AM (Harvard) 1960; Hon. MD (Karolinska Inst.) 1987; Hon. DSc (Naples Univ.) 1991; Hon. PhD (Ludwig Maximillian Univ., Munich) 1995; LinderstrømLang Award and Gold Medal 1980, The Willard Gibbs Gold Medal 1981, William C. Rose Award in Biochemistry 1982, Messenger Lecturer, Cornell Univ. 1988, Raulin Award, Int. Soc. for Trace Element Research in Humans 2002. *Publications:* more than 500 publs on zinc and other metalloenzymes, their structure, function and mechanism of action, emission, absorption, CD and MCD spectroscopy, organic chemical modification of proteins, and organogenesis. *Leisure interest:* riding. *Address:* Harvard Medical School, NRB 930C, 77 Avenue Louis Pasteur, Boston, MA 02115 (office); 300 Boylston Street, Apartment 712, Boston, MA 02116, USA (home). *Telephone:* (617) 432-6577 (office); (617) 432-6595; (617) 695-1701 (home). *Fax:* (617) 432-6580 (office); (617) 695-1702 (home). *E-mail:* bert_vallee@hms.harvard.edu (office); brian_bernert@hms.harvard.edu (office). *Website:* hms.harvard.edu (office).

VALLEE, Rodolphe M. (Skip), BA, MBA; American business executive, politician and fmr diplomatist; *Chairman and CEO, R. L. Vallee, Inc.;* m. Denise Vallee; two s.; ed Williams Coll., Massachusetts, Wharton School, Univ. of Pennsylvania; worked in exec. positions for several cos involved in devt and operation of refuse, biomass, hydro and other renewable energy facilities; Devt Prin., Catalyst Energy Corpn 1986–87, Vice-Pres. Catalyst Waste-to-Energy Corpn 1987–88; f. R. L. Vallee Inc. 1989, Chair. and CEO 1989–2005, 2007–; mem. Bd Dirs MSCI, Inc. 2008–; began his political career in 1982 as regional campaign man. for US Senator Robert T. Stafford and later served as staff asst of Senate Sub-cttee on Educ.; apptd to Advisory Cttee for Trade Policy and Negotiation 2001; mem. Republican Nat. Cttee 1999–2004; Chair. Vt Del. to Republican Nat. Convention 2004; Amb. to Slovakia 2005–07; fmr Dir Mater Christi School; fmr Trustee Nature Conservancy of Vt. *Leisure interests:* skiing, hunting, fishing. *Address:* R. L. Vallee, Inc., 280 South Main Street, Saint Albans, VT 05478-1866, USA (office). *Telephone:* (802) 524-8710 (office).

VALTINOS, Thanassis; Greek writer; *President, Hellenic Authors' Society;* b. 16 Dec. 1932, Karatoula Kynourias; m.; one d.; ed Athens Univ.; Visiting Prof., War Research Inst., Frankfurt 1993–; Pres. Hellenic Authors' Society; mem. European Acad. of Sciences and Arts, Int. Inst. of Theatre, Greek Society of Playwriters; Scenario Award Cannes Festival 1984, Nat. Literary Award 1990. *Address:* Hellenic Authors' Society, Kodrigtonos 8, 112 57 Athens (office); 66 Astidamantos Street, 116 34 Athens, Greece. *Telephone:* (210) 8231890 (office); (210) 7218793. *Fax:* (210) 8232543 (office). *E-mail:* gwrisoc@otenet.gr (office). *Website:* www.dedalus.gr (office).

VALZANIA, Sergio; Italian television journalist, author and broadcasting executive; *Director, Radio 2, Radiotelevisione Italiana SpA (RAI);* b. 1951, Florence; ed Univ. of Genoa; Dir Radio 2, Radiotelevisione Italiana SpA (RAI) 1999–, has directed radio programmes of RAI 2 and RAI 3 2002–. *Television productions include:* Dadaumpa 1984–86, La clessidra, filosofi a confronto 1985, La macchina del tempo 1985–86, La TV delle ragazze 1988–89, Bambini 1989–90 (all for RAI 3). *Publications:* Brodo nero. Sparta pacifica, il suo esercito, le sue guerre 1999, Napoleone 2001, Retorica della guerra. Quando la violenza sostituisce la parola 2002, Una radio strutturalista. Consigli per ascoltare e trasmettere 2002, Tre tartarughe greche 2002, Jutland. 31 maggio 1916: la più grande battaglia navale della storia 2006, Sparta e Atene. Il racconto di una guerra 2006, Austerlitz. La più grande vittoria di Napoleone 2006, Wallenstein. La tragedia di un generale nella guerra dei Trent'anni 2007, La morte dei dinosauri 2007, Le La città degli uomini. Cinque riflessioni in un mondo che cambia (with Fausto Bertinotti) 2007, Le radici perdute dell'Europa. Da Carlo V ai conflitti mondiali (with Franco Cardini) 2007, Amare il vino. Arte natura tecnica estetica (with Luca Maroni) 2007. *Address:* Radio 2, Radiotelevisione Italiana SpA, Viale Mazzini 14, 00195 Rome, Italy (office). *Telephone:* (06) 38781 (office). *E-mail:* info@rai.it (office). *Website:* www.rai.it (office).

VÁMOS, Éva, PhD Habil.; Hungarian museologist; *Senior Researcher, Hungarian Museum for Science and Technology (Országos Műszaki Múzeum);* b. 22 May 1950, Budapest; d. of Endre Vámos and Lilly (née Vigyázó) Vámos; ed Eötvös Loránd Univ. of Budapest, Tech. Univ. of Budapest; affiliated to Hungarian Museum for Science and Tech. (Országos Műszaki Múzeum) 1973–, Curator 1973–78, Scientific Co-worker 1978–86, Head, Ind. Group of History of Science, Scientific Sec. in charge of Public Relations 1986–87, Sr Scientific Co-worker 1987–89, Head of Dept 1989–91, Scientific Deputy Dir-Gen. 1991–93, Dir-Gen. 1994–2004, Sr Researcher 2004–; Memorial Medal, Fed. of Scientific and Tech. Asscns 1997, Justus von Liebig Memorial Medal 2000. *Publications:* Chapters from the History of Communication 1979, History of Writing and Writing Utensils 1980–82, German-Hungarian Relations in the Fields of Science with Special Regard to Chemistry, Chemical Industry and Food Industry 1876–1914 1995, Creative Hungarians 1988, László József Bíró 1996, Women's Opportunities of Studying and Practising Engineering in Hungary 1998, Justus von Liebigs Hungarian Connections by Correspondence 2003, Memorial Sights of Chemistry at Budapest Universities 2007. *Leisure interests:* univ. women's movt, gardening, classical music. *Address:* Hungarian Museum for Science and Technology, Kaposvár 13–15, 1117 Budapest (office); Batthyány u. 3. VI. 32, 1015 Budapest, Hungary (home). *Telephone:* (1) 204-4095 (office); (1) 204-4090 (office); (1) 201-7317 (home). *Fax:* (1) 204-4088 (office). *E-mail:* evamos@nadir.hmst.hu (office); vamos.eva@chello.hu (home). *Website:* www.omm.hu (office).

VÁMOS, Tibor, PhD, DSc; Hungarian research professor; *Chairman, Computer and Automation Research Institute, Hungarian Academy of Sciences;* b. 1 June 1926, Budapest; s. of Miklós Vámos and Ilona Rausnitz; m. Noémi Stenczer; one s.; ed Tech. Univ. Budapest; started in process control automation of power plants and systems, worked later in computer control of processes, robot vision, artificial intelligence; Chief Engineer, Research Inst. of Power System Eng Co. 1950–54, Automation Dept Head 1954–64; Dir Computer and Automation Research Inst., Hungarian Acad. of Sciences 1964–85, Chair. 1986–; Prof. Budapest Tech. Univ. 1969–; Distinguished Visiting Prof., George Mason Univ. 1992–93, Distinguished Affiliate Prof. 1993–94; Corresp. mem. Hungarian Acad. of Sciences 1973, mem. 1979, mem. Governing Bd 1980–; Pres. Int. Fed. of Automatic Control (IFAC) 1981–84, IFAC Lifetime Adviser 1987–; mem. Editorial Bd four int. scientific journals; mem. European Coordinating Cttee for Artificial Intelligence 2004–, Fellow 2006–; Fellow, IEEE Inc. 1986–, IFAC 2006–; Hon. Mem. Austrian Computer Soc. 1992, Austrian Soc. for Cybernetic Studies 1994; Hon. Pres. John v. Neumann Soc. of Computer Science 1986–; Order of Hungarian Repub. 1996; Dr hc (Tallinn Univ.); State Prize 1983, Chorafas Prize, Swiss Acads 1994, World Automation Congress Dedication 2006. *Publications:* Nagy ipari folyamatok irányitása (Control of Large-Scale Processes) 1970, Computer Epistemology 1991; co-author: Applications of Syntactic Pattern Recognition 1977, Progress in Pattern Recognition 1981; co-ed.: The Neumann Compendium 1995; 130 contribs to scientific journals and 170 to other publs. *Leisure interests:* fine arts, mountaineering. *Address:* Lágymányosi u. 11, 1111 Budapest, Hungary (home). *Telephone:* (1) 209-5274 (office); (1) 320-3657 (home). *Fax:* (1) 209-5275 (office). *E-mail:* vamos@sztaki.hu (office). *Website:* www.sztaki.hu/~vamos (office).

VAN AARTSEN, Jozias Johannes, LLB; Dutch politician; *Mayor, The Hague;* b. 25 Dec. 1947, The Hague; m. Henriëtte Warsen; three c.; ed Amsterdam Free Univ.; Supervisory Dir Govt Computer Centre and Printing Office; Ed. Liberal Reveille; worked for Parl. People's Party for Freedom and Democracy (VVD) 1970–74, Dir VVD Research Org. 1974–79; staff mem. Sec.-Gen.'s Office, Minister of the Interior 1979–83, Deputy Sec.-Gen. 1983–85,

Sec.-Gen. 1985–94, Chair. Council of Bd of Sec.-Gens 1994; Minister of Agric., Nature Man. and Fisheries 1994–98, of Foreign Affairs 1998–2002; Leader VVD Parl. Group 2003–06; worked with EC as coordinator of EU project to lay gas pipeline from Turkey to Austria 2006; Mayor, The Hague 2008–; fmr mem. Bd Expertise Centre for Employment among Minorities; fmr Chair. Bd Nat. Inst. for Arts Educ. *Address:* City Hall (Atrium), Spui 70, 2500 DP, The Hague, Netherlands (office). *Telephone:* (70) 3535043 (office). *Website:* www.denhaag .com (office).

VAN AGT, Andries A. M.; Dutch politician; b. 2 Feb. 1931, Geldrop; s. of Frans van Agt and Anna Frencken; m. Eugenie Krekelberg 1958; one s. two d.; ed Catholic Univ., Nijmegen; worked at Ministry of Agric. and Fisheries, then Ministry of Justice 1958–68; Prof. of Penal Law, Univ. of Nijmegen 1968–; Minister of Justice 1971–77; Deputy Prime Minister 1973–77; Prime Minister and Minister of Gen. Affairs 1977–82; Minister of Foreign Affairs 1982; mem. Parl. 1983; Gov. Prov. of Noord-Brabant 1983–87; Amb., Head Del. of European Communities, Tokyo 1987, later Washington, DC –1995.

VAN AGT, Andries A. M. (see Agt, Andries A. M. van).

VAN ASSCHE, Kris; Belgian fashion designer; *Artistic Director, Dior Homme;* b. 1976; ed Antwerp Royal Acad. of Fine Arts; moved to Paris in 1998; worked with Hedi Slimane at Yves Saint Laurent and then for Dior Homme; began to show original creations in 2005; f. own label, Kris Van Assche; Artistic Dir, Dior Homme 2007–. *Address:* August H, Hôtel de Retz, 9 rue Charlot, 75003 Paris, France (office). *Telephone:* 1-48-04-52-42 (office). *Fax:* 1-48-04-03-65 (office). *E-mail:* info@krisvanassche.com (office). *Website:* www.krisvanassche.com (office); www.diorhomme.com (office).

VAN BASTEN, Marco; Dutch football player; b. 31 Oct. 1964, Utrecht; m. Elizabeth Van Basten 1992; one s. two d.; player Ajax 1981–97 (won Golden Boot Award for top-scoring with 37 goals in 1986, three Dutch Championships, three Dutch Cups, Cup Winner's Cup) scoring 128 goals in 143 appearances; player AC Milan 1987–95 (won two European Cups, two World Club Cups) scoring 90 goals in 147 games; player nat. team, 58 caps, 24 goals; coach with Jong Ajax 2003–04, AFC Ajax 2008–09; Head Coach, Dutch nat. team 2004–08; European Footballer of the Year 1988, 1989, 1992, World Footballer of the Year 1988, 1992. *Leisure interest:* golf. *Address:* c/o AFC Ajax, Arena Boulevard 29, 1101 AX Amsterdam, The Netherlands.

VAN BENTHEM, Johannes F. A. K., MA, PhD; Dutch logician and academic; *University Professor of Logic, University of Amsterdam;* b. (Johan van Benthem), 12 June 1949, Rijswijk; s. of A. K. van Benthem and J. M. G. Eggermont; m. Lida Blom 1977; two s.; ed 's Gravenhaags Christelijk Gymnasium and Univ. of Amsterdam; Asst Prof. of Philosophical Logic, Univ. of Amsterdam 1972–77, Chair. Dept of Philosophy 1974–75; Assoc. Prof. of Philosophical Logic, Univ. of Groningen 1977–86, Chair. Dept of Philosophy 1979–81; Prof. of Mathematical Logic, Univ. of Amsterdam 1986–2003, Univ. Prof. of Logic 2003–, Chair. Dept of Math. and Computer Science 1987–89, Scientific Dir Research Inst. for Logic, Language and Computation 1991–98; Chair. European Asscn of Logic, Language and Information 1991–96; Sr Researcher, Center for Study of Language and Information, Stanford Univ., USA 1991–; Bonsall Visiting Chair. in the Humanities, Stanford Univ. 1991–2003, Prof. of Philosophy 2003–; Visiting Univ. Prof., Zhong Shan Univ., Guangzhou, People's Repub. of China; Vice-Pres. Int. Fed. of Computational Logic 1999–; Chair. Nat. Cognitive Science Programme 2001–03, Vienna Circle Foundation 1997–; Man. Ed. Synthese, Logic and Computation, and other journals; Ed.-in-Chief Texts in Logic and Games; mem. Academia Europaea, Royal Dutch Acad. of Sciences, Institut Int. de Philosophie, Hollandse Maatschappij van Wetenschappen; First Hon. Mem. European Asscn of Logic, Language and Information; Dr hc (Liège Univ.) 1998; Spinoza Prize, Netherlands Org. for Scientific Research 1996. *Publications:* The Logic of Time 1983, Modal Logic and Classical Logic 1985, Essays in Logical Semantics 1986, A Manual of Intensional Logic 1988, Language in Action, Categories, Lambdas and Dynamic Logic 1991, Exploring Logical Dynamics 1996; co-author of various textbooks in logic; (ed.) Handbook of Logic and Language 1997, Logic and Games 2001, Handbook of Modal Logic 2006, Handbook of Spatial Logics 2007, Handbook of the Philosophy of Information 2007; more than 300 articles in scientific journals. *Address:* Institute for Logic, Language and Computation, University of Amsterdam, Plantage Muidergracht 24, 1018 TV Amsterdam, Netherlands (office). *Telephone:* (20) 5256051 (office). *Fax:* (20) 5255206 (office). *E-mail:* johan@science.uva.nl (office); johan@csli.stanford.edu (office). *Website:* staff.science.uva.nl/~johan (office).

VAN BERKEL, Ben (Bernard Franciscus); Dutch architect; b. 25 Jan. 1957, Utrecht; s. of Magchiel van Berkel and Maria Therese Mattaar; ed Rietved Acad., Amsterdam, Architectural Asscn, London; graphic designer 1977–82; Co-Founder, Dir Van Berkel & Bos 1988–99; Co-Founder, Dir UN Studio 1999; projects include: switching substation, Amersfoort 1989–93, Erasmus Bridge, Rotterdam 1990–96, Villa Wilbrink, Amersfoort 1992–94, Möbius House, 't Gooi 1993–98, Museum Het Valkhof, Nijmegen 1995–99, Masterplan station area, Arnhem 1996–, City Hall and Theatre, Ijsselstein 1996–2000, switching station, Innsbruck 1998–2001, Music Faculty, Graz 1998–, WTC 2001, Mercedes Benz Museum, Stuttgart; Eileen Gray Award 1983, British Council Fellowship 1986, Charlotte Köhler Prize 1991, winning entry for Police HQ, Berlin 1995, Museum Het Valkhof 1995, music theatre, Graz, Austria 1998, Kunstpreis, Frankfurt. *Address:* UN Studio Van Berkel & Bos, Stadhouderskade 113, 1073 AX Amsterdam, The Netherlands (office). *Telephone:* (20) 5702040 (office). *Fax:* (20) 5702041 (office). *E-mail:* info@ unstudio.com (office). *Website:* www.unstudio.com (office).

VAN BOXMEER, Jean-François, MEcons; Belgian business executive; *Chairman of the Executive Board and CEO, Heineken NV;* b. 12 Sept. 1961, Elsene; ed Facultés Universitaires Notre Dame de la Paix S.J., Namur,

Belgium; traineeship in production, sales and admin areas, Heineken Nederland, assignment in Cameroon 1984–87, Sales and Marketing Man., Heineken Bralima, Rwanda 1987–90, Democratic Repub. of Congo 1990–93, Gen. Man. 1993–96, Pres. and Gen. Man. Zywiec SA, Poland 1996–99, Vice-Pres. and Gen. Man. Grupa Zywiec SA, Poland 1999–2000, Gen. Man. Heineken Italia 2000–01, mem. Exec. Bd Heineken NV, The Netherlands 2001–05, Chair. Exec. Bd and CEO 2005–. *Address:* Heineken NV, PO Box 28, 1000 AA Amsterdam (office); Heineken NV, Tweede Weteringplantsoen 21, 1017 ZD Amsterdam, The Netherlands (office). *Telephone:* (20) 523-92-39 (office). *Fax:* (20) 626-35-03 (office). *E-mail:* info@heinekeninternational.com (office). *Website:* www.heinekeninternational.com (office).

VAN BROECKHOVEN, Christine, BSc, MSc, PhD, DSc; Belgian research scientist and academic; *Professor, Director of the VIB Department of Molecular Genetics and Group Leader of the Neurodegenerative Brain Diseases Group, University of Antwerp;* b. 1953, Antwerp; ed Univ. of Antwerp; postgraduate student, IWONL Fellowship 1975–78, Univ. of Antwerp 1978–80; Researcher, Prov. Inst. of Hygiene 1978–81; high school teacher, Stella Maris Inst., Antwerp 1981–83; Research Asst, Univ. of Antwerp 1983–89; Research Fellow, Nat. Fund of Scientific Research 1989–95; Research Dir Inst. Born-Bunge 1990; Asst Prof., Univ. of Antwerp 1990–94, Assoc. Prof. 1995–96, Scientific Dir and Group Leader of the Neurodegenerative Brain Diseases Group, VIB –Dept of Molecular Genetics 1996–, Assoc. Prof. 1997–98, Full Prof., Univ. of Antwerp 1999–; consultant, Innogenetics Inc. 1990–93, Janssen Pharmaceutics Inc. 1995–2001; mem. Bd Dirs GIMV Belgian Investment Co. 2005–07; Assoc. mem. Royal Flemish Acad. of Sciences and Art 1999; Royal Grand Officer, Order of Léopold 2006, Chevalier, Légion d'honneur 2009; Divry Prize, Belgian Soc. of Neurology 1991, Potamkin Prize, American Acad. of Neurology (co-recipient) 1993, Joseph Maisin Scientific Prize, Nat. Fund for Scientific Research 1995, Marie-Thérèse De Lava Prize, King Boudewijn Foundation 1995, Upjohn Inc. Scientific Prize, NFSR (co-recipient) 1995, Belgian Coll. of Neuropsychopharmacology and Biological Psychiatry Lundbeck Prize (co-recipient) 1997, L'Oréal/UNESCO Special Honour Award for Women in Science 2002, 55th Ark Prize, Belgian Ark Cttee of the Free Word 2005, Zenith Award, Alzheimer Asscn (USAUSA) 2005, L'Oréal-UNESCO Int. Award for Women in Science (Europe) 2006, Award Lecture in the Frontiers in Clinical Neuroscience, Plenary Session of American Acad. of Neurology Annual Meeting, Boston 2007. *Publications:* more than 450 articles in scientific journals. *Address:* VIB – Department of Molecular Genetics, University of Antwerp, CDE, Universiteitsplein 1, Building V, Antwerp B-2610, Belgium (office). *Telephone:* (3) 265-10-02 (office). *Fax:* (3) 265-10-12 (office). *E-mail:* christine.vanbroeckhoven@molgen.vib-ua.be (office). *Website:* www.molgen.ua.ac.be (office).

VAN CAENEGEM, Baron Raoul C.; Belgian academic; *Professor Emeritus, University of Ghent;* b. 14 July 1927, Ghent; s. of Jozef Van Caenegem and Irma Barbaix; m. Patricia Carson 1954; two s. one d.; ed Univs of Ghent, Paris and London; Ordinary Prof., Univ. of Ghent 1964, Prof. Emer. 1992–; Visiting Fellow, Univ. Coll. Cambridge 1968; Goodhart Prof. of Legal Science, Univ. of Cambridge 1984–85; Visiting Fellow, Peterhouse, Cambridge 1984–85; Sir Henry Savile Fellow, Merton Coll. Oxford 1989; Fiftieth Anniversary Fellow, Univ. of Queensland, Australia 1990; Erasmus Lecturer on History and Civilization of the Netherlands, Harvard Univ. 1991; Dr hc (Tübingen) 1977, (Louvain) 1984, (Paris) 1988; Francqui Prize 1974; Solvay Prize, Nat. Fund for Scientific Research, Brussels 1990. *Publications:* Royal Writs in England from the Conquest to Glanvill. Studies in the Early History of the Common Law 1959, The Birth of the English Common Law 1973, Guide to the Sources of Medieval History 1978, English Lawsuits from William I to Richard I (two vols) 1990–91, An Historical Introduction to Private Law 1992, Judges, Legislators and Professors: Chapters in European Legal History 1993, An Historical Introduction to Western Constitutional Law 1995, Introduction aux sources de l'histoire médiévale 1997, European Law in the Past and the Future: Unity and Diversity over Two Millennia 2002. *Leisure interests:* bridge, swimming, wine. *Address:* Veurestraat 47, 9051 Afsnee, Belgium (home). *Telephone:* (9) 222-62-11 (home); (9) 264-68-53 (office). *Fax:* (9) 264-67-07 (office). *E-mail:* karin.pensaert@ugent.be (office). *Website:* www.law.ugent .be (office); www.rechtsgeschiedenis.be (office).

VAN CITTERS, Robert L., MD; American physiologist, cardiologist and academic; *Dean Emeritus, School of Medicine, University of Washington;* b. 20 Jan. 1926, Alton, Ia; s. of Charles J. Van Citters and Wilhelmina T. Van Citters; m. Mary E. Barker 1949; two s. two d.; ed Univ. of Kansas; Intern, Univ. of Kansas Medical Center 1953–54; Medical Officer, Air Research and Devt Command, Kirtland AFB, NM 1954–55; Resident, Internal Medicine, Univ. of Kansas Medical Center 1957–58; Research Fellow Cardiovascular Physiology, Univ. of Washington 1958–62; Research Assoc. Cardiopulmonary Inst., Scripps Clinic and Research Foundation, La Jolla, Calif. 1962; Exchange Scientist, Jt US–USSR Scientific Exchange Agreement 1962; Robert L. King Chair. of Cardiovascular Research 1963–; Asst Prof. of Physiology and Biophysics School of Medicine, Univ. of Washington 1963–65, Assoc. Prof. 1965–68, Assoc. Dean for Research and Grad. Programs 1968–70, Chair. Bd of Health Sciences 1970, Dean, School of Medicine 1970–81, Dean Emer. 1981–, Prof. of Medicine (Cardiology), Prof. of Physiology and Biophysics 1981–; mem. Inst. of Medicine, NAS; Hon. DSc (Northwestern Coll.) 1978. *Publications:* 150 publs in scientific journals. *Leisure interests:* fishing, gardening. *Address:* School of Medicine, University of Washington, Seattle, WA 98195, USA (office). *Telephone:* (425) 774-1770 (office). *Fax:* (206) 543-3639 (office). *E-mail:* vancitters@comcast.com (home). *Website:* www.uwmedicine.org (office).

VAN CREVELD, Martin L.; Israeli academic; *Professor of History, Hebrew University of Jerusalem;* b. 5 March 1946, Rotterdam; s. of L. van Creveld and

M. van Creveld (née Wyler); two step c.; ed Hebrew Univ., London School of Econs; Lecturer, later Prof. in History, Hebrew Univ. of Jerusalem 1971–; Fellow, War Studies Dept, King's Coll. London 1975–76, von Humboldt Foundation, Freiburg 1980–81; Faculty mem. Nat. Defense Univ., Washington DC 1986–87; Prof., Marine Corps Univ., Quantico, Va 1991–92; Sr Fellow, Humboldt Foundation, Postdam 1999–2000; Fellow, Inst. for Contemporary Historical Research, Potsdam 2005–06; Best Book Award, Mil. History Inst. USA 1990. *Publications:* Supplying War 1977, Fighting Power 1987, Command in War 1985, Technology and War 1988, The Transformation of War 1991, The Rise and Decline of the State 1999, The Changing Face of War 2007, The Culture of War 2008. *Leisure interests:* reading, walking. *Address:* Hebrew University of Jerusalem, Mount Scopus, 91 905 Jerusalem, Israel (office). *Telephone:* (2) 5883769 (office); (2) 5344923 (home). *Fax:* (2) 5881118 (office). *E-mail:* msmartin@tms.huji.ac.il.

VAN-CULIN, Rev. Canon Samuel, OBE, AB, DD; American ecclesiastic; *Canon Ecumenist, Washington National Cathedral;* b. 20 Sept. 1930, Honolulu; s. of Samuel Van-Culin and Susie Mossman; ed Princeton Univ. and Virginia Theological Seminary; Curate St Andrew's Cathedral, Honolulu 1955–56; Canon Precentor and Rector Hawaiian Congregation, Honolulu 1956–58; Asst Rector St John's, Washington DC 1958–60; Gen. Sec. Lyman Int., Washington DC 1960–61; Asst Sec. Overseas Dept, Exec. Council of the Episcopal Church USA 1962–68, Sec. for Africa and Middle East 1968–76, Exec. for World Mission 1976–83; Sec. Gen. Anglican Consultative Council 1983–94, Sec. to Lambeth Conf. 1988; Asst Priest All Hallows Church, London 1995–; Canon Ecumenist, Washington Nat. Cathedral 2004–; Hon. Canon, Canterbury, Jerusalem, Honolulu, Ibadan and Cape Town; Hon. DD (Virginia Theological Seminary). *Leisure interests:* music and travel. *Address:* 3900 Watson Place, NW, 5D-B, Washington, DC 20016, USA (home). *Website:* www .cathedral.org.

VAN DAELE, Gen. August; Belgian army officer; *Chief of Defence Staff;* b. 25 Feb. 1944, Sint-Niklaas; ed Royal Cadet Training School, Royal Mil. Acad., Defence Coll.; tech. officer, Proficiency Training Centre, Brustem 1967–69; with Mobile Training Unit 1969–71; assigned as line man. Inspection and Tech. Acceptance Testing Service 1971; CO Air Maintenance Squadron, 10th Fighter-Bomber Wing, Kleine-Brogel 1980–83, CO Maintenance Group 1985–87; Deputy CO of Inspection and Tech. Acceptance Testing Service 1983–84, Head of Service 1987–88; Head of Equipment Inspection Service 1988–89, Inspection Service 1989–92, Aviation Equipment Section 1992–94; apptd Deputy Chief of Staff, Logistics, Air Force HQ 1994; Dir-Gen. for Material Resources, Defence Staff 2000–02; Chief of Defence Staff 2003–; mem. NATO Mil. Cttee; Aide to the King of Belgium. *Address:* Ministry of Defence, 8 rue Lambermont, 1000 Brussels, Belgium (office). *Telephone:* (2) 550-28-11 (office). *Fax:* (2) 550-29-19 (office). *E-mail:* cabinet@mod.mil.be (office). *Website:* mod.fgov.be (office).

VAN DAM, José; Luxembourg singer (bass-baritone)); b. 25 Aug. 1940, Brussels, Belgium; m.; ed Acad. de Musique, Brussels, Conservatoire Royal, Brussels; operatic debut as Don Basilio in The Barber of Seville, Liège; debut in Paris in Carmen (Escamillo) 1961, with Grand Théâtre, Geneva 1965–67, Deutsche Oper, Berlin 1967–, Salzburg Festival, opera and concerts 1966–, Festival d'Aix en Provence 1966–, operatic repertoire includes title roles in St-François d'Assise, Wozzeck, Simon Boccanegra, Elijah, Boris Gudunov, Falstaff, Don Giovanni, The Flying Dutchman, Gianni Schicchi, the Speaker in Die Zauberflöte, Fra Melitone in La Forza del Destino, Germont in La Traviata, the Father in Louise, Claudius in Hamlet, Sachs in Die Meistersinger von Nürnberg, Amfortas in Parsifal, Jochanaan in Salome, Mephisto in Faust, Scarpia in Tosca; recital repertoire includes Verdi's Requiem, La Damnation de Faust; winner, Bel Canto Competition, Liège, Concours Ecole des Vedettes, Paris, Concours de la Chanson, Toulouse, Int. Music Competition, Geneva, Grand Prix de l'Acad. Française du Disque 1979, Orphée d'Or, Académie Lyrique Française 1980, Prix Européen des Critiques 1985, Diapason d'Or, two Grammy Awards. *Address:* Colbert Artists Management, 111 West 57th Street, New York, NY 10019, USA (office). *Telephone:* (212) 757-0782 (office). *Fax:* (212) 541-5179 (office). *E-mail:* nycolbert@colbertartists .com (office). *Website:* www.colbertartists.com (office).

VAN DAMME, Jean-Claude; Belgian actor; b. 18 Oct. 1961, Brussels; m. 1st Gladys Portugues; m. 2nd Darcy LaPier 1994; one s. one d.; fmr European Professional Karate Asscn Middleweight Champion. *Films include:* Monaco Forever 1984, Rue barbare 1984), Breakin' 1984) No Retreat, No Surrender 1986, Bloodsport 1988, Black Eagle 1988, Cyborg 1989, Kickboxer 1989, Lionheart 1990, Death Warrant 1990, Double Impact 1991, Universal Soldier 1992, Nowhere to Run 1993, Hard Target 1993, Timecop 1994, Street Fighter 1994, Sudden Death 1995, The Quest 1996, Maximum Risk 1996, Double Team 1997, Knock Off 1998, Legionnaire 1998, Universal Soldier: The Return 1999, Coyote Moon 1999, The Order 2001, Replicant 2001, Derailed 2002, The Savage 2003, Narco 2004, Wake of Death 2004, Second in Command 2006. *Address:* United Talent Agency, Suite 500, 9560 Wilshire Boulevard, Beverly Hills, CA 90212, USA.

VAN DE KAA, Dirk Jan, PhD; Dutch demographer and academic; *Honorary Fellow, Netherlands Interdisciplinary Demographic Institute (NIDI);* b. 5 Jan. 1933, Scherpenzeel; m. Anna Jacomina van Teunenbroek 1961; one s. one d.; ed Univ. of Utrecht, ANU; Dept Dir, Demographic Research Project, Western New Guinea 1961–66; Research Fellow, Dept of Demography, Research School of Social Sciences, Inst. for Advanced Studies, ANU, Canberra 1966–71; Dir Netherlands Interdisciplinary Demographic Inst. (NIDI), The Hague 1971–87, Hon. Fellow 2003–; Project Dir World Fertility Survey, London 1981–82; Dir Int. Statistical Research Centre, The Hague 1982–84; Prof. of Demography, Univ. of Amsterdam 1977–98; Dir Netherlands Inst. for Advanced Study (NIAS), Wassenaar 1987–95; Vice-Pres. Netherlands Org. for Scientific Research (NWO), The Hague 1988–98; mem. Royal Netherlands Acad. of Arts and Sciences (Vice-Pres. 1984–87); Pres. European Asscn for Population Studies 1983–87, Hon. Pres. 1987–; Dr. hc Instytut Statystyki i Demografii, Warsaw School of Econs 2003 Ridder in de Orde van de Nederlandse Leeuw 1991, Laureate Int. Union for Scientific Study of Population 2001. *Publications:* (author, co-author or ed.) Results of the Demographic Research Project Western New Guinea 1964–67, The Demography of Papua and New Guinea's Indigenous Population 1971, Science for Better and for Worse 1984, Population: Growth and Decline 1986, Europe's Second Demographic Transition 1987. *Address:* Netherlands Interdisciplinary Demographic Institute, POB 11650, 2502 AR The Hague (office); Van Hogenhoucklaan 63, 2596 TB The Hague, Netherlands. *Telephone:* (70) 3565200 (office). *Fax:* (70) 3647187 (office). *E-mail:* vandekaa@nidi.nl (office). *Website:* www.nidi.nl/index.html (office).

VAN DE WALLE, Leslie; French business executive; *President, Shell Europe Oil Products;* b. 27 March 1956, Paris; s. of Philippe Van de Walle and Marie Lucette Van de Walle; m. Domitille Noel 1982; two d.; ed Hautes Etudes Commerciales, Paris; Man. Dir Schweppes Benelux 1990–92, France and Benelux 1992–93, Spain and Portugal 1993–94; Snacks Div., United Biscuits Continental Europe 1994–95 (CEO 1996–97), CEO McVities Group 1998, United Biscuits Group 1999–2000; Pres. Shell Latin America and Africa 2000–03, Shell Europe Oil Products 2003–; mem. Bd of Dirs Aegis plc. *Leisure interests:* golf, travel. *Address:* Shell Centre, London, SE1 7NA (office); 34 Rose Square, Fulham Road, London, SW3 6RS, England (home). *Telephone:* (20) 7934-5226 (office); (20) 7584-1218 (home). *Fax:* (20) 7934-7575 (office); (20) 7584-9339 (home). *E-mail:* Leslie.VandeWalle@shell.com (office).

VAN DEN BERG, Dirk Jan; Dutch economist and diplomatist; *President of the Executive Board, Delft University of Technology;* b. 1953; m. Frederike Mijnlieff; two c.; ed Univ. of Groningen, École Nat. d'Admin, Paris, France; Policy Planner Ministry of Econ. Affairs 1980–84; Head Industrial Policy and Budget Div., Directorate-Gen. for Industry and Regional Policy 1987–88; Deputy Dir-Gen. for Foreign Econ. Relations, Head Trade Policy Div., Directorate-Gen. for Foreign Econ. Relations 1989–92; Deputy Dir-Gen. Directorate-Gen. for Industry and Regional Policy 1992; Dir Public Finance Programme, Erasmus Univ., Rotterdam 1986–88; Sec.-Gen. Ministry of Foreign Affairs 1992–2001; Perm. Rep. to UN, New York 2001–05; Amb. to China 2005–07; Pres. Exec. Bd Delft Univ. of Tech. 2008–. *Leisure interests:* photography, computers, history, sailing and horse riding. *Address:* Executive Board, Delft University of Technology, Postbus 5, 2600 AA Delft, Netherlands (office). *Telephone:* (15) 2783786 (office). *E-mail:* D.J.vandenBerg@tudelft.nl (office). *Website:* home.tudelft.nl (office).

VAN DEN BERGH, Maarten Albert; Dutch business executive; *Chairman, Akzo Nobel NV;* b. 19 April 1942, New York, USA; s. of Sidney James van den Bergh and Maria Mijers; m. Marjan Désirée; two d.; ed Univ. of Groningen; joined the Shell Group 1968, held various man. positions in the Far East and UK, Group Man. Dir Royal Dutch/Shell Group 1992, Dir of Finance 1994–98, Vice-Chair. Cttee of Man. Dirs and Pres. Royal Dutch Petroleum Co. 1998–2000; Dir BT Group plc 2001–, Deputy Chair. 2006–; Deputy Chair. Lloyds TSB Group plc 2000–01, Chair. 2001–06; Chair. Akzo Nobel NV 2006–; Dir British Airways PLC 2002–; mem. Steering Bd and Dutch Co-Chair. Apeldoorn Conf. 2003–; Adviser to Chief Exec. of Hong Kong Special Admin. Region 1998–2002; mem. Int. Bd of Advisers to Pres. of Philippines 2001–05, Advisory Council Amsterdam Inst. of Finance 2001–05; Fellow and Vice-Pres. Inst. of Financial Services 2001–06; mem. Guild of Int. Bankers 2001–06; Companion Chartered Man. Inst. 2001. *Leisure interests:* European history. *Address:* BT Group plc, BT Centre, 81 Newgate Street, London, EC1A 7AJ, England (office). *Telephone:* (20) 7356-5158 (office). *Website:* www.btplc.com (office); www.akzonobel.com (office).

VAN DEN BERGH, Sidney, OC, MSc, Dr rer. nat, FRS; Canadian astronomer; *Researcher Emeritus, National Research Council of Canada;* b. 20 May 1929, Wassenaar, Netherlands; s. of Sidney J. van den Bergh and S.M. van den Bergh; m. 2nd (wife deceased); one s. two d.; m. 3rd Paulette Brown; ed Leiden Univ., Princeton Univ. and Ohio State Univ., USA, Univ. of Göttingen, FRG; Asst Prof., Ohio State Univ. 1956–58; Prof., Univ. of Toronto, Canada 1958–77; Dir Dominion Astrophysical Observatory, Victoria 1977–86, Astronomer 1986–98, Researcher Emer. 1998–; Adjunct Prof., Univ. of Vic. 1978–; Pres. Canadian Astronomy Soc. 1990–92; Assoc. Royal Astronomical Soc.; Hon. DSc 1998, 2001; Killam Laureate 1990, NRC Pres.'s Medal, Henry Norril Russell Lecturer 1990. *Publications:* about 650 scientific publs including Galaxy Morphology and Classification 1998, The Galaxies of the Local Group 2000. *Leisure interests:* archaeology, photography. *Address:* Dominion Astrophysical Observatory, 5071 West Saanich Road, Victoria, BC, V9E 2E7 (office); 418 Lands End Road, Sidney, BC, V8L 5L9, Canada (home). *Telephone:* (250) 363-0006 (office); (250) 656-6020 (home). *Fax:* (250) 363-0045 (office); (250) 363-0045 (office). *E-mail:* sidney.vandenbergh@nrc.ca (office); Sidney .vandenBergh@nrc-cnrc.gc.ca (office). *Website:* www.nrc.ca (office).

VAN DEN BOOGAARD, Hans Albert Dirk; Dutch business executive; b. 5 Nov. 1939, Hengelo; m. Ina Mulder 1967; one s. one d.; ed Rotterdam School of Econs; joined Stork NV 1968, mem. Bd of Man. 1986, Chief Financial Officer –2002, Exec. Vice-Pres., Bd of Man. 1991, Vice-Chair. 2001; Chair. Supervisory Bd NethCorp V, Van der Hoop Effektenbank; mem. Supervisory Bd ICT Automatisering, Royal IBC; Chair. Foundation Certifying Friesland Coberco Dairy Foods, Stork Pension Fund Foundation; retd 2001; mem. Advisory Bd Netherlands Energy Research Foundation (ECN) 1996–; Treas. Exec. Cttee FME-CWM (Employers' Asscn); mem. Bd Coöperatie Achmea, Stichting Continuiteit Polynorm. *Leisure interests:* hockey, skiing, reading. *Address:* c/o Stork Head Office, Stork NV, Amersfoortsestraatweg 7, 1412 KA Naarden,

Netherlands (office). *Telephone:* (35) 695-74-11 (office). *Fax:* (35) 694-11-84 (office). *E-mail:* info@stork.com (office). *Website:* www.stork.com (office).

VAN DEN BROEK, Hans; Dutch institution administrator and fmr politician; b. 11 Dec. 1936, Paris, France; m.; two d.; ed Alberdingk Thym Grammar School, Hilversum, Univ. of Utrecht; attended Sr Man. training, De Baak, Noordwijk; solicitor in Rotterdam 1965–68; Sec. Man. Bd ENKA BV, Arnhem 1969–73, Commercial Man., 1973–76; City Councillor, Rheden 1970–74; mem. Second Chamber, States-Gen. (Parl.) 1976–81; served on Standing Cttees on Foreign Affairs, Devt Co-operation and Justice; Sec. of State for Foreign Affairs 1981–82, Minister 1982–93; Commr for External Relations, Foreign and Security Policy Enlargement Negotiations, Comm. of EC (now European Comm.) 1993–95, for External Relations with Cen. and Eastern Europe, fmr Soviet Union and others for Common Foreign and Security Policy and External Service 1995–99; fmr Pres. Netherlands Inst. of Int. Relations; Chair. Bd of Govs Radio Netherlands (Radio Nederland Wereldomroep); mem. Advisory Bd Global Panel Foundation. *Address:* c/o Radio Nederland Wereldomroep, Witte Kruislaan 55, Postbus 222, 1200 JG Hilversum, Netherlands (office). *E-mail:* letters@rnw.nl (office). *Website:* www.radionetherlands.nl (office).

VAN DEN HOOGENBAND, Pieter; Dutch swimmer; b. 14 March 1978, Maastricht; s. of Astrid van den Hoogenband; mem. PSV Eindhoven club; competed at Olympic Games 1996, 2000, 2004 winning seven medals (three gold, two silver and two bronze) including gold medals at 100m. freestyle, 2000, 2004 and 200m. freestyle (world record); 12 medals at World Championships (one gold, eight silver and three bronze); 28 medals at European Championships (16 gold, eight silver, four bronze). *Address:* Achterdijk 64, 1191 JL, Ouderkerk a/d Amstel, Netherlands. *Website:* www.pietervandenhoogenband.nl.

VAN DEN HOUT, Tjaco T., JD; Dutch lawyer, diplomatist and international organization executive; *Secretary-General, Permanent Court of Arbitration, The Hague;* ed Leiden Univ., Harvard Univ., USA; joined Foreign Service 1974; has served in numerous diplomatic positions including mem. Del. to CSCE, Geneva and at embassies in Africa and Asia; Deputy Dir for Int. Orgs, Ministry of Foreign Affairs 1989–91, Deputy Dir of Foreign Service 1991–94, Deputy Sec.-Gen. 1996-99; Sec.-Gen. Perm. Court of Arbitration, The Hague 1999–. *Address:* Permanent Court of Arbitration, Peace Palace, Carnegieplein 2, 2517 KJ The Hague, Netherlands (office). *Telephone:* (70) 3024165 (office). *Fax:* (70) 3024167 (office). *E-mail:* secgen@pca-cpa.org (office). *Website:* www.pca-cpa.org (office).

VAN DEN WYNGAERT, Christine, PhD; Belgian judge and fmr singer; *Judge, Pre-Trial Division, International Criminal Court;* b. 2 April 1952, Antwerp; ed Free Univ., Brussels; alternative career as singer-songwriter, performing with (among others) Ferre Grignard and Wannes Van de Velde, and resulting in Long Play recording 1970s; Prof. of Criminal Law, Univ. of Antwerp 1985–; Visiting Fellow, Centre for European Legal Studies 1994–96, Research Centre for Int. Law, Univ. of Cambridge 1996–97; Visiting Prof., Univ. of Stellenbosch, S Africa 2001; Ad hoc Judge, Int. Court of Justice in the Yerodia case 2000–02; Ad litem Judge, Int. Criminal Tribunal for the Fmr Yugoslavia 2003–05, Perm. Judge 2005–09; Judge, Pre-Trial Div., ICC, The Hague, Netherlands 2009–; Dr hc (Univ. of Uppsala) 2001; Henri Rolin Prize for PhD thesis 1980, Human Rights Prize, Liga voor Mensenrechten 2006. *Publications include:* Political Offence Exception to Extradition: The Delicate Problem of Balancing the Rights of the Individual and the International Public Order 1980, Strafrecht en strafprocesrecht in hoofdlijnen 1991 (revised 6th edn: Strafrecht, strafprocesrecht en internationaal strafrecht in hoofdlijnen 2006); co-ed.: Criminal Procedure Systems in the European Community 1993, International Criminal Law and Procedure 1996, International Criminal Law: A Collection of International and European Instruments, and other titles. *Address:* International Criminal Court, PO Box 19519, 2500 CM The Hague, The Netherlands (office); Faculty of Law, University of Antwerp, Universiteitsplein 1, 2610 Antwerp, Belgium. *Telephone:* (70) 515-85-15 (office); (3) 820-29-23. *Fax:* (70) 515-85-55 (office); (3) 820-29-40. *E-mail:* chris.vandenwyngaert@ua.ac.be (office); otp.informationdesk@icc-cpi.int (office). *Website:* www.icc-cpi.int (office); www.ua.ac.be.

VAN DER AVOIRD, Ad, PhD; Dutch scientist and academic; *Professor, Institute of Theoretical Chemistry, University of Nijmegen;* b. 19 April 1943, Eindhoven; s. of H. J. van der Avoird and M. A. van der Avoird (née Kerkhofs); m. T. G. M. Lange 1964; two s.; ed Tech. Univ., Eindhoven; Research Fellow, Inst. Battelle, Geneva, Switzerland 1965–67; Section Man. Unilever Research Lab., Vlaardingen 1967–71; Assoc. Prof., Univ. of Nijmegen, Nijmegen 1968–71, Prof. Inst. of Theoretical Chemistry 1971–; mem. Netherlands Acad. of Sciences 1979–, Int. Acad. of Quantum Molecular Sciences 1997–. *Publications:* Interacties tussen moleculen 1989; articles in scientific journals. *Address:* Institute for Molecules and Materials, Theoretical Chemistry, Radboud University Nymegen, Heyendaalseweg 135, 6525 AJ Nymegen, Netherlands (office). *Telephone:* (24) 365-30-37 (office). *E-mail:* a.vanderavoird@theochem.ru.nl (office). *Website:* www.theochem.ru.nl (office).

VAN DER EB, Alex Jan, PhD; Dutch fmr professor of molecular carcinogenesis; *Senior Adviser, Crucell;* b. 16 Jan. 1934, Bandung, Java; s. of Wijnand Jan van der Eb and Gertrude Leonie van der Eb-Blekkink; m. Titia Brongersma 1961; two s. one d.; ed Univ. of Leiden; mil. service 1962–63; Assoc. Prof. of Tumor Virology, Univ. of Leiden 1974–80, Prof. of Molecular Carcinogenesis 1980–99, Prof. Emer. 1999–; Postdoctoral Fellow, Calif. Inst. of Tech., Pasadena, USA 1968–69; Visiting Prof. Nagasaki Univ., Japan 2002–06; Sr Adviser Crucell, Leiden (Netherlands) 2002–; mem. Royal Acad. of Sciences and Letters 1987–, European Molecular Biology Org. 1981–,

Academia Europaea, Royal Holland Science Asscn (Koninklijke Hollandsche Maatschappij van Wetenschappen) 1987; Ridder in de Orde van de Nederlandse Leeuw 1998; AKZO Prize 1975, Korteweg Overwater Fund Award 1977, Beijerinck Virology Medal 1978, Robert Koch Prize 1989, Japan Org. for Promotion Cander Research Award 1989, Hyclone Award 1993, Fedora Award 1996, Inst. of Radiation Pathology IRS Prize 1997. *Publications:* more than 250 publs on molecular carcinogenesis and radiation biology. *Leisure interests:* bird watching, photography, travelling, camping. *Address:* Crucell, POB 2048, 2301 CA Leiden (office); Prinses Beatrixlaan 53, 2341 TW Oegstgeest, Netherlands (home). *Telephone:* (71) 5199162 (office); (71) 5172178 (home). *Fax:* (71) 5199800 (office). *E-mail:* lex.vandereb@crucell.com (office); tvandereb@hotmail.com (home). *Website:* www.crucell.com (office).

VAN DER GEEST, Willem, MPhil, PhD; Dutch research institute director; *Director, European Institute for Asian Studies;* b. 8 June 1954, Leiden; ed Univ. of Leiden, Univ. of Stockholm, Sweden, Univ. of Cambridge, UK; Research Asst Nat. Inst. of Econ. Research, Sweden 1979; Research Officer Inst. of Social Studies, The Hague 1980–82; part-time lecturer at Univ. of Leiden 1981–82; tutor in Econs Cambridge Univ. 1983–84; economist Ministry of Finance, Bangladesh 1984–86; Sr Research Economist Oxford Univ. 1987–91, Research Assoc. 1992–95; Sr Consultant Pakistan Inst. of Devt Econs 1992–95; Sr Economist Int. Labour Org., Geneva 1995–97; Visiting Prof. Univ. Libre de Bruxelles 2001–; Sr Adviser Bangladesh Inst. of Devt Studies 2002–03; currently Dir European Inst. for Asian Studies; mem. Royal Econ. Soc.; Vice-Pres. EU-Japan Assoc., Brussels. *Publications:* Negotiating Structural Adjustment in Africa (ed.) 1994, Adjustment, Employment and Missing Institutions in Sub-Saharan Africa (co-ed.) 1999, Economic Reform and Trade Performance in South Asia (co-ed.) 2004, numerous chapters and articles in books and journals. *Address:* European Institute for Asian Studies, 35 Rue des Deux Eglises, 1000 Brussels, Belgium (office). *Telephone:* (2) 230-81-22 (office). *Fax:* (2) 230-54-02 (office). *E-mail:* w.vandergeest@eias.org (office). *Website:* www.eias.org (office).

VAN DER HEIJDEN, Paul F., LLD; Dutch lawyer, academic and university administrator; *Rector Magnificus and President, University of Leiden;* b. 18 Sept. 1949, Utrecht; m.; three c.; ed Univ. of Amsterdam, Univ. of Leiden; Lecturer, Dept of Law, Univ. of Leiden 1978–85, Univ. of Groningen 1987–90; Lawyer, Court of Law, Amsterdam 1985–89; Prof. of Employment Law, Univ. of Amsterdam 1990–2007, Rector Magnificus 2002–07; Rector Magnificus and Pres. Univ. of Leiden 2007–; Ed.-in-Chief Jurisprudentie Arbeidsrecht; Chair. ILO Governing Body Cttee on Freedom of Asscn; Crown-apptd mem. Social and Econ. Council (SER); Chair. Supervisory Bd Amsterdam Univ. Press; mem. Supervisory Bd NUON NV, Buhrmann Nederland NV, ING Group NV, Dutch Cancer Inst./Antoni van Leeuwenhoek Hosp., AMC-UvA; Chair. De Volkskrant Foundation; mem. Royal Netherlands Acad. of Arts and Sciences. *Address:* Office of the Rektor, Leiden University, Rapenburg 70, PO Box 9500, 2300 Leiden, Netherlands (office). *Telephone:* (71) 527-27-27 (office). *Website:* www.leidenuniv.nl (office).

VAN DER MEER, Jan, MD; Dutch physician; b. 30 Aug. 1935, Leeuwarden; s. of L. van der Meer and G. Bakker; m. Joan Alkema 1962; one d.; ed Univ. of Amsterdam; intern 1968; Sr Registrar in Internal Medicine, Binnengasthuis, Amsterdam 1970–76; Head of Coagulation Lab., Cen. Lab. of Bloodtransfusion Service of Dutch Red Cross 1969–76; Prof. of Internal Medicine, Chair. of Dept, Acad. Hosp. of Free Univ. Amsterdam 1976–2000; Chair. Govs, Cen. Lab. of Blood Transfusion Service, Netherlands Red Cross 1994–98; Chair. Landsteiner Foundation for Blood Transfusion Research 1998–2009. *Publication:* Meting van de plasma renine-activiteit met behulp van een radioimmunologische bepaling van angiotensine I 1969. *Address:* De Wijde Blik 19, 1189 WJ, Amsterdam, Netherlands (home). *Telephone:* (297) 582553 (home).

VAN DER MEULEN, Robert Paul, LLM, MCL; Dutch diplomatist; *Ambassador and Head, European Commission Delegation to Jordan;* b. 25 May 1950, Eindhoven; m. Christine Bayle 1982; two d.; ed Univ. of Leyden; Asst, European Inst., Univ. of Leyden 1974–76; Dir European Integration, Foreign Econ. Relations Dept, Ministry of Econ. Affairs 1976, Head of Bureau, Accession of Greece, Spain and Portugal, Co-operation with Mediterranean cos and EFTA cos 1979; with Perm. Representation of Netherlands to EC, Brussels 1981–82; First Sec. Embassy in Washington, DC 1982–84, Counsellor 1984–85; Deputy Head Office of Vice-Pres. of EC 1985–88; Amb. Head of Del. of European Comm. to Brunei, Indonesia and Singapore 1989–94, to Tunisia 1994–98, to Jordan 2002–; Head, Maghreb Div. (DG RELEX-F3), European Comm. 1998–2001, Acting Dir S Mediterranean and Middle East 2001–02; Grand Officier, Ordre de la Répub. Tunisienne. *Leisure interests:* collecting Chinese porcelain, nineteenth-century paintings. *Address:* Delagation of the European Commission, 15, Al-Jahiz Street, Shmeisani, PO Box 926794, Amman 11110, Jordan (office); 1 rue du Genève (valise diplomatique), 1049 Brussels, Belgium (home). *Telephone:* (6) 5668191 (office); (6) 5931042 (home). *E-mail:* robert.van-der-meulen@cec.eu.int (office); delegation-jordan@cec.eu.int (office); vdmeulen@go.com.jo (home). *Website:* www.deljor.cec.eu.int (office).

VAN DER STOEL, Max, LLM, MA; Dutch politician; b. 3 Aug. 1924, Voorschoten; one s. four d.; ed Univ. of Leiden; Int. Sec. Labour Party (Partij van de Arbeid) 1958–65; mem. Exec. Bd Socialist Int. 1958–65; mem. First Chamber of States-Gen. (Parl.) 1960–63, Second Chamber 1963–65, 1967–73, 1978–80; State Sec. of Foreign Affairs 1965–66; mem. Ass. Council of Europe 1967–72; N Atlantic Ass., European Parl. 1972–73; Minister of Foreign Affairs 1973–77, 1981–82; Perm. Rep. to the UN 1983–86; mem. Council of State 1986–92; OSCE High Commr on Nat. Minorities 1993–2001; Minister of State of the Netherlands 1991; apptd Special Rapporteur of UN Comm. on Human Rights on the situation of human rights in Iraq 1991–99; Special Rep. of Chair.

of OSCE on Macedonia 2001–03; Hon. KCMG, UK 2006; Dr hc (Athens) 1997, (Charles Univ. Prague) 1993, (Utrecht) 1994, (Péter Pázmány Catholic Univ., Budapest) 1999, (Univ. Coll. London) 2001, (SouthEast Europe Univ., Skopje); Gold Medal, Comenius Univ., Bratislava, Slovakia 1998. *Address:* Lubeckstr. 138, 2517 SV The Hague, Netherlands.

VAN DER VEER, Jeroen; Dutch oil industry executive; *CEO, Royal Dutch Shell plc;* b. 27 Oct. 1947, Utrecht; m. Mariette van der Veer; three d.; ed Delft and Rotterdam Univs; joined Royal Dutch Petroleum Co. 1971, Area Co-ordinator Sub-Saharan Africa 1990–92, Man. Dir Shell Nederland 1992–95, Pres. and CEO Shell Chemical Co. USA 1995–97, Group Man. Dir Royal Dutch 1997–, Pres. 2000–04, Chair. Cttee of Man. Dirs Royal Dutch/Shell Group 2004–, CEO Royal Dutch Shell PLC 2004–; Dir (non-exec.) Unilever (mem. Nomination and Remuneration Cttees); World Pres. Soc. of Chemical Industry 2002–04; mem. Supervisory Bd De Nederlandsche Bank; Dr hc (Univ. of Port Harcourt, Nigeria) 2005. *Leisure interests:* visiting museums, playing golf (16 handicap), has twice skated the 200 kilometres 'Elfstedentocht' – 11 cities marathon – in the Netherlands. *Address:* Royal Dutch Shell plc, Postbus 162, 2501 AN The Hague (office); Royal Dutch Shell plc, Carel van Bylandtlaan 30, 2596 HR The Hague, Netherlands (office). *Telephone:* (70) 377-9111 (office). *Fax:* (70) 377-3115 (office). *Website:* www.shell.com (office).

VAN DER WEE, Baron Herman Frans Anna, LLD, PhD; Belgian historian (retd) and academic; *Professor Emeritus of Economic History, Katholieke Universiteit Leuven;* b. 10 July 1928, Lier; s. of Jos Van der Wee and Martha Planckaert; m. Monique Verbreyt 1954; one s. one d.; ed Leuven Univ., Sorbonne, Paris, London School of Econs, UK; Fellow Nat. Foundation for Scientific Research of Belgium 1953–55; lecturer, Leuven Univ. 1955, Assoc. Prof. 1966, Prof. of Econ. History 1969–93, Prof. Emer. 1993–, Sec. Dept of Econs 1970–72, Chair. 1972–74, Chair. Bd of Trustees Leuven Univ. Press 1971–93; Visiting Prof. St Aloysius Univ., Brussels 1972–76, Dean Faculty of Econ., Political and Social Sciences 1972–75; Visiting Prof. Université Catholique de Louvain, Louvain-la-Neuve 1972–80, 1991–92; Research Fellow, Woodrow Wilson Int. Center for Scholars, Washington, DC 1975–76; Francqui Chair, Univ. of Brussels 1980–81; Visiting Fellow, Inst. for Advanced Study, School of Historical Studies, Princeton, NJ, USA 1981–82, 1991, All Souls Coll. Oxford 1985, Inst. for Advanced Study, Indiana Univ., Bloomington, Ind., USA 1986; J. Tinbergen Chair, Erasmus Univ., Rotterdam, Netherlands 1987; Chair of Econ. History, Univ. of Paris IV-Sorbonne, France 1987–88; Ellen MacArthur Chair., Univ. of Cambridge, UK 1989; P.P. Rubens Chair., Univ. of Calif. at Berkeley, USA 1994; Visiting Fellow Inst. for Advanced Study (RSSC), Canberra, Australia 1994; Erasmus Chair, Harvard Univ. (1997); Chair. of Banking History Univ. of St.-Gallen 1999; Guest of the Rector Netherlands Inst. for Advanced Study, Wassenaar 2000; Guest of the Rector Wissenschaftskolleg Berlin, Germany 2004; Visiting Fellow, Wissenschaftszentrum fur Sozialforschung, Berlin, Germany 2004; Pres. Belgian-Luxembourg American Studies Asscn. 1985–92, Int. Econ. History Asscn 1986–90 (Hon. Pres. 1990–); Chair. Leuven Univ. Press 1972–85, Royal Acad. of Belgium (Class of Letters) 1987, Leuven Inst. of Cen. and E European Studies 1990–93, Advisory Council of W European Program at Wilson Int. Center for Scholars, Washington, DC 1986–91, Academic Advisory Council of European Asscn for Banking History 1991–99; mem. Research Council, European Univ. Inst., Florence 1985–94, 1999–2006, Bd of Trustees Cité Int. Universitaire, Paris 1993–; mem. Int. Comm. or accred. research MA Programme in the Humanities at Dutch Univ.; mem. Royal Acad. of Belgium 1977–; Corresp. Foreign mem. Royal Acad. of Netherlands 1983–; Foundation mem. Academia Europaea 1987–; Corresp. Fellow British Acad. 1987, Corresp. Fellow Royal Historical Soc. 1995; Foreign Hon. mem. American Acad. of Arts and Sciences 1993–; Fellow, European Econ. Asscn 2004; Dr hc (Brussels) 1994, (Leicester) 1995; Order of Leopold Belgium, Order of the Crown Belgium, knighted by King Albert II of Belgium (title of Baron) 1994; De Stassart Prize for Nat. History, Royal Acad. of Belgium 1961–67, 1968, Eugène Baie Prize 1966, Fulbright-Hayes Award 1975, 1981, Quinquennial Solvay Prize for the Social Sciences, Nat. Foundation of Scientific Research of Belgium 1976–80, 1981, Amsterdam Biannual Prize for Historical Sciences 1992, Golden Medal for Special Merits, Flemish Parl. 1995. *Publications:* Prix et salaires: Manuel Méthodologique 1956, The Growth of the Antwerp Market and the European Economy (14th–16th centuries), 3 vols 1963, The Great Depression Revisited (ed) 1972, The Rise of Managerial Capitalism (ed) 1974, La Banque Nationale de Belgique et la politique monétaire entre les deux guerres 1975, Monetary, Credit and Banking Systems in Western Europe, 1400–1750, in The Cambridge Economic History of Europe (Part V) 1977, Productivity of Land and Agricultural Innovation in the Low Countries 1250–1800 (ed) 1978, Mint Statistics of Flanders and Brabant 1300–1506 (two vols) 1980, 1985, Prosperity and Upheaval, the World Economy, 1945–1980 1983 (trans. in several languages), The Rise and Decline of Urban Industries in Italy and in the Low Countries (Late Middle Ages–Early Modern Times) (ed) 1988, Histoire économique mondiale (trans. in several languages) 1945–1990 1990, History of European Banking (trans. in several languages) 1991, Winkler Prins. History of the Low Countries, 1500–1800 (ed.) 1992, The Economic Development of Europe, 950–1950 (13 edns) 1982–97, Constructing the World Economy 1750–1990 1992, The Low Countries in the Early Modern World 1993, The General Bank 1822–1997: A Continuing Challenge 1997, Economic Development in Belgium Since 1870 (ed.) 1997, Urban Achievement in Early Modern Europe: Golden Ages in Antwerp, Amsterdam and London (ed.) 2001, A Century of Banking Consolidation in Europe: The History and Archives of Mergers and Acquisitions (ed.) 2001, Cera 1892–1997: The Power of Cooperative Solidarity (ed.) 2002, The Woollen Industries (Cambridge History of Western Textiles) 2003, Monetary and Financial Policy in Occupied Western Europe During the Second World War: Accommodation or Resistance? The Case of the Belgium in its International Context, 1939–1945 2005. *Leisure interests:* literature, music, tennis, skiing. *Address:* Katholieke Universiteit Leuven, Centrum voor Economische Studiën, Naamsestraat 69, 3000 Leuven (office); Ettingestraat 10, 9170 Sint-Pauwels, Belgium (home). *Telephone:* (16) 32-67-25 (office); (3) 776-03-33 (home). *Fax:* (16) 32-67-96 (office); (3) 765-90-28 (home). *E-mail:* ces@econ.kuleuven.ac.be (office); Herman.VanDerWee@econ.kuleuven.ac.be (home). *Website:* www.econ.kuleuven.ac.be/ew/academic/econhist/default.htm.

VAN DEURSEN, Arie Theodorus; Dutch historian and academic (retd); b. 23 June 1931, Groningen; s. of Arie van Deursen and Trijntje Smilde; m. Else Ruth Junkers 1962; two s. two d.; ed Groningen Grammar School and Groningen State Univ.; Research Asst Univ. of Groningen 1957; staff mem. Bureau, Royal Comm. of Dutch History 1958–67; Prof. of Modern History, Free Univ. Amsterdam 1967–96; mem. Royal Acad. of Science 1978; Wijnaends Francken Award 1983. *Publications:* Professions et métiers interdits 1960, Honni soit qui mal y pense 1965, Jacobus de Rhoer 1970, Bavianen en slijkgeuzen 1974, Het kopergeld van de gouden eeuw (four vols) 1978–80, Willem van Oranje (with H. C. de Schepper) 1984, Plain Lives in a Golden Age 1991, Een Dorp in de Polder 1994, Graft: Ein Dorf im 17. Jahrhundert 1997, Maurits van Nassau 2000, De Last van Veel Geluk 2004. *Address:* Tramstraat 320, 2225 PT Katwijk ZH, Netherlands (home). *Telephone:* (23) 5265592 (home). *E-mail:* arievandeursen@12move.nl (home).

VAN DIJK, Petrus, LLM, SJD; Dutch state councillor and fmr professor of international law; *President, Administrative Jurisdiction Division, Council of State;* b. 21 Feb. 1943, De Lier; s. of A. A. M. van Dijk and J. H. van Straelen; m. Francisca G. M. Lammerts 1969; one s. one d.; ed Utrecht and Leyden Univs; Lecturer in Int. Law, Utrecht Univ. 1967–76, Prof. 1976–90; State Councillor 1990–, Pres. Admin. Jurisdiction Div., Council of State 2000–03, 2006–; Judge, European Court of Human Rights 1996–98, Deputy Pres. Admin. Tribunal of Council of Europe 2001–; Fullbright-Hays Scholar, Univ. of Mich. Law School 1970–71; Visiting Prof., Wayne State Univ. Law School 1978; Chair. Netherlands Inst. of Human Rights 1982–97, Netherlands Inst. of Social and Econ. Law 1986–90; Deputy Judge, Court of Appeal of The Hague 1986, Court of Appeal for Business and Industry 1992–, Cen. Appeal Bd Social Affairs 2006–; mem. Perm. Court of Arbitration 2002–; mem. Bd Trustees Inst. of Social Sciences 1992–98, Anne Frank Foundation 1994–; mem. various advisory cttees; mem. Royal Netherlands Acad. of Arts and Sciences; mem. Netherlands Del. to UN Gen. Ass. 1981, 1983, 1986; Kt, Order of the Netherlands Lion. *Publications include:* Theory and Practice of the European Convention on Human Rights (with G. J. H. van Hoof) 1979, The Final Act of Helsinki: Basis for a Pan-European System? 1980, Contents and Function of the Principle of Equity in International Economic Law 1987, Normative Force and Effectiveness of International Economic Law 1988, Access to Court 1993, Universality of Human Rights 1994; book chapters and ed. of numerous legal publs. *Address:* Council of State, PO Box 20019, 2500 EA The Hague, Netherlands (office). *Telephone:* (70) 4264645 (office). *Fax:* 3563217 (office). *E-mail:* pvandijk@raadvanstate.nl (office). *Website:* www.raadvanstate.nl (office).

VAN DÚNEM, Fernando José França; Angolan politician; *First Vice-President, Pan-African Parliament;* fmr Minister of External Affairs; Prime Minister of Angola 1991–98; First Vice-Pres. Pan-African Parl. 2004–; mem. Marxist-Leninist Popular Movt for the Liberation of Angola Workers' Party (MPLA). *Address:* c/o African Union Headquarters, PO Box 3243, Roosvelt Street (Old Airport Area), W21K19 Addis Ababa, Ethiopia.

VAN EEKELEN, Willem Frederik, D.LL.; Dutch politician and diplomatist; *Chairman, European Movement in the Netherlands;* b. 5 Feb. 1931, Utrecht; s. of Dr. Marie van Eekelen and Anna Maria van Eekelen; m. Johanna Wentink; two c.; ed Utrecht Univ. and Princeton Univ., USA; diplomatic service 1957–77; mem. Consultative Ass. Council of Europe and WEU 1981–82; Sec. Gen. WEU 1989–94; Sec. of State for Defence 1978–81, for Foreign Affairs 1982–86; Minister of Defence 1986–88; Senator 1995–; Chair. European Movt in the Netherlands 1995–; mem. Governing Bd Stockholm Int. Peace Research Inst. (SIPRI) 1999–; mem. Advisory Bd Geneva Centre for Democratic Control of Armed Forces (DCAF); Grand Officer Légion d'honneur, Grand Cross of Germany, Belgium, Luxembourg. *Publications:* The Security Agenda for 1996, Debating European Security 1948–1998, From Words to Deeds 2006. *Leisure interests:* old maps, trekking, sailing. *Address:* European Movement in the Netherlands, Het Kleine Loo 414, unit H, 2592 CK The Hague (office); Else Mauhslaan 187, 2595 HE The Hague, Netherlands. *Telephone:* (70) 3541144 (office); (70) 3241103. *Fax:* (70) 3587606 (office); (70) 3241103. *E-mail:* ebn@xs4all.nl (office); derotte@wanadoo.nl (home). *Website:* www.europese-beweging.nl (office).

VAN FRAASSEN, Bastiaan Cornelis, PhD; American/Canadian academic; *Distinguished Professor of Philosophy, San Francisco State University;* b. 5 April 1941, Goes, The Netherlands; s. of Jan Bastiaan van Fraassen and Dina Landman; m. Isabelle Peschard 2005; two s.; ed Univ. of Alberta, Canada, Univ. of Pittsburgh, USA; Asst Prof., Yale Univ. 1966–68, Assoc. Prof. 1969; Assoc. Prof., Univ. of Toronto 1969–73, Prof. 1973–82; Prof., Univ. of Southern Calif. 1976–81; McCosh Prof. of Philosophy, Princeton Univ. 1982–2008, Prof. Emer. 2008–; Distinguished Prof. of Philosophy, San Francisco State Univ. 2008–(11); John Simon Guggenheim Fellowship 1970–71; Fellow, American Acad. of Arts and Sciences; Corresp. Fellow, British Acad.; Foreign mem. Royal Netherlands Acad. of Arts and Sciences; Titular mem. Acad. Int. de Philosophie des Sciences; Hon. DLett. (Univ. of Lethbridge), Hon. LLD (Univ. of Notre Dame), Hon. PhD (Catholic Univ. of Leuven); Franklin Matchette Award (jt recipient) 1982, co-winner Imre Lakatos Award 1986. *Publications:* Introduction to the Philosophy of Time and Space 1970, Formal Semantics and Logic 1971, The Scientific Image 1980, Laws and Symmetry 1989, Quantum Mechanics: An Empiricist View 1991, The Empirical Stance 2002, Scientific

Representation: Paradoxes of Perspective 2008. *Leisure interests:* rock climbing, flying trapeze. *Address:* Department of Philosophy, San Francisco State University, 1600 Holloway Avenue, San Francisco, CA 94132 (office); 1347 Curtis Street, Berkeley, CA 94702, USA (home). *Telephone:* (415) 338-1596 (office). *E-mail:* fraassen@princeton.edu (office). *Website:* fraassen@sfsu.edu (office); www.princeton.edu/~fraassen (office); www.philosophy.princeton.edu/index.php?option=com_faculty=78=fullview=17.

VAN GERVEN, Baron; **Walter M.,** DJur, Lic.not, AgrHE; Belgian lawyer and academic; *Professor Emeritus, Catholic University of Louvain;* b. 11 May 1935, St Niklaas; s. of Willy van Gerven and Germaine van Bel; m. Frieda Sintobin 1959; four s.; ed Catholic Univ. of Louvain; Teaching Fellow, Univ. of Chicago Law School 1959–60; Assoc. Prof. of Law, Catholic Univ. of Louvain 1962–67, Prof. of Law 1967–82, Extraordinary Prof. 1982–, Vice-Rector 1970–76, now Prof. Emer.; Extraordinary Prof., Univ. of Amsterdam 1981–86; mem. Brussels Bar 1970–80; Pres. Banking Comm. of Belgium 1982–88; mem. Bd of Dirs of several commercial cos; Advocate-Gen. Court of Justice of European Communities 1988–95; mem. Ind. Expert Comm. of Investment, EU Comm. 1999, Ind. Review Panel, World Bank 2007; Visiting Prof., Univ. of Chicago 1968–69; Distinguished Arthur & Mark Payne Lecturer, Stanford Univ., USA 2003–04; Distinguished Prof., Tilburg Univ. 2005–; Distinguished Prof., Michigan Univ., USA 2006–07; mem. Royal Belgian Acad., Royal Netherlands Acad., Academia Europaea; Hon. Bencher, Gray's Inn 2003; Commdr, Order of Leopold; Dr hc (Ghent) 2005. *Publications:* Principles of Belgian Private Law 1968, Commercial and Economic Law (three vols) 1973–86, The Policy of the Judge 1973, In Law and Equity 1987, The European Union – A Polity of States and Peoples 2005. *Leisure interests:* modern art, music, golf. *Address:* Demarsinstraat 42, 3012 Wilsele, Belgium (home). *Telephone:* (16) 22-91-54 (home). *E-mail:* walter.vangerven@law.kuleuven.ac.be (home).

VAN GINKEL, Hans J. A., MSc, PhD; Dutch university administrator and academic; *Rector, United Nations University;* b. 22 June 1940, Kota-Radjah, Indonesia; m. Bep Teepen; one s. one d.; ed Utrecht Univ.; Teacher of Geography and History, Thomas à Kempis Coll., Arnhem 1965–68; joined Faculty of Geographical Sciences, Utrecht Univ. 1968, apptd Prof. of Human Geography and Planning 1980, Dean of Faculty 1981–85, mem. Exec. Bd 1985, Rector Magnificus 1986; Treas. Netherlands Foundation for Int. Co-operation in Educ. 1986–97; mem., then Chair. Bd Netherlands Interdisciplinary Demographic Inst. 1986–2000; Ind. Chair. Regional Council of Utrecht 1988–93; Pres. Governing Bd Int. Training Centre for Aerial Survey and Earth Sciences, Enschedé 1990–98; mem. Governing Bd UN Univ. 1992–97, Vice-Pres. 1995–97, Rector 1997–2007 (retd); Vice-Pres. Bd European Asscn of Univs 1994–98; mem. European Science and Tech. Ass., Brussels, Belgium 1994–98; Vice-Pres. Bd Int. Asscn of Univs 1995–2000, Pres. 2000–; mem. Nat. Council, Chair. Organizing Cttee, 28th Int. Geographical Congress, The Hague 1996; Vice-Chair. Bd of Trustees, Asian Inst. of Tech., Bangkok, Thailand 1997–; mem. Steering Cttee, UNESCO World Conf. on Higher Educ. 1998; mem. Academia Europaea; mem. Comm. on Educ. and Communication, World Conservation Union; fmr mem. UNESCO Advisory Group for Higher Educ.; fmr Chair. Co-ordinating Cttee of Advisory Councils on Science Policy; fmr Bd mem. Utrecht Network for Innovation and Economy; fmr mem. Nat. Foresight Cttee on Science Policy; Hon. Fellow, Inst. for Aerospace Survey and Earth Sciences; Hon. mem. Comm. on the History of Geographical Thought, Int. Geographical Union; Kt Netherlands Order of the Lion 1994, Order of the Rising Sun, Grand Cordon (Japan) 2007; Dr hc (Universitatea Babes-Bolyai, Romania) 1997, (Calif. State Univ.–Sacramento) 2003, (Univ. of Ghana) 2005, (Tech. Univ. of Zvolen, Slovakia) 2006. *Publications:* more than 100 publs in academic journals. *Address:* c/o United Nations University, 53–70 Jingumae 5-chrome, Shibuya-ku, Tokyo 150-8925, Japan (office).

VAN HAMEL, Martine; Dutch/American ballerina, choreographer and teacher; *Co-Founder, Kaatsbaan International Dance Center;* b. 16 Nov. 1945, Brussels, Belgium; d. of D. A. van Hamel and Manette van Hamel-Cramer; ed Nat. Ballet School of Canada; started ballet training at age four; debut aged 11 with Nat. Ballet of Venezuela; joined Nat. Ballet of Canada as soloist 1963; moved to New York and danced with Joffrey Ballet 1969–70; joined American Ballet Theatre 1970, as Prin. Ballerina (1973–91) danced classic roles, including Swan Lake, Sleeping Beauty, Raimonda, as well as contemporary works choreographed by Balanchine, Glen Tetley, Anthony Tudor, Kenneth MacMillan, Jiri kylian, Mark Morris, Twyla Tharp, Alvin Ailey; danced with Nederlands Dans Theater III 1993–98; Artistic Dir New Amsterdam Ballet (f. 1986); mem. Founding Bd Kaatsbaan Int. Dance Center, New York Choral Soc.; Gold Medal, Varna Competition 1966, Prix de Varna 1966, Dance Magazine Award, Cue Magazine Award, Award for Excellence, Washington Coll., Dance Educators of America Award. *Films:* Turning point, Little Nikita. *Choreography:* Amnon V'Tamar for American Ballet Theatre 1984 and creator of works for Milwaukee Ballet, Washington Ballet, Royal Winnipeg Ballet and New Amsterdam Ballet. *Leisure interest:* singing. *Address:* Kaatsbaan International Dance Center, PO Box 482, Tivoli, NY 12583 (office); 290 Riverside Drive, New York, NY 10025, USA. *Telephone:* (845) 757-5106 (office); (212) 749-1942. *Fax:* (845) 757-5040 (office); (212) 600-1365. *E-mail:* martinevh@rcn.com. *Website:* www.kaatsbaan.org (office).

VAN HEERDEN, Neil Peter, BA; South African diplomatist; b. 30 July 1939, East London; s. of J. van Heerden and C. Nel; m. Evelin Nowack 1961; one s. one d.; ed Wonderbom High School, Pretoria and Univ. of S Africa, Pretoria; joined Dept of Foreign Affairs 1959; Vice-Consul, Tokyo 1963; opened S Africa's first mission in Taipei 1967–68; opened first S African mission in Tehran 1970–71; First Sec. Washington, DC 1971–75; Amb. to FRG 1980; Deputy Dir Gen., Dept of Foreign Affairs, Pretoria 1985–87, Dir-Gen. of Foreign Affairs 1987–92, Amb. to EC (now EU) 1992–96; Exec. Dir S Africa Foundation (now Business Leadership South Africa) 1996; mem. Bd of Dirs Naspers 1996–, BMW (SA); Trustee Univ. of the Western Cape; councillor Business Unity South Africa; Hon. DLitt et Phil (Rand Afrikaans Univ.) 2000. *Publications:* articles in journals dealing with foreign affairs. *Leisure interests:* music, hiking, sailing, golf. *Address:* PO Box 7006, Johannesburg 2000, South Africa.

VAN HOOFF, Jan A. R. A. M.; Dutch professor of comparative physiology and ethology (retd); b. 15 May 1936, Arnhem; s. of R. A. Th. van Hooff and L. E. Burgers; m. Anna C. M. Bluemink 1964; two s. one d.; ed Canisius Coll., Nijmegen, Univ. of Utrecht; scientific collaborator, Faculty of Biology, Univ. of Utrecht 1963–73, Lecturer in Comparative Physiology 1973–80, Prof. of Comparative Physiology 1980–2001, Dean, Faculty of Biology 1993–96; Dir Science Bd, Burgers Zoo, Arnhem 1969–; Pres. Research Council of Ethology, Netherlands Foundation for Biological Research 1972–78, Dir 1978–83; Pres. Soc. pour l'Etude et la Protection des Mammifères 1985–89, Royal Netherlands Zoological Soc. 1996–2001, Jane Goodall Inst. 1997–2001; Sec. Gen. Int. Primatological Soc. 2000–04; Sec. Lucie Burgers Foundation for Comparative Behaviour Research 1980–; Bd mem. Foundation Prince Bernhard Chair for Int. Nature Conservation; mem. numerous scientific foundations and socs; Fellow, Royal Netherlands Acad. of Arts and Sciences; Hon. Prof., Universitas, Jakarta, Indonesia; Hon. Mem. Assoziazione Primatologica Italiana; Officer, Royal Order of Orange-Nassau 2000; Socio Onorario, La Società di Medicina e Scienze Naturali dell'Università di Parma. *Publications include:* Facial Expressions in Higher Primates 1962, The Comparison of Facial Expressions in Man and Higher Primates 1976, Categories and Sequences of Behavior: Methods of Description and Analysis 1982, Oorlog 1990, Relationships Among Nonhuman Primate Males 2000, Economics in Nature 2001, Laughter and Smiling: the intertwining of nature and culture 2003. *Address:* Department of Biology, Utrecht University, PO Box 80.086, Sorbonnelaan 16, 3584 CB Utrecht (office); Vermeerlaan 24, 3723 EN Bilthoven, Netherlands (home). *Telephone:* (30) 2287639 (home). *E-mail:* jaramvanhooff@planet.nl (home).

VAN HOOVEN, Eckart, DJur; German business executive; b. 11 Dec. 1925; Chair. Supervisory Bd Giesecke & Devrient GmbH, Munich, Mobil Oil AG, Hamburg; Deputy Chair. Supervisory Bd Hapag-Lloyd AG, Hamburg; mem. Supervisory Bd Kaufhof AG, Cologne, Reemtsma Cigarettenfabriken GmbH, Hamburg; fmr mem. Bd Deutsche Bank AG. *Address:* c/o Deutsche Bank AG, Taunusanlage 12, 60325 Frankfurt am Main, Germany.

VAN INWAGEN, Peter Jan, PhD; American philosopher and academic; *John Cardinal O'Hara Professor of Philosophy, University of Notre Dame;* b. 21 Sept. 1942, Rochester, NY; s. of George Butler van Inwagen and Mildred Gloria Knudsen; m. 1st Margery Naylor 1967 (divorced 1988); one d.; m. 2nd Elisabeth Bolduc 1989; ed Rensselaer Polytechnic Inst., Univ. of Rochester; served in US Army 1969–70; Visiting Asst Prof. of Philosophy, Univ. of Rochester 1970–71; Asst Prof., Assoc. Prof., then Prof. of Philosophy, Syracuse Univ. 1971–95; John Cardinal O'Hara Prof. of Philosophy, Univ. of Notre Dame, South Bend, Ind. 1995–; Visiting Prof., Univ. of Ariz. 1981, Rutgers Univ. 1987; research grants, Nat. Endowment for the Humanities 1983–84, 1990–91; delivered the Maurice Lectures, Kings Coll., London1999, the Wilde Lectures, Oxford 2000, the Stewart Lectures, Princeton 2002, the Gifford Lectures, St Andrews 2003; currently Pres. Central Div., American Philosophical Asscn; mem. American Acad. of Arts and Sciences 2005–. *Publications:* An Essay on Free Will 1983, Material Beings 1990, Metaphysics 1993, God, Knowledge and Mystery (essays) 1995, The Possibility of Resurrection and Other Essays in Christian Apologetics 1997, Ontology, Identity and Modality: Essays in Metaphysics 2001, The Problem of Evil 2006. *Address:* Department of Philosophy, 100 Malloy Hall, University of Notre Dame, Notre Dame, IN 46556-4619, USA (office). *Telephone:* (219) 631-5910 (office). *Fax:* (219) 631-0588 (office). *E-mail:* peter.vaninwagen.1@nd.edu (office). *Website:* www.nd.edu/~ndphilo (office).

VAN ITTERSUM, Baron Boudewijn F.; Dutch financial services industry executive; b. 7 June 1939; s. of Paul A. L. A. Van Ittersum and Henriette F. Van Lennep; m. Karin R. W. Van der Ven 1967; three c.; ed Univ. of Amsterdam; joined Ministry of Finance; seconded to IMF, IBRD, Washington, DC 1970–72; subsequently Dir of Int. Affairs, Ministry of Finance; Chair. Amsterdam Stock Exchange 1981–96, Dir 1996–2000 (merged with Paris Bourse and Brussels Exchanges to form Euronext Amsterdam 2000). *Address:* c/o Euronext Amsterdam, Beursplein 5, 1012 JW Amsterdam, Netherlands. *Telephone:* (20) 5504444. *Fax:* (20) 5504897.

VAN LEDE, Cornelis J. A. (Cees), MBA; Dutch business executive; *Chairman of the Supervisory Board, Heineken NV;* b. 1942; ed Univ. of Leiden, Institut Européen d'Admin des Affaires (INSEAD), Fontainebleau, France; joined Akzo Nobel NV as mem. Bd of Man. 1991–2003, Vice-Chair. Bd of Man. 1992–94, Chair. and CEO 1994–2003, mem. Supervisory Bd 2003–; mem. Supervisory Bd Heineken NV 2002–, Chair. 2002–; Chair. Supervisory Bd Dutch Cen. Bank; Chair. INSEAD (also Unit Bd mem. and mem. Supervisory Bd); Exec. Officer, mem. Supervisory Bd and mem. Remuneration Cttee Koninklijke Philips Electronics NV 2003–; mem. Bd of Dirs Air France KLM 2004–, (its subsidiary) Air France 2004–, L'Air Liquide SA (also mem. Supervisory Bd), Sara Lee Corpn 2002–; Dir (non-exec.) Reed Elsevier plc 2003–07, Reed Elsevier Group plc 2003–, Reed Elsevier NV 2001– (also mem. Supervisory Bd 2003–); mem. Supervisory Bd Philips Lighting Co. 2003–, Stork NV 2007–, Philips Electronics N America Corpn 2003–, Philips Electronics Singapore Pte Ltd 2003–, Sara Lee (USA)/DE NV, Scania AB (Sweden), Heineken Holding NV; fmr mem. Bd of Man. Dirs HBG; served as Proposed mem. Supervisory Bd KLM Royal Dutch Airlines; mem. European Advisory Council JPMorgan Chase & Co. 2005–, Int. Council of JPMorgan Chase; Chair. Confed. of Netherlands Industry and Employers (VNO) 1984–91; Vice-Pres. Union of Industrial and Employers' Confeds of Europe (UNICE) 1991–94; mem. European Round Table of Industrialists, Bd of

Trustees of The Conference Bd, Netherlands Pensions and Insurance Supervisory Authority. *Address:* Heineken NV, PO Box 28, 1000 AA Amsterdam (office); Heineken NV, Tweede Weteringplantsoen 21, 1017 ZD Amsterdam, The Netherlands (office). *Telephone:* (20) 523-92-39 (office). *Fax:* (20) 626-35-03 (office). *E-mail:* info@heinekeninternational.com (office). *Website:* www.heinekeninternational.com (office).

VAN LOAN, Peter, MA, MSc, JD; Canadian lawyer and politician; *Minister for Public Safety;* b. 18 April 1963, Niagara Falls; ed Univ. of Toronto, Osgoode Hall Law School; fmr Pnr and Chair Planning and Devt Law Group, Fraser Milner Casgrain LLP (law firm), Toronto; fmr Adjunct Prof. of Planning, Univ. of Toronto; Pres. Progressive Conservative Party of Ont. then Progressive Conservative Party of Canada –2000 (resgnd); MP (Conservative) for York–Simcoe 2004–, Critic for Human Resources and Skills Devt 2004–06, Parl. Sec. to Minister of Foreign Affairs –Nov. 2006, Pres. of the Queen's Privy Council for Canada, Minister of Intergovernmental Affairs and Minister for Sport Nov. 2006–Jan. 2007, Leader of the Govt in the House of Commons and Minister for Democratic Reform Jan. 2007–08, Minister of Public Safety 2008–. *Address:* Public Safety Canada, 269 Laurier Avenue West, Ottawa, ON K1A 0P8, Canada (office). *Telephone:* (613) 944-4875 (office). *Fax:* (613) 954-5186 (office). *E-mail:* communications@ps-sp.gc.ca (office). *Website:* www.pco-bcp.gc.ca/lgc (office).

VAN MIDDELKOOP, Eimert; Dutch politician; *Minister of Defence;* b. 14 Feb. 1949, Berkel en Rodenrijs; m.; three s. one d.; ed Netherlands School of Econs, Rotterdam; Lecturer, Reformed School of Social Work, Zwolle 1971–72; Asst, Calvinist Political Union (GPV) 1973–89; mem. House of Reps (GPV) 1989–2001, for Christian Union 2001–02; mem. Senate 2003–07; Minister of Defence 2007–; fmr mem. Supervisory Cttee, Social and Cultural Planning Office; fmr Chair. Policy Review Cttee European Defence; fmr Sec. Centre for Parl. History, Nijmegen; fmr mem. Advisory Board, East-West Parl. Practice Project, Royal Netherlands Air Force, Netherlands Inst. of Int. Relations, Inst. for Multiparty Democracy. *Address:* Ministry of Defence, Plein 4, POB 20701, 2500 ES The Hague, Netherlands (office). *Telephone:* (70) 3188188 (office). *Fax:* (70) 3187888 (office). *E-mail:* defensievoorlichting@mindef.nl (office). *Website:* www.mindef.nl (home).

VAN MIERLO, Henricus Antonius Franciscus Maria Oliva (Hans), DJur; Dutch politician; b. 18 Aug. 1931, Breda; ed Canisius Coll. Nijmegen and Univ. of Nijmegen; journalist, Het Algemeen Handelsblad, Amsterdam 1960–67; first Chair. newly formed political party Democrats '66 (D66) 1966; mem. Lower House of States Gen. 1967–77, 1986–94; Leader D66 Parl. Party 1967–74, 1986–94; mem. Upper House of States Gen. 1983–86; Deputy Prime Minister and Minister of Foreign Affairs 1994–98; Hon. Minister of State 1998–; fmr mem. Netherlands-Suriname Devt Comm., Advisory Council on Defence; co-producer of TV programmes; various positions in literary and other cultural orgs. *Address:* c/o Ministry of Foreign Affairs, Bezuidenhoutseweg 67, P.O. Box 20061, 2500 EB The Hague, Netherlands.

VAN MIERT, Karel; Belgian international official and politician; *President of Nijenrode University, Netherlands Business School;* b. 17 Jan. 1942, Oud-Turnhout; m.; one c.; ed State University of Ghent; Researcher, Fonds National de la Recherche Scientifique 1968–70; Asst in Int. Law, Free Univ. of Brussels 1971–73; Head. Admin. attached to Pvt. Office of Vice-Pres. of EC 1973–75; part-time lecturer, Free Univ. of Brussels 1978–; Int. Sec. Belgian Socialist Party 1976, Co-Chair. 1977; subsequently Chair. Flemish Socialists; Vice-Chair. Confed. of Socialist Parties of European Community 1978–80; MEP 1979–85; mem. House of Reps 1985–88; Vice-Chair. Socialist Int. 1986–92; EEC (now EU) Commr for Transport, Credit, Investment and Consumer Affairs 1989–94, for Environment (acting) 1992–93, for Competition Policy, Personnel and Admin. 1993–95, for Competition 1992–99, a Vice-Pres. 1993–95; Pres. Nijenrode Univ., Netherlands Business School 2000–; Dir (non-exec.) Anglo-American 2002–. *Address:* Office of the President, Nijenrode University, Netherlands Business School, Straatweg 25, 3621 BG Breukelen, Netherlands (office). *Telephone:* (346) 291211 (office). *Fax:* (346) 264204 (office). *E-mail:* info@nijenrode.nl (office). *Website:* www.nijenrode.nl (office).

VAN MONTAGU, Baron Marc Charles Ernest, PhD; Belgian plant geneticist; *Chairman of Steering Committee, Institute of Plant Biotechnology for Developing Countries, University of Ghent;* b. 10 Nov. 1933, Ghent; s. of Jean Van Montagu and Irene Van Beveren; m. Nora Podgaetchi 1957; ed State Univ. Ghent; Asst, State Univ. Ghent 1962–64, Lab. Dir and Lector, Dept of Histology 1964–78, Assoc. Prof. and Co-Dir Lab. of Genetics 1979–87, Full Prof. and Dir Lab. of Genetics 1987–99; Chair. Steering Cttee IPBO 1999–; Scientific Dir Plant Genetic Systems NV 1983–95; mem. Royal Belgium Acad. of Sciences; Foreign Assoc. NAS; Foreign mem. Russian Agric. Acad., Royal Swedish Acad. of Eng Sciences, Acad. d'Agric. de France; Assoc. Fellow Third World Acad. of Sciences 2001; title of Baron granted by King Baudoin I; Hon. DPhil (Helsinki) 1990 Rank Prize for Nutrition, UK 1987, IBM-Europe Prize 1988, Prize of the Flemish Community 1989, Dr A. De Leeuw-Damry-Bourlart Prize 1990, Charles Leopold Mayer Prize, Acad. of Sciences, Paris 1990, Japan Prize 1998, Theodor Bücher Medal 1999. *Publications:* about 800 articles in specialized journals and books. *Leisure interest:* travel. *Address:* IPBO, Department of Molecular Genetics, University of Ghent, Ledeganckstraat 35, 9000 Ghent (office); Avenue des Sept Bonniers 306, 1190 Forest, Belgium (home). *Telephone:* (9) 264-87-27 (office); (2) 511-25-57 (home). *Fax:* (9) 264-87-95 (office); (9) 264-87-95. *E-mail:* mamon@gengenp.rug.ac.be (office). *Website:* www.ipbo.rug.ac.be (office).

VAN MUNSTER, Hans, DPhil; Dutch ecclesiastic; b. 17 Nov. 1925, Gouda; s. of J. M. van Munster and A. C. B. Faay; ed Univ. of Louvain; entered Order of St Francis of Assisi 1944; ordained priest 1951; Lecturer in Logic and Methodology, Philosophical Inst., Venray 1955–67; Regent, RC Lycee, Venray 1963–67; Prof. of Philosophy, Catholic Theological Faculty of Utrecht 1967–71, Rector 1968–71; Vicar-Gen. of Archdiocese of Utrecht 1970–81; Sec.-Gen. Dutch Bishops' Conf. 1981–91; Pres. Cttee on Justice and Peace 1991–99; Pres. European Conf. of Justice and Peace Comms 1996–99; Pres. Catholic Bible Soc. 1992–98, Franciscan Asscn 1992–98; Officer Order of Oranje-Nassau 1976, Kt of Netherlands Lion 1991. *Publications include:* Kierkegaard een keuze uit zijn dagboeken 1957, De filosofische gedachten van de jonge Kierkegaard 1958, Kierkegaards redevoeringen 1959, Over de vertwijfeling 1963, Sören Aabye Kierkegaard 1963, Naar woorden moet je luisteren 1981, Vanwaar? Waarheen? 1982, Drie prioriteiten voor de kerk van Europa 1983, Kantelt de Koets wel? 1989, Een steen in de vijver, vrede en gerechtigheid na de dood van Marx 1993, Te Doen gerechtigheid 1993, De ware vrede 1993, 't is een vreemdeling zeker 1994, Een ryke heeft het moeilijk 1997, De mystiek van Franciscus 2002, Een mens te zýn op aarde 2004, Wýsheid van Kierkegaard 2006. *Leisure interests:* cycling, literature. *Address:* Jan van Scorelstraat 75, 3583 CL Utrecht, Netherlands (home). *Telephone:* (30) 2510153 (home). *Fax:* (30) 2523326 (home).

VAN NIEKERK, André Isak (Kraai), PhD; South African politician and agricultural scientist; *Chairman, Democratic Alliance Parliamentary Caucus;* b. 7 Oct. 1938, Eshowe, Natal; m. Theresa Claassens 1964; three s.; ed Univ. of Stellenbosch; taught Science and Agric. Eshowe Bantu Training Coll. 1962; specialist officer, Dept of Agric. Tech. Services, Univ. of Stellenbosch 1964–67; Research at Rowett Inst., Aberdeen, UK 1968, Wageningen Agricultural Univ., Netherlands 1969; farmer, Kenhardt Dist 1971–81; elected MP for Prieska 1981; Deputy Minister of Agric. 1986, of Agric. and Water Supply in Ministers' Council 1989, of Agricultural Devt 1989; Minister of Agric. in Cabinet, of Agricultural Devt in Ministers' Council 1991–94, of Agric., Govt of Nat. Unity 1994–96; apptd Leader Nat. Party for the Northern Cape 1994; mem. Senate (for Northern Cape) 1994, Deputy Leader 1994; currently Deputy Chair. Fed. Council, Democratic Alliance and Chair. Parl. Caucus; Hon. Award of S African Agricultural Union 1996, Service to Agric. Prestigious Award, Agricultural Writers' Asscn 1996, Agricultural Leader of the Year, Rand Show Soc. 1996, Golden Ram Award, Nat. Woolgrowers Asscn 1997. *Leisure interest:* bee-farming. *Address:* Democratic Alliance, POB 1475, Cape Town 8000, South Africa (office). *Telephone:* (83) 2616468 (Mobile); (21) 8872596 (also fax) (home). *Fax:* (21) 4032134 (office). *E-mail:* headoffice@da.org.za (office); kraaines@mweb.co.za (home). *Website:* www.da.org.za (office).

VAN PEEBLES, Mario, BEcons; American actor and film director; b. 15 Jan. 1957, Mexico City; s. of Melvin Van Peebles and Maria Marx; ed Columbia Univ.; film debut aged 11; worked as budget analyst in New York Mayor's office; studied acting and script interpretation with Stella Adler. *Theatre:* Champion, Jungle Fever, Midnight, Friday The 13th, Deadwood Dick, Bodybags (also co-dir). *Films include:* Sweet Sweetback's Baadasssss Song 1971, Exterminator 2 1984, Cotton Club 1984, Rappin 1985, Delivery Boys 1985, South Bronx Heroes 1985, 3:15 1986, Last Resort 1986, Heartbreak Ridge 1986, Hotshot 1987, Jaws: The Revenge 1987, Identity Crisis 1989, New Jack City (also dir) 1991, Posse (also dir) 1993, Letter to Dad 1994, Gunmen (also dir) 1994, Highlander III: The Sorcerer 1994, Panther (also dir, producer) 1995, Gang in Blue 1996, Solo 1996, Los Locos (also dir and screenplay) 1997, Stag 1997, Love Kills (also dir, producer) 1998, Crazy Six 1998, Judgment Day 1999, Raw Nerve 1999, Blowback 2000, Guardian 2000, Ali 2001, The Hebrew Hammer 2003, How to Get the Man's Foot Outta Your Ass 2003 (also dir, producer and screenplay), Gang of Roses 2003, Hard Luck 2006 (also dir). *Television includes:* Children of the Night 1985, D.C. Cops 1986, LA Law 1986, The Facts of Life Down Under 1987, The Child Saver 1988, Blue Bayou 1990, Malcolm Takes a Shot 1990, A Triumph of the Heart: The Ricky Bell Story 1991, Stompin' at the Savoy 1992, In the Line of Duty: Street War 1992, Full Eclipse 1993, Mama Flora's Family 1998, Killers in the House 1998, Sally Hemings: An American Scandal 2000, Rude Awakening (series) 2000–01, 10,000 Black Men Named George 2002, The Street Lawyer 2003, 44 Minutes: The North Hollywood Shoot-Out 2003, Crown Heights 2004. *Address:* Vincent Cirrincione Associates, 8721 Sunset Blvd., Suite 205, Los Angeles, CA 90069; United Talent Agency, c/o Steven Small, 9560 Wilshire Blvd., Beverly Hills, CA 90212, USA. *Telephone:* (310) 854-0533. *Fax:* (310) 854-0558. *E-mail:* info@vincentcirrincione.com.

VAN ROIJEN, Jan Herman Robert Dudley, LLM; Dutch diplomatist; b. 17 Dec. 1936, Tokyo, Japan; s. of the late Dr Jan Herman van Roijen and Anne van Roijen (née Jonkvrouwe Snouck Hurgronje); m. Jonkvrouw Caroline H. W. Reuchlin 1963; one s. two d.; ed Groton School, Mass., USA and Univ. of Utrecht; entered foreign service 1963; Third Sec. Jakarta 1965–67; Second Sec. Perm. Mission at NATO, Paris and Brussels 1967–70; Head, Recruitment and Training Section, Foreign Office 1970–73; Chargé d'Affaires, Saigon 1973–75; Counsellor, Athens 1975–78, Ottawa 1978–81; Minister Plenipotentiary, Jakarta 1981–83; Deputy Dir-Gen. Int. Cooperation, Ministry of Foreign Affairs 1983–86; Amb. to Israel 1986–89; Prin. Dir Personnel, Diplomatic Budget and Bldgs, Ministry of Foreign Affairs 1989–91; Amb. to Indonesia 1992–94, to UK 1995–99 (also accred to Iceland); Chair. Netherlands Helsinki Cttee; Kt Order of Netherlands Lion, Officer Order of Orange Nassau, Commdr with Crown, Adolf of Nassau (Luxembourg), Bintang Jasa Utama, First Class (Indonesia), Grand Officer, Order of the Phoenix (Greece). *Leisure interests:* tennis, skiing. *Address:* Jagerslaan 9, 2243 EH Wassenaar, Netherlands (home). *Telephone:* (70) 5144470 (home). *Fax:* (70) 5142751 (home). *E-mail:* vanroijen-reuchlin@hetnet.nl (home).

VAN ROMPUY, Herman; Belgian politician; *Prime Minister;* b. 31 Oct. 1947, Etterbeek; m.; four c.; ed Catholic Univ. of Leuven; research attaché, Nat. Bank of Belgium 1972–75; Vice-Pres. CVP (Christian Democrat Party, now CD&V—Christen-Democratisch en Vlaams) Youth 1973–75, mem. CVP

Nat. Bureau 1975–80, Brussels-Halle-Vilvoorde CVP Dist Chair. 1982–88, Pres. CVP 1988–93; adviser to Prime Minister Leo Tindemans 1975–78, to Minister of Finance 1978–80; Dir Centre for Political, Econ. and Social Studies 1980–88; mem. Senate 1988–95; Sec. of State for Finance and Small and Medium Enterprises May–Sept. 1988; Deputy Prime Minister and Minister of Budget 1993–99; mem. Chamber of Reps 1995–, designated Minister of State 2004, Pres. Chamber of Reps 2007–09; Prime Minister of Belgium 2009–. *Publications:* De kentering der tijden 1979, Hopen na 1984, Het christendom. Een moderne gedachte 1990, Vernieuwing in hoofd en hart. Een tegendraadse visie 1998, De binnenkant op een kier. Avonden zonder politiek, Dagboek van een vijftiger 2004. *Address:* Federal Public Service Office of the Prime Minister, 16 rue de la Loi, 1000 Brussels, Belgium (office). *Telephone:* (2) 501-02-11 (office). *Fax:* (2) 217-33-28 (office). *E-mail:* info@premier.fed.be (office). *Website:* www.premier.be (office).

VAN ROOY, Yvonne Catharina Maria Theresia; Dutch politician and academic administrator; *President of the Executive Board, Utrecht University;* b. 4 June 1951, Eindhoven; ed Jeanne d'Arc Lyceum, Maastricht, Utrecht Univ.; trainee at EC, Brussels 1977; staff mem. Dutch Christian Employers' Union 1978–84; MEP (Christian Democrats) 1984–86; Minister for Foreign Trade 1986–89, 1990–94; Mem. European Parl. (Christian Democrats) 1989–90, 1994–97; Pres. Exec. Bd Tilburg Univ. 1997–2004; Pres. Exec. Bd Utrecht Univ. 2004–; Chair. Bd of Foundation for Promotion of Exports; Crown mem. Social and Econ. Council of the Netherlands; mem. Advisory Bd Deloitte, Selection Cttee for the Judiciary; mem. Supervisory Bd Bank Nederlandse Gemeenten; mem. Bd of Dirs Radboud Foundation; Kt Order of the Netherlands Lion, Commdr Order of Orange-Nassau. *Address:* Utrecht University, Heidelberglaan 8, PO Box 80125, 3508 Utrecht TC, Netherlands (office). *Telephone:* (30) 2535150 (office). *Fax:* (30) 2537745 (office). *E-mail:* y.vanrooy@uu.nl (office). *Website:* www.uu.nl (office).

VAN SANT, Gus, Jr, BA; American film director and screenwriter; b. 24 July 1952, Louisville, Ky; ed Rhode Island School of Design; fmr production asst to Ken Shapiro; Nat. Soc. of Film Critics Awards for Best Dir and Screenplay 1990, New York Film Critics and LA Film Critics Award for Best Screenplay 1989, PEN Literary Award for Best Screenplay Adaptation (jtly) 1989; American Civil Liberties Union (ACLU) of Ore. Freedom of Expression Award 1992. *Albums:* Gus Van Sant 1997, 18 Songs About Golf 1997. *Films include:* Mala Noche (dir, writer), Drugstore Cowboy 1989 (dir, writer, with Daniel Yost), My Own Private Idaho (dir, writer) 1991, Even Cowgirls Get the Blues (dir, writer) 1993, To Die For (dir)1995, Kids (producer) 1995, Ballad of the Skeletons (dir) 1996, Good Will Hunting (dir) 1997, Psycho (dir) 1998, Finding Forrester 2000, Gerry 2002, Elephant (documentary dir, Palme d'Or and Best Dir, Cannes Film Festival) 2003, Last Days 2005, Paris, je t'aime (segment) 2006, Paranoid Park (60th Anniversary Award, Cannes Film Festival 2007) 2007, Milk 2008. *Publications:* 108 Portraits (collection of photgraphs) 1995, Pink 1997. *Address:* William Morris Agency, One William Morris Place, Beverly Hills, CA 90212, USA (office). *Telephone:* (310) 859-4000 (office). *Fax:* (310) 859-4462 (office). *Website:* www.wma.com (office).

VAN SCHAIK, Ben; Dutch business executive; b. 1945; worked in sales for Mercedes Benz in UK, Netherlands, Germany; Chair. Fokker (aircraft maker) 1994–96.

VAN SCHAIK, Gerard, PhD, FCIS; Dutch business executive (retd); b. 29 March 1930, Haarlem; s. of the late Gerard Van Schaik and Maria Mulder; m. Moyra Colijn 1963 (deceased); two s. one d.; ed Free Univ. of Amsterdam, IMEDE, Switzerland; officer Royal Netherlands Air Force 1956–58; joined Heineken's Bierbrouwerij Maatschappij N.V. 1959, mem. Exec. Bd Heineken NV 1974, Deputy Chair. 1983, Chair. 1989–93; Pres. Supervisory Bd Aegon NV 1993–2000; Dir of numerous cos; Vice Chair. CEIBS China European Business School, Shanghai; Hon. Pres. European Foundation of Man. Devt, Brussels, Hon. Fellow, London Business School; Kt, Order of the Dutch Lion; Dr hc (State Acad. for Man., Moscow) 1997. *Leisure interests:* golf, music. *Address:* Duinvoetlaan 7, 2243 GK Wassenaar, Netherlands. *Telephone:* (70) 5179008. *Fax:* (70) 5179008. *E-mail:* gvschaik@wanadoo.nl (home).

VAN SCHALKWYK, Marthinus Christoffel Johannes, MA; South African politician; *Minister of Environmental Affairs and Tourism;* b. 10 Nov. 1959, Pietersburg; m. Suzette van Schalkwyk; one s. one d.; ed Pietersburg High School, Rand Afrikaans Univ.; fmr Nat. Pres. Afrikaanse Studentbond, Chair. Youth for S Africa, Fed. Youth Leader, Nat. Party; mil. service 1978–79; Lecturer in Political Science, Rand Afrikaans Univ., Univ. of Stellenbosch; MP for Randburg 1990–94; mem. Nat. Ass. 1994–, mem. Parl. Portfolio Cttee on Communications, Nat. Party Rep. at Int. Democratic Union and African Dialogue Group; apptd Exec. Dir Nat. Party 1997, Leader New Nat. Party 1997–2005 (party disbanded); Premier of the Western Cape 2002–04; Minister of Environmental Affairs and Tourism 2004–; mem. African Nat. Congress (ANC) 2005–; Pres. African Ministerial Conf. on the Environment 2008–; Abe Bailey Bursary to GB and Europe, Award for Academic Achievement, Transvaal Lawyers' Asscn. *Address:* Private Bag X9154, Cape Town 8000 (office); Private Bag X447, Pretoria 0001, South Africa (office). *Telephone:* (21) 4657240 (Cape Town) (office); (12) 3103611 (Pretoria) (office). *Fax:* (21) 4653216 (Cape Town) (office); (12) 3220082 (Pretoria) (office). *E-mail:* strugel@deat.gov.za (office). *Website:* www.environment.gov.za (office).

VAN SLINGELANDT, Diederik (Rik) Johannes Maximilianus Govert Baron, BBA; Dutch banking executive; *Chairman, Rabobank International;* b. 17 July 1946, Delft; m.; two c.; ed Dutch High School A, Rotterdam, Univ. of Groningen; staff mem. Nationale Investeringsbank NV 1972–80; Head of Finance Dept, Rijn Schelde Verolme 1980–82; Dir of Finance, Treasury, Admin and Information Tech., Verolme Estaleiros Reunidos do Brasil ste, Rio de Janeiro 1982–85; Financial Dir Rodamco Groep 1985–89, also mem. Investment Cttee; Dir of Int. Operations, Rabobank Nederland 1989–96, mem. Bd Dirs 1996–; Chair. Exec. Cttee, Centrale Bank Bedrijf 1989–96; Chair. Rabobank Int. 1996–; Acting CEO of Exec. Bd Rabobank Group 2004; Chair. Supervisory Bd Rabo Australia Ltd, Rabobank Int. Advisory Services (RIAS) BV, Interpolis NV; Chair. Bd Dirs Rabobank Pension Fund; Vice-Chair. Supervisory Bd Bank Sarasin & Cie; mem. Supervisory Bd Robeco Groep NV, SNP Groep NV; mem. Advisory Cttee Issuing Insts (Euronext), Unico Steering Cttee, Bd Dirs Ubbo Emmius Fund, Univ. of Groningen. *Address:* Rabobank Group, Croeselaan 18, 3521 CB Utrecht, The Netherlands (office). *Telephone:* (30) 216-00-00 (office). *Fax:* (30) 216-26-72 (office). *Website:* www.rabobank.nl (office).

VAN SWAAIJ, Willibrordus Petrus Maria, PhD; Dutch chemical engineer and academic; *Professor, University of Twente;* b. 18 Jan. 1942, Nijmegen; s. of Christian van Swaaij and C. Bosman; m. J. J. T. van den Berk 1966; one s. four d.; ed Tech. Univ. of Eindhoven, Univ. of Nancy, France; joined Shell Research 1965, worked in lab. Shell Research BV (KSLA), Amsterdam 1966–72, Section Chief, Gasification 1971–72; Prof. of Chemical Eng Science, Twente Univ. 1972–, mem. of staff Thermo-Chemical Conversion of Biomass Group 1999–; Consultant to DSM, AKZO, Unilever, Netherlands Govt, EEC; mem. Royal Netherlands Acad. of Sciences 1986; Australian European Fellowship Award 1984; Dr hc (Inst. Nat. Polytechnique de Lorraine, France) 1996; Dow Energy Prize 1985, Grand Prix du Génie des Procédés, Inst. de France 1996; Golden Tesla Medal 1999, Golden Hoogewerff Medal for Lifetime Achievement 2000; Australian European Fellowship Award 1984; Kt Order of the Lion (Netherlands) 1997. *Publications:* Chemical Reactor Design and Operation (with Westerterp and Beenackers); about 340 scientific papers, contribs to books etc. *Leisure interests:* sailing, surfing, photography, gardening, history. *Address:* University of Twente, Department of Chemical Technology, Room nr. A1.20, PO B 217, 7500 AE Enschede (office); Sportlaan 60, 7581 BZ Losser, Netherlands (home). *Telephone:* (53) 4892880 (office); (53) 5382677 (home). *Fax:* (53) 4894738 (office); (53) 5384368 (home). *E-mail:* w.p.m.vanswaaij@utwente.nl (office). *Website:* tccb.tnw.utwente.nl/vanswaaij.php (office).

VAN UHM, Gen. P.J.M.; Dutch military officer; *Chief of Defence;* b. 1955, Nijmegen; ed Royal Mil. Acad., Breda, Royal Netherlands Army Staff Coll.; Co. Commdr 43th Armoured Infantry Battalion 1982–84, deployed to Lebanon 1983; Deputy Head of Operations, 1 Div. "7 December" 1986; Head of Training Policy Office, then Head of Training Section, Royal Netherlands Army Staff Coll. 1986–91; Defence Liaison Officer, Ministry of Foreign Affairs 1991; Head of Plans Div., 1 (NL) Corps Staff 1991–94; Commdr 11 Infantry Battalion, Grenadiers and Rifles Guards, Airmobile Brigade 1994–95; Head of Personal Office of C-in-C of Royal Netherlands Army, then Head of Gen. Policy Div., Army Staff, then Head of Mil.-Strategic Affairs Div., Defence Staff 1995–2000; Asst Chief of Staff for Jt Mil. Affairs, UN Stabilisation Force (SFOR), Sarajevo 2000–01; Commdr 11 Airmobile Brigade 2001–02, 11 Air Manoeuvre Brigade 2002–03, Operational Command '7 December' 2005; Commdr Royal Netherlands Army 2005–08; Chief of Defence 2008–. *Address:* Ministry of Defence, Plein 4, POB 20701, 2500 The Hague, The Netherlands (office). *Telephone:* (70) 3188188 (office). *Fax:* (70) 3187888 (office). *E-mail:* defensievoorlichting@mindef.nl (office). *Website:* www.mindef.nl (office).

VAN VUUREN, Jacobus Lukas Jansen, BCom; South African banker; b. 6 June 1931, De Aar; s. of Stephanus van Vuuren; m. Anna van der Merwe 1953; three d.; ed De Aar High School and UNISA; Chief Accountant, Volkskas Bank Ltd 1978, Asst Gen. Man. 1980, Gen. Man. 1981, Sr Gen. Man. 1984, later Man. Dir and CEO; Exec. Dir Volkskas Group Ltd; Chair. MLS Bank Ltd, Volkskas Motor Bank Ltd; Exec. Dir Amalgamated Banks of S Africa Ltd; Dir Bank of Transkei Ltd, United Bank Ltd, Priceforbes Federale Volkskas Holdings (Pty) Ltd. *Leisure interests:* gardening, golf.

VAN WACHEM, Lodewijk Christiaan; Dutch business executive and mechanical engineer; b. 31 July 1931, Pangkalan Brandan, now Indonesia; m. Elisabeth G. Cristofoli 1958; two s. one d.; ed Delft Univ. of Technology; joined Bataafsche Petroleum Maatschappij, The Hague 1953; Mech. Engineer, Cía Shell de Venezuela 1954–63; Chief Engineer, Shell-BP Petroleum Devt Co. of Nigeria 1963–66, Eng Man. 1966–67, Chair. and Man. Dir 1972–76; Head Tech. Admin. Brunei Shell Petroleum Co. Ltd 1967–69, Tech. Dir 1969–71; Head of Production Div. Shell Int. Petroleum Maatschappij, The Hague 1971–72, Co-ordinator Exploration and Production 1976–79; Man. Dir Royal Dutch Petroleum Co. 1976–82, Pres. 1982–92; mem. Presidium of Bd of Dirs, Shell Petroleum NV 1976–92; Man. Dir Shell Petroleum Co. Ltd 1976–92, Chair. Jt Cttee of Man. Dirs of the Royal Dutch/Shell Group 1985–92, Chair. Supervisory Bd Royal Dutch Petroleum Co. 1992–2002; mem. Bd of Dirs Crédit Suisse Holding 1992–96, Zürich Insurance Group (now Zürich Financial Services) 1993–2005 (Vice-Chair. 2001–02, Chair. 2002–05) Supervisory Bd Akzo-Nobel NV 1992–2002, Royal Philips Electronics NV 1993– (Chair. Supervisory Bd 1999–), BMW (Munich) 1994–2002, Bayer AG 1997–2002, Rand Europe (mem. Exec. Bd 2005–); Chair. Global Crossing 2003–07; Dir (non-exec.) IBM Corpn 1992–2002, ATCO Ltd 1993–, AAB Brown Boveri Ltd 1996–99; Hon. Citizen of Singapore 2004; Hon. Commdr and KBE 1989; Kt Order of Netherlands Lion 1981; Commdr, Order of Oranje Nassau 1990; Public Service Star, Singapore 1998. *Address:* Rand Europe, Westbrook Centre, Milton Road, Cambridge, CB4 1YG, England (office). *Telephone:* (1223) 353329 (office). *Fax:* (1223) 358845 (office). *Website:* www.rand.org (office).

VAN WALSUM, (Arnold) Peter, LLB; Dutch diplomatist; *Secretary-General's Personal Envoy for Western Sahara, United Nations;* b. 25 June 1934, Rotterdam; m.; four c.; ed Univ. of Utrecht; First Sec. Perm. Mission to UN 1970–74, First Sec. New Delhi 1974–79, Counsellor, London 1975–79, Counsellor Perm. Mission to EC 1979–81, Head Western Hemisphere Dept, Ministry of Foreign Affairs 1981–85; Amb. to Thailand 1985–89, to Germany

1993–98; Dir-Gen. Political Affairs, Ministry of Foreign Affairs 1989–93; Perm. Rep. to UN 1998–2001, Chair. Iran Sanctions Cttee 1999–2000; UN Sec.-Gen.'s Personal Envoy for Western Sahara 2005–. *Address:* United Nations Mission for the Referendum in Western Sahara (MINURSO), PO Box 80,000, Laayoune, Western Sahara, Morocco (office); United Nations Mission for the Referendum in Western Sahara (MINURSO), PO Box 5846, Grand Central Station, New York, NY 10163-5846, USA (office). *Telephone:* (48) 893828 (office). *Fax:* (48) 892893 (office). *Website:* www.minurso.unlb.org (office).

VAN WIJNGAARDEN, Leendert, PhD; Dutch scientist and academic; *Professor Emeritus of Fluid Mechanics, University of Twente;* b. 16 March 1932, Delft; s. of Cornelis M. van Wijngaarden and Jeanne Severijn; m. Willy F. de Goede 1962; two s.; ed Gymnasium B, Delft and Technological Univ. of Delft; Netherlands Ship Model Basin, Wageningen 1962–66, latterly Head of Hydrodynamics Dept; Prof. of Fluid Mechanics, Twente Univ. 1966–97, Prof. Emer. 1997–; mem. of Bureau and Treasurer Int. Union of Theoretical and Applied Mechanics 1984–88, Pres. 1992–96, Vice-Pres. 1996–; mem. Royal Netherlands Acad. of Science 1988–; Kt in the Order of the Dutch Lion 1995. *Publications:* about 70 publs in professional journals. *Leisure interests:* tennis, chess, literature, music. *Address:* University of Twente, Faculty of Science and Technology, P.O. Box 217, 7500 AE Enschede (office); Von Weberlaan 7, 7522 KB Enschede, Netherlands (home). *Telephone:* (53) 893086 (office); (53) 352078 (home). *Fax:* 53) 4898068 (office). *E-mail:* L.vanWijngaarden@tn .utwente.nl (office). *Website:* www.tn.utwente.nl/pof (office).

VAN WINDEN, Jacobus Cornelis Maria; Dutch ecclesiastic and professor of Greek; *Professor Emeritus, University of Leiden;* b. 10 Oct. 1922, Schipluiden; ed in Franciscan convents and Leiden Univ.; mem. Franciscan Order (OFM) 1941; ordained priest 1948; Asst to J. H. Waszink, Prof. of Latin, Leiden 1954–56; teacher of Greek and Latin, Rotterdam 1956–66; Reader, Leiden Univ. 1966–80, Prof. of Greek of Late Antiquity 1980–87, Prof. Emer. 1987–; Ed.-in-Chief Vigiliae Christianae (review of Early Christian Life and Language) 1977–; mem. Royal Netherlands Acad. *Publications:* Calcidius on Matter: His Doctrine and Sources 1959, An Early Christian Philosopher: Justin Martyr's Dialogue with Trypho (Chapters 1–9) 1971, Tertullianus, De idolatria (critical text, trans. and commentary with J. H. Waszink) 1987, De ware wijsheid: Wegen van vroeg-christelijk denken 1992, Bonaventura, Itinerarium. De Weg die de geest naar God voert 1996, Arche. A Collection of Patristic Studies 1997, Bonaventura, Breviloquium, De theologie in kort bestek 2000. *Address:* Haarlemmerstraat 106, 2312 GD Leiden, Netherlands. *Telephone:* (71) 5120401.

VAN WYK, Andreas Herculas, BA, LLD; South African professor of law and university rector (retd); b. 17 Sept. 1941, Pretoria; s. of Andries Hercules du Preez van Wyk and Hendrina Louise van Wyk (née Kruger); m. Magdalena Krüger 1967; two d.; ed Helpmekaar Boys' High School, Johannesburg, Univs of Stellenbosch and Leiden; Lecturer, then Prof., then Dean, Faculty of Law, Univ. of Stellenbosch 1966–84, Dir Gen. Dept of Constitutional Devt 1984–87, Prof. Faculty of Law 1987–91, Vice-Rector Operations 1991–93, Rector and Vice-Chancellor 1993–2000; Chair. South African Univs Vice-Chancellors Asscn 2001; mem. Bd Comm. of Old Mutual 1992–; guest USA/SA Leadership Exchange Programme 1978; Alexander von Humboldt Foundation Fellowship 1981; mem. SA Akad. vir wetenskap en kuns; Hon. LLD (Leuven); William of Orange Medal (Leiden) 1995. *Publications:* The Power to Dispose of the Assets of the Universal Matrimonial Community of Property 1976, Die Suid-Afrikaanse Kontraktereg en Handelsreg (co-author) 1992, Family, Property and Succession 1983 and numerous articles in academic journals; has drafted various pieces of legislation.

VAN ZYL SLABBERT, Dr F. (see Slabbert, F. Van Zyl).

VANDENBERG, Edwin J., BEng; American chemist and academic; *Research Scientist, Harrington Department of Bioengineering, Arizona State University;* b. 1918, Hawthorne, NJ; ed Stevens Inst. of Tech., Hoboken, NJ; joined Hercules Inc., Wilmington, Del. as Chemistry Researcher 1939, retd 1982; Visiting Prof., Ariz. State Univ. 1982, now Research Scientist, Harrington Dept of Bioengineering; Sec., ACS Div. of Polymer Chem. (POLY) 1975–77, Chair. 1979; Hon. DEng (Stevens Inst. of Tech.) 1965 ACS Award in Polymer Chem. 1981, in Applied Polymer Science 1991, Charles Goodyear Medal 1991, Soc. of Plastics Engineers Int. Award 1994, ACS Priestley Medal 2003. *Achievements:* holder of 116 patents. *Address:* Harrington Department of Bioengineering, Arizona State University, Room ECG334, Tempe, AZ 85287-9709, USA (office). *Telephone:* (480) 9665-3028 (office). *Fax:* (480) 727-7624 (office). *Website:* www.eas.asu.edu/~bme/new (office).

VANDENBROUCKE, Frank, DPhil; Belgian politician; *Vice-Minister-President of the Flemish Government and Flemish Minister for Work, Education and Training;* b. 21 Oct. 1955, Louvain; ed Catholic Univ. of Louvain, Univs of Cambridge and Oxford, UK; Research Asst, Centrum voor Economische Studiën, Catholic Univ. of Louvain 1978–80; staff mem. SEVI (Research Dept of Socialist Party of Flemish Region) 1982–85; MP 1985–96; Leader Socialist Party 1989–94; Leader Parl. Group of Socialist Party 1995–96; Deputy Prime Minister and Minister of Foreign Affairs 1994–95; Minister of Social Affairs and Pensions July 1999–2003; Minister of Employment and Pensions 2003–04; Vice-Minister-Pres. Flemish Govt and Flemish Minister for Work, Educ. and Training 2004–. *Address:* Koning Albert II-Laan 15, 1210 Brussels, Belgium (office). *Telephone:* (2) 552-68-00 (office). *Fax:* (2) 552-68-01 (office). *E-mail:* kabinet.vandenbroucke@vlaanderen.be (office). *Website:* www.ministerfrankvandenbroucke.be (office).

VANDER ESPT, Georges J. H.; Belgian diplomatist; b. 16 Jan. 1931, Ostend; m. Marie-Jeanne Schaeverbeke; two s. two d.; ed Univ. of Ghent; public prosecutor 1957; joined diplomatic service 1961; served in the Netherlands 1963, UK 1969, Portugal 1975, Italy 1979; Dir Cabinet of Minister of Foreign Affairs 1980–88; Amb. to Germany 1988–96; many Belgian and foreign distinctions. *Leisure interests:* reading, swimming, modern painting.

VANDER ZALM, William N.; Canadian politician and business executive; b. 29 May 1934, Noordwykerhout, Netherlands; s. of Wilhelmus Nicholaas van der Zalm and Agatha C. Warmerdam; m. Lillian B. Mihalick 1956; two s. two d.; ed Phillip Sheffield High School, Abbotsford, BC, Canada; emigrated to Canada 1947, became Canadian citizen; purchased Art Knapp Nurseries Ltd, became Co. Pres. 1956; elected to Surrey Municipal Council as Alderman 1965, as Mayor 1969–; elected to Prov. Legis. for Social Credit Party, Minister of Human Resources 1975; Minister of Municipal Affairs and Minister responsible for Urban Transit Authority (now BC Transit) 1978; Minister of Educ. and Minister responsible for BC Transit 1982; est. Fantasy Garden World, major tourist attraction in Richmond 1983; Leader BC Social Credit Party 1986–; Premier of BC 1986–91; Pres. Van's Int. Projects Inc. 1991–, Mitsch Nursery Inc., Oregon, USA 1994–; Leader Reform BC Party 1996–2001; Chair. Water on Net Corpn Inc. 1998–, Chair. Ventures in Paradise Inc. 1999–; Hon. LLD (Univ. of the North, BC) 2004. *Publication:* Northwest's Gardener's Almanac. *Leisure interests:* fishing, swimming. *Address:* 3553 Arthur Drive, Ladner, BC V4K 3N2, Canada. *Telephone:* (604) 946-1774. *Fax:* (604) 946-1981. *E-mail:* vans@lilacking.com (office); billvanderzalm@dccnet.com (home). *Website:* www.lilacking.com (office).

VANDERHAEGHE, Guy Clarence, OC, BA, MA, BEd, FRSC; Canadian writer and playwright; b. 5 April 1951, Esterhazy, SK; s. of Clarence Earl Vanderhaeghe and Alma Beth Allen; m. Margaret Nagel 1972; ed Univ. of Saskatchewan, Univ. of Regina; St Thomas More Scholar, St Thomas More College, Univ. of Saskatchewan 1993–; Saskatchewan Order of Merit 2004; Hon. DLitt (Saskatchewan) 1997; Canadian Authors' Asscn Award for Drama 1996, Saskatchewan Book Award 1996. *Publications:* novels: Man Descending (Gov. Gen. Literary Award for Fiction 1982, Geoffrey Faber Memorial Prize 1987) 1982, The Trouble With Heroes 1983, My Present Age 1984, Homesick (City of Toronto Book Award 1990) 1989, Things As They Are? 1992, The Englishman's Boy (Gov. Gen. Literary Award for Fiction) 1996, The Last Crossing 2004; plays: I Had a Job I Liked, Once (Canadian Authors' Asscn Award for Drama 1993) 1991, Dancock's Dance 1995. *Address:* c/o Department of English, St Thomas More College, University of Saskatchewan, 320 Arts Tower, 9 Campus Drive, Saskatoon, SK S7N 5A5, Canada (office). *Telephone:* (306) 966-5486 (office). *Fax:* (306) 966-5951 (office). *E-mail:* english@usask.ca (office). *Website:* www.usask.ca/english (office).

VANDERHOEF, Larry N., BS, MS, PhD; American biochemist and university administrator; *Chancellor, University of California, Davis;* b. 1941, Minn.; m. Rosalie Slifka Vanderhoef, two c.; ed Univ. of Wis., Purdue Univ.; Asst Prof. of Biology, Univ. of Ill. 1970–77, Prof. and Head of Dept 1977–80; Provost Univ. of Md, College Park 1980–84; Exec. Vice-Chancellor Univ. of Calif., Davis 1984–94, Provost 1991–94, Chancellor 1994–; Dr hc (Purdue) 2000, (Inje Univ., Korea) 2002; Distinguished Community Service Award, Anti-Defamation League 1999, Outstanding Contribution Award, Arts and Business Council of Sacramento 2004, Sacramentan of the Year 2005. *Address:* Fifth Floor, Mark Hall, University of California, Davis, One Shields Avenue, Davis, CA 95616, USA (office). *Telephone:* (530) 752-2065 (office). *Fax:* (530) 752-2400 (office). *E-mail:* lnvanderhoef@ucdavis.edu (office). *Website:* chancellor.ucdavis.edu (office).

VANDEVELDE, Luc; Belgian business executive; *Managing Director, Change Capital Partners;* b. 1951; joined Kraft Gen. Foods Ltd 1971, later apptd CEO Kraft Jacobs Suchard France and Italy –1995, Pres., COO 1995–99, Chair., CEO 1999–2000; participated in merger of Promodès and Carrefour 1999 (apptd Exec. Vice-Chair. new group); Exec. Chair. Marks & Spencer PLC 2000–04, CEO 2000–02; Founder and Exec. Chair. Change Capital Pnrs (pvt. equity firm) 2003–04, Man. Dir 2004–; mem. Bd of Dirs Carrefour SA 2004–07, Chair. 2005–07; fmr mem. Bd of Dirs Vodafone. *Address:* Change Capital Partners, 2nd Floor, College House, 272 Kings Road, London, SW3 5AW, England (office). *Telephone:* (20) 7808-9110 (office). *Fax:* (20) 7808-9111 (office). *E-mail:* lvandevelde@changecapitalpartners.com (office). *Website:* www.changecapitalpartners.com (office).

VANGELIS; Greek composer, musician (keyboards) and conductor; b. (Evangelos Papathanassiou), 29 March 1943, Volos; ed Acad. of Fine Arts, Athens and private tuition with Aristotelis Coudourof; began performing own compositions aged six; moved to Paris in late 1960s; composed and recorded symphonic poem Faire que ton rêve soit plus long que la nuit; returned to Greece, after period in London 1989; formed band Formynx in Greece 1960s; mem., Aphrodite's Child (with Demis Roussos) 1966–71; composer 1972–, in Paris, France, then established Nemo recording studio, London 1974; partnership with Jon Anderson as Jon & Vangelis 1980–84. *Composition for film:* O Adelfos mou o trohonomos 1963, To prosopo tis medusas 1966, 5000 psemata 1966, Sex Power 1970, scores for French wildlife films 1972, Salut, Jerusalem 1972, L'Apocalypse des animaux 1972, Amore 1973, Le Cantique des créatures: Georges Mathieu ou La fureur d'être 1974, Le Cantique des créatures: Georges Braque ou Le temps différent 1975, Ignacio 1975, Ace Up My Sleeve 1976, La Fête sauvage 1976, Prkosna delta 1980, Die Todesgöttin des Liebescamps 1981, Chariots of Fire (Acad. Award for Best Original Score 1982) 1981, Missing 1982, Le Cantique des créature: Pablo Picasso pintor 1982, Blade Runner 1982, Nankyoku monogatari 1983, Wonders of Life 1983, The Bounty 1984, Sauvage et beau 1984, Nosferatu a Venezia 1988, Le Dîner des bustes 1988, Russicum - I giorni del diavolo 1989, Francesco 1989, Terminator II 1990, La Peste 1992, Bitter Moon 1992, 1492: Conquest of Paradise 1992, De Nuremberg à Nuremberg 1994, Rangeela 1995, Kavafis 1996, I Hope 2001, Alexander 2004. *Composition for television:* L'Opera sauvage (series) 1977, Cosmos (series, BBC1) 1980. *Recordings:* albums: with Aphrodite's Child: Aphrodite's Child 1968, Rain & Tears 1968, End Of The World 1969, It's Five O'Clock 1970, 666 1972; solo: Terra, Dragon 1971, L'Apocalypse des animaux 1972, Earth 1973, Heaven and Hell 1975, Albedo 0.39 1976, The Vangelis Radio Special 1976, Spiral 1977, Beauborg 1978, Hypothesis 1978, China 1979, Odes 1979, See You Later 1980, To The Unknown Man 1981, Soil Festivities 1984, Invisible Connections 1985, Magic Moments 1985, Mask 1985, Direct 1988, The City 1990, Themes 1989, Voices 1995, El Greco 1995, Oceanic 1996, Reprise 1990–1999 2000, Mythodea: Music for the NASA Mission – 2001 Mars Odyssey 2001; as Jon & Vangelis: Short Stories 1980, The Friends of Mr Cairo 1981, Private Collection 1983, Page of Life 1991. *Address:* c/o Sony Classical, 550 Madison Avenue, New York, NY 10022-3211, USA. *Website:* www.vangelisworld.com.

VANHANEN, Matti Taneli, MScS; Finnish politician; *Prime Minister;* b. 4 Nov. 1955, Jyväskylä; two c.; journalist, Kehäsanomat (local newspaper) 1985–88, Ed.-in-Chief 1988–91; mem. Centre Party 1976–, mem. Bd and Chair. Youth League 1980–83, Vice-Chair. Party 2000–2003, Chair. 2003–; mem. Espoo City Council 1981–84; mem. Bd Helskinki Metropolitan Area Council YTV 1983–84; mem. Nurmijärvi Municipal Council 1989–; mem. Bd Uusimaa Regional Council 1997–2000; mem. Parl. 1991–; Vice-Chair. Centre Party Parl. Group 1994–2001, Parl. Environment Cttee 1991–95; Chair. Parl. Grand Cttee 2000–01; Rep. of Parl. to European Convention on the Future of the EU 2002–03; Minister of Defence April–June 2003; Prime Minister 2003–; Vice-Chair. Housing Foundation for the Young 1981–97, Chair. 1998–2003; Chair. State Youth Council 1987–90; Vice-Chair. Housing Council 1991–2003; Chair. Union for Rural Educ. 1998–2003; Vice-Chair. Pro Medi-Heli Asscn 1995–2003; mem. Supervisory Bd Neste/Fortum 1991–2003, Helsingin Osuuskauppa (Cooperative) 2002–03. *Address:* Prime Minister's Office, Snellmaninkatu 1A, 00023 Government, Finland (office). *Telephone:* (9) 16001 (office). *Fax:* (9) 16022225 (office). *E-mail:* kirjaamo@vnk.fi (office). *Website:* www.government.fi (office).

VANIN, Mikhail Valentinovich; Russian diplomatist and fmr civil servant; *Ambassador to Slovenia;* b. 1960, Moscow Region; ed Moscow State Univ., Acad. of State Service; Insp., then Head of Div. against Contraband, Deputy Head Customs, Sheremetyevo Airport 1982–91; Chief Counsellor Div. of Contracts and Legal Problems, Ministry of Foreign Affairs 1991–92; Head Div. for Fight Against Contraband and Violation of Customs Law, State Customs Cttee 1992–98, Vice-Chair. 1998, Chair. Customs Inspection 1999, Chair. State Customs Cttee May 1999–2004; Rep. Russian Customs Service, Kyrgyzstan 1998–99; Amb. to Slovenia 2004–. *Address:* Embassy of Russia, Tomšičeva 9, 1000 Ljubljana, Slovenia (office). *Telephone:* (1) 4256875 (office). *Fax:* (1) 4256878 (office). *E-mail:* ambrus.slo@siol.net (office). *Website:* www .rus-slo.mid.ru (office).

VANNI, Carla, LLD; Italian journalist; *Editor-in-Chief, Grazia Magazine;* b. 18 Feb. 1936, Leghorn (Livorno); m. Vincenzo Nisivoccia; two c.; ed Univ. of Milan; joined Mondadori Publrs, working on fashion desk of Grazia magazine 1959, Head fashion desk 1964, Jt Ed.-in-Chief 1974, Ed.-in-Chief 1978–, responsible for launch of Marie Claire magazine in Italy 1987, Publishing Dir Marie Claire until 2002 and Cento Cose-Energy 1987–99, Donna Moderna 1995–, Flair 2003–, Easy Shop 2004–; has created several new supplements of Grazia: Grazia Bricolage, Grazia Blu and Grazia Int., Grazia Accessori and Grazia Uomo, Grazia Profumi e Balocchi and introduced coverage of social problems; also Ed.-in-Chief Grazia Casa; Head, Grazia Int. Network 2005–; mem. juries of several nat. and int. literary awards and many beauty competitions; Montenapoleone d'Oro (Best Journalist) 1970, The Oner (Journalist of the Year) 1987, Gullace (for coverage of women's interest issues) 1995, Letterario Castiglioncello costa degli Etruschi Award 2001, Milan Fashion Award 2003, Fondazione Marisa Bellisario Award 2003, Forte dei Marmi 'Dietro la bellezza' Award 2003, Premio Milano per la Moda 2003, Premio 'Dietro la bellezza', Ponte dei Nariù 2003, Premio Narisa Bellsario 2003. *Address:* Grazia, Arnoldi Mondadori Editore, Via Arnoldo Mondadori 1, 20090 Segrate, Milan, Italy (office). *Telephone:* (02) 754212390 (office). *Fax:* (02) 75422515 (office). *E-mail:* vanni@mondadori.it (office).

VANNI D'ARCHIRAFI, Raniero; Italian fmr diplomatist and business executive; entered diplomatic service 1956; attached to office of Italy's Perm. Rep. to EC, Brussels 1961–66; with Ministry of Foreign Affairs 1966–73; First Counsellor, Madrid 1973; Minister Plenipotentiary 1980; Prin. Pvt. Sec. to Minister of Foreign Affairs 1980; Amb. to Spain 1984–87, 1995–99, to Germany 1987–90; Dir-Gen. for Econ. Affairs 1990, for Political Affairs 1991; mem. Comm. for Institutional Questions, The Internal Market, Financial Services, Enterprise Policy, Small and Medium-sized Enterprises, Trade Services, Crafts and Tourism, EC 1993–95; Pres. RCS Iberica 2002; Dir Telepizza, Finmeccanica. *Address:* c/o Ministry of Foreign Affairs, Piazzale della Farnesina 1, 00194 Rome, Italy (office).

VANRIET, Jan; Belgian artist; b. 21 Feb. 1948, Antwerp; m. Simone Lenaerts 1971; two s. one d.; ed Royal Acad. of Fine Arts, Antwerp; Dir Antwerp Acad. of Fine Arts, Hoboken 1980–2000; works in several museums in Europe, USA and Asia; Special Prize, Art Festival, Seoul 1990, Prize, Van Acker Foundation 2001. *Achievements:* monumental works for KCB-Bank, Brussels, Metro, Brussels, Roularta, Bourla-Theatre Antwerp, UFSIA Univ. *Publications:* poetry: Staat van Beleg 1982, Geen Hond die Brood Lust 1984, Café Aurora 2000, De Reiziger is Blind 2001, Transport 2002. *Address:* Louizastraat 22, 2000 Antwerp 1, Belgium. *Telephone:* (3) 232-47-76; (3) 248-07-03. *Fax:* (3) 226-13-50. *E-mail:* janvanriet@janvanriet.net. *Website:* www .janvanriet.net.

VARADHAN, Srinivasa S.R., MA, PhD, FRS, FAAS; American mathematician and academic; *Professor, Department of Mathematics, Courant Institute of Mathematical Sciences, New York University;* b. 2 Jan. 1940, Chennai, India; s. of S. V. Rangaiyengar and S. R. Janaki; m. Vasundara Narayanan; two s.; ed Madras Univ., Indian Statistical Inst., Courant Inst., New York Univ.; Visiting Member, Courant Inst., New York Univ. 1963–66, Asst Prof. 1966–68, Assoc. Prof. 1968–72, Dir 1980–84, 1992–94, Prof. of Math. 1972–; Assoc. Fellow, Third World Acad. of Sciences 1988; mem. NAS; Abel Prize 2007. *Publications:* Multi-dimensional Diffusion Processes 1979, On Diffusion Problems and Partial Differentiation Equations 1980; Large Deviations and Applications 1984. *Leisure interests:* squash, bridge, travel. *Address:* Courant Institute, New York University, 251 Mercer Street, New York, NY 10012, USA (office). *Telephone:* (212) 998-3334 (office). *Fax:* (212) 995-4121 (home). *E-mail:* varadhan@cims.nyu.edu (office). *Website:* www.math.nyu.edu (office).

VARDA, Agnès; French film writer, film director and photographer; b. 30 May 1928, Ixelles, Belgium; d. of Eugène Jean Varda and Christiane Pasquet; m. Jacques Demy 1962 (died 1990); one s. one d.; ed Sète, Hérault, Univ. of the Sorbonne, Paris, Ecole du Louvre, Paris; Official Photographer, Avignon Festival/Théâtre Nat. Populaire 1951–61; film-maker 1954–; plastician artist, video and installation artist 2003–; Commdr des Arts et des Lettres; Officier, Légion d'honneur, Grand Officier, Ordre nat. du Mérite 2007; César d'honneur 2001. *Full-length films:* La Pointe Courte 1954, Cleo de 5 à 7 (Prix Méliès 1962) 1961, Salut les Cubains (Bronze Lion, Venice Festival 1964) 1962, Le Bonheur (Prix Louis Delluc 1965, David Selznick Award 1965, Silver Bear, Berlin Festival 1965) 1964, Les Créatures 1965, Black Panthers (First Prize, Oberhausen) 1968, Lions Love (...and Lies) (Popular Univs Jury 1970) 1969, Nausicaa 1970, Daguerreotypes 1975, L'une chante l'autre pas (Grand Prix, Taormina, Sicily 1977) 1976, Mur Murs (Grand Prix, Firenze 1981) 1980, Documenteur (An Emotion Picture) 1981, Ulysse (César Award 1984) 1983, 7P. cuis. sdb... 1984, Sans toit ni loi (Vagabond) (Golden Lion, Best Film Venice Film Festival 1985, Prix Méliès 1985, LA Critics Best Foreign Film 1985) 1985, Jane B par Agnés V 1987, Kung Fu Master 1987, Jacquot de Nantes 1990, Les Demoiselles ont eu 25 ans 1992, L'Univers de Jacques Demy 1993, Les Cent et Une nuits 1994, Les Glaneurs et La Glaneuse 2000 (Acad. of European Cinema Award, Prix du Meilleur Film Française), Deux Ans après 2002, Le Lion Volatil 2003, Ydessa, the Bears and etc... 2004, Quelques Veuves de Noirmoutier 2006, Les Plages d'Agnès 2008. *Short-length films:* O saisons, O châteaux 1957, L'opéra-Mouffe 1958, Du côté de la côte 1958, Salut les cubains 1963, Elsa la rose 1965, Uncle Yanco 1967, Black Panthers 1968, Réponse de femmes 1975, Plaisir d'amour en Iran 1975, Ulysse 1982, Les dites Cariatides 1984, T'as de beaux escaliers... tu sais 1986, Le lion volatil 2003. *Video installations:* Patatutopia 2003, L'Ile et elle 2006, Homage aux Justes de France 2007. *Publication:* Varda par Agnès 1994, L'Ile et Elle 2006. *Address:* c/o Ciné-Tamaris, 86–88 rue Daguerre, 75014 Paris, France. *Telephone:* 1-43-22-66-00 (office). *Fax:* 1-43-21-75-00 (office). *E-mail:* cine-tamaris@wanadoo.fr (office). *Website:* www.cine-tamaris.com (office).

VARDANIAN, Ruben, MA; Russian business executive; *Chairman and CEO, Troika Dialog;* b. Armenia; ed Faculty of Econs, Moscow State Univ.; intern Merrill Lynch, New York 1992; Co-founder Troika Dialog (investment bank) 1991, COO 1992–96, Pres. 1996–, CEO 1997–, also Chair. Bd of Dirs Troika Dialog Group 2001–, CEO Rosgosstrakh (insurance co. acquired by Troika) 2002–04, Chair. 2004–05; mem. Russian Union of Industrialists and Entrepreneurs, Head Cttee on Corp. Governance, Arbitrator, Corp. Ethics Cttee; mem. Nat. Council for Corp. Governance; Chair. Bd of Dirs Sukhoi Civil Aircraft 2005–; mem. Bd of Dirs Russian Corp. Competitiveness Council, Russian Trading System (RTS), Nat. Asscn of Stock Market Participants (NAUFOR), OAO NOVATEK 2005–, AK Bars Bank 2006–; mem. Supervisory Bd Higher School of Corp. Governance, Russian Govt Acad. of Nat. Econs; Trustee Moscow State Univ.; Businessman of the Year, US Chamber of Commerce 1999, One of the World's 25 Leaders of the New Generation, Fortune magazine 2001, Russian National Entrepreneur Of The Year 2004. *Address:* Troika Dialog, Romanov Center, 4, Romanov Pereulok, 125009 Moscow, Russian Federation (office). *Telephone:* (495) 258-0500 (office). *Fax:* (495) 258-0547 (office). *E-mail:* webmaster@troika.ru (office). *Website:* www .troika.ru (office).

VAREBERG, Terje, MBA; Norwegian business executive; *Chairman, Norsk Hydro ASA;* b. 1948; ed Norwegian School of Econs and Business Admin; worked for Ministry of Trade and Industry and Ministry of Petroleum –1979; joined Statoil 1979, with Refining and Marketing Div. 1979–83, Exec. Vice-Pres. and mem. Corp. Man. 1989–99, currently Chair. Norsk Hydro ASA (acquired by Statoil); Man. Dir Agro Fellesslakteri 1983–89; mem. Bd of Dirs and Man. Dir Sparebank 1 SR-Bank 1999–; has held several bd positions in Norwegian industry; Chair. Norwegian Savings Bank Asscn. *Address:* Norsk Hydro ASA, Drammensveien 264, 0283 Oslo, Norway (office). *Telephone:* 22-53-81-00 (office). *Fax:* 22-53-27-25 (office). *E-mail:* info@hydro.com (office). *Website:* www.hydro.com (office).

VARFIS, Grigorios; Greek politician; b. 1927, Athens; ed Univs of Athens and Paris; journalist in Paris, 1952–58; on staff of OECD 1953–62; Econ. Adviser to Perm. Greek Del. to the EEC, Brussels 1963–74; apptd Gen. Dir, Co-ordination Ministry, with jurisdiction over Directorate of Relations with the European Communities 1974, resgnd Jan. 1977; contributed to econ. programme of Panhellenic Socialist Movt (PASOK) 1979–; Co-ordination Under-Sec. and Under-Sec. at Foreign Affairs Ministry, responsible for EEC Affairs 1981–83; mem. European Parl. 1984; mem. Comm. of the European Communities (responsible for Regional Policy and Relations with European Parl.) 1985–86, for Structural Funds and Consumer Protection 1986–89. *Address:* Spefsipou 35, 10676 Athens, Greece.

VARGA, Imre; Hungarian sculptor; b. 1 Nov. 1923, Budapest; s. of Mátyás Varga and Margit Csepeli; m. Ildikó Szabó 1944; two s.; ed Budapest Coll. of Visual Arts; Pres. FÉSZEK Artists Club; mem. American Acad. of Arts and

Sciences, Acad. Européenne des Arts et des Sciences, Paris; Hon. Citizen of Budapest 2004; Order of the Flag 1983, Commdr, Ordre des Arts et Lettres (France), Cavaliere dell'Ordine al Merito (Italy), Verdienstkreuz, First Class (Germany) 2004, Officer de l'Ordre Leopold (Belgium) 2004; Munkácsy Prize 1969, Kossuth Prize 1973, Merited Artist 1975, Eminent Artist 1980, Herder Prize 1981. *Works:* Prometheus 1965 and The Professor 1969 in Middelheim, Belgium, Madách Memorial 1968, Radnóti Memorial 1970, Partisans Memorial 1971, Lenin Memorial, Heroes Monument, Oslo 1974, plurifigural St Stephen composition, St Peter's Basilica, Vatican 1980, Bartók Memorial, Paris 1983, Béla Kun Memorial, Budapest 1986, Raoul Wallenberg Memorial 1987; perm. collection of work in Budapest; smaller sculptures: Erőlltetett menet (Forced March), A la Recherche, Baudelaire kedvese (Baudelaire's Sweetheart), Páholy (Theatre box), statue of St Stephen in Aachen Cathedral, Germany 1993, Bartók Memorial, Carrefour de l'Europe Square, Brussels 1995, Ferenc Rákóczi II, commemorative statue, Bad Kissingen, Germany 1992, Memorial to Konrad Adenauer and Charles de Gaulle, Rhöndorf 2004, Memorial to Béla Bartók, London 2004. *Address:* 1126 Budapest XII, Barthautca 1, Hungary. *Telephone:* (1) 2500-274 (Museum) (office); (1) 3951-983 (home). *Fax:* (1) 3951-983 (home).

VARGA, Mihály; Hungarian economist and politician; b. 1965, Karcag; m.; three c.; ed Budapest Univ. of Econ. Sciences; econ. adviser, Water Man. Inst. of East Hungary, Szolnok 1989–90; mem. FIDESZ (Alliance of Young Democrats) 1988, Vice-Pres. 1994, Deputy Head of Parl. Faction 1995–98; mem. Parl. 1990, mem. Parl. Cttee of State Budget and Finances 1990–98, of State Audit; Political State Sec., Ministry of Finance 1998–2001, Minister of Finance 2001–02; mem. Inter-parl. Union 1995, Chair. Parl. Advisory Cttee for Debtors and Banking Consolidation 1995–97; Visiting Prof., Szolnok Business School 1995–97; elder presbyter Reformed Church Community of Karcag and Kt of St John. *Address:* c/o Pénzügyminisztérium, József nádor tér 2/4, 1051 Budapest, Hungary (office).

VARGAS DÍAZ, Marco; Costa Rican politician; *Minister of Economy, Industry and Commerce;* Minister of Inter-Institutional Co-ordination 2006–07, of Agric. and Livestock 2007–08, of Economy, Industry and Commerce 2008–. *Address:* Ministry of Economy, Industry and Commerce, Del Restaurante Princesa Marina 100 m sur, 100 m oeste y 50 m norte, Barrio La Guaria, Moravia, San José, Costa Rica (office). *Telephone:* 2240-5222 (office). *Fax:* 2297-1741 (office). *E-mail:* informacion@meic.go.cr (office). *Website:* www.meic.go.cr (office).

VARGAS LLOSA, (Jorge) Mario Pedro, PhD; Peruvian/Spanish writer and journalist; b. 28 March 1936, Arequipa, Peru; s. of Ernesto Vargas Maldonado and Dora Llosa de Vargas; m. 1st Julia Urquidi 1955 (divorced 1964); m. 2nd Patricia Llosa Urquidi 1965; two s. one d.; ed Colegio La Salle, Lima, Peru, Leoncio Prado Military Acad., Lima, Colegio Nacional San Miguel, Piura, Universidad Nacional Mayor de San Marcos, Lima and Universidad Complutense de Madrid, Spain; journalist on local newspapers, Piura, Peru 1951, for magazines Turismo and Cultura Peruana and for Sunday supplement of El Comercio 1955; News Ed. Radio Panamericana, Lima 1955; Spanish teacher, Berlitz School 1959; journalist, Agence-France Presse 1959; broadcaster, Latin American services of Radiodiffusion Télévision Française 1959; Lecturer in Latin American Literature, Queen Mary Coll., Univ. of London, UK 1967, Prof. King's Coll. 1969; trans. UNESCO 1967; Visiting Prof., Washington State Univ., USA 1968, Univ. de Puerto Rico 1969, Columbia Univ., USA 1975; Prof., Univ. of Cambridge, UK 1977, Harvard Univ., USA 1992, Princeton Univ., USA 1993, Georgetown Univ., USA 1994, 1999; Writer-in-Residence, Woodrow Wilson Int. Center for Scholars, Smithsonian Inst., Washington, DC, USA 1980; Prof. and Chair., Dept of Ibero-American Literature and Culture, Georgetown Univ., Washington, DC 2001–, Distinguished Writer-in-Residence 2003–; Mentor, Literature Program of the Rolex Mentor and Protégé Arts Initative, Second Cycle 2004–05; Weidenfeld Visiting Prof. of European Comparative Literature, St Anne's Coll., Oxford, UK 2004; f. Movimiento Libertad political party and co-f. Frente Democrático (FREDEMO) coalition 1988; cand. for Pres. of Peru 1990; Pres. Jury, Iberoamerican Film Festival, Huelva, Spain 1995, San Sebastian Int. Film Festival 2004; mem. Jury, ECHO Television and Radio Awards 1998, Miguel de Cervantes Prize 1998; Pres. PEN Club Int. 1976–79; mem. Acad. Peruana de la Lengua 1975, Real Acad. Española 1994 (incorporation 1996), Int. Acad. of Humanism 1996, Cervantes Inst. Foundation 1998; Neil Gunn Int. Fellow, Scottish Arts Council 1986; Fellow, Wissenschaftskolleg, Berlin 1991–92, Deutscher Akademischer Austauschdienst, Berlin 1997–98; Hon. Fellow, Hebrew Univ., Israel 1976, Modern Language Asscn of America 1986, American Acad. and Inst. of Arts and Letters 1986; Hon. Prof., Universidad de Ciencias Aplicadas, Lima 2001; Chevalier, Légion d'honneur, Commdr Ordre des Arts et des Lettres 1993, Medal Orden El Sol del Perú (Great Cross of Diamonds) 2001, Medalla de Honor en el Grado de Gran Cruz, Peru 2003; Hon. DHumLitt (Connecticut Coll., USA) 1991; Hon. DLitt (Warwick) 2004; Dr hc (Florida Int. Univ. of Miami) 1990, (Boston) 1992, (Geneva) 1992, (Dowling College (USA) 1993, (Universidad Francisco Marroquin (Guatemala) 1993, (Georgetown) 1994, (Yale) 1994, (Rennes II) 1994, (Murcia) 1995, (Valladolid) 1995, (Lima) 1997, (Universidad Nacional de San Agustin, Peru) 1997, (Ben Gurion) 1998, (Univ. Coll. London) 1998, (Harvard) 1999, (Universidad Nacional Mayor de San Marcos, Lima) 2001, (Rome Tor Vergata) 2001, (Pau) 2001, (Universidad Nacional San Antonio Abad del Cusco) 2002, (Univ. of French Polynesia) 2002, (La Trobe Univ., Melbourne) 2002, (Skidmore Coll., USA) 2002, (Universidad Nacional de Piura) 2002, (Universidad Nacional Pedro Ruiz Gallo) 2002, (Catholic Univ. of Louvain) 2003, (Universidad Nacional de Ingenieria, Lima) 2003, (Oxford) 2003, (Universidad Pedagogica Nacional Francisco Morazan, Tegucigalpa, Honduras) 2003, (Universidad Católica Santa María, Arequipa) 2004; Diploma de Honor, Universidad Nacional Mayor de San Marcos 2000; Crítica Española Prize 1966, Premio de la Crítica, Argentina 1981, Ritz Paris Hemingway Prize 1985, Príncipe de Asturias Prize, Spain 1986, Castiglione de Sicilia Prize, Italy 1990, Miguel de Cervantes Prize, Spain 1994, Jerusalem Prize, Israel 1995, Congressional Medal of Honour, Peru 1982, T.S. Eliot Prize, Ingersoll Foundation of The Rockford Institute, USA 1991, Golden Palm Award, INTAR Hispanic American Arts Center, New York 1992, Miguel de Cervantes Prize, Ministry of Culture (Spain) 1994, Jerusalem Prize 1995, Peace Prize, German Publishers, Frankfurt Book Fair 1996, Pluma de Oro Award, Spain 1997, Medal and Diploma of Honour, Univ. Católica de Santa María, Arequipa, Peru 1997, Medal of the Univ. of Calif. 1999, Jorge Isaacs Award, Int. Festival of Art, Cali, Colombia 1999, Medal "Patrimonio Cultural de la Humanidad", Municipalidad de Arequipa 2000, Certificate of Recognition, Colegio de Abogados 2001, Crystal Award, World Econ. Forum, Davos, Switzerland 2001, Americas Award, Americas Foundation 2001, Son Latinos Festival Prize, Tenerife, Spain 2001, Caonabo de Oro Prize, Dominican Asscn of Journalsits and Writers, 2002, Golden Medal, City of Genoa (Italy) 2002, PEN Nabokov Award 2002, Int. Prize of Letters, Cristobal Gabarron Foundation 2002, Premio Ateneo Americano, on Xth Anniversary of Casa de America 2002, Medal of Honour, City of Trujillo, Peru 2003, Roger-Caillois PEN Club Prize 2003, Budapest Prize 2003, Presidential Medal of Hofstra Univ., New York 2003, Grinzane Cavour Prize: "A Life for Literature International Prize", Turin 2004, Konex Foundation Prize 2004, Medal of the Centenary of Pablo Neruda, Govt of Chile 2004, Medal of Honor of Peruvian Culture, Nat. Inst. of Culture 2004. *Films:* Co-Dir of film version of his novel Pantaleón y las visitadoras. *Television:* Dir La torre de Babel 1981. *Publications:* novels: La cuidad y los perros (Biblioteca Breve Prize) 1963, La casa verde (Premio Nacional de Novela, Peru 1967) 1966, Conversación en la catedral 1969, Pantaleón y las visitadoras 1973, La tía Julia y el escribidor (ILLA Prize, Italy 1982) 1977, La guerra del fin del mundo (Pablo Iglesias Literature Prize 1982) 1981, Historia de Mayta 1984, ¿Quién mató a Palomino Molero? 1986, El hablador 1987, Elogio de la madrastra 1988, Lituma en los Andes (Planeta Prize, Spain 1993, Archbishop Juan de San Clemente de Santiago de Compostella Literary Prize, Spain 1994, Int. Literary Prize, Chianti Ruffino Antico Fattore, Italy 1995) 1993, Los cuadernos de Don Rigoberto 1997, La fiesta del Chivo (first Book of the Year Prize, Union of Booksellers of Spain 2001, Readers of Crisol Libraries Prize, Spain 2001) 2000, El paraíso en la otra esquina (chosen for inclusion in "Books to Remember 2003" by cttee of librarians from The New York Public Library 2004) 2003, Travesuras de la niña mala 2006; short stories: El desafío (Revue Française Prize) 1957, Los jefes (Leopoldo Alas Prize) 1959, Los cachorros 1967; anthologies: Contra viento y marea Vol. I (1962–72) 1986, Vol. II (1972–83) 1986, Vol. III (1983–90) 1990, Desafíos a la libertad 1994, Making Waves (Nat. Book Critics' Circle Award, New York 1998) 1996; plays: La huída del Inca 1952, La señorita de Tacna 1981, Kathie y el hipopótamo 1983, La Chunga 1986, El loco de los balcones 1993, Ojos bonitos, cuadros feos 1994, La verdad de las mentiras (II Bartolome March Prize for revised edn 2002) 1990; non-fiction: El pez en el agua (autobiog.) 1993, La orgía perpetua (criticism) 1975, La utopía arcaica 1978, Cartas a un joven novelista (literary essay) 1997, Nationalismus als neue Bedrohung (in German) 2000, El lenguaje de la pasión (selection of articles) 2001, L'Herne. Mario Vargas Llosa (essays etc.) 2003, Diario de Irak (essays) 2003, La tentación de lo imposible (essay on Les Miserables de Victor Hugo) 2004, Mario Vargas Llosa. Obras Completas, Vol. I Narraciones y novelas (1959–1967) and Vol. II, Novelas (1969–1977) 2004, Un demi-siècle avec Borges (interview and essays on Borges written between 1964 and 1999, in French) 2004; contrib. to El País (series Piedra de Toque), Letras Libres, Mexico (series Extemporaneos). *Address:* Las Magnolias 295, 6° Piso, Barranco, Lima 4, Peru. *Telephone:* (1) 477-3868. *Fax:* (1) 477-3518.

VARIN, Philippe; French steel industry executive; *CEO, Corus Group PLC;* b. 1952; m.; four c.; ed Ecole Polytechnique and Ecole des Mines, Paris; joined Pechiney Group 1978, various positions including researcher, Head of Strategic Studies, Aluminium Br., Vice-Pres. Eng and Research, Project Dir for construction of Dunkirk aluminium smelter 1989–90, Man.-Dir Aluminium Dunkirk 1990–92, Group Financial Controller, Paris and Chicago, 1993–94, Vice-Pres. Rhenlau Div. 1995–99, apptd Sr Exec. Vice-Pres. Aluminium Sector and mem. Exec. Cttee Pechiney Group 1999; CEO Corus Group PLC, London, UK 2003–. *Leisure interests include:* tennis, sailing, clarinet. *Address:* Corus Group PLC, 30 Millbank, London, SW1P 4WY, England (office). *Telephone:* (20) 7717-4444 (office). *Fax:* (20) 7717-4455 (office). *E-mail:* feedback@corusgroup.com (office). *Website:* www.corusgroup.com (office).

VÁRKONYI, Ágnes R., PhD; Hungarian historian and academic; *Professor Emerita, Department of Medieval and Early Modern Hungarian History, Eötvös Lóránd University of Budapest;* b. 9 Feb. 1928, Salgótarján, Nógrád Co.; d. of József Várkonyi and Mária Bérczy; m. Kálmán Ruttkay; two d.; ed Eötvös Lóránd Univ. of Budapest; Asst Prof. Inst. for Historical Research of Hungarian Acad. of Sciences 1951–83; Prof., Head of Dept of Medieval and Early Modern Hungarian History in Eötvös Lóránd Univ. of Budapest 1983–98, Prof. Emer. 1998–; Corresp. Fellow, Royal Historical Soc.; mem. Hungarian-Turkish Friendship Asscn; several awards including Széchenyi Prize. *Publications:* 31 books, including Europica varietas, Hungarica varietas, 1526–1762: Selected Studies 2000; numerous articles. *Leisure interests:* gardening, travelling. *Address:* c/o Hungarian-Turkish Friendship Association (Macar-Turk Dostluk Dernegi), 1062 Budapest, Bajza u. 54 (office); 1021 Budapest, Széher út 24, Hungary (home). *Telephone:* (1) 267-0966 (office); (1) 200-9093 (home). *Fax:* (1) 266-5699 (office). *E-mail:* h7621var@ella.hu (office).

VARKULEVICIUS, Rimas; Lithuanian administrator and engineer; *Director-General, Association of Lithuanian Chambers of Commerce, Industry and Crafts;* b. 10 March 1956, Vilnius; m. Vitalija Zukelyte 1980; one s.; ed

Kaunas Tech. Univ., Moscow Food Industry Tech. Univ., Georgetown Univ., USA; Chief Engineer, Tauras State Brewery 1979–83; Adviser and Chief Engineer, Food Processing Co., Erdenet, Mongolia 1983–85; Exec. Officer, Food Industry Bd of Lithuania 1986; Head of Food Industry Devt Div., Ministry of Agric. 1989–91, Dir Dept of Int. Relations 1991–95, Dir Dept of Int. Integration 1995–97; Chief Consultant, Inst. for Nat. and Int. Meat and Food Industry IFW Heidelberg GmbH 1997–98; Dir-Gen. Asscn of Lithuanian Chambers of Commerce, Industry and Crafts 1998–; has represented the Lithuanian Ministry of Agric. at numerous int. orgs and confs, adviser to the Econ. Cttee of Seimas (Parl.). *Leisure interest:* yachting. *Address:* J. Tumo Vaižganto 9/1 Apt 63A, 2001 Vilnius (office); Mindaugo 16-10, 2029 Vilnius, Lithuania (home). *Telephone:* (2) 335670 (office); (2) 332849 (home). *Fax:* (2) 235338 (office). *E-mail:* rimas.varkulevicius@chambers.lt (office); varkl@post.5ci.lt (home). *Website:* www.lithuaniachambers.lt (office); www.5ci.lt/varkl/ (home).

VARLEY, John S., MA; British banking executive; *Group Chief Executive, Barclays plc;* b. 1 April 1956; m. Carolyn Thorn Pease 1981; two c.; ed Coll. of Law, London; fmr Deputy CEO BZW Equity Div., fmr Head of BZW SE Asia; Chair. Barclays Asset Man. Div. 1995–98, CEO Retail Financial Services 1998–2000, Finance Dir 2000–04, Group Deputy Chief Exec. Barclays plc 2004, Group Chief Exec. 2004–, Exec. Dir 1998–, mem. Group Exec. Cttee 1996–; mem. Bd of Dirs Ascot Racecourse, Astra Zeneca PLC; Chair. Business Action on Homelessness; Pres. Employer's Forum on Disability; mem. Int. Advisory Panel, Monetary Authority of Singapore. *Address:* Barclays plc, One Churchill Place, Canary Wharf, London, E14 5HP, England (office). *Telephone:* (20) 7116-3000 (office). *Fax:* (20) 7116-7780 (office). *E-mail:* info@barclays.com (office). *Website:* www.barclays.com (office).

VARLOOT, Denis; French museum administrator and engineer; *Chairman, Musée des télécommunications de Pleumeur Bodou;* b. 25 Oct. 1937, Lille; s. of Jean Varloot and Madeleine (née Boutron) Varloot; m. Marie J. Kennel 1963; two s.; ed Lycées in Paris, Ecole Polytechnique and Ecole Nat. Supérieure des Télécommunications; Centre Nat. d'Etudes des Télécommunications 1962–68; with Direction Général des Télécommunications, Service des Programmes et des Etudes Economiques 1968–73, deputized for head of service 1973–75; Dir of Telecommunications, Orléans 1975–76; Head of Telecommunications Personnel 1976–81; Dir of Scientific and Tech. Information, Ministry of Educ. 1981–82; Dir Libraries, Museums and Scientific and Tech. Information, Ministry of Educ. 1982–87; Special Adviser to Pres. of France-Télécom 1987, Adviser 1992–98; Chair. and CEO Télésystemes 1988–92; Chair. Admin. Bd Palais de la découverte 1996–2003; Chair. Musée des télécommunications de Pleumeur Bodou 1994–; Chair. Asscn des musées et centres pour le développement de la culture scientifique, technique et industrielle 2001–; mem. Haut Conseil des musées de France 2003–; Chevalier des Arts et Lettres,Officier, Légion d'honneur Ordre nat. du Mérite, Ordre des Palmes Académiques. *Leisure interest:* sailing. *Address:* Musée des télécommunications de Pleumeur Bodou, 86 rue de Lournel, 75015 Paris (office); 14 rue Campagne Première, 75014 Paris, France (home). *Telephone:* 1-43-22-31-31 (home); 1-44-37-06-72 (office). *Fax:* 1-44-37-06-80 (office). *E-mail:* mustel.dv@leradome.com (office); varloot.denis@wanadoo.fr (home). *Website:* www.leradome.com (office).

VARMUS, Harold Eliot, MA, MD; American microbiologist and academic; *President and CEO, Memorial Sloan-Kettering Cancer Center;* b. 18 Dec. 1939, Oceanside, NY; s. of Frank Varmus and Beatrice (née Barasch) Varmus; m. Constance Louise Casey 1969; two s.; ed Amherst Coll., Harvard Univ., Columbia Univ.; physician, Presbyterian Hosp., New York 1966–68; Clinical Assoc., NIH, Bethesda, Md 1968–70; lecturer, Dept of Microbiology, Univ. of Calif. at San Francisco 1970–72, Asst Prof. 1972–74, Assoc. Prof. 1974–79, Prof. 1979–83, American Cancer Soc. Research Prof. 1984–93; Dir NIH 1993–99; Pres. and CEO Memorial Sloan-Kettering Cancer Center 2000–; Consultant, Chiron Corp., Emoryville, Calif.; Assoc. Ed. Cell Journal; mem. Editorial Bd Cancer Surveys; mem. American Soc. of Virology, American Soc. of Microbiology, AAAS; Calif. Acad. of Sciences Scientist of the Year 1982, Lasker Foundation Award 1982 (co-recipient), Passano Foundation Award 1983, Armand Hammer Cancer Prize 1984, Gen. Motors Alfred Sloan Award, Shubitz Cancer Prize (NAS) 1984, Nobel Prize 1989, Nat. Medal of Science 2001, Rave Award, Wired Magazine 2004. *Publications:* Molecular Biology of Tumor Viruses (ed.) 1982, 1985, Readings in Tumor Virology (ed.) 1983, The Art and Politics of Science 2009. *Address:* Memorial Sloan-Kettering Cancer Center, 1275 York Avenue, New York, NY 10065, USA (office). *Telephone:* (212) 639-7317 (office); (212) 639-7227 (office). *Fax:* (212) 717-3125 (office). *E-mail:* varmus@mskcc.org (office). *Website:* www.mskcc.org (office).

VARNEY, Sir David Robert, Kt, BSc, MBA; British telecommunications industry executive and government official; b. 11 May 1946, London; s. of Robert Varney and Winifred Varney; m. Patricia Varney; one d. one s.; ed Univs of Surrey and Manchester; fmrly with Shell, Man. Dir AB Svenska Shell, Sweden, Dir Shell Int.; CEO BG Group (fmrly British Gas) 1996–2000; Chair. mmO2 2001–2004; Exec. Chair. HM Revenue and Customs from 2004–06 (resgnd); Sr Adviser to Gordon Brown on Transformational Govt Strategy (initiative to use information tech. to overhaul UK public services) 2006–, conducted govt review of tax policy in NI 2007, conducting Varney Review of the Competitiveness of NI Dec. 2007–08; Chair. Business in the Community 2002–04. *Address:* Varney Review of the Competitiveness of Northern Ireland, Room 1/E1, HM Treasury, 1 Horse Guards Road, London, SW1A 2HQ; Riverthatch, The Abbotsbrook, Bourne End, Bucks., SL8 5QU (home). *Telephone:* (1628) 521077 (home). *E-mail:* david@varney.uk.com (home).

VARSHALOMIDZE, Levan, LLM, LLD; Georgian lawyer and government official; *Chairman, Council of Ministers of the Autonomous Republic of Adjara;* b. 17 Jan. 1972, Batumi; ed Kyiv Univ., Ukraine; Head, Bilateral Relations Office, Ministry of Foreign Affairs 1998–2000; Chair. Exec. Dept, Ministry of Justice 2000–02; Dir Law Dept, Ministry of Finance 2002; Pnr, Damenia, Varshalomidze, Nogaideli and Kavtaradze (law firm) 2002–04; Dir-Gen. Georgian Railways Ltd Jan.–May 2004; Presidential Envoy to the Autonomous Republic of Adjara May–June 2004; Chair. Council of Ministers of the Autonomous Republic of Adjara 2004–. *Publications:* numerous articles on int. law. *Address:* Office of the Chairman, Council of Ministers of the Autonomous Republic of Adjara, 6010 Batumi, Gamsakhurdia 10, Georgia (office). *Telephone:* (222) 72-006 (office). *Fax:* (222) 77-300 (office). *E-mail:* lvarshalomidze@adjara.gov.ge (office). *Website:* www.adjara.gov.ge (office).

VARSHAVSKY, Alexander J., PhD; American biologist and academic; *Howard and Gwen Laurie Smits Professor of Cell Biology, California Institute of Technology;* b. 8 Nov. 1946, Moscow, USSR; s. of Jacob Varshavsky and Mary Zeitlin; m. Vera Bingham; one s. two d.; ed Dept of Chem., Moscow Univ., Inst. of Molecular Biology, Moscow; Research Fellow Inst. of Molecular Biology, Moscow 1973–76; Asst Prof. of Biology, Dept of Biology, MIT, Cambridge, Mass., 1977–80, Assoc. Prof. 1980–86, Prof. 1986–92; Howard and Gwen Laurie Smits Prof. of Cell Biology, Div. of Biology, Calif. Inst. of Tech., Pasadena, 1992–; Fellow, American Acad. of Arts and Sciences, American Acad. of Microbiology; mem. NAS, American Philosophical Soc., Academia Europaea; Merit Award, NIH 1998, Novartis-Drew Award 1998, Gairdner Int. Award, Canada 1999, Shubitz Prize in Cancer Research, Univ. of Chicago 2000, Hoppe-Seyler Award, Soc. for Biochemistry and Molecular Biology, Germany 2000, Sloan Prize 2000, Merck Award, American Soc. for Biochemistry and Molecular Biology 2001, Wolf Prize in Medicine, Israel 2001, Pasarow Award in Cancer Research 2001, Massry Prize 2001, Horwitz Prize 2001, Max Planck Research Prize, Germany 2001, Wilson Medal, American Soc. for Cell Biology 2002, Stein and Moore Award, Protein Soc. 2005, March of Dimes Prize in Developmental Biology, March of Dimes Foundation 2006, Griffuel Prize in Cancer Research, Asscn pour la Recherche sur le Cancer, France 2006, Gagna and Van Heck Prize, Fonds Nat. de la Recherche Scientifique, Belgium 2006, Schleiden Medal, Deutsche Akad. der Naturforscher Leopoldina, Germany 2007, Gotham Prize for Cancer Research, Gotham Foundation 2008. *Achievements:* discoveries in fields of DNA replication, chromosome structure and segregation, ubiquitin system and regulated protein degradation; inventions of several widely used methods including the chromatin immunoprecipitation (CHIP) assay, the ubiquitin fusion technique, and the split-ubiquitin sensor of protein–protein interactions. *Publications:* more than 200 articles in professional journals in the fields of genetics and biochemsitry; 14 patents in these fields. *Address:* Division of Biology, 145-75, California Institute of Technology, 1200 East California Boulevard, Pasadena, CA 91125, USA (office). *Telephone:* (626) 395-3785 (office). *Fax:* (626) 440-9821 (office). *E-mail:* avarsh@caltech.edu (office). *Website:* www.biology.caltech.edu/Members/Varshavsky (office).

VÁSÁRY, Tamás; Hungarian concert pianist and conductor; *Chief Musical Director and Principal Conductor, Budapest Symphony Orchestra (Symphony Orchestra of the Hungarian Radio and Television);* b. 11 Aug. 1933, Debrecen; s. of Jozsef Vasary and Elizabeth (née Baltazàr) Vasary; m. Henriette Tunyogi 2000; ed Ferenc Liszt Acad. of Music, Budapest under Lajos Hernádi, József Gát and Zoltán Kodály; first solo performance aged eight; studied with Ernst von Dohnányi at Ferenc Liszt Acad. of Music –1954; remained at Ferenc Liszt Acad. as Asst Prof. to Zoltán Kodály; recitals in Leningrad (now St Petersburg), Moscow and Warsaw; settled in Switzerland 1958; London debut 1961, New York 1962; debut as conductor in Menton Festival of Music 1971; has since appeared in Europe, S Africa, S America, USA, Canada, India, Thailand, Hong Kong, Australia, Japan and Mexico; Jt Music Dir Northern Sinfonia, Newcastle, UK 1979–82; Musical Dir Bournemouth Sinfonietta 1988–96; Chief Musical Dir and Prin. Conductor Budapest Symphony Orchestra (Symphony Orchestra of the Hungarian Radio and Television) 1993–; Guest Conductor London Philharmonic, Royal Philharmonic, Philharmonia, New York Philharmonic, Dallas and Houston Symphonies, Detroit Symphony; performances at Salzburg, Edin. and Merano Music Festivals; records for Deutsche Grammophon; Liszt Prizes: Queen Elizabeth (Belgium), Marguerite Longue (Paris); Chopin Prizes: Int. Competition, Warsaw, Int. Competition, Brazil; Bach and Paderewski Medals (London), Kossuth Prize, Presidential Gold Medal 1998, Hungarian Heritage Prize. *Principal recordings:* three records of works of Liszt; eight of works of Chopin and various recordings of works of Rachmaninoff, Dohnányi, Debussy and Mozart; all symphonies and overtures of Beethoven, Schubert and Schumann 1997–98; further records for Hungaroton. *Leisure interest:* writing fiction. *Address:* Magyar Rádió Zenekari Iroda, Bródy Sándor u. 5-1, 1800 Budapest, Hungary (office). *Telephone:* (1) 328-8326 (office). *Fax:* (1) 328-8910 (office).

VÁŠÁRYOVÁ, Magdaléna; Slovak actress, writer, politician and diplomatist; b. 26 Aug. 1948, Banská Štiavnica; d. of Jozef Vášáry and Hermína Vášáry (née Schmidt); m. Milan Lasica; two d.; ed Comenius Univ., Bratislava; actress with Nová Scéna, Bratislava 1971–83, Slovak Nat. Theatre 1984–90; fmr Amb. to Austria, fmr Amb. to Poland; currently mem. of Parl., State Sec. of Ministry of Foreign Affairs 2005–06; mem. Slovak Democratic and Christian Union-Democratic Party (Slovenská demokratická a kresťanská únia-Demokratická strana); Artist of Merit 1988, Prize for Dramatic Performance in ...a pozdravuji vlaštovky, Italy 1972, Gold Crocodile for Za frountou 1974, Andrea 1993, Silver Medal 2000. *Films include:* Senzi mama 1964, Markéta Lazarová 1967, Sladký cas Kalimagdory 1968, Zbehovia a pútnici 1968, Králováská polovacka 1969, Na komete 1970, Radúz a Mahulena 1970, Princ Bajaja 1971, ...a pozdravuji vlaštovky 1972, Rusalka 1977, Postrižiny 1980. *Plays include:* Ubohý moj Marat 1970, Woyzeck 1971, Three Sisters 1972, Hamlet 1074, Clavio 1976, Výnosné miesto 1984, Sleena Júlia 1986, Samovrah 1989. *Publications include:* Short Sheets to One City 1988, Diskrétní pruvodce

- co možná nevíte o spolecesnkém chování. *Leisure interests:* literature, charity fundraising. *Address:* c/o Slovak Democratic and Christian Union-Democratic Party (Slovenská demokratická a kresťanská únia-Demokratická strana), Ružinovská 28, 827 35 Bratislava, Slovakia. *Telephone:* (2) 4341-4102. *Fax:* (2) 4341-4106. *E-mail:* sdku@sdkuonline.sk. *Website:* www.sdkuonline.sk.

VASELLA, Daniel L., MD; Swiss pharmaceutical industry executive; *Chairman and CEO, Novartis AG;* b. 1953; m.; three c.; ed Univ. of Berne; began career as hosp. physician; Head of Corp. Marketing, Sandoz Group 1993, Sr Vice-Pres. and Head of Worldwide Devt, Sandoz Pharma Ltd, COO –1995, mem. Exec. Cttee, then CEO 1995–96, Chair. Bd of Dirs, CEO and Head of Exec. Cttee Novartis AG 1999– (following merger of Sandoz and Ciba-Geigy 1996); mem. Bd of Dirs Crédit Suisse 2000–, PepsiCo Inc.; mem. Chair.'s Council DaimlerChrysler; mem. Supervisory Bd, Siemens AG, Munich; mem. Int. Business Leaders Advisory Council for the Mayor of Shanghai; mem. Bd Inst. Européen d'Admin. des Affaires (INSEAD), Int. Inst. of Man. Devt (IMD), mem. Bd of Dean's Advisors at Harvard Business School; Pres. Int. Fed. of Pharmaceutical Mfrs and Asscns (IFPMA) 2004–06; mem. Global Leaders for Tomorrow Group, World Econ. Forum, Davos, Switzerland; mem. Int. Bd of Govs Peres Center for Peace, Tel-Aviv, Israel; Ordem Nacional do Cruzeiro do Sul (Brazil), Chevalier de la Légion d'honneur; Dr hc (Univ. of Basel Faculty of Medicine) 2002; Harvard Business School's Alumni Achievement Award, Appeal of Conscience Award, AJ Congress Humanitarian Award, numerous other awards. *Leisure interests:* skiing, motorcycles, collecting rare books. *Address:* Novartis AG, Lichtstrasse 35, 4056 Basel, Switzerland (office). *Telephone:* 613241111 (office). *Fax:* 613248001 (office). *E-mail:* info@novartis.com (office). *Website:* www.novartis.com (office).

VASHADZE, Grigol; Georgian business executive and politician; *Minister of Foreign Affairs;* b. 19 July 1958, Tbilisi; s. of Nodar Vashadze and Elene Bakradze; m. Nino Ananiashvili; two c.; ed Moscow State Inst. of Int. Relations; worked in Dept of Int. Orgs, USSR Ministry of Foreign Affairs 1981–88, also worked in Dept of Cosmos and Nuclear Weapons; post-graduate student, Diplomatic Acad. 1988–90; Founder and Dir Georgia Arts Man. and Gregory Vashadze and BR 1990–2008; Deputy Minister of Foreign Affairs Feb.–Nov. 2008; Minister for Culture, Heritage Preservation and Sport Nov. 2008, of Foreign Affairs Dec. 2008–. *Address:* Ministry of Foreign Affairs, 0108 Tbilisi, Sh. Chitadze 4, Georgia (office). *Telephone:* (32) 28-47-47 (office). *Fax:* (32) 28-46-78 (office). *E-mail:* inform@mfa.gov.ge (office). *Website:* www.mfa.gov.ge (office).

VASILE, Radu, PhD; Romanian politician and academic; *Chairman, Romanian People's Party;* b. 10 Oct. 1942, Sibiu; m. Mariuca Vasile; two s. one d.; ed Univ. of Bucharest; historian, The Village Museum, Bucharest 1967–69; scientific researcher, History Inst. Nicolae Iorga, Romanian Acad. 1969–72; Asst Lecturer, Acad. of Econ. Studies, Bucharest 1972; Asst Prof., Vice-Dean, Faculty of Trade, Acad. of Econ. Studies, Bucharest 1990, Prof. 1993; Vice-Pres. Romanian Senate 1996–98, Head Romanian Del. to Parl. Ass. of Council of Europe 1996–98; Vice-Pres. Parl. Ass. of Council of Europe 1997–98; Dir Dreptatea (daily newspaper) 1992–94; mem. Christian Democratic Nat. Peasant Party CDNPP 1990–99 (expelled), Sec. Gen. 1996–98, Pres. Senate Parl. Group 1996–98; Prime Minister of Romania 1998–99; Senator 2000–04; Chair. Romanian People's Party (fmrly Romanian Right Party) 2000–; mem. Editorial Bd Romania and the European Union. *Publications:* World Economy: Avenues and Stages of Modernization 1987, Currency and Economy 1994, Currency and Fiscal Policy 1995, From the Iron Century to the Second World War 1998; author of univ. textbook series: A Handbook of History of Economics –1995; 25 research papers. *Leisure interests:* poetry, satirical literature, chess, football.

VASILEV, Iliyan D.; Bulgarian business executive and fmr diplomatist; Chair. Foreign Investment Agency –1999; Amb. to Russian Fed. 2000–06; currently Chair. Deloitte Bulgaria; Co-founder and Hon. Chair. Bulgarian Econ. Forum and Southeast Europe Econ. Forum; fmr Pres. Bulgarian Int. Business Asscn; Int. Cyril and Methodius Award 2005. *Address:* Deloitte Bulgaria, 103, Al. Stamboliiski Blvd., Sofia Tower, 1303 Sofia, Bulgaria (office). *Telephone:* (2) 80-23-300 (office). *Fax:* (2) 80-23-350 (office). *Website:* www.deloitte.com/dtt (office).

VASILIEV, Vladimir Viktorovich; Russian ballet dancer, choreographer, theatre director, film director and teacher; *President, Galina Ulanova Foundation;* b. 18 April 1940, Moscow; s. of Viktor Vasiliev and Tatiana Kuzmicheva; m. Ekaterina Maximova; ed Bolshoi Theatre Ballet School, State Inst. of Theatrical Arts; with Bolshoi Theatre Ballet 1958–88; toured widely 1988–94; guest appearances with Ballet of Maurice Béjart 1977, 1978, Ballet de Marseille 1987, Teatro di S. Carlo di Napoli 1988–89, Arena di Verona 1988, Opera di Roma, Kirov Ballet, Paris 1988, Metropolitan Opera House, New York 1990; f. Kremlin Ballet 1990; int. tours with Ekaterina Maximova & Vladimir Vasiliev Superstars & Co. 1989–90; Head of Choreographic Dept, State Inst. of Theatrical Arts (now RATI) 1986–95, Prof.; Artistic Dir Arabesque Ballet Competition, Russia 1988–; Man. and Artistic Dir Bolshoi Theatre 1995–2000; Founder and Curator Bolshoi School, Brazil 2000–; freelance choreographer 2000–; Pres. Galina Ulanova Foundation 2000–; Academician, Russian Acad. of Arts; Hon. Prof., Moscow State Univ.; Hon. Citizen, Buenos Aires, Argentina 1983, Tusona, USA 1989; People's Artist of USSR 1973, People's Artist of Russian Fed. 1993, Order of Lenin 1976, Order of People's Friendship 1981, Order of Red Banner of Labour 1986, Chevalier, Ordre nat. du Mérit 1999, State Order of Merit of Russian Fed. 2000, State Order of Lithuania 2002, State Order of Brazil 'Rio Branco' 2004; Hon. DHumLitt (Centre Coll., Danville, Ky, USA); First Prize and Gold Medal, Vienna Int. Youth Festival 1959, Nijinsky Prize, Paris Dance Acad. 1964, Grand Prix, Varna Int. Competition 1964, USSR State Lenin Komsomol Prize 1968, USSR State Lenin Prize 1970, Maruis Petipa Prize, Paris Dance Acad.

1972, USSR State Prize 1977, Jino Tagni Int. Prize, Rome 1989, Together for Peace Prize, Rome 1989, UNESCO Pablo Picasso Medal 1990, 2000, Diagilev Prize 1990, State Prize of Russian Fed. 1991, Moscow Mayor's Office Prize 1997, Crystal Turandot – For Honor and Dignity (Russia) 2001, Premio alla carriera 'Una Vita per la Danza' (Italy) 2001, A Life for Dance Prize (USA) 2003, Premio, Gran Teatro de La Habana 2008. *Principal roles:* Pan (Valpurgis Night), The Poet (Chopiniana), Danila (Stone Flower), Prince Charming/Step Mother (Cinderella), Batyr (Shurale), Andrei (A Page of Life), Basil (Don Quixote), Albert (Giselle), Frondoso (Laurencia), Nutcracker/Prince (Nutcracker), Medjnun (Leili and Medjnun), Ivanushka (The Little Humpbacked Horse), Spartacus (Spartacus), Petrushka (Petrushka) and Icarus (Icarus), Macbeth (Macbeth), Narcissus (Narcissus), Lukash (Song of the Woods), Paganini (Paganini), Romeo (Romeo and Juliet), Prince Desire (Sleeping Beauty), Ivan the Terrible(Ivan the Terrible), Sergey (Angara), Baron (Gaîté Parisienne), Zorba (Greek Zorba) Nijinsky (Nijinsky), Balda (Balda), Pyotr Leontyevich (Anyuta), Professor Unrat (The Blue Angel), Tchaikovsky (Lungo Viaggio Nella Notte de Natale). *Ballets choreographed:* Anyuta, Macbeth, Icarus, These Charming Sounds, Romeo and Juliet, Swan Lake, Cinderella, Paganini, Balda, new version of Giselle, Bolshoi Theatre, Takhir and Zukhra, Uzbek Opera, Macbeth, Novosibisk Opera, Staats Oper Berlin, Budapest Opera, Kremlin Ballet, Anyuta, Teatro di San Carlo Naples, Latvian Opera, Cheliabinsk Opera, Tatar Opera, Perm Opera, Omsk Opera, Romeo and Juliet, Moscow Musical Theatre of K. Stanislavsky and V. Nemirovich-Danchenko, Lithuanian Opera, Latvian Opera, Teatro Municipal of Rio de Janeiro, Don Quixote, Teatro di San Carlo, Naples, American Ballet Theatre, Kremlin Ballet, Lithuanian Ballet, Tokyo Ballet, Giselle, Opera di Roma, pas de quatre in Giselle, Tokyo Ballet, Paganini, Teatro Argentino, Balda, Perm Opera, Cinderella, Kremlin Ballet, Cheliabinsk Opera, Voronezh Opera; choreographer: The Princess and Woodcutter, Sovremennik Drama Theatre, Moscow, Yunona and Avosj (rock opera), Lenkom Drama Theatre, Moscow, F. Zeffirelli's productions of Aida, Opera di Roma, Arena di Verona, La Scala, Khovanschina, Bolshoi Theatre. *Operas staged:* La Traviata, Bolshoi Theatre 1996, Mozart, Mozart..., Novaya Opera of Moscow 1999. *Films:* directed, choreographed and starred in Trapezium, Anyuta, House by the Roadside, Adam and Eva, Icarus, Gospel for the Sly, Gigolo and Gigolette, These Charming Sounds, Fouete, Fragments of One's Biography, I Want to Dance; choreographed Andersen – Life Without Love (Russia); appeared in Franco Zeffirelli's La Traviata; films about Vasiliev: Reflections, Katya and Volodya, ...And there is always something unsaid, Duet. *Television:* starred in USSR with Open Heart, Road to the Bolshoi Ballet, Parade of Numbers, Moscow in Musical Notes, Recollecting Ninjinsky, Glory of the Bolshoi Ballet, Randez-vous with the Bolshoi, Creation of Dance, Choreographic Novellas, Choreographic Symphony, World of Dance, Pages of Modern Dance, The Bolshoi Ballet in Japan, Classical Duets, Grand Pas in the White Night, The World of Ulanova, Ulanova Forever, Commemorating Ulanova, Asaf Messerer, Anna Pavlova, Choreographic Images of Kasyan Goleizovsky, Magic of Giselle, Golden Age of Asaf Messerer, Katya, Ekaterina Maximova, When Dance becomes Life; Olga Lepeshinskaya, Dialogue with a Legend, Vladimir Vasiliev – Dance and Time, The Bolshoi Ballet. *Publications:* poems: The Chain of Days 2000; catalogues of paintings of V. Vasiliev 2004, 2005, 2007. *Leisure interests:* painting, writing poetry. *Address:* Smolenskaya naberezhnaya 5/13 62, 121099 Moscow, Russia (home). *Telephone:* (495) 244-02-27 (home). *Fax:* (495) 244-02-27 (home). *E-mail:* info@vasiliev.com (office). *Website:* www.vasiliev.com (home).

VASILIU, Emanuel Kant, PhD; Romanian professor of linguistics; b. 7 Sept. 1929, Chişinău; s. of Nicolae Vasiliu and Gabriela Vasiliu; m. Maria-Laura Vasiliu 1952; ed Univ. of Bucharest; Assoc. Prof., Univ. of Bucharest 1968, Prof. 1970, Dean Faculty of Letters 1990–92; Visiting Prof., Univ. of Chicago 1964–65, 1970–71, Boston Univ. 1971; Dir 'Al. Rosetti' Inst. of Phonetics and Dialectology 1990–; mem. Editorial Bd Studii şi cercetări lingvistice (Linguistic Studies and Researches), Revue roumaine de linguistique, Fonetică şi dialectologie (Phonetics and Dialectology), Cahiers de linguistique théorique et appliquée; mem. Romanian Acad. 1992, Soc. Linguistica Europaea, Soc. Européenne de Culture, Romanian Linguistic Soc., Romanian Soc. of Romance Linguistics, Int. Cttee of Linguists 1977–87; State Prize (Second Class) 1953, B.P. Hasden Prize, Romanian Acad. 1960. *Publications:* Fonologia limbii române (Romanian Phonology) 1965, Fonologia istorică a dialectelor dacoromâne (Historical Phonology of Daco-Romanian Dialects) 1968, Elemente de teorie semantică a limbilor naturale (Some Principles of a Semantic Theory of Natural Languages) 1970, Outline of a Semantic Theory of Kernel Sentences 1972, Preliminarii logice la semantica frazei (Logic Preliminaries to Compound Sentence Semantics) 1978, Scrierea limbii române în raport cu fonetica şi fonologia (Romanian Writing in Relation to Phonetics and Phonology) 1979, Sens, adevăr analitic, cunoaştere (Meaning, Analytic Truth and Knowledge) 1984, Introducere în teoria textului (Introduction to Textual Theory) 1990, Introducere în teoria limbii (Introduction to the Theory of Language) 1992, Elemente de filosofie a limbajului (Elements of Language Philosophy) 1995, The Transformational Syntax of Romanian (with Sanda Golopentia-Eretescu) 1972, Limba Română în Secolele al XII-lea–al XV-lea. Fonetică–Fonologie–Gramatică (Romanian in the XII–XV Centuries: Phonetics–Phonology–Grammar) (with Liliana Ionescu-Ruxăndoiu) 1986; contrib. to several works on Romanian language. *Leisure interest:* music. *Address:* Institutul de Fonetică şi Dialectologie 'Al. Rosetti', Str. 13 Septembrie 13, Sector 5, 76117 Bucharest (office); Intrarea Lucaci 3, 74111 Bucharest, Romania (home). *Telephone:* (21) 3206337 (home); (21) 6412757 (office).

VASILYEV, Anatoli Aleksandrovich; Russian theatre director; *Founder and Director, School of Dramatic Art;* b. 4 May 1942, Danilovka, Penza Region; m. Nadezhda Kalinina; one d.; ed Rostov State Univ., State Inst. of Dramatic Art, Moscow; Founder and Dir Theatre Co. School of Dramatic Art,

Moscow 1987; staged all works by Pirandello; numerous tours in Europe 1985–2002; Chevalier Ordre des Arts et des Lettres 1989, Honoured Art Worker of Russia 1993; Nuova Realtà Europea Prize, Taormina, Italy 1990, Pirandello Prize, Agrigento, Italy 1992, Stanislavsky Fund Prize 1995, Stanislavsky Prize of Russian Fed. 1998, Golden Mask Prize of Russian Fed. for The Lamentation of Jeremiah (Martynov) 1997, Nat. State Prize of Russian Fed. for creation of School of Dramatic Art 1999, Triumph Prize 2001. *Productions include:* Vassa Zheleznova 1978, Grown-up Daughter of a Young Man (V. Slavkin) 1979, Cerceau (V. Slavkin) 1985, Six Characters in Search of an Author (Pirandello) 1987, Masquerade (Lermontov) at Comédie Française 1992, Uncle's Dream (Dostoyevsky), Budapest 1994, The Lamentation of Jeremiah (Martynov) 1996, The Queen of Spades (Tchaikovsky), German Nat. Theatre, Weimar 1996, Don Juan (Pushkin) 1998, Mozart and Salieri (Pushkin) 2000, Requiem (Martynov) 2000, Medee Materiaux (Heiner Muller) 2001. *Publications:* A propos de bal masqué de Mikhail Lermontov 1997, Szinházi Fuga 1998, Sept ou huit leçons de théâtre 1999, Ione e Menone di Platone 1999, A un unico lettore 2000. *Address:* School of Dramatic Art, Povarskaya 20, Moscow, Russia (office). *Telephone:* (495) 291-50-39 (office); (495) 951-37-71 (home). *Fax:* (495) 291-86-42 (office). *E-mail:* rezy@orc.ru (office).

VASILYEV, Boris Lvovich; Russian writer, dramatist and essayist; b. 21 May 1924, Smolensk; m. Zorya Albertovna Vasilyeva; two adopted s.; ed Mil. Acad. of Armoured Troops; served in Red Army in World War II, seriously wounded; engineer with Acad. of Armoured Troops 1943–54; USSR People's Deputy 1989–91; mem. USSR Supreme Soviet 1991; USSR State Prize 1975; Konstantin Simonov Prize; Dovzhenko Gold Medal. *Publications include:* Dawns are Quiet Here 1969, Do Not Shoot the White Swans 1975, My Horses are Flying 1983, And Tomorrow was War (novel) 1984, The Burning Bush 1987, Regards from Baba Vera 1988, Absent from the Casualty List (novel) 1988, There was Evening, There was Morning 1989, The Short Castling 1989, The Carnival (novel) 1990, The House Built by the Old Man 1991, Kahunk and Prince Prophetic Oleg (novel) 1996, Two Bananas in one Peel (novel) 1996, A Gambler and Rabid Duellist 1998; many screenplays. *Leisure interests:* gardening, history, English literature. *Address:* Chasovaya Str. 58, Apt. 40, 125319 Moscow, Russia. *Telephone:* (495) 152-99-01.

VASILYEV, Sergei Aleksandrovich, PhD; Russian politician; *Chairman, Committee on Financial Markets, Council of the Russian Federation;* b. 8 June 1957, Leningrad; m.; two d.; ed Inst. of Economy and Finance, Leningrad; Head, Research Lab., Inst. of Finance and Economy, Leningrad 1985–90, now Prof.; took part in activities of Moscow-Leningrad group of young economists; mem. Leningrad Political Club Perestroika 1986; Chair. Cttee for Econ. Reform, Leningrad City Soviet 1990–91; Head, Working Centre for Econ. Reform under Russian Govt 1991–94; Deputy Minister of the Economy, Russian Fed. 1994–97; Deputy Head, Office of Russian Govt 1997–98; Chair. Bd Int. Investment Bank, Moscow 1998–99; Pres. Int. Centre for Social and Econ. Research (Leontief Centre), St Petersburg 1999–2001; Rep. of Leningrad Regional Govt to Council of Fed. 2001–, Chair. Cttee on Financial Markets. *Publications:* Economics and Power 1998, Ten Years of Russian Economic Reform 1999, Comparative Analysis of Stabilization Programs of the '90s 2003, Economic Development of the Leningrad Region 2005. *Leisure interest:* travel. *Address:* Council of the Federation, Bolshaya Dmitrovka 26, 103426 Moscow (office); Government of the Leningrad Region, Suvorovsky prosp. 67, 191311 St Petersburg, Russia (office). *Telephone:* (495) 692-67-12 (office); (812) 274-47-23 (office). *Fax:* (495) 926-66-36 (office); (812) 274-47-23 (office). *E-mail:* SAVasilev@council.gov.ru (office); savasiliev@lenreg.ru (office).

VASILYEV, Gen.-Col Vladimir A., Cand.Jur; Russian; *Deputy Minister of Internal Affairs;* b. 11 Aug. 1949, Klin, Moscow region; one d.; m.; ed School of Militia, Acad. of USSR Ministry of Internal Affairs; investigator, inspector, sr inspector, deputy head Bauman district division of internal affairs 1972–83; head of division, deputy head Dept of Property Security, Moscow Dept. of Internal Affairs 1983–87; chief inspector, head of operations dept, deputy head, head of gen. staff, first Deputy Minister of Internal Affairs 1992–98; Deputy Sec. Security Council of Russian Fed. 1999–2001; Deputy Minister of Internal Affairs 2001–. *Address:* Ministry of Internal Affairs, ul. Zhitnaya 16, Moscow 117049, Russia (office). *Telephone:* (495) 237-75-85 (office). *Fax:* (495) 293-59-98 (office). *E-mail:* uimvd@mvdinform.ru (office). *Website:* www .mvdinform.ru (office).

VASILYEVA, Larisa Nikolayevna; Russian poet and writer; b. 23 Nov. 1935, Kharkov, Ukraine; d. of Nikolai Alekseyevich Kucherenko and Yekaterina Vasilievna Kucherenko; m. Oleg Vasiliyev 1957; one s.; ed Moscow Univ.; started publishing 1957; first collection of verse 1966; Sec. of Moscow Br. of Russian Union of Writers; Pres. Fed. of Russian Women Writers 1989–, Int. Publishing League Atlantida 1992–; Moscow Komsomol Prize 1971. *Publications include:* prose: Albion and the Secret of Time 1978, Novel About My Father 1983, Cloud of Fire 1988, Selected Works (two vols) 1989, The Kremlin Wives 1992, The Kremlin Children 1996, The Wives of the Russian Crown; poetry: Fire-fly 1969, The Swan 1970, Blue Twilight 1970, Encounter 1974, A Rainbow of Snow 1974, Meadows 1975, Fire in the Window 1978, Russian Names 1980, Foliage 1980, Fireflower 1981, Selected Poetry 1981, Grove 1984, Mirror 1985, Moskovorechie 1985, Lantern 1985, Waiting For You In The Sky 1986, A Strange Virtue 1991. *Address:* Usiyevicha str. 8, Apt. 86, 125319 Moscow, Russia. *Telephone:* (495) 155-74-86. *E-mail:* muzeiT-34@lobn.ru (office). *Website:* larisavasilyeva.ru.

VASILYEVA, Tatyana Grigoryevna; Russian actress; b. 28 Feb. 1947, Leningrad; two s. one d.; ed Studio-School of Moscow Art Theatre; with Moscow Satire Theatre –1984; actress, Moscow Mayakovsky Theatre 1984–93; People's Artist of Russia, Nika Prize 1992. *Theatre roles include:*

Ordinary Miracle, Pippi Long Stocking, Run, Inspector, The Threepenny Opera, A Place Like the Heavens. *Films include:* Poedinok v tayge (The Fight in the Taiga) 1977, Prezhde chem rasstatsya (Before We Part) 1984, Salon krasoty (Beauty Salon) 1985, Bluzhdayushchiye zvyozdy (Wandering Stars) 1991, Hello, I'm Your Auntie, Uvidet Parizh i umeret (To See Paris and Die) 1992, Zhenikh iz Mayami (The Fiancé from Miami) 1994, Chyornaya vual (The Black Veil) 1995, Tsirk sgorel i klouny razbezhalis 1998, Popsa 2005, Tarif novogodniy 2008, Neporoshchennye 2009. *Address:* 121248 Moscow, Goncharny proyezd 8/40, Apt. 62, Russia.

VASNETSOV, Andrei Vladimirovich; Russian painter; b. 24 Feb. 1924, Moscow; ed Moscow Inst. of Applied Arts; Sec. USSR Union of Artists 1983–88, Chair. 1988–92; First Sec. of Bd RSFSR Union of Artists 1987–88; USSR People's Deputy 1989–91; mem. Presidium, Russian Acad. of Fine Arts; People's Artist of Russia; Hon. Pres. Vasnetsovs' Foundation, USSR State Prize 1979, Pres.'s Prize, Russian Fed. 1998. *Publications:* From Creative Experience, Conquerors of Space, Elkonin's Creative Method. *Address:* Russian Academy of Fine Arts, Prechistenka str. 21, 119034 Moscow (office); Maly Patriarshiy per. 5, Apt. 43, 103001 Moscow, Russia (home). *Telephone:* (495) 201-39-71. *Fax:* (495) 201-39-71 (office).

VASPÁL, Vilmos, BEng; Hungarian business executive; *Chairman, FreeSoft Nyrt.;* m.; two c.; software developer, Videoton 1980s; fmr Chief Information Officer, SZÜV; Founding mem. FreeSoft Nyrt., Chair. 2004–; mem. Bd Asscn of IT Cos 2003–. *Address:* FreeSoft Nyrt., Neumann Janos u. 1/C, Infopark, Budapest 1117, Hungary (office). *Telephone:* (1) 371-2910 (office). *Fax:* (1) 371-2911 (office). *E-mail:* fs.inf@freesoft.hu (office). *Website:* www.freesoft.hu (office).

VÁSQUEZ MORALES, Ricaurte, PhD; Panamanian government official and economist; *Chairman, Panama Canal Authority;* ed Villanova Univ., Pa, N Carolina State Univ., Rensselaer Polytechnic Inst., NY, USA; Minister of Planning and Econ. Policy 1984–88; Pres. Sigma Man. Corpn 1988–96; Vice-Pres. Asesores y Gestores Bursátiles 1992–94; Dir Panama Holdings Inc. 1994–96; fmr econ. analyst Chase Manhattan Bank, econ. consultant Cámara Panameña de la Construcción, economist Corporación de Cobre de Cerro Colorado; Dir Office of Financial Admin, Panama Canal Comm. 1996; Vice-Admin. Panama Canal Authority –2004; Minister of Finance and the Treasury and Chair. Panama Canal Authority 2004–07; has taught econs, econometrics and finance at Universidad Santa María La Antigua, Florida State Univ. Panamá, Universidad del Istmo. *Address:* c/o Ministry of Finance and the Treasury, Edif. Ogawa, Vía España, Apdo 5245, Panamá 5, Panama (office).

VASSANJI, M. G., OC, BS, PhD; Canadian writer; b. 30 May 1950, Nairobi, Kenya; s. of Gulamhussein V. Nanji and Daulatkhanu V. Nanji; m. Nurjehan Vassanji (née Aziz) 1979; two s.; ed Massachusetts Inst. of Tech. and Univ. of Pennsylvania; grew up in Nairobi, Kenya, and Dar es Salaam, Tanzania; Post-doctoral Fellow, Atomic Energy of Canada Ltd 1978–80; Research Assoc., Univ. of Toronto 1980–89; first novel published 1989, full-time writer 1989–; Writer-in-Residence Int. Writing Program, Univ. of Iowa 1989; Hon. DLitt (York) 2005, (McMaster) 2006, (Old Dominion) 2007; Giller Prize for Best Novel (Canada) 1994, 2003, Harbour Front Literary Award 1994, F. G. Bressani Award 1994. *Publications:* The Gunny Sack (novel) (Commonwealth First Novel Award, Africa Region 1990) 1989, No New Land (novel) 1991, Uhuru Street (short stories) 1991, The Book of Secrets (novel) 1994, Amriika (novel) 1999, The In-Between World of Vikram Lall (novel) 2003, When She Was Queen (short stories) 2005, The Assassin's Song (novel) 2007. *Leisure interests:* squash, movies. *Address:* c/o Doubleday Canada Limited, 5900 Finch Avenue East, Scarborough, ON M1B 0A2, Canada (office). *Telephone:* (416) 977-7891 (office). *Fax:* (416) 977-8707 (office). *E-mail:* info@doubledaycanada .ca (office). *Website:* www.doubledaycanada.ca (office); www.mgvassanji.com (office).

VASSILIKOS, Vassilis; Greek writer; b. 18 Nov. 1934, Kavala; s. of Nikolaos Aikaterini; m. Vasso Papantoniou; one d.; ed Anatolia High School of Thessaloniki, Thessaloniki Law School, Yale Drama School, USA, School of Radio and Television, USA; Dir-Gen. of Greek TV (public) 1981–85; Amb. to UNESCO 1996–2004; Pres. Hellenic Authors' Soc. 1999–2005; presenter of weekly TV show on books; mem. Int. Parl. of Writers; mem. Athens Union of Daily Newspaper Journalists; Dr hc (Univ. of Patra, Univ. of Thessaly); Commdr, Ordre des Arts et des Lettres 1999; Prize of 'The Twelve' 1961, Mediterraneo Prize 1971. *Publications include:* (in English trans.): The Plant, The Well, The Angel 1963, Z 1968, The Harpoon Gun 1972, Outside the Walls 1973, The Photographs 1974, The Monarch 1976, The Coroner's Assistant 1986, ...And Dreams Are Dreams 1996, The Few Things I Know About Glafkos Thrassakis 2003. *Address:* Alkyonis 54, 17562 Athens, Greece (home). *Telephone:* (210) 3634868 (office). *Fax:* (210) 3620844 (office). *E-mail:* info@ orama-opera.gr (office).

VASSILIOU, Georghios Vassos, DEcon; Cypriot politician and economist; *Leader, United Democrats Movement;* b. 20 May 1931, Famagusta; s. of Vasos Vassiliou and Sophia Othonos Vassiliou (née Yiavopoulou); m. Androulla Georgiadou 1966; one s. two d.; ed Univ. of Budapest, Hungary; Market Researcher, Reed Paper Group, London 1960–62; Founder Middle East Marketing Research Bureau (now MEMRB Int.) and Ledra Advertising Co. 1962; f. Inst. of Dirs (Cyprus Br.); mem. Exec. Cttee Cyprus Chamber of Commerce 1970–86; mem. Bd and Exec. Cttee Bank of Cyprus 1981–88; mem. Econ. Advisory Council Church of Cyprus 1982–88, Educational Advisory Council 1983–88; Pres. of Cyprus 1988–93; Leader, United Democrats Movt 1993–; Chair. World Inst. for Devt Econ. Research, UN Univ., Helsinki 1995–2000; mem. Parl. 1996–99; Chief Negotiator for the Accession of Cyprus to the EU 1998–2003; Visiting Prof., Cranfield School of Man., UK; mem. InterAction Council 1998–, Trilateral Comm. 2000–; Hon. Prof., Cyprus Int.

Inst. of Man.; Dr hc (Univs of Cyprus, Athens, Salonica, Budapest, Belgrade); Grand Cross, Order of Merit (Cyprus), Grand Cross, Légion d'honneur, Grand Cross of the Saviour (Greece), Grand Cross of the Order of the Repub. of Italy, Grand Star (Austria), Grand Collar, Order of Infante D. Henrique (Portugal), Grand Collar of the Nile (Egypt), Standard (Flag) Order decorated with diamonds (Hungary), and other distinctions, awards and decorations. *Publications:* Marketing in the Middle East 1976, The Middle East Markets Up to 1980 1977, Moyen Orient: Le Consommateur des années '80 1980, Towards the Solution of the Cyprus Problem 1992, Modernisation of the Civil Service 1992, Overcoming Indifference 1994, Tourism and Sustainable Development 1995, Towards a Larger, Yet More Effective European Union 1999, Cyprus-European Union: From the First Steps to Accession 2004; numerous articles in various int. publs. *Leisure interests:* listening to music, reading, swimming, body exercise. *Address:* PO Box 22098, 1583 Nicosia (office); 9A Orpheos Street, 1070 Cyprus (home). *Telephone:* (2) 2336142 (office); (2) 2374888 (home). *Fax:* (2) 2336301 (office). *E-mail:* gvassiliou@memrb.com.cy (office).

VASSILYEV, Alexey Mikhailovich, DrHist; Russian scientist; *Director, Institute of Africa, Russian Academy of Sciences;* b. 26 April 1939, Leningrad; m.; two d.; ed Moscow State Inst. of Int. Relations; with Pravda, political columnist, corresp. in Vietnam, Turkey, Egypt 1962–83; Deputy Dir Inst. of Africa (now of African and Arab Studies), USSR (now Russian) Acad. of Sciences 1983–92, Dir 1992–; Ed.-in-Chief Asia and Africa Today (magazine) 1998–; Pres. Asscn of Cultural and Business Co-operation with African Cos; Pres. Centre of Regional and Civilisation Studies; mem. Council on Foreign Policy, Ministry of Foreign Affairs, Russian Fed.; Visiting Prof. univs in USA, UK, France, Egypt, Saudi Arabia etc.; Medals for Labour Merit, for Labour Heroism, Merited Scholar of the Russian Fed. 1999, Russian Acad. of Sciences E. V. Tarle Prize for Best Studies in History and Int. Relations 2003. *Publications:* more than 30 monographs, numerous scientific works and over 100 articles published in Russia and abroad on Middle East, Central Asia, Africa, Arab-Israeli conflict, Islam including History of Saudi Arabia, Russian Policy in the Middle East, Egypt and the Egyptians, Post-Soviet Central Asia. *Leisure interest:* Russian literature, skiing. *Address:* Institute of Africa, Russian Academy of Sciences, Spiridonovka str. 30/1, 103001 Moscow (office); 11/13-103 Pravda str., 125040 Moscow, Russia (home). *Telephone:* (495) 290-63-85 (office); (495) 214-47-28 (home). *Fax:* (495) 202-07-86 (office). *E-mail:* dir@inafr.ru (office). *Website:* www.inafr.ru (office).

VASTAGH, Pál, PhD; Hungarian politician and jurist; *Director General, College of Management, Budapest;* b. 23 Sept. 1946; m. Erzsébet Fenyvesi; one s. two d.; ed József Attila Univ. of Arts and Sciences, Szeged; Asst Lecturer, later Lecturer, then Sr Lecturer, Dept of Theory of State and Law, József Attila Univ. of Arts and Sciences 1988–89, Dean 1989; mem. of Presidium HSP 1989; mem. Parl. 1990–, Parl.'s Cttee on Constitutional Affairs, Chair. 2002–; mem. Codification and Justice Cttee on European Integration Affairs; Minister of Justice 1994–98; Deputy Leader of Socialist faction 1998–2002; Prof., Budapest School of Man. 1999–; mem. Convention on the Future of Europe 2002–; Observer and mem. European Parl. 2003–04; Chief Advisor to Prime Minister 2004–; Dir Gen. Coll. of Man., Budapest 2004–. *Publications:* articles in nat. newspapers and professional periodicals. *Leisure interests:* reading, hiking, travelling, soccer. *Address:* Képviselői Irodaház, 1358 Budapest, Széchenyi Rkp. 19, Hungary (office). *Telephone:* (1) 441-4484 (office). *Fax:* (1) 441-4823 (office). *E-mail:* pal.vastagh@parlament.hu (office). *Website:* www.parlament.hu (office).

VATOLIN, Nikolay Anatolyevich; Russian metallurgist and academic; *Professor, Institute of Metallurgy, Urals Branch of Russian Academy of Sciences;* b. 13 Nov. 1926, Yekaterinburg; m.; one s.; ed Urals Polytechnical Inst., Sverdlovsk; scientific researcher, scientific sec., Head of Lab., Dir Inst. of Metallurgy, USSR (now Russian) Acad. of Sciences (Urals Br.) 1950–98, Prof. 1973–, Adviser, Russian Acad. of Sciences 1998–; mem. CPSU 1952–91; Corresp. mem. of USSR (now Russian) Acad. of Sciences 1970–81, mem. 1981; USSR State Prize 1982, 1991, Kurnakow Gold Medal, Russian Acad. of Sciences 1995, Govt Prize, Russian Fed. 1997, Demidov's Prize 1997, Russian Fed. State Prize 2000. *Publications:* co-author: Physico-chemical Foundations of Steel Hot Leading 1977, Oxidation of Vanadium Slags 1978, Interparticle Interaction in Molten Metals 1979, Diffraction Studies of High Temperature Melts 1980, Computerization of Thermodynamic Calculations of Metallurgical Processes 1982, Electrical Properties of Oxide Melts 1984, Hydrometallurgy of Ferropowders 1984, Computer Simulation of Amorphous Metals 1985, Vanadium Slags 1988, Thermodynamic Modelling in High Temperature Inorganic Systems 1994, Temperature Dependences of Gibbs Reduced Energy of Some Inorganic Substances 1997, Fire Processing of Integrated Ores 1997, Some Regularities of Changes of Thermochemical Properties of Inorganic Compounds and Computational Methods for these Properties 2001, Lead Wastes Recylcing in Ionic Salt Melts 2002, Diffraction Studies of a Structure of High-Temperature Melts 2003, Nonferrous Metals Recycling in Ionic Melts 2005. *Address:* Institute of Metallurgy, Ural Division of Russian Academy of Sciences, 101 Amundsen Street, 620016 Yekaterinburg (office); 17 Polyanka Street, 620016 Yekaterinburg, Russia (home). *Telephone:* (343) 267-94-21 (office); (343) 267-89-01 (home). *Fax:* (343) 267-91-86 (office). *E-mail:* vatolin@imet.mplik.ru (home).

VAUGHAN, David Arthur John, CBE, QC, FRSA; British barrister and academic; *Visiting Professor of Law, Durham University;* b. 24 Aug. 1938; s. of the late Capt. F.H.M. Vaughan and J.M. Vaughan; m. 1st 1967 (divorced); m. 2nd Leslie A. F. Irwin 1985; one s. one d.; ed Eton Coll. and Trinity Coll. Cambridge; called to Bar, Inner Temple 1962, Bencher 1988; mem. Bar Council 1968–72, 1984–86, Bar Cttee 1987–88; mem. Int. Relations Cttee of Bar Council 1968–86, Bar/Law Soc. Working Party on EEC (now EU) Competition Law 1977– (Chair. 1978–88), UK Del. to Consultative Cttee of Bars and Law Socs of the EC 1978–81 and other cttees etc.; Chair. EC Section, Union Int. des Advocats 1987–91; a Recorder 1994–2001; Chair. Editorial Bd European Law Reports 1997–; a Deputy High Court Judge 1997–; Judge of the Courts of Appeal of Jersey and Guernsey 2000–; Visiting Prof. of Law, Univ. of Durham 1989–; mem. Advisory Bd, Centre for European Legal Studies, Cambridge Univ. 1991–; mem. Council of Man., British Inst. of Int. and Comparative Law 1992–; mem. Editorial Advisory Bd European Business Law Review 1998–; Fellow, Soc. for Advanced Legal Studies 1998; Bronze Medal, Bar of Bordeaux 1985. *Publications:* Gen. Ed. Encyclopaedia of EU Law, Vaughan and Robertson; co-ordinating ed. Halsbury's Laws of England 1986; Vaughan on the Law of the European Communities (ed.) 1986–97; Consultant Ed. European Court Practice 1993, Current EC Legal Development series. *Leisure interests:* fishing, tennis. *Address:* Brick Court Chambers, 7–8 Essex Street, London, WC2R 3LD, England (office). *Telephone:* (20) 7379-3550 (office). *Fax:* (20) 7379-3558 (office).

VAUGHAN, Michael Paul; British professional cricketer; b. 29 Oct. 1974, Manchester; s. of Graham Vaughan and Deirdre Vaughan (née Greenhaugh); m. Nichola Shannon; ed St Marks, Worsley, Dore Junior School, Sheffield, Silverdale Comprehensive School, Sheffield; right-hand opening batsmen, occasional right-arm off-break bowler; teams: Yorkshire 1993–, England Under-19, England A, England 1999– (test debut vs South Africa at Johannesburg; one-day international debut vs Sri Lanka at Dambulla 2001); 54 tests for England (23 as Capt.), scored 3,997 runs (average 44.41, highest score 197 vs India 2002) with 13 hundreds and took six wickets; scored 13,682 runs (average 38.54) with 34 hundreds and took 114 wickets in first-class cricket; 60 one-day ints, scored 1,439 runs (average 27.67); Capt. England A 1998–99, England 2003–08 (retd as one-day int. team 2007); first batsman for 32 years to score 600 runs in a test series in Australia 2002/03; ranked world number one batsman 2003; Professional Cricketer's Asscn Player of the Year 2002, Player of the Series Australia vs England 2002/03, Wisden Cricketer of the Year 2003, Freedom of the city of Sheffield 2005. *Publications:* Michael Vaughan: A Year in the Sun 2003, Calling the Shots: The Captain's Story 2005. *Leisure interests:* golf, football (Sheffield Wednesday). *Address:* c/o Yorkshire County Cricket Club, Headingley Cricket Ground, Leeds, LS6 7QE (office); c/o International Sports Management Ltd, Cherry Tree Farm, Cherry Tree Lane, Rostherne, Cheshire, WA14 3RZ, England (office). *Telephone:* (870) 4296774 (office); (1565) 832100. *Fax:* (0113) 2784099 (office); (1565) 832200. *E-mail:* cricket@yorkshireccc.org.uk (office); ism@golfism.net. *Website:* www.yorkshireccc.org.uk (office); www.michaelvaughan.net.

VAUTRIN, Jean, (Jean Herman); French novelist, film director and photographer; b. 17 May 1933, Pagny sur-Moselle, Meurthe-et-Moselle; s. of Raymond Herman and Maria Schneider; m. 2nd Anne Doat; two s. one d. (and one s. from first m.); ed Lycée Jacques-Amyot, Auxerre, Institut des hautes études cinématographiques; Lecturer in French Literature, Univ. of Bombay 1955; Asst to Roberto Rossellini 1955–57, to Jacques Rivette 1958, to Vincente Minelli 1958; Asst at ORTF, Dir, Armed Forces film div. 1959–61; Asst to Jean Cayrol, then made advertising films and shorts 1958–63, full-length films 1963–; Dir Juilliard 1990–; began writing career 1973; films (made under name Jean Herman) include: Voyage en Boscavie 1958 (Prix Emile Cohl), Actua-Tilt 1960 (Grand Prix, Festival Int. de Tours, Critics' Prize, Oberhausen), La Quille 1961 (Jury's Special Prize, Venice Festival), Le Dimanche de la Vie 1965 (Marilyn Monroe Prize), Garde à vue 1981 (Prix de l'Académie française); several films for TV; Ed. Atelier Julliard series; Conseiller Régional d'Aquitaine; Chevalier, Légion d'honneur, Officier du Mérite, Commdr des Arts et Lettres; Prix Goncourt 1989. *Films:* Le Dimanche de la vie d'après Queneau 1965, Adieu l'ami (with Alain Delon and Charles Bronson) 1968; Garde à vue (scriptwriter) 1981. *Publications:* (under name of Jean Vautrin) include: A bulletins rouges 1973, Billy-Ze-Kick 1974, Bloody Mary (Prix Mystère de la Critique) 1979, Canicule 1982, Patchwork (Prix des Deux-Magots) 1984, Baby Boom (Prix Goncourt de la Nouvelle) 1985, La Vie Ripolin (Grand Prix du Roman de la Société des gens de lettres) 1986, Un grand pas vers le Bon Dieu (Prix Goncourt) 1989, 18 Tentatives pour devenir un saint 1989; (with Dan Franck): La Dame de Berlin 1988, Le Temps des cerises 1991, Romans Noirs 1991, Courage, chacun 1992, Les Noces de Guernica 1994, Symphonie-Grabuge (Prix Populiste) 1994; Mademoiselle Chat (co-author) 1996, Jamais comme avant (co-author) 1996, Le Roi des ordures 1997, Un Monsieur bien mis 1997, Histoires déglinguées 1998, Le cri du peuple 1999, Boro s'en va-t-en guerre (co-author) 2000, L'Homme qui assassinait sa vie 2001, Le Journal de Louise B. 2002, Adieu la vie, adieu l'amour 2004, La femme au gant rouge 2004, New York, 100ème rue Est 2004. *Leisure interest:* drawing cartoons, painting. *Address:* c/o Editions Fayard, 15 rue des Sts Pères 75006, Paris; 6 Allée des oliviers, 33170, Gradignan, France (home). *Telephone:* (5) 56-85-33-87. *Fax:* (5) 56-85-15-23.

VAUZELLE, Michel Marie; French politician and lawyer; *President, Regional Council Provence-Alpes-Côte d'Azur;* b. 15 Aug. 1944, Montelimar, Drome; s. of Fernand Vauzelle and Marine Faure; m. Sylvie Fauvet 1980; two s. one d.; ed Collège St-Joseph, Lyon, Faculty of Law, Paris, Inst. of Political Studies, Paris; barrister 1968; Chargé de mission Prime Minister's Office 1969–72; mem. Finance Section Econ. and Social Council 1972–73; town councillor, Arles 1983–95, Deputy Mayor of Arles 1977–83, 1998–2001, Mayor of Arles 1995–98; Nat. Del. of Socialist Party Council of Civil Liberties 1978–81; Spokesman for the President of the Republic 1981–86; Préfet hors cadre 1985; Socialist Deputy for Bouches-du-Rhône 1986–92, 1997–2002, 2007–; Chair. Comm. for Foreign Affairs Nat. Ass. 1989–92; Minister of Justice and Keeper of the Seals 1992–93; Vice-Pres. Gen. Council Bouches du Rhône 1992–97; Pres. Regional Council Provence-Alpes-Côte d'Azur 1998–; Vice-Pres. ARF (Association des régions de France) 2004–; Pres. Commission Interméditerranéenne, Conférence des Régions Périphériques Maritimes

2007–; Pres. Nat. School of Photography 1982–86. *Publication:* Éloge de Daniel Manin, avocat venitien 1978, La France déroutée. *Leisure interest:* riding. *Address:* Hôtel de la Région, 27 place Jules Guesde, 13481 Marseille cedex 20, (office); 20 Place de la République, BP 196, 13637 Arles Cedex (office); Assemblée nationale, 126 rue de l'Université, 75355 Paris 07 SP, France (office). *Telephone:* 4-91-57-50-57 (office); 4-90-49-67-20 (office); 1-40-63-53-16 (office). *Fax:* 4-91-57-51-51 (office). *E-mail:* mvauzelle@assemblee-nationale.fr (office). *Website:* www.cr-paca.fr (office); www.michel-vauzelle.fr; michelvauzelle.regionpaca.fr.

VAVAKIN, Leonid Vassilyevich; Russian architect; b. 6 April 1932, Moscow; ed Moscow State Inst. of Architecture; fmr Chief Architect, Chair. Moscow Cttee on Architecture and City Construction; Prof. Moscow Inst. of Architecture; Corresp. mem. Russian Acad. of Fine Arts; mem. Int. Acad. of Architecture; Academician-Sec. Russian Acad. of Architecture; USSR Council of Ministers Prize, RSFSR Merited Architect. *Address:* Russian Academy of Architecture, Dmitrova str. 24, 103874 Moscow, Russia (office). *Telephone:* (495) 229-65-26 (office).

VAVILOV, Andrei Petrovich; Russian business executive and politician; b. 10 Jan. 1961, Perm; m. Marina Tsaregradskaya; ed Moscow Inst. of Man.; eng programmer Computation Centre USSR Ministry of Public Health 1982–85; jr researcher, Cen. Inst. of Econs and Math., USSR Acad. of Sciences 1985–88, Head of Lab. Inst. of Marketing Problems 1991–92; sr researcher, Inst. of Econ. Prognosis of Tech. Progress 1988–91; Head Dept of Macroecon. Policy, Ministry of Econs and Finance 1992; First Deputy Minister of Finance 1992–97; Pres. Int. Financial Initiative Bank 1997–; mem. Bd of Dirs RAO Gazprom (Counsellor to Chair. 1998–), Norilsk Nikel; Dir, Inst. of Financial Studies 1998–; mem. Observation Council Savings Bank 1997; Chair. Bd of Dirs N. Oil Co. 2000–2003; Council of Federated Repubs Penza region 2002–. *Publications:* over 20 papers. *Leisure interests:* hunting, skiing, tennis. *Address:* International Financial Initiative, B. Gruzinskaya str. 12, korp. 2, 123242 Moscow, Russia (office). *Telephone:* (495) 725-58-33 (office).

VÁVRA, Otakar; Czech scriptwriter and film director (retd); b. 28 Feb. 1911, Hradec Králové; s. of Alois Vávra and Marie Vávrová; m. 1st Helena Vávrová 1946 (deceased); m. 2nd Jitka Němcová 1997; one s.; ed Czech Tech. Coll.; scriptwriter, Dir Moldavia-film, Elektafilm, Lucernafilm cos 1931–45; scriptwriter, Dir Barrandov Film Studios, Prague 1945–89; art team man. Barrandov Film Studios, Prague 1947–51; teacher, Film Faculty, Acad. of Music and Dramatic Arts, Prague 1949–51, Head, Film and Television Direction Dept 1956–70, Prof. 1963–; mem. collective man. Bd, Barrandov Film Studios, Prague 1951–54; art team man. Barrandov Film Studios, Prague 1954–56; Chair. feature film section, Union of Czechoslovak Film and Television Artists 1965, mem. Cen. Cttee 1966–70; Pro-Rector Acad. of Music and Dramatic Arts, Prague 1967–70; Order of Labour 1961, Order of Repub. 1981; awards from San Sebastián, Acapulco, Moscow, Phnom-Penh, Mar del Plata (Argentina) Film Festivals, Finale Award, Plzen (Special Award for work over previous ten years) 1990, Karlovy Vary Int. Film Festival Prize for contrib. to world film 2001, Czechoslovak Film Prize 1937, 1938, Luce Award for The Guild of Maids of Kutná Hora 1938, Nat. Prize 1941, Czech Land Prize 1948, State Prize 1949, Artist of Merit Award (Edin.) 1955, State Prize of Klement Gottwald 1968, Nat. Artist 1968, Prize of Antonín Zápotocký 1973, State Prize of Klement Gottwald 1977, and various other awards. *Author and co-author of films:* 89 screenplays including The Eleventh Commandment, Maryša 1935, The Lane in Paradise, A Camel through a Needle's Eye 1936, Guard No. 47, Morality Above All 1937, The Case of Jan Masaryk 1998, Dammed Beauty 1998. *Films directed:* 46 films including Gaudeamus igitur, Virginity 1937, scriptwriter and dir of short films Light Penetrates Darkness 1931, We Live in Prague 1934, November 1935 Guild of the Maids of Kutná Hora 1938, Humoresque 1939, The House of Magic 1939, The Enchanted Masqued Lover, The Girl in Blue, The Mistress in Disguise, Dr Hegl's Patient, The May Tale 1940, The Turbine 1941, Come Right Back 1942, Happy Journey 1942, Rozina the Bastard 1945, The Mischievous Bachelor 1946, Presentiment 1947, Krakatit 1948, The Silent Barricade 1949, Deployment 1952, Jan Hus 1955, A Hussite Warrior 1956, Against All 1957, Citizen Brych 1958, The First Rescue Party 1959, The Curfew 1960, August Sunday 1960, The Night Guest 1961, The Burning Heart 1962, The Golden Queening 1965, Romance for a Bugle 1966, 13 Chamber 1968, Witch-Hunt 1969, The Days of Betrayal 1973, Sokolovo 1974, The Liberation of Prague 1977, A Story of Love and Honour 1977, The Dark Sun 1980, Jan Amos Commenius 1982, Comedian 1983, Oldřich a Božena 1984, Veronika 1985, Temptation Catherine, Chief Witness 1985–87, Till 1987, Europe was Waltzing 1989, Genus 1996, Moje Praha 2003. *Publications:* Contemplations of the Film Director 1982, Three Times in Front of the Camera (with M. V. Kratochvil) 1986, Strange Life of the Film Director 1996. *Leisure interests:* literature, cinema, theatre, golf. *Address:* Academy of Music and Dramatic Arts, Faculty of Film and TV, Smetanovo nábřeží 2, 11000 Prague 1, Czech Republic (office). *Telephone:* (2) 24229468 (office). *Fax:* (2) 24230285 (office).

VÄYRYNEN, Paavo Matti, DPolSc; Finnish politician; *Minister of Foreign Trade and Development;* b. 2 Sept. 1946, Keminmaa; s. of Juho Eemeli Väyrynen and Anna Liisa (née Kaijankoski) Väyrynen; m. Vuokko Kaarina Tervonen 1968; one s. two d.; mem. Parl. 1970–; Political Sec. to Prime Minister 1970–71; Vice-Chair. Centre Party 1972–80, Chair. 1980; mem. Nordic Council 1972–75; Minister of Educ. 1975–76, of Labour 1976–77; Minister for Foreign Affairs 1977–82, 1991–93, of Foreign Trade and Devt 2007–; mem. European Parl. 1995–2007, mem. Cttee on Foreign Affairs, Human Rights, Common Security and Defence Policy, Cttee on Regional Devt 2004–07. *Publications:* Köyhän asialla (Speaking for the Poor) 1971, On muutoksen aika (This is a Time of Change) 1974, Kansallisia kysymyksiä 1981, Kansakunta – ihmiskunta 1987, Finlands utrikes politik 1988, Suomen

ulkopolitiikka 1989, Yhteinen tehtävämme 1989, Igenom brytningstid 1993, On muutoksen aika II 1993, On totuuden aika I 1993, On totuuden aika II 1993, Suomen puolueettomuus uudessa Euroopassa 1996, Paneurooppa ja uusidealismi 1997, Itsenäisen Suomen puolesta 1999, Samankeskisten kehien Eurooppa 2000, Etiäisiä vai kaukoviisautta 2004, Pohjanranta 2005. *Address:* Ministry of Foreign Affairs, Merikasarmi, PO Box 176, 00161 Helsink, Finland (office). *Telephone:* (9) 16056302 (office). *Fax:* (9) 16056303 (office). *E-mail:* paavo.vayrynen@formin.fi (office). *Website:* formin.finland.fi; www.vayrynen.com.

VAZ, José Mário; Guinea-Bissau politician; fmr Pres. Assembléia Nacional Popular (Parl.); Minister of Finance 2009–. *Address:* Ministry of Finance, Rua Justino Lopes 74a, CP 67, Bissau, Guinea-Bissau (office). *Telephone:* 203670 (office). *Fax:* 203496 (office). *E-mail:* info@mail.guine-bissau.org (office). *Website:* www.guine-bissau.org (office).

VÁZQUEZ MOTA, Josefina Eugenia; Mexican politician; *Secretary of Public Education;* b. 1961, Mexico City; m. Sergio Ocampo Muñoz; three d.; ed Universidad Iberoamerican, Panamerican Inst. for Exec. Business Admin (IPADE); fmr Head of Women's Secr., Asociación Política Nacional; adviser to Confed. of Nat. Chambers of Commerce and Tourism (Concanaco); fmr adviser to Mexican Patronal Confed. (Coparmex); elected to Congress as mem. of Nat. Action Party (PAN) 2000, Minister of Social Devt 2000–05 (resgnd); man. of successful presidential campaign of Filipe Calderon Hinojosa 2006, then head of transition team; Sec. of Public Educ. 2006–; fmr Deputy Chair., Econ. Policy Cttee; participant, Latin American Social Ministers Forum; Head of Mexican Del., Gen. Conf. of UN Org. for Food and Agric., Rome, Italy; Diploma on Ideas and Insts, Autonomous Technological Inst. of Mexico (ITAM). *Publications:* Dios Mio, Hazme Viuda Por Favor 2001; numerous articles in newspapers including Novedades and El Economista. *Address:* Secretariat of State for Public Education, Dinamarca 84, 5°, Col. Juárez, 06600 México, DF, Mexico (office). *Telephone:* (55) 5510-2557 (office). *Fax:* (55) 5329-6873 (office). *E-mail:* educa@sep.gob.mx (office). *Website:* www.sep.gob.mx (office).

VÁZQUEZ RAÑA, Mario; Mexican business executive and sports administrator; *President and Director-General, Organizacion Editorial Mexicana;* b. 7 June 1932, Mexico City; m. Paquita Ramos; five c.; ed degree in business admin; participated in shooting competitions at nat. and int. level 1960; Pres. Bd Dirs Hermanos Vazquez Co. 1960–80; Pres. and Dir-Gen. Organizacion Editorial Mexicana (largest newspaper co. in Latin America) 1975–, Cartones Ponderosa 2001–; Owner United Press International 1985–88; Pres. Mexican Shooting Fed. 1969–74, American Shooting Confed. 1973–79; Vice-Pres. Mexican Sports Confed. 1973–76; mem. Nat. Olympic Cttee (NOC) 1972–, Pres. 1974–2001; Pres. Pan American Games Org. Cttee 1975, Pan American Sports Org. (PASO) 1975–, Asscn of Nat. Olympic Cttees 1979–; Chair. Int. Olympic Solidarity Comm. for the American Continent 1975–, Vice-Chair. Olympic Solidarity Comm. 1979–96; mem. Exec. Bd IOC as rep. of NOCs 2000–, Deputy Chair. 1997–2001, Chair. 2002–, mem. the following Comms: Olympic Movt 1990–99, Preparation of the XII Olympic Congress 1990–94, Apartheid and Olympism 1990–92, 'IOC 2000' (Exec. Cttee 1999), Marketing 2000, IOC 2000 Reform Follow-up 2002. *Address:* Organizacion Editorial Mexicana, S A De C V, Guillermo Prieto No 7, Ciudad De Mexico, Distrito Federal Mexico, Mexíco, Mexico (home); Association of National Olympic Committees, 54 avenue Hoche, 75008 Paris, France (office). *Telephone:* (55) 5566-2866 (Mexico) (office); 1-56-60-52-80 (office). *Fax:* 1-56-60-55-55 (office). *E-mail:* info@acnolympic.org (office). *Website:* www.acnolympic.org (office).

VÁZQUEZ ROMERO, Antonio; Spanish tobacco industry executive; *CEO and Chairman, Executive Committee, Altadis;* Dir of Subsidiaries and Man. Dir, Osborne Group, Mexico 1978–83; Dir of Subsidiaries, Domecq Mexico and Man. Dir Domecq International 1983–93; Deputy Dir Int. Dept, Tabacalera 1993–96, Dir Cigar Div. 1996–2000, COO Cigar Div., Altadis (tobacco co. cr. out of merger of Seita and Tabacalera) 2000–05, CEO and Chair. Exec. Cttee 2005–. *Address:* Altadis, c/ Eloy Gonzalo 10, Madrid 28010, Spain (office). *Telephone:* (91) 3609000 (office). *Fax:* (91) 3609100 (office). *E-mail:* dircomsp@altadis.com (office). *Website:* www.altadis.com (office).

VÁZQUEZ ROSAS, Tabaré Ramón, PhD; Uruguayan politician, physician and head of state; *President;* b. 17 Jan. 1940, Montevideo; m. Maria Auxiliadora Delgado; three c.; ed Universidad de la Republica, Gustave Roussy Inst., Paris; Prof. Faculty of Medicine, Universidad de la Republica 1987–; Mayor of Montevideo 1990–95; Leader, Encuentro Progresista-Frente Amplio (Broad Front) coalition 2001–; unsuccessful presidential cand. 2000; Pres. of Uruguay 2005–; WHO Dir-Gen's Award for coordinating tobacco control in Uruguay 2006. *Address:* Office of the President, Casa de Gobierno, Edif. Libertad, Avenida Luis Alberto de Herrera 3350, Montevideo; Encuentro Progresista-Frente Amplio, Colonia 1367, 2° Montevideo, Uruguay (office). *Telephone:* (2) 4872110 (office); (2) 9022176 (office). *Fax:* (2) 4809397 (office). *Website:* www.presidencia.gub.uy (office).

VEASEY, Josephine, CBE; British singer (mezzo-soprano) (retd) and vocal consultant; b. 10 July 1930, London; m. Ande Anderson 1951 (divorced 1969); one s. one d.; mem. chorus Covent Garden Opera Company 1948–50, returned as soloist 1955; prin. mezzo-soprano, Royal Opera House, Covent Garden; has sung every major mezzo-soprano role in repertory; many foreign engagements have included Salzburg Festival, La Scala, Milan, Metropolitan Opera House, New York and Paris Opera; Prof., RAM 1982–83; vocal consultant, ENO 1985–94; Hon. RAM. *Recordings:* has made recordings with Karajan, Solti, Bernstein and Colin Davis. *Address:* 5 Meadow View, Whitchurch, Hants., RG28 7BL, England (home). *Telephone:* (1256) 896813 (home).

VEBER, Francis Paul; French screenwriter and director; b. 28 July 1937, Neuilly; s. of Pierre Gilles Veber and Catherine Veber (née Agadjaniantz); m. Françoise Marie Ehrenpreis 1964; two s.; ed Paris Univ. of Science, Paris

Medical School; began career as journalist, also wrote short stories, stand-up comedy material and theatre plays; wrote first film screenplay 1969; Pres. EFVE Films 1976, Escape Film Production Co. 1988; Chevalier, Légion d'honneur, Commdr des Arts et Lettres, Officier de l'Ordre Nat. du Mérite. *Films directed:* first film, Le Jouet, 1976; first American film, Three Fugitives 1989, Le Dîner de Cons 1997 (based on his stage play), Le Placard 2001, Tais-Toi 2003, La Doublure 2006. *Publications:* Le Grand Blond avec une Chaussure Noire 1972, L'Emmerdeur 1973, Le Magnifique 1973, Le Jouet 1976, La Cage aux Folles (adaptation) 1978, La Chèvre 1981, Les Compères 1983, Les Fugitifs 1986, Le Jaguar 1996, Le Dîner de Cons 1998, Le Placard 2001, Tais-Toi 2003. *Leisure interests:* tennis, swimming. *Address:* c/o Artmédia, 20 avenue Rapp, 75007 Paris, France (office); Creative Artists Agency, 9830 Wilshire Boulevard, Beverly Hills, CA 90210, USA (office). *Telephone:* (310) 288-4545 (USA) (office).

VECSEI, Eva Hollo, BArch, FRAIC; Canadian/Hungarian architect; b. 21 Aug. 1930, Vienna, Austria; m. André Vecsei 1952; one s. one d.; ed School of Architecture, Univ. of Tech. Sciences, Budapest; Assoc. Prof., School of Architecture, Univ. of Budapest; designer of various public bldgs and winner of housing competition, Budapest 1952–56; Assoc., ARCOP Architects, Montréal, Canada 1958–71; Assoc. of D. Dimakopoulos, architect, Montréal 1971–73; in pvt. practice, Eva Vecsei, architect 1973–84, in partnership with husband, Vecsei Architectes 1984– (now Prin.); mem. Nat. Capital Comm. Advisory Cttee on Design 1982–87; juror for several architectural competitions; lecture tour in China 1984; Adjunct Prof. and Adviser to Master of Architecture Programme, McGill Univ. 2000; Hon. Fellow, AIA, OAQ; Award of Excellence, The Canadian Architect, for office bldg, McGill Coll. Avenue, Montréal 1983, Prix Orange for renovation of Passage du Musée, Montréal, Médaille du Mérite, L'Ordre des architectes du Québec 2004. *Major projects include:* planning, design devt and design control of Life Science Bldg, Halifax, McGill Univ. Student Centre, Montréal and other projects 1958–71; design and execution La Cité 7-acre redevelopment project, Montréal 1973–76, commercial and financial centre, Karachi, Pakistan, drama faculty and experimental theatre, Sainte-Thérèse, Canada, Inter-Municipal Library and Recreational Centre, Dollard-des-Ormeaux, Canada, Residence Montefiore, Montréal. *Publications:* History of American Literature 1980, Encyclopedia of Contemporary Architects 1980, 1997–98, La Bâtisseuse de la Cité 1993, Designing Women 2000; articles in architectural journals. *Leisure interests:* music, nature. *Address:* Vecsei Architectes, 1425 rue du Fort, Montréal, PQ H3H 2C2 (office); 4417 Circle Road, Montréal, PQ H3W 1Y6, Canada. *Telephone:* (514) 932-7100 (office). *Fax:* (514) 932-7987 (office). *E-mail:* vecsei@total.net (office).

VEDERNIKOV, Alexander Aleksandrovich; Russian conductor; b. 11 Jan. 1964, Moscow; s. of Aleksander F. Vedernikov and Natalya Guryeva; m. Olga Aleksandrovna Vedernikova; ed Moscow P. I. Tchaikovsky State Conservatory; Asst, then Conductor Prin. Symphony Orchestra of Russian TV and Radio 1989–95; Founder and Chief Conductor Russian Philharmonic Orchestra 1995–98, 2000–; Musical Dir and Chief Conductor Bolshoi Theatre of Russia 2001–; conducted opera and ballet productions in European theatres including Covent Garden, London, La Scala, Milan and symphony orchestras in Russia. *Address:* Bolshoi Theatre, Teatralnaya pl. 1, Moscow (office); Pyryeva str. 4, korp. 1, apt. 24, 119285 Moscow, Russia (home). *Telephone:* (495) 292-18-48 (office); (495) 147-52-17 (home).

VÉDRINE, Hubert; French politician and civil servant; *Managing Director, Hubert Védrine Conseil;* b. 31 July 1947, Saint-Silvain-Bellegarde; s. of Jean Védrine and Suzanne Védrine; m. Michèle Froment; two s.; ed Lycée Albert Camus, Univ. of Nanterre, Institut d'Etudes Politiques, Paris, Ecole Nat. d'Admin.; Sr Civil Servant, Ministry of Culture 1974–78, Ministry for Capital Works 1978–79; Co-ordinator for Cultural Relations, Near and Middle East, Ministry of Foreign Affairs 1979–81; Technical Adviser External Affairs, Office of the Sec.-Gen. of the Pres. 1981–86, Legal Adviser, Conseil d'Etat 1986, 1995–96; Spokesman for Presidency of Repub. 1988–91, Sec.-Gen. 1991–95; Minister of Foreign Affairs 1997–2002; Man. Dir Hubert Védrine Conseil 2003–; Pnr, Jeantet et Associés (law firm) 1996–97. *Publications:* Mieux aménager sa ville 1979, Les Mondes de François Mitterrand, A l'Elysée 1981–95 1996, Dialogue avec Dominique Moïsi: Les Cartes de la France à l'heure de la mondialisation 2000, Face à l'Hyperpuissance 2003, Multilateralisme – une reforme possible 2004, François Mitterand – un dessein, un destin 2006. *Address:* Hubert Védrine Conseil, 21 rue Jean Goujon, 75008 Paris (office); 6 rue de Luynes, 75007 Paris, France (home). *Telephone:* 1-45-63-32-82 (office). *Fax:* 1-45-63-38-29 (office). *E-mail:* bureau.hv@hvconseil.com (office). *Website:* www.hvconseil.com (office); www.hubertvedrine.net.

VEGA DE LA CUADRA, Felipe; Ecuadorean politician; *Minister of the Interior;* b. 1961, Cuenca; Gov. of Azuay 1997–2004; Pvt. Sec. to Vice-Pres. Alfredo Palacio 2004–05; Deputy Minister of Labour and Deputy Minister of the Interior 2005, Minister of the Interior 2006–. *Address:* Ministry of the Interior, Calle Benalcázar N4-24 y Espejo, Quito, Ecuador (office). *Telephone:* (2) 2955666 (office). *Fax:* (2) 2955497 (office). *E-mail:* informacion@mingobierno.gov.ec (office). *Website:* www.mingobierno.gov.ec (office).

VEGA DE SEOANE AZPILICUETA, Javier; Spanish mining engineer; *Co-Founder and President, Gestlink;* b. 13 Sept. 1947, San Sebastián; s. of Joaquín Vega de Seoane and Rosa Azpilicueta; m. Mercedes Pérez de Villaamil Lapiedra 1970; two s. one d.; ed Escuela Técnica Superior de Ingenieros de Minas, Madrid and Glasgow Business School, UK; Asst Production Dir, Fundiciones del Estanda SA 1972–75; Asst to CEO, Leyland Ibérica SA 1975–77; Gen. Man. SKF Española SA 1977–83, Pres. and CEO 1983–84; Gen. Man. Instituto Nacional de Industria 1984–86; Pnr TASA AG 1986; Co-Founder Gestlink 1987, Pres. 1991–; Pres. Explosivos Río Tinto, S.A. Cros 1988, Chair. Bd Ercros (following merger) –1991; Pres. Fujitsu España; mem. Bd of Dirs Thyssen Krupp SA, DKV Seguros, AON-Gil y Carvajal, Solvay Ibérica, FYCSA (Formación y Consultoría SA), YDILO Voice Solutions, Ecoralia; mem. Exec. Bd Circulo de Empresarios; mem. Advisory Bd Mining School of Madrid. *Leisure interests:* golf, squash, scuba diving. *Address:* Gestlink, Fortuny 39, Bajo Izqda, 28010 Madrid, Spain (office). *Telephone:* (913) 91-59-10 (office). *Fax:* (913) 19-67-92 (office). *Website:* www.gestlink.es (office).

VEGA GARCÍA, Gen. Gerardo Clemente Ricardo; Mexican politician and army officer; b. 28 March 1940, Puebla City; nat. security studies in USA and Panama and fmr Dir of Mil. Educ.; fmr Rector Army and Air Force Univ.; fmr Deputy Chief of Mil. Doctrine, Estado Mayor of SEDENA; fmr Mil. Attaché, embassies in USSR, Poland, and Germany; fmr Deputy Dir and Dir Nat. Defence Coll.; promoted to Div. Gen. with command of Mil. Zone One 2000; Sec. of Nat. Defence –2006. *Address:* c/o Secretariat of State for National Defence, Manuel Avila Camacho, esq. Avda Industria Militar, 3°, Col. Lomas de Sotelo, Del. Miguel Hidalgo, 11640, México, DF, Mexico (office).

VEIGA, Carlos Alberto Wahnon de Carvalho, PhD; Cape Verde politician and lawyer; b. 21 Oct. 1949, Mindelo; Prime Minister of Interim Govt Jan. 1991, Prime Minister of Cape Verde 1991–2000, also with responsibility for Defence; Presidential cand. 2001; fmr Chair. Movimento para a Democracia (MPD). *Address:* WV Consultones LDA, CP43-A Praia, Santiago, Cape Verde (office). *Telephone:* 60-36-70 (office); 62-12-10 (home). *Fax:* 61-95-83 (office); 62-12-20 (home). *E-mail:* wvjtv@cvtelecom.cv (office); carlos.veiga@cvtelecom.cv (home).

VEIL, Simone, LenD; French politician and fmr lawyer; b. 13 July 1927, Nice; d. of André Jacob and Yvonne Steinmetz; m. Antoine Veil 1946; three s.; ed Inst. d'Etudes Politiques de Paris; Attaché Ministry of Justice 1957–59; Tech. Adviser to Office of René Pleven, Keeper of the Seals 1969; Sec.-Gen. Conseil Supérieur de la Magistrature 1970–74; mem. ORTF Admin. Council 1971–74; Minister of Health 1974–76, of Health and Social Security 1976–79, of Social Affairs, Health and Urban Devt 1993–95; mem. European Parl. 1979–93, (Pres. 1979–82, Chair. of Legal Affairs Cttee 1982–84), Chair. Liberal and Democratic Group 1984–89; mem. Conseil Constitutionnel 1998–; Leader Centre-Right List for European elections 1989; Pres. Fondation pour la Mémoire de la Shoah 2001–, Bd Dirs for Victims Trust, Fund of Int. Criminal Court 2003–, Fondation Gustave Roussy pour la Recherche Médicale 2005; mem. Acad. Française 2008–; Grand Officier, Légion d'honneur 2009, numerous foreign decorations, including Hon. DBE (UK) 1997, Chevalier, Ordre nat. du Mérite, Grand Officer, Nat. Order of the Lion (Senegal), Order of Merit of the Repub. (Ivory Coast), Isabel la Católica (Spain), Grand Cross Order of Merit (FRG), Order of Rio Branco (Brazil), Order of Merit (Luxembourg), Order of the Phoenix (Greece); Hon. LLD (Glasgow) 1995; Dr hc (Princeton) 1975, (Weizmann Inst.) 1976, (Bar Ilan) 1980, (Yale) 1980, (Cambridge) 1980, (Edin.) 1980, (Georgetown) 1981, (Urbino) 1981, (Sussex) 1984, (Yeshiva) 1982, (Free Univ., Brussels) 1984, (Brandeis) 1989, (Pennsylvania) 1997; Onassis Foundation Prize 1980, Charlemagne Prize 1981, Louise Weiss Foundation Prize 1981, Louise Michel Prize 1983, European Merit Prize 1983, Jabotinsky Prize (USA) 1983, Prize for Everyday Courage 1984, Special Freedom Prize 1984, Fiera di Messina 1984, Thomas Dehler Prize 1988, Klein Foundation Prize, Phila 1991, Truman Prize for Peace, Jerusalem 1991, Giulietta Prize, Verona 1991, Atlantide Prize, Barcelona 1991, Prix Grand Siècle 2005, Prix Prince des Asturies 2005 and other prizes, Médaille pénitentiaire, Médaille de l'Education surveillée. *Publication:* Les données psycho-sociologiques de l'adoption (with Prof. Launay and Dr Soule) 1969, Les hommes aussi s'en souviennent 2004, Une Vie (auto-biog.) 2007. *Address:* 10 rue de Rome, 75008 Paris (office); Conseil constitutionnel, 2 rue Montpensier, 75001 Paris; 11 Place Vauban, 75007 Paris, France (home). *Telephone:* 1-42-93-00-60 (office). *Fax:* 1-40-08-03-62 (office). *E-mail:* corinne.adamrix@wanadoo.fr (office).

VEINBERG, Lev Iosifovich, PhD; Russian business executive; *President, SOLEV International Consortium;* b. 6 May 1944, Samara; m. Sofia D. Landau; one d.; ed Moscow Aviation Inst., Moscow State Univ.; scientific research and teaching (automation of tests, metrology), Moscow Aviation Inst. –1987; Founder and Gen. Dir Interquadro (French/Italian/Soviet computer co.—first jt computer venture in USSR) 1987–90; owner and Pres., SOLEV Int. Consortium 1990–; IBM consultant in Russia 1990–92; Vice-Pres., Int. Foundation for Promotion of Privatization and Foreign Investments 1991–93; Chair. Bd of Dirs, AO Centrinvest (reconstruction of Moscow city centre) 1992–, AO Rosvtordragmet 1993–, Russian Bank for Reconstruction and Devt 1993–96; Pres. Asscn of Jt Ventures, Int. Unions and Orgs 1988–, Chair. Supervisory Bd 1998–; Vice-Pres. Scientific-Industrial Union of USSR 1990–91; Vice-Pres. Russian Union of Industrialists and Entrepreneurs 1991–; mem. Presidium, Council on Foreign and Defence Policy of Russia 1992–; Chair. of Bd BAM Credit Bank 1996, AKB Technobank 1997; Order of Friendship 1998; Council of Ministers of the USSR Prize 1988. *Publications:* more than 50 articles in specialized journals. *Leisure interest:* reading history books. *Address:* International Consortium SOLEV, Svetly Proyezd 4, corp. 4, 125080 Moscow (office); Apt. 139, 3 Facultetsky Per., 125080 Moscow, Russia (home). *Telephone:* (495) 158-53-39 (office). *Fax:* (495) 943-00-15 (office). *E-mail:* solev@solev.ru (office). *Website:* www.solev.ru (office).

VEKARIC, Vatroslav, MA, PhD; Croatian research institute director; *Director, Institute for International Politics and Economics;* b. 4 March 1944, Dubrovnik; ed Univ. of Belgrade; began career as journalist with Radio Zagreb 1967–68; Research Fellow, Inst. for Int. Politics and Econs (IIPE) 1968–77, Dir Centre for Regional Studies 1977–80, Deputy Dir IIPE (Dir of Research) 1980–85, Dir IIPE 2000–; Dir Centre for Strategic Studies, Belgrade 1985–2000; conducted UN research projects 1981–83; Lecturer, Univ. of Belgrade 1982–84, Centre for Post-Grad. Studies, Dubrovnik 1985–,

Univ. of Bari 1997, 1999, Univ. of Sant Angelo, Rome 1998, Univ. of Florence 1998; Ed.-in-Chief Review of International Affairs 2001–; mem. Bd Dirs Diplomatic Acad., Serbia and Montenegro 2001–; mem. Int. Advisory Bd Journal of International Relations; mem Int. Studies Asscn, USA 1986–, Cttee for Mediterranean Studies, Sassari, Italy 1983– (Deputy Sec.-Gen. 1984–87), Contemplating Group for Scenarios of Devt of the Mediterranean (UN-UNEP), Cannes, France 1983–87, Governing Bd AIRI, Rome 1989–, Int. Law Asscn 1993–, Editorial Bd Nuova Fase review, Edizioni Democrazia Domani, Rome 1994–, Scientific Council Inst. for the Study of the Greek Economy, Athens 1994–, Programme Cttee Centre for Euro-Mediterranean Studies, Rome 1997–99. *Publications:* seven books and more than 130 essays and articles. *Address:* Institute for International Politics and Economics, Makedonska 25, 11000 Belgrade, Serbia (office). *Telephone:* (11) 3373824 (office); (11) 3110917 (home). *Fax:* (11) 3373835 (office). *E-mail:* amarcord@eunet.yu (office). *Website:* www.diplomacy.bg.ac.yu (office).

VEKSELBERG, Viktor; Russian (b. Ukrainian) oil executive; *Chairman, SUAL Holdings;* b. 1957, Lvov, Ukrain; m.; two c.; ed Moscow Inst. of Railroad Eng; f. Renova 1988, Chair. 1990–; acquired Vlaimir Tractor Factory 1994; merged Siberian Irkutsk Aluminium with Ural Aluminium to form Siberial-Urals Aluminium (SUAL) Co. 1996, Pres. SUAL Group 1996–2003, Chair. 2003–; Deputy Chair. TNK (Tyumen Oil Co.) Man. Bd 1998–2000, Chair. 2000–02, Chair. and CEO 2002–03 (merged with BP Russia to form TNK-BP 2003), COO TNK-BP 2003–; mem. Exec. Bd Dirs Russian Union of Industrialists and Entrepreneurs; mem. Bd Trustees Bolshoi Theatre, Moscow. *Address:* TNK-BP, 18/2 Schipok Street, Moscow 115093, Russia (office). *Telephone:* (095) 745-78-46 (office). *Fax:* (095) 787-96-42 (office). *Website:* www.tnk-bp.com (office).

VELASCO BARAONA, Belisario; Chilean politician; *Minister of the Interior;* b. 5 Feb. 1935, Santiago de Chile; began career at Empresa de Comercio Agrícola (Agricultural Trade Co.) 1953, Man. Dir 1964–70; joined Partido Demócratia Cristiano (Christian Democratic Party) 1957; Man. Dir Radio Presidente Balmaceda 1973–76; co-f. agricultural export co. 1974; Chair. Análisis magazine 1980–86; Deputy Minister of the Interior 1990–99, served as acting Minister of Defence on several occasions; Amb. to Portugal 1999–2003; Minister of the Interior 2006–. *Address:* Ministry of the Interior, La Moneda Palace, Santiago de Chile, Chile (office). *Telephone:* (2) 690-4000 (office). *E-mail:* contact@msgg.gov.cl (office). *Website:* www.interior.gov.cl (office).

VELASCO BRANES, Andres, PhD; Chilean government official and economist; *Minister of Finance;* ed Yale and Columbia Univs, USA; Chief of Staff to Minister of Finance 1990–92, later Dir of Int. Finance; Postdoctoral Fellow in Political Economy, Harvard Univ. and MIT 1994–95; Chief Economist and Deputy Lead Negotiator NAFTA accession team, Chile 1995; fmr adviser to govts of Ecuador and El Salvador; fmr consultant World Bank, IMF, Inter-American Devt Bank, UN Econ. Comm. for Latin America, Fed. Research Bank of Atlanta; fmr Dir Center for Latin American and Caribbean Studies, New York Univ.; Sumitomo-FASID Prof. of Int. Finance and Devt, Harvard Univ. 2000–06; Minister of Finance 2006–. *Publications:* Trade, Development and the World Economy: Selected Essays of Carlos Díaz-Alejandro (ed.) 1988, Vox Populi (novel) 1995, Lugares Comunes (novel) 2003, Free Trade and Beyond: Prospects for Integration in the Americas (co-ed.) 2004. *Address:* Ministry of Finance, Teatinos 120, 12°, Santiago, Chile (office). *Telephone:* (2) 675-5800 (office). *Fax:* (2) 671-8064 (office). *E-mail:* webmaster@minhda.cl (office). *Website:* www.minhda.cl (office); ksghome.harvard.edu/~avelasco.

VELASQUEZ-GÁZTELU RUIZ, Cándido; Spanish business executive; *Director, Telvent GIT SA;* b. 1937, Jerez de la Frontera; ed Univ. of Granada, IESE Barcelona; Dir Coca-Cola and other cos; Head of Sales and Commercial Dir Tabalcera SA 1973, Gen. Dir 1981, Chair. 1982–89; Chair. Compañía Telefónica Nacional de España 1989–96; Dir Telvent GIT SA 2000–; mem. Bd Adolfo Domínguez, Wisdom Lux, Zenith Media, Worldbest Cigars; mem. Advisory Bd Abengoa, Accenture; Pres. Spanish Autism Confed. *Address:* Telvent GIT SA, Valgrande 6, 28108 Alcobendas, Madrid, Spain (office). *Telephone:* (91) 714-70-00 (office). *Fax:* (91) 714-70-01 (office). *Website:* www.telvent.com (office).

VELAYATI, Ali Akbar; Iranian politician, medical scientist and academic; *Professor, Shahid Beheshti University of Medical Sciences and Health Education;* b. 1945, Tehran; s. of Ali Asghar and Zobeideh Asgah; m. Skina Khoshnevisan; four c.; ed Tehran Univ., Johns Hopkins Univ., USA; joined Nat. Front (of Mossadegh) 1961; founder of Islamic Asscn of Faculty of Medicine, Tehran Univ. 1963; underground political activities in support of Ayatollah Khomeini 1979; Vice-Minister, Ministry of Health 1979–80; proposed for Prime Minister by Ayatollah Khomeini Oct. 1981 (candidature rejected by the Majlis); Minister of Foreign Affairs 1981–97; adviser to supreme leader in int. affairs; currently Prof. Shahid Beheshti Univ. of Medical Sciences and Health Educ.; Head, Islamic And Traditional Medicine Dept, Iranian Acad. of Medical Sciences; Pres. Iranian Journal of Infectious Diseases and Tropical Medicine, Iranian Soc. for Support of Patients with Infectious Diseases; mem. Int. Soc. for History of Medicine; Zmaj Od Bosne Gold Medal for Services to Peace in the Balkans 1995; Dr hc (Al-Farabi, Kazakhstan) 1992, (Teflis, Georgia) 1993, (Avecina, Tajikistan) 1995. *Publications:* Infectious Diseases (3 vols) 1979, numerous articles in professional journals. *Address:* Shahid Beheshti University of Medical Sciences and Health Services, Shahid Chamran Highway, Evin, POB 4139-19395, Tehran (office); Iranian Academy of Medical Sciences, PO Box 19395/4655, Pasdaran Avenue, Tehran, Iran. *Telephone:* (21) 220109555 (office). *Fax:* (21) 220109484 (office). *E-mail:* icrd@sbmu.ac.ir (office); vlayati@ams.ac.ir (office); aavelayati@nritld.ac.ir (office). *Website:* www.sbmu.ac.ir (office).

VELDHUIS, Johannes (Jan) G. F.; Dutch university president (retd); b. 4 Oct. 1938, Hengelo; m. Monica M. H. Thier 1969; three s.; ed Univs of Utrecht and Minnesota; Ministry of Foreign Affairs 1968–70; Sec. Univ. Bd Univ. of Leiden 1970–74; Deputy Sec.-Gen. Ministry of Educ. and Science 1974–79, Dir-Gen. and Insp.-Gen. of Educ. and Science 1979–86; Pres. Utrecht Univ. 1986–2003; Chair. Netherlands del. OECD Educ. Cttee 1984–86; Chair. Bd Netherlands-America Comm. for Educational Exchange (Fulbright Comm.) 1984–2001, Netherlands Inst. for Art History, Florence, Fondation Descartes Amsterdam, Museum Catharÿneconvent Utrecht, Stichting Carmelcollege Hengelo; mem. Bd Netherlands History Inst., Rome, Netherlands Archaeological Inst., Cairo, Japan-Netherlands Inst., Tokyo; mem. bds of several hosps in The Hague area; Chevalier, Légion d'Honneur 1997, Officer Order Orange Nassau 1998, Commdr Order Isabel la Católica (Spain) 2001; Dr hc (Florida Gainesville); Univ. of Minn. Distinguished Leadership Award for Ints 2005. *Publications:* various publs in the field of educ. and public admin. *Leisure interests:* comparative educ., literature, botany, tennis, skiing, bridge. *Address:* Roucooppark 12, 2251 AV Voorschoten, Netherlands (home). *Telephone:* (71) 5617696 (home). *Fax:* (71) 5620029 (home). *E-mail:* monica.jan.veldhuis@planet.nl (home).

VELDRE, Vinets; Latvian veterinarian and politician; b. 26 March 1971; ed Latvian Univ. of Agriculture, Faculty of Veterinary Medicine, Uppsala Univ., Sweden, Free Univ. of Berlin, Danish Meat Trade Coll., A & G Univ., Tex., USA, Massey Univ., New Zealand; Lab Asst, Latvian Univ. of Agriculture, Faculty of Veterinary Medicine, Dept of Epizootics 1993–95; Sr Inspector State Veterinary Service, Rīga Dist Veterinary Authority 1995–97, Head, Control Div. for Food of Animal Origin 1997–99, Dir and State Chief Veterinary Inspector 1999–2001, Dir-Gen. Food and Veterinary Service 2001–07; Minister for Health Jan. 2007–Dec. 2007, for Defence Dec. 2007–09; mem. People's Party (TP) (Tautas partija); Award On Diligence, Ministry of Agriculture 2005. *Address:* c/o People's Party, Dzirnavu iela 68, Latvia (office).

VELICHKO, Vladimir Makarovich; Russian fmr politician and business executive; b. 23 April 1937, Mozhaisk, Voronezh Region; s. of Makar Petrovich Velichko and Maria Ivanovna Velichko; m. Eleanora Dmitrievna Bestouzheva 1961, one d.; ed Leningrad Inst. of Mechanics, Leningrad Inst. of Eng and Econs; joined CPSU 1962; started career as foreman, later dir of machine-building plant; First Deputy Minister, Ministry of Power Eng of USSR 1975–83, Minister 1983–87; Minister of Heavy Power and Transport Eng 1987–89; Minister of Heavy Machine-Building Industry 1989–91; USSR First Deputy Prime Minister Jan.–Dec. 1991; Deputy to USSR Supreme Soviet 1984–89; Deputy of the USSR 1989; mem. Political Consultative Council, Sept.–Dec. 1991; Chair. Bd Tyazhenergomash (now jt stock co. TENMA) 1992; Pres. Financial and Industrial Group Heavy Eng Industry 1996; Academician, mem. Presidium Russian Acad. of Eng; USSR State Prize 1974. *Leisure interests:* literature, art. *Address:* TENMA, Nizhni Kislovsky per. 5, GSP, 103906 Moscow K-9, Russia. *Telephone:* (495) 203-15-00. *Fax:* (495) 291-68-26.

VELIKHOV, Yevgeniy Pavlovich; Russian physicist; b. 2 Feb. 1935, Moscow; s. of Pavel Pavlovich Velikhov and Natalia Vsevolodoma Velikhova; m. Natalia Alekseevna Arseniyeva 1959; two s. one d.; mem. of staff, Kurchatov Inst. of Atomic Energy 1958–, Head of Lab. 1962–70, Deputy Dir, then Dir of br. of Inst. 1971–89; Dir Russian Scientific Centre, Kurchatov Inst. 1989–; Founder and Dir Inst. for Security Problems of Nuclear Energy Devt 1988–91; Prof., Moscow Univ. 1973–; mem. CPSU Cen. Cttee 1989–90; mem. USSR (now Russian) Acad. of Sciences 1974, Presidium, Vice-Pres. 1978–96, 2002–, Academician-Sec. Dept of Information Technology, Cybernetics and Automatic Systems 1985–92; mem. Supreme Soviet of USSR; People's Deputy of the USSR 1989–91; mem. Pres. Council 1992–93; Chair. Cttee of Soviet Scientists for Peace against Nuclear Threat; Co-founder Int. Foundation for Survival and Devt of Humanity; del. to numerous scientific and peace confs; Chair. Soviet Nuclear Soc. 1989–; Co-Chair. Jr Achievement of Russia 1991–; Chair. Council, Int. Thermonuclear Experimental Reactor 1992–; mem. Presidential Council of Science and Tech. 1995–; Pres. Shelf-Developing Co. Rosshelf 1992–; mem. American Geophysical Soc. 1981; Foreign mem. Swedish Royal Acad. of Eng Sciences 1989; Dr hc (Notre Dame, Susquachana, Tufts, London); USSR State Prize 1977, Lenin Prize 1984, Hero of Socialist Labour 1985, Science for Peace Prize, Italy, Szillard Award, American Physical Soc.; Order of Lenin (three times). *Publications:* numerous, related both to science and the problems of prevention of nuclear war. *Leisure interests:* skiing, underwater swimming, windsurfing. *Address:* RNTs Kurchatovskiy Institute, Kurchatova pl. 1, 123182 Moscow, Russia. *Telephone:* (495) 196-92-41.

VELJANOSKI, Trajko; Macedonian lawyer and politician; *President, Sobranie (Assembly);* b. 2 Nov. 1962, Skopje; m.; two c.; ed Law Faculty, Ss Cyril and Methodius Univ.; passed Bar examination 1988, est. ind. law office and worked as lawyer 1988–99; began political career by joining Makedonska Revolucionerna Organizacija—Demokratska Partija za Makedonsko Nacionalno Edinstvo (VMRO—DPMNE) 1993, Head of Legal Affairs Cttee for several years, mem. Political System Cttee, also headed VMRO-DPMNE Forum on Legal and Political Affairs and Judicial System; elected Under-Sec., Ministry of Justice 1999, later Deputy Minister; fmr mem. Pres.'s Cttee of Appeals, Man. Bd Centre for European Integration, State Election Comm.; mem. Sobranie (Ass.) 2006–, Chair. Cttee on Election and Appointment Issues 2006–08, Pres. of Sobranie 2008–, Chair. Cttee on Constitutional Issues, Chair. Del. of Ass. to Inter-Parl. Union. *Address:* Sobranie, 1000 Skopje, 11 Oktomvri, Former Yugoslav Republic of Macedonia (office). *Telephone:* (2) 3112255 (office). *Fax:* (2) 3237947 (office). *E-mail:* sobranie@sobranie.mk (office). *Website:* www.sobranie.mk (office).

VELLIDIS, Katerina; Greek publisher; b. 1947, Thessaloniki; d. of Ioannis Vellidis and Anna Vellidis; m. (divorced); one d.; ed Univ. of Geneva and Sorbonne, Paris; Pres. Bd and Man. Dir I. K. Vellidis Press Org. of Northern Greece (publrs of newspapers and magazines, including Macedonia and Thessaloníki) 1980–; Pres. Ioannis and Anna Vellidis Foundation; numerous awards including Silver Medal of Acad. of Athens. *Address:* Thessaloníki, Odos Monastiriou 85, 546 27 Thessaloníki, Greece (office). *Telephone:* (2310) 521621 (office).

VELTCHEV, Milen, MA, MBA; Bulgarian politician; *Vice-Chairman, National Movement for Stability and Progress (Natsionalno dvizhenie za stabilnost i vazhod);* b. 24 April 1966; ed Univ. of Nat. and World Economy, Sofia, Univ. of Rochester, Mass Inst. of Tech., USA; attaché, Ministry of Foreign Affairs, Bulgaria 1990–92; Assoc., Chemical Bank USA 1994, Merrill Lynch & Co., UK 1995–99, Vice-Pres. Emerging Markets 1999–2001; mem. Parl. 2001–; Minister of Finance 2001–05, Gov. for Bulgaria, World Bank, EBRD; currently Vice-Chair. Nat. Movt for Stability and Progress (Natsionalno dvizhenie za stabilnost i vazhod); fmr Chair. Monetary Council, Council for Internal Financial Control, Tax Policy Advisory Council; Euromoney Finance Minister of the Year 2002. *Address:* National Movement for Stability and Progress (Natsionalno dvizhenie za stabilnost i vazhod), 1000 Sofia, ul. Vrabcha 23, Bulgaria (office). *Telephone:* (2) 921-81-63 (office). *Fax:* (2) 921-81-65 (office). *E-mail:* ndsv@ndsv.bg (office). *Website:* www.ndsv.bg (office).

VELTMAN, Martinus J. G., PhD; Dutch physicist and academic; *John D. MacArthur Professor Emeritus of Physics, University of Michigan;* b. 1931; ed Univ. of Utrecht; Prof. of Physics Univ. of Utrecht 1966–81, Univ. of Mich. 1981–, now Prof. Emer.; mem. Dutch Acad. of Sciences; High Energy and Particle Physics Prize (European Physical Soc.) 1993, jt winner Nobel Prize in Physics 1999. *Publications include:* Facts and Mysteries in Particle Physics. *Address:* Randall Laboratory, University of Michigan, 500 East University Avenue, Ann Arbor, MI 48109-1120, USA (office). *Website:* www.physics.lsa .umich.edu (office).

VELTRONI, Walter; Italian politician; b. 3 July 1955, Rome; m.; two c.; ed Film Inst., Rome; fmr journalist and TV Asst Dir; Sec. Rome Br. Fed. of Young Italian Communists 1975, also mem. Nat. Exec.; mem. Rome City Council 1976–81; Deputy in Nat. Ass. 1987–; mem. Nat. Secr. PCI–PDS 1988–1992; Founder mem. Democratici di Sinistra (PDS—Democratic Left) 1991, apptd to Political Co-ordination Bureau 1991, Political Sec. 1998; Ed. L'Unità daily newspaper 1992–96, now Dir; Deputy Prime Minister, Minister for Cultural Heritage, Performing Arts and Sport 1996–98; mem. European Parl. (Party of European Socialists Group) 1999–; Mayor of Rome 2001–08; Exec. Vice-Pres. Council of European Municipalities and Regions 2003–; Vice-Pres. Socialist Int. 1999–; Leader Partito Democratico (formed following the merger of the left wing Socialist Democrats and Margherita parties) 2007–09 (resgnd); Chevalier, Légion d'Honneur 2000. *Publications include:* several books including Il sogno spezzato (on Robert Kennedy), La sfida interrotta (on the ideas of Enrico Berlinguer), Forse Dio è malato (travel book on Africa) and Il disco del mondo – Vita breve di Luca Flores, musicista. *Address:* Partito Democratico, Piazza Sant'Anastasia 7, 00186 Rome, Italy (office); European Parliament, Bâtiment Altiero Spinelli 15G210, 60 rue Wiertz, 1047 Brussels, Belgium (office). *Telephone:* (6) 675471 (office). *Fax:* (6) 67547319 (office); (2) 284-93-45 (Belgium) (office). *E-mail:* wveltroni@europarl.eu.int (office); info@ partitodemocratico.it (office). *Website:* www.partitodemocratico.it (office).

VELYAMINOV, Petr Sergeyevich; Russian actor; b. 7 Dec. 1926, Moscow; m.; four c.; arrested and imprisoned on charge of membership of anti-Soviet org. 1943, acquitted 1952; worked in theatres in Abakan, Perm, Tumen, Cheboksary, Sverdlovsk, Moscow (Sovremennik), St Petersburg (N. Akimov Comedy Theatre 1995–); People's Artist of Russia; USSR State Prize. *Theatre roles include:* Leander Nodan in Men in Her Life, Rodion Nikolayevich in Old-Fashioned Comedy. *Films include:* Komandir schastlivoy 'Shchuki' (Commander of the Lucky Pike) 1972, Yaroslav the Wise, Glass Labyrinth, Zdes nash dom (Here is our Home) 1973, Povest o chelovecheskom serdtse (A Tale about the Human Heart) 1975, Sladkaya zhenshchina (Sweet Woman) 1976, Poema o krylyakh (Poem of Wings) 1979, Dust Under the Sun, Version of Colonel Zorin, Dangerous Friends, Yaroslav Mudry (Yaroslav the Wise) 1981, Nas venchali ne v tserkvi (We Weren't Married in Church) 1982, Vstretimsya v metro (We Will Meet in the Metro) 1985, Zalozhniki dyavola (Devil's Hostages) 1993, Serye volki (The Grey Wolves) 1993, Yermak 1996. *Television:* Vorovka (The Thief) 1995, Banditskiy Peterburg: Advokat (miniseries) 2000, Kavalery morskoy zvezdy (miniseries) 2004. *Address:* N. Akimov Comedy Theatre, Nevski prosp. 56 St Petersburg, Russia. *Telephone:* (812) 314-26-10.

VENABLES, Terry Frederick; British professional football manager and commentator; b. 6 Jan. 1943, London; m. Yvette Venables; two d.; ed Dagenham High School; professional footballer, Chelsea 1958–66 (Capt. 1962), Tottenham Hotspur 1966–68 (FA Cup winners 1967), Queens Park Rangers 1968–73; coach, Crystal Palace 1973–76, Man. 1976–80; Man. Queens Park Rangers 1980–84; Man. Barcelona 1984–87 (winners Spanish Championship 1984, European Cup finalists 1985); Man. Tottenham Hotspur 1987–91 (FA Cup winners 1991); Chief Exec. Tottenham Hotspur PLC 1991–93; coach, England Nat. Team 1994–96; Dir of Football, Portsmouth Football Club 1996–98; coach, Australian Nat. Team 1996–98; head coach Crystal Palace 1998; coach Middlesbrough 2001; Man. Leeds Utd 2002–03; Asst Coach England nat. team 2006–; football analyst BBC BBC –1994, for ITV 1994–; only player to have rep. England at all levels; co-author, Hazell (TV detective series); Hon. Fellow, Univ. of Wolverhampton. *Publications:* They Used to Play on Grass 1971, Terry Venables: The Autobiography 1994, The Best Game in the World 1996, Venables' England—The Making of the Team 1996. *Address:* Terance Venables Holdings Ltd, 213 Putney Bridge Road, London, SW15 2NY, England. *Telephone:* (20) 8874-5001. *Fax:* (20) 8874-0064.

VENDLER, Helen Hennessy, AB, PhD; American academic and literary critic; *A. Kingsley Porter University Professor, Department of English, Harvard University;* b. 30 April 1933, Boston, Mass.; d. of George Hennessy and Helen Conway; m. Zeno Vendler (deceased); one s.; ed Emmanuel Coll. and Harvard Univ.; Instructor Cornell Univ. 1960–63; Lecturer, Swarthmore Coll., Pa and Haverford Coll., Pa 1963–64; Asst Prof. Smith Coll. Northampton, Mass. 1964–66; Assoc. Prof. Boston Univ. 1966–68, Prof. 1968–85; Visiting Prof. Harvard Univ. 1981–85, Kenan Prof. 1985–, Assoc. Acad. Dean 1987–92, A. Kingsley Porter Univ. Prof. 1990–; Sr Fellow, Harvard Soc. of Fellows 1981–92; poetry critic, New Yorker 1978–90; mem. American Acad. of Arts and Sciences, Norwegian Acad., American Philosophical Soc., American Acad. of Arts and Letters (bd mem. 2006–09), Educ. Advisory Bd Guggenheim Foundation, Pulitzer Prize Bd 1990–99; Fulbright Fellow 1954; A.A.U.W. Fellow 1959; Guggenheim Fellow 1971–72; American Council of Learned Socs. Fellow 1971–72; N.E.H. Fellow 1980, 1985, 1994, 2006; Wilson Fellow 1994; Fulbright Lecturer, Univ. of Bordeaux 1968–69; A. W. Mellon Lectures in Fine Arts, Nat. Gallery of Art 2007; Overseas Fellow, Churchill Coll. Cambridge 1980; Parnell Fellow, Magdalene Coll. Cambridge 1986, Hon. Fellow 1996–; 23 hon. degrees; Lowell Prize 1969, Explicator Prize 1969, Nat. Inst. of Arts and Letters Award 1975, Nat. Book Critics Award 1980, Newton Arvin Award, Jefferson Medal. *Publications include:* Yeats's Vision and the Later Plays 1963, On Extended Wings: Wallace Stevens' Longer Poems 1969, The Poetry of George Herbert 1975, Part of Nature, Part of Us 1980, The Odes of John Keats 1983, Wallace Stevens: Words Chosen Out of Desire 1985, Harvard Book of Contemporary American Poetry 1985, The Music of What Happens 1988, The Given and the Made 1995, The Breaking of Style 1995, Soul Says 1995, Poems, Poets, Poetry 1996, The Art of Shakespeare's Sonnets 1997, Seamus Heaney 1998, Coming of Age as a Poet: Milton, Keats, Eliot, Plath 2003, Poets Thinking: Pope, Whitman, Dickinson, Yeats 2005, Invisible Listeners: Lyric Intimacy in Herbert, Whitman, and Ashbery 2005, Our Secret Discipline 2007. *Leisure interests:* travel, music, grandchildren. *Address:* Harvard University, Department of English, Barker Center 205, 12 Quincey Street, Cambridge, MA 02138 (office); 54 Trowbridge Street, Apt. B, Cambridge, MA 02138, USA. *Telephone:* (617) 496-6028 (office). *Fax:* (617) 496-8737 (office). *E-mail:* vendler@fas.harvard.edu (office). *Website:* www.fas .harvard.edu/~english (office).

VENEMAN, Ann M., MA, JD; American government official, lawyer and international organization official; *Executive Director, United Nations Children's Fund (UNICEF);* b. 29 June 1949, Modesto, Calif.; d. of John Veneman (fmr US Under-Sec. of Health, Educ. and Welfare and mem. Calif. State Assembly); ed Univ. of California, Davis, Univ. of California, Berkeley and Univ. of California, Hastings Coll. of Law; staff attorney, Gen. Counsel's Office, Bay Area Rapid Transit Dist, Oakland, Calif. 1976–78; Deputy Public Defender, Modesto 1978–80; Assoc., later Pnr, Damrell, Damrell & Nelson (law firm), Modesto 1980; Assoc. Admin. Foreign Agric. Service, US Dept of Agric. 1986–89, Deputy Under-Sec. of Agric. for Int. Affairs and Commodity Programs 1989–91, Deputy Sec. of Dept 1991–93; with Patton, Boggs & Blow (law firm), Washington, DC 1993–95; Sec., Calif. Dept of Food and Agric. 1995–99; Pnr, Nossaman, Guthner, Knox & Elliott (law firm) 1999–2001; US Sec. of Agric. 2001–05 (resgnd); Exec. Dir UNICEF 2005–; fmr mem. Bd of Dirs Calgene (first co. to market genetically engineered food); mem. Bd Close Up Foundation; Hon. mem. US Afghan Women's Council, US State Dept 2004, Modesto Rotary Club 2008; Dr hc (California Polytechnic State Univ., San Luis Obispo) 2001, (Lincoln Univ. of Mo.) 2003, (Delaware State Univ.) 2004, (Middlebury Coll.) 2006; Outstanding Woman in Int. Trade Award 2001, Outstanding Alumna of the Year Award, Univ. of California, Davis 2001, Food Research and Action Center Award 2001, Nat. 4-H Alumni Recognition Award 2002, Dutch American Heritage Award 2002, Statesman of the Year Award, Jr Statesman Foundation 2002, Alumnus of the Year Award, Goldman School of Public Policy 2003, American PVO Partners Award for Service to People in Need 2004, Richard E. Lyng Award for Public Service 2005, Sesame Workshop's Leadership Award for Children 2006,. *Address:* United Nations Children's Fund (UNICEF), 3 United Nations Plaza, New York, NY 10017, USA (office). *Telephone:* (212) 326-7000 (office). *Fax:* (212) 887-7465 (office). *E-mail:* info@unicef.org (office). *Website:* www.unicef.org (office).

VENESS, Sir David, CBE, MA, LLM; British police officer and UN official; m.; three c.; ed Raynes Park Co. Grammar School, London, Trinity Coll. Cambridge, Royal Coll. of Defence Studies; joined London Metropolitan Police Cadet Corps 1964, Metropolitan Police 1966; apptd Officer, Criminal Investigation Dept (CID) 1969, served as detective in N, E and Cen. London, various specialist depts in Scotland Yard; served as Detective Chief Superintendent in Fraud Squad (5O6) and Crime Operations Group (5O15); trained as hostage negotiator 1979, mem. negotiating team, London Iranian Embassy siege 1980; led negotiations at Libyan Peoples Bureau incident 1984; Instructor, then Dir Scotland Yard Negotiators Course 1980–87; apptd Commdr 1987; served with Royalty and Diplomatic Protection 1987–90; Commdr Public Order, Territorial Security and Operational Support 1990–91; Deputy Asst Commr, Specialist Operations, Crime 1991–94; Asst Commr 1994–2005; Under-Sec.-Gen. for Safety and Security, UN 2005–08 (resgnd); fmr mem. Service Authorities, Nat. Criminal Intelligence Service, Nat. Crime Squad; HM Queen's Police Medal 2000. *Leisure interests:* rugby, reading. *Address:* c/o Office of the Under-Secretary-General for Safety and Security, United Nations, New York, NY 10017, USA (office).

VENETIAAN, Runaldo Ronald; Suriname mathematician and head of state; *President;* b. 1936, Paramaribo; ed Leiden Univ.; moved to Netherlands to further educ.; early career as math. lecturer; fmr Minister of Educ.; fmr mem. Exec. Bd UNESCO; Leader Suriname Nat. Party; Pres. of Suriname 1991–96, 2000–. *Address:* Office of the President, Paramaribo, Suriname.

VENGEROV, Maxim; Russian violinist and violist; *Professor of Violin, Saarbrücken University;* b. 20 Aug. 1974, Novosibirsk, Western Siberia, USSR; s. of Alexander Vengerov and Larissa Vengerov; studied with Galina Tourchaninova and Zakhar Bron; first recital aged five; debut Moscow, playing Schubert's Rondo Brillant 1985; US debut with New York Philharmonic 1990; performs concerts and recitals with all maj. int. orchestras including Concertgebouw, Russian State Symphony, Berlin Philharmonic, London Philharmonic, St Petersburg Philharmonic, Chicago Symphony, Los Angeles Philharmonic, Mozarteum, Vienna Philharmonic, Hallé and English Chamber Orchestras; worked with Abbado, Mehta, Simonov, Barenboim, Menuhin; solo recital programme of Bach, Ysaÿe, Shchedrin and Paganini 2002–03; Prof. of Violin, Musikhochschule des Saarlandes, Saarbrücken Univ.; apptd UNICEF Envoy for Music 1997; 1st Prize Jr Wieniawski Competition Poland 1984, Winner Carl Flesch Int. Violin Competition 1990, Gramophone Young Artist of the Year 1994, Ritmo Artist of the Year 1994, Gramophone Record of the Year 1996, Edison Award 1997, Gramophone Artist of the Year 2002. *Recordings include:* Sonatas by Beethoven and Brahms and Paganini 1st Concerto 1992, Sonatas by Mozart, Beethoven and Mendelssohn 1992, Virtuoso Violin Pieces, Bruch and Mendelssohn Violin Concertos, Britten Violin Concerto and Walton Viola Concerto (Classical BRIT Critics' Award 2004, Grammy Award 2004) 2002. *Address:* c/o Nicola-Fee Bahl, NFBM Ltd, 28 Smalley Close, London, N16 7LE, England (office). *Telephone:* (20) 7254-9606 (office). *Fax:* (870) 0941600 (office). *E-mail:* Nicola-Fee@nfbm.com (office). *Website:* www.nfbm.com (office).

VENIAMIN, Christodoulos; Cypriot government official; b. Sept. 1922; ed in Nicosia and Middle Temple, London; jr officer in govt service 1942, admin. officer 1949; served as Asst Sec. in Depts of Local Govt and Admin, Personnel, Finance, Commerce and Industry, Social Services, Communications and Works, Agric. and Natural Resources; Asst Dist Commr, Larnaca; Asst Sec. Ministry of Interior during transitional period; Dist Officer, Limassol Dist 1960–68; Dir-Gen. Ministry of Foreign Affairs 1968; Minister of Interior and Defence 1975–84, of Interior 1988–93; mem. House of Reps 1997–2001; Grosse Verdienstkreuz mit Stern und Schulterband (Germany), Onorifiecenza di Grande Ufficiale (Italy), Order of the Cedar (Lebanon). *Leisure interests:* reading and walking. *Address:* Kleanthi Ierodiaconou No. 5, 2411 Engomi, Nicosia, Cyprus. *Telephone:* (22) 680339 (office); (22) 352400 (home). *Fax:* (22) 671821.

VENIZELOS, Evangelos, PhD; Greek politician; b. 1957, Thessaloniki; m. Vasiliki Bakatselou; one d.; ed Aristotle Univ. of Thessaloniki, Univ. of Paris II (Paris-Sorbonne); Asst Prof., then Prof. of Constitutional Law, Aristotle Univ. of Thessaloniki 1984–87; Attorney at Law for Council of State and Supreme Court 1984–87; apptd mem. Bd Nat. Centre of Public Admin 1987; apptd mem. Bd Nat. Bank of Greece 1988; mem. Local Radio Cttee; elected to Cen. Cttee of the Panhellenic Socialist Movt (PASOK) 1990; mem. Parl. 1993–; Deputy Minister to the Prime Minister's Office, responsible for Press Affairs 1993–94; Minister for Press and Media Affairs 1994–95; Minister of Transportation and Communications 1995–96; Minister of Justice Jan.–Sept. 1996; Minister of Culture 1996–98, 2000–04; Minister of Devt 1999–2000. *Address:* c/o Ministry of Culture, 20–22 Bouboulinas Sreet, 10682 Athens, Greece (office).

VENNER, Sir K. Dwight, Kt; banker; *Governor, East Caribbean Central Bank;* ed Univ. of the W Indies; Research Asst, Univ. of the W Indies, Jr Research Fellow, Inst. of Social and Econ. Reseach, Lecturer, Dept of Econs; Dir Finance and Planning, Govt of St Lucia; Gov. Eastern Caribbean Cen. Bank 1989–; numerous articles on econs; Chair. Air and Seaports Authority, St Lucia 1981–89, Nat. Insurance Investment Cttee 1981–89, Caricom Cen. Bank Govs, Eastern Caribbean Home Mortgage Bank; Chair. Tech. Restructuring Cttee, Org. of Eastern Caribbean States; Dir St Lucia Devt Bank, Nat. Commercial Bank, St Lucia; mem. Chancellor's Governance Cttee, Univ. of the W Indies; mem. Univ. Strategy Cttee. *Address:* East Caribbean Central Bank, Fairplay Commercial Complex, The Valley, Anguilla (office). *Telephone:* 497-5050 (office). *Fax:* 497-5150 (office). *E-mail:* eccbaxa@aguillanet.com (office). *Website:* www.eccb-centralbank.org (office).

VENTER, J(ohn) Craig, PhD; American scientist; *President, J. Craig Venter Institute;* b. 14 Oct. 1946, Salt Lake City, UT; m. Claire Fraser; ed Univ. of California, San Diego; served in USN, served in Viet Nam 1967; Prof., State Univ. of NY, Buffalo –1984; Section and Lab. Chief, NIH, Bethesda, Md 1984–92; Founder, Chair. and Chief Scientist, The Inst. for Genomic Research 1992–; Founder, Pres. and Chief Scientific Officer, Celera Genomics Corpn, Rockville, Md 1998–2002, Chair. Scientific Advisory Bd 2002–; Pres. J. Craig Venter Inst. 2004–; Founder, Chair., CEO and Co-Chief Scientific Officer, Synthetic Genomics, Inc. 2005–; mem. NAS, American Acad. of Arts and Sciences, American Soc. for Microbiology; numerous hon. degrees; Beckman Award 1999, Chiron Corpn Biotechnology Research Award 1999, King Faisal Int. Prize for Science 2000, Taylor Prize 2001, Paul Ehrlich and Ludwig Darmstaedter Prize 2001, Gairdner Foundation Int. Award 2002. *Publications:* A Life Decoded (autobiog.) 2007; more than 200 articles in scientific journals. *Leisure interest:* sailing. *Address:* J. Craig Venter Institute, 9704 Medical Center Drive, Rockville, MD 20850 (office); Synthetic Genomics, Inc., 11149 North Torrey Pines Road, La Jolla, CA 92037, USA (office). *Telephone:* (301) 795-7000 (Venter Inst.) (office); (858) 754-2900 (Synthetic Genomics) (office). *Fax:* (858) 754-2988 (office). *E-mail:* info@jcvi.org (office); info@syntheticgenomics.com (office). *Website:* www.jcvi.org (office); www.syntheticgenomics.com (office).

VENTO, Sergio, MA; Italian fmr diplomatist; *Senior Advisor, McDermott Will & Emery Studio Legale Associato;* b. 30 May 1938; m.; two c.; ed Univ. of Rome; joined Ministry of Foreign Affairs 1963, Officer, Near East and N African Political Affairs Office 1975–79, Minister Plenipotentiary (Second Class) Office of Econ. Affairs 1985–87, Diplomatic Counsel to Deputy Prime Minister and Minister of Finance 1987–89, apptd Minister Plenipotentiary (First Class) 1988, Diplomatic Counsellor to Prime Minister 1992–95; Second, then First Sec. Embassy in The Hague, Netherlands 1967–70; Consul in Buenos Aires, Argentina 1970–72; Counsellor in Ankara, Turkey 1972–75; Amb. to Yugoslavia 1989–92, to France 1995–99; Perm. Rep. to UN, New York 1999–2003; Amb. to USA 2003–05; currently Sr Advisor, McDermott Will & Emery Studio Legale Associato (law firm), Rome. *Address:* McDermott Will & Emery Studio Legale Associato, Via Parigi, 11, 00185 Rome, Italy (office). *Telephone:* (06) 4620241 (office). *Fax:* (06) 48906285 (office). *E-mail:* svento@europe.mwe.com (office). *Website:* www.mwe.com (office).

VENTURA, Jesse; American fmr politician, radio presenter, actor and fmr professional wrestler; b. (James George Janos), 15 July 1951, Minneapolis; s. of George Janos and Bernice Janos; m. Terry Ventura; two c.; ed N Hennepin Community Coll.; served in USN 1969–73, USNR 1973–75; fmr bodyguard for The Rolling Stones; professional wrestler 1973–84; TV commentator, actor 1984–97; Mayor Brooklyn Park, Minn. 1991–95; radio talk show host 1995–98; Gov. of Minn. 1998–2002; fmr mem. Reform Party; host Jesse Ventura's America TV program 2003; mem. advisory Bd Operation Truth (addresses issues of US Nat. Guard in Iraq) 2004–; Spokesman BetUS.com 2005–. *Films include:* Predator 1987, Running Man 1987, Abraxas, Guardian of the Universe 1991, Demolition Man 1993, Batman & Robin 1997. *Publication:* I Ain't Got Time to Bleed 2000. *Address:* c/o Operation Truth, 770 Broadway, 2nd Floor, New York, NY 10003, USA (office). *Telephone:* (212) 982-9699 (office). *Fax:* (212) 982-8645 (office). *Website:* optruth.org/main.cfm (office); betus.com.

VENTURI, Robert, AB, MFA, FAIA; American architect; b. 25 June 1925, Philadelphia, Pa; s. of Robert C. Venturi and Vanna Lanzetta; m. Denise (Lakofski) Scott Brown 1967; one s.; ed Princeton Univ.; Designer, Oskar Stonorov 1950, Eero Saarinen & Assoc. 1950–53; Rome Prize Fellow, American Acad. in Rome 1954–56; Designer, Louis I. Kahn 1957; Assoc. Prof., School of Fine Arts, Univ. of Pennsylvania 1957–65; Charlotte Shepherd Davenport Prof., Yale Univ. 1966–70; Prin., Venturi, Cope & Lippincott 1958–61, Venturi and Short 1961–64, Venturi and Rauch 1964–80, Venturi, Rauch and Scott Brown (architects and planners) 1980–89; Venturi, Scott Brown and Assocs June 1989–; Fellow American Acad. in Rome, Accademia Nazionale di San Luca, American Acad. of Arts and Sciences; Hon. FRIBA; Hon. Fellow Royal Incorporation of Architects in Scotland, American Acad. and Inst. of Arts and Letters; Hon. DFA (Oberlin, Yale, Penn., Princeton, Phila Coll of Art); Hon. LHD (NJ Inst. of Tech.); Laurea hc (Univ. of Rome La Sapienza) 1994; Pritzker Prize 1991, Nat. Medal of Arts 1992 and numerous other awards. *Works include:* Vanna Venturi House, Phila, Pa 1961, Guild House, Phila 1961, Franklin Court, Phila 1972, Allen Memorial Art Museum Addition, Oberlin, Ohio 1973, Inst. for Scientific Information Corpn HQ, Phila 1978, Gordon Wu Hall, Princeton Univ., NJ 1980, Seattle Art Museum, Seattle, Wash. 1984, Clinical Research Bldg, Univ. of Pa 1985 (with Payette Assocs.), Nat. Gallery, Sainsbury Wing, London, UK 1986, Fisher-Bendheim Hall, Princeton Univ. 1986, Charles P. Stevenson Library, Bard Coll. 1989, Regional Govt Bldg, Toulouse, France 1992, Kirifuri Resort facilities, Nikko, Japan 1992, Univ. of Del. Student Center, Newark, Del. 1992, Memorial Hall Restoration and Addition, Harvard Univ. 1992, The Barnes Foundation Restoration and Renovation, Merion, Pa 1993, Disney Celebration Bank, Celebration, Fla 1993, Irvine Auditorium, Perelman Quadrangle, Univ. of Pa 1995, Princeton Campus Center, Princeton Univ. 1996, Congress Avenue Building, Yale Univ. School of Medicine 1998, Master Plan and Bldgs for Univ. of Michigan 1997–. *Publications:* Complexity and Contradiction in Architecture 1966, Learning from Las Vegas (with Denise Scott Brown and Steven Izenour) 1972, A View from the Campidoglio: Selected Essays, 1953–1984 (with Denise Scott Brown) 1984, Iconography and Electronics upon a Generic Architecture 1996; numerous articles in professional journals. *Leisure interest:* travel. *Address:* Venturi, Scott Brown and Associates, 4236 Main Street, Philadelphia, PA 19127-1696, USA (office). *Telephone:* (215) 487-0400 (office). *Fax:* (215) 487-2520 (office). *E-mail:* info@vsba.com (office). *Website:* www.vsba.com (office).

VENTURONI, Adm. Guido; Italian naval officer and international organization official; *President, Marconi Selenia Communications SpA;* b. 10 April 1934, Teramo; m. Giuliana Marinozzi; two s. one d.; ed Naval Acad. 1952–56; Navigator, Communications Officer, maritime patrol pilot and tactical instructor; Head of Naval Helicopter Studies and Projects Office; Exec. Asst to Chief of Navy Staff, to Chief of Defence at Naval Personnel Directorate; Head of Plans and Operation Dept at Navy Gen. Staff, at Defence Gen. Staff 1982–86; Commdr, First Naval Div. 1986–87; Head Financial Planning Bureau, Naval Gen. Staff 1987–89; Deputy Chief of Staff of Navy 1989–90; Vice-Adm. 1990–91; C-in-C of Fleet and NATO Commdr of Cen. Mediterranean 1991–92; Chief of Staff of Navy 1992–93, Chief of Defence Gen. Staff 1994–99; Over Commdr, Int. Security Mission to Albania 1997; Chair. Mil. Cttee, NATO 1999–2002; Pres. Marconi Selenia Communications SpA 2002–; Kt of Grand Cross of Order of Merit, Silver Medal for sea-duty service, Gold Medal for air service; Medal for Merit (Mauritius); Officer Légion d'honneur; Grand Cross of Orden de Mayo al Mérito Naval (Argentina); First Class Cross of Order of Mérito Naval (Spain); Second Class Decoration of Order of Mérito Naval (Venezuela). *Address:* Marconi Selenia Communications, Pomezia, Via dell'Industria 4, 00040 Pomezia RM, Italy (office). *Telephone:* (06) 910911 (office). *Fax:* (06) 91091339 (office). *Website:* www.seleniacomms.com (office).

VERA BEJARANO, Candido, Lic.; Paraguayan politician; *Minister of Agriculture and Livestock;* b. 16 July 1957, San Pedro de Yeuamandyzú; s.

of Candido Vera and Florencia Bezarano; m.; two s. two d.; ed Escuela Agricola Carlos Pfannl, Universidad del Norte, Asunción, Degree in Farm Man.; elected mem. Nat. Congress (Liberal Party) 1993, re-elected 1998; Pres. Nat. Congress 2000–; Senator 2003–08; Minister of Agric. and Livestock 2008–. *Publications include:* Proyecto de Modificacion del Estatuto Agraiio 2002, Proyecto de ley que creo el Instituto de Desarollo Rural y de la Tierra 2003. *Address:* Ministry of Agriculture and Livestock, Presidente Franco 472, Asunción (office); Pedro Ciancio 1075, Concordia, Asunción, Paraguay (home). *Telephone:* (21) 44-9614 (office); (21) 21-4612 (home). *Fax:* (21) 49-7965 (office); (21) 21-4612 (home). *E-mail:* secretariagral@mag.gov.py (office). *Website:* www.mag.gov.py (office).

VERA CRUZ, Tomé; São Tomé and Príncipe politician; *Secretary-General, Movimento Democrático Força da Mudança (MDFM);* ed in Romania; fmr Head, Water and Electricity Co.; Minister of Natural Resources 2003–04; Prime Minister and Minister of Information and Regional Integration 2006–08 (resgnd); Sec. Gen. Movimento Democrático Força da Mudança (MDFM) 2001–. *Address:* Movimento Democrático Força da Mudança (MDFM), São Tomé, São Tomé and Príncipe (office).

VERANNEMAN DE WATERVLIET, Jean-Michel; Belgian diplomatist; *Ambassador to UK;* b. 1947, Bruges; m. Maria do Carmo Neves da Silveira; three s.; ed Institut d'Etudes Politiques, Paris, Université Libre de Bruxelles, Vrije Universiteit Brussel; six months as trainee European Comm., Brussels; mil. service with Chasseurs Ardennais Regt; joined Diplomatic Corps 1976, postings include Bonn, Brasilia, La Paz, UN, New York, EU, Brussels, Amb. to Mozambique 1983–86, Consul Gen., São Paulo 1991–94, Minister Plenipotentiary, London 1994–97, Amb. to Brazil 2000–03, to Israel 2004–06, to UK 2006–. *Leisure interests:* model ships, archery, reading history books. *Address:* Belgian Embassy, 17 Grosvenor Crescent, London, SW1X 7EE, England (office). *Telephone:* (20) 7470-3700 (office). *Fax:* (20) 7470-3795 (office). *E-mail:* london@diplobel.be (office). *Website:* www.diplomatie.be/london (office).

VERBA, Sidney, PhD; American academic; b. 26 May 1932, Brooklyn, New York; s. of Morris Verba and Recci Salman; m. E. Cynthia Winston 1955; three d.; ed Harvard and Princeton Univs; Asst, then Assoc. Prof. of Politics Princeton Univ. 1960–64; Prof. of Political Science, Stanford Univ. 1964–68; Sr Study Dir Nat. Opinion Research Center 1968–72; Prof. of Political Science, Univ. of Chicago 1968–72; Prof. of Govt, Harvard Univ. 1972–2006, Clarence Dillon Prof. of Int. Affairs 1983–84, Carl H. Pforzheimer Prof. 1984–2006, Assoc. Dean for Undergraduate Educ., Faculty of Arts and Sciences 1981–84, Dir Harvard Univ. Library 1984–2006; Chair. Bd of Dirs Harvard Univ. Press 1991–2006; Pres. American Political Science Asscn 1994–95; mem. NAS, American Acad. of Arts and Sciences; Guggenheim Fellow; Woodrow Wilson and Kammerer Book Awards, James Madison Award (American Political Science Asscn). *Publications:* Small Groups and Political Behavior 1961, The Civic Culture 1963, Participation in America 1972, Participation and Political Equality 1978, The Changing American Voter 1979, Injury to Insult 1979, Equality in America 1985, Elites and the Idea of Equality 1987, Designing Social Inquiry 1994, Voice and Equality 1995. *Address:* Harvard University, Department of Government, Littauer Center (North Yard), Room M–18, 1875 Cambridge Street, Cambridge, MA 02138 (office); 142 Summit Avenue, Brookline, MA 02138, USA (home). *Telephone:* (617) 495-4421 (office); (617) 232-4987 (home). *Fax:* (617) 495-0438 (office). *E-mail:* sverba@harvard.edu (office). *Website:* www.gov.harvard.edu (office).

VERBERG, George H. B., PhD; Dutch energy industry executive; *CEO, NV Nederlandse Gasunie;* b. 2 Sept. 1942, Batavia, Dutch E Indies; ed Netherlands School of Econs, Erasmus Univ., Rotterdam, MIT and Univ. of Calif. at Berkeley; joined Ministry of Educ. and Science 1971, Ministry of Econ. Affairs 1974, positions include Gen. Econ. Policy Dir, Dir-Gen. for Trade, Industry and Services, Dir-Gen. for Energy –1988; joined NV Nederlandse Gasunie 1988, Commercial Man.-Dir 1989–92, CEO 1992–; Chair. Advisory Bd UN-Gas Centre; Vice-Pres. Int. Gas Union; Vice-Chair. Eurogas Asscn; Vice-Chair. Supervisory Bd Univ. of Groningen; mem. Bd Advisory Council ING-Group; mem. Supervisory Bd IKN (Integrated Cancer Centre for N Netherlands). *Address:* NV Nederlandse Gasunie, Concourslaan 17, 9700 MA Groningen, Netherlands (office). *Telephone:* (50) 5219111 (office). *Fax:* (50) 5211999 (office). *E-mail:* communicatie@gasunie.nl (office). *Website:* www.nvnederlandsegasunie.nl (office).

VERBITSKAYA, Ludmila Alekseyevna, PhD; Russian academic administrator and philologist; *President, St Petersburg State University;* b. 17 June 1936, Leningrad (now St Petersburg); m. (deceased); two d.; ed Leningrad State Univ.; lab. asst, then jr researcher, Docent, Chair. of Philology, Leningrad (now St Petersburg) State Univ. –1979, Prof. Chair. of Phonetics 1979–85, Head Chair. of Gen. Linguistics 1985–, Pro-Rector on scientific work, First Pro-Rector 1989, Acting Rector 1993–94, Rector 1994–2008, Pres. 2008–; Vice-Pres. UNESCO Comm. on Problems of Women's Educ.; Rep. to Exec. Council of Int. Asscn of Univs; mem. Russian Acad. of Humanitarian Sciences, Acad. of Sciences of Higher School, Presidium Int. Asscn of Russian Language and Literature Teachers, Presidium Conf. of Rectors of European Univs; mem. of Council Our Home Russia Movt 1996–99; Verbitskaya planet named after her 2000; Hon. Employee of Higher Educ. in Russia, Hon. Citizen of St Petersburg 2006; Order of Friendship, Order for Nat. Service Third Degree and Fourth Degree, Commdr Academic Palm (France), Knight's Cross for Service (Poland), Chevalier, Légion d'Honneur 2005; Dr hc (Bologna Univ., New York Univ., St Petersburg State Tech. Univ., St Petersburg State Medical Univ., Novgorod State Univ. Yaroslav Mudry); Medal of Honour of Saint Grand Duchess Olga III of the Russian Orthodox Church, Medal of Honour of Grand Duchess Olga III (Ukraine), Medal of Merit in Nat. Healthcare, Queen's Anniversary Prize for Higher and Further Educ. (UK) 1997, Woodrow Wilson Award for Public Service 2008. *Publications:* over 300 publs. *Address:* St Petersburg State University, Universitetskaya nab. 7/9, 199034 St Petersburg, Russia (office). *Telephone:* (812) 3200717 (office). *Fax:* (812) 3241250 (office). *E-mail:* president@pu.ru (office). *Website:* www.spbu.ru (office).

VERDONCK, Ferdinand, BEcons, MA, LLD; Belgian financial executive; b. 1942; ed Catholic Univ. of Leuven, Univ. of Chicago; began financial services career at Continental Ill. Bank of Chicago; with Lazard Frères and Co., NY –1984; Head of Operational and Admin Affairs, Bekaert 1984–92; Man.-Dir and mem. Exec. Cttee Almanij NV 1992–2003. *Address:* c/o Almanij NV, Snyderhuis, Keizerstraat 8, 2000 Antwerp, Belgium (office).

VERE-JONES, David, MSc, DPhil, FRSNZ; British mathematician and academic; *Director, Statistical Research Association (NZ) Ltd;* b. 17 April 1936, London; s. of Noel W. Vere-Jones and Isabel M. I. Wyllie; m. Mary To Kei Chung 1965 (died 2000); two s. one d.; ed Cheadle Hulme School, Cheshire, Hutt Valley High School, NZ, Vic. Univ. of Wellington and Univ. of Oxford; emigrated to New Zealand 1949; Rhodes Scholar 1958–61; Sr Scientist, Applied Math. Div. Dept of Scientific and Industrial Research, NZ 1961–65; Fellow, Sr Fellow, Dept of Statistics, ANU 1965–69; Prof. of Statistics Vic. Univ. of Wellington 1970–; Founding Pres. NZ Math Soc. 1975; Chair. Int. Statistical Inst. (ISI) Educ. Comm. 1987–91; Pres. Interim Exec., Int. Asscn for Statistical Educ. 1991–93; Dir Statistical Research Asscn (NZ) Ltd 2001–; several professional affiliations; Hon. mem. ISI, NZ Math. Soc. 2000, NZ Statistical Asscn Henri Willem Methorst Medal 1995, Science and Tech. Medal in gold. *Publications:* An Introduction to the Theory of Point Processes (with D. J. Daley) 1988; about 100 papers on probability theory, seismology, mathematical educ. *Leisure interests:* tennis, walking, languages. *Address:* School of Mathematics and Computing Science, Victoria University of Wellington, P.O. Box 600, Wellington (office); 21A/2 Talavere Terrace, Kelburn, Wellington N2, New Zealand (home). *Telephone:* (4) 463-5662 (office); (4) 473-4745 (home). *Fax:* (4) 463-5045 (office). *E-mail:* dvj@mcs.vuw.ac.nz (office). *Website:* www.statsresearch.co.nz (office).

VEREKER, Sir John (Michael Medlicott), KCB, KStJ, BA, CIMgt, FRSA; British civil servant; b. 9 Aug. 1944; s. of the late Commdr Charles W.M. Vereker and Marjorie Vereker (née Whatley); m. Judith Diane Rowen 1971; one s. one d.; ed Marlborough Coll., Keele Univ.; Asst Prin. Overseas Devt Ministry 1967–69, Prin. 1972, Pvt. Sec. to Minister of Overseas Devt 1977–78, Asst Sec. 1978; Asst Sec. Prime Minister's Office 1980–83, Under-Sec. 1983–88; Prin. Finance Officer Overseas Devt Admin., FCO 1986–88; Deputy Sec. Dept of Educ. and Science, then Dept for Educ. 1988–93; Perm. Sec. Dept for Int. Devt 1994–2002; Gov. and C-in-C of Bermuda 2002–07; Asst Prin. World Bank, Washington, DC 1970–72; Chair. Students Loans Co. Ltd 1989–91; Vice-Pres. Raleigh Int. 2002–; mem. Council, Inst. of Manpower Studies 1989–92, Bd British Council 1994–2002, IDS 1994–2001, VSO 1994–2002, Advisory Bd for British Consultants Bureau 1998–; Hon. DLitt (Keele) 1997. *Address:* c/o Government House, 11 Langton Hill, Pembroke, HM 13, Bermuda (office).

VERES, János, PhD; Hungarian politician; b. 5 Feb. 1957, Nyírbátor; m. Éva Szabó; two c.; ed Univ. of Agriculture, Debrecen and Karl Marx Univ. of Econs; began career in business sector 1981–2002; mem. Nyírbátor local govt 1990–94; mem. Parl. 1994–; Chair., Chamber of Commerce and Trade, Szabolcs-Szatmár-Bereg County 1997–2002; Mayor of Nyírbátor 2002–03; mem. Exec. Cttee, Socialist Party of Hungary 2004–; Sec. of State for Political Affairs, Ministry of Finance 2003–04; Chief of Staff, Office of the Prime Minister 2004–05; Minister of Finance 2005–09. *Address:* c/o Ministry of Finance, 1051 Budapest, József Nádor tér 2–4, Hungary (office).

VERESHCHETIN, Vladlen Stepanovich, DJur; Russian international lawyer and judge; b. 8 Jan. 1932, Briansk; m.; one d.; ed Moscow Inst. of Int. Relations; mem. staff, Presidium of USSR Acad. of Sciences 1958–67; First Vice-Chair. and Legal Counsel, Intercosmos, USSR Acad. of Sciences 1967–81; Prof. of Int. Law, Univ. of Friendship of Peoples 1979–82; Deputy Dir and Head, Dept of Int. Law, Inst. of State and Law, Russian Acad. of Sciences 1981–95; mem. Perm. Court of Arbitration, The Hague 1984–95; judge, Int. Court of Justice, The Hague 1995–2006; Vice-Pres. Russian (fmrly Soviet) UN Asscn 1984–97; Vice-Pres. Russian (fmrly Soviet) Asscn of Int. Law 1985–97; mem. UN Int. Law Comm. 1992–95; Foreign Mem. Bulgarian Acad. of Sciences 2006; Hon. Dir Int. Inst. of Space Law 1995–; Order of Friendship of Peoples 1975, October Revolution Order 1981; Hon. Master of Sciences, Russian Fed. 1995; Hon. Awards from German Acad. of Sciences 1978, Bulgarian Acad. of Sciences 1979, Int. Acad. of Astronautics 1987, 1994, Hugo Grotius Award 2001. *Publications:* books and more than 150 articles on int. law, law of the sea, space law, state responsibility, int. criminal law. *Address:* Profsouyaznaya str. 43, Bldg 1, Apt 255, 117420 Moscow, Russian Federation (home).

VERGE, Pierre, MA, LLD, FRSC; Canadian legal scholar and academic; *Professor Emeritus, Faculty of Law, Université Laval;* b. 9 Jan. 1936, Québec City; m. Colette Habel 1963; two s. one d.; ed Univ. Laval, McGill Univ. and Univ. of Toronto; mem. Québec Bar 1961; QC 1976; Prof. of Law, Univ. Laval 1967–, Dean, Faculty of Law 1973–77, later Prof. Emer.; Commonwealth Fellowship, St John's Coll. Cambridge 1977; mem. Canadian Asscn of Law Teachers (Pres. 1972–73). *Publications:* Le droit de grève, fondement et limites, Le droit et les syndicats (co-author) 1991, Un droit du travail? (co-author) 1997, La représentation syndicale: vision juridique actuelle et future (co-author) 1999, Configuration juridique de l'entreprise et droit du travail (co-author) 2003. *Address:* Faculté de droit, Université Laval, Bureau 2107, Pavillon Charles-De Koninck, Québec, G1K 7P4 (office); 2542 de la Falaise, Sillery, Québec, G1T 1W3, Canada (home). *Telephone:* (418) 656-5009 (office);

(418) 651-4829 (home). *Fax:* (418) 656-7230 (office). *E-mail:* pierre.verge@fd.ulaval.ca (office). *Website:* www.fd.ulaval.ca (office).

VERGÈS, Jacques; French lawyer; b. 5 March 1925, Thailand; m. Djamila Bouhired; two c.; ed legal studies in Paris; served with Free French in World War II in N Africa, Italy, France and Germany; mem. French CP 1945–57; Sec. Int. Union of Students, Prague 1951–55; joined Paris Bar 1955; defended many Algerian FLN militants; pvt. legal practice in Algeria 1965–70; activities unknown 1970–78; returned to Paris Bar 1978; appeared for defence, at trial in Lyons of Nazi war criminal Klaus Barbie who was jailed for atrocities committed during World War II, 1987; adviser to several African heads of state. *Publications:* De la stratégie judiciaire 1981, Pour en finir avec Ponce Pilate: Le Pré aux clercs 1983, Beauté du Crime 1988, Je défends Barbie 1988, La justice est un jeu 1992, Lettre ouverte à des amis algériens devenus tortionnaires 1993, Mon Dieu pardonnez leur 1995, Intelligence avec l'ennemi 1996, Le Salaud lumineux 1996, J'ai plus de souvenirs que si j'avais mille ans 1999, Un procès de la barbarie à Brazzaville (with Dior Diagne) 2000, Les Sanguinaires: sept affaires célèbres J'ai lu 2001, Omar m'a tuer: histoire d'un crime J'ai Lu 2001, L'Apartheid judiciaire (with Pierre Marie Gallois) 2002, Le Suicide de la France 2002, Dictionnaire amoureux de la justice 2002, Que sais-je: les erreurs judiciaires 2002, Justice pour le peuple serbe 2003, La Démocratie à visage obscène 2004, Les Crimes d'État 2004, Passent les jours et passent les semaines: Journal de l'année 2003-2004 2005, Crimes contre l'humanité massacres en Côte d'Ivoire 2006, Que mes guerres étaient belles! 2007. *Address:* 20 rue de Vintimille, 75009 Paris, France (office). *Telephone:* 1-42-81-51-61 (office). *Fax:* 1-42-82-90-30 (office).

VERHAEGEN, Georges, PhD; Belgian scientist and academic (retd); *Professor and Honorary Rector, Université Libre de Bruxelles;* b. 26 March 1937, Brussels; s. of Col J. Verhaegen and L. Nefcoeur; m. M. van de Keere 1965; two s.; ed Ashbury Coll., Ottawa, Canada, Univ. Libre, Brussels, CNRS, France; Pres. Dept of Chem., Univ. Libre de Bruxelles 1973–75, Dean Faculty of Sciences 1978–81, Prof. 1979–, mem. Governing Body 1975–84, 1986–, Rector 1986–90, Pro-Rector 1990, now Hon. Rector; Pres. Belgian Conf. of Rectors (French speaking) 1986–90, Belgian NSF 1990, Network of Univs of Capital Cities of Europe (UNICA) 1989–97; Expert for Univ. Man. (European Univ. Asscn, IBRD, European Comm.) 1993–; winner of three Belgian scientific prizes. *Publications:* more than 60 scientific publs. *Leisure interests:* reading, tennis, handicrafts, travelling. *Address:* C.P. 160/09, Université Libre de Bruxelles, 50 ave. F.D. Roosevelt, B 1050 Brussels (office); 2 rue du Bois des Aulnes, B 7090 Braine le Comte, Belgium (home). *Telephone:* (2) 650-24-24 (office); (6) 763-82-86 (home). *Fax:* (2) 650-42-32 (office); (6) 763-82-86 (home). *E-mail:* gverhaeg@ulb.ac.be (office). *Website:* www.ulb.ac.be (office).

VERHAGEN, Maxime Jacques Marcel; Dutch politician; *Minister of Foreign Affairs;* b. 14 Sept. 1956, Maastricht; m.; two s. one d.; ed Leiden Univ.; began career as Asst at Christian Democratic Alliance (CDA) 1984–87, Head of European Affairs, Devt, Cooperation and Trade Policy 1987–89; mem. Oegstgeest Municipal Council 1986–89; MEP 1989–94; mem. House of Reps 1996–, Chair. Christian Democratic Appeal (CDA) 2002–; Minister of Foreign Affairs 2007–; fmr Vice-Chair. ACP-EU Joint Ass., Parl. Cttee on Foreign Affairs; fmr Bd mem. Eduardo Frei Foundation, Netherlands Atlantic Asscn, European Movt, Univ. of Nijmegen Parl. History Foundation, Free Voice. *Address:* Ministry of Foreign Affairs, Bezuidenhoutseweg 67, POB 20061, 2500 EB The Hague, Netherlands (office). *Telephone:* (70) 3486486 (office). *Fax:* (70) 3484848 (office). *E-mail:* minbuza@buza.minbuza.nl (office). *Website:* www.minbuza.nl (office).

VERHEUGEN, Günter; German politician; *Commissioner for Enterprise and Industry and Vice-President, European Commission;* b. 28 April 1944, Bad Kreuznach; s. of Leo Verheugen and Leni Verheugen (née Holzhaüser); m. Gabriele Verheugen (née Schäfer); ed in Cologne and Bonn; trainee, Neue Rhein-Neue Ruhr-Zeitung 1963–65; Head of Public Relations Div., Fed. Ministry of the Interior 1969–74; Head of Analysis and Information Task Force, Fed. Foreign Office 1974–76; Fed. Party Man., Free Democratic Party (FDP) 1977–78; Gen. Sec. FDP 1978–82; joined Sozialdemokratische Partei Deutschlands (SPD) 1982; mem. Bundestag 1983–99, Chair. EU Special Cttee 1992, mem. Foreign Affairs Cttee 1983–98; Spokesman, SPD Nat. Exec. 1986–87; Ed.-in-Chief Vorwärts (SPD newspaper) 1987–89; Chair. Radio Broadcasting Council, Deutsche Welle 1990–99; Fed. Party Man. SPD 1993–95; Deputy Chair. SPD Parl. Group for Foreign, Security and Devt Policy 1994–97; Chair. Socialist Int. Peace, Security and Disarmament Council 1997–; mem. SPD Nat. Exec.; Minister of State, Fed. Foreign Office 1998–99; EU Commr for Enlargement 1999–2004, for Enterprise and Industry 2004–, Vice-Pres EU Comm. 2004–; Commdr Distinguished Service Cross (Italy). *Publications:* Eine Zukunft für Deutschland 1980, Das Programm der Liberalen Baden-Baden 1980, Der Ausverkauf-Macht und Verfall der FDP 1984, Apartheid-Südafrika und der Deutschen Interessen am Kap 1986. *Address:* European Commission, 200 rue de la Loi, 1049 Brussels, Belgium (office). *Telephone:* (2) 298-11-00 (office). *Fax:* (2) 299-18-27 (office). *Website:* europa.eu (office).

VERHOEVEN, Michael; German screenwriter, director and producer; *Head, Sentana Filmproduktion GmbH;* b. 13 July 1938, Berlin; s. of the late Paul Verhoeven and Doris Kiesow; m. Senta Berger 1966; two s.; actor stage, TV and cinema 1953–; Head Sentana Filmproduktion GmbH, Munich 1965–; medical studies Munich, Berlin and Worcester, Mass., LA, Calif., USA; worked as doctor Munich –1973; taught at Film Acad. Baden-Württemberg; Cross of Merit; Jerusalem Film Festival Award, New York Critics Circle Award, BAFTA Award, Joseph Neuberger-Medaille 1996, Award, Festival Int. de Programmes Audiovisuels, Biarritz 2001; several other awards for writing, directing and producing. *Films:* Dance of Death 1967, O.K. 1970, Great Escape 1973, Sunday Children 1979, The White Rose 1981, Killing Cars 1985, The Nasty Girl 1989, My Mother's Courage 1995. *Plays (director and producer):* The Guns of Mrs Carrar, Believe Love Hope, The Tribades Night, Volpone. *Television (director and producer):* The Challenge 1974, The Reason 1978, Dear Melanie 1983, Gunda's Father 1986, Semmelweis MD 1987, The Fast Gerdi 1989, Land of Milk and Honey 1991, Unholy Love 1993, Tabori – Theatre is Life (documentary) 1998, Room to Let 1999, Metamorphosis 2000, The Fast Gerdi in Berlin 2002, Pictures of an Exhibition (docu-essay) 2004. *Publications:* Liebe Melanie 1974, Sonntagskinder 1979, Die Weisse Rose 1980. *Address:* Sentana Filmproduktion GmbH, Gebsattelstr. 30, 81541 Munich (office); Robert-Koch-Str. 10, 82031 Grünwald, Germany (home). *Telephone:* (89) 4485266 (office). *Fax:* (89) 4801968 (office). *E-mail:* sentana@sentana.de (office). *Website:* www.sentana.de (office).

VERHOEVEN, Paul, PhD; Dutch film director; b. 18 July 1938, Amsterdam; ed Leiden Univ.; worked as a documentary film-maker for the Dutch navy and then for TV; directed: (shorts) A Lizard Too Much 1960, Let's Have a Party 1963, The Wrestler 1971; (feature length) Wat zien ik (Business is Business/Any Special Way) 1971, Turks fruit (Turkish Delight) 1973, Keetje Tippel 1975, Soldaat van Oranje 1940–45 (Soldier of Orange/Survival Run) 1978, Spetters 1980, De vierde man (The Fourth Man) 1984, Flesh and Blood 1985, RoboCop 1987, Total Recall 1989, Basic Instinct 1992, Showgirls 1995, Starship Troopers 1997, Hollow Man 2000, Black Book 2006. *Address:* c/o Beth Swofford, 9830 Wilshire Boulevard, Beverly Hills, CA 90212, USA (office).

VERHOFSTADT, Guy, LLB; Belgian politician; b. 11 April 1953, Dendermonde; s. of the late Marcel Verhofstadt and of Gaby Stockmans; m. Dominique Verkinderen 1981; one s. one d.; ed Koninklijk Atheneum, Ghent and Univ. of Ghent; began career as attorney-at-law Ghent Bar; Pres. Flemish Liberal Students' Union, Ghent 1972–73 and 1974–75; Councillor Ghent 1976–82; Political Sec. to Willy De Clerq, Nat. Pres. Party for Freedom and Progress (PVV) 1977–81; mem. House of Reps Ghent-Eeklo Dist 1978–84; Vice-Pres. PVV Ghent-Eeklo Dist Fed. 1979; Nat. Pres. PVV Youth Div. 1979–81, Nat. Pres. PVV 1982–85; Deputy Prime Minister and Minister for the Budget, Scientific Research and the Nat. Plan 1985–88; Pres. of Shadow Cabinet 1988–91; Nat. Pres. of PVV 1989–92, of Flemish Liberals and Democrats (VLD) 1992–95, 1997–99; Minister of State 1995–99; Senator VLD 1995–99, Vice-Pres. of Senate 1995–99; Prime Minister of Belgium 1999–2007 (resgnd), reappointed Dec. 2007, resgnd March 2008. *Publications:* Het Radicaal Manifest: Handvest voor een nieuwe liberale omwenteling 1979, Burgermanifest 1991, De Weg naar politieke vernieuwing: Het tweede burgermanifest 1992, Angst, afgunst en het algemeen belang 1994, De Belgische Ziekte: Diagnose en remedies 1997, In goede banen: VLD-plan voor meer tewerks telling 1999; De vierde golf – een liberaal project voor de nieuwe eeuw 2002, De verenigde staten van Europa, 2007 (Awarded Best European Book of the Year 2007), Een new age of empires 2009; contribs to books and articles in periodicals. *Leisure interests:* cycling, literature, Italy. *Address:* Vlaamse Liberalen en Demokraten (VLD, Flemish Liberals and Democrats—Liberal Party), Melsensstraat 34, 1000 Brussels, Belgium (office). *Telephone:* (2) 549-00-20 (office). *Fax:* (2) 512-60-25 (office). *E-mail:* contact@openvld.be (office). *Website:* www.openvld.be (office); www.guyverhofstadt.be (home).

VERMA, Om Prakash, LLB; Indian judge; b. 20 March 1937; ed Delhi Univ.; Civil Judge (Jr Div.), UP Civil Judicial Service 1961; Deputy Sec., Deputy Legal Adviser, Ministry of Law 1971–75; Judge, Allahabad High Court 1984–1997; Chief Justice, Kerala High Court 1997–99; Gov. of Punjab 2003–04; Admin. Union Territory of Chandigarh 2003–04. *Address:* R 8/49 Raj Nagar, Ghaziabad, Uttar Pradesh, India. *Telephone:* (172) 2740740.

VERMA, Rajani Kant; Indian government official; b. 23 April 1959; joined Indian Admin. Service; fmr Commr of Sales Tax, Govt of India, New Delhi; fmr Man. Dir Delhi State Industrial Devt Corpn; fmr High Commr in Canada; Admin. Union Territories of Dadra and Nagar Haveli and Daman and Diu 2006–08. *Address:* c/o Office of the Administrator, Silvassa, Dadra and Nagar Haveli, India. *Telephone:* 2642777 (Dadra and Nagar Haveli); 2230700 (Daman and Diu); 2251977 (home). *Fax:* 2642702. *E-mail:* vermark@ias.nic.in (office).

VERNER, Josée; Canadian politician; *Minister for Intergovernmental Affairs and Francophonie;* b. 30 Dec. 1959, Gatineau, Québec; m.; three c.; began career as admin. officer and political adviser, Université du Québec; worked for fmr pres. Robert Bourassa, Deputy Speaker of Ass., Ministry of Health; unsuccessful Conservative Party cand in Fed. election 2004, apptd Opposition Spokesperson on Econ. Devt Agency 2004, on Official Languages 2005, MP for Louis-Saint-Laurent, Québec 2006–, Minister of Int. Co-operation and Minister for La Francophonie and Official Languages 2006–07, for Canadian Heritage 2007–08, for Intergovernmental Affairs and Francophonie 2008–; also currently Chair. Québec Caucus of Conservative Party. *Address:* c/o Office of the Prime Minister, Langevin Block, 80 Wellington Street, Ottawa ON K1A 0A2, Canada (office). *Telephone:* (613) 941-6888 (office). *Fax:* (613) 941-6900 (office). *E-mail:* Verner.J@parl.gc.ca (office). *Website:* www.pm.gc.ca (office); www.joseeverner.ca (home).

VERNIER, Jacques; French politician and environmentalist; *Mayor of Douai;* b. 3 July 1944, Paris; s. of Charles Vernier and Georgette Mangin; m. Bertille Janssen 1968; two s. two d.; ed Ecole Polytechnique and Ecole des Mines, Paris; engineer, Service des Mines, Strasbourg 1968–72; Sec.-Gen. Agence de l'eau Seine-Normandie 1972–74; Dir Agence de l'Eau Artois-Picardie 1974–83, Pres. Comité de Bassin Artois-Picardie (Agence de l'Eau) 1992–2004; Founder and Pres. Asscn Douai-Consommateurs 1976–83; Pres. PACT de Douai 1976–83; Mayor of Douai 1983–; Councillor, Régional du Nord – Pas-de-Calais 1983–90, 1998–, Pres. Communauté d'agglomération du Douaisis 2002–05, Vice-Pres. 2005–; mem. European Parl. 1984–93; Deputy (RPR) to Nat. Ass. 1993–97; Pres. Agence de l'Environnement 1994–97,

Syndicat Mixte pour l'Aménagement et l'Equipement des Zones Industrielles du Douaisis 1995–2001, Comm. interministérielle du transport des matières dangereuses 1998–, Council of Admin Institut nat. de l'environnement industriel et des risques (INERIS) 2003–, Comité départemental de l'UMP du Nord 2003–, Conseil supérieur des installations classées 2004–; Nat. Sec. then Gen. Del., Environnement au sein du RPR 1989–95, mem. Political Bureau RPR 1993–98, Departmental Sec. RPR du Nord 1992–94; Chef de la mission du transport des matières dangereuses 1997–; Officier des Palmes académiques 2001, Chevalier, Légion d'honneur 2002, Commdr, Ordre nat. du Mérite 2005. *Publications:* La bataille de l'environnement 1971, Guide Pratique pour les habitants de Douai 1981–, L'environnement (eighth edn) 2007, Les énergies renouvelables (fourth edn) 2007; several publs on environmental matters. *Leisure interests:* tennis, flying aircraft. *Address:* Hôtel de ville, 59508 Douai (office); 162 quai du Petit Bail, 59500 Douai, France (home). *Telephone:* (3) 27-93-58-00 (office). *Fax:* (3) 27-96-58-22 (office). *E-mail:* cabinet@ville-douai.fr (office). *Website:* www.ville-douai.fr (office); www.jacques-vernier.fr.

VERNON, Sir (William) Michael, Kt, MA, CCMI; British business executive (retd); b. 17 April 1926, Cheshire; s. of the late Sir Wilfred Vernon; m. 1st Rosheen O'Meara 1952 (divorced 1977); one s.; m. 2nd Jane Kilham-Roberts 1977 (died 1998); m. 3rd Penelope Cuddeford 2001; ed Marlborough Coll. and Trinity Coll. Cambridge; joined Spillers (millers and animal food mfrs) as trainee 1948, Dir 1960–80, Joint Man. Dir 1962–67, Deputy Chair. 1967–68, Chair. 1968–80; Chair. Famous Names Ltd 1981–85, Granville Meat Co. Ltd 1981–94; Dir Electrical and Musical Industries (later EMI) Ltd 1973–80, Strong and Fisher (Holdings) PLC 1980–91; Pres. British Food Export Council 1977–79; Vice-Pres. Royal Nat. Lifeboat Inst. 1975–2001, Deputy Chair. 1980–89, Chair. 1989–96, Chair. Emer. 2006–; Bronze Medal, Royal Humane Soc. 1956. *Leisure interests:* travel, shooting. *Address:* Fyfield Manor, Andover, Hants., SP11 8EL, England (home).

VERPLAETSE, Viscount Alphonse Remi Emiel; Belgian central banker; *Honorary Governor, National Bank of Belgium;* b. 19 Feb. 1930, Zulte; m. Odette Vanhee 1954; three s. two d.; ed Katholieke Universiteit Leuven; Nat. Bank of Belgium 1953–81, Dir 1988–, Deputy Gov. 1988–89, Gov. 1989–99, Hon. Gov. 1999–; Office of the Prime Minister 1981–88; Hon. Gov. and Vice-Pres. Higher Finance Council, Admin. BIS, Basle; Gov. IMF 1989–99; Deputy Gov. IBRD 1989–99, IFC 1989–99; Grand Officier, Ordre de la Couronne (Belgium) 1991; Grande Ufficiale, Ordine al Merito (Italy) 1986; Officier, Légion d'honneur 1994. *Address:* c/o National Bank of Belgium, Boulevard de Berlaimont 14, 1000 Brussels (office); Schaveyslaan 25, 1650 Beersel, Belgium (home). *Telephone:* (20) 221-45-82 (office). *Fax:* (2) 221-32-43 (office). *E-mail:* roland.haentjens@nbb.be (office).

VERRETT, Shirley; American singer (soprano); b. 31 May 1931, New Orleans; d. of Leon Verrett and Elvira Verrett; m. Louis Lomonaco 1963; one d.; ed Juilliard School of Music, New York; Prof. of Voice, School of Music, Univ. of Mich. 1996–; operatic début as mezzo-soprano taking title role of Carmen, Spoleto Festival 1962; same role for début at Bolshoi Opera, Moscow 1963, New York City Opera 1966, Florence 1968, Metropolitan Opera, New York 1968; sang at Covent Garden, London in roles of Ulrica in Un Ballo in Maschera 1966, Amneris in Aida 1967, Eboli in Don Carlos 1968, Azucena in Il Trovatore 1970; début at San Carlo, Naples as Elisabetta in Maria Stuarda 1969, at La Scala, Milan as Delilah in Samson et Dalila 1970, at Vienna Staatsoper as Eboli 1970, at Teatro Liceo, Barcelona as Eboli 1971, at Paris Opera as Azucena 1972; other mezzo-soprano roles include Orfeo in Gluck, Dido in Les Troyens, Judith in Bluebeard's Castle, Neocle in Siege of Corinth, Adalgisa in Norma (first performance at Metropolitan, New York 1976); made début as soprano in title role of La Favorita, Dallas Civic Opera 1971; début at San Francisco Opera in title role of L'Africaine 1972; first artist to sing roles of both Dido and Cassandra in one single full-length production of Les Troyens, Metropolitan 1973; other soprano roles: Lady Macbeth, La Scala 1975 and with La Scala at Kennedy Center, Washington, DC 1976, also with Opera Co. of Boston 1976; title role of Norma, Metropolitan Opera 1976 (in the same season took mezzo-soprano role of Adalgisa, being the first singer since Grisi to sing both roles); New Prioress in Dialogues of the Carmelites, Metropolitan 1977; now sings only soprano roles; Amellia, La Scala 1978, title role in Favorita, Metropolitan 1978; in Tosca at Metropolitan, New York 1978; début appearance at Opera Bastille, Paris 1990; appeared in film Maggio Musicale 1990, as Nettie Fowler in Broadway production of Carousel 1994–95; frequent appearances with US and European opera houses, with US symphony orchestras; has appeared as soloist on Milan's RAI; was subject of BBC TV feature Profiles in Music 1971, of documentary Black Diva 1985; Dr hc (Holy Cross Coll., Worcester, Mass., Northeastern Univ.); Commdr des Arts et des Lettres 1984. *Address:* Herbert Breslin Inc., 6124 Liebig Avenue, Bronx, NY 10471 (office); School of Music, University of Michigan, 1100 Baits Drive, Ann Arbor, MI 48109, USA.

VERSACE, Donatella; Italian designer; b. 2 May 1955, Reggio di Calabria; d. of Antonio Versace and Francesca Versace; sister of the late Gianni Versace; m. Paul Beck (divorced); one s. one d.; ed Univ. of Florence; joined Versace 1978, fmrly overseer of advertising and public relations, accessories designer, children's collection designer (Versace Young) 1993, Head Designer for Versus and Isante lines; Style and Image Dir and Vice-Chair. Gianni Versace Group 1997–; solo debut for mainline collection 1998; first couture show for Versace Atelier in Paris Ritz 1998; launched her own fragrance Versace Woman 2001; ranked 43rd by Fortune magazine amongst 50 Most Powerful Women in Business outside the US 2002. *Address:* c/o Keeble Cavaco and Duka Inc., 450 West 15th Street, Suite 604, New York, NY 10011, USA (office); Versace SpA Headquarters, Via Manzoni 38, 20121 Milan, Italy (office). *Telephone:* (02) 760931 (Milan) (office). *Fax:* (02) 76004122 (Milan) (office). *Website:* www.versace.com (office).

VERSHBOW, Alexander R., BA, MA; American diplomatist; *Ambassador to South Korea;* b. 3 July 1952, Boston, Mass; s. of Arthur E. Vershbow and Charlotte Z. Vershbow; m. Lisa K. Vershbow 1976; two s.; ed Yale Coll. and School of Int. Affairs, Columbia Univ.; joined Foreign Service 1977, Bureau of Politico-Military Affairs 1977–79, US Embassy, Moscow 1979–81, Office of Soviet Union Affairs 1981–85, US Embassy, London 1985–88; adviser US Del. to SALT II and START negotiations; Dir State Dept's Office of Soviet Union Affairs 1988–91; US Deputy Perm Rep. to NATO and Chargé d'affaires US Mission 1991–93; Prin. Deputy Asst Sec. of State for European and Canadian Affairs (responsibilities covered the Balkan conflict) 1993–94; Special Asst to the Pres. and Sr Dir for European Affairs at Nat. Security Council 1994–97 (worked on US policy which laid foundations of the Dayton Peace Agreement, adaptation and enlargement of NATO and its new relationship with Russia); Perm. Rep. to NATO 1998–2001; Amb. to Russian Fed. 2001–05, to S Korea 2005–; Anatoly Sharansky Freedom Award, Union of Councils of Soviet Jews 1990, first Joseph J. Kruzel Award for contribs to the cause of peace, US Dept of Defense 1997, Distinguished Service Award for Work at NATO, US State Dept 2001, ABA Amb.'s Award 2004. *Publications:* articles on arms control, speeches on Russia and NATO issues. *Leisure interests:* music, theatre. *Address:* Embassy of the United States, 32 Sejongno, Jongno-gu, Seoul 110-710, South Korea (office). *Telephone:* (2) 397-4200 (office). *Fax:* (2) 725-0152 (office). *E-mail:* EmbassySeoulPA@state.gov (office). *Website:* seoul.usembassy.gov (office).

VERSTRAETE, Baron Marc, MD, PhD, FRCP, FACP; Belgian medical scientist and academic; *Director, Centre for Molecular and Vascular Biology, University of Leuven;* b. 1 April 1925, Bruges; s. of Louis Verstraete and Jeanne Coppin; m. Bernadette Moyersoen 1955; one s. four d.; ed Leuven and Oxford Univs and Cornell Univ. Medical Coll., New York; Lecturer, Univ. of Leuven 1957, Asst Prof. 1961, Assoc. Prof. 1963, Prof. 1968–, Dir Centre for Molecular and Vascular Biology; Visiting Prof., Harvard Medical School, Boston, USA; Past-Pres. Royal Acad. of Medicine of Belgium; mem. Acad. of Medicine of South Africa and of Argentina; Dr hc (Edinburgh, Córdoba (Argentina), Bologna, Bordeaux, London). *Publications:* Arterial Hypertension 1966, 1972, Haemostatic Drugs 1977, Methods in Angiology 1980, Haemostasis 1980, Thrombosis 1982, Thrombolysis 1985, Thrombosis and Haemostasis 1987, Thrombosis in Cardiovascular Disorders 1992; numerous articles in scientific journals. *Leisure interests:* reading, skiing, swimming, tennis. *Address:* Centre for Molecular and Vascular Biology, Campus Gasthuisberg, University of Leuven, Herestraat 29, 3000 Leuven (office); Fac. Geneeskunde, Minderbroedersstraat 17, 3000 Leuven (office); Minderbroedersstraat 29, 3000 Leuven, Belgium (home). *Telephone:* (16) 34-57-75 (office); (16) 22-66-74 (home). *Fax:* (16) 34-59-90 (office); (16) 22-66-74 (home). *E-mail:* marc.verstraete@med.kuleuven.ac.be (office). *Website:* www.med.kuleuven.ac.be (office).

VÉRTES, Attila, EngChem, MEconSc, Dr rer. techn., DChemSci; Hungarian nuclear chemist and academic; *Professor of Chemistry, Eötvös Loránd University;* b. 10 Oct. 1934, Türje; s. of György Vértes and Erzsébet Nagy; m. Irén Vértes 1959; two s.; ed Tech. Univ. of Budapest, Univ. of Econs, Budapest, Lomonosov Univ., Moscow; Prof. of Chem., Eötvös Loránd Univ., Budapest; Visiting Scientist, Univ. of Newcastle, UK 1969; Humboldt Fellow, Tech. Univ., Munich, Germany 1970; Visiting Prof., Lehigh Univ., Bethlehem, Pa USA 1976–77, 1982, 1986, Johannes Gutenberg Univ., Mainz, Germany 1991, 1992, 1993, various univs in Japan 1987, in People's Repub. of China 1989; Chair. Cttee of Radiochemistry, Hungarian Acad. of Sciences 1993–2002; Assoc. mem. IUPAC Comm. on Radiochemistry and Nuclear Techniques, Analytical Chem. Div. 1999–; mem. Int. Bd of Applied Mössbauer Effect 1988–98; mem. Editorial Bd Journal of Radioanalytical and Nuclear Chemistry 1980–, Structural Chemistry 1990–; Corresp. mem., Hungarian Acad. of Sciences 1993–98, Ordinary mem. 1998–; Hon. DSc (Glasgow Caledonian Univ.)1996; Széchenyi Prize 2001, Hevesy Medal 2004. *Publications:* eight textbooks and ten scientific monographs, including Mössbauer Spectroscopy 1979, Nuclear Chemistry 1987, Nuclear Methods in Mineralogy and Geology: Techniques and Applications (co-ed.) 1998, Handbook of Nuclear Chemistry (Ed.-in-Chief) 2003; more than 520 papers in scientific journals. *Address:* Eötvös Loránd University, Department of Nuclear Chemistry, PO Box 32, 1518 Budapest 112, Hungary (office). *Telephone:* (1) 372-2543 (office); (1) 316-9091 (home). *Fax:* (1) 372-2592 (office). *E-mail:* vertesa@ludens.elte.hu (office). *Website:* www.chem.elte.hu (office).

VERWAAYEN, Bernardus J. (Ben), LLM; Dutch telecommunications industry executive; *CEO, Alcatel-Lucent;* b. Feb. 1952, Utrecht; m.; two c.; ed State Univ. of Utrecht; various man. posts with ITT Nederland BV 1975–88, rising to Gen. Man.; joined Koninklijke PTT Nederland (KPN) 1996, Chair. Unisource European Venture 1996–97, Pres. and Man. Dir PTT Telecom 1997–98; Exec. Vice-Pres. of Int. Div., Lucent Technologies Inc. Sept.–Oct. 1997, Exec. Vice-Pres. and COO 1997–99, Vice-Chair. Man. Bd 1999–2002, CEO Alcatel-Lucent (following acquisition of Lucent by Alcatel) 2008–; CEO British Telecommunications PLC (now BT Group plc) 2002–08 (Chair. Operating Cttee); mem. Advisory Council ING; mem. Bd Astro All Asia Networks (ASTRO), Health Center Internet Services Inc.; Chevalier de la Légion d'honneur Medal 2006, Hon. KBE 2007. *Leisure interest:* Arsenal football club. *Address:* Alcatel-Lucent, 54 rue de la Boétie, 75008 Paris, France (office). *Telephone:* 1-40-76-10-10 (office). *Website:* www.alcatel-lucent.com (office).

VERWILGHEN, Marc, BL; Belgian politician and lawyer; b. 21 Sept. 1952, Dendermonde; ed Free Univ. of Brussels; practising lawyer 1975–; Deputy 1991–99; Senator 1999–; Chair. Comms of Inquiry on Dutroux-Nihoul and on

Missing and Murdered Children 1996–98; Chair. Chamber Comm. on Justice; mem. Vlaamse Liberalen en Demokraten-Partij van de Burger (PVV-VLD); Minister of Justice 1999–2003; Dr hc (Univ. of Ghent) 1999. *Publications:* Het V-Plan 1999, Over bruggen bouwen 1999. *Address:* c/o Ministry of Justice, 115, boulevard de Waterloo, 1000 Brussels, Belgium (office).

VESHNYAKOV, Aleksander Albertovich, CandJurSc; Russian government official and lawyer; b. 24 Nov. 1952, Baikalovo, Arkhangelsk Region; m.; two c.; ed Arkhangelsk Navigational School, Leningrad Higher School of Marine Eng, Leningrad Higher Communist Party School, Diplomatic Acad., Russian Ministry of Foreign Affairs; worked for Northern Sea steamship line, Arkhangelsk 1973–87; Sec. Arkhangelsk City CP Cttee 1987–90; Deputy Chair. Council of Repub. Supreme Soviet Russian Fed. 1990–91; Chair. sub-comm., Comm. for Transportation, Communications, Information Science and Space, Council of Repub. 1991–93; Econs Adviser Marine Transport Dept, Ministry of Transportation 1993–94; Consultant Information and Analysis Dept, Cen. Election Comm. 1994, Sec. 1995–99, Chair. 1999–2007; Defender of Free Russia Medal 1997, Medal in Commemoration of 850th Anniversary of Moscow 1997, Class IV Order for Service to the Fatherland 2000, Class II 2007. *Address:* c/o Central Election Commission, Bolshoi Cherkassky per. 9, 109012 Moscow, Russia (office). *Telephone:* (495) 206-86-51 (office). *Fax:* (495) 956-39-30 (office). *E-mail:* intdiv@A5.kiam.ru (office).

VESKIMÄGI, Taavi, BEng; Estonian politician; *Co-Chairman, Res Publica;* b. 28 Nov. 1974, Rapla; m.; one d.; ed Tallinn Tech. Univ., Tallinn Pedagogical Univ.; Head of State Admin Dept and Adviser, Ministry of Finance 1996–2001; Minister of Finance 2003–05; Vice-Speaker of Parliament 2005–; mem. Res Publica Party, Treas. 2001–02, Chair. Parl. Group 2003, Vice-Chair. Res Publica (later Isamaa ja Res Publica Liit–Union of Pro Patria and Res Publica, after merger with Pro Patria Union in 2006) 2003–05, Co-Chair. 2006–; mem. 10th Riigikogu (Parl.) March–Oct. 2003; Lecturer and Consultant in Public Admin and Financial Man. 1998–2003; mem. Rapla City Council and Head of Econ. Cttee 1999–2002; fmr Dir Eesti Post, Tallinn Olympic Sport Centre, Tallinn Harbour, Narva Electricity, Estonian Air Navigation Services. *Leisure interest:* football, restoration of motorbikes. *Address:* Union of Pro Patria and Res Publica, Wismari 11, Tallinn 10136, Estonia (office). *Telephone:* 669-1070 (office). *Fax:* 669-1071 (office). *E-mail:* info@irl.ee (office). *Website:* www.isamaajarespublicaliit.ee (office); www.veskimagi.ee (home).

VESSEY, Gen. John W., Jr, DSC, DSM, BS, MS; American army officer; *Chairman, Advisory Committee, Center for Preventive Action, Council on Foreign Relations;* b. 22 June 1922, Minneapolis, Minn.; s. of John William Vessey and Emily Vessey (née Roche); m. Avis C. Funk; two s. one d.; ed Univ. of Maryland, George Washington Univ.; enlisted in Minn. Nat. Guard 1939; commissioned 2nd Lt, Field Artillery, Anzio May 1944; served successively with 34th Infantry Div., N Africa and Italy, 4th Infantry and 3rd Armoured Div., Germany, 25th Infantry Div., S Viet Nam; promoted Gen. 1976; Commdr US Forces, S Korea 1976–79; Army Vice-Chief of Staff 1979–82; Chair. Joint Chiefs of Staff 1982–85; Presidential Emissary to Hanoi 1987–93; co-founder and Chair. Bd Center for Preventive Action (Council on Foreign Relations) 1995, now Chair. Advisory Cttee; mem. Defense Science Bd 1987–90, 1992–2000, Defense Policy Bd 1990–93, Bd of Dirs Martin Marietta, Illinois Tool Works, Nat. Computer Systems, United Services Life Insurance, Nat. Flag Day Foundation, Youth Services USA, Advisory Bd Gen. Atomics; Trustee AAL Mutual Funds; Distinguished Service Cross, Defense Distinguished Service Medal, Army, Navy and Air Force Distinguished Service Medals, Legion of Merit, Bronze Star, Air Medal, Jt Services Commendation Medal, Purple Heart, Presidential Medal of Freedom 1992, Excellence in Diplomacy Award American Acad. of Diplomacy 1994, and other decorations. *Address:* 27650 Little Whitefish Road, Garrison, MN 56450, USA. *Telephone:* (320) 692-4488. *Fax:* (320) 692-4939.

VEST, Charles Marstiller, MSE, PhD, FAAS; American mechanical engineer, academic and fmr university president; *President, National Academy of Engineering;* b. 9 Sept. 1941, Morgantown, W Va; s. of Marvin Vest and Winifred Buzzard; m. Rebecca McCue 1963; one s. one d.; ed W Va Univ. and Univ. of Mich.; Asst Prof., Assoc. Prof. Univ. of Mich. Ann Arbor 1968–77, Prof. of Mechanical Eng 1977–90, Assoc. Dean of Academic Affairs, Coll. of Eng 1981–86, Dean, Coll. of Eng 1986–89, Provost, Vice-Pres. for Academic Affairs 1989–90; Pres. MIT 1990–2004, Pres. Emer. 2004–; mem. Bd of Dirs Dupont 1993–, Int. Business Machines Corpn; Chair. Advisory Bd TIAX, LLC; Visiting Assoc. Prof., Stanford Univ. 1974–75; Fellow, Optical Soc. of America, AAAS, American Acad. of Arts and Sciences; mem. Nat. Acad. of Eng, Pres. Council of Advisors on Science and Tech., Pres. Nat. Acad. of Eng, Washington, DC 2007–; Nat. Medal of Tech. 2006. *Publications:* Holographic Interferometry 1979; articles in professional journals. *Address:* Office of the President, National Academy of Engineering, 2101 Constitution Ave., NW, Washington, DC 20418, USA (office). *Telephone:* (202) 334-3201 (office). *Fax:* (202) 334-1680 (office). *E-mail:* cvest@nae.edu (office). *Website:* www.nae.edu (office).

VESTERDORF, Bo; Danish judge and international official; b. 11 Oct. 1945; fmr Jurist-Linguist Court of Justice; fmr Admin. Ministry of Justice, later Head Constitutional and Admin. Law Dept, then apptd Dir Ministry of Justice; fmr Legal Attaché with Perm. Representation of Denmark to European Communities; fmr temporary judge Eastern Regional Court; fmr mem. Human Rights Steering Cttee, then Bureau, Council of Europe; Judge Court of First Instance of the European Communities 1989–2007, Pres. 1998–2007.

VETCHÝ, Vladimír, Dr rer. nat, PhD, CSc; Czech politician; b. 8 May 1949, Třebíč; m. Alena Vetchá; one s. one d.; ed Jan Evangelista Purkyne Univ. (now Masaryk Univ.), Brno, Pedagogue Mil. Acad., Brno; Lecturer, Dept of Math., Brno Mil. Acad. 1986–98; mem. Czech Social Democratic Party 1991–, Chair. Defence Cttee 1996–; various functions 1989–98 including mem. Council, Brno, mem. Czecho-Moravian Chamber of Labour Unions; Minister of Defence 1998–2001; Lecturer, Mil. Acad., Brno. *Leisure interests:* sport, especially basketball, volleyball. *Address:* c/o Ministry of Defence, Tychonova 1, 160 00 Prague 6, Czech Republic (office).

VETTRIANO, Jack, OBE; British artist; b. (Jack Hoggan), 1951, Methil, Fife, Scotland; s. of William Hoggan; m. Gail Cormack 1981 (divorced); one adopted d.; fmr mining engineer; self-taught, full-time painter 1989–, adopting pseudonym from his mother's maiden name, Vettrino; represented by Tom Hewlett of The Portland Gallery, London 1994–; Dr hc (Univ. of St Andrews) 2003, (Open Univ.) 2004. *Publications:* Fallen Angels 1999, Lovers and Other Strangers 2000, Vettriano: A Life 2004. *Address:* c/o Tom Hewlett, The Portland Gallery, 9 Bury Street, London, SW1Y 6AB, England (office). *Telephone:* (20) 7321-0422 (office). *Fax:* (20) 7321-0230 (office). *E-mail:* art@portlandgallery.com (office). *Website:* www.portlandgallery.com (office).

VEVERS, Stuart; British fashion designer; *Head Designer, Loewe;* ed Univ. of Westminster; has worked as an accessories designer for Calvin Klein, Louis Vuitton, Givenchy and Bottega Veneta; also collaborates with Luella Bartley and Giles Deacon; Creative Dir, Mulberry, London 2005–06; Head Designer, Loewe, Madrid 2007–; Accessory Designer of the Year Award, British Fashion Design 2006. *Address:* Loewe Hermanos SA, Calle Carrera San Jerónimo 15, Madrid, Spain (office). *Telephone:* (913) 606100 (office). *E-mail:* info@loewe.com (office). *Website:* www.loewe.com (office).

VEYRAT, Marc; French chef and restaurant owner; *Owner and Chef, L'Auberge de l'Eridan;* b. 1950; worked as shepherd before opening first restaurant aged 29; Owner and Chef, restaurants L'Auberge de l'Eridan, Annecy 1987–, La Ferme de Mon Père Megève 1999–2006 (both received three stars from Michelin and Gault Millau magazine 2003), Le Roland Garros 2005–. *Publications include:* Fou de saveurs 1994, Herbier gourmand 1997, La cuisine paysanne 1998, Quatre saisons (à la carte) 2000, L'herbier des montagnes: Tout savoir sur les plantes et les fleurs d'altitude 2000, Déguster les plantes sauvages 2003, L'encyclopédie culinaire du XXIe siècle 2003, L'herbier à croquer 2004, Le gibier en 80 recettes 2004. *Address:* La Maison de Marc Veyrat, 13 Vieille Route des Pensières, 74290 Veyrier du Lac, France (office). *Telephone:* 4-50-60-24-00 (office). *Fax:* 4-50-60-23-63 (office). *E-mail:* contact@marcveyrat.fr (office). *Website:* www.marcveyrat.fr (office).

VEZZAZ, Abderrahmane Ould Hamma, MBA; Mauritanian politician; b. 1956, Tidjikja; m.; six c.; ed Institut Supérieur de Commerce et d'Administration des Entreprises, Casablanca, Morocco and Univ. of Paris IX, France; Dir Overseas Trade Dept, Ministry of Trade 1992–97; Adviser on Public Sector, Office of the Prime Minister 1997–98; Minister of Rural Devt and the Environment Jan.–July 1998; also worked with Arab Bank for Econ. Devt in Africa (BADEA), Tech. Advisor to Prime Minister of Niger 2002–06; Exec. Dir private credit business 2006–07; Minister of the Economy and Finance 2007–08. *Address:* c/o Ministry of the Economy and Finance, BP 181, Nouakchott, Mauritania (office).

VIAL, Martin Marie-Charles François; French civil servant and economist; *Director-General, Europ'Assistance;* b. 8 Feb. 1954, Lyon; s. of René Vial and Thérèse Giuliani; m. Nelly Waldmann 1978; two s. two d.; ed Lycée Ampère, Inst. of Political Studies Paris; Prof. of Econ. and Reform Inst. of Tech. of Commerce Algiers 1977–78, Prof. of Finance Higher School of Applied Commercial Sciences 1978–82; with Office of Gen. Compatibility and Budget for External Services 1982–84, also Head; Head of Office of the Treasury and Financial Man. 1984–86; with Office of Banks and Nat. Financial Cos. 1986–88, tech. adviser Postal Sector 1988–89, charged with reform of Post, Telecommunications and Broadcasting (PTT) 1989–91, Jt Dir office of Minister for Post, Telecommunications and Space 1991, Dir Ministry of Post and Telecommunications 1992–93, Jt Dir for Space Equipment, Accommodation and Transport 1991, Dir 1991–92; Pres. Aéropostale 1993–97; Dir La Poste 1997–2000, Pres. 2000–02; mem. Cen. Cttee Union of Air Transport and Nat. Fed. of Aviation Trade 1994–96, Pres. 1996–; mem. Supervisory Bd Caisse Nat. de Prévoyance (CNP) 1998–, Vice-Pres. 2002–; Conseiller-Maître, Cour des Comptes 2002–; Dir-Gen. Europ'Assistance 2003–; Chevalier, Légion d'Honneur, Ordre National du Mérite. *Publication:* La Lettre et la toile 2000. *Leisure interests:* tennis, skiing. *Address:* Europ'Assistance Holding, 7 boulevard Haussmann, 75309 Paris Cedex 09, France (office). *E-mail:* webmaster@europ-assistance.com (office). *Website:* www.europ-assistance.com (office).

VIAN, Dominique; French government official; *Prefect of Alpes-Maritimes;* Prefect of French Guyana 1997–99, Guadeloupe 2002–04, Alpes-Maritimes 2006–. *Address:* Préfecture des Alpes-Maritimes, Centre administratif départemental, route de Grenoble, 06286 Nice Cedex 3, France (office). *Telephone:* 4-93-72-20-00 (office). *Fax:* 4-93-71-89-20 (office). *E-mail:* dominique.vian@alpes-maritimes.pref.gouv.fr (office). *Website:* www.alpes-maritimes.pref.gouv.fr (office).

VIAN, Giovanni Maria; Italian professor of patristic philology, journalist and editor; *Editor-in-Chief, L'Osservatore Romano;* s. of Nello Vian; m. Margarita Vian 1984 (died 2000); ed Virgilio Classical High School, Rome, Univ. of Rome 'La Sapienza', Inst. for Religious Sciences of Bologna; began to write for Catholic daily newspaper 1973; ed. and scientific adviser with Inst. of the Italian Encyclopedia 1976–; currently Univ. Prof. of Patristic Philology, Univ. of Rome 'La Sapienza'; part-time Prof., Vita-Salute San Raffaele Univ. of Milan, teaches History of Christian Tradition and Identity; mem. Papal Cttee of Historical Sciences 1999–; editorial writer for Avvenire and Giornale di Brescia; has written for various daily papers and periodicals, including L'Osservatore Romano 1977–87 and the fortnightly of the Catholic Univ. of the Sacred Heart Vita e Pensiero; Ed.-in-Chief L'Osservatore Romano 2007–; scholarship from Nat. Research Council 1976. *Publications:* more than 90 specialist studies, including Bibliotheca divina. Filologia e storia dei testi cristiani 2001, La donazione di Costantino 2004; ed. of anthology of writings by Montini with the title Carità intellettuale 2005. *Address:* L'Osservatore Romano, Tipografica Vaticana, Via del Pellegrino, 00120 Città del Vaticano, Rome, Italy (office). *Telephone:* (06) 69899390 (office). *Fax:* (06) 69883252 (office). *E-mail:* ornet@ossrom.va (office). *Website:* www.vatican.va/news_services/or/home_ita.html (office).

VIANA, Marcelo, PhD; Brazilian mathematician and academic; *Professor of Mathematics and Deputy Director, Instituto de Matemática Pura e Aplicada (IMPA);* b. 4 March 1962, Rio de Janeiro; ed Univ. of Porto, Inst. of Pure and Applied Math. (IMPA); Research Asst, Univ. of Porto 1984–91, Asst Prof. 1991–93; Research Asst Instituto de Matemática Pura e Aplicada (IMPA) 1987–91, Asst Prof. 1991–92, Assoc. Prof. 1992–97, Chair. for Scientific Activities 1996–2003, Prof. of Math. 1997–, Deputy Dir 2004–; mem. Brazilian Math. Soc. 1987– (Official 1997–2001), American Math. Soc. 1994–, Brazilian Acad. of Sciences 1997–, Third World Acad. of Sciences 2000–; mem. editorial bd of numerous scientific journals; Calouste Gulbenkian Foundation Fellowship 1988–90, Guggenheim Foundation Fellowship 1993–94; Invited Prof. Coll. de France, Paris 2002; Santaló Distinguished Lecturer, Univ. Complutense, Madrid 2005; Grand Cross of the Order of Scientific Merit 2000; Best Undergraduate in Science, António José de Almeida Foundation, Porto 1984, Third World Acad. of Sciences Award 1998, Math. Union of Latin America and the Caribbean Award 2000, Ramanujan Prize, Int. Centre for Theoretical Physics 2005. *Publications include:* numerous articles in professional journals. *Address:* Instituto de Matemática Pura e Aplicada (IMPA), Estrada Dona Castorina, 110, Jardim Botânico, 22460-320 Rio de Janeiro, Brazil (office). *Telephone:* (21) 2529-5114 (office). *Fax:* (21) 2529-5019 (office). *E-mail:* viana@impa.br (office). *Website:* www.impa.br/~viana (office).

VIAR OLLOQUI, Javier; Spanish arts administrator; *Director, Bilbao Fine Arts Museum;* b. 1946, Bilbao; poet, novelist, art critic and historian; mem. Bd Bilbao Fine Arts Museum late 1980s–, Dir 2002–; fmr mem. Acquisitions Advisory Bd, Guggenheim Bilbao; fmr mem. Dept of Culture, Basque Govt; organizer of numerous int. and nat. exhbns; Euskadi Literature Award, City of Irun Short Story Prize 1992. *Address:* Museo de Bellas Artes de Bilbao, Plaza del Museo 2, 48011 Bilbao, Spain (office). *Telephone:* (94) 4396060 (office). *Fax:* (94) 4396145 (office). *Website:* www.museobilbao.com (office).

VIARDO, Vladimir Vladimirovich, DJur; Russian pianist; *Professor and Artist-in-Residence, College of Music, University of North Texas;* b. 14 Nov. 1949; m. Natalia Viardo; two s.; ed Moscow State Conservatory; Asst Prof., Prof., Moscow State Conservatory 1975–; Grand Prix Marguerite Long Int. Competition; Gold Medal and 1st Prize, Van Clibern Int. Competition, USA 1973; resident in USA 1988–; Prof. and Artist-in-Residence Coll. of Music, Univ. of N Texas 1988–; Visiting Prof. Moscow State Conservatory 1998–2000. *Performances:* played with conductors Mehta, Kitayenko, Maazel, Spivakov, Comissiona, Penderecki; toured in major European, N American and Canadian cities, Asia and S Africa, Israel, Cen. and S America. *Address:* UNT College of Music, PO Box 311367, Denton, TX 76203-1367 (office); 457 Piermont Road, Cresskill, NJ 07626, USA. *Telephone:* (940) 565-4653 (office); (201) 816-1339 (home). *Fax:* (940) 565-2002 (office); (201) 894-5352 (home). *E-mail:* vviardo@music.unt.edu (office). *Website:* www.music.unt.edu/bio/viardo.shtml (office); viardo.com.

VIBE, Kjeld, LLD; Norwegian diplomatist; b. 5 Oct. 1927, Stavanger; s. of Christopher Andreas Vibe and Thordis Amundsen; m. Beate Meyer 1953; one s. three d.; ed Univ. of Oslo; entered foreign service 1954; Sec., Del. to NATO and OEEC, Paris 1956–59; First Sec. Ministry of Foreign Affairs 1959–62; Temp. Head, Norwegian Mil. Mission, Berlin 1961; Personal Sec. to Minister of Foreign Affairs 1962–65; Counsellor, Norwegian Embassy, Wash. 1965–69; Deputy Dir-Gen. for Political Affairs, Ministry of Foreign Affairs 1969–72, Dir-Gen. 1972–77; Amb., Perm. Rep. to NATO 1977–84; Sec.-Gen. Ministry of Foreign Affairs 1984–89; Amb. to USA 1989–97; mem. Norwegian Govt.'s Comm. on Freedom of Speech 1996–2002; Commdr with Star of the Royal Norwegian Order of Sanct Olav; several foreign decorations. *Publications:* regular contribs. on foreign affairs to newspaper Aftenposten 1996–2002. *Leisure interests:* skiing, history, music. *Address:* Holmenkollv 35, Oslo 0376, Norway (home). *Telephone:* 22-14-98-36 (home).

VICARI, Andrew; British artist; b. 20 April 1938, Port Talbot, Wales; s. of Cav. Vittorio Vicari and Italia Bertani; ed Slade School of Art and Univ. Coll. London; works held in many perm. and pvt. collections including Dallas Museum of Fine Arts, Nat. Library of Wales, Museum of Tel-Aviv, Contemporary Arts Soc. of GB, Columbus Museum of Fine Arts, USA, Pezzo Pozzoli Museum, Milan, Petit Palais Museum of Modern Art, Geneva; official painter of King and Govt of Saudi Arabia; Fellow London Zoological Soc.; Freedom of the City of London 2002, Liveryman of Wales 2002, Liveryman of the Guilds of London 2002; European Beaux Arts Prize 1995, Chevalier, Order of Merit (Monaco), Brig. d'honneur, Compagnie Républicaine de Sécurité (France); numerous Int. decorations. *Publications:* Triumph of the Bedouin 1984, The Truth is not Enough (autobiog.) 2003. *Leisure interests:* squash, salsa, food and wine. *Address:* c/o The East India Club, 16 St James's Square, London, SW1Y 4LH, England. *Telephone:* (7976) 310352 (office). *Fax:* (709) 200-6234 (office). *E-mail:* executive@andrewvicari.com (office). *Website:* www.andrewvicari.com (office).

VICKERS, Sir John Stuart, Kt, FBA, MA, DPhil; British economist; *Drummond Professor of Political Economy, University of Oxford;* b. 7 July 1958, Eastbourne; s. of Aubrey Vickers and Kay Vickers; m. Maureen Freed 1991; one s. two d.; ed Eastbourne Grammar School and Oriel Coll. Oxford; Fellow, All Souls Coll. Oxford 1979–84, 1991–; Shell UK Oil 1979–81; Roy Harrod Fellow, Nuffield Coll. Oxford 1984–90; Drummond Prof. of Political Economy, Univ. of Oxford 1991–98, 2005–; Chief Economist, Bank of England 1998–2000; Dir Gen. of Fair Trading 2000–03, Chair. Office of Fair Trading 2003–05; Pres. Royal Econ. Soc. 2007–; Fellow, Econometric Soc. 1998–; Visiting Lecturer, Princeton Univ., USA 1988, Harvard Univ., USA 1989, 1990; Visiting Prof., London Business School 1996;. *Publications:* Privatization: An Economic Analysis (co-author) 1988, Regulatory Reform (co-author) 1994; articles on innovation, competition, regulation, industrial org. etc. *Address:* All Souls College, Oxford, OX1 4AL, England (office). *Website:* www.economics.ox.ac.uk (office).

VICKERS, Jon, CC, RAM; Canadian singer (tenor); b. 29 Oct. 1926, Prince Albert, Saskatchewan; s. of William Vickers and Myrle Mossip; m. 1st Henrietta Outerbridge 1953 (died 1991); three s. two d.; m. 2nd Judith Stewart 1993; began career as concert and opera singer in Canada; joined Royal Opera House, Covent Garden (London) 1957; sang at Bayreuth Festival, Vienna State Opera, San Francisco, Chicago Lyric Opera, Metropolitan Opera, La Scala, Milan, Paris Opera, Boston, Buenos Aires, Athens, Ottawa, Houston, Dallas, Hamburg, Berlin, Munich, Athens Festival, Salzburg Festival, Festival of Orange, Tanglewood Festival, Rio de Janeiro; Hon. LLD (Sask.); Hon. CLD (Bishop's Univ.); Hon. MusD (Brandon, Univ. of Western Ont.); Hon. LLD (Guelph); Hon. Civ. LD (Laval); Hon. DMus (Univ. of Ill.); Critics Award, London 1978, Grammy Award 1979. *Films include:* Carmen, Pagliacci, Norma, Otello. *Recordings:* Messiah, Otello, Aida, Die Walküre, Samson and Delilah, Fidelio, Italian Arias, Verdi Requiem, Peter Grimes, Das Lied von der Erde, Les Troyens, Tristan und Isolde; Enoch Arden (poem by Alfred Lord Tennyson, piano played by Mark Ammelain). *Address:* PO Box 290 WKBX, Warwick, WK 03, Bermuda.

VICTOR, Edward (Ed), MLitt; British literary agent; b. 9 Sept. 1939, New York, USA; s. of the late Jack Victor and the late Lydia Victor; m. 1st Michelene Dinah Samuels 1963 (divorced); two s.; m. 2nd Carol Lois Ryan; one s.; ed Dartmouth Coll., USA, Pembroke Coll., Cambridge; Arts Book Ed., then Editorial Dir Weidenfeld & Nicolson 1964–67; Editorial Dir Jonathan Cape Ltd 1967–71; Sr Ed. Alfred A. Knopf Inc., New York 1972–73, literary agent and Dir John Farquharson Ltd 1974–76; Founding Ed. Victor Agency 1977; mem. Council Aids Crisis Trust 1986–98; Vice-Chair. Almeida Theatre 1994–2002 (Dir 1993–2002); Trustee, The Arts Foundation 1991–2004. *Publications include:* The Obvious Diet 2001. *Leisure interests:* golf, tennis, travel, opera. *Address:* Ed Victor Ltd, 6 Bayley Street, Bedford Square, London, WC1B 3HB (office); 10 Cambridge Gate, Regents Park, London, NW1 4JX, England (home). *Telephone:* (20) 7304-4100 (office); (20) 7224-3030 (home). *Fax:* (20) 7304-4111 (office); (20) 7935-3096 (home). *E-mail:* ed@edvictor.com.

VICTORIA INGRID ALICE DÉSIRÉE, HRH Crown Princess (Duchess of Västergötland); Swedish; b. 14 July 1977, Stockholm; d. of HM King Carl XVI Gustaf and HM Queen Silvia of Sweden; ed Enskilda Gymnasiet, Stockholm, Université Catholique de l'Ouest, Angers, France, Yale Univ., USA and Nat. Defence Coll., Stockholm; internships at Embassy in Washington, DC 1999, UN, New York 2002, Swedish Trade Council, Berlin and Paris 2002; has completed study programmes at Offices of the Swedish Govt and the Swedish Int. Devt Co-operation Agency; participated in state visits to study int. aid efforts. *Leisure interests:* nature and outdoor pursuits. *Address:* c/o Information and Press Department, Kungl. Slottet, Stockholm 111 30, Sweden. *E-mail:* info@royalcourt.se. *Website:* www.royalcourt.se.

VID, Leonard Bernhardovich, CandEcon; Russian banker; *Deputy to the Chairman of the Board of Directors, Alfa-Bank;* b. 9 Nov. 1931, Zaporozhye, Ukraine; m.; two d.; ed Moscow Inst. of Non-ferrous Metals and Gold; with Norilsk Ore Mining and Processing enterprise, master then Deputy Dir 1955–77; First Deputy Chair. USSR State Planning Cttee 1977–91; Deputy Minister of Econs of USSR 1991–92; Dir Cen. of Econ. State of Affairs at Russian Govt 1992–95, Chair. Bd Alfa-Bank 1996–2002, Deputy to Chair. Bd of Dirs 2002–; Exec. Dir Our Home Russia Movt 1995–96; mem. Comm. on Co-ordinating State Programme of Transition to the Int. System of Statistics and Accountancy. *Address:* Alfa-Bank, Mashi Poryvayevoy str. 11, Moscow, Russia (office). *Telephone:* (495) 208-8-42 (office). *Fax:* (495) 913-7142 (office). *Website:* www.alfabank.com (office).

VIDAL, Gore; American writer; b. 3 Oct. 1925, West Point, New York; s. of Eugene L. Vidal and Nina Vidal (née Gore); ed Phillips Acad., Exeter, NH; served in US Army 1943–46; Drama Critic, Reporter (magazine) 1959, Democratic-Liberal Cand. for US Congress from New York 1960; mem. Pres. Kennedy's Advisory Council on the Arts 1961–63; Co-Chair. People's Party 1970–72; writes thrillers under pseudonym Edgar Box; Hon. Citizen, Ravello, Italy 1983; Chevalier, Ordre Nat. des Arts et des Lettres; Edgar Allan Poe Award for Television 1955. *Film and television screenplays:* Wedding Breakfast, The Catered Affair 1956, The Left-Handed Gun 1958, I Accuse 1958, The Death of Billy the Kid (TV) 1958, Suddenly Last Summer 1959, The Best Man (Cannes Critics' Prize) 1964, Is Paris Burning? 1966, The Last of the Mobile Hotshots 1970, Dress Gray 1986. *Publications:* novels: Williwaw 1946, In a Yellow Wood 1947, The City and the Pillar 1948, The Season of Comfort 1949, A Search for the King 1950, Dark Green, Bright Red 1950, The Judgment of Paris 1952, Messiah 1954, Julian 1964, Washington, DC 1967, Myra Breckinridge 1968, Two Sisters 1970, Burr 1972, Myron 1974, 1876 1976, Kalki 1978, Creation (Prix Deauville) 1980, Duluth 1983, Lincoln 1984, Empire 1987, Hollywood 1990, Live from Golgotha 1992, With Honors 1994, Dark Green, Dark Red 1995, The Season of Conflict 1996, The Essential Vidal 1998, The Smithsonian Institution 1998, The Golden Age 2000; short stories: A Thirsty Evil 1956; plays: Visit to a Small Planet 1956, The Best Man 1960, Romulus 1962, Weekend 1968, An Evening with Richard Nixon 1972, Gore

Vidal's Lincoln 1988, On the March to the Sea 2005; non-fiction: Rocking the Boat 1962, Reflections upon a Sinking Ship 1969, Homage to Daniel Shays 1972, Matters of Fact and Fiction 1977, The Second American Revolution 1982, Armageddon? 1987, At Home: Essays 1982–88 1988, A View from the Diners Club: Essays 1987–1991 1991, Screening History (memoir) 1992, United States: Essays 1952–1992 (Nat. Book Award) 1993, Palimpsest (memoir) 1995, Virgin Islands: A Dependency of United States Essays 1992–97 1997, The Last Empire: Essays 1992–2000 2001, Perpetual War for Perpetual Peace: How We Got So Hated 2002, Inventing a Nation: Washington, Adams, Jefferson 2003, Imperial America 2004, Point To Point Navigation (memoir) 2006; criticism in Partisan Review, The Nation, New York Review of Books, Times Literary Supplement. *Address:* c/o Doubleday Publicity Department, 1745 Broadway, New York, NY 10019, USA. *E-mail:* ddaypub@randomhouse.com.

VIDAL, HE Cardinal Ricardo; Philippine ecclesiastic; *Archbishop of Cebu;* b. 6 Feb. 1931, Mogpog, Marinduque; s. of Fructuoso Vidal and Natividad Jamin; ordained priest 1956; consecrated Bishop (Titular Church of Claterna) 1971; Archbishop of Lipa 1973–82, of Cebu 1982–; cr. Cardinal 1985; Chair. Episcopal Comm. on Clergy; mem. Congregation for the Evangelization of Peoples, Congregation for Catholic Educ., Pontifical Council for Pastoral Assistance to Health Care Workers; Pres. Pontificio Collegio Filippino 2000–; Bailiff Grand Cross of Honour and Devotion of the Sovereign Order of Malta 2002; Dr hc (Univ. of Santo Tomas) 1985, (San Carlos Univ.) 1995, Hon. DHumLitt (Manuel S. Enverga Foundation Univ.) 1990, (Ateneo de Manila Univ.) 1993; Univ. of Southern Philippines Rizal Peace Award 2002. *Leisure interests:* walking, classical music, gardening. *Address:* 234 D. Jakosalem Str., PO Box 52, Cebu City 6000, Philippines. *Telephone:* (32) 2533382. *Fax:* (32) 2544458. *E-mail:* rcv@cebu.pworld.net.ph (office).

VIDAL SALINAS, Francisco; Chilean politician; *Minister of National Defence;* b. 20 Sept. 1953; ed Univ. of Chile; Prof. of History and Geography, Univ. of Chile; Sec., Faculty of Econ. Sciences, Univ. Central de Chile 1993–99, Dean, Faculty of Econ. and Admin. Sciences 1998–99; Exec. Dir Fundación Chile 21 1994–2000; mem. Partido por la Democracia 1987–; consultant to Higher Educ. Council and Higher Educ. Div., Ministry of Educ. 1993; Councillor Metropolitan Regional Govt 1993–2000; Under-Sec. for Regional and Admin. Devt, Ministry of the Interior 2000–03; Minister, Sec.-Gen. of the Govt 2003–05, 2007–09; Minister of the Interior 2005–06, of Nat. Defence 2009–; Pres. Directorate, Televisión Nacional de Chile 2006–07; Dir School of Govt, Univ. Alberto Hurtado 2006–. *Address:* Ministry of National Defence, Villavicencio 364, 22°, Edif. Diego Portales, Santiago, Chile (office). *Telephone:* (2) 222-1202 (office). *Fax:* (2) 633-0568 (office). *Website:* www .defensa.cl (office).

VIDEANU, Adriean; Romanian business executive and politician; *Minister of the Economy;* b. 1 June 1962, Crevenicu, Teleorman Co.; m. Mioriţa Videanu; one s. one d.; ed Faculty of Transport, Bucharest Polytechnic Inst.; business exec. in marble and granite industry; Head of Section, SUT Ploieşti 1987–90; Chair. CA Titan Mar SA 2003–04; Deputy (Democratic Liberal Party—DLP) for Teleorman Co. 1990–2003, Vice-Pres. Budget Cttee (Finance-Banks) 2000; Chair. Nat. Youth, DLP 1992–96, Exec. Sec. DLP 1996–2000, Vice-Pres. and Spokesman for DLP, responsible for matters of image and media relations 2001–03; Minister of State and Deputy Prime Minister 2004–05; Mayor of Bucharest 2005–08; Minister of the Economy 2008–. *Address:* Ministry of the Economy, 010096 Bucharest 1, Calea Victoriei 152, Romania (office). *Telephone:* (21) 2025106 (office). *Fax:* (21) 2025108 (office). *E-mail:* dezbateri_publice@minind.ro (office); contact@videanu.ro. *Website:* www.minind.ro (office); www.videanu.ro.

VIDELA, Lt-Gen. Jorge Rafael; Argentine fmr head of state and army officer; b. 2 Aug. 1925, Mercedes, Prov. of Buenos Aires; m. Alicia Hartridge; six c.; ed Nat. Mil. Coll. and War School; commissioned in Infantry 1944; Lt in Vigilance Co., Ministry of War 1946; with Motorized Army Regt 1947–48; Nat. Mil. Coll. 1948; Student, War School, with rank of Army Capt. 1951–54; Staff Officer, Nat. Mil. Coll. 1954–56; Adviser to Office of Mil. Attaché, Washington, DC 1956–58; Staff Officer, Army Gen. Command 1962–65, 1966–68; Col 1965; engaged on course in Strategy, Army Centre of Higher Studies 1965–66; Lt-Col, Chief of Cadet Corps 1968; Second in Command and Chief of Staff, Fifth Infantry Brigade 1968–70; Chief of Operations, Third Army Corps 1970–71; Brig., Head of Nat. Mil. Coll. 1971–73; Chief of Army Gen. Staff 1973–75, of Jt High Command 1975; C-in-C of Army 1975–78; led coup to depose Pres. María Perón (q.v.) March 1976; Pres. of Argentina 1976–81; fmr mem. Inter-American Defence Bd, Washington, DC; arrested Aug. 1984, on trial for human rights offences 1985, sentenced to life imprisonment Dec. 1985, granted pardon Dec. 1990.

VIDENOV, Jan Vassilev; Bulgarian politician; b. 22 March 1959, Plovdiv; m.; one c.; ed Moscow State Inst. for Int. Relations; specialist with Biotech Corpn and Autoelectronics; mem. Supreme Council of Presidency, Bulgarian Socialist Party 1990, Chair. 1994; mem. Parl.; Prime Minister of Bulgaria 1994–97 (forced to resign). *Address:* Bulgarian Socialist Party, 20 Pozitano Str., 1000 Sofia, Bulgaria (office). *Telephone:* (2) 981-57-08 (office). *Fax:* (2) 981-57-08 (office). *E-mail:* foreign@bsp.bg (office). *Website:* www.bsp.bg (office).

VIEGAS FILHO, José; Brazilian politician and diplomatist; *Ambassador to Spain;* b. 14 Oct. 1942, Campo Grande; m. 1st Rosa Maria Amorim (died 1999); three c.; m. 2nd Erika Stockholm; joined Instituto Rio Branco 1964; apptd consul-aid, New York 1969; responsible for Brazilian businesses in Cuba 1987–90; apptd Chief Dept of Int. Bodies within Foreign Office 1992; Amb. to Denmark 1995–98, to Peru 1998–2001, to Russia 2001–02; Minister of Defence 2003–04 (resgnd); Amb. to Spain 2004–. *Leisure interests:* literature, translation. *Address:* Embassy of Brazil, Fernando el Santo 6, 28010 Madrid, Spain (office). *Telephone:* (91) 7004650 (office). *Fax:* (91) 7004660 (office). *E-mail:* adm@embajadabrasil.es (office). *Website:* www.brasil.es (office).

VIEHBACHER, Chris; Canadian/German business executive; *CEO, Sanofi Aventis SA;* b. 26 March 1960, Ottawa; m.; three c.; ed Queens Univ., Ottawa; Chief Financial Accountant, Wellcome GmbH, Germany 1988, Finance Dir 1989–93, Pres. and CEO Burroughs Wellcome Inc., Canada 1993–95, Vice-Pres. Glaxo Wellcome France 1995–96, Gen. Man. 1996–97, Chair. and Man. Dir 1997–2003, Pres. US Pharmaceuticals, GlaxoSmithKline 2003–08, Pres. North American Pharmaceuticals May-Dec. 2008, mem. Bd of Dirs, GlaxoSmithKline Jan.–Sept. 2008; CEO Sanofi Aventis SA 2008–; Bd mem. PhRMA; Chevalier, Légion d'Honneur 2003. *Address:* Sanofi-Aventis SA, 174 Avenue de France, 75013 Paris, France (office). *Telephone:* 1-53-77-42-23 (office). *Fax:* 1-53-77-42-65 (office). *Website:* www.sanofi-aventis.com (office).

VIEIRA, Meredith; American television broadcaster and journalist; *Co-anchor, The Today Show, NBC News;* b. 30 Dec. 1953, East Providence, RI; d. of Edwin Vieira and Mary Elsie Vieira; m. Prof. Richard M. Cohen 1986; two s. one d.; ed Tufts Univ., Medford, Mass; began career as news announcer for WORC Radio, Worcester, Mass 1975; started in TV working as local reporter and anchor at WJAR-TV Providence; later worked in newsroom at WCBS-TV, New York City; first came to nat. recognition as CBS reporter based in Chicago Bureau, later became a corresp. for CBS news-magazine shows including West 57th and 60 Minutes, then Co-anchor of CBS Morning News; corresp. for ABC news-magazine show Turning Point; Moderator and Co-host The View 1997–2006; Host Lifetime's Intimate Portrait 1999–; Host Who Wants to Be a Millionaire? 2002–; Co-anchor The Today Show (NBC) 2006–; seven Emmy Awards for her work on West 57th, 60 Minutes, Turning Point and Daytime Emmy for Outstanding Game Show Host 2005, ranked by Forbes Magazine amongst 100 Most Powerful Women (69th) 2006, (55th) 2007, (61st) 2008. *Address:* The Today Show, NBC News, 30 Rockefeller Plaza, New York, NY 10112, USA (office). *Telephone:* (212) 664-4444 (office). *Fax:* (212) 664-4085 (office). *E-mail:* Today@nbc.com (office). *Website:* www.msnbc.msn.com/id/3032633 (office).

VIÉNOT, Marc, LèsL; French banker; *Honorary Chairman, Société Générale, Paris;* b. 1 Nov. 1928, Paris; s. of the late Jacques Viénot and of Henriette Brunet; m. Christiane Regnault 1953; two s. two d.; ed Nat. Inst. of Politicial Studies and Ecole Nat. d'Admin.; Inspector of Finance 1955; special envoy to Cabinet of Minister of Econ. and Finance April–June 1957, to Cabinet of Minister of Finance, Econ. and Planning June–Nov. 1957; special envoy to cabinet of Pres. of French Parl. 1957–58; special envoy to Treasury Div. July 1958; Chair. Study Cttee OECD 1961–65; Sec. to Bd of Econ. and Social Devt Fund 1963–65; Under-Sec. Treasury Div. 1965; Head, Financial Activities Service, Treasury Div. 1967; Minister (Financial Counsellor), French Embassies in USA and Canada and Dir IBRD and IMF 1970–73; Deputy Gen. Man. Société Générale, Paris 1973, Gen. Man. 1977–86, Chair. and CEO 1986–97, now Hon. Chair, mem. Bd of Dirs –2007; Interim Pres. Alcatel Alsthom April–July 1995; Pres. Paris Europlace 1998–; Chair. Bd Aventis; Dir Alcatel, Ciments Français, Chemin de fer franco-éthiopien, Electricité de France, SNECMA, Vivendi Universal; mem. Supervisory Bd Compagnie bancaire, Carnaud Metalbox; mem. and fmr Vice-Pres. French Banks Asscn; Officier, Légion d'honneur; Commdr, Ordre nat. du Mérite. *Address:* 4 avenue Raymond Poincaré, 75116 Paris, France (home).

VIERA GALLO QUESNEY, José Antonio; Chilean politician; *Minister, Secretary General of the Presidency;* b. 2 Dec. 1943, Santiago; m. María Teresa Chadwick; three d.; ed Univ. Católica de Chile; fmr Prof. of Political Theory, Univ. Católica de Chile; Under-Sec. for Justice during Presidency of Salvador Allende; exiled in Italy following mil. coup 1973; f. Chileamerica magazine (published in Rome during exile); fmr adviser to UNESCO, FAO and World Council of Churches; fmr Deputy Sec.-Gen. Institutional Documentation Service, Rome; Dir Centro de Estudios Sociales 1983–2001; returned to Chile 1985; mem. Chamber of Deputies 1990–98, Pres. 1990–93, mem. Internal Order, Constitutional, Legislation and Justice Perm. Comms, Defence Comm; Senator for Octava 1998–2004, currently Pres. Senate Human Rights, Nationality and Citizenship Comm; Sec.-Gen. of the Presidency 2007–; mem. Cen. Cttee Partido Socialista. *Address:* Office of the Minister, Secretary-General of the Presidency, Palacio de la Moneda, Santiago, Chile (office). *Telephone:* (2) 690-4218 (office). *Fax:* (2) 690-4329 (office).

VIERMETZ, Kurt F.; German banker and stock exchange official; *Chairman of the Supervisory Board, Deutsche Börse AG;* b. 27 April 1939, Augsburg; m. Felicity Viermetz; began career as foreign exchange trader with Deutsche Bank AG, Frankfurt 1960–65; Asst Treasurer, JP Morgan & Co. Inc., Frankfurt 1965–70, Vice-Pres. Paris Br. 1970–75, involved in est. of Saudi Int. Bank Ltd, London 1975–77, Vice-Pres. JP Morgan, New York, responsible for foreign exchange and Euro treasury world-wide 1977–80, Sr Vice-Pres. JP Morgan, Frankfurt, responsible for German and Continental European business 1980–85, Treas. JP Morgan & Co. Inc., New York 1985–90, Vice-Chair. Man. Bd and Supervisory Bd, New York 1990–2000, mem. Bd Dirs 1998–2000; Chair. Supervisory Bd Bayerische Hypo- und Vereinsbank AG, Munich 1999–2002, Vice-Chair. Jan.–Dec. 2003; Chair. Supervisory Bd Hypo Real Estate Holding AG, Munich 2003–; Chair. Supervisory Bd, Deutsche Börse AG 2005–; mem. Supervisory Bd Hoechst AG, Frankfurt 1990–98 (also Chair. Bd Finance Cttee), Advisory Bd Metro Co., Zug, Switzerland 1990–98, Supervisory Bd Veba AG, Düsseldorf 1993–2003, Supervisory Bd E.ON AG, Düsseldorf 1993–2003, Supervisory Bd ERGO Versicherungs AG, Düsseldorf 2003–, Supervisory Bd E.ON-Ruhrgas AG, Essen 2003–05; Dir (non-exec.) Grosvenor Estate Holdings Ltd, London, UK 1996–2004; Chair. Int. Capital Markets Advisory Bd Cttee, New York Stock Exchange 1995–2004; Chair. Bd of Overseers, Univ. of Augsburg 2002–; Founder and mem. Man. Bd,

Förderkreis Schaezlerpalais e.V.; mem. Bd Int. Advisory Cttee Fed. Reserve Bank of New York 1995–, American Council of Germany, New York 1987–; Trustee New York Philharmonic Soc. 1988–2002, Haniel Foundation, Duisberg 1998–. *Address:* Deutsche Börse AG, Neue Börsenstrasse 1, 60485 Frankfurt, Germany (office). *Telephone:* (69) 2110 (office). *Fax:* (69) 2111-1021 (office). *E-mail:* info@deutsche-boerse.com (office). *Website:* deutsche-boerse .com (office).

VĪĶE-FREIBERGA, Vaira, MA, PhD; Latvian fmr head of state and psychologist; b. 1 Dec. 1937, Rīga; m. Imants Freibergs 1960; one s. one d.; ed Univ. of Toronto and McGill Univ., Canada; Prof. of Psychology Univ. of Montréal 1965–98; Prof. Emer. 1998–; Vice-Chair. Science Council of Canada 1988–97; Dir Latvian Inst., Rīga 1998–99; Pres. of Latvia 1999–2007; fmr Pres. Canadian Psychological Asscn; Pres. Social Science Fed. of Canada; Chair. Asscn for Advancement of Baltic Studies, USA; Pres. Acad. des Lettres et des Sciences Humaines, RSC; mem. Latvian Acad. of Sciences, Council of Women Leaders 1999–; lectures and seminars on Latvian culture in USA, Canada, Latvia and numerous countries; Hon. Prof., Victoria Univ., Canada 2000, Latvia Univ.; decorations include Three Star Order of Latvia 1995, Dame of GCB 2006, Officer of the National Order of Québec, Canada 2006; Hon. LLD (Latvia) 1991, Hon. DLitt (Victoria Univ., Toronto) 2000, Hon. DSci (McGill Univ.) 2002, Dr hc (Latvia) 2000, (Vytautas Magnus Univ., Lithuania) 2002, (Eurasian Nat. Univ.) 2004, (Baku, Azerbaijan) 2005, (Tbilisi) 2005, (Yerevan) 2005, (Ottawa) 2006, (Liege) 2006; numerous prizes include Anna Abele Prize 1979, Marcel-Vincent Prize and Medal 1992, Pierre Chauveau Medal 1995, awards from Latvian Acad. of Science 1992, American Acad. of Achievement Gold Plate 2000, McGill Univ., Canada 2002, Kaunas Vytautas Magnus Univ., Lithuania 2002, Georgetown Univ., USA 2002, Free Univ. of Berlin 2003, Grand Prize of Folklore, Ministry of Culture, Latvia 2003, Award of Distinction of the Canadian Psychological Asscn 2004, Forbes Executive Women's Forum Trailblazer Award 2005, Medal of the American Jewish Cttee 2005, Hannah Arendt Prize for Political Thought 2005, Coudenhove-Kalergi Foundation Europa Prize, Pan-Europa Union 2006, Baltic Statesmanship Award of the US-Baltic Foundation 2006, J.W. Goethe Univ. Medal and Walter Hallstein Prize 2006, UN FAO Ceres Medal 2007. *Publications include:* La Frequence Lexicalle des Mots au Québec 1974, Latvian Sun-Songs (co-author) 1988, Linguistic and Poetics of Latvian Folk Songs 1989, On the Amber Mountain 1993, Against the Current 1993, The Cosmological Sun 1997, The Chronological Sun 1999, The Warm Sun 2002, Latvian Sun Song Melodies 2005; contrib. more than 400 articles and papers. *Address:* c/o Chancery of the President, Pils lauk. 3, Rīga 1050, Latvia. *E-mail:* chancery@ president.lv (office). *Website:* www.president.lv.

VIKHAREV, Anatoly Anatolyevich; Russian politician; b. 16 Oct. 1962; ed Ural Polytechnic Inst.; metal worker, mechanic, foreman then head of workshop, Uralenergostroi factory, Sverdlovsk 1982–94; Dir-Gen. Ural Inst. of Heavy Machine Construction 1994–98; Chair. Bd of Dirs Jt-Stock co. Uralgidrotyazhmash 1998–2000; mem. Tutorial Council, Inst. of Human Rights; mem. Council of Feds representing Kurgan Regional Duma 2001, Deputy Chair. 2001, mem. Comm. on Regulation and Organization of Parl. Activities, Comm. on Problems of Youth and Sports. *Address:* Gogol str. 56, Office 63, 640024 Kurgan (office); Council of Federations, Bolshaya Dmitrovka str. 26, 103426 Moscow, Russia (office). *Telephone:* (83522) 4183-94 (office); (495) 292-57-88 (office); (495) 926-63-81 (office).

VIKTYUK, Roman Grigoryevich; Russian/Ukrainian theatre director; b. 28 Oct. 1936, Lvov; ed A. Lunacharcky State Inst. of Theatre Art; Chief Dir Kalinin Theatre of Lenin Komsomol 1968–71; Dir Russian Drama Theatre in Vilnius 1971–77; Artistic Dir Students' Theatre of Moscow Univ. 1977–91; concurrently theatre productions in maj. theatres of Moscow and Leningrad (now St Petersburg); Founder and Artistic Dir Viktyuk Theatre 1991–; directed productions in Swedish Theatre Helsinki, theatres of Brescia, Rome, San Diego; USA tour 1998; several TV productions. *Address:* Roman Viktyuk Theatre, Stromynka str. 6, 107014 Moscow (office); Tverskaya 4, Apt. 87, 103009 Moscow, Russia (office); (095) 268-06-69 (office). *Telephone:* (095) 292-6895 (home).

VILADECANS, Joan-Pere; Spanish artist; b. 1948, Barcelona; s. of Joan-Pere Viladecans and Carme Viladecans; Chevalier, Ordre des Arts et Lettres. *Address:* c/o Galería Joan Gaspar, Plaza Dr. Letamendi 1, 08007 Barcelona (office); Córcega 589, 08025 Barcelona, Spain. *Telephone:* (93) 323-07-48 (office); (3) 455-93-85. *Fax:* (93) 451-13-43 (office). *E-mail:* joangaspar@ galgasparjoan.com (office).

VILÁGOSI, Gábor, DJur; Hungarian lawyer and politician; *Deputy Speaker, Országgyülés (National Assembly);* b. 12 Jan. 1956, Devecser; m.; four c.; ed Univ. of Pécs; legal affairs official, Cen. Transdanubia Water Man. Directorate 1980–83; legal advisor to Alkotmány Agricultural Co-operative, then to Fehérvár Dept Store 1983–89; among first members of Alliance of Free Democrats (SZDSZ) 1989, mem. SZDSZ governing cttee for Székesfehérvár 1989–90, Chair., SZDSZ Fejér County 1999–, mem. Nat. Exec. 2007–; practised law in Székesfehérvár 1990–94; mem., Hungarian Olympic Cttee 1994–98; co-Chair., Lake Velence Regional Council 1995–98; Mem. of Parliament 1990–; State Sec. for Policy, Ministry of Interior 1994–98; mem., Fejér County Ass. 1998–2002; mem. Székesfehérvár Municipal Ass. 2002–06; Keeper of the Minutes of the Országgyülés (Nat. Ass.) 1998–2004; Deputy Speaker, Nat. Ass. 2004–; mem., Cttee on Sport and Tourism 2006–. *Address:* Országgyülés, 1357 Budapest, Kossuth tér 1–3, Hungary (office). *Telephone:* (1) 441-4000 (office); (1) 441-4809 (office). *Fax:* (1) 441-4072 (office). *E-mail:* gabor.vilagosi@parlament.hu (office). *Website:* www.parlament.hu (office).

VILARDELL, Francisco, MD, DSc (Med); Spanish physician and gastroenterologist; b. 1 April 1926, Barcelona; s. of Jacinto Vilardell and Mercedes Viñas; m. Leonor Vilardell 1958; one s. two d.; ed Univs of Barcelona and Pennsylvania; Dir Gastroenterology Service, Hosp. Santa Cruz y San Pablo, Barcelona 1963–; Dir Postgrad. School of Gastroenterology, Autonomous Univ. of Barcelona 1969–; Pres. European Soc. for Digestive Endoscopy 1970–74, European Asscn for Study of the Liver 1975–76; Pres. World Org. of Gastroenterology 1982–90 (Sec.-Gen. 1974–82), now Hon. Pres.; Pres. Council of Int. Orgs in Medical Science 1987–93, Perm. Adviser 1994–; Dir-Gen. Health Planning, Ministry of Health 1981–82, mem. Advisory Council 1997–; Hon. Pres. World Gastroenterology Org.; Chevalier, Légion d'honneur; Gold Medal, Barcelona Acad. of Medicine, Gold Medal, Spanish Soc. of Gastroenterology. *Publications:* ed. of six books; 170 papers in medical journals. *Leisure interests:* music, philology. *Address:* Escuela de Patología Digestiva, Hospital de la Santa Cruz y San Pablo, 08025 Barcelona, Spain (office); CIOMS, c/o World Health Organization, 1211 Geneva 27, Switzerland; Juan Sebastian Bach 11, 08021 Barcelona, Spain (home). *Telephone:* (93) 2197343 (office); (22) 913406 (CIOMS); (93) 2014511 (home). *Fax:* (93) 2010191 (home).

VILARIÑO PINTOS, Daría; Spanish librarian (retd); b. 26 Jan. 1928, Santiago de Compostela; d. of José Vilariño de Andrés and Daría Pintos Castro; mem. staff, state library, museum and archives depts 1957–70; Deputy Dir, Library of Univ. of Santiago 1970–73, Dir 1973–93; Insignia de Oro de la Univ. de Santiago 1993; Medalla de Bronce de Galicia 1993. *Publications:* O Libro Galego onte e hoxe (with Virtudes Pardo) 1981, Hechos de D. Berenguel de Landoria (co-author) 1983, Vasco de Aponte: Recuento de las Casas Antiguas del Reino de Galicìa. Edición crítica (co-author) 1986, Ordoño de Celanova: Vida y Milagros de San Rosendo. Edición crítica (co-author) 1990, Guía do Fondo Antigo de Monografías da Biblioteca Xeral da USC: Literaturas Hispánicas Séculos XV–XVIII (co-author) 2000; articles in professional journals, bibliographical catalogues. *Leisure interest:* reading. *Address:* Calle San Miguel No. 5, 2°, 15704 Santiago de Compostela, La Coruña, Spain. *Telephone:* (981) 583658.

VILELA SAMPAIO, Suely, BSc, MSc, DSc; Brazilian toxicologist and university administrator; *Rector, University of São Paulo;* b. 22 Feb. 1954, Ilicínea, Minas Gerais; divorced; one s.; ed Univ. of Ribeirão Preto; Assoc. Prof., Clinical Analysis, Toxicology and Bromatology Dept, Univ. of Ribeirão Preto 1991, Full Prof. of Pharmaceutical Sciences 1996, Pro-Rector of Post-Graduation 2002; fmr Asst Rector, Univ. of São Paulo, Rector 2005–; Visiting Prof., Univ. of Nice, France 1993, Univ. of Chile 1996, Univ. of Costa Rica 1997, Univ. of London, UK 1999, Univ. of Parma, Italy 2004, Univ. of Havana, Cuba 2004, Rutgers Univ., USA 2004, Univ. of Barcelona, Spain 2004, Ohio Univ., USA 2004; Dir Int. Asscn of Univs. *Address:* Office of the Rector, Universidade de São Paulo, Rua da Reitoria 109, 05508-900 São Paulo, Brazil (office). *Website:* www.universia.com.br (office).

VILHJALMSSON, Thor, Cand. juris; Icelandic judge (retd) and professor of law; b. 9 June 1930, Reykjavik; s. of Vilhjalmur Th. Gislason and Inga Arnadóttir Gislason; m. Ragnhildur Helgadóttir 1950; one s. three d.; ed Reykjavik Grammar School, St Andrews Univ., Scotland, Univ. of Iceland, New York Univ. and Univ. of Copenhagen; Asst Lecturer, Univ. of Iceland 1959–62, part-time Lecturer 1962–67, Prof. 1967–76 and Dean, Faculty of Law 1968–70, Dir Inst. of Law 1974–76; Deputy Judge Reykjavik Civil Court 1960–62, Judge 1962–67; Judge, European Court of Human Rights 1971–98, Vice-Pres. 1998; Assoc. Justice of the Supreme Court of Iceland 1976–93, Pres. 1983–84, 1993; Judge, EFTA Court, Geneva 1994–96, Luxembourg 1996–2002 (Pres. 2000–02); mem. Icelandic Del. to UN Gen. Ass. 1963, UN Sea-Bed Cttee 1972, 1973 to Law of the Sea Conf. 1974, 1975 and other int. confs; Pres. Asscn of Icelandic Lawyers 1971–74; Ed. Icelandic Law Review 1973–83; Commdr, Order of the Icelandic Falcon. *Publications:* Civil Procedure I–IV and several studies and articles on constitutional law, human rights and legal history. *Address:* Midleiti 10, 1S 103 Reykjavik, Iceland (home). *Telephone:* 5535330 (home). *Fax:* 5535330 (home). *E-mail:* thorhv@vortex.is (home).

VILI, Valerie; New Zealand athlete; b. (b. Valerie Adams), 6 Oct. 1984, Rotorua; d. of a Scottish father and Tongan mother; m. Bertrand Vili (discus thrower from New Caledonia); shot putter; Olympic Champion, World Champion and Commonwealth record-holder, having thrown a distance of 20.56m; won World Youth Championships 2001 (with a throw of 16.87m); World Jr Champion 2002 (throw of 17.73m); Silver Medal, Commonwealth Games, Manchester 2002 (throw of 17.45m); finished fifth at World Championships, Paris 2003, eighth at Athens Olympics 2004; Bronze Medal, World Championships, Helsinki 2005 (personal best throw of 19.87m); finished second at World Athletics Final; Gold Medal, Commonwealth Games, Melbourne 2006 (broke 20-year-old Commonwealth Games record with a throw of 19.66m); Gold Medal, World Championships, Osaka 2007 (Commonwealth record throw of 20.54m); one of the few female athletes ever to take Int. Asscn of Athletics Feds (IAAF) World Titles at youth, jr and sr levels; broke the Oceania record in winning her first World Indoor Title in Valencia 2008 (throw of 20.19m); Gold Medal, Olympic Games, Beijing 2008 (throw of 20.56m, personal best, first Olympic gold medal in track and field for New Zealand since John Walker in 1976); New Zealand Sports Award of the Year 2008. *Address:* c/o Athletics New Zealand, PO Box 741, Wellington 6140, New Zealand. *Telephone:* (4) 384-6021. *Fax:* (4) 385-1758. *E-mail:* info@athletics .org.nz. *Website:* www.athletics.org.nz.

VILINBAKHOV, Georgy Vadimovich, D.Hist.SC; Russian historian; b. 13 April 1949; ed Leningrad (now St Petersburg) State Univ.; researcher, later Prof., State Hermitage Museum 1969–, Treas., collection of mil. banners and graphic works 1970–92, Deputy, then First Deputy Dir 1991–; Head, State Heraldic Council 1992–, Head of State Heraldry 1994, then Chair. Herald Council, State Heraldmeister 1999–; mem. Exec. Cttee Int. Asscn of Mil. Museums and Museum of Arms; Order Sign of Honour 1997, Order for Service to Motherland 1999. *Publications:* over 150 articles and publs on Russian history and heraldry. *Leisure interests:* collecting tin soldiers, mil. music. *Address:* State Hermitage Museum, Dvortsovaya nab. 34, St Petersburg, Russia (office). *Telephone:* (812) 710-96-02 (office). *Fax:* (812) 571-90-09 (office). *E-mail:* vilinbakhov@hermitage.ru (office). *Website:* www.hermitagemuseum.org (office).

VILJOEN, Hendrik Christo, PhD (Eng); South African academic and electronics engineer; *Managing Director, Unistel Group Holdings (Pty) Ltd, Stellenbosch University;* b. 31 Aug. 1937, Graaff-Reinet; s. of Hendrik Christoffel Viljoen and Anna Pienaar; m. Hana Stehlik 1965; one s. two d.; ed Univ. of Stellenbosch; engineer, Dept of Posts and Telecommunications, Pretoria 1961–65; Sr Lecturer, Univ. of Stellenbosch 1966–70, apptd Prof. 1970, Dean of Eng 1979–93, Vice-Rector of Operations 1993–98, Man. Dir Unistel Group Holdings (Pty) Ltd; Chair. SABC 1989–93; Visiting Prof., Georgia Inst. of Tech., Atlanta, USA 1975–76, Nat. Chiao Tung Univ., Hsinchu, Taiwan 1981; est. Office for Intellectual Property, Dir –2002; Chair. Task Group on Broadcasting in SA 1987–91, Huguenot Soc. of SA; Deputy Chair. Genealogical Inst. of SA; mem. Council, Univ. Stellenbosch of 2006–09; Sr mem. IEEE, USA 1978–; Fellow, S African Akad. vir Wetenskap en Kuns; Order for Meritorious Service 1991; Sir Ernest Oppenheimer Memorial Trust Award, Engineer of the Year, S African Asscn for Professional Engineers 1991, Merit Medal, S African Acad. for Arts and Science 2000. *Publications include:* Elektronika 1971, Cyber Dictionary 2007. *Leisure interests:* philately, genealogy. *Address:* 6 Hof Avenue, Stellenbosch 7600, South Africa. *Telephone:* (21) 8833754. *Fax:* (21) 8083743. *E-mail:* hcv@sun.ac.za (home); viljoen@mail.com (home). *Website:* www.geocities.com/viljoen_family (home).

VILKAS, Eduardas, DPhys-MathSc, DrHabil; Lithuanian mathematician and economist; *Director, Ekonomikos Institutas, Lithuanian Academy of Sciences;* b. 3 Oct. 1935, Gargzdai; m. Stefa Vilkienė; two s. one d.; ed Vilnius Univ.; researcher, Inst. of Physics and Math., Lithuanian Acad. of Sciences 1958–77, researcher, Inst. of Math. and Cybernetics 1977–79, Deputy Dir 1979–85, Dir Inst. of Econs 1985–; teacher, Vilnius Univ. 1958–78, Prof. 1976; Prof., Vytautas Magnus Univ.; Chair. Parl. Privatization Comm. 1996–2001; mem. Lithuanian Acad. of Sciences, Vice-Pres. 1991–99; Lithuanian Grand Duke Gediminas Order. *Publications:* What is the Theory of Games? 1976, Mathematical Methods in the Economy 1980, Solutions: Theory, Information, Modelling (together with E. Maiminas) 1981, Optimality in Games and Decisions 1991, Lithuanian White Paper for Science and Technology (co-author) 2001, Decision-Making Theory 2003; numerous articles in scientific periodicals on probability theory, game theory, math. econs and their application in nat. econs and the strategy for long-term devt of the Lituanian economy. *Leisure interest:* tennis. *Address:* Ekonomikos Institutas, A. Goštanto 12, 01108 Vilnius (office); Zirgo 20, 10007 Vilnius, Lithuania (home). *Telephone:* (5) 2623502 (office); (5) 2700404 (home). *Fax:* (5) 2127506 (office). *E-mail:* ei@ktl.mii.lt (office); evilkas@takas.lt (home).

VILLA-VICENCIO, Rev. Charles, STM, PhD; South African professor of religion and society; *Executive Director, Institute for Justice and Reconciliation;* b. 7 Nov. 1942, Johannesburg; s. of Charles Villa-Vicencio and Paula Villa-Vicencio; m. Eileen van Sittert 1968; two d.; ed Rhodes Univ. Grahamstown and Natal, Yale and Drew Univs; with Standard Bank of SA 1961–64; Probationer Minister, Methodist Church of Southern Africa 1965–70; ordained Minister 1970; Minister of various congregations in S Africa and USA; Teaching Fellow, Drew Univ. 1974–75; part-time lecturer, Univ. of Cape Town 1976–77; Sr Lecturer, Univ. of S Africa 1978–81, Assoc. Prof. 1981–82; Sr Lecturer, Univ. of Cape Town 1982, Assoc Prof. 1984–88, Head, Dept of Religious Studies 1986–97, Prof. of Religion and Society 1988–97; mem. S African Theological Soc., Nat. Research Dir, Truth and Reconciliation Comm., Exec. Dir Inst. for Justice and Reconciliation 2000–; del. to numerous confs etc; Fellow, Univ. of Cape Town 1996, DHumLitt hc Elmhurst Coll. Chicago 1998. *Publications include:* Between Christ and Caesar: Classical and Contemporary Texts 1986, Trapped in Apartheid 1988, Civil Disobedience and Beyond 1990, A Theology of Reconstruction 1992, A Spirit of Hope: Conversations on Politics, Religion and Values 1993; ed. or co-ed. of and contrib. to several vols of essays; numerous articles including many on the church and politics in S Africa. *Address:* 14 Annerley Road, Rosebank, Cape Town 7700 (home); Institute for Justice and Reconciliation, POB 205, Rondebosch, Cape Town 7700, South Africa (office). *Telephone:* (21) 6597120 (office); (21) 6868643 (home). *Fax:* (21) 6597138 (office); (21) 6592721. *E-mail:* ijr@grove.uct.ac.za (office). *Website:* www.ijr.org.za (office).

VILLAIN, Claude Edouard Louis Etienne, LenD; French civil servant and business executive; *President, Ardo Violaines;* b. 4 Jan. 1935, Paris; s. of Etienne Villain and Marie Louise (née Caudron) Villain; m. Bernadette Olivier 1962 (deceased); two s.; ed Lycée Voltaire, Lycée Louis-le-Grand, Univ. of Paris, Ecole Nat. de la FOM; trainee in French Overseas Admin 1956–59, Officer in Dept of Algerian Affairs 1959–61; Officer for Econ. Studies in Agricultural Devt Bureau 1962–64; Officer in Ministry of Econ. and Finance 1964, Head of Dept 1969, Deputy Dir of Ministry 1973; Tech. Adviser in Office of Valéry Giscard d'Estaing (then Minister of Econ. and Finance) 1973–74; Dir-Gen. of Competition and Prices in Ministry of Econ. and Finance 1974–78; Admin. Soc. Nat. des Chemins de fer Français (SNCF) 1974–78; Admin. Soc. Nat. Elf Aquitaine 1974–79; Dir-Gen. of Agric., Comm. of EEC 1979–85; Dir-Gen. Socopa Int., Vice-Pres. Socopa France 1985–86; Special Adviser to Minister of Econ. and Finance 1986–88; Inspector-Gen. of Finances 1987–2003; Del. Interministerial Mission for Cen. and Eastern Europe (MICECO) 1992–93, for Euro-Disneyland 1993–2003; Chair. Admin. Bd Comilog SA 1996–; mem. Intergovernmental Comm. of the Channel Tunnel 1990–2000, of the Lyon-Turin rail project 1996–2001; Admin. Soc. Nat. RATP 1998–2004; Pres. Ardo Violaines (frozen food enterprise) 2005–; Officier, Légion d'honneur, Commdr, Ordre nat. du Mérite, du Mérite Agricole, Croix de Valeur Mil. *Leisure interests:* tennis, skiing. *Address:* Ardo Violaines, 62138 chemin de la cochiette, 62138 Violaines, France (office); 103 avenue Félix Faure, 75015 Paris, France (home). *Telephone:* 3-20-29-30-30 (office); 1-44-26-01-67 (home). *Fax:* 3-20-29-36-10 (office).

VILLANUEVA SARAVIA, Eladio; Spanish trade union official; *President, General Confederation of Workers;* b. Valladolid; fmr railroad man.; currently Pres. Confederacion General de Trabajo. *Address:* Confederacion General de Trabajo, Sagunto 15, 28010 Madrid, Spain (office). *Telephone:* (91) 4475769 (office). *Fax:* (91) 4453132 (office). *E-mail:* spcc.cgt@cgt.es (office). *Website:* www.cgt.es (office).

VILLAPALOS-SALAS, Gustavo; Spanish university rector; b. 15 Oct. 1949, Madrid; s. of Gustavo Villapalos-Salas and Juana Villapalos-Salas; Prof., Faculty of Law, Universidad Complutense de Madrid 1970–75, Prof. of Law 1976, Dir Dept of History of Law 1980–84, Dean Faculty of Law 1984–87, Rector of Univ. 1987–2000; Research Fellow Instituto de Estudios Jurídcos 1972–74, Centro de Investigaciones Jurídcas, Económicas y Sociales 1975; Visiting Prof. Univ. of Calif. at Berkeley 1976, Univ. of Freiburg 1976–77; Gran Cruz de la Orden de Alfonso X el Sabio, Gran Cruz del Mérito Civil, Hon. CBE; Dr hc (Paris-Sud, St Louis, USA, Guanajuato, Mexico, La Plata, Argentina). *Publications:* Colección Diplomática del Archivo Municipal de Santander: Documentos Reales II (1525–1599) 1982, Los Regímenes Económicos Matrimoniales en la Historia del Derecho Español: Prelección 1983, El Fuero de León: Comentarios 1984, Cortes de Castilla en el siglo XV 1986, La Baja Edad Media, Vol. IV, Historia General de Cantabria 1986, La Alta Edad Media, Vol. III 1987. *Leisure interests:* astronomy, cinema, classical music, reading. *Address:* Calle Alberto Aguilera 11, 28015 Madrid, Spain (home). *Telephone:* (91) 4452929 (home).

VILLARAIGOSA, Antonio, BA; American politician; *Mayor of Los Angeles;* b. (Antonio Villar), 23 Jan. 1953, LA; m. Corina Raigosa; three d. one s.; ed UCLA; mem. Calif. State Ass. 1994, Speaker 1999; Mayoral Cand. 2001; Distinguished Fellow UCLA, Univ. of Southern Calif. 2001–03; mem. LA City Council 2003; Chair. Transportation Cttee, mem. Bd Metropolitan Transportation Authority (MTA) 2003; Mayor of LA 2005–. *Address:* City Hall, 200 North Spring Street, Room 303, Los Angeles, CA 90012, USA (office). *Telephone:* (213) 978-0600 (office). *Fax:* (213) 978-0750 (office). *E-mail:* mayor@lacity.org (office). *Website:* www.lacity.org/mayor (office).

VILLARROEL LANDER, Mario Enrique; Venezuelan international organization official, lawyer and academic; *President, Venezuelan Red Cross;* b. 20 Sept. 1947, Caracas; m. Norka Sierraalta 1969; three s. one d.; ed Cen. Univ. of Venezuela, Santa María Univ., Caracas; joined Venezuelan Red Cross as a volunteer 1967, Nat. Pres. 1978–, Pres. Int. Fed. of Red Cross and Red Crescent Socs 1987–98; Pres. Mirandino Historical Studies Inst., Henry Dunant Inst. 1992–93; Prof. of Penal Law, Chair. of Criminal Law Santa María Univ.; lawyer pvt. legal practice; fmr Dir La Voz del Derecho (legal review); numerous memberships of int. orgs; numerous distinctions from Red Cross orgs. *Publications:* El Cuerpo Técnico de Policía Judicial en el Proceso Penal Venezolano, Habeas Corpus y antejuicio de Mérito; legal articles in Venezuelan and foreign periodicals. *Leisure interest:* journalism. *Address:* Venezuelan Red Cross, Apartado 3185, 1010 Caracas, Venezuela (office). *Telephone:* (212) 571-4380 (office). *Fax:* (212) 576-1042 (office). *E-mail:* dirnacsoc@cantv.net (office). *Website:* www.cruzroja.org.ve (office); www.ifrc.org (office).

VILLAS-BOAS, José Manuel P. de; Portuguese diplomatist and academic; *Professor, Department of Political Science and International Relations, Universidade do Minho;* b. 23 Feb. 1931, Oporto; s. of João de Villas-Boas and Maria Margarida de Villas-Boas; m. Maria do Patrocinio de Almeida Braga 1956; ed Lisbon Univ.; Attaché, Ministry of Foreign Affairs 1954; Embassies, Pretoria 1959, London 1963; Counsellor 1969; Head of African Dept, Ministry of Foreign Affairs 1970–72; Consul-Gen., Milan 1972–74; Minister Plenipotentiary, Asst Dir-Gen. of Political Affairs, Ministry of Foreign Affairs 1974–77, Dir-Gen. of Political Affairs 1977–79; Amb. and Perm. Rep. to NATO 1979–84, Amb. to South Africa 1984–89, to People's Repub. of China 1989–93, to Russia 1993–97; Prof., Dept of Political Science and Int. Relations, Univ. of Minho, Braga 1997–, mem. Strategic Council 2003–; Grand Cross Order of Merit (Portugal), Hon. KCMG (UK), Grand Cross of St Olav (Norway), of Merit (Spain), Cruzeiro do Sul (Brazil), of Rio Branco (Brazil), of Good Hope (S Africa), Grand Officer of the Order of Merit (FRG), of the Lion (Senegal), Commdr, Légion d'honneur (France), Order of Merit (Italy), etc. *Publication:* Orthodoxy and Political Power in Russia 1999, Caderno de Memórias 2003. *Leisure interests:* music, travelling. *Address:* Casa de Esteiro, Vilarelho 4910 Caminha (home); Department of Political Science and International Relations, Universidade do Minho, Campus de Gualtar, 4710-057 Braga, Portugal (office). *Telephone:* (258) 721333 (home); (253) 604518 (office). *Fax:* (258) 921356 (home). *E-mail:* casaesteiro@iol.pt (home). *Website:* www.eeg.uminho.pt (office).

VILLEGAS QUIROGA, Carlos; Bolivian economist and government official; *Minister of Hydrocarbons and Energy;* fmr Researcher, Univ. of San Andres, La Paz; Econ. Adviser to presidential cand. Evo Morales 2005; Minister of Sustainable Devt and Planning –2006, also Gov. IDB and Inter-American Investment Corpn; Minister of Hydrocarbons and Energy 2006–. *Address:* Ministry of Hydrocarbons and Energy, Edif. Palacio de Comunicaciones, Avda Mariscal Santa Cruz, La Paz, Bolivia (office). *E-mail:* minehidro@hidrocarburos.gov.bo (office). *Website:* www.hidrocarburos.gov.bo (home).

VILLELA FILHO, Alfredo Egydio Arruda, MBA; Brazilian engineer and business executive; *Chairman and CEO, Itaúsa-Investimentos Itaú SA;* ed Instituto Mauá de Tecnologia, Fundação Getúlio Vargas; mem. Admin. Council Itaúsa-Investimentos Itaú SA 1995–, mem. Disclosure and Procedure on Insider Trading Cttees, mem. Admin. Council Itautec Philco SA 1997–, mem. Disclosure and Procedure on Insider Trading Cttees Banco Itaú SA, Chair. and CEO Itaúsa-Investimentos Itaú SA 2008–. *Address:* Itaúsa-Investimentos Itaú SA, Praça Alfredo Edydio de Souza Aranha 100, Torre Itaúsa, São Paulo 04344-902, SP, Brazil (office). *Telephone:* (11) 5019-1677 (office). *Fax:* (11) 5019-1114 (office). *E-mail:* info@itausa.com.br (office). *Website:* www.itausa.com.br (office).

VILLELLA, Edward, BS; American ballet dancer; *Artistic Director, Miami City Ballet;* b. 1 Oct. 1936, New York; s. of Joseph Villella and Mildred Villella (née De Giovanni); m. 1st Janet Greschler 1962 (divorced 1980); one s.; m. 2nd Linda Carbonetta 1981; two d.; ed NY State Maritime Coll.; joined NY City Ballet 1957, becoming soloist within a year, now Premier Dancer; originated leading roles in George Balanchine's Bugaku, Tarantella, Stars and Stripes, Harlequinade, Jewels, Glinkaiana, A Midsummer Night's Dream; first danced his famous role of Prodigal Son 1960; has also danced leading roles in Allegro Brillante, Jeux, Pas de Deux, Raymonda Variations, Scotch Symphony, Swan Lake; choreographed Narkissos; has appeared at Bolshoi Theatre, with Royal Danish Ballet and in London and made numerous guest appearances; choreographed and starred in revivals of Brigadoon, Carousel; Chair. NY City Comm. of Cultural Affairs 1978; Artistic Co-ordinator Eglersky Ballet Co. (now André Eglersky State Ballet of New York) 1979–84, Choreographer 1980–84; Choreographer NJ Ballet 1980; Artistic Dir Ballet Okla 1983–86, Miami City Ballet 1985–; Heritage Chair in Arts and Cultural Criticism George Mason Univ. 1992–93, 1993–94; mem. Nat. Council on the Arts 1968–74; Artist-in-Residence Dorothy F. Schmidt Coll. of Arts and Letters 2000–01; Robert Kiphuth Fellow Yale Univ. 2001; Dance Magazine Award 1965; Hon. DFA (State Univ. of New York Maritime Coll.) 1998; Golden Plate Award, American Acad. of Achievement 1971, Emmy Award 1975, Gold Medal Award, Nat. Soc. of Arts and Letters 1990, Nat. Medal of Arts Award 1997, other awards. *Publication:* Prodigal Son (co-author) 1992. *Address:* Miami City Ballet, Ophelia and Juan Js Roca Center, 2200 Liberty Avenue, Miami Beach, FL 33139, USA (office). *Telephone:* (305) 929-7000 (office). *Website:* www.miamicityballet.org (office).

VILLEMÉJANE, Bernard de; French business executive; b. 10 March 1930, Marseille; s. of Pierre Villeméjane and Marie-Thérèse (née Getten) de Villeméjane; m. Françoise Boucheronde 1965; two s.; ed Ecole Polytechnique and Ecole des Mines, Paris; with Direction des Mines et de la Géologie, French W Africa 1955–60; Ministry of Industry 1960–61; Eng Adviser, Banque Rothschild 1961–62; Deputy Man. Dir Société Penarroya 1963, Man Dir 1967, Chair. of Bd and Man. Dir 1971–86, Dir 1986–88, Vice-Pres. Supervisory Bd 1988–91; Man Dir Société Le Nickel 1971–74; Chair. of Bd and Man. Dir SM le Nickel SLN 1974–83, Dir 1984; Dir Imetal (renamed Imerys 1999) 1974, Man. Dir 1974, Chair. 1979–93, Hon. Pres. 1993–; Vice-Chair. Supervisory Bd Metaleurop 1986–91; Dir Copperweld Corpn, USA 1976, Cookson PLC (UK) 1977–86; Dir Financère d'Angers 1989–, Chair. 1989–91; Chair., Man. Dir Gravograph 1994–95; Vice-Pres. Moulinex; Dir of various other European and American cos, including Origny-Desvroise, C-E Minerals Inc., DBK Minerals Inc., Minemet SA; Officier, Légion d'honneur, Officier, Ordre nat. du Mérite, Grand Cross, Orden del Mérito (Spain), Commdr Ordre de l'Etoile Equatoriale (Gabon). *Address:* Imetal, Tour Maine-Montparnasse, 33 avenue du Maine, 75755 Paris Cedex 15 (office); 102 rue d'Assas, 75006 Paris, France (home). *Telephone:* 45-38-48-48 (office).

VILLENEUVE, Jacques, (JV), OQ; Canadian racing driver; b. 9 April 1971, Saint-Jean-sur-Richelieu, Québec; s. of the late Gilles Villeneuve and of Joanne Barthe; m. Johanna Martinez 2006; ed Beau-Soleil School, Villars, Switzerland, Jim Russell Formula Ford School, Mont-Tremblant, Formula 2000 Racing School, Shannonville; first raced in three Alfa Italian touring car races; raced Italian Formula 3 series 1989–91; second place in Japanese F3 series for Team Tom's Toyota with three wins 1992; third place in Macao F3 Grand Prix 1992; Formula Atlantic debut and third place in Player's Grand Prix de Trois-Rivières; Forsythe-Green racing team Formula Atlantic: five wins and three second places in 15 races and third in championship 1993; named Formula Atlantic Rookie-of-the-Year 1993; IndyCar debut with team Players Forsythe-Green, three podiums, finished sixth in championship 1994; finished second in Indianapolis 500 race behind Al Unser Jt 1994; won his first IndyCar race at Elkhart Lake 1994; named IndyCar Rookie-of-the-Year 1994; sole driver for team Players Forsythe-Green 1995; named IndyCar Champion 1995 with seven podium finishes, four wins, one second place, two third places and six poles; first Canadian and youngest driver (aged 24) to win the Indianapolis 500 race 1995; moved to Williams/Renault Fl team 1996; pole position in his first Formula One race at Australian Grand Prix; second in Formula One World Championship 1996 with 78 points, three pole positions, four wins (Europe, GB, Hungary and Portugal), five second places and two third places; named Fl Rookie-of-the-Year 1996; driver for Williams/Renault Fl team 1997; Formula One World Champion 1997 with 81 points, seven wins (Brazil, Argentina, Spain, GB, Hungary, Austria and Luxembourg) and 10 pole positions; driver for Williams/Mecachrome Fl team 1998; fifth in Formula One World Championship with two third places (Germany and Hungary) 1998; driver for B.A.R. Fl team 1999–2003; two third places (Spain and Germany) 2001; moved to Renault Formula One team for last three races of 2004; moved to Sauber Petronas Formula One team in 2005; driver with BMW-Sauber 2006; 150 Formula One Grand Prix races (as at Belgium Grand Prix 2005); Team Peugeot Le Mans 24h 2007; Bill Davis Racing NASCAR Team (Truck Series) 2007, (Sprint Cup) 2008; Owner Newtown restaurant/club, Montreal; Founder and Patron Formula Charity; inductee into Canada's Walk of Fame 1998. *Recording:* first album as singer/songwriter: Private Paradise 2007. *Leisure interests:* reading, music, skiing, ice hockey, computers/gaming. *Address:* c/o Claymore SA, CP 195, 1884 Villars-sur-Ollon, Switzerland (office). *Telephone:* (24) 496-30-40 (office). *Fax:* (24) 496-30-41 (office). *E-mail:* jvmgt@claymore.ch (office). *Website:* www.jv-world.com; www.myspace.com/jvofficial; www.bcv24hvillars.com.

VILLENEUVE, Jeanne Madeleine; French journalist; b. 29 Jan. 1949, Paris; d. of Henry Villeneuve and Jacqueline Picq; ed Inst. d'Etudes Politiques; Financial Analyst, Banque Nat. de. Paris 1974–78; Chef de Service, Soc. Générale de Presse 1978–82, daily newspaper Libération 1982–86, weekly l'Express Feb.–Sept. 1986; Chief Reporter, l'Evènement du Jeudi 1986–91; Asst Ed. Parisien 1991–95; Ed. Libération 1996–97. *Publication:* Le mythe Tapie 1988. *Address:* c/o Journal Libération, 11 rue Béranger, 75003 Paris, France.

VILLEPIN, Dominique Marie François René Galouzeau de, LenD; French diplomatist and civil servant; b. 14 Nov. 1953, Rabat, Morocco; s. of Xavier Galouzeau de Villepin and Yvonne Hétier; m. Marie-Laure Le Guay 1985; one s. two d.; ed Paris Inst. of Political Sciences, Ecole Nationale d'Administration; responsible for Horn of Africa, Office of African Affairs 1980–81, Head of Mission attached to Dir's Office 1981–84, Asst Dir 1992–93; with Centre d'Analyse et de Prévision 1981–84; First Sec. Washington 1984–1987, Embassy Press and Information Dir, Washington 1987–89, Ministerial Councillor, India 1989–92; Deputy Head of African Affairs, Ministry of Foreign Affairs 1992–93, Dir de Cabinet to Alain Juppé (q.v.), Minister of Foreign Affairs 1993–95; Sec. Gen. to Presidency 1995–2002; Minister of Foreign Affairs, Cooperation and Francophony 2002–2004, Minister of the Interior, Internal Security and Local Rights 2004–05, Prime Minister 2005–07; Chair. Admin. Council Nat. Forests Office (ONF) 1996–99; Rep. Convention on the Future of Europe 2002–; Chevalier de la Légion d'honneur. *Publications:* Parole d'Exil 1986 (poetry), Le Droit d'Aînesse 1988 (poetry), Elégies barbares (poetry) 1996, Secession (poetry) 1996, Les Cent-Jours ou l'esprit de sacrifice (Amb.'s Prize) 2001, Le Cri de la Gargouille 2002, In Praise of Those Who Stole the Fire (poetry) 2003, Un Autre Monde – Cahiers de l'Herne 2003, Le Requin et la Mouette 2004. L'Homme européen 2005. *Leisure interest:* marathon running. *Address:* c/o Hôtel Matignon, 57 rue de Varenne, 75007 Paris, France (office).

VILLIERS de SAINTIGNON, Philippe le Jolis de; French politician; b. 25 March 1949, Boulogne; s. of Jacques le Jolis de Villiers de Saintignon and Hedwige d'Arexy; m. Dominique de Buor de Villeneuve 1973; four s. three d.; ed Saint-Joseph Inst., Ecole Nat. d'Admin.; civil servant Ministry of Interior 1978; Prin. Pvt. Sec. to Prefect of La Rochelle 1978; Deputy Prefect Vendôme 1979; f. Alouette FM (regional radio station) 1981, Fondation pour les Arts et les Sciences de la Communication, Nantes 1984; Jr Minister of Culture and Communications 1986–87; mem. Conseil Gen. de la Vendée 1987–, Pres. 1988–; Deputy to Nat. Ass. from Vendée 1988–94 (UDF), 1997– (Ind.); MEP 1994–97, majorité pour l'autre Europe; Nat. Del. UDF (in charge of youth and liaising with cultural groups) 1988; Founder and Pres. Mouvement pour la France 1994; Co-Founder Rassemblement pour la France 1999, Vice-Pres. 1999–2000. *Publications:* Lettre Ouverte aux Coupeurs de Têtes et aux Menteurs du Bicentenaire 1989, La Chienne qui Miaule 1990, Notre Europe sans Maastricht 1992, Avant qu'il ne soit trop tard 1993, La Société de connivence 1994, Dictionnaire du politiquement correct à la française 1996, La machination d'Amsterdam 1998. *Address:* Assemblée nationale, 75355 Paris; Conseil Général de la Vendée, 40 rue Foch, 85923 La Roche-sur-Yon cedex 9, France. *Telephone:* 1-40-63-82-05 (Paris). *Fax:* 1-40-63-82-80 (Paris).

VILLIGER, Kaspar; Swiss former head of state; b. 5 Feb. 1941, Pfeffikon, Lucerne; m.; two d.; ed Swiss Fed. Inst. of Tech., Zürich; Man. of cigar factory Villiger Söhne AG, Pfeffikon 1966; subsequently bought bicycle factory in Buttisholz; fmr Vice-Pres. Chamber of Commerce of Cen. Switzerland and mem. Cttee Swiss Employers' Cen. Asscn; mem. Lucerne Cantonal Parl. 1972–82; mem. Nat. Council, Liberal Party of Switzerland (FDP) 1982; mem. Council of States 1987; Swiss Fed. Councillor 1989–2003; Head, Fed. Mil. (Defence) Dept 1989–95, Dept of Finance 1996–2001, 2003; Vice-Pres. of Swiss Confed. 1994, 2001; Pres. Swiss Confed. Jan.–Dec. 1995, 2002; Dir Nestlé 2004–, Swiss Re 2004–, Neue Zürcher Zeitung. *Address:* c/o Swiss Reinsurance Company, Mythenquai 50/60, PO Box 8022, 3003 Zurich, Switzerland (office).

VILLIS, Hans-Peter; German business executive; *Chairman of the Board of Management and CEO, Energie Baden-Württemberg;* b. 1958, Castrop-Rauxel; Commercial Dir Bergbau AG 1987–89; Man. Planning and Control, VEBA Kraftwerke Ruhr AG 1989–92, Project Man. E Germany VEBA AG 1992–93; Man. Dir Städtische Werke Magdeburg GmbH 1993–99; mem. Bd Gelsenwasser AG 2000–02; Man. Dir Elektrizitätswerk Wesertal GmbH Jan.–Sept. 2003, Chair. Bd of Man. E.ON Westfalen Weser AG 2003–06, Chief Financial Officer and Deputy Chair. Bd of Man. E.ON Nordic AB 2006–07, Chair. Bd of Man. and CEO Energie Baden-Württemberg AG 2007–. *Address:* Energie Baden-Württemberg AG, Durlacher Allee 93, 76131 Karlsruhe, Germany (office). *Telephone:* (7) 21-63-00 (office). *Fax:* (7) 21-63-126-72 (office). *E-mail:* info@enbw.com (office). *Website:* www.enbw.com (office).

VILSACK, Thomas (Tom), BA, JD; American lawyer, government official and fmr politician; *Secretary of Agriculture;* b. 13 Dec. 1950, Pittsburgh, Pa; s. of Bud Vilsack and Dolly Vilsack; m. Christine Bell 1973; two s.; ed Hamilton Coll., NY, Albany Law School; in pvt. law practice, Mt Pleasant, Iowa 1975–98; Mayor of Mt Pleasant 1987–92; elected Iowa Senate 1993–98; Gov. of Iowa 1998–2007; Chair. Democratic Leadership Council 2005-07; Of Counsel, Dorsey & Whitney LLP, Des Moines 2007–08; US Sec. of Agric., Washington, DC 2009–; Distinguished Visiting Prof. of Law, Drake Univ. Law School; mem. Democratic Govs Asscn 1999–2007; Distinguished Fellow, Biosafety Inst. for Genetically Modified Agricultural Products, Iowa State Univ.; mem. Bd of Dirs United Way, Mt Pleasant; unsuccessful cand. for 2008 Democratic party nomination for Pres. of US; Nat. Co-Chair. for Sen. Hillary Clinton's presidential nomination campaign 2007–08; Fellow, Iowa Acad. of Trial Lawyers; mem. ABA, Iowa State Bar Asscn, Iowa Trial Lawyers Asscn (Pres. 1985), Council on Foreign Relations; Democrat. *Address:* Department of Agriculture, 1400 Independence Ave, SW, Washington, DC 20250, USA (office). *Telephone:* (202) 720-5539 (office). *Fax:* (202) 720-9997 (office). *Website:* www.usda.gov (office).

VIMOND, Paul Marcel; French architect; b. 20 June 1922, La Meurdraquière; s. of Ernest Vimond and Marie Lehuby; m. Jacqueline Lefèvre 1945; two s. two d.; ed Lycée de Coutances, Ecole préparatoire des beaux-arts de Rennes and Ecole nat. supérieure des beaux-arts, Paris; Acad. de France at Rome 1950–52; Chief architect, public bldgs and nat. monuments 1954; mem. Jury of Nat. School of Fine Arts; mem. Diocesan Comm. on Sacred Art, Paris; Nat. Expert for Cour de Cassation, Cours d'Appel, Tribuneaux Administratifs and all French courts; Pres. Architecture section, Salon des Artistes Français; Officier Ordre nat. du mérite; Chevalier, Légion d'honneur, des Palmes académiques, des Arts et des Lettres and of Pontifical Order of Merit; Premier Grand Prix de Rome 1949. *Major architectural works:* architect in charge of Int. Exhbn of Sacred Art, Rome 1953; responsible for films and architectural reconstructions of tomb of Saint Peter, Rome; bldgs in Paris for: Assemblée de l'Union française, Conseil économique et social, Union de l'Europe occidentale, Org. de co-opération et de développement économiques; planner and architect for Palais d'Iéna, Paris; town planner for Cherbourg; Atomic Power Station, The Hague; two theatres, three churches in Paris, hotels, restaurants, hospitals and numerous lycées in France; 800 pvt. houses; 15,000 flats in six new towns; tech. insts at Besançon, Montpellier, Paris, Orsay, Nice, Toulon, Troyes; Faculty of medicine, Nice; a hosp. and a coll. in Lebanon; French Lycée, Brussels; numerous telephone exchanges and 14 large postal sorting offices in Paris region and provinces; sorting offices in Riyadh, Jeddah and Dammam and project for TV centre in Saudi Arabia, project for town in Zaïre. *Leisure interests:* painting, golf.

VINCENT, Jean-Pierre, LèsL; French theatre director; b. 26 Aug. 1942, Juvisy-sur-Orge, Essonne; s. of André Vincent and Paulette Loyot; one s.; ed Lycées Montaigne, Louis-le-Grand, Paris, Univ. de Paris (Sorbonne); amateur actor Univ. Theatre, Lycée Louis-le-Grand 1958–64; mem. Patrice Chéreau theatre co. 1965–68, Dir 1968–72; Dir, Admin. Dir Espérance Theatre 1972–74; Dir at Théâtre Nat. and École Supérieure d'art dramatique, Strasbourg 1975–83; Gen. Admin. Comédie-Française 1983–86; Dir Théâtre de Nanterre-Amandiers 1990–2001; Co-Founder Studio Libre 2002; Lecturer Inst. d'études théâtrales de Paris 1969–70; Studio Dir Conservatoire Nat. Supérieur d'art dramatique 1969–70, Prof. 1986–89; Pres. Syndicat nat. de directeurs d'entreprises artistiques et culturelles (Syndeac) 1978–82, Vice-Pres. 1992; mem. Bd of Dirs Festival d'Avignon; numerous critics' prizes, including Molière Prize for Best Dir 1987, Prix de la Critique 1988. *Plays include:* La noce chez les petits-bourgeois 1968, Tambours et Trompettes 1969, Les acteurs de bonne foi 1970, Le marquis de Montefosco 1970, La Cagnotte 1971, Capitaine Eçço 1971, Dans la jungle des villes 1972, Le suicide 1984, Six personnages en quête de l'auteur 1986, Le Mariage de Figaro 1987, Fantasio, Les caprices de Mariane 1991, Woyzeck 1973, 1993, Violences à Vichy 1995, Tartuffe 1998, Pièces de guerre 1999, Homme pour homme, Lorenzaccio 2000, Les Prétendants 2003, Derniers remords avant l'oubli 2003–04, Onze Débardeurs 2004–05, La mort de Danton 2005, Les Antilopes 2006, Le silence des communistes 2007. *Opera includes:* Les Noces de Figaro 1994, Mitridate 2000, Le drame et la vie 2001. *Address:* Bureau du Festival d'Avignon, Cloître Saint-Louis, 20 rue du Portail Bouqier, 84000 Avignon, France (office). *E-mail:* infodoc@festival-avignon.com (office). *Website:* www.festival-avignon.com (office).

VINCENT, Rev. John James, DTheol; British theologian, broadcaster and writer; b. 29 Dec. 1929, Sunderland; s. of David Vincent and Beatrice Ethel Vincent (née Gadd); m. Grace Johnston Stafford 1958; two s. one d.; ed Manchester Grammar School, Richmond Coll., London Univ., Drew Univ., Madison, NJ, USA, Basel Univ., Switzerland; ordained in Methodist Church 1956; Minister, Manchester and Salford Mission 1956–62; Supt Minister, Rochdale Mission 1962–69, Sheffield Inner City Ecumenical Mission 1970–77; Dir, Urban Theology Unit, Sheffield 1969–97, Dir Emer. and Doctoral Supervisor 1997–; Pres., Methodist Conf. 1989–90; Visiting Prof. of Theology, Boston School of Theology, USA 1969, New York Theological Seminary 1970, Theological School, Drew Univ. 1977; elected mem., Studiorum Novi Testamenti Societas 1961; Sec. Regional Working Party, WCC Faith and Order 1958–63; mem., British Council of Churches Comm. on Defence and Disarmament 1963–65, 1969–72; NW Vice-Pres., Campaign for Nuclear Disarmament 1957–69; Founding mem., Methodist Renewal Group 1961–70; Founding mem. and Leader, Ashram Community 1967–; Chair., Alliance of Radical Methodists 1971–74, Urban Mission Training Asscn of GB 1976–77, 1985–90; Co-ordinator, British Liberation Theology Project 1990–; mem. Bd, Int. Urban Ministry Network 1991–; presented Petition of Distress from the Cities to HM the Queen 1993; mem., Ind. Human Rights Del. to Colombia 1994, Partnership Bd Burngreave New Deal for Communities 2001–; Chair., Methodist Report on The Cities 1997; Hon. Lecturer, Biblical Studies Dept, Univ. of Sheffield 1990–, Theology Dept, Univ. of Birmingham 2003–; Fellow, St Deiniol's Library 2003; Centenary Achievement Award, Univ. of Sheffield 2005. *Publications:* Christ in a Nuclear World 1962, Christ and Methodism 1964, Here I Stand 1967, Secular Christ 1968, The Race Race 1970, The Jesus Thing 1973, Stirrings, Essays Christian and Radical 1975, Alternative Church 1976, Disciple and Lord 1976, Starting All Over Again 1981, Into the City 1982, O.K. Let's Be Methodists 1984, Radical Jesus 1986, Mark at Work 1986, Britain in the 90s 1989, Discipleship in the 90s 1991, Liberation Theology from the Inner City 1992, A Petition of Distress from the Cities 1993, A British Liberation Theology (ed.) 1995, The Cities: A Methodist Report 1997, Gospel from the City (ed.) 1997, Hope from the City 2000, Journey: Explorations in Discipleship 2001, Bible and Practice (ed.) 2001, Faithfulness in the City (ed.) 2003, Methodist and Radical (ed.) 2003, Outworkings: Gospel Practice and Interpretation 2005, Mark: Gospel of Action (ed.) 2006, A Lifestyle of Sharing 2009, The City: Biblical Challenges for Today (jtly) 2009. *Leisure interests:* jogging, writing. *Address:* 178 Abbeyfield Road, Sheffield, S4 7AY, England (home). *Telephone:* (114) 243-5342 (office); (114) 243-6688 (home). *Fax:* (114) 243-5356.

VINCENT, John Russell, PhD, FRHistS; British historian and academic; b. 20 Dec. 1937, Cheshire; s. of J. J. Vincent; m. Nicolette Kenworthy 1972; two s. (one deceased); ed Bedales School, Christ's Coll., Cambridge; Fellow of Peterhouse, Cambridge 1962–70, Lecturer in History, Univ. of Cambridge 1967–70; Prof. of Modern History, Univ. of Bristol 1970–84, Prof. of History 1984–2002; Visiting Prof., Univ. of East Anglia, Norwich 2003–08. *Publications:* The Formation of the Liberal Party 1966, The Governing Passion 1974, The Crawford Papers 1984, Disraeli 1990, An Intelligent Person's Guide to History 1995, Derby Diaries, 1869–1878 1995, Derby Diaries 1878–93 2003; various works on political history. *Address:* Senate House, University of Bristol, Bristol, BS8 1TH, England (office).

VINCENT, Olatunde Olabode, BA, CFR, FCIB; Nigerian banker; b. 16 May 1925, Lagos; s. of Josiah O. Vincent and Comfort A. Vincent; m. Edith Adenike Gooding 1958; three s. one d.; ed CMS. Grammar School, Lagos, Chartered Inst. of Secs, London, Univ. of Manchester and Admin. Staff Coll., Henley, England; Nigerian Army 1942–46; Financial Sec.'s Office 1947–56; Fed. Ministry of Finance 1956–61; Asst Gen. Man. Cen. Bank of Nigeria 1961–62, Deputy Gen. Man. 1962, Gen. Man. 1963–66, Adviser 1973–75, Deputy Gov. 1975–77, Gov. 1977–82; co-f., then Vice-Pres. African Devt Bank, Abidjan, Ivory Coast 1966–73; part-time Lecturer in Econs, Extra-Mural Dept, Univ. Coll. of Ibadan 1957–60; mem. Lagos Exec. Devt Bd 1960–61; Dir Nigerian Industrial Devt Bank 1964–66, Nigerian Security Printing and Minting Co. Ltd, Lagos, 1975–77; Chair. Sona Dairies Ltd 1985–90, City Business Computers Ltd 1985–, Equity and Trust Ltd 1986–; Chair. Capital Issues Comm., Lagos, 1975–77, Southern Africa Relief Fund 1977–82, Cttee on Motor Vehicle Advances and Basic Allowance 1978; Chair. Visitation Panel, Lagos State Univ. (LASU) 1993–, Governing Bd, Centre for Environment and Science Educ., LASU 1996–; Chair. Bd of Trustees, Nigerian Lions Charity Foundation 1993–; Life mem. Soc. for Int. Devt; Fellow Nigerian Inst. of Bankers, Inst. of Dirs, Nigerian Inst. of Man.; mem. Nat. Econ. Council 1979–82, Life mem. Nigerian Econ. Soc., Nigerian Stock Exchange, Nigeria-Britain Asscn, Cancer Aid Foundation, Soc. for Prevention of Cruelty to Animals, Nigerian Red Cross Soc., Order of Int. Fellowship; Charter mem. Int. Honour Soc. and World Peace and Diplomacy Forum; Grand Patron, Lagos Diocese of African Church 2000; mem. Nat. Exec. Council Nigerian Conservation Foundation; mem. Bd of Dirs Industrial and Gen. Insurance PLC; Patron Lagos State Chapter, Spinal Cord Injuries Asscn of Nigeria; Patron, African Church, Eye Bank of Nigeria; Commdr Order of Fed. Repub. 1982; Hon. DSc (Lagos State Univ.) 2000; African Church Primatial Honours Award 1981, Distinguished Nigerian Community Leader Award 1983. *Publication:* Ola Vincent's Speeches, Writings and Presentations 2005. *Leisure interests:* reading, listening to African and light classical music, gardening. *Address:* 8 Balarabe Musa Crescent, Victoria Island, PO Box 8780, Lagos, Nigeria (home). *Telephone:* 4617699 (home).

VINCENT OF COLESHILL, Baron (Life Peer), cr. 1996, of Coleshill in the County of Oxfordshire; **Field Marshal The Lord Richard (Frederick) Vincent,** GBE, KCB, DSO, FIMechE, FRAeS, FIC; British army officer; *Chancellor, Cranfield University;* b. 23 Aug. 1931, London; s. of the late Frederick Vincent and Frances Elizabeth (née Coleshill) Vincent; m. Jean Paterson (née Stewart) 1955; two s. (one deceased) one d.; ed Aldenham School, Royal Mil. Coll. of Science; Nat. Service 1950; Germany 1951–55, Gunnery Staff 1959, Radar Research Establishment, Malvern 1960–61, BAOR 1962, Tech. Staff Training, Royal Mil. Coll. of Science 1963–64; Staff Coll. 1965, Commonwealth Brigade, Malaysia 1966–68, Ministry of Defence 1968–70; Commdr, 12th Light Air Defence Regt, Germany, England and NI 1970–72; Instructor, Staff Coll. 1972–73; Mil. Dir of Studies, RMCS 1974–75; Commdr, 19 Airportable Brigade 1975–77; RCDS 1978; Deputy Mil. Sec. 1979–80; Commandant, Royal Mil. Coll. of Science 1980–83; Master Gen. of Ordnance, Ministry of Defence 1983–87; Vice-Chief, Defence Staff 1987–91, Chief 1991–92; Chair., Mil. Cttee of NATO 1993–96; Chair., MoDeM Consortium 1997–99; Chancellor, Cranfield Univ. 1998–; Col Commandant, REME 1981–87, RA 1983–2000; Hon. Col, 100 (Yeomanry) Field Regt RA, TA 1982–91, 12th Air Defence Regt 1987–91; Chair. (non-exec.), Hunting Defence Ltd 1996–2003; Dir (non-exec.), Hunting Eng Ltd 1996–2001 (Chair. 1998–2001), Vickers Defence Systems 1996–2002, R.A. Museums Ltd 1996–2000, INSYS Ltd 2001–05; Pres., Cranfield Trust 1999–, Old Aldenhamian Soc. 1999–2003; Vice-Pres., The Defence Mfrs Asscn 1996–2000, Pres. 2000–05; Vice-Pres., Officers' Pension Soc. 1997–2006; Dir, Hunting-BRAE 1997–2003 (Chair. 1998); Kermit Roosevelt Lecturer 1988; mem. Court, Cranfield Inst. of Tech. 1981–83, Greenwich Univ. 1997–2000; mem. Guild of Freemen of the City of London 1992–, Comm. on Britain and Europe (Royal Inst. for Int. Affairs) 1996–97, Advisory Council, RMCS 1983–91; Fellow, Imperial Coll. London 1996; Gov., Aldenham School 1987–, Ditchley Foundation 1992–2007, Imperial Coll. London 1995– (Chair. Bd Govs 1996–2004); Master Gunner, St James's Park 1996–2000; Patron, Inspire Foundation 1999–; Freeman City of London 1992, Worshipful Co. of Wheelwrights 1997, Fellow, City and Guilds of London Inst.; Jordanian Order of Merit (First Class), USA Legion of Merit (Degree of Cdre); Hon. DSc (Cranfield) 1985. *Publications:* contrib. to journals and publs. *Leisure interests:* seven grandchildren, pursuing a second career. *Address:* House of Lords, Westminster, London, SW1A 0PW, England (office).

VINCENT-ROSTOWSKI, Jacek, BSc, MSc, MA; Polish/British economist, politician and academic; *Minister of Finance;* b. (Jan Vincent-Rostowski), 30 April 1951, London, England; m.; two c.; ed Univ. Coll., London, School of Slavonic and East European Studies, Univ. of London, London School of Econs and Political Science; born into Polish immigrant family in London, grew up and educated in UK; Lecturer, School of Slavonic and East European Studies 1989–95; Adviser, Deputy Prime Minister and Minister of Finance of Poland 1989–91; worked at Centre for Econ. Performance, LSE 1992–95; Prof. of Economy, Cen. European Univ., Budapest 1995–, Dean of Faculty of Economy 1995–2000, 2005–06; Minister of Finance 2007–, Chair. Macro-econ. Policy Cttee 1997–2001; adviser to Pres. Nat. Bank of Poland 2002–04; fmr adviser to Govt of Russian Fed. on macro-econ. policy; adviser to Bd of Bank PEKAO SA 2004–; Co-founder Centre for Social and Econ. Analysis (Centrum Analiz Społeczno-Ekonomicznych—CASE), Warsaw, mem. Supervisory Council 1991–2007, Trustee CASE Foundation; mem. Supervisory Bd Polish Privatization Soc. – Kleinwort Benson (Polskie Towarzystwo Prywatyzacyjne – Kleinwort Benson), Polski Bank Rozwoju SA 1994–95. *Publications:* author or ed. of several books, book chapters and numerous articles in professional journals on an enlarged EU, monetary policy, exchange rates' policy and transformations of post-communist economies. *Address:* Ministry of Finance, ul. Świętokrzyska 12, 00-916 Warsaw, Poland (office). *Telephone:* (22) 694-55-55 (office). *Fax:* (22) 827-27-22 (office). *E-mail:* kancelaria@mf.gov.pl (office). *Website:* www.mf.gov.pl (office).

VINDE, Pierre L. V., JurCand, FilCand; Swedish fmr civil servant, fmr international civil servant and consultant; *Project Director, International Development and Strategies France;* b. 15 Aug. 1931, Paris, France; s. of Victor Vinde and Rita Wilson; m. Lise Le Coeur; ed schools in France, Sweden and UK, Univs. of Uppsala and Stockholm; in Prime Minister's Office 1957–58; Ministry of Trade 1958–60; Ministry of Finance 1961–76, Budget Dir 1970–74, Under-Sec. 1974–76; mem. Bd Devt Assistance Agency 1962–65, Inst. of Defence Org. and Man. 1968–70, Nat. Audit Office 1969–74, Agency for Admin. Devt 1974–76; Deputy Group of Ten 1974–76; Chair. Bd of Dirs Bank of Sweden 1974–76; mem. Police Comm. 1962–64, Defence Comm. 1965–68; Chair. Relocation of Gov. Admin. Comm. 1970–72; Sr Vice-Pres. PKbanken 1977–80; Asst Admin. (Finance and Admin), UNDP 1980–85, Deputy Sec.-Gen. OECD 1985–96; Adviser, Ministry of Finance 1996–97; consultant to OECD 1998, to UNDP 1999–2000, 2003–, to Swedish Ministry of Trade 2002; currently Project Dir, International Development & Strategies France. *Publications:* Frankr av i dag o i morgon 1960, Hur Sverige styres (The Government of Sweden) 1968, Den sv. statsförvaltningen 1969, Swedish Government Administration 1971. *Address:* International Development & Strategies, 22 boulevard Pereire, 75017 Paris, France (office). *Telephone:* 1-53-81-13-35 (office). *Fax:* 1-53-81-01-78 (office). *E-mail:* pierre.vinde@id-strategies.com (office). *Website:* www.id-strategies.fr (office).

VINE, Barbara (see Rendell of Babergh, Ruth Barbara).

VINE, Jeremy, BA; British broadcaster; *Presenter, The Jeremy Vine Show;* b. 17 May 1965, Epsom, Surrey; s. of Guy Vine and Diana Vine; m. Rachel; ed Epsom Coll. and Univ. of Durham; journalist, Coventry Evening Telegraph 1986–87; joined BBC 1987, News Trainee 1987–89, Programme Reporter, Today 1989–93, Political Corresp. 1993–97, Africa Corresp. 1997–99, Presenter, Newsnight 1996–2002 (full-time 1999–2002); Presenter, The Jeremy Vine Show, BBC Radio 2 2003–; Sony Radio Acad. Awards Speech Broadcaster of the Year 2005. *Leisure interest:* Chelsea Football Club, films of Alfred Hitchcock, poems of W. H. Auden. *Address:* Room G680, BBC Television Centre, Wood Lane, London, W12 7RJ, England (office). *Telephone:* (20) 8624-9800 (office). *E-mail:* vine@bbc.co.uk (office). *Website:* www.bbc.co.uk/radio2/shows/vine (office).

VINEN, William Frank, PhD, FRS; British physicist and academic; *Professor of Physics, University of Birmingham;* currently Prof. of Physics, Univ. of Birmingham; mem. Academia Europaea (Physics, Astrophysics and Eng Section); The Simon Prize, Inst. of Physics (co-recipient) 1963, Rumford Medal, Royal Soc. 1980, Guthrie Medal and Prize, Inst. of Physics 2005. *Achievements include:* the observation and measurement of quantized vortices in superfluid helium, the first direct confirmation of the application of quantum mechanics to a macroscopic body. *Publications:* numerous scientific papers in professional journals on superfluids and superconductors. *Address:* School of Physics and Astronomy, University of Birmingham, Birmingham, B15 2TT, England (office). *Telephone:* (121) 414-4667 (office). *E-mail:* w.f.vinen@bham.ac.uk (office). *Website:* www.ph.bham.ac.uk (office).

VINES, David Anthony, PhD; British/Australian economist and academic; *Professor of Economics, University of Oxford;* b. 8 May 1949, Oxford; s. of Robert Vines and Vera Vines; m. 1st Susannah Lucy Robinson 1979 (divorced 1992); three s.; m. 2nd Jane E. Bingham 1995; two step-s.; ed Scotch Coll. Melbourne and Univs of Melbourne and Cambridge; Fellow, Pembroke Coll. Cambridge 1976–85; Research Officer, Sr Research Officer, Dept of Applied Econs, Univ. of Cambridge 1979–85; Adam Smith Prof. of Political Econ. Univ of Glasgow 1985–92; Fellow and Tutor in Econs Balliol Coll. Oxford 1992–, Prof. of Econs, Univ. of Oxford 2000–; Adjunct Prof. of Econs, Inst. of Advanced Studies, ANU 1991–; Dir ESRC Research Programme on Global Econ. Insts 1993–2000; mem. Bd Channel 4 TV 1986–92, Glasgow Devt Agency 1990–92, Analysis, Scottish Early Music Asscn 1988–95; econ. consultant to Sec. of State for Scotland 1988–92; consultant to IMF 1988, 1989; mem. Acad. Panel, HM Treasury 1986–; mem. Research Programmes Bd, ESRC 1990–92; mem. Int. Policy Forum, HM Treasury 1999–; Houblon Norman Fellow, Bank of England 2001–02. *Publications:* Stagflation, Vol. II: Demand Management (with J. E. Meade and J. M. Maciejowski) 1983, Macroeconomic Interactions Between North and South (with D. A. Currie) 1988, Macroeconomic Policy: inflation, wealth and the exchange rate (jtly) 1989, Deregulation and the Future of Commercial Television (with G. Hughes) 1989, Information, Strategy and Public Policy (with A. Stevenson) 1991, North South Macroeconomic Interactions and Global Macroeconomic Policy (ed. with D. A. Currie) 1995, Europe, East Asia and APEC: a Shared Global Agenda (with P. Drysdale) 1998, The Asian Financial Crisis: Causes Contagion and Consequences (ed., with P. Agenor, M. Miller and A. Weber) 1999, Integrity in the Public and Private Domains (ed. with A. Montefiore) 1999, The World Bank: Structure and Policies (ed. with C. L. Gilbert) 2000, papers in professional journals. *Leisure interests:* hillwalking, music. *Address:* Balliol College, Oxford, OX1 3BJ; Department of Economics, Manor Road, Oxford, OX1 3UQ, England. *Telephone:* (1865) 277719 (Coll.); (1865) 271067 (Dept). *Fax:* (1865) 277803 (Coll.); (1865) 271094 (Dept). *E-mail:* david.vines@economics.ox .ac.uk. *Website:* www.economics.ox.ac.uk.

VINES, Sir William Joshua, Kt, AC, CMG; Australian business executive and farmer (retd); b. 27 May 1916, Terang; s. of Percy V. Vines and Isabella Vines; m. 1st Thelma J. Ogden 1939 (died 1988); one s. two d.; m. 2nd Judith Anne Ploeg 1990; ed Haileybury Coll., Victoria; army service, Middle East, New Guinea and Borneo 1939–45; Sec., Alexander Fergusson Pty Ltd 1938–40, 1945–47; Dir, Goodlass Wall and Co. Pty Ltd 1947–49, Lewis Berger and Sons (Australia) Pty Ltd and Sherwin Williams Co. (Aust.) Pty Ltd 1952–55; Man. Dir, Lewis Berger and Sons (Victoria) Pty Ltd 1949–55, Lewis Berger & Sons Ltd 1955–60, Berger, Jensen & Nicholson Ltd 1960–61, Int. Wool Secr. 1961–69, mem. Bd 1969–79; Chair., Dalgety Australia Ltd 1969–80, Carbonless Papers (Wiggins Teape) Pty Ltd 1970–78, Assoc. Pulp & Paper Mills Ltd 1978–82; Deputy Chair. and Dir, Tubemakers of Australia Ltd 1970–86; Dir, Commercial Union Assurance Co. of Australia Ltd 1969–78, Port Phillip Mills Pty Ltd, Conzinc Riotinto of Australia Ltd 1976–89, Dalgety Australia Holdings Ltd 1980–92, ANZ Banking Group Ltd (Deputy Chair. 1980–82, Chair. 1982–89), Grindlays Holdings (now ANZ UK Holdings PLC) 1985–89, Grindlays Bank 1987–89; Chair., Sir Robert Menzies Memorial Trust 1978–92; Chair. Council, Hawkesbury Agricultural Coll. 1975–85; Hon. DSc (Econs) (Sydney) 1993. *Leisure interests:* golf, writing, reading biographies. *Address:* 1/10 West Street, Balgowlah, NSW 2093, Australia (home). *Telephone:* (2) 9948-1147 (home).

VINGT-TROIS, HE Cardinal André Armand; French ecclesiastic; *Archbishop of Paris;* b. 7 Nov. 1942, Paris; ed Catholic Inst., Paris; ordained priest in Paris 1969; after five years in a parish, began teaching at Issy-les-Moulineaux seminary; Vicar Gen. of Paris Archdiocese and Dir of Vocations 1981–88; Auxiliary Bishop of Paris and Titular Bishop of Thibilis 1988–99; Archbishop of Tours 1999–2005, of Paris 2005–; Ordinary of France and Faithful of Eastern Rites 2005–; cr. Cardinal 2007. *Address:* Archdiocese of Paris, 7 rue St Vincent, 75018 Paris Cedex 08, France (office). *Telephone:* 1-49-24-11-11 (office). *Fax:* 1-49-24-10-38 (office). *E-mail:* info@catholique-paris.cef .fr (office). *Website:* catholique-paris.cef.fr (office).

VINKEN, Pierre; Dutch publishing executive (retd); b. 25 Nov. 1927, Heerlen; ed Univs of Utrecht and Amsterdam; consultant neurosurgeon, Univ. of Amsterdam 1964–71; Man. Dir Excerpta Medica Publishing Co. Amsterdam 1963–71, Elsevier Science Publrs, Amsterdam 1971–73; Chair. and CEO Elsevier NV, Amsterdam (now Reed/Elsevier PLC London) 1977–99, Chair. 1993–95; Hon. mem. various scientific asscns; Kt, Order of Netherlands Lion 1983, Commdr Order of Hipólito Unanul (Peru) 1984, Commdr, Order of Orange Nassau 1995; Dr hc (Paris). *Publications:* Handbook of Clinical Neurology (78 vols), The Shape of the Heart 2000; articles on medicine and art history in journals. *Address:* 142 Bentveldsweg, 2111 EE, Aerdenhout, Netherlands (home). *Telephone:* (23) 5246342 (home). *Fax:* (23) 5246032 (home). *E-mail:* vinken@quicknet.nl (home).

VINNICHENKO, Nikolai Alexandrovich; Russian lawyer and politician; *Representative of the President to the Urals Federal District;* b. 10 April 1965, Oktyabrskoye Village, Shemonaikha Dist, Kazakhstan; Chief Prosecutor, St Petersburg 2003–04; Chief Bailiff and Dir Russian Federal Bailiffs Service 2004–08; Plenipotentiary Rep. of Russian Pres. to Urals Fed. Dist 2008–; First Class Councillor in Justice. *Address:* Office of the Plenipotentiary Representative of the President of the Russian Federation, Oktyabrskaya Ploshchad 3, Yekaterinburg 620000, Urals Federal District, Russia (office). *Telephone:* (3432) 77-18-96 (office). *Website:* admhmao.ur.ru (office).

VINOGRADOV, Oleg Mikhailovich; Russian ballet master; *Artistic Director, Universal Ballet;* b. 1 Aug. 1937; ed Vaganov Choreographic School, Leningrad; danced with Novosibirsk Acad. Theatre and Dir Cinderella 1964, Romeo and Juliet 1965; ballet master at Kirov Ballet, Leningrad 1968–72; Chief Ballet Master of Maly Theatre Dance Co. 1973–77; Chief Ballet Master of Kirov (now Mariinsky) Theatre 1977–99; works in USA and S Korea; Artistic Dir Universal Ballet 1998–; People's Artist of USSR 1983; RSFSR State Prize for Kazhlaev's Goryanka 1970, Marius Petipa Prize, Paris 1978, Pablo Picasso Prize 1987. *Productions include:* Useless Precaution (Hérold) 1971, Coppélia 1973, Yaroslavna (B. Tishchenko) 1974, The Hussar's Ballad (Khrennikov), The Government Inspector, The Battleship Potemkin (A. Chaikovsky), Behests of the Past 1983 and numerous others. *Address:* Universal Ballet, 25 Neung Dong, Gwangjin Gu, Seoul 143-847, Republic of Korea (office). *Telephone:* (2) 2204-1041 (office). *Fax:* (2) 458-1791 (office). *E-mail:* ubc@ubcballet.com (office). *Website:* www.universalballet.com (office).

VINOGRADOV, Vasily Valentinovich; Russian diplomatist; b. 19 Sept. 1948, Port Arthur; m.; one s.; ed Moscow Inst. of Int. Relations; with USSR (now Russian) Ministry of Foreign Affairs 1971–; Consulate Dept 1971–79; Third Sec. USSR Gen. Consulate in New York 1979–88; Third, Second Sec. USSR Embassy, USA 1980–84; First Sec., Head of Div., Deputy Head, Head Consulate Dept Ministry of Foreign Affairs 1984–92; Dir Dept of Consulate Service Russian Ministry of Foreign Affairs 1992–96; Amb. to Australia

1997–98; on staff Ministry of Foreign Affairs 1998–. *Address:* Ministry of Foreign Affairs, Smolenskaya-Sennaya 32/34, Moscow 119200, Russia.

VINOGRADOV, Vladimir Alekseyevich; Russian information specialist and economist; b. 2 July 1921, Kazan; s. of Aleksei Alexandrovich and Maria Alexandrovna; m. Marianna B. Antsuta 1943; one s.; ed Inst. of Int. Relations, Moscow; served in Soviet Army 1939–41; mem. staff Presidium of USSR (now Russian) Acad. of Sciences 1948–60, Deputy Chief Scientific Sec. 1961–71, Dir Inst. of Scientific Information on Social Sciences 1972–98, mem. Acad. 1984–, Counsellor 1998–; Lecturer Dept of Political Economy, Moscow Univ. 1954–60; mem. Soviet Cttee of UNESCO 1965–91; Vice-Pres. Int. Asscn for Econ. History 1968–78, Int. Social Sciences Council 1978–81; mem. New York Acad. of Sciences; Hon. Vice-Pres. Vienna Centre 1981–93; USSR State Prize 1982, Chernishevski Prize (Presidium of Acad. of Sciences) and other awards and prizes. *Publications:* numerous books and articles on the genesis of property in Russian and West European countries and on problems of information in the social sciences and the humanities, including Social Sciences and Information 1978, Workers' Control over Production: Theory, History and Contemporaneity 1983, What Type of Privatization Do We Need? 1991, State Property and Privatization in France 1998, Privatization: Global Trends and National Peculiarities 2006. *Leisure interest:* poetry. *Address:* Institute of Scientific Information in Social Sciences, Nakhimovski prosp. 51/21, Moscow 117997, Russia. *Telephone:* (495) 128-89-30 (office); (495) 331-32-16 (home). *Fax:* (495) 420-22-61.

VIOT, Jacques Edmond, CVO, CBE, LèsL; French diplomatist; b. 25 Aug. 1921, Bordeaux; m. Jeanne de Martimprey de Romecourt 1950; ed Bordeaux and Paris lycées, Ecole Normale Supérieure and Ecole Nat. d'Admin; Lecturer in French, Univ. of Dublin 1945–47, Ecole Nat. d'Admin 1948–50; Foreign Office 1951–53, Second Sec., London 1953–57; First Sec., Rabat 1957–61; held various posts in cen. admin 1961–72; Amb. to Canada 1972–77; Gen. Insp. for Foreign Affairs 1977–78; Dir de Cabinet, Ministry of Foreign Affairs 1978–81; Gen. Insp. for Foreign Affairs 1981–84; Amb. to UK 1984–86; Chair. Review Cttee on Foreign Affairs, Paris 1986–87; Chair. France-Grande Bretagne 1987–2000; mem. Admin. Council Alliance-Française 1987–94, Ecole Normale Supérieure 1988–94, Conseil supérieur Agence France-Presse 1988–94; Chair. Franco-British Council (French Section) 1992–2007, Alliance Française 1994–2004; Commdr, Légion d'honneur, Ordre nat. du Mérite. *Address:* c/o Conseil Franco–Britannique, 66 rue de Bellechasse 75005 Paris (office); 19 rue de Civry, 75016 Paris, France (home).

VIOT, Pierre, LèsL, LenD; French barrister; b. 9 April 1925, Bordeaux; s. of Edmund Viot and Irma Viot; m. Monique Fruchier 1952 (deceased); two s. two d.; ed Faculté de droit de Bordeaux, Inst. d'études politiques de Paris, Ecole Nat. d'Admin.; Jr Official, Cour des Comptes 1953, Chief Counsel; Asst, Bureau des Commissaires aux Comptes, NATO 1957–61; Regional and Urban Dept Head, Gen. Planning Office 1961; Spokesman, Nat. and Regional Devt Cttee 1961; Sec.-Gen., Conseil des Impôts 1971; Dir-Gen., Centre nat. de la Cinématographie 1973–84; Pres., Cannes Film Festival 1984–2000, Cinefondation Cannes Film Festival 2000–; Pres. Bd of Dirs, Etablissement public de l'Opéra de la Bastille 1985–89; Commdr, Légion d'honneur, Croix de guerre, Grand Officier, Ordre nat. du Mérite, Commdr Arts et Lettres, Commdr, Ordine al Merito della Repubblica Italiana, Officier, Verdienstorden der Bundesrepublik Deutschland. *Leisure interests:* tennis, gardening. *Address:* 38 avenue Emile Zola, 75015 Paris, France (home).

VIRATA, Cesar Enrique, BS (MechEng), MBA; Philippine politician and banker; *Chairman and President, C. Virata & Associates Inc.;* b. 12 Dec. 1930, Manila; s. of Enrique Virata and Leonor Aguinaldo; m. Joy Gamboa 1956; two s. one d.; ed Univ. of Pennsylvania, USA and Univ. of the Philippines; Dean Coll. of Business Admin., Univ. of the Philippines 1961–69; Chair. and Dir Philippine Nat. Bank 1967–69; Deputy Dir-Gen. Presidential Econ. Staff 1967–68; Under-Sec. of Industry 1967–69; Chair. Bd of Investments 1968–70; Minister of Finance 1970–86; Prime Minister of the Philippines 1981–86; Chair. Land Bank of the Philippines 1973–86; mem. Nat. Ass. 1978–86, Monetary Bd, Nat. Econ. and Devt Authority 1972–86, Comm. on the Future of the Bretton Woods Insts 1992–; Adviser to the Co-ordinating Council for the Philippines Aid Plan 1989–90; Chair. IMF and IBRD Devt Cttee 1976–80; Chair. and Pres. C. Virata & Assocs Inc. (Man. Consultants) 1986–; Chair. Bd of Govs, Asian Devt Bank 1979–80; Dir Philippine Stock Exchange, Inc. 1992; Dir and Corp. Vice-Chair. Rizal Commercial Banking Corpn; Hon. LHD, Hon. DPA, Dr hc (Philippines). *Leisure interests:* tennis, reading. *Address:* C. Virata & Associates Inc., Development Academy of the Philippines Building, San Miguel Avenue, Pasig City, Metro Manila 1600 (office); Rizal Commercial Banking Corporation, 46th Floor, Yuchengco Tower, RCBC Plaza, 6819 Ayala Avenue, Makati City 0727 (office); 63 East Maya Drive, Quezon City, Philippines (home). *Telephone:* (2) 631-2161 (office); (2) 844-8889 (office). *Fax:* (2) 631-2161 (office); (2) 878-3400 (office). *E-mail:* cvirata@pacific.net.ph (office); ceavirata@rcbc.com (office).

VIREN, Lasse; Finnish politician and fmr athlete; b. 22 July 1949, Myrskylä; m. Päivi Kajander 1976; three s.; competed Olympic Games, Munich 1972, won gold medal at 5,000m and 10,000m; Montréal 1976, won gold medal at 5,000m and 10,000m, 5th in marathon; Moscow 1980, 5th in 10,000m; only athlete to retain 5,000m and 10,000m titles at successive Olympics; held world records at two miles, 5,000m and 10,000m; sports promoter in schools at the Union Bank of Finland; elected pres. of his local town council while running own transport business; MP (Conservative Party) 1999–. *Publication:* The Golden Seconds. *Address:* Suomen Urheilulitto ry, Box 25202, 00250, Helsinki 25, Finland.

VIRILIO, Paul; French writer and artist; *Editorial Director, Editions Galilee;* b. 1932, Paris; ed Ecole des Metiers d'Art, Paris, Univ. of the Sorbonne, Paris; worked as artist in stained glass alongside Matisse in various churches in Paris; untrained architect; Chair. and Dir Ecole Spéciale d'Architecture, Paris 1968–98, Prof. Emer. 1998–; Ed. Espace Critique, Editions Galilee, Paris 1973–; Co-Founder and Programme Dir Collège Int. de Philosophie 1990–; mem. French Comm. concerned with housing for the poor (HCLD) 1992–; fmr mem. Editorial Bds Esprit, Cause Commune, Critiques, Traverses; has worked with Fondation Cartier pour l'art contemporain on several exhbns including Bunker Archeology, Pompidou Centre 1975, Speed, Jouy-en-Josas 1991, Unknown Quantity, Paris 2002; Grand Prix Nat. de la Critique 1987. *Publications include:* Bunker Archeologie 1975, L'Insecurité du territoire 1976, Speed and Politics 1977, Popular Defense and Ecological Struggles 1978, L'Esthetique de la disparition 1980, Pure War (with Sylvère Lotringer) 1983, War and Cinema: The Logistics of Perception 1984, L'Espace critique 1984, Polar Inertia 1990, The Art of the Motor 1995, Politics of the Very Worst 1996, Open Sky 1997, The Information Bomb 1998, The Strategy of Deception 1999, A Landscape of Events 2000, Ground Zero 2002, Negative Horizon 2005, The Original Accident 2007; numerous technical works. *Address:* Editions Galilee, 9 rue de Linné, 75005 Paris, France (office). *Telephone:* 1-43-31-23-84 (office). *Fax:* 1-45-35-53-68 (office). *E-mail:* editions.galilee@free.fr (office).

VIRSALADZE, Elisso Konstantinovna; Georgian pianist; b. 14 Sept. 1942, Tbilisi; studied under grandmother, Prof. Anastasia Virsaladze; then at Tbilisi Conservatory; won first prize at All-Union Competition of Performing Musicians, Moscow 1961; Bronze Medal at Tchaikovsky Competition 1962, Prize at Schumann Competition; teacher Moscow Conservatory 1962, Prof.; played as a soloist all over the world and on tour in Europe and USA with Leningrad Philharmonic; soloist with USSR Symphony Orchestra in UK 1983–84, Germany 1984–85; f. Tkvarcheli Music Festival and Summer School; many other tours as soloist in Europe and Japan; teacher Musikhochschule, Munich; USSR People's Artist 1989, Georgian State Prize 1983. *Address:* Artist Management Augstein, Eduard-Schmid-Strasse 30, 81541 Munich, Germany (office). *Telephone:* (89) 26024333 (office). *Fax:* (89) 26024344 (office). *E-mail:* mail@augstein.info (office). *Website:* www.augstein.info (office).

VIRZÌ, Paolo; Italian screenwriter, director and producer; b. 4 March 1964, Livorno, Tuscany; m. Micaela Ramazzotti; ed Univ. of Pisa, studied at Centro sperimentale di cinematografia, Rome under Gianni Amelio and Furio Scarpelli; formed artistic asscn with fmr fellow student Francesco Bruni that became important in later years; later, Furio Scarpelli became his teacher and mentor; f. Motorino Amaranto s.r.l. production house 2007. *Films:* Turnè (writer) 1990, Condominio (Condominium) (story; writer) 1991, Tempo di uccidere (Time to Kill; aka The Short Cut) (writer) 1991, Donne sottotetto (aka Centro storico) (writer) 1992, La bella vita (Living It Up) (writer and dir) (Ciak d'Oro, Nastro d'Argento and David di Donatello Award for Best New Dir 1995, Silver Ribbon for Best New Dir, Italian Nat. Syndicate of Film Journalists 1995) 1994, Ferie d'agosto (story, screenplay) (David di Donatello for Best Film of the Year 1996) 1995, Intolerance (dir segment Roma Ovest 143) 1996, Ferie d'agosto (dir) 1996, Cuba libre – velocipedi ai tropici (writer) 1997, Ovosodo (Hardboiled Egg) (story, screenplay and dir) (Grand Special Jury Prize and Little Golden Lion, Venice Film Festival 1997, Youth Audience Award, Montpellier Mediterranean Film Festival 1997) 1997, Baci e abbracci (Kisses and Hugs) (dir) 1999, Provino d'ammissione (writer and dir) 1999, My Name is Tanino (writer and dir) 2002, Caterina va in città (Caterina in the Big City) (writer, dir and co-producer) (Future Film Festival Digital Award – Special Mention, Venice Film Festival 2002) 2002, 4-4-2 – Il gioco più bello del mondo (all segments) 2006, L'estate del mio primo bacio (writer) 2006, N (Io e Napoleone) (Napoleon and Me) (screenplay and dir) 2006, Il caimano (The Caiman) (actor) 2006, Tutta la vita davanti (writer, dir and producer) 2008. *Television:* Une questione privata (A Private Affair) (writer) 1991. *Address:* Motorino Amaranto s.r.l., Via Miani 40, 00154 Rome, Italy (office). *Telephone:* (06) 5747488 (office). *E-mail:* info@motorinoamaranto.it (office). *Website:* www.motorinoamaranto.it (office).

VISCHER, Ulrich, lic. iur., Dr. iur., PhD; Swiss lawyer and university administrator; *President of the University Council, University of Basel;* b. 1951; m.; two s.; ed Univ. of Basel; began career with Basler Volkswirtschaftsbund (Basel Econ. Fed.); with Schweizerischer Bankverein (Swiss Bank Corpn) 1977–78; fmrly with Baloise Insurance Co.; mem. Basel City Parl. 1980–92 (Pres. 1989); mem. Govt of Canton Basel-Stadt and Minister of Finance 1992–2005; Pnr, Vischer & Assocs (law firm) Basel 2005–; Pres. Univ. Council, Univ. of Basel 2005–; Chair. MCH Swiss Exhibition (Holding) Ltd; Dir Warteck Invest AG 2007–; mem. Soc. of Trust and Estate Practitioners, Basel. *Address:* Office of the President, University of Basel, Leimenstrasse 1, 4001 Basel (office); Vischer, Aeschenvorstadt 4, 4010 Basel, Switzerland (office). *Telephone:* (61) 267-84-05 (office). *Fax:* (61) 267-84-34 (office). *E-mail:* uvischer@vischer.com (office). *Website:* www.unibas.ch (office); www.vischer.com (office).

VISHNEVA, Diana Viktorovna; Russian ballerina; *Principal Dancer, Mariinsky Theatre;* b. 13 July 1976, Leningrad; ed Vaganova Acad. of Russian Ballet; with Mariinsky Theatre 1995–, Prin. Dancer 1996–; Guest Artist, Staatsoper Unter den Linden, Berlin 2002–; Prix de Lausanne 1994, Divine Isadora Prize, Benois de la danse prize 1995, Golden Sophit St Petersburg Theatre Prize 1996, State Prize of Russia, Baltika Prize 1998, Golden Mask 2001, Dance of Europe Prize 2002, Ballet Magazine Prize 2003. *Main roles include:* Masha (Nutcracker), Kitri (Don Quixote), Aurore (Sleeping Beauty), Henriette (Raymonda), Gulnary (Corsare). *Address:* Mariinsky Theatre, 190000 St Petersburg, Teatralnaya pl. 1, Russia (office). *Telephone:* (812) 326-4141 (office). *Fax:* (812) 314-1744 (office). *E-mail:* post@mariinsky.ru (office). *Website:* www.vishneva.ru.

VISHNEVSKAYA, Galina Pavlovna; Russian singer (soprano); b. 25 Oct. 1926, Leningrad (now St Petersburg); m. Mstislav Rostropovich (died 2007); two d.; studied with Vera Garina 1942–52; Leningrad Musical Theatres 1944–52; leading soloist, Bolshoi Theatre 1952–74; left Soviet Union 1974; stripped of citizenship 1978 (citizenship restored 1990); retd from operatic stage as Tatiana in Eugene Onegin, Paris 1982; numerous parts in operas, notably Leonora in Fidelio and Tatiana in Eugene Onegin (also in the film), Aida in Aida, Kupava in Snow Maiden, Liza in Queen of Spades, Cio-Cio-San in Madame Butterfly, Margaret in Faust, Natasha in War and Peace, Cherubino in Marriage of Figaro, Marfa in Tsar's Bridge, Violetta in La Traviata, Liu in Turandot, Katerina in Lady Macbeth of Mtsensk; acted in A. Chekhov Moscow Arts Theatre 1993–94; f. opera School in Moscow 1999. Film: Alexandra 2007. Publication: Galina (autobiog.) 1985. Address: Gazetny per. 13, Apt. 79, 103009 Moscow, Russia. Telephone: (495) 229-04-96 (Moscow); 1-42-27-85-06 (Paris).

VISHNEVSKY, Yuri Georgyevich; Russian geophysicist and civil servant; b. 13 May 1943, Orlovorozka, Kemerovo region; m.; one s.; ed Tomsk Polytech. Inst.; engineer, sr engineer Tomsk-7 (chemical co.), Siberia for Ministry of Machine Construction 1966–85; Head of Volzhsk br., then Cen. Br. State Inspection of Atomic and Energy Safety (Balakovo Nuclear Station) 1985–91; Chair. State Cttee for Inspection of Radiation Safety 1991, Chair. RSFSR State Cttee for Inspection of Nuclear and Radiation Safety at Russian Presidency 1991–92; Dir Fed. Inspectorate of Nuclear and Radiation Safety 1992–2003. Address: c/o Federal Inspection of Nuclear and Radiation Safety of Russian Federation, Taganskaya str. 34, 109147 Moscow, Russia (office).

VITA, Giuseppe, DrMed; Italian business executive; Chairman of the Supervisory Board, Hugo Boss AG; b. 28 April 1935, Sicily; ed in Catania and Rome; qualified as specialist in radiology; Asst Röntgeninstitut, Univ. of Mainz 1962; joined Schering AG as asst in clinical research 1964; Gen. Dir Schering SpA Milan 1965; Deputy mem. Man. Bd Schering AG 1987, mem. 1988, Chair. 1989–2001, Chair. Supervisory Bd 2001–06; Chair. Supervisory Bd Hugo Boss AG 2000–, Axel Springer AG 2002–; Advisor to Bd Dirs Ikonisys 2004–; mem. Supervisory Bd Allianz Lebensvericherungs AG, Vattenfall Europe AG; Cavaliere del Lavoro, Verdienstorden des Landes Berlin, Verdienstkreuz am Bande des Verdienstordens der Bundesrepublik Deutschland. Address: Hugo Boss AG, Dieselstrasse 12, 72555 Metzingen, Germany (office). Telephone: (71) 23940 (office). Fax: (71) 23942051 (office). Website: group.hugoboss.com (office).

VITALE, Alberto; American publishing executive; b. 22 Dec. 1933, Vercelli, Piedmont, Italy; s. of Sergio Vitale and Elena Segre; m. Gemma G. Calori 1961; two s.; ed Turin Univ., IPSOA Business School and Wharton School, Univ. of Pa (Fulbright Scholar); joined Olivetti 1958; moved to USA to assist in Olivetti's acquisition of Underwood 1959; Exec. IFI (Agnelli family holding co.) 1971; Exec. Vice-Pres. for Admin Bantam Books, New York 1975, Co-CEO 1985, sole CEO 1986; Pres. and CEO Bantam-Doubleday-Dell 1987; Chair., Pres. and CEO Random House 1989–96, Chair., CEO 1996–98; Chair. Supervisory Bd Random House Inc., New York 1998; mem. Bd of Dirs Transworld Publrs; mem. Bd of Trustees Mercy Coll. NY; mem. Nat. Advisory Council, Reading is Fundamental; Chevalier, Ordre des Arts et des Lettres 1996. Address: 135 Grace Trail, Palm Beach, FL 33480, USA (home). E-mail: aavitale1@aol.com (home).

VITERBI, Andrew J., BS, MS, PhD, FIEEE; American (b. Italian) telecommunications engineer, business executive and academic; President, The Viterbi Group, LLC; Presidential Chair and Professor of Electrical Engineering, University of Southern California; b. 9 March 1935, Bergamo, Italy; m. Erna Viterbi; two s. one d.; ed Massachusetts Inst. of Tech., Univ. of Southern California; family moved to USA in 1939; began career at Jet Propulsion Lab., Calif. Inst. of Tech. 1968; Prof., School of Eng and Applied Science, UCLA 1963–73; Adjunct Prof. of Electrical Eng and Computer Science, Univ. of California, San Diego 1975, now Prof. Emer.; currently Presidential Chair. and Prof. of Electrical Eng, Andrew and Erna Viterbi School of Eng, Univ. of Southern California, Los Angeles; Co-founder Linkabit Corpn, Exec. Vice-Pres. 1974–82, Pres. M/A-COM Linkabit, Inc. 1982–; Co-founder Qualcomm, Inc. 1985, Vice-Chair. and Chief Tech. Officer –2000; currently Pres. The Viterbi Group, LLC (advises and invests in startup cos in communication, network and imaging technologies); fmr Chair. US Commission C, Int. Radio Scientific Union (URSI), Visiting Cttee, Electrical Eng Dept, Technion, Israel Inst. of Tech.; apptd mem. Presidential Advisory Cttee on Information Tech. 1997–2001; mem. MIT Corpn Visiting Cttee for Electrical Eng and Computer Science; fmr mem. Army Science Bd; fmr mem. or Chair. Bd Govs IEEE Information Theory Group (Transactions Assoc. Ed. for Coding); mem. Nat. Acad. of Eng 1978, NAS 1996, American Acad. of Arts and Sciences 2001; fmr Chair. NAS Computer and Information Sciences Section; developed Viterbi Algorithm, used in wide-ranging applications including mobile phones, DNA analysis and speech recognition; Grande Ufficiale della Repubblica (Italy) 2001; Dr hc (Waterloo, Rome, Technion, Notre Dame); IEEE Information Theory Group Outstanding Paper Award 1968, Christopher Columbus Int. Award, Italian Nat. Research Council 1975, AIAA Aerospace Communications Award (co-recipient) 1980, IEEE Alexander Graham Bell Medal 1984, Marconi Int. Fellowship Award 1990, Claude Shannon Award 1990, Benjamin Franklin Medal in Electrical Eng 2005, James Clerk Maxwell Medal, IEEE and Royal Soc. of Edinburgh (co-recipient) 2007, Robert Noyes Award, Semiconductor Industry Asscn (co-recipient) 2007, Nat. Medal of Science 2007. Publications: Principles of Coherent Communication 1966, Principles of Digital Communication and Coding (co-author) 1979, CDMA: Principles of Spread Spectrum Communication 1995; numerous scientific papers in professional journals. Address: Andrew and Erna Viterbi School of Engineering, University of Southern California, Los Angeles, CA 90089, USA (office).

Telephone: (213) 740-4750 (office). E-mail: viterbi.communications@usc.edu (office). Website: viterbi.usc.edu (office).

VITERI ACAITURRI, Maria Elsa; Ecuadorean economist and politician; Minister of Finance; b. 25 Feb. 1965; ed Univ. Católica de Santiago de Guayaquil, Iowa State Univ., USA; Head of Research, Centre for Econ. Research, Univ. Católica de Santiago de Guayaquil 1989–90, Dir 1992–95, Prof. of Econs 1990–96; Dir of Admin and Finance, Grupo SUPAN 1995–2000; Under-Sec. for the Budget, Ministry of Finance 2007, Vice Minister of Finance 2007–08, Minister 2008–; Premio Benemérita 1971, 1973, 1987. Address: Ministry of the Economy and Finance, Avda 10 de Agosto 1661 y Jorge Washington, Quito Ecuador (office). Telephone: (2) 254-4500 (office). Fax: (2) 253-0703 (office). Website: minfinanzas.ec-gov.net (office).

VITHAYATHIL, HE Cardinal Varkey, MA; Indian ecclesiastic; Archbishop Major of Syro-Malabar Church, Ernakulam-Angamaly; b. 29 May 1927, Parur, Ernakulam; s. of Justice Joseph Vithayathil; ordained priest 1954; Archbishop 1997; Archbishop Major of Syro-Malabar Church, Ernakulam-Angamaly 1999–; cr. Cardinal 2001. Address: Archdiocesan Curia, PO Box 2580, Kochi 682031, Kerala (office); Major Archbishop's House, Ernakulam, PO Box 2580, Kochi 682031, Kerala, India (home). Telephone: (484) 352629, 2352906, 2363664 (office); (484) 2355010 (home). Fax: (484) 366028 (office); (484) 355010 (home). E-mail: Cardinal@ernakulamarchdiocese.org (office). Website: www.ernakulamarchdiocese.org (office).

VITIER, Cintio; Cuban poet and writer; b. 25 Sept. 1921, Key West, FL, USA; s. of Medardo Vitier; m. Fina García Marruz; ed Univ. of Havana; worked on Orígenes magazine 1944–56; Lecturer, Escuele Normal para Maestros, Havana, Universidad Cen. de las Villas; researcher, José Martí Nat. Library 1962–77; Pres. Centre of Martianos Studies; Officier, Ordre des Arts et des Lettres; Dr hc (Univ. of Havana), (Universidad Cen. de las Villas), (Soka Univ., Japan); Nat. Literature Prize 1988, 30th Anniversary Medal, Acad. of Sciences, Order of José Martí 2002, Juan Rulfo Prize for Literature 2002. Publications include: poetry: Vísperas 1953, Testimonios 1968, La fecha al pie 1981, Nupcias 1993; fiction: De peña pobre 1980, Los papeles de Jacinto Finalé 1984, Rajando la leña está 1986; essays: Lo cubano en la poesía 1958, Temas Martianos (with Fina García Marruz) 1969, Crítica Sucesiva 1971, Ese sol del mundo moral 1975, Rescate de Zenea 1987, Crítica cubana 1988. Address: c/o Editorial Letras Cubanas, Ediciones Unión, No. 4, esq. Tacón, Hababa Vieja, Havana, Cuba (office). Website: www.cubaliteraria.cu (office).

VITORGAN, Emmanuil; Russian film and theatre director; b. 27 Dec. 1939, Baku, Azerbaijan; m. 1st Alla Balter (deceased), m. 2nd Irina Mlodek-Vitorgan; one s. one d.; ed Leningrad State Inst. of Theatre Arts; with Leningrad Theatre of Drama and Comedy 1961–63, Leningrad Theatre of Leninsky Komsomol 1964–71, Moscow Stanislavsky Drama Theatre 1971–82, Moscow Taganka Theatre 1982–84, Moscow Academic Mayakovsky Theatre 1984–; f. Vitorgan Foundation 2003–; Merited Artist of Russia 1990, People's Artist of Russia 1998. Films include: King Lear 1972, And This is All About Him 1974, Fortress 1978, Two People in a New House 1979, Profession – Investigator 1982, Devout Marta 1983, The Grown-up Daughter of a Young Man 1990, When Saints are Marching 1990, Lady in Spectacles with a Gun in a Car 2002. Plays include: Westside Story, Humiliated and Insulted, Rain Seller, Shadows, Grown-Up Daughter of a Young Man, Sirano de Berjerac, Circle, The Doll's House. Address: Moscow Academic Mayakovsky Theatre, Bolshaya Nikitskaya str. 19, 103009 Moscow (office); Maly Kislovsky per.7, apt 26, 103009 Moscow, Russia (home). Telephone: (495) 290-30-31 (office); (495) 291-89-89 (office).

VITORINO, António, LLM; Portuguese politician and lawyer; b. 12 Jan. 1957, Lisbon; m.; two c.; ed Lisbon Law School; fmr Prof., Lisbon Autonomous Univ.; mem. Parl. (Partido Socialista) 1981, 2005–; Sec. of State for Parl. Affairs 1984–85, for Admin and Justice of Macao Govt 1986–87; Judge, Portuguese Constitutional Court 1989–94; Minister for Defence and the Presidency 1995–97; Vice-Pres. Portugal Telecom Internacional 1998–99; EU Commr for Freedom, Security and Justice 1999–2004. Address: c/o Partido Socialista, Assembleia da República, Palácio de San Bento, 1249–068 Lisbon, Portugal (office).

VITRENKO, Natalia Mikhailovna, DEcon; Ukrainian politician; Chairman, Progressive Socialist Party of Ukraine; b. 28 Dec. 1958, Kiev; m.; one s. one d.; ed Kiev State Inst. of Nat. Econs; Sr Economist Cen. Dept of Statistics 1973–76; Sr Researcher Research Inst. of Information, State Planning Comm. 1979–89; Docent Kiev Inst. of Nat. Econs 1979–89; Sr Researcher Council on Production Forces, Ukrainian Acad. of Sciences 1989–94; ed. Vybor (journal) 1993–; People's Deputy 1994–; Counsellor on Socio-econ. Problems, Verkhovna Rada; mem. Socialist Party of Ukraine 1991; mem. Progressive Socialist Party of Ukraine (Prohresyvna Sotsialistychna Partiya Ukrainy) 1998–, currently Chair.; Presidium of Political Council 1993–, Acad. of Construction, Acad. of Econ. Cybernetics 1997. Address: Progressive Socialist Party of Ukraine (Prohresyvna Sotsialistychna Partiya Ukrainy), 01011 Kiev, vul. P. Miroho 27/51 (office); Verkhovna Rada, M. Hrushevskogo str. 5, Kiev, Ukraine (office). Telephone: (44) 254-18-40 (office). Fax: (44) 278-54-91 (office). E-mail: pspu@svitonline.com (office). Website: www.vitrenko.org (office).

VITRUK, Nikolai Vasilievich, LLD; Russian lawyer; b. 4 Nov. 1937, Zharovka, Tomsk Region; m. (divorced 1988); one d.; ed Tomsk State Univ.; Man. Legal Advice Bureau, Tomsk Regional Lawyers' Bd 1959; Asst Chair. of Theory and History of State and Law, Tomsk Univ. 1960–63; Asst, Sr Teacher, Asst Prof. Chair. of Theory of State and Law, T. G. Shevchenko Kiev State Univ. 1966–71; Sr Scientific Researcher, Inst. of State and Law, USSR Acad. of Sciences 1971–81; Prof. Chair. of Theory of State and Law and Constitutional Law, Acad. of Ministry of Internal Affairs of USSR 1981–84; Chief, Chair of State and Law Discipline, High Correspondence Law Coll., Ministry of Internal Affairs of USSR 1984–91; Justice, Constitutional Court of Russian Fed. 1991–, Deputy Chair. 1991–96, Acting Chair. 1993–95; mem. Venice Comm., Strasbourg, France 1992; Rep. of Russian Fed., European Comm. for Democracy Through Law; Labour Veteran Medal, Medal for Irreproachable Service, Honoured Scientist of Russian Fed. *Publications:* about 300 legal works. *Leisure interests:* theatre, modern realistic painting, poetry, art, culture of Russia during the 'Silver Age'. *Address:* Constitutional Court, 21 Ilyinka Street, 103132 Moscow, Russia (office). *Telephone:* (495) 206-06-29 (office). *Fax:* (495) 206-17-49 (office).

VITRYANSKY, Vassily Vladimirovich, DJur; Russian lawyer; b. 8 May 1956, Gomel, Belarus; m.; one s. two d.; ed Moscow State Univ.; mem. staff RSFSR State Court of Arbitration 1978–86; Sr Asst Admin. RSFSR Council of Ministers 1986–89, consultant Dept of Law 1989–90; Deputy Chief State Arbiter of RSFSR 1990–92; Deputy Chair. Higher Court of Arbitration of Russian Fed. 1992–; teacher Moscow State Univ., participated in devt of civil law in Russian Fed. *Monographs:* Protection of Property Rights of Businessmen, Protection of Property Rights of Stock Companies and Shareholders, Law and Bankruptcy; numerous publications on protection of civil rights, civil and legal responsibility, bankruptcy, etc. *Address:* Higher Court of Arbitration, M. Kharitonyevsky per. 12, 111001 Moscow, Russia (office). *Telephone:* (495) 208-12-81 (office).

VITTER, David, BA, LLB; American politician; *Senator from Louisiana;* m. Wendy Vitter; four c.; ed Tulane Univ, Oxford Univ UK, Harvard Univ; served over seven years as mem. Louisiana House of Reps –1999, concurrently Adjunct Law Prof. Tulane and Loyola Univs and business attorney; mem. US House of Reps 1999–2004, served on House Appropriations Cttee, House Republican Policy Cttee; Senator from Louisiana 2005–; Republican; Alliance for Good Govt Legislator of the Year, Victims and Citizens Against Crime Outstanding Legislator Award and Lifetime Achievement Award. *Address:* 825A Hart Senate Office Building, Washington, DC 20510, USA (office). *Telephone:* (202) 224-4623 (office). *Fax:* (202) 228-5061. *Website:* vitter.senate.gov (office).

VITUKHNOVSKAYA, Alina Aleksandrovna; Russian poet, writer and journalist; b. 27 March 1973, Moscow; first verses published late 1980s in periodicals; arrested on charge of drugs trafficking, freed Oct. 1995, arrested Nov. 1997; mem. Russian PEN Centre, Writers' Union; Pushkin Scholarship, Hamburg, Germany 1998. *Publications include:* Anomaly 1993, Children's Book of the Dead 1994, Pavlov's Dog (with K. Kedrov) 1996, The Last Old Woman Money-lender of Russian Literature (stories) 1996, Land of Zero 1996, Romance with Phenamine (novel) 1999, Day of Poetry (collaboration with French and Russian poets) 2001, Black Icon 2002. *Address:* Leningradskoye shosse 80, Apt. 89, 125565 Moscow, Russia (home). *Telephone:* (495) 452-15-31 (home).

VIVARELLI, Roberto; Italian historian and academic; *Professor Emeritus of History, Scuola Normale Superiore;* b. 8 Dec. 1929, Siena; s. of Lavinio Vivarelli and Margherita Cosci; m. Ann Sheldon West 1960 (died 1999); two s. one d.; ed Univs of Siena, Florence and Pennsylvania, USA and Istituto Italiano di Studi Storici; Research Fellow, St Antony's Coll. Oxford, UK 1961–62; Asst Prof., Univ. of Siena 1962–70, Full Prof. 1972–75; Assoc. Prof., Univ. of Florence 1970–72, Full Prof. 1975–86; Prof. of History, Scuola Normale Superiore, Pisa 1986–2005, Prof. Emer. 2005–; Visiting Prof., Inst. for Advanced Study, Princeton, USA 1969–70, 1980–81, Harvard Univ. 1976; Visiting Fellow, All Souls Coll. Oxford 1993–94; mem. Editorial Bd, Rivista Storica Italiana; mem. Academia Europaea. *Publications:* Gaetano Salvemini's Scritti sul Fascismo (ed.) 1961, 1974, Georges Sorel's Scritti politici (ed.) 1963, Il dopoguerra in Italia e l'avvento del fascismo 1967, Il fallimento del liberalismo 1981, Storia delle origini del fascismo (two vols) 1991, Profilo di storia (three vols) 1996, La fine di una stagione: Memoria 1943–1945 2000, Storia e storiografia 2004, I caratteri dell'età contemporanea 2005, Fascismo e storia d'Italia 2008. *Address:* Via Dante da Castiglione 1, 50125 Florence, Italy (home). *Telephone:* (055) 223190 (home).

VIVES, Xavier, MA, PhD; Spanish economist; *Professor of Economics and Finance, Institut Européen d'Administration des Affaires (INSEAD);* b. 23 Jan. 1955, Barcelona; m. Aurora Bastida; two s.; ed Autonomous Univ. of Barcelona, Univ. of Calif. at Berkeley, USA; Sr Researcher, Fundación de Estudios de Economía Aplicada (FEDEA); Programme Dir Applied Microecons. and Industrial Org. Programmes, Centre for Econ. Policy Research, London; Dir Institut d'Analisi Económica, Barcelona 1991–2001; Prof. of Econs and Finance, Institut Européen d'Admin des Affaires (INSEAD) 2001–; Visiting Prof., Harvard Univ., Univs of Pa, Calif., Berkeley and New York Univ.; Fellow, Econometric Soc. 1992; Premio Extraordinario de Licenciatura, Autonomous Univ. of Barcelona 1978, King Juan Carlos I Prize for Research in Social Science 1988, Societat Catalana d'Economía Prize 1996. *Publications:* Monitoring European Integration: The Future of European Banking (coauthor) 1999, Oligopoly Pricing: Old Ideas and New Tools 2000, Corporate Governance: Theoretical and Empirical Perspectives (ed.) 2000, Politicas Publicas y Equilibrio Territorial en el Stado Autonomico. *Address:* INSEAD, boulevard de Constance, 77305 Fontainebleau Cedex (office); Bat. C, Royal Paic, Appt 138, 39, Rue Royal, 77300 Fontainebleau France (home). *Telephone:* 1-60-72-42-79 (office); 1-60-72-83-01 (home). *Fax:* 1-60-74-67-19 (office). *E-mail:* xavier.vives@insead.edu (office). *Website:* faculty.insead.edu/vives (office).

VIVES I SICÍLIA, Mgr Joan-Enric, PhD; Spanish/Andorran ecclesiastic; *Bishop of Urgell and Episcopal Co-Prince of Andorra;* b. 24 July 1949, Barcelona, Spain; s. of the late Francesc Vives i Pons and of Cornèlia Sicília Ibáñez; ed Escola 'Pere Vila', Institut 'Jaume Balmes', Barcelona, Barcelona Seminary, Conciliary Seminary of Barcelona, Faculty of Theology of

Barcelona; ordained priest 1974; Prof. of Catalan, Univ. pf Barcelona 1979; apptd Auxiliary Bishop of Barcelona and Titular Bishop of Nona 1993; ordained Titular Bishop of Nona Sept. 1993; Co-Adjutor Bishop of Urgell 2001–03; Bishop of Urgell and Episcopal Co-Prince of Andorra 2003–; Medal of Honour of the City of Barcelona 1999. *Address:* Pati Palau 1-5, 25700 La Seu d'Urgell, Lleida, Spain (home). *Telephone:* (973) 350054 (office). *Fax:* (973) 352230 (home). *E-mail:* bisbevives@bisbaturgell.org (office); secretaricoprincep@bisbaturgell.org (office). *Website:* www.bisbaturgell.org (office).

VIVIAN, Young; Niuean politician; b. 1935; Leader Niue People's Party; Premier Dec. 1992–March 1993, May 2002–08, also Minister responsible for Legis. Ass., Premier's Dept and Cabinet, Civil Aviation, Crown Law Office, Econ. Devt Planning and Statistics, External Affairs and Niueans Abroad, Niue Public Service Comm., Niue Broadcasting Corpn, Finance, Customs and Revenue, Police, Prison and Nat. Security, Environment, Niue Tourism, Public Works (Civil and Quarry, Outside Services and Heavy Plant) and Recovery Task Force. *Address:* Niue People's Party, Alofi, Niue (office).

VIZJAK, Andrej, MEng; Slovenian politician and engineer; *Minister of the Economy;* b. 6 Aug. 1964, Brežice; ed Brežice Gymnasium, Faculty of Electrical Eng and Computing, Univ. of Ljubljana; began career as electrical engineer, Litostroj, Ljubljana; researcher in computer automatisation of industrial processes, Jožef Stefan Inst. –1994; Labour Insp., Krško Unit, Nat. Labour Inspectorate 1994–2000; State Sec., Ministry of Labour, Family and Social Affairs 2000; elected to Nat. Ass. 2000–04, 2004–, Minister of Economy 2004–; Leader of Social Democratic Party (SDP) Parl. Group 2000–04; elected Mayor of Brežice 2002. *Address:* Ministry of the Economy, 1000 Ljubljana, Kotnikova 5, Slovenia (office). *Telephone:* (1) 4783600 (office). *Fax:* (1) 4331031 (office). *E-mail:* info.mg@gov.si (office). *Website:* www.mg-rs-si (office).

VIZZINI, Carlo; Italian politician and academic; b. 28 April 1947, Palermo, Sicily; elected Social Democrat mem. Parl. for Palermo-Trapani-Agrigento-Caltanisetta 1976, now Senator; Nat. Deputy Sec. Italian Social Democrat Party and Head of Econ. Dept 1980–88; Under-Sec. of State in Ministry of Budget and Econ. Planning; Minister for Regional Affairs 1986–87, of Cultural Heritage 1987–88, of the Merchant Navy 1989–91, of Posts and Telecommunications 1991–92; Sec. Partido Socialista Democratica Italiano (PSDI); Pres. Bicameral Comm. for Regional Questions; mem. Parliamentary Comm. of Inquiry into Organized Crime and the Mafia; Prof. of History of Econs, Univ. of Palermo. *Address:* Segretaria Politica, Centro Studi – Laboratorio Politico, Via di Stefano 19, Palermo, Italy (office). *Telephone:* (91) 332697 (office). *Fax:* (91) 321038 (office). *E-mail:* carlovizzini@carlovizzini.it (office).

VLAAR, Nicolaas Jacob; Dutch physicist and academic (retd); *Professor Emeritus of Theoretical Physics, Utrecht University;* b. 17 March 1933, Mijnsheerenland; m. 1st Joanna Lambermont 1956 (died 1976); m. 2nd Everdina den Hartog 1980; three s. (one s. deceased) one d.; ed Bisschoppelijk Coll., Tech. Univ., Delft and Utrecht Univ.; Asst Calif. Inst. of Tech. 1965–66, St Louis Univ. 1966–67, Utrecht Univ. 1963–, Prof. of Theoretical Geophysics 1973; Prof. of Theoretical Geophysics, Free Univ. 1983–, now Prof. Emer., Dean of Faculty 1989–92; mem. Royal Netherlands Acad. of Science 1984–; mem. Hollandsche Maatschappij der Wetenschappen 1983–, Bd Netherlands Science Org. (Biology, Oceanography and Earth Science) 1988–; Hon. Mem. European Geophysical Soc. 1995; Kt, Royal Order of the Lion of the Netherlands 1994; Royal Dutch/Shell Prize 1982, Waterschoot van der Gracht Award 2007. *Publications:* numerous works on seismology and geodynamics. *Leisure interests:* nature, esoterics. *Address:* Mauritslaan 5, 3818 GJ, Amersfoort, Netherlands. *Telephone:* (33) 4613516. *E-mail:* nico.vlaar@planet.nl (home).

VLĂDESCU, Sebastian; Romanian politician and business executive; *Secretary of State on Treasury Issues;* b. 3 April 1958; ed Inst. Acad. of Econ. Studies, Bucharest, Merrill Lynch Inst., USA; economist, COS 1983, IRVMR Co. 1983–90; Shareholder and Dir Gas Prod Com LLC 1990–92, Banc Comp LLC 1992–94, Medist SA 1994–97 (Shareholder and Financial Dir 1998–99, Financial Dir 2001–05); Sec. of State, Ministry of Industry and Commerce Jan.–June 1997 (Advisor to the Minister July–Dec. 1997), Ministry of Finance Jan.–Dec. 2000 (Advisor to the Minister Jan.–April 1998, Oct.–Dec. 1999); mem. Guarantees for External Credits Inter-ministerial Comm., Eximbank Feb.–Aug. 1997, 2000; Chair. Trust Bd Company Bank Assets Recovery Agency 2000, Co. Chamber of Auditors 2000, Supervisory Bd Romanian Commercial Bank 2005– (mem. Privatisation Comm. 2000–01); mem. Bd of Dirs CEC Savings House 2000–01, Petrom Service 2002–03, Upetrom 2002–05, Romanian Centre for Econ. Policies (CEROPE) 2003–05, Petrom SA 2005; Minister of Public Finance 2005–07; Sec. of State on Treasury Issues, Ministry of the Economy and Finance 2007. *Address:* Ministry of the Economy and Finance, 010096 Bucharest 1, Calea Victoriei 152, Romania (office). *Telephone:* (21) 2025106 (office). *Fax:* (21) 2025109 (office). *E-mail:* iuliana-dumitru@minind.ro (office). *Website:* www.minind.ro (office).

VLADIMIR, Metropolitan (Victor Markianovich Sabodan), MTheol; Ukrainian ecclesiastic; *Metropolitan of Kiev and All Ukraine;* b. 23 Nov. 1935, Khmelnitsky Region; ed Leningrad and Moscow Theological Acads.; ordained as deacon, then priest 1962–66; Bishop, Archbishop 1966–82; Metropolitan 1982; taught in Odessa Seminary, then Rector; Deputy Chief Russian Orthodox Mission in Jerusalem 1966–68; Bishop of Pereslavl-Zalessky; Archbishop of Dmitrov, Rector Moscow Theological Acad., Prof. 1973–82; Metropolitan of Rostov and Novocherkassk 1982–86; Patriarch Rep. in West Europe 1986–87; Man. Moscow Patriarchy, Perm. mem. Holy Synod 1987–; Metropolitan of Kiev and All Ukraine 1992–; Dr hc (Christian

Theological Acad., Warsaw) 2008. *Publications:* 10 volumes including Ecclesiology in Russian Theology, Paul the Called Apostle, Christ the Saviour, Principle of the World. *Address:* Ukrainian Orthodox Church, Pechensk Monastery, Sichnevoho Povstannia 25, Kiev, Ukraine. *Telephone:* (44) 280-15-08. *E-mail:* metropolia@svitonline.net (office). *Website:* www.orthodox.org.ua.

VLADIMIROV, Vasiliy Sergeyevich, DSc; Russian mathematician and academic; *Counsellor, Russian Academy of Sciences;* b. 9 Jan. 1923, Djaglevo, Petrograd Region; s. of Sergey Ivanovich Vladimirov and Maria Semyonovna Vladimirova; m. Nina Yakovlevna Vladimirova (née Ovsyannikova) 1948; two s.; ed Leningrad State Univ.; served in Soviet Army 1941–45; Jr Research Worker, Leningrad Dept, V. A. Steklov Inst. of Math., USSR Acad. of Sciences 1948–50; Head, Dept of Computer Math., All Russian Research Inst. of Experimental Physics, Arsamas-16, 1950–55; Sr Research Worker, Steklov Inst. of Math., Moscow 1956–69, Head, Dept of Math. and Physics 1969–2003; Prof. Physico-tech. Inst. 1964–87; Vice-Dir Steklov Inst. 1986–88, Dir 1988–93, Counsellor 1993–; mem. CPSU 1944–91; Corresp. mem. USSR (now Russian) Acad. of Sciences 1968–70, mem. 1970–, Counsellor 1993–; mem. Saxony Akad. der Wissenschaften zu Leipzig 1985, Int. Asscn of Math. Physics 1980, Acad. of Sciences and Arts Voivodina (Yugoslavia) 1987, Serbian Acad. of Science and Arts (Belgrade) 1991; Hon. Mem. Soc. Math. and Physics of the Czech Repub.; Order of Lenin 1975, 1983 (twice), Order of the Great Patriotic War 1985, Gold Star of Hero of Socialist Labour 1983, Gold Medal of N.N. Bogolyubov 1999; State Prize 1953, 1987 (twice), Bogolyubov Prize, Nat. Acad. of Sciences of Ukraine 1997, Gold Medal of A. N. Liapounov 1971, Gold Medal Bernarda Bolzana CSR Acad. of Science 1982, Prize of Russian Govt 2003 and numerous other awards. *Publications:* Mathematical Problems of the One-Velocity Particles Transfer 1961, Methods of the Theory of Functions of Several Complex Variables 1964, Equations of Mathematical Physics 1967, Distributions in Mathematical Physics 1976, Many Dimensional Tauberian Theorems for Distributions (with others) 1986, p-Adic Analysis and Mathematical Physics (with others) 1994, Equations and Mathematical Physics (co-author, in Russian) 2001, Methods of the Theory of Generalized Functions 2002, and works in the field of number theory and numerical methods, analysis of transfer equation, theory of holomorphic functions of several complex variables and distribution theory and their applications in math. physics; about 300 papers and articles. *Leisure interest:* skiing. *Address:* Steklov Institute of Mathematics, Gubkin Street 8, 119991-1 Moscow, Russia (office). *Telephone:* (495) 135-14-49 (office); (495) 124-78-64 (home). *Fax:* (495) 135-05-55 (office). *E-mail:* vladim@mi.ras.ru (office). *Website:* www.pdmi.ras.ru (office).

VLADISLAVLEV, Alexander Pavlovich, DTechSc; Russian politician; b. 21 May 1936, Moscow; m. Karina Lisitsian; one s.; ed Gubkin Petroleum Inst., Moscow, Oil and Gas Inst., Bucharest; mem. CPSU 1959–91; researcher, sr teacher, Docent, Pro-Rector Gubkin Moscow Inst. 1959–74; Vice-Pres. All-Union Soc. Znanie 1974–86; First Vice-Chair. USSR Council of Scientific and Eng Socs 1988–90; Chair. Exec. Cttee, First Vice-Pres. USSR (now Russian) Scientific-Industrial Union 1990–92; Chair. Council of Business of USSR, Pres. 1991; First Deputy Minister of Foreign Econ. Relations of USSR Nov.–Dec. 1991; First Vice-Pres. Russian Union of Industrialists and Entrepreneurs 1990–; USSR People's Deputy 1989–91; Founder and Co-Chair. Democratic Reform Movt 1991–92; a leader of Civic Union 1992–93; mem. State Duma (Parl.) 2000–, Chair. Sub-Cttee on Investment Policy; Chair. Bd, ZIL motor co. 1994–95; mem. Bd of Dirs Moscow CableCom Corpn 2004–; Pres. Ind. Fund for Realism in Politics 1994–; mem. Presidium of Eng Acad., founder and mem. of admin of non-govt foundations and socs; mem. Advisory Council of UNO on Science and Tech.; mem. faction Otechestvo. *Publications:* six books; over 200 articles and papers; 15 patents. *Address:* Novy Arbat prosp. 15, Suite 2424, Moscow, Russia (office). *Telephone:* (495) 202-26-25 (office); (495) 203-55-15 (home).

VLAHOVIĆ, Miodrag; Montenegrin politician and diplomatist; *Ambassador to USA;* b. 1961, Djakovica; m.; three d.; ed Univ. of Montenegro, Podgorica, Univ. of Belgrade, Luxembourg Int. Univ.; f. STUDEKS Cultural Centre, Podgorica 1985; mem. Fed. Presidency and Int. Sec., Socialist Youth Union of Yugoslavia 1986–88; Sec. for Montenegro Asscn for Yugoslav Democratic Unity 1989; co-f. Citizens Cttee for Peace 1991–92, organized first peace rally in Montenegro 1991; mem. Parl., Repub. of Montenegro, mem. Parl. Cttee for Int. Relations, Cttee for Political System, Cttee for Legal and Admin. Matters 1992–94 (resgnd); Liberal Party of Montenegro Int. Sec. 1992–93; columnist for ind. weekly "Monitor" 1991–93, 1999–2000; Founder-mem. Montenegrin Centre for Democracy and Human Rights (CEDEM) 1998; co-author of new Montenegrin law on NGOs; Dir Centre for Regional and Security Studies (CeRS) 1999; Minister of Foreign Affairs, Repub. of Montenegro 2004–06; Amb. to USA 2006–; Owner MConsult Ltd 1990–; mem. Socialiat Democratic Party of Montenegro. *Address:* Embassy of Montenegro, 1610 New Hampshire Avenue, NW, Washington, DC 20009, USA (office). *Telephone:* (202) 234 6108 (office). *Fax:* (202) 234 6109 (office).

VLČEK, Miloslav; Czech politician; *Chairman, Poslanecká sněmovna (Chamber of Deputies);* b. 1 Feb. 1961, Konice; m.; two s. two d.; ed Univ. of Brno; fmr tractor mechanic; mem. Czech SDP (Česká strana sociálně demokratická); mem. Poslanecká sněmovna (Chamber of Deputies) 1996–, Chair. 2006–, Chair. Steering Cttee 2006–. *Address:* Office of the Chairman, 1, Poslanecká sněmovna, 118 26 Prague, Sněmovní 4, Czech Republic (office). *Telephone:* 257171111 (office). *Fax:* 257534469 (office). *E-mail:* vlcek@psp.cz (office); info@miloslavvlcek.cz. *Website:* www.psp.cz (office); www.miloslavvlcek.cz.

VLK, HE Cardinal Miloslav, BSc; Czech ecclesiastic; *Archbishop of Prague;* b. 17 May 1932, Sepekov-Líšnice; ed Faculty of Philosophy, Charles Univ. Prague, Faculty of Theology, Litoměřice; archivist Třeboň and Jindřichův Hradec 1960–61, České Budějovice 1961–64; ordained priest 1968; sec. to Roman Catholic Bishop of České Budějovice 1968–71; parish priest Laiště and Zablatí Romitál pod Třemšínem 1971–78; denied permission to work as priest 1978; window cleaner, Prague 1978–1986; archivist, Czechoslovak State Bank, Prague 1986–88; parish priest, parishes in Šumava Mountains 1989–90; cr. Bishop of České Budějovice 1990, Archbishop of Prague 1991–, cr. Cardinal 1994; mem. Consilium Conferentiarum Episcopalium Europae 1990–2001 (Pres. 1993–2001), Pontificum Consilium de Communicationibus Socialibus 1994–, Congregatio pro Ecclesiis Orientalibus 1994–; Hon. Citizen, Romitál pod Třemšínem 1992, Cedar Rapids, USA 1992, Baltimore, USA 1992, Kłodzko, Poland 1996, Třeboň 1996, Roudnice nad Labem 1997, Mníšek pod Brdy 1998; Hon. LHD (Ill. Benedictine Coll., USA, Univ. of St Thomas, Minn., USA) 1992; Hon. DTheol (Univ. Passau, Germany) 1993, (Pontificia Academia Theologica Cracoviensys, Poland) 2001, (Univ. Opole, Poland) 2002; Grosses Verdienstkreuz, Germany 1999, Görlitz Brückepreis 2001, TGM Order 2002. *Publications:* Reifezeit 1996, Wird Europa neidisch? 1999, Avanti! 1999; numerous ecclesiastical articles. *Leisure interests:* classical and oriental languages, classical music, mountain tourism, skiing, cycling. *Address:* Arcibiskupství praské, Hradčanské nám. 16/56, 119 02 Prague 1, Czech Republic (home). *Telephone:* (2) 20392111 (home). *Fax:* (2) 20515396 (home). *E-mail:* sekretar.vlk@apha.cz (office). *Website:* www.kardinal.cz (office).

VLOK, Adriaan; South African politician; b. 11 Dec. 1937, Sutherland; m. Cornelia Burger; two s. one d.; joined Dept of Justice 1957; became prosecutor and sr magistrate; Asst Pvt. Sec. to Prime Minister John Vorster 1967; subsequently entered pvt. business; later Deputy Sheriff, E Pretoria; MP 1974–94; fmr Deputy Speaker of House of Ass.; Deputy Minister of Defence and Deputy Minister of Law and Order 1985–86; Minister of Law and Order 1986–91, of Correctional Services and the Budget 1991–92, of Correctional Services and of Housing and Works 1992, of Correctional Services 1992–94; Leader House of Ass. 1992–94; mem. Truth and Reconciliation Comm. for amnesty for criminal acts 1998; received suspended ten year sentence for involvement in plot to kill anti-apartheid activist Frank Chikane July 2007. *Leisure interests:* rugby (referee in Northern Transvaal), military history, chewing biltong.

VODIČKA, Jindřich; Czech politician; b. 22 July 1952, Prague; m.; two s.; ed Univ. of Maritime Studies, Odessa; sailed as deck engineer, later First Officer in merchant navy 1977–90; First Deputy Dir, Office for Protection of Constitutional Officials –1990; Dir Job Centre, Prague-West Dist 1990–92; mem. Civic Democratic Party (CDP) 1991–97, 1998–, Unie Svobody Jan.–March 1998; Deputy to House of Nations (Fed. Ass. of ČSFR) June–Dec. 1992; Minister of Labour and Social Affairs of Czech Repub. 1992–97; Minister of Interior 1997–98; Dir-Gen. České přístavy (Czech Ports Ltd). *Address:* Civic Democratic Party, Sněmovní 3, 110 00 Prague 1, Czech Republic (office). *Telephone:* (2) 33334800 (office). *E-mail:* info@ods.cz (office). *Website:* www.ods.cz (office).

VOEVODSKY, Vladimir, PhD; Russian mathematician and academic; *Professor, School of Mathematics, Institute for Advanced Study;* b. 4 June 1966; ed Moscow State Univ., Harvard Univ., USA; held visiting posts at Inst. for Advanced Study and Harvard Univ., USA and Max-Planck-Institut für Mathematik, Germany; mem. Faculty, Northwestern Univ., Evanston, Ill., USA 1996–2002; Prof., School of Math., Inst. for Advanced Study, Princeton, NJ, USA 2002–; Fields Medals, Int. Congress of Mathematicians, Beijing (jtly) 2002. *Publications:* Cycles, Transfers and Motivic Homology Theories 2000; numerous articles in math. journals on algebraic geometry and K-theory. *Address:* School of Mathematics, Institute for Advanced Study, Fuld 116, Einstein Drive, Princeton, NJ 08540, USA (office). *Telephone:* (609) 734-8117 (office). *Fax:* (609) 951-4459 (office). *E-mail:* vladimir@ias.edu (office). *Website:* www.math.ias.edu (office).

VOGEL, Bernhard, DPhil; German politician; *Chairman, Konrad Adenauer Foundation;* b. 19 Dec. 1932, Göttingen; s. of Prof. Dr Hermann Vogel and Caroline Vogel (née Brinz); ed Univs of Heidelberg and Munich; Lecturer, Inst. for Political Sciences, Heidelberg 1961–67; mem. Bundestag (Parl.) 1965–67, Speaker of Bundesrat (Upper House) 1976–77, 1987–88; Minister of Educ. and Culture, Rhineland-Palatinate 1967–76; Chairman / Deputy Chairman of the Joint Commission of the Federal and State Governments for Education Planning and Research Development 1970-1976; mem. Rhineland-Palatinate State Parl. 1971–88, Thuringia State Parl. 1994–2004; Chair. CDU, Rhineland-Palatinate 1974–88, mem. Fed. Exec. Cttee of CDU 1975–, Chair. CDU, Thuringia 1993–2000; Minister-Pres., Rhineland-Palatinate 1976–88, Thuringia 1992–2003, Chair. Conf. of State Prime Ministers 1981–82, 1996–97; Rep. for Cultural Affairs of FRG within framework of Agreement on German-French Co-operation 1979–82; Chair. Advisory Bd of German TV Broadcasting/Second Channel (ZDF) 1979–92, Deputy Chair. 1992–2007; Chair. Konrad Adenauer Foundation 1989–95, 2001–; Pres. Cen. Cttee of German Catholics 1972–76; Hon. Prof., award by State of Baden-Wurttemberg; Grosses Bundesverdienstkreuz; decorations from France, Luxembourg, Poland, UK, and the Vatican; Grosskreuz St Gregorius; Gold Medal of Strasbourg; Dr hc (Catholic Univ. of America, Catholic Univ. of Lublin, German Coll. for Admin. Sciences, Speyer). *Publications:* Die Unabhangigen in den Kommunalwahlen westdeutscher Lander 1960, Wahlen und Wahlsysteme 1961, Kontrolliert der Bundestag die Regierung? 1964, Wahlkampf und Wählertradition. Eine Studie zur Bundestagswahl von 1961 1965, Wahlen in Deutschland 1848–1970 (with D. Noheln and R.-O. Schultze), Schule am Scheideweg 1974, Die Wahl der Parlamente und anderer Staatsorgane 1969–1978 (co-ed. with Dolf Sternberger), Neue Bildungspolitik (ed.) 1975, Federalismus in der Bewahrung (ed.) 1992, Sorge tragen für die Zukunft 2002, Religion und Politik (ed.) 2003, Im Zentrum: Menschenwürde. Politisches Handeln aus christlicher Verantwortung, christliche Ethik als

Orientierungshilfe (ed.) 2006, Deutschland aus der Vogel Perspektive. Eine kleine Geschichte der Bundesrepublik Deutschland (zusammen mit Hans-Jochen Vogel) 2007; Ed. Politische Meinung; numerous essays and speeches. *Leisure interests:* mountaineering, literature, swimming. *Address:* Konrad-Adenauer-Stiftung e.V., Der Vorsitzende, Rathausallee 12, 53757 Sankt Augustin, Germany (office). *Telephone:* (2241) 2462420 (office). *Fax:* (2241) 2462675 (office). *E-mail:* bernhard.vogel@kas.de (office).

VOGEL, Dieter H., DrIng; German business executive; *Chairman of the Supervisory Board, Bertelsmann AG;* b. 14 Nov. 1941; m. Ursula Gross 1970; two c.; ed Tech. Univ. of Darmstadt, Tech. Univ. of Munich; Asst Prof., Thermic Turbo Engines, Tech. Univ. of Munich 1967–69; Vice-Pres., Printing Div., Bertelsmann AG 1970–74, Pegulan AG 1975–85 (Chair. 1978), Chair. Supervisory Bd Bertelsmann AG 2003–; Vice-Chair. Man. Bd Batig (BAT Industries) 1978–85; joined Thyssen Group 1986, Chair. Thyssen Handelsunion AG 1986–96, mem. Exec. Bd 1986–91, Deputy Chair. Thyssen AG 1991–96, Chair. 1996–98; Chair. Supervisory Bd Deutsche Bahn AG 1999–2001. *Leisure interest:* skiing. *Address:* Bertelsmann AG, Carl-Bertelsmann-Strasse 270, 33311 Gütersloh, Germany. *Telephone:* 5241-80-0 (office). *Fax:* 5241-80-9662 (office). *Website:* www.bertelsmann.de (office).

VOGEL, Hans-Jochen, DJur; German politician; b. 3 Feb. 1926, Göttingen; m. 1st Ilse Leisnering 1951 (divorced 1972); one s. two d.; m. 2nd Liselotte Sonnenholzer (née Biersack) 1972; ed Univs of Munich and Marburg; asst, Bavarian Justice Ministry 1952–54; judge, Traunstein Dist Court 1954–55; Bavarian State Chancellery 1955–58; professional mem. Munich City Council 1958–60; Chief Burgomaster of Munich 1960–72; mem. Bundestag 1972–81, 1983–94; Minister for Regional Planning, Building and Urban Devt 1972–74, of Justice 1974–81; Mayor, West Berlin Jan.–June 1981; Chair. SPD Parl. Party 1984–91; Deputy Chair. SPD 1984–87, Chair. 1987–91; Vice-Pres. Org. Cttee for Munich Olympic Games 1972; apptd Chair. Gegen Vergessen (Against Forgetting) Project 1993; mem. Nationalen Ethikrat 2001–05; numerous decorations including Grosses Bundesverdienstkreuz, Bayerischer Verdienstorden, Hon. CBE and honours from France, Italy, etc.; Leo Baeck Prize 2001. *Publications:* Die Amtskette: Meine zwölf Münchner Jahre 1972, Nachsichten: Meine Bonner und Berliner Jahre 1996, Politik und Anstand: Warum wir ohne Werte nicht leben können 2005, Deutschland aus der Vogel Perspektive (with Bernhard Vogel) 2007. *Leisure interests:* mountain walking, history. *Address:* c/o Gegen Vergessen - Für Demokratie e.V., Stauffenbergstraße 13-14, 10785 Berlin (office); Stiftsbogen 74, 81375 Munich, Germany (home). *Telephone:* (30) 2639783 (office). *Fax:* (30) 26397840 (office); (89) 70962211 (home). *E-mail:* info@gegen-vergessen.de (office).

VOGEL, Viola, PhD; German scientist and academic; *Professor, Department of Materials, Swiss Federal Institute of Technology, Zürich (ETH);* ed Max-Planck Inst. for Biophysical Chemistry, Göttingen, Frankfurt am Main Univ.; Postdoctoral Fellow, Univ. of California, Berkeley 1988–90; joined faculty Dept of Bioengineering, Univ. of Washington, Seattle USA 1990, also adjunct appointment in Physics, Founding Dir Center for Nanotechnology 1997–2003; Prof., Dept of Materials, ETH 2004–, also serves as Head, Lab. for Biologically Oriented Materials; Fellow, American Inst. for Medical and Biological Eng, mem. Gordon Research Conf. Selection and Scheduling Cttee; mem. Selection Cttee British Marshall Fund Fellowships 1993–95, German Ministry of Science and Educ. (BMBF) 1998; Max-Planck Soc. Otto-Hahn Medal 1988, NIH First Award 1993, Philip Morris Foundation Research Award 2005, Julius Springer Award for Applied Physics 2006. *Address:* Biologisch-Orientierte Materialwissens, Wolfgang-Pauli-Str. 10, ETH-Hönggerberg, 8093 Zürich, Switzerland (office). *Telephone:* (44) 6320887 (office). *Fax:* (44) 6321073 (office). *E-mail:* viola.vogel@mat.ethz.ch (office). *Website:* www.nanomat.mat.ethz.ch (office).

VOGELSTEIN, Bert E., BA, MD; American oncologist, pathologist and academic; *Clayton Professor of Oncology and Professor of Pathology, Johns Hopkins University School of Medicine;* ed Univ. of Pennsylvania, Pa, The Johns Hopkins Univ. School of Medicine, Baltimore, Md; Pediatric Intern, Johns Hopkins Hosp., Baltimore 1974–75, Pediatric Resident 1975–76; Postdoctoral research at Nat. Cancer Inst. 1976–78; Asst Prof. of Oncology, Johns Hopkins Univ. School of Medicine 1978–83, Assoc. Prof. 1983–89, Clayton Prof. of Oncology 1989–, Jt Appointment in Molecular Biology and Genetics 1992–, Prof. of Pathology 1998–; Investigator, Howard Hughes Medical Inst., Chevy Chase, Md 1995–; Assoc. Ed. Cancer Research 1988–90, Genes, Chromosomes, and Cancer 1988–; mem. Bd of Reviewing Eds Science 1988–; mem. Editorial Bd Cancer and Metastasis 1993–, New England Journal of Medicine 1994–; mem. American Acad. of Arts and Sciences, NAS, American Philosophical Soc., Inst. of Medicine. *Publications:* more than 340 articles in medical and scientific journals on molecular genetics of human cancer. *Address:* Johns Hopkins Oncology Center/HHMI, 1650 Orleans Street, Room 589, Baltimore, MD 21231-1001, USA (office). *Telephone:* (410) 955-8878 (office). *Fax:* (410) 955-0548 (office). *E-mail:* vogelbe@welch.jhu.edu (office). *Website:* www.hopkinsmedicine.org (office).

VOGT, Peter K., PhD; American professor of molecular and experimental medicine; *Professor and Head, Division of Oncovirology, Scripps Research Institute;* b. 3 Oct. 1932; s. of Josef Vogt and Else Vogt; m. Hiroko Ishino 1993; ed Univ. of Tubingen; Asst Prof. of Pathology, Univ. of Colorado 1962–66, Assoc. Prof. 1966–67; Assoc. Prof. of Microbiology, Univ. of Washington 1967–69, Prof. 1969–71; Hastings Prof. of Microbiology, Univ. of Southern California 1971–78, Hastings Distinguished Prof. of Microbiology 1978–80, Chair. Dept of Microbiology 1980–; Chair. Div. of Oncovirology, Prof. Dept of Molecular and Experimental Medicine, The Scripps Research Inst. 1993–; Calif. Scientist of the Year 1975, NAS Award 1980, Alexander von Humboldt Prize 1983, Ernst Jung Prize for Medicine 1985, Howard Taylor Ricketts Award 1991, Charles S. Mott Prize 1991. *Publications:* Genetics of RNA Tumor Viruses 1977, The Genetic Structure of RNA Tumor Viruses 1977 and numerous articles in scientific journals. *Leisure interest:* painting. *Address:* The Vogt Laboratory, Division of Oncovirology, Department of Molecular and Experimental Medicine, The Scripps Research Institute, 10550 North Torrey Pines Road, BCC–239, La Jolla, CA 92037, USA (office). *Telephone:* (858) 784-8079 (office). *Fax:* (858) 784-2070 (office). *E-mail:* pkvogt@scripps.edu (office). *Website:* www.scripps.edu/mem/oncovir/vogt (office).

VOHOR, Serge; Ni-Vanuatu politician; fmr Minister of Econ. Affairs; Pres. Union of Moderate Parties; Prime Minister of Vanuatu 1995–96, 1996–98, July–Dec. 2004; apptd Minister of Foreign Affairs 2000, apptd Deputy Prime Minister 2001; currently Pres. Union of Moderate Parties. *Address:* Union of Moderate Parties POB 698, Port Vila, Vanuatu (office).

VOHRA, Narinder Nath; India politician; *Governor of Jammu and Kashmir;* ed Punjab Univ., Univ. of Oxford; served in Indian Admin. Service 1959–94, positions included Home Sec., Punjab, Additional Sec., Defence, Sec., Defence Production, Home Sec. and Prin. Sec. to Prime Minister, Special Services Bureau in Western Tibet border areas 1962–64; with WHO, Geneva 1982–84; mem. Nat. Security Advisory Bd 1998–2001; Co-Chair. India-European Union Round Table 2001–08; Special Rep. of Govt of India, Jammu and Kashmir Dialogue 2003–08; Gov. of Jammu and Kashmir 2008–; fmr Dir India Int. Centre; fmr Chair. Nat. Task Force on Internal Security, IDSA Review Cttee, Cttee on Review of Mil. Histories; mem. Indian Inst. of Public Admin, United Services Inst., Inst. of Defence Studies and Analysis and Int. House of Japan; Padma Vibhushan 2007. *Address:* Raj Bhawan, Guwahati, India (office). *Telephone:* (361) 540500 (office). *Fax:* (361) 540310 (office). *E-mail:* rakesh.jamwal@nic.in (office). *Website:* jkrajbhawan.nic.in (office).

VOIGHT, Jon; American actor; b. 29 Dec. 1938, Yonkers, New York; s. of Elmer Voight and Barbara (née Kamp) Voight; m. 1st Lauri Peters 1962 (divorced 1967); m. 2nd Marcheline Bertrand 1971 (divorced); one s. one d.; ed Catholic Univ.; f. Jon Voight Entertainment (production co.); Acad. Award (Best Actor) for Coming Home 1979, Best Actor Awards for Midnight Cowboy 1969, Coming Home 1979, Cannes Int. Film Festival, Golden Globe Award for Best Actor for Coming Home. *Theatre includes:* A View From the Bridge (New York); That Summer That Fall (New York) 1966; played Romeo at the San Diego Shakespeare Festival; Stanley Kowalski in A Streetcar Named Desire, Los Angeles 1973, Hamlet 1975. *Films include:* Hour of the Gun 1967, Fearless Frank 1968, Out of It 1969, Midnight Cowboy 1969, The Revolutionary 1970, The All-American Boy 1970, Catch 22 1970, Deliverance 1972, Conrack 1974, The Odessa File 1974, Coming Home 1978, The Champ 1979, Lookin' to Get Out (also wrote screenplay) 1982, Table for Five 1983, Runaway Train 1985, Desert Bloom 1986, Eternity, Heat, Rosewood, Mission Impossible 1996, U-Turn 1997, The Rainmaker 1997, Varsity Blues 1998, The General 1998, Enemy of the State 1998, Dog of Flanders 1999, Lara Croft: Tomb Raider 2001, Pearl Harbor 2001, Ali 2001, Zoolander 2002, Holes 2003, Superbabies 2003, Karate Dog 2003, The Manchurian Candidate 2004, National Treasure 2004, Superbabies: Baby Geniuses 2 2004, Glory Road 2006, The Legend of Simon Conjurer 2006, Transformers 2007, Bratz 2007, National Treasure Book of Secrets 2007, Pride and Glory 2007, Tropic Thunder 2008. *Television includes:* End of the Game 1976, Gunsmoke and Cimarron Strip, Chernobyl: The Final Warning 1991, The Last of His Tribe 1992, The Tin Soldier (also dir), Convict Cowboy 1995, The Fixer 1998, Noah's Ark 1999, Second String 2000, Jasper Texas 2003, The Five People You Meet in Heaven 2004, Pope John Paul II 2005. *Address:* c/o Martin Baum and Patrick Whitesell, CAA, 9830 Wilshire Boulevard, Beverly Hills, CA 90212,; Jon Voight Entertainment, 10203 Santa Monica Blvd, Los Angeles, CA 90067, USA. *Telephone:* (310) 288-4545; (310) 843-0223 (Jon Voight Entertainment). *Fax:* (310) 553-9895 (Jon Voight Entertainment).

VOINEA, Radu, PhD; Romanian civil engineer and scientist; b. 24 May 1923, Craiova; s. of Policarp Voinea and Gabriela Voinea; m. 1st Maria Marta Gorgos 1951 (divorced 1957); one s. one d.; m. 2nd Aurica Daghie 1959 (died 2000); ed Polytechnical School, Bucharest; Asst Prof. 1947; Sr Lecturer, Inst. of Civil Eng, Bucharest 1951; Prof., Polytech. Inst., Bucharest 1962, Pro-Rector 1964–67, Rector 1972–81; Corresp. mem. Romanian Acad. 1963, mem. 1974–, Gen. Sec. 1967–74, Pres. 1984–90; mem. European Acad. of Arts, Sciences and Humanities 1985. *Publications:* Curs de rezistenţa materialelor (Lectures on the Strength of Materials), with A. Beles 1958, Mecanica teoretică (Theoretical Mechanics), with V. Vâlcovici and Ş. Bălan 1959, Metode analitice în teoria mecanismelor (Analytical Methods in the Theory of Mechanisms), with M. C. Atanasiu 1964, Mecanica (Mechanics), with D. Voiculescu and V. Ceausu 1975, 1983, Elasticitate şi Plasticitate (Elasticity and Plasticity), with D. Voiculescu and V. Ceauşu 1976, Vibratii mecanice (Mechanical Vibrations), with D. Voiculescu 1979, Introducere în Mecanica Solidului pentru ingineri (Introduction to mechanics of solids for engineers) with D. Voiculescu and F. Simion 1989, Technische Mechanik (co-author) 1993, Electricity and Plasticity 1994, Aufgabensammlung zur Technische Mechanik 1995, Technical Mechanics (co-author) 1996, Introduction to Mechanics of Elastic Continuous Bodies (co-author) 1997, Mechanics and Mechanical Vibrations 1998, Introducere in Teoria Sistemelor Dinamice (Introduction to the Theory of Mechanical Systems, with Ion Stroe) 1999, Elemente de Mecanica Medülor Continue (Elements of Mechanics of Continuous Media) (jtly) 2000. *Address:* Academia Română, Calea Victoriei 125, 70102 Bucharest 1 (office); Bd Dacia 88, Apt 4, 70256 Bucharest 2, Romania (home). *Telephone:* (1) 2128660 (office); (1) 6105496 (home). *E-mail:* bratosin@acad.ro (office).

VOINOVICH, George V., BA, JD; American politician; *Senator from Ohio;* b. 15 July 1936, Cleveland; m. Janet Voinovich; two s. one d.; ed Ohio State Univ.; called to the Bar, Ohio 1961; Asst Attorney Gen., Ohio 1963–64; mem.

Ohio House of Reps. 1967–71; auditor Cuyahoga Co., Ohio 1971–76, Commr 1977–78; Lt Gov. of Ohio 1979; Mayor of Cleveland 1979–89; Gov. of Ohio 1991–98; Senator from Ohio 1999–, mem. Foreign Relations Cttee.; mem. Nat. Govs' Asscn (Chair. Educ. Action Team on School Readiness 1991, Child Support Enforcement Work Group 1991–92, Co-Chair. Task Force on Educ. 1992–93, mem. Exec. Cttee 1993–; Co-Lead Gov. on Fed. Mandates 1993–; Chair. Nat. Govs' Asscn 1997–98); Certificate of Merit Award, Dist Urban Mayor Award, Nat. Urban Coalition 1987, Ohio Univ. Humanitarian Award, NCCJ 1986 and many others. *Address:* 317 Hart Senate Office Building, Washington, DC, 20510-0001, USA (office). *Telephone:* (202) 224-3353 (office). *Fax:* (202) 228-1382 (office). *Website:* voinovich.senate.gov (office).

VOINOVICH, Vladimir Nikolayevich; Russian writer; b. 26 Sept. 1956, Dushanbe, Tajikistan; m.; one d.; ed Moscow Regional Pedagogical Inst.; active in dissident movt 1960s; freelance writer; mem. USSR Writers' Union, expelled 1974, expulsion revoked 1990; deprived of Soviet citizenship 1981, emigrated and lived in Germany 1980–92; Prof. Princeton Univ., USA; mem. Bavarian Acad. of Fine Arts; Triumph Prize. *Publications:* I Want to Be Honest (short story), We Live Here 1963, The Degree of Confidence 1972, Life and Extraordinary Adventures of the Soldier Ivan Chonkin, Hat, Ivankyada, By Mutual Correspondence, Moscow–2042, Monumental Propaganda 2005. *Address:* Russian Pen-Centre, Neglinnaya str. 18/1, Bldg 2, Moscow, Russia (office). *Telephone:* (495) 209-45-89 (office). *Fax:* (495) 200-02-93 (office).

VOITOVICH, Aliaksander Pavlavich, DR.PHYS-MATH.SCI.; Belarusian physicist and politician; b. 5 Jan. 1938, Radkevichi, Minsk region; s. of Pavel Voitovich and Nadezhda Voitovich; m.; one s.; ed Belarus State Univ.; mem. research staff Inst. of Physics Belarus Acad. of Sciences (BAS) 1962–84 (Deputy Research Dir 1984–92); Deputy Research Dir, then Dir Inst. of Molecular and Atomic Physics, BAS 1992–97; mem. 1996, then Pres. Nat. Acad. of Sciences of Belarus 1997–2000; Chair. Nat. Ass. of Repub. of Belarus Council of Repub. 2000–; author of 24 scientific inventions; State Prize 1966; Badge of Hon. 1981; Order of Francisk Skaryna 1998. *Publications:* Magneto-Optics of Gas Lasers 1984, Lasers with Anisotropic Resonators (with V. Severikov) 1990; some 200 research papers. *Leisure interests:* fishing, carpentry. *Address:* Houses of Government, Council of Republic, 220010 Minsk, Belarus (office). *Telephone:* (17) 226-66-94 (office). *Fax:* (17) 226-67-65 (office).

VOLCHEK, Galina Borisovna; Russian stage director and actress; b. 19 Dec. 1933, Moscow; d. of Boris Volchek and Vera Maimyna; m. 1st Yevgeniy Yevstigneyev 1957 (divorced 1964); m. 2nd Mark Abelev 1966 (divorced 1976); one s.; ed Studio-School of Moscow Art Theatre; co-founder, actress and Stage Dir Theatre Sovremennik 1956–72, Artistic Dir 1972–; Deputy to State Duma (Parl.) 1995–99; over 40 productions including Common Story by Goncharov, On the Bottom by Gorky, Cherry Orchard, Three Sisters by Chekhov, Ascent over Fujiyama by Aitmatov, Echelone by Roshchin, Anfissa by Andreyev, Steep Route by Ginzburg, Pygmalion by George Bernard Shaw, We Go Go... by Kalida, Three Comrades by E. M. Remorque; stage productions in many countries including USA (first Soviet stage dir to work in USA, Alley Theatre, Houston, Echelone by M. Roshchin), Ireland (Abbey Theatre), Hungary, Finland, Bulgaria, Germany, Czechoslovakia; masterclasses in Tisch School, New York Univ.; USSR People's Artist, State Prize, State Orders of USSR, Hungary, Bulgaria and Russia, GA Tovstonogov Prize 2006. *Dramatic roles include:* Martha (Who's Afraid of Virginia Woolf?), Miss Amelia (The Ballad of the Sad Café by Albee), Wife of Governor (Inspector by Gogol). *Films:* roles in films by directors Kozintsev (King Lear), Yutkevich, Danelia and others. *Leisure interest:* designing clothes. *Address:* 101000 Moscow, Chistoprudny blvd 19A, (Theatre); Povarskaya str. 26, Apt 43, Moscow, Russia (home). *Telephone:* (495) 921-25-43 (Theatre). *Fax:* (495) 921-66-29 (office). *E-mail:* teatr@sovremennik.ru (office). *Website:* www.sovremennik.ru (office).

VOLCKER, Paul A., MA; American economist, banker, academic and government official; *Head, President's Economic Recovery Advisory Board;* b. 5 Sept. 1927, Cape May, NJ; s. of Paul A. Volcker and Alma Klippel Volcker; m. Barbara Marie Bahnson 1954 (died 1998); one s. one d.; ed Princeton Univ., Harvard Univ. Grad. School of Public Admin. and London School of Econs, UK; Economist and Special Asst Securities Dept, Fed. Reserve Bank of New York 1953–57; Financial Economist, Chase Manhattan Bank, New York 1957–62, Dir of Forward Planning 1965–69; Dir Office of Financial Analysis, US Treasury Dept 1962–63, Deputy Under-Sec. for Monetary Affairs 1963–65, Under-Sec. Monetary Affairs 1969–74; Sr Fellow, Woodrow Wilson School of Public and Int. Affairs, Princeton Univ. 1974–75; Pres. NY Fed. Reserve Bank 1975–79; Chair. Bd of Govs, Fed. Reserve System 1979–87; Frederick H. Schultz Prof. of Int. Econ. Policy, Princeton Univ. 1988–95, Prof. Emer. 1995–; Chair. James D. Wolfensohn Inc. 1988–96, CEO 1995–96; Henry Kaufman Visiting Prof., Stern School of Business, New York Univ. 1998; Chair. Int. Accounting Standards Cttee Foundation 2000–05; Chair. UN comm. investigating Iraq Oil for Food Program 2004–05; Chair. Bd of Trustees Group of Thirty Consultative Group on Int. Econ. and Monetary Affairs, Inc., Washington, DC –2008; Head of Pres.'s Econ. Recovery Advisory Bd, The White House, Washington, DC 2009–; apptd by World Bank to lead ind. investigation of its Dept of Institutional Integrity 2007; mem. Bd of Dirs (non-exec.) ICI 1988–93, Nestlé 1988–2000, Prudential Insurance 1988–2002; Consultant, Arthur Anderson 2002; Dr hc (Harvard, Yale, Princeton, and other univs); Admin. Fellowship, Harvard, Rotary Foundation Fellow, LSE, Arthur S. Fleming Award, Fed. Govt, US Treasury Dept Exceptional Service Award, Alexander Hamilton Award, Fred Hirsch Memorial Lecture 1978, Public Service Award, Tax Foundation 1981, Courage Award 1989. *Address:* 610 Fifth Avenue, New York, NY 10020, USA (office). *Telephone:* (212) 218-7878 (office). *Fax:* (212) 218-7875 (office).

VOLK, Igor Petrovich; Russian cosmonaut; b. 12 April 1937; m.; two d.; ed Kirovograd Mil. Pilot School, School of Pilot Testers, Moscow Aviation Inst.; army service 1956–63; joined Cosmonauts' Team 1978, first space flight 1984; leading test pilot for Buran aircraft 1984–95; Dir V. Chkalov Test Flights Centre, Gromov Flight Research Centre, M. Gromov Research Flight Inst. (GNC RFLII) 1995–2002. *Leisure interests:* flying, football, skiing, tennis. *Address:* c/o GNC RFLII, Zhukovskiy-2, Moscow 140160, Russia (office).

VOLK, Patricia, BFA; American writer; b. 16 July 1943, New York; d. of Cecil Sussman Volk and Audrey Elayne Morgen Volk; m. Andrew Blitzer 1969; one s. one d.; ed Syracuse Univ., Acad. de la Grande Chaumière, Paris, School of Visual Arts, The New School, Columbia Univ.; Art Dir Appelbaum and Curtis 1964–65, Seventeen Magazine 1967–68; copy-writer, Assoc. Creative Dir, Sr Vice-Pres. Doyle Dane Bernbach Inc. (DDB Needham Worldwide Inc.) 1969–88; Adjunct Instructor of Fiction, Yeshiva Coll. 1991; columnist, Newsday, NY 1995–96; mem. PEN Authors Guild; Yaddo Fellow; MacDowell Fellow; Word Beat Fiction Book Award 1984 and numerous other awards. *Publications include:* The Yellow Banana 1985, White Light 1987, All It Takes 1990, Stuffed: Adventures of a Restaurant Family 2001, To my Dearest Friends 2007; contribs to The New York Times Magazine, The Atlantic, Quarterly, Cosmopolitan, Family Circle, Mirabella, Playboy, 7 Days, Manhattan Inc., The New Yorker, New York Magazine, Red Book, Good Housekeeping, Allure; Anthologies: Stories About How Things Fall Apart and What's Left When They Do 1985, A Reader for Developing Writers 1990, Exploring Language 1992, Magazine and Feature Writing 1992, Hers 1993, Her Face in the Mirror 1994. *Leisure interests:* fly-fishing, tennis. *Address:* c/o Gloria Loomis, 133 East 35th Street, New York, NY 10016, USA.

VOLKOV, Vladimir Konstantinovich, DHist; Russian historian; b. 15 Dec. 1930, Voronezh; m.; two d.; ed Moscow State Univ.; started career as journalist; broadcasting for Bulgaria and Albania 1954–56; researcher, Prof. and Head of Div., Deputy Dir Inst. of Slavonic Studies USSR (now Russian) Acad. of Sciences 1956–87, Dir 1987–; mem. Council Pres. Boris Yeltsin 1993–98; Vice Pres. Nat. Cttee of Historians, mem. several scientific socs. *Publications:* over 160 works on problems of culture and history of Slavic peoples. *Address:* Institute of Slavonic Studies, Leningradsky pr. 7, 125040 Moscow, Russia. *Telephone:* (495) 250-77-08 (office).

VOLLEBAEK, Knut, MSc; Norwegian diplomatist; *High Commissioner on National Minorities, Organization for Security and Co-operation in Europe;* b. 11 Feb. 1946, Oslo; m. Ellen Sofie Aadland Vollebaek; one s.; ed Inst. Catholique de Paris, Univ of Oslo, Univ of California, Santa Barbara, USA, Univ Complutense, Madrid, Spain and, Norwegian School of Econs and Business Admin, Bergen; joined Foreign Service 1973; Second Sec. Embassy of Norway, Delhi 1975–78, First Sec. Embassy of Norway, Madrid 1978–81, Exec. Officer, then Sr Exec. Officer, Ministry of Foreign Affairs 1981–84, Counsellor Embassy of Norway, Harare 1984–86; Head First Political Affairs Div., Ministry of Foreign Affairs 1986–89, State Sec. and Deputy Minister of Foreign Affairs 1989–90; Amb. to Costa Rica 1991–93; Dir Gen. Dept of Bilateral Devt Cooperation, Ministry of Foreign Affairs 1993–94; Gov. Inter-American Devt Bank, Asian Devt Bank and African Devt Bank 1994–97; Deputy Co-Chair. Int. Conf. on the Fmr Yugoslavia, Geneva 1993; Asst Sec. Gen. for Devt Cooperation 1994–97; Minister of Foreign Affairs 1997–2000; Chair. Barents Euro-Arctic Council 1997–98; Chair. Council of Baltic Sea States 1999–2000; Chair.-in-Office OSCE 1999; Amb. to USA 2001–07; High Commr on Nat. Minorities, OSCE 2007–; Commdr of the Royal Norwegian Order of St Olav 2001; Hon. DJur (St Olaf Coll., Minn., USA) 2003; Hon. DHumLitt (Concordia Coll., Minn., USA) 2003. *Address:* High Commissioner on National Minorities, PO Box 20062, 2500 EB The Hague, Netherlands (office). *Telephone:* (70) 3125500 (office). *Fax:* (70) 3635910 (office). *E-mail:* hcnm@hcnm.org (office). *Website:* www.osce.org/hcnm (office).

VOLOCHKOVA, Anastasiya; Russian ballet dancer; b. 20 Jan. 1976, St Petersburg; ed Russian Vaganova Acad. of Ballet; soloist, Maryinsky Theatre, St Petersburg 1994–98; with Bolshoi Theatre 1998–2003; Gold Medal, 2nd Ballet Contest, Kiev. *Roles include:* Odyllia and Swan Princess in Swan Lake, Gisele in Gisele, Raimonda in Raimonda, Niknya in Bayder, Aurora and Lilac Fairy in Sleeping Beauty, Zarema in Fountain of Bakhchisarai, Girl in Spirit of Rose, Medora in Corsair, Carmen in Carmen-Suite. *Leisure interests:* walking, reading, classical and modern music. *Telephone:* (495) 126-17-53 (home). *E-mail:* office@volochkova.ru. *Website:* www.volochkova.ru.

VOLODARSKY, Eduard Yakovlevich; Russian scriptwriter and writer; b. 3 Feb. 1941, Kharkov, Ukraine; s. of Yakov Isaakovich Volodarsky and Maria Yakovlevna Brigova; m. Tagirova Farida Abdurakhmanovna; ed All-Union Inst. of Cinematography; mem. Union of Cinematographers, Sec. 1990–95; mem. Union of Writers; mem. Exec. Bd Studio Slovo 1997; Ed.-in-Chief Cen. Scenario Studio 1998–; Pres. Russian Filmmakers Union (RFU) Guild of Film and TV Scriptwriters 1997–, also Sec. Bd RFU; Merited Worker of Arts; Dr hc (Acad. of Arts, St Marino); USSR State Prize, State Prize of Russian Fed., Dovzhenko Golden Medal. *Film include:* White Explosion 1968, A Road Home 1969, Sixth Summer 1969, Anthracite 1970, Check-up on Roads 1971, Risk 1973, Killed in Performance 1974, Hatred 1975, My Friend Ivan Lapshin 1975, Second Attempt of Victor Krokhin 1976, Eight Days of Hope 1977, Forget the Word Death 1979, Smoke of Motherland 1980, Emelyan Pugachev 1981, People in the Ocean 1981, Look Back 1982, Guilt of Lieutenant Nekrasov 1982, War 1983, Partings 1983, Blackmailer 1984, Appellation 1986, Vagabond 1987, Moonzund 1987, Behind the Deadline 1987, Abyss or Seventh Circle 1992, Lonely Gambler 1993, Ordinary Bolshevism 1999, Marsh-brosok (The Charge) 2003, Dnevnik kamikadze (Diary of a Kamikaze) 2003. *Television includes:* Bayazet (miniseries) 2003, Shtrafbat (miniseries) 2004, Okhota na asfalte (miniseries) 2005. *Plays include:* The Happiest, Moscow Vakhtangov Drama Theatre, Our Debts, Leaving, Look Back, Moscow

Art Theatre, Trap, Moscow Ostrovsky Maly Theatre, Stars for the Lieutenant, Moscow Ermolova Drama Theatre, Run, Run, Evening Star, Tzwilling Theatre. *Publications:* Everyone Has His Own War, A Russian Woman, Diary of a Kamikaze, Skullhunter. *Telephone:* (495) 330-96-64 (home).

VOLODIN, Vyacheslav Viktorovich, DJur; Russian politician; *Deputy Chairman, State Duma;* b. 4 Feb. 1964, Alekseyevka, Saratov region; m.; one d.; ed Saratov Inst. of Agric. Mechanisation, Acad. of Civil Service; teacher, Docent, Saratov Inst. of Agric. Mechanisation 1987–92; Deputy Head Admin. of Saratov 1992–93; Prof., Head of Chair., Pro-Rector Povolzhye Personnel Centre 1993–94; mem., Deputy Chair. Saratov Regional Duma 1994–, Vice-Gov., First Deputy Chair. Saratov Regional Govt 1996–99; Prof. Povolzhye Acad. of Civil Service until 1999; mem. State Duma (Parl.) 1999–; mem. Homeland–All Russia faction, Deputy Sec. Political Council 1999–; mem. United Party Yedinstvo and Otechestvo 2001–2003; re-elected to State Duma as mem. of Yedinaya Rossiya faction 2003–; Deputy Chair. State Duma 2004–. *Leisure interests:* painting, sports. *Address:* State Duma, Okhotny ryad 14, 103265 Moscow, Russia (office). *Telephone:* (495) 292-83-10 (office). *Fax:* (495) 292-94-64 (office). *Website:* www.duma.ru (office).

VOLONTIR, Mikhai; Moldovan actor; b. 9 March 1934; s. of Ermolae Volontir and Feodosia Volontir; m. Eufrosinia Volontir 1961; one d.; ed Actors' Training School; actor and producer with Alecsandri Moldavian Music and Drama Theatre in Beltsy 1957–; work in TV and films 1968–; mem. Pres. Council 1997–2001; USSR People's Artist 1984. *Theatre includes:* Misfortune (producer), The Twilight (actor, producer), Alecsandri's Agaki Flutur, Bayescu's Preshul (actor, producer), Drutsa's Beautiful and Saint (producer), Tanev's The Last Night of Socrates (actor, producer). *Films include:* A Movement of Answer, The Only Man, The Hunting of Deer, Am I Guilty?, Traces of a Wolf, We Shall Remain Faithful, One-Sided Love. *Leisure interest:* protection of animals. *Address:* Str. Independentsei 34, Apt. 4, 3100 Beltsy, Moldova. *Telephone:* (31) 2-80-52.

VOLOSHIN, Alexander Stalyevich; Russian government official; b. 3 March 1956, Moscow; m.; three s.; ed Moscow Inst. of Transport Eng, Ail-Union Acad. of Foreign Trade; Head of Lab. of Scientific Org. of Labour; Sec. Comsomol Org.; Moskva-Sortirovochnaya railway station 1973–83; Researcher, then Sr Researcher, Head of Sector, Deputy Head of Section Ail-Union Research Inst. of Conjuncture 1986–92; Exec. Dir Analysis, Consultations and Marketing 1992–; Pres. ESTA Corpn 1993–96; Pres. Fed. Funds Corpn 1996–97; apptd Asst to Head of Admin. of Presidency (for Econ. Problems) 1997, Deputy Head 1998–99, Head 1999–2003 (resgnd); Chair. Bd of Dirs RAO EES 1999–; Chair. Supervisory Bd Unified Energy Systems (EES) 2004–; Chair. Collegium of Reps, State Bd of Public Radio and TV. *Address:* RAO Unified Energy System of Russia, Bld. 3, 101 Vernadsky Ave., Moscow, 119526, Russia (office). *Telephone:* (495) 220-4001 (office). *Fax:* (495) 927-3007 (office). *Website:* www.rao-ees.ru (office).

VOLPINARI, Antonio Lazzaro, III; San Marino politician; b. 2 Oct. 1943, Domagnano; m. Claudia Berti; one d.; joined Partito Socialista Sammarinese (PSS) 1959, elected to Cen. Cttee 1963–, with Secr. Youth Movt, Vice-Sec. PSS 1980–82, Gen.-Sec. before and after Conf. Socialist Unification 1991, mem. Secr., Pres. of Group of Advisers; elected mem. of Govt 1969–, Mayor of Govt 1974–76, Deputy to Agric., Communications and Transport 1976–78, to Agric. and Commerce 1978–83, to the Territory and Atmosphere 1983–86, Sec. of State for Internal Affairs 1992–2000; Supreme Magistracy of Captain Regent 1973–74, April–Sept. 1977; Head of State (Capt. Regent) 2002; mem. Advisory Comm. on Internal Affairs; Del. to the Council of Europe. *Address:* Partito Socialista Sammarinese (PSS), Via G. Ordelaffi 46, 47890 San Marino (office). *Telephone:* (549) 902016 (office). *Fax:* (549) 906438 (office). *E-mail:* pss@omniway.sm (office). *Website:* www.pss.sm (office).

VOLTEN, Peter M. E., MA, PhD; Dutch research institute director; *Director, Centre for European Security Studies;* m. Karin Deen; four c.; ed Free Univ. of Amsterdam; Visiting Scholar, Stanford Univ., USA 1975–77; Sr Staff mem. Dutch Ministry of Defence 1977–85, Dir of Studies and Strategic Planning 1987–89; Prof. of History, Univ. of Utrecht 1984–89; Sr Research Fellow, Netherlands Inst. of Int. Relations 1985–87; Dir of Research, Inst. for East-West Security Studies 1989–92, Sr Vice-Pres. and Dir Netherlands Centre 1992–93; Prof. of Int. Relations, Univ. of Groningen 1994–, Dir Centre for European Security Studies 1994–; mem. Bd Dirs Free Univ. of Amsterdam. *Publications include:* Brezhnev's Peace Program: a Study of Soviet Domestic Political Process and Power 1982, Uncertain Futures: Eastern Europe and Democracy (ed.) 1990, The Guns Fall Silent: the End of the Cold War and the Future of Conventional Disarmament (co-ed.) 1990, Bound to Change: Consolidating Democracy in East Central Europe (ed.) 1992; numerous articles on security and defence policy in learned journals. *Address:* Centre for European Security Studies, PO Box 716, Groningen, 9700, Netherlands (office). *Telephone:* (50) 3132520 (office). *Fax:* (50) 3132506 (office). *E-mail:* p.m.e.volten@let.rug.nl (office). *Website:* www.let.rug.nl/cess (office).

VON BOMHARD, Nikolaus, DrJur; German insurance industry executive; *Chairman of the Board of Management, Münchener Rückversicherungs-Gesellschaft AG (Munich Re);* b. 28 July 1956, Gunzenhausen; m. Charlotte von Bomhard; two c.; ed Univs of Munich and Regensburg; joined grad. trainee programme, Münchener Rückversicherungs-Gesellschaft AG (Munich Reinsurance Co.) 1985, later worked as underwriter in Operational Div.: Fire/Treat, Deputy Head of Operational Div.: Germany 1992–97, Head, Brazil Office, São Paulo 1997–2000, mem. Bd of Man. 2000–, responsible for Europe 2/Latin America Div. 2001–04, Chair. Bd of Man. 2004–. *Address:* Münchener Rückversicherungs-Gesellschaft AG, Königinstrasse 107, 80802 Munich, Germany (office). *Telephone:* (89) 38910 (office). *Fax:* (89) 399056 (office). *E-mail:* info@munichre.com (office). *Website:* www.munichre.com (office).

VON BRAUN, Joachim, PhD; German agricultural economist, research institute director and academic; *Director General, International Food Policy Research Institute;* b. 10 July 1950, Brakel; m. Dr Barbara von Braun; three d.; ed Univ. of Göttingen; Dir Food Consumption and Nutrition Div., Int. Food Policy Research Inst. (IFPRI), Washington, DC 1990–93, Dir-Gen. IFPRI 2002–; Prof. and Dir Inst. for Food Econs and Consumer Analyses, Univ. of Kiel 1993–97; Dir Centre for Devt Research and Head of Dept of Econs and Technological Change, Univ. of Bonn 1997–2002; Pres. Int. Assen of Agricultural Economists 2000–03; mem. Hunger Task Force, UN Millennium Devt Project 2003–05; Fellow, German Economics Association 1996, AAAS 2006; Hon. Prof., Int. Research Center for Food and Agric. Econs, Nanjing Agricultural Univ., China 2004–; Dr hc (Stuttgart-Hohenheim) 2005; Josef G. Knoll Science Prize 1988. *Publications:* Famine in Africa: Causes, Responses and Prevention (co-author) 1999, Russia's Agro-Food Sector: Towards Truly Functioning Markets (co-ed.) 2000, Agricultural Biotechnology in Developing Countries: Towards Optimizing the Benefits for the Poor (co-author) 2000, Villages in the Future: Crops, Jobs and Livelihood (co-ed.) 2001, Information and Communication Technologies for Development and Poverty Reduction – The Potential of Telecommunications (co-ed.) 2005, Globalization of Food and Agriculture and the Poor (co-ed.) 2008. *Address:* International Food Policy Research Institute, 2033 K Street, NW, Washington, DC 20006, USA (office). *Telephone:* (202) 862-5600 (office). *Fax:* (202) 467-4439 (office). *E-mail:* j.vonbraun@cgiar.org (office). *Website:* www.ifpri.org (office).

VON BÜLOW, Andreas, DJur; German politician and lawyer; b. 17 July 1937, Dresden; s. of Georg-Ulrich Bülow and Susanne von Bülow (née Haym); m. Anna Barbara Duden 1961; two s. two d.; law studies in Heidelberg, Berlin and Munich, studied in France and USA; entered higher admin. service of State of Baden-Württemberg 1966, on staff of Rural Dist Offices of Heidelberg and Balingen, Pres. Admin. Dist of Süd-Württemberg Hohenzollern at Tübingen; mem. Bundestag (Parl.) 1969–94; Parl. State Sec. Fed. Ministry of Defence 1976–80; Fed. Minister for Research and Tech. 1980–82; mem. Social Democratic Party 1960–, Public Services and Transport Workers' Union. *Publications:* Die Überwachung der Erdgasindustrie durch die Federal Power Commission als Beispiel der Funktionen der unabhängigen Wirtschaftsüberwachungskommissionen der amerikanischen Bundesverwaltung 1967 (dissertation), Gedanken zur Weiterentwicklung der Verteidigungsstrategien in West und Ost 1984, Alpträume West gegen Alpträume Ost—ein Beitrag zur Bedrohungsanalyse 1984, Skizzen einer Bundeswehrstruktur der 90er Jahre 1985, Die eingebildete Unterlegenheit—das Kräfteverhältnis West-Ost, wie es wirklich ist 1985, The Conventional Defense of Europe, New Technologies and New Strategies 1986, Im Namen des Staates, CIA, BND und die Kriminellen Machenschaften der Geheimdienste 1998, Die CIA und der 11 September 2003. *Leisure interests:* music, geology, history, swimming, hiking, skiing. *Address:* c/o Sozialdemokratische Partei Deutschlands (SPD), Wilhelmstr. 141, 10963 Berlin, Germany (office).

VON DER DUNK, Hermann Walther; Dutch historian and academic; *Professor Emeritus, University of Utrecht;* b. 9 Oct. 1928, Bonn, Germany; s. of Heinrich M. von der Dunk and Ilse Löb; m. Goverdina Schuurmans Stekhoven 1958; two s. one d.; ed Univ. of Utrecht and Inst. für Europäische Geschichte, Mainz; school teacher, Bilthoven 1961–63; Asst Prof. Dept of History, Univ. of Utrecht 1963–67, Prof. of Contemporary History and Head of Dept 1967–88, Prof. and Head, Dept of Cultural History 1988–90, now Prof. Emer.; mem. Royal Netherlands Acad., Academia Europaea, Dutch Soc. of Science; Grosses Bundesverdienstkreuz 1989, Ridder Nederlandse Leeuw 1991, Vondel Prize 1994, Goethe-Medaille 1995. *Publications:* Der deutsche Vormärz u. Belgien (thesis) 1966, Kleio heeft 1000 ogen (essays) 1974, Conservatisme 1976, De organisatie van het verleden 1982, Voorbij de verboden drempel: de Shoah 1990, Cultuur & Geschiedenis (articles) 1990, Sprekend over identiteit en geschiedenis 1992, Twee buren, twee culturen 1994, Elke tijd is overgangstijd 1996, De verdwijnende hemel. Over de Cultuur van Europa in de twintigste eeuw (two vols) 2000, Mensen, Machten, Mogelijkheden (essays) 2002, In het huis van de herinnering, een cultuurhistorische verkenning 2007, Op schuivende planken.Nederlands perikelen in het licht van zijn verleden.Een essay 2007, Terugblik bij strijklicht.Jeugdherinneringen 2008; articles and contribs to textbooks, journals and newspapers. *Leisure interests:* music (playing piano), drawing and painting, literature. *Address:* Nicolailaan 20, 3723 HS Bilthoven, Netherlands (home). *Telephone:* (30) 2285401 (home). *E-mail:* hwdunk@hotmail.com (home).

VON DOHNÁNYI, Christoph; German conductor; *Chief Conductor, NDR Sinfonieorchester Hamburg;* b. 8 Sept. 1929, Berlin; s. of Hans von Dohnányi and Christine (née Bonhoeffer) von Dohnányi; brother of Klaus von Dohnányi; m. 1st Renate Zillessen; one s. one d.; m. 2nd Anja Silja (q.v.) 1979; one s. two d.; ed Munich Musikhochschule; abandoned legal training to study music 1948; studied in USA under grandfather, Ernst von Dohnányi 1951; répétiteur and conductor under Georg Solti, Frankfurt Oper 1952–56; Gen. Music Dir Lübeck 1957–63, Kassel 1963–66; London debut with London Philharmonic Orchestra 1965; Chief Conductor of Cologne Radio Symphony Orchestra 1964–69; Gen. Music Dir and Opera Dir, Frankfurt 1968–77; Chief Conductor and Intendant, Hamburg State Opera 1977–84; Music Dir (desig.) Cleveland Orchestra 1982–84, Music Dir 1984–2002, Music Dir Laureate 2002–; Prin. Guest Conductor Philharmonia Orchestra 1994, Prin. Conductor 1997–08, Hon. Conductor for Life 2008–; Chief Conductor, NDR Sinfonieorchester Hamburg 2004–(11); numerous guest appearances; numerous recordings of symphonies with Cleveland Orchestra and opera recordings; Commdr, Ordre des Arts et des Lettres; Commdr's Cross, Order of Merit (Germany); Commdr's Cross (Austria); Dr hc (Kent State Univ., Case Western Univ., Oberlin Coll., Eastman School of Music, Cleveland Inst. of Music); Richard Strauss Prize, Bartok Prize, Goethe Medal, Frankfurt, Arts and Science Prize, City of Hamburg, Abraham Lincoln Award. *Address:* Harrison

Parrott, 5–6 Albion Court, London, W6 0QT, England (office). *Telephone:* (20) 7229-9166 (office). *Fax:* (20) 7221-5042 (office). *E-mail:* info@harrisonparrott.co.uk (office). *Website:* www.harrisonparrott.com (office); www.philharmonia.co.uk.

VON DOHNÁNYI, Klaus, DJur, LLB; German politician and political publicist; b. 23 June 1928, Hamburg; s. of Johann-Georg von Dohnányi and Christine (née Bonhoeffer) von Dohnányi; brother of Christoph von Dohnányi; m. Ulla Hahn 1997; two s. one d.; ed Munich, Columbia, Stanford and Yale Univs; fmrly with Ford Motor Co., Detroit, Mich. and Cologne; Dir Planning Div. Ford-Werke, Cologne 1956-60; Dir Inst. für Marktforschung und Unternehmensberatung, Munich 1960–68; Sec. of State, Fed. Ministry of Economy 1968–69; mem. Bundestag 1969–81; Parl. Sec. of State, Ministry of Educ. and Science 1969–72; Minister of Educ. and Science 1972–74; Minister of State and Parl. Sec. of State, Fed. Foreign Office 1976–81, First Burgomaster and Pres. Senate, Hamburg 1981–88; Chair. Bd, TAKRAF AG, Leipzig 1990–94; fmr Co-Chair., Comm. 'Restructuring East Germany'; mem. Club of Rome 1996–, Konvent für Deutschland; mem. SPD; Heuss Medal Theodor Heuss Foundation 1988; Gold Medal for Distinguished Leadership and Service to Humanity, B'nai B'rith 1988, Stolten Medal, Hamburg,. *Publications:* Japanese Strategies 1969, Brief an den Deutschen Demokratischen Revolutionäre 1990, Das Deutsche Wagnis 1990, Im Joch des Profits? (The German Model) 1999. *Leisure interests:* writing, reading. *Address:* Heilwigstrasse 5, 20249 Hamburg, Germany. *Telephone:* (40) 4505789 (office). *Fax:* (40) 4505790 (office).

VON ESCHENBACH, Andrew C., BS, MD; American surgeon and fmr government official; b. Philadelphia, Pa; ed St Joseph's Univ., Phila and Georgetown Univ. School of Medicine, Washington, DC; completed residencies in gen. surgery and urology at Pa Hosp., Phila; fmr Instructor in Urology, Univ. of Pa School of Medicine; served as Lt Commdr in USN Medical Corps; Urologic Oncology Fellow, Univ. of Tex. M.D. Anderson Cancer Center, Houston 1976, mem. Faculty 1977, Chair. Dept of Urology 1983, later Consulting Prof. of Cell Biology and Prof. of Urology, Roy M. and Phyllis Gough Huffington Clinical Research Distinguished Prof. of Urologic Oncology, Vice-Pres. for Academic Affairs and Exec. Vice-Pres. and Chief Academic Officer Univ. of Tex. M.D. Anderson Cancer Center –2002, Founding Dir Prostate Cancer Research Program and Dir Genitourinary Cancer Center; Dir Nat. Cancer Inst., NIH 2002–06; Commr US Food and Drug Admin 2006–09; Founding mem. C-Change; Pres. American Cancer Soc.; mem. editorial bds several leading journals and on several organizational bds; awards from American Medical Writers' Asscn, American Urological Asscn, Uniformed Services Univ. of Health Sciences, included in The Best Doctors in America publs, Medical Award of Excellence, Cancer Counseling, Achievement Awards from 100 Black Men of Metropolitan Houston and Partners in Courage, Julie Rogers 'Spirit of Love' Award. *Publications:* more than 200 articles, books, and book chapters. *Address:* c/o Office of the Commissioner, Food and Drug Administration, 5600 Fishers Lane, Rockville, MD 20857, USA.

VON FIGURA, Kurt, DrMed; German microbiologist, academic and university administrator; *President, Georg-August-Universität Göttingen;* b. 16 May 1944, Heiningen, Baden-Württemberg; m.; four c.; ed Tübingen Univ., Univ. of Vienna; Medical Asst, Bad Wildungen, Tübingen und Munich 1969–70; Scientific Asst, Univ. of Münster Physiologisch-Chemisches Institut 1972–76, Sr Asst 1976–77, Prof. 1977–86; Prof. of Biochemistry, Faculty of Medicine, Georg-August-Universität Göttingen 1986–2004, Pres. 2005–; mem. Deutsche Akademie der Naturforscher Leopoldina 2004–, Max-Planck-Gesellschaft; Dr hc (Namur) 2002; Hoechst AG Prize 1978, Otto-Warburg-Medaille 2002. *Address:* Office of the President, Georg-August-Universität, Wilhelmsplatz 1, 37073 Göttingen, Germany (office). *Telephone:* (551) 39-4311 (office). *Fax:* (551) 39-4135 (office). *E-mail:* praesident@uni-goettingen.de (office). *Website:* www.uni-goettingen.de (office).

VON GRÜNBERG, Hubertus, DSc; German business executive; *Chairman, ABB Ltd;* b. 20 July 1942; ed Univ. of Cologne; began his career with Alfred Teves GmbH (ITT), Frankfurt am Main, various posts in Germany, Brazil and USA 1971–82, Head of Devt and Tech., Frankfurt am Main 1982–84, Chair. Man. Bd 1984–89, Vice-Pres. ITT Corpn, New York, USA 1987–89, Pres. and CEO ITT Automotive Inc., Auburn Hills, Mich., USA 1989–91, Sr Vice-Pres. ITT Corpn; CEO Continental AG 1991–99, Chair. 1999–2007; Chair. ABB Ltd, Zurich 2007–; mem. Bd Dirs Deutsche Telekom AG 2000–, Schindler Holding AG (Switzerland). *Address:* ABB Ltd, Affolternstrasse 44, 8050 Zurich, Switzerland (office). *Telephone:* (43) 317-71-11 (office). *Fax:* (43) 317-44-20 (office). *E-mail:* info@abb.com (office). *Website:* www.abb.com (office).

VON HARBOU, Joachim, 2001; German business executive; *Chairman of the Supervisory Board, Eurohypo AG;* b. 1944; m. Annette von Harbou; three s.; studies in legal science; began career with Dresdner Bank AG 1975, mem. Bd 1996–2001; Chair. of Supervisory Bd Eurohypo AG 2001–; apptd mem. Banking Cttee, Frankfurt Industrie-und-Handelskammer (IHK—Chamber of Trade and Industry) 1998, Chair. and Vice-Pres. 2002–04, Pres. 2004–; mem. Bd of Man. Dirs Dresdner Bank AG; Chair. Frankfurt Arts Soc.; mem. Bd UNICEF Deutschland; Hon. Consul of Czech Repub. for German Fed. State of Hessen. *Leisure interests:* travelling on motorbike through France, French films, spending evenings drinking wine and whisky with friends. *Address:* Eurohypo AG, Helfmann-Park 5, 67760 Eschborn, Germany (office). *Telephone:* 692548-22039 (office). *Fax:* 692548-82039 (office). *Website:* www.eurohypo.com (office).

VON KLITZING, Klaus; German physicist; *Director, Max Planck Institute for Solid State Research;* b. 28 June 1943, Schroda; s. of Bogislav von Klitzing and Anny (née Ulbrich) von Klitzing; m. Renate Falkenberg 1971; two s. one d.; ed Tech. Univ. Brunswick, Univ. Würzburg; Prof., Tech. Univ., Munich 1980–84; Dir Max-Planck Inst. for Solid State Research, Stuttgart 1985–; Nobel Prize for Physics 1985. *Address:* Max-Planck Institut für Festkörperforschung, Heisenbergstr. 1, Postfach 800665, 70506 Stuttgart, Germany (office). *Telephone:* (711) 6891571 (office). *Website:* www.fkf.mpg.de (office).

VON LUCIUS, Wulf D., Dr rer. pol; German scientific publisher; *Publisher and President, Lucius & Lucius Verlag;* b. 29 Nov. 1938, Jena; s. of the late Tankred R. von Lucius and of Annelise Fischer; m. Akka Achelis 1967; three s.; ed Heidelberg, Berlin and Freiburg; mil. service 1958–60; Asst Inst. of Econometrics, Freiburg 1965–66; worked in several publishing houses and as public accountant 1966–69; Partner and Man. Dir Gustav Fischer Verlag 1969–95; mem. Bd of Exec. Officers, German Publrs Asscn (Börsenverein) 1976–86; mem. Bd C. Hanser Verlag 1984–; Publr and Pres. Lucius & Lucius Verlag, Stuttgart 1996–; Chair. Int. Publishers Copyright Council 1995–98, Asscn of Scientific Publrs in Germany 1994–2001; mem. Exec. Cttee Int. Publrs Asscn Geneva 1996–; Bd German Nat. Library 1981–, Bd German Nat. Literary Archive, Marbach 1986–; Friedrich-Perthes-Medaille 1999, Antiquaria Preis 2001, Ludwig Erhard Preis 2004. *Publications:* Bücherlust-Vom Sammeln 2000, Verlagswirtschaft 2005; numerous articles on publishing, copyright and book history. *Leisure interests:* collecting fine prints and artists' books. *Address:* Gerokstrasse 51, 70184 Stuttgart, Germany (office). *Telephone:* (711) 242060 (office). *Fax:* (711) 242088 (office). *E-mail:* lucius@luciusverlag.com (office). *Website:* luciusverlag.com (office).

VON MOLTKE, Gebhardt, LLB; German diplomatist; *Chairman, German-British Society;* b. 28 June 1938, Wernersdorf, Silesia; m. Dorothea von Moltke 1965; one s. one d.; ed Univs of Heidelberg, Grenoble, Berlin, Freiburg im Breisgau; practical legal training 1963–67; with Fed. Foreign Office, Bonn 1968–71, Personnel Admin. 1977–82, Head of US Dept 1986–91; served in Embassy in Moscow 1971–75, in Yaoundé 1975–77, in Washington, DC 1982–86; Asst Sec.-Gen. for Political Affairs NATO 1991–97; Amb. to UK 1997–99; Perm. Rep. to NATO 1999–2003; Chair. German-British Soc. 2003–; Hon. GCVO, Great Cross (Hungary), Grand Cross (Germany), Commdr Cross (Poland), Grand Decoration in Gold with Star (Austria); Hon. DrJur (Birmingham) 2000; US Army Commdr's Award. *Leisure interests:* tennis, music, drawings (old masters).

VON OTTER, Anne-Sofie; Swedish singer (mezzo-soprano); b. 9 May 1955, Stockholm; ed Stockholm Conservatory, Guildhall School of Music and Drama, London, studied interpretation with Erik Werba (Vienna) and Geoffrey Parsons (London), vocal studies with Vera Rozsa; mem. Basel Opera, Switzerland 1982–85; début France at Opéra de Marseille (Nozze de Figaro—Cherubino) and Aix-en-Provence Festival (La Finta Giardiniera) 1984, Rome, Accad. di Santa Cecilia 1984, Geneva (Così fan tutte—Dorabella) 1985, Berlin (Così fan tutte) 1985, USA in Chicago (Mozart's C minor Mass) and Philadelphia (Bach's B minor Mass) 1985, London at Royal Opera, Covent Garden (Le Nozze di Figaro) 1985, Lyon (La Finta Giardiniera) 1986, La Scala, Milan (Alceste) 1987, Munich (Le Nozze di Figaro) 1987, Stockholm (Der Rosenkavalier) 1988, The Metropolitan Opera, New York (Le Nozze di Figaro) 1988, The Royal Albert Hall, London (Faust) 1989, Handel's Ariodante 1997; Glyndebourne (Carmen) 2002, Théâtre des Champs Elysées (Handel's Serse) 2003, Metropolitan Opera, New York (Mélisande) 2005, Santa Fe (Carmen) 2006; repertoire extends from baroque music, German lieder through opera to 20th century music; recorded For the Stars with Elvis Costello 2001; has given recitals in New York, Paris, Brussels, Geneva, Stockholm, Vienna and London; Hon. DSc (Bath) 1992. *Address:* c/o IMG Artists, The Light Box, 111 Power Road, London, W4 5PY, England (office). *Telephone:* (20) 7957-5800 (office). *Fax:* (20) 7957-5801 (office). *E-mail:* sthomson@imgartists.com (office). *Website:* www.imgartists.com (office); www.annesofievonotter.com.

VON PIERER, Heinrich, DrIur, DipEng; German business executive; b. 26 Jan. 1941, Erlangen; m.; three c.; ed Univ. of Erlangen–Nuremberg; Asst, Faculty of Law, Univ. of Erlangen–Nuremberg 1965–69; joined legal dept, Corp. Finance Div., Siemens AG 1969, various commercial assignments in sales and marketing at Kraftwerk Union AG div. and in various corp. depts 1977–1987, apptd Commercial Head Kraftwerk Union AG 1988, Group Pres. Kraftwerk Union AG, mem. Man. Bd Siemens AG 1989, mem. Corp. Exec. Cttee 1990, Deputy Chair. Man. Bd 1991, Chair. Man. Bd, Pres. and CEO 1992–2005, Chair. Supervisory Bd 2005–07; mem. Supervisory Bd Bayer AG 2000–, Hochtief AG 2000–, Münchener Rückversicherungs-Gesellschaft AG (Munich Re) 2000–, Volkswagen AG 2000–; mem. Econ. Cttee RWE AG; Chair. Asien-Pazifik-Ausschuss der Deutschen Wirtschaft (Asia-Pacific Cttee of the German Economy); mem. Bd Bundesverbandes der Deutschen Industrie (Fed. Asscn of German Industry); Chair. Int. Advisory Bd Allianz AG Holding; mem. Senate Max Planck Soc.; Founding mem. UNESCO–Children in Need; Hon. DrIng. *Address:* c/o Siemens AG, Wittelsbacherplatz 2, 80333, Munich, Germany (office).

VON PLOETZ, Hans-Friedrich, DrIur; German diplomatist; *Chairman, Foundation for German–Russian Youth Exchanges;* b. 12 July 1940, Nimptsch; m. Päivi Leinonen; two s.; ed Univs of Marburg, Berlin and Vienna, Austria; Asst Lecturer Univ. of Marburg 1965–66; joined Fed. Foreign Office, Bonn 1966; postings abroad: Trade Mission, German Embassy, Helsinki 1968–73; German Embassy, Washington, DC 1978–80; Perm. Rep. NATO Council 1989–93; Dir-Gen. for European Affairs, Bonn 1993–94; State Sec., Ministry for Foreign Affairs, Bonn and Berlin 1994–99; Amb. to UK 1999–2002, to Russian Fed. 2002–05; Chair. Foundation for German–Russian Youth Exchanges 2006–; mem. Supervisory Bd Bosch GmbH 2008–; strategic business consultant on Russia for several European Cos. *Leisure interests:* music, golf, gardening. *Address:* Schlossstr. 5, 14059 Berlin, Germany (home); Mittelweg 117b, 20149 Hamburg, Germany (office). *Telephone:* (30) 301-091-70 (home); (40) 87 88 679-0 (office). *Fax:* (30) 301 091 72 (office); (40) 87 88 679-

20 (office). *E-mail:* vploetz@web.de (home); info@stiftung-drja.de (office). *Website:* ww.stiftung-drja.de (office).

VON RINGELHEIM, Paul Helmut, BS, MA; American sculptor; b. Vienna, Austria; s. of Henry von Ringelheim and Rosita von Ringelheim (née Altschuler); ed Brooklyn Coll., Fairleigh Dickinson Univ., Art Students League, New York, Acad. of Fine Arts, Munich; teacher of printmaking Brooklyn 1957–58; Prof. of Sculpture School of Visual Arts, New York 1967–71; one-man shows include Niveau Art Gallery, New York 1958, Am Haus, Berlin, Munich and Hamburg 1960–61, Rose Fried Gallery, New York 1964, 1967, Fairleigh Dickinson Univ. 1964, New Vision Galleries, London 1964, New York Cultural Center 1975, O.K. Harris Gallery, New York 1971–73, 1976, 1978, 1980, 1982, Mitzi Landau Gallery, LA 1974, Amarillo Museum of Art 1987, Amarillo Art Center 1987, Robert Berman Gallery, LA 1988, Obelisk Gallery 1992, 1994; has participated in numerous group exhbns internationally; Fulbright scholar 1974–75; mem. Architectural League, New York; Outstanding Young Man of the Year Award, New York World's Fair 1964. *Address:* 9 Great Jones Street, New York, NY 10012-1128, USA. *Telephone:* (212) 777-8757.

VON ROHR, Hans Christoph (see ROHR, Hans Christoph von).

VON ROSSUM, Anton, MBA; Belgian business executive; b. 1945; ed Erasmus Univ., Rotterdam; various consultancy positions in banking and insurance sectors, McKinsey & Co. 1972–2000, co-f. McKinsey & Co. Brussels Office; CEO Fortis 2000–04; mem. Int. Advisory Council, American EC Asscn; mem. Consultative Council, Solvay Business School, Brussels. *Address:* c/o Fortis, Rue Royale 20, 1000 Brussels, Belgium (office).

VON SCHENCK, Michael U. R., DrIur; Swiss diplomatist; b. 21 April 1931, Basel; s. of Dr Ernst von Schenck and Selma Oettinger; ed Humanistisches Gymnasium and Univ., Basel, and in Lausanne; Swiss Trade Fair 1950–55; Die Woche 1950–55; Swiss Foreign Ministry 1957–67, 1973–93, Del. to OECD 1958, Del. to UN 1959–61, UN Narcotics Conf. 1961, Swiss Tech. Assistance Authority 1961–67; Founder and Dir, Swiss Volunteers for Devt 1962–67; Sec.-Gen., Int. Sec. for Volunteer Service 1967–71; Harvard Univ. 1972–73; Rep. to IAEA and UNIDO, Swiss Embassy, Vienna, Austria 1973–77; Head, Econ. Dept, Swiss Embassy, Bonn, Germany 1977–79; Amb. to Ghana (also accred to Liberia, Sierra Leone and Togo) 1979–83, to Finland 1983–86, to Bulgaria 1987–89, to NZ (also accred to Samoa, Tonga and Fiji) 1989–93. *Publications:* Der Statutenwechsel im internationalen Obligationenrecht 1955, Volunteer Manpower for Development 1967, Conferencia Regional sobre Servicio Voluntario 1968, An International Peace Corps 1968, Youth Today 1968, Youth's Role in Development 1968, International Volunteer Service 1969. *Address:* PO Box 641, 4010 Basel 10, Switzerland.

VON SCHLABRENDORFF, Fabian Gotthard Herbert, MA, DrIur; German lawyer; *Partner, Clifford Chance LLP;* b. 23 Dec. 1944, Berlin; s. of Fabian von Schlabrendorff and Luitgarde von Schlabrendorff (née von Bismarck); m. Maria de la Cruz Caballero Palomero 1977; one s. one d.; ed Univs of Tübingen and Berlin, Univ. of Geneva, Switzerland, Univ. of Frankfurt, Univ. of Chicago, USA; service in Bundeswehr 1964–68; Research Co-ordinator, Inst. of Int. and Foreign Trade and Business Law, Frankfurt 1975–82; lawyer with Clifford Chance LLP Frankfurt 1982, Partner 1984; CEPES Award 1987. *Publications:* Mining Ventures in Developing Countries (Parts 1 and 2) (co-author) 1979/81, The Legal Structure of Transnational Forest-Based Investments in Developing Countries (co-author) 1987, Substantive Law in International Long-term Infrastructure Contracts, ADRLJ 3-18 2000, Article 6 of the European Convention on Human Rights and its Bearing upon International Arbitratio, in Liber Amicorum Karl-Heinz Böckstiegel (co-author) 2001, Mehrparteiensituationen und Inter-Omnes-Wirkung, in DIS-Materialien VIII 2001, El Régimen Jurídico del Arbitraje en Alemania, in Anuario de Justicia Alternativa 2003, Geldwäsche in internationalen Schiedsverfahren, in Festschrift Peter Schlosser 2005, Conflict of Legal Privileges in International Arbitration (co-author) in Liber Amicorum Robert Briner 2005, SchiedsVZ (German Arbitration Journal), Parallele Verfahren, Aufnahme von Dritten, Verbindung von Verfahren: Erfahrungen aus der Praxis in der ICC, in Schriftreihe der Deutschen Institution für Schiedsgerichtsbarkeit, Band 16, Die Beteiligung Dritter an Schiedsverfahren (co-ed) 2005, Legal Privilege and Confidentiality in Arbitration (co-author) in Privilege and Confidentiality: An International Handbook 2006. *Leisure interest:* classical music. *Address:* Clifford Chance LLP, Mainzer Landstrasse 46, 60325 Frankfurt am Main, Germany (office). *Telephone:* (69) 7199-01 (office). *Fax:* (69) 7199-4000 (office). *E-mail:* fabian.schlabrendorff@cliffordchance.com (office). *Website:* www.cliffordchance.com (office).

VON STADE, Frederica; American mezzo-soprano; b. 1 June 1945, Somerville, NJ; m. 1st Peter Elkus 1973 (divorced); two d.; m. 2nd Michael G. Gorman 1991; ed Mannes Coll. of Music, New York; opera début with Metropolitan Opera, New York (in Le Nozze di Figaro) 1970; has also sung with Paris Opera, San Francisco Opera, Lyric Opera of Chicago, LA Opera, Salzburg Festival, Covent Garden, London, Spoleto Festival, Boston Opera Co., Santa Fe Opera, Houston Grand Opera, La Scala, Milan, Vienna State Opera; recital and concert artist; Officier, Ordre des Arts et des Lettres 1998; Dr hc (Yale Univ.), (Boston Univ.), (Georgetown Univ. School of Medicine), (Mannes School of Music), (San Francisco Conservatory of Music); two Grand Prix du Disc awards, Deutsche Schallplattenpreis, Premio della Critica Discografica and many other awards and prizes. *Recordings:* over 70 albums include Frederica von Stade Sings Mozart and Rossini Opera Arias, French Opera Arias, Songs of the Cat with Garrison Keillor. *Address:* c/o Matthew Horner, IMG Artists, Carnegie Hall Tower, 142 West 57th Street, 5th Floor, New York, NY 10019, USA (office). *Telephone:* (212) 994-3514 (office). *E-mail:* artistsny@imgartists.com (office). *Website:* www.imgartists.com (office).

VON SYDOW, Björn, MS, PhD; Swedish political scientist, academic and politician; *Principal, School of Social Work and Public Administration;* b. 26 Nov. 1945, Stockholm; s. of Bengt Sköldenberg and Tullia von Sydow; m. Madeleine von Sydow; three s. one d.; ed Stockholm and Linköping Univs; worked as librarian 1970–74; Lecturer in Political Science, Linköping Univ. 1974–78; Assoc. Prof. of Political Science, Stockholm Univ. 1978–83, 1992–96; Prin. School of Social Work and Public Admin 1983–88, 2006–; work on study of gen. election of Bd Dirs Nat. Pension Insurance Fund 1984–86; Visiting Research Scientist, Case Western Reserve Univ., Ohio 1986, Pomona and Scripps Colls Clairmont, Calif. 1992; active in municipal politics in Solna 1979–96, Chair. Swedish Social Democratic Party (SAP), Solna 1983–2000; mem. Editorial Cttee Tiden (political journal) 1983–89; mem. SAP programme comm. 1987–2001; mem. Riksdag (Parl.) 1994–, Speaker 2002–06; mem. Parl. Cttee on Constitutional Affairs 1994–96, mem. SI Cttee on Econ. Policy, Devt and Environment 1995–96, Chair. SAP Cttee on EU Affairs, mem. IGC and EU Enlargement Cttee of Party of European Socialists, Chair. EU Cttee of Nordic Labour Movt (SAMAK) 1996–98; Head of Political Planning responsible for Research and Devt, Econ. Growth and Environment, Office of Prime Minister 1988–91; mem. Cttee on Civil Rights, Ministry of Justice 1993–94; Chair. Cttee on Environmental Protection, Ministry of Environment 1994–96, Parl. Cttee preparing EU Treaty revision, Ministry for Foreign Affairs 1995–96; Minister of Trade at Ministry for Industry and Commerce 1996–97; Minister of Defence 1997–2002; Chair. Univ. Centre for Physics and Astronomy, Stockholm 1992–95, Swedish Research Council 2007–; mem. Swedish Del. to Parl. Ass. of Council of Europe 2007. *Publications:* Parliamentarism in Sweden: Development and Forms up to 1945 1997, The Swedish Defence Decision and the Swedish View of the European Security Structures 1997, Defence up to Date: National and International Hand in Hand 1998, Sweden's Security in the 21st Century 1999. *Leisure interest:* horse riding. *Address:* Sveriges Riksdag, 100 12 Stockholm (office); Riddarhustorget 7–9, Stockholm, Sweden (home). *Telephone:* (8) 70-576-17-29 (mobile); (8) 786-42-10 (office); (8) 786-40-00. *E-mail:* bjorn.von.sydow@riksdagen.se (office). *Website:* www.riksdagen.se (office).

VON TRIER, Lars; Danish film director; b. 30 April 1956; s. of Ulf Trier and Inger Trier; m. 1st Cæcilia Holbek Trier (divorced); two c.; m. 2nd Bente Frøge 1997; ed Danish Film School; Co-founder and Head, Dogme School of Film 1995–. *Films include:* Orchidégartneren (The Orchid Gardener) 1977, Menthe - la bienheureuse 1979, Nocturne 1980, Den Sidste Detalje (The Last Detail) 1981, Befrielsesbilleder 1982, Forbrydelsens element (The Element of Crime; Cannes Film Festival Technical Grand Prize) 1984, Europa (aka Zentropa) 1991, Epidemic 1988, The Kingdom 1994, Breaking the Waves (Cannes Film Festival Grand Prize) 1996, The Idiots 1998, Dancer in the Dark (Cannes Film Festival Palme d'Or) 2000, Dogville 2003, Dear Wendy (script) 2005, Manderlay 2005, Direktøren for det hele (The Boss Of It All) 2006. *Publication:* Trier on Von Trier 2004. *Address:* Zentropa, Filmbyen 22, 2650 Hvidovre, Denmark. *Telephone:* 36868788 (office). *Fax:* 36868789 (office). *E-mail:* zentropa@filmbyen.com (office). *Website:* www.dogme95.dk.

VON TROTTA, Margarethe; German film director and actress; b. 21 Feb. 1942, Berlin; has written scripts for The Sudden Wealth of the Poor People of Kombach 1971, Summer Lightning 1972, Fangschuss 1974, Unerreichbare Nahe 1984. *Films include:* Die Verlorene Ehre der Katharina Blum (The Lost Honour of Katharina Blum) 1975, Das zweite Erwachen der Christa Klages (The Second Awakening of Christa Klages) 1978, Schwestern, oder die Balance des Glücks (Sisters, or the Balance of Happiness) 1979, Die Bleierne Zeit (The German Sisters) 1981, Heller Wahn (Friends and Husbands) 1983, Rosa Luxemburg 1985, Felix 1987, Paura e amore (Love and Fear) 1988, L'Africana 1990, Il lungo silenzio 1992, Das Versprechen (The Promise) 1994, Winterkind (TV) 1996, Dunkle Tage (TV) 1999, Rosenstrasse 2003, Die Andere Frau (The Other Woman) (TV) 2004, Ich bin die Andere 2006. *Television includes:* Jahrestage (miniseries) 2000.

VON WILPERT, Gero, PhD, FAHA; Australian academic; *Professor Emeritus of German, University of Sydney;* b. 13 March 1933, Dorpat, Estonia; s. of Arno von Wilpert and Gerda Baumann; m. Margrit Laskowski 1953; three s.; ed Univs of Heidelberg and NSW; publrs' reader and literary dir, Stuttgart 1957–72; Sr Lecturer in German, Univ. of New South Wales 1973–78, Assoc. Prof. 1978–81; McCaughey Prof. of German, Univ. of Sydney 1982–94, now Prof. Emer. *Publications include:* Sachwörterbuch der Literatur 1955, Deutsche Literatur in Bildern 1957, Schiller-Chronik 1958, Deutsches Dichterlexikon 1963, Der verlorene Schatten 1978, Die deutsche Gespenstergeschichte 1994, Goethe-Lexikon 1998, Deutschbaltische Literaturgeschichte 2005, Goethe 2007, Schiller 2009. *Leisure interests:* 18th century French art and antiques. *Address:* Werrington House, Werrington, NSW 2747, Australia (home). *Telephone:* (2) 9623-1026 (home).

VONDRA, Alexandr, RNDr; Czech diplomatist, academic and consultant; *Deputy Prime Minister, responsible for European Affairs;* b. 17 Aug. 1961, Prague; m. Martina Vondrova; three c.; ed Charles Univ.; worked at Naprstek Museum of Asian, African and American Cultures, Prague 1985–87; also active in Czechoslovakia's democratic opposition mid-1980s; fmr man. rock band Narodni trida; Spokesperson for Charter 77 1989; Co-founder Civic Forum movt 1989; Foreign Policy Adviser to Pres. Václav Havel 1990–92; First Deputy Minister of Int. Affairs 1992, First Deputy Minister of Foreign Affairs 1993–97, chief negotiator in process of preparing Czech-German Declaration 1995–96; Amb. to USA 1997–2001; Czech Govt Commr to Prague NATO Summit (coordinated Prague NATO Summit 2002) 2001–02; Deputy Minister of Foreign Affairs 2003; Asst Lecturer, German Marshall Fund 2003–04; Man. Dir Dutko Worldwide (consulting firm), Prague 2004–06; Minister of Foreign Affairs June–Oct. 2006 (resgnd); elected Senator (ODS) for Litoměřice, Roudnice and Slaný regions 2006; Deputy Prime Minister, responsible for European Affairs 2007–; Adjunct Prof., New York Univ. in Prague; Pres. Czech Euro-Atlantic Council; mem. Bd of Dirs Program of Atlantic Security Studies (PASS), Prague; Hon. Chair. Czech Euro-Atlantic Council 2004–06; Gold Plaque (Slovakia) 2001, Cross of Merit (Czech Repub.) 2002, Cross of Order of Merit (Poland) 2004, Commdr of the Three Stars (Latvia) 2005; US Nat. Endowment for Democracy Medal 1999, NATO Meritorious Service Medal 2005, Award for Human Understanding, Tolerance and Peace 2006. *Address:* Office of the Government, náb. E. Beneše 4, 118 01 Prague 1, Czech Republic (office). *Telephone:* 224002111 (office). *Fax:* 224003090 (office). *E-mail:* posta@vlada.cz (office). *Website:* www.vlada.cz (office).

VONDRAN, Ruprecht, DrIur; German business executive and politician (retd); *Chairman, German-Japanese Industrial Co-operation Committee;* b. 31 Dec. 1935, Göttingen; s. of Rudolf Vondran and Anneliese Unterberg; m. Jutta Paul 1970; two s. two d.; ed Univs. of Göttingen, Bonn and Würzburg; mem. Bundestag 1987–94; Pres., Wirtschaftsvereinigung Stahl 1988–2000, Verband Deutsch–Japanischer Gesellschatten; Chair., German-Japanese Industrial Co-operation Cttee, Poensgen-Stiftung; Order of the Rising Sun (Gold and Silver stars), Japan; Hon. DEng. *Publication:* Der politische Auftrag der Nato und seine Verwirklichung 1966, Wie bewältigt die japanische Wirtschaft ihre Anpassungsprobleme? 1996, Stahl ist Zukunft 1999, Warum Japan? 2005, Deutschland in Japan 2005/2006: was hat es gebracht? 2006, Für ein weltoffenes Deutschland, Japan und China: Auf der Suche nad einer neuen Ordnung. *Leisure interests:* modern graphics, Japanese porcelain. *Address:* Urdenbacher Allee 63, 40593 Düsseldorf, Germany (home). *Telephone:* (211) 7182231 (office). *Fax:* (211) 7118734 (office).

VORA, Motilal; Indian politician; *Member, Rajya Sabha;* b. 29 Dec. 1928, Nagor, Rajasthan; s. of Mohanlal Vora; m. Shanti Vora; two s. four d.; fmr journalist; elected Councillor, Durg Municipality 1968, Congress Party mem. Madhya Pradesh Vidhan Sabha 1972–90; Minister of State for Educ. and Minister for Local Govt 1981–82; Minister of Transport, Science and Tech. 1982–83, of Higher Educ. 1983–84, of Health and Family Welfare and Civil Aviation 1988–89; Pres. Madhya Pradesh Congress (I) Cttee 1984–85; elected Leader Congress (I) Legis. Party 1985; Chief Minister Madhya Pradesh 1985–88, Jan.–Dec. 1989; Gov. of UP 1993–96; mem. Lok Sabha 1998–99, mem. Cttee on Home Affairs; mem. Rajya Sabha 2002–. *Address:* 33 Lodhi Estate, New Delhi 110011, India (office). *Telephone:* (11) 24651313 (office). *E-mail:* vora@sansad.nic.in (office). *Website:* rajyasabha.nic.in (office).

VOROBYEV, Andrei Ivanovich, DrMed; Russian haematologist; *Director, Haematological Scientific Centre, Russian Academy of Medical Sciences;* b. 1 Oct. 1928; m.; two s.; ed First Inst. of Medicine; worked as house-painter 1941–44; practitioner, Head of Polyclinics Volokolamsk Moscow Region 1953–54; Prof. Cen. Inst. of Advanced Medical Studies 1956–66; Head of Div., Inst. of Biophysics 1966–84; mem. Acad. of Medical Sciences 1986; Dir All-Union (now All-Russian) Scientific Cen. of Haematology 1987–91; Minister of Health of Russia 1991–92; Dir Haematological Scientific Centre, Russian Acad. of Medical Sciences 1993–; Ed.-in-Chief Gematologiya i Transfuziologiya; USSR State Prize. *Leisure interest:* history of Russian Acad. of Science. *Address:* Haematological Scientific Centre, Novy Zhukovsky pr. 4A, 125167 Moscow, Russia (office). *Telephone:* (495) 212-21-23 (office). *Fax:* (495) 438-18-00 (office). *E-mail:* tt@blood.ru (office).

VOROBYEV, Yuri Leonidovich; Russian politician and engineer; b. 2 Feb. 1948, Krasnoyarsk; m.: two s.; ed Krasnoyarsk Inst. of Non-Ferrous Metals; mem. staff Krasnoyarsk plant; Sec. Sosnovoborsk dist. CPSU Cttee, Krasnoyarsk 1971–88, instructor Krasnoyarsk regional CPSU Cttee 1988–90; Dir-Gen. Foundation for Protection of Small Business and Devt of Econ. Reforms 1990–91; Deputy Chair. Russian Rescue Corps 1991–92; First Deputy Chair. Russian Fed. State Cttee on Problems of Civil Defence and Emergency Situations 1992–94; First Deputy Minister of Civil Defence and Emergency Situations 1994, now Asst. Dir; Head of Internal Anti-Corruption Comm. 2004; mem. Tech. Comm. at Russian Presidency 1993–; Order for Personal Courage. *Leisure interests:* sports, tourism. *Address:* c/o Ministry of Civil Defence and Emergency Situations, Teatralny pr. 3, 103012 Moscow, Russia (office).

VORONENKOVA, Galina, DPhil, DrHabil; Russian academic; *Professor, Faculty of Journalism, Moscow State University;* b. 30 Jan. 1947, Kostroma Region; d. of late Fyodor Smirnov and Alexandra Smirnova; m. Mikhail Voronenkov; one d.; ed Moscow State Univ., Leipzig Univ., GDR; literary contrib. to local Kostroma Region newspaper 1965–67; mem. staff, Journalism Dept, Moscow State Univ. 1974–87; teacher of Russian language, House of Soviet Science and Culture, Berlin, GDR and Business Man. Journalists' Club, Berlin 1987–90; reporter for Soviet Women, Germany 1990–92; Prof., Faculty of Journalism, Moscow State Univ. 1992–, Dir Free Russian-German Inst. for Publishing 1994–; Corresp. mem. Acad. of Information and Communication; Fed. Council of Russian Fed. Award 1996. *Publications include:* Bürger in der Demokratie (Russian ed.) 1997, Sredstva massovoy Informatii Germanii v 90-e gody 1998, Neue Technologien und die Entwicklung der Medien in Russland und Deutschland (Russian ed.) 1998, Ot rukopisnogo listka do informattonnogo obtschestva 1999, Russland vor den Wahlen: Die Rolle der Medien bei den Wahlen – ein deutsch-russischer Vergleich (Russian ed.) 2000, Put' dlinoju v rjat' stoletij (monograph). *Leisure interests:* classical music, world history, science fiction. *Address:* Faculty of Journalism, Moscow State University, 103009 Moscow, Mochovaya ul. 9, Apt 235, K-9 6SP (office); 125047 Moscow, Fadeyva ul. 6, Apt 60, Russia (home). *Telephone:* (495) 203-26-43 (office); (495) 251-97-76 (home). *Fax:* (495) 251-97-76 (home); (495) 203-26-43 (office). *E-mail:* frdip@journ.msu.ru (office); galina-w@dataforce.net (home). *Website:* www.journ.msu.ru (office); www.frdip.ru (office).

VORONIN, Vladimir Nikolayevich; Moldovan politician and head of state; *President;* b. 25 May 1941, Corjova, Chişinău Dist; m.; two c.; ed Tech. Coll., Chişinău, Union Inst. of the Alimentary Industry, Acad. of Social Sciences, Cen. CPSU Cttee, Acad. of Ministry of Internal Affairs; bakery man., Criuleni 1961–66, Dubăsari 1966–71; fmr Deputy to Supreme Council, Moldovan SSR, First Sec., Party Cttee, Bender (Tighina) 1985–89, Minister of Internal Affairs, Moldovan SSR 1989–90; mem. Police Reserve, Russian Fed. 1989–93; Co-Pres. Organizational Cttee for Consolidation of CP 1993; revived CP Party of Moldova as Party of Communists of the Republic of Moldova 1994; presidential cand. (placed third) 1996; Deputy in Parl. Repub. of Moldova 1998; Pres. of Moldova 2001–. *Address:* Office of the President, 2073 Chişinău, bd Ştefan cel Mare 154, Moldova (office). *Telephone:* (22) 23-47-93 (office). *E-mail:* president@prm.md (office). *Website:* www.president.md (office).

VORONKOV, Mikhail Grigorievich, DrChemSc; Russian chemist; *Head of Department, Institute of Silicate Chemistry, St Petersburg;* b. 6 Dec. 1921, Orel; s. of Grigorii Vasilievich and Raisa Mikhailovna Voronkov; m. Lilia Iliinichna Makhnina 1943; one s. one d.; ed Leningrad Univ.; Sr Scientist, Chemical Dept, Leningrad Univ. 1944–54; Head of Lab., Inst. of Chem. of Silicates, USSR Acad. of Sciences 1954–61; Head of Lab. Inst. of Organic Synthesis, Latvian Acad. of Sciences 1961–70; Dir Inst. of Organic Chem., Siberian Br. of USSR (now Russian) Acad. of Sciences, Irkutsk 1970–94; Scientific Adviser 1994–; Head of Dept, Inst. of Silicate Chem., St Petersburg 2002–; Corresp. mem. USSR (now Russian) Acad. of Sciences 1970, mem. 1990; Corresp. mem. Latvian Acad. of Sciences 1966–91, Foreign mem. 1991–; mem. Braunschweig Scientific Soc., FRG 1976, Asia-Pacific Acad. of Advanced Materials 1992; Prof. Emer., Ulan Bator Univ., Mongolia; mem. Emer. Florida Center of Heterocyclic Chem., USA 1998; Hon. Chemist of the USSR 1983; Honoured Mem. Mongolian Acad. of Sciences; five orders and 20 medals for services to the motherland; Dr hc (Gdansk Tech. Univ., Poland); Laureate, State Prize of Ukrainian SSR 1981, Prize of the USSR Council of Ministers 1991, Laureate, State Prize of Russia 1997, Laureate, A.N. Nesmeyanov Prize of Russian Acad. of Sciences 2003, A.N. Kost Medal for outstanding achievements in the chem. of heterocyclic compounds. *Publications:* more than 3,800 scientific papers, including 45 monographs and 50 patents. *Leisure interests:* numismatics, humour in chemistry. *Address:* A.E. Favorsky Irkutsk Institute of Chemistry, 1 Favorsky Street, 664033 Irkutsk (office); Lermontova Street, 297B-196, 664033 Irkutsk, Russian Federation (home). *Telephone:* (3952) 42-64-00 (office); (3952) 42-85-81 (home). *Fax:* (3952) 51-19-26 (office); (3952) 41-93-46 (office). *E-mail:* voronkov@irioch.irk.ru (office).

VOROSHILO, Aleksander Stepanovich; Russian singer (baritone), theatre manager and business executive; b. 15 Dec. 1944, Dniepropetrovsk region, Ukraine; m. Svetlana Voroshilo; one d.; ed Odessa State Conservatory; served in the army; began vocal studies 1969; soloist Odessa Opera Theatre 1972–75, Bolshoi Theatre, Moscow 1975–91; ended singing career 1991; employee sausage production cos 1992–; owner of two meat processing, sausage production plants 1997–; Exec. Dir Bolshoi Theatre 2000–02; Gen. Dir Moscow Int. House of Music 2002–2003; USSR State Prize, USSR Peoples' Artist. *Opera:* leading roles in Bolshoi Theatre include Onegin in Eugene Onegin, Chichikov in Dead Souls, Iago in Othello and Rigoletto in Rigoletto. *Address:* c/o Moscow Int. House of Music, Kosmodamianskaya Naberezhnaya 52, Bldg 8, 115054 Moscow, Russia (office).

VORRES, Ian, MA; Canadian/Greek art museum president; *President, Vorres Museum;* b. 19 Sept. 1924, Athens; s. of Andrew Vorres and Stephanie Vorres; one adopted c.; ed Queen's Univ. and Toronto Univ.; Founder and Pres. Bd Vorres Museum 1983–; Mayor of Paiania 1991–98; decorations from the govts of Portugal, Austria and Finland; Hon. DFA (American Coll. of Greece). *Publication:* The Last Grand Duchess (biog. of Grand Duchess Olga of Russia) 1964. *Leisure interests:* collection of antiques, collection of contemporary Greek art, writing, architecture, gardening. *Address:* Vorres Museum, 190 02 Paiania, Attica, Greece (home). *Telephone:* (210) 6642520 (home); (210) 6644771 (home). *Fax:* (210) 6645775 (home). *E-mail:* mvorres@otenet.gr (home).

VOSCHERAU, Henning, LLD; German politician; b. 13 Aug. 1941, Hamburg; m.; three c.; qualified as notary public; joined SPD 1966; mem. Borough of Wandsbek Dist Ass. 1970–74, Chief Whip SPD Parl. Group 1971–74; mem. Hamburg City Parl., mem. SPD Parl. Exec. Cttee 1974–, Deputy Chair. 1976–82, Chair. 1982–87, Chair. City Parl. Cttee on Home Affairs 1974–82, Deputy Party Chair. SPD, Hamburg 1981–89; First Mayor and Pres. of Senate, City of Hamburg 1988–97; Pres. Bundesrat 1990–91; Chair. Jt Comm. for Reform of the Fed. Constitution 1992–93; SPD Speaker on Financial Policy 1995–97; Chair. Mediation Cttee 1996–97. *Address:* Alstertor 14, 20095 Hamburg, Germany.

VOSGANIAN, Varujan, PhD; Romanian politician; b. 25 July 1958, Craiova; m. Mihaela Vosganian; one d.; ed Acad. of Econ. Sciences, Bucharest and Bucharest Univ.; Assoc. Prof., Acad. of Econ. Sciences, Bucharest; Sr Researcher, Nat. Inst. of Economy; Deputy, Romanian Parl. 1990–96, Senator 1996–2000, 2004–, Chair. Cttee on Budget, Finances, Banking Activity and Capital Markets 1996–98; mem. Romanian Del. to Parl. Ass. of the Council of Europe (APCE) 2004–, mem. Political and Econ. Comms 2004–; Minister of the Economy 2006–08, also of Finance 2007–08; mem. Nat. Liberal Party (PNL), Vice-Pres. 2007–; Founding mem. Romanian Soc. of the Economy (SOREC); Vice-Pres. Romanian Writers Union 2005–; Hon. mem. Scientific Council, Nat. Inst. of Prognosis, Romania; Dr hc (Vasile Goldis Univ.) 2006, (Leibniz Univ., Milan) 2006; Special Prize for Poetry, Nichita Stanescu Int. Poem Festival 2006, Prize for Excellency for Contrib. to the Devt of Capital Markets in Romania, Bucharest Stock Exchange 2006, Prize for Contrib. to Devt of Romanian Science and Culture, Romanian Acad. 2006. *Publications include:* more then 500 econ., political and literary articles, studies, essays and poems. *Address:* National Liberal Party (NLP), 011866 Bucharest, Bd. Aviatorilor 86, Romania (office). *Telephone:* (21) 2310795 (office). *Fax:* (21) 2310796 (office). *E-mail:* dre@pnl.ro (office); *Website:* www.pnl.ro (office); www.varujanvosganian.ro.

VOTRON, Jean-Paul, MA; Belgian banking executive; b. 1951; m.; two c.; ed Institut Catholique des Hautes Etudes Commerciale, Brussels; began career at Unilever 1975, various man. positions in sales, marketing and gen. man. 1975–91; joined Citibank 1991, served as Pres. Citibank Belgium, Marketing Dir for Europe, Dir for Marketing and Tech. US and European Consumer Bank, Dir of Insurance for USA, Head of US Investment Business, Chair. and CEO Citibank FSB (br. network in USA) –1997; Sr Exec. Vice-Pres. Int. Consumer Banking and E-Commerce, ABN-AMRO 1997–2001; apptd mem. Man. Cttee Citigroup 2002, CEO Citigroup Retail Bank for Western Europe, Cen. Europe, Russia, Middle E and Africa 2002–04; CEO Fortis NV and Chair. Fortis Bank and Fortis Insurance 2004–08 (resgnd); The Business Leader of the Year, European Business Awards Conf. and Ceremony 2007. *Address:* c/o Fortis NV, Archimedeslaan 6, 3584 Utrecht, Belgium. *Telephone:* (30) 2576576. *Website:* www.fortis.com.

VOURLOUMIS, Panagis; Greek business executive and banker; *Chairman and CEO, Hellenic Telecommunications Organization SA;* b. 1937; ed London School of Econs, UK; Head, SE Asia Div., International Finance Corpn 1966–73; Head, Commercial Bank of Greece Group 1979–81; fmr Dir Panagis Vourloumis & Assocs, Financial Advisors; fmr Chair. Askbali.com travel group; Chair. and CEO Alpha Finance, Alpha Mutual Funds and Alpha Bank Romania 1988–2000, Exec. Dir Alpha Bank 1988–2000; Chair. Frigoglass 2000–04, Aegean Baltic Bank 2000–04; Chair. and CEO Hellenic Telecommunications Org. SA 2004–, Cosmote Mobile Telecommunications SA; mem. Trilateral Comm. 1998–. *Address:* Hellenic Telecommunications Organization SA, 99 Kifissias Avenue, Amaroussion, 15181 Athens, Greece (office). *Telephone:* (210) 611-1574 (office). *Fax:* (210) 611-1030 (office). *Website:* www.ote.gr (office).

VOUTILAINEN, Pertti Juhani, MSc; Finnish banker and business executive; *Chairman, Technopolis plc;* b. 22 June 1940, Kuusjärvi; s. of Otto Voutilainen and Martta Voutilainen; m. Raili Juvonen 1963; two s.; ed Helsinki Univ. of Tech., Helsinki School of Econs, Pennsylvania State Univ., USA; joined Outokumpu Oy 1964, Man. Corp. Planning 1973–76, Dir Corp. Planning 1976–78, mem. Bd 1978–91, Pres. 1980–91, Chair. Exec. Bd 1983–91; fmr Chair. and CEO Kansallis-Osake-Pankki (to merge with Unitas Ltd) 1992; fmr Pres. Merita Nordbanken; Vice-Chair. Technopolis plc 2003–05, Chair. 2005–; Commdr Order of Lion of Finland. *Leisure interests:* hunting, fishing. *Address:* Technopolis PLC, Elektroniikkatie 8, 90570 Oulu, Finland (office). *Telephone:* (8) 5513211 (office). *Fax:* (8) 5513210 (office). *Website:* www.technopolis.fi (office).

VOYNET, Dominique; French physician and politician; *Mayor of Montreuil;* b. 4 Nov. 1958, Montbéliard, Doubs; d. of Jean Voynet and Monique Richard; two d.; ed Faculty of Medicine, Besançon; anaesthetist and intensive care specialist, Dole (Jura) public hosp. 1985–89; activist in several ecological and other orgs, Belfort and Besançon 1976–; Co-Founder Les Verts ('Green' Movt) 1984, Gen. Sec. Green Group in European Parl. 1989–91, Nat. Spokesperson 1991–02, Nat. Sec. 2001–02; Municipal Councillor, Dole 1989–2004; mem. regional council Franche-Comté 1992–94 (resgnd); cand. in presidential election 1995, 2007; elected Deputy (Les Verts and Parti Socialiste) for Dole-Arbois, Nat. Ass. 1997, Minister for Town and Country Planning and the Environment 1997–2001; Councillor-Gen. Jura 1998–2004; Senator for Seine-Saint Denis 2004–; Mayor of Montreuil 2008–. *Address:* Sénat, Casier de la Poste, 15 rue de Vaugirard, 75291 Paris Cedex 06, France (office). *E-mail:* d.voynet@senat.fr (office). *Website:* dominiquevoynet.net.

VOYNOVICH, Vladimir Nikolayevich; Russian author, playwright and film scriptwriter; b. 26 Sept. 1932, Stalinabad (now Dushanbe), Tajikistan; s. of Nikolai Pavlovich Voinovich and Rosa (née Goikhman) Voinovich; m. 1st Valentina Voinovich; one s. one d.; m. 2nd Irina Braude 1970; one d.; served in Soviet Army 1951–55; worked as carpenter 1956–57; studied Moscow Pedagogical Inst. 1958–59; started literary activity (and song-writing for Moscow Radio) 1960; various dissident activities 1966–80; expelled from USSR Writers' Union 1974; elected mem. French PEN Centre 1974; emigrated from USSR 1980; USSR citizenship restored 1990; mem. Bavarian Acad. of Fine Arts. *Publications include:* The Life and Unusual Adventures of Private Ivan Chonkin (samizdat 1967) 1975 (English trans. 1977), Ivankiada 1976, By Way of Mutual Correspondence 1979, Pretender to the Throne 1981, Moscow–2042 1987, The Fur Hut 1989, The Zero Decision 1990, Case N3484 1992, The Conception 1994, Tales for Adults 1996, By Means of Mutual Correspondence 1998, Monumental Propaganda 2004.

VOZNESENSKY, Andrey Andreyevich; Russian poet; *Vice-President, Russian PEN Centre;* b. 12 May 1933, Moscow; s. of Andrey N. Voznesensky and Antonina S. Voznesensky; m. Zoya Boguslavskaya 1965; one s.; ed Moscow Architectural Inst.; mem. Union of Soviet Writers, mem. Bd 1967–; Vice-Pres. Soviet (now Russian) PEN Centre 1989–; Hon. mem. American Acad. of Arts and Letters 1972, Bayerischen Kunst Akad., French Acad. Merimé; Int. Award for Distinguished Achievement in Poetry 1978, State Prize 1978. *In English:* Selected Poems 1964, Anti-worlds 1966, Anti-worlds and the Fifth Ace 1967, Dogalypse 1972, Story under Full Sail 1974, Nostalgia for the Present 1978. *Publications:* poems: The Masters 1959, Forty Lyrical Digressions from a Triangular Pear 1962, Longjumeau 1963, Oza 1964, Story Under Full Sail 1970, Ice-69 1970, Queen of Clubs 1974, The Eternal Flesh 1978, Andrey Polisadov 1980, Unaccountable 1981, The Ditch 1981; collections: Parabola 1960, Mosaic 1960, Anti-Worlds 1964, Heart of Achilles 1966, Verses 1967, The Shadow of a Sound 1970, The Glance 1972, Let The Bird Free 1974, Violoncello Oak Leaf 1975, The Master of Stained Glass 1976, Temptation 1978, Metropol (poetry and prose, co-author with 22 others) 1979, Selected Poems 1979, Collected Works (Vols 1–3) 1984, Aksioma Samoiska 1990, Videomes 1992, Rossia-Casino 1997, On the Virtual Wind 2000. *Address:* Kotelnicheskaya nab. 1/15, korp. B., Apt. 62, Moscow 109240, Russia. *Telephone:* (495) 915-49-90.

VRAALSEN, Tom Eric, MEcon; Norwegian diplomatist; *Special Envoy for Humanitarian Affairs for the Sudan, United Nations Department of Peacekeeping Operations;* b. 26 Jan. 1936, Oslo; m.; five c.; ed Århus School of Econs and Business Admin., Denmark; joined Norwegian Foreign Service 1960; various diplomatic positions, Beijing 1962–64, 1969–70, Cairo 1964–67, Manila 1970–71, Jakarta 1971; in charge of Norwegian relations with Africa, Asia and Latin America, Political Dept, Ministry of Foreign Affairs 1971–73, in charge of UN and int. org. affairs 1973–75; Deputy Perm. Rep. to UN 1975–79, Perm. Rep. 1982–89; Dir-Gen. Political Dept, Ministry of Foreign Affairs 1981–82; Minister for Devt Co-operation, for Nordic Co-operation 1989–90; Sr Vice-Pres. Saga Petroleum 1991–92; Asst Sec.-Gen. Ministry of Foreign Affairs 1992–94; Amb. to UK 1994–96, to USA 1996–2001, to Finland 2001–03; UN Special Envoy for Humanitarian Affairs for the Sudan 1998–; Dr hc (Augustana Coll.) 2000. *Publications:* UN in Focus (co-author) 1975, The UN: Dream and Reality 1984. *Address:* Department of Peace-Keeping Operations, Room S-3727-B, United Nations, New York, NY 10017, USA (office). *Telephone:* (212) 963-8079 (office). *Fax:* (212) 963-9222 (office). *Website:* www.un.org/Depts/dpko (office).

VRABIE, Vitalie; Moldovan politician; *Minister of Defence;* b. 2 Oct. 1964, Costuleni Village, Ungheni Dist; m.; two c.; ed Agricultural Inst., Chişinău, Acad. of Public Admin, Moscow; began career as Sr Agronomist, Prut Farm; Dir JSV Garant-impex, Ungheni 1994–99; mem. Ungheni City Council 1995–99, fmr Dir Office of Chamber of Commerce and Industry; elected Mayor of Ungheni 1999, re-elected 2003; Chair. Asscn of Mayors and Local Communities 2003–06; fmr mem. Council of Europe Congress of Local and Regional Authorities, fmr Head Nat. Del.; Minister of Local Public Admin 2006–07; Minister of Defence 2007–. *Address:* Ministry of Defence, 2021 Chişinău, şos. Hînceşti 84, Moldova (office). *Telephone:* (22) 25-22-22 (office). *Fax:* (22) 23-26-31 (office). *E-mail:* ministru@army.md (office). *Website:* www.army.gov.md (office).

VRANITZKY, Franz, DComm; Austrian politician and banker; *President, Vienna Institute for Development and Co-operation;* b. 4 Oct. 1937, Vienna; s. of Franz Vranitsky and Rosa Vernitsky; m. Christine Kristen; one s. one d.; ed Vienna XVII High School, Coll. (now Univ.) of Commerce, Vienna; joined Siemens-Schuckert GmbH, Vienna 1961; Dept of Nat. Econs, Austrian Nat. Bank 1961–69, seconded to the Office of the First Vice-Pres. 1969–70; Adviser on Econ. and Financial Policy to Minister of Finance 1970–76; Deputy-Chair. Bd of Dirs Creditanstalt-Bankverein 1976–81, Österreichische Länderbank 1981, Chair. Bd of Dirs 1981–84; Fed. Minister of Finance 1984–86; Fed. Chancellor 1986–96; fmr Chair. Austrian Socialist Party (now Social Democratic Party of Austria); Pres. Vienna Inst. for Devt and Co-operation 1990–; Hon. KCMG 1995. *Address:* Vienna Institute for Development and Co-operation, Möllwaldplatz 5/3, 1040 Vienna, Austria (office). *Telephone:* (1) 713-35-94 (office). *Fax:* (1) 713-35-94 (office). *Website:* www.vidc.org (office).

VRANKIĆ, Dragan; Bosnia and Herzegovina politician; *Minister of Finance and the Treasury;* b. 23 Jan. 1955, Trebižatu; m.; three c.; ed Univ. of Dubrovnik; fmr Gov. of Herzegovina-Neretva canton; Deputy Prime Minister and Minister of Finance, Fed. of Bosnia and Herzegovina 2003–07; Minister of Finance and the Treasury, Bosnia and Herzegovina 2007–. *Address:* Ministry of Finance and the Treasury, 71000 Sarajevo, trg Bosne i Hercegovine 1, Bosnia and Herzegovina (office). *Telephone:* (33) 205345 (office). *Fax:* (33) 471822 (office). *E-mail:* trezorbih@trezorbih.gov.ba (office). *Website:* www.trezorbih.gov.ba (office).

VUČINIĆ, Boro, PhD; Montenegrin politician; *Minister of Defence;* b. 1954, Podgorica; m.; four c.; ed Faculty of Law, Montenegrin State Univ.; started career at Titograd Civil Eng Org.; Dir Social Fund for Building Land, Business Premises and Roads; Deputy Municipal Ass. of Podgorica; mem. Parl. (Democratic Socialist Party), mem. Constitutional Affairs Cttee, Cttee for Drafting of Constitutional Charter of State Union of Serbia and Montenegro; Minister of Environmental Protection and Urban Planning 2004–06, of Defence 2006–; fmr Chair. Nat. Rifle Ass. of Yugoslavia; fmr Vice-Chair. Yugoslav Olympic Cttee; Head, Yugoslav Sports Del., Mediterranean Games 1997; Chair. Montenegrin Olympic Cttee. *Address:* Ministry of Defence, Jovana Tomasevica 29, 81000 Podgorica, Montenegro (office). *Telephone:* (81) 483561 (office). *Fax:* (81) 224702 (office). *E-mail:* kabinet@mod.cg.yu (office). *Website:* www.vlada.cg.yu/odbrana (office).

VUJANOVIĆ, Filip; Montenegrin politician, lawyer and head of state; *President;* b. 1 Sept. 1954, Belgrade, Serbia; m.; one s. two d.; ed Univ. of Belgrade; began career with First Municipal Court; Official Assoc., Dist Attorney's Office, Belgrade 1978–80; Sec. to Dist Court, Titograd (now Podgorica) 1980–81, mem. Attorney's Chamber, Chair. Chamber 1989; Lawyer, private legal practice 1982–93; Minister of Justice, Repub. of Montenegro 1992–95, of the Interior 1995–98; Prime Minister of the Repub. of Montenegro, with responsibility for Religious Affairs 2001–02; Pres. Parl. Ass. 2002–; Pres. of Repub. of Montenegro 2003–; mem. Democratic Party of Socialists of Montenegro, currently Deputy Chair. *Address:* Office of the President, 81000 Podgorica, Sveti Petar Cetinjski 3, Montenegro (office). *Telephone:* (81) 242388 (office). *Fax:* (81) 246608 (office). *E-mail:* predsjednik@cg.yu (office). *Website:* www.predsjednik.cg.yu (office).

VUKELIĆ, Branko; Croatian politician; *Minister of Defence;* b. 9 March 1958, Karlovac; m. Đurđica Vukelić; one c.; ed Faculty of Electrical Eng, Univ.

of Zagreb; project engineer, Chief of Preparation and Installation, EAB, Karlovac 1982–90; Man. INA Br. Office, Karlovac 1991–97; Pres. Karlovac City Croatian Democratic Union (CDU) Cttee 1993–; mem. Karlovac City Council 1993–97, 2001–, Mayor of Karlovac 1997–2001; Pres. Karlovac Co. CDU Cttee March 2002; Gen. Sec. CDU June 2002; Minister of Economy, Labour and Entrepreneurship 2003–08, of Defence 2008–. *Leisure interests:* football, horticulture, music. *Address:* Ministry of Defence, Trg Petra Krešimira IV. br. 1, 10000 Zagreb, Croatia (office). *Telephone:* (1) 4567111 (office). *Fax:* (1) 4567963 (office). *E-mail:* infor@morh.hr (office). *Website:* www .morh.hr (office).

VULF, Vitaly Yakovlevich, DHist; Russian broadcaster and writer; b. 23 May 1930, Baku, Azerbaijan; s. of Yakov Vulf; ed Moscow State Univ.; barrister, Baku and Moscow 1961–67; Sr, then Leading Researcher Inst. of Int. Workers' Movt (now Inst. of Comparative Politology), USSR (now Russian) Acad. of Sciences 1967–97; Broadcaster VID TV Co. 1997–; creator of Silver Ball TV programme; mem. editorial Bd Ballet (magazine); mem. Union of Theatre Workers. *Publications:* Theatre of the USA of the Seventies and Political Reality, A Little Aside from Broadway, A. Stepanova – Actress of Moscow Art Theatre, Idols, Stars, People, Stars of Difficult Destiny, Theatre Rain and numerous other works on Russian and foreign theatre. *Address:* Panfilovskiy per. 5, Apt. 35, 121099 Moscow, Russia. *Telephone:* (495) 241-97-44.

VUNIBOBO, Berenado, CBE, BAgrSc; Fijian government official and agronomist; *Permanent Representative, United Nations;* b. 24 Sept. 1932, Nukutubu, Rewa; s. of Mateo Vunibobo and Maria Kelekeletabua; m. Luisa Marama Tabumoce 1953; two s. three d.; ed St Joseph's Catholic Mission School, Rewa, Marist Brothers High School, Suva, Queensland State Agric. Coll., Queensland Univ. Imperial Coll. of Tropical Agric., Trinidad; Govt Service 1951–, Dist Agric. Officer 1962–67, Sr Agric. Officer and later Chief Agric. Officer 1968–69; Deputy Dir of Agric. 1969–70, Dir of Agric. 1970–71; Perm. Sec. for Agric., Fisheries and Forests 1971–72, for Works 1973–76; Perm. Rep. to UN, Amb. to USA, High Commr in Canada 1976–80; Perm. Rep. to UN 2008–; Perm. Sec. for Tourism, Transport and Civil Aviation 1980–81; Resident Rep. UNDP, Repub. of Korea 1981–86; Resident Rep. UNDP, Pakistan 1986–87; Minister of Trade and Commerce 1987–92, for Home Affairs, Immigration, Employment, Youth and Sports 1994, of Finance and Econ. Devt 1994–97, for Foreign Affairs and External Trade 1997–99; Chair. UN Visiting Mission to Cayman Islands and US Virgin Islands 1978; Vice-Pres. UN Gen. Ass.; Pres. UN Pledging Conf., Governing Council, UNDP; Chair. UN Observer Mission to New Hebrides (now Vanuatu); Chair. Coconut Pests and Diseases Bd, Banana Marketing Bd, Nat. Marketing Authority 1970–72; Chair. Civil Aviation Authority, Fiji, Air Terminal Services, Fiji; mem. Bd, Fiji Devt Bank 1970–72; mem. Native Lands Trust Bd 1968–75, Fijian Affairs Bd 1968–76, Great Council of Chiefs 1968–76, Cen. Whitley Council 1970–76, Jt Industrial Council 1970–76, Fiji Electricity Authority 1975–76; Gold Medal (Queensland Agric. Coll.) 1986. *Leisure interests:* reading, debating, walking, gardening, swimming, golf. *Address:* Permanent Mission of Fiji to the United Nations, 630 Third Avenue, 7th Floor, New York, NY, 10017, USA. *Telephone:* (212) 687-4130 (office). *Fax:* (212) 687-3963 (office). *E-mail:* fiji@un.int (office). *Website:* www.fijiprun.org/staff.php (office).

VURAL, Volkan, MA; Turkish journalist, business executive and fmr diplomatist; *Counselor to the Chairman, Doğan Şirketler Grubu Holding A.Ş.;* b. 29 Dec. 1941, Istanbul; m.; ed Ankara Coll. and Univ.; early career as journalist; joined Foreign Ministry 1964, Third Sec. Econ. Affairs Dept 1964–65; mil. service 1965–67; Third Sec. Dept of Bilateral and Regional Econ.

Affairs 1967–68, Second then First Sec. Embassy, Seoul 1968–71, Consul then Deputy Consul Gen. Consulate, Munich 1971–73, Acting Head Dept of Int. Econ. Insts, Foreign Ministry 1973–76, Int. Officer Political Dept NATO Headquarters 1976–82, Deputy Dir Gen. for Bilateral Econ. Affairs, Foreign Ministry 1982–87; Amb. to Iran 1987–88, to USSR 1988–93, to Germany 1995–98; Spokesman Foreign Ministry 1993, Chief Adviser to the Prime Minister 1993–95; Perm. Rep. to the UN 1998–2000; Amb. to Spain 2003–06; Counselor to Chair., Doğan Şirketler Grubu Holding A.Ş. 2006–; University Presidential Medal, La Salle Univ., Philadelphia 1999. *Address:* Office of the Chairman, Doğan Şirketler Grubu Holding A.Ş., Oymacı Sok. No:51 Altunizade 34662, Üsküdar İstanbul, Turkey (office). *Telephone:* (216) 5569000 (office). *Fax:* (216) 5569398 (office). *Website:* www.doganholding .com.tr (office).

VY, Lt-Gen. Nguyen Van; Vietnamese politician; b. 16 Jan. 1916, Hanoi; ed Univ., Tong Officers' School and School of Command and Staff, Paris; Chief Mil. Cabinet of Chief of State 1952; Commdr Coastal Interzone 1954; Acting Chief, Gen. Staff, Vietnamese Army Oct. 1954; Insp.-Gen. Dec. 1954; Asst Chief of Staff for Training, Repub. of Viet Nam Air Force (RVNAF) Jan. 1964; Asst to C-in-C Nov. 1964; Commdt Quang Trung Training Centre Feb. 1965; Commdr Training Command, RVNAF June 1966; Chief-of-Staff Jt Gen. Staff RVNAF 1966–67; Minister of Defence 1968–72; Grand Officer Nat. Order of Viet Nam; Army and Air Force Distinguished Service Orders; Officier, Légion d'Honneur.

VYACHIREV, Rem Ivanovich; Russian business executive; b. 23 Aug. 1934, Bolshaya Chernigovka, Kuibyshev Dist; m.; two c.; ed Kuibyshev Inst. of Oil and Gas; worked in Oil Producers' Union, Ozenburg (Ordobycha) 1976–78; Chief Engineer Orenburggazprom 1978–82; Deputy Minister of Gas Industry of USSR 1983–85, 1986–89; Gen. Man. Tyumengazprom 1985–86; Deputy Chair. Bd, State (later Jt Stock) Gazprom Co. 1989–92, CEO 1992–2001, Chair. Bd of Dirs 2001–02; apptd Chair Bd of Dirs Siberian Oil Co. 1996; apptd Chair. Supervisory Bd Promstroybank 1998; mem. Int. Eng Acad. *Address:* c/o RAO Gazprom, Nametkina str. 16, 117884 Moscow, Russia.

VYACHORKA, Vintsuk; Belarusian politician and linguist; *Chairman, Belarusian Popular Front (BPF – 'Revival');* b. 7 July 1961, Bieraście; s. of Ryhor Viačorka and Alaucina Viačorka; m. 1980; two s. one d.; ed Belarus State Univ., Acad. of Sciences; Lecturer, Minsk Pedagogical Univ. 1986–; f. Belarusian Popular Front (BPF) 1988, Chair. BPF – 'Revival' (BPF – 'Adradzhennye') 1999–; Deputy Ed.-in-Chief bi-monthly Spadčyna. *Publication:* Orthography: An Attempt at Comprehensive Standardization 1994. *Leisure interest:* ethno-music. *Address:* BPF – 'Adradzhennye', vul. Varvasheni 8, 220005 Minsk, Belarus (office). *Telephone:* (17) 213-30-09 (office). *Fax:* (17) 284-50-12 (office). *E-mail:* cscsc@user.unibel.by (office). *Website:* www .pbnf.org (office).

VYUGIN, Oleg Vyacheslavovich, CandPhys-MathSc; Russian economist; *Director, Federal Financial Markets Service;* b. 29 July 1952, Ufa, Bashkortostan; m. Irina; one d.; ed Moscow State Univ.; researcher, then Sr Researcher, Head of Lab. Inst. of Prognosis of Nat. Econ., Russian Acad. of Sciences 1989–92; Head Dept of Macroecons Policy, Ministry of Finance 1993–96, Deputy Minister of Finance 1996–99, First Deputy 1999–2000; mem. Bd, Exec. Vice-Pres., Chief Economist Troyka-Dialog investment Co. 2000–2002; First Deputy Chair. Bank Rossii-Central Bank of the Russian Fed. 2002–04; Chair. Fed. Financial Markets Service 2004–. *Address:* c/o Ministry of Finance, ul. Ilinka 9, 103097 Moscow, Russia (office).

WA THIONG'O, Ngugi, (James Thiong'o Ngugi), BA; Kenyan writer, dramatist, critic and academic; *Director of the International Center for Writing and Translation, University of California, Irvine*; b. 5 Jan. 1938, Limuru; m. 1st Nyambura 1961 (divorced 1982); m. 2nd Njeeri 1992; four s. two d.; ed Makerere Univ. Coll., Uganda and Univ. of Leeds, UK; Lecturer in Literature, Univ. Nairobi 1967–69, Sr Lecturer, Assoc. Prof. and Chair Dept of Literature 1972–77; Fellow in Creative Writing, Makerere Univ. 1969–70; Visiting Assoc. Prof., Northwestern Univ., USA 1970–71; arrested and detained Dec. 1977, released Dec. 1978; in exile in London 1982–; Lecturer in Politics and Literature, Yale Univ.; currently Distinguished Prof of English and Comparative Literature and Dir, Int. Center for Writing and Translation, Univ. of California, Irvine; Foreign Hon. mem. American Academy of Arts and Letters; Hon. Llife Mem. Council for the Devt of Social Sciences Research in Africa 2003; Dr hc (Univ. of Leeds), (Univ. of Transkei); Fonlon-Nicholas Award 1996, Medal of the Presidency of the Italian Cabinet; Fourth Memorial Steve Biko Lecture 2003, Grinzane for Africa Heritage Prize 2008. *Publications:* The Black Hermit (play) 1962, Weep Not, Child (novel) 1964, The River Between (novel) 1965, A Grain of Wheat (novel) 1967, This Time Tomorrow: Three Plays 1970, Homecoming: Essays on African and Caribbean Literature, Culture and Politics 1972, Secret Lives and Other Stories 1973, The Trial of Dedan Kimathi (with Micere Githae-Mugo) 1976, Petals of Blood (novel) 1977, Mtwana Mweusi 1978, Caitaani mutharaba-ini (trans. as Devil on the Cross) 1980, Writers in Politics: Essays 1981, Detained: A Writer's Prison Diary 1981, Njamba Nene na mbaathi i mathagu (trans. as Njamba Nene and the Flying Bus) 1982, Ngaahika Ndeena: Ithaako ria Ngerekano (play with Ngugi wa Mirii), (trans. as I Will Marry When I Want) 1982, Barrel of a Pen: Resistance to Repression in Neo-Colonial Kenya 1983, Bathitoora va Njamba Nene, 1984, English trans. as Njamba Nene's Pistol 1986, Decolonising the Mind: The Politics of Language in African Literature 1986, Writing Against Neo-colonialism 1986, Matigari ma Ngirūūngi (trans. as Matigari) 1986, Njambas Nene no Chiubu King'ang'i 1986, Moving the Centre: The Struggle for Cultural Freedoms 1992, Wizard of the Crow 2006. *Address:* International Center for Writing and Translation, School of Humanities, 172 Humanities Instruction Building, University of California, Irvine, CA 92697-3380, USA (office). *Telephone:* (949) 824-1948 (office). *Fax:* (949) 824-9623 (office). *E-mail:* icwt@uci.edu (office). *Website:* www.humanities.uci.edu/icwt (office).

WAAGSTEIN, Finn, MD, PhD; Swedish cardiologist and academic; *Prof. of Cardiology, Inst. of Heart and Lung Diseases, Gothenberg Univ.*; King Faisal Int. Prize for Medicine 2002 (jt recipient). *Achievements inlcude:* pioneered treatment of heart failure with beta-blockers 1973. *Address:* Wallenberg Laboratory, Bruna stråket 16, SU/Sahlgrenska, 413 45 Gothenberg, Sweden (office). *Telephone:* (31) 342-30-14 (office). *Fax:* (31) 82-37-62 (office). *E-mail:* Finn.Waagstein@wlab.wall.gu.se (office).

WACHTMEISTER, Count Wilhelm Hans Frederik; Swedish fmr diplomatist; b. 29 April 1923, Wanås; s. of Count Gustaf Wachtmeister and Countess Margaretha Wachtmeister (née Trolle); m. Countess Ulla Wachtmeister (née Leuhusen) 1947; one s. one d.; ed Stockholm Univ.; Attaché, Foreign Office 1946–47, Embassy in Vienna 1947–49, in Madrid Feb.–May 1949, in Lisbon 1949–50, Foreign Office 1950–52; Second Sec. Foreign Office 1952–55; Second Sec. Embassy in Moscow 1955–56, First Sec. 1956–58; Special Asst to Sec.-Gen. of UN 1958–62; Head of Div. for UN Affairs, Foreign Office 1962–63, Head of Div. 1963–65, Head of Dept July–Oct. 1965, Asst Under-Sec. of State 1965–66; Amb. to Algeria 1966–68; Deputy Under-Sec. of State and Head of Political Div. 1968–74; Amb. to USA 1974–89; Dean of the Diplomatic Corps 1986–89; Sr Adviser to Chair. of AB Volvo 1989–93; Int. Adviser Coudert Bros (law firm) 1989–93; Chair. Swedish-American Chamber of Commerce (US) 1993–96; retd; Hon. LLD (Lund). *Publications:* Som Jag Såg Det (As I Saw It) 1996. *Leisure interest:* tennis. *Address:* Karlavagen 59, 11449, Stockholm, Sweden. *Telephone:* (8) 660-3823 (home).

WADA, Akihiro; Japanese business executive; *Chairman, Aisin Seiki Company Ltd*; b. 1934, Aichi Pref.; m.; one d. two s.; ed Nagoya Univ.; trained as mechanical engineer; joined Toyota 1956, specialised in automotive design, Gen. Man. Product Planning Div. 1978–86, apptd Dir 1986, Man.-Dir 1990–92, Sr Man.-Dir 1992–94, Exec. Vice-Pres. 1994–2001; currently Chair. Aisin Seiki Co. Ltd; mem. Hon. Cttee FISITA. *Leisure interest:* golf. *Address:* Aisin Seiki Company Ltd, 2-1 Asahi-machi, Kariya, Aichi 448-8650, Japan (office). *Telephone:* (5) 6624-8411 (office). *Fax:* (5) 6624-8003 (office). *Website:* www.aisin.co.jp (office).

WADA, Akiyoshi, PhD; Japanese research director and academic; b. 28 June 1929, Tokyo; s. of Koroku Wada and Haruko Kikkawa; m. Sachiko Naito 1958; two s.; ed Gakushūin High School and Univ. of Tokyo; Prof. of Physics, Univ. of Tokyo 1971–90, Prof. Emer. 1990–, Dean Faculty of Science 1989–90; Dir Sagami Chemical Research Center 1991–2001; Vice-Pres. Advanced Tech. Inst. 1988–; Dir Kazusa DNA Research Inst. 1991–; mem. Science Council of Japan 1991–2000; Pres. Nestlé Science Foundation (Japan) 1992–2004; Dir Genomic Sciences Centre (RIKEN) 1998–2004, Adviser 2004–; Dir Yokohama Science Centre 2004–; Dir Ohanomizu Univ. 2005–09; Second Order of the Sacred Treasure 2002; Matsunaga Prize 1971, Shimadu Prize 1983, Polymer Soc. Prize 1995, Purple Ribbon Medal 1995, 10th Anniversary Award, Human Frontier Science Program 1998, Yokohama Prize of Cultural Merit 2003. *Publications:* Macrodipole of α-helix 1976, Molten Globule State of Proteins 1980, Automated DNA Sequencing 1987, Stability Distribution of DNA Double Helix 1987. *Leisure interests:* orchid cultivation, stamp collection.

Address: 11-1-311, Akasaka 8, Minato-ku, Tokyo 107, Japan. *Telephone:* (3) 3408-2932.

WADA, Emi; Japanese costume designer; b. 18 March 1937, Kyoto; d. of Nobu Wada and Sumiko Noguchi; m. Ben Wada 1957; one s.; ed Kyoto City Coll. of Arts (now Kyoto Univ. of Arts); mem. Acad. of Motion Picture Art and Sciences, USA, Costume Designers' Guild, USA; Gold Medal, Cannes Film Festival 1987. *Costumes designed:* theatre: Aoi Hi (Blue Fire) 1957, Image Mandala 1987, King Lear 1993; film: Marco 1972, Ran (Acad. Award, Best Costume Design 1986) 1985, Rokumeikan 1986, Princess from the Moon 1987, Momotaro Forever 1988, Rikyu 1989, Dreams 1990, Prospero's Books 1991, Song jia huang chao (The Soong Sisters) 1997, Fung wan: Hung ba tin ha (The Storm Riders) 1998, 8½ Women 1999, Gohatto (Taboo) 1999, Hero (Best Costumes/Make-Up, Hong Kong Film Awards) 2002, Shi mian mai fu (House of Flying Daggers) 2004, The Go Master 2006; dance: Carmen 1991; TV: Silk Art by Emi Wada (Grand Prix, Montreux Int. HDTV Festival) 1991; opera: Oedipus Rex 1992; (exhbn) Emi Wada Recreates the Momoyama Period, Kyoto 1989. *Publication:* My Costume—Emi Wada 1989. *Leisure interest:* reading. *Address:* 3-31-3-105 Kinuta, Setagaya-ku, Tokyo 157, Japan. *Telephone:* (3) 3417-0425. *Fax:* (3) 3417-1773. *Website:* www.kiryu.co.jp/wadaemi.

WADA, Hiroko; Japanese business executive and consultant; *CEO, Office Wada*; b. 4 May 1952; joined Procter & Gamble Sun Home K.K. (currently Procter & Gamble Far East, Inc.) 1977, Vice-Pres. Corp. New Ventures, Asia, Procter & Gamble 1998–2001; Pres. Dyson 2001-02; Pres. and COO Toys "R" Us (Japan) Ltd 2004; Founder, CEO and Rep. Dir Office Wada (man. consultancy) 2004–; Guest Prof., Momoyama Gakuin Univ. 2009–; mem. Bd of Dirs Aderans Holdings Co. Ltd 2009–; ranked by Fortune magazine amongst 50 Most Powerful Women in Business outside the US (41st) 2004. *Address:* c/o Board of Directors, Aderans Holdings Company Ltd, 1-6-3 Shinjuku Shinjuku-ku, 160-8429, Tokyo, Japan. *Telephone:* (office). *E-mail:* info@wadahiroko01.com (office). *Website:* www.wadahiroko.com (office).

WADA, Isami; Japanese real estate executive; *President and CEO, Sekisui House Ltd*; began career in sales; Pres. and CEO Sekisui House Ltd (real estate firm) 1960–; Pres. Japan Fed. of Housing Orgs. *Address:* Sekisui House Ltd, 1-1-88 Oyodonaka, Kita-ku, Osaka 531-0076, Japan (office). *Telephone:* (6) 6440-3111 (office). *Fax:* (6) 6440-3331 (office). *E-mail:* info-ir@qz.sekisuihouse.co.jp (office). *Website:* www.sekisuihouse.co.jp (office); www.judanren.or.jp.

WADA, Norio, BEcons; Japanese telecommunications executive; *Chairman, Nippon Telegraph and Telephone Corporation*; b. 16 Aug. 1940; ed Kyoto Univ.; joined Nippon Telegraph and Telephone (NTT) Public Corpn 1964, Sr Vice-Pres. and Gen.-Man. Tohoku Regional Communications Sector 1992–96, Exec. Vice-Pres. and Sr Exec. Man. 1996–98, In June 1998, he became an Exec. Vice-Pres. and Sr Exec. Man. of Affiliated Business HQ and Exec. Man. of NTT-Holding Organizational Office 1998–99, Exec. Vice-Pres. and Sr Exec. Man. of NTT-Holding Provisional HQ 1999–2002, Sr Exec. Vice-Pres. NTT 1999–2002, Pres. NTT 2002–07, Chair. NTT 2007–. *Address:* Nippon Telegraph and Telephone Corporation, 3-1 Otemachi 2-chome, Chiyoda-ku, Tokyo 100-8116, Japan (office). *Telephone:* (3) 5205-5581 (office). *Fax:* (3) 5205-5589 (office). *E-mail:* info@ntt.co.jp (office). *Website:* www.ntt.co.jp/index_e.html (office).

WADDELL, (John) Rankin; British photographer; b. 1966, Glasgow; m. Kate Hardie (divorced); one s.; ed Brighton Polytechnic, London Coll. of Printing; co-f. Dazed and Confused magazine; co-f. Vision On Publishing; photographed Queen's Jubilee 2002. *Films:* Perfect (short), The Lives of the Saints 2006. *Publications include:* Nudes, Male Nudes 2000, Fashion Stories 2004, Portraits 2004. *Address:* Rankin Photography, 112–116 Old Street, London, EC1V 9BG, England (office). *Telephone:* (20) 7549-6805 (office). *Fax:* (20) 7336-0966 (office). *E-mail:* info@rankin.co.uk (office). *Website:* www.rankin.co.uk.

WADDINGTON, Baron (Life Peer), cr. 1990, of Read in the County of Lancashire; **David Waddington**, GCVO, PC, QC, DL; British politician; b. 2 Aug. 1929, Burnley; s. of Charles Waddington and Minnie Hughan Waddington; m. Gillian Rosemary Green 1958; three s. two d.; ed Sedbergh and Hertford Coll., Oxford; Pres. Oxford Union Conservative Asscn 1950; called to the Bar, Gray's Inn 1951, Recorder of the Crown Court 1972; MP for Nelson and Colne 1968–74, for Clitheroe (Ribble Valley constituency from 1983) March 1979–91; Parl. Pvt. Sec. to Attorney-Gen. 1970–72; Lord Commr of the Treasury 1979–81, Parl. Under-Sec. of State for Employment 1981–83; Minister of State at the Home Office 1983–87, Parl. Sec. to HM Treasury and Govt Chief Whip 1987–89, Home Sec. 1989–90, Lord Privy Seal and Leader of the House of Lords 1990–92; Gov. and C-in-C of Bermuda 1992–97. *Leisure interests:* golf, sailing. *Address:* House of Lords, Westminster, London, SW1A 0PW (office); Flat 4, 39 Chester Way, London, SE11 4UR; The Clock House, Hadspen, Castel Cary, Somerset, BA7 7BG, England (home). *Telephone:* (20) 7219-6448 (office); (1963) 350987 (home); (20) 7820-9338. *Fax:* (20) 7820-9338 (office). *E-mail:* waddingtond@parliament.uk (office).

WADDINGTON, Leslie; British art dealer; b. 9 Feb. 1934, Dublin; s. of Victor Waddington and Zelda Waddington; m. 2nd Clodagh F. Waddington 1985; two d. by first marriage; ed Portora Royal School, Enniskillen and Ecole du Louvre, Paris; Dir Waddington Galleries 1957, Man. Dir 1966–; Chair. Modern Painting Section Maastricht Art Fair 1994–, Pictura Section 1996–2000; Sr Fellow RCA 1993; Dr hc (RCA) 1993. *Leisure interests:* chess,

2294

reading. *Address:* Waddington Galleries, 11 Cork Street, London, W1S 3LT, England. *Telephone:* (20) 7851-2200.

WADE, Abdoulaye; Senegalese lawyer and head of state; *President;* b. 29 May 1926, Saint-Louis; m.; two c.; ed Univs of Besançon and Dijon, France, Univ. of Dakar; fmr univ. teacher of law in Senegal and abroad; barrister, Court of Appeal, Senegal; Founder and Pres., Senegalese Democratic Party 1974–; mem. Parl. 1974–; Minister of State 1991–92, 1995–97; Pres. of Senegal 2000–; mem. Int. Acad. of Trial Lawyers; Commander, Order of Merit (Senegal); Grand Officer, Légion d'Honneur; UNESCO Félix Houphouët-Boigny Peace Prize 2005. *Publications:* author of several books and essays on law, economics and political science. *Address:* Office of the President, Avenue Léopold Sédar Senghor, BP 168, Dakar, Senegal (office). *Telephone:* 823-10-88 (office). *Website:* www.gouv.sn/institutions/president (office).

WADE, Kenneth, DSc, FRS; British scientist and academic; *Professor Emeritus, Department of Chemistry, University of Durham;* b. 13 Oct. 1932, Sleaford, Lincs.; s. of the late Harry K. Wade and Anna E. Wade (née Cartwright); m. Gertrud Rosmarie Hetzel 1962 (separated); one s. two d.; ed Carre's Grammar School, Sleaford, Lincs., Nottingham Univ.; Postdoctoral Research Asst, Univ. of Cambridge 1957–59, Cornell Univ., Ithaca, NY 1959–60; Lecturer in Chem., Derby Coll. of Tech. 1960–61; Lecturer in Chem., Univ. of Durham 1961–71, Sr Lecturer 1971–77, Reader 1977–83, Head of Inorganic Chem. 1980–98, Prof. 1983–2001, Prof. Emer. 2001–; Chair. Dept of Chem. 1986–89; Visiting Prof., Warsaw 1974, Amsterdam 1977, Univ. of Southern California, Los Angeles 1979, Notre Dame 1983, McMaster 1984, London, Ont. 1990; Pres. Royal Soc. of Chem. Dalton Div. 1995–97; Main Group Award, Royal Soc. of Chem. 1982, Tilden Lecturer 1987, Mond Lecturer 1998, E. Merck Lecturer, Darmstadt 1994. *Publications:* Organometallic Compounds: The Main Group Elements (jtly) 1967, Principles of Organometallic Chemistry (jtly) 1968, Electron Deficient Compounds 1971, Hypercarbon Chemistry (jtly) 1987, Electron Deficient Boron and Carbon Clusters (jtly) 1990. *Leisure interest:* walking. *Address:* Department of Chemistry, University Science Laboratories, South Road, Durham, DH1 3LE (office); 7 Hill Meadows, High Shincliffe, Durham, DH1 2PE, England (home). *Telephone:* (191) 334-2122 (office); (191) 386-5139 (home). *Fax:* (191) 384-4737 (office). *E-mail:* kenneth.wade@durham.ac.uk (office). *Website:* www.dur.ac.uk/chemistry (office).

WADE, Rebekah; British newspaper editor; *Editor, The Sun;* b. 27 May 1968; d. of the late Robert Wade and of Deborah Wade; ed Appleton Hall, Cheshire and Univ. of the Sorbonne, Paris; began career as Features Ed., later Assoc. Ed. and Deputy Ed. News of the World –1998, Ed. 2000–03; Deputy Ed. The Sun 1998–2000, Ed. 2003–; Founder-mem. and Pres. Women in Journalism. *Address:* The Sun, 1 Virginia Street, Wapping, London, E98 1SN, England (office). *Telephone:* (20) 7782-4000 (office). *Fax:* (20) 7782-4108 (office). *E-mail:* news@the-sun.co.uk (office). *Website:* www.thesun.co.uk (office).

WADE, (Sarah) Virginia, OBE, BSc; British broadcaster and fmr tennis player; b. 10 July 1945, Bournemouth, Hants. (now Dorset); d. of the late Canon Eustace Wade (fmr Archdeacon of Durban, SA) and of Joan Barbara Wade; ed Univ. of Sussex; amateur tennis player 1962–68, professional 1968–87; British Hard Court Champion 1967, 1968, 1973, 1974; USA Champion 1968 (singles), 1973, 1975 (doubles); Italian Champion 1971; Australian Champion 1972; Wimbledon Ladies Champion 1977; played Wightman Cup for GB 1965–85, Capt. 1973–80; played Fed. Cup for GB 1967–83 (a record), Capt. 1973–81; won 55 singles titles; commentator BBC 1980–; mem. Cttee All England Lawn Tennis Club 1983–91 (first woman to be elected); Hon. LLD (Sussex) 1985; Int. Tennis Hall of Fame 1989; Fed. Cup Award of Excellence 2002. *Publications:* Courting Triumph (with Mary Lou Mellace) 1978, Ladies of the Court 1984. *Leisure interest:* reading. *Address:* c/o International Management Group, Pier House, Strand on the Green, London, W4 3NN, England.

WADE-GERY, Sir Robert (Lucian), KCMG, KCVO, MA; British fmr diplomatist and banker; *Fellow, All Souls College, Oxford;* b. 22 April 1929, Oxford; s. of Prof. H. T. Wade-Gery and V. Wade-Gery; m. Sarah Marris 1962; one s. one d.; ed Winchester Coll. and New Coll., Oxford; Fellow, All Souls Coll. Oxford 1951–73, 1987–89, 1997–; joined Foreign (now Diplomatic) Service 1951; in Foreign Office (FO) Econ. Relations Dept 1951–54; at Embassy in Bonn 1954–57, Tel-Aviv 1961–64, Saigon (now Ho Chi Min City) 1967–68; FO 1957–60, 1964–67; Cabinet Office 1968–69; Counsellor 1969; on loan to Bank of England 1969; Head of Financial Policy and Aid Dept, FCO 1970; Under-Sec., Cen. Policy Review Staff, Cabinet Office 1971–73; Minister at Embassy, Madrid 1973–77, Moscow 1977–79; Deputy Sec. of Cabinet 1979–82; High Commr in India 1982–87; Vice-Chair. Barclays de Zoete Wedd 1994–98 (Exec. Dir 1987–93), Vice-Chair. Barclays Capital 1998–99; Sr Consultant to Int. Financial Services London 1991–2001 and to Barclays Private Bank 1999–2002; Chair. SOAS 1990–98; Chair. Anglo-Spanish Soc. 1995–98. *Leisure interests:* walking, sailing, travel, history. *Address:* 14 Hill View, 2 Primrose Hill Road, London, NW3 3AX (home); The Old Vicarage, Cold Aston, Cheltenham, Glos., GL54 3BW, England (home). *Telephone:* (20) 7722-4754 (home); (1451) 821115 (home). *Fax:* (20) 7586-5966 (home); (1451) 822496 (home).

WADHWANI, Sushil Baldev, CBE, BSc, MSc, PhD; British economist and investment manager; *Chief Executive Officer, Wadhwani Asset Management;* b. 7 Dec. 1959, Kenya; s. of Baldev Wadhwani and Meena Wadhwani; m. Renu Wadhwani; one s. one d.; ed London School of Econs; Reader in Econs, LSE 1984–91, Visiting Prof. 2000–; Visiting Prof., Sir John Cass Business School, City of London 2000–; Dir of Equity Strategy, Goldman Sachs Int. 1991–95; Dir of Research, Tudor Proprietary Trading LLC 1995–99; mem. Bank of

England Monetary Policy Cttee 1999–2002; CEO Wadhwani Asset Man./Wadhwadni Capital 2002–; Gov. LSE 2004–; Allyn Young Prize, C.S. McTaggart Scholarship, Clothworkers' Co. Exhbn, Gonner Prize, Raynes Undergraduate Prize, Sir Edward Stern Scholarship, Ely Devons Prize, Sayers Prize. *Publications:* numerous articles in academic journals. *Leisure interest:* cricket. *Address:* Wadhwani Asset Management LLP, Warwick Court, 5 Paternoster Square, London, EC4M 7DX, England (office). *Telephone:* (20) 7663-3420 (office). *Fax:* (20) 7663-3410 (office). *E-mail:* sushilw@waniasset.com (office).

WADIA, Jim, FCA, FRSA; British chartered accountant; *Chief Operating Officer, Linklaters;* b. 12 April 1948; m. Joelle Garnier 1972; one s. one d.; ed Le Rosey, Rolle, Switzerland, Inns of Court School of Law; called to Bar, Inner Temple 1969; Pnr Arthur Andersen 1982–2000, Managing Pnr UK 1993–97, Worldwide Managing Pnr 1997–2000; COO Linklaters 2001–. *Leisure interests:* tennis, theatre. *Address:* Linklaters, 1 Silk Street, London, EC2Y 8MQ (office); 28 Eldon Road, London, W8 5PT, England (home). *Telephone:* (20) 7456-4982 (office); (20) 7937-7045. *E-mail:* jim.wadia@linklaters.com (office). *Website:* www.linklaters.com (office).

WADIA, Nusli; Indian industrialist; *Chairman, Bombay Dyeing & Manufacturing Company Ltd;* grandson of Muhammad Ali Jinnah; m. Maureen Wadia; two s.; Chair. Bombay Dyeing & Manufacturing Co. Ltd, Gherzi Eastern Ltd, Bombay Burmah Trading Corpn Ltd, BRT Ltd, NW Exports Ltd, Britannia Industries Ltd, National Peroxide Ltd, Citurgia Biochemicals Ltd, Wadia BSN India Ltd; Chair. and Man. Dir Nowrosjee Wadia & Sons Ltd; Dir Anil Starch Products Ltd, Tata Chemicals Ltd, Atul Products Ltd, Naira Holdings Ltd, Radley Cotton Mills Ltd, ABI Holdings Ltd, Associated Biscuits International Ltd; mem. Bd Oberoi Group. *Address:* Bombay Dyeing, Neville House, J. N. Heredia Marg, Ballard Estate, Mumbai 400 038, India (office). *Telephone:* (22) 22618071 (office). *Fax:* (22) 22614520 (office). *Website:* www.bombaydyeing.com (office).

WADLEY, Veronica; British journalist and editor; b. 28 Feb. 1952, London; d. of Neville John Wadley and Anne Hawise Colleton (née Browning); m. Tom Bower 1985; one s. one d.; ed Francis Holland School, London, Benenden; journalist Condé Nast Publs 1971–74, Sunday Telegraph Magazine 1978–81, Mail on Sunday 1982–86; Features Ed. Daily Telegraph 1986–89, Asst Ed. 1989–94, Deputy Ed. 1994–95; Assoc. Ed. Daily Mail 1995–98, Deputy Ed. (Features) 1998–2002; Ed. London Evening Standard 2002–09. *Address:* c/o The Evening Standard, Northcliffe House, 2 Derry Street, Kensington, London, W8 5EE, England (office).

WAENA, Sir Nathaniel Rahumaea, GCMG; Solomon Islands politician and government official; *Governor-General;* Minister of Prov. Govt and Rural Devt c. 2001; Minister for Nat. Unity, Reconciliation and Peace –2004; Gov.-Gen. Solomon Islands 2004–; Patron St Martins, Tenar 2004, Stuyvenberg Rural Training Centre, Nana 2006, Pawa Prov. Secondary School Fund Raising Drive 2007; Solomon Island Cross (CSI), KStJ. *Address:* Office of the Governor-General, Honiara, Solomon Islands (office).

WAGGONER, Paul Edward, PhD, FAAS; American horticultural scientist; *Distinguished Scientist, Department of Forestry and Horticulture, Connecticut Agricultural Experiment Station;* b. 29 March 1923, Appanoose County, Ia; s. of Walter Loyal Waggoner and Kathryn Maring Waggoner; m. Barbara Ann Lockerbie 1945; two s.; ed Univ. of Chicago and Iowa State Coll., Ames; Asst, then Assoc., then Chief Scientist, Connecticut Agricultural Experiment Station, Dept of Forestry and Horticulture, New Haven 1951–71, Vice-Dir 1969–71, Dir 1972–87, Distinguished Scientist 1987–; lecturer, Yale Forestry School, New Haven 1962–; Guggenheim Fellow 1963; mem. NAS; Fellow American Soc. of Agronomy, American Phytopathological Soc.; Anton-de Bary Medal 1996. *Publications:* Agricultural Meteorology (ed.) 1965, Climate Change and US Water Resources 1990, How Much Land Can 10 Billion People Spare for Nature? 1994 and articles on phytopathology. *Leisure interests:* gardening, bicycling. *Address:* Connecticut Agricultural Experiment Station, Box 1106, New Haven, CT 06504 (office); 314 Vineyard Point Road, Guilford, CT 06437, USA (home). *Telephone:* (203) 974-8494 (office); (203) 453-2816 (home). *E-mail:* paul.waggoner@po.state.ct.us. *Website:* www.caes.state.ct.us/Departments/forestry.htm (office).

WAGNER, Falk (Oskar Paul Alfred), DTheol; German academic; *Professor, Evangelisch-Theologische Fakultät, Institut für Systematische Theologie, University of Vienna;* b. 25 Feb. 1939, Vienna, Austria; s. of Robert Wagner and Friedel Wagner; m. Inamaria Winnefeld 1968; two d.; ed Gymnasium Wiesbaden and Univs of Frankfurt and Mainz; Research Fellow for Economic Ethics and Adult Educ., Karlsruhe 1968–69; Research Fellow, Deutsches Inst. für Int. Pädagogische Forschung, Frankfurt am Main 1969–72; Asst Univ. of Munich 1970–72, Lecturer in Systematic Theology 1972, Prof. 1978–; now Prof. Univ. of Vienna. *Publications include:* Über die Legitimität der Mission 1968, Der Gedanke der Persönlichkeit Gottes bei Fichte und Hegel 1971, Schleiermachers Dialektik 1974, Geld oder Gott? 1985, Was ist Religion? 1986, Die vergessene spekulative Theologie 1987, Was ist Theologie? 1989, Zur gegenwärtigen Lage des Protestantismus 1995, Ende der Religion – Religion ohne Ende? (with M. Murrmann-Kahl) 1996, Religion und Gottesgedanke 1996, Zeitenwechsel und Beständigkeit (co-ed.) 1997; numerous articles on theological, philosophical and ethical questions. *Address:* Universität Wien, Evangelisch-Theologische Fakultät, Institut für Systematische Theologie, Rooseveltplatz 10, 1090 Vienna (office); Kaiserstrasse 32, 1070 Vienna, Austria (home). *Telephone:* (1) 427-73-20-01 (office). *Fax:* (1) 427-79-320 (office). *E-mail:* public@univie.ac.at (office). *Website:* www.univie.ac.at/etf (office).

WAGNER, Heinz Georg, Dr. rer. nat.; German scientist and academic; *Professor Emeritus, Institut für Physikalische Chemie, University of Göttin-*

gen; b. 20 Sept. 1928, Hof, Bavaria; s. of Georg Wagner and Frieda Spiess; m. Renate C. Heuer 1974; ed Tech. Hochschule, Darmstadt and Univ. of Göttingen; Lecturer, Univ. of Göttingen 1960–65, Prof. of Physical Chem. 1971–97, now Prof. Emer.; Prof. Ruhr Univ. Bochum 1965–70; Dir Max-Planck-Inst. für Strömungsforschung, Göttingen 1971–97; Vice-Pres. Deutsche Forschungsgemeinschaft 1983–89; mem. Exec. Council ESF; scientific mem. Max-Planck-Gesellschaft; mem. Göttingen Acad., Acad. Leopoldina, Int. Acad. of Astronautics, Heidelberg Acad., Acad. of Natural Sciences of Russia, Academia Europaea, American Physical Soc., Royal Soc. of Chem. etc.; Hon. Mem. Bunsen-Gesellschaft; Grosses Bundesverdienstkreuz; several hon. doctorates; Fritz-Haber Prize, Bernard Lewis Gold Medal, Achema Medal, Numa Manson Medal, Dionizy Smoleński Medal, Walther-Nernst-Denkmünze, Dechema Medal. *Publications:* articles on combustion, reaction kinetics, thermodynamics of liquid mixtures. *Address:* Institut für Physikalische Chemie, Universität Göttingen, Tammannstr. 6, 37077 Göttingen, Germany (office). *Telephone:* (551) 393100 (office). *Fax:* (551) 393117 (office). *E-mail:* jkupfer@gwdg.de (office). *Website:* www.uni-goettingen.de/de/sh/28451.html (office).

WAGNER, Robert; American actor; b. 10 Feb. 1930, Detroit, Mich.; m. 1st Natalie Wood 1957 (divorced 1962, re-married 1972, died 1981); one d. one step-d.; m. 2nd Marion Marshall Donen; one d. *Films include:* Halls of Montezuma 1951, The Frogmen 1951, Let's Make It Legal 1951, With a Song in My Heart 1952, What Price Glory? 1952, Stars and Stripes Forever 1952, The Silver Whip 1953, Titanic 1953, Star of Tomorrow, Beneath the 12-Mile Reef 1953, Prince Valiant 1954, Broken Lance 1954, White Feather 1955, A Kiss Before Dying 1956, The Mountain 1956, The True Story of Jesse James 1957, Stopover Tokyo 1957, The Hunters 1958, In Love and War 1958, Mardi Gras 1958, Say One For Me 1959, Between Heaven and Hell, All the Fine Young Cannibals 1960, Sail a Crooked Ship 1961, The Longest Day 1962, The War Lover 1962, The Condemned of Altona 1962, The Pink Panther 1963, Harper 1966, Banning 1967, The Biggest Bundle of Them All 1968, Don't Just Stand There! 1968, Winning 1969, Madame Sin 1972, Journey Through Rosebud 1972, The Towering Inferno 1974, Midway 1976, The Concorde: Airport '79 1979, Curse of the Pink Panther 1983, I Am the Cheese 1983, Delirious (uncredited) 1991, Dragon: The Bruce Lee Story 1993, Overdrive 1997, Austin Powers: International Man of Mystery 1997, Wild Things 1998, Something to Believe In 1998, The Kidnapping of Chris Burden 1999, Dill Scallion 1999, Crazy in Alabama 1999, No Vacancy 1999, Love and Fear, Austin Powers: The Spy Who Shagged Me 1999, Play It to the Bone 1999, Forever Fabulous 2000, The Mercury Project 2000, The Retrievers 2001, Sol Goode 2001, Jungle Juice 2001, Nancy and Frank – A Manhattan Love Story 2002, Austin Powers in Goldmember 2002, The Calling 2002, El Padrino 2004, The Fallen Ones 2005, The Wild Stallion 2006, Hoot 2006, Man in the Chair 2007, Netherbeast Incorporated 2007,. *Television series include:* How I Spent My Summer Vacation 1967, Hart to Hart 1979–84, It Takes a Thief (series) 1967–70, City Beneath the Sea 1971, Crosscurrent 1971, Killer by Night 1972, The Streets of San Francisco 1972, Colditz (series) 1972, The Affair 1973, The Abduction of Saint Anne 1975, Switch (series) 1975, Death at Love House 1976, Cat on a Hot Tin Roof 1976, The Critical List 1978, Pearl (mini-series) 1978, Hart to Hart (series) 1979, To Catch a King 1984, Lime Street (series) 1985, There Must be a Pony 1986, Love Among Thieves 1987, Windmills of the Gods 1988, Indiscreet 1988, Around the World in 80 Days (mini-series) 1989, This Gun for Hire 1991, False Arrest 1991, Jewels (mini-series) 1992, The Trials of Rosie O'Neill (series) 1992, Les audacieux 1993, Hart to Hart: Hart to Hart Returns 1993, Hart to Hart: Home Is Where the Hart Is 1994, Heaven & Hell: North & South, Book III (mini-series) 1994, Hart to Hart: Crimes of the Hart 1994, Hart to Hart: Old Friends Never Die 1994, Parallel Lives 1994, Hart to Hart: Secrets of the Hart 1995, Dancing in the Dark 1995, Hart to Hart: Two Harts in Three-Quarters Time 1995, Hart to Hart: Harts in High Season 1996, Hart to Hart: Till Death Do Us Hart 1996, Camino de Santiago (mini-series) 1999, Fatal Error 1999, Die Abzocker – Eine eiskalte Affäre (aka A Sordid Affair, and The Hustle) 2000, Rocket's Red Glare 2000, Becoming Dick 2000, The Retrievers 2001, Mystery Woman 2003, Hope & Faith 2003–06, Boston Legal 2006, Two and a Half Men 2007; numerous other TV appearances. *Address:* c/o William Morris Agency, One William Morris Place, Beverly Hills, CA 90212, USA (office). *Telephone:* (310) 859-4000 (office). *Fax:* (310) 859-4462 (office). *Website:* www.robert-wagner.com (office); www.wma.com (office).

WAGNER, Wolfgang; German opera director; b. 30 Aug. 1919, Bayreuth; s. of Siegfried Wagner and Winifred Wagner (née Williams); grandson of Richard Wagner; m. 1st Ellen Drexel 1943; one s. one d.; m. 2nd Gudrun Mack (née Armann) 1976; one d.; mil. service 1938–40; stage man. at Bayreuth Festival 1940; Asst with Preussische Staatsoper, Berlin 1940–44; returned to Bayreuth after war, worked with brother (the late Wieland Wagner) as dir annual Wagner operatic festival 1951–66, on his own 1967–2008; directed more than 400 performances 1953–2008; numerous guest appearances and int. tours; mem. Bayerische Akad. der Schönen Künste 1986; Ehrensenator Graz 1987, Munich 1988, Tübingen 1988; Bayerischer Maximiliansorden 1984; Dr hc (Univ. of Bayreuth) 1994. *Productions include:* Andreasnacht (Berlin 1944), The Rhinegold (Naples 1952), The Valkyrie (Naples 1952, 1953, Barcelona 1955, Venice 1957, Palermo 1962, Osaka 1967), Lohengrin (Bayreuth 1953, 1967, Taormina 1991, Tokyo 1997), Siegfried (Naples 1953, Brussels 1954, Venice 1957, Bologna 1957), The Flying Dutchman (Bayreuth 1955, Dresden 1988), Tristan and Isolde (Barcelona 1955, Bayreuth 1957, Venice 1958, Palermo 1960, Osaka 1967, Milan 1978), Parsifal (Barcelona 1955, Bayreuth 1975, 1989), Don Giovanni (Brunswick 1955), The Mastersingers of Nuremberg (Rome 1956, Bayreuth 1968, 1981, 1996, Dresden 1985), The Nibelung's Ring (Venice 1957, Bayreuth 1960, 1970), Götterdämmerung (Venice 1957), Tannhäuser (Bayreuth 1985). *Publication:* Acts (autobiog.).

Address: c/o Bayreuther Festspiele, PO Box 100262, 95402 Bayreuth, Germany. *Telephone:* 92178780.

WAGNER TIZÓN, Allan; Peruvian politician and diplomatist; b. 7 Feb. 1942, Lima; s. of Carlos Wagner Vizcarra and Antonieta Tizón Ponce; m. Julia de la Guerra Urquiaga; five d.; ed Nat. Univs of Trujillo and of Engineering, Lima, Universidad Católica and Universidad de San Marcos; joined Ministry of Foreign Affairs 1963; joined Diplomatic Service 1968; Chief of Econ. Dept, Embassy in Washington, DC 1972–74, Deputy Chief of Mission and Chargé d'affaires 1983–85; Chief of Political Dept, Embassy in Chile 1978–79; Minister of Foreign Affairs 1985–88, 2002–03; Amb. to Spain 1988–90, to Venezuela 1991–92 (resgnd); Prof. Diplomatic Acad. 1991; Dir of Devt and Adviser to Latin American Econ. System (SELA) 1992–98; Founder-mem. Peruvian Centre of Int. Studies (CEPEI), Pres. 1999–; Founder-mem. Inst. of European–Latin American Relations (IRELA); Amb. to USA 2001–02; Adviser to Sec.-Gen. of Andean Community of Nations –2002, Sec.-Gen. 2004–06; Minister of Defence 2006–07; Del. of Peru, Int. Court of Justice trying land and maritime boundary dispute with Chile 2007–; Orden Bernardo O'Higgins (Chile) 2001, Orden en el Grado de Gran Cruz (Chile) 2001, Gran Cruz de la Orden El Sol del Perú, Orden al Mérito por Servicios Distinguidos. *Address:* c/o Ministry of Defence, Avda Arequipa 291, Lima 1, Peru.

WAGONER, Dan; American dancer, choreographer and dance company director; *Distinguished Guest Artist, Connecticut College;* b. 1932, West Va; studied pharmacy; joined Martha Graham co. 1957; danced with Merce Cunningham's and Paul Taylor's cos; f. own dance co. 1969, fmr Dir Dan Wagoner and Dancers; has choreographed about 40 works; Artistic Dir London Contemporary Dance Theatre 1989–90; Distinguished Guest Artist, Connecticut Coll. 1999–. *Address:* Department of Dance, Connecticut College, 270 Mohegan Avenue, New London, CT 06320, USA (office). *Telephone:* (860) 447-1911 (office). *Website:* camel.conncoll.edu/academics/web_profiles/wagoner.html# (office).

WAGONER, David Russell, MA; American writer and academic; *Professor Emeritus of English, University of Washington;* b. 5 June 1926, Massillon, Ohio; m. 1st Patricia Parrott 1961 (divorced 1982); m. 2nd Robin H. Seyfried 1982; two d.; ed Pennsylvania State Univ., Indiana Univ.; served in USN 1944–46; Instructor, DePauw Univ., Greencastle, Ind. 1949–50, Pennsylvania State Univ. 1950–54; Assoc. Prof., Univ. of Washington, Seattle 1954–66, Prof. of English 1966–2000, Prof. Emer. 2000–; Elliston Lecturer, Univ. of Cincinnati 1968; Ed. Poetry Northwest, Seattle 1966–2002, Ed. Princeton Univ. Press Contemporary Poetry Series 1977–81; Poetry Ed. Missouri Press 1983–2000; Guggenheim Fellowship 1956, Ford Fellowship 1964, American Acad. Grant 1967, Nat. Endowment for the Arts Grant 1969; Morton Dauwen Zabel Prize (Poetry, Chicago) 1967, Ruth Lilly Prize 1991, Levinson Prize (Poetry, Chicago) 1994, Union League Prize (Poetry, Chicago) 1997; Pacific NW Booksellers Award 2000. *Short Stories:* Afternoon on the Ground 1978, Wild Goose Chase 1978, Mr. Wallender's Romance 1979, Cornet Solo 1979, The Water Strider 1979, Fly Boy 1980, The Bird Watcher 1980, Snake Hunt 1980. *Play:* An Eye for an Eye for an Eye 1973. *Verse:* Dry Sun, Dry Wind 1953, A Place to Stand 1958, Poems 1959, The Nesting Ground 1963, Five Poets of the Pacific Northwest (with others) 1964, Staying Alive 1966, New and Selected Poems 1969, Working Against Time 1970, Riverbed 1972, Sleeping in the Woods 1974, A Guide to Dungeness Spit 1975, Travelling Light 1976, Who Shall Be the Sun? Poems Based on the Lore, Legends and Myths of Northwest Coast and Plateau Indians 1978, In Broken Country 1979, Landfall 1981, First Light 1983, Through the Forest 1987, Walt Whitman Bathing 1996, Traveling Light: Collected and New Poems 1999, The House of Song 2002. *Novels:* The Man in the Middle 1955, Money, Money, Money 1955, Rock 1958, The Escape Artist 1965, Baby, Come On Inside 1968, Where is My Wandering Boy Tonight? 1970, The Road to Many a Wonder 1974, Tracker 1975, Whole Hog 1976, The Hanging Garden 1980. *Address:* 5416 154th Place, SW, Edmonds, WA 98026-4348, USA (home). *Telephone:* (425) 745-6964 (home). *E-mail:* renogawd@aol.com (home).

WAGONER, G. Richard, Jr, BEcons, MBA; American automobile industry executive; b. 9 Feb. 1953, Wilmington, Del.; s. of the late George Wagoner and Martha Wagoner; m. Kathy Wagoner (neé Kaylor) 1979; three s.; ed Duke and Harvard Univs; joined General Motors (GM) 1977, analyst, Office of the Treas., New York 1977, Treas. of GM do Brasil (GMB), São Paulo 1981–84, Exec. Dir of Finance, GMB 1984–87, Vice-Pres. and Finance Man. GM Canada Ltd 1987–88, Group Dir (Strategic Business Planning) Chevrolet-Pontiac-GM, Canada 1988–89, Vice-Pres. Finance, GM Europe, Zürich, Switzerland 1989–90, Pres. and Man. GMB 1991–92, Exec. Vice-Pres. and Chief Financial Officer 1992–94, Head of Worldwide Purchasing 1993–94, Exec. Vice-Pres. and Pres. N American Operations 1994–98, Pres. and COO 1998–2000, Chair. Automotive Strategy Bd, Pres. and CEO 2000–03, Chair. and CEO May 2003–09 (resgnd); Chair. A World in Motion Exec. Cttee, Soc. of Automotive Engineers; mem. Business Council, Business Roundtable; mem. Bd Trustees Duke Univ., Detroit Country Day School; mem. Bd Dean's Advisers, Harvard Business School. *Address:* c/o General Motors Corporation, 300 Renaissance Center, Detroit, MI 48265-3000, USA (office).

WAHID, Abdurrahman, (Gus Dur); Indonesian politician and religious leader; b. 4 Aug. 1940, Jombang, East Java; s. of K. H. Wahid Hasyim (Founder of Nahdlatul Ulama—NU); m. Sinta Nuriyah; four d.; ed Al-Azhar Univ., Cairo, Egypt, Baghdad Univ., Iraq; Lecturer, Hasyim As'yari Univ.; fmr Leader Nahdlatul Ulama 1984; Jt Founder Partai Kebangkitan Bangsa (PKB) (National Awakening Party); Pres. of Indonesia 1999–2001; impeached July 2001. *Address:* c/o Partai Kebangkitan Bangsa (PKB), Jalan Kalibata Timur 12, Jakarta Selatan 12519, Indonesia (office).

WAHL, Jacques Henri; French administrator; b. 18 Jan. 1932, Lille; s. of Abraham Wahl and Simone Kornbluth; m. Inna Cytrin 1969; two s. one d.; ed Inst. d'Etudes Politiques, Paris, Univs of Lille and Paris, Ecole Nat. d'Admin; Insp. des Finances 1961–; Treasury Dept 1965–68; Special Asst to Ministers of Econ. and Finance, François Ortoli 1968–69, Valéry Giscard d'Estaing 1969–71; Asst Dir of the Treasury for Int. Affairs 1971–73; Chair. Invisible Transactions Cttee, OECD 1971–73; Lecturer Inst. d'Etudes Politiques and Ecole Nat. d'Admin., Paris 1969–73; Financial Minister, French Embassies, USA and Canada 1973–78; Exec. Dir IMF, IBRD 1973–78; Sec.-Gen. to the Presidency of the French Repub. 1978–81; Insp.-Gen. des Finances 1981; Dir-Gen. Banque Nat. de Paris 1982 (known as BNP Paribas 2000–), Vice-Chair. 1993–97, Adviser to Chair. 1994–2001; Chair. Banque Nat. de Paris Intercontinentale 1993–97, mem. Bd 1994–; mem. Bd of Dirs BancWest (subsidiary of BNP Paribas) 1998–; Officier, Légion d'honneur, Officier Ordre nat. du Mérite, Commdr Ordre Nat. de Côte d'Ivoire, Officier Ordre du Mérite de la République Centrafricaine, Chevalier Ordre du Mérite de Haute Volta. *Address:* BNP Paribas, 19 boulevard des Italiens, 75009 Paris (office); 15 avenue de la Bourdonnais, 75007 Paris, France (home).

WAHLBERG, Mark Robert; American actor and musician; b. 5 June 1971, Dorchester, Mass; s. of Donal E. Wahlberg and Alma Wahlberg. *Films:* Renaissance Man 1994, The Basketball Diaries 1995, Fear 1996, Traveller 1997, Boogie Nights 1997, The Big Hit 1998, The Corruptor 1999, Three Kings 1999, The Yards 2000, The Perfect Storm 2000, Metal God 2000, Planet of the Apes 2001, Rock Star 2001, The Truth About Charlie 2003, The Italian Job 2003, I Heart Huckabees 2004, Four Brothers 2005, Invincible 2006, The Departed (Best Supporting Actor Nat. Soc. of Film Critics 2007) 2006, Shooter 2007, We Own the Night 2007, The Happening 2008, Max Payne 2008. *Television:* Teen Vid II (Video) 1991, The Substitute 1993. *Recordings include:* albums: Music For the People 1991, You Gotta Believe 1992 (as Marky Mark and the Funky Bunch). *Address:* c/o The Endeavor Agency, 9601 Wilshire Blvd, 10th Floor, Beverly Hills, CA 90212, USA. *Telephone:* (310) 248-2000. *Fax:* (310) 248-2020. *Website:* www.markwahlberg.com (office).

WAHLSTRÖM, Margareta, BA; Swedish international organization official; *Assistant Secretary-General for Disaster Risk Reduction, United Nations;* b. 30 March 1950; ed Univ. of Stockholm; has held numerous positions with non-governmental orgs and pvt. cos in SE Asia, Latin America and Africa; several sr positions with Int. Fed. of the Red Cross and Red Crescent Socs, Geneva 1989–2000, including UnderSec.-Gen. for the Response and Operations Coordination Div.; ind. consultant 2000–02; fmr Chief of Staff of the Special Rep. of the Sec.-Gen., UN Assistance Mission in Afghanistan (UNAMA), Deputy Special Rep. responsible for relief, reconstruction and devt –2004; Asst Sec.-Gen. for Humanitarian Affairs and Deputy Emergency Relief Coordinator, UN 2004–08, concurrently Special Coordinator of the Sec.-Gen. for Humanitarian Assistance to Tsunami-Affected Countries; Asst Sec.-Gen. for Disaster Risk Reduction and Special Rep. of the Sec.-Gen. for Implemen-tation of Hyogo Framework for Action in Secr. for Int. Strategy for Disaster Reduction, Geneva 2008–. *Address:* UN International Strategy for Disaster Reduction, Palais des Nations, Geneva 10, Switzerland (office). *E-mail:* isdr@un.org (office). *Website:* www.unisdr.org (office).

WAIGEL, Theodor, DJur; German politician; b. 22 April 1939, Oberrohr; s. of August Waigel and Genoveva Konrad; m. 1st Karin Hönig 1966 (divorced 1994); m. 2nd Irene Epple 1994; two s. one d.; ed Univs of Munich and Würzburg; with Bavarian Ministries of Finance and of Econ. and Transport 1969–72; mem. Bundestag 1972–2002; Chair. CSU Land (Bavarian) Group in Bundestag 1982–89; Chair. of CSU 1988–98; Minister of Finance 1989–98; Bayerischer Verdienstorden, Dr hc (Univ. of S Carolina) 1997. *Leisure interests:* climbing, theatre. *Address:* c/o Bundestag, 11011 Berlin, Germany.

WAIHEE, John David, III, BA, JD; American fmr state governor; b. 19 May 1946, Honokaa, Hawaii; m. Lynne Kobashigawa; one s. one d.; ed Andrews Univ., Cen. Mich. Univ. and Univ. of Hawaii; admitted to Hawaii Bar 1976; Community Educ. Co-ordinator, Benton Harbor (Mich.) area schools 1968–70; Asst Dir Community Educ. 1970–71; Program Evaluator, Admin. Asst to Dirs., Planner, Honolulu Model Cities Program 1971–73; Sr Planner, Office of Human Resources, City and Co. of Honolulu 1973–74, Program Man. 1974–75; Assoc. Shim, Sigal, Tam & Naito, Honolulu 1975–79; Partner, Waihee, Manuia, Yap, Pablo & Hoe, Honolulu 1979–82; mem. Hawaiian House of Reps 1980–82; Lt Gov. of Hawaii 1982–86, Gov. 1986–95; Democrat. *Address:* 745 Fort Street Mall, # 600, Honolulu, HI 96813, USA.

WAINWRIGHT, Geoffrey, MA, DD (Cantab.), DrThéol; British ecclesiastic and academic; *Robert Earl Cushman Professor of Christian Theology, Divinity School, Duke University;* b. 16 July 1939, Yorks.; s. of Willie Wainwright and Martha Burgess; m. Margaret H. Wiles 1965; one s. two d.; ed Gonville & Caius Coll. Cambridge and Univ. of Geneva; Prof. of Dogmatics, Protestant Faculty of Theology, Yaoundé, Cameroon 1967–73; Lecturer in Bible and Systematic Theology, Queen's Coll. Birmingham 1973–79; Roosevelt Prof. of Systematic Theology, Union Theological Seminary, New York 1979–83; Robert Earl Cushman Prof. of Christian Theology, Duke Univ. 1983–; mem. Faith and Order Comm. WCC 1977–91; Pres. Soc. Liturgica 1985–87; Co-Chair. Jt Comm. between World Methodist Council and Roman Catholic Church 1986–; Sec. American Theological Soc. 1988–95, Pres. 1996–97; Leverhulme European Fellow 1966–67; Pew Evangelical Fellow 1996–97; Hon. DD (North Park Univ.) 2001; Berakah Award, N American Acad. of Liturgy 1999, Festschrift: 'Ecumenical Theology in Worship, Doctrine and Life: Essays Presented to Geoffrey Wainwright on his Sixtieth Birthday' (ed. David Cunningham and others), Oxford Univ. Press 1999, Outstanding Ecumenist Award, Washington Theological Consortium 2003, Johannes Quasten Medal for excellence in theological scholarship, The Catholic University of America 2006. *Publications include:* Christian Initiation 1969,

Eucharist and Eschatology 1971, Doxology 1980, The Ecumenical Moment 1983, On Wesley and Calvin 1987, Methodists in Dialogue 1995, Worship With One Accord 1997, For Our Salvation: Two Approaches to the Work of Christ 1997, Is the Reformation Over? Protestants and Catholics at the Turn of the Millennia 2000, Lesslie Newbigin: A Theological Life 2000, Oxford History of Christian Worship 2006, Embracing Purpose: Essays on God, the World and the Church 2007. *Leisure interests:* music, art, cricket, tennis, travel. *Address:* The Divinity School, Box 90967, Duke University, Durham, NC 27708-0967 (office); 4011 W Cornwallis Road, Durham, NC 27705, USA (home). *Telephone:* (919) 660-3460 (office); (919) 489-2795 (home). *Fax:* (919) 660-3473 (office). *Website:* www.divinity.duke.edu/portal_memberdata/gwainwright (office).

WAISMAN RJAVINSTHI, David; Peruvian politician and business execu-tive; b. 4 May 1937, Chiclayo (Lambayeque); fmr Chair. Cttee for Small Industries and mem. Bd of Dirs Nat. Soc. of Industries in Peru; nat. spokesman Bd of Co-ordination, Corpn of Small and Micro Enterprises; Man. Dir Industrial Gameda; Founder-mem. and Chair. COPEI 1997–2000; mem. and Congressman Perú Posible (PP) party; elected mem. Congreso (Parl.) 2000; Second Vice-Pres. of Peru and Minister of Defence 2000–02. *Address:* c/o Ministry of Defence, Avda Arequipa 291, Lima 14, Peru (office).

WAITE, Terence Hardy, CBE; British fmr religious adviser, author and broadcaster; b. 31 May 1939, Bollington, Cheshire; s. of Thomas William Waite and Lena Waite (née Hardy); m. Helen Frances Watters 1964; one s. three d.; ed Wilmslow School, Stockton Heath, Cheshire, Church Army Coll., London; Lay Training Adviser to Bishop and Diocese of Bristol 1964–69; Prov. Training Adviser to Archbishop of Uganda, Rwanda and Burundi 1969–71; int. consultant working with Roman Catholic Church 1972–79; Adviser to Archbishop of Canterbury on Anglican Communion Affairs 1980–92, Iranian hostages mission 1981, Libyan hostages mission 1985; kidnapped in Beirut Jan. 1987, held for four years in solitary confinement, released 19 Nov. 1991 after 1,763 days; mem. Church of England Nat. Asscn 1966–68; Founder and Co-ordinator Southern Sudan Project 1969–71; fmr mem. Royal Inst. of Int. Affairs; Trustee Butler Trust (Prison Officers Award Project) 1986–; Founder-Pres. Y-Care Int. (YMCA Int. Devt Cttee) 1998–; Pres. Emmaus UK 1998–, Suffolk Br. of Far East Prisoners of War Asscn; Founder-Chair. Hostage UK 2005–; Chair. Prisons' Video Trust 1998–; Amb. for WWF-UK; Vice-Pres. Suffolk Asscn of Local Councils 1999–, East Cheshire Hospice 2001–; mem. Advisory Bd Gorton Monastery 2003–; Patron The Abbeyfield (Ipswich) Soc. 1996–, Canterbury Oast Trust, COFEPOW (Children (and families) of the Far East Prisoners of War), Friends of the Samaritans (Bury St Edmunds Br.), One World Broadcasting Trust 1987–, Strode Park Foundation for the Disabled, Hearne, Kent 1988–, Bury St Edmunds Volunteer Centre 1994–, Able Child Africa (Uganda Soc. for Disabled Children) 1995–, Warrington Male Voice Choir 1996–, The Romany Soc. 1997–, West Suffolk Voluntary Asscn for the Blind 1998–, The Bridge Project Sudbury Appeal 1999–, Save Our Parsonages 1999–,The British Friends of Neve Shalom, Wahat al-Salam 2003–, Underprivileged Children's Charity, Bristol 2003–, Children with Aids Charity 2004–, Habitat for Humanity 2004–, Rapid UK 2004–, Sunderland Counselling Services 2004–, and many other orgs; Trustee FreePlay Founda-tion; Fellow Commoner, Trinity Hall, Cambridge 1992–; Visiting Fellow, Magdalen Coll., Oxford 2006; Freeman, City of Canterbury 1992, Borough of Lewisham 1992; Hon. DCL (Kent) 1986, (City of London) 1992, (Sussex) 1992, (Robert Gordon Univ.) 2007; Hon. LLD (Durham) 1992, (Liverpool) 1992; Hon. LHD (Wittenberg) 1992; Hon. DHumLitt (Southern Florida) 1992, (Virginia Commonwealth) 1996; Hon. DPhil (Anglia Polytechnic) 2001, (Anglia Ruskin) 2005; Hon. DLitt (Nottingham Trent) 2001, (De Montfort) 2005, (Chester) 2008; Dr hc (Yale Univ. Divinity School) 1992; Templeton UK Award 1985, Roosevelt Four Freedoms Medal 1992. *Publications:* Taken on Trust 1993, Footfalls in Memory 1995, Travels with a Primate 2000; numerous contribs to journals and periodicals. *Leisure interests:* music, walking, travel, Jungian studies, int. affairs and politics. *Address:* Trinity Hall, Cambridge, CB2 1TJ, England.

WAITS, Tom; American singer, songwriter, musician (piano, guitar, percus-sion) and actor; b. 7 Dec. 1949, Pomona, Calif.; m. Kathleen Brennan 1980; two s. one d.; recording artist 1971–; Grammy Award for Best Alternative Album 1992, for Best Contemporary Folk Album 2000. *Theatre:* Frank's Wild Years (co-writer, play and music) 1986, The Black Rider 1989, Alice 1992, Woyzeck 2002. *Films:* Paradise Alley 1978, Wolfen 1981, One From the Heart 1982, The Outsiders 1983, Rumblefish 1983, The Cotton Club 1984, Down By Law 1986, Ironweed 1987, Candy Mountain 1988, Cold Feet 1989, Mystery Train 1989, Bearskin: An Urban Fairytale 1989, The Two Jakes 1990, Queen's Logic 1991, The Fisher King 1991, At Play in the Fields of the Lord 1991, Bram Stoker's Dracula 1992, Short Cuts 1993, Mystery Men 1999, Coffee and Cigarettes 2003, Domino 2005, Wristcutters: A Love Story 2006. *Compositions include:* Ol' 55, The Eagles 1974, Angel Wings, Rickie Lee Jones 1983, Downtown Train, Rod Stewart 1990, The Long Way Home, Norah Jones 2004, Tempta-tion, Diana Krall 2004, Jersey Girl, Bruce Springsteen, Domino 2005. *Recordings include:* albums: Closing Time 1973, The Heart of Saturday Night 1974, Nighthawks at the Diner 1975, Small Change 1976, Foreign Affairs 1977, Blue Valentine 1978, Heartattack and Vine 1980, Bounced Checks 1981, One from the Heart 1982, Swordfishtrombones 1983, Anthology 1983, Asylum Years 1984, Rain Dogs 1985, Frank's Wild Years 1987, Big Time 1988, The Early Years 1991, The Early Years Vol. 2 1992, Night on Earth (with Kathleen Brennan) 1992, Bone Machine (Grammy Award for Best Alternative Music 1993) 1992, The Black Rider 1993, Beautiful Maladies 1998, Mule Variations 2000, Used Songs 1973–80 2001, Alice 2002, Blood Money 2002, Real Gone 2004, Orphans: Brawlers, Bawlers & Bastards 2006. *Address:* c/o Anti-Inc, 2798 Sunset Blvd, Los Angeles, CA 90026, USA (office). *Website:* www.anti.com (office).

WAITT, Theodore (Ted) W.; American computer industry executive; *Founder, Waitt Family Foundation;* b. 18 Jan. 1963, Sioux City, Iowa; m. Joan Waitt; four c.; ed Univ. of Iowa; f. Gateway (with Mike Hammond) 1985, Pres. 1985–96, CEO 1993–99, Chair. 1993–2005, relected Pres. and CEO 2001–04; f. Waitt Family Foundation 1993, Waitt Inst. Institute for Violence Prevention 2005, Waitt Inst. for Discovery 2005; Founder, Avalon Capital Group (pvt. investment co.); Vice Chair. Jonas Salk Inst. for Biological Studies; mem. Advisory Council Nat. Geographic Soc.; fmr Chair. Founding Fathers campaign of Family Violence Prevention Fund; Hon. DSc (Univ. of S Dakota); US Small Business Asscn Young Entrepreneur of the Year, US Jr Chamber of Commerce Ten Outstanding Young Americans Award, Nat. Alliance of Business Henry Ford II Award. *Address:* c/o Waitt Family Foundation, PO Box 1948, La Jolla, CA 92038-1948, USA. *Telephone:* (858) 551-4400. *Fax:* (858) 551-6871. *Website:* waittfoundation.org; avalon.com.

WAJDA, Andrzej; Polish film and theatrical director; b. 6 March 1926, Suwałki; s. of Jakub Wajda and Aniela Wajda; m. 1st Beata Tyszkiewicz 1967 (divorced); one d.; m. 2nd Krystyna Zachwatowicz 1975; ed Acad. of Fine Arts, Kraków and Higher Film School, Łódź; Film Dir 1954–; Theatre Dir Teatr Stary, Kraków 1962–98; Man. Dir Teatr Powszechny, Warsaw 1989–90; Senator of Repub. of Poland 1989–91; Pres. Polish Film Asscn 1978–83, Solidarity Lech Wałęsa Council 1981–89, Presidential Council for Culture 1992–94; Founder Manggha Centre of Japanese Art and Technology, Kraków 1987; mem. Inst. de France 1997–, Acad. des Beaux Arts, France 1997–; Hon. mem. Union of Polish Artists and Designers (ZPAP) 1977; Order of the Banner of Labour (Second Class) 1975, Officer's Cross of Polonia Restituta Order, Order of Kirill and Methodius (First Class), Bulgaria 1978, Order of Rising Sun, Japan 1995, Commdr Légion d'honneur 2001, Grosses Verdienstkreuz des Verdienstordens der Bundesrepublik Deutschland 2001; Dr hc (American Univ. Washington) 1981, (Bologna) 1988, (Jagiellonian Univ., Kraków) 1989, (Lyon Univ.) 1995, (Univ. Libre, Brussels) 1995 (Acad. of Fine Arts, Warsaw) 2000, (Polish. Nat. Films, TV and Theatre School, Łódź) 2000; numerous prizes including State First Class Prize 1974, Konrad Swinarski Prize 1976, Premio David di Donatello 'Luchino Visconti' 1978, Prize of Cttee for Polish Radio and TV 1980, Onassis Prize, Greece 1982, Kyoto Prize, Japan 1987, Praemium Imperiale, Japan 1997, BAFTA Fellowship 1982, César Award, France 1983, Pirandello Artistic Award, Italy 1986, 'Felix' European Film Awards (Lifetime Achievement Award) 1990, Golden Lion, Venice 1998, Acad. Award (Oscar) 2000 (donated his Oscar statuette to Museum of Jagiellonian Univ., Kraków 2000). *Films:* Pokolenie (A Generation) (Polish State Prize) 1955, Idę do słońca (I'm Going to the Sun) 1955, Kanal (Jury Special Silver Palm Award, Cannes 1957) 1957, Popiół i diament (Ashes and Diamonds) (Fipresci Prize, Venice 1959, David O. Selznick's 'Silver Laurel' Award 1962) 1957, Lotna 1959, Niewinni czarodzieje (Innocent Sorcerers) 1960, Samson 1961, Sibirska Ledi Makbet (Siberian Lady Macbeth) 1962, L'Amour à Vingt Ans (Love at Twenty) 1962, Popioły (Ashes) 1965, Gates to Paradise 1968, Wszystko na sprzedaż (Everything for Sale) 1969, Polowanie na muchy (Hunting Flies) 1969, Krajobraz po bitwie (Landscape After Battle) (Golden Globe, Milan 1971) 1970, Brzezina (The Birch Wood) (Fipresci Prize, Milan 1970, Golden Medal, Moscow 1971) 1970, Wesele (The Wedding) (Silver Shell, San Sebastián 1973) 1973, Ziemia obiecana (The Promised Land) (Gdańsk Golden Lions 1975, Golden Medal, Moscow 1975) 1975, Człowiek z marmuru (Man of Marble) (Fipresci Prize, Cannes 1978, Jury Special Prize, Cartagena 1980) 1977, Bez znieczulenia (Without Anaesthetic) (OCIC Prize, Cannes 1979) 1978, Panny z Wilka (The Maids of Wilko) 1979, Dyrygent (The Orchestral Conductor) 1980, Człowiek z żelaza (Man of Iron) (Palme d'Or, Cannes 1981) 1981, Danton (Prix Luis Delluc 1982) 1982, Eine Liebe in Deutschland (A Love in Germany) 1983, Kronika wypadków miłosnych (Chronicle of Love Affairs) 1986, Les Possédés (The Possessed) 1987, Korczak 1990, Pierścionek z orłem w koronie (The Crowned-Eagle Ring) 1992, Nastasya 1994, Wielki Tydzień (The Holy Week) (Silver Bear, Berlin 1996) 1995, Panna Nikt (Miss Nobody) 1996, Pan Tadeusz (The Last Foray in Lithuania) 1999, Zemsta (Revenge) 2002, Lekcja polskiego kina (Lesson of Polish Cinema, document) 2002, Katyn 2007. *Television:* Przekładaniec (Roly-Poly) 1968, Macbeth 1969, Pilatus und Andere (for German TV ZDF) (Bambi Award 1972) 1971, Noc listopadowa (November Night) 1975, The Shadow Line (for Thames TV, London) 1976, Z biegiem lat z beiegiem dni (Gone with the Years, Gone with the Days) 1978–79, Zbrodnia i kara (Schuld und Suhne) 1985, Wieczernik (The Last Supper) 1985, Hamlet IV 1989, Silniejsza (The Stronger One) 1990, Mishima 1995, Bigda idzie (Bigda Comes) 1999, Wyrok na Franciszka Kłosa (Judgment on Franciszek Kłos) 2000, Noc czerwcowa (June Night) 2002. *Plays:* Kapelusz pełen deszczu (Hatful of Rain) 1959, Hamlet 1960, 1980, 1989, Dwoje na huśtawce (Two on the Seesaw) 1960, 1990, Demons 1963, Wesele (The Wedding) 1962, 1991, Play Strindberg 1970, Sticks and Bones (Moscow) 1972, Noc listopadowa (November Night) 1974, Sprawa Dantona (The Danton Case) 1975, 1980, Kiedy rozum śpi (When Reason is Asleep) 1976, Emigranci (Emigrés) 1976, Nastasya Filipowna (improvisation based on Dostoyevsky's The Idiot) 1977, Rozmowy z Katem (Conversation with the Executioner) 1977, White Marriage (Yale Repertory) 1977, Z biegiem lat z biegiem dni (Gone with the Years, Gone with the Days) 1978, Antygona 1984, Zbrodnia i kara (Crime and Punishment) 1984, Wieczernik (The Last Supper) 1985, Zemsta (Revenge) 1986, Panna Julia (Miss Julia) 1988, Dybuk 1988, Lekcja polskiego (Lesson of Polish Language) 1988, Romeo and Juliet 1990, The Ghost Sonata (Stockholm) 1994, Mishima 1994, Klątwa (The Curse) 1997, Słomkowy kapelusz (The Straw Hat) 1998. *Publications:* Powtórka z caiosci) 1986, My Life in Film 1989, Wajada mówi o sobie (Wajda Talks about Himself) 1991, Wajda o polityce, o srtuce, o sobie (Wajda about Politics, Arts and Himself) 2000, Podwojne spojnenie (Double Take), Kino i reszta świata (Cinema and the Rest of the World) 2000. *Address:* Manggha Centre of Japanese Art and Technology, ul. M. Konopnickiej 26, 30-302 Kraków, Poland

(office). *Telephone:* (12) 2672703 (office); (12) 2673753 (office). *Fax:* (12) 2674079 (office). *Website:* www.manggha.krakow.pl (office); www.wajda.pl.

WAJED, Sheikh Hasina; Bangladeshi politician; *Prime Minister;* b. 28 Sept. 1947, Tungipara, Gopalganj Dist, East Pakistan (now Bangladesh); d. of the late Sheikh Mujibur Rahman (fmr Prime Minister of Bangladesh) and of Begum Fazilatunnesa; m. M. A. Wazed Miah; one s. one d.; ed Univ. of Dhaka; active in politics as a student; arrested during civil war 1971; assumed leadership of opposition Awami League from her father, first elected Pres. 1981, fifth time in 2002–; lived in exile 1975–81; arrested and placed under house arrest on several occasions during 1980s; Prime Minister of Bangladesh 1996–2001, also Minister of the Armed Forces Div., of the Cabinet Div., of Special Affairs, of Defence, of Power, Energy and Mineral Resources and of the Establishment; charged with corruption and alleged plundering of state funds while in office Dec. 2001; Leader of official parl. opposition 2001–09; arrested on extortion charges July 2007, trial suspended; indicted on extortion charges 2008, High Court stopped trial; Prime Minister 2009–, also Minister of the Armed Forces Div., Cabinet Div., Defence, Power, Energy and Mineral Resources, Establishment, Housing and Public Works, Religious Affairs and Women and Children's Affairs; shared Houphouet-Boigny Peace Prize 1999. *Publications:* several books and numerous articles. *Address:* Prime Minister's Office, Old Sangsad Bhaban, Tejgaon, Dhaka 1215, Bangladesh (office). *Telephone:* (2) 8151159 (office). *Fax:* (2) 8113244 (home). *E-mail:* info@pmo.gov .bd (office). *Website:* www.pmo.gov.bd (office); www.albd.org (office).

WAKABAYASHI, Masatoshi; Japanese politician; b. 4 July 1934; ed Tokyo Univ.; joined Ministry of Agric. and Forestry 1957, Dir Agricultural Policy Planning Div., Agricultural Structure Improvement Bureau 1978–81; Dir Gen. Affairs Div., Agricultural Structure Improvement Bureau, Ministry of Agric., Forestry and Fisheries 1981–83; Dir Gen. Affairs Div., Dir-Gen.'s Secr., Nat. Land Agency 1981; elected to House of Reps 1983, re-elected 1986, 1993, served as Parl. Vice-Minister, Man. and Coordination Agency 1989–90, Dir Cttee on Transport, LDP 1994; elected to House of Councillors 1998, re-elected 2004, Chair. Cttee on Agric., Forestry and Fisheries 1999; Parl. Vice-Minister, Ministry of Finance 1999–2001, Sr Vice-Minister of Finance 2001, Dir Cttee on Financial Affairs 2001, Research Comm. on the Constitution 2002, Special Cttee on Financial Issues and Revitalization of the Economy 2002, Special Cttee on Protection of Personal Information 2003, Chair. Special Cttee on Prevention of Int. Terrorism 2003, Cttee on Discipline 2004, Dir Cttee on the Budget 2004, Chair. Special Cttee on Mountain Villages 2004; Chair. LDP Policy Bd 2005, Acting Chair. LDP Research Comms on the Constitution and Election System 2005; Minister of the Environment 2006–07, Minister in Charge of Global Environmental Problems 2006–07, Minister of Agric., Forestry and Fisheries 2007–08. *Address:* Liberal-Democratic Party (LDP), 1-11-23, Nagata-cho, Chiyoda-ku, Tokyo 100-8910, Japan (office). *Telephone:* (3) 3581-6211 (office). *Website:* koho@ldp.jimin.or.jp (office); www.jimin.jp (office).

WAKEFIELD, Sir Peter George Arthur, KBE, CMG; British diplomatist; b. 13 May 1922; s. of John Bunting Wakefield and Dorothy Ina Wakefield (née Stace); m. Felicity Maurice-Jones 1951; four s. one d.; ed Cranleigh School and Corpus Christi Coll. Oxford; served in Army 1942–47; Mil. Govt, Eritrea 1946–47; Hulton Press 1947–49; entered Diplomatic Service 1949; Middle East Centre for Arab Studies 1950; Second Sec., British Embassy, Jordan 1950–52; Foreign Office 1953–55, 1964–66; First Sec., British Middle East Office, Nicosia, Cyprus 1955–56; First Sec. (Commercial), Egypt 1956, Austria 1957–60, Japan 1960–63; Admin. Staff Coll., Henley 1957; Consul-Gen. and Counsellor, Benghazi 1966–69; Econ. and Commercial Counsellor, Tokyo 1970–72, Econ. and Commercial Minister 1973; seconded as Special Adviser on the Japanese Market, British Overseas Trade Bd 1973–75; Amb. to Lebanon 1975–78, to Belgium 1979–81; Dir Nat. Art Collections Fund London 1982–92; UK Dir, Trust for Museum Exhbns; Gov. European Cultural Foundation 1988–92; Chair. Heritage Co-ordination Group 1993–97, Asia House, London 1994–2000 (Trustee 2000–), Richmond Theatre 1993–2001; Chair. of Judges, Jerwood Painting Prize 1994/95; Hon. LLD (St Andrews) 1991. *Leisure interests:* modern British painting, ceramics, restoring ruins. *Address:* Asia House, 63 New Cavendish Street, London, W1G 7LP, England (office); La Molineta, Frigiliana 29788, nr Málaga, Spain (home). *Telephone:* (20) 7307-5454 (office); (20) 8892-6390 (England) (home); 952533175 (Spain). *Fax:* (20) 7307-5459 (office). *E-mail:* enquiries@asiahouse.co.uk (office); sirpeter@wakefield.biz. *Website:* www.asiahouse.org (office).

WAKEHAM, Baron (Life Peer), cr. 1992, of Maldon in the County of Essex; **John Wakeham,** JP, FCA, PC, DL; British politician; *Chairman, House of Lords Economic Affairs Committee;* b. 22 June 1932, Godalming, Surrey; s. of the late Maj. W. J. Wakeham and Mrs E. R. Wakeham; m. 1st Anne Roberta Bailey 1965 (died 1984); two s.; m. 2nd Alison Bridget Ward 1985; one s.; ed Charterhouse; JP Inner London 1972–; MP for Maldon 1974–83, for Colchester S and Maldon 1983–92; Asst Govt Whip 1979–81, Govt Chief Whip 1983–87; Lord Commr of HM Treasury 1981, Minister of State 1982–83; Parl. Under-Sec. of State, Dept of Industry 1981–82; Lord Privy Seal 1987–88; Leader of House of Commons 1987–89, Sec. of State for Energy 1989–92; Lord Privy Seal and Leader of the House of Lords 1992–94; Chair. House of Lords Econ. Affairs Cttee 2005–; Lord Pres. of Council 1988–89; Chair. Carlton Club 1992–98, Press Complaints Comm. 1995–2002, British Horseracing Bd 1996–98 (mem. 1995–98); Chair. Genner Holdings Ltd 1994–, Alexandra Rose Day 1998–; Chair. Royal Comm. on Lords Reform 1999–2000; Chancellor Brunel Univ. 1998–; Trustee HMS Warrior 1860 1997–. *Leisure interests:* sailing, reading. *Address:* House of Lords, Westminster, London, SW1A 0PW, England (office). *Telephone:* (20) 7219-3162 (office). *Fax:* (20) 8672-8839 (office). *Website:* www.parliament.uk/parliamentary_committees/ lords_economic_affairs.cfm.

WAKELEY, Amanda; British fashion designer; b. 15 Sept. 1962, Chester; d. of Sir John Wakeley; ed Cheltenham Ladies' Coll.; worked in fashion industry, NY 1983–85; began designing for pvt. clients in UK 1986; launched own label 1990; operation includes retail, wholesale worldwide, bridal and corporate-wear consultancy, diffusion range and fine jewellery collection; Co-Chair. Fashion Targets Breast Cancer Campaign 1996–; Glamour Award, British Fashion Awards 1992, 1993, 1996. *Achievements:* raised over £5 million for 'Breakthrough' in 1996, 1998, 2000, 2002 and 2004 as Co-Chair. of Fashion Targets Breast Cancer Campaign. *Leisure interests:* travel, driving, water-skiing, snowskiing, rollerblading. *Address:* Amanda Wakeley Ltd, 26–28 Conway Street, London, W1T 6BQ, England (office). *Telephone:* (20) 7529-0930 (office). *Fax:* (20) 7692-6770 (office). *E-mail:* ajw@amandawakeley.com (office). *Website:* www.amandawakeley.com (office).

WAKIL, Abdul; Afghan politician; b. 1945, Kabul province; ed Kabul Univ.; fmr Sec. Gen. of Afghan Foreign Ministry, Minister of Finance, Amb. to UK and to Viet Nam; mem. People's Democratic Party of Afghanistan (PDPA) 1964, mem. Cen. Cttee 1977; mem. of Revolutionary Council of Afghanistan; Minister of Foreign Affairs 1986–89. *Address:* c/o Ministry of Foreign Affairs, Kabul, Afghanistan.

WAKOSKI, Diane, BA; American poet and academic; *University Distinguished Professor, Department of English, Michigan State University;* b. 3 Aug. 1937, Whittier, Calif.; m. Robert J. Turney 1982; ed Univ. of Calif. at Berkeley; began writing poetry, New York 1960–73; worked as a book shop clerk, a jr high school teacher and by giving poetry readings on coll. campuses; Poet-in-Residence, Prof. of English, Michigan State Univ. 1975–, Univ. Distinguished Prof. 1990–; mem. Authors' Guild, PEN, Poetry Soc. of America; Cassandra Foundation Grant 1970, Guggenheim Fellowship 1972, Nat. Endowment for the Arts Grant 1973, Writer's Fulbright Award 1984, Mich. Arts Foundation Award 1989, Michigan Arts Foundation Distinguished Artist Award 1989, Michigan Library Asscn Author of the Year 2003. *Publications:* Coins and Coffins 1962, Discrepancies and Apparitions 1966, The George Washington Poems 1967, Inside the Blood Factory 1968, The Magellanic Clouds 1970, The Motorcycle Betrayal Poems 1971, Smudging 1972, Dancing on the Grave of a Son of a Bitch 1973, Trilogy (reprint of first three collections) 1974, Virtuoso Literature for Two and Four Hands 1975, Waiting for the King of Spain 1976, The Man Who Shook Hands 1978, Cap of Darkness 1980, The Magician's Feastletters 1982, Norii Magellanici (collection of poems from various vols trans. into Romanian) 1982, The Collected Greed 1984, The Rings of Saturn 1986, Emerald Ice (selected poems 1962–87) (William Carlos Williams Prize 1989) 1988, The Archaeology of Movies and Books: Vol. I Medea The Sorceress 1991, Vol. II Jason The Sailor 1993, Vol. III The Emerald City of Las Vegas 1995, Vol. IV Argonaut Rose 1998, The Butcher's Apron: New and Selected Poems 2000; Towards A New Poetry (criticism) 1980. *Leisure interests:* cooking, films, letters, gambling. *Address:* 607 Division Street, East Lansing, MI 48823 (home); 207 Morrill Hall, East Lansing, MI 48824, USA (office). *Telephone:* (517) 355-0308 (office); (517) 332-3385 (home). *E-mail:* dwakoski@aol.com; wakoski@msu.edu (office). *Website:* www.english.msu.edu (office).

WAKUI, Yoji; Japanese business executive and fmr politician; *Chairman and Representative Director, Japan Tobacco Inc.;* b. 5 Feb. 1942; began career at Ministry of Finance 1964, Deputy Vice-Minister of Finance 1995–97, Dir-Gen. Budget Bureau 1997–99; Vice-Chair. General Insurance Asscn of Japan 1999–2004; Chair. and Rep. Dir Japan Tobacco Inc. 2004–; Auditor Nipponkoa Insurance Co. 2006. *Address:* Japan Tobacco Inc., 2-1, Toranomon 2-chome, Minato-ku, Tokyo, 105-8422, Japan (office). *Telephone:* (3) 3582-3111 (office). *Fax:* (3) 5572-1441 (office). *E-mail:* info@jti.com (office). *Website:* www.jti.com (office).

WALA, Adolf; Austrian banker; b. 18 May 1937, Dürnholz; m.; three c.; ed Commercial School of Vienna Merchants' Asscn; Deputy Supervisor, later Supervisor, Foreign Exchange Dept, Creditanstalt-Bankverein 1957–65; joined Credit and Loans Dept, Austrian Nat. Bank (OeNB) 1965, Head of Office of First Deputy Gov. 1973–80, Deputy Exec. Dir Credit and Loans Dept 1980–88, Gen. Man. 1988–98, Pres. of OeNB 1998–2003; fmr mem. Supervisory Bd Casinos Austria AG 1999, Burgtheater GmbH 1999; Order of Merit; Order of Kts of Malta 1998; Grand Decoration of Honour in Gold with Star for Services to Repub. of Austria 1999; Gold Medal for Outstanding Services to State of Vienna 1994, Arthur von Rosthon Medal 2000. *Address:* c/o Oesterreichische Nationalbank, Otto-Wagner-Platz 3, Postfach 61, 1090 Vienna, Austria (office).

WALCH, Ernest Joseph, M.J., DR.IUR.; Liechtenstein lawyer and politician; *Partner, Walch & Schurti;* b. 1956; ed Univ. of Innsbruck, Austria, New York Univ. School of Law., USA; admitted to Bar, USA 1983, Liechtenstein 1984; Rep. of Progressive Citizens' Party (FBP) to Steering Cttee. of European Democratic Union 1983–93, Pres. FBP 2000–01; mem. Parl. 1989–96, FPB Parl. Spokesman 1992–93, Pres. of Parl. 1993; Minister of Foreign Affairs 2001–05; Co-founder and Pnr, Walch & Schurti (law firm) 1991–; mem. New York State Bar Asscn., Liechtenstein Bar Asscn, Europäische Anwaltsvereinigung e.V., Int. Acad. of Estate and Trust Law, Liechtenstein Asscn of Professional Trustees. *Publications include:* numerous works on int. legal issues. *Address:* Walch & Schurti, Zollstrasse 9, 9490 Vaduz, Liechtenstein (office). *Telephone:* 2372000 (office). *Fax:* 2372100 (office). *Website:* www.walchschurti.net (office).

WALCOTT, Derek, OBE, BA, FRSL; Saint Lucia poet and playwright; b. 23 Jan. 1930, Castries; s. of Warwick Walcott and Alix Walcott; m. 1st Fay Moston 1954 (divorced 1959); one s.; m. 2nd Margaret R. Maillard 1962 (divorced); two d.; m. 3rd Norline Metivier 1982 (divorced 1993); ed St Mary's Coll., Castries, Univ. of Wisconsin, Univ. of the West Indies, Jamaica; teacher, St Mary's Coll., Castries 1947–50, 1954, Grenada Boys' Secondary School, St George's 1953–54, Jamaica Coll., Kingston 1955; feature writer, Public Opinion, Kingston 1956–57; founder-Dir, Little Carib Theatre Workshop, later Trinidad Theatre Workshop 1959–76; feature writer, Trinidad Guardian, Port-of-Spain 1960–62, drama critic 1963–68; Visiting Prof., Columbia Univ., USA 1981, Harvard Univ. 1982, 1987; Asst Prof. of Creative Writing, Brown Univ. 1981, Visiting Prof. 1985–; hon. mem. American Acad. of Arts and Letters; mem. Poetry Soc. (vice-pres.); Rockefeller Foundation grants 1957, 1966, and Fellowship 1958, Ingram Merrill Foundation grant 1962, Eugene O'Neill Foundation Fellowship 1969, Guggenheim Fellowship 1977, John D. and Catherine T. MacArthur Foundation Fellowship 1981; Arts Advisory Council of Jamaica Prize 1960, Guinness Award 1961, Borestone Mountain Awards 1964, 1977, RSL Heinemann Awards 1966, 1983, Cholmondeley Award 1969, Gold Hummingbird Medal, Trinidad 1969, Obie Award 1971, Welsh Arts Council Int. Writers Prize 1980, Los Angeles Times Book Prize 1986, Queen's Gold Medal for Poetry 1988, Nobel Prize for Literature 1992. *Plays:* Cry for a Leader 1950, Henri Christophe: A Chronicle 1950, Robin and Andrea 1950, Senza Alcun Sospetto 1950, The Price of Mercy 1951, Three Assassins 1951, Harry Dernier 1952, The Charlatan 1954, Crossroads 1954, The Sea at Dauphin 1954, The Golden Lions 1956, The Wine of the Country 1956, Ione: A Play with Music 1957, Ti-Jear and his Brothers 1957, Drums and Colours 1958, Jourmard 1959, Malcochon 1959, Batai 1965, Dream on Monkey Mountain 1967, Franklin: A Tale of the Islands 1969, In a Fine Castle 1970, The Joker of Seville (with G. Mcdermott) 1974, O Babylon! 1976, Remembrance 1977, The Snow Queen 1977, Pantomime 1978, Marie Leveau (with G. Mcdermott) 1979, The Isle is Full of Noises 1982, Beef, No Chicken 1985, The Odyssey 1993, The Capeman (musical, jtly) 1997. *Publications:* poetry: 25 Poems 1948, Epitaph for the Young: XII Cantos 1949, Poems 1951, In a Green Night, Poems 1948–60 1962, Selected Poems 1964, The Castaway and Other Poems 1965, The Gulf and Other Poems 1969, Another Life 1973, Sea Grapes 1976, The Star-Apple Kingdom 1979, Selected Poetry 1981, The Fortunate Traveller 1981, The Caribbean Poetry of Derek Walcott, and the Art of Romare Bearden 1983, Midsummer 1984, Collected Poems 1948–1984 1986, The Arkansas Testament 1987, Omeros (epic poem) (WHSmith Literary Award 1991) 1989, Poems 1965–1980 1992, The Bounty 1997, Tiepolo's Hounds 2000, The Prodigal: A Poem 2005, Selected Poems 2007; non-fiction: The Antilles, Fragments of Epic Memory: The Nobel Lecture 1993, What the Twilight Says (essays) 1998, Homage to Robert Frost (jtly) 1998. *Address:* PO Box GM 926, Castries, St Lucia, West Indies (home); c/o Faber & Faber, Bloomsbury House, 74–77 Great Russell Street, London, WC1B 3DA, England (office). *Telephone:* 450-0559 (home). *Fax:* 450-0935 (home).

WALD, Sir Nicholas John, Kt, MBBS, DSc (Med), FRS, FRCP, FFPH, FRCOG, FMedSci, CBiol. FIBiol; British medical scientist and academic; *Director, Wolfson Institute of Preventive Medicine, Barts and The London, Queen Mary's School of Medicine and Dentistry;* b. 31 May 1944; s. of Adolf Max Wald and Frieda Shatsow; m. Nancy Evelyn Miller 1966; three s. one d.; ed Univ. Coll. London, Univ. Coll. Hosp. Medical School; mem. science staff MRC 1971–; mem. science staff Imperial Cancer Research Fund (ICRF) Cancer Epidemiology and Clinical Trials Unit, Oxford 1972–82, Deputy Dir 1982–83, Prof. and Head, Centre for Environmental and Preventive Medicine, Barts and The London, Queen Mary's School of Medicine and Dentistry 1983–, Hon. Consultant 1983–, Dir Wolfson Inst. of Preventive Medicine 1991–95, 1997–; Hon. Dir Cancer Research Campaign Screening Group 1986–2000; Chair. Study Monitoring Cttee of MRC Randomised Clinical Trial of Colo-Rectal Cancer Screening 1986–, Steering Cttee for Multicentre Aneurysm Screening Study 1997–; mem. Scientific Cttee on Tobacco and Health, Dept of Health 1993–2002, Medicines Control Agency Expert Advisory Panel 1996–; mem. Cttee on Ethical Issues in Medicine, Royal Coll. of Physicians 1988–, HPV/LBC Pilots Screening Group 2000–, National Radiological Protection Bd Advisory Group on Nuclear Test Veterans 2000–; mem. Wellcome Trust Physiology and Pharmaceutical Panel 1995–2000; mem. Information Sub-Cttee, Faculty of Public Health 2001–; mem. Council of Trustees, Foundation for Study of Infant Deaths 2001; mem. Council, Action on Smoking and Health 2002–; Ed.-in-Chief Journal of Medical Screening 1994–; Hon. DSc (Med) (London) 2005; Kennedy Foundation Int. Award in Scientific Research 2000, Foundation for Blood Research Award 2000, Obstetrical Soc. of Philadelphia Int. Speakers' Award 2001, BMA Medical Book Competition Award 2001, US Public Health Service and Centers for Disease Control Award 2002, Harvard School of Public Health Award 2004. *Publications:* Alpha-Fetoprotein Screening – The Current Issues (co-ed.) 1981, Antenatal and Neonatal Screening 1984 (2nd edn co-ed. 2000), Nicotine Smoking and the Low Tar Programme (co-ed.) 1989, Passive Smoking: A Health Hazard (co-ed.) 1991, International Smoking Statistics (co-author) 1993 (2nd edn, co-ed.) 2004, Epidemiological Approach 2004. *Leisure interests:* economics, boating. *Address:* Barts and The London, Queen Mary's School of Medicine and Dentistry, Charterhouse Square, London, EC1M 6BQ (office); Centre for Environmental and Preventive Medicine, Wolfson Institute of Preventive Medicine, Barts and The London, Queen Mary's School of Medicine and Dentistry, Charterhouse Square, London, EC1M 6BQ; 9 Park Crescent Mews East, London, W1W 5AF, England (home). *Telephone:* (20) 7882-6269 (office); (20) 7636-2721 (home). *Fax:* (20) 7882-6270 (office). *E-mail:* n.j.wald@qmul.ac.uk (office). *Website:* www.smd.Qmul.ac.uk/wolfson (office).

WALD, Patricia McGowan, LLB; American lawyer and judge; b. 16 Sept. 1928, Torrington, Conn.; d. of Joseph McGowan and Margaret McGowan (née O'Keefe); m. Robert L. Wald 1952; two s. three d.; ed Connecticut Coll. for Women, Yale Law School; Law Clerk, US Court of Appeals for the Second Circuit 1951–52; Assoc., Arnold, Fortas and Porter (law firm), Washington, DC 1952–53; mem. Nat. Conf. on Bail and Criminal Justice 1963–64;

Consultant, Nat. Conf. on Law and Poverty 1965; mem. President's Comm. on Crime in the Dist of Columbia 1965–66, on Law Enforcement and Admin. of Criminal Justice 1966–67; Attorney, Office of Criminal Justice, US Dept of Justice 1967–68, Neighborhood Legal Services Program 1968–70; Co-Dir Ford Foundation Drug Abuse Research Project 1970; Attorney, Center for Law and Social Policy 1971–72, Mental Health Law Project 1972–77; Asst Attorney for Legis. Affairs, Dept of Justice 1977–79; Circuit Judge, US Court of Appeals for the DC Circuit 1979–99, Chief Judge 1986–91; First Vice-Pres. American Law Inst. 1993–98; mem. Exec. Bd CEELI (ABA) 1994–97; Judge Int. Criminal Tribunal for Fmr Yugoslavia, The Hague, Netherlands 1999–2001; Chair. Open Soc. Inst. Justice Initiative 2002–04, now mem. Bd of Dirs; Commr, Pres.'s Comm. on Intelligence Capabilities of US Regarding Weapons of Mass Destruction 2004–05; numerous hon. degrees including Hon. LLD (Yale) 2001; August Voelmer Award, American Soc. of Criminology 1976, Woman Lawyer of the Year, Women's Bar Asscn 1984; Sandra Day O'Connor Medal of Honor (Seton Hall Law School) 1993; Margaret Brent Award for Distinguished Women in the Legal Profession 1994, American Inns of Court Award for Ethics 2003, American Lawyer Lifetime Achievement Award 2004. *Publications:* Bail in the United States (with Daniel J. Freed) 1964, Law and Poverty: Report to the Nat. Conf. on Law and Poverty 1965, Bail Reform: A Decade of Promise Without Fulfillment, Vol. 1 1972, Dealing with Drug Abuse: A Report to the Ford Foundation (with Peter Barton Hutt) 1972, Juvenile Detention in 'Pursuing Justice for the Child' 1977, The Rights of Children and the Rites of Passage in 'Child Psychiatry and the Law' 1980, Provisional Release at the ICTY: A Work in Progress in Essays on ICTY, Procedure and Evidence 2001; and numerous learned articles and contribs to journals. *Address:* 2101 Connecticut Avenue, NW, Apartment 38, Washington, DC 20008-1728, USA (home). *Telephone:* (202) 232-1158 (home). *Fax:* (202) 232-2360 (home). *E-mail:* patwald2@cs.com (home).

WALD, Richard C., BA, MA, AB; American journalist, news executive and academic; *Fred W. Friendly Professor of Media and Society, Graduate School of Journalism, Columbia University;* b. New York City; s. of Joseph S. Wald and Lily Wald (née Forstate); m. Edith May Leslie; two s. one d.; ed Columbia Univ. and Clare Coll., Cambridge, UK; reporter, later Man. Ed. New York Herald Tribune 1955–66; Asst Man. Ed. Washington Post 1967; Exec. Vice-Pres. Whitney Communications Corpn New York 1968; Pres. NBC News, 1968–77; asst to Chair. Bd Times-Mirror Co. LA 1977; Sr Vice-Pres. ABC News 1978–2000; Fred W. Friendly Prof. of Media and Society Columbia Univ. 2000–; Chair. of Bd Columbia Spectator (Columbia Coll. daily newspaper); Chair. Worldwide TV News; mem. Advisory Bd Knight Fellowships Stanford Univ.; mem. Bd of Dirs Correspondents Fund, Center for Communication; mem. Bd of Visitors, School of Communication, Univ. of Colo. *Leisure interests:* reading, running. *Address:* School of Journalism, Columbia University, Mail Code 3801, 701 Journalism, 2950 Broadway, New York, NY 10027, USA (office). *Telephone:* (212) 854-0116 (office). *Fax:* (212) 854-7837 (office). *E-mail:* rcw25@columbia.edu (office). *Website:* www.journalism.columbia.edu (office).

WALDEGRAVE OF NORTH HILL, Baron (Life Peer), cr. 1999, of Chewton Mendip in the County of Somerset; **William Waldegrave,** PC, JP; British banker and fmr politician; b. 15 Aug. 1946; s. of the late Earl Waldegrave, KG, GCVO and Mary Hermione Waldegrave (née Grenfell); m. Caroline Burrows 1977; one s. three d.; ed Eton Coll., Corpus Christi Coll. Oxford, Harvard Univ., USA; fmr Pres. Oxford Union; Fellow All Souls Coll. Oxford 1971–86, 1999–; attached to Cabinet Office as mem. Cen. Policy Review Staff 1971–73; mem. staff political office of Rt Hon. Sir Edward Heath 1973–76; MP for Bristol W 1979–97; Parl. Under-Sec. of State, Dept of Educ. and Science 1981–83, Dept of Environment and Spokesman for the Arts 1983–85; Minister of State, Dept of the Environment (Minister for the Environment, Countryside and Local Govt, subsequently Minister for Housing and Planning) 1985–88; Minister of State, FCO 1988–90; Sec. of State for Health 1990–92, Chancellor of the Duchy of Lancaster 1992–94; Sec. of State for Agric., Fisheries and Food 1994–95; Chief Sec. to Treasury 1995–97; Dir Bank of Ireland Financial Services (UK) PLC 1997–, Corp. Finance, Dresdner Kleinwort Benson 1998–; Man. Dir Dresdner Kleinwort Wasserstein 1998–; Chair. Rhodes Trust 2002–, Nat. Museum of Science and Industry 2002–; several other directorships; worked for GEC PLC 1975–81; Hon. Fellow, Corpus Christi Coll., Oxford 1991. *Publication:* The Binding of Leviathan – Conservatism and the Future 1977. *Address:* House of Lords, London, SW1A 0PW; 66 Palace Gardens Terrace, London, W8 4RR, England (home).

WALDEN, (Alastair) Brian; British broadcaster, journalist and university lecturer; b. 8 July 1932; s. of W. F. Walden; m. Hazel Downes; one s. (and three s. from fmr marriages); ed West Bromwich Grammar School, Queen's Coll. and Nuffield Coll., Oxford; MP (Labour) for Birmingham All Saints 1964–74, Birmingham Ladywood 1974–77; TV presenter, Weekend World (London Weekend TV) 1977–86; mem. W Midland Bd, Cen. Ind. TV 1982–84; columnist London Standard 1983–86, Thomson Regional Newspapers 1983–86, The Sunday Times; presenter, The Walden Interview (London Weekend TV for ITV network) 1988, 1989, 1990–94, Walden on Labour Leaders (BBC) 1997, Walden on Heroes (BBC) 1998, Walden on Villains 1999, A Point of View (BBC Radio 4) 2005–; Chair. Paragon 1994–, Ten Alps 2002–, Capital 2006–; Shell Int. Award 1982, BAFTA Richard Dimbleby Award 1985; Aims of Industry Special Free Enterprise Award 1990; ITV Personality of the Year 1991. *Publication:* The Walden Interviews 1990. *Leisure interests:* chess, reading. *Address:* Landfall, Fort Road, St Peter Port, Guernsey, GY1 1ZU, United Kingdom. *Telephone:* (1481) 722860. *E-mail:* walden@guernsey.net.

WALES, HRH The Prince of; (Prince Charles Philip Arthur George), (Earl of Chester (cr.1958), Duke of Cornwall, Duke of Rothesay, Earl of Carrick, Baron Renfrew, Lord of the Isles and Great Steward of Scotland (cr.1952), KG, KT, GCB, OM, PC, MA; b. 14 Nov. 1948, London; eldest s. of HM Queen Elizabeth II q.v.) and Prince Philip, Duke of Edinburgh (q.v.); m. 1st Lady Diana Spencer (subsequently Diana, Princess of Wales) 29 July 1981 (divorced 28 Aug. 1996, died 31 Aug. 1997); two s., HRH Prince William Arthur Philip Louis, b. 21 June 1982, HRH Prince Henry Charles Albert David, b. 15 Sept. 1984; m. 2nd Camilla Parker Bowles (subsequently The Duchess of Cornwall) 9 April 2005; ed Cheam School, Gordonstoun School, Geelong Grammar School, Trinity Coll. Cambridge and Univ. Coll. of Wales, Aberystwyth; mem. Gray's Inn 1974, Hon. Bencher 1975; Personal ADC to HM the Queen 1973–; Capt. RN 1988, Rear Adm. 1998–, Vice-Adm. 2002–; Maj.-Gen. Army 1998–, Lt-Gen. 2002–; Group Capt. RAF 1988–, Air Vice-Marshal 1998–, Air Marshal 2002–; Col-in-Chief The Royal Regt of Wales (24th/41st Foot) 1969–; Col Welsh Guards 1975–; Col-in-Chief The Cheshire Regt 1977–, Lord Strathcona's Horse (Royal Canadian) Regt 1977–, The Parachute Regt 1977–, The Royal Australian Armoured Corps 1977–, The Royal Regt of Canada 1977–, The Royal Winnipeg Rifles 1977–, Royal Pacific Islands Regt, Papua New Guinea 1984–, Royal Canadian Dragoons 1985–, Army Air Corps 1992–, Royal Dragoon Guards 1992–, Royal Gurkha Rifles 1994–; Deputy Col-in-Chief The Highlanders (Seaforth, Gordons, Camerons) 1994–; Air Cdre-in-Chief RNZAF 1977–; Col-in-Chief Air Reserve 1977–; Pres. Soc. of St George's and Descendants of Knights of the Garter 1975–; Adm. Royal Thames Yacht Club 1974–; High Steward, Royal Borough of Windsor and Maidenhead 1974–; Chair. The Mountbatten Memorial Trust 1979–, The King's Fund 1986; Pres. The Prince's Trust 1976–, The Prince's Scottish Youth Business Trust, Business in the Community 1985, Prince of Wales's Foundation for Architecture and the Urban Enviroment 1992–, Prince of Wales's Business Leaders Forum 1990–; Chancellor, Univ. of Wales 1976–; mem. Bd Commonwealth Devt Corpn 1979–89; Hon. Pres. Royal Acad. Trust 1993–; Trustee Gurkha Welfare Trust 1989; Patron Royal Opera, Oxford Centre for Islamic Studies 1993–, British Orthopaedic Asscn 1993–, Royal Coll. of Music 1993–, Nat. Gallery 1993–, ActionAid 1995–, Help the Aged 1997–, Welsh Nat. Opera 1997–, Guinness Trust 1997–; represented HM the Queen at Independence Celebrations in Fiji 1970, at Requiem Mass for Gen. Charles de Gaulle 1970, at Bahamas Independence Celebrations 1973, at Papua New Guinea Independence Celebrations 1975, at Coronation of King of Nepal 1975, at funeral of Sir Robert Menzies 1978, at funeral of Jomo Kenyatta 1978, at funeral of Rajiv Gandhi 1990, at funeral of King Olav of Norway 1991; Pres. Royal Ballet, Birmingham Royal Ballet 2003–; Hon. FRCS 1978; Hon. FRAeS 1978; Hon. FIMechE 1978; Royal Fellowship of the Australian Acad. of Science 1977; Hon. Fellow, Trinity Coll. Cambridge 1989; Hon. mem. Hon. Company of Master Mariners 1977 (Master 1988), Company of Merchants of City of Edinburgh 1979; Hon. Life mem. Incorporation of Gardeners of Glasgow 1987; Hon. Air Cdre RAF Valley 1993–; received Freedom of City of Cardiff 1969, of Royal Borough of New Windsor 1970, of City of London 1971, of Chester 1973, of City of Canterbury 1978, of City of Portsmouth 1979, of City of Lancaster 1993, of City of Swansea 1994; Liveryman of Fishmongers' Co. 1971; Freeman of Drapers' Co. 1971; Freeman of Shipwrights' Co. 1978; Hon. Freeman and Liveryman of Goldsmiths Co. 1979, Liveryman of Farmers' Co. 1980, of Pewterers' Co. 1982, of Fruiterers' Co. 1989; Hon. Liveryman of Worshipful Co. of Carpenters 1992; Grand Cross of The Southern Cross of Brazil 1978, Grand Cross of The White Rose of Finland 1969, Grand Cordon of the Supreme Order of the Chrysanthemum of Japan 1971, Grand Cross of The House of Orange of the Netherlands 1972, Grand Cross Order of Oak Crown of Luxembourg 1972, Kt of The Order of Elephant of Denmark 1974, Grand Cross of The Order of Ojasvi Rajanya of Nepal 1975, Order of the Repub. of Egypt (First Class) 1981; Grande Croix, Légion d'honneur 1984; Order of Mubarak the Great of Kuwait 1993; cr. Prince of Wales and Earl of Chester (invested July 1969); KG 1958 (invested and installed 1968), KT 1977, PC 1977, GCB and Great Master of Order of the Bath 1975; Dr hc (Royal Coll. of Music) 1981; Hon. DCL (Durham) 1998; Spoleto Prize 1989, Author of the Year 1989, Premio Fregene 1990, Coronation Medal 1953, The Queen's Silver Jubilee Medal 1977, Global Environmental Citizen Prize 2007. *Publications:* The Old Man of Lochnagar 1980, A Vision of Britain 1989, HRH The Prince of Wales Watercolours 1990, Urban Villages 1992, Highgrove: Portrait of an Estate 1993, Prince's Choice: A Selection from Shakespeare by the Prince of Wales 1995, Travels with the Prince 1998, The Garden at Highgrove (with Candida Lycett Green) 2000, The Elements of Organic Gardening (with Stephanie Donaldson) 2007. *Address:* Clarence House, London, SW1A 1BA; Highgrove House, Doughton, Nr Tetbury, Gloucestershire, GL8 8TN, England. *Website:* www.princeofwales.gov.uk (office).

WAŁĘSA, Lech; Polish fmr politician and trade union official; b. 29 Sept. 1943, Popowo; s. of Bolesław Wałęsa and Feliksa Wałęsa; m. Danuta Wałęsa 1969; four s. four d.; ed primary and tech. schools; electrician, Lenin Shipyard, Gdańsk 1966–76, 1983–; Chair. Strike Cttee in Lenin Shipyard 1970; employed Zremb and Elektromontaż 1976–80; Chair. Inter-institutional Strike Cttee, Gdańsk Aug.–Sept. 1980; Co-Founder and Chair. Solidarity Ind. Trade Union 1980–90, Chair. Nat. Exec. Comm. of Solidarity 1987–90; interned 1981–82; Founder of Civic Cttee attached to Chair. of Solidarity 1988–90; participant and Co-Chair. Round Table debates 1989; Pres. of Polish Republic 1990–95, Chair. Country Defence Cttee 1990–95, Supreme Commdr of Armed Forces of Polish Republic for Wartime 1990–95; Founder of Lech Wałęsa Inst. Foundation 1995; Founder Christian Democratic Party of the Third Republic (ChDTRP) 1997, apptd Pres. 1998, Chair. –2000, Hon. Chair. 2000–; retd from politics; resgnd from Solidarity 2006; Order of the Bath 1991, Grand Cross of Légion d'honneur 1991, Grand Order of Merit (Italy) 1991, Order of Merit (FRG) 1991, Great Order of the White Lion 1999, Orden Heraldica do Cristobal Colon 2001; 100 hon. doctorates including Harvard Univ. and Univ. of Paris; Man of the Year, Financial Times 1980, The Observer 1980, Die Welt 1980, Die Zeit 1981, L'Express 1981, Le Soir 1981, Time 1981, Le Point 1981; awarded Let Us Live Peace Prize of Swedish journal Arbetet 1981, Love International Award (Athens) 1981, Freedom Medal

(Philadelphia) 1981, Medal of Merit (Polish American Congress) 1981, Free World Prize (Norway) 1982, Int. Democracy Award 1982, Social Justice Award 1983, Nobel Peace Prize 1983, Humanitarian Public Service Medal 1984, Int. Integrity Award 1986, Phila Liberty Medal 1989, Human Rights Prize, Council of Europe 1989, White Eagle Order (Poland) 1989, US Medal of Freedom 1989, Meeting-90 Award (Rimini) 1990, Path for Peace Award, Apostolic Nuncio to the UN 1996, Freedom Medal of Nat. Endowment for Democracy (Washington USA) 1999, Int. Freedom Award (Memphis USA), and other awards, orders and prizes. *Publications:* autobiogs: Droga nadziei (A Path of Hope) 1987, Droga do wolności (The Road to Freedom) 1991, The Struggle and the Triumph 1992, Wszystko co robię, robię dla Polski (Everything I Do, I Do for Poland) 1995. *Leisure interests:* crossword puzzles, fishing. *Address:* Lech Wałęsa Institute Foundation, Al. Jerozolimskie 11/19, 00 508 Warsaw, Poland. *Telephone:* (22) 622 22 20 (office). *Fax:* (22) 625 14 14 (office). *E-mail:* sekretariat@ilw.org.pl (office). *Website:* www.ilw.org.pl (office).

WALEWSKA, Malgorzata; Polish singer (mezzo-soprano); b. 5 July 1965, Warsaw; one d.; ed Acad. of Music, Warsaw, Nat. Opera, Warsaw; has sung at Bremer Theater 1994, Staatsoper, Vienna 1996–98, Semperoper, Dresden 1999 and Rome (Teatro della Opera), Berlin (Deutsche Open), Düsseldorf (Deutsche Open am Rhein), Florida (Palm Bech Opera) and others; has participated in numerous festivals in Brussels, Seville, London, Bregenz, Nantes and Athens; numerous honours or prizes including 1st Prize Alfredo Kraus Int. Competition 1992, Prize for Best Mezzo-Soprano, Stanislaw Moniuszko Int. Competition, Warsaw 1992, Laureate Luciano Pavarotti Vocal Competition, Phila 1992, Best Graduate, Chopin Acad. of Music, Warsaw, 1994. *Roles include:* Carmen (Carmen), Delilah (Samson and Delilah) Charlotte (Werther), Emilia (Otello), Olga (Eugene Onegin), Jocaste (Oedipus Rex). *Recordings include:* Voce di Donna (a compilation of famous mezzo-soprano arias) 2000, Mezzo (songs and arias in contemporary arrangements) 2000. *Address:* c/o Isabel Wolf, Wolf Artists International LLC, PO Box 492, Gracie Station, New York, NY 10028, USA (office). *E-mail:* bogdanwaskiewicz@wp.pl (office); info@walewska.net (office). *Website:* www .walewska.net (office).

WALI, Yousuf Amin, PhD; Egyptian politician; b. 1930; ed Faculty of Agric., Cairo Univ. and in USA; Reader, later Prof. Faculty of Agric., Cairo Univ.; consultant, Ministry of Scientific Research and Ministry of Agric. and Land Reform; fmr Agric. Planning Consultant in Libya; mem. Nat. Democratic Party, Sec.-Gen. –2002, Deputy Chair. in charge of Internal Affairs 2002; Deputy Prime Minister Sept. 1985; Minister of State for Agric. and Food Security 1982–87, Minister of Agric. and Land Reclamation 1987–2004. *Address:* c/o Ministry of Agriculture and Land Reclamation, Sharia Nadi es-Sayed, Dokki, Egypt.

WALKEN, Christopher; American actor; b. 31 March 1943, Astoria, NY; s. of Paul Walken and Rosalie Walken; ed Hofstra Univ. *Films include:* Me and My Brother 1969, The Anderson Tapes 1971, The Happiness Cage 1972, Next Stop Greenwich Village 1976, Roseland 1977, The Sentinel 1977, Annie Hall 1977, The Deer Hunter (New York Film Critics and Acad. Awards for Best Supporting Actor) 1978, Last Embrace 1979, Heaven's Gate 1980, Shoot the Sun Down 1981, The Dogs of War 1981, Pennies from Heaven 1981, The Dead Zone 1983, Brainstorm 1983, A View to a Kill 1984, At Close Range 1986, Deadline 1987, The Milagro Beanfield War 1988, Biloxi Blues 1988, Homeboy 1988, Communion 1989, The Comfort of Strangers 1989, King of New York 1990, McBain 1991, Mistress 1992, Batman Returns 1992, Day of Atonement 1992, True Romance 1993, Wayne's World II 199, A Business Affair 1994, Scam 1994, Pulp Fiction 1994, Wild Side 1995, Search and Destroy 1995, Things To Do In Denver When You're Dead 1995, The Prophecy 1995, The Addiction 1995, Nick of Time 1995, Celluloide 1996, Basquiat 1996, The Funeral 1996, Last Man Standing 1996, Touch 1997, Excess Baggage 1997, Suicide Kings 1997, Mousehunt 1997, Illuminata 1998, New Rose Hotel (also producer) 1998, Trance 1998, Antz (voice) 1998, Blast from the Past 1999, Sleepy Hollow 1999, Kiss Toledo Goodbye 1999, The Opportunists 2000, Jungle Juice 2001, Scotland, Pa. 2001, Joe Dirt 2001, America's Sweethearts 2001, The Affairs of the Necklace 2001, Poolhall Junkies 2002, The Country Bears 2002, Plots with a View 2002, Catch Me If You Can (BAFTA Award for Best Supporting Actor) 2003, Kangaroo Jack 2003, Gigli 2003, The Rundown 2003, Man on Fire 2004, Envy 2004, The Stepford Wives 2004, Around the Bend 2004, Romance & Cigarettes 2005, Wedding Crashers 2005, Domino 2005, Man of the Year 2006, Fade to Black 2006, Hairspray 2007, Balls of Fury 2007; writer and dir Popcorn Shrimp 2001. *Stage appearances include:* West Side Story, Macbeth, The Lion in Winter (Clarence Derwent Award 1966), The Night Thoreau Spent in Jail (Joseph Jefferson Award 1970–71), Cinders 1984, A Bill of Divorcement 1985, The Seagull 2001. *Address:* ICM New York, 825 8th Avenue, New York, NY 10019, USA. *Telephone:* (212) 556-5600.

WALKER, Alan Cyril, BA, PhD, FRS; British medical scientist and academic; *Evan Pugh Professor of Anthropology and Biology, Pennsylvania State University;* b. 23 Aug. 1938; s. of Cyril Walker and Edith Walker (née Tidd); m. 1st Patricia Dale Larwood 1963 (divorced); one s.; m. 2nd Patty Lee Shipman 1976; ed St John's Coll. Cambridge, Royal Free Hosp., London; Asst Lecturer in Anatomy, Royal Free Hosp. School of Medicine 1965; Lecturer in Anatomy, Makerere Univ. Coll., Kampala, Uganda 1965–69; Hon. Keeper of Paleontology, Uganda Museum 1967–69; Sr Lecturer in Anatomy, Univ. of Nairobi, Kenya 1969–73; Visiting Lecturer, Dept of Anatomy, Harvard Univ. 1973–74, Assoc. Prof. of Anatomy 1974–78, Assoc. Prof. of Anthropology 1974–78; Research Assoc., Peabody Museum 1974–78; Prof. of Cellular Biology and Anatomy, Johns Hopkins Univ. School of Medicine 1978–95 (part-time 1995–97); Prof. of Anthropology and Biology, Pennsylvania State Univ. 1995–96, Evan Pugh Prof. 1996–; Assoc. Ed. American Journal of Physical Anthropology 1974–79, Journal of Human Evolution 1994–98; John Guggenheim Memorial Foundation Fellow 1986, MacArthur Foundation Fellow 1988–93; mem. American Acad. of Arts and Sciences 1996; Foreign Assoc. NAS 2004; Rhône-Poulenc Prize 1997, Int. Foundation Fyssen Prize 1998; Hon. DSc (Univ. of Chicago) 2000. *Publications:* Prosimian Biology (co-ed.) 1974, Structure and Function of the Human Skeleton (co-author) 1985, Nariokotome Homo Erectus Skeleton (co-ed.) 1993, The Wisdom of the Bones (co-author) 1996, numerous papers published in scientific journals. *Address:* Department of Anthropology, 409 Carpenter Building, Pennsylvania State University, University Park, Pittsburgh, PA 16802, USA (office). *Telephone:* (814) 865-3122 (office). *E-mail:* axw8@psu.edu (office). *Website:* www.anthro .psu.edu/faculty_staff/walker.shtml (office); 146.186.95.23/walker.html (office).

WALKER, Alice Malsenior, BA; American writer; b. 9 Feb. 1944, Eatonton, Ga; d. of Willie L. Walker and Minnie Walker (née Grant); m. Melvyn R. Leventhal 1967 (divorced 1977); one d.; ed Sarah Lawrence Coll.; Hon. PhD (Russell Sage Univ.) 1972; Hon. DHL (Univ. of Mass.) 1983; Bread Loaf Writers Conf. Scholar 1966, Ingram Merrill Foundation Fellowship 1967, McDowell Colony Fellowships 1967, 1977–78, Nat. Endowment for the Arts Grants 1969, 1977, Richard and Hinda Rosenthal Pound Award, American Acad. and Inst. of Arts and Letters 1974, Lillian Smith Award 1974, Rosenthal Award, Nat. Inst. of Arts and Letters 1973, Guggenheim Foundation Award 1979, Nat. Book Award (for The Color Purple) 1983, Pulitzer Prize (for The Color Purple) 1983, O. Henry Award 1986, Nora Astorga Leadership Award 1989, Freedom to Write Award, PEN Center West 1990. *Publications:* Once 1968, The Third Life of George Copeland 1970, Five Poems 1972, In Love and Trouble 1973, Langston Hughes, American Poet 1973, Revolutionary Petunias 1974, Meridian 1976, I Love Myself When I am Laughing 1979, You Can't Keep a Good Woman Down 1981, Good Night Willi Lee, I'll See You in the Morning 1979, The Color Purple 1982, In Search of Our Mothers' Gardens 1983, Horses Make a Landscape Look More Beautiful 1984, To Hell with Dying 1988, Living By the Word 1988, The Temple of My Familiar 1989, Her Blue Body Everything We Know: Earthling Poems (1965–90) 1991, Finding the Green Stone 1991, Possessing the Secret of Joy 1992, Warrior Marks (with Pratibha Parmar) 1993, Double Stitch: Black Women Write About Mothers and Daughters (jtly) 1993, Everyday Use 1994, By the Light of my Father's Smile 1998, Alice Walker Banned 1996, Everything We Love Can Be Saved 1997, The Same River Twice 1997, The Way Forward is with a Broken Heart (ed.) 2000, Absolute Trust in the Goodness of the Earth: New Poems 2003, The Third Life of Grange Copeland 2003, Now is the Time to Open Your Heart 2004, We Are the Ones We Have Been Waiting For (essays) 2007. *Address:* Wendy Weil Agency Inc, 232 Madison Avenue, Suite 1300, New York, NY 10016, USA (office). *Website:* www.wendyweil.com (office); www .alicewalkersgarden.com.

WALKER, Charls Edward, MBA, PhD; American economist and academic; *Distinguished Adjunct Professor of Public Affairs, LBJ School of Public Affairs, University of Texas;* b. 24 Dec. 1923, Graham, Tex.; s. of Pinkney Clay Walker and Sammye McCombs Walker; m. Harmolyn Hart 1949; one s. one d.; ed Univs of Texas and Pennsylvania; Pilot instructor, USAF World War II; Instructor in Finance and later Asst and Assoc. Prof., Univ. of Tex. 1947–54; Instructor in Finance, Wharton School 1948–50; Assoc. Economist, Fed. Reserve Bank of Philadelphia 1953–54; Economist and Special Asst to Pres. of the Repub. Nat. Bank of Dallas 1955–56; Vice-Pres. and Financial Economist, Fed. Reserve Bank of Dallas 1958–61; Asst to the Sec. of the Treasury 1959–61; Exec. Vice-Pres., American Bankers' Asscn 1961–69; Under-Sec. of the Treasury 1969–72; Deputy Sec. of the Treasury 1972–73; Adjunct Prof. for Finance and Public Affairs, LBJ School of Public Affairs, Univ. of Texas 1986–, now Distinguished Adjunct Prof.; Distinguished Visiting Prof., Emory Univ.; Adjunct Prof. Texas A & M Univ. 2001; Chair. Walker and Walker LLC; Chair. American Council for Capital Formation; Co-Chair. Presidential Debates 1976; Chair., Pres. Reagan's Task Force on Tax Policy 1980; Co-Founder Cttee on the Present Danger; Founder Chair. Bretton Woods Cttee, Advisory Cttee on Nat. Issues Convention; Chair. Pres. Nixon's Advisory Cttee on Minority Enterprise; Hon. LLD (Ashland Coll.) 1970; Alexander Hamilton Award, US Treasury, Distinguished Alumnus Award, Univ. of Texas, Baber Award for Exemplary Service to Econ. Educ., Distinguished Service Award, Urban League Award for Contributions to Minority Enterprise and Educ. *Publications:* The Banker's Handbook 1978 (co-ed.), New Directions in Federal Tax Policy 1983 (co-ed.), The Consumption Tax: A Better Alternative (co-ed.) 1987, Intellectual Property Rights and Capital Formation in the Next Decade 1988, Saving: The Challenge for the US Economy 1990; numerous articles in newspapers, magazines and economic and other journals. *Leisure interests:* golf, music. *Address:* 10120 Chapel Road, Potomac, MD 20854, USA (home). *Telephone:* (301) 299-5414 (home). *Fax:* (301) 299-5024 (home). *Website:* www .utexas.edu/lbj/faculty/walker.html (office).

WALKER, David Alan, PhD, DSc, FRS; British scientist, academic and author; *Professor Emeritus of Photosynthesis, University of Sheffield;* b. 18 Aug. 1928, Hull; s. of Cyril Walker and Dorothy Walker; m. Shirley Wynne Mason 1956; one s. one d.; ed Univ. of Newcastle; Royal Naval Air Service 1946–48; at Univ. of Newcastle 1948–58, Purdue Univ., Indiana 1953–54; Reader in Botany, Queen Mary Coll., Univ. of London 1963; Reader in Enzymology, Imperial Coll., Univ. of London 1964–70; Prof. of Biology, Univ. of Sheffield 1970–84, Dir Research Inst. for Photosynthesis 1984–88, Prof. of Photosynthesis 1988–93, Prof. Emer. 1993–; Visiting Fellow, Connecticut Agricultural Experimental Station 1965; Scientific Publr Oxygraphics; Corresp. mem. American Soc. of Plant Physiology 1979, Academia Europaea 1994; Hon. DLitt (Sheffield) 2006; von Humboldt Prize 1991, Int. Soc. of Photosynthesis Communications Award 2004. *Publications:* Energy, Plants and Man 1979, 1992, C_3C_4 (with Gerry Edwards) 1983, A Leaf in Time 1999, Like Clockwork

2000, A New Leaf in Time 2007; more than 200 publs on photosynthetic carbon assimilation etc. *Leisure interests:* singing the Sheffield carols and changing the Biddlestone landscape. *Address:* 6 Biddlestone Village, Morpeth, Northumberland, NE65 7DT, England (home). *Telephone:* (114) 230-5904 (home). *E-mail:* d.a.walker@sheffield.ac.uk (office). *Website:* www.dawalker.staff.shef .ac.uk/daw/home/index.htm (office); www.oxygraphics.co.uk (home).

WALKER, Sir David Alan, Kt, MA; British financial executive; *Senior Adviser, Morgan Stanley International Ltd.;* b. 31 Dec. 1939; m. Isobel Cooper 1963; one s. two d.; ed Chesterfield School and Queens' Coll. Cambridge; joined HM Treasury 1961, Pvt. Sec. to Jt Perm. Sec. 1964–66, Asst Sec. 1973–77; seconded to staff IMF, Washington, DC 1970–73; joined Bank of England as Chief Adviser, then Chief Econ. Intelligence Dept 1977, Asst Dir 1980, Dir 1982–88 (non-exec. 1988–93); Chair. Johnson Matthey Bankers Ltd (later Minories Finance Ltd) 1985–88, Financial Markets Group, LSE 1987–95, Securities and Investments Bd 1988–92, Agric. Mortgage Corpn PLC 1993–94, Morgan Stanley (Europe) (now Morgan Stanley Dean Witter (Europe) Ltd) 1994–2000, Morgan Stanley Int. 1995–2000 (Sr Adviser 2001–), Reuters Venture Capital; Deputy Chair. Lloyds Bank Ltd 1992–94; Dir (non-exec.) British Invisibles 1993–, Nat. Power 1990–93; part-time Bd mem. Cen. Electricity Generating Bd 1987–89; mem. Council, Lloyd's of London 1988–92; Gov. Henley Man. Coll. 1993–99, LSE 1993–; Chair. Exec. Cttee of Int. Org. of Securities Comms 1990–92, Cttee of Inquiry into Lloyd's Syndicate Participations and the LMX Spiral; mem. Group of Thirty 1993–; Trustee Cambridge Univ. Devt Foundation; Amb. for Community Links; Hon. Fellow Queens' Coll. Cambridge 1989; Hon. LLD (Exeter) 2002. *Leisure interests:* music, architecture, long-distance walking. *Address:* Morgan Stanley International Ltd, 25 Cabot Square, Canary Wharf, London, E14 4QA, England. *Telephone:* (20) 7425-5400. *Fax:* (20) 7425-8975.

WALKER, David Maxwell, CBE, QC, MA, PhD, LLD, FBA, FRSE, FSAScot, FRSA; British legal scholar, barrister and academic; *Senior Research Fellow, School of Law, University of Glasgow;* b. 9 April 1920, Glasgow; s. of James Mitchell Walker and Mary Paton Colquhoun Irvine; m. Margaret Knox, OBE 1954; ed High School of Glasgow, Univs of Glasgow, Edinburgh and London; army service in India, N Africa and Italy, Capt., Indian Army 1939–46; practised at Scottish Bar 1948–53; Prof. of Jurisprudence, Glasgow Univ. 1954–58, Regius Prof. of Law 1958–90, Dean of Faculty of Law 1956–59, Convener of School of Law 1984–88, Sr Research Fellow 1990–; retd 1990; Chair. Hamlyn Trust 1988–93; Hon. LLD (Edin.) 1974. *Publications:* Law of Damages in Scotland 1955, Law of Civil Remedies in Scotland 1974, The Oxford Companion to Law 1980, Law of Delict in Scotland (2nd edn) 1981, Stair's Institutions (ed.; 6th edn) 1981, The Scottish Jurists 1985, Principles of Scottish Private Law (4th edn, four vols) 1988–90, Legal History of Scotland, Vol. I 1988, Vol. II 1990, Vol. III 1995, Vol. IV 1996, Vol. V 1997, Vol. VI 2001, Vol. VII 2004, Law of Contracts in Scotland (3rd edn) 1994, The Scottish Legal System (8th edn) 2001, Law of Prescription in Scotland (6th edn) 2002. *Leisure interest:* book collecting. *Address:* School of Law, University of Glasgow, Glasgow, G12 8QQ (office); 1 Beaumont Gate, Glasgow, G12 9EE, Scotland (home). *Telephone:* (141) 330-2000 (office); (141) 339-2802 (home). *Website:* www.gla.ac.uk (office).

WALKER, Derek, MArch, RIBA, FRCA; British architect, town planner, university professor and designer; b. 15 June 1931, Ribchester, Lancs.; s. of the late William Walker and Ann Nicholson; m. 1st Honora Jill Messenger 1957; two s.; m. 2nd Jan Larrance 1983; one d.; m. 3rd Evelyn Claire Happold 2003; f. Derek Walker Assocs, Architects & Urban Planners 1960, Walker, Wright, Schofield, Interior Design/Furniture Design 1966; Chief Architect and Planner, New City of Milton Keynes, UK 1969–76; re-formed practices, Sr Partner Derek Walker Assocs, Walker Wright 1976–; Prof. of Architecture & Design, RCA 1984–90, Chair. Design Faculty; Architectural Design Awards, pvt. houses, urban devts, village plans 1965 (two), 1966 (two), 1967, 1968, Civic Trust Awards 1965, 1967, 1968, Financial Times Architectural Awards 1969, first prize numerous nat. and int. competitions for theatres, new towns, shopping bldgs, waterside devts and parks, RIBA Awards 1979, 1980. *Principal projects:* New City of Milton Keynes 1969–82, Sculpture Park, Milton Keynes 1972, Master Planning New City of Jubail, Saudi Arabia 1979–82, WonderWorld Themepark 1982–, StarSite Birmingham Urban Plan 1984, Commodores Point, Jacksonville, Fla Urban Plan, USA 1985, Ski Resort, Telluride, Colo, USA 1986–88, Lijnbaan Shopping Centre, Rotterdam 1987–89, Gyosei Japanese School 1985–87, Kowloon Park, Hong Kong 1985–87, Energy World, Corby 1986, Olympic Pool and Sports Hall, Kowloon 1986–88, Happy Valley Racecourse Re devt, Hong Kong 1990–96, Ushiku New Town Plan, Japan 1991–95, Clarence Dock Master Plan, Leeds 1991, Royal Armouries Museum, Leeds 1992–96, Museum of British History, London 1996–, Newmarket Racing Museum and Stables 1996–, Xanadu Snow and Leisure Dome, Lancashire 1999–2001, Redcar Super Racecourse Devt 2000–, Nat. Museum for the US Army, Washington, DC 2000–03, Leigh Sports Village 2002–09, Calder Valley Racecourse 2002–, Second Gateway Site, Blackpool 2003–06, Earth Angel (Eco friendly global farm) 2003–, Int. Resort Kalpitiya, Sri Lanka 2006–. *Publications:* British Architects 1981, Los Angeles 1982, Architecture and Planning of Milton Keynes 1982, Animated Architecture 1995, The Royal Armouries: The Making of a Museum (with Guy Wilson) 1996, Derek Walker Associates: The View from Great Lindford 1997, New Towns 1999, Happold: The Confidence to Build (with Bill Addis) 1998; numerous articles. *Leisure interests:* fine art, classical music, jazz, literature and most sports. *Address:* Derek Walker Associates, 45 Black Lion Lane, London, W6 9BG; 4 Widcombe Terrace, Bath BA2 6AJ, England (home). *Telephone:* (20) 8563-9435 (office); (20) 8748-48302 (office); (1908) 605883 (office). *E-mail:* derekwalker@dwadesign.com (office).

WALKER, Donald J., BMechEng; Canadian automotive industry executive; *Co-CEO, Magna International Inc.;* ed Univ. of Waterloo; began career with General Motors Corpn, served in numerous mfg and eng positions; joined Magna International Inc. 1987, served as Vice-Pres. for Product Devt and Strategic Planning, COO 1991–92, Pres. 1992–94, mem. Bd of Dirs 1994–2002, 2005–, CEO 1994–2005, Co-CEO 2005–, also Pres. and CEO Intier Automotive Inc. (subsidiary of Magna); Co-Chair. Canadian Automotive Partnership Council; founding mem. Yves Landry Foundation.

WALKER, George Alfred; British business executive; *Chairman, Global Tote;* b. 14 April 1929, London; s. of William James Walker and Ellen Walker (née Page); m. Jean Maureen Hatton 1957; one s. two d.; ed Jubilee School, London; fmr boxer and boxing man.; Chief Exec. Walkers Int. 1992; declared bankrupt April 1993; Chair. Premier Telesports Ltd 1995–, Global Tote; Freeman City of London 1978. *Leisure interests:* skiing, ocean racing, climbing. *Address:* ; Pell House, High Road, Fobbing, Essex, SS17 9JJ, England (home). *Telephone:* 1494 878 960 (office); (1375) 672082 (home). *Fax:* (1494) 878963 (office); (1375) 643315 (home). *E-mail:* admin@globaltote.tv (office). *Website:* www.globaltote.tv (office).

WALKER, Sir John Ernest, Kt, MA, DPhil, ScD, FRS; British scientist; *Director, MRC Dunn Human Nutrition Unit;* b. 7 Jan. 1941, Halifax; s. of Thomas Ernest Walker and Elsie Walker (née Lawton); m. Christina Jane Westcott 1963; two d.; ed Rastrick Grammar School, W Yorks., St Catherine's Coll., Oxford; Visiting Research Fellow, Univ. of Wisconsin, USA 1969–71; NATO Research Fellow, CNRS, Gif-sur-Yvette, France 1971–72; European Molecular Biology Org. (EMBO) Research Fellow, Pasteur Inst., Paris 1972–74; Staff Scientist, MRC Lab. of Molecular Biology, Cambridge 1974–98; Dir MRC Dunn Human Nutrition Unit, Cambridge 1998–; mem. EMBO 1983; Fellow, Sidney Sussex Coll. Cambridge 1997–; mem. Netherlands Acad. of Arts and Science 1998; Foreign mem. Accad. dei Lincei 2003; Foreign Assoc. NAS 2004; Hon. Prof., Peking Union Medical Coll., Beijing 2001, Univ. of Cambridge 2002; Hon. Fellow, St Catherine's Coll. Oxford 1998; Hon. DSc (London) 2002, (Sussex) 2003, (Liverpool) 2004, (East Anglia) 2006, (Moscow State Univ.) 2007; Dr hc (Bradford, Leeds, Oxford, Gröningen, Manchester, Huddersfield, Buenos Aires), (Univ. Paul Sabatier, Toulouse) 2007; Johnson Foundation Prize, Univ. of Pennsylvania 1994, CIBA Medal and Prize, Biochemical Soc. 1996, Nobel Prize for Chem. (co-recipient with Paul Boyer q.v.) 1997, Soc. of Chemical Industry Messel Medal 2000, Royal Soc. of Chem. Award of Biomembrane Chem. 2003. *Publications:* research papers and reviews in scientific journals. *Leisure interests:* cricket, opera music, walking. *Address:* MRC Dunn Human Nutrition Unit, Wellcome Trust/ MRC Building, Hills Road, Cambridge, CB2 2XY, England (office). *Telephone:* (1223) 252701 (office). *Fax:* (1223) 252705 (office). *E-mail:* walker@mrc-dunn .cam.ac.uk (office). *Website:* www.mrc-dunn.cam.ac.uk (office).

WALKER, Martin, MA; British journalist, writer and broadcaster; *Senior Director, Global Business Policy Council;* b. 23 Jan. 1947, Durham, England; m. Julia Watson 1978; ed Balliol Coll., Oxford, Harvard Univ.; staff, The Guardian, Manchester 1972–, Moscow Bureau Chief 1983–88, US Bureau Chief 1989–98; Ed.-in-Chief United Press International 2004–07; Sr Dir Global Business Policy Council 2007–; numerous radio and TV broadcasts; many lectures; Congressional Fellow, American Political Science Asscn 1970–71; Public Policy Fellow, Woodrow Wilson Int. Center for Scholars 2000–01; Sr Fellow, World Policy Inst., New School Univ., New York; mem. Nat. Union of Journalists. *Television:* Martin Walker's Russia (BBC series) 1989. *Publications:* The National Front 1977, Daily Sketches: A History of Political Cartoons 1978, The Infiltrators (novel) 1978, A Mercenary Calling (novel) 1980, The Eastern Question (novel) 1981, Powers of the Press: A Comparative Study of the World's Leading Newspapers 1981, The Waking Giant: Gorbachev and Perestroika 1987, Martin Walker's Russia 1989, The Independent Traveller's Guide to the Soviet Union 1990, The Insight Guide to Washington, DC 1992, The Cold War: A History 1993, The President We Deserve: Bill Clinton: His Rise, Falls, and Comebacks 1996, America Reborn: A Twentieth-Century Narrative in Twenty-Six Lives 2000, The Iraq War 2003; contrib. to anthologies and periodicals. *Leisure interests:* skiing, food, wine. *Address:* Global Business Policy Council, A.T. Kearney, Inc., 8100 Boone Blvd, Suite 400, Vienna, VA 22182, USA (office). *Telephone:* (703) 891-5500 (office). *Website:* www.atkearney.com (office).

WALKER, Melaine; Jamaican athlete; b. 1 Jan. 1983, Kingston; ed St Jago High School; sprinter and hurdler; finished fifth in 200m at World Jr Championships, Annecy, France 1998, Bronze Medal, 4×100m relay; Silver Medal, 200m, World Youth Championships, Bydgoszcz, Poland 1999; Bronze Medal, 400m hurdles, World Jr Championships, Santiago, Chile 2000, Silver Medal, 4×400m relay; Silver Medal, 400m hurdles, World Jr Championships, Kingston 2002; Bronze Medal, 400m hurdles, Cen. American and Caribbean Games, Cartagena, Colombia 2006, Silver Medal, 4×400m relay; Bronze Medal, 400m hurdles, World Athletics Final, Stuttgart 2007; Gold Medal, 400m hurdles, Olympic Games, Beijing 2008 (Olympic record time of 52.64). *Address:* c/o Jamaica Amateur Athletic Association Ltd, PO Box 272, Kingston 5, Jamaica. *Telephone:* 929-6623. *Fax:* 920-4801. *E-mail:* athleticsja@jamweb .net. *Website:* www.jaaaltd.com.

WALKER, Baron (Life Peer), cr. 2006, of Aldringham in the County of Suffolk; **Gen. Michael John Dawson Walker,** GCB, CMG, CBE, DL; British army officer; *Governor, The Royal Hospital Chelsea;* b. 7 July 1944, Salisbury, Rhodesia (now Zimbabwe); s. of William Hampden Dawson Walker and Dorothy Helena Walker (née Shiach); m. Victoria Margaret Holme 1973; two s. one d.; ed Royal Mil. Acad., Sandhurst; joined Royal Anglian Regt 1966, Regimental and Staff Duties 1966–82, with Staff Coll. 1976–77, Mil. Asst to Chief of Gen. Staff 1982–85, CO 1985–87, Col 1996–; Commdr 20th Armoured Brig. 1987–89; Chief of Staff 1 (Br.) Corps 1989–91; GOC NE Dist and Commdr 2nd Infantry Div. 1991–92; Col Commdt Queen's Div. 1991–2000, Army Air Corps 1994–2004; Col Royal Anglian Regt 1997–2002; GOC Eastern

Dist 1992; Asst Chief of the Gen. Staff Ministry of Defence 1992–94; Commdr Ace Rapid Reaction Corps 1994–97; Head NATO Ground Forces, Bosnia 1995–96; C-in-C Land Command 1997–2000; ADC Gen. to the Queen 1997–2006; Chief of the Gen. Staff 2000–03; Chief of the Defence Staff 2003–06; mem. NATO Mil. Cttee 2003–06; Hon. LLD; Hon. DSc. *Leisure interests:* skiing, sailing, golf, shooting, motorcycling. *Address:* c/o House of Lords, Westminster, London, SW1A 0PW, England. *Telephone:* (20) 7219-3000. *E-mail:* walkermjd@parliament.uk (office).

WALKER, Sir Miles Rawstron, Kt, CBE; British politician (retd) and business executive; b. 13 Nov. 1940, Isle of Man; s. of George D. Walker and Alice Rawstron; m. Mary L. Cowell 1966; one s. one d.; ed Castle Rushen High School and Shropshire Agricultural Coll.; co. dir farming and retail trade; mem. and fmr Chair. Arbory Parish Commrs 1970–76; mem. House of Keys (Ind.) 1976–; mem. Bd of Agric., Local Govt Bd, Manx Museum 1976–81; Chair. Broadcasting Comm. 1979, Local Govt Bd 1981–86; mem. Exec. Council 1981–; mem. Assessment Bd 1983–86; Vice-Chair. Post Office Authority 1984–86; Chief Minister, Isle of Man Govt 1986–96; mem. Isle of Man Treasury 1996–2000; Chair. Isle of Man Swimming Asscn 1997–2005; Pres. Rotary Club 2000–01, Southern Amateur Swimming Club, Port St Mary Rifle Club 1988–2006; Hon. LLD (Liverpool) 1994. *Publications:* Isle of Man Government Policy Documents 1987–1996. *Leisure interest:* Rotary Club, charitable fund raising. *Address:* Magher Feailley, Main Road, Colby, IM9 4AD, Isle of Man (home). *Telephone:* (1624) 833728 (home). *Fax:* (1624) 833728 (office). *E-mail:* miles.walker@manx.net (home).

WALKER, Roger Neville, BArch, FNZIA; New Zealand architect; b. 21 Dec. 1942, Hamilton; s. of Andrew Frank Walker and Margaret Clothier; m. 1985; three s. one d.; ed Hamilton Boys' High School, Univ. of Auckland School of Architecture; with corp. architectural practice, Wellington 1968–70; own practice 1970–; designs include Rainbow Springs, Rotorua, Waitomo Visitor Centre, Whakatane Airport, Gardens Park Royal Hotel, Queenstown, City Centre Shopping Devt, New Plymouth, Marist Provincial Bldg, Ropata Medical Centre, Thorndon New World Shopping Devt, Willis Street Village, Wellington, over 120 houses and apartment devts in New Zealand, Australia and UK; lecturer Auckland School of Architecture, Wellington School of Architecture; New Zealand Order of Merit for services to architecture 1999; New Zealand Steel Award 1984, 16 NZ Inst. of Architecture Awards, five NZ Tourism Awards. *Leisure interests:* photography, travel, motor sport, basketball. *Address:* 8 Brougham Street, Mount Victoria, Wellington, New Zealand. *Telephone:* (4) 385-9307. *Fax:* (4) 385-9348.

WALKER, Sarah Elizabeth Royle, CBE, FRCM, FGSM, LRAM; British singer (mezzo-soprano); b. Cheltenham; d. of Elizabeth Brownrigg and Alan Royle Walker; m. Graham Allum 1972; ed Pate's Grammar School for Girls, Cheltenham and Royal Coll. of Music (RCM), London; studied violin and cello and then voice (with Ruth Packer and Cuthbert Smith) at RCM; Martin Musical Trust Scholarship to begin vocal studies with Vera Rozsa 1967; operatic debuts: Kent Opera, Ottavia in Coronation of Poppea 1969, Glyndebourne Festival, Diana/Giove in La Calisto 1970, Scottish Opera, Didon in Les Troyens 1971, ENO, Wellgunde in The Ring 1971; Prin. Singer with ENO 1972–76; debut at Royal Opera House, Covent Garden as Charlotte in Werther 1979; debut at Metropolitan Opera, New York, as Micha in Handel's Samson 1986; has sung opera in Chicago, San Francisco, Göttingen, Geneva, Vienna and Brussels; concert repertoire includes, in addition to standard works, contemporary and avant-garde works by Berio, Boulez, Cage, Ligeti, Xenakis and others; sang Rule Britannia at last night of 1985 and 1989 BBC Promenade Concerts, London; recital début, Wigmore Hall, London 1979; recital tours Australia, N America, Europe; numerous recordings including Handel's Hercules and Julius Caesar and Stravinsky's Rake's Progress; video recordings of Gloriana (title role), Julius Caesar (Cornelia) and King Priam (Andromache); Prince Consort Prof. of Singing, RCM 1993–; vocal performance consultant, Guildhall School of Music and Drama 1999–; Pres. Cheltenham Bach Choir 1986–; Liveryman, Worshipful Co. of Musicians. *Leisure interests:* interior design, gardening, battling against incipient laziness. *Address:* Askonas Holt Ltd, Lincoln House, 300 High Holborn, London, WC1V 7JH, England (office). *Telephone:* (20) 7400-1700 (office). *Fax:* (20) 7400-1799 (office). *E-mail:* info@askonasholt.co.uk (office); megamezzo@sarahwalker.com (home). *Website:* www.askonasholt.co.uk (office); www.sarahwalker.com (home).

WALKER OF WORCESTER, Baron (Life Peer), cr. 1992, of Abbots Morton in the County of Hereford and Worcester; **Peter Edward Walker,** PC, MBE; British politician and banker; b. 25 March 1932; s. of Sydney Walker and Rose Walker; m. Tessa Joan Pout 1969; three s. two d.; ed Latymer Upper School; Chair. Rose, Thomson, Young and Co. Ltd (Lloyd's Brokers) 1956–70; Deputy Chair. Slater Walker Securities Ltd 1964–70; Dir Adwest Ltd 1963–70; mem. Lloyd's 1969–75; parl. cand. for Dartford 1955 and 1959, MP for Worcester 1961–92; mem. Nat. Exec. of Conservative Party 1956–70; Nat. Chair. Young Conservatives 1958–60; Parl. Pvt. Sec. to Leader of House of Commons 1963–64; Opposition Front-Bench Spokesman on Finance and Econs 1964–66, Transport 1966–68, Housing and Local Govt 1968–70; Minister of Housing and Local Govt 1970; Sec. of State for the Environment 1970–72, for Trade and Industry 1972–74; Opposition Spokesman on Trade and Industry 1974, Defence 1974–75; Sec. of State for Agric., Fisheries and Food 1979–83, for Energy 1983–87, for Wales 1987–90; mem. Bd of Dirs NM Rothschild (Wales) 1990–96, DC Gardner 1990–93, Tate and Lyle 1990–2001, British Gas 1990–96, Worcester Group 1990–96, Dalgety 1990–96, Smith New Court 1990–95, Caparo Group Ltd 1995–, ITM Power PLC 2004–; Chair. Thornton and Co. 1991–97, The Vietnam Fund Ltd 1991–2004, English Partnerships (urban regeneration agency) 1992–98, Cornhill Insurance 1992–2003, Kleinwort Benson 1997–99, Allianz Cornhill Insurance 2003–06; Dir (non-exec.) London Int. Financial Futures and Options Exchange 1995–, Kleinwort Benson Group 1996–98; Vice-Chair. Dresdner Kleinwort Benson 1999–2000, Dresdner Kleinwort Wasserstein 2001–06, Dresdner Kleinwort 2006–; Co-Chair. Int. Tax and Investment Centre 1994–; Pres. German–British Chamber of Industry and Commerce 1999–2002, Vice-Pres. 2002–; mem. Conservative Party; Commdr's Cross of Order of Merit (Germany) 1994, Order of Bernardo O'Higgins, Degree Gran Official, Chile 1995, Grand Officer, Order of May, Argentina 2002;Freeman of the City of Worcester 2003; Hon. LLD (Wales) 1991. *Publications:* The Ascent of Britain 1977, Trust the People 1987, Staying Power (autobiog.) 1991. *Address:* Abbots Morton Manor, Gooms Hill, Abbots Morton, Worcester, WR7 4LT, England (home).

WALKER PRIETO, Ignacio, Dr rer. pol; Chilean politician and diplomatist; b. 7 Jan. 1956, Santiago; m. Cecilia Echenique; ed Univ. of Chile, Princeton Univ., USA; visiting prof., Kellog Inst. for Int. Relations, Univ. of Notre Dame 1987; Dir of Political and Institutional Relations, Ministry of the Sec.-Gen. of the Presidency 1990–93; mem. Advisory Council Latin America Studies Program, Princeton Univ. 1994–97; Mem. of Parl. for Demócrata Cristiana party 1994–2002; mem. Advisory Council, Kellog Inst. for Int. Relations, Univ. of Notre Dame 2000; Head of Political Studies Andrés Bello Univ. 2002–03; apptd Amb. to Italy 2004; Minister of Foreign Affairs 2004–06. *Address:* c/o Ministry of Foreign Affairs, Catedral 1158, Santiago, Chile (office).

WALL, Brad, BPA; Canadian politician; *Premier of Saskatchewan and President of the Executive Council;* b. 24 Nov. 1965, Swift Current, Sask.; m. Tami Wall; one s. two d.; ed Univ. of Saskatchewan, Saskatoon, Investment Funds Inst. of Canada; fmr Ministerial Asst, Prov. Govt of Sask.; fmr owner of several businesses, including The Last Stand Adventure Co.; Dir of Business Devt, City of Swift Current 1991; MLA, Sask. Legislature (Swift Current) 1999–; Leader Saskatchewan Party 2004–; Premier of Sask. and Pres. Exec. Council 2007–; Founding mem. and Western Co-Chair. Alliance for the Future of Young Canadians late 1980s; Founding Bd mem. Southwest Centre for Entrepreneurial Devt; active in community service work and on several bds spanning local events, econ. devt, and health care recruitment and retention; Econ. Developer of the Year Award for 1998, Saskatchewan Econ. Developers Asscn 1999. *Address:* Office of the Premier, Room 226, Legislative Building, 2405 Legislative Drive, Regina, SK S4S 0B3, Canada (office). *Telephone:* (306) 787-9433 (office). *Fax:* (306) 787-9433 (office). *E-mail:* premier@gov.sk.ca (office). *Website:* www.gov.sk.ca (office); www.bradwall.com.

WALL, Brian; American sculptor and academic (retd); *Emeritus Professor, University of California, Berkeley;* b. 5 Sept. 1931, London, England; s. of Arthur F. Wall and Dorothy Seymour; m. Sylvia Brown 1973; two s.; ed Luton Coll. of Art, England; Asst Prof. of Art, Univ. of Calif. at Berkeley 1975–77, Assoc. Prof. 1977–81, Prof. 1981–94, Emer. Prof. 1994–. *Address:* 306 Lombard Street, San Francisco, CA 94133, USA. *Telephone:* (510) 652-6042.

WALL, Charles Terence Clegg, PhD, FRS; British mathematician and academic; *Professor Emeritus of Pure Mathematics, University of Liverpool;* b. 14 Dec. 1936, Bristol; s. of Charles Wall and Ruth Wall (née Clegg); m. Alexandra Joy Hearnshaw 1959; two s. two d.; ed Marlborough Coll. and Trinity Coll., Cambridge; Fellow of Trinity Coll. 1959–64; Harkness Fellow, Inst. for Advanced Study, Princeton, USA 1960–61; lecturer, Univ. of Cambridge 1961–64; Reader in Math. and Fellow of St Catherine's Coll. Oxford 1964–65; Prof. of Pure Math., Univ. of Liverpool 1965–99, Prof. Emer. 1999–; Royal Soc. Leverhulme Visiting Prof., CIEA, Mexico 1967; Science and Eng Research Council Sr Research Fellow 1983–88; mem. Council of Royal Soc. 1974–76, Council of London Math. Soc. 1972–80, 1992–96, Pres. 1978–80; Foreign mem. Royal Danish Acad.; Treas. Wirral Area SDP 1985–88, Wirral West Liberal Democrat Party 1988–; Hon. mem. Irish Math. Soc. 2001; Jr Berwick Prize 1965, Sr Whitehead Prize 1976, Polya Prize (London Math. Soc. 1988), Sylvester Medal (Royal Soc. 1988). *Publications:* Surgery on Compact Manifolds 1971, A Geometric Introduction to Topology 1971, The Geometry of Topological Stability 1995, Singular Points of Plane Curves 2004; over 150 research publs in math. journals. *Leisure interests:* reading, walking, gardening, home winemaking. *Address:* Department of Mathematical Sciences, University of Liverpool, Liverpool, L69 3BX (office); 5 Kirby Park, West Kirby, Wirral, Merseyside, CH48 2HA, England (home). *Telephone:* (151) 794-4060 (office); (151) 625-5063 (home). *E-mail:* ctcw@liv.ac.uk (office). *Website:* www.liv.ac.uk/Maths (office).

WALL, Frank A., BCL, LLB, LLM; Irish public official and solicitor; *Director, Fisheries Policy, General Secretariat of Council, European Union;* b. 10 Oct. 1949, Limerick; s. of Frank M. Wall and Eileen Pierse; m. Margot Hourigan 1977; three s. one d.; ed Mungret Coll., Limerick, Univ. Coll., Cork, Inc. Law Soc., Dublin and Free Univ. of Brussels; Adviser Group of European Progressive Democrats, European Parl. 1974–79; Adviser to Minister for Agric., Dublin 1980; Nat. Dir of Elections 1982; Senator 1982–83; mem. Exec. Cttee, Irish Council of the European Movt 1980–91; Gen. Sec. Fianna Fáil 1981–91; mem. Bd, Friends of Fianna Fáil Inc., USA 1986–91; Chair. Irish Council of European Movt 1987–91; Co-Founder Inst. of European Affairs 1990, Chair. Brussels Br. 1998–2001; Dir Inter-Institutional Affairs, Council of the EU 1991–2004, Dir Fisheries Policy 2004–. *Publications:* European Regional Policy (with Sean Brosnan) 1978, Changing Balance between European Institutions 1999. *Leisure interests:* politics, Gaelic football, golf, rugby, gardening. *Address:* Council of the European Union, rue de la Loi 175, 1048 Brussels, Belgium (office). *Telephone:* (2) 285-80-55 (office). *Fax:* (2) 285-82-61 (office). *E-mail:* frank.wall@consilium.europa.eu (office).

WALL, Frederick Theodore, BChem, PhD; American physical chemist and academic; b. 14 Dec. 1912, Chisholm, Minn.; s. of Peter Wall and Fanny Rauhala Wall; m. Clara Vivian 1940; two d.; ed Univ. of Minnesota; Instructor to Prof. of Chem., Univ. of Illinois 1937–64, Dean of Grad. Coll. 1955–63; Prof.

of Chem., Univ. of California, Santa Barbara 1964–66, Vice-Chancellor Research 1965–66; Vice-Chancellor Grad. Studies and Research and Prof. of Chem., Univ. of California, San Diego 1966–69, Adjunct Prof. 1982–90; Ed. Journal of Physical Chem. 1965–69; Exec. Dir ACS 1969–72; Prof. of Chem., Rice Univ. 1972–78, San Diego State Univ. 1979–81; mem. NAS; Corresp. mem. Finnish Chemical Soc.; Fellow, American Acad. of Arts and Sciences; ACS Award in Pure Chem. 1945, Univ. of Minnesota Outstanding Achievement Award 1959. *Publications:* Chemical Thermodynamics 1958; numerous scientific articles on polymers, statistics of macromolecular configurations and theory of reaction probabilities. *Address:* 8515 Costa Verde Blvd, Apt 606, San Diego, CA 92122, USA. *Telephone:* (858) 558-3730. *E-mail:* ftwall@worldnet.att.net (home).

WALL, Jeff D., MA; Canadian artist and academic; b. 1946, Vancouver; ed Univ. of British Columbia, Courtauld Inst., Univ. of London, UK; Asst Prof. Nova Scotia Coll. of Art and Design 1974–75; Assoc. Prof., Simon Fraser Univ., Vancouver 1976–87; fmr Prof. of Fine Arts, Univ. of British Columbia; Int. Photography Prize, Hasselblad Foundation 2002. *Works include:* Destroyed Room 1978, The Children's Pavilion (with Dan Graham), Woman and Her Doctor 1980, Mimic 1982, The Storyteller 1986, Dead Troops Talk 1992, A Sudden Gust of Wind (after Hokusai) 1993. *Publications include:* Jeff Wall: Transparencies 1987, De Duve, Thierry and Boris Groys 1996. *Address:* c/o Tate Modern, Bankside, London SE1 9TG, England (office).

WALL, Sir (John) Stephen, KCMG, LVO; British diplomatist; b. 10 Jan. 1947, Croydon; s. of John Wall and Maria Whitmarsh; m. Catharine Reddaway 1975; one s.; ed Douai School and Selwyn Coll. Cambridge; entered FCO 1968; served Addis Ababa 1969-72, Paris 1972–74; First Sec. FCO 1974–76; Press Officer, No. 10 Downing St 1976–77; Asst Pvt. Sec. to Sec. of State for Foreign and Commonwealth Affairs 1977–79; First Sec. Washington, DC 1979–83; Asst Head, later Head, European Community Dept FCO 1983–88; Pvt. Sec. to Sec. of State for Foreign and Commonwealth Affairs 1988–90, to Prime Minister 1991–93; Amb. to Portugal 1993–95; Perm. Rep. of UK to the European Union 1995–2000; Head European Secr., Cabinet Office 2000–2004; Principal Adviser to RC Cardinal Archbishop of Westminster 2004–; Hon. Fellow Selwyn Coll. Cambridge 2000. *Leisure interests:* walking, photography. *Address:* Archbishop's House, Ambrosden Avenue, London, SW1P 1QJ, England (office). *Telephone:* (20) 7798-9031 (office). *E-mail:* stephenwall@rcdow.org.uk.

WALLACE, Bruce, PhD; American geneticist and academic; *University Distinguished Professor Emeritus of Biology, Virginia Polytechnic Institution and State University;* b. 18 May 1920, McKean, Pa; s. of George E. Wallace and Rose Paterson Wallace; m. Miriam Covalla 1945; one s. one d.; ed Columbia Coll. and Columbia Univ.; Research Assoc., Dept of Genetics, Carnegie Inst. of Washington 1947–49; Geneticist, later Asst Dir, Biological Lab., Cold Spring Harbour, NY 1949–58; Assoc. Prof., Cornell Univ. 1958–61, Prof. of Genetics 1961–81; Univ. Distinguished Prof. of Biology, Virginia Polytechnic Inst. and State Univ. 1981–94, Prof. Emer. 1994–; mem. NAS, American Acad. of Arts and Sciences; Alexander von Humbolt Sr US Scientist Award 1986. *Publications:* Radiation, Genes and Man (with Th. Dobzhansky) 1959, Adaptation (with A. M. Srb) 1961, Chromosomes, Giant Molecules and Evolution 1966, Topics in Population Genetics 1968, Genetic Load 1970, Essays in Social Biology (3 vols) 1972, Basic Population Genetics 1981, Dobzhansky's Genetics of Natural Populations I–XLIII (with others) 1982, Human Culture: A Moment in Evolution (with others) 1983, Biology for Living (with G. M. Simmons, Jr) 1987, Fifty Years of Genetic Load: An Odyssey 1991, The Search for the Gene 1992, The Study of Gene Action (with J. O. Falkinham) 1997, The Environment: As I See It, Science Is Not Enough 1998, The Environment 2: As I See It, The Mold Must Be Broken 2000, The Fringes of Glory: The Cold Spring Harbor Laboratories of the 1950s. *Leisure interest:* promotion of environmental literacy. *Address:* 940 McBryde Drive, Blacksburg, VA 24060, USA. *Telephone:* (540) 951-2464. *Fax:* (540) 951-2464. *E-mail:* kojima@swva.net (home).

WALLACE, Sir David James, Kt, CBE, DL, PhD, FRS, CEng, FREng, FInstP, FRSE, FRSA, CIMgt; British physicist and university vice-chancellor; *Master, Churchill College, Cambridge;* b. 7 Oct. 1945, Hawick, Scotland; s. of Robert Elder Wallace and Jane McConnell Wallace (née Elliot); m. Elizabeth Anne Yeats 1970; one d.; ed Hawick High School and Univ. of Edinburgh; Harkness Fellow, Princeton Univ., USA 1970–72; Lecturer in Physics, Univ. of Southampton 1972–78, Reader 1978–79; Tait Prof. of Math. Physics, Univ. of Edinburgh 1979–93, Head of Physics 1984–87; Vice-Chancellor Univ. of Loughborough 1994–2005; Master of Churchill Coll. Cambridge 2006–, N. M. Rothschild & Sons Prof. of Math. Sciences, Univ. of Cambridge and Dir Isaac Newton Inst. and 2006–); Dir Edin. Concurrent Supercomputer 1987–89, Edinburgh Parallel Computing Centre 1990–93; Chair. Science and Eng Research Council (SERC, subsequently Eng and Physical Sciences Research Council) Physics Cttee 1987–90, mem. SERC Council 1990–98 and Chair. Science Bd 1990–94, Chair. Tech. Opportunities Panel 1994–98; mem. EC Physics Panel, Human Capital and Mobility Programme 1991–94, EC Large Scale Facilities Evaluation Panel 1995–97; mem. European Science and Tech. Ass. 1997–98; Chair. CVCP/SCOP Task Force on Sport in Higher Educ. 1995–97, Value for Money Steering Group, Higher Educ. Funding Council for England 1997–2003; mem. Royal Soc. Scientific and Industrial Award Cttees 1990–95, Scottish Higher Educ. Funding Council 1993–97, LINK Bd, Office of Science and Tech. 1995–98, LINK/Teaching Co. Scheme Bd 1999–2001; Chair. e-Science Steering Cttee, Office of Science and Tech. 2001–06, Teaching Co. Scheme Quinquennial Review 2001; Dir (non-exec.) The Scottish Life Assurance Co. 1999–2001, Taylor & Francis Group PLC 2000–04, UK e-Universities Worldwide Ltd 2001–04; Pres. Physics Section Br. Asscn for the Advancement of Science 1994, Inst. of Physics 2002–04; mem. Council Royal Soc. 2001–, Treas. and Vice-Pres. 2002–; DL for Leics. 2001–06; Hon. DEng (Heriot Watt) 2002; Hon. DSc (Edinburgh) 2003, (Leicester) 2005; Maxwell Medal, Inst. of Physics 1980. *Publications:* numerous publs in research and review journals on a number of areas of theoretical physics and computing. *Leisure interests:* exercise, eating well, mycophagy. *Address:* Churchill College, Cambridge, CB3 0DS, England (office). *Telephone:* (1223) 336142 (office). *E-mail:* david.wallace@chu.cam.ac.uk (office). *Website:* www.chu.cam.ac.uk (office).

WALLACE, George W., Jr; Liberian diplomatist; joined Dept of State (now Ministry of Foreign Affairs) 1954, numerous positions including Amb. to UK, to USA; Sr Amb.-at-Large –2006; Minister of Foreign Affairs 2006–07. *Address:* c/o Ministry of Foreign Affairs, POB 10-9002, 1000 Monrovia, Liberia (office).

WALLACE, Helen, CMG, PhD, FBA; British professor of European studies; *Centennial Professor, European Institute, London School of Economics and Political Science;* b. 25 June 1946, Manchester; d. of the late Edward Rushworth and Joyce Rushworth (née Robinson); m. William Wallace (now Lord Wallace of Saltaire) 1968; one s. one d.; ed Univs of Oxford, Bruges, Belgium and Manchester; Lecturer in European Studies, UMIST 1974–78, Visiting Prof., Coll. of Europe, Bruges 1976–2001; in Public Admin., Civil Service Coll. 1978–85; mem. Planning Staff, FCO 1979–80; Head W European Programme, Royal Inst. of Int. Affairs 1985–92; Prof. of Contemporary European Studies and Dir Sussex European Inst., Univ. of Sussex 1992–2001, Professorial Fellow 2001–06; Dir Robert Schuman Centre for Advanced Studies, European Univ. Inst. 2001–06; Centennial Professor, European Inst., LSE 2006–; mem. Better Regulation Comm. 2006–07; mem. Acad. for Learned Socs for the Social Sciences 2000; Assoc. mem. Acad. Royale des Sciences, des Lettres et des Beaux-Arts, Belgium; Ordre nat. du Mérite 1996; Hon. LLD (Sussex) 2002; Hon. DLitt (Loughborough) 2004; Lifetime Achievement in European Studies, Univ. Asscn for Contemporary European Studies 2006. *Publications:* French and British Foreign Policies in Transition (co-author) 1990, The Wider Western Europe (ed.) 1991, The European Community: The Challenge of Enlargement (co-author) 1992, Participation and Policy-Making (co-author) 1997, Interlocking Dimensions of European Integration (ed.) 2001, Policy Making in the European Union (ed.) 2005, The Council of Ministers (co-author) 2006. *Leisure interests:* gardening, walking. *Address:* Room J216, European Institute, London School of Economics, Houghton Street, London, WC2A 2AE, England (office). *Telephone:* (20) 7955-7301 (office). *Fax:* (20) 7955-7546 (office). *E-mail:* h.s.wallace@btopenworld.com (office); h.wallace@lse.ac.uk (office). *Website:* www.lse.ac.uk (office).

WALLACE, Ian Bryce, OBE, MA, DMus; British singer, actor and broadcaster; b. 10 July 1919, London; s. of the late Sir John Wallace and Mary Temple; m. Patricia Gordon Black 1948; one s. one d.; ed Charterhouse and Trinity Hall, Cambridge; debut, Schaunard in Puccini's La Bohème, London 1946; appeared at Glyndebourne 1948–61 with roles, including Masetto in Don Giovanni, Bartolo in Le nozze di Figaro and Il Barbiere di Siviglia, Don Magnifico in La Cenerentola and Matteo in Arlecchino; continued to appear in opera in Britain and briefly in Italy until 1970s, appearances including Berlin Festwoche 1954, Teatro Reale, Rome 1955, Scottish Opera 1966–75; later appeared on concert platforms and also in plays, reviews, musicals and pantomimes, as well as in many television and radio shows, notably My Music (BBC) 1966–93; Pres. Inc. Soc. of Musicians 1979–80, Council for Music in Hospitals 1987–99; Hon. MusD (St Andrews) 1991; Hon. mem. RAM, Royal Coll. of Music. *Film appearances include* Plenty, Tom Thumb. *Stage appearances* played lead opposite Robert Morley in Harold Rome's musical Fanny, Theatre Royal, London 1956–57, An Evening with Ian Wallace 1965–2000. *Radio:* panellist, 'My Music' (BBC). *Television appearances include:* The Mikado, Singing for Your Supper (opera series, Scottish TV), Porterhouse Blue. *Recordings:* Ian Wallace—My Music, Mikado, Iolanthe, Your Hundred Favourite Hymns, Glyndebourne recordings of Le nozze di Figaro, La Cenerentola, Il Barbiere di Siviglia, Le Comte Ory. *Publications:* I Promise Me You'll Sing Mud (autobiog., vol. I) 1975, Nothing Quite Like It (autobiog., vol. II) 1982, Reflections on Scotland 1988. *Leisure interests:* music, theatre, watching sport, reading. *Address:* PFD, Drury House, 34–43 Russell Street, London, WC2B 5HA, England (office); 18 Denewood Road, Highgate, London N6 4AJ, England (home). *Telephone:* (20) 7344-1000 (office); (20) 8340-5802 (home). *Fax:* (20) 7836-9539 (office). *E-mail:* postmaster@pfd.co.uk (office). *Website:* www.pfd.co.uk (office).

WALLACE-CRABBE, Christopher Keith, MA, FAHA; Australian poet and critic; b. 6 May 1934, Melbourne; s. of Kenneth Eyre Inverell Wallace-Crabbe and Phyllis Vera May Wallace-Crabbe (née Cock); m. 1st Helen Margaret Wiltshire 1957; one s. one d.; m. 2nd Marianne Sophie Feil 1979; two s.; ed Melbourne Univ., Yale Univ., USA; cadet metallurgist 1951–52; then journalist, clerk, schoolteacher; Lockie Fellow in Australian Literature, Univ. of Melbourne 1962; Harkness Fellow, Yale Univ., USA 1965–67; Sr Lecturer in English, Univ. of Melbourne 1967, Reader 1976, Prof. 1987–, Personal Chair 1987–97; Prof. Emer. Australian Centre 1997–; Visiting Chair. in Australian Studies, Harvard Univ., USA 1987–88; Chair. Australian Poetry Centre 2007; Hon. DLitt (Melbourne) 2006; Masefield Prize for Poetry 1957, Farmer's Poetry Prize 1964, Grace Leven Prize 1986, Dublin Prize 1987, Christopher Brennan Award 1990, Age Book of the Year Prize 1995, Philip Hodgins Memorial Medal 2002, Centenary Medal 2003. *Publications:* The Music of Division 1959, Selected Poems 1974, Melbourne or the Bush 1974, The Emotions are not Skilled Workers 1980, Toil and Spin: Two Directions in Modern Poetry 1980, Splinters (novel) 1981, The Amorous Cannibal 1985, I'm Deadly Serious 1988, Sangue è l'Acqua 1989, For Crying out Loud 1990, Falling into Language 1990, Poetry and Belief 1990, From the Republic of Conscience 1992, Rungs of Time 1993, Selected Poems 1956–94 1995,

Whirling 1998, By and Large 2001, The Universe Looks Down 2005, Read It Again 2005, The Thing Itself 2007. *Leisure interests:* drawing, tennis, surfing, making artist's books. *Address:* The Australian Centre, University of Melbourne, Parkville, Vic. 3052 (office); 7 De Carle Street, Brunswick, Vic. 3056, Australia (home). *Telephone:* (3) 8344-6998 (office); (3) 9386-6938 (home). *Fax:* (3) 9347-7731 (office). *E-mail:* ckwc@unimelb.edu.au (office). *Website:* www.hlc.unimelb.edu.au/cwc (office).

WALLACE OF SALTAIRE, Baron (Life Peer) cr. 1995, of Shipley in the County of West Yorkshire; **William John Lawrence Wallace,** BA, PhD; British academic; *Professor of International Relations, London School of Economics;* ed Cambridge Univ., Cornell Univ., USA; Dir of Studies, Royal Inst. of Int. Affairs 1978–90; Walter F. Hallstein Fellow St Antony's Coll., Oxford 1990–95; Prof. of Int. Studies, Central European Univ., Budapest 1994–97; currently Prof. of Int. Relations, LSE; nominated to House of Lords 1995, mem. European Union Cttee 1996–2001, Chair. Sub-Cttee on Justice and Home Affairs 1997–2000; Ordre pour le Mérite, France 1995. *Publications include:* Regional Integration: the West European Experience 1994, Integration in a Larger and More Diverse European Union (jtly) 1995, Policy-making in the European Union (jtly) 2000, Rethinking European Order: West European Responses, 1989–97 (jtly) 2001, Non-State Actors in International Relations (jtly) 2001. *Address:* Department of International Relations, London School of Economics, Houghton Street, London, WC2A 2AE, England (office). *Telephone:* (20) 7955-7166 (office). *Fax:* (20) 7405-1305 (office). *E-mail:* w.wallace@lse.ac.uk (office). *Website:* www.lse.ac.uk (office).

WALLACE OF TANKERNESS, Baron (Life Peer), cr. 2007, of Tankerness in Orkney; **James Robert (Jim) Wallace,** PC, QC, MA, LLB; British politician; b. 25 Aug. 1954, Annan; s. of John F. T. Wallace and Grace Hannah Maxwell; m. Rosemary Janet Fraser 1983; two d.; ed Annan Acad., Downing Coll. Cambridge, Edinburgh Univ.; Chair. Edin. Univ. Liberal Club 1976–77; called to Scots Bar 1979; advocate 1979–83; mem. Scottish Liberal Exec. 1976–85; Vice-Chair. (Policy) Scottish Liberal Party 1982–85; MP for Orkney and Shetland 1983–2001 (Liberal 1983–88, Liberal Democrat 1988–2001), MSP for Orkney 1999–2007; Hon. Pres. Scottish Young Liberals 1984–85; Liberal Spokesman on Defence 1985–87; Deputy Whip 1985–87; Chief Whip 1987–88; first Liberal Democrat Chief Whip 1988–92; Alliance Spokesman on Transport 1987; Liberal Democrat Spokesman on Employment and Training 1988–92, on Fisheries 1988–97, on Scottish Affairs 1992–2001, on Maritime Affairs 1994–97; Leader Scottish Liberal Democrats 1992–2005; Deputy First Minister of the Scottish Exec. 1999–2005, Minister for Justice 1999–2003, for Enterprise and Lifelong Learning 2003–05; Chair. Relationships Scotland 2008–; mem. Comm. on Scottish Devolution 2008–; Hon. DLitt (Heriot Watt Univ.) 2007. *Leisure interests:* golf, music, travel. *Address:* House of Lords, London, SW1A 0PW, England (office); Northwood House, Tankerness, Orkney, KW17 2QS, Scotland (home). *Telephone:* (20) 7219-3526 (office); (1856) 861-383 (home). *Fax:* (20) 7219-4596 (office); (1856) 861-383 (home). *E-mail:* wallacej@parliament.uk.

WALLACH, Eli, MS (Educ); American actor; b. 7 Dec. 1915, Brooklyn, NY; s. of Abraham Wallach and Bertha Schorr; m. Anne Jackson 1948; one s. two d.; ed Univ. of Texas, City Coll. of New York, Neighborhood Playhouse School of Theatre; started theatre career 1946, film career 1955; Donaldson Award, Tony Award, British Film Acad. Award 1956. *Plays include:* The Rose Tattoo, The Teahouse of the August Moon 1954–55, Camino Real, Luv, Typists and Tiger 1964, Promenade All 1973, Waltz of the Toreadors 1974, The Diary of Anne Frank 1978, Opera Comique 1987, The Flowering Peach in Florida 1987, Visiting Mr. Green 1997, Down the Garden Paths 1998–99, Remembered 1999. *Films include:* Baby Doll 1956, The Line-Up 1958, Seven Thieves 1960, The Magnificent Seven 1960, The Misfits 1961, Hemingway's Adventures of a Young Man 1962, How the West Was Won 1962, The Victors 1963, Act One 1963, The Moon-Spinners 1964, Kisses for My President 1964, Lord Jim 1965, Genghis Khan 1965, Poppies Are Also Flowers 1966, How to Steal a Million 1966, The Good, the Bad and the Ugly 1967, The Tiger Makes Out (also producer, uncredited) 1967, I quattro dell'Ave Maria (aka Ace High, USA) 1968, How to Save a Marriage (And Ruin Your Life) 1968, A Lovely Way to Die 1968, Le cerveau 1969, Mackenna's Gold 1969, The Adventures of Gerard 1970, The Angel Levine 1970, The People Next Door 1970, Zigzag 1970, Romance of a Horsethief 1971, ¡Viva la muerte… tua! 1971, Cinderella Liberty 1973, Crazy Joe 1974, L'ultima chance (Last Chance) 1975, Il bianco, il giallo, il nero (White, the Yellow, and the Black) 1975, …e tanta paura 1976, Attenti al buffone (aka Eye of the Cat) 1976, Independence 1976, The Sentinel 1977, The Deep 1977, The Domino Principle 1977, Nasty Habits 1977, Squadra antimafia (aka Little Italy) 1978, Girlfriends 1978, Movie Movie 1978, Circle of Iron 1978, The Silent Flute 1978, Firepower 1979, Winter Kills 1979, The Hunter 1980, The Salamander 1981, The Wall 1982, Sam's Son 1984, Tough Guys 1986, Nuts 1987, The Rose Garden 1989, The Two Jakes 1990, The Godfather: Part III 1990, Nonesense and Lullabyes: Poems (video) 1992, The Godfather Trilogy: 1901–1980 (video) 1992, Nonesense and Lullabyes: Nursery Rhymes (video) 1992, Article 99 1992, Mistress 1992, Night and the City 1992, Caro dolce amore (Honey Sweet Love) 1994, Two Much 1995, The Associate 1996, Uninvited 1999, Keeping the Faith 2000, Advise and Dissent 2002, Merci Docteur Rey 2002, The Root 2003, Mystic River (uncredited) 2003, King of the Corner 2004, The Moon and the Son (voice) 2005, The Easter Egg Adventure (voice) 2005, A Taste of Jupiter 2005, The Hoax 2006, The Holiday 2006. *Television includes:* Where Is Thy Brother? 1958, Gift of the Magi 1958, Lullaby 1960, The Chill Factor 1973, Indict and Convict 1974, Houston, We've Got a Problem 1974, Paradise Lost 1974, Seventh Avenue (mini-series) 1977, The Pirate 1978, Fugitive Family 1980, The Pride of Jesse Hallam 1981, Skokie 1981, The Executioner's Song 1982, Anatomy of an Illness 1984, Murder: By Reason of Insanity 1985, Embassy 1985, Christopher Columbus (mini-series) 1985, Our Family Honor 1985, Our Family Honor (series) 1985, Something in Common 1986, Rocket to the Moon 1986, The Impossible Spy 1987, A Matter of Conscience 1989, Vendetta: Secrets of a Mafia Bride 1991, Legacy of Lies 1992, Teamster Boss: The Jackie Presser Story 1992, Vendetta II: The New Mafia 1993, Naked City: Justice with a Bullet 1998, The Bookfair Murders 2000, Monday Night Mayhem 2002, Character Studies (series) 2005. *Leisure interest:* photography.

WALLBERG-HENRIKSSON, Harriet, MD, PhD; Swedish university administrator, academic and physiologist; *President, Karolinska Institutet;* two c.; ed Karolinska Institutet, Univ. Coll. of Physical Educ. and Sports; fmr Dir of Gymnastics; fmr Assoc. Prof., Karolinska Institutet, Prof. 1998–, Pres. (first female) 2004–, mem. Nobel Ass. 2002–; Dean and Chair., Bd of Research, Royal Swedish Acad. of Sciences 1999–2001, currently mem. Physiology Cttee; Asst Sec.-Gen. Scientific Council for Medicine, Swedish Research Council 1996–98, Sec.-Gen. 2001–03; Vice-Chair. European Asscn for the Study of Diabetes (EASD); has led Swedish dels to Japan and UN; rep. of Sweden on Bds of European Science Foundation, WHO Agency for Cancer Research, Heads of Int. Research Orgs (HIRO); mem. EU Expert Group, EU strategy for competitive research environments. *Publications:* approx. 140 scientific articles on diabetes and clinical physiology. *Address:* Karolinska Institutet, 171 77 Stockholm, Sweden (office). *Telephone:* (8) 524-800-00 (office). *Fax:* (8) 524-866-44 (office). *E-mail:* Rektor@ki.se (office). *Website:* www.ki.se (office).

WALLENBERG, Jacob, BS (Econ), MBA; Swedish business executive; *Chairman, Investor AB;* b. 1956, Stockholm; s. of Peter Wallenberg; m. Marie Wallenberg; three c.; ed Wharton School, Univ. of Pennsylvania, Royal Swedish Naval Acad.; officer in Royal Swedish Naval Reserve; extensive training programmes at several int. banks; joined Skandinaviska Enskilda Banken (SEB) AB 1984, held various posts, primarily in Sweden but also in Singapore, Hong Kong, London and New York, rejoined SEB 1993, CEO 1997, Chair. 1998–2005; Deputy Man. Dir Investor AB (Wallenberg family fund man. firm) 1990–92, Vice-Chair. 2005–; Vice-Chair. Atlas Copco AB, SAS AB; mem. Bd of Dirs ABB; mem. Bd Nobel Foundation, Knut and Alice Wallenberg Foundation AB, Wharton European Advisory Bd. *Leisure interests:* golf, sailing. *Address:* Investor AB, Arsenalsgatan 8C, 103 32 Stockholm, Sweden (office). *Telephone:* (8) 614-20-00 (office). *Fax:* (8) 614-21-50 (office). *E-mail:* fredrik.lindgren@investorab.com (office). *Website:* www.investorab.com (office).

WALLENBERG, Marcus; Swedish international organization executive; *Chairman, International Chamber of Commerce;* s. of Marc Wallenberg; ed Edmund A. Walsh School of Foreign Service, Georgetown Univ., USA; fmr Dir Stora Feldmühle, Düsseldorf; Exec. Vice-Pres. Investor AB –1999, Pres. and CEO 1999–2005; Chair. Saab, Skandinaviska Enskilda Banken (SEB) AB; Vice-Chair. L. M. Ericsson; mem. Bd of Dirs AstraZeneca, Electrolux, Stora Enso Oyj, Knut and Alice Wallenberg Foundation; Chair. ICC 2005–; fmr mem. Advisory Council Stanford Grad. School of Business, Founder Wallenberg Global Learning Center at Stanford Univ.; mem. Royal Swedish Acad. of Eng and Sciences; European Business Leadership Award, Stanford Business School Alumni Asscn 2003. *Address:* International Chamber of Commerce, 38 cours Albert 1er, 75008 Paris, France (office). *Telephone:* 1-49-53-28-28 (office). *Fax:* 1-49-53-28-59 (office). *E-mail:* info@iccwbo.org (office). *Website:* www.iccwbo.org (office).

WALLENBERG, Peter, LLB; Swedish business executive; *Chairman, Knut and Alice Wallenberg Foundation;* b. 29 May 1926, Stockholm; s. of Dr Marcus Wallenberg and Dorothy Mackay; m. (divorced); two s. one d.; ed Univ. of Stockholm; various positions with Atlas Copco Group 1953-74; fmr Chair. Atlas Copco AB, STORA, ASEA, Hon. Chair. Atlas Copco AB; fmr Co-Chair. ASEA Brown Boveri (ABB); First Vice-Chair. Skandinaviska Enskilda Banken 1984–96; mem. Bd Dirs Investor AB 1969–82, Chair. 1982–97, Hon. Chair. 1997–; Chair. Knut and Alice Wallenberg Foundation 1982–; Hon. Kt 1989; Dr hc (Stockholm School of Econs, Augustana Coll. and Uppsala Coll., USA, Uppsala Univ., Royal Inst. of Tech., Stockholm). *Leisure interests:* hunting, tennis, sailing. *Address:* c/o Investor AB, 10332 Stockholm, Sweden. *Telephone:* 86-14-20-00. *Fax:* 86-14-28-15. *Website:* www.investorab.com.

WALLER, Rev. Ralph, PhD; British minister of religion and academic; *Principal, Harris Manchester College, Oxford;* b. 11 Dec. 1945; m. Carol Roberts 1968; one d.; ed John Leggott Grammar School, Scunthorpe, Richmond Coll. Divinity School, Univ. of London, Univ. of Nottingham, King's Coll. London; service in India, teaching math. and physical educ., House Master Shri Shivah Mil. School, Pune 1967–68; Math. Teacher, Riddings Comprehensive School, Scunthorpe 1968–69; Methodist Minister, Melton Mowbray 1972–75; ordained 1975; Minister Elvet Methodist Church, Durham City, Methodist Chaplain, Univ. of Durham 1975–81, Chaplain St Mary's Coll. and St Aidan's Coll. 1979–81; Chaplain, Tutor in Theology and Resident Tutor, Westminster Coll., Oxford 1981–88; Prin. and Tutor in Theology, Harris Manchester (fmrly Manchester) Coll., Univ. Oxford 1988–, Chair. Faculty of Theology, Univ. Oxford 1995–97, mem. Hebdomadal Council 1997–2000; Chair. Environmental Cttee 1997–2000; Dir Farmington Inst. 2001–; Hon. DLitt (Menlo Coll., Calif.) 1994; Hon. DHum (Ball State Univ., Ind.) 1998; Hon. DHL (St Olaf Coll., Minn.) 2001, (Christopher Newport) 2005; Hon. DTheol (Uppsala) 1999; Hon. DD (Hartwick) 2003; Templeton Prize UK 1993. *Publications:* Christian Spirituality (co-ed.) 1999, John Wesley 2003, Basic Texts in Christian Spirituality (co-ed.) 2003. *Leisure interests:* swimming, walking, browsing round second-hand bookshops. *Address:* Principal's Lodgings, Harris Manchester College, Mansfield Road, Oxford, OX1 3TD, England (home). *Telephone:* (1865) 271006 (office). *Fax:* (1865) 281474 (office). *E-mail:* principal@hmc.ox.ac.uk (office). *Website:* www.hmc.ox.ac.uk (office).

WALLER, Robert James; American writer and musician; b. 1 Aug. 1939; s. of Robert Waller Sr and Ruth Waller; m. Georgia A. Wiedemeier; one d.; ed

Northern Iowa and Indiana Univs; Prof. of Man. Univ. of N Iowa 1968–91, Dean Business School 1979–85; singer; guitarist; flautist. *Album:* The Ballads of Madison County 1993. *Publications:* Just Beyond the Firelight 1988, One Good Road is Enough 1990, Iowa: Perspectives on Today and Tomorrow 1991, The Bridges of Madison County 1992, Slow Waltz at Cedar Bend 1994, Old Songs in a New Café 1994, Selected Essays 1994, Border Music 1995, Puerto-Vallarta Squeeze 1995, A Thousand Country Roads 2002, High Plains Tango 2005, The Long Night of Winchell Dear 2006. *Leisure interests:* photography, basketball.

WALLERSTEIN, Ralph O., MD; American professor of medicine; *Clinical Professor, University of California, San Francisco;* b. 7 March 1922, Düsseldorf, Germany; s. of O. R. Wallerstein and Ilse Hollander; m. Betty A. Christensen 1952; two s. one d.; ed Univ. of California Medical School, San Francisco; Chief of Clinical Hematology, San Francisco Gen. Hosp. 1953–81, Clinical Dir of Blood Bank 1955–80; Chief of Staff, Children's Hosp. 1968–72; Clinical Prof., Univ. of Calif. San Francisco 1969–; mem. Exec. Cttee American Soc. of Hematology 1971–78, Pres. 1978; Chair. Bd of Govs American Bd of Internal Medicine 1982–83, Chair. Cttee on Hematology 1974–77; Gov., N Calif., American Coll. of Physicians 1977–81, Chair. Bd of Govs 1980–81, Regent 1981–87, Pres. 1987–88; mem. Residency Review Cttee for Internal Medicine 1985–; Fellow AAAS, ACP; mem. American Medical Asscn, American Fed. for Clinical Research, American Asscn of Blood Banks, American Soc. of Hematology, Inst. of Medicine, American Soc. of Clinical Oncology. *Publications:* Iron in Clinical Medicine (with S. R. Mettier) 1958, 27 articles in specialized journals. *Leisure interest:* photography. *Address:* 3447 Clay Street, San Francisco, CA 94118, USA (home). *Telephone:* (415) 518-5586. *Fax:* (415) 922-6555. *E-mail:* rowmdsf@aol.com (home).

WALLINGER, Mark; British artist; b. 1959, Chigwell, Essex; ed West Hatch High School, Chigwell, Loughton Coll., Chelsea School of Art, London, Goldsmiths Coll., briefly studied architecture at Univ. of Sheffield; tutor at Goldsmiths Coll. since 1986; later works have focused on religion and death and the influence of William Blake; lives and works in London; Hon. Fellow, London Inst. 2002; Dr hc (Univ. of Cen. England) 2003; Henry Moore Fellowship, British School, Rome 1998, DAAD Artists Programme, Berlin 2001–02, Turner Prize 2007. *Address:* c/o Anthony Reynolds Gallery, 60 Great Marlborough Street, London, W1F 7BG, England. *Telephone:* (20) 7439-2201. *Fax:* (20) 7439-1869. *E-mail:* info@anthonyreynolds.com. *Website:* www.anthonyreynolds.com.

WALLIS, Stanley David Martin, BCom, FAIM, FCIS, FCIM; Australian financial services executive; b. 23 July 1939, Melbourne; s. of S. E. Wallis; m. Judith Logan 1962; three s. two d.; ed Wesley Coll., Melbourne, Univ. of Melbourne, Stanford Univ., USA; joined APM/Amcor 1960, Chief Accountant 1986, Financial Man. 1972, Deputy Man. Dir 1975, Man. Dir 1977–96; Chair. Amcor Ltd 1997–2000; Dir AMP Ltd 1990–2003, Chair. 2000–03; Chair. Pineapplehead Ltd 2000–; Dir Coles Myer Ltd 1996–, Chair. 1997–; Dir Walter & Eliza Hall Inst. of Medical Research; Chair. and Dir Santos Ltd 1989–94; Dir Australian Foundation Investment Co. 1987–; fmr Dir Nicholas-Kiwi Australasia Ltd, NZ Forest Products Ltd, Mayne Nickless Ltd, Spicers Paper Ltd; Chair. Inquiry into Australian Financial System 1996–97; Pres. Business Council of Australia 1996–98; fmr Vice-Pres. Melbourne Business School, Univ. of Melbourne; Hon. LLD (Monash); Award for Outstanding Achievement in Business, Melbourne Univ. Grad. School of Man. 1990, Bulletin Deloitte Business Leader Award 1995. *Leisure interests:* tennis, skiing, sailing. *Address:* c/o AMP, AMP Sydney Core Building, 33 Alfred Street, Sydney, NSW 2000, Australia (office).

WALLOT, Jean-Pierre, OC, LèsL, PhD, FRSC; Canadian historian, archivist and academic; *Director, Centre for Research on French Canadian Culture University of Ottawa;* b. 22 May 1935, Valleyfield, Québec; s. of the late Albert Wallot and of Adrienne Thibodeau; m. 1st Rita Girard 1957; m. 2nd Denyse Caron 1990; two s. one d.; ed Univ. de Montréal; Prof. and Dir History Dept Univ. de Montreal 1961–66, 1973–85, Vice-Pres. (Academic) 1982–85; Historian Museum of Man of Canada 1966–69; Prof. Univ. of Toronto 1969–71, Concordia Univ. 1971–73; Nat. Archivist of Canada 1985–97; Dir d'études associé, Ecole des Hautes Etudes en Sciences Sociales, Paris 1975, 1979, 1981, 1983, 1984, 1985, 1987, 1989, 1994; Guest Lecturer Univ. of Ottawa 1986–97, Visiting Prof. Dept of History 1997–2004, Dir Centre for Research on French Canadian Culture 2000–; mem. Bd of Govs Univ. of Ottawa 1988–90; Pres. Int. Council of Archives 1992–96; Pres. RSC 1997–99; Pres. Int. Advisory Cttee on Memory of the World, UNESCO 1993–99; mem. European Acad. of Sciences, Arts and Letters 1997–; Dr hc (Rennes) 1987, (Ottawa) 1996; Jacques Ducharme Prize, Asscn Archiv. du Québec 1997; Marie Tremaine Medal (Canadian Bibliographic Soc.) 1973, RSC Tyrrell Medal 1983, Centenary Medal of RSC 1994; Officier Ordre des Arts et Lettres (France) 1987. *Publications:* Intrigues françaises et américaines au Canada 1965, Les Imprimés dans le Bas-Canada (with John Hare) 1967, Un Québec qui bougeait 1973, Patronage et Pouvoir dans le Bas-Canada (with G. Paquet) 1973, Evolution et Eclatement du Monde Rural, France-Québec, XVIe–XXe Siècles (with Joseph Goy) 1986, Constructions identitaires et pratiques sociales (ed.) 2002, La Commission Cepin-Robart quelque vingtans après (ed.) 2002. *Leisure interests:* reading, hiking, drums. *Address:* 26-635 Richmond Road, Ottawa, Ont., K2A 0G6; Centre for Research on French Canadian Culture, University of Ottawa, Lamoureux Hall, 145 Jean-Jacques-Lussier Street, Ottawa, Ont. K1N 6N5, Canada (office). *Telephone:* (613) 761-7472; (613) 562-5710 (office). *Fax:* (613) 761-9405; (613) 562-5143 (office). *E-mail:* jpwallot@uottowa.ca (office). *Website:* www.uottawa.ca/academic/crccf (office).

WALLS, Gen. (George) Peter, MBE; Zimbabwean fmr army officer; b. 28 July 1926, Salisbury; ed Plumtree School, Royal Mil. Acad., Sandhurst and Camberley Staff Coll., UK; enlisted in Southern Rhodesian Army 1944; commissioned into the Black Watch (Royal Highland Regt), British Army 1946; attested back to Southern Rhodesian Perm. Staff Corps 1948, commissioned 1949; Commdr C. Squadron, 22nd Special Air Service in Malaya 1951–53; Officer Commdg Tactical Wing, later Chief Instructor, School of Infantry 1954–56; Co. Commdr Northern Rhodesian Regt 1956–59; Brigade Maj. Copperbelt Area and later N Rhodesia District 1961–62; Adjutant-Gen. Rhodesian Army 1962–64; CO 1st Bn Rhodesian Light Infantry 1964–67; Commdr 2nd Brigade 1967–68; Chief of Staff, Rhodesian Army 1968–72, Commdr 1972–77; Commdr Combined Operations 1977–80, of Jt Operations 1980; Grand Officer of the Legion of Merit, Defence Cross for Distinguished Service.

WALLSTRÖM, Margot; Swedish politician; *Vice-President and Commissioner for Institutional Relations and Communication Strategy, European Commission;* b. 28 Sept. 1954, Kåge, Västerbotten Co.; m. Håkan Wallström; two s.; Organizing Sec. Värmland br., Social Democratic Youth League; bank clerk, Sparbanken Alfa, Värmland 1977–79; Chief Accountant 1986–88; MP 1979–85; fmr mem. Värmland Co. Council, Directorate of Bd of Civil Aviation, Directorate of Nat. Environment Protection Bd etc.; Minister with responsibility for Ecclesiastical, Consumers, Equality and Youth Affairs, Ministry of Public Admin 1988–92; Minister of Cultural Affairs 1994–96, of Health and Social Affairs 1996–98; EC Commr for the Environment 1999–2004, Vice-Pres. and Commr for Institutional Relations and Communication Strategy 2004–; Chair. of Ministerial Initiative, Council of World Women Leaders 2007; Dr hc (Chalmers Univ.) 2001, (Mälardalen Univ.) 2004, (Univ. of Mass, Howell) 2005. *Publications:* The People's Europe or Why is it so Hard to Love the EU? (with Göran Färm) 2004, EU Elite Project? No! The People's Europe (with Göran Färm) 2008. *Address:* Commission of the European Communities, 200 rue de la Loi, 1049 Brussels, Belgium (office). *Telephone:* (2) 2981800 (office). *Fax:* (2) 2981899 (office). *Website:* ec.europa.eu/commission_barroso/wallstrom/index.htm (office).

WALMSLEY, David George, PhD, DSc, FInstP, MRIA; British physicist and academic; *Professor Emeritus of Physics, Queen's University Belfast;* b. 3 Feb. 1938, Newtownstewart, Northern Ireland; s. of Robert Gwynne Walmsley and Elizabeth Johnston; m. Margaret Heather Edmonstone 1965; two s.; ed Royal School, Armagh, Queen's Univ. Belfast and McMaster Univ., Hamilton, Ont.; NRC Canada Post-doctoral Fellow, MacMaster Univ. 1965; Scientific Officer, Sr Scientific Officer, AERE Harwell 1966–70; Lecturer, Sr Lecturer, Reader in Physics, New Univ. of Ulster 1970–84; Prof. of Physics, Univ. of Ulster 1984–88; Prof. of Physics, Queen's Univ. Belfast 1988–2003, Prof. Emer. 2003–, Dir School of Math. and Physics 1993–98, Dean Faculty of Science and Agric. 1998–2002; Chair. Northern Ireland Regional Medical Physics Agency; Fellow, American Physical Soc. 2001. *Publications:* numerous articles on superconductivity and the electron tunnel effect in scientific journals. *Address:* Department of Physics and Astronomy, Queen's University, Belfast, BT7 1NN (office); 5 Newforge Grange, Belfast, BT9 5QB (home); 25 Swilly Road, Portstewart, BT55 7DJ, Northern Ireland (home). *Telephone:* (28) 90973531 (office); (28) 90664141 (home); (28) 70833257 (home). *Fax:* (28) 90273110 (office). *E-mail:* dg.walmsley@qub.ac.uk (office). *Website:* www.qub.ac.uk/mp (office).

WALPORT, Sir Mark Jeremy, Kt, MB, BChir, MA, PhD, FRCP, FRCPath, FMedSci; British physician, academic and trust executive; *Director, The Wellcome Trust;* b. 25 Jan. 1953; s. of Samuel Walport and Doreen Walport (née Music); m. Julia Elizabeth Neild 1986; one s. three d.; ed St Paul's School, London, Clare Coll. Cambridge, Middx Hosp. Medical School; House Officer, Middx Hosp. and Queen Elizabeth II Hosp., Welwyn 1977–78, House Officer 1978–80; Hon. Registrar, Brompton Hosp. 1980; Registrar, Hammersmith Hosp. 1980–82, Hon. Consultant Physician 1985–, Dir Research and Devt 1994–98; MRC Training Fellow, MRC Mechanisms in Tumour Immunity Unit, Cambridge 1982–85; Harrison–Watson Student, Clare Coll. Cambridge 1982–85; Sr Lecturer in Rheumatology, Imperial Coll. School of Medicine 1985–90, Reader Rheumatological Medicine 1990–91, Prof. of Medicine 1991–2003, Head of Div. of Medicine 1997–2003, Fellow, Imperial Coll. 2006–; Gov. Wellcome Trust 2000–03, Dir 2003–; mem. Scientific Advisory Bd, Cantab Pharmaceuticals, Cambridge 1989–2000, Research and Devt Advisory Bd, Smithkline Beecham 1998–2000; mem. Council, British Soc. for Rheumatology 1989–95, British Soc. for Immunology 1998–2000; Asst Ed. British Journal of Rheumatology 1990–97; Ed. Clinical and Experimental Immunology 1990–97; Series Ed. British Medical Bulletin 1998–; Hon. DSc (Univ. of Sheffield, King's Coll. London); Roche Prize for Rheumatology 1991, Graham Bull Prize in Clinical Science 1996. *Publications:* Immunobiology (co-author); Clinical Aspects of Immunology (co-ed.); numerous papers published in scientific journals on immunology and rheumatology. *Leisure interest:* natural history. *Address:* The Wellcome Trust, 215 Euston Road, London, NW1 2BE, England (office). *Telephone:* (20) 7611-8888 (office). *Fax:* (20) 7611-8545 (office). *Website:* www.wellcome.ac.uk (office).

WALSER, Martin, DPhil; German writer, playwright and poet; b. 24 March 1927, Wasserburg, Bodensee; s. of Martin Walser and Augusta Schmid; m. Käthe Jehle 1950; four d.; ed Theologisch-Philosophische Hochschule, Regensburg and Univ. of Tübingen; writer 1951–; Grosses Bundesverdienstkreuz mit Stern 1997; Group 47 Prize 1955, Hermann-Hesse Prize 1957, Gerhart-Hauptmann Prize 1962, Schiller Prize 1980, Büchner Prize 1981, Orden pour le mérite 1994, Friedenspreis des Deutschen Buchhandels 1998. *Publications:* novels include: Ehen in Philippsburg 1957, Halbzeit 1960, Das Einhorn 1966, Fiction 1970, Die Gallistlische Krankheit 1972, Der Sturz 1973, Jenseits der Liebe 1976, Ein fliehendes Pferd 1978, Seelenarbeit 1979, Das Schwanenhaus 1980, Brief an Lord Liszt 1982, Brandung 1985, Dorle und Wolf 1987, Jagd 1988, Die Verteidigung der Kindheit 1991, Ohne einander 1993, Finks Krieg 1996, Ein springender Brunnen 1998, Der Lebenslauf der

Liebe 2001, Tod eines Kritikers 2002, Der Augenblick der Liebe 2004, Die Verwaltung des Nichts 2004, Leben und Schreiben 2005, Angstblüte 2006, Der Lebensroman des Andreas Beck 2006, Das geschundene Tier 2007, Ein Liebender Mann 2008; short stories: Ein Flugzeug über dem Haus 1955, Lügengeschichten 1964; plays: Der Abstecher 1961, Eiche und Angora 1962, Überlebensgross Herr Krott 1963, Der schwarze Schwan 1964, Die Zimmerschlacht 1967, Ein Kinderspiel 1970, Das Sauspiel 1975, In Goethe's Hand 1982, Die Ohrfeige 1986, Das Sofa 1992, Kaschmir in Parching 1995; essays: Beschreibung einer Form, Versuch über Franz Kafka 1961, Erfahrungen und Leseerfahrungen 1965, Heimatkunde 1968, Wie und wovon handelt Literatur 1973, Wer ist ein Schriftsteller 1978, Selbstbewusstsein und Ironie 1981, Messmers Gedanken 1985, Über Deutschland reden 1988, Vormittag eines Schriftstellers 1994, Messmers Reisen 2003; poetry: Der Grund zur Freude 1978, Die Verwaltung des Nichts 2004. *Address:* Zum Hecht 36, 88662 Überlingen-Nussdorf, Germany (home). *Telephone:* (7551) 4131 (home). *Fax:* (7551) 68494 (home). *E-mail:* nussdorf@t-online.de (home).

WALSH, Arthur Stephen, CBE, MA, FEng, FIEE; British business executive; b. 16 Aug. 1926, Wigan; s. of Wilfrid Walsh and Doris Walsh; m. 1st. Gwendoline Mary Walsh (divorced 1983); m. 2nd Judith Martha Westenborg 1985; one s. one d.; ed Selwyn Coll. Cambridge; joined GEC 1952, various sr appointments, including Tech. Dir of GEC/AEL 1952–79; Man. Dir Marconi Space and Defence Systems 1979–82; Man. Dir The Marconi Co. 1982–85; Chief Exec. STC PLC (now Northern Telecom Europe Ltd) 1985–91; Chair. Telemetrix PLC 1991–97, Simoco Int. Ltd 1997–2001; Dir FKI PLC 1991–99, Deputy Chair. 1993–; Hon. DSc (Ulster) 1988, (Southampton) 1993. *Leisure interests:* sailing, skiing, golf. *Address:* Aiglemont, Trout Rise, Loudwater, Rickmansworth, Herts., WD3 4JS, England.

WALSH, Courtney Andrew, OJ; Jamaican fmr cricketer; b. 30 Oct. 1962, Kingston; s. of Joan Woollaston; right-hand batsman, right-arm fast bowler; player with maj. teams West Indies, Gloucs. and Jamaica; played in 132 Tests; Test debut with West Indies against Australia at Perth 1984–85; world record 519 Test wickets (average 24.44) at time of his retirement in April 2001 and 1,807 first-class wickets (average 21.71); Wisden Cricketer of the Year 1987. *Leisure interests:* cooking, dancing, music, cars.

WALSH, Don, BS, MA, MS, PhD; American business executive, fmr university administrator and fmr naval officer; *President and CEO, International Maritime, Inc.;* b. 1931, Berkeley, Calif.; s. of J. Don Walsh and Marta G. Walsh; m. Joan A. Betzmer 1962; one s. one d.; ed San Diego State Coll., Texas A & M Univ. and US Naval Acad.; entered navy 1950, submarine service 1956–64; became Officer-in-Charge Submersible Test Group and Bathyscaph Trieste 1959, made record dive to 35,780 ft, Jan. 1960; at Dept of Oceanography, Texas A&M Univ. 1965–68; commanded submarine Bashaw 1968–69; Scientific Liaison Officer Submarine Devt Group One 1969–70; Special Asst to Asst Sec. of the Navy for Research and Devt, Washington, DC 1970–73; Resident Fellow, Woodrow Wilson Int. Center for Scholars 1973–74; Deputy Dir Naval Labs. 1974–75; retd from navy with rank of Capt. 1975; Dir Inst. for Marine and Coastal Studies and Prof. of Ocean Eng, Univ. of Southern Calif. 1975–83; Pres. and CEO Int. Maritime, Inc. 1976–; Vice-Pres. Parker Diving Service 1985–94; mem. Marine Bd, Nat. Research Council 1990–93; Exec. Dir Deep Ocean Eng 1990–2000; mem. Bd of Dirs Explorers Club 1994–2000; mem. US Naval Inst., Nat. Advisory Cttee on Oceans and Atmosphere 1979–86, Law of the Sea Advisory Cttee (US State Dept) 1979–83, Soc. of Naval Architects and Marine Engineers, American Soc. for Naval Engineers, Bd of Govs, Calif. Maritime Acad. 1985–94; Ed. Marine Tech. Soc. Journal 1976–80; mem. Nat. Acad. of Eng 2001–; Hon. Life mem. Explorers' Club, Adventurers' Club, Marine Tech. Soc. 1980; American Geographical Soc. 2000; Legion of Merit (two awards); The Walsh Spur (ridge) in the Antarctic, NSF 1973, Gold Medals from City of Trieste and Chicago Geographic Socs, US Coast Guard Meritorious Public Service Medal 1980, Meritorious Service Medal (two awards), Lowell Thomas Award, Explorers' Club 1987, Compass Distinguished Achievement Award, Marine Tech. Soc. 1996, Explorers' Medal, Explorers' Club 2001, L'Etoile Polaire, Jules Verne Aventures 2001. *Publications:* author of more than 200 papers, articles, etc. on marine subjects; ed. and contrib. Law of the Sea: Issues in Ocean Resources Management; Energy and Resource Development of the Continental Margins (co-ed.) 1980, Energy from the Sea: Challenge for the Decade (ed.) 1982, Waste Disposal in the Oceans: Minimum Impact, Maximize Benefits (co-ed.) 1983, Twenty Thousand Jobs Under the Sea: A History of Diving. *Leisure interests:* writing, travel, sailing, flying his aeroplane. *Address:* International Maritime Inc., 14578 Sitkum Lane, Myrtle Point, OR 97458, USA (office). *Telephone:* (541) 572-2313. *Fax:* (541) 572-4041. *E-mail:* imiwalsh@mac.com (office).

WALSH, Edward M., BEng, MSc, PhD, FIEE, FRSA, MRIA; Irish academic administrator; *President Emeritus, University of Limerick;* b. 3 Dec. 1939, Cork; s. of Michael Walsh and Margaret Walsh (née Leonard); m. Stephanie Barrett 1965; three s. one d.; ed Nat. Univ. of Ireland, Iowa State Univ., USA; Assoc., US Atomic Energy Comm. Lab., Ames, Ia 1963–65; Assoc. Prof. Va Polytechic Inst. and State Univ. 1965–69; Dir Energy Research Group Programme, Va 1966–69; Founding Pres. Univ. of Limerick 1970–98, now Pres. Emer.; Founding Chair. Nat. Self-Portrait Collection of Ireland 1979–, Nat. Technological Park 1983–88, Nat. Council for Curriculum and Assessment 1984–90; mem. Bd Nat. Microelectronics Applications Centre 1981–84, Shannon Devt 1976– (Chair. 1987); Vice-Pres. Int. Asscn of Univ. Presidents 1987–99; Chair. Cttee of Heads of Irish Univs 1991–92, Irish Council for Science, Tech. and Innovation 1997–, Citywest Growcorp 1998–; mem. NY Acad. of Science 1988; Hon. mem. Royal Hibernian Acad. of Arts 1994, Nat. Coll. of Art and Design 1997; Fellow Inst. of Engineers of Ireland, Irish Acad. of Eng 1998; Freeman of the City of Limerick 1995; Hon. LLD (Dublin) 1992, (Queen's, Belfast) 1995, (Nat. Univ.) 1998; Hon. DSc (Ulster) 1997. *Publica-*

tions: Energy Conversion: electromechanical-direct-nuclear 1967, Fluid Dynamic Energy Conversion 1967; and over 50 publs in various journals and proceedings. *Leisure interests:* sailing, skiing, gardening, silversmithing, painting, violin. *Address:* University of Limerick, Limerick (office); Oakhampton House, Newport, Co. Tipperary, Ireland (home). *Telephone:* (61) 213198 (office). *Fax:* (61) 213197.

WALSH, Joe; Irish politician; b. May 1943, Ballineen, Co. Cork; m. Marie Donegan; three s. two d.; ed Univ. Coll. Cork; fmr dairy man.; mem. Irish Creamery Mans Asscn, Soc. of Dairy Tech., mem. Cork Co. Council 1974–91; mem. Dáil 1977–81, 1982–2007 (retd); Senator 1981–82; Minister of State, Dept of Agric. and Food 1987, 1989–93; Minister for Agric., Food and Forestry 1993–94, 1997, for Agric. and Food 1997–99, for Agric., Food and Rural Devt 1999–2002, for Agric. and Food 2002–04; Chair. Irish Horse Bd 2005–, Cork Racecourse Mallow 2006–, Horse Sport Ireland 2006–, Hunger Task Force 2007; mem. Fianna Fáil. *Address:* 5 Emmet Square, Clonakilty, Co. Cork, Ireland. *Telephone:* (23) 33575. *Fax:* (23) 34267. *Website:* www.joewalsh.ie.

WALSH, Lawrence Edward, AB, LLB; American lawyer; b. 8 Jan. 1912, Port Maitland, NS, Canada; s. of Dr Cornelius E. Walsh and Lila M. Sanders; m. 1st Maxine Walsh (died 1964); m. 2nd Mary A. Porter; one s. four d.; ed Columbia Univ.; mem. Bar, New York State 1936, Dist of Columbia 1981, Oklahoma 1981, US Supreme Court 1951; Special Asst Attorney-Gen. Drukman Investigation 1936–38; Deputy Asst Dist Attorney, NY Co. 1938–41; Assoc. Davis Polk, Wardwell, Sunderland and Kiendl 1941–43; Asst Counsel to Gov. of New York 1943–49, Counsel to Gov. 1950–51; Counsel, Public Service Comm. 1951–53; Gen. Counsel, Exec. Dir Waterfront Comm. of NY Harbor 1953–54; US Judge, S Dist, NY 1954–57; US Deputy Attorney-Gen. 1957–60; Partner, Davis, Polk & Wardwell 1961–81; Counsel, Crowe & Dunlevy, Oklahoma City 1981–; Independent Counsel, 'Iran-Contra' investigation 1986–93; Pres. American Bar Asscn 1975–76; Trustee Emer., Columbia Univ.; Fellow American Coll. of Trial Lawyers; many other public appointments and mem. numerous bar and lawyers' asscns. *Publication:* The Iran-Contra Conspiracy and Cover-Up 1997. *Address:* Crowe & Dunlevy, 20 North Broadway, Suite 1800, Oklahoma City, OK 73102 (office); 1902 Bedford Drive, Oklahoma City, OK 73116, USA (home). *Telephone:* (405) 235-7789 (office). *Fax:* (405) 272-5919 (office). *Website:* www.crowedunlevy.com/Bio/LawrenceWalsh.asp (office).

WALSH, Patrick Craig, AB, MD; American urologist and academic; *University Distinguished Service Professor of Urology, Johns Hopkins Medical Institutions;* b. 13 Feb. 1938, Akron, OH; s. of Raymond Walsh and Catherine Walsh; m. Margaret Louise Campbell 1964; three s.; ed Case Western Reserve Univ. School of Medicine, Cleveland, OH; internship, Peter Bent Brigham Hosp., Boston, Mass 1964–65, Jr Asst Resident in Surgery 1965–66; Asst Resident in Pediatric Surgery, The Children's Hosp. Medical Center, Boston 1966–67; Resident in Urology, UCLA, Calif. 1967–71, Fellow in Endocrinology, UCLA School of Medicine, Harbor Gen. Hosp. Campus 1968–70; tour of mil. service as Urologist at US Naval Hosp., San Diego 1971–73; Asst Clinical Prof. of Surgery/Urology, Univ. of California, San Diego 1971–73; Visiting Asst Prof. of Medicine, Div. of Metabolism, Univ. of Texas Southwestern Medical School, Dallas 1973–74; David Hall McConnell Prof. and Dir Dept of Urology, Johns Hopkins Univ. School of Medicine, Baltimore, Md 1974, Urologist-in-Chief, The James Buchanan Brady Urological Inst. 1974–2004, Univ. Distinguished Service Prof. of Urology 2004–, fmr Vice-Chair. Exec. Cttee for Medical Institutional Campaign Fund for Johns Hopkins Univ., served on Professional Promotions Cttee, Research Space Planning Cttee, Finance Cttee of Advisory Bd; serves as consultant to US Naval Hosp., Walter Reed Hosp., Clinical Center of NIH, Advisory Bd of Nat. Inst. of Diabetes, Digestive and Kidney Diseases, as well as several local hosps; Trustee, American Bd of Urology; Ed.-in-Chief Campbell's Textbook of Urology 1980–2005 (renamed Cambell Walsh in his honour); mem. Editorial Bd Journal of Urology, New England Journal of Medicine; mem. 14 professional socs, including Inst. of Medicine of NAS, Soc. of Univ. Surgeons, Clinical Soc. of Genitourinary Surgeons (fmr Pres.), American Asscn of Genito-Urinary Surgeons (fmr Pres.), Endocrine Soc., Peripatetic Club; Fellow, American Coll. of Surgeons 1976–80; Paul Harris Fellow, Int. Rotary Foundation 1999; Hon. mem. Urological Soc. of Australasia, German Soc. of Urology, British Asscn of Urologic Surgeons 1998, Royal Coll. of Surgeons of Ireland 2003, Royal Coll. of Surgeons of England 2004, American Urological Asscn 2007; Hon. Dr of Medical Sciences (Masaryk Univ., Brno, Czech Repub.) 2007; prizes for lab. research, American Urological Asscn 1970, 1974, Gold Cystoscope Award, American Urological Asscn 1978, Eugene Fuller Award, American Urological Asscn 1978, Grand Prize, William R. Smart Film Award, American Urological Asscn 1985 and Golden Eagle Award, Council on Nontheatrical Events 1985 for two teaching films, Charles F. Kettering Medal, General Motors Cancer Research Foundation 1996, Robert V. Day Lecturer, Bruce Stewart Lecturer, Southern Lecturer, King Faisal Int. Prize in Medicine, King Faisal Foundation (co-recipient) 2007, Nat. Physician of the Year for Clinical Excellence 2007. *Films:* The Art of Retropubic Prostatectomy 1969, Visits in Urology – Renal Revascularization for Hypertension 1984, Radical Retropubic Prostatectomy and Cystoprostatectomy: Surgical Technique for Preservation of Sexual Function 1985, Radical Cystectomy with Preservation of Sexual Function 'Neuroanatomical Considerations and Surgical Technique' 1987, Radical Retropubic Prostatectomy with Preservation of Sexual Function – An Update after 500 Cases 1987, Radical Retropubic Prostatectomy: Evolution of the Surgical Technique 1993, Radical Prostatectomy, Simultaneous Demonstration by Patrick C. Walsh, M.D. and Fritz H. Schroder, M.D 1993, Alpha Omega Alpha Leaders in American Medicine, Radical Retropubic Prostatectomy: A Detailed Description of the Surgical Technique 2004. *Publications:* Male Infertility (co-ed.) 1977, The Prostate: A Guide for Men and the Women Who Love Them (with Janet F. Worthington) 1995, Campbell's Urology,

Seventh Edn (co-ed.) 1997, Dr. Patrick Walsh's Guide to Surviving Prostate Cancer (with Janet F. Worthington) 2001; more than 500 scientific papers in professional journals. *Leisure interests:* sailing, swimming, cycling. *Address:* James Buchanan Brady Urological Institute, Johns Hopkins Medical Institutions, 600 North Wolfe Street, Baltimore, MD 21287, USA (office). *Fax:* (410) 614-3695 (office). *E-mail:* webmaster@urology.jhu.edu (office). *Website:* urology.jhu.edu (office).

WALSH, Paul S.; British business executive; *Chief Executive Officer, Diageo PLC;* joined GrandMet's brewing div., Watney Mann and Truman Brewers 1982, Finance Dir 1986, Chief Financial Officer Inter-Continental Hotels 1987, GrandMet's Food Div. 1989, CEO Pillsbury 1992, mem. Bd 1995; mem. Bd Diageo PLC (f. after merger of GrandMet and Guinness) 1997–, CEO 2000–; Dir Scottish Whisky Asscn; Dir (non-exec.) Federal Express Corpn, Centrica PLC; Gov. Henley Management Coll. 2003–. *Address:* Diageo PLC, 8 Henrietta Place, London, W1M 9AG, England (office). *Telephone:* (20) 7927-5200 (office). *Fax:* (20) 7927-4641 (office). *Website:* www.diageo.com (office).

WALSH, William (Willie) M., MSc, FRAeS; Irish airline executive; *Chief Executive, British Airways plc;* b. 1961, Dublin; m.; one d.; ed Trinity Coll. Dublin; Cadet Pilot, Aer Lingus 1979, later Capt., CEO Futura (Aer Lingus Spanish charter operation) 1998–2000, COO Aer Lingus 2000–01, CEO 2001–05, mem. Bd 2001–; mem. Exec. Bd and Chief Exec. Designate British Airways plc May–Oct. 2005, Chief Exec. Oct. 2005–; mem. Bd of Dirs Fyffes plc 2004–; Pres. Heathrow Br. of Royal Aeronautical Soc.; mem. Chartered Inst. of Logistics and Transport (UK); Hon. Bd mem. Flight Safety International; Hon. mem. The Aviation Club. *Leisure interests:* all sports, especially soccer, rugby and motor sports. *Address:* British Airways plc, PO Box 365, Waterside, Harmondsworth, London UB7 0GB, England (office). *Telephone:* (844) 493-0787 (from within UK) (office); (191) 490-7901 (from outside UK) (office). *Fax:* (20) 8759-4314 (office). *E-mail:* info@britishairways.com (office). *Website:* www.britishairways.com (office).

WALTER, Bernhard; German banker; joined Dresdner Bank on leaving school; fmr responsibilities include operations in the fmr GDR, corp. finance, Eastern European operations; mem. Bd 1987–2000, Chair. 1998–2000 (resgnd); Chair. Advisory Bd Frauenkirche Dresden Foundation –2005. *Leisure interests:* golf, jogging, music. *Address:* c/o Frauenkirche Foundation Dresden, An der Frauenkirche 12, 01067 Dresden, Germany.

WALTER, Norbert, Dr rer. pol; German economist; *Managing Director, Deutsche Bank Research;* b. 23 Sept. 1944, Weckbach/Unterfranken; s. of Heinrich Walter and Erna Walter; m. Christa Bayer 1967; two d.; ed Johann Wolfgang Goethe Univ., Frankfurt; affiliated to Inst. for Capital Market Research, Frankfurt 1968–71; mem. staff Kiel Inst. of World Econs, Kiel 1971–86, Asst to Pres. and head of various research groups 1971–77, Head, Dept of Business Cycle in the World Economy, subsequently Resource Econs Dept 1977–85; fmr Professorial Lecturer, Christian Albrechts Univ., Kiel; John McCloy Distinguished Research Fellow and Resident Scholar, Johns Hopkins Univ., Washington, DC 1986–87; Sr Economist, Deutsche Bank, Frankfurt 1987–90, Chief Economist, Deutsche Bank Group 1990–, Man. Dir Deutsche Bank Research 1992–; mem. EU Inter-institutional Monitoring Group for Securities Markets 2002–; Forward Thinker of 2008, Plansecur Financial Consulting Firm. *Publications include:* Was würde Erhard heute tun?, Wohin treibt die Wirtschaft? – Die Wende zu mehr Markt (co-author) 1984, Strengths, Weaknesses and Prospects of the German Economy, in The Future of Germany (ed. Gary Geipel) 1990, Weniger Staat – Mehr Markt 1993, Der neue Wohlstand der Nation 1993, Ein Plädoyer für die Marktwirtschaft (with Astrid Rosenschon) 1996, Der Euro – Kurs auf die Zukunft 1997, Mehr Wachstum für Deutschland (with Klaus Deutsch) 2004. *Leisure interests:* jogging, rock/glacier climbing. *Address:* Deutsche Bank Research, Taunusanlage 12, 60325 Frankfurt am Main (office); Bismarckstr. 28, 65812 Bad Soden, Germany (home). *Telephone:* (69) 91031810 (office). *Fax:* (69) 91031826 (home). *E-mail:* norbert.walter@db.com (office). *Website:* www.norbert-walter.com (office).

WALTER, Robert D., MBA; American health care industry executive; *Chairman, Cardinal Health Inc.;* m. Peggy McGreevey 1967; three s.; ed Ohio Univ., Harvard Business School; Engineer, North American Rockwell 1968; Founder Cardinal Foods Inc., Dublin, Ohio 1971–88 (acquired by Roundy's Inc. 1988); Founder and CEO Cardinal Distribution Inc. (wholesale drug and health care products distributor, renamed Cardinal Health Inc. 1994) 1979–2006, Chair. 2006–; mem. Bd of Dirs Bank One Corpn, Viacom Inc., Westinghouse Electric; mem. Bd of Trustees Battelle Memorial Inst., Ohio Univ.; fmr mem. Bd of Trustees Ohio Univ. Foundation. *Address:* Cardinal Health Inc., 7000 Cardinal Place, Dublin, OH 43017, USA (office). *Telephone:* (614) 757-5000 (office). *Fax:* (614) 757-8871 (office). *Website:* www.cardinal-health.com (office).

WALTERS, Barbara, BA; American broadcast journalist and producer; b. 25 Sept. 1929, Brookline, Mass.; d. of Lou Walters and Dena Walters (née Selett); m. 1st Robert Henry Katz (m. annulled); m. 2nd Lee Guber 1963 (divorced 1976); one adopted d.; m. 3rd Merv Adelson 1986 (divorced 1992); ed Sarah Lawrence Coll., Bronxville, NY; fmr writer and producer with WNBC–TV, then with Station WPIX and CBS TV morning broadcasts; Producer, NBC TV; joined Today programme, NBC TV 1961 as a writer, then gen. reporter, regular panel mem. 1963–74, Co-Host 1974–76; moderator, Not for Women Only (syndicated TV programme) for five years; Corresp., ABC News, Co-Anchor of evening news programme 1976–78, Co-Host 20/20 1979–2004; Host Barbara Walters Specials 1976–, Ten Most Fascinating People 1994–; Co.-Exec. Producer and Co-Host The View (ABC), NY 1997–; Hon. LHD (Ohio State Univ., Marymount Coll., New York Temple Univ., Wheaton Coll., Hofstra Univ.); Broadcaster of the Year, Int. Radio and TV Soc. 1975, Emmy

Award of Nat. Acad. of TV Arts and Sciences 1975, 1983, Silver Satellite Award, American Women in Radio and TV 1985, named one of the 100 Most Important Women of the Century, Good Housekeeping 1985, Pres.'s Award, Overseas Press Club 1988, Lowell Thomas Award for Journalism 1990, 1994, Lifetime Achievement Award, Int. Women's Media Foundation 1992, Lifetime Achievement Award, Daytime Emmy Awards 2000, ranked by Forbes magazine amongst 100 Most Powerful Women (25th) 2004, (63rd) 2008, and several other awards. *Publications:* How to Talk with Practically Anybody about Practically Anything 1970, Audition: A Memoir 2008; contribs to Good Housekeeping, Family Weekly, Reader's Digest, and other periodicals. *Address:* Barwall Productions, 320 West 66th Street, New York, NY 10023 (office); c/o 20/20, 147 Columbus Avenue, 10th Floor, New York, NY 10023, USA. *Website:* abc.go.com/daytime/theview.

WALTERS, Carl, BSc, MSc, PhD, FRSC; Canadian marine biologist and academic; *Professor, Fisheries Centre, University of British Columbia;* ed Humboldt State Univ., Colorado State Univ.; currently Prof., Fisheries Centre, Univ. of British Columbia; member several NSERC grant cttees 1970–; has done extensive fisheries advisory work for public agencies and industrial groups; has conducted more than 20 workshops for Int. Canadian Fisheries Service, US Fish and Wildlife Service and Int. Inst. for Applied Systems Analysis 1997–2007; fmr mem. Editorial Bd Journal of Applied Mathematics and Computation, Northwest Environmental Journal, Canadian Journal of Fisheries and Aquatic Sciences; keynote speaker, American Fisheries Soc. 1992, Award of Excellence, American Fisheries Soc. 2006, Volvo Environment Prize, Volvo Environment Foundation (co-recipient) 2006. *Publications:* numerous scientific papers in professional journals on fish population dynamics, fisheries assessment and sustainable man. *Address:* Department of Zoology, University of British Columbia, 2370-6270 University Blvd, Vancouver, BC V6T 1Z4, Canada (office). *Telephone:* (604) 822-6320 (office). *Fax:* (604) 822-2416 (office). *E-mail:* c.walters@fisheries.ubc.ca (office). *Website:* www.fisheries.ubc.ca/members/cwalters (office).

WALTERS, John P., MA; American fmr government official; ed Michigan State Univ., Univ. of Toronto, Canada; Lecturer, Michigan State Univ. and Boston Coll.; acting Asst Dir and Programme Officer, Educ. Programmes Div., Nat. Endowment for the Humanities 1982–85; Asst to US Sec. of Educ., Dept of Educ., Washington, DC 1985–88; Chief of Staff, White House Office of Nat. Drug Control Policy (ONDCP) 1989–91, Deputy Dir Supply Reduction 1991–93, Dir ONDCP 2001–09; Visiting Fellow, Hudson Inst. 1993; Pres. New Citizenship Project –1996; Pres. Philanthropy Round Table 1996–2001. *Publications include:* Body Count: Moral Poverty and How to Win America's War Against Crime and Drugs (with William J. Bennett and John J. Di Iulio Jr). *Address:* c/o Office of National Drug Control Policy, 750 17th Street, NW, Washington, DC 20006, USA.

WALTERS, Julie, OBE, CBE; British actress; b. 22 Feb. 1950, Birmingham; d. of the late Thomas Walters and Mary Bridget O'Brien; m. Grant Roffey 1998; one d.; ed St Pauls Prep. School, Edgbaston, Holly Lodge Grammar School for Girls, Smethwick, Manchester Polytechnic; Variety Club Best Newcomer Award 1980, Best Actress Award 1984, British Acad. Award for Best Actress 1984, Golden Globe Award 1984, Show Business Personality of the Year Variety Club Award 2001. *Stage appearances include:* Educating Rita 1980, Fool for Love 1984–85, When I was a Girl I used to Scream and Shout 1986-87, Frankie and Johnny in the Clair de Lune 1989, The Rose Tattoo 1991, All My Sons (Olivier Award 2001) 2000, Acorn Antiques 2005. *Films include:* Educating Rita 1983, She'll be Wearing Pink Pyjamas 1984, Personal Services 1986, Prick Up Your Ears 1986, Buster 1987, Mack the Knife 1988, Killing Dad 1989, Stepping Out (Variety Club Award for Best Actress 1991) 1991, Just Like a Woman 1992, Sister My Sister 1994, Intimate Relations 1996, Titanic Town 1997, Girls Night 1997, All Forgotten 1999, Dancer 1999, Billy Elliot (Evening Standard Award, BAFTA Award) 2000, Harry Potter and the Philosopher's Stone 2001, Before You Go 2002, Harry Potter and the Chamber of Secrets 2002, Calendar Girls 2003, Harry Potter and the Prisoner of Azkaban 2004, Mickybo and Me 2005, Wah-Wah 2005, Driving Lessons 2006, Becoming Jane 2007, Harry Potter and the Order of the Phoenix 2007, Mamma Mia! 2008. *Television includes:* Talent 1980, Wood and Walters (with Victoria Wood) 1981–82, Boys from the Blackstuff 1982, Say Something Happened 1982, As Seen On TV 1984, 1986, 1987, The Birthday Party 1986, Her Big Chance 1987, GBH 1991, Stepping Out 1991, Julie Walters and Friends 1991, Clothes in the Wardrobe 1992, Wide Eyed and Legless 1993, Bambino Mio 1993, Pat and Margaret 1994, Jake's Progress 1995, Little Red Riding Hood 1995, Intimate Relations 1996, Julie Walters is an Alien 1997, Dinnerladies 1998–99, Jack and the Beanstalk 1998, Oliver Twist 1999, My Beautiful Son (BAFTA Award) 2001, Murder (BAFTA and Royal TV Soc. Awards for Best Actress 2003) 2002, The Canterbury Tales (mini-series, The Wife of Bath) 2003, The Return 2003, Ahead of the Class 2005, The Ruby in the Smoke 2006, Filth! The Mary Whitehouse Story 2007, A Short Stay in Switzerland 2009. *Publications:* Baby Talk 1990, Maggie's Tree (novel) 2006, That's Another Story (auto-biog.) 2008. *Leisure interests:* reading, travel. *Address:* c/o Independent Talent Group, 76 Oxford Street, London, W1D 1BS, England (office). *Telephone:* (20) 7636-6565 (office).

WALTERS, Sir Peter Ingram, Kt, BCom; British business executive; b. 11 March 1931, Birmingham; s. of the late Stephen Walters and of Edna F. Walters (née Redgate); m. 1st Patricia Anne Tulloch 1960 (divorced 1991); two s. one. d.; m. 2nd Meryl Marshall 1992; ed King Edward's School, Birmingham and Univ. of Birmingham; served Royal Army Service Corps 1952–54; joined BP 1954, Vice-Pres. BP N America 1965–67, Gen. Man. Supply and Devt 1969–70, Regional Dir Western Hemisphere 1971–72; Dir BP Trading Ltd 1971–73; BP Chemicals Int. 1972, Chair. 1978–90; Deputy Chair. The British Petroleum Co. Ltd 1980–81, Chair. 1981–90; Vice-Pres. Gen. Council of

British Shipping 1974–76, Pres. 1977–78; Pres. Soc. of Chemical Industry 1978–79, Inst. of Manpower Studies 1980–86; Dir Post Office 1978–79, Nat. Westminster Bank 1981–(Deputy Chair. 1988–89); Dir Thorn EMI (now EMI) 1989, Deputy Chair. 1990–99; Dir SmithKline Beecham PLC 1989–2000, apptd Deputy Chair. GlaxoSmithKline PLC 2000, Deputy Chair. 1990–94, Chair. 1994–2000; Chair. Blue Circle Industries Ltd 1990–96, Midland Bank PLC 1992; Deputy Chair. HSBC Holdings 1992–2001; Adviser Union Bank of Switzerland 1990–92; Dir (non-exec.) Nomura Int. plc, Saatchi and Saatchi 1993–2000; Pres. Police Foundation; Pres. Advisory Council, Inst. of Business Ethics; Chair. Advisory Bd TNK Int. 2002–; mem. of Council, Industrial Soc.; Gov. London Business School 1981–91; Pres. Inst. of Dirs 1986–92; Trustee, mem. Foundation Bd, Nat. Maritime Museum 1982–89; Chair. Int. Man. Inst., Geneva 1984–86; Trustee Inst. of Econ. Affairs; Hon. D. Univ. (Birmingham) 1986, (Stirling) 1987;Commdr Order of Léopold (Belgium). *Leisure interests:* golf, gardening, sailing. *Address:* Institute of Business Ethics, 24 Greencoat Place, London, SW1P 1BE; 22 Hill Street, London, W1X 7FU, England. *Telephone:* (20) 8975-2000. *Fax:* (20) 8975-2040.

WALTERS, Sir Roger Talbot, MSc, KBE, RIBA; British architect; b. 31 March 1917, Chorley Wood, Herts.; s. of Alfred Bernard Walters; m. 1st Gladys Millie Evans 1946 (divorced); m. 2nd Claire Myfanwy Chappell 1976; ed Oundle School, Architectural Asscn School of Architecture, Liverpool Univ. and Birkbeck Coll.; entered office of Sir E. Owen Williams 1936; Directorate of Constructional Design, Ministry of Works 1941–43; served in Royal Engineers 1943–46; Architect, Timber Devt Asscn 1946–49; Prin. Asst Architect, E Region, British Railways 1949–59; Chief Architect (Devt), Directorate of Works, War Office 1959–62; Deputy Dir-Gen. Research and Devt, Ministry of Public Bldgs and Works 1962–67, Dir-Gen. for Production 1967–69, Controller Gen. 1969–71; Architect and Controller of Construction Services, GLC 1971–78; pvt. practice 1981–87; Fellow, Inst. of Structural Engineers; Hon. FAIA. *Address:* 46 Princess Road, London, NW1 8JL, England (home). *Telephone:* (20) 7722-3740 (home).

WALTHER, Herbert, Dr rer. nat; German physicist and academic; *Director Emeritus, Max-Planck Institute für Quantenoptik and Sektion Physik, University of Munich;* b. 19 Jan. 1935, Ludwigshafen; s. of Philipp Walther and Anna Lorenz; m. Margot Gröschel 1962; one s. one d.; ed Univ. of Heidelberg and Tech. Univ. of Hanover; Asst Univ. of Hanover 1963–68, Lecturer in Physics 1968–69; Prof. of Physics, Univ. of Bonn 1971, Univ. of Cologne 1971–75, Univ. of Munich 1975–2003, Prof. Emer. 2003–; Dir Max-Planck-Inst. für Quantenoptik 1981–2003, Dir Emer. 2003–; Vice-Pres. Max-Planck Soc. 1991–96; mem. Bavarian Acad. of Sciences, Acad. Leopoldina, Academia Europaea; Corresp. mem. Acad. of Sciences, Heidelberg, Nordrhein-Westfälische Akad. der Wissenschaften; mem. Convent for Tech. Sciences of the German Acads; Hon. mem. Loránd Eötvös Physical Soc., Hungary, Hungarian Acad. of Science, Romanian Acad., German Physical Soc.; Foreign mem. Russian Acad. of Sciences 1999–; Foreign Hon. mem. American Acad. of Arts and Sciences; Hon. Prof. Academia Sinica, China; Dr hc (Hanover Univ., Lomonosov Univ., Moscow); Max Born Prize, Inst. of Physics and the German Physics Soc. 1978, Einstein Prize 1988, Carl-Friedrich-Gauss Medal 1989, Townes Medal (American Optical Soc.) 1990, Michelson Medal (Franklin Inst.) 1993, King Faisal Prize for Physics 1993, Humboldt Medal, Alexander von Humboldt-Stiftung 1997, Stern Gerlach Medal, German Physical Soc. 1998, Ernst Hellmut-Vits Prize 1998; Willis E. Lamb Medal for Laser Physics, Physics of Quantum Electronics Winter Colloquium, Snowbird, Salt Lake City 1999, EPS Quantum Electronics Prize 2000, Alfried Krupp Prize for Science 2002, Frederic Ives Medal of Optical Society of America 2003. *Publications:* 11 books on laser spectroscopy and high power lasers and applications, including Was ist Licht? Von der Klassischen Optik zur Quantenoptik 1999; 580 articles in professional journals. *Address:* Max-Planck-Institut für Quantenoptik and Sektion Physik der Universität München, 85748 Garching (office); Egenhoferstrasse 7a, 81243 Munich, Germany (home). *Telephone:* (89) 32905704 (office); (89) 8349859 (home). *Fax:* (89) 32905200; (89) 32905314 (office); (89) 8349859 (home). *E-mail:* Herbert.Walther@mpq.mpg.de (office). *Website:* mste.laser.physik.uni-muenchen.de (office).

WALTON, Henry John, MD, PhD, FRCP, F.R.C.PSYCH., DPM; British psychiatrist, physician and academic; *Professor Emeritus of Psychiatry, University of Edinburgh;* b. 15 Feb. 1924, Kuruman, South Africa; m. Dr Sula Wolff 1959; ed Univs of Cape Town, London and Edinburgh and Columbia Univ., New York; Registrar in Neurology and Psychiatry, Univ. of Cape Town 1946–54, Head, Dept of Psychiatry 1957–60; Sr Registrar, Maudsley Hosp. London 1955–57; Sr Lecturer in Psychiatry, Univ. of Edin. 1962–70, Prof. of Psychiatry 1970–85, Prof. Emer. 1990–, Prof. of Int. Medical Educ. 1986–; Ed. Medical Educ. 1976–98, Ed. Emer. 1998–; Pres. Asscn for Medical Educ. in Europe 1972–86, Hon. Life Pres. 1986–; Pres. World Fed. for Medical Educ. 1983–97, mem. Exec. Bd 1997–; frequent consultant to WHO and mem. Advisory Panel on Health Manpower; led worldwide inquiry into training of doctors since 1983; presided at World Summit on Medical Educ., Edin. 1988, 1993, organized six Regional Confs 1986–88, 1994–95; Chair., Bd of Governors Edin. Printmakers; mem. Soc. of Medical Studies of Greece; Academician, Acad. of Medical Sciences of Buenos Aires, Polish Acad. of Medicine, Royal Acad. of Medicine of Belgium; Foundation mem. Nat. Asscn for Medical Educ. of Czechoslovakia; Hon. MD (Uppsala, New Univ. of Lisbon, Tucuman); Hermann Salhi Medal, Univ. of Berne 1976, Thureus Prize, Swedish Acad. of Medical Sciences 1982, De Lancey Prize, Royal Soc. of Medicine 1984, Jofre Medal, Spanish Soc. for Advancement of Psychiatry 1985, WHO Medal 1988, Medicus Magnus Medal 1994, Polish Acad. of Medicine, Grand Medal, Albert Schweitzer World Acad. of Medicine 2003. *Publications:* Alcoholism (with N. Kessel) 1966, 1988, Small Group Psychotherapy (ed.) 1974, Dictionary of Psychiatry (ed.) 1985, Newer Developments in Assessing Clinical Competence (ed. with others), Problem-based Learning (with M. B. Matthews) 1988, Proc. of World Summit on Medical Educ. (ed.) 1994, Psychiatric Education and Training in Contemporary Psychiatry 2001, "Education in Psychiatry", International Encyclopedia of the Social and Behavioral Sciences 2001. *Leisure interests:* literature, visual arts, particularly Western painting, Chinese and Japanese art. *Address:* 38 Blacket Place, Edinburgh, EH9 1RL, Scotland. *Telephone:* (131) 667-7811. *Fax:* (131) 662-0337. *E-mail:* h.walton@ed.ac.uk.

WALTON, Jim; American broadcasting news executive; *President, CNN News Group;* b. 1958; m.; two s.; ed Univ. of Maryland; joined Cable News Network (CNN) 1980, various positions including video journalist, tape editor, exec. producer, launched CNN/Sports Illustrated (all-sports TV channel), served as Pres. 1996–2000, Deputy Pres., Pres. CNN Domestic Networks 2001, Pres. and COO 2001–03, Pres. CNN News Group 2003–; Emmy Award for coverage of 1996 Olympic Park bombing, Atlanta, several Cable Ace awards. *Leisure interests:* Nebraska football, Allman brothers. *Address:* CNN Center, 1 CNN Center, Marietta Street NW, Atlanta, GA 30303, USA (office). *Telephone:* (404) 827-2201 (office). *Website:* www.cnn.com (office).

WALTON, Samuel Robson (Rob), BA, JD; American retail executive; *Chairman, Wal-Mart Stores, Inc.;* b. 1944, Tulsa, Okla; s. of the late Sam Moore Walton (founder of Wal-Mart; died 1992); m. Carolyn F. Walton (divorced); three c.; ed Wooster Coll., Univ. of Ark., Columbia Univ.; fmrly with Conner, Winters, Ballaine, Barry & McGowen (law firm), Tulsa –1969; joined Wal-Mart Stores Inc., Bentonville, Ark. 1969–, Sr Vice-Pres., Sec. and Gen. Counsel 1978–82, Dir and Vice-Chair. Bd 1982–92, Chair. 1992–; Trustee, Wooster Coll. *Address:* Wal-Mart Stores Inc., 702 SW 8th Street, Bentonville, AR 72716, USA (office). *Telephone:* (479) 273-4000 (office). *Fax:* (479) 277-1830 (home). *Website:* www.walmartstores.com (office).

WALTON OF DETCHANT, Baron (Life Peer), cr. 1989, of Detchant in the County of Northumberland; **John Nicholas Walton,** Kt, TD, MA, MD, DSc, FRCP, FMedSci; British neurologist; b. 16 Sept. 1922, Rowlands Gill, Co. Durham; s. of Herbert Walton and Eleanor Watson Walton (née Ward); m. Mary Elizabeth Harrison 1946 (died 2003); one s. two d.; ed Alderman Wraith Grammar School, Spennymoor, Co. Durham, King's Coll., Medical School, Univ. of Durham; served RAMC 1947–49, Col L/RAMC OC 1(N) Gen. Hosp. (TA) 1963–66 (Hon. Col 1968–73); Medical Registrar, Royal Victoria Infirmary, Newcastle-upon-Tyne 1949–51; Nuffield Foundation Travelling Fellow, Mass. Gen. Hosp., Harvard Medical School, Boston, USA, King's Coll. Travelling Fellow, MRC Neurology Unit, Nat. Hosp., Queen Sq., London 1954–55; First Asst in Neurology, Univ. of Durham (Newcastle-upon-Tyne) 1955–58; Consultant Neurologist, Newcastle Hosps 1958–83; Prof. of Neurology, Univ. of Newcastle-upon-Tyne 1968–83, Dean of Medicine 1971–81; Warden, Green Coll. Oxford 1983–89; mem. MRC 1974–78, Gen. Medical Council (Chair. Educ. Cttee) 1971–89, Pres. 1982–89; Chair. Muscular Dystrophy Group of GB 1971–95, Hamlyn Foundation Nat. Comm. on Educ. 1990–96, House of Lords Select Cttee on Medical Ethics 1992–93; Pres. British Medical Asscn 1980–82; Pres. Royal Soc. of Medicine 1984–86; First Vice-Pres. World Fed. of Neurology 1981–89, Pres. 1989–97; Hon. Freeman of Newcastle upon Tyne 1980; Hon. FACP; Hon. FRCP (Edin.); Hon. FRCP (Canada); Hon. FRCPath; Hon. FRCPsych; Hon. FRCPCH; Hon. Fellow Inst. of Educ. (London) 1995; Hon. mem. Norwegian Acad. of Arts and Sciences 1992; Hon. Dr de l'Université (Aix-Marseille) 1975; Hon. DSc (Leeds) 1979, (Leicester) 1980, (Hull) 1988, (Oxford Brookes) 1994, (Durham) 2002; Hon. MD (Sheffield) 1987, (Mahidol Univ., Thailand) 1998; Hon. DCL (Newcastle) 1988; Dr hc (Genoa) 1992. *Publications:* Subarachnoid Haemorrhage 1956, Polymyositis (with R. D. Adams) 1958, Oxford Companion to Medicine (ed.) 1986, Essentials of Neurology (6th edn) 1989, Skeletal Muscle Pathology (with F. L. Mastaglia, 2nd edn) 1992, Brain's Diseases of the Nervous System (ed., 10th edn) 1993, The Spice of Life (autobiog.) 1993, Disorders of Voluntary Muscle (ed., 6th edn) 1994, Oxford Medical Companion (ed.) 1994 and numerous articles in scientific journals. *Leisure interests:* music, golf, reading, cricket. *Address:* 15 Croft Way, Belford, Northumberland, NE70 7ET, England (home). *Telephone:* (1668) 219009 (home). *Fax:* (1668) 219010 (home). *E-mail:* waldetch@aol.com (office).

WALZER, Michael, BA, PhD; American academic, editor and writer; *Professor of Social Science, School of Social Science, Institute for Advanced Study;* b. 3 March 1935, New York, NY; m. Judith Borodovko 1956; two d.; ed Brandeis and Harvard Univs, Univ. of Cambridge, UK; Asst Prof. of Politics, Princeton, NJ 1962–66; Assoc. Prof., Harvard Univ. 1966–68, Prof. of Govt 1968–80; Ed. Dissent 1964–; Prof. of Social Science, School of Social Science, Inst. for Advanced Study, Princeton, NJ 1980–; mem. Conf. on the Study of Political Thought, Soc. of Ethical and Legal Philosophy; mem. Editorial Bd Political Theory; Contributing Ed. The New Republic (weekly newsmagazine); mem. Bd of Govs Hebrew Univ.; Dr hc (Lawrence Univ.) 1980, (Brandeis Univ.) 1981, (Georgetown Univ.) 1992, (Kalamazoo Coll.) 1994, (Tel-Aviv Univ.) 2003, Brandeis Univ. Doctorate Alumni Award 2001; Fulbright Fellow, Univ. of Cambridge 1956–57, Harbison Award 1971. *Publications:* The Revolution of the Saints: A Study in the Origins of Radical Politics 1965, The Political Imagination in Literature (co-ed. with Philip Green) 1968, Obligations: Essays on Disobedience, War and Citizenship 1970, Political Action: A Practical Guide to Movement Politics 1971, Regicide and Revolution: Speeches at the Trial of Louis XVI (ed.) 1974, Just and Unjust Wars: A Moral Argument with Historical Illustrations 1977, Radical Principles: Reflections of an Unreconstructed Democrat 1977, Spheres of Justice: A Defense of Pluralism and Equality 1983, Exodus and Revolution 1985, Interpretation and Social Criticism 1987, The Company of Critics: Social Criticism and Political Commitment in the Twentieth Century 1988, Civil Society and American Democracy (selected essays in German) 1992, What it Means to be an American 1992, Thick and Thin: Moral Argument at Home and Abroad 1994,

Pluralism, Justice and Equality (with David Miller) 1995, Toward a Global Civil Society (ed.) 1995, On Toleration 1997, Arguments from the Left (selected essays in Swedish) 1977, Pluralism and Democracy (selected essays in French) 1997, Reason, Politics and Pasion (The Horkheimer Lectures, in German) 1999, The Jewish Political Tradition, Vol. 1 Authority (co-ed with Menachem Lorberbaum, Noam Zohar and Yair Lorberbaum) 2000, Exilic Politics in the Hebrew Bible 2001, War, Politics, and Morality (selected essays in Spanish) 2001, The Thread of Politics: Democracy, Social Criticism, and World Government (selected essays in Italian) 2002, Erklärte Kriege—Kriegserklärungen (selected essays in German) 2003, Arguing About War (selected essays and articles) 2004, Politics and Passion 2004; contribs to professional journals. *Address:* School of Social Science, Institute for Advanced Study, Einstein Drive, Princeton, NJ 08540, USA (office). *Telephone:* (609) 734-8256 (office). *Fax:* (609) 951-4434 (office). *E-mail:* walzer@ias.edu (office). *Website:* www.sss.ias.edu/home/walzer.html (office).

WAMALA, HE Cardinal Emmanuel, DipEd; Ugandan ecclesiastic; *Archbishop Emeritus of Kampala;* b. 15 Dec. 1926, Kamaggwa; s. of Cosma Kyamcra and Theresa Nnamayanja; ed Minor Seminary, Bukalasa, Major Seminary, Katigondo, Pontifical Urban Univ. and Pontifical Gregorian Univ., Rome, Italy, Makerere Univ., Kampala, Univ. of Notre Dame, South Bend, Ind., USA; ordained priest 1957; worked at parish of Villa Maria, acted as Diocesan School Supervisor in Diocese of Masaka 1960–62; mem. Faculty, Minor Seminary of Bukalasa 1964–68; Chaplain, faculty mem. and Rector Univ. of Makerere 1968–74; Vicar Gen. Diocese of Masaka 1974–81; Parish Priest of Nkoni 1975–77, of Kimaanya 1977–79; Chaplain of His Holiness Pope Paul VI 1977; Bishop of Kiyinda-Mityana 1981; attended Sixth Ordinary Ass. of World Synod of Bishops, Vatican City 1983; Coadjutor Archbishop of Kampala 1988–90, Archbishop of Kampala 1990–2006, Emer. 2006–; Pres. Episcopal Conf. of Uganda 1990–94; First Rector Nuova Uganda Martyrs Univ. 1993–; attended Special Ass. of World Synod of Bishops for Africa, Vatican City 1994; cr. Cardinal (Cardinal Priest of S. Ugo) 1994; Pres. Uganda Joint Christian 1990–. *Address:* Archdiocese of Kampala, PO Box 14125, Mengo-Kampala, Uganda (office). *Telephone:* (41) 270183/4 (office); (41) 342622 (office). *Fax:* (41) 345441 (office).

WAMBAUGH, Joseph, MA; American writer; b. 22 Jan. 1937, East Pittsburgh, PA; s. of Joseph A. Wambaugh and Anne Malloy; m. Dee Allsup 1955; two s. (one deceased) one d.; ed Calif. State Coll., Los Angeles; served US Marine Corps 1954–57; police officer, LA 1960–74; creator, TV series, Police Story 1973; MWA Edgar Allan Poe Award 1974, Int. Asscn of Crime Writers Rodolfo Walsh Prize 1989. *Publications:* The New Centurions 1971, The Blue Knight 1972, The Onion Field 1973, The Choirboys 1975, The Black Marble 1978, The Glitter Dome 1981, The Delta Star 1983, Lines and Shadows 1984, The Secrets of Harry Bright 1985, Echoes in the Darkness 1987, The Blooding 1989, The Golden Orange 1990, Fugitive Nights 1992, Finnegan's Week 1993, Floaters 1996, Fire Lover: A True Story 2002, Hollywood Station 2007, Hollywood Crows 2008. *Address:* c/o Little, Brown Book Group, 100 Victoria Embankment, London EC4Y 0DY, England (office). *Website:* www.littlebrown.co.uk (office).

WAMYTAN, Roch, MA; New Caledonian politician; b. 13 Dec. 1950, Nouméa; s. of the late Benjamin Wamytan and Philomène Pidjot; three s. one d.; ed Grand Séminaire St Paul, Nouméa, Univ. of Lyon II and Centre d'Etudes Financières Economiques et Bancaires, Paris; fmr Head of Office for the Devt of the Interior and Islands; Attaché to Econ. Devt Sec. 1988; mem. Union Calédonienne, now Pres.; Chief, St Louis tribal village; mem. Mt Dore Town Council; mem. Southern Prov. Govt; Deputy Speaker, Congress of New Caledonia, responsible for external relations 1989–; Vice-Pres. Kanak Socialist Nat. Liberation Front (FLNKS) 1990, Pres. 1995–2001; Pres. New Caledonian Diocese Pastoral Council 1996; Chair. Melanesian Spearhead Group –2003. *Address:* BP 288, Mont-Dore, 98810 New Caledonia. *Telephone:* 26-58-83; 27-31-29. *Fax:* 26-58-88; 27-32-04.

WAN, Feng, DEcon, MBA; Chinese insurance executive; *President, China Life Insurance Co. Ltd;* b. 1958; ed Open Univ. of Hong Kong, Nankai Univ.; Dir and Sr Vice-Pres. Tai Ping Life Insurance Co., Hong Kong –1977; fmr Deputy Chief, Life Insurance Div., People's Insurance Co. of China (PICC), Jilin br., becoming Gen. Man. Shenzhen br., PICC Life 1997–99; fmr Asst Pres. China Life Insurance Co. Ltd (CLIC) Hong Kong br., Vice-Pres. and Gen. Man. Shenzhen br. 1999, Dir China Life-CMG 1999, Vice-Pres. CLIC 2003–07, Exec. Dir 2006–, Acting Pres. Jan.-Oct. 2007, Pres. Oct. 2007–, also Chair. China Life Pension Insurance Co. Ltd 2007–; Dir China Life Property and Casualty Insurance Co. Ltd 2006–, China Life Insurance Asset Man. Co. Ltd 2006–. *Address:* China Life Insurance Co. Ltd, 23rd Floor, China Life Building, 16 Chaowai Street, Chaoyang District, Beijing, 100020, People's Republic of China (office). *Telephone:* (10) 85659999 (office). *Fax:* (10) 85252232 (office). *E-mail:* serve@e-chinalife.com (office). *Website:* www.e-chinalife.com (office).

WAN, Guoquan; Chinese politician; b. March 1919, Tao'an Co., Jilin Prov.; ed Zhonghua Univ., May 7th Cadre School; worker, Taxation Bureau, Shenyang City, Liaoning Prov. 1945–47, Lizhong Acid Factory, Tianjin 1947–56; joined China Democratic Nat. Construction Asscn 1950; Deputy Dir Tianjin Dyestuff Chemical Industry Co. 1956–57; Dir Tianjin Fed. of Industry and Commerce 1956–63, Sec.-Gen. 1964, Vice-Chair. 1977; Chair. Hedong Dist Industry and Commerce 1957–63; Perm. mem. Exec. Cttee All-China Fed. of Industry and Commerce 1978–83, Vice-Chair. Tianjin Municipal Cttee 1978; Vice-Chair. 4th China Democratic Nat. Construction Asscn Cen. Cttee 1983–88, Dir Cen. Cttee Exec. Bureau 1985–88, Vice-Chair. 5th Cen. Cttee 1988–92, Vice-Chair. 6th Cen. Cttee 1992–97, Hon. Vice-Chair. 7th Cen. Cttee 1997–2002; mem. 5th CPPCC Nat. Cttee 1978–82, Perm. mem. 6th CPPCC Nat. Cttee 1983–87, 7th CPPCC Nat. Cttee 1988–92, 8th CPPCC Nat. Cttee 1993–98 (Vice-Chair. 1993–98), Vice-Chair. 9th CPPCC Nat. Cttee 1998–2003; Pres. China Council for the Promotion of Peaceful Reunification 1993–99; Vice-Pres. Asscn for Int. Understanding of China 1993–. *Address:* c/o National Committee of Chinese People's Political Consultative Conference, 23 Taipingqiao Street, Beijing, People's Republic of China (office).

WAN, Li; Chinese government official (retd); b. Dec. 1916, Dongping Co., Shandong Prov.; m. Bian Tao; four s. one d.; joined CCP 1936; trained as teacher; various posts in Dongping Co. CCP Cttee; served on Hebei-Shangdong CCP Cttee, Deputy Dir Financial and Econ. Cttee, Nanjing Mil. Control Comm.; Head Econ. Dept and Dir Construction Bureau 1947–49; Deputy Head, then Head Industrial Dept, Southwest China Mil. and Admin. Cttee; Vice-Minister of Bldg, Minister of Urban Construction 1949–58; subsequently Sec. Beijing Municipal CCP Cttee, Deputy Mayor of Beijing, Asst to Premier Zhou Enlai in planning and organizing work of Ten Major Projects of the Capital (including Great Hall of the People) and other important construction projects; persecuted during Cultural Revolution 1966–73; Vice-Chair. Municipal Revolutionary Cttee; fmr Minister of Railways, Head Provisional Leading Party mems' group in Ministry; closely allied with Deng Xiaoping's policies; dismissed as Minister when latter fell from favour 1976; First Vice-Minister of Light Industry 1977; First Sec. Anhui Prov. CCP Cttee, Chair. Anhui Prov. Revolutionary Cttee, First Political Commissar, Anhui Mil. Area 1977–80; Vice-Premier, State Council and Chair. State Agricultural Comm., Sec. Leading Party Group, Chair. Cen. Afforestation Comm. 1982–89, State People's Air Defence Comm. 1980; Deputy to 2nd, 3rd, 4th, 5th and 7th NPC, Chair. Standing Cttee 7th NPC 1988–93; elected mem. CCP 11th Cen. Cttee, mem. Secr. CCP 11th Cen. Cttee; elected mem. Politburo CCP Cen. Cttee and mem. Secr. 1982, 1987; mem. Presidium 14th Nat. Congress CCP 1992; Hon. Pres. Bridge Asscn 1980–, Literature Foundation 1986–, Chinese Youth Devt Foundation 1993–, Greening Foundation 1989–, China Environmental Protection Foundation 1993–. *Leisure interests:* tennis, bridge. *Address:* c/o Standing Committee, National People's Congress, Tian An Men Square, Beijing, People's Republic of China (office).

WAN, Shaofen; Chinese party official, economist and lawyer; b. 1930, Nanchang, Jiangxi Prov.; ed Zhongzheng Univ.; joined CCP 1952; Leading Sec. CCP Cttee, Jiangxi 1985–87; Chair. Prov. Women's Fed., Jiangxi 1983–85; mem. 12th CCP Cen. Cttee 1982–87, 13th CCP Cen. Cttee 1987–92, Deputy Head United Front Work Dept of CCP Cen. Cttee 1988–; mem. CCP Cen. Discipline Inspection Comm. 1992–97, 8th NPC Standing Cttee 1993–98, Preliminary Working Cttee of the Preparatory Cttee of the Hong Kong Special Admin. Region 1993–95; Vice-Chair. Overseas Chinese Affairs Cttee of 8th NPC 1993–98, Cttee for Internal and Judicial Affairs of 9th NPC 1998–2003; Del., 14th CCP Nat. Congress 1992–97. *Address:* c/o Standing Committee of National People's Congress, Beijing, People's Republic of China (office).

WAN, Xueyuan; Chinese administrator; *Vice-President, China Association for International Exchange of Personnel;* b. 1941; ed Jiaotong Univ., Shanghai; joined CCP 1964; Dir Gen. Office and Deputy Dir, later Deputy Sec.-Gen., later Sec.-Gen. People's Govt, Shanghai Municipality; Vice-Gov. Zhejiang Prov. 1992–93, Gov. 1993–97; Deputy Sec. CCP 9th Zhejiang Prov. Cttee 1993–97; Vice-Minister of Personnel, State Admin of Foreign Experts Affairs 1997, Dir State Admin of Foreign Experts Affairs 1997–2006; Vice-Pres. China Asscn for Int. Exchange of Personnel 1999–; Alt. mem. 13th CCP Cen. Cttee 1987–92, mem. 14th CCP Cen. Cttee 1992–97; Del., 15th CCP Nat. Congress 1992–97; Deputy, 8th NPC 1992–97, 9th NPC 1997–2002. *Address:* China Association for International Exchange of Personnel, Beijing, People's Republic of China (office). *Website:* caiep@caiep.org (office).

WAN, Zhexian; Chinese mathematician and academic; b. Nov. 1927; s. of Wan Cheggui and Zhou Weijin; m. Wang Shixiau; two d.; ed Qinghua Univ.; Prof. of Math., Division of Pure Math. and Applied Math., Inst. of Systems Science (now Chinese Acad. of Math. and System Sciences) 1978–; Ed.-in-Chief Algebra Colloquium (journal); mem. Chinese Acad. of Sciences 1992; Hua Lookeng Award for Math. 1995. *Publications:* Classical Groups 1963, Geometry of Classical Groups over Finite Fields 1993, Geometry of Matrices 1996. *Address:* Academy of Mathematics and System Science, 1A Nansi Street, Zhongguancun, Beijing 100080, People's Republic of China (office). *Telephone:* (10) 62553005 (office); (10) 62559148 (home). *Fax:* (10) 62568364 (office). *E-mail:* issb@bamboo.iss.ac.cn. *Website:* www.iss.ac.cn/laboratory/purelab (office).

WANAMAKER, Zoë, CBE; British/American actress; b. New York; d. of the late Sam Wanamaker and Charlotte Wanamaker; m. Gawn Grainger 1994; one step-s. one step-d.; ed Cen. School of Speech and Drama; professional debut as Hermia in A Midsummer Night's Dream, Manchester 1970; repertory at Royal Lyceum 1971–72, Oxford Playhouse 1974–75, Nottingham 1975–76; work with RSC and Nat. Theatre includes Toine in Piaf, London and New York 1980, Viola in Twelfth Night 1983, Adriana in A Comedy of Errors 1983, Kitty Duval in Time of Your Life 1983, Kattrin in Mother Courage 1984, Othello 1989, The Crucible 1990, The Last Yankee 1993, Battle Royal 1999, His Girl Friday 2003, The Rose Tattoo 2007, Much Ado About Nothing 2007; other performances include Fay in Loot, Broadway 1986, Ellie in Terry Johnson's Dead Funny, London 1994, Amanda in The Glass Menagerie, London 1995/96, Sylvia 1996, Electra, Chichester and London 1997, Princeton and Broadway 1998, The Old Neighbourhood, Royal Court 1998, Boston Marriage, Donmar Warehouse, London 2001, New Ambassadors, London 2001–02, Awake and Sing!, Lincoln Center Production, The Belasco Theater, New York, The Rose Tattoo, Royal Nat. Theatre 2007, Much Ado About Nothing, Royal Nat. Theatre 2007–08; Assoc. Royal Nat. Theatre; Patron Prisoners of Conscience; Vice-Patron The Actors Centre; Hon. Pres. Shakespeare's Globe Theatre, Hon. Vice-Pres. Dignity in Dying; Hon. DLitt

(South Bank Univ.) 1993; Dr hc (Richmond American Int. Univ. of London); Soc. of West End Theatres (SWET) Award (Once in a Lifetime) 1979, Drama Award (Mother Courage) 1985, Olivier Award for Best Actress (Electra) 1998, Variety Club Award for Best Actress (Electra) 1998, BAFTA Award for Best Actress (Love Hurts and Wilde), Calaway Award (New York) for Best Actress (Electra) 1998, Gold Hugo for Narration 1998, Award for Excellence in the Arts, Theatre School, DePaul Univ., Chicago 2004; Drama Desk Best Revival, Out of Critics Circle Best Ensemble, Tony Award for Best Revival and Joan Cullman Award for Best Revival (all for Awake and Sing!). *Films include:* The Raggedy Rawney 1987, Wilde 1997, Swept by the Sea 1997, Harry Potter: The Philosopher's Stone 2001, Five Children and It 2004. *Television appearances include:* Inside the Third Reich 1982, The Tragedy of Richard the Third 1983, Edge of Darkness 1985, Paradise Postponed 1986, Poor Little Rich Girl (mini-series) 1987, Morse 1990, Prime Suspect 1990, The Blackheath Poisonings 1992, Love Hurts (series) 1992–94, The Widowing of Mrs. Holroyd 1995, The English Wife 1995, Dance to the Music of Time 1997, David Copperfield 1999, Gormenghast 2000, Adrian Mole: The Cappucino Years 2000, My Family (series) (Best Sitcom Actress, Rose d'Or Awards) 2000–, Miss Marple: Murder is Announced 2004, A Waste of Shame 2005, Dr Who 2005, 2006, Poirot: Cards on the Table 2006, Johnny and the Bomb 2006, The Old Curiosity Shop 2007, Poirot: The Third Girl 2008, Poirot: Mrs McGinty's Dead 2008. *Radio:* The Golden Bowl, Plenty, Bay at Nice, A February Morning, Carol, Such Rotten Luck, The Older Woman. *Address:* c/o Conway van Gelder Grant Ltd, 18–21 Jermyn Street, London, SW1Y 6HP, England. *Telephone:* (20) 7287-0077. *Fax:* (20) 7287-1940.

WANCER, Józef, MA; Polish banker and economist; *President, Przemyslowo-Handlowy Bank;* b. 26 May 1942, Komi, Russia; s. of Jakub Wancer and Edwarda Wancer; m. Krystyna Antoniak; one s. one d.; ed City Univ. of New York City, Webster Univ., Saint Louis, Mo., USA; Vice-Pres. Citibank of New York, managerial posts at Citibank units, including Japan, Austria, UK, France; Vice-Pres., then Pres. Raiffeisen Centrobank, Warsaw 1995–2000; Pres. Man. Bd Przemyslowo-Handlowy Bank (BPH) 2000–01, Pres. BPH PBK (following merger with HVB, now Bank BPH SA) 2001–. *Leisure interests:* cycling, logotherapy, history. *Address:* Bank BPH SA, Al. Pokoju 1, 31-548 Kraków, Poland (office). *Telephone:* (22) 5319230 (office). *Fax:* (22) 5319286 (office). *E-mail:* jozef.wancer@bph.pl (office). *Website:* www.bph.pl (office).

WANG, Anyi; Chinese writer; b. 1954, Tong'an, Fujian Prov.; ed Xiangming Middle School; fmr musician, Xuzhou Pref. Song and Dance Ensemble; Ed. Children's Time; Vice-Chair. Shanghai Writers Assen, Chair. 2001–. *Publications:* Song of Eternal Hatred (Mao Dun Prize for Literature), Xiaobao Village, The Love of a Small Town, The Story of a School Principal, Self-selected Works of Wang Anyi (six vols), Lapse of Time, The Song of Everlasting Sorrow 2008. *Address:* Shanghai Writers Association, Shanghai, People's Republic of China (office).

WANG, Bingqian; Chinese politician; b. 1925, Li Co., Hebei Prov.; Deputy Section Chief, Auditing Div., Dept of Finance 1948–49; Section Chief, later Dir, Vice-Minister, Minister of Finance, Cen. Govt; Dir Budget Dept 1963; Deputy Minister of Finance 1973–80, Minister of Finance 1980–92; mem. 12th Cen. Cttee CCP 1982, 13th Cen. Cttee 1987–92; Pres. Accounting Soc. 1980–; Hon. Chair. Bd of Dirs China Investment Bank 1981–; State Councillor 1983–93; Chair. Cen. Treasury Bond Sales Promotion Cttee 1984–; Vice-Chair. Standing Cttee of 8th NPC 1993–98; mem. State Planning Comm. 1988–92; NPC Deputy Hebei Prov.; Hon. Pres. Auditing Soc. 1984–, China Scientific Research Soc. for Policy Study. *Address:* c/o Standing Committee of National People's Congress, Beijing, People's Republic of China (office).

WANG, Bingzhang, MD; Chinese political activist; b. 30 Dec. 1947; one d.; ed Beijing Medical Univ., McGill Univ., Canada; jailed twice by Chinese authorities during Cultural Revolution; moved to USA 1979; f. China Spring magazine 1980s; Founder and Leader Chinese Alliance for Democracy, New York 1980s; attempted to return to China, but expelled 1998; entered Viet Nam to hold meetings with activists 2002; allegedly abducted by Chinese security forces and held at secret location July 2002; arrested in Fancheng-gang City, S China Dec. 2002; convicted of espionage and leading terrorist group (sentenced to life imprisonment), Guangdong Prov. Court, S China Jan. 2003; imprisoned in Shaoguan Prison, Guangdong Prov.

WANG, Chang-Ching, MSc; Taiwanese politician; b. 22 Sept. 1920, Chingshan Co., Hupeh; s. of C. S. Wang and late Si Teng; m. Hsueh Chen L. Wang; one s. one d.; ed Nat. Chiaotung Univ. and Johns Hopkins Univ., USA; Sr Eng and concurrently Div. Chief, Dept of Communications, Taiwan Provincial Govt 1949–58; Dir Public Works Bureau, Taiwan Provincial Govt 1958–69; Dir Dept of Public Works, Taipei City Govt 1967–69; Vice-Minister, Ministry of Communications 1969–77; Vice-Chair. Council for Econ. Planning and Devt 1977–84; Sec.-Gen. Exec. Yuan 1984–88; Chair. China External Trade Devt Council 1988–; Vice-Chair. Straits Exchange Foundation 1993–. *Leisure interest:* golf. *Address:* 7th Floor, 333 Keelung Road, Sec. 1, Taipei 10548, Taiwan. *Telephone:* (2) 7576293. *Fax:* (2) 7576653.

WANG, Chaowen; Chinese politician; b. 1930, Huangping, Guizhou Prov.; joined CCP 1951; Sec. Guizhou Communist Youth League 1973; Vice-Chair. Prov. Revolutionary Cttee, Guizhou 1977–79; Sec. CCP Guizhou Prov. Cttee 1980–81, Deputy Sec. 1981; Vice-Gov. of Guizhou 1977–83, Gov. 1983–93; Chair. Guizhou Prov. 8th People's Congress 1994–98; mem. 12th CCP Cen. Cttee 1982–87, 13th CCP Cen. Cttee 1987–92, 14th CCP Cen. Cttee 1992–97; mem. 8th Standing Cttee of NPC 1993–98, 9th Standing Cttee of NPC 1998–2003, Chair. Nationalities Cttee 1998–2003; Del., 15th CCP Nat. Congress 1997–2002. *Address:* c/o Standing Committee of the National People's Congress, 19 Xi-Jiaoming Xiang Road, Xicheng District, Beijing 100805, People's Republic of China (office).

WANG, Charles B., BS; Chinese computer executive; *Chairman Emeritus, Computer Associates;* b. 19 Aug. 1944, Shanghai; s. of Kenneth Wang; m. 2nd Nancy Li; ed Queen's Coll.; programming trainee, Reverside Research Inst., Columbia Univ., USA 1976; Founder, Chair., CEO Computer Assocs 1976–2002, Chair. Emer. 2002–; co-owner New York Islanders professional ice hockey team 1999–. *Publications:* Techno Vision 1994, Techno Vision II: Every Executive's Guide to Understanding and Mastering Technology and the Internet 1997. *Leisure interests:* basketball, cooking. *Address:* c/o New York Islanders Hockey Club, L.P., 1535 Old Country Road. Plainview, NY 11803, USA. *Telephone:* (516) 501-6700. *Fax:* (516) 501-6762. *Website:* www.newyorkislanders.com.

WANG, Chen, MScS; Chinese journalist and editor; *President, Renmin Ribao (People's Daily);* b. 1950, Beijing; ed School of Postgraduate Studies, Chinese Acad. of Social Sciences, Beijing; joined CCP 1969; reporter, CCP Yijun Co. Cttee 1970–73, CCP Yan'an Municipal Cttee, Shaanxi Prov.; reporter, Guangming Daily 1974, then successively Ed., Dir Chief Ed.'s Office, Assoc. Chief Ed. 1982–95, Chief Ed. 1995–2000; Deputy Dir Dept of Propaganda, CCP Cen. Cttee 2000–01; Ed.-in-Chief Renmin Ribao (People's Daily) 2001–02, Pres. 2002–; mem. CPPCC Nat. Cttee 1998–2003; mem. 16th CCP Cen. Cttee 2002–07, 17th CCP Cen. Cttee 2007–; Dir State Council Information Office 2008–. *Address:* Renmin Ribao (People's Daily), 2 Jin Tai Xi Lu, Chao Yang Men Wai, Beijing 100733, People's Republic of China (office). *Telephone:* (10) 65092121 (office). *Fax:* (10) 65091982 (office). *E-mail:* info@peopledaily.com.cn (office). *Website:* www.people.com.cn (office).

WANG, Cher, MA (Econs); Taiwanese computer industry executive; *Chairperson, HTC Corporation;* b. 14 Sept. 1958; d. of Wang Yung-ching and Liao Chiao; m. Wenchi Chen; two c.; ed Univ. of California, Berkeley, USA; Gen. Man. PC Div., First International Computer 1982–87; Co-founder and Chair. VIA Technologies 1987–, High Tech Computer (HTC) Corpn 1997–; selected by Business Week as an Innovator in the 2005 Stars of Asia: 25 Leaders on the Forefront of Change and one of the 10 executives to watch in Asia 2005. *Address:* HTC Headquarters, 23 Xinghua Road, Taoyuan 330, Taiwan (office). *Telephone:* (3) 3753252 (office). *Fax:* (3) 3753251 (office). *E-mail:* info@htc.com (office). *Website:* www.htc.com (office).

WANG, Chien-Shien; Taiwanese politician; b. 7 Aug. 1938, Anhwei; m. Fa-jau Su; ed Harvard Univ., USA; Sr Specialist Taxation & Tariff Comm. Ministry of Finance 1971–73; Dir First Div. Dept of Taxation 1973–76, Fourth Dept Exec. Yuan 1976–80; Dir-Gen. Dept of Customs Admin. Ministry of Finance 1980–82, Public Finance Training Inst. 1982–84; Admin. Vice-Minister of Econ. Affairs 1984–89, Political Vice-Minister 1989–90, Minister of Finance 1990–92; mem. Legis. Yuan 1993–, Sec.-Gen. New Party 1994; Asian Finance Minister of the Year 1992. *Publications:* several works on income tax and business. *Address:* c/o New Party, 4th Floor, 65 Guang Fuh S Road, Taipei, Taiwan. *Telephone:* (2) 7562222.

WANG, Dazhong, DSc; Chinese professor of nuclear engineering; b. 1935, Changli, Hebei Prov.; ed Nankai Middle School, Tianjin, Tsinghua Univ., Beijing; Visiting Scholar, Nuclear Research Centre, Juelich (KFA Juelich), FRG 1980–82; fmr Chief Scientist, First Expert Cttee on Energy, Nat. High Tech. Devt Programme; Assoc. Prof., Prof., Research Fellow, Dir of Nuclear Energy Research Inst., Tsinghua Univ. 1958–99, Vice-Chair. Univ. Council, Pres. Tsinghua Univ. 1999–2003; Pres. Beijing Nuclear Soc.; Vice-Pres. China Nuclear Soc.; mem. Chinese Acad. of Sciences 1993–, 4th Presidium of Depts Chinese Acad. of Sciences 2000–; Hon. Dr rer. nat (Aachen Univ. of Tech.) 1982; Nat. Advanced Scientist 1989. *Address:* c/o Tsinghua University, 1 Qinghuayuan, Beijing 100084, People's Republic of China (office). *Telephone:* (10) 62561144 (office). *Website:* www.tsinghua.edu.cn/eng/faculties/wdz.htm (office).

WANG, Demin; Chinese petroleum engineer; b. 9 Feb. 1937, Tangshan, Hebei Prov.; ed Beijing Petroleum Inst.; technician, engineer, Chief Engineer, Daqing Petroleum Admin Bureau, currently Vice Pres.; Prof. Daqing Petroleum Inst.; Fellow, Chinese Acad. of Eng 1994; 10 nat. level and 26 ministerial level awards. *Address:* Daqing Petroleum Administration, Daqing 163453, Heilongjiang Province, People's Republic of China (office).

WANG, Deshun; Chinese mime artist; b. 1938; m. Zhao Aijun; one s. one d.; fmr street performer; with army drama co. 1960–70; joined state-run Changchun Theatre Troupe, NE China 1970; since 1984 has been appearing in 'modelling pantomime' show in which he adopts series of sculpture-like poses to develop a theme; has taken his show to France, Germany and Macao and China's first int. mime festival, Shanghai 1994.

WANG, Deyan; Chinese banker; b. 1931; ed Tsinghua Univ., Cen. Inst. of Finance and Econ., Beijing Foreign Languages Inst.; joined Bank of China 1953, served as Sec., Asst Man., Deputy Gen. Man. 1953–84, Vice-Pres. 1984–85, Pres. 1985–93, Chair. Bd Dirs 1986–93; Dir Council's Office of People's Bank of China, Welfare Fund for Chinese Disabled Persons; Guest Adviser, China Council for Promotion of Int. Trade; Adviser to Coordination Group for Sino-Japanese Econ. and Trade Affairs; Vice-Chair. China Int. Finance Soc.; mem. Leading Group for Introduction of Foreign Capital under State Council; mem. Nat. Geographic Soc., USA; Asian Banker of 1987, Asian Finance; Hon. Dir Research Fund for Prevention of AIDS in China. *Address:* c/o Bank of China, 410 Fuchengmennei Dajie, Beijing, People's Republic of China (office).

WANG, Dianzuo; Chinese metallurgist and academic; *Honorary President, General Research Institute for Nonferrous Metals;* b. 23 March 1934, Linghai, Liaoning Prov.; ed Central-South Univ.; currently Prof. and Hon. Pres. Gen. Research Inst. for Nonferrous Metals; Chair. Int. Mineral Processing Congress Beijing 2008; Dir (non-exec.) Aluminum Corpn of China Ltd

2001–; Foreign Assoc. mem. Nat. Acad. of Eng, USA 1990–; Fellow, Chinese Acad. of Sciences 1991, Chinese Acad. of Eng 1994 (currently Vice-Pres.); made pioneering contribs in flotation theory for mineral processing; many nat., provincial and ministerial awards including He Liang and He Li Prizes 1994. *Publications:* eight monographs and over 300 research papers. *Address:* General Research Institute for Nonferrous Metals, 2 Xinjiekou Wai Street, Beijing 100088, People's Republic of China (office). *Telephone:* (10) 62055356 (office). *Fax:* (10) 62055345 (office). *E-mail:* wangdz@grinm.com (office). *Website:* http://en.grinm.com (office).

WANG, Fosong; Chinese chemist; b. 1933, Xingning Co., Guangdong Prov.; ed Wuhan Univ.; Researcher and Vice-Pres. Chinese Acad. of Sciences 1988, Fellow 1999–, mem. 4th Presidium of Depts Chinese Acad. of Sciences 2000–; Deputy Chair. China Petroleum Asscn; mem. 8th NPC 1993–98; second class Nat. Prize in Nature Science 1982, 1986, third class Nat. Prize in Nature Science 1991, Japanese Soc. of Polymer Science Int. Award 2002. *Publications:* more than 300 scientific papers. *Address:* Chinese Academy of Sciences, 52 San Li He Road, Beijing 100864, People's Republic of China (office).

WANG, Fuli; Chinese actress; b. Nov. 1949, Xuzhou, Jiangsu Prov.; ed Jiangsu Prov. Drama Acad.; actress, Jiangsu Prov. Peking Opera Troupe, then Jiangsu Prov. Drama Troupe 1968–90; with China Broadcasting Art Co. 1990–; TV Gold Eagle Award for Best Actress, Hundred-Flower Award for Best Supporting Actress 1984, Gold Rooster Award for Best Supporting Actress 1986, New Decade Movie Award for Best Actress. *Films:* The Legend of Tianyun Mountain 1980, Xu Mao and His Daughters 1981, Our Niu Baisui, Sunrise 1985, God of Mountains 1992, The Romance of Blacksmith Zhang, The Wooden Man's Bride 1993. *Address:* China Broadcasting Art Company, No 2, Fuxingmen Wai Street, Beijing 100866, People's Republic of China (office). *Telephone:* (10) 66092785 (office).

WANG, Fuzhou; Chinese mountaineer and sports administrator; b. 1931, Xihua, Henan Province; s. of Wang Daikuang and Shen Xiozhen; m. Lia Aihua; one d.; mem. of Chinese mountaineering team that conquered Mt Everest for first time from north 1960; Sec.-Gen. Chinese Mountaineering Asscn 1980–93, Pres. 1993–; Gen. Man. of China Int. Sports Travel Co. 1983–. *Address:* State Physical Culture and Sports Commission, 9 Tiyuguang Road, Beijing (office); Chinese Mountaineering Association, 10 Zuoanmen Nei Street, Beijing, People's Republic of China (office). *Telephone:* 7017810 (office). *Fax:* 5114859 (office).

WANG, Gang; Chinese archivist and party official; *Vice-Chairman, 11th CPPCC National Committee;* b. Oct. 1942, Fuyu Co., Jilin Prov.; ed Jilin Univ.; clerk, Publicity Section, No. 8 Company, 7th Bureau, Ministry of Construction 1968–69, Publicity Div., Political Dept, 7th Bureau 1969–77; joined CCP 1971; Sec. Gen. Office of CCP Xinjiang Autonomous Region Cttee 1977–81; Sec. (rank of Div. Dir) Taiwan Affairs Office of CCP Cen. Cttee 1981–85; Deputy Dir-Gen. Petition Letters Bureau, Gen. Office of CCP Cen. Cttee and Gen. Office of the State Council 1985–87, Exec. Deputy Dir-Gen. 1987–90; Exec. Deputy Dir CCP Cen. Cttee Cen. Archives 1990–93, Sec. Head Office 1990–93, Dir Cen. Archives 1993–99, Dir State Archives Bureau 1993–94, Dir-Gen. 1994–99; Deputy Dir-Gen. Office CCP Cen. Cttee 1994–99, Dir 1999–2007; Chair. Int. Archives Council 1996–; Alt. mem. 15th CCP Cen. Cttee 1997–2002 (Sec. Work Cttee of Dept CCP Cen. Cttee 1999–), mem. 16th CCP Cen. Cttee 2002–07 (Alt. mem. Politburo, mem. Politburo Secr.), mem. 17th CCP Cen. Cttee 2007– (mem. Politburo); Vice-Chair. 11th CPPCC Nat. Cttee 2008–. *Address:* CPPCC National Committee, No. 23, Taipingqiao Street, Beijing 100811, People's Republic of China (office). *Website:* www.cppcc.gov.cn (office).

WANG, Guangtao, MEng; Chinese politician; b. 1943, Shanghai; ed Tongji Univ., Shanghai; technician, Urban Construction Bureau, Xuzhou City, Jiangsu Prov. 1965; engineer, Technique Section, Urban and Rural Construction Cttee, Xuzhou City 1980–81, Chief 1981, Deputy Chief Engineer and Deputy Dir Urban and Rural Construction Cttee 1981–82; joined CCP 1983; Vice-Mayor of Xuzhou City 1988; Dir and Chief Engineer, Urban Construction Dept, Ministry of Construction 1989–95, Minister of Construction 2001–; Deputy Sec. Harbin Municipal Cttee 1995; Acting Mayor, then Mayor of Harbin, Helongjiang Prov. 1995–98; Vice-Mayor of Beijing 1998–2001; mem. CCP Leading Party Group, Ministry of Construction 2001–07; mem. 16th CCP Cen. Cttee 2002–07; Hon. Prof., Dept of Architecture, Chinese Univ. of Hong Kong 2005. *Address:* c/o Ministry of Construction, 9 Sanlihe Dajie, Xicheng Qu, Beijing 100835, People's Republic of China (office).

WANG, Guangying; Chinese business executive; b. 1919, Beijing; s. of Wang Huaiqing; m. 1943; ed Furen Univ., Beijing; Co-founder Xiandai Chemical Factory in Tianjin 1943; f. Lisheng Knitwear Factory, Tianjin 1949; Vice-Chair. China Democratic Nat. Construction Asscn 1954; Man. Knit Goods Manufacturing Co., Tianjin 1956; mem. Standing Cttee All-China Fed. of Industry and Commerce 1956, Vice-Chair. All-China Fed. of Industry and Commerce 1982–93, Hon. Chair. 1993–97; Chair. Tianjin Fed. of Industry and Commerce 1956; jailed for eight years during cultural revolution 1967–75; Vice-Mayor Tianjin Municipality 1980; Founder, Chair. and Pres. China Everbright Co. (China's first trans-nat. corpn), Hong Kong 1983–90; mem. Bd China Int. Trust and Investment Corpn 1983; Exec. Chair. Presidium CPPCC 1983–; Vice-Chair. 6th CPPCC 1983–88, 7th CPPCC 1988–93, Standing Cttee of 8th NPC 1993–98, of 9th NPC 1998–2003; NPC Deputy Tianjin Municipality; Pres. China Council for Promotion of Peaceful Reunification 1990–98; Hon. Vice-Chair. Red Cross Soc. of China 1994–99, Hon. Vice-Pres. 1999; Hon. Chair. China Overseas Friendship Asscn 1997. *Address:* All China Federation of Industry and Commerce, 93 Beiheyan Dajie, Beijing, People's Republic of China (office).

WANG, Gungwu, CBE, PhD, FAHA; Australian historian, academic and university vice-chancellor; *Director, East Asian Institute, National University of Singapore;* b. 9 Oct. 1930, Indonesia; s. of Wang Fo Wen and Ting Yien; m. Margaret Lim Ping-Ting 1955; one s. two d.; ed Nat. Cen. Univ., Nanjing, Univ. of Malaya and Univ. of London; Asst Lecturer Univ. of Malaya, Singapore 1957–59, lecturer 1959; lecturer, Univ. of Malaya, Kuala Lumpur 1959–61, Sr Lecturer 1961–63, Dean of Arts 1962–63, Prof. of History 1963–68; Rockefeller Fellow, Univ. of London 1961–62, Sr Visiting Fellow 1972; Prof. of Far Eastern History, ANU 1968–86, Prof. Emer. 1986–, Dir Research School of Pacific Studies 1975–80; Visiting Fellow, All Souls Coll. Oxford 1974–75; John A. Burns Distinguished Visiting Prof. of History, Univ. of Hawaii 1979; Rose Morgan Visiting Prof. of History, Univ. of Kansas 1983; Vice-Chancellor, Univ. of Hong Kong 1986–95; Chair. Inst. of E Asian Political Economy, Nat. Univ. of Singapore 1996–97, Dir East Asian Inst. 1997–; Distinguished Sr Fellow Inst. of Southeast Asian Studies, Singapore 1996–99, Distinguished Professorial Fellow 1999–2003; Fellow and Hon. Corresp. mem. for Hong Kong of Royal Soc. of Arts 1987–95; Pres. Australian Acad. of the Humanities 1980–83, Asian Studies Asscn of Australia 1978–80; Chair. Australia-China Council 1984–86, Environmental Pollution Advisory Cttee (Hong Kong) 1988–95, Council for the Performing Arts (Hong Kong) 1989–94, Asia-Pacific Council, Griffith Univ. 1997–2001, Inst. of Southeast Asian Studies, Singapore; mem. Exec. Council, Hong Kong 1990–92; Adviser Chinese Heritage Centre, Nanyang Tech. Univ. 1995–2000 (Vice-Chair.) 2000–, Southeast Asian Studies, Academia Sinica, Taipei 1994–; mem. Council Int. Inst. for Strategic Studies, London 1992–2001; mem. Nat. Arts Council, Singapore 1996–2000, Nat. Heritage Bd 1997–99 (Adviser 2000–), Nat. Library Bd 1997–2003; mem. Academia Sinica, Taipei, DD Social Science Research Council, NY 1999–; Foreign Hon. mem. American Acad. of Arts and Science; Hon. Fellow SOAS, London; Hon. Sr Fellow Chinese Acad. of Social Sciences, Beijing; Hon. Prof. Beijing Univ., Fudan Univ., Hong Kong Univ., Nanjing Univ., Tsinghua Univ.; Hon. DLitt (Sydney, Hull, Hong Kong); Hon. LLD (Monash, ANU, Melbourne); Hon. DUniv (Griffith, Soka). *Publications:* 21 books, including The Chineseness of China 1991, China and the Chinese Overseas 1991, Community and Nation: China, South-East Asia and Australia 1992, Zhongguo yu Haiwai Huaren 1994, The Chinese Way: China's Position in International Relations 1995; Hong Kong's Transition: A Decade after the Deal (ed.) 1995, Global History and Migrations (ed.) 1997, The Nanhai Trade 1998, The Chinese Overseas: From Earthbound China to the Quest for Autonomy 2000, Joining the Modern World: Inside and Outside China 2000, Only Connect: Sino-Malay Encounters 2001, Don't Leave Home: Migration and the Chinese 2001, To Act is to Know: Chinese Dilemmas 2002, Bind Us in Time: Nation and Civilisation in Asia 2002, Anglo-Chinese Encounters since 1800: War, Trade, Science and Governance 2003, Ideas Won't Keep: the Struggle for China's Future 2003, Reform, Legitimacy and Dilemmas: China's politics and Society (ed.) 2003, Damage Control: the Chinese Communist Party in the era of Jiang Zeming (ed.) 2004, Diasporic Chinese Ventures 2004; also numerous articles on Chinese and South-East Asian history; Gen. Ed. East Asian Historical Monographs series. *Leisure interests:* music, reading, walking. *Address:* East Asian Institute, Block AS5, 7 Arts Link, National University of Singapore, Kent Ridge, Singapore 117571. *Telephone:* 7752033. *Fax:* 7793409. *E-mail:* eaiwgw@nus.edu.sg (office). *Website:* nus.edu.sg/nusinfo/eai (office).

WANG, Gen. Hai; Chinese army officer; b. 1925, Weihai City, Shandong Prov.; ed China's North-East Aviation Acad.; joined PLA 1945; Group Commdr, air force brigade and sent to Korean battlefield 1950; promoted Col PLA 1964; Commdr, Air Force of Guangzhou Mil. Region 1975–83; Deputy Commdr PLA Air Force 1983–85, Commdr 1985; mem. CCP 12th Cen. Cttee 1982–87, 13th CCP Cen. Cttee 1987–92, 14th CCP Cen. Cttee 1992–97; promoted Gen. PLA 1988. *Address:* Ministry of Defence, Beijing, People's Republic of China (office).

WANG, Hanbin; Chinese state official and party official; b. 28 Aug. 1925, Fujian Prov.; m. Peng Peiyun; two s. two d.; joined CCP in Burma 1941; Deputy Sec.-Gen. NPC Legal Comm. 1979–80; Vice-Chair. and Sec.-Gen. NPC Legal Comm. 1980–83; Deputy Sec.-Gen., Political and Legal Comm. of CCP Cen. Cttee 1980–82, Constitution Revision Cttee of People's Repub. of China 1980–82; Vice-Pres. Chinese Law Soc. 1982–91, Hon. Pres. 1991–; Chair. Legis. Affairs Comm. 1983–87; Vice-Chair. Cttee for Drafting Basic Law of Hong Kong Special Admin. Zone of People's Repub. of China 1985–90, for Drafting Basic Law of Macau Special Admin. Region of People's Republic of China 1988–, Preparatory Cttee, Hong Kong Special Admin. Region 1995–97; mem. 12th CCP Cen. Cttee 1982–87, 13th Cen. Cttee 1987–92, 14th Cen. Cttee 1992–97; Sec.-Gen. NPC Standing Cttee 1983–87, Vice-Chair. NPC 7th Standing Cttee 1988–93; Alt. mem. Politburo CCP 1992–97; Vice-Chair. Standing Cttee 8th NPC 1993–98. *Leisure interest:* bridge. *Address:* c/o National People's Congress Standing Committee, Beijing, People's Republic of China (office).

WANG, J. T., BEng, MBA; Taiwanese computer industry executive; *Chairman and CEO, Acer Inc.;* m.; two d.; ed Nat. Taiwan Univ. and Nat. Cheng-Chi Univ.; sales engineer, Multitech (forerunner of Acer) 1981, held increasingly sr posts until Pres. Acer Sertek 1990–2000, Pres. Acer Inc. 2000–05, Chair. and CEO Acer Inc. 2005–. *Address:* Acer Inc., 9F, 88 Hsin Tai Wu Road, Sec 1, Hsichih, Taipei 221, Taiwan (office). *Telephone:* (2) 696-1234 (office). *Fax:* (2) 696-3535 (office). *Website:* www.acer.com (office).

WANG, Jianzhou; Chinese telecommunications executive; *Executive Director, Chairman and CEO, China Mobile Communication Corporation;* b. Dec. 1958; ed Zhejiang Univ.; served as Dir-Gen. Posts and Telecommunications Bureau, Hangzhou; Dir-Gen. Planning and Construction Dept, Ministry of Posts and Telecommunications 1996–99; Dir-Gen. Gen. Planning Dept, Ministry of Information Industry 1996–99; Dir China Unicom 1999–2001, Exec. Vice-Pres. 2001–02, Pres. 2002–04; Exec. Dir, Chair. and CEO China

Mobile Communication Corpn 2004–. *Address:* China Mobile Communication Corpn, 29 Financial Street, Xicheng District, Beijing 100032, People's Republic of China (office). *Telephone:* (10) 3121-8888 (office). *Fax:* (10) 2511-9092 (office). *E-mail:* info@chinamobile.com (office). *Website:* www.chinamobile.com (office).

WANG, Jida; Chinese sculptor; b. 27 Oct. 1935, Beijing; s. of Wang Sho Yi and Chiu Chen Shin; m. Jin Gao 1971; one s. one d.; ed Cen. Inst. of Fine Arts, Beijing; worked in Nei Monggol 1966, 1976–84; moved to USA 1984; Asst Dir Standing Council, Nei Monggol Sculptors' Asscn; mem., Chinese Artist's Asscn, American Nat. Sculpture Soc. 1988–; Honour Prize, China 1977. *Works include:* The Struggle (commissioned by Exec. Council on Foreign Diplomats) 1987, Natural Beauty (a collection of 18 pieces portraying women and animals) 1987, Statue of Liberty (commissioned by Statue of Liberty/Ellis Island Foundation), several monumental sculptures in Chairman Mao's image, in China. *Leisure interests:* athletics, music, literature. *Address:* Inner Mongolia Artist's Association, 33 West Street, Hohhot, Inner Mongolia, People's Republic of China (office); 76-12 35th Avenue, Apartment 3E, Jackson Heights, NY 11372, USA. *Telephone:* 25775 (China); (718) 651-3944 (USA).

WANG, Jin, PhD; Chinese physicist and academic; *Adjunct Professor of Chemistry, Changchun Institute of Applied Chemistry, Chinese Academy of Sciences;* ed Jilin Univ., Univ. of Illinois, USA; Post-doctoral Research Assoc. (Chem. and Biophysics), Univ. of Illinois 1991–96; Guest Scientist, NIH 1996–97; Adjunct Prof. of Physics, Jilin Univ. 1997–; Adjunct Prof. of Chem., State Univ. of New York at Stony Brook 1999–2004, Adjunct Prof., Dept of Applied Math. and Statistics 2006–, also Adjunct Prof., Harriman School of Man. 2008–; Adjunct Prof., Changchun Inst. of Applied Chem., Chinese Acad. of Sciences 2002–; Nat. Science Foundation Career Award 2005. *Publications:* more than 40 articles in scientific journals on mechanism of biomolecular folding and recognition, especially protein folding and protein-protein/protein-DNA interactions. *Address:* Department of Chemistry, State University of New York, Stony Brook NY 11794, USA (office). *E-mail:* jin.wang.1@stonybrook.edu (office). *Website:* www.sunysb.edu/chemistry/index.html (office).

WANG, Jin-Pyng, BS; Taiwanese politician; *President of the Li-Fa Yuan (Legislative Yuan);* b. 17 March 1941, Kaohsiung Co.; m. Chen Tsai-Lien; one s. two d.; ed Nat. Taiwan Normal Univ.; mem. Legis. Yuan 1975–, various positions including Sec.-Gen. of KMT Caucus, Dir and Dir-Gen. Dept of Party–Govt Co-ordination, Convenor Finance Cttee 1981–88, Vice-Pres. 1993–99, Pres. Li-Fa Yuan (Legis. Yuan) 1999–; Vice-Chair. Cen. Policy Cttee of Kuomintang (KMT) 1990, Chair. Finance Cttee 1990–92; Vice-Chair. KMT 2000–; mem. CSC 1993–; Pres. Sino–Japanese Inter-Parl. Friendship Asscn 1992–99, Taiwan Maj. League of Professional Baseball 1997–2002, Volunteer Fire-Fighter Asscn of the ROC 1997–, Taiwan Foundation for Democracy 2003–; Chair. Nat. Biotech and Health Care Industries Promotion Cttee 2001–, Foundation for the Promotion of Biotech Industries Devt 2001–. *Address:* Legislative Yuan, 1 Chuanshan S. Road, Taipei, Taiwan (office). *Telephone:* (2) 23586011/15 (office). *Fax:* (2) 23955317 (office). *Website:* www.ly.gov.tw.

WANG, Joseph, DSc; American electrochemist and academic; *Distinguished Professor of Chemistry, Regents Professor and Manasse Chair, New Mexico State University;* ed Israel Inst. of Tech.; Research Assoc., Univ. of Wisconsin-Madison 1978–80; faculty mem., New Mexico State University (NMSU) 1980–, currently Distinguished Prof. of Chem., holds Regents Professorship and Manasse Chair; NAS Visiting Scientist Fellowship to People's Repub. of China 1986; Chief Ed. Electroanalysis; mem. Advisory Editorial Bd Analytica Chimica Acta, Analyst, Talanta, Analytical Letters, Electrochemistry Communications, Analytical Instrumentation, Analytical Communications, Analysis Europa, Encyclopedia of Analytical Sciences, Current Topics in Analytical Chemistry, Croatia Chimica Acta, Current Analytical Chemistry; served as instructor ACS Short Course 'Electrochemical Sensors'; mem. IUPAC Comm. for Electroanalytical Chem.; Fellow, Japan Soc. for Promotion of Science 2000; has presented more than 130 invited and plenary lectures in 40 countries; Dr hc (Nat. Univ., Cordoba, Argentina) 2003; Young Faculty Award, Soc. of Analytical Chemists, Pittsburgh 1981, Heyrovsky Memorial Medal (Czech Repub.) 1994, ACS Award for Chemical Instrumentation, ISI 'Citation Laureate' Award as Most Cited Scientist in Engineering in the World 1991–2001, Westhafer Award for Research, NMSU 1990, most-cited electrochemist in the world 1995, 1997, 17th place in ISI list of Most Cited Researchers in Chem. 1992–2002. *Publications:* seven books including Stripping Analysis, Electroanalytical Techniques in Clinical Chemistry and Laboratory Medicine, Biosensors and Chemical Sensors, Analytical Electrochemistry, Biosensors for Direct Monitoring of Environmental Pollutants; 12 book chapters, eight patents and more than 620 articles in scientific journals on nanobioelectronics and electroanalytical techniques. *Address:* Department of Chemistry and Biochemistry, PO Box 30001, MSC 3C, 1175 North Horseshoe Drive, New Mexico State University, Las Cruces, NM 88003-8001, USA (office). *Telephone:* (505) 646-2140 (office). *Fax:* (505) 646-6033 (office). *E-mail:* joewang@nmsu.edu (office). *Website:* www.chemistry.nmsu.edu (office).

WANG, Jun; Chinese business executive; *Chairman and Executive Director, Goldbond Group Holdings Ltd;* b. 11 April 1941, Munan, Human; s. of the late Wang Zhen; joined China Int. Trust and Investment Corpn (CITIC) 1979, served as Deputy Gen. Man. then Gen. Man. Business Dept, Vice-Pres., Vice-Chair. and Pres. CITIC Hong Kong (Holdings), Vice-Pres. CITIC 1986–93, Pres. 1993–95, Chair. of Bd 1995–2006; Chair. Bd of Dirs Poly Group 1991–2007; Chair. Planning Comm. Gansu Prov. People's Govt; Chief Procurator Guangdong Prov. People's Procuratorate; Chair. and Exec. Dir Goldbond Group Holdings 2007–; Chair. China Professional Golfers' Asscn; mem. 10th CPPCC Nat. Cttee. *Leisure interests:* golf, go. *Address:* Goldbond Group Holdings Ltd, 1901-06, Tower 1, Lippo Centre, 89 Queensway, Hong Kong Special Administrative Region, People's Republic of China. *Telephone:* (852) 2111 5666 (office). *E-mail:* www.goldbondgroup.com (office).

WANG, Junxia; Chinese fmr athlete; b. Jan. 1973, Dalian, Liaoning Prov.; m. Zhan Yu; under tutelage of coach Ma Junren set new world record for women's 10,000m race and 3,000m race in 1993; won gold medal in women's 5,000m race (under different coach) in Olympics, Atlanta 1996; retd to study law in Liaoning Prov. 1998; Female Int. Athlete of the Year 1993, Jesse Owens Int. Trophy Award 1994. *Address:* c/o State General Bureau for Physical Culture and Sports, 9 Tiyuguan Road, Chongwen District, Beijing, People's Republic of China (office).

WANG, Gen. Ke; Chinese army officer; *Director, General Logistics Department, People's Liberation Army;* b. Aug. 1931, Xiaoxian Co., Jiangsu Prov.; ed Mil. Acad. of the Chinese PLA; joined CCP-led armed work team 1944; joined CCP 1947; Asst Literacy Teacher, E China Field Army, PLA Services and Arms 1947–48; Deputy Political Instructor, Field Army, Regimental Training Team, PLA Services and Arms 1949; tool part in Jiaozhou Counterattack Battle 1949, Huaihai Campaign 1949; Regimental Staff Officer, Jiangsu Mil. Dist, PLA Nanjing Mil. Region 1949–51; Bn Commdr, PLA, Korea War 1953–56; Deputy Regimental Commdr, later Chief of Staff, Artillery Force, PLA Services and Arms, Korea 1956–61; Section Chief, Training Dept, PLA Artillery School, Beijing 1961–62; Deputy Dir Training Dept, PLA Wuwei Artillery School 1962–64; Deputy Commdr Garrison Div., PLA Lanzhou Mil. Region 1970–72, Political Commissar 1972–78; Div. Commdr PLA 1980–83, Army Commdr 1983–85; Commdr Xinjiang Mil. Dist, Xinjiang Mil. Region 1986–90, Commdr Lanzhou Mil. Region 1990–92; Commdr Shenyang Mil. Region 1992–95; Dir PLA Gen. Logistics Dept 1995–; rank of Lt-Gen. 1988, Gen. 1994; mem. 14th CCP Cen. Cttee 1992–97, 15th CCP Cen. Cttee 1997–2002; mem. CCP Cen. Cttee Cen. Mil. Comm. 1992–97; mem. Cen. Mil. Comm. of People's Repub. of China 1995–. *Address:* People's Liberation Army General Logistics Department, Beijing, People's Republic of China (office).

WANG, Kefen; Chinese dance historian; b. 1 April 1927, Yunyang, Chongqing; d. of Wang Baifan and Liao Huiqing; m. Zhang Wengang 1949; one s. one d.; choreographer and dancer Cen. Nat. Song and Dance Co. 1952–58; Research Fellow Chinese Nat. Dance Asscn 1956–66, Inst. of Dance, China Nat. Arts Acad. (CNAA) 1977–; Academic Prize, Arts Acad. of China 1989, Award for Special Contrib., State Council of China, Award for Outstanding Contribs of Culture and Educ. Exchange, Columbus, USA. *Publications:* The History of Chinese Dance 1980, The Stories of Ancient Chinese Dancers 1983, The History of Chinese Dance: Ming Dynasty, Qing Dynasty 1984, Sui Dynasty and Tang Dynasty 1987 (CNAA Research Excellence Award 1989), The History of Chinese Dance Development (CNAA Research Excellence Award 1994, Chinese Ministry of Culture Art Research Award 1999); Dictionary of Chinese Dance (Chief Ed.) (Nat. Award for Best Dictionary 1995); Chief Ed. on subject of dance in 10-vol. History of Chinese Civilization (Nat. Award for Best Book 1994); Sui and Tang Culture (Co-Ed. and contrib.) 1990 (Social Science Book Award 1992), Chinese Dance of the 20th Century 1991 (Nat. Best Book Award 1993), Buddhism and Chinese Dance 1991, Chinese Ancient Dance History (co-author), The Chinese Contemporary History of Dance 1840–1996 (Ed.-in-Chief), The Music and Dance of the Tang Dynasty recorded in Japanese History 1999, The Culture of the Wei Dynasty, Jin Dynasty, Northern Dynasty and Southern Dynasty (jtly) 2000, Chinese Dance: An Illustrated History (First Prize, Chinese Ministry of Culture Art Research Awards 2006) 2002, The Complete Works of Dunhuang Caves – Dance Vol. 2001, On the Development and Far-reaching Significance of the Chinese Palace Dance 2004, Dance from Heaven to Earth (Dunhuang Myth series) 2007, and other works on Chinese Dance. *Leisure interests:* choreography, writing and dance.

WANG, Kui; Chinese chemist; *Director, National Laboratory of Natural Medicine and Bionic Medicine, Beijing Medical University;* b. 7 May 1928, Tianjin; ed Yanjing Univ.; teaching asst, Beijing Medical Univ., Instructor, Assoc. Prof., Prof., Chair. of Dept, Dean Pharmaceutics School, Dean Coll. of Pharmaceutics, now Dir Nat. Laboratory of Natural Medicine and Bionic Medicine 1950–; Chair. Chem. Dept of Nat. Natural Science Foundation; Fellow, Chinese Acad. of Science 1991–; mem. 4th Presidium, Chinese Acad. of Sciences 2000–; Chinese Acad. of Sciences Award for Advancement in Science and Tech. (2nd Class), State Educ. Comm. Award for Advancement in Science and Tech. (2nd Class). *Publications:* over 100 research papers. *Address:* Beijing Medical University, 38 Xue Yuan Ju, Beijing 100083, People's Republic of China (office). *Telephone:* (10) 62091334 (office). *Fax:* (10) 62015681 (office). *E-mail:* dxb@mail.bjmu.edu.cn (office). *Website:* www.bjmu.edu.cn (office).

WANG, Lequan; Chinese politician; *Secretary, Xinjiang Uygur Autonomous Regional Committee, Chinese Communist Party;* b. Dec. 1944, Shouguang Co., Shandong Prov.; sent to do manual labour, Jiaonan Co., Shandong Prov. 1965–66; joined CCP 1966; Deputy Head, Houzhen Commune, Shouguang Co. 1966–75, mem. Standing Cttee CCP Revolutionary Cttee and Standing Cttee CCP Party Cttee 1966–75, Deputy Sec. CCP Shouguang Co. Cttee and Vice-Chair. CCP Revolutionary Cttee 1975–82; Deputy Sec. CCP Party Cttee, Chengguan Commune 1966–75; Deputy Sec. CCP Communist Youth League of China Shandong Prov. Cttee 1982–86; Deputy Sec. CCP Liaocheng Prefectural Cttee 1986–88, Sec. 1988–89; Vice-Gov. Shandong Prov. 1989–91; Vice-Chair. Xinjiang Uygur Autonomous Regional People's Congress 1991–95; Deputy Sec. CCP Xinjiang Uygur Autonomous Regional Cttee 1992–94, Acting Sec. 1994–95, Sec. 1995–; First Political Commissar, Production and Construction Corps, Xinjiang Uygur Autonomous Region 1995–; Alt. mem. 14th CCP Cen. Cttee 1992–97, mem. 15th CCP Cen. Cttee

1997–2002, 16th CCP Cen. Cttee 2002–07 (mem. Politburo 2002–07), 17th CCP Cen. Cttee 2007– (mem. Politburo 2007–). *Address:* Chinese Communist Party Xinjiang Uygur Autonomous Regional Committee, Urumqi City, Xinjiang Uygur Autonomous Region, People's Republic of China (office).

WANG, Lianzheng, MTAA, PhD; Chinese agronomist and administrator; *President, China Seed Association*; *President, China Agricultural Technology Association;* b. 15 Oct. 1930, Haicheng, Liaoning Prov.; s. of Wang Dianche and Wang Youzhen; m. Li Shuzhen 1959; two d.; ed Northeast Agricultural Coll., Harbin and Moscow Timiryazeev Agricultural Acad.; Asst Prof., Heilongjiang Acad. of Agricultural Sciences (HAAS) 1964–78, Assoc. Prof. 1979–82, Prof. 1983–; Dir Soybean and Crop Breeding Inst. HAAS 1970–78; Vice-Pres. HAAS 1978–82, Pres. 1983–86, Vice-Gov. Heilongjiang Prov. (in charge of Agricultural Production, Science and Tech.) 1983–87; Vice-Minister of Agric. 1988–91; mem. Agricultural Devt Group at State Council 1988–93; mem. and Convenor Plant Genetics, Breeding, Cultivation Academic Degree Cttee at State Council 1991–96; Pres. Chinese Acad. of Agricultural Sciences (CAAS) 1987–94, Pres. and Prof. Grad. School CAAS 1988–95, Hon. Chair. Acad. Cttee of CAAS 1995–; Vice-Chair. Chinese Crop Science Soc. 1988–94, Chair. 1994–2002; Vice-Chair. Scientific Tech. Cttee (Ministry of Agric.) 1988–96, Chinese Cttee for Release of New Crop Varieties 1989–96, Vice-Pres. China Asscn for Science and Tech. 1991–2001, Heilongjiang Asscn of Science and Tech., Chinese Asscn of Agricultural Science Socs; Chair. China Int. Exchange Asscn of Agricultural Science and Tech. 1992–96; mem. Bd IFAD 1988–91, Centre for Agric. and Biosciences (CABI) 1994–97; Co-Chair. Advisory Cttee China-EC Centre for Agricultural Tech. 1992–97; Pres. China Seed Asscn 1998–, China Agricultural Tech. Soc. 2000–; mem. Chinese dels to numerous int. confs; Deputy to NPC; mem. Agricultural and Rural Affairs Cttee of Congress 1998–2003; has developed 24 soya bean cultivars; Foreign mem. Russian Acad. of Agricultural Sciences 1988–; Foreign Fellow Indian Nat. Acad. of Agricultural Sciences 1994–; Second Class Chinese State Prize for Invention, for new soyabean cultivar 'Heinong 26', Second Class Chinese State Prize for Invention, for new potato cultivar 'Kexin No. 1', First Class Prize for Scientific Progress, Ministry of Agric., for collection and investigation of wild soya bean; Second Class Heilongjiang Prov. Prize for Tech. Progress, for high-yielding high-protein soyabean cultivar 'Heinong 35' 1994. *Publications:* Feeding a Billion (co-author) 1987, Soyabean Breeding and Genetics (Ed.-in-Chief) 1992, Agriculture in Modern China (co-ed.) 1992, Soyabean Cultivation for High Yielding (Ed.-in-Chief) 1994 and more than 164 papers. *Leisure interest:* classical music. *Address:* Chinese Academy of Agricultural Sciences, 12 Zhongguancun Nan (Southern) Street, Haidian District, Beijing 100081 (office); Cui wei xili 14-12-2, Haidian District, Beijing, 100036, People's Republic of China (home). *Telephone:* (10) 68975138 (office); (10) 68258061 (home); (10) 68919388. *Fax:* (10) 68975184 (office); (10) 68975138. *E-mail:* wanglz@mail.caas.net.cn (office).

WANG, Linxiang; Chinese business executive; *President and Chairman, Erdos Group;* b. 1951, Baotou, Nei Monggol Autonomous Region; joined CCP 1974; Dir Erdos Cashmere Sweater Mill 1983–89; Pres. and Chair. Bd Erdos Group 1989–; Standing Dir Asscn of Inner Mongolia Import and Export Firms 1997; Vice-Chair. CPPCC Yih Ju Autonomous League Cttee, Inner Mongolia Autonomous Region; Deputy to NPC; mem. All-China Youth Fed.; Hon. Chair. Asscn of Friendship Liaison of Yih Ju League 1999; numerous awards including Sr Economist, Silver Medal of Nat. Frontier Talents, State Econ. and Trade Comm., named Inner Mongolia Most Outstanding Entrepreneur, Model Worker in China's Textile Circle, Nat. Model Worker, Nat. Most Outstanding Young Entrepreneur, Most Outstanding Member of CCP. *Address:* Erdos Group, Baotou, Nei Monggol, People's Republic of China (office). *Website:* www.chinaerdos.com/english (office).

WANG, Liqin; Chinese table tennis player; b. 18 June 1978, Shanghai; began playing aged six and was picked for Chinese men's nat. squad aged 15 in 1993; numerous titles; winner men's singles: Asian Youth Championships 1994, Pro Tour Grand Finals 1998, 2000, Asian Championships 1998, World Championships, Osaka 2001, Asian Games, Busan 2002, World Championships, Shanghai 2005, World Championships, Zagreb 2007; winner men's doubles: Pro Tour Grand Finals 1996, 1998, 2000, 2007, Olympic Games, Sydney 2000 (gold medal), World Championships 2001, 2003; winner mixed doubles: Asian Championships 1998, Asian Games 1998; winner team events: Asian Championships 1998, 2000, Asian Games 1998, 2000, World Championships, Osaka 2001, World Championships 2006, Olympic Games, Beijing 2008 (gold medal); men's singles, Olympic Games, Athens 2004, Beijing 2008 (bronze medal); has won highest number of pro tours, winning more than 20; ranked No. 1 (Int. Table Tennis Fed. —ITTF) in the world 2005, No. 3 2007, No. 4 July 2008; plays for Shanghai city team. *Address:* c/o Chinese Table Tennis Federation, C3 Longtan Road, Chongwen District, Beijing 100061, People's Republic of China.

WANG, Luolin; Chinese economist; *Vice-Chairman, CPPCC Economic Subcommittee;* b. June 1938, Wuchang City, Hunan Prov.; ed Beijing Univ.; joined CCP 1978; Asst Lecturer, Lecturer, Assoc. Prof., Amoy Univ. 1961–84; Deputy Dean, later Vice-Pres. Amoy Univ. 1984; Vice-Pres. Chinese Acad. of Social Sciences 1993–2005, now Special Adviser and Prof.; Vice-Chair. State Academic Degrees Cttee 1999; Alt. mem. 13th CCP Cen. Cttee 1987–92, 14th CCP Cen. Cttee 1992–97, mem. 15th CCP Cen. Cttee 1997–2002, Alt. mem. 16th CCP Cen. Cttee 2002–07; Vice-Chair. CPPCC Econ. Sub-Cttee 2005–; Hon. PhD (Hong Kong Lingnan Univ.). *Publications:* Blue Book of China's Economy (co-ed. annually). *Address:* Chinese Academy of Social Sciences, Jianguomennei Dajie 5 Hao, Beijing 100732, People's Republic of China (office). *Telephone:* (10) 65137744 (office). *Fax:* (10) 65138154 (office). *E-mail:* wangll@cass.net.cn (office). *Website:* www.cass.net.cn (office).

WANG, Maolin; Chinese party and government official; b. 1934, Qidong, Jiangsu Prov.; ed Shanghai Financial and Econ. Coll.; joined CCP 1956; Vice-Chair. Shanxi Prov. Revolutionary Cttee 1977–78; Mayor Taiyuan City, Shanxi Prov. 1979–83; Vice-Gov. Shanxi Prov. 1979–83; Vice-Chair. Shanxi Prov. People's Congress 1981–88; Deputy Sec. Shanxi Prov. Cttee 1988–91, Sec. 1991; Chair. 7th CPPCC Shanxi Prov. Cttee 1993; Sec. 7th CCP Hunan Prov. Cttee 1993–98; mem. 13th CCP Cen. Cttee 1987–92, 14th CCP Cen. Cttee 1992–97, 15th CCP Cen. Cttee 1997–2002; Vice-Chair. 10th NPC Law Cttee 2003–. *Address:* c/o Central Committee of the Chinese Communist Party, Zhongnanhai, Beijing, People's Republic of China (office).

WANG, Gen. Maorun; Chinese army officer; *Political Commissar, National Defence University;* b. May 1936, Rongcheng, Shandong Prov.; ed Mil. Acad. of the Chinese PLA; joined PLA 1951, CCP 1956; staff officer, Qingdao Garrison 1962; various posts in a corps political dept 1969–73; Deputy Sec.-Gen. Political dept Jinan Mil. Region 1973–76; Dir of a corps political dept 1976–83; corps deputy political commissar 1983–85; Dir Political Dept PLA Lanzhou Mil. Region 1985–90; Deputy Political Commissar and Sec. CCP Comm. for Inspecting Discipline, Lanzhou Mil. Region 1990; Political Commissar, Nat. Defence Univ. 1990–; rank of Maj.-Gen. 1988, Lt-Gen. 1993, Gen. 1998; mem. 15th CCP Cen. Cttee 1997–2002; Del., 11th CCP Nat. Congress 1977–82. *Address:* , Beijing, People's Republic of China (office).

WANG, Meng; Chinese politician and writer; b. 15 Oct. 1934, Beijing; s. of Wang Jindi and Tong Min; m. Cui Ruifang 1957; two s. one d.; joined CCP 1948; criticized 1957–76; rehabilitated 1979; Minister of Culture 1986–89; mem. Secr. Chinese Writers' Asscn 1981–86, Vice-Pres. 1986–89, Vice-Chair. 2001; Vice-Pres. China PEN Centre 1982–; Vice-Pres. Asscn for Int. Understanding 1985–; Chief Ed. People's Literature 1983–86; Alt. mem. 12th Cen. Cttee CCP 1982–85, mem. 12th Cen. Cttee CCP 1985–87, 13th Cen. Cttee 1987–92; mem. Standing Cttee 8th CPPCC Nat. Cttee 1993–98, Standing Cttee 9th CPPCC Nat. Cttee 1998–2003. *Publications include:* The Young Newcomer in the Organization Department 1956, Long Live the Youth 1957, Bolshevik State: A Modernist Chinese Novel 1979, The Barber's Tale 1979, A Night in the City 1979, A Spate of Visitors 1980, The Butterfly 1980, The Metamorphosis of Human Nature 1986, Selected Works (Vols I–IV) 1986, Adventures of a Soccer Star 1990, You Can Come into My Dream Again 1991, Revelation from The Dream of Red Mansion 1991, Notes on Styles (collection of literary criticisms) 1991, The Seasons for Love 1992, Hard Gruel (short stories) 1992, The Season for Losing Self-Control 1995, The Season for Hesitation 1997, The Season for Carnivals 2000. *Leisure interests:* swimming, drinking. *Address:* China PEN, Shatan Beijie 2, Beijing, People's Republic of China (office).

WANG, Mengkui; Chinese academic; b. April 1938, Wenxian Co., Henan Prov.; ed Beijing Univ.; joined CCP 1956; Ed. Red Flag Magazine 1964–69; Assoc. Research Fellow then Research Fellow, Research Dept of Secr. CCP Cen. Cttee 1981–87; Exec. Vice-Dir Econs Research Centre of State Planning Comm. 1987; Deputy Dir Research Office of State Council 1990–95, Dir 1995–98, Dir Devt Research Centre of the State Council 1998–2007; Alt. mem. 14th CCP Cen. Cttee 1992–97, mem. 15th CCP Cen. Cttee 1997–2002; Dir (non-exec.) Aluminum Corpn of China 2008–. *Publications:* China's Economic Transformation over 20 Years 2000, China in the Wake of Asia's Financial Crisis 2008, Good Governance in China - A Way Towards Social Harmony 2008. *Address:* Development Research Centre of the State Council, No 225, Chaoyangmen Nei Dajie, Beijing 100010, People's Republic of China (office). *E-mail:* drc@drc.gov.cn (office). *Website:* www.drc.gov.cn (office).

WANG, Nan; Chinese table tennis player; b. 23 Oct. 1978, Fushun City, Liaoning Prov.; started playing aged seven; joined Liaoning prov. table tennis team in 1989 and nat. team in 1993; numerous titles; winner women's singles: Swedish Open 1994, Asian Youth Championships 1994, World Cup 1997, 1998, 2003, Pro Tour Grand Finals 1998, 2001, Asian Games, Bangkok 1998, World Championships 1999, 2001, 2003, Olympic Games, Sydney 2000 (gold medal); winner women's doubles: Asian Championships 1996, Pro Tour Grand Finals 1997, 1998, 1999, Asian Games 1998, World Championships 1999, 2001, 2003, Olympic Games, Sydney 2000 (gold medal), Athens 2004 (gold medal); winner mixed doubles: Asian Games 1998, Asian Championships 1998, World Championships 2003; winner women's team events: Asian Youth Championships 1994, Asian Championships 1996, 1998, World Championships 1997, 2000, 2001, Asian Games 1998, Olympic Games, Beijing 2008 (gold medal); runner-up in women's singles and women's team events, Asian Games, Busan 2002; women's singles, Olympic Games, Beijing 2008 (silver medal); ranked World No. 1 1999–2001; has led Chinese women's table-tennis team following retirement of Deng Yaping. *Leisure interests:* listening to music, watching television, reading, playing tennis. *Address:* c/o Chinese Table Tennis Federation, C3 Longtan Road, Chongwen District, Beijing 100061, People's Republic of China.

WANG, Qimin; Chinese petroleum executive; *President, Daqing Research Institute of Oilfield Exploration and Development;* b. 1937; ed Beijing Petroleum Inst.; joined CCP 1978; technician, Vice-Chief Geologist, Sr Engineer and then Vice-Pres. Daqing Research Inst. of Oilfield Exploration and Devt 1961–96, Pres. 1996–; took part as torch-bearer in Olympic Flame Relay, Daqing July 2008; China Gen. Co. of Oil and Natural Gas Iron Man Achievement Prize. *Address:* Daqing Research Institute of Oilfield Exploration and Development, Daqing 163000, Heilongjiang Province, People's Republic of China (office).

WANG, Qishan; Chinese economist and politician; *Vice-Premier, State Council;* b. July 1948, Tianzhen, Shanxi Prov.; ed Northwest China Univ.; Researcher, Modern History Inst., Chinese Acad. of Social Sciences 1982, Researcher, Secr. (Rural Policies Dept) CCP Cen. Cttee Politboro 1982; joined

CCP 1983; Div. Head, Rural Devt Research Centre of State Council, Acting Dir then Dir Rural Devt Inst. 1982–87; Gen. Man. China Rural Trust and Investment Corpn 1988–89; Vice-Pres. Construction Bank of China 1989–93, Pres. 1994–97; Vice-Gov. People's Bank of China 1993–94, Gov. 1994 (Sec. CCP Party Cttee); Chair. of China Investment Bank 1994–97; Chair. China Int. Capital Corpn Ltd 1995–97; mem. CCP Standing Cttee Guangdong Prov. Cttee 1997–2000; Exec. Vice-Gov. Guangdong Prov. 1998–2000; Dir Econ. Restructuring Office of the State Council 2000–; Sec. Econ. System Reform Scheme Office, CCP Party Cttee 2000–02; Sec. CCP Hainan Prov. Cttee 2002–03; Chair. Standing Cttee Hainan Prov. People's Congress 2003; mem. Standing Cttee CCP Beijing Municipal Cttee 2003–, Deputy Sec. CCP Beijing Municipal Cttee 2003–; apptd Acting Mayor of Beijing 2003–04, elected Mayor and Exec. Chair. . Beijing Organizing Cttee for XXIX Olympiad and Deputy Sec. Leading Party Mem.'s Group 2004–07; Alt. mem. 15th CCP Cen. Cttee 1997–2002, mem. 16th CCP Cen. Cttee 2002–07, 17th CCP Cen. Cttee 2007–; mem. Politburo of CCP Cen. Cttee 2007–; Vice-Premier State Council and mem. Leading Party Members' Group 2008–. *Address:* Office of the Vice-Premier, Great Hall of the People, West Edge, Tiananmen Square, Beijing, People's Republic of China (office). *Website:* english.gov.cn/links/statecouncil .htm (office).

WANG, Gen. Ruilin; Chinese army officer and party official; b. Dec. 1929, Zhaoyuan Co., Shandong Prov.; joined PLA 1946, CCP 1947; copy clerk, Shandong Mil. Dist (Co. Ind. Bn) PLA Jinan Mil. Region 1946–47; decoder and staff officer, Confidential Div., PLA Northeast Mil. Dist 1947–49; Deputy Section Chief, Confidential Div., Govt Admin. Council 1949–52; Sec. Office of Vice-Premier Deng Xiaoping 1973–76; Dir Vice-Chair.'s Office of CCP Cen. Cttee Mil. Comm., then Chair.'s Office; Deputy Dir of Gen. Office, CCP Cen. Cttee 1983–97, Vice-Dir PLA Gen. Political Dept 1992– (concurrently Dir Office of Deng Xiaoping –1997); mem. 13th CCP Cen. Cttee 1987–92 (Sec. Comm. for Discipline Inspection CCP Cen. Cttee Mil. Comm. 1990–93), 14th CCP Cen. Cttee 1992–97 (mem. Cen. Mil. Comm. 1995–97), 15th CCP Cen. Cttee 1997–2002; rank of Lt-Gen. 1988, Gen. 1994. *Address:* Central Office, Chinese Communist Party Central Committee, Beijing, People's Republic of China (office).

WANG, Senhao; Chinese government official; b. 1933, Cixi, Zhejiang Prov.; two s.; joined CCP 1955; Dir Mining Admin, Shanxi Prov. 1970–82; Sec. CCP Party Cttee, Shanxi Prov. 1970–82; Deputy Sec. CCP Party Cttee, Shaanxi Prov. 1983–93; Gov. of Shanxi Prov. 1983–92; Minister of Coal Industry 1993–98; mem. CCP 12th Cen. Cttee 1982–87, 13th Cen. Cttee 1987–92, 14th Cen. Cttee 1992–97; mem. Standing Cttee 9th CPPCC Nat. Cttee 1998–2003, Chair. Society and the Rule of Law Cttee. *Address:* National Committee of Chinese People's Political Consultative Conference, 23 Taipingqiao Street, Beijing, People's Republic of China (office).

WANG, Shenghong; Chinese university administrator; *President, Fudan University;* b. 1942, Shanghai; ed Shanghai Univ. of Science and Tech., Purdue Univ. and Univ. of Tex., USA; fmr Dir and Party Sec., Higher Educ. Bureau, Shanghai, fmr Chair. Shanghai Educ. Asscn for Int. Exchange; fmr Pres. Shanghai Univ. of Science and Tech.; apptd Head, CCP Municipal Cttee, United Front Work Dept, Shanghai 1984, Vice-Chair., CPPCC Municipal Cttee, Shanghai 1995–; Assoc. Dir, China Electro-Mechanical Eng Asscn 1980–90; del. to 15th Nat. CCP Congress, 9th CPPCC 1998–2003, 6th and 7th CCP Congress of Shanghai, 7th and 10th People's Congress of Shanghai; Pres. Fudan Univ. 1998–; mem. Univ. Grants Cttee of Hong Kong, Int. Academic Advisory Panel, Ministry of Educ., Singapore; Dr hc (Univ. of Manchester, UK, Nat. Univ. of Ireland, Waseda Univ., Japan, Chonnam Nat. Univ., South Korea); Chinese Acad. of Sciences Award for Scientific and Technological Breakthroughs 1986, First Prize, Nat. Awards for Scientific and Technological Advancement 1987, First Prize, Shanghai Awards for Scientific and Technological Advancement 1990, Outstanding Worker in the Frontline of Science and Tech. of Shanghai, Outstanding Worker in the Frontline of Educ. of Shanghai, Shanghai Model Worker, President's Medal, George Washington Univ., USA. *Publications:* Structural Design of Electronic Apparatus, Finite Element Method and Its Application; over 40 papers in scientific journals. *Address:* Office of the President, Fudan University, 220 Handan Road, Shanghai 200433, People's Republic of China (office). *Telephone:* (21) 65642222 (office). *Website:* www.fudan.edu.cn (office).

WANG, Shi; Chinese business executive; *Chairman, Shenzhen Wanke Enterprise Ltd;* b. Jan. 1951, Liuzhou, Guanxi Prov.; ed Lanzhou Railway Inst.; worker, Railway Bureau, Guangzhou City (Shenzhen Econ. Special Zone), Guangdong Prov.; f. Modern Scientific and Educational Instrument Exhbn Centre, Shenzhen City, Guangdong Prov., Gen. Man. Shenzhen Vanke Co. Ltd Exhbn Centre 1984, Corp. Rep., Shenzhen Vanke Co. Ltd 1988, Gen. Man. 1988–99, Chair. and CEO Shenzhen Wanke Enterprise Ltd 1988–99, Chair. 1999–; Vice-Chair. Shenzhen Real Estate Asscn, Shenzhen Gen. Chamber of Commerce; Standing Dir China Real Estate Asscn (Vice-Dean City House Devt Cttee); initiated China Urban Real Estate Developers' Collaborative Network 1999; initiated and organized 'New Residence Forum' Shanghai Conf. and promoted New Residence Campaign 2000; elected one of the Top Ten Econ. Figures in China 2000. *Publications:* Wang Shi: Twenty Years with Wanke 2006. *Leisure interest:* mountaineering. *Address:* Shenzhen Wanke Enterprise Ltd, Shenzhen 518003, Guangdong Province, People's Republic of China (office).

WANG, Shouguan; Chinese astronomer and university professor; b. 15 Jan. 1923, Fuzhou; s. of B. L. Wang and S. Y. Gao; m. Lin Zhihuan 1955; one s. one d.; Deputy Head, Div. of Math. and Physics, Chinese Acad. of Sciences 1981–; Prof., Beijing Normal Univ. 1987–, Univ. of Science and Tech. of China 1991–; Chief Ed. Vol. Astronomy, Chinese Encyclopaedia 1980; Chief Ed. Astrophysics Sinica; mem. Chinese Acad. of Sciences 1981; Hon. Dir Beijing Astronomical Observatory 1987–; Hon. Pres. Chinese Astronomical Soc. 1988–; Nat. Science Congress Award 1978, Nat. Science and Tech. Progress Award 1985. *Leisure interest:* poetry. *Address:* Beijing Normal University, Xinyiekouwai Street 19, Beijing 100875 (office); No. 404, Block 808, Zhong-Guan-Cun, Beijing 100080, People's Republic of China. *Telephone:* (10) 62207960 (office). *Fax:* (10) 62200074 (office). *E-mail:* ipo@bnu.edu.cn (office). *Website:* www.bnu .edu.cn (office).

WANG, Shucheng; Chinese politician; b. Dec. 1941, Liyang, Jiangsu Prov.; ed Tsinghua Univ., Beijing; joined CCP 1965; technician, then Deputy Sec. Eng Bureau No. 6, Ministry of Water Resources and Power Industry 1968–84; Deputy Chief, 1st Eng Section, 6th Eng Bureau, Ministry of Power Industry 1980; Deputy Gen. Man. Water Conservancy and Hydroelectric Power Construction Co. 1984–86, Deputy Dir 1986–87, Dir 1987–88; Dir Dept of Hydroelectric Devt, Ministry of Energy 1988–93; Vice-Minister of Power Industry 1993–97; Deputy Gen. Man. State Power Corpn 1997–98; Minister of Water Resources 1998–2007; mem. 16th CCP Cen. Cttee 2002–07. *Address:* c/o Ministry of Water Resources, 2 Baiguang Lu, Ertiao, Xuanwu Qu, Beijing 100053, People's Republic of China (office).

WANG, Shuguo, DEng; Chinese engineer and university administrator; *President, Harbin Institute of Technology;* b. 1958, Hebei Prov.; ed Harbin Inst. of Tech.; joined CCP 1976, Sec., CCP Prov. Cttee, Heilongjiang Prov. Science and Tech. Comm. 1993–2003; Visiting Scholar, Univ. of Paris VI, Pierre et Marie Curie, France 1987–89; Prof. of Mechanical Design, Harbin Inst. of Tech., becoming Deputy Dean, Inst. of Robotics Research 1989–93, Dean, Mechanical and Electrical Eng Coll. 1993–98, Vice-Pres., Harbin Inst. of Tech. 1998–99, Pres. 2003–; Deputy Dir State 863 Project, Intelligent Robot Research Programme 1993–2003; Deputy 10th NPC 2003–08; seven consecutive awards of Advanced Prize in Science and Tech. from Heilongjiang Prov. Govt. *Publications:* over 70 academic papers. *Address:* Office of the President, Harbin Institute of Technology, 92 West Dazhi Street, Nan Gang District, Harbin 150001, People's Republic of China (office). *Telephone:* (451) 86413925 (office). *Website:* en.hit.edu.cn (office).

WANG, Shuo; Chinese writer; b. 1958, Nanjing; spent four years in navy, then worked at various jobs before becoming a full-time writer 1983; first novel Air Stewardesses published 1984; collected works banned by authorities in China 1996; has written over 20 novels with 10 million copies in print, has written scripts for TV and films including work for American Zeotrope, USA. *Film screenplays include:* The Trouble-Shooters 1989, I Love You 2002, Little Red Flowers 2006, Dreams May Come 2006. *Publications include:* Playing for Thrills (translated into English 1997), Please Don't Call Me Human (translated into English 1998), A Sigh 2000, A Conversation with Our Daughter 2008. *Address:* c/o No Exit Press, 16 Capitol Court, 128 School Lane, Didsbury, Manchester, M20 6LB, England (office). *Telephone:* (161) 445 6635 (office). *Website:* www.noexit.co.uk (office).

WANG, Shuwen; Chinese constitutional lawyer; b. 3 April 1927, Qingshen, Sichuan Prov.; ed Sichuan Univ., Univ. of Moscow, USSR; joined CCP 1957; Asst Researcher, Law Research Inst. of Chinese Acad. of Sciences 1957–79; Research Fellow and Dir Nat. Law Research Section of Law Research Inst. of Chinese Acad. of Social Sciences, then Dir of the Inst.; Vice-Chair. Chinese Law Soc. 1979–; took part in drafting the Basic Laws for Hong Kong and Macao and in revising the Chinese Constitution; mem. Standing Cttee 8th NPC 1993–98, Vice-Chair. Law Cttee. *Publications:* Xianfa Jiben Zhishi Jianghua (The ABC of the Constitution), Faxue Jiben Zhishi Jianghua (The ABC of the Science of Law), Wo Guo Renmin Daibiao Dahui Zhidu (The System of China's People's Congress), Xianggang Tebie Xingzheng Qu Jiben Fa Daolun (Introduction to the Basic Law of Hong Kong Special Admin. Region) and Aomen Tebie Xingzheng Qu Jiben Fa Daolun (Introduction to the Basic Law of Macao Special Admin. Region). *Address:* 15 Shatan Bei Jie, Beijing 100720, People's Republic of China. *Telephone:* (10) 64043942.

WANG, Sung; Chinese zoologist and conservationist; b. 1933, Jiangsu; ed Fudan Univ., Shanghai; researcher, Inst. of Zoology, Chinese Acad. of Science, Beijing, later Pres.; was part of first team to catalogue flora and fauna in some of remotest parts of China; work interrupted during Cultural Revolution late 1960s; scientific adviser to Cities Treaty early 1980s; mem. China Council for Int. Cooperation on Environment and Devt; reintroduced Père David deer, extinct in China since 1901, from captive stock in UK; highlighted importance of indigenous domestic stock such as yak of high Tibetan plateau; brought in outside conservation expertise from countries such as UK, Japan and USA; involved with Eco Security Task Force, set up to control 'alien invasive species' in China; Joseph Grinnell Award 1998, Edinburgh Medal 2003. *Publications:* numerous articles in scientific journals. *Address:* c/o Institute of Zoology, Chinese Academy of Sciences, 25 Beisihuanxi Road, Haidan, Beijing 100080, People's Republic of China (office). *Telephone:* (10) 6254-7675 (office). *Fax:* (10) 6256-5689 (office). *E-mail:* wangs@panda.ioz.ac.cn (office). *Website:* www.oiz .ac.cn (office).

WANG, Taihua; Chinese politician; *Director, State Administration for Radio, Film and Television;* b. Oct. 1945, Xingguo, Jiangxi Prov.; ed Jiangxi Teachers' Coll., CCP Cen. Cttee Cen. Party School; worker, No. 9 Regiment, Jiangxi Production and Construction Corps, Jiangxi Prov. 1968–70; joined CCP 1973; Vice-Principal No. 3 Secondary School, Ganzhou City, Jiangxi Prov. 1978; Vice-Pres. Ganzhou City Educ. School 1979; mem. Standing Cttee CCP Ganzhou City Cttee and Head, Publicity Dept 1980; Deputy Commr Ganzhou Prefectural Admin. Office 1983; mem. Standing Cttee CCP Jiangxi Prov. Cttee and Head, Publicity Dept 1985; Vice-Sec. CCP Anhui Prov. Cttee 1992–2000, Sec. 2000–04; Sec. CCP Hefei City Cttee 1992–98; Vice-Gov. Anhui Prov. 1998–99, Gov. 1999–2001; Chair. Standing Cttee Anhui Prov. People's Congress 2003–04; Dir State Admin for Radio, Film and TV 2007–;

Alt. mem. 14th CCP Cen. Cttee 1992–97, 15th CCP Cen. Cttee 1997–2002, mem. 16th CCP Cen. Cttee 2002–07, 17th CCP Cen. Cttee 2007–; Deputy 8th NPC 1983–88; Del., 13th CCP Nat. Congress 1987–92, 14th CCP Nat. Congress 1992–97, 15th CCP Nat. Congress 1997–2002, 16th CCP Nat. Congress 2002–. *Address:* State Administration for Radio, Film and Television, 2 Fu Xing Men Wai Dajie, Beijing 100866, People's Republic of China. *Telephone:* (10) 86092098 (office). *E-mail:* sarft@chinasarft.gov.cn (office). *Website:* www.sarft.gov.cn (office).

WANG, Tao; Chinese geologist; *Honorary Chairman, Sino Union Petroleum & Chemical International Ltd;* b. 1931, Leting, Hebei Prov.; joined CCP 1948; Chief Geologist, Dagang Oil Field; Chief Geologist, Liaohe Petroleum Prospecting Bureau; Gen. Man., South China Sea Eastern Br. of China Nat. Offshore Oil Corpn; Minister of Petroleum Industry 1985–88; Pres. China Nat. Petroleum Corpn 1988–97; Exec. Dir Sino Union Petroleum & Chemical International Ltd, currently Hon. Chair.; Prof. China Univ. of Petroleum; Chair. Chinese Nat. Cttee for World Petroleum Council; Vice-Chair. Chinese-Arab Friendship Asscn, Chair. Chinese-Saudi Arabia Friendship Asscn; mem. CCP 12th Cen. Cttee 1982–87, 13th Cen. Cttee 1987–92, 14th Cen. Cttee 1992–97; mem. Standing Cttee 9th NPC 1998–2003, Vice-Chair. Environment and Resources Protection Cttee 1998–2003; Foreign Academician, Russian Acad. of Natural Sciences; World Petroleum Congress Outstanding Contribution Award 2005. *Address:* Sino Union Petroleum & Chemical International Ltd, Unit 1909A–1912, China Merchants Tower, Shun Tak Centre, 168–200 Connaught Road Central, Hong Kong Special Administrative Region, People's Republic of China. *Website:* www.sunpec.com/english/rel_info.htm (office).

WANG, Tian-Ren; Chinese sculptor, artist and calligrapher; b. 26 July 1939, Henan; s. of Zheng-gang Wang and Shu-zheng Ren; m. Zhang Pei 1969; one s.; ed Xian Acad. of Fine Arts; worked as art designer and sculptor at Shaanxi Exhbn Hall 1963–79, worked on construction 1964–65; cr. sculptures for Yanan Revolution Memorial Hall 1968–71; Dir group sculptures for Shaanxi Exhbn Hall 1972–75; participated in group sculptures for Chairman Mao Memorial Hall 1976–78; calligraphy works exhibited in Chinese and Japanese cities; Pres. Shaanxi Sculpture Inst. 1996–2000; Vice-Dir of Sculpture Art Cttee, Shaanxi Br. Nat. Asscn of Artists; Art Dir, Dir of Creation Office, Shaanxi Sculpture Inst.; mem. Nat. Calligraphers Asscn, Shaanxi Folk Art Inst., Shaanxi Industrial Artists Asscn. *Works include:* Hou Ji 1980–81, Flower, The Morning Rooster, Qin Ox, Zebra, Tang Dynasty Musicians in Nishang and Yuyi (Copper Medal, Nat. City Sculptures Designing Exhbn 1983), Letter Carrier Goose (Copper Medal, Nat. City Sculptures Designing Exhbn 1983), Biaoqi General of Han Dynasty Huo Qu-bing (Excellent Prize, 6th Nat. Art Works Exhbn 1984, First Prize, Shaanxi Art Works Exhbn 1984), Rising to the Sky (for Urumuqi, Xinjing; Prize for Excellence, Nat. Ministry of Urban Construction, Nat. Asscn of Artists 1987) 1985, Qin Unification 1992, Unification of Qin Dynasty (selected for 2nd Nat. City Sculpture, Nat. Prize from Nat. Construction Ministry, Ministry of Culture and Asscn of Nat Artists) 1994, Yu Youren (selected for 8th Nat. Arts Exhbn) 1994, sign sculpture for Xijiang Chemical Fertilizer Factory 1995, civic scenery sculpture for Hejin, Shaanxi Prov. 1995, Soar Aloft (sign sculpture for Xian Yanliang city) 1996, Zhao Hongzhang (granite-sculpture) 1996, Hou Ji (stone sculpture for Shaanxi) 1996, large city sign sculpture for Shanxi 1996, Flying Phoenix 1997, Wang Ding 1997, Surpass 1998, Flying 1998, Fountain 1999, Unlimited 1999, Phoenix Sing 1999, Unrestrained and Far-Ranging 2000, Liang Sicheng 2001, Yu Hua Long 2001, Space Navigation 2001, Li Xiaolong 2002, Happy Fish 2002, Shi Qingyun 2002, Doctor Bethune 2002, A group of little girls and boys 2003, Soul of poetry 2004, Canyon of poetry 2004, A group of figures 2004. *Leisure interests:* Chinese classical literature, poetry, music. *Address:* 9 Wenyibeilu, Wenhua Guangxia 14–1, Xian, Shaanxi 710054, People's Republic of China (home); Shaanxi Sculpture Institute, Longshoucun, Xian, Shaanxi 710016, People's Republic of China (office). *Telephone:* (29) 87855551; (29) 6261002 (office); (29) 6253551 (home). *Fax:* (29) 87855551; (29) 3237768.

WANG, Tianpu, MBA, PhD; Chinese oil industry executive; *President, Sinopec (China Petroleum and Chemical) Corporation;* ed Qingdao Chemical Inst., Dalian Polytechnic Univ., Zhejiang Univ.; Vice-Pres. Qilu Petrochemical Co., Sinopec Group 1999–2000, Vice-Pres. Qilu Co., Sinopec Corpn 2000, Pres. Qilu Co., Sinopec Corpn 2000–01, Vice-Pres. Sinopec Corpn 2001–03, Sr Vice-Pres. 2003–05, Pres. 2005–, Dir 2006–. *Address:* Sinopec Corporation, 22 Chaoyangmen North Street, Chaoyang District, Beijing 100728, People's Republic of China (office). *Telephone:* (10) 6499-0060 (office). *Fax:* (10) 6499-0022 (office). *Website:* www.sinopec.com (office); english.sinopec.com (office).

WANG, Vera; American fashion designer; *Chairman and CEO, Vera Wang Bridal House Ltd.;* b. 27 June 1949, New York; d. of Cheng Ching and Florence Wu; m. Arthur Becker; two d.; ed Chapin School, NY, Sarah Lawrence Coll. and Sorbonne Univ., France; trained as figure skater before moving into fashion; Fashion Ed., Vogue USA 1971–87; Design Dir, Ralph Lauren 1987–89; Founder, Chair. and CEO Vera Wang Bridal House Ltd 1990–; Womenswear Designer of the Year, Council of Fashion Designers of America 2005, André Leon Talley Lifetime Achievement Award, Savannah Coll. of Art and Design 2006. *Publications:* Vera Wang on Weddings 2001. *Address:* Vera Wang Bridal House Ltd., 225 West 39th Street, 9th Floor, New York 10018, USA (office). *Telephone:* (212) 575-6400 (office). *Fax:* (212) 354-2548 (office). *Website:* www.verawang.com (office).

WANG, Wayne; Chinese/American film director; b. 1949, Hong Kong; m. Cora Miao; ed Coll. of Arts and Crafts, Oakland, Calif. *Films directed:* Chan is Mission, Dim Sum, Slamdance, Eat a Bowl of Tea, Life is Cheap... But Toilet Paper is Expensive, The Joy Luck Club 1993, Smoke 1995, Blue in the Face 1995, Chinese Box, Anywhere But Here, The Centre of the World 2001, Maid in Manhattan 2002, Because of Winn-Dixie 2005, Last Holiday 2006, A Thousand Years of Good Prayers (Golden Shell for Best Film, San Sebastian Film Festival 2007) 2007, The Princess of Nebraska 2007. *Address:* 916 Kearny Street, San Francisco, CA 94133, USA (office).

WANG, Weicheng; Chinese party official; b. 1929, Tonglu Co., Zhejiang Prov.; joined CCP 1948; Dir Research Office of the State Council 1977–83; Deputy Head of Propaganda Dept, CCP Cen. Cttee 1987; Dir Cen. Policy Research Center 1989–; Vice-Pres. China Asscn for Int. Exchange of Personnel, Soc. for study of Workers' Political and Ideological Work; mem. 14th CCP Cen. Cttee 1992–97; mem. 9th Standing Cttee of Cttee 1998–2003, Chair. Legal Affairs Cttee 1998–2003. *Address:* c/o Standing Committee of National People's Congress, Beijing, People's Republic of China (office).

WANG, Wenshi; Chinese writer; b. 21 Nov. 1921, Shaanxi Prov.; s. of Wang Zhitong and Cui Jinxiu; m. Gao Bin 1949; two s. one d. *Publications:* Comrade-in-Arms (opera libretto), The Night of Wind and Snow, Hei Feng (novel), The Dunes, New Acquaintance, Yiyun Ji (Echo the Views of Others: essay), Wang Wenshi's Prose, Selected Short Stories, Wang Wenshi Miscellany (four vols). *Leisure interests:* ancient poetry, calligraphy. *Address:* Union of Chinese Writers, Shaanxi Branch, Xian, Shaanxi Province (office); Shaanxi Provincial Writers' Union, Xian, Shaanxi Province; 83 Jian Guo Road, Xian, Shaanxi Province, People's Republic of China (home). *Telephone:* (29) 87451006 (office); (29) 85234873 (home).

WANG, Wenyuan; Chinese politician and economist; b. Feb. 1931, Huangpi, Hubei Prov.; ed Northeast China Inst. of Finance and Econs; teaching asst, Lecturer, Assoc. Prof., Prof. and Pres. Econs Coll., Liaoning Univ. 1958–88; Deputy Sec.-Gen. CPPCC, Shenyang City Cttee, Liaoning Prov., 1982–88; mem. Standing Cttee CPPCC Liaoning Prov. Cttee 1982–92; Vice-Chair. Shenyang City Cttee Jiusan Soc. 1982–88, Liaoning Prov. Cttee Jiusan Soc. 1988–92, Cen. Cttee Jiusan Soc. 1988–; Vice-Gov. of Liaoning Prov. 1988–92; Deputy Procurator Gen. Supreme People's Procuratorate 1992–98; Vice-Pres. China Sr Procurators' Training Centre 1992–98; mem. 7th CPPCC Nat. Cttee 1988–93, 8th CPPCC Nat. Cttee 1993–98, 9th CPPCC Nat. Cttee 1998–2003 (Vice-Chair. 1998); Pres. 6th Council of China Council for the Promotion of Peaceful Reunification 1999. *Address:* c/o National Committee of Chinese People's Political Consultative Conference, 23 Taipingqiao Street, Beijing, People's Republic of China (office).

WANG, Wilfred, BEng; Taiwanese business executive; *Chairman and President, Formosa Petrochemical Corporation;* ed Univ. of London, UK; Exec. Vice-Pres. Formosa Petrochemical Corpn 1998–2003, Pres. 2003–, Chair. 2006–; Chair. Mailiao Harbor Admin Corpn, Formosa Plastics Marine Corpn, Formosa Plastics Maritime Corpn. *Address:* Formosa Petrochemical Corpn, 1-1, Formosa Plastics Group Industrial Zone Mailiao, Yunlin, Taiwan (office). *Telephone:* (2) 27122211 (office). *Fax:* (2) 87128050 (office). *E-mail:* cychiou@fpcc.com.tw (office). *Website:* www.fpcc.com.tw (office); www.fpg.com.tw (office).

WANG, Xianjin; Chinese politician; b. 1930, Haiyang, Shandong; fmr Vice-Sec. Jilin, concurrently Dir State Bureau of Land Admin; Pres. Asscn of Land Valuers of China 1994–. *Address:* Association of Land Valuers of China, Beijing, People's Republic of China (office).

WANG, Xianzhang; Chinese insurance executive; b. May 1942, Hebei Prov.; ed Liaoning Finance & Econ. Inst. (now Northeastern Univ. of Finance and Econs); began career in insurance industry 1965, held positions successively as Gen.-Man. People's Insurance Co. of PICC, Liaoning Br., Vice-Pres. PICC, Vice-Pres. People's Insurance (Group) Co. of China, Pres. China Insurance H.K. (Holding) Co. Ltd, Chair. and Pres. China Life Insurance Co. Ltd 2000–05; Vice-Pres. Insurance Inst. of China; mem. China Enterprise Confed. & China Enterprise Dirs Asscn (CEC-CED); mem. CP, Del. CPC Nat. and mem. People's Political Consultative Congress. *Publications include:* China Insurance Dictionary, Insurance Marketing Psychology, An Insurance Specialist's Comments of Insurance. *Address:* c/o China Life Insurance Company Ltd, 16 Chaowai Avenue, Chaoyang District, Beijing 100020, People's Republic of China (office).

WANG, Xiaochu, DBA; Chinese telecommunications industry executive; *President, China Telecommunications Corporation (China Telecom);* b. 1953, Beijing; ed Beijing Inst. of Posts and Telecommunications, Hong Kong Polytechnic Univ.; fmr Deputy Dir and Dir Hangzhou Telecommunications Bureau, Zhejiang Prov.; fmr Dir-Gen. Tianjin Posts and Telecommunications Admin; Dir China Mobile (Hong Kong) Ltd 1999–, also fmr CEO and Chair.; fmr Vice-Pres. China Mobile Communications Corpn; Gen. Man. China Telecommunications Corpn 2004, Exec. Dir 2005–, Pres. 2004–; Alt. mem. 17th CCP Cen. Cttee 2007–; Class Three National Science and Tech. Advancement Award, Ministry of Posts and Telecommunications Class One Science and Tech. Advancement Award. *Address:* China Telecommunications Corpn, 31 Jinrong Street, Xicheng District, Beijing 100032, People's Republic of China (office). *Telephone:* (10) 6602-7217 (office). *Fax:* (10) 6602-1147 (office). *E-mail:* info@chinatelecom.com.cn (office). *Website:* www.chinatelecom.com.cn (office).

WANG, Xiaodong, BS, PhD; American (b. Chinese) biochemist and academic; *George L. MacGregor Distinguished Chair Professor in Biomedical Science, University of Texas Southwestern Medical Center;* b. 1963, Wuhan, People's Repub. of China; ed Beijing Normal Univ., Univ. of Texas Southwestern Medical Center, Dallas; grew up in Xingxiang, Henan Prov.; Post-doctoral researcher, Univ. of Texas Southwestern Medical Center 1991–95, apptd Asst Prof., Dept of Biochemistry 1996, currently George L. MacGregor Distinguished Chair Prof. in Biomedical Science; at Emory Univ. 1995–96; Asst Investigator, Howard Hughes Medical Inst. 1997, currently Investigator; Co-Dir Nat. Inst. of Biological Sciences, Beijing 2003–; mem. American Asscn of Cancer Research, American Soc. of Biochemistry and Molecular Biology,

American Soc. of Cell Biology, NAS, Soc. of Chinese Biomedical Scientists in America; Damon Runyon-Walter Winchell Cancer Research Fund Postdoctoral Fellowship 1991–94, ACS Eli Lilly Award 2000, Paul Marks Prize, Memorial Sloan-Kettering Cancer Center 2001, Hackerman Award, The Welch Foundation 2002, Shaw Prize in Life Science and Medicine, The Shaw Foundation 2006, NAS Molecular Biology Award 2006, NAS Richard Lounsbery Award 2007. *Publications:* numerous scientific papers in professional journals on biochemical mechanism of programmed cell death, or apoptosis, in human cells. *Address:* Department of Biochemistry, University of Texas Southwestern Medical Center at Dallas, 5323 Harry Hines Blvd, Dallas, TX 75390-9038, USA (office). *Telephone:* (214) 648-6713 (office). *Fax:* (214) 648-8856 (office). *E-mail:* wwwbio@utsouthwestern.edu (office). *Website:* www8.utsouthwestern.edu (office).

WANG, Xiaofeng; Chinese politician; b. Oct. 1944, Cili Co., Hunan Prov.; ed Beijing Mining Inst.; technician, later Deputy Dir, later Dir Changde July 1st Machinery Plant, Hunan Prov. 1970–83; joined CCP 1973; Deputy Sec. CCP Changde Prefectural Cttee 1983–86, Commr Changde Prefectural Admin. Office 1983–86; Dir Hunan Provincial Planning Cttee 1986–90; Vice-Gov. Hunan Prov. 1990–93, Exec. Vice-Gov. 1993–98; Deputy Sec. CCP Hunan Prov. Cttee 1992–93; Deputy Sec. CCP Hainan Prov. Cttee 1993–98, Sec. 2004–06; Vice-Gov. Hainan Prov. 1993–98, Gov. 1998–2003; Pres. Hainan Prov. Entrepreneurs Asscn 1993; Chair. Standing Cttee Hainan Prov. People's Congress 2004–06; Alt. mem. 14th CCP Cen. Cttee 1992–97, mem. 15th CCP Cen. Cttee 1997–2002, 16th CCP Cen. Cttee 2002–07. *Address:* c/o Hainan Provincial People's Congress, Haikou City, Hainan Province, People's Republic of China (office).

WANG, Xiaoguang; Chinese jurist; b. 1924, Anguo, Hebei; Deputy Procurator-Gen. 1983; mem. CCP Discipline Inspection Comm. 1982; Sec. Party Cttee Beijing Univ. 1985; Deputy Procurator Gen., Supreme People's Procuratorate, Pres. Soc. of Procuratorial Work; NPC Deputy Hebei Prov.; mem. 8th NPC 1993–98, Internal and Judicial Affairs Cttee. *Address:* Supreme People's Procuratorate, Beijing, People's Republic of China (office).

WANG, Xiaoshuai; Chinese film director and screenwriter; b. 22 May 1966, Shanghai; ed Beijing Film Acad.; mem. jury BigScreen Italia Film Festival 2006. *Films include:* Dongchun de rizi (The Days) 1993, Da youxi 1994, Jidu hanleng (Frozen) 1996, Biandan, guniang (So Close to Paradise) 1998, The House 1999, Beijing Bicycle (Silver Bear for Best Dir, Berlin Film Festival 2001) 2001, After War (segment) 2002, Drifters 2003, Shanghai Dreams (Jury Prize, Cannes Film Festival 2005) 2005, In Love We Trust (Silver Bear Best Script) 2008.

WANG, Xiji, BEng, MS; Chinese engineer; b. 1921, Dali, Yun'nan Prov.; ed Southwest China United Univ., Virginia Polytechnic Inst., USA; returned to China 1950; fmrly Assoc. Prof. Dalian Polytechnic; Prof., Shanghai Jiaotong Univ. and Shanghai Univ. of Science and Tech.; Chief Engineer, Shanghai Mechanical and Electrical Designing Inst., Chinese Acad. of Sciences; Chief Engineer, Ministry of Aerospace Industry; Vice-Pres. Research Inst. No. 5, Ministry of Aerospace Industry; researcher and adviser, China Aerospace Science and Tech. Corpn, China Space Tech. Research Inst.; Fellow, Chinese Acad. of Sciences 1993–; was in charge of the research and devt of 12 types of sounding rockets and the technical design of China's first launch vehicle Long March I in the 1960s; was first chief designer of Chinese recoverable satellites (CRSAT) and successfully conducted China's micro-gravity space experiments on CRSAT; Special Prize of Nat. Science and Tech. Advancement Award 1985, Meritorious Service Medal for the devt of China's Atomic and Hydrogen Bombs and Satellites by the CCP Cen. Cttee, the State Council and the Cen. Mil. Comm. 1999. *Address:* c/o Chinese Academy of Sciences, 52 Sanlihe Road, Beijing 100864, People's Republic of China (office).

WANG, Xudong; Chinese politician; *Chairman, State Electricity Regulatory Commission;* b. Jan. 1946, Yancheng, Jiangsu Prov.; ed Tianjin Coll. for Advanced Studies in Science and Tech.; joined CCP 1972; fmrly Sec. of Chinese Communist Youth League Cttee; Vice-Sec. CCP Cttee PLA 1418 Research Inst.; Dir Research Inst. No. 18, Ministry of Electronics Industry; Dir Org. Dept, CCP Tianjin Municipal Cttee, also Deputy Sec.; Vice-Dir Org. Dept, CCP Cen. Cttee 1993–2000; mem. Standing Cttee CCP Hebei Prov. Cttee 2000–02, Sec. Prov. Cttee 2000–02; Minister of Information Industry 2003–08; Chair. State Electricity Regulatory Comm. 2008–; Alt. mem. 15th CCP Cen. Cttee 1997–2002, mem. 16th CCP Cen. Cttee 2002–07, 17th CCP Cen. Cttee 2007–. *Address:* State Electricity Regulatory Commission, 86 Xichangan Jie, Beijing 100031, People's Republic of China (office). *Telephone:* (10) 66058800 (office). *E-mail:* manager@serc.gov.cn (office). *Website:* www.serc.gov.cn (office).

WANG, Xuebing; Chinese banker; ed Univ. of Int. Business and Econs, Beijing; Adviser Steering Group, Gold and Exchange Rate Man. of State Council; Gen. Man. US Operations, Bank of China 1988–93; Chair. and Pres. Bank of China 1993–2000; Pres. and CEO China Construction Bank 2000–02 (dismissed following alleged financial irregularities at Bank of China); expelled from CCP 2002; sentenced to 12 years in prison for taking bribes 2003; Alt. mem. 15th CCP Cen. Cttee 1997–2002.

WANG, Ying-Fan, BA; Chinese diplomatist and politician; *Vice-Chairman, Foreign Affairs Committee, National People's Congress;* m.; one d.; ed Beijing Univ.; on staff, Office of Chargé d'Affaires of People's Repub. of China, London 1964; joined Dept of Translation and Interpreting, Ministry of Foreign Affairs 1967; attaché, Embassy, Ghana then Embassy, Philippines; Deputy Div. Dir, Dept of Asian Affairs, Foreign Ministry 1978, Deputy Dir-Gen. 1988; Amb. to the Philippines 1988–90; Dir-Gen. Dept of Asian Affairs, Foreign Ministry 1990–94, Asst Foreign Minister 1994–95, Vice-Minister for Foreign Affairs 1995–2000; Perm. Rep. to UN 2000–03; Vice-Chair. 10th NPC Foreign Affairs Cttee 2003–. *Address:* c/o Foreign Affairs Committee, National People's Congress, Great Hall of the People, Beijing, People's Republic of China (office).

WANG, Yongyan; Chinese doctor; b. Sept. 1938, Tianjin; ed Beijing Chinese Medical Coll.; Assoc. Prof., Prof., Chief Doctor, Pres. Beijing Chinese Medical Univ. 1962; Dir Chinese Acad. of Traditional Chinese Medicine; Fellow, Chinese Acad. of Sciences; Vice-Chair. Chinese Medical Soc. of China; Fellow Chinese Acad. of Engineering 1997–. *Address:* Institute of Basic Research in Clinical Medicine, 16 Nanxiaojie, Dongzhimennei Street, Dongcheng District, Beijing 100700, People's Republic of China (office). *E-mail:* wangyyan@public.bta.net.cn.

WANG, Yongzhi; Chinese aerospace scientist; b. Nov. 1932, Changtu, Liaoning Prov.; ed Moscow Aeronautics Inst.; Dir Research Section, Dir Design Dept, Pres. No. 1 Research Inst. of Ministry of Aerospace Industry; Gen. Designer of Rockets 1961–91; Vice-Dir Science and Tech. Cttee, Ministry of Aerospace Industry 1991–98; designer of rocket launcher series 1991–; Sr Consulting Engineer for manned space programme, including launch of Shenzhou VII spacecraft Sept. 2008; Academician, Int. Astronautical Acad., Foreign Academician Konstantin Eduardovich Ziolkowski Acad., Russia 1992–; Academician Chinese Acad. of Engineering 1994–; Prize of Nat. Scientific Conf., Scientific Advancement Prize, State Pre-eminent Science and Technology Award 2003, Meritorious Scientist of Manned Spaceflight 2005, HoLeung Ho Lee Foundation Technological Science Prize. *Address:* The People's Liberation Army General Equipment Department, 4 Beisanhuan Middle Road, Beijing 100720, People's Republic of China (office). *Telephone:* (10) 66350660 (office). *Fax:* (10) 66061566 (office). *E-mail:* engach@mail.cae.ac.cn (office).

WANG, You-Tsao, MSc, PhD; Taiwanese politician and agricultural adviser; *Chairman, Rural Development Foundation;* b. 2 July 1925, Chinchiang Co., Fukien; s. of Wang Hsiao-kwei and Wang-Huang Pei-feng; m. Jean Eng-ling 1954; two s. one d.; ed Nat. Taiwan Univ., Iowa State Univ., USA; Asst, Instructor, Assoc. Prof., Dept of Agric. Econs, Nat. Taiwan Univ. 1954–60, Prof. 1960–73; Specialist, Rural Econs Div., Jt Comm. on Rural Reconstruction (JCRR) 1960–63, Sr Specialist 1965–66, Chief, Rural Econs Div. 1966–71, Chief, Office of Planning and Programming 1971–72, Deputy Sec.-Gen. JCRR 1972–73, Sec.-Gen. 1973–79; Sec.-Gen. Council for Agric. Planning and Devt, Exec. Yuan 1979, Vice-Chair. 1979–84, Chair. 1984, Chair. and Chief Operating Admin. 1984–88, Adviser 1990–2004; Minister without Portfolio, Exec. Yuan 1988–90; Nat. Policy Adviser to Pres. 1990–96; Dir Asian Agric. Tech. Service Center 1993–95; Pres. Rural Devt Foundation 1995–98 (Chair. 1998–); Chair. Bd of Dirs Harvest (farm magazine) 1995–2002; mem. Agric. Asscn of China, Rural Econs Asscn of China. *Publications:* Statistical Analysis of Resources Productivity in Shihmen Reservoir Area of Taiwan 1963, Technological Changes and Agricultural Development of Taiwan 1946–65 1966. *Address:* Rural Development Foundation, 5F, No. 7, Section 1, Roosvelt Road, Taipei 100 (office); 7F, No. 2, Alley 8, Lane 216, Sect. 4, Chung Hsiao East Road, Taipei, Taiwan (home).

WANG, Yuan; Chinese mathematician; b. 30 April 1930; Dir Inst. of Math., Acad. Sinica March–Oct. 1985; mem. Dept of Math. and Physics, Acad. Sinica 1985–; mem. Nat. Cttee 6th CPPCC 1986; Pres. Chinese Math. Soc. 1989–92; mem. Presidium Chinese Acad. of Sciences 1996–; numerous awards including Hua Loo-Keng Math. Prize. *Leisure interest:* calligraphy. *Address:* Institute of Mathematics, Academia Sinica, Zhong Guan Cun, Beijing 100080, People's Republic of China (office). *Telephone:* (10) 62541846 (office). *Website:* http://infolab.stanford.edu/~wangz/home/link/wangy/.

WANG, Yunkun; Chinese politician; *Chairman, Standing Committee, Jilin Provincial People's Congress Standing Committee;* b. Dec. 1942, Liyang Co., Jiangsu Prov.; ed Tianjin Univ.; joined CCP 1966; Chief, Publicity Section, Chemical Machinery Plant, Jilin Chemical Industry Co., Deputy Dir, later Dir Political Dept, engineer, Refinery, Research Inst. and Organic Synthesis Plant; Vice-Mayor Jilin City 1982–83, Mayor 1983–86; Dir Dept of Electronic Industry, Jilin Prov. 1986–88; Chair. Comm. for Restructuring the Economy, Jilin Prov. 1988; Sec.-Gen. People's Govt, Jilin Prov. 1988–89; Vice-Gov. Jilin Prov. 1989–92, Acting Gov. 1995, Gov. 1996–98; Sec. CCP Changchun City Cttee 1992–95; Deputy Sec. Jilin Prov. Cttee 1995–98, Sec. 1998–2006; Chair. Standing Cttee Jilin Prov. People's Congress 1999–; mem. 15th CCP Cen. Cttee 1997–2002, 16th CCP Cen. Cttee 2002–07. *Address:* c/o Jilin Provincial Government, Changchun City, Jilin Province, People's Republic of China (office).

WANG, Zhaoguo; Chinese party official; *Chairman, All-China Federation of Trade Unions;* b. 1941, Fengrun, Hebei Prov.; ed Harbin Technological Univ.; joined CCP 1965; technician, later Deputy Dir Axle Plant, Second Automotive Works 1968–79 (mem. Standing Cttee, later First Sec. CCP Party Cttee 1968–79), Dir Second Automotive Works 1979–82 (Sec. CCP Party Cttee 1979–82); mem. Standing Cttee CCP Shiyan Municipal Cttee, Hubei Prov. 1968–79; First Sec. CCP Communist Youth League of China and Pres. Party School 1982–84; Deputy for Hubei to 6th NPC 1983; Dir-Gen. Office Cen. Cttee CCP 1984–86; Chief Rep. 21st Century Cttee for Chinese-Japanese Friendship 1984–89; Vice-Gov. and Acting Gov. of Fujian 1987–88, Gov. 1988–90; Dir Taiwan Affairs Office, State Council 1990–96; Chair. All-China Fed. of Trade Unions 2002–; mem. 12th CCP Cen. Cttee 1982–87, 13th CCP Cen. Cttee 1987–92, 14th CCP Cen. Cttee 1992–97, 15th CCP Cen. Cttee 1997–2002, 16th CCP Cen. Cttee 2002–07 (mem. Politburo 2002–07), 17th CCP Cen. Cttee 2007– (mem. Politburo 2007–); mem. Secr., CCP Cen. Cttee 1985–87; mem. Presidium 6th NPC 1983–88, Standing Cttee 6th NPC 1983–88, Vice-Chair. Standing Cttee 10th NPC 2003–08, Standing Cttee 11th NPC 2008–; Head, United Front Work Dept 1992–2007; Vice-Chair. 8th CPPCC Nat. Cttee 1993–98, 9th CPPCC Nat. Cttee 1998–2003; Pres. China Overseas Friendship

Asscn 1997–. *Address:* All-China Federation of Trade Unions, 10 Fu Xing Men Wai Jie, Beijing 100865, People's Republic of China (office).

WANG, Zhenyi, DMed; Chinese haematologist; b. 3 Nov. 1924, Shanghai; ed Fudan Univ. Medical Coll.; fmrly doctor in charge, Shanghai Ruijin Hosp.; currently Prof. of Medicine and Pathophysiology, Shanghai Jiao Tong Univ.; Fellow, Chinese Acad. of Eng 1994–; Dir Shanghai Haematology Research Inst.; mem. Chinese Soc. of Pathophysiology, French Acad. of Sciences, Int. Soc. of Fibrinolysis; numerous awards including Kettering Prize, Prix mondial Cino Del Duca, Charles Rodolphe Brupbacher Prize 1997. *Publications:* more than 300 scientific papers and books. *Address:* Medical School, Shanghai Jiao Tong University, Shanghai, People's Republic of China (office). *Website:* http://www.sjtu.edu.cn/english/academics/wzy.htm (office).

WANG, Zhibao; Chinese administrator; *Chairman, China Green Foundation;* b. July 1938, Zhaoyuan, Shandong Prov.; ed Northeast Electric Power Inst.; joined CCP 1965; Deputy Chief, Machinery and Electrical Div., Yikeshi Forestry Admin 1975; Dir Planning Dept, Ministry of Forestry 1986; Vice-Minister of Forestry 1992–98; Dir State Forestry Bureau 1998–2000; Pres. China Wildlife Conservation Asscn 1998; currently Chair. China Green Foundation; mem. 9th CPPCC Nat. Cttee 1998–2003. *Address:* China Green Foundation, Beijing, People's Republic of China (office). *Telephone:* (10) 84238200 (office).

WANG, Zhixin, PhD; Chinese biophysicist; *Professor of Biological Sciences and Biotechnology, Tsinghua University;* b. 10 Aug. 1953, Beijing; ed Tsinghua Univ., Beijing; Research Fellow, Vice-Dir Biophysics Research Inst. of Chinese Acad. of Sciences 1993–; Prof., Dept of Biological Sciences and Biotechnology, Tsinghua Univ. 2003–; Dir Nat. Biomolecular Lab.; Dir SinoBiomed Inc. 2007–; mem. Chinese Acad. of Sciences 1997–; Chair. Chinese Soc. of Biochemistry and Molecular Biology; mem. Chinese Soc. of Biophysics; Hon. DSc (Biophysics Research Inst. of Chinese Acad. of Sciences) 1988. *Address:* Department of Biological Sciences and Biotechnology, Tsinghua University, Haidan District, Beijing 100084, People's Republic of China (office). *Telephone:* (10) 62785474 (office). *E-mail:* zhixinwang@mail.tsinghua.edu.cn (office). *Website:* www.biosci.tsinghua.edu.cn (office).

WANG, Zhongcheng; Chinese neurosurgeon; b. 20 Dec. 1925, Yantai, Shandong Prov.; ed Peking Univ. Medical School; Chief Surgeon, Beijing Tongren Hosp.; Dir Beijing Neurosurgery Research Inst.; Pres. Beijing Tiantan Hosp.; Pres. and Hon. Dir Beijing Neurosurgical Inst.; Prof., Beijing Second Medical Coll.; Fellow, Chinese Acad. of Eng; neuroscience consultant to WHO; Heliangheli Science and Tech. Achievement Award 1997; State Scientific Award 2009; World Neurosurgery Federation Highest Honour Award; numerous other scientific awards. *Publications:* Cerebral Aneurysms by Angiography, Neurosurgery, Practical Tumourology, Cerebral Vascular Diseases and Surgical Treatment; 278 papers and 24 monographs. *Leisure interests:* table tennis, swimming, calligraphy. *Address:* c/o Chinese Academy of Engineering, 3 Fuxing Lu, Beijing 100008 (office); 6 Tiantan Xili, Beijing Chongwen Qu, Beijing, People's Republic of China (home). *Telephone:* (10) 67014212 (office); (10) 67027880 (home). *Fax:* (10) 67018349 (office). *E-mail:* wang.zhch@mail.cae.ac.cn (office).

WANG, Zhongshu; Chinese archaeologist and academic; *Professor, Institute of Archaeology, Chinese Academy of Social Sciences;* b. 15 Oct. 1925, Ningbo; s. of Wang Xuanbing and Ling Sujuan; m. Chen Kai 1960; one s.; ed Univ. of Beijing; Sr Fellow Inst. of Archaeology, Chinese Acad. of Social Sciences 1979–, Dir 1982–88; Prof. and Tutor for Doctoral Studies, Grad. School Chinese Acad. of Social Sciences 1982–; mem. Nat. Council of Cultural Relics 1983–; Corresp. Fellow, German Archaeological Inst. 1988–; Hon. Prof., Nat. Univ. of San Antonio Abad (Cuzco, Peru) 1973; 7th Fukuoka Grand Asian Cultural Prize, Fukuoka, Japan 1996. *Publications:* Han Civilization 1982, An Outline of Archaeology of the Han Period 1984, Triangular-rimmed Bronze Mirrors with Mythical Figure and Animal Designs unearthed from Japan 1992, Ancient Japan seen from China 1992. *Leisure interests:* Chinese and Japanese classical literature. *Address:* Institute of Archaeology, Chinese Academy of Social Sciences, 27 Wangfujing Dajie, Beijing 100710 (office); 1-2-602 Chang Yun Gong, Zi Zhu Yuan, Beijing 100044, People's Republic of China (home). *Telephone:* (10) 65234003 (office); (10) 68411820 (home). *Fax:* (10) 65135532 (office). *E-mail:* liu.jg@history.cass.net.cn (office); yidan@pku.edu.cn (home). *Website:* www.archaeology.cass.net.cn (office).

WANG, Zhongyu; Chinese politician; *Vice-Chairman, 10th National Committee, Chinese People's Political Consultative Conference;* b. Feb. 1933, Changchun, Jilin Prov.; two s. one d.; ed Light Industry Sr Vocational School, Shenyang City, Liaoning Prov., CCP Cen. Cttee Party School; technician, Deputy Workshop Dir, engineer, Deputy Planning Section Chief, Jilin Paper Mill 1953–67, Deputy Head of Production Man. Group, Deputy Dir, Dir Office of CCP 1970–75, Deputy Dir and Chief Engineer 1975–80; joined CCP 1956; Deputy Dir Light Industry Bureau, Jilin Prov. 1980–81, Dir CCP Leading Party Group, 1982–83; mem. Standing Cttee, Dir Research Office and Sec.-Gen. CCP Jilin Prov. Cttee 1983–85, Deputy Sec. 1985–92; Vice-Gov. Jilin Prov. 1983–85, Acting Gov. 1985–92; Deputy, Jilin Prov., 7th NPC 1988–93; Vice-Gov. Jilin Prov. 1988–89, Gov. 1989–93; Deputy Dir Production Office of the State Council 1992–93 (also Deputy Sec. CCP Party Cttee); Minister in charge of State Econ. and Trade Comm. 1993–98; State Councillor and Sec.-Gen. State Council 1998–2003; Pres. Nat. School of Admin 1998–2003; Head, 5th Nat. Census Leading Group 1998; mem. Govt Del., Macao Hand-Over Ceremony, Macao Special Admin. Region Preparatory Cttee 1999; Alt. mem. 13th Cen. Cttee CCP 1987–92, mem. 14th Cen. Cttee 1992–97, mem. 15th CCP Cen. Cttee 1997–2002, 16th CCP Cen. Cttee 2002–07; Vice-Chair. 10th CPPCC Nat. Cttee 2003–. *Address:* Chinese People's Political Consultative Conference, Beijing, People's Republic of China (office).

WANG, Zikun, DSc; Chinese professor and university administrator; b. 30 April 1929, Jiangxi Prov.; s. of Wang Zhao-ji and Guo Xiang-e; m. Tian Der-Lin 1958; two s.; ed Wuhan Univ., Moscow Univ., USSR; Asst Prof., then Prof., Nankai Univ. 1952–84; Prof. and Pres. Beijing Normal Univ. 1984; Prof., Shantou Univ. 1993–; Dir China Math. Soc.; mem. Standing Bd China Probilistical-Statistics Soc., China Higher Educational Soc.; mem. Editorial Bd Soc., Scientia Sinica, Science Bulletin of China; mem. Chinese Acad. of Sciences 1991–; Hon. DSc (Macquarie Univ., Australia) 1988; China Science Conf. Award 1978, China Natural Science Prize 1982, China Excellent Popular Science Works Award 1981, Ho Leung Ho Lee Foundation Math. and Mechanics Prize, and numerous other awards. *Publications:* Foundations of Probability Theory and Their Applications 1976, Theory of Stochastic Processes 1965, Brownian Motion and Potentials 1982, Probability Theory and Statistical Prediction 1978, Talks on Scientific Discovery 1978, Birth-Death Processes and Markov Chains 1992 and many other math. articles and popular scientific publs. *Leisure interest:* literature. *Address:* Shantou University, Shantou, Guangdong Province, People's Republic of China (office). *E-mail:* web@stu.edu.cn (office). *Website:* www.stu.edu.cn (office).

WANG, Gen. Zuxun; Chinese army officer; b. May 1936, Qujing, Yunnan Prov.; joined PLA 1951; Vice-Commdr, then Commdr Yunnan Mil. Command 1984–89; Commdr Army Group 1989–93; Vice-Pres. PLA Acad. of Mil. Science 1993–99, Pres. 1999; rank of Gen. 2000. *Address:* c/o Xianghongqi, Beijing 100091, People's Republic of China (office).

WANGCHUCK, HM Dasho Jigme Khesar Namgyal, (The Druk Gyalpo — 'Dragon King'— of Bhutan), MPhil; b. 21 Feb. 1980; s. of King Jigme Singye Wangchuck and Queen Ashi Tshering Yandon Wangchuck; ed Cushing Acad. and Wheaton Coll., USA, Magdalen Coll., Oxford, UK; proclaimed Crown Prince Oct. 2004; succeeded to throne 14 Dec. 2006, on the abdication of his father; participated in official visits; officially crowned 6 November 2008; Chair. Bhutan Trust Fund for Environmental Conservation; Pres. Bhutan-India Friendship Asscn; Chancellor Royal Univ. of Bhutan; Chief Patron Scouts Assn of Bhutan; Patron Royal Soc. for the Protection of Nature, Bhutan Chamber of Commerce and Industry, India-Bhutan Foundation, European Convention of Bhutan Socs, Oxford Centre for Buddhist Studies, Bhutan Shooting Fed.; Red Scarf 2002. *Address:* Royal Palace, Thimphu, Bhutan. *Website:* www.bhutan.gov.bt.

WANGCHUCK, HM Jigme Singye; Bhutanese fmr ruler; b. 11 Nov. 1955; s. of the late Druk Gyalpo Jigme Dorji Wangchuk and of Queen Ashi Kesang; m.; ten c. (including HM King Dasho Jigme Khesar Namgyal Wangchuck); ed North Point, Darjeeling, Ugyuen Wangchuk Acad., Paro, also in UK; Crown Prince March 1972; succeeded to throne 24 July 1972, crowned 2 June 1974, abdicated 14 December 2006; Chair. Planning Comm. of Bhutan 1972–; C-in-C of Armed Forces; Chair. Council of Ministers 1972–98. *Address:* Royal Palace, Thimphu, Bhutan (office). *Website:* www.bhutan.gov.bt.

WANGCHUCK, Lyonpo Khandu, BA; Bhutanese politician; *Minister of Economic Affairs;* b. 24 Nov. 1950; ed St Stephen's Coll., India; Asst Sec., Ministry of Trade, Industry and Forests 1974, Deputy Dir 1976, Man. Dir Industrial Devt Corpn 1978, Dir of Trade and Commerce 1980–84; Dir of Agric. 1986, Dir Gen. 1987–89, Sec. 1989–1991; Sec. Royal Civil Service Comm. 1991–94; Prime Minister and Chair. 2001–02, 2006–July 2007 (resgnd); Minister of Trade and Industry 1998–2003, of Foreign Affairs 2003–07 (resgnd), of Econ. Affairs 2008–; mem. Nat. Ass. for Lamgong-Wangchang constituency; mem. Druk Phuensum Tshogpa party; fmr Chair. Bhutan Nat. Bank; Red Scarf 1987, Orange Scarf 1998, Coronation Medal 1999. *Address:* Ministry of Economic Affairs, Tashichhodzong, POB 141, Thimphu (office); Jangsa, Shari Geog, Paro, Bhutan (home). *Telephone:* (2) 322211 (office). *Fax:* (2) 323617 (office). *E-mail:* kdorjee@druknet.bt (office). *Website:* www.mti.gov.bt (office).

WANGCHUK, Dasho Lhatu; Bhutanese diplomatist, government official and airline industry executive; *Chairman, Druk Air (Royal Bhutan Airlines);* fmr Chief of Protocol and Acting Foreign Sec., Ministry of Foreign Affairs; Amb. to Bangladesh –2004; Dir-Gen. Dept of Tourism 2004–07; Chair. Druk Air (Royal Bhutan Airlines) 2007–. *Address:* Druk Air-Royal Bhutan Airlines, Paro, Bhutan (office). *E-mail:* info@drukair.com.bt (office). *Website:* www.drukair.com.bt (office).

WANGDI, Dasho Kunzang, BA, MPA; Bhutanese government official; *Chief Election Commissioner;* b. 17 July 1953; m. Pem Tandi; ed Delhi Univ., India, Pennsylvania State Univ., USA; worked in various capacities in govt ministries for more than 28 years; Auditor-Gen. 1999–2005; Chief Election Commr 2006–, in charge of two rounds of trial elections in 2007 and first ever parl. elections in 2008. *Publications:* drafted Royal Charters, Audit Act, Anti-Corruption Act, Election Acts. *Leisure interests:* reading, photography, cinema. *Address:* Election Commission of Bhutan, Thimphu, Bhutan (office). *Telephone:* (2) 334762 (office). *Fax:* (2) 334763 (office). *E-mail:* kwangdi@druknet.bt (office). *Website:* www.election-bhutan.org.bt (office).

WANIEK, Danuta, DJur; Polish politician and political scientist; b. 26 Oct. 1946, Włocławek; d. of Jerzy Waniek and Jozefina Wisniewski; m. (husband deceased); two s.; ed Warsaw Univ., Institut für Höhere Studien und Wissenschaft, Vienna; with Inst. of Political Studies, Polish Acad. of Sciences (PAN) 1989–; mem. Polish United Workers' Party (PZPR) 1967–90; mem. Social Democracy of Polish Repub. (SDRP) 1990–; Deputy to Sejm (Parl.) 1991–2001, mem. Parl. Cttee of Nat. Defence; Chair. Women's Democratic Union 1990–; Deputy Minister of Nat. Defence 1994–95; Minister of State and Head of Chancellery of Pres. of Poland 1995–97; mem. Nat. Broadcasting Council 2001–, Pres. 2003–05; with Instytut Problemów Strategicznych 2007–; Krzyz Zaslugi (Cross of Merit). *Publications:* Compromise within the Political System of Germany: Partnership or Struggle? 1988, Constitution and

Political Reality 1989, Debate over 'Little Constitution' (ed.) 1992, Creating New Constitutional Order in Poland (ed.) 1993. *Leisure interests:* opera, reading newspapers, embroidering, painting, music (listening and playing). *Address:* Instytut Problemów strategicznych, Al. Ujazdowskie 20/6, 00-478 Warsaw, (office); ul. Protazego 61, 03-606, Warsaw, Poland (home). *Telephone:* (22) 622-07-35 (office). *E-mail:* zarzad@ips.org.pl (office).

WANLESS, Sir Derek, Kt, MA, FCIB; British banker; b. 29 Sept. 1947, Newcastle; s. of the late Norman Hall Wanless and of Edna Charlton; m. Vera West 1971; one s. four d.; ed Royal Grammar School, Newcastle-upon-Tyne, King's Coll., Cambridge and Harvard Univ., USA; joined Nat. Westminster Bank PLC 1970, Marketing Man. Domestic Banking Div. 1980–82, Area Dir North-East Area 1982–85, W Yorks Area 1985–86, Dir of Personal Banking Services 1986–88, Gen. Man. UK Br. Business 1989–90, Chief Exec. UK Financial Services 1990–92, Deputy Group Chief Exec. and Group Head of NatWest Markets (now Hawkpoint Partners Ltd) 1992, Dir 1991–99, Group Chief Exec. 1992–99; Chair. Advisory Cttee on Business and the Environment 1993–95, Nat. Forum for Man. Educ. and Devt (NFMED) 1996–; consultant to Dept of Health 2001–; mem. Investors in People UK Bd, Statistics Comm. 2000–, Inst. of Statisticians; Hon. DSc (City) 1995. *Leisure interests:* all sports, chess, music, walking, gardening.

WANSIRU, Samuel Kamau, (Samuel Wanjiru); Kenyan athlete; b. 10 Nov. 1986, Nyahururu; ed Sendai Ikuei Gakuen High School; long-distance runner; began running aged 15; moved to Japan 2002; joined Toyota Kyushu athletics team, coached by 1992 Olympic marathon silver medallist Koichi Morishita; set 5,000m best time of 13:12.40 in Hiroshima, Japan April 2004; broke half marathon world record in Rotterdam Half Marathon with time of 59:16 minutes Sept. 2005; broke 10,000m World Jr Record at Int. Asscn of Athletics Feds (IAAF) Golden League Van Damme Memorial Race Aug. 2005; broke half marathon world record again in a time of 58:53 minutes in Ras al Khaimah Feb. 2007, and again (58:33) in The Hague March 2007; broke 20km world record with a time of 55:31 2007; made marathon debut at Fukuoka Marathon in course record time of 2:06:39 Dec. 2007; finished second in London Marathon, breaking 2:06:00 for first time April 2008; Gold Medal, marathon, Olympic Games 2008 (Olympic record time of 2:06:32; first male runner from Kenya to win gold in this event); Kenyan Most Promising Sportsman of the Year Award 2005. *Address:* c/o Kenya Athletics Federation, PO Box 46722, Aerodrome Road, Riadha House, 00100 Nairobi West, Kenya. *Telephone:* (2) 605021. *Fax:* (2) 605020. *E-mail:* athleticskenya@gt.co.ke. *Website:* www .athleticskenya.org.

WAPNEWSKI, Peter, DPhil; German academic; *Professor Emeritus of Medieval German Literature, Technical University of Berlin;* b. 7 Sept. 1922, Kiel; s. of Harald Wapnewski and Gertrud (née Hennings) Wapnewski; m. 1st Caroline Gräfin Finckenstein 1950 (divorced 1959); m. 2nd Monica Plange 1971; ed Univs of Berlin, Freiburg, Jena and Hamburg; Prof. of Medieval German Literature, Heidelberg 1959, Free Univ. of Berlin 1966, Univ. of Karlsruhe 1969, Tech. Univ. of Berlin 1982–90 (Prof. Emer. 1990–); Rector, Wissenschaftskolleg, Berlin 1980–86, Perm. mem. 1986–; Vice-Pres. Goethe Inst. 1977–2002; mem. Deutsche Akad. für Sprache und Dichtung, PEN Club, American Medieval Acad.; Grosses Bundesverdienstkreuz 1986, (with star) 1992, Sigmund Freud Prize for Scholarly Prose, German Acad. for Language and Poetry 1996, Rahel Varnhagen von Ense Medal 1999, Ehrensenator, Tech. Univ. Berlin 2002, Ernst Reuter Badge, Berlin Senate 2003, Helmholtz Medal, Berlin-Brandenburg Acad. of Sciences and Humanities 2008; Dr hc (Heidelberg) 2002, (Freiburg) 2004. *Publications:* Wolframs Parzival 1955, Deutsche Literatur des Mittelalters 1960, Walther von der Vogelweide (ed.), Hartmann von Aue 1962, Die Lyrik Wolframs von Eschenbach 1972, Richard Wagner – Die Szene und ihr Meister 1978, Der Traurige Gott 1978, Zumutungen 1979, Tristan der Held Richard Wagners 1981, Minnesang des Codex Manesse 1982, Eduard Hanslick, Aus meinem Leben (ed.) 1987, Götternot und Göttertrauer 1988, Die unerhörten Künste (ed.) 1989, Eduard Hanslick: Aus dem Tagebuch eines Rezensenten (ed.) 1989, Peter Huchel, Gedichte (ed.) 1989, Betrifft Literatur: Über Marcel Reich-Ranicki (ed.) 1990, Richard Wagner Handbook 1992, Zuschreibungen: Gesammelte Aufsätze von P.W. Hildesheim 1994, Weisst Du Wie das Wird? Richard Wagner: Der Ring des Nibelnungen 1995, 2000; about 200 articles on medieval and modern German literature. *Address:* Wissenschaftskolleg zu Berlin – Institute for Advanced Study, Wallotstrasse 19, 14193 Berlin, Germany (office). *Telephone:* (30) 89001150 (office). *E-mail:* arnim@wiko-berlin.de (home).

WAQAR YOUNIS; Pakistani fmr professional cricketer; b. 16 Nov. 1971, Vehari; ed Pakistani Coll. Sharjah and Govt Coll. Vehari; right-hand lower-order batsman, right-arm fast bowler; played for Multan 1987–88 to 1990–91, United Bank 1988–, Surrey 1990–91 and 1993, Glamorgan 1997–98 (took career-best 8 for 17 against Sussex), Warwickshire 2003; played in 87 Tests for Pakistan 1989 –2003 (17 as Capt.) taking 373 wickets (average 23.56); took 956 wickets in first-class cricket; 262 limited-overs internationals (56 as Capt.); retd April 2004; Wisden Cricketer of the Year 1992. *Leisure interests:* football, badminton, squash. *Address:* c/o Pakistan Cricket Board, Gaddafi Stadium, Ferozepur Road, Lahore 54600, Pakistan. *Telephone:* (42) 571-7231.

WARBURTON, Dame Anne Marion, DCVO, CMG, MA; British diplomatist; b. 8 June 1927, London; d. of Capt. Eliot Warburton and Mary Louise Warburton (née Thompson); ed Barnard Coll., Columbia Univ. USA, Somerville Coll. Oxford; with Econ. Co-operation Admin., London 1949–52; NATO Secr., Paris 1952–54; Lazard Bros, London 1955–57; entered Diplomatic Service 1957; Second Sec., Foreign Office 1957–59; Second, then First Sec., UK Mission to UN, New York 1959–62; First Sec., Bonn 1962–65, Diplomatic Service Admin Office, London 1965–67, Foreign Office, then FCO 1967–70; Counsellor, UK Mission to UN, Geneva 1970–75; Head of Guidance and Information Policy Dept, FCO 1975–76; Amb. to Denmark 1976–83, to UN at Geneva 1983–85; Pres. Lucy Cavendish Coll. Cambridge 1985–94, Hon. Fellow 1994–; Equal Opportunities Commr 1986–87; Leader EU Investigative Mission on the Abuse of Bosnian Muslim Women 1992–93; mem. British Library Bd 1989–95, Council of Univ. of East Anglia 1991–97, Cttee on Standards in Public Life (Nolan Cttee) 1994–97; Hon. Fellow Somerville Coll. Oxford 1977–, Lucy Cavendish Coll.; Verdienstkreuz (First Class), FRG 1965; Grand Cross, Order of Dannebrog, Denmark 1979; Order of Isabel la Católica, Spain 1988; Dr hc (Arkansas) 1994. *Leisure interests:* the arts, travel. *Address:* Ansted, Thornham Magna, Eye, Suffolk, IP23 8HB, England (home).

WARCHUS, Matthew, BA; British theatre director; b. 24 Oct. 1966, Rochester; ed Univ. of Bristol; Dir Nat. Youth Theatre 1989, 1990, Bristol Old Vic 1991; Asst Dir RSC 1991–92; Assoc. Dir West Yorkshire Playhouse 1993; freelance dir; Shakespeare's Globe Award 1994, Sydney Edwards Award 1995, Evening Standard Award 1995. *Films directed include:* Simpático (feature film) 1999. *Plays directed include:* (for RSC) Henry V 1995, The Devil is an Ass 1995, Hamlet 1997; (for West Yorkshire Playhouse) Life is a Dream, Who's Afraid of Virginia Woolf?, The Plough and the Stars, Death of a Salesman, Betrayal, True West; other productions The Stuff of Life (Donmar Warehouse) 1994, Volpone (Royal Nat. Theatre) 1995, Art (Wyndhams) 1996, The Unexpected Man (Duchess) 1998, Life x 3 (West End) 2001, Art, True West, Follies (all Broadway), The Lord of the Rings 2007, Boeing Boeing 2008, The Norman Conquests 2008. *Opera:* Troilus and Cressida (Opera North), The Rake's Progress, Falstaff, Cosí fan tutte (ENO). *Address:* c/o Hamilton Asper Management, 24 Hanway Street, London, W1T 1OH, England (office). *Telephone:* (20) 7636-1221.

WARD, Ian Macmillan, MA, DPhil, FRS; British physicist and academic; *Research Professor Emeritus, University of Leeds;* b. 9 April 1928, Stockton-on-Tees; s. of Harry Ward and Joan Ward; m. Margaret Linley 1960; two s. one d.; ed Royal Grammar School, Newcastle-upon-Tyne and Magdalen Coll. Oxford; Tech. Officer, ICI Fibres 1954–61; seconded to Div. of Applied Math., Brown Univ., USA 1961–62; Head, Basic Physics Section, ICI Fibres 1962–65; Sr Lecturer in Physics of Materials, Univ. of Bristol 1965–69; Prof. of Physics, Univ. of Leeds 1970–93, Cavendish Prof. 1987–94 (Chair. of Dept 1975–78, 1987–89, Research Prof. Emer. 1994–; Dir IRC in Polymer Science and Tech. 1989–94); Pres. British Soc. of Rheology 1984–86; Hon. DSc (Bradford) 1993; A.A. Griffith Medal 1982, S.G. Smith Memorial Medal 1984, Swinburne Award 1988, Charles Vernon Boys Medal 1993, Glazebrook Medal 2004, Netlon Medal 2004. *Publications:* Mechanical Properties of Solid Polymers 1971, 1983, Structure and Properties of Oriented Polymers (ed.) 1975, 1997, Ultra High Modulus Polymers (ed.) 1979, An Introduction to Mechanical Properties of Solid Polymers (with D. W. Hadley) 1993, (second edn with J. Sweeney) 2004, Solid Phase Processing of Polymers (ed.) 2000. *Leisure interests:* music, walking. *Address:* IRC in Polymer Science and Technology, School of Physics and Astronomy, University of Leeds, Leeds, West Yorks., LS2 9JT, England (office). *Telephone:* (113) 343-3808 (office); (113) 267-3637 (home). *Fax:* ((113) 343-3846 (office). *E-mail:* i.m.ward@leeds.ac.uk (office).

WARD, Richard, PhD, FRSA; British insurance company executive; *CEO, Lloyd's of London;* m.; two s.; ed Exeter Univ.; Sr Physicist, Science and Eng Council 1982–88; Sr Man., Research, BP plc 1988–91, Head, Business Devt and Marketing, BP Oil Trading Int. 1991–94; Head, Marketing and Business Devt, Tradition Financial Services 1994–95; Dir Product Devt and Research, Int. Petroleum Exchange (ICE) 1995–96, Exec. Vice-Pres. 1996–99, CEO 1999–2005, Vice-Chair. ICE Futures 2005; CEO Lloyd's of London 2006–; mem. Bd of Dirs LCH Clearnet; mem. Royal Inst., Inst. of Dirs. *Address:* Society of Lloyd's, 1 Lime Street, London EC3M 7HA, England (office). *Telephone:* (20) 7327-1000 (office). *Fax:* (20) 7327-5599 (office). *Website:* www .lloyds.com (office).

WARD, Simon; British actor; b. 19 Oct. 1941, Beckenham; s. of Leonard Fox Ward and Winifred Ward; m. Alexandra Malcolm; three d.; ed Alleyn's School, Dulwich and Royal Acad. of Dramatic Art; mem. Nat. Youth Theatre from its foundation (as Youth Theatre) 1956; first professional stage appearance in Hobson's Choice, Northampton Repertory Theatre 1963; London debut in The Fourth of June, St Martin's Theatre 1964; film debut in Frankenstein Must Be Destroyed 1969. *Stage roles include:* Konstantin in The Seagull, Birmingham Repertory 1964; Abel Drugger in The Alchemist and Hippolytus in Phèdre, Playhouse, Oxford 1965–66; Dennis in Loot, Jeannetta Cochrane and Criterion 1966; the Unknown Soldier in The Unknown Soldier and His Wife, Ferdinand in The Tempest and Henry in The Skin of Our Teeth, Chichester Festival 1968; Donald in Spoiled, Haymarket 1971; Romeo in Romeo and Juliet, Shaw 1972; Troilus in Troilus and Cressida, Young Vic 1976. *Other stage performances include:* House Guest 1982, Whose Life is it Anyway?, Birmingham 1982, Heartbreak House 1983, Dial M for Murder 1983, Ross 1986, Paris Match 1988, Henceforward 1990, Rumours 1990, Don't Dress for Dinner 1992, Cell Mates 1995, An Ideal Husband 1997, Mindgame 2000. *Films include:* I Start Counting 1970, Young Winston 1971, Hitler – The Last Ten Days 1972, The Three Musketeers 1973, The Four Musketeers, Deadly Strangers, All Creatures Great and Small 1974–75, Aces High 1975, Battle Flag 1976, The Four Feathers 1978, Zulu Dawn 1979, Supergirl, Around The World in 80 Days, Double X 1992, Wuthering Heights, Ghost Writers. *Television includes:* The Black Tulip, The Roads to Freedom, Holocaust (serials). *Leisure interests:* music, gardening, reading, badminton. *Address:* c/o Shepherd & Ford Associates Ltd, 13 Radner Walk, London, SW3 4BP, England. *Telephone:* (20) 7352-2200. *Fax:* (20) 7352-2277.

WARD, Vincent; New Zealand film director; b. 1956, Greytown; ed Elam School of Fine Art, Christchurch. *Films include:* A State of Siege 1977 (Miami Film Festival Special Jury Prize, Chicago Film Festival Golden Hugo 1978), In Spring one Plants Alone (documentary) 1979 (Silver Hugo at Chicago Film Festival 1980, Grand Prix Co-Winner Cinéma du Réel 1982), Vigil (also co-writer) 1984 (Grand Prix Prades and Madrid Film Festivals), The Navigator: A Medieval Odyssey 1988 (Grand Prix Film Festivals in Rome, Munich, Sitges 1988, Oporto Film Festival 1989, Best Film and Best Director Australian Film Inst. and New Zealand Listener Awards 1989), Alien III (writer) 1991, Map of the Human Heart (also story and co-writer, producer) 1992 (Most Significant Artistic Achievement Tokyo Film Festival 1993), Leaving Las Vegas (actor) 1995, The Shot (actor) 1996, One Night Stand (actor) 1997, What Dreams May Come 1998 (Acad. Award for Best Visual Effects, Best Renting Drama Video Australian Video Ezy Prestige Awards 1999), The Last Samurai (exec. producer) 2003, Spooked (actor) 2004, River Queen (also story and co-writer) 2005. *Publication:* Edge of the Earth 1990. *Address:* PO Box 423, King's Cross, Sydney, NSW 2011, Australia. *Telephone:* (2) 360-2769.

WARDAK, Gen. Abdul Rahim; Afghan government official and military officer; *Minister of Defence;* b. 1945, Wardak Prov.; s. of Abdul Ghani; ed Habibia High School, Ali Naser Acad. of Cairo, Egypt; previous positions include Lecturer Cadet Univ., Asst of Protocol, Ministry of Defence, Mil. Attaché, India, Dir Mil. Officers Soc., Educ. Comm., Disarmament Program; apptd Chief of Army Staff 1992; fmr Deputy Minister of Defence, Minister of Defence 2004–. *Address:* Ministry of Defence, Shash Darak, Kabul, Afghanistan (office). *Telephone:* (20) 2100451 (office). *Fax:* (20) 2104172 (office).

WARDAK, Taj Mohammad; Afghan politician; Gov. of Badakshan Prov. c. 1970s; apptd Gov. of Paktia Prov. 2002; Minister of Interior Affairs 2002–03; govt adviser on tribal matters 2003–; mem. Nat. Security Comm. 2003–. *Address:* c/o Ministry of Interior Affairs, Shar-i-Nau, Kabul, Afghanistan.

WARDHANA, Ali, MA, PhD; Indonesian politician and economist; b. 6 May 1928, Surakarta, Central Java; m. Renny Wardhana 1953; one s. three d.; ed Univ. of Indonesia, Jakarta and Univ. of California at Berkeley, USA; Dir, Research Inst. of Econ. and Social Studies 1962–67; Prof. of Econs, Univ. of Indonesia 1967–, Dean Faculty of Econs 1967–78; Adviser to Gov. of Cen. Bank 1964–68; mem. team of experts of Presidential Staff 1966–68; Minister of Finance 1968–83; Co-ordinating Minister for Econ., Finance, Industry and Devt Control 1983–88; Chair. Cttee of Bd of Govs of the IMF on Reform of the Int. Monetary System and Related Issues 1972–74; Grand Cross Order of Léopold II (Belgium) 1970, Grand Cross Order of Orange Nassau (Netherlands) 1971; Mahaputra Adipradhna II Award (Indonesia) 1973. *Leisure interests:* reading, tennis, bowling, swimming. *Address:* 5, Jalan Brawijaya III, Kebayoran Baru, Jakarta, Indonesia.

WARINER, Jeremy; American athlete; b. 31 Jan. 1984, Irving, Tex.; s. of Danny Wariner and Linda Wariner; ; ed Lamar High School, Arlington, Tex. and Baylor Univ.; coached by Clyde Hart; volunteer asst coach; mem. USA World Jr Team; three-time Jr All-American in 400m 2002; Nat. Collegiate Athletic Asscn (NCAA) Outdoor Champion, 400m 2004, 4×400m relay 2004; NCAA Indoor Champion, 400m 2004, 4×400m relay 2004; US Olympic Trials 400m Champion 2004; Gold Medal, 400m, Olympic Games, Athens 2004, 4×400m relay 2004; first athlete in history to win both collegiate titles, US Championship and Olympic Gold Medal in 400m; turned professional 2004; USA Outdoor Champion 2005; Gold Medal, 400m, World Outdoor Championships, Helsinki, Finland 2005, 4×400m relay 2005; Silver Medal, 400m, Olympic Games, Beijing 2008; Gold Medal, 4×400m relay, Olympic Games, Beijing 2008; current coach Michael Ford; Jesse Owens Award 2004, named by ESPN.com Top Rookie of 2004, named Mondo Track Athlete of the Year 2004. *Address:* c/o USA Track and Field, 1 RCA Dome, Suite 140, Indianapolis, IN 46225, USA. *Telephone:* (317) 261-0500. *Fax:* (317) 261-0514. *E-mail:* Sariyu.Suggs@usatf.org. *Website:* www.usatf.org.

WARLOW, Charles Picton, MD, FRCP, FRSE, FMedSci; British neurologist, epidemiologist and academic; *Professor of Medical Neurology, University of Edinburgh;* b. 29 Sept. 1943, Nottingham; s. of Charles Edward Picton Warlow and Nancy Mary Maclennan Hine; partner Cathie Sudlow; two s. two d.; ed Univ. of Cambridge and St George's Hosp. Medical School, London; Lecturer in Medicine, Aberdeen 1971–74; specialist training in neurology, London and Oxford 1974–77; Clinical Reader in Neurology and Hon. Consultant Neurologist, Oxford 1977–87; Prof. of Medical Neurology, Univ. of Edin. 1987–; Pres. Asscn of British Neurologists 2001–03; Ed. Practical Neurology; Tenovus-Scotland Margaret MacLellan Award 1989–90, Soc. of Authors and Royal Soc. of Medicine Medical Book Award, Advanced Author Book Category 1997, Osler Oration, Royal Coll. of Physicians 1998, Willis Lecturer, American Heart Asscn 2003, Asscn of British Neurologists Medal 2005. *Publications include:* Handbook of Clinical Neurology 1991, Transient Ischaemic Attacks of the Brain and Eye (with G.J. Hankey) 1994, Stroke: A Practical Guide to Management (co-author) (2nd edn) 2001, Lancet Handbook of Treatment in Neurology (ed.) 2006. *Leisure interests:* sailing, photography, mountains. *Address:* Department of Clinical Neurosciences, Western General Hospital, Crewe Road, Edinburgh, EH4 2XU (office); 6 South Gray Street, Edinburgh, EH9 1TE, Scotland (home). *Telephone:* (131) 537-2082 (office). *Fax:* (131) 332-5150 (office). *E-mail:* cpw@skull.dcn.ed.ac.uk (office). *Website:* www.dcn.ed.ac.uk (office).

WARNE, Shane Keith; Australian professional cricketer; b. 13 Sept. 1969, Ferntree Gully, Melbourne; m. Simone Warne; one s. two d.; ed Hampton High School, Mentone Grammar School; leg-break and googly bowler; right-hand lower-order batsman; 125 Tests for Australia 1992–, taking 600 wickets (record) with 2,598 runs scored; took hat-trick vs England, Melbourne, 1994; took 985 wickets and scored 4,768 runs in first-class cricket; toured England 1993, 1997, 2001; 194 limited-overs ints (11 as Capt.); Capt. Vic. Sheffield Shield Team (Bushrangers) 1996–99; received 12-month ban in Feb. 2003 for testing positive for a banned substance; Capt. of Hampshire 2004–; announced retirement from limited-overs ints 2004, from int. cricket 2007; leading wicket-taker in test cricket; Wisden Cricketer of the Year 1994, selected as one

of five Wisden Cricketers of the Century 2000, Overseas Personality of the Year, BBC Sports Personality of the Year Awards 2005. *Publication:* Shane Warne: The Autobiography 2001. *Address:* c/o Hampshire Cricket, The Rose Bowl, Botley Road, West End, Southampton, Hants., SO30 3XH, England; c/o Victorian Cricket Association, 86 Jolimont Street, Vic. 3002, Australia. *Telephone:* (23) 8047-2002 (England). *Fax:* (23) 8047-2122 (England). *E-mail:* enquiries@rosebowlplc.com. *Website:* www.rosebowlplc.com.

WARNER, Bishop Bennie D., MSc, ThM, DD; Liberian ecclesiastic; b. 30 April 1935, Caresburg Dist; ed Monrovia Gbarnga United Methodist Mission School, Booker Washington Inst., Kakata, Cuttington Univ. Coll., Suakoto, Syracuse Univ. and Boston Univ. School of Theology, USA; ordained deacon 1961; Acting Dir Pastors' Inst. of the United Methodist Church 1961; educ. counsellor and maths. and social studies teacher, W.V.S. Tubman Elementary School 1962–68; fmr Chair. Nat. Student Christian Council of Liberia; later ordained Elder; fmr Pastor, St John's United Methodist Church, Gbarnga and Reeves Memorial United Methodist Church, Crozierville; fmr Chair. Interim Cttee for the Admin of the Coll. of W Africa, Bd of Ministry, Liberia Annual Conf. of United Methodist Church; ordained Bishop 1973; later Chair. Bd of Trustees of the Coll. of W Africa; Vice-Pres. of Liberia 1977–80; mem. Bd of Trustees, Cuttington Coll. and Divinity School, Bd of the Booker Washington Inst., Nat. Disaster Comm., Council of Bishops, World Methodist Council; in exile in USA; Grand Band, Order of the Star of Africa.

WARNER, Brian, BSc, MA, PhD, DSc; British astronomer and academic; *Distinguished Professor Emeritus of Natural Philosophy, University of Cape Town;* b. 25 May 1939, Crawley Down, Sussex; s. of Leslie Warner and Edith M. Warner (née Bashford); m. 1st Carole Christian 1965 (divorced 1973); one s. one d.; m. 2nd Nancy Russell 1976 (divorced 1987); ed Univs of London and Oxford; Research Asst, Univ. of London Observatory 1964–65; Radcliffe-Henry Skynner Sr Research Fellow, Balliol Coll. Oxford 1965–67; Asst Prof., Univ. of Texas at Austin 1967–69, Assoc. Prof. 1969–72; Prof. and Head, Dept of Astronomy, Univ. of Cape Town 1972–99, Distinguished Prof. of Natural Philosophy 1999–2004, Distinguished Prof. Emer. 2005–, Fellow 1978–; Alfred P. Sloan Fellow 1969–71; Visiting Fellow, Univ. of Colorado 1977; Visiting Sr Fellow, Dept of Astrophysics, Univ. of Oxford 1985; Visiting Prof., Dartmouth Coll. and Univ. of Texas 1986–87, Univ. of Sussex 1997, Southampton Univ. 2007, 2008, 2009; Visiting Fellow, Univ. of Calif. at Santa Cruz 1990, ANU 1989, 1993, 1996, 1998, 2000, 2003; Visiting Scientist, European Southern Observatory 1996; Sr Fellow, Copernicus Centre, Warsaw 2003; Adjunct Prof., James Cook Univ., Townsville 2006–; Fellow, Univ. Coll., London 2009; Pres. Royal Soc. of S Africa 1981–83, Foreign Sec. 1996–2001, Fellow; mem. Acad. of Sciences of S Africa 1994–; Pres. Comm. of Int. Astronomical Union 1978–82 (Vice-Pres. 2003–09), Astronomical Soc. of Southern Africa 1977–78, The Owl Club 1985–86; mem. Bd of Trustees, S African Museum 1981–99, Deputy Chair. 1988–91, Chair. 1991–99; mem. Council S Africa Library 1991–99; Ernest Oppenheimer Travelling Fellowship 1990; Hon. Fellow, Royal Astronomical Soc. 1994; Hon. mem. Royal Astronomical Soc. of NZ 1995;; Hon. DSc (Univ. of Cape Town) 2009; Boyden Premium, Franklin Inst. 1980; McIntyre Award, Astronomical Soc. of Southern Africa 1983, John F.W. Herschel Medal, Royal Soc. of South Africa 1988, South African Medal, South African Asscn for the Advancement of Science 1989, Gill Medal, Astronomical Soc. of Southern Africa 1992, Univ. of Cape Town Book Award 1997, Science for Society Gold Medal, Acad. of Sciences of South Africa 2004, Gold Medal 2004. *Publications:* Astronomers at the Royal Observatory, Cape of Good Hope 1979, Charles Piazzi Smyth 1983, Maclear and Herschel 1984, The Journal of Lady Jane Franklin 1985, High Speed Astronomical Photometry 1988, William Mann 1989, Lady Herschel 1991, Cataclysmic Variable Stars 1995, Dinosaurs' End 1996, Flora Herscheliana 1998, Cape Landscapes 2006; more than 350 scientific research papers. *Leisure interests:* 19th-century science and exploration, baroque music. *Address:* Department of Astronomy, University of Cape Town, Rondebosch, 7700 Cape (office); 401 Blenheim, Marlborough Park, Claremont, 7700 Cape, South Africa (home). *Telephone:* (2721) 6502391 (office); (2721) 6711850 (home). *Fax:* (2721) 6503342 (office). *E-mail:* warner@physci.uct.ac.za (office). *Website:* mensa.ast.uct.ac.za (office).

WARNER, David; British actor; b. 29 July 1941, Manchester; s. of Herbert Simon Warner; ed Feldon School, Leamington Spa and Royal Acad. of Dramatic Art; worked as bookseller; stage début as Snout in A Midsummer Night's Dream, Royal Court 1962; film début in Tom Jones 1963; joined RSC 1963 and appeared as Trinculo in The Tempest, title role in Henry VI, Edward IV in adaptation of Henry VI (Parts I, II and III) comprising first two parts of trilogy The Wars of the Roses (Stratford). *Other roles include:* Henry VI in The Wars of the Roses, Aldwych 1964; Richard II, Mouldy in Henry IV (Part II) and Henry VI in The Wars of the Roses, RSC, Stratford 1964; Valentine Brose in Eh?, Aldwych 1964; Hamlet, Stratford and Aldwych 1965; the Postmaster in The Government Inspector, Aldwych 1965; Hamlet, Sir Andrew Aguecheek in Twelfth Night, Stratford 1966; Claudius in I, Claudius, Hampstead 1972. *Films include:* Morgan – A Suitable Case for Treatment 1966, Work is a Four Letter Word 1967, The Bofors Gun, The Fixer, The Seagull 1968–69, The Ballad of Cable Hogue 1970, Straw Dogs 1971, A Doll's House 1972, The Omen 1975, Cross of Iron, Providence, Silver Bears 1976, The Disappearance 1977, The Thirty Nine Steps 1978, Nightwing, Time After Time 1979, The Island 1980, Hanna's War 1988, The Secret Life of Ian Fleming 1990, Dark at Noon, Mortal Passions, In the Mouth of Madness, Titanic 1997, Scream 2 1997, Money Talks 1997, Shergar 2000, In the Beginning 2000, Horatio Hornblower 2001. *Television includes:* Clouds of Glory 1977, Holocaust 1977, Charlie 1984, The Choir 1995. *Address:* c/o Julian Belfrage Associates, 46 Albemarle Street, London, W1S 4DF, England.

WARNER, Deborah, CBE; British theatre and opera director; b. 12 May 1959, Oxford; d. of Ruth Warner and Roger Warner; ed Sidcot School, Avon, St

Clare's, Oxford, Cen. School of Speech and Drama, London; Founder and Artistic Dir Kick Theatre Co 1980–86; Resident Dir RSC 1987–89; Assoc. Dir Royal Nat. Theatre 1989–98; Assoc. Dir Abbey Theatre, Dublin 2000; has also staged productions at ENO (Bach's St John Passion, Janacek's Diary of One Who Vanished and Britten's Death in Venice), Glyndebourne Festival Opera (Don Giovanni 1994, Fidelio 2001, 2006), Royal Opera House(Turn of the Screw), Opera North (Wozzeck, La Voix Humaine), London Proms (concert of Honegger's Jeanne d'Arc au Bûcher), and has staged productions for Fitzroy Productions, Odeon Theatre, Chaillot and Bobigny Theatre, Paris, Salzburg Festival (Coriolan), LIFT and Perth Int. Arts Festival, Lincoln Center Festival, New York, Venice Festival (Dido and Aeneas), Bavarian State Opera (The Rape of Lucretia) 2004; Dir Fitzroy Productions; Chevalier, Ordre des Arts et des Lettres 2000; Evening Standard Award 1988, 1998, 2002, Laurence Olivier Award 1989, 1992, New York Drama Desk Award 1997, South Bank Arts Award 1998, OBIE Award 2003. *Productions include:* Titus Andronicus (RSC), King John (RSC), Electra (RSC), Hedda Gabler (Abbey Theatre, Dublin/West End), The Good Person of Sichuan (Royal Nat. Theatre), King Lear (Royal Nat. Theatre), Richard II (Royal Nat. Theatre), The Powerbook (Royal Nat. Theatre), The Waste Land (Fitzroy Productions), Medea (Abbey Theatre/West End/Broadway), The St Pancras Project (LIFT), The Tower Project (LIFT)The Angel Project (Perth Int. Arts Festival and Lincoln Center Festival), Readings (Fitzroy Productions). *Films:* The Waste Land 1996, The Last September 1999. *Television includes:* Richard II (BBC), Hedda Gabler (BBC), Don Giovanni (Channel 4). *Leisure interest:* travelling. *Address:* c/o Askonas Holt, Lincoln House, 300 High Holborn, London, WC1V 7JH, England (office); c/o Leah Schmidt, The Agency, 24 Pottery Lane, London, W11 4LZ (office). *Telephone:* (20) 7400-1700 (Askonas Holt, opera) (office); (20) 7727-1346 (The Agency, theatre) (office). *E-mail:* info@askonasholt.co.uk (office). *Website:* www.askonasholt.co.uk (office).

WARNER, Douglas Alexander III, BA; American banker; b. 9 June 1946, Cincinnati; s. of Douglas Alexander Warner Jr and Eleanor (née Wright) Warner; m. Patricia Grant 1977; two s. one d.; ed Yale Univ.; Officer's Asst Morgan Guaranty Trust Co., New York 1968–70, Asst Treas. 1970–72, Asst Vice-Pres. 1972–75, Vice-Pres. 1975–85, Sr Vice-Pres. Morgan Guaranty Trust Co., London 1983–87, Exec. Vice-Pres. Morgan Guaranty Trust Co., New York 1987–89, Man. Dir 1989–90, Pres. 1990–95, Chair. and CEO 1995–2000; Chair. J.P. Morgan Chase & Co. 2000–01; mem. Bd of Dirs General Electric Co., Anheuser-Busch Cos Inc., Motorola Inc.; Chair. Bd of Man. Overseers Memorial Sloan-Kettering Cancer Center, New York; Trustee Pierpoint Morgan Library, Cold Spring Harbor Lab. *Leisure interests:* golf, tennis, shooting. *Address:* P.O. Box 914, New York, NY 10268, USA (home).

WARNER, Sir Frederick Edward, Kt, FREng, FRS; British engineer and academic; b. 31 March 1910, London; s. of Frederick Warner; m. 1st Margaret Anderson McCrea; two s. two d.; m. 2nd Barbara Ivy Reynolds; ed Bancrofts School, Univ. Coll., London; chemical engineer with various cos 1934–56; partner in firm of consulting chemical engineers working in UK, Ireland, USSR, India, Iran, Jordan, Africa 1956–80; Sr Partner, Cremer and Warner 1963–80; Visiting Prof., Bartlett School of Architecture, Univ. Coll. London 1970, Imperial Coll. London 1970–78, 1993–2001, Univ. of Essex 1983–; Pro-Chancellor Open Univ. 1974–79; mem. Advisory Council on Energy Conservation, Dept of Energy 1974–80; Pres. British Standards Inst. 1980–83, Vice-Pres. 1976–80, 1983–89; Pres. British Asscn for Commercial and Industrial Educ. 1977–90, Inst. of Quality Assurance 1987–90; Chair. British Nat. Cttee on Problems of Environment, Royal Soc. 1973–80, Council of Science and Tech. Insts 1987–90; Treas. SCOPE 1982; Pres. Fédération Européenne d'Asscns Nationales d'Ingénieurs 1968–71; Fellow, Univ. Coll. London 1967; Académico Correspondiente la Academia de Ingeniería, Mexico; Hon. mem. Royal Inst. of Engineers, Netherlands 1972; Hon. Fellow, School of Pharmacy, London 1979, UMIST 1986; Hon. DTech (Bradford) 1969; Hon. DSc (Aston) 1970, (Cranfield) 1978, (Heriot-Watt) 1978, (Newcastle) 1979; Hon. DUniv (Open) 1980, (Essex) 1992; Gold Medal, Czechoslovak Soc. for Int. Relations 1969, Medal, Insinöö riliitto, Finland 1969, Bronze Medal, Associazione Nazionale Ingegneri e Architetti d'Italia 1971, Leverhulme Medal (Royal Soc.) 1978, Buchanan Medal (Royal Soc.) 1982, Tuev Rheinland Prize 1984, Gerard Piel Scientific American Award 1990, Gold Medal World Fed. of Eng Orgs 1993. *Publications:* Problem in Chemical Engineering Design (with J.M. Coulson) 1949, Risk (ed.) 1983, Risk-Analysis – Perception and Management (ed.) 1992, Quality 2000 (ed.) 1992, Radioecology after Chernobyl (with J.M. Harrison) 1993, Nuclear Test Explosions (co-ed. with R. J. Kirchmann) 1999; papers on nitric acid, heat transfer, underground gasification of coal, air and water pollution, contracts, planning, safety, risk, technology transfer, professional and continuous educ., nuclear winter, Chernobyl, nuclear weapons tests. *Leisure interests:* monumental brasses, ceramics, gardens. *Address:* 1 Ropewalk, Southwell, Notts., NG25 0AL, England (home). *Telephone:* (1636) 816483 (home). *Fax:* (1636) 814219 (home).

WARNER, H. Ty; American business executive; *Chairman and CEO, Ty Inc.;* b. Chicago; s. of Harold Warner and Georgia Warner; ed St. John's Military Academy, Wis., Kalamazoo Coll., Mich.; early career selling toys for Dakin LLC, San Francisco; f. Ty Inc. 1986, currently Pres., CEO; creator of Beanie Babies. *Address:* Ty Inc., 280 Chestnut Avenue, Westmont, IL 60559, USA (office). *Telephone:* (630) 920-1515 (office). *Fax:* (630) 920-1980 (office). *Website:* www.ty.com (office).

WARNER, John W., BS, LLB; American lawyer and fmr politician; b. 18 Feb. 1927, Washington, DC; s. of the late Dr John W. Warner and of Martha Warner (née Budd); m. 1st Catherine Conover Mellon (divorced 1973); one s. two d.; m. 2nd Elizabeth Taylor (q.v.) 1976 (divorced 1982); m. 3rd Jeanne van der Myde 2003; ed public schools in Washington, DC, school of Naval Research Lab., Washington, DC, Washington and Lee Univ. and Univ. of Virginia Law School; served in USN, attained rank of Electronic Technician 3rd Class 1944–46; subsequently enlisted in US Marine Corps Reserve, active duty as Communications Officer 1950–52, Capt. in US Marine Corps Reserve 1952–61; admitted to the Bar 1954; pvt. practice 1954–56; served in US Attorney's office as Special Asst 1956, Asst 1957; joined campaign staff of then Vice-Pres. Richard Nixon 1960; Assoc. Hogan & Hartson (law firm) 1960, Gen. Pnr 1964; Dir of Ocean Affairs as rep. of US Dept of Defense 1971; Under-Sec. of US Navy 1969–72, Sec. 1972–74; Dir American Revolution Bicentennial Admin. 1974–76; Senator from Virginia 1979–2009 (retd), Chair. Armed Services Cttee; fmr Head of US Del. to Moscow on Naval Affairs. *Address:* c/o 225 Russell Senate Office Building, Washington, DC 20510, USA (office).

WARNER, Marina Sarah, CBE, MA, FBA, FRSL; British writer and academic; *Professor of Literature, University of Essex;* b. 9 Nov. 1946, London; d. of Esmond Warner and Emilia Terzulli; m. 1st William Shawcross 1971; one s.; m. 2nd John Dewe Mathews 1981; pnr Graeme Segal FRS; ed St Mary's Convent, Ascot and Lady Margaret Hall, Univ. of Oxford; Getty Scholar, Getty Centre for the History of Art and the Humanities 1987–88; Tinbergen Prof., Erasmus Univ., Rotterdam 1990–91; Visiting Prof., Queen Mary and Westfield Coll., Univ. of London 1994, Univ. of Ulster 1994, Univ. of York 1996–, Birkbeck Coll., London; Tanner Lecturer, Yale Univ. 1999; Clarendon Lecturer, Oxford 2001; Prof. of Literature, Univ. of Essex 2004–; Fellow Commonership, Trinity Coll. Cambridge 1998; Visiting Fellow, All Souls Coll. Oxford 2001, Univ. Paris XIII 2003; Fellow, Italian Acad., Columbia Univ., New York, 2003; Sr Fellow, Remarque Inst., New York Univ. 2006; Visiting Prof., Royal Coll. of Art 2008–; Distinguished Visiting Prof., Queen Mary, Univ. of London 2009–; mem. Exec. Cttee Charter 88 –1997, Literature Panel Arts Council of England –1997, Advisory Council British Library –1997, Man. Cttee Nat. Council for One-Parent Families, Bd Artangel, Cttee London Library, Cttee PEN; Trustee, Nat. Portrait Gallery; Chevalier des Arts et des Lettres 2000, Commendatore dell'Ordine della Stella di Solidareità 2005; Hon. DLitt (Exeter) 1998, (Univ. of East London) 1999, (Kent) 2005, (Leicester) 2006, Oxford (2006); Dr hc (Sheffield Hallam, York, N London, St Andrews) 1998, (RCA) 2004, (King's Coll., London) 2009; Fawcett Prize 1986, Harvey Darton Award 1996, Mythopoeic Fantasy Award 1996, Katherine M. Briggs Award 1999, Rosemary Crawshay Prize, British Acad. 2000, Aby Warburg Prize 2004. *Radio:* short stories, criticism. *Publications:* Alone of All Her Sex: The Myth and the Cult of the Virgin Mary 1976, Joan of Arc 1982, Monuments and Maidens: The Allegory of the Female Form 1985, The Lost Father 1988, Indigo 1992, Mermaids in the Basement (short stories) 1993, Wonder Tales (ed.) 1994, Six Myths of Our Time – The 1994 Reith Lectures, From the Beast to the Blonde: On Fairy Tales and Their Tellers 1994, The Inner Eye: Art Beyond the Visible 1996, No Go the Bogeyman: On Scaring, Lulling and Making Mock 1998, The Leto Bundle 2001, Fantastic Metamorphoses, Other Worlds: The Clarendon Lectures 2002, Murderers I Have Known (short stories) 2002, Signs and Wonders: Essays on Literature and Culture 2003, Phantasmagoria: Spirit Visions, Metaphors, and Media 2006. *Leisure interests:* travel, friendship. *Address:* c/o Rogers, Coleridge & White, 20 Powis Mews, London, W11 1JN, England (office); LIFTS, University of Essex, Colchester, CO4 3SQ, England (office). *Telephone:* (20) 7221-3717 (office); (1206) 873073 (office). *Fax:* (20) 7229-9084 (office). *Website:* www.rcwlitagency.co.uk (office); www.marinawarner.com. *E-mail:* mswarner@essex.ac.uk (office).

WARNER, Mark R., BA, BLL; American lawyer and politician; *Senator from Virginia;* b. 15 Dec. 1954, Indianapolis, Ind.; m. Lisa Collis; three d.; ed George Washington Univ., Harvard Law School; Founding Pnr, Columbia Capital Corpn; Gov. of Virginia 2002–06; Senator from Virginia 2009–; Chair. Nat. Govs' Asscn 2004–05; Democrat; fmr Hon. Chair. Forward Together Political Action Cttee. *Address:* c/o Friends of Mark Warner, 1029 North Royal Street, Alexandria, VA 22314, USA.

WARNKE, Jürgen, LLD; German politician; b. 20 March 1932, Berlin; s. of Dr Franz Warnke and Marianne (née Gensel) Warnke; m.; six c.; registered for legal practice 1961; Sec. Chemical Industry Asscn in Bavaria 1962–64; Gen. Sec. Ceramics Industry Assn., Selb, Bavaria; joined Christian Social Union (CSU) 1958, Academic Asst to CSU Group in Deutscher Bundestag 1959–62; mem. Bavarian State Parl. 1962–70; mem. Deutscher Bundestag 1969–; apptd Chair. Bundestag Cttee on Trade Policy 1971, Vice-Pres. Cttee for European and Int. Co-operation 1978; Fed. Minister of Econ. Co-operation 1982–87, 1989–91, of Transport 1987–89; Chair. Supervisory Bd Königliche Porzellan Manufaktur GmbH, Berlin 1995–; mem. Synod, Protestant Church of Germany (EKD) 1985–; Grosses Bundesverdienstkreuz (with Star) 1994. *Address:* Bundestag, Reichstagebäude, Scheidemannstrasse 2, Berlin 10557, Germany.

WARNOCK, John E., MS, PhD; American computer industry executive; *Co-Chairman, Adobe Systems Inc.;* ed Univ. of Utah; fmrly with Evans & Sutherland Computer Corpn, Computer Sciences Corpn, IBM and Univ. of Utah; Principal Scientist Xerox Palo Alto Research Centre (PARC) until 1982; Co-Founder and Jt Chair. Adobe Systems Inc. 1982–; mem. Bd of Dirs Octavo Corpn, mem. Bd, fmr Chair. Tech. Museum of Innovation; mem. Entrepreneurial Bd Advisory Cttee, American Film Inst.; mem Nat. Acad. of Eng, Utah Information Tech. Asscn 2000; numerous awards including Distinguished Service to Art and Design Int. Award and Corp. Outstanding Achievement Award, Rhode Island School of Design 1998; Award for Technical Excellence, Nat. Graphics Asscn; Lifetime Achievement Award for Technical Excellence, PC Magazine; Cary Award, Rochester Inst. of Tech.; ACM Software Systems Award. *Publications:* numerous articles in technical journals and industry magazines. *Address:* Adobe Systems Inc., 345 Park Avenue, San José, CA 95110-2704, USA (office). *Telephone:* (408) 536-6000 (office). *Fax:* (408) 537-6000 (office). *Website:* www.adobe.com (office).

WARNOCK, Baroness (Life Peer), cr. 1985, of Weeke in the City of Winchester; **(Helen) Mary Warnock,** DBE, FCP, FRSM; British philosopher and university administrator; b. 14 April 1924, Winchester; d. of the late Archibald Edward Wilson and Ethel Schuster; m. Sir Geoffrey J. Warnock 1949 (died 1995); two s. three d.; ed St Swithun's, Winchester and Lady Margaret Hall, Oxford; Tutor in Philosophy, St Hugh's Coll. Oxford 1949–66; Headmistress, Oxford High School 1966–72; Talbot Research Fellow, Lady Margaret Hall 1972–76; Sr Research Fellow, St Hugh's Coll. 1976–84; Mistress of Girton Coll. Cambridge 1985–91; Chair. Cttee of Inquiry into Special Educ. 1974–78, Advisory Cttee on Animal Experiments 1979–86, Cttee of Inquiry into Human Fertilization 1982–84, Educ. Cttee Girls' Day School Trust 1994–2001; mem. IBA 1973–81, Royal Comm. on Environmental Pollution 1979–84, Social Science Research Council 1981–85, UK Nat. Comm. for UNESCO 1981–85, Archbishop of Canterbury's Advisory Group on Medical Ethics 1992–; Chair. Planning Aid Trust 2002–; Fellow, Coll. of Teachers (fmrly Coll. of Preceptors); Hon. Master of the Bench, Gray's Inn 1986; Hon. Fellow, Imperial Coll. London 1986, Hertford Coll. Oxford 1997, Lady Margaret Hall Oxford, St Hugh's Coll. Oxford; Hon. FRCM; Hon. Fellow, Royal Soc. of Physicians, Scotland; Hon. FBA 2000; Hon. FRCP 2002; Hon. DUniv (Open Univ.) 1980, (St Andrews) 1992; Hon. LLD (Manchester) 1987, (Liverpool) 1991, (London) 1991; Hon. DLitt (Glasgow) 1988; Dr hc (Univ. of York) 1989; RSA Albert Medal 1998. *Publications:* Ethics since 1900 1960, J.-P. Sartre 1963, Existentialist Ethics 1966, Existentialism 1970, Imagination 1976, Schools of Thought 1977, What Must We Teach? (with T. Devlin) 1977, Education: A Way Forward 1979, A Question of Life 1985, Teacher Teach Thyself (Dimbleby Lecture) 1985, Memory 1987, A Common Policy for Education 1989, Universities: Knowing Our Minds 1989, The Uses of Philosophy 1992, Imagination and Time 1994; Women Philosophers (ed.) 1996, An Intelligent Person's Guide to Ethics 1998, A Memoir: People and Places 2000, Making Babies 2002, Nature and Mortality 2003, Utilitariansim (ed.) 2003, Special Education: A New Look 2005, Easeful Death (with Elisabeth MacDonald) 2008. *Leisure interests:* music, gardening. *Address:* House of Lords, Westminster, London, SW1A 0PW (office); 60 Church Street, Great Bedwyn, Wilts., SN8 3PF, England (home). *Telephone:* (20) 7219-8619 (office); (1672) 870214 (home). *E-mail:* warnock@parliament.uk. *Website:* www.parliament.uk (office).

WARRELL, David Alan, MA, DM, DSc, FRCP, FRCPE, FMedSci; British specialist in tropical medicine and venoms; *Emeritus Professor of Tropical Medicine, University of Oxford;* b. 6 Oct. 1939, Singapore; s. of Mr and the late Mrs A. T. Warrell; m. Dr Mary J. Prentice 1975; two d.; ed Portsmouth Grammar School, Christ Church, Oxford and St Thomas's Hosp. Medical School, London; Oxford Univ. Radcliffe Travelling Fellow, Univ. of Calif. at San Diego 1969; Sr Lecturer, Ahmadu Bello Univ., Nigeria and Lecturer and Consultant Physician, Royal Postgrad. Medical School, London and Hammersmith Hosp. 1970–75; Founding Dir Wellcome-Mahidol Univ., Oxford Tropical Medicine Research Programme, Bangkok and Wellcome Reader in Tropical Medicine, Univ. of Oxford 1979–86; Prof. of Tropical Medicine and Infectious Diseases and Dir Emer. (fmrly Dir) Centre for Tropical Medicine, Univ. of Oxford 1987–2001, Head Nuffield Dept Clinical Medicine 2002–04, Deputy Head 2004–06, Emer. Prof. of Tropical Medicine 2006–; sr adviser to MRC on tropical medicine 2001–; Hon. Consultant in Malariology to British Army 1989–; Hon. Medical Adviser, Royal Geographical Soc. 1993–, Earthwatch Int. 2007–, Foreign and Commonwealth Office 2002–; WHO Consultant 1979–; mem. WHO Expert Advisory Panel on Malaria 1989–; Fellow, St Cross Coll. 1975–2007, Hon. Fellow 2007–; Chair. AIDS Therapeutic Trials Cttee, MRC; Trustee, Tropical Health and Education Trust; Pres. British Venom Group 1992–, Int. Fed. for Tropical Medicine 1996–2000, Royal Soc. of Tropical Medicine and Hygiene 1997–99; Del. Oxford Univ. Press 1999–2006; Marc Daniels, Bradshaw, Croonian and Coll. Lecturer and Harveian Orator 2001, Royal Coll. of Physicians; Runme Shaw Lecturer, Acad. of Medicine, Singapore 1997; Llods-Roberts Lecturer, Royal Soc. of Medicine 2008; Knight Commander, Order of the White Elephant (Thailand) 2004; Hon. mem. Asscn of Physicians GB and NI 2003, American Soc. of Tropical Medicine and Hygiene 2003; Hon. Fellow Ceylon Coll. of Physicians; Ambuj Nath Bose Prize, Royal Coll. of Physicians 1994, Chalmer's Medal, Royal Soc. of Tropical Medicine and Hygiene 1981, Queen's Award for Higher and Further Educ. 2000, Guthrie Medal, Royal Army Medical Corps (RAMC) 2004, Mary Kingsley Medal, Liverpool School of Tropical Medicine 2005. *Publications:* scientific papers and book chapters; Ed.: Oxford Textbook of Medicine, Essential Malariology, Oxford Handbook Expedition and Wilderness Medicine. *Leisure interests:* book-collecting, music, bird-watching, hill-walking. *Address:* Nuffield Dept of Clinical Medicine, University of Oxford, Level 5 – John Radcliffe Hospital, Headley Way, Oxford, OX3 9DU, England (office). *Telephone:* (1865) 234664 (office); (1865) 766865 (office). *Fax:* (1865) 760683 (office). *E-mail:* david.warrell@ndm.ox.ac.uk (office); david.warrell@stx.ox.ac.uk (office). *Website:* www.ndm.ox.ac.uk (office).

WARREN, Chris; Australian international organization executive; *President, International Federation of Journalists;* fmr Gen.-Sec. Australian Journalists Asscn Br., Media Entertainment and Arts Alliance (MEAA), Australia 1999, currently Fed. Sec. MEAA; Pres. Int. Fed. Journalists (IFJ) 2001–. *Address:* International Federation of Journalists, IPC-Residence Palace, Bloc C, Rue de la Loi 155, 1040 Brussels, Belgium (office). *Telephone:* (32) 22352200 (office). *Fax:* (32) 22352219 (office). *E-mail:* christopher.warren@alliance.org.au (office); ifj@ifj.org (office). *Website:* www.ifj.org (office).

WARREN, Sir Frederick Miles, Kt, KBE, FNZIA, ARIBA, DIP.ARCH.; New Zealand architect; b. 10 May 1929, Christchurch; s. of M. B. Warren and J. Warren (née Hay); ed Christ's Coll., Auckland Univ. School of Architecture; worked for the late C. W. Wood, 1946–47, for the late R. C. Munroe,ANZIA 1948; joined partnership with the late G. T. Lucas 1956; started firm Warren and Mahoney 1958, Sr Partner 1958–; Fellow, New Zealand Inst. of Architects (NZIA) 1965; Pres. Canterbury Soc. of Arts 1972–76; Warren and Mahoney awarded NZIA Gold Medal for Dental Nurses' Training School 1960, for Christchurch Memorial Garden Crematorium 1964, for Christchurch Coll. Halls of Residence 1969, for Christchurch Town Hall and Civic Centre 1973; won Architectural Competition for design of Condominium Offices, New Hebrides 1966; Gold Medal NZIA 1980, 1981, 1983, 1984, 1985, 1986, 1988–91. *Publication:* Warren & Mahoney Architects 1990. *Leisure interests:* yachting, water-colouring, sketching. *Address:* 65 Cambridge Terrace, Christchurch 1, New Zealand. *Telephone:* 799-640.

WARREN, John Robin, AC, MB, BS, MD, FAA, FRCPA; Australian pathologist; b. 11 June 1937, Adelaide, S Australia; s. of Roger Warren and Helen Warren (née Verco); m. Winifred Teresa Williams; four s. two d.; ed Univ. of Adelaide and Royal Melbourne Hosp.; Jr Resident Medical Officer, Queen Elizabeth Hosp., Woodville, S Australia 1961; Registrar in Haematology and Clinical Pathology, Inst. of Medical and Veterinary Science, Adelaide 1962; Registrar in Clinical Pathology, Royal Melbourne Hosp. 1964–66, Registrar in Pathology 1966–68; Sr Pathologist, Royal Perth Hosp., Western Australia 1968–99; demonstrated, with Barry J. Marshall, the association of *Helicobacter pylori* and peptic ulcers, particularly duodenal ulcers; Fellow, Royal Coll. of Pathologists of Australasia 1967; Hon. Fellow, Royal Australian Coll. of Physicians 2006; Hon. Mem. Polish Soc. of Gastroenterology, German Soc. of Pathology 2007; Hon. MD (Univ. of Western Australia) 1997; Dr hc (Univ. of Adelaide) 2006, (Univ. of Toyama, Japan) 2007, (Otto-von-Guericke Universität, Magdeburg) 2007; Guest of Honour, Sixth Int. Workshop on Campylobacter, Helicobacter and Related Organisms 1991, Distinguished Fellows Award, Coll. of Pathologists 1995, Inaugural Award, First Western Pacific Helicobacter Congress 1996, Medal of Univ. of Hiroshima 1996, Australian Medical Asscn (WA) Award 1995; jtly with Prof. Barry Marshall: Warren Alpert Foundation Prize, Harvard Medical School 1995, Paul Ehrlich and Ludwig Darmstaedter Award, Goethe-Universität, Frankfurt, Germany 1997, Inaugural Florey Medal Award 1998, Nobel Prize in Physiology or Medicine 2005, Australian Medical Asscn Gold Medal 2006, Western Australian of the Year 2007, Medal of the Hirosaki Univ. School of Medicine 2007, Special Recognition Award for Distinguished Service to Surgical Pathology, American Soc. for Clinical Pathology 2007, Govt of Western Australia Premier's Science Awards, Western Australian Science Hall of Fame 2007. *Publications:* numerous articles in scientific journals. *Leisure interest:* photography. *Address:* Suite 10, 3 Centro Avenue, Subiaco, WA 6003, Australia (office). *Telephone:* (8) 9382-2686 (office). *Fax:* (8) 9382-2313 (office). *E-mail:* mglenn@helicobacter.com (office).

WARREN, Jack Hamilton, OC; Canadian diplomatist and business executive (retd); b. 10 April 1921; m. Hilary J. Titterington; four c.; ed Queen's Univ., Kingston, Ont.; Royal Canadian Navy 1941–45; joined Dept of External Affairs 1945; served in London 1948–51; transferred to Dept of Finance and served as Financial Counsellor, Washington, DC and as Alt. Dir for Canada, IMF and IBRD 1954–57; Canadian Del. to OECD and NATO 1957–58; Asst Deputy Minister of Trade and Commerce 1958–64; Chair. GATT Contracting Parties 1962–65; Deputy Minister of Trade and Commerce 1964–68, of Industry, Trade and Commerce 1968–71; High Commr in UK 1971–74; Amb. to USA 1975–77; Canadian Coordinator for the Multilateral Trade Negotiations 1977–79; Vice-Chair. Bank of Montréal 1979–86; Prin. Adviser on trade policy, Govt of Québec 1986–94; Deputy N American Chair. Trilateral Comm. 1986–90; Hon. LLD (Queen's Univ.) 1974; Outstanding Achievement Award, Public Service of Canada 1975. *Leisure interests:* travel, salmon fishing, food and wine. *Address:* 37 Larrimac Road, Chelsea, PQ J9B 2C4, Canada (home). *Telephone:* (819) 827-3715 (home). *Fax:* (819) 827-3715 (home).

WARRINGTON, Elizabeth Kerr, PhD, DSc, FRS; British academic; *Professor Emerita of Clinical Neuropsychology, National Hospital for Neurology and Neurosurgery;* d. of the late Prof. John A. V. Butler, FRS and Margaret L. Butler; m.; one d.; ed Univ. Coll. London; Research Fellow, Inst. of Neurology 1956; Sr Clinical Psychologist, Nat. Hosp. for Neurology and Neurosurgery 1960, Prin. Psychologist 1962, Top Grade Clinical Psychologist 1972–82, Prof. of Clinical Neuropsychology 1982–96, Hon. Consultant Neuropsychologist to Dementia Research Centre 1996–, Prof. Emer. of Clinical Neuropsychology, Univ. of London 1996–; Fellow, Univ. Coll. London; Dr hc (Bologna) 1998, (York) 1999, (Univ. Louis Pasteur) 2006. *Publications:* Cognitive Neuropsychology (co-author) 1990; numerous papers in professional journals. *Leisure interests:* gardening, entertaining granddaughters. *Address:* Dementia Research Centre, Box 16, National Hospital for Neurology and Neurosurgery, Queen Square, London, WC1N 3BG, England (office). *Telephone:* (20) 7837-3611 (office). *Website:* www.uclh.org/about/nhnn.shtml (office).

WARRIOR, Padmasree, BS, MS; Indian/American engineer and business executive; *Chief Technology Officer, Cisco Systems Inc.;* m.; ed Indian Inst. of Tech. (IIT), New Delhi, Cornell Univ., Ithaca, NY; Vice-Pres. Motorola, Inc. 1999, Motorola's Liaison Exec. for Cornell Univ. 2001, Exec. Vice-Pres. and Chief Tech. Officer, Motorola, Inc. 2003–07; Chief Tech. Officer Cisco Systems Inc. 2007–; mem. Bd of Dirs Corning Corpn 2005–08; mem. Bd Joffrey Ballet, Chicago, Museum of Science and Industry, Chicago, Singapore Agency for Science, Tech. and Research (ASTAR), Chicago Mayor's Tech. Council, Cornell Univ. Eng Council, IIT Advisory Council; mem. Selection Bd for White House Fellows 2001; fmr mem. Texas Gov.'s Council for Digital Economy, Tech. Advisory Council Fed. Communications Comm., Advisory Cttee NSF Computing and Information Science and Eng; Dr hc (New York Polytechnic) 2007; Women Elevating Science and Tech. Award, Working Woman Magazine (co-recipient) 2001, achievements recognized by American Immigration Law Foundation 2003, ranked by The Economic Times as 11th Most Influential

Global Indian 2006, IIT Distinguished Alumni Award 2006,. *Leisure interests:* novels of P. G. Wodehouse, arts and crafts, exercising, meditation. *Address:* Cisco Systems Inc., 170 West Tasman Drive, Bldg. 10, San Jose, CA 95134-1706, USA. *Telephone:* (408) 526-4000 (office). *Fax:* (408) 526-4100 (office). *Website:* www.cisco.com (office).

WARWICK, Dionne; American singer; b. (Marie Dionne), 12 Dec. 1941, East Orange, NJ; m. Bill Elliott (divorced 1975); two s.; pnr Bruce Garrick; ed Hartt Coll. of Music, Hartford, Conn.; as teenager formed Gospelaires; later sang background for recording studio 1966; début, Philharmonic Hall, Lincoln Center, New York 1966; appearances at London Palladium, Olympia, Paris, Lincoln Center; co-host, Solid Gold (TV show); host, A Gift of Music (TV show) 1981; star, Dionne Warwick Special (TV show); appeared in Sisters in the Name of Love on TV 1986; named UN FAO Amb. 2002; Co-founder Carr/Todd/Warwick Production, Inc., Dionne Warwick Design Group Inc.; five Grammy Awards, Luminary Award, American Soc. of Young Musicians 1997, Chairman's Award for Sustained Creative Achievement, Nat. Asscn of Record Merchandisers 1998, History Maker, History Makers Org. of Chicago 2001, Heroes Award, New York Chapter of Recording Acad. 2002, Lifetime Achievement Award, R&B Foundation 2003, named one of Top Faces of Black History 2003. *Films:* The Slaves 1969, No Night, So Long, Hot! Live and Otherwise. *Singles include:* I'll Never Love this Way Again, That's What Friends are For. *Albums include:* Valley of the Dolls and Others 1968, Promises, Promises 1975, Dionne 1979, Then Came You, Friends 1986, Reservations for Two 1987, Greatest Hits 1990, Dionne Warwick Sings Cole Porter 1990, Hidden Gems: The Best of Dionne Warwick (Vol. 2) 1992, Friends Can Be Lovers (with Whitney Houston) 1993, Dionne Warwick and Placido Domingo 1994, Aquarela do Brasil 1994, From the Vaults 1995, Dionne Sings Dionne 1998, I Say a Little Prayer For You 2000. *Publications:* My Point of View 2003. *Address:* c/o Stargirl, Bristol Plaza, 6167 Bristol Parkway, Suite 360, Culver City, CA 90230-6619, USA (office). *Telephone:* (310) 670-4247 (office). *Fax:* (310) 670-3851 (office). *E-mail:* hencarr@aol.com (office). *Website:* www.dionnewarwick.info.

WARWICK OF UNDERCLIFFE, Baroness (Life Peer), cr. 1999, of Undercliffe in the County of West Yorkshire; **Diana Warwick,** BA; British academic; b. 16 July 1945, Bradford; d. of Jack Warwick and Olive Warwick; m. Sean Young 1969; ed Bedford Coll., Univ. of London; Gen. Sec. Asscn of Univ. Teachers 1983–92; mem. RIIA, Inter-Parl. Union, Commonwealth Parl. Asscn, British American Parl. Group, Employment Appeals Tribunal 1984–99; mem. Bd British Council 1985–95, Commonwealth Inst. 1988–95; Chief Exec. Westminster Foundation for Democracy 1992–95; Chair. VSO 1994–; mem. Standing Cttee on Standards in Public Life (Nolan/Neill Cttee) 1994–99, OST Tech. Foresight Steering Group 1997–; Chief Exec. Universities UK (fmrly Cttee of Vice-Chancellors and Prins) 1995; Trustee St Catharine's Foundation, Windsor 1996–; Hon. DLitt (Bradford) 1993, (Open Univ.) 1998. *Address:* House of Lords, London, SW1A 0PW, England. *Telephone:* (20) 7219-5086 (office).

WARWICK-THOMPSON, Paul, PhD; British museum director and university rector; *Rector, Royal College of Art;* b. 9 Aug. 1959, Oxford; s. of Sir Michael Thompson; m. Adline Finlay 1984; one s. one d.; ed Bryanston School, Univ. of Bristol, Univ. of East Anglia; Curator Design Museum, London 1989–92, Dir 1992–2000; Dir Cooper-Hewitt Nat. Design Museum, New York 2001–09; Rector RCA 2009–; Hon. Fellow, RCA 2000. *Leisure interests:* theatre, cinema, gardening. *Address:* Royal College of Art, Kensington Gore, London SW7, England (office). *Telephone:* (20) 7590-4444 (office). *E-mail:* press@rca.ac.uk (office).

WĄSACZ, Emil; Polish economist, business executive and fmr government official; b. 1 Aug. 1945, Zabratówka, Rzeszów Prov.; m.; three c.; ed Łódź Tech. Univ., Main School of Commerce (SGH), Warsaw; employee, Katowice Steelworks 1976–94, Supreme Dir then Chair. Katowice Steelworks SA 1991–94; adviser to Chair. Bank Śląski SA, Bank PeKaO SA and enterprise Stalexport SA; Chair. Szczecin Steelworks SA 1995–97; Vice-Leader Supervisory Bd, later Chair. Progress Nat. Investment Fund 1995–97; Minister of the Treasury 1997–2001; CEO Stalexport Serwis-Centrum S.A. (steel products co.) 2001, then Chair. Man. Bd, suspended from position 2006; mem. Solidarity Trade Union, Leader Plant Cttee in the Katowice Steelworks 1989–90; voluntary worker, Catholic Family Clinic, Sosnowiec 1983–90. *Leisure interests:* tourism, history, astronomy, literature, romantic poetry. *Address:* c/o Management Board, Stalexport Serwis-Centrum S.A, 40-780 Katowice, ul.Owsiana 60a, Poland. *Website:* www.stalexport.katowice.pl.

WASE, Brenson S.; Marshall Islands politician; Minister of Internal Affairs 1997–99, of Transportation and Communications 2000, of Finance 2000–08; Gov. of the Marshall Islands to ADB 2000–, Vice-Chair. Bd of Dirs 2004–; Acting Pres. of Repub. of Marshall Islands 2003. *Address:* c/o Ministry of Finance, POB D, Majuro, MH 96960, Marshall Islands (office).

WASER, Peter Gaudenz, MD, DPhil; Swiss professor of pharmacology; b. 21 July 1918, Zürich; s. of Ernst Waser and Margrit Ruttiman; m. Marion Edmée Bodmer 1946; one s. two d.; ed Univ. of Zürich, Basle Univ. Hosp., Calif. Inst. of Tech., USA; Prof. of Medicine, Univ. of Zürich 1959, Dir Inst. of Pharmacology 1963–87, Prof. of Pharmacy 1965–87, Dean of Faculty of Medicine 1970–72, Rector 1978–80; research in psychopharmacology, Psychiatric Univ. Clinic, Zürich 1987–95; Pres. Engadine Collegium in Philosophy 1967–, Int. Union of Pharmacology 1978–81, Int. Council of Scientific Unions 1981–84. *Publications:* Mechanisms of Synaptic Transmission 1969 (with Akert), Cholinergic Mechanisms 1975, Praktische Pharmakotherapie 1987 (with C. Steinbach), The Cholinergic Receptor 1987, Psychiatrie, Psychopharmaka und Drogen in Zürich 1990. *Leisure interests:* mountaineering, skiing, gardening, painting. *Address:* ETH Zürich, Departement Chemie und Angewandte Biowissenschaften, Oberer Heuelsteig 12, 8032 Zürich, Switzerland (office).

WASHIDA, Kiyokazu; Japanese philosopher, academic and university administrator; *President, Osaka University;* b. 1949, Kyoto; ed Kyoto Univ.; fmr Prof., School of Letters and Dean, Grad. School of Letters, Kyoto Univ., later Vice-Pres. in charge of Educ. and Information; Asst Prof., Faculty of Literature, Osaka Univ. Grad. School 2005, becoming Univ. Vice-Pres., then Pres. 2007–; mem. Kyoto Nat. Festival Planning Cttee; Assoc. mem. Science Council of Japan; Dir Japan Asscn of Nat. Univs; mem. Cabinet Office Council for Science and Tech. Policy Expert Panel on Bioethics; Medal of Honour with Purple Ribbon 2004; Suntory Prize for Social Sciences and Humanities 1989, Kuwabara Takeo Prize 2000. *Publications:* Talking to Myself (co-author) 2002. *Address:* Office of the President, Osaka University, 1-1 Yamadaoka, Suita, Osaka 565-0871, Japan (office). *Telephone:* (6) 6879-7106 (office). *Website:* www.osaka-u.ac.jp/eng (office).

WASHINGTON, Denzel, BA; American film actor; b. 28 Dec. 1954, Mt. Vernon, NY; m. Pauletta Pearson 1983; two s. two d.; ed Fordham Univ. and American Conservatory Theater, San Francisco; worked at New York Shakespeare Festival and American Place Theater; off-Broadway appearances include: Ceremonies in Dark Old Men, When the Chickens Come Home to Roost and A Soldier's Play (Negro Ensemble Co.); played young doctor in TV series St Elsewhere; Harvard Foundation Award 1996. *Films include:* A Soldier's Story 1984, The Mighty Quinn, Cry Freedom 1987, Heart Condition 1989, Glory (Acad. Award for Best Supporting Actor) 1990, Love Supreme 1990, Mo' Better Blues 1990, Ricochet 1991, Mississippi Masala 1991, Much Ado About Nothing, Malcolm X 1992, The Pelican Brief 1993, Philadelphia 1993, Devil in a Blue Dress 1995, Courage Under Fire 1996, The Preacher's Wife 1996, Fallen 1997, He Got Game 1998, The Siege 1998, The Bone Collector 1999, The Hurricane 1999, Remember the Titans 2001, Training Day (Acad. Award for Best Actor 2002) 2001, John Q (Award for Best Actor, Nat. Asscn for the Advancement of Colored People (NAACP) Awards 2003) 2002, Antwone Fisher (also producer and dir; Awards for Best Supporting Actor and Best Dir, NAACP Awards 2003) 2002, Out of Time 2003, Man on Fire 2004, The Manchurian Candidate 2004, Inside Man 2006, Deja Vu 2006, American Gangster 2007. *Leisure interests:* cooking, reading, basketball. *Address:* c/o ICM, 8942 Wilshire Boulevard, Beverly Hills, CA 90211, USA.

WASIM AKRAM; Pakistani fmr professional cricketer; b. 3 June 1966, Lahore; ed Islamia Coll.; left-hand middle-order batsman, left-arm fast bowler; played for Pakistan Automobile Corpn 1984–85, Lahore 1985–86, Lancashire 1988–98 (Capt. 1998), Hampshire 2003; only bowler to have captured more than 400 wickets both in Test and one-day cricket; played in 104 Tests for Pakistan during 1985–2002 (25 as Capt.), scoring 2,898 runs (average 22.64) including 3 hundreds and taking 414 wickets (average 23.6); scored 7,161 runs (7 hundreds) and took 1,042 wickets in first-class cricket; 350 limited-overs internationals (109 as Capt.) taking record 502 wickets; retd 2003; Wisden Cricketer of the Year 1993. *Publication:* Wasim (autobiog.). *Address:* c/o Pakistan Cricket Board, Gaddafi Stadium, Ferozepur Road, Lahore 54600, Pakistan. *Telephone:* (42) 571-7231.

WASMOSY, Juan Carlos, DCE; Paraguayan politician and civil engineer; b. 15 Dec. 1938, Asunción; s. of Dr Juan Bautista Wasmosy and María Clotilde Monti Paoli; m. Maria Teresa Carrasco Dos Santos; five s. (one deceased) one d.; ed San José School, Asunción and Nat. Univ. of Asunción; fmr Asst Prof. Univ. of Asunción; sometime Pres. ECOMIPA, CONEMPA, COCEP, GOYA (pvt. construction and industrial cos); other business affiliations; mem. construction holding which built Itaipú Hydroelectric Power Station; currently engaged in construction of Yacyretá power station; Pres. Int. Fed. of Zebu Cattle Breeders; mem. Colorado Party 1973–; Minister of Integration 1993; Pres. of Paraguay 1993–98, Senator for Life 1998–; Orden de Solidaridad de Brasil; other medals and awards. *Address:* The Senate, Asunción, Paraguay.

WASS, Sir Douglas William Gretton, GCB, MA; British fmr civil servant and business executive; b. 15 April 1923, Wallasey, Cheshire; s. of the late Arthur W. Wass and Elsie W. Wass; m. Dr Milica Pavičić 1954; one s. one d.; ed Nottingham High School, St John's Coll. Cambridge; Scientific Research with Admiralty 1943–46; Asst Prin., Treasury 1946, Prin. 1951; Commonwealth Fund Fellow, USA 1958–59; Fellow, Brookings Inst., Washington 1959; Pvt. Sec. to Chancellor 1959–61; Pvt. Sec. to Chief Sec. 1961–62; Alt. Exec. Dir to IMF and Financial Counsellor, British Embassy, Washington, DC 1965–67; Under-Sec. of Treasury 1968, Deputy Sec. 1970, Second Perm. Sec. 1973, Perm. Sec. 1974–83; Jt Head, Home Civil Service 1981–83; Chair. Econ. Policy Cttee, OECD 1982; Reith Lecturer, BBC 1983; Chair. British Selection Cttee, Harkness Fellowships 1981–84, Governing Body of the Ditchley Foundation, Council of the Policy Studies Inst.; Chair. Nomura Int. PLC 1986–98 (Sr Adviser 1998–2002), Axa Equity and Law Life Assurance Soc. PLC 1986–95, N.C.M. (Credit Insurance) Ltd 1991–95; Gov. Centre for Econ. Policy Research 1983–90; Adviser to Campaign for Freedom of Information; Dir De La Rue Co. PLC 1983–93, Coopers and Lybrand 1984–86, Barclays Bank PLC 1984–87, African Capacity Bldg Foundation, Harare 1991–98, Equitable Cos Inc. New York 1992–95; Administrateur, Cie du Midi SA (now Axa SA) 1987–95; Vice-Pres. Constitutional Reform Centre 1984–92; mem. Council of Univ. of Bath 1985–91; Pres. Market Research Soc. 1987–91; mem. Overseas Devt Council 1990–96; mem. Council British Heart Foundation 1990–96; Dir Soho Theatre Co. 1996–2000; Hon. Fellow, St John's Coll. Cambridge; Hon. DLitt (Bath). *Publications:* The Changing Problems of Economic Management 1978, The Public Service in Modern Society 1982, Government and the Governed 1984, The Civil Service at the Crossroads 1985, What Sort of Industrial Policy? 1986, Checks and Balances in Public Policy Making 1987, Decline to Fall 2008. *Leisure interest:* swimming. *Address:* 6 Dora Road, Wimbledon, London, SW19

7HH, England (home). *Telephone:* (20) 8946-5556 (office). *Fax:* (20) 8241-4626 (home). *E-mail:* douglas.wass@blueyonder.co.uk (home).

WASSENER, Albert; German cultural institute director; b. 25 April 1936, Essen; s. of Albert Wassener and Gertrud Wassener (née Forstbauer); m. Renate Wassener 1962; one s. one d.; ed Univ. of Bonn, Univ. of Munich; Dir Goethe Inst., Tripoli, Libya 1965–66; Officer, Cultural Programmes, Goethe Inst., Rome 1966–74; Head, Teachers' Training Dept, Goethe Inst. Head Office, Munich 1974–78; Dir Goethe Inst., Tel-Aviv 1978–84, Copenhagen 1984–89, Istanbul 1989–90; Head, Talks Dept, Goethe Inst. Head Office, Munich 1990–95; Dir Goethe Inst., London and Regional Dir, Great Britain and Northern Ireland 1995–2000.

WASSERBURG, Gerald Joseph, BSc, MSc, PhD; American geologist, geophysicist and academic; *John D. MacArthur Professor Emeritus of Geology and Geophysics, California Institute of Technology;* b. 25 March 1927, New Brunswick, NJ; s. of Charles Wasserburg and Sarah Levine Wasserburg; m. Naomi Z. Orlick 1951; two s.; ed Univ. of Chicago; served as rifleman, Second Infantry Div. with US Army 1943–46; with Resurrection Mining Co. 1947; Juneau Ice Field Research Project, Alaska 1950; Consultant Argonne Nat. Laboratory, Lamont, Ill. 1952–55; Research Assoc., Inst. for Nuclear Studies, Chicago 1954–55; Asst Prof. of Geology, Calif. Inst. of Tech. 1955–59, Assoc. Prof. of Geology 1959–62, Prof. of Geology and Geophysics 1962–82, John D. MacArthur Prof. of Geology and Geophysics 1982–2002, Prof. Emer. 2002–, Chair. Div. of Geological and Planetary Sciences 1987–89; Adviser to NASA 1968–88; Vice-Chair. Lunar Sample Analysis Planning Team, MSC, NASA 1970; mem. Lunar Sample Review Bd 1970–72, Science Working Panel 1971–73, Physical Sciences Cttee 1971–75; Ed. Earth and Planetary Science Letters 1967–74; Chair. Comm. for Planetary and Lunar Exploration, NAS, Space Science Bd 1975–78; Vinton Hayes Sr Fellow, Harvard 1980; Jaeger-Hales Lecture, ANU 1980; Harold Jeffreys Lecture, Royal Astronomical Soc. 1981; Pres. Meteoritical Soc. 1987–88; mem. NAS; Fellow, American Acad. of Arts and Sciences, American Geophysical Union, Geological Soc. of America; Regents Fellow, Smithsonian Inst. 1982; Geochemistry Fellow Geochemical Soc. and European Asscn for Geochemistry 1996; mem. American Philosophical Soc.; Foreign mem. Norwegian Acad. of Science and Letters 1988; Hon. Fellow Geological Soc. London; Hon. Foreign Fellow European Union of Geosciences (EUG) 1983; Distinguished Visiting Scholar, Harvard Univ. 2001; Dr hc (Brussels) 1985, (Paris) 1986, (Chicago) 1992, (Rennes) 1998, (Torino) 2000; Hon. DSc (Ariz.) 1987; Combat Infantryman's Badge; Exceptional Scientific Achievement Medal, NASA 1970; Arthur L. Day Medal, Geological Soc. of America 1970; Distinguished Public Service Medal, NASA 1972 and with cluster 1978; James Furman Kemp Medal, Columbia Univ. 1973, Leonard Medal, Meteoritical Soc. 1975; V. M. Goldschmidt Medal, Geochemical Soc. 1978, Univ. of Chicago Alumni Asscn Professional Achievement Award 1978; Arthur L. Day Prize, NAS 1981, J. Lawrence Smith Medal, NAS 1985, Wollaston Medal, Geological Soc. of London 1985, Sr US Scientist Award, Alexander von Humboldt-Stiftung 1985, Harry H. Hess Medal, American Geophysical Union, Crafoord Prize, Swedish Royal Acad. 1986, Holmes Medal, EUG 1987, Gold Medal (Royal Astronomical Soc.) 1991, Bowie Medal, American Geophysical Union 2008. *Publications:* research papers in several scientific journals, in the fields of geochemistry, geophysics and astrophysics, cosmology and the application of the methods of chemical physics to problems in the earth and planetary sciences; major researches: determination of the time scale of the solar system, chronology of the moon, establishment of dating methods using long-lived natural radioactivities, study of geological processes using nuclear and isotopic effects as a tracer in nature and the application of thermodynamic methods to geological systems. *Leisure interests:* hiking, music, art. *Address:* California Institute of Technology, Division of Geological and Planetary Sciences, Pasadena, CA 91125 (office); PO Box 2959, Florence, OR 97439, USA (home). *Telephone:* (626) 395-6139 (office); (541) 997-9224 (home). *E-mail:* gjw@gps.caltech.edu (office). *Website:* www.gps.caltech.edu/people/gjw/profile (office).

WASSERMAN, Robert Harold, PhD; American biologist and academic; *James Law Professor Emeritus of Physiology, College of Veterinary Medicine, Cornell University;* b. 11 Feb. 1926, Schenectady, New York; s. of Joseph Wasserman and Sylvia Rosenburg; m. Marilyn Mintz 1950; three d.; ed Mount Pleasant High School, NY, Cornell Univ., Michigan State Univ.; Research Assoc. and Assoc. Prof. of Biochemistry, Univ. of Tenn. Atomic Energy Comm. Agricultural Research Program, Oak Ridge 1953–55; Sr Scientist, Medical Div., Oak Ridge Inst. of Nuclear Studies 1955–57; Research Assoc. in Radiation Biology NY State Veterinary Coll., Cornell Univ. 1957–59; Assoc. Prof. of Radiation Biology, Dept of Physical Biology 1959–63, Prof. of Radiation Biology 1963–80, Prof. of Physiology, Coll. of Veterinary Medicine 1980–89, Prof. and Chair. of Dept and Section 1983–87, James Law Prof. of Physiology 1989–97, Prof. Emer. 1998–; Chair. Cttee Meat and Poultry Inspection, Nat. Research Council 1983–85, mem. Food and Nutrition Bd 1984–87; Visiting Scientist Inst. of Biological Chem., Copenhagen, Denmark 1964–65; Guggenheim Fellowship 1964, 1972; mem. NAS 1980–; Fellow American Inst. of Nutrition 1992; Wise and Helen Burroughs Lectureship 1974, 1987; Mead-Johnson Award in Nutrition 1969; A. Lichtwitz Prize (INSERM) 1982, Merit Status, NIH 1989, Newman Award (American Soc. Bone and Mineral Research) 1990, Career Recognition Award, Vitamin D Workshop 1994. *Publications:* numerous articles in specialist journals. *Leisure interests:* reading, sports, computers, cards, writing. *Address:* Department of Biomedical Sciences, T8-020B VRT, College of Veterinary Medicine, Cornell University, Ithaca, NY 14853; 207 Texas Lane, Ithaca, NY 14850, USA (home). *Telephone:* (607) 253-3437. *E-mail:* RHWZ@cornell.edu (office). *Website:* www.vet.cornell.edu (office).

WASSERSTEIN, Bruce, AB, MBA, JD; American investment banker; *CEO, Lazard LLC;* b. 25 Dec. 1947, New York; s. of Morris Wasserstein and Lola Wasserstein, brother of the late Wendy Wasserstein; m. Claude Becker; four s. one d.; ed Univ. of Mich., Harvard Law School, Harvard Business School and Univ. of Cambridge, UK; Assoc. Cravath, Swaine & Moore, New York 1972–77; Man. Dir First Boston Corpn 1977–88; Pres. Wasserstein, Perella & Co. 1988–2000; Chair. Dresdner Kleinwort Wasserstein (formed after acquisition of Wasserstein, Perella & Co. by Dresdner 2000) 2001–02; CEO Lazard LLC 2002–; mem. Council on Foreign Relations; fmr mem. Visiting Cttees Harvard Law School, Univ. of Mich., Columbia School of Journalism; founding sponsor Arts Connection. *Publications:* Big Deal: The Battle for Control of America's Leading Corporations 2000. *Address:* Lazard LLC, 30 Rockefeller Plaza, New York, NY 10020, USA (office). *Telephone:* (212) 632-6000 (office). *Website:* www.lazard.com (office).

WASSON, Gregory (Greg) D.; American business executive; *President and Chief Operating Officer, Walgreen Company;* ed Purdue Univ.; joined Walgreen as pharmacy intern, Houston, Tex. 1980, managed several drugstores then promoted to dist man. 1986, Regional Vice-Pres. Walgreens store operations 1999–2001, Vice-Pres. and Exec. Vice-Pres. Walgreens Health Initiatives 2001–02, Pres. 2002–04, Sr Vice-Pres. 2004–05, Exec. Vice-Pres. 2005–07, Pres. and COO Walgreen Co. 2007–. *Address:* Walgreen Co., 200 Wilmot Road, Deerfield, IL 60015, USA (office). *Telephone:* (847) 914-2500 (office). *Fax:* (847) 914-2804 (office). *E-mail:* info@walgreens.com (office). *Website:* www.walgreens.com (office).

WÄSTBERG, Olof (Olle), BA; Swedish politician, writer and diplomatist; *Director-General, Swedish Institute;* b. 6 May 1945, Stockholm; s. of Erik Wastberg and Greta Hirsch; m. Inger Claesson 1968; two s.; ed Univ. of Stockholm; Vice-Pres. Liberal Youth Sweden 1968–71; mem. Bd Liberal Party 1972–93, 1997–, Pres. Exec. Cttee 1982–83, teacher of political science, Univ. of Stockholm 1967–68; journalist, political Dept Expressen 1968–71, Ed. 1994–95; Research Fellow, Business and Social Research Centre 1971–76; Pres. Akieframjandet 1976–82; mem. Parl. 1976–82; Pres. Swedish Newspaper Promotion Asscn 1983–91; Under-Sec. of State, Ministry of Finance 1991–93; Consul Gen. of Sweden in NY 1999–2004; Dir-Gen. Swedish Inst., Stockholm 2005–; Dir Stockholm Stock Exchange 1977–82, 1988–94; Pres. Nordic Investment Bank 1992–94; Chair. Bd Swedish Broadcasting Corpn 1996–99, Stockholm City Theatre 1998–99; mem. Govt comms on S African consumer politics, stock market and media; Gold Medal, Swedish Marketing Group 1982. *Publications:* books on African problems, immigration policies and economic topics; articles in professional journals. *Address:* Swedish Institute, Slottsbacken 10, Box 7434, 103 91 Stockholm (office); Bellmangatan 6, 11820 Stockholm, Sweden (home). *Telephone:* (8) 453-78-00 (office). *Fax:* (8) 20-72-48 (office). *E-mail:* margareta.engholm@si.se (office). *Website:* www.si.se (office).

WATANABE, Katsuaki; Japanese automotive industry executive; *Vice-Chairman, Toyota Motor Corporation;* b. 14 Feb. 1942, Mie Pref.; m.; three d.; ed Keio Univ.; joined Toyota Motor Corpn 1964, Man. Dir and mem. Bd 1997–99, Sr Man. Dir 1999–2001, Exec. Vice-Pres. 2002–05, Pres. and Rep. Dir 2005–09, Vice-Chair. 2009–. *Address:* Toyota Motor Corporation, 1 Toyota-cho, Toyota, Aichi 471-8571, Japan (office). *Telephone:* (565) 28-2121 (office). *Fax:* (565) 23-5800 (office). *Website:* www.toyota.co.jp (office).

WATANABE, Kazuhide; Japanese automobile executive; *Chairman and Representative Director, Mazda Motor Corporation;* b. 1941; Man.-Dir in charge of Personnel and Human Affairs, Mazda Motor Corpn 1998, Chair. and Rep. Dir 2001–; mem. Council Japan Productivity Center for Socio-Econ. Devt (JPC-SED); mem. Bd of Dirs The Energy Conservation Center Japan (ECCJ) 2001–03, also Trustee. *Address:* Mazda Motor Corporation, 3-1 Shinchi, Fuchu-cho, Aki-gun, Hiroshima 730-8670, Japan (office). *Telephone:* (8) 2282-1111 (office). *Fax:* (8) 2287-5190 (office). *Website:* www.mazda.com (office).

WATANABE, Ken; Japanese actor; b. 21 Oct. 1959, Koide, Niigata; m. 1st Yumiko Watanabe (divorced 2004); two c.; m. 2nd Kaho Minami 2005. *Films include:* Setouchi shonen yakyu dan 1984, Kekkon annai mystery 1985, Tampopo 1985, Umi to dokuyaku (The Sea and Poison) 1986, Bakumatsu jyunjyoden 1991, Kimitachi ga ite boku ga iru 1992, Rajio no jikan 1997, Kizuna 1998, Oboreru sakana 2000, Supêsutoraberâzu (Space Travelers) 2000, Zawa-zawa Shimokita-sawa 2000, Sennen no koi – Hikaru Genji monogatari 2001, Hi wa mata noboru 2002, T. R. Y. 2003, The Last Samurai 2003, Kita no zeronen 2005, Batman Begins 2005, Memoirs of a Geisha 2005, Ashita no kioku (also producer) 2006, Letters from Iwo Jima 2006. *Television includes:* Sanga moyu 1984, Dokugan-ryu Masamune 1987, Takeda Shingen 1990, Ikebukuro West Gate Park 2000, Hojo Tokimune 2001, Suna no utsuwa 2004. *Address:* c/o The Endeavor Agency, 9601 Wilshire Boulevard, 10th Floor, Beverly Hills, CA 90212, USA (office). *Telephone:* (310) 248-2000 (office). *Fax:* (310) 248-2020 (office).

WATANABE, Shigeo, BS; Japanese business executive; *Member of the Board and Adviser, Bridgestone Corporation;* b. 10 April 1942; ed Keio Univ.; joined Bridgestone Tire Co. Ltd (renamed Bridgestone Corpn) 1965, Tech. Adviser Bridgestone Tire Mfg USA Inc., Gen.-Man. Truck and Bus Devt Dept 1988, Tech. Adviser Firestone Tire and Rubber Co. Int. Tech. Centre 1988–90, Gen. Man. Mfg and Tech. 1990–93, Dir Quality Assurance Div. 1993–94, Dir Tire Devt Div. 1994–97, mem. Bd 1994–, Vice-Pres. and Dir Tire Devt Div. 1997, Vice-Pres. and Dir Commercial Tire Devt and Tire Tech. Admin 1997–98, Sr Vice-Pres. Tire Devt 1998–2000, Sr Vice-Pres. Tire Devt and Quality Assurance 2000–01, Chair., Pres. and CEO 2001–06, Mem. Bd and Adviser 2006–. *Address:* Bridgestone Corporation, 10-1 Kyobashi 1-chome, Chuo-ku, Tokyo 104-8340, Japan (office). *Telephone:* (3) 3567-0111 (office). *Fax:* (3) 3535-

2553 (office). *E-mail:* bfspr@bfusa.com (office). *Website:* www.bridgestone.co.jp (office).

WATANABE, Shuichi; Japanese health care industry executive; *President and Representative Director, Kuraya Sanseido Inc.;* apptd Dir Kuraya Sanseido Inc. 2001, Pres. and Rep. Dir Kuraya Sanseido Inc. (following separation of pharmaceutical distribution from purchasing businesses to form new Kuraya Sanseido Inc. and MEDICEO Holdings Co. Ltd, as parts of MEDICEO Group) 2004–. *Address:* Kuraya Sanseido Inc., 7-15 Yaesu 2-chome, Chuo-ku, Tokyo 104-8464, Japan (office). *Telephone:* (3) 3517-5800 (office). *Fax:* (3) 230-5566 (office). *Website:* www.kurayasanseido.co.jp/english/ (office); www.mediceo-gp.com/english/ (office).

WATANABE, Tsuneo; Japanese newspaper executive; *President, CEO and Editor-in-Chief, Yomiuri Shimbun;* b. 1926; began career with Yomiuri Shimbun newspaper as reporter 1950, fmr Washington DC corresp. USA, chief editorial writer, Pres. 1991–, currently Pres., CEO and Ed.-in-Chief, also Chair. Yomiuri Group. *Publications:* Memoirs of Tsuneo Watanabe 2000. *Address:* Yomiuri Shimbum, 1-7-1, Otemachi, Chiyoda-ku, Tokyo 100-8055, Japan (office). *Telephone:* (3) 3242-1111 (office). *E-mail:* webmaster@yomiuri .co.jp (office). *Website:* www.yomiuri.co.jp (office).

WATANABE, Yoshimi, LLB; Japanese politician; b. 17 March 1952, Nasu Dist, Tochigi; s. of Michio Watanabe; ed Waseda and Chuo Univs; served as pvt. sec. to Minister of Int. Trade and Industry 1986–92, Minister of Foreign Affairs 1992–96; elected to House of Reps 1996, representing Tochigi Pref. Third Dist, re-elected 2000, 2003, 2005, parl. posts have included Chief Sec., Research Comm. on Finance and Banking; Sr Vice-Minister of Cabinet Office 2006, Minister of State for Regulatory Reform 2006–07, Minister of State for Financial Services and Admin. Reform 2007–08 (resgnd); mem. LDP (Liberal Democratic Party), Acting Chair., Public Relations HQ 2004, Acting Dir-Gen., Int. Bureau 2004, Man., Research Comm. on Tax System 2005, resigned from party 2009. *Television:* appears in Takeshi-no-TV-tackle, a humorous political discussion show hosted by comedian Takeshi Kitano. *Address:* c/o Liberal-Democratic Party (LDP), 1-11-23, Nagata-cho, Chiyoda-ku, Tokyo 100-8910, Japan (office).

WATANABE, Youji; Japanese architect; b. 14 June 1923, Naoetsu City; ed Waseda Univ.; Asst to Prof. Takamasa Yosizaka, Architectural Inst., Waseda Univ. 1955–58; Lecturer in Architecture, Waseda Univ. 1959, Special Postgrad. Student of City Planning 1968–73; Visiting Lecturer, Montana State Univ. 1983; Oceanic Architectural Students' Congress, Auckland Univ. 1983; prizes in architectural competitions. *Publication:* Approach to Architecture 1974.

WATARI, Fumiaki, BA; Japanese oil industry executive; *Chairman, Nippon Oil Corporation;* ed Keio Univ.; joined Nippon Oil 1960, numerous positions in Marketing Dept 1960–95, Marketing Dir 1995–98, Vice-Pres. 1998–99, Vice-Pres. Nippon Mitsubishi Oil 1999–2000, Pres. Nippon Oil Corpn 2000–05, Chair. and Rep. Dir 2005–; Pres. Petroleum Asscn of Japan; Dir Japan Cooperation Center for the Middle East. *Address:* Nippon Oil Corpn, 3-12 Nishi Shimbashi 1-chome, Minato-ku, Tokyo 105-8412, Japan (office). *Telephone:* (3) 3502-1131 (office). *Fax:* (3) 3502-9352 (office). *E-mail:* info@eneos.co .jp (office). *Website:* www.eneos.co.jp (office).

WATERHOUSE, (Gai) Gabriel Marie, BA; Australian race horse trainer; b. 3 Sept. 1954, Sydney; d. of the late Thomas John Smith and Valerie Lillian Smith; m. Robert Waterhouse; one s. one d.; ed Univ. of New South Wales; actress 1974–78; journalist, stable foreman 1978–92; racehorse trainer 1992–; Dir Gayval Investments Pty Ltd, Gai Waterhouse Racing Pty Ltd; f. Gai Waterhouse Racing Stables; Australian Racing Personality of the Year 1994–95, fmr NSW Sports Star of the Year, Sarah Kennedy Award for Contrib. to Racing, Silver Horseshoe Award for Best Trainer 1995, NSW Businesswoman of the Year 2000, Nat. Trust Living Treasure 2001. *Publication:* Against All Odds (biog.). *Leisure interests:* skiing, movies, theatre. *Address:* Gai Waterhouse Racing Stables, 16 Bowral Street, Kensington, NSW 2033; Gai Waterhouse Racing Pty Ltd, P.O. Box 834, Kensington, NSW 1465, Australia (office). *Telephone:* (2) 9662-1488 (office). *Fax:* (2) 9662-6328 (office). *E-mail:* Gai.Waterhouse@bigpond.com (office). *Website:* www.gaiwaterhouse .com.au (office).

WATERHOUSE, Keith Spencer, CBE, FRSL; British writer; b. 6 Feb. 1929, Leeds; s. of Ernest Waterhouse and Elsie Edith Waterhouse; m. 2nd Stella Bingham 1984 (divorced 1989); one s. two d. by previous marriage; journalist 1950–, columnist, Daily Mirror 1970–86, Daily Mail 1986–, contrib. to various periodicals; mem. Kingman Cttee on Teaching of the English Language 1987–88; Granada Columnist of the Year Award 1970; IPC Descriptive Writer of the Year Award 1970; IPC Columnist of the Year Award 1973; British Press Awards Columnist of the Year 1978, 1989; Granada Special Quarter Century Award 1982; Press Club Edgar Wallace Award 1996; Gerald Barry Lifetime Achievement Award 2000. *Films (with Willis Hall) include:* Billy Liar, Whistle Down the Wind, A Kind of Loving, Lock Up Your Daughters. *Plays:* Mr. and Mrs. Nobody 1986, Jeffrey Bernard is Unwell (Evening Standard Comedy of the Year 1990) 1989, Bookends 1990, Our Song 1992, Good Grief 1998, Bing-Bong 1999. *Plays (with Willis Hall) include:* Billy Liar 1960, Celebration 1961, All Things Bright and Beautiful 1963, Say Who You Are 1965, Whoops-a-Daisy 1968, Children's Day 1969, Who's Who 1972, The Card (musical) 1973, Saturday, Sunday, Monday (adapted from play by de Filippo) 1973, Filumena (adapted from de Filippo) 1977, Worzel Gummidge 1981, Budgie (musical) 1988. *TV series:* Budgie, Queenie's Castle, The Upper Crusts, Billy Liar, The Upchat Line, The Upchat Connection, Worzel Gummidge, West End Tales, The Happy Apple, Charters and Caldicott. *TV films:* Charlie Muffin 1983, This Office Life 1985, The Great Paperchase 1986. *Others:* Café Royal (with Guy Deghy) 1956, Writers' Theatre (ed.) 1967, The Passing of the Third-floor Buck

1974, Mondays, Thursdays 1976, Rhubarb, Rhubarb 1979, Fanny Peculiar 1983, Mrs Pooter's Diary 1983, Waterhouse At Large 1985, Collected Letters of a Nobody 1986, The Theory and Practice of Lunch 1986, The Theory and Practice of Travel 1988, Waterhouse on Newspaper Style 1989, English Our English 1991, Jeffrey Bernard is Unwell and Other Plays 1992, Sharon & Tracy and the Rest 1992, City Lights 1994, Streets Ahead 1995. *Publications:* (novels) There is a Happy Land 1957, Billy Liar 1959, Jubb 1963, The Bucket Shop 1968, Billy Liar on the Moon 1975, Office Life 1978, Maggie Muggins 1981, In the Mood 1983, Thinks 1984, Our Song 1984, Bimbo 1990, Unsweet Charity 1992, Good Grief 1997, Soho 2001, Palace Pier 2003. *Address:* Daily Mail, Northcliffe House, 2 Derry Street, London W8 5TT, England (office). *Telephone:* (20) 7938-6000 (office). *Fax:* (20) 7937-4463 (office). *Website:* www .dailymail.co.uk (office).

WATERLOW, John Conrad, CMG, MD, ScD, FRS; British scientist and academic; *Professor Emeritus of Human Nutrition, London School of Hygiene and Tropical Medicine, University of London;* b. 13 June 1916, London; s. of Sir Sydney Waterlow and Margery H. Eckhard; m. Angela P. Gray 1939; two s. one d.; ed Eton Coll., Trinity Coll. Cambridge and London Hosp. Medical Coll.; Persia/Iraq force 1943; mem. scientific staff, MRC 1942–70; Dir Tropical Metabolism Research Unit, Univ. of the West Indies 1954–70; Prof. of Human Nutrition, London School of Hygiene and Tropical Medicine 1970–82, Prof. Emer. 1982–; Foreign Assoc. mem. NAS; Murgatroyd Prize for Tropical Medicine, Bristol-Myers Prize for Nutrition, Rank Prize Fund Prize for contribs to nutrition 2000. *Publications:* Protein Turnover in the Whole Body and in Mammalian Tissues 1978, Protein Energy Malnutrition 1992; many papers and reviews on malnutrition and protein metabolism. *Leisure interest:* mountain walking. *Address:* 15 Hillgate Street, London, W8 7SP (home). *Telephone:* (20) 7727-7456 (home).

WATERMAN, Ewen Leith, BEcons; Australian civil servant; b. 2 Dec. 1943, Adelaide, S Australia; s. of Gordon Waterman and Elsie Waterman (née Batty); m. Barbara Prideaux 1966; two s. one d.; ed Pulteney Grammar School, Adelaide, Univ. of Adelaide; Gen. Financial and Econ. Policy Div., Australian Treasury 1967–72, Overseas Econ. Relations Div., 1973–75, Asst Sec. State and Local Govt Finances Br. 1982–84, Prin. Adviser, Gen. Financial and Econ. Policy Div., 1984–85, First Asst Sec., Revenue Loans and Investment Div. 1985–87, Capital Markets Div. 1987–89, Deputy Sec. (Financial) 1989–93; Prime Minister's Dept 1972; Counsellor (Financial), Australian Embassy, Washington, DC 1976–79; Sec. Australian Loan Council 1986–87, Australian Nat. Debt Comm. 1986–87; Exec. Dir IMF, Washington, DC 1993–97; Exec. Dir Access Economics 1997–2001; Man. Dir Export Finance and Insurance Corpn (EFIC) 2001–2003. *Leisure interests:* tennis, golf. *Address:* Export Finance and Insurance Corporation, 22 Pitt Street, Sydney, NSW 2000, Australia. *Telephone:* (2) 9201-2111. *Fax:* (2) 9201-5222. *E-mail:* info@efic.gov .au. *Website:* www.efic.gov.au.

WATERS, John; American film director, actor, producer and screenwriter; b. 22 April 1946, Baltimore, Md; given an 8 mm camera aged 17; formed repertory troupe Dreamland Players to produce films. *Films include:* dir, producer, actor, writer, ed. and cinematographer: Hag in a Black Leather Jacket 1964, Roman Candles 1966, Eat Your Makeup 1968, The Diane Linkletter Story 1969, Mondo Trasho 1969, Pink Flamingos 1972, Hairspray (co-producer) 1988; producer, dir and writer: Multiple Maniacs 1970, Female Trouble 1974, Desperate Living 1977, Polyester 1981; dir, actor and writer: Cry-Baby 1990, Serial Mom 1994, Pecker 1998, Cecil B. DeMented 2000; dir and writer: A Dirty Shame 2004, This Filthy World 2006; actor: Sweet and Lowdown 1999, Blood Feast 2: All U Can Eat 2002, Seed of Chucky 2004. *Television includes:* Family Album (actor) 1994. *Publications include:* Shock Value: A Tasteful Book About Bad Taste 1981, Crackpot: The Obsession of John Waters 1986; articles for National Lampoon. *Address:* c/o Creative Artists Agency, 9830 Wilshire Blvd, Beverly Hills, CA 90212-1825, USA. *Telephone:* (310) 288-4545. *Fax:* (310) 288-4800. *Website:* www.caa.com.

WATERS, Sarah, PhD; British writer; b. 1966, Neyland, Wales; ed Univs of Kent, Lancaster and London; fmr Assoc. Lecturer, Open Univ.; Betty Trask Award 1999, CWA Ellis Peters Historical Dagger 2002, British Book Award for Author of the Year 2002. *Publications:* Tipping the Velvet 1998, Affinity (Sunday Times Young Writer of the Year 2000, Somerset Maugham Award 2000) 1999, Fingersmith 2002, The Night Watch 2006, The Little Stranger 2009; contrib. of articles on lesbian and gay writing, cultural history. *Leisure interests:* cinema, theatre. *Address:* c/o Greene & Heaton (Authors' Agents) Ltd, 37 Goldhawk Road, London, W12 8QQ, England (office). *Telephone:* (20) 8749-0315 (office). *Website:* www.sarahwaters.com.

WATERSTON, Robert Hugh, BSE, MD, PhD; American geneticist and academic; *William H. Gates III Endowed Chair in Biomedical Sciences and Chairman of the Department of Genome Sciences, University of Washington, Seattle;* b. 17 Sept. 1943, Detroit; ed Princeton Univ., courses in biology in Germany, Univ. of Chicago; NIH Predoctoral Trainee 1968–71; American Cancer Soc. Postdoctoral Fellowship 1972–74; Muscular Dystrophy Asscn Postdoctoral Fellowship 1975–76; Postdoctoral Researcher, MRC Lab. of Molecular Biology, Cambridge, UK 1972–74, 1975–76, Sabbatical Visitor, Dir's Div. 1985–86; Postdoctoral Researcher, Children's Hosp. Medical Center, Boston, Mass 1974–75; Asst Prof., Dept of Anatomy and Neurobiology, Washington Univ., St Louis, Mo. 1976–80, Asst Prof. of Genetics, Washington Univ. School of Medicine 1980–81, Assoc. Prof. of Genetics 1981–87, Prof. of Genetics 1987–91, Prof. and Acting Head, Dept of Genetics 1991–93, James S. McDonnell Prof. and Chair. Dept of Genetics 1993–2002; William H. Gates III Endowed Chair in Biomedical Sciences and Chair. Dept of Genome Sciences, Univ. of Washington, Seattle, Wash. 2003–; American Heart Asscn Establ-ished Investigator 1980–85; John Simon Guggenheim Fellowship 1985–86; City of Medicine Award, Dan David Prize, The Dan David Foundation,

Gairdner Award (co-recipient), The Gairdner Foundation, General Motors Prize (co-recipient), George W. Beadle Medal, Genetics Soc. of America, Gruber Genetics Prize, The Peter and Patricia Gruber Foundation 2005. *Publications:* numerous scientific papers in professional journals. *Address:* Department of Genome Sciences, Foege S-350D, Box 355065, University of Washington School of Medicine, 1705 NE Pacific Street, Seattle, WA 98195-5065, USA (office). *Telephone:* (206) 685-7347 (office). *Fax:* (206) 685-7301 (office). *E-mail:* waterston@gs.washington.edu (office). *Website:* waterston.gs.washington.edu (office).

WATERSTONE, Timothy John Stuart, MA; British business executive; b. 30 May 1939; s. of Malcolm Waterstone and Sylvia Sawday; m. 1st Patricia Harcourt-Poole (divorced); two s. one d.; m. 2nd Clare Perkins (divorced); one s. two d.; m. 3rd Mary Rose (Rosie) Alison; two d.; ed Tonbridge School and St Catharine's Coll. Cambridge; Carritt Moran, Calcutta 1962–64; Allied Breweries 1964–73; W. H. Smith 1973–81; Founder, Chair. and Chief Exec. Waterstone's Booksellers Ltd 1982–93; Chair. Priory Investments Ltd 1990–95, Golden Rose Radio (London Jazz FM) 1992–93; Founder and Chair. Chelsea Stores Ltd children's stores 1996–; Chair. HMV Media Group PLC 1998–2001; Deputy Chair. Sinclair-Stevenson Ltd 1989–92; mem. Bd Yale Univ. Press 1992–, Futurestart 1992–, Virago Press 1995–96, Hill Samuel UK Emerging Cos Investment Trust PLC 1996–2000, Downing Classic VCT 1998–; Chair. Dept of Trade and Industry Working Group on Smaller Quoted Cos and Pvt. Investors 1999, Shelter 25th Anniversary Appeal Cttee 1991–92; mem. Bd London Philharmonic Orchestra 1990–97 (Trustee 1995–98), Portman House Trust 1994–96; Chair. Acad. of Ancient Music 1990–95, London Int. Festival of Theatre 1991–92, Elgar Foundation 1992–98, King's Coll. Library Bd 2000–; Co-Founder BOOKAID 1992–93; Advisory mem. Booker Prize Man. Cttee 1986–93; Chair. of Judges Prince's Youth Business Trust Awards 1990. *Publications:* Lilley and Chase 1994, An Imperfect Marriage 1995, A Passage of Lives 1996, Swimming Against the Stream: Ten Rules for Creating Your Business and Making your Life 2006. *Leisure interest:* being with Rosie Alison. *Address:* c/o Ed Victor Ltd, 6 Bayley Street, London, WC1B 3HB, England.

WATERWORTH, Peter; British diplomatist; *Governor of Montserrat;* b. 15 April 1957; m. Catherine Margaret Waterworth; began diplomatic career at NI Office 1979–81, Asst Legal Adviser, FCO 1987–90, First Sec. (Legal Adviser), Bonn 1990–94, Middle Eastern Dept, FCO 1994–96, First Sec., Rome 1996–2000, NI Office 2000–03, Political Counsellor, Islamabad 2003–05, Baghdad 2005, Deputy High Commr and Consul-Gen., Lagos 2005–07, Gov. of Montserrat 2007–; barrister-at-law 1983–86. *Address:* The Governor's Office, Farara Plaza, Brades, Montserrat (office). *Telephone:* 491-2688 (office). *Fax:* 491-8867 (office). *E-mail:* govoffice.montserrat@fco.gov.uk (office). *Website:* www.montserrat-newsletter.com (office).

WATKINS, Alan Keith, PhD; British business executive; b. 9 Oct. 1938, Birmingham; s. of the late Wilfred Watkins and of Dorothy Watkins; m. Diana E. Wynne 1963; two s.; ed Moseley Grammar School and Univ. of Birmingham; Mfg Process Research, Lucas Group Research 1962–69; Mfg and Production Eng Lucas Batteries Ltd 1969–75; Div. Dir Electrical Div. Lucas Aerospace Ltd 1975–82; Man. Dir Lucas Aerospace Ltd 1982–87; Man. Dir Aerospace, Lucas Industries PLC 1987–89; Man. Dir and Chief Exec. Hawker Siddeley Group PLC 1989–91; CEO London Transport 1992–94, Vice-Chair. 1992–93, Deputy Chair. 1993–94, Dir Senior Eng Group (now Senior PLC) 1994–2001, Deputy Chair. 1995–96, Chair. 1996–2001; Dir (non-exec.) Dobson Park Industries PLC 1992–95, Hepworth PLC 1995–98; Chair. High Duty Alloys Ltd 1997–2000; mem. Review Bd for Govt Contracts 1993–. *Leisure interests:* tennis, photography, golf, hot-air ballooning, vintage cars. *Address:* c/o Senior PLC, 59/61 High Street, Rickmansworth, Herts., WD3 1RH, England. *Telephone:* (1923) 714703 (office).

WATKINS, David John, BA, FRSA; British jewellery artist, sculptor and academic; *Head of Department and Professor of Goldsmithing, Silversmithing, Metalwork and Jewellery, Royal College of Art;* b. 14 Nov. 1940, Wolverhampton; m. Wendy Ann Jopling Ramshaw 1962; one s. one d.; ed Wolverhampton Grammar School and Univ. of Reading; sculptor, musician, special effects model maker (including for film 2001: A Space Odyssey) and jewellery designer 1963–71; co-f. with Wendy Ramshaw the fashion jewellery co. Something Special 1965; Visiting Lecturer, Berkshire Coll. of Art, Guildford School of Art 1964–66; own studios for jewellery and sculpture 1971–; est. second studio/workshop for large-scale forged and fabricated steel, utilising combination of eng and hot metal processes for sculpture and public art projects 1980s; mem. Membership Cttee, Crafts Council 1976–78; Artist-in-Residence, Western Australian Inst. for Tech. 1978 Collection Cttee, Crafts Council 1983–84; Visiting Prof., Bezalel Acad., Jerusalem, Israel 1984; mem. Bd of Trustees Haystack Mountain School of Crafts, Me, USA 1999–; Head of Dept and Prof. of Goldsmithing, Silversmithing, Metalwork and Jewellery, Royal Coll. of Art, London 1984–; works in major collections, including American Craft Museum, Australian Nat. Gallery, Birmingham City Museum and Art Gallery, Crafts Council, London, Die Neue Sammlung, Munich, Kunstgewerbe Museum, Berlin, Kunstindustrimuseet, Oslo, Musée des Arts Decoratifs, Paris, Museum für Angewandte Kunst, Cologne, Museum für Kunst und Gewerbe, Hamburg, Nat. Gallery of Victoria, Nat. Museum of Modern Art, Tokyo, Nat. Museums of Scotland, Schmuckmuseum, Pforzheim, Science Museum, London, Stedelijk Museum, Amsterdam, Victoria & Albert Museum, London; Fellow, Chartered Society of Designers 1984; Freeman, Goldsmiths' Co. 1988, Liveryman 1989; De Beers Diamonds Today 1974, Crafts Advisory Cttee Bursary 1976, Japan Foundation Travel Award 1978, Art for Architecture Award, Royal Soc. of Arts 1995. *Publications include:* The Best in Contemporary Jewellery 1994, A Design Sourcebook: Jewellery 1999, The Paper Jewellery Collection 2000. *Leisure interest:* listening to jazz and

classical music. *Address:* Royal College of Art, Kensington Gore, London, SW7 2EU, England (office). *Telephone:* (20) 7590-4261 (office). *E-mail:* david.watkins@rca.ac.uk (office). *Website:* www.rca.ac.uk (office).

WATSON, Emily; British actress; b. 14 Jan. 1967, London; m. Jack Waters; one s. one d.; ed London Drama Studio, Univ. of Bristol. *Films include:* Breaking the Waves (New York Soc. of Film Critics Award, Nat. Soc. of Film Critics Award) 1996, Mill on the Floss 1997, Metroland 1997, The Boxer 1997, Hilary and Jackie 1998, Angela's Ashes 1999, Trixie 2000, The Luzhin Defense 2000, In Search of the Assassin 2001, Gosford Park 2001, Red Dragon 2002, Punch-Drunk Love 2002, Equilibrium 2002, Boo, Zino and the Snurks (voice) 2004, The Life and Death of Peter Sellers 2004, The Proposition 2004, Separate Lies 2005, Corpse Bride (voice) 2005, Wah Wah 2005, Crusade in Jeans 2005, Miss Potter 2006, The Waterhorse 2007, Fireflies in the Garden 2008, Synecdoche, New York 2008, Within the Whirlwind 2008, Cold Souls 2009. *Theatre includes:* Uncle Vanya, Twelfth Night (both at Donmar Warehouse, London 2002, at Brooklyn Acad. of Music, NY 2003). *Television:* The Memory Keeper's Daughter 2008. *Address:* c/o ICM Ltd, Oxford House, 76 Oxford Street, London, W1N 0AX, England.

WATSON, James Dewey, BS, PhD; American biologist and academic; *Chancellor Emeritus, Cold Spring Harbor Laboratory;* b. 6 April 1928, Chicago, Ill.; s. of James D. Watson and Jean Mitchell Watson; m. Elizabeth Lewis 1968; two s.; ed Univs of Chicago and Indiana; Research Fellow, US Nat. Research Council, Univ. of Copenhagen, Denmark 1950–51; Fellow, US Nat. Foundation, Cavendish Lab., Univ. of Cambridge, England 1951–53, 1955–56; Sr Research Fellow in Biology, Calif. Inst. of Tech. 1953–55; Asst Prof. of Biology, Harvard Univ. 1956–58, Assoc. Prof. 1958–61, Prof. 1961–76; Dir Cold Spring Harbor Lab. 1968–93, Pres. 1994–2003, Chancellor 2003–07, Chancellor Emer. 2007–; Assoc. Dir NIH, USA 1988–89, Dir Nat. Center for Human Genome Research, NIH 1989–92; Newton-Abraham Visiting Prof., Univ. of Oxford, UK 1994; mem. NAS, Danish Acad. of Arts and Sciences, American Acad. of Arts and Sciences, American Soc. of Biological Chemists; Sr Fellow, Soc. of Fellows, Harvard Univ. 1964–70; mem. American Philosophical Soc. 1978; Foreign mem. Royal Soc. 1981, USSR (now Russian) Acad. of Sciences 1989; Hon. Fellow, Clare Coll., Cambridge 1967; Hon. KBE 2002; Hon. DSc (Chicago, Indiana, Long Island, Adelphi, Brandeis, Hofstra, Harvard, Rockefeller, State Univ. of New York, Albert Einstein Coll. of Medicine, Clarkson Coll., Stellenbosch, Fairfield, Cambridge, Oxford, Charleston Medical Coll., Washington Coll., Univ. of Judaism, Univ. Coll. London, Wesleyan, Widener, Dartmouth, Trinity Coll. Dublin); Hon. LLD (Notre Dame) 1965; Hon. MD (Buenos Aires) 1986, (Charles Univ., Prague) 1998; Hon. DSc (Rutgers Univ.) 1988, (Bard Coll.) 1991, (Melbourne) 1997; Dr hc (Barcelona) 2005, (Royal Irish Acad.) 2002, (Int. Acad. of Humanism) 2005; Eli Lilly Award in Biochemistry 1959, Lasker Prize (American Public Health Asscn) 1960, Nobel Prize for Medicine (with F. H. C. Crick and M. F. H. Wilkins) 1962, John J. Carty Gold Medal (Nat. Acad. of Sciences) 1971, Medal of Freedom 1977, Gold Medal Award, Nat. Inst. of Social Sciences 1984, Kaul Foundation Award for Excellence 1992, Copley Medal of Royal Soc. 1993, Nat. Biotechnology Award 1993; Lomosonov Medal 1994, Nat. Medal of Science 1997, Liberty Medal Award 2000, Benjamin Franklin Medal 2001, Gairdner Award 2002, Lotos Club Medal of Merit 2004, Othmer Gold Medal, Chemical Heritage Foundation 2005. *Achievements include:* discovered structure of DNA (with Francis Crick) 1953. *Publications:* Molecular Biology of the Gene 1965, The Double Helix 1968, The DNA Story (with John Tooze) 1981, Recombinant DNA – A Short Course 1983 (co-author), The Molecular Biology of the Cell (co-author) 1986, Recombinant DNA (2nd edn) (co-author) 1992, A Passion for DNA 2000, Genes, Girls and Gamow 2001, DNA – The Secret of Life 2003, Avoid Boring People: And Other Lessons from a Life in Science (auto-biog.) 2007, Darwin: The Indelible Stamp (Ed.) 2007; papers on structure of deoxyribonucleic acid (DNA), on protein synthesis and on the induction of cancer by viruses. *Address:* c/o Bungtown Road, Cold Spring Harbor, New York, NY 11724, USA (office). *Telephone:* (516) 367-8311 (office).

WATSON, James Kay Graham, BSc, PhD, FRS, FRSC; British/Canadian research scientist; *Researcher Emeritus, National Research Council of Canada;* b. 20 April 1936, Denny, Scotland; s. of Thomas Watson and Mary C. Miller; m. Carolyn M. L. Kerr 1981; ed Denny High School, High School of Stirling and Univ. of Glasgow; Carnegie Sr Scholar, Dept of Chem., Univ. Coll. London 1961–63; Postdoctoral Fellow, Nat. Research Council, Ottawa, Canada 1963–65; ICI Research Fellow, Univ. of Reading 1965–66, Lecturer in Chemical Physics 1966–71; Visiting Assoc. Prof. in Physics, Ohio State Univ. 1971–75; SRC Sr Research Fellow in Chem., Univ. of Southampton 1975–79, 1980–82; Visiting Scientist, Nat. Research Council, Ottawa, Canada 1979–80, Sr Research Officer 1982–87, Prin. 1987–2007, Researcher Emer. 2008–; Fellow, American Physical Soc. 1990; Chem. Soc. Award 1974, Plyler Prize, American Physical Soc. 1986, RSC Henry Marshall Tory Medal 1999. *Publications:* more than 150 articles on molecular physics in learned journals. *Leisure interests:* music, golf, tree-watching. *Address:* Steacie Institute for Molecular Sciences, National Research Council of Canada, Ottawa, ON K1A 0R6 (office); 183 Stanley Avenue, Ottawa, ON K1M 1P2, Canada (home). *Telephone:* (613) 990-0739 (office); (613) 745-7928 (home). *Fax:* (613) 991-2648 (office). *E-mail:* james.watson@nrc-cnrc.gc.ca (office).

WATSON, Thomas Sturges (Tom), BS; American professional golfer; b. 4 Sept. 1949, Kansas City, Mo.; s. of Raymond Etheridge Watson and Sarah Elizabeth Ridge; m. 1st Linda Tova Rubin 1973; one s. one d.; m. 2nd Hilary Watson; three step-c.; ed Stanford Univ.; professional 1971–; British Open Champion 1975, 1977, 1980, 1982, 1983; record low aggregate for British Open of 268, record two single round scores of 65, lowest final 36-hole score of 130, Turnberry 1977; won US Masters title 1977, 1981; won US Open 1982; won World Series 1975, 1977, 1980; winner numerous other open championships;

top money winner on US Professional Golf Asscn (PGA) circuit 1977, 1978, 1979, 1980; first player ever to win in excess of $500,000 in prize money in one season 1980; Ryder Cup Player 1977, 1981, 1983, 1989 (Capt. 1993); Sr Tour victories: 1999 Bank One Championship, 2000 IR Sr Tour Championship, 2001 Sr PGA Championship, 2002 Sr Tour Championship, Sr British Open 2003; Hon. mem. Royal and Ancient Golf Club of St Andrews 1999; US PGA Player of the Year 1977, 1978, 1979, 1980, 1982; PGA World Golf Hall of Fame 1988, Payne Stewart Award 2003. *Publication:* Getting Back into Basics (jtly) 1992. *Leisure interests:* current affairs, outdoor life, baseball (Kansas City Royals fan). *Address:* PGA America, PO Box 109801, 100 Avenue of the Champions, Palm Beach Gardens, FL 33410; 1901 West 47th Place, Suite 200, Shawnee Mission, KS 66205, USA.

WATT, James Gaius, BS, JD; American fmr politician and lawyer; b. 31 Jan. 1938, Lusk, Wyo.; s. of William G. Watt and Lois M. (née Williams) Watt; m. Leilani Bomgardner 1957; one s. one d.; ed Univ. of Wyoming; Instructor, Coll. of Commerce and Industry, Univ. of Wyo. 1960–62; admitted to Wyo. Bar 1962, US Supreme Court Bar 1966; Legis. Asst, Counsel to Senator Simpson of Wyo. 1962–66; Sec. Natural Resources Comm. and Environmental Pollution Advisory Panel, US Chamber of Commerce 1966–69; Deputy Asst Sec. for Water and Power, Dept of the Interior 1969–72; Dir Bureau of Outdoor Recreation, US Dept of the Interior 1972–75; Vice-Chair. Fed. Power Comm. 1975–77; Founding Pres., Chief Legal Officer, Mountain States Legal Foundation, Denver 1977–80; US Sec. of the Interior 1981–83; practising law, Washington 1983–86, Jackson Hole, Wyo. 1986–; Chair. of Bd Environmental Diagnostics Inc. 1984–87, Disease Detection Int. 1987–90. *Publication:* The Courage of a Conservative (with Doug Wead) 1985. *Address:* P.O. Box 3705, 755 East Paintbrush Drive, Box 3705, Jackson, WY 83001, USA.

WATTS, Charles (Charlie) Robert; British musician (drums); b. 2 June 1941, London, England; m. Shirley Anne Shepherd 1964; one d.; fmr mem., Blues Incorporated; mem., The Rolling Stones 1963–, numerous tours worldwide; toured with Charlie Watts Orchestra 1985–86; Nordoff-Robbins Silver Clef 1982, Grammy Lifetime Achievement Award 1986, Ivor Novello Award for Outstanding Contribution to British Music 1991. *Recordings include:* albums: with The Rolling Stones: The Rolling Stones 1964, The Rolling Stones No. 2 1965, Out Of Our Heads 1965, Aftermath 1966, Between The Buttons 1967, Their Satanic Majesties Request 1967, Beggar's Banquet 1968, Let It Bleed 1969, Get Yer Ya-Ya's Out 1969, Sticky Fingers 1971, Exile On Main Street 1972, Goat's Head Soup 1973, It's Only Rock And Roll 1974, Black And Blue 1976, Some Girls 1978, Emotional Rescue 1980, Tattoo You 1981, Still Life 1982, Undercover 1983, Dirty Work 1986, Steel Wheels 1989, Flashpoint 1991, Voodoo Lounge 1994, Stripped 1995, Bridges to Babylon 1997, Forty Licks 2002, Live Licks 2004, A Bigger Bang 2005; solo: Live at Fulham Town Hall 1986, From One Charlie 1992, Tribute To Charlie Parker With Strings 1991, Warm & Tender 1993, Long Ago and Far Away 1996, Charlie Watts/Jim Keltner Project 2000, Watts At Scott's 2004. *Films include:* Sympathy For The Devil 1969, Gimme Shelter 1970, Ladies and Gentlemen, The Rolling Stones 1977, Let's Spend the Night Together 1983, Flashpoint 1991, Shine a Light 2007. *Publications:* Ode to a High Flying Bird 1965, According to the Rolling Stones (autobiog., jtly) 2003. *Leisure interest:* jazz music. *Address:* Munro Sounds, 5 Wandsworth Plain, London, SW18 1ES, England (office). *Telephone:* (20) 8877-3111 (office). *Fax:* (20) 8877-3033 (office). *Website:* www .rollingstones.com.

WATTS, Donald Walter, AM, PhD, FTSE, FRACI, FACE, FAIM; Australian business executive and academic administrator; *Senior Policy Advisor, University of Notre Dame, Australia;* b. 1 April 1934, Western Australia; s. of Horace Frederick Watts and Esme Anne White; m. Michelle Rose Yeomans 1960; two s.; ed Hale School, Perth, Univ. of Western Australia, University Coll. London, UK; Personal Chair. in Physical and Inorganic Chem., Univ. of Western Australia 1977–79; Dir Western Australian Inst. of Tech. 1980–86; Vice-Chancellor Curtin Univ. of Tech. 1987; Pres. and Vice-Chancellor Bond Univ. 1987–90, Prof. Emer. 1990; CEO Trade Devt Zone Authority, Darwin 1990–91; Chair. NT Employment & Training Authority 1991–93; Prof. of Science and Educ. and Dean Coll. of Arts and Sciences, Univ. of Notre Dame, Western Australia 1995–97, Dean of Research 1998–2004, Senior Policy Adviser (part-time) 2004–; Dir Advanced Energy Systems 1995–96 (Chair. 1997–2003); Chair. and Dir Tech. Training Inst. Pty Ltd 2001–03; Councillor Australian Acad. of Technological Sciences and Eng 2001–; Fellow, Royal Australian Chemical Inst., Australian Acad. of Tech. Sciences and Eng; mem. ACS, Chemical Educ. Sub-Cttee, Australian Acad. of Science; Hackett Scholar 1953, Gledden Fellow 1957, CSIRO Postdoctoral Fellow 1959, Dept of Scientific and Industrial Research Postdoctoral Fellow 1961, Fulbright Scholar 1967; Japan Foundation Visiting Fellow 1984; Hon. Fellow Marketing Inst. of Singapore; Hon. DTech (Curtin Univ. of Tech.) 1987, Hon. DEd (Univ. of Western Australia) 2001; Rennie Medal 1967, Leighton Medal, Royal Australian Chemical Inst. 1987, Australian and New Zealand Asscn for the Advancement of Science (ANZAAS) Medal 1998. *Publications:* The School Chemistry Project – A Secondary School Chemistry Syllabus for Comment (with N. S. Bayliss) 1978, Chemical Properties and Reactions (with A. R. H. Cole and R. B. Bucat) 1978, Chemistry for Australian Secondary School Students (with N. S. Bayliss) 1979, Elements of Chemistry: Earth, Air, Fire and Water 1984, Higher Education in Australia: A Way Forward, Policy Paper No. 8 1986, The Private Potential of Australian Higher Education 1987, A Private Approach to Higher Education 1987; numerous articles. *Leisure interests:* golf, tennis, reading. *Address:* University of Notre Dame Australia, Mouat Street, Freemantle, PO Box 1225, WA 6959 (office); 87 Evans Street, Shenton Park, WA 6008, Australia (home). *Telephone:* (8) 9433-0862 (office); (8) 9381-1667 (home). *E-mail:* dwatts@nd.edu.au (office). *Website:* www.nd .edu.au (office).

WATTS, Sir Philip Beverley, Kt, KCMG, MSc, FInstP, FInstPet, FRGS, FGS; British oil company executive (retd); b. 25 June 1945, Leicester; s. of Samuel Watts and Philippa Watts (née Wale); m. Janet Edna Watts (née Lockwood) 1966; one s. one d.; ed Wyggeston Grammar School, Leicester and Univ. of Leeds; science teacher, Methodist Boys High School, Freetown, Sierra Leone 1966–68; joined Shell Int. 1969; held various posts: seismologist, Indonesia 1970–74, geophysicist UK/Europe 1974–77, Exploration Man., Norway 1978–81, Div. Head, Malaysia, Brunei, Singapore, London 1981–83, Exploration Dir, UK 1983–85; Head EP Liaison—Europe, The Hague 1986–88, Head EP Econs and Planning, The Hague 1989–91; Man. Dir, Nigeria 1991–94, Regional Co-ordinator, Europe, The Hague 1994–95; Dir Planning, Environment and External Affairs, London 1996–97; Chair. Royal Dutch/Shell Group 2001–04 (resgnd) (Group Man. Dir 1997–2004); Chair. Shell Transport and Trading 2001 (Man. Dir 1997–2004); Chair. World Business Council for Sustainable Devt 2001–03 (mem. Exec. Cttee 1998–2004); Chair. ICC-UK 1998–2004 (mem. Governing Body 1997–2004); Worldwide ICC, Exec. Bd 1997–2000. *Leisure interests:* travel, gardening, reading. *Address:* Sunnyridge, Hill Farm Lane, Binfield, Berks., RG42 5NR, England (home). *Telephone:* (1344) 305965 (home). *E-mail:* philbwatts@freeuk.com (home).

WAUGH, John Stewart, PhD; American chemist and academic; *Professor Emeritus of Chemistry, Massachusetts Institute of Technology;* b. 25 April 1929, Willimantic, Conn.; s. of Albert E. Waugh and Edith S. Waugh; m. Susan M. Walsh 1983; one s. one d.; ed Windham High School, Dartmouth Coll. and Calif. Inst. of Tech.; mem. Faculty, MIT 1953–, A. A. Noyes Prof. of Chem. 1973–88, Inst. Prof. 1989–96, Inst. Prof. Emer. 1996–; Visiting Scientist, USSR Acad. of Sciences 1962, Univ. of Calif. 1963, Harvard Univ. 1975; Visiting Prof. Max Planck Inst. for Medical Research 1971, East China Normal Univ., Shanghai 1984, Texas A & M Univ. 1986; Joliot-Curie Prof. Ecole Supérieure de Physique et Chimie, Paris 1985, 1997; Fairchild Scholar, Calif. Inst. of Tech. 1989; Chair. Div. of Chem. Physics, American Physical Soc. 1984–85; Vice-Pres. Int. Soc. of Magnetic Resonance 1996–98, Pres. 1998–2001; mem. NAS, American Acad. of Arts and Sciences 1962–96, Slovenian Acad. of Sciences and Arts; Hon. ScD (Darmouth Coll.) 1989; Von Humboldt Award 1971, Langmuir Award 1974, Pittsburgh Spectroscopy Award 1978, Wolf Foundation Prize in Chem. 1984, Pauling Medal 1985, Richards Medal 1992. *Publications:* numerous scientific research papers. *Leisure interests:* sailing, harpsichord. *Address:* Department of Chemistry, Room 6-231, Massachusetts Institute of Technology, 77 Massachusetts Avenue, Cambridge, MA 02139 (office); 60 Conant Road, Lincoln, MA 01773, USA (home). *Telephone:* (617) 253-1901 (office). *Fax:* (617) 253-7030 (office). *E-mail:* jswaugh@mit.edu (office). *Website:* (office).

WAUGH, Richard (Rick) E., BComm, MBA; Canadian banking executive; *President and CEO, The Bank of Nova Scotia;* m. Lynne Waugh; three s.; ed Univ. of Manitoba, York Univ.; began career with The Bank of Nova Scotia (Scotiabank), Winnipeg 1970, served in investment, corp., int. and retail banking areas, Sr Exec. of US Operations, New York 1985–93, Sr Exec. Vice-Pres. of Corp. Banking, responsible for Global Corp. Banking, Toronto 1993–95, Vice-Chair. of Corp. Banking 1995–98, Vice-Chair. of Int. Banking and Wealth Man. 1998–2003, mem. Bd Dirs, Pres. and CEO 2003–; fmr Chair. Finance Section Campaign Cabinet, United Way of Greater Toronto, Campaign Chair. 2006; fmr Hon. Chair. endMS Capital Campaign, MS Soc. and mem. Bd Scientific Research Foundation; mem. Bd Dirs St Michael's Hosp. (Co-Chair. St Michael's Hosp. Foundation's Advancing Care, Every Day Campaign), Miller Thomson Scholarship Foundation; Patron Pediatric Oncology Group of Ont.; Fellow, Inst. of Canadian Bankers; Honorary Doctor of Laws degrees from York University and Assumption University; Merit of Honor, Council of the Americas. *Address:* The Bank of Nova Scotia, 44 King Street West, Toronto, Ont. M5H 1H1, Canada (office). *Telephone:* (416) 866-6161 (office). *Fax:* (416) 866-3750 (office). *E-mail:* info@scotiabank.ca (office). *Website:* www.scotiabank.ca (office).

WAUGH, Stephen Rodger (Steve), AO; Australian fmr professional cricketer; b. 2 June 1965, Canterbury, Sydney; s. of Rodger Waugh and Beverley Waugh; elder twin of Mark Edward; m. Lynette Waugh; one s. two d.; ed East Hills High School; right-hand batsman and right-arm medium-fast bowler; teams: New South Wales 1984, Somerset 1987–88, Ireland 1998, Kent 2002; 168 Tests for Australia 1985–2004, scoring over 10,927 runs (average 51.06) including 32 hundreds and taking 92 wickets (average 37.44); scored 24,052 first-class runs (average 51.94) with 79 hundreds; shared world record 5th wicket stand of 464 (unbroken) with brother M. E. Waugh for NSW vs Western Australia, Perth, 1990–91; 325 limited-overs internationals (106 as Capt.); Capt. Australian Test Cricket Team 1999–2004; retd Jan. 2004; Patron Camp Quality, Cerebral Palsy Asscn, Udayan Home for Girls, India; Wisden Cricketer of the Year 1989, Australian Cricketer of the Year 2000–01, Allan Border Medal 2001, Laureus Sports Award (World's Best Team) 2001, Australian of the Year 2004. *Publications:* South African Tour Diary 1995, Steve Waugh's West Indies Tour Diary 1996, Steve Waugh's World Cup Diary 1997, Images of Waugh, Never Satisfied, Ashes Summer (co-author), Ashes Diary 1997, 2001, Out of My Comfort Zone: Captain's Diary 2002, Never Say Die 2003. *Leisure interests:* golf, photography, reading, writing. *Address:* c/o Team-Duet, 3 Winnie Street, Cremorne, NSW 2090, Australia. *Telephone:* (2) 9909-2188 (office). *Fax:* (2) 9909-2157 (office). *E-mail:* admin@duetgroup.com (office).

WAX, Ruby, MSc; American comedienne, actress and writer; b. (Ruby Wachs), 19 April 1953, Evanston, Ill.; d. of Edward Wax and Berta Wax (née Goldmann); m. Edward Richard Morison Bye 1988; one s. two d.; ed Evanston High School, Univ. of Calif., Berkeley, Royal Scottish Acad. of Music and Drama; with Crucible Theatre 1976; with RSC 1978–82; Performer of the Year, British Comedy Awards 1993. *Films include:* Chariots of Fire 1981,

Shock Treatment 1981, Things Are Tough All Over 1982, Water 1985, Miami Memoirs 1987, East Meets Wax 1988, Class of 69, Ruby Takes a Trip 1992, Tara Road 2005, Sir Billi the Vet (voice) 2006, Agent Crush (voice) 2008. *Television includes:* Not the Nine O'Clock News (writer) 1982, Romance on the Orient Express 1985, Girls on Top (series) (also writer) 1985–86, Don't Miss Wax 1987–88, Count Duckula (series, voice) 1988, Hit and Run 1990, Ruby Takes a Trip (writer) 1991, The Full Wax (series writer) 1991–94, Ruby Wax Meets … 1996, 1997, 1998, Ruby 1997, 1998, 1999, The Ruby Wax Show (series) (also dir and exec. producer) 1997, Ruby's American Pie 1999, 2000, Hot Wax 2001, The Waiting Game 2001, 2002, Ruby (exec. producer) 2002, Ruby Wax with … 2003, Popetown (series) 2006. *Plays include:* Wax Acts (one woman show) 1992, Stressed (one woman show) 2000. *Publication:* How Do You Want Me? (autobiog.) 2002.

WAY, Kuo, BS, PhD; Chinese engineer, academic and university administrator; *President, City University of Hong Kong;* ed Kansas State Univ., USA, National Tsing-Hua Univ., Taiwan; with Bell Labs 1981–84; Wisenbaker Chair of Eng in Innovation, Texas A&M Univ. 1993– 2003, also Exec. Assoc. Dean of Eng and Head of Dept of Industrial Eng 1993–2000; Univ. Distinguished Prof. and Dean of Eng, Univ. of Tennessee 2003–08; Pres. and Univ. Distinguished Prof., City Univ. of Hong Kong 2008–; Foreign mem. Chinese Acad. of Eng 2008; mem. US Nat. Acad. of Eng, Academia Sinica, Taiwan, Int. Acad. for Quality; Fellow, American Soc. for Quality, IEEE, Inst. for Operations Research and Man. Science, American Statistical Asscn, Inst. of Industrial Engineers; Hon. Prof. at eight univs; numerous awards including David F Baker Distinguished Research Award, Albert G Holzman Distinguished Educator Award, Award for Technical Innovation in Industrial Eng, Pan Wen-Yuan Foundation Award for Outstanding Research, IEEE Millennium Medal, Austin Bonis Award for Outstanding Achievement in the Advancement of Reliability Research. *Publications:* co-author of five textbooks. *Address:* Office of the President, City University of Hong Kong, Level 6, Cheng Yick-chi Building, Tat Chee Avenue, Kowloon, Hong Kong Special Administrative Region, People's Republic of China (office). *Telephone:* (852) 2788-9400 (office). *Fax:* (852) 2788-9020 (office). *E-mail:* Office.President@cityu.edu.hk (office). *Website:* www.cityu.edu.hk (office).

WEAH, George Oppong; Liberian fmr professional football player and politician; b. 1 Oct. 1966, Monrovia; m.; four c.; played for Liberian and Cameroonian clubs; player AC Monaco, Cameroon national team 1988–92 (47 goals, 93 games), Paris St Germain 1992–95 (32 goals, 96 games), AC Milan 1995–99 (34 goals, 78 games); played with Chelsea, Manchester City and Marseille; player Liberia nat. team, also Technical Dir until retired after the African Nations Cup Jan. 2002; signed for Al Jazira, UAE 2001; special rep. for sport UNICEF; Amb. for SOS Children's Villages; unsuccessful cand. for Liberian presidential elections 2005; African Player of the Year 1989, 1994, 1995, World Player of the Year 1995, European Player of the Year 1995, FIFA Fair Player 1996, African Footballer of the Century. *Address:* Liberian National Congress, c/o CDC Headquarters, Bernard Beach Compound, Sinkor, Liberia. *Website:* www.friendsofgeorgeweah.com.

WEAIRE, Denis Lawrence, PhD, FRS, MRIA, MAE; British/Irish physicist and academic; *Erasmus Smith's Professor of Natural and Experimental Philosophy and Head, Physics Department, Trinity College Dublin;* b. 17 Oct. 1942, Dalhousie, India; s. of Allen M. Weaire and Janet E. Rea; m. Colette O'Regan 1969; one s.; ed Belfast Royal Acad. and Cambridge Univ.; Harkness Fellowship 1964–66; Fellow, Clare Coll. Cambridge 1967–69; Instructor, Assoc. Prof. Yale Univ. 1970–74; Sr Lecturer, Prof. Heriot-Watt Univ. 1974–79; Chair. of Experimental Physics, Univ. Coll. Dublin 1980–84; Erasmus Smith's Prof. of Natural and Experimental Philosophy, Trinity Coll. Dublin 1984–, Dean of Science 1989; mem. Academia Europaea, Vice-Pres. 2005–08; Hon. Sec. European Asscn of Deans of Science 1991–93; Vice-Pres. European Physical Soc. 1995–96, 1999–2000, Pres. 1997–99; Vice-Pres. Inst. of Physics 2008–; Dr hc (Tech. Univ., Lisbon) 2001; Cecil Powell Medal 2002, RIA Cunningham Medal 2006, IOP/French Phys Soc Holweck Medal 2008. *Publications:* Introduction to Physical Mathematics (co-author) 1985, The Physics of Foams (co-author) 2000, The Pursuit of Perfect Packing (co-author) 2000; co-ed. of several other vols. *Leisure interests:* sport, sea-fishing, theatre, humorous writing, book collecting. *Address:* School of Physics, Trinity College, Dublin 2; 26 Greenmount Road, Terenure, Dublin, Ireland (home). *Telephone:* (1) 8961675 (office); (1) 4902063 (home). *Fax:* (1) 6711759 (office). *E-mail:* dweaire@tcd.ie (office). *Website:* www.tcd.ie/Physics (office).

WEALE, Martin Robert, CBE, MA, ScD; British economist; *Director, National Institute of Economic and Social Research;* b. 4 Dec. 1955, Barnet, Herts.; s. of R. A. Weale and M. E. Weale; ed Clare Coll., Cambridge; Overseas Devt Inst. Fellow, Nat. Statistical Office, Malawi 1977–79; researcher and lecturer, Faculty of Econs and Politics, Univ. of Cambridge 1979–95, Econs Fellow, Clare Coll. 1981–95; Dir Nat. Inst. of Econ. and Social Research 1995–, Statistics Commr 2000–; mem. Bd for Actuarial Standards 2006–; Hon. Fellow, Inst. of Actuaries 2001; Hon. DSc (City Univ.) 2007. *Publications include:* Macroeconomic Policy: Inflation, Wealth and the Exchange Rate (co-author) 1989, Reconciliation of National Income and Expenditure (co-author) 1995, Econometric Modelling: Techniques and Applications (co-ed.) 2000; numerous journal articles. *Leisure interests:* bridge, walking, art exhbns, music. *Address:* National Institute of Economic and Social Research, 2 Dean Trench Street, London, SW1P 3HE (office); 63 Noel Road, London, N1 8HE, England (home). *Telephone:* (20) 7654-1945 (office). *E-mail:* mweale@niesr.ac.uk (office). *Website:* www.niesr.ac.uk (office).

WEARING, Gillian, BA, RA; British artist; b. 1963, Birmingham, England; ed Chelsea School of Art, Goldsmith's Coll., London; first solo exhbn City Racing, London 1993, numerous exhbns around the world; concentrates on video and photography; New Contemporaries Award 1993, Turner Prize 1997, Prize of Ministry of Employment, Social Affairs and Urban Devt, Culture and Sport, Oberhausen Short Film Festival 1998, British Television Advertising Award, Public Service: Gold 2002. *Publications:* Gillian Wearing City Projects Prague 1996, Signs that say what you want them to say and not signs that say what someone else wants you to say 1997, Gillian Waring 1997, A Woman Called Theresa 1999, Gillian Wearing 1999, 2000, 2001, Broad Street 2001, Unspoken 2001, Sous Influence 2001, Mass Observation 2002, A Trilogy 2002, Living Proof 2006, Family History 2007. *Address:* c/o Maureen Paley, 21 Herald Street, London, E2 6JT, England. *Telephone:* (20) 7729-4112. *Fax:* (20) 7729-4113. *E-mail:* info@maureenpaley.com. *Website:* www.maureenpaley.com.

WEATHERALL, Sir David John, Kt, MD, FRCP, FRS; British medical specialist and academic; *Regius Professor of Medicine Emeritus, University of Oxford;* b. 9 March 1933, Liverpool; s. of the late Harry Weatherall and Gwendoline Weatherall; m. Stella Nestler 1962; one s.; ed Calday Grammar School and Univ. of Liverpool; various resident posts in medicine 1956–58; Jr medical specialist, Royal Army Medical Corps, Singapore 1959–60; Research Fellow, Johns Hopkins Hosp. 1961–65; Reader in Haematology, Univ. of Liverpool 1969–71, Prof. 1971–74; consultant to WHO 1967–82; Nuffield Prof. of Clinical Medicine, Univ. of Oxford 1974–92, Regius Prof. of Medicine 1992–2000, Regius Prof. Emer. 2000–; Chancellor Univ. of Keele 2002–; Fellow, Magdalen Coll. 1974–92, Emer. Fellow 1992, Student, Christ Church 1992–2000; Hon. Dir MRC Molecular Haematology Unit 1979–2000, Inst. of Molecular Medicine 1988–2000; Trustee Wellcome Trust 1990–2000; Pres. British Asscn for the Advancement of Science 1993, Int. Soc. of Haematology 1993; Pres. Kennedy Foundation 2000–02; Trustee Wolfson Trust 2000–, Imperial Cancer Research Fund 2000–02; mem. American Acad. of Arts and Sciences; Watson-Smith Lecture 1974, Croonian Lecture 1984, Foundation Lecture (FRCPath) 1979, Darwin Lecture (Eugenics Soc.) 1979; Sims Visiting Prof. 1982; Fellow Imperial Coll. 1984; Foreign Assoc. NAS 1990, Inst. of Medicine 1991, Founder Fellow Acad. Med. Sci. 1998; Hon. FRCOG; Hon. FACP; Hon. FRCPCH; Hon. MD (Leeds) 1988, (Sheffield) 1989, (Nottingham) 1993; Hon. DSc (Manchester) 1989, (Edin.) 1989, (Aberdeen) 1991, (Leicester) 1991, (London) 1992, (Keele) 1993, (Mahidol Univ., Thailand) 1997, (Exeter) 1999, (McGill Univ., Canada) 1999, (Cambridge) 2004; Hon. DHumLitt (Johns Hopkins Univ.) 1990; Hon. DSc (Oxford Brookes) 1995, (South Bank) 1995, (Exeter) 1998; Hon. LLD (Liverpool) 1992, (Bristol) 1994; Stratton Award and Medal (Int. Soc. of Haematology) 1982, Ballantyne Prize (Royal Coll. of Physicians, Edin.) 1983, Feldberg Foundation Award 1984, Royal Medal (Royal Soc.) 1989, Conway Evans Prize (Royal Soc. and Royal Coll. Physicians) 1991, Gold Medal, Royal Soc. of Medicine 1992, Buchanan Medal (Royal Soc.) 1994, Helmut Horten Int. Prize in Biomedical Science 1995, Manson Medal, Royal Soc. of Tropical Medicine 1998, Prince Mahidol Award, Thailand 2001, Allen Award (American Soc. of Human Genetics) 2003, Genetics Soc. Mendel Medal 2006. *Publications:* The New Genetics and Clinical Practice 1982, The Thalassaemia Syndromes (with J. B. Clegg) 1982, 2001, Oxford Textbook of Medicine (with others) 1983, Science and the Quiet Art 1995, Genomics and World Health (co-author) 2002; over 600 reviews and papers on human genetic disease. *Leisure interest:* music. *Address:* Weatherall Institute of Molecular Medicine, John Radcliffe Hospital, Headington, Oxford, OX3 9DU (office); 8 Cumnor Rise Road, Cumnor Hill, Oxford, OX2 9HD, England (home). *Telephone:* (1865) 222360 (office). *Fax:* (1865) 222501 (office). *Website:* www.imm.ox.ac.uk (office).

WEATHERALL, Vice-Adm. Sir James (Lamb), KCVO, KBE, DL; British naval officer; b. 28 Feb. 1936, Newton Mearns, Renfrewshire; s. of the late Lt Commdr Alwyne Weatherall and Joan Cuthbert; m. Hon. Jean Stewart Macpherson 1962; two s. three d.; ed Glasgow Acad., Gordonstoun School; commanded HM Ships Soberton 1966–67, Ulster 1970–72, Tartar 1975–76, Andromeda 1982–84 (in Falklands Conflict), Ark Royal 1985–87; on staff of Supreme Allied Commander Europe (NATO) as Rear-Adm. 1987–89; Deputy Supreme Allied Commdr Atlantic 1989–91; HM Marshal of the Diplomatic Corps 1992–2001; Extra Equerry to HM The Queen 2001; DL for Hampshire 2004; one of HM The Queen's Commrs of the Lieutenancy for the City of London 2001; Liveryman Worshipful Co. of Shipwrights 1985, Asst to Court 1989, Prime Warden 2001–02; Younger Brother Trinity House 1986; Trustee Marwell Zoological Preservation Trust 1992 (Chair. 1999–); Gov. Box Hill School 1992–2003 (Chair. 1994–2003, Warden 2003–), Gordonstoun School 1994–2003 (Chair. 1996–2003, Warden 2004–); Pres. Int. Social Service 1996–2001; Chair. Lord Mayor of London's Appeal 1997–98; Chair. Sea Cadet Asscn 1992–98; Trustee World Wildlife Fund UK 2001. *Leisure interests:* fishing, stamp collecting. *Address:* Craig House, Street End, Bishop's Waltham, Hants., SO32 1FS, England (home). *Telephone:* (1489) 892483 (home). *E-mail:* weatheralljim@aol.com (home).

WEAVER, Sigourney, BA, MFA; American actress; b. 8 Oct. 1949, New York; d. of Pat Weaver and Elizabeth Inglis; m. James Simpson 1984; one d.; ed Stanford Univ., Yale Univ.; f. Goat Cay Productions (film production co.). *Films include:* Annie Hall 1977, Tribute to a Madman 1977, Camp 708 1978, Alien 1979, Eyewitness 1981, The Year of Living Dangerously 1982, Deal of the Century 1983, Ghostbusters 1984, Une Femme ou Deux 1985, Half Moon Street 1986, Aliens 1986, Gorillas in the Mist (Golden Globe Best Actress Award) 1988, Working Girl (Best Supporting Actress Award Golden Globe) 1988, Ghostbusters II 1989, Aliens 3 1992, 1492: Conquest of Paradise 1993, Dave 1993, Death and the Maiden 1994, Jeffrey 1995, Copycat 1996, Snow White in the Black Forest 1996, Ice Storm 1996, Alien Resurrection 1997, A Map of the World 1999, Galaxy Quest 1999, Get Bruce 1999, Company Man 1999, Airframe 1999, Heartbreakers 2001, Tadpole 2002, The Guys 2002, Holes 2003, The Village 2004, Imaginary Heroes 2004, Snow Cake 2006, The TV Set 2006, Infamous 2006, Happily N'Ever After (voice) 2007, Be Kind Rewind 2007, The Girl in the Park 2007, Vantage Point 2008, Baby Mama

2008, Wall E 2008. *Address:* William Morris Agency, 1 William Morris Place, Beverly Hills, CA 90212; Goat Cay Productions, PO Box 38, New York, NY 10150, USA. *Telephone:* (212) 421-8293 (Goat Cay). *Fax:* (212) 421-8294 (Goat Cay).

WEBB, Sir Adrian Leonard, Kt, BSocSci, MSc, DLitt, FRSA; British academic and university administrator; b. 19 July 1943; s. of Leonard Webb and Rosina Webb; m. 1st Caroline Williams 1966 (divorced 1995); two s.; m. 2nd Monjulee Dass 1996; ed Univ. of Birmingham, London School of Econs; Lecturer, LSE 1966–74; Research Dir Personal Social Services Council 1974–76; Prof. of Social Policy, Loughborough Univ. 1976–93; Dir Centre for Research in Social Policy 1983–90, Dean, later Pro-Vice-Chancellor, 1986–93; Vice-Chancellor, Univ. of Glamorgan 1993–; mem. Nat. Cttee of Inquiry into Higher Educ. (Dearing Cttee) 1996–97, BBC Broadcasting Council for Wales 1998–; Dir (non-exec.) E Glamorgan NHS Trust 1997–. *Publications:* Change, Choice and Conflict in Social Policy 1975; Planning Need and Scarcity 1986; The Economic Approach to Social Policy 1986; Social Work, Social Care and Social Planning 1987; Joint Approaches to Social Policy 1988. *Leisure interests:* birdwatching, walking. *Address:* University of Glamorgan, Pontypridd, Mid Glamorgan, CF37 1DL, Wales (office). *Telephone:* (1443) 482001 (office). *Fax:* (1443) 482390 (office). *E-mail:* alwebb@glam.ac.uk (office).

WEBB, James (Jim) H., Jr, JD; American writer and politician; *Senator from Virginia;* b. 9 Feb. 1946, Arlington, Va; m. Hong Le Webb; three c.; ed US Naval Acad. and Georgetown Univ.; Asst Minority Counsel, House Cttee on Veterans Affairs, Washington, DC 1977–78, Chief Minority Counsel 1979–81; Visiting Writer, US Naval Acad. 1979; Asst Sec. for Reserve Affairs, Dept of Defense 1984–87; Sec. of the Navy 1987–88 (resgnd); Senator from Va 2007–; Fellow, Harvard Inst. of Politics 1992; Dept of Defense Distinguished Public Service Medal, Medal of Honor Soc.'s Patriot Award, American Legion Nat. Commdr's Public Service Award, VFW's Media Service Award, Marine Corps League's Mil. Order of the Iron Mike Award, John Russell Leade-ship Award, Robert L. Denig Distinguished Service Award; Emmy Award for 1983 PBS coverage of US Marines in Beirut. *Film:* Rules of Engagement (wrote story and exec. producer) 2000. *Publications:* Fields of Fire 1978, A Sense of Honor 1981, A Country Such As This 1983, Something To Die For 1991, A Sense of Honor 1995, The Emperor's General 1999, Lost Soldiers 2001, Born Fighting 2004. *Publications include:* A Country Such As This, Something to Die For 1991. *Address:* 144 Russell Senate Office Building, Washington, DC 20510, USA (office). *Telephone:* (202) 224-4024 (office). *Fax:* (202) 228-6363 (office). *Website:* webb.senate.gov (office).

WEBB, Leslie Roy, AO, BCom, PhD; Australian university vice-chancellor (retd); b. 18 July 1935, Melbourne; s. of Leslie Hugh Charles Webb and Alice Myra Webb; m. Heather Brown 1966; one s. one d.; ed Wesley Coll., Melbourne, Univ. of Melbourne, London School of Econs; Sr Lecturer in Econs, Univ. of Melbourne 1964–68, Truby Williams Prof. of Econs 1973–84, Prof. Emer. 1985–, Pro-Vice-Chancellor 1982–84, Chair. Academic Bd 1983–84; Reader in Econs, La Trobe Univ. 1969–72; Vice-Chancellor Griffith Univ. 1985–2002; Chair. Queensland Non-State Schools Accreditation Bd 2001–, Library Bd of Queensland 2002–08; Visiting Prof. Cornell Univ., USA 1967–68; Consultant, UNCTAD 1974–75; Jt Ed. The Economic Record 1973–77; Chair. Cttee of Inquiry into S Australian Dairy Industry 1977, Library Bd of Queensland 2002–; Assoc. mem. Prices Justification Tribunal 1978–79, 1980–81; mem. Council of Advice, Bureau of Industry Econs 1982–84; Chair. Bd of Dirs. Australian-American Educational Foundation (Fulbright Program) 1986–90; mem. Bd of Govs., Foundation for Devt Co-operation 1990–; Dir and mem. Australian Vice-Chancellors' Cttee Bd of Dirs. 1991–94; Pres. Victorian Br., Econ. Soc. of Australia and NZ 1976; Cavaliere, Ordine al Merito (Italy) 1995, Officer of the Order of Australia 2003; Award for Outstanding Achievement, US Information Agency 1987; DUniv (Queensland Univ. Technology) 2002, DUniv (Griffith) 2002, Hon. DLitt (Univ. South Queensland) 2002. *Publications:* Industrial Economics: Australian Studies (Jt Ed.) 1982; articles in learned journals. *Leisure interests:* music, art, gardening. *Address:* 3 Davrod Street, Robertson, Queensland 4109, Australia (home). *Telephone:* (7) 3345-7141 (home). *Fax:* (7) 3344-6797 (home). *E-mail:* roywebb@bigpond.com (home).

WEBBER, Tristan, MA; British fashion designer; ed SE Essex Coll. of Arts and Tech., Cordwainers Coll., London and St Martin's School of Art and Design; work exhibited at Colette, Paris and Powerhouse Exhbn, London 1998; third collection shown at London Fashion Week 1998 and MTV Fashionably Loud event, Miami 1998; fmr Visiting Lecturer Royal Coll. of Art. *Address:* c/o Royal College of Art, Kensington Gore, London, SW7 2EU, England (office).

WEBER, Axel A., PhD; German central banker, economist and academic; *President, Deutsche Bundesbank;* b. 8 March 1957, Kusel; ed Univ. of Constance, Siegen Univ.; Prof. of Econ. Theory, Bonn 1994–98; apptd Prof. of Applied Monetary Econs, Frankfurt 1998; Prof. of Int. Econs, Cologne Univ. 2001–, Dir Centre for Financial Studies 1998–; Pres. Deutsche Bundesbank 2004–; mem. Governing Council, European Cen. Bank 2004–. *Address:* Deutsche Bundesbank, Postfach 100602, 60006 Frankfurt, Germany (office). *Telephone:* (69) 95661 (office). *Fax:* (69) 5601071 (office). *E-mail:* presse-information@bundesbank.de (office). *Website:* www.bundesbank.de (office).

WEBER, Bruce; American photographer, film director and producer; b. 29 March 1946, Greensburg, Pa; ed Hun School at Princeton, Denison Univ., Ohio, New York Univ. Art and Film Schools, New School for Social Research, New York; numerous exhbns in New York, Los Angeles, Chicago, Dallas, San Francisco, Atlanta, New Orleans, St Louis, Paris, London, Dortmund, Basel, Lausanne, Tokyo, Frankfurt etc. 1973–; photographs in perm. collections of Victoria and Albert Museum, London and Photography Div., City of Paris; numerous commercials 1988–; numerous awards including: Council of Fashion Designers of America for Achievement in Photography 1984, 1985, American Soc. of Magazine Photographers Fashion Photographer of the Year 1984, Int. Film and TV Festival of New York Silver Medal 1985, Cannes Int. Advertising Film Festival Silver Lion for Beauty Brothers (commercial) 1988, Int. Center of Photography Award for use of Photography in Advertising 1994, Best Advertising in Print and TV, Fragrance Foundation 1997, First Alfred Eisenstaedt Award for Portrait Photography, Life magazine 1998. *Films as producer and director include:* Broken Noses 1987 (Int. Documentary Asscn Award 1988), Let's Get Lost 1988 (Critics' Award, Venice Film Festival 1988, Int. Documentary Asscn Award 1989), Backyard Movie 1991, Gentle Giants 1994, The Teddy Boys of the Edwardian Drape Society 1996, Chop Suey 1999; music videos: Being Boring, The Pet Shop Boys 1990 (Video of the Year Award, Music Week 1990), Blue Spanish Sky, Chris Isaak 1991, Se A Vida E, The Pet Shop Boys 1996. *Film as director:* A Letter to True 2003. *Publications:* Sam Shepard 1990, Bear Pond 1990, Hotel Room with a View (photographs) 1992, Gentle Giants: A Book of Newfoundland 1994, A House is Not a Home 1996, Branded Youth and other stories 1997, The Chop Suey Club 1999. *Address:* c/o Little Bear Inc., 135th Watts Street, 5th Floor, New York, NY 10013, USA. *Telephone:* (212) 226-0814 (office). *Fax:* (212) 334-5180 (office). *Website:* www.bruceweber.com.

WEBER, George Brian, MA; Canadian national organization official and fmr Red Cross official; *Executive Director, Canadian Dental Association;* b. 18 April 1946, Montréal; s. of Harry Weber and Johanna Alexopoulos; m. Mary Morris 1976; ed McGill Univ., Harvard Univ., USA; voluntary instructor/examiner Canadian Red Cross 1963–73; Field Del. Vietnam, Int. Red Cross 1973–74; Disaster Relief Officer, Chief Del. League of Red Cross Socs 1974–76; Nat. Dir Int. Affairs, Canadian Red Cross 1976–81, Nat. Dir of Programmes 1981–83, Sec. Gen. Canadian Red Cross 1983–93, Hon. Vice Pres. 1993–, Sec. Gen. and CEO Int. Fed. of Red Cross and Red Crescent Socs 1993–2000, Sec. Gen. Emer. 2000–; Chair. Canadian Soc. Assoc. Execs; Exec. Dir Canadian Dental Asscn; CEO Continovation Services Inc.; mem., Dir numerous bodies, including Canadian Inst. of Int. Affairs, Amundsen Foundation, Earth Foundation, American Coll. of Sports Medicine; Vanier Award 1984. *Leisure interests:* diving, tennis, squash, skiing. *Address:* Canadian Dental Association, 1815 Alta Vista Drive, Ottawa, Ont. K1G 3Y6, Canada (office). *Telephone:* (613) 523-1770 (office). *E-mail:* reception@cda-adc.ca (office). *Website:* www.cda-adc.ca (office).

WEBER, Jonathan N., FMedSci, FRCP, FRCPath; British clinical professor; *Jefferiss Professor of Communicable Diseases and GU Medicine, Imperial College London;* Wellcome Clinical Training Fellow, St Mary's Hosp. Medical School 1982–85; Wellcome Trust Lecturer in Cell and Molecular Biology, Inst. for Cancer Research Chester Beatty Labs 1985–88; Sr Lecturer in Infectious Diseases, Royal Postgraduate Medical School, Hammersmith Hosp. 1988–91; Jefferiss Prof. of Communicable Diseases and GU Medicine, Faculty of Medicine, Imperial Coll. London 1990–, also Head of Div. of Medicine; Founding Ed. AIDS (journal) 1987–92; co-f. WHO Network for HIV Characterisation 1992; Adviser on HIV to numerous orgs including WHO, UNAIDS, EC, Elton John Foundation, Wellcome Trust, Dept for Int. Devt, Russian Fed. AIDS Centre, Ivanovsky Inst. of Virology; Collaborator, European Vaccine Effort Against HIV/AIDS, Int. AIDS Vaccine Initiative; Dir Weber Investments 1996–. *Publications:* over 200 scientific papers on HIV and other STIs. *Address:* Faculty of Medicine, Imperial College, St Mary's Hospital, Norfolk Place, London, W2 1PG, England (office). *Telephone:* (20) 7594-3905 (office). *E-mail:* j.weber@imperial.ac.uk (office). *Website:* www1.imperial.ac.uk/medicine/people/j.weber (office).

WEBER, Jürgen, DR. ING.; German business executive; *Chairman of the Supervisory Board, Deutsche Lufthansa AG;* b. 17 Oct. 1941; m. Sabine Rossberg 1965; one s. one d.; ed Stuttgart Tech. Univ., MIT; with Lufthansa Eng Div. 1967–74, Dir Line Maintenance Dept 1974–78, with Aircraft Eng Sub-div. 1978–87, COO (Tech.) 1987–89, deputy mem. Exec. Bd 1989–90, CEO (Tech.) 1990–91, Chair. Exec. Bd Deutsche Lufthansa AG 1991–2003, CEO 1998–2003, mem. Supervisory Bd 2001–, currently Chair.; Chair. Supervisory Bd Deutsche Post AG 2006–; Chair. Supervisory Bd Thomas Cook AG; mem. Supervisory Bd Allianz-Lebensversicherungs AG, Bayer AG, Deutsche Bank AG, Voith AG, Loyalty Pnr GmbH, Tetra Laval Group (Switzerland); Fellow, Royal Aeronautical Soc., London 1997; Hon. DEng (Stuttgart Univ.) 1998; Bambi Award for Industry 1994, Anti-Defamation League Champion of Liberty Award, Man. Magazin Man. of the Year 1999, Wirtschaftswoche Best Man. 2002, L. Welch Pogue Award, Airline Business Award 2003. *Leisure interests:* jogging, skiing. *Address:* Deutsche Lufthansa AG, Von-Gablenz-Strasse 2-6, 50679 Cologne, Germany (office). *Telephone:* (69) 6960 (office). *Fax:* (69) 6966818 (office). *Website:* www.lufthansa.com (office).

WEBER, Lisa M., BA; American business executive; *President, Individual Business, MetLife, Inc.;* ed State Univ. of New York at Stony Brook; Sr Vice-Pres. Human Resources, PaineWebber Group, Inc. 1988–98; Head of Human Resources, Metropolitan 1998–2003, Sr Vice-Pres. MetLife, Inc. Sept.–Nov. 1999, Vice-Pres. Metropolitan Life 1998–99, Exec. Vice-Pres. MetLife, Inc. and Metropolitan Life 1999–2001, Sr Exec. Vice-Pres. and Chief Admin. Officer 2001–04, Pres. Individual Business 2004–; Dir Reinsurance Group of America, Inc. and several MetLife subsidiaries, including MetLife Bank; Dir MetLife Foundation, Rutgers Exec. Advisory Cttee; Trustee, Northeast Region Boys and Girls Clubs of America; ranked by Fortune magazine amongst 50 Most Powerful Women in Business in the US (43rd) 2004, (35th) 2005, (33rd) 2006, (36th) 2007, ranked by Forbes magazine amongst 100 Most Powerful Women (77th) 2008. *Address:* MetLife, Inc., 1 Madison Avenue, New York, NY 10010-3690, USA (office). *Telephone:* (212) 578-2211 (office). *Fax:* (212) 578-3320 (office). *Website:* www.metlife.com (office).

WEBER, Manfred, Dr rer. pol; German banking official; *CEO, Association of German Banks;* b. 18 Dec. 1950, Altenkofen, Landshut; ed Johann Wolfgang Goethe Univ., Frankfurt am Main; Research Asst, Research Dept, Deutsche Bundesbank 1980, Head, Office of Deputy Gov. 1986–91; Monetary and Econ. Dept B.I.S., Basle 1991–92; CEO and mem. Bd of Dirs Bundesverband deutscher Banken, Berlin 1992–; Hon. Prof., Univ. of Potsdam 2004. *Address:* Bundesverband deutscher Banken, Burgstrasse 28, 10178 Berlin, Germany. *Telephone:* (30) 16631000 (office). *Fax:* (30) 16631399 (office). *Website:* www.germanbanks.org (office).

WEBSTER, Paul; British film executive; b. 19 Sept. 1952; Co-Dir Osiris Film, London 1979–81; Founder Palace Pictures 1982–88, launched Working Title Film LA 1990–92; Head of Production, Miramax Films 1995–97; CEO Film Four Ltd 1998–; mem. BAFTA Council, BAFTA Film Council. *Films include:* The Tall Guy 1988, Drop Dead Fred 1990, Bob Roberts (Exec. Producer) 1992, Romeo is Bleeding 1993, Little Odessa (Silver Lion Venice Film Festival) 1994, The Pallbearer 1995, Gridlock'd 1996, The English Patient, Welcome to Sarajevo, Wings of the Dove, The Yards 1998. *Address:* FilmFour Ltd, 76–78 Charlotte Street, London, W1P 1LX, England (office). *Telephone:* (20) 7306-8621 (office). *Fax:* (20) 7306-6457.

WEBSTER, Peter; Irish business executive; joined Jefferson Smurfit Group 1978, fmr Regional Operations Dir, Chair. and Chief Exec. Smurfit Ireland Group 1996, now Dir Smurfit Group Ireland; Pres. Dublin Chamber of Commerce 2002, now mem. Council; Chair. RMI. *Address:* c/o Dublin Chamber of Commerce, 7 Clare Street, Dublin 2, Ireland.

WEBSTER, William Hedgcock, JD, LLB; American fmr government official, judge and lawyer; *Senior Partner, Milbank, Tweed, Hadley and McCloy LLP;* b. 6 March 1924, St Louis, Mo.; s. of Thomas M. Webster and Katherine (née Hedgcock) Webster; m. 1st Drusilla Lane 1950 (died 1984); one s. two d.; m. 2nd Lynda Clugston 1990; ed Amherst Coll., Washington Univ. Law School; admitted to Missouri Bar 1949; attorney with Armstrong, Teasdale, Kramer and Vaughan and predecessors, St Louis 1949–50, 1952–59, Partner 1956–59, 1961–70; US Attorney, Eastern Dist, Mo. 1960–61; Judge, US Dist Court, Eastern Mo. 1971–73, US Court of Appeals 1973–78; Dir FBI 1978–87; Dir CIA 1987–91; Sr Partner, Millbank, Tweed, Hadley & McCloy 1991–; Trustee, Washington Univ. 1974–; Head investigation into police response to LA Riots 1992; served as Lt USNR 1943–46, 1951–52; mem. American, Fed., Mo. and St Louis Bar Asscns, American Law Inst., Council 1978–, Inst. of Judicial Admin Inc.; Fellow, American Bar Foundation; Order of the Coif; Hon. LLD (Amherst Coll.) 1975, (DePauw Univ.) 1978, (Washington Univ.) 1978, (William Woods Coll.) 1979, and numerous others; Washington Univ. Distinguished Alumnus Award 1977, American Legion Distinguished Service Award 1979, St Louis Globe-Democrat Man of the Year 1980, Washington Univ. William Greenleaf Elliot Award 1981, Riot Relief Fund of New York Award 1981, Young Lawyers of the ABA Award 1982, Fordham-Stein Award 1982, William Moss Inst.-American Univ. Award 1983, Freedoms Foundation Medal 1985, Presidential Medal of Freedom 1991, Nat. Security Medal 1991, Justice Award, American Judicature Soc. 2001, ABA Medal 2002, Distinguished Public Service Medal from NASA. *Leisure interest:* tennis. *Address:* Milbank, Tweed, Hadley and McCloy LLP, 1825 I Street, NW, Suite 1100, Washington, DC 20006, USA (office). *Telephone:* (202) 835-7550 (office). *Fax:* (202) 835-7586 (office). *E-mail:* wwebster@milbank.com (office). *Website:* www.milbank.com (office).

WECKMANN-MUÑOZ, Luis, PhD, LLD, MA; Mexican diplomatist and historian; b. 7 April 1923, Ciudad Lerdo, Durango; s. of José Bernardo Weckmann and Ana Muñoz; ed Univ. Nacional Autónoma de México, Univs. of Paris and Calif., Inst. des Hautes Etudes Int. and Ecole des Chartes, Paris; successively Sec. of Legation and Chargé d'affaires, Czechoslovakia, Sec. of Embassy and Chargé d'affaires, France 1952–59; Dir-Gen. for Int. Educ. Affairs and Exec. Sec.-Gen. Mexican Nat. Council for UNESCO 1959–64; Minister Plenipotentiary and Chargé d'affaires, France 1965–66; Amb. to Israel 1967–69, to Austria 1969–72, to Fed. Repub. of Germany 1973–74; Special Rep. of UN Sec.-Gen. to Iran and Iraq 1974; Special Rep. of UN Sec.-Gen. in Cyprus 1974–75; Amb. to Iran 1976–79, to UN 1979–80, to Italy 1981–86, to Belgium and the EEC 1986–88; Consul-Gen. in Rio de Janeiro 1988–90; Vice-Pres. 1st Inter-american Meeting on Science and Tech., Washington; UNESCO's expert for Latin America on Cultural Exchanges. *Publications:* La Sociedad Feudal 1944, Las Bulas Alejandrinas de 1493 y la Teoría Política del Papado Medieval 1949, El Pensamiento Político Medieval y una nueva base para el Derecho Internacional 1950, Les origines des Missions Diplomatiques Permanentes 1953, Panorama de la Cultura Medieval 1962, Las Relaciones Franco-Mexicanas (1823-1885) vol. I 1961, vol. II 1963, vol. III 1972, La Herencia Medieval de México, Vols I and II 1984, new edn in one vol. 1994, Carlota de Bélgica: Correspondencia y Escritos sobre México en los archivos Europeos, 1861–1868 1989, Constantino el Grande y Cristóbal Colón 1992, The Medieval Heritage of Brazil 1993. *Leisure interest:* reading. *Address:* Villa del Cardo, Calzado del Cardo 4, 37700 San Miguel Allende, Gto., Mexico.

WEDDERBURN OF CHARLTON, Baron (Life Peer), cr. 1977, of Highgate; **Kenneth William (Bill) Wedderburn,** QC, MA, LLB, FBA; British lawyer, legal scholar and academic; *Cassel Professor Emeritus of Commercial Law, London School of Economics;* b. 13 April 1927, London; s. of Herbert John Wedderburn and Mabel Ethel Wedderburn; m. 1st Nina Salaman 1951 (divorced 1961); one s. two d.; m. 2nd Dorothy Cole 1962 (divorced 1969); m. 3rd Frances Ann Knight 1969; one s.; ed Aske's (Hatcham) Grammar School, Whitgift School, Queens' Coll., Cambridge; Lecturer in Law, Univ. of Cambridge 1952–64; Fellow, Clare Coll. Cambridge, Hon. Fellow 1996; Cassel Prof. of Commercial Law, LSE 1964–92, Prof. Emer. 1992–, Hon. Fellow 1997; Visiting Prof., Harvard Law School 1969–70, UCLA 1969; Barrister at Law (Middle Temple) 1953–, QC 1990; Gen. Ed. Modern Law Review 1970–88; mem. Civil Service Arbitration Tribunal 1973–; Chair. Trades Union Congress Ind. Review Cttee 1975–; Hon. Pres. Industrial Law Soc. 1996–; Hon. DGiur (Pavia); Hon. DEcon (Siena); Hon. LLD (Stockholm); George Long Prize for Jurisprudence, Univ. of Cambridge 1948, Chancellor's Medal for English Law, Univ. of Cambridge 1949. *Publications:* Employment Grievances and Disputes Procedures in Britain (with P. L. Davies) 1969, Cases and Materials on Labour Law 1967, Company Law Reform 1964, The Worker and the Law 1971, 1986, Industrial Conflict – A Comparative Legal Survey (co-ed. with B. Aaron) 1972, Democrazia Politica e Democrazia Industriale 1978, Discrimination in Employment (co-ed.) 1978, Labour Law and the Community (with W. T. Murphy) 1983, Labour Law and Industrial Relations (with R. Lewis and J. Clark) 1983, Diritto del Lavoro in Europa (with B. Veneziani and S. Ghimpu) 1987, The Social Charter, European Company and Employment Rights 1990, Employment Rights in Britain and Europe 1991, Labour Law and Freedom 1995, I Diritti del Lavoro 1998, The Future of Company Law: Fat Cats, Corporate Government and Workers 2005; numerous articles on legal subjects. *Leisure interest:* Charlton Athletic Football Club. *Address:* London School of Economics, Houghton Street, London, WC2A 2AE (office); 29 Woodside Avenue, Highgate, London, N6 4SP, England (home). *Telephone:* (20) 8444-8472 (home). *Fax:* (20) 8444-8472 (home). *E-mail:* bill.wedderburn@btinternet.com (home). *Website:* www.lse.ac.uk/collections/law (office).

WEDER, Hans, PhD, DHabil; Swiss theologian, university rector and academic; *Rector, University of Zurich;* b. 1946, Diepoldsau; ed Gymnasium, St Gallen, Univ. of Zürich, Univ. of St Andrews, UK; Prof. of New Testament Science, Univ. of Zürich 1980–, Dean Theological Faculty 1986–88, Rector, Univ. of Zürich 2000–, mem. Cttee of Reform UNI2000; Pres. Rectors' Conf. of Swiss Univs 2006–. *Publications:* numerous articles in professional journals on hermeneutics and philosophy. *Address:* Office of the Rector, University of Zurich, Stockargut, Künstlergasse 15, Office 205, 8001 Zürich, Switzerland (office). *Telephone:* (44) 634-22-11 (office). *E-mail:* rektor@uzh.ch (office). *Website:* www.uzh.ch (office).

WEDGEWORTH, Robert, AB, MS, LHD; American university librarian, academic and association executive; *Member, National Commission on Adult Literacy;* b. 31 July 1937; m. Chung-Kyun Wedgeworth; one d.; ed Wabash Coll., Univ. of Illinois; Exec. Dir American Library Asscn (ALA) 1972–85; Dean School of Library Service, Columbia Univ. 1985–92; Librarian, Prof. of Library Admin, Univ. of Ill. at Urbana-Champaign 1993–99; Pres. Int. Fed. of Library Asscns and Insts (IFLA) 1991–97, Hon. Pres. 1997–; fmr interim Pres. Laubach Literacy Int. (LLI), fmr Vice Chair., Bd of Trustees, Pres. and CEO ProLiteracy Worldwide (formed by merger of Laubach Literacy Int.and Literacy Volunteers of America, Inc.) 2000–07; Chair. Advisory Cttee ALA Office of Information Tech. Policy 1995–97; mem. Cttee to Visit Harvard Coll. Library 1994–97; mem. Nat. Comm. on Adult Literacy 2006–; Trustee Newberry Library, Chicago; mem. Bd of Trustees Poetry Foundation; ALA Joseph Lippincott Award 1989, Medal of Honor, Int. Co-operation Admin. 1996, Melvil Dewey Award 1997. *Publications:* World Encyclopaedia of Library and Information Services (ed.) 1993, Issues Affecting the Development of Digital Libraries in Science and Technology (UNESCO) 1996, Courtship, Marriage and Librarianship: A Vision of a 21st Century Profession (IFLA) 1996, Beyond Unification 1997, Reaffirming Professional Values 1997. *Address:* 2626 North Lakeview #3603, Chicago, IL 60614, USA (home). *Telephone:* (773) 525-6609 (home). *E-mail:* rwedge@uiuc.edu (home).

WEE, Cho Yaw; Singaporean banker; *Chairman, United Overseas Bank Group;* s. of Wee Kheng Chiang, founder of United Chinese Bank; m.; five c.; ed high school in China; joined Bd of Dirs of then United Chinese Bank (now United Overseas Bank) 1958, Man. Dir 1960–74, Chair. and CEO United Overseas Bank Group 1974–2007, Chair. 2007–; Pres. Singapore Fed. of Chinese Clan Asscns; Public Service Star, Singapore Govt 1971, named Businessman of the Year 1990, inaugural Credit Suisse-Ernst & Young Lifetime Achievement Award 2006. *Address:* United Overseas Bank, 80 Raffles Place, UOB Plaza, 048624 Singapore (office). *Telephone:* 6533-9898 (office). *Fax:* 6534-2334 (office). *E-mail:* info@uobgroup.com (office). *Website:* www.uobgroup.com (office); www.uob.com.sg (office).

WEEKES, Sir Everton de Courcy, KCMG, GCM, OBE; Barbadian fmr cricketer; b. 26 Feb. 1925, St Michael; ed St Leonard's School, Bridgetown; right-hand batsman; teams: Barbados, West Indies; in 48 Tests scored 4,445 runs (average 58.6) including 15 hundreds; scored 12,010 first-class runs (average 55.3) including 36 hundreds 1944–64; Umpire ICC (four Tests, three One Day Ints); Wisden Cricketer of the Year 1951. *Leisure interest:* int. bridge player. *Address:* c/o West Indies Cricket Board of Control, Letchworth Complex, The Garrison, St Michael, Barbados, West Indies.

WEERAMANTRY, Christopher Gregory, BA, LLD; Sri Lankan judge; *Judge (ad-hoc), International Court of Justice;* b. 17 Nov. 1926, Colombo; ed Univ. of London; advocate Supreme Court of Sri Lanka 1948–65, Commr of Assize 1965–67, Justice of Supreme Court 1967–72; Sir Hayden Starke Prof. of Law, Monash Univ., Melbourne, Australia 1972–91, Prof. Emer. of Law 1991–; Judge Int. Court of Justice 1991–2000 (ad-hoc 1999–2000), Vice-Pres. 1997–99; lecturer and Examiner, Council of Legal Educ. 1951–56; mem. Council of Legal Educ. 1967–72; Visiting Prof. Univs. of Tokyo 1978, Stellenbosch 1979, Papua New Guinea 1981, Fla 1984, Lafayette Coll., Pa 1985, Hong Kong 1989; Hon. Visiting Prof. Univ. of Colombo 1984; Chair Comm. of Inquiry into Int. Responsibility for Phosphate Mining on Nauru 1987–88; mem. Editorial Bd Sri Lankan Journal of Int. Law, Human Rights Quarterly (Johns Hopkins Univ.), Interdisciplinary Peace Research (La Trobe Univ.), Journal of Ceylon Law; mem. Advisory Bd China Law Reports; Vice Chair. UN Centre against Apartheid/Govt. of Nigeria Conf. on Legal Status of Apartheid Regime, Lagos 1984; Co-ordinator UN Univ./Netherlands Inst. of Human Rights Workshop on Science, Tech. and Human Rights, Utrecht 1989;

Assoc. Academician, Int. Acad. of Comparative Law, Paris; Vice-Pres. Int. Comm. of Jurists, Vic.; Past Pres. World Fed. of Overseas Sri Lankan Orgs.; Vice-Patron UN Asscn of Sri Lanka; Chair. Cttee of Chief Justices of Asia and Africa; mem. Europa Mundi (UNESCO project), Club of Rome (Australia), Commonwealth Lawyers' Asscn and other professional bodies; Hon. Life mem. Bar Asscn of Sri Lanka; Hon. LLD (Colombo), Dr. hc (Monash Univ.) 2000; Mohamed Sahabdeen Award for Int. Understanding in the SAARC Region 1993; Order of Deshamanya. *Publications:* numerous books on law, human rights and other topics; numerous articles in law journals worldwide and published lectures. *Address:* 5/1 Roland Towers, Dharmaraja Mawatha, off Alfred House Avenue, Colombo 3, Sri Lanka. *Telephone:* (1) 555028. *Fax:* (74) 720480. *E-mail:* cgw@lanka.ccom.lk.

WEERASOORIYA, Gen. C. S.; Sri Lankan army officer (retd) and diplomatist; m. Dilhani Weerasooriya; commanded Operation Jayasikurui to regain the Liberation Tigers of Tamil Eelam-held Wanni and Mullaitivu areas and subsequently to open a land route through Wanni and Kilinochchi dists to link up with Jaffna Peninsula 1997; Commdr of the Army (rank of Lt-Gen.) 1998–2000; High Commr to Pakistan 2001–07; Rana Wickrama Padakkama, Rana Sura Padakkama, Vishista Seva Vibhushanaya, Uttama Seva Padakkama. *Address:* c/o Ministry of Foreign Affairs, Republic Building, Colombo 1, Sri Lanka. *Telephone:* (11) 2325371. *Fax:* (11) 2446091. *E-mail:* publicity@formin.gov.lk. *Website:* www.slmfa.gov.lk.

WĘGLEŃSKI, Piotr; Polish molecular geneticist; b. 29 June 1939, Swidniki; m. Teresa Juszczyk; two d.; ed Warsaw Univ.; academic, Warsaw Univ. 1961–, Pro-Rector 1985–88, 1990–96, Ordinary Prof. 1989–, Rector 1999–2002, 2002–; Visiting Prof., MIT 1987–88, Univ. Paris-Sud 1991; mem. Polish Genetic Soc., Warsaw Scientific Soc., Corresp. mem. Polish Acad. of Sciences 1994; Officier des Palmes académiques 2002; Dr hc (Prikarpatsky State Univ.) 2002. *Publications:* Genetic Engineering (co-author) 1980, Molecular Genetics (co-author and ed.) 1996; numerous scientific articles. *Leisure interests:* tennis, travel, volleyball. *Address:* Uniwersytet Warszawski, ul. Krakowskie Przedmieście 26/28, 00-927 Warsaw, Poland (office). *Telephone:* (22) 5520355 (office). *Fax:* (22) 5524000 (office). *E-mail:* rektor@mercury.ci.uw.edu.pl (office). *Website:* www.uw.edu.pl (office).

WEI, Christianson, JD; Chinese business executive and fmr lawyer; *Managing Director and CEO, Morgan Stanley China;* m. Jon Christianson; three c.; ed Amherst Coll. and Columbia Univ., USA; fmr attorney Orrick Herrington & Sutcliffe, NY, USA; Assoc. Dir of Corp. Finance, Securities and Futures Comm. of Hong Kong 1993–98; Exec. Dir and Beijing Chief Rep. Morgan Stanley 1998–2002; Country Man., China, Credit Suisse First Boston 2002–04, Chair. China 2004–06; Man. Dir and CEO Morgan Stanley China 2006–; Columbia Law School Medal of Excellence 2006; listed by Fortune Magazine as one of 50 most powerful int. women 2008. *Address:* Morgan Stanley China, 2905 First Avenue, Trade Building 2, Jian'guo Gate, Beijing 100004, People's Republic of China (office). *Telephone:* (10) 65058383 (office). *Fax:* (10) 65058220 (office). *E-mail:* infochina@morganstanley.com (office). *Website:* www.morganstanleychina.com (office).

WEI, Ing-chou; Taiwanese business executive; *Chairman and CEO, Tingyi (Cayman Islands) Holdings Corpn;* m.; three c.; more than 30 years' experience in factory construction, production man. and research in relation to food production; joined Tingyi (Cayman Islands) Holdings Corpn (China's largest instant noodle producer) 1991, currently Chair. and CEO, introduced Master Kong instant noodles to Chinese consumers 1990s. *Address:* Tingyi (Cayman Islands) Holdings Corpn, No. 15 The 3rd Street, Tianjin Economic-Technological Development Area, Tianjin 300457 (office); Tingyi (Cayman Islands) Holdings Corpn, Suite 5607, 56/F, Central Plaza, 18 Harbour Road, Wanchai, Hong Kong Special Administrative Region, People's Republic of China (office). *Telephone:* 2511-1911 (Hong Kong) (office). *Fax:* 2511-7911 (Hong Kong) (office). *E-mail:* info@tingyi.com (office). *Website:* www.tingyi.com (office).

WEI, Jiafu, MEng, PhD; Chinese shipping industry executive; *Executive President and CEO, China Ocean Shipping (Group) Company (COSCO);* b. 1950, Jiangsu; ed Wuhan Marine Coll., Dalian Maritime Univ., Tianjin Univ.; with Guangzhou Ocean Shipping Co. 1967–92; Gen. Man. Chinese-Tanzanian Jt Shipping Co., Tanzania 1992–93; Pres. COSCO Holdings Pte Ltd, Singapore 1993–95; Gen. Man. and CEO Tianjin Ocean Shipping Co. 1995–97, COSCO Bulk Carriers Co. Ltd 1997–98, Exec. Pres. and CEO China Ocean Shipping (Group) Co. (COSCO) Group 1998–; Chair. China Shipowners' Asscn, China Shipowners Mutual Assurance Asscn, China Fed. of Industrial Econs, China Group Cos Promotion Asscn; Vice-Chair. China Merchants Bank; mem. Panama Canal Authority Advisory Bd, Harvard Business School Asia-Pacific Advisory Bd; mem. 17th CCP Cen. Cttee Cen. Comm. for Discipline Inspection 2007–; Hon. Dean, Shanghai Maritime Univ. School of Econs and Man.; Commdr, Order of Leopold II (Belgium); Hall of the Fame, Lloyd's List and Maritime Asia 2003, Port Authority of Long Beach Port Pilot Award 2004, Int. Who's Who Professional, Int. Who's Who Historical Soc. 2004, Valuable Manager of the Year, China's leading media 2004, Economic Booster Award, Massachusetts Alliance for Econ. Devt 2004, Port Pilot Award, Port Authority of Long Beach 2004, Int. Maritime Achievement Award 2005. *Address:* China Ocean Shipping (Group) Company (COSCO), Ocean Plaza, 158 Fuxingmennei Street, Beiing 100031, People's Republic of China (office). *Telephone:* (10) 66493388 (office). *Fax:* (10) 66492266 (office). *E-mail:* info@cosco.com (office). *Website:* www.cosco.com (office).

WEI, Jianxing; Chinese state official; b. Jan. 1931, Xinchang Co., Zhejiang Prov.; ed Dalian Eng Inst., CCP Cen. Cttee Cen. Party School and in USSR; joined CCP 1949; section chief, Northeast China Light Alloy Processing Factory 1961–64, Dir 1977–81; Deputy Sec. Harbin Municipality CCP Cttee 1981–83; Mayor of Harbin City 1981–83; Sec. and mem. Exec. Cttee All-China Fed. of Trade Unions 1983, Vice-Pres. 1983–84, Pres. 1993–02; Deputy Dir CCP Cen. Cttee Org. Dept 1984–85, Dir 1985–87; Minister of Supervision 1987–93; Sec. CCP Beijing Municipal Cttee 1995–97; Alt. mem. 12th CCP Cen. Cttee 1982–87, mem. 13th CCP Cen. Cttee 1987–92, 14th CCP Cen. Cttee 1992–97, 15th CCP Cen. Cttee 1997–2002; mem. CCP Cen. Cttee Politburo, Cttee and Secr. for Inspecting Discipline 1992–2002; Head Cen. Leading Group for Party Bldg Work; Sec. Secr. CCP Cen. Cttee; mem. CCP Standing Cttee Politburo 1997–2002. *Address:* c/o All-China Federation of Trade Unions, 10 Fu Xing Men Wai Jie, Beijing 100865, People's Republic of China (office).

WEI, Jingsheng; Chinese dissident; fmr mem. Red Guards and PLA; active in pro-democracy movt, contrib. to underground magazine Exploration 1978; sentenced to 15 years' imprisonment for allegedly leaking mil. secrets to a foreign journalist and for counter-revolutionary activities Spring 1979, released Sept. 1993; held incommunicado and without charge April 1994; sentenced to 14 years' imprisonment for alleged subversive activities 1995; deported March 1998; Sakharov Prize 1996. *Publication:* The Courage to Stand Alone.

WEI, Wei; Chinese singer; b. Hohhot, Inner Mongolia; m. Michael J. Smith (divorced 2004); three s.; singer at 11th Asian Games, Beijing 1990, performed a duet with Julio Iglesias at East Asian Games, Shanghai 1993; represented Asia at the ceremony of the Olympic Games, Atlanta, USA 1996; performed at closing ceremony, Beijing 2008 Summer Olympics; winner Nat. Young Singers' contest on Chinese TV 1986. *Film appearance:* The Singer's Story. *Recordings include:* albums: Twilight, I Believe In China. *Address:* c/o Björn Bertoft, Kungsgatan 48, 8th Floor, PO Box 22043, 104 22, Stockholm, Sweden (office). *Telephone:* (70) 528-2008 (office). *Website:* www.weiweimusic.com (office).

WEI, Yang, BS, MS, PhD; Chinese engineer and university administrator; *President, Zhejiang University;* b. 16 Feb. 1954, Beijing; ed Tsinghua Univ., Brown Univ., USA; Prof. of Solid Mechanics and Chair., Dept of Eng Mechanics, Tsinghua Univ. –2006; Pres. Zhejiang Univ. 2006–; Visiting Scientist, Univ. of Sheffield, UK 1987–88, Univ. of Calif., Santa Barbara, USA 1993, 1995, Taiwan Univ. 1996–97, Princeton Univ., USA 1998; Visiting Prof. Inst. of Mechanics, Grenoble, France 1988, Brown Univ., USA 1990, Tokyo Inst. of Tech., Japan 2000–01, Univ. of Illinois, Urbana-Champaign, USA 2002; Pres.-elect Far East and Oceanic Fracture Soc.; Vice Pres., Chinese Soc. of Theoretical and Applied Mechanics; Council Mem. China Asscn of Science and Tech.; mem. Scientific Cttee, Ministry of Educ.; mem. Gen. Ass., Int. Union of Theoretical and Applied Mechanics (Chair. Working Party 7); Regional Ed. International Journal of Fracture; mem. Editorial Bds International Journal of Damage Mechanics, Fatigue and Fracture of Engineering Materials and Structures, International Journal of Solids and Structures, Archive in Applied Mechanics; mem. Chinese Acad. of Sciences; three Scientific Achievement Awards, State Educ. Comm., Young Scientists Award 1994, Nat. Natural Science Award 1995, Scientific Achievement Award, Ministry of Educ. 2002. *Publications:* Mesoplasticity and its Applications (jtly) 1993, Macroscopic and Microscopic Fracture Mechanics 1995, Mechatronic Reliability 2001, Interfacial and Nanoscale Failure (co-ed.) 2003; over 240 technical papers. *Address:* Zhejiang University, 38 Zheda Road, Hangzhou 310027, Zhejiang, People's Republic of China (office). *Telephone:* (571) 87951846 (office). *Fax:* (571) 87951358 (office). *E-mail:* zupo@zju.edu.cn (office). *Website:* www.zju.edu.cn (office).

WEICKER, Lowell Palmer, Jr, LLB; American fmr politician; *President, Trust for America's Health;* b. 16 May 1931, Paris, France; s. of Lowell Palmer Weicker and Mary (née Bickford) Paulsen; m. 1st Camille Di Lorenzo Butler; eight c.; m. 2nd Claudia Testa Ingram 1984; ed Lawrenceville School, Yale Univ. and Univ. of Virginia; State Rep. in Conn. Gen. Ass. 1963–69; US Rep., Fourth Congressional Dist, Conn. 1969–71; Senator from Conn. 1971–89; Gov. of Conn. 1991–95; 1st Selectman of Greenwich 1964–68; mem. Select Cttee for Investigation of the Watergate Case 1973; fmr mem. Senate Appropriations Cttee, Senate Labor and Human Resources Cttee, fmr Chair. Senate Small Business Cttee, Sub-Cttee on State, Justice, Commerce, the Judiciary and related agencies, Senate Energy and Natural Resources Cttee; fmr Republican, then Independent; currently Pres. Trust for America's Health; mem. Bd of Dirs Compuware Co. 1996–, Phoenix, Duff & Phelps Mutual Funds, World Wrestling Entertainment, Medallion Financial Corpn; Chair. Pew Foundation Environmental Health Comm. 2000, Century Fund Comm. 2001. *Publication:* Maverick: My Life in Politics 1995. *Leisure interests:* tennis, scuba, history. *Address:* Trust for America's Health, 1707 H Street, NW, 7th Floor, Washington, DC 20006, USA (office). *Telephone:* (202) 223-9870 (office). *Fax:* (202) 223-9871 (office). *Website:* healthyamericans.org (office).

WEIDENBAUM, Murray Lew, BBA, MA, PhD, LLD; American economist, academic and fmr government official; *Mallinckrodt Distinguished University Professor and Honorary Chairman, Weidenbaum Center on the Economy, Government and Public Policy, Washington University;* b. 10 Feb. 1927, Bronx, New York; s. of David Weidenbaum and Rose (née Warshaw) Weidenbaum; m. Phyllis Green 1954; one s. two d.; ed City Coll. New York, Columbia Univ., New York and Princeton Univ.; Fiscal Economist, Budget Bureau, Washington, DC 1949–57; Corpn Economist, Boeing Co., Seattle 1958–62; Sr Economist, Stanford Research Inst., Palo Alto, Calif. 1962–63; mem. Faculty, Washington Univ., St Louis, Mo. 1964–, Dir of Center for Study of American Business at Washington Univ. 1975–81, 1982–95, Chair. 1995–2000, Prof. and Chair. Dept of Econs 1966–69, Mallinckrodt Distinguished Univ. Prof. 1971–; Asst Sec. for Econ. Policy, Treasury Dept, Washington 1969–71; Head, Council of Econ. Advisers, US Govt 1981–82; Chair. Research Advisory Cttee, St Louis Regional Industrial Devt Corpn

1965–69; Pres. Midwest Econ. Asscn 1985; Chair. US Trade Deficit Review Comm 1999–2000; Exec. Sec. Pres.'s Cttee on Econ. Impact of Defense and Disarmament 1964; mem. US Financial Investment Advisory Panel 1970–72; mem. Pres.'s Econ. Policy Advisory Bd 1982–89, Bd of Dirs Harbour Group Ltd 1982–, May Dept Stores Co. 1982–99, Tesoro Petroleum Corpn 1992–2002, Macroeconomic Advisers 1996–; consultant to various firms and insts; Fellow, Nat. Asscn of Business Economists, Int. Acad. of Management; mem. Acad. of Missouri Squires; Hon. Chair. Weidenbaum Center on the Econ., Govt and Public Policy 2001; Hon. Fellow Soc. for Tech. Communication; Townsend Harris Medal for Distinguished Achievement, City Coll. of NY 1970, Treasury Dept Alexander Hamilton Medal 1971, Distinguished Writer Award, Georgetown Univ. 1975, Free Market Hall of Fame 1983, Officier, Ordre nat. du Mérite 1985, Founder's Day Medal, Washington Univ. 1998. *Publications:* Federal Budgeting 1964, Economic Impact of the Vietnam War 1967, Modern Public Sector 1969, Economics of Peacetime Defense 1974, Government-Mandated Price Increases 1975, The Future of Business Regulation 1979, Business, Government and the Public 1990, Rendezvous with Reality: The American Economy After Reagan 1990, Small Wars, Big Defense 1992, Bamboo Network 1996, Business and Government in the Global Marketplace 2004, One-Armed Economist 2004; articles in econ. journals. *Leisure interest:* writing. *Address:* Weidenbaum Center on the Economy, Government and Public Policy, Washington University, Box 1027, One Brookings Drive, St Louis, MO 63130 (office); 303 N Meramec No. 103, St Louis, MO 63105, USA (home). *Telephone:* (314) 727-8950 (home); (314) 935-5662 (office). *Fax:* (314) 935-5688 (office). *E-mail:* moseley@wc.wustl.edu (office). *Website:* wc.wustl.edu (office).

WEIDENFELD, Baron (Life Peer), cr. 1976, of Chelsea in Greater London; **Arthur George Weidenfeld,** Kt; British publisher; *Chairman, Weidenfeld and Nicholson Ltd;* b. 13 Sept. 1919, Vienna, Austria; s. of the late Max Weidenfeld and Rosa Weidenfeld; m. 1st Jane Sieff 1952; one d.; m. 2nd Barbara Skelton Connolly 1956 (divorced 1961); m. 3rd Sandra Payson Meyer 1966 (divorced 1976); m. 4th Annabelle Whitestone 1992; ed Piaristen Gymnasium, Vienna, Univ. of Vienna and Konsular Akademie; came to England 1938; BBC Monitoring Service 1939–42; BBC News Commentator on European Affairs on BBC Empire and N American service 1942–46; Foreign Affairs columnist, News Chronicle 1943–44; Political Adviser and Chief of Cabinet of Pres. Weizmann of Israel 1949–50; Founder of Contact Magazine 1945, George Weidenfeld & Nicolson Ltd 1948–; Chair. George Weidenfeld & Nicolson Ltd 1948–, Wheatland Corpn, New York 1985–90, Grove Press, New York 1985–90, Wheatland Foundation, San Francisco and New York 1985–92; Dir (non-exec.) Orion 1991–; Consultant Bertelsmann Foundation 1991–, Axel Springer AG Germany; Chair. Bd of Govs, Ben Gurion Univ. of the Negev 1996–; Gov. of Tel-Aviv Univ. 1980–, Weizmann Inst. of Science 1964–; Columnist Die Welt, Die Welt am Sonntag; mem., South Bank Bd 1986–99; mem. Bd ENO 1988–98, Herbert Quandt Foundation 1999–; Trustee, Royal Opera House 1974–87, Nat. Portrait Gallery 1988–95, Potsdam Einstein Forum, Jerusalem Foundation; Chair. Cheyne Capital 2000–, Trialogue Educational Trust 1996–; mem. Governing Council, Inst. of Human Science, Vienna; Vice-Chair. Oxford Univ. Devt Programme 1994–99; Pres., Inst. for Strategic Dialogue 2006–; Freeman of the City of London; Hon. Senator, Bonn Univ. 1996; Hon. Fellow, St Peter's Coll. Oxford 1992, St Anne's Coll. Oxford 1993; Golden Kt's Cross of Order of Merit (Austria) 1989; Chevalier, Légion d'honneur 1990; Kt Commdr's Cross (Badge and Star) of Order of Merit (Germany) 1991; Austrian Cross of Honour First Class for Arts and Science, Vienna 2003; Honour of City of Vienna 2003; Hon. MA (Oxon.) 1992; Hon. PhD (Ben Gurion Univ.); Hon. DLitt (Exeter) 2001; Charlemagne Medal 2000, London Book Fair/Trilogy Lifetime Achievement Award 2007. *Publications:* The Goebbels Experiment 1943, Remembering My Good Friends 1994. *Leisure interests:* opera, travel. *Address:* Orion House, 5 Upper St Martin's Lane, London, WC2H 9EA (office); 9 Chelsea Embankment, London, SW3 4LE, England (home). *Telephone:* (20) 7520-4411 (office); (20) 7351-0042 (home). *Fax:* (20) 7379-1604 (office). *E-mail:* george.weidenfeld@orionbooks.co.uk (office).

WEIDENFELD, Werner, DPhil; German political scientist and academic; *Professor of Political Science and Director, Center for Applied Policy Research, Geschwister Scholl Institute for Political Science, Ludwig-Maximilians-Universität München;* b. 2 July 1947, Cochem; s. of Dr. Josef Weidenfeld and Maria Weidenfeld (née Walther); m. Gabriele Kokott-Weidenfeld 1976; ed Univ. of Bonn; Prof. of Political Science, Univ. of Mainz 1976–95; Assoc. Prof., Sorbonne, Paris 1986–88; Co-ordinator for German-American Co-operation 1987–99; Prof. of Political Science, Ludwig-Maximilians-Universität München 1995–, Dir Centre for Applied Policy Research; Perm. Guest Prof., Remnim Univ., Beijing 2000–; mem. Exec. Bd Bertelsmann Foundation Gütersloh 1992–2007; Bundesverdienstkreuz (First Class) 1998, Commdr, Ordinul serviciul Credincios of the Repub. of Romania; Dr hc; Columbus Medal, German-American Soc., Munich 1991, Europe Medal (Bavaria) 1996, Bavarian Europe-Schoolbook Award 1997, Gen. Lucius D. Clay Medal, Assn of German-American Clubs 1998, World of Difference Award, Anti-Defamation League 1999, European Cultural Award, European Cultural Foundation 2001. *Publications:* Die Englandpolitik Gustav Stresemanns 1972, Konrad Adenauer und Europa 1976, Europa 2000 1980, Die Frage nach der Einheit der deutschen Nation 1981, Die Identität der Deutschen 1983, Die Bilanz der Europäischen Integration 1984, Nachdenken über Deutschland 1985, 30 Jahre EG 1987, Geschichtsbewusstsein der Deutschen 1987, Der deutsche Weg 1990, Jahrbuch der Europäischen Integration (ed.), Die Deutschen–Profil einer Nation 1991, Handwörterbuch zur deutschen Einheit 1992, Osteuropa: Herausforderungen-Probleme-Strategien 1992, Technopoly, Europa im globalen Wettbewerb 1993, Maastricht in der Analyse, Materialien zur Europäischen Union (ed.) 1994, Europa '96: Reformprogramm für die Europäische Union (ed.) 1994, Reform der Europäischen Union 1995, Kulturbruch mit Amerika? 1996, Handbuch zur deutschen Einheit 1996, Demokratie am Wendepunkt? (ed.) 1996, Europa öffnen–Anforderungen an die Erweiterung (ed.) 1997, Aussenpolitik für die deutsche Einheit: Die Entscheidigungsjahre 1989/90 1998, Amsterdam in der Analyse: Strategien für Europa (ed.) 1998, Handbuch zur deutschen Einheit 1949–1989–1999 (ed.) 1999, Deutschland-Trendbuch (ed.) 2001, Herausforderung Terrorismus 2004, Wie Zukunft ensteht 2002, Europa-Handbuch (ed.) 2004, Die Europäische Verfassung in der Analyse (ed.) 2005, Managing Integration (ed.) 2005, Rivalität der Partner (ed.) 2005, Die Europäische Verfassung verstehen 2006, Partners at Odds 2006, Werte 2006, Understanding the European Constitution 2007, Europa leicht gemacht 2007, Reformen kommunizieren (ed.) 2007, Reformvertrag in der Analyse (ed.) 2008. *Address:* Center for Applied Policy Research, Geschwister Scholl Institute for Political Science, Ludwig-Maximilians-Universität München, Maria-Theresia-Str. 21, 81675 Munich (office); Oettingenstr. 67, 80538 Munich, Germany. *Telephone:* (89) 21809040 (office). *Fax:* (89) 21809042 (office). *E-mail:* cap.office@lrz.uni-muenchen.de (office). *Website:* www.cap-lmu.de/english/index.php (office).

WEIDINGER, Christine, BA; American singer (soprano); b. 31 March 1946, Springville, NY; m. Kenneth Smith 1976; ed Grand Canyon Coll., Phoenix, studied singing with Marlene Delavan in Phoenix, Adrian de Peyer in Wuppertal, Dean Verhines in Los Angeles; debut as Musetta in La Bohème at Metropolitan 1972, sang at Metropolitan Opera 1972–76, at Stuttgart and Bielefeld Operas, Germany 1979–; roles include Malvina in Heinrich Marschner's Der Vampyr, Anina in Bellini's La Sonnambula, Berthe in Meyerbeer's Le Prophète, Elizabeth I in Donizetti's Roberto Devereux, Inez in L'Africaine, Lucia and Juliet in I Capuleti e i Montecchi, Pamira in Rossini's Siege of Corinth, Eupaforice in Heinrich Graun's Spanish Conquest, Constanze in Abduction from the Seraglio, Electra in Idomeneo, Leonora in Trovatore, Adèle in Le Comte Ory, Vitellia in La Clemenza di Tito, Tancredi, Violetta, Gilda, Donna Anna, Mimi, Liu, and the title roles in Thea Musgrave's Mary, Queen of Scots, Donizetti's Lucia di Lammermoor, Bellini's Norma, Bellini's Beatrice di Tenda; Nat. first prize Metropolitan Opera Auditions 1972. *Recordings:* Handel's Rinaldo with Marilyn Horne, L'Africaine with Caballé and Domingo, Die Freunde von Salamanka by Schubert, Médée with Caballé and Lima, Mitridate by Mozart. *Leisure interests:* yoga, jogging, electric trains. *Address:* Robert Lombardo Associates, 61 W 62nd Street, Suite 6F, New York, NY 10023, USA (office).

WEIKL, Bernd; Austrian singer (baritone); b. 29 July 1942, Vienna; ed Mainz Conservatoire and Hochschule für Musik, Hanover; mem. Hamburg State Opera 1973–, Deutsche Oper Berlin 1974–; guest artist, Bayreuth Festivals 1973–75; Covent Garden debut 1975 as Rossini's Figaro; Metropolitan Opera debut 1977 as Wolfram; guest engagements at La Scala Milan, Bavarian State Opera, Salzburg Festival; performed Iago at Stuttgart 1990, Bovccanegra at Hamburg 1991, Dutchman at Bayreuth 1990, Sachs at the Metropolitan 1993, Jochanaan at San Francisco 1997, Kurwenal in Tristan und Isolde at Munich 1998.

WEILL, Sanford I., BA; American banker; *Chairman Emeritus, Citigroup Inc.;* b. 16 March 1933, New York; s. of Max Weill and Etta (née Kalika) Weill; m. Joan Mosher 1955; one s., one d.; ed Peekskill Mil. Acad., Cornell Univ., School Business and Public Admin.; CEO Carter, Berlind and Weill (now Shearson/American Express Inc.) New York 1960–, Pres. and CEO 1978–85; Chair., Pres., CEO Commercial Credit Co., Baltimore 1986–; Chair., CEO Primerica Corpn 1989–, Pres. 1989–92; Chair., CEO Travelers Group 1996–98; apptd Co-Chair. Citigroup (merger between Citicorp and Travelers Group) 1999, CEO –2003, Chair. –2006, now Chair. Emer.; f. Acad. of Finance; Dir Terra Nova Insurance Co. 1984–; Chair. Carnegie Hall 1991–; mem. Midwest Stock Exchange Bd; Assoc. mem. New York Stock Exchange, Bd of Overseers Cornell Medical Coll., Business Cttee Museum of Modern Art, NY. *Address:* Citigroup, 153 East 53rd Street, New York, NY 10043 (office); Citigroup Inc., 399 Park Avenue, New York, NY 10013, USA. *Telephone:* (212) 559-1000 (office). *Fax:* (212) 793-3946 (office). *Website:* www.citigroup.com (office).

WEINBACH, Lawrence, BS; American business executive; *Chairman, Unisys Corporation;* b. 8 Jan. 1940, Brooklyn, New York; s. of Max Weinbach and Winnefred Weinbach; m. Patricia Lieter 1961; two s. one d.; ed Univ. of Pennsylvania, Wharton; joined Arthur Andersen 1961, Man. Pnr Stamford, Conn. office 1974–83, Man. Pnr New York office 1983–87, COO 1987–89, Man. Pnr and CEO 1989–97; Chair., Pres. and CEO Unisys Corpn 1997–2004; Chair. 2005–; mem. Bd of Dirs Avon Products, UBS. *Leisure interests:* reading, golf. *Address:* Unisys Corporation, Unisys Way, Blue Bell, PA 19424, USA (office). *Telephone:* (215) 986-4011 (office). *Fax:* (215) 986-2886 (office). *Website:* www.unisys.com (office).

WEINBERG, Adam, BA, MFA; American museum director; *Director, Whitney Museum of American Art;* ed Brandeis Univ., State Univ. of NY at Buffalo; Dir of Educ. and Asst Curator, Walker Art Center, Minneapolis 1981–89; Artistic and Program Dir, American Center in Paris 1989–93; Sr Curator of Perm. Collection, Whitney Museum of American Art, NY 1993–99, Dir of Museum 2003–; Dir Addison Gallery of American Art 1999–2003, also Curator of Temporary Exhbns. *Address:* Whitney Museum of Modern Art, 945 Madison Avenue at 75th Street, New York, NY 10021, USA (office). *Telephone:* (212) 570-3633 (office). *Fax:* (212) 570-4169 (office). *E-mail:* pressoffice@whitney.org (office). *Website:* www.whitney.org (office).

WEINBERG, Felix Jiri, PhD, DSc, FRS, MRI, CEng, FInstP, FCGI; British physicist and academic; *Professor Emeritus and Senior Research Fellow, Imperial College London;* b. 2 April 1928, Ústí, Czechoslovakia (now in Czech Repub.); s. of Victor Weinberg and Nelly Marie Weinberg (née Altschul); m.

Jill Nesta Piggott 1954 (died 2006); three s.; ed Univ. of London; Lecturer, Dept of Chemical Eng and Chemical Tech., Imperial Coll. London 1956–60, Sr Lecturer 1960–64, Reader in Combustion 1964–67, Prof. of Combustion Physics 1967–93, Emer. Prof. and Sr Research Fellow 1993–, Leverhulme Emer. Research Fellow 1993–95; Dir Combustion Inst. 1978–88, Chair. British Section 1975–80; Founder and First Chair. Combustion Physics Group, Inst. of Physics 1974–77, Rep. on Watt Cttee on Energy 1979–84; mem. Council, Inst. of Energy 1976–79; Foreign Assoc. US Nat. Acad. of Eng 2001; Hon. DSc (Technion) 1989; Combustion Inst. Silver Combustion Medal 1972, Bernard Lewis Gold Medal 1980, Royal Soc. Rumford Medal 1988, Italgas Prize in Energy Sciences (Turin Acad.) 1991, Smolenski Medal (Polish Acad. of Science) 1999. *Publications:* Optics of Flames 1963, Electrical Aspects of Combustion 1969, Combustion Inst. European Symposium (ed.) 1973, Advanced Combustion Methods 1986; over 210 scientific papers. *Leisure interests:* Eastern philosophies, travel, archery. *Address:* Imperial College, London, SW7 2AZ (office); 59 Vicarage Road, London, SW14 8RY, England (home). *Telephone:* (20) 7594-5580 (office); (20) 8876-1540 (home). *E-mail:* f.weinberg@imperial.ac.uk (office).

WEINBERG, Robert A., PhD; American biochemist and academic; *Member, Whitehead Institute and Professor of Biology, Massachusetts Institute of Technology;* b. 11 Nov. 1942, Pittsburgh, Pa; s. of Dr. Fritz E. Weinberg and Lore W. (née Reichhardt) Weinberg; m. Amy Shulman 1976; one s. one d.; ed M.I.T; Instructor in Biology, Stillman Coll., Ala 1965–66; Fellow Weizmann Inst., Israel 1969–70; Fellow Salk Inst., Calif. 1970–72; Research Assoc. Fellow MIT 1972–73, Asst Prof., Dept of Biology and Center for Cancer Research 1973–76, Assoc. Prof. 1976–82, Prof. Whitehead Inst. for Biomedical Research 1982–, mem. 1984–; mem. NAS; numerous awards including Hon. ScD (Northwestern Univ., Ill.) 1984, Wolf Foundation Prize in Medicine, 2004. *Leisure interests:* house building, gardening, genealogy. *Address:* Whitehead Institute, 9 Cambridge Center, Cambridge, MA 02142 (office); Department of Biology, Massachusetts Institute of Technology, Cambridge, MA 02139, USA (office). *Telephone:* (617) 258-5159 (office). *Fax:* (617) 258-5213 (office). *E-mail:* weinberg@wi.mit.edu (office). *Website:* www.wi.mit.edu/research/faculty/weinberg.html (office).

WEINBERG, Serge, LenD; French business executive; *Chairman, Weinberg Capital Partners;* b. 10 Feb. 1951; Pvt. Prin. Sec. to Budget Minister 1981–82; Deputy Dir-Gen. FR3 1982–83; Chair. Havas Tourisme 1983–87; Dir-Gen. Pallas Finances 1987–90; Chair. Rexel (affiliate of Pinault) 1991–95, mem. Man. Bd Pinault Printemps-Redoute (PPR) 1993–2005, Chair. and CEO 1995–2005, mem. Supervisory Bd PPR Interactive; Founder and Chair. Weinberg Capital Pnrs 2005–; Chair. Supervisory Bd Conforama Holding, France-Printemps, Guilbert SA, Redcats, Accor; mem. Supervisory Bd Boucheron Holding, Gucci Group NV (Netherlands), Yves Saint Laurent Perfumes; Dir Fnac SA, French Asscn of Pvt. Enterprises, ICM (Inst. of Brain and Spinal Cord Disorders), Soc. des Amis du Musée d'Orsay).; mem. National Economic Comm. *Address:* Weinberg Capital Partners, 40 rue La Boétie, 75008 Paris, France (office). *Telephone:* 1-53-53-55-00 (office). *Fax:* 1-53-53-55-19 (office). *E-mail:* serge.weinberg@weinbergcapital.com (office). *Website:* www.weinbergcapital.com (office).

WEINBERG, Steven, PhD; American physicist and academic; *Jack S. Josey-Welch Foundation Chair in Science and Regental Professor and Director, Theory Research Group, Department of Physics, University of Texas;* b. 3 May 1933, New York; s. of Fred Weinberg and Eva Weinberg; m. Louise Goldwasser 1954; one d.; ed Cornell Univ., Univ. of Copenhagen and Princeton Univ.; Columbia Univ. 1957–59; Lawrence Radiation Lab. 1959–60; Univ. of Calif. at Berkeley 1960–69; Prof. of Physics, MIT 1969–73; Higgins Prof. of Physics, Harvard Univ. 1973–83; Sr Scientist, Smithsonian Astrophysical Observatory 1973–83, Sr Consultant 1983–; Josey Chair and Regental Prof. of Science, Univ. of Texas, Austin 1982–, also Dir Theory Research Group; Co-Ed. Cambridge Univ. Press Monographs on Mathematical Physics 1978; Dir Jerusalem Winter School of Theoretical Physics 1983–, Headliners Foundation 1993–; mem. A.P. Sloan Foundation Science Book Cttee 1985–90, Einstein Archives Int. Advisory Bd 1988–, Scientific Policy Cttee, Super-collider Lab. 1989–93, American Acad. of Arts and Sciences 1968–, NAS 1972–, Council for Foreign Relations, President's Cttee on the Nat. Medal of Science 1979–80, Royal Soc. 1982–, American Philosophical Soc. 1983–; fmr mem. Council, American Physical Soc., Int. Astronomical Union, Philosophical Soc. of Tex. (Pres. 1994); Loeb Lecturer, Harvard Univ. and Visiting Prof. MIT 1966–69; Richtmeyer Lecturer of American Asscn of Physics Teachers 1974, Scott Lecturer, Cavendish Lab. 1975, Silliman Lecturer, Yale Univ. 1977, Lauritsen Lecturer, Calif. Inst. of Tech. 1979, Bethe Lecturer, Cornell Univ. 1979, Harris Lecturer, Northwestern Univ. 1982, Cherwell-Simon Lecturer, Oxford Univ. 1983, Bampton Lecturer, Columbia Univ. 1983, Hilldale Lecturer, Univ. of Wisconsin 1985, Brickweede Lecturer, Johns Hopkins Univ. 1986, Dirac Lecturer, Univ. of Cambridge 1986, Klein Lecturer, Univ. of Stockholm 1989, Sackler Lecturer, Univ. of Copenhagen 1994, Brittin Lecturer, Univ. of Colorado 1994, Gibbs Lecturer, American Math. Soc. 1996, Bochner Lecturer, Rice Univ. 1997, Sanchez Lecturer, Witherspoon Lecturer, Washington Univ. 2001.; Tex. A & M Int. Univ. 1998; Hon. DSc (Knox Coll.) 1978, (Chicago, Yale, Rochester) 1979, (City Univ., New York) 1980, (Clark Univ.) 1982, (Dartmouth) 1984, (Weizmann Inst.) 1985, (Columbia) 1990, (Salamanca) 1992, (Padua) 1992, (Barcelona) 1996, (Bates Coll.) 2002, (McGill Univ.) 2003; Hon. DLitt (Washington Coll.) 1985; J. R. Oppenheimer Prize 1973, Dannie Heinemann Mathematical Physics Prize 1977, American Inst. of Physics-U.S. Steel Foundation Science Writing Award 1977, Elliott Cresson Medal, Franklin Inst. 1979, Joint Winner, Nobel Prize for Physics 1979, James Madison Medal (Princeton) 1991, Nat. Medal of Science 1991, Andrew Gemant Award 1997, Piazzi Prize 1998, Lewis Thomas Prize Honoring the Scientist as Poet 1999, Benjamin Franklin Medal,

American Philosophical Soc. 2004. *Publications:* Gravitation and Cosmology 1972, The First Three Minutes 1977, The Discovery of Subatomic Particles 1982, Elementary Particles and the Laws of Physics (with R. P. Feynman) 1987, Dreams of a Final Theory 1993, The Quantum Theory of Fields (Vol. I) 1995, (Vol. II) 1996, (Vol. III) 2000, Facing Up 2001; and over 250 articles. *Leisure interest:* medieval history. *Address:* Department of Physics, University of Texas, Theory Group, RLM 5.208 C1608, Austin, TX 78712-1081, USA. *Telephone:* (512) 471-4394 (office). *Fax:* (512) 471-4888 (office). *E-mail:* weinberg@physics.utexas.edu (office). *Website:* www.ph.utexas.edu/~weintech/weinberg.html (office).

WEINGARTEN, David Michael, BA, MArch; American architect; *Principal, Ace Architects;* b. 22 Jan. 1952, Fort Ord, Calif.; s. of Saul M. Weingarten and Miriam E. Moore; one s.; ed Monterey High School, Yale Univ. and Univ. of Calif. at Berkeley; Pnr Ace Architects 1979–, now Prin.; Lecturer, Univ. of Calif. at Berkeley 1980–81; Graham Foundation for Advances Studies Award 1987, Interiors Magazine '40 under 40' Award 1990, Architectural Digest 'AD 100' Award 1994, 1996. *Publications:* Souvenir Buildings/Miniature Monuments 1996, Monumental Miniatures 1997, Ten Houses: Ace Architects 2000. *Address:* Ace Architects, 330 Second Street, Oakland, CA 94607, USA (office). *Telephone:* (510) 452-0775 (office). *Fax:* (510) 452-1175 (office). *E-mail:* ace@aceland.com (office). *Website:* www.aceland.com (office).

WEINGARTNER, Paul Andreas, DPhil; Austrian academic; *Professor Emeritus of Philosophy, Institut für Philosophie, Universität Salzburg;* b. 8 June 1931, Innsbruck; s. of Karl Weingartner and Maria Weingartner; five s. one d.; ed Univ. of Innsbruck; Research Fellow, Univ. of London 1961–62; Research Asst Inst. für Wissenschaftstheorie, Int. Research Centre, Salzburg 1962–67, Chair. Dept I (Philosophy of Natural Science) 1967–72; Assoc. Prof. of Philosophy, Univ. of Salzburg 1970, Prof. of Philosophy 1971–, now Prof. Emer., Chair. Inst. für Philosophie 1971–79, 1988–90, 1994–98, Chair. Inst. für Wissenschaftstheorie 1972–; mem. Acad. Internationale de Philosophie des Sciences 1975–; New York Acad. of Sciences 1997–; Dr hc (M. Curie Univ., Poland) 1995. *Publications:* Wissenschaftstheorie (two vols) 1976, 1978, Logisch-philosophische Untersuchungen zu Werten und Normen 1996, Zu philosophie-historischen Themen 1996, Basic Questions on Truth 2000; Evil, Different Kinds, In the Light of a Modern Theodicy 2003; Laws of Nature (with P. Mittelstaedt) 2005, Omniscience: From a Logical Point of View 2008; ed of 36 vols; about 150 research articles. *Leisure interests:* sport (climbing, skiing), photography. *Address:* Department of Philosophy, University of Salzburg, Franziskanergasse 1, 5020 Salzburg, Austria (office). *Telephone:* (662) 8044-4070 (office). *Fax:* (662) 8044-4074 (office). *E-mail:* paul.weingartner@sbg.ac.at (office). *Website:* www.uni-salzburg.at/phs (office).

WEINSTEIN, Alan, PhD; American mathematician and academic; *Chair, Department of Mathematics, University of California, Berkeley;* b. 1943, New York; m. Margo Weinstein; ed Massachusetts Inst. of Tech., Univ. of California, Berkeley; conducted postdoctoral research at Institut des Hautes Etudes Scientifiques, France and Univ. of Bonn, Germany; joined faculty of Dept of Math., Univ. of California, Berkeley 1969, Full Prof. 1976, currently also Chair. Dept of Math.; mem. American Acad. of Arts and Sciences 1992–; Dr hc (Utrecht) 2003. *Address:* Department of Mathematics, University of California, Berkeley, CA 94720-3840, USA (office). *Telephone:* (510) 642-4129 (office). *Fax:* (510) 642-8204 (office). *E-mail:* alanw@math.berkeley.edu (office). *Website:* math.berkeley.edu/~alanw (office).

WEINSTEIN, Allen; American historian, academic and archivist; *Archivist of the United States;* Prof. of History, Smith Coll., Chair. American Studies Program 1966–81; Univ. Prof., Georgetown Univ., Washington, DC 1981–84, Exec. Ed. The Washington Quarterly, Center for Strategic and Int. Studies 1981–83; mem. editorial staff, The Washington Post 1981; Univ. Prof. and Prof. of History, Boston Univ. 1985–89; directed research study that led to creation of Nat. Endowment for Democracy, Acting Pres. Endowment 1982–84; founding mem. Bd of Dirs US Inst. of Peace 1985, Dir 1985–2001; founder, Pres. and CEO Center for Democracy 1985–2003; Sr Advisor, Int. Foundation for Election Systems 2003–05; ninth Archivist of the USA, Nat. Archives and Records Admin 2005–; Fellow, Woodrow Wilson Int. Center for Scholars, American Council of Learned Socs; held two Sr Fulbright Lectureships, Commonwealth Fund Lecturer, Univ. of London, UK, among other awards and fellowships; UN Peace Medal 1986, Bicentennial Fourth of July Orator, Faneuil Hall, Boston 1987, Council of Europe Silver Medal 1990, 1996, awards from Presidents of Nicaragua and Romania. *Publications:* The Story of America 2002, The Haunted Wood: Soviet Espionage in America–The Stalin Era 1999, Perjury: The Hiss-Chambers Case (revised edn) 1997, Freedom and Crisis: An American History, Prelude to Populism: Origins of the Silver Issue; eight ed collections; articles and essays have appeared in numerous scholarly and popular publs. *Address:* The National Archives and Records Administration, 8601 Adelphi Road, College Park, MD 20740-6001, USA (office). *Telephone:* 301-837-1600 (office). *Fax:* 301-837-3218 (office). *Website:* www.archives.gov (office).

WEINSTEIN, Harvey; American film industry executive; b. 1952, Buffalo, NY; s. of Mira Weinstein and Max Weinstein; brother of Robert Weinstein (q.v.); Co-Chair. Miramax Films Corpn, New York with brother Robert 1979–2005; co-founder with brother The Weinstein Co. 2005. *Films produced include:* Playing for Keeps 1986, Scandal 1989, Strike it Rich 1990, Hardware 1990, A Rage in Harlem 1991, The Crying Game 1992, The Night We Never Met 1993, Benefit of the Doubt 1993, True Romance 1993, Mother's Boys 1994, Like Water for Chocolate 1994, Pulp Fiction 1994, Pret-A-Porter 1994, Smoke 1995, A Month by the Lake 1995, The Crossing Guard 1995, The Journey of August King 1995, Things To Do In Denver When You're Dead 1995, The Englishman Who Went Up A Hill But Came Down A Mountain 1995, Blue in the Face 1995, Restoration 1995, Scream 1996, The Pallbearer 1996, The Last of the High Kings 1996, Jane Eyre 1996, Flirting with Disaster 1996, The English Patient 1996, Emma 1996, The Crow: City of Angels 1996, Beautiful Girls 1996, Addicted to Love 1997, Shakespeare in Love 1998, Allied Forces, She's All That 1999, My Life So Far 1999, The Yards 1999, Bounce 2000, Scary Movie 2000, Boys and Girls 2000, Love's Labour's Lost 2000, Scream 3 2000, About Adam 2000, Highlander: Endgame 2000, Chocolat 2000, Dracula 2000, Spy Kids 2001, Texas Rangers 2001, Daddy and Them 2001, Scary Movie 2 2001, The Others 2001, Jay and Silent Bob Strike Back 2001, Lord of the Rings: Fellowship of the Ring 2001, Iris 2001, Shipping News 2001, Kate and Leopold 2001, Imposter 2002, Only the Strong Survive 2002, Heaven 2002, Halloween: Resurrection 2002, Full Frontal 2002, Spy Kids 2 2002, Below 2002, Equilibrium 2002, Waking Up in Reno 2002, Lord of the Rings; Two Towers 2002, Gangs of New York 2002, Chicago 2002, Confessions of a Dangerous Mind 2002, Spy Kids 3–D 2003, Human Stain 2003, Duplex 2003, Kill Bill: Vol. 1 2003, Scary Movie 3 2003, Bad Santa 2003, Lord of the Rings: Return of the King 2003, Cold Mountain 2003, The I Inside 2003, Mindhunters 2004, Jersey Girl 2004, Ella Enchanted 2004, Kill Bill: Vol. 2 2004, Paper Clips 2004, Fahrenheit 9/11 2004, Shall We Dance 2004, Cursed 2004, Aviator 2004, Derailed 2005. *Address:* The Weinstein Company, 345 Hudson Street, 13th Floor, New York, NY 10014, USA (office). *Website:* www.weinsteinco.com.

WEINSTEIN, Robert (Bob); American film industry executive; b. 1954, Buffalo, New York; s. of Mira Weinstein and Max Weinstein; brother of Harvey Weinstein (q.v.); co-founder and Co-Chair. Miramax Film Corpn with brother Harvey 1979–2005; co-founder with brother The Weinstein Co. 2005. *Films produced include:* (all with Harvey Weinstein q.v.) Playing for Keeps (with Alan Brewer) 1986, Scandal (with Joe Boyd and Nik Powell) 1989, Strike it Rich 1990, Hardware (with Nik Powell, Stephen Woolley and Trix Worrell) 1990, A Rage in Harlem (with Terry Glinwood, William Horberg and Nik Powell) 1991, The Night We Never Met (with Sidney Kimmel) 1993, Benefit of the Doubt 1993, True Romance (with Gary Barber, Stanley Margolis and James G. Robinson) 1993, Mother's Boys (with Randall Poster) 1994, Pulp Fiction (with Richard N Gladstein) 1994, Pret-A-Porter (with Ian Jessel) 1994, Smoke (with Satoru Iseki) 1995, A Month By the Lake (with Donna Gigliotti) 1995, The Crossing Guard (with Richard N Gladstein) 1995, The Journey of August King 1995, Things To Do In Denver When You're Dead (with Marie Cantin) 1995, The Englishman Who Went Up a Hill But Came Down a Mountain (with Sally Hibbin and Robert Jones) 1995, Blue in the Face (with Harvey Keitel) 1995, Restoration (with Donna Gigliotti) 1995, Velvet Goldmine 1998, Shakespeare in Love 1998, Allied Forces 1999, My Life So Far 1999, The Yards 1999, Music of the Heart 1999, The Cider House Rules 1999, Down To You 2000, Boys and Girls 2000, Scream 3 2000, Love's Labour's Lost 2000, Scary Movie 2000, Highlander: Endgame 2000, Backstage 2000, Malena 2000, Bounce 2000, Chocolat 2000, Dracula 2000 2000, Spy Kids 2001, Texas Rangers 2001, Daddy and Them 2001, Scary Movie 2 2001, The Others 2001, Legend of Zu 2001, Jay and Silent Bob Strike Back 2001, Lord of the Rings: Fellowship of the Ring 2001, Shipping News 2001, Kate and Leopold 2001, Ritual 2001, Imposter 2002, Only the Strong Survive 2002, Halloween: Resurrection 2002, Full Frontal 2002, Spy Kids 2 2002, Darkness 2002, Below 2002, Waking Up in Reno 2002, Lord of the Rings: Two Towers 2002, Equilibrium 2002, Gangs of New York 2002, Chicago 2002, Confessions of a Dangerous Mind 2002, Spy Kids 3–D 2003 Human Stain 2003, Duplex 2003, Kill Bill: Vol. 1 2003, Scary Movie 3 2003, Bad Santa 2003, Lord of the Rings: Return of the King 2003, Cold Mountain 2003, The I Inside 2003, Mindhunters 2004, Jersey Girl 2004, Ella Enchanted 2004, Kill Bill: Vol. 2 2004, Paper Clips 2004, Fahrenheit 9/11 2004, Shall We Dance 2004, Cursed 2004, Aviator 2004, Derailed 2005. *Address:* The Weinstein Company, 345 Hudson Street, 13th Floor, New York, NY 10014, USA (office). *Website:* www.weinsteinco.com.

WEIR, Dame Gillian Constance, DBE, FRCM; British/New Zealand concert organist, harpsichordist and lecturer; b. 17 Jan. 1941, Martinborough, New Zealand; d. of Cecil Alexander Weir and Clarice Mildred Foy Weir (née Bignell); m. 1st Clive Rowland Webster 1967 (divorced 1971); m. 2nd Lawrence Irving Phelps 1972 (died 1999); ed Wanganui Girls' Coll., NZ and Royal Coll. of Music, London, pvt. studies London (organ, piano) 1962–65; with Anton Heiller, Marie-Claire Alain, Nadia Boulanger; winner St Albans Int. Organ Festival Competition 1964; debuts Royal Festival Hall and Royal Albert Hall, London 1965; worldwide career since 1965 as concert organist; has appeared with all leading British orchestras and many abroad, under leading conductors; many radio and TV appearances; adjudicator in int. competitions and artist-in-residence at major univs including Yale; frequent adjudicator at int. competitions; gives lectures and master classes in many countries; organ consultant, Birmingham Symphony Hall; Visiting Prof. of Organ, Royal Acad. of Music, London 1997–98; Prince Consort Prof. of Organ, Royal Coll. of Music, London 1999–; Int. Chair. in Organ Royal Northern Coll. of Music, Manchester 2006–07; Distinguished Visiting Artist Peabody Conservatory of Music, Baltimore, USA 2006; Visiting Tutor Curtis Inst., Philadelphia 2006–; many premières including first British performance of Messiaen's Méditations of 1972; many works written for her including concertos by William Mathias and Peter Racine Fricker; many recordings including 7-CD set complete organ works of Olivier Messiaen 1995 and complete works of César Franck 1997; recognized worldwide as authority on and pre-eminent performer of Messiaen; presenter and performer 6-part BBC TV series 1989; various TV documentaries for NZTV; subject of South Bank Show, ITV 2000; Concerto soloist First Night of the Proms 1967 and Last Night of the Proms 1999, many other Proms appearances; Pres. Inc. Asscn of Organists (first woman Pres.) 1981–83, Inc. Soc. of Musicians 1992–93, Soloists' Ensemble 1998–; mem. Exec. Council, Royal Coll. of Organists (first woman mem.) 1981–85, Council (first woman mem.) 1977–, Pres. (first woman Pres.) 1994–96; mem. Council Royal Philharmonic Soc. 1995–2001; mem. Royal Soc. of Musicians of GB 1996–; Trustee Eric Thompson Charitable Trust

1993–; Hon. FRCO 1975; Hon. Fellow Royal Canadian Coll. of Organists 1983; Hon. mem. RAM 1989; Hon. DMus (Victoria Univ. of Wellington, NZ) 1983, (Hull) 1999, (Exeter) 2001, (Leicester) 2003, (Aberdeen) 2004; Hon. DLitt (Huddersfield) 1997; Hon. DUniv (Univ. of Cen. England) 2001; Countess of Munster Award 1965, Int. Performer of Year Award, American Guild of Organists 1981, Turnovsky Prize for Outstanding Achievement in the Arts 1985, Silver Medal, Albert Schweitzer Asscn (Sweden) 1998, Evening Standard Award for Outstanding Solo Performance in 1998, Lifetime Achievement Award, The Link Foundation 2005, Int. Music Guide Musician of the Year 1982; First musician to receive Turnovsky Foundation Award for Outstanding Contribution to the Arts 1985; Winner of Evening Standard Award for Outstanding Solo Performance 1999; Lifetime Achievement Award from Link Soc. 2005. *Publications:* contrib. to The Messiaen Companion 1995; articles in professional journals. *Leisure interests:* theatre, reading. *Address:* c/o Karen McFarlane Artists Inc., 33563 Seneca Drive, Cleveland, OH 44139-5578, USA (office). *Telephone:* (866) 721-9095 (McFarlane) (office); (191) 384-2437 (office). *Fax:* (440) 542-1890 (McFarlane) (office). *E-mail:* john@concertartists.com (office); gillianweir@gillianweir.com. *Website:* www.concertartists.com (office); gillianweir.com.

WEIR, Judith, CBE, MA; British composer; b. 11 May 1954, Cambridge; ed North London Collegiate School, King's Coll. Cambridge; Composer-in-Residence, Southern Arts Asscn 1976–79; Fellow in Composition, Univ. of Glasgow 1979–82, Creative Arts Fellowship, Trinity Coll. Cambridge 1983–85, Composer-in-Residence, Royal Scottish Acad. of Music and Drama 1988–91; Fairbairn Composer in Asscn with City of Birmingham Symphony Orchestra 1995–98; Artistic Dir Spitalfields Festival 1995–2000; Visiting Prof. in Opera Studies, Univ. of Oxford 1999–2000; Visiting Prof., Princeton Univ., USA 2001; Fromm Foundation Visiting Professor, Harvard Univ. 2004; Distinguished Visiting Research Prof. in Composition, School of Music, Univ. of Cardiff 2007–; mem. Bd of Govs Royal Opera House 2003–; Dr hc (Aberdeen) 1995, (King's College, London) 2007; Critics' Circle Award for most outstanding contrib. to British Musical Life 1994, Queen's Medal for Music 2007. *Compositions include:* King Harald's Saga 1979, Consolations of Scholarship 1985, The Black Spider (children's opera) 1985, A Night At The Chinese Opera 1987, Missa Del Cid 1988, Heaven Ablaze In His Breast 1989, The Vanishing Bridegroom 1990, Music Untangled 1991–92, Heroic Strokes of the Bow 1992, Blond Eckbert 1993, Musicians Wrestle Everywhere 1994, Moon and Star 1995, Forest 1995, Storm 1997, We Are Shadows (South Bank Show Award 2001) 2000, Future Perfect 2000, Really? 2002, The Voice of Desire (British Composer Award for vocal work) 2004, Armida 2004. *Address:* Cardiff School of Music, Corbett Road, Cardiff, CF10 3EB, Wales; c/o Chester Music, 14–15 Berners Street, London, W1T 3LJ, England. *Telephone:* (29) 2087-4816 (Cardiff). *Fax:* (29) 2087-4379 (Cardiff). *E-mail:* music-enq@cardiff.ac.uk. *Website:* www.cf.ac.uk/music.

WEIR, Peter Lindsay; Australian film director; b. 21 Aug. 1944, Sydney; s. of Lindsay Weir and Peggy Barnsley; m. Wendy Stites 1966; one s. one d.; ed Scots Coll., Sydney, Vaucluse Boys' High School, Sydney Univ.; worked in real estate until 1965; worked as stagehand in television, Sydney 1967; dir film sequences in variety show 1968; Dir amateur univ. reviews 1967–69; dir for Film Australia 1969–73; made own short films 1969–73, independent feature-film dir and writer 1973–; Broadcast Film Critics Asscn Passion in Film Award 2004. *Films:* Cars that Ate Paris 1973, Picnic at Hanging Rock 1975, The Last Wave 1977, The Plumber (television) 1978, Gallipoli 1980, The Year of Living Dangerously 1982, Witness 1985, The Mosquito Coast 1986, Dead Poets Society 1989, Green Card 1991, Fearless 1994, The Truman Show (BAFTA Award for Best Dir) 1997, Master and Commander: The Far Side of the World (BAFTA Award for Best Dir) 2003. *Address:* c/o Creative Artists Agency, 2000 Avenue of the Stars, Los Angeles, CA 90067, USA.

WEIR, Stuart Peter, BA; British journalist and academic; *Director, Democratic Audit, Human Rights Center and Visiting Professor, Government Department, University of Essex;* b. 13 Oct. 1938, Frimley, Surrey; s. of Robert H. Weir and Edna F. Lewis; m. 1st Doffy Burnham 1963; two s.; m. 2nd Elizabeth E. Bisset 1987; one s. two d.; ed Peter Symonds School, Winchester and Brasenose Coll. Oxford; Feature Writer, Oxford Mail 1964–67; Diarist, The Times 1967–71; Dir Citizens Rights Office 1971–75; Founding Ed. Roof Magazine (Shelter) 1975–77; Deputy Ed. New Society 1977–84; Ed. New Socialist 1984–87; Political Columnist, London Daily News 1987; Ed. New Statesman 1987–88, New Statesman and Society 1988–90; Founder Charter 88 1988; Dir Democratic Audit and Prof. and Sr Research Fellow Human Rights Centre, Univ. of Essex 1991–, Visiting Prof. 1999–; Series Consultant, The People's Parl. (Channel 4 TV) 1994–97; Consultant, State of Democracy Project, Int. IDEA, Stockholm 1997–2003; Assoc. Consultant (Governance) British Council 1997–; Consultant on Governance Dept for Int. Devt 1999–2002; Sr Int. Facilitator Namibian Govt and Democracy Project 1994–95; UK Facilitator Zimbabwe Parl. Democracy Project; Chair. Parl. Assessment Team, Zimbabwe 2002–03; Lecturer on Politics and the Media, LSE 1994. *Publications:* Manifesto 1981; contributor to: The Other Britain 1982, Consuming Secrets 1982, Defining and Measuring Democracy 1995; Ego Trip (ed.) 1995, Behind Closed Doors 1995, The Three Pillars of Liberty 1996, Making Votes Count 1997, Political Power and Democratic Control in Britain 1998, Voices of the People (jtly.) 2001, The IDEA Handbook on Democracy Assessments (jtly.) 2001, The State of Democracy (jtly) 2002, Democracy Under Blair 2003. *Leisure interests:* children, cooking, walking, football. *Address:* Butts Orchard, Butts Batch, Wrington, Bristol, BS40 5LN, England. *Telephone:* (1934) 863668. *E-mail:* stuart@democraticaudit.demon.co.uk (office). *Website:* www.essex.ac.uk (office).

WEIR, Viscount; William Kenneth James Weir, FRSA, BA; British business executive; b. 9 Nov. 1933, Glasgow, Scotland; s. of Lord Weir and Lady Weir (née Crowdy); m. 1st Diana Lucy MacDougall 1964 (divorced 1972); one s. one d.; m. 2nd Jacqueline Mary Marr 1976 (divorced); m. 3rd Marina Sevastopoulo 1988; one s.; ed Eton Coll., Trinity Coll. Cambridge; served Royal Navy 1955–56; Chair. Weir Group PLC 1972–99, Balfour Beatty PLC (fmrly BICC PLC) 1996–2003, CP Ships Ltd 2001–04; Dir Bank of England 1972–84, British Steel Corpn 1972–76, British Bank of Middle East 1977–79, Canadian Pacific Ltd 1989–2001, St James Place Capital 1990, Canadian Pacific Railway Co. 2001; Pres. British Electrotechnical Mfrs Asscn 1988-89, 1993–95; mem. London Advisory Cttee, Hong Kong Shanghai Bank 1980–92, Export Credit Advisory Cttee 1991–98; Chair. British Water 1999–2000; Hon. FREng; Hon. DEng (Glasgow). *Leisure interests:* shooting, golf. *Address:* Rodinghead, Mauchline, Ayrshire, KA5 5TR, Scotland (home). *Telephone:* (1563) 884233 (home).

WEISFELDT, Myron Lee, BA, MD; American cardiologist and academic; *Director, Department of Medicine, School of Medicine, Johns Hopkins University;* b. 25 April 1940, Milwaukee, Wis.; m. Linda Weisfeldt 1963; three c.; ed Johns Hopkins Univ.; intern then resident, Columbia-Presbyterian Medical Center, New York 1965–67; Fellow in Cardiology, Mass Gen. Hosp., Boston 1970–72; Asst Prof. of Medicine, Johns Hopkins Univ., Baltimore 1972–78, Prof. of Medicine 1978–91, Robert L. Levy Prof. of Cardiology 1979–91, Dir, Cardiology Div., Johns Hopkins Univ. School of Medicine 1975–91, William Osler Prof. of Medicine and Physician-in-Chief, Johns Hopkins Hosp. 2001–, also Dir, Dept of Medicine; Samuel Bard Prof. of Medicine and Chair. Dept of Medicine, Columbia-Presbyterian Medical Center 1991–2001; Pres. American Heart Asscn 1989–90; Fellow, AAAS, American Coll. of Physicians, American Coll. of Cardiology; mem. NAS Inst of Medicine, American Soc. for Clinical Investigation, Asscn of American Physicians, Asscn of Profs of Medicine, Nat. Inst. on Aging Nat. Advisory Council; mem. Bd of Advisers KBL Healthcare Acquisition Corpn; numerous awards including American Heart Asscn Golden Heart Award 1998, Phillips Award in Clinical Medicine, American Coll. of Physicians 2006, Diversity Award, Asscn of Profs of Medicine 2008. *Address:* Office of the Director, Department of Medicine, Johns Hopkins University School of Medicine, 733 N. Broadway, Suite G49, Baltimore, MD 21205-2196, USA (office). *Telephone:* (410) 955-3182 (office). *Website:* www.hopkinsmedicine.org/som (office).

WEISKRANTZ, Lawrence, PhD, FRS; American/British psychologist and academic; *Fellow Emeritus of Magdelen College and Professor Emeritus of Psychology, University of Oxford;* b. 28 March 1926, Philadelphia; s. of Benjamin Weiskrantz and Rose Weiskrantz (née Rifkin); m. Barbara Collins 1954; one s. one d.; ed Girard Coll. of Philadelphia, Swarthmore and Univs of Oxford and Harvard; part-time Lecturer, Tufts Univ. 1952; Research Assoc., Inst. of Living 1952–55; Sr Postdoctoral Fellow, NAS 1955–56; Research Assoc., Cambridge Univ., England 1956–61, Asst Dir of Research 1961–66, Fellow, Churchill Coll. 1964–67, Reader in Physiological Psychology 1966–67; Prof. of Psychology and Head of Dept of Experimental Psychology, Oxford Univ. 1967–93, Prof. Emer. 1993–; Fellow of Magdalen Coll., Oxford, now Fellow Emer.; Kenneth Craik Research Award, St John's Coll., Cambridge 1975–76; Sir Frederick Bartlett Memorial Lecturer 1980; Ferrier Lecturer, Royal Soc. 1989; Hughlings Jackson Lecturer/Medallist (Royal Soc. of Medicine) 1990; Harry Camp Memorial Lecturer, Stamford Univ. 1997; Werner Heisenburg Lecturer, Bavarian Acad. of Science 1998; John P. McGovern Award Lecture, AAAS 2002; Deputy Ed. Brain 1981–91; mem. NAS. *Publications:* Analysis of Behavioral Change (ed.) 1967, Animal Intelligence (ed.) 1985, Neuropsychology of Cognitive Function (ed.) 1986, Blindsight 1986, Thought Without Language (ed.) 1988, Consciousness Lost and Found 1997 and articles in Science, Nature, Quarterly Journal of Experimental Psychology, Journal of Comparative Physiological Psychology, Animal Behaviour and Brain. *Leisure interests:* music, walking. *Address:* Department of Experimental Psychology, University of Oxford, South Parks Road, Oxford, OX1 3UD, England (office). *Telephone:* (1865) 271444 (office). *E-mail:* larry.weiskrantz@psy.ox.ac.uk (office). *Website:* www.psych.ox.ac.uk (office).

WEISS, Ulrich; German banker; b. 3 June 1936; fmr mem. Bd of Man. Dirs, Deutsche Bank AG, Frankfurt; Chair. Supervisory Bd Continental AG, Hanover; Chair. Admin. Council, Deutsche Bank SAE, Barcelona/Madrid, Deutsche Bank de Investimento SA, Lisbon, Deutsche Bank Luxembourg SA; Chair. Admin. Council, Deutsche Bank SpA, Milan; mem. Supervisory Bd Asea Brown Boveri AG, Mannheim, BASF AG, Ludwigshafen, Heidelberger Zement AG, Klein, Schanzlin & Becker AG, Frankenthal, Rheinelektra AG, Mannheim, Südzucker AG, Mannheim; mem. Admin. Council Fiat SpA, Turin. *Address:* c/o Deutsche Bank AG, 60325 Frankfurt am Main, Germany.

WEISSENBERG, Alexis; Bulgarian pianist; b. 26 July 1929, Sofia; studied piano and composition with Pancho Vladigerov aged three, also with Olga Samaroff at Juilliard School, New York 1946; debut aged 14; numerous appearances in Europe, South America, USA, Japan; American debut with New York Philharmonic; soloist with Berlin, Vienna, Japan, Czechoslovak Philharmonics, Philadelphia, Cleveland, Minnesota, Royal Danish and Salzburg Festival orchestras, Boston, Chicago, Pittsburgh Symphony orchestras, Orchestre de Paris and others; recording artist with RCA, Angel; First Prize, Philadelphia Youth competition 1946, First Prize, Int. Leventritt Competition 1947. *Recordings include:* works by Bach, Bartók, Beethoven, Brahms, Chopin, Debussy, Franck, Haydn, Liszt, Mozart, Mussorgsky, Prokofiev, Rachmaninov, Ravel, Saint-Saens, Scarlatti, Schumann, Stravinsky. *Address:* c/o Michal Schmidt, Thea Dispeker Inc., 59 East 54th Street, New York, NY 10022, USA (office). *E-mail:* info@alexisweissenberg.com (office). *Website:* www.alexisweissenberg.com (office).

WEISSER, Alberto, BBA; American business executive; *Chairman and CEO, Bunge Ltd;* b. 26 June 1955, Argentina; ed Universidade de São Paulo, Harvard Business School, Institut Européen d'Admin des Affaires (INSEAD), France; began career with BASF Group, worked in Brazil, Germany, USA and Mexico 1978–93; joined Bunge Ltd as Chief Financial Officer 1993–99, mem. Bd of Dirs 1997–, CEO 1999–, Chair. 2001–; mem. Int. Paper Co. 2006–; mem. North American Agribusiness Advisory Bd of Rabobank; mem. Council on Foreign Relations, Council of the Americas. *Address:* Bunge Ltd, 50 Main Street, 6th Floor, White Plains, NY 10606, USA (office). *Telephone:* (914) 684-2800 (office). *Fax:* (914) 684-3499 (office). *E-mail:* info@bunge.com (office). *Website:* www.bunge.com (office).

WEISSLEDER, Ralph, MD, PhD; German radiologist and academic; *Professor of Radiology, Harvard Medical School;* ed Univ. of Heidelberg; currently Prof. of Radiology, Harvard Medical School, Boston, Mass, USA, Dir Center for Molecular Imaging Research and Attending Interventional Radiologist, Massachusetts Gen. Hosp., Charlestown; Researcher, The Breast Cancer Research Foundation, New York; Founding-mem. Soc. for Molecular Imaging Research, Pres. 2002; J. Allyn Taylor Int. Prize in Medicine 2004. *Publications:* Primer of Diagnostic Imaging (co-author) 2002; 10 US and int. patents and more than 300 articles in medical journals on molecular imaging research in living organisms. *Address:* Center for Molecular Imaging Research, MGH-CMIR, Building 149, 13th Street, Room 5406, Charlestown, MA 02129-2060, USA (office). *Telephone:* (617) 726-8226 (office); (617) 726-8396 (Clinic) (office). *Fax:* (617) 726-5708 (office); (617) 726-4891 (Clinic) (office). *E-mail:* weissleder@helix.mgh.harvard.edu (office); rweissleder@partners.org (office). *Website:* www.mgh-cmir.org (office); www.massgeneralimaging.org (office).

WEISSMAN, Irving L., MD, FAAS; American biologist and academic; *Karel and Avice Beekhuis Professor of Cancer Biology, Professor of Pathology and of Developmental Biology, Professor (By Courtesy) of Neurosurgery and of Biological Sciences, and Director, Stem Cell Institute, Stanford University School of Medicine;* b. 21 Oct. 1939, Great Falls, Mont.; ed Dartmouth Coll., Hanover, NH, Montana State Coll., Univ. of Oxford, UK, Stanford Univ., Calif.; Montana Cancer Soc. Student Research Fellow, Lab. for Experimental Medicine, Montana Deaconess Hosp., Great Falls 1961; Medical Student Research Fellow, Dept of Genetics, Stanford Univ. School of Medicine 1961, NIH Student Traineeship, Dept of Radiology 1961–64, NIH Postdoctoral Fellowship 1965–67, Research Asscn 1967–68, Asst Prof., Dept of Pathology 1969–74, Assoc. Prof. 1974–81, Prof. 1981–, Chair. Stanford Univ. Immunology Program 1986–, Karel and Avice Beekhuis Prof. of Cancer Biology 1987–, Prof. of Developmental Biology 1989–, Investigator, Howard Hughes Medical Inst., Stanford Univ. 1990–92, Prof. (By Courtesy) of Neurosurgery and of Biological Sciences, Dir Stem Cell Inst. 2003–; NIH Student Traineeship, Cellular Immunology Research Unit, Sir William Dunn School of Pathology, MRC, Oxford 1964; Sr Dernham Fellow, American Cancer Soc. (Calif. Div.) 1969–73; Josiah Macy Foundation Scholar 1974–75; Co-Founder and mem. Bd of Dirs SyStemix, Palo Alto, Calif. 1988, Chair. Scientific Advisory Bd 1988–97; Founder Stem Cells, Inc., Palo Alto 1998; mem. Scientific Advisory Bd Amgen, Calif. 1981–89, DNAX, Germany 1981–92, T Cell Sciences, Inc., Mass 1988–92; Pres. American Asscn of Immunologists 1994–95; mem. Nat. Bd of Govs Project Inform; Assoc. Ed. Molecular Therapy 1999–; mem. Editorial Bd Journal of Cellular Biochemistry 1980–, Molecular Marine Biology and Biotechnology 1991–, Biology of Blood and Marrow Transplantation 1995–, Experimental Hematology 1996–, Journal of Clinical Investigation 1998–; mem. NAS 1987, American Acad. of Arts and Sciences 1990, American Acad. of Microbiology 1997, American Asscn of Immunologists, American Asscn of Univ. Pathologists (PLUTO), American Asscn of Pathologists, American Soc. for Microbiology, American Asscn of Cancer Research, American Acad. of Microbiology, Clinical Immunology Soc., American Soc. of Hematology, Int. Soc. of Experimental Hematology, American Soc. for Blood and Marrow Transplantation, Int. Cytokine Soc., Molecular Medicine Soc.; Hon. mem. Israel Immunological Soc. 1995; Hon. DSc (Montana State Univ.) 1992; Faculty Research Award, American Cancer Soc. 1974–78, NIH Outstanding Investigator Award 1986, Kaiser Award for Excellence in Pre-clinical Teaching 1987, Harvey Lecturer 1989, Pasarow Award for Outstanding Contrib. to Cancer Biology 1989, Selected Top 100, Alumni Montana State Univ. 1993, de Villier's Int. Achievement Award, Leukemia Soc. of America 1999, E. Donnall Thomas Prize to Recognize Pioneering Research Achievements in Hematology, American Soc. of Hematology 1999, J. Allyn Taylor Prize in Medicine 2003. *Publications:* more than 410 articles in scientific journals on hematopoietic stem cells, lymphocyte differentiation, lymphocyte homing receptors, normal and neoplastic hematolymphoid devt, phylogeny of stem cells and alloreactivity in protochordates. *Address:* Stanford University School of Medicine, Mail Code 5323, B257 Beckman Center, 279 Campus Drive, Stanford, CA 94305-5323, USA (office). *Telephone:* (650) 723-6520 (office). *Fax:* (650) 723-4034 (office). *E-mail:* irv@stanford.edu (office). *Website:* www.stanford.edu/dept/biology (office); med.stanford.edu/profiles/faculty/Irving_Weissman (office).

WEISSMAN, Myrna M., PhD; American epidemiologists and academic; *Professor of Psychiatry and Epidemiology, College of Physicians and Surgeons and Mailman School of Public Health, Columbia University;* b. (Myrna Milgram), Boston, Mass; d. of Samuel Milgram and Jeanette Milgram; m. Dr Marshall Nirenberg; one s. three d.; ed Yale Univ.; Prof. of Psychiatry and Epidemiology, Yale Univ. School of Medicine, Dir Depression Research Unit –1987; Prof. of Psychiatry and Epidemiology, Coll. of Physicians and Surgeons and Mailman School of Public Health, Columbia Univ. 1987–; Chief of Dept, Clinical-Genetic Epidemiology, NY State Psychiatric Inst. 1987–; Visiting Sr Scholar, Inst. of Medicine, NAS, Washington, DC 1979–80 (mem. 1996–); mem. editorial bd of several journals including Archives of General Psychiatry; mem. Nat. Advisory Mental Health Council, Inst. of Medicine, NAS 1998–, Nat. Inst. of Mental Health 1999–2000, Council, American Coll. of Neuropsychopharmacology 1999–2002; Pres. American Psychopathological

Asscn, New York 1998–99; Fellow, Royal Soc. of Psychiatrists (UK) 1998–, NY Acad. of Sciences; American Psychiatric Asscn Foundation's Fund Prize 1978, Rema Lapouse Mental Health Epidemiology Award, American Public Health Asscn 1985, Research Award, American Suicide Foundation 1990, Joseph Zubin Award, American Psychopathological Asscn 1996 and other prizes and awards. *Publications:* author or co-author of over 500 scientific articles and book chapters and 7 books including The Depressed Woman: A Study of Social Relationships 1974, Interpersonal Psychotherapy of Depression 1984, A Comprehensive Guide to Interpersonal Psychotherapy 2000. *Leisure interests:* running, hiking, family. *Address:* College of Physicians and Surgeons, Nyspi-Unit 24, 1051 Riverside Drive, Columbia University, New York, NY 10032, USA (office). *Telephone:* (212) 543-5880 (office). *Fax:* (212) 568-3534 (office). *E-mail:* mmw3@columbia.edu (office). *Website:* www.mailmanschool.org/sphdir/pers.asp?ID=544 (office).

WEISSMANN, Charles, MD, PhD, FMedSci; Swiss molecular biologist and academic; *Professor and Chairman, Department of Infectology, The Scripps Research Institute;* b. 14 Oct. 1931, Budapest; ed Univ. of Zürich, Switzerland; Prof. and Dir Inst. of Molecular Biology, Zürich –1999, Prof. Emer. 1999–; fmr Sr Researcher, Neurogenetics Unit, Imperial Coll. School of Medicine, London, UK; Sr Research Scientist, Dept of Neurodegenerative Diseases, Inst. for Neurology, Univ. Coll., London 1999–2004; Prof. and Chair. Dept of Infectology, The Scripps Research Inst., Palm Beach Co., Fla 2004–, mem. Scripps Bd of Scientific Govs 2004–; Co-founder Biogen (first European biotechnology co.); Pres. Roche Research Foundation; co-publr several journals; mem. Bd of Dirs F. Hoffman-La Roche –2001, Speedel 2003–, several startup firms in Switzerland and Germany; mem. Bd Govs Tel-Aviv Univ. 1997–; mem. Editorial Bd Proceedings of the Royal Soc. 1999–; mem. Royal Soc., Akad. der Naturforscher Leopoldina, American Soc. of Biological Chem.; Foreign Assoc. NAS; Fellow, American Acad. of Microbiology 1999; first to genetically engineer Interferon-Alpha; Hon. Sr Fellow, Inst. of Neurology, Univ. Coll. London 2004; six hon. doctorate degrees; many leading scientific prizes including Dr H.P. Heineken Prize for Biochemistry and Biophysics 1982, Betty and David Koetser Award, Zürich 2001, Friedrich-Bauer-Prize for Medical Research, Univ. of Munich 2001, Warren Alpert Foundation Prize, Harvard Medical School 2004. *Publications:* numerous articles in scientific journals on interferon and prion diseases. *Address:* Department of Infectology, The Scripps Research Institute, 1555 Palm Beach Lakes Boulevard, West Palm Beach, FL 33401, USA (office). *Telephone:* (561) 297-2257 (office). *Fax:* (561) 297-0329 (office). *E-mail:* charlesw@scripps.edu (office). *Website:* www.scripps.edu/florida (office).

WEISSMANN, Mariana, PhD; Argentine physicist; *Senior Researcher, Argentine National Research Council;* ed Univ. of Buenos Aires; resgnd Univ. of Buenos Aires with 1,000 other profs following mil. coup 1966, moved to Chile, returned and left again after coup in 1976, spent two years in Venezuela before returning to Argentina in 1978; Sr Assoc. Int. Centre for Theoretical Physics, Trieste, Italy 1985–94; currently Sr Researcher, Sección de Matemática, Física y Astronomía, Argentine Nat. Research Council, Buenos Aires; mem. Nat. Acad. of Exact, Physical and Natural Sciences of Argentina (first woman); UNESCO-L'Oréal Award for Women in Science (Latin America) 2003. *Publications include:* numerous papers in scientific journals on condensed matter and solid-state physics. *Address:* c/o Sección de Matemática, Física y Astronomía, Academía Nacional de Ciencias Exactas, Físicas y Naturales, Avda. Alvear 1711, 4° piso, 1014 Buenos Aires, Argentina (office). *Telephone:* (11) 4811-2998 (office); (11) 4815-9451 (office). *Fax:* (11) 4811-6951 (office). *E-mail:* acad@ancefn.org.ar (office). *Website:* www.ancefn.org.ar (office).

WEISZ, Rachel; British actress; b. 7 March 1971, London; one s.; ed Univ. of Cambridge; London Critics Circle Theatre Award for Most Promising Newcomer 1994. *Film roles:* Seventeen, Chain Reaction, Stealing Beauty, Going All the Way, Amy Foster, Bent, I Want You 1998, Land Girls 1998, The Mummy 1999, Sunshine 2000, Beautiful Creatures 2001, Enemy at the Gates 2001, The Mummy Returns 2001, About a Boy 2002, Confidence 2003, Runaway Jury 2003, Envy 2004, Constantine 2005, The Constant Gardener 2005 (Golden Globe Award for Best Supporting Actress, Screen Actors Guild Award for Best Supporting Actress, Acad. Award for Best Supporting Actress 2006), The Fountain 2006, Eragon (voice) 2006, My Blueberry Nights 2007, Fred Claus 2007, Definitely, Maybe 2007. *Plays:* Design for Living 1994, Suddenly Last Summer 1999. *Address:* c/o ICM Ltd., Oxford House, 76 Oxford Street, London, W1N 0AX, England (office). *Telephone:* (20) 7636-6565 (office). *Fax:* (20) 7323-0101 (office).

WEITZMANN, Horst, Dipl.-Ing; German business executive and university administrator; *Chairman, Südweststahl AG;* b. 1941, Riesa, Saxony; m. Marlis Weitzmann 1967; two d.; Man. Dir Vereinigten Schraubenwerke Thyssen/Otto Wolff 1972–77; Man. Dir American Airfilter Co., Düsseldorf 1978–80; Jt Owner Badische Stahlwerke (following man. buyout 1982); Chair. Supervisory Bd Südweststahl AG, BCT Technology AG; Chair. Bd of Trustees Albert-Ludwigs-Universität Freiburg, also Hon. Senator and Chair. Univ. Council; fmr Pres. European Steel Works Asscn. *Leisure interest:* collecting contemporary art. *Address:* Südweststahl AG, Graudenzer Strasse 45, 77694 Kehl, Germany (office). *Telephone:* (7851) 83202 (office). *Fax:* (7851) 72685 (office). *E-mail:* horst.weitzmann@sws-kehl.de (office). *Website:* www.sws-kehl.de (office).

WEIZSÄCKER, Richard von, DJur; German fmr head of state, politician and lawyer; b. 15 April 1920, Stuttgart; s. of the late Baron Ernst von Weizsäcker; m. Marianne von Kretschmann 1953; three s. one d.; ed Berlin, law studies at Oxford, Grenoble, Göttingen; army service 1938–45; prof. lawyer 1955–; fmr mem. Bd Allianz Lebensversicherung-AG, Stuttgart, Robeco-Gruppe, Amsterdam; mem. Robert Bosch Foundation, Stuttgart; mem. Synod and Council of German Protestant Church 1969–84, Pres. Protestant Church Congress 1964–70; mem. Fed. Bd CDU, Deputy Chair. CDU/CSU Party 1972–79; mem. Bundestag 1969–81, Vice-Pres. 1979–81; Governing Mayor of West Berlin 1981–84; Pres. FRG 1984–94; Co-Chair. Ind. Working Group on the Future of the UN 1994–95; Chair. Comm. Common Security and the Future of the German Fed. Army 1999–2000; mem. Nomination Cttee Praemium Imperiale 1998–2006, 'Three Wise Men' Comm. on Institutional Reforms of the EU 1999; mem. Eminent Persons Group requested by UN Sec.-Gen. Kofi Annan to write report Crossing the Divide – Dialogue Among Civilizations 2001; Hon. Pres. Int. Council of Christians and Jews 1994–, Hon. Senator Max Planck Soc.; Hon. DCL (Oxford) 1988; Dr hc (Cambridge) 1994; Theodor Heuss Prize 1983, Leopold Lucas Prize 2000. *Publications:* Die deutsche Geschichte geht weiter 1983, Von Deutschland aus 1985, Die politische Kraft der Kultur 1987, Von Deutschland nach Europa 1991, Vier Zeiten 1997, Drei Mal Stunde Null? 2001, Was für eine Welt wollen wir? 2005. *Address:* Am Kupfergraben 7, 10117 Berlin, Germany (office).

WEK, Alek; Sudanese fashion model; b. 1977, Wau, southern Sudan; b. seventh of nine c., from Dinka ethnic group; fled with her younger sister to UK to escape civil war between Muslim north and Christian south of Sudan 1991; discovered at an outdoor market in Crystal Palace, south London by Fiona Ellis (scout for Models 1) 1995; first appeared on catwalks 1995; appeared in music video for 'GoldenEye' by Tina Turner 1995; later moved to USA; also appeared in 'Got 'Til It's Gone' music video by Janet Jackson 1996; appeared in Lavazza Calendar 1997, Pirelli Calendar 1999, 2004; has done advertisements for Issey Miyake, Moschino, Victoria's Secret and make-up co. Clinique; has modelled for fashion designers John Galliano, Donna Karan, Calvin Klein and Ermanno Scervino; acting debut in The Four Feathers as Sudanese princess Aquol 2002; also designs range of designer handbags called Wek 1933; mem. US Cttee for Refugees' Advisory Council; has helped raise awareness about situation in Sudan and plight of refugees world-wide; named Model of the Year by MTV 1997, ranked 14th in Channel 5's World's Greatest Supermodel, Venus de la Mode Award, honoured by Clutch magazine as one of 21 International Women of Power 2008. *Publication:* Alek (autobiography) 2007. *Address:* c/o Storm Models, 1st Floor, 5 Jubilee Place, Chelsea, London, SW3 3TD, England (office). *Telephone:* (20) 7368-9967 (office). *Fax:* (20) 7376-5145 (office). *E-mail:* info@stormmodels.co.uk (office). *Website:* www.stormmodels.com (office); alek-wek.com; www.alekwek1933.com.

WELCH, C. David, MA; American diplomatist; *Assistant Secretary, Bureau of Near Eastern Affairs;* b. 1953, Munich, Germany; m. Gretchen Gerwe Welch; three d.; ed London School of Econs, UK, Georgetown Univ., Washington, DC, Fletcher School of Law and Diplomacy, Tufts Univ., Medford, Mass; Officer responsible for Syria, Bureau of Near Eastern Affairs and South Asian Affairs, Dept of State, Washington, DC 1981–82, for Lebanon 1982–83, Chief of Political Section, US Embassy, Damascus, Syria 1984–86, Political Counselor, US Embassy, Amman, Jordan 1986–88, mem. staff, Nat. Security Council, White House, Washington, DC 1989–91, Exec. Asst to Under-Sec. of State for Political Affairs 1991–92, Chargé d'Affaires, US Embassy, Riyadh, Saudi Arabia 1992–94, Deputy Chief of Mission 1994–95, Prin. Deputy Asst Sec., Bureau of Near Eastern Affairs 1995–98, Asst Sec. of State for Int. Org. Affairs 1998–2001, Amb. to Egypt 2001–05, Asst Sec., Bureau of Near Eastern Affairs 2005–; mem. Council on Foreign Relations, American Foreign Service Asscn; several State Dept Awards for exceptional service. *Address:* Bureau of Near Eastern Affairs, Office 6242, US Department of State, 2201 C Street, NW, Washington, DC 20520, USA (office). *Telephone:* (202) 647-7209 (office). *Website:* www.state.gov (office).

WELCH, John Francis (Jack), Jr, PhD; American business executive; *Special Partner, Clayton, Dubilier & Rice Inc.;* b. 19 Nov. 1935, Peabody, Mass; s. of John Francis Welch and Grace Welch (née Andrews); m. 1st Carolyn B. Osburn 1959 (divorced 1987); two s. two d.; m. 2nd Jane Beasely 1989 (divorced 2002); m. 3rd Suzy Wetlaufer 2004; ed Univs of Massachusetts and Illinois; joined Gen. Electric Co., Fairfield, Conn. 1960, Vice-Pres. 1972, Vice-Pres. Exec. Components and Materials Group 1973–77, Sr Vice-Pres. Sector Exec., Consumer Products and Services Sector 1977–79, Vice-Chair and CEO 1979–81, Chair. and CEO 1981–2001, Pres. and CEO Nat. Broadcasting Co. 1986–2000; mem. Bd of Dirs Fiat 2002-03, Idealab 2000; Special Pnr, Clayton, Dubilier & Rice Inc. 2001–. *Publications:* Jack Welch and the GE Way 1998, Jack: Straight from the Gut 2000, Winning (with Suzy Welch) 2005. *Address:* Clayton, Dubilier & Rice, Inc., 375 Park Avenue, 18th Floor, New York, NY 10152, USA (office). *Telephone:* (212) 407-5200 (office). *Fax:* (212) 407-5252 (office). *Website:* www.cdr-inc.com (office).

WELCH, Raquel; American actress; b. (Jo Raquel Tejada), 5 Sept. 1940, Chicago, Ill.; d. of Armand Tejada and Josepha Tejada (née Hall); m. 1st James Westley Welch 1959 (divorced); one s. one d.; m. 2nd Patrick Curtis (divorced); m. 3rd Andre Weinfeld 1980 (divorced); m. 4th Richard Palmer 1999 (divorced 2003). *Films include:* Fantastic Voyage 1966, One Million Years BC 1967, Fathom 1967, The Biggest Bundle of Them All 1968, Magic Christian 1970, Myra Breckinridge 1970, Fuzz 1972, Bluebeard 1972, Hannie Caulder 1972, Kansas City Bomber 1972, The Last of Sheila 1973, The Three Musketeers 1974, The Wild Party 1975, The Four Musketeers 1975, Mother, Jugs and Speed 1976, Crossed Swords 1978, L'Animal 1979, Right to Die 1987, Scandal in a Small Town 1988, Trouble in Paradise 1989, Naked Gun 33$^1/_3$1993, Folle d'Elle 1998, Chairman of the Board 1998, The Complete Musketeers 1999, Tortilla Soup 2001, Legally Blonde 2001, Forget About It 2006. *Television includes:* Central Park West (series) 1996, American Family (series) 2002, The Captain (series) 2007. *Plays include:* Woman of the Year (Broadway) 1982, Torch Song 1993. *Videos:* Raquel: Total Beauty and Fitness 1984, A Week with Raquel 1987, Raquel: Lose 10lbs in 3 Weeks 1989. *Publication:* The Raquel

Welch Total Beauty and Fitness Program 1984. *Address:* Innovative Artists, 1999 Avenue of the Stars, Suite 2850, Los Angeles, CA 90067, USA.

WELD, Tuesday Ker; American actress; b. (Susan Ker Weld), 27 Aug. 1943, New York City; d. of Lathrop M. Weld and Aileen Ker; m. 1st Claude Harz 1965 (divorced 1971); one d.; m. 2nd Dudley Moore 1975 (divorced); one s.; m. 3rd Pinchas Zukerman (q.v.) 1985; ed Hollywood Professional School; fashion and catalogue model aged three; regular appearances as magazine cover-girl and in child roles on TV by age twelve; appears in numerous TV programmes and TV films including The Many Loves of Dobie Gillis 1959 and guest roles in Cimarron Strip, Playhouse 90, Climax, Ozzie and Harriet, 77 Sunset Strip, The Millionaire, Tab Hunter Show, Dick Powell Theatre, Adventures in Paradise, Naked City, The Greatest Show on Earth, Mr Broadway, Fugitive. *Films include:* Rock Rock (debut) 1956, Serial, Rally Round the Flag Boys, The Five Pennies, The Private Lives of Adam and Eve, Return to Peyton Place, Wild in the Country, Bachelor Flat, Lord Love a Duck, Pretty Poison, I Walk the Line, A Safe Place, Play it as it Lays, Because They're Young, High Time, Sex Kittens Go to College, The Cincinnati Kid, Soldier in the Rain, Looking for Mr Goodbar, Thief, Author!, Once Upon a Time In America 1984, Heartbreak Hotel 1988, Falling Down 1993, Feeling Minnesota 1996, Chelsea Walls 2001, Investigating Sex 2001.

WELD, William Floyd, JD; American business executive and fmr politician; *Principal, Leeds Weld and Company;* b. 31 July 1945, New York; s. of David Weld and Mary Nichols; m. Susan Roosevelt 1975; two s. three d.; ed Harvard Univ. and Univ. of Oxford, UK; admitted Mass Bar 1970; law clerk, Supreme Judicial Court, Mass 1970–71; Partner, Hill & Barlow, Boston 1971–81; Assoc. Minority Counsel, US House of Reps Judiciary Comm. Impeachment Inquiry 1973–74; US Attorney for Dist of Mass 1981–86; Asst Attorney-Gen. Criminal Div. US Justice Dept, Washington, DC 1986–88; Gov. of Massachusetts 1990–97; currently Principal Leeds Weld and Co. (private equity firm); CEO Decker Coll., Louisville Ky (after acquisition by Leeds Weld) Jan.-Oct. 2005; announced candidacy for NY Gov. Aug. 2005; mem. ABA, American Law Inst., Boston Bar Asscn; Republican. *Address:* Leeds, Weld and Company, 350 Park Avenue, 23rd Floor, New York, NY 10022, USA (office). *Telephone:* (212) 835-2000 (office). *Fax:* (212) 835-2020 (office). *Website:* www.leedsweld.com (office).

WELDON, Fay, CBE, MA, FRSA; British author and academic; *Professor of Creative Writing, Brunel University;* b. 22 Sept. 1931, Alvechurch, Worcs.; d. of Frank T. Birkinshaw and Margaret J. Birkinshaw; m. 1st Ronald Weldon 1960 (divorced 1994); four s.; m. 2nd Nicholas Fox 1995; ed Girls' High School, Christchurch, New Zealand, South Hampstead School for Girls and Univ. of St Andrews; Chair. of Judges, Booker McConnell Prize 1983; Writer-in-Residence Savoy Hotel, London Oct.-Dec. 2002; Prof. of Creative Writing, Brunel Univ. 2006–; fmr mem. Arts Council Literary Panel; mem. Video Censorship Appeals Cttee; Fellow, City of Bath Coll. 1999; Hon. DLitt (Bath) 1989, (St Andrews) 1992, (Birmingham), (Univ. of Connecticut); Women in Publishing Pandora Award 1997. *Theatre plays:* Words of Advice 1974, Friends 1975, Moving House 1976, Mr Director 1977, Action Replay 1979, I Love My Love 1981, Woodworm 1981, Jane Eyre 1986, The Hole in the Top of the World 1987, Jane Eyre (adaptation), Playhouse Theatre, London 1995, The Four Alice Bakers, Birmingham Repertory 1999, Breakfast with Emma, Lyric Hammersmith 2003; more than 30 television plays, dramatizations and radio plays. *Television:* Big Women (series), Channel 4 1999. *Publications:* novels: The Fat Woman's Joke (aka And the Wife Ran Away) 1967, Down Among the Women 1972, Female Friends 1975, Remember Me 1976, Little Sisters (aka Words of Advice) 1977, Praxis 1978, Puffball 1980, The President's Child 1982, The Life and Loves of a She-Devil 1984, The Shrapnel Academy 1986, The Heart of the Country 1987, The Hearts and Lives of Men 1987, The Rules of Life (novella) 1987, Leader of the Band 1988, The Cloning of Joanna May 1989, Darcy's Utopia 1990, Growing Rich 1992, Life Force 1992, Affliction (aka Trouble) 1994, Splitting 1995, Worst Fears 1996, Big Women 1997, Rhode Island Blues 2000, Bulgari Connection 2001, She May Not Leave 2005, The Spa Decameron 2007, The Stepmother's Diary 2008; children's books: Wolf the Mechanical Dog 1988, Party Puddle 1989, Nobody Likes Me! 1997; short story collections: Watching Me Watching You 1981, Polaris 1985, Moon Over Minneapolis 1991, Wicked Women 1995, Angel All Innocence and Other Stories 1995, A Hard Time to be a Father 1998, Nothing to Wear, Nowhere to Hide 2002; other: Letters to Alice 1984, Rebecca West 1985, Godless in Eden (essays) 2000, Auto da Fay (autobiog.) 2002, Mantrapped (autobiog.) 2004, What Makes Women Happy 2006. *Address:* c/o Jonathan Lloyd, Curtis Brown, Haymarket House, 29 Haymarket, London, SW1Y 4SP, England (office); Brunel University, School of Arts, Uxbridge, Middx, UB8 3PH (office). *Telephone:* (1895) 267089 (office). *E-mail:* fay .weldon@brunel.ac.uk (office). *Website:* www.brunel.ac.uk/about/acad/sa (office).

WELDON, William C., BS; American pharmaceutical industry executive; *Chairman and CEO, Johnson & Johnson;* b. 26 Nov. 1948, Brooklyn, NY; m. Barbara Weldon; one s. one d.; ed Quinnipiac Univ., Hamden, Conn.; joined Johnson & Johnson 1971, served in sales and marketing positions with McNeil Pharmaceuticals affiliate 1971–82, led pharmaceutical orgs for Johnson & Johnson in SE Asia and UK 1982–89, Vice-Pres. Sales and Marketing Janssen Pharmaceutica 1989–92, Pres. Ethicon Endo-Surgery 1992–95, Group Chair. 1995–98, mem. Exec. Cttee and Worldwide Chair. Pharmaceuticals Group 1998–2001, mem. Bd of Dirs Johnson & Johnson 2001–, Vice-Chair. 2001–02, Chair. and CEO 2002–; mem. Bd of Dirs JPMorgan Chase & Co.; Chair. CEO Roundtable on Cancer; Vice-Chair. The Business Council; mem. The Sullivan Comm. on Diversity in the Health Professions Workforce, Liberty Science Center Chair.'s Advisory Council; fmr Chair. Pharmaceutical Research and Mfrs of America; Trustee, Quinnipiac Univ. *Address:* Johnson & Johnson, 1 Johnson & Johnson Plaza, New

Brunswick, NJ 08933, USA (office). *Telephone:* (732) 524-0400 (office). *Fax:* (732) 524-3300 (office). *E-mail:* info@jnj.com (office). *Website:* www.jnj.com (office).

WELLAND, Colin; British playwright and actor; b. (Colin Williams), 4 July 1934, Liverpool; s. of John Arthur Williams and Norah Williams; m. Patricia Sweeney 1962; one s. three d.; ed Newton-le-Willows Grammar School, Bretton Hall, Goldsmiths' Coll., London; art teacher 1958–62; entered theatre 1962, Library Theatre, Manchester 1962–64; Fellow Goldsmiths Coll., Univ. of London 2001. *Stage roles:* Waiting for Godot 1987, The Churchill Play, Man of Magic, Say Goodnight to Grandma, Ubu Roi. *Plays written:* Roomful of Holes 1972, Say Goodnight to Grandma 1973, Roll on Four O'Clock 1981. *Film roles:* Kes (BAFTA Award for Best Supporting Actor), Villain, Straw Dogs, Sweeney, The Secret Life of Ian Fleming, Dancing through the Dark. *Screenplays:* Yanks 1978, Chariots of Fire 1980 (Acad. Award), Twice in a Lifetime 1986, A Dry White Season, War of the Buttons 1994. *Television appearances:* Blue Remembered Hills, The Fix, United Kingdom. *Television plays include:* Kisses at 50, Leeds United, Your Man from Six Counties, Bambino Mio, Slattery's Mounted Foot, Jack Point, The Hallelujah Handshake, Roll on Four O'Clock (BAFTA Award for Best TV Screenplay). *Leisure interests:* sport (particularly Rugby League), films, dining out, politics, travel. *Address:* United Agents, 12–26 Lexington Street, London, W1F 0LE, England (office). *Telephone:* (20) 3214-0800 (office). *Fax:* (20) 3214-0801 (office). *E-mail:* info@unitedagents.co .uk (office). *Website:* unitedagents.co.uk (office).

WELLER, Malcolm Philip Isadore, MB, BS, MA, FRCPsych., FCINPsych, FBPsS, CPsychol; British medical practitioner; *Honorary Research Professor, Middlesex University;* b. 29 May 1935, Manchester; s. of Solomon George Weller and Esther Weller; m. Davina Reisler 1966; two s.; ed Perse School, Cambridge, Cambridge and Newcastle Univs; Consultant Emer., Barnet Enfield & Haringey Mental Health NHS Trust, Chartered Neuropsychologist; Hon. Sr Lecturer, London Univ., Royal Free Hosp. School of Medicine –1997; Hon. Research Prof., Middx Univ. 1997–; Chair. N Thames Region Psychiatric Cttee 1997, London Region Psychiatric Cttee 1995–; Vice-Chair. NE Thames Regional Cttee for Hosp. Medical Services 1984–96; Hon. Medical Adviser, Nat. Alliance of Relatives of the Mentally Ill, Jewish Asscn of the Mentally Ill, Nat. Schizophrenia Fellowship and Founder-mem. Parl. Cttee; Chair. CON-CERN 1992–99; co-opted mem. Bd of Studies in Psychology, London Univ. and Higher Degrees Sub-Cttee 1976–; Founder, Ed.-in-Chief Baillière's Clinical Psychiatry series (11 vols); External Examiner for Master in Medicine (Psychiatry) Degree, Nat. Univ. of Singapore 1988, 1989; External Examiner Univ. of Manchester PhD degree 1990; mem. Standing Cttee Bd of Studies in Medicine, Univ. of London 1981–84, Cen. Cttee BMA 1994–96, Gen. Psychiatry Exec. Cttee Royal Coll. of Psychiatry, also of Pharmacology and Social, Community and Rehabilitation Cttees, Council Psychiatry Section Royal Soc. of Medicine, Exec. Psychiatry Cttee, Royal Soc. of Medicine; Examination Officer, Royal Soc. of Medicine; Royal Soc. of Medicine Rep. to Nat. Inst. for Clinical Excellence; Concert organizer, Newcastle Festival 1970–71; co-opted mem. Laing Art Gallery Cttee 1972–73; Chair. Govs Gosforth Middle School 1971–74; Fellow, British Psychological Soc. (elected mem. Neuropsychology Section), Royal Coll. of Psychiatrists, Collegium Internationale Neuro-Psycho-Pharmacologicum (CINP); Mental Health Foundation Undergraduate Scholarship, British Council Travel Award; initiated and ran courses for British Postgraduate Fed.; Invited Fellow, RSA, Ver Heyden de Lancey Prize, Univ. of Cambridge, Wilfred Kingdom Prize, Univ. of Newcastle, Brit Council Travel Award. *Publications:* Scientific Basis of Psychology (ed.) 1983, 1992, International Perspectives in Schizophrenia (ed.) 1989, Dimensions of Community Care 1993, Progress in Clinical Psychiatry 1997; about 150 editorials and papers in learned journals, mainly on schizophrenia, depression, psychological medicine and medico-legal matters; about 100 publs on music in various music journals. *Leisure interests:* fine art, music. *Address:* 30 Arkwright Road, Hampstead, London, NW3 6BH, England (home). *Telephone:* (20) 7794-5804 (home). *Fax:* (20) 7431-1589 (office). *E-mail:* psychiatry@weller .tv (office); malcolm@weller.tv (home).

WELLER, Paul; British musician (guitar, piano), singer and songwriter; b. 25 May 1958, Woking, Surrey; founder mem. and lead singer, The Jam 1972–82, The Style Council 1983–89, The Paul Weller Movement and solo artist 1990–; own record label Freedom High; Ivor Novello Award, BRIT Awards for Best Male Artist 1995, 1996, 2009, Mojo Award for Best Songwriter 2005, Q Award for Outstanding Contribution to Music 2005, BRIT Award for Outstanding Contribution 2006, Silver Clef Award 2007. *Recordings include:* albums: with The Jam: In the City 1977, This is the Modern World 1977, All Mod Cons 1978, Setting Sons 1979, Sound Affects 1980, The Gift 1982; with The Style Council: Introducing The Style Council 1983, Café Bleu 1984, Our Favourite Shop 1985, Home and Abroad 1986, The Cost of Loving 1987, Confessions of a Pop Group 1988, Singular Adventures of the Style Council 1989, Here's Some That Got Away 1993; solo: Paul Weller 1992, Wild Wood 1993, Live Wood 1994, Stanley Road 1995, Heavy Soul 1997, Modern Classics 1998, Heliocentric 2000, Days Of Speed 2001, Illumination 2002, Fly on the Wall: B-Sides and Rarities 2003, Studio 150 2004, As Is Now 2005, Catch-Flame! 2006, Hit Parade 2006, 22 Dreams 2008. *Film:* JerUSAlem 1987. *Address:* c/o William Morris Agency, Centrepoint, 103 Oxford Street, London, WC1A 1DD, England. *Website:* www.paulweller.com.

WELLER, Walter; Austrian conductor; b. 30 Nov. 1939; s. of Walter and Anna Weller; m. Elisabeth Samohyl, 1966; one s.; ed Realgymnasium, Vienna, Akademie für Musik, Vienna; f. Weller Quartet 1958–69; mem. Vienna Philharmonic 1958–60, First Leader 1960–69; Conductor, Vienna State Opera 1969–75; Guest Conductor with all main European, American and Japan Broadcasting Corpn orchestras 1973–; Chief Conductor, Tonkünstler Orchestra, Vienna 1974–77; Principal Conductor and Artistic Adviser, Royal

Liverpool Philharmonic Orchestra 1977–80, Guest Conductor Laureate 1980; Prin. Conductor, Royal Philharmonic Orchestra 1980–85, Chief Guest Conductor 1985–; Chief Guest Conductor, Nat. Orchestra of Spain 1987–; Prin. Conductor, Music Dir Royal Scottish Nat. Orchestra 1992–97, now Conductor Emer.; Chief Conductor and Artistic Adviser, Opera Basel and Allgemeine Musikgesellschaft Basel 1994–95; Medal of Arts and Sciences (Austria) 1968, Grand Prix du Disque, Charles Cross for Duke's Symphony in C, Great Silver Cross of Honour (Austria) 1998. *Leisure interests:* magic, model railways, sailing, swimming, stamp-collecting, skiing. *Address:* Harrison Parrott, 5–6 Albion Court, London W6 0QT, England (office). *Telephone:* (20) 7229-9166 (office). *Fax:* (20) 7221-5042 (office). *E-mail:* info@harrisonparrott.co.uk (office). *Website:* www.harrisonparrott.co.uk (office); www.music.at/walter-weller.

WELLERSHOFF, Dieter, DPhil; German writer; b. 3 Nov. 1925, Neuss/Rhein; s. of Walter Wellershoff and Kläre Weber; m. Dr Maria von Thadden 1952; one s. two d.; ed Gymnasium in Grevenbroich and Univ. Bonn; Ed. 1952–55; freelance writer 1956–59, 1981–; Reader Kiepenheuer and Witsch Publishing House, Cologne 1959–81; author of 11 radio plays and 10 TV plays; Hörspielpreis der Kriegsblinden 1961; Literaturpreis Verband der deutschen Kritiker 1970, Heinrich Böll Prize, Cologne 1988, Hölderlin Prize 2001, Breitbach Prize 2001, Niederrhein Prize, Krefeld 2002, E. R. Curtius Preis, Bonn 2005, Rheinischer Kulturpreis, Köln 2007. *Publications:* Gottfried Benn, Phänotyp dieser Stunde 1958, Der Gleichgültige 1963, Ein schöner Tag 1966, Literatur und Veränderung 1969, Einladung an alle 1972, Die Schönheit des Schimpansen 1977, Die Sirene 1980, Der Sieger nimmt alles 1983, Die Arbeit des Lebens 1985, Die Körper und die Träume 1986, Der Roman und die Erfahrbarkeit der Welt 1988, Pan und die Engel. Ansichten von Cologne 1990, Blick auf einen fernen Berg 1991, Das geordnete Chaos 1992, Angesichts der Gegenwart 1993, Der Ernstfall. Innenansichten des Krieges 1995, Zikadengeschrei 1995, Werke in 6 Bänden 1996–97, Der Liebeswunsch 2000, Der verstörter Eros 2001, Das normale Leben 2006, Der lange Weg zum Anfang 2007, Zwischenreich 2008, Der Himmel ist Kein Ort 2009; (ed.) Gottfried Benn, Gesammelte Werke 1958; works translated into 15 languages. *Address:* Mainzer Strasse 45, 50678 Cologne, Germany. *Telephone:* (221) 388565 (home). *Fax:* (221) 3406127 (office).

WELLINK, Arnout (Nout) H.E.M., PhD; Dutch international banking executive; *President, De Nederlandsche Bank NV;* b. 1943; m. M. V. Volmer; five c.; ed Leyden Univ., Univ. of Rotterdam; teacher, Leyden Univ. 1965–70; staff mem. Ministry of Finance 1970–75, Head of Directorate-Gen. Financial and Econ. Policy 1975–77, Treas.-Gen. 1977–81; Exec. Dir De Nederlandsche Bank NV 1982–, Pres. 1997–; Chair. of Bd and Pres. Bank for Int. Settlements (BIS) 2002–05; mem. Council, European Cen. Bank; mem. Bd of Trustees Museum Mauritshuis, Supervisory Bd Openlucht Museum; Kt, Order of the Netherlands. *Address:* De Nederlandsche Bank NV, Westeinde 1, POB 98, 1000 AB Amsterdam, Netherlands (office). *Telephone:* (20) 5249111 (office). *Fax:* (20) 5242500 (office). *E-mail:* info@dnb.nl (office). *Website:* www.dnb.nl (office).

WELLS, George; Ni-Vanuatu politician; *Minister of Foreign Affairs;* fmr Minister of Internal Affairs, fmr Minister of Nat. Defence; Minister of Foreign Affairs 2007–; mem. Parl. for Luganville; fmr mem. Vanuaaku Pati party, currently mem. Nat. United Party. *Address:* Ministry of Foreign Affairs, PMB 051, Port Vila, Vanuata (office). *Telephone:* 27750 (office). *Fax:* 27832 (office). *Website:* www.vanuatugovernment.gov.vu (office).

WELLS, Rufus Michael Grant, PhD, DSc, FRSNZ; New Zealand marine biologist and academic; *Professor, Marine Biology Group, University of Auckland;* b. 3 July 1947, Cardiff, Wales; s. of Peter F. Wells and Jean Chiles; m. Jane Nelson 1969; one s. one d.; ed Hamilton Boys' High School, Univ. of Auckland, Bedford Coll., Univ. of London, UK; researcher in molecular physiology of haemoglobin and respiration (medical, animal and fisheries science), Antarctic biology; Asst Lecturer in Statistics, Univ. of Auckland 1970–71; Research Asst and PhD student Bedford Coll., London 1971–74; Biochemist and MRC Fellow, Univ. Coll. Hosp., London 1974–75; Lecturer, then Sr Lecturer in Zoology, then Prof., Univ. of Auckland 1975–; biological and editorial consultant, specializing in Antarctic Science and Science Educ.; fmr mem. Nat. Comm. for Antarctic Research; Physiological Soc. of NZ Medal 1983, Royal Soc. of NZ Hutton Medal 1989. *Publications:* 220 scientific papers. *Address:* School of Biological Sciences, Marine Biology Group, Thomas Building, Level 1, Room 138, 3 Symonds Street, City Campus, University of Auckland, Auckland 1, New Zealand (office). *Telephone:* (9) 373-7999 (office). *Fax:* (9) 373-7668 (office). *E-mail:* r.wells@auckland.ac.nz (home). *Website:* www.sbs.auckland.ac.nz (office).

WELSER-MÖST, Franz; Austrian/Liechtenstein conductor; *Music Director, Cleveland Orchestra;* b. 16 Aug. 1960, Linz; m.; ed Musikgymnasium, Linz and Staatliche Musikhochschule, Munich; Chief Conductor, Jeunesse Orchestra, Linz 1982–85, Norrköping Symphony Orchestra 1985, Musikkollegium Winterthur, Switzerland 1986; Music Dir London Philharmonic Orchestra 1990–96; Music Dir Zürich Opera 1995–2002, Principal Conductor 2002–05; Music Dir 2005–08; Music Dir Cleveland Orchestra 2002–(18); Gen. Music Dir designate Vienna Staatsoper (2010–); has also appeared at Deutsche Oper Berlin, Glyndebourne Festival; regularly works with Berlin Philharmonic, Vienna Philharmonic, Bavarian Radio Symphony and Gustav Mahler Youth Orchestra; has conducted all major US orchestras; Outstanding Achievement Award from Western Law Centre, LA, for work for people with disabilities, Musical America's Conductor of the Year 2003, Diasapon d'Or, Japanese Record Acad. Award. *Recordings include:* Mendelssohn Symphonies Nos 3 and 4, Schumann Symphonies Nos 2 and 3, Bruckner Symphony No. 7, Strauss Waltzes, Carl Orff's Carmina Burana, Stravinsky's Oedipus Rex, Bartok's Miraculous Mandarin, Kodaly's Peacock Variations, Kancheli's Symphony No. 3, Pärt's Symphony No. 3, Fratres, Schmidt's Symphony No. 4 (Gramophone Award 1996) (all with LPO), World Premiere Recording of Johann Straus Jr's Simplicius with Zurich Opera Orchestra, Beethoven's Symphony No. 9 (with The Cleveland Orchestra), The Welser-Möst Edition. *Publication:* Kadenzen: Notizen und Gespräche 2007. *Leisure interests:* literature, mountain hiking, marathons. *Address:* IMG Artists, The Light Box, 111 Power Road, London, W4 5PY, England (office); The Cleveland Orchestra, Severance Hall, 11001 Euclid Avenue, Cleveland, OH 44106-1796, USA (office). *Telephone:* (20) 7957-5800 (office); (20) 7957-5801 (office); (216) 231-7300 (office). *E-mail:* amonsey@imgartists.com (office); pmartin@imgartists.com (office); info@clevelandorchestra.com (office). *Website:* www.imgartists.com (office); www.clevelandorchestra.com (office).

WELSH, Irvine, MBA; British writer; b. 1958, Edinburgh, Scotland; ed Heriot-Watt Univ.; co-owner, 4 Way Productions film studio; Amb. for Unicef. *Publications:* Trainspotting (novel) 1993, The Acid House (short stories) 1994, Marabou Stork Nightmares: A Novel 1995, Ecstasy: Three Chemical Romances 1996, The Wedding (with Nick Waplington) 1996, You'll Have Had Your Hole (play) 1997, Filth: A Novel 1998, Glue (novel) 2000, Porno (novel) 2002, Soul Crew (screenplay, also dir) 2003, Meat Trade (screenplay) 2004, The Bedroom Secrets of the Master Chefs (novel) 2006, Babylon Heights (with Dean Cavanagh) 2006, If You Liked School, You'll Love Work (short stories) 2007, Crime (novel) 2008; contrib. to newspapers; contrib. to anthologies, including Children of Albion Rovers 1996, Disco Biscuits 1996, Ahead of its Time 1997, The Weekenders 2002, One City 2006; contrib. to Loaded, Guardian, Daily Telegraph. *Address:* c/o Jonathan Cape, 20 Vauxhall Bridge Road, London, SW1V 2SA, England.

WELSH, Moray Meston, BA, LRAM, ARCM, GradDip; British cellist; *Member, Cropper-Welsh-Roscoe Trio;* b. 1 March 1947, Haddington, Scotland; s. of D. A. Welsh and C. Welsh (née Meston); partner, Jonathan Papp; ed York Univ. and Moscow Conservatoire; debut, Wigmore Hall 1972; cello solo appearances in UK, USA, USSR, Europe and Scandinavia; appeared with major UK orchestras, including London Symphony Orchestra, Royal Philharmonic Orchestra, BBC Symphony; festivals at Bath, Edinburgh, Aldeburgh, Bergen and Helsinki; appeared as soloist internationally under Colin Davis, André Previn, Rafael Frühbeck De Burgos, Bernard Haitink; chamber music performances with Previn, Bashmet, Midori, Galway and Chung; Prin. Cellist, London Symphony Orchestra 1992–2007; mem. Cropper-Welsh-Roscoe Trio; British Council Scholarship 1969, Gulbenkian Fellowship 1970. *Recordings include:* concertos by Boccherini, Vivaldi, Alexander Goehr, Hoddinott, Hugh Wood (Sunday Times record of the year); recorded with James Galway, Kyung-Wha Chung, Allegri Quartet, Alberni Quartet; cello and orchestra music by Herbert Howells with LSO; Rachmaninov Complete Works for Cello and Piano. *Radio:* frequent broadcasts on BBC Radio 3. *Leisure interests:* art, gardening, skiing, writing. *Address:* 32 Dartmouth Road, London, NW2 4EX, England (home). *Telephone:* (20) 8933-3032 (home). *Fax:* (20) 8933-3032 (home).

WELTEKE, Ernst; German economist; b. 21 Aug. 1942, Korbach; ed Univ. Marburg, Univ. Frankfurt am Main; Chair. Parl. Group of Social Democratic Party in Hessen Land Parl. 1984–87, 1988–91; Minister for the Economy, Transport and Tech. in Hessen 1991–94, for Finance 1994–95; Pres. Land Cen. Bank, Hessen 1995–99; Pres. Deutsche Bundesbank Sept. 1999–2004 (resgnd); mem. Governing Council European Central Bank 1999–2004. *Address:* Kennedyallee 76, 60596 Frankfurt am Main, Germany (office).

WELTY, John D., MA, EdD; American university administrator; *President, California State University, Fresno;* b. 24 Aug. 1944, Amboy, Ill.; s. of John D. Welty and Doris E. Donnelly; m. Sharon Brown 1996; three d. two s.; ed Western Illinois, Michigan State and Indiana Univs; Admissions Counsellor, Mich. State Univ. 1966–67; Asst Vice-Pres. for Student Affairs, Southwest Minn. State Univ. 1967–74; Dir of Residences and Asst Prof. SUNY, Albany 1974–77, Assoc. Dean of Students and Dir of Residences 1977–80; Vice-Pres. for Student and Univ. Affairs, Ind. Univ. of Pa 1980–84, Pres. 1984–91; Pres. Calif. State Univ., Fresno 1991–; several distinguished service awards. *Publication:* Alcohol and Other Drugs: A Guide for College Presidents and Governing Boards. *Leisure interests:* golf, jogging, reading, racquetball. *Address:* Office of the President, California State University, 5241 N Maple Ave, Thomas Administration Building, Fresno, CA 93740 (office); 4411 N Van Ness Boulevard, Fresno, CA 93704, USA (home). *Telephone:* (559) 222-2920; (559) 278-2324 (office). *Fax:* (559) 278-4715 (office). *E-mail:* john-welty@csufresno.edu (office). *Website:* www.csufresno.edu (office).

WEN, Carson, MA, JP (Hong Kong); Hong Kong lawyer; *Partner, Heller Ehrman;* b. 16 April 1953, Hong Kong; s. of Sir Yung Wen and Tsi Fung Chu; m. Julia Fung Yuet Shan 1983; one c.; ed Diocesan Boys' School, Hong Kong, Nat. Jr Coll. Singapore, Columbia Univ. New York and Univ. of Oxford; Singapore Govt Scholar 1971–72; partner, Siao, Wen and Leung (Solicitors and Notaries), Hong Kong 1982–; Dir and Sec.-Gen. Hong Kong Kwun Tong Industries and Commerce Asscn 1982–, Pres. Emer. 1989–; Hon. Life Pres. Hong Kong Sze Yap Industry and Commerce Asscn 1983–; mem. Kwun Tong Dist Bd 1983–85; Dir Banco Delta Asia SARL, Macau 1992–; Hon. Pres. Hong Kong Industrial Dists., Industry and Commerce Asscn Ltd 1993–; Attesting Officer apptd. by Ministry of Justice of China 1992–; Special Adviser to China Sr Prosecutors Educ. Foundation under the auspices of the Supreme People's Procurate of People's Repub. of China 1993–; Hong Kong Affairs Adviser to Govt of China 1993–; mem. Selection Cttee for First Govt of Hong Kong Special Admin. Region 1996; Vice-Chair. The Hong Kong Progressive Alliance 1994–; Deputy, Nat. People's Congress, People's Repub. of China 1998–; Partner, Hong Kong Office, Heller Ehrman (pvt. law practice) as Head, China Practice Group 2003–. *Publications:* contribs. to 13 lectures on Hong Kong Law; articles in journals, magazines and newspapers. *Leisure interests:*

reading, golf. *Address:* Heller Ehrman, 35th Fl., One Exchange Square 8 Connaught Place, Hong Kong Special Administrative Region, People's Republic of China (office); 6B, Wealthy Heights, 35 Macdonnell Road, Hong Kong Special Administrative Region, People's Republic of China (home). *Telephone:* (852) 22922288 (office); (852) 28401118 (home). *Fax:* (852) 22922200 (office); (852) 28684179 (home). *E-mail:* cwen@hewm.com (office); wens@netvigator.com (home). *Website:* www.hewm.com (office).

WEN, Jiabao; Chinese party and state official; *Premier of State Council (Prime Minister);* b. Sept. 1942, Tianjin; m. Zhang Beili; one s. one d.; ed Beijing Geological Coll.; joined CCP 1965; technician and political instructor, Geomechanics Survey Team, Gansu Prov. Geological Bureau, Ministry of Land and Resources 1968–1978, Deputy Head 1978–79; Engineer and Deputy Section Head, Gansu Prov. Geological Bureau 1979–81, Deputy Dir-Gen. 1981–82; Dir Reform Research Office of the Geological and Mining Bureau of the State Council 1982–83; Deputy Minister of Geology and Mining 1983–85; Deputy Dir, Gen. Office of 12th CCP Cen. Cttee 1985–86, Dir, Gen. Office of 13th and 14th CCP Cen. Cttee 1986–93; Alt. mem. Secr. of Cen. Cttee 1987; Sec. CCP Cen. Organs Working Cttee 1988; mem. 13th CCP Cen. Cttee 1987–92, 14th CCP Cen. Cttee 1992–97, Alt. mem. CCP Politburo 1992–97, mem. 1997–; Sec. Secr. of Cen. Cttee 1992; mem. 15th CCP Cen. Cttee 1997–2002, 16th CCP Cen. Cttee 2002–07 (mem. Standing Cttee of the Politburo 2002–07), 17th CCP Cen. Cttee 2007– (mem. Standing Cttee of the Politburo 2007–); Sec. Financial Work Cttee of Cen. Cttee 1998–2002; Vice-Premier State Council 1998–2003, Premier State Council (Prime Minister), People's Repub. of China 2003–. *Address:* Office of the Premier, Great Hall of the People, West Edge, Tiananmen Square, Beijing, People's Republic of China (office). *Website:* www.gov.cn (office).

WEN, Shizhen; Chinese party official; b. 1940, Haicheng Co., Liaoning Prov.; ed Faculty of Mechanical Eng, Dalian Inst. of Tech.; Deputy Dir, later Dir Dalian Oil Pump Nozzle Plant, Liaoning Prov. 1965–82; joined CCP 1979; Deputy Dir Dalian City Machinery Bureau 1982–83, Machine Building Industry Dept 1983–85; Asst Gov. Liaoning Prov. 1985–86, Deputy Gov. 1986–93, Vice-Gov. 1993–95, Gov. 1995; Deputy Sec. CCP Liaoning Prov. Cttee 1986–97, Sec. 1997–2004, mem. Standing Cttee 2001–; Chair. Standing Cttee Liaoning Prov. People's Congress 2003–04; Alt. mem. 13th CCP Cen. Cttee 1987–91, mem. 14th CCP Cen. Cttee 1992, 15th CCP Cen. Cttee 1997–2002, 16th CCP Cen. Cttee 2002–07; Deputy, 8th NPC 1993–98, 9th NPC 1998–2003. *Address:* c/o Liaoning Provincial People's Congress, Shengyang City, Liaoning Province, People's Republic of China (office).

WEN, Gen. Zongren; Chinese army officer; *Political Commissar, PLA Military Academy of Sciences;* b. Nov. 1940, Chaoxian Co., Anhui Prov.; ed PLA Tank School, PLA Political Acad., PLA Mil. Acad.; joined PLA 1959, CCP 1961; platoon leader, Tank Regt, PLA Services and Arms, Beijing 1962–67 (also Sec. Political Dept); clerk, Org. Section (Political Dept), Tank Div. and Armoured Force, PLA Services and Arms, Nanjing City Jiangsu Prov. 1967–73; Political Commissar, Tank Regt, PLA Services and Arms 1973–79; Dir 2nd Tank Div. Political Dept 1980–83; Div. Political Commissar 1980–83; Dir 12th Group Army Political Dept 1983–85; 12th Group Army Political Commissar 1985–94; rank of Maj.-Gen. 1988, Lt-Gen. 1996, Gen. 2002; Dir Political Dept of Nanjing Mil. Area Command 1994–96; Political Commissar, Lanzhou Mil. Area Command 1996–2000; Political Commissar, PLA Mil. Acad. of Sciences 2000–; Alt. mem. 14th CCP Cen. Cttee 1992–97, mem. 15th CCP Cen. Cttee 1997–2002, 16th CCP Cen. Cttee 2002–07. *Address:* PLA Military Academy of Sciences, Beijing, People's Republic of China (office).

WENDERS, Wim; German film director; b. 14 Aug. 1945, Düsseldorf; m. Donata Schmidt 1993; ed Filmhochschule, Munich; film critic, Die Suddeutsche Zeitung, Filmkritik 1968–70; Chair. European Film Acad. 1991–96, Pres. 1996–; mem. Akad. der Künste; Hon. Prof., HFF (Acad. of Film and Television), Munich 1993; Dr hc (Sorbonne, Paris) 1989, (Univ. of Freiburg, Switzerland) 1995; Friedrich Wilhelm Murnau Award 1991. *Films include:* Summer in the City 1970, The Goalie's Anxiety at the Penalty Kick 1972, The Scarlet Letter 1973, Alice in the Cities 1974, The Wrong Move 1975, Kings of the Road 1976, The American Friend 1977, Lightning Over Water 1980, The State of Things (Golden Lion, Venice Film Festival) 1982, Hammett 1982, Paris, Texas 1984, Wings of Desire 1987 (Cannes Film Festival Award), Aufzeichnungen zu Kleidern und Städten 1989, Until the End of the World 1991, Faraway, So Close! 1993, Lisbon Story, The Million Dollar Hotel 1999, Buena Vista Social Club 1999, Vill Passiert 2002, Soul of a Man 2003, Land of Plenty 2004, Don't Come Knockin' 2004, Palermo Shooting 2008. *Publications:* Emotion Pictures 1986, Written in the West 1987, Die Logik der Bilder 1988, The Act of Seeing 1992. *Address:* c/o Paul Kohner, 9300 Wilshire Boulevard #555, Beverly Hills, CA 90212, USA. *E-mail:* office@wim-wenders.com. *Website:* www.wim-wenders.com.

WENDT, Albert; Samoan/New Zealand author; b. 1939, Apia; three c.; ed Ardmore Teachers' Coll., Victoria Univ.; fmr Prin., Samoa Coll.; Prof. of Pacific Literature and Pro-Vice Chancellor, Univ. of the South Pacific 1974–88; Prof. of New Zealand Literature, Auckland Univ. 1988–; Order of Merit (Western Samoa), Companion, Order of Merit (New Zealand) 2000; Hon. PhD (Univ. de Bourgogne, France) 1993, Hon. DLit (Victoria Univ.) 2005; Sr Pacific Islands Artist's Award 2003, Nikkei Asia Prize 2004. *Publications include:* novels: Sons for the Return Home 1973, Pouliuli 1977, Leaves of the Banyan Tree 1979, Ola 1991, Black Rainbow 1992, Mango's Kiss 2003; short stories: Flying Fox in a Freedom Tree 1974, The Birth and Death of the Miracle Man 1986; poetry: Inside us the Dead: Poems 1961–1974 1976, Shaman of Visions 1984, Photographs 1995, The Book of the Black Star 2002. *Address:* Department of English, University of Auckland, Private Bag 92019, Auckland 1, New Zealand. *Telephone:* (9) 373-7999. *Fax:* (9) 373-7400. *Website:* www.auckland .ac.nz (office).

WENDT, Henry, III, AB; American business executive; *Managing Director, Caxton Healthcare Acquisition Partners;* b. 19 July 1933, Neptune City, NJ; s. of Henry Wendt and Rachel Lindsey Wendt; m. Holly Ann Peterson 1956; one s. one d.; ed Hackley School, Tarrytown, NY and Princeton Univ., NJ; joined SmithKline and French Labs. 1955; Pres. SmithKline Corpn 1976–89, CEO 1982–89; Chair. SmithKline Beckman Corpn Feb.–July 1989; Chair. SmithKline Beecham PLC 1989–94, Global Health Care Partners –2001, DLJ Merchant Banking 1997–; Dir West Marine Inc. 1997–2001; Man. Dir Caxton Healthcare Acquisition Partners 2004–; Chair. Computerized Medical Systems Inc ., Arrail Dental (China) Ltd; Dir Cambridge Labs. PLC, Bio Partners SA; Propr Quivira Estate Vineyards and Winery 1983–; Order of the Rising Sun with Gold and Silver Star, Japan 1994; Hon. CBE 1995. *Publications:* Global Embrace 1993 Mapping the Pacific Coast 2004; various articles. *Leisure interests:* viticulture, oenology, 16th and 18th century cartography, fly fishing, sailing. *Address:* 4900 West Dry Creek Road, Healdsburg, CA 95448, USA.

WÉNÉZOUI, Charles; Central African Republic politician; fmr Sec. of State for Foreign Affairs, ., Minister of Foreign and Francophone Affairs and Regional Integration 2003–06. *Address:* c/o Ministry of Foreign and Francophone Affairs and Regional Integration, Bangui, Central African Republic (office).

WENG, Yueh-Sheng, DrJur; Taiwanese judge; b. 1 July 1932, Chia-yi; three d.; ed Heidelberg Univ., Germany, Nat. Taiwan Univ.; Assoc. Prof., Nat. Taiwan Univ. 1966–70, Prof. 1970–72; Commr Legal Comm., Exec. Yuan 1971–72, Commr Research, Devt and Evaluation Comm. 1972, Commr and Convenor Admin. Procedure Act Research Comm., Judicial Yuan 1981–92; Grand Justice, Judicial Yuan 1972–99, Presiding Justice, Constitutional Court 1992–99, Pres. Judicial Yuan 1999–2007, Chief Justice of Constitutional Court 2003–07; mem. Council of Academic Review Evaluation, Ministry of Educ. 1998–99; Visiting Prof., School of Law, Univ. of Washington 1991; Commr Academic Consultation Comm., Sun Yat-Sen Inst. of Social Sciences and Philosophy, Academia Sinica 1991–2001, Convenor 1998–2001; mem. Bd Dirs Chiang Ching-kuo Foundation for Int. Scholarly Exchange 2004–(10); Hon. Fellow, Soc. for Advanced Legal Studies (UK) 2002; Order of Propitious Clouds with Special Grand Cordon by Pres. of Taiwan 2000; Golden Medal of the Distinguished Justice, Supreme Court of the Repub. of Guatemala 2000, Chung-Cheng Medal of Honour, Pres. of Taiwan 2007. *Publications include:* Die Stellung der Justiz im Verfassungsrecht der Republik China 1970, Administrative Law and Rule of Law 1976, Administrative Law and Judiciary in a State Under the Principle of the Rule of Law 1994, Administrative Law I and II 1998, Annotation of Administrative Procedure Act (ed. and co-author) 2003. *Leisure interests:* reading, hiking. *Address:* 19, Alley 9, Lane 143, Jiung Gong Road, Taipei 116, Taiwan (home). *Telephone:* (2) 2230-6339 (home). *Fax:* (2) 2230-6339 (home). *E-mail:* weng.ys21@msa.hinet.net (home). *Website:* www.cckf.org.tw (office).

WENGER, Antoine, Rév. Père; French ecclesiastic, theologian and historian; b. 2 Sept. 1919, Rohrwiller (Bas-Rhin); s. of Charles Wenger and Philomène Gambel; ed Sorbonne, Strasbourg Univ.; ordained priest 1943; Dir of Oriental Theology, Univ. Catholique de Lyon 1948–56, Prof. 1956; Chief Ed. La Croix 1957–69; Pres. Fédération Internationale des Directeurs de Journaux Catholiques 1957–65; mem. Pontifical Marian Acad., Rome 1959; Prof. of Ancient Christian Literature, Strasbourg Univ. 1969–73; Ecclesiastical Counsellor to the French Amb. to the Holy See 1973–83; Adviser to Council for Church (Vatican) and Public Affairs 1983–92, to Pontifical Council for non-believers 1987–92, Counsellor for Religious Affairs, French Embassy in Russia 1992–96; mem. Institut Français d'Etudes Byzantines; Croix d'Or du Patriarcat de Constantinople 1964; Officier, Légion d'honneur 1980; Commdr Ordre nat. du Mérite 1984. *Publications:* L'Assomption dans la tradition orientale 1955, Homélies baptismales inédites de St Jean Chrysostome 1957, La Russie de Khrouchtchev 1959, Vatican II, première session 1963, Vatican II, deuxième session 1964, Vatican II, troisième session 1965, Vatican II quatrième session 1966, Upsal, le défi du siècle aux eglises 1968, Rome et Moscou, 1900–1950 1987, Le cardinal Jean Villot, Secrétaire d'Etat de trois Papes 1989, Les trois Romes 1991, Martyrs et confesseurs de l'Eglise catholique en Russie communiste 1917–1980 d'après les archives du KGB 1998, Mgr Petit, archevèque d'Athènes, fondateur des Echos d'Orient 2002, Assomptionnistes 1903–2003: Cent ans en Russie 2004. *Leisure interests:* old books, stamps. *Address:* Le Relars, BP 113, 83510 Lorgues, France. *Telephone:* 4-98-10-10-40.

WENNEMER, Manfred, BSc, MBA; German business executive; *Chairman of the Executive Board, Continental AG;* b. 19 Sept. 1947, Ottmarsbocholt, Münsterland; ed Univ. of Münster, Institut Européen d'Admin des Affaires (INSEAD), Fountainebleau, France; Project Man. Procter & Gamble, Schwalbach 1974–77, Arthur D. Little, Wiesbaden 1978–80; Head of Planning and Controlling Non-Woven Fabrics Div. Freudenberg & Co., Weinheim 1980–82, Gen.-Man. Lady Esther, Weinheim 1982–84, Man.-Dir Freudenberg Nonwovens, Capetown, SA 1984–87, Pres. and CEO Nonwovens N America USA 1987–92, Head of Special Nonwoven Fabrics Business Unit for Europe, Weinheim 1992–93, Head of Spunbounded Fabrics Operations, Kaiserlautern 1993–94; Head Exec. Bd Benecke-Kaliko AG, Hannover 1994–98; joined Continental Aktiengesellschaft (Continental AG) 1998, mem. Exec. Bd ContiTech Group 1998–2001, Chair. Exec. Bd Continental AG 2001–. *Address:* Continental AG, Vahrenwalder 9, 30165 Hanover, Germany (office). *Telephone:* (511) 93801 (office). *Fax:* (511) 9382766 (office). *E-mail:* info@conti -online.com (office). *Website:* www.conti-online.com (office).

WENNER, Jann S.; American publisher; *Editor and Publisher, Rolling Stone;* b. 7 Jan. 1946, New York, NY; m. Jane Schindelheim (divorced); three s.; founder, Ed and Publisher, Rolling Stone magazine 1967–; TV appearances include Crime Story 1987–88; currently oversees Us and Men's Journal magazines; Chair., Wenner Media Inc.. *Film appearances:* Up Your Legs Forever 1970, Perfect 1985, Jerry Maguire 1996, Almost Famous 2000. *Publications include:* Lennon Remembers (ed.) 1972, 20 Years of Rolling Stone: What a Long Strange Trip It's Been 1987, Rolling Stone Environmental Reader 1992, Gonzo: The Life of Hunter S. Thompson (with Corey Seymour) 2007. *Address:* Rolling Stone, Wenner Media Inc., 1290 Avenue of the Americas, New York, NY 10104-0298, USA (office). *Telephone:* (212) 484-1616 (office). *Website:* www.rollingstone.com (office).

WENNING, Werner; German business executive; *Chairman of the Board of Management, Bayer AG;* b. 21 Oct. 1946, Leverkusen-Opladen; m.; two d.; joined Bayer AG, Leverkusen 1966, Commercial Trainee, mem. staff Corp. Auditing Dept, Man. Finance and Accounting Dept Bayer Industrial SA, Lima, Peru 1970–75, Man. Dir and Admin. Head 1978–83, Head of Staff Dept Health Care Sector, Leverkusen 1983–86, Head Marketing Thermoplastics, Plastics Business Group 1986, Head Worldwide Marketing Operations 1987–91, seconded to Treuhandanstalt privatization agency, Berlin 1991–92, Man. Dir Bayer Hispania Industrial SA, Sr Bayer Rep. Spain 1992–96, Head Corp. Planning and Controlling, Leverkusen 1996–97, mem. Bd of Man. Bayer AG 1997–, Chair. 2002–, also Chair. Bd Cttee for Finance, mem. Bd Cttees for Corp. Co-ordination and for Human Resources, Rep. Cen. and S. America, Africa and Middle East regions 1997–2002; mem. Shareholders' Cttee Henkel AG & Co. KGaA; mem. Supervisory Bd E.ON AG, Deutsche Bank AG; Pres. German Chemical Industry Asscn (VCI) 2005–07, Vice-Pres. 2007–. *Address:* Bayer AG, 51368 Leverkusen, Germany (office). *Telephone:* (214) 301 (office). *Fax:* (214) 3058923 (office). *E-mail:* info@bayer.com (office). *Website:* www.bayer.com (office).

WENSLEY, Penelope Anne, AO, BA; Australian diplomatist; *Governor of Queensland;* b. 18 Oct. 1946, Toowoomba; m. Dr Stuart McCosker 1974; two d.; ed Univ. of Queensland; diplomatic service 1968–, Paris 1969–72, Mexico City 1975–77, Wellington, NZ 1982–85, Consul Gen. Hong Kong 1986–88; Head Int. Orgs. Div., Dept of Foreign Affairs and Trade 1991–92, Perm. Rep. to UN, Geneva 1993–95, also Amb. for Environment, UN 1992–95, Head N Asia Div. 1996–97; Perm. Rep. to UN, New York 1997–2002; High Commr to India 2002–04; Amb. to Bhutan 2002–04, to France (also accred to Algeria, Mauritania, Morocco, Monaco) 2005–08; Gov. of Queensland 2008–; Sr Adviser, Australian del. to UN Conf. on Environment and Devt 1992; Vice-Pres. World Conf. on Human Rights, Vienna 1993; Vice-Chair. UN Climate Change Convention Negotiations 1993–96; Coordinator Western Group Negotiations on UN Conventions on Biodiversity and Desertification 1994–96; Chair. Preparatory Process UN Conf. for the Sustainable Devt of Small Island Developing States 1993–94; Chair. Int. Coral Reef Initiative Conf. 1995; Vice-Chair. UN Inst. for Training and Research; mem. WHO High Level Advisory Council on Health and the Environment; Chair. UN Gen. Ass. Fifth Cttee (Admin. and Budgetary) 1999; Co-Chair. Preparatory Process for UN Gen. Ass. Special Session on HIV/AIDS 2001; Patron UN Youth Asscn of Australia; Fellow, Women's Coll., Univ. of Queensland; Adjunct Prof. Univ. of Queensland 2000; Hon. PhD, Alumnus of the Year (Univ. of Queensland) 1994. *Leisure interests:* music, theatre, reading, tennis, bushwalking. *Address:* Government House, GPOB 434, Brisbane, Queensland, 4001, Australia (office). *Telephone:* (7) 3858-5700 (office). *Fax:* (7) 3858-5701 (office). *E-mail:* govhouse@govhouse.qld.gov.au (office). *Website:* www.govhouse.qld.gov.au (office).

WENT, David, BA, LLB, BL; Irish business executive; *Group CEO, Irish Life & Permanent PLC;* b. 25 March 1947, Dublin; s. of Arthur Went and Phyllis Went (née Howell); m. Mary Christine Milligan 1972; one s. one d.; ed Trinity Coll. Dublin; Barrister-at-Law, King's Inns, Dublin; grad. trainee, Citibank, Dublin 1970, Gen. Man. 1975, Gen. Man., Jeddah 1975–76; Dir Ulster Investment Bank 1976, Chief Exec. 1982, Deputy Chief Exec. Ulster Bank Belfast 1987, Chief Exec. 1988–94; CEO Coutts & Co. Group 1994–97; CEO Irish Life Assurance PLC 1998–; Group CEO Irish Life and Permanent PLC 1999–; Brook Scholar, King's Inns 1970; Chair. Trinity Foundation; mem. Bd of Dirs Allianz (Ireland), The Irish Times Ltd; Paul Prize, Trinity Coll. 1969. *Leisure interests:* tennis, reading. *Address:* Irish Life & Permanent PLC, Irish Life Centre, Lower Abbey Street, Dublin 1, Ireland (office). *Telephone:* (1) 7042717 (office). *Website:* www.irishlifepermanent.ie (office).

WERGER, Marinus Johannes Antonius, PhD; Dutch academic; *Professor of Plant Ecology and Vegetation Science, Utrecht University;* b. 3 May 1944, Enschede; s. of Johannes G. Werger and Gezina M. Zwerink; m. Karin E. Klein 1968; one d.; ed Jacobus Coll. Enschede and Utrecht, Groningen and Nijmegen Univs; professional research officer, Botanical Research Inst. Pretoria, S Africa 1968–73; Asst Prof., later Assoc. Prof., Nijmegen Univ. 1974–79; Prof. of Plant Ecology and Vegetation Science, Utrecht Univ. 1979–, Dean Faculty of Biology 1990–93; Consultant Prof., SW China Univ., Beibei 1984–; Visiting Prof., Univ. of Tokyo 1985; mem. Royal Netherlands Acad.; Mid-America State Univs Asscn Award 1986. *Publications:* Biogeography and Ecology of Southern Africa (two vols) 1978, The Study of Vegetation 1979, Man's Impact on Vegetation 1983, Plant Form and Vegetation Structure 1988, Tropical Rain Forest Ecosystems 1989. *Leisure interests:* history, travel, cooking. *Address:* Department of Plant Ecology and Biodiversity, Went Building, Room Z425, PO Box 800.84, 3508 TB Utrecht (office); Nieuwe Gracht 145, 3512 LL Utrecht, Netherlands (home). *Telephone:* (30) 2536843 (office); (30) 311969 (home). *E-mail:* m.j.a.werger@bio.uu.nl (office); m.j.a.werger@uu.nl (office). *Website:* www3.bio.uu.nl/peb (office).

WERLEIGH, Claudette Antoine; Haitian politician, educator, lawyer and organization official; *Secretary-General, Pax Christi International;* b. 26 Sept. 1946, Cap-Haitien; m. Georges Werleigh; two d.; worked for Caritas (Catholic aid org.) 1976–87; Minister of Social Affairs March–Aug. 1990, of Foreign Affairs 1993–95; Prime Minister of Haiti 1995–96; Rep. to OAS summit 1998; Dir of Conflict Transformation Programmes, Life and Peace Inst., Uppsala, Sweden 1999–2007; Sec.-Gen. Pax Christi International 2007–; fmr Vice-Pres. Pax Christi Int.; fmr Bd mem. Forum on Early Warning and Early Response (FEWER), London, UK, Bd mem. Life and Peace Inst., Uppsala, Sweden. *Address:* Pax Christi International, 21 rue Vieux Marche aux Grains, 1000 Brussels, Belgium (office). *Telephone:* (2) 502-55-50 (office). *Fax:* (2) 502-46-26 (office). *E-mail:* claudette@paxchristi.net (office). *Website:* www.paxchristi.net (office).

WERNER, Hans-Joachim, DipChem; German chemist and academic; *Professor and Director, Institute of Theoretical Chemistry, University of Stuttgart;* b. 16 April 1950, Hamburg; ed Univ. of Mainz, Univ. of Göttingen, Univ. of Frankfurt; Visiting Prof., Los Alamos Nat. Lab., Los Alamos, NM, USA 1983–84; Fellow, Churchill Coll., Cambridge, England 1984–85; Heisenberg Fellowship, Deutsche Forschungsgemeinschaft, Univ. of Frankfurt 1985–87; Prof., Univ. of Bielefeld 1987; Prof. and Dir Inst. for Theoretical Chem., Univ. of Stuttgart 1994–; mem. Editorial Bd Zeitschrift für Physikalische Chemie, International Reviews in Physical Chem., Theoretical Chem. Accounts, Physical Chem./Chemical Physics, Molecular Physics; mem. Bd, Arbeitsgemeinschaft Theoretische Chemie; mem. Int. Acad. of Quantum Molecular Science, Akad. der Wissenschaften zu Göttingen, Deutsche Bunsengesellschaft; City of Mainz Gutenbergpreis 1972, Max-Planck Research Award for Int. Collaboration 1996, Deutsche Forschungsgemeinschaft Gottfried Wilhelm Leibniz Award 2000, Akad. der Wissenschaften zu Göttingen Jost Medal 2001. *Address:* Institut für Theoretische Chemie, Universität Stuttgart, Pfaffenwaldring 55, 70569 Stuttgart, Germany (office). *Telephone:* (711) 685-4401 (office). *Fax:* (711) 685-4442 (office). *E-mail:* werner@theochem.Uni-Stuttgart.de (office). *Website:* www.theochem.uni-stuttgart.de/~werner (office).

WERNER, Helmut, Dr rer. nat; German chemist and academic; *Professor Emeritus of Inorganic Chemistry, University of Würzburg;* b. 19 April 1934, Mühlhausen; ed Univ. of Jena, Technische Hochschule, Munich, Calif. Inst. of Tech. (Caltech), Pasadena, Calif., USA; Lecturer in Inorganic Chem., Technische Hochschule, Munich, 1967–68; Asst Prof., Univ. of Zürich, Switzerland 1968–70, Prof. of Inorganic Chem. 1970–75; Prof. of Inorganic Chem. and Head, Inorganic Dept, Univ. of Würzburg 1975–2002, Prof. Emer. 2002–, Dean, Faculty of Chem. and Pharmacy 1987–89; Visiting Prof., Chemical Lab., Univ. of Cambridge, UK 1983; Visiting Prof., Chem. Dept, Universidad Catolica de Chile 1984; Visiting Prof., Research Unit, CNRS, Toulouse, France 1990, Univ. of Zaragoza, Spain 2003; mem. Editorial Advisory Bd Journal of Organometallic Chem. 1988–, Gazzetta Chimica Italiana 1990–97, Comments on Inorganic Chem. 1990–, Monatsheft für Chemie 1993–96, Journal of the Chemical Society 1994–96; mem. German Chemical Soc., ACS, Royal Soc. of Chem. (Fellow 1987–), Swiss Chemical Soc., New York Acad. of Sciences 1997–; Dr hc (Zaragoza) 2001; Lessing Medal 1952, German Chemical Soc. Alfred Stock Memorial Prize 1988, Max-Planck Research Award 1994, Royal Soc. of Chem. Centenary Medal 1994, Spanish Ministry of Science Mutis Award 1995. *Address:* Institut für Anorganische Chemie, Universität Würzburg, Am Hubland, 97074 Würzburg, Germany (office). *Telephone:* (931) 888-5270 (office). *Fax:* (931) 888-4623 (office). *E-mail:* helmut.werner@mail.uni-wuerzburg.de (office). *Website:* www-anorganik.chemie.uni-wuerzburg.de/werner/eng-index.html (office).

WERNER, Karl Ferdinand, DPhil; German historian (retd); b. 21 Feb. 1924, Neunkirchen; s. of Karl Werner and Johanna Kloepfer; m. Brigitte Hermann 1950; one d.; ed schools in Saarbrücken and Dresden and Univs of Heidelberg and Paris; Asst Prof. of Medieval History, Univ. of Heidelberg 1961–65; Prof. of Medieval History, Univ. of Mannheim 1965–68, Hon. Prof. 1968–; Dir Inst. Historique Allemand, Paris 1968–89; mem. Inst. de France 1992–; Corresp. mem. Munich and Dijon Acads, Soc. des Antiquaires, France; Commdr Ordre des Arts et des Lettres; Grosses Bundesverdienstkreuz; Dr hc (Sorbonne, Orléans); Prix Courcel, Acad. des Sciences morales et Politiques (France) 1985, Prix Maurice Baumont, Acad. des Sciences et Politiques 1998, Médaille d'Argent, CNRS (France) 1989. *Publications:* Untersuchungen zur Frühzeit des französischen Fürstentums 9–10 Jh. 1960, NS-Geschichtsbild 1967, Kingdom and Principality in Twelfth Century France 1978, Structures politiques du Monde Franc 1979, L'histoire médiévale et les ordinateurs 1981, Vom Frankenreich zur Entfaltung Deutschlands und Frankreichs 1984, Les origines 1984, (German version Ursprünge Frankreichs 1989), Hof, Kultur und Politik im 19. Jahrhundert 1985, Volk, Nation (in Gesch. Grundbegriffe Vol. 7) 1992, Karl d. Gr. oder Charlemagne? 1995, Marc Bloch 1995, Naissance de la noblesse en Europe 1998, Einheit der Geschichte. Studien zur Historiographie 1999. *Leisure interests:* music, chess.

WERNER, Wendelin, PhD; French (b. German) mathematician; *Professor of Mathematics, Université Paris-Sud;* b. Sept. 1968; ed École Normale Supérieure, Université Paris VI; Research Officer, CNRS 1991–97; Postdoctoral work Univ. of Cambridge, UK 1993–95; Prof. of Math., Université Paris-Sud 1997–, École Normale Supérieure (part time) 2005–; Rollo Davidson Prize 1998, Doisteau-Blutet Prize (Academie des Sciences) 1999, EMS Prize 2000, Fermat Prize 2001, Jacques Herbrand Prize (Academie des Sciences) 2003, Loeve Prize 2005, Soc. for Industrial and Applied Math. Polya Prize (co-winner) 2006, Fields Medal 2006. *Address:* Laboratoire de Mathématiques, Université Paris-Sud, Bâtiment 425, Orsay 91405, France (office). *Telephone:* 8-70-44-70-88 (office). *Fax:* 1-69-15-72-34 (office). *Website:* www.math.u-psud.fr/~werner (office).

WERTENBAKER, Timberlake, FRSL; British playwright; *Artistic Director, Natural Perspective Theatre Company;* m. John Man; one d.; Resident Playwright, Royal Court Theatre 1984–85; Dir English Stage Co. 1991–99; mem. Exec. Cttee PEN 1999–2002; Royden B. Davis Visiting Prof. of Theatre,

Georgetown Univ., Washington, DC 2005–06; Artistic Dir Natural Perspective Theatre Co. 2007–; mem. Artistic Advisory Panel, RADA 2008–; Dr hc (Open Univ.); Guggenheim Fellowship 2004; Plays and Players Most Promising Playwright (for The Grace of Mary Traverse) 1985, Evening Standard Most Promising Playwright, Olivier Play of the Year (for Our Country's Good) 1988, Eileen Anderson Cen. Drama Award (for The Love of the Nightingale) 1989, Critics' Circle Best West End Play 1991, Writers' Guild Best West End Play, Susan Smith Blackburn Award (for Three Birds Alighting on a Field) 1992, Mrs Giles Whiting Award (for gen. body of work) 1989. *Plays include:* (for the Soho-Poly): Case to Answer 1980; (for the Women's Theatre Group): New Anatomies 1982; (for the Royal Court): Abel's Sister 1984, The Grace of Mary Traverse 1985, Our Country's Good 1988, Three Birds Alighting on a Field 1991, Credible Witness 2001; (for Out of Joint): The Break of Day 1995; (for RSC): The Love of the Nightingale 1988; (for Hampstead Theatre): After Darwin 1998; (for Birmingham Rep.): The Ash Girl 2000; (for Theatre Royal, Bath): Galileo's Daughter 2004; (for RSC): trans. Arianne Mnouchkine's Mephisto, trans. Sophocles' Thebans; (for San Francisco ACT): trans. Euripides' Hecuba; (for Peter Hall Co.): trans. Eduardo de Filippo's Filumena (Piccadilly Theatre) 1998, (for Chichester) Jean Anouilh's Wild Orchards 2002, trans. Gabriela Preissová's Jenufa (for Arcola Theatre, London) 2008; other trans. include Successful Strategies, False Admissions, La Dispute (Marivaux), Come tu mi vuoi (Pirandello), Pelleas and Mélisande (Maeterlinck). *Radio includes:* Credible Witness, Dianeira, Hecuba (trans. and adaptation), The H. File (adaptation of novel by Ismail Kadaré), Scenes of Seduction 2005, Divine Intervention 2006. *Television:* Belle and the Beast (BBC). *Films:* The Children (Channel 4), Do Not Disturb (BBC TV). *Publications:* Timberlake Wertenbaker: Plays 1996, The Break of Day 1996, After Darwin 1999, Filumena 1999, The Ash Girl 2000, Credible Witness 2001, Timberlake Wertenbaker: Plays 2 2002, Jenufa (Adaption) 2007. *Leisure interest:* mountains. *Address:* c/o Casarotto Ramsay, National House, 60–66 Wardour Street, London, W1V 4ND, England.

WERTMULLER, Lina; Italian film director; b. (Arcangela Felice Assunta Wertmuller von Elgg), 14 Aug. 1928, Rome; m. Enrico Job; ed Rome Theatre Acad.; toured Europe with a puppet show after graduating; worked in theatre for ten years as actress, director and playwright. *Films as director and screenwriter:* I Basilischi (The Lizards) 1963, Questa Volta parliamo di Uomini (Let's Talk About Men) 1965, Rita la zanzara (Rita the Mosquito) 1966, Non stuzzicate la zanzara (Don't Sting the Mosquito) 1967, Mimi Metallurgio Ferito nell'Onore (The Seduction of Mimi) 1972, Film d'amore e d'anarchia (Love and Anarchy) 1973, Tutto a Posto e Niente in Ordine (All Screwed Up), Travolti da un Insolito Destino nell'Azzurro Mare d'Agosto (Swept Away) 1974, Pasqualino Settebellezze (Seven Beauties) 1976, The End of the World in our Usual Bed in a Night Full of Rain, Shimmy Lagano Tarantelle e Vino 1978, Revenge 1979, Summer Night, On a Moonlit Night, Saturday, Sunday, Monday, Ciao, Professore! 1993, The Nymph 1996, Ferdinando e Carolina 1999, Francesca e Nunziata 2001, Peperoni ripieni e pesci in faccia (dir, TV) 2004. *Address:* Piazza Clotilde 5, 00196 Rome, Italy.

WESKER, Sir Arnold, Kt, FRSL; British playwright and director; b. 24 May 1932, Stepney, London; s. of Joseph Wesker and Leah Wesker (née Perlmutter); m. Doreen (Dusty) Cecile Bicker 1958; two s. one d.; ed mixed elementary schools and Upton House Central School, Hackney, London, London School of Film Technique; left school 1948, worked as furniture maker's apprentice, carpenter's mate, bookseller's asst; RAF 1950–52 (ran drama group); plumber's mate, road labourer, farm labourer, seed sorter, kitchen porter and pastry-cook; Dir Centre 42 1961–70; Chair. British Centre of Int. Theatre Inst. 1978–82; Pres. Int. Cttee of Playwrights 1979–83; Arts Council Bursary 1959; Hon. Fellow, Queen Mary Coll. London 1995; Hon. DLitt (Univ. of E Anglia) 1989; Hon. DHumLitt (Denison Univ., Ohio) 1997; Evening Standard Award for Most Promising Playwright (for Roots) 1959, third prize Encyclopaedia Britannica Competition (for The Kitchen) 1961, Premio Marzotto Drama Prize (for Their Very Own and Golden City) 1964, Gold Medal, Premios el Espectador y la Critica (for The Kitchen) 1973, (for Chicken Soup with Barley) 1979, The Goldie Award (for Roots) 1986, Last Frontier Award for Lifetime Achievement, Valdez, Alaska 1999, Royal Literary Fund annual pension and award for lifetime achievement 2003. *Film scripts:* The Master (free adaptation of An Unfortunate Incident by F. Dostoevsky) 1966, Madam Solario (from anonymous novel of same title) 1969, The Wesker Trilogy 1979, Lady Othello 1980, Homage to Catalonia (from George Orwell's autobiog.) 1991, Maudie (from Doris Lessing's novel Diary of a Good Neighbour) 1995, The Kitchen (for Italian film co.). *Opera librettos:* Caritas (music by Robert Saxton) 1988, Grief (one-woman opera commissioned by Shigeaki Saegusa) 2004. *Plays:* The Kitchen, Royal Court Theatre 1959, 1961, 1994, Chicken Soup with Barley, Roots, I'm Talking about Jerusalem (Trilogy), Belgrade Theatre, Coventry 1958–60, Royal Court Theatre 1960, Chips with Everything, Royal Court 1962, Vaudeville 1962, Broadway 1963, The Four Seasons, Belgrade Theatre and Saville 1965, Their Very Own and Golden City, Brussels and Royal Court 1966, The Friends (Stockholm and London) 1970, The Old Ones, Royal Court 1972, The Wedding Feast, Stockholm 1974, Leeds 1977, The Journalists, Coventry 1977, Germany 1981, The Merchant (later entitled Shylock), Stockholm and Århus 1976, Broadway 1977, Birmingham 1978, Love Letters on Blue Paper, Nat. Theatre 1978, Fatlips 1978, Caritas, Nat. Theatre 1981, Sullied Hand 1981, Edinburgh Festival and Finnish TV 1984, Four Portraits, Tokyo 1982, Edin. Festival 1984, Annie Wobbler, Birmingham 1983, Fortune Theatre 1984, New York 1986, One More Ride on the Merry-Go-Round, Leicester 1985, Yardsale, Edinburgh Festival and Stratford-on-Avon 1985, When God Wanted a Son 1986, Whatever Happened to Betty Lemon, Yardsale, London 1987, Little Old Lady, Sweden 1988, The Mistress 1988, Beorhtel's Hill, Towngate, Basildon 1989, Three Women Talking (now Men Die Women Survive) 1990, Chicago

1992, Letters to a Daughter 1990, Blood Libel 1991, Wild Spring 1992, Tokyo 1994, Denial, Bristol Old Vic 2000, Groupie 2001 (based on radio play), Longitude 2002 (adaptation of book by Dava Sobel), Letter To Myself 2004; 45-minute adaptations for Schools Shakespeare Festival of Much Ado About Nothing and Henry V 2006. *Own plays directed:* The Four Seasons, Cuba 1968, world première of The Friends at Stadsteatern, Stockholm 1970, London 1970, The Old Ones, Munich, Their Very Own and Golden City, Århus 1974, Love Letters on Blue Paper, Nat. Theatre 1978, Oslo 1980, Annie Wobbler, Birmingham 1983, London 1984, Yardsale and Whatever Happened to Betty Lemon, London 1987, Shylock (workshop production), London 1989, The Kitchen, Univ. of Wis. 1990, The Mistress, Rome 1991, The Wedding Feast, Denison Univ., Ohio 1995, Letter to a Daughter, Edin. Festival 1998; also Dir Osborne's The Entertainer, Theatre Clwyd 1983, The Merry Wives of Windsor, Oslo 1989. *Radio includes:* Bluey (Cologne Radio) 1985, (BBC) 1985, Groupie (commissioned by BBC) 2001, adaptation of Shylock (commissioned by BBC Radio 3) 2006. *Adaptations for TV:* Menace 1961, Thieves in the Night (Arthur Koestler) 1984–85, Diary of a Good Neighbour (Doris Lessing) 1989, Phoenix Phoenix Burning Bright (from own story, The Visit) 1992, Barabbas 2000. *Publications:* plays: The Kitchen 1957, Chicken Soup with Barley 1958, Roots 1959, I'm Talking About Jerusalem 1960, Chips with Everything 1962, The Four Seasons 1965, Their Very Own and Golden City 1966, The Old Ones 1970, The Friends 1970, The Journalists 1972, The Wedding Feast 1974, Shylock (previously The Merchant) 1976, Love Letters on Blue Paper (TV play) 1976, (stage play) 1977, Words – As Definitions of Experience 1976, One More Ride on the Merry-Go-Round 1978, Fatlips 1980, Caritas 1980, Annie Wobbler 1982, Four Portraits – of Mothers 1982, Yardsale 1983, Cinders 1983, Bluey 1984, Whatever Happened to Betty Lemon 1986, When God Wanted a Son 1986, Badenheim 1939 1987, Shoeshine & Little Old Lady 1987, Lady Othello 1987, Beorhtel's Hill 1988, The Mistress 1988, Three Women Talking 1990, Letter to a Daughter 1990, Blood Libel 1991, Wild Spring 1992, Circles of Perception 1996, Break My Heart 1997, Denial 1997; essays, stories, etc.: Fears of Fragmentation 1971, Six Sundays in January 1971, Love Letters on Blue Paper 1974, Journey into Journalism 1977, Said the Old Man to the Young Man 1978, Distinctions 1985, As Much As I Dare (autobiog.) 1994, The Birth of Shylock and the Death of Zero Mostel (non-fiction) 1997, The King's Daughters 1998, The Wesker Trilogy 2001, One Woman Plays 2001; novels: Honey 2005, Longitude 2006. *Leisure interest:* listening to music. *Address:* Hay on Wye, Hereford, HR3 5RJ, England (home). *Telephone:* (1497) 820473 (home). *Fax:* (1497) 821005 (home). *E-mail:* wesker@compuserve.com (home). *Website:* www.arnoldwesker.com.

WESSELS, Wolfgang, Dr rer. pol; German academic; *Professor of European Politics, University of Cologne*; b. 19 Jan. 1948, Cologne; s. of Theodor Wessels and Emma Wessels; m. Aysin Wessels 1973; two d.; Dir Institut für Europäische Politik, Bonn 1973–94; Dir Admin. Studies and Prof., Coll. of Europe, Bruges, Belgium 1980–96; Jean Monnet Prof., Univ. of Cologne 1994–; Jean Monnet – European Studies GOLD Lifelong Learning Award, European Comm. 2007. *Publications include:* The European Council, Decision-Making in European Politics (with Simon Bulmer) 1987; Co-Ed.: Die Europäische Politische Zusammenarbeit in den achtziger Jahren—Eine gemeinsame Aussenpolitik für Westeuropa? 1989, Jahrbuch der Europäischen Integration 1980–, Europa vom A–Z. Taschenbuch der Europäischen Integration 1991–, Foreign Policy of the European Union. From EPC to CFSP and Beyond 1997, Die Öffnung des Staates. Modelle und Wirklichkeit grenzüberschreitender Verwaltungspraxis 2000, Das politische System der Europäischen Union. Die institutionelle Architektur des EU-Systems 2008; papers and articles on European integration. *Address:* Forschungsinstitut für Politische Wissenschaft und Europäische Fragen, University of Cologne, Gottfried-Keller-Strasse 6, 50931 Cologne, Germany (office). *Telephone:* (221) 4704131 (office). *Fax:* (221) 9402542 (office). *E-mail:* wessels@uni-koeln.de (office). *Website:* www.wessels.uni-koeln.de (office).

WESSEX, HRH The Earl of; (Prince Edward Antony Richard Louis), (Viscount Severn), KCVO, ADC, KG, MA; British; b. 10 March 1964; s. of Queen Elizabeth II (q.v.) and Prince Philip, The Duke of Edinburgh; m. Sophie Rhys-Jones (now HRH The Countess of Wessex) 1999; one s. one d.; ed Heatherdown Prep. School, Gordonstoun School, Jesus Coll. Cambridge; fmrly Second Lt Royal Marines; worked in theatre production with Really Useful Group, Theatre Div.; f. Ardent Productions Ltd 1993; opened Commonwealth Games, Auckland 1990 and Malaysia 1998, Pres. Nat. Youth Music Theatre, Commonwealth Games Fed.; UK and Int. Trustee, The Duke of Edinburgh's Award; Chair. Int. Council and Trustee, The Duke of Edinburgh's Award Int. Asscn; Patron ADC Theatre Appeal Cambridge, BADMINTONscotland, British Paralympic Asscn, British Ski and Snowboard Fed., Cen. Caribbean Marine Inst., Chetham's School of Music, Manchester, The Church Army 121 Club, City of Birmingham Symphony Orchestra, Glassworks Theatre, Cambridge, Globe Theatre, Saskatchewan, Canada, Gordon's School Stepping Forward Appeal, Haddo Arts Trust, Aberdeen Haddo House Choral and Operatic Soc. (Royal Patron), Headway Dorset, His Majesty's Theatre Aberdeen, The Stage Man. Asscn, UNITEC, Auckland, Nat. Youth Orchestras of Scotland, Nat. Youth Theatre of Great Britain, Northern Ballet Theatre, The Orpheus Trust, Queen Victoria School, Auckland, Real Tennis Professionals Asscn, Royal Exchange Theatre Co., Royal Fleet Auxiliary Asscn, Manchester, Royal Wanganui Opera House, The London Gardens Soc., London Mozart Players, Royal Wolverhampton School; Patron of Appeal, St Thomas Church Appeal, Newport; Col-in-Chief Hastings and Prince Edward Regt, Saskatchewan Dragoons; Royal Hon. Col Royal Wessex Yeomanry; Hon. Chair. The Duke of Edinburgh's Award, Young Canadian's Challenge Charter for Business. *Publication:* Crown and Country 1999. *Leisure interests:* the arts, horse-riding, sailing, skiing, badminton, Real Tennis. *Address:* Buckingham Palace, London, SW1A 1AA; Bagshot Park, Bagshot, Surrey, GU19 5PL, England. *Website:* www.royal.gov.uk.

WEST, Martin Litchfield, DPhil, DLitt, FBA; British academic; *Emeritus Fellow, All Souls College Oxford;* b. 23 Sept. 1937, London; s. of the late Maurice Charles West and Catherine Baker West (née Stainthorpe); m. Stephanie Roberta Pickard 1960; one s. one d; ed St Paul's School, London and Balliol Coll., Oxford; Woodhouse Jr Research Fellow, St John's Coll., Oxford 1960–63; Fellow and Praelector in Classics, Univ. Coll., Oxford 1963–74; Prof. of Greek, Univ. of London (Bedford Coll., then Royal Holloway and Bedford New Coll.) 1974–91; Sr Research Fellow, All Souls Coll., Oxford 1991–2004, Emer. Fellow 2004–; mem. Academia Europaea, London; Corresp. mem. Akad. der Wissenschaften, Göttingen, Accad. dei Lincei; Hon. Fellow, Univ. Coll. Oxford 2001, Balliol Coll. Oxford 2004, St John's Coll. Oxford 2007; Dr hc (Univ. of Cyprus) 2007; Balzan Prize for Classical Antiquity 2000, British Acad. Kenyon Medal for Classical Studies 2002. *Publications:* Hesiod, Theogony (ed.) 1966, Fragmenta Hesiodea (co-ed. with R. Merkelbach) 1967, Early Greek Philosophy and the Orient 1971, Sing Me, Goddess 1971, Iambi et Elegi Graeci (ed.) 1971–72, revised edn 1989–92, Textual Criticism and Editorial Technique 1973, Studies in Greek Elegy and Iambus 1974, Hesiod, Works and Days (ed.) 1978, Theognidis et Phocylidis fragmenta 1978, Delectus ex Iambis et Elegis Graecis 1980, Greek Metre 1982, The Orphic Poems 1983, Carmina Anacreontea 1984, The Hesiodic Catalogue of Women 1985, Introduction to Greek Metre 1987, Euripides Orestes (ed.) 1987, Hesiod (trans.) 1988, Aeschyli Tragoediae 1990, Studies in Aeschylus 1990, Ancient Greek Music 1992, Greek Lyric Poetry (trans.) 1993, The East Face of Helicon 1997 (Runciman Prize 1998), Homeri Ilias (ed.) Vol. I 1998, Vol. II 2000, Studies in the Text and Transmission of the Iliad 2001, Documents of Ancient Greek Music (with E. Pöhlmann) 2001, Homeric Hymns, Homeric Apocrypha, Lives of Homer 2003, Greek Epic Fragments 2003, Indo-European Poetry and Myth 2007. *Leisure interest:* music. *Address:* All Souls College, Oxford, OX1 4AL (office); 42 Portland Road, Oxford, OX2 7EY, England (home).

WEST, Paul, MA; American (b. British) author; b. 23 Feb. 1930, Eckington, Derbyshire, England; s. of Alfred West and Mildred Noden; ed Univ. of Oxford, UK and Columbia Univ.; served with RAF 1954–57; Asst Prof. of English, Memorial Univ., Newfoundland 1957–58, Assoc. Prof. 1958–60; arrived in USA 1961, became naturalized 1971; contrib., Washington Post, New York Times 1962–95, also contributes to Harper's and GQ magazines, Paris Review; mem. of staff Pa State Univ. 1962–, Prof. of English and Comparative Literature 1968–1995, Prof. Emer. 1995–; Crawshaw Prof., Colgate Univ. 1972; Melvin Hill Distinguished Visiting Prof., Hobart and William Smith Colls 1973; Distinguished Writer-in-Residence, Wichita State Univ. 1982; Writer-in-Residence, Univ. of Arizona 1984; Visiting Prof. of English, Cornell Univ. 1986, Brown Univ. 1992; Guggenheim Fellow 1962–63; Nat. Endowment for Arts Creative Writing Fellow 1979, 1984; mem. Author's Guild; Chevalier, Ordre Arts et Lettres; Aga Khan Fiction Prize 1973, Hazlett Memorial Award for Excellence in Arts (Literature) 1981, Literature Award, American Acad. and Inst. of Arts and Letters 1985, Pushcart Prize 1987, 1991, Best American Essays Award 1990, Grand Prix Halpérine Kaminsky Award 1992, Lannan Fiction Award 1993, Teaching Award NE Asscn of Grad. Schools 1994, Art of Fact Prize, State Univ. of NY 2000; Outstanding Achievement Medal, Pa State Univ. 1991. *Publications include:* Byron and the Spoiler's Art 1960, I, Said the Sparrow 1963, The Snow Leopard 1965, Tenement of Clay 1965, The Wine of Absurdity 1966, I'm Expecting to Live Quite Soon 1970, Words for a Deaf Daughter 1970, Caliban's Filibuster 1971, Bela Lugosi's White Christmas 1972, Colonel Mint 1973, Gala 1976, The Very Rich Hours of Count von Stauffenberg 1980, Out of My Depths: A Swimmer in the Universe and Other Fictions 1988, The Place in Flowers Where Pollen Rests 1988, Lord Byron's Doctor 1989, Portable People, The Women of Whitechapel and Jack the Ripper 1991, James Ensor 1991, Love's Mansion 1992, A Stroke of Genius 1995, Sporting with Amaryllis 1996, Terrestrials 1997, Life with Swan 1999, O.K.: The Corral 2000, The Earps 2000, Doc Holliday 2000, The Dry Danube: A Hitler Forgery 2000, The Secret Lives of Words 2000, A Fifth of November 2001, Master Class 2001, Portable People 2001. *Leisure interests:* swimming, astronomy, classical music, cricket, films. *Address:* c/o Elaine Markson Agency, 44 Greenwich Avenue, Floor 3, New York, NY 10011, USA. *Telephone:* (212) 243-8480. *Fax:* (607) 257-0631.

WEST, Richard G., MA, ScD, FRS; British botanist and academic; b. 31 May 1926, Hendon, Middx; m. 1st Janet Abram 1958; one s.; m. 2nd Hazel Gristwood 1973 (died 1997); two d.; ed King's School, Canterbury and Univ. of Cambridge; Fellow, Clare Coll., Cambridge 1954–; Lecturer in Botany, Univ. of Cambridge 1960–68, Reader in Quaternary Research 1968–74, Prof. of Palaeoecology 1974–77, Prof. of Botany and Head, Dept of Botany 1977–91, Dir Sub-Dept of Quaternary Research 1966–87; Hon. mem. Royal Belgian Acad.; Foreign mem. Finnish Acad. of Sciences and Letters 1999; Hon. MRIA; Bigsby Medal, Geological Soc. 1968, Lyell Medal, Geological Soc. 1988. *Publications:* Pleistocene Geology and Biology 1968, The Ice Age in Britain (jtly) 1972, The Pre-glacial Pleistocene of the Norfolk and Suffolk Coasts 1980, Pleistocene Palaeoecology of Central Norfolk 1991, Plant Life in the Quaternary Cold Stages 2000. *Leisure interest:* sailing. *Address:* Clare College, Cambridge (office); 3A Woollards Lane, Great Shelford, Cambridge, CB22 5LZ, England (home). *Telephone:* (1223) 842578 (home).

WEST, Stephen Craig, PhD, FRS, FMedSci; British scientist; *Principal Scientist, Cancer Research UK;* b. 11 April 1952, Hull; s. of Joseph West and Louisa West; m. Phyllis Fraenza 1985; ed Univ. of Newcastle and Yale Univ., USA; Research Scientist, Yale Univ. 1983–85; Sr Scientist, Imperial Cancer Research Fund (now Cancer Research UK) 1985–89, Prin. Scientist 1989–; mem. European Molecular Biology Org. 1994–; Hon. Prof., Univ. Coll. London 1997–; Louis-Jeantet Prize for Medicine 2007. *Publications:* more than 180 research articles. *Leisure interests:* sport, music. *Address:* Cancer Research UK, London Research Institute, Clare Hall Laboratories, South Mimms, Herts., EN6 3LD (office); Meadowbank, Riverside Avenue, Broxbourne, Herts., EN10 6RA, England (home). *Telephone:* (1707) 625868 (office); (1992) 470147 (home). *Fax:* (1707) 625811 (office). *E-mail:* stephen.west@cancer.org.uk (office). *Website:* www.cancerresearchuk.org (office).

WEST, Timothy Lancaster, CBE, FRSA; British actor and director; b. 20 Oct. 1934, Bradford, Yorks.; s. of the late H. Lockwood West and Olive Carleton-Crowe; m. 1st Jacqueline Boyer 1956 (dissolved); one d.; m. 2nd Prunella Scales (q.v.) 1963; two s.; ed John Lyon School, Harrow and Regent Street Polytechnic; repertory seasons, Wimbledon, Hull, Salisbury, Northampton 1956–60; mem. Royal Shakespeare and Prospect Theatre Cos. 1962–79; Artistic Dir, Old Vic 1980–81; Dir-in-Residence Univ. of WA 1982; Assoc. Dir Bristol Old Vic. –1991; Pres. London Acad. of Music and Dramatic Art, Soc. for Theatre Research; Hon. DLitt (E Anglia, W of England) (London), (Hull); Hon. DUniv (Bradford); Hon. LLD (Westminster); Hon. Dr Drama, Royal Scottish Acad. of Music and Drama (RSAMD). *Stage appearances:* (in London): Caught Napping 1959, Galileo 1960, Gentle Jack 1963, The Trigon 1963, The Italian Girl 1968, Abelard and Heloise 1970, Exiles 1970, The Critic as Artist 1971, The Houseboy 1973, A Month in the Country 1974, A Room with a View 1975, Laughter 1978, The Homecoming 1978, Beecham 1980, Master Class 1984, The War at Home 1984, When We are Married 1986, The Sneeze 1988, Long Day's Journey into Night 1991, It's Ralph 1991, Twelve Angry Men 1996, Henry IV Parts 1 and 2 1996, King Lear 1997, The Birthday Party 1999, Luther 2001, King Lear 2003, HMS Pinafore 2003, National Hero 2005, Galileo 2006, The Old Country 2006, A Number 2006, Coriolanus 2007, The Collection 2007; numerous appearances with Prospect Theatre Co., Royal Shakespeare Co. and regional theatres. *Film appearances include:* The Looking Glass War 1969, Nicholas and Alexandra 1971, The Day of the Jackal 1973, The Devil's Advocate 1978, The Thirty-Nine Steps 1978, Agatha 1979, Rough Cut 1980, Cry Freedom 1987, Consuming Passions 1988, The Tempest (voice) 1992, Ever After 1998, The Messenger: The Story of Joan of Arc 1999, 102 Dalmatians 2000, The Fourth Angel 2001, Iris 2001, Shrink 2002, Villa des Roses 2002, Sinbad: Legend of the Seven Seas (voice) 2003, Beyond Borders 2003. *Television appearances include:* Persuasion (mini-series) 1960, Witch Hunt (mini-series) 1967, Feet Foremost 1968, Big Breadwinner Hog (series) 1969, The Tragedy of King Richard II 1970, Edward II 1970, The Edwardians (mini-series) 1972, Horatio Bottomley 1972, Edward the King (mini-series) 1975, Hard Times (series) 1977, Henry VIII 1979, Churchill and the Generals 1979, Crime and Punishment (mini-series) 1979, Masada (mini-series) 1981, Murder Is Easy 1982, Oliver Twist 1982, Brass (series) 1983, The Last Bastion (mini-series) 1984, A Pocket Full of Rye 1985, Florence Nightingale 1985, Tender Is the Night (mini-series) 1985, The Good Doctor Bodkin-Adams 1986, The Monocled Mutineer (series) 1986, When We Are Married 1987, What the Butler Saw 1987, Harry's Kingdom 1987, Breakthrough at Reykjavik 1987, Strife, Beryl Markham: A Shadow on the Sun 1988, The Contractor, Blore M.P. 1989, Lenin: The Train 1990, The Tragedy of Flight 103: The Inside Story (aka Why Lockerbie?) 1990, Bye Bye Columbus 1991, Shakespeare: The Animated Tales (mini-series) (voice) 1992, Framed 1992, Survival of the Fittest, Smokescreen (mini-series) 1994, Reith to the Nation, Eleven Men Against Eleven 1995, Hiroshima 1995, The Place of the Dead 1996, Over Here 1996, Cuts 1996, Rebecca 1997, Animated Epics: Beowulf (voice) 1998, Bramwell: Our Brave Boys 1998, King Lear 1998, The Big Knights (series) (voice) 1999, Midsomer Murders 2000, Bedtime (series) 2001, Murder in Mind 2001, Station Jim 2001, Martin Luther 2002, Dickens 2002, The Alan Clark Diaries 2004, The Inspector Lynley Mysteries: In Pursuit of the Proper Sinner 2004, London 2004, Essential Poems for Christmas 2004, Waking the Dead 2004, Colditz 2005, Bleak House (mini-series) 2005, A Room With a View 2007. *Radio:* has appeared in more than 500 programmes since 1960. *Concerts:* with London Philharmonic Orchestra, Royal Philharmonic Orchestra, Britten Ensemble, Sinfonia 21 etc. *Publications:* I'm Here I Think, Where Are You? 1997, A Moment Towards the End of the Play 2001, So You Want To Be an Actor (with Prunella Scales) 2005. *Leisure interests:* music, travel, inland waterways, old railways. *Address:* c/o Gavin Barker Associates, 2D Wimpole Street, London, W1M 7AA, England.

WESTBROOK, Roger, CMG, MA; British diplomatist (retd); *Chairman, Spencer House;* b. 26 May 1941, Surrey; s. of Edward George Westbrook and Beatrice Minnie Marshall; ed Dulwich Coll. and Hertford Coll., Oxford; Foreign Office 1964; Asst Pvt. Sec. to the Chancellor of the Duchy of Lancaster 1965; held posts in Yaoundé 1967, Rio de Janeiro 1971, Brasília 1972; Private Sec. to Minister of State, FCO 1975; Head of Chancery, Lisbon 1977; Deputy Head, News Dept, FCO 1980, Deputy Head, Falkland Islands Dept 1982, Overseas Inspectorate 1984; High Commr, Brunei Darussalam 1986–91; Amb. to Zaire 1991–92; High Commr in Tanzania 1992–95; Amb. to Portugal 1995–99; British Commr-Gen. EXPO 98; Chair. Spencer House 2000–, Anglo-Portuguese Soc. 2000–04, UK–EC Societies 2004–, Foreign and Commonwealth Office Asscn 2003–; Freeman of the City of London, Liveryman of the Tylers' and Bricklayers' Company 2002. *Leisure interests:* doodling, sightseeing, theatre. *Address:* Spencer House, 27 St James's Place, London, SW1A 1NR (office); 33 Marsham Court, Marsham Street, London, SW1P 4JY, England (home). *Telephone:* (20) 7514-1948 (office).

WESTERBERG, Bengt, MedKand, FilKand; Swedish politician and banker; *Chairman, Financial Board, Financial Supervision Authority;* b. 23 Aug. 1943; s. of the late Carl-Eric and of Barbro Westerberg; m. 2nd Marie Ehrling; one s., two d. from a previous marriage; ed Karolinska Inst., Univ. of Stockholm; joined Liberal Youth League 1965, held elected office at all levels, Chair. Exec. Cttee 1970–71; joined Liberal Party 1965, held municipal office in Södertälje, elected to Nat. Bd 1983, mem. Party Exec. 1983, Chair. 1984–95; Pres. Liberal Party 1993–95; Deputy Sec. to Commr for Greater Stockholm

1969, Sec. to Commr for Municipal Services 1970, Sec. to Stockholm County Council Traffic Commr 1971, Research Dir Traffic Cttee 1972, Adviser Govt Comm. on Traffic Policy 1975, Adviser Ministry of Labour 1976, Liberal Party's Coordination Office 1978; Under-Sec. Ministry of Industry 1978, Ministry of the Budget 1979–82; f. Foundation for a Market-Economy Alternative for Sweden 1983; mem. Parl. 1984–94; Minister of Social Affairs and Deputy Prime Minister 1991–94; Research and Devt Leader, Centre of Gender Studies, Univ. of Karlstad 1995–; currently Chair. Financial Bd, Financial Supervision Authority; Chair. Bd Telia AB 1995–, BTJ 1995–, Media Technology MT AB 1996–; apptd Vice-Chair. Bd Riksbank (Cen. Bank of Sweden) 1994; mem. Bd Morgondagen AB 1995–; Pres. Swedish Athletics Asscn 1995–2004, Swedish Foundation of Dyslexia 1995–2005. *Address:* Financial Supervision Authority, Box 7821, 103 97 Stockholm, Sweden (office). *Telephone:* (8) 787-80-00 (office). *Fax:* (8) 24-13-35 (office). *E-mail:* finansinspektionen@fi.se (office). *Website:* www.fi.se (office).

WESTERBERG, Lars, MSc; Swedish business executive; *Chairman, Vattenfall AB;* b. 1948; ed Univ. of Stockholm, Royal Inst. of Tech.; began career with ASEA 1972, later Sales Man., ASEA Robotics –1984; joined Esab 1984, Pres. and CEO 1991–94; Pres. and CEO Gränges AB 1994–99; Pres. and CEO Autoliv AB 1999–2007, Chair. 2007–; Ind. Chair. Vattenfall AB 2008–; Chair. Husqvarna AB; mem. Bd of Dirs SSAB, AB Volvo, Plastal AB. *Address:* Vattenfall AB, Jamtlandsgaten 99, 162 87 Stockholm, Sweden (office). *Telephone:* (8) 739-50-00 (office). *Fax:* (8) 37-01-70 (office). *E-mail:* info@vattenfall.com (office). *Website:* www.vattenfall.com (office).

WESTERFIELD, Putney, BA; American business executive; b. 9 Feb. 1930, New Haven, Conn.; s. of Ray Bert Westerfield and Beatrice Putney; m. Anne Montgomery 1954; two s. one d.; ed Choate School and Yale Univ.; Vice-Pres. and Co-Founder, Careers Inc. 1950–52; Man. SE Asia Operations, Swen Publs; service with Dept of State in Korea, Washington, Saigon 1953–59; Asst to Publr of Time 1957–59, Asst to Circulation Dir 1959–61, Circulation Dir 1961–66, Asst Publr 1966–68; Asst Publr of Life 1968–69; Publr of Fortune 1969–73; Pres. Chase World Information Corpn 1973–75; Vice-Pres. Boyden Assocs Int. 1976–80, Sr Vice-Pres., Western Man. 1980–84, Pres. and CEO 1984–90, Man. Dir 1990, now Chair. Emer.; Dir East Meets West Foundation 1991; Chair. Bd Dirs Upside Media Inc. *Leisure interests:* reading, music, tennis, swimming. *Address:* c/o Boyden International, 275 Battery Street, Suite 420, San Francisco, CA 94111 (office); 10 Green View Lane, Hillsborough, CA 94010, USA (home).

WESTERWELLE, Guido; German lawyer and politician; *Leader, Free Democratic Party of Germany (FDP);* b. 27 Dec. 1961, Bad Honnef; pnr, Michael Mronz; ed Gymnasium, Univs of Bonn and Hagen; passed First and Second State Law Examinations 1987, 1991 respectively, began practising as attorney in Bonn 1991; joined Freie Demokratische Partei (Free Democratic Party—FDP) 1980, founding mem. Junge Liberale (youth org. of FDP, Chair. 1983–88), mem. Exec. Bd of FDP 1988–, Sec.-Gen. 1994–2001, Chair. 2001–; elected to Bundestag (Parl.) 1996–, Leader of Parl. Group and Leader of Opposition 2006–; FDP cand. in elections for Chancellor 2002. *Address:* Freie Demokratische Partei, Reinhardtstr. 14, 10117 Berlin (office); FDP-Bundestagsfraktion, Platz der Republik 1, 11011 Berlin, Germany. *Telephone:* (30) 2849580 (office); (30) 22771636 (Parl. Group). *Fax:* (30) 28495822 (office); (30) 22776562 (Parl. Group). *E-mail:* guido.westerwelle@bundestag.de (office). *Website:* www.fdp.de (office); www.bundestag.de/mdb15/bio/W/westegu0 .html; www.guido-westerwelle.de.

WESTMINSTER, Archbishop of (see HE Cardinal Cormac Murphy-O'Connor).

WESTON, John Pix, CBE, MA, FRAeS, FRSA; British business executive; *Chairman, Spirent plc;* b. 16 Aug. 1951, Kendal; s. of John Pix Weston and Ivy Weston (née Glover); m. Susan West 1974; one s. one d.; ed Kings School, Worcester and Trinity Hall, Cambridge; under-grad. apprentice, British Aircraft Corpn 1970–74, various positions in Dynamics and Math. Services Div., later Marketing and Gen. Man. 1974–82, seconded to Ministry of Defence 1982–84, Man. Dir British Aerospace Mil. Aircraft Div. 1990–92, mem. Bd 1993–2002, CEO BAe (later BAE Systems following merger with Marconi Electric Systems) 1998–2002; Chair. (non-exec.) Spirent plc 2002–; mem. Dept of Trade and Industry (DTI) Council for Science and Tech.; mem. CBI Pres.'s Cttee, Chair. CBI Europe Cttee 2001–; Vice-Pres. Royal United Services Inst.; mem. Royal Coll. of Defence Studies Advisory Bd; Council mem., European Asscn of Aerospace Industries (AECMA), Soc. of British Aerospace Cos; Fellow, Royal Acad. of Eng; Freeman, City of London. *Leisure interests:* skiing, photography, mountain walking. *Address:* Spirent plc, Spirent House, Crawley Business Quarter, Fleming Way, Crawley, West Sussex, RH10 9QL, England (office). *Telephone:* (1293) 767-676 (office). *Fax:* (1293) 767-677 (office). *Website:* www.spirent.com (office).

WESTON, Sir Michael Charles Swift, KCMG, CVO, MA; British diplomatist (retd); b. 4 Aug. 1937, Crowborough, Sussex; s. of the late Edward C. S. Weston and Kathleen M. Mockett; m. 1st Veronica A. Tickner 1959 (divorced 1990); two s. one d.; m. 2nd Christine J. Ferguson 1990; one s. one d.; ed Dover Coll. and St Catharine's Coll., Cambridge; joined HM Diplomatic Service 1961; Third Sec. Kuwait 1962; First Sec. Tehran 1968; UK mission, New York 1970; Counsellor Jeddah 1977; Royal Coll. of Defence Studies 1980; Counsellor Paris 1981, Cairo 1984; Head S European Dept, FCO 1987–90; Amb. to Kuwait 1990–92; Leader UK Del. to Conf. on Disarmament, Geneva 1992–97; mem. Special Immigration Appeals Comm. 1999–. *Leisure interests:* squash, tennis, walking. *Address:* Beech Farm House, Beech Lane, Matfield, Kent, TN12 7HG, England (home). *Telephone:* (1892) 824921 (home). *Fax:* (1892) 824921 (home).

WESTON, Sir (Philip) John, KCMG; British diplomatist and company director; b. 13 April 1938; s. of the late Philip G. Weston and Edith Ansell; m. Sally Ehlers 1967; two s. one d.; ed Sherborne School and Worcester Coll. Oxford; served Royal Marines 1956–58; entered HM Diplomatic Service 1962; Treasury Centre for Admin. Studies 1964; Chinese language student, Hong Kong 1964–66; Beijing 1967–68; Office of UK Perm. Rep. to EEC 1972–74; Asst Pvt. Sec. to Sec. of State for Foreign and Commonwealth Affairs 1974–76; Counsellor, Head of EEC Presidency Secr., FCO 1976–77; Visiting Fellow, All Souls Coll. Oxford 1977–78; Counsellor, Washington, DC 1978–81; Head, Defence Dept FCO 1981–84, Asst Under-Sec. of State 1984–85; Minister, Paris 1985–88; Deputy Sec. to Cabinet, Cabinet Office 1988–89; Deputy Under-Sec. of State, FCO 1989–90, Political Dir 1990–91; Amb. and Perm. Rep. to N Atlantic Council (NATO) 1992–95; Perm. Rep. to UN 1995–98; Dir (non-exec.) British Telecommunications 1998–2002, Rolls Royce 1998–2005, Hakluyt & Co. 2001–07; mem. Council IISS 2001–05; Chair. Govs Sherborne School 2002–07; Gov. Ditchley Foundation 2000–; Chair. Trustees The Poetry School 2004–08; mem. Council and Trustee The Poetry Soc. 2005–08; Trustee Nat. Portrait Gallery 1999–2008; Hon. Pres. Community Foundation Network (UK) 1998–2008; Hon. Fellow, Worcester Coll. Oxford 2003; Order of Merit (with Star), FRG. *Publications:* Take Five – 04 (poetry anthology) 2004, Chasing the Hoopoe (first poetry collection) 2005; poems published by The Guardian, The Spectator, The London Magazine and other literary magazines. *Leisure interests:* poetry, fly-fishing, running, birds. *Address:* 13 Denbigh Gardens, Richmond, Surrey, TW10 6EN, England (home). *E-mail:* john.weston-pjweston@btinternet.com (home).

WESTON, W. Galen, OC, BA, LLD; Canadian business executive; *Chairman and President, George Weston Ltd;* b. 29 Oct. 1940, grandson of George Weston; m. Hilary Weston (fmr Lt-Gov. of Canada); one s. one d.; ed Univ. of Western Ontario; currently Chair. and Pres. George Weston Ltd (family business est. by grandfather); owns controlling stake in Loblaw Cos Ltd (fmr Chair.) and investments in Holt Renfrew & Co. Ltd (Chair.), Brown Thomas Group Ltd (Chair.), Wittington Investments Ltd, Selfridges & Co. (Chair.); Pres. The W. Garfield Weston Foundation; Dir Associated British Foods PLC, Canadian Imperial Bank of Commerce, Loblaw Cos Ltd; mem. Advisory Bd Columbia Univ., New York. *Leisure interest:* art collecting. *Address:* George Weston Ltd, 22 St Clair Avenue East, Suite 1901, Toronto, ON M4T 2S7, Canada (office). *Telephone:* (416) 922-2500 (office). *Fax:* (416) 922-4395 (office). *E-mail:* info@weston.ca (office). *Website:* www.weston.ca (office).

WESTWOOD, Lee; British professional golfer; b. 24 April 1973, Worksop, Nottinghamshire; s. of John Westwood and Trish Westwood; m. Laurae Coltart 1999; one s., one d.; England Boys, Youths and Srs. amateur teams 1989–93, won Peter McEvoy Trophy 1990, British Youth Championships 1993; turned professional 1993, won Volvo Scandinavian Masters 1996, 2000, Sumitomo Taiheiyo Masters 1996, 1997, 1998, Benson and Hedges Malaysian Open 1997, Volvo Masters 1997, Holden Australian Open 1997, McDermott-Freeport Classic 1998, Deutsche Bank SAP Open 1998, 2000, English Open 1998, Loch Lomond Invitation 1998, Belgacom Open 1998, 2000, Dunlop Phoenix Tournament 1998, Macau Open 1999, TNT Dutch Open 1999, Smurfit European Open 1999, 2000, Canon European Masters 1999, Dimension Data Pro Am 2000, Compaq European Grand Prix 2000, Cisco World Match Play Championship 2000, BMW Int. Open 2003, Dunhill Links Championship 2003; mem. Ryder Cup Team 1997, 1999, 2002, 2004; Volvo Order of Merit 2000. *Leisure interests:* snooker, horse racing (racehorse owner), sports cars, Nottingham Forest football team, cinema, shows. *Address:* International Sports Management Ltd, Cherry Tree Farm, Cherry Tree Lane, Rostherne, Cheshire, WA14 3RZ, England (office). *E-mail:* ism@golfism.net (office). *Website:* www.leewestwood.com (office).

WESTWOOD, Dame Vivienne Isabel, OBE, DBE; British fashion designer; b. (Vivienne Isabel Swire), 8 April 1941, Tintwistle, Derbyshire; d. of Gordon Swire and Dora Swire; m. 1st Derek Westwood 1962, one s.; one s. with Malcolm McLaren; m. 2nd Andreas Kronthaler 1993; worked with Malcolm McLaren 1970–83, developing 'punk' look, and her clothes were sold at McLaren's shop on King's Road, London; designed for the Sex Pistols, Boy George and Bananarama; created first catwalk collection, Pirate (adopted by Adam Ant and Bow Wow Wow) 1981; showed in Paris 1983, in Tokyo 1984; moved to Italy with new business pnr Carlo D'Amario 1984; opened first Vivienne Westwood shop, London 1990; launch of signature fragrance, Boudoir 1998, further fragrances Libertine 2000, Boudoir Sin City 2007, Let it Rock 2007; Prof. of Fashion Acad. of Applied Arts 1989–91, Hochschule der Künste, Berlin 1993–; trustee Civil Liberties Trust 2007–; Hon. Sr Fellow, Royal Coll. of Art 1992; Dr hc (Heriot-Watt) 1995, (Acad. of Art Univ. School of Fashion) 2006; Designer of the Year 1990, 1991, Queen's Award for Export 1998, Moet & Chandon Red Carpet Dresser 2006, Outstanding Achievement in Fashion Award, British Fashion Awards 2007. *Television:* South Bank Show: Vivienne Westwood 1990. *Address:* Vivienne Westwood Ltd, Westwood Studios, 9–15 Elcho Street, London, SW11 4AU, England (office). *Telephone:* (20) 7924-4747 (office). *Fax:* (20) 7738-9655. *E-mail:* info@viviennewestwood .co.uk. *Website:* www.viviennewestwood.com.

WETANG'ULA, Moses Masika, LLB; Kenyan lawyer and politician; *Minister of Foreign Affairs;* b. 13 Sept. 1956, Western Kenya; m.; c.; ed Univ. of Nairobi, Kenya School of Law; Professional Dist. Magistrate, Chief Magistrate's Court, Nakuru 1982, Dist. Magistrate's Court, Rongo, South Nyanza 1983; Sole Practioner, M. M Wetang'ula Advocate Chambers, Nairobi 1983–85, currently Proprietor, Wetang'ula & Co. Advocates; mem. Parl. (FORD–Kenya) 1993–97, 2002–07, fmr mem. Parl. Cttee on Legal and Constitutional Affairs, Foreign Affairs and Standing Orders, Chair Electricity Regulatory Bd 1998–2001; fmr mem. Jt Ass. of African Caribbean and Pacific/EU, Pres. Jt Ass Working Group on Regional Cooperation; Asst Minister for Int. Affairs –2008, Minister of Foreign Affairs 2008–; mem. Law Soc. of Kenya, Commonwealth Parl. Asscn, Int. Bar Asscn, Int. Comm. of Jurists, Kenya Chapter; Parliamentarians for Global Action, Inter-Parl. Union. *Leisure interests:* reading, swimming and other health activities, farming, traveling, intellectual debates and politics. *Address:* Ministry of Foreign Affairs, Old Treasury Bldg, Harambee Avenue, POB 30551, Nairobi, Kenya (office). *Telephone:* (20) 334433 (office). *E-mail:* mfapress@nbnet.co.ke (office); mwetangula@hotmail.com (office). *Website:* www.mfa.go.ke (office).

WETHINGTON, Charles T., Jr, PhD; American fmr university president; b. 2 Jan. 1936, Merrimac, Ky; m. Judy Woodrow 1962; two c.; ed Brescia Coll., Eastern Ky Univ.; Instr. Univ. of Ky 1965–66; Dir Maysville Community Coll. 1967–71; Asst Vice-Pres. for the Community Coll. System, Univ. of Ky 1971–81, Vice-Pres. 1981–82, Chancellor 1982–88, Chancellor for the Community Coll. System and Univ. Relations 1988–89, Interim Pres. Univ. of Ky 1989–90, Pres. 1990–2001, then chief fund raiser; Dir Nat. Coll. Athletic Asscn Foundation 1999–2002. *Address:* c/o University of Kentucky, 5-52 Wm. T. Young Library, Lexington, KY 40506 (office); 2926 Four Pines Drive, Lexington, KY 40502, USA (home). *Telephone:* (606) 257-5646 (office). *Fax:* (859) 323-3777 (office).

WETTER, HE Cardinal Friedrich; German ecclesiastic; *Archbishop of Munich and Freising;* b. 20 Feb. 1928, Landau, Speyer; s. of Peter Wetter and Hedwig Böttinger; ed Univ. Gregoriana Rom; ordained priest 1953; Bishop of Speyer 1968–82; Archbishop of Munich and Freising 1982–; Cardinal-Priest of S. Stefano al Monte Celio 1985; Hon. Prof., Univ. of Mainz 1967–; Grosses Bundesverdienstkreuz mit Stern, Bayerischer Verdienstorden. *Publications:* Zeit-Worte 1993, Er allein trägt 1996, Mit Euch auf dem Weg 1998. *Address:* Postfach 330360, 80063 Munich, Germany. *Telephone:* (89) 21370. *Fax:* (89) 21371585. *Website:* www.erzbistum-muenchen-und-freising.de.

WETTSTEIN, Diter von, Dr rer. nat, Fil.Dr; Danish geneticist and academic; *R. A. Nilan Distinguished Professor, Department of Crop and Soil Sciences, Washington State University;* b. 20 Sept. 1929, Göttingen, Germany; s. of Fritz von Wettstein and Elsa Jesser; m. Penny von Wettstein-Knowles 1967; two d.; ed school in Innsbruck, Austria, Univ. of Tübingen, Germany, Univ. of Stockholm, Sweden; Research Asst, Genetics Dept, Forest Research Inst., Stockholm 1951–54; Asst and Assoc. Prof. in Genetics, Univ. of Stockholm 1954–62; Prof. of Genetics and Head, Inst. of Genetics, Univ. of Copenhagen, Denmark 1962–75; Acting Head, Dept of Physiology, Carlsberg Lab., Copenhagen 1972–75; Prof. of Physiology and Head of Dept 1975–96; R. A. Nilan Distinguished Prof. Washington State Univ. Pullman, Wash., USA 1994–; Rockefeller Fellow 1958; Visiting Prof., Univ. of Calif., Davis 1966, 1972, 1973, 1974, Washington State Univ. 1969; Hon. DrAgr. *Publications:* 300 scientific papers on mutation research, developmental physiology and cell research. *Address:* Department of Crop and Soil Sciences, Washington State University, Pullman, WA 99164, USA (office); Aasevej 13, 3500 Vaerløse, Denmark (home). *Telephone:* (509) 335-3635 (office); 44-48-19-98 (home). *Fax:* (509) 335-8674 (office). *E-mail:* diter@wsu.edu (office). *Website:* css.wsu.edu/people/faculty/crops/Wettstein.htm (office).

WEXLER, Haskell; American cinematographer; b. 6 Feb. 1926, Chicago, Ill.; m. Rita Taggart. *Cinematography:* Stakeout on Dope Street (uncredited) 1958, The Savage Eye 1960, Five Bold Women 1960, Studs Lonigan 1960, Hoodlum Priest 1961, Angel Baby 1961, AmericaAmerica 1963, Lonnie 1963, Face in the Rain 1963, The Best Man 1964, The Bus 1965, The Loved One (also producer) 1965, Who's Afraid of Virginia Woolf? (Acad. Award for Best Cinematography in Black-and-White 1967) 1966, In the Heat of the Night 1967, The Thomas Crown Affair 1968, Medium Cool 1969, Interviews with My Lai Veterans 1971, The Trial of the Catonsville Nine 1972, Introduction to the Enemy 1974, One Flew Over the Cuckoo's Nest 1975, Underground 1976, Bound for Glory 1976, Coming Home 1978, Paul Jacobs and the Nuclear Gang 1978, No Nukes 1980, Second-Hand Hearts 1981, Richard Pryor Live on the Sunset Strip 1982, Lookin' to Get Out 1982, The Man Who Loved Women 1983, Matewan 1987, Uncle Meat 1987, Colors 1988, Three Fugitives 1989, Blaze 1989, Other People's Money 1991, The Babe 1992, The Secret of Roan Inish 1994, Canadian Bacon 1995, The Sixth Sun: Mayan Uprising in Chiapas 1995, Mulholland Falls 1996, The Rich Man's Wife 1996, Limbo 1999, Bus Rider's Union 1999, Good KurdsBad Kurds: No Friends But the Mountains 2000, The Man On Lincoln's Nose 2000, 61* (TV) 2001, From Wharf Rats to the Lords of the Docks 2004, Silver City 2004; miscellaneous: Wild River (additional photographer, uncredited) 1960, Medium Cool (camera operator) 1969, Gimme Shelter (thanks) 1970, THX 1138 (special thanks) (director's cut) 1971, American Graffiti (visual consultant) 1973, Days of Heaven (additional cinematographer) 1978, The Rose (additional photographer: concert scenes) 1979, The Kid from Nowhere (TV) (photographer: Special Olympics) 1982, Blade Runner (additional photographer, uncredited) 1982, To the Moon Alice (TV) (camera operator: second unit) 1990, At the Max (camera consultant, camera operator) 1991, Visions of Light (special thanks from afi) 1992, A Few Good Men (thanks) 1992, Steal Big Steal Little (additional photographer) 1995, Bread and Roses (second camera operator) 2000, Tell Them Who You Are (additional camera operator) 2004. *Films directed:* The Bus (also producer and writer) 1965, Medium Cool (also actor, producer and writer) 1969, Brazil: A Report on Torture 1971, Introduction to the Enemy 1974, Underground 1976, Bus II 1983, Latino (also writer) 1985, Bus Rider's Union (also producer) 1999, From Wharf Rats to the Lords of the Docks 2004. *Film role:* Out of These Rooms 2002. *Address:* c/o ASC, POB 2230, Hollywood, CA 90078, USA.

WEXLER, Nancy Sabin, AB, PhD, FRCP; American neurologist and academic; *Higgins Professor of Neuropsychology, Departments of Neurology and Psychiatry, College of Physicians and Surgeons, Columbia University;* b. 19 July 1945, Washington, DC; ed Radcliffe Coll., Cambridge, Mass, Univ. of the West Indies, Jamaica (Fulbright Scholarship), Hampstead Clinic Child Psychoana-

lytic Training Inst., London, UK, Univ. of Michigan; Psychological Intern and Teaching Fellow, Univ. of Michigan 1968–74; Licensed Psychologist, New York State 1974–; Asst Prof. of Psychology, New School of Social Research, Grad. Faculty, New York City 1974–76; pvt. practice, psychologist, New York City 1974–76; Exec. Dir Congressional Comm. for Control of Huntington's Disease and Its Consequences, based in Nat. Inst. of Neurological, Communicative Disorders and Stroke, NIH, Bethesda, Md 1976–78; Co-organizer Public Forum on Nat. Genetic Diseases Act 1977; Health Science Admin. Demyelinating, Atrophic and Degenerative Diseases Program, Nat. Inst. of Neurological, Communicative Disorders and Stroke, NIH 1978–83; Pres. Hereditary Disease Foundation 1983–; Assoc. Prof. of Clinical Neuropsychology, Depts of Neurology and Psychiatry, Coll. of Physicians and Surgeons, Columbia Univ. 1985–92, mem. Center for Brain and Behavior 1985, Prof. of Clinical Neuropsychology 1992–93, Higgins Prof. of Neuropsychology 1993–; Chair. Jt NIH/DOE Ethical, Legal and Social Issues Working Group of Nat. Center for Human Genome Research, Human Genome Org. (HUGO); Councillor, Soc. for Neuroscience 2000–; mem. Inst. of Medicine, NAS 1997– (mem. Council 2007–); mem. Bd Dirs AAAS, Advisory Cttee on Research on Women's Health, NIH; mem. American Psychological Asscn, American Psychological Soc., American Soc. for Human Genetics, Soc. for Neuroscience, World Fed. of Neurology, Research Group on Huntington's Disease, American Neurological Asscn, American Soc. of Law and Medicine, Inst. of Medicine, NAS, European Acad. of Sciences and Arts 2001, American Acad. of Arts and Sciences 2005; Fellow, New York Acad. of Sciences 1998, AAAS 2002; Order of Merit in Work First Class (Venezuela) 1990; Hon. DHumLitt (New York Medical Coll.) 1991; Hon. DSc (Univ. of Michigan) 1991, (Bard Coll.) 1998; Hon. Doctor of Medical Sciences (Yale Univ.) 2006; PHS-NIMH Fellowship 1969–70, Univ. Fellowship 1973–74, PHS Certificate of Merit 1980, NIH Director's Award 1980, Hon. Declaration, Community of San Luis, Venezuela 1982, 1987, Award for Research, Nat. Huntington's Disease Soc. 1984, Landacre Day Award, Ohio State Univ. 1986, Maracaibo Rotary Club Award (Venezuela) 1986, Award for Research, Huntington's Disease Soc. of America 1986, The SOMA Distinguished Prof. Lecture Series, Univ. of California, San Diego School of Medicine 1987, First Robert J. and Claire Pasarow Foundation Award 1987, Living Legacy Award, Women's Int. Soc. 1988, Esquire Magazine Register 1988, Alumnae Athena Award, Alumnae Council, Univ. of Michigan 1989, Award from Gov.'s Office, State of Zulia, Venezuela 1989, Huntington's Disease Benefit Dinner Honoree 1989, Legislative Resolution of Commendation, New York State 1990, 21st Annual Louis B. Flexner Lecturer, Univ. of Pennsylvania 1992, Dean's Distinguished Lecture in the Clinical Sciences, Columbia Univ. 1992, Distinguished Service Award for Enhancing Educ. Through Biological Research, Nat. Asscn of Biology Teachers 1993, Foster Elting Bennett Memorial Lecturer, 118th Annual Meeting of American Neurological Asscn, Boston 1993, Nat. Health Council Nat. Medical Research Award to Huntington's Disease Collaborative Research Group 1993, Albert Lasker Public Service Award 1993, American Captains of Achievement Golden Plate Award, American Acad. of Achievement 1994, J. Allyn Taylor Int. Prize in Medicine 1994, Asscn of Neuroscience Depts and Programs' Educ. Award 1997, Venezuela Award, Casa Hogar 1999, Soc. for Neuroscience Public Advocacy Award 2003, Distinguished Investigator Award, NARSAD 2006, NARSAD Lieber Investigator 2006, Benjamin Franklin Medal in Life Science 2007. *Achievements include:* important scientific contrib. on Huntington's disease; 20-year study of world's largest family with Huntington's disease, in Venezuela, developing pedigree of more than 18,000 individuals and collecting more than 4,000 blood samples helped lead to identification of Huntington's disease gene on human chromosome 4. *Publications:* numerous scientific papers in professional journals. *Address:* College of Physicians and Surgeons, Columbia University, 1051 Riverside Drive, Unit 6, PI Annex 371, New York, NY 10032 (office); Hereditary Disease Foundation, 3960 Broadway, 6th Floor, New York, NY 10032, USA (office). *Telephone:* (212) 543-5667 (Coll. of Physicians) (office); (212) 928-2121 (Hereditary Disease Foundation) (office). *Fax:* (212) 543-6002 (Coll. of Physicians) (office); (212) 928-2172 (Hereditary Disease Foundation) (office). *E-mail:* wexlern@pi.cpmc.columbia.edu (office); cures@hdfoundation.org (office). *Website:* pi.cpmc.columbia.edu (office); www.hdfoundation.org (office).

WEXNER, Leslie Herbert; American retail executive; *Chairman and CEO, Limited Brands, Inc.;* b. 1937, Dayton, OH; m.; four c.; ed Ohio State Univ.; Founder, CEO and Chair. Limited Inc. fashion chain (now Limited Brands), Columbus, OH 1963–; Dir and mem. Exec. Comm. Banc One Corpn, Sotheby's Holdings Inc.; mem. Business Admin Advisory Council, Ohio State Univ.; Chair. Retail Industry Trade Action Coalition, Columbus Urban League 1982–84, Hebrew Immigrant Aid Soc. 1982–; Co-Chair. Int. United Jewish Appeal Cttee; Nat. Vice-Chair. and Treas. United Jewish Appeal; mem. Bd Dirs and Exec. Cttee American Jewish Jt Distribution Cttee Inc.; founding-mem. and first Chair. The Ohio State Univ. Foundation; mem. Exec. Cttee American Israel Public Affairs Cttee; fmr mem. Governing Cttee Columbus Foundation; Trustee Columbus Jewish Fed. 1972–, Columbus Jewish Foundation, Aspen Inst., Ohio State Univ., Columbus Capital Corpn for Civic Improvement; fmr Trustee Columbus Museum of Art, Columbus Symphony Orchestra, Whitney Museum of American Art, Capitol South Community Urban Redevelopment Corpn; mem. Young Presidents Org.; Cavaliere of Repub. of Italy; Hon. HHD 1986; Hon. LLD (Hofstra Univ.) 1987; Hon. LHD (Brandeis Univ.) 1990; Hon. PhD (Jewish Theological Seminary) 1990; American Marketing Asscn Man of the Year 1974. *Address:* Limited Brands, Inc., PO Box 16000, 3 Limited Way Parkway, Columbus, OH 43216, USA (office). *Telephone:* (614) 415-7000 (office). *Fax:* (614) 415-7440 (office). *Website:* www.limitedbrands.com (office).

WEYERGANS, François; Belgian writer and critic; b. 9 Dec. 1941, Etterbeek; ed Jesuit school, Brussels and Institut des Hautes Études

Cinématographiques, Paris; fmr film dir; literary and film critic, contributing to Cahiers du cinéma. *Films:* Béjart (writer, dir) 1962, Hieronymus Bosch (writer, dir) 1963, Cinéma de notre temps: Robert Bresson - Ni vu, ni connu (TV film; dir) 1965, Beaudelaire est mort en été (dir) 1967, Aline (writer, dir) 1967, Un film sur quelqu'un (dir) 1972, Maladie mortelle (dir) 1977, Je t'aime, tu danses (writer, dir) 1977, Couleur chair (writer, dir) 1979, Une femme en Afrique (writer) 1985. *Publications:* novels: Le Pitre (Prix Roger Nimier) 1973, Berlin, mercredi 1979, Les Figurants (Prix de la Société des Gens de Lettres, Académie Royale de Langue et de Littérature françaises de Belgique Prix Sander Pierron) 1980, Macaire le Copte (Prix Rossel, Belgium, Prix des Deux Magots) 1981, Le Radeau de la méduse (Prix méridien des quatre jurys) 1983, La Vie d'un bébé 1986, Françaises, français 1988, Je suis écrivain 1989, Rire et pleurer 1990, La Démence du boxeur (Prix Renaudot) 1992, Franz et François (Grand prix de la langue française) 1997, Salomé 2005, Trois jours chez ma mère (Prix Goncourt) 2005. *Address:* c/o Éditions Grasset, 61 rue des Saints-Pères, 75006 Paris, France.

WEYLAND, Joseph, DIur; Luxembourg diplomatist; b. 24 April 1943; m.; two s.; ed Institut d'Etudes Politiques, Paris, France; Attaché, Ministry of Foreign Affairs 1967, First Sec., Bonn 1969–72, Deputy Dir of Protocol and Legal Matters, Ministry of Foreign Affairs 1972–76, Deputy Perm. Rep. to EEC, Brussels 1976–79, Dir Econ. Relations and Co-operation, Ministry of Foreign Affairs 1979–83, Amb. and Perm. Rep. to UN, New York 1983–84, to EEC, Brussels 1984–91, Rep. to Inter-Governmental Conf. on Single European Act 1985, Chair. Cttee on Political Union at Inter-Governmental Conf. on Maastricht Treaty 1991, Sec.-Gen. Ministry of Foreign Affairs 1991–92, Amb. to UK (also accred to Ireland and Iceland) 1993–2002, Amb. to Belgium and Perm. Rep. to NATO, Brussels 2003–05, Amb. to USA (also accred to Canada, Mexico and OAS) 2005–08; mem. Bd Luxair 1979–83, 1991–92; mem. Bd SNCI and CFL 1979–83; Grand Officer, Order of Merit (Luxembourg), Commdr, Order of the Crown of Oak (Luxembourg), Commdr, Légion d'honneur, Grand Cross of the Order of Merit (Spain), Grand Cross (Belgium, Italy, Netherlands, Portugal). *Leisure interests:* modern art, sculpture, music, travel. *Address:* Ministry of Foreign Affairs and Immigration, Hôtel St Maximin, 5 rue Notre-Dame, 2240 Luxembourg-Ville, Luxembourg (office). *Telephone:* 478-1 (office). *Fax:* 22-31-44 (office). *E-mail:* officielle.boite@mae .etat.lu (office). *Website:* www.mae.lu (office).

WEYMANN, Gert; German theatre director and playwright; b. 31 March 1919, Berlin; s. of Hans Weymann and Gertrud Israel; ed Grammar School, Berlin and Berlin Univ.; asst dir, later dir Berlin theatre 1947–; worked as dir in several W German cities and New York; Lecturer in Drama Depts, American univs 1963, 1966; Lecturer, Goethe Inst., Berlin 1970–; perm. ind. mem. SFB (radio and TV plays). *Plays:* Generationen (Gerhart Hauptmann Prize 1954), Eh' die Brücken verbrennen, Der Ehrentag; TV plays: Das Liebesmahl eines Wucherers, Familie 1960; radio plays: Der Anhalter, Die Übergabe. *Address:* Karlsruher Strasse 7, 10711 Berlin, Germany. *Telephone:* (89) 11861.

WHALLEY, Joanne; British actress; b. 25 Aug. 1964, Salford; m. Val Kilmer 1988 (divorced 1996); one s. one d.; stage career began during teens and has included season of Edward Bond plays at Royal Court Theatre, London and appearances in The Three Sisters, What the Butler Saw (NW Manhattan Theatre Club), Lulu (Almeida, London). *Films include:* Pink Floyd: The Wall 1982, Dance With a Stranger 1985, No Surrender 1985, The Good Father 1985, Will You Love Me Tomorrow 1987, Willow 1988, To Kill a Priest 1988, Scandal 1989, Kill Me Again 1989, The Big Man 1990, Navy Seals 1990, Miss Helen, Shattered 1991, Crossing the Line, Storyville 1992, The Secret Rapture 1993, Mother's Boys 1994, A Good Man in Africa 1994, Trial By Jury 1994, The Man Who Knew Too Little 1997, A Texas Funeral 1999, Run the Wild Fields 2000, The Guilty 2000, Breathtaking 2000, Virginia's Run 2001, Before You Go 2002, The Californians 2005, Played 2006, Flood 2007. *Television includes:* Coronation Street (series) 1974, Emmerdale Farm (series) 1977, A Kind of Loving (series) 1982, Reilly: The Ace of Spies (mini-series) 1983, Edge of Darkness (mini-series) 1985, The Singing Detective (mini-series) 1986, A TV Dante (mini-series) 1989, Scarlett (mini-series) 1994, Jackie Bouvier Kennedy Onassis (mini-series) 2000, 40 2003, Child of Mine 2005, Life Line 2007, Diverted 2009. *Address:* Creative Artists Agency, 2000 Avenue of the Stars, Los Angeles, CA 90067, USA.

WHARTON, Clifton R., Jr., PhD; American academic, university administrator, financial services executive and government official; *Co-Vice Chairman, Knight Foundation Commission on Intercollegiate Athletics;* b. 13 Sept. 1926, Boston, Mass.; s. of Hon. Clifton R. Wharton Sr and Harriette B. Wharton; m. Dolores Duncan 1950; one s.; ed Boston Latin School, Harvard Univ., Johns Hopkins Univ. School of Advanced Int. Studies and Univ. of Chicago; Head of Reports and Analysis Dept, American Int. Asscn for Econ. and Social Devt 1948–53; Research Assoc., Univ. of Chicago 1953–57; Assoc., Agricultural Devt Council 1957–58, stationed in SE Asia 1958–64, Dir of the Council's American Univs. Research Program 1964–66, Vice-Pres. 1967–69, mem. Bd of Dirs 1973–80; Pres. Mich. State Univ. and Prof. of Econs 1970–78; Chancellor, State Univ. of NY System 1978–87; Chair. and CEO TIAA-CREF 1987–93; Deputy Sec. of State, US Dept of State 1993; Visiting Prof., Univ. of Malaya 1958–64, Stanford Univ. 1964–65; fmr Chair. Bd for Int. Food and Agric. Devt (AID), US Dept of State; mem. Presidential Comm. on World Hunger, Presidential Mission to Latin America, Presidential Mission to S Viet Nam; Chair. Bd Rockefeller Foundation 1982–87; mem. Knight Foundation Comm. on Intercollegiate Athletics 1989–, Co-Vice Chair. 2005–; dir of numerous cos and orgs including Ford Motor Co. 1973–93, 1994–97, Tenneco Inc. 1994–99, NY Stock Exchange 1991–93, 1994–2000, Harcourt Gen. 1994–2001, Equitable Life 1969–82, Overseas Devt Council 1969–79, 1994–2000, Aspen Inst. 1980–93, Time Inc. 1982–89, Federated Dept Stores

1985–88, Rockefeller Foundation 1970–87; Comm. for Econ. Devt 1980–93, 1994–; Deputy Chair. Fed. Reserve Bank, New York 1985–86; mem. Knight Foundation Comm. on Inter-collegiate Athletics 1990–93, Council on Foreign Relations 1983–93, Advisory Comm. on Trade Policy and Negotiations 1990–93; 62 hon. degrees. *Publications:* Subsistence Agriculture and Economic Development (ed.) 1969, Patterns for Lifelong Learning (co-author) 1973. *Address:* c/o Knight Foundation Commission on Intercollegiate Athletics, One Biscayne Tower, Suite 3800, 2 South Biscayne Blvd., Miami, FL 33131-1803, USA (office). *Website:* www.knightcommission.org (office).

WHEATLEY, Glenn Dawson; Australian media executive; *Managing Director, TalentWORKS Pty.;* b. 23 Jan. 1948, Nambour, Queensland; s. of William Dawson Wheatley and Freda Aileen Evans; m. Gaynor Cherie Martin 1982; one s. two d.; guitarist, Purple Hearts 1966, Bay City Union 1966–67, The Master's Apprentices 1967–72; Founder, Man. Dir The Wheatley Org. (TWO Australia Ltd) 1975–92, Hoyts Media (fmrly Wheatley Communications Pty Ltd) 1987–89, Emerald City Records 1991–, TalentWORKS Pty Ltd 1996–; a founding Dir 92.3 EON FM radio station 1980; Man. Dir Radio 2BE Bega NSW 1987–89, Radio 3CV Vic. 1987–89; Co-owner and Dir Sydney Swans Football Club 1988–90; Dir Advantage Int. (fmrly Wheatley Sport Pty Ltd) 1985–88, Sydney Hard Rock Cafe 1988–89; Bd mem. Ausmusic 1993; mem. Tourism Task Force 1990–92; Cttee mem. Austrade (Music) 1986; Trustee AIDS Trust Australia 1990–93; Outstanding Contrib. in Entertainment Industry award, Advance Australia 1987, Marketing Award, Business Review Weekly 1988, Queensland Apprentice of the Year 1965, Aria Hall of Fame 1999. *Leisure interest:* golf. *Address:* TalentWORKS Pty Ltd, Suite 1A, 663 Victoria Street, Abbotsford, Vic. 3067, Australia. *Telephone:* (3) 9429-6933. *Fax:* (3) 9428-7433.

WHEELER, Graeme; New Zealand banker and international organization executive; *Managing Director, World Bank Group;* fmr Dir of Macroeconomic Policy and Strategy, NZ Treasury, fmr Treas. NZ Debt Man. Office and Deputy Sec. NZ Treasury; Dir Financial Products and Services Dept, World Bank (IBRD) 1997–2001, Vice-Pres. and Treas. 2001–05, Acting Man. Dir, then Man. Dir 2005–. *Address:* The World Bank Group, 1818 H Street, NW, Washington, DC 20433, USA (office). *Telephone:* (202) 473-1000 (office). *Fax:* (202) 477-6391 (office). *E-mail:* pic@worldbank.org (office). *Website:* web .worldbank.org (office).

WHEELER, Sir (Harry) Anthony, Kt, OBE, BArch, FRIBA; British architect and town planner (retd); b. 7 Nov. 1919, Stranraer; s. of Herbert G. Wheeler and Laura E. Groom; m. Dorothy J. Campbell 1944; one d.; ed Stranraer High School, Royal Tech. Coll. Glasgow, Glasgow School of Art and Glasgow School of Architecture, Univ. of Strathclyde; Asst City Architect, Oxford 1949; Asst Sir Herbert Baker & Scott, London 1949; Sr Architect, Glenrothes New Town 1949–51; Sr Lecturer, Dundee School of Architecture 1952–58; commenced pvt. practice, Fife 1952; Sr Partner, Wheeler & Sproson, Edinburgh and Kirkcaldy 1954–86, consultant 1986–89; Pres. Royal Scottish Acad. 1983–90; prin. works include St Columba's Parish Church, Glenrothes, reconstruction The Giles, Pittenweem, redevelopment Dysart and Old Buckhaven, Students' Union, Univ. of St Andrews, Leonard Horner Hall and Students' Union, Heriot-Watt Univ., Hunter Bldg Edinburgh Coll. of Art, St Peter's Episcopal Church, Kirkcaldy, Museum of Childhood, Edinburgh, town centre renewal, Grangemouth and Community and Outdoor Educ. Centre, Linlithgow; Past Pres. Royal Incorporation of Architects in Scotland; Hon. Pres. Saltire Soc. 1995; Hon. RA; Hon. Royal Glasgow Inst.; Hon. mem. Royal Hibernian Acad., Royal Soc. of British Sculptors; Hon. Dr Design (Rebort Gordon's Univ. Aberdeen 1991; 22 Saltire Soc. Housing Awards; 12 Civic Trust Awards and commendations. *Leisure interests:* sketching and water-colour painting, fishing, gardens, music, drama. *Address:* South Inverleith Manor, 31/6 Kinnear Road, Edinburgh, EH3 5PG, Scotland (home). *Telephone:* (131) 552-3854 (home).

WHEELER, Gen. Sir Roger Neil, GCB, CBE, MA, FRGS; British army officer; *Constable, HM Tower of London;* b. 16 Dec. 1941, Fulmer, Bucks.; s. of Maj.-Gen. T.N.S. Wheeler, C.B., CBE; m. Felicity Hares 1980; three s. one d. from a previous marriage; ed All Hallows School, Devon and Hertford Coll. Oxford; commissioned Royal Ulster Rifles 1964; early service in Borneo, the Middle East and Cyprus; Chief of Staff, Falkland Islands June–Dec. 1982; Command, 11th Armoured Brig. 1985–87; Dir Army Plans 1987–89; Command, 1st Armoured Div. 1989–90; Asst Chief of Gen. Staff, Ministry of Defence 1990–92; G.O.C. Northern Ireland 1993–96; C-in-C Land Command 1996–97; Chief of Gen. Staff. 1997–2000; ADC Gen. to Queen 1996–2000; Constable HM Tower of London 2001–; Pres. Army Rugby Football Union 1995–99, Army Rifle Assoc. 1995–2000; Col The Royal Irish Regt 1996–2001; Col Commdt Intelligence Corps 1996–2001; Pres. Combat Stress 2001–; Dir Thales UK PLC 2001–, Aegis Specialist Risk Man. 2005–, Serious and Organised Crime Agency 2005–; Patron Police Foundation 2001–; Hon. Fellow, Hertford Coll. Oxford. *Leisure interests:* fly fishing, ornithology, cricket, shooting. *Address:* Constable, HM Tower of London, London, EC3N 4AB, England.

WHELAN, Michael John, PhD, FRS, FInstP; British scientist and academic; *Professor Emeritus and Fellow, Linacre College, University of Oxford;* b. 2 Nov. 1931, Leeds; s. of William Whelan and Ellen Whelan (née Pound); ed Gonville and Caius Coll., Cambridge; Royal Soc. Mr and Mrs John Jaffé Donation Research Fellow 1959–61; Demonstrator in Physics, Univ. of Cambridge 1961–65, Asst Dir of Research 1965–66, Fellow of Gonville and Caius Coll. 1958–66; Reader, Dept of Materials, Univ. of Oxford 1966–92, Prof. 1992–97, Prof. Emer. 1997–; Fellow, Linacre Coll., Univ. of Oxford 1968–; Hon. Prof., Univ. of Science and Tech., Beijing 1995; Hon. Fellow, Royal Microscopical Soc. 2001, Japanese Soc. of Microscopy 2003; C.V. Boys Prize, Inst. of Physics 1965, Hughes Medal, Royal Soc. 1988, Distinguished Scientist Award, Microscope Soc. of America 1998. *Publications:* Electron Microscopy of

Thin Crystals (co-author) 1965, Worked Examples in Dislocations 1990, High-Energy Electron Diffraction and Microscopy (co-author) 2004, numerous papers and articles in scientific journals. *Leisure interests:* gardening, tinkering, Japanese language. *Address:* Department of Materials, Engineering and Technology Buildling, Room 50.14, Parks Road, Oxford, OX1 3PH (office); 18 Salford Road, Old Marston, Oxford, OX3 0RX, England (home). *Telephone:* (1865) 273700 (office); (1865) 273742 (office); (1865) 244556 (home). *Fax:* (1865) 273789 (office); (1865) 244556 (home). *E-mail:* michael.whelan@materials.ox.ac.uk (office). *Website:* www.materials.ox.ac.uk/peoplepages/whelan.html (home).

WHELAN, Noel, BComm, MEconSc, PhD, DPA; Irish civil servant, international public servant, academic and banker; *Vice-President/Dean/Professor Emeritus, University of Limerick;* b. 28 Dec. 1940, Cork; s. of Richard Whelan and Ann Whelan (née Crowley); m. Joan Gaughan 1970; two s. two d.; ed Sacred Heart Coll., Buttevant, Univ. Coll., Dublin; Exec. Officer, Irish Civil Service 1960–62; Sr Admin. Officer and Head of Research Evaluation, an Foras Taluntais (Agricultural Research Inst. of Ireland) 1962–69; Asst Gen. Man. Córas Iompair Éireann (Irish Transport Authority) 1969–74; Deputy Sec. Dept of Public Service and Dept of Finance 1974–77; Special Consultant, OECD (part-time) 1975–80; Sec. Dept of Econ. Planning and Devt 1977–80; Sec. Dept of the Taoiseach (Prime Minister) 1979–82, 1988–; Chair. Sectoral Devt Cttee, Irish Govt 1980–82; Vice-Pres. and Vice-Chair. Bd of Dirs European Investment Bank, Luxembourg 1982–88, Hon. Vice-Pres. 1988–; Vice-Pres. External Univ. of Limerick, Dean, Coll. of Business 1989–, Prof. of Business and Man. 1989–2005; Chair. Sectoral Devt Cttee 1989–97; Special Consultant, UN and World Bank 1989–; Chair./Dir Corp. Bds 1989–; Chair. Nat. Econ. and Social Council of Ireland 1978–84; Adviser to Irish Ministry of Foreign Affairs on Ireland's Foreign Aid Programme 1999–; Chair. Telephone Users' Advisory Council 1993–98; Chair. Caritas Consultative Forum (Health Sector) 1998–, Nat. Adult Learning Council of Ireland 2000–, St Vincent's Healthcare Group 2002–, Dublin Area Teaching Hosps' Group 1998–, State Claims Agency 2002–; Pres. European Univ. Foundation 2002–07, Pres. Emer. 2008–, mem. Strategic Evaluation Panel, European Univ. Asscn; Dir (non-exec.) on various pvt. sector corp. bds; Pres. and Chair. Inst. of Public Admin. (part-time); Council mem. and mem. Exec. Cttee, Econ. and Social Research Inst.; Council mem. Statistical and Social Enquiry Soc.; Council mem. and Fellow, Irish Man. Inst. 1984–. *Publications:* miscellaneous papers and reports in various academic and research journals. *Leisure interests:* reading, photography, music. *Address:* Office of the President External, University of Limerick, Limerick (office); 29 Maxwell Road, Rathgar, Dublin 6, Ireland (home). *Telephone:* (86) 2593019 (mobile) (office); (1) 4960646 (home). *E-mail:* noel.whelan@ul.ie (office); noelwhelan2@yahoo.ie (home). *Website:* www.ul.ie (office).

WHELAN, Peter, BA; British playwright; b. 3 Oct. 1931, Newcastle-under-Lyme, England; two s. one d.; ed Univ. of Keele, Staffordshire; advertising copywriter and Dir 1959–90; Hon. Assoc. RSC 1995; Lloyds Private Banking Playwright of the Year 1996, TMA Regional Theatre Award for Best New Play 1996. *Plays:* Double Edge (with Leslie Darbon, Vaudeville Theatre) 1975, Captain Swing (RSC) 1978, The Accrington Pals 1981, Clay 1982, The Bright and Bold Design 1991, The School of Night 1992, Shakespeare Country 1993, The Tinderbox 1994, Divine Right 1996, The Herbal Bed (West End and Broadway) 1996, Nativity (co-author) 1999, A Russian in the Woods (RSC) 2001, The Earthly Paradise (Almeida, London) 2004. *Address:* The Agency, 24 Pottery Lane, Holland Park, London, W11 4LZ, England (office). *Telephone:* (20) 7727-1346 (office). *E-mail:* info@theagency.co.uk (office). *Website:* www.theagency.co.uk (office).

WHELDON, Dan; British racing driver; b. 22 June 1978, Emberton; began racing go-karts aged four; moved quickly through ranks competing in European formula; moved to USA 1999, competed in F2000 series; finsihed second to Andretti Green Racing team-mate Tony Kanaan in Indy Racing League (IRL) standings 2004; winner, IRL Driver's Championship 2005, six wins in 17 races, breaking Sam Hornish Jr's IRL record for most wins in a season; winner Indianapolis 500 2005 in only his third attempt, first Englishman to win since the late Graham Hill 1966; posted 12 Top-5 finishes and 15 Top-10 finishes 2005; first Englishman and first driver since Jacques Villeneuve in 1995 to win both Indy 500 and major Driver's Championship in same season 2005; tied with Scott Sharp for second all-time in career IRL wins; ranks in IRL's Top 10 for: most Top 5 finishes (5th), races led (5th), most Top 10 finishes (6th), laps led (6th) and career earnings (9th); Rookie of the Year 1999, 2000, 2001, 2003. *Address:* c/o Adrian Sussmann, Vice-President, Client Management North America, CSS Stellar Management, 2801 Youngfield, Suite 210, Golden, CO 80401, USA. *Telephone:* (303) 234-5742. *E-mail:* adrian.sussmann@css-stellar.com. *Website:* www.danwheldon.com; www.css-stellar-management.com.

WHICKER, Alan Donald, CBE, FRSA; British television broadcaster, journalist and author; b. 2 Aug. 1925; s. of the late Charles Henry Whicker and Anne Jane Cross; ed Haberdashers' Aske's; Dir Army Film and Photo Unit, with 8th Army and US 5th Army; war corresp., Korea; Foreign Corresp. Exchange Telegraph 1947–57, BBC TV 1957–68; Founder mem. Yorkshire TV 1968; various awards, including Guild of TV Producers and Dirs., Personality of the Year 1964, Silver Medal, Royal TV Soc., Dimbleby Award, BAFTA 1978, TV Times Special Award 1978, first to be named in Royal Television Soc.'s new Hall of Fame for outstanding creative contrib. to British TV 1993, Travel Writers' Special Award, for truly outstanding achievement in travel journalism 1998, BAFTA Grierson Documentary Tribute Award 2001, Nat. Film Theatre tribute, sixth Television Festival 2002. *Radio includes:* Whicker's Wireless World (BBC Radio series) 1983; Around Whicker's World (six programmes for Radio 2) 1998, Whicker's New World (7 programmes for Radio 2) 1999, Whicker's World Down Under (6 programmes for Radio 2) 2000, Fabulous Fifties (4 programmes for Radio 2) 2000, It'll Never Last—The History of Television (6 programmes for Radio 2) 2001, Fifty Royal Years (6 programmes celebrating Queen's Golden Jubilee, Radio 2), Around Whicker's World (series of Radio 4 essays) 2002. *Television:* joined BBC TV 1957; regular appearances on 'Tonight' programme, then series Whicker's World 1959–60, Whicker Down Under 1961, Whicker in Sweden 1963, Whicker's World 1965–67; made 122 documentaries for Yorkshire TV including Whicker's New World Series, Whicker in Europe, World of Whicker; returned to BBC TV 1982; programmes include: Whicker's World – The First Million Miles! (four programmes) 1982, Whicker's World, A Fast Boat to China (four programmes) 1983, Whicker! (series talk shows) 1984, Whicker's World – Living with Uncle Sam (10 programmes) 1985, Whicker's World – Living with Waltzing Matilda (10 programmes) 1988, Whicker's World – Hong Kong (eight programmes) 1990, Whicker's World – A Taste of Spain (eight programmes) 1992, Around Whicker's World (four programmes, for ITV) 1992, Whicker's World – The Sultan of Brunei 1992, South Africa: Whicker's Miss World and Whicker's World – The Sun King 1993, South-East Asia: Whicker's World Aboard the Real Orient Express, Whicker's World – Pavarotti in Paradise 1994, Travel Channel (26 programmes) 1996, Whicker's Week, BBC Choice 1999; Travel Amb. on the Internet for AOL 2000; One on One 2002, Whicker's War Series (Channel 4) 2004, Comedy Map of Britain (series of 12 programmes) 2007, Comedy Map of Britain (four programmes) 2008, Whicker's World: Journey of a Lifetime (four programmes) 2009. *Publications:* Some Rise by Sin 1949, Away – With Alan Whicker 1963, Best of Everything 1980, Within Whicker's World (autobiog.) 1982, Whicker's Business Travellers Guide 1983, Whicker's New World 1985, Whicker's World Down Under 1988, Whicker's World – Take 2! 2000, Whicker's War 2005, Whicker's World: Journey of a Lifetime 2009. *Address:* Trinity, Jersey, JE3 5BA, Channel Islands.

WHINNERY, John Roy, PhD; American electrical engineer and academic; *University Professor Emeritus, Department of Electrical Engineering and Computer Sciences, University of California, Berkeley;* b. 26 July 1916; s. of Ralph Vincent Whinnery and Edith Bent Whinnery; m. Patricia Barry 1944; three d.; ed Modesto Jr Coll. Calif., Univ. of Calif., Berkeley; student engineer to Research Engineer, Gen. Electric Co. 1937–46; Lecturer, Union Coll., Schenectady, NY, 1945–46; Lecturer, Univ. of Calif., Berkeley, Assoc. Prof., Prof., Chair. of Dept, Dean of Coll. 1959–63, Univ. Prof. 1980–; Guggenheim Fellow ETH, Zurich, Switzerland 1959; Head of Microwave Tube Research at Hughes Aircraft Co., Culver City, Calif. 1952–53; Visiting mem. of Tech. Staff, Bell Telephone Labs 1963–64; Visiting Prof., Stanford Univ. 1969–70; Research Professorship in Miller Inst. for Basic Research in Science 1973–74; mem. Visiting Review Bd, Dept of Electrical Eng, MIT 1968, Div. of Applied Science, Harvard Univ. 1974, 1979, 1980, 1981, 1982, 1983, Dept of Eng and Applied Science, Calif. Inst. of Tech. 1977, 1979, 1980; Hon. Prof. of Chengdu Inst. of Tech., Sichuan, Chengdu, People's Repub. of China 1986; Fellow, Univ. of Calif., Berkeley 1990; IEEE Microwave Theory and Techniques Soc. Distinguished Lecturer for US 1990; mem. Nat. Acad. of Eng 1965, Pres.'s Cttee Nat. Medal of Science 1970–72, 1979–81, NAS 1973, Optical Soc. of America, American Acad. of Arts and Sciences; Life mem. IEEE, American Soc. for Eng Educ.; Fellow AAAS; Okawa Prize in Information and Telecommunications 1997; IEEE Educ. Medal, Outstanding Educators of America Award, Univ. of Calif., Berkeley 1974, Lamme Award of American Soc. on Eng Educ. 1975, IEEE Microwave Career Award 1976, Distinguished Eng Alumnus Award, Univ. of Calif., Berkeley 1980, IEEE Centennial Medallist 1984, IEEE Medal of Honor Award 1985, Founder's Award, Nat. Acad. of Eng 1986, Berkeley Citation, Univ. of Calif., Berkeley 1987, Nat. Medal of Science 1992, American Soc. for Eng Educ. Hall of Fame and Centennial Medal awards 1993, John R. Whinnery Chair in Electrical Eng est. at Univ. of Calif., Berkeley 1994. *Publications:* Fields and Waves in Modern Radio (with Simon Ramo) 1944, 1952, World of Engineering 1965, Fields and Waves in Communication Electronics (with Simon Ramo and T. Van Duzer) 1965, Introduction to Electronic Systems Circuits and Devices (with D. O. Pederson and J. J. Studer) 1966, 140 tech. articles and patents on microwaves and lasers. *Leisure interests:* hiking, skiing, golf, writing poetry and children's stories. *Address:* Department of Electrical Engineering and Computer Sciences, 193M Cory Hall #1770, Univ. of California, Berkeley, CA 94720-1770 (office); 1804 Wales Drive, Walnut Creek, CA 94595, USA (home). *Telephone:* (510) 642-1030 (office); (925) 256-9136 (home). *Fax:* (510) 642-2845 (office). *E-mail:* whinnery@eecs.berkeley.edu (office). *Website:* www.eecs.berkeley.edu (office).

WHISHAW, Anthony Popham Law, RA, ARCA; British artist; b. 22 May 1930, London; s. of Robert Whishaw and Joyce Wheeler; m. Jean Gibson 1957; two d.; ed Chelsea School of Art, Royal Coll. of Art; work for BBC Monitor, work in collections including Arts Council of GB, Bolton Art Gallery, Chantrey Bequest, City Art Galleries, Sheffield, Coventry Art Gallery, Dept of the Environment, European Parl., Strasbourg, Huddersfield Museum and Art Gallery, Leicester City Art Gallery, Museu de Arte da Bahia, Brazil, Museo de Murcia, Spain, Nat. Gallery of Victoria, Melbourne, Australia, Museum of Contemporary Art, Helsinki, Nat. Gallery of Wales, RCA, London, Royal Acad., London, Seattle Museum of Art, USA, Tate Gallery, London, Western Australia Gallery and several pvt. and corp. collections; Hon. mem. Royal West of England Acad.; Royal Coll. of Art Travelling Scholarship 1952, Royal Coll. of Art Drawing Prize 1953, Abbey Minor Scholarship 1954, Spanish Govt Scholarship 1954, Spanish Govt Scholarship 1955, Perth Int. Drawing Biennale Prize 1973, Byer Int. Painting Prize 1973, South East Arts Asscn Painting Prize 1975, Greater London Arts Council Award 1978, Greater London Council Painting Prize 1981, Abbey Premier Scholarship 1982, Lorne Scholarship 1982, Jt Winner, Hunting Group Nat. Art Competition 1986, Korn Ferry Carre Oban Int. Picture of the Year 1996. *Address:* 7A Albert

Place, Victoria Road, London, W8 5PD, England. *Telephone:* (20) 8981-2139 (Studio); (20) 7937-5197 (home). *Fax:* (20) 7937-5197 (home). *Website:* www .anthonywhishaw.com (home).

WHITACRE, Edward E., Jr, BEng; American business executive; b. 4 Nov. 1941, Ennis, Tex.; ed Texas Tech. Univ.; joined Southwestern Bell Telephone Co., Dallas, Tex. 1963, subsequently facility engineer, Lubbock and various posts in operational depts, Texas, Arkansas and Kansas; Pres. Kansas Div. 1982–85; Group Pres., subsequently Vice-Pres. (Revenues and Public Affairs), Vice-Chair. and Chief Financial Officer, Southwestern Bell Corpn 1986–88, Pres. and COO 1988–90, Chair. of Bd and CEO (subsequently called SBC Communications Inc.) 1990–2005, Chair. and CEO AT&T Inc. (after merger of SBC Communications and AT&T) 2005–07; mem. Bd of Dirs Anheuser-Busch Cos Inc., May Department Stores Co., Emerson Electric Co., Burlington Northern Inc.; mem. Bd of Regents, Tex. Tech. Univ. and Tex. Tech. Univ. Health Sciences Center; mem. Bd of Govs, Southwest Foundation for Biomedical Research; Trustee Southwest Research Inst.; Int. Citizen of the Year Award, World Affairs Council, San Antonio 1997, Spirit of Achievement Award, Nat. Jewish Medical and Research Center 1998, Freeman Award, San Antonio Chamber of Commerce 1998. *Address:* c/o AT&T Inc., Room 40, 175 E Houston Street, San Antonio, TX 78205-2233, USA (home).

WHITAKER, Forest; American actor and film director; b. 15 July 1961, Longview, Tex.; m. Keisha Whitaker; two c.; ed School of Theater, Univ. of Southern California; f. Spirit Dance Entertainment (production co.); BET Award for Best Actor 2007. *Films include:* Tag: The Assassination Game 1982, Fast Times at Ridgemont High 1982, Vision Quest 1985, The Color of Money 1986, Platoon 1986, Stakeout 1987, Good Morning, Vietnam 1987, Bloodsport 1988, Bird 1988, Johnny Handsome 1989, Downtown 1990, A Rage in Harlem 1991, Diary of a Hitman 1991, Article 99 1992, The Crying Game 1992, Consenting Adults 1992, Body Snatchers 1993, Bank Robber 1993, Blown Away 1994, Jason's Lyric 1994, Prêt-à-Porter 1994, Waiting to Exhale (dir) 1995, Smoke 1995, Species 1995, Phenomenon 1996, Body Count 1998, Hope Floats (dir) 1998, Ghost Dog: The Way of the Samurai 1999, Light It Up 1999, Battlefield Earth 2000, Four Dogs Playing Poker 2000, Green Dragon 2001, The Fourth Angel 2001, Panic Room 2002, Phone Booth 2002, First Daughter (dir, producer and voice) 2004, Mary 2005, A Little Trip to Heaven 2005, American Gun 2005, The Marsh 2006, Even Money 2006, The Last King of Scotland (Best Actor, Nat. Bd of Review 2006, Best Actor, Los Angeles Film Critics Asscn 2006, Nat. Soc. of Film Critics 2007, Golden Globe for Best Actor (drama) 2007, Screen Actors' Guild Award for Outstanding Performance by an Actor in a Leading Role 2007, Best Actor, London Film Critics' Circle Awards 2007, BAFTA Award for Best Actor 2007, Acad. Award for Best Actor 2007) 2006, Everyone's Hero (voice) 2006, The Air I Breathe 2007, Ripple Effect 2007, The Great Debaters 2007, Vantage Point 2008, Street Kings 2008. *Television includes:* North and South (mini-series) 1985, Strapped (dir) 1993, North and South, Book II (mini-series) 1986, Black Jaq (dir) 1998, Witness Protection 1999, Twilight Zone (series) 2002–03, Deacons for Defense 2003, The Shield (series) 2006. *Address:* Spirit Dance Entertainment, 1023 North Orange Drive, Los Angeles, CA 90038-2317; c/o William Morris Agency, Inc., 1 William Morris Place, Beverly Hills, CA 90212, USA. *Telephone:* (323) 512-7988 (Spirit Dance); (310) 859-4000. *Fax:* (310) 859-4462. *Website:* www.wma .com.

WHITBREAD, Samuel Charles, JP; British business executive; b. 22 Feb. 1937, London; s. of Major Simon Whitbread and H. B. M. Trefusis; m. Jane M. Hayter 1961; three s. one d.; ed Eton Coll.; served Beds. and Herts. Regt 1955–57; Dir Whitbread & Co. 1972, Deputy Chair. 1984, Chair. Whitbread & Co. (Whitbread PLC from 1991) 1984–92, Dir 1972–2001; Chair. Herts. Timber Supplies 2000–; Vice-Pres. East Anglia TA and VRA 1991–; Lord-Lt of Bedfordshire 1991–; Hon. LLB (Bedfordshire). *Publications:* Southill and the Whitbreads 1995, Straws in the Wind 1997, Plain Mr Whitbread 2007. *Leisure interests:* shooting, travel, painting, music. *Address:* Glebe House Southill, Biggleswade, Beds., SG18 9LL, England (home). *Telephone:* (1462) 813272 (home).

WHITE, B. Joseph, DBA; American academic and university administrator; *President, University of Illinois;* b. Detroit; m. Mary White; two c.; ed Georgetown Univ. School of Foreign Service, Washington, DC, Harvard Univ., Univ. of Mich.; Asst Prof. of Organizational Behavior and Industrial Relations, Univ. of Mich. 1975, Assoc. Prof. 1978–80, Assoc. Dean Business School 1987–90, Interim Dean 1990–91, Dean 1991–2001, Pres. William Davidson Inst. 1993–2001, Interim Pres. Univ. of Mich. 2002, Wilbur K. Pierpont Collegiate Prof., Prof. of Business Admin, Research Prof., Life Sciences Inst. and Head, Project for a Positive Healthcare Future 2002–05; Pres. Univ. of Illinois 2005–; Vice-Pres. for Man. Devt, later Vice-Pres. for Personnel and Public Affairs, Cummins Engine Co., Inc. 1981–87; ind. dir or trustee of several cos including Equity Residential, Chicago, Gordon Food Service, Kaydon Corpn, Kelly Services; mem. Bd of Dirs W. E. Upjohn Inst. for Employment Research; fmr chair. several large healthcare orgs including Univ. of Mich. Health System, St Joseph Hosp., Ann Arbor, Catherine McAuley Health System; hon. degree (Wabash Coll.) 2003. *Publications:* numerous articles on leadership, man. and organizational matters. *Address:* President's Office, 364 Henry Administration Building, m/c 346, 506 South Wright Street, Urbana, IL 61801, USA (office). *Telephone:* (217) 333-3070 (office). *Fax:* (217) 333-3072 (office). *E-mail:* bjwhite@uillinois.edu (office). *Website:* www.uillinois.edu (office); www.uiuc.edu.

WHITE, Sir Christopher John, Kt., CVO, PhD, FBA; British arts administrator (retd); b. 19 Sept. 1930; s. of Gabriel Ernest E. F. White; m. Rosemary Katharine Desages 1957; one s. two d.; ed Downside School, Courtauld Inst. of Art, Univ. of London; army service 1949–50; Asst Keeper, Dept of Prints and Drawings, British Museum 1954–65; Dir P. and D. Colnaghi 1965–71; Curator

of Graphic Arts, Nat. Gallery of Art, Washington 1971–73; Dir of Studies, Paul Mellon Centre for Studies in British Art 1973–85; Assoc. Dir Yale Centre for British Art, New Haven 1976–85; Adjunct Prof. of History of Art, Yale Univ. 1977–85; Dir Ashmolean Museum, Oxford 1985–97; Fellow, Worcester Coll., Oxford 1985–97; Prof. of the Art of the Netherlands, Oxford 1992–97; Hermione Lecturer, Alexandra Coll., Dublin 1959; Adjunct Prof., Inst. of Fine Arts, New York Univ. 1973, 1976; Visiting Prof., Yale Univ. 1976; Conf. Dir, European-American Ass. on Art Museums 1975; Reviews Ed., Master Drawings 1967–80; Gov. British Inst. of Florence 1994–2002; Trustee Victoria and Albert Museum 1997–2004; mem. Exec. Cttee NACF 1998, Raad van Toezicht, Mauritshuis, The Hague 1999; Dir Burlington Magazine 1981– (Chair. 1995–2001). *Publications:* Rembrandt and His World 1964, The Flower Drawings of Jan van Huysum 1965, Rubens and His World 1968, Rembrandt's Etchings: a catalogue raisonné (jtly) 1970, Dürer: the Artist and His Drawings 1972, English Landscape 1630–1850 1977, The Dutch Paintings in the Collection of HM The Queen 1982, Rembrandt in Eighteenth Century England (ed.) 1983, Peter Paul Rubens: Man and Artist 1987, Drawing in England from Hilliard to Hogarth (jtly) 1987, Rubens in Oxford (jtly) 1988, One Hundred Old Master Drawings from the Ashmolean Museum (jtly) 1991, Dutch and Flemish Drawings at Windsor Castle (jtly) 1994, Anthony van Dyck: Thomas Howard, the Earl of Arundel 1995, Rembrandt by Himself (jtly) 1999, Ashmolean Museum Catalogue of the Dutch, Flemish and German Paintings 1999, Rembrandt as an Etcher (2nd edn) 1999. *Address:* 34 Kelly Street, London, NW1 8PH, England (home). *Telephone:* (20) 7485-9148 (home).

WHITE, Sir David Harry, Kt; British business executive; b. 12 Oct. 1929, Nottingham; s. of Harry White and Kathleen White; m. Valerie White 1971; one s. four d.; ed Nottingham High School and Master Mariner, Liverpool; Master Mariner's Certificate, HMS Conway; apprentice, Shell Co. 1946–56; Terminal Man., Texaco (UK) Ltd 1956–64; Operations Man., Gulf Oil (GB) 1964–68; Asst Man. Dir Samuel Williams, Dagenham 1968–70; Man. Dir Eastern British Road Services 1970–76; Group Man. Dir British Road Services 1976–82, Pickfords 1982–84; Deputy Chair. Nat. Freight Corpn 1984–89; Group Man. Dir Nat. Freight Consortium Property Group 1984–87; Chair. Pension Fund, Nat. Freight Co. 1985–99; Chair. Nottingham Devt Enterprise 1987–93; Dir (non-exec.) British Coal 1993–94; Chair. Nottingham Health Authority 1986–98, Bd of Govs Nottingham Trent Univ. 1988–99, Mansfield Brewery PLC 1993–99, The Coal Authority 1994–99, EPS Ltd 1997–2000; Dir Hilda Hanson 1997–, James Bell 1998–, Nottingham Forest 1999–2002, Coutts & Co. 1999–, Alkane Ltd 2000–02; DL 1989; Hon. DBA (Nottingham Trent) 1999. *Leisure interests:* football, walking. *Address:* Whitehaven, 6 Croft Road, Edwalton, Notts., NG12 4BW, England (home). *Telephone:* (115) 923-4199 (home). *E-mail:* sdw@pobox.com (home).

WHITE, Edmund Valentine, III, BA; American writer and academic; *Professor of Creative, Princeton University;* b. 13 Jan. 1940, Cincinnati, OH; s. of E.V. White and Delilah Teddlie; ed Univ. of Michigan; writer, Time-Life Books, New York 1962–70; Sr Ed., Saturday Review, New York 1972–73; Asst Prof. of Writing Seminars, Johns Hopkins Univ. 1977–79; Adjunct Prof., Columbia Univ. School of the Arts 1981–83; Exec. Dir, New York Inst. for the Humanities 1982–83; Prof. of English, Brown Univ., Providence, RI 1990–92; Prof. of Humanities, Princeton Univ. 1999, now Prof. of Creative Writing in the Univ. Center for the Creative and Performing Arts; Guggenheim Fellowship; mem. Acad. of Arts and Letters 1998; Officier, Ordre des Arts et des Lettres 1999. *Plays:* Terre Haute. *Publications:* fiction: Forgetting Elena 1973, Nocturnes for the King of Naples 1978, A Boy's Own Story 1982, Aphrodisiac (with others) 1984, Caracole 1985, The Darker Proof: Stories from a Crisis (with Adam Mars-Jones) 1987, The Beautiful Room is Empty 1988, Skinned Alive 1995, The Farewell Symphony 1997, The Married Man 2000, Fanny: A Fiction 2003, Chaos 2007, Hotel de Dream 2007; non-fiction: The Joy of Gay Sex: An Intimate Guide for Gay Men to the Pleasures of a Gay Lifestyle (with Charles Silverstein) 1977, States of Desire: Travels in Gay America 1980, The Faber Book of Gay Short Fiction (ed.) 1991, Genet: A Biography (Nat. Book Critics' Circle Award 1994) 1993, The Selected Writings of Jean Genet (ed.) 1993, The Burning Library (essays) 1994, Sketches from Memory 1994, Our Paris 1995, Proust 1998, The Flâneur 2001, My Lives (autobiog.) 2005, Rimbaud: The Double Life of a Rebel 2008. *Address:* c/o Amanda Urban, ICM, 825 8th Avenue, New York, NY 10019, USA (office); Room 224, 185 Nassau Street, Princeton, NJ 08544, USA (office). *Telephone:* (212) 556-5764 (office); (609) 258-5099 (office). *E-mail:* ewhite@princeton.edu (office). *Website:* www.princeton.edu/~visarts/cwr (office); www.edmundwhite.com.

WHITE, Guy Kendall, AM, MSc, DPhil, FAA; Australian physicist; b. 31 May 1925, Sydney; s. of Perceval George White and Eugenie White (née Kendall); m. 1st Judith Kelly McAuliffe 1955 (divorced); one s. two d.; m. 2nd Belinda Dawson 2005; ed The Scots Coll., Sydney, Univ. of Sydney, Magdalen Coll., Oxford, UK; Research Officer, CSIRO Div. of Physics 1950–54, Prin. Research Scientist 1958–62, Sr Prin. Research Scientist 1962–69, Chief Research Scientist 1969–90, Hon. Fellow 1990–; Assoc. Research Officer, Nat. Research Council of Canada 1955–58; Visiting Fellow, ANU 2000–01; Hon. DSc (Wollongong) 1994; Syme Medal (Melbourne Univ.) 1966, Armco Iron Award, USA 1983, Touloukian Award, USA 1994. *Publication:* Experimental Techniques in Low Temperature Physics 1958, 4th edn jtly 2002, Heat Capacity and Thermal Expansion (co-author) 1999; 200 research papers and review articles. *Leisure interests:* golf, tennis, swimming. *Address:* 6 Abbott Street, Bellerive, Tasmania 7018, Australia (home). *Telephone:* (3) 6244-8256 (home); 417-407-696 (mobile). *E-mail:* guy.white1@gmail.com (office).

WHITE, Adm. Sir Hugo (Moresby), GCB, CBE, DL; British naval officer (retd); b. 22 Oct. 1939, Torquay; s. of the late Hugh F. M. White, CMG and Betty White; m. Josephine Pedler 1966; two s.; ed Dragon School, Nautical Coll.

Pangbourne and Britannia Royal Naval Coll. (BRNC), Dartmouth; served on HMS Blackpool 1960; submarine training 1961; served on HMS Submarines Tabard, Tiptoe, Odin 1961–65; navigation course 1966; Navigator, HMS Warspite 1967; First Lt HMS Osiris 1968–69; CO HMS Oracle 1969–70; staff, BRNC, Dartmouth 1971–72; submarine sea training 1973–74; CO HMS Salisbury (cod war) 1975–76; with Naval Sec.'s Dept 1976–78; Asst Dir Naval Plans 1978–80; CO HMS Avenger (Falklands) and 4th Frigate Squadron 1980–82; Prin. Staff Officer to Chief of Defence Staff 1982–85; CO HMS Bristol and Flag Capt. 1985–87; Flag Officer, Third Flotilla and Commdr Anti-Submarine Warfare Striking Force Atlantic 1987–88; Asst Chief of Naval Staff 1988–89; Flag Officer, Scotland and N Ireland 1991–92; C-in-C Fleet, Allied C-in-C Channel and E Atlantic 1992–94; C-in-C Fleet, Allied C-in-C Atlantic and Naval Commdr NW Europe 1994–95; Gov. and C-in-C Gibraltar 1995–97; DL Devon 1999. *Leisure interests:* sailing, travelling, gardening, reading, biography. *Address:* c/o Naval Secretary, Victory Building, HM Naval Base, Portsmouth, PO1 3AS, England (office).

WHITE, Jack; American singer and musician (guitar, drums); b. (John Anthony Gillis), 9 July 1975, Detroit, Mich.; m. 1st Meg White 1996 (divorced 2000); m. 2nd Karen Elson 2005; one s. one d.; fmrly played in a number of Detroit-based bands; founder and mem. The White Stripes 1997–; founder and mem. The Raconteurs 2006–; MTV Europe Music Award for Best Rock Act 2003, BRIT Award for Best Int. Group 2004, Grammy Awards for Best Rock Song (for Seven Nation Army) 2004, for Best Rock Performance by a Duo or Group with Vocals (for Icky Thump) 2008. *Film appearances:* Cold Mountain 2003, Coffee and Cigarettes 2003. *Recordings include:* albums: with The White Stripes: White Stripes 1999, De Stijl 2000, White Blood Cells 2001, Elephant (Grammy Award for Best Alternative Album) 2003, Get Behind Me Satan (Grammy Award for Best Alternative Music Album 2006) 2005, Icky Thump (Grammy Award for Best Alternative Music Album 2008) 2007; with The Raconteurs: Broken Boy Soldiers 2006, Consolers of the Lonely 2008. *Address:* Monotone Management, 820 Seward Street, Hollywood, CA 90038, USA (office). *Telephone:* (323) 308-1818 (office). *Fax:* (323) 308-1819 (office). *Website:* www.whitestripes.com; www.theraconteurs.com.

WHITE, James Boyd, AM, LLB; American academic; *L. Hart Wright Professor of Law, University of Michigan;* b. 28 July 1938, Boston, Mass.; s. of Benjamin White and Charlotte Green White; m. 1st Constance Southworth 1959; m. 2nd Mary Fitch 1978; two s. two d.; ed Groton School, Amherst Coll. and Harvard Univ.; pvt. practice of law, Foley Hoag & Eliot 1964–67; Prof. of Law, Univ. of Colorado 1967–75, Univ. of Chicago 1975–82; Hart Wright Prof. of Law, Prof. of English Language and Literature and Adjunct Prof. of Classics, Univ. of Mich. 1982–. *Publications:* The Legal Imagination 1973, When Words Lose Their Meaning 1984, Heracles' Bow: Essays on the Rhetoric and Poetics of the Law 1986, Justice as Translation: An Essay in Cultural and Legal Criticism 1990, This Book of Starres: Learning to Read George Herbert 1994, Acts of Hope: Creating Authority in Literature, Law and Politics 1994, From Expectation to Experience: Essays in Law and Legal Education 1999, The Edge of Meaning 2001, Living Speech 2006. *Leisure interests:* reading, walking, swimming. *Address:* University of Michigan Law School, 332 Hutchins Hall, Ann Arbor, MI 48109 (office); 1606 Morton, Ann Arbor, MI 48104, USA (home). *Telephone:* (734) 936-2989 (office); (734) 662-6464 (home). *Fax:* (734) 763-9375 (office). *E-mail:* jbwhite@umich.edu (office). *Website:* www .law.umich.edu (office).

WHITE, Marco Pierre; British chef and restaurateur; b. 11 Dec. 1961, Leeds; s. of the late Frank White and Maria Rosa Gallina; m. 1st Alexandra McArthur 1988 (divorced 1990); one d.; m. 2nd Lisa Butcher 1992 (divorced 1994); m. 3rd Matilda Conejero-Caldera 2000; two s. one d.; ed Allerton High School, Leeds; Commis Chef Hotel St George, Harrogate 1978, Box Tree, Ilkley 1979; Chef de Partie Le Gavroche 1981, Tante Claire 1983; Sous Chef Manoir aux Quat' Saisons 1984–85; Propr and Chef Harveys 1986–93; The Canteen Restaurant, Chelsea Harbour (co-owner Michael Caine) 1992–96, Restaurant Marco Pierre White 1993–, Criterion Marco Pierre White (co-owner Sir Rocco Forte) 1995–, Quo Vadis 1996–, Oak Room, Le Meridien 1997–99, MPW Canary Wharf 1997–, Café Royal Grill Room 1997–, Mirabelle Restaurant, Curzon Street 1998–, L'Escargot, Belvedere 1999, Wheelers of St James 2002, Frankie's Bar and Grill; Catey Award for Newcomer of the Year 1987, Chef of the Year, Egon Ronay 1992, youngest and first British chef to win 3 Michelin stars 1995, Restaurant of the Year, Egon Ronay (for The Restaurant) 1997. *Television:* Hell's Kitchen (presenter) 2007. *Publications:* White Heat 1990, White Heat II 1994, Wild Food from Land and Sea 1994, Canteen Cuisine 1995, Glorious Puddings 1998, The Mirabelle Cookbook 1999, White Slave (autobiog.) 2006, The Devil in the Kitchen 2007, Frankie's: Recipes from an Italian Family (with Frankie Dettori) 2007. *Leisure interests:* fishing, shooting, bird-watching. *Address:* c/o Mirabelle Restaurant, 56 Curzon Street, London, W1J 8PA, England (office). *Website:* www .whitestarline.org.uk.

WHITE, Megan (Meg) Martha; American musician (drums); b. 10 Dec. 1974, Grosse Pointe, Mich.; founder mem., The White Stripes 1997–; MTV Europe Music Award for Best Rock Act 2003, BRIT Award for Best Int. Group 2004, Grammy Awards for Best Rock Song (for Seven Nation Army) 2004, for Best Rock Performance by a Duo or Group with Vocals (for Icky Thump) 2008. *Film appearance:* Coffee and Cigarettes 2003. *Recordings include:* albums: White Stripes 1999, De Stijl 2000, White Blood Cells 2001, Elephant (Grammy Award for Best Alternative Album) 2003, Get Behind Me Satan (Grammy Award for Best Alternative Music Album 2006) 2005, Icky Thump (Grammy Award for Best Alternative Music Album 2008) 2007. *Address:* Monotone Management, 820 Seward Street, Hollywood, CA 90038, USA (office). *Telephone:* (323) 308-1818 (office). *Fax:* (323) 308-1819 (office). *Website:* www.whitestripes.com.

WHITE, Michael Simon; British theatrical and film producer and impresario; b. 16 Jan. 1936; s. of Victor White and Doris White; m. 1st Sarah Hillsdon 1965 (divorced 1973); two s. one d.; m. 2nd Louise Moores 1985; one s.; ed Lyceum Alpinum, Zuoz, Switzerland, Pisa Univ. and Sorbonne, Paris; began career by bringing Cambridge Footlights to London's West End; Asst to Sir Peter Daubeny 1956–61. *Stage productions include:* Rocky Horror Show, Jabberwocky, Sleuth, America Hurrah, Oh, Calcutta!, The Connection, Joseph and the Amazing Technicolour Dreamcoat, Loot, The Blood Knot, A Chorus Line, Deathtrap, Annie, Pirates of Penzance, On Your Toes, The Mystery of Edwin Drood, Metropolis, Bus Stop, Crazy for You, Looking Through a Glass Onion, Me and Mamie O'Rourke, She Loves Me, Fame, Voyeurz 1996, Notre Dame de Paris 2000–01, Contact 2002. *Films include:* Monty Python and the Holy Grail, Rocky Horror Picture Show, My Dinner with André, Ploughman's Lunch, Moonlighting, Strangers' Kiss, The Comic Strip Presents, The Supergrass, High Season, Eat the Rich, White Mischief, The Deceivers, Nuns on the Run 1989, Robert's Movie, The Pope Must Die, Widow's Peak, Enigma 2000. *Publication:* Empty Seats 1984. *Leisure interests:* art, skiing, racing. *Address:* 48 Dean Street, London, W1V 5HL, England. *Telephone:* (20) 7734-7707.

WHITE, Miles D., BA, MBA; American pharmaceutical industry executive; *Chairman and CEO, Abbott Laboratories;* b. 1955, Minneapolis, Minn.; m.; ed Stanford Univ.; began career as Man. Consultant with McKinsey & Co.; Man. Nat. Account Sales and later other Sr Man. posts, Diagnostics Div., Abbott Laboratories 1984–93, Vice-Pres. Diagnostics Systems and Operations 1993–94, Sr Vice-Pres. 1994–98, Exec. Vice-Pres. 1998–99, mem. Bd of Dirs 1998–, CEO Jan. 1999–, Chair. April 1999–; mem. Bd of Trustees Exec. Cttee, Pharmaceutical Research and Mfrs of America; mem. Bd of Dirs Tribune Co., Motorola Inc., Evanston Northwestern Healthcare; mem. Bd of Dirs Fed. Reserve Bank of Chicago 2002–04, Chair. 2005–07; mem. Bd The Museum of Science and Industry, The Joffrey Ballet, Lyric Opera of Chicago; mem. Bd of Trustees Culver Educ. Foundation, The Field Museum, Chicago (currently Chair.), Art Inst. of Chicago, Northwestern Univ.; mem. Int. Advisory Council Guanghua School of Man. at Peking Univ., Advisory Council Stanford Grad. School of Business; Chair. Execs Club of Chicago; Vice-Chair. Chicago 2016; mem. Econ. Club of Chicago, Stanford Advisory Council on Interdisciplinary Biosciences; Distinguished Executive Award from Lake Forest Graduate School of Man. 2004. *Address:* Abbott Laboratories, 100 Abbott Park Road, Abbott Park, IL 60064-6400, USA (office). *Telephone:* (847) 937-6100 (office). *Fax:* (847) 937-1511 (home). *E-mail:* info@abbott.com (office). *Website:* www .abbott.com (office).

WHITE, Norman A., PhD, FIMechE, FRSA; British business executive, academic and international consultant; *Chairman, Spacelink Learning Foundation;* b. 11 April 1922, Hetton-le-Hole, Durham; s. of Charles Brewster White and Lilian Sarah White (née Finch); m. 1st Joyce Marjorie Rogers 1944 (died 1982); one s. one d.; m. 2nd Marjorie Iris Rushton 1983; ed Univs of Manchester and London, Univ. of Philippines, London Polytechnic (now Univ. of Westminster), Harvard Business School, London School of Econs; apprenticeship with George Kent Ltd and D. Napier and Sons Ltd 1936–43; Flight Test Engineer, Mil. Aircraft Devt 1943–45; with Royal Dutch Shell Group 1945–72, numerous posts, including Chair. and Dir of Royal Dutch/Shell Oil and int. mining cos 1963–72; f. Norman White Assocs 1972, Prin. Exec. 1972–92, Chair. 1992–95; tech. consultant to numerous cos 1972–96; Chair. and Dir numerous eng and oil cos 1972–97; Chair. Millennium Satellite Centre 1995–2000, Spacelink Learning Foundation 2000–; mem. Council and Chair. Eng-Man. Div., IMechE 1980–85, 1987–91; mem. Council and Vice-Pres. Inst. of Petroleum 1975–81; Founder, Chair. Jt Bd for Engineering Man., IMechE, ICE, IEE, Inst. of Chemical Engineers 1990–94, Chair. Academic Bd 1994–97; Visiting Prof., Univ. of Manchester, Henley Man. Coll., City Univ. 1971–96; mem. numerous academic and educational cttees including Senate and Advisory Bd in Eng, Univ. of London; Chair. Transnational Satellite Educ. Centre, Univ. of Surrey 1991–94; mem. House of Commons Parl. and Scientific Cttee 1977–83, 1987–92; Chair. British Nat. Cttee of World Petroleum Congresses (WPC) 1987–95 (Deputy Chair. 1977–87), UK Rep. WPC Int. Exec. Bd and Perm. Council 1979–97, Treas. 1983–91, 1994–97, Vice-Pres. 1991–94; mem. Conservation Comm. for World Energy 1979–87; Chair. Int. Task Force on Oil Substitution 1979–84; mem. int. energy/petroleum dels to USSR, People's Repub. of China, Romania, GDR, Japan, Korea, India, Mexico, Argentina, Brazil, Venezuela, Nepal, Indonesia, Southern Africa, Iran 1979–97; Founding mem. British Inst. of Energy Econs; Fellow, Inst. of Man., British Interplanetary Soc.; mem. American Soc. of Petroleum Engineers, Canadian Inst. of Mining and Metallurgy; Liveryman, Worshipful Co. of Engineers, Worshipful Co. of Spectacle Makers, Worshipful Co. of World Traders; mem. numerous professional eng insts; Freeman, City of London; Hon. Calgarian, Alberta, Canada; Hon. DipEM 1998; numerous other honours and awards. *Publications:* Financing the International Petroleum Industry 1978, The International Outlook for Oil Substitution to 2020 1983, Handbook of Engineering Management 1989, articles in professional journals in UK, USA and Canada. *Leisure interests:* family, walking, international affairs, comparative religions, odd-jobbing. *Address:* Spacelink Learning Foundation, PO Box 415, Guildford, Surrey, GU5 7WZ (office); Green Ridges, Downside Road, Guildford, Surrey, GU4 8PH, England (home). *Telephone:* (1483) 855329 (office); (1483) 567523 (home). *Fax:* (1483) 504314. *E-mail:* n.white@spacelink.org (office); normanwhite@norsco-demon.co.uk (home). *Website:* www.spacelink.org (office).

WHITE, Raymond P., DDS, PhD; American oral and maxillofacial surgeon and academic; *Dalton L. McMichael Distinguished Professor of Oral and Maxillofacial Surgery, University of North Carolina;* b. 13 Feb. 1937, New York; s. of Raymond P. White and Mabel S. White; m. Betty P. White 1961; one s. one d.; ed Medical Coll. of Virginia and Washington & Lee Univ.; Asst Prof.

of Oral Surgery, Univ. of Kentucky 1967–70, Assoc. Prof. 1970–71, Chair. Oral Surgery Dept 1969–71; Prof. of Oral Surgery, Virginia Commonwealth Univ. 1971–74; Dalton L. McMichael Prof. of Oral and Maxillofacial Surgery, Univ. of N Carolina School of Dentistry 1974–, Dean 1974–81; Assoc. Dean. Univ. of N Carolina School of Medicine 1981–93; Research Assoc., Univ. of N Carolina Health Services Research Center 1982–98; mem. Inst. of Medicine, NAS; William Gies Award, American Asscn of Oral and Maxillofacial Surgeons 2000, Distinguished Service Award, American Asscn of Oral and Maxillofacial Surgeons 2003, Torch Distinguished Service Award, Oral and Maxillofacial Surgery Foundation 2006. *Publications:* co-author: Fundamentals of Oral Surgery 1971, Surgical Correction of Dentofacial Deformities 1980, Surgical Orthodontic Treatment 1990, Rigid Fixation for Maxillofacial Surgery 1991, Contemporary Treatment of Dentofacial Deformity 2002. *Leisure interests:* tennis, sailing. *Address:* Department of Oral and Maxillofacial Surgery, CB 7450, University of North Carolina, Chapel Hill, NC 27599-7450 (office); 1506 Velma Road, Chapel Hill, NC 27514, USA (home). *Telephone:* (919) 966-1126 (office); (919) 967-4064 (home). *Fax:* (919) 966-6019 (office). *E-mail:* ray_white@dentistry.unc.edu (office). *Website:* www.dent.unc.edu/depts/academic/oms (office).

WHITE, Robert James, AO; Australian banker; b. 18 Oct. 1923, Deniliquin, NSW; s. of the late A. W. White and S. J. White; m. 1st Molly McKinnon 1950 (died 1994); m. 2nd Janice Anne White 1996; ed War Memorial High School, Hay, NSW; joined Bank of NSW 1940, Asst Chief Man., NZ 1965–66, Deputy Chief Accountant 1967–69, Man., Sydney 1970–71, Chief Man., UK and Europe 1972–74, Gen. Man. 1974–77, Dir and CEO Bank of NSW 1977–82, Man. Dir Westpac Banking Corpn (merger of Bank of NSW with Commercial Bank of Australia) 1982–87, Dir 1977–90; Dir ICI Australia Ltd 1987–93, IBM Australia Ltd 1988–95, Atlas Copco Australia Pty Ltd 1989–94; Commr Electricity Comm. of NSW 1989–95; Pres. Australian Inst. of Bankers 1980–86; Chair. Australian Bankers' Asscn 1978–79, 1983–84, 1987; Dir Int. Monetary Conf. 1982–85; Pres. Asian Pacific Bankers' Club 1983–84, Business Council of Australia 1984–86, Australian Coalition of Service Industries 1988–94, Australian Inst. for Int. Affairs 1988–91, German-Australian Chamber of Industry and Commerce 1988–91, Council for Int. Business Affairs 1992–95; mem. Trade Devt Council 1981–84, Australian Pacific Econ. Co-operation Cttee 1984–91; mem. Exec. Bd ICC 1987–90; Fellow Austrialian Inst. of Bankers, Australian Inst. of Co. Dirs; Commdr's Cross, Order of Merit (Germany); Storey Medal, Australian Inst. of Man. 1987. *Publication:* Cheques and Balances (memoir) 1995. *Address:* PO Box 616, Lindfield, NSW 2070, Australia. *Telephone:* (2) 9417-4989.

WHITE, Robert Mayer, BA, MS, ScD; American meteorologist; *Director, The Washington Advisory Group;* b. 13 Feb. 1923, Boston, Mass; s. of David White and Mary White (née Winkeller); m. Mavis Seagle 1948; one s. one d.; ed Harvard Univ., Massachusetts Inst. of Tech.; war service with USAF, exec. at Atmospheric Analysis Lab., Geophysics Research Directorate, Air Force Cambridge Research Center 1952–58, Chief of Meteorological Devt Lab. 1958; Research Assoc., MIT 1959, Karl T. Compton Lecturer 1995–96; Travelers Insurance Cos 1959–60, Pres. Travelers Research Center, Hartford 1960–63; Chief of Weather Bureau, US Dept of Commerce 1963–65; Admin. Environmental Science Services Admin., US Dept of Commerce 1965–70; Perm. Rep. and mem. Exec. Cttee of World Meteorological Org. 1963–77; Admin. Nat. Oceanic and Atmospheric Admin. 1971–77; Chair. Joint Oceanographic Inst., Inc. 1977–79; Chair. Climate Research Bd of NAS 1977–79; Admin. Nat. Research Council, Exec. Officer 1979–80; Pres. Univ. Corpn for Atmospheric Research 1979–83, Sr Fellow 1995–; Pres. Washington Advisory Group 1996–98, now Dir; mem. Exec. Cttee American Geophysical Union, Council Nat. Acad. of Eng, (Pres. 1983–), Marine Tech. Soc., Royal Meteorological Soc., Nat. Advisory Cttee on Oceans and Atmosphere 1979–84, Nat. Advisory Cttee on Govt and Public Affairs, Univ. of Ill. 1987–; Bd of Overseers Harvard Univ. 1977–79; mem. of numerous weather research cttees; Commr Int. Whaling Comm. 1973–77; Hon. DEng (Drexel Univ.) 1985; Cleveland Abbe Award, American Meteorological Soc. 1969, Rockefeller Public Service award 1974, David B. Stone Award, New England Aquarium 1975, Matthew Fontaine Maury Medal, Smithsonian Inst. 1976, Int. Conservation Award Nat. Wildlife Fed. 1976, Neptune Award American Oceanic Org. 1977, Charles Franklin Brooks Award 1978, Int. Meteorological Asscn Prize 1980, Fahrney Award, Franklin Inst. 1983, Tyler Prize, Univ. of California 1992, Vannevar Bush Award 1998, Australian Centenary Medal 2003. *Leisure interests:* gardening, reading. *Address:* The Washington Advisory Group, 1275 K Street, NW, Suite 1025, Washington, DC 20005 (office); Somerset House II, 5610 Wisconsin Avenue, Apt 1506, Bethesda, MD 20815, USA (home). *Telephone:* (202) 682-0164 (office); (301) 652-2901 (home). *Fax:* (202) 682-9335 (office); (301) 052-2901 (home). *E-mail:* qmw@theadvisorygroup.com (office). *Website:* www.theadvisorygroup.com (office).

WHITE, Terrence Harold, PhD; Canadian academic and fmr university president; *Professor of Management and President Emeritus, University of Calgary;* b. 31 March 1943, Ottawa; s. of William H. White and Shirley M. Ballantine; m. Susan E. Hornaday 1968; two d.; ed Univ. of Toronto; Head, Dept of Sociology and Anthropology, Univ. of Windsor 1973–75; Chair. Dept of Sociology, Univ. of Alberta 1975–80, Dean, Faculty of Arts 1980–88; Pres. and Vice-Chancellor Brock Univ. 1988–96, Univ. of Calgary 1996–2001, Prof. of Man. and Pres. Emer. 2001–; Rotary Int. Paul Harris Fellow, Canada 125 Commemorative Medal 1999, Queen's Jubilee Medal 2004. *Publications:* Power or Pawns: Boards of Directors in Canadian Corporations 1978, Quality of Working Life 1984. *Leisure interests:* hockey, skiing, squash, tennis, painting. *Address:* Haskayne School of Business, 452 Scurfield Hall, The University of Calgary, 2500 University Drive NW, Calgary, Alberta, T2N 1N4, Canada (office). *E-mail:* twhite@ucalgary.ca (office). *Website:* www.haskayne.ucalgary.ca (office).

WHITE, Tony L.; American business executive; *Chairman, President and CEO, Applera Corporation;* b. 1947; ed Western Carolina Univ.; Exec. Vice-Pres. Baxter Int. Inc., Group Vice-Pres. 1986–92; Dir and Chair., Pres. and Chief Exec. PE Corpn (Applera Corpn 2000–) 1995–; co-f. Celera Genomics Group 1998, Pres. (acting) 2002; mem. Bd of Dirs C.R. Bard Inc., Ingersoll-Rand Co., Tecan AG, NewCoGen Group, AT&T; mem. Advisory Bd Kellogg Center for Biotechnology, Northwestern Univ.; Trustee N Carolina Univ., Centenary Coll. *Address:* Applera Corporation, 301 Merritt 7, Norwalk, CT 06856-5435, USA (office). *Telephone:* (203) 840-2000 (office). *Fax:* (203) 840-2312 (office). *Website:* www.applera.com (home).

WHITE, Sir Willard Wentworth, Kt, CBE, BA; Jamaican/British singer (bass); b. 10 Oct. 1946, Ewarton, St Catherine, Jamaica; s. of Egbert White and Gertrude White; m. Gillian Jackson 1972; three s. one d.; ed Excelsior School, Kingston and Juilliard School of Music, NY; debut with New York City Opera as Colline in La Bohème 1974–75; European debut as Osmin with Welsh Nat. Opera 1976; has performed in most int. opera houses, including Royal Opera House, Covent Garden, England, La Scala, Italy, Glyndebourne, England, Scotland; roles include: Porgy, Orestes, Banquo, King Henry (Lohengrin), Pizarro, Wotan, Mephistopheles, Boris Godunov, Golau, Leporello, Prince Kovansky, Napoleon; extensive concert appearances; appeared as Othello, RSC, Stratford-upon-Avon; Falstaff at Aix Festival 2001, Klingsor in Parsifal, Covent Garden 2001, Bartok's Bluebeard 2002, Messiaen's St Francis, San Francisco 2002, Wotan in the Ring, Aix and Salzburg 2005; Pres. Royal Northern Coll. of Music 2008–; Patron, London Southbank Scheme for Young Singers; Prime Minister of Jamaica's Medal of Appreciation 1987. *Recordings include:* Porgy and Bess, Mozart Requiem, Orfeo, Die Aegyptische Helena, Acis and Galatea. *Address:* IMG Artists, The Light Box, 111 Power Road, London, W4 5PY, England (office). *Telephone:* (20) 7957-5800 (office). *Fax:* (20) 7957-5801 (office). *E-mail:* bsegal@imgartists.com (office). *Website:* www.imgartists.com (office).

WHITE, William James, BS, MBA; American business executive (retd); b. 30 May 1938, Kenosha, Wis.; s. of William H. White and Dorothy Caroline White; m. Jane Schulte 1960; two s. two d.; ed Northwestern and Harvard Univs; Mechanical Planning Engineer, Procter & Gamble Corpn 1961–62; Corp. Vice-Pres. Hartmarx Corpn, Chicago 1963–74; Group Vice-Pres. Mead Corpn, Dayton, Ohio 1974–81; Pres., COO and Dir Masonite Corpn, Chicago 1981–85; Exec. Vice-Pres. and Dir USG Corpn 1985–88; Pres., CEO Whitestar Enterprises Inc. 1989–90; Chair., Pres., CEO Bell & Howell Co. 1990–95; Chair. CEO Bell and Howell Holdings Co. 1995; Dir Midwest Stock Exchange, Chicago, Evanston Hosp., Evanston, Ill., Ill. Math. and Science Foundation, Business Advisory Council, Univ. of Ill.; mem. The Chicago Cttee, Advisory Council Tech. Inst., Northwestern Univ.; Trustee Northwestern Univ., Evanston. *Publication:* Creative Collective Bargaining (co-author) 1965.

WHITEHEAD, Sir John Stainton, GCMG, CVO, BA, MA; British diplomatist (retd) and consultant; *Chairman, Japaninvest Group Plc;* b. 20 Sept. 1932; s. of John William Whitehead and Kathleen Whitehead; m. Mary Carolyn Hilton 1964; two s. two d.; ed Christ's Hosp. and Hertford Coll., Oxford, Open Univ.; served in HM Forces 1950–52; Foreign Office 1955–56, Third Sec., later Second Sec., Tokyo 1956–61, Foreign Office 1961–64, First Sec. Washington 1964–67, First Sec. Econ., Tokyo 1968–71, FCO 1971–76, Head of Personnel Services Dept 1973–76, Counsellor and Head of Chancery, Bonn 1976–80, Minister, Tokyo 1980–84, FCO, Deputy Under-Sec. of State (Chief Clerk) 1984–86; Amb. to Japan 1986–92; adviser to Pres. of Bd of Trade 1992–96; Sr adviser, Morgan Grenfell Group PLC 1992–99, Deutsche Asset Man. 1999–2000; Chair. Deutsche Morgan Grenfell Trust Bank, Tokyo 1996–2000, Japaninvest 2005–, Daiwa Anglo-Japanese Foundation 2008; Dir (non-exec.) Cadbury Schweppes 1993–2001, Serco PLC 1994–96, BPB Industries PLC 1995–2002; adviser to Cable & Wireless PLC 1992–2001, Guiness PLC 1992–97, Inchcape 1992–96, Sanwa Bank 1993–2000, Tokyo Electric Power Co. 1993–2002; mem. Advisory Bd Powergen Int. 1996–2001, All Nippon Airways 2001–03; Hon. Fellow Hertford Coll. Oxford 1992; Almoner, Christ's Hospital 2005–07. *Leisure interests:* new challenges, music, travel, woodland man., walking, golf. *Address:* Bracken Edge, High Pitfold, Hindhead, Surrey, England (home). *Telephone:* (1428) 604162 (home). *Fax:* (1428) 607950 (home).

WHITEHOUSE, Sheldon; American lawyer and politician; *Senator from Rhode Island;* b. 20 Oct. 1955, New York City; s. of Charles Whitehouse; m. Dr Sandra Thornton Whitehouse; one s. one d.; ed St Paul's School, Concord, NH, Yale Univ., Univ. of Virginia School of Law; worked as clerk for Judge Richard F. Neely, Supreme Court of Appeals of West Virginia 1982–83; Special Asst Attorney Gen., Rhode Island Attorney Gen.'s office 1985–90, Chief of Regulatory Unit 1988–90, Asst Attorney Gen. 1989–90; Exec. Counsel for Gov. Bruce Sundlun of Rhode Island 1991–94, later Dir of Policy, Dir of Business Regulation 1992–94; US Attorney for Rhode Island 1994–98; State Attorney Gen. 1998–2006; cand. for Gov. 2002; Senator from Rhode Island 2007–; f. Rhode Island Quality Inst.; Democrat. *Address:* 502 Hart Senate Office Building, Washington, DC 20510, USA (office). *Telephone:* (202) 224-2921 (office). *Fax:* (202) 228-6362 (office). *Website:* whitehouse.senate.gov (office).

WHITELAW, Billie, CBE; British actress; b. 6 June 1932, Coventry; d. of Perceval Whitelaw and Frances Whitelaw; m. 1st Peter Vaughan (divorced); m. 2nd Robert Muller; one s.; ed Thornton Grammar School, Bradford; Annenberg-Beckett Fellow, Univ. of Reading 1993; Hon. DLitt (Bradford) 1981 (Birmingham, St Andrew's) 1997; Variety Club Silver Heart Award 1961, TV Actress of Year 1961, 1972, British Acad. Award 1968, US Film Critics' Award 1977, Evening News Film Award as Best Actress 1977, Sony Best Radio Actress Award 1987, Evening Standard Best Film Actress Award 1988. *Plays include:* Hotel Paradiso, Winter Garden 1954 and Oxford

Playhouse 1956, Progress to the Park, Theatre Workshop and Saville 1961, England our England, Prince's 1962, Touch of the Poet, Venice and Dublin 1962; with Nat. Theatre 1963–65, Othello, London and Moscow, Hobson's Choice, Play (Beckett), Trelawny of the Wells, The Dutch Courtesan, After Haggerty, Criterion 1971, Not I, Royal Court 1973 and 1975, Alphabetical Order, Mayfair 1975, Footfalls, Royal Court 1976, Molly, Comedy 1978, Happy Days, Royal Court 1979, The Greeks, Aldwych 1980, Passion Play, Aldwych 1981, Rockaby, Nat. Theatre 1982, New York 1982, 1984, Riverside Studios 1986, world tour 1985/86, Tales from Hollywood, Nat. Theatre 1983, Who's Afraid of Virginia Woolf?, Young Vic 1987. *Films include:* No Love For Johnnie 1961, Charlie Bubbles 1968, Twisted Nerve 1968, The Adding Machine 1968, Start the Revolution Without Me, Leo the Last, Eagle in a Cage 1969, Gumshoe 1971, Frenzy 1972, Night Watch 1973, The Omen 1976, Leopard in the Snow, The Water Babies 1977, An Unsuitable Job for a Woman 1981, Slayground 1983, The Chain 1984, Shadey 1985, Maurice 1986, The Dress-maker 1988, Joyriders 1989, The Krays 1990, Deadly Advice 1993, Jane Eyre 1994, Canterbury Tales (animated film), Quills 2000, Hot Fuzz 2007. *Television includes:* No Trams to Lime Street, Lena Oh My Lena, Resurrec-tion, The Skin Game, Beyond the Horizon, Anna Christie, Lady of the Camelias, The Pity of It All, Love on the Dole, A World of Time, You and I, Poet Game, Sextet (8 plays), Napoleon and Love (9 plays, as Josephine), The Fifty Pound Note (Ten from the Twenties), The Withered Arm (Wessex Tales), The Werewolf Reunion (2 plays), Shades by Samuel Beckett, Not I, Eustace and Hilda (2 plays), The Serpent Son, Happy Days (Dir by Beckett), A Tale of Two Cities, Jamaica Inn, Private Schultz, Camille, Old Girlfriends, The Picnic, The Secret Garden, Imaginary Friends, The Entertainer, The 15 Streets, Footfalls, Rockaby, Eh Joe, Duel of Love, Lorna Doone, Murder of Quality, The Cloning of Joanna May, Firm Friends, Born to Run, Shooting the Past, A Dinner of Herbs (miniseries), Last of the Blonde Bombshells 2000. *Plays for radio:* The Master Builder, Hindle Wakes, Jane Eyre, The Female Messiah, Alpha Beta, Marching Song, The Cherry Orchard, Vassa, Beckett's All that Fall, Embers, Beckett Evening (one-woman) 1997. *Publication:* Billie Whitelaw – Who He? (memoirs) 1995. *Leisure interest:* pottering about the house. *Address:* c/o Michael Foster, ICM, Oxford House, 76 Oxford Street, London, W1N 0AX, England. *Telephone:* (20) 7636-6565. *Fax:* (20) 7323-0101.

WHITELAW, James Hunter, PhD, DSc (Eng), FRS, FCGI, FIMechE, FREng; British scientist, mechanical engineer and academic; *Professor of Convective Heat Transfer, Imperial College London;* b. 28 Jan. 1936, Newmains, Scotland; s. of James Whitelaw and Jean Ross Whitelaw (née Scott); m. Elizabeth Shields 1959; three s.; ed High School, Glasgow, Univ. of Glasgow; Research Asst, Univ. of Glasgow 1957–61; Research Assoc., Brown Univ., Providence, RI, USA 1961–63; Lecturer, Imperial Coll., London 1963–69, Reader 1969–74, Prof. of Convective Heat Transfer 1974–; Distinguished Visiting Chair. Prof. of Pollution and Combustion, Dept of Mechanical Eng, Hong Kong Polytechnic Univ. 2000–04; Hon. DSc (Lisbon) 1980, (Valencia) 1996, (Dublin) 1999, (Athens) 2001; Nusselt-Reynolds Prize 1997, AIAA Energy Systems Award 2005. *Publications:* three books (co-author), 30 books (co-ed.) and more than 380 scientific papers. *Leisure interests:* music, reading. *Address:* Department of Mechanical Engineering, Imperial College, London, SW7 2BX (office); 149A Coombe Lane West, Kingston-upon-Thames, Surrey, KT2 7DH, England (home). *Telephone:* (20) 7594-7028 (office); (20) 8942-1836 (home). *Fax:* (20) 7589-3905 (office). *E-mail:* j.whitelaw@ic.ac.uk (office); JHWhitelaw<100773.2135@CompuServe.com (home). *Website:* www.me.polyu.edu.hk/virtual/People/Academic_Staff/whitelaw.htm (office).

WHITEREAD, Rachel, CBE; British artist and sculptor; b. 20 April 1963, London; d. of Thomas Whiteread and Patricia Whiteread; ed Brighton Polytechnic and Slade School of Art, Univ. Coll. London; some works use casts of sinks, baths, beds, mattresses, floors and mortuary slabs; work includes 'Ghost', a white plaster cast of an entire room shown at Chisenhale Gallery, London 1990 and 'House', a cast of an entire London terraced house on show in Bow, East London 1993–94; Hon. DLitt (Brighton Polytechnic) 1998, (Univ. of East London) 1998; Turner Prize 1993, Venice Biennale Award for Best Young Artist 1997. *Publication:* Whiteread 2007. *Address:* c/o Gagosian Gallery, 6–24 Britannia Street, London, WC1X 9JD, England. *Telephone:* (20) 7841-9960. *Fax:* (20) 7841-9961. *E-mail:* info@gagosian.com (office). *Website:* www.gagosian.com.

WHITESIDES, George M., PhD, FAAS; American chemist and academic; *Mallinckrodt Professor of Chemistry, Harvard University;* b. 3 Aug. 1939, Louisville, Ky; ed Harvard Univ., Cambridge, Mass and Calif. Inst. of Tech.; Pasadena; faculty mem., MIT 1963–82; faculty mem., Dept of Chem., Harvard Univ. 1982–86, Chair. 1986–89, Mallinckrodt Prof. of Chem. 1989–; mem. Defense Advanced Research Projects Agency, Defense Science Research Council, US Dept of Defense 1984–, Defense Science Bd 1993–, Threat Reduction Advisory Cttee to Defense Threat Reduction Agency 1998–; Chair. NSF Chem. Advisory Cttee 1986, Nat. Research Council Bd of Chemical Sciences and Tech. 1986–99, NSF Materials Research Advisory Cttee 1993; mem. Scientific Advisory Cttee, Scripps Research Inst. 1993–; mem. NSF Sr Assessment Panel: Int. Assessment of US Math. Sciences 1997; mem. Nat. Research Council Bd on Physics and Astronomy 1997–; Ed. Science Review-ing; mem. Editorial Bd Journal of Applied Biochemistry and Biotechnology, BioOrganic Chemistry, BioOrganic and Medicinal Chemistry Letters, Chem-istry of Materials, Journal of Physical Chemistry, Angewandte Chemie, Chemistry and Biology, Langmuir, Nanotechnology, Colloids and Surfaces B: Biointerfaces; mem. American Acad. of Arts and Sciences, NAS, American Philosophical Soc.; Fellow, New York Acad. of Science; Foreign Fellow, Indian Nat. Science Acad. 2000; Hon. Fellow, Chemical Research Soc. of India 2000; Wallac Oy Innovation Award in High Throughput Screening, Soc. for Biomolecular Screening, ACS (Sierra Nevada Section) Distinguished Chemist Award, Alfred P. Sloan Fellowship 1968, ACS Award in Pure Chem. 1975,

ACS (Rochester Section) Harrison Howe Award 1979, Alumni Distinguished Service Award, Calif. Inst. of Tech. 1980, ACS (Maryland Section) Remsen Award 1983, ACS Arthur C. Cope Scholar Award 1989, 1995, ACS (New England Section) James Flack Norris Award 1994, ACS Madison Marshall Award 1996, Award for Significant Tech. Achievement, Defense Advanced Research Projects Agency 1996, Nat. Medal of Science, Nat. Science Bd 1998, Award for Excellence in Surface Science, Surfaces in Biomaterials Foundation 1999, Von Hippel Award, Materials Research Soc. 2000, Dan David Prize, 2005, Priestley Medal 2007. *Publications:* more than 630 articles in scientific journals on materials science, biophysics, surface science, polyvalency, microfluidics, optics, self-assembly, microfabrication, nanotechnology and cell surface biochemistry. *Address:* Department of Chemistry and Chemical Biology, Harvard University, Mallinckrodt 232, 12 Oxford Street, Cambridge, MA 02138, USA (office). *Telephone:* (617) 495-9430 (office). *Fax:* (617) 495-9857 (office). *E-mail:* gwhitesides@gmwgroup.harvard.edu (office). *Website:* gmwgroup.harvard.edu (office).

WHITHAM, Gerald Beresford, PhD, FAAAS., FRS; American (b. British) mathematician and academic; *Charles Lee Powell Professor of Applied Mathematics, Emeritus, California Institute of Technology;* b. 13 Dec. 1927, Halifax, England; s. of Harry Whitham and Elizabeth E. Whitham; m. Nancy Lord 1951; one s. two d.; ed Elland Grammar School and Univ. of Manchester; Research Assoc. New York Univ. 1951–53; Lecturer in Applied Math. Manchester Univ. 1953–56; Assoc. Prof. of Applied Math., Inst. of Mathemat-ical Sciences, New York 1956–59; Prof. of Math. MIT 1959–62; Prof. of Aeronautics and Math. Calif. Inst. of Tech. 1962–67, of Applied Math. 1967–83, Charles Lee Powell Prof. of Applied Math. 1983–98, Prof. Emer. 1998–; Wiener Prize 1980. *Publications:* Linear and Nonlinear Waves 1974, Lectures on Wave Propagation 1980. *Address:* Applied Mathematics 217-50, California Institute of Technology, Pasadena, CA 91125, USA. *Telephone:* (626) 395-4561. *Website:* www.acm.caltech.edu (office).

WHITLAM, (Edward) Gough, AC, QC, BA, LLB; Australian politician and diplomatist; b. 11 July 1916, Melbourne; s. of the late H. F. E. Whitlam and Martha (née Maddocks) Whitlam; m. Margaret Dovey 1942; three s. one d.; ed Knox Grammar School, Sydney, Canberra High School, Canberra Grammar School and Univ. of Sydney; RAAF 1941–45; admitted to NSW Bar 1947; mem. House of Reps. 1952–78; mem. Parl. Cttee on Constitutional Review 1956–59; mem. Federal Parl. Exec. of Australian Labor Party 1959–77; Deputy Leader of Australian Labor Party in Fed. Parl. 1960–67, Leader 1967–77; Leader of the Opposition 1967–72, 1975–77; Prime Minister 1972–75, concurrently Minister of Foreign Affairs 1972–73; Rep. to UNESCO, Paris 1983–86, mem. Exec. Bd 1985–89; mem. Australian Constitutional Convention 1973–76, Independent Comm. on Int. Humanitarian Issues 1983–86, Constitutional Comm. 1986–88; Chair. Australia-China Council 1986–91, Australian Nat. Gallery 1987–90; Vice-Pres. Socialist Int. 1976–77, Hon. Pres. 1983–; Visiting Fellow (lecturing in Political Science and Int. Relations) Australian Nat. Univ. 1978–80, Nat. Fellow 1980–81; Fellow Univ. of Sydney Senate 1981–83, 1986–89; Pres. Int. Comm. of Jurists (Australian Section) 1982–83; Visiting Prof., Harvard Univ., USA 1979; f. Hanoi Architectural Heritage Foundation 1993; mem. Sydney Olympics 2000 del. to Africa 1993; Corresp. mem. Acad. of Athens 1992; Fellow Australian Acad. of the Humanities; Hon. Pres. Australian Nat. Council for the Celebration of the Bicentenary of the French Revolution 1989; Grand Cross, Order of Makarios III (Cyprus) 1983, Grand Commdr Order of Honour (Greece) 1996, Grand Cross of the Order of the Phoenix (Greece) 1998, Grande Ufficiale nell' Ordine Al Merito (Italy) 1999, Grand Cross of the Apostle Andrew (Greek Orthodox Archdiocese of Australia) 2002, Grand Companion of the Order of Logohu (Papua New Guinea) 2005, Grand Cordon, Order of the Rising Sun (Japan) 2006; Hon. LLD (The Philippines) 1974; Hon. DLitt (Sydney) 1981, (Wollongong) 1989, (La Trobe, Wodonga) 1992, (Univ. of Tech., Sydney) 1995, (Univ. of Western Sydney) 2002; Socialist Int. Silver Plate of Honour 1976, Mem. of Honour Int. Union for Nature Conservation (now World Conservation Union) 1988, Australian Library and Information Asscn Redmond Barry Award 1994. *Publications:* On Australia's Constitution (articles and lectures 1957–77) 1977, The Truth of the Matter 1979, A Pacific Community (Harvard lectures) 1981, The Whitlam Government 1985, Living with the United States: British Dominions and New Pacific States 1990, Hellenism in the Antipodes 1993, Abiding Interests 1997, My Italian Notebook 2002. *Address:* Level 14, 100 William Street, Sydney, NSW 2011, Australia. *Telephone:* (2) 9358-2022. *Fax:* (2) 9358-2753.

WHITMAN, Christine Todd; American consultant and fmr politician; *President, Whitman Strategy Group;* b. 26 Sept. 1946; d. of Webster Bray Todd and Eleanor Schley Todd; m. John R. Whitman 1974; two c.; ed Wheaton Coll.; fmr freeholder, Somerset Co., NJ; fmr Pres. State Bd of Public Utilities; fmr host, radio talk show, Station WKXW, Trenton, NJ; fmr newspaper columnist; Chair. Comm. for an Affordable NJ; Gov. of New Jersey 1994–2001; Admin. US Environmental Protection Agency, Washington, DC 2001–03 (resgnd); Pres. Whitman Strategy Group (consulting firm), Washington, DC 2006–; Co-Chair. Republican Leadership Council 2007–, Clean and Safe Energy; mem. Bd of Dirs S.C. Johnson and Son, Inc., Texas Instruments Inc., United Technologies Corpn, New America Foundation; mem. Steering Cttee Cancer Inst. of New Jersey; mem. Governing Bd Park City Center for Public Policy; Trustee Eisenhower Fellowships; mem. Council on Foreign Relations; advisor, Aspen Rodel Fellowship Program; Republican. *Publication:* It's My Party Too 2005. *Address:* Whitman Strategy Group, 116 Village Boulevard, Suite 200, Princeton, NJ 08540 (office); Whitman Strategy Group, 888 16th Street, NW, Suite 800, Washington, DC 20006, USA. *Telephone:* (609) 524-4068 (NJ) (office); (202) 355-1374 (DC) (office). *E-mail:* christie.whitman@whitmanstrategygroup.com (office). *Website:* www.whitmanstrategygroup.com (office).

WHITMAN, Margaret (Meg) C., AB, MBA; American business executive; b. 4 Aug. 1956, Cold Spring Harbor, Long Island, NY; m. Griffith R. Harsh IV; two s.; ed Princeton Univ., Harvard Business School; Brand Asst, Procter & Gamble, Cincinnati, OH 1979–81; with Bain & Co., San Francisco, Calif. 1982–89, becoming Vice-Pres.; Sr Vice-Pres. Marketing in Consumer Products Div., Walt Disney Co. 1989–92; Pres. Stride Rite Div., Stride Rite Corpn 1993–95, Exec. Vice-Pres. Keds Div.; Pres. and CEO Florists Transworld Delivery 1995–97, leading launch of co.'s internet strategy; Gen. Man. Hasbro Inc.'s Pre-school Div., Brand Man. responsible for global marketing of Playskool and Mr Potato Head brands 1997–98; Pres. and CEO eBay Inc. 1998–2008, mem. Bd of Dirs 1998–2008; mem. Bd Dirs Procter & Gamble 2003–08, DreamWorks Animation SKG, Inc. 2005–08, Gap Inc. 2003–06; Trustee Princeton Univ.; named by Business Week magazine amongst 25 Most Powerful Business Managers annually 2000–, ranked number one by Worth magazine on its list of Best CEOs 2002, ranked by Fortune magazine amongst 50 Most Powerful Women in Business in the US (third) 2002, (second) 2003, (first) 2004, (first) 2005, (third) 2006, (third) 2007, also ranked by Fortune magazine amongst 25 Most Powerful People in Business 2004, ranked by Forbes magazine amongst 100 Most Powerful Women (51st) 2004, (fifth) 2005, (22nd) 2006, (22nd) 2007, named by Time magazine as one of the World's 100 Most Influential People 2004, 2005, named by The Wall Street Journal one of the 50 Women to Watch 2005. *Address:* 24 Edge Road, Atherton, CA 94027, USA (office).

WHITMAN, Marina von Neumann, PhD; American economist and academic; *Professor of Business Administration and Public Policy, Gerald R. Ford School of Public Policy, University of Michigan;* b. 6 March 1935, New York; d. of John von Neumann and Mariette Kovesi (Mrs J. B. H. Kuper); m. Robert F. Whitman 1956; one s. one d.; ed Radcliffe Coll. and Columbia Univ.; Lecturer in Econs, Univ. of Pittsburgh 1962–64, Asst Prof. 1964–66, Assoc. Prof. 1966–71, Prof. of Econs 1971–73, Distinguished Public Service Prof. 1973–79; Sr Staff Economist, Council of Econ. Advisers 1970–71; mem. President's Price Comm. 1971–72; mem. President's Council of Econ. Advisers (with special responsibility for int. monetary and trade problems) 1972–73; Vice-Pres., Chief Econ. Gen. Motors Corpn, New York 1979–85, Group Exec. Vice-Pres. for Public Affairs 1985–92; Distinguished Visiting Prof. of Business Admin. and Public Policy, Univ. of Mich. 1992–94, Prof. 1994–; mem. Trilateral Comm. 1973, Bd of Dirs Council on Foreign Relations 1977–87; mem. Bd of Dirs J. P. Morgan Chase Corpn 1973–2002, Procter and Gamble Co. 1976–2003, Alcoa 1993–2002, Unocal 1993–2005; mem. Bd of Overseers Harvard Univ. 1972–78, Bd of Trustees, Princeton Univ. 1980–90; mem. Consultative Group on Int. Econ. and Monetary Affairs 1979–; more than 20 hon. degrees. *Publications:* New World, New Rules: The Changing Role of the American Corporation 1999; many books and articles on econ. topics. *Address:* Gerald R. Ford School of Public Policy, University of Michigan, Weill Hall, 735 South State Street, Ann Arbor, MI 48109-3091, USA (office). *Telephone:* (734) 763-4173 (office). *Fax:* (734) 763-9181 (office). *E-mail:* marinaw@umich.edu (office). *Website:* www.fordschool.umich.edu (office).

WHITNEY, John Norton Braithwaite, CBE, FRSA; British broadcasting executive; b. 20 Dec. 1930, Burnham, Bucks.; s. of Willis Bevan Whitney and Dorothy Anne Whitney; m. Roma Elizabeth Hodgson 1956; one s. one d.; ed Leighton Park Friends' School, Reading; radio producer 1951–64; set up Ross Radio Productions Ltd 1951, Autocue Ltd 1955; f. Radio Antilles 1963; Man. Dir Capital Radio 1973–82; Dir-Gen. Ind. Broadcasting Authority 1982–89; Man. Dir The Really Useful Group 1989–90, Chair. 1990–95, Dir 1990–97; Dir VCI PLC 1995–98; Chair. The Radio Partnership Ltd 1996–99; Chair. Caspian Publishing Ltd 1996–2002; Dir Galaxy Media Corp PLC 1997–2000, Bird and Co. International 1999–2001, Friends Provident PLC 2001–02; wrote, edited and devised numerous TV series 1956–82; mem. Bd Royal Nat. Theatre 1992–94, City of London Sinfonia 1994–2001; Founder-Dir Sagitta Productions 1968–82; Dir Duke of York's Theatre 1979–82, Consolidated Productions (UK) Ltd 1980–82, Friends' Provident Life Office 1982–2001 (Chair. Friends' Provident Stewardship Cttee of Reference 1985–2000); Chair. Theatre Investment Fund 1990–2001, Trans-World Communications PLC 1992–94, Sony Music Pace Partnership (Nat. Bowl) 1992–95, Rajar Ltd 1992–2002, Friends' Provident Ethical Investment Trust PLC 1992–2001; Trustee Pension and Life Assurance Plan RNT 1994–2003; Chair. and co-f. Local Radio Asscn 1964; Chair. Asscn of Ind. Local Radio Contractors 1973–75, 1980; f. Recidivists Anonymous Fellowship Trust 1962; mem. Films, TV & Video Advisory Cttee, British Council 1983–89, Royal Coll. of Music Centenary Devt Fund 1982–84 (Chair. Media & Events Cttee 1982–94), Royal Jubilee Trusts Industry & Commerce Liaison Cttee 1986–88 (mem. Admin. Council of Trusts 1981–85); mem. Council Royal London Aid Soc. 1966–90, Fairbridge Drake Soc. 1981–96, Intermediate Tech. Group 1982–85; mem. Council for Charitable Support 1989–92; Pres. TV & Radio Industries Club 1985–86, London Marriage Guidance Council 1983–90; Vice-Pres. Commonwealth Youth Exchange Council 1982–85, RNID 1988–2003; Chair. Trustees, Soundaround 1981–2000, Artsline 1983–2000; Chair. Festival Media Cttee 1991–92; Trustee Japan Festival Educ. Trust 1992–2003; Trustee Venture Trust 1982–86; mem. Bd Open Coll. 1987–89; Gov. English Nat. Ballet 1989–91, Performing Arts and Tech. School; Patron Music Space Trust 1990–; Chair. British American Arts Asscn 1992–95, Sony Radio Awards 1992–98, Friends Provident Charitable Foundation 2002–, Royal Acad. of Dramatic Art 2003–; Fellow, Vice-Pres. Royal Television Soc. 1986–89; Hon. FRCM; Hon. mem. BAFTA. *Leisure interests:* chess, photography, sculpture. *Address:* 39 Hill Street, London, W1J 5NA, England. *Telephone:* (20) 7409-7332 (office). *Fax:* (20) 7491-0046 (office). *E-mail:* john@johnwhitney.co.uk (office).

WHITTAM SMITH, Andreas, CBE; British journalist; b. 13 June 1937; s. of Canon J. E. Smith; m. Valerie Catherine Sherry 1964; two s.; ed Keble Coll., Oxford; with N. M. Rothschild 1960–62, Stock Exchange Gazette 1962–63, Financial Times 1963–64, The Times 1964–66; Deputy City Ed. The Telegraph 1966–69; City Ed. The Guardian 1969–70; Ed. Investors Chronicle, Stock Exchange Gazette and Dir Throgmorton Publs 1970–77; City Ed. Daily Telegraph 1977–85; Ed. The Independent 1986–94, Ed.-in-Chief Independent on Sunday 1991–94, Dir Newspaper Publishing PLC 1986–, CEO 1987–93, Chair. 1994–95; Chair., Publr Notting Hill 1995–, Sir Winston Churchill Archive Trust 1995–2000, Financial Ombudsman Service Ltd. 1999–2003; Pres. British Bd of Film Classification 1998–2002; First Church Estates Commr; Vice-Pres. Nat. Council for One Parent Families 1982–86, 1991–; currently commentator, The Independent; Hon. Fellow Keble Coll., Oxford, UMIST 1989, Liverpool John Moores 2001; Hon. DLitt (St Andrew's, Salford) 1989; Wincott Award 1975; Journalist of the Year 1987. *Leisure interests:* music, history, walking. *Address:* c/o The Independent, Independent House, 191 Marsh Wall, London E14 9RS, England (office). *Website:* www.independent.co.uk (office).

WHITTINGTON, Harry Blackmore, PhD, FRS; British palaeontologist and academic; *Professor Emeritus, University of Cambridge;* b. 1916; m. Dorothy Whittington; ed Univ. of Birmingham; went to USA 1940s; taught and researched in China with his wife 1940s; Prof., Agassiz Museum of Comparative Zoology, Harvard Univ. 1949–66; Prof. of Geology, Univ. of Cambridge 1966, now Prof. Emer.; Pres. Palaeontological Soc. 1965; mem. Palaeontological Asscn; Hon. Fellow, Geological Soc. of America; Paleontological Soc. Medal 1983, NAS Mary Clark Thompson Medal 1990, Lapworth Medal, Palaeontological Asscn 2000, Int. Prize for Biology, Japan Soc. for the Promotion of Science 2001, Wollaston Medal, Geological Soc. of London 2001. *Publications:* Treatise on Invertebrate Palaeontology (Ed. Vol. O) 1959, Burgess Shale 1985, Trilobites 1992, The Fossils of the Burgess Shale (co-author) 1995; numerous articles in scientific journals on trilobites, taxonomy, stratigraphic uses and distribution, limb structure, silicified faunas, ontogeny, hypostomes, functional morphology and evolution. *Address:* Department of Earth Sciences, University of Cambridge, Downing Street, Cambridge, CB2 3EQ, England (office). *Telephone:* (1223) 333400 (office). *Fax:* (1223) 333450 (office). *Website:* www.esc.cam.ac.uk (office).

WHITTLE, Peter, PhD, FRS; New Zealand mathematician and academic; *Professor Emeritus, Statistical Laboratory, University of Cambridge;* b. 27 Feb. 1927, Wellington; s. of Percy Whittle and Elsie (née Tregurtha) Whittle; m. Kathe Hildegard Blomquist 1951; three s. three d.; ed Wellington Boys' Coll., Victoria Univ. Coll., NZ, Uppsala Univ., Sweden; NZ Sr Prin. Scientific Officer 1953–59; Lecturer in Math. Univ. of Cambridge 1959–61, Churchill Prof. of the Math. of Operational Research 1967–94, Prof. Emer. 1994–; Prof. of Math. Statistics, Univ. of Manchester 1961–67; Sr Fellow, Science and Eng Research Council 1988–91; mem. Royal Soc. of NZ 1981; Hon. DSc (Victoria Univ. of Wellington) 1987; Lanchester Prize, Operational Research Soc. of America 1987, Sylvester Medal (Royal Soc.) 1994, Guy Medal in Gold, Royal Statistical Soc. 1996, J. von Neumann Theory Medal, Inst. of Operational Research Man. Science 1997. *Publications:* Hypothesis Testing in Time Series Analysis 1951, Prediction and Regulation 1963, Probability 1970, Optimisation under Constraints 1971, Optimisation over Time 1982, Systems in Stochastic Equilibrium 1986, Risk-sensitive Optimal Control 1990, Probability via Expectation 1992, Optimal Control; Basics and Beyond 1995, Neural Nets and Chaotic Carriers 1998. *Leisure interests:* variable. *Address:* Statistical Laboratory, Pavilion D, Centre for Mathematical Studies, Wilberforce Road, Cambridge, CB3 0WB (office); 268 Queen Edith's Way, Cambridge, CB1 8NL, England (home). *Telephone:* (1223) 245422 (home). *Fax:* (1223) 337956. *E-mail:* whittle@statslab.cam.ac.uk (office). *Website:* www.statslab.cam.ac.uk (office).

WHITTLE, Stephen Charles, OBE, LLB, FRSA; British broadcasting executive; *Chairman, Broadcast Training and Skills Regulator;* b. 26 July 1945, London; s. of Charles William Whittle and Vera Lillian Whittle (née Moss); m. 1st Claire Walmsley 1988 (divorced 1999), 2nd Eve Salomon 2004; ed St Ignatius Coll., Stamford Hill, Univ. Coll., London; Asst Ed. New Christian 1968–70; Communications Officer, World Council of Churches, Geneva 1970–73; Ed. One World 1973–77, Asst Head Communications Dept 1975–77; Sr Producer BBC Religious Programmes, Manchester 1977–82, Producer Newsnight 1982, Ed. Songs of Praise and Worship 1983–89, Head of Religious Programmes 1989–93, Chief Adviser, Editorial Policy 1993–96; Dir Broadcasting Standards Council 1996–97, Broadcasting Standards Comm. 1997–2001; Controller of Editorial Policy, BBC 2001–05; Chair. Broadcast Training and Skills Regulator 2007–; Gov. European Inst. for the Media, Düsseldorf 1997–2002; Visiting Fellow, Reuters Inst. for the Study of Journalism, Oxford 2007–; mem. Solicitors Regulation Authority 2005–, Gen. Medical Council 2009–; Freeman, City of London 1990; Personal Award, Sandford St Martin Trust 1993. *Leisure interests:* cinema, theatre, music, reading, walking. *Address:* Flat 4, 34A Sydenham Hill, London, SE26 6LS, England (home). *Telephone:* (20) 8299-8898 (home). *E-mail:* stephen_whittle@btopenworld.com (office).

WHITWAM, David R., BS; American business executive; b. Madison, Wis.; ed Univ. of Wis.; joined Whirlpool Corpn 1968, various sr and marketing positions including Vice-Pres. Whirlpool brand business 1983–85, mem. Bd of Dirs 1985–, Vice-Chair. and Chief Marketing Officer 1985–87, Pres. 1987–92, Chair. and CEO 1987–2004 (retd); mem. Bd of Dirs PPG Industries Inc., Business Roundtable Policy Cttee and Educ. Task Force; Chair. Mich. Business Leaders for Educational Excellence Org.; Trustee Univ. of Wis. Alumni Research Foundation. *Address:* c/o Whirlpool Corporation, 2000 North M-63, Benton Harbor, MI 49022-2692, USA (office).

WHITWORTH-JONES, Anthony, CA; British arts administrator; *General Director, Garsington Opera;* b. 1 Sept. 1945, Bucks.; s. of Henry Whitworth-Jones and Patience Martin; m. Camilla Barlow 1974; one d.; ed Wellington

Coll.; Admin. Dir London Sinfonietta 1972–81; Admin. Glyndebourne Touring Opera 1981–89, Opera Man. Glyndebourne Festival Opera 1981–89, Gen. Dir Glyndebourne 1989–98; Chair. Michael Tippett Musical Foundation 1998–; Gen. Dir The Dallas Opera 2000–02; Artistic Dir Casa da Musica, Oporto, Portugal 2004–05, Artistic Consultant 2007–; Gen. Dir Garsington Opera 2005–; mem. Bd Spitalfields Festival 2003–06 (Hon. Advisor 2006–), Young Concert Artists Trust 2006–; Trustee, Leonard Ingrams Foundation 2006–. *Leisure interests:* the arts, jazz, golf, Greece. *Address:* 81 St Augustine's Road, London, NW1 9RR, England (home). *Telephone:* (20) 7267-3154 (home). *Fax:* (20) 7482-7017 (home).

WHYBROW, John W., BSc, MBA; British business executive; *Chairman, Wolseley PLC;* b. 11 March 1947; m.; two c.; ed Imperial Coll. London, Manchester Business School; joined Philips 1970, apptd Man.-Dir Philips Power Semiconductors and Microwave business 1987, Chair. and Man.-Dir Philips Electronics UK –1995, Pres. and CEO Philips Lighting Holding BV, The Netherlands 1995–2001, Exec. Vice-Pres. Royal Philips Electronics and mem. Bd of Man. 1998–2002; Dir (non-exec.) Wolseley PLC 1997, Chair. Remuneration Cttee 1998–2002, Deputy Chair. April–Dec. 2002, Chair. 2002–, Chair. Nominations Cttee; Chair. CSR PLC 2004–07; Dir (non-exec.) DSG International PLC 2003–; Chair. Petworth Cottage Nursing Home; Order of Merit for Services to Econ. Devt of Poland (Poland) 2002. *Leisure interests:* sailing, shooting. *Address:* Wolseley PLC, Parkview 1220, Arlington Business Park, Theale, West Berks., RG7 4GA, England (office). *Telephone:* (118) 9298700 (office). *Fax:* (118) 9298701 (office). *E-mail:* info@wolseley.com (office). *Website:* www.wolseley.com (office).

WIATR, Jerzy Józef, MPh; Polish politician and sociologist; b. 17 Sept. 1931, Warsaw; s. of Wilhelm Wiatr and Zofia Wiatr; m. Ewa Żurowska-Wiatr; one s.; ed Warsaw Univ.; asst, Warsaw Univ. 1951–59; Mil. Political Acad. 1959–65; Polish Acad. of Sciences (PAN) 1965–69; Prof., Warsaw Univ. 1969–2001, Dean of Social Sciences 1977–80; participant Round Table debates 1989; Deputy to Sejm (Parl.) 1991–2001; mem. Cttee for Nat. Defence and Cttee for Constitutional Responsibility 1991–97; Minister of Educ. 1996–97; Dir Inst. for Social and Int. Studies, Keller-Krauz Foundation 1998–; Pres. Cen. European Political Science Asscn 2000–03; Vice Pres. Int. Political Science Asscn 1979–82; Vice-Pres. Int. Studies Asscn 1980–81; mem. Polish United Workers Party (PZPR) 1949–90; mem. Social Democracy of Polish Repub. (SdRP) 1990–99; mem. Democratic Left Alliance 1999–; Commdr's Cross with Star of Polonia Restituta Order 1996; Dr hc. *Publications:* over 30 books including Education For and In the 21st Century 1997; numerous articles on sociology and political science. *Leisure interests:* tourism, books, chess. *Address:* ul. Komisji Edukacji Narodowej 98/49, 02 777 Warsaw, Poland (home). *Telephone:* (22) 619-90-11 (office); (22) 643-54-41 (home). *Fax:* (22) 643-54-41 (home). *E-mail:* jwiatr@ewspa.edu.pl (office).

WIBERG, Kenneth Berle, PhD; American academic; *Professor Emeritus of Chemistry, Yale University;* b. 22 Sept. 1927, New York; s. of Halfdan Wiberg and Solveig Berle; m. Marguerite Louise Koch 1951; two s. one d.; ed Mass Inst. of Tech. and Columbia Univ., New York; Instructor, Univ. of Washington 1950–52, Asst Prof. 1952–55, Assoc. Prof. 1955–57, Prof. 1958–62; Prof., Yale Univ. 1962–68, Chair. Dept of Chem. 1968–71, Whitehead Prof. of Chem. 1968–90, Eugene Higgins Prof. 1990–97, Prof. Emer. 1997–; Visiting Prof., Harvard Univ. 1957–58; A. P. Sloan Foundation Fellow 1958–62, J. S. Guggenheim Fellow 1961–62; mem. NAS, AAAS; ACS California Section Award 1962, ACS J. F. Norris Award 1973, ACS Arthur C. Cope Award 1988, Linus Pauling Award 1992. *Publications:* Laboratory Technique in Organic Chemistry 1960, Interpretation of NMR Spectra 1964, Physical Organic Chemistry 1964, Oxidation in Organic Chemistry (ed.) 1965, Computer Programming for Chemists 1966, Sigma Molecular Orbital Theory (with Sinanoglu) 1970; approx. 400 articles in scientific journals. *Address:* Department of Chemistry, Yale University, 225 Prospect Street, New Haven, CT 06520 (office); 160 Carmalt Road, Hamden, CT 06517, USA (home). *Telephone:* (203) 432-5160 (office); (203) 288-3408 (home). *Fax:* (203) 432-6144 (office). *E-mail:* kenneth.wiberg@yale.edu (office).

WICKER, Roger Frederick, BA, JD; American lawyer and politician; *Senator from Mississippi;* b. 5 July 1951, Pontotoc, Miss.; m. Gayle Wicker; three c.; ed Univ. of Mississippi; Judge Advocate and Capt. in US Air Force 1976–80, Lt-Col in US Air Force Reserve 1980–2004; Pnr, Sparks, Wicker and Colburn (law firm) 1982–94; public defender, Lee Co., Miss. 1984–87; judge pro tempore judge, Tupelo, Miss. 1986–87; mem. Mississippi State Senate 1987–94; mem. US House of Reps from 1st Miss. Dist 1995–2007, Deputy Majority Whip; Senator from Mississippi 2007–, mem. Armed Services Cttee, Commerce, Science, and Transportation Cttee, Veterans' Affairs Cttee; Republican, mem. Republican Policy Cttee 2001–. *Address:* 487 Russell Senate Office Building, Washington, DC 20510, USA (office). *Telephone:* (202) 224-6253 (office). *Fax:* (202) 228-0378 (office). *Website:* wicker.senate.gov (office).

WICKER, Thomas (Tom) Grey, AB, DJur; American journalist (retd) and author; b. 18 June 1926, Hamlet, NC; s. of Delancey D. Wicker and the late Esta Cameron Wicker; m. 1st Neva J. McLean 1949 (divorced 1973); one s. one d.; m. 2nd Pamela A. Hill 1974; ed Univ. of N Carolina; Exec. Dir Southern Pines (NC) Chamber of Commerce 1948–49; Ed. Sandhill Citizen, Aberdeen, NC 1949; Man. Ed. The Robesonian, Lumberton, NC 1949–50; Public Information Dir NC Bd of Public Welfare 1950–51; copy-ed., Winston-Salem (NC) Journal 1951–52, Sports Ed. 1954–55, Sunday Feature Ed. 1955–56, Washington Corresp. 1957, editorial writer 1958–59; Nieman Fellow, Harvard Univ. 1957–58, Joan Shorenstein Barone Center on the Press, Politics and Public Policy 1993; Assoc. Ed. Nashville Tennessean 1959–60; mem. staff, Washington Bureau, New York Times 1960–71, Chief of Bureau 1964–68; Assoc. Ed. New York Times 1968–85; columnist 1966–91; Visiting Scholar, First Amendment Center, Nashville 1998; Visiting Prof. of Journalism, Davidson Coll. NC, Middle Tenn. State Univ. 1999, Univ. of Southern Calif. 1999. *Publications:* novels (under pseudonym Paul Connolly): Get Out of Town 1951, Tears Are for Angels 1952, So Fair, So Evil 1955; novels (under own name): The Kingpin 1953, The Devil Must 1957, The Judgment 1961, Facing the Lions 1963, Unto This Hour 1984, Donovan's Wife 1992, Easter Lilly 1998; non-fiction: Kennedy without Tears 1964, JFK and LBJ: The Influence of Personality Upon Politics 1968, A Time To Die 1975, On Press 1978, One of Us: Richard Nixon and the American Dream 1991, Tragic Failure: Racial Integration in America 1996, Keeping the Record 2001, Dwight D. Eisenhower 2002, George Herbert Walker Bush 2004, Shooting Star: The Brief Arc of Joe McCarthy 2006; book chapters, contribs to nat. magazines. *Address:* Austin Hill Farm, 688 Austin Hill Road, Rochester, VT 05767, USA (home). *Telephone:* (802) 767-4433 (home). *Fax:* (802) 767-3699 (home). *E-mail:* twicker@sover.net (home).

WICKER-MIURIN, Fields, OBE, FRSA; American/British financial executive; b. 30 July 1958; ed Univ. of Virginia, l'Institut d'Etudes Politiques, Paris, Johns Hopkins School of Advanced International Studies, Bologna, Italy and Washington, DC; CFO and Dir of Global Finance and Strategy, London Stock Exchange 1994–97; fmr Vice-Pres. A. T. Kearney (strategy consultancy), London; fmr Sr Pnr, Mercer Man. Consulting London; fmr Man. Dir Vesta Capital Advisors (venture capital firm); Co-founder and Exec. Dir Leaders' Quest 2002–; mem. Dept of Trade and Industry (DTI) Exec. Cttee, Chair. DTI Investment Cttee, ex officio mem. DTI Tech. Strategy Bd 2002–08; mem. Bd of Dirs D. Carnegie & Co. AB 2003–, Royal London 2003–, Commonwealth Devt Corpn, Savills plc 2002–, United Business Media plc; mem. Nasdaq Tech. Advisory Cttee; apptd Panel of Experts to advise EU Parliament on harmonisation of financial services; Fellow, RSA; fmr Fellow, World Econ. Forum; Gov. King's Coll. London; contrib. Earth Times; awarded Global Leader for Tomorrow (World Econ. Forum). *Address:* c/o Leaders' Quest, 3-5 Richmond Hill, Richmond-upon-Thames, Surrey, TW10 6RE England. *Telephone:* (20) 8948-5200 (office). *Fax:* (20) 8332-6423. *E-mail:* info@leadersquest.org. *Website:* www.leadersquest.org.

WICKRAMANAYAKA, Hon. Ratnasiri; Sri Lankan politician; *Prime Minister, Deputy Minister of Defence and Minister of Internal Administration;* ed Dharmapala Vidyalaya, Pannipitiya, Ananda Coll., Colombo, Lincoln's Inn, London; elected mem. Mahajana Eksath Peramuna for Horana 1960; apptd Deputy Minister of Justice 1970; Gen. Sec. Sri Lankan Freedom Party 1977; won Kalutara Dist seat 1994; apptd Minister of Public Admin, Home Affairs and Plantation and Leader of the House 1994; Prime Minister of Sri Lanka 2000–01; Minister of Buddha Sasana and Religious Affairs 2000–02; Chair. United People's Freedom Alliance; Prime Minister and Minister of Internal Admin 2005–; ex-officio Chair. Bd of Govs Cen. Cultural Fund. *Address:* Prime Minister's Office, 58, Sir Ernest de Silva Mawatha, Colombo 7, Sri Lanka (office). *Telephone:* (11) 2575317 (office). *Fax:* (11) 2575454 (office). *E-mail:* slpm@sltnet.lk (office); pmo@pmoffice.gov.lk (office). *Website:* www.pmoffice.gov.lk (office).

WICKRAMASINGHE, Nalin Chandra, MA, PhD, ScD; British scientist and academic; *Professor of Applied Mathematics and Astronomy, University of Cardiff;* b. 20 Jan. 1939, Colombo, Sri Lanka; s. of Percival H. Wickramasinghe and Theresa E. Wickramasinghe; m. Nelum Priyadarshini Pereira 1966; one s. two d.; ed Royal Coll., Colombo and Univs of Colombo and Cambridge; Research Fellow, Jesus Coll., Cambridge 1963–66, Fellow 1967–73, Tutor 1970–73; Staff mem. Inst. of Theoretical Astronomy, Univ. of Cambridge 1968–73; Prof. and Head of Dept of Applied Math. and Astronomy, Univ. Coll., Cardiff 1973–88; Prof. of Applied Math. and Astronomy, Univ. of Wales Coll. of Cardiff 1988–; Dir Cardiff Centre for Astrobiology 2000–; Dir Inst. of Fundamental Studies, Sri Lanka 1982–83; UNDP Consultant and Scientific Adviser to Pres. of Sri Lanka 1970–81; Visiting Prof., Univs of Ceylon, Maryland, Arizona and Kyoto 1966–70, Univ. of Western Ontario 1974–76, Inst. of Space and Astronomical Science, Japan 1993, Univ. of the W Indies, Mona, Kingston, Jamaica 1994; Dr hc (Soka Univ., Tokyo) 1996, Hon. DSc (Ruhuna Univ., Sri Lanka); Dag Hammarskjöld Laureate in Science 1986, Scholarly Achievement Award of Inst. of Oriental Philosophy, Japan 1989, Sahabdeen Award for Science 1996; Vidya Jyothi (Sri Lanka Nat. Honour) 1992. *Publications:* Interstellar Grains 1967, Light Scattering Functions for Small Particles with Applications in Astronomy 1973, The Cosmic Laboratory 1975; with Sir Fred Hoyle: Life Cloud: The Origin of Life in the Universe 1978, Diseases from Space 1979, The Origin of Life 1980, Evolution from Space 1981, Space Travellers, The Bringers of Life, Is Life an Astronomical Phenomenon? 1982, Why Neo-Darwinism Doesn't Work 1982, Proofs That Life Is Cosmic 1982, Fundamental Studies and the Future of Science 1984, From Grains to Bacteria 1984, Living Comets 1985, Archaeopteryx, the Primordial Bird: a case of fossil forgery 1986, Cosmic Life Force 1987, The Theory of Cosmic Grains 1991, Our Place in the Cosmos: the Unfinished Revolution 1993, Life on Mars? The Case for a Cosmic Heritage 1996; with F. D. Kahn and P. G. Mezger: Interstellar Matter 1972; with D. J. Morgan: Solid State Astrophysics 1976; with Daisaku Ikeda: 2000 A.D. – Emergent Perspectives 1992, Glimpses of Life, Time and Space 1994, Space and Eternal Life 1997, Cosmic Dragons 2001, A Journey with Fred Hoyle 2004. *Leisure interests:* photography, poetry. *Address:* University of Cardiff, Cardiff, CF1 1XL (office); 24 Llwynypia Road, Lisvane, Cardiff, CF14 0SY, Wales (home). *Telephone:* (29) 2087-4201 (office); (29) 2075-2146. *Fax:* (29) 2075-3173. *E-mail:* wickramasinghe@cf.ac.uk (office); xdw20@dial.pipex.com (home). *Website:* (office).

WICKREMASINGHE, Ranil, LLB; Sri Lankan politician and lawyer; *Leader, United National Party;* b. 24 March 1949, Colombo; s. of Esmond Wickremasinghe; m. Maithree Wickremasinghe 1995; ed Royal Coll. of

Colombo, Univ. of Colombo and Sri Lanka Law Coll.; attorney-at-law, Supreme Court; elected mem. Parl. 1977, 1989; Leader of House 1989–93; Deputy Minister of Foreign Affairs 1977–79; Minister of Youth Affairs and Employment 1978–89, of Educ. 1980–89, of Industries 1989–90, of Industries, Science and Tech. 1990–94; Prime Minister of Sri Lanka 1992, 2001–04, also Minister of Policy Devt and Implementation 2001–04; Leader, United Nat. Party 1994–, Leader of the Opposition 1994–2001, 2006–; cand. in presidential elections 1999, 2005. *Address:* United National Party (UNP), 30 Sir Marcu Fernando Mawatha, Colombo 7, Sri Lanka (office). *Telephone:* (11) 5636551 (office). *Fax:* (11) 2682905 (office). *E-mail:* info@unp.lk (office). *Website:* www.unp.lk (office).

WICKS, Malcolm; British politician; *Minister of State, Department for Business, Enterprise and Regulatory Reform;* b. 1 July 1947, Hatfield, Herts.; m. Margaret Wicks; one s. two d.; ed North West London Polytechnic and London School of Econs; Social Policy Analyst, Home Office 1968–74; Univ. Lecturer 1974–77; Dir Family Policy Studies Centre 1980–92; MP for Croydon N (Labour Party) 1992–, Opposition Spokesperson for Pensions 1995–97, Chair. Educ. Select Cttee 1998–99, Parl. UnderSec. of State for Lifelong Learning 1999–2001, Parl. UnderSec. of State for Work 2001–03, Minister for Pensions 2003–05, for Energy 2005–06, for Science and Innovation 2006–07, Minister of State, Dept for Business, Enterprise and Regulatory Reform 2007–; Pres. Carer to Carer; Vice-Pres. Carers UK, Alzheimers Soc. *Publications include:* several books and reports on the welfare state. *Address:* Constituency Office, 84 High Street, Thornton Heath, Surrey, CR7 8LF England (office). *Telephone:* (20) 8665-1214 (office). *Fax:* (20) 8683-0179 (office). *E-mail:* wicksm@parliament.uk (office). *Website:* www.malcolmwicks.labour.co.uk (office).

WICKS, Sir Nigel Leonard, GCB, CVO, CBE; British civil servant (retd); *Chairman, Committee on Standards in Public Life;* b. 16 June 1940; s. of the late Leonard Charles Wicks and Beatrice Irene Wicks; m. Jennifer Mary Coveney 1969; three s.; ed Beckenham and Penge Grammar School, Portsmouth Coll. of Tech., Univ. of Cambridge, Univ. of London; British Petroleum 1958–68; served HM Treasury 1968–75, 1978–83, Second Perm Sec. (Finance) 1989–2000; Pvt. Sec. to Prime Minister 1975–78; mem. Bd BNOC 1980–82; Econ. Minister Embassy, Washington and UK; Exec. Dir IMF and IBRD 1983–85; Prin. Pvt. Sec. to Prime Minister 1985–88; Pres. Monetary Cttee of EC 1993–98; Chair. Cttee on Standards in Public Life 2001–, CRESTCO 2001–02; Deputy Chair. Bd of Dirs Euroclear plc, Euroclear Bank SA/NV; Gov. King's Coll. School, Wimbledon; Grand Officier de l'Order grand-ducal de la Couronne de Chêne (Luxembourg); Hon. LLD (Bath) 1999. *Address:* Committee on Standards in Public Life, 35 Great Smith Street, London SW1P 3BQ (office); Steeple Ashton, Lime Grove, West Clandon, Guildford GU4 7UT, England. *Telephone:* (20) 7276-2595 (office). *Fax:* (20) 7276-2585 (office). *E-mail:* Standards.evidence@gtnet.gov.uk (office); nigel.wicks@bigfoot.com (home). *Website:* www.public-standards.gov.uk (office).

WIDDECOMBE, Rt Hon. Ann Noreen, PC, MA; British politician and writer; b. 4 Oct. 1947, Bath, Somerset; d. of the late James Murray Widdecombe and of Rita Noreen Plummer; ed La Sainte Union Convent, Bath, Univ. of Birmingham, Lady Margaret Hall Oxford; with Marketing Dept Unilever 1973–75; Sr Admin. Univ. of London 1975–87; contested Burnley 1979, Plymouth Devonport 1983; MP for Maidstone 1987–97, Maidstone and The Weald 1997–; Parl. Pvt. Sec. to Tristan Garel-Jones, MP 1990; Parl. Under-Sec. State Dept of Social Security 1990–93, Dept of Employment 1993–94; Minister for Employment 1994–95, Home Office 1995–97; Shadow Health Minister 1998–99, Shadow Home Sec. 1999–2001; Conservative; Spectator/Highland Park Minister of the Year 1996, Despatch Box Best Front Bencher 1998, Talk Radio Straight Talker of the Year 1998. *Publications:* Layman's Guide to Defence 1984, Inspired and Outspoken 1999, The Clematis Tree (novel) 2000, An Act of Treachery 2001, An Act of Peace 2005, Father Figure 2005. *Leisure interests:* reading, researching Charles II's escape. *Address:* House of Commons, Westminster, London, SW1A 0AA (office). *Telephone:* (20) 7219-5091 (office). *Fax:* (20) 7219-2413 (office). *E-mail:* widdecombea@parliament.uk (office). *Website:* www.annwiddecombemp.com (office).

WIDNALL, Sheila Evans, BSc, MS, PhD, FAAS; American astrophysicist and academic; *Institute Professor and Professor of Aeronautics and Astronautics, Massachusetts Institute of Technology;* b. 13 July 1938, Tacoma, Wash.; d. of Rolland Evans and Genevieve Krause; m. William Widnall 1960; one s. one d.; ed Massachusetts Inst. of Technology; Research Staff Engineer, MIT 1961–62, Research Asst 1962–64, Asst Prof. 1964–70, Assoc. Prof. 1970–74, Prof. 1974–86, Abby Rockefeller Mauze Prof. of Aeronautics and Astronautics 1986–93, Assoc. Provost 1992–93, Inst. Prof. 1998–, Dir Fluid Dynamics Research Lab. 1979–90, Chair. of Faculty 1979–80, Assoc. Provost 1992–93; Dir Univ. Research, US Dept of Transportation, Washington, DC 1974–75; Sec. of US Air Force 1993–98, Co-Chair. Dept of Defense Task Force on Sexual Harassment and Discrimination; fmr Dir Aerospace Corpn, Draper Laboratories, ANSER Corp., Chemical Fabrics Inc.; fmr Pres. AAAS; Dir GenCorp Inc.; Vice-Pres. Nat. Acad. of Eng 1998–; Fellow, American Inst. of Aeronautics and Astronautics (AIAA), mem. Bd of Dirs 1975–77, Pres. 2000–01; mem. Nat. Research Council Governing Bd 1999–; Fellow, APS, American Acad. of Arts and Sciences, Royal Aeronautical Soc.; fmr mem. Carnegie Comm. on Science, Council of Smithsonian Inst. of Washington; mem. Exec. Cttee, Nat. Research Council of the Nat. Acads; mem. Int. Acad. of Astronautics, Seattle Mountaineers, Appalachian Mountain Club, Eastern Yacht Club, Charles River Wheelman, Potomac Peddlers; fmr consultant, Macarthur Foundation; fmr Trustee Carnegie Corpn (also Vice-Chair.), Boston Museum of Science; Trustee Sloan Foundation, Inst. for Defense Analysis; Hon. DSc (Princeton) 1994; American Inst. of Aeronautics Lawrence Sperry Achievement Award 1972, Soc. of Women Engineers Outstanding Achievement Award 1975, Boston Museum of Science Washburn Award 1987, Nat. Acad. of Eng Distinguished Service Award 1993, Barnard Coll. Medal of Distinction 1994, Air Force Asscn W. Stuart Symington Award 1995, Air Force Asscn Maxwell A. Kriendler Memorial Award 1995, Boston USO Mil. Award 1995, ASME Applied Mechanics Award 1996, New England Council New Englander of the Year 1996, Women's Int. Center Living Legacy Award 1998, Nat. Space Club Goddard Award 1998, NDIA Hartinger Award 1999, AIAA Reed Aeronautics Award 2000, ASME Spirit of St Louis Medal 2001. *Publications:* contrib. articles to professional journals. *Address:* Room 33-411, Department of Aeronautics and Astronautics, Massachusetts Institute of Technology, 77 Massachusetts Avenue, Cambridge, MA 02139-4307, USA (office). *Telephone:* (617) 253-3595 (office). *E-mail:* sheila@mit.edu (office). *Website:* web.mit.edu/aeroastro/www (office).

WIDOM, Benjamin, PhD; American chemist and academic; *Goldwin Smith Professor Emeritus of Chemistry, Cornell University;* b. 13 Oct. 1927, Newark, NJ; s. of Morris Widom and Rebecca Hertz Widom; m. Joanne McCurdy 1953; two s. one d.; ed Stuyvesant High School, New York and Columbia and Cornell Univs; Research Assoc., Univ. of NC 1952–54; Instructor in Chem., Cornell Univ. 1954–55, Asst Prof. 1955–59, Assoc. Prof. 1959–63, Prof. 1963–, Goldwin Smith Prof. Emer. 1983–; van der Waals Prof., Univ. of Amsterdam 1972; Visiting Prof. of Chem., Harvard Univ. 1975; IBM Visiting Prof. of Theoretical Chem., Univ. of Oxford 1978; Lorentz Prof., Leiden Univ. 1985; Visiting Prof., Katholieke Univ., Leuven 1988, Université d'Aix Marseille III 1995; Kramers/Debye Prof., Univ. of Utrecht 1999; Fellow, American Acad. of Arts and Sciences, New York Acad. of Sciences; mem. NAS, American Philosophical Soc.; Hon. DSc (Chicago); Dr hc (Utrecht); Boris Pregel Award, New York Acad. of Sciences, ACS Langmuir Award, Dickson Prize for Science, Carnegie-Mellon Univ., ACS Hildebrand Award, Hirschfelder Prize in Theoretical Chem., Univ. of Wisconsin, Bakhuis Roozeboom Medal, Royal Netherlands Acad. of Arts and Sciences, Onsager Medal, Univ. of Trondheim, Boltzmann Medal, IUPAP Comm. on Statistical Physics, ACS Award in Theoretical Chem. *Publications:* Molecular Theory of Capillarity (with J. S. Rowlinson) 1982, Statistical Mechanics: A Concise Introduction for Chemists 2002. *Address:* Department of Chemistry, 206C Baker Laboratory, Cornell University, Ithaca, NY 14853, USA (office). *Telephone:* (607) 255-3363 (office). *Fax:* (607) 255-4137 (office). *E-mail:* bw24@cornell.edu (office). *Website:* www.chem.cornell.edu (office).

WIEBE, Rudy Henry, BA, MA, ThB; Canadian writer and academic; *Professor Emeritus of English and Creative Writing, University of Alberta;* b. 4 Oct. 1934, Fairholme, Sask.; m. Tena F. Isaak 1958, two s. one d.; ed Univ. of Alberta, Univ. of Tübingen, Mennonite Brethren Bible Coll., Univ. of Manitoba, Univ. of Iowa; Asst and Assoc. Prof. of English, Goshen College, Ind. 1963–67; Asst Prof., Univ. of Alberta 1967–71, Assoc. Prof. 1971–77, Prof. of English and Creative Writing 1977–92, Prof. Emer. 1992–; mem. Writers Guild of Alberta (Founding Pres. 1980), Writers Union of Canada (Pres. 1986–87); Hon. DLitt Univ. of Winnipeg 1986, Wilfred Laurier Univ. 1991, Brock Univ. 1991; Governor-General's Awards for Fiction, 1973, 1994, Lorne Pierce Medal, Royal Soc. of Canada, 1987, Charles Taylor Prize for Literary Non-fiction 2007. *Publications:* Fiction: Peace Shall Destroy Many 1962, First and Vital Candle 1966, The Blue Mountains of China 1970, The Temptations of Big Bear 1973, Where is the Voice Coming From? 1974, The Scorched-Wood People 1977, Alberta: A Celebration 1979, The Mad Trapper 1980, The Angel of the Tar Sands and Other Stories 1982, My Lovely Enemy 1983, A Chinook Christmas 1992, A Discovery of Strangers 1994, River of Stone: Fictions and Memories 1995, Sweeter Than All the World 2001; Non-fiction (memoir): Of This Earth: A Mennonite Boyhood in the Boreal Forest 2006; Play: Far as the Eye Can See, 1977. Essays: A Voice in the Land, 1981; Playing Dead: A Contemplation Concerning the Arctic, 1989. Editor: The Story-Makers: A Selection of Modern Short Stories, 1970; Stories from Western Canada, 1971; Stories from Pacific and Arctic Canada (with Andreas Schroeder), 1974; Double Vision: Twentieth Century Stories in English, 1976; Getting Here, 1977; More Stories from Western Canada (with Aritha van Herk), 1980; West of Fiction (with Aritha van Herk and Leah Flater), 1983; numerous contribs to anthologies and periodicals. *Address:* c/o Department of English and Film Studies, University of Alberta, 3-5 Humanities Centre, Edmonton, Alberta T6G 2E5, Canada. *E-mail:* rudy.wiebe@shaw.ca. *Website:* www.humanities.ualberta.ca/english.

WIECZOREK-ZEUL, Heidemarie; German politician; *Federal Minister of Economic Co-operation and Development;* b. 21 Nov. 1942, Frankfurt am Main; ed Frankfurt Univ.; teacher, Friedrich Ebert School, Rüsselsheim 1965–74; joined SPD 1965, mem. Nat. Exec. 1984, mem. Presidium 1986, SPD Dist Chair. for S Hesse 1988, Deputy Chair. SPD 1993; City Councillor, Rüsselsheim 1968; mem. Gross-Gerau Dist Council 1972; Fed. Chair. Young Socialists 1974–77; Chair. European Co-ordination Bureau for Int. Youth Asscns 1977–79; mem. European Parl. 1979–87; mem. German Bundestag and SPD Parl. Spokesperson on European Policy 1987; Fed. Minister for Econ. Co-operation and Devt 1998–. *Address:* Federal Ministry of Economic Co-operation and Development, Dahlmannstr. 4, 53113 Bonn, Germany (office). *Telephone:* (228) 995350 (office). *Fax:* (228) 995353500 (office). *E-mail:* info@bmz.bund.de (office). *Website:* www.bmz.de (office).

WIEDEKING, Wendelin, Diplom Ingenieur; German automotive industry executive; *Chairman of the Executive Board, President and CEO, Porsche AG;* b. 28 Aug. 1952, Ahlen; m.; ed Aachen Univ. of Tech.; studied mechanical eng and worked as scientific asst Machine Tool Lab. Rhine-Westphalian Coll. of Advanced Tech. Aachen; Dir's Asst Production and Materials Man. Porsche AG 1983–88; Div. Man. Glyco Metall-Werke KG 1988, advanced to CEO and Chair. Bd of Man. 1990; Production Dir Porsche 1991, CEO 1992–, Chair. of

Exec. Bd 1993–, also Pres.; mem. Bd of Dirs Novartis AG, Eagle Picher Inc. *Publications:* Das Davidprinzip, Anders ist Besser. *Address:* Porsche AG, Porscheplatz 1, Stuttgart, Germany (office). *Telephone:* (711) 9110 (office). *Website:* www.porsche.com (office).

WIEDEMANN, Kent, MA; American diplomatist (retd); m. Janice Weddle 1967; one s.; ed San Jose State Univ., Univ. of Oregon; served with Peace Corps in Micronesia; joined US State Dept 1974; served in Poznań, Shanghai and Beijing; Deputy Chief of Mission, Singapore and Tel-Aviv; on staff Nat. Security Council, White House; on assignment, Bureau of Int. Security Affairs, Dept of Defense; Dir Office of Chinese and Mongolian Affairs, Bureau of East Asian and Pacific Affairs; Deputy Asst Sec., Bureau of East Asian and Pacific Affairs; Chargé d'affaires and Chief of Mission, Rangoon; Amb. to Cambodia 1999–2002. *Address:* c/o US Special Operations Command, 7701 Tampa Point Boulevard, MacDill Air Force Base, FL 33621, USA (office).

WIEGHARDT, Karl Ernst, DipChem, PhD; German chemist and academic; *Director, Max-Planck-Institut für Bioanorganische Chemie;* b. 25 July 1942, Göttingen; ed Univ. of Heidelberg; Postdoctoral Fellow, Univ. Heidelberg 1969–72, Asst Prof. of Inorganic Chem., 1974–75; Postdoctoral Fellow, Univ. of Leeds, UK 1972; Assoc. Prof. of Inorganic Chem., Univ. of Hanover 1975–81; Prof. of Inorganic Chem., Ruhr-Univ. Bochum 1981–94, Hon. Prof. 1994–; Dir Max-Planck-Institut für Bioanorganische Chemie, Mulheim 1994–; Alexander von Humboldt Research Award 1995, Univ. of Ill. John Bailar Medal 2000, German Chemical Soc. Wilhelm-Klemm-Medal 2000, Royal Soc. of Chem. Centenary Medal 2002. *Address:* Max-Planck-Institut für Bioanorganische Chemie, Stiftstrasse 34-36, Postfach 10 13 65, 45413 Mülheim an der Ruhr, Germany (office). *Telephone:* (208) 306-3609 (office). *Fax:* (208) 306-3952 (office). *E-mail:* wieghardt@mpi-muelheim.mpg.de (office). *Website:* www.mpi -muelheim.mpg.de/strneu/staff/wieghardt/wieghardt_home_e.html (office).

WIEHAHN, Nicholas E., LLD; South African academic, labour law scholar and consultant; b. 29 April 1929, Mafeking (now Mafikeng); s. of Johannes Wiehahn and Anna C. Wiehahn; m. Huiberdina J. Verhage 1956; two s.; ed Univ. of OFS, Univ. of S. Africa; research work in Univs. of Hamburg, Cologne, Heidelberg, Munich and London; research visits to labour insts. and univs. in Europe, Israel, Canada, USA and Japan; Advocate, Supreme Court of SA and High Court of Lesotho; Prof. in Labour and Industrial Law at various univs.; Chair. Transkei Nat. Manpower Comm.; Dir Inst. of Labour Relations 1976–77 Univ. of SA, Prof. Extra-Ordinarius, 1980–, Prof. Siemens Chair of Industrial Relations, Unisa School of Business Leadership, Dir Oct. 1984–; mem. Council, Univ. of Port Elizabeth 1973–75, Free State Univ. 1980–; Chair. Council, Univ. of Zululand 1981–90; Dir Bureau for Int. Labour Affairs, Dept of Manpower 1977–78, Ed.-in-Chief EMPACT 1977–78, Labour Adviser to Minister of Manpower 1977–79; mem. Prime Minister's Econ. Advisory Council 1977; Pres. Industrial Court of SA 1979–80, Industrial Court of KwaNdebele; Chair. Comm. of Inquiry into Labour Legis. (Wiehahn Comm.) 1977–80, into Labour Matters (Namibia) 1987–88; Chair. Labour Council, SA Transport Services 1988; Chair. Wiehahn Labour Comm., Transkei 1989, KwaNdebele 1990, Royal Comm. of Inquiry, Swaziland; Chair. Lotteries and Gambling Bd; mem. various Govt comms., advisory cttees., etc.; other public and educational appointments; Chair. and Dir of several public and pvt. cos. 1981–; three hon. doctorates; recipient of several awards and bursaries; Order for Meritorious Service (Gold Class) 1993. *Publications:* articles on labour law and industrial relations in periodicals, commentaries and other publs; Change in South Africa 1983. *Leisure interests:* reading, gardening. *Address:* P.O. Box 5862, Pretoria 0001, South Africa. *Telephone:* (12) 34246014 (office); 474438 (home). *Fax:* (12) 3424609 (office).

WIELGUS, Bishop Stanisław Wojciech, Polish ecclesiastic and professor of history of philosophy; b. 23 April 1939, Wierzchowiska; ed Catholic Univ. of Lublin, Univ. of Munich; ordained priest 1962; curate and parish catechist 1962–69; Prof., Catholic Univ. of Lublin 1969–, Pro-Rector 1988–92, Rector 1989–98; Bishop of Płock 1999–2006; apptd Archbishop of Warsaw Jan. 2007 (resgnd Jan. 2007), Archbishop Emer. 2007–; Head, Dept of the History of Philosophy in Poland, Head, Interdisciplinary Centre of the History of Medieval Culture; Head, Catholic Univ. of Lublin (KUL) Catholic Encyclopaedia Editing Offices; Vice-Pres. Conf. of Polish Univ. of Rectors 1990–93; del. Extraordinary Synod of European Bishops, Rome 1991; canon Lublin Cathedral Chapter; leader Coll. of Rectors, Lublin Region 1992–93; mem. Ethical Team of Scientific Research attached to Minister of Educ. 1998–; Chair. Educ. Council of the Nat. Conf. of Bishops in Poland 2001–; Chair. Council of the Polish Rectors Foundation 2001; mem. KUL Science Soc. (Gen. Sec. 1985–88), Acad. Council of the John Paul Second Inst., mem. numerous socs; Officer's Cross, Order of Polonia Restituta 1993; Award of the Minister of Nat. Educ., Catholic Soc. Civitas Christiana Award 1998, Honour of the Societas Scientiarum Lublinensis Resolutio Pro Laude 1999. *Publications:* Quaestiones Nicolai Peripatetici 1973, Benedykta Hessego Quaestiones super octo libros Physicorum Aristotelis 1983, Bible Research in Ancient Times and in the Middle Ages 1990, Foreign Biblical Literature in Medieval Poland 1990, Mediaeval Biblical Literature in the Polish Language 1991, Mediaeval Polish Bible Studies in the Latin Language 1992, From Research into the Middle Ages 1995, The Medieval Polish Doctrine of the Law of Nations: Jus Gentium 1998, Deo et Patriae, vol. 1 1996, vol. II 1999, Dobra jest więcej 2001, Na Skale budujmy nasz świat 2002, Z obszarów średniowiecznej mysli islamskiej, żydowskiej i chrzescijańskiej 2002, Filozofie w Rzeczypospolitej 2002, Ducha nie gaście 2004. *Leisure interests:* factual literature, memoirs, film. *Address:* c/o Diecezja Płocka, ul. Tumska 3, 09-402 Płock (office); pl. Narutowicza 10, 09-402 Płock, Poland.

WIELICKI, Krzysztof; Polish mountaineer and business executive; b. 5 Jan. 1950, Szklarka Przygodzka; m.; one s. two d.; ed Tech. Univ. of Wrocław; owner of four commercial cos (distribution of alpine and outdoor equipment and garments) and mountain agencies; began climbing 1970; joined 27 high mountain expeditions including Dolomites, Alps, Caucasus, Pamir, Hindukush, Karakoram and Himalayas; leader of 12 expeditions; the fifth man in the world to climb all 14 8,000m peaks; first person to climb in winter: Mount Everest (with partner Leszek Cichy) 1980, Kanchenjunga 1986, Lhotse (solo) 1988; leader climbing expedition on K-2 (Karakoram); mem. The Explorers' Club 1997, Group de Haute Montagne (France) 2001–; Pres. Jury, Piolet d'Or 2004. *Publications:* Talks about Everest (co-author) 1980, The Crown of the Himalayas 1997. *Leisure interest:* travelling. *Address:* ul. A. Frycza Modrzewskiego 21, 443-100 Tychy, Poland (home). *Telephone:* (32) 227-15-00 (home).

WIELOWIEYSKI, Andrzej Jan, LLM; Polish politician, economist and publicist; *Vice-Chairman, Senate;* b. 16 Dec. 1927, Warsaw; m. Zofia Wielowieyska; one s. six d.; ed Jagiellonian Univ., Kraków; trainee, Radomsko Forest Inspectorate 1942–44; Head, Foreign Dept Bratnia Pomoc students' org. Jagiellonian Univ., Kraków 1945–48; mem. Wici Rural Youth Union (ZMW Wici) 1945–48; subsequently councillor and inspector in Ministry of Finance 1948–52; Ed., Słowo Powszechne, Warsaw 1948; inspector, Head Office of Workers' Housing Estates Enterprise Warsaw-South, subsequently Warsaw-Śródmieście 1952–55; inspector, Head Urban Devt Dept, Municipal Comm. of Econ. Planning, Warsaw 1956–62; Head of Section Więź, Warsaw 1961–80; Lecturer, Doświadczenie i Przyszłość (Experience and the Future) Conversatorium, Warsaw 1978–82; Ed. Królowa Apostołów, Warsaw 1982–84, Gość Niedzielny, Katowice 1982–90; mem. Solidarity Ind. Self-governing Trade Union 1980–, adviser to Nat. Comm. of Solidarity 1980–81; Head of Social and Labour Study Centre attached to Nat. Comm. of Solidarity, Warsaw 1981; adviser to Nat. Executive Comm. of Solidarity 1987–89; mem. Civic Cttee attached to Lech Wałęsa (q.v.), Chair. of Solidarity 1988–90; participant Round Table plenary debates, Co-Chair. group for economy and social policy Feb.–April 1989; Senator 1989–91, 2001– (Pres. Freedom Union Group), Vice-Marshal of the Senate 1989–91, currently Vice-Chair. Senate; Chair. Civic Parl. Caucus of Senate 1989–90; Deputy to Sejm (Parl.) 1991–, mem. Parl. Comm. Foreign Affairs 1991–, 2001–; Polish del. and Vice-Pres. Council of Europe Parl. Ass. 1992–; mem. Democratic Action of Civic Movement (ROAD) 1990, Democratic Union 1991–94, Freedom Union 1994–; mem. Pax Romana Catholic Intelligentsia Int. Fed., mem. of Council 1979–83; mem. of European Council 1987–89; co-f. Int. Fed. of Family Life Promotion 1979–; Silver Cross of Merit with Swords, Cross of Valour, Partisan Cross, Cross of Home Army (AK), Victory and Freedom Medal. *Publications:* Przed trzecim przyśpieszeniem 1969, Przed nami małżeństwo 1972, over 300 articles on politics, religion, educ. and history. *Leisure interests:* gardening, skiing, yachting, historical and detective stories. *Address:* Senate, ul. Wiejska 4/6/8, 00-902 Warsaw (office); Biuro Senatora UW, Andrzeja Wielowiejskiego, ul. Marsza łkowska 77/79, 00-683 Warsaw, Poland (home). *Telephone:* (22) 8275047 (office). *Fax:* (22) 8277851 (office). *E-mail:* biuro@unia-wolnosci.pl (office). *Website:* www.uw.org.pl (office).

WIEMAN, Carl E., PhD; American physicist and academic; *Distinguished Professor of Physics, University of Colorado;* b. 26 March 1951, Corvallis, Ore.; ed Mass Inst. of Tech., Stanford Univ.; Asst Research Scientist Dept of Physics, Univ. of Mich. 1977–79, Asst Prof. 1979–84; Assoc. Prof. of Physics, Univ. of Colo 1984–87, Prof. 1987–, Distinguished Prof. 1997–, Fellow Jt Inst. for Lab. Astrophysics 1985–, Chair. 1993–95; Fellow American Physical Soc. 1990, NAS 1995, American Acad. of Arts and Sciences 1998; mem. Optical Soc. of America, American Asscn of Physics Teachers; Hon. DS (Univ. of Chicago) 1997; numerous awards including Sloan Research Fellowship 1984, Guggenheim Fellowship 1990–91, E.O. Lawrence Award in Physics 1993, Fritz London Award 1996, King Faisal Int. Prize for Science 1997, Schawlow Prize for Laser Science 1999, Benjamin Franklin Medal in Physics 2000, Nobel Prize in Physics (jt recipient) 2001. *Address:* Joint Institute for Laboratory Astrophysics, 440 UCB, University of Colorado, Boulder, CO 80309-0440, USA (office). *Telephone:* (303) 492-6963 (office). *Fax:* (303) 492-8994 (office). *Website:* spot.colorado.edu/~cwieman (office); jilawww.colorado.edu (office).

WIESCHAUS, Eric F., PhD; American molecular biologist; *Professor of Biology, Princeton University;* b. 8 June 1947, South Bend, Ind.; s. of Leroy Joseph Wieschaus and Marcella Carner Wieschaus; m. Trudi Schupbach 1982; three d.; ed Univ. of Notre Dame, Yale Univ.; Research Fellow, Zoological Inst., Univ. of Zurich 1975–78; Group Leader European Molecular Biology Lab., Germany 1978–81; Asst Prof. then Assoc. Prof., Princeton Univ. 1981–87, Prof. of Biology 1987–; Visiting Researcher Center for Pathobiology, Univ. of Calif., Irvine 1977; Fellow Laboratoire de Génétique Moléculaire, France, AAAS; mem. Damon Runyon-Walter Winchell Cancer Fund 1987–92, NAS; shared Nobel Prize for Medicine and Physiology 1995. *Publications:* numerous articles. *Address:* Department of Molecular Biology, Princeton University, Princeton, NJ 08544, USA. *Website:* www.princeton.edu (office).

WIESEL, Elie(zer), KBE; American author and academic; *University Professor, Andrew W. Mellon Professor in the Humanities and Professor of Philosophy and Religion, Boston University;* b. 30 Sept. 1928, Sighet, Romania; s. of Shlomo Wiesel and Sarah Wiesel (née Feig); m. Marion E. Wiesel 1969; one s. one step d.; ed Sorbonne, Paris; naturalized US citizen 1963; Distinguished Prof., Coll. of City of New York 1972–76; Andrew Mellon Prof. in Humanities, Boston Univ. 1976–, Prof. of Philosophy and Religion 1988–; Founder The Elie Wiesel Foundation for Humanity 1986; mem. Bd Fund for the Holocaust 1997–; Founding Pres. Universal Acad. of Cultures, Paris 1993; mem. numerous bds of dirs, trustees, govs and advisers including Int. Rescue Cttee, American Jewish World Service, Yad Vashem, Mutual of America, AmeriCares, US Cttee for Refugees; mem. PEN, The Authors' Guild, Foreign Press Asscn, Writers and Artists for Peace in the Middle East, Council of Foreign Relations, American Acad. of Arts and Sciences, American Acad. of

Arts and Letters (Dept of Literature), Jewish Acad. of Arts and Sciences, European Acad. of Arts, Sciences and Humanities, Royal Norwegian Soc. of Sciences and Letters; Grand Officer, Légion d'honneur, Grand Cross of the Order of the Southern Cross, Brazil 1987, Grand Cross of the Order of Rio Branco, Brazil 2001, Grand Officer, The Order of the Star of Romania 2002, Commander's Cross, Order of Merit of Hungary 2004, King Hussein Award, Jordan 2005, Hon. KBE 2006; recipient of over 110 hon. degrees; Prix Rivarol 1964, Jewish Heritage Award 1965, Remembrance Award 1965, Prix Médicis 1968, Prix Bordin (Acad. Française) 1972, Eleanor Roosevelt Memorial Award 1972, American Liberties Medallion, American Jewish Comm. 1972, Martin Luther King Jr Award (Coll. of City of New York) 1973, Faculty Distinguished Scholar Award, Hofstra Univ. 1973–74, Congressional Gold Medal of Achievement 1985, Nobel Peace Prize 1986, Medal of Liberty Award 1986, Ellis Island Medal of Honor 1992, Presidential Medal of Freedom 1993, and numerous other awards. *Publications:* Night 1960, Dawn 1961, The Accident 1962, The Town Beyond the Wall 1964, The Gates of the Forest 1966, The Jews of Silence 1966, Legends of Our Time 1968, A Beggar in Jerusalem 1970, One Generation After 1971, Souls on Fire 1972, The Oath 1973, Ani Maamin, Cantata 1973, Zalmen or the Madness of God (play) 1975, Messengers of God 1976, A Jew Today 1978, Four Hasidic Masters 1978, The Trial of God 1979, One Generation After 1979, Le testament d'un poète juif assassiné 1980 (Prix Livre-Inter 1980, Prix des Bibliothéquaires 1981), The Testament 1980, Images from the Bible 1980, Five Biblical Portraits 1981, Somewhere a Master: Further Tales of the Hasidic Master 1982, Paroles d'étranger 1982, The Golem 1983, The Fifth Son (Grand Prix de la Littérature, Paris) 1985, Signes d'exode 1985, Against Silence 1985, A Song for Hope 1987, Job ou Dieu dans la tempête (with Josy Eisenberg) 1987, A Nobel Address 1987, Twilight (novel) 1988, The Six Days of Destruction (with Albert Friedlander) 1988, L'oublie 1989, Silences et mémoire d'hommes 1989, From the Kingdom of Memory, Reminiscences (essays) 1990, Evil and Exile 1990, A Journey of Faith 1990, Sages and Dreamers 1991, Célébration Talmudique 1991, The Forgotten 1992, A Passover Haggadah 1993, Se taire est impossible 1995, All Rivers Run to the Sea (Memoirs, Vol.I) 1995, Et la mer n'est pas remplie (Memoirs, Vol.II) 1996 (trans. as And the Sea Is Never Full 1999), Célébration prophétique 1998, King Solomon and His Magic Ring 2000, D'où viens-tu? 2001, The Judges 2002, After the Darkness 2002, Wise Men and Their Tales 2003, Et où vas-tu? 2004, The Time of the Uprooted 2005, Un Désir fou de Danser 2006, Confronting Anti-Semitism (with Kofi Annan) 2006, A Mad Desire to Dance 2009. *Address:* Boston University, 147 Bay State Road, Boston, MA 02215, USA (office). *Telephone:* (617) 353-4561 (office). *Fax:* (617) 353-4024 (office). *E-mail:* rstrauss@bu.edu (office). *Website:* www.bu.edu/philo (office).

WIESEL, Torsten Nils, MD; Swedish neurobiologist, university administrator and academic; *President Emeritus, The Rockefeller University;* b. 3 June 1924, Uppsala, Sweden; ed Karolinska Inst. Stockholm; Instructor, Karolinska Inst. 1954–55; Asst, Karolinska Hosp. 1954–55; Fellow in Ophthalmology, Johns Hopkins Univ. Medical School, Baltimore, Md, USA 1955–58, Asst Prof. of Ophthalmic Physiology 1958–59; Assoc. in Neurophysiology/ Neuropharmacology, Harvard Medical School, Boston 1959–60, Asst Prof. 1960–64, Asst Prof. Dept of Psychiatry 1964–67, Prof. of Physiology 1967–68, Prof. of Neurobiology 1968–74, Chair. Dept of Neurobiology 1973–82, Robert Winthrop Prof. of Neurobiology 1974–83; Vincent & Brooke Astor Prof. and Head, Lab. of Neurobiology, The Rockefeller Univ. New York 1983–2001, Gen. Sec. Human Frontier Science Program 2000–, Pres. The Rockefeller Univ. 1991–98, Pres. Emer. 1998–; Pres. Int. Brain Research Org. 1998–; Dir Shelby White & Leon Levy Center for Mind, Brain and Behavior 1999–; Chair. Borderline Personality Disorder Research Foundation 2001–02, New York Acad. of Sciences 2001–; Sec.-Gen. Human Frontiers Science Program 2006–; mem. American Physiology Soc., American Acad. of Arts and Sciences, AAAS, NAS, etc.; Foreign mem. Royal Soc.; Nobel Prize in Physiology or Medicine 1981; numerous honours and awards. *Publications:* more than 80 articles in medical journals. *Address:* The Rockefeller University, 1230 York Avenue, New York, NY 10065, USA (office). *Telephone:* (212) 327-7093 (office). *Fax:* (212) 327-8988 (office). *E-mail:* wiesel@rockefeller.edu (office). *Website:* www .rockefeller.edu/research/abstract.php?id=190=eme (office); nobelprize.org/ nobel_prizes/medicine/laureates/1981/wiesel-autobio.html (office).

WIGDERSON, Avi, MA, PhD; Israeli computer scientist and academic; *Professor, School of Mathematics, Institute for Advanced Study;* b. 9 Sept. 1956; m.; three c.; ed Technion-Israel Inst. of Tech., Princeton Univ., NJ, USA; Visiting Asst Prof. Prof., Dept of Computer Science, Univ. of California, Berkeley 1983–84; Visiting Scientist, IBM Research, San José, Calif. 1984–85; Fellow, Math. Sciences Research Inst., Berkeley 1985–86; Sr Lecturer, Dept of Computer Science, Hebrew Univ. of Jerusalem 1986–87, Assoc. Prof. 1987–92, Chair. Computer Science Inst., 1993–95; Visiting Assoc. Prof., Dept of Computer Science, 1990–92, Prof., Computer Science Inst. 1991–2003; Visiting Prof., Inst. for Advanced Study, Princeton and Dept of Computer Science, Princeton Univ. 1995–96; Prof., School of Math., Inst. for Advanced Study 1999–; mem. Editorial Bd Society for Industrial and Applied Mathematics (SIAM) Journal on Discrete Mathematics, Information and Computation, Complexity Theory; Pres.'s List of Excellence, The Technion 1977–80, IBM Grad. Fellowship, Princeton Univ. 1982–83, Alon Fellowship 1986–89, Bergman Fellowship 1989, Invited Speaker, Int. Congress of Mathematicians, Kyoto 1990, Zürich 1994, Nevanlinna Prize 1994, Yoram Ben-Porat Presidential Prize for Outstanding Research. *Publications:* more than 150 articles in math. journals on complexity theory, parallel computation, combinatorics and graph theory, combinatorial optimization algorithms, randomness and cryptography, distributed and neural networks. *Address:* Simonyi Hall 013, School of Mathematics, Institute for Advanced Study, Einstein Drive,

Princeton, NJ 08540, USA (office). *Telephone:* (609) 734-8115 (office). *E-mail:* avi@ias.edu (office). *Website:* www.math.ias.edu (office).

WIGGINS, David, MA, FBA; British academic; *Professor Emeritus, University of Oxford;* b. 8 March 1933, London; s. of Norman Wiggins and Diana Wiggins (née Priestley); m. Jennifer Hornsby 1980 (separated 1987); one s.; ed St Paul's School and Brasenose Coll., Oxford; Asst Prin. Colonial Office 1957–58; Jane Eliza Procter Visiting Fellow, Princeton Univ. 1958–59; Lecturer, New Coll., Oxford 1959, Fellow and Lecturer 1960–67; Prof. of Philosophy, Bedford Coll., London 1967–78; Fellow and Praelector in Philosophy, Univ. Coll., Oxford 1981–89; Prof. of Philosophy, Birkbeck Coll., London 1989–94; Wykeham Prof. of Logic, New Coll., Oxford Univ. 1994–, now Prof. Emer.; visiting appointments at Stanford Univ. 1964, 1965, Harvard Univ. 1968, 1972, All Souls Coll., Oxford 1973, Princeton Univ. 1980, Univ. Coll., Oxford 1989–; Findlay Visiting Prof., Boston Univ. 2001; Fellow, Center for Advanced Study in Behavioral Sciences, Stanford 1985–86; mem. Independent Comm. on Transport 1973–74, Cen. Transport Consultative Cttee; Chair. Transport Users' Consultative Cttee for South-East 1977–79; Foreign Hon. mem. American Acad. of Arts and Sciences 1992; Dr hc (York) 2005. *Publications:* Identity and Spatio Temporal Continuity 1967, Truth, Invention and the Meaning of Life 1978, Sameness and Substance 1980, Needs, Values, Truth 1987, Sameness and Substance Renewed 2001, Ethics: Twelve Lectures on the Philosophy of Morality 2006, Univ. of Kansas Lindley Lecture: Solidarity at the Root of the Ethical 2008; articles in learned journals. *Address:* New College, Oxford, OX1 3BN, England. *Telephone:* (20) 7584-9009.

WIGHTMAN, Arthur Strong, PhD, FRSA; American mathematician and academic; *Professor of Mathematics and Physics, Princeton University;* b. 30 March 1922, Rochester, NY; s. of Eugene Pinckney Wightman and Edith Stephenson Wightman; m. 1st Anna-Greta Larsson 1945 (died 1976); one d. (died 2001); m. 2nd Ludmila Popova 1977; ed Yale Coll. and Princeton Univ.; Instructor in Physics, Yale Univ. 1943–44; USN 1944–46; Instructor in Physics, Princeton Univ. 1949, Asst Prof., Assoc. Prof., Prof. of Math. Physics, 1960–, Thomas D. Jones Prof. of Math. Physics 1971–92, Prof. Emer. 1992–; Visiting Prof., Sorbonne, Paris 1957, Ecole Polytechnique, Palaiseau 1977–78; mem. NAS, American Math. Soc.; Fellow, American Acad. of Arts and Sciences, American Physical Soc.; Hon. DSc (ETH, Zürich) 1969, (Göttingen) 1987; Dannie Heinemann Prize in Mathematical Physics 1969, Poincaré Prize, Int. Asscn for Math. Physics 1997. *Publication:* PCT, Spin and Statistics and All That (with R.F. Streater) 1964, 1978, 2000. *Leisure interests:* art, music, tennis. *Address:* Physics Department, Princeton University, PO Box 708, Princeton, NJ 08544 (office); 16 Balsam Lane, Princeton, NJ 08544, USA (home). *Telephone:* (609) 921-7779 (home); (609) 258-5835 (office). *E-mail:* wightman@princeton.edu (home). *Website:* www.physics.princeton.edu (office).

WIGLEY, Dafydd, PC, BSc; British politician (retd); b. 1 April 1943, Derby; s. of Elfyn Edward Wigley and Myfanwy (née Batterbee) Wigley; m. Elinor Bennett Owen 1967; three s. (two deceased) one d.; ed Sir Hugh Owen School, Caernarfon, Rydal School, Colwyn Bay, Victoria Univ. of Manchester; Econ. Analyst, Ford Motor Co. 1964–67; Chief Cost Accountant, Mars Ltd 1967–71; Financial Controller, Hoover Ltd 1971–74; Pres. S Caernarfon Creamery 1987–; Co. Borough Councillor, Merthyr Tydfil 1972–74; Vice-Chair. Plaid Cymru 1972–74, Pres. 1981–84, 1991–2000; MP for Caernarfon 1974–2001; Chair. All Party House of Commons Reform Group 1983, Vice-Chair. All-Party Disablement Group 1992–2001; Vice-Chair. Parl. Social Services Group 1985–88; mem. Nat. Ass. for Wales 1999, Leader of the Opposition 1999–2000, Chair Audit Cttee of Nat. Ass. 2002; Chair Ymddiriedolaeth Hybu Gwydoniaeth 2002, now retd; Pres. Spastic Soc. of Wales 1985–90, Mencap Wales 1991–; Vice-Pres. Welsh Asscn of Community Councils 1978–, Nat. Fed. of Industrial Devt Authorities 1981–2001; Sponsor, Disabled Persons Act 1981; Chair. Alpha Dyffryn Cyf/Ltd 1980–91; Dir (non-exec.) Gwernafalau Cyf/Ltd 2001–; Hon. mem. Gorsedd of Welsh Bards; Hon. Fellow Univ. of N Wales Bangor 1995; Hon. LLD (Univ. of Wales) 2002; Grimshaw Memorial Award, Nat. Fed. of the Blind 1982; Freedom of the Borough of Arfon 1994, Royal Town of Caernafon 2001. *Publications:* An Economic Plan for Wales 1970, O Ddifri 1992, Dal Ati 1993, A Democratic Wales in a United Europe 1995, A Real Choice for Wales 1996, Maen i'r Wal 2001. *Leisure interests:* football, tennis, chess, hill walking, writing. *Address:* Hen Efail, Bontnwydd, Caernarfon, Gwynedd, LL54 7YH, Wales (home).

WIGZELL, Hans, MD, PhD; Swedish physician and academic; *Professor of Immunology and Director, Centre for Medical Innovation, Karolinska Institute;* b. 28 Oct. 1938; m. Kerstin Largell 1964; one s. three d.; ed Karolinska Inst., Stockholm; Prof. of Immunology, Uppsala Univ. 1972–82; Prof. of Immunology, Karolinska Inst. 1982–, Pres. 1995–2003, also Dir Centre for Medical Innovation; Dir Nat. Bacteriological Lab., Stockholm 1988–; Chair. Nobel Cttee, Karolinska Inst. 1990–92; scientific adviser to Govt of Sweden 1999–; mem. of seven Academies of Sciences; Anders Jahres Prize, Oslo 1975, Erik Fernstrom Prize, Uppsala 1981; Hon. mem. American Asscn of Immunologists. *Play:* The Gene Scene 1989. *Publications:* about 600 scientific articles, textbooks and popular science books. *Leisure interests:* music, nature, tropical plants, Japanese carp. *Address:* Karolinska Institute, Microbiology and Tumour Biology Centre, 171 77 Stockholm, Sweden. *Telephone:* (8) 5248-6680 (office). *Fax:* (8) 30–05–92 (office). *E-mail:* hans.wigzell@mtc.ki.se (office). *Website:* mtc.ki.se (office).

WIIG, Ole, BArch, MArch; Norwegian architect; *Senior Partner, Narud-Stokke-Wiig AS;* b. 22 Oct. 1946, Trondheim; s. of Thorvald Wiig and Esther-Marie Wiig; m. 1st Alison Wiig 1972; two d.; m. 2nd Cathrine Lerche 2002; ed Harvard Univ., USA, Manchester Univ., Dundee Univ.; joined Kallmann, McKinnel & Wood, Boston 1973; Community Design Services, Boston 1974; City Architects Dept, Edin. 1974–80; lecturer and studio critic, Univ. of Edin.

Dept of Architecture 1979–80, Visiting Lecturer and studio critic 1999–2000; External Examiner, Dublin Inst. of Tech. Dept of Architecture 2000–04; Founding Partner Narud-Stokke-Wiig AS 1979–, now Sr Partner; Pres. Nat. Asscn of Norwegian Architects 1990–94, Council Colletta di Castelbianco, Italy; lecturer at univs and confs in Europe and USA; initiated Ligurian Int. Workshop for architecture students; British Tourist Authority Certificate of Distinction, Museum of the Year Award, Edin. Civic Trust Award 1981, RIBA Award, Civic Trust Award, Disabled Design Award 1983, Homansbyen Environmental Award 1991, Nordic Copper Award 1994, First Prize Int. Competition for Scottish Architecture and Design Centre 1995; several first prizes in Norwegian and int. architecture competitions. *Publications:* numerous articles on architecture and planning topics in books, newspapers and magazines. *Leisure interest:* introducing modern architecture and design into medieval Italian villages. *Address:* c/o Narud-Stokke-Wiig AS, Rådhusgaten 27, 0158, Oslo (office); Bryggegaten 16, 0250 Oslo, Norway (home). *Telephone:* 22-40-37-40 (office); 22-83-41-01 (home). *Fax:* 22-40-37-41 (office); 22-83-21-86 (home). *E-mail:* ow@nsw.no. *Website:* www.nsw.no (office); www.olewiig.no (home).

WIIN-NIELSEN, Aksel Christopher, DrSc; Danish physicist and academic; b. 17 Dec. 1929, Klakring; s. of Aage Nielsen and Marie Petre (née Kristoffersen) Nielsen; m. Bente Havsteen Zimsen 1953; three d.; ed Univs of Copenhagen and Stockholm; staff mem. Danish Meteorological Inst. 1952–55, Int. Meteorological Inst. 1955–58, Jt Numerical Weather Prediction 1959–61, Nat. Centre for Atmospheric Research 1961–63; Prof. (Chair.), Univ. of Mich., USA 1963–73; Dir European Centre for Medium-Range Weather Forecasts 1974–80; Sec.-Gen. WMO 1980–84; Dir Danish Meteorological Inst. 1984–87; Prof. of Physics, Univ. of Copenhagen 1988–94; mem. Danish Acad. of Tech. Sciences 1980 (Vice-Pres. 1989–92), Finnish Acad. of Sciences and Letters 1980, Royal Swedish Acad. of Sciences 1981, Royal Danish Acad. of Sciences 1982; Hon. DSc (Reading, Copenhagen); Ohridsky Medal, Univ. of Sofia, Bulgaria, Buys-Ballot Medal, Royal Netherlands Acad. of Science, Wihuri Int. Science Prize, Wihuri Foundation, Helsinki, Finland, Rossby Prize, Swedish Geophysical Soc., Silver Medal, Univ. of Helsinki, Palmen Medal, Finnish Geophysical Soc. *Publications:* Problems in Dynamic Meteorology 1970, Dynamic Meteorology 1973, Predictability 1987, Chaos and Causality 1992, Fundamentals of Atmospheric Energetics (with C.-T. Chen) 1993 and about 100 articles on dynamic meteorology, numerical weather prediction and atmospheric energetics.

WIJDENBOSCH, Jules Albert, PhD; Suriname fmr head of state; b. 2 May 1941, Paramaribo; one d.; customs officer 1962–66; civil servant, Municipality of Amsterdam 1966–81; mem. State Cttee on Remigration of Surinamese est. by Dutch Govt 1978–81; sr civil servant, Ministry of Dist Admin. and Decentralization 1981, Under-Dir in charge of Bureau for Decentralization of Admin. 1983, Dir of Dist Admin, Ministry of Dist Admin and Decentralization and Nat. Mobilization 1985; Minister of Home Affairs, Dist Admin and Nat. Mobilization and Minister of Justice and Police 1986–87; Prime Minister, Minister of Gen. Affairs and Minister of Foreign Affairs 1987–88; sr civil servant, Ministry of Regional Devt 1988–91; Vice-Pres. Repub. of Suriname and Minister of Finance Jan.–Sept. 1991, Pres. 1996–2000; sr civil servant, Ministry of Regional Devt 1991–; Co-ordinator Jongerengroep (Youth Section) of Suriname Nat. Party 1962–63; Co-ordinator Verenigung van Bestuurskundigen 1982–; mem. and Acting Chair. Political Advisory Group 25th Feb. Movt 1983; mem. Higher Political Council on the Political and Admin. Future of Suriname 1985–87; first Chair. Nationale Democratische Partij (NDP) 1987–91, Deputy Chair. 1992–96; mem. Nat. Ass. and Floor Leader NDP 1991; Deputy Chair. Foundation for the Promotion of Remigration of Surinamese; Chair. Amsterdam Welfare Foundation; Chair. Union of Customs Officers 1962–66; co-f. Algemene Jongeren Organisatie (Youth Org.) 1962, Dir 1963; Chair. Surinamese Basketball Fed., Deputy Chair. Surinamese Football Fed.; mem. Editorial Bd Lanti; Grand Master, Order of the Yellow Star, Order of the Palm. *Publications:* Schets voor de Republiek Suriname eigen stijl (A Personal View of the Republic of Suriname) 1974, Bestuurlijke organisatie in een leefgemeenschap (Administrative Organisation in Surinamese Society) 1980, Politieke orde en legitimiteit (Political Order and Legitimacy) 1981, Statuut van het Koninkrijk der Nederlanden (Charter for the Kingdom of the Netherlands) 1979, Participatie in een waarachtige democratie (Participating in a Modern Democracy) 1983. *Address:* c/o Office of the President, Kleine Combeweg 1, Paramaribo, Suriname.

WIJERS, G. J. (Hans), MA, PhD; Dutch business executive; *Chairman of the Management Board and CEO, Akzo Nobel N.V.;* b. 11 Jan. 1951; ed Univ. of Groningen, Erasmus Univ. of Rotterdam; Asst Prof. of Econs, Erasmus Univ. of Rotterdam 1976–82; participation in two think-tanks for govt ministers 1982–84; sr consultant and pnr for various consulting firms 1984–86; Man.-Pnr Horringa and De Koning 1986–93; Man.-Pnr Amsterdam Office, Boston Consulting Group (BCG) 1993–94; Minister for Econ. Affairs 1994–98; Sr Vice-Pres. BCG and Chair. Dutch Office 1999–2002; adviser to Man. Bd Akzo Nobel 2002, mem. Bd 2002–, Chair. Man. Bd and CEO Akzo Nobel 2003–; Chair. Oranje Fonds; mem. Bd of Dirs Royal Dutch Shell plc 2009–; Vice-Pres. Young Pianist Foundation; mem. European Roundtable of Industrialists. *Address:* Akzo Nobel, PO Box 75730, 1070 AS Amsterdam (office); Akzo Nobel, Strawinskylaan 2555, 1077 ZZ Amsterdam, Netherlands (office). *Telephone:* (20) 502-7833 (office). *Fax:* (20) 502-7604 (office). *E-mail:* media.relations@akzonobel.com (office). *Website:* www.akzonobel.com (office).

WIJESEKERA, Nandadeva, MA, DLitt, PhD; Sri Lankan anthropologist, archaeologist and government official (retd); b. 11 Dec. 1908, Moonamalwatta, Sri Lanka; s. of Muhandiram N. G. de S. Wijesekera and Dona Emaliya de Alwis Gunatilaka; m. Leila Jayatilaka 1941; one d.; ed Ananda Coll., Colombo, Univ. Coll. Colombo, Trinity Coll. Cambridge, England, Univ. Coll. London, Vienna Univ. and Calcutta Univ.; Asst in Ethnology, Colombo Museum 1937–44; war service in civilian duties 1940–44; Deputy Supt of Census 1945–50; Dir Census and Statistics 1950–55; mem. UNESCO Nat. Comm. 1950; Asst Sec., Ministry of Finance 1951; Sec. Royal Comm. on Languages 1951; Sec. Gal-Oya Devt Bd 1952; Liaison Officer, World Bank Comm. 1952–53; Dir Official Language Dept 1956; Deputy Commr Official Language Affairs 1959–60, Commr 1960–67; Amb. 1967–70; Leader Science Del. to China 1964, Ceylon Del. to Colombo Plan Conf. 1967; Adviser to Dept of Archaeology 1983–; mem. Bd of Man. Inst. of Indigenous Medicine 1983–; has been mem. of numerous Govt dels and has held many official appointments; Ed.-in-Chief Mahavamsa (in Pali and Sinhala); represented All-Ceylon cricket team 1932; Pres. Nondescripts Cricket Club 1982; Pundit, Oriental Studies Soc. 1959; Fellow Acad. of Arts, Nat. Acad. of Sciences; mem. Sri Lanka Asscn for the Advancement of Science 1964; Pres. All-Ceylon Football Asscn 1963, Royal Asiatic Soc. 1966–67, 1971, 1973–75; Founder Pres. Archaeological Soc. 1966; Hon. DLitt (Sri Jayawardene-pura); Gold Medal, Royal Asiatic Soc. 1973, Purā vidyā Chakravarti 1986, Desamanya Sri Lanka 1990. *Publications:* many books, including (Sinhala) Lanka Janatawa 1955, Perani Bitusituvam 1964, Perani Murti Kalawa 1970, Proper Names in Sinhala Literature 1988; (English) People of Ceylon 1949, Early Sinhalese Painting 1959, Veddas in Transition 1964, Biography of Sir D. B. Jayatilaka 1973, Selected Writings 1983, Heritage of Sri Lanka 1984, Anthropological Gleanings from Sinhala Literature 1985, Contacts and Conflicts with Sri Lanka 1986, The Sinhalese 1990, Sri Lankave Urumaya 1991, Archaeology Department's Centenary 1890–1990, 5 Vols (Ed.-in-Chief); also (autobiog.) 1995, 25 children's books and 200 articles. *Leisure interests:* reading and writing. *Address:* No. 34 Dudley Senanayake Mawata, Borella, Colombo 8, Sri Lanka. *Telephone:* (1) 694089.

WIJN, Joop, PhD; Dutch politician; b. 20 May 1969, Haarlem; ed Univ. of Amsterdam; taught course for entrepreneurs Schoevers Acad., Amsterdam 1989–94, also taught course in marketing at Netherlands Marketing Inst. and course in business econs at sr secondary vocational level 1991–94; owned and operated personnel recruitment agency, Amsterdam 1992–94; trainee then Investment Man., ABN AMRO Bank 1994–98; mem. House of Reps of the States Gen. 1998–2002; Sec. of State for Econ. Affairs 2002–03, Sec. of State for Finance 2003–July 2006, Minister for Econ. Affairs 2006–07. *Address:* c/o Ministry of Economic Affairs, Bezuidenhoutseweg 30, POB 20101, 2594 AV The Hague, Netherlands (office).

WIJNHOLDS, Johannes de Beaufort (Onno), PhD; Dutch international civil servant and economist; *Permanent Representative, European Central Bank, Washington, DC;* b. 24 Oct. 1943, Amsterdam; m. Jolanthe de Graaf 1968; one s. one d.; ed Univ. of Amsterdam; economist, De Nederlandsche Bank, Amsterdam 1968, various positions in bank 1974–84, Deputy Exec. Dir 1987–94; Asst to Exec. Dir IBRD and IMF, Washington, DC 1972–74, Alt. Exec. Dir IMF 1985–87, Exec. Dir 1994–2003; currently Perm. Rep. of European Central Bank, Washington, DC and its Observer at the IMF; Alt. mem. Social Econ. Council of the Netherlands 1987–94; Prof. of Money and Banking, Univ. of Groningen 1992–95; Order of the Duke of Branimir (Croatia) 2003. *Publications:* The Need for International Reserves and Credit Facilities 1977, The International Banking System (in Dutch) 1985, A Framework for Monetary Stability (ed. and co-author) 1994; numerous articles on int. financial subjects. *Address:* International Monetary Fund, 700 19th Street, NW, Washington, DC 20431, USA (office). *Telephone:* (202) 623-8350 (office). *Fax:* (202) 623-8377 (office). *E-mail:* jwijnholds@imf.org (office). *Website:* www.imf.org (office).

WIJNSCHENK, Harry; Dutch politician; *Leader, Lijst-Pim Fortuyn;* b. 1964; fmr motorcycle and watch magazine publisher; fmr mem. Liberal Party; fmr State Gen. Lijst Pim Fortuyn, Leader 2002–. *Address:* Lijst Pim Fortuyn, Vlaardingweg 62, 3044 CK, Rotterdam, Netherlands (office). *Telephone:* (10) 7507050 (office). *Fax:* (10) 7507051 (office). *E-mail:* info@lijst-pimfortuyn.nl (office). *Website:* www.lijst-pimfortuyn.nl (office).

WIKTORIN, Gen. Owe Erik Axel; Swedish army officer; b. 7 May 1940, Motala; s. of Erik Wiktorin and Ester Wiktorin (née Johnsson); m. Cajs Gårding 1965; two s.; ed AF Flying Training School, AF Acad., Armed Forces Staff and War Coll., USAF Air Command and Staff Coll.; fighter pilot, Skaraborg Wing 1964–69, CO squadron 1969–71; staff officer, Swedish Defence Staff 1973–79, Head of Planning Section 1980–83, Dir of Plans and Policy and Deputy Chief 1986–91, Chief 1991–92; Deputy CO Jämtland (Sector) Wing 1983–84; Head of Planning Section AF Staff 1984–86; CO Southern Jt Command Swedish Armed Forces 1992–94, apptd Supreme Commdr 1994; Fellow Royal Swedish Acad. of War Sciences 1985; Kt Commdr of White Rose of Finland; Chevalier, Légion d'honneur; Gold Medal for Merit, Southern Skåne Regt, Swedish Home Guard; Gold Medal for Merit, Nat. Fed. of AF Asscns. *Leisure interests:* sailing, skiing, cooking, sky-diving, hunting.

WILANDER, Mats; Swedish fmr professional tennis player; b. 22 Aug. 1964, Vaxjo; m. Sonya Mulholland 1987; turned professional 1981; Australian Open Champion 1983, 1984, 1988, French Open Champion 1982, 1985, 1988 (finalist 1983, 1987), US Open Champion 1988; winner Wimbledon Men's Doubles Championship (with Joakim Nystrom) 1986; mem. victorious Swedish Davis Cup Team 1984, 1987, 1988; ranked world No. 1 1988; voted official World Champion 1988; won 33 singles and six doubles titles (including seven Grand Slam titles); coach of Russian player Marat Safin 2001; Capt. Swedish Davis Cup Team 2002–; mem. Sr Tour; International Tennis Hall of Fame 2003. *Music:* released CD 1991. *Leisure interests:* art, music, skiing, golf. *Address:* c/o Tennis HOF, 194 Bellevue Avenue, Newport, RI, 02840-3515, USA. *Fax:* (208) 788-4796 (office).

WILBUR, Richard Purdy, MA; American poet and academic; b. 1 March 1921, New York City; s. of Lawrence L. Wilbur and Helen Purdy Wilbur; m. Charlotte Ward 1942; three s. one d.; ed Amherst Coll. and Harvard Univ.; Asst Prof. of English, Harvard Univ. 1950–54; Assoc. Prof. Wellesley Coll. 1954–57; Prof. Wesleyan Univ. 1957–77; Writer in Residence, Smith Coll., Northampton, Mass. 1977–86; mem. American Acad. of Arts and Sciences, Soc. of Fellows of Harvard Univ. 1947–50; Guggenheim Fellow 1952–53, 1963, Ford Fellow 1961; Chancellor, Acad. of American Poets 1961; Poet Laureate of USA 1987–88; mem. PEN; Pres. American Acad. of Arts and Letters 1974–76, Chancellor 1977–78; mem. Dramatists Guild; Hon. Fellow, Modern Language Asscn 1986; Chevalier, Ordre des Palmes Académiques 1984; Harriet Monroe Prize 1948, Oscar Blumenthal Prize 1950, Prix de Rome from American Acad. of Arts and Letters 1954–55, Edna St Vincent Millay Memorial Award 1956, Nat. Book Award, Pulitzer Prize 1957, co-recipient Bollingen Translation Prize 1963, co-recipient Bollingen Prize in Poetry 1971, Prix Henri Desfeuilles 1971, Brandeis Creative Arts Award 1971, Shelley Memorial Prize 1973, Harriet Monroe Poetry Award 1978, Drama Desk Award 1983, PEN Translation Prize 1983, St Botolph's Foundation Award 1983, Aiken Taylor Award 1988, L.A. Times Book Award 1988, Pulitzer Prize 1989, Gold Medal for Poetry, American Acad. of Arts and Letters 1991, MacDowell Medal 1992, Nat. Arts Club Medal of Honour for Literature 1994, PEN/Manheim Medal for Translation 1994, Nat. Medal of Arts 1994, Milton Center Prize 1995, Robert Frost Medal, Poetry Soc. of America 1996, T. S. Eliot Award 1996, Wallace Stevens Award 2003, Theater Hall of Fame 2003, Ruth Lilly Prize for Poetry 2006. *Publications:* The Beautiful Changes and Other Poems 1947, Ceremony and Other Poems 1950, A Bestiary (anthology, with Alexander Calder) 1955, The Misanthrope (trans. from Molière) 1955, Things of This World (poems) 1956, Poems 1943–1956 1957, Candide (comic opera, with Lillian Hellman and others) 1957, (edition of his poems with introduction and notes) 1959, Advice to a Prophet (poems) 1961, Tartuffe (trans. from Molière) 1963, The Poems of Richard Wilbur 1963, Loudmouse (for children) 1963, Poems of Shakespeare (with Alfred Harbage) 1966, Walking to Sleep (new poems and translations) 1969, School for Wives (trans. from Molière) 1971, Opposites (children's verse, illustrated by the author) 1973, The Mind-Reader 1976, Responses: Prose Pieces 1953–1976 1976, The Learned Ladies (trans. from Molière) 1978, Selected Poems of Witter Bynner (editor) 1978, Seven Poems 1981, Andromache (trans. from Racine) 1982, The Whale (translations) 1982, Molière: Four Comedies (contains 4 plays translated previously listed) 1982, Phaedra (trans. from Racine) 1986, Lying and Other Poems 1987, New and Collected Poems 1988, More Opposites 1991, School for Husbands (trans. from Molière) 1992, The Imaginary Cuckold (trans. from Molière) 1993, A Game of Catch 1994, Amphitryon (trans. from Molière) 1995, The Catbird's Song (prose pieces) 1997, The Disappearing Alphabet (for children and others) 1998, Bone Key and Other Poems 1998, Mayflies (poems) 2000, Don Juan (trans. from Molière) 2000, The Bungler (trans. from Molière) 2000, Opposites, More Opposites and Some Differences (for children) 2000, The Pig in the Spigot (for children) 2000, Collected Poems 1953–2004 2004. *Leisure interests:* tennis, walking, herb gardening. *Address:* 87 Dodwells Road, Cummington, MA 01026; 715R Windsor Lane, Key West, FL 33040, USA. *Telephone:* (413) 634-2275; (305) 296-7499.

WILBUR, Hon. Richard Sloan, MD, JD; American physician and association executive; *Chairman, American Medical Foundation for Peer Review and Education;* b. 8 April 1924, Boston, Mass; s. of Blake Colburn Wilbur and Mary Caldwell Sloan; m. Betty Lou Fannin 1951; three s.; ed John Marshall Law School, Stanford Univ.; Intern, San Francisco County Hosp. 1946–47; Resident, Stanford Hosp. 1949–51, Univ. of Pennsylvania Hosp. 1951–52; mem. of Staff, Palo Alto Medical Clinic, Calif. 1952–69; Deputy Exec. Vice-Pres., American Medical Asscn, Chicago 1969–71, 1973–74; Asst Sec., Health and Environment Dept 1971–73; Sr Vice-Pres., Baxter Labs Inc., Deerfield, Ill. 1974–76; Exec. Vice-Pres. Council Medical Speciality Socs 1976–91, Emer. 1992–; Sec., Accreditation Council for Continuing Medical Educ. 1979–91; Assoc. Prof. of Medicine, Stanford Medical School 1952–69, Georgetown Univ. Medical School 1971–77; Vice-Pres. Nat. Resident Matching Plan 1980–91, Pres. 1991–92; Chair. Bd Calif. Medical Asscn 1968–69; Chair. Calif. Blue Shield 1966–68; Chair. American Medical Foundation 1987–, Professional Advisory Bd, Royal Soc. of Medicine Foundation 1995–; Pres. American Coll. of Physician Executives 1988–89; Pres. American Bd Medical Man. 1992–93; Pres. MedicAlert Foundation Int. 1992–94, MedicAlert Foundation, USA 1992–94, Dir MedicAlert Germany 1992–94, Iberica 1992–94, Europe (UK) 1992–95; Chair. Bd and CEO Inst. for Clinical Information 1994–; Sr Vice-Pres. Healthcare, Buckeye Corpn Pte. Ltd 1997–; Chair. Medical Advisory Bd, Medical City, Bangalore 1997–2000; Pres. Royal Soc. of Medicine Foundation 1998–; mem. numerous other medical asscns; Distinguished Service Medal, Dept of Defense 1973. *Publications:* contribs to medical journals. *Address:* APT Management Inc., 736 North Western Road, Suite 222, Lake Forest, IL 60045 (office); 985 North Hawthorne Place, Lake Forest, IL 60045, USA (home). *Telephone:* (847) 234-6337 (office). *Fax:* (847) 234-5294 (office). *E-mail:* aptmgmnt@aol.com (office). *Website:* www.medicalfoundation.org (office).

WILBY, James; British actor; b. 20 Feb. 1958, Rangoon, Burma; s. of Geoffrey Wilby and Shirley Wilby; m. Shana Louise Magraw 1988; three s. one d.; ed Sedbergh School, Durham Univ., Royal Acad. of Dramatic Art, London; Outstanding Performance by a Cast, Screen Actors' Guild 2001. *Stage appearances:* Another Country (West End début), Who's Afraid of Virginia Woolf (Belgrade Theatre, Coventry), Chips With Everything (Leeds Playhouse), As You Like It (Royal Exchange Theatre, Manchester and tour), Jane Eyre (Chichester), A Patriot for Me (Barbican), Helping Harry (Jermyn Street), Don Juan (Lyric Hammersmith). *Films:* Dreamchild, Maurice (Best Actor, Venice Film Festival 1988), A Handful of Dust (Best Actor, Bari Film Festival 1989), A Summer Story, Howards End 1991, Immaculate Conception 1992, Une partie d'echec, Regeneration, An Ideal Husband, Tom's Midnight Garden, Cotton Mary, Jump Tomorrow, Gosford Park, C'est Gradiva qui vous appelle 2006, The Wreck 2007. *Television:* Sherlock Holmes, The Crooked Man, Dutch Girls, A Tale of Two Cities, Mother Love, Tell Me That You Love Me, Adam Bede, You, Me And It, Lady Chatterley, Crocodile Shoes, Woman in White 1997, The Dark Room, Trial and Retribution IV, Bertie and Elizabeth, Island at War, Jericho 2005, Marple: The Sittaford Mystery 2005, Little Devil 2006, Nero 2006, Lewis 2006, The Last Days of the Raj 2007, Clapham Junction 2007, Impact Earth 2008, A Risk Worth Taking 2008. *Leisure interests:* playing piano, tennis, sailing. *Address:* c/o Sue Latimer, A.R.G., 4 Great Portland Street, London, W1W 8PA, England. *Telephone:* (20) 7436-6400. *Fax:* (20) 7436-6700.

WILBY, Peter; British journalist; b. 7 Nov. 1944, Leicester; m. Sandra James; two s.; ed Univ. of Sussex; reporter, The Observer 1968–72, Educ. Corresp. 1972–75; Educ. Corresp. The New Statesman 1975–77, Ed. 1998–2005, now writes weekly column on policy; Educ. Corresp. The Sunday Times 1977–86; Educ. Ed. The Independent 1986–89, Home Ed. 1989–91, Deputy Ed. 1991–95; Ed. Independent on Sunday 1995–96; Press Commentator, the Guardian newspaper 2007–. *Publication:* Anthony Eden 2006. *Address:* Haus Publishing, 26 Cadogan Court, Draycott Avenue, London, SW3 3BX, England (office). *Telephone:* (20) 7584-6738 (office). *Fax:* (20) 7584-9501 (office). *Website:* www.hauspublishing.co.uk (office).

WILCZEK, Frank, BS, MA, PhD; American physicist and academic; *Herman Feshbach Professor of Physics, Massachusetts Institute of Technology;* b. 15 May 1951, New York; s. of Frank Wilczek and Mary Cona; m. Elizabeth Devine 1973; two d.; ed Univ. of Chicago, Princeton Univ.; Instructor, Princeton Univ. 1974, Asst Prof. 1974–76, 1977–78, Visiting Fellow, Inst. for Advanced Study 1976–77, Assoc. Prof. 1978–80, Prof. 1980–81, R. J. Oppenheimer Prof., Inst. for Advanced Study, School of Natural Sciences 1989–2000; mem. Inst. for Theoretical Physics, Univ. of Calif., Santa Barbara 1980–88, Robert Huttenback Prof. of Physics 1980–88; Visiting Prof., Harvard Univ. 1987–88; Herman Feshbach Prof. of Physics, MIT 2000–; Adjunct Prof., Centros Estudios Cientificos, 2002–; Schrödinger Prof., Vienna 2002; Rudolf Peiriels Visiting Prof., Univ. of Oxford 2008; mem. Editorial Bd, Zeitschrift für Physik C 1981–87, Annual Reviews of Nuclear & Particle Science 1985–89; mem. Scientific Advisory Cttee, CERN 2002–, Perimeter Inst. for Theoretical Physics 2003–; Ed.-in-Chief Annals of Physics 2001–; Editorial Adviser Daedalus 2002–; mem. American Acad. of Arts and Sciences 1993–, NAS 1990–; foreign mem. Royal Netherlands Acad. of Arts and Sciences 2000–; Fellow AAAS 2000–, American Physical Soc. 2004–, American Philosophical Soc. 2005–, Polish Acad. of Arts and Sciences 2007–; hon. lecturerships at numerous int. univs; numerous hon. doctorates; Sakurai Prize, American Physical Soc. 1986, Lorentz Medal, Royal Netherlands Acad. of Arts and Sciences 2002, Michelson-Morley Prize, Case Western Reserve Univ. 2002, Lillienfeld Prize, American Physical Soc. 2003, High Energy and Particle Physics Prize, European Physical Soc. 2003, Nobel Prize in Physics (jt recipient) 2004, King Faisal Prize 2005, Julius Wess Award 2008, Casimir Funk Award 2008. *Publications include:* Longing for the Harmonies 1989, Fantastic Realities: 49 Mind Journeys and A Trip to Stockholm 2006, The Lightness of Being: Mass, Ether and the Unification of Forces 2008; more than 200 contribs to academic journals and books. *Leisure interests:* music, learning things, solving puzzles. *Address:* Department of Physics, Massachusetts Institute of Technology, 77 Massachusetts Avenue, 6-301, Cambridge, MA 02139 (office); 4 Wyman Road, Cambridge, MA 02138, USA (home). *Telephone:* (617) 253-0284 (office). *Fax:* (617) 253-8674 (office). *E-mail:* wilczek@mit.edu (office). *Website:* frankwilczek.com.

WILD, (Royland) Earl; American pianist, composer and teacher (retd); b. 26 Nov. 1915, Pittsburgh, Pa; s. of Royland Wild and Lillian G. Wild; ed Carnegie Tech. Coll., Pittsburgh; studied with Selmar Jansen, Egon Petri, Helene Barrere, Volya Cossack and Paul Doguereau; first and youngest American piano soloist to perform with NBC Orchestra conducted by Toscanini 1942; has performed with symphony orchestras and given recitals in many countries; staff pianist, NBC radio, New York 1937–45; staff pianist, composer, conductor ABC TV, New York 1945–68; has appeared with Sir Malcolm Sargent, Jascha Horenstein, Sir Georg Solti, Arthur Fiedler; played first piano recital on TV 1939; has played for seven US presidents, including inauguration of Pres. J. F. Kennedy; 90th birthday concert, Carnegie Hall, New York 2005; teacher, Penn State 1965–69, Juilliard School of Music 1977–87, Manhattan School of Music 1981–83, Ohio State 1987–94, Carnegie Mellon 1994–2004; numerous recordings for RCA, EMI, Columbia, Nonesuch, Readers Digest, Vanguard Records, Sony Classical and Ivory Classics; hon. docorates (Carnegie Mellon, Grand Valley State Coll.).. *Compositions include:* Piano and Orchestra Variations (Doo-Dah), Piano Sonata 2000, The Turquoise Horse (choral work), ballet music, oratorios, numerous solo piano transcriptions and popular songs. *Radio:* numerous radio performances 1929–60. *Television:* numerous TV performances, including as first pianist to perform on the new medium 1939. *Publications:* more than 35 piano compositions and transcriptions. *Leisure interests:* writing poetry, playing piano. *Website:* www.earlwild.com.

WILDENTHAL, Kern, MD, PhD; American university administrator and physician; *Professor of Internal Medicine and Physiology, University of Texas Southwestern Medical Center;* b. 1 July 1941, San Marcos, Tex.; m. Margaret Wildenthal (née Dehlinger) 1964; two d.; ed Sul Ross Coll., Univ. of Tex. Southwestern Medical Center, Univ. of Cambridge, UK; Intern, Bellvue Hosp., NY 1964–65; Resident, Parkland Hospital, Dallas 1965–67; Asst Prof. then Prof. of Internal Medicine and Physiology, Univ. of Tex. Southwestern Medical School, Dallas 1970–76, Prof. and Dean of Grad. School 1976–80, Prof. and Dean Southwestern Medical School 1980–86, Pres. Univ. of Tex.

Southwestern Medical Center 1986–2008, also Prof. of Internal Medicine and Physiology; fmr Chair. American Section, Int. Soc. for Heart Research, Science Policy Cttee, Asscn of Academic Heart Centers, Basic Science Council, Science Advisory Cttee, American Heart Asscn, Program Project Research Review Cttee, Nat. Heart, Lung and Blood Inst.; mem. NAS Inst. of Medicine, American Soc. for Clinical Investigation, Asscn of American Physicians; mem. Bd of Dirs Dallas Center for the Performing Arts, Dallas Museum of Art, Dallas Symphony Asscn, Dallas Opera, Greater Dallas Chamber of Commerce, Dallas Citizens Council, Southwestern Medical Foundation, Hoblitzelle Foundation, Wendy and Emery Reves Foundation; Hon. Fellow, Hughes Hall, Univ. of Cambridge. *Publications:* 130 scientific papers in basic research and clinical cardiology, numerous articles on health and educ. policy issues. *E-mail:* priscilla.alderman@utsouthwestern.edu (office). *Address:* University of Texas Southwestern Medical Center, 5323 Harry Hines Blvd, Dallas, TX 75390-9002, USA (office). *Telephone:* (214) 648-2508 (office). *Fax:* (214) 648-8690 (office). *Website:* www.utsouthwestern.edu (office).

WILDER, C. John, BS, MBA; American energy industry executive; *Chairman, Bluescape Resources;* b. Missouri; ed SE Missouri State Univ., Univ. of Tex.; joined Royal Dutch/Shell Group 1980, various man. positions including CEO Shell Capital, London, UK –1998; Exec. Vice-Pres. and Chief Financial Officer Entergy Corpn 1998–2004; Pres., CEO and Dir TXU Corpn 2004–07; currently Chair. Bluescape Resources; served as dir of more than 65 Entergy-related cos and 75 Shell-related cos; mem. Bd of Dirs Univ. of Tex. and Tulane Univ. Business Schools; mem. Financial Execs Inst., Edison Electric Inst., United Methodist Church Admin. Bd. *Address:* Bluescape Resources, 200 Crescent Court, Suite 200, Dallas, TX 75201, USA (office). *Telephone:* (214) 855-2260 (office). *Fax:* (214) 855-2265 (office). *Website:* www.bluescaperesources.com (office).

WILDER, Gene, BA; American film actor, director and producer; b. (Jerry Silberman), 11 June 1933, Milwaukee, Wis.; s. of William J. Silberman and Jeanne Silberman (née Baer); m. 1st Mary Joan Schutz 1967 (divorced 1974); one d.; m. 2nd Gilda Radner 1984 (deceased); m. 3rd Karen Boyer 1991; ed Univ. of Iowa, Bristol Old Vic. Theatre School; served with US Army 1956–58; Broadway play: The Complaisant Lover 1962, West End play Laughter on the 23rd Floor 1996. *Films include:* Bonnie and Clyde 1966, The Producers 1968, Start the Revolution Without Me 1970, Quackser Fortune Has a Cousin in the Bronx 1970, Willy Wonka and the Chocolate Factory 1971, Everything You Always Wanted to Know About Sex, But Were Afraid to Ask 1972, Young Frankenstein 1974, The Little Prince 1974, Young Frankenstein 1974, Rhinoceros 1974, Blazing Saddles 1974, Thursday's Game 1974, The Adventure of Sherlock Holmes's Smarter Brother (also writer and dir) 1975, Silver Streak 1976, The World's Greatest Lover (also writer, producer and dir) 1977, The Frisco Kid 1979, Stir Crazy 1980, Sunday Lovers (also writer and dir) 1980, Hanky Panky 1982, The Woman in Red (also writer and dir) 1984, Hanky Panky 1982, Haunted Honeymoon (also writer and dir) 1986, See No Evil, Hear No Evil 1989, Funny About Love 1990, Another You 1991, Stuart Little (voice) 1999, Instant Karma 2005. *Television appearances include:* Death of a Salesman 1966, The Scarecrow 1972, The Electric Company (series) (voice) 1972–77, The Trouble With People 1973, Marlo Thomas Special 1973, Thursday's Games 19741974, Annie and the Hoods, Something Wilder (series) 1994, Murder in a Small Town (film) 1999, Alice in Wonderland (film) 1999, The Lady in Question (film) 1999. *Publication:* My French Whore (novel) 2007. *Address:* c/o Ames Cushing, William Morris Agency, One William Morris Place, Beverly Hills, CA 90212, USA (office). *Website:* www.wma.com (office).

WILDHABER, Luzius, DrIur, LLM, JSD; Swiss judge and professor of law; *President, Administration Tribunal, Council of Europe;* b. 18 Jan. 1937, Basle; m. 1st Simone Wildhaber-Creux 1963 (died 1994); two d.; m. 2nd Gill Reilly 1998 (divorced 2004); ed Basle, Paris, Heidelberg, London and Yale Univs; Int. Law Div. Fed. Dept of External Affairs 1968–71; Prof. of Int. Constitutional and Admin. Law, Univ. of Fribourg 1971–77; Prof. of Int. and Constitutional Law, Univ. of Basle 1977–98, Rector (desig.) 1990–92, Rector 1992–94, Pro-Rector 1994–96; Judge, Supreme Court of Liechtenstein 1975–88, Admin. Tribunal, IDB 1989–94, European Court of Human Rights 1991–2007; Pres. European Court of Human Rights 1998–2007; Pres. Admin Tribunal, Council of Europe 2009–(11); Hon. Bencher of the Inner Temple 2002, Hon. Bencher of the King's Inn Soc. Dublin 2005, Hon. mem. Int. Comm. of Jurists 2008; Star of Romania 2000; Order of Merit of Lithuania 2003, Great Gold Badge of Honour with Sash, Austria 2006, Commander, Order of Orange-Nassau, Netherlands 2007; Dr hc (Charles Univ., Prague) 1999, (Sofia Univ.) 1999, (American Univ. in Bulgaria) 1999, (Bratislava) 2000, (State Univ. of Moldova) 2000, (Bucharest) 2000, (Russian Acad. of Sciences) 2000, (Law Univ. of Lithuania) 2000, (Tbilisi) 2001, (Nat. Law Acad. of Ukraine) 2001, (Neuchâtel); Hon. LLD (McGill Univ., Montreal) 2002; Marcel Benoist Prize 1999. *Publications:* Advisory Opinions – Rechtsgutachten höchster Gerichte 1962, Treaty-making Power and Constitution 1971, Erfahrungen mit der Europäischen Menschenrechtskonvention 1979, Wechselspiel zwischen Innen und Aussen 1996, Praxis des Völkerrechts (with J. P. Müller, 3rd edn) 2001, The European Court of Human Rights: History, Achievements, Reform 2006; more than 200 articles. *Leisure interests:* travel, skiing, hiking, mountaineering. *Address:* Auf der Wacht 21, 4104 Oberwil, Switzerland (home). *Telephone:* 614012521 (home). *E-mail:* luzius.wildhaber@unibas.ch (office).

WILES, Sir Andrew John, KBE, PhD, FRS; British mathematician and academic; *Professor of Mathematics, Princeton University;* b. 11 April 1953; s. of Rev. M. F. Wiles; m.; two d.; ed Merton Coll., Oxford, Clare Coll., Cambridge; fmr Fellow Clare Coll.; Prof. of Math., Princeton Univ., USA 1982–88, 1990–; Royal Soc. Research Prof. in Math. and Professorial Fellow Merton Coll. Oxford 1988–90; Hon. DSc (Oxford) 1999; Jr Whitehead Prize (jtly), London Math. Soc. 1988, Wolf Prize for Mathematics 1995/96, Wolfskehl

Prize (for proving Fermat's Last Theorem), Göttingen 1997, Special Award, Berlin Int. Congress of Mathematicians 1998. *Address:* Department of Mathematics, Princeton University, Fine Hall, Washington Road, Princeton, NJ 08544-1000, USA. *Website:* www.math.princeton.edu/menusa/index0.html (office).

WILEY, John D., BS, MS, PhD; American physicist, university administrator and academic; *Chancellor, University of Wisconsin-Madison;* ed Indiana Univ., Grad. School, Univ. of Wisconsin-Madison (NSF Fellow); mem. tech. staff, Bell Telephone Labs, Murray Hill, NJ 1968–74; at Max Planck Inst., Stuttgart, Germany (awardee of Alexander von Humboldt Sr US Service Award for Research and Training) 1974–75; mem. faculty, Dept of Electrical and Computer Eng, Univ. of Wisconsin-Madison 1975–, Assoc. Dean for Research, Coll. of Eng 1986–89, Dean Grad. School and Sr Research Officer 1989–94, Provost and Vice-Chancellor for Academic Affairs 1994–2000, Chancellor 2001–; Co-founder several research centres, including Center for X-ray Lithography, Eng Research Center for Plasma-Aided Manufacturing; Chair. Materials Science Program 1982–86, Big Ten Council of Pres and Chancellors, Bd for the Council on Higher Educ. Accreditation; mem. Nat. Security Higher Educ. Advisory Cttee; also serves on several local and community bds, including William T. Evjue Foundation, Greater Madison Chamber of Commerce. *Address:* Office of the Chancellor, University of Wisconsin-Madison, 161 Bascom Hall, 500 Lincoln Drive, Madison, WI 53706, USA (office). *Telephone:* (608) 262-9946 (office). *E-mail:* chancellor@news.wisc.edu (office). *Website:* www.wisc.edu (office).

WILHELM, Ivan, CSc; Czech physicist, academic and university administrator; *Government Plenipotentiary, Ministry of Education, Youth and Sports;* b. 1 May 1942, Trnava, Slovakia; m.; one d.; ed Czech Tech. Univ. (CVUT), Prague; Asst, Dept of Nuclear Physics, CVUT 1964–67; study attachment to Neutron Physics Lab., United Inst. for Nuclear Research, Dubna, USSR 1967–71; Sr Research Officer Faculty of Math. and Physics, Charles Univ. 1971–89, Chief Research Officer 1989–91, Dir Nuclear Centre 1990–94, Vice-Rector for Devt 1994–2000, Rector of Charles Univ. 2000–06; Pres. Czech Rectors' Conf. 2000–06; mem. Exec. Council European Univ. Asscn 2000–06, Admin. Council Int. Asscn of Univs 2000–; Govt Plenipotentiary, Ministry of Educ., Youth and Sports 2006–; Dr hc (Univ. of Lyon 1-Claude Bernard) 2003, (Comenius Univ., Bratislava) 2006. *Publications include:* more than 80 research papers on nuclear and neutron physics. *Leisure interests:* cycling, walking. *Address:* Ministry of Education, Youth and Sports, Karmelitska 8, 11812 Prague 1, Czech Republic (office). *Telephone:* (2) 34813104 (office). *E-mail:* ivan.wilhelm@msmt.cz (office); ivan.wilhelm@ruk.cuni.cz (home). *Website:* www.msmt.cz (office).

WILHELMSSON, Hans K.B., DTech; Swedish physicist and academic; *Professor Emeritus, Fondation de France, Ecole Polytechnique, Palaiseau;* b. 4 Oct. 1929, Göteborg; s. of Wilhelm Petterson and Clara M. Johansson; m. 1st Birgitta Fredrikson 1960 (divorced 1995); one s. one d.; m. 2nd Julie Baudin 1995; ed Chalmers Univ. of Tech.; Prof. and Dir Inst. for Electromagnetic Field Theory, Chalmers Univ. of Tech. Göteborg 1971; Prof. of Plasma Physics, Fondation de France, Ecole Polytechnique, Palaiseau 1987–93, Prof. Emer. 1994–; mem. Royal Swedish Acad. of Science, Royal Swedish Acad. of Eng Science, Acad. Nationale des Sciences, Belles-Lettres et Arts de Bordeaux; John Ericson Medal (Chalmers Univ.) 1952, Montesquieu Medal (Bordeaux Acad.) 1999, Hon. Medal of the City of Nantes 2004. *Publications:* Fusion: A Voyage Through the Plasma Universe 2000; more than 200 scientific articles in theoretical and plasma physics. *Leisure interests:* art, travel. *Address:* 2 rue Marcellin Berthelot, 33200 Bordeaux, France. *Telephone:* (5) 56-02-19-80 (home). *Fax:* (5) 56-02-19-80 (home). *E-mail:* lotus15@free.fr (home).

WILKES, Sir Maurice Vincent, Kt, PhD, FRS, FREng, FIEE; British computer engineer (retd); b. 26 June 1913, Dudley; s. of the late Vincent J. Wilkes, OBE; m. Nina Twyman 1947; one s. two d.; ed King Edward VI School, Stourbridge and St John's Coll., Cambridge; Univ. Demonstrator 1937; Radar and Operational Research, Second World War; Univ. Lecturer and Acting Dir of Math. Lab., Cambridge 1945, Dir 1946–70; Head of Computer Lab. 1970; Prof. of Computer Tech., Univ. of Cambridge 1965–80; Staff Consultant, Digital Equipment Corpn 1980–86; Adjunct Prof., MIT 1981–85; mem. for Research Strategy, Olivetti Research Bd 1986–96; Adviser on Research Strategy, Olivetti and Oracle Research Lab. 1996–99; Staff Consultant, AT&T Laboratories, Cambridge 1999–2002; mem. Measurement and Control Section Cttee, Inst. of Electrical Engineers 1956–59; First Pres. British Computer Soc. 1957–60; mem. Council, Int. Fed. for Information Processing 1960–63, Council, IEE 1973–76, Council, Asscn for Computing Machinery 1991–94; Turing Lecturer, Asscn for Computing Machinery 1967; Distinguished Fellow, British Computer Soc. 1973; Foreign Assoc., US Nat. Acad. of Eng 1977, NAS 1980; Foreign Hon. Mem. American Acad. Arts and Sciences 1974; Hon. ScD (Cambridge) 1993; Dr hc (Amsterdam) 1978, (Newcastle-on-Tyne, Hull, Kent, City Univ. London, Linköping, Munich, Bath); Harry Goode Memorial Award, American Fed. of Information Processing Socs. 1968, Eckert-Mauchly Award, American Fed. of Information Processing Socs. 1980, IEEE McDowell Award 1981, IEE Faraday Medal 1981, Pender Award, Univ. of Pennsylvania 1982, C and C Prize, Tokyo 1988, Italgas Prize, Turin 1991, Kyoto Prize 1992, IEEE John von Neumann Medal 1997, Mountbatten Medal, Nat. Electronics Council 1997. *Publications:* Oscillations of the Earth's Atmosphere 1949, Preparation of Programs for an Electronic Digital Computer 1951, 1957, Automatic Digital Computers 1956, A Short Introduction to Numerical Analysis 1966, Time-Sharing Computer Systems 1968, The Cambridge CAP Computer and its Operating System 1979, Memoirs of a Computer Pioneer 1985, Computing Perspectives 1995. *Address:* Computer Lab, University of Cambridge, William Gates Building, 15 J.J. Thomson Road, Cambridge, CB3

0FD, England (office). *Telephone:* (1223) 763699 (office). *Fax:* (1223) 334678 (office). *Website:* www.cl.cam.ac.uk (office).

WILKES, Gen. Sir Michael (John), KCB, CBE; British army officer; b. 11 June 1940, Steep, Hants.; s. of the late Lt-Col Jack Wilkes and of Phyllis Wilkes; m. Anne Jacqueline Huelin 1966; two s.; ed Royal Mil. Acad., Sandhurst; commissioned RA 1960; joined 7 Para Regt, Royal Horse Artillery 1961; served Middle East Troop, Commdr Special Forces, Radfan, Saudi Arabia, Borneo 1964–67; Staff Coll. 1971–72; Brig. Maj. RA, HQ 3 Armoured Div. 1973–74; Battery Commdr Chestnut Troop, 1 Royal Horse Artillery (BAOR) 1975–76, CO 1977–79; Mil. Asst to Chief of Gen. Staff 1980–81; Chief of Staff, 3 Armoured Div. 1982–83; Commdr 22 Armoured Brigade 1984–85; Arms Dir, Ministry of Defence 1986–88; Gen. Officer Commdg 3 Armoured Div. 1988–90; Commdr UK Field Army and Insp.-Gen., TA 1990–93; Middle East Adviser to Ministry of Defence 1992–95; Adjutant-Gen. 1993–95; Lt-Gov. and C-in-C, Jersey 1995–2000; Col Commdt and Pres., Hon. Artillery Co. 1992–98; Pres. Army Cadet Force Asscn 1999–; Kermit Roosevelt Lecturer 1995; Order of Mil. Merit 1st Class (Jordan) 1994, Freeman City of London 1993; KStJ. *Leisure interests:* mil. history, sailing, skiing. *Address:* c/o Le Riche House, PO Box 4, 1-3 l'avenue le Bas, Longveville, St Saviour, JE4 8NB, Jersey (office).

WILKINS, David Horton, BA, JD; American politician and diplomatist; *Ambassador to Canada;* b. 12 Oct. 1946; s. of the late William Walter Wilkins and Evelyn Wilkins; m. Susan Clary; two c.; ed Clemson Univ., Univ. of S Carolina; Chair. Greenville Co. Legis. Del. 1985–86, 1989–94; Chair. Judicial Comm. 1986–92; Chair. Southern Legis. Conf. 1998; Pres. Nat. Speakers Conf. 2001; Speaker Pro Tempore S Carolina Legislature 1992–94, Speaker 1994–2005; State Chair. Bush-Cheney Re-election Campaign; Amb. to Canada 2005–; William M. Bulger Excellence in State Legis. Leadership Award 2004. *Address:* Embassy of the USA, 490 Sussex Drive, PO Box 866, Station B, Ottawa, ON K1P 5T1, Canada (office). *Telephone:* (613) 238-5335 (office). *Fax:* (613) 688-3080 (office). *Website:* www.usembassycanada.gov (office).

WILKINSON, Sir Denys Haigh, Kt, PhD, DSc, ScD, FRS; British physicist, academic and academic administrator; *Professor Emeritus, Sussex University;* b. 5 Sept. 1922, Leeds; s. of Charles Wilkinson and Hilda Wilkinson; m. 1st Christiane Clavier 1947; three d.; m. 2nd Helen Sellschop 1967; ed Jesus Coll., Cambridge; worked on British Atomic Energy Project 1943–46, on Canadian Atomic Energy Project 1945–46; Demonstrator Cavendish Lab., Univ. of Cambridge 1947–51, Lecturer 1951–56 and Reader 1950–57, Fellow, Jesus Coll., Cambridge 1944–59, Hon. Fellow 1961–; Student of Christ Church, Oxford 1957–76, Emer. 1976–79, Hon. 1979–; Prof. of Nuclear Physics, Clarendon Laboratory, Univ. of Oxford 1957–59, Prof. of Experimental Physics 1959–76, Head of Dept of Nuclear Physics 1962–76; Vice-Chancellor Univ. of Sussex 1976–87, Prof. Emer. 1987–; Pres. Inst. of Physics 1980–82, Hon. Fellow 2002–; Rutherford Memorial Lecturer of British Physical Soc. 1962; mem. Governing Bd Nat. Inst. for Research in Nuclear Science 1958–64; Queen's Lecturer, Berlin 1966, Cherwell-Simon Memorial Lecturer, Oxford 1970, Tizard Memorial Lecturer 1975, Lauritsen Memorial Lecturer, Calif. Inst. of Tech. 1976, Schiff Memorial Lecturer, Stanford Univ. 1977, Racah Memorial Lecturer, Univ. of Jerusalem 1977, Solly Cohen Memorial Lecturer, Hebrew Univ. of Jerusalem 1985, Axel Memorial Lecturer, Univ. of Ill. 1985, Breit Memorial Lecturer, Yale Univ. 1987, W. B. Lewis Memorial Lecturer, Chalk River 1989, Humphry Davy Lecturer, Acad. of Science (Paris) 1990, Rutherford Memorial Lecturer, NZ 1991, W. V. Houston Memorial Lecturer, Rice Univ., Houston, Tex. 1994, Hudspeth Lecturer, Univ. of Tex. Austin 1994, McPherson Memorial Lecturer, McGill Univ., Montreal 1995, Pickavance Memorial Lecturer, Rutherford Lab., Oxford 1997, Sargent Memorial Lecturer, Queen's Univ., Kingston, Ont. 1998, Saha Memorial Lecturer, Kolkata 2001; mem. Science Research Council 1967–70; Chair. SRC Nuclear Physics Bd 1968–70, Physics III Cttee CERN, Geneva 1971–75, Radioactive Waste Man. Advisory Cttee 1978–83; Vice-Pres. IUPAP 1985–93; mem. Council of the Asscn of Commonwealth Univs 1981–87; mem. Academia Europaea; Foreign mem. Royal Swedish Acad. of Sciences; Battelle Distinguished Prof., Univ. of Washington 1970; Hon. DSc (Univ. of Saskatchewan, Utah State Univ., Univ. of Guelph, Queen's Univ., Ont.); Hon. FilDr (Univ. of Uppsala); Hon. LLD (Sussex); Hon. DSc (Coll. of William and Mary, Williamsburg); Holweck Medallist of French and British Physical Socs 1957, Hughes Medal of the Royal Soc. 1965, Bruce-Preller Prize of Royal Soc. of Edinburgh 1969, Tom W. Bonner Prize of American Physical Soc. 1974, Royal Medal, Royal Soc. 1980, Guthrie Medal of Inst. of Physics 1986, CCSEM Gold Medal 1988. *Publications:* Ionization Chambers and Counters 1950, Our Universes 1991; Ed.: Isospin in Nuclear Physics 1969, Progress in Particle and Nuclear Physics 1977–84; Mesons in Nuclei (jt ed.) 1979; many articles in learned journals. *Leisure interests:* early music and art, ornithology. *Address:* Gayles Orchard, Friston, Eastbourne, BN20 0BA, England (home). *Telephone:* (1323) 423333 (home).

WILKINSON, Jonathan Peter (Jonny), OBE; British professional rugby football player (rugby union); b. 25 May 1979, Frimley, Surrey; s. of Philip Wilkinson and Philippa Wilkinson, brother Mark Wilkinson (also of Newcastle Falcons); ed Lord Wandsworth Coll., Hants.; fly-half; player for Farnham, Newcastle Falcons 1997–, England Under-18s, England 1998– (debut v. Ireland), apptd Capt. Nov. 2004; 68 tests for England, 1032 points, has also scored 67 points for British and Irish Lions, all-time highest points-scorer in rugby union Test history with 1099 points to 9 March 2008; mem. Grand Slam winning squad 2003, Five Nations Championship winners 1999, Six Nations Championship winners 2000, 2001, World Cup winning squad 2003, 2nd place 2007, 4th place 1995, 1999; mem. British Lions' team Australia 2001 (three test caps), New Zealand 2005 (two test caps); scored most points at World Cup 2003 (113), all-time highest points scorer in history of World Cup with 249 to 2007; Freeman, City of Greater London, Newcastle-upon-Tyne 2004; Hon. DCL (Univ. of Northumbria) 2005; Int. Rugby Board Player of the Year 2003. *Publications:* Lions and Falcons: My Diary of a Remarkable Year 2001, My World 2004, Jonny's Hotshots: How to Play Rugby My Way 2005, Tackling Life 2008. *Leisure interests:* tennis, swimming, basketball, cricket, playing guitar and piano, travelling, speaking and reading French and Spanish. *Address:* c/o Newcastle Falcons, Kingston Park Stadium, Brunton Road, Newcastle upon Tyne, NE13 8AF, England (office). *Telephone:* (191) 2145588 (office). *Fax:* (191) 2142826 (office). *Website:* www.newcastle-falcons.co.uk (office).

WILKINSON, Paul, CBE, MA, FRSA; British political scientist and academic; *Professor of International Relations and Chairman, Centre for the Study of Terrorism and Political Violence, University of St Andrews;* b. 9 May 1937, Harrow, Middx; s. of Walter Ross Wilkinson and Joan Rosemary Paul; m. Susan Wilkinson 1960; two s. one d.; ed Lower School of John Lyon, Harrow, Univ. Coll., Swansea and Univ. of Wales; regular officer RAF 1959–65; Asst Lecturer in Politics, Univ. Coll., Cardiff 1966–68, Lecturer 1968–75, Sr Lecturer 1975–78; Reader in Politics, Univ. of Wales 1978–79; Chair. in Int. Relations, Aberdeen Univ. 1979–89; Head Dept of Int. Relations, Univ. of St Andrews 1990–94, Prof. of Int. Relations 1990–, Head School of History and Int. Relations 1994–96, Dir Centre for the Study of Terrorism and Political Violence 1998–2002, Chair. 2002–; Dir Research Inst. for the Study of Conflict and Terrorism 1989–94; Visiting Fellow, Trinity Hall, Cambridge 1997–98; Hon. Fellow, Univ. Coll., Swansea 1986. *Publications:* Social Movement 1971, Political Terrorism 1974, Terrorism versus Liberal Democracy 1976, Terrorism and the Liberal State (revised edn) 1986, British Perspectives on Terrorism 1981, Terrorism: Theory and Practice (jtly) 1978, The New Fascists (revised edn) 1983, Contemporary Research on Terrorism 1987, Lessons of Lockerbie 1989, Terrorism and Political Violence (co-ed. with David Rapoport) 1990, Technology and Terrorism (ed.) 1993, Terrorism: British Perspectives (ed.) 1993, Research Report (Vol. Two) Lord Lloyd's Inquiry into Legislation Against Terrorism 1996, Aviation Terrorism and Security Versus (co-ed. with Brian Jenkins) 1998, Terrorism Versus Democracy: The Liberal State Response 2000 (second revised edn 2006), Addressing The New International Terrorism (co-author) 2003, Homeland Security in the UK 2007, Very Short Introduction to International Relations 2007; numerous articles in specialist journals. *Leisure interests:* modern art, poetry, walking. *Address:* Department of International Relations, University of St Andrews, New Arts Building, The Scores, St Andrews, Fife, KY16 9AX, Scotland (home). *Telephone:* (1334) 462935 (office). *Fax:* (1334) 461922 (office). *E-mail:* gm39@st-andrews.ac.uk (office). *Website:* (office).

WILKINSON, Tom, OBE; British actor; b. 12 Dec. 1948, Leeds; m. Diana Hardcastle; two d.; ed Univ. of Kent, Royal Acad. of Dramatic Arts; London Critics Circle Theatre Award Best Supporting Actor (for Ghosts) 1986, Best Actor (for An Enemy of the People) 1988; Dr hc (Univ. of Kent) 2001. *Plays:* plays with Royal Nat. Theatre, RSC and Oxford Playhouse include Peer Gynt, Brand, Henry V, Three Sisters, Uncle Vanya, Julius Caesar, Hamlet, The Merchant of Venice, The Crucible, As You Like It. *Films:* Sylvia 1985, Wetherby 1985, Sharma and Beyond 1986, Paper Mask 1990, In the Name of the Father 1993, All Things Bright and Beautiful 1994, Priest 1994, A Business Affair 1994, Sense and Sensibility 1995, The Ghost and the Darkness 1996, Oscar and Lucinda 1997, Smilla's Sense of Snow 1997, Wilde 1997, The Full Monty 1997, Jilting Joe 1997, The Governess 1998, Shakespeare in Love 1998, Rush Hour 1998, Father Damien 1999, Ride with the Devil 2000, Chain of Fools 2000, In the Bedroom 2001, Black Knight 2001, The Importance of Being Earnest 2002, The Gathering Storm 2002, Girl with a Pearl Earring 2003, If Only 2004, Eternal Sunshine of the Spotless Mind 2004, Stage Beauty 2004, Piccadilly Jim 2004, Ripley Under Ground 2005, Batman Begins 2005, The Exorcism of Emily Rose 2005, A Good Woman 2005, Separate Lies 2005, The Night of the White Pants 2006, The Last Kiss 2006, Dedication 2007, Michael Clayton 2007, Cassandra's Dream 2007, RocknRolla 2008, Valkyrie 2008, Duplicity 2009, 44 Inch Chest 2009. *Television includes:* Prime Suspect 1991, Martin Chuzzlewit 1994, Crossing the Floor 1996, Eskimo Day 1996, Cold Enough for Snow 1997, David Copperfield 1999, The Gathering Storm 2002, An Angel for May 2002, Normal 2003, John Adams (series, HBO) (Golden Globe Award for Best Supporting Actor in a Series 2009) 2008–, Recount 2008, A Number 2008. *Address:* The Gersh Agency, 232 North Canon Drive, Suite 201, Beverly Hills, CA 90210, USA (office). *Telephone:* (310) 274-6611 (office). *Fax:* (310) 278-6232 (office). *Website:* www.gershcomedy.com (office).

WIŁKOMIRSKA, Wanda, MMus; Polish violinist; b. 11 Jan. 1929, Warsaw; d. of Alfred Wiłkomirski and Dorota Temkin; divorced since 1976; two s.; ed Higher State of Music, Łódź, Franz Liszt Acad. of Music, Budapest and pvt. studies with Henryk Szeryng, Paris; public debut playing a Mozart Sonata aged seven; first appearance with orchestra aged 15, in Kraków; numerous recordings; concerts in 50 countries with most of the major orchestras throughout the world; toured as soloist with, amongst others, Nat. Philharmonic, Warsaw and Minnesota Symphony; has given world premiere performances of numerous contemporary works including works by Baird and Penderecki; has toured with her sister and brother as the Wilkomirska Trio and has performed with Martha Argerich, Gidon Kremer, Daniel Barenboim, Misha Maisky and others; defected whilst on tour of FRG March 1982; Prof., Hochschule für Musik, Heidelberg-Mannheim 1983–98; Guest Prof. now part-time staff mem. Sydney Conservatorium of Music, Australia 1999–; has also worked with Australian Nat. Acad. of Music, Melbourne 2001–; master classes in Melbourne and Sydney; mem. Jury Hannover Int. Violin Competition 1997, 2000, Kendall Nat. Violin Competition (Australia); Officer's Cross of Polonia Restituta Order 1953, Commdr's Cross with Star 2001, Order of Banner of Labour 2nd Class 1959, (1st Class) 1964; Polish State

Prize 1952, 1964; several foreign prizes, including Second Prize, Leipzig 1950, Bach Competition Award of Democratic German Radio, Culture and Arts Prize (1st Class) 1975, Orpheus Prize, Polish Musicians' Asscn 1979. *Leisure interests:* films, literature, sports. *Address:* Sydney Conservatorium of Music, Building C41, The University of Sydney, Sydney NSW 2006, Australia (office). *Telephone:* (2) 93511222 (office). *Fax:* (2) 93511287 (office). *E-mail:* info@greenway.usyd.edu.au (office). *Website:* www.music.usyd.edu.au (office).

WILLATS, Stephan; British artist; b. 17 Aug. 1943, London; m. Stephanie Craven 1983; three s.; ed Drayton School and Ealing School of Art; Ed. and Publr Control magazine 1965–; Lecturer, Ipswich School of Art 1965–67; Lecturer, Nottingham Coll. of Art 1968–72; Organiser, Centre for Behavioural Art, Gallery House, London 1972–73; numerous group exhbns in the UK, Netherlands, Italy, FRG, Switzerland, Belgium, Australia; numerous project works, including Inside an Ocean, Mile End, London 1979, Two Worlds Apart, Hayes 1981 and Blocks, Avondale Estate, London 1982, Brentford Towers, W London 1985, White Towers, Helsinki 1989, Private Network, Oxford 1990; DAAD Fellowship, Berlin 1979–81. *Publications:* several books, including The Artist as an Instigator of Changes in Social Cognition and Behaviour 1973, Art and Social Function 1976, The Lurky Place 1978, Doppelgänger 1985, Intervention and Audience 1986, Concepts and Projects, Bookworks by Stephen Willats; numerous articles in art magazines. *Address:* c/o Lisson Gallery, 67 Bell Street, London, NW1 5DA, England.

WILLCOCKS, Sir David Valentine, Kt, CBE, MC, MusB, MA, FRCO, FRCM; British musician; b. 30 Dec. 1919, Newquay, Cornwall; s. of T. H. Willcocks; m. Rachel Blyth 1947; two s. (one deceased) two d.; ed Clifton Coll. and King's Coll., Cambridge; served with 5th Bn, Duke of Cornwall's Light Infantry (rank of Capt.) 1940–45; Fellow, King's Coll., Cambridge 1947–51, Fellow and Dir of Music 1957–73, Lecturer in Music, Cambridge Univ. and Cambridge Univ. Organist 1957–74; Conductor Cambridge Univ. Music Soc. 1958–73; Organist Salisbury Cathedral 1947–50, Worcester Cathedral 1950–57; Conductor, Worcester Three Choirs Festival and City of Birmingham Choir 1950–57; Musical Dir Bach Choir, London 1960–98; Pres. Royal Coll. of Organists 1966–68 (Vice-Pres. 1968–), Incorporated Soc. of Musicians 1978–79, Nat. Fed. of Music Socs 1980–90 (Vice-Pres. 1990–), Asscn of British Choral Dirs 1993–; Dir Royal Coll. of Music, London 1974–84 (Vice-Pres. 1984–); conductor in many recordings with the Choir of King's Coll. Cambridge, The Bach Choir (Conductor Laureate 1998–) and the Royal Coll. of Music Chamber Choir; Fellow Royal School of Church Music 1977, Royal Scottish Acad. of Music and Drama 1982; Freeman, City of London 1981; Hon. RAM 1965, Guildhall School of Music and Drama 1980; Hon. FRNCM, FRSAMD; Hon. Fellow Royal Canadian Coll. of Organists 1967, Trinity Coll. of Music 1976, King's Coll., Cambridge 1979; Hon. mem. Royal Philharmonic Soc. 1999; Hon. DMus (Exeter) 1976, (Leicester) 1977, (Westminster Choir Coll., Princeton) 1980, (Bristol) 1981, (St Olaf Coll., Minn.) 1991, (Royal Coll. of Music) 1998, (Univ. of Victoria, BC) 1999, (Rowan Univ.) 2007; Hon. DLitt (Sussex) 1982, (Memorial Univ. of Newfoundland) 2003; Hon. DSL (Trinity Univ., Toronto) 1985; Hon. DFA (Luther Coll., Ia) 1998; Hon. LLD (Toronto) 2001; Hon. MA (Bradford) 1973; Harvard Glee Club Medal 1992, Distinguished Musician Silver Medal, Inc. Soc. of Musicians 1999, Distinguished Visitor Silver Medal, Univ. of Toronto 1999, Silver Medal Worshipful Co. of Musicians 1999. *Address:* 13 Grange Road, Cambridge, CB3 9AS, England (home). *Telephone:* (1223) 359559 (home). *Fax:* (1223) 355947 (home). *E-mail:* david.willcocks3@ntlworld.com (home).

WILLCOX, Peter, MA; Australian oil industry executive; *Chairman, AMP Limited;* began career in oil industry 1975; fmr CEO BHP Petroleum; apptd Dir AMP Ltd 2002, Chair. 2003–; Chair. Mayne Group Ltd 2003–; fmr mem. Bd of Dirs BHP Ltd, Lend Lease Corpn Ltd, Schroders Holdings Australia Ltd, James Hardie Industries Ltd, North Ltd, F.H. Faulding & Co. Ltd, Woodside Petroleum Ltd, Energy Devts Ltd, Tejas Gas Corpn (USA), Hamilton Oil Corpn (USA). *Address:* AMP Limited, Level 24, 33 Alfred Street, Sydney 2000, Australia (office). *Telephone:* (2) 9257-5000 (office). *Fax:* (2) 8275-0199 (office). *Website:* www.ampgroup.com (office).

WILLES, Mark Hinckley, PhD; American media executive and economist; *President and CEO, Deseret Management Corporation;* b. 16 July 1941, Salt Lake City, UT; s. of Joseph Simmons Willes and Ruth Willes (née Hinckley); m. Laura Fayone 1961; three s. two d.; ed Columbia Univ., New York; with Banking and Currency Cttee House of Reps 1966–67; Asst Prof. of Finance, Univ. of Pennsylvania, Phila 1967–69; economist, Fed. Reserve Bank 1967, Sr Economist 1969–70, Dir Research 1970–71, Vice-Pres. 1971, First Vice-Pres. 1971–77; Pres. Fed. Reserve Bank of Minneapolis 1977–80; Exec. Vice-Pres., Chief Finance Officer Gen. Mills Inc. 1980–85, Pres., COO 1985–92, Vice-Chair. 1992–95; Chair., Pres., CEO Times Mirror Co. 1995–2000; Pres. and CEO Deseret Man. Corpn 2009–; Publr LA Times 1997–99; Pres. Hawaii Honolulu Mission, Church of the Latter Day Saints 2001. *Address:* 60 East South Temple, Suite 575, Salt Lake City, UT 84111, USA (office). *Telephone:* (801) 323-4232 (office). *E-mail:* willesmh@deseretmgt.com (office).

WILLETT, Walter C., MD, DrPH; American epidemiologist, nutritionist and academic; *Professor of Epidemiology and Nutrition, Harvard School of Public Health;* b. Hart, Mich.; ed Michigan State Univ., Univ. of Michigan Medical School, Harvard School of Public Health, Boston, Mass; Intern in Medicine, Harvard Medical Service, Boston City Hosp. 1970–71, Fellow, Family and Ambulatory Medicine 1971–73, Physician, Adult Medical Services 1971–74, Assoc. in Medicine 1977–84; Lecturer in Medicine, Faculty of Medicine, Univ. of Dar-es-Salaam, Tanzania 1974–75; Lecturer in Community Medicine and Head of Community Health Dept 1975–77; Research Fellow in Medicine, Harvard Medical School, Boston 1977–80; with East Boston Neighborhood Health Center 1977–85; Research Fellow in Medicine, Peter Bent Brigham Hosp., Boston 1979–80, Jr Assoc. in Medicine, Brigham and Women's Hosp.

1980–82, Assoc. Physician 1982; Asst Prof. of Epidemiology, Dept of Epidemiology, Harvard School of Public Health, Boston 1980–84, Assoc. Prof. of Epidemiology 1984–87, Lecturer in Medicine, Harvard Medical School 1986–92, Prof. of Epidemiology and Nutrition, Harvard School of Public Health 1987–, Chair. Dept of Nutrition 1991, Prof. of Medicine, Harvard Medical School 1992–; D.W. Harrington Visiting Prof., State Univ. of New York at Buffalo 1992; Virginia Beal Lectureship, Dept of Nutrition, Univ. of Massachusetts 1992; Assoc. Ed. International Journal of Oncology 1993, Current Reviews in Public Health 1993, Breast Diseases: An International Journal 1993; mem. American Public Health Asscn 1974, Soc. for Epidemiologic Research 1979, NIH Epidemiology and Disease Control Study Section 1984–86, American Epidemiologic Soc. 1986, American Inst. of Nutrition 1990, NAS Inst. of Medicine 1998; NIH-Research Career Devt Award 1981, Prevention Prize-Nat. Award for Achievements in Preventive Medicine and Health 1992, Charles U. Chapin Award, Rhode Island Medical Soc. 1993, American Cancer Soc. Cancer Prevention Award 1994, Distinguished Alumnus Award, Michigan State Univ. 1994, John Snow Award, American Public Health 1996, Distinguished Achievement Award, American Soc. for Preventive Oncology 1996, Int. Award for Modern Nutrition 1997, Health Advocacy Award, Friends of the Nat. Inst. of Nursing Research 1999, Jill Rose Award for Outstanding Breast Cancer Research, Breast Cancer Research Foundation 2000, Ninth American Asscn for Cancer Research-American Cancer Soc. Award for Research Excellence in Cancer Epidemiology and Prevention 2000, Charles S. Mott Prize for the Most Outstanding Recent Contrib. Related to the Cause or Prevention of Cancer, General Motors Cancer Research Foundation 2001. *Publications:* more than 700 articles in medical and scientific journals. *Address:* Department of Nutrition, Harvard School of Public Health, Building II, Room 311, Boston, MA 02115, USA (office). *Telephone:* 617-432-4680 (office). *Fax:* 617-432-0464 (office). *E-mail:* walter.willett@channing.harvard.edu (office). *Website:* www.hsph.harvard.edu (office).

WILLIAM, HRH Prince (William Arthur Philip Louis of Wales); British; b. 21 June 1982; s. of HRH The Prince of Wales and of the late Diana, Princess of Wales; ed Mrs Mynors' Nursery School, Wetherby School, Ludgrove School, Eton Coll., St Andrews Univ., Royal Mil. Acad., Sandhurst; patron of youth homelessness charity, Centrepoint 2005–; Pres. Designate Football Asscn 2006–; Patron Tusk Trust 2005–. *Address:* Clarence House, London, SW1A 1BA, England. *Website:* www.royal.gov.uk.

WILLIAM, (Bryan) David, BA; British/Canadian director, actor and lecturer; b. 24 June 1926, London, England; s. of Eric Hugh Williams and Olwen Roose; ed Bryanston School, Blandford, Dorset, Univ. Coll. Oxford; nat. service in British Army 1945–48; Artistic Dir New Shakespeare Co., London, England 1962–66, Nat. Theatre of Israel 1968–70; Assoc. Dir Mermaid Theatre, London 1964–66; Founder and first Artistic Dir Ludlow Festival; Artistic Dir Stratford Festival, Stratford, Ont., Canada 1989–93; Visiting Prof. Theatre Dept, De Paul Univ., Chicago 1985–88. *Productions include:* (at Stratford, Ont.): Bacchae, The Importance of Being Earnest, The Winter's Tale, Murder in the Cathedral, Troilus and Cressida, Twelfth Night, Volpone; (elsewhere): A Midsummer Night's Dream, Love's Labour's Lost, Henry V (Open Air Theatre, Regents Park), Richard II (Nat. Theatre of GB), Dear Daddy (Ambassadors Theatre, London), Left-Handed Liberty, The Shoemakers' Holiday, The Canker and the Rose (Mermaid Theatre, London), Albert Herring (Aldeburgh Festival), world premieres of Thérèse (Royal Opera House, Covent Garden), The Lighthouse (Edinburgh Festival), world première of opera Red Emma (Canadian Opera Co.) 1995, Così fan Tutte, Opera St Louis, Tosca (Canadian Opera Co.) 1998, Mrs Mozart, Hartford, Conn. 1999 and many others in London, New York, San Francisco, Washington, DC, Gulbenkian Festival, Lisbon; recent roles performed on stage include Jacques (As You Like It), Serebryakov (Uncle Vanya), Malvolio (Twelfth Night) at Stratford, Ontario, AEH (The Invention of Love), Guthrie Theater, Minneapolis and Studio Theater, Washington DC, Boyet (Love's Labour's Lost), National Arts Centre, Ottawa. *Operas directed include:* Albert Herring, The Fairy Queen, Iphigénie en Tauride, Fennimore and Gerda, Il Re Pastore, Xerxes, The Rake's Progress, A Midsummer Night's Dream, The Knot Garden, La Traviata. *TV roles include:* Richard II in Age of Kings, BBC and Octavius Caesar in Spread of the Eagle, BBC 2. *Publications:* The Tempest on the Stage 1960, Hamlet in the Theatre 1963. *Leisure interests:* walking, dogs. *Address:* 194 Langarth Street, London, ON N6C 1Z5, Canada. *Fax:* (519) 673-3755. *E-mail:* may.king@rogers.com (home).

WILLIAMS, Anthony A., JD; American real estate executive and fmr politician; *CEO, Public Properties Realty Investment Trust;* m. Diana Lynn Simmons; one c.; ed Yale and Harvard Univs; law clerk, US Dist Court Boston 1987–88; Asst Dir Boston Redevelopment Authority 1988–89; Exec. Dir Community Devt Agency St Louis 1989–91; Deputy Comptroller State of Conn. 1991–93; Chief Finance Officer Dept of Agric. 1993–98; Mayor of Washington, DC 1999–2007; Co-founder (with Friedman Billings Ramsey Group) and CEO Public Properties Realty Investment Trust (real estate trust) 2007–; Adjunct Prof. of Public Affairs, Columbia Univ. 1992–93; Nat. Fellow Kellogg Foundation 1991; Democrat. *Address:* c/o Friedman Billings Ramsey Group, 1001 Nineteenth Street, North Arlington, VA 22209, USA. *Telephone:* (703) 312-9500. *Fax:* (703) 312-9501. *Website:* www.fbr.com.

WILLIAMS, Arthur Ronald (Ronnie), OBE; British diplomatist, writer and organization official; *Chief Executive, The Publishers Association;* b. 29 Oct. 1942, Rawalpindi, India (now Pakistan); s. of Alfred Arthur Williams and Marjory Williams (née Heenan); m. 1st Lynne Diana Merrin 1967; m. 2nd Antoinette Catherine Naldrett 1993; two d.; ed Rossall School, Fleetwood, Lancs. and Selwyn Coll., Cambridge; joined diplomatic service 1964, served in Jakarta 1966–67, Singapore 1967–69, Budapest 1971–74, Nairobi 1976–78; Chief Exec. Timber Growers UK 1980–87; Exec. Dir Forestry Industry

Council of GB 1987–97; Chief Exec. The Publrs Asscn 1998–; Dir Digital Content Forum 2002–. *Publications:* Montrose, Cavalier in Mourning 1975, The Lords of the Isles 1985, The Heather and the Gale 1997, Sons of the Wolf 1998. *Leisure interests:* fly fishing, Scottish history, walking, real tennis. *Address:* The Publishers Association, 29B Montague Street, London, WC1B 5BW (office); Starlings, Wildhern, nr Andover, Hants., SP11 0JE, England. *Telephone:* (20) 7691-9191 (office); (1264) 735389 (home). *Fax:* (20) 7691-9191 (office); (1264) 735435 (home). *E-mail:* rwilliams@publishers.org.uk (office). *Website:* www.publishers.org.uk (office).

WILLIAMS, Elizabeth (Betty); Irish campaigner for children's rights, peace and justice; *Founder and President, World Centers of Compassion for Children International;* b. 22 May 1943, Belfast; ed Queen's Univ., Belfast; worked as office receptionist; jt winner of Nobel Peace Prize for launching the Northern Ireland Peace Movt (later renamed Community of the Peace People) 1976, Jt Leader 1976–78; fmr Visiting Prof., Sam Houston State Univ.; Head, Global Children's Foundation; Founder and Pres. World Centers of Compassion for Children Int.; Chair. Inst. for Asian Democracy, Washington DC; Distinguished Visiting Prof., Nova Southeastern Univ.; mem. Bd of Dirs Adoption Options, Inc.; Founding mem. Alliance for the New Humanity; mem. Advisory Bd Dalai Lama Center for Peace and Educ., Camfed Int., Mahatma Gandhi Center for Global Non-violence; mem. Council of Honour UN Univ. for Peace, Costa Rica; mem. Bd of Trustees Pax Natura; Hon. mem. Club of Budapest, World Wisdom Academy, hon. cttee mem. Global Vision for Peace; Hon. DHumLitt (Coll. of Siena Heights, Mich.) 1977, Hon. LLD (Yale Univ.); Nobel Peace Prize (jtly) 1976, People's Peace Prize of Norway 1976, Carl von Ossietzky Medal for Courage (Berlin Section, Int. League of Human Rights), Schweitzer Medallion for Courage, Eleanor Roosevelt Award 1984, Frank Foundation Child Assistance Int. Oliver Award, Together for Peace Foundation Peace Building Award 1995, Gandhi, King, Ikeda Community Builders Prize 2003, Ischia Peace Award 2003, Soka Gakkai Int. Peace and Culture Award 2004. *Leisure interest:* gardening. *Address:* World Centers of Compassion for Children International, Knock Inverin, County Galway, Ireland (office). *Telephone:* (91) 593304 (office). *E-mail:* bwccc@eircom.net (office). *Website:* www.centersofcompassion.org (office).

WILLIAMS, Brian; American television journalist; *Anchor and Managing Editor, NBC Nightly News;* b. 5 May 1959, Elmira, NY; m. Jane Stoddart Williams; one s. one d.; ed George Washington Univ, Catholic Univ of America; intern, The White House; TV reporter KOAM-TV, with WTTG-TV, WCAU-TV; joined WCBS-TV 1993; joined NBC 1993, Chief White House Corresp. 1994–96; anchor, Man. Ed. The News With Brian Williams MSNBC 1996–2004, Anchor and Man. Ed. NBC Nightly News 2004–; mem. Council on Foreign Relations; Emmy Awards for reporting 1987, 1989, 1993. *Address:* NBC News, 30 Rockefeller Plaza, 3rd Floor, New York, NY 10112-0002, USA (office). *Telephone:* (212) 664-4444 (office). *Fax:* (212) 664-4426 (office). *E-mail:* nightly@nbc.com (office). *Website:* www.nbc.com/nbc/NBC_News (office).

WILLIAMS, Sir Bruce (Rodda), KBE, MA; Australian/British economist; b. 10 Jan. 1919, Warragul, Vic.; s. of the late Rev. W J. Williams and of Helen Baud; m. Roma Olive Hotten 1942; five d.; ed Wesley Coll., Melbourne, Queen's Coll., Univ. of Melbourne; Prof. of Econs, Univ. Coll., North Staffordshire 1950–59; Robert Otley Prof., Stanley Jevons Prof., Univ. of Manchester 1959–67; Sec. and Jt Dir of Research, Science and Industry Cttee 1952–59; mem. UK Nat. Bd for Prices and Incomes 1966–67; Econ. Adviser to UK Ministry of Tech. 1966–67; mem. UK Cen. Advisory Council on Science and Tech. 1967; Vice-Chancellor and Principal, Univ. of Sydney 1967–81, Prof. 1967–; Dir Tech. Change Centre 1981–86; Chair. Australian Inquiry into the Eng Disciplines 1987–88; Chair. NSW State Cancer Council 1967–81; mem. Bd of Reserve Bank of Australia 1969–81; Chair. Australian Vice-Chancellors' Cttee 1972–74, Nat. Cttee of Inquiry into Educ. and Training 1976–79; Dir Parramatta Hospitals Bd 1978–81; mem. Commonwealth Working Group on the Man. of Technological Change 1984–85, on Distance Teaching and Open Learning 1986–87; Visiting Fellow ANU 1989–90, 1993–94, Univ. of London Inst. of Educ. 1991–92; Fellow Univ. of Sydney Senate 1994–98; Pres. Sydney Conservatorium of Music Foundation 1994–98, Sydney Spring Festival of New Music 1999–2002; Chair. Exec. Sydney Int. Piano Competition 1986–; Hon. FIE Australia 1989; Hon. DLitt (Univ. of Keele) 1973, (Univ. of Sydney) 1982; Hon. DEcon (Univ. of Queensland) 1980; Hon. LLD (Univ. of Melbourne) 1981, (Univ. of Manchester) 1982; Hon. DSc (Univ. of Aston) 1982. *Publications:* The Socialist Order and Freedom 1942, Industry and Technical Progress (with C. F. Carter) 1957, Investment in Innovation (with C. F. Carter) 1958, Science in Industry (with C. F. Carter) 1959, Technology, Investment and Growth 1967, Science and Technology in Economic Growth 1973, Systems of Higher Education, Australia 1978, Education, Training and Employment 1979, Disappointed Expectations 1981, Living with Technology 1982, Knowns and Unknowns in Technical Change 1985, The Influence of Attitudes to New Technology on National Growth Rates 1986, Review of the Discipline of Engineering 1988, Academic Status and Leadership (with D. Wood) 1990, University Responses to Research Selectivity 1991, Higher Education and Employment 1994, Liberal Education and Useful Knowledge 2001, Making and Breaking Universities 2005, Fortune's Favours 2006. *Leisure interests:* music, theatre. *Address:* 31 Queen Anne's Gardens, Ealing, London, W5 5QD, England (home); 24 Mansfield Street, Glebe, NSW 2037, Australia (home).

WILLIAMS, Charles Kenneth (C. K.), BA; American poet and academic; *Lecturer, Creative Writing, Department of Comparative Literature, Princeton University;* b. 4 Nov. 1936, Newark, NJ; s. of Paul Bernard and Dossie (née Kasdin) Williams; m. 1st Sarah Dean Jones 1966 (divorced 1975); one d.; m. 2nd Catherine Justine Mauger 1975; one s.; ed Univ. of Pennsylvania; Visiting Prof. of Literature, Beaver Coll., Jenkintown, Pa 1975, Drexel Univ.,

Philadelphia 1976, Franklin and Marshall Coll., Pa 1977, Univ. of Calif. at Irvine 1978, Boston Univ. 1979–80, Brooklyn Coll., CUNY 1982–83; Prof. of Writing, Columbia Univ. NY 1981–85; Prof. of Literature, George Mason Univ., Fairfax Va 1982–95; Halloway Lecturer Univ. of Calif. at Berkeley 1986; Lecturer, Creative Writing, Dept of Comparative Literature, Princeton Univ. 1995–; contributing Ed. American Poetry Review 1972–; Fellow Guggenheim Foundation 1975–, Nat. Endowment for Arts 1985, 1993; mem. PEN, American Acad. of Arts and Sciences, American Acad. of Arts and Letters; Pushcart Press Prizes 1982, 1983, 1987, Nat. Book Critics Circle Award for Poetry 1987, Morton Dauwen Zabel Prize, American Acad. of Arts and Letters 1989, Lila Wallace Writers Award 1993, Harriet Monroe Prize 1993, Berlin Prize, American Acad. in Berlin 1998, Voelcker Career Achievement Award, PEN 1998, Pulitzer Prize for Poetry 2000, LA Times Book Award 2000, Weathertop Prize 2000, Nat. Book Award 2003, Ruth Lilly Prize for Poetry 2005. *Publications:* A Day for Anne Frank 1968, Lies 1969, The Sensuous President 1972, I am the Bitter Name 1972, With Ignorance 1977, The Women of Trachis (co-trans.) 1978, The Lark, The Thrush, The Starling 1983, Tar 1983, Flesh and Blood 1987, Poems 1963–1983, 1988, The Bacchae of Euripides (trans.) 1990, Helen 1991, A Dream of Mind 1992, Selected Poems 1994, The Vigil 1997, Poetry and Consciousness (selected essays) 1998, Repair (poems) 1999, Misgivings: A Memoir 2000, Love About Love 2001, The Singing 2004, Pétain (1856–1951) 2005, Collected Poems 2006; contrib. to Akzent, Atlantic, Carleton Miscellany, Crazyhorse, Grand Street, Iowa Review, Madison Review, New England Review, New Yorker, Seneca Review, Transpacific Review, TriQuarterly, Yale Review, Threepenny Review. *Leisure interests:* drawing, piano, guitar. *Address:* 71 Leigh Avenue, Princeton, NJ 08542, USA (home).

WILLIAMS, Sir Daniel Charles, GCMG, QC, LLB; Grenadian government official and fmr lawyer; b. 4 Nov. 1935; s. of Adolphus D. Williams and Clare Stanislaus; m. Cecilia Patricia Gloria Modeste 1970; two s. four d.; ed Univ. of London; called to Bar, Lincoln's Inn, London 1968; barrister 1969–70, 1974–84, 1990–96; magistrate, St Lucia 1970–74; MP (New Nat. Party) 1984–89; Minister of Health, Housing and Environment 1984–89, of Legal Affairs and Attorney-Gen. 1988–89; Acting Prime Minister July 1988; Gov.-Gen. of Grenada 1996–2008; fmrly several lay positions in RC Church; Chief Scout. *Publications:* Index of Laws of Grenada 1959–79, The Office and Duties of the Governor-General of Grenada 1998, A Synoptic View of the Public Service of Grenada 1999, Prescription of a Model Grenada 2000, God Speaks 2001, The Layman's Lawbook 2002, The Love of God 2003, Government of the Global Village 2007; (contrib.) Modern Legal Systems Cyclopedia: Central America and the Caribbean, Vol. 7 1985. *Leisure interests:* lawn tennis, gardening. *Address:* c/o Government House, St George's, Grenada (office).

WILLIAMS, Hon. Danny, QC, JD; Canadian politician; *Premier of Newfoundland and Labrador and Minister Responsible for Business;* m. Maureen Williams; four c.; ed Memorial Univ. of Newfoundland, Univ. of Oxford, UK, Dalhousie Univ.; practiced law in Newfoundland and Labrador 1972; led Cable Atlantic (cable TV co.) in series of acquisitions 1975; Pres. OIS Fisher (offshore oil and gas supply and services co.); apptd QC 1984; MLA for Humber West 2001–; Leader Progressive Conservative Party 2001–, and as Opposition Leader; Premier of Newfoundland and Labrador 2003–; founder and Pres. St. John's Jr Hockey League; fmr mem. Bd of Govs Canadian Sports Hall of Fame; fmr Chair. Canadian Parliamentary Channel, Newfoundland and Labrador Film Devt Corpn, Provincial Govt Offshore Oil Impact Advisory Council. *Address:* Office of the Premier, Confederation Building, East Block, POB 8700, St. John's, NL A1B 4J6, Canada (office). *Telephone:* (709) 729-3570 (office). *Fax:* (709) 729-5875 (office). *E-mail:* premier@gov.nl.ca (office). *Website:* www .premier.gov.nl.ca/premier (office).

WILLIAMS, Sir David Glyndwr Tudor, Kt, MA, LLM; British academic administrator and legal scholar; *Chancellor, Swansea University;* b. 22 Oct. 1930, Carmarthen, Wales; s. of Tudor Williams and Anne Williams; m. Sally G. M. Cole 1959; one s. two d.; ed Queen Elizabeth Grammar School, Carmarthen, Emmanuel Coll. Cambridge, Univ. of California, Berkeley and Harvard Law School; called to Bar, Lincoln's Inn 1956; Commonwealth Fund (Harkness) Fellow, Univ. of California, Berkeley and Harvard Univ. 1956–58; lecturer in Law, Univ. of Nottingham 1958–63; Fellow, Keble Coll., Oxford 1963–67; Fellow, Emmanuel Coll., Cambridge 1967–80, Sr Tutor 1970–76; Pres. Wolfson Coll., Cambridge 1980–92; Rouse Ball Prof. of English Law, Univ. of Cambridge 1983–92, Prof. Emer. 1992–96, 1998–; Vice-Chancellor, Univ. of Cambridge 1989–96, Vice-Chancellor Emer. 1996–, Prof. of Law and Professorial Fellow, Emmanuel Coll. 1996–98; Pres., Univ. of Wales, Swansea 2001–07, Chancellor, Univ. of Swansea 2007–; mem. Royal Comm. on Environmental Pollution 1976–83, Council on Tribunals 1972–83, Sr Salaries Review Body 1998–2004; Chair. Animal Procedures Cttee 1987–89; mem. Int. Jury for the Indira Gandhi Prize for Peace, Disarmament and Devt 1992–2002; Trustee, Rajiv Gandhi (UK) Foundation; mem. American Law Inst.; Hon. Bencher, Lincoln's Inn 1985; Hon. QC 1994; Foreign Hon. mem. American Acad. of Arts and Sciences; Hon. Fellow, Emmanuel Coll., Cambridge 1984, Keble Coll., Oxford 1991, Pembroke Coll., Cambridge 1993, Wolfson Coll., Cambridge 1993; Hon. DLitt (Loughborough, William Jewell Coll., Mo.); Hon. LLD (Hull, Nottingham, Sydney, Davidson Coll., NC, Liverpool, McGill, De Montfort, Duke, Cambridge, Victoria Univ. of Tech., Melbourne); Hon. DCL (Univ. of Western Ontario). *Publications:* Not in the Public Interest 1965, Keeping the Peace 1967; articles in legal periodicals and chapters in books. *Address:* Emmanuel College, Cambridge, CB2 3AP (office); Grange House, Selwyn Gardens, Cambridge, CB3 9AX, England (home). *Telephone:* (1223) 334217 (office); (1223) 350726 (home). *Fax:* (1223) 350726 (home).

WILLIAMS, David J., PhD, DIC; British chemist and academic; *Senior Research Fellow and Professor Emeritus, Imperial College London;* Sr Research Fellow, Computational, Theoretical and Structural Chem. Section, Dept of Chem., Imperial Coll., London, now Prof. Emer. *Publications:* numerous articles in scientific journals. *Address:* c/o Department of Chemistry, Imperial College, London, SW7 2AY, England (office). *Telephone:* (20) 7589-5111 (office). *Website:* www.imperial.ac.uk/chemistry (office).

WILLIAMS, Sir Denys Ambrose, KCMG, MA, BCL; Barbadian attorney-at-law; b. 12 Oct. 1929; s. of George Cuthbert Williams and Violet Irene Gilkes; m. Carmel Mary Coleman 1954; two s. four d.; ed Combermere School, Harrison Coll., Worcester Coll., Oxford and Middle Temple, London; Asst Legal Draftsman, Asst to Attorney Gen., Barbados; Asst Legal Draftsman, Fed. of West Indies; Sr Parl. Counsel, Barbados 1963–67, Supreme Court Judge 1967–86, Chief Justice 1987–2001; Gold Crown of Merit. *Leisure interests:* horse-racing, tennis, gardening, walking. *Address:* 9 Garrison, St Michael, Barbados. *Telephone:* 4271164.

WILLIAMS, Dudley Howard, PhD, ScD, FRS; British organic chemist and academic; *Professor Emeritus of Biological Chemistry, University of Cambridge;* b. 25 May 1937, Leeds; s. of Lawrence Williams and Evelyn Williams; m. Lorna Patricia Phyllis Bedford 1963; two s.; ed Univ. of Leeds, Stanford Univ., USA; Asst Dir Research, Univ. Chem. Lab., Univ. of Cambridge 1966–74, Fellow Churchill Coll. 1964–, Reader in Organic Chem. 1974–96, Prof. of Biological Chem. 1996–, now Prof. Emer.; Visiting Prof. and Lecturer, Univs of California 1967, 1986, 1989, 1997, Cape Town 1972, Sydney 1972, Florida 1973, Wisconsin 1975, Copenhagen 1976, ANU, Canberra 1980, Queensland 1994; consultant to numerous pharmaceutical cos 1966–2002; service on UK Research Councils; co-discoverer of metabolism of vitamin D 1971 and of mechanism of action of glycopeptide antibiotics which inhibit resistant bacteria; mem. Academia Europaea; Meldola Medal, Royal Inst. of Chem. 1966, Corday-Morgan Medal, Chemical Soc. 1968, RSC Award for Structural Chem. 1984, RSC Bader Award in Organic Chem. 1990, ACS Leo Friend Award 1996, Paul Ehrlich Award for Medicinal Chemistry (France) 2001; Tilden Lecturer, Royal Soc. of Chem. (RSC) 1983, Arun Guthikonda Memorial Award Lectureship (Columbia Univ.) 1985, Distinguished Visiting Lecturer, Texas A & M Univ. 1986, Rorer Lecturer, Ohio State Univ. 1989, Univ. of Auckland Foundation Lecturer 1991, Pacific Coast Lecturer 1991, Steel Lecturer, Univ. of Queensland 1994, Lee Kuan Yew Distinguished Visitor, Singapore 2000, Marvin Carmack Distinguished Lecture, Indiana Univ. 2001, Merck Distinguished Lecturer 2001, James Sprague Lecturer, Univ. of Wisconsin 2002, Erasmus Lecturer, Univ. of Neuchatel, Switzerland 2002, RSC Merck Research Prize and Lectureship 2003. *Publications:* ten books, including Spectroscopic Methods in Organic Chemistry (with I. Fleming), more than 400 scientific publs dealing with the devt of mass spectrometry and nuclear magnetic resonance, the structure elucidation of complex molecules, the modes of action of antibiotics and molecular recognition phenomena. *Leisure interests:* music, gardening. *Address:* University Chemical Laboratory, Lensfield Road, Cambridge, CB2 1EW (office); 7 Balsham Road, Fulbourn, Cambridge, CB21 5BZ, England (home). *Telephone:* (1223) 336368 (office); (1223) 740971 (home). *E-mail:* dhw1@cam.ac.uk (office). *Website:* www.ch.cam.ac.uk/staff/dhw.html (office).

WILLIAMS, George Christopher, PhD; American biologist and academic; *Professor Emeritus, Department of Ecology and Evolution, State University of New York, Stony Brook;* b. 12 May 1926, Charlotte, NC; s. of George Felix Williams and Margaret Steuart; m. Doris Lee Calhoun 1951; one s. three d.; ed Univ. of California, Berkeley, Univ. of California, Los Angeles; army service 1944–46; instructor and Asst Prof., Michigan State Univ., East Lansing 1955–60; Assoc. Prof., Dept of Ecology and Evolution, State Univ. of NY, Stony Brook 1960–66, Prof. 1966–90, Prof. Emer. 1990–; Adjunct Prof., Queen's Univ., Kingston, Ont., Canada 1980–, Prof. Emer. 1991–95; Ed. Quarterly Review of Biology; Fellow, AAAS, NAS 1993–; Hon. ScD (Queens Univ.) 1995; Eminent Ecologist Award (Ecological Soc. of America 1989), NAS Daniel Giraud Elliot Medal 1992, Crafoord Prize (co-recipient) 1999. *Achievement:* best known for his vigorous critique of group selection. *Publications:* Adaptation and Natural Selection 1966, Group Selection (ed.) 1971, Sex and Evolution 1975, T.H. Huxley's Evolution and Ethics: with New Essays on its Victorian and Sociobiological Context (with J. Paradis) 1989, Natural Selection: Domains, Levels and Challenges 1992, Why We Get Sick: The New Science of Darwinian Medicine 1994, Plan and Purpose in Nature 1996 (published in USA as The Pony Fish's Glow: and Other Clues to Plan and Purpose in Nature 1997); numerous papers in professional journals. *Leisure interests:* music, swimming, fiction. *Address:* Quarterly Review of Biology, State University of New York, Stony Brook, NY 11794 (office); 1 Jefferson's Ferry Drive, Apt 3322, Sout Setauket, NY 11720, USA (home). *Telephone:* (631) 632-6977 (office); (631) 632-8600 (office); (631) 650-3122 (home). *E-mail:* dcwilliams@ms.ca.sunysb.edu (home). *Website:* life.bio.sunysb.edu/ee/people/williamsindex.html (office).

WILLIAMS, Jody, BA, MA; American international organization official, campaigner, academic and writer; *Chairman, Nobel Women's Initiative;* b. 9 Oct. 1950, Poultney, Vt; d. of John C. Williams and Ruth C. Williams; m. Stephen D. Goose 2001; ed Univ. of Vermont, School for Int. Training, Brattleboro, Vt, Johns Hopkins School of Advanced Int. Studies, Washington, DC; English teacher, Mexico, UK and Washington DC 1978–81; campaigned to spread awareness of US policy in Cen. America 1981–92; Co-ordinator Nicaragua-Honduras Educ. Project 1984–86; Deputy Dir Medical Aid for El Salvador, Los Angeles 1986–92; Founding Co-ordinator Int. Campaign to Ban Landmines (ICBL) 1992, currently ICBL Campaign Amb.; Tech. Adviser, UN Study on Impact of Armed Conflict on Children; Head, UN Human Rights Council High-Level Mission to Darfur 2007; Visiting Prof. of Social Work,

Univ. of Houston 2003–; Founder-mem. and Chair. Nobel Women's Initiative 2006–; more than 15 hon. degrees in USA and Canada, including from the Royal Mil. Coll. of Canada, Smith Coll., Wesleyan Univ., Penn State Univ.; Nobel Peace Prize (jt recipient with ICBL) 1997, Distinguished Peace Leadership Award, Nuclear Age Peace Foundation 1998, Olender Foundation Peacemaker of the Year 1999, Eleanor Roosevelt Global Women's Rights Award 2004, ranked 100th by Forbes magazine amongst 100 Most Powerful Women in the World 2004. *Publications:* After the Guns Fall Silent: The Enduring Legacy of Landmines (with Shawn Roberts) 1995, Banning Landmines: Disarmament, Citizen Diplomacy and Human Security 2008; more than 24 chapters and articles for books and journals; numerous articles for newspapers around the world, including The Wall Street Journal, The Independent (UK), the Economist. *Address:* Nobel Women's Initiative, 151 Slater Street, Suite 408, Ottawa, ON K1P 5H3, Canada (office). *Telephone:* (613) 569-8400 (office). *Fax:* (613) 563-0682 (office). *E-mail:* jwilliams@ nobelwomensinitiative.org (office). *Website:* www.nobelwomensinitiative.org (office); www.icbl.org.

WILLIAMS, John, AO, OBE; classical guitarist; b. 24 April 1941, Melbourne, Australia; s. of Len Williams and Melaan Ket; m. 1st Linda Susan Kendall 1964 (divorced); one d.; m. 2nd Sue Cook 1981 (divorced); one s.; m. 3rd Kathleen Panama 2000; ed Friern Barnet Grammar School and Royal Coll. of Music, London; studied guitar with father, Segovia and at Accad. Chigiana, Siena; has toured widely and appears frequently on TV and radio; numerous transcriptions and gramophone recordings as solo guitarist and with leading orchestras; f. The Height Below (ensemble) with Brian Gascoigne, John Williams and Friends (ensemble) and founder-mem. groups, SKY and John Williams' Attacca; current ensembles include John Williams and Richard Harvey's World Tour and 'Together and Solo' with John Etheridge, as well as solo recitals worldwide; other collaborations with Julian Bream, Itzhak Perlman, Andre Previn, Cleo Lane and John Dankworth, Nat. Youth Jazz Orchestra, Paco Pena and Inti Illimani; Artistic Dir South Bank Summer Music Festival 1984–85, Melbourne Arts Festival 1987; Hon. FRCM, FRAM, FRNCM; Dr hc (Melbourne); Edison Award for Lifetime Achievement 2007. *Films:* composed and played music for film Emma's War. *Recordings:* include Takemitsu Played by John Williams (music by Toru Takemitsu, with the London Sinfonietta) 1991, several of Rodrigo's Conciertos de Aranjuez, Vivaldi Concertos 1991, The Seville Concert/The Film Profile of John Williams (also on laserdisc and VHS) 1993, From Australia (featuring music by Peter Sculthorpe and Nigel Westlake) 1994, The Great Paraguayan 1995, concerti by Richard Harvey and Steve Gray 1996, John Williams Plays the Movies 1997, The Black Decameron (music by Leo Brouwer) 1997, The Guitarist 1998, Schubert and Giuliani 1999, The Magic Box 2002, El Diablo Suelto 2003, The Ultimate Guitar Collection 2004, Places Between (with John Etheridge) 2006. *Leisure interests:* tennis, badminton, chess, table tennis. *Address:* Askonas Holt Ltd, Lincoln House, 300 High Holborn, London, WC1V 7JH, England (office). *Telephone:* (20) 7400-1751 (office). *Fax:* (20) 7400-1799 (office). *E-mail:* info@askonasholt.co.uk (office). *Website:* www.askonasholt.co.uk (office); www .johnwilliamsguitar.com.

WILLIAMS, (John) Gwynn, CBE, MA; British historian and academic; b. 19 June 1924, Wales; s. of the late John Ellis Williams and Annie Maude Rowlands; m. Beryl Stafford Thomas 1954; three s.; ed Holywell Grammar School, Univ. Coll. of North Wales; with RN 1943–46; staff tutor Dept of Extra Mural Studies Univ. of Liverpool 1951–54; Asst lecturer Univ. of North Wales 1955, Prof. of Welsh History 1963–83, Dean Faculty of Arts 1972–74, Vice-Prin. 1974–79, Vice-Pres. 1993–98; Chair. Press Bd Univ. of Wales 1979–91; Dir Gregynog Press 1979–2002; Vice-Pres. Nat. Library of Wales 1984–86, Pres. 1986–96; Pres. Cambrian Archaeological Asscn 1987–88; Vice-Pres. Hon. Soc. of Cymmrodorion 1988–; mem. Royal Comm. on Ancient and Historical Monuments in Wales 1967–91; Hon. mem. Gorsedd of Bards 1983, Hon. Fellow Bangor Univ. 2007; Hon. DLitt (Univ. of Wales) 1999. *Publications include:* The Founding of the University College of North Wales, Bangor 1985, The University College of North Wales: Foundations 1985, University and Nation 1893–1939 (The Thomas Jones Pierce Memorial Lecture) 1992, The Report on the Proposed University of Wales (ed.) 1993, The University Movement in Wales 1993, The University of Wales 1893–1939 1997; numerous articles on 17th-century Wales for learned journals. *Leisure interests:* travelling, walking. *Address:* Llywenan, Siliwen, Bangor, Gwynedd, LL57 2BS, Wales (home). *Telephone:* (1248) 353065 (home).

WILLIAMS, John Peter Rhys (J.P.R.), MBE, MB, BS, LRCP, MRCS, FRCSE; British orthopaedic surgeon (retd) and fmr rugby union player; b. 2 March 1949, Cardiff; s. of Peter Williams and Margaret Williams; m. Priscilla Parkin 1973; one s. three d.; ed Bridgend Grammar School, Millfield, St Mary's Hosp. Medical School; British Jr Tennis Champion, Wimbledon 1966; Welsh int. rugby player 1969–79, 1980–81; 55 caps for Wales; Capt. of Welsh rugby team 1978–79; on tour with British Lions to New Zealand 1971, South Africa 1974; eight test matches for British Lions, winning both series; qualified as medical doctor 1973; surgical Registrar, Cardiff Hosp. 1977–80, Orthopaedic Registrar 1980–82; Orthopaedic Sr Registrar, St Mary's Hosp., London 1982–85; Consultant Orthopaedic Surgeon, Princess of Wales Hosp., Bridgend 1986–2005; Primary FRCS 1976; inducted into Int. Rugby Hall of Fame 1997. *Publications:* Irish Conference on Sporting Injuries, Dublin (ed.) 1975, JPR (autobiog.) 1979, Cervical Neck Injuries in Rugby Football, British Medical Journal 1978, Trans-Oral Fusion of the Cervical Spine, Journal of Bone and Joint Surgery 1985. *Leisure interests:* sport, music. *Address:* Llansannor Lodge, Llansannor, nr Cowbridge, Vale of Glamorgan, CF71 7RX, Wales (home). *Telephone:* (1446) 772590 (home). *E-mail:* jprw15@aol.com (home).

WILLIAMS, John Towner; American composer; b. 8 Feb. 1932, Flushing, NY; ed Juilliard School, UCLA; pianist Columbia Pictures; jazz pianist working with Henry Mancini on television scores; conductor Boston Pops Orchestra 1980–98; numerous hon. degrees; two Emmy Awards, three Golden Globes, 16 Grammy Awards, recipient of Kennedy Center Honors 2004, Classical BRIT Award for Soundtrack Composer of the Year 2005, Grammy Awards for Best Instrumental Composition (for A Prayer for Peace, from Munich) 2007, (for The Adventures of Mutt, from Indiana and Jones and the Kingdom of the Crystal Skull) 2009. *Film scores:* The Secret Ways 1961, Diamond Head 1962, None But the Brave 1965, How to Steal a Million 1966, Valley of the Dolls 1967, The Cowboys 1972, The Poseidon Adventure 1972, Tom Sawyer 1973, Earthquake 1974, The Towering Inferno 1974, Jaws (Acad. Award) 1975, The Eiger Sanction 1975, Family Plot 1976, Midway 1976, The Missouri Breaks 1976, Raggedy Ann and Andy 1977, Black Sunday 1977, Star Wars (Acad. Award) 1977, Close Encounters of the Third Kind 1977, The Fury 1978, Jaws II 1976, Superman 1978, Dracula 1979, The Empire Strikes Back 1980, Raiders of the Lost Ark 1981, E.T.: The Extra Terrestrial (Acad. Award) 1982, Return of the Jedi 1983, Indiana Jones and the Temple of Doom 1984, The River 1985, Space Camp 1986, The Witches of Eastwick 1987, Empire of the Sun (BAFTA Award for Best Score) 1988, 1941 1989, Always 1989, Born on the Fourth of July 1989, Indiana Jones and the Last Crusade 1989, Stanley and Iris 1990, Presumed Innocent 1990, Home Alone 1990, Hook 1991, JFK 1993, Far and Away 1993, Home Alone 2: Lost in New York 1993, Jurassic Park 1993, Schindler's List (Acad. Award) 1993, Sabrina 1995, The Reivers 1995, Nixon 1995, Sleepers 1996, Rosewood 1996, Land of the Giants 1997, Seven Years in Tibet 1997, The Lost World: Jurassic Park 1997, Amistad 1997, Lost in Space 1997, Time Tunnel 1997, Saving Private Ryan 1998, Star Wars: Episode I – The Phantom Menace 1999, Angela's Ashes 1999, Harry Potter and the Sorcerer's Stone 2001, Star Wars: Episode II – Attack of the Clones 2001, Minority Report 2002, Harry Potter and the Chamber of Secrets 2002, Catch Me if You Can 2002, Harry Potter and the Prisoner of Azkaban 2004, The Terminal 2004, Star Wars: Episode III – Revenge of the Sith 2005, War of the Worlds 2005, Harry Potter and the Goblet of Fire 2005, Memoirs of a Geisha (Golden Globe for Best Original Score in a Motion Picture 2006, BAFTA Anthony Asquith Award for Achievement in Film Music 2006, Grammy Award for Best Score Soundtrack Album for Motion Picture 2007) 2005, Munich 2005, Superman Returns 2006, Harry Potter and the Order of the Phoenix 2007, Indiana Jones and the Kingdom of the Crystal Skull 2008, Harry Potter and the Half-Blood Prince 2009. *Recordings include:* John Williams Plays The Movies 1996, Music From The Star Wars Saga 1999, Jane Eyre 1999, Themes From Academy Award Winners, Over The Rainbow: Songs From The Movies 1992, John Williams Conducting The Boston Pops 1996, The Hollywood Sound 1997, From Sousa To Spielberg, Best Of John Williams 1998, Treesong 2001, Call Of The Champions (official theme of 2002 Winter Olympics, Salt Lake City) 2001, John Williams Trumpet Concerto 2002, American Journey 2002; recordings of film scores. *Address:* Michael Gorfaine, Gorfaine & Schwartz, 13245 Riverside Drive, Suite 450, Sherman Oaks, CA 91423, USA (office). *Website:* www.johnwilliams.org (office).

WILLIAMS, Joseph Dalton, BSc; American business executive; b. 15 Aug. 1926, Washington, DC; s. of Joseph Dalton Williams and Jane Day; m. Millie E. Bellaire 1973; one s. one d.; ed Univ. of Nebraska; Sales Rep., Parke-Davis, Kan. City 1950, Field Man. 1956, Asst Man. Market Research 1958, Asst to Dir Sales Research and Devt 1962, Dir Medical-Surgical Market Devt 1967, Dir U.S. Marketing 1968, Group Vice-Pres., Marketing and Sales 1970; following merger of cos., Vice-Pres., Warner-Lambert, mem. Bd, Parke-Davis; Exec. Vice-Pres. and COO, Parke-Davis 1971, Pres. and CEO 1973; mem. Bd of Dirs. Warner-Lambert 1973–97, Sr Vice-Pres. 1973, Exec. Vice-Pres. and Pres. Pharmaceutical Group 1976, Sr Exec. Vice-Pres., mem. Office of Chair. and Pres. Int. Group 1977, Pres., Dir Warner-Lambert Corpn 1979–80, Pres. and COO 1980–84, Chair., CEO 1985–91, Chair. Exec. Cttee 1991–97; Bd Dirs. AT&T, Exxon Corpn, Rockefeller Financial Services Inc.; numerous hon. degrees; Remington Honor Medal, American Pharmaceutical Asscn 1980, Rutgers Univ. Award 1982. *Leisure interests:* golf, antique cars. *Address:* P.O. Box 836, Bernardsville, NJ 07924 (home); c/o Warner-Lambert Co., 55 Madison Avenue, Norristown, NJ 07960, USA (home).

WILLIAMS, Mack Geoffrey Denis, BA; Australian diplomatist; b. 16 July 1939, Sydney; s. of Bernard George Williams and Thelma A. McMillan; m. Carla Lothringer 1966; one s. three d.; ed Fort Street Boys High School, Sydney and Univ. of Sydney; joined Dept of Foreign Affairs 1961; Third Sec. Brussels 1962–65; Second Sec. Saigon 1965–67; First Sec. Phnom Penh 1969–71; Counsellor, Washington, DC 1971–74; Office of Minister of Foreign Affairs, Canberra 1975–76; Deputy High Commr in Papua New Guinea 1977–78; Royal Coll. of Defence Studies, London 1979; High Commr in Bangladesh 1980–82; Dept of Prime Minister, Canberra 1986–87; First Asst Sec. Dept of Foreign Affairs and Trade 1987–89; Amb. to the Philippines 1989–94, to Repub. of Korea 1994–98; Bd mem. Australia-Korea Foundation 1998–; Exec. Australia-Korea Business Council 1998–, Vice-Pres. 2000–; Hon. Investment and Trade Rep., Repub. of Philippines 1999–; Hon. Fellow Senate Univ. of Sydney 1996; Korean Pres. Order of Merit 1998. *Leisure interests:* golf, travel. *Address:* 87 Ferry Road, Glebe, NSW 2037, Australia.

WILLIAMS, Marion V., PhD, FCIB, CMA, GCM; Barbadian economist and banking official; *Governor, Central Bank of Barbados;* ed Univ. of Surrey, UK, Univ. of the West Indies; fmr Deputy Man. Research Dept, East Caribbean Currency Authority; joined Cen. Bank of Barbados 1973–, Adviser, Sr Adviser, Deputy Gov. 1993–99, Gov. 1999–; numerous articles for professional journals; consultant, USAID, Commonwealth Secr., ILO; Pres. Barbados Inst. of Banking and Finance; mem. Barbados Econs Soc., Asscn of Caribbean Econs. *Publications:* Liberalising a Regulated Banking System: The Caribbean Case 1996, Managing Public Finances in a Small Developing Economy—the Case of Barbados 2001, Strategic Repositioning: A Caribbean Perspective on Economic Policy Making 2005. *Address:* Office of the Governor, Central Bank of Barbados, Tom Adams Financial Centre, Spry Street, POB 1016, Bridgetown, Barbados (office). *Telephone:* 436-6870 (office). *Fax:* 427-9559 (office). *E-mail:* cbb.libr@caribsurf.com (office). *Website:* www.centralbank.org.bb (office).

WILLIAMS, Mark J., MBE; British professional snooker player; b. 21 March 1975, Cwm, Wales; s. of Delwyn Williams; commenced professional career 1992; winner of 15 ranking titles: Regal Welsh 1996, 1999, Grand Prix 1996, 2000, British Open 1997, Irish Open 1998, Thailand Masters 1999, 2000, 2002, UK Championship 1999, 2002, Embassy World Championship 2000, 2003, China Open 2002, LG Cup 2003; winner Nations Cup (with Wales) 1999, winner Benson and Hedges Masters 1998, 2003; became second player to hold all four 'major' titles at one time 2003; career prize money: £3,175,730; world ranked one in 1999/2000, 2000/01, 2003/04; secondplayer to regain the top ranking 2003. *Leisure interests:* golf, badminton, cars, fmr amateur boxer. *Address:* c/o 110 Sport Ltd, Spencers Leisure, Kerse Road, Stirling, FK7 7SG, England (office). *Telephone:* (1786) 462-634 (office). *Fax:* (1786) 450-068 (office). *E-mail:* contact@110sport.com (office). *Website:* www.110sport.com (office).

WILLIAMS, Martin John, CVO, OBE, BA; British consultant and diplomatist (retd); *United Kingdom Consultant, New Zealand Antarctic Heritage Trust;* b. 3 Nov. 1941; s. of John Henry Stroud Williams and Barbara Williams (née Benington); m. Susan Dent 1964; two s.; ed Manchester Grammar School, Corpus Christi Coll. Oxford; joined Commonwealth Relations Office 1963; various posts including service at Embassy in Manila 1966–69, Consulate-Gen. in Milan 1970–72, Embassy in Tehran 1977–80, High Comm. in New Delhi 1982–86, Embassy in Rome 1986–90; Head of S. Asian Dept, FCO 1990–92; seconded to NI Office, Belfast as Asst Under-Sec. (Political Affairs) 1993–95; High Commr in Zimbabwe 1995–98, in NZ (also accred to Samoa and Gov. Pitcairn Island) 1998–2001; UK Consultant to New Zealand Antarctic Heritage Trust 2002; Chair. Link Foundation for UK –NZ Relations 2004–. *Leisure interests:* music, gardening, woodwork. *Address:* Russet House, Lughorse Lane, Yalding, Kent, ME18 6EG, England (home). *Telephone:* (1622) 815403 (home).

WILLIAMS, Nigel, MA; British writer and television producer; b. 20 Jan. 1948, Cheshire; s. of the late David Ffrancon Williams; m. Suzani Harrison 1973; three s.; ed Highgate School, Oriel Coll., Oxford; trainee BBC 1969–73, Producer/Dir Arts Dept 1973–85, Ed. Bookmark 1985–92, Omnibus 1992–96, writer and presenter 1997–2000. *Television includes:* Double Talk, Talking Blues, Real Live Audience 1977, Baby Love 1981, Breaking Up 1986, The Last Romantics 1992, Skallagrig (BAFTA Award) 1994. *Stage plays include:* Class Enemy 1978 (Plays and Players Award for Most Promising Playwright 1978), Trial Run 1980, Line 'Em 1980, Sugar & Spice 1980, My Brother's Keeper 1985, Country Dancing 1986, Nativity 1989, Harry & Me 1995, The Last Romantics 1997. *Publications:* novels: My Life Closed Twice 1977 (jt winner Somerset Maugham Award), Jack Be Nimble 1980, Star Turn 1985, Witchcraft 1987, The Wimbledon Poisoner 1990, They Came from SW19 1992, East of Wimbledon 1994, Scenes from a Poisoner's Life 1994, Stalking Fiona 1997, Fortysomething 1999, Hatchett and Lycett 2002; travel: Wimbledon to Waco 1995. *Leisure interests:* dogs, drinking, talking, family, swiming, walking. *Address:* 18 Holmbush Road, Putney, London, SW15 3LE, England (home). *Telephone:* (20) 8964-8811 (home). *Fax:* (20) 8964-8966 (home).

WILLIAMS, Sir Peter, Kt, CBE, MA, PhD, FREng, FRS; British physicist, academic and university administrator; *Chancellor, University of Leicester;* m. 1970; one s.; ed Hymers Coll., Hull, Trinity Coll., Cambridge; Research Fellow, Univ. of Cambridge –1970; Lecturer, Dept of Chemical Eng and Chemical Tech., Imperial Coll., London 1970–75; joined VG Instruments 1975, later Deputy Group Man. Dir; joined Oxford Instruments (first spin-off co. of Univ. of Oxford) 1982, Chief Exec. 1985–91, Chair. 1991–99 (retd); Master, St Catherine's Coll., Oxford 1999–2005; Chancellor, Univ. of Leicester 2005–; Chair. group drawn from Innovation Advisory Bd, Dept of Trade and Industry 1988; Chair. Bd of Trustees Nat. Museum of Science and Industry 1996–2002, Particle Physics and Astronomy Research Council 1990s, Eng and Tech. Bd 2001–06, Advisory Council on Math. Educ., Nat. Physical Lab.; Pres. Inst. of Physics 2000–02, BAAS 2003; Dir (non-exec.) GKN plc (Chair. Audit Cttee), W.S. Atkins plc; Hon. Grad., Univ. of Leicester 1995; Glazebrook Medal, Inst. of Physics 2005. *Leisure interests:* travelling, hiking, skiing, music, collecting wine. *Address:* Office of the Chancellor, University of Leicester, University Road, Leicester, LE1 7RH, England (office). *Telephone:* (116) 252-2522 (office). *Fax:* (116) 252-2200 (office). *E-mail:* chancellor@le.ac.uk (office). *Website:* www.le.ac.uk (office).

WILLIAMS, R. Stanley (Stan), BA, PhD; American physicist, academic and industrial researcher; *HP Senior Fellow and Founding Director, HP Quantum Science Research Group, Hewlett-Packard Laboratories;* b. 1951, Kodiak, Alaska; s. of Bobby L. Williams and Shirley A. Williams; ed Rice Univ., Univ. of California, Berkeley; mem. Tech. Staff, AT&T Bell Labs 1978–80; Asst Prof., Dept of Chem., UCLA 1980–84, Assoc. Prof. 1984–86, Prof. 1986–95, now Adjunct Prof. of Chem.; Adjunct Prof. of Computer Science, Univ. of N Carolina; joined Hewlett-Packard Labs 1995, HP Sr Fellow and Founding Dir HP Quantum Science Research Group 1995–; consultant to several corpns and law firms; mem. Defense Science Study Group; Advisor, Defense Science Bd, Frontier Research Program, Inst. for Physics and Chem. Research (RIKEN), Japan, Nat. Inst. for Materials Science, Japan; Julius Springer Award for Applied Physics 2000, Feynman Prize in Nanotechnology 2000, Dreyfus Teacher-Scholar Award, Sloan Foundation Fellowship, Scientific American Top 50 Technology Leaders 2002, Peter Debye Lecturer, Cornell Univ. 2004, Herman Block Lecturer, Univ. of Chicago 2004, Joel Birnbaum Award 2005.

Achievements: holder of 34 US patents. *Publications:* more than 290 papers in peer-reviewed scientific journals and more than 130 patents world-wide. *Leisure interests:* cookery, long beach walks with wife and dogs. *Address:* Hewlett-Packard Company, 1501 Page Mill Road, MS 1123, Palo Alto, CA 94304-1185, USA (office). *Telephone:* (650) 857-1501 (office). *Website:* www.hpl.hp.com/research/qsr/index.html (office).

WILLIAMS, Richard Edmund; Canadian animated film producer, director and writer; b. 19 March 1933, Toronto, Ont.; s. of Kenneth D. C. Williams and Kathleen (née Bell) Williams; m. 2nd Margaret French 1976; four c. (including two from a previous m.); ed Royal Ontario Coll. of Art; f. Richard Williams Animation Ltd 1962; produced and directed: The Little Island (British Acad. Award, 1st Prize Venice Film Festival) 1958, Love Me, Love Me, Love Me 1962, The Dermis Probe 1965, A Christmas Carol (Oscar for Best Animated Short Subject) 1971, Ziggy's Gift 1982; designed film sequences and titles for: What's New Pussycat 1965, A Funny Thing Happened on the Way to the Forum 1966, The Spy with a Cold Nose 1966, Casino Royale 1967, The Charge of the Light Brigade 1968, Prudence and the Pill 1968, Murder on the Orient Express (uncredited) 1974, The Return of the Pink Panther 1975, The Pink Panther Strikes Again 1976; animation for Raggedy Ann & Andy: A Musical Adventure 1977, Who Framed Roger Rabbit (Special Achievement Oscar) 1988, Arabian Knight (produced and directed) 1995; mem. Acad. of Motion Picture Arts and Sciences; est. Richard Williams Animation Masterclasses for professionals and students worldwide 1995–; mem. Asscn of Cinematographers and TV Technicians. *Publication:* The Animator's Survival Kit 2000.

WILLIAMS, Robert (Robbie) Peter; British singer; b. 13 Feb. 1974, Stoke-on-Trent; s. of Pete Williams and Theresa Janette Williams; played the Artful Dodger in Oliver 1982; mem. group Take That 1991–95; solo artist 1995–; mem. Equity, Musicians' Union, MCPS, PRS, ADAMI, GVC, AURA; nine Smash Hits Awards 1992–98, 14 BRIT Awards (10 solo), Levi's Nordoff-Robbins Music Therapy Original Talent Award 1998, MTV Award for Best Male 1998, Echo Award for Best Int. Male Rock and Pop Artist, Germany 2005, 2006, MTV Europe Music Award for Best Male 2005, MTV Latin America Music Award for Best Int. Pop Artist 2006, Q Idol Award (with Take That) 2006. *Films:* Nobody Someday 2002, De-Lovely 2004. *Recordings include:* albums: with Take That: Take That And Party 1992, Everything Changes 1993, Nobody Else 1995, Greatest Hits 1996; solo: Life Thru' a Lens 1997, I've Been Expecting You 1998, The Ego Has Landed 1999, Sing When You're Winning 2000, Swing When You're Winning 2001, Escapology 2002, Live At Knebworth 2004, Intensive Care 2005, Rudebox 2006. *Publications:* F for English 2000, Robbie Williams: Performance (with Mark McCrun) 2001, Robbie Williams: Somebody Someday 2001, Feel (with Chris Heath) 2004. *Leisure interests:* golf, rollerblading. *Address:* IE Music Ltd., 111 Frithville Gardens, London, W12 7JG, England (office); EMI Music, EMI House, 43 Brook Green, London, W6 7EF, England (office). *Telephone:* (20) 8600-3400 (office). *Fax:* (20) 8600-3401 (office). *E-mail:* info@iemusic.co.uk (office). *Website:* www.iemusic.co.uk (office); www.robbiewilliams.com.

WILLIAMS, Robert Joseph Paton (Bob), DPhil, FRS, FRCS; British chemist and academic; *Professor Emeritus of Chemistry and Fellow Emeritus, Wadham College, University of Oxford;* b. 25 Feb. 1926, Wallasey; s. of Ernest Ivor Williams and Alice Roberts; m. Jelly Klara Buchli 1952; two s.; ed Univ. of Oxford; Rotary Int. Fellow 1951–52; Research Fellow, Merton Coll., Oxford Univ. 1952–55; Tutor and Lecturer (Fellow), Wadham Coll., Oxford 1955–74, Professorial Fellow 1974–93, Prof. Emer. 1991–, Fellow Emer. 1993–, Lecturer, Oxford Univ. 1955–70, Reader 1970–72, Royal Soc. Napier Research Prof. 1974–91; Pres. Dalton Div. Royal Soc. of Chemistry 1991–93; Foreign mem. Royal Swedish Acad. of Science, Lisbon Acad. of Science, Czechoslovak Acad. of Science, Royal Soc. of Science, Liège; Hon. Fellow, Merton Coll., Oxford 1991; Hon. DSc (Louvain, Leicester, East Anglia, Keele, Lisbon); Tilden Medal (Chem. Soc. of England), Liversidge Medal (Chem. Soc. of England), Keilen Medal (Biochem. Soc.), Hughes Medal (Royal Soc.), Sir Hans Krebs Medal (European Biochemical Soc.), Linderstrøm-Lang Medal (Denmark), Sigillum Magna (Univ. of Bologna), Heyrovsky Medal (Int. Union of Biochemistry), Sir Frederick Gowland Hopkins Medal (Biochemical Soc.), Royal Medal (Royal Soc.), Longstaff Medal (Chem. Soc. of England), Lord Goodman Lecturer 1992, J. D. Bernal Lecturer 1993, Canada Lecturer, Royal Soc. 1996, J. D. Birchall Lecturer 1999, Huxley Lecturer 2000, Certificate of Honour for Charity Work, City of Oxford 2003. *Publications:* Inorganic Chemistry (with C. S. G. Phillips), NMR in Biology, Recent Trends in Bioinorganic Chemistry, The Natural Selection of the Chemical Elements (with J.J.R. Frausto da Silva) 1996, Bringing Chemistry to Life (with J. J. R. Frausto da Silva) 1999, The Biological Chemistry of the Elements (with J. J. R. Frausto da Silva) (2nd edn) 2001, The Chemistry of Evolution (with J. J. R. Frausto da Silva) 2005. *Leisure interests:* walking in the country, local planning. *Address:* Wadham College, Oxford, OX1 3QR (office); Corner House, 1A Water Eaton Road, Oxford, OX2 7QQ, England (home). *Telephone:* (1865) 272600 (office); (1865) 558926 (home). *Fax:* (1865) 272690 (office); (1865) 558926 (home). *E-mail:* bob.williams@chem.ox.ac.uk (office). *Website:* www.chem.ox.ac.uk (office).

WILLIAMS, Robin; American actor and comedian; b. 21 July 1951, Chicago; s. of Robert Williams and Laurie Williams; m. 1st Valerie Velardi 1978 (divorced); one s.; 2nd Marsha Garces 1989; one s. one d.; ed Detroit Country Day, Mich., Claremont Men's Coll., Marin Coll., Kentfield, Calif., Juilliard School, New York; f. Blue Wolf Productions Inc. (film production co.); Cecil B. DeMille Award, Golden Globe Awards 2005. *Television appearances include:* Laugh-In, The Richard Pryor Show (also writer), America 2-Night, Happy Days, Mork and Mindy 1978–82, Carol and Carl and Whoopi and Robin (Emmy Award), Royal Gala: Prince's Trust (Emmy Award). *Stage appearances include:* Waiting for Godot. *Films include:* Popeye 1980, The World According to Garp 1982, The Survivors 1983, Moscow on the Hudson 1984, Club Paradise 1986, Good Morning Vietnam 1987 (Golden Globe Award 1988), Dead Poets' Society 1989, Awakenings 1990 (Best Actor, Nat. Bd of Review), The Fisher King 1991 (Golden Globe Award), Hook 1991, Dead Again 1991, Toys 1992, Being Human 1993, Aladdin (voice) 1993, Mrs Doubtfire (also producer) 1993, Jumanji 1996, The Birdcage 1996, Jack 1996, Hamlet 1996, Joseph Conrad's The Secret Agent 1996, Fathers' Day 1997, Deconstructing Harry 1997, Good Will Hunting 1997 (Acad. Award), Flubber 1997, What Dreams May Come 1998, Patch Adams 1998, Jakob the Liar 1999, Bicentennial Man 1999, One Hour Photo 2002, Insomnia 2002, Death to Smoochy 2002, The Final Cut 2004, House of D 2004, Robots (voice) 2005, The Big White 2005, The Night Listener 2006, RV 2006, Everyone's Hero 2006, Man of the Year 2006, Happy Feet (voice) 2006, Night at the Museum 2006, License to Wed 2007, August Rush 2007. *Recordings:* Reality, What a Concept 1979 (Grammy Award), Throbbing Python of Love, A Night at the Met. *Address:* c/o Creative Artists Agency, 9830 Wilshire Boulevard, Beverly Hills, CA 90212; PO Box 480909, Los Angeles, CA 90048; Blue Wolf Productions, Inc. 725 Arizona Avenue, Suite 202, Santa Monica, CA 90401, USA. *Telephone:* (310) 451-8890 (Blue Wolf).

WILLIAMS, Roger Stanley, CBE, MD, FRCP, FRCS, FRCPE, FRACP, FRCPI, FMedSci; British consultant physician; *Director, Institute of Hepatology, University College London; Honorary Consultant Physician, University College London Hospitals NHS Trust;* b. 28 Aug. 1931; s. of Stanley George Williams and Doris Dagmar Clatworthy; m. 1st Lindsay Mary Elliott 1954 (divorced 1977); two s. three d.; m. 2nd Stephanie Gay de Laszlo 1978; one s. two d.; ed St Mary's Coll., Southampton, London Hosp. Medical School, Univ. of London; House Doctor London Hosp. 1953–56; Jr Medical Specialist, Queen Alexandra Hosp. 1956–58; Medical Registrar and Tutor, Royal Postgraduate Medical School 1958–59; Lecturer in Medicine Royal Free Hosp. 1959–65; Consultant Physician Royal S. Hants. and Southampton Gen. Hosp. 1965–66; Consultant Physician and Dir, Inst. of Liver Studies, King's Coll. Hosp. (now King's Coll. School of Medicine and Dentistry), London 1966–96, Prof. of Hepatology; Dir Inst. of Hepatology, Univ. Coll. London, Hon. Consultant Physician, Univ. Coll. London Hosps NHS Trust 1996–; mem. WHO Scientific Group on Viral Hepatitis, Geneva 1972, Transplant Advisory Panel DHSS 1974–83, Advisory Group on Hepatitis DHSS 1980–, European Asscn for the Study of the Liver (Pres. 1983) 1966–, Harveian Soc. of London (Pres. 1974–75), British Asscn for the Study of the Liver (Pres. 1984), Royal Soc. of Medicine, British Soc. of Gastroenterology (Pres. 1989); Vice-Pres. Royal Coll. of Physicians 1991; Hon. Consultant in Medicine to the Army 1988–98; Rep. to Select Cttee of Experts on Organizational Aspects of Co-operation in Organ Transplantation, Congress of Europe; Sir Ernest Finch Visiting Prof., Univ. of Sheffield 1974; Hon. FACP; Hon. FRCPI. *Publications:* Fifth Symposium on Advanced Medicine (ed.) 1969, Immunology of the Liver 1971, Artificial Liver Support 1975, Immune Reactions in Liver Disease 1978, Drug Reactions and the Liver 1981, Clinics in Critical Care Medicine – Liver Failure 1986, Liver Tumours (Baillière's Clinical Gastroenterology) 1987, The Practice of Liver Transplantation 1995, International Developments in Health Care. A review of Health Systems in the 1990s 1995, Acute Liver Failure 1997; author of more than 2,500 papers, reviews and book chapters. *Leisure interests:* tennis, sailing, opera. *Address:* Institute of Hepatology, Royal Free & University College School of Medicine, Harold Samuel House, 69–75 Chenies Mews, London, WC1E 6HX (office); 30 Devonshire Close, London, W1G 7BE, England (home). *Telephone:* (20) 7679-6510 (office); (20) 7679-6511 (office); (20) 7637-2844 (home). *Fax:* (20) 7380-0405 (office). *E-mail:* roger.williams@ucl.ac.uk (office). *Website:* www.ucl.ac.uk/liver-research (office).

WILLIAMS, Ronald A., MS; American business executive; *Chairman and CEO, Aetna Inc.;* b. 11 Nov. 1949, Chicago, Ill.; ed Roosevelt Univ., Sloan School of Management, Massachusetts Inst. of Tech.; Sr Vice-Pres. of Marketing Blue Cross of California 1987–95, Pres. 1995–99; Co-founder and fmr Sr Vice-Pres. Vista Health Corpn; fmr Group Marketing Exec. Control Data Corpn; Co-founder and fmr Pres. Integrative Systems; Group Pres., Large Group Div. WellPoint Health Networks Inc. 1999–2001; Exec. Vice-Pres. and Chief of Health Operations, Aetna Inc. 2001–02, Pres. 2002–07, mem. Bd of Dirs 2002–, Chair. and CEO 2006–; mem. Bd of Dirs American Express Co.; mem. MIT Sloan Dean's Advisory Council, Alfred P. Sloan Man. Soc., Business Council, Business Roundtable, Council for Affordable Quality Healthcare (currently Chair.); Trustee, The Conference Bd, Connecticut Science Center Bd. *Address:* Aetna Inc., 151 Farmington Avenue, Hartford, CT 06156, USA (office). *Telephone:* (860) 273-0123 (office). *Fax:* (860) 273-3971 (office). *E-mail:* info@aetna.com (office). *Website:* www.aetna.com (office).

WILLIAMS, Most Rev., Rt Hon. Rowan Douglas, MA, DPhil, DD, FRSL, FBA; British ecclesiastic and academic; *Archbishop of Canterbury;* b. 14 June 1950, Swansea; m. Jane Paul 1981; one s. one d.; ed Christ's Coll. Cambridge, Wadham Coll. Oxford; deacon 1977; priest 1978; tutor, Westcott House, Univ. of Cambridge 1977–80, Lecturer in Divinity 1980–1986, Dean and Chaplain, Clare Coll. 1984–1986; Canon Theologian Leicester Cathedral 1981–82; Canon Residentiary, Christ Church, Oxford 1986–92; Lady Margaret Prof. of Theology, Oxford Univ. 1986–92; Bishop of Monmouth 1992–2002; Archbishop of Wales 2000–02; Archbishop of Canterbury Dec. 2002–; Fellow, British Acad. 1990; Hon. Fellow, Univ. of Wales, Swansea, Newport, Aberystwyth, Cardiff, Clare Coll., Cambridge, Christ Church, Oxford, Wadham Coll., Oxford, Christ's Coll., Cambridge; Dr hc (Erlangen, Bonn, Nashoteh House, Exeter, Aberdeen, Wales, Open Univ., Roehampton, Cambridge, Oxford); Hon. Curate, St George, Chesterton, Cambridge 1980–1983, Hon. Fellow, Univ. of Wales, Bangor 2003. *Television:* Conversations with Rowan Williams 2003. *Publications include:* The Wound of Knowledge 1979, Resurrection 1982, The Truce of God 1983, Arius: Heresy and Tradition 1987, Teresa of Avila 1991, Open to Judgement: Sermons and Addresses 1994,

Sergei Bulgakov: towards a Russian political theory 1999, Christ on Trial: How the Gospel Unsettles our Judgement 2000, Lost Icons: Reflection on Cultural Bereavement 2000, On Christian Theology 2000, Love's Redeeming Work (ed.) 2001, Ponder These Things: Praying With Icons of the Virgin 2002, Writing in the Dust: Reflections on 11th September and its Aftermath 2002, Silence and Honey Cakes 2003, The Dwelling of the Light 2003, Anglican Identities 2004, Why Study the Past? 2005, Grace and Necessity 2006, Tokens of Trust: An Introduction to Christian Belief 2007, Wrestling with Angels: conversations in modern theology 2007, Dostoevsky: Language, Faith and Fiction 2008; poetry: After Silent Centuries 1994, Remembering Jerusalem 2001, Poems of Rowan Williams 2002, Headwaters 2008. *Leisure interests:* music, fiction, languages. *Address:* Lambeth Palace, London, SE1 7JU, England. *Telephone:* (20) 7898-1200. *Fax:* (20) 7261-9836. *Website:* www .archbishopofcanterbury.org.

WILLIAMS, Serena Jameka; American professional tennis player; b. 26 Sept. 1981, Saginaw, Mich.; d. of Richard Williams and Oracene Williams; sister of Venus Williams (q.v.); turned professional 1995; coached by her father Richard Williams; singles semi-finalist, Sydney Open 1997, Chicago 1998; won mixed doubles (with Max Mirnyi) at Wimbledon and US Open 1998; doubles winner (with Venus Williams) Oklahoma City 1998, French Open 1999, Hanover 1999, US Open 1999, Wimbledon 2000, 2002, 2008, Australian Open 2001, 2003, 2009; winner US Open 1999, 2002, 2008, Paris Indoors 1999, 2003, Indian Wells 1999, 2001, LA 1999, 2000, Grand Slam Cup 1999, Hanover 2000, Tokyo 2000, Canadian Open 2001, French Open 2002, Wimbledon 2002, 2003, Australian Open 2003, 2005, 2007, 2009, Miami 2003; singles finalist, Wimbledon 2004, 2008; US Fed. Cup Team 1999; winner WTA Championship 2001; doubles gold medal with sister, Venus, Olympic Games, Sydney 2000, Beijing 2008; singles quarter-finalist, Olympic Games, Beijing 2008; ranked World No. 1 (singles) 8 July 2002, 8 Sept. 2008, 2 Feb. 2009, No. 5 (doubles) 11 Oct. 1999; 386 career singles wins, 81 defeats, 105 career doubles wins, 17 defeats; 31 WTA Tour singles titles (including ten Grand Slam titles), 11 doubles titles (including eight Grand Slam titles); debuted The Serena Williams Collection by Nike, an apparel and footwear collection 2005; f. clothing label Aneres; numerous appearances as actress on TV programs; Sanex WTA Tour Most Impressive Newcomer Award 1998, WTA Most Improved Player 1999, Teen Awards Achievement Award (shared with sister, Venus) 2000, WTA Player of the Year 2002, ITF World Champion 2002, Associated Press Female Athlete of the Year 2002, World Sportswoman of the Year 2002, WTA Comeback Player of the Year 2004, BET Award for Best Female Athlete 2007. *Leisure interests:* watching movies, playing football and basketball, reading, acting, music, designing clothing. *Address:* c/o William Morris Agency, One William Morris Place, Beverly Hills, CA 90212, USA (office); United States Tennis Association, 70 West Red Oak Lane, White Plains, NY 10604, USA. *Telephone:* (310) 859-4000 (office); (914) 696-7000. *Fax:* (310) 859-4462 (office). *Website:* www.wma.com (office); www.usta.com; www.serenawilliams.com.

WILLIAMS, Stephen, MA, PhD; American anthropologist, archaeologist, academic and museum curator; *Peabody Professor Emeritus of North American Archaeology and Ethnography, Harvard University;* b. 28 Aug. 1926, Minneapolis, Minn.; s. of Clyde G. Williams and Lois M. Williams (née Simmons); m. Eunice Ford 1962; two s.; ed Yale Univ. and Univ. of Michigan; Historical and Archaeological Research on Caddo Indians for U.S. Dept of Justice 1954–55; Research Fellow in N American Archaeology, Peabody Museum of Archaeology and Ethnology, Harvard Univ. 1955–58; Lecturer in Anthropology, Harvard Univ. 1956–58; Asst Prof. of Anthropology 1958–62, Assoc. Prof. 1962–67, Prof. of Anthropology 1967–72, Peabody Prof. of North American Archaeology and Ethnography 1972–93, Prof. Emer. 1993–, Chair. Dept of Anthropology 1967–69, mem. Bd of Freshmen Advisers, Harvard Univ. 1959–60, 1961–65; Asst Curator of N American Archaeology, Peabody Museum 1957–58, Curator of N American Archaeology 1962–93; Dir Peabody Museum, Harvard Univ. 1967–77, Dir Lower Mississippi Survey 1958–93, Hon. Curator N American Archaeology, 1993–; mem. Bd Dirs Archaeological Conservancy 1984–88; Distinguished Fellow School of American Research, Santa Fe 1977–78; Hon. MA (Harvard Univ.); Distinguished Service Award, Southeast Archaeological Conf. 1992, Dean's Distinguished Service Award, Harvard Extension Program 1993. *Publications:* six books and monographs including Excavations at the Lake George Site, Yazoo County, Miss. 1958–60 (with Jeffrey P. Brain), Fantastic Archaeology: The Wild Side of North American Prehistory 1991; numerous articles in journals and magazines. *Leisure interest:* bird watching. *Address:* PO Box 22354, Santa Fe, NM 87502 (office); 1017 Foothills Trail, Santa Fe, NM 87505, USA (home). *Telephone:* (505) 983-8836 (office). *E-mail:* williamsstephen@msn.com (home).

WILLIAMS, HE Cardinal Thomas Stafford, ONZ, STL, BSocSc; New Zealand ecclesiastic (retd); *Archbishop Emeritus of Wellington;* b. 20 March 1930, Wellington; s. of Thomas S. Williams and Lillian M. Williams (née Kelly); ed St Patrick's Coll., Wellington, Victoria Univ., Wellington, St Kevin's Coll., Oamaru, Holy Cross Coll., Mosgiel, Pontifical Urban Coll. de Propaganda Fide, Rome and Univ. Coll., Dublin; ordained priest, Rome 1959; Asst St Patrick's Parish, Palmerston North 1963; Dir of Studies, Catholic Enquiry Centre, Wellington 1965; parish priest, St Anne's, Leulumoega, Western Samoa 1971, Holy Family Parish, Porirua East, Wellington 1976; Archbishop of Wellington and Metropolitan of NZ 1979–2005, Archbishop Emer. 2005–; Bishop of New Zealand, Mil. 1995–2005; cr. Cardinal (Cardinal-Priest of Gesù Divin Maestro alla Pineta Sacchetti) 1983. *Address:* 40 Walton Avenue, Park, Waikanae Park, Kapiti 5036, New Zealand (home). *Telephone:* (4) 293-4684 (home). *E-mail:* t.williams@wn.catholic.org.nz (home).

WILLIAMS, Venus Ebone Starr; American professional tennis player; b. 17 June 1980, Lynwood, Calif.; d. of Richard Williams and Oracene Williams;

sister of Serena Williams (q.v.); ed Art Inst. of Fort Lauderdale; made professional debut Bank of West Classic, Oakland, Calif. 1994; Bausch & Lomb Championships 1996; winner numerous singles titles (WTA Tour) including Oklahoma City 1998, Lipton 1998, 1999, Hamburg 1999, Italian Open 1999, Grand Slam Cup 1998; seven Grand Slam singles titles: Wimbledon 2000, 2001, 2005, 2007, 2008, US Open 2000, 2001; seven Grand Slam doubles titles (with Serena Williams): French Open 1999, US Open 1999, Wimbledon 2000, 2002, 2008, Australian Open 2001, 2003; singles finalist, Wimbledon 2002, 2003, French Open 2002, Australian Open 2003; with Serena Williams, first sisters in tennis history to have each won a Grand Slam singles title; singles Gold Medal, Olympic Games, Sydney 2000; doubles Gold Medal (with sister Serena), Olympic Games, Sydney 2000, Beijing 2008; only sisters in 20th century to win a Grand Slam doubles title together; US Fed. Cup Team 1995, 1999; 499 career singles wins, 118 defeats, 106 career doubles wins, 20 defeats; 37 career singles titles, 12 doubles titles; highest ranking (singles): No. 1 25 Feb. 2002, (doubles): No. 5 11 Oct. 1999; awarded largest-ever endorsement contract for a female athlete by Reebok 2002; Founder and CEO V Starr Interiors (design firm), Jupiter, Fla 2002–; Global Amb. for UNESCO to address worldwide gender issues 2006; teamed up with retailer Steve & Barry's to launch own fashion line EleVen 2007; Sports Image Foundation Award 1995, Tennis Magazine Most Impressive Newcomer 1997, Most Improved Player 1998, Sanex WTA Tour Player of the Year and Doubles Team of the Year (with sister, Serena) 2000, Women's Sports Foundation Athlete of the year 2000, ESPY Awards for Best Female Athlete and Best Female Tennis Player of 2001, 2002, Certificate of Achievement Howard Univ. 2002, Glamour Magazine's Woman of the Year Award 2005. *Leisure interests:* sumo wrestling, surfing, reading, languages, antique furniture, writing poetry. *Address:* c/o IMG Tennis, IMG Center, 1360 East 9th Street, Suite 100, Cleveland, OH 44114-1782, USA (office); V Starr Interiors, 1102 West Indiantown Road, Suite 11, Jupiter, FL 33458, USA (office). *Telephone:* (216) 522-1200 (office). *Fax:* (216) 436-3477 (office). *E-mail:* cleresumes@imgworld .com (office). *Website:* www.imgworld.com (office); www.vstarrinteriors.com; www.venuswilliams.com.

WILLIAMS AGASSE, Vicente; Honduran politician; *Vice-President;* Vice-Pres. of Honduras 2002–. *Address:* c/o Office of the President, Palacio José Cecilio del Valle, Boulevard Juan Pablo II, Tegucigalpa, Honduras (office). *Telephone:* 232-6282 (office). *Fax:* 231-0097 (office).

WILLIAMS-JONES, Michael Robert; British/South African film executive; b. 3 June 1947, Sussex; s. of Hugh E. Williams-Jones and Valerie Lyons; m. 1st. Lynne Williams-Jones 1969 (deceased); m. 2nd Eve Foreman 1994; two s. one step.-s. one step-d.; ed Selborne Coll. East London, S Africa; trainee, United Artists, Southern Africa region 1967, Man. Dir 1969, Brazil 1971, UK 1975; Sr Vice-Pres. United Artists Int. 1978; Pres. United Int. Pictures Film Group 1981; Pres. and CEO United Int. Pictures Corpn 1984–96; owner/co-founder, Merlin Anglesey UK, Ltd 1996–; City of Rio de Janeiro Honour 1974, Golden Horse Lifetime Achievement Award, Taiwan 1986, Lifetime Achievement Award, Locarno 1989, Int. Distributor of the Year 1995. *Leisure interests:* movies, theatre, reading, opera, walking, snorkelling. *Address:* Merlin Anglesey (UK), Ltd, 49C Princes Gate, London, SW7 2PG (office); 11 Kingston House South, Ennismore Gardens, London, SW7 1NF, England (home). *Telephone:* (20) 7584-6065 (office). *Fax:* (20) 7584-7057 (office). *E-mail:* merlina@dial.pipex.com (office).

WILLIAMS OF CROSBY, Baroness (Life Peer), cr. 1993, of Stevenage in the County of Hertfordshire; *Rt Hon. Shirley Williams,* PC, MA; British politician and academic; *Public Service Professor of Electoral Politics, Emerita, John F. Kennedy School of Government, Harvard University;* b. 27 July 1930, London; d. of the late Sir George Catlin and Vera Brittain; m. 1st Bernard Williams 1955 (divorced 1974, died 2003); one d.; m. 2nd Prof. Richard Neustadt 1987 (died 2003); ed Summit School, Minn., USA, St Paul's Girls' School, Somerville Coll., Oxford and Columbia Univ., New York; Gen. Sec. Fabian Soc. 1960–64; Labour MP for Hitchin 1964–74, for Hertford and Stevenage 1974–79; SDP MP for Crosby 1981–83; Parl. Pvt. Sec., Minister of Health 1964–66; Parl. Sec. Minister of Labour 1966–67; Minister of State, Dept of Educ. and Science 1967–69; Minister of State, Home Office 1969–70; Opposition Spokesman on Health and Social Security 1970–71, on Home Affairs 1971–73, on Prices and Consumer Affairs 1973–74; Sec. of State for Prices and Consumer Protection 1974–76, for Educ. and Science 1976–79; Paymaster-Gen. 1976–79; Sr Research Fellow (part-time) Policy Research Inst. 1979–85; mem. Labour Party Nat. Exec. Cttee 1970–81; mem. Council for Social Democracy Jan.–March 1981; left Labour Party March 1981; Co-Founder SDP March 1981, Pres. 1982–88; Public Service Prof. of Elective Politics, John F. Kennedy School of Govt, Harvard Univ. 1988–2000, Prof. Emer. 2000–, Dir Inst. of Politics 1988–89; mem. Social and Liberal Democratic Party 1988–; Deputy Leader Liberal Democrat Party, House of Lords 1999–2001, Leader Nov. 2001–; Visiting Fellow, Nuffield Coll., Oxford 1967–75; Fellow, Inst. of Politics, Harvard 1979–80 (mem. Sr Advisory Council 1986–); Regents Lecturer and Fellow, Inst. of Politics, Univ. of Calif., Berkeley; Dir Turing Inst., Glasgow 1985–90, Learning by Experience Trust 1986–94, Project Liberty 1990–98; Janeway Lecturer, Princeton Univ., NJ; Pick Lecturer, Chicago Univ.; Godkin Lecturer, Harvard Univ.; Montgomery Lecturer, Dartmouth Coll.; Heath Fellow, Grinell Coll.; Rede Lecturer and Darwin Lecturer, Univ. of Cambridge; Hoover Lecturer, Strathclyde Univ.; Dainton Lecturer, British Library; Gresham Lecturer, Mansion House; mem. EC Comité des Sages 1996–97, Council Int. Crisis Group 1998–, Int. Advisory Council, Council on Foreign Relations (US); Chair. EC Job Creation Competition 1997–98; Trustee The Century Foundation, New York, Inst. for Public Policy Research, London, RAND Europe UK; Gov. The Ditchley Foundation; mem. Bd Moscow School of Political Studies; lecture series: Who's Who plus 2001: Erasmus, Notre Dame; Hon. Fellow Somerville Coll., Oxford, Newnham

Coll., Cambridge; Grand Cross (FRG); Hon. DEd, CNAA; Hon. DrPolEcon (Univ. of Leuven, Belgium, Radcliffe Coll., Harvard, USA); Hon. LLD (Leeds) 1979, (Southampton) 1981, (Ulster) 1997; Dr hc (Aston, Bath, Essex, Heriot-Watt, Napier, Sheffield, Washington Coll. (USA)); RSA Silver Medal. *Radio:* Snakes and Ladders – A Political Diary (BBC Radio 4) 1996, Women in the House (BBC Radio 4) 1998. *Television:* Shirley Williams in Conversation (BBC series) 1979. *Publications:* Youth Without Work (OECD Study) 1981, Politics is for People 1981, A Job to Live 1985, 'Human Rights in Europe' for Human Rights: What Work? (ed. Power and Alison) 2000, Making Globalisation Good (Chapter 15: Global Social Justice – The Moral Responsibilities of the Rich to the Poor) (ed. John Dunning) 2003, God and Caesar 2003; pamphlets on EC and economics of Central Africa; articles for The Times, Guardian, Independent, Int. Herald Tribune, Political Quarterly, Prospect etc. *Leisure interests:* riding, rough walking, music. *Address:* House of Lords, Westminster, London, SW1A 0PW, England (office). *Telephone:* (20) 7219-5850 (home); (20) 7219-3242 (home); (617) 495-8866 (Harvard). *Fax:* (20) 7219-1174 (office). *E-mail:* williamss@parliament.uk (office); shirley_williams@ksg.harvard.edu. *Website:* ksgfaculty.harvard.edu/shirley_williams.

WILLIAMS OF ELVEL, Baron (Life Peer), cr. 1985, of Llansantffraed in Elvel in the County of Powys; **Charles Cuthbert Powell Williams,** CBE, MA; British business executive, author and politician; b. 9 Feb. 1933, Oxford; s. of the late Dr Norman P. Williams and Muriel Cazenove; m. Jane G. Portal 1975; one step-s.; ed Westminster School, Christ Church, Oxford and London School of Econs; British Petroleum Co. Ltd 1958–64; Bank of London and Montreal 1964–66; Eurofinance SA, Paris 1966–70; Baring Brothers & Co. Ltd 1970–77, Man. Dir 1971–77; Chair. Price Comm. 1977–79; Man. Dir Henry Ansbacher & Co. Ltd 1980–82, Chair. 1982–85; Chief Exec. Henry Ansbacher Holdings PLC 1982–85; Chair. Acoustiguide UK Ltd 1989–95; Pres. Campaign for the Protection of Rural Wales 1989–95, Vice-Pres. and Pres. Radnor Br. 1995–; Pres. Fed. of Econ. Devt Authorities 1990–96, Vice-Pres. 1996–; parl. cand. (Labour) 1964; Opposition Spokesman for Trade and Industry, House of Lords 1986–92, for Defence 1990–, for Environment 1992–; Deputy Leader of Opposition in House of Lords 1989–92. *Publications:* The Last Great Frenchman: A Life of General de Gaulle 1993, Bradman: An Australian Hero 1996, Adenauer: The Father of the New Germany 2000, Pétain 2005. *Leisure interests:* cricket, music. *Address:* 48 Thurloe Square, London, SW7 2SX, England; Pant-y-Rhiw, Llansantffraed in Elvel, Powys, LD1 5RH, Wales. *Telephone:* (20) 7581-1783 (London); (1597) 823235 (Wales). *Fax:* (20) 7581-1783.

WILLIAMSON, David Keith, AO, BE; Australian playwright and screenwriter; b. 24 Feb. 1942, Melbourne; s. of Edwin Keith David Williamson and Elvie May (née Armstrong) Williamson; m. Kristin Ingrid Lofven 1974; two s. one d.; ed Monash Univ., Melbourne Univ.; Design Engineer Gen. Motors-Holden's 1965; lecturer Swinbourne Tech. Coll. 1966–72; freelance writer 1972–; Hon. DLitt (Sydney), (Monash), (Swinburne); numerous writing, TV and cinema awards. *Plays:* The Removalists 1972, Don's Party 1973, Three Plays 1974, The Department 1975, A Handful of Friends 1976, The Club 1977, Travelling North 1979, The Perfectionist 1981, Sons of Cain 1985, Emerald City 1987, Top Silk 1989, Siren 1990, Money and Friends 1992, Brilliant Lies 1993, Sanctuary 1994, Dead White Males 1995, Corporate Vibes 1999, Face to Face 1999, The Great Man 2000, Up for Grabs 2001, A Conversation 2001, Charitable Intent 2001, Soulmates 2002, Amigos 2004, Influence 2005, Scarlett O'Hara at the Crimson Parrot 2008. *Screenplays:* Gallipoli 1981, Phar Lap 1983, The Year of Living Dangerously 1983, Travelling North 1986, Emerald City 1988, The Four Minute Mile (2-part TV series) 1988, A Dangerous Life (6-hour TV series) 1988, Top Silk 1989, Siren 1990, Money and Friends 1992, Dead White Males 1995, Heretic 1996, Third World Blues 1997, After the Ball 1997, Brilliant Lies 1996, On the Beach 2000. *Address:* Cameron Cresswell Management, Level 7, 61 Marlborough Street, Surry Hills, NSW 2010, Australia (office). *Telephone:* (20) 9319-7199 (office). *Fax:* (2) 9319-6866 (office). *E-mail:* info@cameronsmanagement.com.au (office). *Website:* www.cameronsmanagement.com.au (office).

WILLIAMSON, Sir (George) Malcolm, Kt, FCIB; British banker; *Chairman, National Australia Group Europe Ltd;* b. 27 Feb. 1939, Oldham; s. of George Williamson and Margery Williamson; m. Hang Thi Ngo; one s. one d.; one s. one d. by previous marriage; local dir, Barclays Bank PLC, N London 1978–79; Asst Gen. Man. Barclays Bank PLC 1979–82, Treas. UK 1982–83, Regional Man. 1983–85; Man. Dir Girobank PLC and mem. Bd The Post Office 1985–89; Group Exec. Dir Banking (Eastern Hemisphere), Standard Chartered Bank 1989–90, Group Exec. Dir Banking 1990–91, Group Man. Dir 1991–93, Group Chief Exec. 1993–98; Dir Nat. Grid Group 1995–99; UK Chair. Thai-British Group 1997–; Pres. and Chief Exec. Visa Int. 1998–2004; Chair. Britannic Group 2004–05; Chair. CDC Group PLC 2004–; Dir Group 4 Securicor plc (now G4S PLC) 2004–08; mem. Bd of Dirs Nat. Australia Bank 2004–, Chair. Nat. Australia Group Europe Ltd 2004–, Clydesdale Bank 2004–, (all mems Nat. Australia Bank Group); Deputy Chair. Resolution plc 2005–08; Dir JP Morgan Cazenove Holdings 2005–; Chair. Signet Group plc 2006–; Chair. Advisory Bd Youth Business Int. (now Princes Youth Business Int.) 2005–08; Dir The Prince of Wales Int. Business Leaders Forum 2006–. *Leisure interests:* mountaineering, walking, chess, bridge. *Address:* National Australia Group Europe Ltd, 88 Wood Street, London, EC2V 7QQ, England (office). *Telephone:* (20) 7710-1784 (office). *Website:* www.nabgroup.com (office).

WILLIAMSON, John, PhD; British economist and academic; *Senior Fellow, Peterson Institute for International Economics;* b. 7 June 1937, Hereford; s. of A. H. Williamson and Eileen Williamson; m. Denise R. de Souza 1974; two s. one d.; ed London School of Econs and Princeton Univ.; Lecturer, Reader, Univ. of York 1963–68; HM Treasury 1968–70; Prof., Univ. of Warwick 1970–77; adviser, IMF 1972–74; Prof., Catholic Univ. of Rio de Janeiro 1978–81; Sr Fellow, Inst. for Int. Econs (now Peterson Inst. for Int. Econs) 1981–; Chief Economist South Asia, World Bank 1996–99; Project Dir UN High-Level Panel on Financing for Devt 2001. *Publications:* The Crawling Peg 1965, The Failure of World Monetary Reform 1977, The Exchange Rate System 1983, Targets and Indicators (with M. H. Miller) 1987, Latin American Adjustment: How Much Has Happened? 1990, The Political Economy of Policy Reform 1993, The Crawling Band as an Exchange Rate Regime 1996, A Survey of Financial Liberalization (co-author) 1998, Exchange Rate Regimes for Emerging Markets 2000, After the Washington Consensus: Restarting Growth and Reform in Latin America (co-ed.) 2003, Dollar Adjustment: How Far? Against What? (co-ed.) 2004. *Leisure interest:* birding. *Address:* Institute for International Economics, 1750 Massachusetts Avenue, NW, Washington, DC 20036-1903 (office); 3919 Oliver Street, Chevy Chase, MD 20815, USA. *Telephone:* (202) 454-1340 (office); (301) 654-5312 (home). *Fax:* (202) 328-5432 (office). *E-mail:* jwilliamson@iie.com (office). *Website:* www.iie.com/jwilliamson.htm (office).

WILLIAMSON, Kevin; American screenwriter and producer; b. 14 March 1965, New Bern, NC; ed East Carolina Univ., UCLA; fmr actor, asst dir, music videos; f. Outerbanks Entertainment 1995; Entertainer of the Year, Entertainment Weekly 1997, mem. Power 100 List, Premiere Magazine 1998. *Films include:* Scream (writer) 1996, Scream 2 1997, I Know What You Did Last Summer (writer) 1997, Halloween: H20 (producer) 1998, The Faculty (writer) 1998, Teaching Mrs. Tingle (writer, dir) 1999, Her Leading Man (dir), Cursed (writer, producer) 2005, Venom 2005, Retribution 2006. *TV series include:* Dawson's Creek (creator) 1998–2003, Wasteland (writer, producer) 1998, Glory Days (creator) 2002. *Address:* c/o William Morris Agency, 151 El Camino Drive, Beverly Hills, CA 90212, USA (office).

WILLIAMSON, Matthew, BA; British fashion designer; b. 23 Oct. 1971, Chorlton, Manchester; ed St Martin's School of Art and Design; worked as freelance designer for two years; travelled frequently to India for Marni, Georgina von Ertzdorf and Monsoon fashion retailers; f. and Creative Dir Matthew Williamson (with Joseph Velosa) 1997–; Creative Dir Emilio Pucci 2005–; trademark details are embroidery, beading and sequins;. *Address:* Matthew Williamson Ltd, 46 Hertford Street, London, W1J 7DP, England (office). *Telephone:* (20) 7491-6220 (office). *Fax:* (20) 7491-6252 (office). *E-mail:* press@matthewwilliamson.co.uk (office). *Website:* www.matthewwilliamson.com.

WILLIAMSON, Nicol; British actor; b. 14 Sept. 1938, Hamilton, Scotland; m. Jill Townsend 1971 (divorced 1977); one s.; began career with Dundee Repertory Theatre 1960–61; London debut at Royal Court, That's Us 1961; joined RSC 1962; New York Drama Critics Award for Inadmissible Evidence 1965–66; Evening Standard Award for Best Actor, for Inadmissible Evidence 1964, for Hamlet 1969. *Theatre appearances include:* Satin in The Lower Depths 1962, Leantio in Women Beware Women 1962, Kelly's Eye 1963, The Ginger Man 1963, Vladimir in Waiting for Godot 1964, Bill Maitland in Inadmissible Evidence 1964, 1965, 1978, Diary of A Madman 1968, Hamlet 1969, Uncle Vanya 1973, Coriolanus 1973, Malvolio in Twelfth Night 1974, Macbeth 1974, Rex 1975, Inadmissible Evidence 1981, Macbeth 1982, The Entertainer 1983, The Lark 1983, The Real Thing 1985, Jack – A Night on the Town with John Barrymore 1994, King Lear 2001. *Films include:* Inadmissible Evidence 1967, Laughter in the Dark 1968, Bofors Gun 1968, The Reckoning 1969, Hamlet 1969, The Jerusalem File 1972, The Wilby Conspiracy 1974, Robin and Marian 1976, The Seven Per Cent Solution 1976, The Human Factor 1980, Knights 1980, Excalibur 1980, Venom 1980, I'm Dancing as Fast as I Can 1981, Return to Oz 1984, Black Widow 1986, The Hour of the Pig 1993, The Wind in the Willows 1996, Spawn 1997. *Television includes:* Terrible Jim Fitch, Arturo Ui, I Know What I Meant, The Word 1977, Macbeth 1982, Mountbatten – The Last Viceroy 1985, Passion Flower 1985. *Publication:* Ming's Kingdom (novel) 1996. *Address:* c/o Jonathan Altaras Associates, 11 Garrick Street, London, WC2E 9AR, England (office). *Telephone:* (20) 7836-8722 (office).

WILLIAMSON, Sir (Robert) Brian, Kt, CBE, MA, FRSA; British business executive; b. 16 Feb. 1945; m. Diane Marie Christine de Jacquier de Rosée 1986; ed Trinity Coll., Dublin; Personal Asst to Maurice Macmillan (later Viscount Macmillan) 1967–71; Ed. Int. Currency Review 1971; Man. Dir Gerrard & Nat. Holdings (later Gerrard Group PLC) 1978–89, Chair. 1989–98; Dir London Int. Financial Futures and Options Exchange (LIFFE) 1982–89, Chair. 1985–88, 1998–2003; Chair. GNI Ltd 1985–89; Dir Fleming Int. High Income Investment Trust PLC 1990–96, Deputy Chair. Fleming Worldwide Investment Trust PLC 1996; Dir Bank of Ireland 1990–98 (mem. Bd Bank of Ireland Britain Holdings 1986–90); Dir Electra Investment Trust PLC 1994– (Chair. 2000–), Barlows PLC 1998–; mem. British Invisible Exports Council, Financial Services Authority 1986–98; Gov. at Large Nat. Asscn of Securities Dealers, USA 1995–98; mem. Int. Markets Advisory Bd, NASDAQ Stock Market (Chair. 1997–99); mem. Supervisory Bd Euronext. *Leisure interests:* tobogganing, hot air ballooning. *Address:* 23 Paultons Square, London, SW3 5AP, England (office).

WILLIAMSON OF HORTON, Baron (Life Peer), cr. 1999, of Horton in the County of Somerset; **David Francis Williamson,** GCMG, CB, MA, DCL, DEconSc; British government official (retd); *Convenor, Independent Crossbench Peers, House of Lords;* b. 8 May 1934; m. Patricia M. Smith 1961; two s.; ed Tonbridge School and Exeter Coll. Oxford; army service 1956–58; entered Ministry of Agric., Fisheries and Food 1958; seconded to HM Diplomatic Service as First Sec. (Agric. and Food), Geneva, for Kennedy Round Trade Negotiation 1965–67; Prin. Pvt. Sec. to successive Ministers, Ministry of Agric., Fisheries and Food 1967–70; Head of Milk and Milk Products Div. 1970–74; Under-Sec. 1974; Deputy Dir-Gen. (Agric.), Comm. of European

Communities 1977–83; Deputy Sec. and Head of European Secr. Cabinet Office 1983–87; Sec.-Gen. Comm. of European Communities (now EC) 1987–97; mem. EU Cttee, House of Lords 2000–04; Convenor, Ind. Crossbench Peers, House of Lords 2004–; Visiting Prof., Univ. of Bath 1997–2001; Dir (non-exec.) Whitbread PLC 1998–2005; Trustee, Thomson Foundation; Kt Commdr's Cross of the Order of Merit (Germany); Commdr, Légion d'honneur; Commdr, Grand Cross of the Royal Order of the Polar Star (Sweden). *Address:* House of Lords, Westminster, London, SW1A 0PW, England (office). *Telephone:* (20) 7219-3583 (office). *E-mail:* williamsond@parliament.uk (office). *Website:* www.parliament.uk/about_lords/about_lords.cfm (office).

WILLIS, Bruce Walter; American actor; b. 19 March 1955, Idar-Oberstein, Germany; s. of David Willis and Marlene Willis; m. 1st Demi Moore (q.v.) 1987 (divorced 2000); three d.; m. 2nd Emma Heming 2009; ed Montclair State Coll.; moved to USA 1957; studied with Stella Adler; mem. First Amendment Comedy Theatre; Officier, Ordre des Arts et des Lettres. *Stage appearances:* (off-Broadway): Heaven and Earth 1977, Fool for Love 1984, The Bullpen, The Bayside Boys, The Ballad of Railroad William. *Films:* Blind Date 1987, Sunset 1988, Die Hard 1988, In Country 1989, Die Hard 2, Die Harder 1990, Bonfire of the Vanities 1990, Hudson Hawk 1991, The Last Boy Scout 1991, Billy Bathgate 1991, Death Becomes Her 1992, Striking Distance 1993, Color of Night 1994, North 1994, Nobody's Fool 1994, Pulp Fiction 1994, Die Hard with a Vengeance 1995, 12 Monkeys 1995, Four Rooms, Last Man Standing 1996, The Jackal 1997, The Fifth Element 1997, Mercury Rising 1998, Armageddon 1998, Breakfast of Champions 1998, The Story of US 1999, The Sixth Sense 1999, Unbreakable 2000, Disney's the Kid 2000, Bandits 2001, Hart's War 2002, Tears of the Sun 2003, The Whole Ten Yards 2004, Hostage 2005, Sin City 2005, Alpha Dog 2006, Lucky Number Slevin 2006, 16 Blocks 2006, Over the Hedge (voice) 2006, Hammy's Boomerang Adventure (voice) 2006, Fast Food Nation 2006, The Hip Hop Project 2006, The Astronaut Farmer 2007, Perfect Stranger 2007, Grindhouse 2007, Live Free or Die Hard (also producer) 2007, Planet Terror 2007, Assassination of a High School President 2008, What Just Happened? 2008. *Television:* Trackdown (film), Miami Vice (series), The Twilight Zone (series), Moonlighting 1985–89 (series; People's Choice award 1986, Emmy award 1987, Golden Globe award 1987), Friends (guest) 2000. *Recordings:* The Return of Bruno 1987, If It Don't Kill You, It Just Makes You Stronger 1989. *Address:* 22470 Pacific Coast Highway, Malibu, CA 90265, USA.

WILLIS, Norman David, MA, DipEconPolSc; British trade union official; b. 21 Jan. 1933; s. of Victor J.M. Willis and Kate E. Willis; m. Maureen Kenning 1963; one s. one d.; ed Ashford Co. Grammar School, Ruskin and Oriel Colls, Oxford; Personal Research Asst to Gen. Sec. Transport & General Workers' Union (TGWU) 1959–70; Nat. Sec. Research and Educ. TGWU 1970–74; Asst Gen. Sec. Trades Union Congress 1974–77, Deputy Gen. Sec. 1977–84, Gen. Sec. 1984–93; Councillor (Labour), Staines Urban Dist Council 1971–74; Chair. Nat. Pensioners Convention Steering Cttee 1979–93; Vice-Pres. European TUC 1984–91, Pres. 1991–93; ICFTU 1984–93, Inst. of Manpower Studies 1985–93; Trustee Anglo-German Foundation for Study of Industrial Soc. 1986–95, Duke of Edinburgh's Commonwealth Study Conf. 1986–93; Patron West Indian Welfare (UK) Trust 1986; mem. NEDC 1984, Council, Overseas Devt Inst. 1985–93, Council, Motability 1985–93, Exec. Bd UNICEF 1986–90, Trade Union Advisory Cttee to OECD 1986–93, Council of Prince of Wales Youth Business Trust 1986–93, Employment Appeal Tribunal 1995–2003; Pres. The Arthur Ransome Soc.; Vice-Pres. West Indian Welfare Trust (UK) 1986–93; Patron Docklands Sinfonietta 1986–93; Trustee, Royal School of Needlework 1995–2007; Trustee and Black Bin Bag Operative (grade two), Sunbury Millenium Embroidery Gallery; monthly column 'Cross Stitcher' magazine; Hon. Fellow, Oriel Coll., Oxford; Hon. mem. Poetry Soc., Writers Guild of Great Britain. *Leisure interests:* embroidery, poetry, natural history, architecture, canals, snooker, birding. *Address:* c/o Trades Union Congress, Congress House, Great Russell Street, London, WC1B 3LS, England.

WILLIS, Ralph; Australian politician; b. 14 April 1938, Melbourne; s. of Stanley Willis and Doris Willis; m. Carol Joyce Dawson 1970; one s. two d.; ed Univ. High School and Melbourne Univ.; research officer, Australian Council of Trade Unions 1960, industrial advocate 1970; mem. House of Reps 1972; Minister for Employment and Industrial Relations and Minister assisting Prime Minister in Public Service Industrial Matters 1983–87, Minister for Industrial Relations and Minister assisting Prime Minister in Public Service Matters 1987–88, for Transport and Communications 1988–90, for Finance 1990–91, Treas. 1991, Minister for Finance 1991–93, Treas. 1993–96; Vice-Pres. Exec. Council 1992; mem. Australian Labor Party. *Leisure interests:* tennis, reading, watching football. *Address:* 24 Gellibrand Street, Williamstown, Vic. 3016, Australia.

WILLMOTT, Peter S., BA, MBA; American business executive; *Chairman and CEO, Willmott Services;* ed Williams Coll., Harvard Univ.; began career as sr financial analyst American Airlines; fmr Man. Consultant Booz, Allen & Hamilton; fmr Vice-Pres. ITT Continental Banking Co.; fmr Chief Financial Officer, then Pres. and COO Federal Express Corpn; fmr Chair. and Pres. Carson Pirie Scott, Zenith Electronics Corpn; currently Chair. and CEO Willmott Services (consultancy), Chicago; mem. Bd Fleming Cos Inc. 2002–, interim CEO and Pres. March–Aug. 2003; apptd Man.-Pnr Berkshires Capital Investors (BCI) 2001; mem. Bd Dirs Federal Express, Security Capital Group; mem. bd several civic orgs in Chicago and Berkshires; fmr Chair. Bd Trustees Williams Coll. *Address:* c/o Fleming Companies Inc., 1945 Lakepointe Drive, Lewisville, TX 75075, USA (office).

WILLOCH, Kåre Isaachsen, CandOecon; Norwegian politician (retd); b. 3 Oct. 1928, Oslo; s. of Haakon Willoch and Agnes Saure; m. Anne Marie Jørgensen 1954; one s. two d.; ed Ullern Gymnasium and Univ. of Oslo; Sec. Fed. of Norwegian Shipowners 1951–53, Counsellor Fed. of Norwegian Industries 1954–63; mem. Storting 1958–89; mem. Nat. Cttee Conservative Party 1961–89, Sec.-Gen. Conservative Party 1963–65, Chair. 1970–74, Chair. Conservative Party Parl. Group 1970–81; Minister of Trade and Shipping 1963, 1965–70; Chair. World Bank Group 1967; mem. Nordic Council 1970–86, Pres. 1973; Prime Minister 1981–86; Chair. Int. Democratic Union 1987–89; Chair. Foreign Affairs Cttee of Parl. 1986–89; Co-Gov. of Oslo and Akershus 1989–98; Chair. Norwegian Defence Comm. 1990–92; Chair. Supervisory Bd, Norwegian Bank 1990–96; Chair. Bd of Norwegian Broadcasting Corpn 1998–2000; Chair. Norwegian Comm. on the Vulnerability of Soc. 1999–2000; Dir Fridtjof Nansen Inst. 1999–2001; Commdr with Star, Royal Norwegian Order of St Olav; Dr hc (St Olav's Coll. Minn., USA); Fritt Ords Pris, Norwegian Inst. for Free Speech 1997, Opinion Maker of the Year, Asscn of Norwegian Eds 1996, C.J. Hambro's Prize 2000. *Publications:* Personal Savings 1955, Price Policy in Norway (with L. B. Bachke) 1958, Memoirs (Vol. I) 1988, (Vol. II) 1990, Krisetid 1992, A New Policy for the Environment 1996, Ideas (Tanker i Tiden) 1999, Myths and Realities (Mytirog virkelighet) (memoirs) 2002. *Leisure interests:* skiing, touring. *Address:* Blokaveien 6B, 0282 Oslo, Norway (home). *Telephone:* 22-50-72-89 (home). *E-mail:* fmoa@frisurf.no (home).

WILLOTT, (William) Brian, CB, PhD; British public official; b. 14 May 1940, Swansea; s. of William Harford and Beryl P.M. Willott; m. Alison Leyland Pyke-Lees 1970; two s. two d.; ed Trinity Coll., Cambridge; Research Assoc., Univ. of Md 1965–67; Asst Prin. Bd of Trade 1967–69, Prin. 1969–73; HM Treasury 1973–75; Asst Sec. Dept of Industry 1975–78, Sec. Ind. Devt Unit 1978–80; Sec. Nat. Enterprise Bd 1980–81; CEO British Tech. Group (Nat. Enterprise Bd and Nat. Research and Devt Corpn) 1981–84; Head, Information Tech. Div., Dept of Trade and Industry 1984–87, Head, Financial Services Div. 1987–91; Chief Exec. Export Credit Guarantee Dept 1992–97; CEO Welsh Devt Agency 1997–2000; Chair. Gwent NHS Healtcare Trust; Dir Dragon Int. Studios Ltd; mem. Council Nat. Museums and Galleries of Wales 2001–; Visiting Prof. Univ. of Glamorgan 2000. *Leisure interests:* music, reading, ancient history, gardening. *Address:* Coed Cefn, Tregare, Monmouth, NP25 4DT, Wales (home).

WILLOUGHBY, Christopher R., MA; British economist; *Associate Consultant, Oxford Policy Management;* b. 24 Feb. 1938, Guildford; s. of Ronald James Edward Willoughby and Constance Louisa (née Sherbrooke) Willoughby; m. Marie-Anne Isabelle Normand 1972; ed Lambroke School, Marlborough Coll., Univ. of Grenoble, Jt Services School for Linguists, Balliol Coll., Oxford, Univ. of Calif., Berkeley; served in RN 1956–58, Lt, RNR 1958; New York Times Wash. Bureau 1962–63; economist, World Bank starting 1963, Dir Operations Evaluation Dept 1973–76, Transport, Water and Telecommunications Dept 1976–83, Econ. Devt Inst. 1983–90, Chief, World Bank Mission in Bangladesh 1990–94, in Belarus 1994–97, Infrastructure Lead Adviser Europe and Cen. Asia Region 1997, Lead Specialist Infrastructure Dept 1999, now retd; currently Assoc. Consultant, Oxford Policy Man. *Leisure interests:* running, swimming, house re-modelling. *Address:* Oxford Policy Management, 6 St Aldates Courtyard, 38 St Aldates, Oxford OX1 1BN, England (office). *Telephone:* (1865) 207300 (office). *Fax:* (1865) 250580 (office). *E-mail:* admin@opml.co.uk (office). *Website:* www.opml.co.uk (office).

WILLS, Dean Robert, AO; Australian business executive; b. 10 July 1933, Australia; s. of the late Walter W. Wills and Violet J. Dryburgh; m. Margaret F. Williams 1955; one s. two d.; ed Sacred Heart Coll., S. Australia and S. Australian Inst. of Tech.; Dir W. D. & H. O. Wills (Australia) 1974–, Man. Dir 1977–83, Chair. 1983–86; Dir AMATIL Ltd 1975–, Deputy Chair. 1983–84, Man. Dir Coca-Cola AMATIL Ltd 1984–94, Chair. 1984–99; mem. Business Council of Australia 1984–94, Vice-Pres. 1987–88, Pres. 1988–90; mem. Bd Australian Grad. School of Man. (Univ. of NSW) 1985–92; Gov. Medical Foundation (Univ. of Sydney) 1990–94; mem. Corps. and Securities Panel 1991–94; Vice-Chair. Nat. Mutual Life 1992–97, Chair. 1997–2000; Deputy Chair. Nat. Mutual Holdings 1995–97, Chair. 1997–2000; Chair. Transfield Services Ltd 2001–05, Coca-Cola Australia Foundation Ltd 2002–05; Dir Microsurgery Foundation, Melbourne 1992–, John Fairfax Holdings Ltd 1994–2005 (Chair. 2002–05), Westfield Holdings Ltd 1994–; Gov. Australian Naval Aviation Museum; Deputy Chair. Australian Grand Prix Corpn 1994–2002; Trustee Museum of Applied Arts and Sciences 1986–90. *Leisure interests:* tennis, performance cars. *Address:* 71 Circular Quay East, Sydney, NSW 2000, Australia. *Telephone:* (2) 9259-6420 (office). *Fax:* (2) 9259-6628 (office).

WILLS, Garry, BA, MA, PhD; American writer, journalist and academic; *Professor of History Emeritus, Northwestern University;* b. 22 May 1934, Atlanta, GA; m. Natalie Cavallo 1959; two s. one d.; ed St Louis Univ., Xavier Univ., Cincinnati and Yale Univ.; Fellow Center for Hellenic Studies 1961–62; Assoc. Prof. of Classics 1962–67, Adjunct Prof. 1968–80, Johns Hopkins Univ.; Newspaper Columnist Universal Press Syndicate 1970–; Henry R. Luce Prof. of American Culture and Public Policy 1980–88, Adjunct Prof., later Prof. of History Emeritus 1988–, Northwestern Univ.; mem. American Philosophical Soc., American Acad. of Arts and Letters, American Acad. of Arts and Sciences; various hon. doctorates; Nat. Humanities Medal 1998. *Publications:* Chesterton 1961, Politics and Catholic Freedom 1964, Roman Culture 1966, Jack Ruby 1967, Second Civil War 1968, Nixon Agonistes 1970, Bare Ruined Choirs 1972, Inventing America 1978, At Button's 1979, Confessions of a Conservative 1979, Explaining America 1980, The Kennedy Imprisonment 1982, Lead Time 1983, Cincinnatus 1984, Reagan's America 1987, Under God 1990, Lincoln at Gettysburg (Nat. Book Critics Circle Award 1993, Pulitzer Prize for General Non-Fiction 1993) 1992, Certain Trumpets: The Call of Leaders 1994, Witches and Jesuits: Shakespeare's Macbeth 1994, John Wayne's America 1997, Saint Augustine 1999, A Necessary Evil: A History of

American Distrust of Government 1999, Papal Sin: Structures of Deceit 2000, Saint Augustine's Childhood 2001, Why I Am a Catholic 2002, President 2003, Saint Augustine's Sin 2004, Saint Augustine's Conversion 2004, Bush's Fringe Government 2006, Head and Heart: American Christianities 2007, What the Gospels Meant 2008, Martial's Epigrams (trans.) 2008. *Address:* Department of History, Northwestern University, Harris Hall 202, 1881 Sheridan Road, Evanston, IL 60208, USA (office). *Telephone:* (847) 491-3406 (office). *Fax:* (847) 467-1393 (office). *E-mail:* g-wills@northwestern.edu (office). *Website:* www.history.northwestern.edu/faculty/wills.htm (office).

WILLSON, Francis Michael Glenn, BA, MA, DPhil; British university administrator and academic; *Professor Emeritus, Murdoch University;* b. 29 Sept. 1924, Carlisle; s. of the late Christopher Glenn Willson and Elsie Katrine Mattick; m. Jean Carlyle 1945; two d.; ed Carlisle Grammar School, Univ. of Manchester, Balliol and Nuffield Colls., Oxford; war service in Merchant Navy 1941–42 and RAF 1943–47; seconded to BOAC 1946–47; Research Officer, Royal Inst. of Public Admin. 1953–60; Research Fellow, Nuffield Coll., Oxford 1955–60; Lecturer in Politics, St Edmund Hall, Oxford 1958–60; Prof. of Govt, Univ. Coll. of Rhodesia and Nyasaland 1961–64, Dean of Social Studies 1962–64; Prof. of Govt and Politics, Univ. of California, Santa Cruz 1965–74, Provost Stevenson Coll. 1967–74, Vice-Chancellor Coll. and Student Affairs 1973–74, Visiting Prof. 1985–92; Warden of Goldsmiths Coll., London 1974–75; Prin. Univ. of London 1975–78; Vice-Chancellor Murdoch Univ., Western Australia 1978–84, Prof. Emer. 1985–. *Publications:* Organization of British Central Government 1914–1956 (with D. N. Chester) 1957, 2nd edn 1914–1964 1968, Administrators in Action 1961, A Strong Supporting Cast – The Shaw Lefevres 1789–1936 1993, Our Minerva – The Men and Politics of the University of London 1836–1858 1995, In Just Order Move – The Progress of the Laban Centre for Movement and Dance 1946–96 1997, The University of London – The Politics of Senate and Convocation 1858–1900 2004. *Leisure interests:* listening to music, reading. *Address:* 32 Digby Mansions, Hammersmith Bridge Road, London, W6 9DF, England. *Telephone:* (20) 8741-1247.

WILLUMSTAD, Robert B.; American insurance executive; *Senior Adviser, Brysam Global Partners;* b. Brooklyn, NY; m. Carol Willumstad; two c.; ed Adelphi Univ.; worked in various positions in operations, retail banking and computer systems, Chemical Bank 1967–87; joined Commercial Credit, Baltimore (later CitiFinancial div. of Citigroup) 1987, Chair. and CEO Consumer Financial Services, Travelers Group –1998, Vice-Chair. Global Consumer Group and Chair. Global Consumer Lending, Citigroup Inc. (following merger of Citicorp and Travelers Group in 1998) 1998–2002, Chair. and CEO Citigroup Global Consumer Group 2000–03, Pres. Citigroup Inc. 2002–05, COO 2003–05, also CEO and Pres. Citibank NA 2003–05; mem. Bd of Dirs AIG 2006–08, Chair. 2006–08, CEO June–Sept. 2008; Co-founder and Sr Adviser, Brysam Global Pnrs 2007–; Dir S.C. Johnson & Son Inc., Habitat for Humanity, MasterCard International; mem. Adelphi Univ. Bd of Trustees 2005–; Hon. LLD (Adelphi) 2005; New York City Urban League Frederick Douglass Award 2002. *Address:* Brysam Global Partners, 277 Park Avenue, 35th Floor, New York NY 10172, USA (office). *Telephone:* (212) 622-4378 (office). *E-mail:* marge.magner@brysam.com (office). *Website:* www.brysam.com (office).

WILMOTT, Peter Graham, CMG, MA; British consultant and fmr civil servant; *Director, GlobalLink Border Solutions Ltd;* b. 6 Jan. 1947, Cuckfield, West Sussex; s. of John Wilmott and Violet Wilmott; m. Jennifer Plummer 1969; two d.; ed Hove Grammar School and Trinity Coll. Cambridge; Asst Prin., HM Customs & Excise 1968, Prin. 1973, Asst Sec. 1983, Commr 1988; seconded to UK Perm. Rep. to EC 1971–73, 1977–79, to EC Court of Auditors 1980–82; Dir-Gen. Customs and Indirect Taxation, EC Comm. 1990–96; partner in Prisma Consulting Group 1996–2000; Chair. Int. Value Added Tax Asscn 1998–2000; Pres. Office du Développement par l'Automatisation et la Simplification du Commerce Extérieur (ODASCE), Paris 2000–04, First Vice-Pres. 2004–08; Dir Ad Valorem International Ltd 2002–08, GlobalLink Border Solutions Ltd 2006–; Dir (non-exec.) SITPRO 2001–07. *Address:* GlobalLink Border Solutions Ltd, 31 Wilbury Avenue, Hove, East Sussex, BN3 6HS, England (office).

WILMUT, Sir Ian, Kt, OBE, PhD, FRSE, FRS,; British geneticist; *Director, Centre for Regenerative Medicine, University of Edinburgh;* b. 7 July 1944; s. of Leonard (Jack) Wilmut and Mary Wilmut; m. Vivienne Mary Craven 1967; two d. one adopted s.; ed Univ. of Nottingham and Darwin Coll., Cambridge; Post-doctoral Fellow, Unit of Reproductive Physiology and Biochemistry, Cambridge 1971–73; various research posts, Animal Breeding Research Org. (ARC, now BBSRC Roslin Inst.) 1973–2006, Head of Div. Gene Expression and Devt, jtly responsible (with Keith Campbell) for cloning of Dolly (a sheep, first animal produced from an adult cell) 1996; Hon. Prof., Univ. of Edin. 1998–, Dir, Centre for Regenerative Medicine 2005–; Foreign Assoc. NAS 2004; Hon. DSc (Nottingham) 1998, (North Eastern Univ., Boston) 1999, (Edin.) 2002. *Publications:* The Second Creation (jtly) 2000, After Dolly: The Uses and Misuses of Human Cloning 2006; and contribs to numerous papers on cloning of Dolly the sheep. *Leisure interests:* curling, photography, walking in the countryside. *Address:* Centre for Regenerative Medicine, University of Edinburgh, 1-7 Roxburgh Street, Edinburgh, EH8 9TA, Scotland (office). *Telephone:* 131-650-9090 (office). *Fax:* 131-650-9019 (office). *E-mail:* Research.Innovation@ed.ac.uk (office). *Website:* www.research-innovation.ed.ac.uk (office).

WILSEY, Gen. Sir John, GCB, CBE, DL; British former army officer and business executive; *Chairman, Western Provident Association;* b. 18 Feb. 1939, Frimley, Hants.; s. of the late Maj.-Gen. J. H. O. Wilsey and B.S.F. Wilsey; m. Elizabeth P. Nottingham 1975; one s. one d.; ed Sherborne School and Royal Mil. Acad., Sandhurst; commissioned 1959; served in Cyprus, North Africa, Guyana, USA, Malta, Germany, UK (mem. Blue Nile Expedition 1968),

Staff Coll. 1973; Commdg 1st Bn, The Devonshire & Dorset Regt 1979–82, Col 1990–97; Chief of Staff, HQ, NI 1982–84; Commdg 1st Infantry Brigade and UK Mobile Force 1985–86; Royal Coll. of Defence Studies 1987; Chief of Staff, HQ UK Land Forces 1988–90; GOC and Dir Mil. Operations, NI 1990–93; C-in-C Land Command 1993–96; ADC Gen. to the Queen 1994–96; Chair. Western Provident Asscn 1996–; Hon. Col Royal Jersey Militia, Royal Engineers 1993–; Vice-Chair. Sherborne School 1996–; mem. Council Royal Bath & West 1996–, Commonwealth War Graves Comm. 1998– (Vice-Chair. 2001–); Commr Royal Hosp., Chelsea 1996–; Gov. Suttons Hosp. in Charterhouse 1996–2001, Sherborne School for Girls 1996–2001. *Publications:* Service for the Nation 1987, H. Jones, VC 2002. *Leisure interests:* skiing, fishing, sailing, breeding alpacas. *Address:* Western Provident Association, Rivergate House, Blackbrook Park, Taunton, Somerset, TA1 2PE, England (office). *Telephone:* (1823) 623502 (office).

WILSON, Sir Alan Geoffrey, Kt, MA, DSc, DUniv, LLD, DEd, FBA, FCGI, AcSS; British geographer, mathematician, academic and fmr university vice-chancellor; *Director-General for Higher Education, Department for Education and Skills;* b. 8 Jan. 1939, Bradford, Yorks.; s. of Harry Wilson and Gladys Naylor; m. Sarah Fildes 1987; ed Queen Elizabeth Grammar School, Darlington, Corpus Christi Coll., Cambridge; Chartered Geographer; Scientific Officer, Rutherford High Energy Lab. 1961–64; Research Officer, Inst. of Econs and Statistics, Univ. of Oxford 1964–66; Math. Adviser to Ministry of Transport 1966–68; Asst Dir Centre for Environmental Studies, London 1968–70; Prof. of Urban and Regional Geography, Univ. of Leeds 1970–2004, Pro-Vice-Chancellor 1989–91, Vice-Chancellor 1991–2004; Dir-Gen. for Higher Educ., Dept for Education and Skills 2004–; Ed. Environment and Planning 1969–91; Dir GMAP 1991–2001; mem. Academia Europaea 1991–, Acad. of Learned Socs for the Social Sciences; Dr hc (Univ. of Leeds) 2004; Hon. Fellow, Univ. Coll. London 2003, Corpus Christi Coll. Cambridge 2004; Gill Memorial Award, Royal Geographical Soc. 1978, Hons Award, Asscn of American Geographers 1987, Founder's Medal, Royal Geographical Soc. 1992. *Publications:* Entropy in Urban and Regional Modelling 1970, Urban and Regional Models in Geography and Planning 1974, Spatial Population Analysis (with P. H. Rees) 1977, Mathematics for Geographers and Planners (with M. J. Kirkby) 1980, Models of Cities and Regions (co-ed.) 1977, Catastrophe Theory and Bifurcation: applications to urban and regional systems 1981, Geography and the Environment: Systems Analytical Methods 1981, Mathematical Methods in Geography and Planning (with R. J. Bennett) 1985, Urban Systems (co-ed.) 1987, Urban Dynamics (co-ed.) 1990, Modelling the City: Performance, Policy and Planning (with Bertuglia, Clarke and others) 1994, Intelligent Geographical Information Systems (with Birkin, Clarke and Clarke) 1996, Complex Spatial Systems 2000. *Leisure interests:* writing, miscellaneous fads. *Address:* Department for Education and Skills, Sanctuary Buildings, Great Smith Street, London, SW1P 3BT, England. *Telephone:* (20) 7925-3773 (office). *Fax:* (20) 7925-6133 (office). *E-mail:* alan.wilson@dfes.gsi.gov.uk (office). *Website:* www.dfes.gov.uk/hegateway (office).

WILSON, Alexander (Sandy) Galbraith; British writer and composer; b. 19 May 1924, Sale, Cheshire; s. of George Wilson and Caroline Humphrey; ed Harrow School, Univ. of Oxford and Old Vic Theatre School; contributed to revues Slings and Arrows, Oranges and Lemons 1948; wrote revues for Watergate Theatre, London, See You Later, See You Again 1951–52; wrote musical The Boy Friend for Players Club Theatre 1953, transferred to Wyndhams Theatre and on Broadway 1954 (London revival 1984), The Buccaneer 1955, Valmouth London 1958, USA 1960, Chichester 1982, Divorce me Darling! 1965 (revival Chichester 1997); Dir London revival of The Boy Friend 1967; Composed music for As Dorothy Parker Once Said, London 1969; songs for BBC TV's Charley's Aunt 1969; wrote and performed Sandy Wilson Thanks the Ladies (one-man show) London 1971; wrote His Monkey Wife London 1971, The Clapham Wonder 1978, Aladdin (London) 1979. *Publications:* This is Sylvia 1954, The Poodle from Rome 1962, I Could be Happy (autobiog.) 1975, Ivor 1975, The Roaring Twenties 1977. *Leisure interests:* cinema, cookery, travel. *Address:* Flat 4, 2 Southwell Gardens, London, SW7 4SB, England (home). *Telephone:* (20) 7373-6172 (home).

WILSON, Andrew Norman (A. N.), MA, FRSL; British writer; b. 27 Oct. 1950, England; s. of the late N. Wilson and of Jean Dorothy Wilson (née Crowder); m. 1st Katherine Dorothea Duncan-Jones 1971 (divorced 1989); two d.; m. 2nd Ruth Guilding 1991; one d.; ed Rugby School and New Coll., Oxford; Asst Master Merchant Taylors' School 1975–76; Lecturer St Hugh's Coll. and New Coll., Oxford 1976–81; Literary Ed. Spectator 1981–83, Evening Standard 1990–97; Hon. mem. American Acad. of Arts and Letters 1984; Chancellor's Essay Prize 1975, Ellerton Theological Prize 1975. *Publications:* fiction: The Sweets of Pimlico 1977, Unguarded Hours 1978, Kindly Light 1979, The Healing Art (Somerset Maugham Award) 1980, Who Was Oswald Fish? 1981, Wise Virgin (WHSmith Award) 1982, Scandal 1983, Gentleman in England 1985, Love Unknown 1986, Stray 1987, Incline Our Hearts 1988, A Bottle in the Smoke 1990, Daughters of Albion 1991, The Vicar of Sorrows 1993, Hearing Voices 1995, A Watch in the Night 1996, Hazel the Guinea-pig (for children) 1997, Dream Children 1998, My Name is Legion 2004, A Jealous Ghost 2005, Winnie and Wolf 2007; non-fiction: The Laird of Abbotsford 1980, A Life of John Milton 1983, Hilaire Belloc 1984, How Can We Know? An Essay on the Christian Religion 1985, The Church in Crisis (jtly) 1986, Landscape in France 1987, The Lion and the Honeycomb 1987, Penfriends from Porlock: Essays and Reviews 1977–86 1988, Tolstoy (Whitbread Award for Biography and Autobiography) 1988, Eminent Victorians 1989, John Henry Newman: prayers, poems, meditations (ed.) 1989, C.S. Lewis: A Biography 1990, Against Religion 1991, Jesus 1992, The Faber Book of Church and Clergy (ed.) 1992, The Rise and Fall of the House of Windsor 1993, The Faber Book of London (ed.) 1993, Paul: The Mind of the Apostle 1997, God's Funeral 1999, The Victorians 2003, Beautiful Shadow: A Life of Patricia Highsmith 2003,

Iris Murdoch as I Knew Her 2004, London: A Short History 2004, After the Victorians 2005, Betjeman (biog.) 2006, Harold Robbins: The Man Who Invented Sex 2007, Our Times: The Age of Elizabeth II 2008. *Address:* 5 Regent's Park Terrace, London, NW1 7EE, England.

WILSON, Brian; American musician (bass, keyboards), singer, songwriter and producer; b. 20 June 1942, Inglewood, CA; m. 2nd Melinda Ledbetter 1995; two d.; founder mem., The Beach Boys 1961–; retired from live performance to concentrate on composing and recording 1964; numerous live appearances, tours; band est. Brother Records label 1967–; simultaneous solo artist 1988–; American Music Awards Special Award of Merit 1988, Grammy Lifetime Achievement Award 2001, US Recording Acad. Musicares Award 2004, Kennedy Center Honor 2007. *Recordings include:* albums: with The Beach Boys: Surfin' Safari 1962, Surfer Girl 1963, Little Deuce Coupe 1963, Shut Down Vol. 2; All Summer Long 1964, Christmas Album 1964, The Beach Boys Today! 1965, Summer Days (and Summer Nights) 1965, Beach Boys Party 1966, Pet Sounds 1966, Smiley Smile 1967, Wild Honey 1968, Friends 1968, 20/20 1969, Sunflower 1970, Surf's Up 1971, Carl and the Passions – So Tough 1972, Holland 1973, The Beach Boys in Concert 1973, Endless Summer 1974, 15 Big Ones 1976, The Beach Boys Love You 1977, M.I.U. 1978, LA (Light Album) 1979, Keepin' The Summer Alive 1980, The Beach Boys 1985, Still Cruisin' 1989, Two Rooms 1991, Summer in Paradise 1992, The Sounds of Summer – The Very Best of The Beach Boys 2003; solo: Brian Wilson 1988, I Just Wasn't Made For These Times 1995, Imagination 1998, Pet Projects: The Brian Wilson Productions 2003, Smile 2004, What I Really Want For Christmas 2005, That Lucky Old Sun 2008. *Compositions for stage:* Shine 2002, That Lucky Old Sun (a Narrative) 2007. *Address:* c/o Elliott Lott, Boulder Creek Entertainment Corporation, 4860 San Jacinto Circle West, Fallbrook, CA 92028, USA (office); c/o Capitol Records, 1750 North Vine Street, Hollywood, CA 90028, USA. *Website:* www.thebeachboys.com; www .brianwilson.com.

WILSON, Brian G., AO, PhD; Australian/British physicist and academic (retd); *Professor Emeritus of Physics, University of Calgary;* b. 9 April 1930, Belfast, N Ireland; s. of Charles W. Wilson and Isobel C. Wilson (née Ferguson); m. 1st Barbara Wilkie 1959 (divorced 1975); two s. one d.; m. 2nd Jeanne Henry 1978 (divorced 1988); m. 3rd Joan Opdebeeck 1988; three s.; ed Methodist Coll., Belfast, Queens Univ. Belfast and Nat. Univ. of Ireland; Postdoctoral Fellow, Nat. Research Council of Canada 1955–57; Officer-in-charge, Sulphur Mount Lab., Banff, Alberta 1957–60; Assoc. Prof. of Physics, Univ. of Calgary 1960–65, Prof. 1965–70, Dean of Arts and Science 1967–70; Vice-Pres. Simon Fraser Univ., Burnaby, BC 1970–78; Vice-Chancellor Univ. of Queensland 1979–95; Deputy Chair. Australian Vice-Chancellors' Cttee 1987–88, Chair. 1989–90; mem. Council, Northern Territory Univ. 1988–93, Univ. of the South Pacific 1991–95; Pres. Int. Devt Program of Australian Univs and Colls 1991–92; Chair. Australian Cttee for Quality Assurance in Higher Educ. 1993–95; Fellow, Acad. of Technological Sciences and Eng (Australia); Hon. LLD (Calgary) 1984; Hon. DUniv (Queensland Univ. of Tech.) 1995; Hon. DSc (Queensland) 1995. *Publications:* one book and more than 50 scientific articles in int. journals. *Leisure interests:* golf, viniculture. *Address:* Domaine des Tisseyres, 11270 Fanjeaux, France (home). *Telephone:* (4) 68-24-61-75 (home). *Fax:* (4) 68-24-61-75 (home). *E-mail:* opdebeeck .wilson2@tiscali.fr (home).

WILSON, Charles; British journalist; b. 18 Aug. 1935, Glasgow, Scotland; s. of Adam Wilson and Ruth Wilson; m. 1st Anne Robinson 1968 (divorced 1973); one d.; m. 2nd Sally O'Sullivan 1980 (divorced 2001); one s. one d.; m. 3rd Rachel Pitkeathley 2001; ed Eastbank Acad., Glasgow; copy boy, The People 1951; later reporter with Bristol Evening World, News Chronicle and Daily Mail; Deputy Ed. Daily Mail (Manchester) 1971–74; Asst Ed. London Evening News 1974–76; Ed., Evening Times, Glasgow 1976; later Ed., Glasgow Herald; Ed. Sunday Standard, Glasgow 1981–82; Exec. Ed., The Times 1982, Jt Deputy Ed. 1984–85, Ed. 1985–90; Int. Devt Dir News Int. 1990–91; Ed.-in-Chief, Man. Dir The Sporting Life 1990–98; Editorial Dir Mirror Group Newspapers 1991–92, Group Man. Dir Mirror Group 1992–98; Acting Ed. The Independent 1995–96; Dir (non-exec.) Chelsea and Westminster Hosp. 1999–; mem. Newspaper Panel, Competition Comm. 1999–2007; mem. Jockey Club 1993–, Youth Justice Bd 1998–2004; Trustee World Wildlife Fund-UK 1997–2004, Royal Naval Museum 1999–. *Leisure interests:* current affairs, National Hunt racing, hunting, reading. *Address:* Chairman's Office, Chelsea and Westminster Trust, 369 Fulham Road, London, SW10 9NH (office); 23 Campden Hill Square, London, W8 7JY, England. *Telephone:* (20) 7727-3366 (home).

WILSON, Colin Henry; British writer; b. 26 June 1931, Leicester; s. of Arthur Wilson and Annetta Jones; m. 1st Dorothy Troop 1951; one s.; m. 2nd Joy Stewart 1960; two s. one d.; ed Gateway Secondary Technical School, Leicester; laboratory asst 1948–49, civil servant (taxes) 1949–50; RAF 1950, discharged on medical grounds 1950; then navvy, boot and shoe operative, dish washer, plastic moulder; lived Strasbourg 1950, Paris 1953; later factory hand and dish washer; writer 1956–; Writer in Residence, Hollins Coll., Virginia, USA 1966–67; Visiting Prof., Univ. of Washington 1967–68, Dowling Coll., Majorca 1969, Rutgers Univ., NJ 1974. *Publications include: philosophy:* The Outsider 1956, Religion and the Rebel 1957, The Age of Defeat 1958, The Strength to Dream 1961, Origins of the Sexual Impulse 1963, Beyond the Outsider 1965, Introduction to the New Existentialism 1966; *other non-fiction:* Encyclopaedia of Murder 1960, Rasputin and the Fall of the Romanovs 1964, Brandy of the Damned (music essays) 1965, Eagle and Earwig (literary essays) 1965, Sex and the Intelligent Teenager 1966, Voyage to a Beginning (autobiog.) 1968, Shaw: A Reassessment 1969, A Casebook of Murder 1969, Poetry and Mysticism 1970, The Strange Genius of David Lindsay (with E. H. Visiak) 1970, The Occult 1971, New Pathways in Psychology 1972, Strange

Powers 1973, A Book of Booze 1974, The Craft of the Novel 1975, The Geller Phenomenon 1977, Mysteries 1978, Beyond The Occult 1988; *novels:* Ritual in the Dark 1960, Adrift in Soho 1961, The World of Violence 1963, Man Without a Shadow 1963, Necessary Doubt 1964, The Glass Cage 1966, The Mind Parasites 1967, The Philosopher's Stone 1969, The Killer 1970, The God of the Labyrinth 1970, The Black Room 1970, The Schoolgirl Murder Case 1974, The Space Vampires 1976, Men of Strange Powers 1976, Enigmas and Mysteries 1977; *other works include:* The Quest for Wilhelm Reich 1979, The War Against Sleep: the Philosophy of Gurdjieff 1980, Starseekers 1980, Franken-stein's Castle 1980, The Directory of Possibilities (ed. with John Grant) 1981, Poltergeist! 1981, Access to Inner Worlds 1983, Encyclopaedia of Modern Murder (with Donald Seaman) 1983, The Psychic Detectives 1984, The Janus Murder Case 1984, The Personality Surgeon 1984, A Criminal History of Mankind 1984, Encyclopaedia of Scandal (with Donald Seaman) 1985, Afterlife 1985, Rudolf Steiner 1985, Strindberg (play) 1970, Spiderworld—The Tower 1987, Encyclopaedia of Unsolved Mysteries (with Damon Wilson) 1987, Aleister Crowley: the nature of the beast 1987, The Misfits 1988, Spiderworld—The Delta 1988, Written in Blood 1989, The Serial Killers 1990, Mozart's Journey to Prague (play) 1991, Spider World: the Magician 1992, The Strange Life of P. D. Ouspensky 1993, From Atlantis to the Sphinx 1996, Atlas of Sacred Sites and Holy Places 1996, Alien Dawn 1998, The Books in My Life 1998, The Devil's Party 2000, Atlantis Blueprint (with Rand Fle'math) 2000, Spiderworld—Shadowland 2003, Dreaming to Some Purpose (autobiography) 2004, Crimes of Passion (with Damon Wilson) 2006, Atlantis and the Neanderthals 2006, The Angry Years 2007, Super Consciousness 2009. *Leisure interests:* music, mathematics, wine. *Address:* Tetherdown, Trewal-lock Lane, Gorran Haven, Cornwall, PL26 6NT, England. *Telephone:* (1726) 842708.

WILSON, Sir David Mackenzie, Kt, LittD, FBA, FSA; British fmr museum director; b. 30 Oct. 1931, Dacre Banks; s. of Rev. J. Wilson; m. Eva Sjögren 1955; one s. one d.; ed Kingswood School, St John's Coll., Cambridge, Lund Univ., Sweden; Asst Keeper, The British Museum 1955–64; Reader in Archaeology, Univ. of London 1964–71, Prof. of Medieval Archaeology 1971–76; Dir British Museum 1977–92; Commr English Heritage 1990–97; mem. Royal Swedish Acad. of Science, Norwegian Acad. of Science and Letters; Hon. Fellow, Univ. Coll., London; numerous other honours and awards. *Publications:* The Anglo-Saxons 1960, Catalogue of Anglo-Saxon Metalwork 700–1100 in the British Museum 1964, Anglo-Saxon Art 1964, The Bayeux Tapestry 1965, Viking Art (with O. Klindt-Jensen) 1966, Three Viking Graves in the Isle of Man (with G. Bersu) 1966, The Vikings and their Origins 1970, The Viking Achievement (with P. Foote) 1970, St Ninian's Isle and its Treasure (with A. Small and A. C. Thomas) 1973, The Viking Age in the Isle of Man 1974; Editor: The Archaeology of the Anglo-Saxons 1976, The Northern World 1980, The Art of the Anglo-Saxons 1984, The Bayeux Tapestry 1985, The British Museum: Purpose and Politics 1989, Awful Ends 1992, Showing the Flag 1992, Vikingetidens Konst 1995, Vikings and Gods in European Art 1997; The British Museum – A History 2002; numerous articles and pamphlets. *Address:* The Lifeboat House, Castletown, IM9 1LD, Isle of Man (home). *Telephone:* (1624) 822800 (home). *E-mail:* dmw@mcb.net (office).

WILSON, Donald M.; American journalist and publishing executive; b. 27 June 1925; m. Susan M. Neuberger 1957; one s. two d.; ed Yale Univ.; USAAF navigator, Second World War; magazine assignments in 35 countries 1951–61; fmr Far Eastern Corresp., Life magazine, Chief Washington Correspondent 1957–61; Deputy Dir US Information Agency 1961–65; Gen. Man. Time-Life Int. 1965–68; Assoc. Publisher Life magazine 1968–69; Vice-Pres. Corp. and Public Affairs, Time Inc. 1969–81, Corp. Vice-Pres. Public Affairs Time Inc. 1981–89; Publr NJBIZ 1989–2003. *Address:* 40 Constitution Hl W, Princeton, NJ 08540-6774, USA (home). *Telephone:* (609) 497-4521 (home).

WILSON, Edward Osborne, Jr, BS, MS, PhD; American biologist, academic and writer; *University Professor Emeritus and Honorary Curator of Entomol-ogy, Museum of Comparative Zoology, Harvard University;* b. 10 June 1929, Birmingham, Ala; s. of the late Edward Osborne Wilson, Sr and Linnette Freeman Huddleston; m. Irene Kelley 1955; one d.; ed Univ. of Alabama and Harvard Univ.; Jr Fellow, Soc. of Fellows, Harvard Univ. 1953–56, Prof. of Zoology 1964–76, F.B. Baird Prof. of Science 1976–94, Pellegrino Univ. Prof. 1994–97, Univ. Research Prof. 1997–2002, Prof. Emer. 2002–, Curator of Entomology, Museum of Comparative Zoology 1974–97, Hon. Curator of Entomology 1997–; Founder and mem. Bd Dirs E.O. Wilson Biodiversity Foundation; Fellow, Guggenheim Foundation 1977–78, Advisory Bd 1979–90, mem. Selection Cttee 1982–90; mem. Bd of Dirs World Wildlife Fund 1983–94, Org. for Tropical Studies 1984–91, American Museum of Natural History 1992–, American Acad. of Liberal Educ. 1993–2004, Nature Conservancy 1994–, Conservation Int. 1997–; Foreign mem. Royal Soc. 1990, Finnish Acad. of Science and Letters 1990, Russian Acad. of Natural Sciences 1994; Founding mem. Int. Centre of Insect Physiology and Ecology, Org. for Tropical Studies, Ecosystems Center of Marine Biological Lab.; mem. NAS 1969; Fellow, American Acad. of Arts and Sciences 1959, American Philo-sophical Soc. 1976, Animal Behavior Soc. 1976, Deutsche Akad. der Naturforscher Leopoldina 1977, Royal Soc. of Sciences of Uppsala 1989, World Econ. Forum 2000; Hon. Life mem. American Genetic Asscn 1981, British Ecological Soc. 1983, Entomological Soc. of America 1987, Darwin Soc., Univ. of Bergen 1987, American Humanist Asscn 1989, Zoological Soc. of London 1992, Linnean Soc. of London 1994, Netherlands Entomological Soc. 1995, Asscn for Tropical Biology 1999, European Sociobiological Soc. 2000, Royal Entomological Soc. 2001; mem. Hon. Bd World Knowledge Dialogue and Scientist in Residence for symposium organized in Crans-Montana, Switzer-land 2008; Silver Cross of Columbus (Dominican Repub.) 2003; Hon. DHC (Univ. of Madrid Complutense) 1995; Hon. DPhil (Uppsala University) 1987;

Hon. Dr rer. nat (Univ. of Wurzburg) 2000; Hon. DSc (Duke Univ.) 1978, (Grinnell Coll.) 1978, (Univ. of West Florida) 1979, (Muhlenberg Coll.) 1998, (Yale Univ.) 1998, (Cedar Crest Coll.) 1999, (State Univ. of NY, Albany) 1999; Hon. LHD (Univ. of Alabama) 1980, (Hofstra Univ.) 1986, (Pennsylvania State Univ.), (Lawrence Univ.) 1979, (Fitchburg State Coll.) 1989, (Macalester Coll.) 1990, (Univ. of Massachusetts) 1993, (Univ. of Oxford) 1993, (Ripon Coll.) 1994, (Univ. of Connecticut) 1995, (Bates Coll.) 1996, (Ohio Univ.) 1996, (Coll. of Wooster) 1997, (Univ. of Guelph) 1997, (Univ. of Portland) 1997, (Bradford Coll.) 1997; Hon. LLD (Simon Fraser Univ.) 1982; Nat. Medal of Science 1976, Tyler Prize for Environmental Achievement 1983, Ingersoll Foundation Weaver Award for Scholarly Letters 1989, Crafoord Prize, Royal Swedish Acad. of Sciences 1990, Int. Prize for Biology, Govt of Japan 1993, Carl Sagan Award for Public Understanding of Science 1994, Audubon Soc. Medal 1995, Los Angeles Times Book Prize for Science 1995, Time Magazine's 25 Most Influential People in America 1995, Schubert Prize (Germany) 1996, German Ecological Foundation Book Award 1998, Franklin Prize for Science, American Philosophical Soc. 1999, Humanist of the Year, American Humanist Asscn 1999, Nonino Prize (Italy) 2000, Lewis Thomas Prize for Writing about Science 2000, King Faisal Int. Prize for Science (Saudi Arabia) 2000, Foundation for the Future Kistler Prize 2000, Nierenberg Prize 2001, Addison Emery Verrill Medal, Peabody Museum of Natural History 2007, TED (Tech. Entertainment Design) Prize (co-recipient) 2007, XIX Premi Internacional Catalunya 2007, and others. *Achievement:* coined the term 'sociobiology'. *Publications:* The Theory of Island Biogeography (with R. H. MacArthur) 1967, The Insect Societies 1971, Sociobiology: The New Synthesis 1975, On Human Nature (Pulitzer Prize for Gen. Non-Fiction 1979) 1978, Caste and Ecology in the Social Insects (with G. F. Oster) 1978, Genes, Mind and Culture (with C. J. Lumsden) 1981, Promethean Fire (with C. J. Lumsden) 1983, Biophilia 1984, Biodiversity (ed.) 1988, The Ants (with Bert Hölldobler) (Pulitzer Prize for Gen. Non-Fiction 1991) 1990, Success and Dominance in Ecosystems 1990, The Diversity of Life 1991, Naturalist 1994, In Search of Nature (with Laura Simonds Southworth) 1996, Journey to the Ants (with Bert Hölldobler) 1994, Consilience: The Unity of Knowledge 1998, Biological Diversity: The Oldest Human Heritage 1999, The Future of Life 2002, Pheidole in the New World: A Dominant, Hyperdiverse Ant Genus 2002, From So Simple a Beginning: Darwin's Four Great Books 2005, The Creation: An Appeal to Save Life on Earth 2006, Nature Revealed: Selected Writings 1949–2006 2006, The Superorganism: The Beauty, Elegance, and Strangeness of Insect Societies (with Bert Hölldobler) 2009; numerous articles on evolutionary biology, entomology and conservation. *Address:* Museum of Comparative Zoology, Harvard University, MCZ Room 408, Harvard University, 26 Oxford Street, Cambridge, MA 02138-2902 (office); 1010 Waltham Street, Lexington, MA 02421, USA (home). *Telephone:* (617) 495-2315 (office). *Fax:* (617) 495-1224 (office). *E-mail:* ewilson@oeb.harvard.edu (office). *Website:* www.mcz.harvard.edu/Departments/Entomology (office).

WILSON, Hon. Geoffrey Hazlitt, CVO, BA, FCA, FCMA; British accountant and business executive; b. 28 Dec. 1929, London; s. of Lord Moran and Dorothy Dufton; m. Barbara Jane Hebblethwaite 1955; two s. two d.; ed Eton Coll. and King's Coll., Cambridge; with English Electric Co. Ltd 1956–68, Deputy Comptroller 1967–68; Financial Controller (Overseas), General Electric Co. Ltd 1968–69; Financial Dir, Cables Div., Delta PLC 1969, Group Financial Dir 1972, Jt Man. Dir 1977, Dir 1977, Deputy Chief Exec. 1980, Chief Exec. 1981–88, Chair. 1982–94; Dir Blue Circle Industries PLC 1981–87, Drayton English & Int. Trust PLC 1978–95, Nat. Westminster Bank PLC (W Midlands and Wales Regional Bd) 1985–92 (Chair. 1990–92), Southern Electric PLC 1989–96 (Chair. 1993–96), Johnson Matthey PLC 1990–97 (Deputy Chair. 1994–97); Hon. Treas. mem. Admin. Council The Prince's and the Royal Jubilee Trusts 1979–89; Vice-Pres. Eng Employers' Fed. 1983–86, 1990–94, Deputy Pres. 1986–90; Vice-Chair. King's Coll., Cambridge Campaign Appeal 1994–97; Pres. British Fed. of Electrotechnical and Allied Mfrs' Asscns 1987–88; mem. Court, Worshipful Co. of Chartered Accountants in England and Wales 1982–95, Master 1988–89, Financial Repertoire Council 1990–93; mem. OStJ 1997; Hon. mem. The Hundred Group of Chartered Accountants (Chair. 1979–81). *Leisure interests:* family, reading, vintage cars, skiing.

WILSON, Georges; French actor and theatre and film director; b. 16 Oct. 1921, Champigny-sur-Marne; m. Nicole Mulon 1956; two s.; ed Centre dramatique de la rue Blanche, Paris; acted in two plays in Grenier-Hussenot Company 1947; entered Comédie de l'Ouest 1950; entered Théâtre Nat. Populaire (T.N.P.) 1952, played important roles in almost all the plays; Dir T.N.P. 1963–72; Chair. Interim Action Cttee British Film Authority 1979; several TV appearances; Chevalier, Légion d'honneur, Officier, Ordre nat. du Mérite, Commdr, Ordre des Arts et Lettres. *Films include:* Le Rouge et le noir 1954, Les Hussards 1955, Bonjour Toubib 1957, La jument verte 1959, Le Dialogue des Carmélites 1960, Terrain vague 1960, Le Caïd 1960, Il Federale 1961, Le Farceur 1961, Une aussi longue absence 1961, Tintin et le mystère de la Toison d'Or 1961, Les Sept péchés capitaux 1962, Il Disordine 1962, Leviathan 1962, Carillons sans joie 1962, Le Diable et les dix commandements 1962, The Longest Day 1962, Le Quattro giornate di Napoli 1962, Mandrin 1962, La Noia, 1963, Mélodie en sous-sol 1963, Chair de poule 1963, Dragées au poivre 1963, Lucky Joe 1964, Faites sauter la banque! 1964,, Un monde nouveau 1966, Lo Straniero 1967, C'era una volta 1967, Beatrice Cenci 1969, Max et les ferrailleurs 1970, Blanche 1971, L'Istruttoria è chiusa: dimentichi 1971, Il Generale dorme in piedi 1972, La Violenza: Quinto potere 1972, Non si sevizia un paperino 1972, E di Saul e dei sicari sulle vie di Damasco 1973, Sono stato io! 1973, The Three Musketeers 1973, Nous sommes tous en liberté provisoire 1973, L'Età della pace 1974, Le Mouton enragé 1974, La Gifle 1974, Ecco noi per esempio 1977, L'Apprenti salaud 1977, Tendre poulet 1978, Les Ringards 1978, Lady Oscar 1979, Au bout du bout du banc 1979, Cserepek 1980, Le Bar du téléphone 1980, Le Cheval d'orgueil 1980, Nudo di donna

1981, Asphalte 1981, Les Fruits de la passion 1981, L'honneur d'un capitaine 1982, Itinéraires bis 1983, Tango, l'exil de Gardel 1985, Gandahar 1988, La Passion de Bernadette 1989, La Vouivre (dir) 1989, Le Château de ma mère 1990, La Tribu 1991, Cache Cash 1994, Marquise 1997, Les Destinées sentimentales 2000, Je ne suis pas là pour être aimé 2005. *Television includes:* La Nuit des rois 1957, La Caméra explore le temps 1958, Une nuit orageuse 1959, Merlusse 1965, Sous le soleil de Satan 1971, Frédéric II 1972, Il Giovane Garibaldi 1974, La Dernière carte 1974, Les Jardins du roi 1974, Die Unfreiwilligen Reisen des Moritz August Benjowski 1975, Le Prix 1975, Les Rosenberg ne doivent pas mourir 1975, La Rôtisserie de la reine Pédauque 1975, Léopold le bien-aimé 1975, L'Autre rive 1976, Rossel et la commune de Paris 1977, La Lumière des justes 1979, Les Aiguilleurs 1980, L'Homme des rivages 1981, Frère Martin 1981, La Certosa di Parma 1981,Parole e sangue 1982, Emmenez-moi au théâtre: Un habit pour l'hiver 1982, Emmenez-moi au théâtre: Chêne et lapins angora 1982, L'Homme de la nuit 1983, Christmas Carol 1984, Quo Vadis? 1985, Entre chats et loups 1985, Sarah et le cri de la langouste 1985, Bonjour maître 1987, Un Siciliano in Sicilia 1987, L'Huissier 1991, Jeanne d'Arc au bûcher 1993, L'Affaire Dreyfus 1995, Viens jouer dans la cour des grands 1997, Jeanne et le loup 1998, From the Earth to the Moon 1998. *Plays directed include:* L'école des femmes, Le client du matin (Théâtre de l'Oeuvre), Un otage (Théâtre de France), La vie de Galilée, Lumières de Bohème, La folle de Chaillot, Le diable et le bon Dieu, Chêne et lapins angora, Les prodiges 1971, Turandot 1971, Long voyage vers la nuit 1973, Othello 1975, Un habit pour l'hiver 1979, Huis clos, K2 1983, L'Escalier 1985, Je ne suis Rappaport 1987, Météore (Dir, Actor) 1991, Les Dimanches de Monsieur Riley 1992, Show Bis 1994, Henry IV 1994, Le cerisaie 1999. *Address:* Moulin de Vilgris, 78120 Rambouillet, France (home).

WILSON, Jacqueline, DBE, OBE, FRSL; British writer; b. 17 Dec. 1945, Bath; d. of the late Harry Aitken and of Margaret Aitken (née Clibbons); m. William Millar Wilson 1965 (divorced 2004); one d.; ed Coombe Girls' School; journalist D. C. Thomsons 1963–65; teenage magazine Jackie named after her; Amb. Reading is Fundamental, UK 1998–; mem. Cttee Children's Writers and Illustrators Group, Soc. of Authors 1997–; Advisory mem. Panel Costa (fmrly Whitbread) Book Awards 1997–; Judge Rhône-Poulenc Prizes for Jr Science Books 1999, Orange Prize for Fiction 2006, Prince Maurice Award 2006; mem. Bd Children's Film and TV Foundation 2000–; Children's Laureate 2005–07; Hon. DLitt (Winchester) 2005, (Bath) 2005, (Roehampton) 2007; Hon. DEd (Kingston Univ.) 2006; Hon. LLD (Dundee) 2007; Oak Tree Award 1992, Sheffield Children's Book Award, WHSmith Children's Book of the Year 2002, BT Childline Award 2004, British Book Award for Services to Bookselling 2004. *Plays:* books adapted for the stage include Lottie Project 1999, Double Act 2003, Bad Girls 2004, Midnight 2005, Tracie Beaker Gets Real 2006, Suitcase Kid 2007, Secrets 2008. *Television:* novels Girls in Love, Girls Under Pressure, Girls Out Late and Girls in Tears adapted into 13-part TV series, Granada 2003; The Story of Tracy Beaker adapted into five series on BBC children's TV; The Illustrated Mum adapted for Channel 4 children's TV (two BAFTA Awards, one Emmy Award). *Publications include:* fiction: Hide and Seek 1972, Truth or Dare 1973, Snap 1974, Let's Pretend 1975, Making Hate 1977; juvenile fiction: Nobody's Perfect 1982, Waiting for the Sky to Fall 1983, The Other Side 1984, Amber 1986, The Power of the Shade 1987, Stevie Day Series 1987, This Girl 1988, Is There Anybody There? 1990, Deep Blue 1993, Take a Good Look 1990, The Story of Tracy Beaker 1991, The Suitcase Kid (Children's Book of the Year Award 1993) 1992, Video Rose 1992, The Mum-minder 1993, The Werepuppy 1993, The Bed and the Breakfast Star (The Young Telegraph/Fully Booked Award 1995) 1994, Mark Spark in the Dark 1994, Twin Trouble 1995, Glubbslyme 1995, Jimmy Jelly 1995, The Dinosaur's Packed Lunch 1995, Cliffhanger 1995, Double Act (Children's Book of the Year Award, Smarties Prize) 1995, My Brother Bernadette 1995, Werepuppy on Holiday 1995, Bad Girls 1996, Mr Cool 1996, Monster Story-teller 1997, The Lottie Project 1997, Girls in Love 1997, Connie and the Water Babies 1997, Buried Alive! 1998, Girls Under Pressure 1998, How to Survive Summer Camp 1998, The Illustrated Mum (Guardian Children's Book of the Year Award, Children's Book of the Year Award 1999) 1999, Girls Out Late 1999, Lizzie Zipmouth 1999, The Dare Game 2000, Vicky Angel 2000, The Cat Mummy 2001, Sleepovers 2001, Dustbin Baby 2001, Secrets 2002, Girls in Tears 2002, The Worry Website 2002, Lola Rose 2003, Midnight 2004, The Diamond Girls 2004, Clean Break 2005, Love Lessons 2005, Best Friends (Red House Children's Book Award) 2005, Candyfloss 2006, Starring Tracy Beaker 2006, Kiss 2007, My Sister Jodie 2008, Cookie 2008; other: Jacky Daydream (autobiog.) 2007. *Leisure interests:* reading, swimming, going to art galleries and films, shopping, dancing. *Address:* David Higham Associates, 5–8 Lower John Street, Golden Square, London, W1F 9HA, England (office). *Telephone:* (20) 7434-5900 (office). *Website:* www.jacquelinewilson.co.uk.

WILSON, Jean Donald, MD, FRCP; American endocrinologist and academic; *Professor of Internal Medicine and Charles Cameron Sprague Distinguished Chair in Biomedical Science, Southwestern Medical Center, University of Texas;* b. 26 Aug. 1932, Wellington, Tex.; s. of J. D. Wilson and Maggie E. Wilson (née Hill); ed Hillsboro Coll., Univ. of Texas at Austin and Univ. of Texas Southwestern Medical School, Dallas; Medical Intern and Asst Resident in Internal Medicine, Parkland Memorial Hosp. Dallas 1955–58; Clinical Assoc. Nat. Heart Inst. Bethesda, Md 1958–60; Instr. Univ. of Texas Health Science Center 1960–, Prof. of Internal Medicine 1968–, Charles Cameron Sprague Distinguished Chair in Biomedical Science; Established Investigator, American Heart Asscn 1960–65; Travelling Fellow, Royal Soc. of Medicine, Strangeways Research Lab. Cambridge 1970; mem. NAS, Inst. of Medicine of NAS, American Philosophical Soc., American Acad. of Arts and Sciences; Amory Prize, American Acad. of Arts and Sciences 1977, Henry Dale Medal, Soc. for Endocrinology 1991, Gregory Pincus Award, Worcester Foundation for Experimental Biology 1992, Fred Conrad Koch Award, The

Endocrine Soc. 1993, Kober Medal, Asscn of American Physicians 1999. *Publications:* more than 300 scientific articles in various medical journals. *Leisure interests:* birding, opera. *Address:* Division of Endocrinology and Metabolism, Department of Internal Medicine, University of Texas Southwestern Medical Center at Dallas, 5323 Harry Hines Boulevard, Dallas, TX 75390–8857, USA (office). *Telephone:* (214) 648-3469 (office). *Fax:* (214) 648-8917 (office). *E-mail:* jwils1@mednet.swmed.edu (office). *Website:* www.swmed.edu (office).

WILSON, Kenneth Geddes, PhD; American physicist and academic; *Hazel C. Youngberg Distinguished Professor, Ohio State University;* b. 8 June 1936, Waltham, Mass; s. of Edgar Bright Wilson, Jr and Emily Fisher Buckingham Wilson; m. Alison Brown 1982; ed Harvard Univ., Calif. Inst. of Tech.; Fellow, Harvard Univ. 1959–62, Ford Foundation Fellow 1962–63; joined Cornell Univ., Ithaca, NY 1963, Prof. 1970–88, James A. Weeks Chair in Physical Sciences 1974–88, Dir Center for Theory and Stimulation in Science and Eng (Cornell Theory Center) 1985–88; Hazel C. Youngberg Distinguished Prof., Ohio State Univ. 1988–; Co-Prin. Investigator Ohio's Project Discovery 1991–96; mem. NAS, American Acad. of Arts and Sciences, American Physical Soc.; Heinemann Prize 1973, Boltzmann Medal 1975, Wolf Prize 1980, Nobel Prize for Physics 1982. *Publications:* Redesigning Education 1994; articles in journals. *Address:* Department of Physics, Ohio State University, 191 W Woodruff Avenue, Columbus, OH 43210, USA (office). *Telephone:* (614) 292-8686 (office). *Fax:* (614) 292-3221 (office). *Website:* www.physics.ohio-state.edu (office).

WILSON, Linda S., PhD, FAAS; American chemist and fmr university administrator; *President Emerita, Radcliffe College;* b. (Linda Lee Smith), 10 Nov. 1936, Washington DC; d. of Fred M. Smith and Virginia T. Smith; m. 1st Malcolm C. Whatley 1957 (divorced); one d.; m. 2nd Paul A. Wilson 1970; one step-d.; ed Tulane Univ. and Univ. of Wisconsin; Asst Vice-Chancellor for Research, Washington Univ., St Louis, Mo. 1968–74, Assoc. Vice-Chancellor 1974–75; Assoc. Vice-Chancellor for Research, Univ. of Illinois, Urbana 1975–85, Assoc. Dean, Grad. Coll. 1978–85; Vice-Pres. for Research, Univ. of Michigan, Ann Arbor 1985–89; Pres. Radcliffe Coll., Cambridge, Mass. 1989–99, Pres. Emer. 1999–; Chair. Advisory Cttee Office of Science and Eng Personnel, Nat. Research Council 1990–96; mem. Council on Govt Relations 1971–77, Nat. Inst. of Health Advisory Council on Research Resources 1978–82, Nat. Comm. on Research 1978–80, NSF Dirs Advisory Council 1980–89, Govt-Univ.-Industry Research Roundtable (NAS) 1984–88, Inst. of Medicine Council 1986–89, Inst. of Medicine Cttee on Govt-Industry Collaboration in Research and Educ. 1988–89, Inst. of Medicine Cttee on NIH Priority-Setting 1998–99; mem. Bd of Dirs AAAS 1984–88, Mich. Materials Processing Inst. 1986–89, Mich. Biotechnology Inst. 1986–89, Inst. of Medicine, ACS, AAAS; mem. Bd of Overseers Museum of Science, Boston 1992–2001; Trustee Mass. Gen. Hosp. 1992–99 (Hon. Trustee 1999–2002), Cttee on Econ. Devt 1995–; mem. Bd of Dirs Citizens Financial Group 1996–99, Inacom Corpn 1997–2003, ValueLine Inc. 1998–2000, Myriad Genetics Inc. 1999–, Internet Corpn for Assigned Names and Numbers (ICANN) 1998–2003; Friends of DaPonte String Quartet 2002–; mem. Bd of Admins (Trustee) Tulane Univ. 2002–; elected to Inst. of Medicine 1983; Dr hc (Tulane Univ.), (Univ. of Maryland); Distinguished Contribution to Research Admin. Award, Soc. of Research Admins, Distinguished Service Award, Univ. of Illinois Coll. of Medicine, Centennial Award for Outstanding Accomplishments, Newcomb Coll., Distinguished Alumni Award, Univ. of Wisconsin 1997, Endowed Chair. for Dir of Radcliffe Public Policy Center 1999, Radcliffe Medal 1999. *Publications:* seven book chapters, 10 journal articles, six maj. reports, four commissioned studies, 12 papers on chem., science policy and research policy. *Leisure interests:* cello, reading, music. *Address:* 47 Keene Neck Road, Bremen, ME 04551-3224, USA (office). *Telephone:* (207) 529-2979 (office). *Fax:* (207) 529-2981 (office).

WILSON, Lynton Ronald, OC, BA, MA; Canadian business executive; *Chairman, CAE Inc.;* b. 3 April 1940, Port Colborne, Ont.; s. of Ronald Alfred Wilson and Blanche Evelyn Matthews; m. Brenda Jean Black; two d. one s.; ed Port Colborne High School, McMaster Univ., Cornell Univ., USA; Foreign Service Officer, Dept of Trade and Commerce 1962; Asst Commercial Sec., Embassy in Vienna 1963–65; Second Sec., Embassy in Tokyo 1967–68; Corp. Economist and Dir of Econ. Research, John Labatt Ltd 1969–71; Coordinator, Industrial R & D Policy, Ministry of State, Science and Tech. 1972; Strategic Planning and Devt Officer, MacMillan Bloedel Ltd 1973–74, Vice-Pres. and Dir, MacMillan Bloedel Enterprises Inc. 1974–77; Exec. Dir, Policy and Priorities, Ministry of Industry and Tourism, Govt of Ont. 1977–78, Deputy Minister 1978–81; Pres. and CEO Redpath Industries Ltd, Toronto 1981–88, Chair. Bd 1988–89; Man. Dir N America, Tate & Lyle PLC 1986–89; Vice-Chair. Bank of Nova Scotia, Toronto 1989–90; Pres. and COO BCE Inc., Montreal 1990–92, Pres. and CEO 1992–93, Chair., Pres. and CEO 1993–96, Chair. and CEO 1996–98, Chair. Bd Dirs 1998–2000; Chair. Bell Canada, CAE Inc. 1999–, Nortel Networks Corpn 2001–; Chair. Govt's Competition Policy Review Panel 2007–08; Founding Chair. Historica Foundation of Canada; Dir BCE Mobile Communications Inc., Bell Canada Int. Inc., Northern Telecom Ltd, Bell-Northern Research Ltd, Teleglobe Inc., Chrysler Canada Ltd, Chrysler Corpn, Tate & Lyle PLC, UK, Stelco Inc., CD Howe Inst., Canadian Inst. for Advanced Research; mem. Business Council on Nat. Issues (Policy Cttee), Trilateral Comm., Int. Council JP Morgan & Co., New York, Bd of Trustees Montreal Museum of Fine Arts Foundation; Gov. Olympic Trust of Canada, McGill Univ.; six hon. degrees including Dr hc (Montreal) 1995, Hon. LLD (McMaster) 1995, (Cape Breton) 1998, (Mount Allison) 2000. *Address:* CAE Inc., 8585 Côte de Liesse, Saint-Laurent, Montreal, Quebec H4T 1G6 (office); 2038 Lakeshore Road East, Oakville, Ont. L6J 1M3, Canada (home). *Telephone:* (514) 341-6780 (office). *Fax:* (514) 341-7699 (office). *Website:* www.cae.ca (office).

WILSON, Hon. Margaret, LLB, M.jur; New Zealand politician; *Speaker, House of Representatives;* b. 20 May 1947, Gisborne; ed St Dominic's Coll., Northcote, Morrinsville Coll., Univ. of Auckland; sec. for Legal Employers Union 1970–1971; law clerk and solicitor, Peter Jenkins, barrister and solicitor in Auckland 1970–72; taught at Univ. of Auckland; Founder-mem. Industrial Relations Soc. 1973; Acting Ed. Recent Law 1974; Founding Ed. New Zealand Journal of Industrial Relations 1976–77, mem. Editorial Bd 1994–; Exec. mem., Vice-Chair. and Chair. Auckland Br., Asscn of Univ. Teachers 1976–84; Founder-mem. and Vice-Pres. Auckland Women Lawyers' Asscn 1984, Life mem. 1985–; Convenor, Govt Working Party on Equal Pay and Equal Opportunities 1988; Dir Reserve Bank of New Zealand 1985–89; Chief Political Adviser and Head of Prime Minister's Office 1987–89; Chair. Nat. Advisory Council on Employment of Women 1987–91; Chair. TV3 News Ltd 1988–89; Law Commr of the Law Comm. 1988–89; apptd Foundation Dean and Prof. of Law, Univ. of Waikato 1990; mem. Advisory Cttee to establish the Ministry of Women's Affairs 1985, Advisory Group on restructuring of the Ministry of Justice 1995, team to review the Crown Forestry Rental Trust 1995, Judicial Working Group on Gender Equality 1995–97; Chief Govt Law Officer; Attorney-Gen. 1999–2005; Minister of Labour 1999–2004; Minister in Charge of Treaty of Waitangi Negotiations 1999–2005; Assoc. Minister of Justice 1999–2004, Assoc. Minister of State Services 2000–02; Minister responsible for the Law Comm. 2001–02; Minister for Courts 2002–03, Assoc. Minister 2003–04; Minister of Commerce 2004; Speaker of House of Reps 2005–; Pres. NZ Labour Party 1984–87; Hon. LLD (Waikato) 2004. *Address:* Parliament Buildings, Wellington, New Zealand (office). *Telephone:* (4) 471-9999 (office). *Fax:* (4) 472-2055 (office). *Website:* www.parliament.govt.nz (office).

WILSON, Hon. Michael, PC, OC; Canadian business executive, diplomatist and fmr politician; *Ambassador to USA;* b. 4 Nov. 1937, Toronto; ed Univ. of Toronto, LSE; MP for Etobicoke Centre 1979–93, Minister of Finance 1984–91, Minister of Industry, Science and Tech. and Minister for Int. Trade –1993, represented Canada at IMF, IBRD, OECD, GATT and G-7 Ministers meetings; Vice Chair. RBC Dominion Securities and institutional asset management business 1993; Chair. UBS Canada 2001–06; Amb. to USA 2006–; mem. Bd of Dirs BP plc 1998–2006; Chair. Council for Public-Private Partnerships 2001–06, Canadian Coalition for Good Governance; Chancellor Trinity Coll. (Univ. of Toronto) 2003–06; Dr hc (Univ. of Toronto), (York Univ.). *Address:* Embassy of Canada, 501 Pennsylvania Avenue, NW, Washington, DC 20001, USA (office). *Telephone:* (202) 682-1740 (home). *Fax:* (202) 682-7726 (office). *E-mail:* webmaster@canadianembassy.org (office). *Website:* www.canadianembassy.org (office).

WILSON, Nigel Guy, MA, FBA; British academic; b. 23 July 1935, London; s. of Noel Wilson and Joan L. Wilson; m. Hanneke Marion Wirtjes 1996; ed Univ. Coll. School and Corpus Christi Coll., Oxford; Lecturer, Merton Coll., Oxford 1957–62; Fellow and Tutor in Classics, Lincoln Coll., Oxford 1962–2002; James P. R. Lyell Reader in Bibliography 2003; Hon. LittD (Uppsala) 2001; Gordon Duff Prize 1968, Premio Anassilaos 1999. *Publications:* Scribes and Scholars (with L. D. Reynolds) (third edn) 1991, An Anthology of Byzantine Prose 1971, Medieval Greek Bookhands 1973, St Basil on the Value of Greek Literature 1975, Scholia in Aristophanis Acharnenses 1975, Menander Rhetor (with D. A. Russell) 1981, Scholars of Byzantium 1983, Oxford Classical Text of Sophocles (with Sir Hugh Lloyd-Jones) 1990, From Byzantium to Italy 1992, Photius: the Bibliotheca 1994, Aelian: Historical Miscellany 1997, Pietro Bembo: Oratio pro litteris graecis 2003, Oxford Classical Text of Aristophanes 2007, Aristophanea 2007. *Leisure interests:* bridge, real tennis, wine. *Address:* Lincoln College, Oxford, OX1 3DR, England (office). *Fax:* (1865) 279802 (office).

WILSON, Peter Barton (Pete), LLB, JD; American fmr politician and lawyer; *Distinguished Visiting Fellow, Hoover Institution, Stanford University;* b. 23 Aug. 1933, Lake Forest, Ill.; s. of James Boone Wilson and Margaret (née Callahan) Wilson; m. 1st Betty Robertson (divorced); m. 2nd Gayle Edlund Graham 1983; ed Yale Univ., Univ. of Calif., Berkeley; admitted to Calif. Bar; Asst Exec. Dir Republican Asscn, San Diego Co. 1963–64; Exec. Dir San Diego Co. Republican Cen. Comm. 1964–65; legal service officer, Calif. State Republican Cen. Comm. 1965; mem. Calif. Ass. 1967–71; Mayor of San Diego 1971–83; Senator from Calif. 1983–91; Gov. of Calif. 1991–99; Man. Dir Pacific Capital Group, Calif. 1999–; Distinguished Visiting Fellow, Hoover Inst., Stanford Univ. 1999–; Chair. campaign for Republican Gov. Arnold Schwarzenegger 2003; mem. Presidential Advisory Cttee on Environmental Quality, Task Force Land Use and Urban Growth Policy. *Address:* c/o Hoover Institution, Stanford University, Stanford, CA 94305-6010, USA. *Telephone:* (650) 723-1754. *Fax:* (650) 723-1687. *Website:* www.hoover.org.

WILSON, Peter L., A.A. Diploma; Australian architect; b. 27 Sept. 1950, Melbourne; s. of the late Jack Wilson and of Betty Wilson; m. Julia B. Bolles; one s. one d.; ed Univ. of Melbourne, Architectural Asscn School of Architecture, London; Asst Teacher, Architectural Asscn School of Architecture, London 1974–75, Intermediate Unit Master 1976–79, Diploma Unit Master 1980–88; f. Wilson Partnership, London (with Julia Bolles-Wilson) 1980, Architekturbüro Bolles + Wilson (now Bolles+Wilson GmbH & Co), Münster 1988; Visiting Prof. Kunsthochschule Weisensee, Berlin 1996–98, Accademia di Architettura, Mendrisio, Switzerland 2006–07; winner of more than 20 int. architectural competitions. *Buildings include:* Suzuki House, Tokyo 1993, New City Library, Münster 1993, WLV Office Bldg, Münster 1993, Quay Landscape, Rotterdam 1998, New Luxor Theatre, Rotterdam 2001, BEIC Library and Media Centre, Milan 2001–06, Nord LB Bank, Cathedral Square, Magdeburg, Germany 2002, National Library, Luxembourg 2003–04, Falkenried Urban Quartier, Hamburg 1999–2004. *Publications:* El Croquis No 105 – Bolles and Wilson 1995–2001, Bolles and Wilson

Monograph Electra 2004. *Address:* Bolles+Wilson GmbH & Co., KG, Hafenweg 16, 48155 Münster, Germany (office). *Telephone:* (251) 482720 (office); (251) 43888 (home). *Fax:* (251) 4827224 (office). *E-mail:* info@bolles-wilson.com (office). *Website:* www.bolles-wilson.com (office).

WILSON, (Robert) Gordon, BL, LLD; Scottish politician and solicitor (retd); b. 16 April 1938, Glasgow, Scotland; s. of Robert George Wilson and Robina Wilson; m. Edith Hassall 1965; two d.; ed Douglas High School and Edin. Univ.; Asst Nat. Sec. Scottish Nat. Party 1963–64, Nat. Sec. 1964–71, Exec. Vice-Chair. 1972–73, Sr Vice-Chair. 1973–74, Chair. 1979–90, Vice-Pres. 1992–; MP for Dundee E 1974–87; Party Spokesman on Oil and Energy 1974–87, on Energy 1992–93, on Treasury 1993–94; Jt Spokesman on Devolution 1976–79; Rector, Univ. of Dundee 1983–86; Chair. Marriage Counselling (Tayside) 1989–92; Gov. Dundee Inst. of Tech.; Court mem. Univ. of Abertay Dundee 1991–96; mem. Church and Nation Cttee of Church of Scotland 2000–03, Bd Dundee Age Concern 2001–05; Clerk, St Aidan's Church Congregational Bd 2003–05, (now New Kirk 2005–06). *Leisure interests:* photography, reading, sailing. *Address:* 48 Monifieth Road, Dundee, DD5 2RX, Scotland (home). *E-mail:* gordonwilson10@blueyonder.co.uk.

WILSON, Robert M.; American theatre and opera director and artist; b. 4 Oct. 1941, Waco, Tex.; s. of D. M. Wilson and Velma Loree Wilson (née Hamilton); ed Univ. of Tex., Pratt Inst.; began creating innovative theatre in New York in the 1960s; worked mainly in Europe in the 1980s and 1990s, directing original works as well as traditional opera and theatre; Guggenheim Fellow 1971, 1980; Trustee Nat. Inst. of Music Theatre; mem. Dramatists Guild, Soc. des Auteurs et Compositeurs Dramatiques, Soc. of Stage Dirs. and Choreographers, PEN American Center, American Acad. of Arts and Letters; hon. Dir American Repertory Theatre; has given lectures and workshops at numerous insts.; Dr. hc Calif. Coll. of Arts and Letters, Pratt Inst. New York City; numerous awards and decorations including the Maharam Award for Best Set Design 1975, Lumen Award 1977, First Prize San Sebastian Film and Video Festival 1984, Picasso Award 1986, Inst. Skowhegan Medal for drawing 1987, Grand Prix Biennale, Barcelona Festival of Cinema Art 1989, Germna Theatre Critics Award 1990, Brandeis Univ. Poses Creative Arts Award 1991, Venice Biennale Golden Lion Award for Sculpture 1993, Dorothy and Lillian Gish Prize 1996, Tadeusz Kantor Prize 1997, Harvard Excellence in Design Award 1998, Pushkin Prize 1999; Most Outstanding Theater Designer of the Seventies, U.S. Inst. of Theater Tech. 1977. *Dance created and choreographed:* Snow on the Mesa (for Martha Graham Dance Co.) 1995. *Stage appearances include:* Deafman Glance 1970, The Life and Times of Joseph Stalin (Dir) 1974, A Letter for Queen Victoria 1974, Einstein on the Beach 1976, 1984, Death, Destruction and Detroit 1979, The Golden Windows 1982, 1985, The Civil Wars 1983–85, Hamletmachine 1986, Doktor Faustus 1989, The Black Rider 1990, King Lear 1990, The Magic Flute 1991, Alice 1993, Der Mond in Gras 1994, The Death of Molière 1994, Hamlet: A Monologue 1995, Prometeo 1997, Saints and Singing 1997, Monsters of Grace 1998, Dream Play 1998, Scourge of Hyacinths 1999, The Days Before 1999, Hot Waters 2000, Relative Light 2000. *Plays directed and designed include:* Deafman Glance 1970, Einstein on the Beach 1976, Death, Destruction and Detroit 1979, The Golden Windows 1982, the CIVIL warS 1983–85, Hamletmachine 1986, Doktor Faustus 1989, The Black Rider 1990, The Magic Flute 1991, Doktor Faustus Lights the Lights 1992, Alice 1992, Madame Butterfly 1993, Hanjo 1994, Hamlet: A Monologue 1995, Time Rocker 1996, Lady from the Sea 1998, Das Rheingold 2000, POEtry 2000, Woyzeck 2001, Three Penny Opera, Spoleto Festival, Italy 2008. *Films include:* Overture for a Deafman, Monsters of Grace 1998. *Videos include:* The Spaceman 1976, 1984, Video 50 1978, Stations 1982, La Femme à la Cafétière 1989, Mr. Bojangles' Memory 1991, La Mort de Molière 1994. *Publications include:* The King of Spain 1970, Einstein on the Beach: An Opera in Four Acts (with Philip Glass q.v.) 1976, A Letter for Queen Victoria 1977, Death, Destruction and Detroit 1979, the CIVIL warS 1985, Mr. Bojangles' Memory 1991, RW Notebook 1999. *Leisure interest:* collecting fine art and design. *Address:* RW Work Ltd, 155 Wooster Street, Suite 4F, New York, NY 10012, USA. *Telephone:* (212) 253-7484. *Fax:* (212) 253-7485 (office). *Website:* www.robertwilson.com (office).

WILSON, Sir Robert Peter, KCMG, FRSA, CIMgt; British business executive; *Chairman, BG Group plc;* b. 2 Sept. 1943, Carshalton; s. of the late Alfred Wilson and Dorothy Wilson (née Mathews); m. Shirley Elisabeth Robson 1975; one s. one d.; ed Epsom Coll., Sussex Univ., Harvard Business School; Asst Economist Dunlop Ltd 1966–67; Economist Mobil Oil Co. Ltd 1967–70; with Rio Tinto PLC (fmrly RTZ Corpn PLC) starting 1970, Man. Dir AM & S Europe 1979–82, Project Dir RTZ Devt Enterprise 1982–83, Head of Planning and Devt RTZ Corpn PLC 1984–86, Dir 1987–2003, Chief Exec. 1991–97, Chair. 1997–2003; Dir Rio Tinto Ltd (fmrly CRA Ltd) 1990–2003, Deputy Chair. 1995–98, Chair. 1999–2003; Chair. BG Group 2003–; fmr Dir BP PLC, Dir The Boots Co. PLC 1991–98; Dir Diageo PLC, GSK; Dir The Economist Group Ltd 2002–, Chair. 2003–; Trustee Camborne School of Mines 1993–99; Hon. DSc (Exeter) 1993, (Sussex) 2004; Hon. LLD (Dundee) 2001. *Leisure interests:* theatre, opera. *Address:* BG Group plc, 100 Thames Valley Park Drive, Reading, RG6 1PT, England (office). *Telephone:* (20) 7707-4878 (office). *Fax:* (20) 7707-4858 (office). *Website:* www.bg-group.com (office).

WILSON, Robert Woodrow, PhD; American radio astronomer; *Senior Scientist, Harvard-Smithsonian Center for Astrophysics;* b. 10 Jan. 1936, Houston; s. of Ralph Woodrow Wilson and Fannie May (née Willis) Wilson; m. Elizabeth Rhoads Sawin 1958; two s. one d.; ed Rice Univ., Calif. Inst. of Tech.; mem. of Technical Staff, AT&T Bell Labs, Holmdel, NJ 1963–76, Head of Radio Physics Research Dept 1976–94; Sr Scientist, Harvard-Smithsonian Center for Astrophysics 1994–; mem. NAS, American Astronomical Soc., American Physical Soc., Int. Astronomical Union; Henry Draper Award 1977, Herschel Award 1977, Nobel Prize for Physics 1978. *Publications:* numerous articles in scientific journals. *Address:* Harvard-Smithsonian Center for Astrophysics, 60 Garden Street, #42, Cambridge, MA 02138 (office); 9 Valley Point Drive, Holmdel, NJ 07733, USA (home). *Telephone:* (617) 496-7744 (office); (201) 671-7807 (home). *Fax:* (617) 496-7554 (office). *E-mail:* rwilson@cfa.harvard.edu (office). *Website:* cfa-www.harvard.edu (office).

WILSON, Sandy (see Wilson, Alexander Galbraith).

WILSON, Thomas Joseph, BSc, MSc; American business executive; *Chairman, President and CEO, The Allstate Corporation;* b. St Clair Shores, Mich.; m. Jill Wilson (neé Garling); three c.; ed Univ. of Michigan, J.L. Kellogg Grad. School of Man., Northwestern Univ.; held various financial positions at Amoco Corpn 1980–86; Man. Dir Mergers and Acquisitions, Dean Witter Reynolds 1986–93; Vice-Pres., Strategy and Analysis, Sears, Roebuck and Co. 1993–95; Chief Financial Officer Allstate Corpn 1995–98, Chair. and Pres. Allstate Financial 1999–2002, Pres. Allstate Protection 2002–06, Pres. and COO 2005–06, Pres. and CEO 2007–, Chair. 2008–, mem. Bd of Dirs; mem. Bd Dirs Fed. Reserve Bank of Chicago; mem. Bd Rush Univ. Medical Center, Museum of Science and Industry, Catalyst; mem. Young Presidents' Org., Financial Services Forum, The Business Roundtable, Civic Cttee of Commercial Club of Chicago; CFO Magazine's Excellence Award 1998. *Address:* The Allstate Corpn, 2775 Sanders Road, Northbrook, IL 60062-6127, USA (office). *Telephone:* (847) 402-5000 (office). *Fax:* (847) 326-7519 (office). *E-mail:* directors@allstate.com (office). *Website:* www.allstate.com (office).

WILSON, Trevor Gordon, MA, DPhil, FRHistS, FAHA; New Zealand academic; *Professor Emeritus and Honorary Visiting Research Fellow, School of History and Politics, University of Adelaide;* b. 24 Dec. 1928, Auckland; s. of the late Gordon Wilson and Winifred Wilson; m. Jane Verney 1957; two d.; ed Mount Albert Grammar School, Univs. of Auckland and Oxford; Asst Lecturer in History Canterbury Univ. 1952, Auckland Univ. 1953–55; Research Asst in Govt Univ. of Manchester 1957–59; Lecturer then Sr Lecturer in History, Univ. of Adelaide 1960–67, Prof. 1968–, now Prof. Emer. and Hon. Visiting Research Fellow; Commonwealth Fellow, St John's Coll., Cambridge 1972; Visiting Fellow, Magdalen Coll., Oxford 1987; Drinko Distinguished Visiting Prof., Marshall Univ., W Virginia Fall 1989; Nuffield Dominion Travelling Fellowship 1964–65; Univ. of NZ Overseas Travelling Scholarship 1953; Gilbert Campion Prize (jt winner) 1960, Higby Prize 1965, Adelaide Festival of Arts Literature Award 1988. *Publications:* The Downfall of the Liberal Party (1914–35) 1966, The Political Diaries of C. P. Scott 1911–28 1970, The Myriad Faces of War: Britain and the Great War 1914–18 1986, Command on the Western Front: The Military Career of Sir Henry Rawlinson 1914–1918 (with Robin Prior) 1992, Passchendaele: the Untold Story (with Robin Prior) 1996, The First World War (Cassell History of Warfare) (with Robin Prior) 1999. *Leisure interests:* listening to jazz, watching musical movies, table tennis. *Address:* Department of History and Politics, Room 521, Napier Building, University of Adelaide, North Terrace, S. Australia 5005, Australia. *Telephone:* (8) 8303-5633 (office). *Fax:* (8) 8303-3443 (office). *E-mail:* tjwilson@senet.com.au (home). *Website:* www.arts.adelaide.edu.au/historypolitics (office).

WILSON-JOHNSON, David Robert, BA, FRAM; British baritone; b. 16 Nov. 1950, Northampton; s. of Harry K. Johnson and Sylvia C. Wilson; ed Wellingborough School, Northants., British Inst. of Florence, St Catharine's Coll., Cambridge and Royal Acad. of Music; debut at Royal Opera House, Covent Garden in We Come to the River 1976; has since appeared in Billy Budd, L'Enfant et les Sortilèges, Le Rossignol, Les Noces, Boris Godunov, Die Zauberflöte, Turandot, Werther, Madame Butterfly; Wigmore Hall recital début 1977; BBC Promenade Concert debut 1981; appeared at Edin. Festival 1976, Glyndebourne Festival 1980 and at festivals in Bath, Bergen, Berlin, Geneva, Graz, Netherlands, Hong Kong, Jerusalem, Orange, Paris and Vienna; Paris Opéra debut in Die Meistersinger 1989; played St Francis of Assisi (title role) in Olivier Messiaen's 80th birthday celebrations 1988; American debut in Paulus (title role) 1990; ENO debut (in Billy Budd) 1991, Netherlands Opera debut in Birtwistle's Punch and Judy 1993; Founder Dir Ferrandou Summer Singing School 1985–; Gulbenkian Fellowship 1978–81; Nat. Fed. of Music Soc. Award 1977, Evening Standard Award for Opera 1989. *Films include:* A Midsummer Marriage 1988. *Recordings include:* Schubert's Winterreise, Mozart Masses from King's College, Cambridge, Haydn's Nelson Mass, Schoenberg's Ode to Napoleon, King Priam, Punch and Judy, La Traviata, Lucrezia Borgia and Michael Berkeley's Or Shall We Die?, Belshazzar's Feast, L'Enfance du Christ, The Kingdom (Elgar), The Ice Break (Tippett), Odes (Purcell), Caractacus (Elgar), Black Pentecost (Maxwell Davies), Mass in B Minor (Bach) Peter Grimes, Damnation of Faust. *Leisure interests:* swimming, slimming, gardening and growing walnuts in the Dordogne. *Address:* Prinsengracht 455, 1016 HN Amsterdam, Netherlands (home); 28 Englefield Road, London, N1 4ET, England. *Telephone:* (20) 7254-0941 (London); 5-65-10-94-11 (France); (20) 7728104 (home). *E-mail:* ferrandou@aol.com (office); jumbowj@aol.com (home). *Website:* www.gmn.com (office).

WILSON OF DINTON, Richard Thomas James Wilson, Baron (Life Peer), cr. 2003, of Dinton in the County of Buckinghamshire, GCB, LLM; British civil servant; *Master, Emmanuel College Cambridge;* b. 11 Oct. 1942; s. of the late Richard Ridley Wilson and Frieda Bell Wilson (née Finlay); m. Caroline Margaret Lee 1972; one s. one d.; ed Radley Coll. and Cambridge Univ.; called to the Bar 1965; Asst Prin. Board of Trade 1966, Pvt. Sec. to Minister of State, Board of Trade 1969–71, Prin. Cabinet Office 1971–73, Dept of Energy 1974, Asst Sec. Dept of Energy 1977–82, UnderSec. 1982, Prin. Establishment and Finance Officer 1982–86; on loan to Cabinet Office Man. and Personnel Office 1986–87, Deputy Sec. Cabinet Office 1987–90; Deputy Sec. (Industry) HM Treasury 1990–92; Perm. Sec. Dept of Environment 1992–94; Perm. Under-Sec. of State, Home Office 1994–97; Cabinet Sec. and Head of the Home Civil

Service 1997–2002; Master Emmanuel Coll. Cambridge 2002–. *Address:* The Master's Lodge, Emmanuel College, St Andrew's Street, Cambridge, CB2 3AP, England (office). *Telephone:* (1223) 334248 (office). *Fax:* (1223) 331867 (office). *E-mail:* master@emma.cam.ac.uk (office). *Website:* www.emma.cam .ac.uk (office).

WILSON OF TILLYORN, Baron (Life Peer), cr. 1992, of Finzean in the District of Kincardine and Deeside and of Fanling in Hong Kong; **David Clive Wilson,** KT, GCMG, PhD, FRSE; British diplomatist and public servant; *Master, Peterhouse, Cambridge;* b. 14 Feb. 1935, Alloa, Scotland; s. of Rev. William Skinner Wilson and Enid Wilson; m. Natasha Helen Mary Alexander 1967; two s.; ed Glenalmond and Keble Coll., Oxford; nat. service, The Black Watch 1953–55; entered Foreign Service 1958, Third Sec., Vientiane 1959–60, Second then First Sec., Peking 1963–65, FCO 1965–68 (resgnd 1968, rejoined Diplomatic Service 1972), Cabinet Office 1974–77, Political Adviser, Hong Kong 1977–81, Head S. European Dept, FCO 1981–84, Asst Under-Sec. of State 1984–87; Gov. and Commdr-in-Chief of Hong Kong 1987–92; Chancellor, Univ. of Aberdeen 1997–; Vice-Pres. Royal Scottish Geographical Soc. 1996–; Language Student, Hong Kong 1960–62; Ed. China Quarterly 1968–74; Visiting Scholar, Columbia Univ., New York 1972; Chair. Scottish Hydro-Electric PLC 1993–2000 (Scottish and Southern Energy PLC 1998–2000); mem. Bd of Govs. SOAS 1992–97; mem. Bd British Council 1993–2002 (Chair. Scottish Cttee 1993–2002); Chancellor's Assessor, Univ. of Aberdeen 1993–96; Chair. Council, Glenalmond Coll. 2000–05, Scottish Peers' Asscn 2000–02; Dir Martin Currie Pacific Trust 1993–2003; mem. Advisory Cttee on Business Appointments 2000–; Pres. Bhutan Soc. of the UK 1993–, Hong Kong Asscn 1994–, Hong Kong Soc. 1994–; Registrar of the Most Distinguished Order of St Michael and St George 2001–; Chair. Trustees Nat. Museums of Scotland 2002–06; Hon. Fellow, Keble Coll. Oxford; Hon. Burger of Guild of City of Aberdeen 2003; Hon. LLD (Aberdeen) 1990, (Chinese Univ., Hong Kong) 1996; Hon. DLitt (Sydney) 1991, (Abertay Dundee) 1994, (Univ. of Hong Kong) 2006. *Leisure interests:* mountaineering, reading, theatre. *Address:* The Master's Lodge, Peterhouse, Cambridge, CB2 1QY (home); House of Lords, Westminster, London, SW1A 0PW, England.

WIN, Aung, BSc, PhD; Myanma politician and diplomatist; b. 28 Feb. 1944, Dawei; m. Daw San Yone; two s. one d.; ed Univ. of Yangon; served as Commdr, Staff Officer in Armed Forces and Ministry of Defence 1965–83, Officer in Prime Minister's Office 1983–84; with Myanmar Embassy, Vientiane, Lao People's Democratic Repub. 1986–88, Singapore 1988–90; Amb. to FRG 1990–96, to Belgium, Netherlands and Austria and to UK 1996–98, to Sweden 1997, to Norway 1998; Perm. Rep. to UN, Vienna, IAEA, UNIDO; Chief of Mission to European Comm.; Minister of Foreign Affairs 1998–2004; currently serving jail-term in Insein prison; Naing Ngan Daw Sit Smu Htan Tazeik, Pyi Thu Wun Htan Gaung Tazeik. *Publications include:* Nation of Gold; numerous articles in magazines.

WINBERG, (Sven) Håkan, LLB; Swedish politician and lawyer; b. 30 July 1931, Ånge; s. of Sven Winberg and Sally Angman; m. Ulla Greta Petersson; Justice, Court of Appeal; mem. Parl. 1971–82; mem. Exec. Swedish Moderate Party 1972–, mem. Steering Cttee 1975–; mem. Press Assistance Bd 1971–79, Bd of Council for Prevention of Crime 1974–79, Co. Boundaries Cttee 1970–74, Cttee of Inquiry into the Press 1972–75, New Labour Laws Cttee 1976–78, Nat. Police Bd 1977–79, Nordic Council 1977–82; County Councillor 1974–79; Minister of Justice 1979–81; Pres. Court of Appeal, Sundsvall 1982–; mem. Election Review Cttee of the Riksdag 1983–; mem. Parl. Comm. for Investigation into the murder of Prime Minister Olof Palme 1987–88, new Comm. for same investigation 1994; mem. Security Police Cttee 1989–, Court of Law Cttee 1990–. *Leisure interest:* skiing.

WINBLAD, Ann L., BA, MA, PhD; American investment company executive; *Managing Director, Hummer Winblad Venture Partners;* b. Minn.; ed Univ. of St Thomas, St Paul, Minn.; began career as systems programmer with San Francisco Fed. Reserve Bank; co-f. Open Systems Inc. 1976, sold co. 1983; Co-founder and Man. Dir Hummer Winblad Venture Partners 1989–; Co-Chair. SDForum; serves as adviser to many entrepreneurial orgs; mem. Bd of Trustees Univ. of St Thomas; Hon. LLD (Univ. of St Thomas). *Publication:* Object-Oriented Software (co-author) 1990; numerous articles in industry journals. *Address:* Hummer Winblad Venture Partners, One Lombard Street, Suite 300, San Francisco, CA 94111, USA (office). *Telephone:* (415) 979-9600 (office). *Fax:* (415) 979-9601 (office). *E-mail:* awinblad@humwin.com (office). *Website:* www.humwin.com (office).

WINCH, Donald Norman, PhD, FBA, FRHistS; British academic; *Research Professor Emeritus, University of Sussex;* b. 15 April 1935, London; s. of Sidney Winch and Iris Winch; m. Doreen Lidster 1983; ed Sutton Grammar School, London School of Econs., Princeton Univ.; Visiting Lecturer, Univ. of California 1959–60; Lecturer in Econs., Univ. of Edin. 1960–63; Univ. of Sussex 1963–66, Reader 1966–69, Prof. History of Econs 1969–, now Research Prof. Emer., Dean School of Social Sciences 1968–74, Pro-Vice-Chancellor (Arts and Social Studies) 1986–89; Vice-Pres. British Acad. 1993–94; Visiting Fellow, School of Social Science, Inst. of Advanced Study, Princeton 1974–75; King's Coll., Cambridge 1983, History of Ideas Unit, ANU 1983, St Catharine's Coll., Cambridge 1989, All Souls Coll., Oxford 1994; Visiting Prof., Tulane Univ. 1984; Carlyle Lecturer, Univ. of Oxford 1995, Publr Sec., Royal Econ. Soc. 1971–; Review Ed. The Economic Journal 1976–83; Hon. DLit (Sussex) 2005. *Publications:* Classical Political Economy & Colonies 1965, James Mill, Selected Economic Writings 1966, Economics and Policy 1969, The Economic Advisory Council 1930–39 (with S. K. Howson) 1976, Adam Smith's Politics 1978, That Noble Science of Politics (with S. Collini and J. W. Burrow) 1983, Malthus 1987, Riches and Poverty 1996, Wealth and Life 2009. *Leisure interest:* gardening. *Address:* Arts B, University of Sussex, Brighton, BN1 9QN, England (office). *Telephone:* (1273) 678634 (office); (1273) 400635

(home). *E-mail:* d.winch@sussex.ac.uk (office). *Website:* www .economistspapers.org.uk (office).

WINCKLER, Georg; Austrian university rector and academic; *Professor of Economics, University of Vienna;* b. 27 Sept. 1943, Ostrava, Czechoslovakia; m.; two d.; ed Princeton Univ., USA, Univ. of Vienna; Prof. of Econs, Univ. of Vienna 1978–, Univ. Rector 1999–; with Research Dept IMF 1990–91; Visiting Prof. of Econs, Georgetown Univ., USA 1995; Pres. Austrian Rectors' Conf. 2000–; Vice-Pres. European Univ. Asscn 2001–. *Publications:* Central and Eastern Europe: Roads to Growth 1992, Central Banks and Seigniorage: A Study of Three Economies in Transition (European Econ. Review) 1996, Grundzüge der Wirtschaftspolitik Österreichs (co-author) 2001. *Leisure interests:* mountaineering, skiing, reading. *Address:* Office of the Rector, University of Vienna, Dr Karl Lueger-Ring, 1010 Vienna, Austria (office). *Telephone:* (1) 4277-10010 (office); (1) 328-12-72 (home). *Fax:* (1) 4277-9100 (office). *E-mail:* georg.winckler@univie.ac.at (office). *Website:* www.univie.ac .at (office).

WINDLE, Alan Hardwick, PhD, FRS, FIM, FInstP, ARSM; British scientist and academic; *Professor of Materials Science, University of Cambridge;* b. 20 June 1942, Croydon, Surrey; s. of Stuart George Windle and Myrtle Lillian Windle (née Povey); m. Janet Susan Carr 1968; one s. three d.; ed Whitgift School, Imperial Coll. London, Trinity Coll., Cambridge; ICI Research Fellow, Imperial Coll., London 1966–67, Lecturer in Metallurgy 1967–75; Lecturer in Metallurgy and Materials Science, Univ. of Cambridge 1975–92, Fellow, Trinity Coll. 1978–, Lecturer and Dir of Studies in Natural Sciences, Trinity Coll. 1978–92, Tutor 1983–91, Prof. of Materials Science 1992–, Head of Dept of Materials Science, Univ. of Cambridge 1996–2001; Visiting Prof., N Carolina State Univ., USA 1980; Exec. Dir Cambridge-MIT Inst. 2000–03; Vice-Pres. Inst. of Materials 2001–; Dir Pfizer Inst. for Pharmaceutical Materials Science 2005–; Commr Royal Comm. for Exhbn of 1851 2001–; mem. Indian Acad. of Science; Fellow, American Physical Soc.; Bessemer Medal, Imperial Coll. 1963, RSA Silver Medal 1963, Rosenhain Medal & Prize 1987, Swinburne Medal & Prize, Plastics and Rubber Inst. 1992, Founders' Medal and Prize, Polymer Physics Group, Inst. of Physics and Royal Soc. of Chem. 2007, Royal Soc. Armourers and Braziers Medal and Prize 2007. *Publications:* A First Course in Crystallography 1978, Liquid Crystalline Polymers (with A. M. Donald) 1992 (second edn with A. M. Donald and S. Hanna 2005). *Leisure interest:* flying light aircraft. *Address:* Department of Materials Science and Metallurgy, New Museums Site, Pembroke Street, Cambridge, CB2 3QZ, England (office). *Telephone:* (1223) 334321 (office). *Fax:* (1223) 334366 (office). *E-mail:* ahw1@cam.ac.uk (office). *Website:* (office).

WINDLESHAM, 3rd Baron and Baronet; Baron Hennessy (Life Peer), cr. 1999; **David James George Hennessy,** PC, CVO, MA, DLitt; British politician and fmr college principal; b. 28 Jan. 1932; s. of 2nd Baron Windlesham and Angela Mary Duggan; m. Prudence Glynn 1965 (died 1986); one s. one d.; ed Ampleforth, Trinity Coll., Oxford; Chair. of Bow Group 1959–60, 1962–63; mem. Westminster City Council 1958–62; Dir Rediffusion Television 1965–67; Man. Dir Grampian Television 1967–70; Minister of State Home Office 1970–72; Minister of State Northern Ireland 1972–73; Lord Privy Seal, Leader House of Lords 1973–74; Opposition Leader, House of Lords March–Oct. 1974; Jt Man. Dir ATV Network 1974–75, Man. Dir 1975–81, Chair. 1981; Chair. Ind. Television Cos. Asscn 1976–78; Deputy Chair. Queen's Silver Jubilee Appeal 1976–77 and Trust 1977–80; Prin. Brasenose Coll., Oxford 1989–2002, Hon. Fellow 2002; Pres. Victim Support 1992–2001; Chair. Oxford Preservation Trust 1979–89, Parole Bd for England and Wales 1982–88, Oxford Soc. 1985–88; Vice-Chair. Ditchley Foundation 1987–; sits in House of Lords as Lord Hennessy 1999–; Dir WH Smith 1986–95, The Observer 1981–89; Trustee, Charities Aid Foundation 1977–81, Community Service Volunteers 1981–2000, Royal Collection Trust 1993–2000; Trustee British Museum 1981–96, Chair. 1986–96; mem. Museums and Galleries Comm. 1984–86; Hon. Bencher, Inner Temple 1999; Visiting Fellow, All Souls Coll., Oxford 1986; Visiting Prof. of Public and Int. Affairs, Princeton Univ. 1997, 2002–03; Hon. Fellow, Trinity Coll., Oxford 1982, Brasenose Coll., Oxford 2002; Hon. LLD (London) 2002. *Publications:* Communication and Political Power 1966, Politics in Practice 1975, Broadcasting in a Free Society 1980, Responses to Crime (Vol. 1) 1987, (Vol. 2) 1993, (Vol. 3) 1996, (Vol. 4) 2001, Windlesham/ Rampton Report on Death on the Rock 1989, Politics, Punishment and Populism 1998. *Address:* House of Lords, Westminster, London, SW1A 0PW, England. *E-mail:* windleshamd@parliament.uk (office).

WINDSOR, Colin, DPhil, FRS, FInstP; British physicist and academic; *Consultant, United Kingdom Atomic Energy Authority Fusion;* b. 28 June 1938, Beckenham, Kent; s. of George Thomas and Mabel Rayment; m. 1st Margaret Lee 1963; one s. two d.; m. 2nd Maureen Watkins 2005; ed Magdalen Coll., Oxford, Clarendon Lab., Oxford; Research Assoc., Yale Univ., USA 1963–64; scientist UKAEA 1964–96, Programme Area Man. UKAEA Fusion 1996–98; Visiting Fellow, Japanese Asscn for the Advancement of Science, Sendai 1980; Consultant, UKAEA Fusion 1998–; Sr Consultant, PenOp UK 1998–2000; Hon. Prof. of Physics, Univ. of Birmingham 1990–; Duddell Medal, Inst. of Physics 1986. *Publications include:* Pulsed Neutron Scattering 1981, Four Computer Models 1983, Solid State Science, Past, Present and Predicted (ed.) 1987. *Leisure interests:* singing, playing piano and recorder, composing, cycling to work, naturism. *Address:* D3, UKAEA Fusion, Culham Science Centre, Oxford, OX14 3DB (office); 116 New Road, East Hagbourne, Oxon., OX11 9LD, England (home). *Telephone:* (1235) 466676 (office); (1235) 812083 (home). *Fax:* (1235) 463414 (office). *E-mail:* colin.windsor@ukaea.org.uk (office). *Website:* www.ukaea.org.uk (office); freespace.virgin.net/colin .windsor (home).

WINELAND, David J.; American physicist; *Professor and Group Leader, Time and Frequency Division, National Institute of Standards and Technol-*

ogy (NIST); Prof. and Leader, Time and Frequency Div., Nat. Inst. of Standards and Tech. (NIST), Boulder, Colo, also NIST Fellow; mem. NAS 1992–, mem. NAS Cttee on Atomic, Molecular and Optical Sciences; IEEE Rabi Award 1998, Optical Soc. of America Ives Medal 2004, Nat. Medal of Science 2007. *Address:* National Institute of Standards and Technology, 325 Broadway, Mailcode 847.10, Boulder, CO 80305-3328, USA (office). *Telephone:* (303) 497-5286 (office). *Fax:* (303) 497-6461 (office). *E-mail:* wineland@boulder .nist.gov (office). *Website:* www.nist.gov (office).

WINFREY, Oprah, BA; American broadcaster, actress and producer; *Chairman, Harpo Inc.;* b. (b. (Orpah (sic) Gail Winfrey)), 29 Jan. 1954, Kosciusko, Miss.; d. of Vernon Winfrey and Vernita Lee; ed Tennessee State Univ.; worked for WVOL radio, Nashville, Tenn. while still at school, subsequently as reporter/anchor, WTVF-TV, Nashville; joined WJZ-TV news, Baltimore, as co-anchor 1976, became co-host, People Are Talking 1978; joined WLS-TV, Chicago as host, AM Chicago, subsequently renamed The Oprah Winfrey Show 1985–99; f. Harpo Productions Inc. 1986, Owner and Producer 1986–; Founder and Editorial Dir O, The Oprah Magazine 2000–, O at Home 2004–; f. The Oprah Winfrey Foundation; Partner, Oxygen Media 2000–; launched Oprah & Friends (XM Satellite Radio network) 2006–; est. Leadership Acad. for Girls, S Africa 2007–; initiated US Nat. Child Protection Act 1991, signed by Pres. Clinton ('Oprah's Law') 1993; numerous awards, including Int. Radio and TV Soc.'s Broadcaster of the Year Award 1988, 1995 Individual Achievement Award, George Foster Peabody Awards 1996, Int. Radio and TV Society's Foundation Gold Medal Award 1996, TV Guide Television Performer of the Year 1997, named by Newsweek as the Most Important Person in Books and Media 1997, Nat. Acad. of TV Arts and Sciences Lifetime Achievement Award 1998 (in 1999 Oprah removed herself from future Emmy consideration and the show followed suit in 2000. Oprah and The Oprah Winfrey Show received more than 40 Daytime Emmy Awards: seven for Outstanding Host, nine for Outstanding Talk Show, more than 20 in the Creative Arts categories, and one for Oprah's work as supervising producer of the ABC After School Special Shades of Single Protein), named by Time Magazine amongst 100 Most Influential People of the 20th Century 1998 and amongst 100 Most Influential People in the World 2004, 2005, 2006, ranked by Fortune magazine amongst 50 Most Powerful Women in Business in the US 1998–2001, (10th) 2002, (seventh) 2003, (sixth) 2004, (fourth) 2005, (eighth) 2006, (eighth) 2007, Nat. Book Foundation 50th Anniversary Gold Medal 1999, listed by Life magazine as both the most influential woman and the most influential black person of her generation, and in a cover story profile the magazine called her "America's Most Powerful Woman" 1999, called "arguably the world's most powerful woman" by both CNN and Time.com 2001, also ranked by Ladies Home Journal number one in their list of the most powerful women in America, Broadcasting & Cable Hall of Fame 2002, Bob Hope Humanitarian Award, 54th Annual Primetime Emmy Awards 2002, first African-American woman listed by Forbes Magazine amongst World's Wealthiest People 2003, named the Greatest Pop Culture Icon of All Time by VH1 2003, elected to Nat. Women's Hall of Fame, Seneca, NY, Asscn of American Publrs AAP Honors Award 2003, ranked by Forbes magazine amongst 100 Most Powerful Women (62nd) 2004, (ninth) 2005, (14th) 2006, (21st) 2007, (36th) 2008, Nat. Asscn of Broadcasters Distinguished Service Award 2004, UNA of the USA Global Humanitarian Action Award 2004, Int. Acad. of TV Arts and Sciences Int. Emmy Founders Award 2005, Nat. Asscn for the Advancement of Colored People Hall of Fame 2005, Nat. Civil Rights Museum Nat. Freedom Award 2005, named by Forbes magazine the World's Most Powerful Celebrity 2005, named the Greatest Woman in American History as part of a public poll by The Greatest American and ranked ninth overall on the list of Greatest Americans 2005. *Theatre:* Broadway debut as a producer of The Color Purple 2005. *Films include:* acting roles: Sofia in The Color Purple 1985, Mrs Thomas in Native Son 1986, Throw Momma From The Train 1988, Mattie Michael in The Women of Brewster Place (TV) 1989, Listen Up: The Lives of Quincy Jones 1990, LaJoe Rivers in There Are No Children Here (TV) 1993, Sethe in Beloved 1998, Coretta Scott King (voice) in Our Friend, Martin (video) 1999, Charlotte's Web (voice) 2006, Bee Movie (voice) 2007; producer and/or exec. producer of several TV films including Nine 1992, Overexposed 1992, Beloved 1998, Their Eyes Were Watching God 2005, Legends Ball 2006,. *Publications:* Oprah (autobiog.) 1993, In the Kitchen with Rosie 1996, Make the Connection (with Bob Greene) 1996. *Address:* Harpo Inc., 110 North Carpenter Street, Chicago, IL 60607, USA (office). *Telephone:* (312) 633-1000 (office). *Fax:* (312) 633-1976 (office). *Website:* www.oprah.com (home).

WINGER, Debra; American actress; b. 16 May 1955, Cleveland; d. of Robert Winger and Ruth Winger; m. 1st Timothy Hutton (q.v.) 1986 (divorced); one s.; m. 2nd Arliss Howard 1996; one c.; ed Calif. State Univ., Northridge; served with Israeli army 1972; first professional appearance in Wonder Woman TV series 1976–77. *Films include:* Thank God It's Friday 1978, French Postcards 1979, Urban Cowboy 1980, Cannery Row 1982, An Officer and a Gentleman 1982, Terms of Endearment 1983, Mike's Murder 1984, Legal Eagles 1986, Black Widow 1987, Made in Heaven 1987, Betrayed 1988, The Sheltering Sky, Everybody Wins 1990, Leap of Faith 1992, Shadowlands 1993, A Dangerous Woman 1993, Forget Paris 1995, Big Bad Love (also producer) 2001, Radio 2003, Eulogy 2004, Dawn Anna (TV) 2005, Sometimes in April (TV) 2005, Rachel Getting Married 2008. *Publication:* Undiscovered 2008. *Address:* c/o CAA, 9830 Wilshire Boulevard, Beverly Hills, CA 90212, USA (office). *Telephone:* (310) 288-4545 (office). *Fax:* (310) 288-4800 (office). *Website:* www.caa.com (office).

WINGTI, Rt Hon. Paias, CMG, PC; Papua New Guinea politician; b. 2 Feb. 1951, Moika Village; five s.; ed Univ. of Papua New Guinea; MP 1977–97; apptd. Asst Speaker and mem. Public Accounts Cttee; elected Govt Whip; Minister for Transport and Civil Aviation 1978–80; Deputy Prime Minister

and Minister for Nat. Planning and Devt 1982–84, for Educ. 1984–85; resgnd from Govt, co-f. People's Democratic Movt 1985; Leader of Opposition March–Nov. 1985, 1988–92, 1994; Prime Minister 1985–88, 1992–94; Gov. Western Highlands Prov. *Leisure interests:* playing golf and watching Rugby League. *Address:* People's Democratic Movement, P.O. Box 972, Boroko, Papua New Guinea. *Telephone:* 277631. *Fax:* 277611.

WINID, Bogusław W., MA; Polish diplomatist; *Permanent Representative, NATO;* b. 3 Nov. 1960, Warsaw; m. Beata Winid; one s.; ed History Inst., Warsaw Univ., Indiana Univ., USA; Asst, American Studies Centre, Warsaw Univ. 1984–88; joined Dept of N and S America, Ministry of Foreign Affairs 1991, Deputy Dir 1997–98, Dir 1998–2001; First Sec., later Counsellor, Embassy in Washington, DC 1992–97, Deputy Chief of Mission 2001–06, Under-Sec. of State for Int. Relations, Ministry of Defence 2006–07, Perm. Rep. to NATO and WEU, Brussels 2007–. *Publications:* In the Capitol's Shadow: Polish Diplomacy towards the United States of America 1919–1939, Santiago 1898, NATO Expansion in the United States Congress 1993–1998; numerous journal articles. *Address:* Permanent Mission of Poland to NATO, blvd Léopold III, 1110, Brussels, Brussels (office). *Telephone:* (2) 707-13-88 (office). *Fax:* (2) 707-13-89 (office). *E-mail:* poland@skynet.be (office). *Website:* www.brukselanato.polemb.net (office).

WINIGER, Matthias; Swiss geographer, academic and university administrator; *Rector, Rheinische Friedrich-Wilhelms-Universität, Bonn;* b. 1943, Berne; ed Univ. of Berne; Prof. of Geography, Univ. of Berne 1978–88; Prof. of Geography, Rheinische Friedrich-Wilhelms-Universität, Bonn 1988–, Dean, Faculty of Math. and Natural Sciences 2002–04, Rector 2004–; mem. Acad. Science and Literature, Mainz. *Address:* Office of the Rector, Rheinische Friedrich-Wilhelms-Universität, Meckenheimer Allee 166, 53115 Bonn, Germany (office). *Telephone:* (228) 73-7293 (office). *Fax:* (228) 73-7506 (office). *E-mail:* winiger@uni-bonn.de (office). *Website:* www.uni-bonn.de (office).

WINKLER, Hans Günter; German show jumper and company executive; b. 24 July 1926, Barmen; s. of Paul Winkler; m. 4th Debby Malloy 1994; mem. Exec., German Olympic Riding Cttee 1981–; winner of about 1,000 events, including over 500 int. events, up to 1964; world's most successful Olympic show jumping rider, took part in six Olympiads 1956–76, winning a still (2005) record haul of five gold medals, one bronze medal (Mexico City) 1968, one silver medal (Montreal) 1976; World Riding Champion 1954, 1955 (record of two wins he shares with Raimondo d'Inzeo); European Champion 1957; Winner, King George V Cup 1965, 1968; currently Sports Director, Riders Tour; Hon. Citizen of Warendorf; Hon. mem. Riding Clubs of Warendorf, Ludwigsburg, Herborn, Darmstadt, Bayreuth, Salzburg, Frankfurt am Main, Mitterfels, Kassel, Hünfeld, Deutsche Reiterliche Vereinigung, Aachen-Laurensberger Rennverein; Grand Cross of Honour of FRG 1974; German Rider's Cross in Gold 1950, Best Sportsman of the Decade 1950, 1960, Needle of Honour, Senate of West Berlin 1954, Sportsman of the Year 1955, 1956, Gold Band, German Sports Press Asscn 1956, Needle of Honour, Int. Riding Asscn 1964, FN Award in Gold with Olympic Rings, Laurel Wreath and Diamonds 1976, Media Prize "Bambi" 1990, Prize of Honour of Spoga 1990, Westfälischer Friedensreiterpreis 1997, Golden Sports Pyramid for Lifetime Work in Sport 2000, Silver Horse 2002. *Publications:* Meine Pferde und ich (My Horses and I), Pferde und Reiter in aller Welt (Horses and Riders of the World) 1956, Halla D., Geschichte ihrer Laufbahn (Halla D., A History of Her Career) 1961, Springreiten (Jumping) 1979, Halla die Olympiadiva: Olympiareiter in Warendorf 1981. *Leisure interests:* skiing, hunting, tennis. *Address:* Dr. Rau Allee 48, 48231 Warendorf, Germany. *Telephone:* (2581) 2361. *Fax:* (2581) 62772. *E-mail:* hgwm1@waf-online.de (office). *Website:* www .hgwinkler.de (office).

WINNER, Michael Robert, MA; British film producer and director and screenwriter; b. 30 Oct. 1935, London; s. of the late George Joseph Winner and Helen Winner; ed Downing Coll. Cambridge; Ed. and film critic of Cambridge Univ. paper; entered film industry as film critic and columnist for nat. newspapers and magazines 1951; wrote, produced and directed many documentary, TV and feature films for the Film Producers Guild, Anglo Amalgamated, United Artists 1955–61; Chair. Scimitar Films Ltd, Michael Winner Ltd, Motion Picture and Theatrical Investments Ltd 1957–; Columnist Sunday Times and News of the World; Chief Censorship Officer, Dirs. Guild of GB 1983, mem. Council and Trustee 1983–2007, Sr mem. 1991–2004; Founder and Chair. Police Memorial Trust 1984–; mem. Writers' Guild of Great Britain. *Films:* Play It Cool (dir) 1962, The Cool Mikado (dir, writer) 1962, West 11 (dir) 1963, The System (co-producer and dir) 1963–64, You Must Be Joking (producer, dir, writer) 1964–65, The Jokers (producer, dir, writer) 1966, I'll Never Forget What's 'is Name (producer, dir) 1967, Hannibal Brooks (producer, dir, writer) 1968, The Games (producer, dir) 1969, Lawman (producer, dir) 1970, The Nightcomers (producer, dir) 1971, Chato's Land (producer, dir) 1971, The Mechanic (dir) 1972, Scorpio (producer, dir) 1972, The Stone Killer (producer, dir) 1973, Death Wish (producer, dir) 1974, Won Ton Ton – The Dog Who Saved Hollywood (producer, dir) 1975, The Sentinel (producer, dir, writer) 1976, The Big Sleep (producer, dir, Writer) 1977, Firepower (producer, dir, writer) 1978, Death Wish II (producer, dir, writer) 1981, The Wicked Lady (producer, dir, writer) 1982, Scream For Help (producer, dir) 1983, Death Wish III (producer, dir) 1985, Appointment with Death (producer, dir, writer) 1988, A Chorus of Disapproval (producer, dir, co-writer) 1989, Bullseye! (producer, dir, co-writer) 1990, For the Greater Good (BBC film, actor, dir Danny Boyle) 1990, Decadence (actor, dir Steven Berkoff) 1993, Dirty Weekend (producer, jt screenplay writer) 1993, Parting Shots (producer, dir, writer) 1997. *Theatre:* The Silence of St Just (producer) 1971, The Tempest (producer) 1974, A Day in Hollywood, A Night in the Ukraine (producer) (Evening Standard Award for Best Comedy of the Year 1979). *Radio:* panellist, Any Questions (BBC Radio 4), The Flump (play) 2000.

Television appearances include: Michael Winner's True Crimes (LWT), panellist, Question Time (BBC One), many variety show sketches, starring in and/or directing commercials for different cos 2003–. *Publications:* Winner's Dinners 1999, Winner Guide 2002, Winner Takes All: a Life of Sorts 2004, Michael Winner's Fat Pig Diet 2007; contrib. to Sunday Times, News of the World, Daily Mail. *Leisure interests:* walking around art galleries, museums and antique shops, eating, making table mats, laundry work. washing silk shirts. *Address:* 219 Kensington High Street, London, W8 6BD, England. *Telephone:* (20) 7734-8385. *Fax:* (20) 7602-9217.

WINOCK, Michel, LèsL, DèsL; French historian, academic, writer and publisher; *Professor, Institut d'Etudes politiques;* b. 19 March 1937, Paris; s. of Gaston Winock and Jeanne Winock (née Dussaule); m. Françoise Werner 1961; two s.; ed Sorbonne; teacher, Lycée Joffre, Montpellier 1961–63, Lycée Hoche, Versailles 1963–66, Lycée Lakanal, Sceaux 1966–68; Lecturer, Sr Lecturer Univ. of Paris VIII-Vincennes à St-Denis 1968–78; Sr Lecturer, Institut d'Etudes politiques, Paris 1978–90, Prof. 1990–; Publr Editions du Seuil, Paris 1969–; radio producer, France-Inter 1983–85; Ed.-in-Chief L'Histoire magazine 1978–81, Editorial Adviser 1981–. *Publications:* Histoire politique de la revue esprit 1930–1950 1975, La république se meurt 1978, Les grandes crises politiques 1971–1968 1986, La Fière hexagonale 1986, Nationalisme, antisemitisme et fascisme en France 1990, Le socialisme en France et en Europe XIXe–XXe siècle 1992, Le siècle des intellectuels (essays) 1997, La guerre de 1914–1918 racontée aux enfants 1998, La France politique XIXe–XXe siècle 1999, Les Voix de la liberté 2001, Les écrivains engagés au XIXe siècle 2001, La France et les juifs (Prix Montaigne de Bordeaux 2005) 2004, Pierre Mendès France 2005, Victor Hugo dans l'arène politique 2005, La Gauche au pouvoir: L'héritage du Front populaire 2006, La France antijuive de 1936: L'agression de Léon Blum à la Chambre des députés 2006, L'Agonie de la IVe République 2006, La Gauche en France 2006, La Mêlée présidentielle 2007, Clemenceau 2007. *Leisure interest:* tennis. *Address:* Institut d'Etudes politiques, 27 rue Saint-Guillaume, 75337 Paris Cedex 07, France. *Telephone:* 1-40-46-51-08. *Fax:* 1-40-46-51-75. *E-mail:* wimi@cybercable.fr; wimi@noos.fr.

WINSER, Kim, OBE; British business executive; *President and CEO, Aquascutum Limited;* b. 1959, Helensburgh, Scotland; one s.; ed Purbrook Grammar School, Hampshire; man. trainee Marks & Spencer 1977, various positions including Exec. for Menswear Buying, Div. Dir for Ladies Casualwear Group, est. Corp. Marketing Group 1999, Dir Marks & Spencer (first female in position) –2000; Chief Exec. Pringle of Scotland 2000–06; Pres. and CEO Aquascutum Ltd 2006–; Chair. Charity Events and Exec. mem. Co-operation Ireland 1996–; Hon. DLitt (Heriot-Watt) 2002. *Leisure interests:* being with her family, entertaining, sports, fashion. *Address:* Aquascutum Flagship Store, 100 Regent Street, London, W1B 5SR, England. *Telephone:* (20) 7675-9113 (office). *Website:* www.aquascutum.com (office).

WINSLET, Kate Elizabeth; British actress; b. 5 Oct. 1975, Reading, Berks.; d. of Roger Winslet and Sally Winslet; m. 1st Jim Threapleton 1998 (divorced 2001), one d.; m. 2nd Sam Mendes (q.v.) 2003; one s.; ed Theatre School, Maidenhead; Grammy Award for Best Spoken Word Album for Children 2000, Film Critics' Annual Achievements Award for Best Supporting Actress 2002. *Stage appearances include:* Peter Pan, What the Butler Saw (Manchester Evening News Award for Best Supporting Actress), A Game of Soldiers, Adrian Mole. *Films:* Heavenly Creatures (New Zealand Film and TV Award for Best Foreign Actress, London Film Critics Circle Award for Best British Actress, Empire Magazine Award for Best British Actress 1995) 1994, A Kid in King Arthur's Court 1995, Sense and Sensibility (BAFTA Award for Best Supporting Actress 1996, Screen Actors' Guild Award for Best Supporting Actress 1996, Evening Standard British Film Award for Best Actress 1997) 1995, Jude 1996, Hamlet 1996, Titanic (Variety Club of Great Britain Film Actress of the Year 1998, European Film Acad. Award for Best European Actress 1998, BAFTA Award, Empire Magazine Award for Best British Actress 1998) 1997, Hideous Kinky 1998, Holy Smoke 1998, Faeries (voice) 1999, Quills (Evening Standard British Film Award for Best Actress 2002) 2000, Enigma (Empire Magazine Award for Best British Actress 2002) 2001, A Christmas Carol: The Movie (voice) 2001, Iris (European Film Acad. Award for Best European Actress 2002) 2001, War Game 2001, The Life of David Gale 2003, Plunge: The Movie 2003, Pride (TV film, voice) 2004, Eternal Sunshine of the Spotless Mind (London Film Critics Circle Award, Empire Magazine Award for Best British Actress 2005) 2004, Finding Neverland 2004, Romance & Cigarettes 2005, All the King's Men 2006, Little Children (Desert Palm Achievement for Acting, Palm Springs Int. Film Festival 2007) 2006, The Holiday 2006, Flushed Away (voice) 2006, The Fox and the Child (voice) 2007, The Reader (Golden Globe Award for Best Supporting Actress 2009, BAFTA Award for Leading Actress 2009, Acad. Award for Best Actress 2009) 2008, Revolutionary Road (Golden Globe Award for Best Actress 2009) 2008. *Address:* c/o Dallas Smith, United Agents, 12–26 Lexington Street, London, W1F 0LE, England (office); c/o Hylda Queally, CAA, 2000 Avenue of the Stars, Los Angeles, CA 90067, USA (office). *Telephone:* (20) 3214-0800 (London) (office); (424) 288-2000 (Los Angeles) (office). *Fax:* (20) 3214-0801 (London) (office); (20) 288-2900 (Los Angeles) (office). *E-mail:* info@unitedagents.co.uk (office). *Website:* unitedagents.co.uk (office); www.caa.com (office).

WINSTON, Baron (Life Peer) cr. 1995, of Hammersmith in the London Borough of Hammersmith and Fulham; **Robert Maurice Lipson Winston,** MB, BS, DSc, FRCP, FRCOG, FRCPE, FRCPS, FMedSci, FIBiol, FRSA; British medical researcher; *Professor Emeritus of Reproductive Medicine, Imperial College London;* b. 15 July 1940, London, England; s. of the late Laurence Winston and of Ruth Winston-Fox; m. Lira Feigenbaum 1973; two s. one d.; ed St Paul's School, London and London Hosp. Medical Coll., Univ. of London; Registrar and Sr Registrar, Hammersmith Hosp. 1970–74; Wellcome Research Sr Lecturer, Inst. of Obstetrics and Gynaecology 1974–78, Sr Lecturer 1978–81, Consultant Obstetrician and Gynaecologist 1978–2005; Prof. of Gynaecology, Univ. of Texas at San Antonio, USA 1980–81; Reader in Fertility Studies, Royal Postgraduate Medical School 1982–86, Prof. 1987–97; apptd Prof. of Fertility Studies, Imperial Coll. London 1997, now Prof. Emer. of Reproductive Medicine; Dir NHS Research and Devt, Hammersmith Hosps Trust 1998–2005; Chancellor Sheffield Hallam Univ. 2001–; Visiting Prof., Univ. of Leuven, Belgium 1976–77, Mount Sinai Hosp., New York, USA 1985; Chair. Select Cttee of Science and Tech., House of Lords 1999–2002; Chair. Royal Coll. of Music 2008–; Vice-Chair. Parl. Office of Science and Tech. 2005–; Founder-mem. British Fertility Soc.; mem. Eng and Physical Sciences Research Council 2008–, council mem. Surrey Univ. 2008–; many other professional appointments; Hon. Fellow, Queen Mary and Westfield Coll. 1996; Hon. FRCSE; Hon. Fellow, Royal Coll. of Physicians and Surgeons (Glasg); Hon. FIBiol; 17 hon. doctorates at British univs, including: Hon. DSc (Cranfield) 2001, (UMIST) 2001, (Oxford Brookes) 2001, (St Andrew's) 2003, (Exeter) 2004, (Trinity Coll. Dublin) 2005, (Univ. of Auckland) 2008; Victor Bonney Prize, Royal Coll. of Surgeons 1991–93, Chief Rabbinate Award for Contribution to Society 1992–93, Cedric Carter Medal, Clinical Genetics Soc. 1993, Gold Medal, Royal Soc. of Health 1998, Michael Faraday Award, Royal Soc. 1999, Wellcome Award for Science in the Media 2001, Edwin Stevens Medal, Royal Soc. of Medicine 2003, Gold Medal, North of England Zoological Soc. 2004, VLV Individual Award for Best contribs to UK Broadcasting 2004, Al Hammadi Medal, Royal Coll. of Surgeons, Edin. 2005. *Director:* Each in his Own Way (Pirandello), Edinburgh Festival 1969. *Television:* Presenter, Your Life In Their Hands (BBC) 1979–87, Making Babies 1996, The Human Body 1998, The Secret Life of Twins 1999, Child of our Time (BBC) 2000, Superhuman 2000, Human Instinct 2002, 2003, Threads of Life (BBC) 2003, The Human Mind (BBC) 2004, Story of God (BBC) 2005, Child Against All Odds (BBC) 2006, Superdoctors 2008. *Radio:* Robert Winston's Musical Analysis 2009. *Publications:* Reversibility of Sterilization 1978, Tubal Infertility (jtly) 1981, Infertility: A Sympathetic Approach 1987, Getting Pregnant 1989, Making Babies 1996, The IVF Revolution 1999, Superman 2000, Human Instinct 2002, The Human Mind 2003, What Makes Me, Me? (Aventis Jr Prize, Royal Soc. 2005) 2004, Human (BMA Award for Best Popular Medicine Book) 2005, The Story of God 2005, Body 2005, A Child Against All Odds 2006, It's Elementary 2007, Evolution Revolution 2009; about 300 scientific articles on reproduction. *Leisure interests:* theatre, broadcasting, music, wine, festering. *Address:* Faculty Building, Imperial College, Exhibition Road, London, SW7 2AZ, England (office). *Telephone:* (20) 7594-5959 (office). *Fax:* (20) 8458-4980 (home). *E-mail:* r.winston@imperial.ac.uk (office). *Website:* www.robertwinston.org.

WINTER, William Forrest, BA, LLB; American lawyer and politician; *Senior Partner and Shareholder, Watkins Ludlam Winter & Stennis P.A.;* b. 21 Feb. 1923, Grenada, Miss.; s. of William A. Winter and Inez P. Winter; m. Elise Varner 1950; three d.; ed Univ. of Miss.; Miss. House of Reps. 1948–56; Miss. state tax collector 1956–64; State Treas. 1964–68; Lt-Gov. of Miss. 1972–76, Gov. 1980–84; Sr Pnr, Shareholder, Watkins, Ludlam Winter & Stennis P.A. (law firm), Jackson, Miss. 1985–; Eudora Welty Prof. of Southern Studies, Millsaps Coll. 1989; Jamie Whitten Prof. of Law, Univ. of Miss. 1989; Chair. Advisory Comm. on Intergovernmental Relations 1993–97, Ole Miss Alumni Asscn 1978, Southern Growth Policies Bd 1981, Southern Regional Educ. Bd 1982, Appalachian Regional Comm. 1983, Comm. on the Future of the South 1986, Foundation for the Mid South 1990–92, Kettering Foundation 1990–93, Nat. Comm. on the State and Local Public Service; Fellow, Miss. Bar Foundation; Fellow, Inst. of Politics, Harvard Univ. 1985; mem. American Bar Asscn, DC Bar, Miss. Bar, Hinds Co. Bar Asscn, Nat. Advisory Bd on Race Relations 1997–; Pres. Bd of Trustees Miss. Dept of Archives and History; Dr hc (Univ. of North Carolina, Tougaloo Coll.) 2004; Miss. Bar Lifetime Achievement Award 1998, Martin Luther King, Jr. Memorial Award, Nat. Educ. Asscn 2001. *Address:* Watkins Ludlam Winter & Stennis P.A., 633 North State Street, PO Box 427, Jackson, MS 39202, USA (office). *Telephone:* (601) 949-4800 (office). *Fax:* (601) 949-4804 (office). *E-mail:* wwinter@watkinsludlam.com (office). *Website:* www.watkinsludlam.com (office).

WINTERBOTTOM, Michael; British film director; b. 29 March 1961, Blackburn, Lancs.; ed Univ. of Oxford; fmr ed., Thames TV. *Films include:* Butterfly Kisses 1995, Go Now, Jude 1996, Welcome to Sarajevo 1997, I Want You 1998, Resurrection Man (exec. producer) 1998, Wonderland 1999, With or Without You 1999, The Claim 2000, 24 Hour Party People 2002, In This World (Golden Bear, Berlin Film Festival 2003) 2002, Code 46 2003, 9 Songs 2004, A Cock and Bull Story 2005, The Road to Guantánamo (Silver Bear Berlin Film Festival 2006) 2005, A Mighty Heart 2007. *Television series include:* Cracker Mysteries – The Mad Woman in the Attic 1993, Family 1994, Cinema Europe: The Other Hollywood (mini-series) 1996.

WINTERBOTTOM, Michael, DPhil, FBA; British classicist; b. 22 Sept. 1934, Sale, Cheshire; s. of Allan Winterbottom and Kathleen Mary Winterbottom (née Wallis); m. 1st Helen Spencer 1963 (divorced 1983); two s.; m. 2nd Nicolette Janet Streatfeild Bergel 1986; ed Dulwich Coll., London and Pembroke Coll. Oxford; Domus Sr Scholar, Merton Coll. Oxford 1958–59; Research Lecturer, Christ Church Oxford 1959–62; Lecturer in Latin and Greek, Univ. Coll. London 1962–67; Fellow and Tutor in Classics, Worcester Coll. Oxford 1967–92, Reader in Classical Languages 1990–92; Corpus Christi Prof. of Latin, Fellow of Corpus Christi Coll., Oxford 1993–2001, Fellow Emer. 2001–; Craven Scholar 1954; Derby Scholar 1956; Dr hc (Besançon) 1985. *Publications:* Quintilian (ed.) 1970, Ancient Literary Criticism (with D. A. Russell) 1972, Three Lives of English Saints 1972, The Elder Seneca (ed. and trans.) 1974, Tacitus, Opera Minora (ed. with R. M. Ogilvie) 1975, Gildas (ed. and trans.) 1978, Roman Declamation 1980, The Minor Declamations Ascribed to Quintilian (ed., with commentary) 1984, Sopatros the Rhetor (with D. C. Innes) 1988, Cicero, De Officiis (ed.) 1994, William of Malmesbury, Gesta Regum Anglorum Vol. I (ed. and trans. with R. A. B. Mynors and R. M. Thomson) 1998, William of Malmesbury, Saints' Lives (ed. and trans. with R. M. Thomson) 2002, Quintilian, Institutio Oratoria Book 2 (ed. with T. Reinhardt) 2006, William of Malmesbury, Gesta Pontificum Anglorum Vol. I (ed. and trans.) 2007. *Leisure interests:* travel, geology, hill walking. *Address:* 53 Thorncliffe Road, Oxford, England (home). *Telephone:* (1865) 513066 (home).

WINTERFELDT, Ekkehard, Dr rer. nat; German scientist and academic; *Professor Emeritus of Organic Chemistry, University of Hanover;* b. 13 May 1932, Danzig; s. of Herbert Winterfeldt and Herta Winterfeldt; m. Marianne Heinemann 1958; one s. one d.; ed Tech. Hochschule Braunschweig, Tech. Univ. of Berlin; Asst Prof., Tech. Univ. of Berlin 1959, Assoc. Prof. 1967; Prof. and Head of Dept of Organic Chem., Univ. of Hanover 1970–, now Prof. Emer.; mem. Braunschweigische Wissenschaftliche Gesellschaft, Akad. der Wissenschaften zu Göttingen, Akad. Leopoldina, Halle; Dr hc (Liège) 1991; Dozentenstipendium des Fonds der Chemischen Industrie 1969, Emil Fischer Medal (German Chem. Soc.) 1990, Adolf Windaus-Medaille, Univ. of Göttingen 1993, Richard Kuhn-Medaille (Gesellschaft Deutscher Chem.) 1995, Hans Herloft-Inhoffen-Medaille 1998. *Publications:* 175 publs in scientific journals. *Leisure interests:* music, gardening, history. *Address:* Sieversdamm 34, 30916 Isernhagen, Germany (office). *Telephone:* (511) 9735293 (office); (511) 9734810 (home). *Fax:* (511) 7623011 (office); (511) 9734327 (home). *E-mail:* winterfeldt@mbox.sci.uni-hannover.de (office).

WINTERKORN, Martin, Dr rer. nat; German automotive industry executive; *Chairman, Board of Management, Volkswagen AG;* b. 24 May 1947, Leonberg; m.; two c.; ed Univ. of Stuttgart, Max-Planck-Inst. for Metal Research and Metal Physics; Special Asst in Process Eng, Robert Bosch GmbH 1977, Head, Substances and Processes Group, Bosch-Siemens-Hausgeräte GmbH 1978–81; Asst to Mem. of Bd for Quality Assurance, AUDI AG 1981–83, Head, Measuring Tech./Sampling and Test Lab. 1983–88, Dept Head, Cen. Quality Assurance 1988–90, Head, Audi Quality Assurance 1990–93, Head, Group Quality Assurance, Volkswagen AG 1993, Gen. Man. Volkswagen AG 1994–96, Head, Volkswagen Group Product Man. 1995–96, mem. Brand Bd of Man. for Tech. Devt 1996–2002, mem. Group Bd of Man. for Tech. Devt 2000–02, Chair. Bd of Man. AUDI AG 2002–06, also Chair. Bd of Dirs SEAT, also responsible for AUDI AG Tech. Devt 2003–06, mem. Bd of Man. Volkswagen AG 2002–, mem. Bd of Man. with responsibility for Group Research and Devt and Chair. Bd of Man. Volkswagen AG 2007–, Chair. Supervisory Bd Audi AG 2007–; Hon. Prof., Budapest Univ. of Tech. and Econs 2003, Dresden Univ. of Tech. 2004, Tongji Univ., Shanghai 2007. *Address:* Volkswagen AG, VHH 11. Floor, PO Box 1849, 38436 Wolfsburg, Germany (office). *Telephone:* (5361) 9-86622 (office). *Fax:* (5361) 9-30411 (office). *Website:* www.volkswagen.de (office).

WINTERS, L. Alan, MA, PhD; British economist and academic; *Director, World Bank Development Research Group;* b. 8 April 1950, London; s. of Geoffrey Walter Horace Winters and Christine Agnes Ive; m. 1st Margaret Elizabeth Griffin 1971; m. 2nd Zhen Kun Wang 1997; one s. two d.; ed Chingford Co. High School, Univs. of Bristol and Cambridge; Jr, Research Office, Dept of Applied Econs, Univ. of Cambridge 1971–80; lecturer in econs, Univ. of Bristol 1980–86; economist, World Bank 1983–85, Div. Chief/Research Man. 1994–99; Prof. of Econs, Univ. of Wales at Bangor 1986–90, Univ. of Birmingham 1990–94, Univ. of Sussex 1999–; currently Dir, World Bank Development Research Group, Washington DC. *Publications:* Econometric Model of the British Export Sector 1981, International Economics 1984, Europe's Domestic Market 1987, Eastern Europe's International Trade 1994, Sustainable Development 1995, The Uruguay Round and the Developing Countries 1996, Trade Liberalisation and Poverty 2001. *Leisure interests:* walking, music, cricket. *Address:* World Bank, Mailstop MC3–304, 1818 H Street, NW, Washington, DC 20433, USA (office). *Telephone:* (202) 458-8208 (office). *Fax:* (202) 522-1150 (office). *E-mail:* lwinters@worldbank.org (office). *Website:* econ.worldbank.org (office).

WINTERS, Robert Cushing, BA, MBA; American insurance company executive; *Chairman Emeritus, Prudential Insurance Company;* b. 8 Dec. 1931, Hartford, Conn.; s. of George Warren and Hazel Keith (née Cushing) Winters; m. Patricia Ann Martini 1962; two d.; ed Yale and Boston Univs; with Prudential Insurance Co. of America 1953–, Vice-Pres., Actuary 1969–75, Sr Vice-Pres. Cen. Atlantic Home Office 1975–78, Exec. Vice-Pres., Newark 1978–84, Vice-Chair. 1984–86, Chair. and CEO 1987–94, Chair. Emer. 1995–; Fellow Soc. of Actuaries; mem. and fmr Pres. American Acad. of Actuaries; mem. Business Council, Business Roundtable. *Address:* c/o Prudential Insurance Company, 751 Broad Street, Newark, NJ 07102, USA.

WINTERSON, Jeanette, OBE, BA; British writer; b. 27 Aug. 1959, Manchester; ed Accrington Girls' Grammar School, St Catherine's Coll., Oxford; Whitbread Prize 1985, John Llewellyn Rhys Memorial Book Prize 1987, American Acad. of Arts and Letters E. M. Forster Award 1989, Golden Gate Award, San Francisco Int. Film Festival 1990, Best of Young British Novelists Award 1992, Int. Fiction Award, Festival Letteratura Mantua 1999. *Play:* The Power Book (Royal Nat. Theatre, London, Théâtre de Chaillot, Paris). *Screenplay:* Great Moments in Aviation 1992. *Television:* Oranges Are Not The Only Fruit (BBC) 1990 (BAFTA Award for Best Drama 1990, FIPA d'Argent Award for screenplay, Cannes Film Festival 1991), Orlando – Art That Shook the World (BBC) 2002, South Bank Show 2004. *Publications:* fiction: Oranges Are Not The Only Fruit (Whitbread Prize for Best First Novel 1985) 1985, Boating for Beginners 1985, The Passion 1987, Sexing the Cherry 1989, Written on the Body 1992, Art and Lies 1994, Gut Symmetries 1997, The World and Other Places (short stories) 1998, The Power Book 2000, The King of Capri (juvenile) 2003, Lighthousekeeping 2004, Weight: The Myth of Atlas

and Heracles 2005, Tanglewreck (juvenile novel) 2006, The Stone Gods 2007, The Battle of the Sun (juvenile novel) 2009, The Lion, The Unicorn and Me (juvenile picture book) 2009; non-fiction: Fit for the Future 1986, Art Objects (essays) 1994. *Leisure interests:* opera, ballet, champagne, Paris, motorbikes. *Address:* William Morris Agency, Inc., 1325 Avenue of the Americas, New York, NY 10019, USA (office). *Website:* www.jeanettewinterson.com.

WINTERTON, George Graham, LLM, JSD; Australian barrister, legal scholar and academic; *Honorary Professor of Constitutional Law, University of Sydney;* b. 15 Dec. 1946, Hong Kong; s. of Walter Winterton and Rita Winterton; m. Rosalind Julian 1979; two s. two d.; ed Hale School, Perth, Univ. of Western Australia and Columbia Univ.; Assoc. in Law, Col Univ. 1973–75; joined staff Univ. of NSW 1975, Prof. of Law 1992–2004, Prof. Emer. 2004–; Prof. of Constitutional Law Univ. of Sydney Law School 2004–07, Hon. Prof. of Constitutional Law 2007–; mem. Exec. Govt Advisory Cttee, Australian Constitutional Comm. 1985–87, Repub. Advisory Cttee 1993; del. Australian Constitutional Convention 1998; barrister, NSW; barrister and solicitor, Vic. and W Australia; Hon. LLD (Univ. of Western Australia) 2007; Fulbright Scholarship 1973, Jubilee Medallion, Univ. of NSW 1999. *Publications:* Parliament, The Executive and the Governor-General 1983, Australian Constitutional Perspectives (co-ed.) 1992, Monarchy to Republic: Australian Republican Government 1994, We, the People: Australian Republican Government (ed.) 1994, Judicial Remuneration in Australia 1995, Australian Constitutional Landmarks (co-ed.) 2003, State Constitutional Landmarks (ed.) 2006, Australian Federal Constitutional Law: Commentary and Materials (co-author) (2nd edn) 2007; Gen. Ed. Constitutional Law and Policy Review. *Leisure interests:* music, reading. *Address:* 5 Park Parade, Bondi, NSW 2026 (home); Faculty of Law, University of Sydney, 173–175 Phillip Street, Sydney, NSW 2000, Australia (office). *Telephone:* (2) 9351-0441 (office); (2) 9389-8290 (home). *Fax:* (2) 9351-0200 (office). *E-mail:* georgew@law.usyd .edu.au (office). *Website:* www.law.usyd.edu.au (office).

WINTON, Timothy John; Australian writer; b. 4 Aug. 1960, nr Perth, WA; m. Denise Winton; two s. one d.; ed Western Australian Inst. of Tech.; Vogel Literary Award 1981, Miles Franklin Award 1984, 1992, 2002, Western Australian Premier's Awards 1990, 1991, 2001, Deo Gloria Prize for Religious Writing 1991, Commonwealth Writers Prize 1995, NSF Premier's Awards Christina Stead Prize for Fiction 2002, 2005, Queensland Fiction Prize 2005. *Publications:* An Open Swimmer 1981, Shallows 1985, Scisson and Other Stories 1985, That Eye, The Sky 1986, Minimum of Two 1987, In the Winter Dark 1988, Jesse 1988, Lockie Leonard, Human Torpedo 1990, The Bugalugs Bum Thief 1991, Cloudstreet 1991, Lockie Leonard, Scumbuster 1993, Land's Edge (with Trish Ainslie and Roger Garwood) 1993, Local Colour: Travels in the Other Australia 1994, The Riders 1994, Lockie Leonard, Legend 1997, Blueback 1997, The Deep 1998, Down to Earth 1999, Dirt Music 2001, The Turning 2004, Breath 2008. *Address:* c/o Jenny Darling & Associates, PO Box 413, Toorak, Vic. 3142, Australia (office). *Telephone:* (3) 9827-3883 (office). *Fax:* (3) 9827-1270 (office). *E-mail:* timwinton@jd-associates.com.au (office). *Website:* www.jd-associates.com.au (office).

WINTOUR, Anna; British editor; *Editor, Vogue;* b. 3 Nov. 1949; d. of the late Charles Wintour; m. David Shaffer 1984; one s. one d.; ed Queen's Coll. School, London and N London Collegiate School; deputy fashion ed. Harpers & Queen 1970–76, Harper's Bazaar, New York 1976–77; fashion and beauty ed. Viva magazine 1977–78; contributing ed. for fashion and style, Savvy Magazine 1980–81; Sr Ed. New York Magazine 1981–83; Creative Dir US Vogue 1983–86; Ed.-in-Chief, UK Vogue 1986–87; Ed. House & Garden, New York 1987–88; Ed. Vogue (US) 1988–. *Address:* Vogue, 4 Times Square, 12th Floor, New York, NY 10036, USA (office). *Telephone:* (212) 286-2810 (office). *Fax:* (212) 286-8593 (office). *Website:* www.style.com/vogue (office).

WINWOOD, Stephen (Steve) Lawrence; British musician and composer; b. 12 May 1948, Birmingham; s. of Lawrence Samuel Winwood and Lillian Mary Winwood (née Saunders); m. Eugenia Crafton 1987; one s. three d.; singer and musician, Spencer Davis Group 1964–67, Traffic 1967–74, Blind Faith 1969; British tours with The Rolling Stones 1965, The Who 1966, The Hollies 1967; solo artist 1974–; Dir F.S. Ltd/Wincraft Music Ltd; 14 Gold Record Awards, four Platinum Record Awards. *Recordings:* albums include: three with Spencer Davis Group 1966; with Traffic: Mr Fantasy 1968, Traffic 1968, John Barleycorn Must Die 1970, The Low Spark of High Heeled Boys 1972, When the Eagle Flies 1974; with Blind Faith: Blind Faith 1969; solo: Steve Winwood 1977, Arc of a Diver 1980, Talking Back to the Night 1982, Back in the Highlife 1986, Roll With It 1988 (Grammy Award 1989), Chronicles, Refugees of the Heart 1991, Far from Home 1994, The Finer Things 1995, Junction 7 1997, About Time 2003, Nine Lives 2008; singles: with Spencer Davis Group: Keep On Running 1966, Somebody Help Me 1966, Gimme Some Lovin' 1966, I'm a Man 1967; with Traffic: Paper Sun 1967, Hole in My Shoe 1967, solo singles: While You See A Chance 1980, Freedom Overspill 1986, Higher Love (two Grammy Awards: Record of the Year and Best Pop Vocal Performance 1987) 1986, The Finer Things 1987, Valerie 1987, Roll With It 1988, Don't You Know What the Night Can Do 1988, Holding On 1989, One and Only Man 1990, I Will Be Here 1991, Reach for the Light 1995, Spy in the House of Love 1997; other session work includes: Lou Reed, Berlin 1973, John Martyn, Inside Out 1973, Viv Stanshall, Men Opening Umbrellas Ahead 1974, Marianne Faithfull, Broken English 1979, Talk Talk, The Colour of Spring 1986, Paul Weller, Stanley Road 1995. *Address:* Wincraft Music, Ltd, PO Box 41, Cheltenham, Glos., GL54 4WA, England (office). *E-mail:* management@wincraftmusic.com (office). *Website:* www.stevewinwood.com.

WIRAJUDA, Nur Hassan, MA, LLM, SJD; Indonesian politician; *Minister of Foreign Affairs;* b. 9 July 1948, Tangerang; m.; four c.; ed Univ. of Indonesia, Univ. of Oxford, UK, Tufts Univ., Harvard Univ. and Univ. of Virginia, USA; practising lawyer (legal aid) and univ. lecturer, Jakarta 1972–75; Legal

Council Corp. Sec., Dockyard State Enterprise, Jakarta 1972–73; Head of Section, Secr. of the Foreign Affairs Cttee of the Nat. Council for Political and Security Stabilization, Secr. Gen., Dept of Foreign Affairs 1974–75; Third Sec., then Second Sec. for Political Affairs, Indonesian Embassy, Cairo 1977–81; Head of Section, Politics-Legal Affairs, Directorate of Int. Orgs, Dept of Foreign Affairs 1981, Dir for Int. Orgs 1993–97, Deputy Dir for Territorial Treaties, Directorate of Legal and Treaty Affairs 1998, Dir Gen. for Political Affairs 2000–01; Counsellor, later Minister Counsellor for Political Affairs, Perm. Mission in Geneva 1989–93; Amb. to Egypt (also accred to Djibouti) 1997–98; Amb. and Perm. Rep. to the UN, Geneva, WTO and the Conf. on Disarmament 1998–2000; Personal Rep. of the Pres. to the Group of Fifteen Developing Countries (G-15) 1998–2000; represented the Govt in the sovereignty case concerning Pulau Ligitan and Pulau Sipadan before Int. Court of Justice, The Hague 2000; Leading Govt Negotiator in the Dialogue on Aceh with Free Aceh Movt Reps, Switzerland 2000; Minister of Foreign Affairs 2001–. *Address:* Ministry of Foreign Affairs, Jalan Taman Pejambon 6, 10th Floor, Jakarta 10110, Indonesia (office). *Telephone:* (21) 3813453 (office). *Fax:* (21) 3857316 (office). *E-mail:* ditpen1@deplu.go.id (office). *Website:* www.deplu .go.id (office).

WIRANTO, Gen.; Indonesian politician and army officer (retd); Minister of Defence and Security and C-in-C of Armed Forces –1999; Co-ordinating Minister for Politics and Security 1999–2000; indicted by UN for crimes against humanity in E Timor in 1999 Feb. 2003; unsuccessful presidential cand. for Partai Golongan Karya (Golkar) party 2004 elections. *Address:* c/o Partai Golongan Karya (Golkar), Jalan Anggrek Nellimurni, Jakarta 11480, Indonesia (office).

WIRTH, Iwan; Swiss art dealer; *Director, Galerie Hauser & Wirth;* b. 1971, Zurich; bought first art work at age 13; opened first gallery at age 16; f. Galerie Hauser & Wirth, Zurich (with Ursula Hauser) 1991, represents Louise Bourgeois, Mary Heilman, Pipilotti Rist, John McCracken, Rachel Khedoori, Dan Graham, Fischli & Weiss and estate of Dieter Roth, est. London Br., Piccadilly, UK; f. Zwirner & Wirth Gallery, NY (with David Zwirner) 2000. *Publications:* numerous catalogues and monographs. *Address:* Galerie Hauser & Wirth, Limmatstrasse 270, 8005 Zurich, Switzerland (office); Zwirner & Wirth, 32 East 69th Street, New York, NY 10021-5016 USA (office). *Telephone:* 4468050 (office); (212) 517-8677 (US) (office). *Fax:* 4468055 (office); (212) 517-8959 (US) (office). *E-mail:* zurich@hauserwirth.com (office). *Website:* www.hauserwirth.com (office); www.zwirnerandwirth.com (office).

WIRTH, Timothy Endicott, PhD; American fmr politician and international organization executive; *President, United Nations Foundation;* b. 22 Sept. 1939, Santa Fe, NM; s. of Cecil Wirth and Virginia Maude Davis; m. Wren Winslow 1965; one s. one d.; ed Harvard Coll., Stanford Univ.; served as a Harvard 'Baby Dean' after graduation; Special Asst to Sec. Dept of Health, Educ. and Welfare 1967, Deputy Asst Sec. for Educ. 1969; Asst to Chair., Nat. Urban Coalition 1968; Vice-Pres. Great Western United Corpn, Denver 1970; Man. Arthur D. Little Inc. 1971–73; mem. 94th–99th Congresses from 2nd Dist Colo; Senator from Colorado 1987–92; Counsellor Dept of State 1993–97; Pres. UN Foundation 1998–, Better World Fund 1998–; Ford Foundation Fellow 1964–66; Pres. White House Fellows Asscn 1968–69; mem. Exec. Cttee Denver Council Foreign Relations 1974–75, Harvard Bd of Overseers; mem. Bd of Visitors, USAF Acad. 1978–; Adviser, Pres. Comm. on the 80s 1979–80; Democrat; numerous awards and hon. degrees; honoured by UNEP as a Champion of the Earth 2008. *Address:* United Nations Foundation, 1800 Massachusetts Avenue, NW, Washington, DC 20036, USA (office). *Telephone:* (202) 887-9040 (office). *Fax:* (202) 887-9021 (office). *E-mail:* kmiller@ unfoundation.org (office). *Website:* www.unfoundation.org (office).

WISDOM, Sir Norman, Kt, OBE; British actor and comedian; b. 4 Feb. 1915; m. 1947 (divorced 1969). *Films include:* Trouble in Store 1953, One Good Turn 1954, There was a Crooked Man 1960, The Girl on the Boat 1962, On the Beat 1962, A Stitch in Time 1963, Double X: The Name of the Game 1992, Cosmic Brainsuckers 2000, Five Children and It 2004. *Plays:* Stage musical Walking Happy, The Legendary Norman Wisdom (touring for Johnny Mans Productions) 1982–96, Norman Wisdom and Friends 2002–03; numerous Royal Variety Performances and pantomimes. *Radio:* Robin Hood (six-part series). *Television:* numerous TV series include Wit and Wisdom 1948–50, Norman 1970, Music Hall 1970, Nobody is Norman Wisdom 1973, A Little Bit of Wisdom 1974; TV plays include Going Gently 1981, Between the Sheets (miniseries) 2003; appeared in Bergerac 1982, Casualty 1986, Last of the Summer Wine 1995, Dalziel and Pascoe: Mens Sana 2002, The Last Detective 2003. *Achievements:* Best Newcomer Acad. Award 1953, two Broadway Awards, Lifetime Achievement Award British Comedy Awards 1991, Freeman Tirana, Albania 1995, City of London 1995, Douglas (Isle of Man). *Publications:* Trouble in Store (with Richard Dacre) 1991, Don't Laugh at Me (autobiog. with William Hall) 1992, Cos I'm a Fool (with Bernard Bale) 1996, My Turn (with William Hall) 2002. *Leisure interests:* all sports, especially golf and soccer. *Address:* c/o Johnny Mans, Johnny Mans Productions Ltd, PO Box 196, Hoddesdon, Herts., EN10 7WG, England. *Fax:* (1992) 470516.

WISE, Michael John, CBE, MC, PhD, FRGS, FRSA; British geographer; b. 17 Aug. 1918, Stafford; s. of Harry Cuthbert Wise and Sarah Evelyn Wise; m. Barbara Mary Hodgetts 1942 (died 2007); one s. one d.; ed Saltley Grammar School, Birmingham and Univ. of Birmingham; served with RA and Northamptonshire Regt in Middle East and Italy 1941–46; Lecturer in Geography, Univ. of Birmingham 1946–51, LSE 1951–54; Cassel Reader in Econ. Geography, LSE 1954–58, Prof. of Geography 1958–83, Prof. Emer.; Pro-Dir LSE 1983–85, (Hon. Fellow 1988); Erskine Fellow, Univ. of Canterbury, NZ 1970; Chair. Ministry of Agric. Cttee of Inquiry into Statutory Smallholdings 1963–67; Chair. Dept of Transport Landscape Advisory Cttee 1981–90; Chair. Court of Govs, Birkbeck Coll. 1983–89, Fellow 1990–; Pres. Inst. of British

Geographers 1974, Int. Geographical Union 1976–80, Geographical Asscn 1976–77; Pres. Royal Geographical Soc. 1980–82; Chair. Dudley Stamp Memorial Trust 1986–2007; mem. Univ. Grants Cttee, Hong Kong 1966–73, Social Science Research Council 1976–82; Hon. mem. Geographical Soc., USSR 1975, Paris 1984, Mexico 1984, Poland 1986, Asscn Japanese Geographers 1980, Inst. of British Geographers 1989, Geographical Asscn 1990; Hon. Fellow Landscape Inst. 1991; Hon. DUniv (Open Univ.) 1978; Hon. DSc (Birmingham) 1982; Gill Memorial Award of Royal Geographical Soc. 1958, Founder's Medal 1977, Alexander Csoma Körös Medal of Hungarian Geographical Soc. 1980, Tokyo Geographical Soc.'s Medal 1981, Lauréat d'honneur, Int. Geographical Union 1984. *Publications:* Birmingham and its Regional Setting (Hon. Ed.) 1950, A Pictorial Geography of the West Midlands 1958, R. O. Buchanan and Economic Geography (co-ed. with E. M. Rawstron) 1973, General Consultant, An Atlas of Earth Resources 1979, The Ordnance Survey Atlas of Great Britain 1982; numerous papers on economic and urban geography. *Leisure interests:* music, gardening. *Address:* 45 Oakleigh Avenue, Whetstone, London, N20 9JE, England. *Telephone:* (20) 8445-6057.

WISE, Robert E. (Bob), BA, JD; American politician and lawyer; *President, Alliance for Excellent Education;* b. 6 Jan. 1948, Washington, DC; m. Sandy Wise; one s. one d.; ed Duke Univ., Tulane Univ. Coll. of Law; pvt. law practice, Charleston, W. Va. 1975–80; attorney legis. council for judiciary comm., W. Va. House of Dels. 1977–78; elected to W. Va. State Senate 1980–82, Congress (W. Va. Second Dist.) 1983–2001, whip-at-large 1986–2001, mem. House Transportation and Infrastructure Cttee; Gov. of W. Va. 2001–05; Pres. Alliance for Excellent Education, Washington, DC 2005–; mem. ABA, W. Va. State Bar Asscn. *Leisure interests:* keeping fit, bluegrass music. *Address:* Alliance for Excellent Education, 1201 Connecticut Avenue, NW, Suite 901, Washington, DC 20036, USA (office). *Telephone:* (202) 828-0828 (office). *Fax:* (202) 828-0821 (office). *Website:* www.all4ed.org (office).

WISEMAN, Debra (Debbie), MBE, GGSM; British composer and conductor; b. 10 May 1963, London; d. of Paul Wiseman and Barbara Wiseman; m. Tony Wharmby 1987; ed Trinity Coll. of Music, Kingsway Princeton/Morley Coll., Guildhall School of Music and Drama, London; composer and conductor of music for film and TV productions 1989–; Visiting Prof. of Film Composition, Royal Coll. of Music 1995–; mem. Performing Right Soc., BAFTA, Musicians' Union, British Acad. of Composers and Songwriters; Hon. Fellow, Trinity Coll. of Music London 2006, Hon. Fellow, Guildhall School of Music and Drama 2007. *Compositions include:* Inside Looking Out 1989, Squares and Roundabouts 1989, Echoes of Istria 1989, The Guilty, Lighthouse, Female Perversions, The Dying of the Light, Shrinks (Silents to Satellite Award for Best Original TV Theme Music 1991), The Good Guys (Television and Radio Industries Club Award for TV Theme Music of the Year 1993), Tom and Viv 1994, The Project, Judge John Deed, P.O.W., Wilde Stories, The Upper Hand, The Churchills, Serious and Organised, The Second Russian Revolution, Little Napoleons, Children's Hospital, Death of Yugoslavia, Haunted 1995, Wilde 1997, The Fairy Tale of the Nightingale and the Rose 1999, The Fairy Tale of the Selfish Giant 1999, It Might be You, A Week in Politics, People's Century, What Did You Do In The War, Auntie?, The Cuban Missile Crisis, Vet's School, The Missing Postman, Tom's Midnight Garden, Absolute Truth, My Uncle Silas 2001, Othello 2001, Warriors (Royal TV Soc. Award) 2000, Oscar Wilde Fairy Stories 2002, Freeze Frame 2004, He Knew He Was Right 2004, The Andrew Marr Show, The Truth About Love 2004, Arsène Lupin 2004, Johnny and the Bomb 2005, Middletown 2005, Feather Boy: The Musical 2005, Middletown (film music) 2006, Jekyll 2007, Walter's War 2008, Stephen Fry in America 2008, The Passion 2008, Lesbian Vampire Killers 2009. *Leisure interests:* swimming, snooker. *Address:* c/o Roz Colls, Music Matters International, Crest House, 102–104 Church Road, Teddington, Middx, TW11 8PY, England (office); Kraft-Engel Management, 15233 Ventura Blvd, Suite 200, Sherman Oaks, CA 91403, USA (office). *Telephone:* (20) 8979-4580 (Teddington) (office). *Fax:* (20) 8979-4590 (Teddington) (office). *E-mail:* dwiseman10@aol.com (office). *Website:* www.debbiewiseman.co.uk.

WISEMAN, Frederick, BA, LLB; American documentary filmmaker and theatre director; b. 1 Jan. 1930, Boston, Mass; ed Williams Coll., Yale Univ.; fmr law professor; turned to television documentary film making 1967; Founder and Gen. Man. Zipporah Films Inc. 1971–; mem. Bd of Dirs Int. Documentary Asscn 1986–, Theater for a New Audience (also mem. Artistic Council) 1998–; mem. Advisory Bd New York Documentary Festival 1997–; mem. Advisory Cttee Learning from Performers, Harvard Univ. 1991–, Margaret Mead Film Festival, American Museum of Natural History 1992–; mem. Festival Cttee Human Rights Watch Int. Film Festival 1994–; Fellow, American Acad. of Arts and Letters 1991–; mem. Mass Bar Asscn 1955–; mem. Hon. Advisory Cttee, American Repertory Theatre, Harvard Univ. 1986–; Hon. mem. Les Amis du Cinéma du Réel Association 1987–; mem. Boston Jewish Film Festival, Hon. Cttee 1994–; Fellow, American Acad. of Arts and Letters 1991–; Chevalier de l'Ordre des Arts et des Lettres 1987, Commdr de l'Ordre des Arts et des Lettres 2000; Hon. DHumLitt (Cincinnati) 1973, (Williams Coll.) 1976, (John Jay Coll. of Criminal Justice) 1994; Hon. DFA (Lake Forest Coll.) 1991, (Princeton) 1994, (Bowdoin Coll.) 2005; Peabody Award for Significant and Meritorious Achievement 1990, Rosenberger Medal, Univ. of Chicago 1999, Yale Law Asscn Award of Merit 2002, Dan David Prize Laureate 2003, American Soc. of Cinematographers Distinguished Achievement Award 2006, George Polk Career Award 2006. *Documentary films include:* Titicut Follies 1967, High School 1968, Law and Order 1969, Hospital 1969, Basic Training 1971, Essene 1972, Juvenile Court 1973, Primate 1974, Welfare 1975, Meat 1976, Canal Zone 1977, Sinai Field Mission 1978, Manoeuvre 1979, Model 1980, Seraphita's Diary 1982, The Store 1983, Racetrack 1985, Blind 1986, Deaf 1986, Adjustment & Work 1986, Multi-Handicapped 1986, Missile 1987, Near Death 1989, Central Park 1989, Aspen 1991, Zoo 1993, High School II 1994, Ballet 1995, La Comedie Francaise 1996,

Public Housing 1997, Belfast, Maine 1999, Domestic Violence 2001, La Dernière lettre 2002, Domestic Violence II 2002, The Garden 2005. *Plays include:* as dir: The Last Letter (adaptation from the novel Life and Fate by Vasily Grossman), Hate by Joshua Goldstein, Welfare: The Opera, Oh Les Beaux Jours (Happy Days) by Samuel Beckett. *Publications:* numerous articles in journals and magazines including The Threepenny Review. *Address:* Zipporah Films, One Richdale Avenue, Unit 4, Cambridge, MA 02140, USA (office). *Telephone:* (617) 576-3603 (office). *Fax:* (617) 864-8006 (office). *E-mail:* info@zipporah.com (office). *Website:* www.zipporah.com (office).

WISNER, Frank George, BA; American business executive and fmr diplomatist; *Vice-Chairman for External Affairs, American International Group;* b. 2 July 1938, New York; s. of Frank G. Wisner and Mary E. Knowles; m. 1st Genevieve de Virel 1969 (deceased 1974); one d.; m. 2nd Christine de Ganay 1976; one s. one d. and one step-s. one step-d.; ed Woodberry Forest School, Rugby School and Princeton Univ.; joined US Foreign Service 1961; various posts 1961–75; Special Asst to Under-Sec. for Political Affairs 1975–76; Dir Office of Southern African Affairs 1976–77; Deputy Exec. Sec. 1977–79; Amb. to Zambia 1979–82; Deputy Asst Sec. for African Affairs 1982–86; Amb. to Egypt 1986–91, to Philippines 1991–92, to India 1994–97; Under-Sec. of Defence 1993–94; currently Vice-Chair. for External Affairs, American Int. Group; mem. Bd Dirs Ethan Allen Interiors, EOG Resources; Romanian Order of Merit; Presidential Meritorious Service Awards, Dept of State Honor Awards, Repub. of Vietnam Mil. Medal of Honour, Dept of Defense Service Medal. *Leisure interests:* hunting, horseback riding, golf. *Address:* American International Group Inc., 18th Floor, 70 Pine Street, New York, NY 10270 (office); 164 East 72nd Street, Apt. 5B, New York, NY 10021, USA (home). *Telephone:* (212) 770-5262 (office); (212) 517-2028 (home). *Fax:* (212) 480-5400 (office). *E-mail:* frank.wisner@aig.com (office).

WISSMANN, Matthias; German lawyer and politician; *Partner, Wilmer Cutler Pickering Hale and Dorr;* b. 15 April 1949, Ludwigsburg; s. of Paul Wissmann and Margarete Kalcker; ed Univs of Tübingen and Bonn; practised as lawyer; mem. Fed. Exec. of CDU 1975–; mem. Bundestag 1976–; Pres. European Union of Young Christian Democrats 1976–82; Minister of Research and Technology Jan.–May 1993, of Transport 1993–98; Chair. Parl. Cttee of Econ. and Tech. 1998–2001, Speaker Parl. Group for Econ. and Tech. 2001–02, Chair. Cttee of European Affairs 2002–; Sr Int. Counsellor, Wilmer Cutler Pickering Hale and Dorr (law firm), Berlin 1999–; Pres. German Automotive Industry Asscn; mem. Int. Rolls-Royce Advisory Board; Vice-Chair. Supervisory BD Seeburger AG; Grand Order of Merit of Germany, Grand Order of Merit of Austria, Grand Cross of Chile, Chevalier de Légion d'Honneur. *Publications include:* Zukunftschancen der Jugend 1979, Einsteigen statt Aussteigen 1983, Marktwirtschaft 2000 1993, Soziale Marktwirtschaft 1998. *Leisure interests:* piano, literature, hockey, tennis, skiing, golf. *Address:* Wilmer Cutler Pickering Hale and Dorr, Friedrichstr. 95, 10117 Berlin (office); Am Zuckerberg 79, 71640 Ludwigsburg, Germany (home). *Telephone:* (30) 20226426 (office). *Fax:* (30) 20226500 (office). *E-mail:* matthias .wissmann@wilmerhale.com (office). *Website:* www.wilmerhale.com (office); www.matthias-wissmann.de.

WISZNIEWSKI, Andrzej, PhD, DSc; Polish academic, electrical engineer and politician; *Professor, Institute of Electrical Power Engineering, Technical University of Wrocław;* b. 15 Feb. 1935, Warsaw; s. of Tadeusz Wiszniewski and Ewa Wiszniewski (née Ciechomska); m. Ewa Lutosławska; one d.; ed Tech. Univ. of Wrocław; researcher, Wrocław Univ. of Tech. 1957–, Extraordinary Prof. 1972, Ordinary Prof. 1990–, Rector 1990–96; Univ. of Garyounis Benghazi, Libya 1976–79; Head of Scientific Research Cttee and mem. Council of Ministers 1997–99; Minister of Science 1999–2001; mem. Speech Communication Asscn, USA, Solidarity Trade Union 1980–, Social Movt of Solidarity Election Action 1998–2001; Hon. Mem. Inst. of Electrical Engineers 1999, Distinguished Mem. Int. Conf. on Large Electric Systems 2000; Kt's Cross, Order of Polonia Restituta 1979; Grand Cross, Order of Saint Stanisław with Star 1998; Commdr, Order of Saint Sylvester 1998; Grand Cross, Order of Merit (Peru) 2001, Oficer's Cross of Polonia Restituta 2004; Dr hc (Cen. Conn. State Univ.) 1993, (Tech. Univ. of Lvov) 1999, (Tech. Univ. of Wrocław) 2001; City of Wrocław Award 1996, Council of Rectors Award 1998. *Publications:* Measuring Transformers 1983, Algorithms of Numeral Measurements in Electroenergetic Automatics 1990, Schutztechnik in Elektroenergiesystemen (co-author) 1994, Protective Automatics in Electroenergetics Systems 1998, How to Speak and Make Speeches Convincingly 1994, Aphorisms and Quotations: for Orators, Disputants and Banqueters 1997, Measuring and Decision Making Algorithms (jtly), Art of Writing 2003; over 130 articles on electrotechnics and electroenergetics. *Leisure interests:* contemporary literature, dog-walking, skiing, mountaineering, rhetoric. *Address:* Technical University of Wrocław Institute of Power Engineering, Wybrzeze Wyspianskiego 27, 50-370 Wrocław (office); Krasickiego 18, 51-144 Wrocław, Poland (home). *Telephone:* (71) 3203487 (office); (71) 3726477 (home); (601) 381944 (home). *Fax:* (71) 3202656 (office). *E-mail:* andrzej.wiszniewski@pwr.wroc.pl (office); awiszniewski@wr.home.pl (home). *Website:* www.pwr.wroc.pl/~i-8zas (office).

WIT, Antoni; Polish conductor and academic; *Managing and Artistic Director, Warsaw Philharmonic;* b. 7 Feb. 1944, Kraków; m. Zofia Ćwikilewicz; ed State Higher School of Music, Kraków (conducting and composition), Jagiellonian Univ., Kraków (law), Nadia Boulanger, Paris (composition); Asst Conductor Warsaw Philharmonic, 1967–70, Man. and Artistic Dir 2002–; conductor, Poznań Nat. Philharmonic 1970–72; Artistic Dir Pomeranian Philharmonic, Bydgoszcz 1974–77; Man. and Artistic Dir, Polish Radio Symphony Orchestra and Choir, Kraków 1977–83; Dir Polish Nat. Radio Symphony Orchestra, Katowice 1983–2000; Artistic Dir Orquesta Filarmonica de Gran Canaria, Las Palmas 1987–91; Prof., Fryderyk Chopin Acad. of Music, Warsaw 1997–; has conducted LPO, RPO, BBC Symphony Orchestra, Berliner Philharmoniker, Orchestre National de Belgique, Tokyo Symphony Orchestra, Montreal Symphony Orchestra, Orquesta Nacional de España, Staatskapelle Dresden, Accad. di Santa Cecilia, Rome, Tonhalle-Orchester; numerous prizes include Second Prize, Herbert von Karajan Conducting Competition, Berlin 1971, Orpheus (Warsaw Autumn Festival Critics' Award) 1984, 1996, Diapason d'Or, Grand Prix de Disque de la Nouvelle Académie du Disque 1992, Diamond Baton Award of Polish Public Radio 1998, Cannes Classical Award, Midem Classique 2002. *Compositions:* soundtracks: Kronika wypadków miłosnych (The Chronicle of Love Affairs) 1986, Korczak 1990, Pan Tadeusz (Last Foray in Lithuania) 1999. *Recordings include:* more than 90 recordings for EMI-HMV, CBS, Decca, Naxos, NVS Arts, Pony Canyon, Polskie Nagrania; albums include symphonies by Tchaikovsky, Górecki, Schumann, Penderecki, Lutosławski (all), Olivier Messiaen (Turangalila Symphony) (Cannes Classical Award—Midem Classique 2002), etc. *E-mail:* sekretariat@filharmonia.pl (home). *Website:* www.filharmonia.pl (office).

WITBOOI, Hendrik; Namibian politician; b. 7 Jan. 1934, Gibeon; m. Paulina Joseph 1973; ed Rheinisch Mission School, African Methodist Episcopalian (AME) School, Gibeon, Methodist Church School, Mariental, Wilberforce Inst., S Africa, Augustineum, Okahandja; teacher, Keetmanshoop AME Pvt. School 1955–58, Prin. 1965–67; Sec. to Samuel Witbooi 1958; Prin. State School, Gibeon 1967–77; ordained Deacon in AME Church 1974, Elder Pastor 1976, Presiding Elder for Windhoek Dist 1994–; joined South West African People's Organization (SWAPO) after collapse of Namibian Nat. Convention 1976, mem. SWAPO Del. to NY to take part in talks to draft Resolution 435 1978; elected SWAPO Sec. for Educ. and Culture on Nat. Exec. Cttee; elected Chief of Witboois while in detention; f. pvt. school and initiated community devt projects in Gibeon 1979; Acting Vice-Pres. SWAPO 1983, Vice-Pres. 1991; mem. Constituent Ass. and mem. first Parl. 1989–2004; Minister of Labour and Human Resources Devt 1990–95; Deputy Prime Minister 1995; DHumLitt hc (St Augustine's Coll., NC, USA) 1990; Dr hc (Paul Quin Univ., USA) 1990, (St Augustine Univ., USA) 1990, (Morris Brown Coll., Atlanta, Ga, USA) 1998; Women's Missionary Soc. of the AME Church Award 1990, AME Church Mission Dept Award, Orlando, Fla, USA 1990, Richard Allen Award 1992. *Address:* c/o Office of the Prime Minister, Robert Mugabe Avenue, PMB 13338, Windhoek, Namibia (office).

WITHEROW, John Moore; British journalist; *Editor, The Sunday Times;* b. 20 Jan. 1952, Johannesburg, S. Africa; m. Sarah Linton 1985; two s. one d.; ed Bedford School, Univ. of York, Univ. of Cardiff; voluntary service in Namibia (then SW Africa) after school; posted to Madrid for Reuters; covered Falklands War for The Times 1982; joined The Sunday Times 1984, successively Defence and Diplomatic Corresp., Focus Ed., Foreign Ed., Man. Ed. (news), Ed., The Sunday Times 1995–. *Publications:* The Winter War: The Falklands (with Patrick Bishop) 1982, The Gulf War 1993. *Leisure interests:* sailing, skiing, tennis. *Address:* The Sunday Times, 1 Pennington Street, London E98 1ST, England. *Telephone:* (20) 7782-5640. *Fax:* (20) 7782-5420. *Website:* www .timesonline.co.uk.

WITHERSPOON, Reese; American actress; b. 22 March 1976, Baton Rouge, La; d. of John Witherspoon; m. Ryan Phillippe 1999 (divorced 2007); one s. one d.; ed Harpeth Hall, Nashville, Stanford Univ.; f. production co. Type A Films. *Films:* The Man in The Moon 1991, Wildflower (for TV) 1991, Solomon's Choice (for TV), Return to Lonesome Dove (TV mini-series) 1993, A Far Off Place 1993, Jack the Bear, S.F.W. 1995, Fear, Freeway 1996, (Best Actress, Catalonian Int. Film Festival, Cognac Film Festival) 1996, Twilight, Overnight Delivery, Pleasantville 1998, Cruel Intentions (Best Supporting Actress in a Drama Romance, Blockbuster Entertainment Awards) 1999, Election (Best Actress, Nat. Soc. of Film Critics) 1999, Best Laid Plans 1999, American Psycho 2000, Little Nicky 2000, The Trumpet of the Swan (voice) 2001, Legally Blonde (Best Actress, Cosmo Movie Awards, Best Comedic Performance, MTV Movie Awards) 2001, Sweet Home Alabama 2002, The Importance of Being Earnest 2002, Legally Blonde 2: Red, White & Blonde 2003, Vanity Fair 2004, Just Like Heaven 2005, Walk the Line (Best Actress Critics' Choice Awards 2006, Golden Globe Award for Best Performance by an Actress in a Musical or Comedy, Screen Actors Guild Award for Best Actress 2006, BAFTA Award for Best Actress in a Leading Role 2006, Acad. Award for Best Actress 2006) 2005, Penelope 2006, Rendition 2007. *Television:* Friends, King of the Hill, Saturday Night Live. *Address:* c/o CAA, 2000 Avenue of the Stars, Los Angeles, CA 90067, USA (office).

WITKIN, Joel-Peter, BFA, MA, MFA; American photographer; b. 13 Sept. 1939, Brooklyn, New York; s. of Max Witkin and Mary Pelligrino; ed The Cooper Union, New York, Columbia Univ., New York, Univ. of New Mexico; began photography at age 11; photographer, US Army 1961–64; Commdr des Arts et des Lettres 2000; four Nat. Endowment Awards 1980, 1981, 1986, 1992, Int. Center of Photography Award, New York City 1988, The Augustus Saint Gaudens Medal, The Cooper Union 1996. *Exhibitions include:* Brooklyn Museum 1986, Centro de Arte Reina Sofía Museum 1988, Palais de Tokyo, Paris 1989, Museum of Modern Art, Haifa, Israel 1990, Guggenheim Museum, New York 1995, Il Castello di Rivoli Museum, Turin, Italy 1995, Museum of Fine Arts, Santa Fe 1998, Wildenstein Gallery, Tokyo 1998, Sterburg Museum Prague 1999, Hotel de Sully, Paris 2000, The Louvre, Paris 2001, Graz Museum, Germany 2003. *Publications:* Joel-Peter Witkin (monograph) 1984, Gods of Earth and Heaven 1994, Guggenheim Museum monograph 1995, The Bone House 1998, Joel-Peter Witkin, Disciple and Master 2000; illustrated editions of William Blake's poetry: Songs of Experience 2002, Songs of Innocence 2003, Songs of Innocence and Experience 2004. *Address:* 1707 5 Points Road, SW, Albuquerque, NM 87105, USA (home). *Telephone:* (505) 843-

6682 (office); (505) 842-6511 (home). *Fax:* (505) 842-1611 (home). *E-mail:* jwitkin1@comcast.net (home).

WITKOP, Bernhard, PhD, ScD; American chemist; *Honorary Emeritus Scholar, National Institutes of Health (NIH);* b. 9 May 1917, Freiburg (Baden), Germany; s. of Prof. Philipp W. Witkop and Hedwig M. Hirschhorn; m. Marlene Prinz 1945; one s. two d.; ed Univ. of Munich; Dozent Univ. of Munich 1946; Matthew T. Mellon Fellow Harvard Univ., USA 1947; Instructor and Lecturer 1948–50; Special Fellow U.S. Public Health Service 1950–53; Research Fellow Nat. Heart Inst. 1950; Special Fellow, Nat. Inst. of Arthritis and Metabolic Diseases, NIH 1952, Chief of Section on Metabolites 1956–87, Chief of Lab. of Chem., Nat. Inst. of Arthritis, Metabolic and Digestive Diseases 1957–87; NIH Inst. Scholar 1987–92, Hon. Emer. Scholar 1993–; Visiting Prof., Kyoto Univ. 1961, Univ. of Freiburg 1962; Lecturer, Univ. of Zürich 1972; Ed. (USA) FEBS Letters 1979–; mem. NAS, Acad. Leopoldina-Carolina 1972, NAS Comm. on Int. Relations 1978, American Acad. of Arts and Sciences 1978, Paul Ehrlich Foundation, Frankfurt 1979–96, American Philosophical Soc. 1999, Bd of Dirs, Leo Baeck Inst., New York 1992–; Hon. mem. Pharmaceutical Soc. of Japan 1978, Chemical Soc. 1982–, Japanese Biochemical Soc. 1983–, Academia Scientiarum et Artium Europaea, Salzburg 1993–; Order of the Sacred Treasure, Japan; ACS Hillebrand Award 1959, Paul Karrer Medallist, US Sr A. von Humboldt Award (Univ. of Hamburg) 1979, Golden Doctor Diploma (Univ. . of Munich) 1990. *Publications:* Mushroom Poisons 1940, Curare Arrow Poisons 1942, Yohimbine 1943, Kynurenine 1944, Indole Alkaloids 1947–50, Oxidation Mechanisms, Ozonization, Peroxides 1952, Hydroxyaminoacids, Metabolites, Building Stones and Biosynthesis of Collagen 1955, Mescalin and LSD Metabolism 1958, Pharmacodynamic Amines 1960, Nonenzymatic Cleavage and Modification of Enzymes 1961, Gramicidin A 1964, Rufomycin 1964, Photo-Reductions, -Additions, -Cyclizations 1966, Microsomal Hydroxylations, Arenoxide Metabolites, 'NIH-Shift' 1967, Amphibian Venoms, Batrachotoxin, Pumiliotoxin 1968, Norepinephrine Release, Inactivation, False transmitters 1968, Histrionicotoxin, a selective inhibitor of cholinergic receptors 1970–72, Interaction of Polynucleotides Stimulators of Interferon 1973–74, Gephyrotoxin, a Muscarinic Antagonist 1978, Anatoxin-a: The most potent Agonist at the nicotinic receptor 1980–82, Paul Ehrlich: His Ideas and his Legacy, Nobel Symposium 1981, Amphibian Alkaloids 1983, Forty Years of 'Trypto-Fun' 1984, Mind over Matter (lecture at Israel Acad. of Sciences, Jerusalem) 1987, Paul Ehlich's Magic Bullets Revisited. *Leisure interests:* languages, etymology, literature, piano, chamber music, hiking, skating, mountaineering, history and philosophy of science, Japanese style and culture. *Address:* National Institutes of Health, National Institute of Diabetes and Digestive and Kidney Diseases (NIDDK), Bethesda, MD 20892 (office); 3807 Montrose Driveway, Chevy Chase, MD 20815, USA (home). *Telephone:* (301) 402-4181 (office); (301) 656-6418 (home). *Fax:* (301) 402-0240 (office).

WITTEN, Edward, BA, MA, PhD; American physicist and academic; *Charles Simonyi Professor, School of Natural Sciences, Institute for Advanced Study;* b. 26 Aug. 1951, Baltimore, Md; s. of Louis Witten and Lorraine Wollach Witten; m. Chiara R. Nappi 1979; one s. two d.; ed Brandeis and Princeton Univs; Postdoctoral Fellow, Harvard Univ. 1976–77, Jr Fellow, Harvard Soc. of Fellows 1977–80; Prof. of Physics, Princeton Univ., NJ 1980–87, Prof., School of Natural Sciences, Inst. for Advanced Study 1987–, Charles Simonyi Prof. 1997–; Visiting Prof., Calif. Inst. of Tech. 1999–2001; Fellow, American Acad. of Arts and Sciences 1984, American Physical Soc. 1984, NAS 1988, American Philosophical Soc. 1994; Foreign mem. Royal Soc., 1998; mem. Bd of Dirs Americans for Peace 1992–; MacArthur Fellowship 1982; Dr hc (Brandeis Univ.) 1988, (Hebrew Univ.) 1993, (Columbia Univ.) 1996, (Univ. of Southern Calif.) 2004, (Johns Hopkins Univ.) 2005, (Harvard Univ.) 2005, (Univ. of Cambridge, UK) 2006; Einstein Medal, Einstein Soc. of Berne, Switzerland 1985, Award for Physical and Math. Sciences, New York Acad. of Sciences 1985, Dirac Medal, Int. Center for Theoretical Physics 1985, Alan T. Waterman Award, Nat. Science Foundation 1986, Fields Medal, Int. Union of Mathematicians 1990, Madison Medal, Princeton Univ. 1992, New Jersey Pride Award 1996, Award of the Golden Plate, American Acad. of Achievement 1997, Klein Medal, Stockholm Univ. 1998, Dannie Heineman Prize 1998, Nemmers Prize in Math., Northwestern Univ. 2000, Clay Research Award 2001, Shalom Award, Americans for Peace 2002, Nat. Medal of Science 2003, Harvey Prize, Technion 2006, Poincaré Prize, Int. Assen of Math. Physics 2006, Crafoord Prize (jtly) 2008. *Publications:* Superstring Theory, 2 Vols (with M. B. Green and J.H. Schwarz) 1987; has written more than 300 scientific papers. *Address:* Institute for Advanced Study, School of Natural Sciences, Einstein Drive, Princeton, NJ 08540, USA (office). *Telephone:* (609) 734-8021 (office). *E-mail:* witten@ias.edu (office). *Website:* www.sns.ias.edu/~witten (office).

WITTY, Andrew, BA (Econ); British business executive; *CEO, GlaxoSmithKline plc;* m.; two c.; ed Univ. of Nottingham; joined Glaxo UK 1985, held various positions in UK, including Dir of Pharmacy and Distribution, Int. Product Man. and a variety of other sales and marketing positions, later served as Man. Dir Glaxo South Africa and Area Dir for South and East Africa, then Vice-Pres. and Gen. Man. Marketing for Glaxo Wellcome Inc. (US subsidiary), Sr Vice-Pres., Asia Pacific, based in Singapore –2003, Pres. Pharmaceuticals Europe, GlaxoSmithKline 2003–08, mem. Corp. Exec. Team, CEO Designate 2007–08, CEO 2008–; served as Econ. Advisor to Gov. of Guangzhou, People's Repub. of China 2000–02; mem. Singapore Econ. Devt Bd 2000–02, Econ. Devt Bd Audit Cttee 2000–02, Singapore Land Authority Bd 2000–02; mem. INSEAD UK Council, Interim Bd of Office for Strategic Coordination of Health Research, Imperial Coll. Commercialisation Advisory Bd, London Council for the Advancement of Science and Tech.; mem. Pharma Futures Working Group, Health Innovation Council (UK). *Leisure interests:* tennis, running, watching rugby and cricket. *Address:* GlaxoSmithKline plc, 980 Great West Road, Brentford, London, TW8 9GS, England (office). *Telephone:* (20) 8047-5000 (office); (20) 8990-9000 (office). *Fax:* (20) 8990-4321 (office). *E-mail:* info@gsk.com (office). *Website:* www.gsk.com (office).

WLOSOWICZ, Zbigniew; Polish diplomatist and UN official; fmr UN Rep. from Poland, UN Envoy Feb. 1993; mem. UN Security Council; Special Adviser on Inter-Governmental Affairs UNDP 1998–2000; UN Special Rep. of the Sec.-Gen. in Cyprus and Chief of Mission, UNFICYP 2000–05. *Address:* c/o Ministry of Foreign Affairs, 00-580 Warsaw, Al. Szucha 23, Poland.

WOERTH, Éric; French business executive and politician; *Minister of the Budget, Public Accounts and the Civil Service;* b. 29 Jan. 1956, Creil; m.; two c.; ed HEC School of Man., Paris; legal and tax adviser, Arthur Andersen Int. 1981–82; Head of Internal Audit and Asst Head of Service Operations and Financial Negotiations, Pechiney (aluminium producing co.) 1982–90; Dir, then Pnr Bossard Consultants 1990–97; Assoc. Dir Arthur Andersen 1997–2002; mem. Regional Council, Picardy 1986–2002, Vice-Pres. 1992–98; Mayor of Chantilly 1995–2001; Adviser, Cabinet of the Prime Minister 1995–97; mem. Union pour un Mouvement Populaire (UMP), Treas. 2002–; Deputy for Oise, Nat. Ass. 2002–; Treas., Jacques Chirac's presidential campaign 2002; Sec. of State for Reforms 2004–05; Minister of Budget, Public Accounts and Civil Service 2007–; mem. Finance Comm., Nat. Ass. 2005–07. *Address:* Ministry of the Budget and Public Accounts, 139 rue de Bercy, 75572 Paris, France (office). *Telephone:* 1-40-04-04-04 (office). *Fax:* 1-43-43-75-97 (office). *E-mail:* eric.woerth@wanadoo.fr (home). *Website:* www.minefi.gouv.fr (office); www.blog-ewoerth.com.

WOERTZ, Patricia (Pat) A., BA, CPA; American business executive; *Chairman, President and CEO, Archer Daniels Midland Company;* b. March 1953, Pittsburgh, Pa; ed Pennsylvania State Univ. and Columbia Univ., New York; joined Ernst & Young, Pittsburgh as a certified public accountant 1974; positions in refining and marketing, strategic planning and finance with Gulf Oil Corpn, Pittsburgh 1977–81, head of US upstream audit group, Houston, Tex. 1981–85, worked on asset divestitures during merger of Gulf and Chevron 1985–87, Finance Man. Chevron Information Tech. Co. 1989–91, Strategic Planning Man. Chevron Corpn 1991–93, Pres. Chevron Canada Ltd, Vancouver, BC 1993–96, Pres. Chevron Int. Oil Co. and Vice-Pres. Logistics and Trading for Chevron Products Co. 1996–98, Pres. Chevron Products Co. and Vice-Pres. Chevron Corpn 1998–2001, Exec. Vice-Pres. Global Downstream, ChevronTexaco Corpn 2001–06; Pres., CEO and mem. Bd of Dirs Archer Daniels Midland Co. (ADM) 2006–, Chair. 2007–; mem. Bd of Dirs Procter & Gamble Co., American Petroleum Inst., Bd of Visitors Pennsylvania State Univ.; Vice-Chair. Kennedy Center Corp. Fund; mem. Nat. Petroleum Council, Int. Business Council of the World Econ. Forum, US Chamber of Commerce, The Business Council, Business Roundtable; Trustee, Univ. of San Diego; mem. Bd of Visitors Pennsylvania State Univ.; ranked by Fortune magazine amongst 50 Most Powerful Women in Business in the US (eighth) 2002, (ninth) 2003, (ninth) 2004, (sixth) 2005, (fourth) 2006, (sixth) 2007, named Distinguished Alumna by Pennsylvania State Univ. 2005, ranked by Forbes magazine amongst 100 Most Powerful Women (seventh) 2006, (eighth) 2007, (12th) 2008. *Address:* Archer Daniels Midland Company, 4666 Faries Parkway, Decatur, IL 62526, USA (office). *Telephone:* (217) 424-5200 (office). *Fax:* (217) 424-6196 (office). *E-mail:* info@admworld.com (office). *Website:* www.admworld.com (office).

WOESSNER, Mark Matthias, DrIng; German business executive; b. 14 Oct. 1938, Berlin; m.; two c.; ed Tech. Univ., Karlsruhe; Man. Asst Bertelsmann AG 1968–70; Production Man. Mohndruck Printing Co. 1970–72, Tech. Dir 1972–74, Man. Dir 1974–76; mem. Exec. Bd Bertelsmann AG, Pres. Printing and Mfg Div. 1976–83, Pres. and CEO 1983–98, Chair. Supervisory Bd 1998–2000; Deputy Chair. Exec. Bd Bertelsmann Foundation 1996–98, Chair. Exec. Bd 1998–2000. *Leisure interest:* sport. *Address:* c/o Bertelsmann Stiftung, Carl-Bertelsmann-Strasse 256, 33311 Gütersloh, Germany.

WOESTE, Albrecht, Dipl-Ing; German business executive; *Chairman, Supervisory Board and Shareholders' Committee, Henkel KGaA;* b. 1935; ed Berlin Tech. Univ.; f. Woeste GmbH & Co. KG 1963; Chair. Supervisory Bd and Shareholders' Cttee, Henkel KGaA 1990–; mem. Int. Advisory Bd IESE Business School, Univ. of Navarra. *Address:* Henkel AG & Co. KGaA, Henkelstrasse 67, Düsseldorf 40191, Germany (office). *Telephone:* (211) 797-0 (office). *Fax:* (211) 7982484 (office). *E-mail:* info@henkel.com (office). *Website:* www.henkel.com (office).

WOFFORD, Harris Llewellyn, LLB; American writer, attorney and fmr politician; *Chairman, America's Promise – The Alliance for Youth;* b. 9 April 1926, New York; s. of Harris L. Wofford and Estelle Gardner; m. Emmy Lou Clare Lindgren 1948 (died 1996); two s. one d.; ed Univ. of Chicago and Yale and Howard Univ. Law Schools; admitted DC Bar 1954, US Supreme Court Bar 1958, Pa Bar 1978; Asst to Chester Bowles 1953–54; law assoc. Covington & Burling, Washington, DC 1954–58; legal asst to Rev. T. Hesburgh, Comm. on Civil Rights 1958–59; Assoc. Prof., Notre Dame Law School 1959–60, on leave 1961–66; Special Asst to Pres. John F. Kennedy 1961–62; Special Rep. for Africa, Dir Ethiopian Program, US Peace Corps 1962–64; Assoc. Dir Peace Corps, Washington, DC 1964–66; Pres. Coll. at Old Westbury, State Univ. of NY 1966–70, Bryn Mawr (Pa) Coll. 1970–78; Counsel, Schnader, Harrison, Segal and Lewis, Philadelphia and Washington 1979–86; Sec. Labor and Industry, Commonwealth of Pa 1987–91; Senator from Pennsylvania 1991–95; CEO Corpn for Nat. Service 1995–2001; Chair. America's Promise: the Alliance for Youth 2002–; mem. Bd of Dirs Youth Service America, Points of Light Foundation; mem. Council on Foreign Relations; Democrat. *Publications include:* It's Up to Us 1946, India Afire (with Clare Wofford) 1951, Of Kennedys and Kings 1980. *Address:* America's Promise – The Alliance for Youth, 909 North Washington Street, Suite 400, Alexandria, VA 22314-1556 (office); 955 26th Street, NW, Apartment 501, Washington, DC 20037, USA. *Telephone:* (703) 684-4500 (office). *Fax:* (703) 535-3900 (office). *Website:* www.americaspromise.org (office).

WOGAN, Gerald Norman, PhD; American chemist and academic; *Professor of Chemistry and Biological Engineering, Biological Engineering Division, Massachusetts Institute of Technology;* b. 11 Jan. 1930, Altoona, Pa; s. of Thomas B. Wogan and Florence E. (Corl) Wogan; m. Henrietta E. Hoenicke 1957; one s. one d.; ed Juniata Coll. and Univ. of Illinois; Asst Prof. of Physiology, Rutgers Univ., New Brunswick, NJ 1957–61; Asst Prof. of Toxicology, MIT, Cambridge, Mass. 1962–65, Assoc. Prof. 1965–69, Prof. 1969–, Head of Dept of Applied Biological Sciences 1979–88, Dir Division of Toxicology 1988–99, Prof. of Chem. and Biological Eng 1989–; Consultant to nat. and int. govt agencies and industries; Fellow American Acad. of Microbiology; mem. NAS, Inst. of Medicine. *Publications:* articles and reviews in professional journals. *Address:* Biological Engineering Division, Massachusetts Institute of Technology, 77 Massachusetts Avenue, Room 26-009, Cambridge, MA 02139, USA. *Telephone:* (617) 253-3188 (office). *Fax:* (617) 258-9733 (office). *E-mail:* wogan@mit.edu (office). *Website:* web.mit.edu/be/people/wogan.htm (office); web.mit.edu/gnwlab (office).

WOGAN, Sir Michael Terence (Terry), Kt, KBE, DL; Irish broadcaster; b. 3 Aug. 1938; s. of the late Michael Thomas Wogan and Rose Wogan; m. Helen Joyce 1965; two s. one d.; ed Crescent Coll., Limerick, Belvedere Coll., Dublin; announcer Radio Telefís Eireann (RTE) 1963, Sr Announcer 1964–66; various programmes for BBC Radio 1965–67, 1970–83, 1993–, BBC TV, ITV, Channel 5, UKTV Gold 1972–; now freelance; DL of Buckinghamshire; Hon. DLitt (Limerick Univ.) 2004; Pye Radio Award 1980, Radio Industries Award (Radio Personality three times, TV Personality 1982, 1984, 1985, 1987), TV Times TV Personality of the Year (10 times), Daily Express Award (twice), Carl Alan Award (three times), Variety Club of GB: Special Award 1982, Showbusiness Personality 1984, Radio Personality of Last 21 Years, Daily Mail Nat. Radio Awards 1988, Sony Radio Award, Barcelona Olympics 1993, Best Breakfast Show 1994, Sony Awards 2001, 2002, Best Broadcast Music Show 2002, Sony Gold Achievement Award 2006. *Radio programmes include:* Late Night Extra BBC Radio 1967–69; The Terry Wogan Show, BBC Radio One 1969–73, BBC Radio Two 1973–84, 1993, Wake Up to Wogan, BBC Radio Two 1995–. *Television shows include:* Lunchtime with Wogan, ATV; BBC: Come Dancing, Song for Europe, The Eurovision Song Contest 1983–2008, Children in Need, Wogan's Guide to the BBC, Blankety Blank, Wogan, Terry Wogan's Friday Night, Do The Right Thing 1994–95, Auntie's Bloomers, Wogan's Web, Points of View 2000–01, 2003–, Proms in the Park 1997–; Channel 5: Terry and Gaby Show 2003–04; UKTV Gold: Wogan Now and Then 2006–. *Publications:* Banjaxed 1979, The Day Job 1981, To Horse, To Horse 1982, Wogan on Wogan 1987, Wogan's Ireland 1988, Bumper Book of Togs 1995, Is It Me? (autobiog.) 2000, Musn't Grumble (autobiog.) 2006, Wogan's Year 2007. *Leisure interests:* tennis, golf, swimming, reading, writing, watching rugby. *Address:* c/o Jo Gurnett Personal Management Ltd, 12 Newburgh Street, London, W1F 7RP, England (office). *Telephone:* (20) 7440-1850 (office). *Fax:* (20) 7287-9642 (office). *E-mail:* info@jgpm.co.uk (office). *Website:* www.jgpm.co.uk (office).

WOICKE, Peter L.; German banker and international finance official; *Member, Supervisory Board, Raiffeisen International Bank-Holding AG;* with J. P. Morgan for over 30 years, in particular in Latin America and the Middle East, Head Banking Div., Beirut, Lebanon, Man. Global Gas and Petroleum Group, fmr mem. Exec. Man. Group, Chair. J.P. Morgan Securities Asia, Singapore; Man. Dir Pvt. Sector Operations, IBRD (World Bank) 1999–2005, Exec. Vice-Pres. IFC 1999–2005; mem. Supervisory Bd Raiffeisen International Bank-Holding AG (Raiffeisen International, subsidiary of RZB Group) 2005–, ProCredit Holding 2005–, Anglo American (to begin 2006); Diageo Africa Business Reporting Award 2005. *Address:* Raiffeisen International Bank-Holding AG, Am Stadtpark 9, Vienna, 1030, Austria (office). *Telephone:* (1) 71707-0 (office). *E-mail:* peter.woicke@ri.co.at (office). *Website:* www.ri.co.at (office).

WOJTYŁA, Andrzej Franciszek; Polish politician and paediatrician; b. 1 May 1955, Kalisz; s. Franciszek Wojtyła and Stanisława Wojtyła; m. Ewa Wojtyła; one s. one d.; ed Medical Acad., Poznań, George Washington, Georgetown and La Salle Univs, USA; paediatrician, Children's Ward Municipal Hosp., Pleszew 1980–89; Head, Village Health Service Centre, Jastrzębniki 1985–92; Visiting Researcher, George Washington Univ. 1995, Visiting Prof., Center for Health Policy and Research 1995–96; mem. Solidarity Trade Union 1980–89, Solidarity of Individual Farmers Trade Union 1989–91; Councillor of Commune of Blizanów 1990; mem. Polish Peasant Party Solidarity (PSL Solidarność) 1990–92, Peasant Christian Party (SLCh) 1992–97; Pres. SLCh Voivodship Bd, Kalisz, mem. SLCh Nat. Political Council; mem. Conservative Peasant Party (SKL) 1997–; Deputy to Sejm (Parl.) 1991–93, 1997–, Vice-Chair. Parl. Health Cttee; mem. Parl. Constitutional Responsibility Cttee 1991–93; Minister of Health and Social Welfare 1992–93. *Publication:* Third International Conference: Health Education for Children, International Conference: Health Care Reform in Poland 1995. *Leisure interests:* fitness, walking, history, health care reforms in the world. *Address:* Biuro Poselski, ul. Targowa 24, 62-800 Kalisz, Poland (office). *Telephone:* (62) 7672604 (office). *Fax:* (62) 7672604 (office). *E-mail:* awojtyla@polbox.com.pl (home).

WOLDE-GIORGIS, Girma; Ethiopian head of state; *President;* b. Dec. 1925, Addis Ababa; m.; five c.; ed School of Social Science, Netherlands, Air Traffic Man. School, Sweden, Air Traffic Control Man. School, Canada; served in Ethiopian Army, rank of Lt 1941–45; trainee, Ethiopian Air Force 1946–47; Instructor in Air Navigation and Air Traffic Control 1948–54; Head Civil Aviation Authority, Eritrean Fed. State, Asmara 1955–57; Dir-Gen. Ethiopian Civil Aviation, mem. Bd Ethiopian Airlines 1958; Dir-Gen. Ministry of Commerce, Industry and Planning 1959–60; elected mem. Parl., Pres. 1st Session 1961; Vice-Pres. 52nd Int. Parl. Ass., Belgrade 1961; mem. Bd Ethiopian Chamber of Commerce 1967, Civil Advisory Council 1973; Vice-Commr to Peace Comm. 1974; Rep. of Ministry of Transport and Communications to Northern Region of Eritrea and Tigrai 1974; mem. Int. Cttee of the Red Cross, Head of Logistics to Demobilize ex-Army Personnel 1990; mem. House of People's Reps Econ. Cttee 2000–01; Pres. of Ethiopia 2001–; Medal of Genet, Mil. Officers' Acad. 1944, Haile Selassie Star, Cavalry 1956, Minilik Star, Cavalry 1960, Haile Selassie Gold Medal 1960, City Council Gold Medal 1971, Red Cross Silver Medal 1988. *Publication:* Air and Men (in Amharic) 1954. *Leisure interests:* farming, afforestation. *Address:* Office of the President, PO Box 1362, Addis Ababa, Ethiopia (office). *Telephone:* (11) 1551000 (office). *Fax:* (11) 1552030 (office).

WOLF, Christa; German writer; b. 18 March 1929, Landsberg an der Warthe; m. Gerhard Wolf 1951; two d.; ed Univs of Jena and Leipzig; mem. Deutsche Akademie für Sprache und Dichtung eV, Darmstadt, Freie Akademie der Künste, Hamburg; Art Prize, Halle 1961, Heinrich-Mann Prize 1963, Nationalpreis für Kunst und Literatur (GDR) 1964, 1987, Free Hanseatic City of Bremen Literature Prize 1972, Theodor Fontane Prize for Art and Literature 1972, Georg-Büchner Prize, Deutsche Akad. der Sprache und Dichtung 1980, Schiller Memorial Prize 1983, Austrian Prize for European Literature 1984, Mondello Literature Prize 1990, Rahel Varnhagen von Ense Medal 1994, Hermann Sinsheimer Preis 2005; Officier, Ordre des Arts et des Lettres 1990. *Publications:* Moskauer Novelle 1961, Die geteilte Himmel (trans. as Divided Heaven: A Novel of Germany Today) 1963, Nachdenken über Christa T (trans. as The Quest for Christa T) 1968, Lesen und Schreiben: Aufsätze und Betrachtungen (trans. as The Reader the Writer: Essays, Sketches, Memories) 1972, Unter den Linden: Drei unwahrscheinliche Geschichten 1974, Kindheitsmuster (trans. as A Model Childhood) 1976, J'écris sur ce qui m'inquiète: Débat dans Sinn und Form sur don derneir roman 1977, Kein Ort. Nirgends (trans. as No Place on Earth) 1979, Fortgesetzter Versuch: Aufsätze, Gespräche, Essays 1979, Gesammelte Erzählungen 1980, Neue Lebensansichten eines Katers: Juninachmittag 1981, Kassandra: Vier Vorlesungen: Eine Erzählung (trans. as Cassandra: A Novel and Four Essays) 1983, Störfall: Nachrichten eines Tages (trans. as Accident: A Day's News) 1987, Die Dimension des Autors: Essays und Aufsätze, Reden und Gespräche 1959–86 (trans. as The Author's Dimension: Selected Essays) 1987, Sommerstück 1989, Was bleibt 1990, Im Dialog: Aktuelle Texte 1990, Sei gegrüsst und lebe!: Eine Freundschaft in Briefen 1964–73 1993, Akteneinsicht-Christa Wolf: Zerrspiegel und Dialog 1993, Auf dem Weg nach Tabou, Texte 1990–94 1994, Die Zeichen der Nuria Quevado 1994, Medea: Stimmen 1996, Hierzulande, Andernorts 2000, Ein Tag im Jahr 1960–2000 2003, Mit anderem Blick 2005, Ins Ungebundene gehet eine Sehnsucht 2008. *Address:* c/o Suhrkamp Verlag, Lindenstrasse 29–35, 60325 Frankfurt, Germany (office). *Website:* www.suhrkamp.de (office).

WOLF, Günter, PhD; German particle physicist and academic; *Senior Researcher, Deutsches Elektronen-Synchrotron (DESY);* b. 23 Nov. 1937; worked at Stanford Linear Accelerator Center (SLAC), Stanford Univ., Calif., USA 1960s; co-spokesman for DASP experiment at the Electron-Positron Storage Ring DORIS, Deutsches Elektronen Synchrotron (DESY), Hamburg; spokesman for the TASSO experiment at the Electron-Positron Storage Ring PETRA, (DESY); co-discoverer of the gluon with the TASSO experiment, Hamburg 1979; spokesman for the ZEUS experiment at the Electron-Proton Storage Ring HERA (DESY) 1986–1994; American Physical Soc. Robert R. Wilson Prize 1994, European Physical Soc. High Energy and Particle Physics Prize (jtly) 1995. *Publications:* numerous articles in scientific journals. *Address:* Deutsches Elektronen-Synchrotron DESY, ZEUS/F1, 1B/252, Notkestraße 85, 22607 Hamburg, Germany (office). *Telephone:* (40) 8998-3841 (office). *E-mail:* guenter.wolf@desy.de (office). *Website:* www.desy.de (office).

WOLF, Martin Harry, CBE, MA, MPhil(Econ); British economist and journalist; *Associate Editor and Chief Economics Commentator, Financial Times;* b. 16 Aug. 1946, s. of Edmund and Rebecca Wolf; m. Alison Margaret Wolf; two s. one d.; ed Univ. of Oxford; joined World Bank, Sr Economist in 1974; Dir of Studies, Trade Policy Research Centre, London 1981; Chief Econs Leader Writer, Financial Times 1987–96, Assoc. Ed. 1990, Chief Econs Commentator 1996, currently Assoc. Ed. and Chief Econs Commentator; Visiting Fellow, Nuffield Coll., Oxford; Special Prof., Univ. of Nottingham; Forum Fellow, World Econ. Forum 1999–, mem. Int. Media Council 2006–; Hon. Fellow, Corpus Christi Coll., Oxford; Hon. Fellow, Oxford Inst. for Econ. Policy (Oxonia); NZ Commemoration Medal 1990; Hon. DLitt (Nottingham) 2006; Hon. DSc (Econ) (LSE) 2006; Wincott Foundation Sr Prize for excellence in financial journalism (jtly) 1989, 1997, RTZ David Watt Memorial Prize 1994, Business Journalist of the Year Decade of Excellence Award 2003, Newspaper Feature of the Year Award, Workworld Media Awards 2003, First Magazine Award for Advocacy of Responsible Capitalism 2005, sixth winner, Journalism Prize, Fundacio Catalunya Oberta (Open Catalonia Foundation) 2006, Lifetime Acheivement Award, AMEC 2007. *Publication:* Why Globalization Works 2004. *Address:* Financial Times Group, 1 Southwark Bridge, London, SE1 9HL, England (office). *Telephone:* (20) 7873-3673 (office). *Fax:* (20) 7873-3421 (office). *E-mail:* martin.wolf@ft.com (office). *Website:* www.ft.com (office).

WOLF, Naomi, BA; American writer and feminist; b. 15 Nov. 1962, San Francisco, Calif.; d. of Leonard Wolf and Deborah Wolf; m. David Shipley 1993 (divorced 2005); one c.; ed Yale Univ., New Coll., Univ. of Oxford, UK; Rhodes Scholar 1986; Co-founder Woodhull Inst. for Ethical Leadership 1997–, now Scholar in Residence and Woodhull Fellow; fmr columnist, George magazine; consultant, Al Gore Presidential campaign 2000. *Publications:* The Beauty Myth: How Images of Beauty Are Used Against Women 1990, Fire With Fire:

The New Female Power and How It Will Change in the 21st Century 1993, Promiscuities: The Secret Struggle for Womanhood 1997, Misconceptions: Truth, Lies and the Unexpected on the Journey to Motherhood 2001, The Treehouse: Eccentric Wisdom from my Father on How to Live, Love and See 2006, The End of America: A Letter of Warning to a Young Patriot 2007. *Address:* c/o The Woodhull Institute, 770 Broadway, 2nd Floor, New York, NY 10003; c/o Royce Carlton Inc., 866 UN Plaza, New York, NY 10017, USA. *Telephone:* (646) 495-6060 (Woodhull). *Fax:* (646) 495-6059 (Woodhull). *E-mail:* info@woodhull.org. *Website:* woodhull.org.

WOLF, Siegfried; Austrian automotive industry executive; *Co-CEO, Magna International Inc.;* b. 31 Oct. 1957; trained as tool and die-maker and then as mem. of tech. staff, Quality Lab. at Philips; joined VereinigteMetallwerke Wien (VMW) as Quality Man. and Asst Dir of Quality Control; joined Hirtenberger AG, positions included Dir for Quality Control, then Gen. Man. and Vice Pres.; joined Magna Europe 1994, Pres. 1995–99, mem. Bd Dirs and Vice-Chair. Magna International Inc. 1999–, Pres. and CEO Magna Steyr 2001–02, Exec. Vice-Chair. Magna International Inc. 2002–05, Co-CEO 2005–; mem. Supervisory Bd Verbundgesellschaft (Austria Hydro Power), Österreich Industrieholding AG, Siemens AG Austria, HGI Beteiligungs AG. *Address:* Magna International Inc., 337 Magna Drive, Aurora, ON L4G 7K1, Canada (office). *Telephone:* (905) 726-2462 (office). *Fax:* (905) 726-7164 (office). *E-mail:* info@magna.com (office). *Website:* www.magna.com (office).

WOLF, Stephen M., BA; American business executive; *Chairman, R.R. Donnelley & Sons Company;* b. 7 Aug. 1941, Oakland, Calif.; ed San Francisco State Univ.; American Airlines 1966–81; Pres. and COO Continental Airlines 1982–83; Pres. and CEO Repub. Airlines 1984–86; Chair., Pres. and CEO Tiger Int. Inc. 1986–88; Chair., CEO UAL Corpn 1987–94, also fmr Pres.; Chair. CEO United Airlines 1992–94; Chair. US Air Group Inc. 1996–98 (Pres. 1987–92), Chair. USAIR Inc. (later US Airways) 1998–2002; Sr Adviser Lazard Frères 1994–2003; Man. Pnr Alpilles LLC 2003–; Dir R.R. Donnelley & Sons Co. 1995–, Chair. 2004–; mem. Bd of Dirs Altria Group Inc.; fmr Dir Air Transport Asscn of America. *Address:* R.R. Donnelley Global Headquarters, 77 West Wacker Drive, Chicago, IL 60601-1696, USA (office). *Telephone:* (312) 326-8000 (office). *Website:* www.rrdonnelly.com (office).

WOLFE, Thomas (Tom) Kennerly, Jr, AB, PhD; American author and journalist; b. 2 March 1930, Richmond, Va; s. of Thomas Kennerly and Helen Hughes; m. Sheila Berger; one s. one d.; ed Washington and Lee, and Yale Univs; reporter, Springfield (Mass) Union 1956–59; reporter, Latin American Corresp., Washington Post 1959–62; reporter, magazine writer, New York Herald Tribune 1962–66; magazine writer, New York World Journal Tribune 1966–67; Contributing Ed. New York magazine 1968–76, Esquire Magazine 1977–; Contributing Artist, Harper's magazine 1978–81; exhibited one-man show of drawings, Maynard Walker Gallery, New York 1965, Tunnel Gallery, New York 1974; mem. American Acad. of Arts and Letters 1999; Hon. DFA (Minneapolis Coll. of Art) 1971; Hon. LittD (Washington and Lee) 1974; Hon. LHD (Virginia Commonwealth Univ.) 1983, (Southampton Coll., NY) 1984, (Johns Hopkins Univ.) 1990, (Boston Univ.) 2000, (Duke Univ.) 2002, Yale Univ.) 2004, (Trinity Coll.) 2007; Front Page Awards for Humour and Foreign News Reporting, Washington Newspaper Guild 1961, Award of Excellence, Soc. of Magazine Writers 1970, Frank Luther Mott Research Award 1973, Virginia Laureate for Literature 1977, Harold D. Vursell Memorial Award, American Acad. and Inst. of Arts and Letters 1980, American Book Award for Gen. Non-Fiction 1980, Columbia Journalism Award 1980, Citation for Art History, Nat. Sculpture Soc. 1980, John Dos Passos Award 1984, Gari Melchers Medal 1986, Benjamin Pierce Cheney Medal (E Washington Univ.) 1986, Washington Irving Medal (St Nicholas Soc.) 1986, Theodore Roosevelt Medal 1990, St Louis Literary Award 1990, Yale Graduate School Wilbur L. Cross Medal 1990, President's Humanities Medal 2001, Manhattan Inst. Alexander Hamilton Award 2006, Virginia Library Foundation Lifetime Achievement Award 2007. *Publications:* The Kandy-Kolored Tangerine-Flake Streamline Baby 1965, The Electric Kool-Aid Acid Test 1968, The Pump House Gang 1968, Radical Chic and Mau-mauing the Flak Catchers 1970, The New Journalism 1973, The Painted Word 1975, Mauve Gloves and Madmen, Clutter and Vine 1976, The Right Stuff 1979, In Our Time 1980, From Bauhaus to Our House 1981, The Purple Decades: A Reader 1982, The Bonfire of the Vanities 1987, Ambush at Fort Bragg 1998, A Man in Full 1998, Hooking Up (essays and a novella) 2000, I Am Charlotte Simmons 2004. *Address:* c/o Janklow & Nesbit Associates, 445 Park Avenue, New York, NY 10022-2608, USA. *E-mail:* postmaster@janklow.com. *Website:* www.tomwolfe.com.

WOLFENDALE, Sir Arnold (Whittaker), Kt, PhD, FRS, FRAS, FInstP; British physicist and academic; *Professor Emeritus, Department of Physics, University of Durham;* b. 25 June 1927, Rugby; s. of Arnold Wolfendale and Doris Wolfendale; m. Audrey Darby 1951; twin s.; ed Univ. of Manchester; Asst Lecturer, Univ. of Manchester 1951–54, Lecturer 1954–56; Lecturer, Univ. of Durham 1956–59, Sr Lecturer 1959–63, Reader in Physics 1963–65, Prof. 1965–92, Prof. Emer. 1992–, Head of Dept 1973–77, 1980–83, 1986–89; Chair., Northern Region Action Cttee, Manpower Services Comm. Job Creation Programme 1975–78; Pres. Royal Astronomical Soc. 1981–83, Univ. of Durham Soc. of Fellows 1988–, Inst. of Physics 1994–96, European Physical Soc. 1999–; Prof. of Experimental Physics, Royal Inst. of GB 1996–; mem. Science and Eng Research Council 1988–94; Astronomer Royal 1991–95; Fellow Tata Inst. Fund 1996; mem. Academia Europaea 1998; Foreign Fellow, Nat. Acad. of Sciences of India 1990, Indian Nat. Science Acad.; Foreign Assoc. Royal Soc. of SA 1996; Pres. Antiquarian Horological Soc.; Freeman Worshipful Co. of Clockmakers, Worshipful Co. of Scientific Instrument Makers; Hon. Fellow, Lancs. Polytechnic 1991; Dr hc (Potchefstroom, Łódź, Teesside, Newcastle, Open Univ., Paisley, Lancaster, Bucharest, Durham, Neofit Rilski Southwest Univ. (Bulgaria); Silver Jubilee Medal 1977, Univ. of Turku Medal 1987, Armagh Observatory Medal 1992, Marian Smoluchowski Medal (Polish Physics Soc.) 1992, Powell Memorial Medal, European Physical Soc. 1996, Royal Soc. Bakerian Lecture and Medal 2002, Il Fiorino d'Oro, City of Florence 2004. *Publications:* Cosmic Rays 1963; Ed. Cosmic Rays at Ground Level 1973, Origin of Cosmic Rays 1974, Gamma Ray Astronomy 1981, Progress in Cosmology 1982, Gamma Ray Astronomy (with P. V. Ramana Murthy) 1986, Secular, Solar and Geomagnetic Variations in the last 1,000 years 1988; Origin of Cosmic Rays (co-ed.) 1981, Observational Tests of Cosmological Inflation (co-ed.) 1991; numerous papers on cosmic radiation. *Leisure interests:* walking, gardening, foreign travel. *Address:* Department of Physics, University of Durham, Rochester Building, Science Laboratories, South Road, Durham, DH1 3LE (office); Ansford, Potters Bank, Durham, England (home). *Telephone:* (191) 334-3580 (office); (191) 384-5642 (home). *Fax:* (191) 374-3749 (office). *E-mail:* a.w.wolfendale@durham.ac.uk (office). *Website:* www.dur.ac.uk/Physics (office).

WOLFENSOHN, James (Jim) D., KBE, AO, BA, LLB, MBA; American (b. Australian) international organization official, business executive, arts administrator and diplomatist; *Senior Advisor and Chairman, International Advisory Board, Citigroup Inc.;* b. 1 Dec. 1933, Sydney, Australia; s. of Hyman Wolfensohn and Dora Weinbaum; m. Elaine Botwinick 1961; one s. two d.; ed Univ. of Sydney, Harvard Business School; Pres. J. Henry Schroder Banking Corpn 1970–76; Chair. Salomon Brothers Int. 1977–81; Owner, Pres. James D. Wolfensohn Inc. 1981–95, fmr Chair., also CEO; Pres. World Bank 1995–2005; US Special Envoy for Gaza Disengagement 2005–April 2006 (resgnd); Sr Advisor and Chair. Int. Advisory Bd, Citigroup Inc., New York 2006–; Chair. Wolfensohn and Co. (corp. advisory and investment firm), New York 2005–; Chair. Kennedy Center for the Performing Arts 1990–95, Chair. Emer. 1995–; Chair. Advisory Group, Wolfensohn Center, Brookings Inst.; Chair. Bd Inst. for Advanced Study, Princeton, NJ; mem. Bd Carnegie Hall; Trustee Rockefeller Univ. 1985–94, Howard Hughes Medical Inst. 1987–96; mem. Global Bd of Dirs Endeavor (nonprofit org.), Conservation Int.; mem. Council on Foreign Relations; Montblanc de la Culture Award 1992; sponsor of The Elaine and Jim Wolfensohn Gift. *Achievement:* Capt. Australian Olympic fencing team. *Leisure interest:* playing the cello. *Address:* Citigroup Inc., 399 Park Avenue, New York, NY 10043, USA (office). *Telephone:* (212) 559-1000 (office). *Fax:* (212) 793-3946 (office). *Website:* www.citigroup.com (office).

WOLFENSTEIN, Lincoln, PhD; American physicist and academic; *University Professor of Physics, Carnegie-Mellon University;* b. 10 Feb. 1923, Cleveland, Ohio; s. of Leo Wolfenstein and Anna Koppel; m. Wilma C. Miller 1957; one s. two d.; ed Univ. of Chicago; Physicist, Nat. Advisory Comm. for Aeronautics 1944–46; Asst Prof., Carnegie-Mellon Univ. 1948–57, Assoc. Prof. 1957–60, Prof. 1960–78, Univ. Prof. 1978–; Guggenheim Fellow 1973–74, 1983–84; mem. NAS; J.J. Sakurai Prize, American Physical Soc. 1992. *Publications:* over 100 papers on theoretical particle and nuclear physics, weak interactions, c.p. violation, neutrino physics. *Address:* Physics Department, Carnegie-Mellon University, 5000 Forbes Avenue, Pittsburgh, PA 15213, USA (office). *Telephone:* (412) 268-2752 (office). *Fax:* (412) 681-0648 (office). *E-mail:* lincoln@cmuhep2.phys.cmu.edu (office). *Website:* info.phys.cmu.edu/people/faculty/wolfenstein (office).

WOLFF, Hugh; American conductor; *Stanford and Norma Jean Calderwood Director of Orchestras, New England Conservatory of Music;* b. 21 Oct. 1953, Paris; m. Judith Kogan; three s.; ed Harvard Univ.; began career as Asst Conductor, Nat. Symphony Orchestra, with Mstislav Rostropovich; Musical Dir New Jersey Symphony 1985–92; Prin. Conductor Saint Paul Chamber Orchestra 1988–92, Musical Dir 1992–2000; Prin. Conductor Frankfurt Radio Symphony Orchestra 1997–2006; Stanford and Norma Jean Calderwood Dir of Orchestras, New England Conservatory of Music 2008–; regularly guest-conducts the major orchestras in N America and Europe; Seavor/Nat. Endowment for the Arts Conducting Prize 1985. *Address:* Van Walsum Management Ltd, The Tower Building, 11 York Road, London, SE1 7NX, England (office); New England Conservatory of Music, 290 Huntingdon Avenue, Boston, MA 02115, USA (office). *Telephone:* (20) 7902-0520 (office); (617) 585-1100 (office). *Fax:* (20) 7902-0530 (office). *E-mail:* info@vanwalsum.com (office). *Website:* www.vanwalsum.co.uk (office); www.newenglandconservatory.edu (office); www.hughwolff.com.

WOLFF, Tobias Jonathan Ansell, BA, MA; American writer; *The Ward W. and Priscilla B. Woods Professor, Stanford University;* b. 19 June 1945, Birmingham, Ala; s. of Arthur S. Wolff and Rosemary Loftus; m. Catherine Dolores Spohn 1975; two s. one d.; ed The Hill School, Oxford Univ., (UK) and Stanford Univ. (Calif.); served in US Army 1964–68; reporter, Washington Post 1972; Writing Fellow, Stanford Univ. 1975–78, Prof. of English and Creative Writing 1997–, currently The Ward W. and Priscilla B. Woods Prof.; Writer-in-Residence, Ariz. State Univ. 1978–80; Peck Prof. of English Syracuse Univ. 1980–97; Wallace Stegner Fellowship 1975–76, Nat. Endowment Fellow 1978, 1984; Arizona Council on the Arts and Humanities Fellowship 1980, Guggenheim Fellow 1983; mem. PEN; Hon. Fellow Hertford Coll., Oxford 2000; St Lawrence Award for Fiction 1982, Rea Award for Short Story 1989, Whiting Foundation Award 1989, LA Times Book Prize for Biography 1989, Amb. Book Award 1990, Lila Wallace/Reader's Digest Award 1993, Lyndhurst Foundation Award 1994, Esquire-Volvo-Waterstones Award for Non-Fiction 1994, Award of Merit, American Acad. of Arts and Letters 2001. *Publications:* Ugly Rumours 1975, Hunters in the Snow 1981, The Barracks Thief (PEN/Faulkner Award for Fiction 1985) 1984, Back in the World 1985, A Doctor's Visit: The Short Stories of Anton Chekhov (ed.) 1987, The Stories of Tobias Wolff 1988, This Boy's Life 1989, The Picador Books of Contemporary American Stories (ed.) 1993, In Pharaoh's Army: Memories of a Lost War 1994, The Vintage Book of Contemporary American Short Stories

1994, The Best American Short Stories 1994, The Night in Question (short stories) 1996, Writers Harvest 3 (ed.) 2000, Old School 2003, Our Story Begins (short stories) 2008. *Address:* English Department, Building 460, Room 218, Stanford University, Stanford, CA 94305-2087, USA (office). *Telephone:* (650) 723-0504 (office). *Fax:* (650) 725-0755 (office). *E-mail:* twolff@stanford.edu (office). *Website:* english.stanford.edu (office).

WOLFF, Torben, DSc; Danish biologist; b. 21 July 1919, Copenhagen; s. of Jørgen Frederik de Lichtenberg Wolff and Karen Margrethe Lunn; m. Lisbeth Christensen; two d.; ed Copenhagen Univ.; Curator Zoological Museum, Univ. of Copenhagen 1953–66, Chief Curator 1966–80, 1983–89; External Examiner Aarhus Univ. 1966–75, Copenhagen Univ. 1967–79; Sec. Int. Asscn for Biological Oceanography 1970–76; Vice-Pres. Scientific Cttee on Oceanic Research 1980–84; mem. Panel of NATO Marine Sciences Programme 1981–86; mem. Danish Nat. Council for Oceanology 1964–89, Sec. 1968–85, Chair. 1985–89; mem. Bd Danish Natural History Soc. 1948–50, 1955–68, 1980–85, 1999–2004 (Chair. 1963–68); mem. Adventurers Club of Denmark 1957– (Pres. 1970–73), Bd WWF/Denmark 1980–90, World Innovation Foundation 2001; mem. Bd Denmark's Aquarium 1971–96, Dir 1980–83, 1990–93; Deputy Leader Danish Galathea Deep-Sea Expedition Round the World 1950–52; mem. Danish Atlantide Expedition to West Africa 1945–46; numerous other expeditions; Hon. mem. RSNZ, 1977, Danish Natural History Soc. 1990; Royal Galathea Medal 1955, GEC Gad's Grant of Honour 1964, Popular Science Prize, Danish Asscn of Authors 1983, Sir George Deacon Medal 2003. *Publications:* A Year in Nature 1944, The Systematics and Biology of Isopoda Asellota 1962, Danish Expeditions on the Seven Seas 1967, The History of Danish Zoology 1979, The History of the Danish Natural History Society 1933–83, 1983; numerous scientific and popular scientific papers on crustaceans, deep-sea ecology, history of science, biogs etc. *Leisure interest:* guiding tours abroad to places off the beaten track. *Address:* Zoological Museum, 2100 Copenhagen Ø (office); Hesseltoften 12, 2900 Hellerup, Denmark (home). *Telephone:* 39-62-89-71 (home); 35-32-10-40 (office). *Fax:* 35-32-10-10 (office). *E-mail:* twolff@snm.ku.dk (office).

WOLFOWITZ, Paul Dundes, BA, PhD; American academic, government official and fmr international organization official; *Visiting Scholar, American Enterprise Institute;* b. 22 Dec. 1943, Brooklyn, NY; s. of the late Jacob Wolfowitz and of Lillian Dundes; m. Clare Selgin; three c.; ed Cornell Univ., Univ. of Chicago; Man. Intern Bureau of the Budget 1966–67; Prof., Dept of Political Science, Yale Univ. 1970–73; mem. staff Arms Control and Disarmament Agency 1973–77, also Special Assst Strategic Arms Limitation Talks (SALT); Deputy Asst Sec. of Defense for Regional Programs 1977–80; Dir of Policy Planning, US Dept of State 1981–82, Asst Sec. of State for E Asia and Pacific Affairs 1982–86; Amb. to Indonesia 1986–89; Under-Sec. of Defense for Policy 1989–93, Deputy Sec. of Defense 2001–05; George F. Kennan Prof. of Nat. Security Strategy, Nat. War Coll. 1993; Visiting Prof., Paul H. Nitze School of Advanced Int. Studies (SAIS), Johns Hopkins Univ. 1980–81, Dean and Prof. of Int. Relations 1994–2001; Pres. World Bank Group 2005–07 (resgnd); Visiting Scholar, American Enterprise Inst. 2007–; mem. Advisory Bd Foreign Affairs, National Interest (journals); numerous awards including Presidential Citizen's Medal, Dept of Defense Distinguished Public Service Medal, Distinguished Honor Award, Distinguished Civilian Service Medal, Arms Control and Disarmament Agency's Distinguished Honor Award. *Address:* American Enterprise Institute, 1150 Seventeenth Street, NW, Washington, DC 20036, USA (office). *Telephone:* (202) 862-5948 (office). *Fax:* (202) 862-7177 (office). *Website:* www.aei.org (office).

WOLFRAM, Herwig, DPhil; Austrian historian; b. 14 Feb. 1934, Vienna; s. of Dr. Fritz Wolfram and Rosa Wolfram; m. Adelheid Schoerghofer 1958; three s. one d.; ed Univ. of Vienna; Lecturer 1959–68; Docent, Univ. of Vienna 1967; Assoc. Prof., Los Angeles 1968; Assoc. Prof. of Medieval History, Vienna, 1969, Prof. of Medieval History and Auxiliary Sciences 1971–2002, Dean Faculty of Arts 1981–83; Dir Inst. für österr. Geschichtsforschung, Vienna 1983–2002; Fellow Austrian Acad. of Sciences 1985–; Corresp. Fellow Medieval Acad. of America 1990, Royal Historical Soc. London 1995, British Acad. 1996; Theodor-Koerner Foederungspreis 1962, 1964, Kardinal Innitzer-Foederungspreis 1964, Kardinal Innitzerpreis fuer Geisteswissenschaft 1994. *Television:* adviser to Sturm Ueber Europa I–IV (ZdF, ORF, Arte) 2002. *Publications include:* Splendor Imperii 1963, Intitulatio I 1967, II 1973, III 1988, History of the Goths 1988, Die Geburt Mitteleuropas 1987, Die Goten (7th edn) 2001, Das Reich und die Germanen 1990–92, Salzburg, Bayern, Oesterreich. Die Conversio Bagoariorum et Carantanorum und die Quellen ihrer Zeit 1995, Grenzen und Räume 1995, The Roman Empire and its Germanic Peoples 1997, Konrad II (990–1039): Kaiser dreier Reiche 2000, Die Goten und ihre Geschicte 2001, Die Germanen (7th edn) 2002. *Leisure interests:* sport, music, theatre. *Address:* Institut fuer Oesterreichische Geschichtsforschung, Dr. Karl Lueger-Ring 1, 1010 Vienna (office); Sommeregg 13, 5301, Eugendorf; Wilhelminenstr. 173, 1160 Vienna, Austria (home). *Telephone:* (1) 427-22-72-60 (office); (1) 485-63-28 (home); (6221) 77-43. *Fax:* (1) 427-79-27-2 (office); (1) 485-63-28 (home); (6221) 20277 (home). *E-mail:* herwig.wolfram@univie.ac.at (office). *Website:* www.univie.ac.at/Geschichtsforschung (office).

WOLFSON, Dirk Jacob, PhD; Dutch economist; *Professor Emeritus of Economics, Erasmus University;* b. 22 June 1933, Voorburg; s. of Dirk Wolfson and Gerdina Akkerhuys; m. Anna Maaike Hoekstra 1960; three c.; ed Univ. of Amsterdam; Teaching Asst Univ. of Amsterdam 1961–63; Economist, IMF, Washington, DC 1964–70; Dir (Chief Economist), Econ. Policy Div. Netherlands Treasury Dept 1970–75; Prof. of Public Finance, Erasmus Univ., Rotterdam 1975–86, Prof. of Econs 1992–99, Prof. Emer. 1999–; Rector, Inst. of Social Studies, The Hague 1986–90; mem. Social and Econ. Council 1982–96, Scientific Council for Govt Policy 1990–98; Royal Supervisor, Netherlands Cen. Bank and Chair. Banking Council 1990–99; mem. Senate (Social Democratic Party) 1999–2003; mem. Royal Netherlands Acad. of Arts and Sciences 1989–; Kt, Order of the Netherlands Lion; Commdr, Order of Orange Nassau. *Publications:* Public Finance and Development Strategy 1979; numerous books and articles on econ. theory and policy. *Leisure interests:* theatre, hiking. *Address:* Aelbrechtskolk 41A, 3025 HB Rotterdam, Netherlands (home). *Telephone:* (10) 4779497 (home). *Fax:* (10) 4764667 (home). *E-mail:* dwolfson@xs4all.nl (home).

WOLFSON, Baron (Life Peer), cr. 1985, of Marylebone in the City of Westminster; **Leonard Gordon Wolfson,** Kt, FRS; British retail executive; b. 11 Nov. 1927, London; s. of the late Sir Isaac Wolfson and Lady (Edith) Wolfson; m. 1st Ruth Sterling 1949 (divorced 1991); four d.; m. 2nd Estelle Jackson (née Feldman) 1991; one step-s. one step-d.; ed King's School, Worcester; Chair. Great Universal Stores 1981–96 (Dir 1952, Man. Dir 1962–81); Chair. Burberrys Ltd 1978–96; Founder Trustee Wolfson Foundation 1955–, Chair. 1972–; Pres. Jewish Welfare Bd 1972–82; Patron Royal Coll. of Surgeons 1976; Trustee, Imperial War Museum 1988–94; Fellow, Royal Albert Hall 2004; Hon. Fellow Wolfson Coll., Cambridge, St Catherine's Coll. and Worcester Coll., Oxford, Univ. Coll. London, London School of Hygiene and Tropical Medicine 1985, Queen Mary Coll., Univ. of London 1985, Univ. of Westminster 1991, Imperial Coll. 1991, Royal Coll. of Eng 1997, Somerville Coll., Oxford 1999, LSE 1999, Inst. of Educ., Univ. of London 2001, Israel Museum 2001; Hon. mem. Emmanuel Coll., Cambridge 1996, Royal Coll. of Surgeons, Edin. 1997; Hon. FRCP 1977; Hon. FBA 1986; Hon. FRCS 1988; Hon. PhD (Tel-Aviv) 1971, (Hebrew Univ.) 1978, (Bar Ilan Univ.) 1983, (Weitzmann Inst.) 1988; Hon. DCL (Oxon) 1972; Hon. LLD (Strathclyde) 1972, (Dundee) 1979, (Cantab.) 1982, (London) 1982; Hon. DSc (Hull) 1977, (Wales) 1984, (E Anglia) 1986, (Loughborough) 2003, (Sheffield) 2005; Hon. DUniv (Surrey) 1990, (Glasgow) 1997; Hon. MD (Birmingham) 1992; Dr hc (Technion) 1995, (Edin.) 1996; Sir Winston Churchill Award, British Technion Soc. 1989, Sheldon Medal, Oxford 2003, Pres.'s Award, Hebrew Univ. 2005. *Leisure interests:* history, economics. *Address:* 8 Queen Anne Street, London, W1G 9LD, England (office). *Telephone:* (20) 7323-3124 (office). *Fax:* (20) 7323-3138 (office). *E-mail:* sarah.wishart@wolfson.org.uk (office). *Website:* www.wolfson.org.uk (office).

WOLMAN, M. Gordon, BA, MA, PhD; American environmental scientist and academic; *B. Howell Griswold, Jr Professor of Geography and International Affairs, The Johns Hopkins University;* s. of Abel Wolman; ed The Johns Hopkins Univ., Harvard Univ.; mil. service, USNR 1943–46; hydrologist, US Geological Survey (USGS) 1951–58; Assoc. Prof. of Geography, Johns Hopkins Univ. 1958–62, Chair. Isaiah Bowman Dept of Geography 1958–68, Prof. of Geography 1962–, B. Howell Griswold, Jr Prof. of Geography and Int. Affairs 1975–, Chair. Dept of Geography and Environmental Eng 1970–90, Interim Provost Johns Hopkins Univ. 1987, 1990–91; Fellow, American Acad. of Arts and Sciences 1981, AAAS 1984; mem. NAS 1988, American Philosophical Soc. 1999, Nat. Acad. of Eng 2002, American Geophysical Union; Award of Jt Eng and Architects Socs of Washington, DC 1957, Meritorious Contrib. Award, Asscn of American Geographers 1972, Distinguished Mentor, Nat. Council for Geographic Educ. 1989, Cullum Geographical Medal, Council of the American Geographical Soc. 1989, USGS John Wesley Powell Award 1989, Distinguished Career Award, Asscn of American Geographers Geomorphology Specialty Group 1993, D.L. Linton Award, British Geomorphological Research Group 1994, Rachel Carson Award, Chesapeake Appreciation, Inc. 1995, Medal in Memory of Ian Campbell, American Geological Inst. 1997, Penrose Medal, Geological Soc. of America 1999, Horton Medal, American Geophysical Union 2000, Nevada Medal, Desert Research Inst. 2002, Abel Wolman Award, Chesapeake Water Environment Fed. 2003, Lifetime Achievement Award, Nat. Council for Science and the Environment 2004, Benjamin Franklin Medal in Earth and Environmental Science, The Franklin Inst. 2006. *Publications:* numerous scientific papers in professional journals. *Address:* Department of Geography and Environmental Engineering, Johns Hopkins University, 3400 North Charles Street, Baltimore, MD 21218, USA (office). *Telephone:* (410) 516-7090 (office). *Fax:* (410) 516-8996 (office). *E-mail:* wolman@jhu.edu (office). *Website:* engineering.jhu.edu/~dogee (office).

WOLPE, Howard, BA, PhD; American research director and fmr politician; *Africa Program Director, Woodrow Wilson International Center for Scholars;* b. 11 Feb. 1939, Los Angeles, Calif.; ed Reed Coll., MIT; served in Mich. House of Reps, then seven terms as mem. US Congress, Chair. Sub cttee on Africa, Investigations and Oversight Sub cttee on Science, Space and Tech.; fmr Presidential Envoy to Africa; taught at W Mich. Univ. and Univ. of Mich.; fmr Visiting Fellow Brookings Inst.; currently Africa Program Dir, Woodrow Wilson Int. Center for Scholars, Washington, DC; mem. Council on Foreign Relations; mem. Bd of Dirs Nat. Endowment for Democracy, Africare; African-American Inst. Star Crystal Award for Excellence, Sierra Club Lifetime Achievement Award. *Publications include:* Nigeria: Modernization and the Politics of Communalism (co-ed.) 1971, Urban Politics in Nigeria 1973, The United States and Africa: A Post-War Perspective (co-author) 1998. *Address:* Woodrow Wilson International Center for Scholars, One Woodrow Wilson Plaza, 1300 Pennsylvania Avenue, NW, Washington, DC 20004-3027 (office); 11616 Chapel Cross Way, Reston, VA 20194, USA (home). *Telephone:* (202) 691-4046 (office); (703) 736-0314 (home). *Fax:* (202) 691-4001 (office); (703) 736-0815 (home). *E-mail:* wolpehe@wwic.si.edu (office); hwolpe@aol.com (home). *Website:* www.wilsoncenter.org/africa (office).

WOLPER, David Lloyd; American film and television producer; b. 11 Jan. 1928, New York City; s. of Irving S. Wolper and Anna Wolper (née Fass); m. 1st Margaret Dawn Richard 1958 (divorced); two s. one d.; m. 2nd Gloria Diane Hill 1974; ed Drake Univ. and Univ. of Southern California; Vice-Pres. and Treasurer Flamingo Films TV Sales Co. 1948–50; Vice-Pres. W Coast

Operations 1954–58; Chair. Bd and Pres. Wolper Productions 1958–, Wolper Pictures Ltd 1968–, The Wolper Org. Inc. 1971–; Pres. Fountainhead Int. 1960–, Wolper TV Sales Co. 1964–, Wolper Productions Inc. 1970–; Vice-Pres. Metromedia Inc. 1965–68; Consultant and Exec. Producer Warner Brothers Inc. 1976–; Dir, fmr Chair. Amateur Athletic Foundation of Los Angeles; Dir Acad. of TV Arts and Sciences Foundation, S. Calif. Cttee for Olympic Games, Univ. of S. Calif. Cinema/TV Dept; mem. Acad. of Motion Picture Arts and Sciences, Acad. of TV Arts and Sciences, Producers' Guild of America, Caucus for Producers, Writers and Dirs.; mem. Bd of Govs. Cedars Sinai Medical Center; mem. Bd of Trustees, American Film Inst., Museum of Broadcasting, LA Country Museum of Art and numerous other appointments; Chevalier, Légion d'honneur 1990; seven Golden Globe Awards, five George Foster Peabody Awards, Distinguished Service Award, US Jr Chamber of Commerce, 46 Emmy Awards, Acad. of TV Arts and Sciences, Monte Carlo Int. Film Festival Award 1964, Cannes Film Festival Grand Prix for TV Programmes 1964, two Acad. Awards: Best Documentary Film 1972, Jean Hersholt Humanitarian Award 1985. *Television productions include:* The Race for Space, The Making of the President, Hollywood and the Stars, March of Time Specials, The Rise and Fall of the Third Reich, The Undersea World of Jacques Cousteau, China: Roots of Madness, Primal Man, Welcome Back, Kotter, Roots, Victory at Entebbe, Roots: The Next Generations, The Thorn Birds, North and South—Books I and II, The Morning After, Napoleon and Josephine and numerous TV films including Men of the Dragon, Unwed Father; has produced numerous feature films and several live special events, including Opening and Closing Ceremonies of 1984 Olympic Games, LA, 100th Anniversary of Unveiling of the Statue of Liberty 1986, Legends, Icons and Superstars of the 20th Century, Celebrate the Century, Mists of Avalon, Roots: Celebrating 25 Years. *Film productions include:* Willy Wonka and the Chocolate Factory; If It's Tuesday, This Must Be Belgium; The Hellstrom Chronicle, Visions of Eight, One is a Lonely Number, Wattstax; Birds Do It, Bees Do It; This is Elvis, Victory at Entebbe, Surviving Picasso, Imagine: John Lennon, I Love My Wife, The Animal Within, Four Days in November, The Bridge at Remagen, The Devil's Brigade, L.A. Confidential. *Publication:* Producer: A Memoir (with David Fisher). *Address:* The David L. Wolper Company, 617 North Rodeo Drive, Beverly Hills, CA 90210, USA. *Telephone:* (310) 278-0619 (office). *Fax:* (310) 278-3615 (home). *E-mail:* davidwolper@msn .com (office). *Website:* www.davidwolper.com (office).

WOLPERT, Lewis, CBE, DIC, PhD, FRS, FRSL; British biologist and academic; *Professor Emeritus of Biology as Applied to Medicine, University College and Middlesex School of Medicine;* b. 19 Oct. 1929, South Africa; s. of William Wolpert and Sarah Wolpert; m. Elizabeth Brownstein; two s. two d.; ed Univ. of Witwatersrand, Imperial Coll. London, King's Coll. London; civil engineer S African Council for Scientific and Industrial Research and Israel Water Planning Dept 1951–54; Reader in Zoology, King's Coll. London 1964–66; Prof. of Biology as Applied to Medicine, Dept of Anatomy and Developmental Biology, Univ. Coll. and Middlesex School of Medicine (fmrly at Middx Medical School) 1966–2005, Prof. Emer. 2005–; presenter Antenna (BBC 2) 1988–89, TV documentaries and radio interviews with scientists; Chair. MRC Cell Bd 1984–88; Chair. Comm. on the Public Understanding of Science 1994–; mem. various cttees, scientific panels etc.; Hon. DSc (Leicester) 1996, (Westminster) 1997, (Bath); Hon. DUniv (Open Univ.) 1998; Medanear Lecture, Royal Soc. 1998, Michael Faraday Medal, Royal Soc. 2000. *Publications:* A Passion for Science 1988, The Triumph of the Embryo 1991, The Unnatural Nature of Science 1992, Principles of Development 1998, Malignant Sadness: The Anatomy of Depression 1999, Six Impossible Things Before Breakfast 2006, How We Live and Why We Die 2009. *Leisure interests:* cycling, tennis. *Address:* Department of Anatomy and Developmental Biology, University College London, Gower Street, London, WC1E 6BT (office); 63A Belsize Park Gardens, London, NW3 4JN, England (home). *Telephone:* (20) 7679-1320 (office); (20) 7586-7694 (home). *E-mail:* l.wolpert@ucl.ac.uk (office); lewiswolpert@yahoo.com (home).

WOLSZCZAN, Aleksander, PhD; Polish astronomer; *Evan Pugh Professor of Astronomy and Astrophysics, Penn State University;* b. 29 April 1946, Szczecinek; m.; one d.; ed Nicolaus Copernicus Univ., Toruń; Dir Astronomy Centre, Nicolaus Copernicus Univ. 1997–2000; Evan Pugh Prof. of Astronomy and Astrophysics, Penn State Univ. 2000–; Kt's Cross, Order of Polonia Restituta 1997; Young Astronomer Prize, Polish Astronomical Society 1977, Annual Award, Foundation of Polish Science 1992, Annual Award, Alfred Jurzykowski Foundation 1993, Faculty Scholar Medal, Pa State Univ. 1994, Beatrice M. Tinsley Prize, American Astronomical Society 1996, Casimir Funk Natural Sciences Award, Polish Inst. of Arts and Sciences of America 1996, M. Smoluchowski Medal, Polish Physical Soc. *Publications include:* Interstellar Interferometry of the Pulsar PSR 1237+25 1987 (co-author), Experimental Constraints on Strong-Field Relativistic Gravity 1992 (co-author), A Planetary System Around the Millisecond Pulsar PSR 1257+12 1992 (co-author), Confirmation of Earth-Mass Planets Orbiting the Millisecond Pulsar PSR B1257+12 1994, Binary Pulsars and Relativistic Gravitation 1994. *Leisure interests:* climbing, hiking. *Address:* 501 Davey Laboratory, Department of Astronomy and Astrophysics, Penn State University, University Park, PA 16802, USA (office). *Telephone:* (814) 863-1756 (office). *Fax:* (814) 863-3399 (office). *E-mail:* alex@astro.psu.edu (office). *Website:* www.astro.psu .edu (office).

WOLTER, Frank; German international civil servant; b. 22 Nov. 1943, Seehausen, Bavaria; s. of Dr Hans Wolter and Ilse Wolter (née Henrici); m. Birgit Rein 1975; one s. one d.; ed Univs of Freiburg, Saarbrücken and Kiel; Research Fellow, Kiel Inst. of World Econs 1969–74, Head Research Groups 1974–83; Dir Research Project, German Research Foundation 1977–79; Sr Economist, Econ. Research and Analysis Unit, GATT Secr., Geneva 1983–89, Dir Trade Policies Review Div. 1989–91, Dir Agric. and Commodities 1991–.

Publications: numerous studies and articles on structural change in industry, int. trade and econ. growth. *Leisure interests:* tennis, skiing, classical music, historical literature, golf. *Address:* 154 rue de Lausanne, 1211 Geneva 21, Switzerland (office); 38 La Clé des Champs, 01280 Moens, France (home). *E-mail:* frank.wolter@wto.org (office); wolterfrank@aol.com (home).

WONDER, Stevie; American singer, musician and composer; b. (Steveland Judkins Morris), 13 May 1950, Saginaw, Mich.; step-s. of Paul Hardaway; m. 1st Syreeta Wright 1971 (divorced 1972, died 2004); m. 2nd Yolanda Simmons; m. 3rd Kai Millard Morris; seven c.; ed Michigan School for the Blind; first appeared as solo singer at Whitestone Baptist Church, Detroit 1959; recording artist with Motown, Detroit, initially as Stephen Judkins, 1963–70; f. and Pres. Black Bull Music Inc. 1970–, Wondirection Records 1982–; owner, KJLH, LA; Edison Award 1973, Nat. Asscn of Record Merchandisers Best Selling Male Soul Artist of Year 1974, and Presidential Award 1975, Golden Globe (for I Just Called To Say I Love You) 1985, numerous American Music Awards, including Special Award of Merit 1982, Acad. Award for Best Song 1984, Soul Train Heritage Award 1987, numerous Grammy Awards, including Grammy Award (for Superstition) 1974, Grammy Award (for You are the Sunshine of My Life) 1974, Grammy Award (for Living For The City) 1975, Grammy Award (for Boogie on Reggae Woman) 1975, Grammy Award (for I Wish) 1977, Grammy Lifetime Achievement Award 1990, Nelson Mandela Courage Award 1991, IAAAM Diamond Award for Excellence 1991, National Acad. of Songwriters Lifetime Achievement Award 1992, NAACP Image Award 1992, Polar Music Prize, Swedish Acad. of Music, Grammy Award for Best Male Pop Vocal Performance (for From the Bottom of my Heart) 2006, Grammy Award for Best R&B Performance by a Duo or Group with Vocals (for So Amazing, with Beyoncé) 2006, Grammy Award for Best Pop Collaboration with Vocals (with Tony Bennett) 2007, Library of Congress Gershwin Prize 2009. *Film appearances:* Bikini Beach 1964, Muscle Beach Party 1964. *Recordings include:* albums: Little Stevie Wonder: The Twelve-Year-Old Genius 1963, Tribute To Uncle Ray, Jazz Soul, With A Song In My Heart, At The Beach, Uptight 1966, Down To Earth 1966, I Was Made To Love Her 1967, Someday At Christmas 1967, For Once In My Life 1969, My Cherie Amour 1969, Signed Sealed and Delivered 1969, Music Of My Mind 1972, Talking Book 1972, Innervisions (Grammy Award 1974) 1973, Fulfillingness' First Finale (Grammy Award 1975) 1974, Songs in the Key of Life (Grammy Award 1977) 1976, Journey Through the Secret Life of Plants 1979, Hotter than July 1980, Original Musiquarium 1982, Woman in Red (soundtrack) 1984, Love Songs 1984, In Square Circle 1985, Characters 1987, Jungle Fever (film soundtrack) 1991, Conversation Peace 1995, Motown Legends 1995, Natural Wonder 1996, Song Review 1996, At The Close Of A Century 1999, A Time To Love 2005. *Address:* Steveland Morris Music, 4616 W Magnolia Boulevard, Burbank, CA 91505 (office); c/o Motown Records, 1755 Broadway, New York, NY 10019, USA. *Website:* www.steviewonder.net.

WONG, Anthony Chau-Sang; Hong Kong actor; b. 2 Sept. 1961; m.; one s.; ed Acad. of Performing Arts; began acting career at ATV; film debut in Flower Street Era 1985; writer and dir films New Tenant 1995 and Top Banana Club 1996; lead singer in punk music band. *Films include:* No Risk, No Gain 1990, The Big Score 1990, Dancing Bull 1990, Angel Hunter 1991, Her Fatal Ways 1991, Lucky Encounter 1992, Lady Hunter 1992, The Untold Story (Best Actor Hong Kong Film Award, Golden Horse Award) 1992, Hard Boiled 1992, Executioners 1992, Legal Innocence 1993, The Tigers 1993, Taxi Hunter 1993, Love to Kill 1993, Full Contact 1993, Physical Weapon 1994, Rock n' Roll Cop 1994, Now You See Me, Now You Don't 1994, Highway Man 1994, Husbands and Wives 1995, Another Chinese Cop 1996, Mangkok Story 1996, Blind Romance 1996, Beyond the Cop Line 1996, Young and Dangerous 1996, Armageddon 1997, Midnight Zone 1997, Beast Cops (Best Actor Hong Kong Film Award) 1998, Ordinary Heroes 1998, Haunted Mansion 1998, The Deadly Camp 1999, A Man Called Hero 1999, The Mission 1999, When a Man Loves a Woman 2000, Violent Cop 2000, What is a Good Teacher 2000, Ransom Run 2000, Runaway 2001, U-Man 2002, Just One Look 2002, Infernal Affairs (Best Supporting Actor Hong Kong Film Award, Hong Kong Film Critics Soc. 2003) 2002, The Twins Effect 2002, Princess D (Best Supporting Actor, Taiwan Golden Horse Awards) 2002, Internal Affairs II (Hong Kong Film Award) 2003, Magic Kitchen 2004, Kung Fu Soccer 2004, House of Fury 2005, Initial D 2005, Exiled 2006, The Painted Veil 2006, On the Edge 2006, Sweet Revenge 2007, Great Uncle 2007, Mr Cinema 2007, Simply Actors 2007, Secret 2007, The Sun also Rises 2007. *Leisure interests:* martial arts, kung fu, singing.

WONG, Kan Seng, BA, MBA; Singaporean politician; *Deputy Prime Minister and Minister for Home Affairs;* b. 1946; m. Ruth Wong; two s.; ed Univ. of Singapore, London Business School, UK; began career as trainee teacher, Teacher's Training Coll. 1964–67; joined Admin. Service, Ministry of Labour 1970; called to Nat. Service, Singapore Armed Forces 1970–71; Admin. Officer, Ministry of Defence (MOD) 1971; Head of Navy Personnel, Dir of Manpower Div., then Deputy Sec., MOD 1971–81; Personnel Man., Hewlett Packard, Singapore 1981–85; MP (People's Action Party) for Kuo Chuan Constituency 1984–88, Toa Payoh Constituency 1988–91, Thomson Constituency 1981–97, Bishan-Toa Payoh Constituency 1997–2001, 2001–; Minister of State for Home Affairs, then for Community Devt 1985–86; Minister of State for Communications and Information 1985–87; Acting Minister for Community Devt 1986–87, Minister 1987–91; Leader of the House of Parl. 1987–; Second Minister for Foreign Affairs 1987–88, Minister 1988–94; Deputy Chair. of the People's Asscn 1992–; Minister for Home Affairs 1994–; Deputy Prime Minister 2005–; mem. Cen. Exec. Cttee, People's Action Party 1987–, Second Asst Sec.-Gen. 1992–2004, First Asst Sec.-Gen. 2004–; Adviser to Nat. Transport Worker's Union 1985–; Chair. Chinese Devt Assistance Council 1992–2004; mem. Global Advisory Bd, London Business School 1999–; Public Admin Medal (Silver) 1976, Nat. TUC May Day Medal of Honour 1998.

Leisure interests: working out at gym, golf. *Address:* Ministry of Home Affairs, New Phoenix Park, 28 Irrawaddy Road, Singapore 329560 (office). *Telephone:* 64787010 (office). *Fax:* 62546250 (office). *E-mail:* mha_feedback@mha.gov.sg (office). *Website:* www.mha.gov.sg (office).

WONG, Kar Wai, BA; Chinese film director; b. 1959, Shanghai; ed Hong Kong Polytechnic; TV drama production training programme Hong Kong TV Broadcasts Ltd 1980–82; Pres. 2006 Cannes Film Festival; has also directed numerous TV commercials and music videos; Best Dir Award Cannes Film Festival 1997 (for Happy Together). *Films:* As Tears Go By 1988, Days of Being Wild 1990, Days of Being Wild II, Ashes of Time 1994, Chungking Express 1994, Fallen Angels 1995, Happy Together 1997, In the Mood for Love 2000, 2046 2004, My Blueberry Nights 2007, The Lady from Shanghai 2009. *Television:* scriptwriter Don't Look Now 1981. *Address:* c/o Jet Tone Films, Flat E, Third Floor, Kalam Court, 9 Grampian Road, Kowloon, Hong Kong Special Administrative Region, People's Republic of China (office).

WONG, Penny, BA, LLB; Australian politician; *Minister for Climate Change and Water;* b. 5 Nov. 1968, Kota Kinabalu, Sabah, Malaysia; ed Scotch Coll., Vic., Univ. of Adelaide; moved to Australia aged eight years; began career as industrial officer, Adelaide 1990–96, barrister and solicitor 1996–2000, legal officer 2000–02; fmr Adviser to Carr Govt, NSW; Labor Senator for S Australia 2001–, Shadow Minister for Employment and Workforce Participation and for Corp. Governance and Responsibility 2004–07, also for Public Admin and Accountability 2006–07, Minister for Climate Change and Water 2007–. *Address:* Parliament House, Suite MG 60, Canberra, ACT 2600 (office); Electorate Office, 81 Carrington Street, Adelaide, SA 5000, Australia (office). *Telephone:* (02) 6277-7920 (Canberra) (office); (08) 8223-3388 (Adelaide) (office). *Fax:* (02) 6273-7330 (Canberra) (office); (08) 8223-5588 (Adelaide) (office). *E-mail:* senator.wong@aph.gov.au (office); info@pennywong.com.au. *Website:* www.pennywong.com.au.

WONG YICK MING, Rosanna, DBE, JP, BSc, MS, MA, PhD; Hong Kong administrator and government official; *Executive Director, Hong Kong Federation of Youth Groups;* b. 15 Aug. 1952, Hong Kong; ed St Stephen's Girls' School, Univ. of Hong Kong, Univ. of Toronto, LSE, Chinese Univ. of Hong Kong, Univ. of California, Davis; Exec. Dir Hong Kong Fed. of Youth Groups 1980–; Chair. Hong Kong Housing Authority 1993–2000, Complaints Cttee of Hong Kong Ind. Comm. Against Corruption, Children's Thalassaemia Foundation, Social Welfare Advisory Cttee 1988–91, Comm. on Youth 1990–91, Police Complaints Cttee 1993; mem. Legis. Council 1985–91, Exec. Council 1988–91, 1992–97, Exec. Council of Hong Kong Special Admin. Region 1997–2002; Chair. Educ. Comm. 2001, 2003–07; mem. Judicial Officers Recommendation Comm. 2005–07; Founding Dir Dragon Foundation; Patron Mother's Choice, Children's Kidney Trust Fund; mem. Co-ordinating Cttee for Children and Youth at Risk, Exec. Cttee Hong Kong Council of Social Service; mem. Bd of Dirs Hongkong and Shanghai Banking Corpn Ltd, Cheung Kong (Holdings) Ltd, World Vision Hong Kong; Hon. Fellow, Hong Kong Inst. of Housing 1994; Hon. mem. Chartered Inst. of Housing 1994; Dr hc (Hong Kong Univ.), (Hong Kong Polytechnic Univ.) 2002. *Address:* Hong Kong Federation of Youth Groups, Unit 6-7, G/F., The Center, 99 Queen's Road Central, Hong Kong Special Administrative Region, People's Republic of China (office). *Telephone:* 25756666 (office). *Fax:* 25744000 (office). *E-mail:* yr@hkfyg.org.hk (office). *Website:* www.hkfyg.org.hk (office).

WOO, John; Chinese film director and producer; b. (Yu Sum Woo), 23 Sept. 1946, Guangzhou; m. Annie Woo Ngau Chun-lung 1976; three c.; ed Matteo Ricci Coll., Hong Kong; family moved to Hong Kong 1951; started making experimental 16 mm films in 1967; entered film industry 1969 as Production Asst Cathay Film Co., Asst Dir 1971; later joined Shaw Bros as Asst Dir to Zhang Che; arrived in Hollywood 1992, debut with Hard Target 1993. *Films:* The Young Dragons (debut) 1973, The Dragon Tamers, Countdown in Kung Fu, Princess Chang Ping, From Riches to Rags, Money Crazy, Follow the Star, Last Hurrah for Chivalry, To Hell with the Devil, Laughing Times, Plain Jane to the Rescue, Sunset Warriors (Heroes Shed No Tears), The Time You Need a Friend, Run Tiger, Run, A Better Tomorrow 1986, A Better Tomorrow II, Just Heroes, The Killer 1989, Bullet in the Head, Once a Thief 1990, Hard Boiled 1992, Hard Target 1993, Broken Arrow 1996, Face/Off 1997, King's Ransom, M: I-2 2000, The Last Word (producer), Windtalkers 2002, The Hire: Hostage 2002, Bulletproof Monk (producer) 2003, Paycheck 2003, All the Invisible Children 2005, Red Cliff 2008, 1949 2009. *Television includes:* Once a Thief 1996, Blackjack 1998, The Robinsons: Lost in Space 2004. *Address:* c/o Endeavor Agency, 9601 Wilshire Blvd., 10th Floor, Beverly Hills, CA 90212, USA (office). *Telephone:* (310) 248-2000. *Fax:* (310) 248-2020.

WOO, Peter Kwong Ching, JP, MBA, DLitt, DSC; Chinese business executive; *Chairman, Wheelock & Company Limited;* b. 1946, Shanghai; m. Bessie Pao; ed St Stephen's Coll., Hong Kong, Univ. of Cincinnati and Columbia Business School, USA; family moved to Hong Kong 1949; worked at Chase Manhattan Bank and Worldwide Shipping Group following graduation; Chair. Wheelock & Co. Ltd 1986–96, 2002–; Chair. Wharf (Holdings) Ltd 1986–94, Hon. Chair 1994–; Founding Chair. Wheelock NatWest Ltd 1995–, The Wharf (Holdings) Ltd 1992–; Hong Kong (now Hong Kong Special Admin. Region) Affairs Adviser to People's Repub. of China 1993–; non-official mem. Comm. on Strategic Devt 2007–; mem. Int. Advisory Bd Chemical Banking Corpn 1981–, Nat. Westminster Bank PLC 1992–, Gen. Electric 1994–, Elf Aquitaine 1994–; Dir Standard Chartered Bank PLC 1986–89; mem. Hong Kong (now Hong Kong Special Admin. Region)/US Econ. Co-operation Cttee 1989–95, Hong Kong Gov.'s Business Council 1993–97; Chair. Hong Kong (now Hong Kong Special Admin. Region) Environment and Conservation Fund Cttee 1994–, Hong Kong Hosp. Authority 1995–, Hong Kong Trade Devt Council 2000–08; Deputy Chair. Prince of Wales Business Leaders' Forum 1991–; mem. Court of Hong Kong Polytechnic Univ.; cand. for Chief Exec. of Hong Kong 1996; Grand Bauhinia Star, Cross of Officer, Order of Leopold (Belgium); Leader of the Year (Hong Kong Standard) 1995. *Publication:* The Challenge of Hong Kong Plus 1991. *Leisure interests:* golf, tennis. *Address:* Penthouse, Wheelock House, 20 Pedder Street, Central, Hong Kong Special Administrative Region, People's Republic of China.

WOO, Sir Po-shing, Kt, FCIA, FID; British solicitor; b. 19 April 1929, Hong Kong; s. of the late Seaward Woo and of Ng Chiu Man; m. Helen Woo Fong Shuet Fun (Lady Woo) 1956; four s. one d.; ed La Salle Coll., Hong Kong and King's Coll., London; admitted to practice as solicitor in England and Hong Kong 1960; Notary Public 1966; admitted to practice as barrister and solicitor, Supreme Court of Victoria, Australia 1983; Founder Woo Kwan Lee & Lo, Solicitors and Notaries 1973; Chair. Kailey Enterprises Ltd, Kailey Devt Ltd; Dir Sun Hung Kai Properties Ltd, Henderson Devt Co. Ltd and more than 40 other cos; mem. Inst. of Admin. Man., Inst. of Trade Mark Agents; f. Woo Po Shing Medal in Law (Hong Kong Univ.) 1982, Woo Po Shing Overseas Summer School Travelling Scholarship (Hong Kong Univ.) 1983, The Po-Shing Woo Charitable Foundation 1994, Woo Po Shing Chair of Chinese and Comparative Law (City Univ.) 1995; fmr mem. Council Univ. of Hong Kong; Hon. Voting mem. Hong Kong Jockey Club, Po Leung Kuk Advisory Bd, Tung Wah Group of Hosps; Legal Adviser Chinese Gold and Silver Exchange Soc.; Hon. Pres. and Legal Adviser, South China Athletic Asscn; Patron Woo Po Shing Gallery of Chinese Bronze, Shanghai Museum, The Auckland Observatory (renamed Sir Po-Shing Woo Auckland Observatory Bldg); Fellow, Inst. of Man., King's Coll., London Univ., Hong Kong Man. Asscn; Hon. Prof., Nankai Univ. of Tianjin, China; Chevalier, Ordre des Arts et des Lettres 2004; Hon. LLD (City Univ. Hong Kong); Hon. LLB (King's Coll. London); World Fellowship of Duke of Edinburgh's Award. *Leisure interests:* travelling, viewing and collecting antiques including Chinese paintings, bronzes and ceramics, racehorses. *Address:* 2/F Kailey Tower, 16 Stanley Street, Central, Hong Kong Special Administrative Region, People's Republic of China (home). *Telephone:* 2522-4825 (home). *Fax:* 2537-9747 (home). *Website:* www.kailey.com.hk (office).

WOOD, Adrian John Bickersteth, CBE, MA, MPA, PhD; British economist; *Professor of International Development, University of Oxford;* b. 25 Jan. 1946, Woking; s. of the late John H. F. Wood and of Mary E. B. Brain (née Ottley); m. Joyce M. Teitz 1971; two d.; ed Bryanston School, King's Coll. Cambridge and Harvard Univ.; Fellow, King's Coll. Cambridge 1969–77; Asst Lecturer, Lecturer, Univ. of Cambridge 1973–77; Economist, Sr Economist, IBRD 1977–85; Professorial Fellow, Inst. of Devt Studies, Univ. of Sussex 1985–2000; Chief Economist Dept for Int. Devt 2000–05; Prof. of Int. Devt, Univ. of Oxford 2005–; Harkness Fellowship 1967–69. *Publications:* A Theory of Profits 1975, A Theory of Pay 1978, Poverty and Human Development (with others) 1981, China: Long-Term Development Issues and Options (with others) 1985, North-South Trade, Employment and Inequality 1994. *Leisure interests:* music, art, tennis. *Address:* Queen Elizabeth House, 3 Mansfield Road, Oxford, OX1 3TB, England (office). *Telephone:* (1865) 281837 (office). *Fax:* (1865) 281801 (office). *E-mail:* adrian.wood@qeh.ox.ac.uk (office). *Website:* www.qeh.ox.ac.uk (office).

WOOD, Sir Andrew Marley, GCMG, MA; British diplomatist (retd); b. 2 Jan. 1940, Gibraltar; s. of Robert George Wood; m. 1st Melanie LeRoy Masset 1972 (died 1977); one s.; m. 2nd Stephanie Lee Masset 1978; one s. one d.; ed Ardingly Coll., King's Coll. Cambridge; joined Foreign Office 1961, served in Moscow 1964, Washington 1967, FCO 1970, Cabinet Office 1971, First Sec., FCO 1973, First Sec. and Head of Chancery, Belgrade 1976, Counsellor 1978, Head of Chancery, Moscow 1979, Head of Western European Dept, FCO 1982, Head of Personnel Operations Dept, FCO 1983, Amb. to Yugoslavia 1985–89, Minister, Washington 1989–92, (Chief Clerk) FCO 1992, Amb. to Russia (also accred to Moldova) 1995–2000; Chair. Advisory Council BCB, Russo–British Chamber of Commerce; Dir Foreign and Colonial Investment Trust, PBN Co., Mechel Steel Group; Adviser to BP, Renaissance Capital. *Address:* 15 Platts Lane, London, NW3 7NP, England (home).

WOOD, Anne, CBE, FRTS; British television producer; *Chairman, Ragdoll Ltd.;* b. 1937, Spennymoor, Co. Durham; m. Barrie Wood; one s. one d.; teacher of English Language and Literature 1960s; f. Books For Your Children magazine; co-creator and producer TV programme The Book Tower 1979, Ragdolly Anna; Head of Children's Programmes TV AM (ITV) 1982–84; f. Ragdoll Ltd (TV production co.) 1984, Creative Dir 1984, now Chair.; creator of Pob, Rosie and Jim, Tots TV, Brum, Open a Door, Teletubbies (shown in 120 countries worldwide), Boohbah; Fellow, Royal TV Soc. 1998–; Eleanor Farjeon Award for Services to Children's Books 1969, Ronald Politzer Award 1974; for the Book Tower: BAFTA 1979, 1982, Prix Jeunesse 1980; for Tots TV: Prix Jeunesse 1996, BAFTA 1996, 1997; Baird Medal, Royal TV Soc. 1997; numerous awards for Teletubbies including Grand Prize, Winner Pre-School Educ. Category, Prize Int. Contest (Japan) 1997, Children's BAFTA for Best Pre-School Programme 1998, Indies Nickleodeon UK Children's Award 1999, five awards at Int. Licensing Industry Merchandisers' Asscn 1999, BBC Audiocall Children's Award 2000; Veuve Clicquot Award for Business Woman of the Year 1999; BAFTA Special Award for Outstanding Contrib. in Children's TV and Film 2000, Olswang Business Award, Women in Film and Television 2003, Harvey Lee Award, Broadcasting Press Guild 2007. *Leisure interests:* gardening, reading. *Address:* Ragdoll Limited, 9 Timothy's Bridge Road, Stratford Enterprise Park, Stratford upon Avon, Warwicks., CV37 9NQ, England (office). *Telephone:* (1789) 404100 (office). *Fax:* (1789) 404136 (office). *E-mail:* annew@ragdoll.co.uk (office). *Website:* www.ragdoll.co.uk (office).

WOOD, Charles Gerald, FRSL; British playwright and scriptwriter; b. 6 Aug. 1932, St. Peter Port, Guernsey; s. of John Edward Wood and Catherine Mae Wood (née Harris); m. Valerie Elizabeth Newman 1954; one s. one d.; ed

King Charles I School, Kidderminster and Birmingham Coll. of Art; corporal, 17/21st Lancers 1950–55; factory worker 1955–57; Stage Man., scenic artist, cartoonist, advertising artist 1957–59; Bristol Evening Post 1959–62; mem. Drama Advisory Panel, South Western Arts 1972–73; consultant to Nat. Film Devt Fund 1980–82; mem. Council BAFTA 1991–93; Evening Standard Drama Award 1963 1972, Screenwriters Guild Award 1965, Royal TV Soc. Award 1988, BAFTA Award 1988, Prix Italia 1988, Humanitas Award 2002. *Plays include:* Prisoner and Escort, Spare, John Thomas 1963, Meals on Wheels 1965, Don't Make Me Laugh 1966, Fill the Stage with Happy Hours 1967, Dingo 1967, H 1969, Welfare 1971, Veterans 1972, Jingo 1975, Has 'Washington' Legs? 1978, Red Star 1984, Across from the Garden of Allah 1986; adapted Pirandello's Man, Beast and Virtue 1989, The Mountain Giants 1993, Alexandre Dumas's The Tower 1995. *TV plays include:* Prisoner and Escort, Drill Pig, A Bit of a Holiday, A Bit of an Adventure, Love Lies Bleeding, Dust to Dust. *Screenplays include:* The Knack 1965, Help! 1965, How I Won the War 1967, The Charge of the Light Brigade 1968, The Long Day's Dying 1969, Cuba 1980, Wagner 1983, Red Monarch 1983, Puccini 1984, Tumbledown 1988, Shooting the Hero 1991, An Awfully Big Adventure 1993, England my England (with John Osborne) 1995, The Ghost Road 1996, Mary Stuart 1996, Iris (with Richard Eyre) 1999, Snow White in New York 2001. *TV series:* Don't Forget to Write 1986, My Family and Other Animals 1987, The Settling of the Sun 1987, Sharpe's Company 1994, Sharpe's Regiment 1996, Mute of Malice (Kavanagh QC) 1997, Sharpe's Waterloo 1997, Monsignor Renard 1999. *Publications:* (plays): Cockade 1965, Fill the Stage with Happy Hours 1967, Dingo 1967, H 1970, Veterans 1972, Has 'Washington' Legs? 1978, Tumbledown 1987, Man, Beast and Virtue 1990, The Giants of the Mountain 1994, The Tower 1995, Iris 2002. *Leisure interests:* military and theatrical studies, gardening. *Address:* London Management, 2–4 Noel Street, London, W1V 3RB, England (office). *Telephone:* (20) 7287-9000 (office). *Fax:* (20) 7287-3436 (office). *E-mail:* rdaniels@lonman.co.uk (office); charles@wood4760.fsnet.co.uk (home).

WOOD, Elijah; American actor; b. 28 Jan. 1981, Cedar Rapids, Iowa. *Films include:* Back to the Future Part II 1989, Internal Affairs 1990, Avalon 1990, Paradise 1991, Radio Flyer 1992, Forever Young 1992, The Adventures of Huck Finn 1993, The Good Son 1993, North 1994, The War 1994, Flipper 1996, The Ice Storm 1997, Deep Impact 1998, The Faculty 1998, Black and White 1999, The Bumblebee Flies Anyway 1999, Chain of Fools 2000, The Lord of the Rings: The Fellowship of the Ring 2001, Ash Wednesday 2002, The Adventures of Tom Thumb and Thumbelina (voice) 2002, Try Seventeen 2002, The Lord of the Rings: The Two Towers 2002, Spy Kids 3-D: Game Over 2003, The Lord of the Rings: The Return of the King 2003, Eternal Sunshine of the Spotless Mind 2004, Christmas on Mars 2005, Sin City 2005, Hooligans 2005, Everything Is Illuminated 2005, Paris, je t'aime 2006, Bobby 2006, Legend of Spyro: A New Beginning (voice) 2006, Happy Feet (voice) 2006, Day Zero 2007, The Oxford Murders 2008, 9 2008. *Address:* William Morris Agency, Inc., 1 William Morris Place, Beverly Hills, CA 90212, USA. *Telephone:* (310) 859-4550. *Fax:* (310) 248-5650. *E-mail:* nd@wma.com. *Website:* www.wma.com.

WOOD, Graham Charles, MA, PhD, ScD, FRS, FREng; British scientist, engineer and academic; *Professor Emeritus of Corrosion Science and Engineering, University of Manchester;* b. 6 Feb. 1934, Farnborough; s. of Cyril Wood and Doris Hilda Wood (née Strange); m. Freda Nancy Waithman 1959; one s. one d.; ed Bromley Grammar School, Kent, Christ's Coll., Cambridge; Lecturer, then Sr Lecturer, Reader in Corrosion Science UMIST 1961–72, Prof. of Corrosion Science and Eng 1972–97, now Prof. Emer., UMIST and Univ. of Manchester; Vice-Prin. for Academic Devt UMIST 1982–84, Deputy Prin. 1983, Dean of Faculty of Tech. 1987–89, Pro-Vice-Chancellor 1992–97; Chair. Int. Corrosion Council 1993–96; Pres. Inst. of Corrosion Science and Tech. 1978–80; Hon. DSc (UMIST) 2001; U.R. Evans Award, Inst. of Corrosion, C. Wagner Award of Electrochemical Soc., Beilby Medal, Griffith Medal, Inst. of Materials, Cavallaro Medal, European Fed. of Corrosion, European Corrosion Medal, European Fed. of Corrosion, Hothersall Medal, Inst. of Metal Finishing. *Publications:* more than 400 papers in various learned journals. *Leisure interests:* travel, cricket, walking, history of art, science and politics. *Address:* University of Manchester School of Materials, Corrosion and Protection Centre, PO Box 88, Sackville Street, Manchester, M60 1QD, England (office). *Telephone:* (161) 306-4850 (office); (161) 306-4851 (office). *Fax:* (161) 306-4865 (office).

WOOD, James N., BA, MA; American art historian, museum curator and foundation executive; *President and CEO, J. Paul Getty Trust;* b. 20 March 1941, Boston; son of Charles H. Wood and Helen N. Wood (neé Nowell); m. Emese Forizs 1966; two c.; ed Williams Coll., Inst. of Fine Arts, New York Univ., Universita per Stranieri, Perugia, Italy; Asst to Dir, Metropolitan Museum, New York 1967–68, Asst Curator 20th Century Art Dept 1968–70; Curator Albright-Knox Art Gallery, Buffalo 1970–73, Assoc. Dir 1973–75; Adjunct Prof. of Art History, SUNY at Buffalo 1973–75; Dir St Louis Art Museum 1975–80; Pres. and Dir Art Inst. of Chicago 1980–2004; Pres. and CEO J. Paul Getty Trust, Los Angeles 2007–; Pres. Pulitzer Foundation for the Arts; mem. Bd of Dirs Sterling and Francine Clark Art Inst., Inst. of Fine Arts, New York Univ., Harvard Univ. Art Museums, Museum of the Rhode Island School of Design. *Address:* J. Paul Getty Trust, 1200 Getty Center Drive, Los Angeles, CA 90049-1681, USA (office). *Telephone:* (310) 440-7600 (office). *E-mail:* info@getty.edu (office). *Website:* www.getty.edu (office).

WOOD, John, CBE; British actor; ed Bedford School, Jesus Coll., Oxford; with Old Vic Co. 1954–56, RSC 1971–. *Stage appearances include:* Enemies, The Man of Mode, Exiles, The Balcony 1971, The Comedy of Errors 1972, Julius Caesar, Titus Andronicus 1972, 1973, Collaborators, A Lesson in Blood and Roses 1973, Sherlock Holmes, Travesties 1974 (Evening Standard Best Actor Award 1974, Tony Award 1976), The Devil's Disciple, Ivanov 1976, Death Trap 1978, Undiscovered Country, Richard III 1979, Piaf, The Provok'd Wife 1980, The Tempest 1988, The Man Who Came to Dinner, The Master Builder 1989, King Lear (Evening Standard Best Actor Award 1991), Love's Labours Lost 1990, The Invention of Love 1997. *Television:* A Tale of Two Cities, Barnaby Rudge 1964–65, The Victorians 1965, The Duel 1966. *Films:* Nicholas and Alexandra 1971, Slaughterhouse Five 1972, War Games 1983, The Madness of King George 1994, Sabrina 1996, Richard III 1996, Jane Eyre 1996, The Gambler 1997, Chocolat 2001. *Address:* c/o Royal Shakespeare Company, Barbican Centre, Silk Street, London, EC2Y 8DS, England.

WOOD, L. John, QSO, MA (Hons); New Zealand diplomatist and academic; *Pro-Chancellor, University of Canterbury;* b. 31 March 1944, Kaikoura; s. of Lionel Wood and Margaret Wood; m. 1st Rosemary Taunt 1969 (died 1995); one s.; m. 2nd Rose Newell; ed Lincoln Country Dist High School, Christchurch Boys' High School, Univ. of Canterbury and Balliol Coll., Oxford; joined Ministry of Foreign Affairs 1969; seconded to Treasury 1971–72; Second Sec., later First Sec. Tokyo 1973–76; seconded to Prime Minister's Dept 1976–78; First Sec., later Counsellor and Consul-Gen. Bonn 1978–82; Ministry of Foreign Affairs 1982–83; Minister, Deputy Chief of Mission, Washington, DC 1984–87; Amb. to Iran (also accred to Pakistan and Turkey) 1987–90; Dir N Asia Div. Ministry of External Relations and Trade 1990–91, Deputy Sec. Econ. and Trade Relations 1991–94; Amb. to USA 1994–98, 2001–06; Deputy Sec. External Econ. and Trade Policy, Ministry of Foreign Affairs and Trade 1991–94, 1998–2002; Adjunct Prof. of Political Science, University of Canterbury 2006–, Pro Chancellor 2008–; mem. Advisory Bd, NZ/US Council 2006–; Paul Harris Fellow, Rotary Int. 2005; Trustee, Univ. of Canterbury Foundation 2006–; elected by Court of Convocation to Univ. of Canterbury Council 2007–; Companion of the Queen's Service Order for Public Service 2006; Hon. DLit (Canterbury) 2006; Consumers for World Trade Hall of Fame 2004. *Leisure interests:* rare books and bindings, New Zealand literature, sport, V8 cars. *Address:* 215 Bay Paddock Road, R.D.I Hapuku, Kaikoura (home); School of Political Science and Communications, University of Canterbury, Private Bag 4800, Christchurch, New Zealand (office). *Telephone:* (3) 319-7074 (home). *Fax:* (3) 319-7073 (home). *E-mail:* blue-duck@xtra.co.nz (home). *Website:* www.posc.canterbury.ac.nz (office).

WOOD, Mark William, BA (Hons), MA; British journalist and broadcasting executive; *CEO, Independent Television News (ITN);* b. 28 March 1952, Rochester, Kent; m.; one d. one s.; ed Univs of Leeds, Warwick and Oxford; joined Reuters 1976, Corresp. Vienna, East Berlin and Moscow 1977–85, Chief Corresp., W Germany 1985–87, European Ed. 1987–89, Ed.-in-Chief 1989–2000, Exec. Dir 1990–96, Chair. Visnews Reuters TV 1992–2002, Man. Dir Reuters Contents Partners 2000–02; Dir (non-Exec.) Ind. TV News (ITN) 1993–2002, Chair. 1998–, CEO 2003–; Chair. Meteor GmbH 2000–02; Dir London News Radio 1999–2002; Chair. Museums, Libraries and Archives Council 2003–08; Dir Citywire 2002–, Espresso Education 2005–. *Address:* Independent Television News, 200 Gray's Inn Road, London, WC1X 8XZ, England (office). *Telephone:* (20) 7430-4249 (office). *Fax:* (20) 7430-4868 (office). *E-mail:* mark.wood@itn.co.uk (office). *Website:* www.itn.co.uk (office).

WOOD, Sir Martin (Francis), Kt, OBE, MA, FRS, DL; British engineer and business executive; b. 19 April 1927; s. of Arthur Henry Wood and Katharine Mary Altham (née Cumberlege) Wood; m. Audrey Buxton (née Stanfield) Wood 1955; one s. one d. one step-s. one step-d.; ed Gresham's, Trinity Coll., Cambridge, Imperial Coll., London, Christ Church, Oxford; with Nat. Coal Bd 1953–55; Sr Research Officer, Clarendon Lab., Oxford of Oxford 1956–69; f. Oxford Instruments PLC 1959, Chair. 1959–83, Deputy Chair. 1983–; Chair. Nat. Comm. for Superconductivity 1987–91; mem. Advisory Bd for Research Councils 1983–89, ACOST 1990–93, Central Lab. of Research Councils 1995–98; Dir Orbit Precision Machining Ltd 1965–, Oxford Seedcorn Capital Ltd 1986–, Oxford Ventures Group Ltd 1988–, ISIS Innovation Ltd 1989–, Oxford Innovation Ltd 1989–, Newport Tech. Group Ltd 1989–, FARM Africa Ltd 1985–; Tech. Consultant African Medical and Research Foundation; f. Northmoor Trust (for nature conservation), Oxford Trust (for encouragement of study and application of science and tech.); Trustee Oxon. Council for Voluntary Action 1994–; Fellow Wolfson Coll., Oxford 1967–94, Hon. Fellow 1994; Hon. Fellow UMIST 1989; Hon. DSc (Cranfield Inst. of Tech.) 1983; Hon. DTech (Loughborough Univ. of Tech.) 1985; Hon. DEng (Birmingham) 1997; Hon. DUniv (Open) 1999; Mullard Medal, Royal Soc. 1982. *Address:* c/o Oxford Instruments Group PLC, Old Station Way, Eynsham, Witney, Oxon., OX8 1TL, England. *Telephone:* (1865) 881437.

WOOD, Maurice, MB, BS, MD, FRCGP; American physician and academic; *Physician and Academic Professor Emeritus, Department of Family Practice, Medical College of Virginia;* b. 28 June 1922, Pelton, Co. Durham, England; s. of Joseph Wood and Eugenie Wood (née Lumley); m. Erica J. Noble 1948; two s. one d.; ed Chester-le-Street Grammar School and Univ. of Durham; various hosp. appointments 1945–46, 1949-50; Maj., RAMC 1946–49; Sr Pnr, Medical Practice, South Shields 1950–71; Gen. Practice Teaching Group, Univ. of Newcastle-upon-Tyne 1969–71; Clinical Asst Dept of Psychological Medicine, South Shields Gen. Hosp. 1966–71; Assoc. Prof., Dir of Research, Dept of Family Practice, Medical Coll. of Virginia, Virginia Commonwealth Univ., Richmond, Va 1971–73, Prof. and Dir of Research 1973–87, Prof. Emer. 1987–, now Physician and Academic Prof. Emer.; Career Founding mem. and Pres. N American Primary Care Research Group 1972–83, Exec. Dir 1983–92, Pres. Emer. 1992–; Consultant Adviser, WHO 1979–90; other professional appointments and memberships; mem. US Nat. Comm. on Vital and Health Statistics 1976–79; mem. Inst. of Medicine, NAS; Fellow, American Acad. of Family Physicians, Royal Coll. of Gen. Practitioners, World Org. of Family Doctors 2008; Maurice Wood Award, N American Primary Care Research Group 1995 and other awards and distinctions. *Publications:* International Classification of Primary Care 1987, 2005, The International Classification of Primary Care in the European Community – with a multilanguage layer (co-ed.) 1993, Organization, Funding, Distribution 2003–05; numerous articles in professional journals and book chapters. *Leisure interests:* sailing, gliding, skiing. *Address:* Department of Family Practice, Virginia Commonwealth University, Medical College of Virginia Station, Box 980-257, Richmond, VA 23298-0251 (office); 176 Lakeside Close, Stoney Creek at Wintergreen, Nellysford, VA 22958-8093, USA (home). *Telephone:* (804) 828-9625 (office); (434) 361-1275 (home). *Fax:* (434) 361-1275 (home). *E-mail:* wood150w@earthlink.net (home); nbl4wd@verizon.net (home).

WOOD, Peter, CBE; British insurance industry executive; *Chairman, esure;* m. (divorced); five d.; Founder, CEO Direct Line Insurance 1985–96, Chair. 1996–97; Chair. Privilege Insurance 1993–98; Vice-Chair. Plymouth Rock Co. 1994–; founder and Chair. Esure 2000–, First Alternative 2003–; Dir (nonexec.) The Economist Newspaper Ltd 1998–2004. *Address:* Esure at The Observatory, Reigate, Surrey, RH2 0SG, England (office). *Website:* www.esure.com (office).

WOOD, Peter (Lawrence); British theatre and television director; b. 8 Oct. 1928; s. of Frank Wood and Lucy E. Meeson; ed Taunton School and Downing Coll. Cambridge; Resident Dir Arts Theatre 1956–57; Assoc. Dir Nat. Theatre 1978–89; numerous other productions at theatres in London, Edin., New York, Stratford (Ont.), Vienna etc.; dir of plays for TV in USA and UK since 1970. *Theatre productions include:* (for Nat. Theatre) The Master Builder 1964, Love for Love 1965, 1985, Jumpers 1972, The Guardsman, The Double Dealer 1978, Undiscovered Country 1979, The Provok'd Wife 1980, On the Razzle 1981, The Rivals 1983, Rough Crossing 1984, Dalliance 1986, The Threepenny Opera 1986, The American Clock 1986, The Beaux' Stratagem 1989, The School for Scandal 1990, (for RSC) Winter's Tale 1960, The Devils 1961, Hamlet 1961, The Beggar's Opera 1963, Travesties 1974, The Strange Case of Dr. Jekyll and Mr. Hyde 1991, Indian Ink 1995, (for Chichester) The Silver King 1990, She Stoops to Conquer 1992, Arcadia 2000, On the Razzle 2001. *Opera productions include:* The Mother of Us All, Santa Fe 1976, Il Seraglio, Glyndebourne 1980, 1988, Don Giovanni, Covent Garden 1981, Macbeth, Staatsoper, Vienna 1982, Orione, Santa Fe 1983, Otello, Staatsoper, Vienna 1987. *Leisure interests:* swimming, sailing, travelling. *Address:* The Old Barn, Batcombe, Somerset, BA4 6HD, England.

WOOD, Ronald Karslake Starr, FRS; British biologist, plant pathologist and academic; *Senior Research Fellow, Department of Biological Sciences, Imperial College London;* b. 8 April 1919, Ferndale; s. of Percival T. E. Wood and Florence Dix Starr; m. Marjorie Schofield 1947; one s. one d.; ed Ferndale Grammar School and Imperial Coll., London; Ministry of Aircraft Production 1942; Royal Scholar, Lecturer Imperial Coll. 1947, Reader in Plant Pathology 1955, Prof. of Plant Pathology 1964–86, mem. Governing Body, Head Dept of Pure and Applied Biology 1981–84, Sr Research Fellow 1986–, Prof. Emer. 1986–; Dean Royal Coll. of Science 1975; Dir NATO Advanced Study Insts. 1970, 1975, 1980; Sir C. V. Raman Prof. Univ. of Madras 1980; Regent's Lecturer Univ. of California 1981; Otto-Appel Denkmünster 1978; Sec.-Gen. 1st Int. Congress of Plant Pathology 1968, Hon. Pres. 7th Int. Congress (Edin.) 1998; Founder Pres. Int. Soc. for Plant Pathology 1968, British Soc. for Plant Pathology, now Hon. mem.; Commonwealth Fund Fellow 1950, Research Fellow Conn. Agricultural Experimental Station 1957, Fellow American Phytopathological Soc. 1976, Thurburn Fellow Univ. of Sydney 1979; Vice-Chair. Governing Body E Malling Research Station; Gov. Inst. of Horticultural Research; Corresp. mem. Deutsche Phytomedizinische Gesellschaft 1973. *Publications:* Physiological Plant Pathology 1967, Phytotoxins in Plant Diseases (co-ed. with A. Ballio and A. Graniti) 1972, Specificity in Plant Diseases (co-ed. with A. Graniti) 1976, Active Defence Mechanisms in Plants (ed.) 1981, Plant Diseases: infection, damage and loss (ed.) 1984; numerous papers in scientific journals. *Leisure interest:* gardening. *Address:* Department of Biological Sciences, Imperial College, London, SW7 2AZ (office); Pyrford Woods, Pyrford, nr Woking, Surrey, England (home). *Telephone:* (20) 7589-5111 (office); (19323) 43827 (home). *Fax:* (20) 7584-2056 (office).

WOOD, Ronald (Ronnie); British musician (guitar, bass guitar); b. 1 June 1947, Hillingdon, London, England; m. 1st; one s.; m. 2nd Jo Howard 1985; one s. one d.; guitarist with Jeff Beck Group 1968–69, The Faces 1969–75, The Rolling Stones 1976–; tours worldwide; has also played with Bo Diddley, Rod Stewart, Jerry Lee Lewis; Nordoff-Robbins Silver Clef 1982, Grammy Lifetime Achievement Award 1986, Ivor Novello Award for Outstanding Contribution to British Music 1991. *Recordings include:* albums: with Jeff Beck Group: Truth 1968, Beck-Ola 1969; with The Faces: First Step 1970, Long Player 1971, A Nod's As Good As A Wink... To A Blind Horse 1971, Ooh La La 1973, Coast To Coast Overtures and Beginners 1974; with The Rolling Stones: Black And Blue 1976, Some Girls 1978, Emotional Rescue 1980, Tattoo You 1981, Still Life 1982, Undercover 1983, Dirty Work 1986, Steel Wheels 1989, Flashpoint 1991, Voodoo Lounge 1994, Stripped 1995, Bridges to Babylon 1997, Forty Licks 2002, Live Licks 2004; solo: I've Got My Own Album To Do 1974, Now Look 1976, Mahoney's Last Stand 1976, Gimme Some Neck 1979, 1234 1981, Live At The Ritz 1988, Slide On This 1992, Slide On Live: Plugged In And Standing 1994, Live & Eclectic 2000, Not For Beginners 2002, Live At Electric Ladyland 2002, Always Wanted More 2003, A Bigger Bang 2005. *Film:* Shine a Light 2007. *Publication:* According to the Rolling Stones (autobiog., jtly) 2003, Ronnie Wood: The Autobiography 2007. *Address:* Munro Sounds, 5 Wandsworth Plain, London, SW18 1ES, England (office). *Telephone:* (20) 8877-3111 (office). *Fax:* (20) 8877-3033 (office). *Website:* www.rollingstones.com; www.ronniewood.com.

WOOD, William B., III, PhD; American biologist and academic; *Professor, Molecular, Cellular and Developmental Biology Department, University of Colorado;* b. 19 Feb. 1938, Baltimore, Md; s. of Dr. W. Barry Wood, Jr and Mary L. Hutchins; m. Renate Marie-Elisabeth Hartisch 1961; two s.; ed Harvard Coll., Stanford Univ. and Univ. of Geneva; Nat. Acad. of Sciences–Nat. Research Council Postdoctoral Fellow, Univ. of Geneva 1964; Asst Prof. of Biology, Calif. Inst. of Tech. 1965–68, Assoc. Prof. 1968–70, Prof. 1970–77; Prof. of Molecular Biology, Univ. of Colo, Boulder 1977–, Chair. of Dept 1978–83; mem. NAS, American Acad. of Arts and Sciences, AAAS, American Soc. of Biological Chemists, Soc. for Developmental Biology; U.S. Steel Award in Molecular Biology, NAS 1969. *Publications:* Biochemistry, A Problems Approach (with J. H. Wilson, R. M. Benbow and L. E. Hood) 1974, 1981, Molecular Design in Living Systems 1974, The Molecular Basis of Metabolism 1974, Molecular Biology of Eucaryotic Cells (with L. E. Hood and J. H. Wilson) 1975, Immunology (with L. E. Hood and I. Weissman) 1978, 1984, The Nematode Caenorhabditis Elegans (Ed.) 1988; articles in professional journals. *Leisure interests:* music, tennis, camping. *Address:* Univ. of Colorado, MCDB, 347 UCB, Boulder, CO 80309-0347 USA (office). *Telephone:* (303) 492-6680 (office); (303) 492-8258 (lab) (office). *E-mail:* wood@stripe.Colorado.EDU (office). *Website:* mcdb.colorado.edu/~wood (office).

WOODHEAD, Christopher Anthony, MA; British academic and educational administrator; *Professor, University of Buckingham;* b. 20 Oct. 1946, Middx; s. of Anthony Woodhead and Doris Woodhead; m. 1970 (divorced 1995); one d.; ed Wallington Co. Grammar School, Univs of Bristol and Keele; English teacher Priory School, Shrewsbury 1969–72; Deputy Head of English Newent School, Gloucester 1972–74; Head of English Gordano School, Avon 1974–76; lecturer in English Oxford Univ. 1976–82; English Adviser Shropshire Local Educ. Authority 1982–84, Chief Adviser 1984–86; Deputy Chief Educ. Officer Devon Local Educ. Authority 1988–90; Cornwall Local Educ. Authority 1990–91; Deputy Chief Exec. Nat. Curriculum Council 1990, Chief Exec. 1991–93; Chief Exec. School Curriculum and Assessment Authority 1993–94; HM Chief Inspector of Schools 1994–2001; Prof., Univ. of Buckingham 2002–; Chair. Cognita Schools Ltd 2004–; columnist, Sunday Times. *Publication:* Class War 2002. *Leisure interests:* rock climbing, running. *Address:* Hendre Gwenllian, Llanfrothen, Penrhyndeudraeth, Gwynedd, LL48 6DJ, Wales.

WOODHOUSE, Rt Hon. Sir (Arthur) Owen, Kt, ONZ, PC, KBE, DSC, LLB; New Zealand judge; b. 18 July 1916, Napier; s. of the late Arthur James Woodhouse and Wilhemina Catherine Woodhouse (née Allen); m. Margaret Leah Thorp 1940; four s. two d.; ed Napier Boys' High School and Auckland Univ.; mil. and naval service 1939–45, Lt-Commdr RNZNVR; liaison officer with Yugoslav partisans 1943; Asst to Naval Attaché, British Embassy 1945; joined Lusk, Willis & Sproule, barristers and solicitors 1946; Crown Solicitor, Napier 1953; Judge of Supreme Court 1961–86; a Judge of Court of Appeal 1974–86; Pres. Court of Appeal 1981–86; Founding Pres. Law Comm. 1986–91; Chair. Royal Comm. on Compensation and Rehabilitation in respect of Personal Injury in New Zealand 1966–67, Chair. inquiry into similar questions in Australia 1973–74; Hon. LLD (Victoria Univ. of Wellington) 1978, (Univ. of York, Toronto, Canada) 1981. *Publications:* A Personal Affair (autobiog.) 2004. *Leisure interests:* music, golf. *Address:* 244 Remuera Road, Auckland 1005, New Zealand (home). *Telephone:* (9) 524-4383 (home).

WOODLAND, Alan Donald, PhD, FASSA; Australian economist and academic; *Professor and Australian Professorial Fellow, School of Economics, Australian School of Business, University of New South Wales;* b. 4 Oct. 1943, Dorrigo, NSW; s. of C. J. Woodland and E. Shephard; m. Narelle Todd 1966; one s. two d.; ed Univ. of New England; Lecturer, Univ. of New England 1967–69; Asst Prof., Univ. of British Columbia 1969–74, Assoc. Prof. 1974–78, Prof. of Econs 1978–81; Prof. of Econometrics and Australian Professorial Fellow, Faculty of Econs and Business, Univ. of Sydney 1982–2008; Prof. and Australian Professorial Fellow, School of Econs, Australian School of Business, Univ. of New South Wales 2008–; Jt Ed. The Economic Record 1987–92; Fellow, Reserve Bank 1981; Fellow, Econometric Soc. *Publication:* International Trade and Resource Allocation 1982, International Trade Policy and the Pacific Rim, Institute of Economic Affairs Conference Vol. No. 120, (co-ed.) 1999, Economic Theory and International Trade: Essays in Honour of Murray C. Kemp (ed.) 2002, The Economics of Illegal Immigration (co-author) 2005. *Leisure interests:* bridge, tennis. *Address:* School of Economics, Australian School of Business, University of New South Wales, Sydney, NSW 2052 (office); 5 Rosebery Road, Killara, NSW 2071, Australia (home). *Telephone:* (2) 9385-9707 (office); (2) 9416-3100 (home). *Fax:* (2) 9313-6337 (office). *E-mail:* a.woodland@unsw.edu.au (office). *Website:* www2.economics.unsw.edu.au (office).

WOODROW, Bill (William Robert), DipAD, HDipAD, RA; British artist and sculptor; b. 1 Nov. 1948, nr Henley-on-Thames, Oxon.; s. of Geoffrey W. Woodrow and Doreen M. Fasken; m. Pauline Rowley 1970; one s. one d.; ed Barton Peveril Grammar School and Winchester, St Martin's and Chelsea Schools of Art; numerous solo exhbns in UK, FRG, France, Australia, Netherlands, Belgium, Italy, USA, Canada, Switzerland, Sweden, Ireland and Yugoslavia since 1979; works in many public collections in UK and abroad; Trustee Tate Gallery 1996–2001, Imperial War Museum 2003–; Gov. Univ. of the Arts, London 2003–; elected to Royal Acad. of Arts 2002; finalist in Turner Prize 1986, winner Anne Gerber Award, Seattle Museum of Art, USA 1988. *Publications include:* Bill Woodrow, Sculpture 1980–86, A Quiet Revolution – Recent British Sculpture, Bill Woodrow, Eye of the Needle, Sculptures 1987–1989, Bill Woodrow, XXI Bienal de São Paulo 1991, In Awe of the Pawnbroker 1994, Fools' Gold 1996, Lead Astray 2004, Brood 2007. *Address:* c/o Waddington Galleries, 11 Cork Street, London, W1S 3LT, England. *E-mail:* bill@billwoodrow.com (office). *Website:* www.billwoodrow.com (office).

WOODRUFF, Judy Carline, BA; American broadcast journalist; *Senior Correspondent and Political Editor, The Newshour with Jim Lehrer;* b. 20 Nov. 1946, Tulsa, Okla; d. of William Henry Woodruff and Anna Lee Woodruff (née Payne); m. Albert R. Hunt, Jr 1980; two s. one d.; ed Meredith Coll., Duke

Univ.; News Announcer and Reporter WAGA-TV, Atlanta 1970–75; News Corresp. NBC News, Atlanta 1975–76; White House Corresp., NBC News, Washington 1977–83; Corresp., MacNeil-Lehrer News Hour, PBS, Washington 1983–93, Sr Corresp. and Political Ed. The News Hour With Jim Lehrer 2007—; Anchor and Sr Corresp. Cable News Network (CNN) 1993–2005, also anchored Judy Woodruff's Inside Politics; anchor for Frontline (PBS documentary series) 1983–90; Visiting Fellow, Joan Shorenstein Center on the Press, Politics and Public Policy, Harvard Univ. 2005–; Visiting Prof. of Media and Politics, Duke Univ. 2006; mem. Bd of Advisers Henry Grady School of Journalism, Univ. of Georgia 1979–82, Bd of Visitors Wake Forest Univ. 1982–88, Bd of Advisers Benton Fellowship in Broadcast Journalism, Univ. of Chicago 1984–90, Families and Work Inst. 1989–, Freedom Forum First Amendment Center 1992–, Comm. on Women's Health 1993–, Radio and TV News Dirs' Foundation 1994–; Co-Chair. Int. Women's Media Foundation 1991– (Founder, Dir 1989–); mem. Nat. Acad. of TV Arts and Sciences, White House Corresps Asscn; Trustee, Duke Univ. 1985–97, now Trustee Emer.; Knight Fellowship in Journalism, Stanford Univ. 1985–99, Edward Weintal Award 1987, Joan Shorenstein Barone Award 1987, Helen Bernstein Award for Excellence in Journalism, New York Public Library 1989, Pres.'s 21st Century Award, Nat. Women's Hall of Fame 1994, CableAce Award for Best Newscaster 1995, CableAce Best Anchor Team Award 1996, Allen H. Neuharth Award for Excellence in Journalism 1995, News and Documentary Emmy Award 1997, Int. . Matrix Award, Asscn for Women in Communications 2003, Leonard Zeidenberg First Amendment Award, Radio-TV News Dir Asscn and Foundation 2003; elected to Georgia Asscn of Broadcasters Hall of Fame 2003. *Publication:* This is Judy Woodruff at the White House 1982. *Address:* The Newshour with Jim Lehrer, PBS, 3620 27th Street S, Arlington, VA 22206-2350, USA (office). *Telephone:* (703) 998-2481 (office). *Fax:* (703) 998-4154 (office). *E-mail:* newshour@pbs.org (office). *Website:* www.pbs.org/newshour (office).

WOODS, James Howard; American actor; b. 18 April 1947, Vernal, Utah; s. of Gail Woods and Martha Woods; m. 1st Kathryn Greko 1980 (divorced 1983); m. 2nd Sarah Owen 1989 (divorced 1990); ed Univ. of Calif. at Los Angeles and Massachusetts Inst. of Tech.; first Broadway appearance in Brendan Behan's Borstal Boy; Obie Award for appearance in Brooklyn Acad. of Music Production of Edward Bond's Saved, New York 1971; other stage appearances in 1970s include Moonchildren 1972, The Trial of the Catonsville Nine, Finishing Touches, Conduct Unbecoming; two Emmy Awards. *Films include:* The Visitors 1971, The Way We Were 1972, The Gambler 1974, Distance 1975, Alex and the Gypsy 1976, The Choirboys 1977, The Onion Field 1979, Black Marble 1980, Fast Walking 1982, Split Image 1982, Videodrome 1983, Once Upon a Time in America 1984, Against All Odds 1984, Joshua Then and Now 1985, Best Seller 1987, Cop 1987, The Boost 1989, True Believer 1989, Immediate Family 1989, Straight Talk 1992, Diggstown, Chaplin 1992, The Getaway 1994, Curse of the Starving Class 1994, Casino 1995, Nixon 1996, Killer: A Journal of Murder, Ghosts of Mississippi 1996, Hercules (voice) 1997, Contact 1997, Vampires 1998, True Crime 1999, Virgin Suicides 2000, Race to Space 2001, John Q 2001, Recess, School's Out (voice) 2001, Riding in Cars with Boys 2001, Scary Movie 2 2001, Northfork 2003, This Girl's Life 2003, Ark 2004, Pretty Persuasion 2005, Be Cool 2005, End Game 2006, Surf's Up (voice) 2007. *Television include:* Holocaust 1978, Badge of the Assassin 1985, Promise 1986, My Name is Bill. W. 1989, Citizen Cohn 1992, Jane's House 1994, Next Door 1994, Indictment: The McMartin Trial 1995, The Summer of Ben Tyler 1996, Dirty Pictures 2000, Showtime 2000, Rudy: The Rudy Giuliani Story 2003, Shark (series) 2006. *Leisure interes:* poker. *Address:* c/o Guttman Associates, 118 S Beverly Drive, Suite 201, Beverly Hills, CA 90210, USA.

WOODS, Michael, PhD, DSc; Irish politician; b. 8 Dec. 1935, Bray, Co. Wicklow; m. Margaret Maher; three s. two d.; ed Univ. Coll. Dublin and Harvard Business School, USA; Lecturer, Franciscan Coll. of Agric., Multyfarnham, Co. Westmeath 1958–59; Head of Dept and Prin. Officer, Agric. Research Inst. 1960–70; Man. Dir F11 Produce Ltd 1970–73, Associated Producer Groups Ltd 1974–79; mem Dáil 1977–; Minister of State, Depts of Taoiseach and Defence 1979; Minister for Health and Social Welfare 1979–81, March–Dec. 1982, for Social Welfare 1987–91, for Agric. 1991–92, for the Marine 1992, for Social Welfare 1993–94, Health 1994, Spokesperson on Equality and Law Reform 1994–97, Minister for Marine and Natural Resources 1997–2000, for Educ. and Science 2000–02, Chair. Joint Cttee of Foreign Affairs 2002–; Fianna Fáil. *Publications:* Research in Ireland – Key to Economic and Social Development; numerous tech. and scientific papers. *Address:* Department of Foreign Affairs, 80 St Stephen's Green, Dublin 2 (office); 13 Kilbarrack Grove, Raheny, Dublin 5, Ireland (home). *Telephone:* (1) 8323357 (home); (1) 4780822 (office). *Fax:* (1) 4781484 (office). *E-mail:* library1@iveagh.irlgov.ie (office). *Website:* foreignaffairs.gov.ie (office).

WOODS, Philip (Phil) Wells, BMus; American jazz musician (alto saxophone), composer and teacher; b. 2 Nov. 1931, Springfield, MA; s. of Stanley J. Woods and Clara Markley; m. 1st Beverly Berg 1957 (divorced 1973); one s. one d.; m. 2nd Jill Goodwin 1985; two step-d.; ed studied privately with Harvey LaRose in Springfield, Lenny Tristano in New York, Manhattan School of Music and Juilliard Conservatory; numerous appearances and recordings with own bands and as featured performer; Co-founder Clark Terry Big Bad Band; mem. The European Rhythm Machine 1968–73; Leader, The Phil Woods Quartet 1955–99, The Phil Woods Quintet 1977–, Phil Woods Little Big Band 1988–; mem. Advisory Bd Delaware Water Gap Celebration of the Arts, Bd of Dirs Al Cohn Memorial Jazz Collection, American Fed. of Musicians, Int. Asscn for Jazz Educ.; Hon. LLD (East Stroudsberg Univ.) 1994; Officier, Ordre des Arts et des Lettres; Beacon Jazz Award 2001. *Compositions include:* Three Improvisations (saxophone quartet), Sonata for alto and piano (Four Moods), Rights of Swing, The Sun Suite, I Remember, The Deer Head Suite, Fill the Woods with Light (for Parsons Dance Co.). *Recordings include:* albums: with The Phil Woods Quartet: Woodlore 1955, Leila/Abstraction 1957, Warm Woods 1957, In Paris 1961, Alive and Well in Paris 1968, Gargoyle Wedding 1973, New Music 1973, Phil Woods Broadcasts 1973, The New Phil Woods Album 1975, I Remember 1978, A Live Recording Vol. One 1979, More Live (Grammy Award 1982) 1979, European Tour Live 1980, Sax Today 1980, The Macerata Concert 1980, Birds of a Feather 1981, Live from New York 1982, At the Vanguard 1982, Cool Woods 1999; with The European Rhythm Machine: 9th International Jazz Festival Ljubljana 1968, The Birth of the ERM 1968, Stolen Moments 1968, Freedom Jazz Dance 1969, At the Montreux Jazz Festival 1969, Woods Notes 1969, At the Frankfurt Jazz Festival 1970, Chromatic Banana 1970, Jazz Workshop 1971, Live at Montreux 1972; with The Phil Woods Quintet: Summer Afternoon 1977, Song for Sisyphus 1977, Integrity 1984, Heaven 1984, Dizzy Gillespie Meets The Phil Woods Quintet 1986, Gratitude 1986, Bop Stew 1987, Bouquet 1987, Flash 1989, All Bird's Children 1990, Full House 1991, An Affair to Remember 1993, You and the Night and the Music 1993, Souvenirs 1994, Plays the Music of Jim McNeely 1995, Mile High Jazz 1996, American Songbook 2002, In Her Eyes 2005; with Phil Woods Little Big Band: Evolution 1988, Real Life 1990, This is How I Feel About Quincy 2004; solo: Early Quintets 1954, New Jazz Quintet 1954, Pot Pie (with Jon Eardley) 1954, New Jazz Quartet 1955, Pairing Off (with Gene Quill) 1956, Phil and Quill (with Gene Quill) 1956, The Young Bloods (with Donald Byrd) 1956, Young Woods 1956, New York Scene (with George Wallington and Donald Byrd) 1957, Phil and Quill with Prestige (with Gene Quill) 1957, Bird Feathers (with Gene Quill) 1957, Four Altos (with Gene Quill) 1957, Bird's Night (with Cecil Payne) 1957, The Jazz We Heard Last Summer (with Herbie Mann and Eddie Costa) 1957, Phil Talks with Quill (with Gene Quill) 1957, Rights of Swing 1961, Jazz at the Liberty 1963, Directly from the Half Note 1966, Greek Cooking 1967, What Happens? (with Art Farmer) 1968, Alto Summit (with others) 1968, Round Trip 1969, Born Free (Vols one and two) 1970, A Jazz Life 1970, Gravenstein (with Daniel Humair) 1971, Musique Dubois 1974, Images (with Michel Legrand) (Grammy Award 1976) 1975, Phil Woods and the Japanese Rhythm Machine 1975, Live from the Showboat 1976, Floresta Canto (with Chris Gunning Orchestra) 1976, Crazy Horse (with Chris Swansen) 1979, Three for All (with Tommy Flanagan and Red Mitchell) 1981, The New York–Montreux Connection (with others) 1981, Ole Dude & the Fundance Kid (with Budd Johnson) 1984, Piper at the Gates of Dawn (with Chris Swansen) 1984, Anything Goes (with Stéphane Grappelli) 1987, Embraceable You (with Big Bang Orchestra) 1988, Phil on Etna (with Catania City Brass Orchestra) 1989, My Man Benny My Man Phil (with Benny Carter) 1989, Here's to my Lady 1989, Phil's Mood (with Space Jazz Trio) 1990, Flowers for Hodges (with Jim McNeely) 1991, Live at the Corridonia Jazz Festival (with Space Jazz Trio) 1991, Elsa (with Enrico Pieranunzi) 1991, Ornithology: Phil Salutes Bird (with Franco d'Andrea Trio) 1994, Our Monk (with Franco d'Andrea) 1994, Just Friends (with Renato Sellani) 1994, Alto Summit (with Vincent Herring, Antonio Hart) 1995, The Complete Concert (with Gorden Beck) 1996, Another Time Another Place (with Benny Carter) 1996, Astor & Elis 1996, The Summit (with George Robert) 1997, Celebration! (with the Festival Orchestra) 1997, Chasin' the Bird 1997, The Rev & I (with Johnny Griffin) 1998, Soul Eyes (with George Robert) 2000, Voyage (with the Bill Charlap Trio) 2000, Giants at Play (John Coates) 2001, Beyond Brooklyn (with Herbie Mann) 2002, The Thrill is Gone 2002, Big Encounter at Umbria (Vols 1–4, with Lee Konitz) 2003, Play Henry Mancini (with Carl Saunders) 2003, Unheard Herd 2004, Groovin' to Marty Paich (with Los Angeles Jazz Orchestra) 2004. *Leisure interests:* computer games, reading, public television, movies. *Address:* PO Box 278, Delaware Water Gap, PA 18327, USA (office). *Telephone:* (570) 421-3145 (home). *Website:* www.philwoods.com (home).

WOODS, Eldrick (Tiger); American professional golfer; b. 30 Dec. 1975, Cypress, Calif.; s. of the late Lt-Col Earl Woods and Kultida Woods; m. Elin Nordegren 2004; one s. one d.; ed Stanford Univ.; winner Int. Jr World Championship 1984–91, Nat. Youth Classic 1990, US Jr Amateur Championship 1991 (youngest winner), 1992, 1993, US Amateur Championships 1994 (youngest winner), 1995, 1996, Las Vegas Invitational competition 1996, Walt Disney Classic 1996, Honda Asian Classic 1997, Mercedes Championships 1997, 2000, US Masters 1997 (youngest winner, broke records for lowest score and greatest margin of victory), 2001, 2002, 2005, Bell South Classic 1998, US PGA Championship 1999, 2000, 2006, 2007, Nat. Car Rental Golf Classic 1999, WGC American Express Championship 1999, 2006, AT & T Pebble Beach Nat. Pro-Am. 2000, Bay Hill Invitational 2000, 2001, 2002 US Open 2000, 2002, 2008, British Open 2000, 2005, 2006, winner of numerous other titles; mem. US team World Amateur Team Championship 1994, US Walker Cup team 1995, Ryder Cup 1997, 1999, 2002 (postponed from 2001), 2004; contract with Nike 1999 (biggest sponsorship deal in sporting history); f. Tiger Woods Foundation, Tiger Woods Learning Center; career earnings of more than US$76 million; numerous awards including Sports Star of the Year Award 1997, PGA Tour Player of the Year 1997, 1999–2003, 2005–06; Sports Illustrated Sportsman of the Year 1996, 2000, Mark H. McCormack Award 2006. *Leisure interests:* basketball, fishing, sport in general. *Address:* c/o Tiger Woods Foundation, 4281 Katella Avenue, Suite 111, Los Alamitos, CA 90720; Tiger Woods Learning Center, One Tiger Woods Way, Anaheim, CA 92801; IMG Golf, IMG Center, 1360 East 9th Street, Suite 100, Cleveland, OH 44114, USA. *Telephone:* (714) 765-8000 (Tiger Woods Learning Center); (216) 522-1200 (IMG). *Fax:* (216) 436-3477 (IMG). *Website:* www.tigerwoodsfoundation.org; www.twlc.org; www.tigerwoods.com.

WOODWARD, Robert (Bob) Upshur, BA; American journalist and writer; *Associate Editor, The Washington Post;* b. 26 March 1943, Geneva, IL; s. of Alfred Woodward and Jane Upshur; m. Elsa Walsh 1989; two c.; ed Yale Univ.; reporter, Montgomery Co. (MD) Sentinel 1970–71; reporter, Washington Post

1971–78, Metropolitan Ed. 1979–81, Asst Man. Ed. 1981–2008, Assoc. Ed. 2008–; Pulitzer Prize citation 1972. *Publications:* All the President's Men (with Carl Bernstein) 1973, The Final Days (with Carl Bernstein) 1976, The Brethren (with Scott Armstrong) 1979, Wired 1984, Veil: The Secret Wars of the CIA 1987, The Commanders 1991, The Man Who Would Be President (with David S. Broder) 1991, The Agenda: Inside the Clinton White House 1994, The Choice 1996, Shadow: Five Presidents and the Legacy of Watergate 1999, Maestro, Greenspan's Fed and the American Boom 2000, Bush at War... Inside the Bush White House 2002, Plan of Attack 2004, The Secret Man 2005, State of Denial: Bush at War, Part III 2006, The War Within: A Secret White House History 2006–2008 2008. *Address:* The Washington Post, 1150 15th Street, NW, Washington, DC 20071, USA (office). *E-mail:* woodwardb@washpost.com (office).

WOODWARD, Sir Clive, Kt, OBE, BSc; British professional rugby football coach (rugby union), business executive and former rugby player; *Director of Elite Performance, British Olympic Association;* b. 6 Jan. 1956, Ely, Cambridgeshire; m. to Jayne; two s., one d.; ed degree in Physical Education and Sports Science at Loughborough Univ.; centre; player for Leicester 1979–85, Manly 1985–88, England Under-23, England 1980–84, British Lions (two tours: 1980, 1983); 21 caps for England (mem. Grand Slam winning side 1980), two caps for British Lions in 1980; coach for Henly 1993–95, London Irish 1995, Bath (assistant coach) 1996–97, England Under-21 1996–97, England 1997–2004 (winners Grand Slam 2003, World Cup 2003); coached England to record 14 consecutive victories in 2002–03; apptd Head Coach of British Lions for tour of NZ 2005, resgnd; Dir of Football, Southampton Football Club 2004–06; Dir of Elite Performance, British Olympic Asscn 2006–; freeman, City of Greater London, Royal Borough of Windsor and Maidenhead; Dr hc (Loughborough Univ.) 2004. *Publication:* Winning 2004. *Leisure interests:* golf, skiing, football. *Address:* British Olympic Association, 1 Wandsworth Plain, London SW18 1EH, England. *Telephone:* (20) 8871-2677. *Fax:* (20) 8871-9104. *E-mail:* boa@boa.org.uk. *Website:* www.olympics.org.uk.

WOODWARD, Edward, OBE; British actor and singer; b. 1 June 1930, Croydon, Surrey; s. of Edward Oliver Woodward and Violet Edith Woodward; m. 1st Venetia Mary Collett 1952; two s. one d.; m. 2nd Michele Dotrice 1987; one d.; ed Kingston Coll. and Royal Acad. of Dramatic Art; stage debut at Castle Theatre, Farnham 1946; in repertory cos in England and Scotland; London debut, Where There's a Will, Garrick Theatre 1955; 12 LP records as singer and three of poetry and 14 talking book recordings; numerous int. and nat. acting awards, including Golden Globe Award, Emmy Award, Variety Award (Best Musical Performance). *Other stage appearances include:* Mercutio in Romeo and Juliet, Laertes in Hamlet, Stratford 1958, Rattle of a Simple Man, Garrick 1962, Two Cities (musical) 1968, Cyrano in Cyrano de Bergerac, Flamineo in The White Devil, Nat. Theatre Co. 1971, The Wolf, Apollo 1973, Male of the Species, Piccadilly 1975, On Approval, Theatre Royal Haymarket 1976, The Dark Horse, Comedy 1978, Beggar's Opera (also dir) 1980, The Assassin 1982, Richard III 1982, The Dead Secret 1992; three productions, New York. *Films include:* Becket 1966, The File on the Golden Goose 1968, Hunted 1973, Sitting Target, Young Winston, The Wicker Man 1974, Stand Up Virgin Soldiers 1977, Breaker Morant 1980, The Appointment 1981, Comeback, Merlin and the Sword 1982, Champions 1983, A Christmas Carol, King David 1984, Uncle Tom's Cabin 1989, Mister Johnson 1990, Deadly Advice 1993, A Christmas Reunion 1994, Gulliver's Travels 1995, The Abduction Club 2002, Hot Fuzz 2007. *Television include:* over 2000 TV productions; title role in TV serials Callan 1966–71, The Equalizer 1985–89, Over My Dead Body 1990, In Suspicious Circumstances (series) 1991–94, In My Defence 1991, America At Risk (series) 1991–92, Harrison (series, USA) 1993–95, Common as Muck (BBC TV series) 1994, The Woodward File (series) 1995–96, Gulliver's Travels (mini-series) 1995–96, The New Professionals (series) 1998–99, Emma's Boy 2000, Nikita (series) 2000, Night and Day 2001, Messiah 2001, Night Flight 2002, Murder in Suburbia (series) 2004, Where the Heart Is 2005, Five Days 2007. *Leisure interests:* boating, geology.

WOODWARD, Joanne Gignilliat; American actress; b. 27 Feb. 1930, Thomasville, Ga; d. of Wade Woodward and Elinor Trimmier; m. Paul Newman 1958 (died 2008); three d.; ed Louisiana State Univ.; Trustee, Westport (Conn.) Country Playhouse; numerous awards including Foreign Press Award for Best Actress 1957, Acad. Award 1957, Nat. Bd Review Award 1957, Best Actress Award, Soc. of Film and TV Arts 1974; Franklin D. Roosevelt Four Freedoms Medal 1991, Kennedy Center Honor 1992. *Films include:* Count Three and Pray 1955, A Kiss Before Dying 1956, The Three Faces of Eve 1957, The Long Hot Summer 1958, Rally Round the Flag Boys 1958, The Sound and the Fury 1959, The Fugitive Kind 1959, From the Terrace 1960, Paris Blues 1961, The Stripper 1963, A New Kind of Love 1963, Signpost to Murder 1964, A Big Hand for the Little Lady 1966, A Fine Madness 1966, Rachel Rachel 1968, Winning 1969, W.U.S.A. 1970, They Might Be Giants 1971, The Effects of Gamma Rays on Man-in-the-Moon Marigolds 1972, The Death of a Snow Queen 1973, Summer Wishes, Winter Dreams 1973, The Drowning Pool 1975, The End 1978, The Shadow Box 1980, Candida (Play) 1981, Harry and Son 1984, The Glass Menagerie 1987, Mr and Mrs Bridge 1990, Philadelphia 1993, My Knees Were Jumping: Remembering the Kindertransports (voice) 1998. *Television includes:* All the Way Home, See How She Runs 1978, Streets of LA 1979, Crisis at Central High 1981, Do You Remember Love? 1985, Blind Spot 1993, Breathing Lessons 1994, James Dean: A Portrait 1996, Empire Falls 2005. *Address:* 246 Post Road East, Westport, CT 06880, USA.

WOODWARD, Adm. Sir John Forster (Sandy), Kt, GBE, KCB; British naval officer (retd); b. 1 May 1932, Marazion, Cornwall; s. of the late Tom Woodward and Mabel B. M. Woodward; m. Charlotte M. McMurtrie 1960; one s. one d.; ed Britannia Royal Naval Coll., Dartmouth; Commanding Officer, HMS Tireless 1961–62, HMS Grampus 1964–65; Exec. Officer, HMS Valiant 1965–67; Commdg Officer, HMS Warspite 1969–71; at Royal Coll. of Defence Studies, then in Directorate of Naval Plans, Ministry of Defence; Commdg Officer, HMS Sheffield 1976–78; Dir of Naval Plans, Ministry of Defence 1978–81; Flag Officer, First Flotilla 1981–83; Sr Task Group Commdr during Falkland Islands campaign 1982; Flag Officer, Submarines and Commdr Submarines, Eastern Atlantic, NATO 1983–84; Deputy Chief of Defence Staff (Commitments) 1985–87; C-in-C Naval Home Command 1987–89, rank of Adm.; Flag Aide-de-Camp to HM the Queen 1987–89; Man. consultant Yachtmaster Ocean (Royal Yachting Asscn); Pres. Falkland Island Memorial Chapel Trust 2001–. *Publications:* Strategy by Matrix 1980, One Hundred Days (autobiog.) 1992. *Leisure interests:* sailing, philately, desktop computers. *Address:* c/o The Naval Secretary, Victory Building, HM Naval Base, Portsmouth, Hants., PO1 3LS, England.

WOODWARD, Roger Robert, OBE, AC; Australian pianist, conductor and composer; b. 20 Dec. 1942, Sydney; s. of Francis W. Woodward and Gladys A. Woodward; one s. one d.; ed Conservatorium of Music, Sydney and PWSH, Warsaw; debut at Royal Festival Hall, London 1970; subsequently appeared with the five London orchestras; has performed throughout Eastern and Western Europe, Japan and the USA; has appeared at int. festivals and with the major orchestras throughout world; extensive repertoire and is noted for interpretation of Chopin, Beethoven, Bach and Twentieth Century Music; Artistic Dir Nat. Chamber Orchestra for Contemporary Music in Australia 'Alpha Centaure' 1989 and festivals in London; performs each season at leading int. festivals works by contemporary composers; Nat. Treas. 1998; Fellow Chopin Inst., Warsaw 1976; Kt (Breffini) 1985. *Leisure interests:* cooking, chess, swimming, gardening, painting, design. *Address:* LH Productions, 2/37 Hendy Avenue, Coogee, NSW 2034, Australia. *E-mail:* woodward@metz.une.edu.au.

WOODWARD, Shaun; British politician; *Secretary of State for Northern Ireland;* b. 26 Oct. 1958, Bristol; m. Camilla Davan Sainsbury 1987; one s. three d.; ed Bristol Grammar School, Jesus Coll., Cambridge; Researcher, BBC 1981–91; Dir of Communications, Conservative Party 1991–92; Lecturer on Politics, Queen Mary and Westfield Coll. 1992–94; Fellow, Inst. of Politics, Kennedy School, Harvard Univ., USA 1994; MP (Conservative) for Witney 1997–99, MP (Labour) for St Helens S 2001–, mem. Parl. Jt Cttee on Human Rights 2001–05; fmr mem. Foreign Affairs Select Cttee, EU Scrutiny Select Cttee, Minister for Creative Industries and Tourism and Parl. Under-Sec. of State for NI 2005–06, Parl. Under-Sec., Dept for Culture, Media and Sport 2006–07, Sec. of State for NI 2007–; Dir ENO 1994–2002; fmr Trustee, Homes for Homeless People, Marine Stewardship Council; fmr Chair. Understanding Industry; mem. Advisory Council, Royal Shakespeare Co. *Address:* Northern Ireland Office, 11 Millbank, London, SW1P 4PN, England (office). *Telephone:* (20) 7210-0260 (office). *Fax:* (20) 7210-0213 (office). *E-mail:* info@nio.gov.uk (office). *Website:* www.nio.gov.uk (office); www.shaunwoodward.com (office).

WOOLARD, Edgar Smith, Jr., BSc; American business executive; b. 15 April 1934, Washington, NC; s. of Edgar Smith and Mamie (née Boone) Woolard; m. Peggy Harrell 1956; two d.; ed North Carolina State Univ.; fmr Lt, US Army; industrial engineer, Du Pont at Kinston, NC 1957–59, various supervisory and managerial posts 1959–75, Man. Dir textile marketing div. 1975–76, Man. corp. plans dept 1976–77, Gen. Dir products and planning div. 1977–78, Gen. Man. textile fibers, Wilmington, Del. 1978–81, Vice-Pres. textile fibers 1981–83, Exec. Vice-Pres. 1983–85, Vice-Chair. 1985–87, Pres. and COO 1987–89, Chair., CEO 1989–96, Chair. 1996–98, also mem. Bd of Dirs 1996–2000; mem. Bd of Dirs Telex Communications Inc.; fmr mem. Bd of Dirs Citicorp, New York, Council for Aid to Educ., New York, IBM, New York, Apple Computer Inc., Cupertino, Calif., Jt Council on Econ. Educ., New York, Raleigh, Seagram Co., Canada; mem. Bd of Trustees NC Textile Foundation, Christiana Care Corpn; Int. Palladium Medal Soc. Chimie Industrielle (American Section) 1995. *Address:* c/o Telex Communications Inc., 12000 Portland Avenue South, Burnsville, MN 55337, USA.

WOOLCOTT, Richard, AC, AO, BA; Australian consultant, company director and fmr diplomatist; b. 11 June 1927, Sydney; s. of Dr and Mrs A. R. Woolcott; m. Birgit Christensen 1952; two s. one d.; ed Frankston High School, Geelong Grammar School, Univ. of Melbourne and London Univ. School of Slavonic and E European Studies; joined Australian Foreign Service 1951; served in Australian missions in London, Moscow (twice), S Africa, Malaya, Singapore and Ghana; attended UN Gen. Ass. 1962; Acting Commr to Singapore 1963–64; High Commr to Ghana 1967–70; accompanied Prime Ministers Menzies 1965, Holt 1966, McMahon 1971, 1972, Whitlam 1973, 1974 and Hawke 1988–91 on visits to Asia, Europe, the Americas and the Pacific; Adviser at Commonwealth Heads of Govt Confs London 1965, Ottawa 1973, Kuala Lumpur 1989; Pacific Forum 1972, 1973, 1988; Australia-Japan Ministerial Cttee 1972, 1973, 1988, 1989; Head, S Asia Div., Dept of Foreign Affairs 1973; Deputy Sec. Dept of Foreign Affairs 1974; Amb. to Indonesia 1975–78, to Philippines 1978–82; Perm. Rep. to UN 1982–88; Sec. of Dept of Foreign Affairs and Trade 1988–92; Prime Minister's Special Envoy to develop Asia Pacific Econ. Co-operation 1989; Australian Rep. on UN Security Council 1985–86; rep. of Australia at Non-aligned Summit meeting, Harare 1986; ASEAN Post-Ministerial Conf. 1989, 1990, 1991; Alt. Australian Gov., inaugural EBRD meeting 1991; Chair. Australia Indonesia Inst. 1992–98, Official Establishments Trust 1992–99, Nat. Cttee on Population and Devt 1993–95, Across Asia Multimedia (Hong Kong) 2000–, Cttee to review the Australian Citizenship Test 2008; Dir Auric Pacific (Singapore) 2001–02; mem. int. council of The Asia Soc.; Vice-Pres. Multiple Sclerosis Soc. of Australia 1995–2000; Founding Dir Australasia Centre, Asia Soc. 1997–; Founding Dir or consultant several firms; mem. Bd of Commrs, Lippo Bank, Indonesia 1999–2002; apptd Special Envoy to develop idea of an Asia Pacific community 2008; Life Fellow, Trinity Coll., Melbourne Univ. 1995; Bintang Mahaputra Utama (Indonesia) 2000. *Publications:* Australian Foreign Policy 1973, The Hot Seat: Reflections on Diplomacy From Stalin's Death to the Bali Bombings 2003; numerous articles, including special features for The Australian, articles for International Herald Tribune, Time. *Leisure interests:* writing, cricket, photography. *Address:* Asia Society, AustralAsia Centre, Level 1, 175 Collins Street, Melbourne, Vic. 3000 (office); PO Box 3926, Manuka, Canberra, ACT 2603 (office); 19 Talbot Street, Forrest, Canberra, ACT 2603, Australia. *Telephone:* (2) 6295-3206 (office). *Fax:* (2) 6295-3066 (office). *E-mail:* rwoolcot@ozemail.com.au (home). *Website:* www.asiasociety.org.

WOOLDRIDGE, Hon. Michael Richard Lewis, MB, BSc, MBA; Australian politician; b. 7 Nov. 1956; m. Michele Marion Colman 1988; two s.; ed Scotch Coll., Melbourne, Univ. of Melbourne, Monash Univ.; Resident Medical Staff (Surgical), Alfred Hosp. 1982–85; MP (Liberal Party) for Chisholm, Vic. 1987–88, for Casey, Vic. 1998–; pvt. practice 1985–87; Shadow Minister for Aboriginal Affairs 1990–92; Shadow Minister for Aboriginal and Torres Strait Islander Affairs 1992–93; Deputy Leader of the Opposition, Shadow Minister for Educ., Employment and Training 1993–94, Shadow Minister for Community Services, Sr Citizens and Aged Care 1994–95, for Health and Human Services 1995–96; Minister for Health and Family Services 1996–98, Minister for Health and Aged Care 1998–2002. *Leisure interests:* royal tennis, skiing, reading. *Address:* Parliament House, Canberra, ACT 2600; First Floor, Suite 9, 431 Burke Road, Glen Iris, Vic. 3146, Australia.

WOOLDRIDGE, Richard; British media executive; *Chairman and CEO, International Herald Tribune;* fmr journalist; fmr Ed. Yorkshire Evening Press; Man. Ed. York and Country Press –1992; Dir Westminster Press (regional newspaper group) 1992–96; joined International Herald Tribune 1996, various positions including consultant, Pres. and COO –2003, Chair. and CEO 2003–. *Address:* International Herald Tribune, 6 bis, rue des Graviers, 92521 Neuilly Cedex, France (office). *Telephone:* 1-41-43-93-00 (office). *Fax:* 1-41-43-92-12 (office). *E-mail:* iht@iht.com (office). *Website:* www.iht.com (office).

WOOLF, Baron (Life Peer), cr. 1992, of Barnes in the London Borough of Richmond; **Rt Hon. Harry Kenneth Woolf,** PC, LLB; British judge; b. 2 May 1933, Newcastle-upon-Tyne; s. of Alexander Woolf and Leah Woolf; m. Marguerite Sassoon 1961; three s.; ed Glasgow Acad., Fettes Coll., Edin., Univ. Coll. London; Nat. Service, 15/19th Royal Hussars 1954, Capt., Army Legal Services 1955; called to Bar, Inner Temple 1955, began practising 1956; Recorder, Crown Court 1972–79; Jr Counsel, Inland Revenue 1973–74; First Treasury Counsel (Common Law) 1974–79; Judge, High Court, Queen's Bench Div. 1979–86; Presiding Judge, S Eastern Circuit 1981–84; Lord Justice of Appeal 1986–92; Lord of Appeal in Ordinary 1992–96; Master of the Rolls 1996–2000; Lord Chief Justice of England and Wales 2000–05; Mem. House of Lords, Chair. Parliamentary Standards Sub-Cttee, mem. Constitution Cttee; non-perm. judge, Court of Final Appeal, Hong Kong 2003–; mediator and arbitrator, Blackstone Chambers, London 2005–; founding Pres. Civil, Commercial and Appeal Court, Qatar Financial Centre 2006–; conducted review of working methods of the European Court of Human Rights 2005; Chair. Bank of England Financial Market's Law Cttee; Visiting Prof. of Law and Chair. of Council, Univ. Coll. London; mem. Bd of Man., Inst. of Advanced Legal Studies 1985–94 (Chair. 1986–94); Chair. Lord Chancellor's Advisory Cttee of Legal Educ. 1986–94, Middx Advisory Cttee on Justices of the Peace 1986–90, Magna Carta Trust 1996, Lord Chancellors' Advisory Cttee on Public Records 1996–2000, Council of Civil Justice 1997–2000, Civil Procedure Rules Cttee 1997–2000; Pro-Chancellor London Univ. 1994–2002; Visitor Nuffield Coll., Oxford 1996–2000, Downing College, Cambridge 2000–, Univ. Coll., London 1996–2000; Trustee Butler Trust 1991–96, Chair. 1992–96, Pres. 1996–; Hon. Fellow, British Acad. 2002, Acad. of Medical Sciences, Univ. Coll. London, Coll. of Trial Lawyers, USA; Hon. Visiting Prof. Chinese Univ. of Hong Kong; Hon. LLD (Buckingham) 1992, (Bristol) 1992, (London) 1993, (Anglia Poly Univ.) 1994, (Manchester Metropolitan) 1994, (Hull) 2001, (Cranfield) 2001, (Cambridge) 2002, (Exeter) 2002; Hon. DLitt (London) 2002; Hon. DSc (Cranfield) 2002, Dr. hc (Oxford) 2004. *Publications:* Protection of the Public – The New Challenge 1990, Declaratory Judgement (Ed. with J. Woolf) 1993, Judicial Review of Administrative Action (Jt Eds De Smith, Woolf & Jowell) (5th edn) 1995; reports: Prisons in England and Wales 1991, Access to Justice (Interim) 1995, (Final) 1996, Principles of Judicial Review (jtly) 1999, Pursuit of Justice 2008. *Address:* House of Lords, London, SW1A 0PW, England (office). *Telephone:* (20) 7219-1788 (office). *Fax:* (20) 7219-0785 (office).

WOOLFSON, Michael Mark, MA, PhD DSc, FRAS, CPhys, FInstP, FRS; British physicist and academic; *Professor Emeritus, University of York;* b. 9 Jan. 1927, London; s. of Maurice Woolfson and Rose Woolfson (née Solomons); m. Margaret Frohlich 1951; two s. one d.; ed Jesus Coll., Oxford, UMIST; Nat. Service, Royal Engineers 1947–49; Research Asst, Cavendish Lab., Cambridge 1952–54; ICI Fellow Univ. of Cambridge 1954–55; lecturer, Faculty of Tech. Univ. of Manchester 1955–61, Reader 1961–65; Prof. of Theoretical Physics, Univ. of York 1965–94, Prof. Emer. 1994–; Chair. Royal Soc. Planetary Sciences Subcttee. 1979–83, British Crystallographic Asscn 1985–90, British Nat. Cttee for Crystallography 1985–90; Pres. Yorks. Philosophical Soc. 1985–99; Hughes Medal, Royal Soc. 1986, Patterson Award, American Crystallographic Asscn 1990, Gregori Aminoff Medal and Prize, Royal Swedish Acad. of Sciences 1992, Dorothy Hodgkin Prize, British Crystallographic Asscn 1997, Ewald Prize, Int. Union of Crystallography 2002. *Publications:* Direct Methods in Crystallography 1960, The Origin of the Solar System, The Capture Theory 1989, Physical and Non-physical Methods of Solving Crystal Structures 1995, An Introduction to X-ray Crystallography 1997, An Introduction to Computer Simulation 1999, The Origins and Evolution of the Solar System 2000, Planetary Science 2002. *Leisure interest:* winemaking. *Address:* Department of Physics, University of York, York, YO1 5DD (office); 24 Sandmoor Green, Leeds, LS17 7SB, England (home). *Telephone:* (1904) 432230 (office); (113) 266-2166 (home). *Fax:* (1904) 432214 (office). *E-mail:* mmw1@york.ac.uk (office). *Website:* www.york.ac.uk/depts/phys/staff/academic/woolfson/woolfson.htm (office).

WOOLGAR, Stephen, PhD; British sociologist and academic; *Chair of Marketing, Saïd Business School, University of Oxford;* b. 1950; ed Emmanuel Coll., Cambridge; Visiting Lecturer, McGill Univ., Montréal, Canada 1979–81, MIT 1983–84, École Nat. Supérieure des Mines, Paris 1988–89, Univ. of California, San Diego 1995–96; Prof. of Sociology, Brunel Univ. 1996–2000, Head Dept of Human Sciences –2000, Dir Centre for Research into Innovation, Culture and Tech. Technology 1998–2000; Dir Virtual Society Program, Econ. and Social Research Council 1997–2002; Chair of Marketing, Saïd Business School, Univ. of Oxford 2000–; mem. Man. Bd, Oxford e-Science Centre, Oxford Internet Inst.; mem. Council Consumer's Asscn; mem. Research Assessment Exercise Sociology Panel, Higher Educ. Funding Council for England 1996, 2001; fmr mem. EC (VALUE) Think Tank, Information Tech., Electronics and Communications Foresight Panel for UK Govt, Leisure and Learning Foresight Panel; fmr Adviser to Cabinet Office Better Govt Team; fmr mem. E-Commerce and Consumer Affairs Ministerial Advisory Groups; fmr Adviser to Research Councils of Denmark, Netherlands and Norway; Fulbright Scholarship, Fulbright Sr Scholarship, ESRC Sr Research Fellowship, Econ. and Social Research Council; Bernal Prize 2008. *Publications:* Laboratory Life: The Social Construction of Scientific Facts (co-author) 1979, Science: The Very Idea 1988, The Cognitive Turn: Sociological and Psychological Perspectives on Science (co-author) 1989, Representation in Scientific Practice (co-author) 1990, The Machine at Work: Technology, Work and Society (co-author) 1997, Virtual Society? Technology, Cyberbole, Reality (ed.) 2002. *Address:* Saïd Business School, University of Oxford, Park End Street, Oxford, OX1 1HP, England (office). *E-mail:* steve.woolgar@sbs.ox.ac.uk (office). *Website:* www.sbs.ox.ac.uk (office).

WOOLLEY, Kenneth Frank, AM, BArch, LFRAIA; Australian architect; *Director, Ancher, Mortlock & Woolley;* b. 29 May 1933, Sydney; s. of Frank Woolley and Doris May (Mudear) Woolley; m. 1st Cynthia Stuart (divorced 1979); m. 2nd Virginia Braden 1980; two s. one d.; ed Sydney Boys' High School, Univ. of Sydney; Design Architect, Govt Architect's Office, Sydney 1955–56, 1957–63; Asst Architect, Chamberlin, Powell and Bon, London 1956–57; Partner, Ancher, Mortlock, Murray & Woolley, Sydney 1964–69, Dir 1969–75; Dir Ancher, Mortlock & Woolley Pty Ltd, Sydney 1975–; mem. Quality Review Cttee Darling Harbour Redevt. Authority 1985; Visiting Prof., Univ. of NSW School of Architecture 1983; Visiting Tutor and Critic, Visiting Prof., Univ. of Sydney, Univ. of NSW, NSW Inst. of Tech., Sydney; mem. NSW Bd of Architects 1960–72, NSW Bldg Regulations Advisory Cttee 1960–74, NSW Bd of Architectural Educ. 1969–72, Royal Australian Inst. of Architects Aboriginal Housing Panel 1972–76; Life FRAIA 1976; Sulman Award 1962, Bronze Medal 1962, Wilkinson Award 1962, 1968, 1982, 1987, Blacket Award 1964, 1967, 1969, 1987, Civic Design Award 1983, Gold Medal, Royal Australian Inst. of Architects 1993, numerous other architectural awards. *Major works include:* Australian Embassy, Bangkok, ABC Radio Bldg, Sydney, Hyatt Hotel, Campbell's Cove, Sydney, Control Tower, Sydney Airport, Sydney Town Hall renovations, The Olympics and RAS Exhbn Halls and Hockey Stadium, new offices and city square, three student union bldgs, univs in NSW, numerous urban housing devts, radio stations, Vanuatu, Solomon Islands, over 4,000 production houses, State Govt offices, Sydney, Fisher Library, Sydney Univ., State Library of Vic., Royal Agricultural Showground Dome and Exhbn Halls, Sydney. *Publications:* numerous papers and articles in architectural journals. *Leisure interests:* golf, sailing, music, drawing. *Address:* Ancher, Mortlock & Woolley, Station House, Rawson Place, Level 5, 790 George Street, Sydney, NSW 2000, Australia (office). *Telephone:* (2) 9211-4466 (office). *Fax:* (2) 9211-9733 (office). *E-mail:* amw@amwarchitects.com.au (office). *Website:* www.amwarchitects.com.au (office).

WOOLLISCROFT, James O., BSc, MD; American physician and medical educator; *Dean of the Medical School, University of Michigan;* ed Univ. of Minnesota; Chief Resident, Univ. of Michigan Medical School 1980, Faculty Mem., Dept of Internal Medicine 1980, Prof. of Internal Medicine 1993, Josiah Macy Jr Prof. of Medical Educ. 1996–2001, Lyle C. Roll Prof. of Medicine 2001, Exec. Assoc. Dean 1999–2006, Interim Dean 2006–07, Dean 2007–; Fellow, Council of Deans, Asscn of American Medical Colls 2003–04; Soc. of Gen. Internal Medicine Medical Educ. Award 2004. *Address:* Office of the Dean, University of Michigan Medical School, 1301 Catherine Road, Ann Arbor, MI 48109, USA (office). *Telephone:* (734) 763-9600 (office). *E-mail:* woolli@umich.edu (office). *Website:* www.med.umich.edu/medschool/dean (office).

WOOLSEY, R. James, LLB, MA; American lawyer and fmr government official; *Vice-President, Global Assurance, Booz Allen Hamilton;* b. 1941, Tulsa, Okla; m. Suzanne Haley; three s.; ed Tulsa Cen. High School, Stanford Univ., Univ. of Oxford, UK and Yale Law School; staff mem. Nat. Security Council 1968–70; Adviser US Del. to Strategic Arms Limitation Talks 1969–70; Gen. Counsel to Senate Cttee on Armed Services 1970–73; Under-Sec. of the Navy 1977–79; del.-at-large to US–Soviet Strategic Arms Reduction Talks and space talks 1983–86; Amb. and US Rep. to negotiations on Conventional Armed Forces in Europe Treaty 1989–91; Chair. CIA task force on future of satellite spying 1991; Dir of CIA 1993–95; Pnr, Shea & Gardner 1991–93, 1995–2002; Vice-Pres. Global Assurance, Booz Allen Hamilton 2002–; Chair. Advisory Cttee, Clean Fuels Foundation; Dir USF&G 1995, Sun HealthCare Group Inc. 1995, Yurie Systems Inc. 1996; mem. Bd Govs Philadelphia Stock Exchange; mem. Pres.'s Comm. on Strategic Forces 1983,

Pres.'s Blue Ribbon Comm. on Defense Man. 1985–86, Pres.'s Comm. on Fed. Ethics Law Reform 1989, Comm. to Assess the Ballistic Missile Threat to the US 1998, Nat. Comm. on Terrorism 1999–2000; Trustee Center for Strategic and Int. Studies; Rhodes Scholar 1963–65; mem. Bd Advisors BioDefense Corpn 2004–. *Address:* Booz Allen Hamilton, 8283 Greensboro Drive, McLean, VA 22102, USA (office). *Telephone:* (703) 902-5701 (office). *E-mail:* woolsey_jim@bah.com (office). *Website:* www.bah.com (office).

WOONTON, Robert Philip, PhD; Cook Islands politician; b. 1949; m. Sue Woonton; Minister of Foreign Affairs and Immigration 1999–; Prime Minister Feb. 2002–04, portfolio also includes Police, Parl., House of Ariki, Tourism, Agric., Marine Resources, Transport, Airport and Ports Authorities, Nat. Disaster Man. *Address:* c/o Office of the Prime Minister, Government of the Cook Islands, Private Bag, Avarua, Rarotonga, Cook Islands (office). *E-mail:* rwoonton@oyster.net.ck (home).

WOOSNAM, Ian Harold, OBE; British (Welsh) professional golfer; b. 2 March 1958, Oswestry, Wales; s. of Harold Woosnam and Joan Woosnam; m. Glendryth Pugh 1983; one s. two d.; ed St Martin's Modern School; professional golfer 1976–; tournament victories: News of the World under-23 Matchplay 1979, Cacharel under-25 Championship 1982, Swiss Open 1982, Silk Cut Masters 1983, Scandinavian Enterprise Open 1984, Zambian Open 1985, Lawrence Batley TPC 1986, 555 Kenya Open 1986, Hong Kong Open 1987, Jersey Open 1987, Cepsa Madrid Open 1987, Bell's Scottish Open 1987, 1990, Lancome Trophy 1987, Suntory World Match-Play Championship 1987, 1990, 2001, Volvo PGA Championship 1988, 1997, Carrolls Irish Open 1988, 1989, Panasonic Euro Open 1988, Am Express Mediterranean Open 1990, Torras Monte Carlo Open 1990, Epson Grand Prix 1990, US Masters 1991, USF+G Classic 1991, Fujitsu Mediterranean Open, Torras Monte Carlo Open 1991, European Monte Carlo Open 1992, Lancôme Trophy 1993, Murphy's English Open 1993, British Masters 1994, Cannes Open 1994, Heineken Classic 1996, Scottish Open 1996, Volvo German Open 1996, Johnnie Walker Classic 1996; team events: Ryder Cup 1983–97, Dunhill Cup 1985, 1986, 1988, 1989, 1990, 1991, 1993, 1995, World Cup 1980, 1982, 1983, 1984, 1985, 1987, 1990, 1991, 1992, 1993, 1994, 1996, 1997; finished top Order of Merit 1987, 1990; ranked No. 1, Sony world rankings 1991; World Cup Individual, PGA Grand Slam 1991; Pres. World Snooker Asscn 1999–2002; eighth on all-time European Tour earnings list; 29 European PGA Tour titles; Captain European Ryder Cup Team 2006; now lives in Jersey, Channel Islands; BBC Wales Sports Personality of the Year Award 1987, 1990, 1991. *Publications:* Ian Woosnam's Golf Masterpieces (with Peter Grosvenor) 1991, Golf Made Simple: The Woosie Way 1997, Woosie: My Autobiography 2002. *Leisure interests:* snooker, water skiing, sports, fishing. *Address:* c/o David Barlow, IMG, McCormack House, Hogarth Business Park, Burlington Lane, Chiswick, London, W4 2TH, England (office). *Telephone:* (20) 8233-5077 (office). *Fax:* (20) 8233-5301 (office). *E-mail:* d.barlow@imgworld.com (office). *Website:* www.woosie.com (office).

WORCESTER, Sir Robert Milton, Kt, KBE, BSc, FRSS; American/British company director; b. 21 Dec. 1933, Kansas City; s. of the late C. M. Worcester and Violet Ruth Worcester; m. 1st Joann Ransdell 1958 (deceased); m. 2nd Margaret Noel Turner 1982; two s.; ed Univ. of Kansas; Consultant, McKinsey & Co. 1962–65; Chief Financial Officer, Opinion Research Corpn 1965–68; Man. Dir Market & Opinion Research Int. Ltd (MORI) 1969–94, Chair. 1973–2005; fmr Pres. World Asscn for Public Opinion Research; Visiting Prof., City Univ. 1990–2002, LSE 1992–, Univ. of Strathclyde 1996–2001; Pres. Environmental Campaigns Ltd 2002–06; Vice-Pres. Int. Soc. Science Council, UNESCO 1989–94, European Atlantic Group, UNA 1999–, Royal Soc. for Nature Conservation 1995–; mem. Pilgrims Soc. of GB (Chair. Exec. Cttee 1993–); mem. Court of Govs LSE 1995–, Advisory Bd European Business Journal, Fulbright Comm. 1995–2005, Court Univ. of Middx 2001–, Council Univ. of Kent 2002– (also mem. Court and Chancellor 2006–), Advisory Bd Nat. Consumer Council 2002–, Advisory Council Inst. of Business Ethics; Gov. Ditchley Foundation, English-Speaking Union; Dir (non-exec.) Kent Messenger Group; Chair. Maidstone Radio Ltd (CTR 105.4 fm); Co-Ed. Int. Journal of Public Opinion Research; writes monthly columns for Profile (magazine of Inst. of Public Relations) and Parliamentary Monitor; Trustee WorldWide Fund for Nature (WWF-UK) 1988–94, Natural History Museum Devt Trust 1989–94, Magna Carta Trust 1995–, Wildfowl and Wetlands Trust 2002–; Fellow, Market Research Soc. 1997–; apptd Kent Amb. by Kent Co. Council; Freeman City of London 2001; Hon. Prof. of Politics, Univ. of Kent 2002–; Hon. Prof., Univ. of Warwick 2004–; Hon. Fellow, LSE, King's Coll. London; Hon. DL of Kent 2006; Hon. DSc (Buckingham) 1999; Hon. DLitt (Bradford) 2001; Hon. DUniv (Middlesex) 2001; Hon. LLD (Greenwich) 2002; Helen Dinerman Award, World Asscn for Public Opinion Research 1996. *Publications:* Political Communications (with Martin Harrop) 1982, Political Opinion Polling: An International Review (ed.) 1983, Consumer Market Research Handbook (3rd edn, co-ed. with John Downham) 1986, Private Opinions, Public Polls (with Lesley Watkins) 1986, We British (with Eric Jacobs) 1990, British Public Opinion: History and Methodology of Political Opinion Polling in Great Britain 1991, Typically British (with Eric Jacobs) 1991, Dynamics of Societal Learning about Global Environmental Change (with Samuel H. Barnes) 1992, The Millennial Generation (with Madsen Pirie) 1998, The Next Leaders (with Madsen Pirie) 1999, Explaining Labour's Landslide (with Roger Mortimore) 1999, The Big Turn Off (with Madsen Pirie) 2000, How to Win the Euro Referendum: Lessons from 1975 2000, Facing the Future (with Madsen Pirie) 2000, The Wrong Package (with Madsen Pirie) 2000, Explaining Labour's Second Landslide (with Roger Mortimore) 2001, Explaining Labour's Landslip (with Roger Mortimore and Paul Baines) 2005. *Leisure interest:* castles, choral music, gardening. *Address:* MORI House, 79–81 Borough Road, London, SE1 1FY, England (office). *Telephone:* (20) 7347-3000 (office). *Fax:* (20) 7347-3017 (office). *E-mail:* rmworcester@yahoo.com (office). *Website:* www.ipsos-mori.com (office).

WORMS, Gérard Etienne; French company director; *Vice Chairman, Rothschild Europe;* b. 1 Aug. 1936, Paris; s. of André Worms and Thérèse Dreyfus; m. Michèle Rousseau 1960; one s. one d.; ed Lycées Carnot and Saint-Louis, Ecole Polytechnique and Ecole Nat. Supérieure des Mines, Paris; Engineer, Org. commune des régions sahariennes 1960–62; Head of Dept, Délégation à l'Aménagement du Territoire et à l'Action Régionale 1963–67; Tech. Adviser, Office of Olivier Guichard (Minister of Industry, later of Planning) 1967–69, Office of Jacques Chaban-Delmas (Prime Minister) 1969–71; Asst Man. Dir, Librairie Hachette 1972–75, Man. Dir 1975–81, Dir 1978–81; Prof., Ecole des Hautes Etudes Commerciales 1962–69, Supervisor of complementary courses, Faculty of Letters and Human Sciences, Paris 1963–69; Prof. Ecole Polytechnique 1974–85; Vice-Pres. Syndicat nat. de l'édition 1974–81; Exec. Vice-Pres. Rhône-Poulenc SA 1981–83; Exec. Vice-Pres. Compagnie de Suez 1984–90, Chair. and CEO 1990–95; Pres. Banque Indosuez 1994–95; Pres. Supervisory Bd Rothschild, Compagnie Banque Paris 1995–99, Man. Partner Rothschild et Cie and Rothschild et Cie Banque 1999–, Vice-Chair. Rothschild Europe; Pres. Centre for research into econ. expansion and business Devt 1996–, Supervisory Council for health information systems 1997–2000, History channel 1997–; mem. bd Telecom Italia 1998–2001, Publicis, Métropole Télévision; Chevalier, Ordre nat. du Mérite; Chevalier, Ordre du Mérite maritime; Commdr Légion d'honneur 2007. *Publications:* Les méthodes modernes de l'économie appliquée 1965; various articles on econ. methods in specialized journals. *Address:* Rothschild et Cie, 23bis avenue de Messine, 75008 Paris (office); 61 bis avenue de la Motte Picquet, 75015 Paris, France (home). *Telephone:* 1-40-74-40-31 (office); 1-47-83-99-43 (home). *Fax:* 1-40-74-98-24 (office).

WORRALL, Denis John, PhD; South African business executive, politician and lawyer; b. 29 May 1935, Benoni; s. of Cecil John Worrall and Hazel Worrall; m. Anita Denise Ianco 1965; three s.; ed Univ. of Cape Town, Univ. of SA and Cornell Univ., USA; taught political science, Cornell Univ., Univ. of Calif. at LA, Univ. of Natal, Univ. of SA and Univ. of Witwatersrand; Cornell Research Fellow, Univ. of Ibadan, Nigeria 1962–63; Founder and Ed. New Nation 1967–74; Research Prof. and Dir Inst. for Social and Econ. Research, Rhodes Univ. –1974; Senator for Cape 1974–77; Amb. to Australia 1983–84, to UK 1984–87; Advocate, Supreme Court of SA; MP for Cape Town-Gardens 1977–83; independent cand. for Helderberg in 1987 Election; mem. Pres's. Council 1980–83; f. Ind. Movt 1988; Leader Ind. Party 1988–89; co-founder Democratic Party 1989; MP for Berea, Durban 1989–94; Chair. Omega Investment Research Ltd. *Publications:* South Africa: Government and Politics; numerous articles. *Leisure interests:* reading, cycling. *Address:* Omega Investment Research (Pty) Ltd, P.O. Box 5455, 8000 Cape Town; 4 Montrose Terrace, 5 Montrose Street, (Newlands) 7700 Cape Town, South Africa. *Telephone:* (21) 6897881 (office); (21) 6857502 (home).

WORSTHORNE, Sir Peregrine Gerard, Kt, MA; British journalist; b. 22 Dec. 1923, London; s. of Col A. Koch de Gooreynd and the late Baroness Norman; m. 1st Claudia Bertrand de Colasse 1950 (died 1990); one d. one step-s.; m. 2nd Lady Lucinda Lambton 1991; ed Stowe School, Peterhouse, Cambridge and Magdalen Coll., Oxford; mem. editorial staff, Glasgow Herald 1946–48; mem. editorial staff, The Times 1948–50, Washington corresp. 1950–52, leader writer 1952–55; leader writer, Daily Telegraph 1955–61; Deputy Ed. Sunday Telegraph 1961–76, Assoc. Ed. 1976–86, Ed. 1986–89, Ed. Comment Section 1989–91; columnist, The Spectator 1997–; Granada TV Journalist of the Year 1981. *Publications:* The Socialist Myth 1972, Peregrinations 1980, By The Right 1987, Tricks of Memory (memoirs) 1993, In Defence of Aristocracy 2004. *Leisure interests:* walking, tennis. *Address:* The Old Rectory, Hedgerley, Bucks., SL2 3UY, England (home). *Telephone:* (1753) 646167 (home). *Fax:* (1753) 646914 (home). *E-mail:* therectory.hedgerley@virgin.net (office).

WORTH, Richard, OBE, LLB, MJ, MBA, PhD; New Zealand politician; *Minister of Internal Affairs;* b. 3 July 1948, Auckland; ed Univ. of Auckland, Massey Univ., Royal Melbourne Inst. of Tech.; Pnr, Simpson Grierson 1972–99, Exec. Chair. 1986–99; MP for Epsom 1999–2005, mem. Select Cttees on Regulations Review 1999–2002, on Law and Order 2001–02, on Justice 2005–06, Chair. Regulations Review Cttee 2005–08; Spokesman on Defence 2002–03, on Veterans' Affairs 2002–03, Justice 2003–06; Assoc. Spokesman on Local Govt 2005–06; Minister of Internal Affairs 2008–, also Minister for Land Information, Minister Responsible for Archives New Zealand and for Nat. Library and Assoc. Minister of Justice; Fellow, NZ Inst. of Dirs, NZ Inst. of Man.; Chair. P F Olsen Ltd; Chair. Korea/NZ Business Council, Korean Parl. Group; Trustee, Royal NZ Coastguard Foundation; mem. Council of Legal Educ.; fmr Chair. Willis NZ Ltd; fmr Dir Prada America's Cup NZ Ltd; fmr mem. and Treas. NZ Law Soc. Bd; mem. and fmr Dir Auckland Rotary Club; fmr Pres. The Northern Club, Outward Bound Trust Bd of NZ; Order of St John. *Address:* Department of Internal Affairs, 46 Waring Taylor Street, POB 805, Wellington, New Zealand (office). *Telephone:* (4) 495-7200 (office). *Fax:* (4) 495-7222 (office). *E-mail:* info@dia.govt.nz (office). *Website:* www.dia.govt.nz (office).

WOUK, Herman, AB; American writer and dramatist; b. 27 May 1915, New York, NY; s. of Abraham Isaac Wouk and Esther Levine; m. Betty Sarah Brown 1945; three s. (one deceased); ed Columbia Univ.; radio scriptwriter for leading comedians, New York 1935–41; presidential consultant to US Treasury 1941; served in USNR 1942–46; Visiting Prof. of English, Yeshiva Univ., New York 1952–57; Trustee, Coll. of the Virgin Islands 1961–69; mem. Authors' Guild, USA, Authors' League, Center for Book Nat. Advisory Bd, Library of Congress, Advisory Council, Center for US–China Arts Exchange; Hon. LHD (Yeshiva Univ.); Hon. DLitt (Clark Univ.), (George Washington Univ.) 2001; Hon. DLitt (American Int. Coll.) 1979; Hon. PhD (Bar Ilan) 1990,

(Hebrew Univ.) 1997; Hon. DST (Trinity Coll.) 1998; Pulitzer Prize for Fiction 1952, Columbia Univ. Medal for Excellence, Alexander Hamilton Medal, Columbia Univ. 1980, Ralph Waldo Emerson Award, Int. Platform Asscn 1981, Univ. of Calif., Berkeley Medal 1984, Yad Vashem Kazetnik Award 1990, USN Memorial Foundation Lone Sailor Award 1987, Washingtonian Book Award (for Inside, Outside) 1986, American Acad. of Achievement Golden Plate Award 1986, Bar Ilan Univ. Guardian of Zion Award 1998, Univ. of California at San Diego Medal 1998, Jewish Book Council Lifetime Literary Achievement Award 2000. *Publications:* fiction: The Man in the Trench Coat 1941, Aurora Dawn 1947, The City Boy 1948, Slattery's Hurricane 1949, The Caine Mutiny 1951, Marjorie Morningstar 1955, Slattery's Hurricane 1956, Youngblood Hawke 1961, Don't Stop the Carnival 1965, The Lomokome Papers 1968, The Winds of War (also TV screenplay) 1971, War and Remembrance (also TV screenplay) 1978, Inside, Outside 1985, The Hope 1993, The Glory 1994, A Hole in Texas 2004; plays: The Traitor 1949, Modern Primitive 1951, The Caine Mutiny Court-Martial 1953, Nature's Way 1957; non-fiction: This is My God: The Jewish Way of Life 1959, The Will to Live on: The Resurgence of Jewish Heritage 2000. *Leisure interests:* Hebraic studies, travel. *Address:* BSW Literary Agency, 303 Crestview Drive, Palm Springs, CA 92264, USA (office).

WOUTS, Bernard François Emile; French business executive; *CEO, Éditions Tallandier;* b. 22 March 1940, Roubaix; s. of Emile Wouts and Marie Vanderbauwede; m. Annick Memet 1965; two s. one d.; ed Lycée St Louis, Paris; engineer, then Deputy Dir-Gen. and Man. Bayard Presse and Pres. subsidiaries of Bayard Presse group 1966–81; Dir-Gen. Soc. de Publications et d'Editions Réunies 1980–85; Gen. Man. Le Monde 1985–90; Pres. Coopérative des quotidiens de Paris 1988–90; apptd Pres.-Dir-Gen. Le Point 1990, Chair. and CEO –2004; Pres. SPMI (Syndicat de la Presse Magazine et d'Information) 1995–99, Vice-Pres. 1999–; CEO Éditions Tallendier 2001–; Pres. Diffusion Contrôle 2002–06. *Publication:* La presse entre les lignes 1990. *Leisure interest:* sailing. *Address:* Éditions Tallendier, 2 rue Routrou, 75006 Paris, France (office). *Telephone:* 1-40-46-43-88 (office). *Fax:* 1-40-46-43-98 (office). *E-mail:* atalland@tallandier.com (office). *Website:* www.tallendier.com (office).

WOWEREIT, Klaus, LLB; German politician; *Mayor of Berlin;* b. 1 Oct. 1953, Berlin; adviser to Senator for Internal Affairs, Berlin 1981–84; mem. Regional Cttee and Del. to SPD, Tempelhof Regional Council 1984–95; Chair. SPD Group, Tempelhof Dist 1981–84, Vice-Chair. 1995–99, Chair. SPD Group, Parl. of Berlin 1999–2001; Mayor of Berlin 2001–; Pnr Tempelhof Haus-, Wohnungs- und Grundstückseigentümerverein Berlin-Lichtenrade eV, European Acad.; mem. Tempelhof Art and Cultural Union (TKK); Commdr de la Légion d'Honneur 2004. *Address:* Senate Chancellery, 10871 Berlin, Germany (office). *E-mail:* der-regierende-buergermeister@SKZL.Verwalt-Berlin.de (office). *Website:* www.berlin.de (office); www.klaus-wowereit.de.

WOŹNIAK, Piotr Grzegorz, MSc; Polish business executive and government official; b. 13 Feb. 1956, Warsaw; m.; five c.; ed Warsaw Univ.; Asst Prof. State Geological Inst. 1980–84, 1986–89; head field group Geopol-Polservice in Libya 1985; adviser to Minister of Agric. and Food Economy 1989–90; adviser to Minister of Industry 1990–91; Dir TUW (mutual insurance soc.) 1991; Vice-Chair., mem. of Bd RUCH S.A.; Rep. of Poland UNIDO Programme; Commercial Consul Polish Embassy Ottawa and Montreal Consulate 1992–96; mem. Bd PAKTO S.A. 1997–98; Prime Minister's adviser on infrastructure 1998–2000; mem. Supervisory Bd EkoFundusz Foundation 1998–2001, KUKE S.A. 1998-2002, Polish Oil and Gas Extraction Co. (PGNiG S.A) 1999–2000, Gas Trading S.A. 2000–02, EuRoPol Gaz S.A. 2000–01; mem. Council for Motorways 1998–2002; Vice-Pres. of Man. Bd for Trade and Restructuring PGNiG S.A. 2000–02; Deputy of Warsaw Council, Vice-Chair. Econ. Development and Infrastructure Cttee 2002; econ. adviser on fuel gas trading and power industry 2002–05; Chair. Bd of Dirs Ence.Eko Ltd 2004–05; expert Sejm Investigative Comm. investigating PKN Orlen S.A. 2004–05; Minister of the Economy 2005–07; mem. Catholic Intelligentsia Club. *Address:* c/o Law and Justice Party, ul. Nowogrodzka 84/86, 02-018, Warsaw, Poland (office). *Telephone:* (22) 6215035 (office). *Fax:* (22) 6216767 (office). *E-mail:* biuro@pis.org.pl (office). *Website:* www.pis.org.pl (office).

WOZNIAK, Stephen (Steve) Gary, BS; American computer scientist and business executive; *Chief Scientist, Fusion-io;* b. 11 Aug. 1950; m. 1st Alice Robertson 1980 (divorced); m. 2nd Candice Clark Wozniak 1987 (divorced), three c.; m. 3rd Suzanne Mulkern 1990; ed Univ. of California, Berkeley; joined Hewlett Packard Co. as designer of calculator chips 1976; Co-founder (with Steve Jobs q.v.) Apple Computer Inc. 1976, co-designed world's first personal computers, the Apple I and II, Vice-Pres., Research and Devt 1976–81, Designer 1979–81, Vice-Pres., Eng 1983–85, consultant 1985–; Co-founder and Pres. CL9 Remote Control Co. 1985–89; Co-Chair. Axlon Inc. 1986–; Co-founder Wheels of Zeus (wOz) 2002, CEO and Chair. 2002–04, Pres. 2004–06; Co-founder and Exec. Vice-Pres. Acquicor Tech Inc. (now Jazz Technologies, Inc.) 2005–; mem. Bd of Dirs Fusion-io, Salt Lake City 2008–, Chief Scientist 2009–; Founder, Electronic Frontier Foundation; Founding Sponsor, Tech Museum, Silicon Valley Ballet, Children's Discovery Museum of San Jose; Hon. DSc (North Carolina State Univ.) 2004; Grace Murray Hopper Award, Asscn of Computing Machinery 1979, Nat. Medal of Tech. 1985, Inventors Hall of Fame 2000, Heinz Award for Tech. 2000. *Publications:* iWoz: Computer Geek to Cult Icon 2006. *Address:* Fusion-io, 6350 South 3000 East, 6th Floor, Salt Lake City, UT 84121 (office); Acquicor Tech Inc., 4910 Birch Street, Suite 102, Newport Beach, CA 92660, USA (office). *Website:* www.fusionio.com (office); www.woz.org (office).

WOŹNICKI, Jerzy, DSc, PhD; Polish scientist and business executive; *Chairman, Bank Pekao SA;* b. 22 May 1947, Kotuń; ed Warsaw Univ. of Tech.; Asst Prof. and later Full Prof., Faculty of Electronics and IT, Warsaw Univ. of Tech. 1973, Vice-Dir, Inst. of Microelectronics and Optoelectronics 1984–87, Head, Image Processing Div. 1987–, Dean, Faculty of Electronics and IT 1990–, Chair., Univ. Senate Cttee on Univ. Organization 1990, Rector, Warsaw Univ. of Tech. 1996–2002; Deputy Chair., Supervisory Bd, Bank Pekao SA 1999–2005, Chair. 2005–; mem., Presidential Bd, Polish Section, Int. Soc. for Optical Eng (SPIE); mem. Scientific Council, Inst. of Vacuum Tech.; fmr Polish Govt Scientific Expert, UNESCO; fmr Pres., Conf. of Rectors of Academic Schools in Poland (later Hon. Pres.); Pres., Polish Rectors Foundation; Dir, Inst. of Knowledge Soc.; Deputy Chair., Nat. Council of European Integration; mem. Cttee for Electronics and Telecommunications, Polish Acad. of Sciences; Chair. Poland in the United Europe Cttee, Polish Acad. of Sciences; Kt Cross, Order of Rebirth of Poland, Chevalier, Légion d'Honneur (France); many awards from Ministry of Nat. Educ.; Award of the Stefan Batory Foundation. *Address:* Bank Pekao SA, ul. Grzybowska 53/57 Str., 00–950 Warsaw, Poland (office). *Telephone:* (22) 6210972 (office). *Fax:* (22) 6210973 (office). *E-mail:* frpfund@mbox.pw.edu.pl (office). *Website:* www.frp.org.pl (office).

WRAGG, John, ARCA, RA; British sculptor; b. 20 Oct. 1937, York; s. of Arthur Wragg and Ethel Wragg; ed York School of Art and Royal Coll. of Art; work represented in several public collections including Tate Gallery, London, Contemporary Art Society, Nat. Gallery of Modern Art, Edin., Israel Museum, Wellington Art Gallery, NZ, Sainsbury Centre for Visual Arts, Univ. of East Anglia; Sainsbury Award 1960, winner, Sainsbury Sculpture Competition, Chelsea 1966, Arts Council of GB Major Award 1977, Chantrey Bequest 1981. *Leisure interests:* walking, listening to music, reading. *Address:* 6 Castle Lane, Devizes, Wilts., SN10 1HJ, England. *Telephone:* (1380) 727087. *E-mail:* johnwragg.ra@virgin.net (office).

WRAN, Hon. Neville Kenneth, AC, QC, FRSA; Australian business executive and fmr politician; b. Sydney; m. 2nd Jill Hickson 1976; one s. one d. and one s. one d. by previous marriage; ed Fort Street Boys' High School, Sydney Univ.; solicitor, then admitted to Bar 1957; apptd. QC 1968; mem. NSW Legis. Council 1970–73; Deputy Leader of Opposition 1971–72; Leader of Opposition in Legis. Council 1972–73; mem. NSW Legis. Ass. for Bass Hill 1973–86; Leader of Opposition 1973–76; Premier of NSW and Minister for Arts (and various other ministerial portfolios) 1976–86; Nat. Pres. Australian Labor Party 1980–86; Chair. CSIRO 1986–91, Lionel Murphy Foundation 1986–2000, Wran Partners Pty Ltd, Victor Chang Cardiac Research Inst.; Dir Cabcharge Australia Ltd; Australian rep. Eminent Persons Group, APEC 1993–95; Gov. Australia-Israel Chamber of Commerce; Foundation mem. Australian Republican Movt; Fellow Powerhouse Museum; Life Gov. Art Gallery of NSW; Hon. LLD (Sydney). *Leisure interests:* reading, tennis, walking. *Address:* GPO Box 4545, Sydney, NSW 2001, Australia. *Telephone:* (2) 9223-4315 (office). *Fax:* (2) 9223-5267 (office). *E-mail:* wran@primus.com.au (office).

WRIGHT, Alexander (Alastair) Finlay, MBE, MD; British medical practitioner (retd); b. 19 March 1933, Blantyre, Scotland; s. of Alexander Finlay Wright and Mary Paterson; m. Barbara Lattimer 1957; three s. one d.; ed Hamilton Acad., Univ. of Glasgow; gen. medical practitioner, medical researcher, teacher 1961–92; Council of Europe Fellowship, France 1976; Chair. Clinical and Research Div. Royal Coll. of Gen. Practitioners 1990–91; mem. Scientific Cttee, Jt Royal Coll. 'Defeat Depression' Campaign 1991–98; Ed. British Journal of Gen. Practice 1991–99; Fellow, Royal Coll. of Gen. Practitioners; Hon. Fellow, Royal Coll. of Psychiatrists 1998; Sima/Jansson Prize for Research in Gen. Practice 1981, George Abercrombie Award, Royal Coll. of Gen. Practioners 2000. *Publications include:* Medicine and the New Towns of France 1976, Female Sterilisation: The View From General Practice 1981, Depression: Recognition and Management in General Practice 1993, Psychiatry and General Practice (jtly) 1994. *Leisure interests:* walking, spoken French, grandchildren. *Address:* 5 Alburne Crescent, Glenrothes, Fife, KY7 5RE, Scotland (home). *E-mail:* drafw@blueyonder.co.uk (home).

WRIGHT, Sir David John, Kt, GCMG, LVO, MA; British diplomatist and banker; *Vice-Chairman, Barclays Capital;* b. 16 June 1944; s. of J. F. Wright; m. Sally Ann Dodkin 1968; one s. one d.; ed Wolverhampton Grammar School, Peterhouse, Cambridge; Third Sec., Foreign Office 1966, Third Sec., later Second Sec., Tokyo 1966–72, FCO 1972–75, Ecole Nat. d'Admin., Paris 1975–76, First Sec., Paris 1976–80, Pvt. Sec. to Sec. of Cabinet 1980–82, Counsellor (Econ.), Tokyo 1982–85, Head Personnel Services Dept FCO 1985–88; Deputy Pvt. Sec. to HRH the Prince of Wales 1988–90 (on secondment); Amb. to Repub. of Korea 1990–94, to Japan 1996–99; Deputy Under-Sec. of State, FCO 1994–96; Group Chief Exec. (Perm. Sec.) British Trade Int. 1999–2002; Vice-Chair. Barclays Capital 2002–; Hon. Fellow, Peterhouse, Cambridge 2002; Grand Cordon, Order of the Rising Sun (Japan) 1998; Hon. LLD (Wolverhampton) 1997, (Birmingham) 2000. *Leisure interests:* golf, cooking, military history. *Address:* Barclays Capital, 5 North Colonnade, Canary Wharf, London, E14 4BB, England (office). *Telephone:* (20) 7773-5599 (office). *Fax:* (20) 7773-1806 (office). *E-mail:* david.wright@barcap.com (office).

WRIGHT, James, PhD; American historian, academic and university administrator; *President, Dartmouth College;* b. 1939, Madison, Wis.; m. Susan DeBevoise Wright; two s. one d.; ed Galena High School, Wis. State Univ. (now Univ. of Wis.-Platteville), Univ. of Wis.-Madison; enlisted in US Marine Corps, served for three years in postings that included Calif., Hawaii and Japan; Asst Prof. of History, Dartmouth Coll., Hanover, NH 1969–74, Assoc. Prof. 1974–80, Prof. of History 1980, Dean Faculty of Arts and Sciences 1989–97, Provost and Acting Pres. 1995, Chair. numerous cttees, Acting Provost, then Provost 1997, Pres. Dartmouth Coll. 1998–; Sr Historian, Univ. of Mid-America (consortium of nine Midwestern univs, Lincoln, Neb.) 1976–77; mem. Faculty Dartmouth Inst. 1981–83; Sr Historian for award-winning six-film series on history of the Great Plains 1976–78; participated in confs on 'TV and the Historian' and 'The Historian as Film-Maker' 1978; served as Chair. American Historians' Cttee on TV, Film and Media; mem. American Acad. of Arts and Sciences, Org. of American Historians, Western History Asscn; mem. Bd of Trustees Sherman Fairchild Foundation; fellowships from Danforth Foundation and IBM Corpn, Social Science Research Council Grant, Guggenheim Fellowship, Charles Warren Fellowship, Harvard Univ., American Acad. of Arts and Sciences, Marine Corps Scholarship Foundation's Semper Fidelis Award, New Englander of the Year, New England Council 2007. *Publications:* author or ed. of five books: The Galena Lead District: Federal Policy and Practices, 1824–1847 1966, The West of the American People 1970, The Politics of Populism: Dissent in Colorado 1974, The Great Plains Experience: Readings in the History of a Region 1978, The Progressive Yankees: Republican Reformers in New Hampshire 1987. *Address:* Office of the President, Dartmouth College, 207 Parkhurst Hall, Hanover, NH 03755, USA (office). *Telephone:* (603) 646-2223 (office). *Fax:* (603) 646-2266 (office). *E-mail:* President's.Office@Dartmouth.edu (office). *Website:* www.dartmouth.edu/~presoff (office).

WRIGHT, James Claude (Jim), Jr; American fmr politician; b. 22 Dec. 1922, Fort Worth, Tex.; s. of James C. Wright and Marie (née Lyster) Wright; m. Betty Hay 1972; one s. three d. (by previous m.); ed Weatherford Coll. and Univ. of Texas; army service 1942–45, DFC, Legion of Merit; Partner, advertising and trade extension firm; mem. Texas Legislature 1947–49; Mayor of Weatherford, Tex. 1950–54; mem. League of Texas Municipalities, Pres. 1953; fmr Lay Minister in Presbyterian Church; mem. for Fort Worth (12th District of Tex.), US House of Reps 1954–89, Deputy Democratic Whip –1976, Majority Leader in House of Reps 1976–87; Chair. Democratic Steering and Policy Cttee in House, Vice-Chair. 1976–87, Speaker, House of Reps 1987–89 (resgnd), mem. Budget Cttee 1974–87; Sr Political Consultant, American Income Life Insurance Co. 1989–; Political Consultant, Arch Petroleum 1989–; fmr ranking mem. Public Works and Transportation Cttee; currently Prof. Tex. Christian Univ.; fmr mem. Govt Operations Cttee; fmr Chair. Comm. on Highway Beautification; cand. for US Senate 1961. *Publications:* You and Your Congressman 1965, The Coming Water Famine 1966, Of Swords and Plowshares 1968, Worth It All 1993, Balance of Power 1996; co-author: Congress and Conscience 1970, Reflections of a Public Man 1984. *Address:* c/o Department of Political Science, Texas Christian University, 2800 South University Drive, Fort Worth, TX 76129, USA. *E-mail:* J.Wright@tcu.edu.

WRIGHT, Sir (John) Oliver, GCMG, GCVO, DSC; British diplomatist; b. 6 March 1921, London; s. of Arthur Wright and Ethel Wright; m. Marjory Osborne 1942; three s.; ed Solihull School and Christ's Coll. Cambridge; Royal Navy 1941–45; joined Foreign Office Nov. 1945; served New York 1946–47, Bucharest 1948–50, Singapore 1950–54, Berlin 1954–56, Pretoria 1957–58; Imperial Defence Coll. 1959; Asst Pvt. Sec. to Foreign Sec. 1960–63, Pvt. Sec. Jan.–Nov. 1963; Pvt. Sec. to Prime Minister 1963–66; Amb. to Denmark 1966–69; UK Rep. to Northern Ireland Govt 1969–70; Deputy Under-Sec. of State and Chief Clerk, FCO 1970–72; Deputy Under-Sec. for EEC and Econ. Affairs 1972–75; Amb. to FRG 1975–81, to USA 1982–86; King of Arms, Most Distinguished Order of St Michael and St George 1987–97; Dir Gen. Tech. Systems Inc. 1990–95, Enviromed PLC 1993–97, Berkeley Hotel 1994–96; Clark Fellow, Cornell Univ. 1987; Lewin Prof., Washington Univ., St Louis, Mo. 1988; Trustee British Museum, 1986–91, Bd, British Council, Int. Shakespeare Globe Centre; Co-Chair. Anglo-Irish Encounter 1986–91; Chair. British Königswinter Steering Cttee 1987–97; Pres. German Chamber of Commerce and Industry in London 1988–92; Chair. Govs Reigate Grammar School 1990–97; Hon. Fellow, Christ's Coll. Cambridge 1981. *Leisure interests:* theatre, opera. *Address:* Burstow Hall, Horley, Surrey, RH6 9SR, England (home). *Telephone:* (1293) 783494 (home). *Fax:* (1293) 774044 (home).

WRIGHT, Karen Jocelyn, MA, MBA, FRSA; American editor and journalist; b. 15 Nov. 1950, New York; d. of Louis David Wile and Grace Carlin Wile; m. 1981; two d.; ed Brandeis Univ., Univ. of Cambridge and London Grad. School of Business Studies, UK; Founder and Owner Hobson Gallery, Cambridge 1981–87; co-f. (with Peter Fuller) Modern Painters magazine 1987, Ed. 1990–2006, Ed.-at-Large 2006–; co-f. (with David Bowie, Sir Timothy Sainsbury and Bernard Jacobson) 21 Publishing 1997; mem. Asscn Int. des Critiques d'Art. *Publications:* The Penguin Book of Art Writing (co-ed.) 1998, Colour for Kosovo (ed.) 1999, The Grove Book of Art Writing 2000, Colour 2003; contrib. to Independent on Sunday. *Leisure interests:* looking at art, children, reading, theatre, listening to music, skiing. *Address:* 21 Publishing, Unit 204, Buspace Studios, Conlan Street, London, W10 5AP (office); 39 Portland Road, London, W11 4LH, England (home). *Telephone:* (20) 8964-1113 (21 Publishing) (office). *Fax:* (20) 8964-9993 (21 Publishing) (office). *E-mail:* info@21publishing.com (office). *Website:* www.21publishing.com (office); www.modernpainters.co.uk (office).

WRIGHT, Rt Rev. Nicholas Thomas, BA, MA, DPhil, DD; British theologian and Anglican bishop; *Bishop of Durham;* b. 1 Dec. 1948, Morpeth, Northumberland; s. of Nicholas Irwin Wright and Rosemary Wright (née Forman); m. Margaret Elizabeth Anne Fiske 1971; two s. two d.; ed Sedbergh School, Exeter Coll., Oxford, Wycliffe Hall, Oxford; ordained deacon 1975, priest 1976; Jr Research Fellow, Merton Coll. Oxford 1975–78, Jr Chaplain 1976–78; Fellow and Chaplain Downing Coll. Cambridge 1978–81; Asst Prof. of New Testament Studies, McGill Univ., Montreal and Hon. Prof., Montreal Diocesan Theological Coll., Canada 1981–86; Lecturer in Theology, Univ. of Oxford and Fellow, Tutor and Chaplain, Worcester Coll. Oxford 1986–93; Dean of Lichfield 1994–99; Canon Theologian of Coventry Cathedral 1992–99; Canon Theologian of Westminster 2000–03; Bishop of Durham 2003–; Fellow Inst. for Christian Studies, Toronto 1992–; mem. Doctrine Comm., Church of England 1979–81, 1989–95, Lambeth Comm. 2004; regular broadcasts on TV and radio; Hon. Fellow Downing Coll. Cambridge 2003, Merton Coll. Oxford 2004; Hon. DD (Aberdeen) 2000, (Nashotah House) 2006, (Wycliffe Coll., Toronto) 2006, (Durham) 2007; Hon. DHumLitt (Gordon Coll., Mass) 2003. *Publications include:* Small Faith, Great God 1978, The Work of John Frith 1983, The Epistles of Paul to the Colossians and to Philemon 1987, The Glory of Christ in the New Testament (co-ed.) 1987, The Interpretation of the New Testament 1861–1986 (co-author) 1988, The Climax of the Covenant 1991, New Tasks for a Renewed Church 1992, The Crown and the Fire 1992, The New Testament and the People of God 1992, Who Was Jesus? 1992, Following Jesus 1994, Jesus and the Victory of God 1996, The Lord and His Prayer 1996, What Saint Paul Really Said 1997, For All God's Worth 1997, Reflecting the Glory 1998, The Meaning of Jesus (co-author) 1999, The Myth of the Millennium 1999, Romans and the People of God (co-ed.) 1999, Holy Communion for Amateurs 1999, The Challenge of Jesus 2000, Twelve Months of Sundays, Year C 2000, Easter Oratorio (co-author) 2000, Twelve Months of Sundays, Year A 2001, Luke for Everyone 2001, Mark for Everyone 2001, Paul for Everyone: Galatians and Thessalonians 2002, John for Everyone 2002, Twelve Months of Sundays, Year B 2002, New Interpreter's Bible, Vol. X (contrib.) 2002, The Contemporary Quest for Jesus 2002, Paul for Everyone (The Prison Letters) 2002, Matthew for Everyone 2002, Paul for Everyone (I Corinthians) 2003, Paul for Everyone (II Corinthians) 2003, Quiet Moments 2003, The Resurrection of the Son of God 2003, For All the Saints? 2003, Hebrews for Everyone 2003, Paul for Everyone (The Pastoral Letters) 2003, Paul for Everyone: Romans 2004, Scripture and the Authority of God 2005. *Leisure interests:* music, hill-walking, poetry, cricket, golf. *Address:* Bishop of Durham, Auckland Castle, Bishop Auckland, Co. Durham, DL14 7NR, England (office). *Telephone:* (1388) 602576 (office). *Fax:* (1388) 605264 (office). *E-mail:* bishops.office@durham.anglican.org (office). *Website:* www.durham.anglican.org (office); www.ntwrightpage.com.

WRIGHT, Patrick (Paddy); Irish business executive; joined Jefferson Smurfit 1976, fmrly Chief Exec. UK and Ireland, Pres. and COO 1996–2000 (retd); Chair. RTE Authority 2000–05; fmr Chair. Aon MacDonagh Boland Group; fmr Pres. Confed. of Irish Industry; Chair. Dublin City Univ. Educational Trust 1995–2006; mem. Bd of Dirs Anglo Irish Bank 2000–, Croke Park; Fellow Irish Man. Inst.; Dr hc (Dublin City Univ.) 2004; Hon. Fellow, Nat. Coll. of Ireland. *Address:* c/o Board of Directors, Anglo Irish Bank, Stephen Court, 18/21 St. Stephens Green, Dublin 2, Ireland.

WRIGHT, Sir Peter Robert, Kt, CBE; British ballet director and choreographer; b. 25 Nov. 1926, London; s. of Bernard Wright and Hilda Wright (née Foster); m. Sonya Hana 1954; one s. one d.; ed Bedales School and Leighton Park School, Reading; 1944 debut as professional dancer with Ballets Jooss; during 1950s worked with several dance cos. including Sadler's Wells Theatre Ballet; created first ballet, A Blue Rose, for Sadler's Wells 1957; Ballet Master, Sadler's Wells Opera and teacher, Royal Ballet School 1959–61; teacher and ballet master to ballet co. formed by John Cranko in Stuttgart 1961–65; choreographed several ballets in Stuttgart including The Mirror Walkers, Namouna, Designs for Dancers, Quintet and mounted his first production of Giselle; producer of TV ballets and choreographer of various London West End musicals and revues during 1960s; Asst Dir The Royal Ballet 1969, later Assoc. Dir; Dir Sadler's Wells Royal Ballet (now The Birmingham Royal Ballet) 1977–95; Dir Laureate, Birmingham Royal Ballet 1995–; Gov. Royal Ballet School 1976–2002, Sadler's Wells Theatre 1987–2000; Special Prof. of Performance Studies, Univ. of Birmingham 1990–; Fellow, Birmingham Conservatoire of Music 1991–; Pres. Council of Dance Educ. and Training 1994–99, Friends of Sadler's Wells Theatre 1995–2003, Benesh Inst. of Choreology 1994–; Vice-Pres. Royal Acad. of Dancing 1993–; Hon. DMus (London) 1990; Hon. DLitt (Birmingham) 1994; Evening Standard Award for Ballet 1981, Elizabeth II Coronation Award, Royal Acad. of Dancing 1990, Digital Premier Award 1991, Critics' Award for Services to the Arts 1995, De Valois Award for Outstanding Achievement, Critics' Circle Nat. Dance Awards 2004. *Ballets directed include:* many new productions in various countries of the full-length classics Giselle, Coppelia, Swan Lake, The Sleeping Beauty, The Nutcracker, but particularly for The Royal Ballet and the Birmingham Royal Ballet; original works for Sadlers Wells Royal Ballet include: A Blue Rose, Arpège, El Amor Brujo, Summer's Night, Summertide; for the Stuttgart Ballet: Mirror Walkers, Designs for Dancers, Quintet; for Western Theatre Ballet: Musical Chairs. *Leisure interests:* ceramics, gardens, travel, music. *Address:* 10 Chiswick Wharf, London, W4 2SR, England (home). *Telephone:* (20) 8747-1658 (home). *Fax:* (20) 8400-9939 (home). *E-mail:* petsoprods@aol.com (home).

WRIGHT, Robert C., LLB; American broadcasting executive; b. 23 April 1943, Hempstead, NY; m. Suzanne Wright 1967; one s. two d.; ed Chaminade High School, Holy Cross Coll. and Univ. of Virginia Law School; career in gen. man. marketing, broadcasting, strategic planning and law; fmr Pres. Cox Cable Communications; later Pres. Gen. Electric Financial Services, Vice-Chair. 2001; Pres. and CEO Nat. Broadcasting Co. (NBC) 1986–2001, Chair. and CEO 2001–2004, then Chair. and CEO NBC Universal Inc. (after NBC merger with Vivendi Universal) 2004–07. *Address:* c/o NBC Universal Inc., 30 Rockefeller Plaza, 52nd Floor, New York, NY 10112, USA (office).

WRIGHT, Stuart Pearson, BA; British artist; b. 1975, Northampton; ed Slade School of Fine Art, Univ. Coll. London; award-winning portrait painter; noted persons depicted in paintings include six past-Pres of British Acad., Charles Saumerez Smith (Dir Nat. Gallery, London), H.R.H. The Duke of Edinburgh, Mike Leigh (film dir), Brenda Blethyn, Richard E. Grant, John Hurt, David Thewlis (actors); work has appeared in RA Summer Show 1998, Hunting Art Prize 1998, 1999, BP Portrait Awards 1998, 1999, 2000, 2001, Singer and Friedlander/Sunday Times Watercolour Competition 1998, 1999,

Windsor and Newton Millennium Competition 2000, Royal Soc. of British Painters at the Mall Gallery 2000; BP Portrait Awards (Travel Award 1998, First Prize 2001), Singer and Friedlander/Sunday Times Watercolour Competition (Third Prize 1999, First Prize 2004). *E-mail:* stuart@thesaveloyfactory.com (office). *Website:* www.thesaveloyfactory.com (office).

WRIGHT OF RICHMOND, Baron (Life Peer), cr. 1994, of Richmond-upon-Thames in the London Borough of Richmond-upon-Thames; **Patrick Richard Henry Wright,** KStJ, GCMG, FRCM; British diplomatist (retd); b. 28 June 1931, Reading; s. of the late Herbert H. S. Wright and Rachel Wright (née Green); m. Virginia Anne Gaffney 1958; two s. one d.; ed Marlborough Coll., Merton Coll., Univ. of Oxford; served RA 1950–51; joined Diplomatic Service 1955, Middle East Centre for Arabic Studies 1956–57, Third Sec., British Embassy, Beirut 1958–60, Pvt. Sec. to Amb., later First Sec., British Embassy, Washington 1960–65, Pvt. Sec. to Perm. Under-Sec., FCO 1965–67, First Sec. and Head of Chancery, Cairo 1967–70, Deputy Political Resident, Bahrain 1971–72, Head of Middle East Dept, FCO 1972–74; Pvt. Sec. (Overseas Affairs) to Prime Minister 1974–77; Amb. to Luxembourg 1977–79, to Syria 1979–81, to Saudi Arabia 1984–86; Deputy Under-Sec., FCO 1982–84; Perm. Under-Sec. of State, FCO and Head Diplomatic Service 1986–91; Dir Barclays Bank PLC 1991–96, BP 1991–2000, De La Rue 1991–2000, Unilever 1991–99, British Airports Authority 1992–98; mem. Council, Royal Coll. of Music 1991–2001; Chair. Royal Inst. for Int. Affairs 1995–99, Home-Start Int. 2004–07; Chair. Sub-Cttee F (Home Affairs), House of Lords 2004–07; mem. European Select Cttee 2004–, Sub-Cttee E (Law and Insts), House of Lords 2008–; Gov. Wellington Coll. 1991–2001; Hon. Fellow, Merton Coll. Oxford; Parliamentary Speech of the Year 2004. *Leisure interests:* music, philately, travel. *Address:* House of Lords, Westminster, London, SW1A 0PW, England (office). *Telephone:* (20) 8876-4176 (home). *Fax:* (20) 8876-6466 (home).

WRIGHTON, Mark S., BS, MS, PhD; American chemist, university administrator and academic; *Chancellor, Washington University in St Louis;* b. 1949, Jacksonville, Fla; ed Fla State Univ., Calif. Inst. of Tech.; Asst Prof. of Chem., MIT 1972–76, Assoc. Prof. 1976–77, Prof. 1977–81, Frederick G. Keyes Chair in Chem. 1981–89, Ciba-Geigy Chair in Chem. (first holder) 1989, Head Dept of Chem. 1987–90, Provost of MIT 1990–95; Chancellor Washington Univ. in St Louis 1995–; titular mem. IUPAC Comm. on Photochemistry 1976–83; mem. Chem. Research Evaluation Panel for Air Force Office of Scientific Research 1976–80, American Physical Soc. Study Group on Solar Photovoltaic Energy Conversion 1977–79, Nat. Materials Advisory Bd Study on Battery Materials 1979–80, Energy Research Advisory Bd Solar Panel 1982, Advisory Cttee of Chem. Div., Oak Ridge Nat. Lab. 1983–85, Advisory Cttee for NSF Chem. Div. 1984—87 (Chair. 1986–87), Basic Energy Sciences Advisory Cttee of Dept of Energy 1986–89, Energy Research Advisory Bd Panel on Cold Fusion 1989, Nat. Research Council Bd on Chemical Sciences and Tech. 1986–89, Governing Bd Council on Chemical Research 1988–91, Science Advisory Cttee of Electric Power Research Inst. 1990–92, NSF Materials Research Advisory Cttee 1990–91, Defense Sciences Research Council (fmrly the Materials Research Council) of Advanced Research Projects Agency 1981–97, NSF Advisory Cttee for Directorate for Math. and Physical Sciences 1995–96, Bd of Overseers Boston Museum of Science 1991–97, Corpn of Woods Hole Oceanographic Inst. 1991–95, Corpn of Draper Lab. 1994–96; mem.-at-large Gordon Research Council 1986–89; presidential appointee to Nat. Science Bd 2000–06, Chair. Audit and Oversight Cttee; mem. Bd Dirs Chemical Heritage Foundation 1998–2002, Nat. Asscn of Ind. Colls and Univs 2002–05; mem. Bd Dirs Brooks Automation, Inc., Cabot Corpn, Donald Danforth Plant Science Center, A. G. Edwards, Inc., Nidus Center for Scientific Enterprise, Universities Research Asscn; *ex officio* mem. Bd of Dirs St Louis Regional Chamber and Growth Asscn, Missouri Botanical Garden, Civic Progress; fmr Chair. Business-Higher Educ. Forum, Asscn of American Univs; Ed. (Physical Electrochemistry Division) Journal of the Electrochemical Society 1980–83, two vols of ACS's Advances in Chemistry series; Consulting Ed. General Chemistry (1st, 2nd, 3rd and 4th edns); mem. Editorial Advisory Bd Inorganic Chemistry 1983–89, Chemical and Engineering News 1984–86, Journal of Molecular Electronics 1985–90, Chemtronics 1985–90, Chemistry of Materials 1989–93, Inorganica Chimica Acta 1984–93, Journal of Physical Chemistry 1994–95; Trustee Higher Learning Comm. of North Cen. Asscn of Colls and Schools 1998–2002, Barnes-Jewish Hosp., BJC Healthcare, Innovate St Louis, Saint Louis Art Museum, St Louis Science Center, Saint Louis Symphony Orchestra; Fellow, AAAS 1986, Acad. Academy of Arts and Sciences 1988; mem. American Philosophical Soc. 2001; Hon. Prof., Shandong Univ., Jinan, People's Repub. of China 2002; Hon. DSc (Univ. of West Florida) 1983; Monsanto Chem. Award for outstanding research, Florida State Univ., Alfred P. Sloan Research Fellowship 1974–76, Dreyfus Teacher-Scholar Grant 1975–80, ACS Pure Chem. Award 1981, MIT Chem. Dept Grad. Teaching Award 1981, ACS Award in Inorganic Chem. 1988, MacArthur Prize Fellowship 1983, Gregory and Freda Halpern Award in Photochemistry, New York Acad. of Sciences 1983, E. O. Lawrence Award, US Dept of Energy 1983, Fresenius Award, Phi Lambda Upsilon 1984, named by Science Digest magazine as one of America's brightest scientists under age 40 1984, named by Science Digest magazine as one of America's top 100 innovators of the year 1985, MIT School of Science Teaching Prize 1987, first recipient of Herbert Newby McCoy Award, Calif. Inst. of Tech., Distinguished Alumni Award, Calif. Inst. of Tech. 1992, named by Business Week magazine as one of ten innovators in science 1989, included in Esquire magazine's Register along with 38 other men and women "who are making America a smarter, healthier, wealthier, safer, livelier, prettier, all around more interesting place to live" 1989, named by the Arthritis Foundation's Eastern Missouri Chapter Humanitarian of the Year 2000. *Publications:* Organometallic Photochemistry (co-author) 1979; 14 patents and more than 300 articles published in professional and scholarly journals on transition metal catalysis, photochemistry, surface chemistry, molecular electronics and photoprocesses at electrodes. *Address:* Office of the Chancellor, Washington University in St Louis, Campus Box 1192, One Brookings Drive, St Louis, MO 63130, USA (office). *Telephone:* (314) 935-5100 (office). *Fax:* (314) 935-4744 (office). *E-mail:* wrighton@wustl.edu (office). *Website:* www.wustl.edu (office).

WRIGLEY, Sir Edward Anthony, Kt, MA, PhD, FBA; British academic; b. 17 Aug. 1931, Manchester; s. of Edward Wrigley and Jessie Wrigley; m. Maria Laura Spelberg 1960; one s. three d.; ed King's School, Macclesfield and Peterhouse, Cambridge; William Volker Research Fellow, Univ. of Chicago 1953–54; Fellow, Peterhouse 1958–79, Sr Bursar 1964–74, Hon. Fellow 1996–; Lecturer in Geography, Univ. of Cambridge 1958–74; Assoc. Dir Cambridge Group for the History of Population and Social Structure 1964–95; mem. Inst. of Advanced Study, Princeton 1970–71; Hinkley Visiting Prof., Johns Hopkins Univ. 1975; Tinbergen Visiting Prof., Erasmus Univ., Rotterdam 1979; Prof. of Population Studies, LSE 1979–88; Pres. Manchester Coll. Oxford 1987–96; Sr Research Fellow All Souls Coll. Oxford 1988–94, Acad. Sec. 1992–94, Fellow 2002–05; Prof. of Econ. History, Univ. of Cambridge 1994–97; Master, Corpus Christi Coll. Cambridge 1994–2000; Ed. Econ. History Review 1985–92; Treas. British Acad. 1989–95, Pres. 1997–2001; Pres. British Soc. for Population Studies 1977–79; Chair. Population Investigation Cttee 1984–90; Hon. Fellow, LSE 1997; Hon. DLitt (Manchester) 1997, (Sheffield) 1997, (Bristol) 1998, (Oxford) 1999, (Leicester) 1999, (Queen Mary) 2004; Hon. DScS (Edin.) 1998; James Ford Special Lecturer, Oxford 1986, Ellen Macarthur Lecturer, Cambridge 1987, Linacre Lecturer, Oxford 1998, Laureate of the Int. Union for the Scientific Study of Population 1993, Founder's Medal, Royal Geographical Soc. 1997, Leverhulme Medal, British Acad. 2005. *Publications:* Continuity, Chance and Change 1989, Poverty, Progress and Population 2004, several works on econ. and demographic history. *Leisure interest:* gardening. *Address:* 13 Sedley Taylor Road, Cambridge, CB2 8PW, England (home). *Telephone:* (1223) 247614 (home). *E-mail:* eaw20@cam.ac.uk (office).

WU, Bai; Taiwanese actor and musician; b. 1968, Chaiyi Prov., Taiwan. *Films include:* Zheng hun qi shi 1998, Meili xin shijie 1999, Seunlau ngaklau 2000, San ging chaat goo si 2004. *Music:* singer, songwriter with band China Blue 1993–.

WU, Bangguo; Chinese party official and engineer; *Chairman, 11th Standing Committee, National People's Congress;* b. July 1941, Feidong Co., Anhui Prov.; m. Zhang Ruizhen; ed Tsinghua Univ., Beijing; joined CCP 1964; worked at Shanghai No. 3 Electronic Tube Factory, progressing from freight worker to Factory Dir 1967–78; Deputy Man. Shanghai Municipal Electronics Components Industry Co., Shanghai Municipal Electrical Vacuum Device Co. 1979–81; Deputy Sec. Parl. Cttee Shanghai Municipal Instruments Bureau 1981–83; mem. Standing Cttee Shanghai Municipal CCP Cttee 1983–85, Deputy Sec. 1986–89, Sec. 1991–94; a Shanghai del. to 8th NPC 1993; mem. CCP Secr. 1994–97; Vice-Premier of State Council 1995–2007; Alt. mem. 13th CCP Cen. Cttee 1987–92, mem. 14th CCP Cen. Cttee 1992–97, 15th CCP Cen. Cttee 1997–2002, 16th CCP Cen. Cttee 2002–07, 17th CCP Cen. Cttee 2007–; mem. Politburo CCP Cen. Cttee 1992–, Standing Cttee Politburo CCP Cen. Cttee 2002–; Chair. Standing Cttee 10th NPC 2003–07, Standing Cttee 11th NPC 2008–. *Address:* Quangguo Renmin Daibiao Dahui (National People's Congress), Beijing, People's Republic of China (office).

WU, Boshan; Chinese banker; b. 1940; ed Cen. Coll. of Finance and Econs; joined CCP 1965; Pres. Investment Bank of China 1993. *Address:* c/o Investment Bank of China, Beijing, People's Republic of China (office).

WU, Dechang; Chinese toxicologist; b. 22 Oct. 1927, Beijing; m. Lin Rhi-zhu 1951; one s. two d.; ed Peking Univ. and in USSR; Asst Lecturer, later Lecturer, Xiehe Hosp., Beijing 1949; Prof. of Toxicology, Inst. of Radiation Medicine, Beijing 1981–; Commdt Mil. Medical Science Acad. of PLA 1990–94; Del. to 14th Nat. Conf. CCP 1992–97; mem. 8th Nat. Cttee CPPCC 1993–97; Deputy Rep., UN Atomic Radiation Effectiveness Science Cttee; Pres. Chinese Soc. of Toxicology 1995–; Academician, Chinese Acad. of Eng 1994–; Nat. Science and Tech. Awards 1985, 1993, 1995, Prize for Outstanding Contributions 1991, Ho Leung Ho Lee Medical Sciences and Materia Medica Prize 2003. *Publications:* Radiation Risk and Assessment 1999, Radiation Medicine 2000. *Leisure interest:* classical music. *Address:* Military Medical Science Academy of People's Liberation Army, 27 Tai-Ping Road, Beijing 100850, People's Republic of China (office). *Telephone:* (10) 68186211 (office). *Fax:* (10) 68214653 (office). *E-mail:* wudc@nic.bmi.ac.cn (office); wudc@public.bta.net.cn (office).

WU, Dingfu; Chinese government official; *Chairman, China Insurance Regulatory Commission;* b. July 1946; ed Hubei Univ.; joined CCP 1972; has held numerous govt positions including Magistrate, Guangji Co. 1984, Deputy Commr, Huanggang Pref., Hubei Prov. 1987–90, Auditor-Gen., Prov. Auditing Office, Hubei Prov. 1991–95; joined Nat. Audit Office 1995, Head, Comm. for Discipline Inspection 1998–2000; Vice-Chair. China Insurance Regulatory Comm. 1998–2000, Chair. 2002–; mem. Cen. Comm. for Discipline Inspection, CCP Cen. Cttee 2000–02, Sec.-Gen. 2001–02; Alt. Mem. 16th CCP Cen. Cttee 2002–07, 17th CCP Cen. Cttee 2007–. *Address:* China Insurance Regulatory Commission (CIRC), 410 Fu Cheng Men Nei Dajie, Beijing 100034, People's Republic of China (office). *Telephone:* (10) 66016688 (office). *Fax:* (10) 66018871 (office). *Website:* www.circ.gov.cn (office).

WU, Sir Gordon Ying Sheung, Kt, KCMG, BSc; Chinese real estate executive; *Chairman, Hopewell Holdings;* b. 3 Dec. 1935, Hong Kong; s. of Wu Chung and Wu Sum (née Kang); m. Kwok San-Ping Wu 1970; two s. two d.; ed Princeton Univ., USA; Man. Dir Hopewell Holdings, Hong Kong 1972–2001, Chair. 2001–; responsible for construction of colony's tallest bldg, Hopewell Holdings HQ; projects constructed include China Hotel, Canton, China, coal-fired power station for Prov. of Guangdong, China, motorway linking Hong Kong to Shenzhen and Canton; responsible for design of many of his own bldgs; Vice-Pres. Hong Kong Real Estate Developer's Asscn 1970–; mem. CPPCC 1984–; several hon. degrees; numerous honours including Gold Bauhinia Star 2004, Officer de l'Ordre de la Couronne (Belgium) 2007, Order of Croatian Danica 2007. *Leisure interest:* classical music. *Address:* 64/F, Hopewell Centre, 183 Queen's Road East, Wan Chai, Hong Kong Special Administrative Region, People's Republic of China (office). *Telephone:* 25284975 (office). *Fax:* 28612068 (office). *E-mail:* ir@hopewellholdings.com (office). *Website:* www.hopewellholdings.com (office).

WU, Lt-Gen. Guangyu; Chinese air force officer; b. Dec. 1940, Hongze Co., Jiangsu Prov.; ed middle school and Air Force Aviation School; joined PLA 1958, CCP 1964; air force pilot and squadron leader 1962–70; various posts in Air Force Aviation 1970–85; Commdr Air Force units, PLA Shanghai Base 1985; Commdr PLA Air Force Command Post 1985–90; Deputy Commdr Nanjing Mil. Regional Air Force 1990–93; Deputy Commdr and Air Force Commdr Jinan Mil. Region 1993; Deputy Commdr PLA Air Force 1995; Deputy to 6th NPC 1983; Alt. mem. 14th CCP Cen. Cttee 1992–97, 15th CCP Cen. Cttee 1997–2002. *Address:* c/o Ministry of National Defence, Jingshanqian Jie, Beijing, People's Republic of China (office). *Telephone:* (10) 6370000 (office).

WU, Guanzheng; Chinese government official; b. 25 Aug. 1938, Yugan Co., Jiangxi Prov.; s. of Wu Enshui and Dong Gelao; m. Zhang Jinshang 1959; three s.; ed Tsinghua Univ., Beijing; joined CCP 1962; Deputy Sec. CCP Party Br., Tsinghua Univ. 1965–68; mem. CCP Cttee of Wuhan Gedian Chemical Plant, Deputy Dir Revolutionary Cttee of Wuhan Gedian Chemical Plant 1968–75; Deputy Dir Wuhan Science and Tech. Cttee, Vice-Chair. Wuhan City Asscn of Science and Tech., Deputy Commdr and Dir of Gen. Office, Wuhan City Technical Innovation Headquarters; Dir, Sec. CCP Cttee of Wuhan City Eng Science and Tech. Research Centre 1975–82; Standing mem. CCP Cttee of Wuhan City 1982–83; Sec. CCP Cttee and Mayor of Wuhan City 1983–86; Deputy Sec. Jiangxi Prov. CCP Cttee, Acting Gov., Gov. Jiangxi Prov. 1986–95; Sec. CCP Cttee Jiangxi Prov., First Sec. CCP Cttee Jiangxi Prov. Mil. Command 1995–97, Sec. CCP Cttee Shandong Prov. and Prin. of School for CCP Shandong Cttee 1997–07; Alt. mem. 12th CCP Cen. Cttee 1982–87, mem. 13th CCP Cen. Cttee 1987–92, 14th CCP Cen. Cttee 1992–97, 15th CCP Cen. Cttee 1997–2002, 16th CCP Cen. Cttee 2002–07; mem. CCP Cen. Cttee Politburo 1997–2007, Standing Cttee CCP Cen. Cttee Politburo 2002–07; Sec. 16th CCP Cen. Cttee Cen. Comm. for Discipline Inspection 2002–07. *Leisure interests:* reading, sports. *Address:* 482 Weiyi Road, Jinan City, Shandong, People's Republic of China. *Telephone:* (531) 2033333.

WU, Guanzhong; Chinese painter and university professor; b. 29 Aug. 1919, Yixing Co., Jiangsu Prov.; ed Nat. Inst. of Fine Arts, Hangzhou, Ecole Nat. Supérieure des Beaux Arts, Paris, France; Prof., Cen. Inst. of Applied Arts 1980–; exhbns in Japan, France, Singapore and Hong Kong; mem. 6th CPPCC Nat. Cttee 1982–87, 7th CPPCC Nat. Cttee 1987–92, Standing Cttee 8th CPPCC Nat. Cttee 1993–98, Standing Cttee 9th CPPCC Nat. Cttee 1998–2003; Hon. Pres. China Soc. of Oil Painting 1995; Hon. mem. China Fed. of Literary and Art Circles 1996; Officier de l'Ordre des Arts et des Lettres (France). *Address:* Central Institute of Applied Arts, 34 Dong Sanhuan North Road, Beijing 100020, People's Republic of China (office).

WU, Guoxiong, PhD; Chinese meteorologist; *Academician, Chinese Academy of Sciences;* b. March 1943, Chaoyang, Guangdong; ed Nanjing Meteorological Inst., Beijing Univ., Imperial Coll. London, UK; Research Fellow, Inst. of Atmospheric Physics, Chinese Acad. of Sciences 1985–, currently Sr Scientist; Chair. Academic Cttee, Nat. Key Lab. of Atmospheric Sciences and Geophysical Fluid Dynamics 1993–2000; Sr Visiting Research Prof., Geophysical Fluid Dynamics Lab., Princeton Univ., USA 1989–91; Chair. Chinese Cttee for Int. Asscn of Meteorology and Atmospheric Sciences (IAMAS), Pres. IAMAS; Officer Jt Scientific Cttee, World Climate Research Programme; Academician, Chinese Acad. of Sciences 1997–; Second Nat. Natural Science Prize 2007. *Publications:* Time-Mean Statistics of Global General Circulation 1987, Dynamics of the Formation and Variation of the Subtropical Anticyclones 2002. *Address:* Institute of Atmospheric Physics, Chinese Academy of Sciences, Qijiahuozi, Beijing 100029 (office); Room 1302, Building 801-B, Huangzhuang Dwelling, Beijing 100080, People's Republic of China (home). *Telephone:* (10) 82995266 (office). *Fax:* (10) 82995172 (office). *E-mail:* gxwu@lasg.iap.ac.cn (office). *Website:* www.lasg.ac.cn (office).

WU, Hualun; Chinese artist; b. June 1942, Tianjin; s. of Wu Bing-Zheng and Wang Yaxin; m. Zeng Wan 1985; ed Cen. Acad. of Arts and Crafts; mem. China Artists' Asscn 1982–, China Calligraphists' Asscn 1986–; Sr Art Ed., China People's Fine Art Publishing House; Prof. 1999–; works have been exhibited many times in Japan, Hong Kong and USA; First Prize, Chinese Paintings Competition 1988, Gold Medal, Japan-China Art Exchange Centre 1988. *Publication:* Chinese Paintings by Wu Hualun 1989. *Leisure interests:* travelling, playing badminton. *Address:* People's Fine Arts Publishing House, 32 Bei Zong Bu Hutong, Beijing 100735, People's Republic of China (office). *Telephone:* (10) 65244901 (office).

WU, Jianchang; Chinese engineer and business executive; b. June 1939, son-in-law of Deng Xiaoping; m. Deng Lin; ed Henyang Mining Coll.; fmr Deputy Gen. Man. China Nat. Nonferrous Metals Import and Export Corpn; Vice-Pres. China Nat. Nonferrous Metals Industry Corpn 1984–94, later Pres.; Dir (non-exec.) Jianxi Copper Co. Ltd 2008–, Shanxi Tai Gang Stainless Co., Silver Grant Int. Industries (Hong Kong); Consultant China Iron and Steel Asscn; Hon. Chair. China Council for the Promotion of Int. Trade. *Address:* c/o China Iron and Steel Association, No 46 Dong Si Xi Da Jie, Beijing 100711, People's Republic of China (office). *E-mail:* info-cisa@chinaisa.org.cn (office).

WU, Jichuan; Chinese fmr politician; b. 1937, Changning Co., Hunan Prov.; ed Beijing Inst. of Posts and Telecommunications; joined CCP 1960; technician, later Div. Chief, later Bureau Dir, Ministry of Posts and Telecommunications 1960–84; Vice-Minister of Posts and Telecommunications 1984–90, Minister 1993–98; Minister of Information Industry 1998–2003 (retd); Deputy Sec. Henan Prov. CCP Cttee 1990–93; Vice-Chair. State Radio Regulatory Cttee; Deputy Head, State Leading Group for Information 1996; Dir China Telecom Corpn Ltd 2007–; Alt. mem. 14th CCP Cen. Cttee 1992–97, mem. 15th CCP Cen. Cttee 1997–2002, 16th CCP Cen. Cttee 2002–07. *Address:* c/o China Telecom Corporation Ltd, 31 Jinrong Street, Xicheng District, Beijing 100032, People's Republic of China (office).

WU, Jieping; Chinese urologist and academic; *Professor of Urology, Urinary Surgery Research School, Beijing Medical College;* b. 22 Jan. 1917, Changzhou City, Jiangsu Prov.; s. of Wu Jingyi and Cheng Xia; m. 1st Zhao Junkai 1933; m. 2nd Gao Rui 1984; one s. two d.; ed Huei Wen Acad., Tianjin, Yenching Univ., Beijing, China Union Medical Univ., Beijing; Lecturer, Beijing Medical Inst. 1946–47, Prof. 1957–; Postdoctorate student, Univ. of Chicago, USA 1947–48; Prof., Urinary Surgery Research School, Beijing Medical Univ. 1999–; joined Jiusan Soc. 1952, CCP 1956; Pres. 2nd Medical Coll. Beijing 1960–70; Vice-Pres. Chinese Medical Asscn 1978–84, Pres. 1984–89, Hon. Pres. 1989–; Vice-Pres. Acad. of Medical Sciences 1970–83, Pres. 1983–85, Hon. Pres. 1985–; Vice-Chair. Cen. Council Int. Planned Parenthood Fed. 1986–, Chair. Regional Council 1991–; Chair. China Population Welfare Foundation, China Asscn for Science and Tech.; mem. 5th CPPCC Nat. Cttee 1978–83, 6th CPPCC Nat. Cttee 1983–88; mem. 7th NPC 1988–83, Vice-Chair. Standing Cttee 8th NPC 1993–98, 9th NPC 1998–2003; Chair. Jiusan (Sept. 3) Soc. Cen. Cttee 1992–2002; Hon. Bd Dir, China Foundation for the Devt of Organ Transplantation 1995; mem. Govt Del., Hong Kong Hand-Over Ceremony, Hong Kong Special Admin. Region Preparatory Cttee 1997, Macao Hand-Over Ceremony 1999; Fellow, Chinese Acad. of Science 1980–98, Sr Fellow 1998–; Fellow, Third World Acad. of Sciences 1992–; Fellow Chinese Acad. of Eng 1995–98, Sr Fellow 1998–; Hon. Dean, Science School, China Medical Coll. 1996; Hon. Pres. China Union Medical Coll. 1997; Hon. Dean, Urinary Surgery Research School, Beijing Medical Univ. 1998; Hon. Pres. Chinese People's Asscn for Peace and Disarmament 1998; Hon. Fellow, American Coll. of Physicians 1989, American Urological Asscn 1995–, Royal Coll. of Surgeons, Edin., UK 1996–. *Leisure interest:* reading. *Address:* Urinary Surgery Research School, Beijing Medical University, 38 Xue Yuan Road, Beijing 100083, People's Republic of China. *Website:* (office).

WU, Jinglian; Chinese economist; *Senior Researcher, State Council Development Research Centre (DRC);* b. Jan. 1930, Nanjing, Jiangsu Prov.; ed Fudan Univ.; Asst Research Fellow, Econs Research Inst. of Chinese Acad. of Sciences 1954–79; Assoc. Research Fellow, Econs Inst. of Chinese Acad. of Social Sciences 1979–83, Research Fellow and Prof. 1983–; Vice-Dir Office for Econ. Reform Programmes of State Council; Sr Researcher, State Council Devt Research Centre; mem. Standing Cttee 9th CPPCC Nat. Cttee 1998–2003, Vice-Chair. Econ. Cttee of CPPCC 1998–2003; elected one of China's Top Ten Econ. Figures 2000. *Publications:* Explorations into Problems of Economic Reform, Planned Economy or Market Economy, Fifteen Critical Issues of the Reform of SOEs 1999, Reform: Now at a Critical Point 2001, Understanding and Interpreting Chinese Economic Reform 2005. *Address:* Development Research Center of the State Council, No. 225, Chaoyangmen Nei Dajie, Dongcheng District, Beijing 100010, People's Republic of China (office). *Website:* www.drc.gov.cn/english/ (office).

WU, Liang-Yong; Chinese architect; b. 7 May 1922, Nanjing, Jiangsu Prov.; m. Yao Tong-zhen; two s.; ed Nat. Cen. Univ. China, Cranbrook Acad. of Art, Bloomfield Hills, Mich.; Assoc. Prof. of Architecture and Urban Planning, Tsinghua Univ. 1951–61, Prof. 1961–; Dir Inst. of Architectural and Urban Studies 1983–, Centre for Human Settlements 1995–; Visiting Prof. Centre of Urban Studies and Urban Planning, Univ. of Hong Kong 1983, Ecole de Hautes Etudes Sociales, Paris 1987, Univ. of California, Berkeley 1988, Sydney Univ. of Tech. 1993, Univ. of Cambridge 1995; Vice-Pres. Chinese Soc. for Urban Studies 1984–, Int. Union of Architects 1987–90; Pres. Urban Planning Soc. of China 1993–; mem. Academia Sinica 1980; Fellow, Chinese Acad. of Science 1980–, Int. Acad. of Architecture 1989, Chinese Acad. of Eng 1995–; Hon. mem. Architectural Inst. of Japan 1994; Hon. Fellow American Inst. of Architects 1990, Royal Inst. of British Architects 1998; Chevalier des Arts et Lettres 1999; numerous awards including Gold Medal in Architecture for the Ju'er Project 1992, Jean Tschumi Prize, Int. Union of Architects 1996, Architectural Soc. of China First Prize of Architecture Design Award for Research Institute of Confucius 2006. *Publications include:* A Brief History of Ancient Chinese City Planning 1985, Selected Essays on Urban Planning and Design 1987, Rehabilitating the Old City of Beijing 1999, Reflections at the Turn of the Century: The Future of Architecture 1999, Buildings, Cities and Human Settlements 2003; more than 200 academic papers. *Leisure interests:* fine arts including painting and calligraphy. *Address:* School of Architecture, Tsinghua University, Beijing 100084 (office); No. 12, Apt 10, Tsinghua University, Beijing 100084, People's Republic of China (home). *Telephone:* (10) 62784567 (office); (10) 62784507 (home). *Fax:* (10) 6562768 (office); (10) 62781048 (home). *E-mail:* engach@mail.cae.ac.cn (office); wuly@public.bta.net.cn (home).

WU, Min, DMed; Chinese geneticist; *Director, Cytobiology Section of Tumour Research Institute, Chinese Academy of Medical Sciences;* b. 1935, Changzhou, Jiangsu Prov.; ed Tongji Univ. Medical Coll., USSR Acad. of Medical Science; Research Fellow and then Dir Cytobiology Section of Tumour Research Inst., Chinese Acad. of Medical Sciences 1961–; one of the initiators of nat. Human

Genome project in China; Vice-Pres. Council of Chinese Genetics Soc.; mem. Standing Cttee Biology Dept Chinese Acad. of Sciences; mem. 4th Presidium, Chinese Acad. of Sciences 2000–; several awards including Golden Bull Prize for Devt of Nat. Labs 1990, 1994, China Technology Science Prize 1996, Ho Leung Ho Lee Medical Sciences Prize 1998. *Publications:* The Mitotic Caryotype of the Chinese; more than 300 scientific publications. *Address:* Chinese Academy of Sciences, 52 Sanlihe Road, Beijing 100864, People's Republic of China (office). *Telephone:* (10) 68597219 (office). *Fax:* (10) 68511095 (office).

WU, Poh-Hsiung, BSc; Taiwanese politician; *Chairman, Kuomintang (KMT) Party;* b. 19 June 1939, Taoyuan County; m. Dai Mei-yu; two s. one d.; ed Nat. Cheng Kung Univ., Sun Yat-sen Inst. of Policy and Research and Devt; schoolteacher 1963–65; mem. Taiwan Prov. Ass. 1968–72; Assoc. Prof., Nan Ya Jr Coll. of Tech. 1972–73; Magistrate, Taoyuan Co. 1973–76; Dir Inst. of Industry for Workmen and Friends of Labour Asscn, Dir-Gen. Taiwan Tobacco and Wine Monopoly Bureau 1976–80; Dir Inst. of Industrial and Vocational Training for Workmen 1976–80; Chair. Repub. of China Amateur Boxing Asscn 1981–82; Dir Secr., Cen. Cttee, Kuomintang 1982–84, Chair. Cen. Exec. Cttee, Vice-Chair. Kuomintang 2000–07, Chair. 2007–; Minister of Interior 1984–88, 1991–94; Mayor of Taipei 1988–90; Minister of State 1990–91; apptd Sec.-Gen. Office of the Pres. 1994; Chair. Cen. Election Comm. 1991–94, Political Party Review Cttee 1991–94. *Address:* Kuomintang (KMT), 11 Chung Shan South Road, Taipei 100, Taiwan (office). *Telephone:* (2) 23121472 (office). *Fax:* (2) 23434561 (office). *Website:* www.kmt.org.tw (office).

WU, Renbao; Chinese farmer and business executive; b. Nov. 1928, Jiangyin Co., Jiangsu Prov.; joined CCP 1952; Sec. CCP Huaxi Village br., Huazi, Jiangyin Co. 1961–2003, CCP Jiangyin Co. Cttee 1974–81; mem. Standing Cttee Jiangsu Prov. CPPCC; Gen. Man. Huaxi Agribusiness Co.; Vice-Chair. Chinese Township Enterprises Asscn 1991, China Market Econ. Seminar; currently Chair. Nat. Affluent Village Seminar; Del., 10th CCP Nat. Congress 1972–77, 11th CCP Nat. Congress 1977–82; Deputy, 6th, 7th, and 8th NPC 1983–98, mem. Presidium of 8th NPC 1993–98; named Nat. Model Worker 1989. *Address:* Huaxi Village, Jiangyin, Jiangsu Province, People's Republic of China (office).

WU, Rong-i, MA, MS, PhD; Taiwanese government official and economist; *Vice-Premier and Minister of the Consumer Protection Commission;* b. 15 Dec. 1939; m.; one d. one s.; ed Nat. Taiwan Univ., Université Catholique de Louvain, Belgium; Prof. and Dir Dept of Econs, Nat. Chung Hsing Univ. 1975–93; Visiting Scholar, Yale Univ., USA 1982–83; Vice-Pres. Taiwan Inst. of Econ. Research 1991–92, Pres. 1993–; Commr Fair Trade Comm., Exec. Yuan 1992–93, mem. Science and Tech. Advisory Group 2004–; Nat. Policy Adviser to Pres. 2000–, mem. Econ. Advisory Group to Pres. 2000–; Vice-Premier and Minister of the Consumer Protection Commission 2005–; mem. Eminent Persons Group, Asia-Pacific Econ. Co-operation 1993–94. *Address:* Executive Yuan, No. 1 Jhongsiao East Road, Taipei 10058, Taiwan. *Telephone:* (2) 33566500 (office). *Fax:* (2) 33566920 (office). *Website:* www.ey.gov.tw (office).

WU, Maj.-Gen. Shaozu; Chinese politician and sports administrator; b. 1939, Laiyang Co., Hunan Prov.; s. of Wu Yunfu and Xiong Tianjing; m. Zeng Xiaoqian; two s.; ed Tsinghua Univ., Beijing; Chair. Student Fed. 1965–82; Deputy, 3rd NPC 1964–66; Vice-Minister State Comm. of Science, Tech. and Industry for Nat. Defence 1982–88; promoted to Maj.-Gen. PLA 1988; Minister, State Physical Culture and Sports Comm. 1988–98; Dir-Gen. State Gen. Bureau for Physical Culture and Sports 1998–2000; mem. 12th, 13th, 14th and 15th CCP Cen. Cttee 1982–2002; Chair. Chinese Olympic Cttee 1995–99; Chair. Int. Fed. for Wushu 1995. *Address:* c/o State General Bureau for Physical Culture and Sports, 9 Tiyuguan Road, Chongwen District, Beijing 100763, People's Republic of China.

WU, Lt-Gen. Shuangzhan; Chinese police officer; *Commander-in-Chief, People's Armed Police Force;* b. Feb. 1945, Qingfeng, Henan Prov.; ed PLA Nat. Defence Univ.; joined PLA 1963, CCP 1965; promoted to rank of Maj.-Gen. 1990, Lt-Gen. 1997; Deputy Chief of Staff of Beijing Mil. Area Command 1993; Chief of Staff of the People's Armed Police Force 1993–99, Deputy Commdr-in-Chief 1996–99, C-in-C 1999–200; mem. 16th CCP Cen. Cttee 2002–07, 17th CCP Cen. Cttee 2007–. *Address:* People's Armed Police Headquarters, Suzhou Jie, Beijing 100089, People's Republic of China (office).

WU, Shouing; Chinese economist; b. Jiangyin, Jiangyin Prov.; ed Shanghai East-China People's Revolution Univ.; research student of political econ., Renmin Univ.; fmrly Prof., Pres. of Grad. School, Vice-Pres. Renmin Univ.; Prof., Pres. Peking Univ. 1989–96; mem. Standing Cttee 8th and 9th NPC 1993–2003. *Publications:* Shenme Shi Zhengzhi Jingyixue (What Is Political Economy?), Zhongguo Shehuizhuyi Jianshe (China's Socialist Construction), Moshi, Yunxing and Kongzhi (Model, Operation and Control). *Address:* c/o Peking University, 1 Loudouqiao, Beijing 100871, People's Republic of China (office).

WU, Tianming; Chinese film director; b. Oct. 1939, Shaanxi Prov.; m. Mu Shulan; ed Xian Drama School; Head of Xian Film Studio 1983–89; Visiting Scholar Univ. of Calif., USA 1990–91; returned to China 1994; Telluride Int. Film Festival Award for Outstanding Contributions to Chinese Cinema 1987. *Films:* Kith and Kin 1981, River Without Buoys 1983, Life 1984, The Old Well (Golden Rooster Best Film Award 1986, Tokyo Film Festival Grand Prize 1987) 1986, The King of Masks (Golden Rooster Best Dir Award 1995, Tokyo Film Festival Best Dir 1996) 1995, An Unusual Love 1998, CEO 2002. *Address:* c/o Xi'an Film Studios, Xi'an 710000, Shaanxi Province, People's Republic of China.

WU, Weiran; Chinese surgeon (retd); *Honorary President, Beijing Hospital;* b. 14 Oct. 1920, Changzhou, Jiangsu Prov.; s. of Wu Jingyi and Zheng Zhixia; m. Huang Wuchiung 1951; three d.; ed West China Union Univ.; joined CCP 1956; Deputy Dir Surgery Soc., attached to the Medical Soc. 1972; Deputy Dir Surgery Dept, Beijing Union Medical Coll. Hosp., Chinese Acad. of Medical Sciences 1972; now Prof. of Surgery, Surgical Dept, Beijing Union Medical Coll. Hosp., Chinese Acad. of Medical Sciences; Hon. Pres. Beijing Hosp.; Alt. mem. 12th CCP Cen. Cttee 1982, mem. 1985, 13th Cen. Cttee 1987–92; Del., 14th CCP Nat. Congress 1992–97; mem. 9th CPPCC Nat. Cttee 1998–2003; Nat. Class 2 Award for Scientific and Technological Progress, Nat. Award for his special contribs to work related to health and care, Ministry of Health Class 2 Award for his research into the 'artificial gut' technique. *Publication:* Surgery (co-author). *Leisure interest:* gardening. *Address:* Surgery Department, Beijing Hospital, 1 Dahalu, Dondan, Beijing 100730, People's Republic of China. *Telephone:* 65132266. *Fax:* 65132969.

WU, Wenjun, DrSc; Chinese mathematician and academic; b. 12 May 1919, Jiansu Prov.; ed Jiaotong Univ., Shanghai and Univ. of Strasbourg, France; teacher, Shanghai Univ. 1940–45; returned to China in 1950; Prof., Math. Department, Beijing Univ. 1952–; Deputy Dir, Math. Inst. Chinese Acad. of Sciences 1964, Deputy Dir Inst. of Systems Science 1979–84, Hon. Dir 1984–, est. Math. Mechanization Research Centre 1990, Dir 1990–99, Dir Math. and Physics Div. 1992–96; Pres., Math. Soc. of China 1984–87; mem. Standing Cttee 5th CPPCC 1978–83, 6th CPPCC 1983–88, 7th CPPCC 1988–93, mem. 8th CPPCC Nat. Cttee 1993–98; Fellow, Third World Acad. of Sciences 1991–; Nat. Natural Science Award 1956, Science Congress Prize, Nat. Science Congress 1978, Chen Jiageng Math. and Physics Science Prize 1993, Prominent Scientist Prize, Hong Kong Qiushi Foundation 1994, Herbrand Award in Automated Deduction 1997, First State Supreme Science and Tech. Award 2000, Shaw Prize in Mathematical Science 2006. *Publications include:* Mechanical Theorum Proving in Geometry 1994, Mathematics Mechanisation 2000. *Address:* Zhong Guan Cun, Building 809, Room 303, Beijing 100080; c/o The Chinese Academy of Sciences, 52 Sanlihe Road, Beijing 100864, People's Republic of China (office). *Telephone:* (10) 62555128 (home); (10) 68597289 (office). *Fax:* (10) 62555128 (home); (10) 62630706 (office). *E-mail:* wtwu@mmrc.iss.ac.cn (office). *Website:* www.iss.ac.cn/iss/chinese.html.

WU, Xiaoling, MA; Chinese central banker (retd); b. Jan. 1947; ed Grad. School of People's Bank of China (PBC); Deputy Dir Office of Applied Theory Research, Research Inst., PBC 1985, Deputy Dir-Gen. Financial System Reform Dept, PBC 1991–94, Dir-Gen. Research Bureau 1994–95, Pres. PBC Shanghai Br. 1998–2000, Deputy Gov. PBC 2000–08 (retd); Deputy Chief Ed. Financial News 1988–91; Deputy Admin. State Admin of Foreign Exchange 1995–98, Admin. 1998, 2000; ranked 35th by Forbes magazine amongst 100 Most Powerful Women 2006, (18th) 2007. *Address:* c/o People's Bank of China, 32 Chengfang Street, Xi Cheng District, Beijing, 100800, People's Republic of China (office).

WU, Xichao; Chinese surgeon; b. Aug. 1922, Malaysia; ed Shanghai Tongji Univ. Medical Coll.; Doctor in Charge, Lecturer, Assoc. Prof., Prof., Vice-Pres. PLA Second Medical Univ. 1949; Vice-Chair. Medical Soc. of China; Fellow Chinese Acad. of Sciences; named Model Medical Expert by CCP Cen. Mil. Comm. 1996. *Address:* Chinese People's Liberation Army Second Medical University, Shanghai, People's Republic of China (office).

WU, Xiucheng, PhD; Chinese physicist; *Chief Technology Officer, D-Tech Optoelectronics, Incorporated;* held various sr eng positions with Perkin Elmer, Agere and Finisar; fmr Researcher, Centre for Electrophotonic Materials and Devices, McMaster Univ., Hamilton, Ont., Canada; mem. Man. Team AdTech Optics Inc., USA; Chief Tech. Officer D-Tech Optoelectronics Inc. 2008–. *Publications:* numerous articles in scientific journals. *Address:* D-Tech Optoelectronics Inc., 18007 Cortney Court, City of Industry, CA 91748-1203, USA (office). *Telephone:* (626)581-3755 (office). *E-mail:* xiucheng.wu@atoptics.com (office). *Website:* www.dtechopto.com (office).

WU, Maj.-Gen. Xu; Chinese army officer; b. March 1939, Changsu City, Jiangsu Prov.; ed 5th Artillery School and PLA Mil. Acad.; joined PLA 1954, CCP 1959; various posts in artillery, reconnaissance and training 1956–85; army corps political commissar and army corps commdr 1985–92; Asst Chief of Gen. Staff 1992; Deputy Chief, PLA Gen. Staff 1995–; mem. 15th CCP Cen. Cttee 1997–2002. *Address:* Ministry of National Defence, Jingshanqian Jie, Beijing, People's Republic of China (office). *Telephone:* (1) 6370000 (office).

WU, Yi; Chinese engineer and politician (retd); b. Nov. 1938, Wuhan City, Hubei Prov.; ed Northwest Polytechnic Inst., Dept of Petroleum Refining, Beijing Petroleum Inst.; joined CCP 1962; technician and staff mem. of Political Dept, Lanzhou Oil Refinery 1962–65; technician, Production Div., Production and Tech. Dept, Ministry of Petroleum Industry 1965–67; technician, later Deputy Chief, later Chief, Tech. Section, Beijing Dongfanghong Refinery, later Deputy Chief Engineer and Deputy Dir Beijing Dongfanghong Refinery 1967–83; Deputy Gen. Man. Yanshan Petrochemical Corpn 1983–88; Vice-Mayor of Beijing 1988–91; Vice-Minister of Foreign Trade and Econ. Cooperation 1991–93 (also Deputy Sec. CCP Leading Party Group); Minister of Foreign Trade and Econ. Co-operation 1993–98; Chair. Bd of Dirs Foreign Trade Univ. 1995–98; State Councillor 1998–2003, Vice-Premier State Council 2003–08 (retd); Minister of Public Health 2003–06; Alt. mem. 13th CCP Cen. Cttee 1987–92, mem. 14th CCP Cen. Cttee 1992–97, 15th CCP Cen. Cttee 1997–2002, 16th CCP Cen. Cttee 2002–07; Alt. mem. CCP Politburo 1997–2002, mem. 2002–07; ranked by Forbes magazine amongst 100 Most Powerful Women (second) 2004, (second) 2005, (third) 2006, (second) 2007. *Address:* c/o State Council, Beijing, People's Republic of China.

WU, Yigong; Chinese film director; b. 1 Dec. 1938, Chongqing, Sichuan Prov.; s. of Wu Tiesan and Yu Minhua; m. Zhang Wen Rong 1967; one s.; Dir

Shanghai Film Bureau, Gen. Man. Shanghai Film Corpn, Vice-Pres. China Film Artists' Asscn 1985–; Vice-Chair. China Fed. of Literary and Art Circles 1996–; Alt. mem. 14th CCP Cen. Cttee 1992–97, 15th CCP Cen. Cttee 1997–2002. *Films include:* University in Exile, The Tribulations of a Chinese Gentleman, Bitter Sea, Evening Rain 1980, My Memories of Old Beijing (Golden Rooster Award for Best Dir 1984), A Man Aged 18 (Magnolia Prize 1988), A Confucius Family 1992. *Leisure interests:* music, sports. *Address:* 52 Yong Fu Road, Shanghai, People's Republic of China. *Telephone:* 4332558. *Fax:* 4370528.

WU, Zuqiang; Chinese musician and composer; *Vice-Chairman, China Federation of Literary and Art Circles;* b. 24 July 1927, Beijing; s. of Wu Jingzhou and Wu Qinqi (née Zhou); m. Li-qin Zheng 1953; one s. one d.; Vice-Pres. Cen. Conservatory of Music 1978–82, Pres. 1982–88, now Prof., Hon. Pres.; Vice-Pres. Chinese Musicians' Asscn 1985, now Hon. Chair.; Vice-Exec. Chair. China Fed. of Literary and Art Circles 1988–92, Vice-Chair. 1992–; Adviser to China Nat. Symphony Orchestra 1996; Alt. mem. 12th CCP Cen. Cttee 1982–87; Perm. mem. Nat. Cttee 7th, 8th and 9th CPPCC 1988–2003; artistic adviser for opening and closing ceremonies, Beijing Summer Olympic Games 2008. *Compositions include:* Sunrise at the Tu Mountains – Fighting against the Floods, Little Sisters at the Grasslands, The Moon's Reflection On ErQuan, Listening to the Pines, A Lovely Night, Revival. *Publications:* Musical Form, Analysis of Music Works. *Leisure interests:* literature, fine arts, tourism. *Address:* Central Conservatory of Music, 43 Baojiajie West District, Beijing 100031, People's Republic of China (office). *Telephone:* (10) 66414887 (office). *Fax:* (10) 66417211 (office).

WU SHIHONG, Juliet; Chinese business executive; joined IBM China Co. Ltd 1985, held several exec. positions including Gen. Man. Channel Man. 1997–98; Gen. Man. Microsoft (China) Co. Ltd 1998–99; Vice-Pres. TCL Corpn and Gen. Man. TCL Information Tech. Industrial Group Co. Ltd 1999–2002, mem. Bd of Dirs TCL Multimedia Tech. Holdings Ltd 2007–; mem. Bd of Dirs (non-exec.) Culturecom Group Ltd 2001–; ranked by Fortune magazine amongst 50 Most Powerful Women in Business outside the US (24th) 2002. *Publication:* Up Against The Wind: Microsoft, IBM and I 1999; How to Change the World: Social Entrepreneurs and the Power of New Ideas (trans.) 2006, Banker to the Poor: Microlending and the Battle Against World Poverty (trans.) 2006. *Address:* TCL Holdings Co. Ltd, Huizhou, Guangdong Province, People's Republic of China (office). *Website:* www.tcl.com (office).

WUFFLI, Peter A.; Swiss banking executive; b. 26 Oct. 1957; s. of Heinz Wuffli; m.; three c.; ed Univ. of St Gall; began career as econs journalist, Neue Zurcher Zeitung 1978–84; Man. Consultant, McKinsey & Co. 1984–90, Pnr, McKinsey Switzerland 1990–94; joined Swiss Banking Corpn 1994, Chief Financial Officer, mem. Exec. Cttee 1994–98; Chief Financial Officer UBS Group (following merger with UBS) 1998–99, Chair. and CEO UBS Asset Man. 1999–2001, Pres. and CEO UBS AG 2001–07; mem. Bd of Dirs Inst. of Int. Finance Inc., Zurich Opera House; Vice Chair. Int. Inst. for Man. Devt; Vice Chair. Swiss-American Chamber of Commerce; European Banker of the Year 2005. *Address:* c/o UBS AG, Bahnhofstrasse 45, 8098 Zürich, Switzerland (office).

WULF-MATHIES, Monika, DPhil; German business executive, government official and fmr politician; b. 17 March 1942, Wernigerode; d. of Carl-Hermann Baier and Margott Baier (née Meisser); m. Carsten Wulf-Mathies 1968; ed Univs of Hamburg and Freiburg; Br. Asst Fed. Ministry of Econs 1968–71; Head of Dept for Social Policy, Fed. Chancellery 1971–76; mem. ÖTV (Public Services and Transport Workers' Union) 1971–, mem. Man. Exec. Cttee 1976–95, Chair. of ÖTV (representing around 2.3 million workers) 1982–95; Pres. Public Services Int. 1989–94; Commr for Regional Policies of EU 1995–99; Adviser to the Chancellor on European Policy 2000; mem. Exec. Bd Deutsche Lufthansa AG 1978–95 (Deputy Chair. 1988–95), VEBA 1989–95; mem. SPD 1965–; Exec. Vice-Pres. Corp. Public Policy and Sustainability, Deutsche Post AG 2001–08 (retd); Pres. Netzwerks Europäische Bewegung Deutschland 2001–06, Hon. Pres. 2006–; Founding mem. Policy Fellow, Institut zur Zukunft der Arbeit—IZA, (Inst. for the Study of Labour), Bonn. *Leisure interests:* gardening, cross-country skiing. *Address:* IZA, Schaumburg-Lippe-Str. 5-9, 53113 Bonn, Germany (office). *Telephone:* (228) 38940 (office). *Website:* www.iza.org (office).

WUNDERLICH, Paul; German painter, sculptor and lithographer; b. 10 March 1927, Eberswalde; s. of Horst Wunderlich and Gertud Wunderlich (née Arendt); m. 1st Isabella von Bethmann-Hollweg 1957 (divorced 1959); m. 2nd Karin Székessy 1971; two d.; ed Akad. Hamburg; Prof. of Drawing and Painting, Acad. Hamburg 1963–68; freelance artist 1969–; Premio Marzotto 1967, Kama Kura Prize, Tokyo 1968, Kunstpreis, Schleswig-Holstein 1986. *Publications:* Monographie Paul Wunderlich Vol. I 1978, Vol. II 1980, Werkverzeichnis der Grafik 1982, Skulpturen und Objekte 1988, Skulpturen und Objekte II 2000, Drypoint I 2000, Drypoint II 2001, Grafik II 2002, Schmuck 2002, Portraits 2007, Werboerzeiduis Kaltuadel 2007, Pastelle 2007. *Address:* Haynstrasse 2, 20249 Hamburg, Germany. *Telephone:* (40) 487387. *Fax:* (40) 476312. *E-mail:* www.paul@wunderlich.org (home).

WUNSCH, Carl Isaac, PhD; American oceanographer and academic; *Cecil and Ida Green Professor of Physical Oceanography, Massachusetts Institute of Technology;* b. 5 May 1941, Brooklyn, NY; s. of Harry Wunsch and Helen Wunsch (née Gellis); m. Marjory Markel 1980; one s. one d.; ed Massachusetts Inst. of Tech.; Lecturer in Oceanography, MIT 1966–67, Asst Prof. 1967–70, Assoc. Prof. 1970–75, Prof. of Physical Oceanography 1975–76, Cecil and Ida Green Prof. 1976–, Sec. of Navy Research Prof. 1985–89; Sr Visiting Fellow, Dept of Applied Math. and Theoretical Physics, Univ. of Cambridge, UK 1969, 1974–75, 1981–82; Visitor, Harvard Univ. 1980, 2007–08; Fulbright Scholar 1981–82; John Simon Guggenheim Foundation Fellow 1981–82; Visiting Sr Scientist, GFDL, Princeton Univ. 1993–94; Visiting Scientist, CNES/CNRS, Toulouse, France 1994; Distinguished Visiting Scientist, Jet Propulsion Lab. 1994–; Chair. Ocean Studies Bd, NRC; consultant to NAS, NSF; mem. NAS, Royal Astronomical Soc., Soc. for Industrial and Applied Math.; Foreign mem. Royal Soc. 2002, American Philosophical Soc. 2003; Fellow, American Acad. of Arts and Sciences, American Geophysical Union, American Meteorological Soc.; James R. Macelwane Award 1971, Maurice Ewing Medal 1990, American Geophysical Union, Founders Prize, Texas Instrument Foundation 1975, A.G. Huntsman Prize 1988, NASA Public Service Medal 1993, Henry Stommel Prize, American Meteorological Soc. 2000, Moore Distinguished Scholar, Calif. Inst. of Tech. 2000, Bowie Medal, American Geophysical Union. *Publications:* Evolution of Physical Oceanography (co-ed.), Ocean Acoustic Tomography (co-author), The Ocean Circulation Inverse Problem; many tech. papers. *Leisure interest:* sailing. *Address:* Room 54-1524, Department of Earth, Atmospheric and Planetary Science, Massachusetts Institute of Technology, Cambridge, MA 02139-4307 (office); 78 Washington Avenue, Cambridge, MA 02140, USA (home). *Telephone:* (617) 253-5937 (office). *Fax:* (617) 253-4464 (office). *E-mail:* cwunsch@mit.edu (office). *Website:* eapsweb.mit.edu/people/person.asp?position=Faculty&who=wunsch (office); puddle.mit.edu/~cwunsch (home).

WURTH, Hubert, LLB; Luxembourg painter and diplomatist; *Ambassador to UK;* b. 15 April 1952; m. Lydie Polfer (q.v.); two c.; ed Univ. de Paris II, Inst. d'Etudes Politiques, Paris; called to the Luxembourg Bar 1977; Attaché, Dept of Int. Econ. Relations, Ministry of Foreign Affairs 1978, Deputy Perm. Rep. to Council of Europe 1979, Chief Sec. to Vice-Pres. of the Govt and Minister for Foreign Affairs, Econ. Affairs and Justice 1981, Deputy Dir of Political Affairs 1986; Amb. to USSR (also accred to Poland, Finland and Mongolia) 1988–92, to the Netherlands 1992–98 (also served as rep. for the Pact on Stability in Europe 1993–95 and on special mission in Fmr Yugoslavia 1996), Perm. Rep. to UN, New York 1998–2003, to OECD 2003–, to UNESCO 2003–07, Amb. to France 2003–07, to UK (also accred to Ireland) 2007–. *Publication:* Monography on Hubert Wurth as a Painter 1998. *Address:* Embassy of Luxembourg, 27 Wilton Crescent, London, SW1X 8SD, England (office). *Telephone:* (20) 7235-6961 (office). *Fax:* (20) 7235-9734 (office). *E-mail:* londres.amb@mae.etat.lu (office).

WÜRTH, Reinhold; German trading company executive; *Chairman, Advisory Board, Würth Group;* b. 20 April 1935, Öhringen; m. Carmen Würth; three c.; joined father's wholesale screw business as second employee, Künzelsau 1949, took over man. of business 1954–94, Chair. Advisory Bd Würth Group 1994–; Head Interfacultative Inst. for Entrepreneurship, Univ. of Karlsrühe 1999–2003; Chair. Advisory Bd Entrepreneurs of the Soc. of Int. Cooperation Baden-Württemberg GmbH; Chair. Gesellschaft zur Förderung des württembergischen Landesmuseums e.V., Freunde der Burgfestspiele Jagsthausen e.V., Pro Region Heilbron-Franken; mem. Supervisory Bd IKB Deutsche Industriebank AG, Düsseldorf; mem. Bd Trustees Robert-Bosch-Foundation; made his art collection of over 6,000 items by Edvard Munch, Picasso and others accessible to the public 1991–; est. Kunsthalle Würth, Schwäbisch Hall 2001–; Hon. Senator, Univ. of Tübingen; Distinguished Service Cross (First Class) of the Order of Merit (FRG); Chevalier des Arts et Lettres 2000; Dr hc (Tübingen); Medal of Econ. Merits (Baden-Württemberg); Freedom of Erstein (France) 1997, Künzelsau 2003. *Leisure interests:* flying, motor bikes, art collecting. *Address:* A. Würth GmbH & Co. KG, Reinhold-Würth-Str. 12–17, 74653 Künzelsau, Germany (office). *Telephone:* (7940) 15-0 (office). *Fax:* (7940) 15-1000 (office). *E-mail:* info@wuerth.de (office). *Website:* www.wuerth.de (office).

WURTZ, Robert (Bob) H., AB, PhD; American psychologist, neuroscientist and academic; *Senior Investigator, Laboratory of Sensorimotor Research, National Eye Institute, National Institutes of Health;* ed Oberlin Coll., Univ. of Michigan; Research Asst, Univ. of Michigan 1958–61, PHS Predoctoral Fellow 1961–62, Predoctoral Instructor 1962; Research Assoc., Cttee for Nuclear Information, St Louis, Mo. 1962–63; Postdoctoral Fellow, Dept of Physiology and Research Fellow, Dept of Neurology, Washington Univ. School of Medicine, St Louis 1962–65; Research Psychologist, Spinal Cord Section, Lab. of Neurophysiology, Nat. Inst. of Neurological Diseases and Blindness, NIH 1965–66, Physiologist, Lab. of Neurobiology, Nat. Inst. of Mental Health, NIH 1966–78, Founding Chief, Lab. of Sensorimotor Research, Nat. Eye Inst., NIH 1978–2002, Sr Investigator, Lab. of Sensorimotor Research 2002–, NIH Sr Investigator 2007, apptd to Sr Exec. Service, NIH 1984, apptd to Sr Biomedical Research Service, NIH 1996; Visiting Scientist, Physiological Lab., Univ. of Cambridge, UK 1975–76, Assoc., Neuroscience Research Program 1989–94; mem. Scientific Bd McGovern Inst. for Brain Research, MIT; Pres. Soc. for Neuroscience 1990–91; mem. NAS 1988 (mem. Council 1996), Inst. of Medicine 1997; non-resident Fellow, Salk Inst.; Fellow, AAAS 1990, American Acad. of Arts and Sciences 1990; Grass Foundation Research Fellow, Marine Biological Lab. 1961, Gordon Holmes Lecturer, European Neuroscience Soc. 1985, James M. Sprague Lecturer, Univ. of Pennsylvania 1986, Morris B. Bender Lecturer, Mount Sinai Medical School 1986, Special Lecturer, Soc. for Neuroscience Meeting 1986, W. Alden Spencer Award, Columbia Univ. 1987, George H. Bishop Lecturer, Washington Univ. 1988, Clinton N. Woolsey Lecturer 1991, Keynote Lecturer, Neural Control of Movement Meeting 1992, Presidential Award, Soc. for Neuroscience 1993, Special Lecturer, Soc. for Neuroscience Meeting 1994, AAAS John P. McGovern Award 1995, Karl Spencer Lashley Award, American Philosophical Soc. 1995, NIH G. Burroughs Mider Lecturer 1995, Friedenwald Award, Asscn for Research in Vision and Ophthalmology 1996 Distinguished Scientific Contrib. Award, American Psychological Asscn 1997, Keynote Lecturer, Neurobiology Retreat, Washington Univ. 1999, Plenary Lecturer, Japanese Neuroscience Soc. 2000, Seventh Annual Lecturer, Center for Neural Basis of Cognition, Univ. of Pittsburgh 2001, Eighth Annual American Legion

Lecturer, Univ. of Minnesota Brain Sciences 2002, Keynote Lecturer, Salk Inst. Annual Faculty Meeting 2003, Nat. Eye Inst. Dir's Award 2004, Dan David Prize for the Future Time Dimension: Brain Sciences (with William T. Newsome and Amiram Grinvald) 2004, Ralph W. Gerard Prize, Soc. for Neuroscience 2006. *Publications:* more than 140 scientific papers in professional journals on neurobiology of vision and eye movements. *Address:* National Eye Institute, 2020 Vision Place, Bethesda, MD 20892-3655, USA (office). *Telephone:* (301) 496-9375 (office). *Fax:* (301) 402-0511 (office). *E-mail:* bob@lsr.nei.nih.gov (office). *Website:* www.nei.nih.gov (office).

WÜTHRICH, Kurt, PhD; Swiss scientist and academic; *Cecil H. and Ida M. Green Professor of Structural Biology, The Scripps Research Institute;* b. 4 Oct. 1938, Aarberg; s. of Hermann Wüthrich and Gertrud Bertha Wüthrich-Kuchen; m. Marianne Briner 1963; one s. one d.; ed Univs of Bern, Basel and Calif. at Berkeley, USA; mem. tech. staff Bell Telephone Labs 1967–69; Privatdozent, ETH, Zürich 1970–72, Asst Prof. 1972–76, Assoc. Prof. 1976–80, Prof. of Biophysics 1980– (Chair. Biology Dept 1995–2000); Visiting Miller Research Prof., Univ. of Calif., Berkeley 1988; Scholar-in-Residence, Johns Hopkins Univ., Baltimore, USA 1992; Sherman Fairchild Distinguished Scholar, Caltech, Pasadena, Calif. 1994, Visiting Assoc. in Biology and Chem. 1995; Guest Scientist, The Scripps Research Inst., Calif. 1994, Cecil H. and Ida M. Green Prof. of Structural Biology 2001–; Visiting Prof., Inst. of Physical and Chemical Research (RIKEN), Tokyo, Japan 1997–98, Univ. of Edinburgh, UK 1997–2000; consultant, Hoechst AG, Frankfurt, Germany 1985–92, Sandoz Pharma AG, Basel 1987–96, Hoffman-La Roche AG, Basel 1987–2004, Ciba-Geigy AG, Basel 1989–96, Tripos Inc., St Louis, USA 1992–94, Novartis AG, Basel 1997–; mem. European Molecular Biology Org. (EMBO) 1984, Deutsche Akad. der Naturforscher Leopoldina 1987, Academia Europaea 1989, Schweizerische Akad. der Technischen Wissenschaften 2001, Schweizerische Akad. der Medizinischen Wissenschaften 2002; Foreign Fellow, Indian Nat. Science Acad. 1989; Foreign Assoc. NAS 1992, Acad. des Sciences, Institut de France 2000; Fellow, AAAS 1998; mem. Schweiz Kommission für Molekularbiologie 1973–76, Pres. 1977–82; mem. Council Int. Union of Pure and Applied Biophysics (IUPAB) 1975–78, 1987–90, Sec.-Gen. 1978–84, Vice-Pres. 1984–87; mem. Gen. Cttee Int. Council of Scientific Unions (ICSU) 1980–86, Standing Cttee on the Free Circulation of Scientists 1982–90; mem. Kommission für die Wolfgang Pauli-Vorlesungen, ETH Zürich 1984–92, Pres. 1993–2001; Pres. Züricher Chemische Gesellschaft 1990–91; mem. Exec. Cttee Schweiz Gesellschaft für Biochemie 1986–92, Pres. Biophysics Section 1985–88; mem. IUPAC, Comm. on Biophysical Chem. 1969–99, Chair. 2000–01; mem. Prix Marcel Benoist, Conseil de Fondation, Berne 2001–; mem. Bds Centro Stefano Franscini, Monte Verità and ETH Zürich 1989–98, European Molecular Biology Lab., Heidelberg, Germany 1989–95, Nat. Lab. of Biomacromolecules, Academia Sinica, Beijing, China 1989–, Deutsche Forschungsgemeinschaft, Bonn, Germany: Schwerpunktsprogramm 'Protein Design' 1989–95, Comm. of the European Communities: Human Capital and Mobility Programme 1992–94, Inst. für Molekulare Biotechnologie, Jena, Germany 1993–96, Ciba Foundation, London, UK 1994–96, Institut de Biologie Structurale Jean-Pierre Ebel, Grenoble, France 1994–97, Inst. of Biotechnology, Univ. of Helsinki, Finland 1997–, Novartis Foundation, London 1997–, Triad Therapeutics Inc., San Diego, Calif. 1998–04, Genomics Sciences Centre, RIKEN, Tokyo 2000–, Syrrx Inc., San Diego 2000–04, Groupement d'Intérêt Scientifique 'Infections à Prions', France 2001–, Nat. Inst. of Chemical Physics and Biophysics, Tallinn, Estonia 2001–, Nat. High Field NMR Center (NANUC), Univ. of Alberta, Edmonton, Canada 2001–, Eidogen Inc., Pasadena, Calif. 2002–; Titular mem. European Acad. of Arts, Sciences and Humanities 2003; Foreign mem. Latvian Acad. of Sciences; Hon. Prof., Dalian Inst. of Chemical Physics, Chinese Acad. of Sciences, Dalian Inst. of Light Industry; Profesor Extraordinario con distinción de Académico Ilustre, U.N. de Mar del Plata, Argentina; Hon. Fellow, Nat. Acad. of Sciences, India 1992, Royal Soc. of Chem., UK 2003; Hon. FRSE 2003; Foreign Hon. mem., American Acad. of Arts and Sciences 1993; Hon. mem. Japanese Biochemical Soc. 1993, Nat. Magnetic Resonance Soc. of India 1998, The World Innovation Foundation 2003, Swiss Chemical Soc. 2003, Int. Soc. for Magnetic Resonance in Medicine 2003, Wallisellen Football Club 2003, Hungarian Acad. of Sciences 2004, World Acad. of Young Scientists 2004, World High Tech. Soc., Dalian, China 2004, European Acad. of Sciences and Arts 2004, Groupement Ampère 2004, The Nuclear Magnetic Resonance Soc. of Japan 2004, Indian Biophysical Soc. 2005; Hon. DPhil (Zürich) 1997; Hon. DSc (Sheffield), (King George's Medical Univ., Lucknow, India); Dr hc (Siena, Italy) 1997, (Ecole Polytechnique Fédéral de Lausanne) 2001, (Valencia); Friedrich-Miescher-Preis, Schweizerische Gesellschaft für Biochemie 1974, Shield of the Faculty of Medicine, Tokyo Univ. 1983, Médaille P. Bruylants, Université Catholique de Louvain, Belgium 1986, Stein and Moore Award of the Protein Soc., USA 1990, Louisa Gross Horwitz Prize, Columbia Univ., New York 1991, Gilbert Newton Lewis Medal, Univ. of Calif., Berkeley 1991, Marcel Benoist-Preis, Swiss Confed. 1992, Distinguished Service Award, The Miami Bio/Technology Winter Symposia, USA 1993, Prix Louis Jeantet de Médecine, Fondation Louis Jeantet, Geneva 1993, Kaj Linderstrom-Lang Prize, Carlsberg Foundation, Copenhagen, Denmark 1996, Eminent Scientist of RIKEN, Tokyo 1997, Kyoto Prize in Advanced Tech., Inamori Foundation, Kyoto 1998, Günther Laukien Prize, Experimental NMR Conf., USA 1999, Otto-Warburg-Medaille, Gesellschaft für Biochemie und Molekularbiologie, Germany 1999, Médaille d'Honneur en Argent, Soc. d'Encouragement au Progrès, Paris, France 2001, Nobel Prize in Chem. 2002, World Future Award, The World Awards, Vienna, Austria 2002, Swiss Soc. Award 2002. *Publications:* NMR in Biological Research: Peptides and Proteins 1976, NMR of Proteins and Nucleic Acids 1986, NMR in Structural Biology – A Collection of Papers by Kurt Wüthrich 1995; also published 650 papers and reviews. *Leisure interests:* sports, French literature. *Address:* Institut für Molekularbiologie & Biophysik, ETH Zürich, HPK, 8093 Zürich, Switzerland (office); The Scripps Reseach Institute, MB-44, 10550 North Torrey Pines Road, La Jolla, CA 92037, USA (office); Fliederstrasse 7, 8304 Wallisellen, Switzerland (home). *Telephone:* (44) 6332473 (Zürich) (office); (858) 784-8011 (La Jolla) (office). *Fax:* (44) 6331151 (Zürich) (office); (858) 784-8014 (La Jolla) (office). *E-mail:* wuthrich@mol.biol.ethz.ch (office); wuthrich@scripps.edu (office). *Website:* www.mol.biol.ethz.ch (office).

WYATT, (Alan) Will, CBE, FRTS; British consultant and media commentator; *Chairman, Human Capital Limited;* b. 7 Jan. 1942, Oxford; s. of Basil Wyatt and Hettie Wyatt (née Hooper); m. Jane Bridgit Bagenal 1966; two d.; ed Magdalen Coll. School, Oxford, Emmanuel Coll. Cambridge; trainee reporter, Sheffield Telegraph 1964; Sub-Ed. BBC Radio News 1965; joined BBC TV 1968, Producer, Late Night Line-Up, In Vision, The Book Programme, B. Traven – a mystery solved, etc. 1970–77, Asst Head of Presentation (Programmes) 1977, Head Documentary Features 1981, Features and Documentaries Group 1987, Asst Man. Dir BBC Network Television 1988–91; Man. Dir BBC Network TV 1991–96; Chief Exec. BBC Broadcast 1996–99; Chair. Human Capital Ltd 2001–, Goodwill Assocs (Media) Ltd 2003–; Vice-Chair. Shadow Racing Trust 2003–; Chair. BBC Guidelines on Violence 1983, 1987; Dir Broadcasters' Audience Research Bd 1989–91, BBC Subscription TV 1990–93, BBC Enterprises 1991–93, UKTV 1997–99; Vice-Pres. Royal TV Soc. 1997, Euro Broadcasting Union 1998–99; Gov. Univ. of the Arts, London (fmrly London Inst.) 1990–, Chair. 1999–2007; Huw Wheldon Memorial Lecture 1996; Royal Inst. Discourse 1996; Pres. Royal TV Soc. 2000–; Dir Coral Eurobet 2000–02, Vitec Group plc 2002–, Racing UK 2004–(Chair. 2008–), Racecourse Media Services 2007–(Chair. 2008–); Chair. Teaching Awards Trust 2008–; mem. British Horseriding Bd Comm. into Stable and Stud Staff 2003–04; Gov. Magdalen Coll. School 2000–06; Trustee, Services Sound and Vision Corpn 2007–. *Television:* The Fifties, Late Night Line Up, The Book Programme, Edition, All the Buildings Fit to Print, The Golden Trashery of Ogden Nashery, Robinson's Travels – The Mormon Trail, B. Traven – A Mystery Solved. *Publications:* The Man Who Was B. Traven 1980, Masters of the Wired World (contrib.) 1999, The Fun Factory – A Life in the BBC 2003; articles on broadcasting in Evening Standard, The Times, Daily Telegraph etc. *Leisure interests:* fell walking, horse racing, opera, theatre. *Address:* Abbey Willows, Rayford Lane, Middle Barton, Oxon., OX7 7DD, England (office). *Telephone:* (1869) 340234 (office). *Fax:* (1869) 340145 (home). *E-mail:* ww@dornvalley.net (office).

WYATT, Christopher Terrel, BSc, FREng, FICE, FRSA, FIStructE, DIC, CBIM; British business executive and engineer; b. 17 July 1927, Ewell, Surrey; s. of Lional H. Wyatt and Audrey Vere Wyatt; m. 1st Doreen Mary Emmerson; three s.; m. 2nd Geertruida Willer 1970; one s.; m. 3rd Patricia Perkins 1990; ed Kingston Grammar School, Battersea Polytechnic and Imperial Coll., London; Charles Brand & Son, Ltd, 1948–54; joined Richard Costain Ltd, 1955, Dir 1970–87, Group Chief Exec. 1975–80, Deputy Chair. 1979–80, Chair. Costain Group PLC 1980–87; Chair. W. S. Atkins Ltd 1987–97; Fellow Royal Acad. of Eng, Inst. of Structural Engineers. *Leisure interests:* sailing, music, painting. *Address:* Ryderwells Farm, Uckfield Road, Lewes, East Sussex, BN8 5RN, England (home). *Telephone:* (1273) 812219 (home).

WYDEN, Ronald Lee, JD; American politician; *Senator from Oregon;* b. 3 May 1949, Wichita, Kan.; s. of Peter Wyden and Edith Wyden; m. Laurie Oseran 1978; one s. one d.; ed Univ. of Santa Barbara, Stanford Univ. and Univ. of Oregon; campaign aide, Senator Wayne Morse 1972, 1974; Co-Founder, Co-Dir Oregon Gray Panthers 1974–80; Dir Oregon Legal Services for Elderly 1977–79; Instructor in Gerontology, Univ. of Oregon 1976, Portland State Univ. 1979, Univ. of Portland 1980; mem. 97th–103rd Congresses from 3rd Oregon Dist 1981–95; Senator from Oregon 1996–; mem. ABA; Democrat. *Address:* United States Senate, 516 Hart Senate Office Building, Washington, DC 20510, USA (office). *Telephone:* (202) 224-5244 (office). *Website:* wyden.senate.gov (office).

WYLIE, Andrew, BA; American literary agent; *President, The Wylie Agency;* b. 4 Nov. 1947; m. 1st Christina Meyer 1969; one s.; m. 2nd Camilla Carlini; two d.; ed St Paul's School, Harvard Coll.; founder and Pres. The Wylie Agency, New York 1980–, London 1996–, Madrid 1999–, with over 500 clients. *Address:* The Wylie Agency, 250 W 57th Street, Suite 2114, New York, NY 10107, USA. *Telephone:* (212) 246-0069. *Fax:* (212) 586-8953. *E-mail:* mail@wylieagency.com. *Website:* www.wylieagency.com.

WYLLER, Egil A., DPhil; Norwegian academic; *Professor Emeritus of Philosophy, University of Oslo;* b. 24 April 1925, Stavanger; s. of Trygve Wyller and Anne-Kathrine Wyller; m. Eva Middelthon 1949; three s.; ed Univs of Oslo, Tübingen and Freiburg im Breisgau; fmr Prof. of History of the Ideas of Antiquity, Dept of Philosophy, Univ. of Oslo 1969–95, now Prof. Emer.; Commdr, Order of Phoenix (Greece); Kt First Class, Order of St Olav (Norway) 2000; Gold Medal of HM King of Norway 1958, Cultural Prize of City of Oslo 1986. *Publications include:* Platons 'Parmenides' 1960, Der späte Platon 1965–1970, Enhet og Annethet I–III 1981, Johannes' Aapenbaring 1985, Prinsesse Europa 1989, Platonismus/Henologie in der Antike und im Mittelalter I–II (textbook) 1993, Henologisk Skriftserie I–XX 1994–2002, Henologische Perspektiven I–II 1995, Platon und Platonismus Tre 1996, Henrik Ibsen I–II: 1999–2002, Gestern und Morgen Heute 2005. *Leisure interests:* music, poetry, natural life. *Address:* Institute of Philosophy, University of Oslo, Blindern, Oslo 3 (office); Kaptein Oppegaards v. 15, 1164 Oslo, Norway (home). *Telephone:* 22-84-40-97 (office). *E-mail:* egil.wyller@filosofi.uio.no (office). *Website:* www.hf.uio.no/filosofi/english (office).

WYLLIE, Peter John, PhD, FRS; American geologist and academic; *Professor Emeritus of Geology, Division of Geological and Planetary Sciences, California Institute of Technology;* b. 8 Feb. 1930, London; s. of George W. Wyllie and Beatrice G. Weaver; m. F. Rosemary Blair 1956; two s. one d. (and one d.

deceased); ed Univ. of St Andrews, Scotland; glaciologist, British West Greenland Expedition 1950; geologist, British North Greenland Expedition 1952–54; Asst Lecturer in Geology, Univ. of St Andrews 1955–56; Research Asst to O. F. Tuttle, Pennsylvania State Univ. 1956–58, Asst Prof. of Geochem. 1959–60; Research Fellow in Chem., Univ. of Leeds 1959–60, Lecturer in Experimental Petrology 1960–61; Assoc. Prof. of Petrology, Pa State Univ. 1961–65; Prof. of Petrology and Geochem., Univ. of Chicago 1965–83, Master of Physical Sciences, Collegiate Div., Assoc. Dean Physical Sciences, Assoc. Dean of the Coll. 1972–73, Homer J. Livingston Prof. 1978–83; Chair. Dept of Geophysical Sciences 1979–82; Chair. Div. of Geological and Planetary Sciences, Calif. Inst. of Tech. 1983–87, Prof. of Geology 1983–99, Academic Officer 1994–99, Prof. Emer. 1999–; Vice-Pres. Mineralogical Soc. of America 1976–77, Pres. 1977–78; Foreign Assoc. NAS 1981; Fellow, American Acad. of Arts and Sciences 1982; Corresp. Fellow, Edin. Geological Soc. 1985–; Foreign Fellow (Corresp. mem.) Indian Geophysical Union 1987; Foreign mem. USSR (now Russian) Acad. of Sciences 1988, Academia Europaea 1996; Foreign Fellow Indian Nat. Science Acad. 1991, Nat. Acad. of Science of India 1992, Chinese Acad. of Science 1996; Louis Murray Visiting Fellow, Univ. of Cape Town March 1987; Vice-Pres. Int. Mineralogical Asscn 1978–86, Pres. 1995–99; Vice-Pres. Int. Union of Geodesy and Geophysics 1991–95, Pres. 1995–99; Hon. Prof. China Univ. of Geosciences, Beijing 1996–; Hon. mem. Mineralogical Soc. of GB and Ireland 1986, German Geological Soc. 2001, Mineralogical Soc. of Russia 1987; Hon. DSc (St Andrews) 1974; Polar Medal 1954, Mineralogical Soc. of America Award 1965, Quantrell Award 1979, Wollaston Medal (Geological Soc., London) 1982, Abraham-Gottlob-Werner-Medaille, German Mineralogical Soc. 1987, Roebling Medal (Mineralogical Soc. of America) 2001, Leopold von Buch Medal (German Geological Soc.) 2001. *Sport:* Heavyweight Boxing Champion, RAF Scotland 1949, Pres. Athletic Union, Univ. of St Andrews 1951–52. *Publications:* Ultramafic and Related Rocks (ed.) 1967, The Dynamic Earth 1971, The Way the Earth Works 1976, Solid-Earth Sciences and Society (Chair. NAS Cttee) 1993; numerous articles in scientific journals. *Leisure interests:* writing. *Address:* Division of Geological and Planetary Sciences, California Institute of Technology, Pasadena, CA 91125, USA (office). *Telephone:* (626) 395-6461 (office). *E-mail:* wyllie@gps.caltech.edu (office); wyllie@caltech.edu (office). *Website:* www.gps.caltech.edu/~wyllie (office).

WYMAN, Bill; British musician (bass guitar); b. (William George Perks), 24 Oct. 1936, Lewisham, London; m. 1st Diane Cory 1959 (divorced 1968); one s.; m. 2nd Mandy Smith 1989 (divorced 1991); m. 3rd Suzanne Accosta 1993; three d.; founder mem., The Rolling Stones 1962–91; numerous tours and concerts world-wide; solo artist and mem., Willie and the Poor Boys 1985, Bill Wyman's Rhythm Kings 1998–2004; owner WGW Holdings, WGW Enterprises, Wytel Music, Ripple Records, Ripple Music, Ripple Publications, Ripple Productions, KJM Nominees, Sticky Fingers Restaurant; Lord of the Manor of Gedding and Thormwoods 1968–; Nordoff-Robbins Silver Clef 1982, Grammy Lifetime Achievement Award 1986, Ivor Novello Award for Outstanding Contribution to British Music 1991, Blues Foundation Memphis Literary Award 2002. *Films:* Sympathy for the Devil 1970, Gimme Shelter 1970, Ladies and Gentlemen the Rolling Stones 1974, Let's Spend the Night Together 1982, Digital Dreams 1983. *Recordings include:* albums: with The Rolling Stones: The Rolling Stones 1964, The Rolling Stones No. 2 1965, Out Of Our Heads 1965, Aftermath 1966, Between The Buttons 1967, Their Satanic Majesties Request 1967, Beggar's Banquet 1968, Let It Bleed 1969, Get Yer Ya-Ya's Out 1969, Sticky Fingers 1971, Exile On Main Street 1972, Goat's Head Soup 1973, It's Only Rock And Roll 1974, Black And Blue 1976, Some Girls 1978, Emotional Rescue 1980, Tattoo You 1981, Still Life 1982, Undercover 1983, Dirty Work 1986, Steel Wheels 1989, Flashpoint 1991; solo: Monkey Grip 1974, Stone Alone 1976, Green Ice (film soundtrack) 1981, Bill Wyman 1981, Digital Dreams (film soundtrack) 1983, Stuff 1991, Struttin' Our Stuff 1998, Anyway the Wind Blows 1999, Groovin' 2000, Double Bill 2001, Blues Odyssey 2001, Rude Dudes 2003, Just For The Thrill 2004; singles: with The Rolling Stones: Come On 1963, I Wanna Be Your Man 1963, Not Fade Away 1964, It's All Over Now 1964, Little Red Rooster 1964, The Last Time 1965, (I Can't Get No) Satisfaction 1965, Get Off Of My Cloud 1965, 19th Nervous Breakdown 1966, Paint It Black 1966, Have You Seen Your Mother Baby, Standing In The Shadow 1966, Let's Spend The Night Together/ Ruby Tuesday 1967, We Love You 1967, Jumping Jack Flash 1968, Honky Tonk Women 1969, Brown Sugar 1971, Tumbling Dice 1972, Angie 1973, It's Only Rock 'N' Roll 1974, Fool To Cry 1976, Miss You 1978, Emotional Rescue 1980, Start Me Up 1981, Waiting On A Friend 1981, Undercover Of The Night 1983, Harlem Shuffle 1986, Mixed Emotions 1989, Rock And A Hard Place 1989, Highwire 1991; solo: (Si Si) Je Suis Un Rock Star 1981, Come Back Suzanne 1981, A New Fashion 1981, Groovin' 2000. *Publications:* Stone Alone – The Story of a Rock and Roll Band (with Ray Coleman) 1990, Wyman Shoots Chagall 2000, Bill Wyman's Blues Odyssey (with Richard Havers) 2001, Rolling With The Stones (with Richard Havers) 2002, Bill Wyman's Treasure Islands 2005, The Stones: A History in Cartoons 2006. *Address:* Tony Denton Promotions Ltd, 19 South Molton Lane, Mayfair, London, W1K 5LE, England (office). *Telephone:* (20) 7629-4666 (office). *Fax:* (20) 7629-4777 (office). *E-mail:* mail@tdpromo.com (office). *Website:* www.tdpromo.com (office); www .billwyman.com.

WYNDHAM, Henry Mark; British art expert and company director; *Chairman, Sotheby's;* b. 19 Aug. 1953, London; s. of Hon. Mark Wyndham and Anne Wyndham; m. Rachel Pritchard 1978; three s.; ed Wellesley House, Broadstairs, Eton Coll., Sorbonne, Paris and Sotheby's Fine Art Course; joined Christie's 1974; Head, 19th Century European Picture Dept., Christie's, New York 1978–82, Vice-Pres. 1979; Dir Christie's, London 1983–87; set up Henry Wyndham Fine Art of St James's Art Group 1987–93; set up Portrait Commissions 1992; Chair. Sotheby's UK 1994–, Sotheby's Europe 1997–; Trustee, Glyndebourne Opera, Prince of Wales Drawing School. *Films:* Entrapment 1999, Tomb Raider 2001, And Now Ladies and Gentlemen 2002. *Television:* Antiques Roadshow 1980s, 1990s. *Leisure interests:* cricket, golf, fishing, shooting, travelling, soccer (Brighton & Hove Albion supporter), visiting museums and art, galleries, opera, landscape. *Address:* Sotheby's, 34 New Bond Street, London, W1S 2RT (office); The Old Rectory, Southease, nr Lewes, Sussex, BN7 3HX, England (home). *Telephone:* (20) 7293-5000 (office). *Fax:* (20) 7293-5065 (office). *E-mail:* henry.wyndham@sothebys.com (office). *Website:* www.sothebys.com (office).

WYNNE-MORGAN, David; British public relations executive; *Founding Partner and Chairman, WMC Communications Ltd;* b. 22 Feb. 1931; s. of John Wynne-Morgan and of the late Marjorie Wynne-Morgan; m. 1st Romaine Ferguson; two s.; m. 2nd Sandra Douglas-Home (divorced); m. 3rd Karin E. Stines; two s.; ed Bryanston School; reporter, Daily Mail 1952–55; foreign corresp., later William Hickey, Daily Express 1955–58; contracted to Sunday Times to write biographical features including ghosting autobiog. of the late Pres. Nasser of Egypt; Founder, Chair. and Man. Dir Partnerplan 1964–80; Man. Dir Extel Public Relations 1980–83, Chair. 1983–84; Chair. and Chief Exec. Hill & Knowlton (UK) Ltd 1984–90, Pres. Hill & Knowlton Europe, Middle East and Africa 1990–94; Chair. Worldwide Exec. Cttee 1994, Marketing Group of GB 1989–90; Founding Pnr and Chair. WMC Communications Ltd; Dir Horsham Corpn 1995–97; Council mem. Lord's Taverners 1992–96; mem. Inst. of Public Relations. *Publications:* biogs of Pietro Annigoni, Margot Fonteyn, Sir Malcolm Sargent. *Leisure interests:* squash (fmr Welsh int.), cricket, tennis, riding, golf. *Address:* WMC Communications Ltd, 11–12 Pall Mall, London, SW1Y 5LU (office); Lowndes Flat, 136 Brompton Road, London, SW3 1HY, England. *Telephone:* (20) 7930-9030 (office). *Fax:* (20) 7930-9038 (office). *Website:* www.wmccommunications.com (office).

WYPLOSZ, Charles, PhD, DipEng; French professor of economics; *Professor of Economics, Graduate Institute of International Studies, Geneva;* b. 5 Sept. 1947, Vichy; s. of Jacob Wyplosz and Félicia Zanger; m. Claire-Lise Monod 1967; one s. three d.; ed Univ. of Paris, Harvard Univ.; Asst, Assoc., then Full Prof. of Econs, Institut Européen d'Admin des Affaires (INSEAD), Fontainebleau 1978–, Assoc. Dean (Research and Devt) 1986–89; Directeur d'études, EHESS, Paris 1988–95; Prof. of Econs, Grad. Inst. of Int. Studies, Geneva 1995–; Man. Ed. Econ. Policy 1984–2001; mem. Council of Econ. Advisers to Prime Minister of France 1999–, Comm. Economique, Ministry of Finance, France 1999–; mem. Panel of Econ. and Monetary Experts, Cttee for Econ. and Monetary Affairs, European Parl. 2000–; mem. Group of Econ. Analysis, EC 2001–. *Publications:* numerous publs in professional journals; occasional contribs to press. *Leisure interests:* skiing, music, family. *Address:* Graduate Institute of International Studies, 11 avenue de la Paix, 1202 Geneva (office); 3 rue du Valais, 1202 Geneva, Switzerland (home). *Telephone:* (22) 9085946 (office). *Fax:* (22) 7333049 (office). *E-mail:* charles.wyplosz@graduateinstitute .ch (office). *Website:* www.wyplosz.eu (office).

WYZNER, Eugeniusz, LLM; Polish diplomatist; *Vice-Chairman, International Civil Service Commission;* b. 1931, Chełmno; s. of Henryk Wyzner and Janina Wyzner; m. Elżbieta Laudańska 1961; one s.; ed Jagiellonian Univ., Kraków, Warsaw Univ. and Acad. of Int. Law, The Hague; Deputy Perm. Rep. to UN 1961–68; Deputy Dir of Dept at Ministry of Foreign Affairs 1968–71, Dir of Dept 1971–73; Amb., Perm. Rep. to UN, Geneva 1973–78; Dir of Dept, Ministry of Foreign Affairs 1978–81; UN Under-Sec.-Gen. 1982–94; Deputy Minister for Foreign Affairs and Parl. Sec., Ministry of Foreign Affairs 1994–97, Acting Minister for Foreign Affairs Dec. 1995; Amb. and Rep. to UN 1998–99; Vice-Chair. Int. Civil Service Comm. 1999–; mem. Bd of Dirs Int. Inst. of Space Law, Paris, Int. Peace Acad., New York, Int. Congress Inst. 1987–; Chair. UN Steering Cttee on Status of Women 1989–91, UN Appointments and Promotion Bd 1991–94, UN Exhibits Cttee 1992–94; mem. UN Sr Bd on Services to the Public 1989–94; Amb. ad personam; Gold Cross of Merit; Grand Commdr's Cross, Order of Polonia Restituta; Grand Commdr Order of the Phoenix (Greece); Commdr Légion d'honneur and other decorations. *Publications:* Wybrane zagadnienia z działalności ONZ w dziedzinie kodyfikacji i postępowego rozwoju prawa międzynarodowego, Niektóre aspekty prawne finansowania operacji ONZ w Kongo i na Bliskim Wschodzie, Poland and 50 Years of the United Nations Existence 1995. *Leisure interests:* cross-country skiing, mountain walking, theatre. *Address:* International Civil Service Commission, 2 United Nations Plaza, New York, NY 10017, USA (office). *Telephone:* (212) 963-8465 (office). *Fax:* (212) 963-1717 (office).

X

XHAFERI, Arben; Macedonian politician; *Leader, Democratic Party of Albanians (DPA);* b. 1948; involved in radical student politics; started career as sr ed. at state-run TV station Priština, Kosovo; returned to Macedonia and joined Party for Democratic Prosperity; elected to Parl. 1994; Leader Democratic Party of Albanians 1997–; participated in coalition govts 1998–2002. *Address:* Democratic Party of Albanians, Maršal Tito 2, Tetovo, Macedonia (office). *Telephone:* (44) 7332572 (office). *Fax:* (44) 7332572 (office). *E-mail:* polsh-polsh@yahoo.com.

XHUFI, Pellumb; Albanian diplomatist, politician and academic; *Deputy Chairman, Levizja Socialiste per Integrim (Socialist Movement for Integration);* b. 24 Aug. 1951, Durres; m.; one d.; ed Univ. La Sapienza, Rome, Italy, Univ. of Cologne, Germany; began career with Foreign Affairs Dept, Albanian Radio TV 1977–81; Science Researcher, Inst. of History, Albanian Acad. of Science 1981–97; Dir Regional Dept, Ministry of Foreign Affairs 1997–98; Deputy Minister of Foreign Affairs 1998–2001; apptd Amb. to Malta 2001; fmr Amb. to Italy; Lecturer in Faculty of History, Philosophy and Foreign Languages, Tirana Univ.; currently mem. Parl. and Deputy Chair. Levizja Socialiste per Integrim (Socialist Movt for Integration); Humboldt Scholarship 1992. *Publications:* Albanian Encyclopaedia (co-author) 1986, The Truth About Kosovo (co-author) 1990, History of the Albanian People (co-author) 2002, Gli Statuti di Scutari (co-author) 2002, Albanian Dilemmas: A Study on Medieval Albania 2006, From Palaeologos to Muzakas: Berat and Vlora in XII-XV Centuries 2009; contrib. several academic articles. *Address:* Levizja Socialiste per Integrim, Rr. Sami Frasheri Nr. 20/10, Tirana, Albania (office). *Telephone:* (4) 2270413. *Fax:* (4) 2270412 (office). *E-mail:* pxhufi@yahoo.com (home). *Website:* www.lsi-al.org (office).

XI, Jinping; Chinese politician; *Vice-President;* b. 1953, Fuping, Shaanxi Prov.; s. of the late Xi Zhongxun (fmr Vice-Premier and a founder of Communist guerrilla movt in northern China); m. Peng Liyuan; one d.; ed Tsinghua Univ., Beijing; sent to do manual labour, Yanchuan Co., Shaanxi Prov. 1969; joined CCP 1974; served as Sec. to Geng Biao 1982; Vice-Sec., Sec. CCP Zhengding Co. Cttee 1982–85; First Political Commissar, Chinese People's Armed Police Force; Vice-Mayor of Xiamen, Fujian Prov. 1985–88; Sec. CCP Ningde Pref. Cttee 1988–90; First Sec. Fujian Mil. Dist (Ningde Mil. Sub-Area Command), PLA Nanjing Mil. Region 1988; Sec. CCP Fuzhou Municipal Cttee, Chair. Standing Cttee Fuzhou Municipal People's Congress 1990–96; Deputy Sec. CCP Fujian Prov. Cttee 1995–2002; Vice-Gov. of Fujian Prov. 1999–2000, Gov. 2000–02; Acting Gov. of Zhejiang Prov. 2002–07; Deputy Sec. CCP Zhejiang Prov. Cttee 2002, Sec. 2002–07; Chair. Standing Cttee of Zhejiang Prov. People's Congress 2003–07; Sec. CCP Shanghai Municipal Cttee 2007; Vice-Pres., People's Repub. of China 2008–; Del., 14th CCP Nat. Congress 1992–97; Alt. mem. 15th CCP Cen. Cttee 1997–2002, mem. 16th CCP Cen. Cttee 2002–07, 17th CCP Cen. Cttee 2007– (also mem. Standing Cttee Politburo 17th CCP Cen. Cttee 2007–). *Publications include:* Research on Developing Chinese Rural Market-orientated Economy, Science and Patriotism (Chief Ed.). *Leisure interests:* reading, sports. *Address:* Office of the Vice-President, Beiing, People's Republic of China (office).

XI, Zezong; Chinese astronomer; b. 9 June 1927, Shaanxi Prov.; s. of Xi Renyin and Li Mudan; m. Shi Liuyun 1956; one s. one d.; ed Zhongshan Univ.; Research Prof., Inst. for History of Natural Science 1981– (Dir 1983–88); mem. Chinese Acad. of Sciences 1991–, Int. Acad. of History of Science 1993–, Int. Eurasian Acad. of Sciences 1995–; Pres. Chinese Soc. of History of Science and Tech. 1994–; Hon. Dean, Dept of History of Science, Univ. of Science and Tech. of China Ho Leung Ho Lee Astronomy Prize. *Address:* Institute for History of Science and Technology, 137 Chao-Nei Street, Beijing 100010, People's Republic of China (office). *Telephone:* (10) 64043989 (office). *Fax:* (10) 64017637 (office).

XIA, Peisu, PhD; Chinese computer engineer; b. July 1923, Chongqing; ed Cen. Univ. for Nationalities and Univ. of Edinburgh, UK; Ed.-in-Chief Journal of Computer Science and Tech.; mem. Chinese Acad. of Sciences 1991–, Research Fellow, Computer Tech. Research Inst.; in 1950s designed and successfully trial-manufactured the first universal electronic digital computer independently designed in China; developed the high-speed array processor and successfully developed multiple parallel computers of different types. *Address:* Computer Technology Research Institute, Zhong Guan Cun, Beijing 100080, People's Republic of China (office).

XIAN, Dingchang; Chinese nuclear physicist; *Research Professor, Institute of High Energy Physics, Chinese Academy of Sciences;* b. 15 Aug. 1935, Guangzhou, Guangdong Prov.; s. of Xian Jiaqi and Li Zuoming; m. 1st Ren Mengmei 1966 (died 1994); two s.; m. 2nd Chu Shiuling 2001 (divorced 2005); two s.; ed Beijing Univ.; Research Prof., Inst. of High Energy Physics, Chinese Acad. of Sciences; Chair. Chinese Synchrotron Radiation Soc. 1996–; mem. Chinese Acad. of Sciences 1992–, Acad. of Sciences for the Developing World 2002–; Nat. Science Conf. Prize 1978, State Natural Science Prize 1982, Ho Leung Ho Lee Physics Prize, Supreme Prize for State Science and Tech. Progress 1989. *Publications:* Synchrotron Radiation Applications 1997, Contemporary Scientific and Technological Techniques in Ancient Ceramics Research 1999, Platform for Biomacromolecule Crystal Structure Research with Synchrotron Radiation 2004, Precambrian Fossil Research with Synchrotron Radiation 3D Non-destructive Imaging Fossil Research with Synchrotron Radiation 3D Non-destructive Imaging 2006. *Leisure interests:* literature, music. *Address:* Institute of High Energy Physics, 19 Yuquan Road, Beijing 100049, People's Republic of China (office). *Telephone:* (10) 88235988 (office);

(10) 82661342 (home). *Fax:* (10) 88233201 (home). *E-mail:* xian@ihep.ac.cn (office). *Website:* www.ihep.ac.cn (office).

XIANG, Huaicheng; Chinese politician and economist; b. 1939, Wujiang Co., Jiangsu Prov.; ed Shandong Univ.; Asst Researcher, Inst. of Computing Tech., Chinese Acad. of Sciences 1960–62; Deputy Section Chief, Budget Dept, Ministry of Finance, Deputy Div. Chief, later Deputy Dir Comprehensive Planning Dept 1962–86; joined CCP 1983; Vice-Minister of Finance 1986–94, Minister of Finance 1998–2003; Deputy Head, Leading Group, Three Gorges Project Resettlement 1992; Deputy Head, Leading Group, Aid-the-Poor Projects 1993; Deputy Dir State Admin. of Taxation 1994–98; Pres. Nat. Council for Social Security Fund 2003–07; mem. 15th CCP Cen. Cttee 1997–2002, 16th CCP Cen. Cttee 2002–07; mem. State Steering Group of Science, Tech. and Educ. 1998–. *Publications:* Fiscal System Reform in China, Fiscal System Reform and Macro Economic Management in China, Fiscal Development Strategy in the 1990s, The Theories and Practices on Management of Off-Budget Funds, China: Market Economy and Macro Economic Management. *Address:* Zhongguo Gongchan Dang (Chinese Communist Party), Beijing, People's Republic of China (office).

XIANG, Junbo, MEconSc, LLD; Chinese banking executive; *President and CEO, Agricultural Bank of China;* b. Jan. 1957; ed Peking Univ., Nankai Univ., Renmin Univ. of China; Vice-Pres. Nanjing Audit Inst. 1993–96; Deputy Dir-Gen., Supervision Dept, Nat. Audit Office of China (CNAO) 1996, Special CNAO Attaché to Beijing, Tianjin and Hebei Prov. 1996–99, Dir-Gen. Personnel and Educ. Dept 1999–2000, Dir-Gen. Personnel Dept 2000–02, Deputy Auditor 2002–04; Deputy Gov. People's Bank of China (PBC) 2004–07, also Pres. PBC Shanghai Head Office 2005–07; Pres. and CEO Agricultural Bank of China 2007–; Adjunct Prof., China Europe Int. Business School; Guest Prof., Fudan Econ. Forum 2007; mem. Expert Cttee for Devt of Shanghai as Int. Financial Centre 2007–. *Address:* Agricultural Bank of China, 69 Jianguomennei Road, Dong Cheng District, Beijing 100005, People's Republic of China (office). *Telephone:* (10) 85106660 (office). *Fax:* (10) 85106661 (office). *E-mail:* webmaster@intl.abocn.com (office). *Website:* www.abchina.com (office).

XIAO, Gang, LLM; Chinese banker; *Chairman, Bank of China;* b. 1959; ed Hunan Inst. of Finance and Econs, Renmin Univ. of China; joined People's Bank of China (PBC) 1981, various roles including Gen. Man. China Foreign Exchange Trading Center, Dir-Gen. Policy Research Dept, Asst Gov. PBC 1996–98, Deputy Gov. 1998–2003, also mem. PBC Monetary Policy Cttee 1998–2003; Pres. Bank of China 2003–04, Chair. 2003–, mem. Bd of Dirs BOC Hong Kong Holdings (subsidiary) 2003–; fmr Deputy 9th Nat. People's Congress; fmr Alt. mem. 8th Chinese CP Guangdong Prov. Cttee. *Address:* Bank of China, 1 Fuxingmen Nei Dajie, Beijing 100818, People's Republic of China (office). *Telephone:* (10) 6659-6688 (office). *Fax:* (10) 6659-3777 (office). *E-mail:* info@boc.cn (office). *Website:* www.boc.cn/static (office).

XIAO, Yang; Chinese party and government official; b. Aug. 1938, Heyuan Co., Guangdong Prov.; ed People's Univ. of China, Beijing; joined CCP 1966; imprisoned during Cultural Revolution 1968–71; teacher of political science and law, Heyuan Co. 1969–75; Deputy Dir Qujiang Co. CCP Cttee Office, then various party posts 1971–81; Sec. CCP Cttee of Wujiang Dist, Shaoguan City, Guangdong Prov. 1981–83; Deputy Sec. Qingyuang Prefectural CCP Cttee, Guangdong 1983; Deputy Chief, Guangdong Prov. Procurator's Office, Deputy Sec. CCP Leadership Group 1983–86; Procurator-Gen. Guangdong Prov. Procurator's Office 1986–90; Deputy Procurator-Gen. Supreme Procurator's Office, Deputy Sec. CCP Leadership Group 1990–92; teacher, China Univ. of Political Science and Law, Beijing 1990; Minister of Justice 1993–98; Pres. Supreme People's Court 1998–2008, China Asscn of Judges 1999–; Alt. mem. 14th CCP Cen. Cttee 1992–97, mem. 15th CCP Cen. Cttee 1997–2002, 16th CCP Cen. Cttee 2002–07; Vice-Chair. Cen. Cttee for Comprehensive Man. of Public Security 1998. *Address:* c/o Supreme People's Court, 27 Dongjiaominxiang, Beijing 100745, People's Republic of China (office).

XIAO, Yaqing; Chinese engineer, business executive and academic; *President, China Aluminum Corporation (CHINALCO);* b. 1959, Beijing; ed Cen. South Univ. of Tech.; began working as engineer 1982; fmr Dept Head and Chief Engineer, Tech. Div., Northeast Light Alloy Fabrication Plant; fmr Gen. Man. Northeast High Alloy Corpn Ltd; fmr Factory Man. Southwest Aluminum Fabrication Plant (renamed Southwest Aluminum Industry Group 1999), Chair. and Gen. Man. 1999–2003; Pres. China Aluminum Corpn (CHINALCO) 2003–; Chair. and Gen. Man. Chalco Ltd; Vice-Chair. China Non-ferrous Metals Fabrication Asscn; part-time Prof., Cen. South Univ. of Tech., Chongqing Univ. *Address:* China Aluminum Corpn (CHINALCO), 12B Fuxing Road, Haidian District, Beijing 100814, People's Republic of China (office). *Telephone:* (10) 63971767 (office). *Fax:* (10) 63971690 (office). *E-mail:* webmaster@chalco.com.cn (office). *Website:* www.chinalco.com (office); www .chalco.com.cn (office).

XIE, Heping, DEng, PhD; Chinese mining engineer and university administrator; *President, Sichuan University;* b. Jan. 1956, Shuangfeng Co., Hunan Prov.; ed China Univ. of Mining and Tech.; joined CCP 1986; Prof., China Univ. of Mining and Tech., Beijing 1990, Dean, Postgraduate Dept 1992, Pres. China Univ. of Mining and Tech. 1998, also Deputy Sec., China Univ. of Mining and Tech. CCP Cttee 1999–2000, Sec. 2000; currently Pres. Sichuan Univ.; Alt. mem. 17th CCP Cen. Cttee 2007–; mem. Chinese Acad. of Eng 2001–; numerous awards including Award of Chinese Youth Scientists 1993, Nat. Prize of Natural Sciences 1995, Nat. Prize of Progress in Science and

Tech. 1999, 2000, Ho Leung Ho Lee Prize. *Publications:* five books in English and Chinese and over 150 journal papers. *Address:* Office of the President, Sichuan University, 24 South Section 1, Yihuan Road, Chengdu 610065, Sichuan Province, People's Republic of China (office). *Telephone:* (28) 85403116 (office). *Fax:* (28) 85403260 (office). *E-mail:* wsc@scu.edu.cn (office). *Website:* www.scu.org.cn (office).

XIE, Jun; Chinese chess player; b. 30 Oct. 1970, Beijing; Nat. Jr Champion 1984, 1985; Nat. Women's Champion 1989, World Women's Champion 1991–96, 1999–2001; Grandmaster 1991; f. Xie Jun Chess Skill Centre to promote chess in China 2001; took part as flame bearer, Olympic Torch Relay, Yanji, Jilin Prov. July 2008. *Address:* c/o State General Bureau of Physical Culture and Sports, 9 Tiyuguan Lu, Beijing 100061, People's Republic of China (office).

XIE, Qihua; Chinese steel industry executive; *Chairwoman, China Metallurgical Council;* b. June 1943, Shanghai; ed Tsinghua Univ., Beijing Municipality; trained as engineer; began career in steel industry 1968; joined Shanghai Baoshan Iron & Steel Group 1978, held positions successively as Planning Section Chief, Asst Commdr and Vice-Commdr of Baosteel Project HQ, Dir and Deputy Man. of Group Eng HQ, Dir of Planning and Devt Dept 1993–94, Deputy Pres. and Gen. Man. 1994–98, Vice-Chair. and Pres.; Pres. Shanghai Baosteel Group Corpn (following merger of Baoshan Iron & Steel with Shanghai Metallurgical and Meishan Steel to form new co. 1998) 1998–2004, 2005, Chair. and Pres. 2004–07 (retd); Alt. mem. 16th CCP Cen. Cttee 2002–07; Chair. China Fed. of Industrial Econs Presidium; Chair. China Metallurgical Council; Vice-Chair. China Iron & Steel Asscn (Chair. 2005–), China Women Entrepreneur Asscn, China Group Cos Promotion Asscn, China Investment Asscn, China Enterprise Confed., China Enterprise Dirs Asscn; Shanghai Excellent Entrepreneur 1995, 1995, Outstanding Entrepreneur of Shanghai Municipality, Nat. Outstanding Female Entrepreneur, ranked by Fortune magazine amongst 50 Most Powerful Women in Business outside the US 2002–03, (second) 2004, (second) 2005, (sixth) 2006, Chinese Businesswoman of 2003, ranked by Forbes magazine amongst 100 Most Powerful Women (55th) 2004, (14th) 2005, Outstanding Contrib. to Chinese Enterprise Prize 2004. *Address:* c/o Shanghai Baosteel Group Corporation, Baosteel Tower, Pudian Road 370, Pudong New Distict, Shanghai, People's Republic of China (office).

XIE, Shijie; Chinese administrator; *Chairman, Standing Committee, Sichuan People's Congress;* b. 1934, Liangping Co., Sichuan Prov.; ed South-West Agricultural Coll.; joined CCP 1954; apptd Dir Ya'an Agricultural School, Sichuan Prov. 1959; fmr Deputy Sec., later Sec. CCP Ya'an Prefectural Cttee, Sichuan Prov.; mem. Standing Cttee CCP Sichuan Prov. Cttee 1985–92, Deputy Sec. CCP Sichuan Prov. Cttee 1992–93, Sec. 1993–2000; Vice-Gov. of Sichuan Prov. 1985–1992; Deputy, 8th NPC 1993–98, 9th NPC 1998–2003; Chair. Standing Cttee of NPC, Sichuan Prov. 1998–; mem. 14th CCP Cen. Cttee 1992–1997, 15th CCP Cen. Cttee 1997–2002. *Address:* Standing Committee of Sichuan People's Congress, Chengdu, Sichuan Province, People's Republic of China (office).

XIE, Tieli; Chinese film director; b. 1925, Huaiyin Co., Jiangsu Prov.; joined CCP 1942; film dir, Beijing Film Studio; mem. 5th Nat. Cttee Chinese Fed. of Literary and Art Circles 1988–93, CPPCC, 8th NPC 1993–98; mem. Educ., Science, Culture and Health Cttee; Vice-Chair. Chinese Film Artists Asscn 1985; leading figure in "Third Generation" of Chinese dirs; Golden Rooster Lifetime Achievement Award 2005. *Films include:* Early Spring in February (Zao Chun Er Yue) 1963, Violent Storm, Taking Tiger Mountain by Strategy 1970. *Address:* Beijing Film Studio, 19 Beihuan Xilu Road, Beijing 100088, People's Republic of China (office).

XIE, Xuren; Chinese economist and government official; *Minister of Finance;* b. 1947, Ningbo City, Zhejiang Prov.; ed Zhejiang Univ.; began career as technician, Ningbo Zhenhai Machinery Factory, Ningbo City 1967, served as Section Chief and later Deputy Dir –1981; Magistrate, People's Court, Zhejiang Prov. 1984–85; Dir Investment and Planning Offices, Prov. Planning and Econ. Comm., Zhejiang Prov. 1985–88; Deputy Dir Prov. Planning and Econ. Comm. 1988–90; Deputy Dir Budget Dept, Ministry of Finance 1990–91, Deputy Dir Planning Dept 1990–93, Dir Planning Dept and Asst to Minister 1993–94, Dir Reforms Dept 1994–95, Vice-Minister 1995–98; Pres. Agricultural Devt Bank of China 1998–2000; Vice-Minister, State Econ. and Trade Comm. 2001–03; Dir State Admin of Taxation 2003–07; Minister of Finance 2007–; joined CCP 1980, Deputy Sec., Yinxian Co. Cttee 1984–85, Deputy Sec., Work Cttee Depts, Financial Work Cttee, CCP Cen. Cttee 2000–01, Deputy Sec., Leading Party Group, CCP 2001–03, Alt. mem. 16th CCP Cen. Cttee 2002–07, mem. 17th CCP Cen. Cttee 2007–. *Address:* Ministry of Finance, 3 Nansanxiang, Sanlihe, Xicheng Qu, Beijing 100820, People's Republic of China (office). *Telephone:* (10) 68551888 (office). *Fax:* (10) 68533635 (office). *E-mail:* webmaster@mof.gov.cn (office). *Website:* www.mof.gov.cn (office).

XIE, Zhenhua; Chinese civil servant; *Vice Minister, State Development and Reform Commission;* b. Oct. 1949, Tianjin; ed Tsinghua Univ., Beijing, Wuhan Univ. Environmental Law Research Inst.; joined CCP 1969; Sec. Production and Construction Corps, Heilongjiang Prov. 1979–80; teaching asst, No. 2 Subsidiary School, Tsinghua Univ. 1979–80 (Sec. CCP Revolutionary Cttee); Org. Sec. CCP Party Cttee State Construction Comm. 1980–82; various man. roles, Ministry of Urban and Rural Construction and Environmental Protection 1982–88; Deputy Dir State Environment Protection Bureau 1990–93, Dir 1993–2007; apptd Vice-Chair. and Sec.-Gen. Environmental Protection Cttee of the State Council 1993, Nat. Cttee for the Patriotic Public Health Campaign 1994; apptd Chair. Chinese Comm. for Certification of Produce Conformity and Environmental Standards 1994; apptd Dir Specialists Examination Cttee of Nuclear Environment 1994; Vice-Minister, State Devt and Reform Comm.

2007–; Del., 15th CCP Nat. Congress 1997–2002; mem. 15th CCP Cen. Cttee for Discipline Inspection 1997–2002, 16th CCP Cen. Cttee 2002–07, 17th CCP Cen. Cttee for Discipline Inspection 2007–; Global Environment Facility (GEF) Leadership Award (jt winner) 2002, UNEP Sasakawa Environment Prize (jt winner) 2003. *Address:* State Development and Reform Commission, 38 Yuetannan Jie, Xicheng Qu, Beijing 100824, People's Republic of China (office).

XIMENES BELO, Mgr Carlos Filipe, SDB; Timor-Leste ecclesiastic; b. 3 Feb. 1948, Baucau, Dili; ordained priest 1980; consecrated Titular Bishop of Lorium 1988; Papal Admin. Dili; active in campaign for human rights in Timor-Leste; fmr Apostolic Admin. to Bishopric of Dili (resgnd 2002); Jt winner Nobel Peace Prize (with José Ramos-Horta q.v.) 1996. *Address:* Bishop's Residence, Av. Direitos Humanos, Bidan Lecidere, CP 4, Dili 88010, Timor-Leste. *Telephone:* (390) 321177.

XING, Bensi; Chinese philosopher and academic; b. 7 Oct. 1929, Sheng Co., Zhejiang Prov.; s. of Xing Tinxu and Guei Yuyin; m. Zhou Bangyuan 1953; two d.; ed Special School of Russian Language of CCP Cen. Cttee; joined CCP 1950; teacher, Beijing Inst. of Russian Language 1952–56; Asst Researcher and Academic Sec. Inst. of Philosophy under Chinese Acad. of Sciences 1957–66, Deputy Dir, Dir, Vice-Chair. Academic Cttee, under Chinese Acad. of Social Sciences 1978–82, Academician 1983–85; Guest Prof., Qinghua Univ. 1984–; mem. Council for Int. Cultural Exchange 1984; Deputy Gen. Ed. Philosophy Vol. of Chinese Encyclopaedia 1983–; Vice-Pres. CCP Cen. Cttee Party School 1988–; Ed.-in-Chief Party journal Qiushi 1994–; NPC Deputy, Zhejiang Prov.; mem. NPC Law Cttee; Visiting Scholar Columbia Univ. 1981. *Publications:* The Dualism of Ludwig Feurbach's Anthropology 1963, The Social Theory and Historical Viewpoint of Saint-Simon 1964, Humanism in the History of European Philosophy 1978, Philosophy and Enlightenment 1979, The Anthropology of Ludwig Feurbach 1981, Philosophy and Time 1984, Philosophy (Introduction to Philosophy Vol. of Chinese Encyclopaedia) 1987, The Past, Present and Future of Philosophy (Introduction, Little Encyclopaedia of Philosophy) 1987 and many other essays. *Leisure interests:* music, literature, Peking Opera, Chinese calligraphy. *Address:* Institute of Philosophy, Chinese Academy of Social Sciences, Beijing, People's Republic of China (office).

XING, Huina; Chinese athlete; b. 25 Feb. 1984, Weifang; coached by Wang Dexian 1999–2005, Yin Yanqin 2006–; 10,000m debut 2001; Bronze Medal, Women's 10,000m, Asian Games 2002; set World Jr record of 30:31.55 in finishing seventh at World Championships, Paris 2003; Gold Medal, Women's 1,500m, Chinese Nat. Championships 2004, 5,000m 2004; first Olympic appearance, Athens, Greece 2004; Gold Medal, Women's 10,000m, Olympic Games, Athens 2004; Fifth Place, Women's 5,000m, World Championships, Helsinki, Finland 2005; ranked 12th, 10,000m, Int. Asscn of Athletics Feds (IAAF) World Rankings 2005; mem. Shandong Athletics Club. *Address:* c/o Chinese Athletics Association, A2 Longtan Road, Beijing 100061, People's Republic of China (office).

XING, Gen. Shizhong; Chinese army officer; b. Sept. 1938, Licheng Co., Shandong Prov.; ed Nanjing Eng Army School; joined PLA 1953, CCP 1957; staff officer in a div. engineer section 1959, a div. operational training section 1965, commdr of corps-affiliated eng bn 1969, regt commdr 1975, chief of corps operational training div. 1978, div. chief of staff 1978, div. commdr 1979, corps commdr 1983, Chief of Staff, Lanzhou Mil. Region 1985–88, Deputy Commdr 1988; Deputy Commdr Jinan Mil. Region 1995–96; Commandant Nat. Defence Univ. 1995–2002; mem. 15th CCP Cen. Cttee 1997–2002; mem. 10th Standing Committee of NPC 2003–; Group Leader, State Language Work Cttee 2003–; rank of Maj.-Gen. 1988, Lt-Gen. 1993, Gen. 1998. *Address:* National Defence University, Beijing, People's Republic of China (office).

XIONG, Gen. Guangkai; Chinese diplomatist and army officer (retd); *Chairman, China Institute for International and Strategic Studies (CIISS);* b. March 1939, Nanchang City, Jiangxi Prov.; ed August 1st Middle School, Beijing, PLA Training School for Foreign Languages, PLA Mil. Acad.; joined PLA 1956, CCP 1959; worker, Data Office, Intelligence Dept, PLA HQ of the Gen. Staff, 1957–60; translator, secretarial Asst Office of Mil. Attaché, Chinese Embassy, GDR 1960–72; Asst Mil. Attaché, Chinese Embassy, FRG 1972–80; Asst Div. Chief, Intelligence Dept, Gen. Staff HQ 1983–85, Deputy Dir 1985–87, Dir 1987–88, Asst to Chief of Gen. Staff 1988–92, Deputy Chief of Gen. Staff 1996–2005; Chair. China Inst. for Int. and Strategic Studies (CIISS); Alt. mem. 14th CCP Cen. Cttee 1992–97, mem. 15th CCP Cen. Cttee 1997–2002, 16th CCP Cen. Cttee 2002–07; mem. Cen. Cttee Leading Group on Taiwan 1993; rank of Maj.-Gen. 1988, Lt-Gen. 1993, Gen. 2000; Head of mil. del. to USA 1995. *Address:* China Institute for International and Strategic Studies, No. 3, Toutiao,Taijichang, Beijing 100005, People's Republic of China (office).

XIONG, Shen; Chinese mechanical engineer and academic; b. 13 Sept. 1935, Jiangsu Prov.; s. of Shen Baozhang and Xu Shifeng; m. Xia Xuejian 1965; one d.; ed Tsinghua Univ., Beijing; Prof. Dept of Eng Mechanics, Tsinghua Univ. 1959–; several prizes including State Prize of Science Congress 1978, Prize of Science and Tech. of State Bureau of Instrumentation Industry 1981, Prizes of Science and Tech., State Educational Comm. 1986, 1988, State Prize of Invention 1992, Prize of Zhou Peiyuan Foundation 1992, State Prize of Excellent Book in Science and Tech. 1992. *Publications include:* Modern Techniques and Measurements in Fluid Flows 1989, Fluid Velocity Measurement Techniques (in Chinese) 1987, Laser Doppler Velocimetry and Its Applications (in Chinese) 2004. *Leisure interests:* music, playing piano and accordion. *Address:* Department of Engineering Mechanics, Tsinghua University, Beijing 100084, People's Republic of China (office). *Telephone:* (10) 62784476 (office). *Fax:* (10) 62785576 (office). *E-mail:* shenx@tsinghua.edu.cn (office).

XODJAYEV, Batir Asadillaevich; Uzbekistani politician; *Minister of the Economy;* fmr Prof., Univ. of World Economy and Diplomacy, Tashkent; Minister of the Economy 2006–. *Address:* Ministry of the Economy, 100003 Tashkent, O'zbekiston shox ko'ch. 45A, Uzbekistan (office). *Telephone:* (71) 132-63-20 (office). *Fax:* (71) 132-63-72 (office). *E-mail:* mineconomy@mmes.gov.uz (office). *Website:* www.mineconomy.uz (office).

XONGERIN, Badai; Chinese Inner Mongolia administrator, writer and poet; b. 5 June 1930, Bayinguoltng Prefecture, Hejin Co., Xinjiang; s. of Honger Xongerin and Bayinchahan Xongerin; m. 1952; two s. two d.; Pres. Xinjiang Broadcasting and TV Univ. 1982–; Chair. Cttee of Xinjiang Uygur Autonomous Region of CPPCC 1989; mem. Standing Cttee CPPCC 1991. *Publications:* several books of prose, poetry and history in Mongol language and Chinese. *Leisure interests:* history of poetry, writing plays, Mongol history. *Address:* 15 South Beijing Road, Urumqi, Xinjiang, People's Republic of China. *Telephone:* (991) 2825701 (office); (991) 3839303 (home). *Fax:* (991) 2823443.

XU, Anbi; Chinese potter; b. March 1953, Yixing, Jiangxi Prov.; began practising pottery decoration 1976; exhibited in the USA, Japan, France, Canada, Australia; named one of the ten best handicraftsmen in China 1997. *Address:* Yixing Jingtao Group, Yixing, Jiangxi Province, People's Republic of China (office).

XU, Bing, MFA; Taiwanese artist; b. 8 Feb. 1955, Chongqing; s. of Hua-min Xu and Shi-ying Yang; ed Cen. Acad. of Fine Arts, Beijing; Asst Prof. Printmaking Dept, Cen. Acad. of Fine Arts 1987–, Assoc. Dir 1988–; Hon. Adviser, Dept of Art, Beijing Univ. 1989–; exhbns in China, France, USA, Switzerland, UK, Italy, Japan, Germany, Turkey 1979–; one man exhbns Beijing Art Gallery 1988, Taipei 1988, Taiwan 1990; mem. Chinese Engraving Artists' Asscn 1981–, Chinese Artists' Asscn 1982–, Dir 1985–; Dir Chinese Engraving Artists' Asscn 1986–; mem. Acad. Affairs Cttee, Cen. Acad. of Fine Arts 1988–; mem. Printmaking Artists' Cttee, Chinese Fine Arts Asscn 1989–; mem. Appraisal Cttee, 7th Chinese Nat. Exhbn of Fine Arts 1989; Hon. Fellow, Art Dept, Univ. of Wisconsin at Madison 1990; prizes from Art Exhbns. of Chinese Young Artists' Works 1980, 1985, 8th Exhbn of China's Wooden Paintings 1983, Medal, 9th Chinese Engraving Exhbn 1986, Award for Excellent Prints, Taiwan 1988, Henry E. T. Kok Educ. Foundation Prize for Young Instructors at Insts of Higher Learning 1989, Artes Mundi Prize 2004. *Publications:* Wooden Painting Sketches of Xu Bing 1986, Engravings of Xu Bing; numerous articles in magazines and newspapers. *Leisure interest:* hiking.

XU, Caidong; Chinese administrator and engineer; b. 1919, Fengxin Co., Jiangxi Prov.; ed Tangshan Inst., Jiaotong Univ., Shanghai and Grenoble Inst., France; returned to China 1955; Prof., Guizhou Eng Inst. 1958–; Pres., Science Acad. of Guizhou Prov. 1978, now Hon. Pres.; Vice-Gov. Guizhou Prov. 1983; mem. Dept of Tech. Sciences, Academia Sinica 1985–; Vice-Chair. Jiu San Soc. 1983–; mem. 7th Nat. People's Congress, 8th NPC 1993–98, mem. Educ., Science, Culture and Public Health Cttee; NPC Deputy, Guizhou Prov.; Fellow, Chinese Acad. of Sciences 1980–. *Publication:* The Physical Chemistry of Zinc. *Address:* Guizhou Provincial People's Government, Guiyang, Guizhou Province, People's Republic of China (office).

XU, Gen. Caihou; Chinese army officer; *Vice-Chairman, Central Military Commission, Chinese Communist Party Central Committee;* b. 1943, Wafangdian City, Liaoning Prov.; ed Harbin Inst. of Mil. Eng and PLA Mil. Eng Acad., PLA Inst. of Political Sciences; sent to do manual labour (Farm of the 39th Army) 1968–70; joined CCP 1971; soldier, Jilin Mil. Dist (Third Regt, Second Bn), PLA Shenyang Mil. Region 1970–71; Deputy Political Instructor, Shenyang Garrison (3rd Div., 3rd Artillery Regt, 1st Bn, 2nd Co.), PLA Shenyang Mil. Region 1971–72; Sec., later Deputy Chief, Jilin Mil. Dist (Political Dept), PLA Shenyang Mil. Region 1972–82, Chief of Personnel Div. and of Office for Retired Officers 1982–83, Deputy Dir Political Dept 1983–84, Dir 1985–90; Political Commissar, Army Group, PLA Services and Arms 1990–92; Asst Dir PLA Gen. Political Dept 1992–93, Dir-Gen. PLA Gen. Political Dept 2003–05; Dir Jiefangjun Bao (Liberation Army Daily) 1993, Vice-Dir 1993–99, Exec. Vice-Dir 1999–; Political Commissar, PLA Jinan Mil. Region 1996–99; mem. 15th CCP Cen. Cttee 1997–2002, 15th CCP Cen. Mil. Comm. 1999, 16th CCP Cen. Cttee 2002–07, 16th CCP Cen. Cttee Politburo Secr. 2002, 16th CCP Cen. Mil. Comm. 2002–04 (Vice-Chair. 2004–07), mem. 17th CCP Cen. Cttee 2007–, also mem. Politburo and Vice-Chair. Cen. Mil. Comm. 2007–; rank of Maj.-Gen. 1990, Lt-Gen. 1993, Gen. 1999. *Address:* People's Liberation Army General Political Department, Beijing, People's Republic of China (office).

XU, Guanhua; Chinese scientist and politician; b. 1945, Shanghai; ed Beijing Inst. of Forestry; research intern, teacher, Asst Research Fellow, Chinese Acad. of Forestry Sciences; Researcher, Stockholm Univ., Sweden 1979–81, Research Fellow and Dir Natural Resources Information Inst.; joined CCP 1984; Asst Research Fellow, Inst. of Remote Sensing Application, Chinese Acad. of Sciences 1964–93, Fellow, Chinese Acad. of Sciences 1991, Research Prof., Dir 1993, Vice-Pres. 1994–95, Chair. Div. of Earth Sciences 1996; Vice-Chair. State Science and Tech. Comm. 1995; Vice-Minister of Science and Tech. 1998, Minister 2001–07; mem. 9th CPPCC Nat. Cttee 1998–2003; mem. 16th CCP Cen. Cttee 2002–07; awarded title of Outstanding Scientist. *Address:* c/o Ministry of Science and Technology, 15 B. Fuxing Road, Beijing 100862, People's Republic of China (office).

XU, Houze; Chinese geodesist and geophysicist; b. 4 May 1934, Anhui; s. of Xu Zuoren and Jiang Xinghua; m. Yang Huiji 1967; one s. one d.; ed Tongji Univ., Shanghai; Asst Researcher, Inst. of Geodesy and Geophysics, Chinese Acad. of Sciences 1963, Assoc. Prof. 1978, Prof. 1982–, Dir 1983–, Fellow 1991–; Dir Survey and Geophysics Inst. 1992–; mem. Chinese Geophysics Soc. 1978–; Vice-Pres. Int. Gravimetry Cttee and Pres. Perm. Cttee of Earth Tides,

Int. Asscn of Geodesy 1983–; Vice-Pres. Science-Tech. Soc. of Hubei Prov. 1984–, Chinese Survey and Mapping Soc. 1985–; Prof., Tongji Univ. 1985–, Wuhan Tech. Univ. of Survey and Mapping 1986–, Shandong Univ. of Tech.; NPC Deputy, Hubei Prov.; Ho Leung Ho Lee Foundation Earth Sciences Prize. *Publications:* The Approximation of Stokes' Function and the Estimation of Trunction Error 1981, The Effect of Oceanic Tides on Gravity Tide Observations 1982, The Tidal Correction in Astrometry 1982, Accuracy Estimation of Loading Correction in Gravity Observation 1984, The Effect of Different Earth Models on Load Tide Correction 1985, Representation of Gravity Field outside the Earth using Fictitious Single Layer Density 1984, Collected Papers on Earth Tides 1988, Model of Oceanic Load Tide Correction in Chinese Continent 1988. *Address:* 54 Xu Dong Road, Wuchang 430077, Hubei Province, People's Republic of China. *Telephone:* 813405.

XU, Maj.-Gen. Huaizhong; Chinese writer; b. 1929, Hebei Prov.; s. of Xu Hongchang and Xin Zhuoliang; m. Yu Zengxiang; one s. two d.; mem. Presidium and Bd of Dirs, Chinese Writers' Asscn 1983–; Deputy Cultural Dir, Gen. Political Dept of PLA 1985–88, Dir 1988–; rank of Maj.-Gen. 1988; mem. Nat. Cttee CPPCC 1993–98; Vice-Chair. Chinese Writers' Asscn 1996–; a Deputy Head Propaganda Dept, CCP 5th Fujian Prov. Cttee 1989–96. *Publications:* Rainbow over the Earth, On the Tibetan Highlands, Anecdotes from the Western Front, The Wingless Angel (collection of medium-length novels and short stories), The Selected Works of Xu Huaizhong 1989. *Leisure interests:* playing table tennis and traditional Chinese shadow boxing. *Address:* 21 North Street Andeli, East District, Beijing, People's Republic of China.

XU, Gen. Huizi; Chinese army officer and party official; b. 9 Dec. 1932, Penglai Co., Shandong Prov.; joined PLA 1948, CCP 1950; Deputy Chief of Gen. Staff 1985–95, rank of Lt-Gen. 1988, Gen. 1994; Pres. Acad. of Mil. Sciences 1995–97; mem. Preliminary Working Cttee of the Preparatory Cttee of the Hong Kong Special Admin. Region 1993–97; Vice-Chair. People's Air Defence Cttee 1988–; Deputy Sec. for Discipline Inspection 1994–; mem. 12th CCP Cen. Cttee 1982–87, 13th CCP Cen. Cttee 1987–92, 14th CCP Cen. Cttee 1992–97; Del., 15th CCP Nat. Congress 1997–2002; Deputy, 8th NPC 1993–98, mem. Standing Cttee 9th NPC 1998–2003, Vice-Chair. Cttee of Overseas Chinese Affairs 1998–2003. *Address:* c/o Standing Committee of National People's Congress, Beijing, People's Republic of China (office).

XU, Jialu; Chinese linguist; *Vice-Chairman of 10th Standing Committee, National People's Congress;* b. June 1937, Beijing; ed Beijing Normal Univ.; Prof., fmr Vice-Pres. Beijing Normal Univ. 1959–; fmr Pres. Chinese Soc. for Exegetical Studies of Classical Chinese Literature; joined China Asscn for Promoting Democracy 1987; Vice-Chair. CPPCC Beijing Municipal Cttee 1988; Chair. State Language Work Cttee 1994–; Vice-Chair. 9th Cen. Cttee of China Asscn for Promoting Democracy, Chair. 10th Cen. Cttee 1997–2002; apptd Pres. China Council for the Promotion of Peaceful Reunification 1999; mem. Govt Del., Macao Hand-Over Ceremony, Macao Special Admin. Region Preparatory Cttee 1999; mem. Standing Cttee of 7th and 8th NPC 1988–98, Vice-Chair. Standing Cttee of 9th NPC 1998–2003, of 10th NPC 2003–. *Address:* Beijing Normal University, Xinjiekouwai Street 19, Beijing 100875, People's Republic of China (office).

XU, Jianyi, MBA; Chinese business executive; *CEO, China FAW Group;* Vice-Chair. FAW Car Co. Ltd –2008, Chair. 2008–, fmr Deputy Gen. Man., now Gen. Man. China FAW Group Corpn; mem. Jilin Prov. Standing Cttee and Sec. of Jinlin City. *Address:* China FAW Group, 2259 Dongfeng Street, Changchun 130011, People's Republic of China (office). *Fax:* (431) 87614780 (office). *E-mail:* info@faw.com (office). *Website:* www.faw.com (office).

XU, Jiayin; Chinese real estate executive; *President, Evergrande Real Estate Group Ltd;* b. 1958, Henan; ed Wuhan Univ. of Science and Tech.; founder, Guangzhou Hengda Group 1996, renamed Evergrande Real Estate Group Ltd, currently Pres. and Sec.; mem. CCP; Deputy Chair. China Enterprise Confed., China Entrepreneur Asscn, China Real Estate Asscn, Guangdong Fund for Justice and Courage, Guangdong Private Enterprise Chamber, Guangdong General Chamber of Commerce; Pres. Guangzhou Real Estate Asscn; Hon. Chair. Guangdong Charity Fed.; mem. 11th CPPCC Nat. Cttee; Deputy 12th Guangzhou NPC; numerous awards including one of the People of the Year, Guangzhou Business Circles Award 2005. *Address:* Evergrande Real Estate Group, Tianlun Building, No. 45 Tianhe Road, Guangzhou, Guangdong, People's Republic of China (office). *Website:* www.gzhengda.com.cn (office).

XU, Kuangdi; Chinese politician and educationist; *President Chinese Academy of Engineering;* b. 1937, Tongxiang Co., Zhejiang Prov.; ed Beijing Metallurgy Inst.; asst, Beijing Metallurgy Inst. 1959–63; May 7th Cadre School (Fengyang) 1971–72; Asst, later Lecturer, Metallurgical Dept, Shanghai Inst. of Mechanical Eng 1972–79; Deputy Dean and Assoc. Prof., later Dean and Prof., Metallurgical Dept, Shanghai Polytechnical Univ. 1980–86, Exec. Vice-Pres. Shanghai Polytechnical Univ. 1986–89; joined CCP 1983; Deputy Dir Educ. and Public Health Office, Shanghai 1989–91; Dir Shanghai Higher Educ. Bureau 1989–91; Dir Shanghai Planning Comm. 1991–92; Vice-Mayor of Shanghai Municipality 1992–95, Mayor 1995–2001; mem. Standing Cttee CCP Shanghai Municipal Cttee 1992, Deputy Sec. 1994–2001; Dir Labour and Wages Cttee, Shanghai Municipality 1993; Vice-Pres. China Mayors' Asscn 1996; Sec. CCP Leading Party Group of Chinese Acad. of Eng 2001–, Pres. Chinese Acad. of Eng 2002–, also Chair. China Fed. of Industrial Econs (CFIE); Alt. mem. 14th CCP Cen. Cttee 1992–97, mem. 15th CCP Cen. Cttee 1997–2002, 16th CCP Cen. Cttee 2002–07; Vice-Chair. 10th CPPCC Nat. Cttee 2003–; Fellow, Chinese Acad. of Sciences (Div. of Chemical, Metallurgical and Materials Eng) 1995–; Hon. DEng (NYU Poly) 2007; Hon. Pres. Red Cross Soc. of China 1996; honoured for his achievements in some key projects in 6th Five-Year Plan 1986; Royal Acad. of Engineering (RAE) Int. Medal 2008. *Publication:* The Refining of Stainless Steel. *Address:* Chinese Academy of Engineering, 2 Bingjiaokou Hutong, Xicheng District, Beijing 100088, People's Republic of China (office).

XU, Lejiang, MBA; Chinese steel industry executive; *Chairman, Baosteel Group Corporation;* b. Feb. 1959; ed Jiangxi Metallurgy Inst., Univ. of West Virginia, USA, Fudan Univ.; mem. CCP; joined Baosteel 1982, mem. Bd of Dirs 1998–, Vice-Pres. 1998–2004, Pres. 2004–07, Chair. Baoshan Iron and Steel Co. Ltd 2006–07, 2007–, concurrently Dir and Pres. Baosteel Group Corpn 2005–07, Chair. 2007–; Deputy Chair. HKU Alumni Asscn of Chinese Mainland; Alt. mem. 17th CCP Cen. Cttee 2007–. *Address:* Baosteel Group Corpn, Baosteel Tower, 370 Pudian Road, Shanghai 200122, People's Republic of China (office). *Telephone:* (21) 58350000 (office). *Fax:* (21) 68404832 (office). *E-mail:* info@baosteel.com (office). *Website:* www.baosteel.com (office).

XU, Qin; Chinese politician; b. 1928, Suizhong Co., Fengtian (now Liaoning) Prov.; joined CCP 1949; Deputy for Jiangxi to 5th NPC 1978; Vice-Gov. Jiangxi 1979–83; Deputy Sec. CCP Cttee, Jiangxi Prov. 1981; Vice-Chair. Jiangxi People's Congress 1981, Chair. Feb. 1988; Alt. mem. 12th CCP Cen. Cttee 1982–87; mem. 8th NPC 1993–98; NPC Deputy, Jiangxi Prov. *Address:* Jiangxi Provincial Chinese Communist Party, Nanchang, Jiangxi, People's Republic of China (office).

XU, Rongkai; Chinese politician; b. Feb. 1942, Chongqing; ed Tsinghua Univ., Beijing; joined CCP 1960; engineer, Sichuan Dongfang Steam Turbine Factory, then Dir Sichuan Dept of Light Industry 1966–91; Vice-Minister of Light Industry 1991–93; Vice-Pres. Chinese Nat. Asscn of Light Industry 1993–95; Deputy Dir Research Centre of State Council 1995–98, Deputy Sec.-Gen. of State Council 1998–2001; Deputy Dir China Comm. of Int. Decade for Disaster Reduction 1998–2001, Nat. Leading Group Concerned With Work Supporting the Army and the People 1999–2001; apptd Vice-Chair. China Int. Cttee for Natural Disaster 2000; Deputy Sec. Yunnan Prov. Cttee 2001–02, Vice-Gov. 2001, Acting Gov. 2001–02, Gov. 2002–06; mem. CCP Yunnan Prov. Cttee 2001–, Deputy Sec. 2001–; mem. 16th CCP Cen. Cttee 2002–07. *Address:* Yunnan Provincial People's Government, Wuhuashan, Kunming 650021, Yunnan Province, People's Republic of China (office).

XU, Rongmao, (), MBA; Chinese business executive and property developer; *Chairman, Shimao Corporation;* b. 1951, Shishi, Fujian Prov.; m.; two c.; ed Univ. of South Australia; moved to Hong Kong to work as stockbroker in 1970s; returned to China to export textiles 1980s; Founder and CEO Shimao Group 1985, currently Chair. Shimao Corpn; investor in high-end property market in Fujian Prov., Beijing and Shanghai; Chair. Shanghai Overseas Chinese Chamber of Commerce; Vice-Chair. Shanghai Business Asscn; mem. 10th Chinese People's Political Consultative Conf. (CPPCC), Sub-Cttee Social and Legal Affairs of CPPCC, Standing Cttee Nat. Business Asscn; mem. Standing Cttee All-China Fed. of Industry and Commerce, Vice-Pres. 2007–; Chair. Shanghai Overseas Chinese Chamber of Commerce, Shanghai Real Estate Chamber of Commerce; Vice-Chair. China Real Estate Chamber of Commerce, Hong Kong Chinese Cultural Asscn, Fujan Overseas Friendship Asscn, Beijing Univ. of Chemical Tech.; Life Hon. Chair. Hong Kong Fed. of Overseas Chinese Asscns, Friends of Hong Kong Asscn; Hon. Chair. Conf. on Non-Independence and Pro-Reunification of China; Hon. Vice-Chair. Council of Shanghai Charity Foundation; Vice-Pres. Chinese Red Cross Foundation; mem. Council of Chinese Overseas Friendship Asscns; Hon. JP; Hon. Prof., Tongji Univ.; Shanghai Magnolia Award, Lilac-Bauhinia Golden Award (govt of Heilongjiang) 2006. *Address:* Shimao Group, Jin Mao Tower, 45th Floor, 88 Shi Ji Avenue, Shanghai, 200121 People's Republic of China (office). *Telephone:* (21) 50473399 (office). *Website:* www.shimaogroup.com (office).

XU, Xianming, LLB; Chinese lawyer and university administrator; *President, Shandong University;* b. 1957, Shandong Prov.; ed Jilin Univ., Wuhan Univ.; Vice-Pres. Shandong Univ. 1985–2001, also Head of Grad. School and Dean of Law School, Pres. Shandong Univ. 2008–; Pres. China Univ. of Political Science and Law, Beijing 2001–08; Deputy, 10th NPC 2003–08; Commr, 10th NPC Law Cttee 2003–08; Vice-Chair. China Law Soc.; First Nat. Social Science Achievement Award for Young Scholars, Ministry of Educ. Social Science Achievement Award. *Address:* Office of the President, Shandong University, 27 Shanda Nanlu, Jinan 250100, Shandong Province, People's Republic of China (office). *Telephone:* (531) 8564854 (office). *Fax:* (531) 8565051 (office). *E-mail:* ipo@sdu.edu.cn (office). *Website:* www.sdu.edu.cn/english (office).

XU, Yinsheng; Chinese government official; *President, Chinese Table Tennis Association;* b. 12 June 1938, Suzhou City, Jiangsu Prov.; m. Chen Liwen; one s.; World Table Tennis Champion three times; joined CCP 1961; Vice-Minister State Physical Culture and Sport Comm. 1977–98; Vice-Dir State Gen. Admin. of Physical Culture; Pres. Chinese Table Tennis Asscn 1979–, Chinese Boxing Asscn 1987–; Exec. Vice-Chair. Preparatory Cttee for 6th Nat. Games 1985; Vice-Pres. Chinese Olympic Cttee 1986–89, 1994–, All-China Sports Fed. 1989–; Exec. Vice-Pres. XIth Asian Games Organizing Cttee 1990–; Pres. Int. Table Tennis Fed. 1997; Deputy, 4th NPC 1975–78, 5th NPC 1978–83, 6th NPC 1983–88, 7th NPC 1988–93, 8th NPC 1993–98. *Publication:* How to Play Table Tennis by Dialectics. *Leisure interests:* tennis, fishing. *Address:* Chinese Table Tennis Association, No. 4 Tiyuguan Road, Beijing 100061, People's Republic of China (office). *Website:* http://tabletennis.sport.org.cn (office).

XU, Gen. Yongqing; Chinese army officer; *Political Commissar, Chinese People's Armed Police Force;* b. 1938, Jiande Co., Zhejiang Prov.; joined PLA 1956, CCP 1956; Deputy Army Political Commissar; Army Group Political Commissar; Political Commissar Zhejiang Mil. Provincial Command; Deputy Political Commissar Lanzhou Mil. Area Command 1994; Political Commissar Chinese People's Armed Police Force 1996–; Del., 14th CCP Nat. Congress 1992–97; mem. 15th CCP Cen. Cttee 1997–2002; rank of Gen. 2000. *Address:* Chinese People's Armed Police Force Headquarters, Beijing, People's Republic of China (office).

XU, Yongyue; Chinese politician; b. July 1942, Zhenping Co., Henan Prov.; ed Beijing Municipal People's Public Security School; joined CCP 1972; served consecutively as Sec. Beijing Municipal People's Public Security School, Gen. Office of Chinese Acad. of Sciences, Gen. Office of Ministry of Educ., Gen. Office of Ministry of Culture 1960–83; Political Sec. to Chen Yun 1983–93; Deputy Sec.-Gen. CCP Cen. Cttee Cen. Advisory Comm. 1988; Deputy Sec. Hebei Prov. Cttee 1994–98; Minister of State Security 1998–2007; Alt. mem. 15th CCP Cen. Cttee 1997–2002, mem. 16th CCP Cen. Cttee 2002–07. *Address:* c/o Ministry of State Security, 14 Dongchangan Jie, Dongcheng Qu, Beijing 100741, People's Republic of China (office).

XU, Youfang; Chinese politician; b. Dec. 1939, Guangde Co., Anhui Prov.; ed Anhui Agricultural Coll.; technician, planner and clerk, later Sec. Office of Forestry, Forestry Bureau, Bajiazi, Jilin Prov. 1963–73; joined CCP 1973; Engineer and Deputy Chief, Planning Div., Forestry Bureau 1973–81 (also Deputy Dir CCP Party Cttee); Dir Forestry Bureau, Jilin Prov. 1983–85; Gen. Man. Forestry Industrial Corpn, Jilin Prov. 1983–85; Dir Forestry Industry Bureau, Ministry of Forestry 1985–86; Vice-Minister for Forestry 1986–93, Minister 1993–97; Vice-Chair. Nat. Greening Cttee 1993–98; Deputy Dir State Council Environment Protection Comm. 1996–97; Vice-Chair. Beijing Greening Cttee 1997; Dir China Forestry Science and Tech. Comm.; Vice-Chair. Nat. Afforestation Comm. 1993–1996; Pres. China Wildlife Conservation Asscn 1993–96; Sec. CCP Heilongjiang Prov. Cttee 1997–2004; Chair. Standing Cttee Heilongjiang Prov. Congress 1999–; mem. 15th CCP Cen. Cttee 1997–2002, 16th CCP Cen. Cttee 2002–07. *Address:* c/o Office of the Governor, Heilongjiang Provincial Government, Harbin City, People's Republic of China.

XU, Yuanhe; Chinese philosopher; b. 1942, Rugao, Jiangsu Prov.; ed Peking Univ.; Asst Research Fellow, Assoc. Research Fellow then Research Fellow Inst. of Philosophy, Chinese Acad. of Social Sciences 1980–; Dir Oriental Philosophy Research Centre, Chinese Acad. of Social Sciences; State Council Prize 1993. *Publications:* Origin and Development of Luo Studies, The School of Reason and the Yuan Society, Confucianism and Oriental Culture, Survey of Chinese Civilization. *Address:* 5 Jian guo men wai Street, Beijing (office); 502 F2, 2T Bei tai pin zhuang Road, Haichian District, Beijing (home); Institute of Philosophy, Chinese Academy of Social Sciences, Beijing, People's Republic of China. *Telephone:* (10) 65137744 (office); (10) 63240875 (home). *Fax:* (10) 63240815 (home).

XU, Zhenshi; Chinese photographer, artist and publisher; b. 18 Aug. 1937, Songjiang Co., Shanghai; s. of Xu Weiqing and Jiang Wanying, step-s. of Cheng Shi-fa; m. Zhang Fuhe 1967; one d.; ed No. 1 High School, Songjiang Co., Zhejiang Acad. of Fine Arts; moved to Beijing 1965; Ed. People's Fine Arts Publishing House 1965–86, Dir Picture Editorial Dept 1986–, Ed.-in-Chief 1992–; mem. China Artists' Asscn; Deputy Sec.-Gen. Spring Festival Pictures Research Centre, Publrs' Asscn of China; Deputy Sec.-Gen. and Assoc. Dir Photography Research Centre; mem. Selection Cttee 3rd, 4th and 5th Nat. Exhbns of Spring Festival Pictures and other exhbns; Assoc. Dir Standing Cttee Spring Festival Pictures; Sr Adviser, Office of East China–UN TIPS Nat. Exploit Bureau 1994–; exhbns in China, Japan, Korea, Hong Kong, Thailand; Vice-Ed.-in-Chief Gouache Vol. of Anthology of Contemporary Chinese Fine Arts 1996; Vice-Pres. Chinese Fan Art Soc. 1997; organized 1st Nat. Exhbn of Calligraphy and Paintings to Help the Poor 1998; Dir Foundation for Underdeveloped Regions in China 1998–; prepared 6th Nat. Exhbn of Spring Festival Pictures 1998; union art exhib., St Petersburg, Russia 2006; numerous awards including Bronze Medal for albums of photographs, Leipzig Int. Book Exhbn 1987, Nat. Award 1993, Model Ed. Nat. Press and Publs System 1997, 1998, State Prize for Spring Festival Pictures 2001, two 6th Nat. Exhbn of Spring Festival Pictures Prizes (China) 1998, Chinese Contemporary Art Achievement Prize, Hong Kong, State Prize of Spring Festival Pictures 2001, Prize of A Brilliant Contrib. 2001, Outstanding People's Artist Award. *Publications:* China's Cultural Relics Unearthed during the Great Cultural Revolution 1973, Travel in China (four vols) 1979–80, Tibet 1981, Travel in Tibet 1981, Costumes of China's Minority Nationalities 1981, Travel in Guilin 1981, Travel Leisurely in China 1981, Travel in Yunnan 1982, China's Flowers in Four Seasons 1982, Poet Li Bai 1983, Native Places of Tang Dynasty Poems 1984, Travel along the Yangtse River 1985, Through the Moongate: A Guide to China's Famous Historical Sites 1986, Waters and Mountains in China 1986, Travel in Guangzhou 1986, China 1987, The Chinese Nation 1989, Poet Du Fu 1989, Selected Works of Xu Zhenshi 1990, 1993, Selected Paintings of Xu Zhenshi 1993, 1994, Boat on the Plateau 1998, Album of Xu Zhenshi's Sketches 1999, Love for China 2003; collection of Xu Zhenshi published in 2003, Love for China 2003. *Leisure interest:* sports. *Address:* People's Fine Arts Publishing House, No. 32 Beizongbu Hutong, Beijing, People's Republic of China (office). *Telephone:* (10) 65244901 (office); (10) 65246353 (home).

XU, Zhihong; Chinese plant physiologist, academic and university administrator; *President, Peking University;* b. 14 Oct. 1942, Wuxi, Jiangsu Prov.; ed Peking Univ.; research student, Chinese Acad. of Sciences Shanghai Plant Physiology Research Inst. 1969; Researcher, Assoc. Research Fellow, Research Fellow, Vice-Dir Chinese Acad. of Sciences Shanghai Plant Physiology Research Inst. 1969–91, Dir 1991–94; Vice-Pres. Chinese Acad. of Sciences and Dir Shanghai Life Science Research Centre 1992–2003, mem. 4th Presidium of Depts, Chinese Acad. of Sciences 2000–; Fellow, Third World of Sciences 1995–, Acad. Chinese Acad. of Sciences 1997– (also Deputy Dean); Pres. Peking Univ. 1999–; Hon. Prof. Hong Kong Univ.; Hon. DrSc (De Montfort) 1994, (Nottingham) 2000, (Hong Kong City) 2001, (Wasada) 2002, (McGill) 2003; Hon. DIur (Melbourne) 2003; Natural Science First Prize,

Third Prize (Chinese Academy of Science) 1990, 1991. *Address:* Peking University, 1 Loudouqiao, Beijing 100871, People's Republic of China (office). *Telephone:* (10) 62752114 (office). *Fax:* (10) 62751207 (office). *Website:* (office).

XU, Zhizhan, MSc; Chinese optical scientist; b. Dec. 1938, Changzhou, Jiangsu Prov.; ed Fudan and Beijing Univs; research student of physics, Peking Univ.; Prof., Shanghai Inst. of Optics and Fine Mechanics, Chinese Acad. of Sciences; Chief Ed. Journal of Optics; Vice-Chair. Optical Soc. of China 1992–; Fellow, Chinese Acad. of Sciences 1992–, Third World Acad. of Sciences 2004–; mem. Standing Cttee 9th CPPCC Nat. Cttee 1998–2003; Nat. Award for Natural Sciences numerous times; Ho Leung Ho Lee Foundation Award. *Publications:* over 300 essays on laser and related studies. *Address:* Shanghai Institute of Optics and Fine Mechanics, Chinese Academy of Sciences, Shanghai 201800, People's Republic of China (office).

XU, Zhonglin; Chinese politician; *Chairman, CPPCC Jiangsu Provincial Committee;* b. Dec. 1943, Wujin Co., Jiangsu Prov.; ed PLA Survey and Cartography Inst., Zhengzhou, CCP Cen. Acad., Beijing; teaching asst, PLA Survey and Cartography Inst. 1962; joined CCP 1964; Deputy Sec., City Instrument, Meter and Electronics Bureau, Xuzhou City, Jiangsu Prov. 1975–80; Deputy Dir Planning and Science Cttees, Xuzhou City 1975–80; Deputy Director, CCP Revolutionary Cttee, Xuzhou City 1980; Vice Mayor of Xuzhou 1980-86, Mayor 1986–89; mem. Standing Cttee CCP Xuzhou Muni-cipal Cttee 1984–89, Dir Org. Dept 1984–86, Deputy Sec. Xuzhou Municipal Cttee 1986–89; Deputy Dir Org. Dept, CCP Jiangsu Prov. Cttee 1989–91, Dir 1991–94 (mem. Standing Cttee 1992–99), Deputy Sec. CCP Jiangsu Prov. Cttee 1994–99; mem. Standing Cttee CCP Anhui Prov. Cttee 1999–2002, Deputy Sec. CCP Anhui Prov. Cttee 1999–2002; Gov. Anhui Prov. 2001–02; mem. Standing Cttee CCP Jiansu Prov. Cttee 2002–, Deputy Sec. CCP Jiangsu Prov. Cttee 2002–; Chair. CPPCC Jiangsu Prov. Cttee 2003–. *Address:* c/o Jiangsu People's Government, Nanjing, Jiansu Province, People's Republic of China (office).

XUE, Wei; Chinese violinist; b. 21 Dec. 1963, Henan; s. of Xue-Ming and Shang Yi-qing; ed Shanghai Conservatory, Beijing Conservatory of Music and Guildhall School of Music, London; appears regularly with the major London orchestras; performs in solo recitals and as concert soloist at int. music festivals; guest soloist with Shanghai Symphony on tour in Japan; Prof., RAM, London 1989–; numerous prizes including Silver Medal, Tchaikovsky Int. Competition (violin), Moscow 1986; Gold Medal, Carl Flesch Int. Competition 1986; London Philharmonic Soloist of the Year 1986. *Recordings include:* Great Violin Concertos 2001, Dreamland: Xue Wei Plays Chinese Violin Pieces 2002, Xue Wei and the Romance of Cremona 2003, Jue Ban 2008. *Leisure interests:* reading, chess, poker. *Address:* c/o Royal Academy of Music, Marylebone Road, London, NW1 5HT, England.

Y

YAACOB, Nik Mohamed; Malaysian business executive; *Group CEO, Sime Darby Group;* ed Monash Univ., Asian Inst. of Man.; with Sime Darby, fmrly Regional Dir, Dir of Operations, Malaysia, mem. Bd 1990–, mem. Exec. Cttee, CEO 1993–; Dir, DMIB, Sime UEP Properties, Tractors Malaysia holdings, Consolidated Plantations, Port Dickson Power, SD Holdings, Sime Malaysia Region, SIRIM. *Address:* Sime Darby Group, 21st Floor, Wisma Sime Darby, Jalan Raja Laut, 50350 Kuala Lumpur, Malaysia (office). *Telephone:* (3) 26914122 (office). *Fax:* (3) 26987398 (office). *E-mail:* enquiries@simenet.com (office). *Website:* www.simenet.com (office).

YA'ALON, Lt-Gen. Moshe, BA; Israeli army officer; b. 1950, Kiryat Haim; m.; three c.; ed Command and Staff Coll., Camberley, UK, Univ. of Haifa; drafted into Israeli Defence Forces (IDF) 1968, served in Nahal Paratroop Regt; reserve paratrooper during Yom Kippur War 1973, participated in liberation of Suez Canal; held several command positions in IDF Paratroop Brigade, Commdr reconnaisance unit during Litani Operation 1978, later Deputy Commdr, apptd Commdr 1990; served in elite unit 1979–82, later Deputy Commdr; fought in Operation Peace for Galilee; retrained in IDF Armoured Corps 1989–90; apptd CO Judea and Samaria, promoted Brig.-Gen. 1992; Commdr of Ground Forces, Tze'elim 1993; apptd CO Intelligence, rank Maj.-Gen. 1995; apptd CO Cen. Command 1998, IDF Deputy Chief-of-Staff 2000, Chief-of-Staff 2002–05. *Address:* Ministry of Defence, Kaplan Steet, Hakirya, Tel-Aviv 67659, Israel. *Telephone:* 3-5692010. *Fax:* 3-6916940. *E-mail:* public@mod.gov.il. *Website:* www.mod.gov.il.

YABLOKOV, Alexey Vladimirovich, DSc, DBiolSc; Russian population biologist, ecologist and mammologist; *Chairman, Green Russia faction in Yabloko political party;* b. 3 Oct. 1933, Moscow; s. of Vladimir Yablokov and Tatiana Sarycheva; m. 1st Eleonora Bakulina 1955 (died 1987); one s.; m. 2nd Dil'bar Klado 1989; ed Moscow Univ.; researcher, Head of Lab., Prof. N. Koltsov Inst. of Developmental Biology 1959–89; political activities since late 1980s; Chair. Ichthyological Comm. of USSR Ministry of Fishery 1989–92; USSR People's Congress 1989–91; Deputy Chair. Comm. on Ecology of USSR Supreme Soviet 1989–91; State Counsellor on Ecology and Public Health to Pres. of Russia 1991–93; Chair. Interagency Comm. on Environmental Security, Russian Security Council 1993–97, Pres. Centre of Russian Environmental Policy 1993–2005; Regional Councillor for E Europe, N and Cen. Asia 2005–08; Chair. Green Russia political party 2005–06, Green Russia faction in Yabloko political party 2006–; Corresp. mem. USSR (now Russian) Acad. of Sciences 1984, Counsellor 2003–; Pres. Moscow Soc. for Protection of Animals 1988–; mem. Exec. Cttee Stockholm Environmental Inst. 1994–98; Environmental Adviser to Pres. EBRD 1997–99; Vice-Pres. World Conservation Union 2001–04; Pew Fellowship 1994–97; Severtsev Prize 1976, WASA Prize 1995, Busk Medal 1996, Karpinsky Prize 1997, WWF Gold Medal 2002, Nuclear-free Future World Award 2002. *Publications:* 21 books and numerous articles on population, evolution and conservation biology, zoology, ecology, including Population Biology 1987, Nuclear Mythology 1997, Pesticides as a Toxic Problem 1999, Pesticides – The Chemical Weapons that Kill Life 2003, Non-Invasive Study of Mammalian Populations (co-author) 2004, Chernobyl: consequences for people and nature 2007. *Leisure interests:* writing, fishing, carpentry. *Address:* Centre for Russian Environmental Policy, Room 319, 33 Leninksy Prospect, Moscow 119071, Russia (office). *Telephone:* (495) 952-80-19 (office). *Fax:* (495) 952-30-07 (office). *E-mail:* yablokov@ecopolicy.ru (office). *Website:* www.ecopolicy.ru (office); www.rus-green.ru (office).

YABLONOVITCH, Eli, BSc, AM, PhD; physicist and academic; *Professor of Electrical Engineering and Computing Sciences, University of California, Berkeley;* ed McGill Univ., Montreal, Harvard Univ.; Teaching Fellow, Harvard Univ. 1971, 1972, Asst Prof. of Applied Physics 1974–76, Assoc. Prof. 1976–79, Research Assoc. and Head of Optical Sciences Group; mem. Tech. Staff, Bell Telephone Labs 1972–74; mem. Tech. Staff, Exxon Research Center 1979–84; mem. Tech. Staff Bell Communications Research 1984–90, Distinguished Mem. Staff 1990–93, Dir Solid State Physics Research 1991–93; Prof. of Electrical Eng, UCLA 1992–2007, Univ. of California, Berkeley 2007–; Founder W/PECS series of Photonic Crystal Int. Workshops 1999–; mem. NAS 2003–, Nat. Acad. of Eng 2003–; Fellow, Optical Soc. of America 1982–, American Physical Soc. 1990–, IEEE 1992–; Moore Distinguished Scholar, Caltech 2003–04; Dr hc (Royal Inst. of Tech., Sweden) 2004; Alfred P. Sloan Fellow 1978–79, Adolf Lomb Medal, Optical Soc. of America 1978, IEEE/LEOS W. Streifer Scientific Achievement Award 1993, R.W. Wood Prize, Optical Soc. of America 1996, Clifford Paterson Lecturer, Royal Soc. of London 2000, Julius Springer Prize in Applied Physics 2001, Edison Lecture, Notre-Dame Univ. 2004, Anson L. Clark Memorial Lecture, Univ. of Texas, Dallas 2004, Morris Loeb Lecturer, Harvard Univ. 2005. *Address:* 267M Cory Hall, Electrical Engineering and Computer Sciences Department, University of California, Berkeley, Berkeley, CA 94720-1770, USA (office). *Telephone:* (510) 642-6821 (office). *Fax:* (510) 666-3409 (office). *E-mail:* eliy@eecs.berkeley.edu (office). *Website:* optoelectronics.eecs.berkeley.edu (office).

YACHROUTU, Mohamed Caabi El; Comoran politician; fmr Counsellor to Pres. of Repub.; fmr Amb. to France; fmrly Vice-Pres., with responsibility for Finance, the Budget, the Economy, Foreign Trade, Investments and Privatization. *Address:* c/o Ministry of Finance, the Budget and Privatization, BP 324, Moroni, The Comoros (office).

YACOUB, Sir Magdi Habib, Kt, FRCS, FRS; Egyptian cardiac surgeon and academic; *Professor of Cardiothoracic Surgery, National Heart and Lung Institute, Imperial College London;* b. 16 Nov. 1935, Cairo; m.; one s. two d.; ed Univ. of Cairo; British Heart Foundation Prof. of Cardiothoracic Surgery, Royal Brompton and Nat. Heart Lung Inst., Imperial Coll. London 1986–, also Head, Heart Science Centre; Consultant Cardiothoracic Surgeon, Harefield Hosp., Middx 1969–2001; pioneered techniques of repair of complex congenital heart disease, homograft valve surgery and heart, heart-lung and lung transplantation; Hon. MCh (Wales) 1986; Hon. DSc (Loughborough Univ. of Tech.), (Keele) 1995. *Publications:* numerous medical papers. *Leisure interest:* orchid growing. *Address:* National Heart and Lung Institute, Dovehouse Street, London, SW3 6LY, England (office). *Telephone:* (0)1895828 893 (office); (20) 7351-8534. *Fax:* (20) 7351-8229. *E-mail:* m.yacoub@imperial.ac.uk (office). *Website:* www1.imperial.ac.uk/medicine/about/divisions/nhli (office).

YADAV, Lalu Prasad; Indian politician; *Minister of Railways;* b. 1948; m. Rabri Devi; elected to Lok Sabha 1977; Chief Minister of Bihar 1990–97; Leader Rashtriya Janata Dal (Nat. People's Party); Minister of Railways 2004–. *Address:* Ministry of Railways, Rail Bhavan, Raisina Road, New Delhi 110 001 (office); Rashtriya Janata Dal, 13, V. P. House, Rafi Marg, New Delhi 110 011, India. *Telephone:* (11) 23386645 (office). *Fax:* (11) 23382637 (office). *E-mail:* secyrb@rb.railnet.gov.in (office). *Website:* www.indianrailways.gov.in (office).

YADAV, Mulayam Singh, MA; Indian politician; *President, Samajwadi Party;* b. 22 Nov. 1939, Safayee, Etawah Dist; s. of the late Sudhar Singh; m.; one s.; Minister of Co-operative and Animal Husbandry, UP 1977; Pres. Lok Dal 1980; Leader of the Opposition, UP Legis. Council 1982–85, of UP Legis. Ass. 1985–89; Leader Janata Dal Legis. Party UP 1989; Chief Minister of Uttar Pradesh 1989, 1993–95, 2003–07; Minister of Defence 1996–98; Founder-Pres. Samajwadi Party 1992–; Convenor Rashtriya Loktantrik Morcha (Nat. Democratic Front). *Address:* Samajwadi Party, 18 Copernicus Lane, New Delhi, India (office). *Website:* www.samajwadipartymumbai.org (office).

YADAV, Ram Baran, MBBS, MD; Nepalese physician, politician and head of state; *President;* b. 4 Feb. 1948, Sapahi, Dhanusa dist; s. of the late Thani Yadav and Ramrati Yadav; ed Calcutta Medical Coll., Inst. of Medical Educ. and Research, India; worked as physician for more than two decades in hospitals in south Nepal's Terai region; joined Nepali Congress Party 1987, Gen. Sec. –2008 (resgnd); elected to House of Reps 1991, 1994; Minister for Health 1991–94; Pres. of Nepal (first elected Pres.) 2008–. *Address:* Office of the President, Kathmandu, Nepal (office).

YADAV, Sharad, BSc, BEE; Indian politician; *President, Janata Dal (United);* b. 1 July 1947, Babai Dist, Hoshangabad, Madhya Pradesh; m. Rekha Yadav; one s. one d.; ed Jabalpur Eng Coll.; active youth leader, took part in several mass movements; detained 1969–70, 1972, 1975; mem. Lok Sabha (Parl.) 1974–; Pres. Yuva Janata 1977, Yuva Lok Dal 1979; mem. Rajya Sabha 1986–87; Minister of Textiles and Food Processing Industries 1989–90, of Civil Aviation 1999–2001, of Labour 2001–02, of Consumer Affairs, Food and Public Distribution 2002–04; Gen. Sec. Janata Dal 1989–97, Acting Pres. 1995–97, Pres. 1997–(party merged with Lok Shakti to form Janata Dal—United 1999). *Leisure interests:* reading, music, cricket. *Address:* Janata Dal (United), 7 Jantar Mantar Road, New Delhi, 110 001 (office); 7 Tughlak Road, New Delhi, 110 003 India (home). *Telephone:* (11) 23368833 (office); (11) 23792738 (home). *Fax:* (11) 23368138 (office); (11) 23017118 (home).

YADE, Ramatoulaye (Rama); French politician; *Minister of State, attached to the Ministry of Foreign and European Affairs, responsible for Foreign Affairs and Human Rights;* b. 13 Dec. 1976, Dakar, Senegal; m. Joseph Zimet; ed Institut d'études politiques, Paris; immigrated to France with family 1987; Admin. Sénat Local Authorities Dept 2002–07, Deputy Dir Programmes Public Sénat (Parl. TV channel), becoming Dir of Communication 2005–07; Exec. Sec. France–W Africa Friendship Group; joined UMP (Union pour un Mouvement Populaire) 2005, UMP Nat. Sec. for Francophone Affairs 2006; Minister of State, attached to Ministry of Foreign and European Affairs, responsible for Foreign Affairs and Human Rights 2007–; cand. for municipal elections, Colombes 2008. *Publication:* Noirs de France 2007. *Address:* Ministry of Foreign and European Affairs, 37 quai d'Orsay, 75351 Paris Cedex 07, France (office). *Telephone:* 1-43-17-53-53 (office). *Fax:* 1-43-17-52-03 (office). *Website:* www.diplomatie.gouv.fr (office).

YADLIN, Aharon, BA; Israeli politician and educationalist; b. 17 April 1926, Tel-Aviv; s. of Haim Yadlin and Zipora Yadlin; m. Ada Hacohen 1950; three s.; ed Hebrew Univ.; Co-founder Kibbutz Hatzerim; fmr mem. Presidium, Israel Scouts Movement; mem. Exec. Council Histadrut (Israel Fed. of Labour) 1950–52; Prin. Beit Berl (Labour Party's Centre for Educ.) 1956–58; mem. Knesset (Parl.) 1959–79; Deputy Minister of Educ. and Culture 1964–72; Gen. Sec. Israel Labour Party 1972–74; Minister of Educ. and Culture 1974–77; Chair. Educational and Cultural Cttee, Knesset 1977–79; Chair. Beit Berl Coll. of Educ. 1977–85; Chair. Bialik Inst., Books Publishing House and Acad. for Philosophy, Jewish Studies and World Literature 1990–; Sec.-Gen. United Kibbutz Movt (TAKAM) 1985–89; Chair. Beer-Sheva Theatre, Janush Korczak Asscn in Israel, Scientific Cttee Ben Gurion Research Inst. and Archives 1979–85, Yad Tabenkin (Research Centre of Kibbutz Movt), Beith Yatziv Educational Centre, Beer-Sheva, World Labour Zionist Movt 1992–; Chair. Exec. Cttee, Ben Gurion Univ. of the Negev; lecturer and researcher in EFAL (educ. centre of TAKAM); Dr hc (Ben Gurion Univ. of the Negev) 1988. *Publications:* Introduction to Sociology 1957, The Aim and The Movement 1969, articles on sociology, educ. and youth. *Leisure interests:* stamps, gardening. *Address:* World Labour Zionist Movement, Alcharizi 9, Jerusalem (office); Kibbutz Hatzerim, Mobile Post Hanegev 85420, Israel (home).

Telephone: 2-5671184 (office); 8-6473436 (home). *Fax:* 2-5671182 (office); 8-6473199 (home). *E-mail:* wlzm@jazo.org.il (office).

YADOV, Vladimir Aleksandrovich, DPhilSc; Russian sociologist; *Director, Research Centre of Social Transformations, Institute of Sociology, Russian Academy of Sciences;* b. 25 April 1929, Leningrad; m.; one s.; ed Leningrad State Univ., Univ. of Manchester, London School of Econs; with Inst. of Sociological Studies USSR (now Russian) Acad. of Sciences, Inst. of Social and Econ. Problems USSR (now Russian) Acad. of Sciences, Leningrad br. of Inst. of History of Nat. Sciences and Tech.; Dir, Prof. Inst. of Sociology Russian Acad. of Sciences 1986–99, now Dir Research Centre of Social Transformation; Chief Scientific Researcher 1999–; Dean, Inst. of Sociological Educ. at Repub. Centre of Humanitarian Educ. in St Petersburg 1995–; Pres. Russian Sociological Soc. 1991–; mem. Int. Sociological Asscn 1990– (Vice-Pres. 1990–94); mem. European Asscn of Experimental Social Psychology 1989–, Int. Inst. of Sociology 1990–, Centre for Social Sciences and Documentation, Vienna 1991–; Dr hc (Univs of Tartu and Helsinki). *Publications:* numerous papers on theory and methods of sociology, sociology of labour, social psychology of personality and of science. *Address:* Institute of Sociology, Research Centre of Social Transformations, Krzhizhanovskogo str. 24/35, korp 5, 117218 Moscow, Russia. *Telephone:* (495) 719-09-40 (office).

YAGI, Yasuhiro; Japanese engineer; b. 15 Feb. 1920; m.; one s. two d.; ed Imperial Univ., Tokyo; joined Kawasaki Heavy Industries Ltd 1943; Dir and Asst Gen. Supt Mizushima Works 1971–74, Man. Dir 1974–77, Sr Man. Dir Corporate Tech., Engineering and Tubarao Project 1977–79, Exec. Vice-Pres. Corporate Tech. and Tubarao Project 1979–82; Pres. Kawasaki Steel Corpn June 1982–99. *Leisure interests:* golf. *Address:* c/o Kawasaki Steel Corporation, Hibiya Kokusai Building, 2-3, Uchisaiwaicho 2-chome, Chiyoda-ku, Tokyo 100, Japan.

YAGODIN, Gennadiy Alekseyevich; Russian physical chemist and academic; *First Vice-President, International University, Moscow;* b. 3 June 1927, Vyass, Penza region; s. of Alexei Yagodin and Alexandra Yagodina; m. 1949; one s. one d.; ed Mendeleyev Chemical Tech. Inst., Moscow; mem. CPSU 1948–91; Deputy Dean, Mendeleyev Chemical Tech. Inst., Moscow 1956–59, Dean, Dept of Physical Chemistry 1959–63, Prof. of Chemical Tech. 1959–63, 1966–73, Rector 1973–85; Deputy Dir-Gen. (Head of Dept of Training and Technical Information 1963–64, Head of Dept of Technical Operations 1964–66), IAEA, Vienna 1963–66; USSR Minister of Higher and Secondary Specialized Educ. 1985–89; Chair. State Cttee for Nat. Educ. 1988–91; Rector Int. Univ. in Moscow 1992–2001, First Vice-Pres. 2001–; Head Environmental Science Dept, Mendeleyev Chemical Tech. Univ. 2002–; Deputy, USSR Supreme Soviet 1986–89; mem. Cen. Cttee CPSU 1986–89; Corresp. mem. USSR (now Russian) Acad. of Sciences 1976–; mem. Russian Acad. of Educ.; Order of Lenin; D. Y. Mendeleyev Prize 1981, USSR State Prize 1985, Koptyug Prize 2003. *Leisure interest:* collecting butterflies. *Address:* International University, Leningradsky prosp. 17, 125040 Moscow, Russia. *Telephone:* (495) 250-15-43. *Fax:* (502) 221-10-60; (495) 250-15-43 (office); (495) 332-13-15 (home). *E-mail:* yagodin@interrun.ru (office).

YAHAV, Yona, LLB; Israeli politician and lawyer; *Mayor of Haifa;* b. 9 June 1944, Haifa; ed Univ. of Jerusalem, London Univ.; served as Lt-Col in Israeli Mil. Police; mem. of 14th Knesset (Parl.) 1996–2000, parl. posts included Chair. Subcommittee for Banking, mem. Constitution, Law and Justice Cttee, substitute mem., Finance Cttee; fmr Deputy and Alternating Mayor of Haifa, Mayor of Haifa 2003–; Chair. Haifa Econ. Co.; fmr Chair. Petrol and Gas Resources, Govt Co., Municipal Theatre Exec., Haifa Int. Film Festival Org.; fmr Dir-Gen. Haifa Tourist Devt Org., David Ben-Gurion Foundation; fmr Sec.-Gen. World Jewish Student Union; mem. Israeli Labor Party –2006, mem. Kadima party 2006–. *Publications:* The Anatomy of the Fall of the Labor Party (with Prof. Shevach Weiss) 1977, Libel and Slander 1987. *Address:* Office of the Mayor, Municipality of Haifa, Haifa, Israel (office). *Telephone:* 4-8356767 (office). *Fax:* 4-8356020 (office). *E-mail:* haifa@haifa.muni.il (office). *Website:* www.haifa.muni.il (office).

YAKCOP, Tan Sri Nor Mohamed; Malaysian economist and politician; *Minister of Finance II;* b. 24 Aug. 1947, Butterworth, Penang; m.; ed St Xavier's Inst., George Town, Univ. of Malaya, Kuala Lumpur, Leuven Catholic Univ., Belgium; worked at Bank Negara Malaysia 1968–2000, positions included Deputy Man. in 1985, Man. 1986; Special Econ. Adviser to Prime Minister Tun Dr Mahathir Mohamad 1997–98; Dir Khazanah Nasional 2002–04; Minister of Finance II 2004–; mem. Parl. for Tasek Gelugor 2008–; mem. Exec. Cttee Nat. Econ. Action Council; mem. Bd Khazanah Berhad; mem. Barisan Nasional. *Address:* Ministry of Finance, Kompleks Kementerian Kewangan, Presint 2, Pusat Pentadbiran Kerajaan Persekutuan, 62592 Putrajaya, Malaysia (office). *Telephone:* (3) 88823000 (office). *Fax:* (3) 88823893 (office). *E-mail:* pertanyaan@treasury.gov.my (office). *Website:* www.treasury.gov.my (office).

YAKER, Layashi; Algerian civil servant; b. 1930, Algiers; m.; three c.; ed Ecole de Commerce, Algiers, Ecole des Hautes Etudes at Sorbonne, Inst. d'Etude du Développement Economique et Social, Univ. of Paris and Conservatoire Nat. des Arts et Métiers, Paris; fmr Prof. Nat. School of Admin., Algiers and Inst. of Political, Diplomatic and Int. Studies, Paris; fmr Assoc. Dir Inst. of Strategic Studies, Algiers; Political Sec. Ministry of Foreign Affairs of Provisional Govt of Algeria in Cairo 1960–61; Head of Mission, Provisional Govt of Algeria to India for S. Asia 1961–62; Minister Plenipotentiary, Ministry of Foreign Affairs and Dir-Gen. for Econ. Social and Cultural Affairs and Int. Cooperation 1962–69; mem. Algerian/French Exec. Bd Org. for Exploitation of Saharan Resources 1963–65; mem. Org. for Industrial Cooperation 1965–70; Gov. African Devt Bank and Alt. Gov. IBRD 1966–68; Minister of Commerce 1969–77; Pres. Council of Ministers, Econ. Comm. for Africa (UNECA) 1973–76; Pres. Council of African Ministers of Commerce 1974–77; mem. Council IPU 1977–79; head of del. to numerous int. confs 1961–87; MP 1977–79; Amb. to USSR 1979–82, to USA 1982–84; Amb.-at-Large 1985–87; int. consultant 1988–92; UN Under-Sec.-Gen. and Exec. Sec. Econ. Comm. for Africa (UNECA) 1992–95. *Address:* c/o Executive Secretary of the Economic Commission for Africa, P.O. Box 3001, Addis Ababa, Ethiopia.

YAKIŞ, Yaşar; Turkish politician; *Chairman, EU Committee, Turkish Parliament;* b. 1938, Akçakoca; m.; one c.; ed Ankara Univ.; joined Ministry of Foreign Affairs 1962; Councillor, Turkish Embassy, Damascus, Syria 1980; est. OIC's Standing Cttee for Econ. and Commercial Co-operation 1985; Amb. to Saudi Arabia 1988–92; Deputy Under-Sec., Ministry of Foreign Affairs, responsible for Econ. Affairs 1992–95; Amb. to Egypt 1995–98; Perm. Rep. to UN, Vienna 1998–2002; Minister of Foreign Affairs 2002–03; Chair. EU Cttee in Turkish Parl. 2003–; Decoration of King Abdul Aziz, Saudi Arabia 1992. *Address:* AB Uyum Komisyonu TBMM, Ankara, Turkey (office). *Telephone:* (312) 420-54-01 (office). *Fax:* (312) 420-54-03 (office). *E-mail:* abuyum@tbmm.gov.tr (office). *Website:* www.tbmm.gov.tr (office).

YAKOVENKO, Alexander Vladimirovich, CandJurSc; Russian diplomatist; *Deputy Minister of Foreign Affairs;* b. 1954; m.; one d.; ed Moscow State Inst. of Int. Relations; with USSR Mission to UN, New York 1981–86; Head of Div., Dept on Security and Co-operation in Europe, Ministry of Foreign Affairs, Russian Fed. 1986–92; Deputy Dir Dept on Problems of Security and Disarmament, Ministry of Foreign Affairs 1992–97; Perm. Rep. to int. orgs in Vienna 1997–2000; Dir Information and Press Dept Ministry of Foreign Affairs 2000–04, currently Deputy Minister of Foreign Affairs. *Address:* Ministry of Foreign Affairs, Smolenskaya-Sennaya pl. 32/34, 121200 Moscow, Russia (office). *Telephone:* (495) 244-41-19 (office). *Fax:* (495) 244-41-12 (office). *Website:* www.mid.ru (office).

YAKOVLEV, Aleksandr Maksimovich, DJur; Russian lawyer; *Rector, New Moscow Law Institute;* b. 30 Aug. 1927, Leningrad; s. of Maxim Yakovlev and Maria Yakovleva; m. Eugenia Yakovleva 1950; ed Moscow Inst. of Law; sr research fellow Inst. of Law, USSR Ministry of Internal Affairs, then USSR Ministry of Justice 1957–75; Head Dept of Criminal Law and Criminology USSR (now Russian) Inst. of State and Law, Prof. 1975–94, Chief Researcher 1996–; in democratic movt since late 1980s; USSR People's Deputy 1989–91; mem. Perm. Cttee on Legis. USSR Supreme Soviet 1989–91; Plenipotentiary Rep. of Pres. of Russia at Federal Ass. 1994–96, Expert to Council of Fed. 1997–; Rector New Moscow Law Inst. 1998–; Visiting Prof. Univ. of Manitoba 1990, Rutgers Univ. 1991, Alberta Univ., New York and Toronto Univ. 1992, Emory Univ. Atlanta 1993, 1997; mem. Bd of Dirs Int. Soc. of Social Defence, Paris, UN Cttee Against Torture 1994, Inst. of Sociology of Law for Europe; Hon. LLD (Alberta Univ., Canada) 1991; Merited Lawyer of Russia. *Publications:* The Bear That Wouldn't Dance: Failed Attempts to Reform the Former Constitution of the Soviet Union (with Dale Gibson) 1992, Striving for Law in a Lawless Land 1995, Sociology of Crime 2000, The Social Structure of Society 2003; several other books and more than 100 articles on various aspects of constitutional law, publs in journals. *Leisure interest:* travelling. *Address:* Dolgorukovskaya str. 40, Apt. 153, 127030 Moscow (home); Pogonnyi pz. 78, 107504 Moscow, Russia (office). *Telephone:* (495) 978-84-97 (office). *Fax:* (495) 734-56-03 (office). *E-mail:* yakovlev.27@mail.ru (home).

YAKOVLEV, Veniamin Fedorovich, DJur; Russian politician and lawyer; b. 12 Feb. 1932, Petukhovo, Kurgan Region; s. of Fedor Kuzmich Yakovlev and Domna Pavlovna Yakovleva; m. Galina Ivanovna Yakovleva 1956; two d.; ed Sverdlovsk Inst. of Law; mem. CPSU 1956–91; teacher, then Dir Yakut School of Law 1953–56; Asst Procurator/Attorney-Gen. of Yakut Autonomous Repub. 1956–60; aspirant, teacher, docent, Dean, Pro-Rector Sverdlovsk Inst. of Law 1960–87; Dir All-Union Research Inst. of Soviet Legis. 1987–89; Deputy Chair. Public Comm. of Int. Co-operation on Humanitarian Problems and Human Rights 1988; USSR Minister of Justice 1989–90; Chair. USSR Supreme Arbitration Court 1991, Supreme Arbitration Court of Russian Fed. 1992–. *Publications:* Civil Law Method of Regulation for Social Relations and more than 150 other publs. *Leisure interests:* skiing and other sports. *Address:* Supreme Arbitration Court, Maly Kharitonyevski 12, 101000 Moscow, Russia. *Telephone:* (495) 208-11-19. *Fax:* (495) 208-44-00.

YAKOVLEV, Vladimir Anatolyevich, CandEconSc; Russian politician; *Minister of Regional Development;* b. 25 Nov. 1944, Olekminsk, Yakutia; m. Irina Ivanovna Yakovleva; one s.; ed NW Polytech. Inst.; master on construction sites, Head Repair-Construction Trust 1965–80, Deputy Man. Housing Dept, Leningrad (St Petersburg) 1980–93; First Deputy Mayor of St Petersburg, Russia. Head Cttee on Man. of Municipal Econ. 1993–96; Mayor (Gov.) of St Petersburg 1996–2003; Deputy Chair. (Deputy Prime Minister) Govt of the Russian Fed. 2003–04; Rep. of the Pres. in the S Fed. Dist 2004–05; Minister of Regional Development 2005–; mem. Council of Fed. of Russia 1996–2001; Pres. Ass. of Heads of Regions and Repubs of NW Russia 1997; Pres. Basketball Club Spartacus; Founder and Leader of Vsya Rossiya Movt 1999; Pres. Fed. of Bicycle Sports of St Petersburg; Order of Honour 2000; Merited Constructor of Russia. *Address:* Ministry of Regional Development, ul. Sadovaya-Samotechnaya, 103059 Moscow, Russia (office). *Telephone:* (495) 200-25-65 (office).

YAKOVLEV, Gen. Vladimir Nikolayevich, CAND.MIL.SC.; Russian army officer; *Head of Staff for Co-ordination of Military Co-operation within Commonwealth of Independent States;* b. 17 Aug. 1954, Tver; s. of Nikolai Vassilyevich Yakovlev and Erika Alexeyevna Yakovleva; m. Raisa Anatolyevna Yakovleva; two d.; ed Dzerzhinsky Mil. Acad., Mil. Acad. of Gen. Staff; served with strategic rocket forces incl. Commdr rocket regt 1985–89; Deputy Commdr rocket div. 1989–91, Commdr 1991–93; Head of Staff Rocket Army

1993–94, Commdr 1994–97; Head of Gen. Staff Rocket Troops Jan. 1999–; C-in-C Rocket Strategic Forces of Russian Fed. 1997–2001; Head of Staff for Co-ordination of Mil. Co-operation within CIS 2001–; Prof. Acad. of Mil. Sciences; mem. Russian Acad. of Eng; corresp. mem. Russian Acad. of Rocket and Artillery Sciences; Order of Red Star, Order for Mil. Service, Prize of Russian Pres. for Achievement in Educ. 1998. *Publications include:* Military Work: Science, Art, Vocation 1998, Organizational Activities of General Staff in Rocket Strategic Forces 1999, Rocket Shield of the Motherland 1999, co-author Mil. Encyclopaedic Dictionary of Rocket Strategic Forces. *Leisure interests:* music, reading, tennis, swimming. *Address:* Ministry of Defence, Bolshaya Pirogovskaya str. 23, K-160 Moscow, Russia (office). *Telephone:* (495) 244-62-14 (office).

YAKOVLEV, Yuri Vassilievich; Russian actor; b. 25 April 1928, Moscow; s. of Vassily Vassilievich Yakovlev and Olga Mikhailovna Ivanova; m. Irina Leonidovna Sergeyeva; two s. one d.; ed Shchukin Higher School of Theatre Art; actor Vakhtangov Acad. Theatre 1952–; Order of Lenin 1988, Order of Red Banner of Labour 1978, Order For Service to Motherland 1996; RSFSR State Prize 1970, USSR State Prize 1979, State Prize of Russia, Crystal Turandot Prize 1998, USSR Peoples' Artist. *Films include:* Idiot 1958, Wind 1959, A Man from Nowhere 1961, Unusual Summer, Hussar Ballad 1962, Anna Karenina 1968, A Theme for a Short Story 1970, Irony of the Fate 1975, Love Earthly 1975, Fate 1978, Ideal Husband 1981, Carnival 1982, Idiot 1983, Est-Ouest (East-West) 1999. *Plays include:* Ladies and Hussars, A Play Without Title, My Mocking Happiness, Princess Turandot, Anna Karenina, Great Magic, Casanova, Three Ages of Casanova, Bolingbrook, A Glass of Water, Lessons of the Master, Guilty Without Guilt. *Publications:* Book Album of My Destiny 1997. *Leisure interests:* Russian classical literature, classical music, sports. *Address:* Y. Vakhtangov Academic Theatre, Arbat str. 26, 121002 Moscow (office); Plotnikov per. 10/28, Apt. 28, 121002 Moscow, Russia (home). *Telephone:* (495) 241-09-28 (office); (495) 241-82-71 (home).

YAKOVLEVA, Olga Mikhailovna, ; Russian actress; b. 14 March 1941, Tambov, Russia; ed Moscow Shchukin Theatre School; actress with Moscow Lenkom Theatre 1962–, Moscow Theatre on Malaya Bronnaya 1967–84, Taganka Theatre 1984–, Moscow Mayakovsky Theatre 1991–, Moscow Art Theatre 2004–, and others; People's Artist of Russia; The State Prize 1995, Golden Mask Prize 1996, Crystal Turandot Prize, Golden Lyra Prize, Stanislavsky Prize 2001. *Plays include:* Moscow Lenkom Theatre: Seagull, My Poor Marat, 104 Pages About Love; Moscow Theatre on Malaya Bronnaya: Three Sisters, Othello, Romeo and Juliet, Marriage, Don Juan, A Month in the Country, Brother Alyosha, Summer and Smoke; Moscow Taganka Theatre: The Lower Depths, Misanthrope, A Fine Sunday for a Picnic; Moscow Mayakovsky Theatre: Napoleon 1; In the Bar of a Tokyo Hotel, Descent Down Mount Morgan, Oleg Tabakov Studio-Theatre: The Last Ones, Love Letters; Moscow Art Theatre: The Cabal of Pharisees, Cat-and-Mouse Game, A Little Tenderness, Hay Fever. *Films include:* Za vsyo v otvete (Responsible for Everything) 1972, Beshenoe zoloto (The Golden Fleece) 1976, Otkloneniye - nol (Slope: Zero) 1977. *Television:* Tanya, Four Lubovs, A Few Words in Honour of Mr. Moliére, From Pechorin's Diary. *Publication:* Esly by znat 2003. *leisure interests* fishing, cooking, design. *Address:* Moscow Art Theatre, 3 Kamergersky Str., 125009 Moscow, Russia (office). *Telephone:* (495) 629-33-12 (office). *Fax:* (495) 975-21-96.

YAKUNIN, Gleb Pavlovich; Russian politician and ecclesiastic; b. 4 March 1934; m.; one s. two d.; ed Irkutsk Inst. of Agriculture, Moscow Theological Seminary; sexton, Minister in Zaraisk, Dmitrov; expelled from Moscow Theological Seminary and deprived of the right to be a minister for public protest against collaboration of church admin. with CP; Founder and Leader Christian Cttee for Protection of Believers; sentenced to five years' imprisonment and five-year term of exile for anti-Soviet propaganda 1979; then Minister in St Nicholas Church, Shchelykovo Village, Moscow Region; exonerated 1991; active participant of Movt for Democratic Russia, Co-Chair. Coordination Council; People's Deputy of Russia 1990–93; fmr mem. Supreme Soviet of Russia; Chair. Cttee for Protection of Freedom of Conscience 1996; excommunicated by Holy Synod for political activities Dec. 1993; mem. State Duma (Parl.) 1993–95; Chair. L. Tolstoy Cttee for Defence of Freedom of Conscience. *Address:* Bolshoy Golovin per. 22, 103045 Moscow, Russia. *Telephone:* (495) 207-60-69. *Fax:* (495) 207-60-69.

YAKUNIN, Vladimir I.; Russian transport industry executive; *President and CEO, Russian Railways OAO (RZhD) (Rossiiskiye zheleznyye dorogi);* b. 30 June 1948, Zakharovo, Vladimir prov.; m.; two s.; ed Leningrad Mechanical Inst.; Jr Research Asst, State Inst. of Applied Chem. 1972–75; mil. service 1975–77; worked for Cttee on Foreign Econ. Relations, USSR Ministerial Council 1977–82; Chief of Foreign Dept, Inst. of Physics and Technics, USSR Acad. of Sciences 1982–85; Second then First Sec., Perm. Rep. to UN, New York 1985–91; Co-founder and Chair. Cttee of Dirs CJSC Int. Center For Business Partnership 1991–97; Head North-Western Revision, Chief Control Dept of Pres. of Russian Fed. 1997–2000; Deputy Minister of Transport 2000–02; First Deputy Minister of Communications 2002–03; First Vice-Pres. Russian Railways OAO (RZhD) (Rossiiskiye zheleznyye dorogi) 2003–05, Pres. and CEO 2005–; Chair. Bd Trustees Center of Nat. Glory, Andrew the First-Called Foundation; mem. Council of Co-Chair. World Public Forum—Dialogue of Civilizations, Vienna, Austria;; Order of Saint Equal-to-the-Apostles Grand Duke Vladimir (Second Degree), Russian Orthodox Church. *Address:* Russian Railways OAO (RZhD) (Rossiiskiye zheleznyye dorogi), 107174 Moscow, ul. Novobasmannaya 2, Russian Federation (office). *Telephone:* (495) 262-16-28 (office). *Fax:* (495) 975-24-11 (office). *E-mail:* info@rzd.ru (office). *Website:* www.rzd.ru (office).

YALÁ, Kumba; Guinea-Bissau politician and former head of state; b. 1954; mem. Social Renewal Party (Partido para a Renovação Socia), Pres. 2006–07; Pres. of Guinea-Bissau and C-in-C of the Armed Forces Feb. 2000–03 (deposed in mil. coup). *Address:* c/o Partido para a Renovação Social, c/o Assembléia Nacional Popular, Bissau, Republic of Guinea-Bissau (office).

YALOW, Rosalyn Sussman, PhD; American medical physicist; b. 19 July 1921, New York; d. of Simon Sussman and Clara Sussman (née Zipper); m. Aaron Yalow 1943; one s. one d.; ed Hunter Coll., New York, Univ. of Illinois; Asst in Physics, Univ. of Ill. 1941–43, Instructor 1944–45; Lecturer and temp. Asst Prof. in Physics, Hunter Coll., New York 1946–50; Physicist and Asst Chief, Radioisotope Service, Veterans Admin. Hosp., Bronx 1950–70, Acting Chief 1968–70, Chief Radioimmunoassay Reference Lab. 1969, Chief Nuclear Medicine Service 1970–80, Sr Medical Investigator 1972–92, Sr Medical Investigator Emer. 1992–, Dir Solomon A. Berson Research Lab. Veterans Admin. Medical Center 1973–92; Research Prof., Dept of Medicine, Mount Sinai School of Medicine, New York 1968–74, Distinguished Service Prof. 1974–79; Distinguished Prof.-at-Large, Albert Einstein Coll. of Medicine, Yeshiva Univ. 1979–85, Prof. Emer. 1985–; Chair. Dept of Clinical Sciences, Montefiore Hosp., Bronx, NY 1980–85; Solomon A. Berson Distinguished Prof.-at-Large, Mt Sinai School of Medicine, New York 1986–; Harvey Lecturer 1966, American Gastroenterology Asscn Memorial Lecturer 1972, Joslyn Lecturer, New England Diabetes Asscn 1972, Franklin I. Harris Memorial Lecturer 1973, 1st Hagedorn Memorial Lecturer, Acta Endocrinologica Congress 1973; Pres. Endocrine Soc. 1978–79; mem. NAS 1975–, American Physics Soc., Radiation Research Soc., American Asscn Physicists in Medicine, Biophysics Soc., American Acad. of Arts and Sciences, American Physiology Soc.; Foreign Assoc. French Acad. of Medicine 1981; Fellow, New York Acad. of Science, Radiation Research Soc., American Asscn of Physicists in Medicine; Assoc. Fellow in Physics, American Coll. of Radiology, American Diabetes Asscn, Endocrine Soc., Soc. of Nuclear Medicine; more than 60 hon. doctorates; jt winner AMA Scientific Achievement Award 1975, Albert Lasker Award for Basic Medical Research 1976, jt winner Nobel Prize for Physiology or Medicine for discoveries concerning peptide hormones 1977, Nat. Medal of Science 1988 and more than 30 other awards. *Address:* 3242 Tibbett Avenue, Bronx, New York, NY 10463, USA (home).

YAM, Joseph C. K., CBE, BSc; Hong Kong banker; *Chief Executive, Hong Kong Monetary Authority;* b. 9 Sept. 1948, Canton, China; s. of Shun Yam and Hok-chun Shum; m. Grace Fong 1972; one s. one d.; ed Univ. of Hong Kong, Inst. of Social Studies, The Hague, Netherlands; Demonstrator in Econs, Econs Dept, Univ. of Hong Kong 1970–71; statistician, Census and Statistics Dept, Hong Kong Govt 1971–76, economist, Econ. Services Br. 1976–77, Sr Economist 1977–79, Prin. Asst Sec. (Econ. Services) 1979–82, (Monetary Affairs) 1982–85, Deputy Sec. for Monetary Affairs 1985–91; Dir Office of the Exchange Fund 1991–93; Chief Exec. Hong Kong Monetary Authority 1993–; Banker of the Year in Hong Kong 1995. *Leisure interests:* golf, horse racing, swimming, hiking. *Address:* Hong Kong Monetary Authority, 30/F, 3 Garden Road, Central, Hong Kong Special Administrative Region, People's Republic of China. *Telephone:* 28788196. *Fax:* 28788197. *E-mail:* hkma@hkma .gov.hk (office). *Website:* www.info.gov.hk/hkma (office).

YAMADA, Tadataka (Tachi), BA, MD; American physician, academic and foundation executive; *President, Global Health Program, Bill and Melinda Gates Foundation;* b. Japan; ed Stanford Univ., New York Univ. School of Medicine; emigrated to USA at age 15; started career in Dept of Gastroenterology, UCLA; Chief of Gastroenterology then Chair. Dept of Internal Medicine and Physician-in-Chief, Univ. of Mich. Medical Center 1989-99, now Adjunct Prof. of Internal Medicine, Univ. of Mich. Medical School; mem. Bd of Dirs SmithKline Beecham (now GlaxoSmithKline) 1994–2006, Pres. SmithKline Beecham Healthcare Services 1996–99, Chair. Research and Devt, Pharmaceuticals 1999–2001, Chair. of Research and Devt 2001–06; Pres. Global Health Program, Bill and Melinda Gates Foundation 2006–; mem. Bd of Dirs Research!America; Trustee Rockefeller Brothers Fund; mem. Advisory Bd Quaker BioVentures, Inc.; Sr Advisor Frazier Healthcare Ventures 2006–; mem. Pres.'s Council of Advisors on Science and Tech. 2004–; mem. Advisory Cttee to Dir NIH 2004–; fmr Pres. Asscn of American Physicians, American Gastroenterological Asscn; Master, American Coll. of Physicians; mem. Inst. of Medicine, NAS, Acad. of Medical Sciences (UK); fmr mem. American Bd of Medical Examiners; numerous awards including Distinguished Achievement Award in Gastrointestinal Physiology, American Physiological Soc., Friedenwald Medal, American Gastroenterological Asscn, Distinguished Faculty Achievement Award, Univ. of Mich. and Distinguished Medical Scientist Award, Medical Coll. of Va. *Publications:* Textbook of Gastroenterology (ed.), Yamada Textbook of Medicine (ed.). *Address:* Global Health Program, Bill and Melinda Gates Foundation, POB 23350, Seattle, WA 98102, USA (office). *Telephone:* (206) 709-3100 (office). *E-mail:* info@gatesfoundation.org (office). *Website:* www.gatesfoundation.org/GlobalHealth (office).

YAMAGUCHI, Kenji, MA (Econs); Japanese government official and economist; *Representative, WELL (World Economy and Land Laboratory);* b. 19 July 1933, Yamagata; s. of Futao Yamaguchi and Yoshi Yamaguchi; m. Momoe Matsumoto 1962; one s. one d.; ed Univ. of Tokyo; entered Budget Bureau, Ministry of Finance 1956; Nat. Tax Admin. Agency 1963; Ministry of Interior 1966; Econ. Planning Agency 1968; First Sec. Okinawa Reversion Preparatory Cttee, Foreign Minister's Office and Counsellor, Okinawa Bureau, Prime Minister's Office 1969; Int. Finance Bureau, Ministry of Finance 1971; Consul for Japan, Sydney 1972; Counsellor, Personnel Bureau, Prime Minister's Office 1975; Finance Bureau, Ministry of Finance 1977; Dir-Gen. North East Japan Finance Bureau, Ministry of Finance 1981; Special Asst to Minister of Foreign Affairs 1982–87; Exec. Dir for Japan, IBRD and affiliates 1982–87, Dean IBRD Bd 1985–87; Sr Exec. Dir Water Resources Devt Public Corpn 1988–; Co-ordination Leader, Org. for Industry, Science and Cultural Advancement (OISCA) 1987–99; Exec. Adviser Mitsui Trust

Bank, Tokyo 1993–97; Chair. Mitsui Trust Int. Ltd, London 1993–97, Mitsui Trust Bank Ltd, Switzerland 1993–97; Exec. Adviser Chiyoda Mutual Life Insurance Co., Tokyo 1997–99; f. WELL (World Economy and Land Lab.) a think-tank seeking a balanced relationship between the nat. econ. and land ownership 1998; Human Life Rescue Award 1954, Zuihou Chuujushou conferred by the Emperor 2004. *Publications:* The World Bank – How Can Japan Contribute to the World? 1988, Land Policy for Prosperity – Land as Public Property 1997, Land is to be Owned by the Public 2000, A Cool Observation on the Japanese Economy 2006; and several books on financial matters, foreign affairs, etc. *Leisure interests:* reading, swimming, music. *Address:* 3-16-43 Utsukushiga-Oka, Aoba-ku, Yokohama City 225-0002, Japan. *Telephone:* (45) 901-7309. *Fax:* (45) 901-7309. *E-mail:* well@mx7.ttcn.ne.jp (office). *Website:* www2.ttcn.ne.jp/~well (office).

YAMAGUCHI, Masanori; Japanese business executive; *CEO and President, Kintetsu Corporation;* Vice-Pres., then Pres. Kinki Nippon Railway Co. –2004; currently CEO and Pres. Kintetsu Corpn; Pres. Origin Electric Shoji Co. Ltd; mem. Bd of Dirs Int. Business Org. of Osaka Inc. (IBO). *Address:* Kintetsu Corporation, 6-1-55 Ue-Honmachi, Tennoji-ku, Osaka 543-8585, Japan (office). *Telephone:* (6) 6775-3444 (office). *Fax:* (6) 6775-3467 (office). *Website:* www.kintetsu.co.jp (office).

YAMAGUCHI, Nobuo; Japanese business executive; *Chairman and Representative Director, Asahi Kasei Corporation;* currently Chair. and Rep. Dir Asahi Kasei Corpn (changed name from Asahi Chemical Industry Co. Ltd 2000); Chair. Japan Chamber of Commerce and Industry 2001–, Tokyo Chamber of Commerce and Industry 2001–; Dir Asahi Breweries Ltd 2004–; mem. Pacific Basin Econ. Council. *Address:* Asahi Kasei Corporation, Hibiya-Mitsui Building, 1-1-2 Yurakucho, Chiyoda-ku, Tokyo 100-8440, Japan (office). *Telephone:* (3) 3507-2060 (office). *Fax:* (3) 3507-2495 (office). *Website:* www.asahi-kasei.co.jp (office).

YAMAGUCHI, Shigeru; Japanese judge (retd); b. 4 Nov. 1932, Chiba; ed Kyoto Univ.; Asst Judge, Okayama Dist Court and Okayama Family Court 1957; Judge, Hakodate Dist, Court and Hakodate Family Court 1967; Dir Secr. of Research and Training Inst. for Court Clerks 1969; Judge, Tokyo Dist Court (Presiding Judge of Div.) 1976; Dir Secr. of Tokyo High Court 1980; Dir Gen. Affairs Bureau, Gen. Secr. of Supreme Court 1983; Pres. Kofu Dist Court and Kofu Family Court 1988; Judge and Presiding Judge of Div., Tokyo High Court 1989; Pres. Legal Training and Research Inst. 1991; Pres. Fukuoka High Court 1994; Justice of the Supreme Court 1997, Chief Justice 1997–2002; retd 2002. *Address:* c/o Supreme Court, 4-2, Hayabusa-cho, Chiyoda-ku, Tokyo 102-8651, Japan.

YAMAMOTO, Takuma, BEng; Japanese business executive; b. 11 Sept. 1925, Kumamoto; ed Univ. of Tokyo; joined Fujitsu Ltd 1949, Bd Dir 1975–, Man. Dir 1976–79, Exec. Dir 1979–81, Pres. and Rep. Dir 1981–90, Chair. and Rep. Dir 1990–98; Vice-Chair. Communication Industries Asscn of Japan 1986; Chair. Japan Electronic Industry Devt Asscn 1987–89, Vice-Chair. 1989–; Chair. Cttee on Int. Coordination of Econ. Policies (KEIDANREN) 1988–; Hon. DHumLitt (Chaminade Univ. of Honolulu); Blue Ribbon with Medal of Honour 1984. *Leisure interests:* river-fishing, golf, gardening. *Address:* c/o Fujitsu Ltd, 1-6-1 Marunouchi, Chiyoda-ku, Tokyo 100, Japan.

YAMAMOTO, Yohji; Japanese fashion designer; b. 1943, Tokyo; ed Keio Univ. and Bunkafukuso Gakuin school of fashion, Tokyo; launched first collection Tokyo 1977, Paris 1981, New York 1982, first menswear collection, Paris 1984; costume designer for Opéra de Lyon's production of Madame Butterfly 1990, Wagner Opera's production of Tristan und Isolde, Bayreuth 1993, Kanagawa Art Festival Opera Susanoo 1994; launched first perfume Yohji 1996, second perfume Yohji Essential 1998; participant in 25th Anniversary of Pina Bausch Co., Wuppertal 1998; launched first perfume Yohji Homme 1999; designed costumes for the Ryuichi Sakamoto Opera 'Life' 1999; subject of Wim Wenders' film Notebook on Cities and Clothes 1989; designed costumes for Dir Takeshi Kitano's films, Dolls and Zatoichi; debut of Y-3 line 2003; So-en Award, Endo Award 1969, Fashion Eds Club Award, Tokyo 1982, 1991, 1997, Mainichi Fashion Award, Tokyo 1986, 1994, Chevalier, Ordre des Arts et des Lettres 1994, Night of Stars Award Fashion Group, New York 1997, Arte e Moda Award, Pitti Imagine, Florence 1998, Int. Award Council of Fashion Designers of America 1999. *Publication:* Talking to Myself. *Address:* Yohji Yamamoto Inc., 133 2-2-43 Higashi-Shinagawa, Shinagawa-ku, Tokyo 140-0002, Japan (office). *Website:* www.yohjiyamamoto.co.jp (office).

YAMAMOTO, Yuji, BA; Japanese politician; b. 11 May 1952; ed Waseda Univ.; began career as lawyer; mem. Kochi Prefectural Ass. 1985–90; mem. House of Reps for Kochi Pref. constituency 1990–, State Sec. for Home Affairs 1996, State Sec. for Justice 1999, 2000, Chair. House of Reps Cttee on Economy, Trade and Industry 2001, Cttee on Judicial Affairs 2002, Sr Vice-Minister of Finance 2003, Minister of State for Financial Services 2006–07; Acting Dir Judicial Affairs Div., Policy Research Council, LDP 1995, mem. LDP Gen. Council 1997–, Dir Infrastructure Div., Policy Research Council 1998, Exec. Deputy Sec.-Gen., LDP 2000–. *Address:* Liberal-Democratic Party (Jiyu-Minshuto), 1-11-23, Nagata-cho, Chiyoda-ku, Tokyo 100-8910, Japan (office). *Telephone:* (3) 3581-6211 (office). *E-mail:* koho@ldp.jimin.or.jp (office). *Website:* www.jimin.jp (office).

YAMANAKA, Shinya, MD, PhD; Japanese medical scientist and academic; *Professor, Institute for Frontier Medical Sciences, Kyoto University;* ed Kobe Univ., Osaka City Univ. Grad. School; resident in orthopedic surgery, Nat. Osaka Hosp. 1987–89; postgraduate studies 1989–93; Post-doctoral Fellow, Gladstone Inst. of Cardiovascular Disease, San Francisco, USA 1993–95, Staff Research Investigator 1995–96; Asst Prof., Osaka City Univ. Medical School 1996–99; Assoc. Prof., Nara Inst. of Science and Tech., Nara 1999–2003, Prof. 2003–05; Prof., Inst. for Frontier Medical Sciences, Kyoto Univ. 2004–. *Publications:* numerous articles in professional journals. *Address:* Department of Stem Cell Biology, Institute for Frontier Medical Sciences, Kyoto University, 53 Shogoin, Kawahara-cho, Sakyo-ku, Kyoto 606-8507, Japan (office). *Telephone:* (75) 751-3839 (office). *Fax:* (75) 751-4632 (office). *E-mail:* yamanaka@frontier.kyoto-u.ac.jp (office). *Website:* www.frontier.kyoto-u.ac.jp/rc02/index.html (office); www.med.kyoto-u.ac.jp/E/grad_school/introduction/1517 (office).

YAMANI, Sheikh Ahmed Zaki; Saudi Arabian politician; b. 1930, Mecca; ed Cairo Univ., New York and Harvard Univs, USA; Saudi Arabian Govt Service; pvt. law practice; Legal Adviser to Council of Ministers 1958–60; mem. Council of Ministers 1960–86; Minister of State 1960–62; Minister of Petroleum and Mineral Resources 1962–86; Dir Arabian American Oil Co. 1962–86; Chair. Bd Dirs General Petroleum and Mineral Org. (PETROMIN) 1963–86, Coll. of Petroleum and Minerals, Dhahran 1963–86, Saudi Arabian Fertilizer Co. (SAFCO) 1966–86; f. Centre for Global Energy Studies; Sec.-Gen. OAPEC 1968–69, Chair. 1974–75; mem. several int. law asscns. *Publication:* Islamic Law and Contemporary Issues. *Address:* PO Box 14850, Jeddah 21434, Saudi Arabia.

YAMANI, Hashim ibn Abdullah ibn Hashim al-, PhD; Saudi Arabian politician; b. 1945; ed Harvard Univ., USA; Prof. and later Chair. of Physics Dept, King Fahd Univ. of Petroleum and Minerals; Vice-Pres. King Abdul Aziz City for Science; Minister of Industry and Electricity 1995–2003, Minister of Commerce and Industry 2003–08; Chair. Sabic. *Address:* c/o Ministry of Commerce and Industry, POB 1774, Airport Road, Riyadh 11162, Saudi Arabia.

YAMASHITA, Ryuichi; Japanese automobile industry executive; *Director and Corporate Adviser, Yamaha Motor Company Limited;* ed Tohoku Univ.; joined Yamaha 1962; Sr Gen. Man. Automotive Engine operation 1983–2001, Dir 1983–, Exec. Vice-Pres. 2001, then Chair. Yamaha Motor Co. Ltd –2005, currently Dir and Corp. Adviser; Chair. Motorcycle Cttee, Japan Automobile Manufacturers Asscn, Inc. *Address:* Yamaha Motor Company Limited, 2500 Shingai, Iwata, Shizuoka 438-8501, Japan (office). *Telephone:* (5) 3832-1103 (office). *Fax:* (5) 3837-4252 (office). *Website:* www.yamaha-motor.co.jp.

YAMASHITA, Yasuhiro, MA; Japanese judo player and coach (retd) and academic; *Professor, Department of Sports, Tokai University;* b. 1 June 1957, Kumamoto; m. Midori Ono 1986; two s. one d.; ed Kyushu Gakuin High School, Tokai Univ. Sagami High School and Tokai Univ.; winner nine consecutive times, All Japan Judo Tournament; four-time World Judo Champion; achieved unbroken record of 203 consecutive wins from 1977 till he retd in 1985; gold medallist Olympic Games, Los Angeles 1984; Prof. Dept of Sports, Tokai Univ. 1986–, fmr Team Man. Univ. Judo Team; Man. Japanese Nat. Judo Team 1992–; Dir Int. Judo Fed.; Nat. Honour Prize (Japan, first amateur sportsman to achieve award); mem. Laureus World Sports Acad. *Publications include:* Young Days with Black Belt, Enjoyable Judo, The Moment of Fight, Osoto-Gari, Judo with Fighting Spirits. *Leisure interests:* reading, playing with my kids, karaoke (with family), dining out. *Address:* 1117 Kitakaname, Hitatsuka Kanagawa, 259–1207 (office); 661-104 Higashi Koiso, Oiso-machi, Naka-gun, Kanagawa-ken, Japan (home). *Telephone:* (463) 58-1211 (ext. 3532) (office). *Fax:* (463) 50-2405 (office). *E-mail:* judo1117@keyaki.cc.u-tokai.ac.jp (office).

YAMASSOUM, Nagoum; Chadian politician; b. 1954; s. of Jean Yamassoum and Alice Titingone; m. Brigitte Boukar Belingar; two s.; ed Univ. of Bordeaux, Univ. of Paris XI, France; Prime Minister of Chad Aug. 1999–2002; Minister of State, Minister of Foreign Affairs and African Integration 2003–05; Nat. Order of Chad, Nat. Order of Taiwan. *Leisure interests:* tennis, soccer, gardening. *Address:* POB 4321, N'Djamena, Moursal, Chad (home). *Telephone:* 51-51-59 (home). *Fax:* 51-70-21 (home). *E-mail:* nagoumy@hotmail.com (home).

YAMAUCHI, Yasuhito; Japanese automotive industry executive; *President, Aisin Seiki Company Ltd;* joined Toyota 1968, Man. Dir, also Chair. Plant Production Environmental Sub-Cttee, Overseas Production Environmental Sub-Cttee 1999–2001, Sr Man. Dir 2001–03, Chair. Production Environment Cttee 2003–; Pres. Aisin Seiki Co. 2005–. *Address:* Aisin Seiki Co. Ltd, 2-1 Asahi-machi, Karlya, Aichi 448-8650, Japan (office). *Telephone:* (5) 6624-8239 (office). *Fax:* (5) 6624-8003 (office). *E-mail:* info@aisin.com (office). *Website:* www.aisin.com (office).

YAMEEN, Abdullah; Maldivian politician; brother of Pres. Maumoon Abdul Gayoom; fmr Minister of Trade, Industries and Labour; Chair. State Trading Org., Island Aviation, Electricity Bd; fmr Minister of Higher Educ., Employment and Social Security; left govt's Dhivehi Raiyyithunge Party (Maldivian People's Party) 2007; Founder and Leader People's Alliance party 2008–. *Address:* c/o Ministry of Higher Education, Employment and Social Security, Malé, Maldives.

YAMEY, Basil Selig, CBE, BComm, FBA; British economist and academic; *Professor Emeritus of Economics, London School of Economics;* b. 4 May 1919, Cape Town, South Africa; s. of Solomon Yamey and Leah Yamey; m. 1st Helen Bloch 1948 (died 1980); one s. one d.; m. 2nd Demetra Georgakopoulou 1991; ed Tulbagh High School and Univ. of Cape Town; Prof. of Econs LSE 1960–84, Prof. Emer. 1984–; mem. Monopolies and Mergers Comm. 1966–78; Trustee Nat. Gallery, London 1974–81, Tate Gallery, London 1977–81, Inst. of Econ. Affairs 1987–91; Hon. Fellow LSE 1988. *Publications:* Economics of Resale Price Maintenance 1951, Economics of Underdeveloped Countries (with P. T. Bauer) 1956, Economics of Futures Trading (with B. A. Goss) 1976, Essays on the History of Accounting 1978, Art and Accounting 1989. *Address:* 27B

Elsworthy Road, London, NW3 3BT, England. *Telephone:* (20) 7586-9344. *Fax:* (20) 7586-9344.

YAN, Dongsheng, PhD; Chinese academic; b. 10 Feb. 1918, Shanghai; s. of Chi Yan and Yuhan (née Chu) Yan; m. Bi-Rou Sun 1943; one s. one d.; ed Yanjing and Tsinghua Univs, Beijing, Univ. of Illinois, USA; Deputy Dir Inst. of Chem. Eng, Kailan Mining Admin. 1950–54; Research Prof., Inst. of Metallurgy and Ceramics, Acad. of Sciences 1954–60; Deputy Dir Shanghai Ceramic Inst., Acad. of Sciences 1960, Dir 1977; mem. editorial Bd, Chinese Science Bulletin 1961; Vice-Pres. Shanghai Univ. of Science and Tech. 1980, Hon. Pres. 1985–, mem. Acad. Degrees Cttee 1981, Vice-Chair. Fund Cttee 1981; mem. 12th CCP Cen. Cttee 1982–87; mem. Standing Cttee CPPCC 1987–93, Vice-Chair. Shanghai Municipal CPPCC 1987–93; Pres. Chinese Chemical Soc. 1982–86; Ed.-in-Chief Science in China, Science Bulletin 1987–96, Ceramics Int.; Ed. Material Letters (Int.), Int. Solid State Chem., European Solid State and Inorganic Chem., High Tech Ceramics (Intel); mem. Leading Group for Scientific Work, State Council 1983–88; mem. Chinese Acad. of Sciences (Vice-Pres. 1980–87), Dir Dept of Chem. 1981–93; Party Sec. Chinese Acad. of Sciences 1984–87, Special Adviser 1987–, Sr Fellow 1998–; Sr Fellow Chinese Acad. of Eng 1998–; Pres. Chinese Ceramic Soc. 1983–93, Hon. Pres. 1993–; Pres. Chinese Chemical Soc. 1995–98; Vice-Pres. China–US People's Friendship Asscn 1986–; Titular mem. IUPAC 1987–95; Pres. Fed. of Asian Scientific Acads and Socs 1990–95; Prin. Investigator Climb Project, Nanomaterials Research 1992–97, Adviser Climb Project, Nanomaterials and Devices 1997–2002; Hon. mem. Materials Research Socs, India, Japan, USA, Europe; Hon. DSc (Illinois, Bordeaux) 1986, (Hong Kong Polytechnic) 1993. *Leisure interests:* classical music, bridge. *Address:* Chinese Academy of Sciences, 52 San Li He Road, Beijing, People's Republic of China (office). *Telephone:* (10) 68597289 (office); (10) 62554019 (home). *Fax:* (10) 68512458.

YAN, Haiwang; Chinese politician; b. Sept. 1939, Zhengzhou City, Henan Prov.; ed Harbin Architectural Eng Inst.; joined CCP 1966; Dir Urban and Rural Construction Cttee, Gansu Prov. 1983–87; Vice-Gov. Gansu Prov. 1987–93, Gov. 1993–97; Deputy Sec. CCP Gansu Provincial Cttee 1988–93; Sec. CCP Gansu Provincial Cttee 1993–98; Deputy Gov. People's Bank of China 1998–2000; Deputy Sec. Financial Work Committee, CCP Cen. Cttee Work Cttee Depts 1998–2003; Vice-Chair. China Banking Regulatory Comm. 2003–05; Alt. mem. 14th CCP Cen. Cttee 1992–97, mem. 15th CCP Cen. Cttee 1997–2002, 16th CCP Cen. Cttee 2002–07. *Address:* c/o General Office, China Banking Regulatory Commission, No. 33 Cheng Fang Street, West District, Beijing, People's Republic of China.

YAN, Jiehe; Chinese business executive; *Chairman and CEO, China Pacific Construction Group;* b. 1960, Huai'an, Jiangsu Prov.; taught Chinese language in middle school in Huai'an 1980s; took job as clerk at local cement factory, then apptd man.; expanded into construction materials business by taking over bankrupt state-owned collective; started construction co. in Huai'an 1992; launched his first pvt. business, Jiangsu Pacific Eng Ltd in 1995; currently Chair. and CEO China Pacific Construction Group (leading pvt. co. in building nat. expressways, urban construction and hydraulic projects); purchased ST Zongheng (Shanghai-listed machinery manufacturer based in Jiangsu Prov.) 2003; Chair. Pacific Architect Group; named by a business magazine as one of Ten Best Managers in China and the Ten Famous People in China Economic Field. *Address:* , Nanjing, Jiangsu, People's Republic of China (office).

YAN, Liangkun; Chinese orchestral conductor; b. Oct. 1923, Wuchang City, Hubei Prov.; Artistic Dir and Conductor, Symphony Orchestra of China Cen. Philharmonic Soc.; Vice-Pres. China Musicians' Asscn 1992–; mem. 6th CPPCC Nat. Cttee 1983–88, 7th CPPCC Nat. Cttee 1988–93, 8th CPPCC Nat. Cttee 1993–98. *Address:* Central Philharmonic Society, 11-1 Hepingjie (Peace Street), Beijing 100013, People's Republic of China (office).

YANAGIMACHI, Ryuzo, PhD; American/Japanese biologist and academic; *Professor Emeritus of Anatomy and Reproductive Biology, Institute for Biogenesis Research, John A. Burns School of Medicine, University of Hawaii-Manoa;* b. 27 Aug. 1928, Ebetsu, Hokkaido, Japan; s. of Kyuzo Yanagimachi and Hiroko Yanagimachi; ed Hokkaido Univ., Sapporo; on staff, Worcester Foundation for Experimental Biology, Shrewsbury, Mass 1960–64; returned to Japan 1964–66; Asst Prof., John A. Burns School of Medicine, Univ. of Hawaii-Manoa 1966–74, Prof. of Anatomy and Reproductive Biology 1974–2005, Prof. Emer. 2005–, Founding Dir Inst. for Biogenesis Research 1999–2004; mem. NAS 2001, mem. Editorial Bd Proceedings of the National Academy of Sciences; pioneering work on in vitro fertilization, assisted fertilization and animal cloning; Marshall Medal, Soc. of Study of Fertility 1994, Int. Prize of Biology 1996, Distinguished Andrologist Award, American Soc. of Andrology 1998, Carl G. Hartman Award, Soc. of Study of Reproduction 1999, inducted into Hall of Honor, Nat. Inst. of Child Health and Human Devt 2003. *Publications:* numerous articles in scientific journals on assisted fertilization, freeze-dried sperm tech. and cloning. *Address:* Institute for Biogenesis Research, John A. Burns School of Medicine, University of Hawaii-Manoa, 1960 East-West Road, Honolulu, HI 96822, USA (office). *Telephone:* (808) 956-8746 (office). *Fax:* (808) 956-7316 (office). *E-mail:* yana@hawaii.edu (office). *Website:* manoa.hawaii.edu (office).

YANAGISAWA, Hakuo; Japanese politician; b. 18 Aug. 1935; ed Tokyo Univ.; joined Ministry of Finance 1961; Consul in New York 1971–75; Sec. to Chief Cabinet Sec. 1978–79; mem. House of Reps for Shizuoka 3rd Dist (LDP) 1980–, Parl. Vice-Minister, Ministry of Foreign Affairs 1994–95, Chair. House of Reps Educ. Cttee 1995–96, Health and Welfare Cttee 1998, Minister of State, Dir-Gen., Nat. Land Agency 1998, Minister of State for Financial Reconstruction 1998, Minister of State and Chair., Financial Reconstruction Comm. 1998–99, 2000–2001, Minister of State for Financial Services 2001–02, Minister of Health, Labour and Welfare 2006–07; Man. Chair. LDP Admin. Reform Task Force 1995–98, Chair., LDP Research Comm. on Tax System 2005–06. *Address:* Liberal-Democratic Party (Jiyu-Minshuto), 1-11-23, Nagata-cho, Chiyoda-ku, Tokyo 100-8910, Japan (office). *Telephone:* (3) 3581-6211 (office). *E-mail:* koho@ldp.jimin.or.jp (office). *Website:* www.jimin.jp (office).

YANAYEV, Gennadiy Ivanovich, CAND.HIST.SC.; Russian politician; b. 26 Aug. 1937, Perevoz, Perevozovsky region, Gorky Dist; m.; two d.; ed Gorky Agric. Inst. and All-Union Law Inst.; mem. CPSU 1962–91; began work as foreman of mechanisation unit 1959–63; Komsomol work; Second Sec. Gorky village Komsomol Dist Cttee (Obkom), Second, First Sec. Obkom 1963–68; Chair. Cttee of USSR Youth Orgs, then Vice-Chair. of Presidium of Union of Soviet Asscns for Friendship and Cultural Relations with Foreign Countries 1968–86; trade-union work, Sec., Vice-Chair. All-Union Trades Union Fed. 1986–90; mem. Cen. Cttee CPSU, Sec. 1990–91; fmr People's Deputy; mem. CPSU Politburo 1990–91; Vice-Pres. USSR 1990–91; arrested for participation in attempted coup d'état, charged with conspiracy 1992; on trial 1993–94, released after amnesty 1994.

YAÑEZ-BARNUEVO, Juan Antonio, LLB, DipIL; Spanish diplomatist; *Permanent Representative, United Nations;* b. 15 Feb. 1942, Coria del Río, Seville; s. of the late Luis Yáñez-Barnuevo and Angeles García; m. Isabel Sampedro 1969; one s.; ed Univs of Seville, Madrid and Cambridge, School for Int. Civil Servants, Madrid, Hague Acad. of Int. Law and Diplomatic School, Madrid; Sec. of Embassy, Perm. Mission of Spain to UN, New York 1970–73; Deputy Head, Office of Int. Legal Affairs, Ministry of Foreign Affairs 1975–78; Deputy Perm. Rep. to Council of Europe, Strasbourg 1978–82; Dir of Int. Dept of Presidency of Govt (Foreign Policy Adviser to Prime Minister) 1982–91; Amb. and Perm. Rep. of Spain at UN, New York 1991–96; Deputy Dir Diplomatic School 1996–98; Amb.-at-Large 1998–2004; Head Spanish Del. to UN negotiations on the Int. Criminal Court 1998–2004; Head Legal Dept, Foreign Ministry 2002–04; Perm. Rep. to UN 2004–; mem. Int. Humanitarian Fact-finding Comm. 2002–; Francisco Tomás y Valiente Prize (Seville) 1998, Jurist of the Year (Madrid Law School) 1999. *Publications:* La Justicia Penal Internacional: Una perspectiva iberoamericana 2001. *Leisure interests:* reading, music, nature. *Address:* Permanent Mission of Spain to the United Nations, 345 East 46th Street, New York, NY 10017, USA (office); Carretera de Húmera, 1 (Aravaca), 28023 Madrid, Spain (home). *Telephone:* (212) 661-1050 (office). *Fax:* (212) 949-7247 (office). *E-mail:* spain@spainum.org (office). *Website:* www.spainun.org (office).

YANG, Gen. Baibing; Chinese army officer; b. Sept. 1920, Tongnan Co., Sichuan Prov.; Deputy Political Commissar, Beijing Mil. Region, PLA 1983–85, Political Commissar 1985; Deputy Dir, Bureau under Int. Liaison Dept, State Council 1985–87; Dir Gen. Political Dept 1987; mem. Cen. Mil. Comm., PRC April 1988, Sec.-Gen. 1989; rank of Gen. 1988; mem. 13th CCP Cen. Cttee 1987–92, 14th CCP Cen. Cttee 1992–97; mem. Politburo 1992–97; PLA Deputy to 8th NPC. *Address:* c/o Politburo, Chinese Communist Party, Beijing, People's Republic of China (office).

YANG, Bo; Chinese politician; b. 1920, Shandong Prov.; concurrently Dir Research Office and Comprehensive Dept, State Statistics Bureau, State Council; Deputy Dir then Dir Shandong Prov. Statistics Comm.; Vice-Chair. Prov. Revolutionary Cttee, Shandong 1977; Vice-Minister State Planning Comm., State Council 1979; Deputy Man. 7th Dept, China Nat. Tech. Import Corpn (TECHIMPORT) 1980; Vice-Minister State Energy Comm., State Council 1981; Minister of Light Industry 1982–87; Sec. Party Group 1983; mem. 12th Cen. Cttee, CCP 1982–87; Adviser, China-Japan Personnel Exchange Cttee 1985–, NPC Finance and Econ. Cttee; fmr Adviser Internal and Judicial Affairs Cttee; Deputy 7th NPC, mem. Standing Cttee 1988; Chair. Int. Cttee for Promotion of Chinese Industrial Co-operatives 1992–.

YANG, Chao, MBA; Chinese insurance industry executive; *Chairman, China Life Insurance (Group) Co. Ltd;* ed Shanghai Int. Studies Univ., Univ. of Middlesex, UK; served in various man. positions with People's Insurance Co. of China 1976–96, including Deputy Gen. Man. and Asst Gen. Man. Shanghai Br., Gen. Man. Shanghai Pudong Br.; Chair. and Pres. China Insurance (Holdings) Co., Europe 1996–2000, China Insurance (Holdings) Co. 2000–05, China Insurance HK (Holding) Co. 2000–05; Chair. China Life Insurance (Group) Co. Ltd 2005–; mem. Bd of Dirs Pacific Century Insurance Holdings, CITIC Int. Financial Holdings. *Address:* China Life Insurance (Group) Co. Ltd, 16 Chaowai Avenue, 23rd Floor Chinalife Building, Chaoyang District, Beijing 100020, People's Republic of China (office). *Telephone:* (10) 8565-9999 (office). *Fax:* (10) 8525-2232 (office). *E-mail:* info@chinalife.com.cn (office). *Website:* www.chinalife.com.cn (office).

YANG, Chen Ning (Frank), MSc, PhD; American (b. Chinese) physicist and academic; *Albert Einstein Professor Emeritus of Physics, State University of New York at Stony Brook;* b. 22 Sept. 1922, Hefei; s. of Ke Chuan Yang and Meng Loh Yang; m. Chih Li Tu; two s. one d.; ed Nat. Southwest Associated Univ., Kunming, Tsinghua Univ., Univ. of Chicago, USA; Research Student, Univ. of Chicago, USA 1946, Instructor 1948; joined Inst. for Advanced Study, Princeton, NJ 1949, Prof. 1955–66; Albert Einstein Prof. of Physics, State Univ. of NY at Stony Brook 1966–99, Emer. 1999–; Distinguished Prof.-at-Large, Chinese Univ. of Hong Kong 1986–; Prof., Tsinghua Univ., People's Repub. of China 1998–; Pres. Nat. Asscn of Chinese Americans 1977–80, Asscn of Asia Pacific Physical Socs 1989–94, Asia Pacific Center of Theoretical Physics 1996–; mem. NAS, Chinese Acad. of Sciences, Russian Acad. of Sciences, Brazilian Acad. of Sciences, Polish Acad. of Sciences, Royal Spanish Acad. of Science, Korean Acad. of Science and Tech.; Fellow, American Physical Soc., Academia Sinica (Taiwan); 18 hon. degrees Nobel Prize in Physics 1957, Albert Einstein Commemorative Award 1957, Rumford Prize

1980, Nat. Medal of Science 1986, Benjamin Franklin Medal 1993, Bower Award 1994, N. Bogoliubov Prize 1996, Lars Onsager Prize 1999, King Faisal Int. Prize 2001. *Publications:* numerous articles in scientific journals. *Address:* Department of Physics and Astronomy, State University of New York at Stony Brook, Stony Brook, NY 11794, USA (office). *Telephone:* (631) 632-8100 (office). *Fax:* (631) 632–8176 (office). *E-mail:* yang@insti.physics .sunysb.edu (office). *Website:* insti.physics.sunysb.edu/Physics (office).

YANG, Cheng-Zhi, BSc; Chinese petroleum engineer; b. 8 Aug. 1938, Henan; s. of Yang Xian-zun and Hou Yang; m. Li Yan-qin 1969; one s. one d.; ed Beijing Univ. of Petroleum; Asst Prof., Beijing Univ. of Petroleum 1961–75; Asst Prof., Vice-Dir Dept of Petroleum Eng, Sheng-li Coll. of Petroleum 1976–78; Prof., Sr Research Engineer and Dir of Research for Interface Chem., Research Inst. of Petroleum Exploration and Devt of Beijing 1979–; Dir Jr Lab. for Colloid and Interface Science, Acad. Sinica and China Nat. Petroleum Co. 1990–; Visiting Sr Research Engineer, Inst. Français du Pétrole 1979–80, 1985–87, 1989–90; mem. China Petroleum Soc., Soc. of Petroleum Engineers of USA; research into enhanced oil recovery, the physical chem. of oil reservoirs, surfactant solution properties, absorption of surfactants and polymers, colloid and interface chem. etc.; Hon. Prof., Da-qing Univ. of Petroleum 1988–; Science-Tech. Award in Petroleum Eng 1991, 1996, World Lifetime Achievement Award, ABI, USA 1992 and other awards. *Publications:* Petroleum Reservoir Physics 1975, World Fine Chemical Engineering Handbook (jtly), Enhanced Oil Recovery Theory and Practice 1995, Improved Oil Recovery 1997, Enhanced Oil Recovery by Chemical Flooding 1999; more than 60 articles in professional journals. *Leisure interests:* collecting stamps and badges. *Address:* Research Institute of Petroleum Exploration and Development, PO Box 910, Beijing 100083 (office); No. 1107, West-Beido Lodging House, Zhixing Road, Beijing 100083, People's Republic of China (home). *Telephone:* (10) 62098371 (office); (10) 62397956 (home). *Fax:* (10) 62097181 (office); (10) 62397956 (home). *E-mail:* ylang@public.fhnet.cn.net (office).

YANG, Deqing; Chinese army officer and politician; b. Sept. 1942, Yingcheng, Hubei Prov.; joined PLA 1963, CCP 1964; mem. Secr., Wuhan Mil. Dist, PLA Guangzhou Mil. Region 1973–77, Political Commissar PLA Armoured Force Regt 1977–80, Dir Political Dept, Armoured Force Regt 1982–85; Dir Political Dept, 54th Group Army of Ground Force 1985–89; Dir Political Dept and Political Commissar, Acad. of Mil. Economy 1989–91; Dir PLA Gen. Logistics Dept 1991–94, Sec., later Deputy Sec. CCP Party Cttee Comm. for Discipline Inspection 1994–99; Political Commissar, PLA Chengdu Mil. Region 1999–2005; Sec. CCP Party Cttee, Chengdu City, PLA Guangzhou Mil. Region 1999–; mem. Cen. Comm. for Discipline Inspection; Mayor Zhangjiakou City, Hebei Prov.; mem. 15th CCP Cen. Cttee 1997–2002, 16th CCP Cen. Cttee 2002–07. *Address:* c/o PLA Headquarters, Chengdu Military Region, Chengdu 610000, Sichuan Province, People's Republic of China (office).

YANG, Gen. Dezhong; Chinese army officer and politician; b. 1923, Weinan Co., Shanxi Prov.; joined CCP 1938, First Deputy Dir of Gen. Office 1983, CCP Cen. Cttee, Dir of Garrison Bureau 1982; mem. 12th CCP Cen. Cttee 1982–87, 13th CCP Cen. Cttee 1987–92, 14th CCP Cen. Cttee 1992–97. *Address:* General Office, Chinese Communist Party Central Committee, Zhong Nan Hai, Beijing, People's Republic of China (office).

YANG, Fudong; Chinese artist; b. 1971, Beijing; ed China Acad. of Fine Arts, Hangzhou; Shanghai-based multimedia artist, works include paintings, photography and film.

YANG, Fujia, BSc; Chinese nuclear physicist and university administrator; *Chancellor, Nottingham University;* b. June 1936, Shanghai; ed Fudan Univ.; Lecturer, Dept of Physics, Fudan Univ., later Prof. and Pres. Fudan Univ. 1993; Dir Shanghai Inst. of Nuclear Research 1987–2001; Chancellor, Nottingham Univ., UK 2001– (first Chinese academic to become Chancellor of a UK univ.); fmr Visiting Prof., Niels Bohr Inst., Copenhagen, Rutgers Univ., State Univ. of NY, Univ. of Tokyo; Chair. Shanghai Science and Tech. Union 1992–96; Vice Chair. Chinese Asscn for Science and Tech. 2001–; Pres. Asscn of Univ. Pres. of China 1997–99; Fellow, Chinese Acad. of Sciences; Dr hc (Soka Univ., Tokyo), (State Univ. of NY), (Univ. of Hong Kong), (Univ. of Nottingham), (Univ. of Connecticut). *Address:* Office of the Chancellor, University of Nottingham, University Park, Nottingham, NG7 2RD, England (office). *Telephone:* (115) 951-5151 (office). *Fax:* (115) 951-3666 (office). *Website:* www.nottingham.ac.uk/about/management/chancellor.php (office).

YANG, Fuqing; Chinese computer scientist and academic; *Dean, Faculty of Information and Engineering Sciences and Director, National Engineering Research Center for Software Engineering, Peking University;* b. 6 Nov. 1932, Wuxi, Jiangsu Prov.; ed Tsinghua and Peking Univs; Prof., Dept of Computer Science and Tech., Peking Univ. 1983–, Dean 1983–99, Dean Faculty of Information and Eng Sciences 1999–, Dir Nat. Eng Research Center for Software Eng Research 1997–, Dir Computer Science and Tech. Dept 1983–99; mem. Chinese Acad. of Sciences 1991–, Academic Degree Cttee of the State Council; Fellow, IEEE 2003–; numerous awards and prizes including Special Prize for Advancement of Science and Tech., Electronics Industry Admin. 1996, First Class Prize of the Guang Hua Tech. Fund from the Nat. Defence Tech. Ministry 1996, Science and Tech. Progress Awards of He Liang and He Li Fund 1997, Pioneer of Software Engineering in China. *Publications:* Operating System, Compiler, The Fundamental Theory of Software Engineering, Software Engineering Environment, Software Production Industrialization Technology; more than 150 papers. *Address:* Department of Computer Science and Technology, Peking University, Beijing 100871, People's Republic of China (office). *Telephone:* (10) 62751782 (office). *Fax:* (10) 62751792 (office). *E-mail:* yang@sei.pku.edu.cn. *Website:* www.sei .pku.edu.cn/en/yangfuqing.html (office).

YANG, Gen. Guoliang; Chinese army officer; *Commander, 2nd Artillery Force, People's Liberation Army;* b. March 1938, Zunhua City, Hebei Prov.; ed Beijing Aeronautics Inst.; joined CCP 1961, PLA 1963; Deputy Commdr PLA Second Artillery Force 1985; rank of Maj.-Gen. 1988, Lt-Gen. 1993; Commdr PLA Second Artillery Force 1992–; rank of Gen. 1998; Alt. mem. 12th CCP Cen. Cttee 1985, 13th CCP Cen. Cttee 1987, mem. 14th CCP Cen. Cttee 1992, 15th CCP Cen. Cttee 1997–2002. *Address:* People's Liberation Army Second Artillery Force Headquarters, Beijing, People's Republic of China (office).

YANG, Gen. Guoping; Chinese army officer; *Commander, People's Armed Police;* b. Oct. 1934, Zhongxiang Co., Hubei Prov.; ed PLA Mil. Acad.; joined PLA 1950, fought in Korean War 1951; joined CCP 1956; Staff Officer of Combat Troops, Deputy Section Chief, Section Chief, Deputy Dept Chief, Dept Chief of Combat Troops for Shenyang Mil. Region, Deputy Chief of Staff 1987; Chief of Staff, 14th Army 1983–87; rank of Maj.-Gen. 1988; Chief of Staff, Jinan Mil. Region 1990–94, Deputy Commdr 1994–96; mil. rep. to 14th Cen Cttee CCP 1992–97; rank of Lt-Gen. 1993; Commdr of People's Armed Police 1996–; rank of Gen. 1998; mem. 15th CCP Cen. Cttee 1997–2002. *Address:* People's Liberation Army Headquarters of Armed Police, Beijing, People's Republic of China (office).

YANG, Guoqing, MD; Chinese politician and surgeon; *Chairman, China Association of Taiwan Compatriots;* b. 1936, Taibei City, Taiwan Prov.; ed Beijing Medical Univ., Kobe Medical Univ., Japan; Dir Beijing Overseas Chinese Office 1990; Vice-Chair. China Asscn of Taiwan Compatriots 1993, Chair. 1997–; mem. 8th CPPCC Nat. Cttee 1993–98; Del., 15th CCP Nat. Congress 1997–2002; mem. 9th Standing Cttee of NPC 1998–2003; Vice-Chair. Cttee of Overseas Chinese Affairs, 9th NPC 1998–2003, All-China Federation of Returned Overseas Chinese 1999–. *Address:* China Association of Taiwan Compatriots, Beijing, People's Republic of China (office).

YANG, Henry T. Y., BS, MS, PhD; American engineer and university administrator; *Chancellor, University of California, Santa Barbara;* b. 29 Nov. 1940, Chungking, China; m. Dilling Yang 1966; two d.; ed Nat. Taiwan Univ., West Virginia Univ., Cornell Univ.; Asst Prof., School Aeronautics and Astronautics, Purdue Univ. 1969, Assoc. Prof. 1972–76, Prof. 1976–88, Neil A. Armstrong Distinguished Prof. of Aeronautics and Astronautics 1988–94, Head, School of Aeronautics and Astronautics 1979–84, Dean of Eng and Dir, Computer Integrated Design, Mfg and Automation Center 1984–94; Chancellor and Prof., Dept of Mechanical and Environmental Eng, Univ. of Calif., Santa Barbara 1994–; mem. Nat. Acad. of Eng 1991, Academia Sinica 1992; Fellow, American Inst. of Aeronautics and Astronautics 1985, American Soc. for Eng Educ. 1994; has served on numerous bds and cttees including Defense Science Board, USAF Scientific Advisory Board, Naval Research Advisory Cttee, NASA's Aeronautical Advisory Cttee, NSF Eng Advisory Cttee; Dr hc (Purdue Univ.) 1996, (Hong Kong Univ. of Science and Tech.) 2002, (City Univ. Hong Kong) 2005; numerous awards including USAF Meritorious Civilian Service Award 1989, Centennial Medal, American Soc. of Eng Educ. 1993, Benjamin Garver Lamme Award, Gold Medal, American Soc. of Eng Educ. 1998, South Coast Business and Tech. Award (Exec. of the Year) 2004; recieved 12 outstanding teaching awards from Purdue Univ. *Publications:* Finite Element Structural Analysis; author or co-author of more than 160 articles for scientific journals. *Address:* Office of the Chancellor, 5221 Cheadle Hall, University of California, Santa Barbara, CA 93106-2030, USA (office). *Telephone:* (805) 893-2231 (office). *Fax:* (805) 893-8717 (office). *E-mail:* henry .yang@chancellor.ucsb.edu (office). *Website:* www.chancellor.ucsb.edu.

YANG, Adm. Huaiqing; Chinese naval officer; b. Feb. 1939, Shouguang Co., Shandong Prov.; joined PLA 1958, CCP 1960; served as Asst of Org. Section under political dept of frigate detachment 1964–70; Asst, section chief, deputy Dir and Dir of Cadre Dept of Navy Fleet 1981–85; dir political dept of a naval base; Political Commissar of a naval base 1988–90; Deputy Dir Political Dept of PLA Navy, Dir 1992–95; Political Commissar PLA Navy 1995–2003; rank of Rear-Adm. 1990, Vice Adm. 1994, Adm. 2000; Deputy to 8th NPC 1993; mem. 15th CCP Cen. Cttee 1997–2002, 16th CCP Cen. Cttee 2002–07. *Address:* c/o Ministry of National Defence, 20 Jingshanqian Jie, Beijing 100009, People's Republic of China (office).

YANG, Hyong-sop; North Korean politician; *Vice-Chairman, Presidium of the Supreme People's Assembly;* b. 1 Oct. 1925, Hamhung; ed Kim Il Sung Univ.; Speaker, Supreme People's Ass. 1983, Chair. 1983–98, Assoc. mem. Politburo 1993–, Vice-Chair. Presidium of the Supreme People's Ass. 1998–; Vice-Chair. Peaceful Reunification of Fatherland Cttee 1984–; Chair. Korean Asscn of Social Sciences 1997–; Alt. mem. Political Bureau of Cen. Cttee of the Workers' Party; Head of Del. to China 2004, to S Africa 2005, to Venezuela 2005. *Address:* Presidium of the Supreme People's Assembly, Pyongyang, Democratic People's Republic of Korea (office).

YANG, Jerry, BS, MS; American computer industry executive; *Chief Yahoo, Yahoo! Incorporated;* b. (Yan Chih-Yuan), 1968, Taipei, Taiwan; m. Akiko Yamazaki; one c.; ed Stanford Univ.; moved to San Jose, Calif. at age 10 years; Co-Creator Yahoo! (internet navigational guide) 1994, Co-Founder, Yahoo! Inc. 1995, Chair. Bd of Dirs and Chief Yahoo! 1996–2007, 2009–, CEO 2007–09; mem. Bd of Dirs Cisco Systems Inc. 2000–, Alibaba 2005–, Asian Pacific Fund; mem. Stanford University Board of Trustees; Co-Chair. (with wife) $1B Campaign for Undergraduate Educ., Stanford Univ. *Address:* Yahoo! Incorporated, 701 1st Avenue, Sunnyvale, CA 94089, USA (office). *Telephone:* (408) 349-3300 (office). *Fax:* (408) 349-3301 (office). *E-mail:* CorporateSecretary@yahoo-inc.com (office). *Website:* www.yahoo.com (office).

YANG, Jiechi, PhD; Chinese diplomatist and government official; *Minister of Foreign Affairs;* b. May 1950, Shanghai; m.; one d.; ed Univ. of Bath and London School of Econs, UK; staff mem., later Second Sec. Trans. and Interpretation Dept, Ministry of Foreign Affairs 1975–84, Counsellor, later

Div. Dir 1987–90, Counsellor, later Div. Dir, later Dir-Gen. North American and Oceania Affairs Dept 1990–93, Asst Minister, Ministry of Foreign Affairs 1995–98, Vice-Minister 1998–2000; Second Sec., later First Sec., later Counsellor, Chinese Embassy, Washington, DC, USA 1983–87, Minister and Deputy Chief of Mission 1993–95, Amb. to USA 2001–05; Vice-Minister of Foreign Affairs in charge of region of N America and Oceania and Latin America, foreign-related affairs involving Hong Kong, Macao and Taiwan, work of translation and interpretation 2005–07, Minister of Foreign Affairs 2007–; Alt. mem. 16th CCP Cen. Cttee 2002–07, mem. 17th CCP Cen. Cttee 2007–. *Leisure interests:* playing table tennis, listening to choral music, writing poems. *Address:* Ministry of Foreign Affairs, 225 Chaoyangmen Nan Dajie, Chaoyang Qu, Beijing 100701, People's Republic of China (office). *Telephone:* (10) 65961114 (office). *Fax:* (10) 65962146 (office). *E-mail:* webmaster@mfa.gov.cn (office). *Website:* www.fmprc.gov.cn (office).

YANG, Jike; Chinese scientist and administrator; b. 6 Nov. 1921, Shanghai; m. Wang Anqi; one s. two d.; ed Ohio State Univ., USA; Prof., Chinese Univ. of Science and Tech. 1966–; Vice-Gov. of Anhui Prov. 1979–88; Vice-Pres. Energy Research Asscn 1982–90, Pres. 1990–; Vice-Chair. China Zhi Gong Dang (Party for Public Interests) 1988–97, Hon. Vice-Chair. 11th China Zhi Gong Party (Public Interest Party) Cen. Cttee; Pres. Cen. Coll. of Socialism of China (now Cen. Socialist Acad.) 1991–; Vice-Chair. Environmental and Resources Protection Cttee, 8th NPC 1993–98; mem. Standing Cttee 9th CPPCC Nat. Cttee 1998–2003, Vice-Chair. Population Resources and Environment Sub-cttee 1998–2003. *Address:* c/o Zhi Gong Dang, Taiping Qiao Street, Xi Cheng District, Beijing, People's Republic of China.

YANG, Jingyu; Chinese politician; b. Sept. 1936, Xingyang, He'nan Prov.; ed Beijing Foreign Trade Inst.; joined CCP 1954, Deputy Dir Econ. Law Office, Dir Research Office, Deputy Dir Comm. of Legis. Affairs, Standing Cttee of 5–7th NPC 1981–91; Dir Bureau of Legis. Affairs, State Council 1991–98, Minister, Office of Legis. Affairs 1998–2002, Deputy Sec.-Gen., State Council 1995–98; Del. to 14–16th CCP Nat. Congress 1992–2007; Chair. Law Cttee, 10th NPC 2003–08, Hon. Expert, Standing Cttee of 11th NPC 2008–; Visiting Prof., Renmin Univ. of China, China Univ. of Int. Business and Econs, Nat. Admin School. *Publications:* Rational Explorations in the Process of Rule of Law 2002, My Meditations 2006, Reflections on the Practice of Rule of Law 2008. *Address:* National People's Congress, Beijing, People's Republic of China (office).

YANG, Kaisheng, DEcon; Chinese banking executive; *Vice-Chairman, Executive Director and President, Industrial & Commercial Bank of China Ltd;* b. Nov. 1949, Hubei; ed Beijing Coll. of Chemical Tech., Wuhan Univ.; joined Industrial & Commercial Bank of China (ICBC) 1985, Head of Planning and Information Dept 1985–90, Gen. Man. Shenzhen City Br. 1990–95, Vice-Gov. ICBC 1995–99, Pres. 2005–, also currently Vice-Chair. and Exec. Dir and Deputy ICBC Party Sec. and Chair. ICBC Credit Suisse Asset Man. Co. Ltd; Pres. China Huarong Asset Man. Corpn 1999–; Dir (non-exec.) and Deputy Chair. Standard Bank Group (South Africa) 2008–; Adjunct Prof., Wuhan Univ.; Deputy Dir 16th Cttee, China Int. Econ. and Trade Arbitration Comm. *Address:* Industrial & Commercial Bank of China Ltd, 55 Fuxingmennan Dajie, Xicheng Qu, Beijing 100032, People's Republic of China (office). *Telephone:* (10) 66106070 (office). *Fax:* (10) 66106053 (office). *E-mail:* webmaster@icbc.com.cn (office). *Website:* www.icbc.com.cn (office).

YANG, Lan; Chinese broadcaster; *Chairman, Sunshine-Culture Network Television;* b. 29 March 1968, Beijing; m. Bruno Wu Zheng; two c.; ed Beijing Foreign Studies Univ., Columbia Univ., USA; Presenter, Zheng Da variety show, China Cen. TV Station 1990–94; Producer and Presenter, Chinese Channel Phoenix Satellite TV, Hong Kong 1997–99; Co-Founder and Chair. Sunshine-Culture Network TV (Sun Media Investment Holdings) 2000–; f. Sunshine Cultural Foundation, Hong Kong 2005; creator Her Village website; apptd image Amb. for Beijing 2008 Olympics bid; mem. 10th CPPCC Nat. Cttee 2003–; mem. Columbia Univ. Int. Advisory Council 2005–; Golden Microphone Winner 1994. *Address:* Sun Media Investment Holdings, No. 387 YongJia Road, Shanghai 200031, People's Republic of China (office). *Website:* www.chinasunmedia.com (office).

YANG, Le, (Lo Yang); Chinese mathematician; b. Nov. 1939, Nantong, Jiangsu Prov.; m. Qieyuan Huang; two d.; ed Peking Univ. and Inst. of Math., Chinese Acad. of Sciences; Pres. Acad. of Math. and System Sciences, Chinese Acad. of Sciences 1998–; mem. 4th Presidium of Depts, Chinese Acad. of Sciences 2000–; Research Fellow and Dir Inst. of Math., Chinese Acad. of Sciences; Fellow, Chinese Acad. of Sciences; invited to deliver lectures in 60 univs abroad and to speak at over 20 int. confs; Nat. Natural Science Prize, Hua Luogeng Math. Prize, Tan Kah Kee Prize, Ho Leung Ho Lee Math. Prize. *Publication:* Value Distribution Theory 1993. *Address:* Institute of Mathematics, Chinese Academy of Sciences, Zhongguancun, Haidian District, Beijing, People's Republic of China (office). *Telephone:* (10) 62541848 (office). *Fax:* (10) 62568356 (home).

YANG, Maj.-Gen. Liwei; Chinese astronaut; b. June 1965, Suizhong Co., Liaoning Prov.; m.; one s.; joined PLA 1983, entered No. 8 Aviation Coll. of PLA, became fighter pilot 1987; selected to fly Project 921 (later Shenzhou) spacecraft 1988, in training Astronaut Training Base, Beijing 1988–93; became first Chinese citizen launched aboard a Chinese spacecraft (Shenzhou-5) Oct. 2003; rank of Col 2003, Maj.-Gen. 2008; Dr hc (Chinese Univ. of Hong Kong) awarded title Space Hero 2003. *Address:* c/o China National Space Administration, A8 Fucheng Road, Haidian, Beijing, People's Republic of China (office). *Website:* www.cnsa.gov.cn (office).

YANG, Marjorie M. T., BS, MBA; Hong Kong business executive; *Chairman and CEO, Esquel Group;* ed Baldwin School, Bryn Mawr, Pa, Massachusetts Inst. of Tech. and Harvard Business School, USA; Assoc. in Corp. Finance,

Mergers and Acquisitions, First Boston Corpn, New York 1976–77; Chair. YTT Tourism Advisor Ltd, Hong Kong 1978–87; helped her father to found Esquel Group in 1978, Chair. and CEO 1995–; mem. MIT Corpn; mem. Bd of Dirs of Assocs, Harvard Business School 1997–; Dir Wuxi Int. Man. Services Pte Ltd 1997–, Gillette Co. 1998–, RandD Corpn Ltd, Hong Kong Univ. of Science and Tech. 2000–, Pacific Century Regional Devts 2000–, BlueDot Capital Pte Ltd 2000–, Clarke Quay Ltd 2001–, China Exploration and Research Soc. 2000–; business adviser to Chair. Sembcorp Industries Ltd; Chair. Yang Yuan-Loong Educ. Fund, Suzhou, People's Repub. of China 1995–; mem. All-China Fed. of Industry and Commerce 1995–; Vice-Pres. Exec. Dir Women Entrepreneur Asscn 1995–; Vice-Chair. Fed. of Industry and Commerce, Xinjiang Prov., People's Repub. of China 1997–; Vice-Pres. Friendship Asscn for Overseas Chinese, Xinjiang Prov. 1997–, Asscn of Enterprises with Foreign Investment in Foshan City 1997–; mem. Garment Advisory Cttee 1998–, Hong Kong-US Business Council, Hong Kong Trade Devt Council 1999–; mem. Standing Cttee CPPCC, Xinjian Prov. 1998–, Foshan, Guangdong Prov. 1998–, mem. Cttee CPPCC, Gaoming, Guangdong Prov. 1998–, mem. Hong Kong Exec. Council 2009–; apptd by Gov. of Hong Kong as Immigration Tribunal Adjudicator 1982–88; mem. Asia Advisory Bd of MIT/China Int. Man. Educ. Project, Dean's Council of Advisors, Sloan School of Man., MIT; Hon. Pres. Hong Kong Fed. of Women 1994–; Hon. Citizen of Foshan, Guangdong Prov. 1995, of Turpan, Xinjiang Prov. 1996; Hon. Darjah Setia Pangkuan Negeri, Penang State, Malaysia 1996; Hon. Chargé d'affaires, China Nat. Table Tennis Team 1997–; Commdr of the Star and Key of the Indian Ocean (Mauritius) 1997; Alumnae Award, Baldwin School, Bryn Mawr, Pennsylvania, USA 1996, selected as one of 50 Stars of Asia by Business Week magazine 1998, Owner Operator Award, DHL/South China Morning Post Hong Kong Business Award 1999, selected as one of Six Most Powerful Businesswomen from Asia, Fortune magazine 2000, ranked by Fortune magazine amongst 50 Most Powerful Women in Business outside the US (36th) 2002, (36th) 2003, (44th) 2004, (41st) 2005. *Address:* Esquel Enterprises Limited, 12/F, Harbour Centre, 25 Harbour Road, Wanchai, Hong Kong Special Administrative Region, People's Republic of China (office). *Telephone:* 28118077 (office). *Fax:* 29606988 (office). *E-mail:* questions@esquel .com (office). *Website:* www.esquel.com (office).

YANG, Mianmian; Chinese business executive; *President, Haier Group;* b. 1945; joined Haier Group (fmrly Qingdao Refrigerator Plant) 1984, later Exec. Pres. –2000, Pres. 2000–05, 2006–, Exec. Dir and Chair. 2005–06, a Deputy Dir Technological Centre; Vice-Pres. China Asscn of Women Entrepreneurs; ranked by Fortune magazine amongst 50 Most Powerful Women in Business outside the US (eighth) 2004, (15th) 2005, (20th) 2006, (25th) 2007, ranked by Forbes magazine amongst 100 Most Powerful Women (70th) 2006, (43rd) 2007, (70th) 2008. *Address:* Haier Group Company, No. 1 Haier Road, Hi-tech Zone, Qingdao 266101, People's Republic of China (office). *Telephone:* (532) 8939999 (office), (532) 8938093 (Technology Centre) (office). *Fax:* (532) 8938666 (office);)532) 8938555 (Technology Centre) (office). *E-mail:* tech@ haier.com (office). *Website:* www.haier.com (office).

YANG, Mingsheng; Chinese banking executive; *Vice-Chairman, China Insurance Regulatory Commission;* b. 1952; joined Agricultural Bank of China (ABC) 1980, Deputy Gen. Man., Shenyang Br. 1987–90, Gen. Man., Tianjin Br. 1990–97, Exec. Vice-Pres. 1997–2003, Pres. and CEO 2003–07; Vice-Chair. China Insurance Regulatory Comm. 2007–. *Address:* China Insurance Regulatory Commission, 15 Jin Rong Street, Western District, Beijing 100032, People's Republic of China (office). *Telephone:* (10) 6628-6688 (office). *Website:* www.circ.gov.cn (office).

YANG, Peidong, BA, PhD; Chinese chemist and academic; *Professor of Chemistry, University of California, Berkeley;* b. 1971, Suzhou; ed Univ. of Science and Tech. of China (USTC), Hefei, Harvard Univ., USA; Postdoctoral Fellow, Univ. of Calif., Santa Barbara 1997–99; joined Chem. Dept, Univ. of Calif., Berkeley 1999, Chevron Texaco Asst Prof. 2003–04, Assoc. Prof. 2004, now Prof.; Co-Founder Nanosys Inc.; Assoc. Ed. Journal of the American Chemical Soc.; mem. ACS (Chair., Nanoscience Div. 2003–), American Physical Soc., Materials Research Soc.; USTC Guo Moruo Prize 1993, Camille and Henry Dreyfus New Faculty Award 1999, 3M Untenured Faculty Award 2000, Research Innovation Award 2001, NSF Career Award 2001, Hellman Family Faculty Award 2001, ACS ExxonMobil Solid State Chem. Award 2001, Beckman Young Investigator Award 2002, Camille Dreyfus Teacher-Scholar Award 2004, Materials Research Soc. Outstanding Young Investigator Award 2004, ACS Pure Chem. Award 2005, NSF Waterman Award 2007, Scientific American 50 Award 2008. *Address:* Department of Chemistry, University of California, Berkeley, CA 94720-1460, USA (office). *Telephone:* (510) 643-1545 (office). *Fax:* (510) 642-7301 (office). *E-mail:* p_yang@berkeley.edu (office). *Website:* www.cchem.berkeley.edu (office).

YANG, Rudai; Chinese party official; b. 1926, Renshou Co., Sichuan Prov.; joined CCP 1952; Sec. CCP Renshou Co. Cttee 1952–68; mem. 4th NPC 1975–78; Sec. CCP Leshan Prefectural Cttee, Sichuan Prov. 1977–78; mem. Standing Cttee CCP Sichuan Prov. Cttee 1978–82, Sec. CCP Sichuan Prov. Cttee 1982; Vice-Gov. of Sichuan Prov. 1978–82; mem. 12th Cen. Cttee CCP 1982–87, 13th Cen. Cttee CCP 1987–92; mem. Politburo 1987–92; Political Commissar, Sichuan Mil. Dist 1983–86; First Sec. Party Cttee 1985; Sec. CCP Sichuan 1983–93; mem. Presidium 14th CCP Nat. Congress 1992; Vice-Chair. 8th CPPCC Nat. Cttee 1993–98, 9th CPPCC Nat. Cttee 1998–2003; Hon. Pres. Special Rural Tech. Asscn of China 1995. *Address:* c/o National Committee of Chinese People's Political Consultative Conference, 23 Taipingqiao Street, Beijing, People's Republic of China (office).

YANG, Taifang; Chinese politician and expert in telecommunications technology; b. 30 April 1927, Mei Co., Guangdong Prov.; s. of Yang Shukum and Wen Xinyun; m. Wu Youhong 1957; one s. two d.; ed Zhongshan Univ.,

Vice-Minister of Posts and Telecommunications 1982–84, Minister 1984–92; mem. 12th Cen. Cttee CCP 1982–87, 13th Cen. Cttee 1987–92; Chair. Overseas Chinese Cttee 8th NPC 1993–98; mem. Presidium 14th CCP Nat. Congress 1992–97; NPC Deputy, Guangdong Prov.; mem. Standing Cttee 8th NPC 1993–98; Chair. All-China Fed. of Returned Overseas Chinese 1994. *Leisure interests:* music, bridge, Taiji boxing. *Address:* c/o Overseas Chinese Committee of the National People's Congress, 23 Xijiao Minxiang Road, West District, Beijing 100805, People's Republic of China (office).

YANG, Hon. Sir Ti Liang, Kt, LLB, FCIA; Chinese judge (retd); b. 30 June 1929, Shanghai; s. of Shao-nan Yang and Elsie Chun; m. Eileen Barbara Tam 1954 (died 2006); two s.; ed The Comparative Law School of China, Soochow Univ., Shanghai, Univ. Coll. London, UK; called to Bar (with Hons), Gray's Inn 1954; Magistrate, Hong Kong 1956, Sr Magistrate 1963, Dist Judge, Dist Court 1968, Judge of High Court 1975, Justice of Appeal 1980, Vice-Pres. Court of Appeal 1987, Chief Justice of Hong Kong 1988–96; mem. Exec. Council, Hong Kong Special Admin. Region 1997–2002; Pres. of Court of Appeal of Negara Brunei Darussalam 1988–92; Rockefeller Fellow, London Univ. 1963–64; Chair. Kowloon Disturbances Claims Assessment Bd 1966, Compensation Bd 1967, Comm. of Inquiry into the Rainstorm Disasters 1972, into Lelung Wing-sang Case 1976, into McLennan Case 1980; mem. Law Reform Comm. (Chair. Sub-Cttee on law relating to homosexuality 1980) 1980–96; Chair. Chief Justice Working Party on Voir Dire Procedures and Judges' Rules 1979, Univ. and Polytechnic Grants Cttee 1981–84, Hong Kong Univ. Council 1987–2001; Chair. ICAC Complaints Cttee 1999–2002, Hong Kong Red Cross 2000–; Pro-Chancellor, Hong Kong Univ. 1994–2001; Patron The Soc. for the Rehabilitation of Offenders, Hong Kong; Vice-Patron Hong Kong Scouts Asscn; Hon. Prof., Open Univ. of Hong Kong 2006; Order of Chivalry (First Class), SPMB, Negara Brunei Darus-salam 1990, Grand Bauhinia Medal 1999; Hon. LLD (Chinese Univ. of Hong Kong) 1984, (Hong Kong Polytechnic) 1992; Hon. DLitt (Hong Kong Univ.) 1991. *Publications:* (trans.) General Yue Fei (by Qian Cai) 1995, (trans.) Peach Blossom Fan (novel by Gu Shifân 1948) 1998, (trans.) Officialdom Unmasked (novel by Li Boyuan) 2001. *Leisure interests:* philately, reading, walking, oriental ceramics, travelling, music. *Address:* GPO Box 1123, Central, Hong Kong Special Administrative Region, People's Republic of China (office). *Telephone:* (852) 91373067 (office). *Fax:* (852) 28498099 (home).

YANG, Wei, MS, PhD; Chinese engineer and university administrator; *President, Zhejiang University;* b. 16 Feb. 1954, Beijing; ed Northwestern Polytechnical Univ., Tsinghua Univ., Brown Univ., USA; joined CCP 1976; Faculty mem. and Chair. Dept of Eng Mechanics, Tsinghua Univ., also Acting Dean, School of Aerospace 1978–2004, Dean 2004–05; Dir Ministry of Educ., Postgraduate Educ. Dept 2004–06; Pres. Zhejiang Univ. 2006–. *Address:* Office of the President, Zhejiang University, 388 Yuhangtang Road, Hangzhou 310058, Zhejiang, People's Republic of China (office). *Fax:* (571) 88981358 (office). *E-mail:* zupo@zju.edu.cn (office). *Website:* www.zju.edu.cn/english (office).

YANG, Xizong; Chinese government official; b. 27 Sept. 1928, Dayi Co., Sichuan Prov.; s. of Yang Qunling and Yang Chunbing; m. Zhou Feng; one s. two d.; Alt. mem. CCP Cen. Cttee 1983; Deputy to 6th NPC 1983, NPC Deputy, Sichuan Prov.; Deputy Sec. CCP 4th Prov. Cttee, Sichuan 1983–85; Gov. of Sichuan 1983–85; Chair. Sichuan Prov. 8th People's Congress, Standing Cttee 1993–98; Sec. CCP Prov. Cttee Henan 1985–89; mem. 12th CCP Cen. Cttee 1985–87, 13th CCP Cen. Cttee 1987–92. *Leisure interest:* reading. *Address:* c/o Sichuan Provincial People's Congress, Chengdu, Sichuan Province, People's Republic of China (home).

YANG, Yuanqing, MSc; Chinese computer industry executive; *CEO, Lenovo Group;* ed Univ. of Science and Tech. of China; joined Lenovo Group 1989, CEO 2001, later Pres. and CEO Lenovo Group Ltd, Exec. Chair. 2004–09, CEO 2009–; mem. New York Stock Exchange (now NYSE Euronext) Int. Advisory Cttee, Nat. Youth Asscn Cttee; mem. Bd of Dirs China's Entrepreneurs' Asscn; Guest Prof., Univ. of Science and Tech. of China; named by BusinessWeek magazine as one of the "Stars of Asia", selected by Chinese media as one of China's "Ten Star Entrepreneurs" and "Ten Most Valuable Managers", named by CCTV as a "Man of the Year" 2004. *Address:* Lenovo Group, No. 6 Chuang Ye Road, Shangdi Information Industry Base, Haidian District, Beijing 100085, People's Republic of China (office). *Telephone:* (10) 58868888 (office). *E-mail:* info@lenovo.com (office). *Website:* www.lenovo.com (office).

YANG, Zhengwu; Chinese politician; b. Jan. 1941, Longshan Co., Hunan Prov.; joined CCP 1969; Deputy Sec. CCP Longshan Co. Cttee 1970, Sec. 1970–77; Sec. CCP Tujia-Miao Autonomous Prefectural Cttee, Hunan Prov., Xiangxi 1985–90, Deputy Magistrate, Intermediate People's Court 1985–90; mem. Standing Cttee CCP Hunan Prov. Cttee 1985–90, Deputy Sec. CCP Hunan Prov. Cttee 1990–98, Sec. 1998; Chair. Standing Cttee of People's Congress 1999–; Chair. Comm. for Comprehensive Man. of Social Security 1993–; Gov. of Hunan Prov. 1995–98; Alt. mem. 12th CCP Cen. Cttee 1982–87, mem. 13th CCP Cen. Cttee 1987–92, 14th CCP Cen. Cttee, 15th CCP Cen. Cttee 1997–2002, 16th CCP Cen. Cttee 2002–07. *Address:* Provincial People's Congress, Changsha, Hunan Province, People's Republic of China (office).

YANG, Zhenhuai; Chinese government official; b. Jan. 1928, Anhui; s. of Yang Licuo and Wu Dingshu; m. Yang Duanyi 1960; one s. one d.; joined CCP 1950; Vice-Minister for Water Resources and Electric Power 1983–88, Minister for Water Resources 1988–93; Sec.-Gen. State Flood Control HQ 1986–88, Deputy Head 1988; Deputy Head State Leading Group for Comprehensive Agric. Devt 1990; Vice-Chair. Environmental and Resources Protection Cttee; Vice-Chair. All-China Environment Fed. (ACEF); Alt. mem. 14th CCP Cen. Cttee 1992–97; mem. 9th Standing Cttee of NPC 1998–2003, Vice-Chair. Agric. and Rural Affairs Cttee 1998–2003. *Leisure interests:* reading history, geology, humane studies. *Address:* All China Environment Federation, Beijing, People's Republic of China (office).

YANG, Maj.-Gen. Zhenyu; Chinese air force officer; b. 1931, Chifeng City, Rehe (Jehol) (now Liaoning Prov.); ed Air Force Aviation School, Red Flag Air Force Acad., USSR; joined PLA 1947, CCP 1948; regt literacy teacher of N China Mil. Command 1948–49; joined Chinese People's Volunteers (CPV) in Korea 1951; served in PLA Air Force as Regt Commdr 1962–64, Deputy Commdr of Div. and Chief of Staff, PLA Air Force Shanghai Base 1980–81, Chief of Staff of Corps 1983–85, Deputy Commdr of Command Post of PLA Air Force 1985–86; Vice-Pres. Air Force Command Acad. 1986–90, Pres. 1990; Deputy Commdr PLA Air Force 1994–96; Vice-Pres. China Soc. of Mil. Future Studies 1988–; rank of Maj.-Gen. 1988; a PLA del. to 8th NPC 1993–98. *Address:* c/o Ministry of National Defence, Beijing, People's Republic of China (office).

YANG, Zhiguang; Chinese artist; b. 11 Oct. 1930, Shanghai; s. of Yang Miaocheng and Shi Qinxian; m. Ou Yang 1958; two d.; ed Cen. Acad. of Fine Art; Vice-Pres. and Prof., Guangzhou Acad. of Fine Arts; mem. Council, Chinese Artists' Asscn; mem. Acad. of Traditional Chinese Painting; does traditional Chinese figure painting, calligraphy and seal-making; Artist-in-Residence, Griffis Art Center, Conn., USA 1990; Gold Medal winner, 7th Vienna World Youth Festival, for picture Sending Food in Heavy Snow 1959. *Publications:* Skill of Chinese Traditional Figure Painting, Selections of Portraits, Chinese Water Colours, Yang Zhiguang's Sketches in China's North-west, Portraits of Modern Chinese Artists, Painting Selections of Mr and Mrs Yang Zhiguang. *Leisure interests:* calligraphy, seal-making, poetry. *Address:* Guangzhou Institute of Fine Art, No. 257, Chang Gang Dong Lu Street, Haizhu District, Guangzhou, People's Republic of China (office). *Telephone:* (20) 84017598 (home). *Fax:* (20) 84017417 (home).

YANG, Zhuangsheng; Chinese business executive; *General Manager, Chairman and Chief Executive Officer, Science-Technology Group;* b. Dec. 1942; ed Univ. of Int. Business and Econs; Gen. Man., Chair. and CEO Science-Technology (SCITECH) Group 1991–. *Address:* Saite Dasha, 19 Jianguomenwai Da Jie, Beijing 100004, People's Republic of China (office). *Website:* www.scitechgroup.com (office).

YANGIBOYEV, Baxodir; Uzbekistani politician; *Chairman of the Council of Ministers of the Sovereign Republic of Qoraqalpog'iston;* fmr Minister of Finance, Repub. of Qoraqalpog'iston, Chair. Council of Ministers 2006–, mem. Council of Ministers of Uzbekistan; fmr Gov. To'rtku'l Dist. *Address:* Office of the Chairman, Council of Ministers of the Republic of Qoraqalpog'iston, 230102 Qoraqalpog'iston, Nukus, Dustlik Gazari 96, Uzbekistan (office). *Telephone:* (361) 222-00-14 (office). *Fax:* (361) 222-26-46 (office). *E-mail:* info@sovminrk.gov.uz (office). *Website:* sovminrk.gov.uz (office).

YANGLING, Duoji; Chinese politician and academic; b. 24 April 1931, Batang Co., Sichuan Prov.; s. of Yang Yong-an and Basang-wengmo; m. Qumu-a Ying 1954; two s. one d.; Vice-Gov. Sichuan Prov. 1979–81; Perm. Sec. CCP Cttee, Tibet Autonomous Region 1981–86; Vice-Chair. Tibetan People's Govt 1982–83; Alt. mem. 12th CCP Cen. Cttee 1982–87; Chair. Tibet Br., CPPCC 1983–86; Vice-Chair. and Vice-Sec. of Party, Sichuan CPPCC 1986–; del. to 7th People's Congress of China 1988–92; Del. to 11th Congress of CCP 1980–82, 12th 1982–87, 13th 1987–92; Chair. Tibetan Studies Asscn, Sichuan Prov.; Dean Acad. of Tibetan Studies, Sichuan Prov. 1990–; Ed. Tibetology Research, History of Kong Tibetan 1996–. *Leisure interest:* reading. *Address:* Office of the Vice-Chairman of the Chinese People's Consultative Council, No. 25 Hong Zhao Bi Street, Chengdu, Sichuan, People's Republic of China (office). *Telephone:* (28) 6753780 (home). *Fax:* (28) 663393.

YANIN, Valentin Lavrentyevich, DHist; Russian archaeologist; *Head Chair of Archaeology, Moscow University;* b. 6 Feb. 1929; m.; ed Moscow State Univ.; jr then sr researcher Moscow Univ. 1954–, Prof. 1963–, also Head Chair. of Archaeology, Moscow Univ.; researcher of history and archaeology of Middle Age Russia and of old manuscripts; Chair. of Bd Russian Humanitarian Scientific Fund (RGNF) 1996–; Corresp. mem. USSR (now Russian) Acad. of Sciences 1966, mem. 1990, mem. Presidium 1991–2002; Hon. Citizen of Novgorod; Lenin Prize, USSR State Prize. *Publications include:* Money and Weight Systems of Medieval Russia 1956, Novgorod Posadniki 1962, I Have Sent You a Birch Bark 1965, Act Stamps of Old Russia X–XV Centuries 1970, Novgorod Feudal Ancestral Lands 1982, Novgorod Acts XII–XV Centuries 1991. *Leisure interest:* collecting old vocal recordings. *Address:* RGNF, Yaroslavskaya str. 13, 129366 Moscow, Russia. *Telephone:* (495) 283-55-40 (office); (495) 335-54-28 (home).

YANKILEVSKY, Vladimir Borissovich; Russian artist; b. 15 Feb. 1938, Moscow; s. of Boris Yankilevsky and Rosa Yankilevskaya; m. Rimma Solod 1959; one d.; ed Moscow Secondary Art School and Moscow Polygraphic Inst.; took part in Manège exhbn of 1962; participated in first officially permitted Exhbn of avant-garde artists 1975; first retrospective in Moscow 1978; first retrospectives in the West (New York and Bochum Museum, Germany) 1988; first participation in Sotheby's Auction in Moscow 1988; retrospectives in Moscow 1987, Paris 1991, Tretyakov Gallery, Moscow 1995–96, Neuhoff Gallery, New York 1996, Mané-Katz Museum, Haifa 2001. *Animation work includes:* The World of Tales 1973, I Fly to You 1977, I am with You Again 1977. *Television:* Good Evening, Moscow (Moscow, TV Gallery) 1996, Portraits of Artists-Nonconformists (Moscow, TV Gallery, Culture Channel) 2001. *Publications:* Retrospective 1958–1988 1988, Autoportraits 1992, Retrospective 1995–96, Retrospective 1996, Radierungen 1999; Variations on the Other – A Digital-Analog Monograph on the Work of Vladimir Yankilevsky (ed by David Riff) 2002, I dve figury ... Tales for my Friend (in Russian) 2003. *Leisure interest:* photography. *Address:* 230 rue St Charles, 75015 Paris,

France. *Telephone:* 1-45-58-21-57. *Fax:* 1-45-58-21-57. *E-mail:* vyankilevsky@noos.fr (office). *Website:* www.yankilevsky.net (office).

YANKOVSKY, Oleg Ivanovich; Russian actor; b. 23 Feb. 1944, Jezkazgan; m. Lyudmila Zorina; one s.; ed Saratov Drama School; actor Saratov Drama Theatre 1967–73, Moscow Theatre of Lenin Komsomol (now Lenkom) 1973–; leading roles in many theatre productions; debut in film I am Francisc Skorina 1968; Pres. Russian Nat. Festival Cinotaurus 1992; People's Artist of Russia 1984, State Prize of Russia 1989; winner of many int. and Russian prizes at maj. film festivals. *Films include:* O lyubvi (A Ballad of Love) 1966, Zvezda plenitelnogo schastya (The Captivating Star of Happiness) 1975, Zerkalo (The Mirror) 1975, Obyknovennoye chudo (Ordinary Wonder) 1978, Tot samyy Myunkhgauzen (That Munchhausen) 1979, My, nizhepodpisavshiyesya (We, the Undersigned) 1981, Polyoty vo sne i nayavu (Flights in Dreams and Reality) 1982, Nostalghia (Nostalgia) 1983, Moi Ivan, toi Abraham (Me Ivan, You Abraham) 1993, Mute Witness 1994, Two Hussars, Keep Me, My Talisman, Kitayskiy serviz (Chinese Tea-Set) 1999, The Man Who Cried 2000, Patul lui Procust (Procust's Bed) 2001, Prikhodi na menya posmotret (Come Look at Me) 2001, Lyubovnik (The Lover) 2002, Bednyy, bednyy Pavel (Poor, Poor Pavel) 2003. *Television includes:* Anna Karenina (miniseries) 2005, Doctor Zhivago (miniseries) 2005. *Address:* Komsomolsky prospekt 41, Apt. 10, 119270 Moscow, Russia. *Telephone:* (495) 242-32-85 (home).

YANNARAS, Christos, PhD, DrTheol; Greek philosopher and academic; *Professor Emeritus of Philosophy, Panteion University of Political and Social Studies;* b. 10 April 1935, Athens; ed Univ. of Athens, Univ. of Bonn, Germany, Univ. of Paris (Sorbonne), France, Faculty of Theology, Aristotle Univ. of Thessaloniki, Faculté des Lettres et Sciences Humaines, Sorbonne; Visiting Prof., Catholic Univ. of Paris 1971–73, Univ. of Geneva, Switzerland 1977–79, Univ. of Lausanne, Switzerland 1978–79, Univ. of Crete (Rethymnon) 1979–82; Prof. of Philosophy, Panteion Univ. of Political and Social Studies, Athens 1982–2005, Prof. Emer. 2005–; mem. Hellenic Authors' Soc., Acad. Int. des Sciences Humaines, Brussels, Belgium; Hon. DPhil (Belgrade). *Publications:* more than 40 books, including Critical Ontology (3rd edn) 1995, The Real and the Imaginary in the Political Economy (2nd edn) 1996, Heidegger and the Areopagite (4th edn) 1998, The Linguistic Boundaries of Realism in Metaphysics 1999, The Inhuman Character of Human Rights (3rd edn) 2000, The Freedom of Morality (3rd edn) 2002, Discontinuity in Philosophy (5th edn) 2002, Cultural Diplomacy (2nd edn) 2003, Postmodern Metaphysics (2nd edn) 2004, The Relational Ontology 2004, Variations on the Song of Songs (6th edn) 2005, Culture as the Central Problem in Politics (2nd edn) 2005, Orthodoxy and the West (5th edn) 2006, The Religionization of the Ecclesial Event (2nd edn) 2007, Person and Eros (6th edn) 2007; translated into many languages. *Address:* 84 Plastira Street, 171 21 Nea Smyrni, Athens, Greece (home). *Telephone:* (210) 9353697 (office). *Fax:* (210) 9353697 (office). *E-mail:* anpa@uom.gr (office).

YANO, Akiko; Japanese musician; b. 1955, Tokyo; m. Sakamoto Ryuichi; ed classical training; child piano prodigy; familiar with jazz, pop and R&B at early age; working musician in Tokyo club scene during high school and began singing at this time; played on many albums as session musician in Japan; appeared in concert with Tin Pan Alley; recorded track album by Little Feat, Los Angeles; first solo album Japanese Girl 1976; participated in Yellow Magic Orchestra world tour 1979–80; double solo album co-produced by herself and her husband titled Gohan Ga Dekitayo (Dinner's Ready!) 1980. *Albums include:* Nagatsuki Kan Nazuki 1976, I Rohani Konpeitou 1977, To Ki Me Ki 1978, Gohan Ga Dekitayo 1980, Tadaima 1981, Ai Ga Nakuchane 1982, O.S.O.S. 1984, Brooch 1986, Granola 1987, Welcome Back Akiko Yano 1989, Super Folk Song 1992, Love Is Here 1993, Elephant Hotel 1994, Oui Oui 1997, Ego Girl 1999, Home Journey Girl 2000, Reverb 2002, Honto No Kimochi 2004, Hajimete No Yano Akiko 2006, Akiko 2008. *Address:* c/o Sony Music Entertainment Inc., 550 Madison Avenue, New York, NY 10022-3211, USA. *Website:* www.akikoyano.com.

YANO, Kaoru, MSc; Japanese electronics industry executive; *President and Representative Director, NEC Corporation;* b. 23 Feb. 1944; ed Univ. of Tokyo, Stanford Univ., USA; joined NEC Corpn 1966, based in USA 1985–90, Gen. Man. Transmission Div. 1990–94, Exec. Gen. Man. Transmission Operations Unit 1994–95, Assoc. Sr Vice-Pres. 1995–99, Pres. NEC USA Inc. 1998–2000, Sr Vice-Pres. 1999–2002, mem. Bd of Dirs 2000–, Deputy Pres. NEC Networks Co. 2000–02, Pres. NEC Networks Co. 2002–03, Exec. Vice-Pres. NEC Corpn 2002–04, Sr Exec. Vice-Pres. and Rep. Dir 2004–06, Pres. and Rep. Dir 2006–. *Address:* NEC Corporation, 7-1, Shiba 5-chome, Minato-ku, Tokyo 108-8001, Japan (office). *Telephone:* (3) 3454-1111 (office). *Fax:* (3) 3798-1510 (office). *E-mail:* info@nec.com (office). *Website:* www.nec.com (office).

YANOFSKY, Charles, PhD; American biologist and academic; *Morris Herzstein Professor Emeritus of Biology, Stanford University;* b. 17 April 1925, New York, NY; s. of Frank Yanofsky and Jennie Kopatz Yanofsky; m. 1st Carol Cohen 1949 (died 1990); three s.; m. 2nd Edna Crawford 1992; ed City Coll. of New York and Yale Univ.; Research Asst in Microbiology, Yale Univ. 1951–53; Asst Prof. of Microbiology, Western Reserve Univ. 1954–58; Assoc. Prof., Dept of Biological Sciences, Stanford Univ., Prof., Dept of Biological Sciences 1961–, Morris Herzstein Prof. of Biology 1967, now Prof. Emer.; Pres. Genetics Soc. of America 1969, American Soc. of Biological Chemists 1984; Career Investigator American Heart Asscn 1969–95; mem. NAS, American Acad. of Arts and Sciences; Foreign mem. Royal Soc. 1985–; Fellow, European Acad. of Sciences 2004; Hon. mem. Japanese Biochemical Soc. 1985–; Hon. DSc (Univ. of Chicago) 1980, (Yale Univ.) 1981; Eli Lilly Award in Bacteriology 1959, U.S. Steel Award in Molecular Biology 1964, Howard Taylor Ricketts Award 1966, Albert Lasker Award for Basic Medical Research 1971, Selman A. Waksman Award 1972, Louisa Gross Horwitz Prize 1976, Townsend Harris Medal, City Coll. of New York, Mattia Award, Roche Inst.

1982, Genetics Soc. of America Medal 1983, Gairdner Foundation Award 1985, Thomas Hunt Morgan Medal, Genetics Soc. of America 1990, Passano Award 1992, William C. Rose Award of the ASBMB 1997, Abbott-ASM Lifetime Achievement Award 1998, Nat. Medal of Sciences 2003, 2005. *Publications:* more than 400 scientific articles in Proceedings of Nat. Acad. of Sciences, etc. *Leisure interests:* tennis, growing orchids. *Address:* Department of Biological Sciences, Stanford University, Stanford, CA 94305 (office); 725 Mayfield Avenue, Stanford, CA 94305, USA (home). *Telephone:* (650) 725-1835 (office); (650) 857-9057 (home). *Fax:* (650) 725-8221 (office). *E-mail:* yanofsky@stanford.edu (office). *Website:* med.stanford.edu/profiles/faculty/Charles_Yanofsky (office).

YANUKOVYCH, Viktor Fedorovych, DEcon; Ukrainian politician; *Chairman, Partiya Regioniv (Party of Regions);* b. 9 July 1950, Yenakiyevo, Donetsk Oblast; m. Lyudmyla Oleksandrivna Yanukovych; two s.; ed Donetsk Polytechnic Inst., Ukrainian Acad. of Foreign Trade; worked in a variety of early jobs including welder, Yenakiyevo metal works 1969–70, fitter and mechanic in automobile factory 1972–76, dir of transport depot 1976–84; mem. CP of Soviet Union 1980–91; moved to Donetsk 1984, held exec. positions at transport cos; fmr Dir-Gen. of major production firms including Donbastransremont, Ukrvuhlepromtrans, Donetsk Oblast Motor Transport Territorial Production Asscn 1994–96; Deputy Gov., then First Deputy Gov. of Donetsk Oblast State Admin 1996–97, Gov. 1997–2002; Chair. Donetsk Oblast Council 1999–2001 (resgnd); Prime Minister of Ukraine 2002–07 Dec. 2004, 28 Dec. 2004–5 Jan. 2005, 2006–07; presidential cand. 2004; Chair. Party of Regions 2003–; Prof., mem. Acad. of Econ. Sciences of Ukraine; mem. Presidium Nat. Acad. of Sciences of Ukraine; Orders of Ukraine 'For Merits' of three degrees; Merited Worker of Ukrainian Transport, and other decorations. *Leisure interests:* sport (especially tennis), hunting, pigeon raising. *Address:* Party of the Regions (Partiya Regioniv), 01021 Kyiv, vul. Lypska 10, Ukraine (office). *Telephone:* (44) 254-29-20 (office). *Fax:* (44) 254-33-70 (office). *E-mail:* partreg@ln.ua (office). *Website:* www.partyofregions.org.ua (office).

YAO, Ming; Chinese professional basketball player; b. 12 Sept. 1980, Shanghai; s. of Yao Zhiyuan and Fang Fengdi; m. Ye Li; ed Shanghai Sports Coll.; center; played for Chinese Basketball Asscn Shanghai Sharks 1997–2002; drafted first overall by Nat. Basketball Asscn (NBA) Houston Rockets 2002; mem. Chinese Olympic team 2000 Sydney, 2004 Athens; carried Olympic Flame into Tiananmen Square during Olympic torch relay August 2008; led Chinese delegation during Olympic opening ceremony; mem. Chinese nat. team, Beijing Summer Olympics 2008; Chinese Basketball Asscn (CBA) Most Valuable Player 2001, 2002; CBA Sportsmanship Award 2002; selected for NBA All-Rookie Team 2002; selected for NBA All-Star Game 2003, 2004, 2005, 2006, 2007; Laureus World Newcomer of the Year 2003. *Publications:* Yao: A Life in Two Worlds (with Ric Bucher) 2004. *Address:* Houston Rockets, Toyota Center, 1510 Polk Street, Houston, TX 77002, USA. *Website:* www.nba.com/rockets; www.nba.com/playerfile/yao_ming.

YAO, Zhenyan; Chinese banker; b. 1932, Changsu, Jiangsu Prov.; ed Civil Eng Coll., Jiaotong Univ., Shanghai; joined CCP 1956; Vice-Minister of Water Conservancy and Electric Power 1985–88; Gen. Man. State Energy Investment Corpn 1988–94; Vice-Minister, State Devt and Reform Comm. (fmrly State Planning Comm.) 1991–94; Pres. State Devt Bank 1994–98; Vice-Chair. Financial and Econ. Cttee of NPC 1998–2003; Del., 15th CCP Nat. Congress 1997–2002. *Address:* c/o State Development Bank, 40 Fucheng Lu, Haidian Qu, Beijing, People's Republic of China (office).

YAO, Zhonghua; Chinese artist; b. 17 July 1939, Kunming, Yunnan; s. of the late Yao Penxien and Wang Huiyuan; m. Ma Huixian 1969; two s.; ed Cen. Acad. of Fine Arts; one-man show, Beijing 1980, Cité Int. Arts, Paris 1985 and exhbns in Paris and Eastern Europe; numerous group exhbns in China, also China Oil Paintings of Present Age Exhbn, New York, USA 1987, Melbourne, Sydney, Australia 1987, Wan Yu Tang Art Gallery, Hong Kong 1989; group exhbn Beijing Art Gallery 1992; one-man exhbn Taiwan 1992, Calif., USA 1995; mural for Parl. Hall, Yunnan People's Congress; mem. Council China Artists' Asscn; Vice-Pres. Yunnan Painting Inst. *Works include:* Oh, the Land!, Sani Minority's Festival, The Yellow River, Zhenghe's Voyage, The Jinsha River Flowing beside the Jade Dragon Mountain, Chinese Ink and Water. *Publications:* paper on painter Dong Xi Wen, in Chinese Oil Painting and Art Research 1990, Selected Works of Yao Zhonghua 1993. *Leisure interests:* music, literature. *Address:* c/o China Art Networks, 7/F, Xinzhong Mansion, Gongti Beilu, Beijing, People's Republic of China.

YAP, Emilio; Philippine newspaper publisher and business executive; *Publisher, Manila Bulletin;* Chair. Manila Bulletin Publishing Corpn, Publr Manila Bulletin, other business interests include Philippine Trust Co., Philippine Bank of Communications (PBCom), US Automotive Co. Inc., Bataan Shipyard and Eng Co., Manila Prince Hotel Inc., Philippine Dockyard Corpn, Philippine President Lines Inc., Manila Int. Port Terminal, Liwayway Publishing Inc. *Address:* Manila Bulletin Publishing Corporation, corner of Muralla and Recoletos Streets, Intramuros, PO Box 769, Metro Manila 1002, Philippines (office). *Telephone:* (2) 527-8121 (office). *Fax:* (2) 527-7510 (office). *E-mail:* bulletin@mb.com.ph (office). *Website:* www.mb.com.ph (office).

YAQUB, Muhammad, PhD; Pakistani banker and economist; b. 1937, Jalandar, India; s. of Haji Muhammad Shah and Bibi Karim; m. Nasreen Yaqub; two s. one d.; ed Punjab Univ., Yale Univ., Princeton Univ., USA; Asst Dir, Research Dept State Bank of Pakistan 1966–68, Deputy Dir 1968–69, Sr Deputy Dir 1969–72, Sr Prin. Officer, Dir Research Dept 1975, Gov. 1993–99; Sr Economist and Resident Rep., IMF, Saudi Arabia 1975, Fund Resident Adviser to Saudi Arabian Govt, IMF 1977, Div. Chief, Middle Eastern Dept IMF 1977–80, Asst Dir 1981–82, IMF Rep. to Paris Club, London Club, OECD and co. aid consortia; Consultant IMF, Washington; Prin. Econ. Adviser, Special Section, Ministry of Finance 1992–93; has headed IMF missions to numerous Middle Eastern countries. *Publications:* Major-Macro Economic Policy Issues in Pakistan. *Address:* IMF, 700 19th Street, NW, Washington, DC 20431, USA (office). *Website:* www.imf.org (office).

YAR'ADUA, Alhaji Umaru Musa, MSc; Nigerian politician and head of state; *President;* b. 1951, Katsina; brother of the late Shehu Yar'Adua; m. Hajia Turai Umaru Yar'Adua; ed Barewa Coll., Zaria and Ahmadu Bello Univ.; mem. Nat. Youth Service Corps, Holy Child Coll., Lagos 1975–76; Lecturer in Chem., Katsina Coll. of Arts, Science and Tech. 1976–79, Katsina Polytechnic 1979–83; Gen. Man., Sambo Farms Ltd, Funtua 1983–89; Chair. Katsina State Investment and Property Devt Co. (KIPDECO) 1994–96, Nation House Press Ltd 1995–99; Dir Hamada Holdings 1983–99, Madara Ltd 1987–99, Lodigiani Nigeria Ltd 1987–99, Habib Nigeria Bank Ltd 1995–99; fmr mem. Peoples' Redemption Party (PRP); Founding mem. Peoples' Front (later Social Democratic Party, SDP) 1987–95; mem. Constituent Ass. 1988; f. K34 Political Asscn (later People's Democratic Party, PDP) 1998; Gov., Katsina state 1999–2007; Pres. of Nigeria 2007–, also C-in-C of the Armed Forces and Minister responsible for Petroleum Resources; Nat. Primary Educ. Productivity Merit Award 2004, Cen. Bank of Nigeria Best Gov. Award 2005. *Address:* Office of the President, New Federal Secretariat Complex, Shehu Shagari Way, Central Area District, Abuja, Nigeria (office). *Telephone:* (9) 5233536 (office). *E-mail:* maimaje@yaradua2007.com (office). *Website:* www.yaradua2007.com (office); www.nigeria.gov.ng (office).

YARMOSHYN, Uladzimir Vasilyevich; Belarusian politician and engineer; b. 26 Oct. 1942, Pronsk, Ryazan Region, Russia; m.; two c.; ed Novocherkassk Polytech. Inst., Leningrad Civil Aviation Acad.; turner Electric Locomotive plant, Novocherkassk; sr engineer, chief mechanical engineer, Deputy Dir Minsk Civil Aviation plant 1965–90; Chair. Exec. Cttee Dist Soviet of People's Deputies, Minsk 1990; Deputy Chair. Minsk City Exec. Cttee, also Head Cttee on Housing and Power Eng 1990–92; First Deputy Chair. then Chair. Minsk City Exec. Cttee 1995–2000; mem. Council in Nat. Ass.; Chair. Council of Ministers 2000–01; Head Belorussian Reps, Mobil Telesystems 2002–. *Address:* Mobil Telesystems, Minsk, Belarus (office).

YAROV, Yuri Fedorovich; Russian politician; b. 2 April 1942, Mariinsk, Kemerovo Oblast; m.; one s. one d.; ed Leningrad Tech. Inst., Leningrad Eng Econ. Inst.; worked in factories in Latvia 1964–68, Leningrad oblast 1968–76; Dir factory Burevestnik 1978–85; First Sec. Gatchina City CPSU Cttee (Leningrad oblast) 1985–87; Deputy Chair. Exec. Cttee Leningrad oblast Soviet of Deputies 1987–89, Chair. 1989–90; Chair. Leningrad oblast Soviet of People's Deputies 1990–91; People's Deputy of Russian Fed. 1990–92; Deputy Chair. Supreme Soviet of Russia 1991–92; Deputy Prime Minister 1992–96; Presidential Rep. to Fed. Council; Deputy Head of Presidential Admin 1996–97, First Deputy 1997–98; Plenipotentiary Rep. of Pres. of the Russian Fed. in Federation Council 1998–99; Chair. Exec. Cttee of CIS 1999–2004. *Address:* c/o Executive Committee of Commonwealth of Independent States, 220000 Minsk, vul. Kirava 17, Belarus (office).

YARROW, Sir Eric Grant, 3rd Bt (cr. 1916), MBE, DL, FRSE; British business executive (retd); b. 23 April 1920, Glasgow; s. of the late Sir Harold Yarrow, 2nd Bt and Eleanor Etheldreda Yarrow; m. 1st Rosemary Ann Young 1951 (died 1957); one s. (deceased); m. 2nd Annette Elizabeth Françoise Steven 1959 (divorced 1975); three s.; m. 3rd Joan Botting 1982; ed Marlborough Coll., Glasgow Univ.; served apprenticeship with G. and J. Weir Ltd; army service in Burma 1939–45, Maj. Royal Engineers 1945; trained with English Electric Co. 1945–46; Asst Man., Yarrow and Co. Ltd 1946, Dir 1948, Man. Dir 1958–67, Chair. 1962–85, Pres. 1985–86; Chair. Yarrow (Shipbuilders) Ltd 1962–79; Dir Clydesdale Bank 1962–91, Deputy Chair. 1975–85, Chair. 1985–91; Dir Standard Life Assurance 1958–90, Nat. Australia Bank Ltd 1987–91; mem. Council, Royal Inst. Naval Architects 1957–, Vice-Pres. 1965, Hon. Vice-Pres. 1972; mem. Gen. Cttee Lloyd's Register of Shipping 1960–87; Prime Warden, Worshipful Co. of Shipwrights 1970–71; Deacon, Incorporation of Hammermen of Glasgow 1961–62; fmr mem. Council of Inst. Engineers and Shipbuilders in Scotland; Chair. Exec. Cttee Princess Louise Scottish Hosp., Erskine 1980–86, Hon. Pres. 1986–; Pres. Scottish Convalescent Home for Children 1958–70, Burma Star Asscn in Scotland 1989–; Officer, Most Venerable Order of the Hosp. of St John of Jerusalem. *Leisure interest:* family life. *Address:* Craigrowan, Porterfield Road, Kilmacolm, Renfrewshire, PA13 4PD, Scotland. *Telephone:* (1505) 872067.

YASHIMA, Toshiaki; Japanese energy industry executive; *Chairman, Tohoku Electric Power Company Inc.;* Man.-Dir Tohoku Electric Power Co. Inc. 1997, apptd Pres. 1998, currently Chair.; Chair. Tohoku Econ. Fed.; Vice-Pres. Fed. of Electric Power Cos (FEPC) 1999, Co-Vice-Chair. –2001; Dir Japan Nuclear Fuel Ltd –2001; mem. Bd Energy Conservation Center (ECCJ) 1999–2001, Japan Productivity Center for Socio-Econ. Devt (JPC-SED); mem. Advisory Cttee UNU Global Seminars. *Address:* Tohoku Electric Power Company Inc., 7-1 Honcho 1-chome, Aoba-ku, Sendai, Miyagi 980-8550, Japan (office). *Telephone:* (2) 2225-2111 (office). *Fax:* (2) 2225-2500 (office). *Website:* www.tohoku-epco.co.jp (office).

YASHIRO, Eita; Japanese politician; mem. House of Councillors; fmr mem. House of Reps; Chair. House of Reps Cttee on Judicial Affairs; fmr Parl. Vice-Minister for Science and Tech.; Minister of Posts and Telecommunications 1999–2000. *Address:* c/o Ministry of Posts and Telecommunications, 1-3-2, Kasumigaseki, Chiyoda-ku, Tokyo 100-0013, Japan (office).

YASHIRO, Masamoto, MA; Japanese business executive; b. Feb. 1929, Tokyo; ed Kyoto and Tokyo Univs; joined Esso (now Exxon) 1958, Pres. Esso Sekiyu (affiliate of Exxon Mobile Corpn) –1989; Head of Citicorp, Japan 1989–98 (retd); Pres. and CEO Shinsei (or 'Rebirth') Bank, Ltd (fmrly Long-Term Credit Bank of Japan Ltd) 2000–05 (retd). *Address:* c/o Shinsei Bank Ltd, 1-8, Uchisaiwaicho 2-chome, Chiyoda-ku, Tokyo, 100-8501, Japan.

YASIN, Yevgeny Grigoryevich, DEconSc; Russian politician, economist and academic; *Professor, Higher School of Economics;* b. 7 May 1934, Odessa; s. of Grigory Yasin and Yevgenia Yasina; m. Lydia Yasina (née Fedoulova); one d.; ed Odessa Inst. of Construction Eng, Moscow State Univ.; worked USSR Cen. Dept of Statistics 1963–73, Researcher, Cen. Inst. of Econs and Math., USSR (now Russian) Acad. of Sciences 1973–89; Head of Div. State Comm. on Econ. Reform, USSR Council of Ministers (Abalkin Comm.) 1990–91; one of authors of econ. programme 500 Days; Dir-Gen. Direction on Econ. Policy of Russian Union of Industrialists and Entrepreneurs 1991; f. and Dir Expert Inst. of Russian Union of Industrialists and Entrepreneurs 1992–93; mem. Council of Enterprise of Pres. of Russia 1992; Plenipotentiary Rep. of Govt in Parl. 1992–93; Head of Analytical Centre of Pres. 1994–; Minister of Econs of Russia 1994–97, Minister Without Portfolio 1997–98; Prof., Higher School of Econs 1992–, Scientific Head 1998–; Head of govt legislation drafting teams 1992–97. *Address:* Higher School of Economics, Malaya Yakimanka str. 2/1, Moscow, Russia. *Telephone:* (495) 921-79-83; (495) 928-92-90.

YASSIN, Salim, PhD; Syrian politician and professor of economics; b. 10 Oct. 1937, Lattakia; m. Najwa Ismail 1962; five c.; Dean of Faculty, Aleppo Univ. 1966–68, Vice-Pres. of Univ. 1969–71; Pres. Lattakia Univ. 1971–78; govt minister 1978–85, Deputy Prime Minister in charge of Econ. Affairs 1985–2000; sentenced to ten years' imprisonment for corruption 2001. *Publications:* Theory of Correlation, International Trade, Aggregate Economic Analyses. *Leisure interests:* reading, football, swimming.

YASSUKOVICH, Stanislas Michael, CBE; British/American banker and business executive; *Chairman, S.M. Yassukovich & Co. Ltd;* b. 5 Feb. 1935, Paris, France; s. of Dimitri Yassukovich and Denise Yassukovich; m. Diana Townsend 1961; two s. one d.; ed Deerfield Acad., Mass. and Harvard Univ., USA; U.S. Marine Corps. 1957–61; joined White, Weld and Co. 1961, London Office 1962, Branch Man. 1967–69, Gen. Partner, New York 1969–73, Man. Dir, London 1969–73; Man. Dir European Banking Co. SA Brussels 1983–85, Chief Exec. European Banking Group 1983–85; Chair. Merrill Lynch Europe Ltd 1985–89, Hemingway Properties 1993–; Vice-Chair. Jt Deputy Chair. London Stock Exchange 1986–89, Bristol and West Bldg Soc. (now Bristol & West PLC) 1991–2000, ABC Int. Bank 1993–; currently Chair. S.M. Yassukovich & Co. Ltd; Chair. Securities Asscn 1988–91; Chair. Cragnotti & Partners Capital Investment (UK) 1991–96, Park Place Capital 1994–, Henderson EuroTrust PLC 1995–, Easdaq SA 1997–99, Manek Investment Man. Ltd 1997–; Deputy Chair. Flextech PLC 1989–97, South West Water (now Pennon Group PLC) 1993–2000; Dir Royal Nat. Theatre 1991–96, Chair. City Disputes Panel 1993–99; Dir (non-exec.) Henderson Group PLC 1990–98, Telewest PLC 1998–, Atlas Capital Ltd 1999–. *Leisure interests:* hunting, shooting and polo. *Address:* S.M. Yassukovich & Co. Ltd, 42 Berkeley Square, London, W1J 5AW, England (office). *Telephone:* (20) 7318-0825 (office). *E-mail:* smycoltd@aol.com (office).

YASTRZHEMBSKY, Sergey Vladimirovich, CandHistSc; Russian politician, journalist and diplomatist; *Assistant to the President of the Russian Federation;* b. 4 Dec. 1953, Moscow; m. Anastassia Yastrzhembskaya; three c.; ed Moscow State Inst. of Int. Relations, Inst. of Int. Workers' Movt; jr researcher, Acad. of Social Sciences Cen. Cttee CPSU 1979–81; on staff journal Problems of the World and Socialism (Prague) 1981–89; Sr staff-mem. Int. Div. Cen. Cttee CPSU 1989–90; Deputy Ed.-in-Chief Megapolis (journal) 1990–91, Ed.-in-Chief VIP journal 1991–92; Dir Dept of Information and Press, Russian Ministry of Foreign Affairs 1992–93; Amb. to Slovakia 1993–96; Press Sec. to Pres. Boris Yeltsin 1996; Deputy Head Pres. Yeltsin's Admin. 1997–98; Vice-Chair. Moscow Govt 1998–99; Asst to Pres. Vladimir Putin (q.v.) 2000–; Special Envoy to the EU 2004; Rank II Order of the White Cross (Slovakia); Russian Orthodox Church Order of St Daniil; 850th Anniversary of Moscow Commemorative Medal. *Publications:* Social Democracy in the Contemporary World 1991; essays and articles on current events, contemporary devt of Portugal and European social democracy, and relations between Russia and EU. *Leisure interests:* tennis, stamp collecting, reading, hunting, downhill skiing, photography. *Address:* Office of the President, Staraya pl. 4, 103132 Moscow, Russia (office). *Telephone:* (495) 606-08-31 (office). *Fax:* (495) 606-91-93 (office). *E-mail:* president@gov.ru (office). *Website:* www.kremlin.ru (office).

YASUI, Kaoru, LLD; Japanese jurist and poet; b. 25 April 1907, Osaka; s. of Harumoto Yasui and Harue Yasui; m. Tazuko Kuki 1936; one s. one d.; ed Tokyo Univ.; Asst Prof., Tokyo Univ. 1932–42, Prof. 1942–48; Prof., Hosei Univ. 1952, Dean Faculty of Jurisprudence 1957–63, Dir 1963–66, Prof. Emer. 1978–; Leader (Chair. etc.) Japan Council Against Atomic and Hydrogen Bombs 1954–65; Pres. Japanese Inst. for World Peace 1965–; Dir Maruki Gallery for Hiroshima Panels 1968–; Chair. Japan–Korea (Democratic People's Repub.) Solidarity Cttee of Social Scientists 1972–; Dir-Gen. Int. Inst. of the Juche Idea 1978–; mem. Lenin Peace Prize Cttee; Hon. mem. Japanese Asscn of Int. Law 1976–; Hon. DJur (San Gabriel Coll., USA); Lenin Peace Prize 1958; Gold Medal (Czechoslovakia) 1965. *Publications:* Outline of International Law 1939, Banning Weapons of Mass Destruction 1955, People and Peace 1955, Collection of Treaties 1960, My Way 1967, The Dialectical Method and the Science of International Law 1970, A Piece of Eternity (poems) 1977. *Address:* Minami-Ogikubo 3-13-11, Suginami-ku, Tokyo, Japan.

YASUKAWA, Hideaki; Japanese business executive; *Chairman, Seiko Epson Corporation;* trained as engineer and watch designer; joined Suwa Seikosha (renamed Seiko Epson Corpn) 1955, apptd Dir 1976, Man.-Dir 1981–85, Sr Man.-Dir 1985–87, Exec. Vice-Pres. 1987–91, Pres. 1991–2001,

Chair. 2001–; Chair. Nagano Employers' Asscn; mem. Nippon Keidanren, Japan Business Fed.; Order of the Sacred Treasure, Gold and Silver Star 2002 Medal of Honour with a Blue Ribbon 1996. *Address:* Seiko Epson Corporation, 3-3-5 Owa, Suwa, Nagano 392-8502, Japan (office). *Telephone:* (2) 6652-3131 (office). *Fax:* (2) 6653-4844 (office). *Website:* www.epson.com (office).

YASUOKA, Okiharu; Japanese politician; *Minister of Justice;* b. 11 May 1939; ed Hibiya High School, Tokyo, Legal Trainee of Supreme Court of Japan (grad. of 19th Class), Faculty of Law, Chuo Univ.; mem. House of Reps (Kagoshima Dist 1) 1972–; Judge, Kagoshima Dist Court 1972–78; Parl. Vice-Minister, Nat. Land Agency (Ohira Cabinet) 1978–80, Parl. Vice-Minister of Finance (Suzuki Cabinet) 1980–84; Chair. Standing Cttee on Construction, House of Reps (second Nakasone Cabinet) 1984–87, Deputy Sec.-Gen. LDP 1987, Chair. Cttee on Planning, HQ for Political Reform, LDP 1989, Special Cttee on Relocation of the Diet, House of Reps 1993, Finance Cttee, LDP 1996, Sr Dir Finance Cttee, House of Reps 1996, Sr Deputy Chair. Policy Research Council, LDP 1997, Acting Chair. HQ for Implementation of Educational Reform, LDP 1997, Chair. Research Comm. on Judiciary System, LDP 1998, Special Comm. on Promotion of Comprehensive Plan for Financial Revitalization, LDP 1998, Sr Dir Special Cttee on Financial Stabilization, House of Reps 1998, Chair. Research Comm. on Constitution, House of Reps 2000, Chief Sec. Nat. Vision Project HQ, LDP 2001, Acting Chair. HQ on Urgent Countermeasures to Stabilize the Financial System, LDP 2003, Chair. Research Comm. on Constitution, LDP 2003, Sr Dir Special Cttee for Research on Constitution of Japan, House of Reps 2005–07, Chair. Research Comm. on Antimonopoly Laws, LDP 2005–07, Deputy Chair. Jt Gen. Meeting of Both Houses 2007–08, Supreme Adviser, Research Comm. on Antimonopoly Laws 2007, Acting Chair. Council on Constitution 2007–08; Chief Judge, Judge Impeachment Court 2007–08; Minister of Justice 2000–01, 2008–. *Leisure interests:* jogging, swimming. *Address:* Ministry of Justice, 1-1-1, Kasumigaseki, Chiyoda-ku, Tokyo, 100-8977 Japan (office). *Telephone:* (3) 3580-4111 (office). *Fax:* (3) 3592-7011 (office). *E-mail:* webmaster@moj.go.jp (office). *Website:* www.moj.go.jp (office).

YATES, Peter; British film and theatre producer and director; b. 24 July 1929; s. of Col Robert Yates and Constance Yates; m. Virginia Pope 1960; two s. two d. (one deceased); ed Charterhouse, Royal Acad. of Dramatic Art (RADA); entered film industry as studio man. and dubbing asst with De Lane Lea; Asst Dir The Entertainer, The Guns of Navarone, A Taste of Honey, etc; Golden Globe Best Film Award 1979, Evening Standard Film Award Special Achievement 2001. *Films directed include:* Summer Holiday 1962, Danger Man, Saint (TV series) 1963–65, Robbery 1966, Bullitt 1968, John and Mary 1969, Murphy's War, Mother, Jugs and Speed 1975, The Deep 1976, Breaking Away (also produced) (Golden Globe Best Film) 1979, The Janitor (Eyewitness in USA; also produced) 1980, Krull 1982, The Dresser (also produced) 1983, Eleni 1984, The House on Carroll Street (also produced) 1986, Suspect 1987, An Innocent Man 1989, The Year of the Comet 1992 (also produced), Roommates 1995, The Run of the Country 1996 (also produced), It all Came True 1997, Curtain Call 1999, Don Quixote 1999, A Separate Peace 2002. *Plays directed:* The American Dream 1961, The Death of Bessie Smith 1961, Passing Game 1977, Interpreters 1985. *Leisure interests:* tennis, sailing, skiing. *Address:* Judy Daish Associates, 2 St Charles Place, London, W10 6RG, England.

YATIM, Dato' Rais bin, MA, LLB, PhD; Malaysian politician; b. 15 April 1942, Jelebu, Negeri Sembilan; m. Datin Masnah Mohamat; three s. one d.; ed Univs of Northern Illinois, Singapore and London; lecturer at ITM, School of Law and also managed own law firm in Kuala Lumpur 1973; mem. Bar Council 1973; mem. Parl. 1974; Parl. Sec. Ministry of Youth, Sport and Culture 1974; Deputy Minister of Law 1976, of Home Affairs 1978; elected to State Ass., Negeri Sembilan 1978; Menteri Besar, Negeri Sembilan 1978; Minister of Land and Regional Devt 1982, of Information 1984–86, of Foreign Affairs 1986–87; Advocate and Solicitor, High Court of Malaysia 1988–; returned to law practice, Kuala Lumpur 1988–; mem. United Malays' Nat. Org. (UMNO) Supreme Council of Malaysia 1982–; Deputy Pres. Semangat 1989–; Minister in Prime Minister's Dept 1999; Minister of Foreign Affairs 2008–09; mem. Civil Liberty Cttee Bar Council, Kuala Lumpur 1996–98. *Publications:* Faces in the Corridors of Power 1987, Freedom under Executive Power in Malaysia 1995, Zaman Beredar Pesaka Bergilir 1999. *Leisure interests:* photography, writing, travel. *Address:* 41 Road 12, Taman Grandview, Ampang Jaya, 68000 Ampang, Selangor, Malaysia (home). *Telephone:* (3) 4569621 (home). *E-mail:* drrais@pc.jaring.my (home).

YATSENYUK, Arseniy Petrovych, PhD; Ukrainian lawyer and politician; b. 22 May 1974, Chernivtsi; m.; two d.; ed Chernivtsi State Univ. and Kyiv Univ. of Trade and Econs; Pres. Yurek Ltd (law firm), Chernivtsi 1992–97; consultant to credit dept, Aval Jt Stock Postal Pensions Bank, Kyiv 1998, Advisor to Chair. of Bd 1998–2001, Deputy Chair. of Bd Aug.–Sept. 2001; Minister of Economy, Autonomous Repub. of Crimea, Simferopol 2001–03; First Deputy Chair. Nat. Bank of Ukraine 2003–05; First Deputy Gov. Odesa Region Feb.–Sept. 2005; Minister of Economy 2005–06, of Foreign Affairs 2007; Deputy Head, Presidential Secr. 2006–07; Chair. Verkhovna Rada 2007–08; mem. Nat. Security and Defence Council –2008. *Address:* c/o Office of the Chairman, Verkhovna Rada, 01008 Kyiv, vul. M. Hrushevskoho 5, Ukraine. *Telephone:* (44) 255-21-15. *E-mail:* Yatseniuk.Arsenii@rada.gov.ua (office).

YATSKEVICH, Boris Alexandrovich, CandGeol; Russian geologist; b. 7 Jan. 1948, Lignice, Poland; ed Voronezh State Univ.; Sr Technician, Sr Geologist, Chief Geologist Ukhta geological expedition, Komi Autonomous Repub. 1972–86; chief geologist Polar–Urals production geological co. Vorkuta 1986–90; Head of Div. State Cttee on Geology RSFSR 1990–92; Deputy Chair. State Cttee on Geology and use of Mineral Wealth 1992–96; First

Deputy Minister of Natural Resources Russian Fed. 1996–99, Minister 1999–2001; mem. Observation Council ALROSA (Diamonds of Russia and Sakha). *Address:* c/o Ministry of Natural Resources of Russian Federation, Bolshaya Gruzinskaya str. 4/6, 123812 Moscow, Russia (office).

YAU, Carrie, BSocSc; Hong Kong civil servant; *Permanent Secretary for Home Affairs;* b. (Tsang Ka Lai), 4 June 1955; d. of Tsang Hin Yeung and Tsang Choon Kwa; m. Francis Yau; one s.; ed Maryknoll Sisters' School, Diocesan Girls' School, Univ. of Hong Kong; joined Hong Kong Govt as an Admin. Officer 1977, various posts in maj. policy areas, Govt Spokeswoman, Chief Sec.'s Office 1994–95, Dir of Admin. 1997–2000, Sec. for Information Tech. and Broadcasting 2000–02, Perm. Sec. for Health, Welfare and Food 2002–06, Perm. Sec. for Food and Environmental Hygiene of Health, Welfare and Food 2006–07, Perm. Sec. for Home Affairs 2007–; Chair. Bd of Review (Film Censorship), Steering Cttee on Cyberport; Vice-Chair. Broadcasting Authority; mem. Business Advisory Cttee, Services Promotion Strategy Group, Steering Cttee for Third Generation Mobile Service. *Leisure interests:* singing, hiking, family activities. *Address:* Office of the Permanent Secretary of Home Affairs, 31/F, Southern Centre, 130 Hennessy Road, Wanchai, Hong Kong Special Administrative Region, People's Republic of China (office). *Telephone:* 2835-2056 (office). *Fax:* 2591-6002 (office). *E-mail:* hab1@hab.gov.hk (office). *Website:* www.hab.gov.hk (office).

YAU, Shing-tung, PhD, FAAS; Chinese mathematician and academic; *William Casper Graustein Professor of Mathematics, Harvard University; Director, The Institute of Mathematical Sciences, The Chinese University of Hong Kong;* b. 4 April 1949, Kwuntung; s. of Chen ying Chiu and Yeuk Lam leung; Yu-yun Kuo, Isaac Chiu Yau and Michael Chiu; ed Univ. of California, Berkeley; Asst Prof. of Math., State Univ. of New York, Stony Brook 1972–73, Distinguished Visiting Prof. 1990; Prof. of Math., Stanford Univ. . 1974–79; Prof. of Math., Inst. for Advanced Study, Princeton NJ 1979–84; Chair and Prof. of Math., Univ. of California, San Diego 1984–87; Visiting Prof. and Sid Richardson Centennial Chair in Math., Univ. of Texas, Austin 1986; Prof. of Math., Harvard Univ. 1987–, Higgins Prof. (Chair Prof.) 1997–2000, William Casper Graustein Prof. 2000–, Chair. Math. Dept 2008–; Fairchild Distinguished Scholar, Calif. Inst. of Tech. 1990; Wilson T. S.Wang Distinguished Visiting Prof., The Chinese Univ. of Hong Kong 1991–92, Adjunct Prof. of Math. 1994–2003, Dir Inst. of Math. Sciences 1994–; Distinguished Prof.-at-Large 2003–; Special Chair, Nat. Tsinghua Univ., Hsinchu, Taiwan 1991–92; Eilenberg Visiting Prof., Columbia Univ., New York 1999; mem. Bd of Math. Sciences, National Acad. of Science –1989); Mem.-at-Large Council of the American Math. Soc. 1990–92; mem. Scientific Advisory Council Math. Sciences Research Inst. –1989; Ed.-in-Chief Journal of Differential Geometry 1980–, Methods and Application of Analysis 1994–, Asian Journal of Mathematics 1997–; Ed. Communications in Mathematical Physics 1982–99, Mathematical Research Letters, 1993–, Advances in Mathematics 1994–, Journal of Mathematical Physics 1997–; mem. Editorial Advisory Bd Methods and Applications of Analysis, 1993–, Communications in Analysis and Geometry 1993–; mem. American Acad. of Arts and Sciences 1982; Academic Sinica 1984, NAS 1993, New York Acad. of Science, American Physical Soc., Soc. for Industrial and Applied Math.; Foreign mem. Chinese Acad. of Sciences 1995, Russian Acad. of Sciences 2003; Hon. Prof., Fudan Univ. 1983–, Chinese Acad. of Sciences 1983, Hangzhou Univ. 1987–, Tsinghua Univ. 1987–, Nankai Univ. 1993–, Beijing Univ. 1998–, Univ. of Science and Tech. of China 1999–, Zhejiang Univ. 2002–; hon. mem. Academic Cttee Inst. of Math., Chinese Acad. of Sciences 1980–; Hon. Ed. Communications in Information and Systems, 2001–; Hon. PhD (Chinese Univ. of Hong Kong) 1981, (Chao Tung Univ.) 1997, (Nat. Tsinghua Univ., Beijing) 2000, (Macao Univ.) 2002, (Zhejing Univ.) 2003, (Hong Kong Science and Tech. Univ.) 2004, (Cen. Univ. of Taiwan) 2005, (Taiwan Univ.) 2006; Hon. MA (Harvard); Sloan Fellow 1975–76, California Scientist of the Year 1979, Veblen Prize 1981, Carty Prize, Nat. Acad. 1981, Guggenheim Fellowship 1982, Fields Medal, Int. Math. Union, Warsaw 1982 (presented 1983), America's 100 Brightest Scientists Under 40, Science Digest 1984, MacArthur Fellow 1985, American Math. Soc. Lecturer 1986, Crafoord Prize, Royal Swedish Acad. 1994, John Harvard Fellow, Univ. of Cambridge 1996, US Nat. Medal of Science 1997, Bowen Lecturer, Univ. of California, Berkeley 1997, Run Run Shaw Distinguished Lecturer, The Chinese Univ. of Hong Kong 1998, Bergman Lecturer, Stanford Univ. 1999, Radamacher Lecture, Univ. of Pennyslvania 1999. *Publications:* numerous articles in math. journals on partial differential equations, the Calabi conjecture in algebraic geometry, the positive mass conjecture of general relativity theory, and real and complex Monge-Ampère equations. *Address:* Harvard University, Department of Mathematics, One Oxford Street, Cambridge, MA 02138, USA (office); The Institute of Mathematical Sciences, Unit 601, 6/F, Academic Building No. 1, The Chinese University of Hong Kong, Shatin, Hong Kong Special Administrative Region, People's Republic of China. *Telephone:* (617) 495-0836 (Harvard) (office); 2609-8038 (Hong Kong) (office). *Fax:* 2603-7636 (Hong Kong (office). *E-mail:* yau@math.harvard.edu (office); yau@ims.cuhk.edu.hk (office). *Website:* math.harvard.edu (office); www.math.cuhk.edu.hk (office).

YAVLINSKII, Grigorii Alekseevich, PhD, CEconSc; Russian politician and economist; *Leader, Yabloko Russian Democratic Party (Rossiisskaya demokraticheskaya partiya);* b. 10 April 1952, Lviv, Ukrainian SSR; m.; two s.; ed Plekhanov Inst. of Econ., Moscow; electrician Lviv Co., Raduga 1968–69; Sr Researcher, Research Inst. of Man., Ministry of Coal Industry, Moscow 1976–80; Head of Div. Research Inst. of Labour 1980–84; Deputy Chief, Chief of Div., Chief of Dept of Man. USSR State Labour Cttee 1984–89; Chief of Div. State Cttee on Econ. Reform USSR Council of Ministers 1988–90; mem. Pres.'s Political Advisory Council 1990–; Deputy Chair. Council of Ministers of Russian Fed., Chair. State Cttee on Econ. Reform 1990, author of econ. programme 500 days July–Nov. 1990; Econ. Counsellor of Prime Minister of

Russia 1991; Chair. of Council of Scientific Soc. EPI-CENTRE (Cen. for Political and Econ. Studies) 1991–; mem. Econ. Council of Pres. of Kazakhstan 1991–; Deputy Chair. USSR Cttee on Operational Man. of Nat. Econ. Aug.–Dec. 1991; mem. Political Advisory Council of Pres. Gorbachev Oct.–Dec. 1991; co-leader (with Y.U. Boldyrev and V. Lukin) of pre-election bloc (later political movt then political party) Yabloko Russian Democratic Party (Rossiisskaya demokraticheskaya partiya 'Yabloko') 1993, Leader 1995–, currently also party Chair. in Duma; mem. State Duma (Parl.) 1993–; cand. in presidential elections 1996, 2000; Int. Prize for Freedom 2004. *Achievements:* Ukraine Jr Boxing Champion 1967, 1968. *Publications:* Russia–The Search for Landmarks 1993, Incentives and Institutions: The Transition to a Market Economy in Russia 2000; over 60 books on economy of USSR, numerous articles. *Address:* Yabloko Russian Democratic Party (Rossiisskaya demokraticheskaya partiya 'Yabloko'), 119034 Moscow, per. M. Levshinskii 7/3, Russia (office). *Telephone:* (495) 201-43-79 (office). *Fax:* (495) 292-34-50 (office). *E-mail:* info@yabloko.ru (office). *Website:* www.yabloko.ru (office).

YAWER, Ghazi Mashal Ajil al-; Iraqi engineer and business executive; b. 1958, Mosul; m.; three c.; ed Petroleum and Minerals Univ., Saudi Arabia, Georgetown Univ., USA; prominent mem. of Shammar tribe; left Iraq in mid-1980s; Vice-Pres. Hicap Tech. Co., Riyadh, –2003; apptd to Governing Council 2003, Interim Pres. 2004–05; Vice-Pres. of Iraq 2005–06. *Address:* c/o Office of the Vice-President, Baghdad, Iraq (office).

YAZDI, Ibrahim, PhD; Iranian politician; *Secretary-General, Liberation Movement of Iran;* b. c. 1933; m.; two s. four d.; studied and worked as physician in USA for sixteen years; close assoc. of Ayatollah Khomeini during exile in Neauphlé-le-Château, France Oct. 1978–Feb. 1979; mem. Revolutionary Council during Feb. 1979 revolution; Deputy Prime Minister with responsibility for Revolutionary Affairs Feb.–April 1979; Minister of Foreign Affairs April–Nov. 1979; Special Emissary of Ayatollah Khomeini on Prov. Problems 1979; Supervisor Keyhan Org. 1980–81; Deputy in Parl. for Tehran 1980–84; mem. Foreign Affairs, Health and Welfare Parl. Comms; WHO Adviser 1991; Sec.-Gen. Liberation Movt of Iran 1995–; arrested Dec. 1997. *Publications:* Final Efforts in Terminal Days: Some Untold Stories of the Islamic Revolution of Iran 1984, Principles of Molecular Genetics 1985, Mutational Changes in Genetic Materials and Repair Systems 1989, The Ills of the Human Heart 1994; papers on herbal and traditional medicine, carcinogenics, the nucleic acid of cancer cells and Islamic and social topics. *Address:* 21 Touraj Lane, Valiasr Avenue, Tehran 19666, Iran. *Telephone:* (21) 2042558. *Fax:* (21) 2042558.

YAZGHI, Muhammad al-, LenD; Moroccan politician, lawyer and newspaper executive; *Minister of State;* b. 28 Sept. 1935, Fez; m. Balafrej Souada 1972; two s.; ed Moulay Youssef Coll., Lycée Gouraud, Univ. of Rabat and Ecole Nat. d'Admin., Paris; Dir of Budget, Ministry of Finance 1957–60; Dir Al-Moharir (daily paper) 1975–81, Liberation (daily paper) 1989–; First Sec. Moroccan Press Union 1977–93; Deputy in Parl. 1977–; mem. Political Bureau, Union Socialiste des Forces Populaires (USFP) 1975–91, Joint Vice-Sec. 1992, First Sec. –2007 (resgnd); Minister of Territorial Admin, the Environment, Urban Planning and Housing, then Minister of Territorial Administration, Water Resources and the Environment –2007; Minister of State 2007–. *Publications:* articles in magazines and journals. *Leisure interests:* reading, travel. *Address:* Parliament of Morocco, Chambre des Représentants, Avenue Mohamed V, Rabat (office). *Telephone:* (3) 7679700 (office). *E-mail:* parlement@parlement.ma (office). *Website:* www.parlement.ma (office).

YAZICI, Hayati, BS; Turkish politician and lawyer; *Minister of State;* b. 1952, Rize; m.; two c.; ed Istanbul Univ.; served as judge and freelance lawyer 1976–2002; elected mem. Grand Nat. Ass. representing Istanbul 2002; Deputy Prime Minister 2007–09, Minister of State 2009–; Co-founder, Bd Mem. and Deputy Chair. (Organizational Affairs), AKP (Adalet ve Kalkinma Partisi/Justice and Devt Party). *Address:* c/o Prime Minister's Office, Başbakanlık, Bakanlıklar, Ankara, Turkey (office).

YAZOV, Marshal Dmitri Timofeevich; Russian military official (retd); b. 1923; ed Frunze Mil. Acad. and Mil. Acad. of Gen. Staff; entered Soviet army 1941–; active service 1941–45; command posts 1945–76; Deputy Commdr of Far Eastern Mil. Dist 1976–79; Commdr of Cen. Group Forces in Czechoslovakia 1979–80; Deputy to USSR Supreme Soviet 1979–89; Commdr of Cen. Asian Mil. Dist 1980; Deputy Minister of Defence Feb.–June 1987, Minister of Defence and Head of Armed Forces 1987–91; mem. of Cen. Cttee of Kazakh CP 1981–87; mem. Presidential Council 1990–91; Cand. mem. of Cen. Cttee of CPSU 1981–91; fmr mem. Politburo; rank of Marshal 1990; arrested 1991, for participation in attempted coup d'état, charged with conspiracy 1992; on trial 1993; released 1994; Chief Mil. Adviser, Ministry of Defence 1998; Chair. Marshal G. Zhukov Memorial Cttee. *Leisure interests:* theatre, poetry. *Address:* Ministry of Defence, ul. Myasnitskaya 37 Moscow 105175, Russia (office). *Telephone:* (495) 296-39-66 (office). *Fax:* (495) 296-84-36 (office). *Website:* www.mil.ru (office).

YBARRA Y CHURRUCA, Emilio de; Spanish banker; b. 1936, San Sebastián; m.; four c.; ed Jesuit Deusto Univ., Bilbao; joined Banco de Bilbao 1964, mem. Bd of Dirs 1971, Chief Exec. 1976, Vice-Pres. and Chief Exec. 1986; Sole Vice-Pres. Banco Bilbao-Vizcaya (BBV) (following merger of Banco de Bilbao with Banco de Vizcaya) 1988, Pres. 1990–99, Co-Pres. (following merger with Argentaria SA) Banco Bilbao Vizcaya Argentaria SA (BBVA) 1999–2002. *Address:* c/o Banco Bilbao-Vizcaya Argentaria SA, Paseo de la Castellana 81, 28046 Madrid, Spain.

YE, Gongqi; Chinese administrator; b. 1930; joined CCP 1948; Deputy Dir of Shanghai Light Industry Bureau 1976–; Vice-Mayor Shanghai 1985; Chair. Shanghai Municipal 10th People's Congress 1986; Chair. Shanghai Consumers Asscn 2004–; Sr Consultant China Shipping (Group) Co. *Address:* Shanghai Consumers Association, 14th Floor, No. 301 Zhaojiabang Road Shanghai 200032, People's Republic of China (office).

YE, Liansong; Chinese politician and engineer; b. 1935, Shanghai; ed Jiaotong Univ., Shanghai; engineer, Shijiazhuang Municipal Diesel Plant 1960–80; Vice-Mayor Shijiazhuang 1982–85; mem. Standing Cttee Hebei Prov. CCP Cttee 1983–2000, Deputy Sec. 1998–2000; Vice-Gov. Hebei Prov. 1985–93, Gov. 1993–98; Alt. mem. 13th Cen. Cttee CCP 1987–92, mem. 14th Cen. Cttee 1992–97, 15th CCP Cen. Cttee 1997–2002; Deputy to 8th NPC 1993–98. *Address:* c/o Office of the Governor, Hebei Provincial Government, 1 Weiming Jie Street, Shijiazhuang City, People's Republic of China (office).

YE, Rutang; Chinese politician; *Vice-Chairman, Environment and Resources Protection Committee, National People's Congress;* b. 20 March 1940, Wenling Co., Zhejiang Prov.; s. of Ye Mei and Chen Jiaoru; m. Liu Wenbin 1968; one s. two d.; ed Tsinghua Univ.; Minister of Urban and Rural Construction and Environmental Protection 1985–88; Vice-Chair. Environmental Protection Cttee of State Council 1985–88; Vice-Minister of Construction 1988–98; Vice-Chair. Chinese Soc. of Science and Tech. for Social Devt 1991–2001; Vice-Chair. Environment and Resources Protection Cttee, 10th NPC 2003–; apptd Pres. Architectural Soc. of China 1992. *Leisure interests:* calligraphy, swimming. *Address:* c/o Ministry of Land and Natural Resources, 3 Guanyingyuanxiqu, Xicheng Qu, Beijing 100035, People's Republic of China (office). *Telephone:* (10) 66127001 (office). *Fax:* (10) 66175348 (office).

YE, Shaolan, (Ye Qiang); Chinese singer, actor and playwright; b. Sept. 1943, Beijing; s. of Ye Shenglan; ed China Acad. of Traditional Operas, Cen. Acad. of Drama; started learning Peking Opera at age of 9; actor, dir, playwright; Art Dir Zhanyou Peking Opera Troupe, PLA Beijing Mil. Command; mem. Exec. Council of Chinese Dramatists Asscn; won 1st Nat. Theatre Plum Blossom Award 1984; Fulbright Int. Scholar; New York Lincoln Center Life Achievement Award. *Peking operas include:* Lu Bu and Diao Chan, Luo Cheng, Story of the Willow Tree, A Meeting of Heroes, Butterfly Lovers. *Recordings include:* Selected Arias of Ye Shaolan 1995. *Address:* c/o Zhanyou Peking Opera Troupe, People's Liberation Army, Beijing Command, Beijing, People's Republic of China (office).

YE, Weilin; Chinese writer; b. 1935, Huiyang Co., Guangdong Prov.; s. of Ye Wei; m. Chen Jieni; two c.; joined PLA 1950; Chair. Hainan Writers' Asscn 1990–; also writes film screenplays. *Publications:* The Blue Mulan Rivulet, On the River without Navigation Marks, The First Farewell, Passing the Night at Meiziguo. *Address:* Hunan Branch of the Writers' Association, Changsha City, Hunan Province, People's Republic of China (office).

YE, Wenling; Chinese writer; *Chairman, Zhejiang Writers' Association;* b. 1942, Yuhuan, Zhejiang Prov.; ed Literature Inst., Chinese Writers' Asscn; worked as kindergarten nurse, school teacher, farm worker, factory worker, govt office worker, factory clerk before becoming professional writer; fmrly Vice-Chair. He'nan Prov. Fed. of Literary and Art Circles; Chair. Zhejiang Prov. Writers' Asscn, Vice-Chair. Fed. of Literary and Art Circles, Zhejiang Prov.; mem. CPPCC Cttee 2007. *Publications:* Father-Mother Official, The Proud Son of the Sun, Dreamless Valley, Qiu Jin, The Twisting Golden Bamboo Pond, The Brook with Nine Twists, Silent Valley, Selected Short Stories by Ye Wenling, Selected Prose of Ye Wenling, Collected Works of Ye Wenling (eight vols). *Address:* Zhejiang Writers' Association, Hangzhou, Zhejiang Province, People's Republic of China (office).

YE, Xiaogang; Chinese composer; b. 23 Sept. 1955, Shanghai; s. of Ye Chunzi and Ho Ying; m. Xu Jing 1987; ed Eastman School of Music, USA (postgraduate); Lecturer, Cen. Conservatory of Music, Beijing; Fellow Metropolitan Life Foundation, Pennsylvania Council of the Arts 1996; piano concerto Starry Sky was premiered during opening ceremony of Beijing Olympic Games by pianist Lang Lang, August 2008; Alexander Tcherepnin Prize 1982, Japan Dance Star Ballet Prize 1986). *Compositions:* Xi Jiang Yue Symphony 1984, Horizon Symphony 1985, Piano Ballade 1987, Dance Drama: The Love Story of Da Lai VI 1988. *Address:* Central Conservatory of Music, 43 Baojiajie, Beijing, People's Republic of China (office).

YE, Xuanping; Chinese state official; b. Nov. 1924, Meixian Co., Guangdong Prov.; s. of the late Marshal Ye Jianying and Zeng Xianzhi; ed Yan'an Coll. of Natural Sciences, Harbin Polytechnic Univ., Tsinghua Univ., Beijing, studies in USSR 1950–53; joined CCP 1945; trainee, Machine-Building Bureau, Shenyang, Liaoning Prov. 1960–61; Deputy Dir and Chief Engineer Beijing No. 1 Machine-tool Factory 1962–73; Bureau Dir State Science and Tech. Comm. 1978–80; Vice-Gov. Guangdong Prov. 1980–85, Gov. 1985–91; Chair. Guangdong Prov. Scientific and Tech. Cttee 1980–85; Deputy Sec. CCP Cttee, Guangzhou Municipality 1983–85; Acting Mayor Guangzhou 1983, Mayor 1983–85; Alt. mem. 12th CCP Cen. Cttee 1982, mem. 1985, 13th CCP Cen. Cttee 1987–92, 14th Cen. Cttee 1992–97; mem. 5th NPC 1978–83, Deputy for Guangdong Prov. to 6th NPC 1983–88; Exec. Chair. Preparatory Cttee for 6th NPC Games 1985–89; Chair. Zhongkai Inst. of Agricultural Tech. 1987; Vice-Chair. 7th CPPCC Nat. Cttee 1991–93, 8th Nat. Cttee 1993–98, 9th Nat. Cttee 1998–2003; attended Macao Handover Ceremony as mem. of Chinese Govt Del. 1999; Pres. Soc. for the Promotion of Chinese Culture 1992; Hon. Pres. Soc. for Study of the Chinese Revolution of 1911 1993; Hon. Chair. Bd of Trustees, Beijing Science and Eng Univ. 1995–. *Address:* c/o National Committee of Chinese People's Political Consultative Conference, 23 Taipingqiao Street, Beijing, People's Republic of China (office).

YE, Yonglie; Chinese writer; b. 30 Aug. 1940, Wenzhou, Zhejiang Prov.; ed Peking Univ. *Publications:* Xiao Lingtong's Travels in the Future (science fiction) 1978, Ten Thousand Why's, The Biography of Jiang Qing, The Biography of Zhang Chunqiao, The Biography of Yao Wenyuan, The

Biography of Wang Hongwen, The Real DPRK 2008. *Address:* Shanghai Science Education Film Studio, Shanghai, People's Republic of China (office).

YEANG, Dato' (Darjah Mulia Panguan Negeri) Ken, AADipl, PhD, RIBA; Malaysian architect and academic; *Principal, Llewelyn Davies Yeang and T. R. Hamzah & Yeang Sdn. Bhd.;* b. 6 Oct. 1948, Penang; ed Architectural Asscn, London, UK, Univ. of Pennsylvania, USA, Wolfson Coll., Cambridge, UK; Prin. T. R. Hamzah & Yeang Sdn. Bhd. 1976–; External Examiner, Univ. of Moratuwa 1986–87, Universiti Sains Malaysia 1988–89, 2000–01; Adjunct Prof. Univ. of Malaya, Royal Melbourne Inst. of Tech. 1993–, Univ. of Hawaii at Manoa 1999–, Univ. of NSW 2000–; AIA Assoc. Prof. (Graham Willis Visiting Professorship), Univ. of Sheffield 1994–2004; Provost's Distinguished Visitor, Univ. of Southern California 1999; Hon. Fellow, Singapore Inst. of Architects 1998; Hon. FAIA 1999; Hon. Academician Int. Acad. of Architecture (Sofia) 2000; Norway Award 1992, Far Eastern Econ. Review Innovation Award 1998, Auguste Perret Prize 1999, Asia Pacific Distinguished Scholar Award 1999, Enterprise 50 Award 1999, Prinz Claus Fonds Award 1999, Sir Robert Mathew Award 2000. *Publications:* Bioclimatic Skyscrapers 1994, Designing with Nature 1995, The Skyscraper Bioclimatically Considered: A Design Primer 1997, The Green Skyscraper: The Basis for Designing Sustainable Intensive Buildings 1999. *Address:* Brook House, Torrington Place, London, WC1E 7HN, England (office). *Telephone:* (20) 7637-0181 (office). *Fax:* (20) 7637-8740 (office). *E-mail:* trhy@tm.net.my (office). *Website:* www.trhamzah-yeang.com/main.htm (office); www.ldavies.com (office).

YEARWOOD, Robin; Antigua and Barbuda politician; MP for St Phillips North 1976–; Minister for Transportation, Aviation and Housing; Deputy Prime Minister of Antigua and Barbuda 2002–04. *Address:* c/o Office of the Prime Minister, Queen Elizabeth Highway, St John's, Antigua (office).

YEDDYURAPPA, B(okanakere) S(iddalingappa), BA; Indian politician and government official; *Chief Minister of Karnataka;* b. (b. Bokanakere Siddalingappa Yediyurappa), 27 Feb. 1943, Bookanakere village, Mandya Dist, Karnataka; s. of Siddalingappa Yediyurappa and Puttathayamma Yediyurappa; m. Smt. Maithra Devi Yediyurappa 1967 (died 2004); two s. three d.; mem. Bharatiya Janata Party (BJP); represents Shikaripura in Karnataka Legis. Ass.; first-div. clerk in social welfare dept 1965; clerk, Veerabhadra Shastri's Shankar rice mill, Shikaripur 1965–67; set up hardware shop in Shimoga; Sec. Rashtriya Swayamsevak Sangh's Shikaripur unit 1970–72; Pres. Taluk unit, Jan Sangh 1972–75; Pres. Town Municipality of Shikaripur 1975; imprisoned during Emergency in India 1975–77, lodged in Bellary and Shimoga jails; Pres. Shikaripur Taluk unit of BJP 1980–85, Pres. Shimoga Dist unit of BJP 1985–88, Pres. BJP unit, Karnataka 1988; first elected to Lower House of Karnataka Legislature 1983, has represented Shikaripur constituency five times, mem. Eighth, Ninth, Tenth and Eleventh Legis. Ass (Lower House) of Karnataka, Leader of Opposition, Tenth Ass., lost election 1999, nominated by BJP to become mem. Legis. Council (Upper House) of Karnataka; helped H. D. Kumaraswamy of Janata Dal (Secular) party bring down coalition govt of Dharam Singh, Kumaraswamy formed govt with help of BJP in Karnataka; Deputy Chief Minister and Minister of Finance in Kumaraswamy's Govt 2006–07, Chief Minister of Karnataka (prior to collapse of coalition govt) 12–19 Nov. 2007 (first BJP mem. to become Chief Minister of a South Indian state) 2008–. *Address:* Office of the Chief Minister, Room No. 323, Vidhana Soudha, Bangalore 560 001, Karnataka, India (office). *Telephone:* (80) 22253414 (office), (80) 22253424 (office). *E-mail:* info@karnataka.gov.in (office). *Website:* www.karnataka.gov.in (office).

YEFIMOV, Air Marshal Aleksandr Nikolayevich, MSc; Russian air force officer (retd); b. 6 Feb. 1923, Kantemirovka, Voronezh Oblast; ed Voroshilovograd Mil. Air Acad., Mil. Acad. of Gen. Staff; joined CPSU 1943; served in Soviet army 1941; fought on the Western and on 2nd Byelorussian Fronts at Vyazma, Smolensk, in Byelorussia, Poland and Germany 1942–45; by July 1944 had flown about 100 missions and was made Hero of the Soviet Union; completed his 222nd mission on 8 May 1945; awarded second Gold Star; held various command posts 1945–69; First Deputy C-in-C, Soviet Air Defence Forces 1969–91; Deputy to Supreme Soviet 1946–50, 1974–89; rank of Air Marshal 1975; Commdr of Soviet Air Force and Deputy Minister of Defence 1984–91, Mil. Insp.-Adviser, Ministry of Defence 1991; Chair. CIS Interstate Comm. on use of space and control of air services 1992–96, Council for co-operation with war veterans' unions 1995–; mem. CPSU Cen. Cttee 1986–90; USSR People's Deputy 1989; Hero of the Soviet Union 1944, 1945, Order of Lenin (twice), Order of the Red Banner (five times), Aleksandr Nevsky Order, Merited Mil. Pilot of USSR 1970 and other decorations. *Publication:* Over the Field of Battle 1976. *Address:* c/o Ministry of Defence, Myasnitskaya str. 37, 101000 Moscow, Russia. *Telephone:* (495) 293-31-76.

YEFUNI, Sergey Naumovich; Russian anaesthesiologist and physiologist; *Director-General, Institute of Hyperbaric Medicine;* b. 24 Jan. 1930; m.; two s.; ed Second Moscow Inst. of Medicine; head of surgery div., municipal hosp. 1954–56; researcher First Moscow Inst. of Medicine 1959–63; Sr Researcher, Head of Lab. All-Union Research Cen. of Surgery, USSR Acad. of Medical Sciences 1963–78, Head of Dept 1978–93; Dir-Gen. Inst. of Hyperbaric Medicine 1993–; Corresp. mem. USSR (now Russian) Acad. of Sciences 1979, mem. 1992; research in physiology of breathing, practical problems of anaesthesia, effect of anaesthesia on cardio-vascular system; mem. United Scientific Council on complex problem Physiology of Man and Animals; Chair. Comm. Acad. (now Inst.) of Sciences Problems of Hyperbaric Oxygenation; lives in USA; USSR State Prize. *Address:* Institute of Hyperbaric Medicine, 119435 Moscow, Russia (office). *Telephone:* (495) 246-49-87 (office); (495) 201-43-68 (home).

YEGOROV, Sergey Yefimovich; Russian banker; *President, Association of Russian Banks;* b. 4 Oct. 1927, Orenburg Region; m.; one s. one d.; ed Saratov Inst. of Econ., Acad. of Finance; economist Altai territory branch USSR Gosbank 1950–60; instructor, Head of Sector Dept of Planning and Finance Bodies Cen. CPSU Cttee 1960–74; Chair. of Bd Russian Repub. Bank 1973–; Deputy to RSFSR Supreme Soviet 1973–88; consultant Exec. Bd USSR Gosbank 1988–91; Pres. Asscn of Russian Banks 1991–; mem. Int. Acad. of Information Processes and Tech.; Corresp. mem. Acad. of Man. and Market. *Leisure interests:* theatre, painting. *Address:* Association of Russian Banks, Skatertny per. 20, St 1, Moscow, Russia. *Telephone:* (495) 291-66-30 (office). *Fax:* (495) 291-66-66 (office). *E-mail:* arb@arb.ru (office).

YEGOROV, Adm. Vladimir Grigoryevich; Russian politician; *Governor of Kaliningrad;* b. 26 Nov. 1938, Moscow; m.; one s., one d.; ed M. Frunze Mil. Naval Higher School, Mil. Naval Acad., Mil. Acad. of Gen. Staff; officer service, Baltic Navy 1964–74, Head of Staff, Deputy Commdr, Torpedo-boat Brigade 1974–76, Head, Rocket-boat Brigade 1976–83, Commdr, Motor Rocket-boat Brigade 1983–85, Commdr, Baltic Mil. Navy Base, Mediterranean Fleet of Black Sea Navy 1985–86, First Deputy Commdr, Baltic Navy 1986–91, Commdr 1991–2000; Head of Admin, Gov. of Kaliningrad region 2000–; Hon. mem. Swedish Royal Mil. Navy Soc.; Hon. mem. St Petersburg Navy Ass.; Service to the Motherland Order, Mil. Service Order, Arms of Honour. *Address:* Administration of Kaliningrad Region, Office of the Governor, Dmitry Donskogo str. 1, 236007 Kaliningrad, Russia (office). *Telephone:* (112) 46-75-45 (office). *Fax:* (112) 46-35-54 (office). *E-mail:* ako@ako.baltnet.ru (office). *Website:* www.gov.kaliningrad.ru (office).

YEGOROV, Vladimir Konstantinovich; Russian politician, philosopher and journalist; *Rector, Russian Academy of State Service;* b. 30 Oct. 1947, Kanash, Chuvash ASSR; m.; one s.; ed Kazan State Univ.; Deputy Ed. Molodoi Komsomolets, also Head, Dept of Propaganda, Cen. Comsomol Cttee 1974–85; Rector, Gorky. Inst. of Literature in Moscow 1985–87; Deputy Head, Div. of Culture, Ideological Dept, CPSU Cen. Cttee 1987–90; Asst to Pres. Mikhail Gorbachev (q.v.) on Problems of Culture and Religion 1990–91; Chief Scientific Researcher, Analytical Centre at Ministry of Science 1992–96; Prof. Russian Acad. of State Service 1993–; mem. Co-ordination Council, My Motherland; Dir Russian State Library 1996–98; Minister of Culture Russian Fed. 1998–2000; Rector Russian Acad. of State Service 2000–. *Publications:* books including History in our Lives, Intelligentsia and Power, The Star Turns Pale: Reflections on Russian History, From Deadlock to Uncertainty, Many Faces of Russia, numerous articles. *Address:* Academy of State Service, Vernadskogo prosp. 84, 117606 Moscow, Russia. *Telephone:* (495) 436-90-12 (office).

YEH, Chu-Lan, LLB; Taiwanese politician; b. 13 Feb. 1949, Miaoli Co.; m. Cheng Nan-jung (died 1989); one d.; ed Fu Jen Catholic Univ.; Dir Business Dept, United Advertising Co. Ltd 1979–89; mem. Legislative Yuan 1990–2000, Convener Home and Nations Cttee, Foreign and Overseas Chinese Affairs Cttee, Judiciary Cttee, Deputy Convener Democratic Progressive Party Caucus 1992, Gen. Convener 1995; Minister of Transportation and Communications 2000–02; Chair. Council for Hakka Affairs 2002–04; Vice-Premier and Minister of Consumer Protection Comm. 2004–05; Acting Mayor of Kaohsiung 2005–06; mem. Cen. Standing Cttee, Democratic Progressive Party. *Address:* c/o Democratic Progressive Party, 10/F, 30 Beiping East Road, Taipei 10051, Taiwan. *Telephone:* (2) 23929989. *E-mail:* foreign@dpp.org.tw. *Website:* www.dpp.org.tw.

YEHOSHUA, Abraham B., MA; Israeli writer and academic; *Professor of Comparative and Hebrew Literature, University of Haifa;* b. 9 Dec. 1936, Jerusalem; s. of Yakov Yehoshua and Malka Rosilio; m. Rivka Kirsninski 1960; two s. one d.; served in paratroopers unit 1954–57; Dir Israeli School in Paris 1964; Gen. Sec. World Union of Jewish Studies, Paris 1963–67; Dean of Students, Haifa Univ. 1967–72, Prof. of Comparative and Hebrew Literature 1972–; Visiting Prof., Harvard Univ., USA 1977, Univ. of Chicago 1988, 1997, 2000, Princeton Univ. 1992–; Co-Ed. Keshet 1965–72, Siman Kria 1973–, Tel Aviv Review 1987–; active mem. Israeli Peace Movt; Dr hc (Hebrew Union Coll., Tel-Aviv Univ., Univ. of Turin, Bar Ilan Univ.); Brener Prize 1983, Alterman Prize 1986, Bialik Prize 1989, Booker Prize 1992, European B'nai B'rith Award 1993, Israel Prize 1995. *Film adaptations of novels and stories include:* The Lover, Facing the Forests, Continuing Silence, Mr Mani, Open Heart, A Voyage to the End of the Millennium, Early in the Summer of 1970. *Plays:* A Night in May 1969, Last Treatments 1973, Possessions 1992, The Night's Babies 1993. *Publications:* Death of the Old Man (short stories) 1963, Facing the Forest (short stories) 1968, Three Days and a Child (short stories) 1970, Early in the Summer of 1970 (novella) 1973, Two Plays 1975, The Lover (novel) 1977, Between Right and Right (essays) 1980, A Late Divorce (novel) (Flaiano Int. Poetry Prize, Italy 1996) 1982, Possessions 1986, Five Seasons (novel) (Nat. Jewish Book Award 1990, Cavour Prize, Italy 1994) 1988, The Wall and the Mountain (essays) 1988, Mister Mani (novel) (Israeli Booker Prize 1992, Nat. Jewish Book Award 1993, Wingate Prize, UK 1994) 1990, The Return from India 1994, Open Heart (novel) 1994, A Voyage to the End of the Millennium (novel) (Koret Prize) 1997, The Terrible Power of a Minor Guilt (essays) 1998, The Liberated Bride (novel) (Napoli Prize, Lampedusa Prize) 2001, The Mission of the Human Resource Man (novel) 2004, A Woman in Jerusalem (Los Angeles Times Book Prize for Fiction) 2006, Friendly Fire (novel) 2007. *Address:* 33 Shoshanat Ha-Carmel, Haifa, 34322, Israel. *Telephone:* 4-8370001. *Fax:* 4-8375569. *E-mail:* bulli@research.haifa.ac.il (home).

YEKHANUROV, Yuriy Ivanovych; Ukrainian politician and economist; *Minister of Defence;* b. 23 Aug. 1948, Belkachi, Yakut ASSR (now the Repub. of Sakha—Yakutiya) Russian Fed.; s. of Ivan Mikhailovich Yekhanurov and Galina Mikhailovna Yekhanurova; m. Olena Lvivna Yekhanurova; one s.; ed Kyiv Construction Tech. Coll.; Higher School of Econ. State Planning, Kyiv Inst. of Nat. Econs, Academic Research Econ. Inst. of State Planning; master, then head of workshop, Chief Engineer, Dir, Kyivmiskbur Co. 1967–77, Head of Kyivmiskbudkomplekt Co. 1977–88; Head, Buddetal Co. 1977–88; Deputy Chief, Golovkyivmiskbud Co. 1988–91; elected to Kyiv City Rada (Council) 1990; Head of State Econ. Council, Cabinet of Ministers 1991–92; Deputy Head of Bd of Verkhovna Rada 1992; Deputy Head of Kyiv City Admin. 1992–93; Deputy Minister of the Economy 1993–94; Head of State Property Fund 1994–97; Minister of Economy Feb.–July 1997; Head of State Cttee on Entrepreneurship Devt 1997–98; mem. Verkhovna Rada (Parl.) 1998–, Deputy Head, Cttee on Econ. Policy, Man. Economy, Property and Investment 1998–99; First Deputy Prime Minister 1999–2001; Deputy Head of Presidential Admin 2001, 2004, re-elected mem. Verkhovna Rada for Our Ukraine bloc 2002, Head of Parl. Cttee on Industrial Policy and Entrepreneurship 2002; Deputy Head of Viktor Yushchenko's presidential campaign team 2004; Head of Cen. Exec. Cttee, Our Ukraine People's Union party March 2005; Gov. Dnipropetrovsk Oblast April–Sept. 2005; apptd Acting Prime Minister Sept. 2005, Prime Minister Sept. 2005–06; Minister of Defence 2007–. *Publications:* more than 60 publs on econs. *Address:* Ministry of Defence, 03168 Kyiv, Povitroflotskyi pr. 6, Ukraine (office). *Telephone:* (44) 226-26-56 (office). *Fax:* (44) 226-20-15 (office). *E-mail:* pressmou@pressmou.kiev.ua (office). *Website:* www.mil.gov.ua (office).

YELLAND, David, BA, AMP; British business executive and fmr journalist; *Partner, Brunswick Group LLP;* b. 14 May 1963, Harrogate; s. of John Michael Yelland and Patricia Ann McIntosh; m. Tania Farrell 1996 (died 2006); one s.; ed Brigg Grammar School, Lincs., Univ. of Coventry, Harvard Business School, USA; grad. trainee, Westminster Press 1985; trainee reporter, Buckinghamshire Advertiser 1985–87; industrial reporter, Northern Echo 1987–88; gen. news and business reporter, North West Times and Sunday Times 1988–89; city reporter, Thomson Regional Newspapers 1989–90; joined News Corpn 1990; city reporter, then City Ed. The Sun 1990–92, New York Corresp. 1992–93; Ed. 1998–2003; Deputy Business Ed. Business Ed., then Deputy Ed. New York Post 1993–98; Sr Vice-Pres. News Corpn, New York 2003–04; Vice-Pres. Weber Shandwick Worldwide (public relations consultancy) 2004–06; Partner, Brunswick Group LLP 2006–. *Leisure interests:* contemporary art, Manchester City Football Club. *Address:* Brunswick Group LLP, 16 Lincoln's Inn Fields, London, WC2A 3ED, England (office). *Telephone:* (20) 7404-5959 (office). *Fax:* (20) 7936-7730 (office). *E-mail:* dyelland@ brunswickgroup.com (office). *Website:* www.brunswickgroup.com (office).

YELLEN, Janet Louise, PhD; American economist, academic and central banker; *President and CEO, Federal Reserve Bank of San Francisco;* b. 13 Aug. 1946, Brooklyn, NY; d. of Julius Yellen and Anna Ruth Yellen (née Blumenthal); m. George Arthur Akerlof 1978; one s.; ed Brown Univ., Yale Univ.; Grad. Fellow, NSF 1967–71; Asst Prof. of Econs, Harvard Univ. 1971–76; consultant, Div. of Int. Finance, Bd of Govs of US Fed. Reserve System 1974–75; economist, Trade and Financial Studies section 1977–78; consultant, US Congressional Budget Office, Washington, DC 1975–76; Research Affiliate, Yale Univ. 1976; economist, with the Federal Reserve's Board of Governors in 1977– 1978; Lecturer, LSE 1978–80; Asst Prof. of Econs, School of Business Admin., Univ. of California, Berkeley 1980–82, Assoc. Prof. 1982–85, Prof., Haas School of Business 1985, Bernard T. Rocca Jr Prof. of Int. Business and Trade 1992, Eugene E. and Catherine M. Trefethen Prof. of Business Admin., now Prof. Emer., fmr mem. Haas Econ. Analysis and Policy Group; mem. Bd of Govs US Fed. Reserve System 1994–97; Chair. Council of Econ. Advisers 1997–99, also Chair. Econ. Policy Cttee of OECD; Pres. and CEO Fed. Reserve Bank of San Francisco 2004–; Research Fellow, MIT 1974; mem. Panel of Econ. Advisers, US Congressional Budget Office 1993; mem. Advisory Panel on Econs NSF 1977–78, 1991–92; mem. Brookings Panel on Econ. Activity 1987–88, 1990–91, Sr Adviser 1989–; Lecturer on Macroeconomic Theory, Yrjö Jahnsson Foundation, Helsinki 1977–78; mem. Council on Foreign Relations 1976–81, American Econ. Asscn; Guggenheim Fellow 1986–87; Fellow, American Acad. of Arts and Sciences 2001–, Yale Corpn 2000–; Assoc. Journal of Econ. Perspectives 1987–91; Hon. Woodrow Wilson Fellow 1967; Maria and Sidney Rolfe Award for Nat. Econ. Service, Women's Econ. Roundtable 1997, Wilbur Lucius Cross Medal, Yale Univ. 1997. *Publications:* The Limits of the Market in Resource Allocation (co-author) 1977, contrib. articles to professional journals. *Address:* Federal Reserve Bank of San Francisco, 101 Market Street, San Francisco, CA 94105, USA (office). *Telephone:* (415) 974-2000 (office). *Website:* www.frbsf.org (home).

YEMBA, Adolphe Onusumba; Democratic Republic of the Congo politician; Leader Rassemblement congolais pour la démocratie (RCD—Goma) 2000–03; Minister of Defence, Demobilization and War Veterans' Affairs 2005–06. *Address:* c/o Ministry of Defence, Demobilization and War Veterans' Affairs, BP 4111, Kinshasa-Gombe, Democratic Republic of the Congo (office).

YEMELYANOV, Aleksei Mikhailovich, DEcon; Russian politician and economist; b. 15 Feb. 1935; ed Moscow Univ.; mem. CPSU 1959–90; Lecturer, Prof., Head of Chair Moscow Univ.; mem. Russian Agric. Acad.; USSR People's Deputy 1989–91; Deputy Chair. Cttee on Agric. Problems, USSR Supreme Soviet 1989–91; mem. Pres. Council 1992–; Pres.-Rector Russian State Acad. of State Service 1994–2000, Prof. Dept of Econs 2000–; active participant of democratic movt; mem. of State Duma (Parl.) 1993–95. *Publications:* scientific works and articles on agricultural reforms in Russia. *Address:* Russian Agricultural Academy, Bolshoi Kharitonyevsky per. 21, 107814 Moscow; Academy of State Service, Vernadskogo prosp. 84, 117606 Moscow, Russia. *Telephone:* (495) 923-40-90 (Agricultural Acad.); (495) 436-94-24 (Acad. of State Service).

YEMELYANOV, Stanislav Vasilevich, DTechSc; Russian management specialist; b. 18 May 1929, Voronezh; s. of Vasilii Yemelyanov and Ludmila (née Chepkova) Yemelyanova; m. Olga Yemelyanova 1952; one s. one d.; ed

Moscow Univ.; with Inst. of Control Problems, USSR (now Russian) Acad. of Sciences 1952–76, with Inst. for Systems Analysis 1976– (Dir 1991–), mem. Acad. 1984, mem. Presidium 1988, Acad.-Sec., Dept of Informatics, Computer Science and Automation 1990–; Gen. Dir Int. Inst. for Man. Science 1976–; Head of Chair of Nonlinear Dynamics and Control Processes, Moscow State Univ.; Chair of Engineering Cybernetics, Moscow Steel and Alloys Inst.; mem. editorial Bd Differential Equations, Automatic and Remote Control, Problems of Theory and Practice of Management, Dynamics and Control; research into variable structure control theory; holder of about 100 patents; Lenin Prize 1972, USSR State Prize 1980, Council of USSR Ministers Prize 1981, Russian Fed. State Prize 1994. *Publications:* 7 books; 250 journal articles. *Address:* International Institute for Management Science, Shchepkina Street 8, 129090 Moscow (office); Academic Zelinskii str. 38/8, Apt 69, Moscow, Russia (home). *Telephone:* (495) 208-91-06 (office); (495) 135-54-69 (home). *Fax:* (495) 938-16-74.

YEMENIDJIAN, Alex, MA; American business executive; *Chairman and CEO, Armenco Holdings LLC;* ed California State Univ., Northridge, Univ. of Southern California; Man. Partner Parks, Palmer & Yemenidjian; joined Metro-Goldwyn-Mayer (MGM) Grand Inc., Las Vegas 1989, Chief Financial Officer 1994–98, Pres. and COO 1995–99, mem. Bd Dirs 1999–2005, Dir MGM Grand Inc. (now MGM MIRAGE), Santa Monica 1989–, Chair. and CEO 1999–2005; Chair. and CEO Armenco Holdings LLC 2005–; Exec. Tracinda 1990–97, 1999; Chair. United Armenian Fund; mem. Bd of Dirs Guess? Inc. 2005–, Kirk Kerkorian's Lincy Foundation. *Address:* c/o Board of Directors, Guess? Inc., 1444 South Alameda Street, Los Angeles, CA 90021, USA (office).

YEN, Ching-Chang, LLB, MA; Taiwanese politician; b. 7 April 1948, Tainan; m.; one s. one d.; ed Nat. Taiwan Univ., Univ. of Michigan, USA; joined Ministry of Finance 1972, Sr Customs Officer, Taipei Customs Bureau 1972–73, Specialist, Dept of Customs Admin. 1973–77, Sr Specialist in Secr. 1977–78, 1980–84, Exec. Sec. Legal Comm. 1984–85, Taxation and Tariff Comm. 1985–92, Deputy Minister of Finance 1996–2000, Minister of Finance 2000–02; Deputy Dir-Gen. First Bureau, Office of the Pres. 1992–93, Dir-Gen. 1993–96; Prof., Nat. Taiwan Univ., Nat. Chengchi Univ. and Soochoe Univ. 1981–86; first Amb. of Taiwan WTO 2002–05; Chair. and CEO Yuanta Financial Holding Co., Ltd (fmrly Fuhwa Financial Holding Co.) 2005–; Eisenhower Fellowship, USA 1995; Chevalier Ordre nat. du Mérite 1998; Class One Merit Medal, Exec. Yuan 2000, Order of Brilliant Star with Grand Cordon in 2005. *Publications:* Anti-dumping Act and Customs Policy 1981, Legal Problems of Sino-American Trade Negotiations 1987, Unveiling GATT: Order and Trend of Global Trade 1989, International Economic Law 1991, Laws and Regulations of International Economic Relations 1995, Taxation Law 1998, Understanding and Appreciating French Wines 1997; (in English) Taiwan Trade and Investment Law 1994. *Address:* Yuanta Financial Holding Co., Ltd, 9F, No. 4, Section 1, Chung-Hsiao W. Road, Taipei, Taiwan (office).

YENTOB, Alan, LLB; British television executive; *Creative Director, BBC;* b. 11 March 1947, London; s. of Isaac Yentob and Flora Yentob (née Khazam); one s. one d. by Philippa Walker; ed King's School, Ely, Univ. of Grenoble, France, Univ. of Leeds; BBC gen. trainee 1968, Producer/Dir 1970–, including Omnibus 1973–75, Ed. Arena 1978–85, Head of Music and Arts, BBC-TV 1985–88, Controller, BBC 2 1988–93, BBC 1 1993–96, BBC Dir of Programmes 1996–97, BBC Dir of TV 1997–2000, of Drama, Entertainment and Children's Programmes 2000–04, Creative Dir, BBC 2004–; presenter of arts series Imagine (BBC 1) 2003–; mem. British Film Inst. Production Bd 1985–93, British Screen Advisory Council, Advisory Cttee, Council Royal Court Theatre; Chair. Inst. of Contemporary Arts; Gov. Nat. Film School 1998–; mem. S Bank Bd 1999–, Int. Acad. of Television Arts and Sciences; Trustee Architecture Foundation 1992–, Timebank 2001–; Hon. Fellow RCA, RIBA, Royal TV Soc. *Leisure interests:* swimming, books. *Address:* BBC Television, Television Centre, Wood Lane, London, W12 7RJ, England (office). *Telephone:* (20) 8743-8000 (office). *Website:* www.bbc.co.uk (office).

YEO, Cheow Tong, BEng; Singaporean politician; b. 1947; m.; three d.; ed Anglo-Chinese School, Univ. of Western Australia; worked in Econ. Devt Bd 1972–75; joined LeBlond Makino Asia Pte. Ltd (LMA) as Staff Engineer 1975, subsequently promoted to Eng Man., then Operations Dir; Man. Dir LMA and subsidiary co., Pacific Precision Castings Pte. Ltd 1981–85; MP for Hong Kah 1984–; Minister of State for Health and for Foreign Affairs 1985–87; Acting Minister for Health, Sr Minister of State for Foreign Affairs 1987–90, of Health 1990–94, for Community Devt 1991–94, for Trade and Industry 1994–97, of Health and for the Environment 1997–99; Minister for Communications and Information Tech. 1999–2001; Minister of Transport 2001–06 (resgnd). *Address:* Yew Tee PAP Branch, Block 608, #01-103, Choa Chu Kang Street 62, Singapore 680608, Singapore (office). *Telephone:* 67606233 (office). *Fax:* 6760 2133 (office). *E-mail:* ctyeo@yewtee.org.sg (office). *Website:* www .parliament.gov.sg (office).

YEO, George Yong-Boon, BA, MBA; Singaporean politician; *Minister of Foreign Affairs;* b. 13 Sept. 1954, Singapore; m. Jennifer Leong Lai Peng 1984; one d. three s.; ed Univ. of Cambridge, UK, Singapore Command and Staff Coll., Harvard Business School, USA; fmr Signals Officer, Singapore Air Force, later Head Air Plans Dept, Chief of Air Staff 1985; Dir Jt Operations and Planning, Ministry of Defence 1986–88, rank of Brig.-Gen. 1988; mem. Parl. 1988–; Minister of State for Finance and Minister of State for Foreign Affairs 1988–90; Acting Minister for Information and the Arts and Sr Minister of State for Foreign Affairs 1990–91; Minister for Information and the Arts 1991–99; Second Minister for Foreign Affairs 1991–94; Minister for Health 1994–97; Second Minister for Trade and Industry 1997–99, Minister for Trade and Industry 1999–2004; Minister of Foreign Affairs 2004–; mem. Harvard Business School Visiting Cttee 1998–2004; Adviser Sun Yat Sen Nanyang Memorial Hall. *Leisure interests:* reading, swimming, jogging. *Address:*

Ministry of Foreign Affairs, Tanglin, 248163 Singapore (office). *Telephone:* 63798000 (office). *Fax:* 64747885 (office). *E-mail:* mfa@mfa.gov.sg (office). *Website:* www.mfa.gov.sg (office).

YEOH, Michelle, BA; Malaysian actress; b. (Nee Yeoh Choo-Keng (sometimes credited as Michelle Khan, Ziqiong Yang or Chi-King Yeung)), 6 Aug. 1962, Ipoh, Perak; m. Dickson Poon 1988 (divorced 1992); ed Royal Acad. of Dance, London; Chevalier, Légion d'Honneur 2007. *Films:* Owls vs. Dumbo 1984, In the Line of Duty 2 1985, The Target 1985, Magnificent Warriors 1987, Easy Money 1987, The Heroic Trio 1993, Police Story 3 1992 (Part 2 1993), Butterfly Sword 1993, Heroic Trio 2: Executioners 1993, Seven Maidens 1993, Tai-Chi 1993, Wonder Seven 1994, The Stunt Woman 1996, The Soong Sisters 1997, Tomorrow Never Dies 1997, Moonlight Express 1999, Crouching Tiger, Hidden Dragon 2000, The Touch 2004, Fei ying 2004, Memoirs of a Geisha 2005, Sunshine 2007, Babylon A.D. 2008, Far North 2008. *Address:* c/o United Talent Agency, Inc., 9560 Wilshire Blvd., Suite 500, Beverly Hills, CA 90212, USA. *Telephone:* (310) 273-6700. *Fax:* (310) 247-1111.

YEOH, Tan Sri Dato' Seri Tiong Lay; Malaysian chartered builder and business executive; *Executive Chairman, YTL Corporation Berhad;* m.; seven c.; ed Chong Hwa Ind. High School, Kuala Lumpur; Founder and Exec. Chair. YTL Corpn Berhad (conglomerate with interests in construction, utilities, hotels, property Devt and technology); Fellow, Chartered Inst. of Building, Australian Inst. of Building, Faculty of Building (UK); PSM, SPMS, DPMS, KMN, PPN, PJK, Order of the Rising Sun, Gold Rays with Neck Ribbon 2008; Hon. DEng (Heriot-Watt), Hon. DBA (Universiti Malaysia Sabah). *Address:* YTL Corporation Berhad, 11th Floor, Yeoh Tiong Lay Plaza, 55 Jalan Bukit Bintang, 55100 Kuala Lumpur, Malaysia (office). *Telephone:* (3) 2142-6633 (office). *Fax:* (3) 2143-3192 (office). *E-mail:* info@ytl.com.my (office). *Website:* www.ytl.com.my (office).

YÉPEZ NAJAS, Mauricio; Ecuadorean economist; ed Pontificia Universidad Católica de Quito, Univ. of Colorado, Williams Coll., USA; Gov. Cen. Bank of Ecuador –2004, Dir 2004–; Minister of the Economy and Finance 2004–05. *Address:* c/o Ministry of the Economy and Finance, Avda 10 de Agosto 1661 y Jorge Washington, Quito, Ecuador (office).

YEREMIN, Yuri Ivanovich; Russian theatre director and drama instructor; *Acting and Directing Instructor, Institute for Advanced Theatre Training;* b. 9 March 1944, Kolomna, Moscow Region; s. of Evdokiya Fillippovna Yeremina; m. Nina Petrovna Yeremina 1974; one s. one d.; with Youth Theatre, Rostov-on-Don 1973–77; Gorky Drama Theatre, Rostov-on-Don 1978–80; Cen. Army Theatre, Moscow 1981–87; Dir Pushkin Theatre, Moscow 1987–2000; Acting and Directing Instructor, Inst. for Advanced Theatre Training, Harvard Univ., USA 1997–; mem. Faculty Moscow Art Theater School USA; US debut with production of The Paper Gramophone, Hartford Stage Co. 1989; Ward No. 6, dramatic adaptation of Chekhov story, performed at int. drama festivals in USA, France, Italy, Switzerland, Belgium, UK and Canada 1989–91; Vice-Pres. Int. Asscn of Theatre Producers 1991–; People's Artist of Russia 1986, Order for Literature and Art (France) 1989. *Recent productions include:* The Possessed (Dostoevsky adaptation) 1989, Black Monk (Chekhov adaptation) 1990, At Kingdom Gate (Hamsun) 1991, Erick XIV (Strindberg) 1992, The Ghosts (De Filippo) 1992, The History of one Staircase (Buero Valejo) 1993, To Moscow! To Moscow! (adaptation of Chekhov's Three Sisters) 1994, Madame Bovary (Flaubert adaptation) 1994, The Inspector (Gogol) 1994, King Oedipus (Sophocles) 1995. *Productions at American Repertory Theater (Cambridge, Mass.):* The Idiot (Dostoevsky) 1998, Ivanov (Chekhov) 1999, Three Farces and a Funeral (based on Chekhov's comedies) 2000, Othello (Shakespeare) 2001, Silver Age (Roshchin) 2001. *Leisure interests:* painting, writing. *Address:* A. R. T./MXAT Institute, Loeb Drama Center, 64 Brattle Street, Cambridge, MA 02138, USA (office); 7 Soviet Army Street, Apt. 213, 01827 Moscow, Russia. *Telephone:* (617) 496.2000 ext. 8890 (Cambridge) (office); (495) 281-83-20 (home); (495) 299-41-36. *E-mail:* institute@amrep.org (office); yuryer@mail.ru (home). *Website:* www.amrep.org/iatt (office).

YERGIN, Daniel, PhD; American writer and business executive; *Chairman, Cambridge Energy Research Associates;* ed Yale Univ., Univ. of Cambridge (Marshall Scholar), UK; taught at Harvard Business School and John F. Kennedy School of Govt, Harvard Univ.; Chair. Cambridge Energy Research Assocs; Dir US-Russian Business Council, Atlantic Partnership, New America Foundation; Global Energy Analyst, NBC, CNBC; mem. Bd US Energy Asscn, Advisory Bd US Sec. of Energy; mem. Nat. Petroleum Council, Russia Acad. of Oil and Gas; mem. Cttee on Studies, Council on Foreign Relations; Trustee Brookings Inst.; fmr Chair. US Dept of Energy Task Force on Strategic Energy Research and Devt; Pres.'s Medal, Repub. of Italy 2005; Dr hc (Univs of Houston and Missouri); US Energy Asscn Award. *Publications:* Shattered Peace: Origins of the Cold War and the National Security State 1978, Energy Future: Report of the Energy Project at the Harvard Business School (with Robert Stobaugh) 1981, Dependence Dilemma 1984, The Prize: The Epic Quest for Oil, Money and Power (Pulitzer Prize for Gen. Nonfiction 1992) 1993 (also PBS/BBC documentary series), Russia 2010 and What It Means for the World (with Thane Gustafson) 1995, Commanding Heights: Battle for the World Economy (with Joseph Stanislaw) (also PBS/BBC documentary series— CINE Golden Eagle Award, New York Festivals Gold World Medal). *Address:* Cambridge Energy Research Associates, 55 Cambridge Parkway, Cambridge, MA 02142, USA (office). *Telephone:* (617) 866-5000 (office). *Fax:* (617) 866-5900 (office). *E-mail:* akipp@cera.com (office). *Website:* www.cera.com (office).

YERIN, Army Gen. Victor Fedorovich; Russian politician; b. 17 Jan. 1944, Kazan; m.; two c.; ed Higher School, USSR Ministry of Internal Affairs; regional militiaman; mem. Criminal Investigation Dept Ministry of Internal Affairs, Tatar Autonomous Repub., Chief of Dept 1980–83; Chief of Div. Admin. of struggle against embezzlement of social property 1983–88; First

Deputy Minister of Internal Affairs of Armenian SSR 1988–90; Deputy Minister of Internal Affairs of RSFSR, Chief Service of Criminal Militia 1990–91; First Deputy Minister of Internal Affairs of USSR Sept.–Dec. 1991; First Deputy Minister of Security and Internal Affairs of Russian Fed. 1991–92; Minister of Internal Affairs of Russian Fed. 1992–95; Deputy Dir of Foreign Intelligence (SVR) 1995. *Address:* 101000 Moscow, Kolpachni per. 11, Russia (office).

YEROFEYEV, Victor Vladimirovich; Russian writer and critic; b. 19 Sept. 1947, Moscow; m. Veslava (née Skura) Yerofeyeva; one s.; ed Moscow Univ.; expelled from USSR Writers' Union for participation in almanac Metropol, membership restored in 1986; lecturer Maxim Gorky Literature Inst.; seminars on Modern Russian Literature at Univ. of South Calif.; contribs to Moscow News, Moscow Magazine, New York Review of Books; mem. Bd Russian PEN Centre; named Man of the Year by Moscow Magazine 1990. *Publications:* Anna's Body and End of the Russian Avant-garde (collection of short stories) 1980, Life with an Idiot (novel) 1980, Russian Beauty (novel) 1981, In the Maze of Cursed Questions (collection of essays) 1990, The Pocket Apocalypse 1993, Collected Works (3 vols) 1994–95, The Doomsday 1996, Men 1997, Five Rivers of Life 1998, Encyclopedia of the Russian Soul 2000. *Leisure interest:* travelling. *Address:* 1st Smolensky per. 9, Apt 1, Moscow, Russia. *Telephone:* (495) 241-02-08.

YERSHOV, Yuri Leonidovich, DMathSci; Russian scientist and mathematician; b. 1 May 1940, Novosibirsk; m.; three c.; ed Novosibirsk State Univ.; jr, sr researcher, then Head of Div. Inst. of Math., Siberian br., USSR (now Russian) Acad. of Sciences 1963–85, corresp. mem. Russian Acad. of Sciences 1970, mem. 1991; Rector Novosibirsk Univ. *Publications:* numerous scientific publs including monographs. *Address:* Novosibirsk State University, Pirogova str. 2, 630090 Novosibirsk, Russia (office). *Telephone:* (3832) 35-78-08 (office); (3832) 35-51-75 (home).

YESENBAYEV, Mazhit Tulenbekovich; Kazakhstani politician, engineer and economist; b. 28 April 1949, Pavlodar; ed Kazakh Polytech. Inst., Almaty; fmr Gov. Cen. Karaganda Region; apptd Minister of Finance 1999–2001, of Economy and Trade 2002–03; Presidential Aide on Econ. Affairs 2003–; Order of Parasat 1999. *Publications:* 34 publs on problems of territorial org. of production and optimization of teaching and educational process. *Address:* c/o Ministry of Economy and Trade, Beibitshilik 2, 473000 Astana, Kazakhstan (office).

YESIMOV, Akhmetzhan S.; Kazakhstani politician; *Minister of Agriculture;* ed Kazakh Inst. of Agric., Acad. of Social Sciences, Moscow, Russia; mechanical engineer 1979–80; worked for econ. orgs in Almaty Region 1979–90; First Vice-Chair., State Agricultural and Industrial Cttee 1990–91; First Deputy Minister of Agric. of Kazakh SSR 1991–92; Head of Almaty Regional Admin 1992–94; Deputy Prime Minister of Kazakhstan 1994–96, State Sec. of Kazakhstan 1996, First Deputy Prime Minister and Chair. of State Cttee on Investments 1996–06; Minister of Agriculture 2007–; fmr Amb. and Head of Perm. Del. of Kazakhstan to NATO, Brussels, Belgium. *Address:* Ministry of Agriculture, pr. Abaya 49, 010000 Astana, Kazakhstan (office). *Telephone:* (7172) 32-37-63 (office). *Fax:* (7172) 32-62-99 (office). *E-mail:* mailbox@minagri.kz (office). *Website:* www.minagri.kz (office).

YESIN, Sergey Nikolayevich; Russian writer; *Rector, Maxim Gorky Literary Institute;* b. 18 Dec. 1935, Moscow; s. of Nikolai Yesin and Zinaida (née Afonina) Saprykina; m. Valentina Ivanova; ed Moscow State Univ.; debut as journalist, corresp. Moskovsky Komsomolets, Ed.-in-Chief Krugozor 1972–74; ed. Drama Broadcasting Div. State TV and Broadcasting Cttee 1974–81; Rector Maxim Gorky Literary Inst. 1992–, Prof. 1993; a Founder Club of Ind. Writers 1992; Founder and Vice-Pres. Acad. of Russian Literature 1996; Chair. Int. Union of Social Asscns of Bibliophiles 1997–; State Order of Friendship 1996, Sholohov Literary Award 2000, Moscow Literary Award. *Publications include:* Recollections of August, Memoirs of a Forty-Year-Old, The Imitator, The Spy, Standing in the Doorway, Gladiator 1987, Characters 1990, Selected Stories 1994, In the Season of Salting Pickles 1994, The Current Day 1994, The Mars Eclipse 1994, Tutor 1996, The Power of Culture 1997, Selected Stories 1998, Literary Diaries 1999, 2000, 2001, 2002, Death of Titan 2002, Companion Thoughts 2002, Marburg. *Leisure interests:* building dachas, home maintenance. *Address:* Maxim Gorky Literary Institute, Tverskoy Boulevard 25, 103104 Moscow; Stroiteley str. 4, korp. 6, Apt. 43, 117311 Moscow, Russia (home). *Telephone:* (495) 202-84-22 (office); (495) 930-35-45 (home); (495) 203-01-01. *Fax:* (495) 202-76-88 (office); (495) 203-60-91. *E-mail:* liternity@litinstitut.ru (office); rectorat@litinstitut.ru (home). *Website:* www.litinstitut.ru (office).

YESSENIN-VOLPIN, Alexander Sergeyevich; Russian mathematician, philosopher and poet; b. 5 Dec. 1924, Leningrad (now St Petersburg); s. of poet Sergey Esenin and Nadiezhda Volpina; m. 1st V. B. Volpina; m. 2nd I. G. Kristi; m. 3rd 1994; one c.; studied at Faculty of Math., Moscow Univ. 1941–46; arrested for his poetry and committed to mental asylum 1949; in exile Karaganda, Kazakh SSR 1950; amnestied 1953; wrote numerous articles on logic and math. and translated extensively; worked at USSR Acad. of Sciences Inst. of Scientific and Tech. Information 1961–72; dissident activity 1959–; emigrated 1972. *Publications include:* A Free Philosophical Treatise 1959, A Leaf of Spring 1959, 1961, Open Letter to Solzhenitsyn 1970, Report on Committee on Rights of Man 1971, On the Logic of Moral Sciences (in English) 1988; numerous articles in Western and Russian scientific journals (after 1990s). *Leisure interests:* logic, philosophy. *Address:* 1513 North Shore Road, 2nd Floor, Revere, MA 02151, USA. *Telephone:* (781) 289-1072.

YEUTTER, Clayton K., BS, JD, PhD; American lawyer, business executive and fmr government official; *Senior Adviser, Hogan & Hartson LLP;* b. 10 Dec. 1930, Eustis, Neb.; m. 1st Lillian Jeanne Vierk (died); two s. two d.; m. 2nd